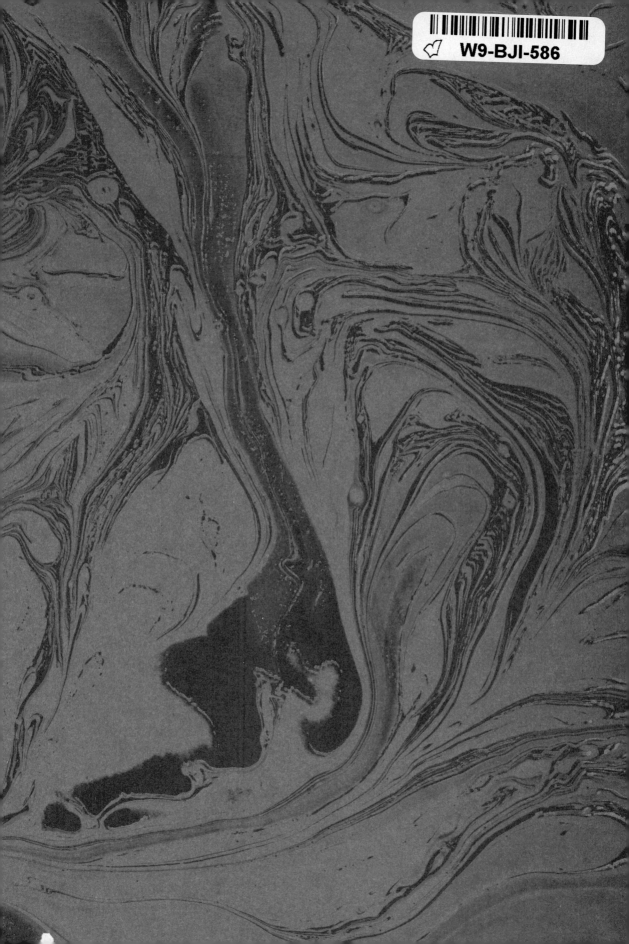

THE INTERPRETER'S ONE-VOLUME COMMENTARY ON THE BIBLE

Introduction and Commentary
for Each Book of the Bible
Including the Apocrypha

With General Articles

Edited by
CHARLES M. LAYMON

ABINGDON PRESS—Nashville and New York

CONTRIBUTORS

PETER R. ACKROYD
Samuel Davidson Professor of Old Testament Studies, University of London, King's College, England

G. W. ANDERSON
Professor of Hebrew and Old Testament Studies, University of Edinburgh, Scotland

HUGH ANDERSON
Professor of New Testament, University of Edinburgh, Scotland

WILLIAM BAIRD
Professor of New Testament, Brite Divinity School, Texas Christian University, Ft. Worth, Texas

EDWARD L. BEAVIN
Professor of Religion, Kentucky Wesleyan College, Owensboro, Kentucky

HARRELL F. BECK
Professor of Old Testament, Boston University School of Theology and Graduate School, Boston, Massachusetts

CYRIL BLACKMAN
Professor of New Testament Exegesis, Emmanuel College, Toronto, Canada

EDWARD P. BLAIR
Harry R. Kendall Professor of New Testament Interpretation, Garrett Theological Seminary, Evanston, Illinois

ROBERT G. BRATCHER
Translations Consultant, American Bible Society, New York, New York

WILLIAM HUGH BROWNLEE
Professor of Religion, Claremont Graduate School and University Center, Claremont, California

GEORGE A. BUTTRICK
Professor of Preaching Emeritus, Garrett Theological Seminary, Evanston, Illinois

ROGER N. CARSTENSEN
Dean of the College, Christian College of Georgia, Athens, Georgia

BRUCE T. DAHLBERG
Professor of Religion, Smith College, Northampton, Massachusetts

ROBERT C. DENTAN
Trinity Church Professor of Old Testament Literature and Interpretation, General Theological Seminary, New York, New York

SIMON J. DE VRIES
Professor of Old Testament, Methodist Theological School in Ohio, Delaware, Ohio

L. HAROLD DeWOLF
Dean and Professor of Systematic Theology, Wesley Theological Seminary, Washington, D.C.

GORDON B. DUNCAN
United Methodist Research Specialist, The Methodist Publishing House, Nashville, Tennessee

FRANCES W. EASTMAN
Secretary for Special Program Development, Division of Christian Education

iii

of the United Church Board for Homeland Ministries, Boston, Massachusetts

MORTON S. ENSLIN
Professor of Christian Thought and Literature, Dropsie College, Wynnewood, Pennsylvania

FLOYD V. FILSON
Dean Emeritus and Professor Emeritus of New Testament, McCormick Theological Seminary, Chicago, Illinois

CHARLES T. FRITSCH
Professor of Hebrew and Old Testament Literature, Princeton Theological Seminary, Princeton, New Jersey

STANLEY BRICE FROST
Professor of Old Testament Studies and Dean of the Faculty of Graduate Studies and Research, McGill University, Montreal, Canada

VICTOR PAUL FURNISH
Associate Professor of New Testament, Perkins School of Theology, Southern Methodist University, Dallas, Texas

S. MACLEAN GILMOUR
Late Norris Professor of New Testament, Andover Newton Theological School, Newton Centre, Massachusetts

NORMAN K. GOTTWALD
Professor of Old Testament and of Biblical Theology and Ethics, American Baptist Seminary of the West and Graduate Theological Union, Berkeley, California

JOHN GRAY
Professor of Hebrew and Semitic Languages, University of Aberdeen, Aberdeen, Scotland

JONAS C. GREENFIELD
Department of Near Eastern Languages, University of California, Berkeley, California

JAMES C. G. GREIG
Lecturer in Religious Education, Jordanhill College of Education, Glasgow, Scotland

KENDRICK GROBEL
Late Professor of New Testament, Vanderbilt Divinity School, Vanderbilt University, Nashville, Tennessee

HARVEY H. GUTHRIE, JR.
Dean, Episcopal Theological School, Cambridge, Massachusetts

DOROTHEA W. HARVEY
Professor of Religion, Urbana College, Urbana, Ohio

JAMES PHILIP HYATT
Professor of Old Testament, Vanderbilt Divinity School, Vanderbilt University, Nashville, Tennessee

SHERMAN ELBRIDGE JOHNSON
Dean and Professor of New Testament, The Church Divinity School of the Pacific, Berkeley, California

FRANCIS E. KEARNS
Bishop, Ohio East Area, The United Methodist Church

LEANDER E. KECK
Professor of New Testament, Vanderbilt Divinity School, Vanderbilt University, Nashville, Tennessee

HOWARD CLARK KEE
Rufus Jones Professor of the History of Religion, Bryn Mawr College, Bryn Mawr, Pennsylvania

GEORGE A. F. KNIGHT
Principal (President) of the Pacific Theological College, Suva, Fiji

CHARLES FRANKLIN KRAFT
Professor of Old Testament Interpretation, Garrett Theological Seminary, Evanston, Illinois

G. W. H. LAMPE
Gonville and Cains College, Cambridge University, Cambridge, England

CHARLES M. LAYMON
Chairman, Department of Religion, Florida Southern College, Lakeland, Florida

S. VERNON MCCASLAND
Late Professor Emeritus of Religion, University of Virginia, Charlottesville, Virginia

JOHN L. MCKENZIE, S.J., S.T.D.
Professor of Old Testament Studies, University of Notre Dame, Notre Dame, Indiana

CLYDE L. MANSCHRECK
Director, Center for Reformation and Free Church Studies, Chicago Theological Seminary, Chicago, Illinois

JOHN H. MARKS
Associate Professor of Oriental Studies, Princeton University, Princeton, New Jersey

HERBERT G. MAY
Professor Emeritus of Old Testament Language and Literature, Oberlin College, Oberlin, Ohio, and Vanderbilt Divinity School, Vanderbilt University, Nashville, Tennessee

JACOB MILGROM
Associate Professor, Department of Near Eastern Languages, University of California, Berkeley, California

LUCETTA MOWRY
Professor of Religion and Biblical Studies, Wellesley College, Wellesley, Massachusetts

ROLAND E. MURPHY, O. Carm.
Professor of Old Testament, Catholic University of America, Washington, D.C.

FREDERICK A. NORWOOD
Professor of History of Christianity, Garrett Theological Seminary, Evanston, Illinois

LINDSEY P. PHERIGO
Professor of New Testament and Early Church History, Saint Paul School of Theology, Kansas City, Missouri

JAMES L. PRICE
Professor of Religion, Department of Religion, Duke University, Durham, North Carolina

JAMES B. PRITCHARD
Assistant Director, The University Museum, Professor of History of Old Testament Religion, University of Pennsylvania, Philadelphia, Pennsylvania

WARREN A. QUANBECK
Professor of Systematic Theology, Luther Theological Seminary, St. Paul, Minnesota

JOHN H. P. REUMANN
Ministerium of Pennsylvania Professor —New Testament, Lutheran Theological Seminary at Philadelphia, Philadelphia, Pennsylvania

ARNOLD B. RHODES
Professor of Old Testament, Louisville Presbyterian Theological Seminary, Louisville, Kentucky

H. NEIL RICHARDSON
Professor of Old Testament, Boston University School of Theology, Boston, Massachusetts

RICHARD L. SCHEEF, JR.
Professor of New Testament, Eden Theological Seminary, Webster Groves, Missouri

MASSEY H. SHEPHERD, JR.
Hodges Professor of Liturgics, The Church Divinity School of the Pacific, Berkeley, California

Lou H. Silberman
Hillel Professor of Jewish Literature and Thought, Vanderbilt University, Nashville, Tennessee

Robert Houston Smith
Professor, The Department of Religion, The College of Wooster, Wooster, Ohio

David M. Stanley, S.J.
Professor of New Testament Studies, Regis College, Willowdale, Ontario, Canada

Albert C. Sundberg, Jr.
Professor of New Testament Interpretation, Garrett Theological Seminary, Evanston, Illinois

Samuel Terrien
Davenport Professor of Hebrew and the Cognate Languages, Union Theological Seminary; Adjunct Professor of Religion, Columbia University, New York, New York

Claude H. Thompson
Professor of Systematic Theology, Candler School of Theology, Emory University, Atlanta, Georgia

Eric Lane Titus
Professor of New Testament, Southern California School of Theology, Claremont, California

Lawrence E. Toombs
Professor, School of Religion, Waterloo Lutheran University, Waterloo, Ontario, Canada

John C. Trever
Professor of Religion, Baldwin-Wallace College, Berea, Ohio

John W. Wevers
Professor of Near Eastern Studies, University College, University of Toronto, Toronto, Canada

Robert McLachlan Wilson
Professor of New Testament Language and Literature, St. Mary's College, University of St. Andrews, St. Andrews, Fife, Scotland

G. Ernest Wright
Parkman Professor of Divinity (Old Testament), Harvard Divinity School, Harvard University, Cambridge, Massachusetts

EDITOR'S PREFACE

A significant commentary on the Bible is both timely and timeless. It is timely in that it takes into consideration newly discovered data from many sources that are pertinent in interpreting the Scriptures, new approaches and perspectives in discerning the meaning of biblical passages, and new insights into the relevancy of the Bible for the times in which we live. It is timeless since it deals with the eternal truths of God's revelation, truths of yesterday, today, and of all the tomorrows that shall be.

The Interpreter's One Volume Commentary on the Bible has been written within this perspective. Its authors were selected because of their scholarship, their religious insight, and their ability to communicate with others. Technical discussions do not protrude, yet the most valid and sensitive use of contemporary knowledge underlies the interpretations made of the several writings. It has been written for ministers, lay and nonprofessional persons engaged in studying or teaching in the church school, college students, and those who are unequipped to follow the more specialized discussions of biblical matters, but who desire a thoroughly valid and perceptive guide in interpreting the Bible.

The authorship of this volume is varied in that scholars were chosen from many groups to contribute to the task. In this sense it is an ecumenical writing. Protestants from numerous denominations, Jews, and also Roman Catholics are represented in the book. Truth cannot be categorized according to its ecclesiastical sources. It is above and beyond such distinctions.

It will be noted that the books of the Apocrypha have been included and interpreted in the same manner as the canonical writings. The value of a knowledge of this body of literature for understanding the historical background and character of the Judaic-Christian tradition has been widely recognized in our time, but commentary treatments of it have not been readily accessible. In addition, the existence of the Revised Standard Version and the New English Bible translations of these documents makes such a commentary upon them as is included here both necessary and significant.

An important section of the Interpreter's One Volume Commentary on the Bible contains the General Articles. These deal with various approaches to biblical interpretation—historical, literary, linguistic, geographical, archaeological, and theological—as well as with the contemporary use of the Scriptures in the life of the Church. They will be useful in understanding and assessing the thought movements of our time as these relate to biblical interpretation. For instance, the emphases of form criticism, bibli-

cal myth, and biblical theology are considered, as is also the significance of the Dead Sea Scrolls. In the several interpretations of the material throughout the commentary, these will also be evident in passage after passage.

The major section of full-color maps as well as numerous spot-map sketches significantly placed throughout the volume are intended to assist the biblical interpreter in locating movements and events. The several charts dealing with such matters as weights, measures, and dates will also be useful. And the inclusion of numerous pictures will further enable the users of this volume to bring to life the biblical passages at hand.

In editing, it has been our purpose to represent each author's viewpoint as he would wish it to be presented. Any changes in wording have been made in line with the general style manual for the entire volume. This would include such matters as abbreviations, the use of other languages—which has been discouraged except in rare instances—footnotes, the readability and availability of books in the bibliographies, and the aptness of literary expression in view of the anticipated level of readership. Each author read and approved his edited material in galley form before it was placed in the volume.

The commentary as a whole avoids taking dogmatic positions or representing any one particular point of view. Its authors were chosen throughout the English-speaking field of informed and recognized biblical scholars. Each author was urged to present freely his own interpretation and, on questions where there was sometimes a diversity of conclusions, each was also asked to define objectively the viewpoints of others while he was offering and defending his own. The dates of the biblical kings and kingdoms were brought into line with the chronological table carried in the Commentary on pp. 1271-75, although the authors were free to argue for a date more acceptable to them.

Many persons have contributed to the writing and production of this volume. One of the most rewarding of my personal experiences as editor was corresponding with the authors. On every hand there was enthusiasm for the project and warmth of spirit. The authors' commitment to the task and their scholarly sensitivity were evident in all of my relationships with them. The considerate judgments of the manuscript consultants, Morton S. Enslin, Dwight M. Beck, W. F. Stinespring, Virgil M. Rogers, and William L. Reed, were invaluable in the making of the character of the commentary. The copy editors who have worked under the careful and responsible guidance of Mr. Gordon Duncan of

Abingdon Press have contributed greatly to the accuracy and readability of the commentary.

In addition, acknowledgment must be made specifically to Herbert G. May, professor emeritus of Old Testament language and literature at Oberlin College and Vanderbilt University, for providing many of the fine illustrations for the commentary.

My thanks also go to Oxford University Press and Dr. May for the creation of accurate and readable maps, and to the editorial and production staffs of Abingdon Press.

—Charles M. Laymon, Editor

ABBREVIATIONS AND EXPLANATIONS

ABBREVIATIONS

Add. Esth. — Additions to Esther
Apoc. — Apocrypha
ASV — American Standard Version

ca. — *circa* (about)
cf. — *confer* (compare)
ch. — chapter
Chr. — Chronicles
Col. — Colossian, Colossians
Cor. — Corinthian, Corinthians

D — Deuteronomic; Deuteronomist
  source*
Dan. — Daniel
Deut. — Deuteronomy

E — east, eastern; Elohist source*
Eccl. — Ecclesiastes
Ecclus. — Ecclesiasticus
ed. — edited by, edition, editor
e.g. — *exempli gratia* (for example)
Eph. — Ephesian, Ephesians
ERV — English Revised Version
esp. — especially
Esth. — Esther
Exod. — Exodus
Ezek. — Ezekiel

Gal. — Galatian, Galatians
Gen. — Genesis

H — Holiness Code*
Hab. — Habakkuk
Hag. — Haggai
Heb. — Letter to the Hebrews
Hos. — Hosea

i.e. — *id est* (that is)
intro. — introduction

Isa. — Isaiah
ill. — illustration

J — Yahwist source*
Jas. — James
Jer. — Jeremiah
Josh. — Joshua
JPSV — Jewish Publication Society
  Version
Judg. — Judges

KJV — King James Version

L — Lukan source*
Lam. — Lamentations
Lev. — Leviticus
lit. — literally
LXX — Septuagint, the earliest Greek
  trans. of the OT and Apoc. (250
  B.C. and after)

M — Matthean source*
Macc. — Maccabees
Mal. — Malachi
Matt. — Matthew
Mic. — Micah
MS — manuscript

N — north, northern
Nah. — Nahum
NEB — New English Bible
Neh. — Nehemiah
NT — New Testament
Num. — Numbers

Obad. — Obadiah
OT — Old Testament

P — Priestly source*

p. — page
Pet. — Peter
Phil. — Philippian, Philippians
Philem. — Philemon
Prov. — Proverbs
Ps., Pss. — Psalm, Psalms
Pss. Sol. — Psalms of Solomon
pt. — part (of a literary work)

Q — "Sayings" source*

Rev. — Revelation
rev. — revised
Rom. — Roman, Romans
RSV — Revised Standard Version

S — south, southern
Sam. — Samuel
Song of S. — Song of Solomon

Thess. — Thessalonian, Thessalonians
Tim. — Timothy
Tit. — Titus
trans. — translated by, translation,
  translator

viz. — *videlicet* (namely)
vol. — volume
vs. — verse
Vulg. — Vulgate, the accepted Latin
  version, mostly trans. A.D. 383-405
  by Jerome

W — west, western
Wisd. Sol. — Wisdom of Solomon

Zech. — Zechariah
Zeph. — Zephaniah

* For explanation of these sources see "The Compiling of Israel's Story," pp. 1082-89, and "The Literary Relations Among the Gospels," pp. 1129-35.

QUOTATIONS AND REFERENCES

In direct commentary words and phrases quoted from the RSV of the passage under discussion are printed in boldface type, without quotation marks, to facilitate linking the comments to the exact points of the biblical text. If a quotation from the passage under discussion is not in boldface type, it is to be recognized as an alternate trans., either that of another version if so designated (see abbreviations of versions above) or the commentator's own rendering. On the other hand, quotations from other parts of the Bible in direct commentary, as well as all biblical quotations in the intros. and general articles, are to be understood as from the RSV unless otherwise identified.

A passage of the biblical text is identified by book (see abbreviations above), ch. number, and vs. number or numbers, the ch. and vs. numbers being separated by a colon (e.g. Gen. 1:1). Clauses within a vs. may be designated by the letters *a, b, c,* etc. following the vs. number (e.g. Gen. 1:2*b*). In poetical text each line as printed in the RSV—not counting runovers necessitated by narrow columns —is accorded a letter. If the book is not named, the book under discussion is to be understood; similarly the ch. number appearing in the boldface reference at the beginning of the paragraph, or in a preceding centered head, is to be understood if no ch. is specified.

A suggestion to note another part of

the biblical text is usually introduced by the abbreviation "cf." and specifies the exact vss. To be distinguished from this is a suggestion to consult a comment in this volume, which is introduced by "see above on," "see below on," or "see comment on," and which identifies the boldface reference at the head of the paragraph where the comment is to be found or, in the absence of a boldface reference, the reference in a preceding centered head. The suggestion "see Intro." refers to the intro. of the book under discussion unless another book is named.

CONTENTS

I. COMMENTARY ON THE BOOKS OF THE OLD TESTAMENT

II. COMMENTARY ON THE BOOKS OF THE APOCRYPHA

III. COMMENTARY ON THE BOOKS OF THE NEW TESTAMENT

IV. GENERAL ARTICLES

Biblical Interpretation

Geographical and Historical Setting

The Making of the Literature

The Religion of the Bible

Text, Canon, and Translation

COMMENTARY ON THE BOOKS
of the OLD TESTAMENT

GEN.
EXOD.
LEV.

THE BOOK OF GENESIS

John H. Marks

Introduction

In the Hebrew the books of the Law, the first 5 of the OT, had no individual titles. The name Genesis, "beginning," was given to the first of them in the earliest Greek translation. This book may be described as the story of Hebrew origins. It is the introductory section to the compilation of the historical, cultural, and legal traditions which circulated among the tribes of Israel concerning the time before their political establishment in Palestine. Gen. cannot be studied by itself, therefore, as though it were a special unit of divine revelation. On the contrary, just as the exodus from Egypt and the conquest of Canaan are best understood when one knows the traditions contained in Gen. (cf. e.g. Josh. 24:2-13), so Gen. can be properly understood only when one does justice to the larger framework of which it is an essential part.

The Traditions of Israel. Israel had traditions about her past which to her were crucial to an understanding of her life in Palestine. The motive for collecting these traditions was neither idle curiosity nor a desire to codify abstract truth. It was rather the attempt to come to terms with her own existence as a divinely chosen people who formed a small state clinging precariously to political independence on the arid land lying between the great fertile river valleys of Egypt and Mesopotamia. Gen. contains some of the oldest of those traditions.

The mass of diverse material in Gen. is arranged according to a simple chronological scheme. First the traditions about the origins of the world and mankind (chs. 1–11) are presented according to time-honored chronological sequence: the Creation and the mythology about the first men, then the Flood, and finally the establishment of civilization in the E. In each of these cycles of tradition the compiler adheres to his final purpose, the telling of Israel's story. Thus when the reader comes to the 2nd section of the book, the stories of the patriarchs and the descent into Egypt, the transition from the primeval to the patriarchal history is natural and logical, so carefully has the main thread of the "sacred history" been followed. Gen. concentrates attention on the direct line of Israel's forebears from Adam to Jacob and his family, and from this genealogical line hangs the mass of varied traditions about Israel's own past and that of her contemporaries.

The Compiling of the Traditions. Where did these traditions originate and what was the process of their final compilation? The answers to such ques-

tions about the origin and composition of the materials in Gen. necessarily involve literary analysis of the larger work of which it is a part and therefore are treated elsewhere in this volume (see "The Hebrew Community and the OT," pp. 1072-76, and "The Compiling of Israel's Story," pp. 1082-89). Since, however, the evidence for such analysis must largely be drawn from Gen., a brief explanation is advisable here.

A serious reading of Gen. reveals that the book is not the homogeneous work of a single author, for no writer would be guilty of discrepancies like those, e.g., between the accounts of Creation (cf. 1:26 with 2:7, 18, 19, 22) or of the Flood (cf. 7:1-3 with 6:18-21). The book is rather a compilation in which we recognize at least 3 strands of tradition. Though these strands can no longer be isolated precisely in their original form, it is possible to assign most of the content of Gen. to one or another of them (see table, p. 2). The traditions have behind them a long history of formulation, elaboration, revision, and combination until they received their final form in Gen.

These sources of tradition are known as "J" (Yahwist), "E" (Elohist), and "P" (Priestly); and there are in addition traditions like those of ch. 14 which do not seem to belong to any of these sources. The symbols J, E, and P signify, not individual authors, but rather clusters of traditional material which are distinguished from one another by their use of differing names for God (Yahweh, translated as "the LORD"; Elohim, translated as "God") and by other preferences for favorite words, phrases, and facts. E.g. the Priestly tradition was much concerned with genealogies and precise dates, while the Elohist was interested in dreams and divine revelations through intermediaries. The traditional accounts of J were in many instances early combined with those of E so that the original accounts have become almost inextricably entwined.

The exact process by which this mass of traditional material assumed its final form is unknown. Clearly the compilers were unwilling to remove the obvious discrepancies between the various accounts in the interest of a uniform presentation. It seems likely that they worked with existing documents, themselves final formulations of earlier oral traditions which circulated among "schools" in Judah (J) and Ephraim (E) or were taught by the priests (P). When these documents were combined, the Priestly chro-

Sources of Genesis

Most of the content of Gen. has been attributed by scholars to one or another of the
3 strands of tradition in the columns below. Certain passages which cannot be assigned to one strand only are listed in both columns followed by the letters indicating
their composite structure. Passages esp. difficult to assign are indicated by question
marks. Ch. 14 appears to come from an independent source. Longer editorial additions
and glosses are recognized in 15:19-21; 16:9-10; 18:17-19; 19:17-22; 30a; 20:18; 22:15-
19; 31:47; 48:7.

J (Yahwist)	E (Elohist)	P (Priestly)
		1:1-31
2:4b-25		2:1-4a
3:1-24		
4:1-26		
		5:1-32
6:1-8		6:9-22
7:1-5, 7, 8-9JP, 10, 12, 16b, 17b, 22-23		7:6, 8-9JP, 11, 13-16a, 17a, 18-21, 24
8:2b-3a, 6-12, 13b, 20-22		8:1-2a, 3b-5, 13a, 14-19
9:18-27		9:1-17, 28-29
10:1b, 8-19, 21, 24-30		10:1a, 2-7, 20, 22-23, 31-32
11:1-9, 28-30		11:10-27, 31-32
12:1-4a, 6-20		12:4b-5
13:1-5, 7-11a, 12b-18		13:6, 11b-12a
15:1(?), 3-4(?), 7-12, 17-18	15:2(?), 5, 6(?), 13-16(?)	
16:1b-2, 4-8, 11-14		16:1a, 3, 15-16
		17:1-27
18:1-16, 20-23		
19:1-16, 23-28, 30b-38		19:29
	20:1-17	
21:1a, 2a, 6b-7, 25-26, 28-30, 32-33	21:6a, 8-24, 27, 31, 34	21:1b, 2b-5
22:20-24	22:1-14	
		23:1-20
24:1-67		
25:1-6, 11b, 18, 21-26c, 27-34		25:7-11a, 12-17, 19-20, 26d
26:1-33		26:34-35
27:1-45JE	27:1-45JE	27:46
28:10, 13-16, 19	28:11-12, 17-18, 20-22	28:1-9
29:2-14, 31-35	29:1, 15-23, 25-28, 30	29:24, 29
30:1-43JE	30:1-43JE	
31:1, 3, 17-18a, 43-44, 46, 48, 50	31:2, 4-16, 19-42, 45, 49, 51-55	31:18b-d
32:3-13a, 24-32	32:1-2, 13b-23	
33:1-17	33:18a, 18c-20	33:18b
34:1-31JE(?)	34:1-31JE(?)	
35:21-22a	35:1-8, 14-20	35:9-13, 22b-26, 27-29
36:20-30(?), 31-39(?)		36:1-19, 40-43
37:3-4JE, 12-20JE, 21, 25b-27, 28c, 31-35JE	37:3-4JE, 5-11, 12-20JE, 22-25a, 28ab, 28d-30, 31-35JE, 36	37:1-2(?)
38:1-30(?)		
39:1-23		
	40:1-23	
41:29-44JE, 45, 46b-57JE	41:1-28, 29-44JE, 46b-57JE	41:46a
42:2-7JE, 27-28a, 38	42:1, 2-7JE, 8-26, 28b-37	
43:1-13, 15-34	43:14	
44:1-34		
45:1a, 4-5a, 9-14, 28	45:1b-3, 5b-8, 15-27	
46:1a, 28-34	46:1b-5	46:6-27
47:1-5a, 6cd, 12, 13-26(?), 27a, 29-31		47:5b-6b, 7-11, 27b-28
48:9b-10a, 13-14, 17-19	48:1-2, 8-9a, 10b-12, 15-16, 20-22	48:3-6
49:1b-28a		49:1a, 28b-33
50:1-11, 14	50:15-26	50:12-13

nology became the final framework around which were worked the formulations of the traditions about Israel's early history. The scope and form of the story, however, had been laid down by the literary and religious genius whose work is conspicuous in the J source. Customary dates for the documents are *ca.* 950 for J, 750 for E, and after 539 for P; but these dates do not indicate the age of individual traditions, which are often much older. Material in P e.g. may antedate the supposed documentary formulation of J in the 10th cent.

The literary genres represented in Gen. indicate the diverse and independent origins of the material (see "The Literary Forms of the OT," pp. 1077-81). Folklore (e.g. the story of the Flood, chs. 6–9), local traditions (e.g. about Bethel, 28:19), tribal traditions (e.g. about Simeon and Levi, ch. 34), traditions about Israel's neighbors, songs, and lists—all are incorporated into the book and doubtless owe their origin as well as their inclusion to political and religious events and concerns which we can no longer determine. The long and complicated history which lies behind Gen. as we have it cannot be encompassed by neat phrases or simple theories. An elucidation of the history of this book would also mean the unfolding of Israel's history, and that is what makes the literary problem of Gen. so fascinating.

Religious Values. The values to be derived from reading Gen. are not scientific or primarily historical; they are religious. The stories of creation do not contain scientific materials of use to geology, biology, or zoology; and the primeval history as a whole (chs. 1–11) contains no historical records of primitive man. Rather this primeval history poses the perennial riddles of human life: man's dominion over animals, the nature and cause of evil, the reason for death, the meaning of life, the values of civilization. These riddles are posed in the language and form of mythology and are answered from the faith by which Israel learned to live. The patriarchal stories undoubtedly contain historical material and are meant to convey historical fact, but the curious interest shown today in "proving the Bible true" reveals their dearth of historical information apart from the mass of knowledge made available through archaeology. Archaeology does not simply confirm biblical statements—it clarifies them first and foremost.

The patriarchal stories combine historical fact, tradition, poetry, and symbolism, according to what today is recognized as unscientific historical method. Their value lies not so much in the bits of historical information they provide as in the religious insights they disclose. These insights are the more cogent for being clothed in credible historical garb. Whether the Abraham of Gen. actually lived or not is an idle question for which an answer is unavailable. What this Abraham is reported to have done and believed, however, receives added significance from the probability that the traditions about him were not invented. The milieu in which he is said to have lived is established for the 2nd millennium by historical research, and Abraham's story thus becomes exemplary for a life of faith.

The theme which the materials of Gen. elaborate, and around which they cluster, is the remarkable story of Israel's ancestors who were chosen mysteriously by God, the Creator of the universe and Lord

of history, to be the "founders of a holy nation." The fact of this choice in the tangled web of Palestine's history in the 2nd millennium became clear to the prophetic writers who assembled these traditions. Israel, they believed, did not exist as a happenstance, and they were interested in tracing Israel's ancestry. But more decisively than that they wanted to confess their faith in Yahweh as unique among the gods of the nations. The Lord of their history must indeed be the Creator of the universe and the Lord of all history, revealing himself to the man he had made and establishing justice and mercy in the world. What they emphasize is a conception of God which remains worthy of man's noblest thought and profoundest reverence wherever the mysteries of life are soberly and steadfastly accepted.

For Further Study. John Skinner, *A Critical and Exegetical Commentary on Gen.,* 1910; the basic work in English. H. E. Ryle, *The Book of Gen.,* 1914. S. H. Hooke, *In the Beginning,* 1947. C. A. Simpson in *IB,* 1952. Alan Richardson, *Gen. I–XI,* 1953. S. Moscati, *The Face of the Ancient Orient,* 1959. Gerhard von Rad, *Gen.: A Commentary,* 1961. Otto Eissfeldt in *IDB,* 1962. A. S. Herbert, *Gen. 12–50,* 1962. J. M. Holt, *The Patriarchs of Israel,* 1964.

I. The Primeval History (1:1–11:32)

A. Creation of the World (1:1–2:4a)

1:1-5. The Beginning. Creation begins when God imposes order on primeval, nonpersonal chaos by calling **light** into existence. This P account has obvious parallels in the Babylonian creation and flood epics (cf. also Pss. 74:13-15; 89:10; Isa. 51:9). It seems to picture a chaotic storm churning over the primordial dark and mysterious abyss of infinite and formless waters. Out from this God summons order, thus creating the universe (cf. Job 26: 10-14; Pss. 29:10; 93:3-4; 104:5-9). Time begins with that creation. Nothing is said of the origin of the chaos or of God's activity prior to creation (cf. Ps. 90:2). The question about whether creation is out of nothing (*creatio ex nihilo*) is also irrelevant to the story. God's creation **in the beginning** is unique and inexplicable, and appropriately the Hebrew word *bara,* here translated "create," is applied in the OT only to God's activity (see below on vss. 20-23, 24-30; 2:2-4a; cf. Isa. 40:26, 28; 45:18). An ordered universe is conceivable only as a divine act of creation.

1:4-5. The most obvious sign of order is the gift of **light** and its daily separation from the **darkness.** God's lordship is expressed further in his naming of his works. The **one day** seems to be reckoned from morning to morning; i.e. God works all day till **evening** and begins his work again the next **morning.**

1:6-8. The Firmament. A translucent dome, like an inverted basin, placed **in the midst of the waters** defines the spatial boundaries of God's further work. This God-given vault sets limits to the universe and provides focus for the story of man which follows, for the author is interested ultimately in the phenomenon of man, not that of nature. The solid, "hammered-out" firmament restrains **the waters** of chaos from above and receives its blue color from them (cf. 7:11-12; 8:2). **Heaven** is therefore the upper protective limit of created order (cf. Job 38:8-11). The contradictions in terminology between creation by word (vss. 6, 14, 20, 24, 26) and creation by act (vss. 7, 16, 21, 25, 27) may reveal parallel original accounts of creation. Significantly both conceptions have been preserved.

1:9-13. Earth and Vegetation. God further restrains the waters of chaos and there appears the earth, which is thought to be a disk resting on waters (cf. Exod. 20:4; Ps. 24:2). Order has by now so replaced chaos that the earth can produce vegetation and achieve part of her destined, God-ordained function (cf. vs. 24) as "mother earth." One observes that the author does not impute "life" to vegetation.

1:14-19. Celestial Lights. Time too is ordered. Light is assigned to luminaries **in the firmament,** which are to preside over **day** and **night** and to provide convenient guideposts for marking time and regulating activity. The **stars** and planets are denied any divine character or potency. Their primary function is to give light at their appointed times, thus restraining the darkness in an ordered fashion.

1:20-23. Sea Creatures and Birds. The waters likewise are freed to their destined purpose, and they bring forth swarms of **living creatures.** Also **birds** can exist where chaos is restrained. But all these are conceivable only as the creation of God, since the watery remnants of chaos are incapable of producing life. To insure continuation of this life God blesses the creatures with reproductive functions (vs. 22).

1:24-30. Land Creatures and Man. Everything is thus ready for the appearance of land creatures and man. The creatures are the offspring, as it were, of the earth (vs. 24), and their reproductive functions derive from the earth; nevertheless God makes them (vs. 25; see above on vss. 6-8). Man, however, has a different position in the world (cf. Ps. 8; Ezek. 28:12). He is unique among the creatures of the universe, resembling but not to be equated with members of the heavenly court (vs. 26; cf. I Kings 22:19-22; Ps. 82:1). He is to rule living things on earth as he in turn is ruled by God. But such a creature must be created by God. Order (vs. 1), birds and fish (vs. 21), and man (vs. 27) are thus considered unique, unthinkable apart from God's special creative activity, expressed in the Hebrew word *bara*.

1:27-28. God creates man **male and female;** i.e. this act of God's creation embraces mankind as a whole. God also blesses mankind with reproductive capacity, thus removing sexuality from being either the divine spark in man or the terror to which he is subject. Procreation is both God's gift and his command, and man's task from creation is to **fill the earth and subdue it,** to join in God's will for order.

1:29-30. For **food** men are given every grain and pulse and every fruit; to animals are assigned as food **every green plant.** The eating of meat by animals or men is passed over in silence and therefore presumed to be absent at creation.

1:31-2:1. Creation Finished. God now surveys his work and is well pleased. It has come from his hand precisely as he intended it and is therefore **very good.** The chaos has been effectively restrained, and order prevails; the world is furnished and populated, and mankind has been brought into being to maintain God's created order.

2:2-4a. The Day of Rest. One work remains to fill out the week of creation (the measurement of time by weeks is taken for granted); it is called God's rest. God takes delight in his creation, and in sanctifying **the seventh day** he wills that mankind shall take similar delight. This rest is thus considered to be God's climactic work and man's highest good (cf. Mark 2:27). The text says nothing explicit about the cultic institution of the sabbath, the origins of which are unknown. Implicitly, however, the institution of the sabbath is traced to God's creative act. Significantly, the formula **there was evening and there was morning** (1:5 etc.) is omitted. The work of creation has ended; there is to be no new 7-day cycle.

Various interpretations of the significance of sabbath observance are given in the OT: it is a sign that one keeps God's covenant (Isa. 56:2-8), a memorial of Israel's deliverance from Egypt (Deut. 5:12-15), a memorial of God's rest after creation (Exod. 20:8-11). Here, however, the author is content to record the fact of God's rest as the climax to his work of creation and God's blessing and hallowing of the day of rest. Apparently the 7th day of God's rest is to be fruitful in a fashion analagous to that stated in the blessing of sea creatures, birds, and mankind (1:22, 28). So ends the P account of the creation **of the heavens and the earth** (2:4a).

This account of creation is best described in both narrative and doctrinal terms. The sequence of days provides the narrative framework for recounting God's creative activity at the beginning of time. The author, claiming the legitimate freedom to tell his story in a form most appropriate to his purpose, probably meant for the days to be understood literally as 24-hour periods. But he desired also to propagate doctrine. He used terms which reflect the "scientific" attitude and understanding of his time, and he incorporated the religious truths which in P circles had become accepted as dogma: "God created"; "God said, . . . and it was so"; "God saw that it was good"; "God blessed them"; "God created man in his own image . . . to have dominion . . . over all the earth, and over every creeping thing that creeps upon the earth"; "God rested on the seventh day [and] blessed the seventh day and hallowed it." Here is a view of man and the universe which, while taking account of accepted theories of natural origins of that day, sees life in religious, theological perspective. The reader is given a theological view of primeval history, not a scientific account of nature. The setting is provided for the drama of man. The account thus presents with soberness and exaltation something of the grandeur of man, the beauty of creation, and man's joy in the gift of life.

B. The Story of Paradise (2:4b-3:24)

2:4b-9. Creation of Man. The J story which follows differs from the preceding account in both form and content. The form is no longer pedagogical, strictly chronological, or liturgical. Stylized expression and doctrinal repetition yield place to charmingly simple narration. In the first story the reader saw the world of nature created day by day before his eyes in increasing complexity with mankind as the culmination. Now the reader is again taken to the beginning of time to see God form the first man from the damp soil of a barren plain, prepare a garden to place him in, and then find a companion for him. The setting for this 2nd story has been said to be Palestinian, in contrast to the Mesopotamian background of the previous account. The parabolic, mythical nature of this story differentiates it sharply from the formal, doctrinal account which precedes; but the view of man's relationship to God presented by each is essentially the same.

2:4b-7. When God made the world, this J story begins, the **earth** was barren for lack both of **rain** and of cultivation. The narrator, taking for granted other features of the universe, focuses attention at once on man's immediate physical environment, the fields from which he lives. The barren land is moistened by some underground source of water. Nothing is said about the chaos of ch. 1, and water appears to be not a vestige of chaos but a necessity for vegetation. To end the unproductiveness of the earth, God molds a man from clay of the plain and **breathed into his nostrils the breath of life.** This animated **dust,** man, therefore bears a unique relationship of immediacy to and dependence on God (cf. vs. 19), and all creation is for his enjoyment and well-being.

2:8-9. God prepares a park, a paradise, **in the east** to be man's home; and there God places him **to till it and keep it** (vs. 15; cf. Ezek. 28:12-19). The location of **Eden** is unknown (cf. II Kings 19: 12), if indeed the author considered it a geographically identifiable haven (cf. Isa. 51:3). A derivation of the name from Babylonian *edinu,* "plain" or "steppe," is possible, in which case the meaning might be that God miraculously created an oasis in the desert plain. The park contains all trees of aesthetic charm and practical value, and in their midst **the tree of life.** Also present, according to vs. 9, is **the tree of the knowledge of good and evil,** i.e. knowing (by experience, personal acquaintance) everything (cf. 24:50; 31:24; II Sam. 14:17, 20). Two traditions have been combined here. It is the tree of knowledge about which the story centers (2:17; 3:3-12, 17). The tree of life is not mentioned again till 3:22, 24 (cf. Rev. 22:2).

2:10-14. *A Geographical Note.* This digression, which interrupts the story and appears also to place the garden outside Eden (cf. vss. 8, 10), indicates that the world is watered by **four rivers** which are branches of the one great **river** originating in Eden. Only the 3rd and 4th of the branch rivers, **Tigris** and **Euphrates,** can be identified; and their known sources in the mountains of Armenia make it appear that the author located Eden in the N rather than in the E. Proposed identifications of **Pishon** (the Indus or a river in Arabia) and of **Gihon** (the Nile or "Nubian Nile") lack cogent support. **Cush** here probably refers, not to Ethiopia, but to the land of the Kassites in the mountains E of Mesopotamia (see below on 10:8-12 and color map 7). On this basis it has been suggested that originally the rivers flowed into rather than out of Eden and that the garden was therefore located at the head of the Persian Gulf. The paragraph reveals the vague knowledge about rivers and oceans which was common in the ancient world and persisted at least to the era of Alexander the Great.

2:15-25. *Creation of Woman.* The garden provided for man's enjoyment is also the arena of his responsible obedience. The author here suggests the problem of human freedom as the proper relationship between obligation and unrestrained and unrestricted enjoyment and conceives man's destiny soberly in terms of his pleasure in creation, his work in the garden, and his obedience to God. He sees the question about obedience to God as the larger context within which the problem of human knowledge must be considered, and he concludes that (*a*) knowledge without obedience is perverse, and (*b*) such perversion means death (not mortality; see below on 3:4-5). An implied thesis is the bliss of ignorance. There is no mention of the tree of life. The symbolic nature of the story must be taken earnestly, and questions, therefore, about God's purpose in making his prohibition must be treated as unanswerable.

2:18-20. Having created man's physical world and established the limits of his destiny, God decrees an end to man's solitude and thus provides opportunity for the widest range of human fulfillment. God determines to provide man with **a helper fit for him**—i.e. corresponding to him as his opposite. None of the animals, though obviously akin to man, fulfill this function, for man cannot find fellowship with them. By giving the animals their names the man exerts his rule over them (cf. 1:26-28).

2:21-23. Man's relationship with his woman involves not only authority (in naming her) but also irrepressible joy (in at last finding her) and dependence and companionship (she was made from his rib). The statement that the creation of woman from man's **rib** may derive from a Sumerian pun. The goddess created to heal Enki's rib is called Nin-ti, i.e. "the lady of the rib" and/or "the lady who makes live."

2:24-25. Man's sexual drive results from God's creative activity: a man and woman belong to each other because originally they were **one flesh.** The man and the woman were **naked** before each other, un-self-conscious and unashamed. Nudity is here the symbol for mutually frank and honest self-giving, which is now impossible except rarely and imperfectly among young children.

3:1-24. *Temptation and Fall.* Temptation through the medium of the **serpent** next enters the story. The question of time is here irrelevant; it does not become relevant to mankind until the Fall conditions man's future life. In Christian symbolism the serpent usually stands for evil (but cf. Matt. 10:16). Here, however, the serpent represents cleverness and magical power (cf. II Kings 18:4), not the devil (cf. Wisd. Sol. 2:24; Rev. 12:9; 20:2), a god, or the dragon of chaos.

3:1b-3. With an innocent question the serpent awakens the woman's dormant desire for the forbidden tree and arouses her inchoate feelings of rebellion at being denied its **fruit.** God's prohibition has been a trial to her, and her exaggerated answer to the serpent is the avenue to her further temptation.

3:4-5. The serpent uses the occasion to deny the death penalty for disobedience and to impute ulterior, selfish motives to God. It insinuates that God has deceived the woman about the real properties of the tree: eating the fruit will bring man not death but knowledge. In the light of man's final expulsion from the garden, the precise meaning both of that knowledge and of the threatened death penalty seems relatively clear. The idea that man here lost immortality, though parallel with the notion in the Babylonian myths of Adapa and Gilgamesh, is not consonant with biblical ideas about man. The OT thinks in terms, not of man's immortality, but of his life as fulfillment rather than mere existence. The serpent speaks of death as the end to mortal existence and therefore in a sense speaks truly: the man does not die. But the author obviously means to express by "life" more than existence, and the death threatened by God (2:17) thus can be understood as separation from the possibility of free and perfect enjoyment of life, expulsion from the garden where fulfillment was granted. Death is separation from God, the giver of "life."

3:6-7. Thus man exchanged "life" for knowledge, and the first pair **knew** at once with shame **that they were naked;** i.e. they experienced their nudity as embarrassing. The suggested interpretation of the passage to mean that man received sexual knowledge from eating the forbidden fruit is improbable— in spite of the parallel of Enkidu and the harlot in the Gilgamesh epic and the usage in Deut. 1:39; II Sam. 19:35; Isa. 7:15. This interpretation is too restrictive of the knowledge acquired and degrades human sexual experience by viewing it as unplanned by God and acquired only at the price of man's disobedience. A more satisfactory interpretation would be the knowledge about the increase and mastery of life which was reserved for God, the Creator. Further light may be shed in terms of Hamlet's lament that "conscience does make cowards of us all."

3:8-19. The instinctive reaction to guilt is to hide, to cover one's nakedness, to exculpate oneself. But the gulf of separation cannot be concealed, and the consequences of this alienation are inescapable. Suffering and misery enter the world: motherhood and **childbearing** become painful, fatherhood and labor become wearisome, and futility hangs like a pall over life. The serpent becomes a symbol of evil, and hostility between man and beast begins.

3:20-24. Nevertheless, paradoxically, man affirms life in the naming of his wife. He has indeed become like a god, refusing to think of himself as creature. The author thinks of God's gift of clothing as a special act of grace. Paradise and perfect fulfillment are, however, irretrievably lost. **Cherubim** are known from ancient Near Eastern lore as mythological winged animals, usually with human faces (see comment on I Kings 6:23-28).

C. The Spread of Population (4:1–6:4)

4:1-16. *Cain and Abel.* The penalty for man's rebellion against God is separation both from God and, as the narrative will show, from other men. The story of Cain and Abel, which illustrates further the consequences of the Fall, does not agree in detail with the narrative of ch. 3 and probably derives, therefore, from a different source of tradition which the J author incorporated into his material. The account assumes the existence on earth of other people who are presumably unrelated to Cain (vss. 14-16), of an accepted institution of sacrifice, and

therefore of settled community life. In addition, 2 pictures of Cain are preserved side by side, one of Cain the agriculturalist turned nomad (vss. 1-16) and one of Cain the city builder (vss. 17-24). Both narratives are embraced within the genealogical statements of vss. 1, 25.

4:1-2a. The man **knew . . . his wife,** i.e. had sexual intercourse with her. This euphemism reveals both the Hebrew attitude toward knowledge and the OT ideal of marriage. Knowledge and sexual union are elevated above the plane of mechanical and academic detachment to the realm of spiritual commitment and fulfillment. The first son of this union is named **Cain** (meaning "spear" as in II Sam. 21:16? or "smith"?) under circumstances which are obscure (vs. 1b can scarcely be translated, still less understood). His younger brother is named **Abel,** which suggests the Hebrew word for "breath."

4:2b-7. The boys represent 2 ways of life, the agricultural and the pastoral. Both seek divine favor by means of sacrifice, but only Abel receives a favorable omen. Does the author intend to suggest that seminomadic pastoral life is superior to settled agricultural community? (For a NT interpretation cf. Heb. 11:4.) Cain, angry and sullen, apparently inquires the reason for the failure of his sacrifice and receives a reply which can no longer be understood (vs. 7) but which in its present form stresses Cain's responsibility with regard to his sin and guilt. The interesting suggestion has been made that originally vs. 7 referred to a specific demon, "the croucher," who lay in wait secretly for his victim.

4:8-16. Cain's subsequent action in killing Abel seems to be premeditated, but his motivation cannot be unmistakably discerned from the text. The usual interpretation that it was jealousy and chagrin accords most readily with the present context; but the hypothesis that the text is the remnant of an original cult-ritual story of human sacrifice, performed to secure fertility of the soil, cannot be easily dismissed.

4:9-16. A man is responsible, however, for his brother's life. Cain, the first to rob another of life, becomes as a consequence **a fugitive** both from the soil which has drunk his **brother's blood** (cf. Isa. 26:21) and from the family which he has also deprived of a life. But God protects the accursed man with a **mark** (tattoo?), a kind of sign often used to distinguish members of a class, e.g. prophets (cf. Zech. 13:6). Cain, who is usually recognized as the name ancestor of the Kenites (cf. Num. 24:21-22), goes to dwell in **Nod,** a land of "wandering" (?) which is geographically unknown. Thus the theme of alienation unfolds.

4:17-26. *Genealogy of the Kenites.* In the genealogical account which follows, **Cain,** not a nomad but a settler (in the land of Nod?), is considered to be the father of civilization (vss. 20-22). But culture, with all the benefits it brings to mankind, does not close the spiritual rift which has opened between men and God. The consequences of alienation can be frightful, as the account of Lamech shows.

4:17-22. A comparison of this 7-generation genealogical list (vss. 17-18) with the parallel P 10-generation list (5:3-27) reveals the range of Hebrew traditions about the descendants of the first man.

4:23-24. The song of **Lamech** may originally have explained the origin of tribal blood revenge: **seventy-**

sevenfold vengeance is required to satisfy justice because of harm done to one mighty man (cf. Judg. 8: 18-21; 16:28; II Sam. 21:1-9).

4:25-26. The final genealogical notice is fragmentary and suggests the beginnings of what might be called "true religion"—**to call upon the name of the LORD** (Yahweh). The notice may have been included here to show that as the beginning of civilization led to further alienation of a man from his neighbor, so the beginning of Yahweh worship opened an avenue of reconciliation between man and God and thus between man and man. Here the worship of Yahweh is considered to derive from antediluvian antiquity, in contrast to the traditions in Exod. 3:14 (E); 6:3 (P), which consider Moses to be the first recipient of this revealed personal name of God.

5:1-32. *Adam's Descendants Until the Flood.* This enumeration of the 10 human generations between the Creation and the Flood is the sequence to the P account of creation in chs. 1–2:4a. According to the Hebrew text the account covers a period of 1656 years (Greek and Samaritan totals differ from the Hebrew and from each other), during which the human span of life is about 900 years. Thereafter it is reduced to 200-600 years for the period from Noah to Abraham (11:10-32), to 100-200 years for the patriarchal period (25:7; 35:28; 47:28; 50:22), and finally to 70-80 years as the normal limit (Ps. 90:10). At least one scholar has suggested this account of man's gradually diminished life span as the P equivalent to the J story of the Fall (cf. Isa. 65:20 for a statement about longevity in the messianic age), but the significance of the numerical systems is unknown.

This is the book of the generations of . . . was doubtless originally the title of an actual book, from which the genealogical formula repeated at 6:9; 10:1; 11:10, 27; 25:12, 19; 36:1, 9; 37:2 may derive. The formula in 2:4a was artificially fitted into the system. Together the genealogies provide a structural pattern for arranging the manifold material in Gen.

The genealogical list resembles the Sumerian king lists of the antediluvian period: 10 names are given; both lists conclude with the hero of the flood story; and in each text a new era begins after the Flood. Both this P list and the parallel J list (4:17-22) reflect indirectly, therefore, Mesopotamian prototypes.

Curiosities regarding the longevity figures here and in 11:10-26 have often been noted. Adam lived to see the birth of Lamech; Seth died shortly before the birth of Noah; Enoch lived 365 years, which may somehow be related intentionally to the number of days in a sun year; Noah died in Abraham's 60th year; Shem outlived Abraham to see the birth of Esau and Jacob; and according to one Greek manuscript Methuselah died 14 years after the Flood. The consequences, if any, to be drawn from these facts are not intimated in the text.

5:21-24. Enoch (the same person as in 4:17?) receives special notice as one who **walked with God** (cf. 6:9; 17:1), i.e. one who led an exemplary life (cf. Mic. 6:8). As a result of his exemplary life, apparently, he did "not see death" (Heb. 11:5), **for God took him** (cf. II Kings 2:10-11). Only a fragment of the original Enoch tradition is preserved here (cf. Jude 14-15).

5:28-31. The etymology of the name **Noah** (a form of Hebrew *naham,* "he comforted") is an allusion to 3:17, 19 and is therefore from the J source of tradition. The reference is to Noah's discovery of the cultivation of the vine (9:20) and the cheer which wine gives mankind (cf. Judg. 9:13; Ps. 104:15). The suggested derivation, however, leads obviously to the name Naham, not Noah. Is **Lamech** to be identified with the Lamech of 4:23-24?

6:1-4. *The Birth of Demigods.* The J source now emphasizes the cosmic nature of man's fall: the heavenly beings (cf. e.g. 28:12; Job 1:6; Ps. 29:1) wantonly marry mortal women (cf. Matt. 22:30). The text of vs. 4, the interpretation of which is not entirely clear, seems to imply that the gods married existing gigantic earthly women and that these marriages produced the **mighty men** (heroes) of saga and legend (cf. Deut. 2:10-11; 3:11; 9:2; Amos 2:9), i.e. demigods of gigantic size and superhuman strength. Vs. 4 has also been interpreted to mean that the **Nephilim** (i.e. giants) on the earth were the offspring of the divine-human marriages, but this interpretation seems less cogent in the light of other OT references to giants (cf. Num. 13:33; Ezek. 32: 27; II Pet. 2:4; Jude 6).

The passage suggests the early existence of a race of supermen on earth, the destruction at that time of the created bounds between heavenly beings and men, the explanation for the popular hero tales about an age long past, and the further weakening of primeval man's original stature and strength. The difficult vs. 3 seems to mean that man did not achieve immortality through his union with the heavenly beings but rather as a consequence had his life span reduced to **a hundred and twenty years.**

D. THE FLOOD (6:1–9:29)

The account of the Flood is an interweaving of the J and P versions, both of which in turn derive from Mesopotamian originals. The fullest Babylonian account is preserved on the 11th tablet of the Gilgamesh epic, where the context is man's vain search for immortality; but the proper context of the Babylonian flood story is probably to be found in the epic of Atrahasis, in which the flood is the climax of a series of punishments inflicted on mankind. The biblical story reveals the use which the Hebrews made of traditional mythological material to illustrate and reinforce their conceptions both of God's judgment and mercy and of human dignity and recalcitrance. The popularity of the story among the Hebrews is suggested by allusions like that in Isa. 54:9.

The composite character of the story is apparent from its repetitions and discrepancies. Repetitions include the following: God sees the corruption on earth (6:5, 11-12); he announces the imminent destruction (6:17; 7:4); Noah enters the ark (7:7, 13); the Flood comes (7:10, 11); the waters increase (7:17, 18); all flesh dies (7:21, 22-23); the Flood ceases (8: 2a, 2b); there will never be another flood (8:21-22; 9:9-17).

Startling inconsistencies are not removed. The animals entering the ark are one pair of every species in P (6:19-20; 7:15-16), 7 pairs of clean animals and one pair of unclean in J (7:2-3). In J the Flood is caused by heavy rain (7:4 etc.), in P by the release of the waters above the sky and beneath the earth (see below on 7:11). Yet the composite account is remarkably unified and loses little of its force as a result of its uneven composition. For a listing of the vss. in each account see table, p. 2.

6:5-13. Man's Corruption. In vss. 5-8 J summarizes succinctly and with pathos man's condition as the antediluvian eon ends: complete and continued corruption of will and thought, which apparently has also corrupted the animal world (vs. 7)! And God is heartsick at man's ruin; he is **sorry,** i.e. repents (cf. e.g. Exod. 32:14; Num. 23:19; I Sam. 15:11, 29), **that he has made them.** His solution is to begin again with man and beast (in contrast to his solution in vs. 3?), but not in such a way as to obliterate the past. Nevertheless the emphasis falls, not on continuity with the past, but on a new beginning and on God's grace in allowing it at all.

6:9-13. This P passage is parallel to the J summation in vss. 5-8, yet the difference in representation is clear. As in the paradise story J has emphasized the human aspects of the situation, but P states facts without comment or explanation. God has decided to put an end to **all flesh** (a favorite expression in this account) because of corruption and **violence** on earth. Man's rebellion against God has brought a return to chaos. Only Noah is **righteous** and **blameless,** the last of those about whom it is reported that he **walked with God.**

6:14-22. The Building of the Ark. Noah is commanded by God, continues P, to construct a large (*ca.* 450 by 75 by 45 ft.), watertight, 3-storied boat (the same Hebrew word is used in Exod. 2:3, 5) **of gopher** (cypress ?) **wood.** The reason for building the ark is then explained to Noah. The word **flood** in this story is not that used elsewhere of overflowing rivers but refers to the **waters** of the heavenly ocean (Ps. 29:10; cf. 1:6-7). These waters are to inundate the earth in a catastrophe of cosmic proportion (cf. vss. 13; 9:11). But in the ark Noah and his immediate family together with one pair of every kind of living creature will be spared. God will establish his **covenant** with Noah, who will become thereby the new father of mankind, virtually replacing Adam. He will be bound by the covenant to recognize in gratitude and obedience God's sovereignty and grace.

7:1-16. The Entrance into the Ark. After the decision to destroy life on earth (6:5-8) the J story proceeds with Yahweh's command to Noah to **go into the ark.** Noah has no doubt built it according to a divine command once related in the J story but now omitted in favor of the P version (6:13-22). J clearly suggests that Noah learns only after he has finished building the boat the purpose it is to serve (vs. 4; cf. Heb. 11:7), and Gerhard von Rad accordingly concludes that "the Yahwist did not simply assert Noah's righteousness, as P did (6:9), but he described it." The distinction, which is religious rather than hygienic, between **clean** and unclean animals (vss. 2-3; contrast 1:31) is doubtless primeval; for biblical legislation cf. Lev. 11; Deut. 14. The Flood is to result from **forty days** of **rain,** which will begin to fall **seven days** after the command to enter the ark and will destroy **every living thing** (vs. 4). Noah and his family go aboard as commanded (vss. 5, 7), and after 7 days the Flood

begins (vs. 10). Vs. 6 is from P, and vss. 8-9 are mixed.

7:11-16. P dates the catastrophe with apparent precision, a mark no doubt of the importance he attaches to its occurrence at the end of an era. The destructive waters are released from their bounds on the **seventeenth day** of the **second month** of Noah's **six hundredth year** (see below on 8:1-19). The waters come, not from rain as in the J account, but from the **fountains of the great deep** (i.e. the great underworld ocean; see comment on Ps. 18:7-18) and the **windows of the heavens** (i.e. the ocean above the firmament; see above on 6:14-22). **On the very same day** the waters are released Noah and his family and the animals enter the ark (vss. 13-16a). In vs. 12 the **rain** falling for **forty days** and in vs. 16b the use of the LORD (Yahweh) identify interspersed bits of the J story.

7:17-24. The Ark on the Waters. J tells briefly that the ark rises **high above the earth** on the swelling waters (vs. 17b) and that **every living thing** except those in the ark is destroyed (vss. 22-23). With characteristic statistical interest P reports in repetitious detail how the waters reach a depth of **fifteen cubits** (*ca.* 22½ ft.) above the highest mountains. Thus if the ark can be assumed to draw 15 cubits of water it just floats above the mountain peaks and is ready to ground as soon as the waters slightly abate. P's period for the Flood's duration is **a hundred and fifty days.**

8:1-19. The Subsiding of the Waters. The P account of the Flood's end (vss. 1-2a) is reminiscent in some respects of this account of creation (cf. 1:2, 7, 9). God's remembrance of Noah (vs. 1a) carries the theological force of his creative will for order over chaos, and his remembering is thus synonymous with his faithfulness (cf. 19:29; 30:22). By God's action the Flood ends as abruptly as it began and immediately the waters recede so that the ark grounds the same day **upon the mountains of Ararat,** i.e. probably in NE Armenia (see color map 2). The date is the **seventeenth day** of the **seventh month,** precisely 5 solar months of 30 days each after the Flood's beginning (vs. 4; see above on 7:11-16). On the **first day** of the **tenth month,** i.e. *ca.* 2½ months later, dry land is visible (vs. 5). Vss. 2b-3a, telling how the **rain** stopped and **the waters receded . . . continually** is a part of the J account.

8:6-12. Noah, J continues, opens a **window,** which evidently is so placed that he cannot look out of it on the world. Hence he releases first a **raven** and then a **dove** in order to discover whether the earth is habitable. The **olive leaf** perhaps has some mythological or symbolic value, but it is unknown.

8:13-19. P gives further dates for the conclusion of the Flood. It is not clear how vss. 13a, 14 are to be harmonized, but according to the latter the cataclysm has required one year and ten days to run its course (see above on 7:11-16). Thereupon Noah, his family, and the animals disembark. Vs. 13b is from J.

8:20-9:17. God's Covenant with Noah. J concludes the story (vss. 20-22) with a report of God's resolve never again to **curse the ground** (scarcely a reference to 3:17 or 4:12) and **destroy every living creature** by a flood (cf. 6:6-7). The reason for this resolve (vs. 21) is the same as that for sending the

Flood (6:5), and a similar paradoxical statement about God's resolves is made by the prophets (cf. Hos. 11:8-9; Isa. 54:9-10). Noah's gratitude for his life, as expressed in his sacrifice of propitiation, may summarize J's view of man's proper relationship with God.

9:1-7. P considers the postdiluvian age to be guided by divine moral enactments which have been modified from their original form at creation (vss. 2-3; cf. 1:28-30). God now permits the eating of **flesh** from which the **blood,** the symbol of **life,** has been drained (cf. Lev. 7:26; Deut. 12:16) and specifically enjoins blood vengeance. No distinction is drawn between clean and unclean animals. In contrast, J has recognized blood vengeance as existing before (4:11, 23) and therefore does not regard the Flood as having significantly altered either God's purpose or created order. Regarding P's account an observation of Paul Tillich that "law is the form love takes when we are estranged from it" is relevant. God's original purpose, expressed in the command to be **fruitful,** is here repeated immediately after Noah's deliverance from destruction and forms a parenthesis within which the new divine enactments are contained. **Man,** not God (cf. 4:11), is made legal guardian and avenger of the sanctity of human life (vs. 6).

9:8-17. The P account closes with God's covenanted assurance (cf. 6:18) that **never again** will **a flood . . . destroy the earth** and **all flesh** (cf. 8:21-22, J). The composite nature of the P account here is revealed by the doublets, vss. 9 and 11a, 12 and 17, 14 and 16. The use of the term **covenant** seems out of place, unless the author intends vss. 1-7 to be included in it, as appears unlikely. A covenant is made to clarify the relationship between 2 parties and puts an obligation on each. Since no living creature is here called on to affirm God's ordinance, the "covenant" cannot be broken except by God (cf. Isa. 24:5). The **sign** serves to remind all participants in the covenant relation of its existence. The rainbow (here seen for the first time?) is the sign of God's everlasting mercy toward his creation; he has laid aside his **bow** of war.

E. The Discovery of Wine (9:18-29)

The Noah who discovers wine and its properties in this J story is distinct from the Noah of the Flood. Here he (a nomad?) has **three** apparently unmarried **sons** (cf. 7:7) living with him **in his tent.** The passage reveals a combining of 2 genealogies, a Palestinian and an ecumenical. In the Palestinian, Noah's youngest son is **Canaan** (vss. 24-25), whose brothers are **Shem** and **Japheth** (vss. 26-27). According to the other (vs. 18a) the brothers are **Shem, Ham, and Japheth.** Vs. 18b and the words **Ham, the father of** in vs. 22 are harmonizing glosses.

9:20-21. Noah is here apparently considered to be **the first tiller of the soil** (cf. 4:2). The text of vs. 20 is difficult to understand, however. "Tiller of the soil" is lit. "man of the ground." Does this mean the first farmer or the first man (cf. 2:7)? Cf. JPSV: "Noah, the tiller of the soil, was the first to plant a vineyard." The fruit of the vine was greatly esteemed in Israel (cf. 5:29; 49:11-12; Amos 9:13; see above on 5:28-31).

9:22-27. Canaan's wrongdoing probably consists in ridiculing his father in what he reports to his brothers (vss. 22, 24), though more may be implied in vs. 24. Noah's curse and blessings are doubtless meant to describe the conditions prevailing in Palestine at the time the poetic lines originated (cf. ch. 49). Canaan is enslaved to Shem and Japheth (vs. 25), Shem's God is Yahweh (vs. 26, RSV footnote), and Japheth occupies **the tents of Shem** (vs. 27). The references may be to the Canaanites, Israelites, and Philistines; but historical precision is impossible.

9:28-29. The P account of Noah's death is the conclusion of the genealogical statements of 6:9-10; 7:6.

F. The Table of Nations (10:1-32)

The composite genealogical table of nations suggests 2 questions: (a) According to what principle are the peoples arranged? (b) Why is the table included here at all? In regard to the first, the ch. is an obvious attempt to classify geographically the peoples of the world into 3 groups who are unified as families because of their descent from Noah's 3 sons. The list is not organized racially or linguistically but rather territorially and politically; and it is not always certain whether the names refer to land (e.g. vs. 4) or people (e.g. vs. 7). The geographical horizon of the P table (for list of vss. see table, p. 2) is that of the 7th cent. B.C. in the Near East, Japheth representing the peoples of the W and N, Shem the peoples of the E, and Ham those of the S.

In regard to the 2nd question, the account is transitional; it sketches the political background from which the holy people of God is to emerge. Israel is not mentioned in the table, though its existence must be presupposed as part of the geographical picture of the 7th cent. The anachronism of a world inhabited e.g. by Medes (**Madai**), Ionians (**Javan**), Etruscans (**Tiras,** vs. 2), and Arameans (vs. 23) where the nation of Israel is presumed to be as yet nonexistent cannot be overlooked. The transition from mythical tradition to history cannot be made with precision. On the other hand Israel had no illusions about her origins in the world family of nations; kingship did not come down from heaven to Jerusalem as the Sumerian king list declared it had first come to Eridu.

The parts of the table assigned to J are, when compared with P, more narrowly oriented geographically and are also at some variance—cf. e.g. vss. 7 (P) and 28-29 (J); also **Cush** in vss. 6-7 (Ethiopia, P) and **Cush** in vs. 8 (the Kassites, J; see below on vss. 8-12). The postulate, therefore, of a "much older Yahwistic table of nations" more or less parallel with and basic to that of P as assumed by some scholars is questionable. The P interest in genealogy (see above on 5:1-32) would account for the collecting of various genealogical bits, the original significance of which was either unknown or disregarded, to be fused into a larger, presumably complete, composite account. The so-called J sections enumerate sons of Shem (vss. 21, 24-30), presumably Ham (vss. 13-19) and perhaps Japheth (vss. 8-12); but the evidence for an original complete genealogy in J, descending from Shem, Ham, and Japheth, is inconclusive.

10:2-7. These vss. and vs. 20 give the **Japheth** and **Ham** sections of the P table.

10:8-12. The J passage about **Nimrod** refers to the Assyrian Empire (cf. Mic. 5:5-6) and its Kassite (**Cush**) founder who **built Nineveh** and 3 other cities (vss. 11-12). The editor evidently inserted the passage here because he thought it dealt with the **Cush** (Ethiopia) of vss. 6-7. The Kassites from the E ruled Mesopotamia for several cents. ending *ca.* 1150 (see above on 2:10-14). The relationship between Nimrod's fame as **the first on earth to be a mighty man** and the mighty men of 6:4 is not clear. Nimrod's Mesopotamian prototype may perhaps be found in the Babylonian god Ninurta or the Assyrian king Tukulti-Ninurta I (*ca.* 1246-1206). **Shinar** is probably the Hebrew form of Sumer (S Mesopotamia) and **Accad** is Agade, capital of the first Akkadian dynasty (see "The People of the OT World," pp. 1005-17). On **Babel** see below on 11:1-9.

10:13-20. That **Egypt** and **Canaan** are "sons" of Ham according to J can be assumed only in the light of the P table (vss. 6, 20). The J conception of the extent of Canaanite territory (cf. vs. 19 with vss. 15-18*a*) is obscure.

10:20-32. Hebrews (**Eber**) and Semites (**Shem**) are according to J 2 names for the same people (vs. 21), who are represented by sons of **Peleg** (vs. 25) and **Joktan,** the father apparently of the peoples of S Arabia (vss. 26-30), whom P thinks of as stemming from Ham (vss. 6-7). Vss. 22-23, 31 present the **Shem** section, followed by vs. 32 as the conclusion, of the P table.

G. The Tower of Babel (11:1-9)

This J story is independent of the preceding table of nations—not merely of the P table, in which diversity of **language** is specifically stated (10:5, 20, 31), but even of the J table, in which **Babel** already exists (10:10) and the various descendants are assumed to **spread abroad** gradually (10:18, 30; but cf. 10:25). Here the confusion of tongues and the consequent dispersal of mankind over the earth are an immediate result of divine judgment (vss. 7-8). Two stories appear to have been combined to form the present account: (*a*) the building of a **tower** to gain fame, and (*b*) the building of a **city** to preserve the unity of mankind (cf. the doublets in vss. 3*a*, 3*b;* 5, 7, 8*a*, 9*b*).

On **Shinar** see above on 10:8-12. The **tower** is obviously a ziggurat, a Mesopotamian type of temple consisting of a number of stories forming a stepped pyramid (see ill. this page). **Babel** (Hebrew name for Babylon), according to this erroneous popular etymology (vs. 9), derives its name from the Hebrew root *balal,* "confusion," referring to the confusion of tongues which occurred there. The Akkadian *Bab-ilu* means "gate of the god."

The narrative in its present form suggests that civilization, which seeks to bring order out of cultural, economic, and political chaos, can become an end in itself, thus amounting to rebellion against God and resulting in self-defeat. In Gen. man's will to be like God (vs. 6; cf. 3:5-6; 6:2) has ended in separation from God, a return to chaos in the Flood, and an alienation among men which makes communication and cooperation between them extremely difficult if not impossible. Having treated the problem of human origins, the authors now offer an in-

terpretation of history which speaks to man knowing himself as "a possibility entrapped in failure but yearning toward the long light." (John Ciardi).

H. Genealogies of Shem and Terah (11:10-32)

The authors abruptly narrow their field of vision from **the face of all the earth** (vs. 9) to the world of **the descendants of Shem** (vs. 10), concentrating their attention on Abraham (**Abram;** see below on vss. 20-27), by whom according to J **all the families of the earth will bless themselves** (12:3). The account in its final form as we have it obviously is meant to have significance beyond the confines of Israel, and in some sense Israel's experience is considered a model for the nations of the world.

11:10-19. According to the P figures in 5:32 (where "after" should read "when" as in this ch.) and 7:11 Shem was **a hundred years old** when the Flood began. The discrepancy cannot be removed without deleting the phrase **two years after the flood.** P sees **Eber** (vss. 14-17) as the name ancestor of the Hebrews (see below on 14:13); according to J (10:21, 25-30) he is the father of all Semites.

11:20-27. In spite of the P view that Abraham was born in Ur on the lower Euphrates (see below on vss. 31-32) the setting of this genealogy is around Haran in NW Mesopotamia (see color map 2). **Serug . . . , Nahor . . . , Terah** are all known from nonbiblical tablets as place names in this region (Sarug, Nahur, Turahi). It was the focal point of the Aramean migrations in the first half of the 2nd millennium (cf. Deut. 26:5). That **Nahor** appears as both father and son of **Terah** indicates that more

Courtesy of the Oriental Institute, University of Chicago

Ziggurat at Ur (see comment on Gen. 11:31-32)

than one tradition of this genealogy came down to P. **Abram,** originally Abi-ram, means "the (my) father is exalted." In 17:5 (see comment) this name is changed to Abraham. **Haran** the man is in Hebrew spelled differently from the city of Haran.

11:28-30. This is all that remains of the J genealogy which presumably once connected Peleg (10:25) with Abraham. Two traditions about Abraham's original home were known in Israel (cf. Josh. 24:2; Neh. 9:7). In the view of J it is clearly Haran (24:2-7, 10, 15, 29; 27:43). For this reason, and because apparently the Chaldeans were not in possession of Ur till the 8th cent., **in Ur of the Chaldeans** in vs. 28 (cf. 15:7) is probably a harmonizing insertion

of the editor or a later gloss. **Sarai,** meaning "princess" (perhaps the title of a moon goddess in Haran), is changed to Sarah in 17:15 (see comment). The information that she is **barren** is given to heighten the effect of the promise in 12:2-3.

11:31-32. P follows the tradition that Abraham originally came from **Ur of the Chaldeans** but harmonizes with the rival tradition (see above on vss. 28-30) by reporting that he and his family **settled** for a time in Haran on their way to Canaan. Archaeology has revealed that Ur was a center of probably the first great civilization on earth, the Sumerian, and in Abraham's time was still a city of notable wealth and culture. The implication here is that **Terah** was prevented by death from going on to Canaan, but from the figures in vs. 26; 12:4b he survives 60 years after Abraham's departure.

II. Patriarchal History (12:1–50:26)

The preceding stories of human origins (chs. 1–11) are symbolic, mythical accounts of man's position in a universe believed to be created and ordered by God. They are not historical; i.e. they do not record events which can be validated by contemporary evidence. Rather they record truth in a way more akin to poetry. They provide the background which the Hebrews created as the setting for their conceptions of man and of the history of God's relationship to him. These writings are considered divinely inspired because the truths they proclaim have been experienced as true wherever the tales have been heard. In the stories which follow (chs. 12–50) the symbols in which the understanding of man's life is expressed are more historical. They are drawn from history—which in some respects can be and in fact has been verified by archaeology—rather than from poetry, from events rather than from accepted religious constructions. We therefore distinguish between myth and saga, neither of which can be described in strictly historical categories, but both of which nevertheless have credible historical aspects. Myth describes in historical language the cosmic design overarching and determining history, while saga recounts in historical detail traditionally accepted events which may be used to illustrate accepted myth. Saga often accurately reflects customs and historical events as the environment in which its story unfolds.

Various interpretations of the patriarchal stories have dominated eras of OT study. Julius Wellhausen, whose work in tracing and dating the sources J, E, and P has become classic, declared in 1886 that the patriarchal legends reflected only the beliefs and customs of the period in which they were written, viz. after Solomon, and were therefore historically useless for the period they seemed to describe. Others have treated the patriarchs as figures from Palestinian or Mesopotamian myths, as legendary founders of Canaanite sanctuaries, as personifications of tribes, as folk heroes about whom cycles of legends tended to circulate at specific locations, or as combinations of these. On the whole, however, contemporary scholars, recognizing the contributions made by archaeology to our knowledge of the 2nd millennium, tend more and more to find historical elements in these traditions and to forsake purely mythical and legendary interpretations.

A. The Story of Abraham (12:1–25:18)

One can glimpse perhaps in the story of Abraham the purpose for which Gen. was written. The compiler of these traditions desired to present an account of the Hebrews which would reveal and confirm his conception of God's unfolding purpose for his people. In order to do "righteousness and justice" (18:19) Israel must become a nation (12:2), yet not so as to be reckoned among the community of nations (Num. 23:9). To this end, and within God's purpose, a land set apart as the seat of such a nation was needed.

Two traditions about God's call to nationhood existed: (a) the account in Gen., according to which God's call to Israel began with Abraham (cf. Isa. 51:2); and (b) the account in Exod., according to which God's call to Israel came through Moses in Egypt. These 2 traditions were united literarily by means of the Joseph story and theologically through the "God of the Fathers" who continually revealed himself. Abraham, therefore, who set out for the Promised Land, became the ideal man of faith and obedience (Heb. 11:8-10), the type of the "righteous man."

12:1-9. *Abraham's Migration to Canaan.* The story of Abraham's response to the summons to make a complete break with his past so that he might become the founder of a nation in a land as yet unknown to him suggests certain of the J author's religious conceptions:

a) Abraham is the representative figure who truly apprehends the demand of the God of Truth for absolute commitment, in the interest of future generations. All who respond to the "divine imperative" as Abraham did **will bless themselves** by him, i.e. account Abraham as their spiritual father (cf. 48:20; Ps. 72:17). Those who refuse the divine command will suffer the consequences (cf. Jer. 29:22).

b) The community of those who have accepted the divine summons must possess its own land and become a nation, in order both to preserve its identity and to give light to the nations of the world (contrast the expectation of the tower builders in 11:1-9). Abraham is therefore the type of the true Israelite, and Israel is to be the type of the true nation of God.

c) God's blessing is his promise of fruitfulness (cf. 1:22), which for Abraham is impossible of fulfillment so long as Sarah remains barren. The facts of God's promise and Abraham's patient and apparently futile waiting (cf. ch. 22) give dramatic content to the entire Abraham saga.

12:4b-5. According to this bit from the P account, Abraham leaves his home for the Promised Land at **seventy-five years** of age. Thus he roams through the land for 100 years until he dies at the ripe old age of 175 (25:7). In his 100th year he begets a son, Isaac (21:5). The figures suggest perfection — 100 years to claim the promise both of a son and of the land.

12:6-7. Abraham's nomadic wandering from Syria S follows the routes used by migrating peoples in the 2nd millennium. Indeed the stories of the patriarchal movements are in substantial accord with what is known of the nomadic migrations of that period. Abraham's first recorded stopping place in Palestine is **the place at Shechem**, i.e. a sacred place (cf. 22:3; Jer. 7:12). Shechem was a Canaanite city located *ca.* 40 miles N of Jerusalem and 1 mile E of the pass between the mountains Ebal and Gerizim (1½ miles E of modern Nablus; see color map 3). Excavation of the site has revealed that the city flourished during the Hyksos period, perhaps

Courtesy of Herbert G. May

Burnt-offering altar at Megiddo probably dating from the time of Abraham (*ca.* 1900 B.C.); cf. Gen. 12:7

the time of Abraham's visit (see below on 14:1). It owed its importance to its location at the crossroads of the main N-S and E-W routes of travel in Palestine, its good water supply, and the fertile fields adjoining it on the E. Rehoboam's journey to Shechem to be crowned king (I Kings 12:1) attests its religious and political importance in Israel (cf. 33:18-20). The Sychar of John 4:5 may be Shechem. The **oak of Moreh** was apparently a Canaanite holy place, certainly religiously important to Israel (cf. 35:4; Deut. 11:29-30; Judg. 9:37).

12:8. Abraham's next stop is **the mountain on the east of Bethel**—modern Beitin, located *ca.* 10 miles N of Jerusalem (see color map 3). Bethel, earlier named Luz (28:19), doubtless owed its importance to an excellent water supply (cisterns were not required for the city until the increase in population during Roman times). It was an ancient Canaanite sanctuary of the god El (the oldest excavated stratum is dated 2000-1600) and was associated with the traditions of Jacob (28:10-22; 35:1-15) before it became an Israelite cultic center (Judg. 20:18). Jeroboam I found it important enough to set up as the rival of the Jerusalem temple in his establishing of the N kingdom of Israel (I Kings 12:26-33). It served as a royal sanctuary (cf. Amos 4:4) and continued as a shrine until destroyed by Josiah (II Kings 23:15). The site of **Ai on the east** is uncertain.

12:9. The **Negeb** is the S dry highland of Palestine which can be marked out roughly by a triangle drawn with its points at Gaza, the N tip of the Gulf of Aqaba, and the S tip of the Dead Sea (see color map 4). By careful and ingenious systems of water conservation and irrigation its ancient inhabitants were able to cultivate the land more extensively than today seems feasible.

12:10–13:1. Abraham's Visit to Egypt. The story of a patriarch's stratagem of sacrificing his wife's honor to save his own life occurs 3 times in Gen. (20:1-18; 26:6-16). Its occurrence here in the J narrative breaks the connection between 12:8 and 13:2, 5, 7 ff. and raises several related questions. Where did Lot go when Abraham entered Egypt? Was **Sarah** really so **beautiful** as this incident implies (cf. the P idea of her age in 12:4; 17:17)? Did Abraham wander so aimlessly between Bethel and Hebron (13:18)? In spite of its incongruities, however, the incident does reinforce the reader's awareness of Abraham's growing despair regarding God's promise. The promise of 12:7 is jeopardized by the Canaanites (12:6b) and that of 12:1-3 by the measures Abraham adopts to save himself first from starvation and then from death (12:10-20).

12:13. The wife-sister motif of this story and its parallel versions has been shown to be based on Hurrian laws whereby sistership was a transferable relationship; accordingly a woman given in marriage by her brother became legally her husband's sister and insured prestige for herself as well as purity for her children. The notice about **camels** (cf. 24:10; 30:43; 31:34; 32:16) is believed by many scholars to be an anachronism because archaeological evidence points to *ca.* the 12th cent. for the domestication of the camel (cf. Judg. 6:5).

12:17. But what of God's righteousness? Why does God afflict with plagues the **Pharaoh** rather than the craven Abraham? The plagues in this instance appear to have been considered not penal but portentous of impending evil to Egypt unless Sarah is returned immediately to her husband.

13:2-18. Abraham's Separation from Lot. After his unfortunate Egyptian trip, J continues, Abraham returns **to the place where his tent had been at the beginning, . . . to the place where he had made an altar.** The words seem to contain a judgment on Abraham's Egyptian excursion, which is now illuminated and emphasized by Lot's decision to settle in the Jordan Valley. To Israel both Babylon and Egypt represented bondage, and Lot's settlement in **Sodom** would illustrate the nature of that bondage. From **the mountain on the east of Bethel** (12:8) one can survey the lush green of the Jordan rift, and the contrast of this prospect with the memory of the arid hills over which Abraham and Lot wandered is not lost on either man. In selecting the land which is **like the land of Egypt** (vs. 10) Lot chooses what Abraham rejected when he set out from Haran and what his stay in Egypt has seemed to offer him: the enticements, complexities, and compromises of civilization. Abraham here remains faithful to his original call and in dealing with his nephew becomes an exemplary, magnanimous figure. The contrast with his behavior in Egypt is noteworthy. Also significant is the virtual elimination of Lot as recipient of the divine promise.

13:14-18. Since the view from Bethel does not provide a panoramic prospect of Palestine, vss. 14-17 may be a later insertion into the story; vs. 18 follows most naturally after vs. 12.

14:1-24. Abraham's Victory over the Eastern Kings. This difficult ch., which is completely independent from all other biblical sources, is apparently inserted here to establish (a) Abraham's place in the history of the 2nd millennium and (b) his relationship to Jerusalem.

14:1. With regard to the first of these goals we must admit that none of the invading kings can be identified for certain with rulers known to us from contemporary sources. **Amraphel** is a Babylonian name (on **Shinar** see above on 10:8-12), but it cannot be equated, as was once thought possible, with Hammurabi. **Arioch** can perhaps be identified with an Amorite-Hurrian name, Arriwuku, known as king of the city of Mari on the middle Euphrates (see color map 2). The once-accepted identification of **Ellasar** with Larsa in lower Mesopotamia then becomes impossible, however. A well-known but still undiscovered Hurrian city, Alziya, has been proposed for Ellasar. **Chedorlaomer** could be the Hebrew form of an otherwise unattested Elamite name Kudur-Lagamar. **Tidal** has been identified with the Hittite king, Tudhalias.

These suggested identifications place the kings in the late 18th or early 17th cent., i.e. at the time of unrest in the Near East caused by invading Hurrians, Kassites, and Elamites (see "The People of the OT World," pp. 1005-17). It is known, e.g. that Transjordan experienced cultural and political upheaval during the first half of the 2nd millennium. The Hyksos, who invaded Egypt (see Intro. to Exod.) during the first half of the 18th cent., are also part of this picture, and one suggestion is that this account describes a phase of their campaign. On the other hand recent archaeological study of the Negeb has convinced some scholars that Abraham could not have lived in this region later than the 19th cent. (see "Chronology," pp. 1271-82).

14:2-4. There is no way as yet of identifying the Canaanite kings, but the report of a coalition of Palestinian city-states in revolt against their NE overlords during this period is credible enough, though unsupported by nonbiblical evidence.

14:5-12. The battle takes place in the vicinity of the Dead Sea, after a surprisingly circuitous route which the invading kings follow. Coming from the N they move through places (**Ashteroth-karnaim, . . . Ham, . . . Shaveh-kiriathaim**) along the E side of the Jordan–Dead Sea rift, S through Edom (**Mount Seir**) to the Gulf of Aqaba (**El-paran**), thence NW to **Kadesh** in the Negeb, and finally NE to **Hazazontamar** and on to meet their rebellious vassals in the **Valley of Siddim** (see color maps 3, 4). The purpose of this excursion, it has been suggested, is to keep the route open for travel and trade. The invaders defeat the Canaanite coalition, sack **Sodom and Gomorrah,** and capture Lot. The repetition of vs. 11 in vs. 12 suggests that the ch. is not a literary unit. Cf. also the break between vss. 17, 21.

14:13. Abraham is here **the Hebrew** and one of his allies is an **Amorite.** The use of the place name **Mamre** as a personal name is contrary to the usage either of J (a sacred grove) or P (Hebron). **Hebrew,** which occurs here for the first time in the OT, normally was used either by non-Israelites or by Israelites to distinguish themselves from Egyptians. It should probably be connected with the term "Habiru," which has been widely attested in ancient Near Eastern documents, and which designated a wanderer. The appellative here may identify Abraham as a leader of the Habiru in Palestine. According to the Amarna documents, however, the Habiru were disrupting Palestine in the 15th and 14th cents., i.e. 200 or 300 years after the presumed date of the events in vss. 1-12. The telescoping of events in this account thus prevents assigning a more certain date for Abraham than sometime between the 19th and 14th cents. and reduces the possibility of precise historical interpretation of the ch.

Clearly aspects of the political turmoil of the 2nd millennium in Palestine are here sketched in vague fashion, but the claim that Abraham is thus removed from the realm of saga to that of history is unwarranted. The account may with reason be considered either a postexilic literary product or an ancient document of uncorroborated historical value. Evidence for either view is inconclusive; explanatory glosses in vss. 2, 3, 7, 17 seem to suggest an early date for the ch., but then one would also expect to find the older name Laish instead of **Dan** in vs. 14 (cf. Judg. 18:29).

14:14-16. Abraham and his **trained men** pursue the retreating, victorious kings to the vicinity of **Dan,** rout them in a **night** attack, follow them on beyond **Damascus,** and rescue goods and captives, including **Lot.** This portrayal of Abraham as a military leader is in striking contrast to all other traditions recorded about him

14:17-24. Regarding Abraham's relationship to Jerusalem we have only the **Melchizedek** story as evidence. The account is puzzling. Vss. 18-20 interrupt the connection between vss. 17, 21-24 and stand in some contradiction to them. One wonders how Abraham can give **a tenth** of the spoil to Melchizedek and still claim (vss. 22-23) not to be taking anything belonging to **the king of Sodom.** One is also surprised to find the king of Sodom still alive after vs. 10.

Salem (cf. Ps. 76:2) is considered to be an ancient name for Jerusalem, though the Amarna tablets attest the antiquity of the full name (for another variant cf. Judg. 19:10; I Chr. 11:4). **Shaveh, ... the King's Valley** was apparently close to Jerusalem (cf. II Sam. 18:18). The name **Melchizedek** may mean either "king of righteousness" or "my king is Zedek" (cf. the similar formation of the name Adonizedek, Josh. 10:1). The recurrence of Melchizedek in Ps. 110 (which is evidently based on this passage) suggests that Melchizedek as both priest and king of Jerusalem was to be the true prototype of the ideal Davidic ruler (cf. Heb. 7).

The story may originally have told the role which the king of Jerusalem played in the defeat of the E kings, possibly as leader of the Palestinian coalition. As it stands, however, the episode may be regarded as etiological, i.e. as an explanation for the Jerusalem tithes and position of the Zadokite priesthood. It may also be symbolic. Abraham, the "friend" of God (Isa. 41:8), accepts the blessing of a Canaanite priest and accepts the priest's God as his own (vs. 22); i.e. Yahweh, God of revelation, the God of Abraham, is also to be recognized as **God Most High** (El Elyon), God of the universe, the God of Melchizedek (vs. 18).

15:1-21. God's Covenant with Abraham. The narrative, after describing Abraham's initial relationship to the land of promise, turns to a 2nd of its themes (cf. 12:1-3), the promised heir, who is necessary to Abraham's becoming the father of a great nation. Abraham has begun to possess the land (chs. 13-14), but still he has no son. Some hint of his anxiety may be implied in the vague reference **after these things,** but cf. e.g. 22:1; 40:1.

Literary analysis of the ch. is difficult because of a number of peculiarities: (a) Vss. 2, 3 are doublets. (b) The prophetic phrase **the word of the LORD came** (vss. 1, 4) occurs only here in the Pentateuch. (c) Vs. 7 seems a new introduction to the story. (d) Vs. 5 (night) contradicts vss. 12, 17 (**as the sun was going down**). We seem to have at least 2 originally distinct accounts interwoven in this ch. The first is a promise to Abraham of numerous descendants (vss. 1-6), with a possibly related prediction of their future bondage and release (vss. 13-16); the 2nd is a description of God's covenant with Abraham regarding the Promised Land (vss. 7-12, 17-21).

A fragment of the beginning of the E source is probably to be found in the first of these; but editors have interwoven it so thoroughly with other material, perhaps substituting Yahweh for E's characteristic name Elohim, that it is impossible to make a clear separation (the analysis in the table, p. 2, is only one of many that have been suggested). The portion most likely to represent E is vs. 5, in which Abraham is promised **descendants** as numerous as **the stars.** The occasion for this promise is no doubt to be found in vs. 2 or vs. 3, or parts of them. The word translated **continue** (vs. 2) is lit. "go" and has been generally taken to mean either "die" or "live," but a recent suggestion is that here it means "set out"; i.e. the E story is that while still in his original home (see below on 29:1) Abraham on receiving God's call protests, "I am setting out childless," and is reassured by the promise of vs. 5. Some scholars think the E account is continued in the prediction of vss. 13-16, or parts of it.

15:1-5. Abraham's **fear** in vs. 1 may be caused by his apprehension of Yahweh's presence, by some antecedent experience like that of ch. 14, or, if the connection with elements in the following vss. is original, by his growing despair at having no son. The prospect in vs. 3, and presumably in vs. 2 (the name **Eliezer** is textually uncertain, and **of Damascus** is impossible), is that a **slave** in his household will be his **heir.** Contracts of adoption dating from the 15th cent. found at Nuzi in Mesopotamia show that a slave was often adopted by a childless master to inherit his property. These suggest that we here have to do with an accepted legal safeguard to a man's dying intestate.

15:6. The conclusion is a comment on Abraham's faith, which Yahweh **reckoned ... to him as righteousness** (cf. Hab. 2:4 and Paul's interpretation in Rom. 4:13-25). Abraham is adjudged righteous when he accepts and affirms the divine promise. The accent rests on the state of mind which makes acts of justice and mercy (obedience) possible.

15:7-11. If the account of the covenant ritual is from J, as most scholars believe, **Ur of the Chaldeans** must be an editorial revision (see above on 11:28-30). The incident begins with Abraham's doubts about possessing the Promised Land. These doubts conflict with the preceding statement about his faith

and indicate either a different source from vss. 6 or an editorial rearrangement of material from the same source. The doubts are apparently to be stilled by the vision of the completed covenant ceremony. Abraham prepares the elements. **A heifer . . . , a she-goat . . . , and a ram,** each **three years old,** are **cut in two** and the halves placed on the ground opposite one another in 2 rows. An undivided **turtledove** in the one row and **a young pigeon,** also undivided, on the opposite side, complete the rows. The **birds of prey** which swoop **down upon the carcasses** were probably interpreted as evil omens of Israel's Egyptian bondage, though the text allows no precise interpretation of details.

15:12. God causes to fall on Abraham **a deep sleep.** The same word is used in 2:21; I Sam. 26:12; Job 4:13; 33:15; Isa. 29:10; and seems to mean a God-given trance which opens the mind to revelation and ecstasy.

15:13-16. God's extensive speech here may be an E expansion on the idea of vs. 5, as noted above, but is more generally viewed as a later interpolation, inserted to explain Israel's long bondage in Egypt. As it now stands, the passage appears to interpret the evil omen of vs. 11. The Palestinians, as the **Amorites** of vs. 16 must be understood, still have not filled to overflowing their cup of **iniquity** (cf. Lev. 18:24-30; Deut. 9:5) and Abraham's descendants must therefore wait in Egypt until judgment for Palestine is ripe. Nevertheless the stay in Egypt will not be without its benefit (vs. 14), and Abraham will himself die at a ripe **old age** in peace. The time **four hundred years** (vs. 13) does not agree with Exod. 12:40 (430 years) or with vs. 16 (**they shall come back here in the fourth generation,** i.e. 120 years). It has been suggested that vs. 13 be read "they will be oppressed four generations" and Exod. 12:40 "The time . . . in Egypt was three generations, yea four generations." This would mean a date ca. 1510-1470 for Abraham's generation. The passage is remarkable for its view of history: God rules the world according to his plan, which he reveals to Abraham and Israel; the chosen people inherit the land because of the evildoing of its former inhabitants.

15:17-18a. In his trance (vss. 12) Abraham sees **a smoking fire pot and a flaming torch** pass down the aisle formed by the divided carcasses, and the account ends with the affirmation that **on that day the Lord made** (lit. "cut") **a covenant with Abram** to give his descendants the land. This ceremony can be interpreted as being both retributive (the man who breaks the covenant will perish like the slaughtered animal; cf. Jer. 34:18-19) and sacramental (walking between the halves of the carcasses results in identification of the persons with the victim, endowing them with certain qualities which the victim is regarded as possessing). Two difficulties with such an explanation, however, are its inapplicability to Yahweh and Abraham's nonparticipation in the ritual. Since the purpose of the vision is to reassure the doubting Abraham, and since Abraham's role in the ceremony consists only in preparing the elements while Yahweh's role is not explicitly mentioned at all (only a fire passes between the pieces), the incident may have something in common with Yahweh's self-vindication in Elijah's contest with the prophets of Baal: "Then the fire of the Lord fell, . . . and . . . all the people . . . said, 'The Lord, he is God; the Lord, he is God' " (I Kings 18:20-39). It seems fairly clear that the primary significance both of the ritual and of the covenant itself is here strained, but the account suggests many questions to which at present no answers can be given. The sense is that Yahweh obligates himself to keep his promise of land to Abraham in a way which Abraham can accept with renewed confidence.

15:18b-21. The extent of the Promised Land is idealized. These boundaries were approximated only in the reigns of David and Solomon. **River of Egypt** (i.e. the Nile) is probably a scribal error for "brook of Egypt," a wadi ca. 50 miles SW of Gaza (cf. I Kings 8:65; Isa. 27:12; see color map 4). Vss. 19-21 are thought by many to be an editor's addition (cf. Exod. 3:8).

16:1-16. *The Flight of Hagar.* The Israelites acknowledged their kinship with the Ishmaelites (a name for all Arabs to the late Jews), whose presence in Palestine antedated their own; but they looked down on them as descendants of an Egyptian mother (cf. 21:21, where Ishmael marries an Egyptian wife). This people may have been part of the larger group of Hagrites (Ps. 83:6) or perhaps identical with them since 2 of Ishmael's sons (25:15) are identical with 2 of the Hagrites (I Chr. 5:19). The name **Hagar** is perhaps related to an Arabic word meaning "flee." This J story, of which the E version is found in 21:8-21 (vs. 9 provides the connecting link), records Abraham's attempt to solve the problem of his childlessness. On another level, however, it explains both Israel's relationship to her neighbors in the south, the Ishmaelites, and the sacredness of a famous well near **Kadesh** in the Negeb.

16:1-6. Sarah, despairing of having a child, gives Abraham her personal maid in the hope that through her slave she herself may become "mother" (cf. 30:3, 6). This procedure, as is known from both Hurrian and Babylonian law, was both legally and morally acceptable. When Hagar becomes pregnant she turns haughtily against her mistress (cf. Prov. 30:23). In following his wife's suggestion Abraham has apparently gained ownership of Hagar. Sarah's complaint, therefore, is that Abraham alone can deal with Hagar since she is his and justice is his responsibility. The unhappy man's reply is simply to restore to his wife her arrogant slave (vss. 5-6). Sarah thereupon makes life so miserable for the pregnant girl that she flees toward Egypt, and the question of an heir for Abraham again confronts the reader.

16:7-16. Hagar has almost reached the Egyptian frontier (**Shur;** cf. 25:18; see color map 4), when at an oasis she is confronted by the **angel** (i.e. messenger) of Yahweh—clearly a circumlocution for Yahweh himself (cf. vs. 13). The triple repetition of **the angel of the Lord** probably indicates editorial insertions in vss. 9-10. Only gradually does Hagar recognize her visitor as he reveals her condition and foretells her future. She will **bear a son,** to be called **Ishmael** ("God hears") because Yahweh has paid heed to his mother's distress. The description **a wild ass of a man** was no doubt meant to characterize Israel's seminomadic neighbors (cf. Job 39:5-8), who were a constant source of irritation (vs. 12; cf. 25:18).

16:13-14. The well where the encounter takes place was probably associated with a sanctuary (cf. 24:62; 25:11*b*) whose name **Beer-lahai-roi** could no longer be explained. The translation of vs. 13 is uncertain (see RSV footnote).

16:15-16. The original J story of Ishmael's birth, probably at the oasis, has been suppressed in favor of these laconic statements which complete the P account of vss. 1*a*, 3. In its present context the Hagar story emphasizes Abraham's apparently vain expectation of the fulfillment of God's promise and casts some light on the way Israel viewed the history of her neighboring kinsmen, the Ishmaelites (Arabs), who also worshiped Yahweh and were blessed by him.

17:1-27. *The Covenant of Circumcision.* This new account of God's covenant with Abraham belongs to P, from which we have thus far had only 2 extended accounts, the Creation and the Flood. Here the interest centers in circumcision as the sign of a new covenant between God and Abraham. The purpose is to distinguish a new era in God's self-revealing witness to his people, an era which is signified by certain changes in name as well as by the appropriation of new significance to an old rite.

17:1-8. The passage begins with a call to Abraham (cf. 15:1, 7) in which the covenant promises are stated (cf. 12:1-3), and God reveals himself as El Shaddai. The name, which is either new (so Exod. 6:3) or a familiar name which now receives special meaning for Abraham, has been variously interpreted —usually with the LXX as **God Almighty,** but recently as "God all-knowing." Either meaning would be appropriate to the context of Abraham's despair of having the promised son at his age. The command to **walk before me, and be blameless** requires that Abraham conduct himself before God in complete obedience (cf. 18:19; Deut. 10:12; Mic. 6:8); this is to be his response to God's covenant. Implied specific covenantal requirements may be sabbath observance (2:1-3), abstinence from eating blood (9:4), and circumcision (vs. 10).

Probably to avoid any suggestion of anthropomorphism, the P writers affirm that God "gives" (so lit., vs. 2) or "establishes" (vs. 7) rather than "cuts" (see above on 15:17-18*a*). The promises are (*a*) numerous descendants, (*b*) a permanent relationship of his descendants to God as God's own people, and (*c*) **all the land of Canaan, for an everlasting possession.** The change of the name **Abram** (see above on 11:20-27) to **Abraham** is probably the result of combining 2 originally independent traditions, one about Abram, the other about Abraham. The etymology in vs. 5 would produce, not the name Abraham, but rather Abhamon. The covenant clearly extends to the **nations** of Palestine (vss. 4-7; cf. 12:3) and is not meant specifically for Israel alone (but cf. vss. 20-21).

17:9-14. The sign of the covenant is to be circumcision, and perhaps this passage is intended as an interpretation of vs. 1, i.e. as man's part in the covenant. Observe the antithesis between vs. 4, which begins "As for me" (omitted in the RSV), and vs. 9, **as for you.**

Circumcision is extremely old; it is known to have been practiced in Egypt in 3000 B.C. The tradition that it was to be performed with stone knives (Exod.

4:25; Josh. 5:3) may attest its extreme antiquity. It was practiced by a number of Israel's neighbors, but not in Mesopotamia or among the Philistines.

Probably the rite began as an initiation ceremony at puberty. Its significance to the P authors as a sign of Abraham's acceptance of God's promise, and at the time of the Exile (Jer. 9:25-26) as a sign of allegiance to Yahweh, is quite different from its original cultic significance (cf. **he that is eight days old**). The authors may intend to suggest that only after Abraham's acceptance of God's covenant, signified in his own circumcision, is he eligible to receive the promised heir.

17:15-21. Inserted between the accounts of the covenant and of Abraham's obedience to it is the renaming of **Sarah** (cf. vs. 5; **Sarai** is simply an older form; see above on 11:28-30) and the promise that she will bear a **son,** which is in general parallel to the J account in 18:1-15. The name **Isaac** is associated with laughter (vs. 17; cf. 18:12; 21:6), and the name **Ishmael** is again connected with God's hearing (vs. 20; cf. 16:11). The **covenant** is not to be with Ishmael, however, but with Isaac (vs. 21).

17:22-27. The P account concludes with detailed assurance that Abraham and all males associated with him are circumcised in accordance with the covenant. Perhaps the statistic that **Ishmael was thirteen years old** reflects the customary time for circumcision among Israel's nomadic neighbors, an age more consonant with the original significance of the rite.

18:1-33. *God's Visit to Abraham at Mamre.* This resumption of the J story has properly been regarded as the immediate sequel to ch. 13 in the cluster of legends which places Abraham's dwelling in Hebron. The P narrative of ch. 17 is continued at ch. 21. Nevertheless the unity imposed on the mass of material is partially indicated by the 7-fold reiteration of the promise to Abraham (12:2; 13:16; 15:5, 18; 17:5, 15; 18:10) and the fulfillment at last in 21:1.

18:1-15. The appearance of Yahweh at midday **by the oaks of Mamre** (the men are suddenly there) is apparently unrecognized by Abraham; not until the promise of **a son** is made (vs. 10) and affirmed (vs. 14) can Abraham suspect who his visitors are. The relationship of the 3 visitors to Yahweh is difficult. Yahweh **appears** (vs. 1); but Abraham, who sees **three men** (vs. 2), addresses only one in vs. 3 (the leader?) and several in vs. 4. The men accept Abraham's hospitality (vss. 5, 8) and apparently ask together for Sarah (vs. 9), but only Yahweh speaks in vss. 10, 13. The visitors go to Sodom (all 3? vss. 20-22), but Abraham talks with Yahweh (who remains behind?). A later interpretation considers Yahweh to be one of the 3 (19:1), but clearly the tradition is confused on the point. The object of the visit is to predict the birth of a son to Sarah in 9 months (vs. 10), a promise that evokes in Sarah a **laugh** (cf. Abraham's laugh in 17:17) which she then fears to confess (vss. 15, cf. 3:9). The incident incorporates the remarkable affirmation of Yahweh's omnipotence (vs. 14).

18:16-21. Abraham accompanies the men a short way on their journey and is told that their destination is **Sodom** (vs. 16), to determine its fate (vss. 20-21). Since in vs. 17 the destruction of Sodom appears certain while in vs. 20 it will be decided after Yahweh's personal inspection, vss. 17-19 are generally considered to be an insertion. Here Yahweh proposes to tell Abraham what is about to happen in Sodom, both so that in the future, when Abraham is instructing his children, he may realize the didactic usefulness of the judgment on Sodom, and so that nothing will hinder fulfillment of Yahweh's promise to Abraham (vs. 19*b*). Abraham is thus considered a prophet (cf. Amos 3:7), and Yahweh the Lord of history.

18:22-23. The ch. concludes with Abraham's intercession for Sodom, toward which he stands looking with Yahweh from the hills E of Hebron. His problem is not primarily the fate of the city. What troubles Abraham (i.e. the author) is the ambiguity of history. Does the fate of Sodom hinge on the righteousness of the majority only? To what limits can God's mercy be pushed? What is justice? **Shall not the Judge of all the earth do right?** (vs. 25). The problem cannot be solved, but the author is satisfied to conclude that for the sake of a handful of righteous people God would spare a wicked city.

19:1-38. *The Destruction of Sodom.* The reputed wickedness of the inhabitants of Sodom (cf. 18:20) is immediately exposed in their depraved treatment of the divine messengers. Lot, who knows the customs of these city dwellers, cannot permit the strangers to pass the night unprotected from the unchaste designs of his neighbors. He is even willing to sacrifice his **daughters** for the sake of the well-being of the travelers, whom he treats as his own guests; and he is finally rescued from his plight only by the superhuman intervention of the strangers themselves (vss. 10-11). The evil of Sodom was not considered by all the OT writers to have been sodomy. Ezekiel defines it: "She . . . had pride, surfeit of food, and prosperous ease, but . . . did not aid the poor and needy" (Ezek. 16:48-50; cf. Isa. 1:10; 3:9; Jer. 23:14). This fact and the similarity of the attempted assault to the outrage at Gibeah (Judg. 19:22-26) suggest that this episode may originally have been an independent tradition. Cf. the visitors' reception by Abraham (18:2-8) and by Lot (vss. 1-3), also the effect of their message on Sarah (18:12) and on Lot's sons-in-law (vs. 14). The judgment apparently is to be accomplished at sunrise (vs. 23), and Lot therefore has to hasten the escape of his family.

19:15-29. The city of **Zoar** is traditionally located SE of the Dead Sea (see color map 3). The episode in vss. 17-22 is usually considered a later addition to the original story, with vs. 30*a*, which seems slightly to contradict vs. 21, a transitional, harmonizing gloss. The statement about Lot's wife (vs. 26) is clearly etiological; it was suggested by the strange pillars found everywhere in the vicinity of the Dead Sea and explains in all probability one pillar which remarkably resembled a human female figure. The story of destruction of the **cities, and all the valley** (vss. 24-28), which perhaps was considered to have resulted in the formation of the Dead Sea (cf. 13:10; 14:3, 10), may contain a recollection of some natural catastrophe; but the occurrence in folklore of the motif of angel visitation prior to catastrophic destruction suggests a mythological rather than a historical origin of the story. Abraham, 40 miles away near Hebron, could see the signs of the disaster.

19:30-38. One further incident in Lot's story (chs. 13; 18-19) remains to be told. Alone with his 2 unmarried and childless daughters in a cave in the hills E of Zoar, Lot is victimized by them and becomes the father of their sons, **Moab** and **Ammon.** The etymologies (*ab*, "father"; *am*, "people") are linguistically false. The story may have been told originally to show Israelite contempt for E neighbors. It has also been suggested in the light of vs. 31, **there is not a man on earth to come in to us,** that in the original account a universal catastrophe had occurred, in which all mankind except Lot and his daughters had perished, and that the women resorted to this expedient to repopulate the earth. In its present context, however, the account summarizes Lot's bankruptcy.

20:1-18. *Abraham and Sarah at Gerar.* This E narrative—the first material of any length from this source—about Abraham and Sarah at Gerar (SE of Gaza; see color map 3; cf. 10:19; 26:1) clearly resembles the J account of Abraham and Sarah in Egypt (12:10-20). Certain ambiguities of the earlier story have here been removed (cf. vss. 4, 12, 16) and the moral offensiveness is thereby softened. The E author is concerned with the problem of guilt (both Abraham's, vss. 11-12, and Abimelech's, vss. 4-5, 16), and no doubt the editor included the story at this point as an appropriate sequel to the determination of Sodom's guilt and the question of God's righteousness. Abimelech's question, **LORD, wilt thou slay an innocent people?** is reminiscent of Abraham's dialogue with God in 18:22-32. Certainly Abraham's honor is tarnished, in spite of the author's attempts at extenuation. The story may reveal Israel's early awareness that her life in the world was not one of exemplary piety, in spite of her conviction that she was God's chosen people, and that some of her "heathen" neighbors were also God-fearing (vs. 11), to Israel's shame and humiliation (vs. 6). Abraham, the **prophet** (vs. 7), appears morally inferior to the God-fearing non-Israelite king; and God mercifully preserves both Sarah's honor and Abimelech's innocence. Technically a compromising incident is whitewashed, but the moral problems of the dilemma are emphasized with uncompromising exposure.

It seems fairly obvious that a familiar story was variously used in the religious and literary circles of Israel to emphasize aspects of Israel's history. In 12:10-20 it emphasizes Yahweh's omnipotent purpose in spite of Abraham's departure from the Promised Land. In this ch. the account struggles with the problem of guilt and righteousness. The final occurrence of the story (26:6-11), perhaps its oldest version, indicates some of the difficulties Isaac found in settling in Palestine.

21:1-7. *The Birth of Isaac.* The story of Isaac's birth is a conflate of the 3 sources J, E, P (to E belongs only vs. 6*a*) and brings together the narrative threads of chs. 17-18. The motif of **laughter** which has dominated the story is here finely developed as a sign of unexpected joy (vs. 6*a*) finally replacing skeptical incredulity (17:17; 18:12). The neighbors' laughter (vs. 6*b*) need not be considered the result of jesting; they too will rejoice with the happy parents.

21:8-21. *The Expulsion of Ishmael.* The story of Ishmael's expulsion from Abraham's household is the E version of the J account in ch. 16. Whereas J placed the event before Ishmael's birth, E has it at the time Isaac is **weaned** (i.e. when he is about 3 years old; cf. II Macc. 7:27) and thinks of Hagar's son, who has not yet been named (see below on vss. 15-21), as only slightly older (vss. 14-16), in contrast with P's statistics (vs. 5; cf. 16:16; 17:25), which make Ishmael 14 years older than Isaac. Sarah discovers the 2 children playing together, and the sight of this equality of status angers the jealous mother. There is no need to suspect the slave's son of any unchaste or arrogant behavior (cf. Gal. 4:29); in Sarah's eyes he threatens her son's position and therefore must go. Abraham's indignation at his wife's demand is removed by God's approval of Sarah and promise of the future of **the son of the slave woman.**

21:15-21. The skillful account of the child's desert plight and rescue originally also included his naming (vs. 17; cf. 16:11). He becomes the ancestor of the Ishmaelites, here represented as living S of the Negeb (see comments on 12:9; 25:12-18 and color map 4). Thus the narrative has disposed of another of Israel's related neighbors, and the central concern with Abraham's own freeborn son (cf. Gal. 4:30) can be developed further.

The responsibility which rests on the bearer of the promise (12:1-3) to be the agent of divine blessing is steadily emphasized, as all human considerations of deserving are stripped one by one from Abraham, Sarah, Isaac, Jacob, and even Joseph. God's inexplicable and vaguely apprehended purpose in history becomes an object in turn of incredulity, despair, outrage, joy, and hope as human values seem overturned; and the bearers of promise are more and more enjoined to follow Abraham, who believed God in spite of everything.

21:22-34. The Covenant with Abimelech. The section concerning Abraham and Abimelech can be separated into 2 distinct narratives. One account (vss. 22-24, 27, 31, 34) which concerns Abimelech's anxiety to make an agreement with Abraham to insure his continued loyalty, is the sequel to the E story of ch. 20 and concludes with an explanation of the place name **Beer-sheba** as the well (**beer**) where the oath (**sheba**) was made. The other (vss. 25-26, 28-30, 32-33), apparently from J, concerns the settlement of a dispute **about a well;** it concludes by identifying Beer-sheba as the well where Abimelech received **seven** (another meaning of *sheba*) **ewe lambs** guaranteeing Abraham access to the water forever (cf. 26:33). **Beer-sheba,** located in the Negeb *ca.* 50 miles SW of Jerusalem (see color map 3) was a famous sacred place, devoted to the **Everlasting God** (vs. 33; cf. 26:25; Amos 5:5; 8:14). **Philistines** is an anachronism, as this people did not enter Palestine till the time of Joshua or later.

22:1-19. Abraham's Temptation to Sacrifice Isaac. The story of what we must call the brutal trial of Abraham's faith is a literary masterpiece. In this simple, moving account Abraham appears indeed as the father of the faithful. The trial of his faith involved in God's command that he sacrifice **your son, your only son Isaac, whom you love,** marks the climax of the Abraham cycle of stories. With fine perception it has been said that Abraham had to cut himself off from his entire past when he left his homeland and now is summoned to give up his entire future. The testing goes to the heart of his life, his hope for meaning, and his trust in Yahweh;

he is asked to give up the child of his old age, on whose life the fulfillment of God's promise depends.

God's incredible command and Abraham's unwavering obedience are bearable only because the reader knows the situation is a trial: **God tested Abraham** (vs. 1); **now I know that you fear God** (vs. 12). An inescapable conclusion is that Abraham's fear of God is revealed in his steadfast obedience, whether or not it results in his son's death. Isaac's deliverance neither invalidates Abraham's act nor serves as his reward (as suggested in the later addition, vss. 15-19) for risking everything. The thought is close to Paul's on justification by faith (Rom. 4; cf. Heb. 11:17-22; Jas. 2:21).

22:1-14. The original story, which belongs to E, consists of these vss. It may have been told to explain the substitution of animal for human sacrifice at some cultic center, the name of which is now lost. The words of vs. 14 are explanatory, but they do not yield the original place name. The Hebrew has been reconstructed and rendered "Abraham called the name of that place Jeruel [cf. II Chr. 20:16], for he said, 'Today, in this mountain, God provides.'" This suggestion is the best we have, but the name of the cultic center cannot be satisfactorily determined.

References to human sacrifice in the OT indicate that the Hebrews knew and practiced it (see comment on Deut. 18:9-14). Mesha of Moab caused the Israelite armies to withdraw by sacrificing his son in their presence (II Kings 3:27); Ahaz sacrificed his son (II Kings 16:3); and all Israel is accused of practicing this barbarity (II Kings 17:17). The sacrifice of Jephthah's daughter (Judg. 11:29-40) and Hiel's sons (I Kings 16:34) are additional instances (cf. II Kings 21:6; 23:10; Isa. 57:5; Jer. 7:31; etc.). The prophetic reflection on proper worship of God is perhaps best summarized in Mic. 6:6-8; but the narrative in its present context is best interpreted, not as illustrating general truths about child sacrifice or surrender of the will, but rather as describing the supreme test of Abraham's life.

22:2. The **land of Moriah** (vs. 2) cannot be identified. On the basis of II Chr. 3:1 the place where Isaac was spared is often said to be the hill in Jerusalem on which the temple was later built. This, however, does not accord with the specification here of a **land** containing several **mountains,** or with the fact that Jerusalem was already settled in Abraham's time (cf. 14:18). Perhaps the text has been corrupted from an original "land of the Amorites" (cf. 10:16, where Canaan is father of the Amorites).

22:20-24. The Genealogy of Nahor. This J genealogy has probably been included here to prepare for the story in ch. 24. The names of Nahor's 12 sons—like those of Ishmael's 12 sons (25:13-16), Esau's (36:15-19), and Jacob's—represent tribes or tribal territories. They are located in Aram, NE of Palestine, i.e. in either N Syria or the Syro-Arabian desert. **Bethuel,** Rebekah's father (cf. 24:15, 24, 47), is Nahor's son; but Laban, Rebekah's brother (24:29; 25:20; 28:2), is also Nahor's son (29:5; but cf. 28:5, where Laban and Rebekah are both children of Bethuel). At least 2 traditions appear to have been confused, one about Bethuel's children from Haran and the other about Nahor's from NW Arabia.

23:1-20. Abraham's Purchase of a Grave for Sarah.
The account of Abraham's purchase from the Hittites of a grave for his family is generally credited to the P tradition and is the 4th extensive narrative in Gen. from this source (see above on 17:1-27).

23:2. The burial site was near **Kiriath-arba,** later known as **Hebron** (cf. Josh. 14:15; Judg. 1:10). The name may mean "city of 4 [quarters]" or, as legend suggests, the city of the person Arba (Josh. 15:13).

23:3. The mention of **Hittites** has usually been considered an anachronism, but continued research indicates that isolated Hittite settlements may have been made in S Palestine early in the 2nd millennium. Nevertheless references in Gen. to pre-Israelite inhabitants of Palestine suggest that the term "Hittite" is often a vague designation for "Palestinian" in P as are the terms "Canaanite" in J and "Amorite" in E (cf. Ezek. 16:3, 45).

23:4-11. The negotiations for the sale of the property are illuminated by a passage from a Hittite legal code found in Turkey, according to which the possession of property carried definite feudal obligations unless only a part of it was transferred. This may explain Abraham's original request for only the **cave** and Ephron's insistence that Abraham purchase the entire **field.**

23:12-16. The **silver** is **weighed out** on a balance, with shekel weights of stone or metal in the other

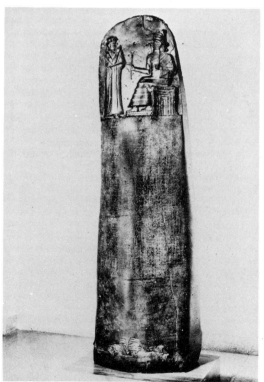

Courtesy of the Oriental Institute, University of Chicago

Hammurabi's laws, predated by Hebrew law *ca.* 150 yrs.

pan. Archaeologists have discovered many such weights. Perhaps **current among the merchants** refers to some sort of weight standard (see "Measures and Money," pp. 1283-85). The price is no doubt

meant to be understood as exorbitant (cf. Jer. 32:9).

23:17-18. The final transaction is precisely recorded, the property described, and the witnesses attested in contractual, legal terms. **Machpelah,** derived perhaps from a word meaning "double," seems to refer to the district rather than to the cave only (cf. vs. 9).

23:19-20. The interest of the P authors in this transaction is difficult to determine. Nothing indicates either that the place was considered sacred, unless it be connected with **Mamre** (cf. 13:18), or that the story was told to settle a dispute about who owned the cave. The theory that Abraham's purchase of this piece of "promised land" was a pledge of the future possession of the entire land by Abraham's descendants is scarcely satisfactory. The story reemphasizes Abraham's faith in God's promise, which goes unrewarded (cf. Acts 7:5; Heb. 11: 13); at the end he possesses a grave.

24:1-67. Isaac's Marriage to Rebekah. The charming story about the arrangement for Rebekah's marriage to Isaac is usually attributed to J, though several discrepancies in the account suggest a conflation of variant traditions. Twice **Laban** goes out to meet **Abraham's servant** (vss. 29*b*, 30*b*). The relatives agree to the servant's request (vs. 51), but later Rebekah is given freedom of choice (vss. 57-58). In vs. 59 Rebekah is accompanied by her **nurse,** in vs. 61*a* by **her maidens.** These and other inconsistencies, however, do not seriously mar the story, much less prove the existence of original parallel accounts.

24:1-9. Abraham's concern that his son not marry a Canaanite woman but obtain a wife from his father's family is not simply an example of normal oriental custom. Rather it must be understood as the aged Abraham's final act of faith in God's promise. His demand for an oath indicates that he expects to die before his steward returns. It is not unlikely that an account of his death was originally a part of this story but was removed by an editor in favor of the P account in 25:7-11. The practice of swearing by the genital organ (vs. 2; cf. 47:29) was doubtless an ancient custom, the significance of which had been forgotten at the time the story was incorporated into Gen.—or else was so well known that no interpretation was considered needed. Abraham's will is that (*a*) Isaac shall marry only a girl from his relatives in the land from which he came (see above on 11:28-30), and (*b*) Isaac shall not go to that land. He is convinced that God himself will choose Isaac's wife and prosper his servant's journey (vs. 7; cf. vss. 21, 42, 56).

24:10-27. On **camels** see above on 12:16. **Mesopotamia** translates the Hebrew *Aram-naharaim,* "Aram of the 2 rivers," i.e. the Aramean or NW part of Mesopotamia, called Paddan-aram in the P source (e.g. 25:20). **The city of Nahor** is presumably Haran (cf. 29:4-5; but see above on 11:20-27). With the meeting at the well cf. the stories of Jacob and Rachel (29:2-12) and Moses and Zipporah (Exod. 2:15*c*-17). Abraham's trust in Yahweh is echoed and confirmed by the faith of his steward (vss. 12, 21, 27).

24:28-51. The reference to **her mother's household** and the fact that **Laban** takes the lead in hospitality, as well as later in the negotiations for Rebekah's departure (vss. 55-59), suggest that her father is to be understood as no longer living, and that **and Bethuel** in vs. 50 is a later insertion. This narrative may preserve a tradition about a later wave of settlement in Canaan, an Aramean wave represented in the Jacob stories, which supplemented the first migration described in the Abraham saga. Since Laban figures so prominently here and in Jacob's attempts to find a wife, it seems likely that this story is intended to provide the link between the Abraham cycle of stories and the Jacob, or Aramean, cycle. The steward's statement that Abraham **has given all that he has to Isaac** (vs. 36; cf. 25:5) confirms the implication that Abraham is to die before his return.

24:52-61. Oriental custom would call for a period of celebration of the betrothal before Rebekah's departure. The steward's insistence on returning at once points up his fear that Abraham may not survive his journey. The bridal blessing (vs. 60) corresponds to oriental custom (cf. Ruth 4:11-12). It is reflected in the late addition of 22:17.

24:62-67. The details of the conclusion to the story are obscured by several textual corruptions. Isaac has apparently moved (from Hebron?) to **Beer-lahai-roi** (cf. 25:11b). There, while out for an evening stroll, he meets the returning caravan and his bride. The steward's identification of him as **my master** again indicates that Abraham's expected death has occurred and suggests that originally the marriage with Rebekah **comforted** Isaac, not for **his mother's death,** but for his father's. Because of the uncertain text, however, this suggested reconstruction is only a conjecture.

25:1-6. Abraham's Descendants by Keturah. This passage, a distinct element in the traditions about Abraham, is a footnote to the main narrative. It is probably from J; but Abraham's marriage to another wife and the naming of his descendants born of her does not follow easily after ch. 24, nor does an earlier position for it fit with the uniqueness of Isaac's birth (cf. 15:3-4; 18:10-12). The passage preserves a tradition about Israel's relationship to her neighbors on the SE, on the borders of the N Arabian desert. Perhaps the name **Keturah,** almost identical with the Hebrew word for "incense," contains an allusion to the trade in frankincense carried on among Arabia, Palestine, and Egypt. Vss. 5, 11b may be fragments from a J account of Abraham's death originally part of ch. 24 (cf. 24:36, 62; see above on 24:1-9).

25:7-11. The Death of Abraham. According to the P source Abraham dies 100 years after his entrance into the Promised Land (cf. 12:4b). He is buried in the family grave by **Isaac and Ishmael.** The sons of Keturah are not present, and Ishmael's presence does not accord with the E story of his expulsion (ch. 21). God's blessing is reserved for Isaac (vs. 11a). On vs. 11b see above on vss. 1-6.

25:12-18. Ishmael's Genealogy. The P genealogy of Ishmael, like those of Nahor, Esau, and Jacob, consists of 12 members. The known tribes and places in vss. 13-15 indicate a territory covering most of N Arabia; but possibly the Hebrews used the name "Ishmaelites," not of a specific tribal group, but of bedouin in general. Vs. 18 may be the conclusion to the suppressed J story of Ishmael's birth (cf. 16:7, 12; see above on 16:15-16).

B. THE STORY OF JACOB (25:19-36:43)

The Jacob stories—i.e. the story of **the descendants of Isaac** (25:19; cf. "the history of the family of Jacob," 37:2a)—comprises the next large body of material in Gen. Aside from ch. 26, which may be called the Isaac story, and ch. 36, which contains Edomite genealogies, the saga of Jacob is related in 25:19-36:43.

The material may be divided conveniently though inaccurately into 3 cycles: (a) Jacob and Esau, (b) Jacob and Laban, and (c) Jacob's return to Canaan. Several cult legends interspersed throughout the material cannot easily be integrated into the tripartite scheme. The saga is unified by a strong biographical interest which is not so evident in the Abraham stories. Whereas Abraham emerges as an ideal figure rather than a historical person, Jacob is clearly an individual, the "real Israel" as opposed to the "ideal Israel" (S. H. Hooke). The stories may reflect historical traditions about Israel's relations with her neighbors, the Edomites on the S and the Arameans on the N.

25:19-28. The Birth of Esau and Jacob. Except vss. 19-20 and the notice in vs. 26d about Isaac's age, which are from P, the account of the twins' birth comes from J.

25:20. Noteworthy is the divergence between P and J in the genealogy of **Bethuel.** P considers him an **Aramean,** i.e. a descendant of Aram, the brother of Arpachshad (10:22), who is the ancestor of Abraham (11:10-27). J considers Bethuel to be Abraham's nephew (22:20-23), his brother Nahor's son (but see above on 22:20-24). On **Paddan-aram** see above on 24:10-27.

25:21-24. Rebekah, like Sarah (11:30) and Rachel (29:31), is **barren;** and it is only in answer to Isaac's pleading that Yahweh grants her children. The activity in her womb during pregnancy leads Rebekah, fearing perhaps an evil omen, to consult Yahweh at a sacred shrine (Beer-sheba? cf. 21:33; 26:23-25). There she receives an oracle proclaiming that she will bear twins who will become **two** rival **nations,** the **younger** and **stronger** (?) of which will dominate the elder (cf. 27:40; II Sam. 8:14; Rom. 9:10-12).

25:25-28. The nations are characterized in their ancestors: Esau, **red** (a play on "Edom") and **hairy** (a play on "Seir," the mountain range SE of the Dead Sea where the Edomites lived; see color map 4), is a clever **hunter.** Jacob (here connected with the noun **heel** and the related verb "overreach"), grasping for first place, is a civilized herdsman. Actually the name "Jacob" is extremely old, meaning probably "God protects" (Yaqob-el).

25:29-34. Jacob Acquires Esau's Birthright. The story of the birthright, which continues the J account, doubtless delighted the descendants of Jacob with pride in the way their ancestor outwitted the Edomite ancestor, Esau. It has been suggested that Esau may have thought he was bargaining for some kind of magical stew and learned of his brother's treachery (cf. 27:36) only when he discovered the prized dish to be nothing but lentil soup. The precise significance of the birthright is not clear from this passage. The presupposition is that it gave the firstborn claim to a double share of his father's property, as is known from Assyrian law (cf. Deut. 21:15-17), as well as the leadership of the tribe. Clearly, however, Jacob becomes the bearer of God's promise to Abraham.

26:1-35. Traditions About Isaac. The cluster of Isaac traditions contained in this ch. is attributed to J, except for the account of Esau's Hittite wives (vss. 34-35), which is from P. Most of the episodes are closely parallel to stories already related of Abraham. The story of Isaac and Rebekah in **Gerar** (vss. 1, 6-16) duplicates 12:10-16; 20:1-18; the renewal of God's promise (vss. 2-5) is similar to 12:2-3, 7; 15:7; 22:17; and the incident about the **wells** (vss. 17-33) is like 21:22-34. Why these duplicates exist cannot be explained. If there once was an extensive cycle of Isaac legends, it has been largely lost in favor of the Abraham cycle. Yahweh blesses Isaac **for Abraham's sake** (vss. 3, 5, 24). Nevertheless the revelation at **Beer-sheba** (vss. 23-25) is recorded as though Isaac were the discoverer of the sacred place (cf. 21:33), and in vs. 33 its name receives yet another etymology (cf. 21:25-32).

26:34-35. This P notice about Esau's wives is out of accord not only with the narrative in ch. 27 (where he is still an unmarried member of Isaac's household) but even with 36:1-3, which also comes from the P tradition. It leads into the P account of Jacob's leaving home (27:46–28:9; see comment).

27:1-45. Jacob's Theft of Isaac's Blessing. The story of the treacherous deception perpetrated by Rebekah and Jacob on the blind and aged Isaac appears to be a conflation of parallel narratives from J and E. The most striking evidence of at least 2 original accounts is the doublet in vss. 44b, 45a. There have been many proposed analyses of these sources, with fair agreement on certain elements— e.g. that the smell of Esau's garments is from J while the hairy kidskins are from E—but the strands are too closely interwoven for precise separation. This narrative is the continuation from either 25:28 or 25:34. Since there appear to be 2 traditions about Esau's home territory—one (J, P) considering him the ancestor of the Edomites (25:29-34; 36:9), the other (E) apparently placing him in Transjordan, (vss. 39-40; chs. 32–33)—the precise relationship between the traditions of this story and 25:21-34 cannot be determined.

Five superbly drawn scenes reveal the depths of hostility and bitterness in Isaac's family (vss. 1-5a, 5b-17, 18-29, 30-40, 41-45). His determination to bless his favorite son is foiled by Rebekah's skillful courage (vs. 13) and Jacob's blasphemous audacity (vss. 20, 24, 27), and in the end he finds himself in effect cursing Esau (vss. 39-40). The blessing, once given, is irrevocable and effective, an objective, independent reality; and Isaac is incapable of providing a remedy for his unwitting role in the monstrous crime (vs. 37). The animosity between Edom and Israel is unmistakably attested in the OT (cf. e.g. Ps. 137:7). David conquered Edom and made it a vassal state (II Sam. 8:14), but Edom won its independence from Israel in the mid-9th cent. (II Kings 8:22).

Moral judgments are absent from the story. The drama is enacted in its tragic dimensions, with no suggestion that any member of the family is mindful of or unduly concerned with God's promise to Abraham. Humor and pathos are skillfully blended in

the stark revelation of Jacob's character, Rebekah's reckless cunning, Esau's joy in the chase, and the manipulation of Isaac over which he is helpless. The compiler almost seems to suggest that the righteous Abraham never found a worthy successor, that Israel's history moved between the poles of faithful obedience to divine summons and the crassest self-seeking and irresponsibility. No one in the story can escape condemnation; but also in God's providence the more reprehensible, less likable brother becomes the bearer of promise, while the victimized, legitimate heir is passed over without recognition or recourse. The story can be interpreted as an illustration of God's providence which overarches and comprehends in its purpose both the best and worst that men can do (cf. 50:20).

27:46–28:9. Jacob's Departure. This section from the P material continues the notice at 26:34-35 about Esau's marriage to **Hittite women** which distresses Isaac and Rebekah. Jacob is sent away, therefore, not to escape Esau's anger as in vss. 41-45, but rather to find a suitable wife among his mother's relatives (cf. the note about **Bethuel,** 25:19-20). Esau's hostility to Jacob is ignored in this account. On **Paddan-aram** see above on 24:10-27. Isaac invokes on Jacob God's blessing of Abraham (cf. 17:4-8). Esau, in an attempt to please his father too, marries another wife (cf. 36:3) from his father's family. The reference to **Ishmael** may recall tribal kinship between Edomites and Ishmaelites (see above on 16:1-16).

28:10-22. Jacob's Dream at Bethel. The Bethel story, which appears to be a conflate of J (vss. 10,

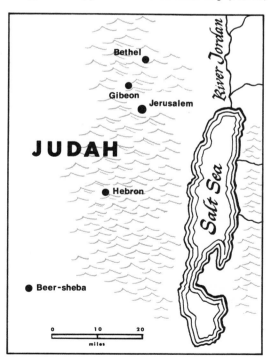

13-16, 19) and E (vss. 11-12, 17-18, 20-22, with a later insertion in vs. 21b) traditions, continues the narrative of 27:45.

28:11-12. The vision of the **ladder** (more accurately "stairway" or "ramp") **to heaven** suggests a Mesopotamian temple tower (ziggurat; see ill. on p. 10), at whose summit, which was accessible by a ramp, the god was supposed to dwell. The story, therefore, tells how Jacob accidentally (vs. 11a) discovers the place where God's **angels** (i.e. messengers) set out upon earth on their divinely appointed missions (cf. John 1:51).

28:13-16. God renews his promise to Jacob as previously he has given it to Abraham (13:14-17) and Isaac (26:1-5).

28:17-22. Originally the narrative explained the sanctity of a **pillar** at Bethel—it marked the place where Jacob saw in a dream **the gate of heaven** and received a manifestation of God (cf. 35:1-15). Jacob's great strength, attested in his single-handed

Courtesy of Herbert G. May

Sacred pillars in a sanctuary at Gebal, 18th cent. B.C.; cf. the pillar erected by Jacob at Bethel

erection of this monolith, must have been legendary (cf. 29:10; 32:25-26). On **Bethel** see above on 12:8.

29:1-14. Jacob's Arrival at Laban's House. The cycle of stories about Jacob and Laban (chs. 29-31) preserves traditions about Israel's relationship with her NE kinsmen. Its context is Jacob's search for a wife among his mother's Aramean kinfolk, and the cycle concludes with Jacob's return to the Land of Promise (31:13).

29:1. The goal of Jacob's journey according to J was Haran (28:10) and according to P was Paddan-aram (28:7), but in this vs., which probably continues the E account of 28:20-22, it is **the land of the people of the east.** This designation and the speed with which Jacob later arrives with his flocks in Gilead (Transjordan) after leaving Laban (31:22-23) suggest that the setting for this cycle of stories in the E traditions is not NW Mesopotamia but Aramean territory somewhere in the Syrian desert (cf. 22:20-24). The stories reflect the movement of the Arameans over NW Mesopotamia and NW Arabia in the 14th cent.

29:2-14. This story of Jacob's arrival at his uncle's house is usually attributed to J. The **well in the field** is quite different from the well "outside the city" of ch. 24. Evidently a cistern, it is covered by a large **stone,** which is to be removed only when all who are entitled to draw water are present—both to help in lifting the stone and to avoid any unfair access to the limited supply of water. Jacob is able to lift the stone by himself (cf. 28:18; 32:25-26).

29:15-30. Jacob's Marriages. Though some consider these vss. a continuation of the preceding J account, the implication in vs. 15 that Jacob has already started serving Laban and especially the new introduction of Rachel in vs. 16 suggest that the editor has here shifted to the E account. This coarse story about how the cunning Jacob is outwitted by his scheming uncle is a fitting sequel to the account of Jacob's own trickery. Jacob is unable to pay the bride price (for the custom cf. e.g. I Sam. 18:25) and offers to work for Rachel **seven years.** Laban's reply to Jacob's proposal is noncommittal (vs. 19). Seven years later on the wedding night the heavily veiled bride, **Leah** (meaning "cow") instead of **Rachel** (meaning "ewe"), is escorted to Jacob, who discovers the shameless deception only in the morning. He is then obliged to conclude the week of festivity before he can marry Rachel, for whose hand he obligates himself to another 7 years' service. Laban's reason is that **the younger** Rachel cannot be given in marriage **before the first-born,** Leah (vs. 26). The parentheses in vss. 24, 29 are generally considered insertions from P, though a similar statement about assignment of a slave girl to a bride in a Nuzi tablet (see above on 15:1-5) has been cited as evidence that these notices may have been part of the original tradition.

29:31–30:24. The Birth of Jacob's Children. That this narrative is a conflation of the J and E source is evident from the varying divine names and the duplicate explanations of the names of Issachar, Zebulun, and Joseph. The account undoubtedly preserves traditions about Israel's tribal history. It has been suggested that this bit of family history symbolizes a new Aramean influx into Canaan, there to be united with the earlier migration symbolized by Abraham (see above on 24:28-51). Eleven sons return with Jacob from Aramean territory; only Benjamin is born in Canaan (35:16-21). The order in which the sons are listed may be traditional: first 4 sons of Leah (29:31-35), then 4 sons of Jacob's concubines (30:4-13), 2 more sons of Leah (30:17-20), a daughter (vs. 21), and finally Joseph of Rachel (31:23-24). Cf. ch. 49; Num. 26. Whether this arrangement indicates superior and inferior tribes or has some other significance is unknown. The explanations attached to the names are not and probably were not meant to be strictly etymological. The series is rather a sort of game with words which derives its point from the rivalry between Leah and Rachel, Jacob's neglected and cherished wives.

30:1-13. Rachel's demand for children leads her to a solution similar to Sarah's (cf. 16:2), but Jacob is not as understanding as Abraham (vs. 2). Leah also follows the same custom.

30:14-24. In spite of Rachel's preferential status before Jacob (vs. 15) she does not bear children, even with the aid of **mandrakes,** thought to be a stimulant to conception. Perhaps Joseph's birth was originally related to her eating of the mandrakes (cf. vs. 22, **then God remembered Rachel**).

Jacob's sons, who are to become the fathers of the chosen people, are conceived in passionate rivalry and bitterness, born of preferred and despised wives and concubines, in startling fulfillment of God's promise to make of Abraham a great nation. The sons and daughter are said to be born within the brief span of only 7 years (cf. 29:20; 30:25; 31:41).

30:25-43. Jacob's Wealth. After 14 years of service for his wives Jacob is ready to go home. Laban, however, wants him to stay. The 2 clever and mistrusting men therefore strike a bargain. The doublets such as vss. 25, 26, the discrepancy between vss. 33, 35, and the difficulty of vs. 40 reveal the composite nature of this narrative (J and E). For this reason the precise terms of the bargain are not clear.

30:31-36. According to vss. 32-34 Jacob is to receive at once as his wage for a further term of service all the speckled sheep and goats and all the black lambs from Laban's flocks, presumably a small number among the generally white sheep and black goats (cf. Song of S. 4:1-2). According to vss. 35-36, however, Laban does not give these animals to Jacob but entrusts them to his own sons, whom he sends away a distance of three days' travel; and he places Jacob in charge of the normally colored animals. The agreement therefore turns out to be that all the abnormally colored offspring born to the normally colored animals in Jacob's care will belong to Jacob.

30:37-43. What appears as a bargain favorable to Laban is turned by Jacob to his own advantage through skillful breeding technique. Laban's distance from Jacob keeps him ignorant of Jacob's stratagem and eventual flight (31:22). Thus Jacob becomes wealthy.

31:1-42. Jacob's Flight from Laban. The story of Jacob's departure from Laban, though composite, as revealed by the doublets (vss. 1, 3 from J and vss. 2, 13 from E) and the P name **Paddan-aram** (vs. 18), is essentially from E. Both human and divine causes motivate his return to Canaan, indications of the narrator's interpretation of history.

31:4-16. The pious, honest Jacob of this ch. ill accords with the scheming, wily man of chs. 29-30. Clearly another conception of the man is here presupposed. Jacob's trickery is bypassed in this narrative in favor of an assertion of God's activity on Jacob's behalf (vss. 5b, 7b, 9, 11-13, 16). The wives speak (vs. 16) as though they were Laban's sole heirs. Jacob requires their consent to accompany him to Canaan to avoid legal difficulties (cf. vss. 26, 29, 43), since his wives are still considered members of the household of Laban, who must be induced to give them up (cf. vss. 31, 43; also the case of Timnah, who remains at home after her marriage to Samson, Judg. 14:2–15:1). The daughters' complaint that Laban has spent the bride price (vs. 15) seems to imply that Laban owes them the equivalent of Jacob's 14 years of service. For Jacob's vow at **Bethel** (vs. 13) cf. 28:18-22.

31:17-20. Jacob chooses the busy shearing season, which normally culminated in a feast (cf. I Sam. 25: 8; II Sam. 13:23-29), as the opportune time for his flight. The significance of Rachel's theft (vs. 19) of her father's **household gods** (teraphim; cf. I Sam. 19: 13-17; Ezek. 21:21) is not unmistakably clear. A Mesopotamian document of adoption from Nuzi (see above on 15:1-5) suggests that the possessor of these images was the legitimate heir to the family property. This explanation would account for both Laban's agitation at losing the images and Jacob's decree of death for the discovered offender (vss. 30-35).

31:21-25. The distance of the **hill country of**

Gilead on the E of the Jordan from the closest point beyond the **Euphrates** (vs. 21) is some 300 miles, and from Haran nearly 100 miles farther (see color map 7). Since Jacob could not drive his flocks this distance in 10 days (vss. 22-23; cf. 33:13-14) the phrase about crossing the Euphrates is probably a bit from the J account inserted in the E narrative. E's short time for the journey fits with the evidence of 29:1 (see comment) that this tradition located Laban's home in NW Arabia.

31:26-42. Laban overtakes Jacob and accuses him both of wrongfully taking away his daughters and grandchildren (see above on vss. 1-16) and of stealing his household gods (see above on vss. 17-25). Rachel saves herself from being discovered with the latter and in the process renders the idols temporarily unclean (cf. Lev. 15:19-24). Thus Laban is tricked, and Jacob in his long speech (vss. 36-42) emerges as a faithful and generous servant unjustly treated (cf. Exod. 22:9-11).

31:43-55. Jacob's Covenant with Laban. Laban yields his claims, and the 2 men agree on a formal compact, which they confirm by setting up a monument. This formality seems unrelated to the situation in the narrative (note the abrupt transition from vs. 43 to vs. 44); and the doublets, which are obvious despite considerable editorial harmonizing, indicate the incorporation of 2 independent traditions about a landmark in the hill country between the Yarmuk and Jabbok rivers E of the Jordan (see color map 1).

One tradition concerns a **heap** (cairn) of **stones** (vs. 46), which according to J is named **Galeed** (probably meant to be the source of the name Gilead, vs. 48) and is the **witness** to Laban's permitting his daughters to leave his household (see above on vss. 1-16) in return for Jacob's promise to treat them well and marry no rival wives (vs. 50). Since the 2 men have been speaking the same language all along, vs. 47 (see RSV footnotes; contrast vs. 48b) is probably a later insertion. Vs. 50b probably should read: "When no man of (father's) kin is watching, God will be witness."

The other tradition concerns a treaty setting a territorial boundary (vs. 52; see above on vss. 17-25 and 29:1-14), which according to E is marked by a **pillar** (vs. 45; cf. 28:18) located at **Mizpah** (vs. 49), probably a play on the Hebrew word for "pillar," *mazzebah*. The men seal their compact by a sacred meal (vs. 54; cf. vs. 46), each invoking his own god (vs. 53) to witness the agreement and punish any violation of the boundary by the other. Thus a definite break is made between Jacob (the Israelites) and Laban (the Arameans).

32:1-23. Jacob's Preparation to Meet Esau. Having concluded the Jacob-Laban cycle of stories, the compiler returns to the Jacob-Esau cycle. Jacob's preparations for meeting with his brother reveal his wealth, his uneasy conscience, and his awareness of the need for reconciliation before his own future in Canaan can be secure. The story may reflect some of the tensions with bordering nomadic people attending the Aramean migratory moves into Palestine, but the compiler's main interest lies in Jacob's awakening consciousness of his relationship to the God of his fathers (vss. 9-12).

32:1-2. Jacob's return to his own territory according to E is marked by an encounter with God's angels (i.e. messengers; cf. 28:12), the meaning of which seems to be that Jacob is now again in God's realm. It is uncertain whether the explanation of the name **Mahanaim** (the dual form of the word for "camp," "company," or "army") is based on the 2 groups of God's and Jacob's attendants or simply on the divine **army.** The site of this city, so important in Israel's history (cf. II Sam. 2:8 ff.; 17:8 ff.; I Kings 2:8; 4:14), has not yet been identified by archaeologists.

32:3-13a. In the J narrative Jacob invites Esau to meet him by sending **messengers** to **Seir,** some 100 miles to the S (see color maps 4, 7). This account may think of Jacob as headed toward his old home in Beer-sheba (cf. 28:10) by a route to the E and S of the Dead Sea which would come near Esau's home in Edom (cf. 33:12-14). When the messengers return with news of Esau's approach with **four hundred men** Jacob becomes frightened and as a precaution divides his companions and property into **two companies.** This may have been the basis for a J explanation of the name Mahanaim that was suppressed by an editor in favor of the E explanation (vs. 2).

32:13b-23. In the E account Esau's home territory seems to lie, not in Edom, but E of the Jordan (see above on 27:1-45) directly athwart Jacob's route toward central Palestine. Fearing an unavoidable immediate encounter, Jacob sends ahead a series of gifts to **appease** his brother while he and his wives and children linger behind.

32:24-32. Jacob's Wrestling. The experience at **Penuel** is Jacob's 2nd critical encounter with God (cf. 28:10-22), and it seems clear that these 2 incidents are the poles around which the material of the Jacob cycle is meant to revolve. The God who promised to bring Jacob back to the land of Canaan when he left (28:15) finally encounters him in deathly struggle on his return and changes his name and cripples him before blessing him. One may indeed find struggle to be the dominant theme of the Jacob cycle. The story as told by J has lost its original significance in favor of explanations for the place name **Peniel** (i.e. "face of God," vs. 30), the name **Israel** (which has been derived from roots meaning "God struggles," or "rules," or "heals," vs. 28), and the law against eating the sciatic muscle (vs. 32).

Courtesy of William L. Reed

Jabbok River at traditional site of Jacob's wrestle with the angel

Perhaps in its original form the tale was an account of how Jacob(?) in a gigantic struggle was able at night to wrest from the Canaanite god El permission to cross the Jabbok into his territory. (For another account of physical struggle between God and man cf. Exod. 4:24-26.) The site of **Penuel** (of which **Peniel** is a variant used only in vs. 30; cf. Judg. 8:8; I Kings 12:25) is said to be the E one of 2 mounds where the Jabbok River enters the Jordan Valley (see color map 3).

33:1-17. Jacob's Meeting with Esau. Esau's attitude on meeting Jacob is surprisingly magnanimous (cf. Luke 15:20), in contrast with his previous murderous intent (cf. 27:41), while Jacob's remains suspicious and wary. The presence of Esau's **four hundred men** was no doubt reason for pause. The story (from J) follows the previous narrative almost inevitably, and Jacob's remark that seeing Esau's face was **like seeing the face of God** (vs. 10) is probably meant to bind the 2 incidents together (but cf. the similar usage at II Sam. 19:27). After the meeting, the only purpose of which is apparently the reconciliation of the 2 brothers, Esau proceeds alone to Edomite territory, while Jacob moves on only a few miles. **Succoth** has been identified with a mound in Jabbok and Jordan, but recent excavation there has brought the identification into question.

33:18-20. Jacob's Arrival at Shechem. According to E and P (vs. 18b) Jacob on his return re-enters

Courtesy of Herbert G. May

Ruins of east gate of ancient Canaanite city of Shechem *ca.* 40 miles N of Jerusalem

the central part of **the land of Canaan** and stops first at Shechem (see above on 12:6-7). His purchase of land near the city (cf. Josh. 24:32) is the 2nd recorded patriarchal land acquisition in Canaan (cf. ch. 23). **Pieces of money** (cf. Job 42:11) probably designates a weighed amount of precious metal (see above on 23:12-16), but archaeologists have not yet discovered an inscribed example of this weight.

34:1-31. The Rape of Dinah. This narrative presents many problems. It does not fit the chronology of Jacob's career, since at his return to Canaan Dinah would be a child of 6 or 7, with her oldest brothers in their early teens (cf. 30:21; 31:41). Jacob is portrayed in a passive role, with his sons taking the lead in both negotiations and actions. This and the fact that the story concerns the capture and despoiling of a major city (see above on 12:6-7) suggest that it was originally a tradition, not of Jacob and his family, but of the Israelite tribal confederacy.

The inconsistencies in the story perhaps reveal the conflation of 2 parallel accounts. In one, attributed to

J, Shechem violates Dinah and then offers to marry her, but Simeon and Levi take vengeance by killing him and his family. In the other, assigned to E or by some to P, Hamor seeks a treaty with the clan of Jacob, including intermarriage in general and the marriage of his son with Dinah in particular; and all the sons of Jacob employ the circumcision ruse to disable the Shechemites so that they may sack the entire city. On the other hand a number of scholars explain the inconsistencies as the result of successive expansions of an original tale and assign the entire story to J. Views have also been advanced deriving this ch. and ch. 38, with various other passages, from a written source independent of J, E, and P.

The historical substance of the events described is anything but clear. The story preserves a tradition of tribal history, perhaps alluded to in 49:5-7, which no doubt explained both the independence of Shechem and the virtual disappearance at an early time of the tribes of Simeon and Levi from Israel's military history. Perhaps the Shechemites offered Israelite tribes the opportunity of settling in their territory on conditions involving **trade** (vs. 10) and intermarriage, to which the Israelites added the requirement of circumcision (which here appears as an obligatory tribal custom, a prerequisite to marriage, unrelated to faith in Yahweh; see above on 17:9-14). It is not clear whether the Israelites involved in the treaty negotiated it **deceitfully** (vs. 13) or the tribes of Simeon and Levi violated an agreement entered on in good faith by other tribes.

The story scarcely fits into the patriarchal age but suggests rather the period of the judges or, if we can accept the theory of many scholars that only the Joseph tribes sojourned in Egypt and returned under Moses and Joshua (see Intro. to Josh. and "The History of Israel," pp. 1018-25), the period in which there was an Israelite confederacy in Canaan consisting of the Leah tribes. Jacob's reproach (vs. 30), based on considerations of prudence rather than morality, reflects perhaps the animosities between Canaanites and invading Habiru (see above on 14:13) which arose when Canaanite conciliatory conditions for settlement were flouted by the invaders.

One notes the emphasis on the great value of female chastity as well as on the danger to Israel of adopting Canaanite ways of life, a process which could be followed only by compromising Israel's moral principles.

35:1-15. Jacob's Return to Bethel. Jacob's journey **to Bethel** in order to fulfill his vow (28:20-22) as described by E is a pilgrimage which requires renunciation of everything unholy (earrings were used as magical amulets, cf. Hos. 2:13) and ritual purification (vss. 2-4) by washing (cf. Exod. 19:10) and changing clothes. Such pilgrimages were probably common in the period of the judges, after the sanctuary was transferred from Shechem (Josh. 24:1, 25) to Bethel (Judg. 20:26-28). Jacob's pilgrimage may reflect a tradition of the original transfer of the central shrine, perhaps as a result of the events recorded in ch. 34. **Terror from God** (cf. Exod. 23:27; II Chr. 14:14; Ps. 14:5) prevents the Canaanites at that time from molesting the Israelites as they take leave of their misdeed at Shechem.

35:9-15. The notice about God's appearance to Jacob (vss. 9-13) is from the P tradition (cf. 32:28,

J). The section simply records the change of Jacob's name, without giving an etymology of the new name, **Israel,** and the renewal of the promise made to Abraham and Isaac (cf. 17:3-8). The command to **be fruitful and multiply** (cf. 1:28) is scarcely appropriate at this stage in Jacob's life after he has already begotten 11 of his traditional 12 sons. For this reason it has been suggested that vss. 11-13 may have been transposed from a location following 28:1-9. Vss. 14-15 probably continue the E account of vss. 1-8, though vs. 15 has often been assigned to P. Since Jacob has already set up a **pillar** at Bethel (28:18) vs. 14 may be an editorial corruption of the marking of the grave of **Deborah** (vs. 8; cf. vs. 20).

35:16-20. The Birth of Benjamin. In this continuation of the E account Jacob moves S from Bethel toward **Ephrath**—erroneously identified by an editorial insertion with **Bethlehem** (vs. 19; 48:7; cf. Mic. 5:2) but actually a town near Ramah in Benjaminite territory (I Sam. 10:2; Jer. 31:15), possibly the same as Ophrah (Josh. 18:23). In this vicinity **Rachel** dies in childbirth, fulfilling her hope for **another son** (cf. 30:24). Jacob changes the ill-omened name "Son of My Sorrow" to "Son of the South" (or "Right"). A marauding tribe of "Southerners," perhaps meaning Benjaminites, is known to have molested the area around Haran in the 18th cent., and it may be that part of that tribe migrated into Palestine (note that the P tradition places the birth of Benjamin in **Paddan-aram,** vs. 26). The story in Judg. 19–21 may preserve an explanation of how the once powerful tribe of Benjamin became the smallest of the Israelite tribes.

35:21-22b. The Sin of Reuben. From this point on, the J source regularly uses the name **Israel** for Jacob. The phrase translated **tower of Eder** (lit. "flock") is used of Jerusalem in Mic. 4:8, but such reference here seems improbable. Reuben's offense may have been an attempt to usurp his father's authority (cf. II Sam. 16:21-22), but the passage is incomplete. The reference is included here no doubt to explain the primacy of Judah after Simeon, Levi (cf. ch. 34), and Reuben disqualified themselves for leadership (cf. 49:3-7; I Chr. 5:1).

35:22c-29. The Death of Isaac. Vss. 22c-26 give the P record of Jacob's sons. That all 12 were **born . . . in Paddan-aram** contradicts vss. 16-18. According to the P chronology **Isaac** was 100 years old when Jacob left home for Paddan-aram (25:26; 26:34; 27:46–28:5). That he should have survived 80 more years is in surprising contrast to the JE view in ch. 27 (cf. esp. 27:41). Esau and Jacob bury their father just as Isaac and Ishmael bury Abraham (25:9).

36:1-43. Edomite Genealogies. The collection of Edomite genealogies (cf. I Chr. 1:35-54) contains 6 lists which are surprising both for their similarities and for their discrepancies. The most obvious difficulty concerns their relation to the lists of Esau's wives in 26:34; 28:9. The names in the 2 lists of vss. 1-8, 15-19 closely parallel those of vss. 9-14 with the supplement in vss. 40-43. The words **these are the descendants of Esau** (vss. 1, 9) indicate that the original lists were collected to form a part of the P traditions. The lists of **Horites** (vss. 20-30) and Edomite **kings** (vss. 31-39) may derive from the J tradition, though this is far from demonstrable. The collection rounds off the Jacob cycle of stories in similar fashion to the completion of the Abraham stories by the addition of the Ishmaelite genealogy (25:12-18).

The historical value of these lists must be determined in the light of future archaeological investigation. They attest the early presence in S Palestine and Edom of the Hurrians (**Horites**), who entered Mesopotamia in the 2nd millennium (see "The People of the OT World," pp. 1005-17), and suggest their overthrow by an incursion of Edomite nomads (cf. Deut. 2:12, 22). They further indicate the formation in Edom of a monarchy in which kingship was not dynastic but elective, perhaps 2 cents. or more before its development in Israel. The kinship of the Edomites with the tribe of Judah is shown by some of the names, e.g. **Zerah** (cf. 38:30), **Shammah** (cf. I Sam. 16:9). Numerous references in the OT indicate the relations between Edomites and Israelites, e.g. Exod. 15:13-18; Num. 20:14-21; Ps. 137:7; Jer. 49:7-22; Amos 1:11-12.

C. The Story of Joseph (37:1–50:26)

The final section of Gen., except chs. 38; 49, is devoted to the story of Joseph. This narrative is distinguished from those of Abraham, Isaac, and Jacob both by its length and by its unified construction. The scenes together form a dramatic unity, in contrast with the disparate and often conflicting traditions about the other patriarchs. Cult legends, revelations of deity, and tribal history, which are prominent elsewhere in Gen., are here secondary; and Joseph emerges as an ideal figure of a wise man, whom the pharaoh finds fitted "to instruct his princes at his pleasure, and to teach his elders wisdom" (Ps. 105:22).

The narrative shows discrepancies and duplications and is generally considered a conflation of J and E; only a few fragments from P are to be found. Use of the name Israel and emphasis on Judah among the brothers identify J material, while use of Jacob and the leadership of Reuben characterize E. These and other clues make it possible to identify the strands with confidence in many passages, but at other points all attempts to isolate the 2 sources have proved unsatisfactory. So skillfully has the editor combined the parallel narratives that the successive scenes build up to a moving climax to which both accounts contribute.

The historical period in which the Joseph story is set is difficult to determine. Details about Egypt in it are accurate but give no indication of a probable date. The pharaoh is not identified, and the only personal names mentioned (37:36; 41:45) are characteristic of the 10th cent. Geographical references (45:10; 47:11; see comments) point at the earliest to the 13th cent., the probable time of Moses. Of other suggested clues the most significant is mention of a chariot (41:43; see comment); this, however, could be expected at any time after the latter half of the 18th cent. In sum, the picture of Egypt which emerges from the Joseph story seems to be contemporary with the J and E authors; there is no internal evidence for determining when the original events occurred. On the Egyptian background see Intro. to Exod., "The People of the OT World," pp. 1005-17, and "Chronology," pp. 1271-82.

37:1-11. Joseph Arouses His Brothers' Jealousy. The beginning of the narrative presents 3 reasons for the brothers' dislike of Joseph. In vs. 2 it is his bearing **an ill report** of some of them to his father. If this vs. is all from P—the evidence is contradictory—it suggests that this source contained some account of the brothers' crime against Joseph which the final editor omitted in favor of the much fuller JE narrative. The other 2 reasons are his preferential treatment by his father (vss. 3-4) and his dreams of preeminence (vss. 5-11). It is uncertain whether these were originally cumulative or represent different sources—in which case the statements that they **hated him the more** (vss. 5, 8) would be harmonizing additions of the editor.

37:3-4. Joseph is here apparently considered to be much younger than his brothers, though according to 30:22-24 he was scarcely the child of Jacob's **old age** (see below on 43:3-10). The exact meaning of the words translated **long robe with sleeves** (cf. II Sam. 13:18-19) is uncertain. The familiar KJV "coat of many colours," which comes from the LXX, seems unlikely. The gift is a symbol of Joseph's privileged status and probably indicates that he stands above the necessity of manual labor. Laborers wore shorter garments to free their arms and legs.

37:5-11. This paragraph is attributed predominately to E (cf. chs. 40–41; 42:9; but contrast **mother,** vs. 10, with 35:19). **Dreams** play an important role in the story of Joseph, but these dreams are distinguished from those recorded earlier (e.g. 20:3-7; 31:11, 24) in that neither God nor an angel appears or speaks in them. No one in the story takes Joseph's dreams to be divine revelations, and the realization that they convey more than Joseph's youthful vanity is confirmed only in 42:6; 50:18. The story proceeds without the aid of special divine intervention. God's providence, which is a basic premise to the entire story (cf. 50:20), is made known in human terms which must be interpreted and can be misunderstood.

37:12-36. Joseph's Transfer to Egypt. Surprisingly Jacob seems unaware of his sons' hostility toward Joseph and naïvely delivers him into their power. The site of **Dothan** lies about 15 miles N of **Shechem,**

Courtesy of Herbert G. May

Plain of Dothan. The Ishmaelites, to whom Joseph may have been sold by his brothers, were following an ancient caravan route over this plain toward Egypt

well over 60 miles from **Hebron** (cf. 35:27; see color map 3). The incongruity of wearing the princely robe of vs. 3 on a long foot journey may indicate differing sources, but attempts to identify the 2 strands in vss. 12-20 are mostly unsatisfactory. It is evident, however, that in both the brothers plot to kill Joseph (vss. 18, 20).

37:21-30. In these vss. the account is clearly composite. According to vss. 21 (if, as many scholars believe, Judah was originally the speaker), 25b-27, 28c, from J, **Judah** persuades the other brothers not to kill Joseph but instead to **sell him** to passing **Ishmaelites**—his 2nd cousins! According to vss. 22-25a, 28ab, 28d-30, from E, **Reuben** prevails on the others to throw Joseph alive into a **pit** (i.e. an empty cistern), from which **Midianites** kidnap him while the brothers are eating lunch.

37:31-35. Analysis of the sources in these vss. has led to little agreement. The brothers' report to their father has been anticipated in vs. 20, and the **long robe with sleeves** has been mentioned in vss. 3, 23 but may be an editorial harmonization at one or more points. Jacob's reaction on hearing of Joseph's supposed death is to embark on life-long **mourning.** He finds no comfort in the thought of a reunion with his son in **Sheol** (see comment on Ps. 6:4-5).

37:36. The **Midianites** who according to the E account have kidnapped Joseph (vs. 28ab) and taken him to Egypt (vs. 28d) sell him to **Potiphar,** a high official of **Pharaoh.**

38:1-30. *Judah and Tamar.* This story, perhaps from J (but see above on 34:1-31), interrupts the Joseph story, with which it has no connection. Judah is here separated from his brothers and living in S Palestine with the Canaanites, among whom he has found a wife and had sons, who have now reached the age of marriage. The chief interest of the narrative lies in Tamar's relationship to Judah. This story about 2 persons is apparently intended to indicate the way in which the tribe of Judah established itself in S Palestine and produced the important families of Perez and Zerah, mentioned in Matt. 1:3 (cf. Ruth 4:18-22).

38:6-10. Judah arranges the marriage of his oldest son, **Er,** to Tamar, who is evidently also a Canaanite. When Er dies his brother **Onan** is required to beget by Tamar a son to become the heir of Er (cf. Deut. 25:5-10, a codification of the laws of the levirate, i.e. marriage to a brother-in-law, a widespread ancient custom). This Onan refuses to do. Whether it is this refusal to perform the duty of a brother-in-law or the sexual act by which he evades the responsibility that is **displeasing in the sight of the LORD** is not clear. It has been suggested that in the original tradition Onan's act may have been a practice associated with the Canaanite fertility cult (cf. the reference to Tamar as a cult prostitute, vss. 21-22). After Onan's death Judah is required by the levirate to give his 3rd son, **Shelah,** to Tamar. He fears for his son's life, however, assuming that Tamar has been responsible for the deaths of the other 2 (cf. Tobit 3:7-8; 8:9-10). Therefore he tries to keep Shelah from her by indefinite postponement.

38:12-23. Tamar, becoming aware of Judah's dishonesty (vs. 14b), and determined to continue the name of her dead husband, takes matters into her own hands. She abandons her **widow's garments** and disguises herself as a **harlot.** The Hebrew word used in vss. 15, 24 is the general term for a prosti-

tute, whereas the word used in vss. 21-22 denotes a cult prostitute. Though some have tried to differentiate the terms in this story, the latter meaning probably should be understood in vs. 15. The precise significance of the **veil** (cf. 24:65) and wrapped figure has not been discovered, but they evidently are the marks of a woman offering herself as a religious rite. For Tamar they are also a means to avoid recognition by Judah. The practice of cult prostitution was later forbidden in Israel (Deut. 23:17-18; Hos. 4:3-14) but obviously sanctioned at the time described in this story (cf. vs. 26), though Judah later takes pains to avoid any publicity. His **signet** (vs. 18) is a cylinder of wood, ivory, stone, or metal carved so that when rolled on moist clay it impresses a distinctive design identifying the owner. Near one end is a hole for a **cord** so that it may be hung around the neck. Archaeologists have found examples throughout the Near East.

38:24-30. When discovered to be pregnant, Tamar is deemed worthy of death (cf. Lev. 20:10; 21:9), apparently because she was considered Shelah's betrothed and therefore guilty of adultery. She is vindicated by the exposure that because of Judah's refusal to give her Shelah she has tricked him into fulfilling the levirate obligation himself. The account of the birth of her twin sons is reminiscent of 25:24-26.

39:1-23. *Joseph and His Master's Wife.* The account of Joseph's unjust imprisonment comes entirely from J except the words **Potiphar, an officer of Pharaoh, the captain of the guard** (vs. 1), which are no doubt a repetition from 37:36 to harmonize this story with that of E. Joseph is sold by the **Ishmaelites** to a man identified by J simply as **an Egyptian,** whose personal attendant he becomes, as well as **overseer of his house.** Because **the LORD was with him** (vss. 2, 3, 5, 21, 23) Joseph gains the complete confidence of his master, and the Egyptian needs to care only about his own food (cf. 43:32).

39:6c-10. The harmonious state of affairs is disturbed when the mistress of the house solicits Joseph's affection. Joseph's refusal of her advances is based on honest regard for his master and a morality which Joseph considers God-given (cf. Deut. 22:22). His respect for his master and mistress as well as his fear of God determines his resistance to this temptation. Joseph is portrayed in this story as the ideal wise man (cf. Prov. 7). The use of **God** rather than Yahweh in vs. 9 is not a sign of another source but normal usage when an Israelite is speaking to a foreigner.

39:11-18. The woman's thwarted persistence discovers opportunity for revenge when she cunningly procures damaging evidence against Joseph by forcing him to flee from her and leave his robe in her possession. On **Hebrew** (vss. 14, 17) see above on 14:13. The term, which occurs 3 more times in the Joseph story (40:15; 41:12; 43:32), denotes here not an ethnic but a social group of low status. Only gradually did it come to designate the people of Israel as a national entity (40:15 may contain something of this later meaning).

39:19-23. The punishment meted out to Joseph, a slave, for his presumed adultery is surprisingly mild when one considers that in Israel death was the usual penalty for adultery among free men. A story similar to Joseph's experience with his master's wife is the Egyptian "Story of 2 Brothers," the manuscript of which can be dated to the 13th cent. B.C. In it the older brother's wife tries unsuccessfully to seduce the unmarried younger brother and then accuses him. The woman's husband is finally persuaded of her guilt and kills her.

40:1-25. Joseph the Interpreter of Dreams. Joseph's gift for interpreting dreams is told by E (cf. 37:5-11). The situation differs from that in the preceding J account, where Joseph is in prison but has become supervisor of his fellow prisoners (39:22-23). Here he is a slave assigned to wait on 2 prominent officials (vss. 2-4) who are **in custody in his master's house** (vss. 3a, 7). Joseph's statement in vs. 15a that he was **stolen out of the land of the Hebrews** agrees with 37:28ab and leads to the assumption that the E narrative passed directly from his purchase from the Midianites by Pharaoh's **captain of the guard** (37:36) to the events of this ch. The J incident of the false accusation of Joseph by his master's wife (ch. 39) was apparently not known to E; the references here to **prison** (vss. 3b, 5b) and **dungeon** (vs. 15b) were inserted by the editor in an attempt to smooth the connection between the 2 accounts.

40:5-19. Dreams were thought in ancient times to be divine communications, and their interpretation was considered a science. Joseph is not trained in its techniques; rather he believes that God-given dreams must be interpreted through God-given inspiration, of which he himself may be the recipient. For the 2 similar dreams he presents opposing interpretations and thus demonstrates his gift. His requested payment for his service (cf. Num. 22:7; I Sam. 9:7-8) is only that he be remembered to **Pharaoh** (vs. 14). He is confident the king will rescue from slavery a freeborn man who has been kidnapped (vs. 15a).

40:20-23. The confirmation of Joseph's interpretation is stated in the same words Joseph has used (vs. 20; cf. vss. 13, 19); events occur precisely as he has said they would. But his chance for freedom is delayed 2 years (41:1) because of the happy butler's short memory (vs. 23).

41:1-57. Joseph Becomes Vizier of Egypt. The account of Pharaoh's dreams and Joseph's interpretation of them is a continuation of the narrative begun in ch. 40 and is therefore from E. Discrepancies and doublets in the 2nd half of the ch., however, reveal the existence of originally parallel narratives: Pharaoh is to **select a man** in vs. 33, but in vs. 34 **overseers;** a **fifth** of the produce is to be gathered in vs. 34, but in vs. 35 **all the food;** vs. 45b is parallel to vs. 46b. That **Potiphera** (vs. 45; cf. 46:20) and Potiphar (37:36) bear practically the same name may be the result of independent traditions of Joseph's experience in Egypt; since 37:36 is from E, vs. 45 may be from J. The notice about Joseph's age (vs. 46a) is from P. This source apparently allowed 13 years to elapse between Joseph's descent into Egypt (37:2) and his appointment as administrator (see below on 43:3-10).

41:33-36. Public storing of grain was common practice in Egypt from early times. The narrative seems to represent Joseph as the originator of this policy.

41:37-41. Joseph's sudden elevation from slave to virtual ruler of Egypt is essentially a success story, showing that true wisdom comes from God (vs. 38; contrast the **wise men** who could not interpret the dreams, vs. 8). Such wisdom is self-authenticating, and its possessor is ultimately rewarded (cf. 40:14). It carries its own responsibility, which Joseph also recognizes and assumes (cf. vss. 33-36). Pharaoh needs no other interpretation of his dreams, nor does he seek further advice for official policy. He respects Joseph's charismatic gift and entrusts to him responsibility for providing grain for the country.

41:42-44. Pharaoh's **signet ring** is similar to Judah's signet (see above on 38:12-23) but shaped to be worn on a finger. Its possession is a "blank check" to issue orders in the king's name (cf. Esth. 3:10, 12; 8:2, 8). The other insignia of Joseph's official position are authentically Egyptian: the splendid **garments of fine linen,** the **gold chain** of honor, the **chariot,** and the criers who precede Joseph when he goes out. The horse and **chariot** were introduced into Egypt by the Hyksos invaders in the 18th cent. Previously dignitaries were carried in sedan chairs. The precise meaning of the Hebrew word translated **Bow the knee!** is unknown. It may mean simply "make way."

41:45-57. Though the meaning of Joseph's new **name** is uncertain, it probably refers to an Egyptian god. **On,** Greek Heliopolis, "City of the Sun" (cf. Jer. 43:13), was a cult center of the sun god Re located a few miles NE of modern Cairo (see color map 4). The new name and marriage into the ranking priestly family in Egypt are reported simply, with no hint either of a change of religion or of constancy to his father's faith (contrast 24:2-4). The impression is that Joseph becomes completely "at home" in Egypt, as the naming of his 2 sons suggests. Strange that he makes no effort to communicate with his father!

42:1-38. Joseph's Brothers Visit Egypt. The way is now prepared for Joseph's reunion with his father's family, the theme of chs. 42-45. The bulk of this ch. is generally credited to E, but the presence of several doublets (vss. 1a and 2a, 5a and 6b, 7a and 8) reveals again the existence of originally parallel accounts.

42:1-25. Since Benjamin is not permitted to go with his brothers to Egypt (vs. 4), one of Joseph's intentions is a reunion with his younger brother (vs. 15). His treatment of his brothers cannot be rationally accounted for. They are now in his power, not he in theirs. Revenge is clearly a motive, but scarcely dominant, especially in the light of 50:20. Joseph has to satisfy himself about the attitudes and motives of his brothers, and the methods he employs are psychologically credible. He accuses them of being **spies** and intimidates them with a 3-day **prison** sentence. Thereafter, overhearing how Reuben meant to rescue him, he keeps the 2nd oldest brother, **Simeon,** as hostage for the return of the others with Benjamin.

42:26-35. The finding in the grain sacks of the money (see above on 23:12-16), which Joseph has meant to be a gift (vs. 25), is an enigmatic and ominous sign to the troubled family. Vss. 27-28a, which relate how one of the brothers opens his sack and discovers his money **at the lodging place,** contradict both vs. 25, in which Joseph supplies provisions that make using the grain along the way unnecessary, and vs. 35, in which the brothers are dismayed to find the money after arriving home. That vss. 27-28*a* are an insertion from the J account is evidenced by the reference to them in 43:21 and the use in them of an unusual Hebrew word for "sack" which is used also in the J narrative of chs. 43-44. Probably vs. 28*b* originally followed the discovery of the money in vs. 35.

42:36-38. On hearing of the vizier's demand to see **Benjamin,** Jacob accuses his sons of sacrificing his children one by one, and **Reuben** (cf. 43:8) offers to sacrifice his own **two sons** if Benjamin does not return in safety from Egypt. Because the narrative in this ch. looks forward to an immediate 2nd trip to release Simeon (cf. vss. 18-20), it is likely that in the original E account Jacob acceded to Reuben's offer (his response is no doubt to be found in 43:14). To harmonize with the J idea of a delayed 2nd trip (cf. 43:2) the editor rearranged Jacob's replies and placed here vs. 38 from J. The result is to make Jacob appear unconcerned about what happens to his son Simeon so long as Benjamin is safe.

43:1-34. *The Brothers' Return to Egypt.* The story of the brothers' 2nd trip to Egypt comes from J, as shown by the name **Israel** (vss. 6, 8, 11) rather than Jacob (cf. 42:1, 4, 29, 36). The journey occurs only after the grain secured the first time has been **eaten,** and the reason for it is the severity of the **famine,** not the freeing of Simeon (cf. 42:19, 24*b*, 36). It is clear that in this account the only pressure exerted by Joseph was a refusal to sell more grain unless Benjamin should come on the next trip (vss. 3, 5) and that the release of Simeon in vs. 23 is an editorial harmonization (on vs. 14 see above on 42:36-38).

43:3-10. It is **Judah** rather than Reuben (cf. 42:37) who according to J speaks for the brothers and offers himself as surety for Benjamin's safe return. Later in this account Judah takes the lead in all negotiations with Joseph (44:14-34; 46:28; cf. 37:26-27). The conversation seems to call for a reply by the father after vs. 7; perhaps 42:38 originally appeared at this point (see above on 42:36-38). Benjamin is here called a **lad** (vs. 8; cf. **my son,** vs. 29). Evidently his age is reckoned on a different basis from the P chronology, according to which Joseph has been in Egypt over 20 years (cf. 37:2; 41:46*a*, 53-54). Some have conjectured that in the original J story Benjamin was born only after Joseph was in Egypt (cf. vs. 7; 37:3).

43:11-15. Having yielded to Judah's plea, the anxious father spares no pains in seeking to assure the favor of the Egyptian vizier. He sends some of the precious products of Palestine and **double the money** for grain, i.e. what Joseph returned and an equal amount for the impending purchase.

43:16-25. The brothers present themselves to Joseph at his office, where he sees Benjamin and directs that they be received at his **house.** The frightened brothers speak anxiously with the **steward** and offer to return all the money they found in their sacks (cf. 42:27-28*a;* on **in full weight** see above on 23:12-16). The steward, who apparently knows Joseph's purpose, congratulates them on their good fortune and informs them of Joseph's invitation to dine **at noon.**

43:26-34. Joseph's emotion on seeing Benjamin is effectively described (vss. 29-31). At the meal the guests are seated **by themselves** (vs. 32), apart from Joseph and separated from the other Egyptians (on **Hebrews** see above on 14:13; 39:6*b*-18). Much to their astonishment the brothers are placed according to their age. They are honored by **portions** of food served **from Joseph's table,** but Benjamin receives **five times** the honor. The number 5 is prominent in this story (cf. 41:34; 45:22; 47:2, 24); its significance is not understood. In pleasant conviviality the brothers forget their anxiety and enjoy their feast.

44:1-34. *Joseph Sets the Climactic Trial.* Joseph, however, has one more test for his unsuspecting brothers, and the J narrator records it with dramatic skill. In the evening (cf. vs. 3) Joseph instructs the steward to place his **silver cup** in Benjamin's sack of grain and then, after the brothers have departed, to overtake them and accuse them, specifically Benjamin, of stealing it. The note about placing the money in the sacks (vs. 1) is apparently a gloss, since there is no mention in vss. 11-12 of finding it. Though the precise way in which a cup was used to **divine** is not known, in general it appears that water or oil was poured into it and conclusions were drawn from the figures suggested by the motion of the liquid when small objects were dropped into it. The theft of such an object was a serious crime (cf. 31:30-32).

44:17. Joseph's insistence, when the brothers are brought before him, that only the guilty man suffer for the crime is designed to make the brothers reveal decisively their solicitude for their father. Will they again confront him coldly with the death of his favorite son?

44:18-34. Judah's speech is a paragon of Hebrew eloquence. He recounts the events which have led up to the present dilemma (naturally omitting the circumstances surrounding the death of Benjamin's brother, vs. 20), describes his father's fear of losing Benjamin and what confirmation of that premonition would do to him, and offers to take Benjamin's place **as a slave** in Joseph's household if only his brother may be redeemed. The effect of this speech on Joseph is overpowering, and the narrator moves swiftly to his conclusion.

45:1-27. *Joseph's Self-Disclosure.* The climactic ch. of the Joseph story is a scene of such dramatic impact that only on 2nd reading does one notice the signs that the J and E narratives have again come together. Though precise separation is not possible at every point, the major blocks can be readily recognized.

45:3-5*a*. Joseph twice announces his identity, and in each case his following words reveal the source. Since in J Joseph has already asked about his **father** and been reassured (43:27-28), vs. 3 must be from E. In vss. 4-5*a* his reference to being **sold,** i.e. to the Ishmaelites (37:28*c*), shows the source is J.

45:5*b*-8. The name **God** identifies these vss. as from E. In them Joseph reinforces his forgiveness of his brothers by his generous insistence that God has providentially ordered his fate for the sake of Jacob's family. Not the brothers' evil intent was responsible for Joseph's transference to Egypt, but God's will **to preserve life.** This interpretation of their experience will deliver the brothers both from fear of revenge (vs. 3) and from mutual recrimination (vs. 24) of the kind illustrated in 42:22. They are not absolved of their guilt, but it now can be accepted in the light of God's overarching, all-inclusive providence. This is the recurring theological theme of the Joseph story (cf. 50:20).

45:9-28. In vss. 9-11 Joseph on his own authority invites his entire family to move to Egypt and settle **in the land of Goshen.** In vss. 16-20 **Pharaoh** hears of the brothers and is delighted at the opportunity to show his gratitude to Joseph by inviting the family to come and enjoy **the best of the land of Egypt.** The 2 invitations might seem compatible except that later (46:31–47:6) it is told how after the family arrive Joseph carefully coaches his brothers in what to say to Pharaoh in order to secure his permission to settle in Goshen. Thus in one account, which can be identified as J, Joseph informs Pharaoh of his family only after they have arrived in Egypt; in the other, the E account, it is Pharaoh himself who proposes the migration. **Goshen,** evidently to be located in the NE part of the Nile delta, is probably the modern Wadi Tumilat, between Port Said and Suez. The Egyptian capital was not **near** this region (vs. 10) till the time of Moses (see comment on Exod. 1:11).

45:28–46:27. *Israel Goes to Egypt.* The traditions now provide an answer to the question, How did our people ever come to be in Egypt? In contrast to the J conception of the decision to visit Egypt as an independent choice (45:28–46:1a), E represents it as obedience to God's special command, characteristically revealed in a dream, to leave the Promised Land (vss. 1b-5). Carefully the narrator emphasizes the divine purpose which brings the chosen people down into Egypt, from famine and destruction to food and prosperity, and which later will bring them out of slavery into freedom.

46:6-27. These vss. bear the unmistakable marks of P. The list of the descendants of Israel entering Egypt appears with some change in Num. 26:5-50 (cf. I Chr. 2–8; also Exod. 6:14-16 for Reuben, Simeon, and Levi). Its artificiality is apparent: Jacob's concubines are each credited with half as many male descendants as their mistresses (Leah 33, Zilpah 16; Rachel 14, Bilhah 7). Benjamin, the "lad" (see above on 43:3-10), already has a large family (vs. 21). The author got his total of **seventy** from a tradition (cf. Deut. 10:22) in which it was a conventional round number (cf. Num. 11:16; Judg. 8:30) and stretched the facts a bit to make it exact by counting **Er and Onan,** who **died in the land of Canaan** (vs. 12; cf. 38:7, 10), and Joseph's 2 sons, who were born **in the land of Egypt** (vs. 20; cf. vs. 27; 41:50-52). The subtotal **sixty-six** (vs. 26) may be a gloss pointing out that these 4 do not fit. **Dinah** (vs. 15), like the **sons' wives** (vs. 26), is apparently not included in the count.

46:28–47:12. *The Arrival in Egypt.* Vs. 28 is the continuation of vs. 1a in the J narrative and therefore **He** means **Israel.** The purpose of sending Judah ahead is obscured by a textual corruption for which the ancient versions offer little help (see RSV footnote). In contrast with the E story that it was Pharaoh who suggested the migration to Egypt (see above on 45:9-28) Joseph here has already settled his family in Goshen and must now use his skill as

a courtier to inform the king of their presence and secure consent for them to stay. He carefully instructs his brothers to stress that they are **shepherds** in order to be assigned to **Goshen,** which as a border territory might otherwise seem a risky place to settle aliens. The explanation of an Egyptian prejudice against shepherds cannot be confirmed from Egyptian sources and seems to be an unwarranted exaggeration. The intent may be to underscore Egyptian suspicions of immigrants from the N.

47:1-12. The continuation of the preceding J story is found in vss. 1-4, and a P story of Jacob's interview with Pharaoh appears in vss. 7-11; but in vss. 5-6 the ending of one and the beginning of the other have been confused in transmission. The LXX apparently preserves the correct order and also original explanatory material which has dropped out of the Hebrew text. Thus the proper ending of the J story is that Pharaoh tells Joseph (vs. 5a) that his brothers may settle in Goshen (vs. 6c) and that some may be appointed as royal herdsmen (vs. 6d). Then the P account should begin as added in the LXX: "And Jacob and his sons came into Egypt to Joseph. And Pharaoh, king of Egypt, heard of it. And Pharaoh said to Joseph." After this follow vss. 5b-6b, 7-11. Vs. 12 returns to the J account. **The land of Rameses** (vs. 11) is anachronistic. Evidently it was the region around the city of Rameses (or Raamses, Exod. 1:11; 12:37; see color map 4), which was built by Ramses II (1290-1224), probably with the help of Hebrew slaves, as described in Exod. 1:8-14 (see Intro. to Exod.).

47:13-26. *Joseph's Agrarian Policy.* This section, which tells how all Egypt except priestly possessions became Pharaoh's property and all Egyptians his slaves, is unconnected with the Joseph story. Is one to imagine that Jacob's sons are exempted from this enslavement, or is this incident perhaps a neglected parallel to Exod. 1:8 in accounting for Israel's enslavement in Egypt? Though this material is often attributed entirely to J, its literary analysis and its connection with 41:34-35, 55-57 are quite uncertain. The statements concerning the 20% tax follow strangely after vs. 23, according to which land and people belong to Pharaoh.

47:27–48:22. *Jacob's Last Words.* The various accounts of Jacob's deathbed sayings from the 3 sources bring the Joseph story to its close.

47:27-31. According to P (vss. 27b-28) Jacob survives his journey to Egypt by **seventeen years.** The other sources imply, however, that his death follows soon after his arrival. That vss. 27a, 29-31 are from J is suggested by the oath by the genital organ (vs. 29; see above on 24:1-9). Jacob desires to be buried **out of Egypt,** but about the place traditions vary; there may be some editorial harmonizing in vs. 30 (see below on 49:28b–50:14). Vs. 31b is obscure. The Hebrew consonants for **bed** can be read with different vowels to give the LXX translation quoted in Heb. 11:21, "over the head of his staff." The significance of the gesture is unknown (cf. I Kings 1:47).

48:1-7. The account of Jacob's blessing of Joseph's sons derives from all 3 sources. That a new source begins in vss. 1-2 is obvious: in 47:29-31 Israel, knowing his death is approaching, has called Joseph and given him instructions for his burial; now Joseph is told of Jacob's illness and goes to him, taking his two sons. Here, then, is the beginning of the E story of Jacob's deathbed blessing of the 2 boys. Vss. 3-6 present the P account of the blessing, which is strictly tribal rather than personal. Jacob gives to **Ephraim and Manasseh** the status of full tribes (vs. 5) and orders that future sons of Joseph are to be counted as clans of those 2 tribes (vs. 6). The notice about Rachel's death (vs. 7) has no connection with what precedes or follows. Since it contains both P and E material derived from 35:9, 16, 19, it must be an insertion by the final editor or a later glossator.

48:8-12. Despite the use of **Israel** throughout the rest of this ch., the marks of conflation are evident. Though closely interwoven, the J and E strands can for the most part be traced. The implication of vss. 8-9a that Jacob is meeting his grandsons for the first time fits the situation of the E narrative, in which he has just arrived in Egypt (46:5). The explanation of his blindness in vs. 10a, however, contradicts the statement that he **saw** the boys (vs. 8) and is therefore from J. The E account continues in vss. 10b-12, with Jacob rejoicing to **see** Joseph's sons. The ceremony of placing the children on their grandfather's **knees** (vs. 12) is part of the rite of adoption (cf. 30:3; 50:23), which was so well known apparently as to require no description.

48:13-19. The reason for the J mention of Jacob's dim eyesight (vs. 10a) is now seen in Joseph's care to guide the sons to him so that his **right hand,** conferring the greater blessing, will be placed on the head of the **first-born** (vs. 13). But Jacob insists on **crossing his hands** (vs. 14) in spite of Joseph's efforts to **remove** them (vss. 17-18), and explains his action by predicting that the **younger brother** will become the **greater** (vs. 19)—i.e. the tribe of Ephraim will play a superior role in Israel's history (cf. Ephraim as the usual name for the N kingdom in Hos.). Since vss. 15-16 interrupt this account, they are either out of order or, more probably, from E. In them Jacob's care in identifying the God of blessing as the God of his fathers, who has led and redeemed him (i.e. delivered him as a kinsman; cf. Lev. 25:25-28; II Sam. 4:9), is noteworthy. For Jacob's experiences of the **angel** of God see 28:12; 31:11-13; 32:1-2.

48:20-22. Though the connection is by no means certain, vs. 20 appears to be the conclusion of the blessing of vss. 15-16. If so, E joins J and P (vs. 5) in attributing Ephraim's preeminence to Jacob's dying words. **Mountain slope** (lit. "shoulder," vs. 22) evidently refers to Shechem (the same Hebrew word; see above on 12:6-7), but the saying comes from a tradition different both from that in ch. 34, where Jacob condemns his sons for their deed at Shechem (34:30), and from that in 33:19, where Jacob purchases a piece of ground at Shechem. It seems also to imply that Jacob has already allotted to his other sons their inheritances.

49:1-28a. The Blessing of Jacob. This careful compilation of oracles concerning the tribes of Israel contains sayings which differ in significance, type, and age. The oracles taken as a whole refer to no single historical period and seem to be arranged partly by the sons' ages and partly by geography. The statements are unified in a single poem, not by virtue of content or genre, but only because of their artificial setting as the words of the aged Jacob to his sons (vss. 1-2, 28a), a picture which is not consistently maintained throughout. The final collecting of this ancient material was done probably during the era of David or Solomon, since the implicit situation is the tribal confederacy during the period of the judges rather than the patriarchal family. The collection should be compared with the tribal descriptions in the Song of Deborah (Judg. 5:14-18), which are unified and may be older, and the Blessing of Moses (Deut. 33:6-25), which is later.

49:3-4. Reuben, Jacob's **first-born,** because of his crime against his father (cf. 35:22) is destined for political obscurity (cf. Judg. 5:15-16). This tribe, which once must have been powerful, apparently lost interest in the Israelite confederacy, preferring nomadic life E of the Jordan (cf. Josh. 13:16-23).

49:5-7. Simeon and Levi were responsible for the massacre at Shechem (34:25, 30), to which this oracle may refer. They are represented as cruel and dangerous men (tribes) who lost whatever land they originally possessed. Simeon, if it ever existed independently as a tribe, was absorbed by Judah (cf. Josh. 19:1-9 with 15:26-32, 42). The connection between the tribe of Levi and the Levitical priesthood is far from clear.

49:8-12. Judah, after the elimination of the 3 oldest sons, assumes the leading position among the tribes. The oracle extols Judah's prowess in war and the respect which his obedient and grateful brothers give him. The prosperity of his people will be like that of Paradise (vss. 11-12). An unsolved difficulty is the proper understanding of vs. 10c. The translations "until Shiloh come" (KJV) and **until he comes to whom it belongs** illustrate the 2 possibilities for interpreting the crucial Hebrew word *shiloh* —either as a proper name or as a combination of words. Neither possibility is free of objections, and agreement on the interpretation of the passage is therefore impossible. A messianic interpretation, in view of the situation in vss. 11-12 and the presumed royal symbols in vs. 10ab, is often urged; but against this view one must add that the symbols may be tribal rather than monarchical and that the literary unity of the passage is not assured. The thought seems to be that Judah will exercise tribal authority (cf. Judg. 1:1-2) until the monarchy is established with a Judahite on the throne, at which time peace and prosperity will become proverbial.

49:13. Zebulon is simply located on the Phoenician coast, in contrast with its position as stated in Josh. 19:10-16 or presupposed in Judg. 12:11-12. The tribe was at one time apparently forced to move.

49:14-15. Issachar too gave up its original territory, exchanging freedom for servitude with a promise of ease and comfort (cf. 30:18). The tribe is not mentioned in Judg. 1, but its courage in war was well known (Judg. 5:18).

49:16-18. Dan was apparently one of the weakest of the tribes, but it used its strength as effectively as a snake against a horse and **rider.** The Danites were among the last of the Israelites to secure permanent territory and had to change their area of settlement several times (cf. Judg. 1:34; 18:1-31; also Josh. 19:47-48). Vs. 18 bears no relation to the oracles; it marks the middle of the song.

49:19. Gad on the E side of the Jordan, could effectively repulse marauding bands of nomads, but eventually succumbed to them (Jer. 49:1). A. G. Herbert has reproduced in English the word play of the Hebrew by changing the tribal name to "Rad" and translating: "Raiders shall raid Rad, but he shall raid at their heels."

49:20. Asher has a **rich** land which produces **royal dainties** (cf. Deut. 33:24); therefore he is "happy" (cf. 30:11).

49:21. Naphtali was situated on the W shore of Lake Gennesaret in a fertile area (cf. Deut. 33:23). The oracle about the tribe cannot be interpreted.

49:22-26. Joseph is treated in a text corrupt and difficult to translate. The oracle was apparently composed when it was still a single tribe, before the emergence of Ephraim and Manasseh. The vss. stress Joseph's importance (cf. I Chron. 5:2)—his economic and military prosperity (vss. 22-23) because of God's **help** (vss. 24-25a) and the **blessings** invoked on him (cf. Deut. 33:13-16).

49:27-28a. Benjamin, whose warriors included 700 left-handed sharpshooters (Judg. 20:16), was renowned for its predatory abilities. Vs. 28a (through **said to them**) is the conclusion to the collection.

49:28b-50:14. Jacob's Death and Burial. At least 2 traditions of the location of Jacob's grave existed: (a) the cave of **Machpelah** (49:30), where the other patriarchs were buried, as reported in P; (b) a **tomb** prepared by Jacob himself (50:5) **beyond the Jordan** (50:10), found in material generally attributed to J (but contrast "in their burying place," 47:30). According to P Jacob's last words (49:29-32) are an injunction to his sons to bury him in the **cave . . . in the field of Machpelah,** that small parcel of the Promised Land which thus far has been acquired by Israel (ch. 23; cf. the garbled reference in Acts 7:16), along with **Sarah** (23:19), **Abraham** (25:9), and the rest of his family, whose burials are not elsewhere recorded (except Rachel's, 35:19; cf. 48:7). Jacob then dies (49:33), and the sons obey his request (50:12-13). According to J Jacob has given his burial instructions to Joseph alone (47:29-31) before blessing his sons and grandsons. On his death Joseph

orders the body **embalmed** according to Egyptian practice, and he is mourned **seventy days,** the period reported by the Greek historian Diodorus as normally allotted to a royal funeral in Egypt (50:1-3). Joseph then secures permission from Pharaoh for all the family, as well as Egyptian officials, to journey to Transjordan—to **the threshing floor of Atad,** the location of which is unknown—and return after the burial (50:4-11, 14). In combining the accounts the editor has given the impression that Atad is merely a stopping place for **mourning** on the way from Egypt to Machpelah, whereas Transjordan is actually far beyond **Mamre** (see color map 3).

50:15-21. Conclusion of the Joseph Story. After Jacob's death the brothers' anxiety mounts—Joseph may have been waiting for this moment to seek revenge. The E narrator, however, emphasizes again (cf. 45:5b-8) God's providence. The matter of the brothers' guilt is included in their deliverance from famine and death. The final verdict has been given; nothing further need be said: **You meant evil . . . ; God meant . . . good** (vs. 20). How can Joseph add to or detract from what God has done (vs. 19)? The mystery of human freedom and necessity here receives classic statement, and the paradox humbles Joseph and his brothers before one another and before God. Joseph's forgiveness is his acceptance of that divine providential care which includes his brothers' evil deed. There is no possibility of accepting the one without the other, and "brotherly love" thus becomes an expression of humble gratitude for the mystery of divine providence.

50:22-26. Joseph lives to see his great-grandchildren in Egypt and dies after what was considered an ideal life span, **a hundred and ten years** (cf. Josh. 24:29). The E narrative concludes the story of Joseph with the reminder of God's promise of land to the patriarchs and the certainty of the exodus of their descendants from Egypt. Later in this account Joseph's mummy in its sarcophagus is to be carried out of Egypt by Moses (Exod. 13:19) and buried at Shechem (Josh. 24:32).

THE BOOK OF EXODUS

John Gray

Introduction

Scope and Significance. The title Exodus, Greek for "going out," comes from the LXX. It indicates that the book enshrines the fundamental experience of God's active power and grace and moral purpose which formed the factual basis of Israel's faith, viz. the deliverance from Egypt. The law and the covenant are here placed in the context of history, which Israel continued to experience sacramentally in her drama of salvation at the great central sanctuaries when the various tribal groups met to realize their unity in the common faith. Thus the book presents not only the deliverance itself (chs. 1–15) and certain traditions of the desert wandering (chs. 16–18) but the encounter with Yahweh at Mt. Sinai (chs. 19–40).

After the saving act which was the genesis of Israel, even as the event of Jesus Christ was the genesis of the Christian church, God engaged Israel in her divine destiny through the covenant, revealing his nature and his will for her in the law—moral principles and ritual observances designed to emphasize and maintain her distinctive status as his "peculiar people." These comprise (*a*) the categorical imperative of moral law in the nucleus of the Decalogue (20:2-17), (*b*) commands to safeguard the worship and ethic of the distinctive people in the Ritual Code (34:14-26), and (*c*) regulations for a comparatively complex society in the Book of the Covenant (20:23–23:33). The disproportionately long passage on the sanctuary and its service (chs. 25–31; 35–40) reflects the interest of late priestly editors in the rehabilitation of people and cult after the Exile.

The book is epitomized in the Decalogue and its historical intro. (20:2), where law and grace are associated in a formula relating directly to the covenant. The recurrence of these associated themes in the OT indicates the main source of the tradition of the law in the context of covenant and esp. in the covenant sacrament, which is as old as Israel's self-consciousness in the Mosaic age.

Sources. Exod. is a composite work assembled during at least half a millennium (see "The Compiling of Israel's Story," pp. 1082-89). There are doublets and discrepancies, as well as differences in style—e.g. hymn, narrative prose, legal formula, saga, and cult drama—and in theology. These and other clues in the book distinguish the components of 3 of the main literary sources of the Pentateuch: Yahwist (J), Elohist (E), and Priestly (P). There are evidences of 2 stages of P, with a final fusion of the 2 that supplied the framework of the Pentateuch.

The traces of Deuteronomic (D) elaboration in this book are very slight. The passages attributed to the several sources are shown in the table on p. 34.

J, E, and P are the literary crystallization of earlier traditions of miscellaneous character and worth. The originally independent bodies of tradition underlying J, E, P in this book include: (*a*) the exodus tradition proper, developed with accretions from secular saga as the cult legend of the passover when it was a public festival, perhaps at Gilgal (cf. Josh. 5:10; II Kings 23:22); (*b*) the tradition of the covenant with the law at Sinai, which developed also with saga accretions as the cult legend of the feast of tabernacles or booths (cf. Deut. 31:10-11), originally at Shechem (cf. Deut. 27; Josh. 8:30-35; 24); and (*c*) the tradition of the desert wandering, including a hero saga about Moses at Kadesh and a number of self-contained traditions associated simply on grounds of common locality about Kadesh and not necessarily the record of a sequence of events. J and E endeavor, not too successfully, to combine these components into a consecutive narrative; and P completes a topographical framework, the late and artificial nature of which precludes our assuming a consistent unity for the whole.

The fact that these traditions developed in cult legends, which were important sources of J and E, does not argue against their genuine historical origin. The frank admission that the Hebrews shared the desert sanctuary of Yahweh with the Midianites—or Kenites (cf. Judg. 1:16; 4:11)—whose cult was actually longer established, is a very strong argument for the historicity and genuine antiquity not only of the worship of Israel here but indeed of the covenant whereby she was constituted as a distinctive sacral community. Her continued affinity in historical times with the Kenites (cf. Judg. 1:16; 4:17-22; 5:24-30; I Sam. 15:6; 30:29) seems to corroborate the tradition of their common association with the worship of Yahweh at the holy mountain. Similarly the inveterate enmity of Israel toward Amalek and the memory in the narrative of Saul late in the 11th cent. that Amalek waylaid Israel on her way up from Egypt (I Sam. 15:2) supports the historicity of the tradition in 17:8-16.

Historical Background. The history of the Hebrews in Egypt and the date of their departure and settlement in Palestine are problems with no simple solution. The biblical traditions speak only of "Pharaoh," and explicit chronological statements of

Sources of Exodus

Most of the content of Exod. appears to come from the 3 strands of tradition in the columns below. The Decalogue (20:1-17) and Book of the Covenant (20:22–23:33), and perhaps the Ritual Code (34:14-26), seem to have been inserted from other ancient sources. Other probable insertions in the 2 earlier sources are: 1:20b-21; 3:19-22; 4:14-16; 9:1-7, 14-16, 31-32; 10:1b-2; 11:2-3, 9-10; 12:25-27a(D), 35-36; 13:3b-d, 5, 8-9(D), 14-16(D); 14:25, 27b; 15:19-21a, 26(D); 16:8; 18:2-4; 19:3b-6(D), 9b, 23-24a; 24:2, 12c, 14-15a; 32:8bc, 13, 34b, 35b; 33:2, 5a, 18, 19b; 34:1b, 11b-13, 14b-16(D).

J (Yahwist)	E (Elohist)	P (Priestly)
1:6, 8-12	1:15-20a, 22	1:1-5, 7, 13-14
2:11-23a	2:1-10	2:23b-25
3:2-4a, 5, 7-8, 16-18	3:1, 4b, 6, 9-15	
4:1-13, 19-20a, 22-26, 29-31	4:17-18, 20b-21, 27-28	
5:3, 5-23	5:1-2, 4	
6:1		6:2-30
7:14-15a, 16-17a, 18, 20a, 21a, 22, 24-25	7:15b, 17b, 20b	7:1-13, 19, 21b, 23
8:1-4, 8-15a, 20-32		8:5-7, 15b-19
9:13, 17-21, 23b, 24b-30, 33-34	9:22-23a, 24a, 35ab	9:8-12, 35c
10:1a, 3-11, 13b, 14-15a, 15c-19, 24-26, 28-29	10:12-13a, 13c, 15b, 20-23, 27	
11:4-8	11:1	
12:21-24, 27b, 29-34, 38-39		12:1-20, 28, 37, 40-50
13:3a, 4, 6-7, 10-13, 21-22	13:17-19	13:1-2, 20
14:5-7, 9a, 10-14, 19b-20a, 21b, 24, 27cd, 30, 31	14:19a, 20b	14:1-4, 8, 9b, 15-18, 20c-21a, 21c-23, 26-27a, 28-29
15:1-18, 21bc, 22b-25a	15:25b	15:22a, 27
16:4-5, 13b-15a, 27-30		16:1-3, 6-7, 9-13a, 15b-26, 31-36
17:2c-3, 7a, c	17:1b-2b, 4-6, 7b, 8-16	17:1a
	18:1, 5-27	
19:9a, 11b-13a, 15, 18, 20-22, 24b-25	19:2b-3a, 7-8, 10-11a, 13b-14, 16-17, 19	19:1-2a
	20:18-21	
24:1, 9-11	24:3-8, 12ab, 13, 18b	24:15b-18a
		25:1–31:18a
	31:18b	
32:7-8a, 9-12, 14	32:1-6, 15-34a, c, 35a	
33:1, 3-4, 7-17, 19a, c, 20-23	33:5b-6	34:29-33
34:1a, 2-11a, 14a, 17-28, 34-35		35:1–40:38

the latest source are contradicted by evidence implicit in the earlier strands. References in Egyptian records from the 20th, 14th, and 13th cents. to the passage of nomads to and from the Delta "after the manner of their fathers from the beginning," as one inscription states, confirm the historical probability of a Hebrew sojourn in this area but show that identification of a particular group is hardly to be expected in these sources. Archaeological findings in Palestine are also significant but inconclusive, and basically we must rely on analysis of the biblical traditions.

I Kings 6:1 synchronizes the foundation of the temple in Solomon's 4th year (*ca.* 965) with the 480th year after the Exodus, pointing to a 15th-cent. date (*ca.* 1445; cf. Judg. 11:26). This fits with the theory of some scholars that Joseph rose to power while Egypt was under the Hyksos, "rulers of foreign lands" (*ca.* 1750-1570)—kings who came from Asia and employed some persons with Semitic names as officers, as attested by papyrus documents—and that

the rise of a "new king . . . who did not know Joseph" (1:8) refers to the overthrow of the Hyksos by the founder of the native Egyptian 18th dynasty. On this assumption the oppression of the Hebrews became esp. severe under Thutmose III (1490-1439), who while extending his empire into N Syria carried on a large building program at home; and their escape occurred perhaps in the reign of his son Amenhotep II (1439-1406).

The cuneiform tablets discovered at Tell el-Amarna, site of Akhetaton (see color map 2), the capital of Amenhotep IV (Akhenaton, 1369-1353), include letters from vassals in Palestine asking for help in withstanding attacks by Habiru. If the Hebrews led by Moses left Egypt in the 15th cent. they presumably began their occupation of Palestine early in the 14th cent. and thus might be the Habiru of the Amarna tablets. For these and other reasons a number of scholars have favored a 15th-cent. date for the Exodus.

There are certain serious difficulties, however. The pharaohs of the 18th dynasty had their capital at Thebes, *ca.* 400 miles up the Nile (see color map 2), and they apparently did little if any building in the E Delta region, where the biblical traditions clearly locate the events leading up to the Exodus. Thutmose III and most of his successors down to near the end of the 13th cent. were engaged in constant military campaigns in Palestine; on the assumption of a 15th-cent. date for the Exodus this activity must have extended well into the age of the Israelite judges, yet there is no reflection of it in the OT. Archaeological research E and SE of the Dead Sea has shown no settled occupation there during the 19th-14th cents., yet the traditions tell of established nations of Edom and Moab which the Israelites had to skirt around in their trek through this territory.

Though the terms "Habiru" and "Hebrew" are probably related, references to Habiru in documents from widely scattered times and places prevent our identifying all of them with the Hebrews who left Egypt with Moses. The term seems to have denoted, not an ethnic group, but a social class of displaced persons, including political refugees. The Habiru of the Amarna letters may represent elements later incorporated in Israel—e.g. with the references to the Habiru near Shechem cf. Gen. 34—but not necessarily those involved in the Exodus. Thus the only strong support for a 15th-cent. date seems to be the figure in I Kings 6:1.

The author of I Kings 6:1 may have calculated his 480 years by multiplying a tradition of 12 generations (cf. I Chr. 6:4-10, 50-53) by the conventional 40 years for a generation. If so, recalculation with the more realistic average of 25 years per generation gives the date 1265, which is within the period of the 19th dynasty now favored by most scholars. The 2nd king of this dynasty, Seti I (1302-1290), fortified the E Delta area as a base for operations through Palestine against the Hittites in Syria. Ramses II (1290-1224) continued and enlarged his father's program in that region, building Pithom and Raamses (1:11), or Rameses (12:37; Num. 33:3-5), which he made his chief residence and capital. He was one of several pharaohs whose records mention forced labor by Apiru, probably the Egyptian equivalent of Habiru. His son Merneptah (1224-1214) in a stele of his 5th year boasts of conquering several cities in Palestine and also the people of Israel.

The biblical traditions speak of 2 pharaohs as oppressing the Hebrews (cf. 1:8; 2:23; 4:19) and represent Moses as born and growing up during the reign of the first and effecting the deliverance from the 2nd. Since the P source regularly gives exaggerated ages, the statement that Moses was 80 years old when he appeared before the 2nd (7:7) is not to be taken seriously, but he was evidently a mature man. Therefore at one time it was widely accepted that Ramses II was the pharaoh who initiated the oppression and that the internal and external troubles which marked the succession of his son Merneptah made possible the escape of the Hebrew serfs *ca.* 1220. A few scholars, ignoring the Palestinian context of the reference to the Israelites in Merneptah's stele, even suggested that it was his effort to claim their escape into the desert as a victory over them.

From *The Ancient Near East in Pictures*, by James B. Pritchard, copyright 1954 by Princeton University Press; by permission of Princeton University Press

Stele of Mer-ne-Ptah evidencing the only extant mention in Egyptian writing of the name "Israel"

Archaeological evidence of a major disturbance in Palestine *ca.* the time of Merneptah's accession, however, including the destruction of the cities of Lachish, Debir, and Hazor (cf. Josh. 10:31-32, 38-39; 11:10-11), now seems to indicate that the escaping Hebrews were in Palestine by this time and therefore that the Exodus must be dated earlier, during the reign of Ramses II. Some scholars, taking the death of Seti I as the occasion for Moses' return to Egypt (cf. 2:23; 4:19), date the event early in Ramses' reign, *ca.* 1290-1280. This view of course requires assuming that the tradition either has erred in representing Moses' birth and upbringing in the Egyptian court as occurring during the oppression begun by Seti or else has telescoped a change in policy toward the Hebrews by one of the kings of the 18th dynasty with Seti's inauguration of forced labor on building projects in the E Delta region.

Though the evidence, both in the tradition and from archaeology, is too complex and contradictory

35

for any certainty, the most probable date for the Exodus now seems to be *ca.* the middle of the 13th cent. On this assumption Seti I, the "new king . . . who did not know Joseph" (1:8), began impressing the Hebrews of the E Delta area for his nearby building operations at the beginning of the cent. After his death, which the tradition has misplaced to a later point in the narrative (2:23), Ramses II stepped up the forced labor for a massive building program in this region, which included esp. Pithom and Raamses (1:11) and extended over many years. *Ca.* 1250 a sizable group of the serfs managed to escape into the desert. There they spent a number of years, which the tradition later magnified to the conventional round number 40. At length they made their way into Palestine and, with the help of kindred elements already in the land, attacked some of the Canaanite city-states which were vassals of Egypt. On one occasion a body of the attackers, which may or may not have represented the group that escaped from Egypt, engaged the army of Merneptah, with results that the pharaoh commemorated on his stele.

For Further Study. S. R. Driver, *Exod.*, 1911. A. H. McNeile, *Exod.*, 1917. J. C. Rylaarsdam in *IB*, 1952. Roland de Vaux, *Ancient Israel: Its Life and Institutions*, Eng. trans. 1961. Benno Rothenberg, *God's Wilderness*, 1961. Martin Noth, *Exod.*, Eng. trans., 1962. G. E. Wright in *IDB*, 1962.

I. THE GREAT DELIVERANCE (1:1–15:21)

A. BEGINNING OF THE OPPRESSION (1:1–2:25)

1:1-7. Transition. To link the patriarchal history with the originally independent exodus theme the P source (vss. 1-5, 7) renames the 12 sons of Jacob who came to Egypt with their families (on **seventy**

Courtesy of Herbert G. May

Rose granite statue of Ramses II, pharaoh of the oppression and the Exodus. Found at Memphis, the statue weighs seventy tons, stands *ca.* thirty-two feet high

Courtesy of Herbert G. May

Temple at Thebes (modern Luxor) built by Ramses II; statues of Ramses can be seen in the foreground

36

see comment on Gen. 46:6-27) and notes the large number of their descendants, reflecting the promise to Abraham (cf. Gen. 12:2; 17:6) and anticipating the oppression. The traditions assume that all the tribes sojourned in Egypt and were delivered in the Exodus, but probably only a few of them were involved. Vs. 6 may be the ending of the J story of Joseph, and **they multiplied and grew exceedingly strong** (vs. 7; cf. vs. 20*b*) is apparently a fragment from an omitted portion of J leading up to the hostility of Pharaoh in vss. 9-10. **The land** is actually

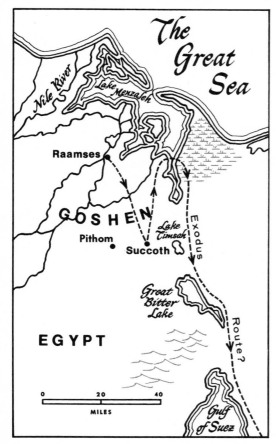

not the whole land of Egypt but the E Delta, including Goshen (cf. Gen. 47:4), which was frequented by nomads for seasonal grazing, as Egyptian military records indicate (see Intro.).

1:8-14. *Forced Labor.* On the **new king** see Intro. During the 18th and 19th dynasties Egypt's empire in Palestine and Syria required continual military action against invasion from the outside and rebellion within. Remembering the Hyksos (see Intro.) the pharaohs had reason to be sensitive to the danger of potential foreign agents among the aliens settled near their military bases in the E Delta. State slavery is well attested throughout the ancient Near East, embracing esp. the displaced persons known as Habiru, Egyptian Apiru (see Intro.), who might be exploited as impressed soldiers or as forced laborers on building projects.

1:9-10. The name **Israel,** which denotes the community based on a common stock and even more on a common religion, is an anachronism as used here of the scattered groups in Egypt, a "mixed multitude" (12:38), and anticipates the founding of the community through the experience of the covenant. **Deal shrewdly** indicates cunning rather than wisdom and visualizes exploitation of the Hebrews which would break their spirit and reduce their numbers through hardship.

1:11. The Egyptian word **Pharaoh,** lit. "great house," i.e. palace, by the time of the Exodus had come to mean the king, though not till much later was it used as a title prefixed to his name (cf. II Kings 23:29; Jer. 44:30). The **store cities** were regional capitals like those of Solomon (cf. I Kings 9:19) for storing provisions no doubt primarily for the repeated military campaigns in Palestine and Syria. **Pithom,** Egyptian for "House of Atum," has been located at a site in the Wadi Tumilat between the E arm of the Nile and Lake Timsah where monuments of Ramses II were discovered (see color map 4). **Raamses,** or Rameses (12:37; Num. 33:3-5), is an abbreviation of the Egyptian name meaning "The House of Ramses Beloved of Amon." The city was built by Ramses II as his main seat on the site of the former Hyksos capital, Avaris; and 2 letters from his reign mention the provisioning of Apiru (Habiru) who were hauling stones for the work. The city was later given another name which appears in the OT as Zoan and in Greek writings as Tanis. These 2 cities specifically associate the oppression with the reign of Ramses II. Those who favor a different date (see Intro.) must therefore view this reference to them as not an original part of the tradition.

1:13-14. The Hebrews' **hard service** includes not only work with **mortar and brick** (see below on 5:6-21) but also labor **in the field**—no doubt mostly raising water from the canals and wells by weighted lever and bucket, treadwheel, or revolving shaft (cf. Deut. 11:10) and digging and damming channels by which it would irrigate the growing plants.

1:15-22. *The Order to Kill Infants.* Anticipating the death of the firstborn of Egypt (12:29-30) in the literary plan of the exodus narrative, E introduces a popular Moses saga by setting the stage for the infant Moses' concealment and preservation. **Birthstool** (vs. 16) with slightly different vowels may be read as "two stones," which may reflect a custom of sitting or kneeling during labor found today among primitive Arab villagers; but the LXX "when they give birth" is probably to be preferred. **Vigorous** (vss. 19) might be better rendered "like wild creatures." The common humanity of the **midwives** accentuates the inhumanity of **Pharaoh,** the archenemy in the cult legend.

1:20-22. Vs. 20*b* seems to be a repetition of vs. 7*b* inserted by an editor, and vs. 21 may also be an insertion. Vs. 22 is viewed by some scholars as a parallel J account of Pharaoh's attempt to stem the growth of Hebrew population, but more probably it is a further step in the E story—since his private instruction to the midwives has failed Pharaoh broadcasts an order for **all his people** to aid in the slaughter.

2:1-10. *Moses' Birth and Adoption.* In contrast to the full P genealogy (6:16-27) the E tradition knows nothing of Moses' parentage beyond the fact that he was of Levitical family. Of his mother the Hebrew reads lit. "the daughter of Levi" (cf. 6:20), as if following her name; but the original sense was no doubt simply that she was a Levite woman, as in the LXX, "one of the daughters of Levi." The language of vs. 2a is that regularly used of a firstborn son but is contradicted by the older sister of vs. 4. The fact that nothing is said here of Moses' brother Aaron, whom the P account makes 3 years older (7:7), suggests that this passage is drawn from a saga of Moses and that the relation with Aaron and with Miriam, the "sister of Aaron" (15:20), is secondary. This relation and even Moses' Levitical affinity possibly arose from his role in the revelation of the divine ordinances at Sinai.

2:2b-9. With its directness and naïve detail this story suggests a hero legend. Cf. esp. that of the Akkadian conqueror Sargon (*ca.* 2300), said to have been committed by his mother, a temple votaress, to the river in a reed box sealed with bitumen, recovered by a temple gardener, and cherished by the goddess Ishtar, who raised him to the throne. Even so the **daughter of Pharaoh** saves the infant Moses; in God's providence the adversary is thwarted by his own daughter. There is archaeological evidence from Egypt and Palestine of the wide diffusion of Mesopotamian myths and legends, probably by professional storytellers. The **reeds** amid which the baby is hid are papyrus, the Egyptian plant from which writing material was made as early as the 4th millennium.

2:10. The popular etymology of **Moses** here (see RSV footnotes) is quite unreliable; if Hebrew the name would mean "drawing" rather than "drawn." Instead it is probably Egyptian, meaning "son," and was originally preceded by the name of a deity —cf. e.g. Ramses, "son of Ra," Thutmose, "son of Thut" (Thoth). Though adoption as Pharaoh's grandson may be legendary, the Egyptian name and upbringing are elements of the tradition which Israelites would not naturally invent.

2:11-15a. Stirring of Conscience. With fine susceptibility the J writer portrays the sympathy of the quasi-Egyptian Moses awakened by the mistreatment of **one of his people** and contrasts with it the apathy to which slavery has reduced the Hebrews. This incident provides the motive for his flight to the desert with its important consequences.

2:15b-22. Sojourn in Midian. Ancient extrabiblical sources locate the **land of Midian** E of the Gulf of Aqaba (see color map 4); but here it may mean simply the place where a group of the nomadic Midianites has settled (see below on 3:1). In this place Moses comes in contact with the desert sheik-priest whose sacred traditions seem to have played a significant part in the development of Israel's religion (see below on 18:12). He is called Jethro in E narratives (3:1; 4:18; 18:1-12)—though in each case the name seems to have been inserted later (see below on 18:1-12)—but in the J tradition he was apparently known as Hobab (see comment on Num. 10:29; cf. Judg. 4:11). Possibly this name was originally included in vs. 16; **Reuel** (vs. 18) appears to be a later gloss based on a misunderstanding of Num. 10:29.

2:16-20. With this story of Moses' meeting with

his future wife cf. Gen. 24:11-28; 29:2-12. The sheik's **seven daughters** indicate the saga. Care of the flocks is still a task of the girls and boys among the bedouin.

2:21-22. In staying with the Midianites Moses becomes a **sojourner** (*ger*), i.e. a protected alien such as one finds in many bedouin tribes, usually as a refugee in a blood feud. **Zipporah** means "bird" and **Gershom** is taken to mean "sojourner there," but this popular etymology is quite unlikely. The tradition of Gershom as Moses' son is reflected in the claim of the priests at Dan to be descended from Moses through him (Judg. 18:30).

2:23-25. The Cry for Deliverance. On the **king** who **died** see Intro. Vss. 23b-25 from P reflect the general Pentateuchal theme of promise under **covenant** to the patriarchs **Abraham** (Gen. 15:18; 17:1-14), **Isaac** (Gen. 26:2-4), and **Jacob** (Gen. 28:13-14).

B. Moses' Call (3:1–4:31)

3:1. The Mountain of God. On Jethro see above on 2:15b-22. The sacred mountain called **Horeb** in E and D is evidently the same as Mt. Sinai in J and P, where the law is given (19:10-23). Traditionally it has been identified since the 4th cent. A.D. with the peak Jebel Musa (*ca.* 7,500 feet; see color map 4) near the S tip of the Sinai Peninsula.

Courtesy of Jay and Mary Smith

Traditional Mount Sinai

This location is supported by the note in Deut. 1:2 that it was 11 days' journey from Kadesh-barnea and perhaps by the P list of stopping places in Num. 33, though scarcely any of them can be located. Against it, however, is the tradition that Palestine and Midian lay in different directions from the holy mount (cf. Num. 10:29-32).

Because the signs of the divine descent on Mt. Sinai in 19:16, 18 suggest a volcano in eruption, some scholars have placed the holy mountain E of the Gulf of Aqaba, in the traditional land of Midian, which is the only area in the entire region where there have been active volcanoes in historical times. But this is too far from Egypt to fit other elements of the tradition. It is more likely, therefore, that the place was somewhere NW of the Gulf of Aqaba. If the mountain was already sacred to the Midianites (see below on 18:12) they might well transfer to it a tradition of Yahweh's manifestation in smoke and fire and earthquake at a volcanic mountain in their original homeland.

The narrative of the desert wandering breaks off after ch. 17, giving way to the block of material about the stay at Sinai, and then resumes in Num. 10:11 with incidents which repeat some of the same themes —viz. the manna and quails (ch. 16; Num. 11) and the springs of Massah and Meribah (17:1-7; Num. 20:2-13). The setting in Num. is clearly near Kadesh (see color map 4) and suggests that this is where the wandering narrative has brought us in ch. 17. The tradition of the supporting of Moses' hands at Rephidim (17:11-12), meaning "supports," authenticates the association of this place, said to be the last station before Mt. Sinai (19:2), with the battle against the Amalekites, who were nomads of the Kadesh region (cf. esp. Gen. 14:7; I Sam. 15:7; 27:8).

Among the mountains near Kadesh the most likely peak seems to be Jebel Helal (*ca.* 3,000 feet), *ca.* 25 miles W of the Kadesh oasis. Moses' taking his flocks to the **west side of the wilderness** fits with this location, where the W exposure to the prevailing wind from the Mediterranean affords better pasture.

3:2-6. *The Burning Bush.* The **angel,** lit. "messenger," of God as a manifestation of the divine presence is characteristic of, though not confined to, the E source, where usually a palpable personal presence is visualized. Here in J, however, **the angel of the LORD** expresses a lively sense of personal confrontation and the urgency of the call. It is perhaps more than a coincidence that the Hebrew word for **bush,** lit. "thornbush," probably comes from the same root as Sinai. The **burning** may have been due to a natural phenomenon—e.g. the discharge of atmospheric electricity from pointed objects during a storm known as St. Elmo's fire—but in popular religion fire was a sign of a theophany, i.e. a deity's manifestation of his presence (cf. e.g. 13:21; 19:16; Gen. 15:17; Judg. 6:21). The bush is mentioned elsewhere in the OT only in Deut. 33:16. The sanctity of the place is indicated by the divine command for Moses to remove his sandals—a convention still observed by Muslims on entering a mosque.

3:7-10. *Moses' Commission.* The J account (vss. 7-8) visualizes not only liberation from Egypt but also the occupation of Canaan, the land of promise which is the subject of the covenant with the patriarchs in J. The emphasis of E (vss. 9-10) is rather on Moses' immediate mission, the encounter with Pharaoh and the actual Exodus. **Broad** (vs. 8) refers, not to the size of Palestine, but to the variety of terrain and the scope for settlement, esp. for nomads with sheep and goats, in the marginal lands on the thinly populated E slopes. **Flowing with milk and honey,** a conventional description of the land in the Pentateuch, reflects the ideal of the nomad, for whom even the poorest part was a contrast to the desert with its brief spring grazing. **Honey** may refer to the product of wild bees but more probably means a syrup reduced from grape juice, still used by Arab peasants. On the pre-Israelite inhabitants of Palestine see "The People of the OT World," pp. 1005-17.

3:11-15. *Divine Authentication.* Moses' diffidence emphasizes God's authority behind the human agent —cf. the divine assurance in the call of Gideon, also authenticated by a **sign** (Judg. 6:14-18). The sign offered to Moses must have dropped out, for the promise that the **mountain** on which he is standing will become an Israelite sanctuary after the mission is accomplished could scarcely give assurance while it is being carried out.

3:13. Moses is to base his claim to authority in his mission on this divine encounter and commission, which, revealing God's particular purpose, reveals also his nature and personality in his **name.** To ask Moses the name of the God whom both he and the Hebrews acknowledge is not merely to test his claim to a special call but to seek to know the immediate purpose of God according to the new revelation, in accordance with which one can invoke his presence and aid.

3:14-15. In reply we might expect a succinct oracle. Instead we have the well-known word play on the divine name Yahweh. In E this is the first revelation of this name, whereas in J it is represented as known since antediluvian times (Gen. 4:26). The meaning is obscured by the conventional translation **I am who I am,** which implies that God is the ground of his own existence. The Hebrew verb denotes, not abstract being, but manifestation in a definite character, or name; and its form indicates habitual manifestation in past, present, or future. Since English requires a tense, the best rendering is "I will be as I will be." The famous declaration signifies that God is known in his dynamic confrontation of man and in man's active response to God. This truth may well have been apprehended by Moses and expressed in the development of the divine name with this verbal sense from an original exclamatory "Yah" or "Yahu."

3:16-18. *The Way of Fulfillment.* Having announced the liberation and the fulfillment of the promise to the patriarchs (vss. 7-8) the J source turns to the immediate task of Moses in Egypt, to assemble the **elders** and with them confront Pharaoh. **Three days' journey** is certainly a round number. The destination possibly is the holy place where Moses is now standing, though in this source the locale of the burning bush is not identified with Mt. Sinai. The occasion for **sacrifice** is perhaps a spring festival in the pastoral cycle. The Egyptian frontier police would be quite familiar with pilgrimages for such occasions by the nomads who passed to and from the Delta in their seasonal grazings.

3:19-22. *Predictions of Details.* In vss. 19-20 an editor anticipates Pharaoh's intensifying opposition and God's convincing **wonders.** The curious tradition of the borrowed ornaments in vss. 21-22 (cf. 11:2; 12: 35-36) seems gratuitous, awkwardly interrupting the narrative, and is probably a secondary embellishment of the original exodus tradition. It may echo the Egyptian poem of Ipuwer describing the social upheaval in Egypt after the invasions at the end of the 3rd millennium, when "gold and lapis-lazuli, silver and turquoise, carnelian and bronze [were] hung about the necks of slave girls" (see below on 7:14–11:10).

4:1-9. *Further Authentication.* The **sign** of the divine power and determination to a certain end was often a miracle. In the prophetic experience it is both a token of the effective will of God proclaimed by the prophet and a confirmation of the prophet's authority as an agent of the will of God, as here. In the saga form of the tradition Moses' signs are miracles.

4:2-5. According to J the **rod** is the ordinary shepherd's staff of Moses; according to E it is esp. given by God (vs. 17), hence called in E the "rod of God." In P the rod is Aaron's (7:9-12) when the miracle, now considerably elaborated, is used to convince Pharaoh. The "rod of God" which became a serpent may reflect the bronze serpent on a pole as the ancient cult symbol of Yahweh (cf. Num. 21:6-9; II Kings 18:4; see below on 17:9).

4:6-7. The phrase **leprous, as white as snow** is a conventional description (cf. Num. 12:10; II Kings 5:27) for a skin disease, "whiteness," which Herodotus distinguishes from true leprosy.

4:8-9. The fact that the last of the 3 signs, the **water from the Nile** turned to **blood,** is also the first of the plagues (7:17-21) probably indicates a fusion of 2 literary traditions earlier than J.

4:10-17. *The Association with Aaron.* To Moses' plea of lack of eloquence Yahweh replies in poetic cadence that the creator is able to make what he has created effective for his purpose (vss. 11-12). When Moses still demurs, Yahweh, now exasperated (vs. 14), promises **Aaron** as spokesman. The reference to Miriam as the "sister of Aaron" (15:20) must cast doubt on the tradition that Aaron was the **brother** of Moses and suggests that vss. 14-16 are a later addition to J. **Levite** here probably signifies priestly office rather than tribal affinity. It has been suggested that the source of the Aaron tradition may have been the role of a priestly caste which during the preparation for liberation moved to and fro between the desert shrine and the Hebrews in Egypt in cooperation with Moses; cf. the E tradition of Aaron's meeting with Moses **at the mountain of God** (vs. 27). On vs. 17 see above on vss. 2-5.

4:18-23. *Departure for Egypt.* E depicts Moses as taking the initiative to see his **kinsmen** (vs. 18), obviously as a pretext for setting out on his mission. J represents Moses as leaving in response to a divine call (vs. 19), and the fact that Yahweh says nothing of his mission but only that **the men who were seeking your life are dead** seems to reflect a variant tradition that the revelation at the burning bush occurred later, i.e. on the way back to Egypt. If so, presumably vss. 19-20a, 24-26 originally followed 2:23a and were transposed here to fit with the order in the E tradition. The variant traditions are esp. obvious regarding Moses' family, who in E are left with Jethro to be reunited with Moses after the deliverance (18:5) whereas in J they accompany him (vs. 20a). The plural **sons,** even though the birth of only one has been mentioned (2:22), and only one is implied in vs. 25, may indicate that J has only partially drawn on the details of a Moses saga; or it may be due to editorial harmonizing with the E idea of 2 sons (18:6).

4:20b-21. This may be E's editorial summary of the whole encounter with Pharaoh culminating in the Exodus. It keeps the theme of the passover cult legend in perspective amid the variety of incidents and traditions. The recurring statement that God will **harden** Pharaoh's heart does not imply moral determinism but emphasizes the fact that willful obduracy to the good intention of God makes a man callous to his own welfare (cf. Isa. 6:10).

4:22-23. This passage has been variously attributed but is probably a misplaced fragment of J. The con-cept of Israel as the **first-born son** of Yahweh (cf. Jer. 31:9; Hos. 11:1), suggested by the prediction of the death of Pharaoh's firstborn son (cf. 12:29), is the expression of one of the central J themes, the election of Israel.

4:24-26. *The Circumcision of Moses.* This is perhaps the J version of an older Kenite tradition. The repeated phrase **bridegroom of blood** suggests premarital circumcision, probably a Midianite custom. Moses, who would no doubt be already circumcised in infancy either as a Hebrew or as an adoptive Egyptian, now is said to undergo the rite vicariously at the circumcision of his son, the blood of the severed skin being put on his **feet,** a euphemism for genitals (cf. e.g. Isa. 6:2; 7:20). The localization at an unknown place in the desert and the hostility of the demonic power, which the orthodoxy of J identifies with Yahweh, indicate an independent local tradition which fits ill with the context. The incongruity is perhaps slightly mitigated if it is assumed that in the original J narrative the incident preceded Moses' commissioning (see above on vss. 18-23). A **flint** blade for the operation (cf. Josh. 5:2-3) reflects the primitive inhibition against metal when it was still a novelty; cf. the ban on metal-hewn stones on the altar (Deut. 27:5; Josh. 8:31).

4:27-31. *Meeting of Moses and Aaron.* On the association of Aaron with the **mountain of God** see above on vss. 10-16. The spokesman to the **elders** (cf. 3:16-17) is Aaron, who also performs the **signs** (cf. 4:1-9). The people **heard,** i.e. accepted the fact, that Yahweh **had visited** them, i.e. had taken stock of their particular situation.

C. Confrontation with Pharaoh (5:1-6:1)

5:1-5. *First Appeal to Pharaoh.* According to E (vss. 1-2) **Moses and Aaron** demand release of the serfs on the pretext of a pilgrimage **feast** at a desert shrine, presumably the mountain of God (see above on 3:1). According to J (vs. 3) **they,** i.e. Moses and Aaron and the elders (cf. 3:18), follow the divine instruction to propose a **three days' journey into the wilderness** for a **sacrifice** (see above on 3:16-18). **Pestilence** and the **sword** were natural evils in the corridor between Africa and Asia, where caravans or armies might carry plague and bedouin raids were a constant menace. **Hebrews** here means the social class of Apiru, or Habiru (see Intro.).

5:4-6. Blandly Pharaoh does not question the existence of the Hebrews' God; he contemptuously ignores him. The stage is thus set for the conflict between Yahweh and the archenemy—the theme of the cult drama. Emendation of **many** (vs. 5) to "idle" (cf. vss. 8, 17) has been suggested; but since **people of the land** in the sense of the laborers, or lowest stratum of the free population, is a usage later than either J or E, the reading of the Samaritan Pentateuch, "they are more numerous than the people of the land," i.e. than the native Egyptians, is to be seriously considered.

5:6-6:1. *The Oppression Intensified.* The black mud of the Delta was puddled and molded into **bricks,** which were dried in the sun. The **straw,** chopped small, preserved the consistency during these operations. The whole process, including the supervision of taskmasters and the tallying of the

Brickmaking in Egypt: workmen with hoes knead clay moistened with water as laborers carry material to two brickmakers

number by scribes, is illustrated in a 15th-cent. mural painting at Karnak (Thebes; see ill., above).

5:16. For **the fault is in your own people** we may read with different vocalization of the same consonants either as in the LXX "you will wrong your own people," i.e. the Hebrews as state serfs, or as in the later Greek version of Symmachus "and yours is the fault."

5:19-21. The Hebrew foremen realize that their people are **in evil plight;** hence their bitter remonstrance with Moses and Aaron (vs. 21), which is almost as strong as a curse. **Made us offensive,** lit. "made our smell to stink," is a common expression in the OT narratives (e.g. Gen. 34:30; II Sam. 10:6; 16:21).

5:22–6:1. Moses' expostulation with God introduces a renewed divine assurance of the coming deliverance.

D. The P Account of Moses' Call (6:2-7:7)

6:2-3. *The Divine Name.* The name Yahweh is represented in P as being revealed to Moses for the first time, as it is in E (see above on 3:13), but P does not elaborate on its significance. Instead the patriarchs' experience of the same God is emphasized, esp. in the covenant and promise of Canaan, which is a prelude to Moses' commission. For P the specific name of God to the patriarchs was *El Shaddai*, translated **God Almighty** in the LXX. El was the ancient Semitic high god, now known very explicitly from the myths and legends in the 14th-cent. Ugaritic texts found at Ras Shamra in N Syria. In Gen. the name El appears with several qualifiers according to the content and places of his theophanies in the experience of the patriarchs. *Shaddai* as a divine title is predominantly late but may reflect

earlier usage, possibly coming from an old root meaning "mountain." This patriarchal name may have been selected here because of its use in Gen. 17:1 in the context of God's covenant with Abraham, now to be fulfilled.

6:6-9. *Assurance to the Hebrews.* The reiterated declaration of vss. 6-8 reflects the revelation of the divine name as a new dynamic self-manifestation of God. Here P foreshadows the drama of salvation in its widest scope, including the Sinai covenant (vs. 7) and culminating in the occupation of the promised land (vs. 8). The word **redeem** (vs. 6) is also used of the great deliverance in 15:13 and in Pss. 74:2; 77:15; 78:35; 106:10 and regularly of the 2nd exodus from Babylon in Isa. 40-55. The verb means primarily "play the part of a kinsman," as in reclaiming property (cf. e.g. Ruth 4:1-8), revenging a murder, or buying back one who has forfeited his freedom for debt. The Exodus involves both vengeance and rehabilitation from slavery. **Acts of judgment** in the light of the Ras Shamra texts means acts that show kingly power or impose regular government. The word is a leading motif in passages in Pss. and in the prophetical books which, like passages in the Ras Shamra Baal myth, deal with the establishment of order against the menace of chaos. Thus in the cult drama of the Exodus the term means the establishment of God's order against the menace of chaos in history personified in Pharaoh.

6:10-13. *Moses' Commission to Pharaoh.* According to P Moses is instructed to demand complete liberation rather than merely leave to perform religious rites as in J and E (cf. 5:1, 3). **Uncircumcised lips** is a daring figure, signifying the secondary sense "defective"—cf. "uncircumcised heart" (Lev. 26:41; Jer. 9:26; Ezek. 44:7) and "ears" (Jer. 6:10 RSV footnote).

6:14-27. Genealogy of Moses and Aaron. The recapitulation of vss. 10-12 practically verbatim in vss. 28-30 indicates that this intervening passage was inserted as a later supplement to P. Loosely incomplete lists are given only of the first 3 Hebrew tribes—through **Levi,** in which is included the genealogy of Moses and Aaron. The continuation of Aaron's line to **Phinehas** reveals the characteristic interest of the P editor in the family of Aaron as the only legitimate priesthood. This list reflects the relationships among the Levites after the Babylonian exile, but the Egyptian names **Phinehas,** "Negro," and **Putiel,** "El has given," indicate early historical traditions.

6:28–7:7. The Mission of Aaron. P elaborates on the E idea in 4:16 by stating that Aaron shall be Moses' **prophet,** Hebrew *nabi,* related to Akkadian *nabu,* "proclaim." In Mesopotamian mythology Nabu was the messenger of the gods and patron of the arts of speech and letters. The fact that the P source is oblivious of all but the declaratory function of the prophet indicates the decline of prophecy after the Exile. The note on the ages of Moses and Aaron (vs. 7) is characteristic of P and obviously artificial, to fit the idea that Moses died at the age of 120 (Deut. 34:7) after 40 years of wandering in the wilderness.

7:8-13. Victory Over Pharaoh's Magicians. The wonder wrought here by **Aaron's rod** to impress Pharaoh is obviously prompted by the first of the signs of Moses' rod by which he is to convince the Hebrews (4:1-5). The word translated **serpent** here usually means "dragon"; a young crocodile may be visualized (cf. Ezek. 29:3; 32:2). In a popular Egyptian tale a wax image of a crocodile is magically animated to the great consternation of an illicit lover. The swallowing of the other reptiles may have been suggested by an Egyptian snake charm: "The mottled knife, black, green, and gold, goes forth against it; it has swallowed up for itself that which it tasted." The word for **magicians** is probably Egyptian, as it is always applied to Egyptians in the OT except in Dan. (e.g. 1:20; 2:2), where it was evidently picked up from the Pentateuch. Later Jewish tradition named the magicians Jannes and Jambres (cf. II Tim. 3:8).

E. THE PLAGUES OF EGYPT (7:14–11:10)

Each of the 3 sources J, E, and P presents the plagues with its own peculiar emphasis, and none by itself describes all 10; but all 3 agree on the general theme of a conflict between Yahweh and Pharaoh, a series of natural disasters, and the obtuseness of Pharaoh leading to the last fatal stroke which breaks his will (12:29-32). It may be noted that in J the plagues are sent directly from Yahweh, with Moses merely announcing them; in E Moses is the agent, usually with the rod (cf. 4:17, 20); in P Aaron manipulates the rod and competes with the Egyptian magicians as in 7:8-13.

All of the plagues are natural phenomena, some esp. characteristic of Egypt. The Hebrew tradition may have been influenced by Egyptian literature referring to such disasters. In an Old Kingdom papyrus from late in the 3rd millennium Ipuwer laments the eclipse of Egypt by Asian invaders (see above on 3:19-22) and states, obviously figuratively, that the "river was blood." Of the same events Nefer-rohu declares: "The sun is veiled and will not shine so that men may see." In their sequence, however, the plagues are not naturally explicable; they must be understood in the context of Israel's sacramental experience of the great deliverance as elements in a cult drama.

7:14-25. Pollution of Water. The first plague, like the last, is included in all 3 sources. In J Yahweh kills all the **fish in the Nile** and as a result the water becomes undrinkable. In E and P, by the manipulation of the rod wielded by Moses and Aaron respectively, the water is **turned to blood**—a miracle which on a smaller scale appears earlier in J as a sign by which Moses convinces the Hebrews (4:9). In J and E only the Nile is affected, but in P the plague extends to all waters in the land. Egypt, the "gift of the Nile," is cultivable only where the water of the river reaches in its annual summer flood or can be channeled for irrigation. The Nile was also the source of drinking water, as still among the peasantry. During its flood stage the river water regularly has a reddish coloration from mud and algae, but this would not have been regarded as a portent. What is intended is a miracle as a demonstration of God's power and purpose expressed in the cult drama. The word translated **loathe** means rather "weary themselves," i.e. in digging wells (vs. 24). **Vessels of** (vs. 19) is supplied by the translators; the meaning may be rather "on wood and on stone," i.e. either sap and springs issuing from the rocks or dew on bushes and rocks.

8:1-15. Frogs. In J the frogs come from the Nile, in P (vss. 5-7) from all the waters in the land. The

Courtesy of Herbert G. May

Nile River at flood-tide

baking **ovens** (vs. 3) were open clay cylinders heated from without, the bread being baked within on hot pebbles. In vss. 8-11 J introduces the theme of Pharaoh's bargaining with Moses as a beginning to his reluctant but progressive relenting which sustains the dramatic tension—a feature of both cult drama and saga.

8:16-19. Gnats. This 3rd plague, from P only, is perhaps a variant of the 4th plague of flies from J (vss. 20-32). **Dust** has been thought by some to identify the insects as sand flies; but if there is any naturalistic significance in this association it may denote the breeding in the drying stagnant waters of mosquitoes, which molest both **man and beast** (vs. 18). Though the tradition is colored by local conditions, again a miracle is intended. The striking of the dust with Aaron's **rod** and the consequent dust cloud suggests imitative magic, like the ashes and boils (9:8-10). This may have been a rite in the Israelite cult drama. The narrative moves nearer a climax with the first failure of the Egyptian **magicians** (cf. 7:22; 8:7) and their admission that the miracle was by the **finger of God.**

8:20-32. *Flies.* On the relation of this J account to the 3rd plague see above on vss. 16-19. Isa. 7:18 takes flies as a symbol for Egypt, where they are numerous in the congested areas and are potent disease carriers. Some have viewed the flies as a result of the dead frogs (cf. vs. 14) but the association is rather in the saga or cult legend. The separation of **Goshen** is a significant amplification of the miracle to emphasize the power of the God of the Hebrews, who are settled there.

8:25-32. Pharaoh now concedes that the Hebrews may **sacrifice.** But in Egypt the cow was sacred to Isis; the Apis bull was sacrificed only when it was ritually clean by Egyptian standards; the ram was sacred to Amon of Thebes. Thus the sacrifice of any of these animals by the Hebrews would be **abominable to the Egyptians.** The sudden removal of the flies, so that **not one remained** (vs. 31), is a greater miracle than their appearance and emphasizes the inadequacy of any naturalistic explanation.

9:1-7. *Disease Among the Cattle.* This account appears to be from J but the absence of the characteristic motif of Pharaoh's bargaining for the removal of the plague suggests that it may be a later addition to this source. The statement that **all the cattle of the Egyptians died** (vs. 6) is contradicted by later references to such cattle in the J narrative (vss. 19-21; 11:5; 12:29).

9:8-12. *Boils.* This P account is possibly a late tradition developed from an earlier variant of either the disease of the cattle (vss. 1-7; cf. vs. 10) or the darkness (10:21-29), in which the tossing up of soot may be a rite of imitative magic. The connection between darkness and the boils may be based on skin irritation caused by the hot sirocco, a wind heavily charged with fine sand particles which obscure the sun—cf. "darkness to be felt" (10:21). The compiler who inserted this tradition so far appreciated the dramatic pattern as to note that the **magicians** not only were unable to control this plague (cf. 8:18) but were themselves affected (vs. 11). At this point they disappear from the scene.

9:13-35. *Hail, Thunder, and Lightning.* This narrative is mostly from J but includes a brief E account (vss. 22-23a, 24a, 35ab). The final clause (vs. 35c) was added by a P editor.

9:14-16. The homiletic and apologetic tone of this part of the address to Pharaoh suggests that it is a later addition by one who, uneasy at Pharaoh's defiance of Yahweh, felt it necessary to explain that he was allowed to persist in it only to enhance Yahweh's final victory. **Name** (vs. 16) denotes "reputation."

9:17-18. The verb translated **exalting** is the root of the word meaning "siege mound" (cf. e.g. II Kings 19:32; Jer. 6:6) and therefore has the sense of raising himself in opposition. **People** is used here in its specific sense of a religious community analogous to a kin group together with their God, to whom they stand in a moral relationship as tribesmen to a sheik or a common ancestor.

9:19-21. The inconsistency in the repeated killing of the Egyptian **cattle** (cf. vs. 6; 12:29) raises the question whether all 3 passages belonged to the original J narrative. In favor of the originality of this passage is the likelihood that the warning and the presumed obedience of certain of the **servants of Pharaoh** are intended to show that the Egyptian people, in contrast with Pharaoh, are beginning to be impressed—an anticipation of the appeal of Pharaoh's servants to release the Hebrews (10:7).

9:22-26. The rarity of **very heavy hail** in Egypt would make its occurrence a portent. In Palestine hail is usually accompanied by **thunder** and **fire,** i.e. lightning. The exemption of the Hebrew settlements in **Goshen** (cf. 8:22) emphasizes the miracle.

9:27-30. Pharaoh's admission **I have sinned** means lit. "I have missed the mark," i.e. proved the loser (cf. I Kings 1:21). **The LORD is in the right, and I and my people are in the wrong** is in the technical language of the law court and does not necessarily have a moral connotation. The spreading out of the **hands,** palms up, was the common attitude of prayer in the ancient Near East (cf. e.g. I Kings 8:22; Isa. 1:15).

9:31-32. This parenthetical note about the season was probably added by an editor anxious to explain how vegetation completely destroyed by the hail (cf. vs. 25) could still be left for the locusts to destroy (cf. 10:5, 12, 15). **In the ear** renders the Hebrew *abib,* the name of the first spring month in the Canaanite calendar (cf. 13:4), but in Egypt the **barley** would have heads a month earlier. **Spelt** is an inferior variety of wheat; it is not certain whether this grain is referred to by the Hebrew word.

10:1-20. *Locusts.* The J narrative continues, again with intermingling of a brief E account (vss. 12-13a, c, 15b, 20). It describes one of the grimmest of all natural catastrophes in the Near East, because of the impossibility of coping with the enormous swarms and the immediate and prolonged effects of their ravages (cf. Joel 2:3).

10:1-6. Vss. 1b-2 are generally regarded as a later insertion, both because of their style and content and because the J pattern elsewhere is to give in full Yahweh's instruction to Moses of what to say to Pharaoh, as in vss. 3b-6b, which thus may originally have followed immediately after vs. 1a. The didactic note in **that you may tell in the hearing of your son** is a new feature. It is characteristic of the D style and viewpoint (cf. Deut. 4:9; 6:7) and thus may come from the editor who added Deut. to JE, but more probably it reflects the recital of the cult legend at the sacramental celebration where the experience of the great salvation was communicated to succeeding generations (cf. 12:26-27).

10:7-11. The dramatic tempo now increases as Pharaoh's **servants,** i.e. presumably the members of his court, urge him to release the Hebrews. Their attitude emphasizes his own obduracy. He gives his consent with a qualification—that only the **men,** who alone could participate in the ritual, may go on the pilgrimage; their wives and **little ones** must remain behind. His imprecation **the LORD be with**

you, if ever I let you . . . go! is really a threat. Cf. the Arabic dismissal "With Allah!"—as distinct from the customary "With peace!"—to signify inability or reluctance to guarantee one's safety.

10:12-20. Locusts are brought into both Egypt and Palestine by the **east wind.** It is no exaggeration that they **covered the face of the land,** as evidenced from attacks in modern times—e.g. a swarm is reported covering an area of 10 by over 20 miles. In **I have sinned against the LORD** (vs. 16) the sense of guilt is apparently stronger than in 9:27; but **forgive my sin** (vs. 17) may mean simply "relieve my disability," without any significant consciousness of guilt, as the sequel indicates. **Not a single locust was left** (vs. 19), as is characteristic in the J narrative, emphasizes the miracle. On **Red Sea** see below on 13:18a.

10:21-29. *Darkness.* The 9th plague is described only by E (vss. 21-23, 27). On **darkness to be felt,** i.e. the concomitant of the sirocco, see above on 9:8-12. But the darkness may also portend the ultimate disaster, the reign of chaos in Egyptian mythology, where the inveterate enemy of the sun god Re, of whom Pharaoh was thought to be the incarnation, was Apophis, the serpent of chaotic darkness. Again the tradition may reflect the figurative description of the disasters of the Asian invasions in the papyrus of Nefer-rohu (see above on 7:14-11:10).

10:24-29. In the dramatic J narrative of the negotiations between Moses and Pharaoh this is the final climactic interview. Pharaoh makes his last offer: the Hebrews may go with their families but must leave their **flocks and . . . herds.** In alleging in reply that **we do not know with what we must serve the LORD until we arrive there** Moses is referring to the inspection of the sacrificial victims before and after slaughter. In saying **I will not see your face again** he may speak ambiguously, for to see the face of a monarch meant to depend on his favor (cf. e.g. Esth. 1:14). This statement seems to be contradicted by 11:4-8, but in the original J narrative the passage was the continuation of Moses' speech begun in vs. 29, now interrupted by 11:1-3.

11:1-10. *Warning of the Final Plague.* On vss. 2-3 see above on 3:19-22. Vss. 4-8 continue the J account of Moses' speech to Pharaoh beginning in 10:29 and ending with his departure **in hot anger,** matching that of Pharaoh (10:28). The final stroke **about midnight** (vs. 4) relates to the nocturnal rite of passover. The language of vs. 5 is repeated with a variant in 12:29. The narrative prose here is influenced by the cadence and style of Hebrew poetry, perhaps reflecting original poetic cult legends. The slave girl grinding grain into meal represents the lowest status in society (cf. Judg. 16:21; Isa. 47:2). **Behind the mill** suggests a rubbing stone pushed back and forth along a shallow stone mortar. On **cattle** see above on 9:19-21. **Growl** (vs. 7) is lit. "sharpen his tongue" (cf. Josh. 10:21). **Dog** may be a corruption for "all," i.e. "no one." Vss. 9-10 come from a P editor.

F. Memorials of the Deliverance (12:1–13:16)

The traditions associate with the Exodus 3 religious observances of Israel: passover, the feast of unleavened bread, and dedication of the firstborn. It is clear that they were originally separate. Passover, as bedouin analogies suggest, is most readily intelligible as a nomad rite on the eve of departure from the desert for summer grazings, but it may also have been associated with the return to the desert by nomads who had seasonal grazings in Egypt. Unleavened bread was an agricultural festival inaugurating the barley harvest, evidently adopted from the Canaanites after the settlement in Palestine. In the P source, both here and in Lev. 23:5-8; Num. 28:16-25, these 2 observances are associated; but in the ancient festal calendars in 23:15; 34:18-23 the commands to observe the feast of unleavened bread say nothing about the passover. Hence there is question of how soon the 2 came to be connected.

The elevation of the passover from a family observance in the home to the status of a pilgrimage feast in the temple is described as an innovation by Josiah late in the 7th cent. (II Kings 23:21-23). Though this account makes no mention of unleavened bread, it ascribes Josiah's action to a written ordinance, presumably Deut. 16:1-8, which combines the 2 festivals, though it shows consciousness that this combination is an innovation. In emphasizing the novelty of Josiah's passover II Kings 23:22 states that it was a reversion to a practice in the time of the judges. This is borne out in the association of the 2 festivals at Gilgal in Josh. 5:10-12, which appears to be a late passage but may preserve an early tradition. At any rate it would be natural for the Israelite tribes, in coming together at a common sanctuary to realize their solidarity on the basis of their common experience of the Exodus, sacramentally preserved, to associate with this the feast of unleavened bread, and perhaps also the passover.

This association was designed to preserve Israel from assimilation to Canaanite religion in the settlement in Palestine, when the settlers were most prone to appropriate with the new techniques of agriculture the rites and ideology of the festivals at the great seasonal crises. Thus also Hebrew elements which had not been in Egypt were associated with the historical experience of the Exodus and the covenant, which were the bases of the Israelite confederacy.

12:1-13. *The P Passover Ordinance.* This passage is an expansion of the older ordinance in J (vss. 21-27). The old agricultural and civil year in Israel apparently began in the autumn (cf. 23:16; 34:22; see Chronology, pp. 1271-82) but during, or possibly before, the Exile the Mesopotamian calendar with a spring new year was adopted. The postexilic P author here assumes that the calendar used in his day dated back to the Exodus. Sometime before the Exile, perhaps for convenience in international trade, the months came to be known by numbers beginning with a spring new year (see comment on Jer. 28:17) and thus in P the passover is regularly dated in the **first month.** This month was earlier known by the Canaanite name Abib (cf. 13:4) and later by the Babylonian name Nisan (cf. Neh. 2:1; Esth. 3:7).

12:3-6. Characteristically P regards the Hebrews as already a **congregation,** i.e. a compact religious community. The keeping of the **lamb,** or kid (vs. 5; cf. Deut. 16:2), from the **tenth day** (vs. 3) to the **fourteenth** (vs. 6), whatever its origin, is incongruous with a hurried departure and reflects the later rite in a settled community. In the public festival in the 2nd temple units of 10 shared a lamb, but no such strict **count** is visualized here; rather the number is to be reckoned by what each can eat, taking account of the age, sex, and health of the members of the family. That the victim must be **without blemish,** i.e. ritually perfect, implies inspection both before and after killing—again inconsistent with hurried departure. The significance of this domestic ceremony for the whole community is conserved by the simultaneous slaughter. The lambs are to be killed **in the evening,** lit. "between the two evenings." The Pharisees interpreted this as meaning between midafternoon, when the sun's heat abated, and sunset, whereas the Sadducees took it to mean between sunset and dark (cf. "at sunset," Deut. 16:6).

12:7-10. The sprinkling of **blood** on the **doorposts** and **lintel,** which were specifically associated with supernatural influences (cf. 21:6; Deut. 6:9; 11:20; Isa. 57:8), as a prophylactic rite (cf. vss. 13, 23) has analogies in ancient Mesopotamia and among the Arabs, who smear blood on the door of a house during an epidemic. The victim in this rite is called a "redemption." Such a sacrifice is made also before such new enterprises as the completion of a house or the digging of a well, and among the Rashaideh bedouin of the Syrian desert in connection with their early summer migration. **Night** (vs. 8) is the transitional period when evil influences are esp. active. The Hebrew word translated **roasted** emphasizes fire, the firepit of primitive desert cooking, as still at the Samaritan passover at Nablus. In Deut. 16:7 the victim may be **boiled.** In addition to the roasting the **unleavened bread** (see below on vss. 14-20), the normal bedouin bread, and the **bitter herbs,** the normal bedouin seasoning, are primitive features. Later they were artificially connected with the hasty departure (vs. 34) and the bitter treatment in Egypt. The prohibition against eating the meat **raw** grows out of the blood taboo in Israel and may reflect an earlier custom of eating raw meat in the rite. Nothing is to be left over until the next day (vs. 10) lest the sacrifice be profaned by persons in an unsanctified state or at an unsanctified time.

12:11-13. The departure of migrant nomads is reflected in **loins girded,** i.e. the long robe tucked up in the belt, **sandals on** instead of lying at the entrance to the house, and **staff in . . . hand.** The word translated **in haste** implies trepidation; Isa. 52:12 promises that the 2nd exodus, from Babylon, will not be "in haste." The derivation of *pesach,* **passover,** from an assumed Hebrew verb **pass over** (cf. vs. 27), i.e. "jump," the houses to be spared is unlikely. The etymology has not yet been determined but the most feasible suggestion is that it is related to an Arabic verb meaning "separate." In associating the **first-born** of **man and beast** the P source, following J (cf. vs. 29; 13:11-16), connects the passover with the dedication and redemption of the firstborn.

12:14-20. The P Unleavened Bread Ordinance. The leavening of bread was accomplished by mixing with the dough a piece of old dough in which yeast had been allowed to develop. Thus the **leaven** was in a sense a corruption (cf. Matt. 16:6; I Cor. 5:6-8). The elimination of leaven was designed to preserve

the new crop, with its direct association with the supernatural, from contact with the profane until its due desacralizing through the ritual. Being **cut off from Israel** probably means the equivalent of excommunication, but see comment on Lev. 20:2-9. **Holy** denotes the condition resulting from ritual contact with what has been consecrated by the divine presence. Hence work was suspended not only as a precaution against the contamination of the holy by the profane but also as a protection of the profane against the dread influence of the holy—cf. Uzzah's touching the ark (II Sam. 6:6-7). The terms **sojourner** (see above on 2:21-22) and **native of the land** clearly refer to the conditions after the settlement in Palestine.

12:21-28. The J Passover Ordinance. Since the last sentence of vs. 27 is the natural conclusion to vss. 21-24, evidently vss. 25-27*a* are a later addition, possibly D. In contrast to P (cf. vss. 1-14, 43-49) the J author assumes familiarity with the rite requiring no specific description. Therefore there is greater significance to the few details given, viz. the sprinkling with **blood** (vss. 22-23), the injunction that no one leave the house **until the morning** (vs. 22), and the **destroyer** (vs. 23). This last, obviously some demonic power, is the supernatural agent in J; in the secondary didactic exposition (vss. 26-27*a*) the slayer is Yahweh himself. In vs. 28 the association of **Aaron** with Moses (contrast vs. 21) indicates P.

12:29-36. The Last Plague. The dramatic pattern of the J narrative is resumed with the sequel to the warning in 11:4-8. The stroke falls **at midnight** (cf. Ps. 91:6; on the poetic language in vs. 29 see above on 11:1-10). Pharaoh now capitulates unconditionally, seeking the favor of Yahweh, whom he has so arrogantly ignored. This skillfully constructed dramatic narrative, best preserved in J, betrays its origin in saga and in cult legend, the latter predominating as the natural association of the ritual of passover and unleavened bread indicates. Some interpreters have suggested that historically only the oldest son of the king himself died, affording the Hebrews an opportunity to escape during the period of mourning; and others theorize about an epidemic of some children's disease. But the suddenness and completeness of the disaster in the traditions admit of no such naturalistic explanation. The incident of the spoiling of the Egyptians (vss. 35-36) is the fulfillment of 3:21-22 (see comment; cf. 11:2).

12:37-39. The Departure. This passage is generally viewed as a continuation of the J narrative from vs. 34; but the fact that hereafter only P particularizes on localities in the exodus itinerary, as well as the exaggerated and artificial statistics, while not excluding an earlier tradition, suggests the possibility that vs. 37 comes from P or has been rewritten by a P editor. **Journeyed,** lit. "pulled up tent pegs," is reminiscent of Israel's nomadic origins. **Rameses** is the same as Raamses (see above on 1:11). **Succoth,** though spelled like the Hebrew word for "booths," probably represents an Egyptian name denoted by its hieroglyphic determinative as a border town in a district inhabited by foreigners. Its probable site has been located in the E part of the Wadi Tumilat, *ca.* 30 miles SE of Rameses (see color map 4). **About six hundred thousand men** far exceeds the strength even of imperial armies in the records of the ancient Near East. Even with the crudest weapons such a force could surely have overpowered Ramses II's army of *ca.* 20,000. With **women and children** the population would have totaled over 2 million, much more than any oasis in the Sinai region could sustain. The figure may be a round number derived from the census total in 38:26 (see comment).

12:38-39. The **mixed multitude,** as the use of the same adjective in Neh. 13:3 indicates, consisted of non-Israelites, including no doubt Canaanite deportees in Egypt (see Intro.). With the association of the passover and unleavened bread in mind the J author notices the completion of **unleavened cakes.** The LXX and the Vulg. say that these were **baked** in hot embers (cf. I Kings 19:6).

12:40-42. *A P Chronological Note.* The length of the sojourn in Egypt, **four hundred and thirty years** (cf. 400, Gen. 15:13; Acts 7:6), is artificial, like all P statistics, and fits poorly with the P genealogy in 6:16-20, where Moses is Levi's great-grandson. Feeling this difficulty the LXX and the Samaritan Pentateuch include in the 430 years the earlier sojourn of the patriarchs in Canaan. The word translated **watching** has the sense both of guarding (vs. 42*a*) and of observing a commemoration (vs. 42*b*).

12:43-50. *Further P Passover Regulations.* Unlike a **hired servant,** assumed to be a **foreigner,** a **slave,** being a permanent member of the household, is permitted to participate in the passover if made a member of the religious community by being **circumcised.** The word translated **sojourner** in vs. 45 means rather "settler," one of a foreign group who may have penetrated the land and taken up residence there, e.g. the Edomites who moved into S Judah after 586. On the other hand **stranger** in vs. 48 renders the word usually translated "sojourner" (see above on 2:21-22). In his special relation to the Israelite tribe he is to be admitted to the passover rite if he is circumcised, since he comes under the protection of Yahweh, whose power he thus practically confesses. The eating of one lamb in **one house,** nothing being taken **outside** (vs. 46), prevents unlawful participation. The injunction not to **break a bone** probably reflects association of the rite with the health of the flocks. Some interpreters have taken this to be the scripture said in John 19:36 to have been fulfilled when Jesus' legs were not broken after his crucifixion, but the quotation there is rather from Ps. 34:20.

13:1-2. *The P Ordinance of the Firstborn.* Fuller P regulations for the dedication and redemption of the firstborn appear in Lev. 27:26-27; Num. 3:11-13, 44-51; 8:17-18; 18:15-18. Here P simply endorses the connection the Exodus already made by J (vss. 11-13) and D (vss. 14-16; cf. Deut. 15:19-23, where the ordinance is stated as the prelude to the passover ordinance). Like other peoples of the ancient Near East the ancestors of the Israelites probably at one time actually sacrificed their firstborn children, as Gen. 22:1-14 (cf. Mic. 6:7) implies, though perhaps only in critical emergencies. Num. 3:47; 18:16 specify 5 shekels of silver as the redemption price, to be the perquisite of the priests.

13:3-10. *The J Unleavened Bread Ordinance.* No date for the rite is given in J beyond the month of the Exodus, **Abib** (see above on 9:31-32; 12:1-13),

but cf. **at its appointed time from year to year** (vs. 10). This passage has been expanded by a D editor (vss. 3*b-d*, 5, 8-9), whose pleonastic style, stereotyped description of the promised land, emphasis on the law in the context of sacramental history, and didactic interest are unmistakable.

13:8-9. Both the corporate consciousness of the ancient Israelite and the continued sacramental experiencing of the Exodus are reflected in **what the LORD did for me when I came out of Egypt.** The language and thought in these vss. suggest Deut. 6:4-9 (cf. Deut. 11:18-19), according to the literal interpretation of which orthodox Jews after confirmation attach to their foreheads and arms during morning prayer boxes containing miniature scrolls of vss. 1-10, 11-16; Deut. 6:4-9; 11:13-21—the phylacteries of Matt. 23:5. The **law of the LORD . . . in your mouth** indicates the law, or a résumé of it, in the context of the great deliverance, which reflects Israel's sacramental experience of the covenant. Law in Israel implied the gospel of God's grace in the deliverance and his election of Israel sealed by the covenant. The law was not the condition of the covenant; it was the expression of Israel's status as the covenanted people.

13:11-16. *The J Ordinance of the Firstborn.* This ordinance is repeated elsewhere in J (34:19-20) and appears also in the Book of the Covenant in E (22:29-30) and in D (Deut. 15:19-23) and P (see above on vss. 1-2). Vss. 14-16 here are an expansion by a D editor. As belonging to Yahweh the firstborn is **set apart** as holy or sacrosanct (see above on 12:14-20) and must be either sacrificed or desacralized, i.e. released for common life and use, by a substitute sacrifice. The word translated **redeem** here is not that used in 6:6; 15:13, which involves the duty of a kinsman; this verb denotes simply an impersonal transaction of substitution. An **ass** must be redeemed by sacrifice of a **lamb** because it is ritually unclean; for this reason its **neck** must be broken if it is not redeemed, lest its blood be shed as in a sacrifice. Cuneiform tablets found at Mari on the middle Euphrates (see color map 2) mention an Amorite rite involving sacrifice of an ass; though not attested in Palestine such a pagan custom may lie behind the ban here. The association of dedication of the firstborn with the Exodus may have originated with its observance at the pilgrimage feast of unleavened bread (cf. 23:15), when the solidarity of the community was realized by the sacramental experiencing of the deliverance.

G. THE RESCUE AT THE SEA (13:17–15:21)

In the grand climax of the drama of salvation the effect of the J narrative based on the cult legend is again marred by combination with P amplifications and geographical notes. Only a limited amount of E material appears. Whatever the historical nucleus may have been, the tradition was transmitted to the older sources, not as factual annals, but as the substance of faith in a highly dramatized cult legend and saga emphasizing the miraculous action of Yahweh. The dominance of the deliverance at the sea as the supreme divine act of might and mercy and the genesis of the religious community of Israel recurs through scripture, esp. in Isa. 40; 43, and is

taken by Paul as the prototype of Christian baptism (I Cor. 10:1-2).

13:17-18a. Route of the Departure in E. Apparently relying on the saga form of the tradition, E notes the avoidance of the **way of the land of the Philistines.** The name is an anachronism, since Egyptian records show that the Philistines did not settle in Palestine till the first half of the 12th cent., but the coastal route had been long the regular military road to the N. The fleeing Hebrews would **see war** if they attempted to pass its fortifications. The mention of it suggests Rameses (cf. 12:37; see above on 1:11) as at least one point of departure.

13:18a. The **way of the wilderness** may have been an alternative inland caravan route. The Hebrew words translated **Red Sea,** following the LXX, mean lit. "Papyrus Sea" or "Lake." The term is the Hebrew name for the sea on the S side of the world known to Israel, including the Gulf of Suez (10:19; Num. 33:10-11) and the Gulf of Aqaba (23:31; Num. 14:25; 21:4; Deut. 1:40; 2:1; I Kings 9:26; Jer. 49:21); but this usage, though ancient, is evidently secondary and arose from the tradition that Israel crossed in the Exodus a body of water of this name on the E border of Egypt. There has been much debate about the body actually crossed:

a) Traditionally the N end of the Gulf of Suez has been assumed. Such a location, however, would involve too long a journey through desert country;

geological evidence has disproved the theory that in ancient times the sea extended farther N than at present. No reeds grow along this shore.

b) The name "Papyrus Lake" indicates fresh water and therefore suggests the N or S end of Lake Timsah, or possibly the N end of the Great Bitter Lake. Such a location is suggested by the older tradition reflected in the P itinerary (see below on vs. 20). This route would lead directly into the wilderness of Shur (15:22).

c) An arm of Lake Menzaleh (see color map 4) may be indicated by an Egyptian text mentioning a Papyrus Lake near Rameses.

d) E of Lake Menzaleh on the Mediterranean is the salt marsh of Bardawil (Lake Sirbonis; see color map 4), separated from the sea by a narrow sandspit which is generally a dry salt crust capable of bearing men and light animals but occasionally is flooded. The situation fits with a naturalistic explanation of the sea crossing but is less easy to fit with the traditions about the route of the departure. Whether or not Bardawil was the site of the actual crossing, acquaintance with it by travelers to Egypt may have influenced the later elaboration of the narrative (see below on 14:1-4).

13:18b-19. It is unlikely that the escaping serfs were **equipped for battle.** Probably the word means "by fives" or possibly "by fifties" and thus refers to a regular formation. On the **bones of Joseph** cf. Gen. 50:25.

13:20. A P Itinerary. On **Succoth** see above on 12:37-39. **Etham** has not been located but was probably an Egyptian border fortress. Possibly it was the redoubt on the desert edge E of Succoth mentioned in a police report of the late 13th cent. concerning 2 fugitive slaves. This document is doubly significant for the tradition of the Exodus, indicating the concern of the pharaoh for escaping slaves and the existence in this locale of a route into the wilderness of Shur (cf. 15:22). Here P seems to reflect earlier traditions of a Hebrew departure from Egypt at the E end of the Wadi Tumilat (see below on 14:1-4).

13:21-22. The Pillar of Cloud and Fire. This feature of the J account has been naturalistically explained as a glowing brazier carried by guides, with which analogies may be cited from desert experience. Fire, however, is a sign of the divine presence (cf. e.g. 3:2; 9:23; 19:18) as is a cloud (cf. e.g. 19:9; 33:9-10; 40:34-38).

14:1-4. A Change of Itinerary. The divine command to **turn back** is represented by the P author as for the purpose of encouraging pursuit so that Yahweh may **get glory over Pharaoh,** but this explanation is evidently his attempt to reconcile 2 different traditions of the itinerary—one starting in the Wadi Tumilat around Succoth (cf. 12:37; 13:20), with a crossing of Lake Timsah or possibly the Great Bitter Lake, the other starting no doubt in the NE Delta near Rameses (cf. 12:37) and involving the places named in vs. 2, with a crossing of an arm of Lake Menzaleh or more probably the sandspit between the Bardawil salt marsh and the Mediterranean (see above on 13:18a). It is likely that the S route preserves an older tradition and the N reflects the memory of Jewish refugees who came that way to Egypt after 586. Each version, however, may reflect the traditions of various groups at the time of the Exodus and at the time of the postexilic settlement in Egypt.

Migdol was probably a fortress on the military road to Palestine (cf. 13:17) which is depicted with its fort and well in a sculpture of Seti I at Karnak. Probably it was located *ca.* 12 miles NE of the modern city of Qantara on the Suez Canal, though an alternative location in the Wadi Tumilat has been suggested. **Baal-zephon** evidently took its name from the shrine of a Canaanite god. Inscriptions from the Roman imperial period found amid remains *ca.* 12 miles N of the supposed site of Migdol identify a shrine of Zeus Kasios, certainly the Greek adaptation of Baal-Zephon. Some scholars, however, believe that the shrine of Baal-zephon was at Tahpanes (see color map 4). **Pi-hahiroth** may come from an Egyptian name meaning "mouth of the canals"; if so, in this context it suggests a site near the E-most mouth of the Nile. A location in the Wadi Tumilat which is at least etymologically feasible has also been proposed. **The wilderness has shut them in** probably means that the desert with its lack of water has confined the Hebrews to established routes, where they are easily followed.

14:5-18. The Pursuit. The J narrative now moves forward, with some P material (vss. 8, 15-18 and at least the locations in vs. 9b; cf. vs. 2). **Officers over all of them** (vs. 7) means rather "charioteers in each of them"; the word originally denoted the 3rd man in a chariot team of 3. The dismay of the Hebrews (vss. 10-12) is effectively used by the J author to heighten the approaching climax. Moses' prophetic assurance in response, **Fear not, stand firm, and see the salvation of the LORD,** focuses attention on the coming great act of God. **Salvation** here preserves something of the word's primary physical connotation of width or freedom (see comment on Ps. 3), which redeems it from deterioration into glib homiletic jargon. The suspense of the J narrative is ruined by the P synopsis (vss. 15-18) giving away the climax of the story. With theological rather than dramatic interest the P author sees the final event as a convincing demonstration of divine power rather than as the merciful deliverance of the people. P alone particularizes on the actual dividing of the sea (vs. 16).

14:19-31. The Passage of the Sea. This account is a highly complex interweaving of the 3 literary sources, though the E contribution is very small. Having depicted the Hebrews menaced by the Egyptians but reassured of divine aid (vss. 10-14), J states that Yahweh's presence symbolized by the **pillar of cloud** shifted position and **stood behind** them, i.e. between them and the Egyptians (vs. 19b). E agrees in the same shift but embodies the divine presence in the **angel of God** (vs. 19a). Vs. 20 probably includes all 3 sources, but the only clearly identifiable element is the **darkness,** mentioned also in Josh. 24:7, which probably represents the preliterary tradition behind E.

In spite of their variations all the sources agree in emphasizing the element of miracle. This agreement should discourage all attempts at naturalistic interpretation. Even if natural phenomena contributed to the deliverance, their coincidence with Israel's need was in itself a miracle.

14:21-22. In P Moses controls the action by holding out his **hand** (vs. 21a; cf. vss. 26-27). In J, however, the event is entirely the work of Yahweh, who **drove the sea back by a strong east wind all night, and made the sea dry land** (vs. 21b). Here it is probably the J author rather than his sources who essays a naturalistic explanation—the drying up by a sirocco of a moist depression, which is all that the Hebrew word for **sea** need signify (see above on 13:18a). In P the **waters** of the sea are **divided** (vs. 21c; cf. vs. 16) and form a **wall** on each side of the Hebrews as they walk between (vs. 22). This may be an elaboration of a tradition visualizing passage along the narrow sandspit between the salt marsh of Bardawil and the Mediterranean, but more probably it is a prose paraphrase of the hyperbolic poetical representation in the hymnic celebration of the deliverance (cf. 15:8). This is a good example of the principle that the problem of miracle is not to be solved either by naturalistic explanation or by dogmatic approach without the preliminary discipline of analysis of the literary sources and the traditions behind them.

14:23-30. In vs. 24 J transmits what is probably the original tradition, that **in the morning watch,** i.e. toward morning, **the LORD in the pillar of fire and of cloud looked down upon . . . the Egyptians . . . and discomfited them,** i.e. threw them into a panic. The theme of the sea in vs. 27cd seems to represent a different tradition, which the J author may have drawn from the hymnic version in the cult, e.g. the Song of Miriam (15:21b) and its development in the ps. attributed to Moses (15:1b-18). The note that God bound up **their chariot wheels so that they drove heavily** (vs. 25a) seems secondary, as is suggested by the statement that only thereafter did the Egyptians decide to flee (vs. 25b) whereas they have apparently already panicked (vs. 24b). This detail may indicate the swamping of a depression with ground water by a sudden rainstorm, the looking forth of Yahweh from the pillar of fire suggesting thunder and lightning with rain, which was sufficiently rare in the Delta to be considered a miracle, esp. when coinciding with the need of the Hebrews. The statement that the sea **returned to its wonted flow** (vs. 27b), probably secondary, may be an instance of the saga motif of a striking phenomenon and its reverse—cf. e.g. the rod and serpent (4:3-4), Moses' leprosy (4:6-7), Gideon's fleece (Judg. 6:37-40). **When the morning appeared** possibly relates to the cult legend of the nocturnal passover festival.

14:31. This conclusion, perhaps editorial, clearly indicates the subject of cult legend, a miracle which confirms the faith of Israel in Yahweh and his prophet. Nevertheless the substantial agreement of all sources, in spite of variations, in the deliverance from an Egyptian chariot force at the sea indicates a historical nucleus for the tradition, however this may have been modified in its transmission in saga and cult legend.

15:1-21. The Song of the Sea. This poem consists of a hymn on the theme of the deliverance at the sea (vss. 1b-12) developed from the older "Song of Miriam" (vs. 21bc), which is apparently contemporary with the event itself, and a further development on the themes of the occupation of Palestine (vss.

13-16) and **thy own mountain** and the **sanctuary** where Yahweh **will reign** as King (vss. 17-18). It is clear that vss. 13-18 date from after the settlement in Palestine, specifically after the subjection of the Philistines (vs. 14) under David and probably after the development of the cult of Yahweh as King in the new year festival in Solomon's temple.

Many scholars have taken vss. 1, 20-21 as parallel J and E versions of the original victory song and regarded vss. 2-18 as a much later composition, late preexilic or even postexilic, inserted by an editor. Recently, however, certain scholars have noted points of prosody which appear to be an early development from Canaanite poetry attested in 14th-cent. Ugaritic texts found at Ras Shamra in N Syria. Certain archaic grammatical forms also give evidence of an early date. Accordingly it may well be that vss. 1b-12, 21bc formed the hymnic culmination of the cult legend of the sacrament of the deliverance at the central shrine of the Israelite tribes before David's occupation of Jerusalem. If so, the addition of vss. 13-18 may represent the adaptation of the old hymn to the service of the temple in Jerusalem in the time of Solomon. Thus the whole may have been incorporated intact as the culmination of the J narrative of the deliverance.

The theme of the kingship of Yahweh (vs. 18), symbolized by the establishment of his **abode** (vs. 13), the **sanctuary** (vs. 17), after his triumph in conflict with the forces of chaos represented by the sea, reproduces with historical adaptation the theme of the Canaanite new year festival illustrated in the Ras Shamra texts. This relationship seems to connect the whole composite ps. to the Israelite festival involving renewal of the covenant with Yahweh and its historical prelude in the exodus theme.

15:1b-5. Praise of Yahweh for what he has done in the deliverance at the sea forms the intro. to the ancient ps. in vss. 1b-12 and the refrain which punctuates it in vss. 5, 10, 12—perhaps in response to prompting such as is attributed to Miriam in vss. 20-21a. Thus introduced and epitomized, the song declares the elation in which the singer praises his **father's God,** who is personally experienced. Vs. 2a expresses the consciousness of possession by the divine spirit, which inspires the poet with supernatural insights and powers of expression. **My strength** indicates assurance, urge, and ability to praise Yahweh, whose nature as a **man of war** is revealed by his overthrow of the Egyptians. The **floods** (vs. 5) are the subterranean waters of Semitic cosmology, conceived sometimes naturally (e.g. Gen. 7:11; 8:2; Deut. 8:7; Amos 7:4), sometimes mythologically (e.g. Pss. 46:2-3; 89:8-9; 93:3-4). The Hebrew word is related to Tiamat, the Mesopotamian mythological monster of chaotic waters overcome by the god Marduk in the liturgy of the Babylonian new year festival.

15:6-10. The 2nd strophe expresses the confidence and eager anticipation of the pursuers by the staccato of verbs in vs. 9. The boastful **desire,** i.e. greed, of the **enemy** points up the might of Yahweh, which is elaborated with poetic hyperbole in the piling up of the **waters** by the **blast of thy nostrils**—a phrase that suggests at once the sirocco, i.e. the hot E wind (cf. 14:21), associated with Yahweh as a desert god, and the figurative sense of the Hebrew word for "nostrils," his anger.

15:11-12. In the Hebrew **holiness** is the proper and exclusive nature of God, the wholly Other. The word itself has no moral connotation, though as relating to the God of Israel it has secondarily a moral sense. If textually correct here it emphasizes the exclusiveness of Yahweh's majesty, but the LXX reading "among the holy ones" probably preserves the original parallel to **among the gods.** The recognition of the God of Israel as one among other gods indicates an early date. Thus the defiant rhetorical question **Who is like thee . . . among the gods?** expresses preeminence over rivals. The basis of it is Yahweh's effective action, **doing wonders** in nature and history, esp. in the overthrow of the Egyptians. **The earth swallowed them** may allude to the bogging down of Pharaoh's chariots (cf. 14:25a); on the other hand the detail in the narrative may have been suggested by this passage in the hymn. If so, the prose author probably misinterpreted it, for by **earth** the poet evidently intended to denote Sheol, the underworld abode of the dead (see comment on Ps. 6:4-5). Vs. 12 may have been followed originally by the call **Sing to the LORD** and the remainder of vs. 21bc, reechoing the opening couplet of the ps. (vs. 1bc; see above on vss. 1-21).

15:13-18. The form of these vss., which are not in strophes and lack the refrain on the victory at the sea, gives further evidence that they are a later addition to the hymn of vss. 1b-12 (see above on vss. 1-21). The opening couplet on God's guidance of his people introduces and epitomizes their subject, viz. the desert wandering and occupation of Canaan (vss. 13-16) and the occupation of Jerusalem, denoted probably in **thy holy abode** (vs. 13) and certainly in vss. 17-18. The Hebrew word translated **steadfast love** (vs. 13) always implies the concept of loyalty to the covenant. On **redeemed** see above on 6:6-9. The sudden collapse of **Edom** and **Moab** (vs. 15) does not correspond to Pentateuchal tradition and evidences a date when the effective resistance of both was long forgotten, i.e. after their conquest by David. **Purchased** (vs. 16) is a possible translation but the word may also mean "created" (cf. e.g. Deut. 32:6c).

15:19-21. The prosaic summary in vs. 19 indicates how a late P editor, no longer conscious of the original cultic context of the hymn, interprets its figures lit. Probably vss. 20-21a accurately describe the ritual in which the poem originated, with prompting by women in a high state of elation to **sing to the LORD** and response by the worshipers in the remaining words of vs. 21bc. **Miriam,** here mentioned for the first time, is identified as the **sister of Aaron** (see above on 2:1-10) and said to be a **prophetess,** i.e. an inspired, ecstatic female like the prophets of early times (see comments on Num. 11:16-25; I Sam. 10:1c-13; cf. Deborah, Judg. 4-5). A **timbrel** was a small percussion instrument made of skin stretched tightly over a frame used primarily to accompany **dancing** (cf. Judg. 11:34; I Sam. 18:6-7; Ps. 150:4).

II. The Desert Wandering (15:22–18:27)

The independence and continuity of the traditions of Yahweh's provision of food (ch. 16; cf. Num.

11:4-35) and water (15:22-27; 17:1b-7; cf. Num. 20:2-13) in the desert, with the related themes of murmuring against Moses and the vital significance of Moses and his rod before and after the tradition of the giving of the law at Mt. Sinai, suggest an originally independent tradition of the desert wandering, if not an independent Moses saga, as a basic source.

15:22-27. The Spring at Marah. This passage, introduced and concluded by geographical details in the style of P (vss. 22a, 27), is basically a J narrative explaining the name of the spring **Marah,** meaning **bitter,** to which has been joined an E fragment (vs. 25b) related to a spring named Massah, "proving" (cf. 17:1-7), that has been elaborated by a D editor (vs. 26). The **wilderness of Shur** was apparently the N Sinai area immediately E of the modern Suez Canal (cf. Gen. 25:18; I Sam. 15:7; 27:8; see color map 4). The name may be a dialectic word, "wall," used by the Semites in Sinai or possibly a version of the Egyptian name Taru, the key fortress E of the Delta in the chain of fortresses called the "Wall of the Prince." The period of **three days** without **water** seems saga convention rather than history. Despite reports of Near Eastern shrubs capable of sweetening brackish water no such plant is certainly known.

15:25b-27. The statement that Yahweh **made for them a statute and an ordinance and . . . proved them,** which makes his preservation of Israel conditional on obedience, seems displaced from some point after the giving of the law at the holy mountain. The preservation from **diseases,** abruptly introduced and associated with the observance of the commandments, may have been suggested by the concept of Yahweh as **healer,** participle of the verb used of sweetening water at Jericho (II Kings 2:21-22) and the Dead Sea (Ezek. 47:7-8). **Elim** may be the plural of either "terebinth," a species of tree common in Palestine, or "god." If the latter, the name evidently refers to local spirits such as the Arabs often associate with oases, springs, and isolated trees. **Twelve** and **seventy** suggest the stylization of saga, which must qualify any attempt at localization.

16:1-36. Manna and Quails. This ch. is mainly from P but includes a briefer account of the manna only (vss. 4-5, 13b-15a, 27-30) from one of the early sources—probably J, though some scholars connect **that I may prove them** (vs. 4b) with 15:25b and attribute the material to E. That the incident is chronologically out of order (cf. the J quail narrative, Num. 11:4-35) is shown by the references to Yahweh's **glory** in the **cloud** (vs. 10), which P associates with the tabernacle (cf. 40:34-38), and to the **Testimony** (vs. 34), i.e. the tablets of the Decalogue placed in the ark (cf. 25:16).

16:1. Representation of the Hebrews as a **congregation** is characteristic of P. Location of the **wilderness of Sin** depends on the location of Mt. **Sinai.** Those who accept the traditional identification with Jebel Musa in the S part of the Sinai Peninsula assume the wilderness of Sin to lie NW of that peak (see color map 4). But the probability that the holy mountain should be located in the N Sinai region near Kadesh (see above on 3:1) points rather to Sin's being a variant form of Zin, perhaps by association with Sinai. The wilderness of Zin is men-

tioned in connection with Kadesh (Num. 20:1; 27:14; Deut. 32:51; Josh. 15:3) and is described as W of Edom (Num. 34:3; Josh. 15:1) and at the S limit of the settled land of Palestine (Num. 13:21).

16:2-12. The murmuring against Moses is one of the themes of the tradition of the desert wandering. **Bread from heaven** (vs. 4) is not spiritual food as allegorized by Paul (I Cor. 10:3) but food in a general sense coming from the sky, as the manna was thought to come. The cessation of manna on the sabbath, anticipated by the double portion on the **sixth day** (vs. 5), may be a secondary elaboration suggested by the special sanctity of the sabbath noted both in the Decalogue (20:8) and in the Ritual Code (34:21). Apparently vss. 9-12 should precede vss. 6-7, and vs. 8 is an editorial addition.

16:13a. P has inserted the **quails** in this story from the J account in Num. 11:31-34. Like manna, quails are a natural phenomenon of the N Sinai region, where they come as autumn migrants from S Europe. Making their landfall on the coast of Egypt and S Palestine, they are so exhausted that they are easily netted and sent in large numbers to the cities. The quail tradition shows that the Hebrews came near the Mediterranean coast (cf. Num. 11:31), perhaps preserving the memory of a seasonal expedition from the inland area generally occupied.

16:13b-15a. In Sinai and other desert regions manna is a sweet substance found, not **on the ground,** but on the low tamarisk shrubs. It has generally been assumed to be an exudation of the plant, perhaps after perforation by an insect, but according to one study it is an excretion of certain plant lice which solidifies in the dry desert air. The popular etymology which J essays—*man hu,* Aramaic rather than Hebrew for **What is it?**—is obviously unlikely.

16:15b-30. In contrast to the general sense of J in vs. 4, P uses **bread** in the specific sense—cf. Num. 11:8, where the manna is said to be actually ground with the millstone. The **omer,** defined as the **tenth part of an ephah** (vs. 36; see "Measures and Money," pp. 1283-85), i.e. *ca.* 1.6 dry quarts, occurs only here. It is to be distinguished from the homer, which was 10 ephahs. The disappearance of the manna **when the sun grew hot** (vs. 21) is due, not to melting, but to its being eaten by ants which come out with the warmth. On the **sabbath** see below on 20:8.

16:31-35. On **honey** see above on 3:7-10. J compares the **taste** to "cakes baked with oil" (Num. 11:8). In N Sinai manna (Arabic *mann*) is still valued for its sugar content, in which the desert diet is deficient. The tradition that a pot of manna was preserved **before the Testimony,** i.e. with the 2 tables of the Decalogue, is specifically denied in a D statement that the ark contained nothing but these tables (I Kings 8:9).

17:1-7. Water from the Rock. After the intro. about the itinerary from P (vs. 1a; on **wilderness of Sin** see above on 16:1; on **Rephidim** see below on vss. 8-16) the narrative is an interweaving of similar traditions about 2 different springs from J and E. In the J account (vss. 2c-3, 7a, c) the spring is named **Massah,** "proving" or "ordeal," explained on the basis that there the people tested Yahweh. A fragment of the E tradition of Massah, in which Yahweh tests the people, has been preserved in 15:25b, being confused with the story of the spring of Marah from J. In the E narrative here the spring is called **Meribah,** "contention," reflecting the competition for precious water among desert nomads (cf. Gen. 21:25-32; 26:19-22). The parallel narrative combined from J and P associates Meribah with Kadesh (Num. 20:2-13; cf. Num. 27:14; Deut. 32:51) and suggests that it was one of the minor springs within the Kadesh oasis, an area *ca.* 5 miles in radius from Ain el-Qudeirat, where there is a fort of the 8th-7th cents., probably occupied earlier. **Bring us up** (vs. 3) is a regular expression for the Exodus, i.e. coming up from the Delta to the mountains of N Sinai and Palestine. As in the plague narrative E is distinguished by the use of the **rod** (vs. 5). **The rock** (vs. 6) probably means "this rock," **at Horeb** (see above on 3:1) being a later addition.

17:8-16. *The Battle with Amalek.* This narrative was possibly incorporated as a unit in the E source from a hero saga about Moses, the leader on whose raised or lowered hands the fortunes of war depend. The sudden appearance of **Joshua** as a warrior, whereas in 33:11 he is introduced as Moses' **servant** and a **young man,** indicates that the incident really belongs to a later phase of the desert wandering, probably following the initial defeat by the Amalekites near Hormah SE of Beer-sheba (Num. 14:43-45; cf. Num. 21:1-3). It was perhaps part of a Joshua saga secondarily associated with Moses. The tradition has become an explanatory legend for the names of **Rephidim,** "supports," and the **altar** called **The LORD is my banner** (vs. 15) in the neighborhood of Kadesh.

17:9-10. The **hand** of Moses on the **rod of God** (see above on 4:2-5) is the same motif as Joshua's spear stretched out toward Ai until the enemy was defeated (Josh. 8:18, 26). The rod may actually have been a standard of Yahweh with the serpent symbol as in the incident of the serpent plague (Num. 21:6-9), where the Hebrew word for the pole or staff is that translated **banner** in vss. 15-16. If this was the standard after which the altar was named, and which was the subject of the poetic fragment about Amalek, the fact that it is twice attested in undoubtedly old traditions strongly suggests its originality.

17:11-13. The function of Moses' **hands** is probably a later modification of the primitive concept of the rod or standard as a symbol of the divine presence. The intro. of the hands may be related to the local tradition explaining the name **Rephidim** as "supports" for the arms. Here Moses is the inspired intermediary between Yahweh and the people, his reputation being the effective source of confidence or dismay. **Steady** is lit. "steadiness," an emphatic usage with the meaning "steadiness itself." The noun, used here in its primary physical sense, came also to mean "faith."

17:14-16. The recording of the curse against Amalek **in a book** and its commission to Joshua may have been suggested to the E author by a collection under the name of Joshua extant in his day, perhaps the source underlying Josh. 1-11. That the word translated **banner** means rather a standard (see above on vss. 9-10) is borne out by its use in Isa. 30:17 in parallelism with "flagstaff," a word that elsewhere is used of the mast of a ship (Isa. 33:23; Ezek. 27:5). Such a standard on a hilltop

served as a rallying signal (cf. Isa. 18:3; 62:10; Jer. 4:21). The **altar** was not only a memorial; it was also a place where the people might look for the rallying signal pole, so vital when they were diffused over the Kadesh oasis and constantly menaced by the Amalekites. The couplet in vs. 16 may be a relic of the originally poetic version of the saga source. It might better be translated:

As [my] hand is on the standard of Yahweh,
Yahweh will be at war with Amalek for every generation.

The "disabling oracle" against Amalek which might be expected here is perhaps to be found displaced among the oracles of Balaam (Num. 24:20).

18:1-12. *Meeting with Jethro.* This passage is from E, but an editor has added vss. 2-4 and perhaps other phrases in an effort to harmonize with the J material about Moses' family (2:21-22; 4:20a, 24-26). Since the name **Jethro** is usually followed both here and elsewhere (3:1; 4:18) by **Moses' father-in-law,** which is the only designation used in vss. 13-27, it gives the impression of having been inserted later. Thus the father-in-law may have been nameless in the E tradition. He is called Hobab in at least one J passage (see above on 2:15b-22) but some scholars attribute Jethro to a 2nd J source. Moses' being already **encamped at the mountain of God** (vs. 5) indicates that this passage should follow 19:2.

18:6-11. The approach of Jethro is announced as of a man of consideration, a sheik and a **priest** (vs. 1). Moses goes to **meet** him, bowing to him as his elder, his father-in-law and head of his household, and greeting him in bedouin fashion with a kiss. Then follow the interminable inquiries and reassurances of health so familiar in Arab society. In the tent Moses tells Jethro of the deliverance and the desert wandering, and Jethro acknowledges the power of Yahweh.

18:12. A fellowship meal is characteristic of such encounters in the desert. This, however, is no common meal but a communion meal **before God** in connection with **sacrifices.** Thus the family idyl is quite incidental to this narrative; rather Jethro's initiative in the sacrifices and his direction to Moses in the sequel indicate that it transmits the tradition of the formal adoption of the Hebrews into the cult of Yahweh at the desert sanctuary, probably at Kadesh, where Jethro was priest. This view that the Kenites, or Midianites, were the original Yahweh worshipers is rejected by some scholars, who regard this incident as instead the occasion on which Jethro identified his god with Yahweh. Moses' narration of the deliverance and saving acts of Yahweh (vs. 8), however, and Jethro's acknowledgment of these indicate a decisive development of the cult at the Midianite sanctuary, which was transformed after its adoption by the Hebrews. The omission of Moses in the notice of the ritual may be due to his being already a member of Jethro's family and of the Midianite religious community, whereas **Aaron** and **all the elders of Israel,** representing the people as a whole, are being brought into the community for the first time.

18:13-27. *Administration of Justice.* Though this passage is now linked by **On the morrow** to vs. 12 it relates a separate tradition of a later event, after the giving of the law (see below on vss. 15-16), and perhaps belongs at the position of the J contradiction of vs. 27 (Num. 10:29-36). Jethro's question about Moses' judicial activity and Moses' explanation follow a common saga convention for introducing a new subject. Here they serve to emphasize Moses' conscientious fulfillment of the ideal of the tribal sheik and ruler in the ancient Near East. In the Ras Shamra legends 2 kings hear cases and dispense justice as described here, and Muhammad and the early caliphs acted similarly in a much larger and more complex society.

18:15-16. The phrase **inquire of God** seems to anticipate the institution of the priestly oracle—i.e. the use of the sacred lots Urim and Thummim to determine the divine will (see comment on I Sam. 14:36-46)—as the final resource in deciding cases (cf. Deut. 17:8-9). No doubt the purpose of this passage is to introduce this practice. **Statutes** refers to decrees which have acquired the permanency of statutory law. **Decisions** are directives applied to specific cases. These terms imply the law only later communicated at Mt. Sinai and show that this passage belongs later in the narrative (see above on vss. 13-27). Moses' role here may reflect the office of expounder of the law in the tribal assembly, the judge of Israel in the narrower judicial sense during the settlement in Palestine in the period of the judges.

18:17-26. In the original tradition vss. 19-20 may have described Jethro's ordination of Moses as an oracle priest. The distinction between this office and that of secular arbitrators, who handled cases that could be decided mechanically by the application of customary law (cf. Deut. 16:18), is significant. **At all times** (vss. 22, 26) refers to everyday cases and suggests by contrast solemn occasions when the parties came either before an oracle priest or before the judge at the tribal assembly at statutory times and after due ritual preparation. This distinction underlies the difference between the categorical imperatives of the apodictic or absolute laws and the casuistic or conditional laws with their many qualifications in the Book of the Covenant (20:22–23:33; see "The Law Codes of Israel," pp. 1090-94). The divisions in vss. 21, 25 reflect the administrative organization for the military levy projected back into the period of the militant tribal confederacy, which is now assumed to be brought into being.

18:27. Jethro's **own country** may mean the Midianite homeland E of the Gulf of Aqaba (see above on 2:15b-22; 3:1). But more probably it was nearer Kadesh. If he was of the smith caste known as Kenites, his clan during the cooler season may have worked the copper ores of the Arabah, the rift valley extending from the Dead Sea to Aqaba, and during the summer taken their flocks to the Kadesh oasis. In the J tradition Moses' father-in-law and some of his clan seem to have stayed with the Hebrews and settled with them in Palestine (see comment on Num. 10:29-36).

III. The Law and Covenant at Mt. Sinai (19:1-24:18)

The theme of the first half of Exod. is the creative divine act of deliverance. That of the 2nd half

is the constitution of a distinctive community, Israel, on the basis of a divine covenant with explicit provisions, both ritual and moral, for Israel's expression of her distinctive status as the people of Yahweh. These provisions comprise the law, which is thus primarily the consequence rather than the condition of the covenant and is also a revelation of the nature of the God of Israel. This account of the awakening of Israel's consciousness as a people of divine destiny is therefore central in scripture. The prospect of the great J work that after the fall (Gen. 3) all families of the earth should be blessed in the seed of Abraham (Gen. 12:3) now comes near its realization in the adoption of Israel as God's covenanted people, **a kingdom of priests and a holy nation** (19:6; cf. I Pet. 2:5-9; Rev. 1:6; 5:10; 20:6).

In its present form the material is arranged with the theophany, i.e. the physical manifestation of the divine presence, on the holy mountain (ch. 19) followed by the giving of the law (chs. 20–23) and in turn by the making of the covenant (ch. 24, continued in chs. 32–34). This is the order of E, which predominates in this section. In the J tradition the making of the covenant (24:1-2, 9-11) may have preceded the giving of the law (ch. 34). In J it involves a communion meal on the mountain in which elders of the people participate. In the later E account Moses is the sole mediator and other details enhance his authority. The theophany is exceedingly complicated, reflecting not only the liturgical variations at the various sanctuaries which preceded Jerusalem as central shrines of Israel—Shechem, Bethel, Gilgal, Shiloh, and perhaps Hebron—but also the development of the theme in pss. of praise (e.g. Deut. 33:2-4; Judg. 5:4-5; Pss. 18:7-16; 50:3; 97:3-5; Hab. 3:3-6, 10-11). The law, consisting of the Decalogue (20:2-17) and the Book of the Covenant (20:22–23:33), is set loosely in this tradition complex in such a way as to suggest that these traditions are independent of the narrative.

The general pattern of admonition before the approach to God (19:4-6; cf. Josh. 24:14-15), response of the people (19:8; cf. Josh. 24:16, 24), proclamation of the law (20:23-26; cf. Josh. 24:25; Deut. 27:15-26), the formality of the covenant (24:4-8; cf. Josh. 24:27), and blessings and curses as a sanction of the law (34:6-7; cf. Josh. 8:34; Deut. 28:3-6, 16-19) is so well attested in various parts of the OT as to indicate that it derives from an established covenant sacrament. If the relevant passages in the OT reflect the covenant tradition as it developed in Palestine, that tradition was itself probably determined by an older experience at the desert sanctuary. This experience, however, may be recovered in chs. 19-24; 33-34 only in general outline.

A. The Manifestation of Yahweh's Presence (19:1-25)

19:1-2a. The Journey to Mt. Sinai. The P itinerary is here resumed from 17:1. Perhaps vs. 2a should precede vs. 1. **On the third new moon** is reckoned inclusively and thus denotes an interval of 2 months, probably to agree with the late tradition of the giving of the law at the feast of weeks (Pentecost) 50 days after the passover. On the location of **Sinai** see above on 3:1.

19:2b-8. *Admonition and Response.* Into this section of E narrative a D editor has inserted the words of admonition (vss. 3b-6). God's sure, swift succor of his people **on eagles'** wings (cf. Deut. 32:10-11) probably reflects the hymnic language of the liturgy of the covenant sacrament. On Israel as God's **own possession** cf. Deut. 7:6; 14:2; 26:18. On the monotheistic concept **all the earth is mine** cf. Deut. 10:14. **A kingdom of priests** indicates that the government of Israel is to be theocratic, her executives dedicated intermediaries between God and the community as befits **a holy nation,** i.e. a dedicated people. As a commonwealth of priests appropriated by Yahweh Israel is a community where all have insight into the divine will through immediate fellowship with him—cf. the concept of the new covenant (Jer. 31:34), under which all should know the divine direction previously the specific province of the priests. **Holy,** properly a sacro-physical term, gains moral content in the context of the law and the covenant.

19:9-15. *Ritual Precautions.* In preparation for the theophany E emphasizes the need for ritual purity by the washing of clothes (vss. 10-11a, 13b-14; cf. Gen. 35:2, which also reflects the covenant sacrament at Shechem). Special clothes worn in worship are familiar in Semitic antiquity and are represented today in the simple shift of Muslim pilgrims entering the sacred territory about Mecca. Another tradition, probably J, calls for abstention from sexual intercourse (vs. 15; cf. I Sam. 21:4, indicating this practice by warriors in the holy war). Clearly from J is the delimitation of the holy area around **Mount Sinai** by **bounds** (vss. 11b-13a). The sacred boundary is a well-known concept; cf. the present walled area around the Dome of the Rock, the site of the temple in Jerusalem. The idea of contact with the holy as fatal is primitive; cf. the death of Uzzah for touching the ark (II Sam. 6:6-7). The ram's-horn **trumpet** (*shophar*) was used to convoke a solemn assembly and to punctuate ritual (see comment on Ps. 81:1-5b).

19:16-25. *Yahweh's Descent on Mt. Sinai.* The J description of the theophany (vs. 18) strongly suggests a volcano in eruption, and accordingly some scholars have tried to identify Mt. Sinai with one of the volcanic peaks E of the Gulf of Aqaba in the Midianite homeland (see above on 2:15b-22; 3:1). It is more probable, however, that a Midianite tradition of a volcanic theophany originating in this region was transferred to a sacred mountain near Kadesh. On the other hand the theophany in the E tradition (vs. 16) is evidently a thunderstorm, developed from the cult legend of the Canaanite Baal as adapted by Israel in Palestine in the autumnal new year festival. In the Ras Shamra texts thunder and lightning are the concomitants of the manifestation of Baal as king (cf. Ps. 29).

Instead of **the whole mountain** (vs. 18) certain Hebrew manuscripts and the LXX have "all the people." This is supported by the fact that the word translated **quaked,** the same verb as **trembled** (vs. 16), is ordinarily used of the emotional reactions of persons; but the figure of the earth's trembling at the presence of Yahweh, expressed with other verbs, is common in poetic descriptions of theophanies (cf. e.g. Judg. 5:4-5; Pss. 18:7; 68:8; 77:18). In vs. 19

the word translated **thunder** possibly is intended in its lit. sense of "a voice" (so KJV) but more probably refers to thunder, as it obviously does in vs. 16. Moses' impertinence in vs. 23 is evidently an editor's attempt to reconcile the conflicting instructions of J and E.

B. THE 10 COMMANDMENTS (20:1-21)

The Decalogue is an insertion into the E narrative between 19:19 and 20:18, both of which describe the theophany at the holy mountain. The relation of the sabbath to the ordinance in the P account of Creation (Gen. 2:1-3) indicates that, whatever the antiquity of the Decalogue, in its present form it is the product of P editing. It relates to the sacrament of the renewal of the covenant. In fact it is an epitome of apodictic laws, categorical imperatives relating to purity of worship and social morality, distinguished by their form from casuistic laws in the Book of the Covenant (20:22-23:33). The characteristically terse nature of these apodictic laws indicates that the Decalogue has been expanded by comment and explanation, reflecting a harangue after the declaration of the law in the absolute form at the tribal assembly.

In the past many scholars believed that the high morality of the Decalogue must stem from a later time, under the influence of the great prophets of the 8th cent. Now, however, there is a growing tendency to relate to Moses the primitive 10 words, apart from the secondary additions, or at least to admit that his authorship can be neither denied nor proved by scientific methods. In its form the Decalogue resembles treaties imposed by Hittite kings on their vassals in the 14th-13th cents. In these the suzerain declares his name and status (cf. vs. 2a) and enumerates his benefits to his vassal (cf. vs. 2b) as a claim to absolute and exclusive obedience (cf. vs. 3) introducing the detailed obligations (cf. vss. 4-17). Heaven and earth and various natural features are called to witness in the Hittite treaties (cf. Deut. 30:19) and adjurations are added as sanctions (cf. Deut. 27:15-26). The covenant formula of the Decalogue seems to reflect this convention of international treaty law at the central shrines of Israel in Palestine; but the apodictic laws themselves, which have no parallel in the Hittite covenants, quite conceivably relate to the early religious community at Kadesh.

The numbering of the commandments in most Protestant and Eastern Orthodox churches, followed here, derives from Jewish tradition known to Philo and Josephus in the first cent. A.D. Modern Jewish usage, following another tradition, counts vs. 2 as the first commandment and vss. 3-6 as the 2nd. In the Roman Catholic tradition, derived from Augustine and followed by some Lutherans, vss. 3-6 comprise the first commandment and, based on the order in the LXX (cf. Deut. 5:21), the prohibition against coveting one's neighbor's wife is the 9th and the rest of vs. 17 the 10th.

20:1-2. *Preamble.* In the context of the apodictic laws which distinguished the religious community of Israel **I am the LORD your God** indicates a regular sacramental occasion. The historical declaration of God's grace and power in the drama of salvation (vs. 2b; cf. Josh. 24:2-13) is a prelude to the moral demands of the prophets (cf. e.g. Amos 2:6-10). God's grace to Israel in the Exodus is the basis of his claim on her exclusive worship and unconditional obedience. The former bondmen have a new status as a religious community whose distinctive character is expressed by their keeping of the principles declared in the following commandments, the ethical elements of which reveal also the nature of their God.

20:3. *The First Word.* The meaning of **before me** is "above [or "beside"] my presence," or possibly "against my presence." While not excluding the recognition, as distinct from the worship, of other gods (cf. e.g. 15:11; Deut. 32:8) the Decalogue is practically, if not theoretically, monotheistic.

20:4-6. *The 2nd Word.* The original short commandment was no doubt simply the opening clause, the rest being later expansion. **Graven image** probably visualizes a material representation of Yahweh as well as such conventional figures of other deities in human or animal form as are known from excavations in the whole Near East. Not only must Yahweh not be portrayed with the attributes of neighboring deities, but there must be no particularization of the concept of him which might lead through emphasis on his several attributes to distinct objects of worship. The later explanation of this prohibition in Deut. 4:15 probably expresses the idea implied in the revelation of the name Yahweh (see above on 3:14-15). God is known through his action; thus what expresses his whole and indivisible character defies material representation. The suggestion that this 2nd commandment, like the 3rd (see below on vs. 7), was designed to prevent any attempt to control God by magical means is also feasible.

Insofar as representations of other supernatural powers may be implied, the reference may be to such images as the figurines of the fertility goddesses of Canaan and the Egyptian amulets which archaeology attests even in Israelite houses. Even if such cult objects as the ephod (Judg. 8:27) and Jeroboam's golden calves (see comment on I Kings 12:26-33) are regarded as images of Yahweh, their existence does not militate against the antiquity of the 2nd commandment any more than David's adultery with Bathsheba does against the antiquity of the 7th. More problematic is the tradition attributing the bronze serpent to Moses himself (Num. 21:8-9; II Kings 18:4). Though the early use of this image is well attested (see above on 17:9-10) Moses' connection with it is less certain; it may have been a Kenite element adopted by certain of the S Hebrews as a visible expression of their solidarity with the Kenites.

20:5. Yahweh's being a **jealous God**, demanding exclusive worship and resenting all that impairs his sole dignity, reflects the whole motive of the Decalogue to preserve the integrity of Israel as exclusively the people of God. This point belongs with the first commandment (vs. 3) as in the Ritual Code (cf. 34:14) rather than with the 2nd. The punishment of descendants **to the third and the fourth generation,** repeated in 34:7, probably reflects the formula of the ban, under which certain delinquents were put to death with their families—e.g. Achan (Josh.

7:22-26). Thus man's communal responsibility is emphasized. Cf. the Arab tribal convention of blood revenge, which includes all kindred within 5 generations.

20:6. The concept of the **love** of God as the obverse of his effective wrath (cf. 34:6-7) probably reflects the genuine early practice of the amplification of the blessing and curse in public harangue after the adjurations which concluded the presentation of the law in the covenant sacrament (cf. Deut. 28-30 after Deut. 27:15-26).

20:7. *The 3rd Word.* Vs. 7b is a homiletic expansion. On the significance of the **name** see above on 3:13. The divine name must not be "lifted for vanity," i.e. for any frivolous or malicious purpose, as in magic. God must be obeyed, not controlled. While primarily relating to magic, the commandment also probably visualizes perjury—cf. the oath by Allah among the Arabs, which is so trite as to be of no value. Since perhaps as early as the Exile Judaism has revered the name of God to the extent of refraining from pronouncing Yahweh and using circumlocutions instead—e.g. "the LORD," "the Name," "the Place," "the Holy One."

20:8-11. *The 4th Word.* The original short commandment (vs. 8) is to note the special significance of the **sabbath** as a day dedicated to God. Its elaboration in vss. 9-10, probably D, and in 23:12; Deut. 5:13-14 emphasizes the weekly rest day for the whole community, with a humanitarian motive for slaves and cattle. The P expansion in vs. 11 connects it with the P scheme of creation (Gen. 1:1–2:4a).

The original commandment does not specify how often the sabbath is to be kept, but the 7th day is stated in the apodictic commandment in 23:12; 34:21. The root of the word denotes "abeyance," i.e. suspension of normal activities. This was felt to be necessary at the transitional lunar phases, when the untoward powers of the supernatural were esp. dreaded. In Mesopotamia the king on behalf of the community suspended his normal activities on the 7th, 14th, 19th, 21st, and 28th days of the month. It is not stated how the sabbath is to be observed apart from the suspension of work to delimit between the sacred and the profane. It may have been designed to facilitate visits to the sanctuary or business with holy persons (cf. II Kings 4:23) and to afford a means for the religious community to realize its solidarity at the local shrine.

The exclusive worship of the God of Israel being defined, the distinctive character and integrity of his people are now safeguarded by laws affecting their freedom.

20:12. *The 5th Word.* This commandment is directed to adults as members of the religious community, possibly reflecting life at the subsistence level, where the old might be neglected as economically useless. The injunction to **honor your . . . mother** was the more natural in a polygamous society, where an aging wife might well depend on her son rather than on her husband. In the broader sense discipline in the family, where the mature wisdom of parents overrules the impulse and prejudice of youth, is the basis of an ordered society. The D expansion in vs. 12b connects the covenant and law with the fulfillment of the promise of the **land** (cf. Deut. 28:63-68).

20:13. *The 6th Word.* Here and generally the verb translated **kill** denotes premeditated homicide (but cf. Deut. 4:42). In view of the admission of the vendetta (Deut. 19:11-13; Num. 35:6-21) the prohibition refers primarily to murder as a breach in the sacral community, but possibly also to the mitigation of the blood feud in the case of accidental death, for which sanctuaries were provided pending decision by the community (Deut. 19:1-10; Num. 35:1-15). The commandment does not prohibit killing in war or capital punishment.

20:14. *The 7th Word.* As addressed to a man this commandment visualizes **adultery** primarily as sexual relations with a woman married or betrothed to another—a capital offense (cf. Deut. 22:22-27)—but irregularity with others is not condoned (see below on 22:16-17). The law conserved, not the dignity of the woman, but the right of her husband or father.

20:15. *The 8th Word.* The use of the verb translated **steal** by Joseph (Gen. 40:15) indicates that it refers specifically to kidnapping and selling into slavery—a capital offense in the apodictic law in 21:16; Deut. 24:7 and an offense against the community as the people of God.

20:16. *The 9th Word.* This commandment prohibits false evidence, implying perjury, which might damage the status and even the life of a man (e.g. Naboth, I Kings 21:12-16) in the community of the people of God and impair the whole order on which it was founded. In Deut. 19:16-19 the convicted perjurer incurs the penalty of the crime he has alleged.

20:17. *The 10th Word.* The original short commandment is the opening clause. By Arabic analogy **house** includes all the possessions mentioned in the amplification. Generally the verb translated **covet** denotes inordinate desire, but in view of the palpable nature of the social offenses in the rest of the Decalogue it more likely refers here to practical measures taken to secure the desired object. Cf. Mic. 2:2, where the context indicates violent seizure, and in the Ritual Code 34:24, which implies a fear that one's land will be taken during absence at a pilgrimage festival.

20:18-21. *Reaction to Yahweh's Manifestation.* This is a continuation of the E narrative from 19:19, except for the J phrase **and the mountain smoking.** The account of the theophany immediately before and after the Decalogue enhances the solemnity of the law. The request of the people that Moses rather than God should speak to them clearly demarcates the categorical imperatives of the Decalogue from the detailed laws of the Book of the Covenant, which to a large extent is the development of the social law of Canaan in the general legal tradition of the ancient Near East.

C. The Book of the Covenant (20:22–23:33)

The title "Book of the Covenant" for this collection of laws, also called the Covenant Code, was suggested by the allusion in 24:7, which evidently refers instead to the Decalogue. That the collection is not complete is indicated by comparison with Deut. 12–26. That it is not a unity is shown by doublets, by the address in 2nd person plural (e.g. 20:22-23) and singular (e.g. 20:24), and generally by the different superscriptions (20:22a; 21:1) and the different forms in which the laws are communicated, viz. apodictic and casuistic (see above on 18:17-26). A ritual code, more completely represented in 34:17-26, may be another independent element. The concluding appendix (23:20-33) is not the conclusion of a self-contained body of laws—cf. the solemn adjurations with blessings and curses in Deut. 27–30; Lev. 26—but is really an adaptation of the conclusion to the whole Sinai episode.

The Book of the Covenant, then, is a compilation made over a considerable period which was inserted somewhat awkwardly into the E Sinai narrative. It may go back to the first cents. after the settlement in Palestine, for the fact that there is no mention of political institutions points to a time before the monarchy. In the subject matter there is nothing to suggest Sinai or desert society but much to indicate settlement, esp. the casuistic laws, which in form and content reflect the common law of the Near East in the 2nd millennium—cf. e.g. the Code of Hammurabi. On the other hand, in view of the years when the Israelites lived a seminomadic life around Kadesh, where agriculture on a very limited scale was possible, certain laws, esp. the ethical commandments, may have been associated with Moses.

20:22-26. *Ritual Ordinances.* The prohibition against the representation of strange **gods** and the provisions for an **altar** safeguard the purity of the worship of Yahweh and belong with the apodictic laws, though in what precise context cannot now be determined. Altars are to be built **in every place** where a theophany occurs (vs. 24; cf. 17:15), as in patriarchal times—contrast the later D restriction to a single altar (Deut. 12:5-14). God's presence is to be invoked in the confidence inspired by the revelation of his nature and will in the event the altar commemorates. The altar rather than an image symbolizes the presence of God and reminds men that he is known by his interventions in history.

The **altar of earth** was probably made of compacted clay or crude brick, which would have the added advantage of absorbing the blood of the sacrifices. The motives for prohibiting **stone** dressed with an edged **tool** (cf. Deut. 27:5; Josh. 8:31, which say "iron tool") probably combine the desire to avoid materials contaminated by man and the early superstitious fear of iron as a trade secret of an alien smith caste. The **steps** now familiar to archaeologists from Canaanite altars of the Bronze Age are prohibited on the basis of modesty, which determined the intro. of breeches for the priests at a later period (28:42-43) and the use of a ramp instead of steps in Herod's temple.

The 2 main sacrifices made with the effusion of blood are mentioned: **burnt offerings,** in which the whole animal was burned as a sacrifice to God, and **peace offerings,** better "communion offerings," in which the blood, fat, and vital organs were burned on the altar to God and the rest was eaten by the worshipers, who thus effected solidarity with one another and with God.

21:1. *Intro. to the Casuistic Law.* Following the apodictic ritual ordinances (20:23-26) this intro. significantly demarcates a solid block of civil law (21:2–22:17) communicated in casuistic form except for certain insertions of more primitive laws (21:12,

15-17). This casuistic matter is logically arranged and gives the impression of an extract from a civil code.

21:2-11. Slavery. The laws regarding slaves within the community indicate a comparatively developed society with fixed property rights. In view of the affinity of the casuistic laws in the Book of the Covenant with general Near Eastern law in the Late Bronze Age it is doubtful whether **Hebrew** (vs. 2) has an ethnic significance. It may rather refer to the Habiru (see Intro.), an alien and underprivileged class who might in fact sell themselves into temporary or permanent slavery, as is well known from Mesopotamian texts. Except for this possible reference there is no evidence of such a class in Israel after the settlement in Palestine, but there was the practice of enslavement for debt (cf. II Kings 4:1; Neh. 5:5; Isa. 50:1) and Israelite slave debtors were apparently regarded as the Habiru had been. The release in the **seventh year** is related to the septennial cancellation of debts (Deut. 15:1-2). Deut. 15:12-18 also enjoins release in the 7th year on grounds of humanity, the status of the Hebrews in Egypt corresponding to that of the Habiru.

21:3-6. If the master provides a **wife** for the slave, she and their children are the property of the master and need not be released when the 6-year term ends. For this reason or because of poverty or insecurity as a freeman a man may choose to become a permanent slave. If so, the master brings him **to God,** i.e. probably to the sanctuary, to ratify his wish and declaration by oath. Alternative suggestions are that "God" should be rendered "gods," signifying the household gods, or that it is a corruption of "judges," as indicated by the Targums and Syriac version—cf. the LXX reading "tribunal of God," indicating familiarity with both the standard Hebrew text and a variation. Probably the **doorpost** to which the slave's ear is to be fixed is that of the master's dwelling—cf. the association with supernatural influences in the family (12:23; Isa. 57:8). Thus 2 distinct transactions are visualized.

21:7-11. Vs. 7 explicitly discriminates between slaves of this class and a female sold into slavery by her father (cf. Neh. 5:5)—probably in discharge of debt, though this is not stated. The master may take her himself as wife or concubine or allow his son to do so. In either case her marital status must be recognized and she cannot be reduced to the position of a slave; if he does not wish to keep her she may be **redeemed** by her father. If the master remarries he may not deprive her of her maintenance or her conjugal rights; otherwise she may claim her freedom without a redemption price. The institution of slavery within the Hebrew community, like that of concubinage (cf. e.g. Judg. 8:31; 9:18; 19; II Sam. 3:7; 5:13) reminds us that we must study the OT against its own background as the records of a community developing over a millennium and not assume that all scripture has equal and absolute authority.

21:12-17. Capital Offenses Against Persons. The general principle of capital punishment for manslaughter (vs. 12) is stated in only 5 Hebrew words. This and the similarly terse statements in vss. 15-17 are probably part of a brief apodictic code like the nucleus of the 10 Commandments or the 12 Curses of Deut. 27:15-26, probably taken from such a summary as headings for the casuistic modifications which follow.

21:13-14. In blood revenge nomad society does not discriminate between murder and accidental homicide; thus the principle in vs. 12 may indicate an early stage in Israelite society. But in the relative congestion and complexity of sedentary life unlimited vengeance became intolerable and discrimination must be made. According to the solution which was developed the death penalty for murder was not waived (vs. 14) but sanctuary was provided for the homicide (vs. 13) at the altar of a shrine until it could be determined whether **God let him fall into his hand,** i.e. whether the death was an "act of God" or the willful act of a killer. Among the Arabs in the desert today such sanctuary may be sought in any tent and may be recognized either for the conventional period of a few days or perpetually, according to tribal pride or power. In Israel this sanctuary was eventually limited to 6 cities of refuge (Num. 35:6-11; Deut. 4:41-43; 19:1-13; Josh. 20)—possibly when the local cult centers were suppressed under Josiah.

21:15-17. Among the capital crimes is disrespect for parents, here specified as striking (vs. 15) or cursing (vs. 17; cf. Lev. 20:9; Deut. 27:16), which for the ancient Semite had as much force as a palpable act. Also a capital crime is kidnapping (vs. 16; see above on 20:15). In Deut. 24:7 an Israelite victim is specified and such is probably to be assumed here. The selling of a man to such ready merchants as the seafaring Phoenicians and the Edomite caravaneers (cf. Amos 1:6, 9) would impair the religious community by removing one of its members.

21:18-32. Compensation for Injuries. Here is a series of casuistic qualifications on the damages to be assessed in cases of bodily injury.

21:18-19. That a quarrel is sudden and unpremeditated is proved by the use of makeshift weapons. **Fist** translates a rare word (cf. Isa. 58:4) which possibly means some sort of implement. If one injured in such a situation recovers, the other is punished only by having to compensate **loss of his time,** a single Hebrew word from the root of "sabbath," which therefore refers to the interruption in his work. **Have him thoroughly healed** probably refers to the expense of a physician and other medical care.

21:20-21. The life of a **slave** also is protected in Israelite law. Though it is not explicitly stated how the master who beats his slave to death is to be **punished,** the verb implies blood revenge, probably executed by the community. On the other hand the survival of the slave even **a day or two** is taken as evidence that. the master did not intend to kill him, and the loss of valuable personal property is treated as sufficient penalty.

21:22. Even the life unborn is protected. In case of a **miscarriage** suffered by a woman who intervenes in a fight, presumably on behalf of her husband, the right of the family to compensation is recognized. **As the judges determine** is a rather free translation of a word that probably should be slightly emended to read "for the miscarriage."

21:23-25. The law of retaliation (*lex talionis*), well known from its rejection by Jesus (Matt. 5:38), ostensibly is applied to injury suffered by a pregnant woman; but the abrupt change from the general hypothesis to the direct categorical command in the 2nd person singular is noticeable. Thus the passage may be displaced, as some believe, and should follow vs. 19. On the other hand the similar formula in Deut. 19:21 suggests that this may be the quotation of a principle which applies to any case of injury personally caused to the person of a freeman.

21:26-27. The master who injures his **slave** is exempt from the principle of retaliation, being held to be sufficiently deprived by the compulsory release of the slave, who is also his capital. Here Israel endorses the general principle of common Near Eastern law that a slave has not the same legal worth as a freeman.

21:28-32. A similar distinction is made in the provisions for cases of fatal goring by an **ox.** In any case the ox is to be publicly stoned to death and its flesh may not be eaten, being taboo by blood guilt. If an ox has been notoriously vicious the owner who neglects to confine it is responsible when it kills someone. In such case a freeman's life demands the life of the owner—though he may ransom himself, apparently at the discretion of the community—but a slave's life demands only the payment to his master of **thirty shekels of silver** (see "Measures and Money," pp. 1283-85), apparently the usual price of a slave.

21:33–22:17. *Compensation for Property Loss.* Underlying the laws of this section is the general principle of requiring equivalent restitution for accidental injury to livestock or other property, with multiple restitution where a theft is involved. Thus the man responsible for loss of an animal in an uncovered pit (21:33-34) must simply exchange a live animal for the dead one. If one ox kills another unexpectedly the 2 owners divide the loss, but the owner of an ox known to be vicious who fails to confine it must bear the full loss (21:35-36; cf. vss. 28-29).

22:1-4. The distinction here between **ox** and **sheep** reflects the added value of the ox for labor as well as meat. The thief who kills or sells stolen beasts is penalized much more heavily than one who keeps them so that they may be recovered. If a thief has neither the money nor the beast to pay his fine—probably the more common situation—he is to be **sold** as a slave.

22:2-3a. This law is an interpolation (see RSV footnote) and belongs in a different context, since it concerns homicide rather than restitution for theft. If the thief is killed in **breaking in,** lit. "digging through," presumably at night, when he himself might have killed the occupants of the house and remained undetected, **no bloodguilt** ensues. But killing the thief in daylight is regarded as a vindictive act and demands blood revenge. Some interpreters take **if the sun has risen upon him** to mean simply "at a later time"; i.e. a burglar caught in the act at any time may be killed, but one apprehended afterward may not.

22:5-6. If crops are destroyed, either by animals or by fire, the man responsible must make the equivalent compensation to the owner. Apparently no distinction is made between accidental and malicious damage.

22:7-9. Lacking banks, ancient people had frequent need of pledges for loan or safe deposit. Among the Arabs today these are usually deposited under the oath locally most binding, though good faith in pledges is also a point of honor. Here it is provided that one alleging theft of a deposit must **come near to God,** i.e. at the local shrine, probably to take an oath (see below on vss. 10-13) as the LXX interprets. If **breach of trust,** i.e. deliberate infringement of the law of the community, is alleged and a man claims that any of his property is in another's possession, the **case,** lit. "word," **of both parties shall come before God,** i.e. at the local shrine, and the one there declared guilty shall make **double** restitution. Possibly some ordeal is understood, as when a wife is accused of adultery (Num. 5:11-28).

22:10-13. One who alleges the legitimate loss of a beast in his care must take an **oath by the LORD,** i.e. a declaration attested by a ritual invoking severe punishment by Yahweh if it is not true (cf. I Kings 8:31-32). If he satisfies the priests and witnesses of his oath no compensation is to be demanded. Vs. 12 seems inconsistent with vss. 10-11 and may be from a different source. Perhaps the distinction is that **driven away** refers to a raid which would be common knowledge in the neighborhood even though the taking of the particular animal was not seen, whereas **stolen** refers to alleged theft by an individual. In the latter case the likelihood of negligence if not collusion was considered such as to require restitution as a safeguard. Another suggestion is that **is driven away** may be an erroneous duplication of **is hurt,** which differs by only one letter in the Hebrew, so that vss. 10-11 apply only to death or injury of the animal. If so, **accept the oath,** lit. "accept it," may mean "accept the dead or injured animal." If the ravaging of wild **beasts** (vs. 13) can be proved by the evidence of mangled remains, compensation is waived (cf. Amos 3:12).

22:14-15. Restitution is demanded for the death or injury of a borrowed beast unless the owner was present and thus could have prevented abuse. For casualties from natural causes no one is liable. The final clause of vs. 15 is ambiguous. Possibly it means that if the animal is not lent but **hired** no compensation is due because the owner has allowed for such risks in setting his fee. Another possibility is that if the beast is in the charge of a hired man, the compensation must come out of his wages.

22:16-17. The seduction of an unbetrothed **virgin,** who is expected to bring a **marriage present,** i.e. bride-price, to her father, is treated in the context of damaged property rather than family law. This is in fact the only sexual case in the Book of the Covenant, surely evidence of its fragmentary nature. Seduction or rape of a betrothed virgin ranks as adultery and is a capital offense (Deut. 22:23-27). Seduction of an unbetrothed virgin is a lesser offense for which the penalty is simply payment of the bride-price and regular marriage to her. If the father refuses such marriage the bride-price must be paid nevertheless, since the loss of virginity, which must be publicly attested if challenged by the bridegroom (cf. Deut. 22:13-21), would prejudice the eventual marriage of the girl. The bride-price was paid to the parents but might in part or whole be remitted to the bride as a dowry.

22:18-31. *Miscellaneous Ordinances.* This section consists generally of laws in apodictic form, some of them expanded with admonitions. Except for the 3 capital offenses at the beginning (vss. 18-20) and a later threat of death after invasion (vs. 24) it differs from the preceding material in that, as in the Decalogue, no penalties are stated.

22:18. Deut. 18:10*b*-11 includes the masculine form of **sorceress** in a list of terms for practitioners of various forms of sorcery—attempts to secure information from the beyond or to bring supernatural influence to bear on situations or persons by other than the regular means of religion. All such practices are recognized as antisocial and punishable by death (cf. Lev. 20:6, 27).

22:19. Bestiality (cf. Lev. 20:15-16; Deut. 27:21) is covered also in the ancient Hittite laws, where it is specified as a capital offense, though subject to royal pardon, with most domestic animals but not punishable with a horse or mule.

22:20. The utter destruction demanded for one who sacrifices to gods other than Yahweh possibly included his family and possessions, as in the case of Achan (Josh. 7:15, 24-25; cf. I Sam. 15:3).

22:21-24. The word here translated **stranger** is *ger* (see above on 2:21-22), which the RSV more often renders as "sojourner," i.e. a protected alien. Humanitarian concern for the sojourner, the **widow,** and the **orphan** as persons in need of special consideration is repeatedly enjoined in the legal codes (e.g. 23:9; Lev. 19:33-34; Deut. 14:28-29; 24:17-22) and cited as a prime example of righteousness by the prophets (e.g. Isa. 1:17; Jer. 7:6; Ezek. 22:7; Zech. 7:10; Mal. 3:5).

22:25-27. Further humanitarian ordinances deal with lending **money,** lit. "silver," which until postexilic times was reckoned by weight, to the **poor.** The prohibition against **interest** refers, not to commercial investment, where the interest is simply a share of the borrower's profit, but to exploitation of a poor man's need. In no way might the religious community of Israel be impaired. One might lend with interest to a resident foreigner (Deut. 23:20), who would own no land but live by trade and might use the loan to his personal advantage. **Garment** refers to the long loose robe which served as both overcoat and blanket and therefore was needed at nightfall (cf. Deut. 24:17; Job 22:6; Amos 2:8). In view of the ancient conception of the garment as peculiarly representative of the person, the pledging of it may have signified that in the event of the debtor's selling himself into slavery the holder should have the first option.

22:28. To **revile,** lit. "lighten," i.e. divest of weight or honor, the deity or **curse** the civil authority menaced the community at its source. Though it is not explicitly stated here, this was a capital offense (cf. Lev. 24:15-16; I Kings 21:9-10). **Ruler,** lit. "one raised up," probably denoted originally the tribal representative to the common assembly (cf. e.g. Num. 1:16, 44; 7:2, where "leaders" renders the same Hebrew word) and later was understood to mean the king (cf. I Kings 11:34).

22:29-31. *Ritual Ordinances.* These apodictic commandments and their continuation in 23:10-19 are probably fragments of a ritual code parallel to 34:14-26 (see comments). Though apparently in-congruous with the moral and civil ordinances of the context, the ritual ordinances actually provided for the visible expression of the solidarity of the people of God and afforded occasions for the public declaration and application of the law. Vs. 29*a* refers to the offering of first fruits (cf. 23:19*a*; 34:26*a*). On the **first-born** (vss. 29*b*-30) see above on 13:1-2, 11-16. The prohibition in vs. 31 probably grew out of the taboo against eating blood.

23:1-9. *Ordinances About Justice.* The series of apodictic injunctions in vss. 1-3 amplifies the commandment against false witness (20:16) by naming particulars: creating prejudice by rumors, being suborned to perjury, deferring to the majority despite one's true conviction, and partiality. The prohibition against favoring a **poor man** (vs. 3), if correct, presumably forbids letting pity for him subvert the justice due a richer opponent. "Poor," however, may be a corruption of "great," which differs by only one consonant, or possibly both words were originally included as in Lev. 19:15.

23:4-5. These are casuistic injunctions to neighborliness in the cases of an enemy's straying animals or ass foundered under an awkward burden. **Help him lift it up** (vs. 5) represents an emendation of the Hebrew text, which is an apparent repetition of the verb translated **leaving.** Probably instead it is a word play—a different verb with the same consonants meaning "loose"; though not found elsewhere in the OT it is attested in the Ras Shamra texts. Thus the effect is somewhat like "not leave but relieve." These injunctions are motivated by social considerations rather than by consideration for the beasts, which would be exceptional in the ancient Near East.

23:6-9. These vss. continue the injunctions about justice in vss. 1-3. With vs. 6 cf. vs. 3. With vs. 8 cf. 18:21; Deut. 16:19. With vs. 9 cf. 22:21.

23:10-19. *Further Ritual Ordinances.* These are a continuation of 22:29-31, probably the fragments of a ritual code parallel to 34:14-26 (see comments). Here in the context of humanitarian pleas the injunction to let fields **lie fallow** in the **seventh year** (vss. 10-11) is said to be for the purpose of providing food for the **poor.** Here alone also the sabbath (vs. 12) is given a humanitarian rather than a religious explanation. Mentioning the **names of other gods** (vs. 13) means invoking their presence; cf. the later substitution of *bosheth,* "shame," for such names at some points in the OT text (see comment on II Sam. 2:8-11; Jer. 7:16-20). **Feast of harvest** (vs. 16) is probably the original name of what is called the feast of weeks elsewhere in the OT.

23:20-33. *Hortatory Epilogue.* In this exhortation stressing God's conditional grace the law is related to the occupation of the promised land (see above on 20:12). Actually the section may be a conclusion to the whole Sinai episode, introducing the departure for Canaan, which has been adapted as a conclusion to the Book of the Covenant. Here there are no curses on disobedience as in the epilogues to the law in Lev. 26:14-39; Deut. 28:15-68. Rather there are both admonitions and assurance (vss. 20-22) for the journey to Canaan and the settlement there (vss. 25-31*a*).

23:20-26. Guidance is promised by an **angel,** i.e. the presence of God, whose **name** (vs. 21) indicates his presence in character. The **voice** of the angel and his commands, however, indicate a human intermediary, a "messenger," the lit. meaning of "angel," such as Moses. On the other hand vs. 23 suggests that the angel means the ark, which went before Israel in battle (cf. Num. 10:35). Possibly the passage shows several stages of elaboration. The familiar list of the inhabitants of Canaan, the prohibition against worshiping their gods, and the injunction to eradicate their worship and to make no covenant with them (cf. vss. 32-33) suggest expansion by a D editor. **Pillars** were stones set on end either to symbolize the presence of a deity at the place where he had manifested himself or to commemorate a noted or favored ancestor.

23:27-33. The **terror** of God is the supernatural panic which causes the enemy's morale to break in the crisis of battle, a familiar concept in the idea of the holy war (see comment on Deut. 20; Ps. 14:5-7). The partial settlement of Israel in Canaan, frankly admitted here as in Judg. 1:19, 21, 27-35, is explained theologically as according to the divine economy to keep the land in cultivation—contrast Judg. 2:20-23, where the survival of the Canaanites is explained as for the discipline and training of Israel. Here only in the OT the land occupied by Israel is defined as **from the Red Sea,** i.e. the Gulf of Aqaba (see above on 13:18a), **to the sea of the Philistines,** i.e. the Mediterranean, **and from the wilderness,** i.e. the S desert, **to the Euphrates**—the extent of David's control if not occupation.

D. The Making of the Covenant (24:1-18)

Combined here are 2 accounts of the covenant. In the J account (vss. 1, 9-11) **Moses with Aaron, Nadab, and Abihu, and seventy . . . elders** representing Israel celebrate a communion meal on the mountain in the presence of God, and this effects the covenant (cf. Gen. 31:46, 54). Contradicting this are the words **and worship afar off** (vs. 1) and all of vs. 2, which declare that Moses alone is to **come near** God and therefore must be a later addition. The E account (vss. 3-8) which is more circumstantial, also includes a communion meal shared with God, the **peace offerings** (vs. 5). This tradition, however, is distinct from that of J in that it is celebrated at a regular sanctuary with an **altar at the foot of the mountain** and **pillars** (vs. 4) and involves a public recitation and endorsement of the **book of the covenant** (vs. 7). Possibly some of these elements were originally included in the J account but were omitted by the editor to avoid duplication.

24:3-8. *Ritual at an Altar.* This account reflects in several details the tradition of the sacrament of the renewal of the covenant in the period of the judges at Shechem (cf. Deut. 27; Josh. 24), but there are older traditions here also. **All the words of the LORD**—omitting **and all the ordinances** as a later expansion after the composition of the Book of the Covenant—probably denotes a short collection of apodictic law like the 10 Commandments in their original form. The formal endorsement of the terms of the covenant (vs. 3b) is a regular element of the ritual—cf. the popular assent to the 12 curses in Deut. 27:15-26—which is found in the Hittite vassal treaties (see above on 20:1-21). Moses' recording of the law (vs. 4) is also paralleled in the Hittite vassal

treaties by the recording without which the treaty was not valid. Cf. the recurrent tradition of the recording of the law in the covenant ceremony at Shechem (Deut. 27:3; Josh. 8:32; 24:26). The **twelve pillars** (see above on 23:20-26) are probably an anachronism reflecting the 12-tribe confederacy in Palestine—cf. the single stone as witness to the covenant at Shechem (Josh. 24:27; Judg. 9:6).

24:5-8. The role of **young men of the people of Israel** instead of priests in killing the sacrificial victims clearly indicates an early tradition in this account. Its antiquity is further suggested by the fact that here only is the rite of sprinkling **blood** mentioned in connection with the covenant ceremony. The blood is dashed on the **altar,** symbolizing the presence of God, and on the **people** as the parties to the covenant. This unique tradition may reflect the formal adoption of members to the covenant community. Certainly it is not a literary composition merely written as an epilogue to the Book of the Covenant.

24:9-11. *A Communion Meal.* The simpler tradition in this J account may reflect the covenant ceremony at Kadesh in which S elements of the Hebrews were involved with the Midianites or Kenites (see above on 18:12). **Nadab** and **Abihu,** introduced abruptly here and not mentioned elsewhere in J or E, are identified in P as the 2 older sons of Aaron (6:23), who were later destroyed for offering "unholy fire" (Lev. 10:1-2). They may represent a priesthood displaced by Aaron. Their presence here with Moses, Aaron, and the elders of Israel possibly indicates that they were representatives of the Kenites. Though it is twice stated that the whole company **saw . . . God** his appearance is not described except for the **pavement** under his feet. **Sapphire** probably refers to the blue sky. **Chief men** means lit. "corners," hence "supports" (cf. I Sam. 14:38).

24:12-18. *Moses Alone on the Mountain.* In this passage P reappears for the first time since 19:1-2a. Vss. 15b-18a evidently are the P version of the theophany on **Mount Sinai** described by J and E in 19:16-19; 20:18-21. The rest of the passage has generally been attributed to E as an intro. to the golden calf story in ch. 32. Certain elements that seem unrelated to the E narrative have been explained by some scholars as coming from a 2nd J source; but probably these are due to development by a P editor, who used the passage as an intro. to the account of the tabernacle and its service in chs. 25-31; 35-40, where the concern is to associate the reestablished cult of the 2nd temple with the Mosaic tradition. The **tables of stone** inscribed with the law may reflect the tradition of a monument with a summary code at a central sanctuary in the time of the judges, e.g. at Shechem (cf. Deut. 27:2-8; Josh. 8:32). The assignment to **Aaron and Hur** of judicial duties during Moses' absence (vs. 14) adds to the evidence that the appointment of judges at Jethro's suggestion (18:13-27; see comment) originally came later in the narrative.

24:15-18. In the P version of the theophany the **cloud** is the symbol of the divine presence, but with studied avoidance of the anthropomorphisms of the earlier sources (cf. 13:21; 14:24; 19:9; 20:21). P still retains, however, the traditional symbolism of **fire** as the sign of the theophany as well as the old narrative convention of **six days** before the climax on the **seventh.** Possibly **forty days and forty nights** is also a typical P statistic, but more probably this detail is part of the E narrative providing time for the making of the golden calf (32:1-6).

IV. INSTRUCTIONS FOR THE SANCTUARY AND THE SERVICE (25:1-31:18)

Chs. 25-31 are all characteristically P in both content and style; but that they are nevertheless composite is evident from doublets and discrepancies, from the alternation between 1st and 3rd persons in the references of Yahweh to himself, and in the belated descriptions of the incense altar and the laver, which logically belong in chs. 25; 27 respectively (see below on 30:1-38). Various theories of editorial supplementation have been proposed, but the most plausible explanation is that 2 independent versions have been combined by an editor, who added supplementary material.

The tabernacle is generally regarded as the retrojection into the desert period of a later shrine which housed the ark, generally assumed to be Solomon's temple, though the dimensions and some other details are different. The differences may be due to fusion of the conception of the temple with that of the genuine old tradition of a much simpler tent of meeting in 33:7-11 (see comment), which is an oracle shrine where God condescends to meet man occasionally. The P description preserves continuity with the old tradition by continuing to use the term "tent of meeting" (cf. esp. 29:42-44; 30:36) and specifically elaborates on the idea that God will meet with his people there (25:22). The word for "tabernacle" is derived from the verb translated "dwell" in 25:8; 29:45-46. Evidently the promise of God's dwelling in the tabernacle is to be understood in this sense of his occasional presence in the place of meeting rather than a localization of the transcendent God of postexilic Judaism (cf. I Kings 8:27).

A. THE SANCTUARY AND ITS FURNITURE (25:1-27:21)

25:1-9. The Materials. The tabernacle is to be provided by a freewill **offering,** as in the rebuilding of the temple after the Exile (Ezra 1:4; 2:68-69)— in contrast to the forced labor used by Solomon (I Kings 5:13-18). Dyes of **blue and purple,** i.e. respectively bluish and reddish purple, the classical royal purple, both obtained from a Mediterranean shellfish, the murex, at various stages of decomposition, and **scarlet** dye from the cochineal insect, which lives on the Syrian evergreen oak, were as unlikely in the desert as olive **oil** and balsam **spices,** i.e. perfumes, and Egyptian **linen** and dressed leather, which is probably denoted by the rare word translated **goatskins.** On the other hand the webs of **goats' hair,** still the material of the bedouin tent, the framework of **acacia wood** which grows in the desert, in contrast with the cedar used in the temple, and the **tanned,** lit. "reddened," **rams' skins** may have pertained to the primitive tent of meeting (33:7-11). The red skins suggest an analogy to the red leather portable tent sanctuary of Mecca before Islam, with which the tent of meeting has been compared by various scholars. On **ephod** and **breastpiece** see below on 28:6-35.

25:10-22. The Ark. That the first article in the tabernacle to be described is the ark reflects its significance in the temple, where it was the only object kept in the inmost shrine. In the older narrative sources in the Pentateuch the ark is mentioned only twice (Num. 10:35-36; 14:39-45) and in neither passage is it associated with the tent of meeting. In the narrative of Eli and Samuel at Shiloh in I Sam. 1-3 the ark is housed in a temple (I Sam. 1:9; 3:3) and the mention of the tent of meeting in I Sam. 2:22b is an obvious later insertion (see comment). In the detailed history of the ark in I Sam. 4:1-7:2; II Sam. 6:1-19 there is no reference to a tent until David provides one in Jerusalem (II Sam. 6:17). Therefore it seems probable that the ark and the tent of meeting belong to 2 independent traditions originally related to different tribal groups among those who composed the later Israel (see below on 33:7-11). For an alternative suggestion see below on 33:1-6.

The construction of the ark can only be surmised from the earlier sources (see comments on I Sam. 4:4; Ps. 99:1-5). This is the only detailed description and it is unfortunately late and idealistic; obviously the profusion of **gold** would be far beyond the resources of nomadic Israel. The dimensions of vss. 10 are credible—*ca.* 45 by 27 by 27 inches according to the common **cubit** of *ca.* 18 inches, though possibly a longer cubit of up to 21 inches is meant (cf. Ezek. 40:5; 43:13; see "Measures and Money," pp. 1283-85)—but they may be no more reliable than many other P statistics.

The developing theological interpretation of the ark is noteworthy. In Num. 10:35-36; 14:39-45; I Sam. 4 it symbolizes the divine presence and activity in battle; cf. the Philistine reaction, "a god has come into the camp" (I Sam. 4:7). Deposited in the temple built at Shiloh and later in the temple at Jerusalem, it is considered the throne of the invisible God (cf. e.g. I Sam. 4:4; II Kings 19:15), as indicated by the **cherubim**—winged sphinxes (see comment on I Kings 6:23-28) familiar to archaeologists as side supports of thrones in Palestine (e.g. at Megiddo, *ca.* 1350-1150) and Syria (e.g. at Byblos, 12th cent.). In the ark narratives in I Sam. 4:1-7:2; II Sam. 6:1-17 it is regularly called the "ark of God," sometimes "of Yahweh"; but in the D writings it is termed "ark of the covenant," no doubt because it reputedly contained the 2 stone tablets on which the 10 Commandments were written (cf. Deut. 10:1-5). This may be the revival of a genuine old tradition; cf. the deposit of agreements in sanctuaries beneath the feet of statues of Hittite and Egyptian gods. In the P material the ark is the repository of the **testimony** (vss. 16, 21), i.e. the 2 tables of the law (31:18), and is accordingly called the **ark of the testimony** (vs. 22). The tabernacle as the shelter for the ark is sometimes called the "tabernacle of the testimony" (e.g. 38:21). Here God at his own discretion meets with and declares himself to man (vs. 22; cf. 29:42-46) in revelation, as in the law, and in mercy. The lid of the ark is called the **mercy seat,** and on it the blood of atonement was to be sprinkled by the high priest on the Day of Atonement (Lev. 16:2-16).

25:23-30. The Table. The **bread of the Presence**

for which the table is to be provided (vs. 30) was according to Lev. 24:8 a symbol of the everlasting covenant between God and Israel. The 12 cakes (Lev. 24:5-9), possibly symbolizing the 12 tribes, remained with **incense** (vs. 29) on the table for 6 days and then were eaten by the priests on the sabbath while the incense was burned as an offering. The purpose of the rite was evidently either to realize the presence of God by the mention of his name or to keep him mindful of Israel in a symbolic communion meal. Its antiquity is indicated by David's eating of the holy bread (I Sam. 21:4-6). The table with 2 incense vessels (vs. 29) is depicted among the spoils of Herod's temple on the Arch of Titus in Rome.

25:31-40. The Lampstand. The 7-branched lampstand (*menorah*) shown on the Arch of Titus (see above on vss. 23-30) agrees with the description here, which is thus evidently based on that used in the 2nd temple. In Solomon's temple there were 10 single lampstands (I Kings 7:49), and Zech. 4:2 describes a lampstand shaped like a bowl with spaces for 7 lamps around its rim. A **talent**—not less than 62½ pounds (see "Measures and Money," pp. 1283-85)—**of pure gold** is unlikely in the desert.

26:1-37. The Tabernacle. On the relation of the tabernacle to the tent of meeting (33:7-11) and to Solomon's temple see above on 25:1–31:18. On the materials see above on 25:1-9. The dimensions total 30 by 10 by 10 cubits (see above on 25:10-22), the length and width being exactly half those of Solomon's temple (I Kings 6:2). A few details of the structure remain obscure, but Arabic etymology has authenticated that the **frames** (vss. 15-30) are to be understood as sections of trelliswork. As in the temple, the interior is to be divided into 2 rooms. That farther from the entrance, corresponding to the room in the temple which in I Kings 6:16-31 is called the "inner sanctuary," lit. "back part," is in P invariably termed the **most holy place,** whereas the other room is called the **holy place** (vss. 33-34). Only the **ark of the testimony** is to be placed in the most holy place, while the **table** for the bread of the Presence (25:23-30) and the **lampstand** (25:31-40) are to be placed in the holy place (vs. 35). Separating the 2 rooms is to be a **veil** (vss. 31-35), which was given a theological significance in early Christian allegory (Heb. 6:19; 9:3; 10:20; cf. Mark 15:38).

27:1-8. The Great Altar. This description is evidently intended to portray a portable model of the great "bronze altar" (I Kings 8:64; cf. 38:30; 39:39) in the court of Solomon's temple. Probably it is based on a description of Solomon's altar originally included in I Kings 7:15-44 but later deleted or inadvertently omitted (with vs. 3 cf. I Kings 7:45). The construction of **acacia wood** encased in sheet **bronze** would hardly be fireproof, and it is incompatible with the ordinance requiring earth or undressed stone (20:24-25). The **horns** (vs. 2) were upward protuberances at the corners. They were smeared with the blood of the sin offering (29:12) and a refugee from blood revenge grasped them to claim the sanctuary of the altar (cf. I Kings 1:50; 2:28; see above on 21:13-14). Perhaps this feature was the survival of the horns of a sacrificial animal as the point of contact between God and man. The reference to the **ledge** (vs. 5) apparently means that

the upper half of the altar was to be smaller and that the **network** (vs. 4), i.e. grating, was to surround the larger base.

27:9-19. The Court. The sacred area surrounding an ancient Semitic sanctuary is so regular a feature that it is often synonymous with "temple" in the OT and the Ras Shamra texts. Here a court measuring 100 by 50 cubits, i.e. *ca.* 150 by 75 feet, is to be fenced by **hangings** 5 cubits, i.e. *ca.* 7½ feet, in height. The number of **pillars** on each side is simply a 5th of the number of cubits—evidence that the author did not test his theory by drawing a plan.

27:20-21. Oil for a Constant Light. This instruction substantially duplicates Lev. 24:2-4 (see comment) and is probably a late editorial insertion.

28:1-4. The Priestly Family. The selection of **Aaron . . . and his sons** to be **priests** reflects the hereditary high priesthood of the family of Zadok and esp. the status of the high priest as the head of the Jewish community after the Exile. Restriction of the priesthood to the descendants of Aaron is characteristic of P, in contrast with the D emphasis on descent from Levi. On **Nadab and Abihu** see above on 24:9-11. The family of **Ithamar** served as custodians of the ark at Shiloh and after its capture and the death of Eli were priests at Nob until massacred at the order of Saul. Abiathar escaped and became David's priest but was later deposed by Solomon in favor of Zadok, who had supported his succession to the throne. According to the Chronicler (I Chr. 6:4-8, 50-53; 24:3; Ezra 7:2-5) Zadok was a descendant of **Eleazar;** but since there is no mention of his origin in the early sources (see comment on II Sam. 8:15-18) some scholars question his Aaronite descent and suggest instead that he may have been the hereditary Jebusite priest of Jerusalem (cf. Gen. 14:18-20; Josh. 10:1-3) when David captured the city. According to I Chr. 24:1-4 the priesthood consisted of 16 families descended from Eleazar and 8 from Ithamar.

The word "priest," here first mentioned in Exod., is probably cognate with an Arabic word denoting a functionary who might officiate at sacrifices but was better known as the medium of oracles and divination. In view of the association of the primitive tent of meeting with oracles Moses may have had such a function. The tradition of the consecration of Aaron as priest may reflect the divergence of the sacrificial office from that of the agent of oracles represented by Moses.

28:5-14. The Ephod. References to the ephod as a priestly vestment in the historical texts (cf. esp. I Sam. 2:18; II Sam. 6:14, 20) indicate that it was a ritual loincloth, such as was worn also by Egyptian priests. The ephod of the high priest described here is a relic of this, now worn over elaborate other vestments (cf. 29:5; Lev. 8:7) perhaps as a sort of apron. Gradual enlargement no doubt led to the later development of **two shoulder-pieces** (vs. 7) and a **band** (vs. 8) around the waist. **Two onyx stones** engraved with the names of the 12 tribes are to be attached to the shoulder straps (vss. 9-14). The idea that the priest thus will **bear their names before the LORD** may reflect the calling of the tribal names in the common assembly in the time of the judges (cf. Gen. 49; Judg. 5; Deut. 33). On the materials and colors see above on 25:1-9.

28:15-30. The Breastpiece of Judgment. In other passages in the historical texts **ephod** evidently refers to an article used in divination which contained a receptacle for the sacred lots, **the Urim and the Thummim** (vs. 30; see comment on I Sam. 14:2-3, 16-23, 36-46; cf. I Sam. 23:9-12; 30:7-8; Hos. 3:4). Possibly this was some sort of sacred robe, which might be a casing of sheet metal, if not something more substantial (cf. Judg. 8:27; I Sam. 21:9). The significance of this meaning of the term possibly survived in the high priest's **breastpiece of judgment,** better "decision," which apparently included a bag for the sacred lots. The **twelve stones** engraved with the names of the **twelve tribes** may be a variant tradition of the 2 stones so engraved on the shoulder straps (vss. 9-12). The Hebrew names of the stones evidently refer to semiprecious stones, some of which cannot now be identified.

28:31-35. The Robe of the Ephod. The outer vestment worn immediately under the breastpiece and ephod is to be **blue,** i.e. bluish purple (see above on 25:1-9). The immature **pomegranate** was a fertility symbol in Canaanite art; cf. the capitals of the pillars Jachin and Boaz in front of Solomon's temple (I Kings 7:18-20). On the **skirts** of the priest's robe, however, they may simply denote tassels. The **bells** may have been originally designed to scare off evil influences—**lest he die** (vs. 35). Practically they warned the laity of the priest's approach and prevented the dangerous contact with the holy (cf. II Sam. 6:7).

28:36-39. The Sacred Emblem. Vss. 36-38 logically belong after vs. 39, where the instruction to make a **turban** appears, and may originally have followed vs. 40 (cf. 39:27-31). The Hebrew word inadequately rendered **plate,** though from a root that may mean "shine," usually means "flower" and here probably denotes a representation of a flower. The word translated **crown** in 29:6, from a root meaning "separate" or "dedicate," evidently refers to this emblem or possibly to its mounting (cf. 39:30; Lev. 8:9). That it was a symbol of dedication is further indicated by the inscription **Holy to the LORD.** Almost certainly it was inherited by the high priest from the king (cf. II Sam. 1:10; II Kings 11:12; Pss. 89:39; 132:18).

28:40-43. Vestments for Other Priests. The instruction for the dress of **Aaron's sons** is that applicable to priests in general in the postexilic period. On vs. 41 see below on 29:1-26. On vss. 42-43 see above on 20:22-26.

29:1-37. The Consecration of Priests. This passage is apparently based on the account of the consecration of Aaron and his sons in Lev. 8 and assumes the sacrificial regulations of Lev. 1–7. There is no detailed account of the installation of a priest before this postexilic passage, and the only feature in common with earlier passages (e.g. Judg. 17:5-12; I Kings 13:33) is the idea expressed in the word translated **ordain** (vs. 9), lit. "fill the hand"—either the handing over of a sacrificial victim to the priest (vss. 24-25; cf. Lev. 8:27-28) or, as suggested by a secular text from Mari on the middle Euphrates, the assignment of perquisites as reward for service (cf. vss. 27-28; Judg. 17:10; 18:4; I Sam. 2:13-14).

The limitation of the hereditary priesthood to the family of **Aaron** reflects postexilic usage. Through-out the historical period up to the Exile the priestly status of the Levites was recognized (cf. e.g. Deut. 27:9; 33:8; Judg. 17:13) but the office was not limited to them—e.g. Samuel was an Ephraimite and the highest priestly office was held by the king.

29:4-9. After ceremonial washing of all the candidates, **Aaron,** i.e. the candidate for high priest, is to be invested with the high priestly **garments** (cf. ch. 28) and then anointed as a symbol of his being set apart from common associations. His **sons,** i.e. those to be lesser priests, are then to be invested in their garments (cf. 28:40). On **crown** see above on 28:36-39.

29:10-14. A young **bull** is then to be sacrificed, the **blood** being partly smeared on the **horns of the altar** (see above on 27:1-8) and partly poured at **the base of the altar** as in the sin offering for the community (Lev. 4:25, 30, 34). The **flesh** is to be burned **outside the camp** since it is a **sin offering** for the priestly candidates, who are not yet fully consecrated (cf. Lev. 4:11; 9:11). Their ritual disability is communicated to the victim by their placing their **hands** on its **head** (cf. Lev. 4:4).

29:15-18. The offering of the first **ram** as a **burnt offering,** i.e. one made wholly over to God in smoke and **pleasing odor,** was probably considered as a gift to put God in a good humor with Aaron and his family, who are to make the gift theirs by their hands on its head.

29:19-25. The 2nd ram is properly the **ram of ordination** (vs. 22). The **tips of the right ears** and **thumbs** and **great toes** of the ordinands are to be touched with the **blood,** which is then to be dashed **against the altar.** The priests will thus be attached to God, as in a blood-smearing rite in the Ras Shamra texts. The application to the extremities, by which supernatural influences were thought to have access, as in the case of a cleansed leper (Lev. 14:14), indicates a prophylactic rite. The smearing of the **garments** with blood and oil (vs. 21) is surely a later elaboration, for contact with the sanctified person would itself sanctify the vestments.

29:26-37. Priestly Perquisites. Vss. 27-28 are a secondary expansion on the **priest's portion.** Vss. 29-30 provide, apparently incidentally, for the hereditary high priesthood by specifying that Aaron's **holy garments** are to be passed on to his sons in an act of consecration lasting **seven days.** The instructions of vss. 1-26 are resumed in vs. 31; but the sudden mention of the atoning significance of the 2nd ram (vs. 33) and of the repeated **sin offering** (vss. 36-37) indicates a later expansion reflecting the atonement for the imperfection of the priest and the **altar** on the Day of Atonement (cf. Lev. 16).

29:38-42a. The Daily Offering. The custom of a **burnt offering** every **morning** and a **cereal offering** every **evening** was already established in preexilic times (II Kings 16:15). Described here is a more elaborate practice of postexilic times. **Fine flour** was that ground from the inner kernels of the wheat. **Beaten oil** was the finest grade, the olives being patiently pounded in a mortar rather than squeezed in a press. The pulp was strained into water, from which the oil was skimmed after settling and hence was called "washed oil."

29:42b-46. The Divine Presence. The sudden divine

address in the first person, in contrast with the 3rd person **before the LORD** in vs. 42*a,* indicates literary disunity. The P editor expresses the theological conception that God's presence is evoked by the daily offering agreeable to him and symbolic of the receptive and submissive spirit of the inquirer. Thus he will **meet** with his people in this place and in this sense may be said to **dwell** in the sanctuary even though not restricted to it (see above on 25:1–31:18). This assurance, reflecting the covenant formula (vs. 45) and Israel's historical confession (vs. 46), forms a natural conclusion to the ritual ordinances.

30:1-10. *The Incense Altar.* The omission of this altar from the furniture of the sanctuary in ch. 25; 26:35 indicates that the instruction for it is a later addition. The proportions—1½ feet **square** and 3 feet high—and the **horns** are illustrated in incense altars from archaeological sites in Syria and Palestine, e.g. from Megiddo *ca.* 10th or 9th cent. This fact and the apparent correspondence with the "golden altar" in Solomon's temple (I Kings 6:22; 7:48) suggest that it may have been revived in later postexilic times because of a tradition of its earlier use. The ritual involving this altar on the Day of Atonement (vs. 10) is probably also described in Lev. 16:15-19.

30:11-16. *The Poll Tax.* The capital numbering of the people insofar as it focused the divine attention on every individual, the moral or ritual defect of any one of whom would impair the community, was always dangerous (cf. II Sam. 24). Hence atonement for the community was required to divert God's wrath to the expiatory sacrifice, for which the poll tax is now stated to be levied. This explanation is apologetic and secondary, the actual purpose being to provide for the regular cult (vs. 16), which was the charge of the king before the Exile and was later defrayed out of the revenue of the province in the Persian period (cf. Ezra 6:8-10). All alike eventually paid a **half shekel** (cf. Matt. 17:24); there was neither pauper nor patron in the cult in Israel. **Shekel** and **gerah** refer to weights of silver (see "Measures and Money," pp. 1283-85).

30:17-21. *The Laver.* The inclusion of this instruction here rather than with the description of the bronze altar and its accessories (27:1-8) indicates that it is a later addition. Solomon's temple had a "molten sea" and 10 lavers for priestly ablutions (I Kings 7:23-39).

30:22-38. *Holy Oil and Incense.* The ingredients of both these recipes are perfumes which were highly valued in ancient times. Except the Arabian myrrh they came from India and the Far East, probably by way of S Arabia. The anointing of the **tent** and its furnishings indicates that the rite signified separation rather than delegation of authority (see above on 29:4-9). The instruction in vs. 30 that not only **Aaron,** as in 29:7, but **his sons** also are to be anointed shows that this is a later addition. Probably the difference is due to the symbolism used by the respective authors rather than a reflection of a change in practice; i.e. in 29:7 (cf. 29:29; Lev. 6:20-22; 8:12-13) the sons symbolize priests in general as distinguished from the high priest, symbolized by Aaron himself, whereas here (cf. 28:41; 40:15; Lev. 7:36; 10:7; Num. 3:3) they symbolize Aaron's hereditary successors in the office of high priest.

31:1-11. *The Craftsmen.* This passage was probably derived from 35:10-19, 30–36:1 and inserted here by an editor with antiquarian interests. Included are the **altar of incense** (vs. 8; cf. 35:15) and the **laver** (vs. 9; cf. 35:16) which were added later to the instructions of chs. 25-29 (see above on 30:1-10, 17-21). The skill and intelligence of the craftsmen are attributed to the **Spirit** of God, that invasive divine influence which is the source of initiative and preeminence in thought and action in any field, physical, intellectual, or spiritual. It is symptomatic of the practical interest of the Hebrews and their wholesome integrated view of life that they related the skill of the craftsman, no less than the wisdom of the sage, the artistry of the poet, and the insight of the prophet, to the Spirit of God.

31:12-18. *The Sabbath Ordinance.* Insertion here of this P version of the sabbath commandment (cf. 20:8-11) was no doubt suggested by the instruction for work on the sanctuary. The passage is loosely constructed, vss. 15, 17*b* being later expansions, as shown by the naming of Yahweh in the 3rd person. Noteworthy features are the sabbath as the distinctive **sign** of the covenanted community (vss. 14, 16, 17; cf. Ezek. 20:12), the penalty of **death** for its breach (vs. 14), and the relation to the P account of creation (vs. 17; cf. 20:11; Gen. 2:2-3). Vs. 18 brings to a close the P version of the instructions given to Moses on **Mount Sinai** (chs. 25–31). On **tables of the testimony** see above on 25:10-22. The concluding phrases are probably a fragment of E linking the material in 24:12-18 (see comment) with the golden calf narrative of ch. 32.

V. Conclusion of the Early Sinai Narratives (32:1–34:35)

Having presented all of the P material alleged to have been revealed to Moses on Mt. Sinai (chs. 25–31), the compiler returns to the remainder of the JE Sinai narrative. Both literary analysis of this section and recovery of the complex traditions underlying it are very difficult.

32:1-6. *Making of the Golden Calf.* The bull was the cult animal of the Canaanite god Baal, whose season of triumph, as shown by the Ras Shamra texts, was the new year festival on the eve of the early winter rains, at which time he was worshiped as king. The enthronement of Yahweh as King, an important element in the autumn festival in Jerusalem and in Bethel (cf. I Kings 12:32), was an adaptation of this Canaanite festival. The centering of apostasy in a **molten calf,** i.e. bull, and esp. the saying in vs. 4*b* (cf. I Kings 12:28) suggest that the story reflects the opposition to the establishment by Jeroboam I of Yahwist shrines at Dan and Bethel which included bull images. Because these images, like the cherubim in the Jerusalem temple, were probably thrones for the invisible Yahweh rather than representations of the deity, and because the only other passages earlier than the D writings which criticize them are Hos. 8:5-6; 10:5; 13:2, some scholars have assumed that this passage comes from the same period and have cited it as evidence for dating the E source in the middle of the 8th cent. It is possible, however, that Jeroboam's cultic innovations, esp. his appointment of priests "from among all the people" (I Kings 12:31; cf. Deut. 33:11), aroused immediate opposition among the Levites whose authority was thus challenged. Such a reaction may well have influenced the final E tradition. On the other hand the unfavorable role of Aaron in the story points to an underlying authentic tradition of the Mosaic age which involved a cult object in the form of a bull—cf. the serpent image of Num. 21:8-9 (see above on 20:4-6). **Play** (vs. 6) refers to sexual license (cf. Gen. 26:8, where "fondling" translates the same Hebrew verb), reflecting Canaanite fertility rites and similar rites of imitative magic practiced at some Yahwist shrines, e.g. at Bethel (cf. Amos 2:7).

32:7-14. Moses' Intercession. The author who so skillfully composed the dramatic scene of Moses' discovery of the calf (vss. 17-19) obviously never intended that he should be forewarned of the situation. Probably, therefore, this passage comes from a J parallel to the tradition of apostasy immediately following the covenant. Editorial elaboration is evidently responsible for the summary of vss. 1-6 in vs. 8bc and the use of phrases from Gen. 22:17, a late passage, in vs. 13. Some scholars have viewed the whole passage as a late insertion; but the differences of form and argument here and in vss. 30-34, as well as of divine retribution in vss. 25-29, 35, indicate variant traditions. The appeasing of the divine wrath by the mediation of Moses exemplifies an important aspect of the prophetic office (cf. Gen. 20:7; I Sam. 7:5; 12:19-25; Amos 7:1-6).

32:15-24. Destruction of the Calf. This is the dramatic continuation of the E narrative begun in vss. 1-6. The P phrase **tables of the testimony** (see above on 25:10-22) indicates editorial expansion of vs. 15. Moses' words in vs. 18 are in poetry and may come from a saga. The breaking of the **tables** probably expresses the idea that apostasy abrogates the covenant. The Hittite vassal treaties (see above on 20:1-21) state that destruction of the record will invalidate the treaty. For the editor who combined J and E the breaking provided an opportunity to use the J account of the making of the tables (ch. 34) as a restoration. Moses' compelling the people to **drink** the **water** with the powdered gold (vs. 20) seems to involve a confusion of motifs: (a) an ordeal (cf. Num. 5:11-28) to discriminate between the innocent and the guilty, of which the plague of vs. 35 seems to be the immediate consequence, and (b) the ritual of the sin offering, which involved the destruction of the offending object by powdering and mixing with water to carry it away (cf. Deut. 9:21). The absence of any retort by Moses to Aaron's very lame excuse (vss. 22-24) suggests a glossing over of Aaron's part in the episode out of respect to the established Aaronite priesthood—possibly the supression of a part of the narrative which linked it to the following vss. 25-29.

32:25-29. The Massacre by the Levites. The loose connection of the passage with its context suggests that it represents an independent tradition, and for this reason some scholars have attributed it to the J source. Certain details of phraseology, however, and esp. its affinity with the folk oracle on Levi in Deut. 33:9, which probably comes from N Israel, make the E source more probable. Viewed in the light of the ancient poem in Deut. 33:8-11 both this

account and the preceding calf story seem to preserve traditions of a conflict at Kadesh between 2 Levitical groups led respectively by Moses and Aaron. It has been suggested that Aaron and his adherents had not been in Egypt and had adopted Yahwism from the Kenites separately from Moses and his followers (see above on 18:12).

32:30-35. Another Intercession. This is probably the E parallel to vss. 7-10, despite the view of some scholars that the concept of Yahweh's **book** (cf. Ps. 69:28; Mal. 3:16) represents the theology of a later time. The thought here is not necessarily that of judgment in an afterlife but may simply imply foreordination for life or death within the normal life span, as in I Sam. 25:29; Isa. 4:3. Moses' willingness to be sacrificed for the sake of his people expresses a concept of vicarious atonement that is developed later in the suffering servant of Isa. 52:13–53:12 and in the theology of the Qumran sect, which regarded itself as working atonement for the rest of Israel. Instead Moses is given the practical task of leading his people to the promised land. The guiding **angel** (vs. 34b; cf. 23:20) seems to come into the context as an afterthought and may be a later insertion. Vs. 35 indicates variant tradition not only about the divine retribution but also about who made the calf —the awkward structure is no doubt due to an editor's effort to harmonize.

33:1-6. Preparations for Departure. The J source introduces this new phase of the narrative by recalling the promise to the patriarchs (cf. e.g. Gen. 12:2); but vs. 2, which is contradicted by vs. 12a, seems to be a later elaboration based on 23:23 (cf. 32:34b). Different sources are indicated by the 2 explanations of the discarding of the **ornaments:** according to J as a mourning rite after Yahweh's refusal to go with Israel (vss. 3-4), according to E in obedience to a divine command (vss. 5b-6). The latter probably visualizes the ornaments as amulets or even figurines of gods such as are familiar from archaeological sites (cf. Hos. 2:13). This and the reference to Jacob's burying such ornaments at Shechem before his pilgrimage to Bethel (Gen. 35:4) may point to a regular rite of renunciation corresponding to the divine claim to purity of worship in the sacrament of the covenant. The association of this with the problem of continuing **presence,** lit. "face," of God on leaving his cult place (vss. 15-16) has suggested to some scholars that originally the ornaments were used in construction of the ark and that this account was omitted in favor of that in 25:10-22. Another theory is that later orthodoxy has suppressed here a genuine old tradition of their use in the making of a cult mask to be worn by Moses in communicating the divine oracle, later communicated through the ephod and sacred lots (see below on 34:29-35).

33:7-11. The Tent of Meeting. The tent sanctuary of this passage is quite different from the P tabernacle described in ch. 26 but not yet constructed (cf. ch. 36). Unlike the tabernacle it is pitched **outside the camp.** It is used for oracles (vs. 7b; cf. Num. 11:24-25; 12:4-8) and is served, or kept, by **Joshua** alone (vs. 11). It has been compared to the portable shrine, both tent and litter, in pre-Islamic Mecca, which was also used among other things for sacred oracles. The contrast of this simple tent with the elaborate P tabernacle is strong evidence of its genuine antiquity, though Joshua's connection with it may be a secondary tradition.

The P concept of the tabernacle as the housing for the ark is obviously based on the place of the ark in Solomon's temple. Before the building of the temple, however, David placed the ark in a tent on bringing it to Jerusalem (II Sam. 6:17). Some scholars have taken this to be a revival of an original association of the ark with the tent in the desert. But this is by no means certain. The early traditions of the Pentateuch speak of them only separately, and indeed the ark as the symbol of the permanent presence of Yahweh is counter to the concept of his occasional presence in the tent of meeting. Thus the ark and this oracle tent may belong to the traditions of different groups in the Israelite confederacy —the ark associated with the tribes which settled near Shechem, Bethel, and Shiloh, the tent no doubt with those in the S whose center was Hebron (see above on 25:10-22; the references in Josh. 18:1; 19:51 to a tent of meeting at Shiloh are the work of a P editor who had in mind the tabernacle). On this assumption David's bringing of the ark to Jerusalem and housing it in a tent would be, not the revival of an older association, but the new idea of a political genius for uniting the religious symbols of N and S.

This passage has characteristics of the J source, but independence of its present J context is indicated both by Yahweh's presence in the pillar of cloud (vss. 9-10), in contrast with the problem about the presence in vss. 12-16, and by Moses' speaking with Yahweh **face to face** (vs. 11), in contrast with his being allowed in vss. 22-23 to see, and that exceptionally, only the back of God. Accordingly this and other early references to the tent (Num. 11:16-17, 24b-30; 12:1-16; Deut. 31:14-15) have often been attributed to E. On the other hand the passage may well be editorially displaced, as the abrupt beginning suggests, and in another position would be no more inconsistent than certain other traditions assembled in J—cf. e.g. 24:9-11, where not only Moses but all his companions see Yahweh. Probably the tent of meeting tradition, whether from Hebron or elsewhere, was originally independent of the main tradition of both J and E but came into association with one or the other through connection with David's tent.

33:12-17. *The Continuing Divine Presence.* This J passage is loosely connected with vss. 1-4 through the theme of the departure; perhaps a closer link containing the assurance quoted by Moses in vs. 12b has dropped out. Some have suggested that vs. 17 should precede vs. 12, but then an antecedent for **this very thing** would be lacking. Another suggestion is that 34:9 should precede vs. 14. Moses' request for the divine **presence,** lit. "face," to accompany Israel probably meant originally a concrete token. If this does not refer to the ark (see above on vss. 1-6) it may anticipate sanctuaries of Yahweh in Palestine where one might see the "face" of God, thus pursuing the theme of the accessibility of Yahweh once his cult place in the desert has been left behind.

33:18-23. *Moses' Vision.* The revelation of God's **glory** (vs. 18) or his **back** (vs. 23) is not the assurance of his continuing presence Moses has been requesting. Therefore it is probable that **this very thing** (vs. 17) originally introduced a story of the giving of a concrete token and that the sight of the back of God represents an effort to modify the cruder concept of an earlier time. As indicated by the 3-fold intro. to the speech of Yahweh, the passage is not a unity. Later modifications are the vision of the divine **glory,** i.e. worth or honor (vss. 18, 22), and the declaration of the **name** Yahweh (vs. 19), with its implications of divine self-disclosure in the crises of history (see above on 3:14-15). The tradition of the revelation in vss. 21-23 is certainly reflected in the tradition of Elijah at Horeb (I Kings 19:9a, 11-13a). Perhaps the passage is continued in 34:6-9.

34:1-5. *The Tables of Stone.* No doubt E included some notice of replacement of the tablets broken by Moses (32:19), and possibly phrases from it helped the editor who turned the J account of the making of the tablets into this story of their remaking. In contrast to the E emphasis on their total divine manufacture (24:12; 31:18b; 32:16) the J tradition was that Moses both **cut** the tablets and **wrote** the words on them (vss. 27-28) at Yahweh's instruction. Originally the making of the tablets must have come earlier in J—certainly before the order to depart (33:1)—and the restrictions in vs. 3 suggest closer connection to 19:12-13a, 20-22 than to the covenant meal which included Aaron, Nadab, Abihu, and 70 elders (24:9-11). Some scholars have separated vs. 5b from what precedes and joined it to vs. 6, but this proclamation of the **name** Yahweh is needed to introduce the **covenant** of vss. 10-28. The initial element in the vassal treaties of the ancient Near East was a declaration of the name of the suzerain who imposed the treaty (see above on 20:1-21).

34:6-9. *Yahweh's Mercy and Justice.* This passage is probably from J but has been transposed into the context, perhaps because of the similar wording in vss. 5b, 6. It is connected rather with 33:12-23 by the dominating themes of Yahweh's presence, the favor Moses finds in his sight, and esp. his discretionary mercy (cf. 33:19). This last is expanded in a style reminiscent of Deut. to emphasize his retributive justice as well as his **love.** The close analogy with 20:5b-6 suggests that this is the language of the liturgy of the covenant. Israel's incompatibility with God prompts Moses' prayer for pardon (vs. 9; see above on 33:12-17) as the basis for the renewed covenant—a prayer which probably reflects actual usage in the sacrament of the covenant.

34:10-16. *Announcement of the Covenant.* Vss. 10-28, continuing vss. 1-5, consist of J material with D expansion. The framework is the making of a covenant that, like the Decalogue, follows the literary scheme of Hittite vassal treaties of the 14th-13th cents. (see above on 20:1-21), which probably reflect the general convention of the Near East in these and succeeding cents. In such a treaty the suzerain proclaims his name (cf. vs. 5) and declares that he makes a covenant with his vassals (cf. vs. 10a). He then lists his past exploits to remind them of his benefactions and his power to punish. Departing at this point from the usual pattern (cf. 20:2) vs. 10b instead promises future display of Yahweh's **marvels** and **terrible** deeds.

34:11-16. The suzerain demands of his vassals

absolute obedience to the terms he imposes (cf. vss. 11a), of which the first is exclusive allegiance (cf. vs. 14a; see above on 20:3, 5). The rest of vss. 11-16 is D exhortation to obey this command by avoiding any **covenant** with the Canaanites—e.g. to secure rights of seasonal grazing and sojourn in the settled land. Their **altars** and **pillars** (see above on 23:20-26) are to be destroyed, and also their **Asherim**—probably trees, either natural or stylized, which symbolized the tree of life and ultimately the mother goddess Asherah. Lest they be drawn into participation in the local cult with its sexual rites of imitative magic, Israelites must esp. avoid making marriage contracts with the Canaanites.

34:17-26. The Ritual Code. In the vassal-treaty pattern the comprehensive first command of exclusive allegiance (vs. 14a) is followed by a list of specific demands. Here the series constitutes a Ritual Code, of which the items are parallel to the ritual ordinances of the Decalogue, the Book of the Covenant, and the sequel to the passover ordinance, as follows:

vs. 14a	20:3	vs. 20c	23:15b
vs. 17	20:4	vs. 21	23:12a
vs. 18	23:15a	vss. 22-23	23:16-17
vss. 19-20b	13:12-13	vss. 25-26	23:18-19

These ritual ordinances in the covenant sacrament are designed to preserve the distinctive cult and community of Yahweh (cf. vss. 12-13, 15-16; 33:16) against assimilation to Canaanite cult practices, esp. at the 3 agricultural festivals. Therefore they must have arisen in Palestine rather than at Kadesh. Because "Yahweh the God of Israel" (vs. 23) seems to have been a form of address used at the early tribal center at Shechem (cf. Gen. 33:20; Josh. 8:30; 24:2) and transferred to the shrine at Shiloh (cf. I Sam. 1:17), it has been suggested that the Ritual Code originated at Shiloh during the time of the judges. On the other hand it may reflect the period of the early monarchy, when Canaanite areas were incorporated under David and the danger of assimilation became acute.

34:17-20. On vs. 17 see above on 20:4-5; 33:1-6; cf. Lev. 19:4. On vs. 18 see above on 12:1-13:16. On vss. 19:20b see above on 13:1-2, 11-16. **Appear before me** (vs. 20c), lit. "see my face," indicates a concrete symbol of Yahweh's presence, probably the ark, at the central shrine. The statutory pilgrimages thrice a year with offerings were an economic necessity for the support of cult and priesthood.

34:21-24. On vs. 21a see above on 20:8-10; 23:10-19. The addition here of specific mention of **plowing and harvest** safeguards the observance even in the busy seasons when urgency might encourage its suspension. The 2nd pilgrimage festival, at the end of the **wheat harvest,** took its name from being 7 **weeks** (cf. Deut. 16:9-10)—or 50 days (cf. Lev. 23:16), whence the Greek name Pentecost—after the feast of unleavened bread inaugurating the barley harvest. Thus it was the time for offering **first fruits.** The 3rd pilgrimage festival—the greatest and probably earliest (cf. Judg. 21:19), thus sometimes called simply "the festival" (Ezek. 45:23)—celebrated the autumn **ingathering** of all fruits, including the last of the grapes, olives, and grain from the threshing floor, **at the year's end** (see above on 12:1-13). The occasion thus came to be both harvest festival and new year festival. It is also called the feast of booths or tabernacles (Lev. 23:34; Deut. 16:13). **Desire** (vs. 24), in the Hebrew the same verb as "covet" in 20:17, obviously has here a more palpable significance than either English word denotes. The assurance, which surely stems from the early period of the occupation of Canaan, reflects the reluctance of the seminomadic settlers to leave their **land** for pilgrimages lest the dispossessed take advantage of their absence.

34:25-26. The ban on **leaven,** i.e. old dough, contaminated by common use (see above on 12:14-20), in bread offered with a **sacrifice** involving effusion of **blood** was known to Amos (4:5). The following **passover** regulation has the same purpose of delimiting strictly the holy and the profane (see above on 12:7-10) but is evidently a later modification, for the passover was not an established **feast,** i.e. pilgrimage festival, till the time of Josiah (see above on 12:1-13:16). Cf. 23:18, which probably preserves the original ordinance applying to the pilgrimage feasts. **First fruits of your ground** (vs. 26a) may mean the first crop of freshly broken, or occupied, land rather than an annual offering as in vs. 22. **The house of the LORD your God** probably refers to the temple at Shiloh (cf. I Sam. 1:7, 24) or another early central sanctuary. The injunction not to **boil a kid in its mother's milk**—the basis for orthodox Jewish maintenance of 2 sets of cooking utensils to segregate meat and dairy products—was probably directed against a Canaanite practice which may be referred to in a Ras Shamra text describing spring agricultural rites. The association with first fruits suggests that the first kid may have been sacrificed thus to insure the future fertility of the mother. Adoption of this rite would infringe the dedication of the firstling to Yahweh. Israel's prosperity depends on his grace rather than on manipulative magic.

34:27-28. Recording of the Covenant. As the Hittite vassal treaties (see above on vss. 10-16) were given final validity by being recorded, Moses is instructed to **write** the terms of the covenant on the **tables** he has prepared (vss. 1, 4). The process visualized may be simply application of ink with a brush rather than the divine engraving of the E tradition (32:16). The covenant is said to be based on **these words,** identified as the **ten commandments.** Accordingly various attempts have been made to arrange the ordinances of vss. 14-26 into a "Ritual Decalogue," which some scholars have viewed as more primitive than the "Ethical Decalogue" (20:1-17). But since the Palestinian origin of the Ritual Code is obvious (see above on vss. 17-26) it could not have been the basis of the Sinai covenant. More probably it was modeled on the Decalogue as a priestly summary of the cultic duties of the laity. Possibly the compiler of JE, having used the Decalogue earlier, omitted a J version of it here and substituted the Ritual Code. If not, the final phrase may be a later addition by one concerned to make clear that the 10 Commandments were the basis for the covenant.

34:29-35. The Shining of Moses' Face. The verbs in this curious passage indicate 2 parts: vss. 29-33, the P continuation from 31:18*a,* describing what happened once at the conclusion of the Sinai theophany; vss. 34-35, a genuine old tradition of a continuing custom of Moses, probably connected with the tent of meeting (33:7-11). The word translated **veil,** used only here, probably means a cult mask —such as is well attested in antiquity and among the Arabs in connection with prophecy—which Moses used to use when speaking an oracle from Yahweh. Since the tradition was embarrassing to later orthodoxy (cf. Ezek. 13:18) the P author explains the mask as worn on only one occasion to cover the awesome afterglow on Moses' face resulting from the divine encounter (cf. Paul's explanation, II Cor. 3:13). In vs. 35*a,* however, omission in the LXX of **the skin of Moses' face** suggests that these words were repeated by an editor from vss. 29-30 and that the meaning is rather that the **face of Moses . . . shone** when he was wearing the mask. No doubt it was made of burnished metal—cf. an Arab cult mask of gold—or decorated with metal pieces, perhaps from the ornaments contributed by the people (see above on 33:1-6). **Shone** translates a rare word which contains the consonants of "horn" and was so rendered in the Vulg.—whence Michelangelo's famous statue of Moses with horns. Possibly vs. 35*a* originally described the mask as having horns.

VI. Execution of the Instructions for the Sanctuary and the Service (35:1-40:38)

This account of the establishment of the cult largely repeats in narrative form the detailed instructions which according to P were given to Moses on Mt. Sinai (chs. 25-31), with a few summary abridgments and secondary elaborations. Inclusion in their proper order of items added in chs. 30-31 (see comments) shows that most of this section is also a later addition.

35:1-3. *The Sabbath Ordinance.* See above on 31:12-18. Unique here, though implied in 16:23, is the prohibition of **fire** on the sabbath. It has been suggested that this may be a vestige of the religion of the Kenites, desert smiths (see above on 18:27), who were no doubt forbidden to smelt or work metals on the sabbath.

35:4-36:7. *The Contributions.* This section is an elaboration of 25:1-9 (see comment), mostly by repetition and summary. Added is the enlistment of **every able man** to contribute labor (35:10), under the leadership of **Bezalel and Oholiab** (35:30-36:3*a;* see above on 31:1-11). Added also is the account of having to stop the contributions (36:3*b*-7) because the people have offered **much more than enough**—the depiction of an ideal situation, obviously as a stimulant rather than as a narration of fact.

36:8-38:20. *The Sanctuary and Its Equipment.* De-

parting from the order in the instructions of chs. 25-27, the narrative describes first the construction of the **tabernacle** (36:8-38; see above on 26:1-37). An added detail is that the **pillars** have **capitals** (vs. 38; cf. 26:32, 37), presumably of carved work (cf. I Kings 7:16-20). On the **ark** (37:1-9), **table** (37:10-16), and **lampstand** (37:17-24) see above on 25:10-22, 23-30, 31-40. The **altar of incense** (37:25-28) and **anointing oil** and **incense** (37:29), the instructions for which are later additions (30:1-10, 22-38; see comments), are here included with the furnishings of the tabernacle. Because of inclusion of the incense altar the main altar is now identified as the **altar of burnt offering** (38:1-7; see above on 27:1-8). In the mention of the **laver** (38:8; see above on 30:17-21) the reference to **women** serving **at the door of the tent of meeting** does not fit this context, since the tabernacle is not yet in use (cf. 40:17); neither does it suit the early tradition of a simple tent for oracles to which only Moses and Joshua have access (33:7-11). It is apparently related to I Sam. 2:22*a,* also an insertion into its context (see comment). Possibly female singers of the temple are visualized. In the **court** (38:9-20; see above on 27:9-19) **capitals** for the **pillars** (vss. 17, 19) are also added.

38:21-31. *A Statistical Summary.* That this section is a late expansion is indicated by the mention of **Ithamar** as supervising the service of the **Levites** in the sanctuary (cf. Num. 4:28, 33; 7:8) and by the calculation on the basis of the poll tax (see above on 30:11-16) and the **census** (Num. 1:1-46). The census total (vs. 26; see above on 12:37-39), taken from Num. 1:46 (see comment and above on 12:37-39), was probably calculated from the phrase "the children of Israel" by gematria, i.e. giving each letter its numerical significance. On the weights of the metals see "Measures and Money," pp. 1283-85.

39:1-43. *The Priestly Vestments.* See above on 28:5-43. The most significant variation is the omission of the Urim and Thummim from the description of the **breastpiece** (vss. 8-21), which accordingly is not called the "breastpiece of judgment" (cf. 28:15). On **plate of the holy crown** (vs. 30) see above on 28:36-39.

40:1-38. *Consecration of the Tabernacle.* Construction of the tabernacle with its appurtenances having been completed, it is now erected and consecrated (vss. 1-33) and occupied by Yahweh's **glory** (vss. 34-38). The separation from common use is effected by anointing with the holy **oil** (see above on 30:22-38). The **cloud** (vs. 34) covering the tabernacle, signifying the presence of Yahweh according to the promise of 29:43-45 (see comment), sets the seal on the final episode of the book. The note on the cloud's significance for the **journeys** (vss. 36-38) is really supplementary, anticipating the next phase, the desert wandering.

THE BOOK OF LEVITICUS

JACOB MILGROM

INTRODUCTION

The name Leviticus comes from the Vulg., based on the LXX title meaning "The [Book] of the Levites" or, as the rabbis more accurately described it, "The Priests' Manual." By its own definition the priests here teach the distinctions "between the holy and the common, and between the unclean and the clean" (10:10; cf. 15:31; Ezek. 22:26; 44:23). We would be mistaken, however, to expect just a book of ritual. On the contrary in Lev. the ethical fuses with and even informs the ritual so that we are justified to assume a moral basis behind almost every ritual act. This is so because Israel's cult is the product of the monotheistic revolution. Even though its outward expression is often similar to the surrounding pagan world, its spirit is ethically different.

Lev. is not the whole of "The Priests' Manual"; it actually begins in Exod. (chs. 25-31; 35-40) and continues through most of Num. Moreover it is part of a larger historical narrative that runs from Gen. through Num., with a brief conclusion in Deut. or perhaps Josh. This narrative with its incorporated legal material is the latest of the 4 literary sources of the Pentateuch (see "The Compiling of Israel's Story," pp. 1082-89) and because of its content and viewpoint is known as the "Priestly" (P) source.

Though literary analysis of Lev., as well as the other parts of P, reveals evidence of strata—esp. the unit known as the Holiness Code (chs. 17-26; see "The Law Codes of Israel," pp. 1090-94)—all the material has been so thoroughly assimilated to the P viewpoint and is so indistinguishable in ideology that such study offers little help in interpreting the book. Because the text has been so excellently preserved, textual study has likewise been of comparatively little value. The significant problems of interpretation lie in the one area of terminology. We are dealing here with the cult, a hoary institution with its peculiar conservative vocabulary, the meaning of which was sometimes lost on those of the postexilic age, not to speak of later generations. It is a wonderful paradox that we today understand more of the older terminology of Lev. than they did, because of recently unearthed cultic and legal texts of other ancient Semitic peoples of the 2nd millennium. The most notable of these come from Mari on the middle Euphrates, Nuzi in E Assyria, and Ras Shamra in N Syria, site of the old Canaanite city of Ugarit (see color map 2). In view of these discoveries it may be safely hazarded that most if not all of the peculiarities of vocabulary and style in Lev. will prove to be obsolete technical terms from Israel's early history.

It is clear, therefore, that the legislation of Lev. is old. That this is invariably true is indicated by the fact that no part of it can be identified as reflecting a postexilic innovation. Though the book in its present form is the work of the late P school, its members have here done little more than fit the older material into their narrative framework as instructions given to Moses for the service of Aaron and his sons, representing the high priest and his assistants, at the tent of meeting, representing the temple.

For Further Study. Nathaniel Micklem in *IB*, 1953. J. B. Pritchard, ed., *Ancient Near Eastern Texts*, 1955; contains translations of cultic and legal texts from Israel's neighbors. Yehezkel Kaufmann, *The Religion of Israel*, abridged and trans. by Moshe Greenberg, 1960; a thorough study which argues that, contrary to the usual view, P preceded D. Roland de Vaux, *Ancient Israel: Its Life and Institutions*, 1961. Gwynne Henton Davies in *IDB*, 1962. *The Torah*, 1962; vol. I of the new Jewish Publication Society Version (JPSV), which because of recent scholarship contains the most accurate translation of Lev. thus far achieved. Martin Noth, *The OT Library*, 1965.

I. THE SACRIFICIAL SYSTEM (1:1-7:38)

The sacrifices described here are to be brought by the individual Israelite of his own volition; they must be sharply distinguished from the mandatory requirements of public feasts and fasts in chs. 9; 16; 23; Num. 28-29. Even when their motivation is clearly recognition of wrongdoing (4:1-6:7) no outside force compels them, only the urging of conscience and a sense of guilt. The emphasis is on offenses committed involuntarily, and even in cases of premeditation (6:1-7) there is no indication that the offender is in fear of being apprehended. His desire for atonement is assumed to be spontaneous and his sacrifice but the culmination of a penitential process of contrition, confession, and compensation. Thus the sacrificial system practiced by the ancient Israelite is an incontestable tribute to his moral sensitivity.

That the sacrificial regulations are incorporated here should occasion surprise. In the pagan world this could not have happened. Sacrifices were exclusively a priestly prerogative and their laws a jealously

68

guarded secret. But in Israel, certainly by post-exilic times, they were exposed and taught to the laity (cf. 10:10-11); there were no esoteric mysteries to frighten the people into obedience to the temple cult and its functionaries. Priests and laymen alike learned and practiced their respective responsibilities as partners and, to judge by the witness of scripture (cf. e.g. Pss. 43; 65; 84; Ecclus. 50:1-21), effected a ritual of worship that fully answered the people's spiritual needs.

A. Instructions for Laymen (1:1–6:7)

That the emphasis of this section is on the layman is shown by the pronouns, which consistently refer to the donor of the sacrifice. A difference in the Hebrew conditional particles suggests that chs. 1; 3 were originally a unit—as confirmed by the linking of their 2 offerings in the oldest records (cf. e.g. Exod. 20:24; 24:5; 32:6; Judg. 20:26; I Sam. 10:8)—to which chs. 2; 4–5 were added later.

1:1-2. An Invitation to All. In the P narrative the **tent of meeting,** i.e. tabernacle, houses the ark, from above which God speaks to Moses (cf. Exod. 25:22; Num. 7:89). The conditional construction **When any man of you brings an offering** underscores the voluntary basis of these individual sacrifices. Though the instructions are addressed to **Israel,** we know from this book (e.g. 17:8) and elsewhere (e.g. I Kings 8:41-43) that the sacrificial system was made available to the sojourner, i.e. resident alien, and even the foreigner. **Offering** means lit. "that which is brought near," i.e. to God, for it is not always placed on the altar (cf. e.g. 23:16-20).

1:3-17. The Burnt Offering. The Hebrew word translated **burnt offering**—lit. "that which goes up," i.e. in smoke—is used exclusively of a sacrifice entirely consumed on the altar. To distinguish it from other offerings of which only a part is burned this sacrifice might better be called a "whole burnt offering" (Deut. 33:10; I Sam. 7:9; Ps. 51:19) or simply "whole offering." Within Israel, both for individuals (cf. e.g. Gen. 8:20; 22:2; Judg. 13:16) and for the community (cf. e.g. Exod. 10:25; Josh. 8:31; I Kings 3:4), it is the oldest and most typical sacrifice.

1:4. The laying of the **hand upon the head** designates the animal as representative of the worshiper. Involved is the transmission of power (cf. e.g. Num. 8:10; 27:18-20) or, in this case, of sin (cf. 24:14). Though the whole burnt offering can have connotations of a tribute (cf. e.g. Num. 15:3; Ps. 66:13-16), here its expiatory function is emphasized (cf. 9:7; 14:20; I Sam. 13:12; Job 1:5; 43:8). Indeed expiation is the fundamental purpose of the sacrificial system as a whole (cf. 14:18-20; but see below on 3:1-17). Thus **atonement** is better translated "expiation" (cf. 17:11; Exod. 32:30).

1:5-9. The text does not identify who is to **kill the bull** and **flay** and **cut it into pieces.** Apparently anyone could qualify, even a foreign slave (cf. Ezek. 44:6-14). Slaughter by priests and also Levites was limited to their personal (9:8, 12; 16:11) and public sacrifices (9:15, 18; 16:5; II Chr. 29:24; 30:17; 35:6, 11). But the priests only were permitted to "go up to my altar" (I Sam. 2:28; cf. II Kings 23:9) and therefore to **present the blood** (see below on 17:10-16), prepare the **fire,** and **lay the pieces**

on it. For his service the priest received the hide of the animal (7:8). **Pleasing odor** (vs. 9) harks back to an era when sacrifices were thought to be food for the gods.

1:14-17. For the poor (cf. 5:7; 12:8) a whole burnt offering of **birds** is provided, without the requirement that they be male and unblemished (cf. vss. 3, 10). Since not mentioned in vs. 2, this may be a later addition. **Turtledoves** and **pigeons** were esp. abundant in Palestine.

2:1-16. The Cereal Offering. The word translated **cereal offering** denotes a gift to gain favor (cf. e.g. Gen. 32:21) or a tribute of subjects to their overlord (cf. e.g. Judg. 3:15-18; I Kings 4:21). Such tribute to the divine Overlord might be either animal or vegetable (cf. e.g. Gen. 4:3-4; I Sam. 2:17), but in time the term came to be used specifically of an offering of grain or its products. This restriction of the meaning emphasizes man's tribute to God brought from the fruit of his labors on the soil which God has entrusted to his care, but in practice the aspect of a gift for appeasement may also have been present. As Israel developed from a pastoral to an agricultural community the tribute offering of grain may have largely replaced the private whole burnt offering of an animal in function and popularity (cf. e.g. I Sam. 3:14; 26:19; Joel 1:9, 13). The cereal of the tribute offering may take 3 forms: **fine,** i.e. choice, **flour** (vss. 1-3), **cakes** or **wafers** cooked from such flour (vss. 4-10), or roasted **grain** (vss. 14-16). For other cereal offerings cf. 5:11-13; 6:20-23; 23:13; Num. 5:15; 15:1-12.

2:2b-3. By definition a tribute offering was the property of the deity and originally was entirely consumed on the altar as food for him—as suggested by the equivalence of **offerings by fire** with "bread of their God" (21:6). For the pagan the cereal tribute was the staple of the divine diet. But in Israel—as an example of the changes wrought by the monotheistic revolution—all but a **memorial portion,** i.e. a token, of the food was transferred to the **priest.** A similar development took place with the bread of the Presence (24:5-9). The priest's portion of this and certain other offerings is **most holy** (cf. 6:17), meaning that it may be eaten only by priests within the sacred precinct near the altar (cf. 6:26-29; 10:12-13; 24:9; Num. 18:9-10), whereas merely "holy" perquisites may be eaten by all clean members of the priest's household in any clean place (10:14-15; 22:1-16; Num. 18:11-19). The Hittites made the same distinction.

2:11-13. The prohibition of **leaven,** i.e. old dough containing yeast, and **honey,** a term including fruit syrup, is probably based on their fermentation. **First fruits** in vs. 12 translates a different Hebrew word from that in vs. 14; since these are not **offered on the altar** leaven and honey are permissible. On the other hand **salt** is a preservative and thus a symbol of the abiding. It was used in sealing a **covenant** (cf. Num. 18:19), as among the Arabs to this day.

2:14-16. Because **first fruits** had to be offered up before the new grain crop could be eaten (23:14) they were brought roasted rather than milled.

3:1-17. The Peace Offering. The Hebrew word for "peace" meant much more than absence of conflict; it included health, prosperity, and general well-being. This broad meaning should be understood in the designation **peace offering.** Because this offering is shared by the deity (vss. 3-5, 9-11, 14-16), the priest (7:31-34), and the worshiper (7:11-18), it is often said to be for the purpose of bringing about unity with God. The scriptural language, however, gives no basis for any notion of mystical union with God—one is to "eat before the LORD" (Deut. 12:7), not with him. Rather the original function of the peace offering, as is clear from ch. 17, was simply to permit the eating of meat. Since quick spoilage required consumption of an entire animal within 2 days (cf. 7:16-18; 19:6) beef and mutton were luxuries all too rare for any but the most wealthy in ancient times. Such a sacrifice would usually be prompted by some special occasion for rejoicing, of which 3 types are cited in 7:11-18: thanksgiving, fulfillment of a vow (cf. e.g. Ps. 116:12-19), and freewill sacrifice, which is always mentioned in a happy context (cf. e.g. Num. 15:3; Deut. 16:10-11).

In view of the joyous character of such occasions it is not surprising that in P the word "atonement," i.e. "expiation," which is regularly used of the other 4 private offerings (cf. e.g. 14:18-20), never occurs in connection with the peace offering. True, in Ezek. 45:15, 17 the peace offering is included in a list of sacrifices said to be for atonement, and among the many historical references to it a few are in times of crisis—even in a situation that elicits wailing and fasting (Judg. 20:26). In each of these cases, however, the peace offering follows a whole burnt offering (see above on 1:3-17) and thus may be recognized as the joyous conclusion to a series of propitiatory rites (cf. II Chron. 29:31-36), a festive meal enjoyed in gratitude or at least hope that a reconciliation with God has finally been effected.

The sacrificial rules enumerated here are similar to those for the whole burnt offering (ch. 1) with certain exceptions. The victim may be either **male or female,** and the requirement here that it be **without blemish** is modified in 22:23 for a freewill offering. There is no provision for the poor to present birds (cf. 1:14-17) for a peace offering. Some of the internal organs and the internal fat—i.e. suet, which should be understood throughout in distinction from the muscular fat—including the broad tail of the sheep, are burned on the altar, for **all fat is the LORD's** (vs. 16b; cf. 7:22-24; I Sam. 2:15-16). Deut. 32:37-38 gives biblical attestation to the universal pagan belief that animal suet, as well as blood (cf. 17:11), was a source of cosmic vitality and nourishment for the gods. The reference to divine **food** (vss. 11, 16), like that to **pleasing odor** (see above on 1:5-9), is a linguistic vestige of such belief that survived in Israel's cult.

4:1-21. *The Public Sin Offering.* The most common Hebrew verb for "sin" in some of its forms has the reverse meaning "cleanse" (14:49; Num. 19:12; Ezek. 43:20-23), "purge" (Ps. 51:7), or "purify" (8:15; Num. 8:21; 31:19-20). Its noun form also has this sense in the phrase translated "water of expiation" (Num. 8:7), where a purificatory function is clear. That this is the sense of the word likewise in its application to the **sin offering** is shown by the purposes for which this sacrifice is specified: to mark recovery from childbirth (12:6-8), leprosy (14:19, 22b, 30-31), and gonorrhea (15:14-15), to complete the Nazirite vow (Num. 6:13-17), to sanctify new

objects (8:14-15; Exod. 29:35-37), and to consecrate new priests and Levites (9:8-11; Exod. 29:10-14; Num. 8:8, 12). The name might therefore be more accurately rendered "purification offering."

4:2. The sin which this offering is intended to remove is "uncleanness" (cf. e.g. 14:19), i.e. ritual impurity, rather than any ethical offense. Thus **any of the things which the LORD has commanded not to be done** (cf. vss. 13, 22, 27) refers to the prohibitive commandments between man and God, not those between man and man. The sacrifice is efficacious for such violations committed **unwittingly** —better "inadvertently" or "unintentionally," for one is aware of them and acknowledges them. The point is that, as the root meaning, "miss," of the word "sin" suggests, they are errors or shortcomings rather than deliberate misdeeds; sacrifice cannot expiate what one does "with a high hand" (Num. 15:30).

4:3. The first situation for which this offering is prescribed presumes that the **anointed priest,** i.e. the high priest, has inadvertently erred and thereby caused harm to his **people** (cf. Num. 18:5). Normally he is able to "take upon himself any guilt [i.e. unintentional ritual error] incurred in the holy offering which the people of Israel hallow as their holy gifts" (Exod. 28:38). I.e. while officiating he possesses the holiness to absorb all the accidental impurity of the people. But if the impurity is due to his own error only his personal purification offering can expiate for him, as well as for his fellow priests (cf. 16:6, 11).

4:4-12. The distinctive features of the procedure for this sacrifice are the smearing of **blood** on the **horns of the altar** (vs. 7; cf. vss. 18, 25, 30, 34; 8:15; 9:9; 16:18; Exod. 29:12; 30:10; Ezek. 43:20) and the removal of all but the blood and suet of the victim to be burned **outside the camp** (vs. 12; cf. vs. 21; 6:30; 8:17; 9:11; 16:27; Exod. 29:14; Ezek. 43:21)—or, in the case of an individual's sacrifice, to be eaten by the priests under special safeguards (see below on 6:24-30). The smearing of blood purifies the sanctuary of the impurity transmitted to it by the worshiper's inadvertent error and immunizes it against future contamination. It is clearly akin to the application of blood to lintel and doorposts in Egypt to keep away the "destroyer" (Exod. 12:23). The unique disposition of the victim, considered along with the detailed descriptions of 2 other specific purificatory rites—the sanctuary purification (16:26-28) and the red heifer (Num. 19:6-10, 21-22)—leads to the deduction that this offering causes defilement to its handlers. From both these distinctive features, therefore, we must conclude that the purificatory sin offering has its roots in an apotropaic rite—i.e. a magical procedure for warding off evil. It has come down from an era when the domain of evil was believed to be so powerful and pervasive that it could even invade and overwhelm the temples of the gods.

Though the forms of such a rite have persisted, there is no longer any trace of the belief in an independent, primordial evil. Here the only demonic influence is within man—his own error. It is man's sin which impairs the holiness of the camp (cf. Num. 5:2-5) and the sanctuary (cf. 15:31; Num. 19:13, 20) and even necessitates cleansing of the Holy of Holies (cf. ch. 16). The rite now follows awareness of the sin and acknowledgment of it. Because the sin, though inadvertent, has been committed a miasma of impurity has been released to defile the community and the sanctuary. Purification is thus required before forgiveness is assured (cf. 14:19-20).

4:13-21. These instructions assume that the offering of the **whole congregation** or **assembly**, i.e. community, is to follow that of the high priest (vss. 3-12), as shown by: (a) the emphasis on identical procedure (vss. 20-21); (b) the specification of a **bull** rather than a goat (cf. 9:15; 16:5; Num. 15:24), and (c) the inclusion of the concluding formula **shall make atonement . . . shall be forgiven** only at the end of the people's sacrifice (vs. 20b; cf. vss. 26b, 31c, 35c; 5:10b, 13a). No doubt the reason is recognition that the **sin,** i.e. ritual error, committed **unwittingly** by the people is probably the result of the high priest's improper guidance.

4:22–5:13. *Private Sin Offerings.* Whereas the impurity resulting from the inadvertent error of high priest and community penetrates to the sanctuary and requires purificatory action there, that involving a layman requires smearing **blood** only on the **horns of the altar of burnt offering** in the outer court. Furthermore, whereas the sin transferred to the victim by the high priest or the elders of the community can be removed only by destroying it at a distance, the priests can absorb that of the layman's offering and therefore may eat the flesh of the victim as something "most holy" (6:24-30; see comment thereon and above on 2:2b-3; 4:3). The general term **ruler** in the P material is the archetype and synonym of the king. The goat he offers must be **male,** but **one of the common people** offers a **female,** either **goat** (4:27-31) or **lamb** (4:32-35). Offerings of money are mentioned in II Kings 12:16. The poor may offer **two turtledoves** or **pigeons** (5:7-10) or even **flour** (5:11-13). The fact that only this and the whole burnt offering (1:14-17) have such alternatives is further indication of their similar purpose—expiation of sin, a need that had to be made available to all levels of the populace.

5:1-6. There is apparent confusion in the terminology here, in that the same sacrifice seems to be called both a **guilt offering** and a **sin offering** (vs. 6). A possible explanation is that the P editors introduced the confusion because they no longer understood the distinction between the 2 sacrifices. More probably, however, they accurately transmitted an older text which is confused only in translation. The verb translated **be guilty** in this passage has the extended meaning "suffer guilt" and its consequence, "punishment" (cf. e.g. Ps. 34:21-22; Prov. 30:10). With a personal indirect object the verb has the further meaning "incur liability" to that person—e.g. in Gen. 42:21, where these 2 senses are combined: "In truth we are guilty concerning our brother," i.e. "we are being punished for our liability to our brother." In this sense the noun form refers to liability and its cost, i.e. a payment or restitution or reparation—e.g. in Num. 5:6-7, where the word in verb and noun forms appears 3 times: "When a man or woman . . . *is guilty* . . . he shall make full *restitution* . . . to him to whom he *did the wrong.*" The noun also sometimes has the specific meaning **guilt offering** (see below on 5:14–6:7), but the confusion of terminology is cleared up if we recognize that in

vs. 6, as well as vs. 7, the meaning is instead "his reparation to the LORD."

There is also apparent confusion of function in that some at least of the cases in vss. 1-4 seem not to fit the specification in 4:27 of **sins** committed **unwittingly.** No doubt it is precisely because these are borderline cases that they are included here as an appendix to the procedures for this sacrifice. Since one who **utters . . . a rash oath** (vs. 4) knows it at the time, the phrase **hidden from him** must refer in this case to a lapse of memory. Probably it has the same meaning in vss. 2-3. Simply becoming **unclean** as described in these 2 cases requires no sacrifice but merely washing (cf. 11:24-40; 15:1-12, 16-27). The offense requiring sacrifice lies in forgetting the uncleanness and taking some action permissible only for one who is ritually clean, e.g. touching holy things, thus allowing his impurity to contaminate the sanctuary. An **adjuration** (vs. 1), lit. "curse," if assented to by the **witness,** or even if directed to him specifically, would make him guilty of perjury if he should keep silent—indeed in an earlier time such a curse would be considered effective without his assent or even awareness (cf. I Sam. 14:24-28, 36-45). Here, however, his ignoring of the adjuration, like the forgetting of an oath (vs. 4), is classed as a profanation of the name of God (cf. 19:12) for which confession and purification are needed.

5:7-13. These provisions for the poor are presented as relating only to the cases of vss. 1-4 (cf. vs. 13 with vs. 5a). On the other hand the lack of a special intro. to vs. 1 (contrast 6:1) may indicate that 4:27–5:13 should be considered as a single unit, the scaled sacrifices thus applying to the general statement of 4:27. On **guilt offering** (vs. 7) see above on vss. 1-6. **Two birds** are required so that one may be treated as a **burnt offering** to take the place of the suet available in a larger victim. For an offering of **flour** the procedure is the same as for a cereal **offering** (vs. 13b) except that **oil** and **frankincense** are to be omitted. On **ephah** see "Measures and Money," pp. 1283-85.

5:14–6:7. *The Guilt Offering.* Though "guilt" is the root meaning of the Hebrew word translated **guilt offering** it does not convey the distinctive function of the sacrifice, since guilt is a prerequisite also of the purificatory sin offering (cf. 4:13, 22, 27; 5:2-5). The sense of the word as it is applied to this offering is more accurately expressed by the name "reparation offering," for in every case its purpose is to discharge liability for material damage or loss, either to God or to man (see above on 5:1-6). Restitution for the damage, plus 20%, must be supplemented by a sacrificial fine in expiation (cf. Num. 5:6-8).

That the offering is a sacrificial fine commutable into **silver** (see below on 5:15) is evidence of its antiquity. The Nuzi texts from E Assyria, reflecting customary law that goes back at least to the middle of the 2nd millennium, state that in certain cases fines are to be imposed in terms of fixed ratios of animals for which specified amounts of precious metal may be substituted. In the story of the Philistines' return of the ark (I Sam. 6:2-18) a guilt offering of gold is described, and in connection with Jehoash's repair of the temple guilt offerings of money are mentioned (II Kings 12:16).

The distinction between the sin offering for purification and the guilt offering for reparation is illustrated in the regulations for the Nazirite, one who takes a vow of temporary "separation to God" (Num. 6:1-21). If during his period of holiness he touches a corpse he becomes defiled and the time he has spent is voided. Thus a sin offering is required to purify his defilement (Num. 6:11) and a guilt offering to compensate for the loss he has inflicted on God by thus depriving him of the promised term of service (Num. 6:12). A Nazirite who completes his period of separation brings a sin offering for purification (Num. 6:14) but, having fulfilled his vow, is not liable for a guilt offering.

5:15. The Hebrew word translated **breach of faith** is usually rendered "faithlessness" or "treachery" in the RSV. Here, however, it is defined as sinning **unwittingly in any of the holy things of the LORD**, i.e. withholding, misappropriating, or profaning his sacred property (cf. 22:14-16). This may involve material objects (e.g. Josh. 7:1), the temple (e.g. II Chr. 26:16-18), his chosen people (e.g. Ezra 9:2), or the loyalty due him (e.g. Num. 31:16; Ezek. 20:27)—all holy things of God whose misuse requires reparation. The word is used exclusively of a sin against God except once (Num. 5:12, 27), where it is applied to the wrong an adulterous wife does her husband. Thus the older translation "trespass" (e.g. KJV, ASV, JPSV) comes closer to the true meaning as the sort of offense against God to be expiated by a guilt offering.

The procedure for sacrificing the **ram** is described in 7:1-7. The obscurity of **valued by you in shekels of silver** may be due to postexilic ignorance of the ancient ordinance. In view of the history of the guilt offering as a sacrificial fine (see above on 5:14–6:7) and the similar regulations in ch. 27, the meaning is evidently that an equivalent monetary payment may be substituted for the sacrifice. Until the Persians introduced coins into Palestine after the Exile **silver** used as currency had to be weighed in balances (cf. e.g. Jer. 32:9). The **shekel of the sanctuary** had a different weight from the commercial shekel adjusted to foreign trade (see "Measures and Money," pp. 1283-85).

5:16. Though the word **also** is not in the Hebrew its insertion is justified to make clear that the sacrificial fine of vs. 15 is in addition to the **restitution,** plus a **fifth** penalty, due to God for the loss or damage, just as in the case of a wrong done to a neighbor (6:5). The restitution is made to the **priest** because ordinarily the **holy thing** involved would be a priestly perquisite.

5:17-19. The language of vs. 17 is almost the same as that describing the occasion for a sin offering for purification (4:1, 22, 27). The significant difference is that, whereas the sin offering is predicated on later discovery of the cause of guilt (4:14, 23, 28), here the person still **does not know it.** Nevertheless he feels **guilty,** usually because suffering **his iniquity,** i.e. punishment—e.g. illness, axiomatically viewed as the result of sin—and to obviate the possibility of further divine wrath he brings a guilt offering. This provision is witness to the psychological truth that he who does not know the exact cause of his suffering will imagine the worst; he will assume that he has incurred liability

for damage or loss to holy things rather than mere ritual error and therefore make the more expensive reparation offering.

6:1-7. The sacrificial laws here reach their ethical summit. The same reparation due for damage to God's property is specified for one's neighbor—with the significant priority that only after rectification has been made with man can it be sought from God. Though the guilt offering originated as a fine for civil damages it is here clearly outside the jurisdiction of the court—a voluntary sacrifice like the others of chs. 1-5. The crime could not be proved and the offender has escaped the usual penalty for his embezzlement or theft (cf. Exod. 22:1-4, 7-13). Nevertheless he has **become guilty** (see above on 5:17-19) and in contrition he comes forward to **restore** his wrongful gain, with an added **fifth,** and offer a reparation sacrifice to God. Probably **swearing falsely** should follow the dash in vs. 3 and be joined to the following phrase (cf. vs. 5a) as the common element in all the examples cited. Violation of an oath before God (cf. 19:12) constitutes a **breach of faith** (see above on 5:15) **against the LORD** needing expiation by a guilt offering.

B. SUPPLEMENTARY INSTRUCTIONS FOR PRIESTS (6:8–7:38)

The reference to these laws as given **on Mount Sinai** (7:38) shows that they are independent of 1:1–6:7, said to have been spoken "from the tent of meeting" (1:1). Being addressed to the officiating priest, the series groups together the cereal, sin, and guilt offerings, of which all not burned on the altar is "most holy" and must be eaten by the priests themselves in the environs of the sanctuary, and places last the peace offering, of which the priest's limited portion is merely "holy" and may be taken home to his family. Included with this last is an appendix addressed to the laity (7:22-36).

6:8-13. *The Burnt Offering.* These instructions concern esp. the daily whole burnt offerings of the community (Exod. 29:38-41). The **fire of the altar** is to be **kept burning** and the fat-saturated **ashes** are to be cleared each morning. The **linen garment** worn for this chore is perhaps the coat of Exod. 28:40; on the **breeches** cf. Exod. 28:42-43. The clothing worn while approaching the altar is holy and must be changed before a trip outside the sacred precinct. The altar is thus prepared for voluntary offerings (vss. 14-18, 24–7:36; cf. 1:1–6:7) whenever brought by individuals. Of these only **peace offerings** are mentioned (vs. 12), perhaps because of their ancient affinity with whole burnt offerings (see above on 1:1–6:7) or perhaps because of their greater frequency.

6:14-23. *The Cereal Offering.* This explains what **most holy** means as applied to the priestly portion of cereal offerings brought by laymen (see above on 2:2b-3). It must be **eaten unleavened** by **male** descendants of **Aaron,** i.e. priests, **in the court of the tent of meeting** (vss. 16-18; cf. Ezek. 42:13; 46:20). On the other hand cereal offerings brought by priests—both those of the high priest which accompany the daily public burnt offerings (vss. 19-22; cf. II Kings 16:15; Ecclus. 45:14) and voluntary offerings of ordinary priests (vs. 23)—must be **wholly burned** on the altar. **On the day** (vs. 20) should be translated rather "from the day" (cf. 7:35-36).

6:24-30. *The Sin Offering.* On **most holy** (vss. 25-26, 29) see above on vss. 14-23. The resemblance of vss. 27-28 to the laws of uncleanness of 11:32-33 shows that holiness and ritual impurity, though opposites, are alike in their contagion. Not only does the **flesh** of this purification offering render **holy,** i.e. withdrawn from ordinary use (cf. 27:9-10), all objects it touches—in common with all most holy offerings (cf. vs. 18; Ezek. 46:20; Hag. 2:12) and the equipment of the sanctuary (cf. Exod. 30:29) —but it singularly infects the **vessel** in which it is cooked and the **garment** on which its **blood** is splattered. The contagion must be washed out; and porous earthenware, from which it cannot be extracted, must be **broken.** No other passage so clearly indicates both the pagan background of Israel's sacrificial system and severance from it. The contamination which in paganism was an active demon has been transformed into a "most holy" substance. Thus apotropaic magic (see above on 4:4-12) has emerged as ritual purification. Vs. 30 reinforces the distinction between the sin offering of priest (4:3-21) and layman (4:22-5:13; see comment).

7:1-10. *The Guilt Offering.* The procedure omitted in 5:14-6:7 is described here. It is the same as that for the **sin offering** (cf. 4:27-31; 6:25-26, 29) except that it lacks the purificatory ritual with the blood of that offering. The references to the officiating **priest** in the singular reflect the early days when a single priest would see the sacrifice through from beginning to end. The failure of Josiah's effort to bring the country priests into the the centralized worship of the temple (II Kings 23:9) indicates that there were no vacancies in the Jerusalem priesthood at that time. Perhaps by then the priests were already organized into "divisions" and "fathers' houses" (I Chr. 24) which multiplied the number of officiants at each sacrifice.

7:11-36. *The Peace Offering.* These instructions make clear what is assumed but never explained in ch. 3 (see comment), that the peace offering is essentially a feast of the worshiper and his family and guests. After the sprinkling of the blood and the burning of the suet on the altar (ch. 3) and the payment of certain choice pieces to the officiating priest (vss. 31-36) the rest of the flesh of the victim is to be **eaten.**

7:12-15. The motivation for such a feast would nearly always include gratitude to God, but if the worshiper specifically calls it a **thanksgiving** he must observe certain additional formalities. The **bread,** which in any case he would certainly provide for the feast, must include 4 specified types (vss. 12-13), from each of which he must give the officiating priest **one cake** (vs. 14). His guest list must be large enough to consume all the meat **on the day of his offering** (vs. 15).

7:16-18. For a less formal offering—whether **votive,** i.e. in fulfillment of a vow, or **freewill,** i.e. without the compulsion of a previous promise (cf. 22:23)—the donor and his guests may take 2 days to consume the meat. **On the third day** any leftover is an **abomination,** lit. "stinking thing," i.e. putres-

cent, and must be **burned;** eating any of it would make the whole sacrifice unacceptable.

7:19-21. Anyone who is ritually **unclean** (cf. chs. 11-16) must not participate in the feast. **Cut off from his people** probably means, not banishment or ostracism by the community, but an early death by divine action (see below on 20:2-9). One who joins in without recognizing his uncleanness until afterward, however, can obtain purification and forgiveness by a sin offering (cf. 5:2-3). **Abomination** (vs. 21)—lit. "filthy thing," a different word from that in vs. 18—is evidently a scribal error for "swarming thing" (cf. 5:2), found in several manuscripts and the ancient versions.

7:22-27. The general prohibition of eating **fat,** i.e. suet, and **blood** stated in 3:17 (see comment) is here made more explicit for the benefit of the **people of Israel,** i.e. the laity. The detailed statement fails to cover all species, e.g. the suet of birds and game (cf. 17:13) and the blood of fish, which inferentially might thus be exempted. The negative implication of vs. 24 is that the suet of a slaughtered animal must not be **put to any other use** and therefore, since it cannot be eaten either, must be burned on the altar. If so, this is another vestige of the days before Josiah's adoption of the D law (Deut. 12:15-16, 20-25) permitting slaughter of animals without sacrifice. Inclusion of these prohibitions in this context indicates that before that time all meat of domestic animals was prepared as a peace offering.

7:28-36. These instructions, also addressed to the laity, emphasize the worshiper's obligation to make all the preparations for the sacrifice himself up to the point of delivering the suet for the priest to burn on the altar and the choice pieces which are the priest's perquisites. In the Canaanite temple at Lachish in SW Judah archaeologists found the bones of 4 animals clustered about the altar: sheep or goat, ox, and 2 wild species, either gazelle or ibex. All identifiable bones were from the upper part of the right foreleg. In Israel this desirable portion (cf. I Sam. 9:24) is here reserved for the priests (vs. 32). **Offered** in vs. 34 means lit. "lifted up" and has been thought to refer to a specific gesture of the sacrificial ritual in contrast to another gesture represented by **waved.** More likely, however, since the 2 terms are used interchangeably (cf. e.g. 9:21; 10:15; Exod. 25:2; 35:22*b*) they are simply synonyms for "offered." In vss. 35-36 **on the day** should be translated "from the day" (cf. 6:20).

7:37-38. *A Summary.* This list corresponds exactly to the order of the sacrifices in 6:8-7:36 except that **consecration,** i.e. the ordination offering, is added. The addition has been generally assumed to be a marginal notation which a scribe erroneously copied into the text, but it may be evidence that the instructions about the peace offering (vss. 11-36) were originally preceded by similar instructions about the ordination offering. The inclusion of such material here would give the references to ordination in 6:20; 7:35-36 more point; and adaptation of it by the author of Exod. 29 would help explain the parallels between that ch. and vss. 11-36 (e.g. with vss. 12, 14*a,* 15-17, 30*b*-34 cf. Exod. 29:2, 23-24, 34, 26-28 respectively), as well as its omission by the compiler of Lev. On **Mount Sinai** see above on 6:8-7:38.

II. The Inaugural Services at the Sanctuary (8:1-10:20)

This section of P narrative resumes the story following the interruption of the legal material in chs. 1-7 after the construction of the sanctuary and its appurtenances (Exod. 35-40). The priests are inducted into service and perform their initial sacrifices. It is noteworthy that Moses rather than Aaron dominates the scene. It is he who conducts the inaugural service, consecrates the priests, and apportions all tasks. Aaron is clearly answerable to him, as seen from their confrontation in 10:16-20. Thus a P author insists on the superiority of prophet over priest.

8:1-36. The Installation of the Priests. This account of the ordination of Aaron and his sons largely duplicates in narrative form the instructions in Exod. 29 (see comment), as indicated by the repeated reminder as the **LORD commanded Moses** (vss. 9, 13, 17, 21, 29, 36). On the priestly vestments mentioned in vss. 7-9 see comment on Exod. 28.

8:10-13. Middle Assyrian laws of the 2nd millennium dealing with the marriage of patricians mention pouring **oil** on the head of a prospective daughter-in-law as a sign of betrothal. In Israel this ancient custom indicated the consecration to divine use of both things (vss. 10-11; cf. e.g. Gen. 28:18) and persons—e.g. prophets and kings (cf. e.g. I Kings 19:15-16) as well as the high priests symbolized by Aaron (vs. 12). **Aaron's sons** (vs. 13) are clothed in the vestments of ordinary priests. Though only Aaron is anointed, the sons participate in all other elements of the ordination.

8:14-30. On the **sin offering** (vss. 14-17) see above on 4:1-21. On the **burnt offering** (vss. 18-21) see above on 1:3-17. The procedure for sacrificing the **ram of ordination** (vss. 22-29) is quite similar to that for a peace offering for thanksgiving (cf. ch. 3; 17:11-15, 28-36; see above on 7:37-38), with Moses in the role of the officiating priest, who receives his portion (vs. 29), and Aaron and his sons corresponding to the lay donor of a peace offering. As priests, however, they may offer only **unleavened bread** (vs. 26; contrast 7:13). On the special rites with the **blood** and the **anointing oil** see comment on Exod. 29:19-26.

8:31-36. The **flesh** and the **bread** of the ordination offerings brought by Aaron and his sons are viewed as "most holy" (see above on 2:2b-3) and therefore are to be eaten **at the door of the tent of meeting,** where the priests are required to stay for **seven days.** The Hebrew phrase translated **ordain** means lit. "fill the hand of" and is used exclusively for the ordination of priests (cf. e.g. Exod. 32:29; Judg. 17:5, 12; I Kings 13:33). In archives from Mari on the middle Euphrates dating from early in the 2nd millennium this idiom is used of the distribution of booty taken in battle. Thus the original sense as applied to priests was that their ordination entitled them to a share of the sacrifices brought to the sanctuary. That such a priestly share was an ancient custom in Israel is shown by the story of Eli's sons (I Sam. 2:13-14).

9:1-24. The Priests' Initiatory Sacrifices. Following the week of consecration, during which Moses has officiated, the priests begin their official duties.

Aaron now officiates in offering special sacrifices for the people, with Moses' promise that God's presence will be revealed (vss. 4, 6). Thus the **eighth day** is a climax to the ordination (cf. I Kings 8:66-9:2; Ezek. 43:27). Indeed the whole purpose of the sacrificial system is revelation, the assurance that God is with his people. But here there is no pagan idea of the cult as controlling the revelation; rather God's presence is recognized as always an act of his grace.

9:8-21. The procedure narrated here departs from the prescriptions of chs. 1-7 in 2 details: (a) the people's sin offering is a **goat** (vs. 15; cf. vs. 3; Num. 15:24) instead of a bull (cf. 4:14); (b) the **blood** purification rite is performed at the main **altar** (vss. 9, 15; cf. 8:15) rather than in the "inner part of the sanctuary" (10:18; cf. 4:5-7, 16-18). The first of these, at least, probably indicates strata in the P material reporting the practices of different periods. But purifying of the sanctuary (see above on 4:4-12) may have been omitted from these initiatory sacrifices on the assumption that following its consecration (8:10) no impurity has entered it.

9:22-24. Aaron's blessing of the people is an invocation of God's presence with them (cf. e.g. Exod. 20:24; Num. 6:22-27; I Kings 8:55-61). Such a blessing regularly concludes the offering on the altar and precedes the sacrificial meal (cf. I Sam. 9:13). In this case, however, Moses and Aaron enter the sanctuary, presumably for a further prayer that God will reveal himself (cf. e.g. I Kings 18:36-38; II Chron. 7:1-3). Then before the people they again invoke God's presence in a final blessing, after which the revelation occurs. **Glory** generally refers to a cloud (cf. e.g. Exod. 33:9-10; 40:34-38; I Kings 8:10-11), which often contains **fire** (cf. e.g. Exod. 24:16-17; 40:38). Because the usual fire on the altar is implied throughout the narrative, some have taken vs. 24 to be an interpolation based on earlier accounts of divine igniting of a sacrificial flame (Judg. 6:21; I Kings 18:38). Here, however, the **fire . . . from before the LORD** is an essential climax of the promised revelation and is to be understood as a supernatural flame which immediately **consumed,** i.e. totally reduced to ashes, the offering being slowly burned by the ordinary process.

10:1-11. The Sin of Nadab and Abihu. The reason for the death of Aaron's two older sons (cf. Exod. 6:23) is not clear and has been variously interpreted. Probably they are punished for offering **fire** which is **unholy,** lit. "alien," because taken from elsewhere than the altar (cf. 16:12; Num. 16:46). Other suggestions are that their **incense** is improperly prepared (cf. Exod. 30:9, 34-38); that these 2 sons, though specially privileged (cf. Exod. 24:1, 9-11), are not authorized to offer incense **before the LORD,** i.e. in the Holy of Holies (cf. 16:1-2); and that the 2 are drunk, as indicated by the injunction against drinking intoxicants before the service (vss. 8-9), which otherwise seems irrelevant in the context. That the destroying fire comes **from the presence of the LORD** may mean that it shoots out from the Holy of Holies. Perhaps it is to be understood as the same fire which consumes the offerings on the altar (9:24).

10:4-7. Aaron and his 2 remaining sons are forbidden to show their grief lest it appear as a protest against God's justice and bring further punishment.

10:8-11. On vs. 9 see above on 10:1-11. The priests are more than officiants at sacrifices; they are to be Israel's chief teachers. The Hebrew word translated **teach** (vs. 11) is the verbal form of *torah,* the usual term for the divine law. The priestly educational duty embraces not only ritual (vs. 10) but also ethics, as implied in **all these statutes** and confirmed by the prophets (cf. e.g. Jer. 2:8; Hos. 4:6; Mal. 2:6-8).

10:12-20. *The Eating of the Initiatory Offerings.* Moses' instructions for the eating of the **cereal offering** and the **peace offerings** (vss. 12-15) repeat in substance those of 6:16; 7:28-34. In vss. 16-20 a genuine part of the Nadab and Abihu tradition has been elaborated by an editor concerned to justify the discrepancy between this narrative and the rules of 6:24-30 and also to emphasize the duty of the high priest to **bear the iniquity of the congregation** (see above on 4:3). In 9:15 it is implied that the **goat of the sin offering** was treated in all respects **like the first sin offering** and thus that the **flesh** was **burned** immediately **outside the camp** (9:11; cf. 4:21). Here it appears, however, that the meat was originally retained for eating by Aaron and his sons (cf. 6:26) and it was only after the death of the 2 older sons that Aaron followed the more stringent procedure of destroying rather than eating it. Moses' objection to this implies that the meat must be **eaten** for the **atonement,** i.e. expiation, to be complete. In reply Aaron points out that in spite of the purificatory and expiatory sacrifices just completed his 2 older sons died. Fearing that their ritual error has added priestly sin to the lay sin with which the flesh of the goat is laden, he has not dared to eat it (see above on 4:4-12; 4:22-5:13) lest it not be **acceptable** (cf. e.g. 1:3-4; 7:18). The emergency purgation rites necessitated by the dangerous defilement of the sanctuary are described in ch. 16, which at one time probably followed immediately.

III. The Laws of Uncleanness (11:1-15:33)

On the meaning of "unclean" see above on 4:2, 3, 4-12. An empirical knowledge of contagion must be credited to biblical man. E.g. though the symbolism of cleansing may have influenced the use of washing as a part of purificatory rituals, the ways it is used reveal some recognition of its practical value. Washing is prescribed only for those types of impurity arising from dead bodies (11:25, 28, 40; Num. 19:11-19) and from certain skin diseases (chs. 13-14) and discharges (ch. 15)—all prime sources of putrefaction and infection. Contact with an animal carcass or a diseased person calls for washing immediately—such antisepsis would be effective only during the first hour or so—rather than at nightfall when the impurity ends, as symbolism would suggest. On the other hand the one afflicted with a disease is quarantined (13:4-6, 31-34, 46; 14:9; 15:13; cf. Num. 5:2-3) and washes only after he has been healed—washing would serve no medical purpose once infection has set in.

11:1-47. *Unclean Animals.* The food prohibitions are certainly older than the rationale given them in scripture. No doubt their origins were quite varied. Some creatures were disgusting in appearance or habits, while others were discovered from experience

to be carriers of disease—attributed to demonic forces. Taboos against some were no doubt the remnants of long-forgotten associations with tribal enemies. Recent research has pointed to the possibility that some dietary prohibitions were directed against the cultic practices of pagan neighbors.

Regardless of individual origins, however, the development within Israel of the diet laws as a total system must be attributed to the one reason offered by all 4 scriptural passages referring to these laws, viz. holiness (vss. 44-45; 20:22-26; Exod. 22:31; Deut. 14:21). It is noteworthy that no punishment for violating these laws is ever mentioned. The prohibited foods are simply declared **unclean,** and it is understood that anyone absorbing their impurity would be cut off from all contact with the **holy** and therefore from God. The concept of holiness bears a dual connotation: not only separation from impurities—esp. those of the pagans (cf. 20:23-26)—but also sanctification, the emulation of God's nature (vs. 44a; see below on 18:1-20:27).

The food prohibitions taken together with the blood prohibition (see below on 17:1-16) form a unified dietary code whereby man may indulge his appetite for meat and not be brutalized in the process. At his creation he was meant to be a vegetarian (Gen. 1:28-29). Later the sons of Noah, i.e. all races of men, were permitted meat on the condition that they not eat the blood (Gen. 9:3-4). Now the sons of Jacob, as a "holy nation" (Exod. 19:6a), are directed to a higher level of holiness; they are to narrow their menu to a few living creatures of the tame, herbivorous species. They are to recognize that the taking of animal life is a divine concession and that the spilling of its life source, the blood, is a divine injunction. Thus they are disciplined to revere all life.

The **living things** covered by the regulations about food are classified into 4 categories (cf. vs. 46): (a) **animals,** i.e. larger mammals, the same word as **beast** in vs. 46 (vss. 3-8); (b) aquatic creatures (vss. 9-12); (c) **birds,** a term that takes in all flying creatures (vss. 13-23); and (d) **swarming things,** i.e. small creatures, including mammals (cf. vs. 29), **upon the earth** (vss. 41-43). Interrupting the food laws is a passage (vss. 24-40) on impurity from contact with animal carcasses evidently inserted from another source.

11:2-8. Here the rule for distinguishing clean from unclean **animals** is given but only those forbidden are named; contrast the parallel in Deut. 14:4-8, where those permitted are named also. The **rock badger** is the hyrax, which looks rather like a groundhog but does not burrow. Like the **hare,** it frequently moves its jaws in a way that gives the appearance that it **chews the cud.**

11:9-12. That no aquatic creatures are named, either here or in Deut. 14:9-10, may be explained by the little contact Israel had with the sea.

11:13-23. No classification is given for **birds,** probably because none was known. Identification of a number of the species named is conjectural. **Winged insects,** lit. "swarming birds," are included in the same category. For these a rule is given to permit the eating of certain varieties of **locust.**

11:24-40. This interpolation into the food laws deals with the impurity arising from touching the dead body of an animal—no living animal is unclean to the touch. Among larger mammals the distinction is like that of the food laws (cf. vss. 3-7); i.e. the **carcass** of one forbidden as food transmits impurity on contact. So too does the body of a permitted animal if it died naturally (vss. 39-40). Nevertheless a carcass must be removed, and so touching it is not prohibited (contrast vs. 8); instead one who **carries** it away must go through the ritual of washing and avoid contact with holy things until nightfall. Apparently no impurity attaches to the bodies of aquatic or aerial creatures, or of earthbound **swarming things** other than the 8 named in vss. 29-30. **Mouse** was a general term for mice, rats, moles, hamsters, etc.; and **weasel** was similarly inclusive. Nonporous articles defiled by the carcasses of these 8 household pests must be washed; but absorbative pottery, including the usual earthenware **oven or stove,** must be destroyed (cf. 6:28). **Food** and **seed** grain are immune to the impurity when dry but absorb it if moist.

11:41-47. This is the original continuation of vs. 23, completing the food laws with the 4th category and a summary (vss. 46-47). Isa. 66:17 has been taken by some to refer to a pagan cultic practice of eating "mice," i.e. perhaps rats or some other rodents. Possibly the extra emphasis given to the ban on eating **swarming things** is due to their involvement in pagan sacrifice, but more likely it grew out of experience of their transmission of disease (see above on 11:1-15:33). On **holy** see below on 19:1-37.

12:1-8. *Uncleanness from Childbirth.* For the mother of a newborn son a period of impurity lasts for 40 days. During the first **seven days** no conjugal relations are allowed (vs. 2c; cf. 15:19-24) and during the rest of the time she must not **touch any hallowed thing**—e.g. meat (cf. 7:19-21). If the child is a girl the periods are doubled. That her sacrifices are brought after her defilement has passed is evidence that their purpose has become purificatory rather than magical (see above on 4:4-12); the puerperal period is no longer feared as under demonic control. There remains only ritual impurity, which time alone removes, and which a purification rite certifies. The offering is scaled to economic circumstance (cf. 5:7-13).

13:1-14:57. *Uncleanness from Skin Diseases.* Considering the ancient view of illness as a punishment for sin, we might expect the priest in Israel to be a physician, as was his pagan counterpart. Aside, however, from officiating in sacrificial rites—which would include special public offerings in time of epidemic (cf. e.g. Num. 16:46; II Sam. 24:25) and private voluntary expiations motivated by illness (cf. esp. 5:17-19)—the only responsibility for health assigned him in scripture is that described here in connection with contagious skin diseases. Here the priest's role is that of a quarantine officer, an ecclesiastical minister of public health, who determines whether the afflicted person is a menace to the community. Only God can cure (cf. II Kings 5:7). The sufferer on his own initiative must pray (cf. e.g. I Kings 8:37c-39; II Kings 20:2-3) and fast (cf. e.g. II Sam. 12:16) to win healing from God, who may act either directly (cf. e.g. Gen. 20:17; Exod. 15:26; Pss. 30:2-3; 103:3) or through a prophet (cf. e.g.

II Kings 5:10-14; 20:7). It is only after the disease has passed that the priest imposes sacrificial rites (14:1-32); and these are not for healing but for purification, i.e. to purge the convalescent and the sanctuary of their ritual impurity, and immunization against future incursions.

13:1-44. The word translated **leprosy** covers a variety of skin diseases in addition to Hansen's disease, to which "leprosy" refers in modern usage. Most of the afflictions apparently described are curable, and comparatively few cases would actually warrant separation from society.

13:45-46. The unfortunate **leper,** as determined by the priest's diagnosis, must be removed from the community and live **outside the camp,** i.e. city (cf. Num. 5:2-4), and must give notice of his impurity by the dress of a mourner and by a voiced warning.

13:47-59. The symptoms of a **leprous disease in a garment** are probably the effects of mildew or other fungus.

14:1-32. *Purification of a Healed Leper.* Recovery from some of the skin diseases described in 13:1-44, even without special treatment, was common enough that a method of restoring the person to the community became established. The procedure involves 3 separate ceremonies, on the first day (vss. 4-8), the **seventh** (vs. 9), and the **eighth** (vss. 10-32).

14:4-9. The ritual of the first day is also applied to "leprosy" of houses (vss. 48-53). Originally it was no doubt the method of exorcising the demon responsible for the disease by means of **blood** and **scarlet** dye and a flying **bird** to carry the demon away. With the monotheistic transformation the demonic element is gone and the rite is entirely purificatory (see above on 4:4-12). After this partial purification the healed leper is admitted to the **camp** but cannot yet enter his **tent.** The ritual of shaving and washing on the 7th day (vs. 9) resembles the purification of the Levites before their ordination (Num. 8:7).

14:10-20. The sacrificial ritual of the 8th day is quite similar to that for the consecration of priests (ch. 8) and even the differences between them underscore the purificatory purpose underlying both. The healed leper brings a **guilt offering** as reparation for the trespass against God which must be presumed as the cause for his punishing affliction (see above on 5:17-19). In contrast the new priest has no such taint and so his ordination ram is treated procedurally as a thanksgiving offering to be climaxed by a joyous feast. The smearing of **blood,** common to both rituals, is probably apotropaic in origin (see above on 4:4-12); the priest needs protection against harm during his ministry and the leper against a recurrence of his disease. The daubing of the healed leper with **oil** reemphasizes the purification motif. In ancient Ugarit a female slave was freed when the officiant announced: "I have poured oil upon her head, and I have declared her pure." On **ephah** and **log** see "Measures and Money," pp. 1283-85.

14:21-32. The **poor** are permitted a less costly sacrifice, but only for the **sin offering** (cf. 5:7-13); the reparation of the **guilt offering** cannot be reduced.

14:33-57. *"Leprosy" in a Building.* The appearance of a **leprous disease in a house** might be due either to chemical action, e.g. saltpeter, or the growth of a moss or fungus. Unusual consideration for property is reflected in the provision that the priest should clear the house before his inspection (vs. 36) lest the contents be condemned along with the building. The procedure for purifying a house that has been **healed** (vss. 49:53) is adapted from the first ritual for purifying a healed person (vss. 4-7). The separation of this section from the section on leprous garments (13:47-59) has been taken to indicate it was inserted later, but inclusion of the purificatory ritual would explain its placement after the rituals of vss. 1-32 (cf. vs. 55).

15:1-33. Uncleanness from Genital Discharges. In this ch. **body,** lit. "flesh," is a euphemism for the genital organs (cf. e.g. Gen. 17:14; Ezek. 23:20, where the same Hebrew word is used). A discharge from any other part of the body, e.g. the nose or ear, is not **unclean.** The regulations apply to 4 cases: (a) male pathological discharges (vss. 2-15), usually due to gonorrhea; (b) normal **emission of semen** (vss. 16-18); (c) normal menstruation (vss. 19-24); (d) female pathological discharges (vss. 25-30). The impurity from a pathological discharge is presumed to have contaminated the sanctuary, which thus requires sacrificial purification after recovery (vss. 14-15, 29-30; cf. 5:7-10). Impurity from normal discharges or from contact with another person having a pathological discharge is a lesser matter and is removed by washing and passage of the specified time. On vs. 12 see above on 11:24-40. The effect of vs. 18 is to prohibit marital relations on the eve of worship at the sanctuary (cf. vs. 31; Exod. 19:15; I Sam. 21:6). The language of vs. 24 (cf. 18) appears to mitigate the absolute prohibition of the Holiness Code (cf. 18:19; 20:18) but may refer to accidental contamination from mere proximity.

IV. The Purification of the Sanctuary and the Nation (16:1-34)

This chapter is identified (vs. 1) as a sequel to ch. 10. Nadab and Abihu create double defilement of the sanctuary (10:1-2)—in life by their sin, in death by their corpses. Thus purification of the sanctuary, including the Holy of Holies, is required. Instruction for this emergency rite is given in vss. 1-28 and then transformed into a yearly procedure by vss. 29-34. Chs. 11-15 were no doubt inserted by an editor who viewed them as a relevant listing of specific impurities inhibiting contact with the sanctuary (15:31) and its holy things (12:4b) which would be expiated by the ritual described.

16:1-28. The Purificatory Ritual. This procedure represents a fusion of 2 rites: (a) purging the sanctuary of priestly and lay defilement through sacrifices (cf. 4:3-21) and (b) expiating the sins of the people through their confession and transfer to a live animal banished into the desert. The first of these rites seems to have been performed without the other in Hezekiah's purgation of the temple (II Chr. 29:15-24; cf. Ezek. 45:18-22). The sins expiated by both rites are clearly of the same character and thus are exclusively within the religious sphere, i.e. between man and God (see above on 4:2). Ethical violations would require rectification with the person wronged before God's forgiveness could be expected (see above on 6:1-7).

16:2-5. The **mercy seat,** the cover of the ark containing the **testimony** (vs. 13), i.e. the tablets inscribed with the 10 Commandments, represents God's throne in the Holy of Holies. The **cloud** over it is here apparently not the divine revelation of 9:23-24 but a **cloud of incense** (vs. 13) brought in

Courtesy of Herbert G. May

Acacia tree in the Edomite Desert near the King's Highway; wood from the acacia tree was used in constructing the Ark of the Covenant, the table of shewbread, altars and other wooden objects used for worship

by Aaron to hide the symbol of God's presence from his human gaze. Instead of his usual elaborate vestments Aaron is to wear the simple white **linen** garments prescribed for a priest tending the altar (cf. 6:10). White linen is assumed to be worn by divine beings (cf. Ezek. 9:2; 10:2; Dan. 10:5; 12:6) and symbolizes the highest degree of purity.

16:6-28. On the **goat** rather than a bull for the people's **sin offering** see above on 9:8-21. Some interpreters take **Azazel** to be the name of a place E of Jerusalem where in later times it was customary to push the 2nd goat off a cliff. But the parallelism of **for Azazel** with **for the LORD** (vs. 8) and the instruction to **let the goat go in the wilderness** (vs. 22), i.e. set it free rather than kill it, favor the view of most scholars that Azazel is the name of a demon. Originally the rite may have been for the purpose of driving away a demon of this name in the goat, but now Azazel has come to be merely a symbol of a no-return to which the people's impurities are consigned. During the Babylonian spring new year festival an animal loaded with the temple's exorcised evil was thrown into the Euphrates, and those who handled it were rendered impure. Other temple purification rituals of the ancient Near East are also known.

16:29-34. The Annual Day of Atonement. The purpose of the merger of the 2 rites of vss. 1-28 is now given, viz. the joint purification of sanctuary and nation on a specified day in the autumn of each year (cf. 23:27-32; Num. 29:7-11). Thus the editor tacitly admits that an emergency rite of purgation prescribed for such extraordinary cases of defilement of the sanctuary as the sin of Nadab and Abihu has later become regularized into Israel's cultic calendar. **Afflict yourselves** refers to fasting and other forms of self-denial. **Sabbath** here has its root meaning of cessation from ordinary pursuits (see comment on Exod. 20:8-10).

V. THE HOLINESS CODE (17:1-26:46)

This lengthy insertion into the P material seems to be an independent legal code; and because of its repeated call for Israel to be **holy**, as God is holy (e.g. 19:2; 20:7-8; cf. 11:43-45, which may be a displaced fragment of it), it has become known as the Holiness (H) Code. Like the Covenant Code (Exod. 20:22-23:33) and the Deuteronomic Code (Deut. 12-28; see "The Law Codes of Israel," pp. 1090-94) it opens with a law about the place of sacrifice and closes with an exhortation, and like them it contains a mixture of ethical and ritual laws and appears to be a compilation of several older collections.

The closing exhortation seems to point to a date of compilation in preexilic times (see below on 26:3-46), which is supported by the apparent allusions in Ezek. 22 to laws found in chs. 18-20. Aside from the compiler's hortatory contributions the content is essentially similar to the other legal material incorporated by the P editors.

In Semitic polytheism **holy** referred to what was separated from common use by a supernatural quality that made it dangerous to touch or even approach except under certain conditions. Material objects—e.g. specific trees, stones, rivers—were believed to be invested with this quality of themselves.

For Israel, however, holiness stems solely from God. If certain things are holy—a land, Palestine; a place, the sanctuary; times, the festivals; persons, the priests—they are so by divine dispensation.

Only for Israel is holiness known to have been enjoined on a whole people. Mankind, Israel, and the priesthood form 3 concentric rings of increasing holiness about the center, God. The scriptural ideal is that all Israel shall be "a kingdom of priests and a holy nation" (Exod. 19:6). Israel is to observe a more rigid code of behavior than other nations, just as the priest lives by more stringent standards than his fellow Israelites. Holiness therefore requires separation from all defiling contact with man, e.g. through sharing in idolatrous practices (cf. 20:6-7, 23-24), or beast, e.g. through eating forbidden meats (cf. 11:43-45; 20:25-26).

Holiness for Israel means more than separation, however. It is a positive concept, an inspiration and a goal associated with God's nature and his desire for man: **You shall be holy; for I . . . am holy** (19:2). What man is not and can never fully be, yet what he is commanded to emulate and approximate—this is the life of godliness called "holy."

A. LAWS ABOUT MEAT (17:1-16)

17:1-14. Slaughter of Animals. This passage is of one piece and presents 2 related laws: (a) all slaughtered domestic animals must be brought to the altar as **peace offerings** (see above on 3:1-17; 7:22-27); (b) the **blood** must not be eaten. The centralization of worship demanded in the D Code was practical only if slaughter for food was permitted without sacrifice (Deut. 12:15-25). Before Josiah's adoption of the D Code (II Kings 23) there were many local shrines to which anyone desiring to slaughter an animal could bring his peace offering (cf. Exod. 20:24). Since **to the door of the tent of meeting** is characteristic P language adapting to the setting of Moses' day, this law may originally have commanded bringing the animal to an established shrine with a priest in attendance rather than slaughtering at an improvised altar (cf. e.g. Judg. 6:20-21; 13:19; I Sam. 6:14-15; 14:32-35; I Kings 1:9) with a non-priest officiating (cf. e.g. Judg. 6:25-28; I Sam. 9:12-14).

Bloodguilt, i.e. murder, is charged against anyone who kills an animal without sacrifice (vs. 4); on **cut off from among his people** see below on 20:2-9. The **atonement**, i.e. expiation, gained by bringing the blood to the **altar** (vs. 11)—or, in the case of game, by draining it and covering it with earth (vs. 13)—is not for general sin but for the slaughter which without such expiation would be murder.

17:15-16. Uncleanness from Eating Carrion. In P the carcass of an animal that dies naturally or by mishap is not forbidden as food, except to priests (22:8); but it transmits impurity (cf. 11:39-40), even to the **sojourner**, i.e. resident alien. That the absolute prohibition of Exod. 22:31; Deut. 14:21 was not obeyed may be inferred from Ezek. 4:14 and the laws of Exod. 21:28, 34-36.

B. ETHICAL AND RITUAL LAWS (18:1-20:27)

18:1-30. Illicit Sexual Relations. The laws of this ch. are framed by opening and closing exhortations by the H compiler (vss. 1-5, 24-30) which castigate the Egyptians and Canaanites for the depravity of their sexual mores. The pagan world of the ancient Near East worshiped and deified sex. It reserved the term "holy ones" for its cult prostitutes. No wonder Israel is charged with an exacting code of family purity whose violation means death (cf. 20:11-16).

18:6-18. In these laws against incest relation by marriage has the same force as blood relationship. Each partner in the marriage transfers his set of incest taboos to the other. The list prohibits unions that were customary in patriarchal and Mosaic times and even during the early kingdom (cf. e.g. Gen. 20:12; 29:21-30; Exod. 6:20; II Sam. 13:13).

18:19-23. Amid the prohibitions of sexual aberrations is a condemnation of subjecting **children** to the cult of **Molech,** lit. "the King." Since the Hebrew text here omits **by fire** from the usual formula referring to a god with this title (see RSV footnote to Deut. 18:10 and comment), it is possible that a different meaning is intended—that **devote them . . . to** should read "serve" as in the LXX. If so, in this context cultic prostitution might be meant. More probably, however, this is the usual reference to the child sacrifices practiced by certain neighbors of Israel (cf. II Kings 3:27). With the approval of some of Judah's later kings an apparatus for this practice was set up in the valley on the S side of Jerusalem (II Kings 16:3; 21:6; cf. Jer. 7:31; 32:35), but it was never incorporated into Israel's worship and did not spread beyond this solitary shrine.

18:24-30. The H Code is the only source which proclaims the holiness of the **land** of Palestine—a doctrine which explains the equal responsibility of both Israelite and **stranger,** i.e. resident alien, to maintain its sanctity (vs. 26; cf. 20:2; see below on 19:1-37) as well as the moral justification for its conquest (vss. 27-28; cf. 20:22-23). But Israel's ideological sword is 2-edged; if guilty of the same infractions she too will be **vomited out.** On **cut off from among their people** see below on 20:2-9.

19:1-37. *Positive Holiness.* How can man imitate the holiness of God? The answer of this ch. is given in a mingled series of ethical and ritual commands; no distinction is made between them. Throughout the ancient Near East morality was inseparable from religion. Indeed it is precisely within a ritual context that scriptural ethics rise to their summit.

Not only is the Decalogue encompassed here— the first half in vss. 3-8, the 2nd in vss. 9-22—but soaring above it is the commandment to **love** all men, fellow Israelites (vs. 18) and aliens (vs. 34) alike. This leveling of society stems partly from the sanctity which in the view of the H compiler God's **land** imposes on all its inhabitants (see above on 18:24-30). But there is more. The law of love is probably not one of the older laws assembled by the H compiler but his own composition—his generalization of the meaning of the laws. Yet it is no mere verbal ideal of one man. It is the principle underlying many of the laws collected not only in the H Code but throughout the P material and indeed the whole Pentateuch. The law of love must be expressed in deeds: equality in justice, both civil (cf. e.g. 20:2; 24:16, 22; Num. 35:15) and religious (cf. e.g. 16:29; 17:15; Exod. 12:19, 49; Num. 9:14), and

equality in mercy, e.g. free loans (25:35-55; cf. Deut. 10:18) and free gleanings (vss. 9-10; cf. Deut. 24:9-12). That the law of love may be implemented, the vitiating components in the nature of man, callousness (vss. 14, 33) and hatred (vss. 16-18), are also proscribed.

19:5-18. On vss. 5-8 see comments on 7:16-18; 20:2-9. On vss. 9-10 cf. 23:22; Deut. 24:19-22. Since the **sojourner,** i.e. resident alien, was not permitted to own land, he had to subsist by hiring out his services (cf. Deut. 24:14). He is often classified with the **poor** as a ward of God (cf. e.g. Deut. 10:18; Ps. 146:9; Mal. 3:5), for whom Israel must provide. The context in vs. 16 favors the translation **stand forth,** i.e. stand up to make a false accusation; but the Hebrew verb, lit. "stand," may mean here "stand still," i.e. fail to take action to help one in peril. Another possibility is "profit by the blood of your neighbor" (JPSV). Also obscure is **bear sin** (vs. 17; cf. 22:9; Num. 18:32). On vs. 18b see above on vss. 1-37.

19:19-25. A **cloth made of two kinds of stuff,** wool and linen, is prescribed for the curtains of the tabernacle (Exod. 26:1, 31, 36) and the vestments of the high priest (Exod. 28:5-6, 8, 15). Such a mixture is holy and therefore forbidden to the laity. Similarly a field sowed with 2 kinds of seed becomes holy (Deut. 22:9b) and cannot be used by the lay owner. Though the prohibition against cross-breeding animals was no doubt observed, mules were imported and used (cf. e.g. II Sam. 13:29; I Kings 10:25; Ezra 2:66). The Hebrew word for **betrothed** (vs. 20) is not that used of a free woman but means rather "assigned" or "designated," as in Exod. 21:7-11. **An inquiry shall be held** should be translated "an indemnity shall be paid." The case involves a 2-fold offense: (*a*) since the woman is no longer a virgin her value as a concubine has been reduced and her owner is entitled to damages and (*b*) since the designation included a vow before God its violation is a trespass against him requiring a **guilt offering** (see above on 6:1-7).

19:26-37. The juxtaposition in vs. 26 of eating **blood** and practicing **witchcraft,** i.e. divination, is not accidental. These pagan practices rank with idolatry and homicide (cf. 17:4, 14; Ezek. 33:25). Shaving the head and face except for a circle of hair as a magical rite was also a pagan practice (cf. Deut. 14:1; Jer. 9:26; 25:23). Removing hair and beard and gashing the flesh were common ancient ways of mourning (cf. Ezra 9:3; Isa. 22:12; Jer. 16:6; 41:5; Ezek. 7:18; Amos 8:10; Micah 1:16) and were a prominent part of the annual rites in observance of the seasonal death of Baal (cf. I Kings 18:28). **Mediums** and **wizards** (vs. 31; cf. 20:6, 27) practiced divination by communication with the dead (cf. I Sam. 28:3-7; II Kings 21:6; 23:24; Isa. 8:19). On vss. 33-34 see above on vss. 1-37, 5-18. The **ephah** (vs. 36) was a measure for grain, the **hin** for oil and wine (see "Measures and Money," pp. 1283-85).

20:1-27. *Penalties for Certain Infractions.* In this ch. a number of the absolute commands of chs. 18–19 are duplicated in conditional form with punishments specified. Evidently the H compiler here turned to a different source.

20:2-9. On the giving of **children to Molech** see above on 18:19-23. One who commits this sin is to be **stoned** by the **people,** but if they fail to act God himself will **cut him off from among his people.** Elsewhere in the P writings this expression appears in passive form and is often taken as an injunction for the religious community to banish the guilty person (cf. Ezra 10:8). The usage here, however, suggests that in all cases the idiom refers to divine rather than human punishment, viz. an early death through sickness or accident. The offenses for which this punishment is threatened involve ritual impurity—**defiling my sanctuary and profaning my holy name.** Vss. 4-5 are not a mere repetition but add that all who do not bring the Molech worshiper to judgment are likewise implicated and will suffer the same punishment. So too will those who consult **mediums and wizards** (vs. 6; see above on 19:26-37). On vs. 9 see comment on Exod. 21:15-17.

20:10-21. These sexual prohibitions duplicate those in ch. 18 except for the cases of grandchild, stepgrandchild, and marriage with 2 sisters (18:10, 17*b*, 18). No doubt the difference in form and esp. the inclusion of penalties in this series induced the H compiler to incorporate both collections. In vss. 10-16 the penalty is death by human agency, but in vss. 17-21 it is to be **cut off** by divine action (see above on vss. 2-9). Most of the offenses noted in vss. 17-21 involve marriages known to have been acceptable in Israel's early history (see above on 18:6-18). No doubt with such notable precedents the ordinances could not be humanly enforced and must be left to God's action. To the ancient Israelite to **die childless** (vss. 20-21) was the supreme penalty (cf. e.g. Num. 27:2-4; Deut. 25:6; Ruth 4:10; Pss. 109:13).

20:22-27. The H compiler's exhortation in vss. 22-24 largely repeats 18:24-30 (see comment). Vs. 25 seems closely related to 11:43-45, which perhaps at one time was included here along with a set of diet laws. The **medium** or **wizard** (vs. 27; see above on 19:26-37), as distinct from the one who merely consults such a person (vs. 6), must be **stoned.**

C. LAWS ABOUT PRIESTS AND SACRIFICES (21:1–22:33)

The priest, ranking highest in human holiness, could enter the sanctuary to handle its objects and eat of its gifts. These privileges had commensurate restrictions, the more so for the high priest. They were intended as safeguards against moral and ritual defilement which might inflict dire consequences on him and his people (22:9, 15-16; cf. 15:31).

21:1-15. *Mourning and Marriage.* In marked contrast to the modern clergyman the ancient priest was virtually isolated from death in the community and even among his relatives (vss. 1-6; cf. 10:6; Ezek. 24:15-18). The Israelite view, indeed obsession, was that death imparted a most severe impurity (cf. Num. 19:11-19). Probably this was a violent rejection of the opposite premise basic to Egyptian religion, that the dead and his burial place were equal to the temple in their sanctity. Vs. 4 is obscure and perhaps textually corrupt. Probably **as a husband among his people** means "as a kinsman by marriage" (JPSV). On vs. 5 see above on 19:26-37.

21:7-9. The priest's household must be protected from any sexual defilement through either his wife or his daughter. Marriage with a woman whose husband has died is not forbidden to the ordinary priest, but he must not marry a woman who has been **divorced,** lit. "driven away," by her husband —perhaps on the assumption that her dismissal would probably be due to "some indecency" (Deut. 24:1).

21:10-15. The greater holiness of the high priest —identified as **chief among his brethren** by his anointment and special vestments—requires more severe restrictions. He is forbidden any show of mourning or any contact with the **dead,** even his closest relatives, and must not even **go out of the sanctuary** to attend burial rites (cf. 10:6-7). He is prohibited from marrying a **widow;** his wife must be a **virgin of his own people,** i.e. from a priestly family (so the LXX; cf. Ezek. 44:22).

21:16-24. *Physical Disqualifications.* Like the sacrificial victim the officiating priest must be **without blemish.** The exact meaning of some of the blemishes is uncertain; e.g. **mutilated face** may mean "limb too short" (JPSV; cf. 22:23). The disfigured male descendant of a priestly family is permitted to share in eating the priests' portions of offerings, even the **most holy** (see above on 2:2*b*-3), but is forbidden to enter the sanctuary or have access to the altar.

22:1-16. *Eating of Holy Food.* The priest is subject to the same laws of uncleanness as the layman (cf. esp. chs. 11–15) and while in a state of impurity must avoid **holy things**—specifically, must not eat the priest's portion of offerings (cf. 7:19-21; 15:31). Obviously a qualification such as **while he has an uncleanness** is to be understood with **keep away** (vs. 2). On vs. 8 see above on 17:15-16.

22:10-13. The priestly perquisites, except those classified as "most holy" (see above on 2:2*b*-3), are to be eaten by all members of the priest's family. This includes a **slave** (vs. 11) but not an **outsider,** i.e. guest who is not a priest, or a **sojourner,** i.e. resident alien, or other **hired servant** (vs. 10). A **widow** with a **child** (vs. 13) would be supported by her husband's relatives and therefore not qualify as a member of her father's family.

22:14-16. These vss. are somewhat obscure. A layman who unintentionally **eats of a holy thing** can thereafter scarcely **give** it to the priest. The sense is evidently that he is to give its equivalent, with an added **fifth,** and also bring a guilt offering —so **guilt** should be translated (vs. 16; see above on 5:1-6, 16). Looking for his own gain, an unconscionable priest might deliberately allow an unsuspecting layman to eat of holy food (cf. Hos. 4:8) and thus commit a profanation which would require repayment with an extra 5th and a guilt offering for himself. Vss. 15-16 forbid such venality.

22:17-33. *Sacrificial Animals.* The regular rule that an animal offered for sacrifice must be **without blemish** (cf. e.g. 1:3; 3:1; 4:3; 5:15) is here elaborated and some of the unacceptable blemishes are specified (vs. 22). Though only a **burnt offering** and **peace offerings** are mentioned, it is to be understood that other offerings would require if anything a stricter standard. Some exception is made for a **freewill offering** (vs. 23) but is not permitted for a **votive offering,** since a perfect animal is assumed to have been promised by the vow. Castration of edible animals is effectively forbidden by vs. 24

since, before adoption of the D Code, which permitted slaughter without sacrifice, an animal not eligible for sacrifice could not be eaten (see above on 17:1-14).

22:26-33. On vs. 27 cf. Exod. 22:30. On vs. 28 cf. Deut. 22:6-7. On vss. 29-30 see above on 7:12-15. Vss. 31-33 are the compiler's concluding exhortation for this section.

D. THE FESTIVALS (23:1-44)

That this ch. is composite is obvious from the new beginnings in vss. 9, 39. Closer analysis suggests that the component introduced by vss. 2, 4 and summarized by vss. 37-38 includes vss. 5-8, 21, 23-36. The connection of vss. 26-32 with ch. 16 suggests further that this component comes from the P narrative source. Vs. 3 is probably a later interpolation; most of vss. 13, 18-20 seem to be variants of Num. 28:5, 7, 27-30; and vs. 22 is a duplication of 19:9-10. The rest is presumably from the H Code and was taken by the compiler from a preexilic source.

These instructions are addressed to the **people of Israel,** i.e. the lay farmers, rather than to the priests. Thus except in the later interpolations in vss. 13, 18-20 only the offerings of the individual farmer are enumerated. Probably it is for this reason that the new moon observance (cf. Num. 28:11-15) is not mentioned here, since on that day the lay Israelite had no special duties or prohibitions.

23:5-14. _The Feast of Unleavened Bread._ The **passover** and unleavened bread observances were originally quite separate, the former a pre-Israelite nomad shepherd rite and the latter an agricultural holiday of Canaan marking the beginning of the barley harvest (vs. 10; see comment on Exod. 12:1-13:16). The 2 fell at the same season and early in Israel's history came to be linked to each other and to the Exodus. Bread was leavened by including a piece of dough from an earlier batch in which yeast had developed. The first bread of the new crop is to be eaten **unleavened,** i.e. without anything from the previous year's crop in it (vs. 14). The **first month** is numbered according to the Babylonian calendar, in which the year began at the spring equinox (see below on vss. 23-25).

23:9-14. According to the older law in the H Code the first **sheaf** of the barley **harvest** is to be brought to the local sanctuary—not on a fixed date but on the first day of reaping (cf. Deut. 16:9)—for the **priest** to **wave** (see above on 7:28-36) as a thank offering for the new crop. None of it may be eaten till after this offering (vs. 14). The obvious agricultural setting of this ordinance is evidence of its antiquity. Vs. 13 is a later interpolation based on the public cult. On **ephah** and **hin** see "Measures and Money," pp. 1283-85.

23:15-22. _The Feast of Weeks._ This festival, unnamed here (cf. Exod. 34:22; Num. 28:26; Deut. 16:10), is called the feast of harvest in Exod. 23:16 —a recognition that it celebrates the harvesting of the wheat, the last grain to ripen. It comes **fifty days** after the ceremony of the first sheaf of the barley harvest—hence the name Pentecost, from the Greek for 50. An offering of **loaves of bread** is to be brought in thanksgiving—**leavened** to indicate that

the new crop is sanctioned for ordinary use. On vss. 18-22 see above on vss. 1-44.

23:23-25. _The New Year._ For the postexilic P authors the year began in the spring, according to the Babylonian calendar, which was followed also by the Persians. Thus the first month fell in the spring and the **seventh month** in the autumn. This numbering of the months seems to have been used in Judah before the Exile (see comment on Jer. 28: 17), perhaps for commercial convenience, even though her own new year came in the fall (cf. II Kings 22:3; 23:23). In early times the feast of booths (cf. vs. 34), or ingathering, apparently marked the "end of the year" (Exod. 23:16); but development of a more precise calendar fixed the opening of the new year before that festival (cf. I Kings 8:2; 12:32-33), with an observance of its own. In postexilic times this observance was continued at the traditional time but without the new year designation, which was revived only at a later time. The observance includes **rest,** special **blast of trumpets,** and additional public offerings (Num. 29:1-6). Perhaps pss. in which trumpeting is prominent (e.g. Pss. 47; 95-100) may have been used on this day and its theme of cosmic judgment, "he comes to judge the earth," incorporated as a permanent feature.

23:26-32. _The Day of Atonement._ The essential purpose of this day is to purify the sanctuary of its year-long defilement by man (see above on 16:1-34). Since the expiation rituals are confined to the sanctuary and performed exclusively by the priests (cf. ch. 16; Num. 29:7-11) this lay calendar omits the cultic aspects. This day is often said to be a postexilic innovation because it is not mentioned in preexilic sources, esp. Deut. 16. But the obvious antiquity of the purification ritual from which it developed makes its early establishment as an annual occasion probable, while the fact that it involves no participation by the laity would keep it from mention in such a passage as Deut. 16, which describes the festivals requiring the people to bring offerings to the central sanctuary. On this day they do not go to the temple; they **rest** from work, **afflict** themselves, i.e. fast, and rejoice that their year-long sins against God—the ritual sins causing the sanctuary's contamination (cf. 15:31; see above on 4:2)—have been forgiven.

23:33-44. _The Feast of Booths._ This festival is also called the feast of ingathering (Exod. 23:16; cf. vs. 39), the **feast of the LORD** (vs. 39), and simply "the feast" (Ezek. 45:25)—indication that in preexilic times it was the most important of the festivals. On the date see above on vss. 23-25.

23:39-43. This description, placed after the P summary of vss. 37-38, evidently represents a preexilic source copied by the H compiler (see above on vss. 1-44). The date in vs. 39 is an editorial harmonization, as is the reference to the **eighth day** —cf. the similar alteration of I Kings 8:66 in II Chr. 7:9-10. The 4 types of **branches** (vs. 40)— **fruit** can mean "boughs"—are presumably for festal processions around the local altar (cf. Ps. 118:27). The people are to live during the week in the fields in **booths** (vs. 42), temporary shelters such as are put up to this very day in Palestine to facilitate the grape and fruit harvest. This strictly rural and neighborhood celebration of the end of the agricultural year was radically altered by the author of Deut. 16:13-17 to enjoin a pilgrimage to the centralized sanctuary, with no mention of branches and booths. Neh. 8:14-17, reflecting an age which probably had the complete Pentateuch, harmonizes the conflicting traditions of H and D by calling for the use of branches—5 in number, a variant tradition—as construction materials for the booths, which are to be built on the roofs of the houses in Jerusalem. Like the passover this festival has been historicized (vs. 43) as a memorial of the Exodus. Num. 29:12-38 supplies the order of public sacrifices in the temple for each day.

23:44. This vs. is either the sequel to the P summary in vss. 37-38—cf. **appointed feasts** (vss. 2, 4, 37)—or the insertion of a later editor. It is at odds with the viewpoint of the H Code, which is represented as a continuous series of instructions given to Moses on Mt. Sinai (26:46).

E. Miscellaneous Laws (24:1-23)

This ch. is again composite; only vss. 15-21, 22b appear to come from the H Code. The rest is P material.

24:1-4. The Lamp Oil. Vss. 2-3 substantially duplicate Exod. 27:20-21. The **lampstand of pure gold** (vs. 4) is described in Exod. 25:31-40. Since it is inside the sanctuary, its greater sanctity requires **pure oil**—unlike the oil for anointing (Exod. 30:22-33)—and its lighting by **Aaron,** i.e. the high priest (cf. Exod. 30:7-8; Num. 8:2-3); "his sons" in Exod. 27:21 probably symbolize his successors as high priests. The lamp is to burn **from evening to morning,** i.e. only through the night; **continually** means "regularly" rather than "continuously."

24:5-9. The Bread of the Presence. This bread, translated also as "showbread" (e.g. I Chr. 9:32; II Chr. 2:4), consists of **twelve cakes,** symbols of God's covenant with the 12 tribes, made from the best wheat **flour,** probably without leaven. The loaves are to be placed along with **pure frankincense** in **two rows** of **six** on the **table** which stands before the Holy of Holies (cf. Exod. 25:23-30). Being within the sanctuary, they are to be tended only by **Aaron,** i.e. the high priest. **Every sabbath** he is to renew the bread and incense, burning the previous week's incense as a token offering and joining with other priests in eating the old loaves as a **most holy portion** (see above on 2:2b-3). The bread is thus considered as the priestly share of **offerings by fire,** reflecting the probability that originally, as Mesopotamian and Egyptian parallels indicate, it was entirely burned on the altar. It was a widespread pagan belief that the gods dined at the sanctuary table, as illustrated by the mockery in Isa. 65:11 and Bel and the Dragon. That the rejection of this belief and the transfer of the eating from deity to man took place early in Israel's history is shown by the account of David's eating such bread (I Sam. 21:6).

24:10-23. The Penalty of Blasphemy. Two laws about blasphemy in a brief series from the H Code (vss. 15-21) are here emphasized by a P narrative illustrating the enormity of this offense. The supreme blasphemy spotlighted by the narrative—and by the elaboration in vs. 16bc, probably added by the P editor, since **congregation** is a characteristic P term

—is not mere cursing of God (vs. 15) but doing so while speaking the **name of the LORD** (vs. 16a; cf. Exod. 20:7), i.e. the unique name Yahweh by which he revealed himself to his covenant people. Because of the derogatory context the P author dares not even write "Yahweh" and substitutes **Name** (vss. 11, 16c).

24:13-16. The power of the blasphemy affects not only the speaker but his hearers; their contamination must be transferred back to the blasphemer by the ritual of laying **their hands upon his head** (vs. 14; see above on 1:4). The injunction to enforce this particular law against the non-Israelite **sojourner** (vs. 16c) may have been suggested by the identification of the culprit in the narrative as only half Israelite.

24:17-23. The remainder of the brief series from the H Code (vss. 17-21) states the law of retaliation (lex talionis; cf. Exod. 21:23-25; Deut. 19:21), limiting vengeance to punishment equivalent to the damage caused by the original crime. The granting of the protection of this limitation to **sojourner** as well as **native** (vs. 22a) might well be attributed to the H compiler (see above on 18:24-30) except that the statement of it is quoted from other P material (Exod. 12:49; Num. 15:15-16, 29) and thus must be an insertion by a P editor. No doubt the insertion was suggested by that in vs. 16c, but it is noteworthy that the principle of the resident alien's equality before the law is stated for as well as against him. The extension of this justice to the sojourner is one of the great moral achievements of the P legislation. Not only is distinction eradicated between the powerful and the helpless but even between the Israelite and the non-Israelite.

F. The Sabbatical and Jubilee Years (25:1–26:2)

A number of commentators have taken the references to the jubilee year (vss. 8-13, 15-16, 26-34, 40b-41, 44-46, 50-52, 54, with minor variations) to be a late P editorial insertion, primarily because they assume the jubilee to be a utopian proposal rather than an actual practice (see below on vss. 8-34). Yet Deut. 15:1-11 (cf. Deut. 31:10), which enjoins a similarly "utopian" cancellation of debts every 7th year, is clearly an integral part of the D Code. Thus there seems no strong reason to suppose that this material is not an original part of the H Code.

25:2-7. The Sabbatical Year. Each **seventh year** is to be a **sabbath of solemn rest for the land** (see above on 18:24-30). Exod. 23:10-11 makes a similar provision, with the stated purpose of providing food for the poor (cf. 19:9-10). There it might be supposed that each plot of ground could have its own schedule but here it is obvious that all Israel is to observe the same sabbatical year. Leaving fields fallow was practiced in early times (cf. Prov. 13:23; Jer. 4:3; Hos. 10:12) and a 7-year cycle for it may be reflected in the 7 years of plenty and of famine in the Joseph story (Gen. 41:25-36). Of early observance of a simultaneous sabbatical year for the land there is no proof outside the codes; but 26:35, 43 (cf. II Chron. 36:21) seems to indicate that it was recognized as an obligation before the Exile even though not always faithfully observed. Its observance in later times is evidenced in Neh. 10:31b; I Macc. 6:49, 53.

25:5-7. Vss. 6-7 have been thought by some to be a later interpolation amending the strict prohibition of vs. 5 (cf. vss. 20-22); but the meaning may be that, though a **harvest of what grows of itself** is forbidden, eating from it from day to day is permissible.

25:8-34. *The Jubilee Year.* At the sound of the **trumpet,** i.e. the ram's-horn shophar—**jubilee** means ram or ram's horn—a year of **liberty** is to be proclaimed. The liberty includes: (*a*) leaving the land fallow (vss. 11-12; cf. vss. 2-7), (*b*) restoring landed property to its original owner (vss. 13-17, 28-34), and (*c*) setting free all Israelite slaves (vss. 40b-41, 50-54). The basis for the jubilee is clearly stated: the land belongs solely to God (vs. 23; see above on 18:24-30) and so do the people of Israel (vs. 42); absolute human ownership of either is forbidden.

Since the rabbinic literature indicates that the jubilee, unlike the sabbatical year, was not observed in later times, some scholars have viewed it as a theoretical scheme for alleviating poverty which was never actually put into practice. It is true that there are no early references to it, but in addition to the P references (27:18, 23-24; Num. 36:4) Ezek. 46:17 takes it for granted and Isa. 61:1-2 is a literary allusion to it. The patrimonial system of land ownership which it reflects and the tribal inheritances which it protects (cf. Num. 36:4) were outmoded institutions by the time of the early monarchy and would hardly be useful in a new proposal in the time of the H compiler or the P authors. The exclusion of town houses from redemption (vss. 29-31) is clearly an amendment to the original law to meet changing economic conditions—as is probably also the omission of the early limitation of an Israelite slave's service to 6 years (Exod. 21:2-6), of which Deut. 15:12-18 was no doubt a revival (cf. Jer. 34:13-14). Amendment is the sign of a living rather than a theoretical law. It should be noted also that the jubilee year begins in the fall according to the pre-exilic calendar (vs. 9; see below on vss. 8-12) rather than in the spring according to the Babylonian calendar followed by the P authors (see above on 23:23-25).

25:8-12. There is uncertainty how the jubilee cycle is calculated. The most plausible theory is that the author figures from the standpoint of the Babylonian calendar with a spring new year (see above on 23:23-25) so that the **day of atonement** inaugurating the jubilee year falls in the middle of his year. By the common ancient inclusive method of counting ("antedating"; see Chronology, pp. 1271-82) he takes the half year at the beginning as the first year and thus comes out at the end with a half year as the **fiftieth,** even though the actual interval has been only **forty-nine years.** Thus the jubilee year coincides with the 7th sabbatical year. This theory avoids assuming 2 successive fallow years, which would be impossible without famine, and is supported by the 49-year cycles used in the apocalyptic Book of Jubilees, written in the Maccabean period, and in the Dead Sea scrolls.

25:13-17. Since all land reverts to the original owner at the jubilee, any sale is actually a lease for the remaining years of the cycle and the price is to be calculated accordingly.

25:18-22. The calculation here is probably to be explained on the basis that the author's numbered years begin in the spring (see above on vss. 8-12) whereas the observance of the sabbatical year begins after the end of the harvest in the fall. Thus there is actually no problem about what to **eat in the seventh year** (vs. 20) because the people **gather** during the spring and summer of that year the **crop** sowed during the **sixth year,** which must provide the food for parts of **three years.** The sabbatical year begins with the fall of the 7th year and extends through the summer of the **eighth year,** after which the people sow a crop that does not come to harvest **until the ninth year,** i.e. the first half of it.

25:23-28. All the **land** in Palestine belongs to God, and he is assumed to have assigned it in the days of Joshua—by the casting of lots, believed to be divinely controlled—to the families of Israel. There is to be no absolute sale of this property. Any transfer of it is subject to **redemption** by the current heir of the family to which it was originally allotted, or if he is too **poor** by **his next of kin**—a technical term for the member of his family obligated to be the avenger of blood (cf. Num. 35:19-20) as well as the redeemer of property (cf. Ruth 4:1-10; Jer. 32:6-9) and of the person from slavery (vss. 48-49). In view of the approaching jubilee the sale is just a lease (see above on vss. 13-17) and so the redemption price is reduced year by year.

25:29-34. With the growth of urban life and an economic class engaged in trade rather than agriculture an exception has to be made for a **house in a walled city,** which cannot be kept in the same family indefinitely. An exception to the exception, however, is made for the **Levites,** who in the beginning were assigned the nonagricultural occupation of religious leadership and allotted special cities.

25:35-55. *Debt and Slavery.* The Israelite farmer who has had to sell his land must become a hired hand for one of his more fortunate neighbors and thus fall to the status of a landless **stranger** or **sojourner**—technical terms for 2 classes of resident aliens, the sojourner having limited citizenship rights (see above on 24:17-23). If unable to pay his debts he has no recourse but to sell himself and his family into slavery. Exod. 21:2-6 (cf. Deut. 15:12-18) limits the term of service of a Hebrew slave to 6 years unless he voluntarily chooses to remain for the rest of his life, but no doubt that law was not always enforced (cf. Jer. 34:13-14). Perhaps it had become a dead letter when this passage was written.

25:35-38. Parallels to the terminology of this passage in Old and Middle Babylonian laws from the time of the patriarchs found at Alalakh in N Syria and Nuzi in E Assyria (see color map 7) help to clarify the obscurity in vss. 35:36a. Probably they mean: "If your brother, being in straits, comes under your authority, and you hold him as though a resident alien, so that he remains under you, do not exact from him advance or accrued interest" (JPSV). Cf. Exod. 22:25; Deut. 23:19-20.

25:39-55. An Israelite enslaved for debt is to be treated like a **hired servant** rather than a slave and is to be released in the jubilee year. But a non-Israelite slave, whether imported or born in the land, is not subject to the jubilee release. On the other hand a resident non-Israelite master must release an Israelite slave in the jubilee year and must let him be **redeemed** earlier by a **kinsman** (see above on vss. 23-28), the amount depending on the **number of years** till the jubilee. Masters sometimes allowed slaves to earn income and keep part of it, so that in time a slave might save enough to **redeem himself** (vs. 49).

26:1-2. *Prohibition of Idols.* Cf. 19:3*b*-4. **Idols** here is lit. "things of naught." **Pillar** is coupled with **graven,** i.e. sculptured, **image** because it served not only as a commemorative stele (cf. e.g. Gen. 31:45) but also as a cultic symbol of the deity (cf. e.g. II Kings 3:2). Such pillars have been found at various places in Palestine, e.g. in an Israelite sanctuary at Arad in S Judah (see color map 3), whose destruction is tentatively dated at the end of the 7th cent., the time of Josiah's reform (cf. II Kings 23:14).

G. The Concluding Exhortation (26:3-46)

Like the promises at the end of the Covenant Code (Exod. 23:20-33) and the blessings and curses at the end of the D Code (Deut. 28) this final admonition with both promise and threat follows a pattern common in ancient law codes—cf. e.g. the epilogue to Hammurabi's code.

26:27-45. The detailed threat of devastation and exile and the final promise to **remember the covenant,** as well as the parallels in thought and language to Ezek., have caused a number of commentators to date this passage, and accordingly the compiling of the H Code as a whole, during the period of the Exile. On the contrary, however, the discrepancy between the description in vss. 36-39 and the actual life of the exiles in Babylonia (cf. Jer. 29:5-7) shows that this passage must have been written before the event. Furthermore the plural **sanctuaries** in vs. 31 points to a time before Josiah's centralization of worship. From the middle of the 8th cent. on the possibility of conquest and exile was never very remote. The parallels with Ezek., therefore, must come from the prophet's acquaintance with the code. It should be noted that the H compiler's view that children are punished **because of the iniquities of their fathers** is repudiated both by Ezekiel (Ezek. 18) and by the P authors (Num. 14:31; 26:11).

26:46. This sentence declares what precedes to be the basis of the covenant on **Mount Sinai.** Many scholars have taken it to be the conclusion to the H Code, but the parallelism with 25:1 indicates rather that it applies only to chs. 25-26.

VI. Commutation of Votive Gifts (27:1-34)

A **vow** was a promise to God, usually of an offering, made contingent on his aid in response to some petition—e.g. for success in achieving some goal (cf. Gen. 28:20-22; II Sam. 15:7-12) or for recovery from illness or other distress (cf. Ps. 66:13-15). Originally a **vow of persons** called for a human sacrifice (cf. Judg. 11:29-40) but in very early times substitution of an animal (cf. Gen. 22:13) or a payment of silver (cf. II Kings 12:4) became established (see above on 5:14–6:7). The word translated **valuation** is thus an ancient technical term for the equivalent in commutation (see above on 5:15).

27:9-25. A vow to sacrifice a specific clean animal must be fulfilled. An attempt to substitute another renders both beasts **holy,** i.e. subject to sacrifice. But an equivalent payment plus a **fifth** may be substituted for an **unclean animal,** e.g. an ass or camel, or for a **house** or **land.** Since a **homer,** *ca.* 5 bushels, **of barley** would sow a vast area and make the land ridiculously cheap, it is likely that **seed** and **sowing** —the same word—here mean "grain" and refer to the yield (cf. vs. 30). The land is subject to release in the **year of jubilee** and thus must be appraised on the basis of the number of years remaining (cf. 25:13-17).

27:26-34. Since a **firstling** belongs to God anyway it cannot be the fulfillment of a vow. On vs. 27 cf. Exod. 13:13. A **devoted thing** in early times was irrevocably condemned to death or destruction, usually in connection with holy war (cf. e.g. Num. 21:1-3; Deut. 13:13-18; I Sam. 15:3), but now is **most holy,** i.e. the unredeemable property of the sanctuary and its priests (cf. Num. 18:14). A devoted person, however, is still to suffer **death** without a way to be **ransomed.** Like firstlings, the **tithe** already belongs to God and cannot fulfill a vow, but an equivalent payment plus a **fifth** may be substituted for it if it is **seed,** i.e. grain, or **fruit.** On the other hand an animal tithe—mentioned only here (vss. 32-33) and in II Chr. 31:6—cannot be **exchanged.** Vs. 34 probably sums up this ch. rather than the entire book (cf. 1:1).

THE BOOK OF NUMBERS

Harvey H. Guthrie, Jr.

Introduction

Like the other books of the Pentateuch, Numbers is designated in the Hebrew Bible by a word from its opening sentence, "In the wilderness." Its English title originated with the LXX and refers to the census described in its opening chapters.

Neither in its final form nor in any of the sources underlying it is Num. a separate unit. It is part of a larger unit the division of which into books is largely arbitrary (see "The Compiling of Israel's Story," pp. 1082-89). The rationale by which Num. is set off in this division is that it narrates the movement of Israel from Sinai to the borders of Canaan, beginning with the census of the tribes taken before the journey. In other words it covers the traditional 40 years of wandering in the wilderness.

Sources. The literary sources J, E, and P are the basis of Num. as they are of Gen.-Lev. The separation of J and E in Num. is difficult, and there is no general agreement about it. The following commentary, for the most part, simply refers to JE sections. P is usually fairly easily recognized. Many of the P portions of Num. are secondary supplements to the basic P work, inserted rather haphazardly into the narrative. Tradition seems to have been vague about the wilderness period, and the era covered in Num. became a convenient peg on which to hang presettlement traditions which editors wished to get into the record. A table of the sources appears on this page.

Behind the literary sources, and alongside them, lay traditions from various places and groups in Israel. As a larger unity Israel undoubtedly came into existence later than the period of which Num. speaks, after her constituent groups were established in Palestine. After this establishment the traditions of the Exodus and the Sinai covenant became creative of and normative for the theology of the entire united federation of tribes that preceded the monarchy. The experiences underlying the traditions, however, were originally undergone by the ancestors of only parts of united Israel, not by those of all the tribes and clans. Likewise the many other traditions later recounted and revered by the whole of Israel arose out of the past of only segments of the united people. If the narrative of Num. seems disjointed and haphazard (esp. in 10:11–20:29), it is due to the way in which a subsequently united people remembered and organized originally separate traditions as part of a common history. In the same way today a citizen of the United States thinks of the traditions of the Massachusetts pilgrims and the Virginia cavaliers as

Sources of Numbers

The early and late strands of tradition in Num. are shown in the 2 columns below. Since the most prominent distinguishing marks of the 2 early strands, J and E, do not appear in Num., they can rarely be separated with assurance. Accordingly probable J and E elements are noted in the commentary where recognizable but are not distinguished in this table. Strata apparent in the P material are indicated by the letter s to mark later additions. The combined initials after 32:1-42; 33:1-49 point to the probability that traditions from all 3 sources have been combined by a later editor.

JE (early)	P (Priestly)
	1:1-47, 48-54s
	2:1-34
	3:1-13s, 14-51
	4:1-15, 16-20s, 21-49
	5:1–7:89s
	8:1-4s, 5-22, 23-26s
	9:1-14s, 15-23
10:29-33, 35-36	10:1-10s, 11-12, 13-28s, 34s
11:1–12:16	
13:17b-20, 22-24, 26b-31	13:1-17a, 21, 25-26a, 32-33
14:1b, 4, 11-25, 39-45	14:1a, 2-3, 5-10, 26-38
	15:1-41s
16:1b-2a, 12-15, 25, 26b, 27b-34	16:1a, 2b-11, 16-24, 26a, 27a, 35, 36-50s
	17:1–19:22s
20:14-22a	20:1-13, 22b-29
21:1-35	
22:2-41	22:1
23:1–24:25	
25:1-5	25:6-18
	26:1-65s
	27:1-11s, 12-23
	28:1–31:54s
32:1-42JEP	32:1-42JEP
33:1-49JEP	33:1-49JEP, 50-56s
	34:1–36:13s

his heritage without considering when his own ancestors came to America. This process does not devaluate or discredit the biblical narrative properly understood. Rather it leads to an understanding of the real nature of Num. and of what Israel's tradition meant to her.

Theological Significance. Only by engaging in allegorical interpretation can one gain inspiration and edification from the bulk of Num. Its theological significance for the Christian lies simply in the fact that both the church and the civilization of which it is a part have, for good and for ill, been produced by an empirical history of which Israel and Israel's remembrance and interpretation of her past as found in Num. are part. Furthermore the uniqueness of Israel and the church lies in their affirmation that it is precisely in that empirical, conditioned history that God has acted to reveal himself and to redeem his world. Thus, using the results of historical method as applied to the Bible, the Christian can read Num. for what it really is, not in spite of, but precisely because of, the nature of the Christian affirmation. To read into Num. relevance or edification that is not really there or to reject Num. because of the lack of those things, is to misunderstand what the Bible as a whole is really saying.

For Further Study. G. B. Gray, *Num.*, 1903; though old, the most complete commentary in English. John Marsh in *IB*, 1952. Roland de Vaux, *Ancient Israel*, 1961; a study of Israel's institutions which figure so much in Num. R. C. Dentan in *IDB*, 1962. Murray Newman, *The People of the Covenant*, 1962; a suggestive study of the period.

I. FINAL DAYS AT SINAI (1:1–10:10)

This section is the conclusion of the P account of Israel's sojourn at Mt. Sinai, which began at Exod. 25:1 and, excluding Exod. 32–34, continues through Exod. and Lev. As elsewhere, P is obviously composite, its basic account of Israel's sacred institutions having been expanded and supplemented. The dates in 1:1; 10:11 indicate that P conceives of this section as covering a period of 19 days.

1:1-46. The Census of Israel. The purpose of this census is military, but in no secular sense. Israel in premonarchic days was an amphictyony (sacral league) consisting of independent tribes with allegiance to a common God, Yahweh, and all were obligated to maintain his sanctuary and to send men to his army when holy war was declared.

1:1. Though the **wilderness of Sinai**, i.e. desert around Sinai, is traditionally located at Jebel Musa in the S of the Sinai Peninsula, many scholars, for sound reasons, locate the holy mountain farther N, near Kadesh-barnea (see comment on Exod. 3:1 and color map 4). Like J, P always refers to the mountain as Sinai, while E and D call it Horeb. This may indicate a more radical difference in traditions than is allowed by the usual simple equation of the 2. P generally uses the term **tent of meeting** for the sacred central shrine of the tribes, and speaks of the **tabernacle** (vs. 50) as being inside the tent (Exod. 26:7) as a housing for the ark (3:31; 4:5). Both tent and ark are used in the present literary sources, but they may originally have been associated with the traditions of separate groups which came together within Israel only after the settlement in Palestine (see comments on Exod. 25:10-22; 33:7-11).

1:2-16. Though usage is sometimes confused, the tribe consisted of a number of **families** ("clans" might be better), each of which consisted of a number of **fathers' houses,** the smallest social units (cf. Josh. 7:16-18). **Company** (vs. 3) and **clans** (lit. "thousands," vs. 16) are military divisions.

1:20-46. The statistics are unbelievably large for this period and are generally considered artificial (see comment on Exod. 38:21-31). They may, however, represent the results of a census at some later point in Israel's history and, like much in P, be material much older than the finished document itself.

1:47-54. The Levites. P agrees with all early traditions in associating the Levites closely with Moses and the shrine of Yahweh but reflects their status in the postexilic temple in representing them as a group separate from and subordinate to the priests (cf. 3:5-10). A long, complicated, and debated history of the Israelite priesthoods lies behind the situation assumed here, which is like that described in Chr. The Levites' function is said to be simply to care for and protect the **tabernacle.** They are not one of the 12 tribes (as in e.g. Gen. 35:23; 49:5-7; Exod. 1:2) but a caste outside the tribes, the number having been filled by the division of Joseph into 2 tribes (vss. 32-45).

2:1-34. The Sacred Encampment. The plan of Israel's camp in the wilderness is pictured by P as quadrilateral. The 12 tribes are arranged, 3 on each side, to form the perimeter. Inside, the priests are to the E of the tent, and the 3 divisions of the Levites are on the other 3 sides (cf. 1:50-53; 3:23, 29, 35, 38). While the symbolism of God's tabernacling presence in Israel's midst is significant to P, what is described here is probably not sheer invention from the exilic or postexilic period. Behind this ch. may lie very ancient, premonarchic cultic tradition. It has been held that the source of traditions such as this was the most ancient form of the feast of booths, an annual occasion on which the tribes would camp in the desert around the tent of meeting to recall their ancient days.

3:1-4:49. The Levites and Their Duties. In designating the Aaronic priests alone as those to whom the priestly office belongs (3:1-4) P differs from preexilic sources. Vs. 4 refers to Lev. 10:1-2. On vss. 5-10 see above on 1:47-54.

3:11-13. A different tradition from that in the preceding vss. claims that the Levites were taken from **among the people of Israel** as substitutes for the **first-born** sons of Israel, who belong to Yahweh (cf. Exod. 22:29; 34:20, both JE; and Exod. 13:2, P). See further below on vss. 40-51.

3:14-39. These vss. describe a census of the Levitical families (contrast 1:47-49) and the stations in camp and duties of the 3 divisions of the Levites. Vs. 38 designates the priests' place in the camp. The discrepancy between the total of Levites in vs. 39 and the sum of the figures in vss. 22, 28, 34 may be due to an early scribal error dropping a letter from vs. 28.

3:40-51. The count of **first-born males** of all Israel includes those **from a month old and upward** because it was at the age of one month that the parents of a first-born son were required to pay **five shekels** to the priests (cf. 18:16; on **shekel of the sanctuary** see comment on Exod. 30:13). A Mosaic origin for this requirement is here claimed. In all this P, or a supplement to it, may be utilizing ancient tradition about the encampment, but cultic conditions of postexilic times are certainly read back into the account. Thus it is asserted that what Israel is, originated with Moses. There may have been polemical reasons for such an assertion at the time of writing.

4:1-49. Another **census** is made of men aged 30-50 in the 3 groups of Levites for the purpose of assigning their duties in the camp and on the march. Various tasks of the priests are also mentioned. Again premonarchic cultic traditions are read in the light of postexilic times. This accounts for discrepancies and inconsistencies in the passage. The results of the census are summarized in vss. 34-49. We have no way of knowing the source or date of the figures.

5:1-6:27. *Various Laws.* Though supplements may obscure the connection, this section logically follows what precedes it. Sacral army, camp and sanctuary, priestly and Levitical duties having been described, P now turns to the conditions of ritual purity incumbent on all Israel. This is the point of the bulk of OT law.

5:1-4. Specified bodily disqualifications bar one from inclusion in the sacral congregation. Such ritual requirements still prevail in Roman Catholic and Eastern Orthodox qualifications for physical soundness in members of the priesthood.

5:5-10. Ritual disqualification results when an oath or pledge is violated, and one must make **restitution.** Such a violation constitutes **breaking faith with the LORD**—sacred and secular are not distinguished (cf. Lev. 6:1-7). In modern terms, ritual law is also ethical.

5:11-31. Adultery defiles the ritual purity of the congregation. A woman suspected of the offense must undergo an ordeal in connection with a sacrifice by her husband and her own oath of purgation. This is the only OT specification of a trial by ordeal, an attempt to obtain a direct divine verdict in ambiguous cases, but the custom must have been used by Israel in other situations (cf. ch. 16). In vs. 23 **book,** a general term for writing material, probably means a piece of pottery, stone, or wood from which the priest could wash the ink.

6:1-21. Regulations are laid down for the **Nazirite,** one separated from others by a **special vow.** The dietary and tonsorial customs of Nazirites, found all through Israel's history (cf. Judg. 13–16; Amos 2:11-12; I Macc. 3:49) may indicate that one of their motives was protest against agricultural, Canaanite society. P places the Nazirite under priestly authority.

6:22-27. This familiar priestly blessing might more logically have come in Lev. 9:22. It is probably very ancient, and has continued to be used in temple (cf. Ecclus. 50:20), synagogue, and church. Its essence in ancient Israel lay, not primarily in the predicates, but in the placing of the divine **name** (note its 3-fold repetition) on God's **people** (vs. 27).

7:1-89. *Offerings at the Dedication of the Altar.* Out of order chronologically (Exod. 40 has the altar anointed a month before the date in 1:1) and repetitive in its enumeration of the offerings by tribal leaders, this ch. must be the product of a late supplementer of P. Its basis in fact may have been found in lists of temple equipment and offerings, and it may have been placed here because of the census lists in chs. 1-4, but it must be largely fancy. Possibly its writer thought of the ancient leaders as models of generous supporters of the sanctuary. Vs. 89 is a fragment from a lost narrative; it has no connection with its context here (cf. Exod. 25:22).

8:1-4. *The Golden Lampstand.* This prototype of the well-known Jewish *menorah,* which stood before the table for the bread of the presence in the temple, is described in P at greater length in Exod. 25:31-40; 37:17-24. The motive behind ch. 7 probably accounts for the allusion to it here.

8:5-26. *Consecration of the Levites.* Like the two

preceding sections, this shows how P was expanded and supplemented. It repeats what is already found in 3:5-13, and vss. 23-25 do not agree with 4:3. At several points it repeats itself (vss. 6, 11, 13, 15). The original part is in vss. 5-13, the procedure by which Levites were set apart for their service. This has attracted elements from 3:5-13 and has been expanded in P style.

9:1-14. *The Supplemental Passover.* Also a supplement in P, this passage provides for the keeping of the passover a month later than its regular date by those found ritually unclean at the appointed time. It was probably placed here by attraction to the date in 1:1, which places chs. 1-10 in the 2nd month, the time of the supplemental passover it describes (cf. II Chr. 30).

9:15-23. *The Fiery Cloud.* Again, this section is repetitive—of Exod. 40:34-38—and must be a supplement in P. In Exod. 40:35 the cloud is connected with the "glory" of Yahweh, i.e. his presence. P, Isa., and Ezek. come from a tradition in which "glory" designates Yahweh's presence, Deut. from a tradition emphasizing Yahweh's "name."

10:1-10. *The Silver Trumpets.* P holds that the last act before leaving Sinai was the manufacture of silver trumpets with which the tribes of Israel were to be summoned to various sacral functions. These are described to account for the trumpets mentioned in II Kings 12:13; Ps. 98:6; and often in Chr.; Ezra; Neh. The use of these instruments—straight tubes *ca.* 2 feet long—in the postexilic cult probably was an elaboration of the solemn sounding of the rams-horn *shophar* in the preexilic, and even premonarchic, cult at the point of Yahweh's manifestation of his presence (cf. Exod. 19:13, 16, 19; 20:18). Thus, this time with real warrant, P again attributes the institution of postexilic procedures to the time of Moses.

II. The Period in the Wilderness (10:11–20:29)

Any outline of Num. is arbitrary, the final form of the book having resulted from a sometimes haphazard combination of various traditions. Underneath it, however, seem to lie 2 traditions of how Palestine proper was entered by the tribes: (*a*) a push upward from the S, completed in Judg. 1; (*b*) a movement N into Transjordan, completed in the account of the conquest in Josh. The present form of Num. combines these originally separate traditions—if such they are—into a unified narrative.

Tradition holds that the period covered in this section was 40 years—a generation (cf. 14:33). The chronology of P strictly followed makes the exact figure 38 years (cf. 10:11 with 20:23-29; 33:38). Major attention is devoted to the beginning (10:11-14:35) and end (20:1-29) of the period.

In spite of the various places mentioned by P (cf. the catalogue in ch. 33), the traditions seem to indicate that actually the center of Israel's life in this period was the oasis-sanctuary of Kadesh-barnea (see color map 4), by which were located Massah and Meribah (cf. Exod. 17). Near this area, rather than at the site fixed on by postbiblical tradition, was Mt. Sinai (see comment on Exod. 3:1). Thus the traditions in chs. 1-20 have to do, not with "wandering," but with the life of an association of tribes at a common center.

A. The Departure from Sinai (10:11-36)

10:11-28. The P Account. P here recounts how instructions given previously are followed as the march from Sinai begins. The **cloud** (cf. 9:15-23) signals the time to move, and the order of march specified in ch. 2 is followed, with the Levites (cf. chs. 3-4) and the tribes under their leaders (cf. 1:5-15) in proper place.

10:29-36. The JE Account. Here for the first time in Num. is taken up the thread of narrative from the preexilic sources, J and E, continuing from Exod. 34:28. Though the wording here is ambiguous, the total evidence suggests that in the E tradition **Moses' father-in-law** was a **Midianite** who returned to his own land (cf. Exod. 18:27) whereas in the J tradition he was **Hobab** the Kenite of the clan of **Reuel** and accompanied the Israelites, or at least part of them, into Canaan (cf. Judg. 1:16; 4:11; see comment on Exod. 2:15b-22; 18:1-12). At any rate the traditions indicate that Moses, and therefore the origins of Israelite religion, were closely connected with a nomadic group, itself very probably a part of the tribal complex to the S of Canaan before the occupation. This is one of the indications that behind the traditions of the Pentateuch lies a long and complex history not now recoverable in all its details.

10:33-34. JE denotes the portable sanctuary as the **ark of the covenant,** as opposed to the "tabernacle" and "tent of meeting" in P, and says that it **went before** the people on the march (contrast vss. 11-28). Again variant traditions from groups which actually merged only later on in Palestine underlie the text. The 2nd **three days' journey** seemed to be a scribal error duplicating the first. Vs. 34 is probably a P supplement.

10:35-36. This is an ancient poetic invocation of Yahweh's presence with the ark, by which Israel was led in holy war until it was placed by Solomon in the Jerusalem temple (cf. e.g. I Sam. 4:3-7; Pss. 68:1; 132:8).

B. Problems and Dissension in Israel (11:1-12:16)

The traditions of the Pentateuch stress that the Israel being led by her God to a homeland was by no means a cooperative people. Her rebelliousness during the trek from Egypt to Canaan is the subject of a number of stories (cf. Exod. 16:1-3; 17:1-4; 32). Israel's sacred songs cited these stories as examples of the terrible decision demanded by God's election of her (e.g. Ps. 95:8-11; cf. I Cor. 10:1-15). It is not reading subsequent theology into the OT to say that Israel stressed divine grace as opposed by human sinfulness. That is the theological motive behind the presence of such stories in the earliest strata of the Pentateuch. This whole section is from JE.

11:1-3. Taberah. Though the **fire of the LORD** can mean lightning (cf. II Kings 1:10; Job 1:16), this story implies a direct divine act in punishment of Israel's complaining. The story gives an explanation of the name of a place—though Taberah could mean "pasture" as well as "burning." It also serves as an example of the effectiveness of prophetic intercession, a motif stressed in E (cf. Gen. 20:7, 17). Deut. 9:22 indicates that this place, along with Massah, was in the vicinity of Kadesh.

11:4-35. The People's Craving for Meat. Two

stories are now interwoven in these vss. The account of Israel's complaint about having to subsist only on the manna of the desert (vss. 4-15, 18-24a, 31-35) is a parallel to the story from P in Exod. 16. Aside from being the JE account of Yahweh's provision for Israel in the desert, the story explains the name of a place (vs. 34). It has been generally attributed to J but may contain fragments from E, especially in vss. 11-15, which seem to manifest the interest of E in the power of prophetic intercession.

11:4-6. The word **rabble** comes from a root meaning "gathering" (a different term is used of this group in Exod. 12:38; see comment). The traditions are conscious that elements not later reckoned as part of Israel were involved in her preconquest history (see above on 10:29-32). The catalogue of Egyptian food is accurate. The preexilic sources seem to have had an acquaintance with Egypt and its ways.

11:7-9. This story does not suggest, as does Exod. 16 (cf. Deut. 8:3, 16; Neh. 9:15, 20; Pss. 78:23-25; 105:40), that the manna was miraculous, but sees it as a natural product of the desert. The miracle is rather in the provision of quail.

11:16-25. The interwoven story of **seventy ... elders of the people** and the prophetic **spirit** (vss. 16-17, 24b-30) betrays the interests of E. As in Exod. 18; 24 the elders are associated with Moses in his leadership of Israel—E seeming to reflect the more antimonarchic tendencies of N tradition. Present also is the tendency of E to stress Moses' great spiritual powers, as well as its interest in prophecy.

Though it has been maintained that the story here is but a variant of that in Exod. 18, or that in Exod. 24:1-11, its motive seems to be different, in that the endowment of the elders with the spirit of prophecy is only the setting for the Eldad-Medad incident in vss. 26-30. **Prophesied** here refers to the ecstatic behavior implied in I Sam. 10:9-12; 18:10 (where "raved" is in Hebrew the same verb; cf. I Kings 18:29). This behavior was the outward sign of the elders' possession of divine power (spirit), and the conclusion of vs. 25 implies that it took place on only one occasion.

11:26-30. The point of the story is Moses' attitude toward the 2 men who prophesy **in the camp** while he and the elders are at the sanctuary (note that E, contrary to P in chs. 2-3, places the **tent** outside the camp). Moses' reply to Joshua's indignation is more than a claim for magnanimity. In it is expressed an ideal which Joel 2:28-29 declares will be realized in the final time (cf. Acts 2:17-21), and which finds expression in a different way in Jer. 31:31-34.

11:31-35. Large flocks of migrating **quails** often stop to rest in this region and, when exhausted from flight, can be easily caught. Deut. 9:22 indicates that **Kibroth-hattaavah** was near Kadesh, but its exact location is not known. The location of **Hazeroth** is also unknown.

12:1-16. The Rebellion of Miriam and Aaron. The point of this story, probably from E (except vs. 16 from J), is quite simple, and it is easy to see how it was preserved in close connection with the Eldad-Medad story in 11:26-30. Miriam and Aaron question Moses' unique, divinely granted authority and are solemnly reproved by Yahweh, who proclaims Moses' authority in a poetic oracle and punishes Miriam with leprosy.

The story is one strong indication of a rift that developed among the Israelites at Kadesh, other hints of the same thing being provided in the accounts all through chs. 11–16 of discontent, differences over entering Canaan from the S, and challenges to Moses' authority. Combined with traditions of 2 entries into Canaan, one from the S and one from Transjordan (cf. Judg. 1 with Josh. 1–12), all this may indicate some kind of split into separate groups which were reunited tenuously again later on in Canaan only to break up once more after Solomon's reign. If this is what happened, however, later tradition has forgotten it, and Num. now treats the past as a series of successive events involving all the ancestors of the Israel of later times.

12:1-2. Though **Cushite** usually means Ethiopian (e.g. Jer. 13:23) or Kassite (see comment on Gen. 10:8-12), Hab. 3:7 suggests that here it may mean Midianite and refer to Zipporah (cf. Exod. 2:15-22; see comment on II Chr. 14:9-15). There is no mention elsewhere of a tradition that Moses had a 2nd wife, and vs. 1*b* probably is a later insertion. In any case the reference is a puzzle. Vs. 2 locates the root of the incident in offended pride.

12:6-8. The semipoetic form of this pronouncement argues for its antiquity. The lines may come from the premonarchic cult in which Moses' "covenant mediator" successors played a central role.

C. Spies Sent into Canaan (13:1–14:45)

Now told in such a way as to show why Israel journeyed around the E side of Canaan to enter across the Jordan, the traditions here may indicate that the elements of later Israel entered the land in various ways and at various times (see above on 12:1-16). The present account is manifestly, with its incongruities and repetitions, composite. Scholars differ in their analyses of J and E, but there is substantial agreement on what is JE and what P.

According to JE Moses dispatches men to enter Canaan from the S for reconnaissance (13:17*b*-20). Through the Negeb they penetrate as far as Hebron and obtain samples of the excellent crops of the country (13:22-24). They report to Moses at Kadesh the desirability of the land and the forbidding strength of its inhabitants, but Caleb insists that it can be taken (13:26*b*-31). Discouraged and disappointed at this frustration (14:1*b*), the people advocate overthrowing Moses and returning to Egypt (14:4). Yahweh, enraged at the people's response and ready to reject them and reserve his election for Moses and his descendants, accedes to Moses' plea for pardon, but says that of those concerned only Caleb shall enter Canaan, and commands Israel to turn back into the desert in order to circumvent S Canaan (14:11-25). Reversing their former reaction, the people insist on an invasion, only to be defeated and routed (14:39-45).

The P account states that the spies include a representative from each of the 12 tribes (13:1-17*a*) and that they explore the whole of Palestine (13:21). After 40 days they return to Paran (13:25-26*a*) with a discouraging report of the land itself and of the size of the inhabitants (13:32-33), which causes the people to complain (14:1*a*, 2-3). Joshua and Caleb declare that the land is good and with Yah-

weh's help they can conquer it, but the people reject their counsel (14:5-10). Therefore Yahweh decrees that Israel must wander in the desert for 40 years, until all the murmurers have died and only Joshua and Caleb are left to lead the new generation into the Promised Land (14:26-38).

13:1-16. The listing of the 12 spies as representatives of their tribes accords with the constitution of the tribal league described in chs. 1; 26; 34 and betrays the usual interest of P in genealogy.

13:17-21. According to JE the spies are to explore simply the **Negeb** (the arid steppe S of Beer-sheba; see color map 4) and the **hill country** (the rough, mountainous area of Judah). In the P account, however, they survey the whole land from **the wilderness of Zin** surrounding Kadesh to **Rehob**, i.e. Beth-rehob near Dan (cf. Judg. 18:28; see color map 5). This illustrates the P tendency to emphasize the nation as a whole and play down local and tribal traditions.

13:22-29. The JE traditions contain probably accurate remembrance of which clans were pre-Israelite inhabitants of the **Hebron** area (vs. 22) and of the **Negeb** and the **hill country** (vs. 29). On **Zoan** see comment on Exod. 1:8-14. On **Anak** see below on vss. 32-33. The **Amalekites** were desert nomads remembered by Israel as archetypal enemies (cf. Exod. 17:8-16; I Sam. 15:1-33). The **Hittites** were remnants of an empire in Asia Minor that had penetrated into Palestine before the Israelite occupation (see ill., p. 90). The **Jebusites** were the Canaanite group still holding Jerusalem in David's time (cf. Josh. 15:63; Judg. 1:21; II Sam. 5:6-9). The **Amorites,** mentioned often in various areas both in the OT and in other ancient sources, were desert peoples who penetrated into all parts of the Fertile Crescent in the 18th and 17th cents. B.C. The name is regularly used by E instead of **Canaanites** as the general term for the pre-Israelite inhabitants of Palestine. Note the characteristic interest in telling the supposed origin of a place name, **Eshcol** (vss. 23-24).

13:30-31. The depiction of **Caleb** in the JE account—probably from J—as the one spy expressing confidence in Israel's ability to **overcome** the land seeks to explain why elements of Judah, including Calebites (cf. Judg. 1:10-20), occupied the Hebron area long before the conquest of central and N Palestine.

13:32-33. In contrast to the JE report of fertility (vss. 23-24, 26*b*-27) the spies in the P account declare that the country **devours its inhabitants,** apparently meaning that it starves them. Vs. 33, probably from P though many scholars attribute it to JE, expands the tradition that the **sons of Anak** (cf. vs. 22) were of unusual size by interpreting them to be descendants of the **Nephilim** (cf. Gen. 6:1-4). This probably represents a legendary or mythological tradition that the original inhabitants of Israel's land were more-than-human giants.

14:6-9. P portrays not only Caleb but also **Joshua** in a good light. This is in line with the emphasis of P on the unified movement of the tribes in the wilderness until the conquest led by Joshua and on the inclusion of the N tribes (Joshua) in the favor with which Yahweh looks on the S tribes (Caleb) in the JE account. It is also in line with a tendency to emphasize an orderly, divinely ordained chain of

Courtesy of the Oriental Institute, University of Chicago

Faience tile of a Hittite prisoner; note shaved face, long hair, and tattooing on the belly

command, since tradition denoted Joshua as Moses' valid lieutenant.

14:11-20. Once again the JE account stresses the divine approval of Moses and the power of his intercession as a prophet (cf. Ps. 99:6; Jer. 15:1). Moses' plea that Yahweh's reputation demands an action which seemingly violates his justice touches a problem present also to later prophets (cf. Ezek. 36; Isa. 48). The real basis of pardon is Yahweh's **steadfast love,** his abiding, loving loyalty to his covenant with his people (cf. Exod. 34:6-9).

14:21-38. The purpose of the story of the spies in both JE (vss. 21-25) and P (vss. 26-38) is to explain why tradition held that Israel, after escaping so successfully from Egypt, spent a generation wandering in the wilderness between Sinai and the Conquest. The answer here is that those who came out of Egypt failed to trust Yahweh to lead them to victory and were punished by being forbidden to enter the Promised Land, only Caleb as one who trusted (and Joshua, according to P) being permitted to survive and enter with the new generation. On **the way to the Red Sea** (vs. 25) see below on 21:4-9.

14:39-45. In contrast to the Calebites (see above on 13:30-31) other Israelite groups did not succeed in occupying the hill country of Judah (on Hormah cf. 21:1-3). Again there is indication of differences between elements of Israel at Kadesh and of a more disparate and gradual possession of Canaan than the finished biblical tradition recognizes.

D. Various Ritual Laws (15:1-41)

This section as a whole bears no perceptible relation to its context, and the 4 laws and an incident of which it consists bear no relation to one another. It probably represents additions to P which were included after the completion of that document simply because they were not found elsewhere in it. Why they were inserted at this point is hard to say, though vs. 1 provides a link with what has gone before.

15:1-16. The amounts of **fine flour** (ground from the hearts of the wheat kernels), **oil,** and **wine** to be offered with various kinds of sacrifices are specified (on **ephah** and **hin** see "Measures and Money," pp. 1283-85. Similar regulations are found in Ezek. 46:5-7, 11, 14. Vss. 14-16, in line with many other passages in P, assert that this law applies to the **stranger** or **sojourner** (resident alien) as well as to the native Israelite. Such passages indicate that even at a very late time Israel consisted of various elements and membership in the worshiping congregation was not simply hereditary.

15:17-21. The meaning of the key word in this instruction about an offering is unknown. **Coarse meal** is only a guess at translation.

15:22-31. Propitiatory offerings are provided for those breaking the law **unwittingly** (cf. Lev. 4:2-21). It should be noted, however, that sins committed **with a high hand** (i.e. intentionally, vs. 30) are not covered by any sacrifice. Properly understood, Israel's complicated system of sacrifices was not a crass ritualism but expressed the gracious provision of a forgiving God for those who sincerely sought to obey his law.

15:32-36. This narrative is apparently introduced

to underline the fact that there is no atonement for sins committed "with a high hand."

15:37-41. This provision, also found in Deut. 22:12, is still followed by Jews in the wearing of the tallith, or prayer shawl, with **tassels on the corners.** Vss. 39-40 give a rationale for a custom which undoubtedly originated in ancient superstition. Vs. 41 concludes the section with the divine assertion characteristic of the Holiness Code (Lev. 17-26).

E. RIGHTS AND DUTIES OF LEVITES AND PRIESTS (16:1–18:32)

The purpose of this section in P is seen in ch. 18, which outlines the duties of Levites and the sources of income reserved for priests and Levites. The stories in chs. 16–17 are illustrations of the exclusive claims of these orders to the tasks appointed them. While P (undoubtedly supplemented) is wholly responsible for chs. 17–18, a story from JE has been worked into the narrative in ch. 16.

16:1-50. *The Rebellion of Korah, Dathan, and Abiram.* That this ch. is composite in origin is indicated not only by internal repetitions and inconsistencies but by the fact that the 2 basic elements in it are elsewhere (27:3; Deut. 11:6) referred to separately. In its present composite form the story was well known (cf. 26:9-11; Ps. 106:16-18; Ecclus. 45:18; Jude 11). The JE element (vss. 1b-2a, 12-15, 25, 26b, 27b-34) seems to be the conflation of a J narrative about **On the son of Peleth** (vs. 1) with a brief E account of **Dathan and Abiram.** The P story of **Korah** (vss. 1a, 2b-11, 16-24, 26a, 27a, 35-50) is likewise itself composite; a supplement by a later P author or authors has changed a story of general rebellion into a challenge of priestly authority by the Levites.

16:1-2a. This introduction contains bits from all 4 sources. **Korah** from the basic P account is given a genealogy making him a Levite by the P supplement. **On,** if not a corruption in the text, is perhaps a fragment of the J story. **Dathan and Abiram** are identified as **sons of Reuben** who **rose up before Moses**—indicating that in the E source, and probably also in J, the revolt centers in the tribe of Reuben (cf. the tradition of loss of primacy of this tribe in Gen. 35:22; 49:3-4) and represents a challenge to Moses' authority as leader of the tribal league. The constitution of premonarchic Israel was that of an amphictyony, a sacral league of independent tribes to which the constituent tribes owed certain duties and by whose laws certain boundaries were set around their own independence. This story in JE recalls some occasion on which the tribe of Reuben refused to submit to the league's authority and perform its appointed duties.

16:2b-11. The basic P story has to do with a sort of "laymen's revolt" against the religious leadership of Moses and Aaron. Korah's centention is that **all the congregation are holy** and that sacred functions should therefore not be reserved to a few (vs. 3). Moses proposes a way to test the objection by having the **two hundred and fifty** rebels offer incense so that Yahweh can choose **the holy one** (vss. 4-7a). The P supplement has added vss. 7b-11 to change the basic P story of a revolt by **leaders** from all the tribes (vs. 2) into an account of the challenge of priestly authority by the Levites. Some contro-

versy, probably postexilic, in the long and complicated history of the Israelite priesthoods must underlie this version.

16:12-15. The JE story is here continued from vs. 2a. **Come up** is probably a technical term referring to the tribal obligation (see above on vss. 1-2a). **Put out the eyes** is a figurative expression for "deceive." Vs. 15 perhaps refers to a part of the story omitted by the editor.

16:16-24. In vss. 16-17, from the P supplement, the **company** of Korah is actually the same Hebrew word as **congregation** but is here applied only to the group of Levites joined with Korah in his rebellion. In the basic P story, on the other hand, **all the congregation,** i.e. all the Israelites except Moses and Aaron, are sympathetic to Korah, as shown by the intention of Yahweh to consume them all (vss. 19-20). In response to the intercession of Moses and Aaron, however, Yahweh tells them to instruct the people to leave so that they may be saved. **Dwelling** (vs. 24) means the tabernacle (cf. vs. 19); **of Korah, Dathan, and Abiram** is an editorial addition.

16:25-35. In these vss. the climaxes of the JE and P stories are confusingly interwoven. The P story of the assemblage before the tabernacle is continued in the words **And he said to the congregation** (vs. 26a), but Moses' warning has been omitted by the editor in favor of the similar order from the JE story (vs. 26b). The people leave the **dwelling,** i.e. the tabernacle (vs. 27a; **of Korah, Dathan, and Abiram** is another editorial addition), and those presuming to offer **incense** are **consumed** by fire (vs. 35). The JE story into which these bits have been inserted portrays a solemn gathering of the tribal league, with **all Israel** present (vs. 34) and Moses accompanied by the **elders of Israel** (vs. 25) as he confronts the offending Reubenite clans represented by Dathan and Abiram. At his word a miraculous divine judgment is wrought on them—**the ground opens its mouth, and swallows them up** (a misguided editorial insertion in vs. 32b includes Korah and his followers in this catastrophe so that they are killed twice; cf. vs. 35). This JE story thus goes back to very ancient times and institutions (also recalled in Judg. 19–20), in spite of its present position in a narrative with a different point to make.

16:36-40. This is a further addition by the P supplement. The **censers** of the rebels are made into a **covering for the altar** to act as a continual warning to anyone not a priest—e.g. a Levite—not to approach it.

16:41-50. In the conclusion of the basic P story **all the congregation** continue the complaint begun by Korah and are saved from total annihilation by Yahweh only when Moses and Aaron again intervene. In contrast to the offering of the 250 laymen the **incense** carried by Aaron is effective to halt the **plague** and save Israel. The story thus drives home the reservation of sacred acts for Moses and Aaron as representatives of the Levites (cf. the story with a similar point in I Sam. 13:5-15). It is typical of the P viewpoint.

17:1-13. *Authentication of Aaron's Authority.* The close connection of this story with the P narrative in ch. 16 is evident—the Hebrew Bible even begins ch. 17 with 16:36. This story must come from P itself rather than from the later supplement in ch. 16, for

91

its point is the vindication of the Levitical claims, not of the priesthood in distinction from the Levites (cf. vss. 3, 8). Here, in contrast with chs. 1; 26, Levi is apparently reckoned as one of the 12 tribes, not as a separate caste. Thus P maintains a confusion present in early traditions (cf. Gen. 29:31–30:24; 49).

18:1-32. Duties and Income of Levites and Priests. More logically connected with the narrative than many laws in Num., this ch. forms a conclusion to chs. 16–17 by giving specific regulations concerning Levites and priests. It is a valuable source of information for compiling a history of the Israelite priesthoods.

18:1-7. In view of the preceding stories it is provided that only the priests shall directly approach the sanctuary, in order that the rest of Israel may be saved from perishing. The Levites, in accord with postexilic practice, are assistants to the priests.

18:8-20. The priests and their families are to be maintained from the various offerings to Yahweh. As he has allotted the land as the **portion** of the tribes, so he allots what is offered to him as the priests' portion. Various regulations to be observed in the practice of this allotment are set down. On the **redemption** of the **first-born** see above on 3:40-51.

18:21-24. The **tithe** (cf. Lev. 27:30-33; Deut. 14:22-29; 26:12-15) is to provide the income for the Levites, who like the priests have no landed inheritance.

18:25-32. The Levites must give to the priests a tithe of their income from the people's tithe—**a tithe of the tithe** (cf. Neh. 10:38).

F. Purification of Uncleanness from Contact with the Dead (19:1-22)

This ch. is from P, in part probably from a supplement to the basic work. Vss. 1-10, 20-22 provide for a ritual washing in a solution the basic ingredient of which is the ashes of a red heifer, while vss. 11-19 describe the various ways in which ritual uncleanness is contracted through contact with the dead. The ch. represents late priestly regulation of a practice which must have been very ancient. The belief that pollution results from contact with a corpse is common in many cultures. Aside from the conjecture that the large number of deaths reported in chs. 16–18 brought the subject to an editor's mind, it is difficult to see why the ch. is inserted at this point. For other discussion of the subject see Lev. 5:2; 11:8, 24-28; 21:1-4, 10-11; Num. 5:2; 6:6-12; 9:6-14. Cf. also 31:19-24.

G. End of the Stay at Kadesh (20:1-29)

This ch. marks the transition from the stay in the wilderness to the journey through Transjordan to the point where the tribes enter Canaan under Joshua.

20:1. The Death of Miriam. In spite of the tradition that Israel "wandered" in the wilderness for 40 years after the events of chs. 13–14, the narrative is almost completely silent about what happened during such a period. It is P that holds this theory, and its difficulties may be the reason P cites here only **the first month** without specifying the year. On the other hand, since P supposes that Israel only now arrives in the **wilderness of Zin,** the region in

which Kadesh is located (see map, p. 93) some scholars suggest that an editor may have omitted the year to avoid contradicting the JE account of an earlier arrival in this area. The older sources, J in particular, remember Kadesh as the center of Israel's life all through this period. It is for this reason that the geography of chs. 1–20 is confused. The latter half of this vs., naming **Kadesh** and reporting the death of **Miriam,** of whom P has not recounted any incidents, is probably from JE.

20:2-13. Water from the Rock. The coming to the wilderness of Zin is no doubt the reason for the inclusion here of this incident associated with Kadesh, of which a JE version is found in Exod. 17:1-7. This account is mostly from P but seems to contain some fragments from a J story. As in the earlier version, the name of a spring, **Meribah** ("contention"), is accounted for by this ancient tradition—another indication that controversy at Kadesh resulted in some kind of division there among the Israelites. The wording of vss. 12-13 suggests that originally the story also accounted for the name Kadesh, the root of which is **sanctify** or **holy.** But for P it serves as an explanation of the fact that both Moses and Aaron died without entering the promised land. The obscurity of this explanation is due to the attempts of later editors to soften criticism of such holy men. It may be that **did not believe** in vs. 12 refers to the question of vs. 10, which was perhaps originally addressed to God.

20:14-22a. Rebuff by Edom. This JE narrative begins the account of Israel's trials and battles on the journey from Kadesh to the Jordan by recounting how the Edomites refused passage through their territory. **Your brother** indicates Israel's consciousness of kinship with Edom (cf. Gen. 25:21-34; 27; 36), but the story also bespeaks the traditional enmity between the two. **The King's Highway** (vs. 17; see color map 4) is the road from Damascus to the Gulf of Aqabah in use from time immemorial, known still

Courtesy of Herbert G. May

In the Edomite Desert; view of Wadi Hismeh (foreground) at S end of Edomite plateau as seen from the King's Highway

by that name in Arabic (cf. 21:22; Deut. 2:27). Vs. 22a is the transition in JE to the incidents in ch. 21.

20:22b-29. Death of Aaron. This section of P concludes with an account of Aaron's death and his replacement by his son **Eleazar.** P locates **Mount Hor on the border of the land of Edom,** and tradition locates it near Petra, but the antiquity and obscurity

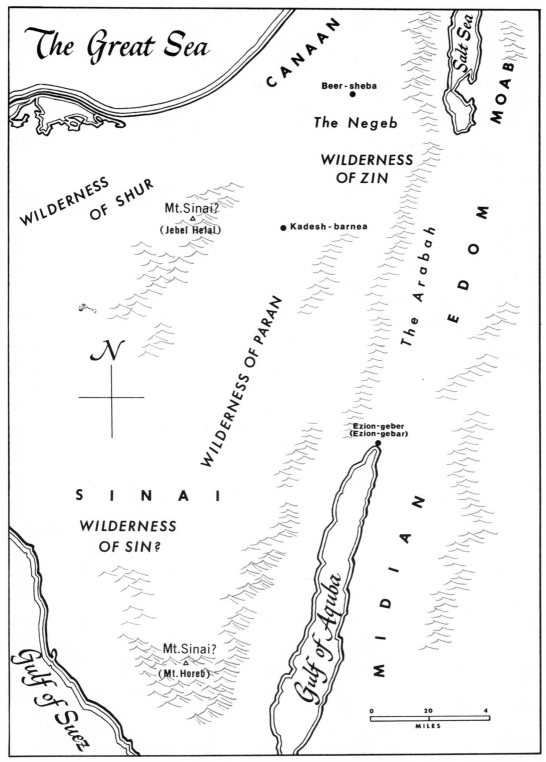

of the tradition make exactitude impossible. P takes no interest in Israel's subsequent adventures on the march to Canaan, its continuation of the narrative being found in the note in 22:1.

III. THE OCCUPATION OF TRANSJORDAN (21:1–36:13)

Entry into Canaan from the S having failed and permission to pass through Edom having been de-

93

nied, Israel skirts Edom and Moab through the desert to the S and E and then conquers an Amorite kingdom across the Jordan from central Palestine and the kingdom of Bashan just to its N. Num. closes with Israel in the **plains of Moab** in that conquered territory. The narrative presupposes that the Moabite kingdom is E of the Dead Sea, with its N border marked by the river Arnon and the plains of Moab actually lying in the territory of the Amorite kingdom. Here as elsewhere the narrative is composite, the result of the preservation, modification, and combination of various traditions through more than 7 cents. Even the earliest written document is some 2 cents. younger than the events here reported.

A. THE BATTLE AT HORMAH (21:1-3)

This isolated piece of tradition from JE does not belong with the main thread of the narrative in this section. Probably it originated with the group that entered Palestine directly from the S (cf. Judg. 1:17, where important differences in associated place names complicate a simple equation of the 2 places). **Arad** apparently lay between Kadesh and Hebron, and 14:45 locates **Hormah** in the same area. Its name is explained here by its connection with **utterly destroy,** the technical term for laying a place under a sacred ban.

B. FROM EDOM'S BORDER TO THE REGION OF MOAB (21:4-20)

In a short space, and with only 2 incidents briefly recounted, the Israelites are brought by JE from the far S desert around inhabited Transjordan to the area adjacent to central Palestine.

21:4-9. *The Bronze Serpent.* The opening words of vs. 4 are from a P editor, connecting this part of the finished narrative with 20:22a-29, but the account itself is from JE and continues from 20:14-21. The Israelites are setting out from Kadesh (20:16) to **go around the land of Edom** to the S before going E and N (see color map 4). Thus **the way to the Red Sea** obviously means the caravan route from Kadesh to the head of the Gulf of Aqaba (cf. 14:25; Deut. 1:40; 2:1; I Kings 9:26). The same Hebrew name, lit. "Sea [or "Lake"] of Reeds," elsewhere designates the body of water miraculously crossed by Israel in escaping from Egypt (see comment on Exod. 13:18a). Its use here indicates that at the time of this writing the 2 bodies were thought to be the same, i.e. that already the exodus tradition had been interpreted as describing a crossing of some part of the arm of the ocean between Africa and Arabia (cf. 33:10-11). The English "Red Sea" comes from the LXX, where the Greek name for these waters replaced the Hebrew term. Though the incident here described displays motifs present in many of the stories in Num. (the people's complaints, Yahweh's punishment of them, relief at Moses' intercession), it has been preserved to account for the **bronze serpent** in Solomon's temple (cf. II Kings 18:4; Wisd. Sol. 16:1-7).

21:10-20. *Progress Through Transjordan.* This section seems to consist of bits and pieces from various sources and traditions. Its list of stations on Israel's trek is not as complete as the one in ch. 33 and is rather confused because of the combination of sources. It could be derived from lists of pilgrimage sites existing in the period of the judges and into the monarchy. The confusion indicates that the movements of the Israelites were not as unified as the finished narrative assumes.

21:10-13. Vss. 10-11a about **Oboth** and **Iye-abarim** are apparently a misplaced duplication of a bit from P (cf. 33:44-45). Vss. 11b-13, probably from E, seem to view the route of Israel as skirting Edom on the S and E (vs. 4), then N through the desert E of **Moab** (vs. 11b) across the **Zered,** which flows into the SE end of the Dead Sea, to a stop somewhere near the **Arnon,** which flows into the E side of the Dead Sea (see color maps 4, 5). **Other side** probably is to be understood from the viewpoint of the author in central Palestine, i.e. on the S side of the Arnon, in Moab.

21:14-15. This very ancient fragment of a poem is cited to show that the Arnon was indeed the border of Moab in a much earlier time, for when the context was written Moab extended farther to the N. The poem is said to come from the **Book of the Wars of the LORD.** Like the Book of Jashar (Josh. 10:13; II Sam. 1:18), this must have been an ancient collection of poetry. The wars of Yahweh were sacral affairs for the tribal league (cf. Deut. 20; Judg. 5; I Sam. 18:17; 25:28), and this collection must have been a sacred book of premonarchic Israel. **Ar** (cf. vs. 28) was evidently a major city of Moab on the S bank of the Arnon but its site has not yet been identified.

21:16-18c. Another ancient piece of poetry is this song at the digging of a **well.** Vs. 16 preserves a tradition that the song originated in the time of Moses when water was sorely needed in the desert. **Beer** simply means "well" and is too general a term to permit any location of a place.

21:18d-20. This fragment of itinerary records Israel's movement N into Sihon's kingdom. **Mattanah** has been identified with El-Medeiyineh E of the Dead Sea. **Nahaliel** could denote either a stream (Wadi Zerka Main?) or a town. **Bamoth** simply means "high places," but probably refers here to some specific place (cf. 22:41; Josh. 13:17). None of these places is mentioned in ch. 33, and their identification is uncertain. Again there is reason to believe that different elements of later united Israel brought traditions of different kinds and from different places into the common heritage. Vs. 20 agrees with 33:47 in locating the final stop in Sihon's territory in the headlands of the Moabite plateau (**Pisgah** and Nebo; see comment on Deut. 3:23-29 and color map 5) opposite the N end of the Dead Sea. **Desert** is probably a proper noun, Jeshimon, referring to the waste area of the Jordan where it enters the Dead Sea (cf. I Sam. 23:19, 24; 26:1, 3).

C. CONQUEST OF THE AMORITE KINGDOM (21:21-31)

Israel's earliest possession was the territory associated with the tribes of Gad and Reuben, bordered by the **Arnon** on the S, the Jordan on the W, the **Jabbok** on the N, and the **Ammonites** on the E (vs. 24). This territory had been controlled by **Sihon** from his city-kingdom of **Heshbon** (vs. 26; see color map 5), having been won by him from the Moabites (vs. 26), so that part of his territory could continue to be called **the region of Moab** (vs. 20). On **Amorites** see above on 13:22-29.

21:21-25. Israel's request to Sihon is described as like the one to Edom (cf. 20:17). The exact location of **Jahaz,** site of the decisive battle (vs. 23), is not known, but other references indicate that it was near the desert to the E (cf. Deut. 2:32; I Chron. 6:78; Jer. 48:21). The Hebrew text of vs. 24, that the Ammonite boundary was "strong," has been defended as showing why Sihon's territory extended no farther to the E; but the RSV **Jazer,** following the LXX, must be correct (cf. vs. 32; Josh. 13:25; Isa. 16:8-9; Jer. 48:32; I Macc. 5:8). Jazer was evidently a few miles W of the Ammonite capital, Rabbah, now Amman (see color map 5).

21:26-31. Vs. 26 betrays that this narrative has to do with more than a mere incident on the way to Canaan. Like many of the Pentateuchal traditions, this one undoubtedly belonged originally to only one part of the Israelite tribal league. It nevertheless was revered by Israel as the record of the first victorious step in possessing a land of her own. She took over an ancient song in praise of the city of Heshbon (vss. 27-30), celebrating a victory over Moab, just as she later took over songs praising Jerusalem (cf. Pss. 46; 48), and her literature again and again recalls this victory (e.g. Deut. 31:4; Josh. 2:10; Pss. 135:11; 136:19). On **Ar** see above on vss. 14-15. **Chemosh** was the god of the Moabites, here said to have let his children be defeated. **Dibon** and **Medeba** were between Heshbon and the Arnon (see color map 5).

D. Conquest of Bashan (21:32-35)

Apparently much of Transjordan was held by **Amorites.** Vs. 32 records the conquest of Jazer (see above on vss. 21-25), perhaps another city-kingdom and its territory. Vss. 33-35 record the conquest of **Og the king of Bashan.** Og was apparently another Amorite (cf. Deut. 31:4; Josh. 2:10), and Bashan lay E and N of the Jordan. **Edrei** lay in the extreme NE of Israel's territory. This account, also originally concerning a part of Israel, seems to have been incorporated into Num. from Deut. 3:1-2.

E. The Balaam Stories (22:1-24:25)

The narrative now turns back to the Moabites, who occupied the remaining territory to the E of the Jordan. The derivation of the stories in Num. from the traditions of various groups is manifest in the geographical confusion. While it has been stated that Sihon's kingdom extended S to the Arnon (21:24; cf. 22:36), some of the incidents recounted in this section as occurring in Moabite territory (23:14, 28) are definitely located N of the Arnon.

Moab's defeat is not really recounted but assumed (proleptically? — 24:15-19 refers to David) in the famous and fascinating stories about the diviner Balaam, unlike anything else in Num. Very ancient material from preliterary oral tradition is preserved here, and its popularity is evident not only in the fullness of the parallel J and E narratives but also in their agreement on the main points of the story despite differences in details. The evidences of the interwoven strands are rather clear even in the En-

glish translation, and except in a few passages the narrative threads can be traced. P is represented in this section only by 22:1, which is the continuation of 20:22b-29; 21:4a. Later allusions to Balaam in P (31:8, 16; see below on 25:6-18) reveal a quite different tradition about him.

In the view of E a non-Israelite would not be acquainted with the divine name Yahweh revealed to Moses (Exod. 3:13-15), and accordingly E often uses Elohim ("God") in the narrative portions (e.g. 22:9-10, 38; 23:4, 27), whereas J, as in Gen., regularly identifies the God who speaks to Balaam as Yahweh ("the LORD"). That this distinction is not consistent throughout may be due to the editor. It should be noted, however, that Balaam's oracles all contain both divine names, with Elohim predominating. These pronouncements are evidently very ancient poems which J and E have incorporated in their accounts.

22:2-21. Balak Sends for Balaam. Though closely intertwined in this part of the story, the J and E portrayals can for the most part be recognized. According to the J account the Moabite king Balak sends **messengers** (vs. 5) to summon the diviner Balaam to **curse** Israel (vs. 6). These **elders of Moab** bring **fees for divination** (vs. 7) and promise **great honor** (vs. 17), but Balaam declares that even for a **house full of silver and gold** (vs. 18) he cannot disobey Yahweh. Though the editor has evidently omitted part of the J narrative following this, we may infer that after the messengers leave the thought of the fee becomes too great a temptation for Balaam to resist (cf. II Pet. 2:15; Jude 11).

In E the representatives sent by Balak are **princes of Moab** (vs. 8), and the inducement they offer is not mentioned — in this account Balaam does only what God commands. Balaam keeps the princes overnight while he receives divine instruction not to go and then sends them back to Balak (vss. 8-10, 12-14). When Balak dispatches a larger and more honorable delegation of princes (vss. 15-16), Balaam keeps them waiting also until the divine word comes to him **at night,** making clear that he may go to Balak but only to speak what God commands (vss. 19-20). Accordingly Balaam sets out for Moab with the princes (vs. 21).

22:4. Here and in vs. 7 (where the phrase may be a harmonizing editorial insertion) **elders of Midian** are associated with Moab in sending for Balaam, but no further mention of them occurs. Such an association was entirely possible, as Midian ranged over the S and E desert (cf. Gen. 36:35), but the hanging reference is curious. It may have come in under the influence of 31:8, or may be a remnant of something more prominent in one of the sources.

22:5. Balaam is said to have lived **at Pethor, which is near the River** (i.e. the Euphrates), **in the land of Amaw.** Pethor apparently is a site in Upper Mesopotamia where the Sajur joins the Euphrates, near Carchemish (see color map 2), and Amaw has been found in inscriptions as a name for this region. This area is some 400 miles from Moab. On the other hand instead of Amaw several Hebrew manuscripts and most ancient versions read "Ammonites," which would put Balaam's home much nearer Moab; and in 23:7 he says he has come from **Aram** (i.e. Syria). It has been suggested that Amaw may be a scribe's harmonizing of the J and E accounts. At any rate the traditions have Balaam come from some place in the NE.

22:22-35. The Talking Ass. This colorful account seems to be entirely from J except in vs. 35, where the editor has inserted an adaptation of E material, leaving the original J conclusion of the episode in some doubt. There is some uncertainty about the original beginning also (see above on vss. 2-21), since in vs. 18 Balaam has refused the offer of Balak's messengers, declaring that he must obey Yahweh's command, but in vs. 22 he is setting out with his **two servants,** apparently after the messengers have left and without the permission of Yahweh. It is clear enough, however, that he is strikingly reminded that he must obey and declare the word which Yahweh gives to him. The theme also present in Jonah, that God has his way in spite of the recalcitrance of his spokesman, informs this whole story. It arises out of Israel's conviction of her election and accounts for Balaam's prominence in later tradition (cf. Deut. 23:3-5; Josh. 24:9-10; Neh. 13:1-3; Mic. 6:5).

22:36-40. Meeting of Balaam and Balak. This part of the story is hard to follow because of the fusion of J and E, which here cannot be isolated with certainty. The **city of Moab** (vs. 36) probably means Ar (see above on 21:14-15) since it is said to be on the Arnon, though the rest of the story, at least in the E account, seems to take place farther N near Mt. Pisgah (cf. 23:14). **Kiriath-huzoth** is otherwise unknown.

22:41-23:12. Balaam's First Oracle. This part of the story seems to be entirely from E. The exact location of **Bamoth-baal** (lit. "high places of Baal"; cf. Josh. 13:17) is not known, but it must have been in the mountainous area E and N of the Dead Sea. The point is that the diviner is being brought in sight of those he is to curse. Vss. 1-4 relate preparations calculated to dispose God favorably toward the cursing. In some ancient versions Balak alone offers the sacrifices in vs. 2, and it has been suggested that originally vs. 4b may have followed this as his report to Balaam of what he has done. The poem of vss. 7-10 must be at least as old as the 10th cent. It bespeaks Israel's fierce conviction of the involvement of divine revelation in her own historical destiny—note esp. vs. 9cd. Vss. 11-12 (cf. vs. 5) re-emphasize the chief motif of this story, that regardless of all efforts to the contrary Balaam must speak the word of Yahweh.

23:13-26. Balaam's 2nd Oracle. The humor of Balak's repeated frantic efforts to obtain a curse on Israel in both the J and E versions is no doubt one reason for the story's popularity. This portion seems to be a continuation of the E account. Balak takes Balaam to another place where he can **see** the people of Israel (vs. 13; cf. 22:41); perhaps this originally read "may see them all" but was modified by the editor to prepare for the J account in ch. 24. **Zophim** (lit. "watchers") is not otherwise known and may be a common noun here. On **Pisgah** see above on 21:18d-20. In the poem vss. 18-21 are clearly an ancient companion to vss. 7-10, but doubts have been raised about vss. 22-24. Vs. 23 is obscure (**against** in the first 2 lines probably should be translated "in"), and vss. 22, 24 largely duplicate 24:8-9.

Vss. 25-26 bring to a close the Balaam story of E (though perhaps 24:25 is its final sentence) with a repetition of its theme.

23:27-24:13. Balaam's 3rd Oracle. The remainder of the narrative is taken primarily from J. Vss. 27-30 seem to be largely a composition of the editor to fit the new source into the pattern of what has preceded. On **Peor** see below on 25:1-5. The narrative which follows is, like that in ch. 23, the framework for an ancient poem, found in vss. 5-9, with vss. 3-4 as a poetic prelude. Vs. 7 seems, however, to place this poem in the time of the monarchy. The reference to **Agag** is obscure, as the Amalekite king of I Sam. 15 was no model of royal power. On vss. 8-9 see above on 23:13-16. The conversation in vss. 10-13 refers to the beginning of the story (cf. 22:17-18), and emphasizes that in J also Balaam speaks, not for himself, but for Yahweh.

24:14-25. Balaam's 4th Oracle. The J narrative continues with Balaam pronouncing a farewell oracle that Balak has not asked for, in which the future conquest of Moab by Israel is predicted. Vss. 15-19 (esp. vs. 17) clearly glorify the monarchy and are a prophecy after the event. It may be no accident that both this poem and that in vss. 5-9 occur in the framework of J, the Jerusalemite source in which the Davidic monarchy is seen as the fulfillment of God's promise. It may also be that the reason the story about Moab is the framework for prophecy, whereas the stories about the Amorites tell of conquest, is that Israel subdued Moab (as well as Edom, vs. 18) only in the time of David. **Sons of Sheth** (lit. "tumult," or perhaps "pride"; cf. Isa. 16:6) seems to be simply a poetic designation of the Moabites. **Seir** is the mountain range covering most of the land of Edom.

24:20-25:24. These 3 brief oracles cursing other nations seem to have little relation to the context, and many scholars consider them a later insertion. The curse on **Amalek** is in line with tradition (cf. Exod. 17:8-16; I Sam. 15). The curse on the **Kenite** is harder to understand since the Kenites are usually pictured as friends and allies of Israel. The reference of vs. 22b to Assyria's capturing them is obscure, and the text is difficult to translate. Our distance from these lines makes it impossible to know what their meaning was. The curse on **Asshur** (i.e. Assyria) **and Eber** (cf. Gen. 10:21-25; its association with Assyria is puzzling) must have originated in the 8th or 7th cent. It seems to predict a defeat of the Assyrians by **Kittim** (i.e. Cyprus, though the name later was applied generally to maritime peoples of the Mediterranean). Again the meaning is irrecoverable.

F. Apostasy at Peor (25:1-18)

This ch. recounts 2 originally separate pieces of tradition, one from JE (vss. 1-5), the other from P (vss. 6-15). They have been linked together by a P editor in vss. 16-18.

25:1-5. Baal of Peor. Israel is now in **Shittim,** or Abel-Shittim (33:49), the place in Transjordan from which was made the final move across the Jordan (cf. Josh. 2:1; 3:1; Mic. 6:5). Its location is not certain, but it must have lain in the territory taken from Sihon. The appearance of the **daughters of**

Moab is evidence that boundaries fluctuated and that formerly dominant elements would remain in a conquered territory (as Canaanites did when Israel dominated Palestine). The incident recounted here previews the pattern repeated in the stories in Judg. —Israel's apostasy to the gods of the land. The meaning here is that Moabite women led their Israelite paramours into worship of the local deities. **Baal** is a general title meaning "lord." **Peor** here may refer to a mountain near Pisgah and Nebo (cf. 23:27-28), or it may mean a city named Beth-peor (cf. Deut. 4:46; Josh. 13:20). The Moabites may have identified the god of Peor with their national god, Chemosh. Two traditions of the punishment meted out to the offenders seem to be represented in vss. 4, 5. The incident is frequently cited as an example of apostasy (Deut. 4:3; Josh. 22:17; Ps. 106:28; Hos. 9:10; I Cor. 10:8).

25:6-18. Phinehas' Zeal. The combination of the JE story in vss. 1-5 with this P story has resulted in the mutilation of the end of the first and the beginning of the 2nd. There is no account of the carrying out of the punishment commanded in vss. 4-5, and vss. 6 (Israel **weeping at . . . the tent of meeting**) and 8-9 require some account of the origin of the **plague.** 31:16 hints at a lost beginning of this story in which Balaam was responsible for the introduction of Midianite women into Israel that resulted in disloyalty to Yahweh punished by a plague (cf. Rev. 2:14).

25:6-13. This story is typical of P in accounting for a sacral institution by narrating an incident in justification of it. Phinehas, identified as 3rd in line in the Aaronic priesthood (vs. 7), by his quick action against an Israelite who has married a Midianite woman (vss. 6, 8) both stays the plague (vss. 8b-9; cf. Ps. 106:30-31; Ecclus. 45:23-24; I Macc. 2:26, 54) and obtains a **perpetual** priestly status for his family (vss. 10-13). Though connected by P with the Aaronic priesthood, Phinehas seems to represent an originally N and very important priesthood (cf. the notice of a town belonging to the family in Josh. 24:33 and the traditions in Num. 31:6; Josh. 22:10-34; and Judg. 20:27-28; cf. also Ezra 8:2; I Esd. 5:5; 8:29) later subsumed in the Aaronic line.

25:14-18. The typical P genealogical interest shows in vss. 14-15. The editorial addition in vss. 16-18 connects the 2 stories of this ch. with the account in ch. 31 of the holy war against Midian in which Phinehas again leads in vengeance.

G. The 2nd Census (26:1-65)

The reason for a repetition of what was done in chs. 1-2 is that the wilderness period is now at an end and Israel is about to take possession of her land. The tribes are to be allotted territory according to their size (vss. 52-66), and so P records another census. The total number of adult male Israelites is given here as 601,730 (vs. 51) as compared with 603,550 in 2:32. As in chs. 1-2, the data here must come from records of some period during the monarchy, and the listing of only men capable of military service may indicate the purpose of the census. The Levites are numbered separately as before (vss. 57-62; cf. 1:47; chs. 3-4). The section closes with the note that only **Caleb** and **Joshua**

survive of those numbered in the first census (vss. 63-65; cf. 14:26-35). P thus ties things up according to its theories.

H. A Law Concerning Inheritance (27:1-11)

Logically following the census preparatory to the division of Canaan among the tribes, this section makes the point—as usual P backs up a law with narrative—that a man's property (land) may be inherited by a daughter if no son survives. Further legislation connected with this situation is found in ch. 36, and the execution of Moses' verdict is recorded in Josh. 17:3-4. Behind this lies the Israelite conviction that a family's land was its gift from God, from which the family should not be separated (cf. I Kings 21; Isa. 5:8; Micah 2:1-2; also the law of jubilee, Lev. 25:8-17).

I. The Selection of Joshua (27:12-23)

Referring to the cryptic tradition in 20:2-13, P here relates how Moses, having viewed the land he is not to enter, requests Yahweh to designate his successor before he dies. **Abarim** is the general term for the headlands of the plateau of Moab at the N end of the Dead Sea, and Deut. 32:49; 34:1 designate Nebo as the particular mountain associated with Moses' last days (see comment on Deut. 3:23-29). Actually the P material now in Deut. 34 must have followed this section directly at one time, before supplementers added the bulk of the material now found in chs. 28-36, and before the other Pentateuchal sources were worked into P.

The basic tradition about Joshua is preserved in Josh. 1-12. He was a hero of the N tribes in the sacred wars in which central Palestine was won, and the phraseology of vss. 17, 21b preserves the memory of his military leadership. Historically it is doubtful that his connection with Moses was as close as the Pentateuch now pictures it, if it existed at all. But already in the earliest written sources the history that led to the united Israel of the period of the judges and the monarchy is read in the light of the later unity, and P carries the process to its final conclusion with a concern for orderly and valid succession (cf. vss. 19, 23 and the role of the priesthood in vss. 19, 21, 22).

The account makes clear that no successor is Moses' equal—note **some of your authority** (vs. 20). Whereas Moses has spoken with God directly (cf. 12:8, JE), Joshua is to receive divine direction through priestly manipulation of the **Urim,** the sacred lot (vs. 21; cf. Exod. 28:30; Lev. 8:8). P thus makes priestly authority final.

J. Public Offerings (28:1-29:40)

From a supplement to P, this section treats of the sacrifices to be made by the whole community, as opposed to private offerings of individuals as in ch. 15. Its subject is not treated elsewhere in the Pentateuch, but is in Ezek. 45:18–46:15. The calendar of sacred seasons to which the regulations apply is paralleled in Lev. 23. The section, coming as it does from the priestly school, must reflect the practice of the postexilic temple, though the practices it outlines go back to ancient custom. The calendar is essentially that still followed in Judaism. **Due seasons** are important to P, which holds in Gen. 1:14 that the heavenly bodies, rather than being objects for superstitious reverence as among Israel's neighbors, exist to mark the proper occasions for worship of Israel's God.

Definite regulations for sacrifices are provided for the following occasions: daily, 28:3-8; sabbath, 28:9-10; new moon, 28:11-15; passover and unleavened bread, 28:16-25; weeks (Pentecost), 28:26-31; new year, 29:1-6; day of atonement, 29:7-11 (cf. Lev. 16); booths, 29:12-38. The paradox of a new year observance **on the first day of the seventh month** reflects the fact that in the postexilic period the Jews used the Babylonian calendar, which began in the spring. The conclusion of the section makes clear that these provisions are for public, not private offerings (29:39-40).

K. Vows of Women (30:1-16)

While vows made by men are binding once made (vs. 2), among women the same rule applies only to the widowed and divorced (vs. 9). The vows of unmarried women living in their father's houses are subject to the approval of their fathers (vss. 3-5), as those of married women are subject to the approval of their husbands (vss. 6-8, 10-15). The regulations reflect the fact that in a society in which women have little legal status (but cf. vs. 9 with 27:1-11; ch. 36). Regulations for vows are set down elsewhere (cf. 6:1-21; Lev. 5:4-6; 27:1-33; Deut. 23:1-23), but only here are women's vows treated. The section is a supplement to P.

L. Annihilation of Midian (31:1-54)

Though closely related to Israel (Gen. 25:2) and to Moses (Exod 2:15; Num. 10:29-32) according to JE, the Midianites are enemies of Israel in Transjordan according to P (25:6-18; cf. JE in 22:4, 7). The present chapter is a P supplement's largely fictional account of how the command of 25:16-18 was carried out before Moses' death. The list of Midianite kings in vs. 8 (cf. Josh. 13:21-22) undoubtedly goes back to authentic tradition. On **Phinehas** (vs. 6) and **Balaam** (vss. 8, 16) see above on 25:6-18. Vss. 19-54 betray the real purpose of the story—to show how legal provisions for the purification of warriors (vss. 19-24) worked out in practice.

M. Settlement of the Transjordan Tribes (32:1-42)

This ch. has defied any generally agreed analysis into sources. Certainly part of it represents the conclusion of the JE narrative in Num., the continuation of which is found in Deut. 34. P elements are also present. It may be that an editor has recast the narrative on the basis of JE and P rather than merely combining them.

Behind the account lies the fact that the elements of later united Israel by which Transjordan was occupied were not really a part of the groups by which central Palestine proper was won. Yet when premonarchic Israel was established in the land those elements were parts of the 12-tribe league, obligated to go to war on behalf of their brethren and of Yahweh (note the picture of Gad in Deut. 33:21).

Since the past that had led to united Israel was viewed as a common, unified history, this account came to be given of the relation of the Transjordan tribes to their Palestinian colleagues. Not sheer fiction, it may represent the entry of the Transjordan tribes into the league (see Intro.).

32:1-5. Apparently **Jazer** (see above on 21:21-25) was the city marking the E boundary of the territory of **Gilead,** which was and is famous for its **cattle** (vs. 1; cf. Song of S. 4:1; 6:5; Mic. 7:14). The towns listed in vs. 3 were authentic places in this area (see color map 5).

32:6-32. Underneath this discussion lies authentic remembrance of the duties incumbent on members of the old tribal league, from which frequent allusions to the holy war come (cf. e.g. Judg. 5). Vss. 6-13 recall elements in the tradition as recounted by both JE and P in chs. 13-14.

32:39-42. These vss. seem to contain a separate piece of tradition from that in vss. 1-38 concerning Reuben and Gad. **Machir** apparently had a complicated history, being listed as a clan of Manasseh in 26:29 and as a full part of the tribal federation in Palestine proper in Judg. 5:14. Possibly incorporating Aramean elements (cf. I Chr. 2:21-23), Machir came to be dominant in NE Transjordan to the extent that Gilead could be characterized as Machir's son (e.g. 26:29; 27:1; 36:1). **Jair** (vs. 41) is associated by tradition with Manasseh, as is Machir (cf. I Chr. 2:23); and the fact that a place in Gilead bore the name **Nobah** (vs. 42; cf. Judg. 8:11) indicates that this was a clan associated with Machir. These vss. recall a tradition only on the fringe of Israel's history, but they indicate how complicated that history was.

N. A Summary (33:1-49)

Elements of the traditions preserved both in JE and in P are present in this résumé of Israel's progress from Egypt to Canaan, the chief point of which is to list the 40 **stages,** or stopping places, along the way (cf. the tradition of 40 years). In its final form the ch. must be a supplement produced by the P school. In addition to JE and P the author probably drew on another source going back, through a literary and oral history not now traceable, to cultic practice of premonarchic times in which Israel reenacted the tradition of her years of wandering in the wilderness. In its present form the section is dominated by P style and interest—e.g. the chronological framework in vss. 3, 38-39.

In the introduction (vss. 1-4) the traditions in vss. 2 and 4a are peculiar to this ch. Likewise lacking in any of the other Pentateuchal sources are 17 of the 40 stations listed: **Dophkah** (vs. 12), **Alush** (vs. 13), **Rithmah** (vs. 18), **Rimmon-perez** (vs. 19), **Libnah** (vs. 20), **Rissah** (vs. 21), **Kehelathah** (vs. 22), **Mount Shepher** (vs. 23), **Haradah** (vs. 24), **Makheloth** (vs. 25), **Tahath** (vs. 26), **Terah** (vs. 27), **Mithkah** (vs. 28), **Hashmonah** (vs. 29), **Abronah** (vs. 34), **Zalmonah** (vs. 41), and **Punon** (vs. 42). Most of the places cannot be located.

O. Israel's Landed Inheritance (33:50-34:29)

Israel's point of view and her theology were concrete and not abstract. What modern man would call spiritual things were manifest for her in visible, tangible realities. Thus in all the strata of the OT the land of Canaan (Palestine) is Israel's **inheritance** from Yahweh, the outward sign of his choice of Israel, of his continuing sovereignty over her, and of his power to work his will. All this is what lies behind the present section, cast in the form of instruction to Israel through Moses on the eve of her entry into Canaan, and of the numerous other places stressing the land. This section comes from a P supplement, but ancient tradition underlies it.

33:50-53. The non-Israelite inhabitants of the land and their sanctuaries and cult objects are to be eliminated. The point of this—and it underlies the ancient institution of the holy war—is that no concession can be made by which Yahweh's sovereignty over the inheritance exclusively designated for his people would be compromised. Deut. and Judg. are dominated by this motif.

33:54-56. The distribution of the land to tribes and families is to be by lot. Since this process involved no human decision, it meant that the land of an Israelite family was its own in a way that was rooted in Israel's theology. Even kings could not alter it (cf. I Kings 21).

34:1-15. These vss. designate the boundaries of Israel's land W of the Jordan (cf. Ezek. 47:13-20). That the picture must come from P in postexilic times is indicated by its idealistic nature and by its omission of a division of Transjordan. The S boundary (vss. 3-5; cf. Josh. 15:1-4; Ezek. 47:19) corresponds to what was Judah's S extremity, and goes some distance beyond the traditional line at Beersheba (cf. Deut. 11:24). The W boundary is naturally the Mediterranean (vs. 6; cf. Josh. 15:12; Ezek. 47:20); actually Israel never substantially occupied the coast. The N boundary runs from some point on the Mediterranean up into Syria (vss. 7-9; cf. Ezek. 47:15-17), and probably reflects David's conquests extending beyond Dan, the traditional N terminus. The E boundary is marked by the E shores of the Sea of **Chinnereth** (Galilee) and the Dead Sea and the Jordan (vss. 10-12; cf. Ezek. 47:18).

34:13-15. To harmonize with ch. 32 it is pro-vided that the foregoing boundaries apply only to the tribes W of the Jordan. In vs. 15 the author forgets that Moses is on the E side of the Jordan.

34:16-29. Tribal representatives are designated to superintend the division of the land in accord with the census procedure of 1:1-15.

P. LEVITICAL CITIES AND CITIES OF REFUGE (35:1-34)

35:1-8. *Land for the Levites.* The OT contains in different places provisions for support of priests and Levites, the variety in which indicates a long and changing history. This section outlines provisions quite different from those in ch. 18 (cf. 18:20, 24); 26:62; Deut. 10:9. Furthermore the lists of cities set aside are different in Josh. 21; I Chr. 6. The institution as described probably arose during the monarchy but is definitely idealized here. Again it arises from the theological insistence that all property is God's.

35:9-34. *Cities of Refuge.* This provision is connected with that of Levitical cities by vs. 6. The names of the cities are listed in Deut. 4:41-43; Josh. 20:1-9. Their purpose is to provide for setting aside the law of blood revenge in cases where the death is not due to intentional murder (vss. 15, 22-28). If, however, intentional murder is committed, the **avenger of blood,** i.e. the next of kin of the slain, must carry out the law of retaliation (vss. 16-21). The basis of the custom of blood revenge in the ancient taboo on shedding blood (cf. Gen. 4:1-16; 9:1-7) is outlined in vss. 29-34. The institution of cities of refuge, an early form of courts of appeal, probably dates from the period of the united monarchy.

Q. SUPPLEMENT TO THE LAW OF INHERITANCE BY DAUGHTERS (36:1-13)

The purpose of this supplement to 27:1-11 is to keep property in the family to which it originally belonged (see above on 33:50–34:29). It subordinates women's rights to the Israelite theology of land as the inheritance of Yahweh. This P supplement gives an ancient law a narrative framework.

THE BOOK OF DEUTERONOMY

Norman K. Gottwald

INTRODUCTION

Deuteronomy is the 5th book of the OT and the last in the division known as the Law, Torah, or Pentateuch. Externally tradition regards Moses as the author—except for the account of his death, often attributed to Joshua—and internally he is stated to have written the greater part (31:24). The indefensibility of this tradition is evident in the fact that the book presupposes the Conquest and, at points, even the Exile.

Deut. is also the first in a series of books—written in the same style and vocabulary—which tells the story of Israel from the wilderness wandering to the Babylonian exile. The others are Josh., Judg., Sam., and Kings. By subject and period Deut. is joined to the books that precede it, but in style and theological outlook it is linked to those that follow. Because both the style and the theological outlook originated in Deut., the writings which exhibit them are known as "Deuteronomic" (often abbreviated as "D").

Contents. The book is set in the form of a speech of Moses delivered in Moab just before his death and the entry of Israel into Canaan led by Joshua. Its core (chs. 12-26) is a collection of "laws" (referred to in other parts of the book as "this law" and "the statutes and the ordinances"). Some of the subunits of this collection are laws in the technical sense, but many are either totally or largely moral exhortation and amount to brief admonitions or sermons based on legal texts or precedents.

The laws of chs. 12-26 are most closely related to those of the Covenant Code of Exod. 20:22-23:33 (see "The Law Codes of Israel," pp. 1090-94). Approximately half the laws in the Covenant Code are duplicated in Deut., but the differences are sufficient to cast serious doubt on the hypothesis that Deut. used the Covenant Code directly and on the otherwise attractive view that Deut. was intended to replace the Covenant Code. It appears rather that both codes drew on a larger body of laws.

The 11 chs. preceding the laws and the 8 following are almost entirely cast in the form of a Mosaic address (exceptions are 4:41-43; 31:14-23; 32:44-52; 34). The materials are of 3 types: (*a*) historical résumés, recalling Israel's experience from Horeb (Sinai) to Moab and the final events in the life of Moses, including the commissioning of Joshua, the writing of the law, and Moses' death and burial; (*b*) threats and appeals for Israel to love and obey God, which are either loosely constructed sermonic admonitions or technically formed blessings and curses; (*c*) liturgical directions for writing and recitation of the laws and for rites to accompany the periodic renewal of the covenant.

Deut. is very largely in prose. At times the style is crisply legal and formulaic, like that of the parts of the Covenant Code which seem to have been drawn from the same source. More frequent, however, is an expansive, verbose, and sonorous style used in narration and admonition—the characteristic D style that pervades not only Deut. but also the work of the compilers of Josh., Judg., Sam., and Kings. Two long poems attributed to Moses, entitled "song" (32:1-43) and "blessing" (ch. 33), have been inserted toward the end of the book.

Cultic Purity at a Central Sanctuary. To place Deut. in the literary and religious history of Israel it is necessary to consider certain prominent features of the book. Of these the sharpest ideological feature is the demand for exclusive worship at a central sanctuary (see below on ch. 12). In the fierce reiteration of this point Deut. and the D portions of Josh.-Kings are unique. Other parts of the OT legislate for, or report without condemnation, practices of worship at various sanctuaries throughout the land, or else assume that centralization of worship has existed all along. Deut. and its related D writings alone propagandize for centralization—and do so in a way that reveals the novelty of the program and the intensity of the opposition.

Is there historical evidence of any sustained attempt to enforce worship at one site? II Kings 22-23 tells of just such an endeavor in the reign of King Josiah of Judah, beginning in 622. Of course the account itself is from the D tradition and thus is not beyond question. Yet no basis exists for denying its essential outlines, viz. that after discovery of a "book of the law" in the temple Josiah enforced centralization of worship at Jerusalem and also celebration in the temple of the passover previously observed in homes, removal of astral worship and sacred poles and pillars, and proscription of magic and divination and the immolation of children. All these are features of the laws of chs. 12-26.

That this account is not simply a gross idealization of the king and his religious accomplishments is suggested by an admission that his success was incomplete (II Kings 23:9, which reads like an apology for the failure to carry out Deut. 18:6-8). He seems to have been unable to get the Jerusalem Levites to accept the Levitical priests from the countryside, who were in effect defrocked when the reform closed down their shrines. The undoubted fact that in the period 609-586 idolatrous practices are reported in Judah does not disprove Josiah's reforms. It only shows how much they depended on his forceful personality and how revulsion and disillusionment at the pious king's death led to repeated and widespread breach of the laws he had enforced.

It is possible that some features of Deut. are reflected in reforms carried out by earlier kings—esp. by Hezekiah (late 8th cent.), who according to II Chr. 29-31 decreed a passover at Jerusalem to which even the survivors of the fall of the N kingdom were invited. It is difficult to be certain, however, since the reports of them tend to be conventional and lack the specificity of the Josianic records.

The many affinities of Deut. with Hos. and the E source of the Pentateuch (see "The Compiling of Israel's Story," pp. 1082-89) strongly suggest that D traditions derive at least in part from the 8th cent. Furthermore allusions to worship at Shechem (see below on 11:29; 27:1-13) argue that at least some segments of the book stem from N Israel, probably while it was still an independent nation. Thus Hezekiah may have been motivated by D traditions in his reforms, even though there is no direct evidence of it.

Composite Structure. Deut. is a deceptive work as literature. Its style is so distinctive that the first impression is monolithic solidarity. Yet when one passes from the language to the narrative flow and the sequence of the parts he is at once confronted with proliferating cracks in its facade.

The "statutes and the ordinances" of chs. 12-26 are not consistently grouped by form or subject—as is true of all Israelite law compilations (see "The Law Codes of Israel," pp. 1090-94). Again and again topical or formal clusters of laws are broken by material on a different topic or in a different form or in a similar but greatly expanded form. Though in chs. 12-20 a certain logic in the arrangement can be made out, the individual laws have obviously been drawn from various circles and treated in divergent ways. In chs. 21-26 the unity is even more precarious, so that 23:15-25:19 appears as a miscellaneous catchall at the end of the laws, which are capped off by 2 rites in ch. 26. It is clear that the laws have had a considerable prehistory, and that in this respect Deut. is like all the other bodies of law in the OT.

The intro. and conclusion to the laws are marked by the same gaps and inconsistencies; because narrative is involved these are even more noticeable than in the laws. It has often been noted that chs. 1-4 and 5-11 are 2 separate intros. There is an obvious difference in the 2 sections, and both end with formal headings to the laws of chs. 12-26. But these larger entities easily subdivide. The admonition of 4:1-40 is strikingly different in character from the historical résumés and reflections of chs. 1-3. On analysis chs. 5-11 fall into 3 admonitions, each beginning with "Hear, O Israel!" (5:1-33; 6:4-8:20; 9:1-11:25). In addition to the law headings in 4:44-49; 11:26-32, another occurs in 6:1-3. It is therefore not altogether convincing to say that there are 2 intros. in chs. 1-11; we may need to identify at least 3 and possibly more.

Much the same can be said of chs. 27-34. The 2 poems in chs. 32-33 have obviously been grafted into literary contexts to which they are foreign. In 27:1-13 there is a natural link with 11:26-32, but the transition to ch. 28 is broken by the dodecalogue of curses in 27:14-26 (see comment). Chs. 29-30 have been consciously added to the preceding (cf. 29:1, 20-21). Still more complex is the further appendix (31:1-32:47) in which the commissioning of Joshua, the writing of the law, and the writing of the Song of Moses are very awkwardly interwoven.

Thus there are abundant signs that Deut. has known a complicated history, that the book was not created as a totality by a single mind.

Cultic Origin. At several points in Deut. cultic rites are either directly described or strongly implied. Some of these are connected with particular festivals or specific types of sacrifice. Others are rites at which the law is read and affirmed or sanctions are imposed to insure obedience to it. These sanctions are of particular interest because they give valuable clues for the origins and structure of the book.

A ceremony of blessings and curses recited from the summits (or slopes) of Mts. Ebal and Gerizim (see color map 5) is described in 11:26-32; 27:1-13, and a text of the blessings and curses with hortatory expansion is given in ch. 28. At this same ceremony "all the words of this law" (at least chs. 12-26) are to be written on large plastered upright stones. Later, after Moses writes the law and gives it to the priests, he instructs Israel to read the law every 7th year at the feast of booths (31:9-13). How the blessings-curses ceremony and the law recitation at the feast of booths are related, if at all, is not explained.

Overt references to public reading or enforcement of the law are not the whole of the pertinent evidence. Throughout many of the admonitions put in the mouth of Moses sounds the note of urgent decision. Again and again Israel is said to stand "this day" before Yahweh, and "this day" she must decide for him as he has decided for her. It takes little imagination to see that speeches of this sort have their origin in the cult. The cultic foundations show through in spite of literary expansion and rearrangement which have served to disguise the original situation.

Not only is it clear that the cultic event shaping Deut. is a recitation of the law, but it is evident that this event was also an entering anew into covenant with God. This constant contemporaneity of the covenant, and its cultic reenactment, is articulated in Deut. by the continuity and tension between the "covenant at Horeb" and the "covenant in Moab" (see below on chs. 29-30). The 2 covenants are continuous in the purposes of God but they are in tension in their varying legal instruments—"new occasions teach new duties." The shape of the covenant renewal ceremonies may be seen in the speeches of Moses (i.e. the cultic figure who speaks for Moses) in 29:10-15 and in 26:16-19, which states, "You have declared this day concerning the LORD that he is your God . . . ; and the LORD has declared this day concerning you that you are a people for his own possession."

Thus it emerges that back of Deut. lies a liturgy

of covenant renewal in which Israel was addressed by a leader representing Moses. Elements in the ceremony included: historical retrospect of God's deeds and Israel's relation to him, recitation of the law, pronouncement of sanctions for obedience (blessings and curses), decision to enter (or re-enter or reaffirm) covenant with God. When Deut. is viewed as a totality precisely this sort of structure stands out as its skeleton. Into this liturgical covenant renewal pattern, however, a vast amount of material has been intruded, so that the result is a literary composite which probably was never employed in the cult in its entirety.

We are thus confronted with a paradox—Deut. is both a highly cultic and a highly "bookish" or "scriptural" work.

Prominence of the Levitical Priests. To identify more fully the liturgical milieu of Deut. it is necessary to consider the official personnel of the cult in whose hands the covenant ceremony and its admonitory and legal materials rested.

Various Israelite cult functionaries are mentioned in Deut. in one of 3 ways: (*a*) sometimes associated with Moses in the narratives or speech headings; (*b*) on other occasions alluded to in the laws; and (*c*) still more fully treated in a section that describes at least some of their duties (see below on 16:18-18:22). Among those prominently involved are elder, judge, prophet, and king. More prominent than all the others, however, are "the Levitical priests" (lit. "the priests the Levites"; sometimes simply "the priests").

A rather full profile of the Levitical priests may be drawn from the data of the book. The Levites live "in your towns" and, being landless, must be provided for by the other tribes (12:12, 18; 14:27, 29; 16:11, 14). They are to receive designated parts of sacrificed animals and the first fruits (18:1-5) as well as triennial tithes (26:12-15). They are scattered throughout Israel, but with the centralization of worship they are to come to Jerusalem if they wish to continue functioning as priests (18:6-8). The double role of Levite as priest at Jerusalem who receives offerings and Levite as layman who worships is seen in the account of the first-fruits ceremony (26:3, 11).

Additional duties of the Levitical priests, as attested in the laws, are: (*a*) membership on and co-chairmanship of a central tribunal or court of appeals at Jerusalem (17:8-13; 19:15-21); (*b*) guardianship of an authoritative copy of the D law, from which the king makes a copy (17:18); (*c*) address to the military muster to assure Israel of victory (20:2-4); (*d*) application of leprosy laws (24:8-9; cf. Lev. 14:54-57). In the narrative sections and brief headings of chs. 27-34 the Levites also appear as functionaries in the cultic renewal ceremonies. Moses and the Levitical priests declare the covenant in effect (27:9-10); Levites declaim curses over Israel (27:14-26); and the priests convene a gathering of elders and officers so that Yahweh can "witness against them" (31:28). Moses delivers the written law to the priests and directs them to read it every 7th year (31:9-13). The priests carry the text of the law beside the ark as a witness to Israel (31:25-26). In the somewhat cryptic poetry of the Blessing of Moses, Levi is portrayed as controlling the sacred lots (Urim and Thummim) and as a leader in the 2-fold role of teacher and priest (33:8-11).

In many of these references the connection of the Levitical priests with law is unmistakable, and not merely in the general sense that they uphold it. More specifically the priests (*a*) keep the standard text of the law, (*b*) read it, and (*c*) pronounce sanctions and admonitions concerning it. In short, public recitation of the law in solemn ceremony is their particular prerogative. It is logical, therefore, to regard Levitical priests as the earliest creators and proponents of the D traditions in their capacities as functionaries at the covenant/law renewal ceremonies.

This hypothesis of Levitical cultic reading of the law as the origin of Deut. receives external confirmation from the report of the reading of the law by Ezra and its reacceptance by the returning exiles. As Ezra read from the book to a public assembly, it is said, the Levites "helped the people to understand the law. . . . And they read from the book, from the law of God, clearly; and they gave the sense, so that the people understood the reading" (Neh. 8:7*b*-8). Regrettably there are difficulties in the text. It seems probable, however, that the Levites on that occasion translated the Hebrew text of the law into Aramaic, the vernacular of the postexilic Jews, and that they explained the meaning by paraphrase, expansion, illustration, etc. That the Levites had this role of public reading and explanation of the law *ca.* 450-400 suggests a similar role during the period 750-600 and corroborates the internal evidence of Levitical responsibility for Deut.

Deut. as a Book. However obvious its oral cultic origins, Deut. now stands before us as a book. More than that, in its present form it stresses that "this book of the law" is so authoritative that it may not be altered by addition or subtraction and must be obeyed unequivocally (4:2; 12:32; 28:58; 30:10; 31:12). Even if we assume exaggeration—allowing e.g. that the other law codes may have been binding—the preeminence of Deut. is unquestionably asserted. At all disputed points its view, notably that of centralization of worship, will have to prevail.

It is necessary, therefore, to account for the development in the D traditions from the oral-cultic milieu to the written-didactic milieu. It is further necessary to take account of the relation between the book itself and the several D-oriented books which follow it and carry the story of Israel into the Babylonian exile. All questions about authorship and date have to take into account the entire D complex, Deut.-Kings, and not alone the passage concerned with Josiah's reform (II Kings 22-23).

The one hard date is the year of Josiah's reform, 622. But the origins of Deut. are older than the reform. Levitical reading and preaching of the law did not begin in 622; considering the allusions to Shechem the practice must have extended back at least a cent. into N Israel. The shock of the discovery of the law in 622 does not mean that such traditions were unknown in Israel previously; it means rather that the Judean monarchy had lost touch with them for as much as 50 or 75 years (assuming that Hezekiah knew of them and used them in his reforms).

The attempt to reconstruct the Deut. found in the temple, in contrast to its later amplifications, has not yielded solid results; the criteria of separation are too uncertain. We can be sure only that the law book of II Kings 22–23 contained many of the laws of chs. 12–26 and that they were accompanied by warnings similar to the curses of ch. 28.

Was the law written specifically for the purpose of "planting" it in the temple? Perhaps—if we assume that only in this way could its claims be brought to the king convincingly and without danger to the law's advocates. Yet it is striking that even with the written law before him Josiah was unconvinced until specific supporters of the law had assured him of its validity (II Kings 22:8-20).

It is more likely that the writing and rewriting of D laws and admonitions was going on underground throughout the reign of Manasseh (ca. 687-642). If we visualize the Yahwistic cultic calendar as lapsing or at least suffering from neglect, the old patterns of cultic renewal of covenant and law would be strained and even threatened with extinction. Oral materials remembered from year to year would no longer be recited, and authoritative texts of the laws inscribed at cult sites (cf. 27:2-3) would become defaced or even destroyed. Thus both oral and written records of D traditions were driven underground and fostered there until they broke to the surface in 622.

This interpretation does away with the view that the planted Deut. was a "pious fraud." No one needed to concoct a book purporting to be by Moses; all he had to do was collect materials long attributed to Moses, through the device of the cult functionary speaking on behalf of Moses, and to assert that these traditions should once again be binding in Israel.

The radically new thing in 622 was the tying of the D traditions to the single sanctuary of Jerusalem. Previously centralization had meant no more than concentration of official Yahwistic worship at the tribal center in Shechem (see below on ch. 12), and it did not rule out all other types of worship at local shrines and temples. The transfer of D traditions to Judah after Samaria's fall, together with the shrinking of the land area in which politically independent Yahwists lived, created a situation where a total centralization policy could be realized at Jerusalem. But this new policy was merely a marriage of convenience with D materials.

Precisely this elevation of the single cult at Jerusalem as the sole valid cult is what cut the former strong Israel-wide cultic roots of the Levitical D traditions. The various speeches, admonitions, songs, etc. that were used at various sites for the celebration of covenant renewal no longer had their original homes but were brought to Jerusalem. These old cultic materials—greatly reworked to fit the guise of a Mosaic narrative—were finally given a "bookish" setting (chs. 1–11; 27–34, with appropriate expansions in 12–26).

At the same time a concern with the post-Mosaic history of Israel, which previously had been left to JE circles (see "The Compiling of Israel's Story," pp. 1082-89), now emerged decisively in D circles. So strongly did it emerge that a whole new history of Israel, the Deut.-Kings corpus, was created. Probably it drew in some measure on JE materials, but it was shaped in a wholly distinctive way. The basic aim of this "history," which was in fact moral and cultic admonition, was to connect Israel's life in Canaan and her historical vicissitudes with the taproot of her existence in Yahwism. Specifically it was intended as a sketch of Israel's prevailing apostasy lightened only by the counterpoint of priestly and prophetic warnings, occasional favorable minority responses, and the dramatic but sporadic acts of a Hezekiah or a Josiah. But for the persistent purpose of God, his loyalty to his "word," Israel's history would have been waste and void.

Deut. thereby becomes the basis not only for centralization of worship at Jerusalem but also for an extended reading of Israel's post-Mosaic history—the record of greater Israel's faithlessness balanced against Yahweh's faithfulness and the commitment of an Israelite minority.

Thus the parodox of Deut. was that traditions it sought to appropriate solely for Jerusalem were, with the Exile, sown abroad in book form to all the faithful. Materials originally read and celebrated in scattered holy places and subsequently restricted to Jerusalem became available to the Jewish believer in private or in reading conventicles such as probably formed the basis for the later synagogues. When we speak of the cultic character of Deut. we need to recognize how profound a transition occurred in the use of the traditions, from the earlier cult setting rooted in oral recitations accompanying sacrifice to the later cult setting rooted in the reading of a book or books from which sacrifice and other activities unrealizable in exile had been eliminated. It is a useful simplification to think of Deut. under the rubric "from altar to synagogue." What serves to give continuity to both aspects is the abiding covenant relationship and God's communication of his will by the "word" and by the "instruction."

In sum, then, Deut. represents a gathering of old cultic laws, admonitions, songs, etc. developed in Levitical priestly circles from at least the 8th cent., transferred from Israel to Judah, appropriated for Jerusalem in a reform to centralize worship, and finally structured as the intro. to a religious evaluation of the history of Israel from Moses to the Exile.

The writing down of the book began in a sense when the first text of laws was set up at a cult site such as Shechem (see below on 27:1-13), but in the literary sense it began in the 7th cent. when Yahwism was driven underground. The version of 622 included laws and admonitions, but the present form is doubtless due to expansions as older D material was added to that sparser 622 version. This process was mainly one of supplementing a single edition from varying sources that may have been both written and oral. We have no firm evidence of parallel or opposing editions of Deut. Rather it appears that the laws of chs. 12–26 were expanded by the prefixing and suffixing of Levitical cultic materials in a process of agglomeration. Probably this expanding was done by the same hand that prepared the first edition of Deut.-Kings before Josiah's death in 609. The later edition carries the story down to Jehoiachin's release from prison in 561, and sections of Deut. which presuppose the Exile may have been added at that time or even later.

Theological Ideas. In defining the theological point of view of Deut. it is usual to stress its moral earnestness and urgency, its ringing appeals for love and obedience, and its solemn equations of piety with prosperity and impiety with adversity. These are important, but they are subordinate to the dynamics of the relations among Yahweh, Israel, the land, and the nations.

Yahweh, according to Deut., is the Lord of history, who determines the geopolitical position and the worship of the nations. Israel's God has also given territories to the Moabites, Ammonites, and Edomites, which they seized by destroying the previous inhabitants (2:1-23). Thus Israel must not attempt to dispossess those Transjordanian peoples, who also have a place in Yahweh's design. The Amorites led by Sihon and Og are not included in this exemption, however, for God has hardened their hearts that they may be given over to Israel and exterminated in "holy war" (2:26-3:11). Israel must have no truck with worship of the heavenly bodies, objects which Yahweh "has allotted [for worship] to all the peoples under the whole heaven" (4:19). In the Song of Moses a cryptic passage (32:8) says that in determining the territorial status of the various peoples God matched them with "the number of the sons of God," i.e. minor deities who are his servants (cf. e.g. I Kings 22:19-23; Job 1:6; Pss. 29:1; 82:1). The idea seems to be that Yahweh has assigned each people to one of these godlings but has chosen Israel for himself. Israel alone knows of the historical revelation at Sinai. Thus God deals indirectly with all the nations but directly with Israel only.

As Yahweh has ordained a special cult for his special people Israel, so he grants them a special geopolitical place in Canaan. From early times Yahwism entailed not only a cult but a land. It is the land-giving and land-keeping which occupies the D mind. The extent of the land promised to Israel varies considerably in the OT traditions, and the accounts in Deut. are vague (e.g. 12:20). But it is assumed that Yahweh will not rest until he has helped Israel to take the land.

Such views create an inevitable tension. How can God's guidance of all the nations be reconciled with his particular guidance of a single nation? Specifically, what is to happen when the nations and Israel claim the same land? It is highly probable that this question pushed more and more into the forefront as Assyrian domination extended farther into Palestine. With the collapse of N Israel and the vassalage of Judah beneath Assyria, and with the consequent action of Manasseh to ignore or suppress Yahwism, maintenance of the land and of the cult became increasingly interlocking issues. The effort of Josiah at Israelite independence, followed by further vassalage to Egypt and Neo-Babylonia, intensified the illogicalities and moral enigmas of Israel's position in the land. Deut. offers 2 explanations.

The first explanation is in the nature of an unargued premise. Yahweh has by decree given Canaan to Israel because "he loved your fathers and chose their descendants after them" (4:37). This is really no explanation but the assertion of a dogmatic proposition. It is rooted in the general Near Eastern belief that a god has the right and power to will the fate of peoples. It also assumes that every

people must have a land, even the people of Yahweh. In one sense Yahweh's gift of Canaan to Israel is no more inexplicable than his gift of Transjordanian territories to Ammon, Moab, and Edom. In each case earlier inhabitants had to be annihilated or expelled. Israel is merely the supreme instance of God's choosing a land for a people.

The 2nd explanation follows from the first and introduces the uniqueness of Yahweh's cultic connection with Israel. Israel must occupy her land in such a way as to remain true to Yahweh, i.e. she cannot share it with the Canaanites because their worship of Baal will tempt Israel into apostasy and cause her to surrender her sole worship of Yahweh.

At one point Israel is warned not to assume that Yahweh's expulsion of the Canaanites is due to her own righteousness, since it is rather "because of the wickedness of these nations" (9:4). This is a curious bit of reasoning. Read in one way it would appear merely to reinforce Israel's confidence—"We are at least relatively more righteous than those Canaanites!" But if the urgent question underlying the passage is cultic rather than moral, then its phrasing is entirely intelligible. "The wickedness of these nations" here means their cultic practices which will entice Israel if they are allowed to remain in the land. The sober warning against Israel's depending overly on her own righteousness has as its background her notorious weakness for non-Yahwistic worship. Followed strictly, the logic of Deut. says: Baal worship is in keeping with Yahweh's will to assign various forms of worship to the nations and for the Canaanites it is not wickedness. The wickedness lies rather in its insidious appeal to Israel. Being so cultically fickle, Israel must morally and religiously sanitize her territory by centralized worship and by holy war.

It becomes evident in Deut. that centralized worship and holy war are highly rationalized theological concepts as well as cult practices. They are the means appointed by God for Israel to maintain her cultic purity, i.e. her identity in covenant with God. Deut. has gathered snippets of information about older forms of centralized worship at Shechem and about holy war practices, but these are not presented as historical information. Rather the historical context is obscured by the device of concentrating the mass of tradition in the mouth of Moses. Thus the sporadically and variously practiced forms of centralized worship and of holy war are elevated to the level of dogmatic principles commanded of God. All that we know of the course of Israelite history from the occupation onward, however, shows that the Canaanites, far from being annihilated, remained in the land to mix with Israel and to form a constant cultic threat to Yahwism. All that we know of the history from Solomon on shows that Jerusalem, though a very important cultic site, was not the sole place of legitimate worship of Yahweh until Josiah's (or possibly Hezekiah's) reform.

In a sense, then, Deut. is saying: This is the way history should have gone if we had really wished to remain faithful to God. If we had wiped out the Canaanites and worshiped only at Jerusalem, we would have avoided apostasy, and we would have kept our land. Deut. therefore explains why the land has been partly or wholly lost and offers a foundation for exilic hopes that the land and the kingship will be restored. If Israel is again to possess the land it can be only through the strictest cultic purity.

The essence of Deut. is a total and indivisible interpenetration of morality and cult: one God for one people through one cult in one land.

For Further Study: G. A. Smith, *The Book of Deut.*, 1918. A. C. Welch, *The Code of Deut.*, 1924. R. H. Pfeiffer, *Intro. to the OT*, 1941. G. E. Wright in *IB*, 1955. N. K. Gottwald, *A Light to the Nations*, 1959. Gerhard von Rad in *IDB*, 1962; *Deut.: A Commentary*, 1966.

I. INTRODUCTION PLACING MOSES IN THE S ARABAH (1:1-2)

This apparent superscription to the entire book locates Moses **in the wilderness** (i.e. desert), **in the Arabah,** the deep Jordan–Dead Sea rift and its extension to the S. **Suph** (lit. "reed") may refer to the Gulf of Aqabah (so the LXX; see comment on Num. 21:4-9). On **Paran** cf. 33:2; Num. 10:12; 12:16; 13:3. On **Hazeroth** cf. Num. 10:12; 33:17-18. These suggest an area far to the S of the Dead Sea on the W side of the Arabah (see color map 4). This impression is strengthened by vs. 2, which speaks of the travel time between **Horeb** (Sinai) and **Kadesh-barnea.** Such a site is far from the region **beyond the Jordan** (cf. vs. 5).

II. SPEECH OF MOSES IN MOAB (1:3-4:49)

The first major subunit is presented formally, like the rest of the book, as a speech of Moses. In reality it consists, rather unevenly, of a lengthy historical résumé of the trip from Horeb to Moab (1:4-3:29), an admonition to obey the law of God (4:1-40), a brief account of Moses' appointment of cities of refuge (4:41-43), and what appears to be a superscription to the laws of chs. 12–26 (4:44-49).

A. REVIEW OF THE JOURNEY FROM HOREB (1:3-3:29)

1:3-5. *Setting of the Speech.* The speech is dated in the **fortieth year** after leaving Horeb, following the defeat of **Sihon** and **Og** (cf. Num. 21:21-35). The place is the **land of Moab,** in 3:29 more closely defined as the "valley opposite Beth-peor," i.e. at the edge of the Arabah a few miles NE of the Dead Sea (see color map 5). Moses is said to have begun to **explain this law,** lit. "instruction" (*torah*). It is clear that the instruction, presumably chs. 12–26, is to be distinguished from the explanation, the speech of 1:6-4:43. It is not impossible, however, that this intro. was intended by the editor to apply to the entirety of chs. 1–11, and even to chs. 27–34 since at the end Moses is buried in the same "valley in the land of Moab opposite Beth-peor" (34:6).

1:6-8. *Command to Leave Horeb.* Israel is abruptly ordered to leave the covenant mountain of Horeb and to possess the land promised to the patriarchs. In E and D **Amorites** is the general term for the pre-Israelite inhabitants of Palestine and **Canaanites** is restricted to inhabitants of the N coastal region of Phoenicia, whereas in J and P "Canaanites" is the general term and "Amorites" are found only in the hill country of Judah and in Transjordan. If the translation **neighbors** is correct, **hill country of the**

Amorites means specifically the mountain heartland of Judah, given preeminence among the surrounding regions because it was the site of Jerusalem. Since the root meaning of the Hebrew word is simply "inhabitants," however, "hill country of the Amorites" may here refer loosely to the whole area of Palestine and Syria occupied by "Amorites," with the other regions named as subdivisions of it. The **Arabah** is the Jordan–Dead Sea rift, the **hill country** the central mountainous region, and the **lowland** the foothills to the W. The **Negeb** is the desert to the S, and the Phoenician **seacoast** (the **land of the Canaanites**) and **Lebanon** are on the N, with the promised territory extending to the **Euphrates.**

1:9-18. *Appointment of Officials.* Moses tells how, overburdened with the people and their **strife,** he appointed men to assist him (cf. Exod. 18:13-27; Num. 11:16-17, 24b-30). This account seems to distinguish between newly appointed officials called **commanders** (lit. "rulers"; cf. Exod. 18:21) and **officers** (cf. Num. 11:16)—2 terms used loosely in the OT to refer to various types of civil and military leaders—and **judges** who are being newly **charged** but have been previously appointed. The functions of the officials are not discussed, but the judges are said to deal with legal cases, the difficult ones being referred to Moses himself (vss. 16-17).

1:19-46. *An Attempt to Enter Canaan.* Moses relates the sending of a scouting party from Kadesh-barnea into Canaan. In general the story parallels the accounts in Num. 13–14; 32:8-13, but it varies in that here Moses gives an explicit command to **take possession** of the land (vs. 21) and the people temporize by suggesting the scouting party, whereas in Num. Moses sends out the spies but Caleb and Joshua urge the invasion on their return and are therefore exempted from the decree that their generation must die in the wilderness. Here no reason is given for exempting these 2 except that Caleb **has wholly followed the LORD** (vs. 36). Moses himself is said to be excluded from entrance into Canaan because **the LORD was angry with me also on your account** (vs. 37; cf. 3:26; 4:21). This contrasts with the view in 32:48-52 (see comment) that his debarment was a punishment because he "broke faith" with Yahweh. Here he is not personally guilty but is the representative of his people and suffers with them the consequences of their faithlessness.

2:1-23. *Passage Through Edom and Moab.* This version is only loosely related to Num. 20:14-21; 21:4-20 (see comment). Here the emphasis is on the order that Israel is not to **contend** with the Edomites (**sons of Esau;** cf. Gen. 36:9) or with the Moabites and Ammonites (**sons of Lot;** cf. Gen. 19:36-38) since it is Yahweh who has awarded these nations their land. Nothing is said about Edomite hostility to Israel. This is a different outlook from that in 23:3-8, where Edomites of the 3rd generation may become worshipers of Yahweh but not Ammonites or Moabites. The explicit award of land by Yahweh to non-Israelites assumes importance in the total theological structure of Deut. (see Intro.).

2:1. On **Red Sea** see comment on Num. 21:4-9. **Mount Seir** was the mountain range covering most of the Edomite territory (see color map 4).

2:10-12. A note gives anthropological and historical data on the previous populations of Moab, some of whom tradition viewed as giants (see comment on Num. 13:32-33). On **Horites** see "The People of the OT World," pp. 1005-17.

2:20-23. A similar note is included on Ammon. **Caphtorim** refers to the Philistines (cf. Jer. 47:4; Amos 9:7).

2:24-3:11. Defeat of Sihon and Og. The Amorite kings of **Heshbon** and **Bashan,** who control Transjordan from the Arnon River N toward Damascus, refuse passage to Israel and are soundly defeated (cf. Num. 21:21-35; see comment). The holy war "ban" (see below on 20:10-18) is imposed on all the citizens, who are killed, but the livestock and goods are kept. Antiquarian notes comment on various names for **Mount Hermon** (vs. 9) and on the legendary gigantic iron **bedstead** of Og (vs. 11; on **cubits** see "Measures and Money," pp. 1283-85).

3:12-22. Allotment of Land in Transjordan. The tribes of Reuben and Gad and **half-tribe of Manasseh** are given the former territories of Sihon and Og (cf. Num. 32). **Machir** (vs. 15) and **Jair** (vs. 14) are specified as the 2 chief clans of Manasseh (cf. Num. 32:39-42) whereas in Judg. 5:14 Machir appears to be the name of the tribe otherwise called Manasseh. Care is to be taken not to intrude on the neighboring territories of the Moabites (S of the **Arnon** River) or of the **Ammonites** (E of the upper **Jabbok** River) or of the **Geshurites** and **Maacathites** (N of Bashan; see color map 3). The Transjordanian tribes are enjoined to send their warriors with the other 9½ tribes to complete the conquest of W Canaan (cf. Josh. 1:12-18). The book adheres tenaciously to the concept of a united 12-tribe conquest of all Canaan (see Intro.).

3:23-29. Moses Told to Survey the Land. Moses is denied entrance to W Canaan because of his identification with the sinful people (see above on 1:19-46). He may only **behold** it from the **top of Pisgah.** Three names are used of this height: Abarim, Nebo, and Pisgah. Abarim was apparently the name of the mountainous region in which Nebo was one peak (32:49; Num. 27:12; 33:47). Pisgah was either an alternate name for the same summit or a spur or promontory of it (34:1). It is traditionally identified with a peak about 12 miles E of the outlet of the Jordan into the Dead Sea.

B. Admonition to Obey the Law (4:1-40)

This impassioned exhortation contains historical reflection but in style and mood resembles the admonitions of chs. 5-11. In its harking back to the character of the revelation at Horeb it is esp. close to 5:1-6:3.

4:1-8. Call to Obedience. The caution not to **add to or take from** the following instruction strikes a note of verbal strictness unprecedented in ancient Israel (cf. 12:32). It doubtless reflects the new stress during the Exile on the written traditions as the objective focus for the deported community. Temple and king might fail but not the law of God. The point is probably not so much a new concept of literal inspiration as it is a practical insistence on obedience to laws that have been too frequently ignored. Evidence that this caution should not be taken too lit. may be seen in the fact that chs. 12-26 lack guidance for many areas of life, e.g. marriage practices, which would have to be supplied not only

from the earlier law collections (some of which may now appear in Exod.; Lev.; Num.) but also from instructions which were never included in the Hebrew Bible.

4:3. The warning against disobedience is underscored by a recollection of the Israelites who were **destroyed** by plague when they followed the **Baal of Peor** by engaging in licentious rites with Moabite women (cf. Num. 25:1-9).

4:7-8. The section culminates with rhetorical questions about the uniqueness of Israel's God that set the pattern for the rest of the speech.

4:9-24. The Revelation at Horeb. How the fearful Israelites drew near to the smoking mountain at Horeb is described in terms closest to the E account in Exod., but if E is the source it is freely paraphrased and expanded. The thrust of the reminiscence is that only Yahweh's **voice** was perceived; **no form** was seen (vs. 12). Therefore Israel is to make no images of Yahweh.

4:13-14. Particularly illuminative of the D outlook is the virtual equation of the **covenant** and the **ten commandments,** which Yahweh himself **wrote . . . upon two tables of stone.** This focusing of the covenantal act and relationship on the covenantal legal instrument moves considerably beyond Exod. 24, where, though the written instrument can be called the "book of the covenant," a distinction is clearly maintained (Exod. 24:7-8). In another respect, however, Deut. is freer than Exod. in its interpretation of the relation between the covenant event at Horeb-Sinai and the law. The "book of the covenant" of Exod. 24:7 is apparently regarded as containing not only the 10 commandments but also the Covenant Code of Exod. 20:22-23:24, whereas vs. 14 treats the **statutes and ordinances** of chs. 12-26 as additional laws which Moses was to teach Israel on its way from Horeb to Moab (cf. 5:31).

4:15-24. With vss. 16-18 cf. 5:8. The prohibition of worship of the astral bodies (vs. 19) reflects the influx of Assyrian astral worship in the last of the 8th and throughout the 7th cent. in Judah. On the idea that worship of these objects is permitted to other peoples see Intro. On vss. 21-22 see above on 1:19-46.

4:25-31. Consequences of Apostasy. Continued idolatry in the land of Canaan will lead to Israel's deportation, enforced idolatry in foreign lands, the eventual repentance of the people, and their return to the land. The full description probably stems from the Babylonian exile, but the core of the passage may well come from any time after 722, when N Israel was scattered. The expression **in the latter days** (vs. 30) shows how language often used to refer to the end of history (cf. e.g. Dan. 10:14) could be used about an important turning point in history. The aim of the passage is not only to warn against idolatry but to assure Israel that God is **merciful** and will not **forget the covenant.**

4:32-40. Yahweh's Unique Revelation. The admonition comes to a head in one of the most eloquent appeals of the book. In all known experience has a god ever saved a people or revealed himself or given such a law as Yahweh has done with and for Israel? His goal in this tremendous historical display was to form a disciplined people who would obey him. Since he has shown his love for Israel and demonstrated that he alone is God, Israel has every reason to keep his commandments. The passage closes with the conventional D promise of long life **in the land,** but the real force of the unit is in the evocation of God's numinous presence and power, with which Israel is joined in awesome intimacy.

C. Cities of Refuge in Transjordan (4:41-43)

This brief section departs from the prevailing pattern of historical retrospect. In straightforward 3rd-person narrative Moses is said to have designated **Bezer, . . . Ramoth, . . . and Golan** in Transjordan as places of asylum for **manslayers** until their cases could be fairly tried. Josh. 20:7-9 states that these three cities were appointed by Joshua along with 3 in W Palestine only after the whole land was conquered. See below on 19:1-13, where the provision for such cities is outlined.

D. Introduction to the Law (4:44-49)

This brief section states simply: **This is the law . . . ; these are the testimonies, the statutes, and the ordinances** spoken by Moses **in the valley opposite Beth-peor,** and then summarizes 2:24-3:17. Given other allusions in the book to "this law," it is almost certain that these vss. are a caption to the laws of chs. 12-26 rather than to the 10 Commandments (5:6-21) or to any other part of the introductory speeches of chs. 1-11. If so, it is apparent that at one stage in the compilation of the book, or in one version in which it circulated, these vss. immediately preceded ch. 12. This intro. is analogous to the one in 6:1-3.

III. Three Admonitions to Obey the Law (5:1-11:32)

A. First Admonition (5:1-6:3)

5:1-21. The 10 Commandments. In its reference to the circumstances of the covenant revelation at Horeb this section is related to 4:9-14, but it has its own peculiarities, esp. the prominent role of Moses as mediator. Though Yahweh **spoke with you face to face,** i.e. directly and commandingly, it was in fact Moses who stood **between** the people and Yahweh **to declare to you the word of the LORD.** Then follows the full text of the 10 Commandments.

5:2-3. The emphatic declaration that Moses' hearers are the same persons who accepted the covenant at Horeb contradicts the statements of 1:35-39; 2:14 (cf. Num. 14:20-35; 26:64-65; 32:11-13) that the generation that came out of Egypt was condemned to die in the wilderness. It is unlikely that the author did not know the tradition of 40 years of wandering (cf. 8:2-4; 29:5). Rather he must have chosen to ignore it in order to make his point more vivid to his own generation: **Not with our fathers** solely **but with us . . . this day** does Yahweh make his covenant as we recite the traditions and undertake the ceremonies of covenant renewal (see Intro. and below on 11:2-7).

5:6-21. This version of the 10 Commandments is substantially the same as that in Exod. 20:2-17 (see comment) except that the motivation for sabbath observance here is the memory of Israel's hard labor in Egypt, which enables her to appreciate the value of a fixed 7th day of rest (cf. Exod. 20:11).

5:22-33. Moses as Mediator. The mediatorial function of Moses as the communicator and expounder of the law which emerges clearly in the E tradition of Exod. 19-24 (esp. Exod. 20:18-20) is here enlarged on. In one E tradition ambiguous sounds from Horeb are heard by Moses as "these words" (i.e. the 10 Commandments, Exod. 20:1-17) and "ordinances" (Exod. 20:22-23:33), and he writes them in the "book of the covenant" (Exod. 24:4, 7). Here the sound from the mountain is heard directly by Israel as **these words** (i.e. the 10 Commandments, vss. 6-21), which are written by God on **two tables of stone** (cf. Exod. 24:12; 32:16, which appear to be later E attempts to harmonize the 2 traditions). The people are so frightened by this numinous revelation that they insist that Moses in the future be the go-between in relaying Yahweh's words to them. Moses agrees and is told to stay at hand while Yahweh tells him **all the commandment and the statutes and the ordinances which you shall teach them** (vs. 31), yet another reference to the laws of chs. 12-26.

6:1-3. Another Intro. to the Laws. This is an intro. to the body of laws of chs. 12-26 similar to the one in 4:44-49. The fact that the reader may move directly from these vss. to ch. 12 suggests that 5:1-6:3 existed at one time as an independent preface to chs. 12-26, and consequently that 6:4-11:32 was later inserted in its present position because it begins with the imperative "Hear, O Israel!" while further developing certain topics not mentioned or only briefly referred to in earlier chs., esp. the ground and import of Yahweh's choice of Israel.

B. Second Admonition (6:4-8:20)

6:4-7:5. Love for and Obedience to Yahweh. The so-called Shema ("hear"), **Hear, O Israel: The LORD our God is one LORD,** is set in the context of an injunction to teach one's children love and obedience by inculcating the **words** of Yahweh regularly through working them into the routine of daily life. This section contains 2 statements (vss. 13, 16) quoted by Jesus in replying to Satan's temptations (Matt. 4:7, 10; Luke 4:8, 12). The precise meaning of the Shema is debatable—in fact it may intentionally combine 2 meanings: (*a*) Yahweh is one, in contrast to the many Baals; (*b*) Yahweh is the only one for Israel, in contrast to other peoples who are permitted, even by Yahweh (see Intro.), to worship other real or imagined beings.

The following enlargement of the Shema is structured by 3 "whens": (*a*) what Israel must do **when the LORD your God brings you into the land** (6:10), viz. renounce all connections with pagan worship; (*b*) what is to be said **when your son asks** the meaning of God's law (6:20; cf. the father-son exchange in the passover service, Exod. 12:26-27); (*c*) the complete destruction of the Canaanites **when . . . the LORD your God gives them over to you** (7:1-2; see below on 20:1-20), for only in this way can the future generations be kept faithful to Yahweh.

7:6-26. Israel Set Off by Yahweh's Love. Yahweh's choice of Israel is attributed to his inexplicable love and his **oath . . . to your fathers,** i.e. the patriarchs Abraham, Isaac, and Jacob. Specifically excluded is the reasoning that Israel was chosen for her great strength, for she was in fact **the fewest** (or "least") **of all peoples.** But the continuation of God's favor depends on Israel's keeping the covenant by obeying the ordinances about to be given. Vss. 12-16 contain a brief recital of blessings Israel can expect to receive if she is obedient, a list considerably expanded in 28:2-14. Israel is not to fear the Canaanites, for Yahweh will destroy them as he has destroyed the Egyptians (vss. 17-21). He will do so **little by little,** however, since too sudden a removal of the former population would return the land to wilderness and set back civilization (vs. 22). The metal-adorned idols of Canaan may not be kept by Israelites, even for their ornamental value, but must be burned by fire (vss. 25-26).

8:1-20. Israel's Probation. These vss. present a strong case for Israel's wilderness wandering as a period of **testing** rather than simply a time of punishment. The verbs **humble** ("humiliate," or "weaken") and **test** ("try" or "prove") are repeated (vss. 2, 16). From vs. 5 we may conclude that the author thinks also of the settlement in Canaan as a continuing probation to determine if Israel will keep God's commandments. The 2 probationary periods differ strikingly; in the wilderness it was testing by privation, but in Canaan it is to be testing by abundance. The earlier bitterness and churlishness of the people may all too easily give way to self-righteousness and overconfidence (vss. 11, 17). The aim of the wilderness experience is summarized eloquently: "in order to teach you that man does not live on bread alone, but that man may live on anything that the LORD decrees" (vs. 3b JPSV). This is another word quoted by Jesus to answer Satan's temptation (Matt. 4:4; Luke 4:4).

8:19-20. The unit closes with a terse but sharp reminder that disobedience will cause Israel to **perish** like the nations they are to destroy—a point expanded greatly in the curses of 28:15-57. This raises the question whether the author believed that these nations would not have perished had they not been idolatrous. Since he does not speak of their having any practical alternatives to idolatry it is a moot point. Yet, logically considered, how could the nations be blamed for idolatry unless they had a choice? Nor does this section face the question of the status of Edom, Moab, and Ammon, who according to 2:1-23 were given land by Yahweh in perpetuity, apparently by virtue of their genealogical connection with Israel as sons of Esau and Lot, yet were certainly idolators in the biblical sense.

C. THIRD ADMONITION (9:1–11:32)

9:1-10:11. Election by God's Promise. The core of this unit is 9:1-5, which calls Israel to confident courage in seizing Canaan because God has **promised** it. The ground of Israel's confidence, as of the promise, is not her **righteousness** but Canaanite **wickedness** and God's wish to **confirm** his promise to the **fathers.** The criteria for comparing and estimating the moral culpability of Israel and Canaan are problematic since on no points of ethical or cultic conduct are comparisons drawn between the 2. We are told nothing about Canaanite betrayal of moral standards (contrast the denunciations of the nations in Amos 1-2). The only tenable explana-

tion of the passage's rationale is that the **wickedness of these nations** refers to the lure of the Canaanite cult for Israel. The other nations are wicked, not in their own right, but in their temptation of Israel, since they continually draw her away from her sole allegiance to Yahweh. He has given Canaan to Israel simply because he wants to plant his people there in order to keep them cultically pure. Thus the gift of the land and the displacement of the Canaanites is an irrational and arbitrary decree. For the implications of this D view of Israel and the nations see Intro.

9:6-10:11. The remainder of this unit illustrates Israel's apostasy from earliest times, in a manner not unlike Ezek. 16; 23. Moses reviews the story of the **tables of the covenant** and the **molten calf** (cf. Exod. 24:12-18; 31:18–32:24; 34:1-5, 28) and mentions the incidents at **Taberah** (cf. Num. 11:1-3), **Massah** (cf. Exod. 17:1-7; Num. 20:2-13), and **Kibroth-hattaavah** (cf. Num. 11:31-34) and the failure to attack Canaan from **Kadesh-barnea** (cf. 1:19-40; Num. 13–14). He sums it up by saying: **You have been rebellious against the LORD from the day that I knew you** (9:24). For the most part these traditions are either identical with or close to the E accounts of Exod.; Num.

10:12-11:25. Love and Obey God and Keep the Land. The hortatory intro. to the laws of chs. 12–26 comes to a climax with a drawing together of previously introduced themes such as the unique election of Israel by Yahweh (10:15; cf. 7:6-8) and the importance of teaching the law to one's children (11:19; cf. 6:7, 20-25). In the Hebrew the imperative form prevails in series of verbs commanding adherence to Yahweh. Israel must **fear, . . . serve, . . . cleave to, . . . love** Yahweh; she must **keep, . . . lay up, . . . teach** his commandments.

10:17-22. A note of social justice enters for the first time in vss. 17-19 in anticipation of the same emphasis in several of the laws of chs. 12–26. On **seventy persons** (vs. 22) see comment on Gen. 46:6-27.

11:2-7. The syntax of this long sentence is dubious. In an effort to make sense the RSV supplies in vs. 2 **I am . . . speaking** and the 2nd **consider,** which are not in the Hebrew. JPSV has a preferable rendering: "Take thought this day that it was not your children, who neither experienced nor witnessed the lesson of the LORD your God—[long apposition, vss. 2c-7]—but that it was you who saw with your own eyes all the marvelous deeds that the LORD performed." The meaning of this is uncertain. It seems to envision the first generation from Egypt as still alive, contrary to the tradition that they perished during the 40 years in the wilderness. Possibly here the author slips from historical guise to the contemporary ceremony of covenant renewal and with cultic existentialism contrasts all who directly experience Yahweh's deeds (in the traditions properly recited and observed) with those **children who have not known or seen** them (because of either callousness or immaturity). See Intro. and above on 5:2-3. On **Dathan and Abiram** cf. Num. 16:1-34.

11:8-17. The thrust of the whole passage is in the necessity of love and obedience if Israel is to possess and keep the land. A specific point is made of Palestine's dependence on the **rain from heaven**

in contrast to Egypt's secure reliance on water provided **with your feet,** i.e. by irrigation from the Nile. The rains will depend on Israel's faith and conduct. The D belief in a direct correlation between morality and prosperity, immorality and want, is one line of development that is extremely strong in the Bible. Another line, represented by Job, some pss. and prophets, and Jesus, sees all such correlations as strained or frankly broken.

11:26-32. *Blessing or Curse.* The admonition closes with a sharp posing of the moral contingencies before Israel: **if you obey . . . , if you do not obey.**

11:29. Moses gives order for a ceremony in which **you shall set the blessing on Mount Gerizim and the curse on Mount Ebal.** Its execution is described in ch. 27. This is one of the clearest evidences that the original setting of at least some of the D traditions was Shechem, located in the saddle between these twin peaks (see color map 5).

11:30. This note on the location of the mountains is rather obscure. The **oak of Moreh** (or "Instructor's oak") was an ancient shrine near Shechem (Gen. 12:6; cf. Gen. 35:4; Josh. 24:26; Judg. 9:37). Some scholars take **over against Gilgal** to mean that there was a Gilgal close to Shechem, whereas others understand it as referring to the familiar Gilgal near Jericho (cf. e.g. Josh. 4:19-20). On the latter basis the meaning may be that from where Moses is assumed to be speaking Mts. Gerizim and Ebal can be seen by looking in a line with Gilgal, or perhaps can be reached by journeying through it.

11:31-32. This subunit is not only the summit of the admonition beginning at 9:1 but is yet another —at least the 3rd—intro. to **the statutes and the ordinances** of chs. 12–26.

IV. THE DEUTERONOMIC LAWS (12:1–26:19)

A. CENTRALIZATION OF WORSHIP (12:1-32)

The core legislation of Deut. is found here in vss. 2-7 restricting worship to a central sanctuary and vss. 15-19 concomitantly permitting profane slaughter of animals anywhere in the countryside. Only these vss. are cast in strictly legal style. The remainder of the ch. is exhortation in a form that maintains the fiction of Moses delivering the law on the verge of the Promised Land. Most of the hortatory material either repeats or expands elements of the basic stipulations.

12:5. The site of the central sanctuary is not named. It is simply **the place which the LORD your God will choose.** From II Kings 22–23 we note that this unnamed place was early understood to be Jerusalem. This seems to have been the view not only of the reforming King Josiah in 622 but also of Hezekiah a hundred years earlier (cf. II Kings 18:4; II Chr. 29–31). It is doubtful, however, that Jerusalem was originally **the place.** That Mts. Gerizim and Ebal are specified as settings for recitation of the laws (11:26-32; ch. 27) strongly suggests that before the fall of Samaria in 722 the D central sanctuary was at Shechem (see above on 11:29). On the other hand the Hebrew for **out of all your tribes** may be taken to mean "from each of your tribes," which could be construed as an original provision for 12 tribal centers of worship.

It may have been to rule out just such ambiguity when the law was applied to Shechem, and later to Jerusalem, that an addition was made in vs. 14 reading **in one of your tribes** (vs. 14).

12:6. The law gives a brief inventory of the main types of sacrifice that Israelites could offer (cf. 14:22-29; 15:19-23; 18:4; 23:21-23; 26:2).

12:15-16. The limitation of offerings to one place of worship meant the end of the close bond that had existed between sacrifice and all forms of animal slaughter. It was manifestly impossible to require that all meat be slaughtered at Shechem or at Jerusalem. Therefore permission is given for slaughter **within any of your towns** (i.e. anywhere throughout the land) of domestic animals as if they were game (e.g. a **gazelle** or **hart**) being killed in a hunt. Since no cultic act is involved one need not be ritually **clean** to eat the meat. The only restriction is that the **blood** must be drained from the carcass before it is eaten (cf. vss. 23-25).

12:17-19. It is repeated that, in contrast to such slaughter simply for food, all religious offerings, whether of meat or of agricultural produce, whether regular or occasional (e.g. **votive** or **freewill offerings**), must be brought directly to Jerusalem. The animal must be slaughtered there and eaten there.

12:29-32. The motivation for centralization of worship is the risk of becoming **ensnared to follow** Canaanite religion. With the establishment of a central place for Israelite worship all the other holy places are to be destroyed as remnants of paganism. This is to be done in order to preclude Israel's asking **How did these nations serve their gods?** and then following their practices. On vs. 31*c* see below on 18:9-14.

B. WARNINGS AGAINST APOSTASY (13:1-18)

This unit is composed of 3 laws constructed in mixed conditional and categorical forms. The prohibition against following each type of apostate is stated conditionally—**If he says, . . . you shall not listen**—and then the death penalty for the apostate is prescribed categorically.

13:1-5. Though the **prophet** or **dreamer of dreams**—possibly a synonym for "prophet" (cf. Num. 12:6) but more probably a type of soothsayer (cf. 18:10-11)—is discussed here only as one form of enticement to apostasy, the practical religio-political problem of discerning the true from the false prophet is involved. The general criterion of success in prediction (18:15-22; see comment) cannot be trusted too far. Even though the **sign or wonder . . . comes to pass** it may be only Yahweh's way of **testing** loyalty. If the successful prophet or soothsayer advises departure from the worship of Yahweh he must be recognized as false and put to death. Presumably the person here castigated is a Canaanite prophet or a former Yahwist prophet who has transferred allegiance to a pagan god.

13:6-11. Loyalty to Yahweh must supersede even love for family.

13:12-18. Whereas the first 2 cases conceive of individual direct enticements that are stopped before becoming widely influential, the 3rd deals with the situation where **base fellows** (JPSV "scoundrels") have already **drawn away** a whole **city** into pagan worship. The penalty is that the town is to be put under the ban of holy war and all its inhabitants and their possessions are to be destroyed (see below on 20:10-18). By their failure to **purge the evil** from their community (vs. 5) all share in the guilt.

C. Funerary and Dietary Laws (14:1-21)

This section consists of a series of brief categorical laws, perhaps originally part of a cultic decalogue or dodecalogue, which has been amplified by a list of permitted and prohibited foods and by D exhortation.

14:1-2. That shaving the head as a sign of mourning was widely practiced is shown by many allusions in prophetic writings (e.g. Isa. 3:24; Jer. 7:29; Ezek. 7:18; Amos 8:10; Mic. 1:16), and cutting gashes in the flesh is mentioned in Jer. 16:6; 41:5. Cf. Lev. 19:28; 21:5.

14:3-20. The treatment of clean and unclean animals is roughly divided into mammals, marine creatures, birds, and insects. The similar list in Lev. follows the same order and specifies most of the same mammals and birds that may not be eaten. Chief differences are that the Lev. list permits eating certain insects and treats "swarming creatures," i.e. rodents and reptiles, whereas this list names a number of clean mammals. Probably the 2 lists were developed independently from a common source.

14:6-10. The only criteria offered for determining what is a clean animal are that it both **parts the hoof** and **chews the cud,** or, for marine life, has **fins and scales.** Efforts to find a clear sanitary or cultic or moral rationale for the distinctions have not yielded convincing results. It appears that the factors contributing to Israel's sense of the unclean were highly eclectic and often so ancient that they had become uncritical custom and were thus totally lost to the view of the law compilers. Among the operatives in the distant or near background may have been: (*a*) fear of some animals as potential disease carriers; (*b*) revulsion at the appearance or habits of certain animals; (*c*) totemic taboos; (*d*) symbolic or sacramental use of animals in pagan worship. This eclectic potpourri of dietary prohibitions was given arbitrary status as the law of God and thereby was put beyond the realm of rational inquiry or personal taste.

14:21*a-c*. The prohibition against eating any animal that **dies of itself** is based on the fact that the blood would not be properly drained from the carcass (cf. 12:16, 23-25). A secondary motive was doubtless to prevent the eating of spoiled meat, but note that it might be given to the **alien** or sold to **foreigners.**

14:21*d*. This final law forbidding one to **boil a kid in its mother's milk** (cf. Exod. 23:19; 34:26) is understandable as abhorrence at a Canaanite cult practice. By extension it has become the basis for modern Jewish separation of meat and milk foods and of the dishes in which they are prepared and served.

D. Tithing Laws (14:22-29)

14:22-27. Every year a 10th of the agricultural produce and a token offering (**firstlings**) from the flock are to be dedicated at the central sanctuary and eaten there. To allow for the **long** distance that some must travel to Jerusalem it is permitted to turn the tithe **into money** and to purchase equivalent produce in Jerusalem for the sacrificial meal. The Levites are to share in the food with the worshipers (cf. 12:12).

14:28-29. Every 3rd year the tithe is to be kept **within your towns** instead of brought to Jerusalem, and the Levites and the poor are to be fed from it. That this segment of the law envisions the Levites as still living throughout Israel, in contrast to the larger framework of D, which legislates their transfer to Jerusalem, is yet another indication of the older origin of some of the book's contents. Whether this tithing ceremony is the same as the first-fruits ceremony of 26:1-11 is uncertain. The P version of the tithing law (Num. 18:21-32) conceives the entire tithe as given to the Levites, who in turn are to give a 10th of the tithe to the Aaronic priesthood. Perhaps D represents the N practice and P that of Jerusalem. Early Judaism harmonized the discrepancy by adding the D tithe to the P tithe. Whether the 2 were harmonized before the Exile, or whether D simply replaced P at Jerusalem after 622, or whether the P law did not originate until after the Exile—all are possibilities, but none can be demonstrated.

This offering of tithes and first fruits at the central sanctuary is widely thought to have been in conjunction with one of the 3 annual fixed feasts, esp. the feast of weeks (see below on 16:9-12). This may well be true at least in the sense that the feast of weeks marked the beginning of the period, continuing on through the summer, when such offerings were made. If so, on every 3rd feast of weeks the tithing ceremony was not observed at Jerusalem.

E. The Year of Release (15:1-18)

Two laws are juxtaposed here which have in common release of contractual obligation in the 7th year.

15:1-11. *Release of Debtors.* The first law specifies that every 7th or sabbatical year there shall be a cancellation of all debts owed by fellow Israelites. **At the end of every seven years** probably means that the law covers loans outstanding at the close of the year. The sense of the passage is that the entire principal ceases to be owed, not merely the year's payment on the principal. In Exod. 23:10-11; Lev. 25:1-7 a sabbatical year is enjoined on the land so that it may lie fallow, but Lev. 25:8-55 reserves cancellation of debts for the 50th or jubilee year. One practical problem in such a release of debt is demonstrated in the exhortation of vss. 7-11 to ignore the approach of the **year of release** and thus in effect make a gift rather than a loan. How widely this law was observed is unknown, but we can easily imagine disregard or even outright rejection of it.

15:12-18. *Release of Slaves.* The 2nd law applies the sabbatical principle to **Hebrew** slaves. The 7th year in this case, however, is not a fixed period but refers to the 7th year of the slave's service (cf. Exod. 21:2-11). There was an intimate connection between debts and slavery in that the last resort of a debtor unable to repay was to offer himself and his physical labor to his creditor (cf. Neh. 5:1-13).

F. Firstlings (15:19-23)

This provision for each first-born male animal to be given to God rightly belongs with the tithing laws of 14:22-29, as is evident not only from the subject matter but also from the reference in 14:23 to the **firstlings of your herd and flock.** The intrusion of 15:1-18 may be due to an editorial desire to parallel **At the end of every three years** (14:28) with **At the end of every seven years** (15:1).

G. Annual Feasts (16:1-17)

The stated annual festivals of ancient Israel are here summarized. The prescriptions stand midway in detail between the terse law of Exod. 23:14-17 and the expanded specifications, esp. of the offerings, in Lev. 23; Num. 28-29. Common to all the lists of festivals is the centrality of the 3 agricultural feasts: **passover . . . unleavened bread** in the first month (Mar.-Apr.); **weeks** (harvest, NT Pentecost) in the 3rd month (May-Jun.); **booths . . . ingathering** in the 7th month (Sep.-Oct.). The D emphasis is on the observance of these 3 feasts at the central sanctuary, **at the place which the LORD your God will choose,** and on the obligation of worshipers to come with suitable offerings, not to **appear before the LORD empty-handed.**

H. The Office of Judge (16:18-17:13)

Administration of justice is provided for in the primary categorical law of 16:18. This is expanded by a hortatory call climaxed with **Justice, and only justice, you shall follow** (16:19-20) and by 2 conditional amplifications (17:2-7, 8-13).

16:21-17:1. *Two Cultic Laws.* Intruded here are 2 brief laws which topically belong to cultic provisions such as 14:1-21 or 18:9-14. One prohibits planting a **tree** (i.e. installing a wooden pole or image) dedicated to the Canaanite goddess **Asherah** or setting up a stone **pillar,** perhaps a symbol of Baal, as a part of Yahweh worship. The other prohibits sacrifice of an animal with a **blemish.** Possibly an editor conceived of these 2 laws as illustrations of the "abominable" pagan practices referred to in the following vss.

17:2-7. *The Requirement for Witnesses.* When one is suspected of a crime, e.g. apostasy (cf. ch. 13), the judges must **inquire diligently** and secure the **evidence of two witnesses or of three;** the accused may not be executed because of one man's charge (cf. 19:15; Num. 35:30).

17:8-13. *The "Supreme Court."* Provision is made for handling cases **too difficult** for the local judges, e.g. a thorny case of **homicide,** property **right,** or **assault.** These complicated or disputed cases are to be referred to a central tribunal in Jerusalem, whose verdict is final (vss. 10-11), with death as the penalty for contempt (vs. 12). The composition of the tribunal is both clerical (**Levitical priests**) and lay (**judge**). Though its organization is touched on only obscurely here, comparison with 19:15-21; II Chr. 19:8-11 indicates that the tribunal had 2 presiding officers, a priest who presided over ecclesiastical cases and a lay judge who presided over civil cases. The D law assumes the tribunal as already in existence (**in office in those days,** vs. 9); the aim is

not to initiate it but to insure that its supreme jurisdiction will be honored and its procedures for appeal regularly utilized.

I. The Office of the King (17:14-20)

Technically the law about kingship in Israel is framed, not as an injunction, but as a subjunctive: **You may . . . set as king over you** (vs. 15). The warnings and appeals that follow show the monarchy as a given but embarrassing factor in Israel's life.

17:14-15. *Selection of a King.* Presupposed by the permission to have a king **whom the LORD your God will choose** are the various measures for popular choice and ratification of a king by the assembly of the people or their representatives by means of which they enter a covenant with the new leader. Though never directly described, such protocols are alluded to in the accounts of Sam. and Kings. That the present section is not a political document per se is evident in its failure to detail the mechanism of choice and the means of formal ratification. We can only speculate as to whether the author, or editor, thought that the long-established principle of hereditary kingship could be reversed, esp. in Judah. If the older form of this provision is from N Israel before 722, the call for extreme care in the choice of a king would be more intelligible since in that kingdom there were several dynasties and transient claimants to the throne in contrast to the endurance of the Davidic dynasty in the S.

17:15b. The one firm requirement in the choice of a king, that he be **one from among your brethren,** comes as something of a superfluity. There is no report that a **foreigner** ever held the throne in Israel or Judah. Some have suggested, however, that Omri (cf. I Kings 16:15-22) is a non-Israelite name and that the apparently Ammonite "son of Tabeel" (Isa. 7:6), whom the kings of Israel and Syria intended to install in Judah in place of Ahaz, may have had Judean support. Given the theocratic character of the book, the prohibition may rather be a dramatic way of warning against the allure of foreign worship and custom which the kingship might introduce.

17:16-20. *Rules for the King's Conduct.* The law declares that the king **must not multiply horses, . . . wives, . . . silver and gold.** But how much is too much? This is no precise legal instrument but a solemn warning: too many armaments (horses for cavalry), too many alliances (wives to seal political pacts), too much revenue would lead toward monarchic autonomy and absolutism and away from Israel's unique "congregational" faith. Solomon was a famous example of just such antitheocratic tendencies, but he was not alone in baleful effects on Israel. According to II Kings 22-23 it is Josiah who exemplifies the D ideal of a king, for his political actions are modest and directly related to his cultic and religious goals of rebuilding the Israelite community of faith.

17:18. The stipulation that the king must retain and frequently study **a copy of this law** shows the vital interest of the section. The monarchy must not act in a manner that will jeopardize the D law, for that would bring about the ultimate catastrophe of alienation from Yahweh. After a fashion we can speak of a constitutional monarchy, but only very loosely. The laws of chs. 12-26 supply a constitution, not for the monarchy, but for Israel's theocratically guided life. The king must avoid intruding into the theocratic sphere, where the priests and prophets and judges preside. These laws are not of the sort that the king would directly execute; they do not describe the authority or the functions of his office. Indeed such laws would be at cross purposes with economic, political, and military policies of monarchy as generally practiced in the ancient world.

J. The Office of Priest (18:1-8)

The Levitical priests, already introduced as the landless clients of the other tribes and as members of the central tribunal, are here discussed in their own right.

It is significant to note that in Deut. **all of the tribe of Levi** may be priests, though they may not all be officiating at once. This is in contrast to the view in the P writings, which regard only those of Aaron's stock as full priests, the rest of the Levites being merely assistants or cultic menials (cf. e.g. Num. 3:1-10).

18:3-5. The support of the priests is the duty of the other tribes. It is to be provided regularly by giving them specified portions of each animal **sacrifice** and the **first fruits of . . . grain, . . . wine, . . . olive oil, . . . fleece.** An additional measure for the support of the Levites is that those from any of the **towns** may come to Jerusalem, **minister** at the temple, and receive equal maintenance along with the indigenous Jerusalem Levites. This express permission for the migration of Levites into Jerusalem is doubtless an attempt to mitigate the drastic effect of closing outlying sanctuaries (12:17). Obviously if the Levites were to function as priests at all they would have to do so at Jerusalem. It takes little imagination, however, to picture the immense difficulties in the way of realizing such an idealistic program. The practical problems stemming from interpersonal frictions and institutional jealousies are reflected in an aside in the account of Josiah's destruction of the high places in 622: "However, the priests of the high places did not come up to the altar of the Lord in Jerusalem, but they ate unleavened bread among their brethren" (II Kings 23:9).

18:8. The clause translated **besides what he receives from the sale of his patrimony** renders an obscure Hebrew text that refers imprecisely to "sales according to the fathers." The most that can confidently be said is that it alludes to a limited source of private income that Levites would bring with them when they moved to Jerusalem, perhaps no more than their personal possessions.

K. Condemnation of Pagan Cult Practices (18:9-14)

The sequence of laws about offices in Israel, ending with the prophet in vss. 15-22, is broken by this proscription of pagan religious **abominable practices** of 2 sorts. The first sort (vs. 10a) is denoted by a phrase lit. meaning "makes . . . pass through the fire" (cf. e.g. Lev. 18:21; II Kings 17:17; 21:6; Jer. 32:35; Ezek. 20:26). This was apparently under-

stood by the Chronicler as referring to child sacrifice (II Chr. 28:3; cf. II Kings 16:3) and has been generally so interpreted—e.g. in the translation **burns . . . as an offering.** Some scholars claim, however, that it refers rather to an ordeal by fire and that occasional failures to survive the test explain such references to it as 12:31; Jer. 7:31; 19:5; Ezek. 16:20-21; 23:37-39. The other sort of condemned practices (vs. 10b) includes various forms of communication with the occult, such as **divination** of the future, fixing of curses or spells, and communication with the dead. It may well have been the editor's intent to place this piece as a foil to the description of the true prophet which follows it.

L. The Office of Prophet (18:15-22)

The subject is introduced under the guise of Moses announcing his prophetic successors. Though he speaks of **a prophet** the context implies that the prophetic office is to be filled by a succession of prophets. The common messianic view that this refers to a single prophet yet to come is challenged by the following criteria for distinguishing true from false prophets (vss. 20-22). Obviously more than one prophet is involved and they are currently vying for the people's credence.

18:20-22. Criteria of prophetic validity are discussed more inclusively here than in 13:1-5. There is agreement on the point that any prophet who prophesies **in the name of other gods** than Yahweh is disqualified. But this passage goes on to consider the knotty problem of the prophet who speaks falsely in Yahweh's name. Some interpreters take this to refer to those who deliberately claim Yahweh's inspiration when they know they do not have it. Religious certitude being what it is, however, it is far more likely that the reference includes precisely those who are sincere in their Yahwistic claims but who are nonetheless mistaken according to the D view.

How are claims of prophetic inspiration to be judged? The D author answers in a somewhat heavy-handed way that the thing to do is to wait to see if what the prophet says does **come to pass.** In the long run this is probably an argument of some force. Religious claims can often best be judged by how they help us to interpret events; they have an objective social and historical reference. But it is scarcely a very helpful criterion for taking immediate action—the sort of choice that Israelites often had to make between competing prophetic claims (cf. e.g. I Kings 22:1-40; Jer. 27-28). At very best then this can only have been an exceedingly rough indicator of validity and goes to show how little amenable prophecy was to testing by legalistic formulations. Yet the very fact that Deut. is the only law compilation that deals with prophecy shows how profoundly that movement had impressed the D authors, even to the extent that they regarded the prophet as Israel's equivalent of the omnipresent diviner or soothsayer in surrounding religions.

M. Criminal Laws (19:1-21)

Three crimes are treated. Procedures for ascertaining guilt and administering punishment are given only for the first and 3rd.

19:1-13. Homicide. The problem of protecting an

innocent **manslayer** from the vengeance sanctioned by ancient custom is to be handled by establishing **cities of refuge**—places of asylum to which the accused can flee for a cooling-off period. If the homicide was committed **unintentionally** he can thus save himself from death at the hands of the victim's relatives. Cf. Exod. 21:12-14; Num. 35:9-34; Josh. 20.

19:7-10. This passage does not name any cities of refuge or explicitly take account of Moses' designation of 3 such cities in Transjordan in 4:41-43. Two interpretations are possible: (a) The Transjordanian cities of 4:41-43 are tacitly presupposed, the 3 cities of vs. 7 are in W Palestine, and the 3 cities of vs. 9 are to be in enlarged territory of Israel N from Mt. Hermon to the Euphrates, thus making a total of 9 cities of refuge. (b) The designation of 4:41-43 is ignored and therefore duplicated in vs. 7, and the additional cities of vs. 9 are those in W Palestine, making a total of 6. There are difficulties in the way of either view but the weight of evidence tends toward the first.

19:11-13. A city of refuge will not protect one who kills with malice and premeditation. The **elders of his city** are to take him from the place to which he has fled, presumably judge his guilt (cf. I Kings 21:9-13), and hand him over for execution to the **avenger of blood,** i.e. the relative of the victim who by murdering the murderer restores balance to society and the divine order.

19:14. Removal of Boundary Markers. In quoting an old law against stealing land by moving the stone **landmark** indicating its border (cf. 27:17) the D author placed it in the setting of Moses' speech by adding the opening clause but apparently did not feel free to modify **which the men of old have set** to fit Moses' point of view.

19:15-21. False Witness. To the requirement for **two** or **three witnesses** (see above on 17:2-7) is added a provision about **malicious** perjury (cf. 5:20; Exod. 20:16; 23:1-2; Lev. 19:16). If such is suspected the case must be taken **before the LORD,** i.e. to the **priests** and **judges** of the central tribunal (see above on 17:8-13). The false witness is to suffer the penalty which he sought for his victim.

N. Holy War (20:1-20)

The provisions for the conduct of holy war in this passage must be read in conjunction with similar laws in 21:10-14; 23:10-14; 24:5; 25:17-19. They belong to a pattern of thought which underlies the entire book and permeates the accounts of the conquest and settlement of Palestine in Josh., Judg., Sam. The essence of that pattern is the protection of Israel's cultic purity by extermination of the Canaanites, whose intermixture with Israel would lead inevitably to her apostasy.

20:1-9. The Muster to Military Service. The **priest** is to instruct the army not to fear a more powerful enemy inasmuch as God will **fight** for Israel. The conscription **officers** are to announce exemptions for those who have **built a new house, . . . planted a vineyard, . . . betrothed a wife** recently. They are even to dismiss those who are simply **fearful** so that others may not be infected (cf. Judg. 7:2-3). **Commanders** are to be chosen after this weeding-out process.

20:10-18. Terms of Peace. A besieged **city** outside Canaan is to be offered an opportunity to surrender. If it is accepted, the populace is to be enslaved. If it is rejected, captured males are to be killed and women, children, livestock, and goods are to be taken. No terms of peace are to be offered to Canaanite cities; the entire populace, livestock, and possessions are to be destroyed lest pagan religious practices infect Israel.

20:19-20. Preservation of Fruit Trees. The short-range military advantage of securing wood to **build siegeworks** does not overrule the long-range productivity of fruit-bearing trees.

O. Expiation for an Unsolved Murder (21:1-9)

A murder in the **open country** becomes the responsibility of the **nearest** town if the murderer cannot be identified. Its **elders** are to conduct a ceremony of expiation by killing a **heifer** over **running water.** The washing of hands over the heifer, whose blood is in turn washed away in the stream, symbolizes the removal of the **guilt of innocent blood** from the town. The regulation cogently illustrates the Israelite notion of communal solidarity in guilt and in the expiation of guilt.

P. Miscellaneous Laws (21:10–22:12)

Ten laws of mixed form and subject matter have been arbitrarily assembled at this point. Since they are without hortatory expansion they give the impression of being from an early collection which the author or editor did not choose to redistribute topically. The motivations for these laws range from conscious efforts to achieve complete fairness in human dealings (e.g. 21:15-17) to uncritical feelings about what is appropriate or natural and vice versa (e.g. 22:9-11).

21:10-14. Female Prisoners of War. A captive woman (cf. 20:14) may be taken as a wife only after she is allowed to mourn **a full month** for her parents. If later her captor is displeased with her, she must be released rather than sold or enslaved. This law rightly belongs to the holy war regulations of ch. 20.

21:15-17. Right of the First-born. The oldest son's claim to a **double** share of the inheritance is inalienable. The father may favor one wife above another but cannot alter the status of their sons.

21:18-21. Rebellious Sons. The death penalty is prescribed for the son who does not **obey** his parents (cf. 5:16; Exod. 21:15, 17). They must bring the charge for trial by the **elders of his city.**

21:22-23. Burial of Executed Criminals. Publicizing the punishment of a criminal by displaying his body (cf. e.g. Josh. 8:29; 10:26-27; I Sam. 31:10; II Sam. 4:12) is permitted only on the day of execution. The body must be buried before nightfall, for an exposed corpse is **accursed by God** and would **defile your land** (cf. Num. 19:11-14; Tob. 1:17-18).

22:1-4. Care for Lost Property. Duty toward a **brother** (i.e. fellow Israelite) requires not merely avoiding injury to him but positive aid when his livestock or other property is lost or endangered. Cf. Exod. 23:4-5.

22:5. Distinction of Sexes. In addition to an obvious feeling about what is proper to the respective sexes this regulation possibly involves condemnation of pagan cultic practices (**abomination**).·

22:6-7. *Protection of Mother Birds.* This law perhaps grows out of the same attitude toward animal reproduction as Lev. 22 :27-28.

22:8. *Parapets on Roofs.* Most Palestinian houses were built with flat roofs. Their common use necessitated this safety regulation (cf. Exod. 21:33).

22:9-11. *Prohibition of Mixtures.* The basis for these rules is historically obscure and may be merely a feeling that mixing species violates their natural purity. Cf. Lev. 19:19.

22:12. *Tassels on Garments.* See comment on Num. 15:37-41.

Q. SEXUAL LAWS (22:13-30)

The first of these 6 laws concerns chastity of a wife (vss. 13-21), and the next 4 legislate against various types of extramarital sexual intercourse: with a married woman by consent (vs. 22; cf. Lev. 18:20; 20:10), with a betrothed woman by consent (vss. 23-24), with a betrothed woman by rape (vss. 25-27), and with a virgin by rape (vss. 28-29; cf. Exod. 22: 16-17). The 6th law—the only one in categorical form—appears to prohibit any sexual intercourse with one's mother or stepmother, including marriage to a stepmother following the father's death (vs. 30; cf. Lev. 18:8; 20:11).

The penalties for violation of these laws range from death for both parties through death for the man alone to payment to the father of the violated girl (cf. Exod. 22:16-17). On close examination it is clear that the fabric of sexual values and practices in ancient Israel was fundamentally intended as a cloak for the institution of the patriarchal family. Whatever threatens the rights of the male-dominated family must be firmly rejected. The double standard is clearly expressed in the penalties accompanying the first law. The wife shown to be unchaste stands to lose her life, whereas the most that a falsely accusing husband will suffer is a public whipping, payment of compensation to his father-in-law, and forfeiture of the right of divorce. Such checks would prevent his making charges lightly. The woman has protection but even this is an extension of the honor of her father—note that the compensation goes to him and not to her. It is evident that any adulterous liaison means death for the wife, whereas a husband who consorts with a virgin will, if caught, only pay compensation and be required to take her as his wife (assuming that vss. 28-29 include married men, since polygamy was not prohibited in Israel until postexilic times).

R. EXCLUSIONS FROM THE RELIGIOUS COMMUNITY (23:1-8)

A series of brief categorical regulations specifies those who are to be excluded from the **assembly of the LORD,** i.e. from participating in the gathering of the nation for religious purposes, not from living in the land of Israel.

23:1-2. *Sexual Bars.* The language of vs. 1 evidently intends to exclude a eunuch whether emasculated accidentally or deliberately (cf. Lev. 21:17). Rabbinical tradition applied the word translated **bastard** to one born of marriage between persons of a prohibited degree of affinity (cf. Lev. 18:6-20; 20: 10-21) but presumably it means any child of an illicit union (cf. Judg. 9:1-3; Hos. 2:4).

23:3-8. *Ethnic Bars.* Anyone descended from an **Ammonite** or a **Moabite** is prohibited from entering the Israelite religious community, but a descendant of the **third generation** from an **Edomite** or an **Egyptian** may become a member. The reasons offered are historical: Ammon and Moab did not help Israel through the wilderness but instead hired **Balaam** to **curse** Israel. Edom (i.e. Esau) is Israel's **brother** (cf. Gen. 25:23-26; 36:8) and Israel was a **sojourner** in Egypt, apparently implying that during part of Israel's stay the Egyptians treated the Hebrews well (cf. Gen. 39–50). However, none of the Pentateuchal accounts (including 2:8*b*-19) agree in picturing Ammon as rebuffing Israel or involved in Moab's hiring of Balaam. The laws themselves seem very old and it may be that the motivations were added later by someone whose memory lapsed or who knew of other traditions about Ammon. It is possible that the contrasting attitudes are simply based on those which predominate in Gen., where Ammon and Moab are born of incestuous unions between Lot and his daughters (Gen. 19:30-38; cf. Lev. 18:9) but Esau (Edom) is held in affection in spite of his uncouthness and witlessness and Egypt is the benefactor of Joseph and his family. No period is known in Israel's history when Ammon and Moab were her enemies while Edom and Egypt were cordial or neutral.

S. MILITARY CAMP LAWS (23:9-14)

These laws, designed to keep the Israelite soldier **from every evil thing** while in camp, belong to the rules of holy war (see above on ch. 20). They reflect profound abhorrence of uncovered semen and excrement—an abhorrence naïvely projected on the deity. If Yahweh, who **walks in the midst of your camp,** should encounter **anything indecent** (lit. "naked") he would necessarily **turn away from you.** The underlying view is that Yahweh is himself powerless before such elemental magical realities and that therefore to hold on to her God Israel must be clean. Understood simply as sanitary measures the rules make sense.

T. MORE MISCELLANEOUS LAWS (23:15–25:19)

This is by far the largest block of miscellaneous laws in the book. As in 21:10–22:12 the miscellany extends to form and to subject matter. The inclusion of such D exhortations as 24:8-9; 25:17-19 argues against the view that this section was drawn as a whole from another source. It is possible of course that one or more smaller collections were incorporated but the lines of demarcation do not remain. That these varied items occur at the virtual close of the law code suggests that they were remaining materials which the D author wanted to include but did not see reason to organize topically within themselves or to combine with earlier segments of his work.

23:15-16. *Shelter of Fugitive Slaves.* A runaway slave is to be given asylum. The provision could apply equally to one who flees to Israel from another land or to one who leaves an Israelite master, but vs. 16 seems to envision only the first situation.

23:17-18. Cult Prostitution. Among Israel's cultic functionaries there is to be no **cult prostitute** (lit. "holy one"), i.e. one devoted to miming the fertility of the gods and communicating it to men and nature. Furthermore money acquired from payment to secular prostitutes may not be offered to fulfill a religious vow.

23:19-20. Interest. Charging interest on a loan to a fellow Israelite is forbidden (cf. Exod. 22:25; Lev. 25:35-38) but on a loan to a **foreigner** it is allowed. This may be simply an instance of in-group-out-group bias, but it may equally reflect the fact that loans to fellow Israelites were mainly to those in desperate straits (cf. 15:7-11) whereas loans to foreigners were normally to tradesmen for the expansion of business. If so, behind the seeming ethnic discrimination lies an attempt to differentiate on the basis of need.

23:21-23. Vows. Vows to God—esp. promises to make contributions to the temple in return for divine favor—are optional. Once made, however, they must be paid (cf. Lev. 27; Num. 30). This "law" is illustrative of the hortatory type common in Deut., and we may well wonder how it could be enforced. It would seem to depend on individual conscience and community persuasion, esp. if the vow was not heard by others or if God's favor was in doubt.

23:24-25. Eating from a Neighbor's Crops. A passer-by may take food from a **vineyard** or field of **grain** sufficient to meet his immediate need, but he may not carry anything away (cf. 24:19-22).

24:1-4. Remarriage After Divorce. This is as near as the OT comes to containing a divorce law. It is in fact a law presupposing divorce but attempting to control its abuse. A woman who is divorced and remarries may not be retaken by her first husband should the 2nd husband die or divorce her. The apparent intent is to reduce the frequency of divorce by cautioning the husband that he may not reacquire a wife he divorces impetuously. The **indecency** (lit. "nakedness of a thing") mentioned as the cause of divorce is probably not adultery since that offense was punishable by death; it refers rather to immodesty or too open relations with other men.

24:5. Exemption from Military Service. The law exempting a betrothed man from military service (20:7) is here extended to include one **newly married**, i.e. within **one year**.

24:6. Pledges on Loans. A borrower was expected to provide a **pledge**, i.e. security for repayment of the loan. The lender is here forbidden to take in pledge an object which the debtor needs in order to live, the family **millstone** used to grind grain into flour (cf. vss. 10-13).

24:7. Forced Enslavement. Kidnapping a fellow Israelite in order to retain or sell him as a slave is strictly forbidden (cf. Exod. 21:16).

24:8-9. Leprosy. This is not a law at all but an exhortation to observe the leprosy laws as interpreted by the Levitical priests. Precisely that sort of guidance, "to show when it is unclean and when it is clean," is contained in Lev. 13-14 (cf. esp. Lev. 14: 54-57). The D author's counsel presupposes a Levitical tradition of the same general type and thus shows familiarity with the antecedents of Lev. 13-14 or with parallel tradition. On **Miriam** cf. Num. 12:10-15.

24:10-13. Pledges on Loans. Another law on pledges is in the same mood as vss. 6, 17. A creditor may not enter the debtor's **house** to take any pledge he likes. If the debtor is reduced to the point of offering his **cloak** as pledge, it must be returned to him for night use as a blanket (cf. Exod. 22:26-27; Amos 2:8). In effect this means that no pledge at all is to be taken or that it is merely to be taken ceremonially for one day or on periodic occasions as a reminder that the debt is still due (cf. Ezek. 18:7).

24:14-15. Payment of Hired Laborers. Israelites or **sojourners** (i.e. resident aliens) who hire out are not to be taken advantage of, but are to be paid at the end of each day (cf. Lev. 19:13). This seemingly small point probably took on importance because much hiring was for seasonal agricultural work on a day-to-day basis (cf. Matt. 20:1-16).

24:16. Individual Criminal Guilt. This categorical law specifically excludes executing a father for his children's crimes or children for their father's crimes (cf. Jer. 31:29; Ezek. 18). Josh. 7:16-26; II Sam. 21: 1-9 show that collective guilt (see above on 21:1-9) was sometimes translated into legal guilt and punishment. Even if such cases were exceptional the very possibility would be a source of uneasiness in the community and an occasion for misuse. II Kings 14:5-6 notes that King Amaziah of Judah executed only the assassins of his father Joash and not their children. His leniency seems to have been sufficiently exceptional—at least for political crimes in the 8th cent.—to draw the special attention of the D historian.

24:17. Justice for the Weak. Israel is cautioned not to **pervert the justice due** the weakest elements of society (cf. Exod. 22:21-22; 23:6-9; Lev. 19:33-34). This is illustrated by the heinous crime of taking a **widow's garment in pledge** (see above on vss. 10-13). Such solicitude for the weak is to be based on the remembrance that Israel was herself once a **slave in Egypt**; as God **redeemed** her so Israel must "redeem" her poor.

24:19-22. Gleanings for the Poor. When a **field** of grain, orchard of **olive trees**, or **vineyard** is harvested, sufficient of the produce is to be left that the provisionless **sojourner, the fatherless, and the widow** may gather the gleanings for food (cf. Lev. 19:9-10; 23:22; Ruth 2:2-7). The slavery-in-Egypt motif is again urged as the basis for this humanitarianism.

25:1-3. Regulations for Judicial Beatings. Beatings for crimes are to be administered only after trial and in view of the **judge**. The number of blows may not exceed **forty**; in later times it was limited to 39 (cf. II Cor. 11:24) lest there be a miscount. The remark that the offender is **to lie down** suggests that the blows may have been applied to the soles of the feet.

25:4. The Unmuzzled Ox. The concern for domestic animals succinctly expressed in this law that the ox used for threshing must not be prevented from eating of the grain seems genuine (cf. Prov. 12:10) in spite of Paul's argument to the contrary (I Cor. 9:3-12; cf. I Tim. 5:18).

25:5-10. Levirate Marriage. When a married man dies without a son, the **husband's brother** (*levir* in Latin—the word "levirate" has nothing to do with "Levite"!) living on the same estate is expected to

Courtesy of Herbert G. May

Gleaners on the Plain of Esdraelon (see comment on 24:19-22)

marry the widow. The **first son** born of the union is to take the **name** of the deceased man; any further offspring are presumably reckoned to the living brother. The surviving brother who **refuses** this obligation is to be publicly rebuked in a ceremony in which the widow will remove his **sandal** and **spit in his face.** The aim of levirate marriage was not primarily to provide for the widow since other means were available for that purpose, but rather (a) to secure the survival of the deceased's line (the only form of immortality known to ancient Israel) and (b) to keep in the family estate property which might otherwise be sold to pay debts. This is the only biblical stipulation on the practice, but it is presupposed in the account of Judah and Tamar (Gen. 38), and the story of Ruth and Boaz is based on an extension of it to the nearest consenting relative when no brother is available (Ruth 4:1-8). Levirate marriage is also known in India, Madagascar, and Brazil.

25:11-12. Protection of an Assailant's Genitals. So important are offspring to a man that his genitals must be protected at all costs. For this reason even a woman protecting her husband against an assailant may not harm the aggressor's genitals. Presumably the application to women is not exclusive but simply recognizes that, lacking the strength to fight a man by other means, a woman might be more tempted to attack the vulnerable male genitals. It is possible the passage refers to a wrestling match which a zealous wife tries to help her husband win.

25:13-16. Honest Weights and Measures. False weights and measures were a tempting form of commercial misconduct (cf. Amos 8:5). Israelites are warned not to have **two kinds . . . , a large and a small,** meaning either (a) correct ones for purchase and false ones for defrauding customers or (b) 2 false

sets, one large for fixing quantities bought and another small for fixing quantities sold. Cf. Lev. 19:35-36. See "Measures and Money," pp. 1283-85.

25:17-19. Extermination of Amalek. Amalekites from the desert region S of Canaan attacked Israel in the wilderness shortly after the Exodus (Exod. 17:8-16). In the time of the judges they raided Palestine alongside the Midianites (Judg. 6:3, 33; 7:12) and Saul and David fought several engagements with them (I Sam. 15; 27:8-9; 30; II Sam. 8:12). Though a "remnant of the Amalekites" are said to have been destroyed during Hezekiah's reign (I Chr. 4:42-43; cf. Ps. 83:7) they seem not to have been a serious threat after David's reign. Therefore this vehement command to **blot out the remembrance of Amalek** (cf. Exod. 18:14) is best understood as a tradition from premonarchic times that lived on as an expression of the holy war obligation (see above on 20:1-20). By the 7th cent. it was no more than a liturgical archaism.

U. RITES FOR FIRST FRUITS AND TITHES (26:1-15)

The law proper in Deut. is brought to a close by descriptions of how to conduct annual first-fruits offerings and triennial tithes. The heart of each ceremony is a declaration to be made by the worshiper, each with its own special character: the one a collective statement of Israel's faith, the other an affirmation of individual compliance with the tithe law of 14:22-29. The "confessions" have been placed in their present position to give an appropriately resounding liturgical conclusion to the compilation.

26:1-11. First-Fruits Ceremony. The offering of **some of the first of all the fruit of the ground** (cf. 18:4; Exod. 22:29; 23:19a; 34:26a; Lev. 23:10-11; Num. 15:20-21; 18:12-14; Neh. 10:35-37) may be one form of the tithing obligation cited in 14:22-29 (see comment), or it may be an earlier form of practices that developed into tithes, i.e. an original token "first fruit" which developed into a fixed tenth of the produce. An open question also is whether the ceremony was at one of the fixed public festivals. Though our information is hazy, the feast of weeks (cf. 16:9-12) seems to have inaugurated a period extending to the feast of booths (cf. 16:13-15) during which first fruits could be offered. The actions and set words described here could certainly represent a part of one of the great festivals—this may well be the plain sense of **rejoice** (vs. 11), i.e. "celebrate publicly and collectively." On the other hand the presentation of a **basket** of fruit before the **priest** could easily be repeated at Jerusalem as often as landowners appeared there during the summer. The fact that crops ripen at differing times in Palestine, depending on altitude, soil, and rainfall patterns, suggests flexibility in the timing of the first-fruits ceremony.

26:5-11. The liturgical affirmation begins **A wandering Aramean was my father** (JPSV "a fugitive Aramean") and is exemplary of a number of biblical restatements of the people's history (cf. e.g. 6:20-25). The worshiper identifies with his ancestor Jacob and the past experience of his people, and he concludes on the note of responsibility for maintaining the land by loyalty to his God.

26:12-15. Tithe Ceremony. After the triennial tithing observance in each of the **towns,** when the tithes are distributed locally to **the Levite, the sojourner, the fatherless and the widow** (see above on 14:28-29), the worshiper is to give an oath of clearance asserting his compliance with the law and explicitly denying ritual defilement of the tithe through contact with anything **unclean.** That the oath is to be a sign **before the LORD** suggests that it is to be offered at Jerusalem following the tithing season, possibly at the feast of booths. Since the actual transactions of this triennial tithe were all carried out away from Jerusalem, this would constitute a formal report at the central sanctuary verifying that the tithe laws had in fact been properly observed.

V. Hortatory Conclusion to the Laws (26:16-19)

The **statutes and ordinances** of chs. 12–26 are rounded out with exhortations placed in the mouth of Moses and replete with D religious and moral terminology. Israel's holiness is to be demonstrated in observance of the law and in her consequent position **high above all nations.**

VI. Renewal of the Covenant and the Death of Moses (27:1–34:12)

As in the introductory exhortations and résumés of chs. 1–11, so in these final chs. the aim is to inculcate fundamental loyalty to Israel's God and esp. obedience to the laws of chs. 12–26. The distinctive feature of the conclusion, however, is the open or implied reference to ratification of the covenant in Moab and to subsequent renewal ceremonies to be observed in Canaan after the occupation of the land.

The distinction between the covenant at Horeb and the covenant in Moab is sharply stated in 29:1. The reason for the 2nd covenant is not that the first was annulled through faithlessness, nor that the 2nd

is to have a different content or orientation. It seems rather that the 2nd covenant is a reaffirmation and an elaboration of the first. It is necessitated partly by the rebellion of the people and partly by the demands of the new situation which they are to face in Canaan. There is thus a certain recognition of the development of historical and legal traditions, even though the development is compressed dramatically into the lifespan of Moses. Not everything was given to Israel at one time and place. The "covenant" is in fact a series of covenants, a growing and changing relation with God. This is expressed in Deut. by quoting the decalogue of 5:6-21 as the legal instrument of the first covenant in such a way as to show that it remains in effect under the 2nd; to it the "statutes and ordinances" are added as instruments of the 2nd covenant. It is in essence 2 phases or stages of one covenant relationship to God.

Of particular interest is the reference to renewal ceremonies to be held in Canaan, one on Mts. Gerizim and Ebal at which blessings and curses are to be recited (27:11-13) and another at every 7th feast of booths at the central sanctuary (31:10-13). On the relation between the renewal ceremonies and the growth and structure of the book see Intro.

A. Ceremony of Covenant Renewal (27:1–28:68)

All of chs. 5–26 in their present form appear as a long speech of Moses, introduced in 5:1 by "Moses . . . said." In contrast, ch. 27 contains 3 such 3rd-person introductions (vss. 1, 9, 11), each followed by a brief speech, whereas ch. 28 again presents at some length a speech of Moses in characteristic D hortatory style without such interruptions. These and other literary phenomena have led many scholars to view ch. 27 as a composite of unrelated materials interpolated between chs. 26 and 28.

Such a view, however, gives too little consideration to the evidence that not only chs. 27–28 but the core of the whole book grew out of a periodic cultic celebration in which a priest in the role of Moses recited the terms of the covenant and called on the people to ratify it anew "this day" (see Intro.). In this light the 3rd-person introductions may be recognized as "stage directions" for the person portraying Moses and for the elders (vs. 1) and priests (vs. 9) participating in the dramatic rite. The climax of this ceremony was the intoning of blessings and curses by the tribes facing each other on opposite mountainsides (27:11-13); and the text of their blessings and curses is to be found, not in 27:14-26 (see comment below), but in ch. 28, where it is much amplified by D exhortation. Ch. 28 is thus the continuation, not of 26:16-19, as often said, but of 27:1-13.

Nearly all interpreters agree that the consternation of King Josiah on reading the edition of Deut. found in the temple in 622 (II Kings 22:11-13) proves that it contained the blessings and curses of ch. 28 (probably most of vss. 1-46; see below on 28:47-68). That these were preceded in this edition by 27:1-13 is strongly suggested by the probability that not long afterward the D compiler-author of Josh.-Kings (see Intro.) composed an account (Josh. 8:30-35) of how Joshua carried out the instructions "written in the book of the law of Moses" (cf. II Kings 22:8; 23:25) by building an altar on Mt. Ebal (cf. 27:5-7), writing the law on stones (cf. 27:2-4), and conducting a ceremony with the people standing on the 2 mountainsides (cf. 27:11-13) in which a reading of the law (cf. 27:9-10) was followed by blessing and cursing (cf. ch. 28, esp. vss. 3-6, 16-19).

27:1-8. *The Sanctuary at Shechem.* The first instruction, by **Moses and the elders,** is to **write . . . all the words of this law** on large plaster-coated **stones** to be raised **on Mount Ebal,** near Shechem (see above on 11:25). Examples found in Egypt show that the **plaster** was used to provide a smooth light-colored surface on which letters could be painted **very plainly** (vs. 8). The custom of displaying public decrees, reports, or statutes on walls or on stone or metal steles (i.e. free-standing slabs or pillars) is a familiar one in the ancient world—e.g. Hammurabi's code was inscribed on a large diorite stele. The intent was to insure compliance with the laws by publicizing a standard text for recitation and instruction. The command for an **altar . . . of unhewn stones** (cf. Exod. 20:25) to be built **there,** i.e. on or perhaps at the foot of Mt. Ebal, could be explained as a temporary provision pending Yahweh's choice of Jerusalem as the exclusive center of worship; but it seems rather to give evidence that the original central sanctuary of Deut. was at Shechem (see above on 11:29; 12:5).

27:9-10. *A Renewed Covenant.* Moses is joined by the **Levitical priests** in addressing to the people the solemn pronouncement **This day you have become the people of the LORD your God.** Since the D author does not picture the covenant in Moab as a new one, we should understand these words as typical of the reaffirming actions of the renewal ceremonies. As the people relived the original covenant events, recited the laws, and promised their fidelity, the presiding religious officials would announce Yahweh's acceptance of them as happening at that moment. The liturgical existentialism of the affirmation is evident; each new generation and each new year or cycle of years witnesses to the people's continual "becoming" the people of God.

27:11-13. *A Ceremony of Blessing and Cursing.* When Israel reaches Shechem (see above on 11:29) 6 of the tribes are to declaim blessings on the people from Mt. Gerizim and 6 are to declaim curses from Mt. Ebal. All the most important tribes are among those who **bless** but there is no reason to believe that the tribes who must **curse** are thereby demeaned or contaminated. Manasseh and Ephraim are here treated as a single tribe, **Joseph** (their father), as in 33:13-17 (cf. Gen. 49:22-26). These vss. lead on directly to ch. 28, where the blessings and curses are recorded.

27:14-26. *A Dodecalogue of Curses.* This dodecalogue has the look of an old preexilic list which has been awkwardly interpolated into a context in which it does not belong—apparently for 2 reasons: (a) association of **Cursed** as the initial word of each stipulation with "curse" in vs. 13 and (b) association of **the Levites** (vs. 14) with "Levi" in vs. 12. In actual fact the 2 passages clash. In vss. 11-13 Levi, along with 5 other tribes, pronounces blessings and the remaining tribes reply with curses. Here Levi alone addresses all the other tribes with curses, to each of which they are to respond **Amen.**

The 12 curses condemn various religious, social, and criminal offenses. All are specific except the last, which curses **whoever does not confirm the words of this law by doing them.** This suggests either that (a) an original series of 10 curses followed by a summarizing reinforcement was built up to 12 by adding a curse (perhaps vs. 15) or that (b) the series of 12 was formed from various older materials with chs. 12-26 in mind.

28:1-68. *The Blessings and Curses.* This ch. presents in expanded form the content of the blessings and curses which 27:11-13 instructs the tribes to intone from the 2 mountains overlooking Shechem. If 27:14-26 is deleted (see comment above) the transition from 27:13 to this ch. is smooth, requiring only the briefest introduction, e.g. "And they [i.e. the respective tribes on Mts. Gerizim and Ebal] shall say . . ."

The core blessings (vss. 3-6) and curses (vss. 16-19) are in parallel form, being directed specifically to human, agricultural, and pastoral fertility. The D author has amplified these by spelling out in 2 lists of uneven length the consequences of obedience (7-14) and disobedience (vss. 20-46). The amplifications are replete with illustrations of types of good and evil and with vivid exhortations to obedience.

28:47-68. These vss. are very likely a later addition to the original unit. They extend the curses into lurid descriptions of military and natural disaster, including threats of cannibalism during siege. **The LORD will bring a nation against you from afar** (vs. 49) may refer to either Assyria or Babylonia, but taken altogether this section appears to come from the Babylonian exile. It is so detailed and repetitive that it has the marks of after-the-event condemnation —a kind of "I told you so" cast.

B. A Covenant in Moab (29:1–30:20)

These 2 chs. comprise a unit which has marks of being one of the latest in the book and certainly comes from sometime during or after the Exile (see below on 30:1-10). The expression **the curses of the covenant written in this book of the law** (29:21) shows that the author knew Deut. as a compiled work and that he composed his work as an admonition to be added to it. The unit has as its focus the ceremony of ratification of the law in Moab and evidently reflects the liturgy of periodic ceremonies of renewal of the covenant (see Intro. and above on 27:1–28:68).

29:1. In the Hebrew Bible this vs. is numbered as the last of ch. 28, and some scholars believe it was written to be the final sentence of the book as compiled at that time. More probably, however, it is an intro. to chs. 29–30. **These are the words of the covenant** may mean the contents of this unit but more likely is a suture to join the unit to the rest of the book by summarizing what has preceded. It refers not only to the laws of chs. 12–26 but also to the blessings and curses of chs. 27–28 and probably also to portions if not all of chs. 1–11.

29:2-15. The recital of Yahweh's past favors to Israel in vss. 2-9 presents at every point ideas and often phraseology found earlier in the book (cf. esp. 2:32-3:13; 4:9, 34-35; 5:3; 6:21-22; 8:4; 11:1-7). On the other hand the climactic call in vss. 10-15 to **enter into the sworn covenant . . . this day** does not show any direct awareness of the covenant transaction account of 27:9-10 and is presumably a parallel account. Such data present problems if we attempt to explain them by literary dependence. They are best put into a meaningful perspective if the separate units are seen as compilations of texts drawn from or imitative of renewal ceremonies which have been edited only in part and with no attempt to create complete consistency at the expense of liturgical diversity.

29:16-27. With this warning against apostasy cf. ch. 13. **Admah and Zeboiim** (vs. 23) were cities near **Sodom and Gomorrah** destroyed in the same catastrophe (cf. Gen. 10:19; 19:24-25; Hos. 11:8).

29:29. This unusual view of the law contrasts it with **secret things** God has reserved from mankind, implying that the **revealed** law is sufficient for all human need (see below on 30:11-14).

30:1-10. The late date of this unit is supported by the concern of these vss. for the fate of those who have disobeyed and gone into exile. The refugees are pictured as coming to their senses, returning to God, being restored to Palestine, and being purified by God so that they will henceforth **love** and **obey** him. The curses under which Israel suffered will be transferred to her foes. This highly moralistic assessment contrasts with the presumably contemporary notion that God would restore Israel in spite of her disobedience, for his own name's sake, which was articulated by Ezekiel and 2nd Isaiah.

30:11-14. A 2nd unusual claim about the law (cf. 29:29) characterizes it as being **exceedingly close, in your mouth and in your heart** instead of enigmatic or remote. God has not left his will in doubt. It is not necessary to employ soothsayers or magicians to penetrate the future or to unlock mysteries. Everything that matters hinges on this easily accessible law, which the people carry in their very persons, and which the Levitical priests can always interpret if there is question.

C. Moses' Final Preparations (31:1–32:47)

That this literarily complex block of material comprises a unit is indicated by the reference to 31:1 in the intro. to the closing speech, **when Moses had finished speaking all these words to all Israel** (32:45). The section is split up by headings into subunits that some have regarded as independent additions to the book. Binding them together, however, is a concern for continuation of the work of Moses through his final acts—passing the leadership to his successor and ordering preservation of "this law" (chs. 12–26 at the least) and his "song" (32:1-43) for future "witness" against the people.

Allusions to a communal liturgical setting are scattered throughout the unit: Moses gives the written law to the Levitical priests, who keep it beside the ark (31:9, 26); his successor is addressed in view of the whole assembly (31:7); Moses and Joshua present themselves in the sacred tent (31:14-15); the elders and officers of Israel are assembled to affirm their oath of allegiance to God (31:28-29). In a kind of "play within a play," similar to the blessing-curse rite of ch. 27, the priests are advised to read the law before the people every 7th year at the feast of booths (31:10). It is not difficult to imagine that circum-

stantial details of the imagined congregation in Moab are actually supplied from ceremonies of covenant renewal known to the author(s). We may go so far as to say that this unit, cast in Mosaic form, is intended to describe the origin of contemporary practice at the feast of booths, i.e. to assure readers that present liturgical practice has a validly ancient foundation.

31:7-8. Cf. 1:38; 3:28. See below on vss. 14-15.

31:9-13. *Sabbatical Feast of Booths.* The custom of joining a special celebration to an annual festival is familiar from the tithing procedures at the feast of weeks for 2 out of every 3 years (14:22-29). In this passage the celebration involving reading of **this law** at the feast of booths is only every 7th year and is to coincide with the **year of release** (15:1-11). Such gatherings for the purpose of Levitical reading and interpretation of the laws would stimulate the growth and elaboration of the D traditions.

31:14-15. *Commissioning of Joshua.* These vss. are apparently continued in vs. 23. Their position after Joshua's selection (vs. 3) and presentation before the people (vss. 7-8) as Moses' successor has been cited against the unity of 31:1–32:47. The commissioning may be understood, however, as a ritual of transference of Moses' power to his chosen successor which occurs only when Moses is about to die. The passage has been attributed to the E source (cf. Exod. 33:7-11; also the P account, Num. 27:15-23).

31:16-22. *Intro. to Moses' Song.* This subunit appears to interrupt the continuity of vss. 15, 23 and it might more logically follow vss. 24-29 and immediately precede the text of Moses' **song** (32:1-43; note that vs. 30 largely duplicates vs. 22). It provides further glimpses into the D literary circles. Moses' writing of the song and its recitation in successive generations means that it is to **confront them as a witness (for it will be unforgotten in the mouths of their descendants).** Far from being a piece of archaic poetry, it is a vehicle for constantly reconfronting Israel with her obligation to God. Obviously the covenant renewal ceremonies included not only reading of the law but singing of liturgical compositions that recalled the past and summoned to present commitment. The double action of Moses in writing the song and then reciting it to the people (vs. 22; cf. vs. 30; 32:44) is analogous to the writing of the law (vs. 9) and the priests' reading of it in Israel's hearing (vs. 11). A standard text and a public reading bring the intimate relation between written and oral traditions into focus. Deut. may be understood as an attempt to bring various textual versions together with a minimal loss of any of them.

31:23. See above on vss. 14-15.

31:24-29. *The Law as a Witness.* See above on vss. 16-22. The phrase **to the very end** (vs. 24), perhaps meaning "in their totality," may well be an allusion to the various forms in which the law circulated orally and literarily until finally compiled in this book.

31:30. See above on vss. 16-22.

32:1-43. *The Song of Moses.* This poem is not at all exclusively or even dominantly D in phraseology and outlook. It was apparently adopted in D circles because it was recited at renewal ceremonies in conjunction with D laws. There is nothing to identify Moses as the speaker. The situation reflected in the poem is probably late preexilic, *ca.* 800-600 B.C. The conception behind use of the song and its attribution to Moses is that of Moses as liturgical leader, which lends support to the view that the chief Levitical priest functioned in the renewal ceremonies as Moses-substitute or covenant mediator who spoke on behalf of God to the people and vice versa.

The song shows a broad affinity with D thought on such points as the election of Israel as the select son among the various peoples of the earth, idolatrous abuse of God's gift of the land, and adversity as the judgment of God. There are, however, notable differences; negatively it lacks any reference to the law; positively it asserts that God will vindicate his people, not because of their repentance, but because of his own urge to manifest his strength and glory before the nations—a view shared with Ezekiel and 2nd Isaiah. Perhaps we are to account for the song's prominent place in the book on the basis that in D circles during the Exile the prophetic view of God's "amoral" initiative in restoring Israel for his own glory made considerable headway against the older and more moralistic view that restoration would only follow repentance.

On vs. 8 see Intro. **Jeshurun** (vs. 15; cf. 33:5, 26; Isa. 44:2), meaning lit. "upright," is a term for Israel possibly based on similarity in the written appearance of the 2 words. On the cosmology of vs. 22 see comment on Ps. 18:17-18.

D. Moses' Blessing and Death (32:48–34:12)

32:48-52. *The Order to Ascend Mt. Nebo.* These vss. and their continuation in ch. 34 comprise a narrative unit, generally seen as containing elements of all 4 Pentateuchal sources, which was displaced by editors from its logical place at the end of Num. so that Moses' death might come after his farewell speech as presented in Deut. Moses is instructed to go up to a mountaintop (on **Abarim** and **Mount Nebo** see above on 3:23-29) and **view the land of Canaan** (see ill., this page). There he is to **die** as **Aaron** did on **Mount Hor** (contrast 10:6; cf. Num. 20:22-29; 33:37-39) because both of them **broke faith** in the incident of the striking of the rock at **Meribath-kadesh** (cf. Num. 20:11-12; 27:12-14). This reason for Moses' exclusion from Canaan follows the P tradition and is in tension with the explanation of it in 1:37; 3:26; 4:21 (see above on 1:19-46).

33:1-29. *The Blessing of Moses.* This poem has as little of the peculiarly D style and vocabulary as the "song" of 32:1-43, but in subject it refers more explicitly to the Mosaic age, even referring overtly to the law in the blessing on the Levites. That Moses was not its author is evident, not only in the fact that the Conquest is plainly in the past, but also in the 3rd-person reference to Moses in vs. 4. The inclusion of the blessing here may be explained as follows: One feature of the covenant renewal ceremony was a recitation of blessings on the tribes. The practice continued into monarchic times even when the tribes had lost political and social significance. The connection between the blessings pronounced on the individual tribes (vss. 6-25) and the affirmation of the covenant and law is sharply stressed in the preamble (vss. 1-5) and in the epilogue (vss. 26-29), which were probably already added in the liturgical

celebrations. This association of the tribal blessings with Moses made it an easy matter for a D editor to insert it as the deathbed blessing of Moses in a manner analogous to the blessing of Jacob in Gen. 49.

The milieu of the blessing is most likely the late period of the judges (after the migration of Dan, vs. 22; cf. Judg. 18) or the early monarchy. There are no identifiable historical allusions and, being liturgical poetry, it does not lend itself to confident dating.

33:2-5. The absolute distinction of Yahweh as God and Israel as **his people** is stressed in this poetic intro. to the individual blessings and in the conclusion (vss. 26-29). Israel alone has such a deity and such a relation to him through the **law** that he is her **king** (see "The Kingdom of God in the OT," pp. 1159-66) and she holds the land in prosperity and security. **Seir** (vs. 1) was the mountain range covering most of Edom, and **Mount Paran** was evidently the highland S of Kadesh-barnea (cf. 1:1; Num. 10:12; 12:16; 13:3; see color map 4). On **Jeshurun** (vs. 5) see above on 32:1-43.

33:6-25. Simeon is omitted from the tribal blessings, presumably because it no longer existed as a tribe, and **Reuben** (vs. 6) has become **few** and about to **die** as an independent group. **Judah** (vs. 7) is on the defensive—perhaps the Philistines are **his adversaries**—whereas **Joseph** (i.e. **Ephraim** and **Manasseh**, vss. 13-17) prospers. **Levi** (vss. 8-11) is already a priestly tribe discharging the double function of teacher and priest in broad agreement with the D description of the office (see above on 17:8-13, 18; 18:1-8). If we could be certain that vss. 8-10 are as old as the 11th or 10th cent. we would be in possession of important data on the early history of the Levites, but some interpreters suspect that the original blessing of Levi was vs. 11 alone, the preceding vss. having been added later. **Thummim** and **Urim** (vs. 8*bc*) were sacred lots used to ascertain Yahweh's will (see comment on I Sam. 14:36-46). The allusion to **Massah** and **Meribah** (vs. 8*de*) is obscure, since Levi is not mentioned in the other references to these places (6:16; 9:22; 32:51; Exod. 17:1-7; Num. 20:2-13). **In the bush** probably alludes to the burning bush but may be a textual error for "on Sinai" (see comment on Exod. 3:2). Vs. 21*c-e* seems to be out of place; possibly it belongs in vs. 4.

33:26-29. See above on vss. 2-5.

34:1-12. *The Death of Moses.* This ch. is a continuation of the narrative unit begun in 32:48-52 (see comment; on **Mount Nebo** and **Pisgah** see above on 3:23-29). The extent of Canaan which **the LORD showed** Moses is of course far wider than the human

Courtesy of Herbert G. May

View from Mt. Nebo

eye could see from a peak in Moab (see color map 3). Moses looks first N across **Gilead** (Transjordan) over 100 miles to **Dan**—as the city will be known after the tribe captures it (Judg. 18:29). From Dan his gaze moves SW to the area to be occupied by **Naphtali** W of the Sea of Galilee and by **Ephraim and Manasseh** in central Palestine. Due W he sees over the highland of N **Judah** to the **Western Sea** (the Mediterranean). To the SW he views the **Negeb** (the dry region S of Beer-sheba) and the **Plain** (the Jordan–Dead Sea rift) **as far as Zoar** near the former site of Sodom (cf. Gen. 19:22-23). After this view of the land and renewal of the promise Moses dies. **He buried him** means almost certainly that Yahweh buried Moses and accounts for the otherwise strange fact that **no man knows the place of his burial to this day.**

34:9-12. A concluding passage pictures Joshua's authority as deriving from Moses but maintains the preeminence of Moses over any subsequent **prophet.** On the surface vs. 10 looks like a contradiction to 18:15, where "a prophet like me" is promised. The nuances of the 2 "like's" are quite different, however. In 18:15 the similarity is in office or function whereas here it is in directness of revelation; i.e. no prophet has known God so directly as Moses knew him. **Signs and wonders** performed by Moses are cited as evidence that he is an unparalleled spokesman for God. Obviously the accounts of prophetic calls and performance of marvels by some of the Israelite prophets are here subordinated to the primacy of the Mosaic revelation. Prophecy is assimilated to Mosaic Yahwism in a manner which the D author already has attempted to do in the legal formulations of 13:1-5; 18:15-22. As a counter to Canaanite prophetism the force of the motif is clear, but how it stands in relation to the special revelatory claims of Yahwistic prophets such as Isaiah, Jeremiah, and Ezekiel is not clear. Indeed one of the unresolved issues in the history of Israel's religion is the precise relation between the great prophets and the D movement.

THE BOOK OF JOSHUA

Robert Houston Smith

Introduction

A story of conquest, a testimony to faith, a statistical record, a geography—Joshua is all of these. Beginning where Deut. ends it narrates how, under the leadership of Josh. and the protection of Yahweh ("the LORD"), Israel entered Canaan and there carved out a place for herself. The early chs. deal mainly with military aspects of the Conquest; the later ones concern the apportionment of Canaan to the tribes of Israel and episodes revolving around Josh.'s impending death.

Literary History. In spite of the simplicity of its overall arrangement Josh. is a complex document. It did not spring into existence full blown—whether from the hand of Josh. himself or of any other single author—but grew by a process which spanned many centuries. The earliest traditions of the Conquest were apparently songs which commemorated the victories of Israel under Yahweh. Only fragments of these songs have survived—notably Josh.'s famous utterance at the battle for Gibeon (10:12c-13a). By studying other bits of early poetry in the OT, e.g. Judg. 5; Exod. 15:1-18; Ps. 68, we see that such songs arose not so much in folk tradition as in the cultic worship of Israel's God (see comment on Judg. 5).

By a process familiar to students of the history of literature these songs came to be replaced during the early centuries of the Hebrew occupation of Palestine by prose accounts of the same events.

Like the poetic traditions these prose narratives seem to have had as their home not so much the campfire as the sanctuary. Of great importance in the early traditions in Josh. are the shrines at Shiloh, Gilgal, and Shechem. Perhaps this connection with the cult accounts for the emphasis on religious ceremonies in the work, esp. in chs. 3–5; 24. Some of these stories may seek to explain the origin of certain religious practices or to justify the importance of the traditional places of worship. Occasionally the stories show an interest in explaining the existence of certain places or place names, but that interest seems to be relatively minor.

Such traditions form the basis of chs. 2–11 and parts of the remainder of Josh. For many decades scholars supposed that these early stories came from the J and E sources, on which much of the first 4 books of the OT are based (see "The Compiling of Israel's Story," pp. 1082-89). There are indeed many similarities, but the evidences of relationship are much less clear than in the earlier books. Recently, therefore, a number of scholars have come to doubt

that the categories of Gen.-Num. can be appropriately applied to Josh. The final word on the early sources of this book has not yet been said, and perhaps never will be, but we can no longer use the terms J and E quite so confidently as did former generations of scholars.

The J and E sources are generally believed to date respectively from the 10th and 8th cents. and to have been combined to form JE after the fall of the N kingdom, probably early in the 7th cent. If the supposed JE portions of Josh. were not part of this process, however, their content suggests rather that they should be attributed to an author who in the later years of the N kingdom—i.e. in the 8th cent., or possibly earlier—brought together a number of the stories about the conquest and settlement of Palestine and wove them into a single account. This work may have included also the nucleus of Judg., since a vs. found at the end of the Greek translation of Josh. but now missing from the Hebrew text (see below on 24:32-33) constitutes a transitional sentence which leads directly into Judg. 3:15.

The sanctuaries of Israel were the repositories not only of old narratives but also of statistical records of various sorts. Some of these records, mainly descriptions of tribal boundaries and lists of cities within these tribal areas, appear prominently in chs. 13–21. Detailed study of these lists has shown that they date from different periods, all much later than the time of the Conquest, ranging perhaps from the early monarchy to the end of the 7th cent.

The editor-author responsible for shaping the major part of Josh. essentially in the form in which it has come down to us probably lived in the last quarter of the 7th cent. or the first half of the 6th cent. and had close connections with both the religious traditions of N Israel and the temple in Jerusalem. Some scholars find 3 editions of Josh. by this editor or his colleagues, but in any case the style remains remarkably uniform throughout. Working at a time when there was a resurgence of interest in the N Palestinian traditions, to which much of the content of Josh. belongs, he was a man of consuming religious passion, whose concern was not to preserve old traditions in an academic manner but to present the Conquest in such a way that it would have clear theological significance for his readers. To this end he added introductions, transitions, summaries, conclusions, and blocks of theology in the form of speeches. His theology can be seen most clearly in chs. 1; 23, where in speeches attributed to Yahweh and to Josh. he expresses the concept that Yahweh has unfailingly carried out all of his promises to his chosen people. It is this conviction which prompts the editor to portray the conquest of Palestine under Josh. as more extensive than the older traditions indicate. His message also carries the warning that Yahweh's kindness will continue only so long as his people obey him.

Because these convictions are expressed in a much fuller way in Deut., those who share them are known as Deuteronomists or the Deuteronomic ("D") school. It may well be that the editor-author of Josh. was the originator of these ideas, who compiled the laws of Deut., composed the framework for them, and then proceeded to demonstrate historically the necessity of obedience to them. The commoner view is that it was the publication of the core of Deut. in 622 (II Kings 22–23; see Intro. to Deut.) which inspired another person or persons to compile Josh. and also Judg., I-II Sam., I-II Kings. Since the last event recorded in II Kings occurred during the Exile, in 561, opinions differ on whether the compilation involved 2 or more editions or was prepared only after this last event (see Intro. to I Kings). In any case recent study seems to make clear that the bulk of the entire series Josh.-Kings was the work of a single compiler, or possibly a small group working together, who intended that it should be joined to Deut. to form a history of Israel from Moses to his own time. The affinities of Josh. tend to be as much with the other books of this D history as with the first 4 books of the OT.

There are inconsistencies and other signs that the tribal boundary and city lists of chs. 13–21 were added to the original D edition of Josh. It was long assumed that they came from the P source and were idealized postexilic creations of the P authors. As noted above, however, recent study has shown that these are genuine preexilic records, and it therefore seems probable that they were added by another D editor early in the Exile. Several scattered sentences with P characteristics are apparently individual insertions by later editors rather than signs of a substantial P contribution to the book.

Historical Reconstruction. At the time of the Israelite conquest the dominant people in Palestine were the Canaanites, a Semitic people who lived mainly in the valleys and coastal regions where water was relatively plentiful and farming was fairly easy. The lives of the Canaanites revolved around sturdy walled cities scattered throughout the lowlands. There was no central government; each city was virtually a little kingdom with its own ruler, aristocrats, military establishment, commercial enterprises, religious institutions, and serfs. This feudal culture had been in existence for more than 6 cents.; at its height it had been technologically advanced and artistically refined, but by the 14th cent. it had lost much of its vigor and creativeness.

The hill country, which runs like a backbone down the middle of Palestine, was only sparsely settled, for water was scarcer and farming more difficult on the stony hillsides. The Canaanites could not exercise strong military control there, and merchants did not wish to take their caravans into the hills if they could go by way of the coast and valleys. As a result, the mountains became a refuge for dispossessed people of various sorts, e.g. the Jebusites, Hivites, and Perizzites, of whom we know little but their names. These people seem generally to have lived a more rural life than their neighbors in the plains. In Transjordan seminomadism was a long-established pattern of life.

It was against this background that the Israelite conquest took place. Though Josh. presupposes that all of the Israelites who settled in Palestine came in from Transjordan in one surge, there are indications both in this book and in other OT materials that the number of Israelites who entered Palestine in this manner was not large. Rather it appears that the great majority of those who called themselves Israelites did not take part in the descent into Egypt and in the Exodus but continued living in Palestine. These people, like those who participated in the Exodus, were descendants of wandering traders called "Habiru" who had come into the country early in the 2nd millenium and eventually settled down. Though perhaps consisting largely of related Semitic tribes, these Habiru were apparently not an ethnic group as such. As they had settled down in Palestine they had learned the ways of the Canaanites and adopted their language, which became the parent of the Hebrew language. But the Canaanites seem to have never allowed these landless people to forget that they were outsiders, and treated them as a lower class. They continued to call them Habiru, or Hebrew, which became a term of scorn synonymous with "serf" or even "slave"—a connotation which some OT passages still recall (e.g. Gen. 39:14; 43:32; I Sam. 4:9).

Aware of the hopelessness of their situation within the closed society of the Canaanites, these Habiru or Hebrews began to wander off to the sparsely settled hill country, where they were largely free of Canaanite oppression. Already by the early 14th cent. the Egyptian Amarna letters (see "The People of the OT World," pp. 1005-17) show they were disrupting some of the city-states by living as brigands and, in some cases, by maneuvering to force the grudging cooperation of certain hill-country cities, e.g. perhaps Shechem, Tirzah, and Tappuah. The majority of Hebrews probably settled down, however, to building villages and tilling the soil. In each locality conditions were different, and there were many local Hebrew leaders. The number of villages and cities taken by outright battle was probably small, for the Hebrews lacked the strength to take the populous and relatively well-defended lowland cities of Canaan. It is true that many Canaanite cities show destruction during the period 1400-1200, but much of this can reasonably be regarded as the result of warfare among the cities, not to mention destructive invasions by Egyptian armies from time to time.

This picture of how the Hebrew nation began is strongly supported by excavated Palestinian artifacts from late Canaanite and early Hebrew times. Archaeologists have found that the remains of early Hebrew settlements show no significant cultural infusions but only a normal development from late Canaanite culture. Far, then, from being a nomadic people encountering civilization for the first time, as biblical interpreters have long assumed, most of the Hebrews were people who left the urbanized Canaanite environment for a more rural life in the hills.

Though the Hebrew conquest of Palestine seems to have gone on for at least 2 cents., *ca.* 1400–1200, the earliest traditions in Josh. may come from the latter part of that time, when the Israelite immigrants from Egypt joined their relatives who were already in Palestine. This later phase perhaps fell *ca.* 1250–1200, the period to which most scholars now date the Conquest, rather than the traditional 1450–1400. It may be, as the biblical accounts indicate, that these incoming Israelites brought with them the faith in Yahweh, though it is unlikely that the name of this God was entirely unknown to the Hebrews who had stayed in Palestine. In any case the memories of the 2 groups of Hebrews were remarkably similar: both had originally had the same background as traders and free people, both had settled in foreign lands and eventually become serfs, and both had at last broken free and fled to the hill country of Palestine seeking land and freedom. United in these experiences and in their belief in Yahweh, and sharing a common distrust of oppressive human rule of all sorts, these dissidents lived in a loose confederation cemented by treaties, welcoming all who wished to join their ranks. These relationships were later to be systematized by Israelite thinkers into the picture of 12 tribes which has come down to us in the OT.

Josh. the Man. The role of Josh. in this process of Israelite settlement is difficult to assess, so extensive is the legend which has grown up around him. To judge from the earliest traditions, Josh.'s raids seem to have been chiefly on enemies in the territory traditionally occupied by Benjamin, below the S border of his own tribe of Ephraim. These may have been blows inflicted on the Benjaminites themselves (cf. Judg. 19–20) or strikes against independent strongholds which threatened Ephraim (cf. Judg. 1:22-26). Josh. may have carried out raids farther S, in the territory of Judah (cf. ch. 10), but there is no indication that he attempted by this to expand Ephraim's frontiers. The tradition of his military activity in the N (ch. 11) may reflect raids carried out to protect the N border of Ephraim's sister tribe, Manasseh. Thus Josh.'s military activities can be seen as deeds defending the territories of the closely related tribes of Ephraim, Manasseh, and Benjamin. Not entirely without reason some scholars have suggested that Josh. was not involved in the Israelite entry into Palestine from Transjordan and that the stories of his leading the crossing of the Jordan are early editorial harmonizing of the Josh. traditions with those about Moses, cycles which otherwise are separate.

Of Josh. as a person the traditions have little to say. In Exod., Num., Deut. he appears as Moses' military assistant, but the allusions do not seem to have been a part of the earliest Mosaic stories. The representation of him is highly stylized; later editors, influenced by their knowledge of Hebrew kingship, have tended to portray him as a king in all but the title. In only one scene, where Josh. joins his soldiers in a dangerous ruse outside the walls of Ai (ch. 8), does one get a personal glimpse of the man. Here he seems to be a daring, clever warrior, not unlike some of the judges, Jonathan, and the young David.

Religious Outlook. The question of the religious values in Josh. merits careful attention. It is evident that the book hammers out an impressive statement of the conviction that God is active in history. Mod-

ern readers, however, are apt to be disturbed by the way Yahweh is depicted as callously indifferent to non-Israelites. It may be pointed out, though it is perhaps small comfort, that throughout history devout persons have often scorned other races and cultures and assumed that they were serving God rightly when they suppressed all viewpoints contrary to their own. With regard specifically to Josh. one may recognize that the concept of God and morality presented in the work is part and parcel of its time. Just how true this is can be seen by comparing an inscription which King Mesha of Moab ordered cut on a commemorative slab in the mid-9th cent. Mesha, whose name comes from the same root, "save," as the name Josh. ("Yahweh saves"), uses language similar to that in Josh. when he tells how, in the process of extending Moab's boundaries and settling new areas, he defeated his enemies—in this case Israel—and utterly destroyed their towns as an act of devotion to his god Chemosh, to whose help he attributes his victories. In recognizing the thought world from which Josh. arises one necessarily becomes less demanding that its theological outlook conform to later standards.

Historical events are sometimes greater than those who pass on the record of them recognize. In some ways the actual circumstances of the conquest of Canaan, as reconstructed above, offer religious insights which may be more meaningful to the modern reader than the interpretations of it which the biblical editors give. The Hebrews who settled in the hill country of Canaan were a free association of serfs fleeing from the stifling environment of the Canaanite city-states. United in their rejection of the ancient system of human overlords, they insisted that no man is inherently better than any other and thus came remarkably near a concept of a democracy under God. Far from building their nation on the extermination of all those outside their group, they welcomed into their confederation any people who shared this longing for a new society; thus their society was inclusive, not exclusive. Likewise inclusive was the worship of their God; G. E. Mendenhall has pointed out that early Yahwism was "an ecumenical faith, a catholic religion in the best sense of the term the very purpose of which was to create a unity among a divided and warring humanity." These views stand in sharp contrast to those later ones which saw Israel as an ethnic group, which believed that loyalty to God could be measured by conformity to cultic requirements, which assumed that some men could be made serfs, and which asserted that God revealed himself only to selected leaders rather than communicating his will in Israel's collective deliberations.

For Further Study. John Bright in *IB*, 1953; *A History of Israel*, 1959, ch. 3. Martin Noth, *History of Israel*, 2nd ed., 1960, Pt. 1. E. M. Good in *IDB*, 1962. W. F. Albright, *The Biblical Period from Abraham to Ezra*, 1963, ch. 3.

I. ISRAEL'S CONQUEST OF PALESTINE (1:1–12:24)

A. JOSHUA'S ACCESSION TO LEADERSHIP (1:1-18)

1:1-9. *Yahweh's Commission to Josh.* The story of the conquest of Palestine begins where Deut. 34 ends. Israel is encamped at the foot of the Moabite hills at the SE end of the Jordan Valley. **Moses** has just died. In vss. 2-9 Yahweh commissions **Joshua,** Moses' former lieutenant, and instructs him to cross the **Jordan** and enter Palestine. This speech presupposes a scene very much like that of an ancient oriental coronation, with implications of a covenanting ceremony similar to those in Gen. 15 and elsewhere. Yahweh promises to give Israel **the land,** described idealistically in vs. 4, and other benefits in return for Israel's obedience. The passage is reminiscent of the commissioning of Josh. in Deut. 31, but bears marks of the hand of the D editor, esp. in its stress on the keeping of the Torah, or divine **law** (vss. 7-8). The editor thus makes clear at the outset that this book is not to be a matter-of-fact annal but a religious document. He intends, furthermore, that these ancient happenings shall have relevance in his own day, stressing that Yahweh will continue to be beneficent to those who follow Josh.'s example in obeying the divine commandments (vs. 8; cf. Ps. 1:2-3).

1:10-18. Josh.'s First Council. In ancient Near Eastern concepts and practices of royal investiture the private encounter between the new ruler and the deity was followed by acclamation by the people, who were sometimes represented by members of the nobility or royal council. The D editor maintains this convention. In a scene which is virtually one of covenanting the **officers of the people** pledge their loyalty to Josh. Vss. 10-11 are basically from a pre-D source; the rest is the composition of the D editor.

1:12-17. From the tribes of Reuben, Gad, and Manasseh, which have already settled in Transjordan (cf. 13:7-8; Num. 32; Deut. 3:12-17), Josh. demands troops who will aid the rest of Israel in conquering Palestine (cf. Deut. 3:18-20). The leaders agree to this, cautioning only that if Josh. is to be their leader the LORD must remain with him (vs. 17). By stressing the participation of the Transjordanian tribes the editor presents the conquest of Palestine as the unified undertaking of Israel, a matter of theological importance to him. The emphasis on their willingness may be an attempt to counteract a common opinion that these tribes tended to be reluctant to fight on behalf of the rest of Israel (cf. Judg. 5:15b-17a).

1:18. The threat of **death** to rebels may have originated under the influence of the story of Achan's disobedience (ch. 7), but possibly is only an expression of the traditional demand of loyalty which, on penalty of death, oriental rulers placed upon their subjects.

B. The Reconnaissance of Jericho (2:1-24)

This story is one of several extended narratives in Josh. which have descended from early traditions. Two or more accounts have been interwoven, as certain differences of detail reveal; many scholars identify these sources as J and E, but the complex history of the early traditions is difficult to unravel. Judg. 1:22-25 preserves a brief narrative which shows some broad similarities to this story, prompting some interpreters to suspect that the 2 traditions may be related. The place name **Shittim** (vs. 1) has previously appeared in Num. 25:1 (cf. Num. 33:49) —a reminder that the intervening material in Num.

25-36; Deut.; Josh. 1 is largely an expansion by D and P writers.

While the people are making preparations for the crossing of the Jordan, Josh. acts as a good tactician by sending spies to survey his first object of attack (cf. the spies sent to Canaan, Num. 13). **Jericho** (see color map 5) was the only important city in the arid region at the S end of the Jordan Valley, whereas in the central and N part of the valley lay a number of powerful Canaanite cities. If one may judge from the reference to **stalks of flax** laid on the **roof** (vs. 6), presumably to dry, the season was spring, the usual time for military campaigns. The motif of the story, which appears also in the account of the fall of Sodom (Gen. 18-19), is a familiar one in folk tradition: divine agents come incognito to a hostile region and find hospitality in the home of the humblest persons in the community; to these righteous people they promise salvation while preparing the destruction of the rest.

A modern reader, inclined to want a tightly constructed plot, will perhaps wonder how the spies got into Jericho, why their speech failed to betray them, how the king came to know of their presence, etc.; but the ancient storytellers focused on dramatic effect, realizing that their audience would delight in the vivid sequence of images, e.g. the rush of the bumbling Jericho police in the wrong direction and the escape of the spies down the wall.

The story gives informative glimpses into the life of an ancient Palestinian city, details which archaeological discoveries largely confirm. Jericho was an independent city-state with its own king, just as most other pre-Israelite cities of Palestine were. Houses at Jericho were crowded right up to the city wall, even as they are today in Damascus (cf. Acts 9:25). The city's **gate** was closed at dusk. The roofs of at least some—and probably all—of the houses were flat and were put to such practical uses as drying and storing produce. Prostitution was a tolerated practice, possibly—one suspects—in connection with the local religion. The **scarlet cord** which Rahab ties in her **window** hints at a magical practice intended to keep evil from the house (cf. the blood on Israelite houses on the night of the slaughter of the firstborn in Egypt, Exod. 12:7, 13, 22-23).

By portraying Rahab not simply as a brave and clever woman but as an apostate from her native religion the storyteller made possible her later veneration not only by Hebrews but also by Christians (cf. Heb. 11:31; Jas. 2:25). Rahab's words in vss. 10-11a are a D addition (cf. 5:1). Her description of Israel's God as **he who is God in heaven above and on earth beneath** (vs. 11b) also has a D ring, but recently discovered Canaanite texts sometimes use similar expressions for the god El—evidence either that the D language has ancient roots or that Rahab's words are not so anachronistic as previously assumed.

C. The Crossing of the Jordan (3:1–5:1)

This episode seems to be set in April, during the spring harvest (cf. 3:15; 4:19), a time consistent with that of the preceding story. Behind this lengthy account with its occasionally confusing details lie 2 or more old traditions, often assumed to be from J and E, which have been compiled in one narrative.

The crossing is described as a religious rite involving purification, a solemn procession, a sermon, and the erection of memorial stones. Because these rites take place at or near **Gilgal** (4:19-20) on the W side of the Jordan, some interpreters have felt—with some justification—that the story reflects a rite at Gilgal in which the crossing was reenacted from time to time. With its stress on the passing of Israel through parted waters the episode is also reminiscent of the exodus tradition (Exod. 12-15). If some rite was performed, it was possibly at the passover festival in the spring (cf. 5:10). The ritualistic passing between the cleft waters is also reminiscent of the practice of passing between the cleft halves of an animal in a covenanting ceremony (cf. Gen. 15:7-17), esp. since not long afterward Josh. does institute a covenant (8:30-35). These motifs combine to make the story a subtle but compelling statement of the important OT themes of God's covenanted relationship with Israel and his deliverance of his people from the dangers which beset them.

The D editor, concerned as always with the contemporary significance of the events in Israel's past, has added to the old tradition several short indications of what he feels to be the religious values of the story. The miraculous crossing takes place, he says in 3:7 (cf. 4:14, 23), in part so that Josh., in whom he has great theological interest, will be remembered even as Moses was remembered for his part in the crossing of the Red Sea. In 4:4-7, 21-24 he explains the importance of the stones set up in memorial. The overall significance of the stopping of the Jordan's flow is, he concludes in 4:24, that **all the peoples of the earth may know that the hand of the LORD is mighty; that you may fear the LORD your God forever.**

3:1-17. The Preparation and the Crossing. The crossing of the Jordan by a large number of people at one time would naturally present a problem, since in biblical times there were no bridges and few fords. The later storytellers undoubtedly presupposed a vast populace (cf. 4:13; Exod. 12:37; Num. 1:46; etc.), but most modern commentators estimate that not more than a few thousand persons could have been involved; similar exaggeration of numbers appears in Canaanite and other ancient Near Eastern literature. The **ark** plays an important role in the story, though its existence in the earliest traditions has been questioned. The storytellers assume that from it emanates power, somewhat like—one might say—an electric current or a laser beam. To this power only authorized priests and Levites are immune; the layman must stay a respectful distance away—**two thousand cubits** (*ca.* 1,000 yards) according to a later editorial insertion in vs. 4—lest he be harmed (cf. II Sam. 6:6-7). The power resident within the ark is apparently intended to be that which holds back the waters of the Jordan.

Many interpreters have accepted the idea that the stopping of the Jordan was a natural phenomenon, e.g. a temporary damming of the river by a landslide, but this explanation leaves unanswered the question of why such a rare occurrence happened so opportunely. Many readers may wish to conclude that a miracle did occur. Others will prefer to see the account as the Israelite thinkers' way of expressing, in a day when both philosophical and scientific

Courtesy of Herbert G. May

Tell ed-Damiyeh in the Jordan valley, site of the city of Adam where the waters of the Jordan were dammed

language did not yet exist, their deep faith in their God as the Lord of nature and as one who saves his people from peril. The use of the image of water to represent all that threatens a man is a very ancient one which often finds expression in the OT, as does the concept of Yahweh as he who pushes back the waters to make dry land and a place of safety (e.g. Gen. 1:9; Ps. 18:15).

4:1-24. The Memorial of Stones. The **twelve stones** which Josh. orders set up—according to one tradition, on the bank of the Jordan (vs. 8); according to another, in the Jordan itself (vs. 9)—have long fascinated readers. The fact that the name of the place where Josh. makes camp, **Gilgal** (vs. 19), may mean "[sacred] circle"—rather than **rolled away** as 5:9 declares—suggests that the episode may be based on the tradition of a shrine at Gilgal containing a group of sacred stones, perhaps set up in pre-Israelite times but taken over by the Israelites and linked with their religious traditions. The earliest sources in ch. 4 offer no explanation for the stones, but the D editor, who is probably responsible for vss. 5-7, understands them to be a memorial of the crossing of the Jordan. Gilgal has not conclusively been located, but it must have been within a few miles of Jericho (see color map 5).

5:1. An Editor's Conclusion. In an appended note the D editor describes the reaction which the Israelite crossing produced among the rulers of Palestine (cf. Rahab's words in 2:10-11). That the Israelites disturbed rulers of the city-states is likely, as the 14th-cent. Egyptian Amarna letters suggest (see Intro.). but subsequent battles in Canaan show that not all **spirit** deserted the inhabitants of the land. The editor himself recognizes this in 9:1-2.

D. THE INAUGURATION OF A NEW ERA (5:2-12)

5:2-9. Circumcision of Israel. In preparation for the coming passover (vss. 10-12) Josh. circumcizes the Israelites (cf. Exod. 12:43-50). Here, as elsewhere in the book, Josh. is shown as the chief officiant in religious rites; Near Eastern rulers were often the titular heads of the religious institutions of their lands. The OT is not entirely clear about the origins of circumcision. The P tradition attributes this rite to Abraham (Gen. 17:9-27); the J source first speaks of it in connection with Moses (Exod. 4:24-26). The tradition here, which some scholars link with the E source, shows Josh. as instituting the rite (omitting **again the second time** in vs. 2 as a later addition). Vss. 4-7 are an editor's attempt to reconcile the differing traditions by explaining that circumcision had not been instituted as a perpetual rite but only ordered for the generation of Israelites who left Egypt. Several ancient Near Eastern peoples practiced circumcision, sometimes in mass ceremonies at irregular intervals in a way similar to that suggested in this passage. On the explanation of the name **Gilgal** see above on 4:1-24.

5:10-12. *Celebration of the Passover.* This passage, which is the work of an author with P interests, links the passover with the entry into Canaan—as well it might in view of the similarity of motif between the exodus from Egypt and the crossing of the Jordan. The celebration of the passover is presented as marking the end of one era in Israelite history and the beginning of another, as does also the cessation of manna (vs. 12). The connection of the passover with Gilgal may be very ancient. If, as some scholars have suggested, the Hebrew word for "passover" originally came from the verb "limp," it may originally have alluded to a dance performed in the passover rites (cf. I Kings 18:21, 26). In any case it is possible that the passover was a pre-Israelite agricultural festival.

E. The Conquest of Jericho (5:13–6:27)

5:13-15. *The Divine Manifestation to Joshua.* This is one of several bits of old tradition in the OT which allude to manifestations by heavenly military leaders (cf. e.g. Gen. 32:1-2, II Sam. 24:15-17). The scene is reminiscent of the burning bush in Exod. 3: 2-5. The preservation of the story may be due in part to its presentation of Josh. as a new Moses, but as it stands it serves as a prologue to the story of the taking of Jericho. The episode ends without narrating the divine instructions; perhaps it is a fragment of a longer tradition, or the compiler may intend 6:2-5 to continue the scene.

6:1-27. *The Siege and Fall of Jericho.* Two somewhat differing traditions, commonly said to come from J and E, have been interwoven here, as is evident from the repetition and divergence of some details. **Jericho** lay at the intersection of important trade routes in the Jordan Valley (see color map 1) and had been a commercial center thousands of years before Josh. came on the scene. Small by modern standards, the city could not have been more than a few acres in size nor have contained more than a few thousand inhabitants.

6:1-14. For an unspecified time the Israelites have been enforcing an embargo on Jericho (vs. 1). The final stage of the siege begins as Josh.'s army marches **around the city** each day for a week (vss. 8-14). There is an interesting parallel in a 14th-cent. Canaanite story in which King Keret captures a city by surrounding it and cutting off its supplies. Many of the details of Josh.'s siege seem to be based on reasonable military strategy: devices for insuring complete blockade of supplies to the city, ways of unnerving the enemy while keeping up the morale and physical condition of Israel's army, signals to indicate the maneuvers to be executed, etc. But the marching, ark carrying, horn blowing, and shouting

also seem to have overtones of religious ritual—such as might perhaps be performed as an act of sympathetic magic before a siege in hope of influencing the course of the battle, or perhaps be enacted at a shrine in the repeated commemoration of a great victory.

6:15-20. In light of the above military and cultic considerations the question of whether or not the wall of Jericho actually **fell down flat** seems almost beside the point. To explain its collapse as due to an opportune earthquake is to stretch probability. Possibly the reference is only a bit of dramatic exaggeration—especially if the story was first told in song —of what was actually a victory by ordinary military procedures. It is also possible that the story means to hint that **Rahab** played traitor to her people and opened the gates to Israel when she heard the **great shout** outside; the Amarna texts of the 14th cent. tell of traitors who by some means handed their cities over to the Habiru (see Intro.). Still another possibility is that in an earlier stage the tradition assumed that some of Israel's spies remained in Jericho and at the signal opened the gates of the city; an Egyptian text from the 15th cent. tells how Egyptians took Joppa (see color map 3) by bringing in soldiers hidden in baskets, who later opened the city's gates. Conclusions about how Jericho fell are made the more difficult because archaeology has revealed little trace of habitation of the city at the time of the Israelite conquest. What excavators of 1930-36 thought to be the wall that fell down was shown in excavations of 1952-57 to be of much earlier date; of the wall of Josh.'s day there is no trace—possibly because of erosion in that part of the ruins.

6:21-27. The Israelites completely destroy Jericho and its inhabitants except for Rahab's household (vss. 22-25). To destroy everything in a captured city, save perhaps the precious metals, was regarded as an act of high devotion to Yahweh. The Israelites were not alone in practicing, or claiming to practice, this kind of piety; in a later century King Mesha of Moab declares on his commemorative stele that he slew all of the Israelite inhabitants of Nebo because he had dedicated their city to his god Ashtar-Chemosh (see Intro.). In vs. 26a Josh. lays a curse on anyone who **rebuilds** Jericho. To this curse an editor has added a bit of poetry (vs. 26b) which seems rather unrelated to the story, since it concerns the Canaanite practice of offering a child as a sacrifice to the gods when erecting a building (cf. I Kings 16:34). This appears to be a fragment from some longer poem, possibly not originally connected with Jericho.

F. The Conquest of Ai (7:1–8:29)

Next the Hebrews attack **Ai**, generally identified as the modern et-Tell, a mound in the hill country of Palestine about 15 miles W and a little N of Jericho (see color map 5). But archaeologists excavating in 1933-36, while finding that Ai was occupied during the Early Bronze Age (3rd millennium) and again in a modest way *ca.* the 11th cent., discovered no evidence that a city existed there in Josh.'s time. To explain this puzzling fact some scholars, taking "Ai" to mean "ruin" (cf. 8:28), have suggested that the story of the conquest of Ai grew up to explain the presence of ruins which the early Hebrews saw. Others, however, have more recently noted that in the OT "Ai" is the name of inhabited places, not ruins, and that the word can better be translated "heap" or "pile of stones." If Ai was a thriving city at the time of the Israelite conquest, it should perhaps be sought elsewhere than at et-Tell, possibly—as some have suggested—at the nearby site usually assumed to be Bethel (cf. the story of the conquest of Bethel in Judg. 1:22-26, which may be related to this story). As to the ancient name of et-Tell, it has been suggested that it was Beth-aven, mentioned in 7:2. There are so many uncertain factors that the question must be regarded as unresolved.

7:1-26. Achan's Disobedience. As in the previous narratives, at least 2 underlying traditions can be detected, often identified as from J and E.

7:2-9. Josh. sends spies to Ai, who on their return predict an easy conquest and suggest that the entire army need not make the steep climb to the city (which must have been some 3,000 feet higher in altitude than Gilgal). Josh. sends out a detachment of **three thousand men.** In the disastrous battle which follows the Israelites lose **thirty-six men**—a figure which suggests that the attacking force was perhaps in the low hundreds rather than in the thousands. News of the disaster prompts Josh. to conclude, in accordance with the outlook of his day, that Yahweh is in some way displeased. Josh. tears his garments, throws dust on his head, falls to the earth and prays—all traditional gestures of sorrow and humility intended to evoke the compassion of the deity.

7:10-26. Yahweh tells Josh. that someone has **stolen** part of the forbidden spoil from Jericho (cf. 6:18-19). Josh. devises a test by lot in order to uncover the wrongdoer. The selection narrows to Achan, who confesses his guilt and then undergoes death by stoning or, according to the other source, burning. The story ends with an explanation of the place name **Valley of Achor** (vs. 26).

Though this account is fairly straightforward as it stands, there may be more behind it than first appears. When Hittites suffered military defeat they assumed that the gods were displeased and performed a human sacrifice to appease them. Other peoples, e.g. apparently the early Greeks, sometimes performed human sacrifice before a major battle in hope that this supreme sacrifice would bring victory (cf. Agamemnon's sacrifice of his daughter Iphigenia). The story of Jephthah's daughter (Judg. 11:29-40) shows that on occasion Israelites followed such a practice. Achan's execution may thus be primarily a sacrifice to try to insure victory in the coming battle for Ai; as a confessed criminal (vss. 20-21) he is the most expendable person.

The modern reader may well feel that Achan's death could not really please God and that in any case his fate was not commensurate with his crime, esp. since his household perished with him (vs. 24). The concept of the family as so unitary that all had to perish for the offense of one member was eventually rejected by the Israelites themselves in favor of the idea that each man should be judged as an individual, whether by man or by God (cf. Ezek. 18), though the older idea reappeared from time to time (cf. John 11:50). The belief that Yahweh demanded human sacrifice was also rejected in time, as the story of Abraham's attempt to sacrifice his son Isaac (Gen. 22) seems to want to teach. But the belief that religious leaders had the right to determine capital punishment for the violation of religious regulations persisted for a much longer time (cf. the stoning of Stephen in Acts 7 and perhaps even the story of Ananias and Sapphira in Acts 5:1-11); against this view one may place the teaching of Jesus that judgment belongs to God alone (e.g. Matt. 7:1-5).

8:1-29. The Successful Attack on Ai. The way is now clear for the conquest of Ai. Unlike the first attack, which did not proceed by instruction from Yahweh, the fresh assault is divinely commanded (vs. 1; cf. a similar instruction by the god Chemosh which King Mesha of Moab reports on his commemorative stele; see Intro.). Vs. 2 is a D addition. The number of soldiers (vs. 3) seems to be exaggerated. Some of the details of the attack are not clear because of the editorial linking of the 2 sources, but the general plan is that Josh. lures the defenders of Ai outside with a small body of soldiers as a decoy, enabling the main body of the Israelite soldiers to enter the city and take it. In telling of his role in the ruse the storyteller gives a few personal glimpses of Josh. as a daring hero not unlike some of Israel's later great warriors. The public execution of the **king of Ai** and the display of his body (vs. 29) follow the standard Near Eastern practice of disconcerting the conquered people and emphatically indicating the end of the old regime.

G. Josh.'s Altar (8:30–9:2)

8:30-35. A Ceremony at Shechem. Here we find Josh. at **Mount Ebal** and **Mount Gerizim,** the twin mountains flanking Shechem in central Palestine, over 20 miles N of Ai (see color map 5). The story is unexpected, since Josh. has not yet attempted the conquest of this region. Clearly an editorial addition, the passage is D throughout, showing Josh.'s fulfillment of Moses' instructions (Deut. 11:29-30; 27; see comment). Though not called such, the scene is one of covenanting and has affinities with the account of Josh.'s covenant at Shechem in ch. 24 (see comment), which some interpreters suspect once stood at this point and was later replaced by this passage. In stressing Josh.'s writing of the **law of Moses** on stones the D author shows, as elsewhere, his assumption that Josh.'s experiences often parallel those of Moses. These **stones** (vs. 32; cf. Deut. 27:2-4) are apparently freestanding rather than part of the **altar** (vs. 31; cf. Deut. 27:5-7) and as such may be compared with the stones set up at Gilgal (ch. 4).

9:1-2. An Editorial Conclusion. The D editor summarizes the effect of Josh.'s victory over Ai on the indigenous peoples of Palestine. As elsewhere (2:9-11; 5:1), he pictures consternation among them, but here—as not previously—he reports, not despondency, but willingness to withstand Israel. The statement serves as a foil to the story which follows. **Beyond the Jordan** here refers to Palestine, not Transjordan as the expression usually does.

H. Israel's Covenant with Gibeon (9:3-27)

Gibeon was an important town 6 miles NW of Jerusalem (see color map 5). Its inhabitants in Josh.'s time were apparently not of Canaanite stock. Vs. 7 speaks of them as **Hivites,** perhaps the same as Horites (see "The People of the OT World," pp. 1005-17), while another source calls them Amorites (II Sam. 21:2)—but contrast the story of an Amorite attack on them in 10:1-27. Excavations at the site in 1956-62 revealed evidence of Late Bronze Age occupation not long before the time of the Hebrew conquest of Canaan. The story of how the Gibeonites save themselves by deceiving the leaders of Israel into making a treaty with them comes from 2 major accounts, usually identified as J and E, which have been woven together. The episode originally followed the conquest of Ai (8:29). There is a bit of D embellishment in vss. 24-25 and an addition in vss. 17-21 which many interpreters assume, perhaps correctly, to be from a P source.

9:6-15. The **covenant** which the Gibeonites seek is of the suzerainty type, in which they agree to accept political subservience to Israel in return for protection of their peace. The covenant may have been accompanied by a solemn feast (cf. Gen. 26:30), but the food which the Gibeonites bring (vss. 12-13; cf. vss. 4-5) is probably not to be understood as provisions for such a meal, since it was customarily offered by the dominant party—in this case Israel. The food must therefore be part of the ruse.

9:16-27. The Gibeonites' deception is successful, and they accept the role of **hewers of wood and drawers of water** which the covenant imposes on them. This terminology appears in the Canaanite Keret text of the 14th cent. as a designation of the village pursuits of women; in this context it seems to imply that the Gibeonites are to disband their army and rely on Israel for their defense. Hebrew storytellers, unwilling to concede that the Gibeonites went unpunished for their deception, have modified the tradition so that the role appears to be some sort of disgrace which Josh. imposes on the Gibeonites after he learns of the deception; indeed they speak of the Gibeonites as becoming **slaves** (vs. 23) and having to serve in the **congregation** (i.e. the temple in Jerusalem) as servants of an esp. low class (vs. 27); such modifications largely reflect conditions of later cents. The Gibeonites seem eventually to have merged with the Israelite population. Part of the reason for the preservation of this story was undoubtedly that it served as a background for the following episode and for II Sam. 21:1-14.

I. The Conquest of S Palestine (10:1-43)

10:1-27. *Defeat of a Coalition of S Kings.* For the first time since the conquest began the Canaanite rulers attempt to take offensive action, though it is directed, not toward Israel, but toward Israel's new vassal, **Gibeon.** The tendency of kings to band together for warfare was natural, since each city-state was too small to exert strong military power alone. Most of the cooperating cities had been yokefellows under Egypt's rule in previous cents. and had known the threat of the Habiru, or Hebrews. The name of the leader of the coalition, **Adoni-zedek,** resembles that of Adoni-bezek in Judg. 1:5-7, and it is possible that the 2 stories are in some way related.

10:6-11. When Gibeon is threatened, Josh. fulfills his responsibility as the protector of the vassal city (cf. the covenant in 9:15) and comes to the rescue.

Following a practice successfully employed at Ai (8:3) Josh. directs a forced nighttime march from his base at Gilgal. Surprising the enemy, he not only wins a victory but drives deep into S Palestine (vs. 10; see color map 5). The narrative, in which more than one source can be detected, bears some resemblance to the story of the coalition of 5 kings against 4 kings in Gen. 14; perhaps both traditions are based on a common old motif.

10:12-15. Like perhaps other parts of chs. 2-11 (see Intro.) this story may originally have been cast as a poem; the 4 lines of vss. 12c-13b may be a fragment from that poem as it once existed in the now-lost **Book of Jashar.** The standing still of **Sun** and **Moon** has long fascinated readers, who have often attributed to it far more significance than the original storyteller probably intended. Possibly there is nothing more complicated here than a wish to defeat the enemy before nightfall (cf. the wish of Agamemnon, *Iliad* II. 412-18). The prose writer of vs. 13cd takes the poem literally, explaining that the sun stopped its movement until the battle was won. Assuming that some unusual but natural phenomenon occurred during the battle, modern interpreters have often sought to explain that event as an eclipse, a hailstorm, the presence of sun and moon in the sky together at dawn, a clouding of the sky, etc.; but these interpretations seem strained. The poet is probably speaking metaphorically, like the author of the Song of Deborah when he speaks of the stars fighting against Sisera (Judg. 5:20).

Behind the metaphor may lie interesting concepts of cosmology (cf. Hab. 3:11) and perhaps even astrology. Indeed it is possible, as some interpreters have suggested, that Josh. was uttering an incantation to the sun and moon to help him defeat his enemies, since vs. 13a (which may, however, be an early addition) and the prose explanation imply that the command to sun and moon occurred before the battle. On the other hand the fact that the song is placed (like that of Moses, Exod. 15:1-18) after rather than before the battle suggests that it was originally a song of victory, related to a religious celebration and possibly to the establishment of a special commemorative ceremony. To what extent, however, these cultic associations belong with the original tradition cannot be determined.

10:16-27. This is a relatively lengthy description, somewhat separate from the preceding episode, of the pursuit and execution of the **five kings** who fought against Israel. As usual, 2 sources have been interwoven, resulting in some confusion in detail. One suspects that originally there was a good deal of significance to this story which can no longer be discovered. The scenes show considerable stylization. The idea that defeated kings hid in caves is widespread, not only in Hebrew tradition (cf. I Sam. 22:1) but in Egyptian as well. Josh.'s command to his associates to come forward and place their **feet upon the necks of these kings** as a symbol of their utter defeat follows ancient oriental custom (cf. e.g. Ps. 110:1; I Cor. 15:25-27). It is interesting to note that Josh. shares the heady moment of triumph with his lieutenants. As in 8:29, Josh. orders the bodies of the kings displayed publicly.

10:28-43. *Further Conquests in S Palestine.* This section, which builds directly on the preceding narrative, is D. Apparently the earlier tradition said nothing of any conquests of Josh., other than possibly raids, in S Palestine, but the D editor, looking back from a vantage point many cents. later, knew that Israel had come to occupy S Palestine. Perhaps drawing on certain older traditions available to him, he here attributes to Josh.'s conquests a number of S cities (see color map 5), which in every case he shows as suffering utter destruction at Josh.'s hands. Accurately enough, he does not say that Josh. actually took **Gezer** (vs. 33).

10:40-43. This is the D editor's summary of the S campaign. The **Negeb** is the dry region S of Beersheba. The **country of Goshen** here is not in Egypt but the S hill country surrounding the town of Goshen (cf. 15:51; see color map 5). Many scholars have doubted that Josh. conquered any of S Palestine, preferring instead the traditions in Judg. 1:1-20, which suggest that this region was conquered by various groups, probably over an extended period.

J. The Conquest of N Palestine (11:1-15)

Vss. 1, 4-5, 7, 8b are generally recognized as coming from an old tradition, often identified as J or JE. They tell briefly of Josh.'s defeat of **Jabin king of Hazor** and his 3 confederates at the **waters of Merom,** a place NW of the Sea of Galilee (see color map 5). The remaining vss. are a D amplification of the story which shows Josh. as conquering virtually all of Galilee.

11:1-5. On **Jabin** see comment on Judg. 4:1-24. The **Arabah** is the deep valley of the Sea of Galilee, Jordan River, and Dead Sea. **Chinneroth** (or Chinnereth, NT Gennesaret) may mean either the town on the NW shore of the Sea of Galilee (cf. 19:35) or the lake itself (cf. 12:3; 13:27).

11:6-9. Josh. defeats the confederates and pursues them apparently to the N border of Palestine. **Great Sidon** is generally taken to mean the boundary of Sidonian territory. The **valley of Mizpeh** is probably the same as the **land of Mizpah** at the foot of Mt. **Hermon** (vs. 3).

11:10-15. That **Hazor** was a chief Canaanite city is confirmed by references in Egyptian and Meso-

potamian records. Excavation has revealed that it was destroyed and rebuilt a number of times, one destruction possibly occurring in the 13th cent. As often, this D section contains some old material—e.g. that Josh. destroyed **none of the cities that stood on mounds** (vs. 13), i.e. none of the powerful old Canaanite walled cities of the lowlands. Behind this statement lies the recollection that the Israelites, settling in the rural hill country, did not have the strength or technological knowledge to enable them to defeat the chariot armies of the Canaanite cities. That Israel carried out so extensive a program as the D author describes (vss. 12, 14) is unlikely and may be attributed to his zeal in showing the success of Israel under Yahweh.

K. Summary of Joshua's Conquests (11:16–12:24)

11:16-23. An Editorial Summary. This passage is largely, and perhaps entirely, D. Eager to show that Yahweh fulfilled his promise that Israel would make its home in Canaan, the author declares that **Joshua took all that land,** from **Lebanon** to **Mount Halak** in the **Negeb** (see above on 10:40-43). He probably represents the conquest as far bloodier than it was, and he devotes only passing attention to the fact that some regions remained outside Israelite control (vs. 22; on the **Anakim** see comment on Num. 13:32-33). The concluding sentence (vs. 23) serves as a transition to the 2nd half of Josh., which begins in ch. 13.

12:1-24. A Statistical Summary. Though brought into Josh. by the D editor, this ch. seems largely to be an independent record compiled by an unknown archivist.

12:1-6. This is a summary of the Transjordanian kings and kingdoms said to have been defeated by the Israelites under Moses (cf. Num. 21:21-35; Deut. 2:24–3:11; see comments) and Moses' allotment of these territories to Gad, Reuben, and Manasseh (cf. 1:12-18; 22:1-34; Num. 32; Deut. 3:12-17). On **Sea of Chinneroth** see above on 11:1-5. **The sea of the Arabah, the Salt Sea** is the Dead Sea.

12:7-24. The **kings** and peoples defeated by the Israelites under Josh. in Palestine proper are listed.

Courtesy of Yigael Yadin: The James A. de Rothschild Expedition at Hazor, The Hebrew University, Jerusalem, Israel

Sacred pillars in the temple at Hazor

The fact that many of these names have not previously been mentioned indicates that this section is not simply a summary of the preceding stories. The cities of vss. 10-16a are in S Palestine. Some of the places of vss. 16b-24 are in the territories of Ephraim and Manasseh in central Palestine, where no conquests have previously been narrated. Many scholars believe that the lack of traditions about Josh.'s conquests in Ephraim and Manasseh indicates Hebrew settlement in that region well before his time.

II. The Apportionment of the Land (13:1–22:34)

The content of this large division differs considerably from that of chs. 2-11. Though it contains some D editorial materials, it consists mainly of statistical information about persons, places, and tribes which Israelite archivists gathered from various sources. Some of the data may have their roots in the Conquest, but as they stand they seem to reflect conditions of later cents. Such records must have been compiled for cultic or administrative use, and they have affinities with the P traditions of the OT (see Intro.). Some of these materials were undoubtedly first preserved in N Palestinian sanctuaries, but sometime after the centralization of Yahwist religion in the temple they were transferred to Jerusalem. Not surprisingly, the sections dealing with S Palestine, in which Jerusalem lay, are more detailed than those concerning N Palestine and Transjordan. The statistical records which have been preserved here probably represent only a small part of the total body of archives which once existed. Parts of these chs. have shorter parallels in Judg. 1:1–2:5. The places named in the allotments which have been located appear on color map 5.

A. Preface to the Allotment (13:1–14:15)

13:1-7. Summary of Unconquered Areas. Except for vs. 1 this passage is D and is the fullest D statement in Josh. of those parts of Canaan which the Israelites were not able to conquer. The author idealistically includes not only the coastal lands of the **Philistines** and **Sidonians** (Phoenicians) but other territories to the S and N never occupied by Israel (cf. 1:4; I Chr. 13:5). The **Geshurites** of vs. 2 are a S people different from the Aramean Geshurites of vs. 13. Yahweh instructs Josh. to allot to the tribes of Israel even those portions admittedly not then under Israelite control, along with the rest of the land.

13:8–14:5. Review of Tribal Allotments Under Moses. This section reviews the traditional allotment of Transjordan by Moses to the tribes of Gad, Reuben, and Manasseh (cf. 1:12-18; 12:1-6; 22:1-34; Num. 32; Deut. 3:12-17). Vss. 8-12, 14 are usually recognized as D; the remaining material is from one or more archivistic records. The D editor takes note of the fact that the **tribe of Levi,** which had a religious function and presumably lived throughout the country, received no allotment (13:14, 33; cf. 18:7; 21:1-45). 14:1-2 prepares for the allotment of the land W of the Jordan described in 14:6–19:51. Some interpreters believe that 18:1 originally stood before 14:1 and therefore that the locale of the allotment tradition was originally Shiloh. The reference to **Eleazar the** (chief) **priest** in 14:1, next to whom

Josh. takes 2nd place, seems to reflect P interests.

14:6-15. Caleb's Inheritance at Hebron. In view of Josh.'s prominence, the place which Caleb occupies in the exodus and conquest traditions is remarkable. This story tells of Josh.'s gift of land to Caleb, the only other Israelite of the exodus generation who has lived on into the conquest period (cf. Num. 14:20-24). Variant traditions in 15:13-19; Judg. 1:11-15 (see comments) indicate that Caleb actually gained his territory by military conquest. The account here, apparently D, retains a hint of this tradition (vs 12; on the **Anakim** see comment on Num. 13:32-33) but portrays Josh. bestowing the land as if it had already been taken (vss. 13:14; cf. 10:36-37; 11:21-22). The time span of **forty-five years** (vs. 10) is notable because it implies that the Israelites conquered all Canaan, including Transjordan, within 7 years (cf. vs. 7; Deut. 2:14). The author could compress and simplify happenings in this way because he was greatly removed from them in time.

B. The Allotment to Judah (15:1-63)

15:1-12. The Boundaries of Judah. This, the first and most complete of the boundary lists, indicates that the compiler not only had fuller records for Judah but gave that tribe preeminence. The limits of Judah are set at their greatest possible extent, including desert and coastal regions which were not historically a part of the tribe's territory.

15:13-19. An Interpolation on Caleb's Territory. Since the portion given to Caleb and his family lay within Judah, the editor can now introduce an old tradition about Caleb's inheritance which some interpreters identify as from J. A parallel account is found in Judg. 1:11-15. In both passages Caleb is shown as taking his territory by force. Contrast 14:6-15, composed in D circles (see comment).

15:20-63. The Cities of Judah. This list presents a number of difficulties both of geography and of dating, but many scholars would agree that it is based on a list of districts within Judah and was drawn up for governmental administrative purposes sometime after the time of David—several cents. later, some would say—but perhaps based on records of pre-Davidic times. The list presupposes the existence of major cities, each surrounded by villages subservient to it. Among the more noteworthy later modifications of the list are the addition of Philistine cities in vss. 45-47 and the omission of a block of cities between vss. 59-60—fortunately preserved in the Greek text.

15:63. This appended bit of ancient tradition is important for the history of **Jerusalem.** Though 12:10 asserts that Josh. vanquished the king of Jerusalem and Judg. 1:8 tells of the capture of the city, these traditions seem to grow out of S interests in monarchical times—the editorial **to this day** here. This passage supports the more likely tradition that Jerusalem remained a stronghold of the **Jebusites** until David captured it (II Sam. 5:6-9; cf. Judg. 19:10-12). The city was closely bounded by both Judah (vs. 8) and Benjamin (18:16; see color map 5) and was apparently open to both tribes. This vs. mentions men of **Judah** living in Jebusite Jerusalem, whereas a similar passage in Judg. 1:21 speaks of Benjaminites. If one must choose between the traditions, that which speaks of Benjaminite connections with Jerusalem perhaps has the stronger claim.

C. The Allotment to the Joseph Tribes (16:1–17:18)

The borders of the territories allotted to Joseph's **descendants** are not entirely clear. No lists of cities, as such, are given. It is evident that the compiler did not have the same kind of detailed resources for these tribes as he did for Judah.

16:1-4. The Area Broadly Defined. The tribes of **Manasseh and Ephraim,** traditionally linked as the sons of **Joseph,** are treated together in vss. 1-3, which come from an old tradition of the JE kind. Interpreters are not agreed on whether this treatment of Joseph as a single tribe is older than the treatment of Ephraim and Manasseh separately (vss. 4–17:13) but most assume that it is.

16:5-10. The Allotment to Ephraim. This brief notice, in which tribal boundaries are confusingly delineated, ends with a fragment from an earlier tradition (vs. 10; cf. Judg. 1:29) which explains why Canaanites continue to live among the Israelites. Cf. the story in ch. 9 which explains the presence of Gibeonites in Israel. In both instances the aboriginal population is said—probably anachronistically—to be reduced to slavery.

17:1-18. The Allotment to Manasseh. This treatment is more extensive than the preceding section on Ephraim because it includes 2 segments of narrative (vss. 3-6, 14-18). Other materials can also be detected in this section, e.g. the list of Manasseh's descendants in vs. 2. Concerning boundaries, however, the details (vss. 7-11) are sketchy.

17:3-6. This story of the **daughters** of Zelophehad and their claim to an **inheritance** may be based on Num. 27:1-11 (cf. also vs. 3 with Num. 26:33), which is generally attributed to the postexilic P source.

17:11-13. This notice about the Canaanite cities which the Manassites were unable to take (cf. Judg. 1:27) is informative. The statement that they **put the Canaanites to forced labor** (cf. 9:23-27; 16:10; Judg. 1:28) probably reflects conditions of a later time.

17:14-18. Ephraim and Manasseh are here treated as one tribe, **Joseph,** as in 16:1-3. This passage consists of 2 versions of the same tradition, vss. 14-15, 16-18. Both traditions recall that the Joseph tribes could inhabit only the **hill country** during the conquest. They were not sufficiently strong or mechanized to challenge the Canaanite cities, which were defended with **chariots of iron** (i.e. having iron armor plates; cf. 11:6; Judg. 1:19; 4:3; etc.). Thus they had to be content to wrest a livelihood from the rugged, unfarmed hills, forgoing the better alluvial territory of the Canaanites. Though the passage says nothing of their leaving their **too narrow** territory, it may be derived from an earlier tradition which told of the migration of these tribes to Transjordan, where Ephraim later had certain connections and part of Manasseh is traditionally said to have lived. Such a tradition would naturally tend to be modified in the face of that other tradition which showed the Joseph tribes coming first to Transjordan, before the conquest of W Canaan. On the lack of space for expansion cf. the story of the migration of the tribe of Dan to the far N of Palestine (Judg. 17-18).

D. The Allotments to the Other Tribes (18:1–19:51)

18:1-10. The Allotment Ceremony at Shiloh. Having dealt with the major tribes of Judah, Ephraim, and Manasseh, which together occupied a large part of the hill country possessed by Israel, the D compiler turns to the remaining **seven tribes**—omitting Gad and Reuben, who are assumed to be settled in Transjordan, and Levi, who is not given a territorial allotment, as he explains in a note (vs. 7; see above on 13:8–14:5). He describes their allotments as being determined at a single gathering of Israel at **Shiloh,** one of the important shrines where Israelites worshiped. Some interpreters, however, have argued that vs. 1 originally stood before 14:1 and that the original site of the present episode was Gilgal (reading "Gilgal" for "Shiloh" in vss. 8-10; cf. 14:6). In preparation for the ceremony Josh. orders representatives of the tribes to survey the remaining land and divide it into **seven portions.** He then proceeds to **cast lots . . . before the LORD** (cf. 7:14-18; 15:1; 16:1) in order to allot one portion to each tribe. That these tribes actually received their traditional territories in such a manner is unlikely; the process was probably a more complex one of historical settlement which took place at various times.

18:11-19:48. The Individual Allotments to the Seven Tribes. Beginning with Benjamin and continuing with Simeon, Zebulun, Issachar, Asher, Naphtali and Dan, Josh. allots the remaining land. The descriptions, most of which consist of boundary delineations and lists of cities, are brief and frequently confusing. Behind them may lie various tribal records which the D editor, perhaps not entirely understanding them, has modified. The tribal boundaries of **Simeon** are lacking (19:1-9), probably because the tribe long had lived within the territory of Judah. The boundaries of **Dan** are likewise missing (19:40-48), perhaps because the tribe had only a few towns squeezed in among the surrounding tribes. To the treatment of Dan the editor has added a brief note derived from an old tradition of the Danites' subsequent loss of their land and migration to the N of Palestine (19:47; cf. Judg. 17-18).

19:49-51. Josh.'s Inheritance; Conclusion. The D editor appends a note, drawn from a separate tradition often identified as from E, that Israel gave Josh. the city of **Timnath-serah** (called Timnath-heres in Judg. 2:9) in **Ephraim** at his request. That Josh., an Ephraimite (cf. Num. 13:8) would choose to settle in his tribe's territory is not surprising, but one may observe that the gift is apparently not arranged by lot as were the lands for the tribes, being given instead as a reward for services well performed (cf. Caleb's portion, 14:13). The reference to **Eleazar the priest** in vs. 51 is a P embellishment which reflects cultic interests (cf. 14:1; 21:1; etc.).

E. The Cities of Refuge (20:1-9)

A Semitic common law, still prevalent in some Arab villages in Palestine, held that one **who kills any person,** even unintentionally, is guilty of bloodshed and may be immediately executed by the family of the slain person. This passage provides that certain **cities of refuge** are to be "off limits" to vengeful relatives, thereby giving time for tempers to cool and a sober inquiry to be made. The P tradition of Num. 35:9-15 attributes the establishment of such cities to instructions of Moses. It is likely, however, that at least some of the cities set aside—3 W of the Jordan and 3 E—had functioned as havens in Canaanite times, presumably because of the particular nature of the cults located in them. There is no need to assume, as scholars often have, that the provision for these cities should be traced to Bedouin practice. D circles were also interested in the cities of refuge, as Deut. 19:1-13 shows; cf. also the earlier tradition in Exod. 21:13.

F. The Allotment of Cities to Levites and Aaronic Priests (21:1-42)

This passage shows P interests more clearly than perhaps any other in Josh., but is not necessarily to be taken to be a postexilic creation. It attempts to show priests and Levites sharing in the divine promise of the inheritance of Canaan by receiving certain **cities** within the territories of the other tribes (cf. I Chr. 6:54-81). The D view, as expressed in 13:14; 18:7, seems to be that the Levites have no territorial allotment at all. This episode again is set at **Shiloh** and is described as apportionment by lot (see above on 18:1-10). The Levitic groups mentioned in vss. 4-7 and elsewhere were traditionally said to be descended from Kohath, Gershon, and Merari, sons of the patriarch Levi.

21:9-42. This is a more extensive version of the allotment. Most attention is given to the Levites, but vss. 13-19 list **thirteen cities** assigned to the **descendants of Aaron,** who himself is presented as a descendant of Kohath (vs. 4). The scheme is highly idealistic; that Levites ever effectively controlled many of these cities is unlikely, though they may have served in the religious establishments in many cities. All of the Levitic cities are in N Palestine and Transjordan, while all of the Aaronic cities are in S Palestine and the vicinity of Jerusalem. The cities of refuge (cf. ch. 20) are listed among the 35 Levitical cities.

G. The Completion of the Apportionment of the Land (21:43–22:34)

21:43-45. *Summary of the Apportionment.* In this concise, idealized summary the D editor brings the apportionment of Canaan to its completion. This graceful statement shows his firm conviction that Yahweh has faithfully fulfilled all that he promised to Israel.

22:1-9. *Dismissal of the Transjordanian Tribes.* This continuation of the D editorial addition begun in 21:43 draws, it seems, on earlier materials. Josh.'s words in vs. 8 are reminiscent of those in the D passage at the beginning of the Conquest (1:12-15). On this note the Transjordanian tribes depart. Vs. 9, from a non-D source, serves as a transition to the story which follows.

22:10-34. *The Altar at the Jordan.* This lengthy appendix to the narrative of the division of the land

tells how the Transjordanian tribes, as they are returning home, build **an altar of great size** on the W side of the Jordan. Taking this act to be contrary to proper religious practices, the other tribes send a delegation which criticizes the E tribes. On being assured, however, that the altar was erected, not for sacrifices, but solely as a memorial of faithfulness to Yahweh, the W tribes are mollified. Behind this tradition apparently lies the memory of a conflict of religious practices, though not necessarily one which occurred at the time to which it is attributed—note that Josh. does not appear in the account and that the chief **priest** is **Phinehas,** rather than **Eleazar** who has appeared several times previously. Though commentators often assume that this story attempts to show the importance of one central shrine for Israelite worship (i.e. at Jerusalem), the story seems rather to attempt to justify the continued veneration of an old local shrine which would otherwise have been forbidden following the centralization.

III. The Last Acts of Josh. (23:1-24:33)

23:1-16. *Josh.'s Farewell Speech.* With this speech cf. the farewell addresses attributed to Jacob (Gen. 49:1-27) and to Moses (Deut. 31-33). It is entirely D. In an earlier edition of Josh. it may have constituted the conclusion of the book, ch. 24 perhaps having been added later. In the speech Josh., now an old man, assures the assembled Israelites that although the land is not yet entirely conquered (vs. 4) Yahweh will ultimately give total possession of it to Israel if the people remain steadfast in keeping **the law.** Ignoring as insignificant the fact that the conquest was only partial, Josh. emphasizes that **not one** of Yahweh's good promises **has failed** (vs. 14; cf. 21:45).

The D author wrote, of course, with knowledge of the events which had occurred during the cents. after Josh.'s time. Anticipating the period of the judges, he has Josh. mention that **evil things** will come upon Israel through failure to live by Yahweh's commandments. As elsewhere, he shows concern for contemporary problems and values. Notable is his warning to the Israelites not to **marry** among the other inhabitants of the land (vss. 12-13)—a topic which was esp. lively in the postexilic period. Like many other D speeches, this passage is gracefully written but shows a narrow concept of the nature of the proper worship of Yahweh and a highly particularistic view of his actions with Israel. For the author other peoples have little or no significance.

24:1-28. *The Covenant at Shechem.* Because Josh.'s speech in ch. 23 forms an appropriate conclusion to the original D edition of Josh., ch. 24 seems to be an appendix, perhaps added by a later editor of the D circle. The core of the story is older material which many interpreters identify as belonging to the E source. The fact that the review of Israelite history in vss. 2-11a, c (vss. 11b, 12-13 being largely D embellishment) concludes with a reference to the fall of **Jericho** suggests that the episode may once have stood approximately where the D story of covenanting at Ebal-Gerizim (near **Shechem**) now stands in 8:30-35.

The account first tells how Josh. summons the leaders of Israel to Shechem. This city was obviously not hostile to the Israelites (cf. Gen. 34), but it is not necessary to assume that it was controlled by Israel at this time or that its religion was Israelite. Judg. 8:33; 9:4, 46 suggest that the cult was that of El-berith (i.e. "El-covenant"), the Canaanite god of covenanting, and that the Israelites were able to gather because of the covenant peace which gave them protection (cf. Shechem as a city of refuge, ch. 20). Here, flanked by the mountains of Gerizim and Ebal, and using language solemn enough that it could have been inscribed on a stele, Josh. acts as hierophant, i.e. interpreter of sacred history, in a ceremony of covenanting. Customarily we would expect a covenant among the tribes themselves with Yahweh as a witness, but Josh.'s covenant is between Yahweh as the dominant party and Israel as the subservient one.

Of the ceremony itself little information is given; but by comparing other covenants described in the OT, as well as various covenants now known in ancient Near Eastern literature, we may deduce the kind of rite lying back of the account. At some early point, in keeping with Near Eastern covenant forms, Josh. reviewed the historical relationship between Yahweh and Israel (vss. 2-13)—a "history of salvation," one may call it, or very nearly a creedal affirmation (cf. e.g. Deut. 26:5-11; Acts 7:2-53). This was followed by a proclamation of the stipulations of the covenant, here given very briefly (vss. 14-15) and limited to the general demand for loyalty to Yahweh and rejection of other gods—an interest possibly reflecting later concerns more than those of Josh.'s day. To these the people responded (vss. 16-18). Josh. then tested Israel's resolve by pointing out risks which this servitude involved (vss. 19-20), and the people again responded (vs. 21). A final series of declarations and responses solemnly ratified the covenant (vss. 22-24).

It is possible that there was a place for ceremonial blessings and curses such as appear in the covenanting scene in 8:30-35 (cf. Deut. 27:11-28:19). The Israelites may also have performed the ritual of cutting sacrificial animals in 2 and passing between them (cf. Gen. 15:9-17), though standing between Gerizim and Ebal may have served the same function. They may also have eaten a sacred meal (cf.

Gen. 26:30) and participated in a symbolic transfer of gifts (cf. Gen. 21:27-30). That a public record of the covenant was set up is strongly implied by the reference to the **stone** erected **under the oak** (vs. 26). It is interesting to note that there is no mention of the ark, which was traditionally associated with Shiloh (cf. e.g. I Sam. 3:3) rather than Shechem.

The extent to which it is likely that such a covenant including all the tribes of Israel was actually made in Josh.'s time has been much debated, but there can be little doubt that early tribal relationships were often cemented with treaties. With its great stress on Josh.'s speech and the omission of all but a few descriptive details of the ceremony itself, the account clearly reveals that a long development lies behind the tradition. This development, as well as the very preservation of the tradition, may have occurred within the context of a ceremony of covenant renewal enacted at intervals among the tribes of Israel.

24:29-31. *Josh.'s Death.* His work finished, Josh. dies and is **buried** at **Timnath-serah,** the Ephraimite town which the Israelites gave to him for his services (19:49-50); cf. the parallel tradition in Judg. 2:7-9. He is said, like the patriarchs before him, to have lived an exceptionally long time. The D editor adds a sentence (vs. 31) which may be intended as a transition to the period of the judges which is to follow.

24:32-33. *Appended Notes.* Later editors have added brief notes, from earlier traditions, concerning the reburial of the remains of **Joseph** (vs. 32; cf. Gen. 50:26; Exod. 13:19) at **Shechem** (cf. Gen. 33:19) and the death of **Eleazar,** the chief priest (vs. 33). Both burials, we may assume, were in family tombs, cut into the bedrock, as was the practice throughout most of the Israelite times in Palestine. The Greek version of Josh. adds that the Israelites took the ark about with them with **Phinehas** as priest until his death and that Israel began to worship foreign gods so that the Lord gave them into the hands of Eglon, king of Moab, who dominated them for 18 years. This latter statement leads directly into Judg. 3:15 and may be a survival of a pre-D edition (see Intro.) in which Josh. and Judg. formed a single account, Judg. 1:1-3:14 not yet having been added.

THE BOOK OF JUDGES

Robert Houston Smith

INTRODUCTION

The history of Israel between the death of Joshua and the rise of the prophet Samuel is the subject of the book of Judges. The story is told in a series of episodes which revolve around a half dozen heroes, or "judges." Attached to this core are traditions dealing with the conquest of Palestine, 6 minor judges, the attempt of a leader named Abimelech to become king of Shechem, the migration of the tribe of Dan to the N, and a war between Benjamin and the other tribes.

Literary History. Among the earliest forms which the stories of Israel's judges took was undoubtedly song (see "The Compiling of Israel's Story," pp. 1082-89). Some songs were apparently ballads, sung by minstrels who had a keen sense of what would delight an audience of simple people; traces of these are preserved in several poetic utterances in the stories of Samson (chs. 13–16). More serious in tone were didactic poems, such as Jotham's fable (ch. 9) originally may have been. Most majestic of all were the cult poems, such as the Song of Deborah (ch. 5), which by its formal content, ancient rhythm, and archaic language reveals that it was composed by one or more professional musicians in the service of a sanctuary. It is not implausible to trace poetic elements in Judg. back to as early as the 12th cent., though their very nature precludes close dating.

Concurrent with the rise of songs was the appearance of prose accounts which dealt with the same, or similar, subjects. Like the songs, these prose accounts probably often had their origin in Israelite cults, serving in some cases to present a historical, or seemingly historical, basis for existing ideas and practices, as do the story of Jephthah's sacrifice of his daughter and perhaps the stories of Gideon's rites. More efficient than poetry in handling matter-of-fact details, these stories became increasingly popular as Israel's interest in historical records developed, and eventually they became the nucleus of Judg.

There were probably many more stories in circulation than have come down to us. Several versions of some stories came into being, as we can see in the tales of Gideon, Abimelech, and others. As the old accounts in Judg. still show, these stories concerned deliverers of individual tribes rather than of all Israel. It is therefore reasonable to suppose that these traditions—and for that matter the poems too—were best known within the tribes of the judges with which they were concerned. If there were accounts concern-

ing the S tribes of Judah and Simeon, no clear trace of them has survived, for all of the old stories in Judg. concern the N tribes.

Editors in N Palestine began making collections of stories of the judges no later than the 9th cent. and may have continued through the 8th cent. The relationship of these collections to other sources in the OT is not entirely clear. Many scholars find behind the present accounts 2 major collections of stories, which they identify with the J and E sources in Gen.-Num. Others find the evidence for specific collections unconvincing and prefer simply to recognize that old sources underlie the nucleus of Judg.

This nucleus reached its essential form *ca.* the 8th cent. It consists of most of 3:15–16:31 and may also have included chs. 17–18. The compiler added various brief summaries and transitions, among which were probably the number of years of each judge and each period of oppression, the total of which is 410 years. He may also have been responsible for the addition of 6 minor judges (3:31; 10:1-5; 12:8-15). Where the compiler got his information about these minor personages is not known. Possibly he summarized fuller traditions which he knew but felt had only limited usefulness; it is perhaps more likely, however, that he constructed these minor judges out of names he found in old lists.

The compiler's concern with the minor judges may have arisen from a desire to show that each of the 10 N tribes had one great deliverer—an early form, one might say, of the idea that the judges delivered all Israel. In their present form the stories still show a considerable distribution among the tribes, but subsequent alterations have largely obscured any pattern which may once have existed. The compiler seems also to have wished to show a different enemy—the Moabites, the Canaanites, the Midianites, the Ammonites, and the Philistines—in each of the stories of the major judges. The completed work seems to have followed directly on Josh. and to have led directly into the stories about Samuel, the last judge.

In the latter part of the 7th cent. or the first half of the 6th cent. the Deuteronomic school, affiliated in some way with the Jerusalem cult but deeply informed about the religious traditions of N Palestine, took over this core of stories as a part of its extended history of Israel from Deut. through II Kings (see Intro. to Josh. and "The Compiling of Israel's Story," pp. 1082-89). Leaving the older material unaltered

135

save for a few transitions and summaries (notably 3: 12-14; 4:1-3; 6:1; 13:1) the D editor—or editors—prefaced it with a long introductory section drawn in good part from older materials (2:6–3:6) and with an opening story (3:7-11) and possibly omitted chs. 9; 17-18. This editor saw the judges as deliverers of all Israel and assumed that men from all Israel joined in battling the enemy.

In the postexilic period one or more editors with priestly associations expanded Judg. by prefacing the D text with a block of materials (1:1–2:5) taken from an old source which surveyed the conquest of Palestine. This P editor also reintroduced chs. 9; 17-18 —if indeed these chs. had been omitted from the D edition—and added chs. 19-21 as well. To the same editor may also perhaps be attributed the separation of Judg. from Josh. and I Sam.

After this final state of accretion the text of Judg. began a trend toward abridgment and minor modification which seems to have continued down to the time when the present Hebrew text was standardized by Jewish rabbis ca. A.D. 100. These late alterations have done little except to obscure the text. Interpreters are sometimes able to discover an earlier and clearer form of a passage by consulting the LXX version of Judg., which is unique among OT books in that the 2 oldest manuscripts differ greatly in wording. Also helpful are fragments of a slightly different Hebrew text found at Qumran (see "The Dead Sea Scrolls," pp. 1063-71).

Israelite History. This analysis of the process by which Judg. came into its present form has direct relevance for the understanding of Israelite history during the period of the judges. Freed from having to suppose that each judge delivered all Israel, that the judges followed one another in orderly sequence, and that the total length of the period was 410 years, the interpreter is able to reconstruct the history in broad outline and place it within the larger framework of Hebrew and ancient Near Eastern history.

The time of the judges, most scholars now agree, was ca. 1200-1050. By the beginning of this period the traditionally stabilizing Egyptian, Hittite, and Mesopotamian powers had faded into insignificance in Palestine and Transjordan, leaving the small nations of the region to pursue policies of expansion. From the N and W came a seafaring people known as the Philistines, who settled the S coast of Palestine. The Israelite tribes were already established in the hill country and perhaps in parts of N Transjordan. By this time they were occasionally having to fight off hostile forces of Midianites, Ammonites, Moabites, and others who wished to press W across the Jordan. The Canaanites continued to occupy many of their old lowland city-states and a few isolated cities such as Shechem and Jerusalem in the hill country.

Israel's history during this period was mainly one of consolidating settlements previously made, a process which involved defending the tribal territories from aggression by adjoining peoples. The tribes were largely pursuing independent courses, though they shared a sense of common heritage and were bound by various treaties, or covenants, with one another. Life centered around tribal relationships rather than cities. Judg. mentions Israelite cities, but these must have been small and rural by comparison

with the great Canaanite and Philistine cities. Borders remained fluid and the people were relatively mobile. Marriages among the tribes were frequent, and intermarriage with Canaanites and Philistines was tolerated to a considerable degree. Most Israelites were tillers of the soil, cultivating such plants as wheat, olives, grapes, and figs.

Tribal leaders, apparently selected by the leading men of the clans—in principle on the basis of qualities of leadership but in practice sometimes on the basis of familial status—came and went. They sometimes engaged in feuds and power struggles as they pursued their careers. Whether they were called "judges" in their own time is uncertain. The D editor so designates collectively the heroes of the book (2: 16-19), and sometimes says that so-and-so "judged Israel"; but no individual hero is actually called a judge, or is portrayed as rendering a courtroom verdict. Yet the judge in ancient Canaanite and Israelite usage was not so much a legal expert as one who upheld the customs of his people; consequently he became a deliverer of wronged persons who were not strong enough to obtain justice for themselves —widows, orphans, and victims of military aggression. Indeed the D editor several times refers to one or another of the heroes as a "deliverer." Clearly the tribal leaders did not conform to any one narrow role—cf. e.g. Jephthah, a military commander (11:6, 11), and Deborah, a prophetess (4:4). Some of them may have had ties with certain sanctuaries—e.g. Samuel (I Sam. 1–12), considered by the D editor the last of the judges.

The Israelite tribes resisted kingship of the Canaanite kind, of which they continued to have a deep distrust born of long and unhappy experience (see Intro. to Josh.). Nevertheless the process of consolidation of tribal areas and defense against organized enemies gradually pushed them toward a more centralized government. The large and powerful tribes of Ephraim and Manasseh seem esp. to have moved in this direction, as the attempt by Abimelech to extend his authority to the old Canaanite city of Shechem (ch. 9) suggests. Development in this direction was at first slow because the Israelites lacked the technological knowledge to enable any one leader to have the military force necessary for a strong central government. This lack is clearly reflected in the stories of victories in Judg., which stress, not formal battlefield tactics, but raids by small bands of brave men, individual acts of prowess, and assassination. The final phases in the development of a centralized government would come quickly only a short time later, under Saul, David, and Solomon.

Religious Outlook. The religious concepts and practices of the Israelites during the period of the judges were extremely diverse and frequently linked with the Canaanite religion. There is ample evidence of the survival of primitive concepts of reverence for trees, stones, wooden pillars, and idols, not to mention crude prebattle rites involving magical ceremonies, the reading of signs, and human sacrifice. But this is only a relatively minor aspect of Israelite religion.

Canaanite religious texts of the 14th cent. found at Ras Shamra in N Syria have shown in recent decades that the Canaanite religion as it was practiced in major cultic centers was remarkably advanced at the time the Israelites settled in Palestine. Using a developed poetic style Canaanite thinkers set forth in their myths an elaborate attempt to understand the world which they knew. Though far from the heights of religious insight which were to characterize Israelite religion in its classical form, they nevertheless had reached a level that enabled them to make signal contributions to the religious quest of Israel. Amid their cluster of ancient deities such as El, Anath, and Dagon these Canaanite thinkers were already stressing a god whom they called by the title Baal, i.e. "Lord." They proclaimed Baal's dominance over his fellow gods and his beneficence to the earth as he gave fertilizing rain and acted as "king and judge" in the universe. Already they tended to subsume under the one deity Baal a host of old local deities—e.g. El-berith (i.e. "El-covenant"), the god of covenanting at Shechem (cf. 8:33; 9:4, 46).

It is not surprising that the Israelites could recognize in such a deity their own God, Yahweh—who e.g. was also a god of covenanting—nor is it surprising that they could take names such as Jerubbaal without sensing any incongruity. The early traditions in Judg. thus do not bear out the D editor's presupposition that the worship of Baal and the worship of Yahweh were completely different things at this time. Indeed, it was to be several cents. before the worship of Yahweh had become sufficiently unique that a total distinction between the 2 religions was possible. The extent of this process of differentiation by the end of the period of the judges can best be seen in the Song of Deborah (ch. 5), which, though heavily Canaanite in some ways, shows a theological sensitiveness unparalleled elsewhere in Judg.

To say this is to suggest the broader significance of Judg. The contemporary value of the book hardly lies in the moral example which the judges set, for these heroes on occasion display such vices as lying, cruelty, murder, hatred, and sexual immorality. It is certainly not convincing to try to turn these vices into virtues—as interpreters have sometimes tried to do by praising e.g. Jael's bravery, Samson's vigor, and Jephthah's devotion to God. The D editor attempts to find a lasting value in the stories by depicting the sole issue as one of apostasy versus obedience to Yahweh, but his explanation—though perhaps of value in principle—does not do justice to the early traditions themselves. What Judg. does show is the Israelites at an early stage of their search for their self-identity under Yahweh, a search which was to continue throughout the whole of OT times. It is to the lasting credit of the editors of Judg. that they did not expunge or rewrite the stories of Israel's first uncertain steps in this process of religious discovery.

For Further Study: J. M. Myers in *IB*, 1953. Martin Noth, *History of Israel*, 2nd ed., 1960, Pt. 1, Pt. 2, ch. 1. John Bright, *A History of Israel*, 1959, ch. 4. C. F. Kraft in *IDB*, 1962. W. F. Albright, *The Biblical Period from Abraham to Ezra*, 1963, ch. 4.

I. Prologue (1:1–3:6)

A. Summary of the Conquest (1:1–2:5)

This section constitutes a survey of the Israelite conquest of Palestine with which a postexilic editor has prefaced the D edition of Judg. The material

which the late editor used is quite old and resembles parts of Josh., but it is actually a compilation of traditions from various early sources not identical with those in Josh. The passage agrees with Josh. in admitting that large areas of Palestine were not taken by Israel during this period, but it shows no acquaintance with the D idea that the Conquest was accomplished by a united army of Israel, stressing rather that the tribes settled individually in their respective areas. Because it offers this independent picture the passage has great value. It cannot, however, be uncritically accepted as necessarily the most accurate record of the Conquest in every detail, for some portions of it seem to be less primitive than the corresponding materials in Josh.

1:1-21. Conquests by Judah. The editor seems to assume that Israel is still camped at Gilgal in the Jordan Valley (cf. 2:1; Josh. 4:19; 10:43; 14:6; see color map 5) and that the territorial allotment has already been made (vss. 1-3; cf. Josh. 13-21); of these matters the earlier traditions probably knew nothing. He also assumes that there was a 2nd kind of allotment which determined the sequence in which the tribes would conquer their assigned regions. That Judah goes first shows the editor's presupposition that Judah was the preeminent tribe, as does the undue proportion of space given to the stories of Judah's conquests. The tendency of Hebrew storytellers to personify tribes as individual persons can be seen vividly in these stories connected with Judah.

1:5-7. This short account of the defeat of **Adoni-bezek** is reminiscent of the story of Adoni-zedek of Jerusalem in Josh. 10. Vs. 7 hints that Adoni-bezek may have been king of **Jerusalem** rather than of **Bezek**; indeed many interpreters have concluded that "Adoni-bezek of Bezek" was originally "Adoni-zedek of Jerusalem" and that the 2 stories stem from a single event. Cutting off the **thumbs** and **great toes** was apparently intended to render the king unfit as a military leader, and perhaps as a religious leader as well (cf. Lev. 21:16-23); more broadly it was an act of humiliation. Adoni-bezek's plaintive statement in vs. 7 indicates that such barbarity was not uncommon, and that it reduced conquered kings to a life no better than that of dogs who ate **scraps** dropped from the king's table (cf. Matt. 15:27). **Seventy** is a round number, used esp. often in connection with noblemen (cf. e.g. 8:30).

1:8-9. Vs. 8, which tells of Judah's conquest of Jerusalem, appears to be a later addition to the account, and cannot easily be reconciled with vs. 21; 19:10-12 (see comment on Josh. 15:63). The **Negeb** (vs. 9) is the arid region to the S of Palestine (see color map 5).

1:10-15. This account duplicates, with variations, Josh. 14:6-15; 15:13-19 (see comments). It is concerned in part to explain the ownership of important sources of water in arid S. Palestine.

1:16-18. On the **Kenite, Moses' father-in-law** see comments on Num. 10:29-32. **The city of palms,** though usually taken to be Jericho (cf. 3:13), was apparently a city in the S and may reflect a tradition that elements of Judah invaded Canaan from the S. Only one city, **Zephath** (vs. 17), is said to have been put under the sacred ban of total destruction (the meaning of **Hormah;** cf. Num. 21:3), in contrast to the numerous cities which the D editor of Josh. supposes were so destroyed. Vs. 18 is generally regarded as a late addition, inasmuch as the Philistine cities of **Gaza . . . Ashkelon . . . Ekron** remained outside Israelite control throughout this period, as the D editor knows (3:3; cf. Josh. 13:3). The LXX resolves this difficulty by reading "did not take" instead of **took.**

1:19-21. On vs. 19 see comment on Josh. 17:14-18. On vs. 20 see above on vss. 10-15. On vs. 21 see comment on Josh. 15:63.

1:22-36. Conquests by Other Tribes. The conquest of **Bethel** is by the **house of Joseph,** a term used in old traditions in Josh. 16:1-3; 17:14-18. Usually the 2 Joseph tribes are treated separately as Ephraim and Manasseh. It is not certain which of the forms is the earlier. With its reference to **spies** the story has a ring similar to that of the reconnaissance of Jericho in Josh. 2. The entrance into the city which the spies ask to have shown to them (vs. 24) may have been a secret water tunnel from the city to the spring (cf. II Sam. 5:8). Vs. 26 seems to allude to a fuller tradition which is now lost; where **Luz** was no one knows, but a S Syrian site is implied by the reference to the **land of the Hittites.** This story may be connected with the account of the capture of Ai (Josh. 7:1-8:29; see comment), esp. since it is possible that Bethel was originally called Ai.

1:27-36. This unit deals almost entirely with those peoples whom the Israelites did not conquer. It seems to differ in origin from vss. 22-26, since it treats **Manasseh** and **Ephraim** as separate tribes (vss. 27-29). The Transjordanian tribes of Reuben and Gad are not mentioned in the list, nor are Issachar, Benjamin, and Levi. As a tribe of priests, however, Levi was never thought to have a territory (but cf. Josh. 21). No battles are mentioned, a fact which implies a largely peaceful settlement in the areas named (see color map 5). Only Dan gets special notice (vss. 34-35) as unable to dominate a territory; the **Amorites** mentioned appear to be Canaanites. Eventually the Danites migrated to N Palestine (ch. 18). Vs. 36 concerns the region S of the Dead Sea and is not related to vss. 34-35. That the Canaanites were put to **forced labor** for Israel, as vss. 27-36 several times say, was probably not true until the time of David and Solomon.

2:1-5. Significance of the Incomplete Conquest. Borrowing an old tradition (vss. 1a, 5b) which told of the transfer of the Israelite sanctuary from **Gilgal** to Bethel—here called **Bochim**—the editor explains the meaning of the survey of the Conquest which he has given in ch. 1. Speaking through an angelic intermediary (cf. Josh. 5:13-15) Yahweh declares that because the Israelites have allowed the Canaanites to live peacefully among them rather than exterminating them (cf. Exod. 23:31-33) he will not give Israel complete possession of the Promised Land. The editor links the name Bochim ("weepers") with the weeping of Israel over its plight.

B. The D Intro. (2:6-3:6)

2:6-10. The Last Years and Death of Joshua. Derived from an old tradition which interpreters have often associated with E, this material appears to have been used by the D editor as a transition from the narrative in Josh. to the editorial preface to the stories of the judges. The content is almost identical with Josh. 24:28-31. If the D edition of Josh. ended with Josh. 23, this passage dealing with the death of Joshua served to link it to the D edition of Judg.

2:11-3:6. State of Affairs After Joshua's Death. Drawing on earlier materials, the D school offers 3 interpretations of Israel's vicissitudes following Joshua's death. These are now interwoven into a single text. That Israel was beset with threats to her peace is assumed throughout, but the explanation of what the affliction was, why it occurred, and how Israel responded differ.

a) The simplest explanation, probably taken from a very early source, suggests that Yahweh allowed Israel to be oppressed in order to teach the people the art of warfare (3:2).

b) A more elaborate view sees Israel as falling into the worship of Canaanite gods (2:13) and Yahweh as consequently giving Israel **over to plunderers** (2:14a). Since this produces no effect on the people, who refuse to respond to **judges** whom he raises up, Yahweh declares he will not **drive out** Israel's enemies from the land (2:20-21) but leave them to **test Israel** (2:22).

c) The most typically D view sees Israel turning to the **gods** of neighboring peoples (2:12) and Yahweh handing Israel over to these nations for punishment (2:14b-15), with the result that Israel repents and obeys for a time **judges** whom Yahweh sends to rescue them (2:18), falling back into apostasy only after each judge's death (2:19). This 3rd view recurs several times in Judg. (esp. 3:7-11, 12-14; 4:1-3; 10:6-16). As in Josh. the D editor's attack on apostasy reflects his interest in showing the lasting relevance of the events in Israel's history.

II. Israel's Deliverance by the Judges (3:7-16:31)

A. Othniel (3:7-11)

In contrast to the accounts which follow, the first story of a judge is cast in D form. The D editor's reason for introducing this story is not clear; some interpreters have suggested that he wished to show that the first judge was from Judah. If so, he was unable to find a strong figure, for Othniel was from the Caleb clan (cf. 1:13), a group only loosely associated with Judah. Behind the highly stylized D wording of the story may lie the memory of an actual judge, but of him the editor has preserved only his name and the name of his opponent, **Cushan-rishathaim king of Mesopotamia.** This king is an unknown figure, and there is little likelihood that any invasion of Palestine from Mesopotamia occurred at this time. Of the various solutions proposed for this difficulty the most plausible is that Cushan was a desert tribe from the SE (cf. Hab. 3:7) which foraged into S Palestine and was repulsed by the Caleb clan.

B. Ehud (3:12-30)

Vss. 12-13 are a D introduction to the story of Ehud. **The city of palms** (vs. 13) seems to be Jericho, the city W of the Jordan closest to **Moab** (see color map 5). Apparently the D editor believed that the city was taken by the Moabites and made a tribute-paying vassal, but there is no archaeological evidence that Jericho was inhabited at this time.

Presumably the original setting was some other city in the lower Jordan Valley, probably E of the river, where the Moabites had established headquarters. That **Ammonites** and **Amalekites** joined Moab in oppressing Israel is not suggested in the older tradition which follows. Vs. 14 is the work of the pre-D compiler of the stories of the judges (see comment on Josh. 24:32-33).

3:15-25. *The Assassination of Eglon.* This story has been drawn from 2 slightly differing accounts, but the tradition is essentially unitary. **Eglon the king of Moab** is exacting tribute from Israel—or, probably more accurately, from the tribes of Reuben and Gad in Transjordan and Benjamin just across the Jordan from them. Already established by the 13th cent., Moab had become a strong little nation which for the next several cents. was to live in tension with Israel, Israel sometimes becoming the oppressor of Moab very much as Moab is here shown as Israel's oppressor. Israel's **tribute** would consist largely of produce—e.g. oil, wine, hides, and wool—carried in by porters (vs. 18). **Ehud,** who is a **Benjaminite,** supervises the delivery of the tribute. Being **left-handed** (cf. 20:16; I Chr. 12:2) he is able to hide a **sword** under his robe by fastening it to his **right thigh,** where a weapon would be unexpected. **Cubit** here translates *gomed,* a word not found elsewhere. Since the sword was probably shorter than a cubit, which was originally the distance from elbow to fingertips, a gomed may have been from elbow to knuckles, i.e. *ca.* 13½ inches.

3:19-25. After ostensibly setting out for home and reaching the **sculptured stones near Gilgal** (cf. Josh. 4), Ehud returns on the pretext of having a divine message for Eglon—perhaps one allegedly received at the shrine at Gilgal—and slays the king with his concealed sword. The fatal audience takes place on the **roof** of the house, where there is a room with a veranda. As he flees Ehud pulls the latch string on the outside of the **doors of the roof chamber,** thus drawing shut a wooden bolt on the inside; in order to enter the king's **servants** have to use a **key** which pushes back the bolt (vs. 25).

3:26-30. *The Defeat of Moab.* Ehud hastens to gather an army **in the hill country of Ephraim.** This may be simply a geographical name for the central highlands (cf. 4:5) where he rallies his own Benjaminite tribesmen, or it may mean that he secures the help of the Ephraimites adjoining them on the N. Under Ehud's leadership they blockade the Jordan to cut off any retreat of the Moabite forces occupying Benjaminite territory and proceed to kill them all. The pre-D compiler's addition in vs. 30 assumes that this victory freed all Israel from Moabite domination. There is no evidence that Ehud's leadership continued after the battle.

C. Shamgar (3:31)

This allusion is tantalizingly brief. Like Ehud, **Shamgar** is remembered for his unusual method of exterminating Israel's enemies. Their identification as **Philistines** seems to give the episode a setting relatively late in the period of the judges, when this people had become a major threat to Israel. This element may account for the fact that the LXX places this vs. at the end of the Samson stories in 16:31. It will be noted that Samson also battles Philistines, and slays them with a similarly improvised weapon (15:15-17); on the lack of proper weapons among the Israelites at this time cf. 5:8*b;* I Sam. 13:22. On the other hand, since 5:6 places Shamgar before Deborah the name **Philistines** may be a later addition or alteration.

If Shamgar was indeed a hero of Israel, a fuller story of his dramatic deed probably once existed. Some interpreters, however, have doubted that Shamgar was an Israelite, in part because his name does not seem to be Semitic; indeed it has been suggested that he was one of Israel's oppressors or a Canaanite warrior hero (cf. 5:6). The name of his father, **Anath,** is unusual in that it is the name of a Canaanite goddess mentioned often in the Ugaritic texts from Ras Shamra in N Syria. Possibly the name was originally Shamgar of Beth-anath (cf. 1:33; Josh. 19:38).

All in all, the passage seems rather contrived. Its lateness is indicated by the fact that the customary statement of the pre-D editor about the length of the judge's reign is lacking. The vs. came into its present position after the major editions of Judg. were completed; 4:1 shows no knowledge of it but builds directly on 3:30. No doubt it was placed just before the story of Deborah because of the reference to Shamgar in 5:6.

D. Deborah and Barak (4:1–5:31)

4:1-24. *The Prose Account.* Vss. 1-3 constitute a D transition of the familiar sort (cf. e.g. 3:12-14). The account in this ch. appears to be a composite of 2 originally separate stories. One account may have dealt with Jabin, king of Hazor in the far N of Palestine, and involved Heber the Kenite, the city of Kedesh, and the tribes of Zebulun and Naphtali. The other perhaps concerned Sisera, king of Harosheth-ha-goiim in the valley of the Kishon, and involved Deborah, Barak, Jael, Mt. Tabor, and Issachar. The Jabin tradition, the less prominent of the 2, appears to be related to the account of Jabin of Hazor in Josh. 11:1-15; Jabin was apparently so noted a foe that his name became legendary in Israel. In the process of conflation Jabin has become **king of Canaan** (vs. 2) and Sisera has become his general.

In addition to this combination of traditions the story has also undergone expansion, esp. in the role of Deborah, who was probably represented in the earliest tradition only as a prophetess whose favorable oracles aroused Barak to go into battle (cf. the role of Samuel). Deborah's tribal connections are obscure; vs. 5 associates her with the **palm of Deborah,** located in the territory of either **Ephraim** or Benjamin (see above on 3:26-30 and color map 5) —possibly by confusing her with Rebekah's nurse Deborah, who was buried under an oak near **Bethel** (Gen. 35:8)—but 5:15 suggests that she was of the tribe of Issachar.

4:6-16. Because of the combination of the 2 stories the details of the battle are not entirely clear. It seems that the Sisera tradition told of an encounter in the valley of the Kishon, not far from Sisera's city of Harosheth-ha-goiim. Since this region was still in Canaanite hands, it appears that Sisera was defending his territory from an Israelite attack. Barak, hav-

Courtesy of Herbert G. May

Mount Tabor rising above the Plain of Jezreel, lying *ca.* six miles E-SE of Nazareth and twelve miles W-SW of the S end of the Sea of Galilee

ing gathered his army on **Mount Tabor**—perhaps, it has been suggested, for prebattle religious rites—marches into the valley, where he is at a disadvantage since Sisera's **chariots** (see comment on Josh. 17:14-18) operate most effectively on the plain. The description of the battle (vs. 15) is almost entirely devoid of detail but implies that Barak's soldiers win their victory by combat. The enemy flee, as one would expect, to Harosheth-ha-goiim. The statement that Sisera **fled away on foot** may be a conventional way of indicating the king's utter defeat, for it occurs in other ancient Near Eastern texts. It will be noted that the Israelites do not attack the city itself.

4:17-22. The framework of the account of Sisera's flight **to the tent of . . . the wife of Heber the Kenite** and his subsequent assassination may come from the Jabin tradition, since it is set near Kedesh (vs. 11), some 40 miles NE of the site of the battle. If so, this part of the tradition may originally have belonged at the end of the Jabin story in Josh., which presently has only a D conclusion (Josh. 11:9-15). The details of Jael's slaughter (see below on 5:24-27) are presumably taken from the Sisera tradition, but the material has been so interwoven with the Jabin tradition that the 2 stories cannot be entirely disentangled.

5:1-31. *The Song of Deborah.* This is the only deliverance story in Judg. which is told in poetry. The poem in form and diction is archaic and possibly was so intended even at the time of its composition in the 11th—some say 12th—cent. It is certainly one of the most magnificent works of art in the OT. Its text, however, is replete with obscurities, partly because of its archaic vocabulary and partly because of alterations which seem to have crept in as it was transmitted.

Though virtually all interpreters regard the poem as a spontaneous, natural outburst by an eyewitness of the battle, it is actually highly stylized and contains almost no specific information. Features of both the Jabin and the Sisera traditions (see above on 4:1-24) can be seen in it; they appear in a manner which suggests that the coalition took place before the composition of the poem, which thus may date from 2 or 3 generations after the battle. It was probably composed by professional musicians in the

service of one of the major Israelite sanctuaries in N Palestine. Their craft had been evolving for centuries—perhaps originally under the influence of Egyptian musicians in the courts of Canaanite kings.

The song is built around a complex standard pattern consisting of the interwoven theological motifs of the glory of Yahweh, the Sinai experience, the conquest of Canaan, and the worship of Yahweh. This pattern is seen most clearly in Ps. 68, a ps. adapted for the Jerusalem sanctuary from older traditions of premonarchic times. If one may judge from other passages, the reputation of a poet was based on his brilliance in expanding this pattern with historical or pseudohistorical details. One can see this clearly in Exod. 15:1-18, where the theme is that of the Exodus. In contrast the Song of Deborah has been historicized with imaginary details pertaining to a battle of Israel with the kings of Canaan, a subject which continually slips into the more general interest in the conquest of Canaan as a whole. In his historicizing of this pattern the poet has not bothered to arrange all of his events in a fully natural sequence, much to the confusion of generations of scholars.

5:1-3. The prose ascription to **Deborah and Barak** in vs. 1 is not original to the poem, as shown by the allusions to these heroes in the 2nd and 3rd persons (vss. 7, 12, 15). Vs. 2c indicates the hymnic nature of the poem at the outset (cf. Ps. 68:26a, 35d). Vs. 3 is a solemn rhetorical address to the rulers of the world (not Israel's nobility; cf. e.g. Ps. 2:2; Prov. 8:15; Hab. 1:10), who are warned to learn from the song that they should not interfere with Israel lest they suffer the same fate as the opponents described in vss. 19-21. Ancient Near Eastern rulers sometimes used similar expressions in the opening lines of monumental inscriptions which they set up for passers-by to see. Vs. 3b-d is reminiscent of Ps. 68:4ab (cf. Exod. 15:2).

5:4-5. These vss. are a solemn hymn of praise similar to Ps. 68:7-8. The allusion is not only to God as a storm deity but to the army of God (Israel) as well, which appears like a myriad of raindrops (cf. Deut. 33:2). The poet has partially historicized this theological affirmation about God by suggesting the march of Israel through the wilderness before the settlement in Palestine. **Yon Sinai** in vs. 5b should read "the One of Sinai" and be placed with the first half of the couplet.

5:6-11. Vss. 6-9b are esp. difficult to interpret because the text seems to have suffered alteration. The poet attempts to introduce a historical prologue to the coming battle, but he deals chiefly in generalities; the names which he introduces only confuse the passage. On **Shamgar** as a judge see above on 3:31. In vs. 9c a hymnic tenor reappears, which continues in vss. 10-11c, where the riders, marchers, and musicians seem to be in a great procession (cf. Ps. 68:24-25), celebrating not so much a particular battle as the conquest of Palestine in general. The RSV translation of vs. 11 makes the best of an obscure passage, but the allusion actually seems to be to the antiphonal singing of **musicians** which rings out loudly and clearly in the procession, not at the **watering places** themselves. Vs. 11d anticipates vs. 13.

5:12. This vs., which seems to be out of sequence if the song is taken as a historical reminiscence, appears to be a historicizing of the motif "Let God arise, let his enemies be scattered," which finds expression in Ps. 68:1 (cf. Ps. 68:18); this motif also implies the exodus tradition (cf. Num. 10:35).

5:13-18. These vss. are reminiscent of Ps. 68:24-27, where the setting is that of a cult procession in which representatives of the tribes of Israel march in fixed order with **Benjamin** in the lead (cf. Exod. 15:16*cd*). Allusions to the coming battle are almost entirely lacking; in historicizing the description the poet seems to have in mind, not any particular battle, but the conquest of Palestine as a whole. It will be noted that the tribes—those of Transjordan and the far N of Palestine—which are reproached for not participating are ones which, by and large, had a minor role in the conquest traditions. In its enumeration of those tribes to be praised and those to be castigated, the list is almost identical with the list of tribes for blessing and cursing given in Deut. 27:12-13 (omitting the S tribes, which do not figure in the Song of Deborah, and taking vs. 18 of the song as an addition). **Machir** in vs. 14 is the tribe of Manasseh. **Deborah** and **Barak** are awkwardly brought into vs. 15*ab*, but the reference may preserve a genuine tradition that these heroes were from the tribe of **Issachar**; cf. 4:6, 10, which show only Naphtali and Zebulun going to battle. Vs. 16*a* has an interesting parallel in Ps. 68:12*b*-13*a*. Vs. 18 may have been introduced under the influence of 4:6, 10.

5:19-22. These vss. are a historicizing of the motif which appears in Ps. 68:11-14 (cf. Exod. 15:1, 4-10). The poet has little information to draw on—perhaps none at all except the knowledge of the general locale of the battle. He is probably thinking in part of the whole conquest of Palestine, as the reference to the enemy as **the kings of Canaan** (vs. 19*b*) suggests. The region between **Taanach** and **Megiddo** (see

Courtesy of Herbert G. May

Horned incense altar made of limestone found at Megiddo

color map 5) had probably been celebrated as the scene of a great battle ever since Thutmose III of Egypt won a notable victory there cents. earlier. The allusion to **spoils** (vs. 19*c*) was a standard element in such songs (cf. Ps. 68:12*b*-13; Exod. 15:9).

The description of the **stars** fighting **against Sisera**

(vs. 20) cannot be regarded as anything other than a poetic generalization intended to indicate the hopelessness of the enemy's cause (cf. Josh. 10:12). The reference to the **torrent Kishon** as sweeping away the enemy (vs. 21), which interpreters almost always take to be an allusion to a sudden flooding of the river near Megiddo, should probably be understood as a figurative statement based on the theological motif of the destruction of Israel's enemies by God, a concept found most prominently in the traditions of the Exodus (cf. esp. Exod. 15:1-18; Hab. 3:7-15). It is related to the theme of God's coming with a flood of water (vs. 4). The prose account of the battle (4:15-16) knows of no such miraculous occurrence. Vss. 21*c*, 22 are obscure both in content and in their position in the narrative.

5:23. The cursing of **Meroz** is an unexpectedly specific allusion, the original significance of which is unfortunately unknown. The motif seems to be related to the enumeration of the tribes in vss. 13-18. Cf. the curses implied against certain tribes in Deut. 27:13.

5:24-27. Here the poet is exercising his—or her—skill to the fullest. The inspiration for this hypnotically repetitive stanza—some parts of which seem to have undergone expansion—is probably that which finds expression in Ps. 68:21: "God will shatter the heads of his enemies, the hairy crown of him who walks in his guilty ways" (cf. also Exod. 15:6*b*). The poet contributes essentially no information that is not in the prose account; his contribution is in the dramatic telling of the episode.

5:26-27. Jael improvises a murder weapon from bedouin equipment. Vs. 26 seems to say that she grasped a **tent peg** in her left **hand** and a **mallet** for driving the tent peg in her **right** and so **pierced his temple**—as indeed the prose account describes (4:21) except that here Sisera is apparently standing (cf. vs. 27) rather than lying asleep. On the other hand the word translated "mallet" is less precise than the English suggests, and the word translated "tent peg" might possibly be an editorial harmonization with 4:21. In poetic parallelism the 2 words could well be intended as synonyms for only one weapon, just as **pierced** is evidently a synonymous parallel to **crushed**—probably **shattered** is a gloss to explain the archaic word translated "crushed." On this basis the meaning seems to be that Jael used a single object as a club to strike the death blow. Most scholars have assumed this latter meaning, but it is possible that both the poet and the author of 4:21 were trying to interpret a tradition that Jael killed Sisera by driving a tent peg into his head.

5:28-30. The scene of women awaiting spoil is likewise a historicization of a familiar motif, one which appears in Ps. 68:12b-13; Exod. 15:9 (cf. II Sam. 1:24). A simpler statement of the same theme has already appeared in vs. 19c. The artificiality of the scene is evident, not only in the fact that no Hebrew would have been present to witness the scene but also in the mother's expectation of maidens and splendid garments—appropriate if Sisera had been besieging a city but less to be anticipated amid the Israelite army.

5:31. This vs., taken by some scholars as a late addition, may be as old as the rest of the song (cf. Ps. 68:2-3, 35c; Deut. 33:29).

E. GIDEON (6:1–8:35)

The story of **Gideon** is based on 2 or more old traditions, at least one of which seems to have concerned a warrior named **Jerubbaal** (6:32; 7:1; 8:29, 35; ch. 9), who was later identified with Gideon. The hand of the D editor can be seen only in 6:1 and perhaps in 8:33-35. Israel's new enemy is the **Midianites,** a nomadic or seminomadic people from the desert region SE of Palestine who do not appear elsewhere in Judg.

6:1-10. *Midian's Oppression of Israel.* Vss. 2-5 describe the Midianites' encroachments into the hill country of Palestine. The comparison of the invaders' army to **locusts** (vs. 5; cf. 7:12) is an ancient one which can be found in the Canaanite Keret text. 8:18-19 suggests some kind of feud between Gideon and the leaders of Midian, but of that nothing is said here. The **Amalekites and the people of the East** (cf. Gen. 29:1) seem to be Transjordanians. Vss. 8-10, apparently an addition to the story, contain the only reference to a **prophet** in Josh. and Judg., though this fact does not necessarily mean that prophets were unknown in the period of the judges. The prophet's speech, which is a polished summary of God's salvation of Israel in the Exodus and Conquest, holds out no hope for the wayward Israelites.

6:11-24. *The Call of Gideon.* Gideon, of the tribe of Manasseh, is—like other early Israelites—a farmer by occupation and a soldier on occasion. Unable to thresh **wheat** openly, lest the dust cloud draw a raid from the Midianites, Gideon has resorted to beating out his grain by hand in the narrow confines of the rock-cut **wine press** in the floor of his father's house. The divine call of Gideon, which has similarities to the story of Samson's birth (ch. 13), seems to have been handed down in 2 traditions, one in vss. 11-24 and another in vss. 25-32. As Moses (Exod. 3:1–4:17), prophets (e.g. Isa. 6:5), and newly chosen kings (e.g. Saul, I Sam. 9:21) often do, Gideon protests his inadequacy when the **angel** of Yahweh summons him to lead Israel. The authenticity of the divine revelation is attested by a **sign** (vss. 17-23) not unlike that given to Moses (Exod. 3:2-5; cf. I Sam. 10:1-9). Mingled with the motif of divine sign is that of hospitality which one offers to a guest (vs. 19; cf. Gen. 18:1-8) and that of a ceremonial offering (vss. 18, 20-24). The idea that seeing Yahweh was fatal appears several times in the OT (e.g. Exod. 19:21; 33:18-23).

6:25-32. *Gideon's Attack on the Baal Cult.* This story shows Gideon acting much as a fiery prophet, but not yet as a military leader. The scene may be regarded as a variant tradition of the divine call of Gideon, an event marked by an act which throws Gideon into the forefront as a leader. The story presupposes that Gideon's family worships the Canaanite god **Baal** (perhaps identified with Yahweh, the Israelite god?), for whom there was a household **altar** and an **Asherah** (a sacred wooden pole of some sort). Like the first account of Gideon's call, this episode shows Gideon erecting an **altar** to Yahweh (vs. 26; cf. vs. 24). The use of a **bull,** the symbol of Baal, to destroy Baal's altar would strike the ancient hearer of the story as humorous and ironical. The point of the story, at least as the compiler uses it, may be the idea that Gideon cannot hope to deliver Israel from its enemies unless the worship of foreign gods is purged from his clan. The story also serves to explain the reason Gideon was also known by the name **Jerubbaal** (vs. 32); the name actually means "Baal contends," or perhaps "establishment of Baal," and is clearly Canaanite in origin. The passage appears to be a harmonistic one which arose—or at least was preserved—to explain the reason that Gideon had 2 names.

6:33–7:18. *Gideon's Preparations for Battle.* Manasseh's enemies approach and camp in the Valley of **Jezreel,** which slopes E toward the Jordan Valley (see color map 5). Gideon becomes divinely inspired (vs. 34; cf. e.g. 11:29). The reference to participation by the tribes of **Asher, Zebulun, and Naphtali** (vs. 35) may not be original to the text. Gideon performs 4 acts of preparation for battle: he obtains an oracle, he selects his men, he scouts the enemy's camp, and he arms his men for the battle.

6:36-40. Gideon seeks to know if he has divine approval for the coming battle. Oracles before battles were commonplace (cf. 4:6-7; Josh. 6:2-5; 7:10-15; 8:1-2). The use of **fleece** to obtain such prebattle oracles may have been an accepted practice. The first oracle is inconclusive, since fleece might well collect **dew** even if the **ground** appeared **dry.** The 2nd oracle, in which the fleece is dry while the ground is wet, is regarded as conclusive proof that the outcome of the battle will be favorable to Gideon. There is no need to suppose that the story intends to describe a new call of Gideon.

7:1-8. Vs. 1 uses the name **Jerubbaal** in a way which suggests that the story of the battle with Midian may have originally been told about that hero rather than Gideon. The 2nd stage of preparation appears in vss. 2-8, where Gideon selects a small band of men to participate in a daring ruse. The principle of selection has long puzzled readers, in good part because the text of vss. 5-6 has probably been expanded by an editor. The basic idea seems to be that Gideon chooses those who lap water like dogs, i.e. those who are so reckless that they do not bother to keep a watchful eye as they drink. Possibly there is also an undertone of sympathetic magic here, the lapping of water like dogs being symbolic of the men's lapping of the blood of their enemies as dogs would do (cf. Ps. 68:23). This stress on daring and viciousness well accords with the act which the soldiers will be asked to perform. Vs. 8 seems to want to explain how the **three hundred men** got enough **jars** and **trumpets** to make possible the stratagem, viz. by collecting those items from among the larger group of 32,000 men of the original fighting force.

7:9-14. The account of a **dream** which Gideon overhears during his reconnaissance is the sort of story which a commander would gladly be able to report to his troops in order to stir them into zeal for the imminent battle. This daring foray into the Midianite camp reminds one of stories told of heroes such as Jonathan (I Sam. 14:1-15) and David (I Sam. 26:6-12).

7:15-18. Gideon rouses his men and gives them their unusual implements of **trumpets** and **torches** in **jars.**

7:19-23. *The Battle.* Creeping up to the Midianites' tents an hour or 2 before midnight, Gideon's soldiers, on signal, create panic among the sleeping soldiers by blowing their rams' horns, breaking their jars, exposing their lighted torches, shouting, and charging about with drawn swords. Readers are likely to wonder how a soldier could possibly perform all these actions at once. The easiest solution is to suppose that 2 traditions of the attack have been interwoven, one of which spoke of horns and swords, the other of which knew only of jars, torches, and shouts. Since Gideon's band was so small, the main purpose of the attack can hardly have been the killing of the enemy. Presumably the original tradition understood that Gideon wished to chase the frightened enemy into the hands of a larger body of waiting troops; vss. 23-25 indeed suggest this, though the account is confused by the implied delay required for the new call to Naphtali, Asher, and Manasseh (cf. 6:35).

7:24-8:3. *Ephraim's Complaint.* In this section, apparently from a separate tradition, it is the **men of Ephraim** who intercept the Midianites. Ephraim's irritation at having entered the scene belatedly presupposes a covenant relationship between Ephraim and Manasseh in which unilateral military action was prohibited. The anger should therefore not be attributed simply to quarrelsomeness. Gideon's soothing words are a typical example of oriental diplomacy in which one flatters the offended person and deprecates oneself. The Midianite leaders **Oreb and Zeeb** appear only in 7:25; 8:3; subsequently other names are given.

8:4-21. *Gideon's Punishment of Offenders.* This passage comes from a different tradition from 7:24-8:3, with the result that Gideon seems to cross the **Jordan** a 2nd time. It shows no knowledge of Ephraim's participation or of any troops other than

Gideon's original **three hundred men.** Here the Midianite leaders, implausibly called **kings,** are **Zebah and Zalmunna.**

8:5-12. Pursuing the fleeing men, Gideon passes **Succoth** and **Penuel** on the E side of the Jordan, where the elders of the cities refuse to supply provisions for Gideon's hungry men. Gideon continues his pursuit and successfully attacks the Midianite survivors and takes their leaders captive.

8:13-17. Returning to Succoth, Gideon plans punishment of the unfriendly cities, which he accomplishes with the aid of a learned **young man of Succoth,** who writes down the names of the city's leaders so that Gideon can later punish them. That the art of writing was widely known is unlikely, if one may judge from the lack of inscriptional materials from this period in Palestine; but it need not be doubted that writing was used for commercial, governmental, and cultic records. Capturing Succoth, Gideon tortures its **elders** and ravages the city.

8:18-21. Gideon executes the captured Midianite leaders, first asking his son to perform the act — as an honor to the son and a dishonor to the kings — then doing the deed himself when his son hesitates. According to this tradition Gideon's warfare has been undertaken in order that he might have vengeance on the Midianites for a specific act of aggression which they had perpetrated on his family (vss. 18-19). Reference to blood vengeance of this kind can be found in Canaanite texts many cents. earlier. The **crescents** which Gideon takes from the slain kings' **camels** perhaps were amulets (cf. vs. 26).

8:22-23. *Gideon's Rejection of Kingship.* These vss. appear to be an editorial addition in preparation for the story of Abimelech in ch. 9. They tell briefly of the men of Israel's wish to make Gideon **king** over them, and of Gideon's refusal on the ground that Yahweh should rule. A similarly negative view of kingship is found in the "Samuel source" in I Sam. 8; 12.

8:24-28. *Gideon's Ephod.* Gideon collects a share of the jewelry of the defeated Midianites, who are here called **Ishmaelites.** As nomadic people the Midianites would carry a good deal of their wealth around with them. The booty hardly amounts to a 20th of that which Thutmose III took at the rich city of Megiddo several cents. earlier. On **shekels** see "Measures and Money," pp. 1283-85. The **ephod** was a cult object used in obtaining oracles (see comment on Exod. 28:15-30). The original story probably saw nothing wrong with Gideon's ephod, but the author of vs. 27*b*, speaking from a later time, deplores the act. Like the Canaanite name Jerubbaal, the making of the ephod shows how different early Hebrew religion was from that of later times.

8:29-35. *Gideon's Later Life.* Gideon, or **Jerubbaal,** gives up his leadership of the army, which is presumed to be disbanded, and settles down at home. The number of sons attributed to him, **seventy,** is a round number esp. popular in stories dealing with kings and nobles and may allude to Gideon's family as a whole (cf. 1:7; 12:14; Exod. 1:5; Num. 11:16; II Kings 10:1). **Abimelech** is mentioned separately (vs. 31), perhaps in anticipation of the story in ch. 9. Vss. 33-35 are an editorial transition to ch. 9, or perhaps are the D editor's substitute for that ch. The reference to **Baal-berith** in vs. 33 is derived from the story which follows (9:4; cf. 9:46; see Intro.).

F. ABIMELECH (9:1-57)

These episodes illuminate more clearly than perhaps any others in Judg. the kind of activity in which some Israelite leaders were engaging during this period. **Abimelech** was an ambitious Israelite who apparently gained control of the countryside near the Canaanite city of **Shechem** (see color map 5), maintaining his headquarters in the insignificant town of **Arumah** (vs. 41) and occasionally venturing out to conquer some vulnerable city in the region, e.g. **Thebez** (vss. 50-55). His most audacious plan was to take over Shechem itself, which for cents. had been ruled by the dynasty of **Hamor** (vs. 28; cf. Gen. 34; Josh. 24:32). This was not the first time Shechem had encountered Hebrews, for as early as the 14th cent. the Habiru had been stirring up trouble in the vicinity, apparently less by battle than by persuasion and treachery.

Like other Canaanite cities Shechem had lost much of its former vigor. The ruling house was so effete that Abimelech was apparently able to threaten, drive away, and kill its males to the point that none of them dared to occupy the throne. In his project he was aided by the report, true or false, that his mother was a Shechemite. Proclaimed king by the elders of the city, Abimelech maintained his authority in spite of a rebellion by conservative elements which occurred a few years after he gained control. Though triumphant over Shechem, Abimelech finally met his end in an ignominious yet brave way at Thebez as he sought to quell a revolt there. Not without justification one interpreter has called Abimelech an early-day Macbeth.

Such, in brief, is the course of Abimelech's career as it can be reconstructed from the stories in this ch. The stories themselves contain a number of obscurities, due in part to the storyteller's confusion about certain details and in part to the fact that at least 2 different traditions have been interwoven. Editors did not find Abimelech particularly commendable. The pre-D compiler regarded him as a wicked man (vss. 1-5, 24, 56). The D editor may have omitted the account from his edition of Judg., and the postexilic editor who reintroduced the story may have seen it as an example of the evils of kingship (cf. 8:22-23). The original story itself contained no suggestion that kingship, at least at Shechem, was evil or that Abimelech himself was acting wrongly.

9:1-21. *The Investiture of Abimelech at Shechem.* The pre-D compiler has compressed the opening of the story to the point that the details of Abimelech's rise to power at Shechem can no longer be fully understood. **Jerubbaal,** Abimelech's father, was an Israelite (cf. chs. 6-8), but the role which Jerubbaal and his **seventy . . . sons** (see above on 8:29-35) play in vss. 1-5 seems more appropriate as a description of what happened to the ruling dynasty of the sons of Hamor at Shechem. On **Baal-berith** (vs. 4) cf. 8:33; 9:46; see Intro. In any case, having been declared **king** by the **citizens of Shechem,** Abimelech goes to the sacred precinct in the city and is there invested with his new office (vs. 6).

9:7-21. The fable which **Jotham** tells, though presented by the storyteller as a speech of the surviving son of Jerubbaal on hearing of the murder of his brothers, is not unfavorable to Abimelech, but simply warns the Shechemites of their own duty to support Abimelech. It should therefore probably be regarded as a speech originally thought to have been delivered by some prophet or priest at the ceremony of investiture. The fable accurately describes the situation in which Shechem finds itself: its ruling house (called **cedars of Lebanon,** vs. 15; cf. II Kings 14:9) cannot provide a man willing to rule—perhaps, one may suspect, because Abimelech has brought pressure to bear on them—and a candidate of nonaristocratic birth (the **bramble**) is willing to be king. The point of the fable is that all will go well if the people serve Abimelech faithfully, but that otherwise destruction will come upon them. The similarity of this idea to that in Samuel's speech at the investiture of Saul (I Sam. 12) is noteworthy. Vss. 17-18 were not a part of the original story.

9:22-49. *The Revolt Against Abimelech.* Two traditions can be seen here. In the first of these, vss. 22-25, 42-45, one sees how **the men of Shechem** do indeed act treacherously toward Abimelech, without any apparent provocation on his part. **Israel** (vs. 22) should probably read "Shechem." The outcome of the brigandry of the Shechemites (vss. 42-45) is that Abimelech ambushes the insurgents, slays them, and razes the city. Abimelech's sowing of the city with salt is a graphic declaration that the city should remain uninhabited. Archaeological evidence has thus far not supported this story, for there was no destruction of Shechem (modern Tell Balatah, not Nablus, as scholars used to think) during this period.

In the 2nd account of the revolt, vss. 26-41, 46-49, there is a great deal more specific detail. The rebellion is instigated by one **Gaal,** whose appeal to the memory of the old ruling dynasty of **Hamor** (vs. 28) suggests that he may have been one of that dynasty who had initially fled from Abimelech. As in the alternate tradition, Abimelech battles the insurgents outside Shechem and wins the battle. Vs. 41 is an intrusive editorial comment. The conclusion to the story seems to be found in vss. 46-49, which tells of Abimelech's destruction of a large number of persons who had fled to the sanctuary of the city for refuge (on **El-berith** cf. 8:33; 9:4; see Intro.). Of the fate of the city as a whole the story says nothing. In every way this tradition seems to be the more historical of the 2.

9:50-57. *Abimelech's Death at the Siege of Thebez.* To conclude the story of Abimelech the storyteller tells of his attack on the city of Thebez. Like many another person in Judg., Abimelech meets his end in an unusual way. Struck by a **millstone** which a **woman** throws, Abimelech asks his **armor-bearer** to dispatch him lest he die disgracefully at the hands of a woman (cf. I Sam. 31:4; II Sam. 1:9). Vss. 55-57 are the work of one or more editors, who mistakenly suppose that Abimelech was supported by an army of men from all Israel (vs. 55).

G. TOLA (10:1-2)

This is the first of 2 brief notices about otherwise unknown judges. Nothing is recorded about **Tola** except his ancestry, home, and length of judgeship. The family connections seem rather contrived. Gen. 46:13 (cf. I Chr. 7:1-2) names Tola and Puvah as sons of **Issachar,** and Num. 26:23 lists these persons as heads of clans.

H. JAIR (10:3-5)

Jair is a family name (cf. Num. 32:41; Deut. 3:14; I Kings 4:13) which appears here to have been individualized. The allusion to Jair's **thirty sons**—who should perhaps be understood to mean noblemen, not lit. sons—with their **thirty asses** and **thirty cities** is stylized and is probably derived from an earlier tradition which spoke only of 30 cities. The implication is that Jair was overlord of a number of cities (or villages), each of which—somewhat like Shechem under Abimelech (ch. 9)—maintained its own government. Several OT passages (e.g. Josh. 13:30; I Chr. 2:22) allude to the "cities of Jair," the number of which varies from 23 to 60.

J. JEPHTHAH (10:6-12:7)

10:6-18. *An Editor's Transition.* This unusually long editorial statement anticipates the story of Jephthah. Like 2:11-23, which it resembles, the passage is largely D though the editors utilize pre-D materials. Israel's enemies are now the Ammonites, dealt with in the following story, and the Philistines, appearing in the stories of Samson, which begin in ch. 13. That the list of peoples from whom Yahweh has delivered Israel (vss. 11-12) does not correspond to the enumeration of Israel's enemies in the stories of the judges indicates that this passage is not a summary of the contents of Judg. The **Maonites** were probably an Arab tribe living E of Edom (cf. "Meunites," II Chr. 20:1; 26:7). As usual the editor presupposes that all Israel is involved in the oppression and deliverance rather than individual tribes.

10:17-18. This is a specific transition to the story of Jephthah; it seems to come from a different source from the rest of the passage (cf. vs. 9). **Mizpah** is not the Benjaminite city but a cult center of uncertain location in N Gilead (cf. 11:11, 29; Gen. 31:49).

11:1-11. *Jephthah's Rise to Leadership.* Jephthah has dubious genealogical credentials, his father having been an unknown Gileadite whom the storyteller calls simply Gilead and his mother a prostitute (vs. 1). Rejected by his fellow tribesmen (vs. 7; cf. vs. 2) Jephthah turns to brigandry in the border region around **Tob** (vs. 3; see color map 5). He earns such a reputation as a leader that the **elders of Gilead** call on him as their deliverer when the **Ammonites** commence war against them.

11:9-11. Vs. 11 alludes to an investiture of Jephthah in the sanctuary at **Mizpah** (see above on 10:17-18). The ceremony probably involves a covenant between Jephthah and the Gileadites, as vss. 9-10 imply, in which each party agrees to certain conditions. The final words of the elders (vs. 10) are similar to those used in the pledge between Jacob and Laban when they covenant at this same shrine (Gen. 31:49); it was customary to call on the deity to witness covenants and to punish any violators of the agreement.

11:12-28. *Jephthah's Futile Diplomatic Overtures.*

This section consists largely of a message which Jephthah, acting as king in all but name, delivers to the Ammonites as a defense of Israel's occupation of certain disputed lands in Transjordan. It is clearly intrusive, for it speaks of all Israel rather than Gilead alone and of **Moab** more than Ammon; Jephthah's mild tone also contrasts with that in vss. 29-33.

11:15-22. This historical summary is basically in agreement with Num. 20-24 and shows how effectively Israelite archives could be utilized in international diplomacy. The message argues that the territory in dispute does not belong to either Ammon or Moab but is part of the former kingdom of **Sihon,** which the Israelites conquered under Moses. In style and content the passage seems to reflect conditions around 850, when King Mesha of Moab (see Intro. to Josh.) began to try to regain this territory, which had belonged to Moab before Sihon took it (Num. 21:26) and had been recaptured by the Moabites a time or two thereafter (e.g. under Eglon, 3:12-30), but which had been occupied by Israel at least since the time of David (cf. II Sam. 8:2). It is possible that we have here a transcript of a letter sent to Mesha by King Jehoram of Israel (cf. II Kings 3:4-7).

11:23-28. The Moabite god **Chemosh** (vs. 24) is referred to as if he actually existed, and many interpreters have assumed that this usage represents Israelite thought of the time. However, if this passage is indeed a transcript of a letter sent to the king of Moab it would necessarily be phrased in diplomatic language calculated to put the Israelite and Moabite gods on an equal plane. Ostensibly **three hundred years** (vs. 26) refers to the time between the conquest of the kingdom of Sihon and Jephthah's message, but the figure is too high to be historically accurate. It would be approximately correct as the time from Sihon to Mesha's day. The unusual reference to Yahweh as a **Judge** (vs. 27) is an ancient expression which appears in Canaanite religious texts in connection with Baal.

11:29-40. *Jephthah's Sacrifice of His Daughter.* After the interlude of vss. 12-28 the narrative commences approximately where it was interrupted. Becoming divinely aroused for battle, Jephthah is willing to perform the most extreme of all prebattle rites—offering human sacrifice (see comment on Josh. 7). But Jephthah is also a shrewd man who does not wish to make his sacrifice in vain; so he cleverly promises Yahweh a human offering only if he wins the battle. As yet a further safeguard Jephthah does not choose his victim in advance but agrees to sacrifice the first person who comes to meet him as he arrives home in triumph. But Jephthah cannot cheat Yahweh, who, having granted him victory, arranges—one must suppose—that Jephthah is met by his virgin **daughter.** The storyteller heightens the pathos by presenting the girl as an **only child.** The whole episode, from Jephthah's attempt to cheat Yahweh to his final sad fulfilling of his vow, moves like a Greek tragedy; indeed it has its parallel in the story of Agamemnon's sacrifice of his daughter Iphigenia.

That the story presupposes a primitive concept of what God demands of man is evident, and one should not try to soften its harshness by emphasizing the fidelity with which Jephthah and his daughter carry out the grisly deed. One may legitimately point out, however, that the story is less a historical recollection than a moral tale teaching the futility of a man's scheming against God. It also seems to have served as a pseudohistorical explanation (vss. 37-40) for the existence of religious rites performed at some stage in Israel's history in which virgins went about ceremonially mourning—probably over the death of growing things which occurred each winter, here symbolized by the descent of a virgin to the realm of the dead (cf. the Greek myth of Persephone). Traces of a cult of this sort, sometimes involving a male who dies, can be found throughout the ancient Near Eastern and Mediterranean world. Lacking in the story, of necessity, is any allusion to the revivification of the slain person such as is presupposed in the ancient fertility myths (cf. Ps. 126:5-6).

12:1-7. War Between Gilead and Ephraim. This episode begins like 8:1-3, but because Jephthah makes no diplomatic overtures the outcome is war between Gilead and Ephraim, in which Gilead is victor. Vs. 4 is obscure but seems to allude to a covenant between the 2 tribes in which Gilead was the lesser party, forbidden to take unilateral military action (vss. 1-3; cf. 8:1-3; see comment on Josh. 9:6-27). The Gileadites identify fleeing Ephraimites (vss. 5-6) by their inability to pronounce "sh." Vs. 7, which tells of Jephthah's death, is the compiler's conclusion to the Jephthah stories.

K. IBZAN (12:8-10)

This is the first of 3 brief notices concerning minor judges (cf. 10:1-5). **Thirty sons** is a conventional indication of the judge's importance. **Marriage** outside one's tribe or clan seems to have been a standard practice (cf. 19:1; chs. 14; 16; 21). Of Ibzan's acts of deliverance nothing is said. Since the stories in the basic collection in Judg. concern only the N tribes, some interpreters have suggested that **Bethlehem** here is not the well-known Judahite city but a locale in Zebulun (cf. Josh. 19:15; see color map 5). It is possible, however, that Bethlehem in Judah had an Ephraimite population, as the expression "Bethlehem Ephrathah" (i.e. "Ephraimite"; Ruth 4:11; Mic. 5:2) seems to imply.

L. ELON (12:11-12)

All that one learns of this judge is that he was a **Zebulunite** whose home was in **Aijalon**—presumably an Aijalon other than that in central Palestine (1:35; Josh. 10:12). Possibly, however, the place name is not original to the account, since in Hebrew it is almost identical with the name Elon.

M. ABDON (12:13-15)

The author stresses the numerous progeny of this leader (cf. 8:30; 10:4; 12:9), a sign of his prominence in society. Abdon appears to have been an Ephraimite. The reference to **Amalekites** here is unusual. Elsewhere they are described as nomads ranging over an area S and SE of Palestine. They are mentioned, however, as aiding other groups in attacks on central Palestine from Transjordan (3:13; 6:3) and possibly on one of these occasions some of them settled in Ephraimite territory.

N. SAMSON (13:1-16:31)

The stories about Samson constitute the most extensive cycle of traditions in Judg. They are heavily influenced by legendary, cultic, and folk elements, with the result that little or nothing can be said about Samson as a historical person. The Samson who does appear in these tales is a typical folk hero, abounding in fascinating contrasting characteristics such as roughness and gentleness, cleverness and naïveté, good-naturedness and irritability, and having above all an extraordinary strength and passion for life. The D editor evidently found little of interest in Samson. The pre-D compiler apparently did see a moral value to the stories and may be responsible for adding the account of Samson's birth (ch. 13). By presenting Samson as a **Nazirite** he leaves the reader to draw the conclusion that Samson failed to live according to his Nazirite calling when he contacted dead bodies, ate unclean food, drank wine, and allowed his hair to be cut—not to mention the times when he consorted with Israel's enemies, the Philistines. In the final story, in which the blind Samson pulls down the Philistine building, the compiler wishes to suggest that Samson finally was reconciled to God; his willingness, however, to let the stories speak for themselves is notable.

In the older materials which the compiler used, and which may have originally circulated in poetic form, little or no concern with moral values appears, but there does seem to be a certain interest in old solar myths. Samson, whose very name appears to be related to the Hebrew word for "sun," appears suspiciously like a sun-god hero in several episodes. The extent to which one may legitimately discover this motif has long been debated by scholars and perhaps can never be finally decided. What all scholars can agree on, however, is that these old stories contain a wealth of information about life in W-central Palestine during the period of the judges. Particularly valuable are the references to the Philistines, who appear clearly for the first time as neighbors of the Israelites. The stories thus share much with the cycle of Samuel stories in I Sam. 1-12. Some of the Samson stories may have been influenced by Philistine traditions, but even more they may have influenced Philistine stories, which in turn perhaps passed across the Mediterranean on Philistine ships to the Greeks, whose legends about Hercules bear occasional resemblance to those about Samson.

13:1-25. The Birth of Samson. This ch., apparently belonging to the latest pre-D stage of the formation of the Samson cycle, is prefaced by a D editor's formula (vs. 1); thereafter no trace of D influence appears.

13:2-7. Samson's father, who is unnamed in ch. 14, is here called **Manoah,** a man of the tribe of Dan living in the town of **Zorah** on the W edge of the hill country (see color map 5). His unnamed wife, who is childless, prays for a **son;** the author probably supposes that the woman, like the childless Hannah not long afterward (cf. I Sam. 1:9-18), goes to a sanctuary to make her petition. An **angel** appears to the woman and directs her to rear her son as a **Nazirite,** one dedicated to an ascetic life (vss. 3-5, 7; cf. Num. 6). She herself must keep Nazirite purity until the child is born (cf. vs. 14).

13:8-20. Manoah is also granted a vision of the

angel. He offers the visitor the hospitality of a meal (cf. Gen. 18:1-8), but the food which he sets out is clearly an offering (cf. 6:11-24). The **name** of the angel (vss. 17-18), who may originally have been thought of as a god, possibly even Yahweh himself, is so sacred that one dare not pronounce it (cf. vs. 22). The departure of the angel in the **flame** of the sacrifice (vs. 20) has no close parallel elsewhere in the OT.

13:21-25. The reply of the wife (vs. 23) to Manoah's expression of fear is refreshingly practical. In time she bears a son, Samson, who thrives under the Lord's blessing (vs. 24). The storyteller adds, as a transition to the story which follows, an allusion to the divine power which begins to stir in Samson. This ch., one may note, strongly influenced the infancy stories of John the Baptist and Jesus in Luke 1-2.

14:1-15:20. Samson's Wife at Timnah. These 2 chs. consist of a series of closely related stories which revolve around Samson's marriage to a Philistine woman.

14:1-4. Of marriageable age, Samson goes down the slopes a few miles to **Timnah** (see color map 5), which is apparently a Philistine city. The **Philistines,** a seafaring people who settled on the S coast of Palestine around 1200, are living in close contact with the Hebrews to the E, over whom they exert both physical and cultural dominance (vs. 4b; cf. 15:11). Samson does not hesitate to ask for a Philistine woman as a **wife,** but his parents hold the conservative view that he should marry among his own people. The storyteller, who does not approve of Samson's wishes, justifies his behavior on the ground that Yahweh put the idea into his mind for an ulterior purpose (vs. 4).

14:5-9. The story of Samson's slaying of the **lion** was long ago noted to be suggestive of the ancient Near Eastern motif of a struggle between a hero-god and the lion as a sun symbol, as well as also having a broad affinity with Hercules' slaying of the Nemean lion. The lion image, however, was rather widely diffused; e.g. the Canaanite god Baal was on occasion called a lion. Samson's parents appear in this narrative rather awkwardly and should probably be removed from vs. 5. The whole process of Samson's coming and going to Timnah is rather obscure, but much of the difficulty disappears if one regards this passage as originally having stood at the opening of the story (vs. 1). Samson's eating **honey from the carcass of the lion** (vss. 8-9) prepares for the episode which follows.

14:10-20. This passage tells of Samson's marriage, at which in good oriental style he entertains the party with a **riddle.** The seriousness with which the Philistines take the challenge, as if suspecting that Samson seeks to humiliate them, indicates tension between the Israelites and the Philistines. When the answer to the riddle is eventually wheedled from him by his bride, Samson denounces the Philistines in a poetic couplet which is inapt but a not uncommon element of folk tales. Vs. 20 prepares for the story which is to follow. The motif of the disloyal wife who cajoles a secret from her husband reappears in the story of Samson and Delilah (ch. 16).

15:1-8. His anger later abated, Samson takes a gift and goes to Timnah **at the time of wheat harvest. . . to visit his wife.** Discovering that her father has given her to another (cf. 14:20) he takes revenge by tying lighted **torches** to the **tails** of **foxes** and allowing the distraught animals to run through the fields setting fire to the **grain.** This episode has parallels elsewhere in the ancient world, particularly in a religious rite which the Romans annually performed. Behind such imagery, or perhaps reflecting it, may be the idea that the red-coated fox is a symbol of fire; the Greeks sometimes called the fox a "torch-tail." Such concepts and practices have suggested to some interpreters that this story is a historicized version of a harvest rite practiced among some of the ancient peoples of Palestine, a rite which was perhaps connected with the concept of the sun as a scorching brand hurtling through the summer sky. Samson's deed sets off a fast-moving feud in which the Philistines retaliate by killing Samson's erstwhile wife and her father. Samson returns the attack and then flees to the hills.

15:9-17. When the Philistines seek Samson at the Judahite locality of **Lehi,** a few miles to the S, the men of Lehi find Samson and persuade him to let them hand him over to the Philistines. Brought to Lehi, Samson is seized by divine power, breaks his bonds, and slaughters the Philistines with a **fresh jawbone of an ass** (cf. 3:31; II Sam. 23:11-12). The bit of poetry in vs. 16 may be a fragment of an older poem which perhaps alluded, not to an actual ass's jawbone, but to a curved sickle or scimitar resembling a large jawbone; weapons were sometimes likened to objects in daily life (cf. I Sam. 17:7).

15:18-20. In a further scene Samson, having grown **thirsty,** receives **water** from a rock which God splits open. Vs. 20 is the compiler's summary of Samson's years as judge (cf. 16:31b).

16:1-3. Samson at Gaza. This brief story is not closely related to what precedes or follows but, like the other episodes, is built on one of Samson's amorous adventures. The story may be a historicized account of some now obscure cult rite or concept; Samson's picking up the **doors of the gates** of **Gaza** (see color map 5) and carrying them some 40 miles to the ridge of central Palestine may allude to the commencement journey of the sun god as he daily breaches the gates of the underworld. With this one may compare Samson's pulling down the 2 pillars in 16:23-30, an episode which is also said to occur at Gaza.

16:4-31. Samson and Delilah. Samson's 3rd and fatal encounter with a woman involves, like the other episodes, the Philistines. His long hair, attributed in 13:5 to his role as a Nazirite, here is probably understood as the mark of a hero-warrior. There is a strong element of magic in the story, perhaps derived from a legend concerning the sun hero, whose fiery locks represented his strength, and who was finally trapped when night (Hebrew laylah; cf. **Delilah**) wove his locks fast in a magic loom as he rested in the underworld, thus preventing him from rising. If this interpretation is correct—not all scholars would accept it—the 3rd of Delilah's attempts to make Samson captive may be the one which originally was said to have succeeded, the 4th having been added under the influence of the idea that Samson wore his hair long because he was a Nazirite.

The idea that Samson's strength was permanent and lay in his hair is at variance with the idea that

Courtesy of the Israel Department of Antiquities

Philistine jug from the Iron Age found at Gezer

he got his strength only on specific occasions by a divine infusion of power (14:6, 19; 15:14). The Philistines' blinding of Samson (vs. 21)—suggestive of the idea of putting out the eye of the sun (cf. vs. 28, which speaks of one eye)—seems to imply a different idea as to how he could be rendered harmless.

The reference to the regrowth of Samson's **hair** (vs. 22) seems to prepare for vss. 28-30, where, however, the stress is on God's sending sudden power to Samson when he prays for it. Possibly this final story was the addition of the compiler—perhaps based on an earlier tradition—who wished to show that Samson was ultimately rehabilitated. Samson's seizing of the **two . . . pillars** is reminiscent of 16:3, also set at **Gaza.**

The god **Dagon** (vs. 23) was a deity of grain, not a fish god as earlier interpreters supposed; Dagon (or Dagan) is named a number of times in old Semitic texts (cf. also I Sam. 5:2-5).

Vs. 31 appears to be editorial (cf. 15:20).

III. Supplementary Stories (17:1–21:25)

The stories of these chs. do not concern judges and are not included in the book's pattern of judgeships, but most of the materials in them seem to be as old as anything else in Judg. Chs. 17–18 and parts of chs. 19–21 may have been included in the pre-D edition of the book. Some interpreters believe that the D editor did not wish to use these materials and ended his edition with the Samson stories; if so, then a postexilic editor reintroduced this section, adding certain elements of his own, esp. 20:1-21:14.

The editorial statement that **in those days there was no king in Israel; every man did what was right in his own eyes** (17:6; 21:25; cf. 18:1; 19:1) seems to be a counterpart of the D formula that "whenever the judge died [Israel] turned back and behaved worse than their fathers, going after other gods" (2:19). It implies not only that the editor felt that the deeds narrated in the stories were not commendable, occurring in one or more of the interims between judges, but also that the institution of kingship was a necessary stabilizing power in Israel. Since this formula appears only in connection with the earlier stories in these chs., one may suppose that it is the work of the pre-D compiler, writing when the N Israelite monarchy still existed, before 722.

A. The Establishment of the Danite Cult (17:1–18:31)

17:1-13. Micah and the Levite. Based on 2 differing accounts which an editor has interwoven—or, according to some interpreters, a single account which has been awkwardly expanded—this story seems to serve chiefly as a background for ch. 18. The reader will value it, however, for its information about religious practices in the period of the judges. One learns that at least some families have household shrines at which the father, or someone acting for him, officiates.

17:3-6. The references to the **graven image** and **molten image** and the **ephod and teraphim** (cf. 18: 17-18) may come from 2 separate sources, but all 4 objects seem to be idols (cf. 8:24-27). The editor's comment in vs. 6, while possibly implying disapproval of household cults, is notable for its historical perspective; he recognizes that customs have not always been as in his own day (cf. 18:1; 19:1; 21:25).

17:7-13. A Levite from **Bethlehem** appears on the scene. That this man is a Judahite suggests that at this time **Levite** denoted a profession rather than a tribe. Bethlehem may at this time have been an Ephraimite settlement (see above on 12:8-10). Micah's concern to have a Levite as his priest suggests that Levites were more skilled in cult matters than ordinary persons.

18:1-31. The Danites' Migration. This story commences as though it were a separate tradition; in any case it seems to consist of 2 interwoven accounts. Interest has shifted to the Danites, an Israelite tribe which lacked a well-defined territory of its own, living crowded in by Judah, Benjamin, Ephraim, and Philistia (cf. Josh. 19:40-48). This story, telling how the Danites—or part of them—migrated to the far N of Palestine constitutes, as it were, a concluding ch. in the story of the conquest of Palestine.

18:2-6. In an episode reminiscent of Num. 13 the Danites send out spies to locate a suitable object of conquest. Heading N, the spies pass Micah's **house,** where they discover the Levite and obtain a favorable oracle.

18:7-26. Receiving a good report from the spies, the Danites set out for the N. As they pass Micah's house they steal Micah's cult objects and the Levite who is his **priest.** Micah pursues the Danites in vain, for their forces outnumber his.

18:27-31. Taking **Laish** by sudden assault the Danites settle, rename the city **Dan,** and establish a cult with the cult objects and the Levite. Vs. 30, which names the Levite for the first time, is an editor's attempt to link the Danite cult with the mainstream of Hebraic cultic tradition. The reference to **the captivity of the land** suggests that the Danite cult continued until the Assyrian invasion of the region about 733. Vs. 31 seems to be a different editorial conclusion. It is not known how long **the house of God was at Shiloh;** the allusion may be to the presumed destruction of Shiloh under the Philistines about 1050, to the centralization of the Hebrew religion at Jerusalem under David and Solomon, or just possibly to a destruction of Shiloh during the Assyrian invasion.

19:1-30. *The Episode at Gibeah.* Here a new cycle of materials begins. As an explanation of the war which ensues between Benjamin and other Israelite tribes (ch. 20) the storyteller narrates how a **Levite** of **Ephraim** goes to Bethlehem (see above on 12:8-10) for **his concubine** and on the way home stays overnight at the Benjaminite town of Gibeah (see color map 5), where he suffers a gross indignity which arouses first his anger and then that of all Israel.

19:10-15. Clearly **Jerusalem** was not yet under Israelite control (see above on 1:8). It is doubtful that the city was ever called **Jebus,** since extrabiblical texts of earlier cents. know only the name **Jerusalem.** The **open square** of Gibeah would be just inside the city's gate.

19:16-30. The details of the hospitality of the sojourner and the attempted assault by the men of Gibeah are reminiscent of the story of Lot at Sodom (Gen. 19); but the solution of the problem (vss. 22-26) is unique. The Levite's anger does not arise out of compassion for his abused concubine, for whom he seems to show no personal concern, but out of the feeling that his own dignity and property rights have been violated (vss. 27-29). The distribution of **pieces** of the woman's body throughout Israel (vs. 29) resembles Saul's distribution of the pieces of a yoke of oxen (I Sam. 11:5-7) and appears to be drawn from customs of covenanting (cf. Gen. 15:9-17). The implication is that the tribes of Israel must come to help the Levite take revenge, on penalty of suffering a fate like that of the dismembered woman. The earlies form of the story probably told only of a call to the men of Ephraim.

20:1-48. *Israel's Punishment of Benjamin.* Dealing as it does with Israel acting as a whole, this passage appears to be relatively late, though it seems to be based on 2 earlier accounts of the same episode, traces of which appear from time to time. **From Dan to Beersheba** indicates the whole of Palestine. The tribes—except of course Benjamin—gather at **Mizpah** in Benjamin; possibly an earlier version of the episode set the assembly at Bethel (cf. vs. 18).

20:12-28. The Benjaminites stand solidly behind the offenders of Gibeah. Vs. 16 speaks of the frequency of **left-handed** persons among them (cf. 3:15; I Chr. 12:2) and their proficiency with the slingstone. The number of Israel's soldiers (vs. 17) is vastly exaggerated. **Judah** receives the lot to go first (vs. 18; cf. 1:1-2; Josh. 15), a convention which shows the S background of the storyteller. When the men of Israel are defeated twice they perform acts of penitence (vss. 23, 26; cf. Josh. 7), and a divine oracle promises victory in the next battle (vss. 27-28). The parenthetical reference to the **ark** is a later addition; nowhere else in Judg. is the ark mentioned.

20:29-48. Lured from the city in a maneuver reminiscent of that in Josh. 8, the **Benjaminites**—more plausibly the Gibeahites—see their city go up in **smoke;** cut off, they are mostly slain. The details of this battle are not entirely clear; some interpreters take vss. 36b-44 as a separate and earlier version of the taking of Gibeah. Only **six hundred** Benjaminites escape, and the Israelites destroy **all the towns** of Benjamin (vss. 47-48). That such wholesale extermination of Benjamin actually occurred is of course highly improbable; the idea is the work of the late editor who, long removed from the days of the judges, presents a highly stylized narrative.

21:1-25. *The Rehabilitation of Benjamin.* This ch. consists of two separate accounts describing how it was that, after the near annihilation of Benjamin told in the preceding ch., the tribe survived.

21:1-14. This explanation, like ch. 20, is a late composition which shows the tribes of Israel going to **Jabesh-gilead** in the Transjordanian territory of Gad and slaughtering every person in the city except **four hundred young virgins** who then become brides for a part of the surviving Benjaminites. The sparing of virgins as spoil for warriors was not an unfamiliar practice (cf. 5:30b; Num. 31:17-18). The account is highly artificial, but behind it may lie the remembrance that Jabesh-gilead, a city which had long had ties with Benjamin, esp. through Saul (cf. I Sam. 11:1-11; 31:11-13), was attacked as an ally of Gibeah.

21:15-25. These vss. seem much nearer to old traditions, though they show late editorial influence. According to this account some of the Benjaminites got wives by capturing them at an annual vintage festival at **Shiloh** (cf. perhaps I Sam. 1:3, 21). The story hints that this practice was not entirely novel. Indeed it may be that during the period of the judges it was a regular practice for young men to choose partners from among the girls dancing at the festival, if not permanently at least for the duration of the celebration. Similar rites, known in many parts of the ancient world, had the serious purpose of attempting to induce fertility for the coming year.

THE BOOK OF RUTH

Herbert G. May

INTRODUCTION

The Story. The book of Ruth is an exciting short story, possessing almost rustic simplicity and charm. Unlike the story of Joseph, with which it may be compared for literary excellence, it contains no note of dissension or intrigue. Unlike the story of Esther, it has no villain. It maintains the reader's interest through the credibility of events and persons; the characters appear as real folk, and the author has remarkable sensitivity in depicting motivation. He draws no moral, but leaves his teaching obviously implicit.

The story is dramatic, but there are no spectacles. No miracles are wrought. The action shifts naturally from Moab to Bethlehem, from a day scene in the fields of grain to a night scene on the threshing floor, from the gateway of the city to the home where a child is born. There are 2 heroines, Naomi the Jewess and Ruth the Moabitess, and there is 1 hero, Boaz their kinsman. The other figures are properly subordinated, briefly playing their parts and unobtrusively slipping into the background. It is a story of tragedy overcome by love and loyalty—but also much more than that. The time is a quiet period in the hectic days of the judges.

The Purpose of the Story. Ruth is something more than a novel, even though it appears to teach nothing directly. The author's main reason for telling the story has to be determined from what seems to be its central theme. It is the tale of a Gentile woman who is consistently commended for her actions, and who enters into the community of Israel and becomes an important ancestress within that community. She is a Moabitess who, in words that give the impression of a keynote to the entire story, says to her Judean mother-in-law: "Your people shall be my people and your God my God" (1:16; see below on 1:16-17).

The author does not allow us to forget that his heroine was a foreigner (1:4, 15, 22; 2:2, 6, 10, 21; 4:5, 10). His viewpoint clashes with that expressed in Deut. 23:3, that "no Ammonite or Moabite shall enter the assembly of the Lord." It is contrary to that of Ezra and Nehemiah, who led reforms in which foreign wives, including women of Moab, were ousted from the community of Israel (Ezra 9–10; Neh. 13:23-27). He would find more congenial Isa. 56:6-8, which welcomes into Israel "the foreigners who join themselves to the LORD," or (though he was no legalist) the P code in the Pentateuch, which carefully prescribes "one law" for both

the sojourner (=proselyte) and the native born (Num. 15:15-16). He would find support in the tradition that 2 leading tribes sprang from the marriage of Joseph with the daughter of an Egyptian priest (Gen. 41:45), that Judah married a Canaanite woman (Gen. 38:2), and that Abraham took an Egyptian girl as a 2nd wife (Gen. 16:1-2).

He is not a theologian, intent like 2nd Isaiah on proclaiming the uniqueness of one God whom all people should worship. He is not an eschatologist, visioning a future when all peoples will acknowledge Israel's God (cf. Isa. 2:1-4; 19:21-25; 45:22-25). He does not condemn Orpah for returning to her gods (see below on 1:15-18). His is not a mission of conversion of Gentiles to Judaism. Rather, he writes to answer the question whether it is right and good that a Gentile woman be welcomed through marriage into the community of Israel.

The author has several secondary motives. He wants to tell a story about the ancestry of David. He intends his book to be a part of the history of Israel in the period of the judges. It is written as a continuation of that which has gone before. Its opening words are lit.: "And it was in the days of the judging of the judges." The setting in Bethlehem suggests the originality of the allusions to David, although some scholars think them later additions. David's family associations with Moab are perhaps hinted in I Sam. 22:3-4. The contemporaries of the author doubtless found his message more meaningful because his story concerned ancestors of the ruler from whose line they expected the Messiah to come.

The book is also a story of the loyal friendship of 2 women, Ruth and Naomi, recalling that other great friendship tale in the OT, the story of David and Jonathan. Further, it is a story of divine providence manifesting itself in critical circumstances, a tale of what happens when one seeks refuge in the shadow of the wings of the Lord (2:2). This theme runs through the book.

The Date of Composition. There is a Talmudic tradition that the author of Ruth was Samuel. The book is obviously later than that, but modern scholars have dated it all the way from the beginning of the Hebrew monarchy to the 3rd cent. B.C. The nature of the theme, the literary style, the numerous Aramaisms in the Hebrew text (although this in itself is not conclusive), and its position in the Hebrew Bible among the Writings—all these when taken together speak strongly for a postexilic origin, and this is the more general view. Although not written in a polemic spirit, it does involve the issues at stake in the 5th-cent. marriage "reforms" of Ezra and Nehemiah. Many scholars have taken the book as a tract written in opposition to those reforms. As noted above, the viewpoint is congenial with the attitude of the post-exilic writers toward the proselyte in Isa. 56 and in the P legislation. The general spirit is consonant with that in Jonah. The author refers to a day long before his own when he speaks of "the custom in former times in Israel" (4:7). His opening sentence has almost a "once upon a time" flavor. A late-5th- or 4th-cent. date of composition seems most probable.

Despite its lateness, and even though it cannot be shown that an earlier written form of the story lies behind the present work, the book seems generally to be based on a solid historical tradition. The story of David's Moabite ancestry is hardly something that would have been invented in the postexilic period. The book does, of course, reflect the author's religious viewpoint. He wrote it to teach his contemporaries by gentle persuasion.

The Place of the Book in the Bible. In our English Bibles following the Greek and Latin versions, Ruth is placed between Judg. and I Sam. This is in accord with the historical setting of the story. In the Hebrew Scriptures it is found among the Writings as one of the 5 Scrolls (Song of S., Ruth, Eccl., Lam., Esth.), which are read at various festivals of the Jewish religious calendar. Ruth is appropriately read at the feast of Weeks, the harvest festival, which is also considered the anniversary of the giving of the Sinai covenant. The rabbis said that Ruth was used at this festival because it was at that time that the Torah, which was intended for all men, was given.

For Further Study: Israel Bettan, *The Five Scrolls*, 1950, pp. 49-72. George A. F. Knight *Ruth and Jonah* (Torch), 1950. H. H. Rowley, "The Marriage of Ruth," in *The Servant of the Lord*, 1952, pp. 161-86. Samuel Sandmel, *The Hebrew Scriptures*, 1963, pp. 488-93.

I. Naomi's Bereavement and Return to Bethlehem (1:1-22)

The main sections of the narrative are adequately indicated by the ch. divisions. This first section introduces the situation for which the rest of the story is the unfolding solution. Naomi, bereaved of her husband and sons, returns to Bethlehem with her widowed and childless daughter-in-law.

1:1-5. Naomi's Emigration and Loss. As Abraham and Jacob went to Egypt in time of famine (Gen. 12:10; 47:4), so Elimelech with his wife Naomi and their 2 sons took refuge in Moab. **Ephrathites** is a term also associated with Bethlehem in I Sam. 17:12; Mic. 5:2. **Elimelech** means "God is King" and **Naomi** "my pleasant one." The meanings of the other names are uncertain, although **Mahlon** has been taken to mean "weakness," **Chilion** "pining," **Orpah** "stiff-necked" or "rain cloud," and **Ruth** "rose" or "companion." It has even been noted that "Ruth" in Hebrew spelled backwards means "turtledove." These are not fictitious but real names and persons. "Elimelech" is found as early as the 14th cent. B.C. in Canaanite inscriptions. The story carefully notes that Mahlon and Chilion married **Moabite** (i.e. Gentile) women. The status of a childless widow was unfortunate (cf. Isa. 1:23; 10:2), and the law demanded fair treatment of the widow (Deut. 14:29; 24:17, 19-21). She is often classed with the sojourner and fatherless. God is the protector of widows (Ps. 68:5).

1:6-14. Naomi Entreats Orpah and Ruth to Remain. The 3 widows set out to return to Bethlehem. Their route would lead them N and W to the lower Jordan crossing, and then perhaps down to the spring at modern Ain Feshkna and up through the rugged and desolate Wilderness of Judah where, near the present monastery of Mar Saba, the road turns up toward Bethlehem. Jerusalem was at that time still in the hands of the Canaanites. The solicitude of Naomi for the welfare of her Moabite daughters-in-law is notable (vss. 8-9). She seeks the blessing of her God, Yahweh, upon them, that he may **deal kindly** with them and grant that they **find a home** (rest and security) **each . . . in the house of her husband,** thus looking forward to their remarriage. The affection of Ruth and Orpah for their Judean mother-in-law is shown by their desire to go with her and by their tears (vs. 10).

1:11-14. Naomi's plea refers to the levirate marriage practice, the law for which occurs in Deut. 25:5-10. It involved marriage between the deceased husband's brother (or next of kin) and his childless widow. The first child born to the remarried widow was considered the son of the deceased husband. The story of Tamar (Gen. 38), an ancestress of Boaz, likewise involves levirate marriage, and Mark 12:19-23 also refers to it. The bitterness of Naomi is not self-pity, but arises out of consideration for her **"daughters"** (vs. 13*b*). The Lord himself has brought this calamity upon her (cf. Isa. 45:7; Job 2:10). Orpah's decision to turn back sets in sharp relief Ruth's persistent loyalty (vs. 14). The parting may have been on the Plains of Moab before the Jordan River.

1:15-18. Ruth Insists on Accompanying Naomi. The persistence of Naomi in trying to dissuade Ruth from accompanying her emphasizes her concern for Ruth's welfare. Naomi would have Ruth return, like Orpah, **to her people and to her gods.** The chief god of Moab was Chemosh (Num. 21:29), who is mentioned on the Moabite Stone (see p. 198). Naomi does not chide Orpah for returning to her own gods; her interest is in her daughters-in-law, not in making proselytes. Ruth's motivation is not loyalty to Yahweh, but devotion to Naomi. The story moves on a personal rather than a theological plane, although there are, of course, theological presuppositions and implications.

1:16-17. These words of Ruth are regarded by some as poetry; at the least they are poetic prose. In the OT it is unusual for a Gentile to take an oath by the sacred name Yahweh (cf. the oath formula in I Sam. 20:13). Ruth affirms that Naomi's home, people, God, and tomb will be hers. Family tombs with multiple burials are frequently found in excavations (cf. the patriarchal family tomb in Gen. 23; 49:29-33). Even in death Ruth would not be separated from Naomi.

1:19-22. Naomi and Ruth Arrive at Bethlehem. From Bethlehem Ruth could lift up her eyes and see the steep slopes of the hill country of Moab to the E beyond the Wilderness of Judah and the valley of the Dead Sea. Elimelech and Naomi had been persons of importance in Bethlehem; Naomi returns a childless, sorrowing widow, accompanied by her childless widowed daughter-in-law. She uses an ancient name for God, Shaddai, translated **the Almighty** (cf. Exod. 6:3; also Job 27:2, of which vs. 20*b* may be a reflection). **Mara** is an Aramaic feminine form. The change in name indicates a change in status, as when Abram became Abraham (Gen. 17:5), Jacob became Israel (Gen. 32:28), etc. So "my pleasant one" becomes "bitter." Like Job, Naomi accepts her lot as from the Lord (vs. 21; Job 1:21).

1:22. The **barley harvest** came in late April or early May. A 10th-cent. B.C. agricultural calendar found in the Gezer excavations designates a spring month as "his month of the harvest of barley." Barley ripened a couple of weeks earlier than wheat (2:23), could be grown on poorer soil, and was cheaper.

The Hebrew word translated **return, turn back, go back** is a key word in this ch., occurring 12 times.

II. Ruth Gleans in the Field of Boaz (2:1-23)

Boaz is the instrument for the resolution of the calamity set forth in ch. 1. As that ch. centered around Naomi, this one has Boaz as its key figure.

2:1-7. Ruth, the Gleaner, Meets Boaz. Boaz, **kinsman** of Elimelech, is a man of wealth and influence. Rabbinic sources make him a cousin, but the story does not specify his exact relationship. There is no known connection between Boaz here and the name of one of the pillars of Solomon's temple (I Kings 7:21). Boaz appears in the genealogy of Jesus (Matt. 1:5; Luke 3:32). The meaning of the name is uncertain. For the legal right of the widow and sojourner to **glean** (i.e. to pick up and keep the stalks of grain left by the harvesters) see Lev. 19:9-10; 23: 22; Deut. 24:19-22. The **reapers** cut the grain with small hand sickles, the blade of which was formed by a row of serrated flints set into a rounded haft. Ruth sought permission from Naomi to go gleaning. The obedient subservience of Ruth to Naomi is a part of the author's fine character depiction. Her industriousness receives special comment (vs. 7). She **happened to come** into the field of Boaz (vs. 3); thus was the providence of God at work. Boaz singled out Ruth immediately. The piety of oaz and of his people is evident in his greeting to the reapers and in their response (vs. 4); cf. Ps. 129:8, also in a harvest context (see ill., p. 116).

2:8-16. The Solicitude of Boaz for Ruth. (2:8-9) Boaz permitted Ruth to glean **close to** his **maidens** who were gathering up the sheaves to take to the threshing floor (cf. Mic. 4:12). Often reapers would yell at gleaners when they came too close (cf. vs. 16), and gleaners would normally have to wait for a signal from the reapers before they could gather the leavings. Boaz also invited her to **drink** from the large water jars which were in the field for the use of the reapers. The water may have come from the well beside the gate at Bethlehem. Ruth's descendant, the battle-weary David, was to yearn for water from that well (II Sam. 23:15).

2:10-13. Ruth was surprised that she, a **foreigner,** should be so favored, but Boaz had heard of her loyalty to Naomi (vs. 11). His motive was more one of respect than of love. He was a devout, kindly, older farmer, and Ruth a humble, obedient, and grateful girl. In the name of the Lord, **under whose wings** she had **come to take refuge,** Boaz invoked a blessing on her (vs. 12; cf. Ps. 36:7).

2:14-16. The work day began at dawn, and **at mealtime** there was a light repast, late in the morning. According to the Talmud, the 5th hour, *ca.* 11 A.M., was the mealtime for laborers in the field. This gave Boaz opportunity to show further favors to Ruth. The Moabitess was permitted to sit with the reapers and was provided with food and drink. She moistened the pieces of **bread** from the thin, flat loaves by dipping them into the fermented sour **wine** (or "vinegar," as the word is elsewhere translated). Boaz personally gave to her **parched grain**—fresh heads of grain lightly roasted over the fire, from which the husks were then rubbed off. As she went back to her gleaning, she was permitted to **glean even among the sheaves,** and the workers were instructed to **pull out** stalks from the sheaves to leave for her.

2:17-23. Ruth Reports the Day's Events to Naomi. As a result of the special treatment she received, Ruth returns to Naomi in the city with **an ephah** (*ca.* a half bushel) of barley. On learning the name of the man with whom Ruth has worked, Naomi invokes on him a 2nd blessing from the Lord, **whose kindness has not forsaken the living and the dead;** for she has immediately seen in Boaz the solution to the problem of preserving the name of the dead. **Nearest kin** (vs. 20*b*) is a technical term, Hebrew *go'el,* lit. "redeemer." It may designate the one who redeems the name of the dead through the levirate marriage custom (see above on 1:11-13) or the one who redeems the property of a poor relative by buying it (Lev. 25:25-28) or the avenger of blood (Num. 35:12, 19-21). Both name and property are involved in this situation. *Go'el* is also a title used of God the Redeemer (e.g. Ps. 19:14; Isa. 41:14). The providence of God is working things out **for the living and the dead** (vs. 20*a*). Keeping unobtrusively in the background, Naomi through her wise counseling helps the situation along to its desired end (cf. 3:1-5, 16-18).

III. Ruth's Night Visit to the Threshing Floor (3:1-18)

In this threshing-floor scene Boaz agrees to act as next of kin and marry Ruth, providing the one who is actually next of kin should be unwilling to do so.

3:1-5. Naomi Instructs Ruth. Naomi again affirms her responsibility for the welfare of Ruth (cf. 1:9). The sheaves were brought to the **threshing floor,** where they were crushed by a threshing sledge or by the feet of oxen. The **winnowing** was done toward evening, when the cool breezes were blowing in from the Mediterranean. The crushed sheaves were tossed into the air with a winnowing shovel or fork, and the wind blew the chaff away (cf. Isa. 30:24; Matt. 3:12), while the **heap of grain** (vs. 7) grew larger near the feet of the winnower (see ill., p. 153). Ruth was instructed to **anoint** herself and put on her **best clothes,** much as a bride (cf. Ezek. 16:9-10). Boaz planned to spend the night at the threshing floor to guard the grain.

Winnowing grain at the threshing floor; note the "heap of grain"

3:6-13. Ruth and Boaz at the Threshing Floor. After the evening meal, after the feasting and drinking which were a part of the happy occasion of a harvest, in a merry mood Boaz went to lie down at the end of the pile of grain on the threshing floor. Apparently as he slept, Ruth came quietly and lay down at his feet. With characteristic reserve, she did not awaken him, and he discovered that she was there only when something startled him. It was then midnight, and Boaz could not recognize Ruth in the darkness. Ruth's words to him were a clear request that he take her as his wife under the levirate marriage custom. He was her *go'el* (see above on 2:20*b*). Cf. the use of the expression "to spread one's skirt over" in Ezek. 16:8. The use of the words **young men** by Boaz suggests that he himself was not a young man; in vs. 10 he calls Ruth his daughter. Although Boaz was honored by Ruth's **kindness** (Hebrew *hesed,* which also implies loyalty, faithfulness) in coming to him, he must give the nearer kinsman the opportunity to exercise his right. Boaz might in any case be reticent in expressing any emotional involvement with Ruth, since he could not yet be certain that Ruth would be free to marry him.

3:11-13. The phrase **all my fellow townsmen** is lit. "all the gate of my people"—i.e. all the responsible citizens who have concern for community affairs, who might gather in the broad place before the city gate (cf. 4:1-2, 11; Prov. 31:23, 31; Amos 5:10). Boaz requested Ruth to **remain** the rest of the night, perhaps because he feared she might be molested by the festal-spirited harvesters.

3:14-18. Ruth Returns to Naomi in the Morning. Boaz would protect the good reputation of Ruth. Threshing floors were not always scenes of rustic innocence, especially at harvest festival time under the influence of Canaanitish fertility rites (cf. Hos. 9:1). Boaz would not let Ruth leave **empty-handed;** his gift of barley was perhaps both a present for Naomi and a token of the validity of his promise. **Six measures** probably means 6 seahs (cf. Gen. 18:

6), equal to 2 ephahs (cf. 2:17) or about 1⅓ bushels. The ch. ends with Naomi counseling patience, in confident assurance that before the day was over the matter would be settled. Thus the reader is prepared for the consummation of the story.

IV. The Marriage and the Birth of a Son (4:1-17)

The story comes to a satisfying conclusion with all the problems happily solved.

4:1-6. The Next of Kin Refuses His Right. (4:1-2) Boaz **went up** (for Bethlehem is on a hill) to the city gate (see above on 3:11) and chose **ten . . . elders** to act as a court of decision. This incident provided a precedent for the later view that 10 men formed a quorum and was the smallest possible number for a synagogue. Among the Essenes (the Dead Sea Scroll sect) 10 men formed a quorum.

4:3-4. Boaz presented the case to the next of kin, whose name is not given. For the first time it is noted that the case involves redeeming by purchase a **parcel of land** belonging to Elimelech which Naomi has put up for sale. See Lev. 25:25-28 for the law of redemption of land by the next of kin; an illustration of the law in practice appears in Jer. 32. Naomi's control of the land seems inconsistent with the later law in Num. 27:8-11, which presumes that the property of a man who dies without a son does not go to the widow.

4:5-6. The next of kin, apparently a man of limited wealth, was willing to buy the land until he learned that it involved acquiring Ruth to restore the name of the dead to his inheritance. This would mean that the land would go to Ruth's son; he would thus diminish his own estate, and there would be less **inheritance** for his other sons. If Boaz had no sons, the son born to Ruth would perhaps be the legal heir of both the deceased and of Boaz. The situation, however, is not entirely clear. In any case, the next of kin was not willing to take whatever loss there might be. **You are also buying Ruth** (vs. 5) should perhaps be rendered "you are also acquiring Ruth"; the verb has both meanings, and may be used in 2 senses in this vs. Ruth is not the property of anyone, but must go with the land, which will belong to her son.

4:7-12. Boaz Assumes the Right of Redemption. (4:7-10) Through the ceremony of the removal of his **sandal** and presenting it to Boaz, the next of kin attested to his relinquishing of the right of redemption. It was thus a symbol of renunciation and transfer of rights. A quite different custom is involved in Deut. 25:5-10, where the widow pulls off the sandal of her husband's brother who has refused to do the duty of a husband's brother and spits in his face. There it is a symbol of disgrace. An earlier practice is represented in Ruth. In ancient Mesopotamia sandals (shoes) or other articles of clothing might be used as tokens to validate special transactions. This is not quite analogous, for the next of kin is not the one who has bought something; yet the action does in some way validate the agreement between the 2 parties. On **Ruth . . . I have bought** (vs. 10) see above on vs. 5.

4:11-12. With the good wishes given to Boaz cf. those to Rebekah in Gen. 24:60 and especially those to the royal groom in Ps. 45:16-17. It is prayed that Ruth may be like **Rachel and Leah,** who with their handmaidens had produced the ancestors of the 12 tribes of Israel. **Perez** was a son of **Tamar** (Gen. 38:27-30), and from him could be traced the line of David (vss. 18:22; cf. Matt. 1:3; Luke 3:33); this suggests the author did intend to tell a tale about the ancestry of David. Tamar was also involved in a levirate marriage situation (see above on 1:11-13). She was probably a Canaanite woman and so, like Ruth, a Gentile married to a Hebrew.

4:13-17. *Obed Is Born.* The congratulatory role of the women of Bethlehem is set in deliberate contrast with their reaction in 1:19-21. This exemplifies the fine literary sensitivity of the author. Ruth was more to Naomi than **seven sons.** This was an ideal number of sons; the blameless Job had 7 sons and 3 daughters (Job 1:2; cf. I Sam. 2:5). The women recognized the child as Naomi's, for through him the name of Elimelech had been redeemed, and also that of Mahlon. Ruth has in part acted as a substitute for Naomi in the levirate marriage practice (see above on 1:11-13), and her son is also Naomi's. Naomi's action in vs. 16 symbolizes and perhaps legitimizes this fact.

4:17. The name **Obed,** meaning "he who serves," does not provide the usual word play that one might expect (cf. Gen. 4:1; 25:25-26; etc.). This has led some scholars to conclude that in the earlier form of the story there was a different name beginning with Ben ("son of") or one containing a play on Naomi's name and that therefore the Davidic genealogy is an intrusion. On the other hand, the author may deliberately have avoided a word play to make more startling the punch-line of his composition: **he was the father of Jesse, the father of David.** The narrow-minded particularists would get the point: Obed, the son of a Gentile woman, was the grandfather of David who instigated the dynasty; God's covenant was with him, and from his line would come the Messiah.

4:18-22. *The Genealogy of David.* Is this a later addition or the work of the original author? If the author wrote as late as the end of the 5th or the beginning of the 4th cent., it may be his, for he could then have had before him the genealogical lists in the Pentateuch, after which this genealogy is patterned. The list is obviously too brief by several generations to fill the period between the patriarchal age and the time of David. The same genealogy, with differences in spelling, is presumed in I Chr. 2:5-15. The Ruth and Chr. lists have provided the data for the genealogical tables in Matt. 1:2-6; Luke 3:31-33. In Matt. 1:5 the mother of Boaz is identified with Rahab, a Canaanite woman of Jericho (Josh. 2). Through this genealogical list at the end of the book, the author or editor indicates that the story of Ruth is an important part of the sacred history of Israel.

THE FIRST BOOK OF SAMUEL

John William Wevers

INTRODUCTION

Originally the books of Samuel and Kings constituted one book, but because of their length they were divided into 2. The LXX further divided them into 4 and called them appropriately "Concerning the Kingdoms." The 4-fold division has been adopted down to the present, but the name has not.

Name and Place in the Canon. The name "Samuel" for the first pair of books comes from the Hebrew text; it was probably chosen since Samuel is the first major character appearing in it. In the Hebrew canon Sam. is grouped along with Josh., Judg., and Kings to make up the Former Prophets (see "The Making of the OT Canon," pp. 1209-15). As opposed to Chr., Ezra, and Neh., which constitute a priestly view of Israel's history, the Former Prophets show a prophetic viewpoint. In content they cover Israel's history from the conquest of Canaan to the destruction of Jerusalem in 586 B.C.

The Deuteronomic Edition. In its final form Sam. seems to have formed a part of a large work, containing also Josh., Judg., Kings, and perhaps Deut., which recounted the history of Israel from the Conquest to the compiler's own day. It was put together by an editor (or editors) of the Deuteronomic school (see "The Compiling of Israel's Story," pp. 1082-89) during the Exile, *ca.* 560 B.C., as shown by the last event recorded in II Kings; other scholars maintain that it was done during the reign of Josiah, *ca.* 610, with revision or supplementation by others of the D school *ca.* 560. The work of the D editor is not as apparent in Sam. as in Kings (see Intro. to I Kings) since he adopted materials from various earlier sources without change, and only here and there did he add his own comments, e.g. in II 7. He was, however, responsible for the present arrangement of the materials in large part, except where his source in turn already had collected and arranged materials which the editor took over.

Earlier Sources. The problem of literary sources in Sam. is incredibly complicated, and only a sketch of these can be given. By the time the D editor began his work various collections of traditions were already in existence which in turn had been collected from earlier sources. Some of these sources are extremely early, even contemporary to the events described, e.g. the Military Source and the Succession Document described below. Certain lists and summaries of campaigns, e.g. II 8; 23:8-39 must go back to official court records kept in the time of David. Cf. also the family lists of II 3:2-5; 5:13-16.

Local Traditions. Originally many of the early stories concerning Samuel and Saul were traditions rooted in a particular area. Such sanctuaries as Mizpah, Gilgal, Ramah, and Shiloh in particular were centers of traditional lore about those ancient heroes. Sometimes the same story was told in 2 different centers, with the result that both were taken over by later collectors of traditions into their collections, and divergent or doublet accounts obtain. This is particularly striking in the account of Saul's becoming king. Involved are at least 2, if not 3, cycles of stories centered respectively at Ramah, Mizpah, and Gilgal.

Shiloh Stories. I 1-3 is obviously centered in the important sanctuary of Shiloh and is from an independent source, which in turn contains divergent traditions. 2:27-36 is an insertion from the D editor which parallels 3:10-14. The Song of Hannah, 2:1-10, is a hymn from monarchical times; cf. vs. 10 with its reference to the king, inserted much later and put into the mouth of Hannah. The stories center about a permanent sanctuary with its cult and show no hint of its destruction. The picture of Sam. as a young ministrant to Eli finds no parallel elsewhere. Later Sam. stories contain no mention of his Shiloh apprenticeship.

Ark Stories. These stories, I 4:1-7:2; II 6:1-19, seem to be unrelated in origin to the Shiloh stories. There too no reference to the Philistine destruction of that sanctuary is told even though it would have been germane. The center of interest here is the fortunes of the ark and its holy character. Thus it is quite clear that the story of Uzzah in II 6:6-7 is of the same type as those in I 5; 6:19-7:2 and belongs with them. It could not, however, be placed immediately after 7:2 because it concerned David after the capture of Jerusalem. The present form of II 6 is possibly an amalgamation of a tradition from the ark stories and one from the Succession Document, to which it also belongs. The stories were probably collected in the time of David.

Sam. Stories. These stories are found in I 7-12 and combine 2 quite distinct sources in turn. Though in both the account of the origin of the monarchy is given, Sam. is the actual hero. He is the great judge, prophet, and charismatic leader; and his words are definitive. Source A is in general unfavorably disposed to the monarchy, which its author views as rebellion against Yahweh. It probably originated in Mizpah, though ch. 8 details a Ramah event. The following stories clearly belong to this source: 8:1-22; 10:17-27; 12:1-25. Ch. 7, which has been some-

155

what editorialized, also belongs to this source. Sam. is judge over all Israel and universally respected, even though his advice is not heeded. The age of the stories cannot be determined; they come from the N, probably from the time shortly after the division of the kingdom. There is no good reason for considering these as a late source as many commentators do.

Source B, found in 9:1-10:16; 11:1-15, represents a favorable view of Saul and the monarchy. Sam. is presented as a man of God only locally prominent, and Saul is a young man of great promise. The story of the charismatic actions of Saul against the Ammonites is an excellent sequel to God's giving Saul "another heart" in 10:9, as the Gilgal coronation is a sequel to Sam.'s earlier instructions in 10:8.

Saul Stories. These are found in I 13-15; 28; 31. Independent traditions concerning Saul are almost nonexistent in view of the dominance of David. Even the Saul stories in which David plays no part betray a judgment on his career quite at variance with the picture of him given in Source B of the Sam. stories. From the start the stories of his early successes against Philistines and Amalekites in chs. 13-15 are told under the shadow of his rejection and lack of good royal judgment. From the D editor's point of view this nemesis was important—Yahweh's spirit was not on Saul even though he was zealous for Yahweh. Some of these stories have often been related to the Sam. ones, and this is possible. Thus the rejection of Saul twice told in different contexts (chs. 13; 15) would fit with Source A. Both are Gilgal stories; the former is, however, much more sympathetic toward Saul, whereas the latter is a complete rejection of a disobedient king. In all these stories the tragic figure of a rejected king is central. His reign begins in error (13:8-15) and ends with the despairing events at Endor and Gilboa (chs. 28; 31).

Stories About David. The stories about David in I 16-27; 29-30; II 1:1-5:5 present more difficulties than any other complex. These concern David's fortunes from his secret anointing by Sam. at Bethlehem to his election as king over the 12 tribes. The traditions are varied in origin and do not present a consistent chronological pattern. At times doublet accounts are given, e.g. David's sparing Saul's life (I 24 in Engedi, but ch. 26 in Ziph; cf. 18:10-11; 19:8-10). At times stories that obviously belong in sequence are separated: in I 17 vss. 32-54 should follow vs. 11; the David and Jonathan story of I 20 cannot follow 19:24, but follows on 19:10; the story of David at the Nob sanctuary is also out of order, properly constituting a sequel to 19:18-24. There are numerous instances of contradictory accounts; e.g. David's flight to Gath (I 21:10-15) can hardly be harmonized with the story of his slaying of a Gath champion (I 17), or with his later stay near Gath in Achish's employ (I 27; 29-30).

Nonetheless the stories must have been brought together by a collector of David stories no later than the time of Solomon. The collector's method was typically oriental: when variant accounts were found, all were written down so that no traditions would be lost. The arrangement of materials that resulted from this kind of collection is undoubtedly confusing.

The motivation of the collector is perfectly clear. He wanted to show that David's rise to power was not his own doing but strictly that of Yahweh. David does not fight Saul or his forces; he evades them. When David can easily stretch out his hand against Yahweh's anointed he never does; in fact he reprimands those who wish to do so and kills those who do. His phenomenal popularity in his early days at court is due, not to his own planning, but to Yahweh's spirit. Even in his military exploits he seeks oracles to ascertain Yahweh's will. He does not win the kingdom; it comes to him from Yahweh. After Saul's death at Yahweh's direction he goes up to Hebron, where the Judeans anoint him as their king. Later, after the death of Saul's heir, the united tribes anoint him as Israel's king (II 2:1-4; 5:1-5). With few exceptions the David stories are basically Judean in origin.

The Succession Document. One of the finest historical sources which the editor took over is the account of court intrigues involving the problem of David's eventual succession. The core of this document is II 9-20 (except for 10:1-19; 12:26-31, on which see the next section); I Kings 1-2. It would seem likely that the document originally had parts of II 5-7 as a preface. Certainly some early version of God's covenantal promise of the prosperity of David's house, i.e. of a succession (ch. 7), must have preceded the document.

The document must have been composed by an eyewitness no later than the early years of Solomon's reign. Various names—e.g. Ahimaaz, Nathan, Gad, Zadok—may be suggested, but these are only guesses. Characteristic of the author is his failure to gloss over David's weaknesses as a husband and a father. That his chief interest is the royal succession is clear from his choice of stories. Ammon, the eldest, is rejected as immoral. After his death the 3rd son, Absalom (the 2nd was Chileab, who probably died in early life; at least he is never mentioned beyond the list of sons born in Hebron, II 3:3), makes an attempt to take over the throne and is killed in the civil war that results. Joab subsequently has to save the kingdom for David (ch. 20). Finally Adonijah, the 4th son, attempts a *coup d'état* but is thwarted by the Solomonic party (I Kings 1-2).

A Military Source. The account of the Ammonite war in II 10:1-19; 12:26-31 is taken over by the author of the Succession Document to give a proper setting for the David-Bathsheba story. Its vividness in describing the military operations and its lack of religious interest clearly brand it as a separate source. It probably constitutes an eyewitness account of the battle; in any event it is contemporary, earlier than the Succession Document.

Stories of Divine Affliction. The origin of 2 stories, II 21:1-14; 24:1-25, is unknown. They seem to represent the same genre. In both Yahweh is displeased, in both some form of expiation is demanded, and in both Yahweh is appeased.

Poems. Four longer poems are inserted into the historical traditions. One, the Song of Hannah, has been discussed above. Two may well be Davidic in origin, the elegy over Saul and Jonathan (II 1:19-27) and David's last words (II 23:1-7). A 4th, found in II 22, is taken from the body of cultic poetry; it is a variant of Ps. 18. The origin of I 15:22-23 is not clear; two others, I 18:7; II 3:33-34, are popular refrains (cf. also I 29:15).

Religious Significance. Sam. stands in the middle of the D history. The historian's purpose was to show how Yahweh directed the course of Israel's affairs. As Israel's God he guided her destinies in a special way. Canaan was given to Israel under Joshua, and after his death charismatic rulers judged Israel. Eventually Yahweh directed his people through, kings for whom the norm was David, the man after God's heart. Sam. shows the change from judge to Davidic king. Saul's reign was a misguided attempt to combine charismatic rule with kingship. David was the first genuine king.

But Yahweh's direction is based also on ethical demands. When David sins he is punished. Saul is rejected because he is disobedient. Eli's house is destroyed because of the immorality of his sons. On the other hand David's reign is prosperous because he follows the proper course of action. Before embarking on any venture he consults the oracles. He is not chosen for outward appearance, as Saul was, because Yahweh "looks on the heart." It is he who captures Jerusalem, the city where Yahweh has chosen "to put his name" (as throughout Deut.), and brings the ark there, not only making Jerusalem a political center but also translating it into Zion, the cultic center.

For Further Study: H. P. Smith, *A Critical and Exegetical Commentary on the Books of Sam.,* 1899. S. R. Driver, *Notes on the Hebrew Text and the Topography of the Books of Sam.,* 1913. A. R. S. Kennedy, *The Book of Sam.,* n.d. G. B. Caird in *IB,* 1953. Martin Noth, *A History of Israel,* 1958. John Bright, *A History of Israel,* 1959. Stephen Szikszai in *IDB,* 1962.

I. Shiloh Stories (1:1-4:1a)

A. Sam.'s Birth and Dedication (1:1-2:11)

1:1-20. Birth of Sam. The story is laid in **Ephraim,** appropriately in **Ramah** ("height," vs. 19) or **Ramathaim** ("2 heights," vs. 1). **Zophim** should read "a Zuphite" as in the LXX. The town was probably modern Beit-Rima, 12 miles W of **Shiloh** (see color map 5), not the better known Ramah in Benjamin, 5 miles N of Jerusalem. The story concerns a favored but childless wife who is taunted by the other wife (who of course has children). Barrenness was considered the greatest of misfortunes. The occasion is the annual pilgrimage made by the family to **Shiloh,** modern Seilun, almost halfway from Bethel to Shechem, a holy place where the ark was housed. There **Elkanah** would offer a thank offering, and the family would eat together at the feast. Finally the desperate wife, who can take the gibes of **her rival** no longer, rises and enters the sanctuary to pray.

1:9-20. Silently the distraught **Hannah** proclaims a vow to Yahweh **of hosts** (i.e., the armies of Israel), the full name of Israel's God. If he will give her a **son** she will devote him as a Nazirite (cf. Num. 6:1-21; Judg. 13:2-14). **Eli,** the sanctuary priest, after an embarrassing misunderstanding is cleared up, blesses her; and she is cheered knowing that she has been heard. **In due time** she has a son, whom she names **Samuel.** The explanation given is peculiar. Sam. means "name of God" rather than **asked.** However, "Saul" does mean "asked"; an explanation of that name seems to have been inappropriately transferred to Sam.

1:21-2:10. Dedication of Sam. Until the baby **is weaned** Hannah stays home from the annual pilgrimage, but eventually the time comes for redeeming her vow. The story has been confused by the insertion of the Song of Hannah (2:1-10). Originally it must have concerned the woman only. The RSV has hidden the difficulty by changing vs. 28b to the plural. The Hebrew reads "he worshiped." Since Elkanah is not part of the story at all, "he" would have to refer to the infant Sam. Originally the story must have read "and she worshiped Yahweh there and went home to Ramah" (2:11a). Hannah brings for the occasion a particularly large offering and leaves the child in Shiloh as a sanctuary servant (2:11b).

2:1-11. The Song of Hannah is a hymn of praise to Yahweh, inappropriate in its present context. For similar insertions of a cultic poem cf. the pss. of Hezekiah (Isa. 38:10-20) and Jonah (Jon. 2:2-9). Its insertion here was no doubt due to the reference to **the barren** (vs. 5; cf. Jer. 15:9). It is clearly a later composition from the time of the monarchy, as the reference in vs. 10 shows. The song is in praise of Yahweh's power, against which mortal opponents can do nothing. Life and death, honor and dishonor, all these and more are under his direction. His power is not despotic, however; he will judge men by moral standards and will give strength to the Davidic king. This song was probably the model for the Song of Mary (Luke 1:46-55).

B. The House of Eli (2:12-4:1a)

2:12-17. The Sins of Eli's Sons. Though priests at Shiloh, Eli's sons are guilty of **contempt** for the **offering.** Shiloh **custom** is described as being for the priest to take as much as could be **brought up** on a **fork** thrust into the vessel where the **meat was boiling.** Eli's sons, however, prefer to take **raw** meat. Most scholars feel that vss. 13-14 should be corrected to read that the taking of the meat from the container was contrary to Shiloh custom and thus also evidence of the wickedness of the priests, but such a change would be at odds with vss. 15-16. On the priestly portion cf. Lev. 7:28-36; Deut. 18:3-4.

2:18-21. Hannah's Annual Visit to Shiloh. Sam. does service in the sanctuary as a ministrant wearing the **linen ephod** appropriate for cultic service (cf. II 6:14). Annually Hannah visits her son and brings him new clothing, and she receives priestly blessing. On **the loan** cf. 1:28. The blessing is successful; Hannah has 5 more children.

2:22-25. Eli's Rebuke of His Sinful Sons. This passage, as well as vss. 27-36, is intended to depreciate the Elid house. Inconsistent to the narrative is vs. 22b (cf. Exod. 38:8), which was probably added later to emphasize the immorality of the priests. The sanctuary here was not a **tent** but a building with doorposts (cf. 1:9). Eli's rebuke is ineffectual because Yahweh wanted **to slay them.** Even the sins of the Elids are part of the divine plan. In contrast to the evil sons Sam. is pictured as favored by God.

2:27-36. House of Eli Denounced. An oracle from an unnamed prophet is typical of the D editor (see Intro. to I Kings). The denunciation of the Elid house reflects the rivalry of the Zadokite and Aaronite priesthoods. Vs. 28 refers to the choice of Aaron (cf. Num. 3:2-3) to perform the priestly offices, one of which was to carry (not **wear**) the **ephod,** here an instrument of divination (see below on 14:2-3, 16-23) and not a garment as in vs. 18. Because of the cultic sin (cf. vss. 15-17) of Eli's sons Yahweh will destroy his house and raise up a **faithful priest,** Zadok, in his place.

2:32-36. Vs. 32 is difficult. Eli died, according to 4:18, when he heard the news that the ark was taken and his sons were killed. What then is meant by **prosperity?** The text is probably corrupt. The **man** who alone is **spared** is Abiathar (see comment on I Kings 2:26-27). For the language of vs. 35 cf. II 7. Vs. 36 probably reflects the conditions of Josiah's reform (cf. II Kings 23:8-9).

3:1–4:1a. Yahweh's Appearance to Sam. This passage combines the call of Sam. to prophethood with another denunciation of the Elid house. The setting for the story emphasizes the rarity of such an oracle, the auditory and visual nature of which is emphasized (3:1). Sam. as a young ministrant is asleep when he hears his name called and naturally waits on Eli, his master, who on the 3rd occasion realizes that Yahweh is **calling the boy.**

3:10-18. The oracle summarizes the divine intent to destroy Eli's house, not only because of the sins of his sons but also because of the father's slackness in rebuke (in contrast to 2:22-25). The sin is unpardonable.

3:19–4:1a. In the years that follow, Sam.'s reputation as a **prophet** (note that elsewhere this word is not used of him; elsewhere it designates ecstatics; cf. 9:9; 10:5-6) increases throughout **all Israel.** The phrase **from Dan to Beersheba** means from the N to the S limits of the country (cf. Judg. 20:1).

II. Stories About the Ark (4:1b–7:2)

The exact nature of the **ark of the covenant of the LORD of hosts,** as the D editor calls it, is not clear. It was probably a plain oblong box which dated from desert days before Israel's arrival in Canaan. It was in some special way a symbol of Yahweh's presence, possibly intended to portray the throne for the invisible deity. As such it was carried into battle, showing that Yahweh was the God of the armies of Israel. About its ultimate fate nothing is known.

4:1b-11. The Capture of the Ark. The site of **Aphek** is in the Plain of Sharon (see color map 5), thus near the border between Philistine and Israelite territory. **Ebenezer** must have been near by, though it remains unidentified (see below on 7:5-17). When battle is joined the Israelites are disastrously **defeated** but hold ground. Wise counselors suggest bringing the ark from Shiloh to insure Yahweh's presence.

4:4. The ark is given the full cultic name **ark of . . . the LORD of hosts, who is enthroned on the cherubim.** These were winged creatures (see comment on I Kings 6:23-28) who guarded the ark (possibly represented decoratively on the sides of the ark) and served to support the divine throne.

4:5-11. The Israelites, as well as their enemies, mistakenly confuse the symbol with the reality. The **Philistines** are full of superstitious dread—the storyteller even attributes to them an acquaintance with early Hebrew traditions of the plagues in Egypt—nonetheless they are determined to fight **like men.** The results are again disastrous for Israel, esp. the capture of the ark and the death of Eli's sons. That this is central to the story is clear from the failure of the author to refer to the fate of Shiloh (cf. Jer. 7:12-14; 26:6), which was apparently destroyed by the Philistines.

4:12-18. The Death of Eli. A Benjaminite runner with traditional display of mourning arrives at Shiloh with the news. Blind old Eli, alarmed at the outcry, inquires for news. He is sitting near the gate overlooking the **road,** and when he hears about the capture of the ark he **fell over backward** in shock and **died.** The D editor, in accordance with the artificial scheme in Judg., speaks of Eli's serving **forty years** as judge, whereas the original tale knows only of Eli as priest at Shiloh.

4:19-22. The Birth of Ichabod. Eli's **daughter-in-law** is pregnant. The news of the loss of the ark brings on **her pains** and she dies in childbirth. The **son** is named—by the attendants, not by the unconscious mother—**Ichabod,** meaning "there is no glory," to commemorate the disaster. Yahweh was Israel's **glory,** and the loss of the ark symbolized to the Israelite Yahweh's departure from Israel.

5:1-12. A Terror to the Philistines. The heathen take the sacred trophy to **Ashdod** (see color map 5), evidently at this time the chief of the 5 Philistine city-states, and place it in the temple of their god. The name **Dagon** means "grain," rather than "fish" as formerly supposed, and indicates a vegetation deity. Yahweh, however, is not defeated. The first morning finds the Dagon statue in a position of obeisance before the ark, and the next morning it is shattered. Vs. 5 is an antiquarian note to explain a Philistine **threshold** rite.

5:6-12. Shortly thereafter the city suffers a plague —possibly bubonic since mice are carriers of the disease (cf. 6:4-5). On consultation the Philistine **lords** (*seranim,* perhaps akin to *turannoi,* the "tyrants" of the later Greek city-states) decide to send the ark to **Gath,** another of their 5 cities. After the same dread result ensues, the ark is in turn sent to a 3rd city, **Ekron,** where the inhabitants greet its arrival with **panic.** The plague, the **hand of God,** also breaks out here.

6:1–7:2. The Return of the Ark. The situation after **seven months** is critical. The experts, viz. **priests and diviners,** are consulted. They recommend its return together with a **guilt offering**—a kind of payment for infringement on the rights of deity. By sympathetic magic **five** (for the 5 city-states; cf. vss. 17-18) **golden tumors and . . . mice** (symbolizing the plague and its cause) are to effect the deliverance. To determine whether the plague is Yahweh-inspired or coincidence the ark with the guilt-offering is placed on a **new cart** drawn by a pair of fresh **cows.** If against nature the cows leave their sucking **calves** and proceed to Israelite land, the plague is obviously from Yahweh. They do so, going directly to **Bethshemesh,** *ca.* 12 miles to the E (see color map 5), and stopping near a large **stone.** Here the cows are sacrificed as a **burnt offering,** the cart being used for fuel. In vs. 15 the interest of the author (or probably of a later editor) in correct cultic procedure is evident; only **Levites** can handle the ark—though why they should be on the spot at the **wheat harvest** (vs. 13) is not explained. Vs. 18b is an antiquarian note identifying a large memorial stone as the site of this event.

6:19-21. The ark retains its dreadful power even on Israelite soil. Some people inspect with unhealthy interest (lit. "looked at," not **looked into**) the holy object and are killed. The Hebrew text says 50,070 men, a fantastic number; **seventy** is likely correct. The ark is immediately transferred to **Kiriath-jearim,** *ca.* 9 miles NW of Jerusalem (see color map 5). This is to be its temporary abode (Shiloh having been destroyed by the Philistines) till David can transfer it to its permanent location in Jerusalem. In view of the death of the Elids a new priest, **Eleazar,** is given **charge of the ark.** 7:2 is an editor's connecting link between the ark stories and the following section.

III. SAM. TRADITIONS (7:3–12:25)

In the main these stories have Sam. as their hero. They reflect 2 divergent views of the monarchy—one unfavorable (Source A), the other favorable (Source B; see Intro.). The D editor has added his comments. Traditions about Sam. seem to have been numerous. He acts as priest, judge, intercessor, and prophet. As with Moses, a firm historical picture of Sam is difficult to reconstruct.

A. SAM. AS LEADER OF ALL ISRAEL (7:3–8:22)

7:3-17. *Sam. the Last Judge.* This passage is based on Source A but has been rewritten by the D editor, with the result that it conflicts with other sources. Thus the picture of a Philistine rout and the idyllic recovery of lost **territory** contradicts the more historical accounts of continuous conflict. Vs. 14 might be more accurately applied to David.

7:3-4. These vss. are typical of the D editor and recall the framework of Judg. (see Intro. to Judg.). The Israelites are warned against idolatry and promised relief from the enemy if they will serve Yahweh only. They do so and the stage is set for the great victory of vss. 10-11. The people take part in a water-pouring ceremony apparently symbolizing contrition (cf. John's baptism of repentance, Matt. 3:11).

7:5-17. Israel gathers at **Mizpah,** 5 miles N of Jerusalem in Benjaminite territory (see color map 5). Here Sam. **judged,** probably meaning that he rendered legal decisions. On Sam.'s intercessory powers cf. Jer. 15:1. That Yahweh is the victor is the point of the story; the Israelites simply engage in mopping up exercises. The location of **Beth-car** is unknown. The location given for the memorial **Ebenezer,** meaning "stone of help," indicates a different place from the town Ebenezer mentioned in 4:1*b;* but some have conjectured that this story reflects a variant tradition of the battle of 4:1*b*-2 in which an Israelite defeat has been turned into a victory. **Amorites** here is another name for Canaanites. Apparently Sam. served as sanctuary judge in various places in central Palestine. On **Ramah** see above on 1:1-20. On **Bethel** see comment on Gen. 12:8-9; 28:18-22. **Gilgal** here refers to a town 7 miles N of Bethel rather than the tribal center near Jericho prominent elsewhere in the Sam. and Saul traditions.

8:1-22. *The People's Demand for a King.* This account expresses most forcefully the bias against the monarchy which is characteristic of Source A. A deputation of **elders** comes to Sam. at his home in **Ramah** to plead for a **king.** Their plea is based on the misconduct of Sam.'s own **sons** as judges in **Beer-sheba,** an important sanctuary in the far S. The point of the request, however, is to be **like all the nations.** Sam. recognizes this as a rejection of his own role as judge, but the narrator criticizes it as a rejection of God's kingship over Israel. This rejection is typical of Israel's past history from the time they became a people and is characterized in the typical language of the D editor as idolatry (vs. 8).

8:10-18. The picture that Sam. presents of royal prerogatives is a reflection, not of later practice among the kings of Israel, but rather of the practice of oriental despots among **all the nations.** Such absolute monarchs not only despised their subjects' property rights but also impressed them into service, both military and domestic (cf. the strictures on kings in Deut. 17:14-17).

8:19-22. The elders, however, insist on a king, since having such a leader will unite the people for military purposes.

B. SAUL'S ANOINTING (9:1–10:16)

All of this account comes from Source B, which contrasts with the preceding in that it considers Sam. a local leader only and views the founding of the monarchy as the means of saving Israel in a time of crisis.

9:1-4. *The Search for Lost Asses.* Saul is a Benjaminite of exceptional stature and fine appearance,

Courtesy of Herbert G. May

Hill country of Ephraim showing type of terrain through which Saul and his servant passed

in the prime of life (rather than **young**), and thus an ideal candidate for the kingship. He and a **servant** set out to find lost **asses** and travel for 3 days (vs. 20). Both **Shalisha** and **Shaalim** are unknown, and the text of vs. 4 may well be corrupt, since obviously they start from **Benjamin** and arrive in **Ephraim.**

9:5-14. *Steps Toward Consulting a Seer.* When the travelers reach **Zuph,** the region of Sam.'s home town of Ramah (see above on 1:1-20), the servant suggests a visit to the **man of God in this city**—the author builds up suspense by keeping him unidentified till the 2 actually meet him (vs. 14). This man of God is reputed to be trustworthy; he can predict correctly (cf. Deut. 18:21-22). When Saul brings up the fee customary for such consultation, the servant provides a small piece of **silver,** valued by its weight (see pp. 1284-85). Vs. 9 is an explanatory note on the word **seer,** which does not occur in the story till vs. 11. In early times this term was distinct from **prophet,** which referred to roving ecstatics (cf. 10:5-13), whereas the seer simply saw what others could not—i.e. he had 2nd sight. In the author's time the 2 terms had fallen together; Sam. traditionally was the father of prophecy, and as such was to anoint Saul to kingship (cf. 16:1-13; I Kings 1:34; II Kings 9:1-10).

9:11-14. Near Eastern cities were always on the hill, but the spring would be lower down the slope. Girls going for water tell the inquirers that the seer has just arrived (cf. 7:16-17). The **high place** was apparently outside the town walls on the brow of the hill. To slaughter meat was to **sacrifice** it, and Sam. as priest first has to bless it before the communal meal is eaten.

9:15-25. Sam.'s Encounter with Saul. Sam. has received a prior revelation that Saul is coming and that he is to **anoint him** as the one designated by God, i.e. as **prince,** to deliver Israel. When Saul approaches Sam., he is invited to the sacrificial feast as the seer's special guest. The narrative throughout emphasizes Yahweh's direction of events. Saul is parenthetically told not to worry about the lost asses; there are more important things in the wind. Sam. hints obscurely at Saul's future royal role in vs. 20b, to which Saul replies with typical oriental modesty.

9:22-25. Saul is entertained in the **hall** of the high place—where the sacrificial feasts were held—and accorded the place of high honor. Who the other guests are is not indicated; they are probably important men of the city. Saul is also given a **bed** for the night on the **roof** of Sam.'s home, a common place for sleeping in the Near East.

9:26-10:1b. The Anointing. At the **break of dawn** Sam. escorts Saul out of the city and anoints him secretly. The anointing of kings was a religious rite common among both the Egyptians and the Hittites. Though a priest or prophet could be anointed to office, it was the king esp. who was set apart by this rite and sacramentally endowed with royal powers, so that in a real sense he became another man (cf. 10:6, 9). Now the obscure "all that is desirable in Israel" (9:20) is made clear. Saul is the divinely designated one to rule and **save** the people. It is clear that the kingship was set up in the first place to give military leadership in view of the Philistine crisis.

10:1c-13. Signs Given to Saul. Signs were often given as an attestation for what was otherwise incredible. Three are given to Saul, each of increasing value. First he **will meet two men by Rachel's tomb** (near Bethel; see comment on Gen. 35:19-20; **Zelzah** remains unidentified) who will inform him about his domestic affairs. Next he will meet **three men** carrying provisions for a sacrificial feast at the **Bethel** sanctuary. They will give him **two loaves of bread,** which Saul is secretly to take as earnest of his future royal state. Finally he is to meet a **band of prophets** and temporarily become one of them. This is to occur at **Gibeath-elohim** ("hill of God"), probably simply his home town of Gibeah (cf. vs. 26), 3 miles N of Jerusalem (see color map 5). The word translated **garrison** here and in 13:3-4 (differing from that in 13:23-14:15) is believed by most scholars to refer rather to an official (cf. RSV footnote), one of a number stationed by the Philistines

throughout Israel for collecting tribute. In early times **prophets** were ecstatics, spirit-filled men, who used music (on the instruments see comment on Ps. 150) to bring on a state of ecstasy during which they **prophesied.**

10:8. Sam. ends his statement with instructions to **go down . . . to Gilgal,** the tribal center in the Jordan Valley near Jericho (cf. Josh. 4:19-20; etc.; see color map 5), where he is to wait for Sam. and receive further instructions. This is probably intended by the author to harmonize with the story of the popular acclaim of Saul as king at Gilgal (11:15; see below on 13:7b-15a).

10:9-13. All 3 signs are said to take place as Sam. has predicted, but only the 3rd is described. The surprise of Saul's acquaintances at his joining in the ecstatic behavior of the **band of prophets** gives rise to a proverbial saying. What is meant is that Saul as a farmer has no business being a prophet (cf. 19:18-24 for another explanation of the saying). Vs. 12 probably is intended to cast aspersions on prophets as a class whose parentage is unknown, whereas that of Saul is well known. **The high place** (vs. 13) is probably a scribal error and should read "his house."

10:14-16. Saul's Discretion. Saul's uncle asks about the experiences of the journey. Saul reveals that they inquired of Sam.—apparently a familiar name to the uncle—but refers only to the lost asses, keeping to himself the **matter of the kingdom.**

C. Saul's Election by Lot (10:17-27)

Source A resumes again with this story from Mizpah (see above on 7:5-17), which is quite at variance with the preceding tradition. If Saul were anointed he would hardly now have to be divinely

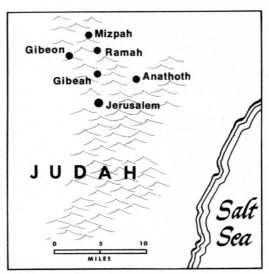

chosen once again. The story may be a cult legend portraying the first coronation: the divine choice by lot, the popular acclaim, and the recital of the privileges and duties of kingship and their incorporation into a book and its subsequent deposit in the sanctuary. This passage originally followed 8:22a.

10:17-24. In distinction from the elders of ch. 8 all the **people** are involved here. **Thousands** (vs. 19) has the sense of "clans." The sacred priestly **lot** is cast by Sam., finally isolating Saul. The incident in vss. 21c-23 is peculiar. Possibly it represents a variant tradition of the choice (like that in 16:6-13) in which the lot falls on no one and so Sam. asks, "Is there still another man to come here?" (as in the Hebrew text rather than the **LXX Did the man come hither?**). Saul eventually becomes king by popular acclaim.

10:25-27. The final act in the drama is the "testimony" (cf. II Kings 11:12) or recital which vs. 25 relates. Apparently coronation involved, at least in later times, such a statement of royal **rights and duties.** For a similar recital which the D editor would certainly know cf. Deut. 17:14-20. This may well be the D editor at work in keeping with the requirement set out there. The passage concludes with the disclosure of only partial acceptance of the king by the populace as he returns home.

D. Saul's Coronation at Gilgal (11:1-15)

This section is from Source B and thus is a sequel to the secret anointing of 9:1-10:16. It gives a variant Gilgal version to the coronation described in 10:17-27.

11:1-4. The Ammonites were a nomadic people living in Transjordan N of Moab and E of the Israelite tribe of Gilead. **Jabesh** of Gilead, or **Jabeshgilead,** was a town on the E edge of the Jordan Valley (see color map 5). The besieged inhabitants ask for terms, but the Ammonites make insulting demands instead of the usual **treaty.** To highlight the general plight of Israel they give a week's **respite** in which the **elders** can seek help.

11:5-11. Saul hears the news purely by chance. He has been secretly anointed, but now the **spirit** of Yahweh falls on him, and he becomes a charismatic leader like Samson (Judg. 14:19; 15:14). For a parallel to Saul's symbolic act uniting all tribes in a common venture cf. Judg. 19:29-20:11. The result is a universal **dread** of Yahweh; i.e. Israel recognizes Saul's action as divinely inspired. Failure to take part would mean being under a curse. The numbers of vs. 8 are incredibly high. **Bezek,** 13 miles NE of Shechem on a hill overlooking the Jordan Valley almost opposite the town of Jabesh, provided an excellent rallying place. The day began at sundown; therefore **the morrow** (vs. 11) means "that night." The **morning watch** was the final 3rd of the night.

11:12-15. Vss. 12-13 belong as a postscript to 10:27 and are out of place here. Vss. 14-15 are the real point of the story. Sam. is pictured as summoning the people to **Gilgal** (see above on 10:8). At the sanctuary the victorious Saul is made king by popular acclaim.

E. Sam.'s Covenantal Discourse (12:1-25)

This ch. is from source A and belongs with 8:1-22; 10:17-27. It has been rewritten in large part by the D editor.

12:1-6. Sam.'s Protestation of Integrity. In contrast to 8:3-5 the mention of Sam.'s **sons** (vs. 2) is simply to show his age. The new institution of kingship has not been made necessary by the failure of the former charismatic leaders. Before God and the new king the people declare unambiguously that Sam. has judged rightly.

12:7-15. Yahweh's Redemptive Acts. Sam.'s survey of Yahweh's **saving deeds** includes not only the Exodus and the gift of Canaan but also deliverance from the various enemies by the judges. **Jerubbaal** is another name for Gideon (cf. Judg. 8:29). Also listed is Sam. himself, considered by the D editor to be the last of the great judges. Time and time again the people have rebelled (vs. 9), but always God has **delivered** them when they **cried** to him. Now the Ammonites have threatened and the Israelites have demanded a king. This was quite unnecessary since **God was your king.** That this demand was occasioned by the Ammonite threat contradicts ch. 8.

12:16-25. Sam.'s Intercession. Sam. shows his great power by calling on Yahweh to confirm his displeasure by bringing on **thunder and rain** during the **wheat harvest,** a period when Palestine never sees rain. The people, fearing this phenomenon, are repentant and beg Sam.'s intercession. For an interesting parallel of a prophet's intercessory power cf. I Kings 13:1-6. Sam. assures the people that they can cancel the effects of their sin by faithful adherence to Yahweh and his demands. Yahweh **will not cast away his people, for his great name's sake** (vs. 22)—i.e. his reputation is at stake. In typical D language the earlier admonitions of vss. 14-15 are repeated in vss. 23-25.

Apparently the ch. reflects some kind of rite of contrition connected with the royal covenant, but beyond the materials of this ch. little is known of its character.

IV. Saul's Reign and Rejection (13:1-15:35)

A. The Revolt Against Philistine Domination (13:1-14:46)

13:1-22. The Outbreak of Hostilities. The original story of how Saul's war for independence from the Philistines began is found in vss. 2-7a, 15b-18. The remainder consists of 2 additions by the D editor, vss. 1, 7b-15a, and a 3rd passage, vss. 19-22, which is probably an insertion.

13:1. The D editor has supplied the usual formula for kings' reigns, but textual corruption has produced an incomplete record. The number of years for Saul's age is lacking. The LXX has 30 years, but this may simply be a guess. His having a son with the prowess described in the following story, which clearly must be assigned to the beginning of his reign, indicates that actually Saul must have been 40 or older (cf. 9:2). Similarly a word is obviously missing in the number for the length of the reign. Probably either 10 or 20 must be inserted to make 12 or 22 years. Acts 13:21, as well as Josephus, has 40 years, which is certainly too long.

13:2-4. Saul recruits an army of 3,000 and assigns a 3rd of it to **Jonathan,** who is here introduced for the first time and is later (vs. 16) identified as the **son** of Saul. **Michmash** (see color map 5) lay 7 miles NE of Jerusalem on the N slope of a steep and narrow wadi (river course dry except in the rainy season) and **Geba** lay on the higher S slope, overlooking the pass where the action of 14:1-15 takes place. **Gibeah** lay 5 miles SW of Geba. Scribes have confused the 2 places at several points in chs. 13-14. Jonathan and his troops are at Geba rather than Gibeah (vs. 2); and he precipitates the revolt by killing the Philistine officer (not **garrison**; see above on 10:1c-13) stationed at Gibeah rather than Geba (vss. 3; cf. 10:5). Further textual corruption is evident in vs. 3, since Saul would not summon his compatriots by the name **Hebrews**, which in early times was a contemptuous term used primarily by outsiders (cf. 14:11; 29:3; see Intro. to Josh.). The rumor spreading through **all Israel** (vs. 4) assumes that the new king ordered his son's rash deed. On Gilgal (vs. 4c) see below on vss. 7a-15b.

13:5-7a. The Philistines muster an army to put down the uprising, and they occupy **Michmash**. The numbers are probably exaggerated; certainly **chariots** in this precipitous wadi would be useless. The Israelites are terrified. Many of them, fearing Philistine revenge, either hide or flee to Transjordan.

13:7b-15a. When the D editor took over this account he inserted a story to support his conviction that Saul's reign was a reject kingdom and that the acceptable rule began only with David, his successor. By adding to vs. 4 a reference to **Gilgal** he gives the impression that Saul is in the Jordan Valley while Jonathan remains on the battlefield. It would have been military suicide to retire to such a distance at this time.

This Gilgal story details a version of Saul's rejection as king by Yahweh. The D editor ties it in with Sam.'s instruction in 10:8, which was intended to be fulfilled by Saul's coronation at Gilgal. In this story Saul is placed in an impossible position. The army is **scattering** but he must wait for Sam. He waits the stipulated **seven days** (cf. 10:8) and then himself performs the necessary sacrifices. As soon as he has finished Sam. arrives and upbraids him. Saul was being tested (cf. Gen. 3) and has failed to meet the arbitrary requirement (contrast e.g. 14:35; II 24:25). Had he passed the test, Sam. says, the dynasty of the future would have been his rather than David's. For another version of Saul's rejection cf. ch. 15.

The D editor may have placed the story in this context to prove that Saul was rejected before undertaking his first act of kingship. Could the 2 years of vs. 1 then be intended as the length of time that he ruled before his rejection?

13:15b-18. Desertions have reduced Saul's army to about **six hundred men.** They are at Geba on the S side of the wadi (see above on vss. 2-4). Opposite them at **Michmash** the Philistines send most of their force in 3 companies of **raiders** to ravage the countryside to the N, W, and E respectively.

13:19-22. This parenthetical note may be part of the original story, but since there is no other indication that the Israelites were handicapped by lack of weapons it is generally considered a later insertion. Even if they were ill equipped before, booty from the Ammonite war (ch. 11) must have provided a considerable supply. However, the note has a historical basis in the fact, confirmed by archaeology, that at this period early in the Iron Age the Philistines far surpassed the Israelites in production and utilization of iron. Archaeological discovery of small weight stones inscribed **pim** (used in balances to weigh silver for payments; cf. 9:8; see table, p. 1285) underlies the RSV reconstruction of vs. 21 from the obscure Hebrew.

13:23-14:15. Jonathan's Exploit. From the height

at Geba Jonathan sees across the wadi the **Philistine garrison** come out from **Michmash** to the N side of the **pass.** He suggests to the boy who serves him as **armor-bearer** a madcap venture. Of course he does not inform his **father** what he plans.

14:2-3. Saul is also at Geba (not **Gibeah**; cf. 13: 16; see above on 13:2-4) with his reduced army. **Migron** is unknown and may be a scribal error for "the threshing floor." **Ahijah** is the **son of Ahitub,** as is also Ahimelech, the father of David's priest Abiathar (chs. 21-22). The 2 names may identify brothers or, as many scholars believe, the same man. In either case the genealogy is probably intended to relate the prophecies concerning the house of **Eli** (2:27-36; 3:11-14) to Solomon's expulsion of Abiathar (I Kings 2:26-27). Ahijah is carrying, not **wearing,** the **ephod,** which in this story is not a priestly garment (as in 2:18) but a container for the Urim and Thummin (vs. 41) used to obtain oracles from Yahweh (see below on vss. 16-23).

14:4-5. The jutting crags on either side of the forbidding **pass** have names. **Bozez** means "shining," i.e. baldfaced, and **Seneh** "thorny."

14:6-15. The slur **uncircumcised** is the regular Israelite designation of the Philistines, who alone among their neighbors did not share the practice of circumcision. In return the Philistines call the Israelites **Hebrews** (vs. 11; see above on 13:2-4). Jonathan proposes an arbitrary **sign** to his lackey, who fully concurs. When the sign is positive, they clamber up the steep slope and with sublime faith fall on the garrison. Apparently the shock of the attack throws the army into panic. Yahweh helps the 2 attackers by an earthquake, which increases the panic even more.

14:16-23. Defeat of the Philistines. From Geba (not **Gibeah**; see above on vss. 2-3) Saul's sentries, overlooking the enemy's camp, note the confusion. Saul immediately undertakes a roll call. Jonathan and his aide are discovered missing. The text of vs. 18 is confused. Saul calls on the priest **Ahijah** to bring forward the **ark of God**—but at this time the ark was at Kiriath-jearim (7:2). The LXX represents a clearer tradition: " 'Bring hither the ephod,' for he was carrying the ephod at that time before Israel." Thus Saul asks Ahijah to bring the ephod (see above on vss. 2-3) and secure an oracle but, observing the growing **tumult** among the Philistines on the other side of the wadi (vs. 19), interrupts the priest's manipulation and orders an immediate attack (vs. 20). The Israelites fall on the enemy camp, which is now in complete **confusion.** Their force of 600 men is swelled by **Hebrews** who have been with the Philistines, as well as by stragglers who panicked earlier (cf. 13:6). Israel is victorious, and the Philistines flee. **Beth-aven** is unidentified but must have been W of Michmash in the direction of Philistine territory.

14:24-35. Saul's Taboo. The text of vss. 24-26 is corrupt, but the general intent is clear. Saul is apparently concerned lest the people fail to set aside Yahweh's part of the booty first and so imposes a taboo against eating before **evening.** It turns out to be a tactical error since the weakened troops find it difficult to pursue their military advantage with sufficient energy. Jonathan, not having heard the **oath,** breaks the taboo by eating some wild **honey** and is refreshed (**his eyes became bright**). The last sentence in vs. 28 is probably copied from vs. 31 by error.

14:31-35. The pursuit extends to **Aijalon,** *ca.* 15 miles W of Michmash toward the Philistine border. By now the sun has gone down and the taboo is no longer in effect. The famished soldiers fall on the prey, eating flesh **with the blood.** This is forbidden practice (cf. Deut. 12:16), and Saul is alarmed. A **great stone** is brought up to serve as **altar** and the people are ordered to **slay** their animals properly and then eat. Saul is much concerned with religious observance.

14:36-46. *The Silent Oracle.* Saul is determined to follow up his advantage and smite the enemy **by night.** When **the priest** seeks an oracle from Yahweh there is no **answer,** and Saul realizes that someone must have broken the taboo that day. He swears an oath that the guilty **shall surely die.** The sacred lot is cast by means of **Urim** and **Thummin** (meaning "lights" and "perfections"). Exactly what these were is not known; possibly they were flat objects carried in the ephod (see above on vss. 2-3) dark and light on opposite sides. The **lot** eventually falls on Jonathan, who confesses that he ate some **honey.** That he was unaware of the taboo makes no difference; he realizes that only his death will wipe out the effects. The people, to whom Jonathan is obviously the great hero of the day, stand between Saul and his son, pointing out that if God really were displeased with Jonathan he would hardly have saved Israel through him. A sense of fairness triumphs over superstition. Jonathan is **ransomed,** presumably by the sacrifice of an animal in his stead (cf. Exod. 13:13; 34:20, where "redeem" renders the same Hebrew word). Nonetheless the pursuit of the Philistines, which in Saul's eyes would demand the removal of the taboo, is abandoned.

B. CONCLUSION AND FINAL REJECTION (14:47–15:35)

14:47-52. *Summary Notices.* Vss. 47-48 are a short summary, similar to that of David's reign in II 8. **Zobah** was an Aramaean kingdom (see below on II 8:3-8). That this is simply a summary is clear from vs. 48*a,* which summarizes ch. 15 in a single sentence. Vs. 52 refers to constant war with the Philistines and Saul's building of a standing army. Vss. 49-51 interrupt the summary with genealogical notices concerning Saul's family. The list is incomplete, since 31:2 mentions another son, Abinadab. **Ishvi** (probably a textual corruption of "Ishiah," meaning "man of Yahweh") is evidently the same as Ishbosheth in II 2:10–4:12; his name was actually Ishbaal (see comment on II 2:8-11). **Abner,** Saul's commander of the army, was his cousin (cf. vs. 51 with 9:1).

15:1-35. *Saul's Rejection.* To the D editor this tradition confirmed his belief that the real kingdom started with David and it was fitting that the David stories should follow immediately. The story has a parallel in 13:7*b*-15*a;* here also the setting is **Gilgal,** but the occasion is transferred to an Amalekite war of extermination. It presents the prophetic view on Saul and his kingdom.

15:1-3. Sam. is here a prophet. Saul receives through him a divine mandate to conduct a holy war against the Amalekites in fulfillment of the

curse in Deut. 25:17-19 (see comment). A holy war was a war of complete extermination presumably under Yahweh's orders. The **Amalekites** were nomads living in the wilderness area S of Judah, and Saul may well have embarked on such a punitive expedition to insure Judean support of his throne.

15:4-9. Saul accordingly musters an army; note the overly large numbers. **Telaim** lay somewhere in the S of Judah; its location is uncertain. Nor is the **city of Amalek** known; in fact Amalekites did not dwell in cities. Probably a winter encampment is visualized. On the **Kenites** cf. Judg. 1:16. The Amalekites are completely defeated and their chief captured. The dimensions of their territory given are ideal rather than actual—from the boundaries of **Havilah** (i.e. Arabia) to those of **Egypt!** Saul, however, does not carry out the barbaric demands of a holy war. **Agag** is spared, as well as a large amount of cattle.

15:10-21. In the next scene Yahweh tells Sam. that he has rejected Saul from being king because of his disobedience. Sam.'s reaction is to be **angry;** having anointed Saul he is disappointed and tries to change God's mind (cf. Jonah 4:1-2). **Carmel** (not Mt. Carmel) was 7 miles S of Hebron (see color map 6), on the edge of Amalekite territory. There Saul has erected a victory stele. When Sam. and Saul meet at the Gilgal sanctuary, Sam. is not deceived; he hears all the **sheep** and **oxen.** But, says Saul, the people have saved some as a **sacrifice**— an inane subterfuge since all the cattle are under the ban, i.e. declared profane and doomed to destruction, thus not fit for sacrifice. Sam. rebukes Saul, rightly placing all the responsibility on him as the **anointed** king.

15:22-23. This oracle of rejection has become classic as presenting the prophetic viewpoint over against the priestly. Cult is always second to morality; sacrifice never takes precedence over obedience. Vs. 23*ab* is difficult. The Hebrew text has: "The sin of divination is surely rebellion; and iniquity and idols a presumption." Their condemnation does not seem esp. appropriate here. The 3 terms used are all connected with pagan cult, and Saul's sin seems to be compared with these evil practices. On the other hand **idolatry** here is lit. "teraphim," and it has been suggested that originally **iniquity** read "ephod" (cf. e.g. Judg. 17:5; Hos. 3:4; see above on 14:2-3) and the lines condemned sin *against* divination by ephod and teraphim—i.e. disobedience to the command of holy war against Amalek which at an earlier stage of the tradition was received through this medium rather than prophetically as now in vss. 1-3.

15:24-35. Saul is portrayed as a pathetic character groveling before Sam. For a symbolic act of tearing similar to that in vss. 27-28 cf. I Kings 11: 30-31. On the hidden reference to David cf. 13:14. The term **Glory of Israel** (vs. 29) refers to Israel's God; it fits strangely with vs. 11. Eventually Sam. gives in to Saul and for the sake of appearance accompanies the king for the sacrifice (vs. 31). Possibly Sam.'s killing of **Agag** was originally a separate tradition from that ending with vs. 23. On the other hand vs. 28 seems important to the story. What is clear is that after this the break is complete; Sam. never sees Saul again.

V. David's Rise to Power (16:1–II 5:5)

A. Introduction of David (16:1–18:5)

16:1-13. David's Anointing. It is appropriate that the collector of David stories should have begun with this one, since it determines the outcome, viz. David's succession to the throne, from the beginning. The story centers around Sam., though the hero is David. Vs. 1 connects it with the preceding ch.; Saul is **rejected,** and thus a new king must be chosen by Yahweh. **Bethlehem** lies *ca.* 5 miles S of Jerusalem (see color map 5). The statement that Sam. **consecrated Jesse and his sons** (vs. 5) refers to a purificatory rite otherwise unknown.

16:6-13. Successively **seven** sons of Jesse are viewed by Sam. but **not chosen** by Yahweh, who **looks on the heart** (vs. 7). Even so, when the **youngest,** a shepherd, is called it is noted that he is **handsome** and **ruddy**—a word used also of the newborn Esau (Gen. 25:25) and interpreted by some to mean that both he and David were redheaded. Sam. is told to **anoint** the youth. From vs. 2 it appears that his real purpose in coming is to remain secret, but **in the midst of his brothers** (vs. 13) would seem to make the anointing a public ceremony. Possibly the phrase is not to be taken as meaning "in the sight of," so that, as in the case of Saul, Sam. takes David aside; or possibly he performs the act in such a way that those present do not recognize what he is doing. Throughout the stories there is no hint that knowledge of it is public. Now God's **Spirit** inspires David, i.e. makes him qualified to rule when the time comes. This ability is amply shown in subsequent stories, e.g. vs. 18.

16:14-23. David's Arrival at Court. The rejection of Saul means that God's Spirit has abandoned him; he is no longer qualified for rule. Saul was apparently a psychiatric case who progressively worsened. This is put in theological rather than psychological terms: **an evil spirit from the LORD tormented him.** His **servants** suggest the therapeutic value of music, and someone proposes David, who is described in glowing but exaggerated terms. David arrives at court with his **lyre** and a present for the king from his father. The lyre was a stringed instrument later popular in the cult (see comment on Ps. 150:3). David's musical therapy is successful, and Saul is enamored of his new servant, even making him his personal military aide. The story is but one version of David's introduction to Saul.

17:1-11. A Philistine Champion's Challenge. A Philistine army again is arrayed against Israel, this time in Judah 14 miles W of Bethlehem **between Socoh and Azekah** (see color map 5). **Ephesdammim** may be a site *ca.* 4 miles NE of Socoh. The Israelite army is encamped by a wadi, the **valley of Elah.** Instead of beginning a pitched battle the Philistines send out a **champion** to challenge any Israelite to fight with him. This peculiar custom is well known from pre-Islamic desert days in Arabia. In II 21:19 it is stated that one of David's heroes, Elhanan, killed **Goliath** the Philistine giant. If that tradition is correct, it is likely that originally the champion of this story was anonymous and later was given the name of a known giant, though some interpreters have argued instead that a tradition of Elhanan's exploit came to be associated with the more famous hero David.

The giant champion is unbelievably huge and strong. He is about 9½ ft. tall and completely equipped with **bronze** armor of great weight and a large **iron** spear (see above on 13:19-22) which reminded one of a **weaver's beam.** Ancient weights were not standardized throughout the Near East, and the figures given cannot be confidently translated into modern equivalents, but the impression given of impregnability and tremendous strength is intentional.

17:12-31. Introduction of David. This section contradicts ch. 16 and is not part of the story represented by vss. 1-11, 32-54. Along with 17:55–18:5 it is omitted by the LXX. Its author knew neither of David's anointing nor of his introduction to court. It thus is a doublet to 16:14-23. Its purpose is to bring David forward as Saul's legitimate successor, on whom God's favor rests. This is esp. clear from 17:55–18:5, which belongs to this same tradition.

17:12-16. David is introduced anew. Throughout the narrative editorial changes have been brought in to harmonize this account with the other. Thus reference is made to **eight sons** of Jesse, though the story presupposes only 4 (vs. 14). Vs. 15 is also an addition to make concessions to 16:14-23, as though David is traveling **back and forth** from his **sheep** to the court. Since vss. 55-58 show that in this source Saul does not know David at all, vs. 15 cannot have been part of the original story.

17:17-19. Jesse sends David with food for his 3 soldier **brothers** as well as a substantial present for their **commander.** An ephah is *ca.* a half bushel. Volunteer soldiers had to provide their own provisions. The **token** (vs. 18) must be some agreed sign of their continued welfare. Vs. 19 is part of Jesse's instructions and should not begin a new paragraph.

17:20-31. As David arrives the 2 armies are drawing into their **battle lines,** as they do every morning, retiring to their camps at night. As usual the Philistine champion struts between the drawn lines challenging the Israelites. Rumor circulates that anyone who successfully defies him will receive a princess' hand in marriage—a common folk motif. No one dares to take up the challenge except the young visitor. David puts his finger on the real problem, the insult that this heathen should **defy the armies of the living God.** Like a typical older brother **Eliab** scolds David for his impertinence. Eventually Saul hears about young David's bold words.

17:32-54. David's Victory. The original story again is resumed. David offers his services as champion, but Saul is doubtful. David assures him of his prowess as a courageous shepherd. Furthermore Yahweh will fight for him, since this is really Yahweh's battle, not his own. Saul eventually gives in and tries to equip him as a soldier with armor; the term **his armor** (vs. 38) hardly means Saul's own. David goes out as a shepherd, without armor, with **his sling.** The sling could be an extremely effective weapon (cf. Judg. 20:16). David's lack of armor is important to the story; David is simply an instrument in God's hands (cf. Zech. 4:6).

17:41-47. As the unequal contestants meet they both make speeches. The Philistine's is insulting and uncouth, a typical speech of a warrior who glories in his own strength and intends to put fear into the heart of an opponent. David's speech shows that the spirit of Yahweh is on him (cf. 16:13). His weapon is an invocation. Yahweh will today defeat the Philistines through David.

17:48-54. Vss. 50 and 51 both state that David **killed** the giant, the former by the **stone,** the latter by decapitation. They need not be conflicting, since vs. 51 simply supplies fuller details to the general summary of vs. 50. On **Gath** and **Ekron** see above 5:6-12. **Shaaraim** is unidentified. Vs. 54 remains a mystery; **Jerusalem** was still a Jebusite city and David could hardly have brought the grisly trophy there. Mention of David's **tent** conflicts with vss. 12-31, but may be original. The Philistine's armor was later removed to the sanctuary at Nob (cf. 21:8-9).

17:55–18:5. *Postscript to the Story.* Saul again does not recognize David—in spite of vs. 31! The story is another version of David's introduction to the court, not as a musician (16:14-23) but as a military hero. Saul's son **Jonathan** becomes attached to David and makes a **covenant** of friendship with him, giving him clothing and **armor** as a seal on their friendship. Such a covenant was often made among Semites for mutual protection; it was intended as a covenant of clan adoption, as is evident from the one-sided gift of the wealthy prince to David. The verbal phrase **was successful** in vs. 5 really means "acted wisely." Accordingly Saul gives him a military captaincy—which seems to please everyone.

B. Rivalry Between Saul and David (18:6–28:2)

18:6-16. *Saul's Jealousy.* The RSV rightly paragraphs this section as 3 stories. Throughout the narrative the tragic figure of the king whom Yahweh has abandoned is contrasted with the rising star of David whom Yahweh prospers. In the first story the impulse to jealousy is aroused by the chanting of **women** giving greater honor to David than to Saul. **Timbrels,** or tambourines, were commonly used by women to accompany dancing, as were the three-stringed lutes (better than **instruments of music,** vs. 6). The LXX has the women meeting David instead of **King Saul,** which makes better sense. Possibly the original reading had both.

18:10-11. The 2nd scene is out of context since David is now pictured as a musician rather than as a warrior, but an editor felt rightly that the tradition fitted the mood of Saul and David's relations. Vs. 10 shows Saul's mental instability in an interesting way. When an evil spirit attacks him he acts like a prophet, i.e. **he raved,** a reference to the ecstatic frenzy of prophetic bands (cf. 19:23-24).

18:12-16. The last scene shows the king trying to solve his problem by getting rid of it. Saul sends David out as an army officer—at least he would not see the object of hatred any more—but this too boomerangs. By being in the public eye David is fast becoming a popular idol. Small wonder that Saul is awestricken!

18:17-30. *David's Marriage to a Princess.* This section is composed of 2 stories, originally separate. The first fits as sequel to 17:25. It shows Saul breaking his promise to give his daughter to anyone defeating the Philistine giant. Saul is pictured as promising David his **elder daughter Merab** as wife on condition that he remain a good soldier. The end of vs. 17 may not be original to the story and may have crept in on the basis of vs. 21*a* or 25*b*. Saul, however, gives her to someone else.

18:20-30. The 2nd story concerns **Michal,** the daughter who does become David's wife. Saul wants to take advantage of the situation to incite David to a dangerous mission, hoping that he may be killed. A **marriage present** was a kind of bride purchase given by the husband to the father-in-law. Saul is again frustrated in his attempt to get rid of David. Saul is really powerless against David because Yahweh is with him. David is now a most successful soldier as well as his **son-in-law.** Vs. 21*b* is editorial; the collector added this to harmonize the 2 stories.

19:1-7. *Jonathan's Mediation.* Saul now comes out in the open and gives general orders to **kill David.** Jonathan intercedes with Saul successfully, and so David continues in service at court. The passage seems to be another version of ch. 20, probably placed here by the collector of the David stories to show why David is still in the court. The story is also confused. If Jonathan spoke to Saul **in the field where you are,** why did he have to inform him of his success afterward? And if Saul was there, why must David be **brought** to Saul as though the latter were at court?

19:8-24. *Saul's Attempts on David's Life.* The first attempt (vss. 8-10) is a doublet version of 18:10-11. The story belongs here rather than in ch. 18.

19:11-17. The 2nd attempt follows hard on the first, according to the present arrangement. David flees to his home, apparently on the city wall, and Michal lowers him **through the window** outside the wall (cf. the story of Rahab, Josh. 2:15). To delay pursuit she puts **an image** in the **bed** to deceive the casual onlooker. Surprising is Michal's possession of an idol—if this is in fact the meaning of the term (lit. "teraphim"; see above on 15:22-23). When Michal's ruse is discovered, she evades her father's anger by a face-saving lie. David is now no longer safe and remains at large as an outlaw until Saul's death.

19:18-24. The 3rd attempt finds David in **Ramah** under Sam.'s protection. The story is clearly legendary. It seems to be a tale to give another explanation for the origin of the proverb in vs. 24 (cf. 10:10-12). The picture of Sam. as head of a band of ecstatics is quite at variance with the Sam. stories of chs. 7–12. Nor would one expect David to escape to the N but rather to Judah. Three times messengers come to capture David and remain to prophesy, and finally Saul himself suffers a similar fate. Vs. 24 gives a startling picture of the uncontrolled frenzy of the prophets. **Secu** and **Naioth** are unknown; possibly the latter is simply the name for the dwelling of the confraternity of prophets. The story probably came from the Ramah sanctuary and was eventually incorporated by the collector of the David stories.

20:1-42. *David and Jonathan.* The collector of these stories has connected the preceding story to this one by vs. 1*a,* but they do not follow chronologically. That Jonathan is unaware of his father's hostility toward David is hardly credible subsequent to the events of 19:1-7. It may, however, be subsequent to 19:9-10. Jonathan is astounded at his father's attitude and in accordance with his covenant of brotherhood (18:3-4) is willing to do anything for his friend. The following day will be a feast day—the **new moon** was, like the sabbath, a day of rest and of special religious significance. On the new moon David, as well as Abner and Jonathan will be expected to eat with Saul. If Saul inquires about David's absence, Jonathan is to present his excuse, viz. an annual family feast in Bethlehem. Saul's reaction will be definitive.

20:10-23. One problem occurs to David. Should Saul be angry and suspicious it will be impossible for the friends to meet. But Jonathan has a novel solution. They **go out into the field,** presumably somewhere near Gibeah. He suggests that 3 days hence David is to hide himself near a **stone heap** in the field (the phrase in vs. 19 **when the matter was in hand** lit. means "in the day of the affair," but the allusion is now lost). Jonathan will give the bad news by means of a code, and David can escape without endangering his friend.

20:14-17. Jonathan's instructions have been rendered considerably more difficult by a later editor's insertion of these vss., intended to explain David's later care for Mephibosheth (II 9:6-7; 21:7). Jonathan makes David **swear** that when he becomes king he will remain **loyal** to their covenant of brotherhood. That such a promise was not superfluous is clear from the common Near Eastern custom of a new royal house exterminating all members of the superseded house.

20:24-34. The arrangements are carried out without a hitch. On the first day Saul attributes David's absence to some ritual uncleanness, but the following day he inquires concerning him. The agreed excuse sends Saul into a rage, and he vilifies Jonathan. The real cause for his hatred slips out. He suspects that David will be the next king. When Jonathan tries to defend him, Saul throws **his spear** at Jonathan, who escapes.

20:35-42. The following morning Jonathan enacts his little scene with an unsuspecting partner in the hearing of David. Unnecessary to the story are vss. 40-42a. If the friends could meet and speak, the shooting-arrows episode would be horseplay. This probably represents another version of the parting. David is now an outcast.

21:1-9. David at Nob. This story is a fitting sequel to 19:11-17. It contrasts with 19:18-24, where he seeks refuge with the prophets; here it is with the priest. **Nob** was near Jerusalem, possibly on Mt. Scopus, in any event between Anathoth and Jerusalem (cf. Isa. 10:32). The priest there is **Ahimelech,** probably the same as Ahijah, of Elid descent and formerly at Shiloh (see above on 14:2-3). David, unarmed and **alone,** presents a startling sight to the priest, of whom he demands food under guise of being on a secret and hurried mission for the king. **Holy bread,** which could only be eaten by those ritually clean, is provided on David's assurance that he (and his fictitious **young men**) have been sexually continent and thus are clean. **Bread of the Presence** according to the late P legislation was renewed weekly and was reserved for the priests (Lev. 24:5-9), but here there is no such reservation. David is given the weapon of the Philistine champion he killed (see above on 17:1-11). Present on this occasion is a certain **Doeg the Edomite,** of whom the next ch. relates dastardly action.

21:10-15. David's Flight to Gath. This is another version of ch. 27 and belongs at that point. It does not fit here. David has just received the **sword** of the

Philistine champion and would hardly go to Gath with it. He is also called **king of the land,** which must be the reflection of a later situation—unless it is the Philistines' application of the song recalled in vs. 11b. Possibly the tale is here retold in order to make certain that any possible idea of friendship with **Achish** is refuted.

22:1-5. David's Brigand Band. David now flees to **Adullam,** possibly a town 10 miles SW of Bethlehem, near the border between Judah and Philistine territory (see color map 5). According to vs. 5 it is in Philistine hands. Here his relatives as well as a large number of malcontents and oppressed come to his support. David thus becomes the leader of a band of outlaws. His relatives naturally join him for fear of royal reprisal. Adullam is called a **cave** (vs. 1), probably because of the many caves in that area, but in vss. 4-5 more appropriately a **stronghold.** Eventually a prophetic word orders him back to danger in **Judah.** This is intended to show that he must remain under Yahweh's protection rather than seek refuge in an alien land. The **forest of Hereth** is unknown but must have been in the SW part of Judah, NW of Hebron.

22:3-4a. Inserted into this account is the strange reference to David's entrusting his parents to the care of the **king of Moab.** On the close relations of Bethlehem and Moab see Intro. to Ruth. On the other hand David's severe treatment of the Moabites in II 8:2 makes this story questionable. **Mizpeh of Moab** is unknown.

22:6-19. Saul's Revenge on the Priests of Nob. This is the sequel to 21:1-9, with vs. 6 written by the collector as a connecting link but anticipating vs. 9. Saul as king sits in the place of judgment, with the **spear** as symbol of royalty **in his hand,** and harangues his fellow tribesmen standing about.

22:9-19. In response **Doeg the Edomite** now informs on the priests of Nob (cf. 21:7). So Ahimelech and his fellow priests are summoned and accused of abetting the enemy. Ahimelech, who apparently knew nothing of the vendetta between Saul and David, stoutly affirms his good faith. The irrational Saul immediately condemns them all to death and commands his **guard** to carry out the sentence. They refuse, but Doeg is quite willing and wipes out the entire priestly contingent and sacks their **city.** Saul is not only abandoned by Yahweh; he now uses holy war tactics against Yahweh's priests.

22:20-23. A Priest's Escape. Only one, **Abiathar,** son of Ahimelech, escapes the slaughter. He joins David's forces. From now on Abiathar becomes David's close friend, personal priest, and confidant.

23:1-13. David at Keilah. Keilah was ca. 9 miles NW of Hebron and just a little S of Adullam (22:1-2; see color map 5). David is here portrayed in his later role of deliverer of Israel. The Philistines have come with transport to raid the people of Keilah and take their harvest.

23:2-5. David twice inquires by the ephod (cf. vs. 6; see above on 14:2-3) and Yahweh commands him to deliver Keilah. His men are dubious but David persists and is victorious. The Philistines are defeated, **their cattle** (for transport of spoils) are taken, and the city is delivered.

23:6. According to this vs. it is here at Keilah that Abiathar joins David (cf. 22:20-23) but in view of vss. 2, 4 it seems more likely to have been prior to this. In any event the **ephod,** the means for inquiring an answer from Yahweh, is now no longer with Saul but with David.

23:7-13. Meanwhile Saul has heard of David's stay in Keilah and is determined to attack the city in order to capture him. David asks 2 questions of Yahweh by means of the ephod and discovers that Saul is intent on coming to Keilah and that its inhabitants will give him up rather than defend him. By now the number of his band has swelled to **six hundred.** From now on David is to stay out of walled towns and remain in **wilderness** areas. There David as a native has the advantage over Saul.

23:14-29. Saul's Pursuit of David. The **Wilderness of Ziph** is the rugged area E and SE of Hebron around Ziph, ca. 5 miles SE of Hebron (see color map 5). The emphasis in the story is on God's care for David so that Saul is frustrated throughout. **Horesh** was less than 2 miles S of Ziph. The visit of **Jonathan,** though historically difficult, shows the increasing certainty of future events. David's succession to the throne is openly acknowledged (cf. 20:14-16) and Jonathan will then take 2nd place.

23:19-24a. The citizens of Ziph betray David's presence to Saul. The **hill of Hachilah** and **Jeshimon** are not identified but must have been S of Hebron, i.e. near Ziph. **Thousands** (vs. 23) has the meaning of "clans." A more detailed doublet account of Saul's pursuit of David in the Wilderness of Ziph is found in ch. 26.

23:24b-29. David meanwhile has gone somewhat further S to the area around **Maon** 3 miles S of Horesh (see color map 5). Reference to the **Arabah** (the great depression from the Sea of Galilee to the Gulf of Aqaba) is out of order here; the event takes place in **mountain** territory. Saul is on the point of capturing David when he is recalled by news of a Philistine **raid.** After this hairbreadth escape David seeks refuge in the area around **Engedi,** the wild mountain area overlooking the Dead Sea, which lies in the desolate region ca. 20 miles S of Qumran (see color map 5).

24:1-22. Saul's Life Spared. David and his men are in a large **cave** when Saul comes in alone unaware of danger. David's men are jubilant. They quote an oracle (vs. 4), not attested elsewhere, predicting David's victory over his enemy; but he refuses to do Saul harm because he is Yahweh's **anointed.** Instead he removes a piece of Saul's outer garment as evidence that the king has been in his power. Vss. 4d-5 should be understood as occurring between vs. 7a and b. Saul remains completely unaware of what has happened until later when David calls out after him and makes a speech of defense.

24:16-22. Saul settles the issue by admitting his own guilt and blessing David for his good action. The statement of Jonathan in 23:17 is confirmed (vs. 20). David promises that contrary to common Near Eastern custom, he will not kill off the members of his predecessor's family (vss. 21-22). Then they go their separate ways. The point of the narrative is not merely to exalt David's fine character and show his respect for God's anointed, but to bring out with increasing clarity the inevitableness of the establishment of the Davidic dynasty. For a more detailed doublet cf. ch. 26.

25:1-44. David and Abigail. Vs. 1a gives an obituary notice of Sam. which seems out of place here and may have crept in from 28:3.

25:2-4. The **wilderness of Paran** seems to be a general designation for the desert area W of Edom, S of Judah, and extending down to Aqaba; it may be an error here. In any event David is once again S of Hebron near Maon (see above on 23:24b-29). A wealthy shepherd, **Nabal** (meaning "fool"), is engaged in sheepshearing at **Carmel,** ca. 1 mile NW of his home in Maon. The Calebites were a small clan around Hebron, a subclan within Judah (cf. Josh. 14:13-14). Sheepshearing was occasion for a **feast day,** and the owner would be expected to provide liberally for the servants and guests. Now Nabal the dolt has a **wife** wise and **beautiful;** it is she who is the heroine, with David the hero, and Nabal the villain, of the story.

25:5-13. David sends **ten young men** to ask for a gift, a brigand's payment for protection. Nabal not only refuses payment but returns an insulting reply: David and his men are but renegade slaves, men of no account; why should he give them anything? **Water** (vs. 11) probably should read "wine" as in the LXX. David in true oriental fashion gives orders to prepare to wipe out the insult. Two 3rds of his band are mustered for attack, the rest remaining to guard the baggage.

25:14-17. Meanwhile Nabal's servants inform **Abigail** of her husband's foolhardy retort to David's men, insisting that David's band deserves better treatment, having protected them against danger.

25:18-31. The next scene shows Abigail with a large present (cf. Gen. 32:13-21) hurrying to intercept the hot-blooded David, without of course informing her churlish spouse. Meanwhile David has sworn an oath that he will wipe out the insult by blood. Suddenly the 2 meet and Abigail intercedes for Nabal, asking David not to take revenge. Nabal is a fool indeed; she will bear his **guilt.** Accordingly she has brought a small gift; let David be generous. She is the instrument in Yahweh's hands to keep him from incurring **bloodguilt,** which would be a stain on his record when he eventually becomes king. With perfect charm she ends her plea by asking for favor when Yahweh has prospered him, a harbinger of the romantic outcome of the story!

25:32-35. David can hardly resist the winsome charms of the heroine and blesses her for her intercession, informing her of the intention he had had of wiping out every male of Nabal's household before morning.

25:36-42. The denouement comes quickly. On Abigail's return Nabal is completely **drunk.** The next **morning** when he is sober Abigail gives him the full story. The shock apparently brings on a stroke, and a 2nd stroke **ten days later** removes him. David sees Nabal's death as Yahweh's intervention through the good Abigail, who has kept him from bloodguilt. David thereupon woos and wins the widow.

25:43-44. David is becoming a man of parts in the area, also taking **Ahinoam** as wife. **Jezreel** is not to be confused with the famous N city; it lay in the vicinity of Ziph. Meanwhile Saul has given **Michal,** David's first wife, to someone else. **Gallim** was a small town N of Jerusalem, ca. 1 mile E of Gibeah.

26:1-25. Saul's Life Spared Again. This is another version of 23:19-24:22 (see comment). As in 23:19-

167

20 the Ziphites are the informers. In this version Saul and his men are encamped, and David and his nephew **Abishai** (whose mother, **Zeruiah**, was David's sister, I Chr. 2:16) sneak **into the camp . . . by night,** into the tent of Saul. There lies the **sleeping** king with the upright lance beside him as symbol of the presence of the king. As in 24:6 David will not harm Yahweh's **anointed** one. So they simply take the **spear** and a **water** jug from the tent and creep away unnoticed.

26:13-16. Once David is at a safe distance he shouts to **Abner,** taunting him with his failure to guard the king; the spear and the water jug are gone!

26:17-20. Meanwhile Saul has **recognized David's voice,** and David reproaches Saul for his pursuit of the innocent. The argument is somewhat different from that in 24:9-15. Who has incensed Saul to pursue David? If it is Yahweh, may he be placated by an **offering?** That God could stir men up to sin is often said in the OT (e.g. II 24:1; I Kings 22:17-23). But **if it is men,** then may they be effectively **cursed** in Yahweh's name. That such men are driving David out of Yahweh's land (an anticipation of the next ch.) means he cannot share in Yahweh's heritage; only in Yahweh's land can he take part in the blessing of Yahwism. Popular belief had it that a god was closely allied to his land; in fact exile meant to **serve other gods,** because other lands meant other gods.

26:21-25. Saul's response, like that in 24:17-21, admits his guilt and David's innocence, but is shorter. They then go their separate ways, never to meet again.

27:1–28:2. David's Service to the Philistines. This passage shows no awareness of a prior visit of David to Achish (see above on 21:10-15). Aware that life in Judah is becoming increasingly dangerous for him, David goes to Philistine territory and offers his services to Achish, **king of Gath.** This is a daring step since it may weaken his cause in Israel to join the traditional enemy's side and be absent from the land (see above on 22:1-5). David attempts the tightrope course of using his stay to persuade both Philistines and Judeans that he is loyal to their respective causes. He lays the basis for the deception of his host by making numerous raids on Bedouin tribes, killing everyone—dead men tell no tales—then bringing back booty and reporting raids against Judeans. So successful is this deceit that Achish not only wants to appoint David as his personal **bodyguard,** even in battle **against Israel,** but also gives David the town of **Ziklag,** a border town *ca.* 12 miles N of Beer-sheba, as a reward for and token of his loyalty to the Philistines. Vss. 5-7 are chronologically out of order and should be understood as following vs. 12.

David is now free of Saul's persecution, and on foreign soil he is able to consolidate his position. His raids against the neighboring Bedouin tribes bring in wealth for both himself and Achish, and also relieve his relatives by marriage. The **Negeb** (vs. 10; cf. 30:14) refers simply to the dry steppe land extending from Beer-sheba over to the desert. Unfortunately David is overly successful in convincing Achish of his loyalty (28:1-2). What would have happened had David been put to the test is not known (see below on 29:1-11).

C. The Final Battle of Saul (I 28:3–II 1:27)

28:3-25. The Witch of Endor. This story, which concerns only Saul and is a fitting sequel to ch. 15, is not really a part of the David stories; but chronologically it does belong within their framework. Properly it should come between chs. 30; 31. Chs. 29–30 continue the narrative of ch. 27. The advance of the Philistines also becomes reasonable if ch. 28 follows ch. 30. They are at Aphek in 29:1, go up to Jezreel in 29:11, and now encamp at **Shunem** (vs. 4). For a parallel tale in which a departed spirit reappears to a former acquaintance see the translation of an ancient Sumerian story in Gilgamesh XII, 84. There the spirit of Enkidu appears to Gilgamesh.

28:3. The notice of Sam.'s death belongs here as a setting for the story rather than in 25:1. Also preparatory to the story is the fact that Saul has earlier banished necromancy as an illegal and superstitious means of determining the future (cf. vs. 9; Deut. 18: 10-11).

28:4-6. But the situation is now critical. The armies are drawn up in battle array, the **Philistines** at **Shunem** overlooking the Jezreel valley on the SW slope of Nebi Dahi, and the Israelites on Mt. **Gilboa** (see color map 5) at the E end of the valley. The fear-ridden and divinely abandoned king naturally wishes an oracle before proceeding to battle the next morning, but none of the legal means—**dreams,** the **Urim** (see above on 14:36-46), and **prophets**—give him an answer. Yahweh has now completely abandoned him.

28:7-14. So Saul seeks out a female necromancer at **Endor,** on the N slope of Nebi Dahi, thus only a short distance away. Israel believed that man could have communication with the dead through mediums, though such communication was illegitimate. The disguised king is not recognized by the **medium** until he requests her to bring up the shade of Sam. The narrator undoubtedly believed in the reality of the scene, but note that Saul never sees the spirit. The medium states that she sees the ghostlike figure (a **god,** lit. "gods") of an **old man . . . wrapped in a robe.** Saul recognizes Sam. from her description.

28:15-19. Now the medium is no longer necessary. Saul's distress is reiterated; he can get no divine instructions. Sam. also refuses to give advice; **tomorrow you and your sons** will die and Israel will be defeated. An editor expanded the original statement of Sam. by adding vss. 17-19a, thus tying it in with ch. 15.

28:20-25. Saul is now without any hope. He returns to camp, a doomed man wrapped in despair.

29:1-11. David's Dilemma Resolved. This section is the sequel to 28:1-2. On **Aphek** see above on 4:1b-11. The **fountain . . . in Jezreel** ("spring of Harod," Judg. 7:1) was probably at the foot of Mt. Gilboa. As the Philistine **lords** (see above on 5:6-12) pass their troops in review, David and his men also pass by. The commanders recall his military prowess against the Philistines in former days and are naturally suspicious of his turncoat loyalties (on **Hebrews** see above on 13:2-4). Achish defends David on the double ground that he is a Judean rebel and has proved his loyalty for the past 2 years (LXX, better than **days and years,** vs. 3). The **commanders** overrule Achish, who advises David of his dismissal, assuring him of his own faith in his loyalty with an oath formula in the name of Yahweh, David's God. David protests this questioning of his devotion (doubtless with tongue in cheek), but Achish insists that he and his men leave the ranks before **morning.** The LXX amplifies vs. 10 as an order to "go to the place where I stationed you and do not devise some evil plan in your heart because you are a good man in my opinion, and go directly."

30:1-6a. *An Amalekite Raid on Ziklag.* On their return to Ziklag David and his men find it completely despoiled and all the women and children, including David's two wives (cf. 25:39-43), **taken captive** by raiding Amalekites. The raid was probably retaliatory (cf. 27:8-12). Each bewails his loss, and then in anger the men turn on their leader David, a natural reaction. He had left no males to guard the town.

30:6b-20. *David's Rescue of the Captives.* David, however, turns to the oracle for guidance. At his request **Abiathar,** his priest-friend (cf. 22:20-23), consults the **ephod.** Yahweh answers David (in contrast to Saul, 28:6) affirmatively.

30:9-10. David immediately sets out with his band of 600 men in spite of the exhausting march from Aphek to Ziklag (*ca.* 80 miles) in less than 3 days which they have just finished. When they arrive at the **brook Besor,** a 3rd (i.e. 200 men) are **too exhausted** to make the crossing, and they are left with the baggage (vs. 24). David continues with the remaining 400.

30:11-15. Fortunately they find an **Egyptian** slave abandoned by the Amalekites. Abandonment in the desert meant inevitable death through starvation and thirst. Their kindness to him is amply repaid, since he not only informs them of the extent of the raids but also serves as a desert guide to lead them to the Amalekite encampment. On **Negeb** see above on 27:8-12. The Negeb of the **Cherethites** was at the S end of Philistine territory, that of **Caleb** S of Hebron (cf. 25:1b-3).

30:16-20. They come on the Amalekites engaged in a great feast, probably a religious celebration because of their successful raids. It is not exactly clear when the attackers arrive. Vs. 17 probably should read "from dawn" rather than **from twilight.** The point is that on the following day (they wait until dawn) they attack and the slaughter lasts until sunset. The **four hundred** cameleers escape; all the rest are killed. The captives are rescued and the spoil is taken. Vs. 20 is not entirely clear; the intent seems to be to show that David took not only the spoil from Ziklag but also all that had been taken on their other raids (cf. vs. 14). Vss. 26-31 seem to suggest this as well. This spoil was considered to be the possession of the chieftain, who had absolute control over its division.

30:21-31. *The Division of the Spoil.* On the return journey the victors join with the 200 who stayed with the **baggage.** When it comes to the division of the booty, some men selfishly want the 200 to have no share. David decrees that all shall share alike, quartermasters as well as warriors. This generous decision becomes binding precedent for later Israelite practice (cf. e.g. Num. 31:25-47).

30:26-31. On arrival in Ziklag David repairs his political fences in S Judah by sharing the **spoil** with leaders in the various places in the Negeb where he has been, symbolizing thereby his identification with their situation. David has become the effective defender of the area. Not all the places mentioned in vss. 26-31 have been identified, but all are in the same general area. **Racal** (vs. 29) should probably be changed to "Carmel" as in the LXX.

31:1-13. *The Death of Saul.* This account is the sequel to ch. 28 (see comment). Battle between the two armies is joined and Israel is defeated. Three of Saul's 4 **sons** are killed—Ishbaal is not present at the battle apparently (see above on 14:49-52)—and Saul himself is hard pressed, **wounded,** and in despair. When his aide refuses to kill him he commits suicide, a rare occurrence among Israelites. Initial Philistine success results in panic even across the Jordan. **Cities** and towns are abandoned by their inhabitants and occupied by the invading Philistines. Saul, in spite of his many shortcomings, had been the hope of Israel and his death precipitated political chaos. Occupation E of the Jordan, however, must have been minimal; e.g. **Jabesh-gilead** (see above 11:1-11) remained free. The parallel account in I Chr. 10 omits reference to **those beyond the Jordan,** but this is not so to be trusted.

31:8-13. The following morning the victors return to the battlefield to despoil the **slain** and find the royal corpses, which they strip of **armor.** Saul is decapitated (cf. 17:51) and his armor is displayed in the **temple** of Astarte (for **Ashtaroth,** vs. 10), probably in **Beth-shan,** a strong Canaanite city at the E end of the Valley of Jezreel (see Beth-shan on color map 5). Astarte was the Canaanite fertility goddess, consort of Baal. Saul began his reign with the rescue of Jabesh-gilead (11:1-11); now it ends with the men of Jabesh as an act of piety taking his defiled corpse and those of his sons to Jabesh and interring them after cremation, an uncommon practice in Israel. It has been plausibly suggested that the Hebrew word for **burnt** (vs. 12) actually means "anointed"; this would remove the difficulty. They then mourn for the dead Saul by fasting for a week.

THE SECOND BOOK OF SAMUEL

John William Wevers

For introduction see Intro. to I Sam. The outline of the contents indicated by the headings continues that in I Sam.

1:1-16. *News of Saul's Death.* This account is a sequel to I 30. An **Amalekite** messenger comes to David at **Ziklag** with signs of mourning to notify him that **Saul** and **Jonathan** are dead. His account conflicts with that of the preceding ch.; he is trying to gain favor by pretending to be responsible for Saul's death. Vs. 9 is not clear. The word translated **anguish** may mean "giddiness" or possibly "fainting." The Amalekite must actually have been on the battlefield at Gilboa, since he robbed Saul's body of **crown** and **armlet** and brought them to David.

1:11-16. The double reaction of David to this news (vss. 11-12, 13-16) has led many to think that 2 traditions are here intertwined. This theory is unnecessary if vss. 11-12 are understood to follow vs. 16. David's immediate reaction (vss. 13-16) is anger against the Amalekite for daring to lay hands on Yahweh's **anointed.** The surprised Amalekite is killed forthwith at David's order (cf. 4:10). The Amalekite is a **sojourner,** i.e. a non-Israelite who lived in Israel. By his violent death the curse of Saul's death was wiped out. The 2nd reaction (vss. 11-12) is one of mourning for Saul, Jonathan, and the defeated Israelites—a mourning imposed on the entire camp for the day.

1:17-27. *A Dirge over the Fallen Heroes.* David's poetic genius is here beautifully shown. The **lamentation** was preserved in the **Book of Jashar** (see comment on I Kings 8:12-13). The poem is completely secular and is unquestionably from David's hand. It is full of difficulties and the RSV rendering is much clearer than the original. The Hebrew of vs. 18*a* has "and he said that the people of Judah should be taught the bow," which makes no sense. Possibly the word for "bow" is a corruption for some word meaning a "dirge" or "poem."

1:19-21. David first bewails the defeat of the Israelites in battle. Israel's **glory** refers to its leaders, the **mighty.** Then he curses the place of battle (vs. 21) as the place where the heroes were slain. There Saul's **shield** lies in the sun, its leather drying out for lack of **oil.** For **upsurging of the deep** the Hebrew has "fields of offering," which probably should be retained as a reference to productivity of the fields.

1:22-27. Here begins the actual dirge over Saul and Jonathan. They have been mighty warriors and now are together **in death.** The women normally led mourning as well as festal rites, and their grief is

esp. evoked since they have received costly booty from Saul's campaigns. But to David the loss of **Jonathan** is personal. With him he has had a covenant of brotherhood (cf. I 18:3-4; 20:42; 23:18), and the bond of love between them is now broken. **Weapons of war** (vs. 27) refers to Saul and Jonathan.

D. David's Ascent to the Throne (2:1–5:5)

2:1-7. *David's Anointing as King of Judah.* With divine approval (cf. I 30:7-8) David can return to **Judah** now that Saul is dead. He is appropriately

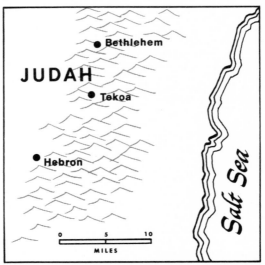

directed to **Hebron** (see color map 6) since it lies more or less central to the area where he has roamed and has in-laws. He is there **anointed** by Judean representatives as king. Apparently the Philistines felt that David would really extend their control over Judah. Later their eyes were opened to David's real loyalties when he became king over the united tribes (5:17-25). The action described in I 30:26-31 immediately paid off.

2:4b-7. David begins strengthening his position immediately. The **loyalty** of the citizens of **Jabesh-gilead** (cf. I 31:11-13) to Saul's memory might create eventual friction to his successor. David promises them his protection, a fairly clear statement of his ambitions. Protection of Jabesh from Hebron would be a meaningless promise!

170

2:8-11. *Saul's Son as King in the N.* A surviving son of Saul is **Ishbosheth.** His actual name was Ishbaal (Eshbaal in I Chr. 8:33; 9:39), meaning "man of baal"—in his time apparently used as a title ("master" or "lord") of Yahweh. Later editors replaced "baal" with "bosheth," meaning "shame," or in I 14:49 probably with "iah," meaning "Yahweh" (see comment on I 14:47-52). **Abner** now sets up Ishbaal as puppet king over the N tribes, but so insecure is his position that he has to rule from **Mahanaim** in **Gilead** in Transjordan; its location is not known. **Ashurites** probably means the tribe of Asher. **Jezreel** may be a general term for some of the N tribes. Ishbaal's rule over these tribes, **Ephraim,** and **Benjamin** was certainly more nominal than real. The Philistines still occupied the land W of the Jordan. Vss. 10-11 contain 2 difficulties. Ishbaal was certainly younger than **forty years** and, like his father, Saul, reigned more than **two years** (cf. I 13:1). He must have reigned *ca.* 7 years. Ishbaal probably was too young to fight with Saul at Gilboa and was still a minor when Abner made him king.

2:12-3:1. *The Battle of Gibeon.* Gibeon was 6 miles NW of Jerusalem (see color map 6). Here Abner's forces meet the Judean forces under **Joab,** son of David's sister **Zeruiah** (cf. I Chr. 2:16), at the **pool,** a huge water cistern. Joab is already in a commanding position, a position he is to retain throughout his uncle's reign. The 2 leaders agree to a jousting tournament, **twelve** to a side, as a form of sport. When this leads to fatal consequences (just how all 24 could kill each other is not clear), battle is joined in which

Abner's forces are beaten. The meaning of the place name commemorating the tournament is not certain (see RSV footnote).

2:18-28. Joab's younger brother, **Asahel,** a runner, is determined on military honors and tries to catch **Abner.** The seasoned warrior warns the youth, knowing that his death will evoke an undying blood feud with his brothers. When Asahel nevertheless tries to take on Abner he is killed. The 2 remaining brothers, **Joab and Abishai,** take up the pursuit until sunset, when Abner is able to reassemble his forces on some defensible **hill.** Neither **Ammah** nor **Giah** has been identified, nor does the **wilderness of Gibeon**—after all the flight started at Gibeon—make good sense. Possibly Geba should be read for Gibeon here; it lay 5 miles E on the way toward the Jordan. Abner appeals to Joab to put an end to the blood feud and Joab agrees to the truce.

2:29-3:1. Both sides then return to their respective capitals. Abner's men are called Benjaminites, probably because most of Saul's support came from fellow tribesmen (cf. I 9:1). The concluding statement shows that David is obviously going to win the struggle.

3:2-5. *David's Sons.* This is the first list of David's offspring (cf. the supplement in 5:13-16). Six wives are listed (on the first 2 see comment on I 25:36-44), each with her first-born son. Oddly, one, **Eglah,** is specifically called **David's wife.** Only 3 of the 6 occur in later stories. **Chileab** is called Daluia in the LXX and Daniel in I Chr. 3:1.

3:6-11. *Abner's Quarrel with Ishbaal.* When a king

Courtesy of James B. Pritchard, University Museum, University of Pennsylvania

The Pool at Gibeon; worker at top of picture is ascending the seventy-nine rock-cut steps; bottom of pool is thirty-three feet down

died his harem became the possession of the new king. Abner, the strong man of the N kingdom, has taken one of Saul's concubines, **Rizpah** (cf. 21:8-14), for himself; and Ishbaal (see above on 2:8-11) upbraids him for it. Abner then loses his temper and swears an oath to throw his support from Saul's to David's house. Abner is aware, as were Jonathan, Saul, and Abigail, that Yahweh intends David to rule over united Israel (cf. I 20:13-16; 24:20-21; 25:30-31).

3:12-21. Abner's Attempt to Fulfill His Oath. Vss. 12-16 fit badly into the context. Abner immediately makes representation to David for some agreement by which he will make David king over united Israel. David, however, demands the return of **Michal,** his **wife,** whom Saul gave to another (cf. I 25:44), as a precondition to negotiation. But then David makes the demand of Ishbaal, who accedes, and Abner is also involved in the removal of Michal from her 2nd husband. Possibly these vss. are a later insertion intended to render David's political action legitimate; as son-in-law of Saul he was a legitimate successor, and this needed establishment before he proceeded with negotiations. Abner meanwhile has a number of conferences with Israelite leaders, including the recalcitrant Benjaminites, urging them to transfer their loyalties to David. With their agreement in hand he goes to Hebron, where he is festively received by David. Doubtless Abner expects something in return, but about this nothing is said.

3:22-30. Joab's Slaying of Abner. Joab has been absent when David received Abner, possibly by David's careful arrangement. In any event on his return from some successful raiding party he discovers what has happened and expostulates with David over the foolishness of letting Abner depart peaceably. Unknown to David, Joab sends men to overtake Abner at the well of **Sirah,** 1½ miles to the NW, and bring him back to Hebron. Pretending to speak with him privately, Joab treacherously stabs Abner in the **belly.** So Abner had fatally wounded Joab's brother Asahel (cf. 2:23). The narrator insists that the murder is purely a brother's **blood** revenge for the killing of Asahel and not instigated by David. In fact David avoids the bloodguilt resulting from Abner's slaying by insisting that he himself is **guiltless** and calling an eternal curse on Joab's **house.** The involvement of **Abishai** (vs. 30) seems secondary to the story, an editorial insistence that the deed is the result of a blood feud.

3:31-39. Abner Mourned and Buried. David completely dissociates himself from Joab's deed by ordering national mourning rites for the fallen leader. David effectively convinces the people of his own innocence in various ways: by taking part in the funeral procession, by composing a dirge, and by fasting. The short dirge (vss. 33-34) emphasizes the tragedy of Abner's death. A **fool** brings about his own death by folly; Abner did not die as a prisoner or in warfare but was killed by guile. David again absolves himself (vs. 39) from complicity in the guilt of his nephew. Since it was a blood feud he can hardly kill Joab, as was his normal practice (cf. 1:15; 4:12); he contents himself with a general curse on the **evildoer.** David realizes that this may well cause civil war and that his dream of ruling over united Israel has received a severe setback. His prompt action, however, averts further trouble.

4:1-12. The Murder of Ishbaal. The death of Abner precipitates a crisis in N Israel. He has been the power behind the throne, and **all Israel** knows it. Ishbaal (see above on 2:8-11) is shortly thereafter murdered during the **noonday rest** by 2 of his officers, who take his **head** to David in expectation of reward. David, however, immediately has the 2 murderers **killed** and their bodies publicly displayed, thereby dissociating himself from the action.

4:2-3. The story has been amplified by a note explaining how Beeroth could be Benjaminite. According to Josh. 9:17 Beeroth was one of the 4 cities of the Gibeonite confederacy. It was probably *ca.* 9 miles N of Jerusalem (see color map 6), though this location has been challenged. Why the citizens should have fled to **Gittaim** (location unknown) is not clear; possibly David later took further revenge on the Beerothites for Ishbaal's murder, thereby causing their flight.

4:4. This vs. is out of context here. It belongs to ch. 9, probably after 9:3. It refers to **Mephibosheth,** the son of Jonathan, and the reason for his lameness. His real name was Meribaal (cf. I Chr. 8:34; 9:40). As in Ishbaal, "baal" was changed to "bosheth" (see above on 2:8-11); "Mephi" is a scribal error for an original "Meri."

4:6. The text here is uncertain. The RSV follows the LXX rather than the Hebrew which does not make good sense.

5:1-5. David's Anointing as King of Israel. Vss. 1-2 relate how after Ishbaal's death the **tribes** gather to David at his S capital to plead his kingship on the basis of blood relationship, his past military leadership, and the divine prediction of his rule (cf. 3:9-10, 18). Vs. 3 then specifies the actual kingmaking. The **elders** gather, agree to a **covenant,** and anoint David king over united **Israel.** The account is merely a summary of what was probably an involved negotiation and ceremony. Vss. 4-5 are probably from the D editor (cf. the chronological notices in I, II Kings; see Intro. to I Kings). David's dreams are now fulfilled; God has made him king.

VI. EARLY SUCCESS AS KING OF ISRAEL (5:6–8:18)

A. MILITARY VICTORIES (5:6-25)

5:6-12. The Capture of Jerusalem. Obviously David could hardly rule from Hebron over the N tribes. Nor could he deny his own Judean kinsmen by moving his capital to the N. What he needed was neutral ground on the border between Judah and Benjamin. No better place could be found than **Jerusalem** (see color map 6). It was still in Canaanite (Jebusite) hands, and it was an easily defensible fortress. Jerusalem was an ancient city, mentioned in Egyptian texts of the 19th cent.; it is called Salem in Gen. 14:18. That Jerusalem was considered impregnable is clear from the taunting words of the inhabitants.

5:8. This vs. would seem to be some explanation of the method of taking Jerusalem, but the text is full of difficulties. The original text has David saying: "Whoever would smite the Jebusite let him touch the lame and the blind, whom David's soul hates, in the water shaft." This makes no sense. The parallel passage in I Chr. 11:6 has a simpler version, omitting all reference to water shafts and the lame and the blind. If by **water shaft** the text intends an ancient tunnel known as Warren's Shaft (as is commonly

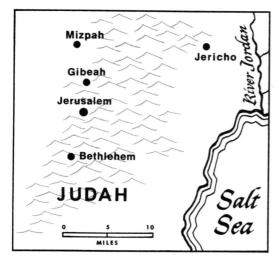

suggested) to be understood as the path of the Judean entrance to the city, the feat was a tremendous undertaking. How the saying of David could explain the proverbial saying of vs. 8*b* is also a mystery. Undoubtedly the text is corrupt.

5:9-10. On the **Millo** see comment on I Kings 9: 15-23. **Zion** became the sacral name, whereas Jerusalem was the political name, but popularly it could be called the **city of David.**

5:11-12. The Phoenician **Hiram** (cf. I Kings 5:1) sends workmen and lumber to David to build a palace. David's reputation against the Philistines would be the basis for his gaining international respect, and so Hiram's actions are more natural after vss. 17-25.

5:13-16. *Postscript.* This note is certainly out of place, being a sequel to the list of David's sons in 3:2-5. **Solomon** was certainly born later since he was the son of Bathsheba (cf. 12:24). The list is probably taken from some later court record and inserted here to show David's royal status. Kings had many consorts.

5:17-25. *Defeat of the Philistines.* Two stories of Philistine defeat are here told serially in vss. 17-21, 22-25, but it is likely that the events of vss. 6-10 intervened.

5:17-21. The **Philistines** did not mind David's ruling over Judah, but as king over all **Israel** he threatened their control over Palestine. David realized that Hebron was hardly defensible and accordingly **went down to the stronghold.** This cannot refer to Jerusalem, which was on a hill. The stronghold must have been that of Adullam (cf. I 22:1-5; II 23:13-14; see color map 6), a favorite place of David. The Philistines, however, go N to the plain of **Rephaim,** immediately SW of Jerusalem, probably with the intention of cutting the N tribes from Judah. David as usual consults the oracle—probably the ephod at the hand of Abiathar (cf. I 23:6)—which yields a positive response. David attacks and breaks through the Philistine army, thereby once and for all uniting the N and S tribes militarily. The place of breakthrough is memorialized by the name **Baal-perazim,** i.e. "the Lord of the breaking through." It was probably located *ca.* 2½ miles NW of Jerusalem.

5:22-25. The 2nd encounter—possibly after Jeru-

salem was in David's hands—is again in **Rephaim.** This time David receives divine instruction not to attack but to **go around to their rear.** Only when the divine sign is given is David to attack. The rendering **balsam trees** is uncertain; some kind of shrub is undoubtedly meant. David is again successful, and the Philistines are driven back to their borders. **Gezer** was on the edge of the coastal plain (see color map 6). **Geba** should probably be Gibeon, as the LXX reads.

B. Jerusalem as Religious Center (6:1-7:29)

6:1-11. *The First Move of the Ark.* This passage is the sequel to the taking of Jerusalem, since it shows how David strengthens his new capital by making it a religious capital as well. He means to unite even more firmly the N tribes to his rule by bringing their sacred palladium to Jerusalem. The account is full of obscurities.

6:1-2. The assemblage of **thirty thousand men** seems grossly exaggerated; nor is it clear why **chosen men,** i.e. warriors, should take part in the ceremony. The ark has been housed in Kiriath-jearim (see above on I 6:21-7:2), which according to I Chr. 13:6 was also called Baalah. Somehow this latter name must have fallen out of vs. 2 as the identification of the place to which **from there** refers. **Baale-judah** cannot be a variant form of Baalah, for Kiriath-jearim was not in Judah but in Benjamin. Rather the phrase should be translated "of the lords of Judah." On the cultic name of the ark see comment on I 4:4.

6:3-5. The name **Ahio** is strange and could simply be translated as "his brother." If this is correct, however, it is odd that the brother is unnamed. Apparently the bringing up of the ark was an important cultic ceremony, possibly connected with some feast. It seems probable that it gave the impetus for some later recurrent feast in which the bringing up of the ark became an important ritual (cf. e.g. Ps. 24). Music and the sacral dance were part of the ritual (cf. vs. 14; on the musical instruments see comment on Ps. 150:3-5).

6:6-11. The unfortunate incident which puts an abrupt end to the festivities is particularly obscure. All that is clear is that **Uzzah** dies suddenly next to the ark. Apparently he does something thought to incur divine displeasure. The RSV rendering of vss. 6-7 is based on the parallel text of I Chr. 13:9-10, which in turn was based on this passage. There is no word for **his hand** in either vs. The site of the tragedy is also unknown; in I Chr. it is called Chidon instead of **Nacon.** In any event David is too terrified to continue; and a nearby Philistine (**Gittite** means "man of Gath"), **Obed-edom** by name, is conscripted to care for the ark in his home.

6:12-19. *Bringing of the Ark to Jerusalem.* The presence of the ark apparently has no further bad results, and so David resolves on its transfer to the Jerusalem sanctuary, i.e. **the tent** (vs. 17). After the first **six paces** (not every 6 paces) a sacrifice is made by the king. God is apparently willing to let the ark proceed. David is clad, not in his royal robe, but in a **linen ephod** (cf. I 2:19), and performs some kind of whirling dance to the accompaniment of music and ritual shouting.

6:16-19. Vs. 16 has been put into the story here to

prepare for vss. 20-23. David has prepared a **tent** and altar for the ark. Once it is housed he offers sacrifices and pronounces the benediction over the people. The king here performs priestly functions, since in the early monarchy the king could act as priest (cf. 8:18*b*). To end the festive occasion the people receive a royal gift of food.

6:20-23. *Michal's Quarrel.* This episode has been combined with the ark story but belongs to the Succession Document of chs. 9-20; I Kings 1-2 (see Intro.). On David's return his wife **Michal,** Saul's daughter (cf. I 18:20-27), speaks sarcastically of his role in which he divested himself of his royal robe. David's reply is corrupt in the Hebrew and must be corrected from the LXX to read "Before Yahweh I am dancing. Blessed be Yahweh who chose me. . . ." David is not interested in his wife's opinion of him as long as he remains popular with the common people. The quarrel apparently led to complete estrangement between the 2; it is noted that there was no offspring from the union to perpetuate the house of Saul.

7:1-29. *God's Promise to David.* This story of Nathan's prophecy probably was placed here to follow the story of the ark's removal to Jerusalem in ch. 6. Its core belongs to the Succession Document of chs. 9-20; I Kings 1-2 (see Intro.), as does at least part of ch. 6, whereas the intervening ch. 8 is peculiarly placed. The struggle for the succession presupposes the divine promise of a dynasty.

The ch. is composite and thus not fully consistent. There is a mixture of the promise to David with a statement concerning Israel's future. The D editor added the introductory words of vs. 1 to give a setting for the story, vs. 13 to make the temple prophecy consistent with Solomon's building of the temple, and vss. 22-24 as a hymnodic prayer praising God, who redeemed and established his people.

Nor was the source used by the D editor completely original. The oldest form is probably found in vss. 2-7, 11*b*, 16, 18-21, 25-29. According to this, David tells **Nathan** of his desire to build a permanent shrine for the **ark** (vs. 2). Nathan first approves (vs. 3) but later receives an oracle forbidding David's building of a temple (vss. 4-7). Rather God will build David a **house** (vs. 11*b*), i.e. establish the Davidic dynasty, which will be unending (vs. 16). This promise became a cornerstone of the D editor's view of the history of the S kingdom.

7:4-7. The argument used in the oracle is that Yahweh has never lived in or demanded the construction of a permanent **dwelling.** Its basis is not strictly historical since a permanent structure did house the ark in Shiloh. Of course Shiloh was destroyed and was not therefore permanent. Probably intended by the oracle is the idea that Yahweh is not to be bound to a particular location or structure—a doctrine which a temple might endanger.

7:8-17. Most of this section represents a somewhat later amplification of the original promise in vss. 11*b*, 16. The point of view, however, is somewhat different. Though the promise of succession remains in vss. 12, 14-15, it is limited to Solomon rather than applied to an eternal dynasty. The promise is also conditional on Solomon's good behavior—a principle which the D editor endorsed and used in his view of the Davidic dynasty. Furthermore the promise has been made somewhat secondary to national interests by insistence on the future greatness of Israel

(vss. 10-11*a*). Vs. 13, with its reference to Solomon's building the temple and his (rather than David's) establishment of a dynasty, ill fits the context and was not part of it before the D editor's time. I Chr. 22:6-16 in turn builds on this vs. a case for David's instructions to his son concerning temple building.

7:18-29. This is the royal prayer of praise to God for his promise. David goes **before the LORD,** i.e. to the sanctuary. Not only has God blessed David wonderfully in the past; he has now given him a view of his descendants in the future. The end of vs. 19 is corrupt. The RSV has changed the Hebrew "this is the law of mankind" to **and hast shown me future generations,** which is only a guess. The prayer reflects the divine promise of a Davidic dynasty—except for vss. 22-24, which are typically D and praise God for himself and for his redemption of his people (cf. Deut. 4:34-39). Vs. 25 logically follows vs. 21, asking for confirmation of the knowledge given David in vss. 19-21.

C. DAVID'S CAMPAIGNS AND CHIEF OFFICIALS (8:1-18)

8:1-14. *Summary of Davidic Wars.* This ch. belongs logically after ch. 5. It is an annalistic account of David's various military successes which may at one time have concluded the source dealing with David's rise to power, though it has also been thought of as an independent record. In any event it does not belong after ch. 7, which presupposes "rest from all his enemies." The opening words, **after this,** can apply only to ch. 5, possibly to the taking of Jerusalem.

8:1. First reference is to the subjection of the **Philistines. Methegh-ammah** is probably not a place name but a Hebrew phrase referring to sovereignty, lit., "the reins of the metropolis."

8:2. That **Moab** was treated with particular severity is strange in view of I 22:3-4 (but see comment). Two 3rds are killed; whether of captives, males, or the entire populace is not stated. On Moabite **tribute** cf. II Kings 3:4.

8:3-8. There is a fuller parallel in 10:6-19, whereas this simply summarizes David's campaign against the Aramean states. The location of **Zobah** is uncertain, though an area N of Damascus has been suggested by some; others place it between the Lebanons and the Anti-Lebanons. Since the territory of **Hadadezer** extended toward the **Euphrates,** the former is more likely. The numbers in vss. 4-5 are exaggerated (cf. 10:6, 18). David cripples most of their **horses,** presumably capturing **a hundred chariots** and sufficient horses. Chariots were of little military value in the hilly regions of Palestine. Conquest of the state of **Damascus** and imposition of **tribute** on it marks David's military successes. The locations of **Betah** and **Berothai** are unknown.

8:9-12. The congratulatory message and gifts from **Hamath,** 120 miles N of Damascus, are a token of voluntary submission. Precious metals are all **dedicated** to Yahweh, and apparently used by Solomon in the building of the temple. In the summary list of subjects (vs. 12) are also listed **Amalek** (cf. I 27:8) and the **Ammonites** (cf. 10:1-19; 12:26-31). For Toi's son **Joram** I Chr. 18:10 has Hadoram, which in turn is an error for "Hadad-ram." Joram is a Hebrew, not an Aramean, name.

8:13-14. David also is able to subdue **Edom;**

Israelite prosperity could always be gauged by its ability to hold this land of nomads. It was not only difficult to hold—note that David keeps the land under occupation—it was also most important as giving access to the Gulf of Aqaba. For the **Valley of Salt** see comment on II Kings 14:7.

8:15-18. The Chief Officials. For a similar list cf. 20:23-26. David himself serves as ultimate judge by virtue of his royal office. The military is under double command: **Joab** is commander in chief of the **army,** and **Benaiah** is captain of David's foreign bodyguard, which is composed of **Pelethites,** i.e. Philistines. On **Cherethites** see above on I 30:11-15. The **recorder** was probably some kind of press secretary and adviser on state affairs, whereas the **secretary** kept the official annals and records (cf. II Kings 25:19). The name of the secretary, **Seraiah,** is uncertain; in 20:25 it is given as Sheva and at I Chr. 18:16 as Shavsha. In connection with the priests a curious error has crept in. **Zadok** was probably an earlier Jebusite king-priest; he is now placed on a par with "Abiathar the son of Ahimelech the son of Ahitub," David's old companion (see above on I 22:20-23), but the text has been disarranged to read **Zadok the son of Ahitub and Ahimelech the son of Abiathar.**

VII. David and His Court (9:1–20:26)

A. Some Royal Acts (9:1–12:31)

9:1-13. David's Care for Jonathan's Son. This ch. should be preceded by 21:1-14 (see comment). David, probably recalling his earlier covenant of brotherhood with Jonathan (cf. I 18:3-4; 20:42; 23:18), seeks information concerning possible offspring. A servant loyal to the **house of Saul** named **Ziba** informs him about the lame son of Jonathan living in hiding in Gilead in Transjordan. **Lo-debar** remains unidentified. **Mephibosheth** was actually named Meribaal (see above on 4:4). He is brought to the court, and all Saul's former possessions are restored to him. He is kept under David's eye at court, where he is well treated. Ziba is appointed steward of Meribaal's restored lands.

10:1–11:1. War with the Ammonites. This section has been inserted into the narrative (see Intro.). On **Nahash** cf. I 11. David's ambassadors are grossly insulted; the **beard** was the pride of Semitic manhood, and nakedness was considered most shameful. Such an insult demands immediate revenge, and the Ammonites know it. They make hurried preparations by hiring various Syrian troops. **Beth-rehob** lay near Dan in the N; its exact location is unknown. On **Zobah** see above on 8:3-8. **Maacah** lay somewhere S of Mt. Hermon in the W of Bashan, whereas **Tob** lay further S in the Hauran, probably near the Yarmuk River. None of these sites is exactly identified. The numbers given are all exaggerated. **Joab** overcomes them with **the mighty men,** i.e. the professional army.

10:9-14. As the battle lines are drawn Joab is the victim of a pincer attack with **Syrians** on one side, the **Ammonites** on the other—the scene was probably at the entrance of **Rabbah** (11:1), modern Amman, the capital **city** of Ammon. Joab divides his army into 2 parts—he leads the force against the Syrians, **Abishai** the one against Ammon. The

Syrians are defeated, and the Ammonites panic and retreat into the city. A siege being impractical, the Israelite soldiery returns to Jerusalem.

10:15–11:1. This account of a subsequent attempt to fight **David** is parallel to that in 8:3-8, with different and contradictory details (e.g. cf. vs. 18 with 8:4). **Hadadezer,** in company with **Syrians** from the **Euphrates** region, comes to **Helam** (of unknown location but probably in N Gilead), where David's army meets and completely defeats them. The Syrians now become subjects to David, and the **Ammonites** are isolated militarily for the next phase in the conflict, which is begun in 11:1 and continued in 12:26-31. **In the spring of the year** (11:1) is incorrect. The Hebrew means "at the turning of the year," which means fall, not spring. **Kings** did not do battle until after the harvest. This sets the stage for the David and Bathsheba story, which interrupts the account.

11:2-27a. David's Great Sin. David has not accompanied his army (vs. 1), and **one afternoon** after the rest period he goes to the palace **roof** and sees **a woman bathing.** He learns on inquiry that she is **Bathsheba,** probably granddaughter of his royal counselor Ahithophel (cf. 23:34) and wife of one of his professional soldiers. **Uriah** is a **Hittite** proselyte to Yahwism, as his name, meaning "Yahweh is light," shows. David then commits adultery with Bathsheba, and she becomes pregnant.

11:6-13. David in panic tries to avoid the consequences of his sin by recalling her husband, under the pretext of wanting news of the campaign, but actually to have him spend a night at home with his wife. But soldiers on an expedition were required to remain in a sanctified state, i.e. might have no relations with women (cf. I 21:4-5), and Uriah simply beds down at the palace **door.** When the anxious David inquires, Uriah replies as a doughty soldier. The **ark** still accompanied Israel into battle (vs. 11; cf. I 4:3-9). David has him stay an extra night, making him drunk, but to no avail.

11:14-27a. David then sends a **letter** by Uriah to **Joab** ordering him to place Uriah in a place of danger. Joab does so and Uriah is killed. After the traditional short period of **mourning** Bathsheba becomes David's wife. On **Abimelech** cf. Judg. 9:50-57.

I Chr. omits this entire account as derogatory to David. Not only does this account show David's sin to be adultery and murder, but there is an implied criticism of failure to go to battle with his army.

11:27b–12:15a. Nathan's Rebuke. The account of David's sin was told, not for its own sake, but to show Yahweh's displeasure, even though it was his own anointed who did wrong. Accordingly the court prophet **Nathan** is sent to David. Since David is in his royal capacity supreme judge (cf. 8:15) Nathan presents to him a blatant, though imaginary, case of injustice. David's anger is stirred at such injustice, and he calls for **fourfold** (the LXX has "sevenfold," which may be correct) repayment by this man, who really ought **to die.**

12:7-13a. At Nathan's reply, **You are the man** (vs. 7a), David is conscience stricken (vs. 13a). Intervening are later amplifications (vss. 7b-12) which take subsequent disasters in David's life and explain them as punishment for this sin. The sin is one of despising Yahweh's word by doing evil. Vs. 8 is the only reference to David's taking over his predecessor's harem (that of Ishbaal?). This was common evidence of royal dignity (cf. 3:7-11; I Kings 2:13-25). The punishment, according to the amplified version, is the trouble he is to have with his own sons (Amnon, Absalom, and Adonijah). On vss. 11-12 cf. 16:20-23.

12:13b-15a. In Nathan's original prophecy David is restored to favor with God, i.e. he is forgiven. Nevertheless the actual effects of the sin cannot be voided. The **child** of the adulterous union must **die**. The RSV of vs. 14a is a conjecture. It probably should read "you have caused the enemies of Yahweh to blaspheme." Yahweh's cause has been degraded.

12:15b-25. The Judgment Effected. The punishment is the illness and eventual death of the child. David, by strict fasting and intercessory prayer, tries to dissuade Yahweh. Even the chieftains of his family are unable to persuade David to **eat**. When the child does die after 6 days David's servants are afraid that he may be deranged by grief; but to their surprise, and contrary to oriental custom, he ends his fast, arises from the ground, washes, and changes. David explains his action by stating that he was hoping to sway Yahweh to spare the child. Now it is too late. Rather he will eventually join his child. David is now fully reconciled with God. As signal of his atoned status David and Bathsheba have a 2nd child, who is named **Solomon,** i.e. "peace." A prophetic word by Nathan names the child **Jedidiah,** meaning "beloved of Yahweh." Nathan originally brought the divine condemnation and sentence; now he brings the word that David is restored, that the incident is closed.

12:26-31. The Ammonite War Continued. This is a continuation of 11:1. Joab eventually takes the walled capital city, though **royal city** should probably read **city of waters** as in vs. 27. This would mean that he has captured Rabbah's water supply, so that the actual taking of the city itself is a matter of course, which he diplomatically leaves to David. The citadel is taken and plundered and the populace reduced to slave labor. Particularly mentioned as booty is a **crown** of special splendor containing a gem of some kind which David takes for his own crown. The crown could hardly be **their king's** crown since it weighed a **talent,** ca. 63 pounds (see table, p. 1285). Rather it belonged to their idol Milcom, confused with *malkam,* meaning "their king."

B. Family Struggles (13:1–14:33)

13:1-22. The Rape of Tamar. With this story David's family troubles explode. The crown prince **Amnon,** son of Ahinoam, has a sexual passion for his **virgin** half sister **Tamar,** sister of **Absalom** (children of Maacah; cf. 3:2-3). Marriage between half brother and sister was forbidden in later legislation (Lev. 18:9, 11; Deut. 27:22) but at this time was still acceptable. On the advice of a **crafty** cousin, **Jonadab,** he pretends illness; then when David visits him, he asks his father for Tamar's attendance. Apparently Amnon has a separate dwelling with at least 2 rooms.

13:7-14. Accordingly Tamar is ordered to **prepare food** for her sick brother. When the food is set out he refuses to eat until all the servants clear out. Then when she brings the food he betrays his passion, which she renounces as both **folly** and against the social mores. If Amnon will ask for her, surely David will give her to him.

13:15-22. After he has had his way with her, Tamar as a violated woman is no longer eligible for marriage—hence her signs of mourning (vs. 19) and her remaining **desolate** in her brother's house (vs. 20). Absalom is furious and determines on vengeance, but cunningly he does not betray his feelings.

13:23-30. Absalom's Revenge. Only after **two full years** can Absalom wreak his revenge on Amnon. The occasion is his sheepshearing—a festival occasion (cf. I 25:2-8)—at **Baal-hazor,** 6 miles NE of Bethel (see color map 6), to which he invites his father and brothers. David declines but gives his blessing. When Absalom asks his father to send Amnon, David is suspicious but on being pressed allows all the princes to attend. At the festival Absalom orders his **servants** to **kill** Amnon as soon as he is drunk. When the deed is done, the other brothers flee for their lives, each on his **mule** (the animal for royalty), probably assuming that Absalom is intent on a *coup d'état.*

13:30-36. Exaggerated rumors quickly reach the court that Absalom has killed **all** his brothers. But David's nephew, the "crafty" **Jonadab** (cf. vs. 3), advises him that only Amnon has been killed. Eventually the princes return along the road from **Horonaim** (i.e. the 2 Horons, Upper and Lower Beth-horon, NW of Gibeon).

13:37-38. The text of these vss. is badly corrupt. Three times it is said that **Absalom fled** (vss. 34, 37, 38). The first statement is out of place, whereas these vss. are repetitious and do not fit with vs. 39, which belongs with the next story. Vs. 37b should precede vs. 37a, with only the last phrase of vs. 38 retained. **Geshur** was an Aramean state NE of Galilee, and its king, **Talmai,** with whom Absalom sought refuge for **three years,** was his maternal grandfather (cf. 3:3).

13:39–14:33. Absalom's Return. David may be a brilliant military strategist and the anointed of God, but he is a poor parent, alternating between severity and laxity. He realizes that Absalom has incurred bloodguilt and should be put to death, but the 3-year exile makes David long for his son. **Joab,** who always has David's best interests in mind, devises a stratagem by which David may be persuaded to do what in his **heart** he really wants. He sends for a **wise woman** of **Tekoa** (ca. 6 miles S of Bethlehem; see color map 6) to act as a mourning widow with an appeal case to present to David as supreme judge.

14:4-11. The woman tells David a fictitious tale about a fratricide son. His interest is awakened, and he promises that no one shall harm her or her son. When she still persists, he swears an oath in Yahweh's name that her son will not suffer.

14:12-17. Now the woman applies David's oath-bound decision to the case of Absalom. David has become the family avenger in not allowing Absalom to return. Amnon is dead and cannot return. Vs. 14b should be rendered: "but God does not simply take away life, but rather desires means not to keep an exile banished from him"; i.e. God is not interested in pure vengeance but rather in having the exile return. Having made the application, she returns to the original tale, probably to cover up her real aim.

14:18-24. David shrewdly sees through her subterfuge and asks her bluntly whether she is speaking at Joab's direction. With crafty flattery and courtesy she compares his shrewdness to that of an **angel of God,** but fully admits Joab's direction. David then informs Joab that he has won his case; Absalom may return to **his own house,** but must remain away from the court.

14:25-27. These vss. interrupt the narrative but relate some popular rumors about the handsome prince. Cf. the exaggerated fiction about his **heavy** head of **hair** (*ca.* 4 pounds; see "Measures and Money," p. 1285). Reference to **three sons** conflicts with 18:18, where it is said that he has no sons. Concerning **Tamar** the LXX adds that she became Rehoboam's wife, but I Kings 15:2, 10 states that the queen's name was Maacah, Absalom's mother's name. Tamar was the name of his violated sister. Thus both were family names appropriate for Absalom's daughter.

14:28-33. Absalom remains 2 years but his nonrecognition at court galls him. Twice he summons Joab, who refuses to come. Thereupon the imperious prince sets Joab's **barley** field on **fire.** When Joab comes to expostulate he is ordered to obtain full pardon from David for Absalom. Joab complies, and so the murderer is again fully accepted in court society.

C. Absalom's Rebellion (15:1–19:8b)

15:1-6. *Absalom's Subversion.* Absalom is determined on a well planned *coup d'état.* Amnon is dead; and Chileab, the 2nd son, has apparently died also, since he is not mentioned except in the list of David's sons born at Hebron (3:2). Absalom is the 3rd son, thus in line for the succession (though the eldest was not necessarily the crown prince; cf. e.g. I Kings 1:11-13). His princely state is exemplified by his obtaining a **chariot and horses** and runners—pomp which David has always avoided. Absalom cleverly propels himself forward as a man more interested than his father in the cause of the common man. This kind of propaganda naturally **stole** (i.e. won) **the hearts,** esp. when he refuses obeisance and greets suppliants as brothers.

15:7-12. *The Coup.* After **four years** (not 40, as the Hebrew has it) of propaganda Absalom is ready. **Hebron,** his birthplace, is to be the center for his move. Secretly messengers distribute invitations to take part in the revolt. **Two hundred** unsuspecting Jerusalem hostages accompany Absalom as **guests** at the rites used as a cover. **Ahithophel,** who is David's counselor (and probably Bathsheba's grandfather; cf. 11:3; 23:34), is summoned from his home at **Giloh,** *ca.* 5 miles N of Hebron (see color map 6), to serve Absalom. Some dissatisfaction at David's removal of the capital to Jerusalem probably explains the reason for the choice of Hebron.

15:13-16:14. *David's Flight from Jerusalem.* When David hears the news he immediately prepares to flee from the city, both to spare it and to choose his own form of defense.

15:16-23. At the **last house,** i.e. probably the ex-

treme S of the city, David pauses to marshal his forces. The term **all the people** in vs. 17 must refer to his forces rather than to the populace. Accompanying David are his loyal officers, the mercenary guard, **his household** (except for **ten concubines**) and a special Philistine troop from **Gath** under **Ittai.** On **Cherethites** and **Pelethites** see above on 8:18. And so David and his followers leave the city, cross the **Kidron** and proceed E up the **Mount of Olives** (vs. 30) toward the Judean **wilderness.**

15:24-29. A 2nd leave-taking scene concerns the priests and the **ark.** David orders the 2 priests to return to the **city** with the ark. Later they are to serve as spies for David in the city and send word to him secretly. Questionable is the reference to **Levites** (vs. 24) serving in this way in David's time; it may come from a later editor. Leaving the ark in Jerusalem is to be David's touchstone. His return to worship there will be determined by whether God is gracious to him. **Fords of the wilderness** refers to fords of the Jordan, probably those a few miles above the Dead Sea.

15:30-37. David's departure is accompanied by signs of mourning and distress (cf. 13:19). News of the defection of **Ahithophel** is a staggering blow to David, since his wisdom and cunning were proverbial (cf. 16:23). But at the **summit** of the **Mount of Olives** (at a shrine; cf. I Kings 11:7) **Hushai,** another wise man, comes as a loyal friend to David. The **Archite** clan was Benjaminite, living S W of Bethel (cf. Josh. 16:2). David presents a plan by which Hushai is to return to Jerusalem and pledge false allegiance to Absalom so that he may counteract the **counsel of Ahithophel.** The sons of the 2 loyal priests are to inform David secretly.

16:1-4. Proceeding E beyond the summit David meets **Ziba** (cf. ch. 9), bringing presents for the king but at the same time craftily intimating that his master, Meribaal (**Mephibosheth;** see above on 4:4), is also revolting. David naïvely believes the insinuation and gives him his master's property (cf. 19: 24-30).

16:5-14. The final scene takes places at **Bahurim,** just E of Mt. Scopus. **Shimei,** a member of the **house of Saul,** heaps curses and insults on David. Obviously there still remained a great deal of hatred and bitterness in the followers of the former king. **Abishai** (on **Zeruiah** see comment on I 26:1-25) proposes to kill the offender, but David restrains him. He hopes that Yahweh may in righteousness eventually grant him a similar amount of blessing to offset the present **cursing.** The fleeing king and his supporters finally arrive at some place with water for refreshment, presumably the **Jordan** (as the LXX reads).

16:15-17:23. *Hushai's Advice.* Absalom and his followers have by now entered Jerusalem in triumph. Hushai also presents himself to Absalom and feigns adherence to his cause.

16:20-22. Absalom's first action, on the advice of his counselor **Ahithophel,** is publicly to take over the royal harem, thereby symbolizing his succession to the throne (see above on 3:6-11; 12:7-13a). The **tent** pitched on the **roof** was the wedding tent.

16:23-17:4. Absalom immediately convenes a council of strategy, both Ahithophel and Hushai being invited to give counsel. Ahithophel's advice is to **pursue** David immediately and to concentrate on him **only**. Once David is killed, the followers will no longer oppose. Sound advice!

17:5-14. Hushai then proceeds to counteract Ahithophel's advice in order to win time for David. To pursue David now when he and his **mighty men**, i.e. professionals, are **enraged** like a mother **bear robbed of her cubs** would be foolish. Besides, the seasoned old campaigner is still wily; he would hardly be in an obvious place during the night. Should they attack now and some slaughter occur, it would be the unseasoned troops of Absalom who would panic since they are only too aware of the valor of David's bodyguard. Thus far the refutation. With vs. 11 begins Hushai's positive suggestion. Let **all Israel** from N to S be collected together as one great army to be led **in person** by Absalom (subtle flattery!). Should David withdraw into a walled city, the great army will simply dismantle the city. Bad advice! But Yahweh had **ordained** that the **counsel of Hushai** should win the day (vs. 14).

17:15-22. Hushai has done his best for David, but not knowing how effective his advice has been he immediately sends word to David not to stay at the **fords** of the Jordan (see above on 15:24-29). On **En-rogel** see comment on I Kings 1:5-10. The messengers are seen leaving the area and pursued. They manage to escape through the connivance of a **woman** at **Bahurim** (see above on 16:5-14). Details of the ruse employed by the woman are obscure. The word rendered **grain** (vs. 19) is completely unknown, nor is her reply clear. **Brook** (vs. 20) is purely a guess; since it is followed by **of water** it may be correct.

17:23. Meanwhile **Ahithophel** sees the handwriting on the wall. The rejection of his **counsel** means the eventual triumph of David. Rather than fall into David's hands, he goes home and commits suicide.

17:24-29. *David's Arrival at Mahanaim.* Hushai's strategy was sound. David has time to regroup and to entrench himself in Mahanaim (see above on 2:8-11). Absalom has appointed **Amasa**, a cousin of **Joab**, over his forces. Amasa's forebears are not certain. In the Hebrew text his father is "the Israelite." I Chr. 2:16-17 says his father was Jether the Ishmaelite and his mother Abigail, sister of David. **Daughter of Nahash** is probably an error that crept in from the mention of Nahash in vs. 27.

17:27-29. David is greeted by friends with supplies. **Shobi** was a brother of Hanun (cf. 10:1-5), king of the Ammonites. On **Rabbah** see above on 12: 26-31. **Machir** earlier provided hospitality for Meribaal (9:4-5). **Rogelim** lay E of Mahanaim, but its location is uncertain.

18:1-8. *The Victory of David's Men.* David's active forces are divided equally under the command of faithful officers, **Joab** and **Abishai** and the Philistine exile **Ittai** (cf. 15:19-22). The king is dissuaded from taking part in the fight; rather he stays with the reserves in the **city**. As the army leaves, David gives orders to **deal gently** with his rebel son. The battle is easily won by David's forces, and **twenty thousand** are killed. The field of battle is the **forest of Ephraim**. This designation of some Gilead woodland is surprising but not impossible. The treacherous forest contributes heavily to the casualties.

18:9-18. *Absalom's Death.* Trying to escape on his royal **mule**, Absalom loses control of the animal and is left helpless with his **head** wedged firmly in the branches of a large **oak**. When news of it is brought to Joab, he puts common sense above sentimentality. David is guided by a father's heart, but Joab knows that only Absalom's death can bring stability to David's kingdom. Thus he takes **three darts** (vs. 14, lit. "clubs," which could hardly be thrust into the heart) and smites him, after which 10 military aides finish him off. Joab then gives signal to stop the battle while his aides (**they** in vs. 17 probably refers to the 10 aides of vs. 15) throw Absalom's corpse into a nearby **pit** and cover it with a large **heap of stones**—the mark of an evil person (cf. Achan's grave, Josh. 7:26).

18:18. This vs. tells of a different type of monument to Absalom's memory. This stele was placed in the **King's Valley** (probably the Kidron Valley). The vs. contradicts 14:27. Had the 3 sons born to him all died in infancy and this funeral stele been erected as **Absalom's monument?**

18:19-19:8b. *David's Reaction.* Zadok's son **Ahimaaz**, who has been David's faithful link with Jerusalem during the revolt, again wishes to be bearer of **tidings** to the waiting David. But Joab, knowing his king, sends a **Cushite** (i.e. Ethiopian) slave. Ahimaaz is insistent, however, wanting to soften the blow. By choosing a better road he is able to reach Mahanaim first.

18:24-19:8b. Meanwhile David is waiting at the city entrance between the outer and inner **gates**. A **watchman** reports a solitary runner approaching, whom David rightly interprets to be a messenger (numerous men running would mean flight). Ahimaaz, on arrival, informs the king of the victory but dissimulates on being asked about Absalom's welfare. Not so the Ethiopian, who gives a full report. David's excessive grief was as much for his own failure as parent as lament for his dead son. **Joab** with characteristic bluntness rebukes the king. The king's lament in the hearing of the people is sheer ingratitude and dangerous for the future of the newly saved kingdom. Unless quick action is taken David will lose all popular support. Joab is right and David's good sense takes over.

D. THE RETURN TO POWER (19:8c-20:26)

19:8c-43. *David's Return to Jerusalem.* The battle has been won, but the kingdom still has to be wooed. The first scene finds **Israel**, i.e. the N tribes, aware of the new situation: Absalom is **dead** and David is not. To gain some psychological and political advantage they make plans for escorting the king to the capital.

19:11-15. David has heard about the plans; the last clause of vs. 11 belongs at the end of vs. 10 and should be read "and the word of all Israel came to the king." With his old energy he quickly sends word to his **priests** to persuade the Judeans who were party to revolt to be the first to welcome him back. His argument is based both on clan membership and on his promise to demote Joab in favor of **Amasa** (cf. 17:25). This strategy accomplishes 2 things: winning over Absalom's military commander and demoting Joab, over whom he has never had full control. The result is immediate capitulation. Judah is on hand to **bring the king over the Jordan.**

19:16-23. The next scene highlights a much-chastened **Shimei** (cf. 16:5-13), as well as the sycophantic **Ziba.** Ziba and his household assist in the fording of the Jordan, and Shimei apologizes humbly for his former reviling. Both of these attendants are Benjaminites, members of Saul's clan. When **Abishai** wants to kill Shimei, David declares an amnesty for him. Abishai, as brother of Joab, is hardly in favor with David. **House of Joseph** (vs. 20) means the N tribes.

19:24-30. Meribaal (**Mephibosheth;** see above on 4:4) also meets David to welcome him and is upbraided for lack of support at the time of David's departure. His defense contradicts the earlier statement of Ziba, and David gives final judgment on the property settlement (cf. 9:7-10; 16:4 for earlier dispositions). The evidence of Meribaal's personal distress (vs. 24) and his response to the king's questions (vs. 30) demonstrate his real loyalties. Where this meeting took place is uncertain.

19:31-40. David's gracious but **aged** host, **Barzillai,** accompanies him to the Jordan (cf. 17:27-29). David urges him to come to the palace to live, but he with courtly courtesy declines and suggests that **Chimham** (probably a young son) serve as his substitute.

19:41-43. David's return is not without its difficulties. The N tribes and Judah are equally eager to show their greater share in David's triumph. The stage is set for the revolt described in ch. 20.

20:1-22. *Sheba's Revolt.* Opposition to Davidic rule is spurred by Sheba, whose rallying cry is a return to tribalism. This was to be more effective after Solomon's death (I Kings 12:16). The call served temporarily to isolate Israel from Judah.

20:3. This vs. is a digression, a note on David's dealing with the **concubines** defiled by Absalom (16:20-23). The phrase **living as if in widowhood** is a technical phrase for marriage without sexual relations.

20:4-13. The account of Joab's treachery is necessary to show why it was Joab who put down the rebellion rather than **Amasa,** his successor (19:13). Amasa is ordered to muster **Judah** but is ineffective. So David orders **Abishai** to take the professional troops and pursue Sheba to prevent his preparing adequate defense. For parallel strategy cf. 17:1-3. On the composition of the mercenaries (vs. 7) see above on 8:15-18. Joab naturally accompanies his brother and automatically assumes command.

The details of Joab's deed are uncertain. Vs. 8 seems to say that Joab has a **sword** sheathed and hidden in his **girdle.** Then as he approaches Amasa he greets him, taking him **by the beard with his right hand to kiss him.** Meanwhile the sword falls out into his left hand and with it he kills Amasa. Joab murders Amasa simply because he is a rival. Without pause Joab and his brother continue the pursuit of Sheba, one of the men being left to deal with the dying Amasa.

20:14-22. Sheba meanwhile hurries N with his clan, the Benjaminite **Bichrites,** and holes up in **Abel of Beth-maacah,** 12 miles N of Lake Huleh and 4 miles W of the city of Dan (see color map 6). The rebellion is now limited to a single clan. When the city is attacked in earnest a **wise woman** intercedes with Joab, with the result that the city is spared on giving up the **head** of the rebel. The state-

ment in vss. 18-19 is difficult. Abel has apparently been of old a traditional center of wisdom. Why then use force when at such a place consultation will probably yield good results? **A mother in Israel** means a city with daughter villages around it, i.e. an important city.

20:23-26. *A List of Chief Officials.* A parallel list appears in 8:15-18 (see comment). Differences are the mention here of **Adoram,** chief of the **forced labor** (see comment on I Kings 4:1-6) and of an otherwise unknown **Ira the Jairite** (a clan in Manasseh). The list was probably placed here to show that Joab was again commander of the army.

VIII. Appendixes (21:1-24:25)

21:1-14. *Gibeonite Revenge on the House of Saul.* Chronologically this section belongs before ch. 9 since both ch. 9 and 16:7-8 presuppose it (see Intro.). A 3-year drought needs explanation. David seeks an oracle concerning it and discovers that there is **blood guilt** in Israel (cf. a similar story about Achan, Josh. 7). Saul in his early zeal for Yahweh put to death Gibeonites, with whom Israel had a covenant of friendship (Josh. 9:3-27), as we are told in a parenthetical remark in vs. 2*b*. This bloodguilt has to be removed before rain will come.

21:3-9. The Gibeonites demand retaliation; i.e. **seven** of Saul's **sons** are to be delivered to them to be **hanged** (i.e. exposed after execution as a public disgrace; cf. vs. 12; I 31:10; II 4:12; Deut. 21:22-23). **Gibeon on the mountain of the LORD** in the light of vs. 9 is probably better than the Hebrew "in Gibeah of Saul, the chosen of Yahweh." The statement in vs. 7 is a gloss to explain the action detailed in ch. 9 and to show that the Meribaal (**Mephibosheth;** see above on 4:4) of vs. 8 is not Jonathan's son. The victims are 2 sons of **Rizpah** (cf. 3:7) and 5 of **Merab,** Saul's elder daughter (cf. I 18:17-19). **Barzillai** is not to be confused with David's aged host in 17:27-29; 19:31-40.

21:10-14. How long Rizpah kept the death watch is uncertain. Normally the **beginning of barley harvest** is in April and the fall rains do not begin until the end of October. But spring rains do occasionally come in May. The coming of the **rain** proves that the expiation is complete, i.e. the bloodguilt is removed. David's gathering of the 7 corpses, along with the transfer of Saul's and Jonathan's bones from Jabesh (cf. I 31:11-13), is an act of piety. **Zela** is unknown; it is probably simply a rock tomb in Gibeah.

21:15-22. *Warrior Exploits.* Four successful exploits against Philistine **giants** are recorded. These events belong to the early period of the Philistine wars (cf. 5:17-25). These giants presumably belonged to the pre-Israelite occupants of Canaan, considered to be of large stature. The text of the first anecdote is corrupt. The name in vs. 16 is simply a transliteration of the Hebrew for "and they dwelt in Nob," which makes no sense; probably **Gob** (cf. vs. 18). is intended. On the large **spear** cf. I 17:7. **Gob** (vs. 18) is still unidentified. **Hushathite** was probably a Bethlehem clan (cf. I Chr. 4:4). On the conflict of tradition about **Goliath** see above on I 17:1-11. I Chr. 20:5 reconciles the 2 accounts by changing Goliath to "Lahmi, the brother of Goliath," but that is incorrect. The 4th giant (vss. 20-21) is described as deformed.

22:1-51. *A Thanksgiving Ps.* This ps. is almost word for word the same as Ps. 18 (see comment). An editor has taken it as peculiarly appropriate to David after he was at rest from **all his enemies.**

23:1-7. *The Last Words of David.* This text has suffered a great deal. Whether it actually came from David or not is uncertain, but it is an early poem celebrating his rule as a Yahwist king. **Sweet psalmist of Israel** (vs. 1) should be "the favorite of Israel's songs," i.e. the favorite hero of popular songs. Both as singer and as **anointed** he is the vehicle of divine inspiration. Vss. 3c-4 give the content of the divine message: God prospers the righteous and God-fearing ruler. The Hebrew of vs. 4 reads lit.: "Then he shall be as the morning light, when the sun shines, a cloudless morning—when because of the brightness due to rain grass comes from the earth." Then vs. 5 applies this figure for prosperity to God's **covenant** with the Davidic **house** (cf. ch. 7). The last 2 vss. show the fate of wickedness. Wicked men are compared to the thorny bramble.

23:8-39. *David's Heroes and Their Exploits.* The parallel text in I Chr. 11:11-47 is often better. The list of the 30 heroes is preceded by the exploits of the 3 heroes.

23:8-12. The name of the first in I Chr. 11:11 is Jashobeam; originally it must have been Ishbaal. In vs. 9 **when they defied the Philistines who** can be corrected from I Chr. 11:13 to read "at Pasdammim when the Philistines." The site is unknown. The exploits of the 3 champions were all individual heroic deeds in the holy war against the Philistines.

23:13-17. These vss. relate an act of bravery by 3 unidentified heroes. The occasion for the exploit is 5:17-21. The Philistines have a **garrison** at Bethlehem. In his **stronghold** David expresses longing for fresh **Bethlehem** water. The heroes **broke through** enemy ranks to fulfill David's wish. He then refuses to **drink** that for which men's lives have been endangered.

23:18-23. The commander of the **thirty** is Abishai, Joab's brother, of whom a heroic deed is recounted (cf. 21:15-17). Of **Benaiah,** captain of the **bodyguard,** a number of deeds are told. **Kabzeel** was in the SE part of Judah on the Edomite border (Josh. 15:21) but is unidentified. What **two ariels of Moab** were is unknown. Possibly the words "sons of" should be inserted after "two." The word "ariel" means "lion of God." Could it here mean "strong lions" in view of the reference to **lion** in the next line?

23:24-39. The number of the mighty men is given in vs. 39 as **thirty-seven** but the list contains only

32. I Chr. 11:26-47 expands the list to 47. The number 37 is intended to include not only the 32 but also the 3 of vss. 8-11, as well as Abishai and Benaiah. The list does not include Joab, probably because he was commander of the army and thus not in the special list. It has been plausibly suggested that the list goes back to David's days in Ziklag and originally contained 30, the last 7 being added later.

24:1-25. *A Pestilence from Yahweh.* This story logically belongs with 21:1-14. The reason for Yahweh's anger is not given. I Chr. 21:1 attributes the incitement to Satan in order to avoid charging Yahweh as the author of sin. The Sam. text, however, is the original. All historical movement was attributable to God, according to the ancients. Why a military census should be universally recognized in David's time (even by **Joab**) as sin is not clear. Yahweh did not save by large numbers, according to Judg. 7:2-7; possibly it was thought to be invading divine secrets.

24:5-9. The census is begun at **Aroer** on the Arnon River E of the Dead Sea (see color map 6) and proceeds N in Transjordan to **Jazer,** *ca.* 10 miles W of Rabbah on the border of Ammonite territory. More likely than **Kadesh in the land of the Hittites** (i.e. on the Orontes in Syria; see color map 9) would be Kedesh in Naphtali, NW of Lake Huleh (see color map 5), more or less on the way from **Gilead** to **Dan** and **Sidon.** In this case **Tyre** would be the N point of the census. Then the commanders work their way S through W Palestine to **Beer-sheba** at the edge of the **Negeb,** the arid region S of **Judah.** The final count is probably exaggerated, though not as much as in I Chr. 21:5. The census lists in Num. 1:46, often thought to be based on David's census, show a total of 603,550.

24:10-17. David's repentance follows on the lengthy census, and God presents him with a choice of 3 forms of punishment. David rejects the 2nd (flight before the enemy) and throws himself on Yahweh's mercy—either **famine** or **pestilence.** The severe pestilence throughout the land kills 70,000 people before Yahweh relents. Vs. 17 seems to have little to do with the context and may be an editorial expansion to enhance David's piety.

24:18-25. The point of the episode is to be found in the divine command to purchase the **threshing floor of Araunah** ("Ornan" in I Chr. 21), a **Jebusite,** i.e. a pre-Israelite inhabitant of Jerusalem. There he is to build an **altar** on which a sacrifice is to be made in order to stay the **plague.** On the typical oriental bargaining cf. Gen. 23:1-16. The importance of this purchase lies in the fact that the land is destined to be the site for the temple (cf. I Chr. 22:1; II Chr. 3:1).

THE FIRST BOOK OF THE KINGS

John William Wevers

Introduction

The books of Kings were originally one book, the last of the Former Prophets. In fact the 4 books of the Former Prophets (i.e. Josh., Judg., Sam., Kings) were composed as a single history of Israel from Joshua's conquest of Palestine down to the Exile, and its division into various books was probably only for convenience. The division of Kings into 2 was introduced by the LXX but was not accepted in Hebrew until the text was printed.

Authorship and Date. In 622 B.C. the Deuteronomic (D) Code was discovered in the course of temple renovations and King Josiah inaugurated a thoroughgoing D reform (see "The History of Israel," pp. 1018-25; "The Religion of Israel," pp. 1150-58, and Intro. to Deut., pp. 100-05). The code was adopted as national law (see below on II 23:3-20). Judah now had a word of God, a standard by which she might examine not only her practices but her history as well. Prior to this there had existed S and N sacred histories from earliest times to the Conquest—now known respectively as J and E (see "The Compiling of Israel's Story," pp. 1082-89). In the course of the 7th cent. these 2 had been united into a single JE history. But these were not as yet canon, whereas D had now officially been adopted as such (see "The Making of the OT Canon," pp. 1209-15).

It was thus expedient that the history of Israel on Palestinian soil be examined from this new point of view. This task was undertaken by a historian who was thoroughly imbued with D ideas. Because a few passages (esp. II 22:20) seem to have been written during Josiah's lifetime, some scholars maintain that the main body of the work he produced was completed in the decade immediately following discovery of the D Code and then was supplemented by others of a D school over the next half century. The consistency of thought and style, however, overweigh the evidence of such passages, which may be explained as coming from the author's source. It seems more likely that this historian lived and worked during the early years of the Babylonian exile and that he completed his history immediately following the last event he records (II 25:27-30), *ca.* 560.

Jerusalem, the sole legitimate sanctuary, had been destroyed in 586, and the leading people of Judah had been exiled to Babylon. Now, after a reign of many years, the hated conqueror king had died, and his son and successor seemed more favorably disposed toward the exiles. Perhaps he would allow a restoration. If so, it was appropriate, even imperative, that the history of the kingdoms be examined from the D point of view, so that the people might be given guidance and warning.

The D historian had available for his use various sources; some he adapted to his own ends and others he took over with little change. The result gives the appearance of an anthology of materials with a superficially imposed overall structure and point of view. He has combined materials from annals with prophetic legends, temple archives with popular stories and pure D creations.

The D Structure. I 1-11 deals with the reign of Solomon, after whose death the kingdom was divided. The remaining chs. deal with the history of the divided kingdoms as a series of reigns of individual kings. Each reign is begun with an accession notice detailing the year of its beginning, its length, and an evaluation of it from the D viewpoint. The reign is then completely dealt with before the next reign, or that of the next king of the sister kingdom, is taken up. This shuttlecock method is disconcerting, but it was probably the simplest method available to the author-editor. Each reign ends as well with an obituary and succession notice and a reference to the "chronicles" of the reign for further details.

Into this formal structure have been inserted various stories, all of which are not necessarily germane to the reign in question. Thus not all the stories of Elisha (II 2-8) are to be taken as part of the reign of Jehoram of Israel. Furthermore the story concerning Ahaziah of Israel in II 1 probably belongs to the Elisha rather than the Elijah cycle.

The synchronization of reigns throughout gives a superficial impression of scholarly exactness to the book. Unfortunately this has created one of the most difficult historical problems. Many scholars have proposed solutions to the chronologies of the kings of Israel and Judah. Coregencies, changes in dating systems (postdating and antedating), and textual errors have all been suggested. In this commentary the chronology proposed by E. R. Thiele (see "Chronology," pp. 1271-82) has been followed in the main as necessitating the fewest changes in the biblical text.

Named Sources. Three sources are mentioned as providing materials for the history of the kingdoms: the "book of the acts of Solomon" (I 11:41), the "Book of the Chronicles of the Kings of Israel" (I 14:19, etc.), and the "Book of the Chronicles of the Kings of Judah" (I 14:29, etc.). These were apparently official court annals available at the time of composition but now lost. It should be noted that mention of a court annalist or recorder is first made for the reign of David (II Sam. 8:16; cf. I 4:3).

The first of these sources may have contained not only extensive archival materials from Solomon's reign but also legendary biographical materials intended to enhance the glory of his reign, e.g. the stories of his wisdom (I 3) and of his fabulous wealth and connection (I 10). The chronicles of the 2 kingdoms are mentioned for all kings except Jehoram and Hoshea of Israel and Ahaziah, Jehoahaz, Jehoiachin, and Zedekiah of Judah, the last 4 being omitted because they were not buried in Judah.

These annalistic sources are esp. important since they were contemporary. Such materials may often be recognized by the absence of editorial judgment, the use of temporal expressions such as "then," "in that day," "at that time," or of exact dating such as at I 14:25. These sources dealt mainly with such items as wars, amounts of tribute imposed, relations with other states, buildings and fortifications, alliances, commercial traffic, and lists of officials.

One further source is mentioned in the LXX of I 8:12-13 as being the "Book of Songs," which may be the same as the "Book of Jashar" of Josh. 10:13; II Sam. 1:18 (see below on I 8:12-13).

Prophetic Sources. Prophetic sources center largely around 3 figures: Elijah, Elisha, and Isaiah. These cycles of stories probably circulated independently at one time. The Elijah cycle (I 17-19; 21; II 1) was of special interest to the D historian because of Elijah's central position in the crucial struggle between Baalism and Yahwism under the Omri dynasty.

Like the Elijah cycle, the Elisha cycle (found mainly in II 2-8) is basically N in origin, but it is far more folkloric in character. Most of the tales (except for the anointing of Jehu, II 9:1-13) are miracle stories, some of which parallel the Elijah stories (raising of a dead child to life, the unfailing cruse of oil, the parting of the Jordan waters) and were included by the historian to enhance the prophetic office.

The Isaiah cycle (II 18:17-20:19) is repeated, with some variants and the addition of a complaint prayer, in Isa. 36-39. This cycle is Jerusalem based and shows the position of the great prophet in the court of the righteous King Hezekiah. As a historical source it is unreliable, since the few historical data have been extensively colored by legendary stories.

Other prophetic stories were kept alive by the "sons of the prophets." These are skillfully used by the author-editor to illustrate his D point of view. Such are the tales of Ahijah of Shiloh (I 11:29-39), the unnamed prophets at Bethel (I 13), and Jehu the son of Hanani (I 16:1-4, 7; cf. also Jonah, II 14:25). Not to be confused with this source are the references to prophets in II 17:13; 21:10-15, which are the creation of the D historian himself.

Special mention should be made of I 20; 22, which though preserved by prophetic circles are excellent historical sources, possibly from Ahab's own days. They are comparatively friendly toward Ahab, in contrast to the Elijah cycle into which they were inserted.

Other Sources. David's court memoirs, continuing the Succession Document of II Sam. 9-20 (see Intro. to I Sam.), come to an end with I 2:46.

Architectural description of Solomon's building operations, esp. of the temple and the temple furniture, in I 6-7 (cf. I 8:1-11, 62-66) is based on some contemporary official account, usually called temple archives. These documents may well have been preserved in the temple, but they included descriptions of other buildings as well.

Stories of cultic reform in Jerusalem may have come from the official chronicles but more likely represent another source connected with the temple, though nonpriestly in origin. Thus the story of the revolt against Athaliah (II 11:4-20) in one of its forms (see comment) comes from this source—as do the stories of Jehoash's repair of the temple (II 12:4-16), Ahaz' introduction of a Syrian altar (II 16:10-16), and the finding of the book of the law (II 22:3-20).

The D Point of View. The D historian wrote history from the point of view of the D Code. Central to its cultic demands was a purified cult at a single national sanctuary, viz. the Jerusalem temple. Before the building of the temple the historian expresses no criticism of Solomon's sacrifices at Gibeon (I 3)—though even here he has Solomon return to Jerusalem to stand before the ark and offer sacrifices at the end of the story. Once the temple is standing, however, he condemns out of hand all pre-D shrines outside Jerusalem and holds worship at such places to be illegitimate. He judges every succeeding reign by its fidelity to the cult of the central sanctuary.

After the division of the monarchy the N kings remained officially Yahwist but naturally did not worship at the Jerusalem temple, a shrine on foreign soil. For this the D historian condemns them all as doing "evil" in the eyes of Yahweh. He brands Jeroboam I as the one who "made Israel to sin," i.e. encouraged worship at shrines in his own country. Even Jehu, the ardent champion of Yahwism who ruthlessly stamped out Baalism, he condemns, though with regret (II 10:28-31).

For the Davidic kings in the S the temple was the royal shrine. But in the eyes of the D historian these kings were not all faithful to the book of the law. Only the great cult reformers, Hezekiah and Josiah, does he approve as doing "right" in the eyes of Yahweh. Five others he conditionally approves as doing "right. . . . Nevertheless the high places were not removed." All others he summarily condemns.

The role of the prophetic word as regulatory in human affairs is also characteristic of the D historian's point of view. Prophets again and again issue warnings and predict disaster, and events confirm their words. Thus Elijah predicts drought and the end of the house of Omri; Elisha the end of famine in Samaria, Hazael's future harsh rule in Damascus, and Israelite victory over the Syrians; Ahijah the division of the kingdom and the downfall of Jeroboam's house; Jehu the son of Hanani the end of Baasha's house; and anonymous prophets the ruin of the Bethel sanctuary, Ahab's death, and the end of the Judean state.

The historical problem that particularly plagued the D historian was the end of the Davidic dynasty and the destruction of temple and city. God had promised David an eternal dynasty. True, this was conditional on the good behavior of David's descendants, but God had constantly been gracious; in spite of this the monarchy had come to a disastrous end. Furthermore the law demanded public worship at the Jerusalem temple only, and now it lay in ruins. To this problem he found a solution in the reign of Manasseh. Manasseh's reign was so evil that Judah's existence could no longer be condoned. Even the reign of good Josiah could not avert the divine intention to destroy Judah and Jerusalem. Eventually God might restore his people, but for the moment they must bear the punishment.

For Further Study: C. F. Burney, *Notes on the Hebrew Text of the Books of Kings,* 1903. John Skinner, *Kings,* 1904. W. E. Barnes, *The First-Second Book of the Kings,* 1911. J. A. Montgomery and H. S. Gehman, *A Critical and Exegetical Commentary on the Books of Kings,* 1951. N. H. Snaith in *IB,* 1954. Martin Noth, *History of Israel,* 1958. John Bright, *The History of Israel,* 1959, chs. 5–8. Stephen Szikszai in *IDB,* 1962. E. R. Thiele, *The Mysterious Numbers of the Hebrew Kings,* rev. ed., 1964.

I. SOLOMON'S SUCCESSION TO THE THRONE (1:1–2:46)

1:1-4. *David's Senility.* That the powers of a senile male could be restored by contact with a virgin was a common primitive belief. David's personal attendants provide such a young girl, **Abishag the Shunammite.** She has often been wrongly equated with the Shulammite of Song of S. 6:13. The story emphasizes that she simply served as **nurse** to the aged king.

1:5-10. *Adonijah's Attempt to Seize Power.* Adonijah, the crown prince—with the connivance of **Joab** and **Abiathar,** David's military commander and chief priest respectively—determines to take over the throne from his old father, using tactics similar to those of his late brother **Absalom** (cf. II Sam. 15:1). The court is divided in its loyalties. Those who do not take part in the attempt are listed in vs. 8; among them are the **mighty men,** i.e. the mercenaries. The planned *coup d'état* is well supported by the court and the Judean officials, and might have succeeded but for the prompt intervention of those of the pro-Solomon party, who are naturally not invited to the feast. **En-rogel** is usually identified with a spring near the juncture of the Kidron and Hinnom valleys (see color map 13).

1:11-31. *Nathan's Counterplot.* Nathan, the prophet who once reproved David for his relations with **Bathsheba** (II Sam. 12:1-15), now advises her as Solomon's **mother** to inform David immediately, since their lives are at stake, and to urge the king to immediate action.

1:15-21. Bathsheba informs David of Adonijah's attempt to seize the throne. She suggests that **all Israel** awaits royal direction in the matter; if affairs are allowed to drift Adonijah will be successful and she and **Solomon** will, after David's death, lose their lives as unsuccessful pretenders to the throne.

1:22-27. Nathan enters and asks whether this situation represents David's pleasure and why the king's intimates have not been informed on the matter. This scene is separate from the preceding, since the queen has left. Nathan then also retires from the royal presence.

1:28-31. Bathsheba is recalled by the king, who repeats his oath and swears that Solomon is to **reign.** She leaves the scene after paying her respects.

1:32-40. *The Crowning of Solomon.* The king summons Nathan and the faithful **Benaiah** to give them detailed instructions for the immediate coronation of Solomon. These steps are to be taken: Solomon is to ride on David's **own mule** (vs. 33); they are to go down into the Kidron Valley to the Spring of **Gihon** (see color map 13); there he is to be anointed (only **Zadok** as priest is to do the actual anointing, vs. 34; cf. vs. 39); the **trumpet** is then to be blown (vs. 34) and the coronation salute **Long live King Solomon** cried aloud. Finally the new king must come to the palace with his followers (vs. 35) and take his place on the **throne** itself. To these instructions Benaiah makes a fitting response.

1:38-40. The royal wishes are immediately carried out. Those actually involved include not only Zadok, Nathan, and Benaiah—representing priest, prophet, and soldier respectively—but also the foreign bodyguard, composed of David's old comrades (cf. I Sam. 27), **the Cherethites and the Pelethites,** i.e. Cretans and Philistines. These have remained loyal to the old king and can be relied on to carry out his wishes. The **tent** is the shrine of Yahweh which David built earlier to contain the ark (II Sam. 6:17), and in which the Jerusalem cult has since been carried on. The coronation is popular with the people, who eagerly take part in the gala event, making a great deal of noise.

1:41-53. *Collapse of Adonijah's Attempt.* While Adonijah and his fellow plotters are prematurely **feasting** they hear the noise accompanying Solomon's coronation. A runner brings the fateful news, and adds that Solomon is receiving pledges of loyalty from his courtiers and that the bedridden David has given his blessing to the coregency.

1:49-53. The disconcerting news quickly breaks up the feast. The ex–crown prince, fearing for his life, flees for sanctuary to the tent of Yahweh, where he touches the **horns of the altar.** By this symbolic act he invokes God's protection. Solomon is told of Adonijah's action and sends a message to him promising him royal pardon for his treachery if he remains fully loyal to the new king. But at the first sign of **wickedness,** i.e. disloyalty, he will be put to death. Adonijah then follows the suit of the courtiers and pledges his loyalty to his brother, who dismisses him curtly.

2:1-12. *David's Dying Counsel.* This passage represents a favorite Hebrew literary genre (cf. Gen. 27; 49; Deut. 33; Josh. 24). David, realizing that he is about to die, advises his son to continue his own **strong** rule.

2:3-4. These vss. are an amplification with typical D references to **statutes . . . commandments . . . ordinances . . . testimonies,** as well as to the **law of Moses.** They are the work of the D historian, reflecting on the later disastrous history of the dynasty. The divine oracle probably refers to II Sam. 7.

2:5-9. David gives detailed instructions about 3 cases: (*a*) **Joab** wreaked private vengeance in wartime (cf. II Sam. 3:27; 20:10). This endangered the security of the dynasty, since by this action guilt was attached to the royal house. Joab was David's appointee, and thus his act of barbarity involved the peace of his master's house. This breach of communal health can be healed only by Joab's violent death in turn. (*b*) David owes a debt of gratitude to **Barzillai** (cf. II Sam. 17:27-29; 19:31-39) which Solomon is told to pay to his family. (*c*) The curse of **Shimei** still lies on David's house (cf. II Sam. 16:5-

14). In a moment of weakness David swore (cf. II Sam. 19:18-23) that he would not kill him, but meanwhile the curse is still effective. Again only Shimei's violent death can render the evil inherent in the curse inoperative. Since Solomon is free of his father's oath, he is told to take care of the matter.

2:10-12. The D Editor's Note. Both David and Solomon (cf. 11:42) are said to have reigned **forty years,** a round number meaning a full career. **City of David** now appropriately becomes the new term for Jerusalem.

2:13-25. Adonijah's Death. Adonijah asks the queen mother to intercede with Solomon on his behalf in order to obtain **Abishag** as his wife. Bathsheba is somewhat leery of Adonijah but is willing to speak to her son on the matter.

2:19-25. Though Solomon accords his mother full courtesy, he chooses to interpret Adonijah's request as a challenge to his throne. Abishag has been a member of David's harem, and whoever inherits the harem is king (cf. II Sam. 16:22). On Solomon's order **Benaiah,** the chief of his bodyguard, immediately goes out and kills Adonijah.

2:26-27. Abiathar's Demotion. Abiathar was a fellow conspirator with Adonijah, but because he is a priest and a close friend of David's youth his life is spared. He is removed from his position, however. Thereby the status of the Zadokites as sole priests of the Jerusalem shrine is consolidated (vs. 35; see comment on II Sam. 8:15-18). The D editor adds a note stating that this was a divine judgment on the **house of Eli** (cf. I Sam. 2:27-36).

2:28-35. Joab's Death. Joab flees for sanctuary as did Adonijah (see above on 1:49-53) but to no avail. Solomon orders Benaiah to kill him. Benaiah is somewhat fearful when Joab refuses to leave the shrine and returns to the king for further instructions. Solomon with a long apology commands Benaiah to violate the right of asylum on the basis of Joab's murder of the 2 commanders of the N and S armies. Bloodshed demands bloodshed in return before the health of the Davidic dynasty can be assured. Joab is therefore killed at the altar and buried on his own property E of Bethlehem (cf. II Sam. 2:32).

2:36-46. Shimei's Death. Shimei is told to remain **in Jerusalem** for life, in spite of the fact that he is a native of Transjordan. Should he as much as **cross the brook Kidron,** just outside the E wall of the city, he will be killed.

2:39-46. For **three years** Shimei obeys Solomon's order, but there comes a day when 2 runaway slaves of his are reported found in **Gath,** one of the Philistine cities where **Achish,** David's onetime ally (cf. I Sam. 27:2-12), is still king. Shimei goes to get them, and on his return Solomon uses this as a pretext for legally killing him. He is charged with violating his **oath** and disobeying the king's command and is reminded of, if not taunted with, his old **evil** (i.e. curse) against David and then killed by Benaiah. With these threats removed Solomon's position as David's successor is firmly **established,** and the Succession Document continued from II Sam. 9–20 (see Intro. to I Sam.) comes to an end.

II. SOLOMON'S REIGN (3:1–11:43)

With the notice of Solomon's marriage to an Egyptian princess begins the actual account of his reign—in distinction from its establishment. To the D editor the building of the **house of the LORD,** i.e. the temple, was the great event of this reign, since through it the eventual centralization of worship at Jerusalem became possible.

A. HIS WISDOM AND RICHES (3:3–4:34)

3:3-15. Solomon's Dream at Gibeon. The D editor has a high opinion of Solomon's piety but admits that he worshiped **at the high places**—from the viewpoint of a later age an illegitimate act, since only Jerusalem was permitted as a true place of public worship. Solomon goes to **Gibeon,** an important shrine in Benjamin about 6 miles NW of Jerusalem (see color map 6). The king's pilgrimage to Benjamin undoubtedly had political overtones as well. The story of his **dream** at the high place, probably an incubation ritual (see Intro. to Pss.), is certainly ancient, though the dialogue is typical of the D editor. The dream story is told to account for the wisdom attributed to Solomon. The earlier version (2:6) has it that the young king's wisdom is an innate quality rather than a divine gift made at his own request.

3:15. On awakening the king returns to **Jerusalem** to engage in the proper cult, viz. sacrifices before the **ark.** This would hardly seem to be original to the story but rather a D revision. The story originally may well have referred to the sacrifices and the concluding **feast** as part of the Gibeon pilgrimage.

3:16-28. Solomon's Wise Judgment. The gift of wisdom at Gibeon is immediately applied in the story of Solomon's judicial decision in the case of the 2 mothers and the one live baby. This folklore motif is a favorite one among various cultures, and it illustrates the Hebrew admiration for practical wisdom. The result of the king's wise decision is universal popular acclaim. The concluding vs. emphasizes the Hebrew conception of Solomon's **wisdom**—it is for rendering **justice** and its source is **God.**

4:1-6. Solomon's Chief Officials. The officials' names are given along with their offices. The reference to **Zadok and Abiathar** is an intrusion from the list of David's officials in II Sam. 8:17. The royal "cabinet" consists of the following officers: the **priest,** 2 **secretaries,** a **recorder** (probably the official court annalist), commander in chief of the **army,** head of the officers' staff, **priest and king's friend,** royal chamberlain, and chief of the **forced labor** corps. This ch. emphasizes Solomon's undoubted genius at organization.

4:7-19. The 12 Governors and Provinces. Solomon divides his kingdom roughly along the lines of the old 12 tribal boundaries. The paragraph mentions 13 districts, and many have suggested that **Judah** (vs. 19*b*) was outside the levy, being Solomon's own tribe. Admittedly the governor of Judah is not named, and if this supposition is correct it would mean that **all Israel** refers only to the N tribes. But **Gilead** is mentioned twice, once with **Ben-geber** (i.e. the son of Geber) as governor (vs. 13) and once with **Geber** (vs. 19*a*). Obviously one of these is repetitive and not original. The list is partially defective in that the first 4 governors' names are missing; only their fathers' names are given (i.e. "the son of Hur," etc.).

4:20-28. Solomon's Wealth. The text is somewhat

confused, since vss. 27-28 are a conclusion to the previous section. The passage contains 2 ideal descriptions of the extent of Solomon's kingdom, vss. 20-21, 24-25. They each introduce a statement on the extent of the royal supplies, the first listing the daily provisions, the second the number of **stalls of horses** and **horsemen.** The number given for the stalls is much exaggerated (cf. 10:26). On **cors** see "Measures and Money," pp. 1283-85. **Tiphsah** was the nearest point on the **Euphrates** to Palestine (see color map 9); **Gaza** was the Philistine city farthest S.

4:29-34. Solomon's Wisdom. The term **wisdom** refers to a particular type of oral and written literature consisting of **proverbs,** riddles, **songs,** and the like (see "The Wisdom Literature," pp. 1101-05). These might deal with any subject; particularly mentioned here is botanical and zoological lore. Just as a later age attached the name of Moses to law and that of David to psalmody, so it attributed wisdom to Solomon. Particularly noted in the Near East for such wisdom were the **people of the east,** i.e. the Arabs and Edomites, as well as the Egyptians, among whom were the wise men named in vs. 31.

B. THE BUILDING OF THE TEMPLE (5:1-7:51)

5:1-12. Solomon's Treaty with Hiram of Tyre. Ch. 5 serves as an intro. to the building of the temple. Preparations have to be made; esp. wood has to be imported from **Lebanon.** The language has been expanded greatly by the D editor on the basis of II Sam. 7.

5:7-12. Hiram's woodcutters are to fell the timbers of **cedar and cypress** (perhaps pine) and ferry them as **rafts** down the Mediterranean coast (II Chr. 2:16 says to Joppa, which seems the logical port). There Solomon's men are to **receive** them. In payment for the wood Solomon is to export **wheat** and **oil** to Lebanon. The number of **cors of beaten oil** required is not certain since the Hebrew of vs. 11 says only 20; **twenty thousand** is taken, probably rightly, from the LXX and II Chr. 2:10. On **cors** see "Measures and Money," pp. 1283-85.

5:13-18. Solomon's Forced Labor Corps. Solomon raises a **levy** of **thirty thousand men** to work in shifts every 3rd month. The 150,000 workers added by the D editor (vs. 15) necessitate **three thousand three hundred** foremen (vs. 16), in contrast to only 550 in 9:23. Solomon's laborers are skilled in **stone** but not in **timber**—a situation still true in Palestine today. Hiram's craftsmen are from **Gebal,** i.e. Byblos (see color map 7), a famous Phoenician seaport in ancient times.

6:1-10. The Temple Structure. The account of the building of the temple in chs. 6–7 is largely a contemporary document, and evidence of later additions is infrequent. One such is the opening chronological statement, part of which was adapted from vs. 37. **Four hundred and eightieth** is an artificial number —12 generations of 40 years each. The actual interval from the Exodus to the building of the temple probably did not exceed 325 years at the most (see Intro. to Exod.). On **Ziv** see below on vss. 37-38. The temple dimensions are given as 90 feet long, 45 feet high, and 30 feet wide—assuming the common cubit of *ca.* 18 inches, though a long cubit of *ca.* 21 inches may have been used (cf. Ezek. 40:5; 43:13; see "Measures and Money," pp. 1283-85). To this

Courtesy of Herbert G. May

"Dome of the Rock"; this famous Muslim shrine, completed 691 A.D., occupies the site on which stood Solomon's, Zerubbabel's, and Herod's temples in Jerusalem

must be added the vestibule 15 feet in width running along the front or E side. On the sides are built **side chambers** 3 stories in height, the successive stories upward being widened by correspondingly narrowing the main wall with **offsets.** These chambers were for use by the priests, probably for provisions and storage.

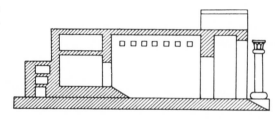

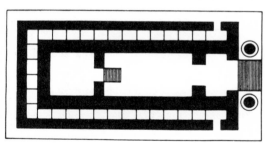

0 10 20 30 40 Cubits
(1 cubit = c. 1½ ft.)

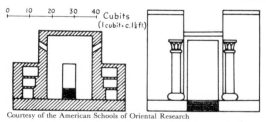

Courtesy of the American Schools of Oriental Research

Steven's reconstruction of Solomon's Temple; from specifications prepared by W. F. Albright and G. Ernest Wright

6:11-13. A Prophetic Oracle to Solomon. This passage interrupts the architectural description and is a D addition based on II Sam. 7. The editor's concern for explaining how God could have permitted the exile of the people in his own day is clear. Solomon and his descendants did not keep God's ordinances and so God forsook his people.

6:14-22. Woodwork and Other Decoration. The temple proper consists of 2 parts, the **nave** or holy place, and the **inner sanctuary** or holy of holies. The latter is a 30-foot cube and contains the **ark.** Emphasis is laid on the use of wood throughout, since wood, esp. **cedar and cypress,** was scarce and therefore precious. The lavish use of **gold** overlay throughout as well as carved decorative motifs is described. Apparently everything in the **inner sanctuary**—walls, altar, and cherubim—is completely **overlaid** with gold.

6:23-28. The Cherubim. Canaanite and Mesopotamian carvings of **cherubim** (Hebrew plural of "cherub") show them as winged creatures, usually with human heads and animal bodies (cf. II Sam. 22:11); they appear esp. on the thrones of kings. Two such figures are said to have been placed in the **inner sanctuary.** Appropriately they fill the lower half of the W wall, their height being 15 feet, and their outspread wings reaching from one side to the other. The empty upper half thus symbolizes the throne for the invisible deity (cf. e.g. II 19:15; Ps. 80:1). Other passages (e.g. Exod. 25:18-20; 37:6-9; Num. 7:89) describe the ark as decorated with cherubs forming Yahweh's throne, but these may represent a later tendency to seek earlier origins for features of the temple.

6:29-36. Decorations and Doors. Not only carvings of cherubs, **palm trees,** and **flowers** are mentioned, but extravagant use of **gold** throughout, even to overlay all the **floor.** Both the 5-sided **entrance** to the sanctuary and the **square** entrance to the nave have elaborate doors. Outside the temple is a court where the people congregate.

6:37-38. Chronology of the Building. The construction takes *ca.* **seven years,** i.e. either 6½ or 7½ since **Ziv** is Apr.-May, **Bul** Oct.-Nov. (see "Chronology," pp. 1271-82). The use of these old Canaanite names shows the antiquity of the reference.

7:1-12. Other Buildings. Solomon's building continues for 13 more years after the temple is finished (cf. 9:10). Since the architectural details are sparse and at times technical, it is not always clear what the records intend.

7:2-5. The first of these buildings is the **House of the Forest of Lebanon,** probably intended as an armory (cf. Isa. 22:8). It is 150 feet long, 75 feet wide, and 45 feet high, thus considerably larger than the temple. It is likely that there were not **three** (LXX) but 4 (Hebrew) rows of **cedar pillars,** with the outer rows against the sides, forming 3 aisles. This would total 60 pillars in all, not **forty-five.** That this is correct appears from the added reference to **three rows** and **three tiers** which have **windows**—an apparent allusion to the aisles. The building evidently received its name from its complete construction of cedar.

7:6. The **Hall of Pillars** may simply be a covered portico in the front of the preceding building, i.e. an extension of it by **thirty cubits.** If so, vss. 6*b* should read "even a portico in front with pillars and a roof over them."

7:7-12. The **Hall of Judgment** is apparently another part of this architectural complex, whereas Solomon's palace and the house of **Pharaoh's daugh-**

ter (cf. 3:1) are in the harem complex, nicely called the **other court.**

7:13-14. Hiram, Workman in Bronze. This paragraph serves as an intro. to all the bronze furniture to be made for the temple recorded in vss. 15-47. There is some doubt about the name of this Tyrian craftsman since II Chr. 2:13-14 calls him Huramabi and states that his mother was from Dan rather than **Naphtali.**

7:15-22. The 2 Pillars of Bronze. It was common practice in antiquity to erect 2 independent pillars flanking the entrance to a temple. Their precise purpose is unknown. The pillars for Solomon's temple are huge in size, each nearly 6 feet thick and *ca.* 27 feet high, plus an elaborately decorated **capital** of almost 8 feet made of bronze 3 inches thick (see above on 6:1-10). The 2 pillars have names, **Jachin** (meaning "he sets up") and **Boaz** (meaning unknown, though with different vowels it would mean "with strength"). Why these names were given and what they signified is unknown.

7:23-26. The Bronze Sea. The huge **molten sea,** according to II Chr. 4:6 a basin for priestly ablutions, is almost 15 feet in diameter and 8 feet deep and is made of **cast** bronze 3 inches thick. It rests on 12 bronze **oxen** facing outward, 3 in each direction.

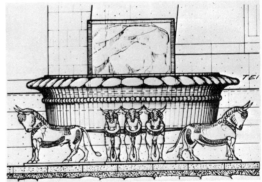

Reconstruction of the Bronze Sea; made of cast bronze, this 15-foot diameter bowl rested on the backs of 12 oxen; estimated weight: 25-30 tons

Why oxen were used is unknown; some have conjectured that they were actually bulls and thus symbols of fertility, but the text gives no basis for this. The basin is set **on the southeast corner of the house** (vs. 39). Its capacity, **two thousand baths**—over 10,000 gallons according to fragments of jars marked "bath" which have been excavated (see "Measures and Money," pp. 1283-85)—is much too great for the dimensions given and probably is an interpolation.

7:27-39. The Stands and Lavers. Ten large wheeled stands are made, into which 10 lavers are set. These are arranged 5 on the N and 5 on the S of the temple. The water in the lavers must have been used in connection with the sacrificial rites (cf. II Chr. 4:6). Some of the technical terms of the description, e.g. **panels** and **frames,** are not understood; but the dimensions and capacity stated seem to make the objects too large and heavy to be movable.

7:40-47. Summary of Bronze Objects. Not only the large objects described above but also many small vessels and decorations are made. All the bronze work is done in the **Jordan** Valley—in an area **between Succoth and Zarethan** (see color map 6) where **clay** is available to make molds for the casting—and then brought to Jerusalem.

7:48-51. *The Furnishings of Gold.* This passage—except the concluding statement (vs. 51) about final transfer of temple furniture and **vessels** to the temple **treasuries**—constitutes a later reflection, possibly by postexilic writers, rather than a contemporary document, as can be seen by comparison with the P account of the tabernacle furnishings in Exod. 37:10–38:7.

C. THE DEDICATION OF THE TEMPLE (8:1-66)

For an earlier parallel to this ch. cf. II Sam. 6. The **feast** of dedication is coincident with the feast of ingathering, or booths (cf. Deut. 16:13-15). It has often been suggested that it was actually the New Year festival (see Intro. to Pss.) according to the calendar beginning in the fall (see "Chronology," pp. 1271-82). According to the later spring calendar **Ethanim** was the **seventh month**. In any event it was the month preceding Bul; thus the feast was held either one month before or 11 months after the actual completion date (cf. 6:38).

8:3-13. *The Ark Brought into the Temple.* The main event is the pilgrimage with the ark, symbolizing Yahweh's invisible presence among his people, and its entrance into the **inner sanctuary.** The passage has been considerably amplified by later additions, esp. vss. 7-11. On the **cherubim** see above on 6:23-28. On the **cloud** cf. the late tradition in Exod. 40:34-35. Vss. 12-13 are a fragment of a song which according to the LXX comes from the "Book of Songs" (see Intro.).

8:14-21. *Explanation for the Building Enterprise.* This is the D editor's interpretation of the fact that Solomon rather than David built the temple. It is an expansion of the first part of the dedicatory prayer, i.e. vss. 22-26. Emphasis is placed on **David** as the object of Yahweh's choice rather than on a **city** where the temple was to be built.

8:22-53. *Solomon's Dedicatory Prayer.* This great prayer is also a late composition. It begins with praise for divine faithfulness to the terms of the Davidic **covenant** (II Sam. 7).

8:27-30. These vss. are a general intro. The temple is an effective place for prayer, since Yahweh has said that his **name shall be there.** His name is the greatest gift that he can give, since by this he gives man power. This gift is divine condescension, for no house can **contain** the infinite deity.

8:31-34. The author believes that calamity is the result of sin. Accordingly, when the people suffer military defeat at the hands of their foes, they must repent. When they confess their sins **in this house,** God may **forgive** and restore them **again to the land**—a phrase that seems to presuppose a knowledge of the Exile.

8:35-40. Similarly when natural calamities overtake the people—e.g. drought, **famine,** or other **plague**—they are the result of sin and can be removed only by divine pardon, attendant on confession.

8:41-43. These vss. are a prayer for the non-Israelites who may be attracted to the temple because of the fame of Israel's God. This passage is typical of a much later age, esp. after the Exile when proselytes to the Jewish faith were much more welcome.

8:44-53. The last part of the prayer is a **supplication** for restoration from exile and an interpretation by the D editor of the meaning of exile as a national calamity. Such an event also lies under divine direction. Implied in the prayer, by its emphasis on God's past deliverance of his **people** from **Egypt,** is the hope that he will again restore them.

8:54-61. *Solomon's Benediction.* At the end of the prayers it is said that Solomon **arose.** This is in apparent contradiction to vs. 22, where he stands and prays. II Chr. 6:13 removes the contradiction by describing a bronze platform on which he first stands and then kneels for the actual prayer. Basic to this prayer is the realization that without divine help the people cannot keep God's laws (vs. 58). Gradually what begins as benediction changes into a pleading with the assembly to remain faithful.

8:62-66. *The Feast of Dedication.* The feast of **seven days** is marked mainly by a large number (surely exaggerated) of sacrifices by which the building is officially dedicated. The passage, like the rest of the ch., is editorial, and may actually describe postexilic practices. The **middle of the court** probably means the area of the altar. Here occurs the first mention of the **bronze altar,** though the bronze furnishings were fully described earlier as of Hiram's workmanship. At least 3 kinds of sacrifices are mentioned; only the **peace offerings** involved the common sacrificial meal. The **assembly** is described as representing the whole of ideal Israel, from the **entrance of Hamath** (the boundary of the city-state of Hamath on the Orontes; see color map 9) to the **Brook of Egypt** (a seasonal stream *ca.* 60 miles SW of Beer-sheba; see color map 4). The passage ends with the bias typical of the D editor, viz. the importance of the Davidic dynasty.

D. SOLOMON'S APEX AND DECLINE (9:1–11:43)

9:1-9. *Solomon's 2nd Vision.* Yahweh appears to Solomon in answer to his dedicatory prayer to state that the continuance of the dynasty and of Israel is conditional on the faithfulness of Solomon and his successors to God's law. Like ch. 8 this is D material and constitutes the editor's explanation for the Exile as due to the people's idolatry.

9:10-14. *Solomon's Bargain with Hiram.* The building operations are finally completed (see above on 7:1-12) and Solomon's treasury is empty. In order to refill it he finds it necessary to sell Hiram **twenty cities in . . . Galilee** bordering on the Tyrian state for a huge amount of gold (vs. 14; on **talents** see "Measures and Money," pp. 1283-85). An editorial parenthesis (vs. 11*a*) sugarcoats this unpalatable bit of history by the implication that Solomon simply gave the villages in appreciation for past favors, but the building materials had already been paid for (cf. 5:11). The ceded area was named **Cabul** (meaning uncertain) and an early folk etymology ("like nothing") has it that Hiram was dissatisfied with his new possession and gave it this derogatory name.

9:15-23. *Solomon's Labor Force.* In contradiction to the true record in 5:13-18, confirmed by the complaint in 12:4, the levy of forced labor is here apolo-

Courtesy of the Oriental Institute, University of Chicago

Ruins of stables at Megiddo, formerly ascribed to Solomon, but more probably from the time of Ahab

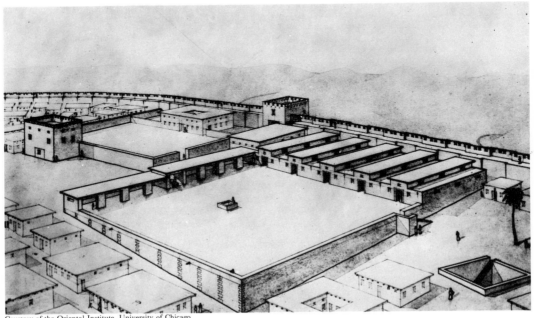

Courtesy of the Oriental Institute, University of Chicago

Reconstruction of stables at Megiddo probably from the time of Ahab; a walkway *ca.* eight feet wide ran down the center of each unit; rows of pillars on each side of the passage supported the roof and served for hitching; between the pillars were mangers and stalls; cf. Solomon's cities for his chariots and horses (horsemen) in I Kings 9:19 and 10:26

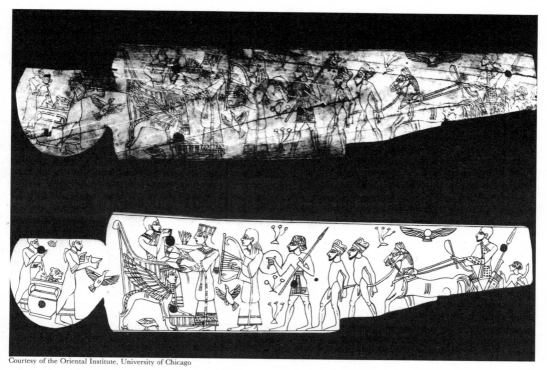

Courtesy of the Oriental Institute, University of Chicago

Ivory plaque from Megiddo (*ca.* 1350-1150 B.C.) incised with scene depicting a king seated on a cherub throne celebrating a victory by feasting while a musician plays a lyre; two bound and naked prisoners are tied to horses of the royal chariot; cf. I Kings 11:18

getically described as applied only to the non-Israelite population, with Israelites pictured as officers. Into the framework of this account has been inserted an early, probably archival, summary of Solomon's building operations (vss. 15*b*-19). Solomon also builds up Jerusalem by extending the city **wall** —presumably N to enclose the palace and temple structure—and constructing the problematic **Millo,** which was some kind of stone or earth work in the city that needed constant repair possibly a kind of stone terracing at the crest.

9:24-25. *A Miscellany.* Vs. 24 is probably taken from Solomon's court annals, whereas vs. 25 shows him as dutifully performing the cultic rites of major concern—esp. to a later age—the celebration of the 3 annual feasts prescribed for all Israelites.

9:26-28. *Solomon's Navy.* The fleet is stationed at **Ezion-geber** at the N end of the **Red Sea** (i.e. the Gulf of Aqaba; see comment on Num. 21:4-9 and color map 7), the control of which was conditional on the subjection of **Edom.** Its purpose was purely commercial. Various locations for **Ophir** have been proposed—E Africa, SW Arabia (see color map 7), but SE Arabia, where it is known that **gold** was produced is the most likely. On **talents** see "Measures and Money," pp. 1283-85.

10:1-13. *Visit of the Queen of Sheba.* This account describes a diplomatic visit by the monarch of a distant state to Solomon's court—no doubt to negotiate trade relations. Archaeologists have discovered that a highly developed Sabean kingdom existed in Solomon's time in SW Arabia (see color map 7) while Assyrian inscriptions seem to confirm biblical references (e.g. Gen. 25:3; Job 1:15) to Sabeans

in N Arabia. The interchange of munificent gifts was part of oriental etiquette on such an occasion. There is no reason to doubt the historicity of the event, though details are probably exaggerated in order to enhance Solomon's fame.

10:11-12. The story is interrupted by these vss., which amplify the account of Solomon's commercial navy in 9:26-28, calling attention to the importation of **precious stones** and **almug** wood. The meaning of the latter is unknown; it apparently could be used for making musical instruments.

10:14-25. *Various Laudatory Details.* Solomon's commercial exploits bring in a huge quantity of **gold** used for all kinds of displays. Since gold is a soft metal the **shields** would be useless in warfare and serve only to exhibit the splendor of Solomon's reign. They are hung in the national armory (cf. 7:2-5). The **large shields** of vs. 16 are long and curved to cover the body, whereas those of vs. 17 are small and round. On the weight terms see "Measures and Money," pp. 1283-85. On **Tarshish** see comment on Jonah 1:1-3.

10:23-25. This exaggerated summary of Solomon's **riches** and **wisdom** finds parallels in ancient oriental royal inscriptions. A later age made Solomon the wisest man of all times, a judgment contradicted by ch. 11.

10:26-29. *Solomon's Cavalry.* For **horsemen** in vs. 26 read "horses." Trade in horses and chariotry was with Asia Minor. In vs. 28 **Egypt** (Hebrew *Misraim*) must be corrected to Musri, ancient Cappadocia (see color map 9), which together with **Kue,** i.e. Cilicia, was a center of horse breeding. It is possible that in vs. 29 Egypt is correct as a center for chariot building, though this too may have been intended as Musri.

11:1-8. Solomon's Large Harem. The D editor has placed all of Solomon's difficulties in a final ch., thereby creating the impression that these all occurred in the final years of his reign as a direct result of his idolatry, though this is hardly true, as vss. 21, 25 show. This idolatry, the editor insists, was due to his large harem that included many foreigners. Many of these, primarily those of subject states, were probably political hostages. These foreign wives have their own **gods,** and Solomon provides for the cult of these gods. Specifically mentioned are **Ashtoreth** (i.e. Astarte), the Phoenician fertility goddess, and **Milcom** (meaning "the king" and sometimes shortened to **Molech,** "king," vs. 7) and **Chemosh,** astral deities, for whom he builds altars on the **mountain east of Jerusalem,** i.e. the Mt. of Olives (cf. II Sam. 15:32).

11:9-13. Yahweh's Judgment on Solomon. Here we have the D editor's explanation for the division of the kingdom at the end of Solomon's reign. Yahweh has warned Solomon in dreams against idolatry. Because of his disobedience Yahweh will remove all but **one tribe,** Judah, from the Davidic house after his death—a classic case of prophecy after the event.

11:14-22. Hadad's Revolt. Edom was conquered by David (cf. II Sam. 8:13-14), and on that occasion the young Edomite prince fled first S to the desert of **Midian,** E of the Gulf of Aqaba (see color map 4), then managed to make his way through the wilderness (or possibly oasis) of **Paran,** in the Sinai Peninsula, to **Egypt.** The circumstances of the Edomite invasion are not fully clear from the text. Obviously a general massacre occurred, though vs. 16 is exaggerated—Edom was to remain for centuries! Hadad eventually intermarries with Pharaoh's house and returns to Edom at the news of David's and Joab's deaths and apparently revolts against Solomon.

11:23-25. Rezon's Revolt. Syria was also defeated by David (cf. II Sam. 8:3-12; 10), quite thoroughly. On **Zobah** see comment on II Sam. 8:3-8. An escapee from that slaughter, Rezon, becomes a bandit chief and, when the weaker Solomon becomes king, is able to establish an independent Syrian state at **Damascus** which long remains a military opponent to Israel.

11:26-40. Jeroboam's Revolt. Jeroboam is from the N—an **Ephraimite** from **Zeredah** (of uncertain location, though see color map 6). Because of his ability he is given supervision of the **forced labor** in Ephraim, the **house of Joseph.** The form which his rebellion takes is not shown, but he is forced to flee to **Egypt,** where he becomes friendly with **Shishak,** the ruler there. Into this story is inserted the prophetic story of a prediction by **Ahijah** of the division of the kingdom. The language is characteristically D, with its emphasis on the continuation of the Davidic house in Jerusalem and the warning to keep the laws of God. The symbolic tearing action is typically prophetic (cf. I Sam. 15:27-28), but also reflects a later period when Judah had assimilated Simeon, thereby making **one tribe** out of 2.

11:41-43. Obituary Notice. The regular D notice for change of ruler (see Intro.) occurs here for the first time. **Forty years** is not an exact number (see above on 2:10-12).

III. History of the 2 Kingdoms (I 12:1-II 17:41)

A. The Division (12:1-24)

12:1-20. The Revolt of the 10 Tribes. The story as told here is strangely inconsistent. According to vss. 2, 3, 12 Jeroboam is a ringleader in the revolt, but vs. 20 pictures him as summoned to the kingship. The LXX omits vss. 2-3a and the reference to Jeroboam in vs. 12, thus making a consistent story.

12:1-15. Significantly, and unlike Solomon, **Rehoboam** cannot be crowned at Jerusalem and has to

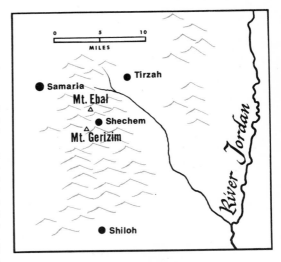

meet delegates in the N at **Shechem** (see color map 6), an old center of the sacral tribal union for premonarchic days. They propose an end to the forced labor levy as a condition of their loyalty. The young king-elect foolishly follows the advice of his contemporaries and advises the assembly of his intended despotism with autocratic bravado. The D editor adds an interpretative note (vs. 15) that Rehoboam's foolishness was a fate divinely inspired in accordance with 11:29-39.

12:16-20. The result is immediate revolt against the Davidic dynasty by all the tribes except **Judah.** Sheba's old watchword is revived (cf. II Sam. 20:1) and Rehoboam has to **flee** for his life to his capital. The 10 tribes then elect **Jeroboam** as king, and the old rupture between Judah and the N is again complete. Politically the 2 kingdoms now go their own way, the S under dynastic rule, the N under a strong-man rule. ·

12:21-24. An Attempt to Quell the Revolt. Here the name of **Benjamin** is added to that of Judah, reflecting the later extension of Judah N. Rehoboam's military action is stayed by a prophetic oracle, according to a late prophetic story, intended to show that the Davidic dynasty was obedient to the divine intent.

B. Early History of the Kingdoms (12:25-16:34)

12:25-33. Jeroboam's Cultic Innovations. The account of Jeroboam's reign in Israel is given first and at some length (12:25–14:20). The first capital of the rebel kingdom is established at **Shechem**. The fortification of **Penuel** in Transjordan near the Jabbok (see color map 8) was probably intended both to interrupt the N-S trade route and to serve as a frontier post against invaders from the E.

12:26-33. Of more concern to the D editor is the necessary condemnation of Jeroboam, "who made Israel to sin" by his attempt to break with the Jerusalem cult. Jeroboam realizes the danger inherent to his new kingdom in the cultic dominance of Jerusalem and seeks to promote local shrines, esp. that at **Bethel,** known in Amos' time as "the king's sanctuary" (Amos 7:13). At least 2 of these shrines he sets up golden **calves,** actually bulls, as images of Yahweh—though some scholars surmise that these figures were really thrones for the invisible Yahweh, like the cherubim in the Jerusalem temple (see above on 6:23-28). These symbols were particularly dangerous in view of the Canaanite use of the bull as a fertility symbol. Other measures concern the clergy for these centers, or **high places,** as well as a change in the cultic calendar. Here the Judean bias is esp. evident. The celebration of the **feast** (presumably ingathering, or booths) in the **eighth month** was simply an adherence to ancient custom, whereas the Judean observance in the 7th month was a later change (see above on 8:1-66).

13:1-10. *Jeroboam Warned by a Divine Word.* This is a prophetic legend not earlier than the time of Josiah, since the author is acquainted with the reforms of 622. According to the story a Judean **man of God** utters an oracle against the **Bethel** altar, saying that one day **Josiah** will defile the **altar** by slaying the **priests** of the illegitimate shrines on it. The angry king tries to order the arrest of his rebuker, but his arm is paralyzed, and the prophetic sign of the altar tumbling into ruins immediately takes place. On the holy man's intercession the king's arm is **restored.**

13:11-32. *The Sequel.* In accordance with instructions the Judean holy man refuses to accept hospitality in Bethel. A Bethel **prophet** (so called in the N corresponding to "man of God" in Judah) intercepts him and by a lying oracle persuades him to accept food and drink. The prophet then gives a true oracle reproving the holy man for his disobedience and predicting his violent death. The prediction is fulfilled; a **lion** kills him. The prophet then buries him and mourns for him, requesting **his sons** to bury his own body in the same tomb. The story is homiletic and ties in with that in II 23:17-20. On lying prophets see below on 22:5-28.

13:33-34. *The D Editor's Judgment on Jeroboam.* Not only has Jeroboam created an illegitimate cult but he has himself **consecrated** the illegitimate priesthood—to the D editor an unpardonable crime which can be corrected only by extermination of the royal **house.**

14:1-18. *Ahijah's Prophecy.* Another prophetic saga is told to insure the complete denunciation of the actions of the renegade king. The long speech of Ahijah is the D editor's interpretation of the N kingdom's ruin as due to its apostate cult. The editor considers it peculiarly appropriate that the prophet who predicted Jeroboam's rebel kingship many years previously (11:29-39) should now predict his doom. The condemnation is put into the framework of a tale about a hopelessly **sick** child of Jeroboam. The queen disguises herself at the king's behest to seek guidance from the now aged and blind prophet. But the prophet, divinely warned, reprimands her and predicts the child's death before her return. The older form of the story is probably contained in vss. 1-6, 12, 17.

14:15. The term **Asherim** (Hebrew plural of Asherah) probably refers to male and female fertility symbols associated with the worship of the Canaanite goddess Asherah (cf. e.g. 15:13; 18:19).

14:17. The mention that the queen returned to **Tirzah,** if historically accurate, indicates that Jeroboam early in his reign moved his capital from Shechem (cf. 12:25) to that city. Tirzah probably lay *ca.* 7 miles NE of Shechem (see color map 8). Some interpreters believe it was rather Baasha who established the N capital at Tirzah (cf. 15:33), where it remained till Omri built Samaria (16:23-24).

14:19-20. *Obituary Notice of Jeroboam.* This is given in the usual annalistic terms (see Intro.): reference to the court records, the length of his reign, his death, and the name of his successor.

14:21-31. *Rehoboam's Reign in Judah.* Rehoboam's reign is introduced with the common formula giving his age at accession, the length of his reign, and his mother's name (given only for Judean kings). Rehoboam's mother is one of the foreign wives of Solomon, an **Ammonitess** (repeated by error in vs. 31).

14:22-24. The particular accusations are stereotyped: the erection of illegitimate shrines, **pillars,** and **Asherim** (see above on vs. 15) and the existence of **male cult prostitutes** (cult devotees in Canaanite religion)—all strictly forbidden in the later D legislation which guided the editor's evaluation.

14:25-28. Sheshonk, or **Shishak,** was the first ruler of the 12th dynasty of Egypt and Jeroboam's patron (cf. 11:40). His invasion, however, was not to support Jeroboam but simply to gain booty, as proved by the well-known Karnak inscription with its long list of plundered Palestinian cities of both N and S.

14:29-31. This is the usual obituary notice for Judean kings (see Intro.). Almost all of them are said to have been buried in Jerusalem, but the site of the royal tomb area has not as yet been found.

15:1-8. *Abijam's Reign in Judah.* Abijam, the 2nd king of Judah, reigns only **three years.** The name **Abishalom** is a variant form of Absalom (cf. II Chr. 11:20-21; but contrast II Chr. 13:2) and has sometimes been taken to mean David's son. This identification is supported by the appropriateness of **Maacah** as a name for the **daughter** of Absalom the son of David (see comment on II Sam. 14:25-27) but otherwise seems unlikely because (*a*) any child of his would apparently be considerably older than Solomon's son Rehoboam and (*b*) after the rebellion his children would probably be in disfavor with the rest of David's family. Though Josephus, Jewish historian of the first cent. A.D., suggests a solution to the age problem by making Maacah the granddaughter of Absalom through his daughter Tamar (cf. II Sam. 14:27), it appears more probable that Abishalom was a different man from David's rebel son.

15:3-8. Abijam's rule is condemned as an evil one by the D editor. Typical of his point of view are vss. 4-5, enhancing the promise of a dynasty to **David.** Vs. 6 is a repetition of 14:30 and quite out of place here. Vss. 7-8 give the usual obituary (cf. 14:29-31).

15:9-24. *Asa's Reign in Judah.* Asa is said to have ruled the S kingdom **forty-one years.** A problem arises regarding the name of his mother, who is given the same name as the mother of Abijam, his father (see above on vss. 1-8). Probably the explanation is that **Maacah** retained the status of queen mother, since Asa must have been a minor when he became king.

15:11-15. Because of the cultic reforms of his reign Asa is judged by the D editor to have done **right** in Yahweh's **eyes,** though it must be noted that he did not remove the shrines outside Jerusalem. The Canaanite practices have apparently been continued from the time of Rehoboam chiefly under Maacah's influence, and the young king courageously demotes his grandmother from her harem leadership and destroys her idol. On **Asherah** see above on 14:15.

15:16-22. These vss. describe Asa's military and political accomplishments. **Baasha** of Israel (cf. 15:33-16:7) fortifies **Ramah** of Benjamin, only 5 miles N of Jerusalem (see color map 8). By a large bribe Asa persuades **Ben-hadad** I of **Damascus** to relieve the pressure by attacking the N borders of Israel. The establishment of this treaty with Judah means breaking a similar treaty with Israel, a treachery which appeals to Ben-hadad's raiding instincts. The attack on Israel's N frontier is extensive, permitting Asa to regain the Benjamin territory in question. Instead of taking over Ramah as a fortress, Asa has it dismantled as a national work project in order to fortify **Geba**—probably an error for Gibeah, Saul's old capital, 2 miles S of Ramah—and **Mizpah,** 3 miles to the N. The passage ends with the usual obituary notice but adds that in his latter days he was **diseased in his feet.**

15:25-32. *Nadab's Reign in Israel.* Jeroboam I of Israel is succeeded briefly by his son Nadab, who as a N king is naturally judged by the D editor as **evil.** After less than **two years** a military *coup d'état* under **Baasha** of Issachar results in the assassination of Nadab along with the entire family of Jeroboam. Such wholesale wiping out of a royal house in order to destroy all possible opposition was common ancient practice. It is interpreted by the D editor as the fulfillment of Ahijah's prophecy to Jeroboam's wife (cf. 14:14). Vs. 32 is a repetition of vs. 16; either it is out of place or Nadab should be read for Baasha.

15:33-16:7. *Baasha's Reign in Israel.* Baasha is reported as ruling from **Tirzah** (see above on 14:17-18) for **twenty-four years.**

16:1-7. Nothing is told of Baasha's career except a prophetic doom oracle by **Jehu the son of Hanani.** The oracle is similar to that of Ahijah against the house of Jeroboam (14:7-16) but in abbreviated form. Somewhat puzzling is the condemnation of Baasha's destruction of the **house of Jeroboam** in vs. 7*b*, since this was considered the fulfillment of the prophetic word according to 15:29. Possibly this is simply the judgment of the exilic D editor (cf. "blood of Jezreel," Hos. 1:4).

16:8-14. *Elah's Reign in Israel.* Baasha is succeeded by his son Elah, who in turn is assassinated

by one of his military commanders during his 2nd year. Like Baasha, **Zimri** inaugurates a bloodbath of his predecessor's house—interpreted again as the fulfillment of a prophetic oracle.

16:15-22. *Zimri's Reign in Israel.* Zimri's assassination of Elah touches off civil war. On hearing of it **all Israel** (i.e. the army) elects **Omri** king. He immediately marches on **Tirzah.** Zimri, besieged in his castle, burns it to the ground and dies, having reigned only one week.

16:21-22. Omri's victory over Zimri is merely the first stage in his campaign. The people are **divided** in support of Omri and an otherwise unknown **Tibni.** Over 4 years of civil war end with Omri's victory, laconically described by **so Tibni died and Omri became king.**

16:23-28. *Omri's Reign in Israel.* Zimri's death is dated **in the twenty-seventh year of Asa** and Omri's reign is said to begin **in the thirty-first year.** In the LXX the interval is apparently attributed to Tibni (see "Chronology," pp. 1271-82). That Omri was an extremely capable ruler is known from nonbiblical sources. He conquered Moab, made a marriage alliance with Sidon (i.e. Phoenicia), and built

Courtesy of Herbert G. May

Hill on which Omri built ancient Samaria (modern Tell Sebasteyeh)

Samaria (see color map 8) as the new permanent capital of Israel. A cent. later Assyrian kings still referred to the kingdom as the "land of Omri." The biblical writers recall only his purchase and building of Samaria midway during his reign. Samaria became as important politically for Israel as Jerusalem was for Judah.

16:29-34. *Introduction to Ahab of Israel.* Omri is succeeded by Ahab, in whom the D editor is particularly interested. Almost all the remainder of I Kings deals with events of his reign. Information concerning his period came to the editor mainly through prophetic stories, this passage being the only exception. It relates his unpardonable marriage with **Jezebel,** daughter of **Ethbaal king of the Sidonians,** who according to Josephus was a priest of Astarte. It was her influence and ardor in attempting to substitute the worship of **Baal** for that of Israel's God that evoked the wrath of later historians in Judah.

16:32-33. The title **Baal** (lit. "master" or "lord"), which in earlier times was often used of Yahweh (see comment on II Sam. 2:8-11), is at least from the time of Ahab on used specifically of the Syrian god Hadad (cf. Ben-hadad, i.e. "son of Hadad," 15:16-24), worshiped as "Lord of the heavens." Under Ahab, because of the influence of Jezebel,

Courtesy of the Palestine Exploration Fund

Excavations at Samaria showing foundation walls of temple courtyard built by Herod the Great with the walls of the Israelite palace area at a lower level

Baalism became established in Samaria as an officially approved cult. On **Asherah** see above on 14:15.

16:34. This incidental historical note refers to the official refortification of **Jericho** by **Hiel.** He suffers the loss of 2 children, which the D editor interprets as the fulfillment of an ancient curse (cf. Josh. 6:26). Excavation at Gezer of a foundation containing skeletons of persons apparently sacrificed to secure divine favor for the construction has led many to conjecture that this verse records such a foundation sacrifice. But the text is more naturally understood as reflecting a popular interpretation of an unwary builder's double misfortune.

C. Elijah Stories (17:1-19:21)

Chs. 17-19; 21 contain a series of stories, largely miracle stories, in which Elijah is the chief figure, and his name (which means "Yahweh is God") is the central theme.

17:1-7. Elijah and the Drought. The first scene shows Elijah, in obedience to Yahweh, predicting to Ahab a terrible drought. For this audacity he has to flee to an area beyond Ahab's jurisdiction, again by divine direction. He goes to the **brook Cherith** in Transjordan (see color map 8). There God commands **ravens** to feed him twice daily. This suffices until the drought dries up the brook.

17:8-16. Elijah at Zarephath. Again at divine bidding Elijah goes to **Zarephath,** *ca.* 10 miles S of **Sidon** (see color map 8), to be fed by an impoverished **widow.** The widow at Elijah's request hospitably provides **water** but she lacks sufficient food. Miraculously the **meal** and **oil** are multiplied

in accordance with a divine oracle given by the prophet.

17:17-24. *The Revival of the Dead Boy.* When the widow's son dies, she is afraid of the prophet. Ancients felt that holy men could detect hidden faults as well as perform wonders and predict events. Elijah takes the child to his room and prays to Yahweh, remonstrating with him on this seeming injustice. Elijah then performs a ritual prayer for a return to life of the child. The revived lad is restored to **his mother,** who affirms her faith in Elijah's prophethood. This kind of story is a common folktale; a similar version about Elisha appears in II 4:32-37.

18:1-19. Elijah's Challenge to Ahab. The drought is now to come to an end, but first the superiority of God over Baal must be decisively demonstrated. This occurs **in the third year.** Later Jewish traditions speak of a drought of 3½ years (cf. Luke 4:25; Jas. 5:17). As always Elijah moves only by divine order. Because of the severity of the famine Ahab orders his chamberlain **Obadiah** to help search throughout the land for food for the royal animals.

18:7-16. Later Elijah meets Obadiah, who is surprised that Elijah should openly appear in Israel. Ahab holds the prophet personally responsible, because of his operative word, for the drought and has conducted a frantic search everywhere for him. Elijah bids Obadiah summon the king, but the chamberlain reacts in fear. He knows that the prophet suddenly appears and disappears by the **Spirit of Yahweh.** He himself has been loyal to Yahweh rather than to Baal, and should Elijah again disappear he fears for his life. Only when Elijah promises that he will remain, swearing by the full cultic name of the God of Israel, i.e. Yahweh **of hosts,** does Obadiah obey.

18:17-19. Finally the 2 foes, king and prophet, meet. Ahab, too full of animosity to greet his foe, calls him the one who troubles Israel. Elijah sternly corrects him by placing the blame for the famine directly on the king's idolatrous proclivities. Without further ado he imperiously orders Ahab to sum-

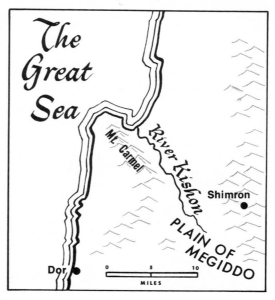

mon Israel, together with the prophets of **Baal** (see above on 16:32-33) and **Asherah** (see above on 14: 15), to **Mount Carmel** (see color map 8). This famous mountain on the N Palestinian coast was an old shrine, as appears from Thutmose III's reference to it as "the holy promontory."

18:20-40. *Yahweh vs. Baal.* Ahab obeys Elijah and summons the popular assembly, which is to be judge and jury. The contest will be between Elijah and the Baal prophets. **The God who answers by fire,** i.e. lights the sacrifice without human instrumentality, is to be adjudged God. On Elijah's feeling of solitude cf. 19:9-18.

18:25-29. The prophets of Baal are to have the first opportunity. They engage in various cultic manipulations—a ritual limping dance about the unlit **altar,** wounding themselves with **swords** to produce **blood,** and calling on Baal ecstatically (**raved on**). Elijah, certain of the outcome, mocks the devotees (vs. 27) by suggesting that their Baal is busy, **has gone aside** (i.e. to relieve himself), is traveling, or is sleeping. The Baalists persist until midafternoon, the time of the evening sacrifice.

18:30-35. Now Elijah's turn has come. As the people gather about, he prepares an **altar.** It is not clear whether this is a new altar (vs. 32a) or an old altar that has been ruined, possibly through Jezebel's fanaticism (vs. 30b). In any event vs. 31 referring to **twelve** (rather than 10) **tribes** is a much later insertion hardly appropriate to a N Israel story. To avoid any trickery the sacrifice and the altar are thoroughly drenched with **water.** Some have suggested that this was a magical rainmaking ceremony, but rather it is evidence of good faith.

18:36-40. The crucial moment is at hand. Elijah prays. Suddenly God's **fire** falls from heaven. God has spoken; the sacrifice, even **the stones, and the dust,** are consumed. Awestricken, the people render their decision: Yahweh is God. It is foolish to try to rationalize the story by calling the fire lightning. The whole point is the miraculous intervention, which is the way the Hebrews saw the way God acts. In fact, in view of vs. 44 it could not have been lightning at all. In the flush of this dramatic denouement Elijah has the idolatrous **prophets,** all 450, slain.

18:41-46. *The End of the Drought.* Now that Elijah's name, "Yahweh is God," has been vindicated, rain may be expected. Elijah goes to the **top of Carmel** to engage in a 7-fold rain ritual. Ahab is warned to hurry back to **Jezreel,** *ca.* 17 miles to the SE (see color map 8), at the foot of Mt. Gilboa. Endowed with supernatural strength, Elijah is able to outrun Ahab's steeds. The rains descend. Yahweh's victory would now seem to be complete.

19:1-3. *Jezebel's Vow.* When Jezebel hears of the outcome at Carmel, she swears an oath by **the gods** that she will kill Elijah and so informs him. In fear he flees **for his life,** passing through Judah and beyond **Beer-sheba** into the desert.

19:4-8. *Elijah in Despair.* Out in the desert the prophet sits in the shade of a **broom** shrub and, completely discouraged, begs to be allowed to **die.** Falling asleep, he is awakened by the **angel** of Yahweh—i.e. God appearing in human form, an apparition typical of the J and E writers. He eats divinely provided food and after another rest is told to continue. He is thus able to journey for **forty days and forty nights** without further nourishment. His

destination is the holy mountain of revelation, called Sinai in J but **Horeb** in the D and E sources.

19:9-18. *God's Revelation to Elijah.* On arrival at the holy mountain Elijah goes **to a cave.** There is some confusion in the story. Vss. 13b-14 repeat almost word for word vss. 9b-10. Furthermore vs. 11a commands Elijah to stand outside, whereas vs. 13 finds Elijah still inside the cave. It seems best to consider vss. 9b-11a as a later addition to the original story. In the original story Elijah is in the cave when a **strong wind,** an **earthquake,** and a **fire** take place successively; but contrary to expectation Yahweh appears in none of these. It is the contrasting sound of a gentle whisper which Elijah recognizes as the voice of deity, causing him like Moses of old (Exod. 3:6) to hide **his face** lest he look on God. To Yahweh's reproving inquiry about his business here far outside Israel he, in an orgy of self-pity, complains that all have forsaken God and that he the fugitive is the sole true worshiper **left.** As though Carmel had never happened!

19:15-18. Before replying directly to Elijah's complaint Yahweh gives him a 3-fold mission—the anointing of **Hazael** as **king** in **Damascus** (cf. II 8:7-15), **Jehu** as **king** of **Israel** (cf. II 9:1-10), and **Elisha** as his own successor. Since Elijah carries out only the last, it is possible that part of the Elisha cycle has here intruded into the Elijah story. In such case vs. 17 is a judgment by an editor subsequent to that confusion. Finally Yahweh addresses himself to Elijah's complaint by correcting the facts; he is far from being his sole surviving worshiper.

19:19-21. *The Call of Elisha.* Elijah now carries out his assignment by finding Elisha, a young farmer of substance, and throwing on him his own hairy prophetic **mantle**—thought to be invested with great power (cf. II 2:13-15). Elisha recognizes this action as a call to service and asks permission to take leave of his parents. Elijah's peculiar answer is puzzling. It may be a mysterious way of saying: Do take leave of your parents if you recognize the intent of what I have done, i.e. invested you as my successor.

D. War with Syria (20:1-43)

This ch. gives an account of the constant wars between Israel and Damascus *ca.* the middle of the 9th cent. It is from a source completely separate from chs. 17-19; 21-22 and is the only account at all favorable to Ahab. It makes no reference to Elijah and Elisha, though unnamed prophets are mentioned.

20:1-12. *Ben-hadad's Audacious Demands.* Ben-hadad of Damascus (cf. 15:16-24; but see below on vss. 30c-34) heads a large federation of troops, probably a group of Aramean kinglets. He has laid siege to **Samaria,** and it is in desperate straits. Ben-hadad sends in heavy demands, to which Ahab accedes, but then comes the malicious 2nd demand to open up the city to pillage. This is refused, and Ben-hadad states his intention to pulverize the city. Ahab answers defiantly with a proverb roughly parallel to "Don't count your chickens before they're hatched."

20:13-21. *Israel's Victory.* On the advice of an unnamed **prophet** Ahab determines on attack. At **noon,** an uncivilized time to begin a battle, a small group of **two hundred and thirty-two** men leave the city to draw on the besiegers. Then, when the "suicide squad" is engaged, the full army of **seven thousand** falls on the **Syrians,** and panic turns the tide. The Syrians flee leaving their equipment behind them.

20:22-34. ***Ben-hadad's 2nd Attack.*** Ben-hadad's military council suggests 2 changes in strategy for the next campaign: (*a*) Attack on the **plain,** since Israel's gods are thought to be mountain **gods.** For this rash statement a divine oracle through another prophet (vs. 28) promises Ahab complete victory. (*b*) Substitution of military **commanders** for **kings** to lead the Syrian forces. Accordingly battle is joined in the plain, at **Aphek** (location uncertain but placed by some scholars E of the Sea of Galilee; see color map 8). The Syrians are completely routed, though the numbers in vss. 29-30*b* are probably much exaggerated. **In the spring** (vss. 22, 26) can hardly be right. Warfare was not conducted until the fall, when the harvest was finished. The phrase probably should be rendered "at the beginning of the year," i.e. in the fall.

20:30c-34. The surrender, though complete, is conducted with oriental cunning. Execution of a defeated king was normal procedure; but Ahab, flattered by the abjectness of the conquered, not only spares Ben-hadad but courteously takes him into his own **chariot.** Ben-hadad then proposes economic concessions in his capital for Israelite merchants and the return of **cities** earlier taken by the Syrians during the reign of Baasha (15:20). **My father** (vs. 34) has led many scholars to believe that this Ben-hadad is not the same as that in 15:16-24, but this is by no means certain.

20:35-43. ***Rebuke of Ahab's Leniency.*** Another unnamed **prophet,** after having a comrade wound him, disguises himself so as to hide the prophetic brand on his forehead and tells the king a tale. He was trusty for a Syrian captive who has escaped, he says, and he now fears the consequences. Ahab refuses to listen to his appeal. Thereupon the prophet drops his disguise and predicts Ahab's death as penalty for having released Ben-hadad.

E. Elijah Stories, Continued (21:1-29)

21:1-16. ***Naboth's Vineyard.*** The story of royal violation of peasant property rights is told as a setting for the curse on Ahab and his house by Elijah, and is thus part of the Elijah cycle. The scene of the incident is **Jezreel** (see above on 18:41-46). Naboth refuses to sell his patrimony to the king, who goes home in a fit of pique. His wicked queen takes the matter in hand by ordering trumped-up charges brought against Naboth by 2 false witnesses (cf. Deut. 17:6; 19:15). Accordingly a **fast** is proclaimed—something done only in a great crisis. The false witnesses then present their charge that Naboth has **cursed God and the king** (cf. Exod. 22:28). This was a heinous crime, since a curse was thought by ancients to have inherent power. A spoken word was believed to be immediately effective. Such a curse could only be wiped out by stoning and state confiscation of goods. Thus Ahab takes over the coveted **vineyard.**

21:17-29. ***The Curse on Ahab's House.*** This story belongs to the Elijah cycle, as its intro. shows. **Elijah** is directed by a divine oracle to **meet Ahab** and pronounce doom on the king for his perfidy. The D

editor has expanded the original story by extending the curse to cover Ahab's **house** (vss. 20*b*-26) and in the process has dropped Elijah's original words which caused Ahab to show remorse.

21:27-29. Because of the king's outward repentance a 2nd oracle mitigates the doom by postponing the complete extermination of his house to a succeeding generation.

F. A 2nd Account of the Syrian War (22:1-53)

This ch. records Ahab's final battle, which must have taken place less than a year after the battle of Qarqar (853), in which Assyrian records report Ahab's fighting as an ally of Ben-hadad and the Syrians against the Assyrians (see "The History of Israel," pp. 1018-25).

22:2-4. The fact that **Jehoshaphat** is pressed into military service seems to indicate that Judah at this time was a vassal state of Israel.

22:5-28. ***The Story of Micaiah.*** Before going to battle men were accustomed to seek an oracle to see whether God would help them (cf. I Sam. 23:1-5). **Four hundred** prophets predict success for the venture. Jehoshaphat suspects this unanimity and asks whether there is **another prophet** who may be consulted. So **Micaiah the son of Imlah,** otherwise unknown, is summoned.

22:13-23. When the fearless Micaiah appears he too, with tongue in cheek, echoes the reply of the 400. Adjured to speak the **truth** only, he poetically predicts the death of the king in battle. Then he continues with an account of a heavenly vision dramatizing a primitive view of the false prophet: God is sitting in conclave embarrassed by the continued existence of the evil **Ahab.** How can Ahab be misled into going to battle? Eventually one **spirit** has a suggestion; he will be a **lying spirit** for the band of prophets. Micaiah does not deny the sincerity of his fellow prophets; he simply states that they were intentionally deluded by God.

22:24-28. For such treason Micaiah is **struck** by **Zedekiah,** leader of the false prophets, and ironically asked how this lying spirit transported himself to speak to him. Micaiah replies ambiguously that this will be clear when Zedekiah must flee for his life. Ahab then gives Micaiah into custody, to be held prisoner until his safe return. Vs. 28*b* is a late editorial quotation from Mic. 1:2*a* which incorrectly identifies Micaiah with the prophet Micah of the late 8th cent.

22:29-40. ***Ahab's Death.*** To avoid the dire fate predicted by Micaiah, Ahab goes into battle **disguised** as a common soldier, but to no avail. The chance shot of a bowman fells him in fulfillment of the prophetic word, and by **sunset** he dies. Ahab is **buried** in **Samaria** and the account ends with the usual obituary and succession notice. The D editor added vs. 38 to show the correctness of Elijah's prophecy in 21:19. **The ivory house which he built** (i.e. palace decorated with ivory inlays; cf. Ps. 45:8) has been substantiated by archaeological finds of the Samarian ivories.

22:41-50. ***Jehoshaphat's Reign in Judah.*** Jehoshaphat becomes sole ruler in Ahab's **fourth year** after a coregency with **Asa,** his father, for 3 or 4 years which must be assumed to complete his total reign of **twenty-five** years (see "Chronology," pp. 1271-82).

On vs. 44 see above on vss. 2-4. Another early detail is described in vss. 47-49. **Edom** is subject to Judah, being ruled by a Judean governor. Jehoshaphat's attempt to rebuild Solomon's fleet (cf. 9:25-28) is ill fated because of lack of naval experience. He astutely rejects an Israelite offer of help as interference.

22:51-53. *Accession of Ahaziah in Israel.* The accession date of Ahaziah is based on Jehoshaphat's sole rule and ignores his coregency (see above on vss. 41-50).

THE SECOND BOOK OF THE KINGS

JOHN WILLIAM WEVERS

For the introduction see Intro. to I Kings. The outline of the contents indicated by the headings continues that in I Kings.

G. ELIJAH STORIES, CONCLUDED (1:1-18)

The ch. begins with a statement taken from 3:5. The remainder, except for the obituary and succession notice at the end, is a story from the prophetic cycle. In general tone it is far more like the Elisha stories than like those of the Elijah cycle.

1:2-16. The Sickness of Ahaziah of Israel. The occasion for the tale is Ahaziah's illness resulting from a fall and his consequent search for an oracle from Baal instead of from Israel's God. Probably the name here given Baal was originally Baal-zebul (cf. Beelzebul, Mark 3:22 and parallels, where he is called "prince of demons"; see comment on Mark 3:22-26, 27) and was intentionally changed in early times to ridicule the idol by calling it **Baal-zebub,** meaning "lord of flies." **Ekron** was the Philistine city nearest to Samaria (see color map 8).

1:5-16. The king's messengers report being intercepted by a man pronouncing a doom oracle. Ahaziah recognizes Elijah and sends 2 consecutive military detachments to apprehend the impertinent prophet, with disastrous results. A 3rd, whose **captain** pleads with the prophet, is spared. Elijah then predicts death to the king in person. The tale is but another stage in the story of Elijah as Yahweh's prophet in the struggle between Israel's God and the Canaanite Baal.

1:17-18. Obituary of Ahaziah of Israel. The succession notice states that Ahaziah was succeeded by **Jehoram, his brother,** in the 2nd year of **Jehoram** of **Judah,** whereas 3:1 states that this took place in the 18th year of Jehoshaphat. Apparently Jehoram of Judah had begun a coregency with his father during the preceding year (see "Chronology," pp. 1271-82).

H. ELISHA STORIES (2:1-8:29)

2:1-12b. Elijah's Ascent into Heaven. Though Elijah is the central figure of this story, it really belongs to the Elisha cycle. **Elisha** is here introduced as the successor to Elijah's **spirit.** He receives not only Elijah's **mantle** with its mystic powers but also the legacy of a firstborn son, a **double portion** of his spirit. He thus becomes the leader of the prophetic bands.

2:1-8. The 2 prophets walk **from Gilgal . . . down to Bethel . . . to Jericho . . . to the Jordan.** Gilgal here can hardly mean the well-known sanctuary site near Jericho but must refer to the town of this name *ca.* 7 miles N of Bethel (see comment on I Sam. 7:5-17). When they reach the Jordan Elijah, like a 2nd Moses or Joshua, miraculously parts the Jordan by smiting it with **his mantle.**

2:9-12b. Suddenly the fiery **horses** and **chariot** come and Elijah is transported heavenward. Elisha cries out in despair; Elijah is equal to Israel's entire cavalry. The story of Elijah's miraculous translation probably originally had something to do with the myth of the chariots of the sun. In later legend Elijah is ranked with Moses as one whom God personally cared for, and for this reason no one knows their graves (cf. Deut. 34:6; Mal. 4:5; Matt. 17:3; Mark 9:4-5; Luke 9:30-33).

2:12c-18. Elisha as Elijah II. That Elisha now is fully endowed with the spirit of and is successor to Elijah is clear from his performing the miracle of parting the Jordan with Elijah's **mantle.**

2:15-18. On Elisha's return to Jericho the prophetic band recognize him as their new leader. In spite of his warning they send a group to search for the departed Elijah, for Yahweh's **Spirit** has often removed him suddenly in the past.

2:19-22. The Healing of the Waters. This is the first of a series of miracle stories about Elisha. **Water** from the Jericho **spring** is blamed for making women barren. Elisha by means of **salt** and a divine oracle heals the waters. Note the point of view of the later writer in the phrase **to this day.**

2:23-25. The Curse on the Jeering Boys. Elisha has his head shaved in tonsure as a sign of his prophetic function. When **boys** of **Bethel** rail at this prophetic mark, he utters an awful **curse** in Yahweh's name. The curse is immediately effective when **two she-bears** kill 42 of the lads. The legend emphasizes the awful consequences of profaning that which is holy, whether it be God himself or the person of his prophet.

3:1-3. Accession of Jehoram in Israel. On the accession date see above on 1:17-18. The usual judgment on N kings is made, but one mitigating fact is mentioned, viz. his removal of the Baal image made by his father Ahab.

3:4-27. War Against Moab. According to the famous Moabite Stone, a stele erected by **Mesha** to celebrate his accomplishments, esp. against Israel,

Courtesy of the Oriental Institute, University of Chicago

Cast of the Moabite Stone, providing a contemporary record of the relations between Israel and Moab; original in Louvre, Paris

Moab was conquered by Omri and remained a vassal state for 40 years, after which Mesha rebelled in the days of Omri's "son"—evidently to be understood as meaning "grandson," i.e. **Jehoram.**

3:4-8. That the yoke imposed on Moab was a galling one is evident from the huge periodic tribute required of Mesha. When he rebels, Israel naturally has no intention of giving up this lucrative income without a struggle. Jehoram invites—a polite way of ordering a vassal—**Jehoshaphat** of Judah and the latter's vassal, **Edom** (see comment on I 22:41-50) to help him put down the rebellious shepherd king of Moab.

3:9-12. Perhaps because of fortifications in N Moab which Mesha boasts of on his stele, the allies make a **circuitous march,** apparently around the S end of the Dead Sea through **Edom** (vs. 8), in order to attack Moab from the S. On the border of Moab the expected **water** supply does not materialize and the attackers are in desperate straits. Jehoshaphat inquires whether any **prophet** is present and Elisha is discovered.

3:13-20. The prophetic story is again tinged with the miraculous. A **minstrel** is brought to play in order to induce ecstasy—a practice common in

various cultures. The oracle given by Elisha predicts **water** in the **dry stream-bed** (i.e. wadi) without benefit of **wind or rain,** as well as victory over the Moabites. He further commands complete destruction of Moab, entailing the cruel practice of cutting down trees and despoiling all water holes. At dawn the stream is rushing with water.

3:21-25. The **Moabites** are encamped on the N edge of the wadi, and when they look down on the unexpected **water** it looks **red**—probably a word play on the word "Edom," which means "red." They rush down to plunder, but are badly beaten and flee in panic. The ensuing devastation of the countryside is told in terms of the prophetic command in vs. 19. Finally only one fortress is left to Mesha in S Moab, **Kir-hareseth** (see color map 8). This is "attacked," not **conquered,** by the **slingers** of the allies.

Courtesy of Herbert G. May

Kir-Hareseth (modern Kerak) ancient capital of Moab located *ca.* 17 miles S of Arnon and 11 miles E of the Dead Sea

3:26-27. Mesha, seeing that even this stronghold is on the point of falling, makes a concerted effort to break through the line of besiegers but fails. He then determines on a desperate course. In full view of the attackers he sacrifices **his eldest son,** the crown prince, as a **burnt offering** to Chemosh, his god. This action causes the attackers to panic, and the siege is lifted. On sacrifice of offspring cf. 16:3; see comments on Deut. 18:9-14; Judg. 11:29-40; I Kings 16:34.

4:1-7. *The Unfailing Jar.* Here begins a series of prophetic miracle stories which show Elisha as a worker of wonders. Some of these have parallels in the Elijah cycle. On this story cf. I 17:8-16. Enslavement for debt was practiced in Israel, though later legislation mitigated the practice (cf. Lev. 25:39-41; Deut. 15:12-18).

4:8-37. *Restoration of the Dead Boy.* This story is much more elaborate than the parallel from the Elijah cycle (I 17:17-24). A **wealthy woman** of **Shunem,** i.e. a **Shunammite** (vs. 11; cf. I 1:3; I Sam. 28:4; see color map 8), provides a specially built and furnished guest room for Elisha. For this kindness Elisha wishes to repay her, but she proudly asserts her independence. **Gehazi,** Elisha's **servant,** notes that **she has no son, and her husband is old.** Elisha then promises her a son **when the time comes round,** i.e. after a normal period of pregnancy.

4:18-25a. The next scene shows the young lad out in the field. He is suddenly stricken with sunstroke and taken to the house, where he dies in his mother's arms. She lays the corpse on Elisha's **bed** and immediately sets out for **Mount Carmel,** *ca.* 25 miles away.

4:25b-31. When she arrives, Elisha sends his servant with his wonder-working **staff,** which he is to **lay** on the **face** of the corpse. He is to maintain complete silence on the journey so as to lose none of the wonder-working power of the staff. The magic, however, does not work. Meanwhile the woman with correct intuition has refused to leave the prophet.

4:32-37. In the final scene Elisha enters his chamber. There he both prays to Yahweh and performs a magical life-transference rite, which is finally successful.

4:38-41. *The Poisoned Food.* Elisha is visiting Gilgal (see comment on 2:1-8) in a time of **famine.** There at the confraternity of **prophets** a common meal is being provided. A large **pot** of vegetables is being cooked, but unfortunately someone has by error collected some poisonous **gourds** (probably colocynthis). Elisha throws in some good **meal,** thereby rendering the food edible.

4:42-44. *Multiplication of Loaves.* Again the prophetic confraternity's food is involved. Custom demanded that Yahweh receive the **first fruits** of the harvest at his shrine. Apparently in early days a prophet might receive such as well as a priest. **Baal-shalisha** was probably a village SW of Shechem (see color map 8).

5:1-19a. *The Healing of Naaman.* Naaman is military **commander** of Damascus and in **high favor** with his **master,** an unnamed **king of Syria—but he was a leper.** Leprosy was a term used to designate a wide variety of skin diseases. It is doubtful whether modern leprosy (Hansen's disease) was prevalent in ancient Palestine or Syria.

5:2-7. An Israelite slave girl mentions to her mistress, **Naaman's wife,** that a **prophet** in **Samaria** can **cure** the leprosy. Elisha is pictured as having a house there. The Elisha stories have various locales throughout the N: Mt. Carmel, Shunem, Gilgal, Jericho, Dothan, and the Jordan. Naaman proceeds to Samaria with a fabulous load of presents (on the weights see table, p. 1285). He comes to the **king of Israel**—apparently a Syrian vassal—to whom he gives his master's **letter** ordering the healing of Naaman. The Israelite king is greatly disturbed at this impossible demand.

5:8-14. Elisha meanwhile hears about the king's distress and sends him an ironical note bidding the leper come to him. When Naaman arrives the prophet simply sends him a message to bathe **seven times** in the Jordan. Naaman is indignant. Damascene rivers—the **Abana** and the **Pharpar**—are far finer than the muddy Jordan. Better counsel prevails, however, and he carries out Elisha's prescription and is cured.

5:15-19a. Naaman now recognizes Yahweh to be the true God and vows to be his worshiper. The story here involves some curiously primitive ideas. He wishes to take Israelite **earth** along to Damascus so that he will be able to worship Israel's God there, the theory being that a god could be worshiped only on his own soil. He asks pardon for one exception to his vow, viz. his necessary accompaniment of the Syrian king to worship his god on state occasions.

Rimmon was a Syrian title (meaning "thunderer") of the god Hadad (see comment on I 16:32-33).

5:19b-27. *Gehazi's Greed.* Elisha has refused to accept any gifts from Naaman. Gehazi secretly follows the Syrian and by means of a falsehood secures for himself money and clothing. These he hides, presumably in his own quarters, though exactly what is meant by **hill** (vs. 24) is not known. Elisha's prophetic sight reveals the deception. As punishment Gehazi is to be afflicted with Naaman's **leprosy,** a fitting retribution. In line with ancient conceptions of corporate involvement in guilt this leprosy is to be suffered by his offspring as well.

6:1-7. *A Floating Axe Head.* On an expedition to get logs from the banks of the Jordan a **borrowed** axe head made of **iron** falls into the water. Elisha by his magical powers makes it **float,** thus enabling the borrower to recover it.

6:8-23. *Capture of a Syrian Army.* This is another miracle story about Elisha's 2nd sight. Syrian military plans are inexplicably and repeatedly made known to the Israelite king, and the **king of Syria** naturally suspects treachery. On inquiry he is told that Elisha is the informer. Accordingly when he discovers that Elisha is in **Dothan** (about 10 miles N of Samaria; see color map 8), he dispatches a large force to besiege the city and seize the informer.

6:15-19. The following morning Elisha's **servant** is dismayed at the sight. At Elisha's prayer the servant is able to see the **horses and chariots of fire** (cf. 2:11-12a) surrounding and protecting the prophet. Again at Elisha's prayer the Syrians are struck **with blindness** and led . . . **to Samaria.**

6:20-23. The Syrians are now helpless captives, and at Elisha's word their sight is restored. Elisha orders the king to treat them hospitably and release them. The story has a happy but quite unhistorical ending, viz. that the Syrians remain at peace with Israel after this.

6:24-7:20. *Siege of Samaria.* In contrast to the statement in vs. 23, **Ben-hadad** (perhaps not Benhadad I but the son of Hazael; cf. 13:24-25) lays effective siege to **Samaria,** with the result that the city is in extreme straits. Prices have soared and people are paying exorbitantly for garbage. A **kab** was slightly more than a dry quart. The king's reply in vs. 27 is better rendered "No! may Yahweh help you." An instance of cannibalism incites the distressed king to swear an oath that he will kill Elisha, whom for unexplained reasons he holds responsible.

6:32-7:2. Immediately someone is sent to effect Elisha's capture; but the prophet, aware of the situation by 2nd sight, has already barred the **door.** The **king** follows his **messenger** and is apparently allowed to enter, whereupon he expresses complete skepticism of any divine help. Elisha then gives an oracle that within 24 hours the siege will be lifted and food will be on sale at normal prices. A **captain** of the king expresses disbelief, and his death is predicted for the following day.

7:3-15. During the night rumor spreads through the Syrian camp that **Hittites** and Musrites (for **Egypt;** see above on I 10:26-29) are approaching to help the Israelites. The rumor has been divinely inspired in order to fulfill the prophet's oracle. Panic sets in and, abandoning all their arms and provisions, the Syrians flee without the besieged city's knowing it. Meanwhile at daybreak (**twilight,** vs. 5, refers to the first break in the night's darkness, in contrast to **morning light,** vs. 9, which means the full dawn) **four . . . lepers** go over to the Syrian camp, which they find deserted. They immediately eat their fill and gather some plunder before reporting the **good news** to the city. The king suspects a trap but in view of the desperate situation is persuaded to risk a few cavalrymen for reconnoitering. They report that the Syrians are nowhere in sight.

7:16-20. So the siege comes to an end. There still remains the skeptical **captain** to deal with. He is on duty at the gate that day and loses his life in the trample of the excited people. So the word of the prophet is again vindicated.

8:1-6. Restoration of the Shunammite's Property. Elisha's hostess at Shunem (cf. 4:8-37), as a result of his warning of **famine,** has spent **seven years** in Philistia. On her return she finds her possessions confiscated, and she appeals to the king at the exact moment when **Gehazi** is relating to him Elisha's restoration of her son to life. When she confirms the story, the king orders the return of her property, including its **produce** during her 7-year absence.

8:7-15. Elisha in Damascus. The aged **Ben-hadad** is ill and, hearing that the great prophet Elisha is in the city, sends **Hazael** to him for an oracle. That a fee had to be paid for such a service is clear from I Sam. 9:5-10, but the gift in this story seems much exaggerated. Elisha replies ambiguously with an oracle which probably means "the sickness is not fatal." He predicts Hazael's succession and his cruel treatment of Israelites in future warfare. Hazael politely protests but nonetheless returns to the palace and implements Elisha's prediction. He mollifies the bedridden king with the ambiguous oracle and the following day assassinates him and assumes the Syrian throne.

8:16-24. Jehoram's Reign in Judah. The name **Joram** is a shortened form used of both Jehoram of Israel (vs. 16; cf. 3:1-8) and Jehoram of Judah (vss. 21-24). The accession notice takes no account of the coregency indicated by 1:17 (see comment).

8:20-24. Politically the reign of Jehoram of Judah was calamitous, as 2 historical notes from contemporary annals (vss. 20-22a, 22b) show. **Edom** revolts and throws off its vassalage in a sortie from which the king extricates himself with difficulty. The location of **Zair** is uncertain; some have placed it near Hebron (see color map 8), but the context points rather to the S end of the Dead Sea. Apparently the Israelite army is surrounded, the infantry deserts, and the king and the chariotry manage to break through and escape. **Libnah** was a frontier town on the Philistine border. Later it seemingly was regained by Judah (cf. 19:8; 23:31).

8:25-29. Ahaziah's Reign in Judah. For the accession date see "Chronology," pp. 1271-82. Ahaziah's mother was **Athaliah,** Ahab's daughter. **Son-in-law** is of course not to be taken lit., since it was his father who was son-in-law to Ahab. The son is then said to be **son-in-law to the house of Ahab.** Vss. 28-29 are a doublet to 9:14-16.

I. Jehu's Revolt (9:1–10:28)

9:1-13. Jehu's Anointing as King of Israel. The first scene details the secret anointing by an emissary of Elisha (cf. I 19:16). Jehu is a commander of the Israelite army on guard duty at **Ramoth-gilead.** Prophets were often involved in anointing—e.g. Samuel (I Sam. 10:1; 16:12-13) and Nathan (I 1:34). Elisha's command in vs. 3 is carried out by the neophyte **prophet** in vss. 6, 10b, but the D editor has inserted an addition (vss. 7-10a) based on I 21: 21-24.

9:11-13. After the ceremony Jehu returns to the meeting of the chiefs of staff from which he has been summoned and is eventually persuaded to tell his comrades about the rite. They thereupon proclaim him **king** on the spot (cf. I 1:38-40). The prophet is called a **mad fellow** since prophets were held in some contempt because of their ecstatic behavior (cf. I Sam. 19:18-23).

9:14-29. Jehu's Successful Attack. Since the success of a revolution depends in part on surprise, Jehu asks his followers to guard the secret. He immediately sets out in **his chariot** for **Jezreel,** where Joram is convalescing in his palace. **Ahaziah** of Judah is also there visiting his royal cousin.

9:17-26. Jehu and his company are seen at a distance by the **tower** guard and 2 successive advance scouts are sent, who desert to Jehu. When finally the guard recognizes the party, by reason of Jehu's mad **driving,** the royal cousins go out in their chariots expecting news from the Ramoth-gilead front. When Joram meets Jehu he realizes his danger for the first time, calls out a warning to his cousin, and tries to flee. Jehu kills him and orders the corpse thrown into Naboth's vineyard as appropriate to the prophetic doom predicted to Ahab.

9:27-29. In the meantime Ahaziah of Judah flees toward **Beth-haggan,** 7 miles S of Jezreel (see color map 8). He is shot on the way between there and **Ibleam,** a mile farther S. The wounded king then changes his course to the NW and dies in **Megiddo,** almost 12 miles away. His body is brought to **Jerusalem** and **buried.** On vs. 29, which does not belong here, see "Chronology," pp. 1271-82.

9:30-37. Assassination of Jezebel. The proud queen mother, realizing that she is not to escape, takes great pains to beautify herself for death; and when Jehu approaches she taunts him. She is flung from an upper **window** and her crushed body is **trampled** (vs. 3) by the **horses** and chariots. Later Jehu orders her burial, but only remnants of the corpse remain, in accordance with Elijah's word (cf. I 21:23).

10:1-17. Extermination of the House of Omri. The capital city of **Samaria** is not yet in Jehu's hands, and a **letter** is sent to the military and civil authorities, as well as to the palace officials, challenging them to civil war. The officials immediately communicate their capitulation.

10:6-11. Jehu now demands that they bring him the **heads** of all the king's **sons** within 24 hours. This gruesome demand is complied with and the heads are thrown in **two heaps at the entrance** of the city, the traditional place of judgment. Jehu impudently attributes this slaughter to Yahweh's separate doing and proceeds to a bloodbath of the **house of Ahab** in Jezreel.

10:12-14. Now Jehu can proceed to the capital city itself. On the way he meets some relatives of **Ahaziah** of Judah, who are all ruthlessly killed as well. Shortly thereafter he meets **Jehonadab,** a prophet and leader of the Rechabites. The Rechabites were particularly bitter opponents of Canaanite culture (see comment on Jer. 35:1-19) and natural foes of the house of Omri. Jehu is assured of cooperation. On arrival he kills off **all that remained to Ahab** in Samaria.

10:18-28. Massacre of the Baal Devotees. By a ruse Jehu assembles all the officials, i.e. **prophets** and **priests** (omit **all his worshipers** from vs. 19), together in the Baal temple which Ahab built (cf. I 16:32). Ostensibly an important cultic feast for Baal is to be held. To make the ruse more convincing the king himself offers the sacrifice. Once it is clear that only Baal devotees are present, the order is given to slaughter them all. The temple and all its cultic paraphernalia are destroyed and defiled.

J. FROM JEHU TO THE FALL OF SAMARIA (10:29–17:41)

10:29-36. The Remainder of Jehu's Reign. Because of Jehu's effective destruction of the Baalists the D editor's judgment on him (vss. 29-31) is not as condemnatory as on other N kings. A prophetic oracle (vs. 30) promises dynastic succession to the **fourth generation** for his zeal.

10:32-36. Jehu's reign marks the beginning of Syrian incursions on Israelite territory. All of Transjordan is lost to **Hazael,** not to be retaken until the reign of Jeroboam II (cf. 14:23-29). Jehu reigns **twenty-eight years.**

11:1-3. Athaliah's Interregnum in Judah. Ahaziah's mother, Athaliah, daughter of Ahab, immediately seizes the throne by killing off the entire royal family. Only the infant **Joash** escapes the bloodbath. The baby's aunt, **Jehosheba** (wife of the priest Jehoiada according to II Chr. 22:11), hides the baby in the priestly quarters of the temple. Athaliah rules for **six years,** unaware of the crown prince's existence.

11:4-20. Athaliah's Overthrow. This account is based on 2 contemporary sources, one official (vss. 4-12, 18b-20), the other popular (vss. 13-18a). Both detail the slaying of Athaliah; vs. 20 actually says "the city was quiet and Athaliah they slew with the sword." The 2 accounts supplement each other nicely.

11:4-8. The *coup d'état* is thoroughly planned by **Jehoiada** the priest. The **Carites,** i.e. mercenary elite (cf. "Cherethites," I 1:38), are organized for the revolt and sworn to secrecy. Apparently **on the sabbath** a 3rd of the guard is on duty and stationed at 3 posts (the 2 gates are named but their location is unknown). The other 2 groups are to remain on duty in the temple to protect the young **king.**

11:9-12. Only when the stage is fully prepared is the crown prince brought out and the public coronation rite enacted. The meaning of **testimony** is uncertain; possibly some scroll delineating the covenantal responsibilities of the ruler is meant.

11:13-18a. The popular account adds details concerning the killing of Athaliah, the royal covenant, and the religious reform sparking the restoration of the Davidic king. Only the **noise** of the public coronation ceremony makes the queen aware that her plans have gone awry. She is roughly seized as she approaches the temple and led away to an area near the palace, where she is executed.

11:17. That coronation in Judah involved a covenant ceremony is first mentioned here. It is presented as 2-fold: (*a*) a sacral bond renewing the covenant between Yahweh and the people and (*b*) a popular contract between **the king and the people.** It is not certain what this latter involved, but from now on **the people of the land** (i.e. the populace) take a more important part in political affairs.

11:18a. The renewal of the sacral bond is immediately applied when the populace demolishes all the cultic objects and shrines associated with Baalism. The chief **priest of Baal,** whose possible Phoenician background is apparent from his name, **Mattan,** is also slain.

11:18b-20. The official account is now concluded. Jehoiada leaves **watchmen** to guard the temple, while the boy king is escorted under heavy guard to the palace, where he assumes the **throne** amid rejoicing of the populace. Then Athaliah is killed.

11:21-12:21. Jehoash's Reign in Judah. Jehoash rules for **forty years.** The D editor judges him a good king but notes that he did not remove the local shrines.

12:4-8. Most of the account of Jehoash's reign deals with his attempt to **repair** the Jerusalem temple, by this time fallen into a sad state. By royal edict both the temple tax and the freewill offerings are to be used solely for this purpose. But the cupidity of the priests frustrates the pious wishes of the king, and so he takes the matter out of their hands and directs affairs personally. The term **acquaintance** (vss. 5, 7) makes little sense; possibly some official receiver of tithes is meant.

12:9-16. To avert misappropriation of funds a **chest** is made with a **hole in the lid** where worshipers can deposit their funds directly. Periodically Jehoiada and the king's personal representative empty the chest and weigh out **money** for the repairs after making a careful record of the accounts. A note (vs. 16) is added that the priests did not really suffer since they still received their usual income from **guilt** and **sin offerings.**

12:17-18. One disastrous event during the reign of Jehoash is an invasion by the Syrians. They are able to penetrate to **Gath,** a Philistine city to the SW, and then turn toward Jerusalem (see color map 8). Jehoash is able to buy off the Syrians only by ransacking the temple and the royal **treasuries,** leaving them empty.

12:19-21. Like Jehoram (see above on 8:16-24) the name Jehoash is shortened and becomes **Joash.** Though this king is assassinated, there is no change of dynasty, as in the N kingdom; **his son** succeeds to the throne. On **Millo** see above on I 9:15-23. **Silla** is unknown.

13:1-9. Jehoahaz' Reign in Israel. Jehu is succeeded by his son Jehoahaz in a time of all but utter subjection to the Syrians. The cavalry is almost completely wiped out. With the **ten chariots** left to the army cf. the 2,000 attributed to Ahab 40 years earlier in Shalmaneser's inscription. It is usually suggested that vss. 4-6 are a later addition contradicting the context in vss. 3, 7. Possibly **savior** (vs. 5) is a misplaced reference to 14:27.

13:10-25. Jehoash's Reign in Israel. On the discrepancy between the figures for Jehoash's reign and those of his father (vs. 1) see "Chronology," pp. 1271-82. His premature obituary (vss. 12-13) reappears in its proper place in 14:15-16. Two stories from the Elisha cycle are inserted in the account of his reign.

13:14-19. The first story concerns the visit of **Joash** (shortened form of Jehoash; see above on 12:19-21) to the aged prophet's deathbed. On Joash's cry (vs. 14) see above on 2:9-12b. By an act of sympathetic magic Elisha insures victory over Syria. The king is told to **shoot** an **arrow**; this insures victory in a battle at **Aphek** (see comment on I 20:23-24). Then the king is told to **strike the ground** with arrows and does so **three times**; this insures similar victories 3 times. Indeed the king should have struck more often!

13:20-21. The 2nd legend concerns Elisha's corpse. When a sudden raid by Moabites interrupts a funeral the deceased is hastily thrown into the tomb of the prophet. Touching the holy **bones** revives the man.

13:22-25. In fulfillment of Elisha's last prediction Jehoash now defeats Syria **three times** and recovers thereby some of the territory lost to the Syrians. Vs. 23 shows the attitude of the D editor. External sources show that Damascus was weakened during this period by Adad-nirari III of Assyria, who besieged and looted Damascus in 805. **Ben-hadad** II's declining power is also demonstrated by an inscription of Zakir, king of Hamath and Laash.

14:1-22. Amaziah's Reign in Judah. Amaziah is said to have **reigned twenty-nine years,** but apparently during ca. 10 years of this time he was a captive (vss. 13, 17) and his son Azariah ruled instead (vs. 21; see "Chronology," pp. 1271-82).

14:5-6. Amaziah executes his father's **murderers** (cf. 12:20-21) but spares their **children**—a clemency so unusual in this time that it is entered in the record. The D editor's comment on it quotes from Deut. 24:16.

14:7. An isolated event early in Amaziah's reign is a successful invasion of Edom. The places mentioned are unknown. Some have identified the **Valley of Salt** with a wadi near Beer-sheba (see color map 8) but an area near the S end of the Dead Sea would seem more appropriate (cf. II Sam. 8:13). **Sela** is often identified with the acropolis overlooking Petra (see color map 7)—a romantic identification for which there is no proof.

14:8-14. Amaziah's success leads him foolishly to challenge **Jehoash** of Israel to battle. Jehoash replies with a contemptuous parable, but Amaziah persists. The king of Israel quickly invades Judah toward the W. At Beth-shemesh, on the Philistine frontier 24 miles W of Jerusalem (see color map 8), the armies meet and Judah is disastrously defeated. Amaziah is captured and presumably taken as a prisoner to Samaria. Jerusalem is taken, part of its walls being demolished and its treasures pillaged.

14:15-22. When Jehoash dies **Jeroboam** II apparently releases the captive Amaziah, who lives another **fifteen years** before he is assassinated. **Lachish** was about 30 miles SW of Jerusalem (see color map 8). The election of **Azariah** at the age of 16 (vs. 21) evidently refers to the occasion, not of Amaziah's

death, but of his capture (vs. 13). The antecedent of **He** in vs. 22 is not certain. In the present context it must be Azariah, but in view of vs. 7 the sentence is often thought of as being misplaced and originally applying to Amaziah. On **Elath** (or Eloth) cf. I 9:26.

14:23-29. Jeroboam II's Reign in Israel. Apparently Jeroboam was coregent with his father, Jehoash, for ca. 12 years before beginning **in the fifteenth year of Amaziah** his sole reign (see "Chronology," pp. 1271-82).

14:25-27. The reign of Jeroboam was politically one of expansion. From Amos 6:13 it appears that Transjordan was again won for Israel. The old N **border** at the **entrance of Hamath** (i.e. probably the end of the Lebanons and the Anti-lebanons) is **restored** and Israel is extended S to the **Sea of the Arabah** (i.e. the Dead Sea; see below on 25:4-7). Vss. 26-27 must originally have been the content of the oracle referred to in vs. 25. **Jonah** is the prophet about whom the book of Jonah was written (cf. Jonah 1:1). **Gath-hepher** was in Zebulon, ca. 3 miles NE of Nazareth (see color map 8).

14:28-29. This obituary notice contains a difficulty. **Damascus and Hamath** never belonged to Israel. The Hebrew says lit. "recovered Damascus and Hamath for Judah in Israel," which is absurd. Possibly the author meant subjection of these cities by Jeroboam, but the reference to **Judah** remains a puzzle.

15:1-7. Azariah's Reign in Judah. Azariah is the throne name for the king known also by his popular name Uzziah (cf. e.g. 15:13, 30-34; II Chr. 26; Isa. 1:1). On his age of **sixteen** see above on 14:15-22. On the other data of vss. 1-2 see the "Chronology," pp. 1271-82. During the latter part of his long life Azariah becomes a **leper** (see above on 5:1-19a), and his son **Jotham** governs as coregent. For a fuller account of Azariah's reign see II Chr. 26.

15:8-12. Zechariah of Israel. Here begins the account of civil war in the N (vss. 8-31). After only **six months** Zechariah is murdered by **Shallum** and the dynasty of Jehu comes to an end. On **Ibleam** see above on 9:27-29. On vs. 12 cf. 10:30.

15:13-16. Shallum's Brief Reign in Israel. After a reign of only **one month** (see "Chronology," pp. 1271-82) Shallum is in turn assassinated by **Menahem,** who savagely puts down all opposition. On **Tirzah,** the former capital, see comment on I 14:17-18. **Tappuah,** evidently the center of Shallum's support, lay about 13 miles S of Samaria (see color map 8). On the barbarism of ancient warfare cf. Amos 1:13.

15:17-22. Menahem's Reign in Israel. The outstanding event recorded of Menahem's reign of **ten years** is the W march of Tiglath-pileser III (745-727) and his extraction of a huge tribute. The Assyrian king is here mentioned by his Babylonian name, **Pul** (or "Pulu"). His annals give independent confirmation of Menahem's tribute along with that of Syrian states. In order to pay the tribute Menahem assesses the **wealthy men** a heavy tax. A talent equaled 3,000 shekels; thus 60,000 men are forced to contribute.

15:23-26. Pekahiah's Reign in Israel. Pekahiah follows his father peaceably, but after **two years** he is assassinated by **Pekah,** at the head of a small band of **Gileadites.**

15:27-31. *Pekah's Reign in Israel.* A reign of twenty years for Pekah beginning in the fifty-second year of Azariah, i.e. at the time of Pekahiah's assassination, is impossible. Rather this figure dates the beginning of his reign back by 12 years. The synchronisms in vs. 32; 16:1 seem to indicate that Pekah's regnal years were numbered on this basis during his lifetime. Pekah may well have made such a claim as a way of denying the legitimacy of the Menahem dynasty and thus justifying his murder of Pekahiah. Or possibly (see "Chronology," pp. 1271-82) he may have dated his reign from the death of Zechariah and claimed to be the rightful successor of the house of Jehu. On the other hand it has been suggested that Pekah may have been a partisan of Shallum who, like Tibni (I 16:21-22), held control over part of the country as a rival to Menahem. Possible support for this theory may be found in vs. 32, which, if contemporary, would indicate early Judean recognition of such a regime; but a problem is the identification of Pekah as Pekahiah's captain (vs. 25). The records of this period of civil war are so fragmentary that any explanation of Pekah's claimed overlapping reign can be only conjecture.

15:29-31. The outstanding event during Pekah's reign was the Syro-Ephraimitic War (see comment on Isa. 7:1-25) against Assyria and its disastrous effects on Israel. The Assyrians came W in 734 and put down the revolt, capturing the areas of Galilee and Gilead, and limiting Israel to the province of Samaria itself. Shortly thereafter Pekah was in turn assassinated by Hoshea. In his annals Tiglath-pileser states that the Israelites overthrew their king, Pekah, and that he "placed Hoshea as king over them." Presumably the *coup d'état* had his blessing. Hoshea was to be the last N king.

15:32-38. *Jotham's Reign in Judah.* The beginning of Jotham's reign is dated at his taking over the government because of his father's leprosy (vs. 5; see above on vss. 27-31). On its length see "Chronology," pp. 1271-82. On his reign 2 historical notes are given: his rebuilding the upper gate of the temple—also called the Benjamin Gate (Jer. 20:2), probably because it faced N (Ezek. 9:2)—and the beginning of the Syro-Ephraimitic coalition against Judah (vs. 37; cf. 16:5), an offensive ascribed to Yahweh.

16:1-20. *Ahaz' Reign in Judah.* On the dating and length of this reign see "Chronology," pp. 1271-82. Ahaz was king of Judah at the time of the destruction of the N kingdom. The D editor condemns him more severely than any other ruler except Manasseh. Nor does he name the queen mother, as is otherwise done for Judean rulers.

16:3-4. The phrase burned his son as an offering is lit. "made his son to pass through the fire." Some scholars maintain that this refers to an ordeal by fire (see comment on Deut. 18:9-14) but it has generally been interpreted as meaning child sacrifice. It has been suggested that Syro-Ephraimitic attack on Jerusalem may have driven Ahaz, like Mesha (3:27), to sacrifice his son, but this is not certain.

16:5-9. In the Syro-Ephraimitic War Rezin of Syria and Pekah of Israel unite to revolt against Assyria and try to force Judah to join. When Judah refuses they besiege Jerusalem (cf. Isa. 7:1-9), intending to kill Ahaz and install a puppet ruler. Ahaz appeals to Assyria for help and sweetens the

appeal with as large a bribe (vs. 8) as he can muster. The Assyrians respond by capturing Damascus and executing Rezin (in 732) and by capturing most of Israel (see above on 15:29-31; cf. Isa. 8:4-8a). Interrupting the account is the record of the loss of Elath (vs. 6), which was captured by Amaziah (or Azariah, 14:22), to the Edomites and the consequent ejection of Judeans from that area. The Hebrew mistakenly has "Aram," i.e. Syria, for Edom here.

16:10-16. On Ahaz' visit to Tiglath-pileser in Damascus he sees an Assyrian altar which strikes his fancy. He orders it copied for the Jerusalem temple, and it is built by Uriah (cf. Isa. 8:2). The old bronze altar (cf. I 8:64) is relegated to the north side of the new altar and is to be reserved for the king's divinatory rites, whereas the new altar is to serve for the various sacrifices detailed in vs. 15. The dedicatory rites of the altar are performed by the king himself—a practice legitimate before the Exile. The D editor makes no condemnatory statement on these innovations; the passage as a whole must be largely contemporary.

16:17-20. Ahaz has purchased survival from the Assyrians at great cost. To pay the necessary tribute all the bronze accessories of the temple furniture (cf. I 7:23-39) are melted down and sent off to Assyria. What is meant by the covered way for the sabbath and the outer entrance for the king is not known. Palace is lit. "house" and probably means the temple rather than the king's house.

17:1-6. *Hoshea, the Last King of Israel.* On the erroneous synchronism in vs. 1 see "Chronology," pp. 1271-82. The usual absolute judgment of evil is strangely mitigated by the D editor. Tiglath-pileser has been succeeded by his son Shalmaneser V (727-722) and against him Hoshea conspires with So (Sibu), king of Egypt. Shalmaneser comes W, imprisons Hoshea, and lays siege to Samaria for three years, until at length it is captured. His successor, Sargon II (722-705), in an inscription claims the victory over Samaria as an achievement of his own reign, though many scholars believe the city fell some months before his accession (see "Chronology," pp. 1271-82). Sargon's account amplifies the biblical record: "I led away as prisoners 27,290 inhabitants, and 50 chariots I collected for my royal force. I rebuilt the city and made it more populous by settling there peoples from lands I had conquered. I set up one of my officers as their governor and imposed taxes customary to Assyrian citizenry." The Israelite deportees are taken to N Mesopotamia and to Media far to the E (see color map 10) and quickly lose their identity.

17:7-23. *An Editorial Sermon.* The D editor's attitude toward the N kingdom is expressed here at length. The people of Israel separated themselves from the worship at the central sanctuary at Jerusalem. This in turn meant worship at various high places (vs. 9) or shrines of the Canaanite type, where they served idols and practiced divination and sorcery. Which the kings of Israel had introduced is lit. "of the kings of Israel that they made" —i.e. kings set up by the people rather than by Yahweh. On Asherim and Asherah see comment on I 14:15b-16. On the two calves see comment on I 12:25-31. The host of heaven refers to astral deities. On **Baal** see comment on I 16:32-33. On **burned their sons and daughters as offerings** see above on 16:3-4.

17:19. The application to **Judah also** obviously comes from after the Babylonian exile and probably dates the whole sermon in this period, though scholars who believe the principal D editor worked during the reign of Josiah naturally regard this vs. as an addition (see Intro.).

17:21-23. All of Israel's **sin** is rooted in the **sins** of **Jeroboam.** Now the logical consequence has come about; the people are broken up and **exiled** to **Assyria.**

17:24-41. *The Mixed People of the N.* The ravaged country is forcibly repopulated by settlers from other areas conquered by the Assyrians. **Cuthah** was a town N of **Babylon,** and **Hamath** was in Syria (see color map 9). **Avva** and **Sepharvaim** were probably also Syrian cities. When the countryside is overrun by **lions** (vss. 25-26), the new settlers attribute it to failure to propitiate the **god of the land.** They petition for the return of some exiled native **priests** to teach them proper cult. This is granted (vs. 28), and a priest returns to **Bethel** to teach.

17:29-41. Nonetheless the worship in the N country becomes a peculiar mixture of ancestral and local cult. The immigrants continue to worship their own gods as well as Yahweh. Thus the Babylonians worship **Succoth-benoth,** possibly 2 deities, **Sakkuth** (Saturn) and Benoth (probably Sarpanitu, the wife of Marduk, Babylon's chief god). **Nergal** was the well-known god of the underworld in Cuthah. **Ashima** was a Syrian goddess (cf. Amos 8:14). **Tartak** is a corruption of the famous goddess Atargatis, worshiped throughout Syria. The name **Nibhaz** has not been identified with certainty, though a corruption of the altar god Madbacha has been suggested. The **gods of Sepharvaim** have been identified as Adad-melekh and Anu-melekh respectively. On Adad (Hadad) see comment on I 18:20-40. Anu was the chief Babylonian sky god. Both were apparently worshiped under Melekh (or "Molech") rites which included human sacrifice. Inserted into this account of the syncretistic religion of the **Samaritans** (as the populace is now called for the first time, vs. 29) is a diatribe composed of D phrases against these people (vss. 34b-40). It is of later origin and probably intended to condemn the later Samaritans as idolatrous from the beginning.

IV. Judah After the Fall of Israel (18:1–25:30)

A. The Threat from Assyria (18:1–21:26)

18:1-8. *Evaluation of Hezekiah's Reign.* The synchronism in vs. 1 seems to be based on incorrect data (see "Chronology," pp. 1271-82), for Hezekiah began his reign some years after the fall of Samaria, i.e. *ca.* 716. His great religious reforms are briefly listed in vs. 4. Removal of the **high places** seems to imply an early attempt at centralizing all public cult in Jerusalem (cf. 23:4-25). The **bronze serpent** was an old fetish which tradition attributed to **Moses** (cf. Num. 21:4-9), and which the Judeans venerated by acts of worship. The name **Nehushtan** is a word play since it means either "serpent" or "bronze object." Hezekiah and Josiah (22:2; 23:25) are the D editor's 2 great Judean heroes, and Hezekiah is

extravagantly eulogized in vss. 5-7a. His religious reforms go hand in hand with his nationalism. Politically he **rebelled against the king of Assyria** by attacking Philistine territory, which Sargon of Assyria had captured in 713-711. Hezekiah lived dangerously but managed somehow to avoid the full consequences of his rebellion, and for this the D editor shows unbounded admiration.

18:9-12. *Duplication of the Fall of Samaria.* Because of chronological miscalculation (see "Chronology," pp. 1271-82) the fall of Samaria was thought by one author to have taken place during Hezekiah's reign, and so the data from 17:5-6 are repeated here together with the D editor's judgment of the reasons for it.

18:13-16. *Tribute Paid Sennacherib.* This is a short account from contemporary royal and temple annals. Sennacherib's annals give a detailed account of the 46 cities taken, and the large tribute imposed on Hezekiah, including the **three hundred talents of silver** (vs. 14) and **thirty talents of gold** recorded here. Only abject submission saves Hezekiah from a traitor's death. Submission involves denuding the royal and temple treasuries of precious metals. The only thing left to Hezekiah is his throne and the capital city.

18:17–19:37. *The Assyrian Siege of Jerusalem.* Apparently there are 2 parallel popular accounts of the same siege: 18:17–19:9a; 19:9b-37. Both are prophetic stories connected with the Isaiah cycle. The 2 accounts disagree on certain details, esp. on the cause for the lifting of the siege. The stories are further complicated by the mixture of traditions concerning 2 campaigns, one in 701 and the other toward the end of Sennacherib's life. Later tradition does not distinguish between them, and the stories here have conflated the events into a single dramatic episode of miraculous deliverance of the holy city. That 2 different campaigns are actually involved is clear from the reference in 19:9a to Tirhakah, who did not become king of Egypt and Ethiopia until *ca.* 689. The 2nd campaign must have taken place in 688 or even somewhat later. The annals of Sennacherib are incomplete for the latter years, and since the outcome of the 2nd campaign was inglorious for him it was not recorded. Unfortunately the biblical stories are prophetic legends and mix fictional elements with already confused facts.

18:17–19:9a. *First Account of the Siege.* In this first story the Assyrian army makes loudmouthed demands for immediate surrender. Vs. 17 introduces us to 3 Assyrian officers. The exact distinctions are not clear; in the subsequent story only the **Rabshakeh** occupies the position of spokesman for the besiegers. Apparently the interchange takes place outside the walls near the end of Hezekiah's tunnel, though why such an unlikely spot should be chosen is not clear (cf. Isa. 7:3, from which this geographical note may have been borrowed). Three representatives of Hezekiah speak for the besieged.

18:19-25. This speech seems to be more applicable to the later campaign in view of its references to **Egypt,** though Egyptian involvement in the earlier campaign makes it difficult to unscramble the actual state of affairs. The argument of the Assyrian spokesman is most persuasive: (*a*) Egyptian promises are untrustworthy as always (vs. 21); (*b*) trust in Yahweh is hardly wise in the light of Hezekiah's cultic reforms (vs. 22), which to the speaker, and perhaps to the original author, seem to interfere with accustomed worship; (*c*) Judean weakness in cavalry makes opposition ludicrous (vss. 23-24); and (*d*) Yahweh has actually ordered Assyria to destroy Jerusalem.

18:26-37. Since **Aramaic** was the *lingua franca* of the day it could be understood by Judean and Assyrian alike. That the Assyrian could speak Hebrew is most unlikely. The offensive description in vs. 27 refers to the privations of the coming siege. The address to the populace in vss. 29-35 is largely dependent on 19:10-13. The direct challenge to Yahweh's power to **deliver** out of Assyrian hands is of course the point of the story. The reference to the failure of heathen gods to deliver **Samaria** (vs. 34) is further condemnation of the Samaritans (cf. 17:24-41).

19:1-9a. When Hezekiah hears the demands of the Assyrians, he engages in a communal rite of lament. In **sackcloth,** a garb denoting great distress, Hezekiah goes to the temple and seeks the advice of **Isaiah** the prophet. An oracle is sent to the king counseling courage since Yahweh will deliver Jerusalem by creating a **rumor** (vs. 7) among the Assyrians which will send them hurrying back to Assyria, where the king will be assassinated. The original conclusion to this must have been vss. 36-37, but its fulfillment here is interpreted as news concerning the advance of **Tirhakah king of Ethiopia** and of Egypt. On **Libnah** see above on 8:16-24.

19:9b-37. *A 2nd Account of the Siege.* This account is tied to the preceding one as a 2nd message from the Assyrians to Hezekiah but is actually a parallel to the first popular account. The message arrogantly states the superior strength of the Assyrian king to that of Yahweh. Subject peoples listed are **Gozan** near the Euphrates, **Haran** (cf. Gen. 11:31), **Rezeph** NE of Palmyra, and the children of **Eden** (rather Beth-eden) S of Haran near the Euphrates (see color map 9). **Tel-assar** is unknown. Vs. 13 is the source of 18:34.

19:14-19. Hezekiah responds by presenting the problem to Yahweh in the temple and offering a complaint prayer. The prayer, its actual form indicating exilic composition, is directly applicable to the taunting message.

19:20-28. The reply spoken by **Isaiah** is a taunt song against Assyria. With this poem cf. Isa. 10:5-11. Assyria is proud of her prowess in warfare and arrogantly attributes her conquests to her own strength. By this she has **mocked** Israel's God, who **long ago . . . planned** that Assyria should be the rod of his anger. Now for her proud insolence God will **turn** her **back.**

19:29-34. Isaiah gives also 2 prose oracles. God will give a **sign** (vss. 29-31; cf. Isa. 7:10-14) to demonstrate the promise of the song. This sign will be the abundance of natural growth, i.e. of the unsown, for 2 years. Not until the 3rd year will normal seed and harvest occur. So decimated Judah will repopulate and **bear fruit.** As for the present siege, the arrogant Assyrian will not take the **city,** for God himself is fighting for Jerusalem.

19:35-37. The outcome is that an **angel** of destruction kills off 185,000 Assyrians that night. A parallel story in Herodotus tells of a plague of mice attacking Sennacherib's army; what really happened cannot be reconstructed. The Assyrians withdraw, and some years later Sennacherib is killed by **Adrammelech and Sharezer,** 2 of **his** sons. Another son, **Esarhaddon** (681-669), then governor of Babylon, succeeds him. **Nisroch** is probably a corruption of Marduk, the Babylonian god. The **land of Ararat** is the kingdom of Urartu referred to in Assyrian inscriptions, which was centered around Lake Van (see color map 9).

20:1-11. *Hezekiah's Sickness.* On the occasion of Hezekiah's illness Isaiah comes with a divine oracle advising him to prepare for death. Hezekiah pleads his cause before Yahweh successfully and receives an extension of **fifteen years.** The prophet then prepares a poultice of **figs** (vs. 7) to bring about the recovery. To this account has been appended a miracle story from the Isaiah legends concerning the **sign** of the **shadow** receding on the sundial.

20:12-21. *The Embassy from Babylon.* A long-time foe of Assyria, **Merodach-baladan** (Babylonian Marduk-abal-idinna), has seized the throne of Babylon. The embassy is sent undoubtedly to foment a W coalition against Sennacherib, and Hezekiah's sympathy is shown by his demonstrating the possible extent of support he could give in the rebellious venture. The reference in vs. 12 to this embassy as congratulatory on his recovery is editorial; vss. 12-19 are not necessarily subsequent to the event of vss. 1-11 at all. The date of the embassy must have been shortly after Sennacherib became king of Assyria.

20:16-19. Isaiah's rebuke is in line with his isolationist attitude. For the specific reference to a Babylonian (not Assyrian!) exile the events of 586 seem best fitted to the occasion which the D editor has in mind. Vs. 19 apparently gives 2 responses on the part of Hezekiah. The 2nd is better rendered: "Is it not the case that there will, however, be peace and security in my days?" This is a commentary on the word **good.**

20:20-21. The final obituary and succession notice specifically refers to the building of the famous **conduit,** i.e. water tunnel, from the Virgin Spring to the Pool of Siloam (see color map 13).

21:1-18. *Manasseh's Reign.* Manasseh must have ruled as coregent with his father for *ca.* 10 years and thus was an adult when he became sole ruler on the death of Hezekiah, *ca.* 687 (see "Chronology," pp. 1271-82). His long reign is condemned as completely **evil.** In fact the account deals only with the evil practices which Manasseh reintroduces into Judean cult. This is the period of Assyrian strength, and Manasseh holds onto his position by a thoroughgoing Assyrianization of cult practice in Jerusalem—rebuilding the **high places** (vs. 3) and **altars for Baal** (see comment on I 16:32-33), placing an **Asherah** image in the temple (see comment on I 14:15*b*-16), and worshiping the **host of heaven** (i.e. astral deities) there. The D editor, responsible for the entire account, also mentions human sacrifice (vs. 6; see above on 16:1-20), divination practices of various kinds, familiar spirits, and **wizards.** The reference to **two courts** (vs. 5) is puzzling; probably the outer court was the building complex referred to as the "middle court" in 20:4, the area between palace and temple.

21:7-15. To the D editor the evil reign of Manasseh is the explanation for the exile of 586. Yahweh promised to David a perpetual dynasty in Jerusalem (II Sam. 7), but this was conditional on its good behavior (vss. 7-8). Time and again evil kings occupied the throne, but for the sake of his servant David Yahweh did not bring the dynasty to an end. But Manasseh is far worse (vs. 9). The cup of iniquity is now full, and the prophetic word now makes an exile certain (vss. 10-15). **Jerusalem** will be completely destroyed.

21:16. To this indictment is added the statement that the evil king also slew many of the faithful. This vs. may be the source for the late but unhistorical tradition that Isaiah the prophet was martyred by Manasseh.

21:19-26. *Amon's Reign.* Amon reigns only **two years.** His reign is also condemned by the editor as wholly **evil.** He is assassinated by some underlings in the palace, who are in turn killed by the populace. It is also the **people of the land** who place Amon's son **Josiah** on the throne as his successor. The accuracy of Amon's age of **twenty-two years** at accession may well be questioned, since 2 years later he has a son 8 years old (cf. 22:1).

B. THE D REFORM (22:1–23:30)

22:1-2. *Introduction to Josiah's Reign.* Josiah is (along with Hezekiah) the hero to the D editor, and his rule is completely approved (cf. 23:25). His age at accession is given as **eight years.** The accuracy of this statement may well be questioned.

22:3-20. *The Law Code Found.* In 622 Josiah orders temple repairs in terms similar to the reforms commanded by Jehoash (12:9-16), from which the D editor probably borrowed the account. In any event it simply serves to introduce the real point of the story, the finding of the **book of the law** in the temple by **Hilkiah the priest** (not **high priest** as in vss. 4, 8). When it is read to the king, it is said that he **rent his clothes,** a sign of national calamity. He appoints a committee of 5 to seek divine direction. They go to a cult **prophetess** who lives in the area directly N of the palace and temple complex. **Huldah** gives them an oracle reiterating the divine intention expressed in 21:10-15. This prophecy is largely the D editor's interpretation of the later exile, though the statement that Josiah shall die **in peace** in vs. 20 is a slip. On the other hand it may preserve an oracle from Josiah's own day.

The book of the law found has generally been recognized as the original corpus of Deut., esp. chs. 5; 12–26; 28 (see Intro. to Deut.). Ch. 5 probably constituted the original intro. to the actual laws of chs. 12–26, and ch. 28 contains the curses on those who disobey the law, curses which promoted Josiah to such a display of penitence and sorrow. The reforms described in the next ch. all find their basis in Deut. and in no other book of the law in the OT.

The book had probably been in existence at least since the early days of Manasseh, but the Assyrianizing reign of that king was obviously not the time to propose its social and cultic reforms, and it was deposited in the temple and lost. Now the time was

ripe. Assyrian power had been broken, and nationalist reactions in subject states were again possible. Nationalism and true piety went hand in hand.

23:1-3. *The Covenant with Yahweh.* The first stage of the reform is the public ceremony of covenant renewal. Josiah convokes an assembly of all Judeans and has the **book of the covenant** read to them. The king and the people then solemnly reconsecrate themselves to complete obedience to all the demands found in the book.

23:4-14. *The Reforms of the Cult.* The reform naturally begins in the temple itself, where the heathen paraphernalia introduced by Manasseh (cf. 21:3-7) are removed and burned in the valley of the **Kidron** (see color map 13). Appropriately, though rather absurdly, the **ashes** are carried to **Bethel**—an editorial note probably based on vss. 15-16. Priests engaged in illegitimate cult in the **high places** are now out of work (and unemployable). **Constellations** (vs. 5) actually means the "signs of the zodiac." One characteristic of the cultic reform throughout is that heathen cult objects are **defiled,** taken forever out of the sphere of the holy. Thus the **Asherah** image is powdered (vs. 6) and scattered on **graves,** and heathen cult **places** (vs. 14) are filled with **bones.** Cultic prostitution has its home in the temple area; here women weave robes (not **hangings**) for the Asherah, i.e. ritual garments to be used in the fertility cult.

23:8-14. Vss. 8*a*, 9 seem, with vs. 5, out of place in the list of defilings, but are nonetheless central to the reform. All shrines except **Jerusalem** are to be illegal. The priests of the shrines are now to live in Jerusalem and eat priestly rations but can hardly take part in the Jerusalem cult (vs. 9)—there were too many of them! The reference to **gates** in vs. 8*b* makes no sense, and most scholars translate as "satyrs," i.e. evil spirits or demons. The locations of the **gate of Joshua** (vs. 8), the **chamber of Nathan-melech the chamberlain** and the **precincts** (vs. 11), and the **upper chamber of Ahaz** (vs. 12) are all unknown. The **mount of corruption** (vs. 13) is the Mt. of Olives, "corruption" being a Hebrew pun on "olives." **Topheth** (vs. 10) was a heathen cult place in the S end of the **Hinnom Valley** (near the Pool of Siloam) dedicated to the cult of **Molech** (see above on I 11:1-8; cf. Jer. 7:31-32). The idea that the sun god drove winged **chariots** with horses across the sky was widespread. Just how horses were used in the solar cult is, however, not clear. The **altars on the roof** (vs. 12) were used for astral worship (possibly of Venus the morning star?). On the altars of **Manasseh** cf. 21:4-5. The heathen high places built by **Solomon** (vs. 13) for his foreign wives (I 11:1-8), still existing on the S end of the Mt. of Olives, are also destroyed.

23:15-20. *The Reform Beyond Judah.* Particularly the **altar at Bethel** has to be profaned since it epitomizes to the D editor the sin of the N kingdom in breaking away from the cult at Jerusalem. So that it may be **defiled** effectually it is turned into a garbage dump for **bones.** Only the bones of the 2 prophets (vss. 17-18) involved in the story of I 13 escape desecration. All this according to the D editor is to fulfill the ancient prophecy uttered on that occasion. The 2nd prophet, however, was not from **Samaria** but from Bethel. The same reform is carried out throughout the N, i.e. **the cities of Samaria.**

23:21-23. *The Passover Celebration.* In accordance with Deut. 16:1-8 what was essentially a domestic feast is now celebrated at the temple at **Jerusalem**— a complete innovation, and one which was to fall into disuse quickly. This is the climax of the great reform.

23:24-27. *Summary and Editorial Judgment.* Josiah makes a complete reform based on the book of the law, i.e. Deut. The eulogy of vs. 25 flatly contradicts that concerning Hezekiah in 18:5. Appropriately the judgment is put in actual D terms (cf. Deut. 6:5). Some have viewed this vs., minus the final clause, as the ending of an assumed first edition of Kings completed during Josiah's lifetime (see Intro.). On vss. 26-27 cf. 21:10-15.

23:28-30. *Josiah's Death.* Though Assyria was now in a state of collapse, the Neo-Babylonian Empire was quickly taking its place. Meanwhile **Egypt,** to keep a balance of power, joined a weakened Assyria against the Babylonians. For some misguided nationalistic reason Josiah tries to oppose the Egyptian army at **Megiddo** and loses his life. His son **Jehoahaz** is democratically made **king** to succeed him.

C. The Last Days of Judah (23:31–25:30)

23:31-35. *Jehoahaz' Reign.* The great reform of Josiah dies with him, and his successors are all judged to have done **evil** in the sight of Yahweh! After only **three months** as king Jehoahaz is imprisoned by **Neco** of Egypt at his Syrian headquarters and taken to Egypt, where he dies. **Riblah** was strategically located on the Orontes just at the pass above the Lebanons (see color map 9). Judah now becomes an Egyptian province. Neco places Jehoahaz' older brother on the throne with the throne name of **Jehoiakim** and imposes a heavy tribute on the country.

23:36–24:7. *Jehoiakim's Reign.* In 605 Neco was severely defeated and Egyptian hopes for Asiatic power were completely deflated. Judah now becomes a Babylonian province and Jehoiakim a puppet prince under **Nebuchadnezzar** (more accurately spelled Nebuchadrezzar in Jer., Ezek.) **king of Babylon.** The incursion of the Babylonians into Judah (vs. 1) is undated, and may have been as late as 601. Jehoiakim foolishly rebels after **three years** but loses his life apparently at the hands of roving tribes. The D editor interprets this all in line with the earlier condemnation of Manasseh in 21:10-15 (cf. 23:26-27). No reference is made to his burial in the obituary notice (cf. Jer. 22:18-19).

24:8-17. *Jehoiachin's Reign.* The young king has ruled only **three months** when the Babylonian army lays siege to the city. Jehoiachin quickly surrenders, and he, his court, his harem, and his military and social leaders are exiled to Babylon. The city fell on March 16, 597, as is now known from the Babylonian Chronicle. Vs. 15 originally followed vs. 12, the intervening vss. being later additions more ap-

propriate to the final sack of the city 11 years later. Nebuchadnezzar thereupon places a 3rd son of Josiah on the puppet throne (vs. 17) with the throne name **Zedekiah.** On the number of deportees cf. Jer. 52:28. Here only round numbers are given.

24:18–25:7. *Zedekiah's Reign.* Zedekiah is destined to be the last Judean king (597-586; see "Chronology," pp. 1271-82). On 24:20 cf. 21:10-15. For a fuller account of the final days of Jerusalem cf. Jer. 37–39. As long as Judah remains loyal to the Babylonians life can continue, but eventually the pro-Egyptian party wins and Zedekiah rebels, i.e. withholds the tribute.

25:1-7. The final **siege** begins Jan. 15, 588, and 30 months later, July 19, 586, the walls are breached. The city is deserted (25:4) by its leaders. The **king's garden** was probably near the Pool of Siloam. The escape route lay at the lower end of the Valley of Hinnom (see color map 13). The **two walls** (or "double wall") has not been certainly located but it must have been at the S tip of the city. The **Arabah** refers to the deep valley of the Jordan River and the Dead Sea. The king is captured near **Jericho** and brought captive to **Riblah** (see above on 23:31-35). Apparently Nebuchadnezzar himself has remained there (but cf. vs. 1).

25:8-21. *The City Destroyed.* The following month (Aug. 15) Jerusalem is razed. The palace, the temple, and **every great house** in the city are **burned.** The **walls** are broken by the army, thereby making any future resistance impossible. Many **people** are exiled to **Babylon** and only peasants are left.

25:13-17. Large **bronze** furnishings of the temple are broken up, smaller metal vessels are left intact, and all are carried off as loot. Vss. 16-17 are simply the D editor's summary of I 7:15-39.

25:18-21. The Babylonian commander, **Nebuzaradan,** arrests 72 (cf. Jer. 52:24-27) ringleaders in the revolt and brings them to military headquarters at Riblah, where they are executed by royal decree. These include 5 temple personnel, as well as 7 military officials.

25:22-26. *Gedaliah as Governor.* For a fuller account cf. Jer. 40:7–43:7. Nebuchadnezzar appoints a Judean noble as his viceroy. On Gedaliah's father, **Ahikam,** cf. 22:12; Jer. 26:24. Gedaliah is treacherously slain by a few hotheaded nationalists, who also brutally kill the inhabitants of the new provincial capital, **Mizpah** (see above on I 15:16-22).

25:27-30. *A Final Note of Hope.* Nebuchadnezzar finally dies (562) and is succeeded by his son **Evilmerodach** (Babylonian "Amil-marduk"), who releases the captive **Jehoiachin** after 37 years of imprisonment (Mar. 21, 561). The ex-king is given an increased living **allowance** (vs. 30) and a great deal of preferment. Was Amil-marduk about to restore him to his rightful place as subject ruler in Judah? This will never be known, since a year later he was assassinated by Nergal-sharezer (560–556), who thereby dashed any possible Jewish hopes for immediate restoration.

THE FIRST BOOK OF THE CHRONICLES

Charles T. Fritsch

INTRODUCTION

Name. In the Hebrew Bible the Chronicles, which form a single volume, are called "the things [or "events"] of the days [i.e. history]." The LXX, to which we owe the division of the book into 2 parts, has the title "the things which have been passed over," referring to those events which were omitted in the former history books of Sam. and Kings. The name "Chronicles," found in German and English Bibles, is derived from Jerome's statement that these books are a "chronicle of the whole of sacred history."

Place in the Canon. I, II Chr., which originally formed one book, were part of a larger work that included Ezra and Neh. The proof for this is found, not so much in the fact that the conclusion of II 36 and the beginning of Ezra 1 are the same, as in the common linguistic and stylistic features of the books and in the fact that Ezra-Neh. describes the restoration of that which has been lost at the end of I Chr. In the Hebrew Bible, where these books are found in the Writings, the 3rd division of the Jewish canon, Ezra and Neh. precede I, II Chr., which close the canon. In the LXX, however, the chronological order is preserved—I, II Chr., Ezra, Neh.—the order followed in the English Bible.

Content and Purpose. In these 4 books the history of Judah is traced from the beginning of the world (Adam) to the restoration of Judaism under Ezra and Nehemiah. According to the Chronicler the rule of God on earth was most perfectly realized in the Davidic monarchy and the postexilic cultic community. The genealogies which introduce the history (I 1–9) and set the stage for the appearance of David and his dynasty not only legitimatize the Jews as the lineal descendants of the chosen people of God but indicate that they have been in the center of God's redemptive plan for the world since the beginning of time.

The brevity of the genealogical tables in I 1, esp. vss. 1-4, 24-27, shows that the Chronicler takes for granted his readers' acquaintance with these lists in Gen. He likewise passes over the accounts of Israel's early history because he is interested mainly in the theocracy—i.e. God's rule over his people through chosen leaders—which for him begins, not with Abraham, or even Moses, but with David. This special concern for David and the worshiping community of Israel is already reflected in these introductory chs., where Judah and his descendants, including David, come first in the genealogical history of Israel's sons (I 2:3–4:23; cf. 5:1-2). Also more space is given to Judah and Levi (I 6) in these tables than to all of the other sons of Israel combined.

After a brief account of Saul's ignominious death (I 10) the history of Israel begins with the glorious reign of David, the ideal ruler of God's people (I 11–29). According to the Chronicler, the true Israel, i.e. the worshiping community, was founded by David in Jerusalem, not by Moses in the desert. He was the spiritual founder of the temple, for he made the most detailed preparations for its construction and gave to Solomon the money, building materials, and model for its erection. He was also the organizer of the elaborate temple service and the numerous offices among the temple personnel. In Chr. the political and social history of Israel gives way to the history of the cultic community. For the first time the annals of a nation are scored to the accompaniment of musical instruments and singing choirs, with the result that these books sound more like an opera than history (cf. esp. II 13:14; 20:18-28, where trumpets and choirs win the victories for Abijah and Jehoshaphat).

Solomon's reign was more magnificent than his father's (II 1–9). He was extremely powerful, wealthy, and wise. But his main claim to fame in the Chronicler's view was the fact that he built the temple in Jerusalem and organized its affairs. In the accounts of both these rulers the Chronicler has omitted the more sordid details of their reigns, recorded in Sam. and Kings, in order to portray them as the ideal kings of God's people.

Now follows the history of the S kingdom from Rehoboam to the fall of Jerusalem in 586 B.C. (II 10–36). Because of the sin of Jeroboam I the N kingdom became apostate (cf. II 13:4-12) and thus was contemptuously ignored by the Chronicler. The regnal records of Jehoshaphat, Hezekiah, and Josiah are greatly expanded beyond those of the older history because of their interest in religious reforms. Yet the sins of rulers like Ahaz, Manasseh, and Zedekiah far outweighed the pious efforts of these religious heroes and brought God's wrath on the nation "till there was no remedy" (II 36:15-16). With the fall of Jerusalem God's plans for the redemption of the world appear to be shattered.

The book concludes, however, on a hopeful note (II 36:22-23). All is not lost. God's eternal purposes will not be thwarted by sinful men. The day of restoration will come when God's people will return from captivity to Jerusalem, the temple will be rebuilt, and songs of praise will once again resound from the holy hill of Zion.

Date. In the continuation of the Chronicler's work in Ezra-Neh.—which we may assume for the reasons given above—he goes on to relate the return from captivity and rebuilding of the temple under Zerubbabel late in the 6th cent. and a further return and renewal of strict observance of the law under Nehemiah and Ezra a cent. later. In view of the content and evident purpose of the total work it is natural to conclude that the author has brought it down to his own day. On this basis the writing is to be dated during the lifetime of Ezra or a short time thereafter, i.e. in the last decades of the 5th cent. or the early part of the 4th. In fact the Chronicler may well have been Ezra himself or one of his close disciples. This dating is supported by the fact that both the Davidic genealogy of I 3:19-24 (see comment) and the list of priests in Neh. 12 come down to *ca.* 400.

There has been serious disagreement among scholars about the date of Chr., however, and many have placed it in the Greek period, i.e. after the overthrow of the Persian Empire by Alexander the Great in 333. Chief reasons for the later date are: (*a*) The Aramaic in Ezra 4:8–6:18; 7:12-26, an integral part of the Chronicler's work, has been thought to be late. (*b*) In the LXX and other versions the genealogy of David (I 3:19-24) is continued to the 11th generation after Zerubbabel. (*c*) The reversal of the evident historical order of the careers of Nehemiah and Ezra suggests a time when the events of the period had been blurred by distance.

The first of these reasons has been largely broken down by recent comparative study of extrabiblical sources which shows that the Aramaic of Ezra fits into the latter part of the Persian period and that certain unusual words assumed to be derived from the Greek are rather of Persian origin. Both the extended Davidic genealogy in the versions and the confusion about Nehemiah and Ezra may be attributed to later revision, and other considerations often mentioned in discussion of the date—e.g. the author's anti-Samaritan bias and his emphasis on the place of the Levites in the organization of the community—are applicable to either period. Therefore an increasing number of scholars now favor an earlier date for Chr., in the late Persian period if not specifically *ca.* 400.

Sources. The data in the genealogies (I 1-9) come from the Pentateuch for the most part. For the history of David and Solomon the Chronicler depends almost entirely on Sam.; Kings; any differences or additions may be attributed to the Chronicler himself. In II 10-36, however, he seems to have used an expanded version of Kings—perhaps the "Commentary [Midrash] on the Book of the Kings" mentioned in 24:27. Citations from prophetic books are found in II 16:9 (Zech. 4:10); 20:20 (Isa. 7:9) and the Psalter is quoted in I 16:8-36 (Pss. 105:1-15; 96; 106:1, 47-48); II 6:41-42 (Ps. 132:8-9).

For Further Study: E. L. Curtis and A. A. Madsen, *A Critical and Exegetical Commentary on the Books of Chr.*, 1910. A. C. Welch, *The Work of the Chronicler*, 1939. I. W. Slotki, *Chr.*, 1952. C. C. Torrey, *The Chronicler's History of Israel*, 1954. W. A. L. Elmslie in *IB*, 1954. R. H. Pfeiffer in *IDB*, 1962.

I. Genealogies from Adam to David (1:1–9:43)

Genealogies are the backbone of history. In biblical history they are particularly important because they show how God's redemptive purpose has been carried on from one generation to another. For the Chronicler the genealogical tables of the first 9 chs. are not just prelude or intro. They are an integral part of the divine plan of redemption which has been gradually unfolding since the beginning of human history, i.e. Adam, until its climax in the radiant splendor of the Davidic kingdom and the glory of the Solomonic temple, where God is rightfully worshiped.

The genealogical lists include the descendants of Adam (1:1-3) and Noah and his sons (1:4-26); Abraham and his descendants are traced through Ishmael and Keturah (1:27-33) and through Isaac and his sons Esau (1:34-54) and Israel (2:1-2). Then follow the genealogies of the individual tribes of Israel (2:3–8:40), with special emphasis on Judah and the line of David (2:3–4:23), Levi (ch. 6), and Benjamin (ch. 8).

The section closes with a list of the postexilic inhabitants of Jerusalem (9:1-16), of temple personnel (9:17-34), and the genealogy of Saul (9:35-44).

A. Patriarchal Genealogies (1:1-54)

1:1-4. From Adam to Noah and His Sons. Cf. Gen. 5. Relationship is not mentioned in this list. The godless line of Cain has been purposely omitted. The stylistically similar vss. 24-27 carry the line from Shem to Abraham (cf. Gen. 11:10-26). The mere citation of names in these 2 lists (vss. 1-4, 24-27) indicates that the Chronicler takes for granted his readers' acquaintance with the sources.

1:5-23. Descendants of the Sons of Noah. Cf. Gen. 10. Vs. 6 probably should read "Riphath" instead of **Diphath.** The explanation of the name **Peleg** in vs. 19 is not clear.

1:28-34. Sons of Abraham. This list consists of Isaac and Ishmael and their offspring (cf. Gen. 25:13-16) and the sons of Keturah, the **concubine** of Abraham (cf. Gen. 25:1-4, where she is called his wife).

1:35-42. Sons of Esau and Seir. Cf. Gen. 36. Esau, who became identified with Edom (Gen. 25:30), is the ancestor of the Edomites (Gen. 36:9).

1:43-54. Kings of Edom. Cf. Gen. 36. Vs. 43*b* reads lit. "before there reigned a king of the children of Israel [over Edom?]." **Baal-hanan** (vs. 49) is equivalent to Hannibal—cf. Johanan (John), "Yahweh is gracious." By adding vs. 51*a* (not in Gen. 36:39-40) the Chronicler wants to make clear that the kings of Edom are replaced by the **chiefs,** who are listed in vss. 51*b*-54.

B. Genealogies of the Sons of Jacob (2:1–8:40)

2:1-2. Sons of Israel. Cf. Gen. 35:23-26. In the Chronicler's list **Dan** is placed before the sons of Rachel, **Joseph** and **Benjamin.**

2:3–4:23. Genealogies of Judah. The sons of Judah come first in accordance with the Chronicler's interest in the S kingdom and the ideal rule of David (cf. 5:1-2). He devotes 100 vss. to this genealogy, which is longer than any of the others. The royal line of David springs from the union of Judah and **Tamar,** a Canaanite woman and daughter-in-law of

Judah (cf. Gen. 38; 46:12; Lev. 18:15). Her name appears in the genealogy of Jesus (Matt. 1:3). **Achar, the troubler of Israel,** is also found in the line of David (vs. 7; cf. Josh. 7, where the name is given as Achan), as well as **Ethan, Heman, Calcol, and Dara** (better Darda), famous for their wisdom (vs. 6; cf. I Kings 4:31).

2:9-55. Descendants of Hezron. This, according to the Chronicler, is the most important clan of Judah. From Hezron springs the royal family of **David** (vss. 9-17), as well as the 2 important clans of Caleb (so read **Chelubai,** vs. 9; cf. vss. 18-24, 42-55) and Jerahmeel (vss. 25-41). According to the Chronicler, David is the **seventh** son of Jesse (vs. 15); in I Sam. 16:10-11; 17:12 Jesse has 8 sons, of whom David is the youngest.

3:1-9. Descendants of David. Those born to David in **Hebron** are listed in vss. 1-4 (cf. II Sam. 3:2-5). **Daniel,** the **second** son, is called Chileab in II Sam. 3:3. The length of David's reign in Hebron and in **Jerusalem** (vs. 4; contrast 29:27) is taken from II Sam. 5:5. Those born to David in Jerusalem are listed in vss. 5-9 (cf. II Sam. 5:14-16). For **Bathshua** (vs. 5) read Bathsheba.

3:10-16. Kings of Judah. Athaliah, who was not of the line of David (cf. II Kings 8:26), is not mentioned. **Johanan the first-born** of Josiah (vs. 15) is mentioned nowhere else. **Jeconiah,** son of **Jehoiakim,** was known also as Coniah (Jer. 22:24) and Jehoiachin (II Kings 24:6). **Zedekiah** (vs. 16) was the uncle of Jehoiachin (cf. vs. 15), whom he succeeded. **Son** here is a conventional term of relation.

3:17-24. The Davidic Line After the Exile. This is the only place where **Zerubbabel** is the son of **Pedaiah** (vs. 19) and nephew of **Shealtiel** (vs. 18); elsewhere he is called the son of Shealtiel (e.g. Ezra 3:2; Neh. 12:1; Hag. 1:1). Perhaps he may have been the real son of Pedaiah and the legal son of Shealtiel by levirate marriage (see comment on Deut. 25:5-10). For **sons of Pedaiah** in vs. 19 the LXX reads "sons of Shealtiel." **Shenazzar,** a brother of Pedaiah (vs. 18), is probably to be identified with Sheshbazzar, who was put in charge of restoring the temple (Ezra 1:7-11). The difficult Hebrew text of vs. 21 seems to list 6 **sons of Hananiah,** but the LXX and other versions make each the son of the preceding, thus adding 5 generations (see Intro.).

4:1-23. Additional Genealogies of Judah. In vs. 1 for **Carmi** read Caleb (cf. 2:18-19, 50-51). A popular etymology of the name **Jabez** is found in vs. 9. Jabez prays away the curse of his name (vs. 10). **Mered** (vs. 17; cf. 2:34-35) must have been a man of distinction to marry the **daughter of Pharaoh.**

4:24-43. Sons of Simeon. Geographically and historically Simeon is closely connected with Judah (cf. Josh. 19:9, Judg. 1:3). The names of Simeon's offspring (vss. 24-27; cf. Num. 26:12-14) and their places of dwelling (vss. 28-33; cf. Josh. 19:2-8) are followed (vss. 34-38) by a list of princes from the time of **Hezekiah** who lead their people in a search for more grazing ground into the peaceful **valley of Gedor** (LXX "Gerar"; see color map 8), somewhere in the territory of Philistia, and into the territory of Edom, where they smite the **Amalekites** who have survived attacks by Saul and David (vss. 39-43; cf. I Sam. 14:48, II Sam. 8:12). **Meunim** (vs. 41), name

of an Arabian tribe living E of Edom, is here probably a scribal error for "their dwellings."

5:1-26. Sons of Reuben, Gad, and Manasseh. The **sons of Reuben** are given (vs. 3; cf. Gen. 46:9) after the Chronicler states why he began the genealogies of the tribes of Israel with Judah (vss. 1-2). Reuben lost his **birthright,** i.e. the status of **first-born,** because he defiled his father's bed (cf. Gen. 35:22a; 49:4). In Gen. 48:8-22 it was not the birthright but a "blessing" (as the LXX reads here) that Jacob gave to the **sons of Joseph,** Ephraim and Manasseh. Nevertheless **Judah** achieved preeminence and produced a **prince,** i.e. David (cf. Ps. 78:67-68, where Judah is chosen above Joseph).

5:4-10. The captivity of **Beerah** (vs. 6) is not recorded elsewhere. **Tilgath-pilneser** is the Chronicler's misspelling for Tiglath-pileser III, who in 734/33 overran Transjordan and Galilee and exiled many of the people (cf. vs. 26; II Kings 15:29). The Reubenites are said to live E of the Jordan in **Gilead** (vs. 9) and have spread S to the Moabite cities named in vs. 8 (see color map 6). The **Hagrites** (vs. 10; cf. vss. 19-20; Ps. 83:6) were bedouins living in N Arabia.

5:11-17. The **sons of Gad** live in **Gilead** (vs. 16) and in **Bashan** to the N (but cf. Josh. 13:25-27) and have spread E to **Salecah** in the desert (see color map 9).

5:18-22. This is a more detailed account of the war on the **Hagrites** (see above on vss. 4-10). On **Jetur** and **Naphish** cf. 1:31. The **exile** (vs. 22) is that of vs. 6.

5:23-24. The **half-tribe of Manasseh** is the portion of the tribe living E of the Jordan. It is a prolific group, occupying land to the N of Gad, as far as the Lebanon mountain range.

5:25-26. Because of apostasy Reuben, Gad, and the half-tribe of Manasseh are taken into captivity by **Tilgath-pilneser** (see above on vss. 4-10). **Pul,** a usurper, assumed the throne name Tiglath-pileser; only one king is referred to. On the cities of exile cf. II Kings 17:6, 18:11.

6:1-81. Sons of Levi. The list of preexilic high priests from **Aaron** to **Jehozadak,** who was taken into captivity by **Nebuchadnezzar** (vss. 3b-15), is preceded by a genealogical record of descendants from Levi to Aaron (vss. 1-3a). Abiathar, of the line of Eli, is not mentioned with **Zadok** (vs. 8) as a priest under David, since he supported another aspirant to the throne rather than Solomon (I Kings 1:7; 2:26-27).

6:16-30. In vss. 16-19a the sons and grandsons of Levi are named. Then the descendants of the sons are listed: **Gershom** (vss. 20-21), **Kohath** (vss. 22-24), and **Merari** (vss. 29-30). The descendants of **Elkanah,** of the line of Kohath, are given (vss. 25-28; cf. vss. 33b-38) in order to show that **Samuel** came from the line of Levi, though according to I Sam. 1:1 he was an Ephraimite. Cf. 9:22; 11:3 for the Chronicler's high opinion of Samuel.

6:31-48. These vss. contain the genealogies of the chief singers of David: **Heman** (vss. 33b-38), **Asaph** (vss. 39-43), and **Ethan** (vss. 44-47). According to vs. 33 **Samuel** was the grandfather of Heman, one of David's chief musicians (cf. 16:41-42).

6:49-53. The duties of the priests are described, as **Moses . . . commanded** (vs. 49), followed by an additional genealogy of the sons of Aaron (vss. 50-53; cf. vss. 4-8). Though the Chronicler begins his history of Israel with the reign of David, he recognizes the important role that Moses played in Israel's earlier history in cultic and legal matters (cf. e.g. 15: 15; II 8:13; 23:18).

6:54-81. The names of these Levitical cities are taken from Josh. 21, with many corruptions in the spellings and a few inadvertent omissions.

7:1-5. Sons of Issachar. Cf. Num. 26:23-25.

7:6-12a. An Uncertain Genealogy. A list of Benjamin's descendants is found in ch. 8, whereas there is none for Zebulun, which according to 2:1 should follow Issachar. In the Hebrew **The sons of** is missing from vs. 6 but would be the same as the opening letters of **Benjamin**—suggesting a copyist's error in writing "Benjamin" for "The sons of Zebulun." On the other hand this list does not match other genealogies of Zebulun (Gen. 46:14; Num. 26:26) and it is possible that the genealogy for this tribe has been lost in the transmission of the text. In vs. 12a read "Shupham and Hupham" (cf. Num. 26:39).

7:12b. The Son of Dan. On the basis of Gen. 46:23 and the LXX this fragment should read: "The sons of Dan, Hushim his son, one."

7:13. Sons of Naphtali. Cf. Gen. 46:24-25.

7:14-19. Sons of Manasseh. According to Gen. 50: 23 **Machir** and his sons were born in Egypt. Here they are associated with an **Aramaean** background. The genealogy is based on Num. 26:29-33. Elements of the tribe living both E and W of the Jordan are included in this genealogy (cf. 5:23-24).

7:20-29. Sons of Ephraim. Cf. Num. 26:35. Included in this genealogy (vss. 25-27) are the forebears of Joshua. A disastrous **raid** of Ephraimites (vss. 21b-23) into Philistine territory is also recounted. A list of cities (vss. 28-29; see color map 6) belonging to Ephraim and Manasseh has been added.

7:30-40. Sons of Asher. Cf. Gen. 46:17; Num. 26: 44-46. The source from which many of the names recorded here are taken is not known.

8:1-40. Genealogy of Benjamin. Cf. Gen. 46:21. Benjaminites in **Geba** (vss. 3-7), in **Moab** and **Ono and Lod** (vss. 8-12), in **Aijalon** and **Jerusalem** (vss. 13-28), and in **Gibeon** (vss. 29-32) are noted. The genealogy of the house of **Saul** is found in vss. 33-40 (cf. I Sam. 14:49). **Eshbaal** (vs. 33) should be Ishbaal (see comments on I Sam. 14:49-51; II Sam. 2:8-11). On **Meribbaal** see comment on II Sam. 4:4.

C. The Postexilic Families of Jerusalem (9:1-18a)

After 2 introductory vss., the postexilic residents of Jerusalem are given in the following order: Israelites, i.e. laymen of the tribes of **Judah** and **Benjamin** (vss. 4-9); **priests** (vss. 10-13); **Levites** (vss. 14-16); and **gatekeepers** (vss. 17-18a). A similar list is found in Neh. 11:3-19. The **Book of the Kings of Israel** (vs. 1) is not canonical Kings (see Intro.). The **exile** refers to the captivity of the Jews after the fall of Jerusalem in 586 to Nebuchadnezzar. Though Ephraimites and Manassites are mentioned as citizens of postexilic Jerusalem, they are not included in the lists of this ch.

D. Temple Personnel (9:18b-34)

The **gatekeepers** (vss. 18b-32) are of special interest to the author. Their office goes back to the time of Moses (vss. 18b-20) and was sanctioned by Samuel and David (vs. 22). They are reckoned among the Levites (vs. 26). Other duties (vss. 28-32) are ascribed to them besides keeping the gates. The **singers** in the temple (vs. 33) are **on duty day and night.**

E. The Genealogy of Saul (9:35-44)

Repeated from 8:29-38, this is an intro. to the opening vss. of ch. 10, which describe Saul's tragic end.

II. The Reign of David (10:1–29:30)

For the Chronicler David and his rule is the all-important subject in his history of the Hebrew nation. Not only does he omit the whole period of the judges and the events of Saul's life up to his death, but he also idealizes the life of David by omitting all references to his life of exile from the court of Saul, his reign in Hebron, and the Bathsheba incident. He ignores even the history of the N kingdom except where it impinges on the affairs of Judah. In his view Saul's attempt to found a kingdom ended in failure; God's redemptive purpose was realized in the history of the S kingdom, which to all intents and purposes was founded by David, the Lord's anointed.

A. The Death of Saul (10:1-14)

The reason for beginning the history of David with the death of Saul is given in vss. 13-14. With this ch. cf. I Sam. 31. As far as the Chronicler is concerned, Saul's whole **house** perished with him (vs. 6; cf. I Sam. 31:6); he tells nothing of David's later dealings with Ishbaal (Ishbosheth, II Sam. 2:8–4:12), Meribaal (Mephibosheth, II Sam. 9; 19:24-30), and others (II Sam. 21:1-14) remaining of Saul's family. Because of religious scruples he avoids any references to Ashtaroth (I Sam. 31:10), the hanging of the bodies of Saul and his sons on the walls of Bethshan (I Sam. 31:10; cf. Deut. 21:22-23), and the burning of the bodies by the men of Jabesh (I Sam. 31:12; cf. Lev. 20:14; 21:9). As he sums it up (vss. 13-14), Saul's miserable failure as king of Israel was due to his disobedience to the Lord's commandments (cf. I Sam. 15:17-35) and his trafficking with a **medium** (cf. I Sam. 28:8-14). This dark picture of Saul (cf. also 13:3) is in sharp contrast with the glorious reigns of David and Solomon which he portrays.

B. Establishment of the Davidic Kingdom (11:1–22:1)

11:1-9. David's Anointing. David becomes king of all Israel and captures Jerusalem. On vss. 1-3, which describe the anointing of David as king over **all Israel,** cf. II Sam. 5:1-3. His 7½-year rule over Judah at **Hebron** and his long warfare with the house of Saul are passed over (cf. II Sam. 1-4). On vss. 4-9, in which the capture of **Jerusalem** by David and all Israel is described, cf. II Sam. 5:6-10.

11:10-47. David's Mighty Men. Cf. II Sam. 23:8-39, which has been expanded here by the addition of vss. 41b-47. These mighty men, by their bravery and loyalty, help David establish his kingdom in accordance with the divine purpose.

12:1-22. David's Supporters Against Saul. The sources from which this material is derived are not known. Men from Benjamin (vss. 1-6, 16-18), Gad (vss. 8-15), and Manasseh (vss. 19-22) attach themselves to David at different times during this period.

12:23-40. David's Army at Hebron. Large numbers of fighting men from every tribe join David at Hebron to make him king. All Israel joins in the coronation festivities (vss. 38-40), which seem to have messianic overtones.

13:1-14. An Attempt to Return the Ark. Cf. II Sam. 6:1-11. The Chronicler places this narrative immediately after the capture of Jerusalem (11:4-9) to show David's concern for the worship of God. Note the different order of events in II Sam. 5:6–6:10. In Chr. the **priests and Levites** join in the procession which accompanies the **ark** (vs. 2), but they do not appear in the II Sam. narrative. After the introductory vss. 1-5 there follows the story of the unsuccessful attempt to bring the ark to Jerusalem from **Kiriath-jearim** (vss. 6-14; cf. II Sam. 6:2-11).

14:1-17. Miscellaneous Matters. This ch. concerns David's dealings with **Hiram king of Tyre** (vss. 1-2), additions to the royal household (vss. 3-7), and wars with the Philistines (vss. 8-17). These events are described in II Sam. 5:11-25, before the removal of the ark from Kiriath-jearim. The Chronicler places them after the removal of the ark, during the 3 months it is resting in the house of Obed-edom. In vs. 12 David has the idol **gods** of the Philistines **burned** (cf. Deut. 7:3, 25); in II Sam. 5:21 they are simply carried away by David and his men.

15:1–16:3. The Ark Brought to Jerusalem. The parallel story in II Sam. 6:12-19 is greatly expanded here. The additional material includes elaborate plans for bringing the ark to Jerusalem in which the **Levites** play the dominant role. The Levites **carry the ark** (vss. 2-15); bands of Levitical **singers** and musicians accompany the procession (vss. 16-24); and the Levites sacrifice **seven bullocks and seven rams** (vs. 26) whereas in II Sam. 6:13 David sacrifices only "an ox and a fatling." God looks with favor on these preparations, and the ark is successfully transferred to Jerusalem and into the **tent which David had pitched for it** (15:26–16:3).

16:4-43. The Service of Joy Before the Ark. None of this material is found in II Sam. except the last vs. (cf. II Sam. 6:19b-20a). The Levites, who have carried the ark up to Jerusalem (15:27), are now **appointed** by David to minister **before the ark** with praise and thanksgiving (vss. 4-7). By tracing this appointment back to David the Chronicler assures the Levites, in whom he is esp. interested, a legitimate place among the temple personnel in Jerusalem (cf. II 5).

16:8-36. The psalm of praise is composed of several elements from the Psalter: vss. 8-22 = Ps. 105: 1-15; vss. 23-33 = Ps. 96:1-13; vss. 34-36 = Ps. 106: 1, 47-48.

16:37-43. Two holy places are mentioned: one at Jerusalem, where **Asaph and his brethren** minister **before the ark** (vss. 37-38); and one at **Gibeon** (cf. I Kings 3-4), where **Zadok the priest** and his Levitical assistants offer the sacrifices in the **tabernacle** (vss. 39-42; cf. 21:29; II 1:3-4).

17:1-27. David's Desire to Build a Temple. This passage is taken with slight variations from II Sam. 7. David desires to build a temple for God, and **Nathan the prophet** agrees (vss. 1-2). But God tells Nathan in a dream that he does not approve of this plan (vss. 3-6). Instead God promises to **build** David a **house,** i.e. a dynasty, through the house of God which his son will build (vss. 7-15). "When he [i.e. David's son] commits iniquity I will chastise him with the rod of men, with the stripes of the sons of men" (II Sam. 7:14b) is omitted in the Chronicler's account (vs. 13) because it does not fit in with his ideal view of David's successor. Also "your [David's] house and your kingdom" (II Sam. 7:16) becomes **my** [God's] **house and . . . my kingdom** (vs. 14), showing the Chronicler's idea that David is ruler over God's kingdom (cf. 28:5; 29:23; II 9:8; 13:8). David's prayer of thanksgiving follows (vss. 16-27).

18:1–20:8. David's Military Victories. These accounts follow closely the older sources. Ch. 18 = II Sam. 8. 19:1–20:3 = II Sam. 10:1–11:1; 12:26-31. 20:4-8 = II Sam. 21:18-22.

David's successful encounters with the **Philistines** (18:1), the **Moabites** (18:2), the kingdom of **Zobah** (18:3-4), **Damascus** (18:5-10), **Edom** (18:12-13), the **Ammonites** and the **Syrians** (19:1–20:3), and the Philistine **giants** (20:4-8) are related and his administrative officers are listed (18:14-17).

The story of David's kindness to Meribaal (Mephibosheth; cf. II Sam. 9) is omitted here, probably because the Chronicler has stated in 10:6 that all of Saul's house perished with him at the battle of Gilboa. Also omitted are the odious story of David and Bathsheba (cf. II Sam. 11:1–12:25) and the accounts of family intrigues and revolts against David (cf. II Sam. 13:1–21:14) since they do not fit the Chronicler's idealized figure of David.

20:5. Here **Elhanan** slays **Lahmi the brother of Goliath the Gittite.** According to II Sam. 21:19 "Elhanan . . . , the Bethlehemite, slew Goliath the Gittite," but in I Sam. 17 David kills the giant. The Chronicler's account of this episode is probably an attempt to reconcile the 2 narratives in Sam.

21:1–22:1. David's Census and the Plague. This passage derives from II Sam. 24, with some important variations:

a) **Satan,** a supernatural evil emissary (cf. Job 1:6-12; Zech. 3:1-2), is said to have **incited David to number Israel,** whereas in II Sam. 24:1 God himself does the inciting. The Chronicler avoids the idea that a holy God can perpetrate a sinful act.

b) **Levi and Benjamin** (vs. 6) are not included in the census. On Levi cf. Num. 1:49. Benjamin may have been omitted because Jerusalem lay in Benjaminite territory (cf. Josh. 18:28).

c) The frequent references to the **angel**—9 times as compared with 3 times in Sam.—reflect the Chronicler's belief in a transcendent God who deals with man more and more through intermediaries. The divine nature of this angelic emissary is indicated by the fact that he stands **between earth and heaven** (vs. 16).

d) David pays **six hundred shekels of gold by weight** (i.e. in a balance; see below on 29:1-22a and table, p. 1285) for the **site of the threshing floor.** In Sam. he pays only 50 shekels of silver for it. By exaggerating the cost the Chronicler emphasizes the great value of the temple site.

e) The burning of the offering by **fire from heaven** (vs. 26) indicates the divine approval of the site for the future temple.

f) The authenticity of the site is further emphasized by the words of 22:1, which have a polemical ring. Jerusalem is the true center of worship as opposed to **Gibeon**, but perhaps even more as opposed to any Samaritan holy place. Because of this, David cannot sacrifice any more at the high place of Gibeon, where, according to the Chronicler, the **tabernacle** has been (21:28–22:1; but cf. II 1:1-6).

C. Preparations for the Temple and the Cult (22:2–29:30)

There are no parallels for this section in either Sam. or Kings. The Chronicler would like to make David builder of the temple. Since history stands in his way, he stresses David's preparations so strongly that the temple ideally appears to be his work.

22:2-19. *David's Preparation for the Temple.* After the consecration of the site the Chronicler describes some of the building **materials** (vss. 2-5) which David provides for the temple—stone, metal, and wood.

22:6-16. David charges his son **Solomon** to build the temple. Cf. the prophecy of Nathan (17:1-15) to which David refers. In I Kings 2:1-9 David gives his last instructions to Solomon without mentioning the temple. Note the astronomically high figures in vs. 14 to describe the amounts of **gold** and **silver** which David sets aside for the building of the temple.

22:17-19. David also exhorts the **leaders of Israel** to help Solomon in this important task of building a **sanctuary** for the **ark** of the Lord.

23:1-32. *Organization of the Levites.* After the Levites are counted (vs. 3-5) they are organized into 3 divisions according to the **sons of Levi**: Gershonites (vss. 7-11), Kohathites (vss. 12-20), and Merarites (vss. 21-23).

23:24-32. The Levites are no longer required to **carry the tabernacle** (vs. 26) and its equipment since there is now a central sanctuary. This appears to be the reason the age limit for Levites is increased 10 years (vss. 24, 27; cf. vs. 3). The main work of the Levites is to **assist** (vss. 28-32) the Aaronic priests in the temple services.

24:1-19. *Divisions of the Aaronic Priesthood.* The **sons of Aaron**, through **Eleazar and Ithamar**, are divided into 24 classes, with their duties being determined **by lot**.

24:20-31. *An Additional List of Levites.* The relation to 23:6-24 is not clear. The Gershonites are omitted and some new names are added.

25:1-31. *Divisions of the Temple Singers.* The leaders of the musical guilds come from the Levitical families of **Asaph**, of **Heman**, and of **Jeduthun** (vss. 1-7). That these singers **prophesy with lyres, with harps, and with cymbals** seems to indicate that they are closely related to prophetic circles.

Heman is called **the king's seer** (vs. 5) whereas in II 29:30 Asaph is called "the seer" and in II 35:15 Jeduthun is called "the king's seer." In II 20:14 "the Spirit of the Lord" comes upon "a Levite of the sons of Asaph," who then gives a message to King Jehoshaphat in the same manner as the prophets of old. And in II 34:30 "Levites" is substituted for "prophets" in the parallel passage in II Kings 23:2. This seems to indicate that in the days of the Chronicler prophetic inspiration had been transferred to the Levitical singers. The subdivisions, with their order of succession in the service, are given in vss. 9-31.

26:1-32. *Further Levitical Offices.* The doorkeepers are descended from 3 families (vss. 1-11); their duties are assigned by **lots** (vss. 12-19). The financial officials (vss. 20-28) are responsible for the **treasuries of the house of God** and the **gifts** dedicated to the temple, including spoils of war. Officials are chosen as **officers and judges** (vss. 29-32) in the areas both E and W of the Jordan.

27:1-34. *Military and Civil Administration.* The army (vss. 1-15) is organized with 12 officers, each with **twenty-four thousand** men. They are appointed for military duty, one for each **month**. The names of the officers are taken from 11:11-12.

27:16-24. David appoints leaders **over the tribes of Israel.** For some reason Gad and Asher are omitted. **Zadok**, who is said to come from Aaron (vs. 17), represents all the people.

27:25-34. The officials in charge of David's personal affairs oversee his **treasuries**, fields, and flocks, and serve as his personal counselors.

28:1–29:30. *David's Last Words and Acts.* David announces to the assembled officials of Israel that Solomon is to be his successor, according to God's own choosing (28:1-10). All of the palace intrigues, violence, and murder associated with Solomon's accession in I Kings 1-2 are not mentioned by the Chronicler.

28:11-21. David has received the **plan of the . . . temple** from God (cf. Exod. 25:9, where the plan of the tabernacle is given to Moses by God) and this is given over to Solomon with parental words of encouragement.

29:1-22a. David asks the assembled congregation to give freely toward the construction of the temple, as he has done. The response is overwhelming, and David pours out his heart in prayer and praise to God. **Darics** (vs. 7) were Persian gold coins used in the Chronicler's day but of course an anachronism for the time of David, when precious metal used for money had to be tallied by weight (cf. 21:25). On **talents** see table, p. 1285.

29:22b-30. Solomon is made king **the second time** (cf. 23:1). The book closes with a résumé of David's rule.

THE SECOND BOOK OF THE CHRONICLES

Charles T. Fritsch

For the introduction see Intro. to I Chr. The outline of the contents indicated by the headings continues that in I Chr.

III. The Reign of Solomon (1:1–9:31)

The underlying purpose of the Chronicler's history is clearly revealed in his description of Solomon's reign. He idealizes Solomon by omitting certain unfavorable events recorded in I Kings: the troubles connected with his accession (I Kings 1–2), his marriage to Pharaoh's daughter (I Kings 3:1), his worship of foreign deities, his love for foreign women, and the political and military troubles at the end of his reign (I Kings 11). Instead he emphasizes the building of the temple and the organization of its affairs.

A. The Establishment of Solomon's Kingdom (1:1-17)

1:1-13. *Solomon at Gibeon.* The story of Solomon's prayer for wisdom is based on I Kings 3:4-14. Gibeon is said to be the place where the Mosaic tabernacle and the **bronze altar** are at this time (cf. I 16:39; 21:29). David has **brought up the ark** to Jerusalem (I 15) but no provision has been made for sacrificial offerings there (cf. I 16:4-6).

1:14-17. *Solomon's Wealth and Power.* Cf. I Kings 10:26-29. The **horses,** which come from Asia Minor (vs. 16; see color map 7), bring less money than the **chariots** from **Egypt.**

B. The Building and Dedication of the Temple (2:1–7:11)

2:1-18. *Preparations for the Temple.* This account is based on I Kings 5. Solomon receives building materials and **skilled** labor for the temple from **Huram** (Hiram) **the king of Tyre.** He conscripts the laborers from the **aliens** in Israel (cf. I Kings 5: 13, 15, where Israelites are conscripted). On **Huram-abi** (vss. 13-14) cf. I Kings 7:13-14; also Exod. 35: 30-35.

3:1-17. *The Construction.* Cf. the longer account in I Kings 6–7. The site of the temple is said to be **Mount Moriah,** where God appeared to David (cf. I 21), and where Abraham offered up Isaac (Gen. 22:2). **A hundred and twenty cubits** (vs. 4) for the **height** of the **vestibule** should probably read "twenty cubits" since the temple itself is only 30 cubits high (cf. I Kings 6:2). On the **cherubim** (vss.

10-14) see comment on I Kings 6:23-28. The 2 bronze **pillars** (vss. 15-17), named **Jachin** and **Boaz** (see comment on I Kings 7:15-22), were symbolic, free-standing columns which stood outside the inner chamber.

4:1-22. *The Furniture and Vessels.* Cf. I Kings 7: 23-51.

5:1–7:11. *The Dedication.* After the **gold** and **silver** and all the **vessels** which belonged to David are brought into the temple treasury (5:1) the **ark of the covenant** is transported from the tent which David pitched for it in the Jebusite stronghold of **Zion** (cf. I 16:1) to its permanent resting place in the **inner sanctuary** of the temple (cf. I Kings 8:1-11). According to the Chronicler the **Levites** carry the ark (5:3); in I Kings 8:3 it is the priests. Only the priests, however, may place it in the sanctuary (5:7).

5:11-14. As the chief musicians of the temple, appointed by David (I 16:4), the Levites sing joyful songs of **praise and thanksgiving** to the accompaniment of **musical instruments** (see comment on Ps. 150:3-5). The climax of this outburst of praise is reached when the **glory of the LORD** filled the **house of God.**

6:1-42. This ch. is taken almost verbatim from I Kings 8:12-50. It contains Solomon's words to the people (vss. 3-11) and the prayer of dedication (vss. 12-42). Significant differences in the Chronicler's account are few. That the **covenant** is **with the people of Israel** (vs. 11) rather than "with our fathers, when he brought them out of the land of Egypt," as in I Kings 8:21, indicates the Chronicler's view that the covenant relationship with Israel did not begin at Sinai but existed from the very beginning of Israel's history. The **bronze platform** (vs. 13) on which Solomon kneels in prayer before the congregation is not mentioned in Kings.

6:40-42. The conclusion of the prayer is strikingly different from that in I Kings 8:50b-53. A quotation from Ps. 132:8-10, eulogizing **David** and the temple tradition, fittingly concludes the dedicatory prayer according to the Chronicler's view. Here Solomon asks that God be **attentive** to the prayers offered in (or toward) **this place** because of his love for David, his **servant,** whereas in the older account he is to give ear because of his love for Moses, who led Israel out of Egypt. The bringing of the ark into the temple is the climax of the service of dedication for the Chronicler. God now dwells in his holy place in the temple, where priest and Levite minister before his presence and the people worship in holy array.

7:1-11. Divine approval of the new temple is shown by the **fire** which **came down from heaven and consumed** the sacrifices and the **glory** which **filled** the **house.** The great **feast** is concluded with sacrifices offered by king and people, and with great thanksgiving.

C. THE REMAINDER OF SOLOMON'S REIGN (7:12-9:31)

7:12-22. *Solomon's Dream.* Following the dedication ceremonies Solomon has a dream at **night** in which God assures him that his prayer will be answered. The divine blessing will be his if he keeps God's **statutes;** if he does not, the people will be uprooted from the **land,** and the magnificent temple will be deserted (cf. I Kings 9:2-9).

8:1-18. *Solomon's Activities.* Cf. I Kings 9:10-28. Cities are built (vss. 1-6), laborers are conscripted from the alien peoples living in Canaan (vss. 7-9), the religious **feasts** are duly observed (vss. 12-16), and the journey of Solomon's navy to **Ophir** for **gold** is noted (vss. 17-18). The Chronicler speaks of **cities** being **given** to Solomon by **Huram** (Hiram, vs. 2), reversing the historical record of I Kings 9:11-14 that Solomon sold "twenty cities in Galilee" to Hiram for 120 talents of gold. **Tadmor** (vs. 4), an oasis 120 miles NE of Damascus later known as Palmyra (see color map 7), is defended by some scholars as a place where Solomon would establish protection for his trading operations, but it is more likely that the Chronicler confused the reference in I Kings 9:18 to Tamar S of the Dead Sea (see color map 6).

8:11. The Chronicler's great respect for the ark is shown in Solomon's statement that his foreign-born wife must not dwell **in the house of David king of Israel, for the places to which the ark of the LORD has come are holy** (cf. I Kings 9:24, where this religious note is not found).

9:1-12. *The Queen of Sheba's Visit.* This story is taken from I Kings 10:1-13 with little change. The theocratic viewpoint of the Chronicler is strikingly brought out in vs. 8, however, where **set you on his** [i.e. God's] **throne as king for the LORD your God** contrasts with the parallel in I Kings 10:9, which simply has "set you on the throne of Israel" (see comment on I 17:1-27).

9:13-28. *Solomon's Wealth.* Cf. I Kings 10:14-28.

9:29-31. *Solomon's Death.* Cf. 1 Kings 11:41-42. In accordance with his idealization of Solomon the Chronicler omits any mention of his love for foreign women, his idolatries, and his military and political problems described in I Kings 11.

IV. THE KINGS OF JUDAH (10:1-36:21)

This portion of the Chronicler's history deals with the kings of the S kingdom. He ignores the history of the N kingdom except where it impinges on the affairs of Judah. The reason for doing this is found in 13:5-11. New material, not in Kings, is introduced into his accounts of Judah's rulers, with special attention being given to the activities of prophets and priests in the life of the nation.

A. REHOBOAM (10:1-12:16)

10:1-19. This ch. is an almost exact duplication of I Kings 12:1-19, but the crowning of Jeroboam (I Kings 12:20) is not mentioned by the Chronicler.

11:1-23. New material in this ch. includes: the building activity of Rehoboam (vss. 5-12), esp. the fortification of **cities** in the S part of Judah, evidently as a protection against Egypt; the immigration of **priests** and **Levites** (vss. 13-17) to Judah from the N tribes; and a record of the members of Rehoboam's family (vss. 18-23).

12:1-12. The invasion of **Shishak king of Egypt** is described with the addition of theological comments (cf. I Kings 14:25-28). The ch. concludes with some general remarks concerning Rehoboam's rule and the notice of his death (vss. 13-16; cf. I Kings 14:29-31).

B. ABIJAH (13:1-22)

On the basis of I Kings 15:7, which simply states that "there was war between Abijam [Abijah] and Jeroboam," the Chronicler proceeds to give a detailed account of one of the battles between the 2 kings. **Zemaraim** (vs. 4) is unknown as a mountain, but a town of this name in the territory of Benjamin (Josh. 18:22) was probably located *ca.* 5 miles NE of Bethel (see color map 8).

13:4b-12. In Abijah's speech the N kingdom is condemned because it has broken away from the Davidic dynasty and the legitimate cult. Judah, on the other hand, with the true God on her side and the **priests with their battle trumpets** at the head of her army, is assured of victory (cf. 20:22, where another battle is won by songs of praise and musical instruments). The **covenant of salt** (vs. 5; see comment on Lev. 2:11-13) probably refers to the eternal duration of God's covenant with David. The Davidic covenant is a favorite theme with the Chronicler (cf. 21:7).

13:13-22. In spite of the overwhelming number of the enemy's forces and Jeroboam's military tactics, Abijah wins the battle. The report of Jeroboam's death (vs. 20) is premature, since according to I Kings 15:8-9 he outlived Abijah. In contrast with Jeroboam's humiliating defeat Abijah increases in strength (vs. 21).

C. ASA (14:1-16:14)

The basis of this section is I Kings 15:9-24, which has been greatly expanded. Asa's piety (14:2) and zeal for cultic reform (14:3-5; 15:1-19) are the reasons for the peace which prevails during most of his reign (cf. I Kings 15:16).

14:9-15. Asa's military power is tested by **Zerah the Ethiopian**—lit. "Cushite," which here may refer instead to an Arabian tribe (cf. Hab. 3:7), since the name Zerah is philologically related to a Sabean (Sheba) princely title (see comment on Num. 12:1-2). God routs the enemy in response to the king's fervent prayer. On the place names see color map 8. There is no parallel account of this battle in the older history.

16:1-12. The generally peaceful reign of Asa is shattered at the end by a battle with **Baasha king of Israel** (cf. I Kings 15:17-22). His successful rule ends in shame and disgrace as the prophet **Hanani** (perhaps to be taken as the father of the prophet

Jehu; see below on 18:1–19:3) rebukes him for relying on the king of Syria in fighting Baasha rather than on God. Asa puts the prophet in jail for his condemnation and this, in the Chronicler's mind, is the reason for Asa's fatal disease **in his feet.**

16:13-14. In spite of his apostasy Asa receives a magnificent burial at which precious **spices** are burned in his honor.

D. JEHOSHAPHAT (17:1–20:37)

The Chronicler's account of this glorious reign is based on I Kings 22, with several important additions. In ch. 17 the piety of Jehoshaphat and his military power are noted. Of special interest is his appointment of 5 lay **princes,** 9 **Levites,** and 2 **priests** (17:7-9) to go throughout the cities of Judah and teach the people the **law** of God.

18:1–19:3. *Alliance with Israel.* Taken with few changes from I Kings 22:1-35a, this is the only extensive reference to the history of the N kingdom in Chr. The 2 kingdoms are brought close together through the **marriage** of Jehoram the son of Jehoshaphat to Athaliah the daughter of Ahab (18:1; cf. 21:6)—an alliance which led to the introduction of idolatry into Judah and the near extinction of the royal family (cf. 22:10-12). Jehoshaphat is severely rebuked by a prophet for making this alliance, but is promised that divine retribution will be averted because of his inherent goodness (19:2-3). According to I Kings 16:1 **Jehu the son of Hanani** was a prophet of the N kingdom in the time of Baasha, *ca.* 35 years earlier (see above on 16:1-12).

19:4-11. *Civil Reforms.* Courts are set up throughout the land over which judges of impeccable character preside. In Jerusalem a higher court of appeal is established to deal with both religious and secular matters (see comment on Deut. 17:8-13).

20:1-30. *Jehoshaphat's Victories.* On news that a vast army of **Moabites and Ammonites** is invading Judah from Edom, Jehoshaphat prays for deliverance. God answers through **Jahaziel,** a Levite, who is moved by the **Spirit** to prophesy **victory** in the ensuing battle (see above on I 25:1-31). With words of assurance (vs. 20; cf. Isa. 7:9) and songs of **praise** the army of Judah marches out into the **wilderness of Tekoa** (see color map 8) to meet the enemy, whom they find already destroyed because of internal dissension. In vs. 1 **Meunites** (probably a desert tribe living E of Edom) is a guess, based on 26:7, at correcting a corruption in the text and may identify the **inhabitants of Mount Seir** (the mountain range of Edom) attacked by their allies (vs. 23). **Hazazon-tamar** (vs. 2) should probably be identified, not with **Engedi** on the W shore of the Dead Sea, but with Tamar farther S (see above on 9:1-12).

20:31–21:1. *The Conclusion of Jehoshaphat's Reign.* Of special interest here is the account of the king's naval activities. His alliance with the wicked king **Ahaziah** of Israel is given as the cause of the wrecking of his fleet at **Ezion-geber** on the Gulf of Aqaba (see color map 4). The prophet **Eliezer** is not mentioned elsewhere. Cf. a different account of this episode in I Kings 22:48-49.

E. JEHORAM (21:1-20)

Cf. II Kings 8:17-22. The new material emphasizes the wickedness of Jehoram.

21:2-4. Jehoram has 6 **brothers,** all of whom he kills. The duplication of **Azariah** is probably an error in copying one of the names. **Princes** (vs. 4) means, not members of the royal family, but men in positions of authority. For **Judah** (LXX) the Hebrew text reads "Israel." Some scholars, taking this as correct, suggest that it reflects an authentic record that certain N officials were stationed in Judah during this period.

21:7. Sounding a favorite note (cf. 13:5) the Chronicler revises II Kings 8:19 to declare that, in spite of Jehoram's great wickedness, God will **not destroy the house of David, because of the covenant which he had made with David.** The **lamp** which God gave to David and his sons is a figure of life which has messianic overtones (cf. I Kings 11:36; 15:4; II Kings 8:19; Ps. 132:17).

21:11-20. Jehoram's introduction of pagan rites into Judah, as well as his murders, will bring disasters on the nation, his family, and himself, according to a **letter** (vss. 12-15) purportedly written by **Elijah**—who actually was no longer alive at this time (cf. II Kings 3:11-12). In fulfillment God sends the **Philistines** and **Arabs** against Judah (vss. 16-17) and Jehoram suffers heavy personal losses, which leave him only one son. In the Hebrew **Jehoahaz** is a transposition of the elements composing the name Ahaziah (cf. 22:1; on **youngest son** see below on 22:1-9). Finally (vss. 18-20), as predicted in the letter, Jehoram dies of a dreadful **disease** and is buried in dishonor.

F. AHAZIAH (22:1-9)

Cf. II Kings 8:26-29. **Forty-two years old** would make Ahaziah 2 years older than his father (cf. 21:20) and is no doubt a copyist's error. II Kings 8:26 in the Hebrew has 22, in the LXX 20—a somewhat more credible age for Jehoram's **youngest son** (vs. 1; cf. 21:17). His brief but wicked reign is under the domination of the queen mother **Athaliah,** the daughter of **Ahab.** The alliance between the 2 kingdoms involves Ahaziah in the revolt of **Jehu** and brings about his death (cf. II Kings 9).

G. ATHALIAH (22:10–23:21)

Athaliah, the daughter of Ahab and wife of Jehoram, on hearing of the death of her son Azariah (22:10-12; cf. II Kings 11:1-3), destroys the **royal family of . . . Judah.** Only one escapes, the infant **Joash** (a shortened form of Jehoash), who is hidden by his aunt, **Jeho-shabeath** (Jehosheba in Kings) —the Chronicler adds that she is the **wife of Jehoiada the priest.** The means by which after 7 years the boy is brought forth from hiding and anointed king and Athaliah is assassinated are described in ch. 23 (cf. II Kings 11:4-20). The Chronicler's account emphasizes the role of the **Levites** in the plot, as well as the reorganization of the temple services. Note that David's organization of the Levites was based on Mosaic legislation (23:18).

H. JOASH (24:1-27)

The reign of Joash may be divided into 2 parts. In his earlier years he **did what was right** under the influence of **Jehoiada** (vss. 1-16; cf. II Kings 12:4-16), restoring the temple with the help of a **chest** for contributions. After the death of Jehoiada, Joash turns to evil ways. He orders the death of **Zechariah the son of Jehoiada,** who has proclaimed judgment on Judah (vss. 20-22) and as a result is defeated by a small force of **Syrians** (vss. 23-24; cf. II Kings 12:17-18). Note that when God is not with Israel's forces the enemy with few men can defeat a very large army, but a small army with God's help can defeat a much larger enemy force (cf. 13:3, 13-19). Bedridden because of wounds received in battle (vs. 25), Joash is assassinated by **his servants.** The Chronicler adds that he was not buried in the **tombs of the kings,** as a further sign of his degradation (vss. 25-27; cf. II Kings 12:19-21).

I. Amaziah (25:1-28)

This account is based on II Kings 14, with an expanded description of the battle with **Edom** (vss. 5-13; cf. II Kings 14:7). Two unnamed prophets with words of warning are introduced by the Chronicler (vss. 7-8; 15-16).

J. Uzziah (26:1-23)

Uzziah's prosperous reign was one of the longest in Judah history. The short account of it in II Kings 15:1-7, where he is called Azariah, is expanded by the Chronicler. Uzziah's military victories, building activities, and great interest in husbandry and agriculture are graphically described (vss. 6-15). On the places named see color map 8. On **Meunites** see above on 20:1-30. According to the Chronicler, Uzziah is stricken with **leprosy** because he burns **incense on the altar** in the temple in defiance of the **priests** (vss. 16-23).

K. Jotham (27:1-9)

Jotham, having ruled as coregent during his father's affliction (26:21), becomes king at Uzziah's death (cf. II Kings 15:32-38). The Chronicler expands the earlier account of Jotham's reign by noting his building activities and his warfare with the **Ammonites,** whom he conquers. He, like his father, **did what was right in the eyes of the LORD.** On **cors** see "Measures and Money," pp. 1283-85.

L. Ahaz (28:1-27)

This ch. is based on II Kings 16, with many alterations. The attacks on Judah by the Syrians and by the Israelites (in II Kings the **king of Syria,** i.e. Rezin, and **Pekah** invade Judah together) are brought about by the heinous apostasies of Ahaz (vss. 1-8). Then follows the curious account of the release of the Judean prisoners by the Israelites at the instigation of **Oded** the **prophet** (vss. 9-15). Ahaz asks the Assyrian king, **Tilgath-pilneser** (see comment on I 5:1-26), to intervene against the invading **Edomites** and **Philistines** (in II Kings against the coalition of Syria and Israel), but he comes as an oppressor rather than a deliverer (vss. 16-21; on the places named see color map 8). The iniquitous reign of Ahaz comes to an end with the introduction of Syrian deities into Judah and the closing of the temple at Jerusalem (vss. 22-27; but cf. II Kings 16:10-18).

M. Hezekiah (29:1–32:33)

Because Hezekiah was a God-fearing man and great reformer, the Chronicler found his reign of special interest. Whereas the account of it in II Kings 18-20 deals mainly with political events, the Chronicler emphasizes its religious reforms, expanding one vs. (II Kings 18:4) into 3 chs. (29-31).

29:3-19. At the very beginning of Hezekiah's reign the **doors** of the temple are **opened** and the sanctuary is **cleansed.** Notice the prominent place given to the **Levites** in this operation, in accordance with the Chronicler's religious outlook.

29:20-36. A happy day of rededication follows, with sacrifices, songs of praise led by the Levites, and personal consecration of the members of the congregation. When the people bring more offerings than the priests can handle, the Levites help them, and are noted as having been **more upright in heart . . . in sanctifying themselves,** i.e. preparing themselves ritually for such service.

30:1-27. After the temple is in order, Hezekiah orders a national observance of the **passover** at **Jerusalem,** to which are also invited the subjugated Israelites of the N kingdom. Those in the territory occupied by the Samaritans in the Chronicler's day scorn the invitation, but those farther N accept (vss. 10-11). The observance is held in the **second month** of the year rather than the first (vss. 13-22) because many **priests** remain unsanctified and the people, esp. those from the N, have to have more time to come to Jerusalem. The postponement is allowed by law (see comment on Num. 9:1-14). The enthusiasm is such that the feast is prolonged **another seven days** (vss. 23-27). Cf. another great passover festival in Josiah's time described by the Chronicler (35:1-19).

31:1-21. Hezekiah's religious zeal is further manifested in his destruction of pagan cultic centers in both N and S kingdoms, his reorganization of the temple personnel, and his efforts to get adequate support for the maintenance of the clergy.

32:1-33. The Chronicler's account of Sennacherib's invasion is abbreviated from II Kings 18:13–20:21 (cf. Isa. 36–39). Vss. 2-8, which describe the

Courtesy of Jay and Mary Smith
Entrance to Gihon Spring

king's frantic efforts to build up the defenses of **Jerusalem** against the imminent Assyrian attack, are taken from an independent source.

Courtesy of Jay and Mary Smith

Inside Gihon Pool with opening of Siloam tunnel on left

Courtesy of Jay and Mary Smith

Inside the Siloam Tunnel at point where Hezekiah's laborers, working from both ends, converged

N. Manasseh (33:1-20)

Vss. 1-9, describing Manasseh's idolatrous practices, parallel II Kings 21:1-9. The Chronicler then adds new material (vss. 10-19) decribing Manasseh's captivity, repentance, and return to purify Jerusalem. In light of Assyria's troubles within and without her vast empire during the last part of Ashurbanipal's reign there may be some historical basis for the Chronicler's statement that Manasseh was brought to **Babylon** in chains and later released, though no mention of this incident is found either in Kings or in the Assyrian records. The repentance of Manasseh and his reforms in Jerusalem, however, seem contrary to the evidence, since the pagan practices which he introduced into Israel's religion were still prevalent in the days of Josiah. On the **outer wall** described in vs. 14 see color map 13. The

prayer mentioned in vs. 19 is purportedly preserved in the Prayer of Manasseh in the Apoc.

O. Amon (33:21-25)

Amon follows in his father's **evil** ways and is assassinated in the palace (cf. II Kings 21:19-24).

P. Josiah (34:1–35:27)

This section parallels quite closely II Kings 22–23, with some abridgment and addition.

34:3-33. According to the Chronicler, Josiah's reforms start **in the twelfth year** of his reign (vss. 3-7; cf. II Kings 23:4-20) whereas in Kings the reforms are not undertaken until after the discovery of the **book of the law** (vss. 8-33; cf. II Kings 22:3–23:3). The Chronicler emphasizes the role of the **Levites** in the **repairing** of the temple and in its services (vss. 8-13; cf. II Kings 22:3-7).

35:1-19. As one expects, the Chronicler describes in great detail the celebration of the **passover,** which is simply mentioned in II Kings 23:21-23. Notice again the prominent part played by the Levites in the passover rites.

35:20-27. The tragic death of Josiah is treated in more detail by the Chronicler than in the earlier history (cf. II Kings 23:29-30). In 609 B.C. Pharaoh **Neco** set out with his Egyptian army to **Carchemish** on the upper Euphrates (see color map 9) to join Assyrian remnants attempting to hold out against the Babylonian mop-up of the overthrown Assyrian Empire. The Chronicler is probably correct in saying that Josiah offered military opposition to Neco at the pass of **Megiddo** (see color map 8) and was mortally **wounded** in the battle. The unhappy defeat and death of this ideal young king was difficult to justify according to the orthodox dogma of retribution. The Chronicler attempts to do it by stating that Josiah sinned by ignoring a divine oracle given to him by Neco himself which forbade him to oppose the pharaoh in battle.

Q. JEHOAHAZ (36:1-4)

Cf. II Kings 23:31-35. A younger son of Josiah named Shallum (cf. I 3:15; Jer. 22:10-12) is crowned by the **people of the land** and takes the throne name Jehoahaz. He reigns only **three months** before he is deposed by Neco and deported to Egypt. In his place Neco sets up his brother **Eliakim** under the throne name **Jehoiakim** and demands a large **tribute.**

R. JEHOIAKIM (36:5-8)

Cf. II Kings 23:34–24:7. In 605 **Nebuchadnezzar** (better Nebuchadrezzar as in Jer., Ezek.) defeated Neco at Carchemish (see above on 35:20-27; cf. Jer. 46:2) and drove him back to Egypt. Soon after this he succeeded to the Babylonian throne and began laying tribute on the little W states, including Judah. Possibly at this time he came to Jerusalem and **bound** Jehoiakim **in fetters** and despoiled the temple (vss. 6-7), though there is no hint of such an attack elsewhere in the OT or in Nebuchadnezzar's own chronicle. *Ca.* 601 an apparent Babylonian attempt to invade Egypt failed with heavy casualties, and this event may have encouraged Jehoiakim to withhold his tribute to Babylonia (cf. II Kings 24:1-2). As a result Nebuchadnezzar besieged Jerusalem in 598, and during the course of the siege Jehoiakim died, probably by assassination (cf. Jer. 22:18-19; 36:30).

S. JEHOIACHIN (36:9-10)

Cf. II Kings 24:8-17; 25:27-30. Jehoiachin was the throne name of Jeconiah (cf. I 3:16-17). That he was more than **eight years old** is indicated by his having wives (cf. II Kings 24:15) and children (cf. Jer. 22:28). Perhaps the word **ten** was somehow displaced from his age and came to be added to the **three months** of his reign (cf. II Kings 24:8). **In the spring of the year**—March 16, 597, according to Nebuchadnezzar's chronicle—Jehoiachin capitulated to the siege started before his father's death. He and his family and the leading citizens of Judah were taken to Babylon in the first deportation of exiles. According to II Kings 24:17; Jer. 27:1 **Zedekiah** (throne name of Mattaniah) was not Jehoiachin's **brother** but his uncle, another son of Josiah (cf. I 3:15-16).

T. ZEDEKIAH (36:11-21)

Cf. II Kings 25:1-21; Jer. 52:1-27. Like his brothers and nephew, Zedekiah does wickedly, and he refuses to heed the words of **Jeremiah the prophet.** The **leading priests and the people** join him in scorn of the **prophets,** and as a result **the wrath of the LORD rose against his people, till there was no remedy.** Jerusalem is captured by the Babylonians after a long siege and the temple is destroyed. The survivors are taken into exile to Babylon—though Jer. 52:16, 29 states that the Babylonians left the "poorest of the land" and took only 832 persons. The exile is to last for a **sabbath** consisting of **seventy years**—apparently considered as ending, not with the overthrow of the Babylonian Empire by **Persia** in 539 and the decree allowing Jewish exiles to migrate to Jerusalem which was issued the following year, but with the completion of the 2nd temple over 20 years later.

U. THE DECREE OF CYRUS (36:22-23)

This repetition of Ezra 1:1-3*a* (see comment) may have been added to show that at one time Ezra followed II Chr. (see Intro.). More likely, however, its purpose is to bring the book, and the Hebrew Bible, to a hopeful conclusion (cf. the similar hopeful ending in II Kings 25:27-30).

THE BOOK OF EZRA

Charles T. Fritsch

Introduction

Place in the Canon. Ezra and Nehemiah were originally part of a larger work that included I, II Chr. (see Intro. to I Chr.). In the Hebrew Bible Ezra and Neh. precede I, II Chr. to comprise the last 4 books of the final division, the Writings; but it is clear for several reasons that they were originally attached to the end of the Chronicler's history, in the correct chronological order. This original order is preserved in the LXX as well as in English Bibles.

The separation of Ezra and Neh. in our English Bibles rightly emphasizes the importance of the 2 title personages in the restoration period of Jewish history but obscures the original unity of the writing. This is indicated by the subject matter and by the usage in the Hebrew manuscripts, where the 2 are found as a single book up until 1448. That they remained one book in the LXX at first is shown by their being in this form in the Codex Vaticanus (4th cent.). But Origen (died A.D. 254) already knew of their separation in Greek, and in the Vulg. Ezra is called "Esdras I" and Neh. "Esdras II." Under the influence of the Vulg. the Christian practice has been to treat them as 2 books.

Contents and Sources. The history of postexilic Judaism as related in these 2 books centers around certain leaders as follows:

a) The return of exiles to Jerusalem in 538 under Sheshbazzar with the permission of Cyrus (Ezra 1–2). The list of returning exiles in ch. 2, repeated with minor variations in Neh. 7:6-73a, actually refers to those returning with Zerubbabel (cf. 2:2).

b) The rebuilding of the temple under Zerubbabel, beginning in 520, the 2nd year of Darius I (Ezra 3–6). The confusion between Sheshbazzar and Zerubbabel persists in the representation that the latter began the building in 538 but because of opposition—including correspondence with Artaxerxes (4:7-22) actually pertaining to the later rebuilding of the walls—had to postpone it till 520, when rediscovery of the decree of Cyrus cleared the way for its completion.

c) A return and reforms under Ezra (Ezra 7–10) and the reading of the law by Ezra and its acceptance by the people (Neh. 7:73b–10:39—a misplaced excerpt belonging with Ezra 7–10). There is uncertainty about the date of Ezra's activity, as will be discussed in the following section.

d) The rebuilding of the walls of Jerusalem under Neh., beginning in 445, the 20th year of Artaxerxes I, under whose authority Neh. acts (Neh. 1:1–7:73a; 11–13, with interpolations).

The reader of these books is impressed by the number of sources the Chronicler has used in them. The most important of these are:

Temple records: "the book of the genealogy" (Neh. 7:5) and "the Book of the Chronicles" (Neh. 12:23), which is not the canonical work of the same name.

The decree of Cyrus, in Hebrew (Ezra 1:1-4) and in Aramaic (6:3-5).

Aramaic sources: mostly correspondence between the enemies of the Jews and the Persian court (Ezra 4:7-22; 5:6-17; 6:2-12) and the letter given to Ezra by Artaxerxes (7:12-26).

Neh.'s "memoirs" (Neh. 1:1–7:73a and portions of chs. 11–13), written in the first person in a style distinct from other parts of the books and universally recognized as the authentic composition of Neh. himself.

Ezra's narrative (Ezra 7–10; Neh. 7:73b–10:39), part of which is written in the first person and has the appearance of being autobiographical (Ezra 7:27–8:34; 9:1-15).

The Chronicler's interest in records of all kinds, esp. genealogies, is shown by the various lists found in the 2 books: Ezra 2:2-69; 7:1-5; 8:1-14; 10:18-43; Neh. 7:7-22; 10:1-26; 11:4–12:26.

Date and Authorship. One of the most puzzling problems in these books is the historical order of the 2 men Ezra and Neh. and the relation between their contributions toward establishing the Jewish community after the Exile. From the order of the books in the canon it is natural to assume that Ezra appeared in Jerusalem before Neh.; and the dates given in the text—for Ezra the 7th year of Artaxerxes (7:7) and for Neh. the 20th year of Artaxerxes (Neh. 2:1)—seem to corroborate this view. But this apparently simple chronology raises a number of problems.

If Ezra preceded Neh. it is strange that Neh. nowhere mentions Ezra's work in his memoirs. In all of Neh.'s reforms there is no indication that he is enforcing the law introduced by Ezra and accepted by the people. If Ezra came first then we must conclude that his reforms were a miserable failure and that Neh. had to come just a few years later to reinstitute them. On the other hand if Neh. used his political authority to enforce certain provisions of the Mosaic law, it is understandable that Ezra later should call for acceptance of this law in its entirety, including more stringent measures than those of Neh. about intermarriage with non-Jews.

Eliashib, the high priest when Neh. arrives (Neh. 3:1), is said to be the father (Ezra 10:6) or grandfather (Neh. 12:10-11, 22) of Jehohanan, who is apparently the high priest in the time of Ezra (10:6).

In the light of these and other evidences many scholars are convinced that Neh. must have preceded Ezra, and they have attempted to solve the chronological problems on this basis. Besides the dates mentioned above these problems include references (Neh. 8:9; 10:1; 12:26, 36) which appear to make the 2 men contemporaries. To allow for an overlap in their careers some scholars have conjectured that there may be a textual error in the date of 7:7 and have suggested that Ezra came to Jerusalem later in the reign of Artaxerxes, probably in his 27th or 37th year. Much more widely accepted, however, is the view that, whereas Neh. 2:1 means the 20th year of Artaxerxes I (445), Ezra 7:7 refers to the 7th year, not of this king (458), but of Artaxerxes II (397). According to this view Neh. and Ezra were not contemporaries at all, and the references indicating that they were—some of them suspect for other reasons—must be considered erroneous.

As noted in the Intro. to I Chr., the confusion about the order of Neh. and Ezra has been one of the factors influencing many scholars to date the Chronicler at a later time when the sequence of the 2 leaders was forgotten. But the reversal is not necessarily evidence that the Chronicler was ignorant of their correct order. Rather it is probable that, wanting to include Neh.'s important role in his overall plan, he appended the memoirs at the conclusion of his own work. Later copyists are no doubt responsible for several dislocations—most noticeably the placing of part of the Ezra narrative within the Neh. memoirs (Neh. 7:73b–10:39)—and for insertion of the references associating Ezra and Neh. With the removal of other reasons for a background in the Greek period (see Intro. to I Chr.) an increasing number of scholars now recognize that the most natural date for the Chronicler's writing is soon after the last event he describes—i.e. in the first decades of the 4th cent. Assuming such a date, it is not unlikely that the Chronicler was a disciple of Ezra—or possibly even Ezra himself, since the portion of Ezra's narrative in the first person (7:27–8:34; 9:1-15) displays to some extent the Chronicler's characteristic style.

In these 2 books which form the conclusion and climax of his work the Chronicler proclaims with unshakable assurance the saving acts of God in the days since the Exile whereby the Jewish community, delivered from bondage, was brought again into the Land of Promise.

For Further Study: H. W. Ryle, *The Books of Ezra and Neh.,* 1901. C. C. Torrey, *Ezra Studies,* 1910. L. W. Batten, *A Critical and Exegetical Commentary on the Books of Ezra and Neh.,* 1913. A. C. Welch, *Postexilic Judaism,* 1935. R. A. Bowman in *IB,* 1954. R. H. Pfeiffer in *IDB,* 1962.

I. The Return Under Sheshbazzar (1:1–2:70)

1:1-4. *The Decree of Cyrus.* Cf. I Esdras 2:1-7. Vss. 1-3a are repeated in II Chr. 36:22-23. In fulfillment of the prophecy of **Jeremiah** (cf. Jer. 29:10) God **stirred up the spirit of Cyrus** to proclaim an edict of deliverance for the Jewish people. The **first year** refers to Cyrus' first regnal year (538) as ruler of the former Babylonian Empire; he had been **king of Persia** *ca.* 20 years and had added to his realm Media and other lands extending as far as Lydia in Asia Minor before capturing Babylon in 539.

1:2-4. The decree not only orders the rebuilding of the temple but also permits **whoever is among you of all his people** to go to Jerusalem. **All** here fits in with the Chronicler's idea that N Israelites who had been in preexilic Jerusalem were also among those who returned. Jews remaining in Babylon are invited to assist the venture with their contributions. Another version of this decree in Aramaic is found in 6:3-5. There is no reason to doubt the essential authenticity of either account, since the Hebrew document may represent the oral **proclamation** made throughout the empire to all Jews, while the Aramaic text is in the form of a written memorandum of an oral decree or decision of a king or other public official.

1:5-11. *The Return.* Cf. I Esdras 2:8-15. Those who return are the family heads of the tribes of **Judah and Benjamin,** who according to the Chronicler constitute the postexilic community, and the **priests** and **Levites,** who are the religious personnel needed for the temple services. In accordance with the decree (vs. 4) the returning exiles are given gifts of money and **goods** by their neighbors who remain behind (cf. Exod. 3:22; 11:2; 12:35). As a royal gesture of good will Cyrus returns the precious **vessels** taken by **Nebuchadnezzar** when he destroyed the temple. They are put into the hands of **Sheshbazzar,** who is probably to be identified with Shenazzar, a younger son of Jehoiachin (Jeconiah), the king of Judah taken into exile by Nebuchadnezzar in 597 (cf. I Chr. 3:16-17; II Chr. 36:9-10; Jer. 24:1). Some of the Hebrew terms for the vessels in vss. 9-11 are not clear, and the figures in the Hebrew text are hopelessly confused (those in the RSV are taken from I Esdras).

2:1-70. *The List of Returning Jews.* Cf. I Esdras 5:7-46. The text assumes (vs. 1; cf. 1:11) that this list refers to those who returned to Jerusalem under Sheshbazzar in the days of Cyrus, but the list itself does not include his name. Actually a careful study of the document indicates that it is a composite census list, made of data drawn from different sources. It is repeated with minor variations in Neh. 7:6-73a and may possibly come, in its present form, from Neh.'s day.

2:2a. *A List of Leaders.* Eleven names are given here (there are 12 in Neh. 7:7) without any genealogy, indicating perhaps that they are well-known people. **Zerubbabel,** grandson of Jehoiachin and nephew of Sheshbazzar (cf. I Chr. 3:17-19; see above on 1:5-11), and **Jeshua,** called "Joshua the high priest" in Hag., Zech., are known to have been leaders of the postexilic Jewish community in the time of Darius I during the rebuilding of the temple (520-515; cf. 4:24–5:2; Hag. 1; Zech. 4:9; 6:11-12). Their position at the head of this list may indicate that they led a group of returning exiles shortly before the rebuilding, or simply that at one time they were leaders of the returned exiles, since possibly the 11 men named were not contemporary but successive—note e.g. **Nehemiah,** and **Bigvai,** mentioned in nonbiblical sources as governor of Judah *ca*. 410. It is evident that the Chronicler, however, assumed either that Zerubbabel and Jeshua accompanied Sheshbazzar in 538 and took over the leadership from him on arriving in Jerusalem or, more probably, that Sheshbazzar and Zerubbabel were alternate names for the same man.

2:2*b*-35. *A List of Laymen.* These are classified by families (vss. 3-20) and by cities (vss. 21-35). The numbers often differ from those in the Neh. list (cf. e.g. vss. 5-6 with Neh. 7:10-11). **Sons of** should be understood as "descendants of," since the list refers to rather remote ancestors. There are various types of personal names included in this list, some being of Babylonian and Persian derivation. **Gibbar** (vs. 20) is given in Neh. 7:25 as Gibeon, which as a place name should not appear before vs. 25 in a list which works N. It may be the personal name Gaber, as the LXX vocalizes it.

2:21-35. The cities mentioned here (see color map 11) fall into 3 major groups: those in the mountainous area from **Bethlehem** N to **Harim** (vss. 21-32), those to the W in the coastal area (vs. 33), and

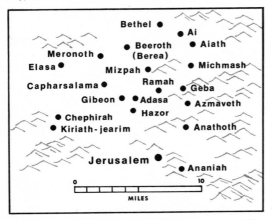

those to the E in the Jordan Valley (vss. 34-35). **The other Elam** (vs. 31) is in contrast with the Elam in vs. 7.

2:36-58. *Lists of Temple Personnel.* First the **priests** are mentioned. They belong to 4 families. **Jeshua** (vs. 36) is probably to be identified with the high priest who was a contemporary of Zerubbabel (cf. vs. 2; 10:18). The number of priests (4,289) is extremely large, almost a 10th of those returning to Jerusalem.

2:40. In Ezra-Neh. the priests are generally distinguished from the **Levites** (but cf. 10:5), who are here mentioned next. They number only **seventy-four** (cf. also 8:15-20). Evidently Levites were not inclined to leave Babylonia for Jerusalem, where they would be doing menial tasks in the temple (cf. Ezek. 44:9-14; Neh. 10:13), or else only a few Levites had been taken into captivity by Nebuchadnezzar.

2:41. Next in order come the **singers,** who are the descendants of **Asaph** (cf. I Chr. 16:4-6; according to I Chr. 6:31-47; 15:16-19 Heman and Ethan were also leaders of musical guilds). In 3:10, throughout Chr., and in several vss. of Neh. 11-12 the singers are identified with the Levites. In this

passage and in several others (e.g. 10:23-24; Neh. 10:28) the Levites are carefully distinguished from the singers.

2:42. The **gatekeepers** follow next in order. Their duties are described in I Chr. 9:17-32, where they are identified with the Levites. In this passage, as well as in others (e.g. 10:23-24; Neh. 10:28), they are distinguished from the Levites.

2:43-54. After the gatekeepers the **temple servants** are listed. According to 8:20 they were "set apart" (i.e. given) by David and his officials to serve the Levites. The large number of foreign names in the list probably indicates that most of this group were captives of war (cf. Josh. 9:27). Their special place of residence was on the Ophel mount, opposite the Water Gate, which probably led out to the spring of Gihon (Neh. 3:26; see color map 13). In I Chr. 9:2, as well as here, they are distinguished from the Levites, though like the singers and gatekeepers they were eventually incorporated into the Levitical order (cf. I Chr. 23:28).

2:55-58. The last list of temple personnel identifies the **sons of Solomon's servants.** The origin and duties of this special class of people are somewhat obscure. They may have been descended from Solomon's levy of forced labor who were drafted for the building of the temple (cf. I Kings 5:13-18). It is noted that they are included in the total in vs. 58 and also among the temple servants in Neh. 10:28.

2:59-63. *Persons Lacking Genealogies.* The presence of this brief list reveals the keen interest of the people in racial and religious purity. The uncertainty of the priests' genealogies (vss. 61-63) posed a special problem since they might contaminate the holiness of the temple. **Governor** here is a Persian title, *tirshatha* (cf. I Esdras 5:40 and see comment). It is applied specifically to Neh. in Neh. 8:9; 10:1 but no doubt was applicable also to Sheshbazzar and Zerubbabel, who had similar authority from Persian rulers. The person designated here depends on the date of this part of the list. The **Urim and Thummim** refer to the sacred lot (see comment on I Sam. 14:36-46); there is no other clear evidence that this method of ascertaining the divine will was in use in postexilic times.

2:64-67. *Numerical Summaries.* The total number of returnees, 42,360, is found also in Neh. 7:66; I Esdras 5:41, though the preceding figures in the 3 lists disagree at various points and in no case add up to the total. The **male and female singers** (vs. 65) were professional entertainers employed at banquets, feasts, and funerals (cf. II Sam. 19:35; II Chr. 35:25; Eccl. 2:8) and are not to be confused with the temple singers (vs. 41).

2:68-70. *Summaries of Gifts.* These **offerings** are reported as given by the people for the purpose of rebuilding the temple. The parallel passage in Neh. 7:70-73*a* differs markedly in details and the stated amounts of the gifts. **When they came to the house of the LORD** must refer to the **site** of the temple, which now lies in ruins. **Darics** were Persian coins first issued by Darius I and probably not in use during the early years of his reign when the temple was being built. **Minas** were weights (see "Measures and Money," pp. 1283-85). Vs. 70 describes ideally the restored condition of the land.

II. THE RECONSTRUCTION OF THE TEMPLE UNDER ZERUBBABEL (3:1-6:22)

3:1-6a. Reestablishment of Altar and Sacrifices. Cf. I Esdras 5:47-53. The restoration begins with the resumption of the cult, the rebuilding of the altar of **burnt offerings** being the first step. In David's time there was an altar in Jerusalem before the temple was built (II Sam. 24:25), and after the destruction of the temple sacrifices were still offered there (Jer. 41:5). Now it is of utmost importance at this critical moment in the life of the people that an altar be set up in Jerusalem before the temple is rebuilt.

3:1-2a. In what year the **seventh month** falls is not clear. The Chronicler apparently has in mind the first year of Cyrus (cf. 1:1; 3:8a). But since **Jeshua** and **Zerubbabel** are said to have built the altar, his source probably meant a year in the time of Darius I. Once again the Chronicler has telescoped the work of Zerubbabel with that of his uncle, Sheshbazzar (see above on 2:2a). Here Jeshua precedes Zerubbabel (cf. vs. 8; 2:2; 4:3; 5:2; Neh. 12:1, where Zerubbabel is mentioned first), probably because this passage deals with cultic matters and Jeshua is the high priest of the restored community (cf. Hag. 1:1). On **son of Shealtiel** see comment on I Chr. 3:17-24.

3:2b-3. The altar is built **as it is written in the law of Moses the man of God** (cf. 6:18; see comment on I Chr. 6:49-53; the Mosaic regulation is in Exod. 20:25; cf. Deut. 27:6). The reason for the hasty erection of the altar is said to be **the fear** which **was upon them because of the peoples of the lands.** In this way the returnees will be assured of God's help against their foes.

3:4-6a. In line with the Chronicler's special interest in cultic matters, the regulations for the sacrifices and set feasts are reinstituted before work is started on rebuilding the temple. The sacrifices for the **feast of booths,** or tabernacles, are described in Num. 29:12-38. On the **continual burnt offerings** cf. Exod. 29:38-42; Num. 28:3-8; on the sacrifices connected with the celebration of the **new moon** cf. Num. 28:11-15; on the **appointed feasts** cf. Lev. 23:2-37; II Chr. 8:13. The **freewill offering** could be offered by individuals on great feast days or on any other occasion (cf. Num. 29:39; Deut. 16:10).

3:6b-13. The Laying of the Foundation. Cf. I Esdras 5:54-65. This account is strongly reminiscent of the building of the Solomonic temple (I Kings 5-6; II Chr. 2-3). The **grant . . . from Cyrus** probably refers simply to the permission given by Cyrus to rebuild the temple and his promise of help. Here Zerubbabel and Jeshua are said to have begun the work by laying the foundation, though in 5:16 this is ascribed to Sheshbazzar (see above on 2:2a; 3:1-2a for an explanation of this apparent confusion). The Chronicler's special interest in the **Levites** is shown by the important role they play in the work in spite of the small number that have returned from Babylonia (cf. 2:40). On the minimum age limit of the Levites cf. I Chr. 23:24, 27.

3:10-13. The people rejoice when the **foundation** is laid. **Priests and Levites** lead the service of praise and thanksgiving instituted by David (cf. I Chr. 15:16; II Chr. 29:25-26). The refrain, from Ps. 136:1, is used frequently by the Chronicler (I Chr. 16:34;

II Chr. 5:13; 7:3; 20:21). Intermingled with the **joyful shout** is the **sound of . . . weeping,** for **many** of the people remember the magnificence of the old temple destroyed by Nebuchadnezzar (cf. Hag. 2:1-3).

4:1-5. Samaritan Opposition. Cf. I Esdras 5:66-73. The **adversaries of Judah and Benjamin** are the descendants of the mixed population of the province of Samaria, formerly the N kingdom of Israel. When the Assyrians took this area in 722 they deported many Israelites and resettled the land with foreigners (cf. II Kings 17:24). **Esarhaddon** (681-669) evidently followed the same policy since the present adversaries claim to have been in the land since his time. These Samaritans offer assistance in building the temple on the basis of worshiping the same God as the Jews. Zerubbabel and Jeshua refuse their offer on the technicality that Cyrus has given permission only to the Jews to rebuild the temple (cf. 1:3). This exclusiveness of the Jews arouses the hostility of the **people of the land,** who oppose them **all the days of Cyrus . . . , even until the reign of Darius.**

4:6-24. Later Samaritan Interference. Cf. I Esdras 2:16-30. Since chs. 5-6 deal with the building of the temple in the reign of Darius I this section, which describes further Samaritan opposition in the days of Darius' son **Ahasuerus** (Xerxes I, 486-465) and grandson **Artaxerxes** I (465-424), is chronologically out of order. The correspondence with Artaxerxes about the rebuilding of Jerusalem and its walls must have occurred only a short time before Neh. came to the city in 445. No doubt the Chronicler displaced this material *ca.* 70 years too early to reinforce his idea that the delay in completing the rebuilding of the temple was entirely due to Samaritan interference.

4:7-16. A **letter** addressed to **Artaxerxes** accusing the Jews is described and quoted in full in the **Aramaic** language, which begins in vs. 8 and continues through 6:18. It appears from vss. 7-8 that there may originally have been 2 letters which have been combined by the Chronicler. Because of the **rebellious** nature of the Jewish people the king is advised to halt the **rebuilding** of Jerusalem, which in its restored state would pose a threat to the Persian overlords. This concern with the **city** and its **walls** of course does not fit the Chronicler's context, which has to do with opposition to rebuilding the temple. **Bishlam** (vs. 7) is probably not a man's name; it may be a greeting, "in peace," as in the LXX, though a miscopying of "against Jerusalem" has been suggested. **Osnapper** (vs. 10) is probably a corruption of Ashurbanipal, an Assyrian king (669-*ca.* 629). **Beyond the River** refers to the country W of the Euphrates River.

4:17-24. In his **answer** Artaxerxes reports that investigation of the records has confirmed that Jerusalem has been rebellious throughout its history and he decrees that all work on the rebuilding of the city must stop. **Plainly** (vs. 18; cf. "clearly," Neh. 8:8) means "in translation." In vs. 24 the Chronicler attempts to tie all this into his account by declaring that as a result the work on the temple is halted **until the second year of the reign of Darius** (cf. vs. 5).

5:1-6:22. The Completion of the Temple. Cf. I

Esdras 6–7. The temple narrative, interrupted after
4:5, now continues. The **Jews,** discouraged by the
Samaritans in their first attempt to rebuild the temple (4:4), are spurred on to resume their work by
Haggai and Zechariah. The exhortations of these
prophets are recorded in the books bearing their
names. According to Zech. 1:1 Zechariah was not
the **son** but the grandson of **Iddo.**

5:3-5. When the people start to work a new difficulty immediately develops. The officials of the
Persian satrapy, **Tattenai** and **Shethar-bozenai,**
come to investigate and want to know who has given
permission to rebuild the temple. On receiving a
reply, which is not reported till vss. 11-16, they let
the work proceed pending consultation with the
king.

5:6-17. Tattenai writes a **letter** to Darius about
the situation, noting his own concern about it and
reporting the answer the Jewish **elders** gave him on
being questioned about their building activity. In
a remarkable confession of guilt they have admitted
that God **gave them into the hand of Nebuchadnezzar** because of their unfaithfulness (vs. 12). They
claim that **Cyrus** issued a **decree** authorizing **Sheshbazzar** to rebuild the temple, on the basis of which
he **laid the foundations of the house of God** (vs.
16; contrast 3:8-10, where Zerubbabel and Jeshua
are said to have begun the work on the temple).
The letter closes with the suggestion that the **royal
archives** be searched for this decree. The Aramaic
word translated **huge** (vs. 8) and **great** (6:4) is of
uncertain meaning; discovery of an inscription
applying it to small objects has shown that it does
not refer to the size of the **stones.**

6:1-12. Darius orders a search for the document,
which is discovered in **Ecbatana** (see color map 10),
the summer **capital** of Cyrus and his successors.
The Aramaic form of the edict, given here, differs
slightly from the Hebrew text in 1:2-4. This version
seems to be an expansion of the simple permission to
return. Cf. the measurements of Solomon's temple
(I Kings 6:2; II Chr. 3:3), which differ from those
given here (vs. 3; one dimension is missing). **Three
rows of stones** (on **great** see above on 5:6-17) and
one row of timber (vs. 4) are specified for the walls
of the inner court. Darius then issues a new decree

Courtesy of George G. Cameron, the American Schools of Oriental Research
and the University of Michigan

Close-up of Darius wearing a war crown; note the twirled
mustache, the hair in a bun and the square beard;
vandal's bullets have scarred the image

Courtesy of George G. Cameron, the American Schools of Oriental Research
and the University of Michigan

Persian god Ahuramazda above Darius' enemies, his right
hand raised in blessing

Courtesy of George G. Cameron, the American Schools of Oriental Research
and the University of Michigan

King Darius I graces a panel ordered cut by him in the
side of Bisitun Mtn., one foot upon his archenemy,
Gaumata. Darius receives nine other captive kings,
their hands tied and necks roped together; the whited
area is a latex rubber solution used by archaeologists
to preserve the 2,500-year-old carving

that the Persian officials are to support the work
with funds and threatens those who attempt to **alter**
this decree with severe punishment.

6:13-22. In accordance with the decree of Darius,
and with the cooperation of the Persian officials,
the Jews complete the temple on the **third** (23rd

in I Esdras 7:5) **. . . of Adar, in the sixth year . . . of Darius,** i.e. March 12, 515. The joyful **dedication** ceremonies (vss. 16-18) are not to be compared with Solomon's dedicatory service, where thousands of animals were sacrificed (cf. I Kings 8; II Chr. 5-7). Hebrew is resumed in vs. 19, following the Aramaic section (4:8-6:18). A fitting climax to these ceremonies is the celebration of the 2 great feasts, **passover** (vss. 19-21) and the **feast of unleavened bread** (vs. 22). **King of Assyria** is an anachronism in the Persian period; in the context the phrase would naturally refer to Darius.

III. THE RETURN UNDER EZRA (7:1–8:36)

7:1-28. Ezra's Commission. Cf. I Esdras 8:1-27. The interval denoted by **after this** (lit. "after these things") extends from the completion of the temple in 515 (6:15) to the coming of Ezra to Jerusalem **in the reign of Artaxerxes,** probably over a cent. later, in 397 (see Intro.).

7:1-10. The genealogy of Ezra traces his ancestry back to **Aaron** (cf. I Chr. 6:2-15, 50-53). He is not only a priest (cf. vss. 11-12, 21) but also a **scribe skilled in the law of Moses** (vs. 6). Originally an official of the royal court (cf. II Sam. 8:17), the scribe became associated with the studying and copying of the law. Ezra is the ideal representative of this later type of scribe (cf. vs. 11; Neh. 8:1). His deep devotion to the law throughout his life is shown (vs. 10) by his studying, obeying, and teaching it.

7:11-26. In a **letter** in the Aramaic language (vss. 12-26) **King Artaxerxes** authorizes Ezra to go to Jerusalem with a party of compatriots (vs. 13) in order to investigate the moral and religious conditions of the Jews in the homeland (vs. 14) and deliver gifts gathered in **Babylonia** for the support of the temple (vss. 15-19). The king promises additional funds, if needed, from the royal **treasury** (vs. 20) and orders the provincial **treasurers** to provide Ezra with any further funds and supplies he requires (vss. 21-23; on the weights and measures of vs. 22 see tables, p. 1285). He also exempts the temple personnel from taxes and forced labor (vs. 24; cf. 4:13). He directs Ezra to **appoint magistrates and judges** with full authority to enforce **the law of your God and the law of the king** (vss. 25-26).

7:27-28. In this hymn of praise Ezra for the first time appears as the speaker. From here through ch. 9 (except 8:35-36) the so-called Ezra memoirs are in the first person. In ch. 10 and the continuation in Neh. 7:73b–10:39 the narrative is in the third person.

8:1-36. Ezra's Journey to Jerusalem. Cf. I Esdras 8:28-67. Just as a list of returnees under Zerubbabel and Jeshua is given in ch. 2, so a list of those who return under Ezra is given here. Unlike the earlier list, this begins with the priests (vs. 2), though there is no heading to identify them, and then names the lay families. Many of the names duplicate those in 2:1-15.

8:15-20. When Ezra gathers his group at **Ahava,** an unknown site by a **river** in Babylonia (cf. vs. 31), in order to make final preparations for the trip, he discovers that there are no Levites in the company. Relatively few joined Zerubbabel's group

(2:40); now **none of the sons of Levi** have volunteered to return to Jerusalem. Through the efforts of **Iddo** from **Casiphia** (both unknown) 38 Levites are recruited for the trip, as well as 220 **temple servants** (see above on 2:43-54).

8:21-36. After fasting and prayer to insure a safe journey (vss. 21-23), Ezra entrusts the precious gifts of **gold** and **silver** to the **priests** for safekeeping during the trip (vss. 24-30). The exaggerated amounts are reminiscent of the Chronicler's extravagant figures where the temple is concerned (cf. I Chr. 21:25; 29:1-9; on **darics** see above on 2:68-70). Ezra and his party set out and arrive at Jerusalem (vss. 31-32) after a 4-month journey (7:9). The gifts are handed to the priests and Levites in the temple (vss. 33-34), sacrifices are offered in thanksgiving for bringing the group safely to Jerusalem (vs. 35), and the king's orders are delivered to the provincial authorities (vs. 36).

IV. RELIGIOUS REFORMS (9:1–10:44)

The reforms attributed to Ezra include the dissolution of mixed marriages narrated here and the reading of the law and its acceptance by the people described in Neh. 7:73b–10:39. The order in which they belong is uncertain. In I Esdras 8:68–9:55 the account of the mixed marriages is followed by the reading of the law, indicating that Neh. 7:73b–10:39 belongs after Ezra 10. On the other hand, whereas the assembly about mixed marriages is dated in the 9th month (10:9), the reading of the law is placed in the 7th month (Neh. 8:2). The absence of a year date in either case may mean that the 7th year of Artaxerxes, when Ezra arrived in Jerusalem, is still to be understood (cf. 7:7-9; 8:31). On this basis Neh. 7:73b–8:18, at least, should be inserted before Ezra 9 (see comment on Neh. 9:1-5a). Historically it seems likely that Ezra would acquaint the people with the law and win their acceptance of it before undertaking the severe measure of demanding that a considerable number of leading citizens divorce their foreign wives.

9:1-5. The Problem of Mixed Marriages. Ezra is informed by the **officials** of the community that many Jews, including **priests and Levites,** have been intermarrying with **the peoples of the lands,** who are described in terms of Israel's enemies of old. By these mixed marriages pagan practices are being introduced into the community which corrupt both religion and society. On hearing this news Ezra tears his clothes and pulls out his hair as signs of his deep remorse. After the people have **gathered round** him throughout the day to see this strange spectacle, Ezra falls on his **knees** and lifts his **hands** in prayer.

9:6-15. Ezra's Prayer. This prayer of confession and intercession stands in line with the great prayers of the Bible (e.g. Gen. 18:22-33). Ezra reviews the past sins of his people which brought on their suffering and humiliation under foreign rulers. Even now, when their condition is better because of the beneficent rule of the Persian kings, the people **have forsaken** the **commandments** of God again and by intermarrying with the surrounding peoples have incurred his wrath. How can this **remnant** stand before a just God in this sinful condition? The Hebrew word rendered **protection** (vs. 9) means "wall" and should probably be so translated since Ezra is listing things which the returnees have actually accomplished. The laws ascribed to the prophets (vss. 10-12) are more properly derived from the Deuteronomic tradition (cf. Deut. 7:1-3, 12; 23:6), which of course was deeply influenced by the prophets.

10:1-5. *Public Confession of Guilt*. Ezra's prayer, which ends on the note of fear that God can no longer do anything for his people, produces the immediate effect that Ezra has wanted: **the people wept bitterly** because of their sins. Through their representative, **Shecaniah,** they confess their guilt and propose that drastic action be taken. They vow before God that they will **put away** the foreign **wives and their children** in accordance with the regulations set up by Ezra.

10:6-17. *The Public Assembly*. After Ezra has **spent the night** in continual fasting, a proclamation is sent forth to the **returned exiles** to **assemble at Jerusalem** (vs. 7), attendance being mandatory under threat of severe punishment. The **chamber of Jehohanan** (vs. 6) to which Ezra withdraws for the night probably refers to a temple chamber or cell where Jehohanan, the high priest, has his living quarters (cf. 8:29). The assembly meets in the **ninth month** (i.e. Dec.; see above on 9:1–10:44), the beginning of the rainy season. Ezra simply repeats the recommendation of Shecaniah (cf. vs. 3) and the people acquiesce. The procedure of the reform is outlined (vs. 14) and carried out with but little opposition.

10:18-44. *A List of Offenders*. The list of those who have **married foreign women** includes **priests** (vss. 18-22), **Levites** (vs. 23), together with one of the **singers** and 3 **gatekeepers** (vs. 24), and certain lay families of Israel (vss. 25-44). All these give up their wives and **children.**

THE BOOK OF NEHEMIAH

Charles T. Fritsch

For the introduction see Intro. to Ezra.

I. Neh.'s Coming to Jerusalem (1:1–7:73a)

1:1-11a. *Neh.'s Concern for Jerusalem.* From his brother **Hanani** (cf. 7:2) and a group of companions who have just come from **Judah** Neh. receives word that there is **great trouble** in the **province,** i.e. Judah, and that the **wall of Jerusalem** is breached and **its gates are destroyed by fire.**

1:1b-3. The date is given as **Chislev,** i.e. the 9th month (Dec.), **in the twentieth year,** whereas in 2:1 later events are dated in **Nisan,** i.e. the first month (Apr.), in the same year. Some scholars explain this apparent discrepancy as indicating that the author counted from an autumn new year, as was the custom in preexilic Judah, even though the Babylonian calendar beginning in the spring was the standard throughout the Persian Empire. Others assume a copying error in the first date—that it should read "in the 19th year of Artaxerxes." In either case the first date is Dec. 446 and the 2nd Apr. 445 (see Intro. to Ezra). **Susa,** the capital of ancient Elam (see color map 10), became the **capital** of the Persian Empire. Whereas Ezra and the Chronicler emphasize returned exiles, Neh. views the inhabitants of Judah as those **who escaped exile,** i.e. the descendants of those left in the land by Nebuchadnezzar.

1:4-11a. Overcome with grief at the news of the shocking conditions in Judah, Neh. prays to the **Lord God of heaven** for his **people.** Neh.'s prayer, like Ezra's (Ezra 9:6-15), is largely composed of Deuteronomic phrases, including confession of past sins and an appeal to God to **hear the prayer of thy servant.** Some scholars believe the prayer was inserted into Neh.'s memoirs by the Chronicler. Since **this man** (i.e. the king) has not previously been mentioned, it has been suggested that vs. 11a, or a part of it, originally followed 2:4.

1:11b-2:10. *Permission to Go to Jerusalem.* Neh., as **cupbearer to the king**—and **queen** (vs. 6)—holds one of the highest positions in the Persian court. As an intimate servant he was probably a eunuch. According to Deut. 23:1 this would exclude him from the Jewish community, but in postexilic times a more lenient attitude was taken (cf. Isa. 56:3-5). On the date (vs. 1) see above on 1:1b-3. Neh.'s request to visit Jerusalem is granted by the king. Letters of introduction to **governors of the province Beyond the River** (i.e. W of the Euphrates) are given to him, as well as permission to use **timber**

from the **king's forest** in Lebanon for construction work in Jerusalem.

2:9-10. Opposition is immediately encountered. **Sanballat,** a Samaritan leader from Beth-horon in Ephraim, and **Tobiah,** from Ammon in Transjordan (see color map 11), are displeased when they hear that **someone had come to seek the welfare of the children of Israel.** Actually they are afraid that the power which they exercise over Judah will be curtailed with the coming of a royally supported official such as Neh.

2:11-20. *Inspection of the Wall.* Under cover of night Neh., who alone is mounted, secretly sets out with a few servants to inspect the battered **walls of Jerusalem** in order to formulate his plans for reconstruction.

2:13-16. Locating the gates is a difficult problem because of uncertainty about the area of Jerusalem in Neh.'s day (cf. Barrois' drawing, p. 228)—whether, as some scholars believe, the ruined walls surround only the E hill, with little enlargement from the time of Solomon (black and red lines on color map 13), or, as others maintain, had been extended by later kings of Judah across the central valley and around the W hill (blue lines on color map 13). If the smaller limit is correct, the **Valley Gate** probably was on the W side of the old City of David, opening into the central valley; if this valley was already within the walls, this gate must have been on the S or W side of the newer wall opening into the Hinnom Valley. The **Jackal's Well** (Hebrew "Dragon Well") could be a name for the spring En-rogel (cf. I Kings 1:9). Through the **Dung Gate** in the S part of the wall the refuse of the city was carried to the Valley of Hinnom. The **Fountain Gate** on the SE led either to En-rogel or to the Gihon Spring, and the **King's Pool** was no doubt a reservoir collecting water from Gihon.

2:17-20. When Neh. informs the Jewish leaders and the people of the city of his plans to **build the wall** they enthusiastically respond, **Let us rise up and build.** Added to the opposition noted before (vs. 10) is **Geshem** from the province of Arabia S of Judah. Probably unaware of Neh.'s official capacity as an emissary of the king, the 3 enemies consider this new effort of the Jews as rebellion.

3:1-32. *Workers Rebuilding the Wall.* The reconstruction of the wall and its gates begins at the **Sheep Gate,** which was probably in the NE part of the city wall, near the temple, since **Eliashib the high priest . . . with his brethren the priests** works on this gate (vss. 1-2). The mention of Eliashib here

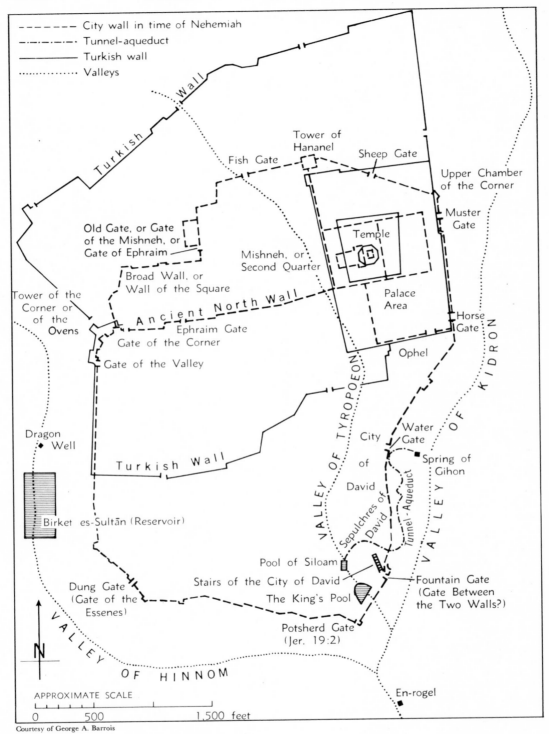

- - - - - - - City wall in time of Nehemiah
- ·- ·- ·- ·- Tunnel-aqueduct
———— Turkish wall
·············· Valleys

Turkish Wall

Tower of
Hananel

Fish Gate

Sheep Gate

Upper Chamber
of the Corner

Muster
Gate

Old Gate, or Gate
of the Mishneh, or
Gate of Ephraim

Temple

Mishneh, or
Second Quarter

Broad Wall, or
Wall of the Square

Tower of the
Corner or
of the
Ovens

Ancient North Wall

Palace
Area

Ephraim Gate
Gate of the Corner

Horse
Gate

Gate of the Valley

Ophel

Dragon
♦ Well

Turkish Wall

City
of
David

Water
Gate

Spring of
Gihon

Birket es-Sultān (Reservoir)

Sepulchres of David

Tunnel-Aqueduct

VALLEY OF TYROPOEON

VALLEY OF KIDRON

Pool of Siloam

Dung Gate
(Gate of the
Essenes)

Stairs of the City of David
The King's Pool

Fountain Gate
(Gate Between
the Two Walls?)

Potsherd Gate
(Jer. 19:2)

N

VALLEY OF HINNOM

En-rogel

APPROXIMATE SCALE

0   500   1,500 feet

Courtesy of George A. Barrois

Probable outline of Jerusalem in the time of Nehemiah

as high priest in the days of Neh. is important for the dating of Neh. and Ezra (see Intro. to Ezra).

3:3-32. Next in order come the **Fish Gate,** on the N part of the wall (vss. 3-5); the **Old Gate,** or more accurately the "Gate of the Old," presumably on the W side (vss. 6-12); the **Valley Gate,** the **Dung Gate,** and the **Fountain Gate** (vss. 13-15; see above on 2:13-16); the **Water Gate** on the E, probably leading to the Gihon Spring (vs. 26); and the **Horse Gate** (vs. 28) and the **Muster Gate** (vs. 31), also on the E, near the temple area. Finally the **Sheep Gate** is mentioned again (vs. 32), a full circuit having been made counterclockwise around the walls of the city. On the problem of locating these and other places mentioned in this ch. see above on 2:13-16. It is interesting to note that women (vs. 12) also take part in the work of restoring the walls.

4:1-12. *Opposition of Sanballat and Tobiah.* The opposition, noted before (2:10, 19), now takes on more concrete form with the increased activity of the Jewish workers. Neh.'s reaction to the taunting questions of Sanballat and Tobiah (vss. 2-3) is an imprecatory prayer (vss. 4-5) which is reminiscent of certain pss. (cf. e.g. Pss. 54; 64) and prophetic outbursts against the enemy (cf. e.g. Jer. 18:23; 20:11-12). Insults soon give way to threats of attack (vss. 7-8). A lament by **Judah** (i.e. the community) shows the inner weakness of the people (vs. 10; contrast vs. 6). The enemy from without is planning a secret attack (vs. 11); the rumor of attack is confirmed (vs. 12) by those coming into Jerusalem from outlying areas.

4:13-23. *Neh.'s Measures of Defense.* But Neh. cannot easily be discouraged. In the face of danger he sets up certain measures of defense for the workers. He sets armed groups in the **open places** under the cover of the **wall** where they can maneuver more freely if attacked. Armed men also take their places among the workers. The workers themselves labor **with one hand** and hold their weapons in the other. A special alarm system is set up to **rally** the people to any place of attack along the wall. Finally Neh. orders those who live outside the city to come within its protecting walls during this time of danger. As the leader of the people he sets the example of devoted service and hard work for all to follow.

5:1-19. *Relief for the Poor.* The poor, who far outnumber the rich in the land, cry out to Neh. that they desperately need food for their families. They have no **money** to buy the bare necessities of life, and they cannot borrow because they have no property to put up as collateral. They refuse to see their families starve while their rich brethren prosper and refuse to give them aid. Those with some property have mortgaged it **to get grain,** while others have even sold their children into slavery in order to pay their creditors the money they have **borrowed** for the **king's tax.**

5:6-13. When Neh. hears these protests he becomes **very angry** and proposes that **interest** no longer be charged on borrowed money and that everything that has been taken on pledges be restored. The people agree to Neh.'s proposal and the bargain is sealed by an **oath.** Neh.'s symbolic act in emptying his **lap** (better "sash," which was used like a pocket for carrying money, etc.) emphasizes the penalties which will occur if the pledge is broken.

5:14-19. During Neh.'s administration as governor —lasting **twelve years,** i.e. 445-433—he claims that he has not taken any money from the people for his own support and has never even taken the money allowed him for his household expenses.

6:1-14. *Plots Against Neh.* On hearing of the progress on the wall **Sanballat** and **Geshem** (cf. 2:19) try to lure Neh. out of the city for a meeting in **Ono,** on the plain of Sharon, near Lydda (see color map 11). Neh. anticipates danger and refuses the invitation on the basis of the **work** he has to do in Jerusalem.

6:5-9. Sanballat next accuses Neh. of planning a rebellion against the king and setting himself up as **king** in Judah. This is vehemently denied by Neh.

6:10-13. Finally **Shemaiah,** probably a priest, is **hired** by Tobiah and Sanballat to invite Neh. to find shelter **within the temple** to protect his life. He refuses to do this because (*a*) he is no priest and would violate the sanctity of the temple if he entered it and (*b*) he will not put his own personal safety above that of his fellow Jews.

6:14. Just as Neh. prayed to God to remember his good deeds, presumably for reward (5:19), so now he prays that his enemies may be remembered by God for punishment.

6:15-19. *Completion of the Wall.* The period of time for the completion of the wall is given as **fifty-two days.** The success of the project is a witness to the **nations** of the zeal of the people and the goodness of God. **Tobiah** still remains a thorn in the flesh for Neh., however, since his marriage into an eminent Jewish family gives him contact with many important people in Judah, who serve his evil ends as spies and propagandists.

7:1-73a. *A List of Returning Jews.* After the city is secured (vss. 1-4) Neh. decides to take a census, probably to replenish the population of Jerusalem (vs. 5a; cf. vs. 4; 11:1-3). It is in the course of taking the census that the list of those who returned to Jerusalem under **Zerubbabel** is found, presumably in the temple (vs. 5b). The list largely duplicates Ezra 2:1-70 (see comment); the differences are very slight.

II. FURTHER REFORMS OF EZRA (7:73b–10:39)

At this place in the narrative the Neh. memoirs break off and Ezra reappears as the main character. Apparently this section is a misplaced part of the Ezra narrative (see comment on Ezra 9:1–10:44 and below on 9:1-5a).

7:73b–8:12. *The Reading of the Law.* Cf. I Esdras 9:37-55. The people gather before the **Water Gate** (cf. 3:26) to have the law read to them by Ezra **on the first day of the seventh month.** If this refers to Ezra's first year in Jerusalem the time is only 2 months after his arrival (cf. Ezra 7:7-9). **The book of the law of Moses** (vs. 1; cf. vss. 2, 5, 8) was probably not the Pentateuch as we know it but certain portions of it. Ezra reads the text in Hebrew (vs. 3), and the Levites translate it aloud in Aramaic, the common speech in postexilic Palestine (vss. 7-8; see comment on Ezra 4:17-24). From this procedure developed the Targums, the Aramaic translation of the OT.

8:9-12. The people, on hearing the law read, **weep** because of their sins and the punishment which is to come upon them. They are enjoined to rejoice, however, because **this day is holy**—a day on which they have come to hear again the words of the law. If, as is probable, Ezra and Neh. were not contemporaries (see Intro. to Ezra) **Nehemiah, who was the governor** (vs. 9) must be a later addition.

8:13-18. *Celebration of the Feast of Booths.* A closer reading of the law by the secular and ecclesiastical leaders of the community leads to the discovery that they have not kept the **feast of the seventh month,** i.e. the feast of booths, or tabernacles, as prescribed by Moses (cf. e.g. Lev. 23:39-42). The observance described here is different in some details from that prescribed in the Mosaic law. That the feast has not been observed since the days of **Jeshua** (i.e. Joshua) **the son of Nun** (vs. 17) must refer to some special phase of the ritual—perhaps that it is now centralized in Jerusalem—since the Chronicler has mentioned its observance earlier (II Chr. 8:13; Ezra 3:4). The **Gate of Ephraim** (vs. 16), from which the road led to Ephraim, was located in the N section of the city wall.

9:1-5a. *A Time of Mourning.* Some scholars have suggested that this ch. should follow Ezra 9-10, since the deep mourning of the people is more understandable if due, not to the reading of the law (cf. 8:12), but to concern over mixed marriages. **Separated themselves from all foreigners** (vs. 2) makes no sense following ch. 8, but it does mean something if it refers to the divorce proceedings described in Ezra 10. The date in vs. 1 would then be the **twenty-fourth day** of the first month (i.e. Nisan, or Apr.; cf. Ezra 10:17). A **fourth of the day** (vs. 3) means 3 hours.

9:5b-37. *A Confession of Sin.* This penitential ps. is an independent unit introduced here because it seems to reflect generally the attitude of the people. **And Ezra said** (vs. 6), which is not found in the Hebrew text, is supplied from the LXX. The recital of God's mighty acts from creation to the conquest of Canaan (vss. 5b-25) is followed by confession of sin and the acknowledgment of God's mercy, even in time of punishment (vss. 26-37). The ps. ends on the note of despair (vss. 36-37) as the writer describes the sad plight in which the people find themselves.

9:38-10:39. *A Renewed Covenant.* The people, **because of all this,** or better "in spite of all this"—i.e. the sorrow and suffering which they are enduring—renew their covenant relationship with God and **set their seal** to the pledge they make.

10:1-39. A list—beginning with Neh. and **Zedekiah,** the secular authorities of the community, and including **priests** (vss. 3-8), **Levites** (vss. 9-13), and laymen (vss. 14-27)—is incorporated here as naming those connected with the covenant ceremony. Closer study shows, however, that the list is from a different source; e.g. Ezra's name is not found, and the order of the groups in 9:38 is the reverse of that found in the listings themselves.

10:28-39. The covenant obligations of the community, assumed under a **curse** and **oath** formula **to walk in God's law** (vs. 29), include avoidance of mixed marriages (vs. 30), observance of the **sabbath,** as well as the sabbatical year (vs. 31), and support of the temple and its personnel (vss. 32-39). Because of the similar topics it has been suggested that the author of this material based it on Neh.'s account in ch. 13.

III. FURTHER ACTIVITIES OF NEH. (11:1-13:31)

11:1-12:26. *Various Lists.* Since this material has no relationship with what immediately precedes, it probably is to be connected with 7:73a or, more specifically, with 7:4-5a. The problem of repopulating Jerusalem would certainly have something to do with Neh.'s desire to take a census. It is proposed that a 10th of the population live in the **holy city.** There follow lists of the **chiefs of the provinces who lived in Jerusalem** (11:3-24; cf. I Chr. 9:2-17) and of the **villages** and towns settled by Jews outside of Jerusalem (11:25-36). In 11:23 **the king** may refer to a Persian ruler.

12:1-26. This is a list of **the priests and the Levites** serving under the various high priests, whose genealogy is given in vss. 10-11. **Jonathan** (cf. vss. 22-23) or Jehohanan, the high priest in Ezra's time (Ezra 10:6; see Intro. to Ezra). **Darius the Persian** (vs. 22) may refer to either Darius II (423-404) or Darius III (336-331). Since according to Josephus **Jaddua** was the high priest when Palestine was taken by Alexander the Great (333), Darius III may be meant. This reference has been cited as evidence that the Chronicler wrote during the Greek period (see Intro. to Ezra), but it may be a later addition to his text. The **Book of the Chronicles** (vs. 23) is not the canonical book but one of the Chronicler's postexilic sources. Vs. 26b is probably an interpolation, since Neh. and Ezra do not fit into a list dated **in the days of** respective high priests.

12:27-43. *Dedication of the Wall.* After the **Levites** and **singers** are gathered together in Jerusalem from the surrounding areas (vss. 27-29), the ceremony of purifying the wall takes place (vs. 30). Though the specific rites of this ceremony are not mentioned, it may be surmised that sacrifices are offered and probably blood or holy water is sprinkled on the wall.

12:31-43. Next 2 groups, moving **in procession** in opposite directions, walk around the top of the wall to the accompaniment of **musical instruments** and singing choirs. Apparently starting at the Valley Gate (cf. 2:13; 3:13), the first group marches around the S of the city and the 2nd around the N till they come near the temple on the NE (on the places named see above on 2:13-16; 3:1-32; 8:13-18). According to the present text **Ezra** (vs. 36) leads the first company and Neh. (vs. 38) accompanies the second; but if Ezra and Neh. were not contemporaries, as seems likely (see Intro. to Ezra), the clause about Ezra must be a later addition. The 2 groups converge in the temple court (vs. 40), where **sacrifices** are offered (vs. 43) and all **rejoice with great joy.**

12:44-13:3. *The Ideal Community.* The **contributions** for the temple personnel fill the storehouses because the people are pleased with the service that the **priests** and **Levites** are rendering. The ideal cult, founded by **David,** has continued throughout the postexilic period from **Zerubbabel** to Neh.

13:1-3. During a reading of the **book of Moses**—i.e. some portion of the Pentateuch (cf. 8:1)—a passage is noted stating that an **Ammonite or Moabite** is to be excluded from the **assembly of God** (cf. Deut. 23:3-5). On the basis of this Mosaic law the people exclude **all those of foreign descent,** either from the temple services or possibly from the entire community.

13:4-9. *Expulsion of Tobiah.* In opposing the rebuilding of the wall Tobiah gave Neh. particular trouble by corresponding freely with friends and in-laws among the Jews (6:17-19). Now after an administration of 12 years (445-433, vs. 6; cf. 5:14) Neh. returns to Persia, and Tobiah proceeds to move into the temple quarters with the permission of **Eliashib the priest,** one of those with whom he is **connected.** Many interpreters have taken this to mean the high priest who helped Neh. in rebuilding the wall (3:1, 20-21; cf. 12:10, 22; 13:28), but the description suggests rather a priest of lower rank. **After some time**—perhaps on hearing of such irregularities—Neh. asks the **king** for permission to go back to Jerusalem. The date and length of his 2nd sojourn there are not known. Discovering Tobiah's trespass on his arrival, Neh. is **very angry** (cf. 5:6) and ejects him and his belongings from the temple quarters. As an Ammonite (cf. 2:10) Tobiah must be excluded from the temple (vss. 1-3); more seriously, as an enemy of Neh. he cannot be allowed to live in the heart of the city.

13:10-14. Restoration of Tithes. In contradiction to the claim of 12:47 the people are failing to support the temple personnel by giving their tithes, and as a result the **Levites** have had to leave their duties in the temple to work in the fields. Neh. organizes a group of **officials** to oversee the **storehouses** and **distribute** the food to the temple personnel.

13:15-22. Sabbath Reforms. The observance of the sabbath was one of the distincttive features of Jewish religion. Because it set the Jews apart from their Gentile neighbors it was a cause of constant friction. The desecration of the sabbath both by Jews and by Gentile traders in Neh.'s day brings drastic action to keep the day **holy.** The **gates** of Jerusalem are to be closed on the sabbath and guarded by the Levites. Vs. 18 probably refers to a passage like Jer. 17:21-27.

13:23-29. Mixed Marriage Reforms. Neh.'s violent reaction against his countrymen who have married **foreign women** is in sharp contrast with Ezra's actions when faced with the same problem (Ezra 9:1-5). An appeal is made to the example of **Solomon,** who sinned in taking foreign wives (cf. I Kings 3:1; 11:1-8). Neh. makes the people **take oath** that they will not indulge in this practice any more. One offender singled out for special notice (vs. 28)—apparently because related to **Sanballat,** Neh.'s inveterate enemy (cf. 2:10; 4:1-2, 7-8; 6:1-14)—is **chased,** i.e. banished from the city.

13:30-31. Conclusion. The book closes with a brief review by Neh. of his work and a prayer for God's remembrance of him **for good** (cf. 5:19; 6:14; 13:14, 22, 29).

THE BOOK OF ESTHER

H. Neil Richardson

Introduction

Esther is a historical novella written to explain the origin of the Jewish festival Purim, here said to commemorate a victory of the Jews of the Persian Empire over their enemies.

In the story Ahasuerus, king of Persia, deposes his queen, Vashti, for disobedience and selects Esth. as her successor without knowing that she is a Jewess. Esth.'s cousin and guardian, Mordecai, incurs the animosity of the prime minister, Haman, who in consequence secures the king's consent to a decree that all the Jews in the empire are to be killed on an appointed day. At Mordecai's urging Esth. invites the king and the prime minister to a dinner, at which she pleads for her people and accuses Haman. The outcome is that Haman is executed and Mordecai is permitted to issue a 2nd decree authorizing the Jews to defend themselves and kill their attackers on the appointed day. At the conclusion of the slaughter Esth. and Mordecai order an annual observance, henceforth to be known as Purim.

The book is the work of a skilled literary artist, who keeps the reader in suspense as he unfolds the successive stages of the plot and brings it to an effective climax with Esth.'s accusation of Haman.

Authorship and Date. The statement that "Mordecai recorded these things" (9:20) has been taken by some in ancient times and even today as attributing authorship of the book to Mordecai. The reference, however, seems to be merely to the document sent out to urge annual commemoration, so that the work should be viewed as anonymous. In any case the viewpoint of the storyteller is not that of a contemporary but of one who looks back to the reign of Ahasuerus, i.e. Xerxes I (486-465; see below on 1:1), from a much later time. The author makes no mention of the known historical events of Xerxes' career; indeed during the time of the Persian invasion of Greece he represents the king as in Susa testing candidates for the queenship (see below on 2:12-14). Various historical and chronological inaccuracies (e.g. see below on 1:9; 2:6) and improbabilities lead to the conclusion that the book is something less than dependable history and was written a long time after the events its describes. This is borne out by the reference to the Jews as "scattered abroad and dispersed among the peoples" (3:8), which was much more true in later times than under Xerxes.

It is probable that the LXX translation of Esth. was made before 77/76 B.C. (see comment on Addi-

tions to Esth. 11:1), and acquaintance with the book *ca.* that time is confirmed by II Macc. 15:36. Jeshua ben Sira, however, writing *ca.* 180, describes a long list of heroes of Israelite history (Ecclus. 44-49) but makes no mention of Esth. and Mordecai, whom he could be expected to include if he knew about them. Significant also is the fact that as yet no fragment of the book has been found among the Dead Sea scrolls, produced by the Qumran community that existed *ca.* 150 B.C.–A.D. 70; nor is there any quotation or allusion to it in the NT. The book's attitude of vindictiveness toward Gentiles fits well in the Maccabean age—not so much the early years of religious zeal but rather the materialistic reign of John Hyrcanus (134-104), who beginning *ca.* 128 forcibly proselytized the peoples of Idumea, Samaria, and Galilee (cf. 8:17; 9:27). Such considerations lead many scholars to date Esth. *ca.* 125.

On the other hand there is much in the book that suggests that it was written in Persia. There is a high degree of accuracy in the presentation of the details of Persian court life, and scattered throughout are a considerable number of words borrowed from the Persian language. One might explain the former, as some scholars do, by saying the author had traveled in Persia or had read a great deal about the country and its people; but such explanations fail to come adequately to grips with the problem of word borrowings. Thus there seems a strong possibility that the book was written by a Jew living in geographical proximity to the setting of his story even though at some chronological distance—e.g. living in or near Susa (see below on 1:2-8) in the latter days of the Persian Empire, *ca.* 350. This supposition would explain the book's combination of accuracy and inaccuracy and also the general unfamiliarity with it in Palestine until its sudden popularity in the first cent. A.D.

Purpose and Significance. It has been argued that the festival of Purim originated simply as a literary invention of the author of Esth. and came to be celebrated because of the popularity of the story. To the contrary, however, most scholars agree that celebration of the festival came first and that the book was written to justify it. Justification was needed since such a festival is nowhere mentioned in the other books of the Bible. Like other holy days of Judaism it is here given a setting in a historical event—one in which Jews were delivered from virtual annihilation.

In all likelihood Purim was originally a non-Jewish celebration. A body of Jews no doubt adopted it from their neighbors, presumably in some part of the Persian Empire, and made it their own by interpreting it as the commemoration of a victory over persecutors. Whether some historical incident underlies this connection is uncertain. The striking though superficial resemblance of the names Mordecai and Esth. to those of the Babylonian deities Marduk and Ishtar has led some scholars to assume a mythological basis for the book. A similar possible connection of Vashti and Haman with names of Elamite gods has suggested to them a myth of rivalry between the 2 sets of national deities with the Babylonian gods coming out victorious. The discovery, however, of a cuneiform text mentioning a high official at Susa during the early years of Xerxes' reign with the name Marduka, along with the fact that Esth. is a credible Persian feminine name with the meaning "star," seems to indicate that the characters of the story are intended to represent historical persons rather than deities. It is possible that a local incident of conflict in connection with celebration of the festival was remembered on later anniversaries and, as the celebration spread, was magnified to involve the whole Persian Empire.

Purim is still observed on the 14th-15th of Adar (cf. 9:21), i.e. ca. Mar. 1, as a wholly secular holiday. Its only religious aspect is the reading of Esth. in the synagogue, and even that is in a nonreligious atmosphere, being accompanied by considerable noisemaking. Otherwise Purim is a time of merrymaking, feasting, visiting, and giving gifts (cf. 9:22).

Aside from its purpose of explaining Purim the book may be seen as a protest against persecution of minority groups, whether religious or ethnic. Haman has become the prototype of one motivated by prejudice and blind hatred against his neighbor of another faith, race, or nationality. In this sense the book has an important religious significance. It is true that in a specific sense it makes no mention of religion; the word "God" never appears and nothing is said of prayer at the points in the story where pleas for divine aid would be expected—though fasting is practiced at one time of crisis. Indeed the book expresses a vindictive spirit at odds with the ethical teaching of both OT and NT. On the other hand it does reveal God's will by showing the terrible consequences of hatred. An attitude and an act which brings about the denial of justice to other human beings and the massacre of God's children must be wrong in his sight.

Unity and Canonicity. Most scholars regard 9:20-10:3 as a later addition, on the basis of both differences in language and inconsistencies in thought. The arguments are not decisive, however, and one may not unjustly view the entire book as the work of one author. On the other hand there is little question that the several sections which make the LXX *ca.* a 3rd longer than the Hebrew are insertions by other hands, mostly intended to make up for the religious deficiencies. Though scattered through the Greek text, these passages were relegated by Jerome to an appendix in the Vulg. and thus came to be included in the Protestant Apoc. under the title "The Additions to the Book of Esther."

In the Hebrew Scriptures Esth. is included among the Writings, the 3rd and latest division, as the last of the 5 scrolls—Song of S., Ruth, Lam., Eccles., Esth.—read in the synagogue on the respective feast and fast days. Neither Jews nor Christians, however, have been happy with the presence of the book in the canon of holy scripture. Its status was hotly debated by the rabbis all through the first 2 cents. A.D., and they obviously accepted it only because of the demand of the masses. Among Christians also there was question about its status. Martin Luther declared that he wished it did not exist. It must be admitted that without the popularity of the festival of Purim the book would have had little to recommend it for a place in the canon. At the same time, as already noted, Esth. does have a message, even though stated negatively, concerning God's will for man.

For Further Study. L. B. Paton, *Esth.*, 1908. R. H. Pfeiffer, *Intro. to the OT*, 1949, pp. 732-47. B. W. Anderson in *IB*, 1954. D. W. Harvey in *IDB*, 1962.

I. The Deposing of Vashti (1:1-22)

1:1-8. Ahasuerus' Banquets. The author at once gives his story a setting of grandeur by giving historically accurate information about the vast size of the Persian king's empire and the magnificence of his palace along with fantastic exaggeration of the size and length of his feasts—a 6-months-long house-party for all the officials of the empire followed by a week-long party for all the common people of the city.

1:1. The name **Ahasuerus** is an English approximation of the Hebrew and Aramaic *Ahashwerosh*, which has been found in inscriptions as the equivalent of the Persian *Khshayarsha*, known also through classic Greek transcription as Xerxes. Xerxes I (486-465) inherited from his father Darius I an empire which truly extended **from India to Ethiopia.** According to the contemporary Greek historian Herodotus it was divided into 20 major administrative areas known as satrapies, which may well have been subdivided into **one hundred and twenty-seven provinces** (cf. 120 in Dan. 6:1).

1:2-8. The governmental center of the Persian Empire was Persepolis (see color map 10). The phrase translated **Susa the capital** refers rather to the "citadel of Susa," a large acropolis which was formerly the capital of Elam. There Darius built a luxurious palace as a winter residence. Excavation of its court has shown that the description here is based on accurate information about it. The banquets also have some foundation in the reputation of the Persians in the ancient world for lavish entertaining.

1:9-12. Vashti's Disobedience. Herodotus states that Xerxes' queen was Amestris, daughter of a Persian general; but the fact that **Vashti** is an Elamite name suggests that it may represent a historical person—possibly a local princess who was added to the royal harem. The author gives no motivation for her refusal to appear at the king's bidding. Early rabbinic interpreters concocted the explanation that she was ordered to appear wearing only the **royal crown.**

1:13-22. An Example to All Women. The detail accorded this episode, in contrast with the bare statement preceding, reveals not only the author's judgment of his ancient readers' sensibilities but also his skill in establishing in advance the idea of the irrevocability of the **laws of the Persians and the Medes** (vs. 19) needed later to explain why the conflict could not be simply called off (cf. 8:8). The same idea is similarly essential to the story of Daniel and the lions' den (Dan. 6:8, 12, 15) and, being contrary to historical evidence, seems to indicate literary relationship; but which work is dependent on the other is not clear.

1:22. The sending out of the decree in every **language** of the empire is a literary device to emphasize its wide dissemination. Actually the official correspondence of the Persian imperial administration was all in Aramaic, the international language of trade and diplomacy throughout the Near East during this period. The provincial governors would be responsible for translating proclamations into the many local vernaculars. Cf. the inscription carved on a cliff near Bisitun (Behistun; see color map 10) which boasts of the victory of Darius I over a rival claimant to the throne in Elamite, Akkadian, and Persian (see ill., p. 224).

II. Intro. of Mordecai, Esth., and Haman (2:1–3:6)

2:1-18. The Selection of a New Queen. The shrewdness of the 7 counselors in advising an irrevocable deposition and thus protecting themselves from the vengeance of a restored queen becomes evident as the king sobers up and regrets losing her. To distract him his **servants** propose an ancient counterpart of a modern beauty contest to pick Miss Persia—with the significant difference that all the contestants are to be added to the royal **harem** as **concubines** (vs. 14). Early rabbinic commentators, viewing Esth.'s voluntary marriage to a Gentile as unthinkable, declared **all the beautiful young virgins** of the empire were drafted; but the author does not make this point clear.

2:5-6. On the name **Mordecai** see Intro. **Jeconiah** is the alternate name of Jehoiachin (cf. II Kings 24:6; I Chr. 3:16-17; Jer. 24:1), who was taken to Babylon with the first body of exiles in 597 (II Kings 24:10-16). Some defenders of the author's historical accuracy have taken vs. 6 to apply to **Kish**, whom they assume to be Mordecai's great-grandfather. But in normal Hebrew usage it must apply to Mordecai (cf. Additions 11:2-4). The author has telescoped the time between 597 and the 3rd year of Xerxes (1:3), i.e. 483. Perhaps he shared the reversed notion of the author of Dan. that Ahasuerus was the father of Darius (Dan. 9:1) and both preceded Cyrus (Dan. 6:28) and thus thought of his story as set during the Exile rather than after it (cf. Tobit 14:15). **Shimei** (cf. II Sam. 16:5-14) and **Kish** (cf. I Sam. 9:1-2) were prominent early Benjaminites and probably are named as remote rather than immediate ancestors.

2:7-11. The Hebrew name **Hadassah** means "myrtle." On **Esther** see Intro. Reflected here is a practice which still prevails to some extent among the Jews of giving both a Hebrew and a non-Hebrew name to their children. Esth. is Mordecai's young cousin—not niece as in the Latin versions—whom he has reared. On his instruction she keeps secret her relationship to him and the fact that she is a Jewess (vs. 10)—an important element in the plot

—even though to do so she must eat unclean **food** (vs. 9; contrast Dan. 1:8-16) and otherwise ignore the distinctive observances of the Jewish law. Yet inconsistently Mordecai himself risks almost certain recognition of the relationship by his solicitude (vs. 11) and does not hesitate to display his own Jewishness (3:4). His access to the vicinity of the harem suggests that he holds some minor official position (cf. vs. 19). This and the means of maintaining contact without revealing the secret are details the author has not cared to clarify.

2:12-18. After **twelve months** of **beautifying** herself each girl is permitted to spend a night with the king (vs. 14). Since it has been implied that the number of virgins assembled is quite large, we are evidently to understand that the king is in his palace in Susa engaged in this process throughout a period of *ca.* 3 years (cf. 1:3) ending when he selects Esth. in the **tenth month** of his **seventh year**, i.e. Jan. 478. Historically Xerxes spent most of this period in Asia Minor and in Greece, which he attacked unsuccessfully in 480-479. **Granted a remission of taxes** is lit. "caused a rest." The idiom is not found elsewhere and its precise meaning is uncertain (see RSV footnote).

2:19-23. Mordecai's Service to the King. Vs. 19a is obscure and probably corrupt. It has been suggested that it is intended to refer to transfer of the **virgins** who have not yet had a turn to the 2nd harem (cf. vs. 14). Mordecai's **sitting at the king's gate** seems to imply that he is a minor official of the court (see above on vss. 7-11). In the LXX a duplicate version of the incident in vss. 21-23, with differences in detail, is found near the beginning of the book (Additions 12:1-6). **Hanged on the gallows** refers, not to strangulation by a rope as in modern times, but probably to impalement on a sharp stake and slow death by starvation—a Persian mode of execution from which the Romans got the idea of crucifixion. The **Book of the Chronicles** is of course not the biblical book but the royal annals of the Persian court.

3:1-6. The Origin of Haman's Hatred. The villain of the story is now introduced. **Agagite** is probably intended to identify him as a descendant of the king of the Amalekites who was the occasion of Saul's losing the kingdom (cf. I Sam. 15) and thus heighten the conflict between him and Mordecai, who is a descendant of the family of Saul (see above on 2:5-6). The reason for Mordecai's refusal to pay homage to the new prime minister is not given. In the LXX he states that he will not bow to anyone but God (Additions 13:14) and rabbinic interpreters explained that Haman wore an idol on his robe. Perhaps the Hebrew text implies that Haman understands Mordecai's attitude as arising from religious views shared by other Jews and accordingly wants to **destroy all the Jews.**

III. The Danger to the Jews (3:7–5:14)

3:7-15. The Edict of Extermination. Haman casts a **lot** to discover the most propitious day for his planned annihilation of the Jews. Evidently "till the thirteenth day" has accidentally been dropped following **day after day** (vs. 7; cf. LXX and vs. 13); the idea is that the lot is first cast to determine the day of the month and then again to determine the month. **Pur** is a Persian word borrowed from the Akkadian and thus must be explained by the Hebrew word for "lot."

3:8-11. The Jews have always observed **laws**—dietary and otherwise—which have prevented their assimilation with their neighbors. To such laws rather than civil laws Haman refers. The bribe he offers with his petition is a tremendous sum (on **talents** see table, p. 1285). The king's apparently casual reply (vs. 11) is probably to be understood as accepting it—i.e. **as it seems good to you** is no doubt the ancient Near Eastern courtly equivalent of "if you please" (cf. 4:7). The **signet ring** was used to impress a distinctive design into the seal of a document and thus would serve as the king's signature (cf. e.g. I Kings 21:8; I Macc. 6:15).

3:12-15. The **edict** is issued in the king's **name** and sent out in every **language** (see above on 1:22). The **couriers** are an authentic reference to the empire-wide postal system established by Cyrus *ca.* 535. The ordering of the massacre 11 months in advance (cf. vss. 12*a*, 13*b*) is clearly a literary device to give Mordecai and Esther an opportunity to come to the aid of their people. In the LXX a purported copy of the letter in the king's name (Additions 13:1-7) is inserted following vs. 13.

4:1-17. *Mordecai's Appeal to Esth.* Torn **clothes,** a rough **sackcloth** garment, **ashes** scattered over the head, and **wailing** are common mourning customs of the ancient Near East known from both literature and art. Mordecai's behavior at the palace **gate** and his refusal to put off his sackcloth (vs. 4) are obviously designed to impress on Esth. the seriousness of the situation and motivate her to take action. On the other hand the **mourning among the Jews,** which includes **fasting** (vs. 3), surely would involve a plea for divine pity and deliverance and therefore would include prayer and other religious practices of Judaism. The author's avoidance of mentioning these is quite noticeable (see below on vss. 15-17).

4:5-9. Through an intermediary Mordecai reports to Esth. all the details of the **decree** and its issuance, including the **exact** amount of the bribe (3:9), which he has no doubt learned from court gossip. He urges

Esth. to appeal to the king on behalf of her people.

4:10-12. The frequency of political assassinations in ancient times gave reason for strict security precautions surrounding all monarchs, and anyone suspiciously aggressive in approaching one would put his life in danger. But accounts by Herodotus and other ancient historians of persons who initiated audiences with Persian kings mention no extreme restrictions such as Esth. here describes. Of course harem rivalries might cause even an official queen to fear making a nuisance of herself at a time when she appears to be out of favor (cf. 1:14). It is evident, however, that by assuming only one possible way for Esth. to speak to the king the author has formalized and exaggerated the danger in order to enhance her heroism. An authentic touch is the **golden scepter** (see ill., this page), which Persian kings no doubt symbolically extended to those permitted to approach the throne.

4:13-14. Mordecai's final plea to Esth. is very persuasive, though she might well doubt his threat that she would be killed along with **all the other Jews.** The expression **from another quarter** is strange and has been much discussed. Any other book of the Bible would say "God" here. Most ancient interpreters and some today have taken the phrase to mean "God," in line with the practice in rabbinic Judaism of avoiding use of divine names by substituting such terms as "heaven." But the author's apparent deliberate avoidance of religious references elsewhere in the book suggests that here he is referring to human help, perhaps without any particular source in mind. Mordecai's concluding question, **Who knows whether you have not come to the kingdom for such a time as this?** challenges what little courage Esth. possesses. It is often quoted to emphasize each individual's responsibility.

4:15-17. The **fast** which Esth. requests of the Jews of the city can aid her approach to the king only as a religious observance soliciting divine help. As such it would naturally be accompanied by verbal expression of the help desired, i.e. prayer. Thus some commentators have declared that in referring to fasting the author intends to imply prayer. On the contrary, however, it is evident that he has intentionally avoided any hint of a religious purpose in

Courtesy of The Oriental Institute, The University of Chicago

Ahasuerus (Xerxes) stands behind his father King Darius I receiving a visiting dignitary; relief from the ruins of the palace at Persepolis excavated by the Oriental Institute

the fast. To make up for this omission the LXX includes lengthy prayers by Mordecai and Esth. following vs. 17 (Additions 13:8–14:19).

5:1-14. Esth.'s First Dinner. Feeling let down by the author's simple account of Esth.'s easy approach to the king and immediate reception, someone composed an expanded version of vss. 1-2, found in the LXX (Additions 15:1-16), in which Esth.'s fears for a time seem justified. When the king promises **half of my kingdom**—a proverbial hyperbole of royal generosity (cf. Mark 6:23)—Esth. sensibly invites him and the prime minister to a **dinner** as the best occasion for presenting her concern. But interpreters have long been troubled to explain why, having arranged a perfect after-dinner setting, she does not come right to the point instead of inviting the 2 to a 2nd dinner. The explanation is purely literary—to provide suspense and opportunity for further developments of the plot before the climax. Thus Haman is given a chance to gloat (vss. 10-12) and deepen the contrast between his own exalted opinion of himself and his ultimate fall. The excessive height, **fifty cubits,** i.e. *ca.* 75 feet, of the **gallows** (see above on 2:19-23) which he orders for Mordecai (vss. 13-14) would serve little practical purpose, but as a literary exaggeration it sounds impressive.

IV. The Tables Turned (6:1–8:2)

6:1-13. The Glorification of Mordecai. The sleeplessness of a king is a familiar literary device. Here it affords occasion for the reading of royal records throughout the night in an effort to put him to sleep and the resulting coincidental reminder of his unpaid debt to Mordecai. The question **Who is in the court?** inquires about any high official that at the moment may be available for consultation. Ironically it is Haman coming at dawn to request Mordecai's execution. The unsuspecting prime minister in his conceit plans the honor to be paid the man he is expecting to destroy—and as a final stroke is ordered to carry out his plan in person. That the king commands this honor for a Jew indicates he does not know that the edict of extermination recently issued in his name is directed against the Jews. Authenticity of the **royal crown** on the horse's head (vs. 8) is suggested by Assyrian monuments depicting horses wearing crowns with tall plumes.

6:14-7:10. Esth.'s 2nd Dinner. The story reaches its climax as Esth. now states her petition. Her explanation is somewhat obscure (7:4). Apparently the **loss to the king** refers to the huge bribe (3:9), which she fears he may be reluctant to forgo. The **wrath** which drives him into the **garden** on hearing her accusation may be inspired not so much by his prime minister's misdeeds as by the realization that he himself has been used in a plot without knowing what was going on. Haman's **falling on the couch** is for the purpose of grasping and perhaps kissing Esth.'s feet in a common ancient Near Eastern gesture of humble petition (cf. e.g. 8:3; Additions 13:13; II Kings 4:27; Ps. 2:12; Matt. 28:9; Luke 7:37-38). The king mistakes Haman's abject groveling for a sexual attack and, if undecided before, is stirred to immediate action. Unmoved by her enemy's plea, Esth. shows no compunction about bearing false witness by silence. An opportunist attendant calls attention to the **gallows** Haman has prepared for Mordecai, and the king orders his execution on it.

8:1-2. Completion of the Reversal. In ancient times execution of a criminal was usually accompanied by confiscation of his property. In this case the king gives Haman's **house,** i.e. estate (cf. 7:9), to Esth., who in turn gives it to Mordecai. To complete the turning of the tables the king also gives Mordecai the **signet ring** (see above on 3:8-11), thus elevating him to Haman's former office of prime minister—a post for which his now-revealed relationship to the queen is apparently considered sufficient qualification.

V. The Revenge of the Jews (8:3–9:19)

8:3-8. The Irrevocable Edict. At this point all that seems needed to bring the story to a happy ending is withdrawal of the decree for extermination of the Jews. But so simple a solution would not explain the annual celebration of Purim. For that a conflict and victory in which all the Jews of the empire participate is needed. Therefore the author now makes use of the fiction he has set up at the beginning of the story (see above on 1:13-22), that under Persian law a royal decree **cannot be revoked.** In response to Esth.'s renewed plea for her people the king can only tell her and Mordecai to **write as you please** a new decree to circumvent the unrevoked **edict** ordering the Jews' destruction. Despite what has come to light he seems as unconcerned as before (cf. 3:11) over what the result may be for the citizens of his empire.

8:9-14. The Counter Edict. Following the same procedure as his predecessor (cf. 3:12-15) the new prime minister sends out an edict designed to counteract that issued by Haman 2 months and 10 days earlier. As before it is distributed in the various languages (see above on 1:22) by means of the imperial postal service (see above on 3:12-15), but this time the author emphasizes its urgency by adding a reference to **swift horses** from the royal stable—mentioned also by other ancient authors. Some commentators have claimed that Mordecai's decree merely allows the Jews to **defend their lives** (vs. 11), lit. "stand for their life"; but the following duplication of the wording of the earlier decree (cf. 3:13) clearly gives them the same right as their opponents to take the initiative (cf. 9:2) and to **avenge themselves upon their enemies** (vs. 13). In the LXX the purported full text of the decree (Additions 16:1-24) is inserted after vs. 12.

8:15-17. Public Acclaim of Mordecai. The author continues to contrast Mordecai and Haman; whereas the people of **Susa** were "perplexed" (3:15) by Haman's issuance of the earlier decree they now greet Mordecai with loud cheers as he walks forth in his official regalia. The **Jews** throughout the empire of course rejoice at this turn in their favor. **Declared themselves Jews** has been taken by some to mean that **many** merely pretended to be Jews, but since the Jews themselves would scarcely be deceived by false claims the reference is more probably to proselytes. Some scholars have taken this to be an allusion to forced conversions to Judaism in the time of John Hyrcanus (see Intro.).

9:1-10. The Day of Slaughter. Thus far in the story only Haman has been presented as an enemy of the

Jews—though perhaps Mordecai's instruction to Esth. to keep her Jewishness a secret (2:10) has hinted at the existence of prejudice. Now it appears that the Jews have large numbers of **enemies** throughout the empire. The identity of these enemies is unclear. In defiance of the **king's command and edict** issued by Haman, supposedly irrevocable, the **royal officials** change to the side of the Jews (vs. 3); and thus the assumption of some interpreters that the attackers are soldiers of the Persian army acting under orders seems unjustified. Rather the enemies of the Jews must be understood as neighboring peoples within the empire who of their own accord **sought their hurt** (vs. 2) because they **hated them** (vs. 5). It is evident that the author is writing at a time when he can expect that his Jewish readers will be accustomed to having enemies and will take them for granted in the story without explanation.

9:11-19. An Added Day. In view of the acclaim which Mordecai has received from the people of Susa (8:15) it is surprising that within the limited area of the **capital,** i.e. citadel (see above on 1:2-8), which includes the palace itself, the Jews have so many enemies that **five hundred** are killed. Undoubtedly the low point in the book comes when Esth., not satisfied with this number, requests a 2nd day of slaughter. The reason for the additional day, however, is not to increase the statistics by **three hundred** but to explain why the date of Purim varies in different places. As indicated here, Jews in the **villages** observe it on the **fourteenth** of Adar whereas those **in Susa** and presumably other cities have their festival on the **fifteenth.** The hanging of Haman's **ten sons** who have already been killed (vss. 7-10) is probably not an inconsistency but simply confirmation that the **gallows** served not only for execution of criminals but also for public display of their bodies (see above on 2:19-23). Remembering that the book is fiction we need not be concerned by the empirewide report of **seventy-five thousand** killed—esp. since the LXX reduces it to 15,000—or be surprised that there are no Jewish casualties.

VI. Annual Observance of Purim (9:20–10:3)

9:20-32. Instructions for the Festival. Whereas vss. 17-19 clearly assume a one-day festival observed on different dates by rural and urban Jews, this section calls on all Jews to celebrate a 2-day festival taking in both dates. Because of this inconsistency and differences in style and vocabulary many scholars believe this section comes from a different author (see Intro.). Its purpose is to emphasize the legality of Purim. The repeated stress on **letters to all the Jews** is to insure that this festival, which has no basis in the Pentateuch, will be recognized as official in the life of Judaism. It is not enough that it have its basis in a historical event; it must be legalized by official documents. This reflects a characteristic view of postexilic Judaism. The addition here of **gifts to the poor** (vs. 22) is a natural aspect of such an occasion of joyousness and remains a part of the observance to this day.

9:23-28. Possibly vss. 24-25 are intended to summarize part of what **Mordecai had written to them,** but if so it probably does not mean that the whole book is to be understood as a transcript of Mordecai's letter. In vs. 25 the name **Esther** has been supplied by many translators because the verb **came** is feminine, i.e. equivalent to "she came"; but probably this is a scribal error and should read "he came" as in the LXX, referring to Haman. The name **Purim** (vs. 26) by which the festival came to be known is a Hebrew plural form, which is now explained as the plural of **Pur,** the **lot** used by Haman to select the day for destroying the Jews (see above on 3:7-15). **All who joined them** (vs. 27) refers to proselytes (see above on 8:15-17).

9:29-32. The legality of Purim is further emphasized by a **command of Queen Esther** in a joint letter with Mordecai. The reference to **fasts** may indicate that this letter was added to establish the custom of fasting on the day before Purim in commemoration of Esth.'s fast (4:16).

10:1-3. Exaltation of Mordecai. The wealth and **power** of Ahasuerus enhance the **honor** of his prime minister, Mordecai. The reference to the official annals of **Media and Persia** (vs. 2) is patterned after similar statements in I, II Kings (e.g. I Kings 14:19, 29) and is intended to authenticate the historicity of the book. Probably the best thing that can be said for Mordecai—and the best thing in the book—is that **he sought the welfare of his people and spoke peace to all his people.** This is a fitting conclusion, but the LXX follows it with an interpretation of the dream of Mordecai described at the beginning of that version and a colophon authenticating the Greek translation (Additions 10:4–11:1; see Intro.).

THE BOOK OF JOB

Hugh Anderson

INTRODUCTION

Literary Character. Job is one of the noblest works of world literature; it should be classed with the Greek tragedies of Aeschylus and Sophocles, with Dante's *Divine Comedy*, Milton's *Paradise Lost,* and Goethe's *Faust.* The "Prologue in Heaven" in Goethe's *Faust* is in fact modeled on the interview of Satan with God in the preface of Job (chs. 1-2). Tennyson called Job "the greatest poem of ancient or modern times."

Whereas the literary grandeur of Job is supreme beyond doubt, the question of what kind of literature it is has been the subject of protracted discussion. Does it belong primarily to the order of drama? Is it epic or lyric poetry? Is it a philosophical and reflective composition? Or is it didactic, intended to teach and instruct? Perhaps the wisest course is not to try to fit Job into any one literary category but to acknowledge it for what it is, a vast literary complex containing in addition to a prose narrative (chs. 1-2; 42:7-17), a remarkable variety of poetic pieces, many of which could be read as separate literary units complete in themselves. The range of the author's poetic imagination is extensive and expresses itself in such forms as hymns of praise to the power of the Almighty (e.g. 5:8-16), laments of Job over his dire fate (e.g. ch. 3), proverbs (e.g. 4:8-11; 5:1-7; 12:11-12; 14:1-2), and descriptions of the blessedness of the righteous and the destruction of the wicked (e.g. ch. 8).

The last 2 of these literary forms are part of the stock in trade of the wisdom writers of the OT and of the Apoc. (see "The Wisdom Literature," pp. 1101-05). Job is normally grouped with Prov. and Eccl. under the heading of wisdom literature. The wise men or sages of Israel were a special class characterized by their rationalistic and calculating approach to ethics, religion, and the problems of human life. When Elihu addresses Job's 3 friends as wise men (34:2) the title is to be construed in this specialized sense. In their disputation with Job his friends often appeal to an apparently well-established norm of wisdom.

We must, however, exercise some caution about straightforwardly calling Job a book of wisdom in the same sense as Prov. or Eccl. In this book the segments of proverbial wisdom and the reckonings of the contrasting destinies of the righteous and the wicked are nearly always found on the lips of the friends, whereas the hero himself tirades in vehement protest against the cold calculations of their normative wisdom point of view. So there is dis-cernible what may be called an anti-wisdom strain. Yet, on the positive side, the author's theology resembles that of the wisdom literature in general, in that it is expressed in utterances about creation (chs. 38-39), and we may be sure that he was very much influenced by contact with the wise men or sages.

Wisdom, in the technical sense indicated above, went far beyond the boundaries of the nation of Israel. The wise men of Israel had their counterparts in Egypt and beyond the E borders of Palestine (cf. I Kings 4:30-31). Each of the 4 main human characters in Job is a foreigner. Eliphaz, one of the friends, comes from Teman in Edom, and Edom apparently had a special reputation for wisdom (cf. Jer. 49:7). Fortunately modern archaeological discoveries have increasingly clarified for us the wider canvas of the cultural background of Job. We recognize today that the book belongs to a family of literary works of the ancient Near East. These were generally constructed as dialogues permeated with complaints about suffering, esp. innocent suffering, and dealing with the problem of theodicy, which may be roughly defined as the problem of how to square belief in a good God with the existence of evil in the world.

E.g. the Babylonian ps. "I Will Praise the Lord of Wisdom" (often called the Babylonian Job) is a prayer of thanksgiving for deliverance from misfortune. The author tells how he was wrongfully removed from his priestly office, banished from home, and reduced to slavery. He called on the gods for help. When they did not respond, he concluded that their conception of goodness must be different from that of men. He was smitten with a serious illness for which no cure could be found, and all the while his enemies rejoiced. Thereupon he had 2 visions promising him both help and cure, and in the sequel his health was restored, his innocence vindicated, and his release from slavery achieved. The god Marduk took him by the hand and his persecutors were punished. He then went back to Babylon and in the temple of Marduk the people joined with him in praising the god for his mercy.

Alongside this ps. we may place a Babylonian dialogue between a sufferer and his friends, who address each other as scholars eminent for their wisdom and insight, and another earlier poem from the same milieu, entitled "A Pessimistic Dialogue Between Master and Slave," which is concerned with the seeming meaninglessness of life. Comparable with these is an Egyptian work, written probably before 2000 B.C., in which a sufferer converses with his own soul and contemplates death by suicide as a justifiable way out of the afflictions of this life.

Of all these ancient works perhaps the one most closely related to Job is a Sumerian poem recovered recently from fragments discovered at Nippur and dating from soon after 2000 B.C. Sumer, the land which came to be known in classical times as Babylonia (see color map 2), was the scene of probably the first high civilization in the history of man. The hero of the Sumerian poem is a nameless man who was suddenly reduced from health, wealth, and happiness to severe illness and pain. Though he laments his fate, he does not chide his god for it. Rather he confesses his own guilt, with the result that the god delivers him from his ordeal.

While the author of Job may not have been directly dependent on such writings as these, he nevertheless inherited their tradition and outlook. In terms of both literary form and content, therefore, his book was not produced "out of the blue" and should not be too narrowly judged as emanating from a purely Hebrew environment.

Authorship. Despite our richer acquaintance with the background of Job, the name of the author remains quite unknown to us, nor do we possess any information about him save the few hints we can glean from the book itself. One of its most striking features is that its setting is not Hebrew and that it is pervaded by foreign elements. The action and characters are most closely associated with Edom, the land neighboring Israel to the SE, which was inhabited by a seminomadic people in touch with both the Arabian peninsula and Egypt (see color map 4). The author seems to avoid both the divine name Yahweh and the other common Hebrew designation for God, Elohim, and employs instead such "outside" names as El, Eloah, and Shaddai. Such civil and moral prescriptions as are alluded to appear to be not so much specifically Hebrew in character as common to all ancient civilized nations. Works of ancient oriental wisdom, as we have seen, furnished a literary, poetic, and religious background for the author. His Hebrew language has been greatly influenced by Arabic. Accordingly a few scholars have argued that he could hardly have been a Jew at all and was indeed most probably an Edomite.

On the other hand the author does reveal some familiarity with the prophetic and wisdom literature of the OT. E.g. Job's dirge in ch. 3 recalls Jer. 20: 14-18 and certain pss. of lamentation (Pss. 38; 88; 102). Failing, therefore, more concrete evidence than we possess to connect the author's life with a particular foreign locale, it is perhaps better to assume, with the majority of critics, that he was a Jew, albeit a Jew who, as a member of the intelligentsia, had traveled very widely and had amassed an encyclopedic knowledge of the lore of the ancient Near East. Evidently he was esp. well versed in the lore of Egypt. His work contains a number of Egyptian loan words and many echoes of Egyptian language. Moreover the whole tenor of ch. 31 is reminiscent of the so-called "negative confession" of the Egyptian Book of the Dead.

The author coupled with his expert knowledge of folklore a keen observation of the natural world and a remarkably scientific understanding of its working, as we gather most of all from the majestic nature poem of ch. 38 and the portrayal of the wonders of the animal world in ch. 39.

His gifts of intellect appear to have been matched only by his gifts of heart. The whole book bears the authentic stamp of a profoundly religious spirit, sensitive to the world's sin and sorrow. Job's violent reaction to his agony and ordeal is depicted with such realism that we cannot but feel that the author himself knew what it was to be "battered with the shocks of doom" and really poured himself into his hero's doubts and fears and protests.

Date. The question of when Job was written is a very open one. The difficulty is compounded by the fact that the book consists of 2 separate portions: 1:1-2:13; 42:7-17 are prose and may be recognized as the beginning and end of an old folk story, while the long section in between is in poetic form. The prose narrative takes us back to a great antiquity, reflecting as it does the genuine coloring of the patriarchal age—e.g. wealth consisting of cattle and slaves (1:3; 42:12; cf. Gen. 12:16; 32:5) and Job's great length of years (42:17). Therefore, perhaps not surprisingly, there arose an ancient view (in the Jewish Talmud) that the author of Job was Moses himself. But we have no means whatever of confirming this tradition. There is in fact one feature of the prose prologue, viz. the prominent part played by Satan, that may be as late as the 6th or 5th cent., a time when Persian influences were infiltrating Hebrew religious thinking. Probably the safest inference is that the author—or, as some believe, the editor—employed a very old folk legend regarding a pious sufferer, which, as we have seen, had ancient Sumerian-Babylonian and Egyptian parallels, and adapted it slightly as a setting for the poetical composition.

Can we go further in defining a date for the extensive poetical section of Job? Significantly enough, there is not a single allusion in it to any event in Hebrew history. Yet this very lack may afford us some clue to the time of writing, for it implies that the earlier faith in God's lordship and rulership over the history of his people Israel had broken down and been replaced by the questioning and anxiety that followed the catastrophe of 586, when God's judgment on the nation was executed. Since the book was known to Ben Sira (Ecclus. 49:9; Hebrew text only) it can scarcely be later than 250. Thus we may tentatively place the writing somewhere between the 6th and 3rd cents.

Structure. The Hebrew text of Job as it has come down to us is the most corrupt of all biblical documents. In addition the structure, or disposition, of the whole work is in a very disturbed state. There is abundant evidence that the original has repeatedly been worked over and revised by a number of different editors. The poetical portion is in the form of a dialogue consisting of a soliloquy by Job, followed by 3 cycles of 6 speeches, one from each of Job's friends in turn and an immediate reply to each by Job himself. The 3rd cycle of speeches, however, is confused and incomplete. Chs. 24-27 are particularly garbled. Bildad's 3rd speech (ch. 25) is very brief and is not in accord with his earlier utterances. Job's reply (chs. 26–27) brings forward ideas to which he had previously been opposed, and Zophar's 3rd speech is missing altogether. The poem that follows in praise of wisdom (ch. 28) is a separate literary unit. Though it may possibly be from the hand of the author, it is certainly out of context where it stands, and is generally recognized as an addition to the original poem.

The majority of scholars are also agreed that the speeches of Elihu (chs. 32–37) are an addition to the original work. The youthful Elihu (32:6) takes up the better part of 2 chs. apologizing for his intrusion into the debate. When he does eventually say something positive, he mainly reiterates or supplements points already made by Job's 3 friends. Then again (chs. 36–37) the words of Elihu simply anticipate the reply made to Job by God out of the whirlwind (chs. 38–40). We may accordingly assume that the Elihu speeches were composed and inserted by an editor who felt constrained to counter Job's defiance more effectively than the friends had done and to improve on the arguments presented in the divine discourse. They should not be dismissed as entirely insignificant, however, since they provide us with an interesting early commentary on certain aspects of the original poem by someone who did not share the author's philosophy.

Of the many problems connected with the structure of the book the most crucial is that of the relationship between the prose prologue and epilogue (1:1–2:13; 42:7-17) and the great poem of 3:1–42:6. At first sight they seem to be both quite separate from and contradictory to each other. The prose narrative centers on a pious sufferer who remains faithful and submissive to God's will and is rewarded in the end for his patience. The Job of this folktale must indeed have become widely known in antiquity as an outstanding example of quiet and brave endurance under trial (cf. Ezek. 14:14, 20; Jas. 5:11). The Job of the poem, on the other hand, is a rebel who, even after his confrontation with God, seems to be left still in his distress and suffering. The poem is hostile to the notion of the final reward of the suffering righteous; the prose epilogue endorses it. Because of this conflict many scholars have concluded that the author initially wrote only the poem and that the prose prologue and epilogue were added later by some editor or editors out of a natural propensity for a happy ending and a desire to encourage the afflicted to hold on to the last.

Nevertheless there are good reasons for thinking that the author of the poem was himself responsible for combining it with the prose narrative so as to produce what the Jewish scholar Tur-Sinai has called a "framework-poem," patterned after early Sumerian-Babylonian and Egyptian models. In the prose section the "plot" is unfolded. We are allowed a glimpse of the righteous Job in the halcyon days of his prosperity (1:1-5) and are introduced to the actions taken in the heavenly court for his trial. Against the background of this prelude the disintegration of Job's faith and the desperate cry he utters in ch. 3 are all the more heartrending for us. So at the end, after the Job of the poem has been stilled and silenced by his encounter with the God of the whirlwind (42:1-6), the epilogue appears to make good sense by drawing down the curtain on his

misery and depicting his final restoration (42:7-17). The whole book, therefore, prose narrative and poem together, may be taken as a single and unified work of great dramatic force and urgency.

Theme. If Job is a dramatic unity, is there also one great theme running through the whole work? The question is not so simple as might at first appear. The modern reader in the W world has great difficulty with the long poetical section. He is troubled by the lack of any logical progression of thought and by the fact that the poet does not seem to define any clearly fixed subject for conversation in the speeches. Job's speeches range rapidly from topic to topic and are marked by sudden changes of tone and mood. The speeches of the friends do not consist of rationally developed arguments, but rather of a series of loosely connected sections. E.g. Eliphaz offers Job 5 different and largely separate propositions to think over (chs. 4–5). The difficulties presented by the poetical portion may, in part at least, account for the traditional interpretation of the book. The popular view has fastened on the prose folk story's simple and edifying picture of a moral hero and patient saint, whose faith in God remains undimmed through every tribulation, and has affirmed that the real theme of the work is "the fortitude of a good man under testing." But we can take that to be the theme of Job only at the cost of ignoring or neglecting what the poetry actually says, for it tells us of one who shakes his fist against God in fiery *impatience* and gives vent to blasphemous utterance.

Nearer the point is the claim that the author is dealing with the problem of suffering, esp. innocent suffering, and its meaning. The reader is told in the prologue that Job was an innocent man and that this innocent man was smitten with a dread physical disease. How is the seeming injustice of this experience to be explained? In the body of the poem the friends move around this question and attempt to answer it out of their own traditional belief in a God who rewards or punishes men according to their moral deserts. They assert that, in face of the majesty of this "tit-for-tat" God, Job must simply resign himself to the calamities that have befallen him.

But is this all the author of Job intends to say? Not if the Job of the poem himself, rather than the friends, is the author's spokesman. The question raised by this Job is both broader and deeper than the question of how to account for the infliction of physical adversity on the innocent. His physical predicament has become merely the outward symbol of an intense inward agony, the agony of all humanity in those tortured hours when they feel themselves the victims of a meaningless and evil universe, when faith is swallowed up in the abyss of doubt and God seems to have vanished. The anguished Job speaks the language of those whose complacency has been shattered by staggering events that reason cannot grasp or fathom: "What kind of God is this who hides himself from me?" "Let me but meet him face to face that I may justify myself to him." What is at stake for Job—and for the author—is the 2-fold question of the justice of God and the justice and honor of man before God.

Job's inextinguishable longing to recover his justification before God, which he thinks has been lost, finds its answer at length in his direct encounter with the Most High God of the whirlwind. Before this God Job is silenced; he has not one plea or claim left; he has no longer any merit of his own. He has found the God *who is God,* who is higher than all human reckoning, who can only be adored, and in whose presence man is fit only to repent in dust and ashes (42:1-6). Through his repentance Job's estrangement from God, the world, and men is ended; he is restored; he has become a "new man."

Precisely because its theme is the possibility of finding the sovereign God amid the whirlwind of despair, anxiety, and desolation, this book is peculiarly relevant to our own age, which is justly called the "age of anxiety." The hero is, after a fashion, an oriental beatnik of his own day, remote and uncouth in his garb and visage. He is an angry man, an insubordinate campaigner against conventional doctrine. In the darkness of his night of agony Job protests, with Promethean arrogance, against heaven. The consolations of his would-be ministering friends, with their glib utterances about a God who metes out justice, reward, and punishment by human rather than divine standards, Job cannot endure and violently rejects. Vanished for him is the little God whose only role in the world is thought to be that of guarding our inferior ethical judgments and man-made systems and adjusting our human grievances.

Job is living in that awful period between the demise of the old gods of formal religion and the coming of that other God who is higher than all human systems and calculations and deeper than all human anguish. Only at last, in the pit of despair, is Job given his reply. The answer he receives is not an all-embracing philosophical solution to his torment of soul. Rather, as we have seen, it is an experience, a direct confrontation with the sovereign God, in whose presence Job's self-righteousness and pride are broken, so that he is now given a new power of being and a new self.

In our own generation, we too, like Job, are living precariously between the times. "Where is God?" sensitive men are asking in this critical interim. Deep down they have lost the support of the old gods of culture, history, and progress. No God created in the image of man can satisfy their hunger. No version of religion that equates it simply with human wishes and ambitions or with the cult of individual happiness and success can meet their need. For our generation has known the wreckage of human hopes and has tasted the bitterness of doubt and despair. Job speaks to our situation because it speaks of the God who is found, through the night of man's doubt and sorrow, at the center of the storm, even as the God and Father of our Lord Jesus Christ is found by needy men amid the darkness of the cross of Calvary.

For Further Study. E. G. Kraeling, *The Book of the Ways of God,* 1939. Anthony and Miriam Hanson, *The Book of Job,* 1953. H. W. Robinson, *The Cross of Job,* 1955. Samuel Terrien in *IB,* 1954; *Job: Poet of Existence,* 1957. N. H. Tur-Sinai, *The Book of Job,* 1957. M. H. Pope in *IDB,* 1962. Roger Carstensen, *Job: Defense of Honor,* 1963.

I. The Prologue (1:1–2:13)

1:1-5. *The Righteous and Prosperous Job.* The opening is in true folk-story style: **There was a man**

in the land of Uz. Uz probably lay in the desert **east** (vs. 3) of Palestine and NE of Edom (cf. Lam. 4:21). The author, though a Jew, has given his work a foreign setting. That is fitting, since the problems Job faces transcend national boundaries and the language he speaks is the language, in crisis hours, of Everyman. The sheik of Uz is depicted in his heyday, sustained by an enlightened moral conscience and by religious faith (vs. 1), as rich in his possessions (vs. 3) as he is blessed in his family (vs. 2). No father is more devoted to his children, for when they feast together in celebration of a birthday Job, fearful perhaps of some irreverent conduct on their part, **continually** makes intercessory sacrifices to God on their behalf (vss. 4-5). The curtain rises then on an idyllic scene—Job in the day of his affluence and faithfulness. Set against this, how stark are the tragedies that are to invade his life!

1:6-12. *Conspiracy in Heaven.* The scene now shifts suddenly from earth to heaven. The **sons of God,** i.e. the "angelic beings," are assembled in convocation before the divine Presence. **Satan** (lit. "the Adversary"; cf. e.g. Num. 22:22; I Kings 11:14) has slipped in among them. Though here he stands on the side of the servants of God and plays the part of prosecuting attorney for the heavenly court, the reader can hardly avoid picturing him as the fiendish "devil" of later cents. (cf. I Chr. 21:1 and NT references) and quickly feels that "toil and trouble" are not far away. Sensing the challenge in God's inquiry about the **blameless** Job (vs. 8) Satan retorts sardonically that Job would not be the good and pious man he is if there were no profit in it (vss. 9-11). So Satan is commissioned to strike down **all that he has** (vs. 12).

1:13-22. *The Testing of Job.* A grim series of disasters hammers Job's prosperity into the dust. All his wealth, his flocks, and his servants are destroyed either by the **fire of God** (i.e. lightning, vs. 16) or by marauders who come miraculously at Satan's behest from the ends of the earth—**Sabeans** (vs. 15) from Sheba in the S and **Chaldeans** (vs. 17) from Babylonia in the E (see color map 7). But even the crowning blow, the death of all his children (vss. 18-19), leaves Job's faith in his God quite unshaken (vs. 21). When Job speaks about returning **naked** he means to the earth, which is the common **womb** of all men. Job's superb refusal, under the iron rod of Providence, to relinquish his faith has become a rallying call for countless people in days of catastrophe.

2:1-13. *Further Testing.* Job's initial victory is followed by a repetition of the opening scene in heaven. God points out that Job has so far remained steadfast. Satan's reply, **Skin for skin!** (vs. 4), is usually taken to be a metaphor from barter or exchange, but it is more likely a very terse popular proverb meaning that "the heart of a man is enclosed by skin after skin." Satan is therefore saying that if Job's fidelity is to be taken away, every protection he has must be penetrated and access gained to his inmost soul. So the new strategy is the affliction of Job himself with a dreadful malady. Job is brought near to death, for the fact that he sits **among the ashes** (vs. 8) is a mark of mourning. Yet, despite his wife's entreaty, he will not recant his faith (vss. 9-10). Finally his **three friends** from neighboring desert tribes, having heard of his misfortune, come to **comfort him** (vs. 11) and to mourn with him (vs. 12). **Seven days** was the time appointed for mourning (cf. Gen. 50:10; I Sam. 31:13).

Though full account must be taken of the discrepancies between them (see Intro.) the introductory folk story prepares us for the poem to come in 2 ways: (*a*) It connects God with the fact of Job's agony; though the Job of the poem is unaware himself of what has occurred in the heavenly court, the reader knows, and for him this intensifies Job's predicament. (*b*) It shows us a man who has reached the last limits of human endurance and who yet remains secure in his faith in God. Just when the prologue has prompted us to ask whether this faith of Job's can last forever, we are shocked by his discordant outcry in ch. 3.

II. The First Round of Speeches (3:1–11:20)

3:1-26. *The Flint in Job's Heart.* When the Job of the poem first opens his mouth to speak, it is in a mood vastly different from the pious utterances of the prologue. The flint has struck into his soul, and he curses his life in the way men frequently do in their darkest hours: "I wish I had never been born!"

3:4-10. From the shelter of his former God-protected life Job has now passed into all the depths of apparent abandonment by God. His once peaceful and ordered existence has become a chaos, and he summons the powers of chaos to join him in his cursing. **Leviathan** (vs. 8; cf. Ps. 74:14; Isa. 27:1) was the primeval serpent monster of the sea, symbol of confusion, corresponding to Tiamat, mentioned repeatedly in Babylonian epics. Job is probably conjuring up the notion of the war of the forces of **darkness** and disorder against the God of heaven and light, or the notion of the return of chaos.

3:11-19. Job's life has become such a terrifying and meaningless void that he would prefer the ghostly and bloodless existence of the departed shades in the underworld of Sheol (see comment on Ps. 6:4-5), where death is the great leveler.

3:20-26. Vss. 20-22 revert to the question of vs. 11: **Why did I not die at birth?** In his agony of body and soul ("moans are served as my food and groans poured out as my drink," as vs. 24 should probably be translated) Job feels trapped—as one **whom God has hedged in.** His first tentative charge against the justice of God, implicit in the question of vs. 23, will subsequently become a raging storm of protest.

4:1-5:27. *Eliphaz' Reply.* The 7 days and nights of silent mourning observed by the 3 friends (2:13) are now ended when Eliphaz feels constrained to reply to Job's outburst.

It should be noted that the author makes little attempt to develop the character of any of the 3 friends as individuals. They appear simply as special pleaders, each coming to court with already fixed ideas and set speeches. There is hardly any interchange of ideas, nor do the speakers really pick up the threads of conversation from one to the other. Within each speech there is a good deal of detail not strictly relevant to the main issue. The speeches are in fact mostly composite, made up of separate or loosely connected units and lacking any rationally developed argumentation. We must therefore avoid manufacturing imaginary connections of thought which might appeal to our sense of logic but are not in the text. The author's method is to use the word images of the friends as so many windows through which we may look at the chief problem raised by Job and come at the end to understand it better in its totality.

4:1-11. Eliphaz' first speech illustrates a number of these points. He offers for consideration several largely unrelated propositions. Initially he gives Job a curt reminder that a man of his faith and uprightness (vs. 6), who has once been a tower of strength to the **weak** in his society (vss. 3-4), should be the last person to succumb to despair. He propounds the philosophy (vss. 7-8) that the righteous retain their material prosperity in this life while the wicked are inevitably brought down to ruin **by the breath of God** (cf. Ps. 18:16-24). Eliphaz thus insists that history makes sense and that the universe is ruled by God on moral lines (cf. 5:13; 8:3, 20). Vss. 10-11 apparently portray the breaking up of a den of **lions** and are usually understood to be a graphic figure for the sudden discomfiture of the wicked.

4:12-21. Vss. 12-17 purport to be Eliphaz' account of his ecstatic visionary encounter with God in the waking hours **of the night.** The question put by the divine visitor makes clear that no **mortal man** can make a convincing case for his own righteousness **before God.** But this really contradicts the whole viewpoint of Eliphaz in the remainder of his speech, which is that the good man *is* just in the sight of God and will as surely be rewarded for his righteousness as the guilty will be punished. Throughout the dialogue it is not the friends but Job himself who is apprehensive that he will never be able to convince God of his righteousness. Probably, therefore, the night vision was originally related, not by Eliphaz, but by Job (cf. 7:14, where he speaks of being "scared by dreams"). If so, vss. 18-21 should also be taken as Job's words, pleading that men in their weakness have little chance to persuade God of their merits when he will not recognize those even of his **angels,** i.e. heavenly attendants. Certainly vss. 12-21 accord more with Job's situation and philosophy than with the friends'.

5:1. If the night vision of the **spirit** or **form** of God (4:15-16) was told by Job, then this is Eliphaz' jeer at one who claims to have visits from supernatural beings.

5:2-27. Eliphaz now presents a series of pictures on the theme of the reward of the good and the ruin of the evil. The man who murmurs against his lot comes at last to a sorry end (vss. 2-4) and suffers dire calamities—e.g. **his sons . . . are crushed in the gate,** the city gate being the place where justice was administered (cf. Isa. 29:21; Amos 5:10). God is portrayed by Eliphaz as the great adjuster (vss. 8-16), who dispenses a retributive justice. Eliphaz then seems to address Job more directly (vss. 17-27), saying that if Job will accept his affliction as a merited divine **chastening** he can yet win the favor of God and enjoy a life of pastoral peace and plenty—the **stones** will not accumulate to spoil his fields nor the wild **beasts** raid his farm (vs. 23). But the promise of a long and happy life if only he will acknowledge his guilt before God can only outrage further the sentiments of one who now believes that the processes of divine justice have miscarried in his case.

6:1–7:21. _Job's Alienation from God and Men._ There is a greater progression of thought in the speeches of Job than in those of the friends. In his first speech there was the hint that his desire for the oblivion of death rather than life amounted to a charge against God and God's justice. Now in this long 2nd speech his words become increasingly filled with acrimony and irreverence and convey with gripping realism the horror of his journey into the twilight zone of human existence. His tragic situation is one not only of physical suffering but of complete disruption of his existence. He is cut off from his friends. They do not understand him (6:24-27). He has become, for no reason he can discover, the victim rather than the favorite of heaven (6:4; 7:20).

6:1-7. The vehemence of his words, Job claims, does but match the awful severity of his sufferings. His outcry against God as the grand inquisitor who tortures him is an instinctive reaction, as natural as the protest of animals against an unaccustomed diet or the complaint of men against insipid and repulsive food.

6:8-13. These vss. reveal the nature of Job's struggle with God; he is caught between 2. He still accepts the reality of **the Holy One** and cannot admit that by any sin of his he has broken the old intact relationship. But at the same time he knows God now as his crushing enemy, who is pushing him beyond all human capacity to bear pain.

6:14-23. Job has to wage this struggle with God in awesome loneliness. These vss. convey the dereliction of one estranged completely from his friends. He has never asked from them any tangible gifts or benefits (vss. 22-23), but their sympathy at least he has had every reason to expect, and they are a bitter disappointment to him. He compares them to a wadi, a stream that runs in spate in wintertime but come summer, when the thirsty desert traveler's need is greatest, has not a drop of water to offer.

6:24-30. Job challenges the friends to regard him, not according to his **words**, which are born only of despair and are no true index of his normal state (vss. 25-26), but according to his life, which is innocent and free from error (vs. 24). There is nothing in it, so far as he is able to **discern** (vs. 30), to justify the disasters that have come to him.

7:1-10. Job becomes the spokesman for all disillusioned men, protesting vehemently how empty life is and how puny man's standing is before God. He compares, or rather contrasts, himself with the laborer who waits longingly for the dusk of evening to get some rest and receive his **wages** for the day —all that Job has got for waiting is sleepless nights of agony that remind him of the hopelessness of life and of the near approach of death (vss. 1-6). He therefore looks on death as but the grim underscoring of life's futility (vss. 7-10).

7:11-21. These vss. are important for understanding what is at issue for Job in his struggle. His anguish of soul arises, not from the fact that he feels Godforsaken, but that he is God-haunted. He cannot understand why the all-powerful God does not mercifully overlook frail man, why instead he maintains a close watch over him (vs. 12) and lies in wait to **test** him (vs. 18). Why will he not **let me alone till I swallow my spittle?** Vss. 17-18 are a bitterly ironical reminiscence of Ps. 8. The psalmist rejoices over the gracious care of God the friend. Job bewails the unwanted but inescapable care of God the enemy. The question posed in ch. 7 is the question of how God deals with man or the question of man's existence before God.

8:1-22. _Bildad's Reply._ Indignant at Job's violent complaints against God, Bildad enters the lists as champion of the **justice** of God. For Bildad there is no problem; men's destinies are measured by God exactly according to their merits; the good fare well, the wicked ill. After the storm of Job's speech, Bildad's utterance is like a great calm. The simplicity of his words betokens the simplicity of his theology: those who suffer must have sinned; those who sin receive their due reward. As an advocate of this simple orthodox philosophy Bildad, like all defenders of orthodoxy, appeals to antiquity, to the tradition of the ancients to support his view (vss. 8-10).

9:1–10:22. _Job's Contention with God._ Instead of taking up in detail any of the points made by the friends, Job, who has shown by his previous speech that he has encountered God as an enemy (e.g. 7:19), nevertheless presses on to have communication with him and is clearly thinking of engaging him in a legal contest (9:3, 15-16, 19-20, 32-33). Though Job feels that in such a lawsuit he will not stand a chance (9:15-20), he does not shrink from wishing to bring God into court and face him there (10:2).

9:1-12. In offering the picture of a God who unfailingly rewards the righteous and punishes the guilty the friends, as Job now sees, are really scaling God down to human size by making him dispense his justice according to their own _quid pro quo_ concept of morality. Over against the too-small God of the friends, the God of Job's experience, the God whom he describes here, is an absolute Lord, whose deeds cannot be controlled by any human reason. So Job appeals to God's irresistible might in initiating natural calamities (vss. 5-7) and in creating and controlling the heavenly constellations (vss. 8-10). Before his sovereign freedom in regulating the fearful workings of nature man is helpless (vss. 11-12).

9:13-31. But the main question Job has to face is whether his suffering is God's verdict of guilt. He simply will not allow himself to be declared guilty in this way (vss. 15, 20, 21; cf. 10:2, 7); he defends his own integrity and innocence. In pointing to himself as a good man who has suffered affliction Job is really demolishing the friends' notion that God deals with men in terms of a retributive justice. The God of whom and to whom Job speaks here has the incomparable freedom to root justice, not as and where men please, but as and where he pleases. How in legal contest could Job ever hope to stand before this God, who has vanquished even the chaos dragon of the sea (here called **Rahab,** vs. 13; see above on 3:1-26) and her retinue of deities?

9:32-35. This new awareness of the awful gap between himself and God suggests to Job the need for an **umpire**—an arbiter or referee who might listen to the complaints of both man and God. Vss. 32-33 may be taken as expressing his inextinguishable longing for an intermediary between the God who in his majesty is inaccessible and the man who feels the need to communicate with him. But his plight is that he knows there can be no arbiter; the absolute God is so powerful that he himself determines cases and is always in the right against man.

10:1-2. Even so Job refuses to be silent. Life has so little left to offer him that he may as well speak out. The whole of the speech which is introduced by **I will say to God** (vs. 2) tells us what Job would say to God if there were any opportunity. We are to picture Job, in his fevered imagination, projecting himself into a situation of face-on encounter with God in the law court. It is as if a jilted lover, fancying himself in his beloved's presence, were seeking from her explanations of her quarrel with him.

10:3-7. These vss. are somewhat disjointed and difficult to interpret. The hypothetical shortness of God's life implied in Job's rhetorical question in vs. 5 is hardly a probable reason for the pursuit of his quarrel with Job in vs. 6. Some have understood God's being short-lived in the sense of his being limited in experience like men, but that is a forced interpretation. Possibly, therefore, in the process of editing vs. 5 has been misplaced from its proper context alongside vss. 20-22. Vs. 4 connects well with vs. 6: **Dost thou see as man sees . . . that thou dost seek out my iniquity?**

10:8-22. Job goes on to charge God with fickleness toward his creature. Why should God bestow such lavish care on bringing a man like Job to birth (vss. 8-12) and yet of set intent (vs. 13) brand him as guilty and convict him of sin (vss. 14-15), becoming his terrible enemy and hunting him like a wild beast (vs. 16)? Why should the God who gave him birth not leave him alone at least to go down to the grave in peace (vss. 18-22)?

Knowing that there is no umpire between God and himself (9:33), Job's only option is to accost directly the opponent who so outrageously fouls him (10:2-22). The poignant questions he puts to God, out of his yearning to understand the secrets of God's dealings with him, articulate very well man's perennial need for a mediator with God. It is instructive to contrast Job's portrayal here of God as the great enemy, who chases man endlessly for a verdict of guilty against him, with Francis Thompson's poem "The Hound of Heaven," where from the standpoint of Christian faith God appears as the great lover, pursuing sinful man forever with his mercy.

11:1-20. *Zophar's Cold Comfort.* Angered by Job's garrulousness, Zophar takes him to task. Like Bildad, Zophar is one of those who must have neat, practical, and easily understood explanations for life's problems. Job's claim to be innocent, as Zophar thinks, is demonstrably without foundation: Job cannot measure his innocence or guilt, for man has no access to **wisdom**, the place of which is known only to God (vss. 4-6). We can guess what the reaction of a person in Job's position would be to Zophar's saying in effect (vs. 6c) that if he but knew it—if he could but stand on God's side—he would realize that he has in fact got off much more lightly than he deserves.

11:7-12. In this series of questions Zophar is reminding Job that God's ways are inscrutable and

therefore he must simply accept what has come to him without blasting the gates of heaven as he is doing. Vs. 12 is difficult to translate. The meaning may be that the incorrigible stupidity of a man like Job has as much chance of being remedied as **a wild ass's colt** has of being **born a man.** By a slight change in the Hebrew text, however, we may obtain another translation: "And man is an offspring which a donkey produces; an ass begets a man." The vs. would then be a harsh verdict on man's ignorance (the ass being the symbol of ignorance) in contrast with God's omniscience. Clearly this vs. is an old proverb, and its original form and meaning are not now easy to recover.

11:13-20. Zophar addresses a nice little sermon to Job on the friends' favorite theme of God's treatment of the righteous and the wicked. Whereas the wicked perish without **hope** (vs. 20), if Job will only rid his household of all **iniquity** (vss. 13-14), pleads Zophar, then he will enjoy a new day of security and blessedness. But the promise of a "better day coming if you're good" is cold comfort indeed to a man in desperate torment of body and soul. The medicine of forgetfulness (vs. 16) offered by Zophar can only sharpen the present anguish of one who has lost all his children, his property, his health.

In Zophar's whole speech there is a radical inconsistency that never dawns on him, so impregnable is the logic of his own belief in the divine distribution of rewards and punishments according to men's deserts. He insists that neither Job nor any man can understand the ways of God (vss. 4-12). Yet at the same time he presumes to make his own fairly rigid mathematical calculations about how God dispenses his justice to men (vss. 13-20). So it becomes clear that Job, in his agony, is pressing toward a profounder and more adequate view of God's dealings with men than the friends seem to possess.

III. THE 2ND ROUND OF SPEECHES (12:1-20:29)

12:1-14:22. *Job's Plea for Life.* With biting sarcasm Job asks in his opening remark (12:2) whether his friends think they are the whole **people** and so have a monopoly of all **wisdom.** He then pours cold water on their intellectual arrogance by reminding them that their ideas are but part of the common stock of human knowledge. Between Job's question **Who does not know such things as these?** (12:3c) and his contention **Lo, my eye has seen all this, my ear has heard and understood it. What you know, I also know; I am not inferior to you** (13:1-2), we may presume, he is not expressing any fresh thought or any new presentation of his case before God but rather is echoing the views and opinions expressed by the friends.

12:4-25. The text of vss. 4-6 is so disordered that it is almost impossible to achieve a translation that makes sense, and a number of indications (e.g. the use of Yahweh, vs. 9b) suggest that vss. 7-12 may be an interpolation. Vss. 13-25, however, clearly bear out that in this early part of Job's 3rd speech he is alluding to the views of the friends rather than developing his own thought. In vs. 13 he makes a somewhat laconic concession to the friends' opinion that **wisdom and might** belong only to God and not to man. Then he proceeds to make his own ironic recapitulation and extension of some of the friends' arguments. "You tell me God is wise and mighty," Job appears to be saying; "I will show you just how mighty." Then in a sequence of graphic images he describes how God intervenes indiscriminately and destructively in history, changing the normal course of things by swift and unexpected dispensations.

13:1-19. But talk of God's irresistible might is irrelevant to the **case** Job wants to **argue** with **the Almighty** (vss. 1-3). Indeed the friends have been no better than quack doctors (**worthless physicians,** vs. 4). Convinced that his contest with God is unequal enough without his so-called friends' taking up arms on God's side (vss. 5-12), Job entreats them to be silent so that he may, at whatever cost, further state his case against God (vss. 13-15). He dares to go on only because he believes that his very readiness to confront God is the sign of his innocence and the pledge of his ultimate victory (vss. 16-19).

13:20-28. Job is back once again in the law court with God, so to speak, and addresses him directly. He asks only that his case be decided in a fair and legal way (vss. 20-26) and not by the exercise of that arbitrary divine power which hems him in helplessly as a prisoner (vs. 27).

14:1-12. This book is marked by swift transitions of mood and feeling, like many of the pss. Throughout the dialogue with the friends Job both rails against God and presses on toward him; he both utters fiery protests against God's ordering of life and holds on to the fitful but lingering hope that justice will prevail (cf. 6:2; 13:18). So within this ch. he seems to waver between despair and hope. His solemn lament over the dreadful futility that overshadows the common lot of men recalls the cynicism of the Preacher's cry "All is vanity" (Eccl. 1:2). Job's entreaty for but a brief snatch of happiness before death (vs. 6) is awakened by his certainty of the finality of death. A man's present life can never be restored beyond death; he is not like a **tree** (vss. 7-12), able to regenerate life from the wasted **stump** of a dead body.

14:13-22. But then suddenly into the darkness of his brooding pessimism there breaks the light of a momentary new expectation (vss. 13-15), the expectation of a possible personal reconciliation with God, in the end, beyond death. Job asks for life, the real life of unbroken communion with God instead of the death of alienation from God. He is willing to be hidden in **Sheol** (see above on 3:11-19) for ages if only he can be sure of a **time** appointed for the termination of God's wrath and the granting of his mercy. However, Job's dream of future restoration is cherished only to be abandoned. He turns in a moment (vss. 18-22) to bemoan the sure and steady decay of human hopes and aspirations.

15:1-35. Eliphaz' Hardening Toward Job. The gently persuasive tone of Eliphaz' first speech now gives way to caustic criticism of Job as of one who, with consummate arrogance (vss. 7-8), has become the foe of true religion (vs. 4) by his blasphemous talk (vss. 5-6), and who claims to possess an innocence before God which not even his angels have (vss. 14-16).

15:17-19. Accordingly the strategy employed here by Eliphaz to "convert" Job is to try to frighten him with a daunting picture of the fate of the wicked.

As is usual with the friends, Eliphaz first seeks corroborating testimony to his own presentation in the wisdom of the ancients (vss. 18-19). In vs. 19 he may be alluding, in good Arab fashion, simply to the earliest and purest days of his own tribe of Teman. But the Hebrew of this vs. allows us also to take it, together with vss. 17-18, in another way: "I will declare what wise men have told, and their fathers have not hidden: 'To them alone the land is given, and no stranger passes among them.'" Vs. 19 then becomes the quotation of an old saying about the prosperity of the righteous, who are given to dwell peacefully in the land without any strangers or enemies to disturb them (cf. Joel 4:17).

15:20-24. Eliphaz now tells Job that while on the surface the **wicked** may appear to prosper, they are in reality perpetually agitated in their inward life and forever haunted by the thought of their impending doom. Eliphaz' argument here is of course a weak one—just as weak as the argument that the wicked always suffer and the righteous always prosper externally in this life. As we know, many of the arch evildoers in the history of our 20th cent. have by no means been plagued with remorse of conscience.

15:25-28. As if to strike further terror into Job's heart, Eliphaz confronts him with a picture of wickedness on a lavish or monstrous scale. The images of these vss. may be taken as metaphorical descriptions of the rampant evil of the godless man (vss. 25-26), insolent in his pride (vs. 27; **fat** is often a symbol of arrogance in the OT; cf. e.g. Ps. 73:7; 119:70), at home amid ruin and devastation (vs. 28). On the other hand Eliphaz may here be describing some mythological titan king, taking up arms against God (vss. 25-26), smearing himself with grease to swim the sea (vs. 27), making his quarters in ruined cities (vs. 28).

15:29-35. After this picture of flagrant evil Eliphaz returns to the customary theme of the friends, the impermanence of the wicked.

16:1-17:16. Job at His Tether's End. Rejecting the futile consolations of his friends and outraged by them (16:1-5), Job now reaches an unsurpassable dread of God. Here the God of Job's experience is portrayed as a demon-God (16:6-14) who has **gnashed his teeth** at Job and **sharpens his eyes** over him (16:9)—the LXX speaks of "eye-daggers." God has become his devilish enemy, setting him up as a **target** for practice (16:12). Staggered at the incompatibility between his own innocence (16:16-17) and the fiendish persecutions of this devil-God, Job has now apparently sunk down into an abyss of complete estrangement from the God he once knew as friend.

16:18-21. The tension of Job's struggle is nowhere more clear than when he adjures the **earth** not to let his **blood** trickle away, that his **cry** may not come to rest (vs. 18). The ancients believed that blood which soaked into the ground became silent, but that if it lay on a rocky place unabsorbed it cried out to heaven perpetually for vengeance. In appealing to God, therefore, as the avenger of blood, Job is really harking back to the very old idea that God is the owner of all life, and that wherever life is threatened or taken by violence God must concern himself with it, as when the blood of Abel calls to God (Gen. 4:10). From this Job suddenly comes to the startling confidence that he has after all a **witness . . . in heaven** (vs. 19). In ch. 16 Job is thus appealing *to* God *against* God—to the God whom, even at the last limit of his rebelliousness, he still can recognize as friend against the God who, in the bitterness of his experience, has become his foe.

Other explanations of these vss. are possible. But their obscurity, largely because of textual difficulties, will not allow us to base on them, as some interpreters have done, the notion that Job is here expressing the hope that in a life beyond death (in the depth of Sheol) he will yet come to know a heavenly Redeemer.

16:22-17:16. In the remainder of his speech Job returns to a mood of extreme pessimism. The whole passage presents us with many complex textual problems. E.g. the meaning of 17:3-5 is most uncertain, esp. vs. 5, which has received widely different interpretations. One commentator translates: "To flattery he said: 'Friends!'—and the eyes of his children failed." He takes it to refer to the ancient fable of the fox who by flattery cajoles a pair of birds into trusting him and thus giving him a chance to kill their young; Job's mocking friends are like the fox. Others understand the vs. to be a proverb by which they are compared to a man who invites guests to share his goods while "the eyes of his children languish," i.e. while they are starving.

Aside from textual difficulties, some sections of ch. 17 have obviously been displaced—e.g. vss. 8-9, which seem to be out of place on Job's lips and would be much more typical of the friends.

However, we can gather with some assurance that, in his estrangement from God, Job feels himself also alienated from time. He is severed from his **past** (vs. 11). He knows no future—**Where then is my hope?** (vs. 15). Without past and without future, with only a seemingly meaningless present, Job has in fact suffered the same shattering of existence as many of the displaced persons of our time.

18:1-21. *Bildad's Description of the Wrongdoer's Downfall.* Bildad begins by taunting Job about his interminable talk (vs. 2), his treating the friends as dolts when all the time he himself is like the angry fool who destroys himself in his wrath (vss. 3-4*a;* cf. 5:2-5), and his apparent desire that God should change the natural order of things just for his sake (vs. 4*bc*). What Bildad implies here is that the law of suffering as the result and proof of sin is inexorable and no exception can possibly be made in Job's case.

18:5-21. For the rest Bildad confines himself to a gloomy account of the fate of the wicked, harried by all manner of adversity during his life (vss. 5-13), and disappearing completely in death without remembrance or posterity (vss. 14-21).

18:15*b*. The **brimstone** may refer to the sulphur **scattered** as a disinfectant on the house of the wicked man smitten with leprosy (vs. 13). The ancients were well acquainted with the curative properties of sulphur. More probably this line depicts desolation of the homestead through brimstone falling on it from heaven as a mark of the curse of God and recalls the story of the destruction of Sodom and Gomorrah (Gen. 19:24). Indeed throughout Bildad's whole description of the fearful destiny of the wicked there may well be features drawn from

some old story of wicked primeval men destroyed by God in punishment for their sin.

19:1-29. *Job's Fleeting Moment of Trust.* Job suggests that by their supposed consolations the friends are only shattering him the more (vs. 2). Whereas they repeatedly construe his suffering as God's just punishment on his wickedness (vss. 3-5), Job himself in his innocence is still convinced that God is in fact perverting justice and is waging cruel war against him (vss. 6-12).

19:13-22. Alienated from God and from time (ch. 17), Job now reveals his alienation from his fellow men. He is filled with that eerie feeling of not belonging which calamity often brings to men. His account of his abandonment by the whole human community ends in a vain plea for his friends' pity.

19:23-29. With this Job at once begs that his words be **graven in the rock for ever** (vs. 24) and declares **I know that my Redeemer lives** (vs. 25*a*). At this point we instinctively feel that Job has reached the climax of his struggle; nowhere else do such solace and certainty seem to enfold him. Christian interpreters have long seen here a positive belief in the resurrection of the body—e.g. in many editions of the KJV we find over this ch. the heading "He believeth in the resurrection." Unfortunately, however, the Hebrew of vss. 25*b*-26*a* is too obscure to draw any sure conclusion from it, and in vs. 26*b* the all-important words **without my flesh** are lit. "from my flesh"—an ambiguous phrase which can mean either "away from my flesh" (i.e. after death) or "from the vantage point of my flesh" (i.e. in this present life). Nor do vss. 27-29, the text of which is so corrupt that we can only conjecture what the original may have been, afford any help in determining the meaning of vss. 25-26. Accordingly we cannot infer from this passage that Job hoped for a resurrection of the body.

We have also been inclined to look at Job's assertion **my Redeemer lives** from the standpoint of faith in Jesus Christ as Savior. But in order to grasp the real force of Job's words here we should compare them with other passages in which in his ongoing struggle *against* God Job is nevertheless pressing on *to* God and is momentarily expressing the wistful hope that through a heavenly friend justice will prevail for him, esp. 9:33 and 16:19. The umpire for whom Job appeals in 9:33 is not to be connected with the Jewish Messiah nor taken as a prophetic signpost pointing to Jesus Christ. Rather there probably lies behind Job's appeal for an umpire the ancient Sumerian idea of a personal god on whom each man relied to present his cause to the greater gods in the divine assembly. So also it is a mistake to see in the ally or witness of 16:19 or in the Redeemer of 19:25 the figure of Christ. In fact the word translated "Redeemer" is better rendered as "vindicator." The Hebrew word refers to the next of kin who has the duty of avenging the blood of a brother or protecting his title to property after his death. The role of the vindicator is to insure justice for his own kinsfolk, bound to him by ties of blood.

In this passage then, so far as we can be at all sure of the text, Job first insists on the strength of his case. Since the friends have shown no sympathy with his words, and God has made no response, he wishes his case to be preserved, as if engraved **with an iron pen** in the rock forever. And in the same instant, in a bright flash of expectancy, he believes that if only his case is fairly represented in the divine court his claims for justice must eventually be fulfilled and he himself vindicated.

For all the comfort to which Job has won through here, the matter is not ended yet. If this assurance of ultimate justice were the last word of the book, then its significance would be that, in voicing his expectation of a day of God in which there would be righteous redress of ancient wrongs, Job has come through this ordeal to a more refined faith than the friends in a God of ethical religion. But this is not the last word. Job has still to discover that he is living in the fateful period between the twilight of the old God of formal moralism, who dispenses justice as men measure it and understand it, and the dawn of that other God who is higher than all human reckoning.

20:1-29. Zophar's Speech on the Wicked Man's Portion. The opening of Zophar's speech is somewhat obscure, but he appears to be giving voice to his inward agitation and frustration with Job. For the most part he concentrates on the thought that the success and prosperity of the wicked are quite ephemeral; they are not given long to enjoy the fruits of their shameful labors (vss. 6-11, 16, 20-21). Whereas in their earlier descriptions of the terrible fate of the wicked the friends have been concerned mainly with crimes against God, Zophar is concerned chiefly with crimes against society. His arrows are directed at the racketeer who thinks nothing of crushing the poor for profit (vs. 19). But no more than Job can we of today derive much comfort from Zophar's view that the racketeer is doomed to get no pleasure from his stolen riches.

IV. The 3rd Round of Speeches (21:1–31:40)

21:1-34. Job's Refutation of the Friend's Philosophy. After rejecting the consolations of the friends and asserting his right to speak (vss. 2-5) Job expresses his resentment and impatience that, contrary to the friends' philosophy of just divine retribution, the evildoers prosper in all their undertakings and in fact enjoy a gay life (vss. 6-13) despite their open defiance of God and his commandments (vss. 14-15).

21:16-22. Job's words have clearly been interspersed with 2 ejaculations of piety (vss. 16b, 22) that are out of context on his lips and can be traced rather to some devoutly orthodox editor or scribe. These pious intrusions aside, the rest of the ch. shows that Job has begun to reflect on the general injustices found in the world, on the anomalies and incongruities of common human experience. He alludes to and overthrows the contention of the friends that a day of doom is always in store for the wicked (vss. 17-18). He refuses to be taken in by the argument that even if the wicked seem to prosper now **God stores up** calamity for their children or their homes after their death (vss. 19-20). **What do they care,** Job asks ironically (vs. 21), when they are dead?

21:23-33. In vss. 23-26 Job is not so much complaining that the divine justice is unfairly distributed as bemoaning the emptiness and irrationality of all

existence—dusty death awaits all men, rich and poor. Thereafter Job maintains that even "the man in the street" (presumably from his common-sense observation of life) could tell the friends that, far from the wicked man's home being invariably destroyed, he very often remains safe and secure (vss. 27-31). Perhaps with mingled wistfulness and irony, Job goes on to say that the wicked may even have a lovely funeral, a most honorable burial, and a pleasant last resting place (vss. 32-33).

21:34. If any confirmation were needed at this juncture that the theme of the book cannot be restricted to the problem of human suffering, we have it in this ch. Grievously offended by the friends' belief that the wicked inevitably are punished, demonstrably untrue to the facts of experience, Job is obsessed with the question of justice: he has been just, but he has been unjustly treated.

22:1-30. Eliphaz' Indictment. Eliphaz maintains—and in so doing reveals how shallow is his theology —that it is of no profit to God whether men are good or bad; only men themselves stand to gain from being righteous (vss. 2-3). So Eliphaz regales Job with what seems to him to be an irrefutable logic hard as nails: the righteous reap benefits, the wicked losses; Job is wicked and therefore a loser (vss. 4-11). Eliphaz brands Job as indeed a basely antisocial man (vs. 6-7, 9). But from all we learn elsewhere of Job's highly sensitive social conscience (e.g. ch. 31) we can only suppose that Eliphaz is compelled by the logic of his theory—that a big loser must be a big sinner—to conjure up out of his imagination the most dastardly crimes for Job.

22:8-20. Vs. 8 can hardly be taken to mean that part of Job's crime against society has been to leave the powerful unscathed in their power. This vs. should probably be transferred to the end of vs. 14 and be understood as part of the words of Job cited by Eliphaz. "Job holds," observes Eliphaz, "that God is indifferent to men's deeds [vss. 13-14] and that one practical consequence of his indifference is that the powerful lord it on the earth [vs. 8]." Eliphaz tries to counter Job's argument, of course, in the only way he knows: the proof of God's interest is that the good are automatically blessed with prosperity and the bad punished (vss. 15-20).

22:21-30. Apparently believing that Job still has some chance, Eliphaz proceeds to preach him a neat little sermon on repentance and its fruits: "Turn, Job, humble yourself; find all your riches in God and he will restore to you your old prosperity." But, as we discover from Job's next utterance, what he really wants is not the return of his old prosperity or the old creature comforts for his own sake but to engage in such conversation with God as would make genuine reconciliation possible.

23:1-24:25. Job's Quest for God. The friends have their God in their hand, so to speak. They presume to know exactly how he orders and measures the world's affairs. By contrast, in his anguish and restlessness of spirit Job is awaiting the coming of a high and unknown God far above the small God of the friends: **Oh, that I knew where I might find him** (23:3). Job is thus among the number of those profounder souls of the Bible who wait for God to come toward them, to reveal himself to them (cf. Isa. 45:15; Matt. 5:3-6; Luke 2:25, 38).

23:4-17. In his moment of waiting for that other God, Job almost thinks himself into his presence (vs. 4) and, in yet another of his outbursts of confidence, asserts that if once he could get God's ear he would win acquittal (vss. 5-7). But, as previously, his hope of being vindicated in a fair trial (vss. 10-12) is quickly swallowed up in his continued terror in the presence of God, the unsearchable God (vss. 8-9) of arbitrary and inflexible judgments (vss. 13-17).

24:1-25. In this ch. Job reverts to his theme of ch. 21: the wicked all too often get off scot-free. In the midst of his account of the various crimes of the wicked (vss. 2-4*a*, 13-17) there comes a series of poignant pictures of the terrible plight to which the **poor** are reduced by their cruel persecutors (vss. 4*b*-12). Vss. 18-24 are, through textual corruption, quite obscure or ambiguous. Following the RSV rendering we may take it that in vss. 18-20 Job is quoting the friends' view that evildoers are quickly destroyed, only to refute it in vss. 22-23. But that in vs. 24 Job should immediately contradict himself by speaking of the transitoriness of the wicked seems impossible; this vs. must be out of place.

25:1-27:23. The Dialogue Continued. This subject heading is vague, but so badly dislocated is the text of this final part of the 3rd cycle of speeches that we can hardly say anything more precise than simply that the dialogue is going on.

25:1-26:14. The 6 verses of ch. 25 are clearly but a fragment of Bildad's original speech. Ch. 26 is assigned to Job (vs. 1); but though the utterances about the marvelous handiworks of God in nature (vss. 5-14) could come from either Job or the friends, it is only by interpreting vss. 2-4 in a most unnatural way—as Job's ironical acknowledgment of the help he has received from Bildad's speech—that we can attribute them to Job. It seems better to take vs. 1 as an editorial insertion and think of ch. 26 as a continuation of Bildad's address in ch. 25. Thus Bildad is sarcastically charging Job with scaling God down to such a pygmy size that Job, a mere man, can dare to instruct him. James Moffatt translates vs. 2: "What a help you are to poor God! What a support to his failing powers!" Vss. 2-4 then connect naturally with what follows in vss. 5-14; after teasing Job about his presuming to help "poor God" Bildad chastens him with an account of the might and majesty of God in nature. **Abaddon** (26:6) is a poetic synonym for **Sheol** (see above on 3:11-19). On **Rahab** see above on 9:13-31.

27:1-23. In this ch. vss. 2-6 do sound like another genuine *cri du coeur* from Job—**Till I die I will not put away my integrity from me.** But vss. 7-23 once again express the philosophy of the friends that the trophies amassed by the wicked are taken away from them overnight. Perhaps they are the words of the missing Zophar, who does not appear at all for the 3rd round of speeches. Some scholars, accepting the text as it is—i.e. ch. 25 as Bildad's and the whole of chs. 26-27 as Job's—suggest that the author has greatly abbreviated Bildad's speech and has left Zophar out in order to show that the friends are now running out of arguments. The suggestion is more ingenious than convincing.

28:1-28. An Interpolated Hymn of Praise to Wisdom. The consensus of opinion among scholars is that this ch. is completely out of accord with its context. The frame of mind represented here is too tranquil and submissive to be Job's; we find him in fact as rebellious as ever in his next speech (cf. e.g. 30:20-23). Moreover, if Job had already attained to this view of things, he would, as it were, have reached his "conversion," and there would be no need of the divine speeches (chs. 38-41), since Job would already have learned the lesson contained in them.

Though we must regard ch. 28 as an interpolation, we should certainly have been the poorer for not having it. It ranks with Prov. 8 as one of the most magnificent poetical pieces in the whole range of the wisdom literature. The author of the poem (whether the author of the book or some other writer) is clearly an expert in ancient mineralogy and mining (vss. 2-11). In drawing a sharp contrast between man's unlimited genius for material achievement and his strictly limited understanding of the ways in which God orders the world and of the ways of men the poem has a direct applicability to our own age. We have come to exult in our technological genius and in our ever-increasing mastery and control over the physical universe, but **wisdom** eludes us, that wisdom which consists in the **fear of the Lord** and empowers both men and nations **to depart from evil.** The poet reminds us that that wisdom is with God and is always and only God's gift.

Assuming that this ch. is an interpolation, we have to ask why some editor should have inserted it at this point in the dialogue. Was there a reply by Job to Zophar's speech (27:7-23) which he found so outrageous that he felt the need to delete it and substitute this poem? Or did he think of this as a suitable place in the movement of the dialogue for a pause for quiet reflection before the denouement of God's direct confrontation of Job? A few scholars believe that the divine speech of chs. 38-41 is incomplete and affords no real solution to Job's problem. Accordingly they propose that ch. 28 is the true conclusion of God's address to Job and should follow ch. 41. But that is only a surmise, and a rather unlikely one.

29:1-25. Job's Remembrance of Happier Days. There is a deep pathos in Job's reminiscences of the "good old days" of his prosperity, when God looked on him with favor (vss. 2-5*a*), when he was secure in the companionship of his family and the possession of his wealth (vss. 5*b*-6), when he was most highly respected on every hand, even by the **princes** and **nobles** of the land (vss. 7-11), when he championed the cause of the afflicted and triumphed for them by outsmarting their oppressors (vss. 12-17), and when he dreamed hopeful dreams of a serene and peaceful end to his life (vss. 18-20). His return in vss. 21-25 to the theme of vss. 7-11, the esteem in which he was once everywhere held, prepares the way for the contrast he is about to make in ch. 30, the contempt now poured on him, and makes that contrast the more poignant.

30:1-31. The Contrast of His Present Misery. In the course of his speeches as we have seen, Job strikes up an abundance of themes and often changes rapidly from one to the other. So in vss. 1-15 it is far from easy to grasp the real point of his long description of the rogues and vagabonds who, excommunicated from all normal society, live like animals in the wilderness (vss. 3-8) and sally forth to attack him (vss. 9-15). Perhaps we should take these vss. as yet another indication of how acute and agonizing is Job's sense of alienation not only from God but from men. He is despised now even by the meanest of his fellows.

30:16-19. Job turns next to what most interpreters take to be an account of his own grievous bodily **affliction.** But the Hebrew of these vss., esp. vs. 18, is so confused that we can scarcely recover the original. Cf. the translation of vs. 18 by the eminent Jewish scholar N. H. Tur-Sinai: "In my cloth he disguiseth himself as an attorney; as 'my mouth' he clotheth himself in my coat." Tur-Sinai thinks of vss. 17-19 as depicting a dream in which Job sees a figure "disguised" as God's attorney, who in fact makes Job accuse himself.

30:20-31. With vss. 20-23 we are on surer ground. Job once more addresses God directly and charges him with deliberately turning a deaf ear to his pleas and making sport of him by tossing him around on the winds of suffering. In vss. 24-31 Job defends his right to **cry** to God for **help.** Who, left pitilessly to bear the burden of his own suffering, would not emit moans or howls as melancholy as those of **jackals** or **ostriches?**

31:1-40. *Job's Final Challenge to God.* This ch. is one of the most significant and moving in the whole book. Job issues his final challenge to God, not, as we might have expected from his previous Promethean outbursts, by a last gigantic thrust of the battering-ram against the ramparts of heaven, but by the more effective weapon of a quiet and sensitive defense of the honor and integrity of his own character and life. Job here utters his "negative confession"—so called because it resembles that found in the ancient Egyptian Book of the Dead —or his "oath of purgation."

However we entitle this ch., we cannot fail to see that it embodies a most exalted ethic, highlighting the inward wellsprings of genuine obedience to God's demand rather than any mere outward fulfillment of the prescriptions of a moral code or any exercise of a formal piety diligent in prayers and sacrifices. In this respect indeed it is worthy to be set beside the Sermon on the Mount—cf. e.g. vss. 1, 9 with Matt. 5:27-28; vs. 29 with Matt. 5:21-22; vs. 33 with Matt. 7:5; vs. 34 with Matt. 5:11-12.

Job's stress throughout is in fact on his own abiding concern for the welfare of others. He would not assault the honor of any woman (vs. 1), least of all the honor of his **neighbor's** wife (vss. 9-12), or refuse to listen to the case of his servant (vss. 13-15), or close his eyes to the needs of the **poor** (vss. 16-21). He would not make money his god nor secretly worship the **sun** and the **moon** (vss. 24-27). He has taken no joy in the downfall of his enemies (vss. 29-31). He has not been hypocritical nor impelled by **fear** of what the public might say (vss. 33-34). He has been honest and faithful in his dealings with his **land** (vss. 38-39).

Armed with this goodness that goes beyond the line of duty or any written code, Job is ready to approach God with head held high, **like a prince** (vs. 37) rather than a worm (cf. 25:6). Here is the climax of Job's contention with God, when by a

majestic self-assertion he even lords it over God himself. Job's whole defense of his honor and integrity in fact implies his conviction that he has dealt more faithfully with *his* world than God has done with his.

Job's ultimate protest should really set the stage for God's reply; ch. 38 follows most naturally immediately after this ch. The continuity is broken, however, and God's reply is held up for 6 chs. by the interruption of the long-winded Elihu.

V. Elihu's Intervention (32:1–37:24)

Nearly all scholars are now agreed that the Elihu speech has been interpolated into the original poem of Job. Elihu is mentioned nowhere else in the book. In the rest of the dialogue the friends' speeches alternate with those of Job, but Elihu stands out on his own and continues for 6 chs. without a break.

Most likely these chs. were composed by a later poet whose point of view was quite different from that of the original author. He felt the need to build a bridge between Job's challenge and God's response, dissatisfied as he was on the one side with the friends' efforts at countering Job (32:3, 5) and on the other side with the terms of God's reply.

32:6-33:7. *Elihu's Assertion of His Right to Speak.* Protocol has up to now imposed silence on Elihu. But now that the friends and Job are through he seizes his chance to talk. Though the friends have apparently capitulated to Job's arguments as unanswerable by man (32:13), Elihu will not; with irrepressible bombast he declares himself to be **full of words** (32:18) and bursting to speak (32:19-20). That he has something new and relevant to contribute he does not for a moment doubt, something communicated directly to him from God and superior to the traditions of the past (32:8-10). Job has asked for an umpire to mediate between God and himself (9:33) and we may reasonably suppose that the author of this interpolation intends his spokesman to fulfill some such mediatorial role, since he presents Elihu as a skilled exegete of the ways of God on the one hand (32:8-9) and on the other as sympathetic in his understanding of men— **Behold, no fear of me need terrify you** (33:7).

33:8-33. *God's Communication with Man.* His right to speak established, Elihu goes on to confute Job's assertion that God does not answer him (vss. 12-13). He insists that God does have his various ways of communicating with man, even though man may not understand them, e.g. by dreams or visions (vss. 15-17) or by the discipline of suffering itself (vss. 19-22). One of Elihu's most distinctive emphases is the disciplinary aspect of suffering. As part of his defense of God's overall strategy in human affairs Elihu is prepared to argue that in man's suffering God is no absentee but may be speaking most profoundly and effectively just there and then. He maintains that an **angel** of God (vs. 23) may enable a man even on the threshold of death to grasp the logic of God's ways with him. So he may see in his sufferings the hand of God and God's call to that repentance which leads to the recovery of new life and health. Eventually he may sing songs of thanksgiving, a healed and forgiven penitent among the worshiping congregation.

34:1-37. God's Justice. But the foundation pillar of Elihu's whole edifice of arguments is his exposition of the impartial justice of God, over against Job's complaint that God had **taken away** his **right** (vs. 5). God is no ordinary despot (vss. 10-12). He is the one who deigns to govern the universe (vss. 13-15), and all his works and dispensations are absolutely just, since in no way does he show regard to **human** pretensions (vss. 16-28).

34:29-37. This is another of those sections where the text is so corrupt it is almost impossible to reconstruct it. E.g. the Hebrew of vs. 31 reads lit.: "For to God one says, 'I have carried; I will not act corruptly.'" The Jewish scholar Tur-Sinai makes of this: "For he hath said unto God: 'I have lent but I ask no surety.'"

35:1-16. God's Independence of Man. In ch. 9 Job argued that it is all one whether a man is righteous or wicked, for the limitless power of a God beyond sanction makes justice for man impossible. Elihu now inverts Job's argument, asserting that the very fact which insures the impartiality of God's justice is his majestic detachment from the world of men (chs. 35-37). God is higher above man than the **clouds;** he can be neither affected nor coerced by **wickedness** or **righteousness.** Man's actions have consequences only for himself (vss. 5-8). But consequences they do have, as Elihu seems to argue in the rest of this ch. (the text of vss. 9-16 is once again confused and problematical). In human relationships there are both oppressors and victims of oppression. If the victims cry to God for help and are not answered, that is not so much a slur on God's justice as a sign that the victims—like Job (vss. 15-16)—are lacking in genuine religious feeling.

36:1-23. God's Revelation in Affliction. Elihu maintains that the storms of affliction blow on **wicked** and **righteous** men alike (vss. 5-9). Everything depends on the temper in which the suffering man receives his affliction. Those who perceive God's **instruction** in their anguish are turned away from impending moral disaster (vss. 10-11). But if they do not hear the call of God within the very urgency of pain itself, they separate themselves from the God who is to be found in the order of things and become broken and defeated men (vss. 12-15). Job's great fault, declares Elihu, has been his inability or unwillingness to see past his struggle to the reality of God or to sense the meanings of God in his agony (vss. 17-23).

36:24-37:24. God's Power. So Elihu summons Job to turn and magnify the God whose works are ineffably great, past finding out. His description of the irresistible force of storms and the grandeurs of the natural world anticipates the speech of God (chs. 38-41), in which God himself describes the wonders of the cosmos. But there is one salient difference. While the speech of God simply sets forth the glories of nature in staggering array and leaves the hearer to draw his own conclusions, Elihu philosophizes and makes his own applications—e.g. the **lightning** brings warning of God's judgment (36:33) and the **clouds** he uses at will either to reveal the flashing of his anger or to dispense showers of blessing (37:11-13).

The author of the Elihu interpolation has set himself the task of going deeper than the friends in meeting Job's case. In a measure he succeeds. He is a less naïve retributionist than the friends (35:3-16). He appeals to man's rational capacity for discerning in his suffering the very hand of God. For him Job's error lies in his ignorance; he does not know how to decipher the communications from God in his agony (34:35-36). But the Elihu author's solution could never have satisfied the original author. In that author's view what Job is seeking is not a moralizing answer to the problem of his suffering but, as a representative of Everyman, the recovery before God of that justification of himself which he feels has been lost.

VI. GOD'S CONFRONTATION OF JOB (38:1–42:6)

Originally, as we have noted (see above on 31:1-40), the challenge to God presented by Job (31:35-37) must have been immediately followed by God's answer. The response of God, when it does come, issues from the **whirlwind** (38:1), the traditional accompaniment of God's appearances in the OT (cf. e.g. I Kings 19:11; Ps. 18:9-10; Ezek. 1:4). Job has complained about God's silence (e.g. 9:11). God now breaks the silence and addresses Job, but not really on equal terms as man to man, for the divine voice is wrapped in the mystery of the storm's center. If anything, the unbridgeable distance between God and man is increased. Job, who wants to come before God like a prince (31:37), is scaled down to less than beggar's stature, dwarfed by the opening fusillade of God's questions.

38:2-41:34. God's Majesty and Mystery in Creation. As God's speech develops, it becomes clear that the divine voice is strangely noncommittal. God passes no verdict on Job as either innocent or guilty. Nor does he prescribe any nostrum of salvation or medicine of immortality for him. Instead he simply overwhelms Job with his infinite power as it is manifested first in his majestic control of all natural phenomena: in his measuring the earth at creation's dawning (38:4-7); in his command over the chaos monster of the **sea** (38:8-11; see above on 3:4-10), **light** and **darkness** (38:12-21), and **snow** and **rain** and **ice** (38:22-30); in his ordering of the movements of the constellations (38:31-33) and of the **clouds** (38:34-38).

38:39-39:30. The divine discourse has its own singular shape and form. The veil is lifted on one riddle of the cosmos and Job is challenged to penetrate it, only to find another more baffling riddle lying behind the first, waiting to stretch his comprehension and imagination to the utmost. From the marvels of earth and sky Job is drawn on to contemplate the marvels of the animal creation: the **lion** (38:39-40), **raven** (38:41), **mountain goats** (39:1-4), **wild ass** (39:5-8), **wild ox** (39:9-12), **ostrich** hen (39:13-18), **horse** (39:19-25), **hawk** (39:26), and mountain **eagle** (39:27-30)—all creatures beyond man's ken but within the universal scope of God's providential care (cf. Pss. 104; 145:16).

40:15-41:34. Two other marvels of the animal creation are described at length in terms partly realistic and partly mythological. **Behemoth** (40:15-24) seems to be the hippopotamus—known in the Nile but not the **Jordan**—and **Leviathan** (ch. 41; see above on 3:4-10) the crocodile. Many scholars believe part or all of these 2 descriptions to be a later addition to the book.

The first instinct of the modern reader is to wonder what kind of sublime irrelevance all this is with which God regales Job. And perhaps our first inclination is to "Christianize" the conclusion of Job. Such interpretations of the book have tended to translate the Christian's saving experience of the grace of God in the cross of Jesus Christ into Job's situation, as if Job too were made at last, through the divine encounter, the recipient of God's grace and love. But to do so is to transgress the proper limits of the book by moving it some cents. ahead of its own true time and place.

We have in fact to acknowledge that the whole of the divine speech betrays nothing of God's loving concern for man or of the possibility of restoration. If the "solution" of Job's plight consists only in God's finally stretching out before him the canvas of the incomprehensible cosmos, and if such a solution seems inadequate to the present-day reader, esp. the Christian reader, we must remember that the theology of the author moves within the same orbit as that of the wisdom literature generally, and that wisdom theology expressed itself in utterances about the greatness of God in creation.

So much for the negative side of the concluding divine discourse. There is, however, a more positive —if yet not Christian—side. Job's endless yearning to be confronted with God is answered. God does speak to him. Harsh and intimidating as are the questions God puts to him, they are demands for a response, and God's recognition of Job's freedom to respond is at the same time an acknowledgment of his responsibility. The dignity of his being is thus respected by God; he counts enough to be approached and interrogated. More than that, the God who interrogates him is one who turns his face in concern toward his whole creation. This much we can say is implicit in the picture of God's limitless power over the works of nature. From God's just governance of all his creatures, glorified in the divine discourse, there may also be inferred his justice toward the greatest of his handiworks, man himself. Of course this overarching universal justice of God cannot be comprehended by man; man can only adore it, like the morning stars which sang together when God laid the foundation of the earth (38:7).

42:1-6. Job's Response. The divine discourse has offered nothing to consolidate Job's vestigial faith (cf. 6:2; 13:18; 19:25) that human righteousness would be vindicated in the end. Instead its import has been that the measurements of the Creator are not those of his creature, that God is not the custodian of our man-made systems or the guardian of our inferior ethical judgments. Before the God of the whirlwind the little God of retributive justice to whom the friends cling has been reduced to what he really is, an idol fabricated by men, designed to adjust life's inequalities and anomalies and to administer justice as men understand it and measure it. Before the God of the whirlwind Job's momentary hopes of a vindicator have been dashed. The insistent defender of his own self-righteousness is crushed at last by the conviction of his own creaturely finitude. Before this Most High God he has no claim left, no merit of his own. He has found the God before whom all conditioned questions and complaints and pretensions disappear. In confrontation with this God he can only **repent in dust and ashes.**

42:3-4. In 2 lines of this final brief speech of submission Job uses almost the very words with which God first questioned him out of the whirlwind (vss. 3a, 4b; cf. 38:2, 3b). Conceivably Job repeats the opening question addressed to him by God as if to admit the rebuke implied in it—"Yes, I have hidden counsel without knowledge." Conceivably he cites the challenge to **declare** the answers to God's questions before confessing his inability to meet it. But more probably, since the intrusion of these short segments mars the poetic structure here, some scribe wrote them down as marginal comments beside Job's own final words and they were incorporated into the text by a later copyist.

42:5-6. Unfortunately the last 2 lines of Job's recantation, **Therefore I despise myself, and repent in dust and ashes** (vs. 6), are of very uncertain translation. It is not impossible, with some commentators, to take the words in a quite different way: "Therefore, though I am melting away, I am comforted in regard to dust and ashes." Perhaps the best translation is: "Therefore I abhor and repudiate [all my words, sitting] on dust and ashes" (on ashes as a sign of grief and mourning see above on 2:1-13; cf. Isa. 58:5; Jonah 3:6).

However, the general sense of Job's confession and submission is not in doubt, and is well summed up in the quite unambiguous vs. 5: **I had heard of thee by the hearing of the ear, but now my eye sees thee.** In the outcome, through the dark night of anxiety and despair, Job has encountered the answer to his predicament. The answer Job finds is no theoretical or philosophical or moralistic solution to his problem, but an experience. The vision spoken of is not, of course, the actual sight of any form or appearance of God. Job could not "see" the God shrouded in the mystery of the storm's center. What is meant is that for him hearsay has now been transformed into firsthand personal confrontation with the God who, on the last frontier of Job's existence, bestows on him a new power in a new way.

VII. THE EPILOGUE: JOB'S RECOVERY OF SELF
(42:7-17)

The majority of interpreters hold that the prose narrative of the epilogue, which belongs to the same folk-tale world as the prologue, cannot have been part of the original book and in fact ruins its unity. They claim that its fairy-story ending, with all living happily ever after, flagrantly contradicts the message the author intended to convey, his condemnation of the friends' theory of divine reward and punishment. There is moreover, it is pointed out, a radical inconsistency in that in the divine speech climaxing the poem Job is condemned but in the epilogue he is praised (vs. 7).

But this view that the prose epilogue is no integral part of the original work may be questioned first on literary grounds. Such inconsistency as there is may be accounted for by the assumption that in adopting the old folk tale as the framework for his own composition the author was working with prefabricated materials which he did not feel free to alter too extensively.

The majority view may also be questioned on thematic or theological grounds. The hard reality of Job's plight has been his alienation. Alienated from his family, from his friends, from time, from God, Job's anguish is the anguish of the dissolution of his existence, the anguish of self-estrangement. When Job's tragedy is understood thus, the epilogue can be construed as a meaningful conclusion to his encounter with the Absolute Being of the whirlwind. It may be taken as symbolizing, in characteristic Hebrew mythopoeic fashion, Job's recovery of his own true existence through his meeting with this transcendent Being. His family is restored (vs. 11). The people and things from which he was alienated are returned to him. Time is no longer excruciatingly out of joint for him, for he lives in felicity for length of days (vss. 16-17). The dislocation of his existence is healed. Before God he has become a whole man once more. He has recovered his own being through his experience of Being.

Among OT books this is perhaps most of all a book for our time. Job could find no solace in the traditional little predictable God of the friends. No more can our generation find any genuine solace in the small God of many a church square and market place, who is no bigger or better than the perpetuator of our human values, the custodian of our particular way of life, the preserver of our national prosperity, the protector of our religious denomination. Such idol-gods as this, we should know, have died a thousand deaths in our cent., in the carnage of the Pacific Islands, in the North African deserts, in the battlefields of Europe, in the gas chambers, in the nuclear fallout that drifts eerily across our skies, in the barriers at the Brandenburg Gate of Berlin. Craving an answer in our darkening history as Job did in his own thick darkness, we may remember that Job's answer was found, not in the friends' talk about a God who puts everything to right in the world's affairs, nor even in what God says and does, but in God himself.

Precisely at this point, where the book shows us a man encountering, to the recovery of his true life and selfhood, the God who is God out of the darkest places of anguish and despair rather than out of the habitations of comfort and security, it both speaks a trenchant word to us and anticipates the heart of the NT message. The Most High God is to be found in unexpected ways and places, and none more unexpected than Golgotha, the place of a skull, where there is neither comfort nor security but a great agony, where Jesus of Nazareth is crucified and God may be met in his grace and truth.

THE PSALMS

Lawrence E. Toombs

Since the Psalter, like any hymnbook, has no continuity of thought, a running commentary on its content is impossible. In order to deal with the many repetitions of words, ideas, and situations in ps. after ps. numerous cross references are necessary. To minimize the confusion which the welter of references is likely to cause, the reader is advised first to read the ps. in which he is interested without commentary, next to study the commentary skipping the parenthetical references, and finally to read ps. and commentary side by side, checking all references and biblical quotations.

Authorship and Date. The titles of many of the pss. reflect the view which prevailed for cents. that David was their author. It is now clear that the theory of Davidic authorship cannot be maintained. Many scholars have even insisted that the majority of the pss. are postexilic and that a large number date to the Maccabean period (2nd cent. B.C.). Within the last half cent., however, archaeological discoveries in the Near East have placed at our disposal the literatures of Israel's neighbors: the Babylonians, Assyrians, Egyptians, and Canaanites. This new knowledge makes clear that Israel originated neither the poetic form of the pss. (see "The Literary Forms of the OT," pp. 1077-81) nor their use in worship. Poetic technique and vocabulary were borrowed from peoples who had attained a high degree of culture before Israel emerged as a nation.

In the light of this ancient Near Eastern literature it is probable that the original of almost every ps. was composed in preexilic times for use in public worship during the period of the monarchy. Once introduced into worship, however, a ps. would naturally be adapted and revised to make it appropriate to changing circumstances. Pss. originally spoken by the king at a time of national stress came to be used by individuals for crises in their personal lives. An ancient prisoner-of-war song might be sung by the exiles in Babylon to express their homesickness for Jerusalem and the temple. The Psalter is thus the product of cents. of Israelite worship. It grew, changed, and shifted in emphasis under the stimulus of a changing political and religious environment. For most of the pss., therefore, a search for clues to date and author does not repay the effort.

A more fruitful approach is to investigate the literary type to which each ps. belongs and the worship setting in which it was used. In this way the ps. ceases to be a sentimental lyric or a relic from a lifeless past and is seen as a vital part of dynamic and meaningful worship, affirming the faith of living men in the face of the triumphs and disasters of real life. Accordingly this commentary does not attempt to date individual pss. except in the rare cases where a specific historical allusion gives a substantial clue to the date. Unless otherwise noted the pss. are assumed to belong to the period of the monarchy before the exile of 586 B.C. and to be of unknown, and often of composite, authorship.

Poetic Form. Judged by any standard the pss. are poetic compositions of the highest order, but unfortunately the full beauty of the poetry does not appear in translation. The most obvious loss is the *rhythm* of the original. Hebrew meter did not take account of all the syllables in the sentence, but for metrical purposes counted only those which carried an accent. Thus a Hebrew metrical foot consists of one accented syllable and an indefinite number of unaccented syllables associated with it. The result is a rhythm which has, not the mathematical regularity of a ticking clock, but the irregular beat of waves upon a shore.

English translations do, however, preserve the most conspicuous characteristic of Hebrew poetry, its *parallelism.* This literary device consists of a repetition of the same idea, or a balancing contrast to it, in 2 or more successive statements. In its simplest form the members of the parallelism correspond word for word to one another:

> No man who practices deceit
> shall dwell in my house;
> no man who utters lies
> shall continue in my presence (101:7).

Several types of parallelism, with examples of each, are described in the article "The Literary Forms of the OT" (see pp. 1077-81). A skillful poet could weave these threads of parallelism into a brilliant tapestry of words. The changing patterns capture the attention of the reader and lead his mind effortlessly from one idea to the next, now lingering on a significant thought, now leaping boldly forward to a new insight.

The literary principles by which the pss. were divided into longer units are unknown. Occasionally there is a built-in guide to the place where the stanza division should fall—a refrain (e.g. Pss. 42-43), the occurrence of "selah" (see below) at the end of a stanza (e.g. Ps. 3), or a change in speaker signalized by a shift in the pronouns (e.g. 85:7-8). Usually, however, the division into strophes must be made conjecturally on the basis of major breaks in the sense.

The acrostic poem is an outstanding exception to this general uncertainty about strophes. Several pss., usually of late date, were composed using the artificial technique of beginning each successive unit with the letters of the alphabet in sequence. The acrostic poems in the Psalter are Pss. 9–10; 25; 34; 37; 111; 112; 119; 145. Ps. 119 is the most complex acrostic. It has a stanza for each letter of the Hebrew alphabet, and each line of the stanza begins with the appropriate letter.

The recent discovery of a large body of Canaanite poetic literature at the site of the ancient city of Ugarit shows clearly that the Hebrews did not originate their poetic technique. Although they went to school to the Canaanites in poetic matters, the Israelites outstripped their teachers. Nothing in Canaanite literature approaches the majestic style and elevated religious thought of the Psalter.

Ancient Near Eastern Background. Lyric poetry and sacred dance are ancient aspects of man's approach to God in worship, probably reaching back to prehistoric times. The great centers of culture in the Near East refined the primitive poetic expression and gave it artistic forms. Except for the Hymn to the Sun God, attributed to Pharaoh Akh-en-Aton (1369-1353 B.C.), Egyptian religious poetry had little direct influence on Israel. The sacred literature of the Tigris-Euphrates Valley, however, contributed strongly to Hebrew poetic tradition. Beginning in remote antiquity with the sensitive and artistic Sumerians, Mesopotamian poetic forms developed in a straight line through the Assyrians and Babylonians and produced a wealth of hymns, songs of penitence and thanksgiving, prayers, odes, and wisdom poems used in the daily service of the temples and at the state festivals as well as in the private worship of individuals.

The state festivals were the occasions which called forth the richest expression of ancient poetic art. At these times the entire community gathered to affirm its faith and to draw from its religious resources. At the high points of the festival epic poems were recited while king, priests, and people dramatically enacted the events which the poems described.

Throughout the Near East in Sumerian, Assyrian, Babylonian, Hurrian, Hittite, and Canaanite cultures the crucial festival was that of the new year. Human society was not regarded as autonomous or self-determining. Mysterious but potent forces controlled the destiny of men and states, and no society could prosper unless it brought itself into harmony with those invisible powers. The turn of the year, when a new cycle of existence began, was fraught with potentialities for good or evil. Society therefore brought all its resources to bear on insuring that in the new cycle of days the human world would be favorably related to the superhuman order.

In Babylon the new year festival lasted 11 days, most of its ritual taking place in the forecourt of the temple, where it could be viewed by the people. On each of the first 7 days of the feast the images of the god and his consort were carried from the temple to their pleasure house. These gay and colorful processions were accompanied by joyful hymns of praise.

The next phase of the ceremonial was a period of mourning for the dead god. The ancients interpreted their cycle of 2 seasons as a struggle, perpetually renewed, between the rain-bearing god of fertility and the sinister lord of death and drought. During the dry season the fertility god was in the underworld and the earth was under the rule of the god of death. During the period of mourning the king assumed the role of a penitent and was struck and humiliated by the priests in the temple. The city and its sacred places were purified by ritual means from all uncleanness in preparation for the return of the god. When he reappeared, the people greeted him with joy and carried his idol in triumph to the temple.

But the evil powers which threatened the community were not yet overcome, and the worshipers accordingly recited and enacted an epic poem describing the combat between the high god and the monster of chaos. The monster was destroyed and the ordered universe established. Recitation of this myth brought the creative powers which had been operative at the beginning into renewed activity against the destructive forces which threatened the ordered life of society. The god was then formally enthroned in his temple for another year, and his first act was to fix the "destinies" of nature and society for the days ahead.

This pagan ritual, in which poetry and song played so spectacular a part, has direct relevance for the study of the pss. The religious procession, the lamentation, the sorrow and penitence, the central role of the king, the emphasis on creation, and the determination by the deity of the destiny of man, society, and nature are all strongly present in the Psalter. Through the Canaanites, Israel inherited from Mesopotamia the themes and vocabulary, the technique and cultic use of poetry. They put this borrowed apparatus into the service of their distinctive covenant faith (see "The Religion of Israel," pp. 1150-58) and out of old material created a new thing, a body of religious poetry of unparalleled beauty and insight.

Covenant Renewal and Holy War. In the premonarchical period Israel was a loosely organized association of tribes, each of which conducted its own affairs and lived in almost complete independence of the other members of the league. Annually, however, the tribes came together to renew their common allegiance to the Lord and to his covenant. The ritual of covenant renewal has not come down to us, but it may be tentatively reconstructed as follows:

The tribes assembled at the designated place, probably the sacred area of the city of Shechem, and as they came they identified themselves as authentic members of the covenant league. The leader, serving as a kind of mediator of the covenant, recounted God's mighty acts in delivering Israel from Egypt and giving her a homeland in Canaan (cf. Josh. 24:1-15). The assembly responded to God's deed by hearing the covenant law and by pledging allegiance to it. The ceremony concluded with blessings for those who obeyed and curses on those who violated the covenant.

God's mighty acts in the formation of his people are the starting point of all distinctively Israelite theological thought (see "The Religion of Israel," pp. 1150-58), and many pss. reflect one or more portions of the covenant renewal ritual.

The tribes came together also to fight the wars of the LORD. If any member of the tribal league was threatened, messengers sped to all the tribes to sound the ram's horn (see below on 81:1-5b) and gather the warriors together. Once assembled, the soldiers sought a sign that the battle was one of which God approved. When this had been obtained, perhaps through a prophet (cf. I Kings 22), the army was consecrated as a band of sacred persons and awaited the coming of the LORD and his heavenly hosts to lead the troops into battle (cf. II Sam. 5:24). The trust in the LORD, which was essential to success in the holy war (see below on 14:5; 20:6-9), and his theophany, or appearance to his people (see below on 11:4-7a; 18:7-19), are only 2 of the many influences of the assembly for battle upon the structure and thought of the Psalter.

Agricultural Festivals. As Israel settled in Canaan and became increasingly a farming community, it adopted and adapted the agricultural feasts of the Canaanites, which in their turn reflected the ritual patterns and ideas of general Near Eastern culture. The earliest Hebrew calendars indicate 3 principal festivals: unleavened bread, to which passover was attached; weeks at the beginning of the grain harvest; and ingathering at the end of the fruit harvest (Exod. 23:14-17; 34:18-23). Ingathering was later called tabernacles, or booths, from the practice of living in temporary shelters erected in the fields (Deut. 16:13-16). These were pilgrimage festivals at which every male Israelite was expected to present himself; and the sacred places must at these times have overflowed with pilgrims, joyful or sad depending on the state of the crops for that year.

The biblical descriptions of ancient festivals are so sketchy that we can form no precise idea of the ritual by which they were celebrated. Combining knowledge gained from Near Eastern studies with indications in the biblical text, scholars have reconstructed a new year festival and a feast of the enthronement of the LORD. It is impossible to demonstrate conclusively the ritual, or even the existence, of these festivals; but they provide a theoretical setting in which the pss. have living meaning, and undoubtedly in some respects at least they correspond to the facts.

An Israelite Festival. In earliest times the Hebrew new year began in autumn at the feast of ingathering. When Judah became a vassal of Babylon (609 B.C.) she adopted the Babylonian year, which began in the spring. Let us assume that during the monarchy Israel observed an autumnal new year festival and attempt to reconstruct a tentative and theoretical outline of its ritual.

This would be a pilgrimage festival, and throngs of pilgrims would crowd into the sacred place. As they came they would sing of their adventures along the road and of the guiding power of God by which they had been brought safely to their journey's end. The priests would meet the procession at the steps leading to the temple and welcome them with songs of praise and calls to worship. Those about to enter the sanctuary would question the priests as to the qualifications for admission, and the priests would reply with appropriate answers. This question-and-answer ritual before the gates gave rise to such "entrance liturgies" as Pss. 15; 24:1-6.

The assembled congregation would then expose itself to the purifying judgment and justice of God. Prophetic spokesmen declared God's verdict concerning the nation's loyalty to or violation of the covenant, and the people confessed their national and personal sin. Now the ritual of covenant renewal (see above) would be conducted, binding every Israelite to wholehearted allegiance to the covenant God for the year which lay ahead. In this part of the ritual God's dealings with Israel from the time of the patriarchs to the conquest of Canaan were recalled in dramatic recitation (e.g. Ps. 105).

The festival then passed into a mood of rejoicing as the people, newly pledged to the covenant, welcomed the LORD as king. This was not an enthronement ritual in the strict sense of the word, since, unlike the dying-and-rising gods of paganism, the LORD had never relinquished his rule. It was rather the nation's recognition of the kingly majesty of God and acknowledgment of his rule over Israel. At this point in the ceremonial the ark of the covenant, the symbolic throne of the LORD, was carried in procession up the slope of Mt. Zion to its resting place in the temple, the glad crowds singing the praise of God the King, mighty ruler of the universe and of human history.

The Jerusalem Cult. This theoretical description of the Israelite new year festival combines motifs of the premonarchical covenant renewal ceremony with themes similar to those of the Babylonian and Canaanite new year feasts. Where would such a fusion take place? The most reasonable answer is, in Jerusalem. The city was not conquered until the reign of David, but soon after it was added to his possessions it became the religious center of his realm, a change in status signalized by the bringing to it of the ark.

Before its capture by David Jerusalem was already an important religious center. Hebrew tradition concedes that its priest-king was an authentic minister of Abraham's God (Gen. 14:17-24). The deity worshiped there was "God most High." He was revered as the king of the gods, the God above the gods, and his sovereignty expressed itself particularly in his creative activity. Faith in God as creator was not a crucial part of Israel's covenant religion, which focused instead on God's saving acts in history and in particular on the events of the Exodus. In the Jerusalem temple the Jebusite creation faith and Israel's historically oriented religion were brought into a splendid unity.

The theological basis of this unity was incorporated in the formula, repeatedly used in the pss., the LORD's "steadfast love and faithfulness" (e.g. 25:10; 26:3). The first term refers properly to God's mighty acts of deliverance in Israel's history by which he created and sustained his people, but under the influence of the Jerusalem cult the concept was broadened to include every aspect of his government of the world. (cf. Ps. 136). God's faithfulness is his absolute reliability in word and deed. Consistent with himself and his own purpose, he will never abandon or deceive his people.

This formula may be rendered by a single word, "righteousness," or "justice." The divine justice is the decree, unalterable and perfect, by which the LORD enforces his order in nature and human nature, in world history and in the life of the covenant people. In the natural world God's righteousness is manifested by his conquest of the unruly powers of chaos and disorder, often symbolized by the sea. In the world of men divine justice characteristically takes the side of the downtrodden and oppressed, for exploitation in any form was to the Hebrew mind a violation of the ordering and harmonizing purpose of God. Thus Israel's national enemies will be destroyed because they interpose their will against God's purpose for his people, and the Israelite who places himself in a position of oppressive superiority to his fellow citizens stands in the path of God's destructive judgment.

The creation faith of the Jerusalem cult looked forward to the time when by the destruction or conversion of the LORD's enemies creation would be complete and the divine order established and recognized universally. Before that consummation the nations would gather against Jerusalem; but, invulnerable under God's protection, the city would survive and her enemies perish. This aspect of Jebusite theology contributed not a little to the development of eschatological thought in Israel (see "The Apocalyptic Literature," pp. 1106-09).

The combination of Israelite and Jebusite themes which went on so vigorously in the temple can be seen in the way the Zion pss. (discussed below) play on and combine a variety of divine names. Yahweh ("the LORD," the personal name of Israel's God, to be distinguished from occasional occurrences of the title Adonai, "Lord," meaning "master" or "ruler") is also called El (general Semitic name for the father and king of the gods, translated "God"), Elohim (a plural form of El, also translated "God"), and El elohim ("God of gods"). He is given the title "LORD of Hosts" (i.e. armies), a name stemming from the holy war tradition. On occasion the names given him connect him with the traditions of the patriarchs and of the 12-tribe league—"God of Abraham" and "God of Jacob." In addition, and often in the same ps., titles which suggest his creative and world-ruling power are used, e.g. "God Most High" and "God Almighty."

A striking aspect of Jebusite religious practice was the priest-king who was head both of the state and of the cult, the leader in war and in worship. The kings of the Davidic line took up the traditions of the priest-kings of Jerusalem and frequently appear in the pss. as mediators between God and man. The special status of the king accounts for the presence in the Psalter of a number of songs in praise of the Davidic monarchy (the "royal pss." discussed below).

The ancient traditions of holy war were attached to the temple worship through the figure of the king, who replaced the judge as the leader of the LORD's armies. This transfer was made easier by the fact that in both the Jerusalem cult and the holy war ideology the expectation of God's theophany—his self-revelation to his people—played a large part. The consciousness of God's willingness to draw near to his people, one of the most pervasive theological assumptions of the pss., arises from this expectation.

Ps. Types. Modern research on the pss. begins with Hermann Gunkel's attempt (1926) to classify the pss. according to literary type, employing literary criteria and using content and idea only as minor

and supporting evidence. The scheme presented here follows that of Gunkel with only minor modifications.

Hymns. This category includes Pss. 8; 19:1-6; 33; 65; 100; 103-105; 111; 113; 114; 115; 117; 134-136; 145-150. The hymn consists of 3 elements: (a) a call to praise, (b) a statement of the motive or reason for praise, and (c) a renewed summons to praise. The fundamental expression of Israel's approach to God, the hymn is almost startlingly God-centered. It lifts the eyes and heart of the worshiper from his own crises and problems to the God whom the congregation has assembled to honor. It follows, therefore, that God is praised, not so much for what he gives to his people, as for what he is and for what, out of his majestic nature, he does. Praise is most frequently directed to the "name" and the "glory" of God. The first of these words refers to his active, mighty, saving presence with his people, the 2nd to his absolute authority as ruler of the world and of human events.

It is not possible to specify a single cultic setting for the hymns. They were used in the daily service, in connection with sacrifices of all kinds, frequently during every festival, and probably also by individuals in their private worship. Ideally praise, publicly offered in the temple, was merely the climax of a national and individual life which was in every part an act of praise, being lived in the presence and under the authority of God.

Hymns of Zion. These hymns include Pss. 46; 48; 76; 87. In them the worship of the congregation seems to be directed, not to God, but to the temple on Mt. Zion. Closer examination shows, however, that the temple is valued, not for its own sake or for any power intrinsic to it, but as the earthly "dwelling place" of the LORD. He chose this site to be the point of contact between himself and his people, and although the heavens cannot contain him, he graciously causes his saving presence (his "name") to dwell in the temple. There he appears to his people in judgment and deliverance, and within the courts of the temple they find his protection and draw near to him in worship. The hymns of Zion are therefore in reality praises of the presence of the God of Zion.

Enthronement Pss. The cultic setting of these specialized hymns—Pss. 29; 47; 93; 95-99—has been described above in connection with the New Year festival. As the festal procession bearing the ark approaches the temple, the people pour out their praise of God's sovereignty over the world and men. His triumph over chaos in every form rings through the poems. Majestic in holiness and power, he is the supreme warrior-king who will overcome all who oppose his universal rule. This group of pss. provides the classic statement of the OT doctrine of the sovereignty of God.

Lament Pss. These poems, which form the largest group in the Psalter, are constructed in 4 sections: (a) a brief invocation of God, often no more than the divine name; (b) a cry for hearing and help; (c) a statement of the nature and causes of the misfortune; and (d) a prayer for deliverance. The pathos of these pss. is due in no small measure to the pendulumlike swings of the poetry from despair to confidence, from the psalmist's personal misery to the greatness and love of God. A single ps. may have several such oscillations.

Suffering or disaster of any kind may provide the occasion for a lament, but the underlying motive for the prayer is not the disaster itself but the alienation from God which it produces. Disease, poverty, abuse, sin, oppression break the mood of praise and cut man off from God in radical loneliness. This was especially true for the Israelite, who regarded suffering as punishment for sin. Anyone under affliction was likely to be mocked by his enemies and shunned by his friends as a sinner under the wrath of God. The Hebrew could not sweep aside his sense of guilt as something unreal or unworthy; he had to deal with it in the context of worship, and consequently he was frequently in the mood of lamentation.

The prayer for deliverance often includes a "vow." The sufferer pledged that if he obtained relief from his anguish he would make such and such an offering or perform some specified service. His vow was not an attempt to bribe God but evidence of the seriousness of his desire for deliverance and the reality of his confidence in God.

Laments were sung both by individuals during personal crises and by the community in times of national disaster.

Individual Laments. This literary type includes Pss. 3–7; 13; 17; 22; 25; 26; 28; 31; 35; 38; 39; 42–43; 51; 54–57; 59; 61; 63; 64; 69–71; 86; 88; 102; 109; 120; 130; 140–143. The lament form probably originated in the ancient function of the temple as a place of asylum or sanctuary. Ordinary legal cases were dealt with by the elders of the village courts or the judges of the royal courts in the principal cities. When a case was too difficult for these bodies, it could be brought to the temple for adjudication by God himself. The problem might be one which did not lend itself to purely legal solution, such as malicious gossip or the lying accusations of a whispering campaign against a prominent citizen. Or the contention might be directly between God and the sufferer. If he felt himself to be afflicted with disease because of his sin, no human court could acquit him. His only recourse was to the LORD's tribunal in the temple.

The ritual for the presentation of a legal case in the temple is unknown, but indications in the pss. permit us to attempt a reconstruction. In the presence of the priests the one who had sought sanctuary stated his case. He did so in conventional language which portrayed him in the grip of death, drowning in the sea, slipping into the underworld, entangled in the hunter's net, mired in a bog, or torn to pieces by savage beasts. He declared his innocence of the specific charges against him, inviting the searching scrutiny of God to determine his guilt or innocence.

During his defense the victim often denounced his enemies in vigorous terms and heaped terrible curses upon them. These passages are couched in the traditional language of Near Eastern denunciations. The violence of the words is due to the fact that in the pagan cultures in which this literary form originated the enemies were often sorcerers attempting to destroy the sufferer by magical means. He sought to turn the evil back upon its perpetrators. In early times the innocence of the suppliant may have been tested by means of an ordeal, but only faint traces of this practice remain in the lament pss.

After presenting his case in the correct ritual form, the suppliant spent the night in the temple precincts awaiting a sign of divine favor, which might be given in a dream or orally by a priest or cult prophet. Some of the pss. contain examples of the "oracles of salvation" spoken for the comfort and encouragement of the sufferer (e.g. 55:22). Since the assurance of salvation came after a night's vigil in the temple, the morning was regarded as the time when God revealed his salvation. Assured of deliverance, the suppliant paid his vows, usually a thank offering and a public testimony to the goodness of God, and departed.

When the ritual of sanctuary was no longer practiced, the various elements of the pattern broke apart and often appear in isolation in the later pss. The language of the suppliant's appeal became the accepted language of lamentation and was used freely in poems of suffering and sorrow quite apart from the ritual of sanctuary.

Although the broken relationship between man and God results most frequently from the attack of enemies or the onset of disease, alienation caused by sin is occasionally the focus of attention. More rarely still the psalmist feels himself to be separated from God by geographical remoteness from the temple. Pss. with this emphasis may have originated as prisoner-of-war songs, for in ancient thought to be held captive in a foreign land was to be denied access to the god of one's own country. The Babylonian exiles used ancient prisoner songs as particularly appropriate means of describing their own plight. In the spiritual isolation of sin or the physical isolation of captivity the sufferer has no defense except his confidence in the saving love of the LORD.

The *dramatis personae* of the laments is interesting. The psalmist and his associates seem always to be "poor," "needy," "afflicted," "meek," and "righteous," and their enemies inevitably are "wicked," "proud," "arrogant," "liars." These two sets of terms should not be taken too literally. They are conventional designations for 2 groups opposed in spirit and often in fact: those who adhered loyally to the covenant, obeyed its laws, and honored its God; and those who rejected the covenant law and held the power of the God of the covenant in contempt.

Community Laments. In Pss. 12; 44; 58; 60; 74; 79; 80; 83; 90; 106; 123; 126; 137 the whole community seeks the sanctuary of the temple and the protection of its mighty God. Expressions of national sorrow were called forth by a sense of the nation's sin and of the degradation and decay of the covenant community, by crop failure, by the threat of military attack, by defeat in war, or by the mockery of victorious enemies.

Songs of Confidence. These songs include Pss. 11; 16; 23; 62; 125; 129; 131. Complete and unrelieved alienation from God would make prayer impossible, and the sufferer would be able only to "curse God, and die" (Job 2:9). But in the Psalter the deepest anguish is lighted by faint rays of confidence. God has saved and will save again. Thus a note of assurance, often muted and far away, sounds in the bitterest laments. Sometimes, however, the assurance of salvation becomes so strong that it pushes suffering and despair into the background and almost out of the picture. This mood gives rise to the song of confidence—a halfway house, as it were, between lamentation and thanksgiving. The pss. of this group have no definite literary pattern and are recognized mainly by their use of vocabulary and images suggestive of trust and assurance. All except Pss. 125; 129 are sung by individuals. Taken together, this group of pss. is a splendid study of those qualities of the divine nature upon which man may anchor his hope.

Thanksgiving Pss. These poems, which are in effect extensions of the lament form, look back on distress and sorrow from the calm and security of deliverance. The period of alienation is still vividly remembered, but its bitterness has been removed by the restoration of communion with God. As the 4-fold structure indicates, the thanksgiving ps. is a complete act of worship, beginning and ending with praise: (a) An introductory passage blesses God for his saving power. (b) This is followed by a poetic narrative, patterned closely on the lament form. Here the psalmist recalls how in a period of deep distress he cried out to God for help. The suffering is described in detail; but, unlike the laments, the thanksgiving pss. weave an account of the deliverance into the description of trouble. (c) This leads to a specific acknowledgment that the source of the psalmist's restoration and joy is the saving love of God. (d) The ps. concludes with thanksgiving and praise.

Pss. of this category were probably used in the temple ritual just before the sacrifice of the thank offering. They were the public testimony of individual or community to the goodness of God which had touched and transformed their lives.

The individual thanksgiving pss. are: 30; 32; 34; 41; 66; 92; 116; 138. There are 3 community thanksgiving pss.: 65; 67 (both connected with the agricultural feasts); and 124 (for victory in war).

Royal Pss. These include Pss. 2; 18; 20; 21; 45; 72; 89; 101; 110; 132; 144. Solomon's temple stood side by side with the palace, and the king had direct access to the sacred building from his chambers. In many respects the temple was the chapel of the palace. The close proximity of palace and temple suggests the intimate relationship which was believed to exist between the Davidic monarchy and the God of Israel. The line of David had been chosen by God and was bound to him by a perpetual covenant (I Sam. 16:1-13; II Sam. 7:4-17). The reigning king was the adopted son of God, his representative, almost his vicegerent, on earth. Through the king's person the divine blessing was channeled to the nation, and what happened to him happened to all his subjects. His 2 principal functions are reflections of attributes of God: (a) maintaining the covenant law, the revelation of God's will and justice, and (b) defending Israel against her enemies. It is not surprising, therefore, that the Psalter contains poems dealing with the person and office of the earthly king.

The monarch's status was conferred on him when the sacred oil of anointing was poured on his head during his coronation. It is not unlikely that when the king dies his successor was not formally crowned

until the new year, so that his coronation formed part of the great feast and was seen in close conjunction with the enthronement of the LORD, as described above. Thus every new year was an anniversary of the coronation, and appropriate rituals undoubtedly marked this fact. Six of the royal pss. (2; 21; 72; 101; 110; 132) have their cultic setting in the coronation ceremony. Ps. 101 gives the king's response to the prayers made in his behalf.

The king's function as leader in war gave rise to 2 prayers for victory (Pss. 20; 144) and a thanksgiving after victory (Ps. 18). The royal marriage, a significant event for king and nation, as Solomon's matrimonial adventures show, is celebrated in the most secular of the pss. (45). In addition to these specifically royal pss. the king appears as speaker in several laments and thanksgivings.

Wisdom Pss. Included in this category are Pss. 1; 37; 49; 73; 112; 127; 128; 133. The priests were teachers of the religious traditions of which they were custodians and guardians. The festivals to which people came from all parts of the realm provided the priests with a unique opportunity for instruction. Many of the pss. contain instructional passages, but a small number bear the marks of the formal teacher and are closely related to the wisdom literature of Israel and the ancient Near East. For the nature of Semitic wisdom, its main themes, and its relation to ancient Near Eastern wisdom writing see "The Wisdom Literature," pp. 1101-05, and the introductions to Prov., Job, and Eccl., the great OT representatives of this type of writing.

The principal aim of the wisdom pss. is to teach the doctrine that faithful obedience to the revealed will of God brings material and spiritual prosperity but rejection of his will means destruction, no less complete because sometimes long delayed. Ps. 73 deals with the problem of the prosperity of the wicked at a deeper level than the other wisdom psalms and reminds one irresistibly of Job. Pss. 127; 133 treat of family problems, a favorite topic of the writers of proverbs.

Liturgies. These are Pss. 15; 24; 50; 75; 85; 118; 121. Ancient Near Eastern literature contains several detailed accounts of rituals conducted in pagan temples, of which the most important is the Babylonian description of the new year festival. By contrast the OT never outlines precisely the ritual setting in which the pss. were used. Some pss., however, display such abrupt changes of thought and mood that they appear to be composed of disconnected fragments. In certain pss. it is possible to detect changes of speaker corresponding to the changes in sense. These phenomena can best be explained on the assumption that the pss. of this group were the spoken parts of now-unknown rituals. If it is remembered that our knowledge of the accompanying rituals is far from exact, they may conveniently be classified as liturgies. When the following commentary speaks of 3- or 5-part liturgies, it refers to the number of changes in speaker or mood which can be identified with reasonable certainty.

The cultic setting of the liturgies is by no means always clear. Pss. 15; 24 are entrance liturgies used at the gates of the temple. Pss. 50; 75; 85 appear to belong to the new year festival and to express God's judgment on the nation, Israel's penitence, and God's final judgment on world history. Ps. 121, though considered by many a pilgrim ps. (see below) sung during the dangerous journey to Jerusalem, is more likely for the dismissal of pilgrims leaving the temple on their homeward journey. Ps. 118, which gives thanks for victory in war, is closely related to the community thanksgiving pss. Liturgical elements are present in many pss. not classified as liturgies.

Pilgrim Pss. The pilgrims who gathered for the great annual festivals came singing. Most of their hymns are included in other ps. categories, but Pss. 84; 122 belong so distinctively to the pilgrims as to form a separate group. The keynote of these pss. is joy. Ps. 84 expresses the pilgrim's delight at his safe arrival among the splendors of the Holy City and his gratitude to God for guidance and protection during the dangerous journey. Ps. 122 is a song of the departing pilgrims, radiant with their love for Zion, God's earthly dwelling place.

Pss. of Mixed Type. Under this heading fall Pss. 9-10; 14; 27; 36; 40; 77; 94; 107. Poems of this category appear to consist of 2 or more pss. of different literary type loosely joined together. Their apparent disunity may be the result of their use in rituals the details of which are now unknown. The movement of the ps. would then correspond to the various phases of the ritual. For discussion of these pss. see the commentary on each.

Because of their free composition the following pss. have not been classified: 19:7-14; 52; 68; 78; 81; 82; 91; 108; 119; 139.

The "I" of the Pss. In most of the OT the religious unit is the nation, but the Psalter appears to be an exception to this general rule, and many readers turn to it as the richest expression of the personal piety of the individual Israelite. Recent scholarship has called this evaluation into question on the basis of the ancient Semitic concept of "corporate personality." Groups of any size from family to nation were regarded as possessing unity and solidarity, a common mind and will, which conferred on them a personality as real and definite as that of an individual. The group could speak and be spoken to as if it were a single person. The "I" of the pss. may therefore in most cases be the worshiping community speaking with one voice out of its unified corporate life.

"Corporate personality," however, does not exclude individual piety, but fosters and deepens it. The ancient individual was not lost in the crowd, his personality submerged and obliterated by that of the group. He was a living representative of his society, carrying in himself the history, ideals, and qualities of the total community. When the pss. were sung in corporate worship his consciousness that they described his personal condition was not lessened, but enhanced, by the realization that he shared his condition with all who stood around him in the temple.

In several pss. where the corporate interest is clear the pronouns suddenly shift from the plural "we" to the singular "I" (e.g. Ps. 85). In these cases we must assume that an individual has stepped forward as representative and spokesman of the congregation. Because of his office the king was the most significant representative figure in the nation (e.g.

44:4, 6, 15), but in war pss. the single voice which spoke for the nation might be the commanding general or other high-ranking officer. The priests, and in particular the high priest, could represent the entire congregation (e.g. 85:1-3), calling them to worship and pronouncing "oracles of salvation" and blessings.

The representative function cannot, however, be limited to these officials. Any person of status or authority in the community could speak for the whole group (e.g. Pss. 30; 94). The "I" of the pss. is sometimes clearly a prophetic figure. The personnel of the ancient temple included prophets whose duty it was to announce the decisions of the deity to whom they were dedicated and of whom they were the spokesmen. The "cultic prophets" of the Jerusalem temple took part in the worship whenever the ritual contained a direct word of God (e.g. 81:5b-15). Sometimes they pronounced oracles handed down in set traditional form from ancient times (e.g. 60:6-8). On other occasions their words sound the notes of judgment and direct personal inspiration characteristic of the great prophets of Israel (e.g. 50:7-15; 75:2-5).

Superscriptions. Most of the pss.—all except 34 untitled "orphans"—carry a superscription added at some time during the process of collecting and editing. These titles bristle with difficulties, and we can do no more here than indicate the elements which make up the superscriptions and a possible interpretation of their meaning.

Authorship. In some cases the editors evidently intended to indicate whom they believed to be the author of the ps. The majority are attributed to David, and the editors tended to assign any ps. which dealt directly or indirectly with the monarchy to his authorship. Pss. are also attributed to Moses (90), Solomon (72; 127), Ethan the Ezrahite (89), and Heman the Ezrahite (88). The last 2 "authors" were leaders of temple choirs and men renowned for their musical skill (I Kings 4:31; I Chr. 15:16-19). The temple choirs, composed of Levites and named after their founder, had collections of pss. which formed their special repertoire and were sung in their distinctive style. Contributions have come from the hymnbooks of Asaph (Pss. 50; 73-83; cf. I Chr. 6:39; 15:17) and the Sons of Korah (Pss. 42; 44-49; 84; 85; 87; 88; cf. Num. 16; I Chr. 9:19). Jeduthun was the founder of a 3rd choir (I Chr. 25:1-7), and the pss. which show his name in the title (39; 62; 77) were either attributed to his authorship or, more probably, sung in the style which he originated.

Type of Composition. A "Song" (Pss. 30; 46 etc.) is a sacred musical composition for use in worship, and "Psalm" (Pss. 3-6 etc.) has much the same meaning. A "Prayer" (Pss. 17; 86 etc.) is a poem of lamentation and petition. "Love song" (Ps. 45) and "Song of Praise" (Ps. 145) are self-explanatory. Several enigmatic words may belong to this category. A "Maskil" (Pss. 32; 42-45 etc.) is probably a ps. of instruction, designed to inculcate wisdom. "Miktam" (Pss. 16; 56-60) may refer to a ps. which commemorates an event of permanent significance or, if it relates to a root meaning "to cover," a ps. for atonement rituals.

Cultic Occasion. Certain pss. are said to be used:

"for the memorial offering" (Pss. 38; 70; cf. Lev. 2:1-3), "for the thank offering" (Ps. 100; cf. Lev. 7:11-15), "for the Sabbath" (Ps. 92), "for instruction" (Ps. 60), and "of one afflicted, when he . . . pours out his complaint before the LORD" (Ps. 102. "At the dedication of the Temple" (Ps. 30) may refer to a ritual conducted annually as part of the New Year festival. It probably does not apply to any historic dedication of a new temple building. The title "A Song of Ascents" (Pss. 120-134) probably belongs to this category. "Ascents" (lit. "goings up") relates to both "staircase" and "pilgrimage," and these pss. were probably sung during the pilgrimage feasts on the stairway leading up to the temple at the times when the pilgrims were arriving or departing. "Mahalath" (Pss. 53; 88) and "Leannoth" (Ps. 88) may mean respectively "'in time of sadness" and "for affliction," but the first term may equally well refer to the sad mood of the music or the accompaniment of flutes, in which case "Mahalath Leannoth" would be a flute song rendered in a melancholy mood.

Musical Direction. The ambiguities of the last 2 terms point to this 4th element in the superscriptions. "To the choirmaster," which occurs in 55 pss. (4-6; 8-14 etc.), tells us that the musical directions are intended for him, but does not inform us of the significance of the directions. Some scholars believe that the Hebrew expression should rather be interpreted, in the light of a root meaning "to shine," as indicating a ps. for propitiation rituals, i.e. for making God's face shine. Certain phrases are clearly catch words identifying the popular song to the tune of which the ps. was sung: "Muth-labben" (possibly 'Die for the Son," Ps. 9), "The Hind of the Dawn" (Ps. 22), "Lilies" (Pss. 45; 69; 80) or "Shushan Eduth" ("Lily of Witness," Ps. 60), and "The Dove on Far-off Terebinths" (Ps. 56). "Do Not Destroy" (Pss. 57-59; 75) was evidently the song for the grape harvest from which a line is quoted in Isa. 65:8. "For the flutes" (Ps. 5), a word not found elsewhere, may actually mean to the tune "Inheritances." "According to The Gittith" (Pss. 8; 81; 84) may mean to the tune "The Wine Presses" or may refer to a musical instrument or style of music imported from the Philistine city of Gath. "According to The Sheminith" (lit. "eighth," Ps. 6:12) is enigmatic and has been interpreted as a particularly deep tone or an 8-stringed instrument. "According to Alamoth" (Ps. 46) seems to mean "in the style of the women," hence a high-pitched melody. "Shiggaion" (root meaning "to wander," Ps. 7) possibly describes a fast-paced melody, but the word is quite obscure.

References to David's Life. The several superscriptions referring to an episode in the career of David as the occasion on which the ps. was composed are guesses of late editors and have no historical value. The pss. in which these notes appear and the passages in the historical books on which they most closely depend are:

3—II Sam. 15	54—I Sam. 23:19-23
7—II Sam. 18:31-33	56—I Sam. 21:10-11 or 27:1-4
18—II Sam. 7:13-16	57—I Sam. 22:1 or 24:1
34—I Sam. 21:10-15	59—I Sam. 19:11
36—II Sam. 23:10-11	60—II Sam. 8:3-14
51—II Sam. 11-12	63—I Sam. 24:1-4
52—I Sam. 22:9	142—I Sam. 22:1 or 24:1

Selah and Higgaion. These obscure terms occur in the body of pss. "Higgaion" (9:16) has the root meaning "sigh" or "meditate." It probably refers to a pause in the singing for meditation or for a musical interlude. "Selah" (3:2, 4, 8 etc.) is one of the greatest puzzles of the OT. Its meaning seems to be connected with rising or lifting; but it is not clear whether the congregation rises or lifts up its hands, head, or eyes, or whether the voices or the music rise at the indicated points. The word probably instructs the worshipers that the singing should stop to allow the congregation an interlude for presenting its homage to God by some gesture or act of worship.

The Compilation of the Psalter. As it lies before us the Psalter consists of 5 books (Pss. 1-41; 42-72; 73-89; 90-106; 107-150), each clearly marked off by a closing doxology (41:13; 72:18-19; 89:52; 106:48). Ps. 1 is a prologue to the Psalter, giving a brief summary of its theology and religious significance. Ps. 150 is an extended doxology, a fitting conclusion to the whole collection. This arrangement is an artificial division made late in the history of the Psalter in order to produce 5 books of pss. parallel to the 5 books of the Law.

Examination of the superscriptions shows that Pss. 2-41 and 51-72 generally bear the title "A Psalm of David." The intervening group, 42-50, are almost all pss. of the Sons of Korah, and 73-83 are pss. of Asaph. The first and 2nd Davidic collections show noteworthy repetitions. Ps. 14 appears again as 53, and 40:13-17 is repeated as 70. The first Davidic collection prefers "the LORD" (Yahweh) as its principal divine name, whereas the 2nd favors "God" (Elohim). These observations indicate that at one stage in the history of the Psalter 4 small hymnbooks were in circulation: 2 Davidic, 1 Korahite, and 1 Asaphite collection. The first major compilation probably consisted of bringing together these 4 collections of pss. into a single book, roughly corresponding to our Pss. 2-83.

Since this first edition left out many familiar and well-loved hymns, an appendix was added consisting of Pss. 84-89 (4 Korahite pss., 1 attributed to David, and 1 to Ethan the Ezrahite). This 2nd edition closed with a doxology and a 2-fold "Amen."

At a still later date, and perhaps in several stages, another appendix of miscellaneous pss. (90-150) was added to the growing Psalter. Of these 17 are ascribed to David and 1 each to Moses and Solomon, but many are without superscription. This appendix incorporated several smaller, originally independent collections. One of these is the block of 15 "Songs of Ascents" (120-134) already mentioned. There are 2 "Hallel" collections (111-113; 146-150) in which each ps. begins with "Praise the LORD" (Hebrew *hallelujah*) and a trio of "Give thanks" (Hebrew *hodu*) pss. (105-107).

It is possible, therefore, to outline the literary history of the Psalter in 6 stages. (a) The pss. existed as independent poems, preserved in the Jerusalem temple and other Israelite shrines for use in the rituals of the festivals and other acts of worship. (b) Small collections of pss. were made—in order to facilitate the preservation of accurate texts, because they were used in the same ritual setting, because they belonged to the repertoire of a particular guild of singers, or for some other reason. (*c*) Four of these collections were combined to produce the first edition of the Psalter (Pss. 2-83). (*d*) This work was subsequently enlarged by the addition of Pss. 84-89 with a closing doxology. (*e*) The process of growth continued with the addition of Pss. 90-149. (*f*) A prologue (Ps. 1) and a closing doxology (Ps. 150) were provided, and the completed work was divided into 5 books. This development, which began in very early times, reached its conclusion sometime between 400 and 200 B.C.

Religious Teaching. The pss. have no unified theological viewpoint; they represent all shades and varieties of religious thought which could exist in the context of Israel's covenant faith. The main themes of this compendium of theological thinking have been indicated above. Readers who wish to pursue them further must turn to the individual pss. Orientation for this task is given by the article "The Religion of Israel" (pp. 1150-58), and a good concordance is an invaluable aid in following the use of a particular word or concept through the Psalter. The cross references included in the commentaries on specific pss. will guide the reader to companion statements of the same theme.

For Further Study: W. O. E. Oesterley, *The Psalms,* 1939. Elmer A. Leslie, *The Psalms,* 1949. John Paterson, *The Praises of Israel,* 1950. Samuel Terrien, *The Psalms and Their Meaning for Today,* 1952. Artur Weiser, *The Psalms,* 1962; the best commentary in English. Sigmund Mowinckel, *The Psalms in Israel's Worship,* 2 vols., 1963.

Ps. 1. The Man Whom God Approves

This titleless ps. was added at a late date as an introduction to the Psalter as a whole. Its emphasis on the reward of virtue and the punishment of godlessness connects it with Israel's wisdom teachers, the compilers of Prov., Job, and Eccl. The "beatitude" with which it begins, **Blessed is** (Oh the manifold happinesses of) **the man,** is a wisdom formula (cf. Prov. 8:34; Eccl. 10:17). However, the ps. is late in the history of the wisdom movement, dating from a time when wisdom and the law were virtually identified. God's guidance, not human instruction, is the source of wisdom. This suggests a date after the reform of Ezra (ca. 400 B.C.; cf. Neh. 8:1-8).

The ps. is artistically constructed of two carefully balanced strophes: vss. 1-3, 4-6.

1:1-3. The first strophe describes the character of the one who wins God's approval (**the righteous,** vs. 6) negatively, positively, and by means of a metaphor. Negatively, he shuns evildoers, refusing to direct his life by the advice of those whom God condemns (**the wicked**), to conform to the example of those who wander from the road (**sinners**), or to join company with the arrogant who sneer at God and man (**scoffers**). Positively, his life is pervaded and ruled by **law,** not a written legal code, but the guidance and instruction of God (the original meaning of *torah,* "law"). This obedience is not a yoke or burden but a **delight,** for in the divine guidance the psalmist finds a stable foundation for his life. The metaphor of the **tree** (cf. Jer. 17:8) suggests abundant prosperity, productivity, usefulness, and ability to endure the hardships of life, all made possible by the nourishing **streams** of God's guidance.

1:4-6. The 2nd strophe shows the impermanence, worthlessness, and meaninglessness which by contrast characterize the wicked. Like **chaff** tossed in the air by a winnower he is blown away, destroyed —not by natural weakness but by divine action. Tried and found guilty, he is barred from the community (**congregation**) of those with whom God is pleased, and the present condemnation will be confirmed at the final judgment.

1:6. The metaphor changes to that of a **way**— lit. "trodden path." The path followed by the **righteous** is broad and safe, because the LORD **knows** it, i.e. it is under his protection. In contrast the path of the **wicked,** like a desert trail, leads nowhere and will soon peter out (**perish**), perhaps beside a dry water hole marked by the skeletons of those who followed it.

Ps. 2. Universal God and Universal King

This untitled royal ps. (on this category see Intro.) was composed by a court poet for use at the coronation of a king or at the annual enthronement festival (see Intro.). It was inspired by the hope that the geographical limits and political glory of the kingdom of David would be restored to his successors. But it goes beyond this to assert the *worldwide* sovereignty of the Davidic king. However, the ps. is more than an example of the inflated "court style" of an oriental monarch. It rests on the theological premises of the universal creativity of God and his sovereignty over world history. Because God rules all men in all ages, the Davidic king will enjoy worldwide dominion.

The ps. dates from a time after the reign of Solomon and before the fall of Jerusalem (931-586 B.C.). The NT gives it a messianic interpretation (Acts 4: 25-26; Heb. 1:5; 5:5), but in its original intention it did not refer to a future ruler. The four strophes (vss. 1-3, 4-6, 7-9, 10-12) were spoken by the reigning king in reference to himself.

2:1-3. *World Rebellion.* In the ancient world the accession of a king was the opportunity for his vassal states to assert their independence. In accents of shocked wonder the Israelite king pictures this happening on a world scale. The **kings of the earth** plot revolt against the LORD and against the one who, by the sacred oil of anointing, was set apart as his earthly representative.

2:4-6. *God's Decision.* Their scheming is **in vain** and makes the occupant of the heavenly throne laugh. To plot the destruction of the king whom the ruler of the universe has established is ludicrous. God's calm, self-assured words (vs. 6) sound to the plotters like the crack of doom. They know that by their scheming they have exposed themselves to the destructive judgment of God, **his wrath.** The Hebrew poets spoke of God in human terms (he laughs and is angry) in order to reinforce their conviction that the LORD was actively, vigorously, and personally involved in man's history.

2:7-9. *A Promise of Dominion.* The LORD's decree (vs. 6) means that the Israelite king is God's **son** by adoption, brought into that intimate relationship **today,** i.e. at the time of his coronation. A similar theory of kingship was held by Babylonian rulers. Since his Father is lord of the universe, the king can have worldwide authority for the asking; and his scepter, the symbol of his royal power, will **break** the rebels as easily as a **rod of iron** shatters an earthen **vessel.**

2:10-12. God's Ultimatum. The king warns the rebels that they must learn to recognize the LORD as ruler of the universe and must do homage to him —figuratively **kiss his feet,** as the subjects of an oriental ruler did to their king. The alternative is destruction, for only those who acknowledge their dependence on the LORD can hope for the blessings of prosperity and peace (vs. 12*b*). The Hebrew of vss. 11*b*-12*a* is obscure, but the interpretation given is more in keeping with the context than either alternative: "rejoice with trembling, kiss with purity," or "kiss the son."

Ps. 3. A GOD OF DELIVERANCE

This individual lament (on this category, the title, and **selah** see Intro.) is based on one of the fundamental tenets of Israel's exodus faith: the God who saved Israel from Egypt is a God of **deliverance** (vs. 8). The root word means "make wide" or "give room to" (see below on 18:19) and is particularly appropriate to the psalmist's condition, hemmed in by enemies. The military metaphors (vss. 3, 6) suggest that the speaker is the king, but many pss. which originally belonged to the setting of the court were "democratized" and used by the people, the royal language being understood figuratively.

3:1-4. Oppressed by enemies who scornfully declare that God cannot help him, the psalmist does not lose confidence in the LORD. Recognizing that he owes his protection (**shield**) and his worth as a man (**glory**) to the LORD, he recalls how in the past he bowed before God, like a subject before his king, and the LORD answered him favorably (lifted up his **head**). He feels assurance that the LORD in his dwelling place in the temple will hear his servant and answer by action.

3:5-8. In this confidence the psalmist can **sleep** peacefully in the midst of **ten thousands** of armed enemies. Some have assumed from vs. 5 that the ps. is a morning prayer, offered after a night spent in the sacred place (a practice technically called "incubation"), but the language hardly forces this conclusion. The psalmist bases his call to the LORD to **arise** from his throne and act on his belief that God gives tit for tat to those who insult him, striking their cheeks (cf. I Kings 22:24) and smashing their scornful mouths.

Ps. 4. THE ONLY SECURITY

At first reading this individual lament (on this category, the title, and **selah** see Intro.) appears to be a haphazard collection of disconnected vss., and scholars vary widely in their interpretations. With considerable emendation the ps. may be read as a pious man's reproof of those who have been led to apostasy by a succession of bad harvests. Other commentators understand the poem as the defense of a high official (king or high priest) against charges that he has abused his office. Still others regard it as the exhortation of a man of faith to those who have been disheartened by hard times.

The speaker, however, seems to be a poor man who faces the lying accusations of the wealthy (vs.

7). The designation translated as **men** (vs. 2) is used in Egyptian and Babylonian literature to refer to persons of standing or wealth. These facts suggest that the ps. belongs to a legal context. In Israel, as throughout the ancient Near East, legal cases which could not be resolved by direct evidence were taken to the temple, where the accused swore an oath of innocence in the presence of the god (cf. Exod. 22:11; Num. 5:19). This ps. was probably originally a liturgy for use in a temple trial and was subsequently slightly modified to make it generally serviceable as a hymn of confidence.

4:1-5. The ps. begins, as usual in a lament (see Intro.), with a cry to God for aid. Significantly it addresses the **God of my right,** i.e. the God who declares me innocent. By lying words the psalmist's accusers have attacked his dignity as a man (vs. 2; cf. 3:3), but he remains confident that the LORD, who has heard him in the past, will respond again to his prayer (vs. 3). Calmly he urges his persecutors to keep their anger and their plots against him to themselves, and so avoid the sin of lying publicly (vs. 4), and he enjoins them to true worship and to trust in the LORD (vs. 5).

4:6-8. The psalmist's numerous accusers display their lack of trust by complaining about their lot, piously using words reminiscent of the priestly benediction (vs. 6; cf. Num. 6:26; in ancient thought the god signified rejection of his worshiper by averting his eyes). But the psalmist's consciousness of innocence and his fellowship with God give him more inner joy than his enemies derive from the material possessions which they covet (vs. 7). Confident in the LORD's protection, he sleeps peacefully as soon as he lies down, possibly in the temple itself during the ordeal of the trial (vs. 8; cf. 3:5).

Ps. 5. ALIENATION AND ACCEPTANCE

This beautifully constructed individual lament (on this category and the title see Intro.) unfolds in 4 stages. It begins with a repeated appeal to God for hearing and help. He is addressed with the cultic formula **my King and my God** (vss. 1-3). The ps. goes on to describe the alienation from God of the psalmist's enemies and his own acceptance by the LORD (vss. 4-7). This leads to a prayer for guidance and justification (vs. 8), to a condemnation of the enemies and a cry for vengeance (vss. 9-10), and finally to a meditation on the joy and blessing of the righteous (vss. 11-12).

5:1-7. The setting is the **morning** service of the temple (Exod. 29:39; Lev. 6:12-18; Num. 28:4-7), to which the psalmist brings his offering and waits expectantly for an answer from the LORD (vs. 3). Two qualities of the divine nature assure the worshiper that his prayer will be heard: (*a*) God's hatred of **evil** in any form (vss. 4-6), and (*b*) his **steadfast love** (i.e. his nature as one who acts to save) toward the weak and helpless (vs. 7*a*). Because of the first, the proud, violent, deceitful men who oppose the psalmist are denied entrance to the temple, i.e. are cut off from fellowship with God (vss. 4-5; cf. vs. 10). By virtue of the 2nd the psalmist himself has free access to the sanctuary, which he enters with **fear** (i.e. reverential awe, vs. 7).

5:8-12. His prayer is 3-fold: (*a*) for himself, that he may be guided in the **way** approved by God from which his **enemies** try to divert him (vs. 8); (b) against those who plot violence even while they speak flattering words (vss. 9-10); and (c) on behalf of all who trust in the LORD for their defense, that they may receive **joy** and blessing (vss. 11-12). The vengeance called down on the enemies will be both the judgment of God and the consequence of their crimes, just as the joy of the righteous is both the natural outpouring of their gratitude and the direct gift of God.

Ps. 6. IN THE FACE OF DEATH

This typical individual lament (on this category and the title see Intro.), is a patchwork of traditional cultic phraseology. Because implicitly the psalmist acknowledges that his suffering is the result of his sin—i.e. has been visited on him by the wrath of God—it is traditionally regarded as the first of the 7 penitential pss. (along with 32; 38; 51; 102; 130; 143), although it contains no word of confession.

6:1-3. The psalmist, pleading for relief from the divine **wrath** (vs. 1), complains of sickness (vs. 2) and mental anguish (vs. 3). His **bones,** the most stable part of his physical frame, and indeed his **soul**—i.e. not his immortal spiritual part but his total personality as a living being—are in disorder.

6:4-5. On the basis of the LORD's **steadfast** (delivering) **love** (see above on 5:1-7) he begs for his life. He is in terror because **death** will plunge him into **Sheol** (the underworld), where his existence will be reduced to just short of the vanishing point. The LORD's presence does not reach this dark and cheerless place far beneath the surface of the earth (see below on 18:7-18), and the shades even lack **remembrance** of their God (cf. 30:9; 88:10-11; 115:17). Vs. 5 is a fair representation of the hopelessness with which the Hebrews of the classical period, in common with the ancient Mesopotamians and Hittites, faced death as the effective end of meaningful human experience, including fellowship with God. (see "The Religion of Israel," pp. 1150-58).

6:6-7. With characteristic oriental exaggeration the psalmist describes his **bed** as soaking wet from his **tears** and his **eye** as worn out with weeping. His distress is due also to human **foes.**

6:8-10. So confident is the psalmist of God's willingness to answer his **prayer** for the thwarting of his **enemies** that he regards it as already accomplished.

Ps. 7. AN OATH OF INNOCENCE

This is an individual lament (on this category and the title see Intro.). On the basis of changes in style and mood some have viewed vss. 6-11 as a separate poem interpolated in vss. 1-5, 12-17; but such a division is unnecessary, for the ps. can be read as the unified utterance of one man.

7:1-5. Pursued by savage enemies the psalmist has fled to the temple for sanctuary (vss. 1-2; cf. I Kings 2:28). In the sacred place he swears an oath of purgation (vss. 3-5; cf. I Kings 8:31-32), in which he declares his innocence—not of all sin but only of the crimes with which he is falsely accused—and asks that, if he is guilty, his enemies be allowed to **trample** him to death.

7:6-11. The scene in the divine court, where the LORD sits enthroned among his courtiers and messengers, is a common motif in the OT (cf. I Kings

22:19-23; Job 1:6-12; see below on 58:1-5; 82:1-5). The psalmist prays that the court be convened and the LORD, who judges the nations, sit in **judgment** between himself and his **enemies** (vss. 6-8). He wishes not only that he be found not guilty but also that his enemies be utterly destroyed. His plea for vengeance is based on the belief that the judge of the earth is a **righteous God,** i.e. a God of moral perfection, and is therefore always moved to anger by evil or injustice (vss. 9-11; on **minds and hearts** see below on 16:7-8; 26:1-3). In his concentration on the judgmental character of God he does not entertain the possibility that the LORD may love the evildoer.

7:12-16. These vss. are a meditation on the nature of the righteousness of God and involve a Semitic ideal of justice found in many Near Eastern law codes. In the code of Hammurabi of Babylon (ca. 1750 B.C.) the perjurer receives the punishment which he tried to bring on his victim, and in this ps. the **wicked** are trapped in their own plots and tumble into the **pit** which they prepared for the psalmist. This "poetic justice" of God is swift as war **arrows** and deadly as the cut of a **sword.**

7:17. Certain of vindication by the righteous God, the psalmist concludes with a vow to acknowledge his gratitude publicly in the temple by means of a thank offering and songs of **praise.** The vow is a common feature of pss. of lament or thanksgiving.

Ps. 8. THE DIGNITY OF MAN

This familiar hymn (on this category and the title see Intro.) belongs to the evening service of the temple, when the night sky was visible above the open courts of the building. It was sung antiphonally.

8:1-2. *Ascription of Glory.* This part was sung by the people (note **our Lord**). In Hebrew a **name** is more than a title by which a person or thing is designated. It summarizes and *contains* the nature and character of its bearer. The key to the LORD's character is his **glory.** This means: (a) "weight" as measured by a scale; (b) figuratively "honor," "dignity," or "reputation"; and (c), when applied to God, his authoritative presence in creation, salvation, or judgment. This authoritative presence of God fills the whole **earth,** and is the object of Israel's praise.

8:1c-2. The Hebrew of this passage is difficult. Punctuated as in the RSV, it may contain a mythological reference—i.e. angelic hosts, innocent as **babes,** who surround the throne of the LORD **above the heavens,** overcome the dark demonic powers of the universe by the harmony of their praise to the King of kings. It is probably better, however, to put a semicolon after vs. 1 and read the passage as meaning that the stars in the sky (vs. 1c) and children on earth (vs. 2) both proclaim the divine glory. Another possibility is to regard **above the heavens** as an adjectival phrase defining **glory** and thus confine the whole scene to earth. In the latter sense the passage contains the familiar OT idea that the LORD uses the humble and weak to carry out his great designs and can make the songs of **infants** a fortress strong enough to hold back the wicked and reduce them to silence.

8:3-8. *The Glory and Insignificance of Man.* This part was sung by a solo voice (note I). Contemplation of the night sky makes man acutely aware of his humanity. He seems too insignificant to merit the attention, much less the loving care, of the Creator, who shaped the heavenly bodies one by one with his **fingers** and fastened them in the vast dome of the sky. But size is not everything, and for all his earthbound littleness man has a crown of kingly authority and a dignity which place him just below the level of God himself. In the phrase **little less than God** (vs. 5) the Hebrew word *elohim* may be translated "judges," "heavenly beings," "gods,": or "God." The LXX took it to mean "angels," but since it is a normal OT word for "God" this seems the best translation here. Man is Godlike in his ability to control the rest of the created order. This mastery over the world in which he lives is the "image of God" of which Gen. 1:26 speaks. But it does not belong to man as a possession. His **crown** of dignity and his **dominion** are bestowed on him as a gracious gift by the Creator of earth and heaven.

8:9. *Ascription of Glory Repeated.* The refrain was sung again by the people. Contemplation of the dignity of man, understood in the terms of the ps., leads, not to pride, but to renewed praise of the **majestic** nature of God—an observation not without value in a technologically oriented society.

Pss. 9–10. Thanksgiving and Lamentation

In the LXX these pss. appear as one. The correctness of this tradition is indicated by the facts that Ps. 9 ends with **selah** (on this word and **higgaion** see Intro.), which rarely concludes a ps. (only Pss. 24; 46), and that Ps. 10 has no title (on the title to Ps. 9 see Intro.). Similar in subject matter, the 2 pss. taken together once formed a single poem in which the strophes began with successive letters of the Hebrew alphabet (an alphabetic acrostic; see Intro.), although the pattern is now much disturbed. In form 9:1-12 is a thanksgiving hymn, and 9:13–10:18 is an individual lament (on these categories see Intro.).

9:1-12. *Praise for God's Justice.* The hymn, an extended invocation introducing the lament, begins with praise of the wonderful deeds of the **Most High**—an ancient divine name going back to the pre-Mosaic era (cf. Gen. 14:19). The wonderful deeds are the LORD's acts of judgment (vss. 3-10). He turned back the psalmist's **enemies** at the gates of the temple and overthrew them (vss. 3-4). He **destroyed** the turbulent **nations** of the earth, blotting out their **name** and **memory** (vss. 5-6)—a Hebrew idiom for total annihilation. The heavenly court of the divine King-Judge figures prominently in these vss. (see comment on 7:6-11; 58:1-5; 82:1-5). To those whom the world-controlling justice of God finds guilty he is a ruthless destroyer (vs. 12), but to those who trust in him and know his true nature (**name**) he is a sure defense (vss. 9-10). His every decision is scrupulously correct (vss. 7-8). The thanksgiving hymn closes with praise of this perfect justice (vss. 11-12).

9:13-17. *Former Blessings from God.* Appropriately the lament begins with remembrance of past blessings (vss. 13b-18). The LORD restored the psalmist to his people after his enemies had pushed him to the point **of death** (vs. 13; see above on 6:4-5). **Daugh-**

ter of Zion (vs. 14) is a poetic personification of Jerusalem. The **I** of the ps. may be the king, speaking as the representative of the nation. God's treatment of the enemy nations is marked by poetic justice (see above on 7:14-16). He sends them to **Sheol** (i.e. the underworld, vs. 17; see above on 6:4-5), whither they have tried to dispatch the psalmist. The **net** (9:15; 10:9) is an animal trap triggered when the victim steps on a release mechanism.

9:18–10:18. *The Question of Theodicy.* This portion deals with the thorny question of the apparent reversal in actual life of the justice of God. The wicked prosper (10:5a), the poor are afflicted (9:18), and the obvious inequity makes even the persecuted righteous doubt that God is at all concerned over their plight (10:10-11). **The wicked** are atheists in practice (10:4). They deny, not God's existence, but his effective control over the world (10:6, 13), contending that he cannot, or will not, take action against them. The psalmist recognizes that their attitude is in fact self-deification. Forgetting their humanity, they behave as if they were God (9:20). In characteristic Hebrew fashion the psalmist does not try to settle the problem of the prosperity of the wicked by logical argument. Instead he reaffirms his faith—the basic OT conviction, derived from the Exodus, that the eternal **king** (10:16) will oppose the powerful and aid the helpless and **oppressed** (10:17-18). **Poor** (10:2, 9), **afflicted** (10:12) and **meek** (10:17) are alternative translations of the same Hebrew word (see Intro.).

Ps. 11. Sanctuary in the Temple

This song of confidence (on this category and the title see Intro.) is the work of an unknown refugee who sought sanctuary in the temple (see above on Ps. 7).

11:1-3. The wicked are on the warpath and his friends advise him to **flee . . . to the mountains,** because justice and right dealing, **the foundations** of stable society, **are destroyed** (cf. Amos 5:7), and the persecuted **righteous,** of which he is perhaps a leader, are helpless.

11:4-7a. The psalmist views plight as a denial of his trust in the LORD. He comes instead to the **temple,** to await the theophany (i.e. manifestation or revelation of the deity to man; see Intro.). He hopes that the "coming" of the LORD celebrated in the cult will now be actualized. He bases his expectation on his understanding of the nature of God. The LORD, who is present in the temple with his people, is at the same time enthroned as judge above the earth (see above on 7:6-11). His unhindered vision **tests** the deeds of men (vss. 4-5), and he reacts to what he sees with a vigor which can be described only by analogy with the most intense of human emotions, hate and love (vss. 5b, 7a). The LORD's appearance in judgment is described in traditional metaphors of theophany (cf. 18:7-19; 29:3-9)—the volcanic **fire** which destroyed Sodom and Gomorrah (vs. 6a; cf. Gen. 19:24) and the E **wind** from the desert (sirocco) which can kill the spring grass in a day (vs. 6b, cf. 90:5-6; Isa. 40:6-7). **Cup** (vs. 6) probably alludes to the practice of trial by ordeal: the accused was given a cup of sacred liquid to drink; if he was guilty its contents destroyed him (Num. 5:23-28).

11:7b. The reward of the **upright** at the coming

of the LORD will be fellowship with him—to **behold his face.** In paganism to "behold the face" of a god was to enter the inner shrine where the idol stood. In the OT it is a technical term for entrance to the sanctuary (cf. Exod. 24:11), but with the wider connotation of communion with God and the consciousness of being accepted by him.

Ps. 12. VILENESS EXALTED

In this community lament (on this category and the title see Intro.) the God-fearing congregation cries for **help** (vs. 1a) and prays for vengeance against its enemies (vss. 1b-4). Lying and boasting are symptoms of the decay and disintegration of society. A prophetic voice interrupts the congregational prayer to assure the people that God's long-awaited response (see Intro.) is at hand (vss. 5-6). In answer the congregation renews its petition for protection (vss. 7-8).

The ps. displays an extreme pessimism concerning the condition of society (vss. 2, 8). The reason for this emphasis is that in eschatological thought the complete triumph of evil is the signal for the LORD to break into history in his final act of salvation and judgment (vs. 5; see Intro.).

12:6. The **promises of the LORD** are lit. his "words," and the reference is to passages such as Deut. 27–28 in which curses are directed against the wicked and blessings promised to the righteous. Such passages were recited in the temple cultus as part of the ritual of the covenant renewal festival (see Intro.). By contrast with the lying speech of **the wicked** the LORD's words are true, pure as molten **silver** fresh from the refiner. **In a furnace on the ground** presents difficulties and many commentators suggest that it is a marginal gloss. Others emend to read "in a crucible" or "in a workshop." It is probably a metal workers' technical term, perhaps referring to the pouring of the melted silver into an earthen mold.

Ps. 13. AN APPEAL FOR DELIVERANCE

This individual lament (on this category and the title see Intro.) conforms perfectly to the pattern: appeal to the LORD (vss. 1-2), reason for the lamentation (vss. 3-4), hymnic expression of confidence (vss. 5-6).

13:1-4. The meaning can best be seen by following the thought backward from vs. 4 to vs. 1. For a long time his enemies have oppressed the psalmist and brought him near death (see above on 6:4-5). But his bitter anguish and inner turmoil (vs. 2) are caused, not so much by the triumph of his foes, as by his theological assumption that the LORD rewards the righteous with prosperity. In the light of that conviction his suffering is evidence that the Lord has forgotten him—hidden his face (cf. 6:1-3). The cry **how long?** is a cultic formula of lamentation appearing in the Babylonian Lament of Nebuchadnezzar and frequently in the OT.

13:5-6. The psalmist grounds his confidence in the Lord's saving action toward the weak (**steadfast love**) and his readiness to save. Both qualities of the divine nature are derived from Israel's historic exodus faith.

Ps. 14. THE REIGN OF FOLLY

Of mixed type and basically a community lament (on this category and the title see Intro.), this ps. incorporates prophetic (vss. 1, 5-6) and wisdom (vss. 1, 2b) characteristics. Like Ps. 12 this poem is a prayer that the heavenly Judge will enter history in his final act of judgment against the wicked (vs. 5) and of salvation for Israel (vs. 7). The total corruption of society indicates that the divine action will soon take place (vss. 1, 3; see above on 12:2, 8).

14:1-4. The portrait of the wicked is sharply drawn. The Hebrew word for **fool** refers, not to simpleminded people, but to coarse, brutal, self-centered rogues. They deny God, not by intellectual arguments, but by a corrupt life (vs. 1, see above on 9:18–10:18). Their tragic failure in **knowledge,** i.e. in intimate, personal experience of the LORD's nature and will, arises from refusal to seek or to **call upon** him, a radical assertion of their independence (vss. 2-4). It issues in violence toward the true **people** of God (vs. 4) and in **abominable deeds,** i.e. actions hateful to the LORD (vs. 1).

14:5-7. The term **terror** is drawn from the ancient tradition of the holy war (see Intro. and on 20:6-9). At the crucial moment of the battle dread of the LORD seized his enemies and brought them to ruin (cf. Exod. 23:27; Deut. 11:25; Josh. 11:8). For the descendants of Jacob-Israel the appearance of the LORD means salvation. The **deliverance . . . out of Zion** (vs. 7) is brought, not by the messianic king, but by the LORD himself, coming forth from his temple. The congregation prays that he may soon appear. On **restore the fortunes** see below on 85:1.

Ps. 15. DEMAND FOR MORAL PURITY

This entrance liturgy (on this category and the title see Intro.) reflects the ancient Near Eastern insistence that certain conditions be fulfilled before admission to the sacred place (cf. 24:3-5; Isa. 33:14-16). Egyptian and Mesopotamian stipulations for entrance to the sanctuary were usually of a ritual nature. By contrast this ps. demands moral purity. The pilgrims, approaching the temple during the great festivals (see Intro.), formally inquire of the priests who meet them at the gates what the requirements for admission are (vs. 1). The priests reply with a poetic description of the character pleasing to God (vss. 2-5), ending with a promise of blessing for those who conform to their instructions (vs. 5c). Entrance liturgies of this kind (cf. Ps. 24) are adaptations to community use of the practice of settling disputes or solving problems by asking the priest for a "directive" (Hebrew torah) from the LORD (cf. Hag. 2:10-14).

15:1. The use of **tent** as an archaizing term for the Jerusalem temple on the **holy hill** preserves the memory of the tabernacle or tent of meeting of the Mosaic era. Its use in vs. 1 shows how the Sinai covenant dominates the thought of the ps. from beginning to end.

15:2-5. Vs. 2 gives a general description of the man whose whole being and every outward act accords with the requirements of the covenant. Vss. 3-5 show how this character expresses itself in specific social situations. The blameless man avoids **slander** or the passing on of malicious gossip (vs. 3).

He values his fellow citizens on the basis of their relationship to the God of the covenant, not the size of their bankroll (vs. 4ab). He keeps his word even if to do so puts him at a disadvantage (vs. 4c). He will not exploit his wealth by exacting **interest** from a fellow Israelite (vs. 5a; cf. Exod. 22:25; Lev. 25:36-37; Deut. 23:19; among Israel's pagan contemporaries the going interest rate was 33⅓ to 50 percent). Neither will he exploit his influence in the community by accepting a **bribe** (vs. 5b). This kind of loyalty to the covenant is rewarded by permanent prosperity within the covenant community (vs. 5c).

Ps. 16. THE DECISIVE CHOICE

This song of confidence (on this category see Intro.) is a classic example of the doctrine that virtue and reward go hand in hand.

16:1-2. The psalmist begins in the mood of lamentation, but declares that good fortune came to him because he submitted his life voluntarily and unreservedly to the LORD.

16:3-4. This is a digression from the main theme, and its meaning is obscure because of difficulties in the text. As the RSV translates it, vs. 3 expresses the psalmist's **delight** in the nobility of the **saints** (i.e. the true members of the covenant community). Perhaps, however, we should read with the LXX: "The Lord deals gloriously with the saints in the land." Numerous other emendations have been suggested. Vs. 4 contrasts the depravity of the idolater with the nobility of the saints and specifically rejects 2 pagan practices, pouring out offerings of blood to the gods and using their names in magical incantations.

16:5-6. The psalmist expands on the consequences of his decisive choice of vs. 2. With the exception of **cup,** which is a cultic metaphor for "destiny," the vocabulary—**portion . . . lot . . . lines** (i.e. a measured plot of ground) **. . . heritage**—recalls the division of the Holy Land among the 12 tribes after the conquest of Canaan (cf. Num. 26:52-56; Josh. 14:1-5). As the LORD gave his people an inheritance in Canaan, so he gave the psalmist a goodly and pleasant place in the covenant community.

16:7-8. The psalmist moves to the less tangible results of his choice—guidance and inspiration. The LORD is like a guide before him and a companion at his side. He reveals his will to the psalmist, and **in the night** the psalmist's inner being responds to the revelation. **Heart** is lit. "kidneys"; in OT thought the vital organs were regarded as the seat of man's private inner life.

16:9-12. In vss. 9-10 we learn the source of the psalmist's confidence. He was near death and the LORD rescued him from **Sheol** and **the Pit** (i.e. the underworld; see above on 6:4-5). No doctrine of resurrection is involved. After a close brush with death the poet rejoices in a sound **heart** and **soul** and **body** (vs. 9; on **soul** see above on 6:1-3) and exults because the LORD has given him **life,** showed him how to live it (vs. 11a), and crowned it with **joy** and endless delight (vs. 11bc).

Ps. 17. SAVAGE INNOCENCE

This individual lament (on this category and the title see Intro.), in which a fugitive comes to the temple to present his case before the divine Judge and spends the night in the sacred place awaiting the verdict (see above on Pss. 3; 4; 7), follows the pattern of a legal argument:

17:1-2. *Address to the judge,* stressing the justice of the psalmist's **cause,** his sincerity in setting it forth, and his demand for **vindication**—a word which means not only the recognition of innocence but also the reward which innocence merits.

17:3-5. *Oath of purgation* (see above on 7:3-5). The psalmist swears that he is guiltless of deceit and violence, the specific charges against him, and claims complete innocence in thought and word by whatever test the Lord wishes to apply.

17:6-9. *Prayer for deliverance,* based on his proved innocence, and appealing to the LORD's concern for the weak and his willingness to save **those who seek refuge** in the temple (vs. 7; see above on 13:5-6). **Apple of the eye** is an obsolete English idiom for "eyeball." The Hebrew here is lit. "the little man in the eye"—the pupil which reflects the image of anyone who looks into it, and which its owner carefully protects from injury (cf. Deut. 32:10; Prov. 7:2; Zech. 2:8). **The shadow of** God's **wings** may be a reference, not to the mother bird's care for her young, but to the Persian and Egyptian practice of representing the deity as a winged solar disc, or to the outspread wings of the cherubim on the ark of the covenant (see below on 99:1-5).

17:10-12. *Countercharges,* declaring that the psalmist's enemies are corrupt outwardly and inwardly (**mouths** and **hearts,** vs. 10) and fierce as a hunting **lion** (vs. 12; cf. 7:2; 10:9).

17:13-14. *Prayer for vengeance,* based on the countercharges, and blending 2 motifs of OT religion. The God who cuts down his enemies with the sword comes from the holy war tradition (see Intro. and below on 20:6-9), and the sacred food or drink which swells the **belly** of the guilty and kills him is derived from the trial by ordeal (see above on 11:5-6). The demand for vengeance is as extreme as the protestation of innocence, "Let the family of the wicked suffer to the 3rd generation."

17:15. The closing *expression of confidence* corresponds to the opening cry for justice. When morning comes the psalmist will receive a vision of God—**behold . . . thy form,** as Moses did in the tabernacle (Num. 12:5-8). The divine revelation will satisfy him by establishing his innocence (see Intro.).

This ps. exposes the dangers inherent in a sense of innocence. It breeds intolerance, spiritual superiority, and the tendency to equate one's own enemies with the enemies of God. The cry for vengeance is then inevitable. Cf. Matt. 5:43-48.

Ps. 18. THE LORD AT WAR

Although the title (see Intro.) has little historical significance, it is correct in connecting the ps. with the monarchy, for it is a royal hymn of thanksgiving (on this category see Intro.), a liturgy spoken in the temple by the king after a military triumph and possibly repeated annually in the enthronement festival. Its archaic language indicates that it may be as old as the 10th cent. B.C. A somewhat later version of it appears in II Sam. 22.

Some commentators regard this as 2 pss.; vss. 1-30, the lament of a man beset by enemies, and vss. 31-

50, a royal thanksgiving hymn. However, the poem is a tightly knit artistic unit. It has a hymnic passage at the beginning (vss. 1-3) and at the end (vss. 46-50). The body of the ps. contains 2 accounts of the king's victory. In the first (vss. 4-19) God is the chief actor, breaking into the human scene to rescue his king from certain defeat. In the 2nd (vss. 31-45) the king plays the leading role, but the victory is still the LORD's. Vss. 20-30 are a meditative interlude on the relationship between the LORD and the Davidic king. The imagery of the ps. reflects the holy war tradition (see Intro. and on 14:5-7; 20:6-9).

18:1-3. The metaphors here are all military: the **rock** is a promontory on which a fortress is built; the **horn** (i.e. of a bull) is the symbol of strength; and **salvation** in this context means "victory."

18:4-6. The king is portrayed as driven to the edge of disaster. **Sheol** (see above on 6:4-5) is compared to a bird net made of **cords** which has all but entrapped him (vs. 4a) and to a flash flood rushing toward him (vs. 4b). In this extremity he prayed in the **temple** and the LORD heard his **cry** for deliverance (vs. 6).

18:7-18. The wonder of God's delivering action transcends ordinary speech and is described as a battle between heaven and Sheol for the life of the king. It involves upheavals of nature traditionally associated with a theophany—the manifestation of a god to man (see above on 11:4-7a). Attended by earthquake (vs. 7; cf. Judg. 5:4-5) and volcanic **fire**, the LORD thrusts his way through the dome of the sky (vs. 9a). Surrounded and supported by storm **clouds** (vss. 9b, 11) and carried along by the **wind** (vs. 10b), preceded by hail and thunder (vss. 12-13) and with his **arrows** of lightning striking down his enemies (vs. 14), the LORD cleaves his way through the **sea** . . . **and the foundations of the world** to Sheol itself and lifts the beleaguered king to safety through the subterranean **waters** (vss. 15-17). The cosmology involved in this description is the ancient Mesopotamian conception of the 3-storied universe: heaven, the abode of God, above the dome of the sky (the firmament); the inhabited world, a flat disk, anchored or founded over the subterranean waters; and Sheol, the realm of the dead, within the waters and far below the earth.

18:19. The metaphor **brought me forth into a broad place** (vs. 19; cf. vs. 36) is based on the root meaning, "make wide," of the Hebrew word for "save" (see above on Ps. 3).

18:20-30. The meditation turns on the fact that the Israelite king was not an absolute monarch, but like the other members of the covenant community was obligated to obey the covenant law (**ways of the LORD . . . ordinances . . . statutes,** vss. 20-24). The LORD, whose every action is above reproach (vss. 25b, 30), rewards such **humble** loyalty with his steadfast support (vss. 25a, 26a, 27a), guides the king, and renews his life and strength (vss. 28-29).

18:31-45. The 2nd account of the victory is introduced by general statements of the LORD's saving and strengthening power (vss. 31-33), but it quickly moves into the military sphere and describes in violent poetry the overthrow of the king's enemies. Emphasis falls on the superhuman speed, agility, and **strength** which the LORD gives to the king (vss. 33-34, 39), but it is the LORD, not the king, who wins the victory (vss. 39-40). The ensuing peace is a com-

plete triumph for the Davidic monarch and inaugurates his worldwide rule (vs. 43-45; see above on Ps. 2).

18:46-50. The conclusion is a hymn of praise to God for his goodness to the king, and the last line refers to the fact that the LORD's covenant with the house of David was an agreement in perpetuity (cf. II Sam. 7:16).

Ps. 19. WITNESSES TO GOD'S AUTHORITY

Two poems, different in age, meter, and subject matter—a pre-exilic nature psalm (vss. 1-6) and a late poem in praise of the law (vss. 7-14)—have been forged into a single hymn (on these categories and the titles see Intro.). The 2nd reflects an age when the written law was the object of religious veneration and is therefore probably later than the legalizing reform of Ezra (*ca.* 400 B.C.; cf. Neh. 8:1-8). The concept of the **glory of God** (his authoritative presence, vs. 1; see above on 8:1-2) gives these diverse poems a theological unity. The **firmament** (i.e. the dome of the sky; see above on 18:7-18) bears witness to God's creative power in nature, and the law declares his authoritative presence in history, in particular in the history of the covenant people, of which also he is the creator (Isa. 43:1).

19:1-6. *The Testimony of Nature.* Although they have no audible voice and speak no intelligible language (vs. 3), the stars are custodians of a mysterious **knowledge** which day after day they proclaim to **all the earth** (vss. 2, 4, emending "measuring line" to **voice;** cf. RSV footnote). They know and declare that they were created and are kept in their places by the authoritative word of God. These vss. reflect the world view of the ancient Near East. This is particularly true of the hymn to the **sun** (vss. 4c-6), which is closely related to similar poems in Babylonian and Egyptian literature, especially the Babylonian Hymn to Shamash. The sun waits the night in his **tent** at the extremity of the earth—or, by a slight emendation of the word translated **in them,** "in the sea" (vs. 4c). At the time appointed he emerges, glowing with the radiance of a **bridegroom** and the strength of an athlete (a Babylonian hymn calls the sun "warrior and champion"), to follow his path across the sky and sink in the evening into the W sea. He completes the **circuit** by returning to his tent at night through the waters of the underworld (see above on 18:7-18). The psalmist, like the pagan poets, personifies the heavenly bodies, but unlike them he does not give them the status of gods. To him they are examples of God's craftsmanship and witnesses to his glory.

19:7-14. *Hymn to the Law.* This hymn consists of 6 beautifully balanced statements of the nature of the law and its effect on human life (vss. 7-9) followed by a prayer for aid in keeping the law (vss. 10-14). Vs. 7 is the basic statement on which the rest is commentary. The law is no mass of lifeless ordinances, but a living expression of the totality of God's will. To obey it is to have one's life renewed. It is God's self-witness to his will (**testimony**), his standing orders to and detailed demands upon his people (**commandment** and **precepts**), the justice by which he rules history (**ordinances**), and the speech by which he makes his purpose known to Israel (emending **fear** to "word" in the interest of the parallelism). **Perfect** and **enduring,** the law is the fountain from which flows everything of supreme value to men. The connection with wisdom (vs. 7*b*) recalls Ps. 1 (see comment).

19:11-13. The **reward** is not gross material prosperity but the kind of life which the law promotes and produces. But man's inadequate self-understanding keeps him from this life-giving obedience. He cannot recognize his own **errors.** He unknowingly violates God's will (**hidden faults**). He flouts it consciously because of cocky self-confidence (**presumptuous sins**). The law can be obeyed only on the nonlegalistic ground of reliance on God's sustaining power.

19:14. This is a dedicatory formula (cf. 104:34; 119:108) of the type spoken at the presentation of a sacrifice (cf. Lev. 1:3-4). Here the offering is not an animal sacrifice but a hymn expressive of the total dedication (**mouth** and **heart**) of the worshiper to his God.

Ps. 20. A Prayer for Victory

This royal ps. (on this category, the title, and **selah** see Intro.) is a prayer for **victory** (vss. 5, 9) offered on behalf of the king by a choir of priests on the eve of battle.

20:1-5. The **name** of the Lord is his divine presence residing in the temple (cf. I Kings 8:17). The ambiguity of identifying his dwelling as both the temple and heaven (vs. 6) may be noted in other pss. (see above on 11:4-7*a*). In the temple the king presents a grain offering and a whole burnt offering (vs. 3; cf. I Sam. 7:9; I Kings 8:44-45). Sacrifice and prayer belonged together in the temple ritual. To set up the standards on a battlefield (vs. 5) may be a sign of victory, but in the interest of parallelism it may be better to emend the word translated **set up our banners** to "delight."

20:6-9. A solo voice among the choir sings vss. 6-8, or at least vs. 6. The ideology of the holy war (see Intro.) which informs vss. 7-8 goes back to the period of the tribal confederacy (*ca.* 1250-1000 B.C.). The size and equipment of the army has no bearing on the outcome of the battle, since the Lord, the real commander of the host, *gives* the victory (cf. Judg. 7:2). Absolute trust in his power to overthrow the enemy (see above on 14:5-7) is all that is required of Israel. Calculating relative strength indicates a failure of trust and invites disaster. The RSV translation of vs. 9 is taken from the LXX and other versions as fitting the sense of the ps. much better than the Hebrew text translated in the footnote.

Ps. 21. A Coronation Liturgy

Analysis of this royal ps. (on this category, the title, and **selah** see Intro.) shows that it is appropriate to a variety of cultic occasions. Vss. 1-7 are a thanksgiving hymn sung by the priests in acknowledgment that the king's prayer has been answered. In vss. 8-12 a priest or cultic prophet pronounces an oracle assuring the king of victory over his enemies. Vs. 13 is a doxology offered by the congregation. The ps. would fit the coronation of the king (vs. 3) or the annual festival commemorating the king's enthronement, the eve of a battle (vss. 8-12) or the festival of the enthronement of the Lord (vs. 13; see Intro.).

21:1-7. This hymn expresses the Israelite theory of kingship. The monarch's well-being (**blessings,** vss. 3, 6) and authority to rule (**glory,** vs. 5) are derived from his relationship to God, from the divine **strength** (vs. 1) and **presence** (vs. 6). The king's trust in the Lord is answered by God's **steadfast** (i.e. helping and delivering) **love** (vs. 7). The supreme blessing which the king receives in consequence of this relationship is a long and successful reign. **For ever** (vs. 4) signifies, not immortality (see above on 6:4-5), but the inviolable sanctity and complete fulfillment of life which the Lord bestows on the king.

21:8-12. In the tradition of the holy war this oracle declares that the king's victories are due to the Lord's intervention on behalf of Israel (see above on 20:6-9). The extravagant language of the ps., the oriental "court" style, emphasizes the irresistible power of the covenant God and of his chosen king.

Ps. 22. Dereliction and Deliverance

This individual lament (on this category and the title see Intro.) begins with radical despair (vss. 1-21) and ends in thanksgiving and praise (vss. 22-31). Its setting is any cultic occasion marked by the mood of rejoicing after sorrow.

22:1-21. *Despair.* Three times the psalmist struggles through sorrow toward confidence only to be overwhelmed again by despair:

22:1-5. To the tormented mind of the psalmist his suffering is proof that the Lord has **forsaken** him and that his passionate and continuous prayer falls into an unhearing void. In this overpowering sense of alienation, shared by Jesus on the cross (Matt. 27:46; Mark 15:34), the psalmist draws comfort from reflection on the history of his people. This sacred history witnesses to a God who is **holy** (i.e. other than and different from man), but who is always present with his people, **enthroned** on their hymns of praise as on the cherubim above the ark (cf. 99:1-5; Isa. 37:16), and who has never disappointed those who put their trust in him.

22:6-11. With gestures of derision the psalmist's enemies mock his confidence. Their cruel taunts, confirming his belief that God has abandoned him, strip him of his humanity and reduce him to the lowest form of animal existence. He obtains temporary relief from this agony by remembering his personal history. From his first stirrings in **the womb** God has protected him.

22:12-21. The thought of his enemies, tearing at his legs like a pack of **dogs** and charging him with the fierceness of wild **bulls of Bashan** (the grasslands of N Transjordan), wear him down like a wasting disease, strip the flesh from his **bones,** and leave him dry, brittle, and useless as a broken pot. Some commentators believe that the animal imagery refers to the demonic creatures who, according to pagan mythology, brought disease to men (e.g. the 7 Udugs of Sumerian literature; see below on 91:5-10) and point out that vss. 14-15 describe the effects of fever. Crowding around this emaciated body, the psalmist's enemies treat him as if he were already dead by confiscating his **garments** and dividing the plunder by casting **lots** (cf. John 19:24). This time the psalmist can find no external ground for confidence and simply utters a naked appeal for **help.**

22:22-31. *Rejoicing.* The psalmist looks back on his torment from the tranquility following deliverance.

22:22-24. The psalmist offers public testimony before the worshiping **congregation** in the temple to the salvation which God has brought to him and exhorts all true worshipers and genuine Israelites to praise the LORD for his delivering power (his **name**).

22:25-26. The psalmist acknowledges that his ability to praise is the consequence of his deliverance. In payment of his **vows** (see Intro.) he provides a sacrificial meal to which his friends are invited. **The afflicted** are the God-fearing Israelites of which the psalmist is a leader, and not the materially poor or downtrodden (see Intro.). **Live for ever** is an oriental exaggeration meaning "live long" (cf. I Kings 1:31; Neh. 2:3) and does not refer to immortality (see above on 6:4-5).

22:27-31. The Hebrew text of these vss. is difficult, and numerous emendations have been suggested. The readings accepted by the RSV seem best, except that in vs. 29a "those who sleep in the earth" is preferable to **the proud of the earth.** Under the inspiration of his deliverance the poet's vision broadens to include all time and space. The whole **earth,** the **generation** yet to be born, and the dead in the underworld will accept the rule of the LORD and proclaim his saving acts. The conviction that God's power extends beyond death and reaches even to Sheol is the first theological step toward a doctrine of resurrection (see above on 6:4-5).

Ps. 23. SHEPHERD AND HOST

This poetic gem is a song of confidence (on this category and the title see Intro.) in which a worshiper, grateful for deliverance from human **enemies** (vs. 5) and unnamed perils (vs. 4), presents a thank offering in the temple. Some interpreters hold that the ps. involves only the metaphor of the shepherd. Others see in it an interweaving of 3 images: shepherd, vss. 1-3a; guide, vss. 3b-4; and host vss. 5-6. Because, however, **rod** and **staff** tie vs. 4 to the shepherd metaphor, whereas vss. 5-6 clearly describe a sacred meal, it seems best to regard the ps. as based on the double imagery of shepherd (vss. 1-4) and host (vss. 5-6).

23:1-4. The poet's choice of metaphors is determined by the structural and theological center of his ps.—the triumphant affirmation of faith, **Thou art with me** (vs. 4). In ancient Near Eastern literature kings are called shepherds of their people, and in the OT this language is applied primarily to the LORD's relationship to Israel (cf. 80:1; 95:7; 100:3). Because of his place in the covenant community the psalmist lacks nothing (vs. 1). The Shepherd-God leads him by the right paths to nourishment and rest (vss. 2b-3), and if the way leads through a dark, precipitous defile (**the valley of the shadow of death,** i.e. deathly shade), the sheep fears neither pitfalls nor enemies, for the shepherd with club and staff is near at hand to defend him (vs. 4). **For his name's sake** (vs. 3) may mean "in order that his name may be exalted" or, more probably, "because that is the kind of God he is."

23:5-6. Vs. 5 probably refers to the sacrificial meal associated with the presentation of thank offerings (Lev. 7:11-17). In the thought of the ps., however, the LORD, not the worshiper, is the host, and he provides for his guests with lavish generosity. Ancient laws of hospitality required that the host take his guests under his protection. The psalmist has come to the temple followed by enemies. Now he will be followed by God's saving **goodness and mercy** (i.e. "steadfast love," as the Hebrew word is usually translated elsewhere in the RSV). Vs. 6 is probably a Levitical confession, originally expressing the priest's joy because of his permanent residence in the temple; but to the psalmist God's presence *is* the holy place, and in that protecting presence he will live the rest of his life. **For ever** here is lit. "for length of days" (cf. RSV footnote; see above on 6:4-5).

Ps. 24. AT THE GATES OF THE TEMPLE

This tripartite liturgy (on this category, the title, and **selah** see Intro.) consists of a hymn (vss. 1-2), an entrance liturgy for the people (vss. 3-6), and an entrance liturgy for the LORD's coming to his temple as king (vss. 7-10).

24:1-2. During the festival of the enthronement of the LORD (see Intro.) a cultic procession bearing the ark, the LORD's throne (Exod. 25:10-22), moves up **the hill of the LORD** toward the great gates of the temple and sings in praise of the world-embracing sovereignty and creative power of God (vss. 1-2). For the concept of the inhabited world anchored in the ocean and above the subterranean waters see above on 18:7-18; 19:1-6.

24:3-6. The procession asks the priests for the conditions of entrance to the temple and is answered with a general requirement and 2 concrete illustrations (see above on Ps. 15). He who would worship in the temple must be **clean** not only ritually but also morally in both outer and inner life (**hands** and **heart**). He must **not lift up his soul to** (i.e. worship; cf. 25:1) **what is false** (i.e. idols; cf. 31:6) and must practice honesty in his social relationships. Perjury is a flagrant violation of the integrity which makes possible a stable society. On vs. 6 see above on 11:7b.

24:7-10. Twice the procession calls on the temple **gates** to open and admit the LORD, symbolized by the ark. The Hebrew word translated **ancient** may mean either "everlasting" or "very old." The Egyptians believed that when the **doors** of the earthly temple opened the portals of heaven (eternal gates) swung wide as well, and the ps. may reflect a similar concept. The God who seeks entrance is the **King of glory**—the ruler whose power and authority are unlimited. From within the temple the priests demand further identification of the deity. The procession answers that he is the God of the old holy war tradition, the **mighty** warrior and commander of Israel's **hosts** (i.e. army; see Intro. and on 20:6-9). This tradition was originally associated with the ark at Shiloh (I Sam. 4:1-9) and was transferred to Jerusalem when the ark was brought there at the order of David (II Sam. 6:12-15).

Ps. 25. GUIDANCE AND FORGIVENESS

This individual lament interspersed with expressions of confidence (vss. 8-10, 15), is in places reminiscent of the wisdom pss. (on these terms and the title see Intro.). The ps. is an alphabetic acrostic (see Intro.), and adherence to the form has taken precedence over logical development of the thought. It can therefore best be discussed topically rather than vs. by vs.

The immediate cause of the psalmist's lamentation is the violent attack of treacherous **enemies** (vss. 2, 19), who have isolated him and plunged him into loneliness and despair (**troubles,** lit. "narrowness," **of my heart;** vss. 16-17). Is he, he wonders, being punished for his present sins and those of his wayward youth (vss. 7, 18; cf. Job 13:26)? He is able to approach God, however, because the LORD has revealed himself not only in Israel's history but also in the covenant as a God who pardons **sinners,** saves the afflicted, and removes the barriers (**salvation** comes from a root meaning "make wide"; see above on 18:19) which restrict the lives of his people (vss. 5, 8, 10, 11).

The psalmist bases his prayer on his own character as well as on the name (nature) of God (vs. 11a). He will **lift up** his **soul to** (i.e. worship) and **trust** only the LORD (vss. 1-2a). Eagerly and expectantly he will **wait** (i.e. hope) for divine aid (vss. 5, 21). He will **fear** the LORD (i.e. worship him humbly and with reverential awe, vss. 12, 14). Strengthened by these considerations he prays that God will **deliver** him from his enemies (vss. 2, 15, 19-20; on the **net** of vs. 15 see above on 9:13-17). Beyond physical deliverance he prays that God will **forgive all** his **sins** which have caused his distress (vss. 7, 11, 18) and **teach** and **lead** him in the true meaning of the **covenant,** which will keep him from further offenses (vss. 4-5, 8-10).

Above all other gifts the psalmist craves admission into God's **friendship** (a weak translation of *sodh,* which means a circle of intimate companions, vs. 14; cf. Job 19:19; Jer. 15:17 and see the Intro. to Jer.). If he is granted this relationship, **integrity and uprightness** will be like guardian angels, preserving his life (vs. 21). Vs. 22 was added outside the acrostic pattern to make this highly personal ps. suitable for congregational use.

Ps. 26. A Plea of Innocence

In this individual lament (on this category and the title see Intro.) the psalmist asks that God declare him not guilty of charges made against him by his enemies (vss. 1-2), takes an oath of innocence (vss. 3-5), performs an appropriate ritual (vss. 6-7), renews his prayer for vindication (vss. 8-11), and affirms his confidence (vs. 12). On the setting and theology of this type of ps. see above on Pss. 7; 17.

26:1-2. The psalmist prays for vindication on the ground that his **heart** and **mind** (lit. "kidneys" and "heart," i.e. his inner life; see above on 16:7-8) will pass the test of the LORD's searching examination, possibly during a night spent in the temple (cf. Pss. 3; 4; 7; 17).

26:3-5. Inspired by God's **steadfast** (saving) **love,** he conducts himself in firm loyalty to the LORD. On the negative side he has nothing to do with those who conceal their real thoughts in order to deceive others, and he hates the society of the wicked and godless (see above on 1:4-6).

26:6-7. In confirmation of his oath he washes his **hands**—an ancient means of declaring one's innocence (cf. Deut. 21:6; Matt. 27:24)—and joins in a solemn procession around the **altar, . . . singing** of God's mighty acts in Israel's history (or perhaps of the wonderful deliverance which God will perform for him).

26:8-12. The psalmist professes his love for the temple, the place where Israel confronts the majestic, authoritative presence of the LORD—his **glory** (cf. I Kings 8:11). This moves him to renew his prayer for vindication: may his **integrity** be recognized, and may he not receive the penalty merited by the violence, sexual immorality (**evil devices**), and graft of which his enemies accuse him. In view of his exemplary life he is confident that God will deliver him and establish his position in the community. The **foot** that slips is a frequent OT metaphor for destruction.

Ps. 27. The Conquest of Fear

The song of confidence (vss. 1-6; cf. Ps. 23) and individual lament (vss. 7-14; cf. Ps. 13; on these categories and the title see Intro.) is believed by most scholars to be 2 independent pss. It is possible, however, to view the ps. as a unity describing the experience of a fugitive who seeks refuge in the temple (see above on Pss. 7; 11). While still at a distance and beset by enemies he sings of his confidence in the LORD. Arrived at the temple he pours out his distress in the traditional lament form and receives an encouraging answer from a priest or cult prophet (vs. 14).

27:1-6. *Song of Confidence.* The psalmist has reason to be afraid. His enemies rip at his flesh like a pack of wild beasts (vs. 2 footnote) and come against him like a hostile army (vs. 3). **Uttering slanders against me** (vs. 2) is a questionable translation based on evidence that in later times "to eat up my flesh" (the lit. translation) was a common metaphor for malicious accusation (cf. Dan. 3:8). The psalmist's complete trust in the LORD as his **light,** his deliverer, and his fortress (vs. 1) casts out his **fear.** His **one** prayer and desire is to reach the **temple** (vs. 4a). There he will find permanent refuge and will contemplate the beauty of the sacred place, which is the beauty of the LORD. **To inquire** may be a technical term for offering a sacrifice in the expectation of receiving an oracle from God. **Behold the beauty of the LORD,** which in pagan religion meant viewing the idol (see above on 11:7b), perhaps signifies looking at the ark.

27:5-6. These vss. reflect the function of the temple as a place of refuge for fugitives and describe it in archaic terms reminiscent of the tent of meeting of the wilderness period (see above on 15:1). **In the day of trouble,** when his enemies come forward to condemn him, the psalmist will be exalted over them, as the **rock** on which the temple stood was exalted over Jerusalem. In gratitude he will present the thanksgiving offering with singing and merrymaking.

27:7-14. *Individual Lament.* Vss. 7-13 are a prayer for hearing (vss. 7-9a), acceptance (vs. 9b-10), guidance (vs. 11), and deliverance (vs. 12), followed by a brief cry of confidence (vs. 13). **To seek** the **face** of the LORD is a technical term for entering the temple (see above on 11:7b), and **servant** is a common Near Eastern word for "worshiper." The psalmist has been rejected by all human society, even his parents, but he will be adopted by the LORD (vs. 10). The metaphor may have been suggested by the royal pss. in which the king is the LORD's adopted son. As in many lament pss. the enemies are those who bring false charges against the psalmist (cf. 7:3-4; 35:11). **I believe** is a powerful word signifying "I have anchored my life on the conviction that I will live and receive good from the God in whom I trust."

27:14. This closing oracle in response to the psalmist's lament urges him to show strength and inner **courage** and to **wait** (i.e. hope) expectantly and eagerly for the saving power of the LORD (cf. 25:5, 21).

Ps. 28. If God Be Silent

This individual lament (on this category and the title see Intro.) has a cultic setting like Pss. 7; 17 (which see).

28:1-2. These vss. are a prayer for hearing. If the psalmist receives no answer he is as good as dead and in the lowest part of Sheol (**the Pit;** see above on 6:4-5). Lifting up the **hands** is an ancient gesture of supplication and appeal, directed in this case toward the innermost room (Holy of Holies) of the temple, where the LORD was enthroned above the ark (cf. I Kings 8:6-7). On **rock** see above on 18:1-3.

28:3-5. The psalmist appeals against enemies who greet him as friends while plotting his ruin. **Peace** (*shalom*), meaning total well-being rather than mere absence of conflict, is still the common word of greeting among Semitic peoples (cf. e.g. I Sam. 25:6; John 20:19; Rom. 1:7). They have disqualified themselves from membership in Israel by their unconcern for God's mighty acts in the nation's history. On God's "poetic justice" see above on 7:12-16.

28:6-9. After hearing an oracle of assurance from a priest or cult prophet (cf. 27:14) the psalmist expresses his thanksgiving and joy (vss. 6-7). To bless God is to acknowledge his might and saving power. Unlike his enemies the psalmist is an authentic Israelite and cannot rejoice in his own salvation without recognizing his involvement with the nation and its anointed king (vss. 8-9). On **shepherd** see above on 23:1.

Ps. 29. Praise in Heaven

The background of this hymn for the enthronement of the LORD (on this category and the title see Intro.) is the ancient Near Eastern concept of the council of the gods (see below on 58:1-5; 82:1-5).

29:1-2. In monotheistic Israel the lesser deities (**heavenly beings,** lit. "sons of God" or "sons of gods") have only the status of servants and choir boys. They are exhorted to praise the **glory** of the LORD's **name** (see above on 8:1-2) and to fall down before him "when he appears in his holiness"—a translation, based on an Ugaritic parallel, which seems more probable than the RSV's **in holy array** (i.e. clad in holy garments) or "in the beauty of holiness" (KJV).

29:3-8. The song of the heavenly beings is modeled on Canaanite hymns to the weather god, Baalhadad. **The voice of the LORD** (i.e thunder; cf. 18:13) sounds above the celestial ocean (vs. 3; cf. Gen. 1:7; 6:17), heralding the approach of the storm. The tallest trees are broken, and the land is shaken from end to end, from the N mountains (**Lebanon** and **Sirion,** the Phoenician name for Mt. Hermon) to the desert of **Kadesh,** 50 mi. S of Beer-sheba (see color maps 4, 5).

29:9. The Hebrew text of vs. 9a with vowel points says that the thunder makes the does writhe (i.e. in the throes of giving birth; cf. RSV footnote); but the consonants alone, as written during biblical times, spell either "does" or **oaks.** With slight emendation vs. 9b can be read "and causes the goats to give birth." The irresistible power of the LORD moves those assembled in the heavenly palace (in Hebrew the same word as **temple**) to shouts of acclamation (vs. 9c).

29:10-11. The congregation prays to the God of the sevenfold thunder, who rules **for ever** from his throne above the celestial ocean, for **strength** and **peace** (i.e. well-being; see above on 28:3-5).

Ps. 30. Joy in the Morning

The occasion for this thanksgiving ps. (on this category and the title see Intro.) is the presentation of a thank offering in the temple (see above on 23:5).

30:1-3. The psalmist says he will **extol** (lit. "lift up") the LORD, because his God has raised him from a deadly sickness (vs. 3) and from the callous rejoicing of his enemies over his misfortune (vs. 1b). For **Sheol** and **the Pit** as synonyms for death see above on 6:4-5.

30:4-5. The psalmist invites the worshipers gathered in the temple (**saints**) to join his songs of praise for the God whose wrath is a secondary and transient aspect of his nature, and whose true and permanent purpose for men is gracious and favorable.

30:6-10. From the vantage point of deliverance the psalmist looks back on his trouble. In good times he had been proud and self-satisfied (vs. 6; cf. 10:6). Perhaps to teach him humility God withdrew his protecting presence (vs. 7b) and he fell desperately ill. He appealed to God on the ground that since the dead cannot **praise** God (vs. 9; see above on 6:4-5) his passing into **the Pit** (Sheol) would be all loss and no gain for the Lord.

30:11-12. He acknowledges that this prayer was abundantly answered. God completely reversed his condition of misery, giving him a festal robe instead of the **sackcloth** garment of the mourner. He is sure that his new estate will be permanent. On **soul** and **for ever** see above on 6:1-3; 22:25-26 respectively.

Ps. 31. In the Hand of the Lord

Basically an individual lament, this ps. incorporates features of the hymns and thanksgiving pss. (on these categories and the title see Intro.; for the cultic setting see above on Pss. 7; 17; 22).

31:1-8. After a typical opening prayer (vss. 1-2) the lament appeals to God to act in accordance with his revealed character (**for thy name's sake,** vs. 3; see above on 23:1-4). In describing the divine character the psalmist emphasizes protection, guidance, justice, hatred of idolatry, and **steadfast** (delivering) **love.** Into the hands of this reliable and **faithful** (consistent) **God** he commits his life (**spirit** means "wind" or "breath" and hence life power in man; cf. Luke 23:46). He has complete confidence (vs. 6b) that the LORD, whose saving power he has already experienced, will save him once more. The hunter's **net** (vs. 4; see above on 9:13-17) is a metaphor for hidden peril which strikes without warning, and salvation is appropriately symbolized by **a broad place** (vs. 8; see above on 18:19).

31:9-13. Despair temporarily overcomes the psalmist's confidence. Ridden with disease (vss. 9-10; cf. Ps. 22), mocked and falsely accused by enemies who are openly plotting to do away with him (vss. 11, 13), isolated from his fellow citizens (vs. 11) and from God (vs. 22), he is as much forgotten as if he were in his grave (vs. 12). This acute sorrow has been with him for a long time (vs. 10).

31:14-18. These vss. begin with the congregational confession of faith, **Thou art my God,** and represent a return of confidence. At all stages (**times**) of the psalmist's life the LORD has kept him (vs. 15). He prays that the LORD will again make his **face shine** (i.e. show himself gracious and favorable, vs. 16), and will bring deliverance to him and total destruction to his enemies (vss. 17-18; on **Sheol** see above on 6:4-5).

31:19-24. The final confession of faith in vss. 19-22 is in the mood of a thanksgiving ps. sung by one who has already experienced deliverance. The clump of bushes and the hut which shelter the wayfarer from the driving sand of the desert storm (vs. 20) are powerful metaphors for the protecting power of the LORD. The didactic note of vs. 23 is a common feature of thanksgiving pss. Vs. 24 may be an addition, perhaps reflecting the oracle of assurance spoken by a priest or cult prophet (see above on 27:14).

Ps. 32. Repentance and Forgiveness

This individual thanksgiving (on this category, the title, and **selah** see Intro.) is one of the 7 penitential pss. (see above on Ps. 6). It was probably sung in the temple in connection with the presentation of a guilt offering (Lev. 6:1-8). After 2 beatitudes (vss. 1-2) the psalmist tells of his experience of alienation and forgiveness (vss. 3-5) and confesses his indebtedness to the grace of God (vss. 6-7). He then instructs his fellow worshipers in the style of a wisdom teacher (vss. 8-10) and invites them to join him in praise (vs. 11).

32:1-5. Three words are used to describe man's alienation from God: **transgression,** lit. rebellion; **sin,** lit. wandering from the road or missing the mark; and **iniquity,** lit. distortion or perversion. By concealing his true condition from himself and God the psalmist incurred a heavy weight of guilt which **wasted** his **body** and sapped his **strength** like a disease (vss. 3-4). But when, no longer hiding his guilt, he acknowledged it to God and figuratively cast it upon him (**confess**), God **covered** his **sin** (vs. 1), thought no more of his **iniquity** (vs. 2a), and, healing the broken relationship, received him back into fellowship without prejudice and without reservation (**forgive,** vs. 5d). This forgiveness brought healing, blessing, and purification of the vital power of his life (**spirit;** see above on 31:1-8) so that he no longer misled or dealt treacherously with his fellow men (**deceit,** vs. 2).

32:6-7. In vs. 6b **distress** (lit. "evil") is a conjectural emendation for 2 Hebrew words meaning "finding" and "merely" or "at the least" (cf. RSV

footnote, also KJV ". . . in a time when thou mayest be found: surely in the flood . . ."). The text can be interpreted without emendation as meaning that one who calls on the LORD at the appropriate times (i.e. those prescribed by law and practice? cf. Isa. 49:8; 55:6) will not be overwhelmed when trouble rushes upon him like a flash flood (cf. 124:4) or like an outbreak of the chaotic waters of the underworld (see above on 6:4-5; 18:7-18). Suffering may lead not only to prayer (vs. 6) but also to confidence in God's saving power (vs. 7).

32:8-9. Opinions differ as to whether the speaker here is the psalmist or God. The warning against brutish indifference to religion (vs. 9; cf. Prov. 26:3) would have more weight as a divine word mediated through a priest or cult prophet (see above on 27:14). The eye of God on the worshiper would then be an assurance of his saving presence, not an expression of the psalmist's interest in the welfare of his hearers.

32:10-11. Vs. 10 recapitulates the psalmist's experience. When, like **the wicked,** he withheld his confession of guilt, he suffered. When he opened his life to God he felt the **steadfast** (saving) **love** of the LORD surrounding him.

Ps. 33. God's Word and Work

This typical hymn (on this category see Intro.), suitable for any cultic occasion where the predominant theme was praise, was especially appropriate to the New Year festival (see Intro.), which throughout the ancient Near East centered in the motif of creation (cf. vss. 6-9).

33:1-3. The call to **praise** summons the congregation, conventionally called the **righteous** and **upright,** to join in the hymn to the accompaniment of stringed instruments and festal cries of joy. **New song** does not necessarily mean one originating in the recent past. It could be a familiar hymn renewed in the present experience of God's majesty and the present impulse to praise. On the musical instruments see below on 92:1-4; 150:3. **On the strings** is not in the Hebrew text but is one of several proposed emendations to fill out the meter of the line.

33:4-5. A generalized summary introduces the reasons for praise—not what God gives but what he is and does. The LORD's creative **word** is above reproach and his **work** absolutely trustworthy. He loves **justice,** displaying it in his own actions and demanding it of his servants; and he fills **the earth** with acts of **steadfast** (saving) **love** (cf. Isa. 6:3).

33:6-9. The general statements of vss. 4-5 are illustrated first by the LORD's control of nature. Creation by the word of God is not unknown in ancient mythology. The official theology of Old Kingdom Egypt, e.g., taught that the natural order came into being by the command of Thoth. But in these theologies creation by the word is one concept among many. In Israel it was the ruling, if not the only, doctrine of creation (vs. 9, cf. Gen. 1). Vs. 7 has a mythological ring. God collected as if in a **bottle** (i.e. waterskin) the great ocean above the sky (cf. Gen. 1:7; see above on 18:7-18) and stored it to pour out as rain (cf. Gen. 7:11).

33:10-15. The summary of vss. 4-5 is further illustrated by the LORD's control of history. **Counsel** (vss. 10-11) is a considered decision or plan of action. When God's plans and those of men collide, the human schemes come to nothing. In the OT the **heart,** rather than the brain, is considered to be the organ of thought (vs. 11). On God's judgment throne in heaven see above on Ps. 7. The decisions of that judge are the determining force in history (vss. 13-15).

33:16-19. The summary of vss. 4-5 is again illustrated by the LORD's saving power. On the holy war ideology which underlies vss. 16-17 see Intro. and on 20:6-9. Not human power, calculated in military terms, but humility and reverence (**fear**) are the prerequisites of deliverance.

33:20-22. As the plural pronouns indicate, the conclusion is a congregational response to God's **holy name** (i.e. his nature which sets him apart from and above man) and to his **steadfast** (delivering) **love** extended to his people. The response consists of expectant **hope** (cf. **waits,** vs. 20) and **trust.**

Ps. 34. The Fear of the Lord

This individual thanksgiving has the form of an alphabetic acrostic (on these terms and the title, which has no historical value, see Intro.). It shows how the temple service could combine instruction and worship. After a hymnic introduction (vss. 1-3) and a narrative of deliverance (vss. 4, 6), the ps. teaches the faithful the meaning and saving value of the **fear** of the LORD. Hence it has strong affinities with the wisdom literature (cf. Ps. 1; Prov. 1:7; 9:10).

34:1-3. The introduction provides an epitome of the OT language of praise. To **bless the LORD** is to acknowledge his preeminence and authority over every aspect of life, and to **exalt his name** is to extol his nature by reciting his saving acts.

34:4-10. The psalmist has recently experienced the LORD's saving power. He was delivered from an unnamed anxiety which had set his life in turmoil (vss. 4, 6). The counterpart of his experience is available to all who come into the LORD's presence as humble suppliants. This meaning underlies the rich vocabulary of the approach to God found in this passage—especially the metaphor of tasting (vs. 8), which may have been suggested by the sacrificial meals in the temple. The **angel** (lit. "messenger," vs. 7) is probably the commander of the LORD's heavenly army (cf. Josh. 5:13-15), who includes the God-fearer within the protective circle of his camp (cf. II Kings 6:17).

34:11-22. Despite the impression created by vss. 10, 12, 17, the fear of the LORD is not naïvely presented as a means to prosperity and long life. Basically, as the overall impact of this passage shows, to fear the LORD is to be humble in his presence. Such a life is marked by an orientation toward what God approves (**good**) and what makes for well-being (**peace,** vs. 14; see above on 28:3-5). Outwardly it manifests itself in honesty of speech (vs. 13), but it gives no guarantee against trouble. **Many . . . afflictions** (vss. 18-19) may shatter the inner being (**broken-hearted;** see above on 16:7-8; 33:10-15) of the **righteous** and crush his vital powers (**spirit;** see above on 31:1-8), but his real existence and security are at a depth that suffering cannot reach, and at that level God's presence restores and preserves him. **The wicked** (vs. 21; see above on 1:4-5), lacking this depth, are destroyed by the surface phenomenon of **evil** (i.e. suffering). God's absence from their lives,

which is the real cause of their destruction, thus takes on the appearance of his wrath (vs. 16).

Ps. 35. A Plea for Vindication

The background of this individual lament (on this category and the title see Intro.), like that of Pss. 7; 22, is the prayer of a hunted man for his vindication and for the destruction of his enemies.

35:1-18. The word **contend** is a technical term meaning to enter a legal controversy. The standard imagery and language of the lament dominate the ps.: the **pursuers** (vs. 3; cf. 7:1), the hunter's metaphors of **net** and **pit** (vss. 7-8; see above on 9:13-17), the outcry for poetic justice (vs. 8; cf. 7:12-16), the false **witnesses** (vs. 11; cf. 27:12), the comparison of the enemy with wild beasts (vs. 17; cf. 22:12-13, 16), the mockery in word and gesture (vss. 15-16; 19; cf. 22:7). Vss. 5-6 ask that a warrior **angel** from the LORD's heavenly army be sent to drive the enemies **like chaff** from the threshing floor.

35:19-28. The psalmist's anger against his enemies (vss. 15-17, 20-21) and the intensity of his prayer (vss. 13-14, 22-24) increase until he is demanding that God **awake** and do something (vs. 23). Like all sufferers he sees the world through the narrow window of his own agony, praying for the destruction of his enemies (vs. 26) and for the happiness of those who side with him (vss. 27-28).

Ps. 36. Man's Evil and God's Love

This ps. of mixed type, with features of the hymn (vss. 7-9) and the lament (vss. 10-12; on these categories and the title see Intro.) consists of 3 sections. The first 2 (vss. 1-4, 5-9) contrast the wickedness of the psalmist's enemies with the love of God, and the 3rd (vss. 10-12) prays for the blessing of God's love on those who live in fellowship with him and divine judgment on those who reject him.

36:1-4. Because evil has captured his **heart** (i.e. the very center of his nature), **the wicked,** having neither reverence for God nor **fear** of his judgment, devotes himself to **mischief and deceit.**

36:5-9. The **steadfast love** of God, not the depravity of man, rules the universe. The psalmist makes skillful use of ancient cosmology (see above on 18:7-18) to show the universality of divine love, which is also God's steadfastness and justice (vss. 5-6). It reaches from the **heavens** to the clouds that brood over the earth and from the highest **mountains** to the **great deep** of the underworld. The **children of men** (i.e. all mankind) may shelter in that love and enjoy its bounty (vss. 7-9). The imagery of these vss. was suggested by the temple—the outspread **wings** of the cherubim over the ark and the abundant food and drink of the sacrificial meals. From the living God all life flows, like water from a **fountain** (i.e. a natural spring), and in the light of his presence people of God **see light** (i.e. live). The ps. shows clearly that God's steadfast love is delivering love.

Ps. 37. Trust vs. Envy

This repetitious acrostic poem (on this term and title see Intro.) reinforces by means of a series of proverbs the main tenet of Israel's wisdom teachers (cf. Ps. 1).

Though temporarily shaken and distressed, **the righteous** will be rewarded with long life and prosperity; but **the wicked,** though they may live well and lord it over the righteous, will be destroyed as the spring grass perishes before the first hot wind of summer (vss. 2, 20). In the experience of a long life the psalmist has never seen an exception to this rule (vs. 25).

The synonymous terms **righteous, meek, poor, needy, upright, blameless,** and **saints** refer to the faithful adherents to Israel's covenant faith whose chief characteristic is unshakable confidence in the God of the covenant (they **trust in** and **wait for the LORD**). As a result of this attitude they are **generous** (vss. 21, 26), speak with **wisdom** and **justice** (vs. 30), and obey the **law** (vs. 31).

The repeated warning **fret not yourself** (vss. 1, 8) shows why the ps. was included in the temple service. The prosperity of the wicked might arouse the envy of the faithful and tempt them away from the trust which was the foundation of their lives.

Ps. 38. Under God's Wrath

The background of this individual lament (on this category and the title see Intro.), which is one of the 7 penitential pss. (see above on Ps. 6), is given in the comment on Pss. 7; 22.

The lament begins (vss. 1-2) and ends (vss. 21-22) with a cry to God for **help.** The body of the psalm is an extended account of the psalmist's plight, brought about by deadly sickness (vss. 1-11) and the attack of enemies (vss. 12-20). Expressions of confidence appear in the midst of the lamentation at vss. 9, 15-16. The festering **wounds** (vs. 5), the wasted **flesh** (vs. 7), and the fact that the sufferer is able to move about (vs. 6) indicate leprosy.

The Babylonian prototype of this kind of ps. was used as a magical incantation to remove a spell cast by one's enemies, but in the theology of the psalmist illness and persecution were evidence of the **anger** of God (vs. 1) and proof of the sufferer's guilt. Like Apollo in Greek mythology, the LORD shoots **arrows** of sickness (vs. 2; cf. 91:5).

Convinced his suffering is caused by his **sin** and **foolishness** (i.e. rejection of God's discipline, vss. 3, 5), the psalmist is alienated from himself (vs. 8) and from his **friends** (vs. 11) and is like a **deaf** mute before his enemies (vss. 13-14). All he can do is **confess** the sin he cannot name (vs. 18) and cast himself on the mercy of the God of **salvation** (vss. 21-22).

Ps. 39. Forced to Pray

The key vss. (10-11) show that this individual lament (on this category, the title, and **selah** see Intro.), like Ps. 38, is the cry of a man who attributes his suffering to the wrath of God, brought on him by his sin. For background and general discussion see above on Ps. 38.

39:1-6. Vss. 1-3 are an unusual biographical note. In order not to compound his **sin** or to hearten his enemies the psalmist resolved to keep **silent** (cf. also vs. 9), but the unspoken complaint **burned** within him and forced its way to utterance (cf. Jer. 20:9). The words thus wrung from him (vss. 4-6) are as darkly pessimistic as Eccl. **Life** is short, man's strength a **shadow,** and his efforts futile.

39:7-11. From his own hopelessness the psalmist turns to the one ground of **hope** left to him (vss. 7-11), but he sees God only as wrath, as a deity who **like a moth** consumes the sinner's dearest possession, his life (vs. 11). He therefore prays only to be delivered from the consequences of his sin and from the derision of those who mock his faith (**the fool;** see above on 14:1-4).

39:12-13. The concluding prayer returns to the transience of human life. The psalmist is a **guest** in God's tent and a **sojourner** (resident alien) in his land. He could claim hospitality and protection, but whereas other psalmists pray for the presence of God, he asks only that God withdraw and leave him a brief period of happiness before he is finally cut off by death (see above on 6:4-5).

Ps. 40. Out of the Pit

This ps. of mixed type begins with thanksgiving (vss. 1-10) and ends with lamentation (vss. 11-17; on these terms and the title see Intro.).

40:1-3. In deep distress the psalmist remembers the LORD's goodness in the past. The **pit** "of tumult" (RSV footnote) and **the miry bog** are common Near Eastern metaphors for the underworld (see above on 6:4-5). When the psalmist was at the point of slipping into the realm of the dead the LORD entered into his misery and delivered him. His ability to praise is thus the gift *of* God, and not a gift *to* God (vs. 3*a;* on **new song** see above on 33:1-3). His deliverance obligates him to testify to others (vs. 3*b;* cf. vss. 9-10).

40:4-5. The "new song," his testimony to the congregation, may be quoted in these vss. Unshakable confidence in God is seen to imply not only blessing but also rejection of arrogant self-confidence and its near relative, idolatry. Prideful self-assurance necessarily involves rejection of the LORD. Recitation of the LORD's saving **deeds** (vs. 5) was the chief feature of the covenant renewal ceremony (see Intro.).

40:6-8. The offering acceptable to the God of the covenant is the worshiper himself (**Lo, I come**). The sacrificial system—the **sacrifice** of an animal killed for the common meal, the cereal **offering** of homage to the LORD as King, the **burnt offering** consumed in its entirety on the altar, and the **sin offering**— is secondary and unessential. What is required is **an open ear,** itself a gift of God (vs. 6), and conformity of the whole personality to God's **will** (vs. 8) as it is recorded in the sacred scrolls (vs. 7).

40:9-10. The **law** is not a burden but **glad news of deliverance,** because it reveals a God who acts consistently in **saving . . . love.**

40:11-12. Recollection of the divine **mercy** to himself and others emboldens the psalmist to ask a renewal of that mercy in his present plight. He is acutely conscious that his **iniquities** have so distorted his mind as to rob him of his power of discernment and leave him helpless.

40:13-17. The psalmist here quotes a traditional supplication—almost identical with Ps. 70. It does not continue the theme of sin but reverts to a motif familiar in lament pss. (cf. Pss. 7; 22; 38; 39)—the attack of enemies. The plea of vss. 13-15 is that these foes, who are to be equated with the proud apostates of vs. 4, be stripped of their honors and struck with terror because of their idolatry. **Shame** is a common OT circumlocution for idol worship. **Aha** expresses an unpleasant combination of mockery and delight. The psalmist prays (vss. 16-17) that joy may reside where it properly belongs, in the community of the faithful worshipers of the LORD. The cultic cry **Great is the LORD** suggests the amazing condescension of God, whose majesty does not prevent him from bending his thoughts toward his **needy** servants. This emphasis, missing in 70:5, conforms the traditional lament to the trustful spirit of vss. 1-10.

Ps. 41. INTEGRITY SUSTAINED

This individual thanksgiving (on this category and the title see Intro.) praises God for deliverance from the onslaughts of malicious enemies (cf. Pss. 7; 22; 38; 39).

41:1-3. The opening beatitude indirectly provides the reason for the psalmist's deliverance—his concern for the helpless and needy (vs. 1a). This kind of action results in salvation, the providential care of God, a good reputation, and protection from **illness** and **enemies.**

41:4-10. Because he **sinned** (see above on Ps. 38) the psalmist fell ill and was tormented by malicious enemies who desired his death and the extinction of his **name** (i.e. family, vs. 5). Hypocritically they visited him with **empty words** of comfort, only to go away and spread rumors of what a thoroughgoing sinner he was (vss. 5-7). "**A deadly thing**" (lit. "thing of Belial") **has fastened upon him**" (vs. 8) has the ring of a sorcerer's formula. It reflects the original connection of this type of ps. with Babylonian incantation texts (see above on Ps. 38). Thinking the psalmist a man cursed by God, his closest **friend** joined ranks with his tormentors (vs. 9). The psalmist prayed for recovery in order that he might revenge himself on his enemies and turncoat friends (see above on Ps. 17).

41:11-12. The LORD has been **pleased** with his endurance under trial and granted his prayer. He is able again to enter the temple and can now look forward to a life of continuous fellowship with God (on **for ever** see above on 22:25-26).

41:13. An added benediction closes Book I of the Psalter (see Intro.).

Pss. 42-43. A MAN'S DIALOGUE WITH HIMSELF

Pss. 42-43 were originally a single individual lament (on this category and the title see Intro.) divided into 3 strophes by a refrain of haunting melancholy and soaring hope (42:5, 11; 43:5). Thrice the psalmist sinks into depression and rises again to faith.

42:1-2a. The psalmist begins abruptly with the memorable metaphor of a thirst-crazed deer frantically searching the desert for a stream of water. With the same intensity as the animal seeks the "living water" the psalmist seeks the **living God,** from whom life and hope come. **My soul** (see above on 6:1-3) is an emphatic equivalent for "me."

42:2b-4. The psalmist's sorrow arises from his inability to get to Jerusalem, where alone the living God may properly be worshiped. **Behold the face of God** is a technical term for ceremonial entrance into the temple (see above on 11:7b). The psalmist's depression is aggravated by the taunts of his neigh-

bors, who call in question the existence and activity of his God. Memories of the temple service which in former days he attended on festival days with joyous pilgrims singing pss. rescue him from this slough of despond. The Hebrew of vs. 4b is corrupted and should be emended with the LXX to read:

> how I went into the tent of the Glorious One,
> in procession to the house of God.

On the use of "tent" for the temple see above on 15:1.

42:5. Under the inspiration of these memories the psalmist in his refrain gently chides his soul for its restlessness and expresses the confident **hope** that he will again sing the LORD's **praise** in the temple.

42:6-11. Despair returns and the psalmist's vital power (**soul**) is at a low ebb (vs. 6a). He is an exile, or more likely a prisoner of war (cf. 43:1-2), far to the N of Jerusalem near the source of the **Jordan** River on the slopes of Mt. **Hermon** (see color map 5). **Mount Mizar** is one of the peaks in the Hermon range. Lonely and isolated among enemies, he feels his homesickness beat in his ears like the noise of the chaotic underworld ocean rushing to overwhelm him and carry him down to the realm of death (vs. 7; see above on 6:4-5; 18:7-18). He seems to be forsaken by God (vs. 9), and the pagans around him wound him like a fatal sword thrust by their mocking denial of the reality of his God (vs. 10). **Hope** comes from memory of the hymns of the temple and from prayer, but especially from meditation on the **steadfast** (saving) **love** of God (vs. 8). This is his **rock**—solid ground amid the shifting sands of his loneliness.

43:1-5. The last strophe, phrased in part in bitter questions, is a prayer for vindication before his pagan tormentors. This will take the form of a return to the temple. The psalmist prays that the LORD's **light** (guiding power) and **truth** (the certainty of his salvation) will stream across the intervening miles to bring him home to the **holy hill** in Jerusalem. Restored to the temple, he will place the thank offering on the **altar** and join the congregation in the joyful singing of the pss. of thanksgiving. On **lyre** see below on 150:3.

Ps. 44. WAKE UP, O LORD!

This ps. is a community lament (on the category, the title, and **selah** see Intro.) over military defeat (vs. 10). The "I" of vss. 4, 6, 15 is the leader of worship, possibly the king, speaking as representative of the nation.

44:1-8. Vss. 1-3 refer to the recitation of God's saving acts during the exodus period, which was the chief feature of the ritual of covenant renewal (see Intro.) The ideology of the holy war (see Intro. and on 14:5-7; 20:6-9) fills the ps. **Victory** is won by the LORD (vss. 3-5), who leads the army to battle (vs. 9). The LORD's **countenance** brings terror on the enemy (vss. 3c, 7b). Absolute **trust** is required of Israel's army and king (vss. 6-8).

44:9-16. Past deliverances (vss. 1-3) and victories more recently granted (vss. 4-8) notwithstanding, the LORD has absented himself from the battle just concluded (vs. 9). Fighting in an unholy war the people have been slaughtered **like sheep** (vs. 11), plundered (vs. 10), taken prisoner (vs. 11), and like every defeated nation of antiquity exposed to the

taunt songs of the enemy (vss. 13-16; cf. Judg. 5:28-31). The LORD has **sold** out his **people** and gained no profit (vs. 12).

44:17-22. The LORD'S action is inexplicable, since Israel has rejected idolatry, kept the terms of the **covenant,** and preserved the purity of worship. The defeat has figuratively thrust the nation into the underworld, the realm of death (vs. 19; see above on 6:4-5). **Place of jackals** (*tannim*), if correct, refers to wasteland abandoned to wild animals (cf. Isa. 34:13; Jer. 9:11); but parallelism with the following line makes more likely "place of the dragon" (*tannin*; cf. 74:13; Isa. 27:1; 51:9). God must be asleep rather than arbitrarily opposed to his people. Hence the *demand* that he **rouse** himself and behave like a God of saving love. **Soul** in vs. 25 has its physical meaning "upper chest."

PS. 45. A ROYAL MARRIAGE

This royal ps. (on this category and the title see Intro.) in the flamboyant oriental court style was probably composed for the wedding of Ahab to the Tyrian princess Jezebel (see below on vs. 12a; cf. I Kings 16:31). The poem gained such popularity that it was used at later royal weddings and probably also at the festival of the enthronement of the king (see Intro.).

45:1-9. After a vainglorious introduction (vs. 1) the poet addresses the royal bridegroom, stressing the 2 principal functions of the king—to lead in war (vss. 2-5) and to maintain justice (vss. 6-7). Vs. 6a begins lit. "Your throne, O god." Although the Israelite monarch was never regarded as an incarnate god, as were the pharaohs of Egypt, he could be given a divine title because at his coronation he became the son of God by adoption (see above on 2:7-9). His adoption, symbolized by **the oil** of anointing, and the attendant blessing of God were the sources of his majesty (vss. 2a, 7b). The catalogue of his royal splendors (vss. 6-9) climaxes in the gold-decked figure of the new **queen** standing in the place of honor beside him. On **ivory palaces** see comment on Amos 3:15 (cf. I Kings 22:39). On **Ophir** see color map 7 (cf. I Kings 9:28; 10:11; 22:48).

45:10-17. The latter half of the poem is addressed to the bride. She is admonished to **forget** her foreign origin and to devote herself to her new master. If she does so, she will receive the homage of her Israelite subjects (vss. 10-13a). In vs. 12a the text probably should read, "The people, O daughter of Tyre." The poet then reminds the queen of her glorious entrance into **the palace** (vss. 13b-15) and assures her that her permanent fame will rest, not with her pagan ancestry, but with her children who will occupy the Israelite throne **for ever and ever** (vss. 16-17).

PS. 46. A MIGHTY FORTRESS

This hymn of Zion (on this category, the title, the divine names, and **selah** see Intro.) consists of 3 balanced strophes, each ending with a majestic refrain (vss. 7, 11, but missing after vs. 3). The God who dwells on Mt. Zion is a sure defense for his people even in the catastrophic events of the end of the world. The theme of the end of the age

(eschatology) is rare in the Psalter, but common in prophecy.

46:1-3. The imagery of the first strophe has mythological origins. The chaotic **waters** of the underworld break forth, shaking and submerging **the mountains** and overwhelming **the earth,** so that it reverts to the chaos from which God created it (Gen. 1:2; see above on 18:7-18).

46:4-7. In Jerusalem, where **a river** of life and health flows from the temple, all is quietness and security (vss. 4-5; cf. Joel 3:18; Ezek. 47:1-12). At the end of the age the heathen will **rage** against the Holy City (vs. 6), but the sight of its God-given majesty makes them reel, and at the sound of the LORD'S **voice, the earth melts.**

46:8-11. The last strophe invites Israel to **behold** the result of these cataclysmic events. The earth is covered with broken and burned weapons of war, and God's eternal reign of peace has begun. The goal to which history moves is universal knowledge of God and the submission of all men to him. The direct word of God in vs. 10 was probably spoken by a cult prophet.

PS. 47. THE ENTHRONEMENT OF THE LORD

The theme of this hymn for the enthronement festival, celebrated along with covenant renewal rituals at the New Year feast (on this category, the title, the divine names, and **selah** see Intro.) is God's sovereignty over world history. The repeated claim that the LORD rules **all the earth** (vss. 2, 7-9) is not political wishful thinking but the result of the faith that, since God's authority governs the whole sweep of history, it will eventually be recognized by all mankind.

47:1-4. The people are invited to raise the festal cry as they remember how their **terrible** (i.e. awe-inspiring; see above on 14:5-7) God overcame the Canaanites and gave them the land which he promised to their ancestor **Jacob.**

47:5-7. After the recitation of these mighty acts of God during the covenant renewal ritual the people formed a procession to bear the ark, the throne of the LORD, into the temple (see above on 24:1-2). The blowing of the ram's-horn **trumpet** (*shophar;* see below on 81:1-5b) and the singing of these vss. probably accompanied the procession.

47:8-9. As the ark entered the Holy of Holies the congregation sang the concluding vss. Here the universalism of the hymn is magnificently expressed. History moves toward the time when the rulers of foreign **nations** and the covenant **people,** the heirs of **Abraham,** will form a single congregation, paying homage to the king of the earth, to whom all world power (**shields**) belongs.

PS. 48. THE STRENGTH OF ZION

This hymn of Zion (on this category, the title, and **selah** see Intro.) praises both **Mount Zion** and the **great King** who dwells there. The 2 themes are combined in a single shout of praise. Jerusalem is surrounded by precipices on 3 sides, and the heights were crowned by massive stone walls and numerous defense towers. The palace and the temple were formidable fortresses (vss. 3, 13). The visible fortifications symbolized Jerusalem's unseen defense, the protecting presence of her God, which set her apart from other cities and made her **holy**. Canaanite mythology placed the home of the gods on a mountain **in the far north** (vs. 2). Sacrificing geographical accuracy, the psalmist took over this traditional phrase to describe the home of the one God **of all the earth**.

48:4-8. These vss. reflect the cultic recitation of God's saving acts in which the worshiper could "see" and "hear" (vs. 8) the defeat of Israel's enemies by land and sea. **Ships of Tarshish** were deep-water vessels capable of sailing to Tarshish (probably on the SW coast of Spain; see comment on Jonah 1:3). The terror inspired by God is a feature of the holy war ideology (see above on 14:5-7; 44:1-8).

48:9-14. Vss. 9-11 express the universal rule of Zion's King, whose fame and **praise** have spread from the temple throughout the earth. In holy war contexts God's **steadfast love** (vs. 9) is his power to bestow **victory**. Vss. 12-14 emphasize the community's responsibility to educate its children in the traditions of God's guiding and protecting actions (cf. Deut. 6:20-25).

Ps. 49. The Delusions of Wealth

This wisdom psalm (on this category and the title see Intro. and on Pss. 1; 37) exposes the futility of trust in wealth.

49:1-6. The wisdom teacher calls for a universal audience to consider a universal problem (**riddle**, vs. 4). His personal experience (vs. 5) forced him to ask, "How can one maintain trust in God when the wicked prosper and use their power to exploit the weak?" (cf. Ps. 73). By meditation and as a revelation from God (vss. 3-4) he has obtained an answer which he has cast in the form of a poem and recites to the accompaniment of a **lyre** (see below on 150:3).

49:7-19. Equanimity, says the teacher, can be preserved by contemplation of the common **fate** of mankind. A multimillionaire cannot buy escape from death (vss. 7-9). Death, the great leveler, makes all men—**wise**, godless (**the fool**), boors, and kings— equal and brings them to the same permanent **homes** (vss. 10-12). Led by **Death** (an oblique reference to Mot, the Canaanite god of death) like **sheep** by a **shepherd**, stripped of their possessions, their shades troop to the dark underworld (vs. 14; see above on 6:4-5) while their bodies rot in the family **grave** (vss. 13-14, 17-19).

49:15. This vs. is a faintly sounded intimation of immortality (cf. 73:23-24). Money cannot **ransom** a man from **Sheol**, but God may. How God will buy him back from the power of death he does not know, but even beyond the grave he will be in communion with God and that suffices him.

Ps. 50. God Judges His People

This prophetic liturgy belongs to the New Year festival (on these terms, the title, the divine names, and **selah** see Intro.).

50:1-6. The theophany of the LORD from the temple is accompanied by light and storm (vss. 2-3; see above on 11:4-7*a*; 18:7-18). He comes as **judge** (vs. 6) to bring his people to trial before they enter into the ritual of **covenant** renewal, and his mighty voice calls the whole universe to witness his judgment (vss. 1, 4).

50:7-15. These vss., probably spoken by a cult prophet, give the verdict against the whole congregation. The covenant making at Sinai was accompanied **by sacrifice** (vs. 5; cf. Exod. 24:3-8), but the people have developed a false faith in their sacrifices, believing that the sacrificial meals and **burnt offerings** bind God to them and minister to his needs. To think that the creator and ruler of the world needs gifts or feeds on animal flesh is ridiculous (vss. 9-13). What God requires is his people's grateful acknowledgment of their total dependence on him (vss. 14-15). To **pay . . . vows**—pledges made **in the day of trouble**—is to acknowledge publicly one's debt to God. The psalmist's insight that sacrifices which bind the worshiper to God are valid, but those which attempt to bind the deity to the worshiper are not, is still too easily forgotten.

50:16-23. The Judge's 2nd verdict, again probably spoken by a cult prophet, denies the right of **the wicked** to participate in the covenant renewal. They have rejected the terms of the covenant by word and deed and have mistaken God's patience for approval (vs. 21). He makes a last attempt to reform them by showing the deadly peril in which their conduct has placed them.

Ps. 51. Repentance and Cleansing

This individual lament (on this category and the title, which has no historical value, see Intro.) is one of the 7 penitential pss. (see above on Ps. 6, and for the vocabulary of sin and forgiveness see on Ps. 32).

51:1-2. God's **mercy** and **steadfast** (saving) **love** create the *possibility* of forgiveness.

51:3-5. The 4 aspects of repentance are detailed: (*a*) recognition that **sin** has obtained control over one's life (vs. 3); (*b*) understanding that sin is directed, not against self or others, but against God (vs. 4*a*); (*c*) willingness to assume full responsibility (vs. 4*b*); and (*d*) abandonment of all claim to merit (vs. 5). Vs. 5 does not condemn the sexual act or reflect on the chastity of the psalmist's **mother**. It recognizes that life is lived in an environment of temptation and at no point from his conception can a man claim innocence.

51:6-9. It is the nature of God to desire sincerity in man's inner life. He alone can implant **truth** there and **purge** (lit. "unsin") the sinner. The deeply ground-in stain of sin can be removed only by vigorous scrubbing (cf. vs. 2) and a cleansing agent as potent as the herb **hyssop**, used in the purification of lepers (Lev. 14:4).

51:10-12. The new life is the creation, as miraculous as the formation of the universe, of a new inner life (**clean heart**) and a new life power (**right spirit**; see above on 31:1-8). It is characterized by a marvelous **joy** (cf. vs. 8).

51:13-17. The one valid missionary motive is desire to share the experience of God's saving love with others. The psalmist does so by teaching, by public testimony, and by participation in the temple services. Vss. 16-17 make the same point concerning sacrifice as 50:7-15. **A broken spirit** is one in which the self-assertive craving for autonomy has been shattered and replaced by conformity to God's will.

51:18-19. This ending was added during the Exile by an enthusiastic advocate of sacrifice, who longed for the day when the ruined temple and its sacrificial system would be restored.

Ps. 52. THE FINAL CONDEMNATION

This ps. is an announcement in the prophetic style (cf. Isa. 22:15-25) of God's judgment on the wicked. Possibly it is a formula for the expulsion of an offender from the covenant community (the **godly** or **righteous**). On the title, which has no historical value, and **selah** see Intro.

52:1-7. The **mighty man** (Hebrew term for a hero, used sarcastically) is described as so steeped in **evil** that all his values are reversed. He takes pride in oppression (vs. 1), loves vicious deeds and **lying** words (vss. 2-4), and trusts completely in his possessions (vs. 7). Rather vindictively vss. 5-7 predict his total destruction and the pleasure this will give to his victims. **Tent** (vs. 5) may mean "temple" (see above on 15:1) and refer to expulsion from the religious community, or it may signify simply "household."

52:8-9. The conclusion sounds the theme of the preserving power of trust in God's **steadfast** (saving) **love,** but the psalmist is too sure of his own innocence (see above on Ps. 17 and contrast Ps. 51). Trees, symbols of the goddess of fertility, often grew in pagan sacred places. In the temple the worshiper, secure in God's **presence,** is the symbol of his power, the **green olive tree.**

Ps. 53. THE FATE OF THE WICKED

53:1-6. This ps. is almost identical with Ps. 14. It uses **God** instead of "the LORD" (see Intro.). Vs. 5 has major variations from 14:5-6, drawing more directly on the holy war concept of the terror of the LORD (see above on 14:5-7). To **scatter the bones,** the most permanent part of the body, signifies complete destruction.

Ps. 54. RINGED BY FOES

This is an individual lament (on this category, the title, and **selah** see Intro.; on the cultic setting see on Pss. 4; 7).

54:1-3. The cry for help is based on the **name** (i.e. the saving nature) of God, here equated with his **might.** The psalmist is under attack by foreign enemies ("strangers," as most Hebrew manuscripts read, rather than **insolent men;** cf. 86:14) who do not reverence Israel's God. Perhaps, therefore, the original suppliant was the king.

54:4-5. The expression of confidence presents a textual difficulty in vs. 4b. If the speaker is the king we should probably follow the Hebrew text, rather than the LXX as does the RSV, and read "The Lord is with those who uphold my life," i.e. the armies of Israel. **Requite** (vs. 5) means pay the reward due for their deeds.

54:6-7. These vss. are a vow, a pledge made in time of **trouble.** To **give thanks** means in this context to offer a thank offering (Lev. 7:12). **A free-will offering** is one which is not prescribed by law but is presented voluntarily as an act of homage to God. The psalmist's memory of past deliverances makes him confident of God's present help (vs. 7).

Ps. 55. THE TREACHEROUS FRIEND

Many commentators regard this individual lament (on this category, the title, and **selah** see Intro.; on its cultic setting see on Pss. 4; 7) as 2 poems joined together, but they rarely agree on the limits of each. It may be taken, however, as a single composition, disjointed in structure because of the intense emotion of its author.

55:1-11. The appeal for hearing (vss. 1-2) arises from the attack of vicious enemies (vss. 3-11). **Horror** of the dread realm of **death** oppresses the psalmist's mind (vss. 4-5; see above on 6:4-5). He expresses his desire to escape in the splendid **dove** metaphor. **In the wilderness** (vss. 7-8) he could find refuge from the violence of nature; **in the city** (vss. 9-11) he can find none from the cruelty of men. In prophetic disgust he condemns the total depravity of a community where rogues continually walk the **walls** and wait in the **market place** to cheat and defraud the citizens.

55:12-23. The ranks of his unruly enemies include one who was his best **friend** (vss. 12-14, 20-21), but who has broken the unwritten, mutual bond of friendship (**covenant,** vs. 20). To the Hebrew **fellowship** in worship (vs. 14) is the most intimate of human relationships, the real seal of friendship. Going down **alive** to **Sheol** (vs. 15; see above on 6:4-5) was the punishment of Dathan and Abiram (Num. 16:31-33). **Evening and morning and at noon** (vs. 17) were the customary hours of prayer. Vs. 22 is an "oracle of salvation," probably spoken by the priest for the comfort and encouragement of the sufferer.

Ps. 56. TRUST CASTS OUT FEAR

This individual lament (on this category and the title see Intro.) has a refrain at vss. 4, 10-11. Some interpreters believe the refrain originally appeared at the end of each strophe (i.e. after vss. 7, 13 also); some others consider a refrain inappropriate and explain the inclusion of vs. 4 as a copying error. Since the cry for help (vss. 1-2) uses military language and vs. 7 identifies the enemy as **the peoples,** the original speaker may have been the king.

56:1-4. The word translated **be gracious** is a specific term for a monarch's willingness to hear and act on the petition of one of his subjects. The expression of confidence in vss. 3-4 voices the faith that complete **trust . . . in God** casts out **fear** (cf. vss. 10-11). **Flesh** is man in his humanity and weakness in contrast to the majesty of God.

56:5-7. The reason for the lament is the lying charges and malicious plots of the psalmist's enemies. The fear of death is present, but in a muted form (vs. 6; cf. vs. 13).

56:8-11. The renewed expression of confidence is an impressive metaphorical description of the depth of God's concern for men. He counts how many times the psalmist tosses on his bed. The sufferer's **tears** are not lost. God collects them in a **bottle** (waterskin) and enters each drop in his ledger.

56:12-13. The psalmist pledges a thank offering if his prayer is answered (see above on 54:6-7). The perfect tense in vs. 13 indicates that the ps. was sung just before the presentation of the offering.

Ps. 57. PRAISE AFTER PERSECUTION

This individual lament (on this category, the title, which has no historical value, and **selah** see Intro.)

follows the usual lament pattern: cry for help (vs. 1), description of the trouble (vss. 4, 6, interrupted by a refrain in vs. 5), and expression of confidence and vow (vss. 7-10, followed by the refrain in vs. 11). The normal elements of the lament are present: appeal to the divine mercy (vs. 1), comparison of the enemy to wild beasts and of their machinations to a hunter's traps (vss. 4, 6), God's poetic justice (vs. 6b), oath of innocence (vs. 7), and vow (vss. 8-10). On these features see above on Pss. 7; 17; 22; 31.

57:1-6. On the shadow of thy wings (vs. 1) see above on 17:6-9. Vs. 3, looking forward to the theophany (see above on 11:4-7a), personifies God's **steadfast** (saving) **love and his faithfulness** (self-consistency) as ministering angels (cf. vs. 10, which marvels at the magnitude of these divine qualities that fill the universe). On **net** (vs. 6) see above on 9:13-17.

57:7-10. The closing expression of confidence is especially fine. The psalmist declares that he has responded to God's faithfulness by consistent loyalty to his Lord. He then pictures the joy of the morning (cf. Ps. 30) when, after his night's vigil in the temple, he awakes to the assurance that he has been vindicated at the bar of God's justice. He greets the new day with music (see below on 150:3), song, and sacrifice which will be heard in foreign lands (vs. 9), or perhaps by Jews from other parts of the world gathered in the temple.

57:11. The psalmist's universal outlook appears in the refrain in the prayer that God's **glory** (authority) be recognized in **the heavens** and on **earth.**

Ps. 58. Demons in Heaven and Earth

This community lament (on this category and the title see Intro.) is unusual in structure and rich in varied word pictures.

58:1-5. The question and answer of vss. 1-2 are spoken by God to the members of his heavenly court (see above on 7:6-11; 29:1-2). In Babylonian mythology the council of the gods met annually to determine the fates and inscribe them upon the Tablets of Destiny. In OT thought the divine council is an assembly, not of gods of roughly equal status, but of the Lord and his angelic messengers and servants whose duty is to maintain his justice in the world (cf. 82:1-5). God charges them with rebellion and with corrupting his moral order. **The wicked** (vss. 3-5) are the human agents of these demonic beings. They are like viper's **venom** in the bloodstream of society (vs. 4) and heed warnings and entreaties no more than a **deaf adder** responds to the **voice** of snake **charmers** (vs. 5).

58:6-9. The psalmist appeals to God to destroy the wicked in heaven and on earth as quickly as a housewife's cooking **pots** heat up over a fast-burning fire of **thorns** (vs. 9). Dry thorn bushes are still gathered for fuel in the Holy Land. The slimy track of **the snail** (vs. 8) suggested to the prescientific mind that the animal was dissolving as it crept along.

58:10-11. The faithful members of the covenant community (**the righteous**) will see in the extinction of the wicked their own **vengeance** and the operation of the perfect justice of God. The bloodbath is an ancient symbol of vengeance. In Canaanite mythology the goddess Anath walked knee-deep in the blood of her enemies.

Ps. 59. A Prayer Against the Nations

This individual lament (on this category, the title, which has no historical value, the divine names, and **selah** see Intro.) alternates between prayers (vss. 1-2, 4b-5, 8-13, 16-17) and descriptions of the psalmist's distress (vss. 3-4a, 6-7, 14-15).

The ps. has many of the standard features of Hebrew lament poetry: fear of death (vs. 3a; cf. 6:4-5), oath of innocence (vs. 3b; cf. Ps. 4), appeal to God to **come** (vss. 4b, 10, cf. 18:4-9), comparison of the enemy to wild beasts (vss. 6-7, 14-15; cf. 22:12-21), cry for vengeance and the destruction of the enemy (vss. 10b-13; cf. Ps. 17), and pledge of songs of praise in the morning after God has made clear his intention to save (vs. 16, cf. 4:7; 5:3). Less usual are the references to the Lord as God of the covenant people (vss. 5, 13) and as ruler of history who laughs at the would-be world powers (vs. 8).

God is described in military terms (**strength . . . fortress,** vss. 9, 17; **shield,** vs. 11); and the psalmist identifies his enemies as **nations** (vss. 5-8), accusing them of bloodthirstiness, pride, and treachery (vs. 2), and denial of the sovereignty of God (vs. 7). He calls Israel **my people** (vs. 11). These facts indicate that the king was the suppliant who originally offered this prayer in the temple.

Ps. 60. A Nation Rejected

This ps. is a community lament in liturgical form (on this category, the title, which has no historical value, and **selah** see Intro.). Its date is uncertain, but since Shechem is in enemy hands (vs. 6), it was perhaps composed after the Assyrian conquest of the N Kingdom (722 b.c.). On the holy war ideology see Intro. and on 14:5-7; 20:6-9.

60:1-3. After military defeat the nation, broken and reeling like a drunken man, gathers in the temple for a ceremony of national lamentation. The belief that disaster in war was caused by the anger of the national deity was widespread in antiquity. A commemorative stele of Mesha, king of Moab, attributes his defeat at the hands of the Israelites to the fact that the Moabite god "Chemosh was angry with his land."

60:4-5. Already God's **banner** has been raised to rally the scattered troops. The peasant soldiers of Israel, mostly spearmen, naturally feared **the bow,** the weapon of trained warriors. The people pray for victory in order that God's **beloved** (i.e. Israel) may be saved and appeal to God for an answer.

60:6-8. The response comes in an oracle spoken by a priest or cult prophet. The central highlands around **Shechem** and the **Vale of Succoth** E of the Jordan will be reconquered and reapportioned as in the days of the original conquest (vs. 6). All the land E of the Jordan (**Gilead** and **Manasseh**) belongs to Israel's God; and on the W the 2 great tribes, **Ephraim** in the N and **Judah** in the S, are his battle armor. Judah holds the supremacy since she is God's **scepter,** the symbol of his royal power (vs. 7). God's rule extends to the vassal states of **Moab, Edom,** and **Philistia** (vs. 8; see color maps 6, 8). The Dead Sea (Moab's sea, since that nation occupied its E shore) is God's **washbasin,** and he casts his **shoe** (an ancient symbol for claiming possession) over Edom.

60:9-12. Assured of God's sovereignty over the

whole territory, the king or the commanding general seeks God's guidance for a campaign against Edom (vs. 9) and reflects on the reason for the recent defeat (vss. 10-11). God rejected his people and did not go with them to battle. If, however, he will accept his people's prayer and fight for them, defeat will be turned to victory.

Ps. 61. A Prisoner's Lament

This individual lament (on this category, the title, and **selah** see Intro.) was sung by one far from the temple and surrounded by enemies. Since it assumes that a king is reigning in Jerusalem, it must date from before the Exile, and the singer is likely a prisoner of war.

61:1-4. After a cry for hearing (vss. 1-2a), the psalmist, conscious that he cannot reach the temple (**the rock,** vs. 2b) by his own power, prays for the guidance and protection of God. He longs to live the rest of his days in the environs of the sacred place (vs. 4; on **tent** and the **wings** of God see above on 15:1; 17:6-9 respectively).

61:5. Externally and inwardly the psalmist is a true Israelite, one of those whose ancestors received the Holy Land as a heritage from God, and one who reverences God's **name,** i.e. his mighty nature and saving deeds. He is therefore certain that God has heard his pledge of sacrifice and praise to be rendered in the temple and will enable him to fulfill his **vows** (cf. vs. 8; see above on 7:17).

61:6-8. Prayers for **the king** in language like that of vss. 6-7 are frequent in ancient Near Eastern religious poetry.

Ps. 62. What Supports Trust?

This song of confidence has features of the lament and wisdom pss. (on these categories, the title, and **selah** see Intro.).

62:1-7. The ps. begins in a mood of serene confidence that God will deliver the psalmist from his trouble (vss. 1-2). Virtually the same words reappear in vss. 5-7. On **my soul** see above on 6:1-3; 42:1-2a. The psalmist then castigates his enemies (vss. 3-4) for taking advantage of his weakness and trying to topple him like a shaky stone **wall.** He was evidently a man of authority whom his political opponents tried to unseat by slander and lies.

62:8-10. The psalmist adopts the stance of a wisdom teacher toward those who look to him as leader and exhorts them to **trust** and prayer. Human nature, no weightier than a **breath,** cannot be trusted. Crime and confidence in **riches** delude but do not save.

62:11-12. The conclusion has the form of a numerical proverb (e.g. Prov. 6:16-17; cf. Job 5:19; Amos 1:3). In the deliverance of Israel from Egypt God revealed himself, and the psalmist has heard the message repeated in the temple worship. God is a God of justice (vs. 12b), whose deeds of **steadfast** (saving) **love** are backed by unlimited **power.** *He* can be trusted to save.

Ps. 63. A Thirst for God

This individual lament (on this category and the title, which has no historical value, see Intro.)

weaves the customary phrases and ideas of lament poetry into a composition of uncommon beauty. It is spoken by one who has sought **sanctuary** in the temple (vss. 1-3) and found refuge and a renewal of joy (vss. 5-8). At the end his vision broadens beyond his own situation, and he reaches the certainty that the king, the lord of the temple, and the nation of which he is the earthly representative will prosper (vss. 9-11).

63:1-4. As a desert wanderer longs for water, the psalmist yearns with his whole being for the protective presence of God. **Looked upon thee** (vs. 2) is a technical term for God's self-revelation to his worshipers (theophany; see above on Ps. 11). To experience God's **steadfast** (saving) **love** and to witness to it in worship **is better than life** (vs. 3). Standing with **hands** extended, palms upward (vs. 4b), was the traditional posture for prayers of petition.

63:5-11. During a night vigil the psalmist is given the certainty that he is safe under God's protection, and this satisfies him as if it were the richest of foods (vss. 5-6). On the **wings** of God see above on 17:6-9. Poetic justice (see above on 7:12-16) will overtake his enemies. They seek his life but will themselves **go down** to the realm of death (see above on 6:4-5). The **sword** and the scavenging **jackals** are common OT symbols of destruction (cf. Jer. 7:33; Lam. 5:18). As in Babylon and Egypt, oaths were taken in Israel **by . . . the king** (vs. 11).

Ps. 64. The Destroyer Destroyed

This ps. is an individual lament (on this category and the title see Intro.).

64:1-6. The prayer for hearing (vs. 1) is followed by a bitter description of the enemies who, like archers **shooting from ambush** or hunters setting **snares,** try to destroy the psalmist by **secret plots** and lying charges (vss. 2-5a). They hold God's justice in contempt and trust the profundity of their own scheming minds (vss. 5b-6; on the elements in this description see above on Ps. 59 and references listed there).

64:7-10. God will destroy the destroyers (vss. 7-8; see above on 7:12-16). The **arrow** of God (vs. 7) usually refers to sickness (cf. 38:2). Others will profit by the fate of the malicious liars, learning to reverence God and to meditate on his mighty deeds (vs. 9). The **righteous** and **upright** (i.e. the faithful members of the covenant community) will **rejoice** and will extol the authority of God.

Ps. 65. Creation, Providence, and Salvation

This is a hymn of thanksgiving (on this category and the title see Intro.). In a time of drought the congregation pledged that if God would send rain they would offer him a sacrifice of praise. The ps. is the payment of that vow (see above on 7:17).

65:1-4. Since the drought was regarded as punishment for national sin, strophe 1 appropriately praises God for his willingness to hear **prayer** and to **forgive** sin. The **temple** on Mt. **Zion,** the dwelling of God, is the source of the prosperity of the land, and any member of the chosen people who enters its courtyards comes within the sphere of blessing (vs. 4).

65:5-8. Strophe 2 draws a universal lesson from

the deliverance from drought (cf. vs. 2). Israel's God is the hope of the whole earth, for he is its creator. Vs. 7 refers to the Babylonian belief that before they created the ordered universe the gods had to subdue the raging sea of chaos, personified as the dragon-monster Tiamat (see below on 74:12-14). The ps. historicizes this mythological concept by equating the turbulent sea with the unruly nations, Israel's historic enemies (vs. 7c). Dawn and sunset are visible signs of God's authority over the world from end to end. The pagans recognize that this is so, but wrongly attribute the movement of the heavenly bodies to the activity of their many gods (vs. 8).

65:9-13. Strophe 3 pictures the rejoicing of nature at the coming of the rain, which streams from **the river of God,** i.e. the ocean above the heavens (cf. Gen. 1:7; 7:11; see above on 18:7-18; 33:7-9). The Canaanites believed that their fertility God, Baal, the rider of the clouds, brought the rain. Vs. 11 retains the pagan imagery but identifies the cloud **chariot,** in whose rain-soaked **tracks** the land springs to life, with the chariot of the LORD (cf. 104:3). The bountiful harvest is a crown on the head of the **year** (vs. 11).

Ps. 66. Deliverance Acknowledged

This ps. is an individual thanksgiving (on this category, the title, and **selah** see Intro.) to accompany the payment of a vow (see above on 7:7).

66:1-4. The psalmist summons **all the earth** to praise the **glory** (authority) of God's **name** (nature) as revealed in his historic acts of salvation and his triumph over his **enemies.** Vs. 4 might be better translated: "Let all the earth worship thee; let them sing praises. . . ."

66:5-7. The congregation is invited to dramatic recollection of God's greatest saving deed, the deliverance from Egypt, especially the drying up of the **sea** (Exod. 14:21-29) and the **river** (Josh. 3:14-17) and the defeat of the **nations** who opposed Israel.

66:8-15. The hardships and defeats of the wilderness period were a test of Israel's loyalty to her God (vs. 10), but in the end he brought the nation safely into the **spacious place** of Canaan (vs. 12; see above on 18:19). The psalmist regards these events as typical of all God's saving deeds, including the deliverance which he has personally experienced. While in distress he vowed to offer **burnt offerings** in the temple and is now ready to pay his vows with costly sacrifices (vss. 13-15).

66:16-20. The psalmist in his testimony to the congregation (vss. 16-19) claims, not that he was sinless, but that sin did not gain control of his inner life (vs. 18) and that even in his distress he did not lose the spirit of praise (vs. 17). Therefore God heard him and delivered him by an act of **steadfast** (saving) **love** (vs. 20).

Ps. 67. A Harvest Thanksgiving

This community thanksgiving for the harvest festival (on this category, the title, and **selah** see Intro.) contains 2 principal themes: praise to God for his bounty (vs. 6) and prayer that all nations will reverence Israel's God (vs. 7 and the refrain, vss. 3, 5).

67:1-3. In words reminiscent of the Aaronic benediction (Num. 6:26) the congregation recalls the prayer for blessing which was offered at seedtime (vs. 1), in which Israel sought prosperity as a visible sign to the whole world of the **power** of her God (vs. 2).

67:4-5. In the same universal spirit the 2nd strophe extols God's perfect justice, which, although not universally recognized, in fact rules and guides all history and all men.

67:6-7. The congregation gratefully acknowledges that its prayer for blessing has been answered by a good harvest and renews its prayer for the conversion of the world.

Ps. 68. Themes from the Theophany

In both text and interpretation this ps. is the most difficult in the Psalter. Some regard it as a unified composition used in a procession (vs. 24), others as a mere index of first lines. It seems to be a collection of fragments united around the idea of the theophany —God's appearing to his people (see Intro. and on 11:4-7a). The dominant motif is the warrior God leading the holy war (see above on 14:5-7; 20:6-9), found in 5 of the poems. On the title, divine names, and **selah** see Intro.

68:1-3. The first poem calls on God to destroy Israel's enemies in the holy war (cf. Num. 10:35) and bring joy to the nation.

68:4. A hymnic fragment of praise to the God **who rides upon the clouds** (see above on 65:9-13).

68:5-6. A minor motif of the ps. but one appropriate to the theophany is God's justice (see above on 7:12-16). Essentially that justice is the protection of the needy and easily exploited classes of society and hatred of self-will and highhandedness.

68:7-14. This longest of the poems in the collection recalls the classic instance of holy war, the conquest of Canaan. It is reminiscent of the ancient Song of Deborah (Judg. 5). Amid rain and earthquake God comes from his traditional home on Mt. **Sinai** to conquer a homeland for his **people** (vss. 7-10). His word of command shatters the enemy, and hosts of angelic beings hasten to report the victory (vss. 11-12). **The spoil** enriches even the humblest Israelite. A shepherd woman receives a **gold**-and-**silver**-encrusted statuette of a **dove,** the emblem of the Canaanite love goddess Astarte (vs. 13). The victory is accompanied by natural wonders. **Snow,** a rarity in Palestine, falls on Mt. **Zalmon** in the central highlands near Shechem (cf. Judg. 9:48).

68:15-16. A hymn in praise of the temple, the place of the theophany, denies the claim of some **mountain of Bashan** in the N Transjordan region (Hermon, or the mythological mountain of the gods?) to be called the home of the LORD. He has himself chosen the temple **mount** in Jerusalem as his dwelling.

68:17-18. Another reminder of the conquest of Canaan, this fragment tells how, after his victory over the Canaanite kings, the LORD transferred his residence from **Sinai** to the **holy . . . mount** in Jerusalem, traveling like an oriental monarch surrounded by his angelic charioteers, leading his **captives,** and receiving the homage of his subjects.

68:19-20. This is another brief hymn of praise to the God who comes to save his people.

68:21-23. This holy war fragment quotes an ancient promise of God to bring the fugitive Canaanites back from Bashan on the E or from the sea on the W in order that Israel's revenge might be complete. Long hair, a symbol of strength, was the mark of the soldier (vs. 21b). On the bloodbath see above on 58:10-11; cf. I Kings 21:19.

68:24-27. This poem describes the cultic procession at the enthronement festival (see Intro.). Two S tribes, **Benjamin** and **Judah,** and 2 from the N, **Zebulun** and **Naphtali,** are mentioned to indicate the presence of the whole 12-tribe confederacy by specifying its extremes. **Fountain** (vs. 26) is probably a scribal error for "assembly."

68:28-31. This holy war poem calls on God to reenact the ancient victories over Canaan against Israel's present enemies and to bring even Egypt and Ethiopia under his rule (cf. Isa. 18:7). Vs. 30 is almost impossible to translate, but **beasts . . . among the reeds** probably represents Egypt along the marshy banks of the Nile.

68:32-35. The final poem is a hymn of praise to the God who **rides in the heavens** (see above on 65:9-13) and is **terrible** (awe-inspiring) **in his sanctuary,** the temple.

Ps. 69. Piety Mocked

This individual lament (on this category, the title, and the divine names see Intro.) alternates between prayer (vss. 1a, 6, 13-18, 22-29) and lamentation (vss. 1b-5, 7-12, 19-21).

69:1-5. After a stark, bare cry for help (vs. 1a) the first lament employs with unusual power the customary metaphors for deep distress (cf. 6:4-7; 40:2). The psalmist's enemies have got the better of him by **lies** and false accusations (vs. 4). God, who sees all his sins, knows that he is innocent of those for which he is being punished (vs. 5).

69:6-12. The psalmist prays (vs. 6) that he may be delivered from his enemies in order that the faith of the God-fearing folk who look to him as leader may not be shaken. His second lament tells how even his relatives shun him as a sinner (vs. 8) and the village wiseacres and tavern haunters make witty **songs** about him as a pious pretender (vs. 12). Thus his **zeal** for God and his temple (vss. 7, 9) has become the main cause of his misery.

69:13-18. The psalmist calls on God for help on the basis of his **steadfast love** and **abundant mercy.**

69:19-29. The psalmist laments again that those from whom he expected comfort have given him heartbreaking insults and **poison for food** (vss. 19-21). Then he voices a terrible prayer for vengeance (vss. 22-29). His enemies have tried to poison him; may their hypocritical participation in the **sacrificial feasts** poison them, glazing **their eyes** and making their limbs shake (vss. 22-23). May their families be destroyed (vs. 25). May their **punishment** be endless, without hope of acquittal (vs. 27). May their names be erased from God's ledger of **living** men and from the rolls of **the righteous** (i.e. the covenant community, vs. 28).

69:30-33. If deliverance from his enemies is forthcoming the psalmist vows to **praise** God with a grateful heart—a more acceptable offering than costly sacrifices. Others in peril or need will **see** his deliverance and will have their faith renewed.

69:34-36. The concluding call for universal praise may have been added during the Exile by a poet who saw in the psalmist's plight a parallel to the sufferings of the exiles in Babylon and used the ps. to pray for the restoration of **Zion** (i.e. Jerusalem) and **Judah.**

Ps. 70. A Plea for Help

For comment see above on 40:13-17, where this ps. is quoted almost verbatim. On the title see Intro.

Ps. 71. Distress in Old Age

This individual lament (on this category and the divine names see Intro.) is spoken by an old man (vss. 9, 18) so hard pressed by the lying charges of **cruel . . . enemies** (vss. 4, 10-11, 13) and by the sense of alienation from God (vss. 11, 18) that he has become for many the symbol of what the wrath of God can do to a man (vs. 7). In this extremity he seeks sanctuary in the temple and vindication from the God of justice—the **refuge** of every needy soul (vs. 3), who has watched over his **birth,** supported him in his **youth** (vs. 6), and educated him in the sacred traditions of the covenant people (vs. 17).

The psalmist's single appeal for vengeance is comparatively mild (vs. 13; cf. 69:22-29), and his expressions of confidence are frequent (vss. 3, 5, 19-21). In his trouble he makes 2 vows: public testimony to God's **deeds of salvation** in Israel's history and in his personal experience (vss. 15-19) and joyful songs of **praise** (vss. 22-24).

For background and further details see above on Pss. 4; 7; 9-10; 22. On **harp** and **lyre** see below on 150:3.

Ps. 72. A Coronation Hymn

This royal psalm (on this category and the title see Intro.) was composed in the inflated style of the court poets for the accession to the throne of a crown prince.

72:1-7. The **son** of his predecessor in the divinely chosen line, the new **king** is the human agent through whom God's **justice** reaches the nation (vss. 1-4; cf. vss. 12-14; on the concept of justice see above on 7:12-16; 85:5-6). The poet prays that the royal justice will fill both society and nature (vs. 3). The king's intimate relationship to God makes him the bearer also of the blessings of prosperity and fertility to the land (vs. 6; cf. vs. 16). In his prosperity the nation flourishes, and the poet prays for his long life (vss. 5, 7).

72:8-17. The poet further prays that the king may be blessed with victory (vs. 9), worldwide **dominion** (vss. 8-11, 17), and wealth (vs. 15). According to ancient geography the inhabited earth was bounded by **sea** on all sides (vs. 8a). **The River** (vs. 8b) is the Euphrates. The places mentioned in vs. 10— **Tarshish,** probably on the SW Spanish coast (see comment on Jonah 1:3); the **isles** of the Mediterranean; **Sheba** in S Arabia (see color map 7); and **Seba,** probably in Ethiopia—stand for the remote, the foreign, and the exotic. On the theological implications of the claim to world domination see above on Ps. 2.

72:18-20. Vss. 18-19 are the closing benediction to Book II of the Psalter, and vs. 20 probably marks the end of an early compilation (see Intro.).

Ps. 73. THE PILGRIMAGE OF A SOUL

This wisdom psalm (on this category and the title see Intro.) depicts a journey from the dark night of doubt to the dawn of faith.

73:1-3. The psalmist, a priest or leader of the religious community, **had well nigh slipped** (vs. 2) from the established doctrine that loyalty to God means prosperity (vs. 1). In the world as he saw it arrogance and brutality paid dividends, and to his horror he found himself envying **the prosperity of the wicked** (vs. 3).

73:4-14. The social situation which created his doubts is described. Free from pain and **trouble** (vss. 4-5) the oppressors wear **pride** and **violence** as badges of distinction (vs. 6), and instead of shunning them **the people** rush to do them honor (vs. 10). They blaspheme God and exploit their neighbors (vs. 11) and grow daily fatter and more self-satisfied (vs. 7), while the psalmist has been loyal and devout to no purpose (vss. 13-14).

73:15-17. The psalmist's first reaction was to publicize his doubts before the congregation, but that would solve nothing and merely injure the congregation of which he was leader (vs. 15). He sought the solution of his problem by earnest thought, but his intellectual processes were rendered incompetent by the nagging pain and bitterness of his mind (vs. 16). At the end of his resources he entered the temple to lay his case before God, and there he discovered the answer to his problem (vs. 17).

73:18-28. At one level the answer is simply that wealth is a precarious foundation for life. Standing on the **slippery** edge of an abyss, the wicked will suddenly disappear over the edge and be forgotten **like a dream** (vss. 18-20). At a deeper level the psalmist learned that material prosperity is religiously irrelevant. In his envy of the wicked he was **like a beast** displaying exclusive concern for its own comfort (vss. 21-22). The center of life must be God, not possessions, and the one who possesses fellowship with God is richer than any plutocrat (vss. 25-26, 28). Communion with God is permanent, guiding this life and enduring into the mysterious **afterward** beyond death, where God's **glory** (authority) still rules (vss. 23-24). This passage, for which some interpreters have suggested other meanings, seems to be one of the rare exceptions to the usual view in the Psalter that death brings only a shadowy existence in Sheol far removed from God's presence (see above on 6:4-5; 49:15).

Ps. 74. THE DESTRUCTION OF THE TEMPLE

This community lament (on this category and the title see Intro.) bewails the destruction of the temple, probably by the Babylonians in 586 B.C. though some have argued for the desecration by Antiochus IV in 168 B.C. (see "The History of Israel," pp. 1026-31).

74:1-11. God is bluntly accused of abandoning his people in anger and forgetting his covenant and his own dwelling place on **Mount Zion.** The **enemy** (vss. 4-8) have set up their battle standards in the temple, **hacked** away the woodwork for its gold and ivory inlay, burned the **sanctuary,** and **destroyed** the places of assembly in the outlying towns. During this disaster God has kept his delivering **right hand** tucked in his robe (vs. 11), and no **signs** of deliverance (cf. Judg. 6:14-18) or prophetic word of assurance have come from him to dispel the anxiety of his people.

74:12-14. In Babylonian mythology the god Marduk split in half the dragon monster Tiamat, symbolized by the chaotic ocean, and from her carcass created the universe. The Canaanite Baal was said to have broken **the heads** of the unruly Judge River (Hebrew **Leviathan**) with a magic club. But it was the LORD, rather than the pagan deities, who in the beginning overcame all forces of disorder.

74:15-23. He who controls the **springs** and rivers, **day** and **night,** the stars and the seasons (vss. 15-17) can easily dispose of a puny human enemy. By his known merciful character (vs. 21), by the promises of the **covenant** (vs. 20), and by the shame to which inactivity exposes him (vss. 22-23) the nation calls on God to act.

Ps. 75. GOD'S COMING IN JUDGMENT

This is a liturgy (on this category, the title, and **selah** see Intro.) for the ritual of covenant renewal, when the congregation recited God's wonderful deeds of the past and looked for new manifestations of his power.

75:1-5. After a congregational thanksgiving (vs. 1) a cult prophet gives a direct word from God (vss. 2-5). **At the . . . time** determined by his own sovereign will he will come in final judgment of the **wicked.** Meanwhile when the foundations of society tremble the creator of the world holds them **steady.** On the **pillars** of the world see above on 18:7-18; 19:1-6. The **horn,** the armament of the powerful bull, is an ancient oriental symbol for might.

75:6-10. The congregation responds to the word of God (vss. 6-8), acknowledging that justice can be found nowhere in the world but in God alone. The concept of the **cup** of God's wrath which crazes and destroys the wicked (vs. 8; cf. Jer. 25:15-16; Obad. 16) probably originated in the ordeal in which a suspected criminal was made to drink a cup of sacred liquid (Num. 5:16-32; see above on 11:6). A solo voice leads the concluding thanksgiving to the God of justice (vss. 9-10).

Ps. 76. THE TERRIBLE GOD

This hymn of Zion (on this category, the title, and **selah** see Intro.) celebrates the theophany of God in his temple (see Intro. and on 11:4-7a; 18:7-18).

76:1-6. Though God dwells in heaven (vs. 8), his point of contact with the world is Mt. **Zion** in the midst of **Salem** (a pre-Israelite name for Jerusalem; cf. Gen. 14:18), where his **name** (i.e. saving nature) is **known** and proclaimed. His presence makes Zion **more majestic than the everlasting mountains** (vs. 4). He is a warrior God, and the terror of his presence makes his enemies fall unconscious (vss. 3, 5-6; on this terror in the holy war ideology see above on 14:5-7).

76:7-9. The God who appears on Mt. Zion is the heavenly God whose authority embraces the whole **earth.** The theophany is the revelation of his **judg-**

ment, which means peace for the world and deliverance for the oppressed (see above on 7:14-16).

76:10-12. God makes even the hostility of his enemies a source of praise, and those who survive the residue of wrath (i.e. his judgment) worship him (vs. 10). To this kingly and victorious God it is appropriate to pay vows (see above on 7:17; 50:7-15) and offer homage (vs. 11). On spirit (vs. 12) see above on 31:5.

Ps. 77. The Deeds of the Lord

This individual lament passes at vs. 11 into a hymnic meditation on Israel's deliverance from Egypt (on these categories, the title, and selah see Intro.).

77:1-10. In an agony of body and mind the psalmist tosses sleepless on his bed, searching his inner being for the reason God has deserted the covenant people, canceled his promises, and apparently denied his own gracious and saving nature (steadfast love). Instead of answering these desperate questions he turns to reflection on what it was like before God's right hand (i.e. delivering power) changed (vs. 10).

77:11-20. The deliverance from Egypt demonstrated the uniqueness of Israel's God, his difference from all other deities—i.e. he is holy (vs. 13). Vss. 15, 20 are conventional statements, but the description of the miracle of the sea passage (Exod. 14:21-29) in vss. 16-19 is alive with poetic imagery. Vs. 16 compares the event to God's victory over the primeval ocean of chaos (see above on 74:12-14) and vss. 17-19 contain all the accompaniments of the theophany of the warrior God (see above on 11:4-7a; 18:7-18; 68:7-10). Himself invisible, he cuts a path through the great waters for his people (vs. 19).

Ps. 78. The Riddle of Rebellion

This ps. belongs to none of the basic types. On the title and the divine names see Intro.

78:1-8. In the style of the wisdom teacher the psalmist propounds a problem (dark sayings, or "riddles," as the same word is translated in 49:4) raised by Israel's historic traditions (vss. 1-4; cf. 49:1-4). Passed on from father to son, these traditions are God's testimony to himself and the means of the education of the nation (vss. 5-6). They teach 2 sharply contrasting lessons: the saving power of God (vs. 7) and the persistent rebellion of the people (vs. 8).

78:9-55. The evidences of God's saving power were many: the plagues in Egypt (vss. 12, 43-51); the miracle at the sea (vss. 13, 53); the pillar of cloud and fire (vss. 14, 52); provision of water and manna and quails (vss. 15-29); and the conquest of Canaan (vs. 54). Zoan (vss. 12, 43) was a city in the delta region of Egypt, probably the same place as Raamses (Exod. 1:11) and Rameses (Exod. 12:37; see color map 4). According to Gen. 10:6 Egypt was descended from Noah's 3rd son, Ham (vs. 51). God opened the doors of the storehouses in heaven and poured out the food of the angels for Israel (vss. 23-25). The people greeted these wonderful deeds with the ultimate blasphemy. Taking to themselves the role of God, they tested the Lord's faithfulness to the nation (vss. 18, 41, 56). When their presumption was punished they feigned repentance but had no

real loyalty to his covenant (vss. 34-37), even though repeatedly he was compassionate and forgiving (vss. 38-39).

78:56-64. The record of apostasy climaxes in the worship of idols in Canaan (vss. 56-58). The shrine at Shiloh was destroyed (vs. 60); its priests, Hophni and Phinehas, were killed (vs. 64); and the ark, the power and glory of the Lord, was captured by the Philistines (vs. 61; cf. I Sam. 4).

78:65-72. Then God rose with power to solve the riddle of history (vss. 65-66). He rejected the N tribe of Ephraim, the ringleader of revolt (vs. 67; cf. vs. 9), and chose the tribe of Judah. He selected Mount Zion as his dwelling in preference to the Ephraimite shrine at Shechem, and appointed David as king and benign shepherd of the people. The ps. is thus a piece of royalist propaganda. The Davidic kingship, the city of David, and the temple are God's own answer to the rebellion of his people.

Ps. 79. Lament over Jerusalem

Although it is a patchwork of stock phrases, this community lament (on this category, the title, and the divine names see Intro.) gives a powerful impression of the intense emotions aroused by the destruction of the Holy City (see above on Ps. 74).

79:1-7. After describing the sack of Jerusalem (vss. 1-4) the psalmist complains that God's vigorous anger (for jealous in vs. 5 a more accurate translation would be "zealous") is operative in the wrong direction, falling on his own servants instead of the pagan invaders who do not worship him (vss. 5-7).

79:8-10. The nation's plight may be due to its own sin (vs. 9) or that of its ancestors (vs. 8; cf. Exod. 20:5), but the prayer for pardon (vs. 9) is perfunctory. God is asked to defend his glory (authority) and his name (reputation for saving deeds) against the contempt of the conquerors. Speedy vengeance will convince them and the world that the Lord has not abandoned Israel (vs. 10).

79:11-13. In ancient times prisoners of war could be, and often were, slaughtered at the whim of the captors. Sevenfold vengeance is vengeance in its extreme form (cf. Gen. 4:15; Lev. 26:18). If the prayer is answered, the nation promises to establish a thanksgiving service in perpetuity.

Ps. 80. Israel the Vine

This community lament (on this category, the title, and the divine names see Intro.) contains 4 strophes (vss. 1-2, 4-6, 8-13, 15-18) and a congregational refrain (vss. 3, 7, 19, modified in 14 to accord with the allegory of the vine).

80:1-7. Strophes 1 and 2 combine the metaphors of Shepherd and King. The Shepherd, angry at his flock, feeds it on tears (vs. 5; cf. 23:1-3). The national sorrow is occasioned by a military defeat in which his bewildered people God seems to be destroying his own creation. On God enthroned upon the cherubim see below on 99:1-5. Benjamin and Joseph were the children of Jacob's favored wife, Rachel, and Ephraim and Manasseh were Joseph's sons. Benjamin, Ephraim, and Manasseh were the principal tribes of the N Kingdom, and their mention together in vs. 2 indicates that the ps. had a N origin.

80:8-19. Strophes 3 and 4 describe God's mighty acts in Israel's history under the allegorical figure of the vine: the Exodus (vs. 8); the conquest of Canaan (vs. 9); and the empire of David and Solomon, extending from **the River** (the upper Euphrates) to **the sea** (the Mediterranean, vss. 10-11). Now the stone **walls** of God's protecting presence are gone, and enemies crowd in to strip the vine of **its fruit** and to uproot it like wild pigs (vss. 11-13). The psalmist prays for the return of God's saving presence (vss. 14-16) and for the coming of the divine power on the king, who though a mere mortal (**son of man**) is **the man of thy right hand** (cf. 110:1), endowed by the LORD with more than human power (vs. 17). Because of the names in vs. 2 some have dated this ps. before 722 B.C. and applied it to a N king. More probably, however, it comes from a later time, and vss. 17-18 are a prayer for the restoration of united Israel under the Davidic king in Jerusalem.

Ps. 81. A Prophet at a Feast

This is an unclassified ps. On the title, the divine names, and **selah** see Intro.

81:1-5b. The hymnic beginning reminds pilgrims approaching the temple with music, songs, and shouts of joy that the festival to which they come was specifically prescribed in the Sinai covenant. A 15-day feast, it begins **at the new moon** and ends **at the full moon,** opening and closing to the sound of the ram's-horn **trumpet** (the *shophar,* still used in the synagogue in the autumn new year service and at other special times; cf. 47:5; on the instruments of vs. 2 see below on 150:3, 4). The description suggests the new year festival (ingathering or booths; see Intro.).

81:5c-10. In the ancient Near East the new moon was considered a favorable time for prophecies; and here a prophet, inspired by the mysterious **voice** of God (vs. 5c), recalls the nation's deliverance from **basket**-carrying slave labor in Egypt, God's answer to their cries for help in the wilderness, his revelation in **thunder** from Sinai, and his testing of the nation at **Meribah** (vss. 6-7; cf. Exod. 17:1-7; Num. 20:1-13). The covenant established by these events requires unswerving obedience to the first commandment (vss. 8-9), vividly reinforced by reference to the ancient covenant formula (vs. 10; cf. Exod. 20:2-3).

81:11-16. In its desire for self-determination, continues the prophet, the nation turned a deaf ear to God (vs. 11). He allowed them their independence, and they were overrun by enemies (vs. 12; see above on 7:12-16). If they would now obey God, their enemies would be permanently subdued, and the nation would be satisfied by a miracle greater than those of the wilderness period—**honey,** not water, **from the rock** (vss. 14-16).

Ps. 82. The Judgment of the Gods

This ps. is a prophetic vision of the heavenly **council** (see above on 7:6-11; 29:1-2; 58:1-5), meeting as a legal body to hear the case of divine beings accused of dereliction of duty. On the title, the divine names, and **selah** see Intro.

82:1-5. The high God, king of the gods (cf. 86:8; 97:7c; 135:5) has entered and **taken his place** of honor (vs. 1). He states the case against the rebels (vss. 2-4). They have failed to be his agents in the administration of his **justice** in the world (see above on 7:12-16; 68:5-6). The accusation (vs. 5) asserts that they have willfully preferred the **darkness** of their own ignorant and incapable minds, and that the resulting perversion of justice has shaken **the foundations of the earth,** since in Hebrew thought the justice of God maintains both the stability of nature and the order of society.

82:6-8. The divine beings are **sons of the Most High,** not by physical generation, but by sharing in divine qualities, the most decisive of which is freedom from death. Their sentence (vss. 6-7) is that, their divinity taken away, they will **die like men.** The congregation responds to this vision by calling for a similar just and final judgment on **the earth** and its **nations** (vs. 8).

Ps. 83. A Covenant Against God

This community lament (on this category, the title, the divine names, and **selah** see Intro.) was composed in the face of a threat from a coalition of nations against Israel. The description does not fit any known historical situation and probably involves poetic exaggeration of the actual crisis.

83:1-8. Surrounding **enemies** have conspired under solemn oath (vss. 3, 5) to destroy Israel. Throughout the ancient Near East the wiping out of a **name** from memory (vs. 4) signified complete extinction. The league against Israel includes most of her neighboring states: **Edom . . . , Moab . . . , Ammon . . . , Philistia . . . , Tyre** (i.e. Phoenicia; see "The People of the OT World," pp. 1005-17, and color maps 6, 8). Included also are various desert tribes: **the Ishmaelites** (cf. Gen. 16:10-12; 21:18; 25:16-18) . . . , the **Hagrites** (probably meaning descendants of Ishmael's mother Hagar; cf. Gen. 16:10), **Gebal** (here not Byblos in Phoenicia but a bedouin tribe from S of the Dead Sea) **. . . , and Amalek** (cf. Gen. 36:15-16; Exod. 17:8-16; Num. 13:29). The Assyrian invasions of 732-722 B.C. gave these lesser powers the opportunity to plunder Israel, but since **Assyria** here seems to be a secondary menace, it may be a figurative name for some later Mesopotamian power (cf. Ezra 6:22). **Children of Lot** means specifically Moab and Ammon (cf. Gen. 19:36-38; Deut. 2:9, 19) but is used as a slur on all who are in collusion with them.

83:9-18. The prayer for vengeance refers to 2 of the LORD's victories over those who tried to take possession of Israel's territory (vs. 12) during the period of the judges: over the Canaanites led by **Sisera and Jabin,** by means of a flash flood of **the river Kishon** (Judg. 4-5); and over the Midianite generals **Oreb and Jeeb** and their kings **Zebah and Zalmunna** (Judg. 8). **En-dor** (vs. 10) has been suspected by some as a scribal error because not mentioned in Judg. 4-5 but is probably used because it is near Mt. Tabor (see color map 5), where the Israelite army assembled before the battle against Sisera. The congregation calls on God to come as victorious storm God and sweep away the present enemies of his people like **a tumbleweed** (RSV footnote) or **chaff** and destroy them as lightning sets forested **mountains** aflame (vss. 13-17). This final victory will establish God's worldwide rule (vs. 18).

Ps. 84. The Pilgrim Way

This is one of the most popular of the pilgrim pss. (on this category, the title, and divine names, and **selah** see Intro.).

84:1-4. The pilgrim cries out in admiration of the beauty of the temple (vs. 1) and recalls with the vividness of present experience how he has longed to see it (vs. 2; on **my soul** see above on 6:1-3; 42:1-2a). The birds nesting among the beams instruct him that to be in the presence of the God whose house shelters even the swallow's **young** is life's greatest good (vss. 3-4).

84:5-7. God's blessing is not confined to the temple but radiates outward to those in remote places whose minds are set on the pilgrimage **to Zion** (vs. 5). The fall **rain** and **springs** of water convert an arid valley, fit only for balsam trees (the meaning of **Baca**), into an oasis before them (vs. 6). Defying fatigue, they get stronger as they approach Zion, where God makes himself known (vs. 7).

84:8-9. The festival to which the pilgrim has come is the autumn New Year feast, during which the enthronement of God as king was celebrated (cf. vs. 3, and see Intro.). The **prayer** for the human king (**our shield**) is appropriate to this occasion.

84:10-12. This is a lyrical statement of the conventional OT doctrine that trust in God means spiritual and material prosperity. A single **day** spent as a pilgrim before the temple gate (lit. "stand at the threshold" rather than **be a doorkeeper;** cf. I Chr. 26:1-19) **is better than a thousand** in the homes of those who reject God (vs. 10). The **sun** (vs. 11) was a common ancient symbol for divine lifegiving power, but is nowhere else used of the Lord, perhaps because of pagan associations (cf. 27:1; Mal. 4:2).

Ps. 85. A Plea for Restoration

This liturgy (on this category, the title, and **selah** see Intro.) is in 5 parts.

85:1-3. A solo voice praises God for his mercy in forgiving Israel's **sin** and removing the destructive effects of his **anger** (on the vocabulary of sin and forgiveness and on the **wrath** of God see above on 32:1-5; 34:16). Most recent translators have accepted **restore** (lit. "turn") **the fortunes** (vs. 1b) rather than the traditional "turn the captivity" wherever this phrase appears in the OT (e.g. 14:7; 53:6; 126:1, 4; Deut. 30:3; Job 42:10; Hos. 6:11). However, the 2 variant spellings of the Hebrew word for "fortunes-captivity" may indicate that scribes confused 2 words which originally differed in different passages (e.g. Jer. 29:14; 30:3; Ezek. 29:14; 39:25). If "turn the captivity" was original here, the ps. is postexilic, and the return from Babylon is the great example of God's forgiving love.

85:4-7. The congregation pleads for a new manifestation of God's **steadfast love.** His wrath has placed the people in the realm of death; hence the prayer "Restore us to life again" (vs. 6).

85:8-9. A priest or prophet asks leave to listen for God's answer to the nation's prayer, confident that he will assure his **saints** (i.e. faithful people) of **peace** (i.e. complete spiritual and physical well-being; see above on 28:3-5) and **salvation,** and of his **glory** (i.e. authoritative presence) in their midst.

85:10-11. God's answer indicates that salvation is a joyous meeting, like that of friends long separated, between God's saving love and his people's loyalty (vs. 10a), God's justice and man's well-being (vs. 10b), **faithfulness** from the earth and **righteousness . . . from the sky** (vs. 11).

85:12-13. In response the congregation acknowledges that all its welfare is God's gift and expresses confidence that he will come in justice and that the land will prosper. The Hebrew of vs. 13b makes little sense and probably should be emended to "and salvation in the way of his footsteps."

Ps. 86. From Self to God

This is the individual lament (on this category, the title, and the divine names see Intro.) of a man who, pursued by godless enemies, has fled to the temple to seek hearing and help from God.

86:1-7. At first the psalmist concentrates on his need, his piety, and his trust (vss. 1-3), but the act of exposing his life before the God of **forgiving . . . love** (vs. 5) shifts his vision from himself to God.

86:8-13. Thinking about God changes the psalmist's mood to one of praise. In Israel's history her unique God (vss. 8a, 10b) has performed unparalleled deeds (vss. 8b, 10a); and to him, creator God and Lord of history, all men will eventually come (vs. 9). To **glorify thy name** is to acknowledge the authority of God's nature as revealed in his acts of saving love. Thoroughly humbled, the psalmist recognizes the need for divine instruction, so that his disturbed life may be unified by reverence for God (vs. 11). He gratefully recalls that God's love has rescued him from death (vss. 12-13; on **soul** and **Sheol** see above on 6:1-3, 4-5). As the psalmist thinks of his **ruthless** enemies (vs. 14; cf. 54:3) and prays for **a sign** which by showing God's **favor** to him will rebuke them (vs. 17), he keeps an ancient cultic description of the goodness of God in the forefront of his mind (vs. 15; cf. Exod. 34:6). Just as the child of a female slave was the property of her master, the psalmist will remain God's **servant** as long as he lives (vs. 16; cf. Exod. 21:4).

Ps. 87. Zion's Children

This hymn of Zion (on this category, the title, and **selah** see Intro.) dates from the postexilic period when the Jews were scattered throughout the ancient world. The order of the lines has been disturbed in the transmission of the text, but scholars are not agreed on a reconstruction.

87:1-3. Standing on Mt. **Zion** the psalmist watches a procession of pilgrims approach the gates of the temple with singing and dancing (vs. 7) and thinks of the **glorious** traditions of the Holy City (vs. 3). God has favored this spot over all the cities and shrines of Israel (vs. 2) and by establishing his dwelling there has guaranteed the security of the city (vs. 1; cf. vs. 5b).

87:4-6. Among the pilgrims are Jews from many lands, and seeing them the psalmist reflects that Jerusalem is the true home of every Jew. He hears God himself declare that in the book which contains the list of living men (cf. 69:28) he is writing after the name of each pilgrim "A native Jerusalemite." **Rahab** (vs. 4; cf. 89:10) is a Hebrew name for the dragon monster of chaos, corresponding to the Babylonian Tiamat (see above on 74:12-14), here applied metaphorically to Egypt (cf. Isa. 30:7; 51:9). Some interpreters believe that the names to be written in the book are those, not of Jews, but of the foreign nations that will eventually acknowledge God's rule (cf. 86:9).

87:7. The pilgrims in their hymn speak of the river of blessing which flows from the temple (cf. 46:4).

Ps. 88. Unrelieved Sorrow

This individual lament (on this category, the title, and **selah,** see Intro.) contains no expression of confidence or hope.

After an intense plea for hearing and **help** (vss. 1-2), the psalmist bitterly describes his plight (vss. 3-18). A deadly disease which has plagued him **from my youth up** has now brought him to the point of death (vss. 4, 15). God has turned away his favor (vs. 14) and unleashed his **wrath** (vs. 7), which attacks the psalmist (vs. 16), floods over him like the sea (vss. 7, 16-17; cf. 42:7), and pursues him with nameless horrors against which he has no defense (vs. 15*b*). This incomprehensible anger of God (vs. 14) has shut him in a narrow prison (vs. 8*c*), the opposite condition to salvation (see above on 18:19). His friends, horrified at his loathsome condition, have abandoned him to comfortless loneliness (vss. 8, 18).

88:10-12. The psalmist's chief dread is that he will be plunged forever into the deepest part of **Sheol** (i.e. the underworld; see above on 6:4-5). In that dark realm, also called **the Pit** and **Abaddon** (lit. "destruction"), **the shades** cannot remember God's saving love, and hence cannot worship him (vs. 10; cf. 30:9). They are beyond the reach of his **steadfast love . . . , faithfulness . . . , and saving help** (vss. 11-12). **The grave** terminates man's relationship with God.

Ps. 89. The King Rejected

To an ancient royal ps. (vss. 1-37) has been added a later lament over the defeat and humiliation of the king (vss. 38:51; on these categories, the title, the divine names, and **selah** see Intro.). The historical occasion for the lament is described in some detail; though other possibilities have been suggested, none fits so well as the surrender and exile of Jehoiachin in 597 B.C. (cf. II Kings 24:8-15).

89:1-4. The introduction states the 2-fold theme to be developed in the royal ps.: God's permanent, consistent **love** and his indissoluble **covenant** with the family of **David.**

89:5-18. The God of Israel is infinitely superior to the angelic beings of the heavenly council (vss. 5-8; see above on 58:1-5; 82:1-5). He overcame the powers of chaos and created the universe (vss. 9-11; see above on 74:12-15; 87:1-4). The entire land of Palestine including its great mountains, is his creation and is protected by his might (vss. 12-13). The justice and saving love on which his heavenly authority (**throne;** see above on 7:6-11) is founded bring blessing and power (**horn;** see above on 75:1-5) to his worshiping people and establish the throne of the Davidic monarchy (vss. 15-18).

89:19-37. These vss. purport to repeat God's promise to David through Nathan (vs. 19; cf. II Sam.

7) but are in fact a compilation of several older oracles concerning the Davidic king. God chose David and adopted him as son (vs. 26; cf. 2:7-9; 18:20-30) by the sacred ritual of anointing (vs. 20), giving him victory (vss. 22-24), empire (vss. 25-26), and the eldest son's preeminence over other kings (vs. 27). The relationship thus described in the royal covenant will be inherited by David's descendants as long as the universe endures (vss. 28-29, 35-37). Rebellion by the king will bring punishment, but will not cancel the promise to which God has pledged himself on oath (vss. 30-34).

89:38-51. The Babylonian armies have devastated Jerusalem, and the youthful Jehoiachin has surrendered the city and been taken prisoner to Babylon (vss. 38-45). The impossible has happened. God has broken his word and stripped a descendant of David of **crown** (vs. 39), **scepter,** and **throne** (vs. 44), the symbols of his kingly office. The lament calls on God to withdraw his **wrath** (vs. 46), to **remember** man's frailty and bondage to death (vss. 47-48; cf. 6:4-5), and to reinstate his covenant with the family of David (vs. 49).

89:52. This vs. is not a part of the ps. but the benediction closing Book III of the Psalter (see Intro.).

Ps. 90. The Brevity of Life

In this community lament (on this category, the title, and the divine names see Intro.) praise for the creator of time and space (vss. 1-12) leads up to a plea for pity and renewed favor (vss. 13-17).

90:1-12. God is the true, eternal home of his people; from the remotest imaginable past to the furthest conceivable future he remains the same (vss. 1-2). His independence of time and space exposes the dreariness of man's fleeting, dreamlike existence (vss. 4-6). God has decreed death for man, commanding him to return **to the dust** from which he was made (vs. 3; cf. Gen. 2:7; 3:19). His brief, miserable life is the result of his chronic sinfulness standing face to face with God's moral purity (vss. 7-8). He cannot throw off his sin and therefore must live perpetually under its consequence—the **wrath** of God which brings him under the control of death (vss. 9-10). Understanding man's position and its causes is wisdom (vss. 11-12).

90:13-17. Such wisdom leads man to recognize that his deepest need is for God's presence and his **steadfast** (saving) **love,** for which in the lament proper the congregation prays. God's love will not bring escape from death, but it makes possible joyful acceptance of the limitations of life (vss. 14-15). Undergirded and supported by God's saving **work** (vs. 16), the **work** of the nation will endure (vs. 17), though the workers perish.

Ps. 91. Security in Trust

This psalm of trust was spoken for the instruction of the congregation by a priest or by a worshiper who had experienced God's delivering power (see above on Ps. 34; on the divine names see Intro.).

91:1-4. To be in the temple is to be in God's **shadow** and under the protection of **his wings** (see above on 17:6-9). The worshiper whose confidence is complete is safe from his enemies (**the snare of the fowler**) and from disease (vs. 3).

91:5-10. These vss. reflect the ancient belief that **pestilence** is the work of demons, like the plague god Nergal, the night hag Lilith, and the 7 Udugs (see above on 22:12-21) who prowl the earth at **noonday** and dark of **night,** shooting **the arrow** of sickness. Ancient man trusted for his protection against these evil powers to magical incantations and spells. But the psalmist believes that the man who trusts in God is safe in person and family though **ten thousand** should **fall** around him. The plague is God's instrument for **the recompense of the wicked** and is under his control (vss. 7-8).

91:11-13. God sends **angels** (i.e. messengers from the heavenly council; see above on 58:1-5; 82:1-5) to keep the man of trust from stumbling on life's road and to allow him to walk triumphantly over every peril. Snakes and wild beasts were regarded as agents or incarnations of the demonic powers.

91:14-16. God declares that the man who holds fast to him **in love** and is intimately acquainted with his **name** (i.e. his saving nature) will enjoy a 3-fold salvation: deliverance, **honor** and **long life.**

Ps. 92. Righteousness Rewarded

This individual thanksgiving was probably used during the presentation of a thank offering (on these terms, the title, and the divine names see Intro.). It is a beautiful but naïve expression of the doctrine that righteousness brings prosperity and sin disaster (cf. Ps. 73).

92:1-4. The opening hymn gives the psalmist's reason for thanksgiving: the character of God as it is publicly declared in the morning and evening worship of the temple. This nature is invoked in 4 ways: God's **name** (i.e. his authoritative presence), his **steadfast** (saving) **love,** his **faithfulness** (i.e. his unalterable self-consistency), and his **works** (i.e. his historic acts through which he makes himself known). **Lute** (lit. "ten," vs. 3) may mean a 10-stringed instrument different from the usual **harp;** or possibly the line should be emended to read with the LXX: "to the music of the ten-stringed harp" (cf. 33:2; 144:9; see below on 150:3).

92:5-9. The psalmist isolates one aspect of God's dealings with men in which his wisdom is most evident. **The wicked** may prosper for a time, and their success may confuse and mislead **dull** (i.e. brutish) men, but their final fate is eternal **destruction.**

92:10-11. In strophe 3 the psalmist offers personal thanksgiving for the downfall of his **enemies** and his own present strength and joy. **Oil** is a symbol of rejoicing (cf. 45:7) and the **horn . . . of the wild ox** of strength (see above on 75:1-5).

92:12-15. Strophe 4 takes a wide view and embraces the prosperity, long life, and productive vigor of all righteous men, of whom the psalmist himself is but one instance. Their well-being is not, however, their own achievement, but the gift of God's justice and the illustration of its perfection. On trees in the temple see above on 52:8-9.

Ps. 93. The Majestic King

This ps. is a hymn for the enthronement festival (on this category see Intro. and on Ps. 47).

93:1-2. Strophe 1 announces that the LORD, attired in kingly **majesty** as in a royal robe, has ascended his **throne.** Because his authority, symbolized by his throne, is eternal, the order of nature and society which he has **established** will endure.

93:3-4. Strophe 2 depicts the struggle of the forces of chaos, represented by the **floods** (see above on 74:12-14) to disrupt the order and harmony of his creation, a struggle which goes on even to the present (vs. 3c). God is **mightier than** chaos, and his order stands fast. His rule guarantees that the world will not be overwhelmed by cosmic or political catastrophe.

93:5. Strophe 3 insists once more on the security of what God has ordained. His utter majesty adorns the temple, where the worshiping congregation continuously proclaims his absolute power.

Ps. 94. Confidence in the Lord

This ps., which combines lament (vss. 1-11) and confidence (vss. 12-23; on these categories see Intro.) was spoken by an individual who felt his cause to be so closely allied with that of the people that he could come forward as their spokesman (vss. 4-7, 14-15, 21.)

94:1-3. The psalmist calls on God to appear as **judge** (see above on 7:6-11; 11:4-7a) and avenger (cf. Deut. 32:35).

94:4-15. The **evildoers** who oppress Israel, exploit the helpless (see above on 7:12-16; 68:5-6), and mock God (vss. 4-7) are evidently Israelites in positions of power; but they do not really belong to the people of God. They are gross, godless, and bestial (vs. 8), incapable of understanding that their acts and motives cannot be hid from the creator of **ear, eye,** and mind (vss. 9-11). The righteous—those who endure God's discipline and are instructed by his **law** (vs. 12)—are God's chosen heritage. When their enemies temporarily have the upper hand, he upholds them (vs. 13), and he will give them the **justice** for which they long (vs. 15).

94:16-23. The psalmist's experience gives substance to this confidence. Note the dramatic introduction by means of 2 questions. On **soul** see above on 6:1-3; 42:1-2a; on **land of silence** see above on 6:4-5; 88:10-12. When the psalmist was at the end of his resources God's **steadfast** (saving) **love** sustained him with the assurance that in spite of appearances the just God does not take the side of the oppressor. He defends the righteous; and the cruelty of **the wicked,** recoiling upon them, destroys them.

Ps. 95. Worship of the Creator-King

This ps. is an invitation to participate in the enthronement festival and the ritual of covenant renewal (see Intro. on Ps. 47).

95:1-5. With song and festal cry the procession bearing the ark approaches the temple and hails God, who rules the divine beings of the heavenly council (see above on 58:1-5; 82:1-5), the creator and owner of the universe who dwarfs his creation.

95:6-7c. These vss. state the God-man relationship on which **worship** is based. The congregation owes its collective and individual existence to the creator God (vs. 6) and must accept his absolute authority (vs. 7a). As **sheep** survive only because of

PSALMS 99:6-9

the shepherd who finds pasturage for them, the congregation lives by God's continuous guidance (vs. 7bc).

95:7d-11. This passage, a direct speech of God mediated to the worshipers by a priest or prophet, describes the sin which negates the relationship between God and people. It is an evil mixture of stubbornness (hardness of heart) and the attempt to coerce God into satisfying the wants of his people (testing him, vss. 8-9) The incident **at Meribah and Massah** during the exodus period (Exod. 17:1-7; Num. 20:1-13) is the classic example of this rebellion. There the people demanded water in the desert. They received the water but lost the greater blessing of entering Canaan (**my rest**). All died **in the wilderness** under God's wrath and loathing during the 40 years of wandering.

Ps. 96. The Universal King

This ps. was composed for the enthronement festival (see Intro. on Ps. 47). The leading themes of the festival, creation (vss. 1-5) and judgment (vss. 10-13), come together in an invitation to all nations to join the sacred procession (vss. 7-9).

96:1-9. The creator and judge of the earth requires the worship of all its inhabitants (vss. 1, 7). On **new song** see above on 33:1-3. God's **name** is his authoritative presence with his people (cf. I Kings 8:44). The worshipers are urged to see in this presence the source of all blessing (vs. 2) and the authority to which they must submit (vss. 7-8; cf. 29:1-2). Since *all* divine power is included within the might of the Lord, the **gods of the peoples** (i.e. other nations) can have no reality beyond the images which represent them (vss. 4-5). On **in holy array** (vs. 9) see above on 29:1-2.

96:10-13. No distinction is recognized here between nature and history. The same decrees of God establish the ordered universe and judge the nations. The description of the Lord's coming in judgment (vss. 11-12) draws on the pagan imagery of the annual resurrection of the fertility god. In Canaanite mythology when Baal escaped from the underworld, bringing the lifegiving rain, the gods in heaven rejoiced and the earth exulted in the rebirth of its powers. In this ps. God's stabilizing and order-producing justice causes the universal **joy.** Even the chaotic **sea** joins the rejoicing (vs. 11; see above on 74:12-14).

Ps. 97. King Above the Gods

This hymn for the enthronement festival (see Intro. and on Ps. 47) celebrates God's coming to his people as king.

97:1-5. The whole **earth,** including the **many coastlands** (i.e. the remote islands and peninsulas of the Mediterranean), is summoned to rejoice in the Lord's universal kingship. Using the standard imagery of the theophany, vss. 2-5 describe God's coming to reign over his people (see above on 18:7-19). God's **justice** is the dais on which his heavenly **throne** stands (see above on 7:6-11).

97:6-9. The harmony of the heavenly bodies testifies to his ordering justice, and by observing them men of all races can see his authority in action

(vs. 6; see above on 96:10-13). Pagan deities are mere **worthless idols** (cf. 96:4-5); the only divine beings other than the Lord are the members of his heavenly council, who are his servants and **bow down before him** (vs. 7; see above on 58:1-5; 82:1-5). Hearing God's world-ruling majesty declared in the temple, **Zion** (Jerusalem) and the **daughters** (smaller cities) **of Judah rejoice** (vs 8).

97:10-12. God's moral government of the universe is fraught with meaning for the covenant community. He **loves those who hate** what is opposed to his will and protects the loyal adherents to the covenant faith against their enemies, filling their lives with **light** and joy. All their songs of thanksgiving are therefore responses to his **"holy name"** (i.e. his majestic, awe-inspiring presence with them).

Ps. 98. The Warrior-King

This hymn for the enthronement festival emphasizes the coming of God to his people as warrior-king (on these terms and the title see Intro.).

98:1-3. In the holy war context (see above on 20:6-9) **steadfast** (saving) **love** and **faithfulness** refer to God's **victory** over his and his people's enemies. The fame of these triumphs fills **the earth.** On **new song** see above on 33:1-3.

98:4-9. The worldwide rejoicing is localized in and symbolized by the **song** and instrumental music of the festal procession. **Trumpets** here are straight metal tubes blown by priests in concert (cf. Num. 10:2, 8; II Chr. 5:12-13; the **horn** is the solo curved ram's-horn *shophar,* less accurately translated "trumpet" in 47:5; 81:3; 150:3 (see above on 81:1-5a); on the **lyre** see below on 150:3. Since the procession carries the ark its rejoicing is **before the King** (vs. 6; see below on 99:1-3). Vss. 7-9 closely parallel 96:11-13.

Ps. 99. The Holy King

In this hymn for the enthronement festival (see Intro.) the refrain (vss. 3, 5, 9) emphasizes that the Lord's presence with his people in awe-inspiring majesty places a gulf between himself and his worshipers—he is **holy.** This "otherness" confers a sacred distinctiveness on the **holy mountain** (i.e. the temple, vs. 9), where it is revealed to men.

99:1-5. These verses celebrate God's worldwide dominion (vs. 1a) and the **justice** by which he establishes the universe and rules history (vs. 4; see above on 7:12-16; 68:5-6; 96:10-13). His heavenly throne (see above on 7:6-11) has its earthly counterpart in the ark which the festal procession carried into the temple. It was a portable box, surmounted by 2 **cherubim** (winged figures with animal bodies and human heads). They formed the sides of a throne of which the outstretched wings were the seat (vs. 1b). The golden lid of the box served as **footstool** for the invisible King (vs. 5; cf. Isa. 66:1). For further description of the ark see comments on Exod. 25:10-22; I Sam. 4:4.

99:6-9. God's justice is manifested in the covenant with Israel. **Moses and Aaron** and **Samuel** were mediators of that covenant, interceding with God on behalf of the people and mediating his self-revelation and law to them. Since the covenant in-

289

volved both blessing and curse, God's action through his mediators was sometimes forgiveness and sometimes punishment (vs. 8). The **pillar of cloud** (vs. 7), symbol of God's presence, was associated with the tabernacle, the place of revelation in the time of Moses (cf. Exod. 33:9-10; 40:34). It was transferred successively to Samuel's shrine at Shiloh and the Jerusalem temple, the heirs of the tabernacle as Israel's central shrine.

Ps. 100. REJOICING IN GOD

This hymn for the presentation of a thank offering (on this category and the title see Intro.) shows that at its best OT thanksgiving arises, not from benefits received, but from the character of God.

100:1-2. The procession approaching the temple is reminded that worship is an occasion for **gladness.** The worshipers are called on to **know** (i.e. experience for themselves) **that the LORD is** their **God** (i.e. the final authority of their lives), their creator, and the one who shepherd-like provides for their needs (cf. 95:7). Though "and not we ourselves" (vs. 3b, RSV footnote) is the reading of most Hebrew manuscripts, **and we are his,** differing by one letter, seems the more likely original.

100:3-5. As the singing procession nears the temple **gates** it is exhorted to **enter . . . with praise** which will acknowledge that God's presence (**his name**) is the source of their blessing. His nature is to perform acts of **steadfast love,** and his character remains consistent and reliable throughout all time. For the Hebrew time was neither an abstract concept nor the mere ticking of a clock but was the flux and flow of human experience. Hence **for ever** equals **all generations.**

Ps. 101. A 7-FOLD PLEDGE

This royal ps. (on this category and the title see Intro.) is the king's response to prayers offered on his behalf at his coronation (cf. Ps. 72). The king's conduct was of vital concern to the nation. If he incurred divine wrath by failure to mediate the LORD's justice to his people, all would suffer. Hence, addressing himself to God, the king here proclaims before his people the principles of private life and public administration by which he will live.

101:1-3b. The king summarizes his guiding principles as **loyalty** (the word usually translated "steadfast love," "mercy," or "kindness") and **justice** (cf. Hos. 12:6; Mic. 6:8). He promises to fix his mind on **blameless** conduct and unswerving trustworthiness (slightly emending vs. 2b to the more probable reading "truth will abide with me"). Even in the privacy of his palace his inner life will be upright and free of anything pertaining to evil (vss. 2c-3b).

101:3c-8. The king will despise the deed of those who violate the covenant and the distorted thinking which leads to rebellion (vss. 3c-4). His justice will fall hard on slanderers and haughty oppressors (vs. 5). He will form his government of loyal men devoted to **blameless** conduct (vs. 6) and exclude crooks and liars from his court (vs. 7). He will purge Judah and Jerusalem of all whose crimes show that they are guilty before God (**wicked,** vs. 8). His justice, like God's, will be exercised in the **morning** (cf. 59:16).

Ps. 102. EXILE AND ILLNESS

This individual lament (on this category and the title see Intro.) includes 2 prophecies (vss. 13-22, 28), each introduced by a hymn (vss. 12, 25-27). Since the prophecies are concerned with the coming of God as king, the introductory hymns are similar to enthronement pss. (see above on Pss. 95-97). This is one of the penitential pss. (see above on Ps. 6).

102:1-11. The psalmist, stricken in the prime of life (vss. 23-24) by a deadly disease and harassed by mocking **enemies** who use magic spells against him (vs. 8), describes his plight in the conventional language of the lament (see above on Ps. 22), but with vivid images: an inner life blighted like sunwithered **grass** (vs. 4a), the loneliness of a bird in the desert (vs. 6), the total abandonment of being tossed aside by God (vs. 10).

102:12-28. In his mind his suffering and salvation are bound up with those of the nation, and in a prophetic vision he announces that **the time** of deliverance has come (vs. 13). The exiles, no longer rebellious, yearn for Jerusalem and mourn over her ruins (vs. 14). On his heavenly throne (see above on Ps. 7) God hears **the groans** of the exiles and will come to save them from national death (vss. 19-20) and to bring all **nations** under his rule (vss. 15, 22). This great salvation will be recorded as a witness to later generations and will, like the events of the Exodus, be recited in the worship of the temple (vss. 18, 21; cf. Ps. 105; Isa. 43:18-21).

Ps. 103. A FATHER'S COMPASSION

This hymn is for the presentation of a thank offering (on this category and the title see Intro.).

103:1-5. The psalmist summons his whole being to grateful acknowledgment of the saving presence of God (**his holy name**), which has touched his life in many ways: forgiveness, healing, rescue from death, and long life which has retained the vigor of a soaring eagle (cf. Isa. 40:31). On **my soul** and **the Pit** (Sheol) see above on 6:1-3, 4-5.

103:6-18. He has received these benefits from God's **justice** toward the **oppressed** (vs. 6), which in the OT is the same as his saving love. The gracious God described in Israel's ancient confession of faith (vs. 8; cf. 86:15; Exod. 34:6) delivered his people from Egypt and gave them his law through **Moses** (vs. 7). Though he may punish, **anger** is a transient quality of his nature; in contrast, his **steadfast love** is immense, eternal, and unchanging (vss. 9-11, 17-18). **He** knows man's frail, death-dominated existence (vss. 14-16) and **pities** those who reverence him with a father's compassion (vs. 13). Because he understands he forgives to the uttermost (vs. 12).

103:19-22. The final call to praise embraces all that exists: the members of the heavenly council who hear the LORD's commands and do his work (vss. 19-20; see above on 58:1-5; 82:1-5), the creation over which he rules, and the psalmist's own joy-filled **soul** (vss. 21-22). On God's **throne in the heavens** (vs. 19) see above on 7:6-11.

Ps. 104. THE WONDERS OF CREATION

This hymn (on this category see Intro.) praises the majesty of God the creator (cf. 19:1-6). Older than

Gen. 1, it demonstrates that creation-thought was not a late phenomenon in Israel but formed part of the cult traditions of Jerusalem from an early date. The poet's natural science is that of Mesopotamia and Canaan. Vss. 1-5 are based on the Mesopotamian picture of the universe and on the Canaanite conception of the weather god as the "rider of the clouds" (see above on 18:7-18; 65:9-13). Vss. 10-24 also celebrate the LORD's power to give the rain. Vss. 20-30 closely resemble sections of the Egyptian Hymn to the Sun attributed to Pharaoh Akh-en-Aton, but many scholars believe that the Egyptian poem is itself based on Canaanite models. In Israel, as in the rest of the Near East, interest centered, not in the creation of matter out of nothing, but in the conferring of order upon chaos; and the psalmist unfolds the ordering of the universe in 7 stages:

104:1-4. *The Organization of the Heavens.* God "pitches" the sky **like a tent** and founds his palace on the unstable surface of the heavenly ocean (cf. Gen. 1:7). He creates **clouds** and **winds** and **fire and flame** (i.e. lightning) to serve him. On the cloud **chariot** see above on 65:9-13.

104:5-9. *Formation of the Earth.* The earth is firmly anchored in the ocean. Originally the primeval sea covered the land, but at the command of God's thunder-voice it retreated, revealing the **mountains** and **valleys** (see above on 74:12-14; cf. Gen. 1:9).

104:10-13. *Provision of Water.* The underground ocean surges up in the form of **springs,** and the heavenly ocean is released as rain.

104:14-18. *Food for Man and Beast.* God provides

Courtesy of Herbert G. May

Cedars of Lebanon with summer snow on hill in background

vegetation, both wild and cultivated. Even the **wild goats** and rock **badgers** of the **high mountains** find sustenance. Olive **oil** (vs. 15) was used for cleansing the skin.

104:19-23. *Organization of Time.* In ancient Israel, where the lunar calendar was in use, the **moon** controlled the **seasons** and the **sun** day and night. **Darkness** was a real thing, created by God.

104:24-26. *The Sea.* The most marvelous work of God's wisdom was the taming of the primeval ocean, now become a home for God's creatures and a highway for commerce. Grim old **Leviathan** (see above

Courtesy of Ewing Galloway, New York

An old cedar at Lebanon; cedar was used for pillars, roofing, beams, ceilings, paneling and carvings

on 74:12-14), thoroughly domesticated, plays in the water.

104:27-30. *Control of Life.* When God withdraws his presence the animals suffer want. He takes away their life and by his creative **spirit** (lit. "breath"; cf. Gen. 2:7; 6:17) forms their successors.

104:31-35. The hymnic conclusion prays that the rule of God whose presence is accompanied by earthquake and volcano will continue **for ever** and expresses the psalmist's joy in contemplating the wonders of God's work. Those who rebel against one who creates such a perfection of order have forfeited their right to live.

Ps. 105. GOD'S SAVING DEEDS

This is a hymn for covenant renewal (on this category see Intro.). Vss. 1-15 are quoted in I Chr. 16:8-22.

105:1-6. The priests command the heirs **of Abraham** to pray for God's presence (vss. 1*a*, 6), to be diligent in their attendance at the feast (vs. 4), and to hear the story of Israel's beginnings on which their worship is centered and from which their theology has come (vss. 2, 5). As told in the cult, "history" is the record of what God **has done,** every episode being represented as his deliberate act (vss. 1*b*, 5; detailed throughout vss. 9-44).

105:7-15. The priests' account of Israel's formative history devotes more space than usual to the patriarchs (vss. 7-22; cf. Deut. 6:20-25; 26:5-11; Josh. 24:2-13). The **covenant . . . with Abraham** is an act of God's justice (vs. 7). It is not an **agreement** between 2 parties but a divine **promise** which was **sworn** to by God (vss. 8-9). Since it depends solely on God's faithfulness to his oath it endures **for ever.** Vs. 14*b* refers to the protection of Sarah from abuse by foreign **kings** (Gen. 12:10-16), and vs. 15 suggests that the **prophets** and **anointed** kings of Israel were present by anticipation in the patriarchs.

105:16-22. The patriarch **Joseph** is the model of an Israelite wise man. Because of his righteousness he passed the hard testing of God and became capable of teaching the rulers of Egypt, the traditional home of **wisdom.** The **staff of bread** (vs. 16b) is a small stake on which loaves were placed for transport or storage.

105:23-44. The account of the Exodus includes the sojourn in Egypt (vss. 23-25), the plagues (vss. 26-36), the miracles in the wilderness (vss. 37-42), and the entrance into Canaan (vss. 43-44) but omits the deliverance at the sea, the revelation at Sinai, and the rebellion in the wilderness. On **the land of Ham** (vs. 23) see above on 78:9-55. In the description of the plagues the 5th and 6th (cattle disease and boils) are omitted, and the order differs from that in Exod. 7:20–12:50.

105:45. The purpose of God's historic acts was to create a people obedient to his revealed will. The congregation responds with one word, "Hallelujah" (i.e. **Praise the LORD!**).

Ps. 106. A RECORD OF REBELLION

This ps. is a community lament for covenant renewal (on this category see Intro.). In its present form it is postexilic (vss. 27, 47). In describing the Essene covenant ceremony the Manual of Discipline (see "The Dead Sea Scrolls," pp. 1063-71) says, "The priests shall recount God's saving deeds, and the Levites shall recount 'the sins of the Israelites.'" This double use of the formative exodus event probably reflects ancient practice, Ps. 105 being the part spoken by the priests and Pss. 78; 106 that of the Levites.

106:1-5. The ps. begins with "recognition of God's righteousness and mercy" (Manual of Discipline) and a personal prayer for prosperity as a member of a prospering nation.

106:6-46. The lament is a confession of national sin which uses the exodus period to set up a contrast between the saving and forgiving God (vs. 45) and his rebellious people (vss. 13, 21). As in Ps. 78, Israel's sin is her disposition to test God by his willingness to fulfill her demands promptly on order and, when he does not do so, to turn to more amiable deities. The ps. is full of the idea of God's poetic justice (vss. 15, 24-27, 34-36; see above on 7:12-16).

On **his name's sake** (vs. 8), **the land of Ham** (vs. 22), and **Moses** as intercessor (vs. 23) see above on 23:1-4; 78:9-55; 99:6-9 respectively. On the identification of pagan gods with the demonic powers who rebelled against God in the heavenly council (vs. 37) see above on 58:1-5. On the specific instances of Israel's rebellion cf. as follows: **the Red** (lit. "Reed"; see comment on Exod. 13:17-22) **Sea** (vss. 6-12) Exod. 14:10-12; quails and manna (vss. 13-15) Num. 11:4-33; **Dathan** and **Abiram** (vss. 16-18) Num. 16:1-35; the golden **calf** (vss. 19-23) Exod. 32:1-14; the spies (vss. 24-27) Num. 13:1–14:10; **the Baal of Peor** (vss. 28-31) Num. 25:1-13; **Meribah** (vss. 32-33) Num. 20:1-13; **the idols of Canaan** (vss. 34-39) Exod. 34:11-16; Lev. 18:21; the pattern of rebellion, foreign invasion, repentance, and deliverance (vss. 40-46) Judg. 3:7–16:31.

106:47-48. The lament ends with a prayer for the return of the dispersed Jews to their homeland. Vs.

48 is the benediction and doxology closing Book IV of the Psalter (see Intro.) and is not a part of this ps.

Ps. 107. SALVATION AND LORDSHIP

This ps. consists of a community **thanksgiving** (vss. 1-32) and a hymn (vss. 33-43; on these categories see Intro.). Though some interpreters have argued for the unity of the ps., it seems more probable that the hymn (vss. 33-43) and vs. 3, which presupposes the dispersion, are postexilic additions to an earlier poem. This is borne out by the strophic arrangement of the first part, with a double refrain in vss. 6, 13, 19, 28 and 8, 15, 21, 31.

107:1-32. The community thanksgiving is a liturgical introduction to the presentation of individual thank offerings. The priests lead the congregation in calling on those who have experienced God's salvation to bring their offering and testify to God's saving **love** (vss. 2, 22, 32). The summons to thanksgiving is addressed to wayfarers who have received divine guidance (vss. 4-9), liberated **prisoners** (vss. 10-16), the **sick** who have been **healed** (vss. 17-22), and seafarers rescued from the **storm** (vss. 23-32). The sovereignty of God is emphasized throughout. Imprisonment and illness are his punishment of sin (vss. 11, 17), and he raises the storm which he eventually stills (vss. 25, 29; on the allusion here to God's victory over the primeval ocean see above on 74:12-14). In ancient thought the underworld was entered by 7 **gates** (vs. 18; see above on 6:4-5; 18:7-18).

107:33-43. Elaborating the emphasis on God's sovereignty, the hymn insists on his lordship over the powers of fertility (vss. 33-38) and the course of history (vss. 39-43). This is an effective and complete denial of the power of the pagan deities to whom ancient mythology assigned precisely these functions. The wise man will **consider** how God's justice supports **the needy** and overthrows the powerful, for in these actions his **steadfast** (saving) **love** is revealed.

Ps. 108. AWAKE, GIVE THANKS

This ps. is a composite of 57:7-11 (vss. 1-5) and 60:5-12 (vss. 6-13). See comment on these pss. On the title see Intro.

Ps. 109. CURSED BUT CONFIDENT

In this individual lament (on this category and the title see Intro.) a suppliant in the temple seeks vindication from the LORD (see above on Ps. 7).

109:1-5. The psalmist cries for help to the God whom he worships. He is beset by enemies who bring **lying** charges against him, although he has done them good and prayed for them when they were in trouble.

109:6-19. In the ancient Near East the curse was a potent means of attacking an enemy. The magical formula might be recited over a statue of the victim which incorporated cuttings of his hair or nails. The potent words brought the contents of the curse to reality. These vss. are a series of such curses, but it is not clear against whom they are directed. Many have understood them as the psalmist's curses against his enemies, collectively designated by singular pronouns, or against a leader among them; but it is more likely that he is here repeating before God the terrible curses against himself by which his enemies have sought to destroy him utterly. They wish, he reports, that he be found **guilty** of a crime and executed, that his sons be robbed of their inheritance and die childless (vss. 10-13), and that his very **name be blotted out** (vss. 13, 15; see above on 83:1-8).

109:20-31. Basing his petition on the **steadfast** (saving) **love** of the LORD (vss. 21, 26; on **thy name's sake** see above on 23:1-4) the psalmist prays that the curses of his enemies may recoil on their own heads (vs. 26). Their power has already reduced him to a pitiable condition of weakness, over which they gloat (vss. 22-25). He pleads that God will cancel their curses with his blessing (vss. 27-29) and vows that he will publicly proclaim God's goodness if his prayer is answered (vss. 30-31; see above on 7:17).

Ps. 110. The Priest-King

This royal ps. (on this category and the title see Intro.), probably used at the coronation ritual, consists of 2 divine speeches (vss. 1, 4), spoken by a priest or prophet, and the congregational response to each (vss. 2-3, 5-7).

110:1-3. The LORD invites the king to **sit at my right hand**—probably at the right side of the ark. This position of honor indicates that the king is God's vicegerent. Mesopotamian art often depicts the king with his foot on the neck of a conquered enemy. The congregation prays that the king's power, symbolized by his **scepter,** will spread outward from Jerusalem and overthrow his enemies. The people will fight for him in the sacred battle array of the holy war (RSV footnote; see above on 20:6-9), and the king's vigor will be renewed as the dew refreshes the earth at dawn.

110:4-7. The 2nd oracle (vs. 4) refers to Gen 14: 17-24, in which Abraham recognizes **Melchizedek,** king of Salem (Jerusalem), as both king and **priest** by offering him tribute and participating in a sacrifice conducted by him. The Davidic monarch is in the direct line of the kings of pre-Israelite Jerusalem and like them combines the offices of priest and sovereign. The Jerusalem cult stressed the justice of God (Melchizedek means "my king is righteousness"). The LORD has condemned **the nations,** and his priest-king will carry out the sentence (vss. 5-6). During the ceremony the king replenishes his strength by drinking from a sacred spring—possibly Gihon (cf. I Kings 1:28-40)—a practice attested in the old Canaanite texts from Ugarit.

Ps. 111. The Beginning of Wisdom

This ps. is a hymn in the form of an alphabetic acrostic (on these terms see Intro.).

111:1-4. The opening "Hallelujah" (i.e. **Praise the LORD;** cf. 112:1; 113:1) sets the mood of the hymn, in which an individual offers public thanksgiving for **the works of the LORD** (vss. 1-2). In them are revealed his majestic power and perfect justice, his grace and mercy (vss. 3-4).

111:5-9. Like all OT theologians the psalmist concentrates on the exodus events which brought Israel into existence: the miracles of **food** in the wilderness, the conquest over the **nations** of Canaan, and the giving of eternally valid **precepts** (i.e. the law) which demand steadfastness and integrity. The whole complex of events is summarized as **redemption** and the establishment of the **covenant,** a binding agreement **commanded** by God and accepted by the people. Contemplating these wonders the psalmist cries out that God's **name** (i.e. presence) is unique and awe-inspiring.

111:10. This is the basic doctrine of Israel's wisdom teachers. In OT thought **wisdom** is the ability to deal successfully with the tensions and problems of practical life, and **understanding** is the capacity to discern among the conflicting possibilities what values and courses of action ought to be followed. The source of these qualities is not brain power but reverence for God, **the fear of the LORD.** The hymnic conclusion echoes the opening mood of **praise.**

Ps. 112. He Will Not Be Moved

This alphabetic acrostic, similar in form to Ps. 111, is related in content to Ps. 1 and hence is to be classed as a wisdom ps. (on these terms see Intro.). It is a bold statement of the familiar OT doctrine that righteousness is rewarded and wickedness punished in this life. Having no hope of personal immortality (see above on 6:4-5; 88:10-12) the psalmist looks for the continuation of his life in his family and the memory of his friends (vss. 2, 6).

112:1-4. The man who reverences God by joyfully keeping **his commandments** will have **wealth** and children who will be honored and influential in the community. When trouble comes the **light** of God's saving presence will shine into his **darkness.** God's saving power is directed especially to the helpless and oppressed, and so directed is his justice.

112:5-9. A similar **justice** characterizes all the social activity of the man who reverences God. In particular it is expressed in his use of his money. Firmly anchored in the reality of God's nature, his inner life is stable and his **righteousness** lasts, even when he is the victim of **evil tidings** (better "rumors," vs. 7) spread by his enemies. His **adversaries** will go down, but his **horn** (i.e. power) will increase (vss. 8-9). Even as he perishes **the wicked man gnashes his teeth** in envy of the good man.

Ps. 113. King Above the Heavens

This ps. is a congregational hymn (on this category see Intro.).

113:1-6. The priests call on the worshipers in the temple (**servants**) to **praise** God for his saving presence with them. He is worthy to be praised continuously by all the inhabitants of the earth because he is enthroned in **glory,** i.e. authority over nature, man, and history. Ps. 7 speaks of God's throne in heaven, but here God towers over heaven itself with an authority which cannot be confined within the bounds of the universe.

113:7-9. God's throne is founded on justice (cf. 97:2) and that justice is particularly concerned with the protection of the helpless and oppressed (see above on 68:5-6). When his loyal worshipers (the **poor** and **needy;** see Intro.) are crushed and mourn in **dust** and ashes, God **raises** them to the highest places in the land. To have **children** was one of God's greatest blessings, since the only immortality for which a Hebrew could hope was the continuation of his name and memory in his family (see above on 6:4-5). **A barren woman** was in danger of being divorced and dismissed from her home. But God opens the womb of the childless (cf. I Sam. 2:5) and makes her a **joyous mother.**

Ps. 114. THE SEA FLED

This artistically constructed hymn was probably used in the covenant renewal ritual of the new year festival, when worship centered on the exodus event (on these terms see Intro.).

114:1-2. Strophe 1 emphasizes the unity of the people of God. Both the N and S divisions of the nation (**Israel** and **Judah**) were chosen by God, led out of **Egypt**—a land so foreign that its **language** was unintelligible—and made God's holy place of residence and kingdom.

114:3-4. Strophe 2 dwells on the miracles which accompanied the Exodus: the crossings of the **sea** (Exod. 14:21-29) and the **Jordan** (Josh. 3:14-17) and the earthquake at Sinai (Exod. 19:18) when the mountains **skipped** like frolicsome **lambs.** The nature religion of Canaan depicted a vicious battle between Baal and Judge River (see above on 74:12-14), but here the sea flees at the mere approach of the LORD. The pagan myth has been historicized, the defeat of the sea being equated with the deliverance of Israel at the beginning of her national life.

114:5-6. The poet feels himself so much a part of the events recreated in the worship of the temple that he asks the questions of strophe 3 in the present tense.

114:7-8. Strophe 4 reverts to the earthquake at Sinai and adds the miracle of **water** from **the rock,** heightening the wonder by declaring that the rock itself became a **pool.**

Ps. 115. A LITURGY OF PRAISE

This hymn in liturgical form (on this category see Intro.) was sung during a time of national distress.

115:1-8. The ps. begins with a congregational prayer that God will help his people, not to enhance their power, but to show the world-wide authority of his **steadfast** (saving) **love** and consistent **faithfulness** (see below on Ps. 117). Even though **the nations** deny that the LORD can save Israel, the worshiping congregation boldly affirms the universal sovereignty of its God. He is the God who acts, and he does what **pleases** him. The pagan deities are manmade **idols,** without life or power (cf. 96:4-5), and the idolaters are likewise impotent and futile.

115:9-15. As Israel, the priesthood, and the non-Israelite worshipers of the LORD (those who **fear** him) are called on to commit themselves wholly to him, each group replies with a confession of faith in his saving power (vss. 9-11). The congregation affirms that the LORD has blessed and will bless again (vss. 12-13), and a priest pronounces a benediction on the congregation (vss. 14-15).

115:16-18. The concluding strophe portrays the 3-storied universe of ancient cosmology (see above on 18:7-18). In heaven God's rule is supreme, but he has given control of **the earth** to human beings, and because of man's freedom inequities and oppression exist. In the underworld the shades, sunk in

forgetfulness, cannot **praise the LORD** (see above on 6:4-5; 88:10-12). In spite of the ambiguity of human existence and the long silence of death Israel will continuously praise her God.

Ps. 116. GRATITUDE FOR DELIVERANCE

This ps. is an individual thanksgiving (on this category see Intro.).

116:1-4. Unless interpreted in the light of vss. 5-6, 15, the opening cry of deeply felt gratitude sounds grossly self-centered—love in return for services rendered. The psalmist was near death, possibly from disease, and the LORD **heard** his desperate cry. On **snares** and **Sheol** see above on 9:13-17; 6:4-5 respectively.

116:5-11. The psalmist rejoices to think that his deliverance is evidence of the **gracious** nature of the LORD. He is the champion of the **simple,** those who lack the capacity to fend for themselves (vs. 6), and acts toward them with the justice which saves the oppressed and the mercy which understands their sorrow (vs. 5; cf. 103:13). The psalmist invites his **soul** (i.e. his vital powers; see above on 6:1-3) to **rest** after its turmoil. Even in his distress he lost neither his **faith** nor his life, but learned that trust in human power is deceitful and **a vain hope** (vss. 8-11).

116:12-19. These vss. are spoken just before the presentation of the thank offering. The **cup of salvation,** the opposite of the "cup of wrath" (75:8), was probably held aloft before the altar and then poured out as libation (cf. Exod. 29:40). The worshiper pays his **vows** (see above on 7:17; 50:7-15) and offers the thank offering (Lev. 7:12). Vs. 15 means that the LORD is not indifferent to whether or not his faithful servants are killed. On **son of thy handmaid** see above on 86:14-17.

Ps. 117. A CALL TO PRAISE

This ps. is a hymn (on this category see Intro.) for the beginning of a temple service. It calls on **all nations** to **praise the LORD,** whose creative power and control is world wide (see above on Ps. 97), and extols his **steadfast** (saving) **love** abundantly revealed to Israel (**us**) in the nation's history. As frequently in the Psalter (e.g. 36:5; 40:10; 88:11; 89:1), God's love is united to his **faithfulness,** i.e. his consistency to his own nature, a quality which guarantees that none of his actions will be arbitrary or inconsistent with his declared will.

Ps. 118. THANKSGIVING FOR VICTORY

This is a thanksgiving liturgy for the king's victorious return from battle (on this category see Intro.). The abrupt changes in thought result from changes in speaker and mood as the ceremony progresses.

118:1-4. The procession approaches the temple, and the priests call the congregation to general thanksgiving. Vs. 1 is the same as 107:1, and the groups mentioned in vss. 2-4 correspond to those of 115:9-11 (see comment).

118:5-14. The king offers his personal thanksgiving. Hard pressed by numerous enemies he **called on the LORD** for aid (vs. 5; cf. vss. 10-12). In the tradition of the holy war (see Intro. and on 20:6-9) he is confident that **with the LORD on my side** he has nothing to **fear** (vss. 6-7) and that his trust is better than manpower or generalship (vss. 8-9). The LORD, who has always been his **strength** and the object of his praise, has given him victory (vs. 14). **In the name** (i.e. saving presence) **of the LORD** he has destroyed his enemies (vss. 10-13).

118:15-18. The camp of the Israelites is resounding with **songs of victory,** praising **the right hand** (i.e. might) **of the LORD.** The king predicts a long reign in which he will tell of what God has done for him. His temporary setbacks and troubles were God's discipline.

118:19-25. Arrived at the temple gates the king requests admission (see above on Ps. 24). He calls the doors **gates of righteousness** because the temple is the place where God's justice is revealed. The priests remind him that only those whom God has declared innocent can enter (vs. 20), and he replies that his recent victory is sufficient evidence of God's favor (vs. 21). The procession chants its praise of God's **marvelous** deed. He has made the building **stone** which the nations despised the most important in the structure and has made possible this **day** of national rejoicing. The congregation prays for continued divine blessing.

118:26-29. A benediction is pronounced by the priests, who then bid the procession with its garlands and palm **branches** to form a human chain of dancers up to the **altar.** The **horns** were projections at the corners of the altar which stood in the temple court (cf. I Kings 8:64). The king then concludes his thanksgiving within the temple (vs. 28), and the congregation answers with the words with which the ritual began.

Ps. 119. Veneration of the Law

This skillfully contrived composition expresses a deep piety centered in the **law** (see above on 19:7-14). It consists of 22 sections, one for each letter of the Hebrew alphabet. Each section contains 8 lines, all beginning with the same letter.

The number of lines per section was perhaps suggested by the 8 synonyms for law used in the poem. Four of these—**precepts, statutes, commandments, ordinances**—refer to separate legal units, commands and prohibitions in the strict sense. **Testimonies** is more general, signifying that the law is God's own witness to his will for men (cf. vs. 72). The use of **word** shows that the psalmist regarded the law, not as an impersonal mass of legislation, but as the dynamic utterance of God. **Way** (lit. "path") has the same connotation—guidance through the complex and infinitely varied landscape of life. "Law" itself means basically "guidance" or "instruction."

The law, so conceived, is perfect (vs. 96). It brings the promise of **salvation** (vs. 41) and is therefore the sure ground of **hope** (vs. 49) and the source of **life** (vss. 50, 93). Although it fills the worshiper with fear of God's terrible justice, it means **liberty** (vss. 44-45), **peace,** and protection (vs. 165). It can be spoken of in these terms because it is the same creative word by which the universe (vss. 89-90) and the psalmist himself (vs. 73) were made and because it represents God's **name** (i.e. his lifegiving presence,

vs. 55) and his **steadfast** (saving) **love** (vss. 41, 64, 76).

Man obeys the law, not as a duty, but because it is true, and indeed is **truth** itself (vs. 160). Such obedience cannot be mechanical. The servant of the LORD loves the law (vss. 48, 97, 113, 119, 131); it is his **delight** (vss. 77, 103), and he values it above all treasure (vs. 72).

But devotion is not sufficient to insure obedience. The psalmist acknowledges that he wanders from the way, but his sin is never the result of willful rejection of the law (vs. 176). Even in his erring the law is in his heart and at the center of his vital concern. Obedience produces wisdom (vss. 32, 98, 100, 130), but obedience also *requires* wisdom (vss. 32, 125), and the **understanding** prerequisite to obedience is the gift of God. The law can be obeyed only as God's presence enables the worshiper to hold fast to God's will.

This divine support is sorely needed, for many in the community hold the law in contempt and hinder the servants of God in their obedience (vss. 113, 115, 134). As the psalmist thinks of these enemies he passes into the style and mood of the lament (vss. 25, 41-43, 53, 69-71, 78-80, 81-88; on this category see Intro.). The psalmist's obedience in spite of the difficulties which surround him becomes the basis of his cry for help (vss. 143, 153-154).

It is impossible to say definitely whether "law" in this ps. refers to oral legal tradition, Deut., the Law (i.e. the Pentateuch), or the Law and the Prophets (see "The Making of the OT Canon," pp. 1209-15). However, the clear affinities of the ps. with the thought of the wisdom teachers (see above on Ps. 1) and the fact that the individual's, rather than the nation's, relationship to the law is the main theme indicate a postexilic date, and the "law" is probably the Pentateuch in written form.

Ps. 120. Irreconcilable Foes

In this individual lament (on this category and the title see Intro.) a pilgrim, ascending toward the temple, prays for deliverance from the accusations of malicious enemies.

120:1-4. The psalmist's **distress** is caused by **lying lips,** and he wishes for these adversaries the fate which they have tried to bring on him. Vss. 3-4 have the structure of a curse formula (see above on 109:6-19). The **arrows** shot by a professional soldier were war's deadliest weapon, and the wood of **the broom tree** burned hottest and longest.

120:5-7. The psalmist's enemies are members of his own people who as citizens of the covenant community should live at **peace** with one another. Instead they behaved to him like rough mountaineers of **Meshech** (a region between the Black and Caspian seas) or wild tribesmen of **Kedar** (the Syrian desert; see color map 10). When he tries to be reconciled to them they redouble their attacks.

Ps. 121. A Ritual of Dismissal

This liturgy (on this category and the title see Intro.), though viewed by some scholars traditionally as a pilgrim ps. sung on approaching Jerusalem, was more probably used for the dismissal of pilgrims leaving the temple on their homeward journey.

121:1-2. Looking E over the arid **hills** of the Judean wilderness the pilgrim wonders what **help** he can rely on to complete the arduous journey and affirms that the God who created the universe is able to sustain him on his way. These vss. may, however, refer to the hills that surround Jerusalem and state the confidence which fills the departing pilgrim as he contemplates the dwelling place of the mighty God (cf. 125:2).

121:3-8. The priests dismiss the wayfarer with a threefold benediction. Guarded by the ever-vigilant God he will suffer no disaster on the road (vss. 3-4). Sickness will not assail him, either from the heat of the **sun** or the baleful effects of the **moon,** which according to Mesopotamian thought could cause such diseases as leprosy and fever (vss. 5-6; cf. our "lunacy"). The LORD will preserve his life and keep him from every peril from the time he leaves the temple until he enters his home, and continuously thereafter (vss. 7-8; on **for evermore** see above on 22:25-26).

Ps. 122. MEMORIES OF JERUSALEM

This is a pilgrim ps. (on this category and the title see Intro. and on Ps. 84). Vs. 5 seems to indicate that it dates from postexilic times.

122:1-2. A pilgrim taking leave of Jerusalem expresses the joy which his visit to the city has brought him. He recalls his pleasure at being invited to join a group of travelers banded together for the dangerous journey (vs. 1; cf. vs. 8).

122:3-5. Three impressions of his visit are strongly with the pilgrim: the imposing structure of the **city** (vs. 3; cf. the **walls** strengthened at intervals by defense **towers,** vs. 7), the procession of pilgrims from all the **tribes** of **Israel** (vs. 4), and the site where in former times the **thrones** of the Davidic kings stood (vs. 5). The law required that every male Israelite present himself at the sanctuary 3 times a year (vs. 4; cf. Exod. 23:17; Deut. 16:16). Since the main function of the Davidic king was to mediate the justice of God to the nation (see above on 72:1-7; Ps. 101), his throne was preeminently one of **judgment** (vs. 5).

122:6-9. The psalmist concludes with a moving prayer for the complete spiritual and material well-being of the city and of those **who love** her. His motive is not patriotism but religious faith. He values the city, not because it is the nation's capital, but because it is the place where God's temple, his earthly **house,** is established.

Ps. 123. GORGED WITH CONTEMPT

In this community lament (on this category and the title see Intro.) a pilgrim, smarting under the mockery and insult heaped on his nation by foreign oppressors, pours out his complaint on the threshold of the temple. The most probable historical setting is the postexilic period, when Israel was under the direct rule of foreign powers.

123:1-2. The psalmist raises his **eyes** to God's heavenly throne, founded on righteousness (97:2), from which he administers his justice to men and nations (see above on 7:6-11). Speaking for faithful Israel the psalmist describes the nation's eager longing for God's delivering justice. As a slave, knowing

that his life depends on his master's good will, watches his **hand** for some sign of favor, so Israel waits expectantly for God's response to her prayers.

123:3-4. The psalmist prays that God will quickly respond to the nation's petitions. The oppressors have lorded it over them so long that they are "fed up" with **contempt.**

Ps. 124. A VICTORY SONG

This community thanksgiving for victory (on this category and the title see Intro.) contains strong overtones of the holy war ideology (see Intro. and on 20:6-9).

124:1-5. Except for the LORD **on our side** the threatened attack of a foreign enemy, like some ravening monster, **would have swallowed us up alive.** The attacking host resembled nothing so much as the primeval ocean raging to engulf the ordered universe in chaos (see above on 74:12-14). Vss. 4-5 are a striking example of the historicizing of motifs borrowed from Near Eastern mythology (cf. 114:3, 5).

124:6-8. Israel was already between the **teeth** of the monster and enmeshed in the net of the **fowlers.** With immense relief and gratitude the congregation exclaims, **The snare is broken, and we have escaped!** Vs. 8 ascribes the victory to the **name** (i.e. saving presence) of the creator of the universe, who is also Lord of history.

Ps. 125. THE TRUE ISRAEL

This community song of confidence (on this category and the title see Intro.) was composed in a time of foreign domination, probably after the Exile. Pagan control of the nation put a premium on cooperation with the conquerors, and the Jew had to summon all his powers to hold fast to the traditional faith against the pressure of conformists within and foreigners in positions of authority.

125:1-3. The opening vss. are an assurance that **those who trust** the LORD have a stability of life which no power can move and the permanent protection of God's saving presence. The burning question was, "What will happen to the Holy Land? Will pagans and traitors continue to rule it?" The psalmist answers that those who remain true to the covenant faith (**the righteous**) are the true Israel, and **the land** belongs to them. The **scepter** (i.e. domination) of the foreigner will not long continue.

125:4-5. The concluding prayer asks that God **do good** (i.e. restore the land) to those who in their inner being adhere to the straight way of his will, and that the oppressors (**evildoers**) and those who follow **their crooked ways** perish together. Then Israel will know **peace** (i.e. complete well-being; see above on 28:3-5).

Ps. 126. A HARVEST OF JOY

This community lament (on this category and the title see Intro.) probably dates from the difficult times after the return from the Babylonian exile (*ca.* 538 B.C.). Many commentators, however, render vss. 1-3 in the present or future tense and thus read the ps. as a prediction of restoration (vss. 1-3) followed by a prayer for its fulfillment (vss. 4-6)—in which case it could have been composed during any time of difficulty in Israel's history. On **restored the fortunes** see above on 85:1.

126:1-3. Assuming the early postexilic date, these vss. recall the joy with which the exiles greeted the decree of Cyrus of Persia permitting them to return to Palestine. In that event even the foreign **nations** recognized the power of the LORD. But drought, locusts, and bad harvests have reduced the returned community to poverty (cf. Isa. 59:9-11; Hag. 1:9-11).

126:4-6. The people pray for a new manifestation of God's restoring power which will bring renewed life to the nation like the winter rains filling the dry **water-courses in the Negeb,** the semidesert in the S of Palestine (see color map 1). Then the sower, who went out with his bag of seed at his belt and sorrow in his heart, will return with **shouts of joy** from the bountiful harvest.

Ps. 127. WISDOM FRAGMENTS

In this wisdom psalm (on this category and the title see Intro.) 2 independent proverb-like sayings are brought together, probably for use at the birth of a son.

127:1-2. No product of purely human effort can survive, neither a man's **house** (i.e. family) nor the **city** in which it lives. Labor from dawn to dusk brings no lasting result, for the LORD can give more good gifts to those he loves during a night's **sleep** than they could accumulate in a life **of anxious toil.**

127:3-5. Nothing is really done unless the LORD does it. Like all else good in life sons are God's gift —an **inheritance** but also, in accordance with a basic doctrine of the wisdom teachers (see above on Ps. 1), a **reward** (lit. "wage") for righteousness. Through them the house which God has built is continued and the name and memory of the father are kept alive (see above on 113:7-9). Moreover, sons born in the vigor of **youth** protect their father **like arrows** of a professional soldier, and it is well to come into battle with a **quiver full.** The law courts at which the elders presided in the open space at the city **gate** were often corrupt (cf. Amos 5:12), but enemies would not dare to rig a case against a man who came backed by stalwart sons.

Ps. 128. A PRIESTLY BLESSING

This wisdom psalm (on this category and the title see Intro.) was probably used as a priestly blessing on pilgrims arriving at the temple. Its theological basis is the OT doctrine, favored by the wisdom teachers (see above on Ps. 1), that righteousness brings material reward.

128:1-4. Vs. 1 states that the blessing is given to those who reverence God and live in obedience to his revealed will. Vss. 2-4 specify the nature of the blessing, apparently for a group of small farmers. They will not be robbed of the **fruit** of their **labor** by crop failure or the exactions of the tax collector. Their wives will receive the gift of many **children,** who will stand **around your table** like young **shoots** at the base of an **olive** tree (vs. 3; see above on 127:3-5).

128:5-6. These vss. indicate that the **prosperity** of the individual depends on the welfare of the community and on the God who resides in **Zion.** A prosperous Jerusalem is a center radiating well-being to the whole land. May the pilgrim live to be a grandfather and all his days see Israel enjoying **peace** (cf. 125:5c; see above on 28:3-5).

Ps. 129. NOT WORTH HARVESTING

This community song of confidence (on this category and the title see Intro.) was composed in a time of foreign domination (see above on Ps. 125).

129:1-4. Israel's enemies have often overrun the Holy Land, scarring the covenant people as a plow scars a field. But the God of justice (see above on 112:1-4) remained true to the covenant. He **cut the cords** (i.e. harness) so that the plowmen could work no more.

129:5-8. The congregation prays that those who now oppress the people of God may be dealt with like her enemies of the past. The flat roofs of Palestinian houses were made of mud plastered on reeds. A little **grass** could grow there, but the first hot wind of summer killed it so that it was not worth harvesting. Vs. 7 reflects ancient harvesting techniques. The **reaper** grasped a handful of grain and cut it with his sickle. Then, holding it against his chest, he tied it into a sheaf. It was customary to greet reapers with a **blessing** (cf. Ruth 2:4), but those **who hate Zion** (vs. 5)—foreign oppressors, native traitors, and all who set any value upon them —are outside the sphere of the LORD's blessing and stand under his curse (vs. 8).

Ps. 130. OUT OF THE DEPTHS

This individual lament (on this category and the title see Intro.) is one of the 7 penitential pss. (see above on Ps. 6).

130:1-4. Almost submerged in the watery deep, a common OT synonym for death or deep distress (cf. 42:7; see above on 6:4-5; 18:7-18), the psalmist calls on God for aid. Vss. 3-4 reveal the ground of his hope. He knows himself to be a sinner and realizes that if God were to keep a record of deviations from his will, all would **stand** guilty before him. But the LORD is no bookkeeper of offenses. It is his nature to forgive, and because of his forgiving love, even more than his power, he is to be **feared** (i.e. worshiped with reverence).

130:5-8. Vss. 5-6 state the attitude of true repentance. With the tense, strained expectancy of **watchmen** on the wall of a besieged city, the psalmist **waits** for the assurance of forgiveness. **The morning** was the traditional time when God revealed his salvation (cf. 59:16). Like the young Isaiah the psalmist recognizes the universality of sin and his own oneness with a sinful people (Isa. 6:5). He therefore calls on the nation of **Israel** to join him in penitence and in confident **hope** in the LORD's **steadfast** (saving) **love** and power.

Ps. 131. REPOSE OF SOUL

In this individual song of confidence (on this category and the title see Intro.) the psalmist asserts that he does not indulge in pretentious claims to greatness. He is not proud of himself, nor does he pretend to understand the profound mysteries of the universe. Nevertheless his life was deeply troubled until he brought his turbulent **soul** (see above on 6:1-3) to quietness and repose. This was not an exercise in self-mastery. He stilled his restless and disturbed spirit by holding fast to the LORD, as **a child** quiets its fears by clinging to its mother. He invites all **Israel,** with which he is intimately at one, to share his unquestioning confidence in the God of the covenant.

Ps. 132. THE UNITY OF TEMPLE AND COURT

This royal ps., in dramatic liturgical form, was probably sung during the annual ritual of the enthronement of the LORD when the ark was carried in procession into the temple (on these terms and the title see Intro.). It provides theological and historical justification for the close relationship between the Jerusalem temple and the Davidic monarchy. **David,** the first king of united Israel and the conqueror of Jerusalem, was also the reputed planner though not the builder of the temple. This ps. consists of 2 parts, vss. 1-10, 11-18, which were probably once independent poems; they may have been combined because both relate to the narrative in II Sam. 7.

132:1-5. A solo voice calls on the Lord to remember to David's credit the difficulties he surmounted in finding a site for the temple. David's oath (vss. 3-5) does not occur elsewhere in the OT (cf. I Kings 8:17), but it graphically illustrates the story in II Sam. 7 of the king's desire to provide a temple for the LORD. The use of the ancient name **Mighty One of Jacob** (cf. Gen. 49:24) emphasizes that under David all the descendants of Jacob lived in a political unity.

132:6-7. A choir takes the part of David and his followers. In his home town, Bethlehem **Ephrathah** (cf. Mic. 5:2) they learn that the ark, which has been captured by the Philistines (cf. I Sam. 4:10-11), is at **Jaar** (i.e. Kiriath-jearim, also called Baale-judah, I Sam. 7:1-2; II Sam. 6:2) and decide to go there and **worship** at the **footstool** of God's throne, the golden lid of the ark. For a description of the ark see above on 99:1-5.

132:8-10. The tradition of David's bringing the ark to Jerusalem (II Sam. 6) blends with the cultic procession now carrying **the ark** into the temple as the congregation prays that the LORD will enter the sacred place with his throne. Since the ark was a portable shrine which traveled with Israel during the Mosaic period, the permanent structure of the temple provides the LORD with a **resting place** (cf. vs. 14). Since it was carried into battle with the armies of Israel (I Sam. 4:1-9) it is the throne of God's military **might.** The procession bearing the ark consists of the king, the **priests,** and the people. A solo voice prays (vss. 9-10) that the priests' robes of office be the **righteousness** and salvation of God, which they mediate to the people, that the loyal members of the covenant community (**saints**) be filled with **joy,** and that the reigning king enjoy God's favor, not only for his own sake, but because of the devotion of his ancestor David (cf. vss. 1-5).

132:11-12. The 2nd poem deals with 2 decisive and closely related choices of the God of Israel. He chose David as king and pledged **a sure oath** that his descendants would occupy the **throne . . . for ever.** The condition of obedience to the law attached to the promise does not appear in the narrative of II Sam. 7:10-17 and may have been written into the

tradition after a succession of bad rulers had shown the weakness of an unconditional promise.

132:13-18. The LORD's 2nd act of election was the choice of Jerusalem as his dwelling place. Because of his presence the land is blessed with abundant food, its **poor** are cared for, its **priests** channel the **salvation** of God to the nation, and its people rejoice. God will make the successor of David, his **anointed** one, a **horn,** symbol of strength, and a **lamp,** symbol of illumination and life, for his people. God will crush the king's **enemies,** and his kingly authority will gleam like his golden **crown.**

Ps. 133. BROTHERS TOGETHER

This wisdom ps. (on this category and the title see Intro.) was intended to combat a practice which threatened to destroy the traditional structure of Israelite society. If brothers continued to **dwell** "together" (the lit. meaning, rather than **in unity;** cf. Gen. 13:6; 36:7; Deut. 25:5) after the death of their father the estate remained undivided and the family's inheritance in the Holy Land was kept intact. The development of commerce and the urbanization of society induced many young men to sell their share of the inheritance and go off on their own. The psalmist urges that the old custom is **good and pleasant** (vs. 1), decreed by the LORD and followed by his blessing (vs. 3c), the continued **life** and vigor of society (not personal immortality, vs. 3d; see above on 22:25-26).

Two metaphors illustrate the beauty of the ancient way: the holy **oil** of anointing **running down** the hair and **beard** of the high priest, the successor of Aaron (cf. Exod. 29:7; 30:22-33; Lev. 21:5); and the **dew** gathering copiously on the slopes of Mt. **Zion.** Mt. Hermon in the far N was a region of heavy dew, and the expression **dew of Hermon** had become proverbial. Some commentators delete vs. 2bc as an interpolation not fitting the poetic meter, and thus make the metaphor merely a reminder of the beneficial effect of olive oil on the hair. Some also, regarding the flow of dew from Hermon to Zion as a geographical impossibility, emend one letter of vs. 3b to give "which flows down on the arid highlands."

Ps. 134. EVENING WORSHIP

This hymn (on this category and the title see Intro.) is a call to worship for the evening service of the temple (vs. 1; cf. Isa. 30:29). The priests summon the people to praise (vss. 1-2) and pronounce a blessing on the congregation (vs. 3). To **bless the LORD** is to acknowledge that all good is the gift of his might and grace. To be blessed by him is to receive the gifts from that power which created the universe.

The temple is the center of the sphere of blessing. The worshipers are called **servants,** a term applied throughout the Near East to slaves, subjects of a king, or worshipers of a god. They stand in the temple courtyard with their **hands** held up toward the inner court containing the shrine, the dwelling of the LORD.

Ps. 135. LORD OF NATURE AND HISTORY

This hymn (on this category see Intro.) begins and ends with "Hallelujah" (**Praise the LORD**).

135:1-4. On the opening call to praise see above on Ps. 134. Because **he is gracious,** i.e. because of his kingly quality of hearing and acting on the petitions of his subjects, the LORD's **name** is a saving presence, as witnessed by the most conspicuous example of his grace—the election of **Israel** in the deliverance of the nation from Egypt.

135:5-7. The hymn proper begins with a solo voice praising the power of God in nature. He rules supreme over the members of the heavenly council (see above on 58:1-5; 82:1-5) and his authority over his creation from the highest **heaven** to the lowest **deeps** of the ocean is unlimited (see above on Ps. 95). The LORD, not the pagan weather gods, gives the **rain** on which the fertility of Palestine depends, gathering the **clouds** from afar, fashioning **lightnings** to accompany the storm, and unleashing the **wind** from the heavenly **storehouses.**

135:8-14. The Lord of nature is also Lord of history. Vss. 8-12 are a condensation of 136:10-22 (see comment) describing how in the formative period of Israel's history he brought her out of **Egypt** and gave her **Canaan . . . as a heritage.** Since God's power is independent of time he will likewise deliver **his people** from their present troubles (vss. 13-14; cf. Exod. 3:15; Deut. 32:36).

135:15-21. Contemplation of the LORD's greatness leads the psalmist to pour scorn on the pagan deities (see above on 115:1-8). The closing call to praise resembles 115:9-11 (see comment). The Levites (**house of Levi**) were the temple singers and servants.

Ps. 136. God's Saving Love

This is a hymn (on this category see Intro.) in praise of God's **steadfast love,** manifested in his control over nature (vss. 4-9) and his rule in human affairs as typified by the deliverance from Egypt and the giving to Israel of her homeland (vss. 10-22). The antiphonal response which follows each line was a regular part of the temple liturgy (cf. I Chr. 16:41; II Chr. 5:13; 7:3, 6; 20:21; Ezra 3:11; Jer. 33:11; I Macc. 4:24).

Israelite theology and worship arose from the same source. The nation was the creation of the LORD, brought into being by a series of mighty acts which both defined and illustrated his *hesed*—a Hebrew word which can be only partially translated by "steadfast love." It meant his consuming concern for a worthless slave people that led him to come to their rescue and his unshakable loyalty to the relationship between the people and himself which his saving act had created.

136:1-3. Vs. 1 is the call to thanksgiving commonly used in the temple worship, source of the antiphonal response, as already noted (cf. vs. 1 of Pss. 106; 107; 118). Vss. 2-3 are an expansion of this.

136:4-9. The pre-Israelite Jerusalem cult focused on the Most High God, whose power was revealed in his creation and control of the universe. When the temple was established in Jerusalem, Israel adopted this feature of Jebusite worship as a preliminary and prefatory statement of its traditional historic faith and another manifestation of the LORD's steadfast love. On the creation thought of this section, which closely parallels Gen. 1:1-19, see above on Ps. 104.

136:10-22. The recital of the LORD's mighty acts in the nation's founding includes the events in which he broke the power of Pharaoh **with a strong hand and an outstretched arm,** saved his people at the **Red** (lit. "Reed"; see comment on Exod. 13:17-22) **Sea,** preserved them in **the wilderness,** destroyed the **kings** of the E Jordan region who opposed their march (on **Sihon** and **Og** see Num. 21:21-35), and gave them a **heritage** in the Holy Land. This account omits the revelation at Sinai and the people's rebellion in the wilderness (see above on Pss. 105; 106).

136:23-26. Hearing these deeds of the LORD dramatically recited at the covenant renewal festival (see Intro.) the worshipers felt them to be, not traditions from the remote past, but events taking place in the living present and involving every true Israelite for all time. **He remembered,** not "our forefathers," but **us.** The concluding verse continues the opening call to thanksgiving.

Ps. 137. No Song of Zion

This is a community lament (on this category see Intro.).

137:1-4. The exiles in **Babylon** gather on the banks of the irrigation canals which bring the **waters** of the Euphrates to the fields of the city (cf. Ezek. 1:1) for a ceremony of mourning over the destruction of Jerusalem and prayer for her restoration. There is no music. The **lyres** (see below on 150:3) hang silent on the poplar trees (RSV footnote), because the **songs of Zion** (cf. Pss. 95–99) with their emphasis on the might and majesty of the LORD would only arouse the contempt and amusement of the conquerors. **The LORD's song** belongs to the ritual of a temple that is no more.

137:5-6. An individual testifies that, though he cannot sing the sacred songs, he will never **forget** the place of their origin and will regard the opportunity to return as life's **highest joy.**

137:7-9. The ps. ends with 2 curses. **The Edomites,** who lived S and E of the Dead Sea, joined the Babylonian armies in the sack of **Jerusalem** (cf. Obad. 8-14)—an especially heinous offense since as descendants of Jacob's brother Esau they were the nation most closely related to Israel. Vss. 8-9 are a wish of blessing on the world power which shall destroy Babylon as she destroyed Jerusalem. The gruesome practice of vs. 9 was a common feature of ancient warfare (cf. II Kings 8:12; Hos. 10:14).

Ps. 138. The Divine Presence

This is an individual thanksgiving (on this category and the title see Intro.).

138:1-3. The psalmist, standing in the forecourt of the **temple,** prostrates himself toward the sanctuary in the inner court (vs. 2) and gives thanks to God with his **whole heart** (i.e. inner being). **Before the gods** may mean either that he praises the LORD's infinite superiority over the pagan deities or that he calls the heavenly council (see above on 58:1-5; 82:1-5) to witness his act of devotion. He gives thanks to the **name** (i.e. the mysterious presence in the temple) of God for his **steadfast** (saving) **love** and **faithfulness** to his declared purpose and for the supremacy of his creative and judging **word.** He has been through severe trouble, but the LORD has restored strength to his life (on **soul** see above on 6:1-3).

138:4-6. These reflections lead the psalmist into a hymn to the greatness of the LORD. Israel's testimony to her God has been heard by the nations, and their **kings** will eventually worship the LORD, who rejects the **haughty** and exalts the **lowly** (see above on 112:1-4).

138:7-8. The ps. closes with an expression of confidence that the LORD will deliver the psalmist from his **enemies** and a prayer that he will **not forsake** the one who owes life itself to his saving work.

Ps. 139. The Ever-present God

This ps. expresses the abstract concepts of the omniscience (vss. 1-6), omnipresence (vss. 7-12), and creative power (vss. 13-18) of God in remarkably personal and concrete language. It defies classification, but vss. 19-24 suggest that it may have been used by a suppliant seeking God's vindication and help (see above on Pss. 4; 7). On the title see Intro.

139:1-6. God knows the psalmist's every movement, reads his **thoughts** before he thinks them, and understands the full meaning of each **word** he utters. Like a city wall God surrounds, and his protecting **hand** is always near. **Such** perfect **knowledge** is quite beyond the psalmist's comprehension.

139:7-12. Even if he would, the poet could not escape God's mighty presence. The meaning of **wings of the morning** is not clear, but it may refer to an ancient personification of the dawn as a winged creature. Since the **sea** lies to the W of Palestine, vss. 8-9 mean that the universe from top to bottom and from side to side is filled with the presence of God and is under his control. On the cosmology of these vss. see above on 18:7-18. **Even the darkness** has no reality for the God whose presence is **light.**

139:13-15. The psalmist's creation thought centers, not in the formation of the universe, but in the making of his own person and personality. His being holds no mystery for the God who formed his **inward parts** (lit. "kidneys," which in OT psychology are organs of thought) and **knit** his frame together with bone and sinew. The ancient world believed that children were formed in mother **earth** before they entered the womb, and Egyptian art shows the potter-god fashioning a child of clay on his wheel.

139:16-18. Vs. 16 develops the theme of the "book of the living" (see above on 69:19-29). Before the psalmist was born the LORD recorded the number of days given him. This is a poetic statement of the comprehensive knowledge of God, incomprehensible, but **precious,** to the psalmist (vss. 17-18). Vs. 18 is obscure (cf. RSV footnote) but appears to mean, "If I were to count God's thoughts till my strength failed, the task would remain unfinished."

139:19-24. That men should defy such a God and hold him in contempt fills the psalmist with passionate hatred and loathing. He realizes that some **wicked way** may lurk unrecognized and undetected in himself and prays that God will expose him with divine wisdom, eradicate the evil, and lead him in the way of permanent peace (see above on Ps. 1).

Ps. 140. Plots of Violent Men

This individual lament (on this category, the title, and **selah** see Intro.) closely resembles Pss. 59; 64 (see comments).

140:1-8. Three prayers describe the psalmist's predicament and seek divine aid (vss. 1-3, 4-5, 6-8). He is beset by enemies, **evil men** bent on violence, godless and proud (vss. 1, 4-5). In a **plot** to bring him to ruin (vss. 2, 8) they have brought lying charges against him. He compares their malicious **lips** to those of a serpent which has **poison** under its **tongue** (vs. 3), their violence to that of a hostile army (vs. 2), and their cunning to that of a hunter laying snares (vs. 5; see above on 9:13-17). Vs. 7 recalls former occasions when God protected the psalmist from hostile men.

140:9-11. This cry for vengeance has a form reminiscent of ancient Near Eastern curse formulas (see above on 17:13-14; 109:6-19). The **burning coals** suggest the fate of Sodom (Gen. 19:24). The other curses have the character of poetic justice, especially the personification of **evil** as a hunter stalking the hunters (see above on 7:12-16).

140:12-13. The closing expression of confidence states the psalmist's certainty of the **justice** of God which supports the helpless against the oppressor (see above on 68:5-6; 112:1-4). Because this is God's nature the faithful in Israel will remain forever in his saving **presence** and will have continuous cause for thanksgiving.

Ps. 141. Temptations

This is an individual lament (on this category and the title see Intro.).

141:1-2. The psalmist offers his prayer at the time of the **evening sacrifice** of grain and frankincense (cf. Lev. 2:1). Holding his **hands** out palms upward—the ancient gesture of supplication—he asks that his **prayer** be considered as itself a sacrifice. In this request we can see the beginning of the spiritualization of the sacrificial system.

141:3-7. These vss. relate in the form of a prayer the reason for the psalmist's cry for help. Many Israelites have renounced their allegiance to the LORD and have prospered (see above on Pss. 73; 125). They are friendly with the psalmist, inviting him to their feasts (vs. 4) and offering to anoint him with **oil** like an honored guest (vs. 5). Fearing that this association will lead him to some corrupt word (vs. 3), thought, or deed (vs. 4) he prays for divine protection from all temptations, declaring that he would rather take harsh discipline from **a good man** than lavish hospitality from an apostate. Vss. 5-7 are obscure but apparently contain a **prayer** that those who spurn the covenant law will be condemned in God's heavenly council (vs. 6; see above on 7:6-11), broken as a field stone shatters under a farmer's hammer, and given over to the dark power of the underworld (see above on 6:4-5; 88:10-12).

141:8-10. The concluding vss. renew the appeal for help. On **the snares of evildoers** see above on 9:13-17.

Ps. 142. No Human Helper

This is an individual lament (on this category and the title see Intro.).

142:1-3b. A note of confidence breaks through the call for help. The God of perfect knowledge (cf. 139:1-6) already knows that the psalmist's **spirit** (i.e. vital power; see above on 31:1-8) is at a low ebb.

142:3c-6b. The cause of the psalmist's distress is the plots hatched by his enemies against him. On the trap set by the enemy see above on 9:13-17. The helper traditionally appeared on the **right** side (cf. 110:5; 121:5), but though the psalmist looks anxiously no human defender comes (cf. 60:11). Therefore he renews his appeal for aid to the LORD, the only **portion** (i.e. possession) he has among **living** men.

142:6c-7. The psalmist acknowledges his helplessness before his enemies. The **prison,** like the underworld, is a common symbol for distress. Both are narrow and confining, and the root meaning of "salvation" is "to make wide" (see above on 18:19). The psalmist pledges the vow of a thank offering if his prayer is answered (see above on 50:7-15). He imagines the scene as he presents the offering. The worshiping community will crowd around him, sharing his joy in God's goodness.

Ps. 143. Justice for a Sinner

This individual lament (on this category, the title, and **selah** see Intro.) is the last of the penitential pss. (see above on Ps. 6).

143:1-6. Persecuted by vicious enemies the psalmist seeks vindication and vengeance from the LORD. He cannot base his appeal on his innocence (contrast Ps. 17) since any human being brought to trial before God would be found guilty (vs. 2). He therefore appeals because of his need (vss. 3-4). His foes have reduced his **life** and his **spirit** (i.e. his vital powers; see above on 31:1-8) to the vanishing point so that he is already as if in the realm of death (see above on 6:4-5). God's justice (vs. 1) is known to act most vigorously in just such a case (see above on 68:5-6; 112:1-4), as his wonderful deliverance of Israel from Egypt testifies (vss. 5-6; see above on Ps. 136).

143:7-10. The renewed cry for help expresses the psalmist's alienation from God (cf. 22:1-21), almost as complete as that of the shades in **the Pit** (i.e. the underworld; see above on 88:10-12). He prays for instruction and the guidance of God's **good spirit** (i.e. his mighty but beneficent presence). On **soul** see above on 6:1-3.

143:11-12. His closing prayer appeals to God's justice and **steadfast love** (see above on Ps. 136) to **preserve** his **life** and **destroy** his **enemies.** On **thy name's sake** and **servant** see above on 23:1-4; 27:7-14 respectively.

Ps. 144. Before Battle

This royal ps. (on this category and the title see Intro.) was spoken by the king on the eve of battle (cf. Ps. 20).

144:1-4. In a series of military metaphors the king acknowledges that the LORD is the source of his power in war (vss. 1-2). The theological basis is the ancient holy war concept, "The LORD is a soldier" (cf. Exod. 15:3; II Sam. 22:35). The holy war requires absolute trust in the LORD and none in the troops or their officers (see Intro. and on 20:6-9). Hence the meditation on the frailty of human nature (vss. 3-4; cf. 39:4-6; 90:4-6).

144:5-11. The king then calls on God to **come down** as he had in old time and rescue him from enemies whose **right hand** (i.e. power) is founded on treachery (vss. 5-8, 11). On the accompaniments of the theophany see above on 11:4-7a; 18:7-18; cf. Judg. 5:4-5. If the victory is granted the king promises a thanksgiving service in which he will himself lead the singing of a ps. of the type of Ps. 124, accompanying himself on the **ten-stringed harp** (see below on 150:3). On **new song** see above on 33:1-3.

144:12-15. Looking beyond the victory the king prays for the general welfare of his nation in its population, crops, and cattle (12-14). He confidently expects that the covenant **people** of the LORD, the ruler of nature and history, will enjoy these **blessings.**

Ps. 145. The Name of the Lord

This hymn for a solo voice is in acrostic form (on these terms and the title see Intro.). The vs. beginning with "n," missing in the Hebrew, is supplied in the RSV from the LXX as vs. 13cd.

145:1-7. The singer praises the various qualities which unite in the **name** of God, i.e. his saving presence with his people (vss. 1-2; cf. vs. 21). The unlimited power of his kingly majesty (vss. 1, 3) is revealed in his wonderful **works** (vss. 4-7)—an expression usually used of the exodus event (see above on Ps. 136). The deeds of the LORD also make plain his **goodness** and his **righteousness,** i.e. his faithfulness to his covenant with Israel.

145:8-13b. The merciful character of the covenant God is reinforced by the quotation of an ancient covenant formula (vs. 8; cf. 103:8; Exod. 34:6) and by the insistence that **his compassion** is as wide as the world he created (vs. 9). **Kingdom** in vss. 11-13b is not a geographical or political unity but God's kingly authority which rules all time and space (see above on 100:3-5).

145:13c-21. Vss. 13c-20 describe God's consistency to his **words** and **deeds** of salvation and judgment: upholding the weak, feeding man and beast, protecting those who sincerely call on him, preserving **all who love him,** and destroying inveterate enemies against his authority. These deeds are manifestations of his justice (vs. 17; see above on 68:5-6; 112:1-4). Such a God is worthy to be praised by everything he has made, especially by the members of the covenant community (**saints,** vs. 10), by the singer himself, and by every human being (**all flesh,** vs. 21; cf. vs. 6).

Ps. 146. The Justice of God

This is a hymn for a solo voice (on this category see Intro.). Pss. 146-50 are called "Hallelujah Pss." because they begin and end with this one-word call to praise (**Praise the LORD**).

146:1-4. The psalmist summons his **soul** (i.e. all his vital powers; see above on 6:1-3; 42:1-2a) to the praise of the LORD. He declares that **no help** can be expected from any human being (**son of man**), since all are subject to death, and their **plans** are as fragile and fleeting as their bodies (see above on 6:4-5; 88:10-12).

146:5-10. The theme of this hymn is the **justice** of God which reaches out to deliver the helpless and to destroy **the wicked** (see above on 68:5-6). God's justice, in which alone man's hope and happiness are grounded, is the operation among men of that kingly power which created the universe and rules it eternally (vss. 6, 10; see above on 96:10-13). Vss. 7-9 show God's justice in action on behalf of easily exploited or defenseless members of society: **the hungry, ... prisoners** (see above on 79:11-13), **... the blind, ... sojourners** (i.e. resident aliens), **the widow and the fatherless.**

Ps. 147. The Paradox of God's Deeds

This hymn (on this category see Intro.), one of the "Hallelujah Pss." (see above on Ps. 146), consists of 3 brief poems (vss. 1-6, 7-11, 12-20) expressing the paradoxical nature of God's dealing with his world.

147:1-6. The God who gathers the **outcasts** (i.e. exiles) **of Israel,** tenderly caring for the sorrowful and weak, counts the countless **stars** and calls them by **their names.** Infinite in wisdom toward the universe, he is infinite in compassion toward its weakest inhabitants.

147:7-11. By his unlimited power the LORD summons the **rain** to bring fertility to the soil and **food** to the animals, but he does not respect power in **man** or beast. He delights in the reverent devotion of those who anchor their lives on his **steadfast love.** On **lyre** see below on 150:3.

147:12-20. The God who rules the universe has taken up his residence in **Zion** and made it a center of blessing and strength. His **word** is all-powerful. When he speaks the **snow,** the **hoarfrost,** and biting **cold** grip the land (rarely enough in Palestine to be regarded as a natural wonder); then at his command the warm **wind** releases the imprisoned **waters.** This world-controlling **word** was given to Israel in the covenant, and the command that sends forth the snow has been enshrined in **his statutes and ordinances** (i.e. the law).

Ps. 148. Praise in Heaven and Earth

This hymn (on this category see Intro.), one of the "Hallelujah Pss." (see above on Ps. 146), calls for **praise** to the LORD **from the heavens** (vss. 1-6) and **from the earth** (vss. 7-14).

148:1-6. The psalmist summons the members of the heavenly council (see above on 58:1-5; 82:1-5), the heavenly bodies, and the heavenly ocean (see comment on Gen. 1:6-8) with the purpose of forming a great choir for the praise of the God who created them by his word (cf. Gen. 1:6, 14-15), gave them permanence, and established the limits of their movements and powers.

148:7-13. This heavenly choir should have an equally inclusive earthly counterpart. Such marvelous creations of God as **fire** (i.e. lightning), **snow,** the **stormy wind,** and the deep sea with its mysterious creatures (see above on 104:5-9, 24-26) should join the more mundane landscape and creatures of the earth and its human inhabitants of all ranks and ages to praise the LORD, whose **name** (i.e. saving presence) **is exalted** in power and whose **glory** (i.e. authority) rules the universe.

148:14. Israel has special reason to praise the LORD. He has exalted her by drawing her **near to him** and binding her to himself in the covenant and by taking up his residence with her in Jerusalem (see above on 68:15-16; 87:1-3). On **horn** and **saints** see above on 75:1-5; 16:3-4 respectively.

Ps. 149. A Hymn of Victory

This hymn (on this category see Intro.) is one of the "Hallelujah Pss." (see above on Ps. 146).

149:1-3. The call to praise summons the **faithful** members of the covenant community, **the sons of Zion,** to song and sacred dance in praise of Israel's **Maker,** who created her by the deliverance from Egypt and the covenant at Sinai (cf. Isa. 44:2; 51:6). On **new song** see above on 33:1-3. On the musical instruments see below on 150:3, 4.

149:4-9. The worshipers are celebrating a **victory** (vs. 4) and appear in the temple with **swords in their hands** (vs. 6). As part of the ritual they recline on **couches,** possibly for a sacred meal (vs. 5). The titles **humble** (vs. 4) and **faithful** (vs. 5) are appropriate to soldiers in the holy war, where trust in the LORD was more important than military skill (see Intro. and on 20:6-9). The victorious warriors rejoice in the acclaim of their fellows (vss. 4*b*-5*a*) and in the flush of victory dream of a greater triumph to come. The LORD's **judgment** on the pagan nations has been **written** (i.e. is unequivocally determined), and Israel will be his instrument for the execution of the sentence (vss. 7-9). The treatment of the foreign rulers here is less harsh than that sometimes visited on defeated princes (cf. Num. 31:8-12; Josh. 10:24-27).

This ps. could belong to any period of Israel's history, but the kind of thought it contains gave birth to the idea, common in apocalyptic literature, of the final battle at the end of the age.

Ps. 150. The Last Hallelujah

This hymn (on this category see Intro.), one of the "Hallelujah Pss." (see above on Ps. 146), was possibly used as an introduction to the covenant renewal ritual (see Intro.) when the mighty acts of God in delivering the nation from Egyptian bondage were recited.

150:1-2. The praise in the **sanctuary** is echoed by the heavenly choir above the **firmament,** the blue dome of the sky (see above on 148:1-6).

150:3. The raucous blast of the ram's-horn **trumpet** (the *shophar;* see above on 81:3) opened and closed the worship. There is less certainty about the other instruments of the impressive temple orchestra (cf. I Chr. 15:16-22; 16:4-6; 25:1-8; II Chr. 5:12-13; 29:25-30). The word here translated **lute** is elsewhere in the RSV rendered "harp" (e.g. 57:8; 71:22; Isa. 23:16; Amos 6:5). If it was like the harps found in Egyptian tombs, it consisted of strings stretched from a long soundbox to an arm curving from one end of the box. Josephus, Jewish historian of the first cent. A.D., describes it as having 12 strings, but in earlier times it may have had only 10 (see above on 92:1-4). On the other hand **harp** here represents the word usually translated "lyre" in the RSV (e.g. 49:4; 137:2; Gen. 4:21; Isa. 24:8). From representations in Mesopotamian reliefs the Semitic lyre seems to have been quadrilateral in shape, with strings stretched over a bridge on a soundbox to a crosspiece at the other end. Josephus says it had 10 strings and was played with a pick, but the reliefs show fewer strings, and David played the lyre "with his hand" (I Sam. 16:23). Both harp and lyre were made of wood (I Kings 10:12).

150:4. The **timbrel** was a small hand drum to accompany the **dance** (cf. 149:3; Exod. 15:20; Judg. 11:34; I Sam. 18:6). **Strings** are mentioned also in 45:8 (and perhaps 33:3; see comment), but the instruments so designated are not known. The **pipe** was probably a sort of flute—a tube of cane or metal with finger holes, sounded by blowing across the end, or perhaps transversely across a hole (cf. Gen. 4:21).

150:5. Two kinds of **cymbals** are mentioned. The difference between them is uncertain, but it has been suggested that those of one type were flat and struck horizontally, of the other cone-shaped and struck vertically. Probably both kinds were of bronze.

150:6. The ps. and the Psalter end with a "Hallelujah"—a call to every living thing to **praise the Lord.**

THE PROVERBS

Robert C. Dentan

Introduction

Name and Character. The proverbs in the book of Proverbs were not written, as the common reader might suppose, in the style of folk sayings. The Hebrew word translated "proverb" can indeed mean a folk saying (e.g. I Sam. 10:12), but it is also used to designate a variety of other, more artificial literary forms. It can mean a parable or allegory (Ezek. 17:2), a taunt song (Isa. 14:4), or a prophetic oracle (Num. 23:7); it can also mean a polished apothegm or a more lengthy moral essay. It is in the last 2 senses that the word is chiefly used in Prov., especially in chs. 1–29; in chs. 30–31 the term is extended to cover such diverse forms as a meditation, or private revelation (30:2-4), a prayer (30:7-9), numerical lists of interesting things (30:11-31), and a descriptive poem (31:10-31).

All the material in Prov. 1–29 is educational in character, composed with conscious literary art for the instruction of the young—the larger part in the form of terse maxims running to no more than a vs. or 2, a smaller part in the form of short essays covering as much as a whole ch. Its pedagogic purpose explains in large part why the book was written in poetic form, since poetry, with its regular rhythmic patterns, unusual turns of phrase, and striking images, is more easily memorized than prose. The schoolroom setting is also the chief clue to the interpretation of the book and should be continually in the reader's mind.

Authorship. The book is traditionally ascribed to Solomon, but this is a mere convention. It was in Solomon's court that ancient oriental "wisdom" was first introduced to Israel, and it later became customary to attribute all books belonging to this particular literary genre to him. The actual authors of Prov. were the successive generations of wisdom teachers (or "wise men") who had charge of the moral and practical training of young men of the court and upper classes as they were being prepared for positions of responsibility in society, business, politics, and diplomacy. The best description we have of such a wisdom teacher, though from long after the time of Solomon or even the later monarchy, is that found in Ecclus. 51:13-30 (see comment), where both the teacher's early training (vss. 13-22) and the subsequent practice of his profession (vss. 23-30) are described.

From the time of Solomon on, these wisdom teachers played an important role in Israel and were recognized, along with the prophets and priests, as spiritual leaders to whom men might look for religious instruction and moral insight (cf. Jer. 18:18). Because they operated more within the traditional framework of society and based their teaching chiefly on rational and experiential premises, there was frequently tension between them and the prophets (cf. Jer. 9:23), who were often social radicals claiming immediate divine inspiration. Nevertheless on many points the teaching of the wise men and the prophets is strikingly similar (cf. 11:1; 15:8; 17:5, 15; 21:3, 30, 31).

The wise men were the intellectuals of the ancient world and like all intellectuals sometimes strayed into dangerous, certainly unorthodox, realms of speculation. Eccl. and Job are products of this kind of private, unconventional intellectual activity. Prov. however—with the possible exception of chs. 30–31—is a collection of maxims and essays composed by wisdom teachers of unimpeachable orthodoxy. Its component units were designed for practical use in instruction, each one presumably intended to be memorized by the pupil and further expounded orally by the teacher.

Date of Composition. The book in its present form cannot be older than the time of King Hezekiah (late 8th cent. B.C.), who is mentioned in 25:1. In actual fact it is probably much younger than that. Individual "proverbs" may, of course, be as old as Solomon, or even older, but it is generally agreed that the book as we have it comes from the postexilic age, perhaps as late as the 4th cent. B.C. The developed style of chs. 1–9, as well as the social and intellectual milieu they suggest, strongly point to this period. The dating of the other, smaller collections of which the book is composed is of course a further problem.

Contents. The book falls into certain natural divisions, for the most part marked off by separate subtitles. The nucleus consists of the 2 collections particularly designated as "The Proverbs of Solomon" (10:1; 25:1; the similar phrase in 1:1 is intended to cover the whole book). The first of these, 10:1–22:16, can be further subdivided on the basis of form and subject matter into 2 collections, chs. 10–15 and 16:1–22:16. The 2nd collection, chs. 25–29, "Proverbs of Solomon which the men of Hezekiah king of Judah copied," is likewise to be divided into 2 collections, chs. 25–27 and chs. 28–29. The most exhaustive study yet made of the content, literary form, and cultural background of these 4 collections led its author to the conclusion that chs. 10–15 are the oldest, chs. 28–29 the next oldest, with 16:1–22:

16 and chs. 25–27 coming somewhat later, all of them preexilic. Interesting and important as these conclusions are, however, they offer only a reasonable working hypothesis and cannot be taken as definitive.

Between the 2 "Solomon" collections an editor has inserted 2 smaller sections, each entitled "The words of the wise" (22:17; 24:23). The first of these (22:17–24:22) is of special interest since it was apparently written in deliberate imitation of an Egyptian work, The Instruction of Amen-em-Opet, even to the extent of its division into "thirty sayings" (22:20). In 22:17–23:11 nearly all the material has direct parallels in Amen-em-Opet's book, which probably dates from the end of the 2nd millenium B.C. The 2nd collection of "words of the wise" (24:23-34) is apparently just an appendix to the first and is too brief to provide any clue as to date.

Chs. 1–9, a collection of extended essays (for the most part) dating in all probability from the postexilic period, was prefixed to chs. 10–29 as a general introduction.

The last 2 chs. (30–31) are a miscellaneous appendix, containing material of entirely different character from the rest of the book. Each ch. has at its head the name of an otherwise unknown foreign wise man (Agur and Lemuel). In the LXX some of this material is placed in the middle of the book rather than at the end (see below on 30:1–31:31).

Wisdom. Prov. belongs to the general class of wisdom literature (see "The Wisdom Literature," pp. 1101-05). This means, from one point of view, that it was produced by a group of teachers collectively called the wise men; it also means that the theme of the book is something called "wisdom." This concept is important not only for the exegesis of Prov. and the history of the wise men in OT times but also for the development of NT Christology. In I Cor. 1:24 Christ is called "the wisdom of God," and in Col. 2:3 he is said to contain "all the treasures of wisdom." In John 1:1-14; Col. 1:15-18; and Heb. 1:2-3 the underlying idea is likewise clearly dependent on the concept of "wisdom" as developed in the canonical and apocryphal wisdom literature, though the word "wisdom" does not actually appear.

The wisdom literature, taken as a whole, is the philosophical literature of the Hebrews, being concerned with the proper governance of life through an understanding of ultimate goals and general principles. It is distinguished from the philosophical literature of the Greeks by its predominant concern for practical activity rather than metaphysical speculation. The word "wisdom" in its basic, non-philosophical use (outside the wisdom literature) means merely skill, e.g. in dressmaking (Exod. 28:3), the art of government (Gen. 41:39-40), or even wickedness (II Sam. 13:3). Even in its highest philosophical development the Hebrew word never quite lost its connection with this basic sense of practical skill.

In the wisdom literature proper, "wisdom" means primarily skill in the management of one's life, a knowledge of the true ends of human existence, the general rules which enable one to attain them, and the ability to put those rules into practice. Since these goals and rules can be learned and taught, it also becomes possible to designate as "wisdom" the totality of such knowledge conceived as a body of learning that has been handed down from ancient days and can be transmitted as a sacred trust to posterity. From this point on it is not difficult to see how the concept developed into an almost metaphysical idea—Hebrew thinkers' closest approach to Greek philosophy—so that wisdom came to be thought of as a constituent part of the universe and, indeed, of God himself. This is the stage represented by 8:22-31. There is further development in a genuinely metaphysical direction in Wisd. Sol. (see comment on Wisd. Sol. 6-9), and the writings of Philo. It was from the use of it by these later writers that the term became available to the early Christian church as it searched for a suitable vocabulary in which to express its judgment as to the meaning of Christ's character and work.

Although this theologically and cosmically significant "wisdom," personified and almost hypostatized, appears only in the latest parts of Prov., notably in chs. 8–9, the whole book takes on added meaning when it is seen that this was the direction in which the wisdom movement had been tending from the first.

The Influence of Foreign Wisdom. The wisdom movement did not originate in Israel. It was introduced from abroad and never entirely lost the marks of its foreign derivation. In Egypt and Mesopotamia, where civilized societies had long been highly organized, there had grown up a class of skilled officials, educated men who had mastered the art of government as well as the complex and mysterious arts of reading and writing. They had long been engaged in developing a philosophy of how men should live and work in society. When Israel first aspired, under Solomon, to be a civilized people among the other great nations of the world, it was from these other nations that she had to borrow the techniques, and almost certainly the personnel, for establishing the elaborate governmental organization which was necessary. Along with the methods of organization of foreign courts came also the educational procedures and the moral philosophy which animated them.

The most striking example of foreign influence in Prov. is that already mentioned in 22:17–23:11, in which every proverb but one can be paralleled in The Instruction of Amen-em-Opet. In addition the book as a whole exhibits many affinities with other well-known Egyptian wisdom books, such as The Instruction of Ptah-hotep and The Instruction of King Meri-ka-Re, and with various Mesopotamian wisdom texts. Recent studies have also disclosed a large Phoenician influence on the book. Two sections of Prov. are explicitly attributed to otherwise unknown foreign wise men: "Agur son of Jakeh of Massa" (30:1) and "Lemuel, king of Massa" (31:1).

The foreign origin of wisdom explains the absence in Prov. (as well as in Job and Eccl.) of any reference to the distinctive ideas or institutions of Israel or the facts of its history (3:9-10 is hardly an exception). In the wisdom literature of the Apoc. (Tobit, Wisd. Sol., Ecclus., Baruch), which represents a later stage of the movement, the situation is altogether different. These books present wisdom as an integral part of traditional Hebrew religion. But the canonical wisdom literature shows no conscious effort in this direction. It makes no attempt to harmonize the universal truths taught by the wise men of the ancient orient with the particular revelation given by God to Israel.

To say this, however, is not to minimize the unconscious transformation that foreign thought necessarily underwent as it passed through the filter of the Hebrew mind. Careful study of ancient Hebrew wisdom shows that even the early parts of Prov. have subtle differences of emphasis from their foreign prototypes (e.g. see below on 1:1-6; 21:1-3), but the general reader is likely—at least on first approach—to find the similarities more striking than the differences.

The Philosophy and Theology of Prov. The character of wisdom thinking was largely determined by its foreign origin. It is this that gives it, first of all, the stamp of *universalism*. It is concerned with man as such and the general principles that govern his life everywhere, not specifically with Israelite man and the divinely revealed laws to which Israel was subject under a special covenant with God.

Another characteristic, partly to be explained by the practical, educational function of the wise men, is their apparent *utilitarianism*. Wisdom teaching, with a few notable exceptions (e.g. 15:16, 17; 23:4-5; 28:6), is concerned with pragmatic success in ordinary life, not with response to supernatural challenges or the search for transcendent goals. It aims to produce good citizens rather than saints or spiritual heroes.

The need to have clear-cut sanctions for conduct, easy to use in classroom intruction, leads the wise men, further, to present on the whole *a mechanical view of retribution.* They are inclined to speak of immediate temporal and material success as the reward of the good life and immediate and tangible disaster as the punishment for wickedness. Both reward and punishment are represented as resulting from the operation of an impersonal law inherent in the sequence of human events although certainly subject to God's overruling sovereignty.

The wisdom philosophy also, for pedagogical reasons, tends toward *oversimplification of human character,* dividing all men roughly into 3 sharply defined classes: (*a*) the "wise" or "righteous," who know and do what is right and are successful (e.g. 10:1, 2); (*b*) the "simple," who are capable of becoming wise although they are not yet (e.g. 9:4, 16); and (*c*) the "fools," who are utterly corrupt, incapable of moral growth, and doomed to destruction (e.g. 10:21; 17:16; 27:22).

Finally, because of their upper-class mentality and their concern for the stability of human institutions, the wise men incline—in contrast to the prophets—toward *conservativism* in their political and social views.

The wise men of Prov., unlike those responsible for Job, Eccl., or the wisdom literature of the Apoc., show little specific concern for theological matters. This is not to say that they were indifferent to theology, but their immediate task did not seem to involve the application to any great extent of theological principles. That they considered themselves thoroughly orthodox is shown by the fact that they normally refer to God under his distinctive Israelite name Yahweh ("the LORD"). This is their one direct point of contact with official Hebrew religion, but it is certainly a significant one.

Since the purpose of the wise men is practical, the only attributes of God they mention are those connected with creation and the moral government of the universe: viz. his omniscience (15:3, 11; 20:12; 24:12), power (16:1, 3, 4, 7, 9, 33; 18:10; 21:1, 30, 31; 22:2), and justice (11:1; 12:22; 14:31; 15:8; 16:11; 17:2, 5, 15; 19:17; 21:3; 28:5). While the law of retribution functions on the whole impersonally, Yahweh is presumably its author, certainly its guarantor, and on occasion is represented as setting it in operation.

Because of its pedagogical concern with God as guardian of the moral order Prov. has little to say of his love and mercy (only in 28:13 and perhaps 3:12), but it would be an error to suppose the wise men were unconscious of these aspects of the divine nature or indifferent to them. God's merciful overruling of men's plans in order to deliver even the wicked is the major theme in the Joseph story (Gen. 50:20; cf. Prov. 16:9), which is a typical product of the older wisdom school. The thought of God's compassion is a recurrent one in the wisdom literature of the Apoc. (e.g. Wisd. Sol. 11:24-26; Ecclus. 18:11-14).

A direct concern with theological speculation for its own sake is found in Prov. only in the poem on cosmological wisdom in 8:22-31 and in the enigmatic words of Agur (30:1-4).

That the wise men became increasingly concerned with religion and theological matters as the movement developed is shown by the fact that the latest part of Prov. (chs. 1-9) is much more explicitly religious than the earlier. The latest editor, furthermore, was so profoundly religious in outlook that he placed the whole book under the motto "The fear of the LORD [i.e. Israel's religion] is the beginning of knowledge" (1:7). This tendency would ultimately lead to the complete identification of universal wisdom with national Hebrew religion, signalized by the equation of wisdom and the law in Ecclus. (19:20; 24:23; cf. Baruch 4:1).

The Poetry of Prov. The entire book is written in the common patterns of Hebrew poetry (see "The Literary Forms of the OT," pp. 1077-81). Each vs. therefore normally falls into 2 parts, the 2nd of which "rhymes" in thought with the first, either by way of repetition ("synonymous parallelism," e.g. 27:2) or by stating the converse ("antithetic parallelism," e.g. 15:1) or by simply completing the sentence ("synthetic parallelism," e.g. 22:6). That the antithetic type overwhelmingly predominates in chs. 10-15; 28-29 seems to mark these collections as the oldest, whereas in the later collections (including 16:1-22:16; 25-27) there is greater variety, and the antithetic type is in the minority.

The acrostic, a type of poem in which each line begins with a successive letter of the Hebrew alphabet, although well represented in the Psalter (e.g. Pss. 111; 112; 119), is found in Prov. only in the "praise of the good wife" (31:10-31).

A distinctive wisdom type of poetry is the numerical proverb, which calls attention to a certain number of similar objects or phenomena (e.g. 6:16-19; 30:11-31; cf. Amos 1:3, 6, etc.). It is thought that this type may have originated in the telling of riddles. There are many examples of it in the Ras Shamra texts, clay tablets excavated at the ancient Canaanite city of Ugarit in Syria.

Each proverb, whether long or short, is designed to give aesthetic pleasure as well as moral instruction. Each is polished like a jewel, with the most careful attention being paid to alliteration, assonance, puns, and other subtleties of sound and association, few of which, unhappily, can even be suggested in translation. The individual proverbs are meant to be read, not in rapid succession, but leisurely, separately, with a careful savoring of all the nuances of each. The wise man's aesthetic delight in his art is shown by the remark of one of them that

> A word fitly spoken
> is like apples of gold in a setting
> of silver (25:11; cf. 15:23).

The wise men believed that truth should be adorned with beauty.

For Further Study: W. O. E. Oesterley, *The Book of Prov.,* 1929. A. Cohen, *Prov.,* 1945. C. T. Fritsch in *IB,* 1955. E. D. Jones, *Prov. and Eccl.,* 1961. S. H. Blank in *IDB,* 1962. R. B. Y. Scott, *Prov.; Eccl.,* 1965. R. N. Whybray, *Wisdom in Prov.,* 1965.

I. COMMENDATION OF WISDOM (1:1–9:18)

It is generally agreed that these chs., in which teaching takes the form of developed essays rather than brief maxims, contain the latest material in the book and were assembled in order to provide an introduction to the other collections. They consist in large part of the praise of wisdom and rise to a climax in chs. 8–9 with the eloquent and universal appeal spoken by wisdom herself, personified as a woman. The extended warnings against the "loose [or "strange"] woman" which are also so characteristic of these chs. (2:16-19; 5:1-23; 6:20-35; 7:1-27), although meant quite literally to put young men on their guard against sexual immorality, also serve to furnish the scene with a counterpart figure who acts as a dramatic foil to personified wisdom. The background is obviously that of a developed, sophisticated society.

A. INTRODUCTION (1:1-7)

1:1. Title. The name of **Solomon** is an indication of the kind of book rather than of authorship (see Intro.).

1:2-6. Preface. The Instruction of King Amen-em-Opet (see Intro.) begins with a preface very similar in character. It is notable, however, that the Egyptian book was intended only for court officials, whereas Prov. obviously has a more democratic outlook and offers wisdom to all who are capable of receiving it.

1:7. Motto. This was placed by the latest editor over the whole book. **The fear of the LORD** means simply "religion" (or more specifically "Israel's religion"), a concept for which Hebrew had no special word (see below on 29:25). The word translated **beginning** can also mean "best part."

B. THE DANGER OF BAD COMPANIONS (1:8-19)

1:8-9. Parental Instruction. When well received, training by parents is the basis for later happiness. Fathers and mothers are the first and most important teachers (cf. 4:3-4; 31:1-9; Deut. 6:7).

1:10-19. *A Warning Against Gangsters.* The wis-

dom teacher, who is responsible for the later education of youth, takes the role of father and addresses his pupil as **my son.** In the ancient world, as today, the promise of quick wealth had great appeal for many young men, and organized robber bands existed to exploit their impatience. The pledge of brotherhood and equal shares (vs. 14) was no doubt as hollow then as it is now. Vs. 17 seems to say that even a **bird** will avoid a trap set for him, yet foolish men rush into an evil life however obvious the consequences. The prominence given to the warning seems to indicate that gangsterism was a particular problem at the time when the final editing of the book took place.

C. WISDOM'S PUBLIC CALL TO REPENTANCE (1:20-33)

For dramatic appeal **wisdom** is personified as a prophetess, the word "wisdom" being feminine in Hebrew. Like the older prophets she is represented as appearing in the principal place of public concourse, around **the city gates,** to threaten those who will not listen to her message and, incidentally, to promise security to those who accept her (vs. 33). In vs. 22 **simple ones** are callow youths who are capable of learning, **scoffers** are skeptics who reject the principle of retribution (like "the wicked" in Ps. 10:4, 11), and **fools** are the incorrigibly wicked in morals as well as mind (cf. Matt. 5:22).

D. THE BLESSINGS OF WISDOM (2:1–3:35)

2:1-22. *The Benefits of Pursuing Wisdom.* In Hebrew ch. 2 is one long, loosely constructed sentence in which the wisdom teacher describes to his pupil the advantages that will come from the diligent pursuit and apprehension of wisdom. The pupil must listen to his teacher and exercise his intelligence (**heart**) to grasp the meaning of his words (vs. 2), but he must also **seek** for wisdom passionately on his own initiative (vss. 3-4). If he does this he will come to a genuine personal **knowledge of God** (vss. 5-8), acquire an understanding of what is good and right among men (vss. 9-11), be delivered from the influence of criminals (vss. 12-15; cf. 1:10-19) and immoral women (vss. 16-19), and finally, in a positive sense, be set firmly on the right way and given the companionship of those **good men** who will ultimately possess **the land** of Israel (vss. 20-22).

2:16-19. These vss. introduce the reader to the **loose woman,** who is so prominent in this part of Prov. Like the gangsters of ch. 1, the adulterous wife seems to have been a special problem of the period in which these chs. were written. More will be said of her in connection with chs. 5; 7. Vs. 17 is particularly remarkable for the high view of marriage that it implies. The wife is not the property of her husband but stands to him in a relation of companionship; marriage is not a legal-economic contract but a **covenant** solemnly witnessed before God (cf. Ezek. 16:8; Mal. 2:14), requiring lifelong loyalty.

3:1-12. *Wisdom the True Religion.* While the older Hebrew wisdom, partly because of its foreign origin (see Intro.), had little to say about specifically religious attitudes and obligations, there was obviously an increasing tendency toward connecting traditional wisdom teaching with the precepts of Israel's faith.

This poem is the most religious section in the book; every one of its 6 2-vs. strophes except the first, which is merely introductory, contains the name of God. In vs. 1 **teaching** represents the word more commonly, but less accurately, translated elsewhere in the OT as "law." The qualities particularly praised in this section are **loyalty** (the word usually translated "steadfast love" or "kindness") and **faithfulness** (vs. 3), qualities which are also attributed to God (Exod. 34:6), and humility (vss. 5-8). The fulfillment of cultic obligations is commended in Prov. only in vss. 9-10. The offering of **first fruits** to the deity was not, of course, unique to Israel.

3:13-26. The Value of Wisdom. The opening clause, **Happy** (or "Blessed") **is the man,** is typical of the wisdom teachers (cf. 14:21; 16:20; 28:14; Ps. 1:1; Matt. 5:3-11). The transcendent value of wisdom is shown by the fact that it is useful not only to man (vss. 13-18) but even to God (vss. 19-20). Here one can see the first steps in the direction of the idea of cosmic wisdom, which will be developed at such length in 8:22-31. Belief in God as creator was a fundamental article in the faith of the wise men (see Intro.). The rewards of wisdom are **long life** (vs. 16), prosperity and happiness (vss. 16-17), and protection from various forms of disaster (vss. 23-26; cf. Ps. 91:3-13).

3:27-30. Love for Neighbors. For all their utilitarianism the wise men are insistent on the obligation of unselfish generosity toward other men, especially the poor and helpless (cf. e.g. 14:21, 31; 19:17; 22:9; 28:27).

3:31-35. The Justice of God. With the growth of reflective thought in Israel came the problem of reconciling the frequent apparent success of the wicked and the suffering of the innocent with the wise men's teaching of inevitable retribution. It became acute in Job and Eccl., but from vs. 31 it is evident that many had long been troubled about it. This wise man, like his colleague in Ps. 37 and the "friends" of Job, answers doubts by simply reaffirming the fact of God's justice.

E. In Praise of Wisdom (4:1-27)

This ch. contains three lectures, or essays, in general praise of wisdom. While their thought is similar, there are slight differences of emphasis. Each one begins with a renewed address to the **sons** or **son** (vss. 1, 10, 20).

4:1-9. The Best Possession. The opening vss. make clear the traditional character of wisdom. It is not something which each man must dig out for himself but is passed on as a tradition from generation to generation (vss. 3-4). This poem assumes that a young man entering on an independent career will be interested in building up his estate and acquiring valuable possessions; the point the teacher wishes to impress is that wisdom is the most valuable possession of all (vss. 5, 7). It has been suggested that vss. 6-9 view wisdom as a bride and her acquisition as a wedding ceremony (note esp. vs. 9; cf. Wisd. Sol. 8:2, 9, 16).

4:10-19. The Way of Wisdom. The idea of **the righteous** as those who belong to the **light** while **the wicked** belong to **darkness** is familiar from the NT, especially in the Johannine literature (cf. John 3:19-21; I John 2:10-11; also Eph. 5:8-14) and is now

known also from the literature of the Dead Sea community. We find the same contrast here in ancient Hebrew wisdom (vss. 18-19). The righteous lives his life in a **dawn** which is becoming continually brighter, while the wicked is like a man stumbling around through the night in impenetrable darkness.

4:20-27. The Sure Path. The comparison of life to a journey is a commonplace of ethical teaching. In rabbinical literature the rules of conduct are called Halakah ("a way of walking"); Jesus spoke of the need of choosing the right road (Matt. 7:13-14). The wise man here makes use of the same imagery (vss. 25-27; cf. Deut. 5:32-33; Ps. 119:1, 5, 105; Jer. 6:16).

F. Warnings Against Immoral Women (5:1-7:27)

5:1-23. The Loose Woman. This part of the book is particularly concerned with the problem of sexual immorality. This concern is undoubtedly an indication of the later date of the collection, which comes from a time when the strict moral standards of ancient Hebrew society were being threatened by contact with new influences from abroad. It is striking that the word translated **loose** is lit. "strange," meaning at least that the woman's moral standards seemed foreign to the people of Israel (see below on 7:1-27). Vss. 9-10 imply, and 6:26-35; 7:19-20 make clear, that the problem is not prostitution but adultery. The ch. falls in 3 parts.

5:1-6. These vss. are introductory. After the usual general exhortation (vss. 1-2) the specific problem is set forth and the woman described (vss. 3-6). Her charm is acknowledged, but the student is warned that beneath the charm there is concealed a deadly poison. **Sheol** is the dark underworld to which all the dead must go.

5:7-14. The exhortation becomes more explicit. In ancient Hebrew society the punishment for adultery was death (Deut. 22:22); but the law was evidently no longer carried out, for this passage mentions only the danger that the adulterous young man may lose his property to the injured husband and fall into the hands of moneylenders in order to pay the damages imposed (vss. 9-10; cf. 6:33).

5:15-20. These vss. speak positively of the need of confining sexual attention strictly to one's own wife. The language is picturesque, at one point reminiscent of the Song of S. (cf. vs. 19 with Song of S. 4:5; 7:3). The emphasis on the sexual side of marriage is due to the context, not to a purely physical conception of the marriage relationship (cf. 2:17).

5:21-23. This section concludes with an appeal from the level of mere human, prudential considerations to the authority of God and the validity of an unchangeable, universally valid moral law.

6:1-19. Digression: Various Moral Precepts. These vss. which are more closely related to later collections than to chs. 1-9, are probably an intrusion in this section, since 6:20-7:27 continues the theme of ch. 5.

6:1-5. Against Suretyship. While the wise men were emphatic in proclaiming the obligation of charity, they were equally emphatic in declaring that young men must curb their generous, but rash, impulses to guarantee debts for friends (cf. 11:15; 22:26-27). From a common-sense point of view, this could lead only to disaster.

6:6-11. Laziness. Observation of nature was one

of the interests of the wise men (I Kings 4:33), sometimes for its own sake (e.g. 30:18-19, 24-31) and sometimes, as here, in order to draw moral lessons from it. Sloth was a vice particularly obnoxious to them, since it is obviously so natural to the young and so objectionable to employers (10:26). It can lead only to failure and poverty (cf. 12:24; 19:15; 20:4; 24:30-34).

6:12-15. Crookedness. The wise men believed in straightforwardness of speech and honesty in behavior. They warn against the person who says one thing with his lips but through sly signals indicates that he means something quite different.

6:16-19. Seven Things God Hates. The numerical proverb (see Intro.) is a favorite device in wisdom poetry (cf. 30:15-31). This one begins with a list of 5 organs of the body sometimes used in detestable ways: **eyes . . . tongue . . . hands . . . heart** (i.e. the mind) **. . . feet.** The last 2 items are the **false witness** (cf. Exod. 20:16) and the **man who sows discord,** who deliberately creates antipathy among those who would otherwise be at peace.

6:20-35. Another Warning Against Adultery. The exhortation begins, as usual, in general terms (vss. 20-23). **The evil woman** of vs. 24 is identified as an **adulteress** in vss. 26, 29. Vss. 27, 28 resemble folk proverbs: both are commonsense warnings that one cannot play with fire without getting **burned.** The proper translation of vs. 30 is not quite certain; but vss. 30-31, 32-35, when compared, certainly mean to suggest that adultery is far more dangerous from a prudential point of view than stealing. The thief may lose no more than his property; but the adulterer, confronted by an enraged husband, may be beaten, lose his position in the community, and even lose his life. No bribe can save him (vs. 35).

7:1-27. The Wiles of the Adulteress. This is the most elaborate of the 4 warnings against adulterous women found in chs. 1-9. In a vivid and extended narrative the wise man pictures the wiles she makes use of to lead callow, impressionable youth astray. Certain details in this ch. have led one scholar to suppose that the **loose** (lit. "strange") **woman** of these passages is a non-Israelite, wife of a foreign merchant resident in Israel, whose debased fertility-cult religion requires her to have intercourse with a stranger, as described by the Greek historian Herodotus. While the arguments have considerable merit, it seems on the whole more natural to understand her as a wealthy Hebrew woman of the late postexilic period whose morals have been corrupted through contact with the pagan world.

7:1-5. Anticipating the introduction of the **loose woman** (vs. 5) the wise man advises his pupil to make wisdom his female companion (vs. 4).

7:6-23. These vss. describe a typical seduction scene. Some interpreters believe the LXX is right in making the woman the person who **looked out** (vs. 6). The woman, in the absence of her **husband** (vs. 19), goes out into the city street at the time of the evening promenade to find herself a lover. Acting like an ordinary prostitute she makes shameless advances to an inexperienced **young man.** Her arguments are: (a) There is a banquet waiting to be consumed at her home, for she has just been offering a votive sacrifice in the temple and the accompanying meal is not yet eaten (vs. 14; in the so-called peace

offering only a small part of the animal was sacrificed, the rest being eaten by the worshipers, Lev. 3: 3-4). (b) She is able to offer luxuries such as only great wealth can provide (vss. 16-17). (c) Since her husband, evidently a successful merchant, is away on a long business trip there will be no danger (vss. 19-20). Finding the lure irresistible the foolish youth goes to his doom. The result of such folly, described in matter-of-fact terms in 6:33-35, is here portrayed only in metaphorical language (vss. 22-23).

7:24-27. The conclusion makes use of the familiar idea that the pursuit of loose and foolish women is **the way** that leads **to Sheol** (see above on 5:1-6).

G. THE CONTRAST BETWEEN WISDOM AND FOLLY (8:1–9:18)

8:1-36. Wisdom Speaks. As in 1:20-33, wisdom herself, rather than the wise man, is represented as speaking. Standing at the city gate, where the streets come together, she declares her worth and offers her blessings. No doubt this is the way prophets and other religious teachers of ancient Israel often presented their message. Wisdom characteristically directs her appeal to all **the sons of men,** not just to men of Israel.

8:4-21. Particularly notable in wisdom's speech is her emphasis on straightforwardness as opposed to crookedness (vss. 8-9) and humility as opposed to **arrogance** (vs. 13). Her high dignity is shown by the fact that **kings** rule by means of her (vss. 15-16; cf. Isa. 11:2).

8:22-31. Wisdom was present with God at the creation of the world (cf. 3:19). As indicated in the Intro., this passage is of primary importance for the development of a doctrine of cosmic wisdom, such as is found e.g. in Wisd. Sol. 7:22–8:1, and for the later doctrine of the Logos (Word), so basic to an understanding of NT Christology. Here, however, the conception seems to be not yet philosophical but merely poetic. The dignity of wisdom as the most important of possessions is enhanced by representing her as the first of God's creations. Poetically she is pictured as standing by God's side when the rest of the world was made (cf. John 1:1).

The meaning of the word translated **master workman** in vs. 30 is uncertain (cf. RSV footnote). Nothing else in the passage suggests that wisdom played an active role in creation, although she undoubtedly does so in the later development of the doctrine. In view of the unusual number of Canaanite-Phoenician expressions in this remarkable passage it seems probable that the conception derives ultimately from Canaanite sources and that "wisdom" was originally a pagan goddess of wisdom.

8:32-36. The note of direct appeal returns at the end of the poem (vss. 32-33). The **life** promised in vs. 35 is not everlasting life but a rich and full life in man's present existence.

9:1-6. The Invitation of Wisdom. This section of Prov. closes appropriately with a challenge to choose between the 2 ways open to man: the way of wisdom and the way of folly (vss. 13-18; cf. Deut. 30:19; Matt. 7:13-14). Wisdom, again personified, is represented as inviting guests to a rich banquet she has prepared (cf. 7:14; Matt. 22:1-14). Since only the most luxurious houses have pillars her 7-pillared house is evidence of the wealth at her command. **Seven** is possibly derived from some originally cosmological or mythological conceptions, for this passage, like 8:22-31, shows traces of Canaanite influence. If the picture is that of a house, rather than a temple, the **pillars** are to be understood as ranged around an interior courtyard. Wisdom's final invitation (vss. 5-6) forms the ultimate pattern for the similar appeals in Ecclus. 24:19; 51:23-26; Matt. 11: 28-30.

9:7-12. *Digression: Incorrigibility of the Scoffer.* This passage is plainly a later addition, obscuring the intended parallelism of vss. 1-6, 13-18. The tone is pessimistic. While the appeal in vss. 1-6 is addressed to the **simple,** i.e. the young and inexperienced, this paragraph is chiefly concerned with the **scoffer,** i.e. the skeptic and hardened evildoer, for whom wisdom's appeal always falls on deaf ears.

9:13-18. *The Invitation of Folly.* As wisdom was personified, so here is folly. Her portrait is evidently modeled on that of the "loose woman" who has been so prominent in the preceding chs. In contrast to wisdom, who sends out her messengers to summon guests to a magnificent feast, she **sits** lazily **at the door** and, like a common prostitute, loudly invites passers-by to a meal that consists only of **bread** and **water.** She suggests, perhaps quoting a proverb, that her food is more delightful because forbidden (vs. 17). There is nothing to warn the unwary youth that her house is only the entrance chamber of **Sheol** (see above on 5:1-6).

II. THE FIRST SOLOMONIC COLLECTION (10:1–22:16)

Following chs. 1-9, which are to a large extent general and introductory, the main part of Prov. (chs. 10-29) consists of several collections of brief moral apothegms, most of them consisting of a single vs., occasionally, as in ch. 24, of 2 vss., and only rarely of longer units (e.g. 23:29-35). In a few instances (e.g. 10:18-21; 11:24-26; 26:1-12, 20-28) an attempt has been made to arrange the proverbs according to subject matter, but on the whole their arrangement within the collections is unsystematic. The commentary deals only with vss. of particular interest or presenting some particular problem. The first Solomonic collection is marked by the title **The proverbs of Solomon** (10:1*a;* on "Solomon" see Intro.), which applies to all of the material through 22:16. The style and content of the proverbs show, however, that this collection is made up of 2 smaller collections which were originally independent—chs. 10-15 and 16:1–22:16.

A. PART I OF THE FIRST SOLOMONIC COLLECTION (10:1–15:33)

This collection consists overwhelmingly of proverbs composed in antithetical parallelism and may well be the oldest collection in the book (see Intro.). The predominant theme of the proverbs is the contrast between the wise man and the fool, the righteous man and the wicked. They are concerned more with general attitudes than with specific acts.

10:1*b*-2. *The Wise Man and the Fool.* These vss. introduce the 2 pairs of contrasted terms which provide the theme of the whole collection: wisdom vs. folly; righteousness vs. wickedness. Wisdom and folly are intellectual-moral terms. They imply the ability or inability to apprehend the principles by which life should be lived and to order one's life accordingly. **Righteousness** and **wickedness,** on the other hand, are in Hebrew essentially legal terms. The righteous is the one who is "innocent" of any violation of the legal norm, while the wicked is "guilty." In the practice of the wise men the 2 pairs of terms are really equivalent and generally used interchangeably. In vs. 1 no distinction is intended between **father** and **mother;** the variation is merely for the sake of parallelism.

10:3. *Retribution.* The retribution doctrine is plainly stated and its operation put under the control of God (cf. vss. 27-32).

10:4-5. *Sloth.* Laziness is one of the vices most frequently condemned by the wise men (cf. vs. 26; see above on 6:6-11). Vs. 5 illustrates the fact that the background of this collection, so far as it can be determined, is that of an agricultural society (cf. 12: 10, 11; 13:23; 14:4).

10:7. *A Lasting Name.* For the pious Hebrew the only possible immortality was that of his **memory,** kept alive by his children. This will be achieved only by the wise and righteous.

10:12. *Love Above Hatred.* The wise men of Israel, like those of Egypt, regarded the calm, cool, unargumentative life as the best. Better than **hatred,** which **stirs up strife** on every side (cf. 6:19), is **love,** which "is not irritable or resentful" (I Cor. 13:5), seeks to promote harmony and finds excuses for the misdeeds of others (cf. 17:9). The vs. is quoted in Jas. 5:20 and probably alluded to in I Cor. 13:4-7; I Pet. 4:8.

10:15. *The Advantages of Wealth.* A number of proverbs in this book appear to be merely cynical when taken out of context (e.g. 13:7, 8; 14:20; 18:11; 19:4, 6, 7; 22:7), but their purpose is pedagogical: to make the young man realize how important it is to preserve his patrimony and not allow it to be dissipated by sloth and luxurious living (but cf. 11:28).

10:18-21. *Controlling the Tongue.* The wise men were characteristically concerned with the importance of keeping one's speech (**tongue . . . lips**) under proper control (e.g. 12:16-19, 22, 23; 15:28; 17:27, 28; 18:2, 4). The NT wisdom book shows the same concern (Jas. 3:1-12). Simply talking too much was regarded as evil (vs. 19).

11:1. *Honesty.* Like the prophets (e.g. Mic. 6:11) and the lawgivers of ancient Israel (e.g. Deut. 25:13) the wise men were concerned with promoting honest practice in business. Significantly they are not content merely to say it "is the best policy" but also place it under divine sanctions (cf. 20:10, 23).

11:2. *Pride.* Since a willingness to learn is an essential quality of the seeker after wisdom, it is evident that pride—the confidence that one already possesses the requisite knowledge—is a prime deterrent in the quest. Therefore humility is a basic virtue (cf. 12:15; 13:10; 16:18; 26:12; 29:23).

11:8. *Dramatic Retribution.* The thought of a reversal in the lots of the good man and the sinner is a common feature of didactic literature (cf. 14:19; 21: 18; 26:27; 28:10; Esth. 7:9-10; Ps. 7:15; Luke 16: 25).

11:9-14. *Wisdom's Social Value.* The wise man is a source of advantage not only to himself but also to the society of which he is a part. These vss. are good evidence that in spite of their individualistic emphasis the wisdom teachers had by no means forgotten that man is a creature who lives in society and is responsible for it. Vss. 12, 13 show that the emphasis on silence (cf. 10:18) is not merely self-regarding but includes an aversion to malicious gossip because of the injury it causes to others.

11:15. See above on 6:1-5.

11:16, 22. The Need for Good Sense in Women. Though most proverbs are concerned with men, a few deal with qualities desirable in women, probably to provide the young man with guidance in his search for a wife (cf. 12:4). The meaning of vs. 16 is not entirely clear, but vs. 22 is a good example of how humor can be used to inculcate a lesson. Here it is that intelligence is a far more important quality in a wife than beauty.

11:24-26. Generosity. The man who is generous with his goods will receive generously in return (cf. 21:26; 22:9; Matt. 5:7; 7:2). Vs. 26 refers to the practice of hoarding **grain** in time of famine.

11:28. Life's Ultimate Aim. Despite their generally utilitarian point of view (cf. 10:15) the wise men were quite aware that the achievement of wealth and security is not the ultimate aim of life (cf. 15:16, 17; 23:4, 5; 28:6, 11). To be **righteous** (i.e. the right kind of person) is far more important. On the image of the **green leaf**, a favorite one in a dry country, cf. Ps. 1:3; Jer. 17:8.

12:1. Discipline. The word translated "discipline" means both "chastisement" and "education"—an indication that the wise men believed that severity was part of the educational process (cf. 13:24). The intelligent pupil will understand why his teacher is strict and will submit himself gladly (cf. 13:18; 15:32; 29:1).

12:4. Value of a Good Wife. A young man's success in life will be greatly abetted by the wise choice of a wife (cf. 11:16, 22; 21:9, 19). The most elaborate treatment of this theme is in 31:10-31.

12:9. Comfort Above Ostentation. The common sense of the wise men shows itself in their advice that one should not dissipate his resources in trying to keep up with neighbors. Comfort and basic necessities are more important (cf. 13:7).

12:10. Kindness to Animals. While kind treatment of animals is obviously good business, since it means taking care of one's own property (cf. 14:4), the maxim is not prudential but a natural expression of the kindly and generous ethical philosophy of the wise men (cf. Deut. 25:4).

12:11. Industry. Hard work is the price of success (cf. vss. 24, 27). Vss. 10, 11 both show the interest in agriculture that is characteristic of this section.

12:16-23. Reticence, Truth, and Kindliness. A considerable number of vss. in this ch. exhibit the wise men's concern with self-control in speaking (cf. 10:18-21). Vs. 16 recommends reticence in showing bad temper; vs. 23 advises against garrulity in any situation. Vss. 17, 19, 22 all assert that a man's word must be absolutely dependable (cf. 13:5); God himself requires it (vs. 22). Vs. 18 says the **words** of the wise are always kindly.

12:25. The Effect of a Good Word. As in vs. 18 the emphasis is a positive one. Kind words create health and joy.

13:2-3. Words Have Power. Vss. 2a, 3a both assert that the proper use of speech brings great benefits (cf. 12:25). Vs. 3b (and perhaps vs. 2b) says that its improper use brings one to **violence** and **ruin.**

13:7-8. The Value of Money. Though vs. 7 might seem purely empirical, it is intended to teach the same moral as 12:9: better to be **rich** and act **poor** than to be foolishly ostentatious and have nothing. The meaning of vs. 8b is uncertain, but the RSV makes a good guess. As in 10:15 the purpose is to commend habits of thrift to young men inclined to dissipation, not to represent the attainment of wealth as the chief purpose of life (cf. 11:28; see below on 14:20-21, 31).

13:11. Easy Come, Easy Go. As in modern society there was always a tendency for young men to prefer get-rich-quick schemes to laborious toil (cf. 1:10-19). This proverb represents one aspect of the wise men's attempt to inculcate habits of industry, more conventionally advocated in vs. 4. The translation in the RSV is based on the LXX rather than the Hebrew, but it gives the probable meaning: what comes too easily is likely to vanish just as easily (cf. 19:2; 20:21; 28:20, 22).

13:12. Longing and Fulfillment. This is a good example of the wise men's capacity for psychological observation. Though primarily occupied as teachers of the good **life** they were also interested in studying the world and men's behavior as objects of interest in their own right. Just as 30:18-19, 24-31 illustrate their interest in the world of nature, this vs. shows their interest in the operations of human nature (cf. 14:10, 13; 16:26; 25:25; 27:7-9, 17, 19; 30:15-16, 21-23). Anxiety and unfulfilled longing result in psychological depression and even physical illness, but a desire suddenly satisfied often seems to release new psychic and physical energies (cf. 15:13). The idea of vs. 12b is repeated in vs. 19a, but vs. 19b has no obvious connection and is perhaps misplaced.

13:17. Dependability. The pupils of the wise men were being prepared for positions of trust in society, where they would frequently be employed as messengers for others and in later life might be trusted with important missions of state. No quality was more important than absolute fidelity to their employers and to the commissions given them (cf. 25:13; 26:6).

13:19. See above on vs. 12.

13:20. Good Companions. A man's character is deeply affected by those with whom he habitually associates (cf. I Cor. 15:33), hence the great importance of choosing them carefully (cf. 14:7; 22:24-25; 24:1).

13:23. Misfortunes of the Poor. The meaning is uncertain, but may be that, although God has provided adequately for the poor, man's **injustice** often deprives him of his due. Possibly the moral is the same as in 10:15.

13:24. Strictness with Children. This vs. is a classic statement of the wise men's theory of pedagogy (cf. 12:1; 20:30; 22:6, 15; 23:13-14; 29:15). The insistence that strict **discipline** is an expression of love is specially noteworthy (cf. 3:12).

14:6. The Scoffer. Education implies both capacity and receptivity; the scoffer has neither and is wasting his time (cf. 9:7-12).

14:10, 13. Man's Natural Solitude and Sadness.

These are 2 further examples of the wise men's keenness of observation (see above on 13:12). Every **heart** has depths that are inaccessible to others (vs. 10). Though the wise men were, on the whole, cheerful and optimistic (cf. 13, 15; see below on vs. 30), they were by no means unaware that even the greatest joys of life are tinged with sadness (vs. 13).

14:15. Credulity. While one should be open to truth and willing to learn, only the fool **believes everything** he is told.

14:20, 21. Concern for the Poor. Vs. 20 is a purely prudential proverb, similar to 11:15; 13:8, 23; but vs. 21 (cf. 15:27; 21:26; 22:9) shows how unfair it would be to draw from this fact the conclusion that the wise men were mere materialists, interested only in success and unconcerned for the poor (see below on vs. 31).

14:26, 27. True Religion Means Life. On the **fear of the LORD** (cf. vs. 2) see above on 1:7. **Life** means a full life in the present world; **death** means premature death that comes before life has been fully lived. On the **confidence** which comes from righteousness cf. 28:1.

14:28. The King. This vs. and vs. 35 contain the only references to the king in the older collection of chs. 10-15, and these are merely incidental. Contrast the frequent references to the king and court life in 16:1-22:16 (e.g. 16:10-15; 19:10; 20:2; 22:11). Vs. 28 says that the fortunes of the king are involved in those of his **people;** vs. 35 says that he prefers courtiers who have acquired wisdom.

14:30. Health Through Calmness. This vs. may constitute a first essay in psychosomatic medicine (see above on vss. 10, 13; 13:12). The wise men were aware that there is close interrelationship between the states of the spirit and of the body. Tranquility and cheerfulness incline toward health; **passions** such as anger and fear produce sickness (cf. 15:13, 15, 30; 17:22; 18:14).

14:31. More on the Poor. This vs. is particularly significant because it makes the care of the poor a religious duty, based on God's special care for them (see above on vss. 20, 21; cf. 15:25; 17:5; 19:17; 22: 22-23; Job 31:15; also Gen. 9:6; Mal. 2:10; Matt. 25:40, 45). To abuse God's creatures is an affront to their **Maker.**

14:34. See above on 11:9-14.

14:35. See above on vs. 28.

15:1. Anger. Calmness and self-control are among the principal virtues admired by the wise men (cf. vss. 4, 18; 12:16; 14:17, 30; 16:32; 19:11; 25:15). In the famous formula of Exod. 34:6 God himself is said to be **slow to anger** (vs. 18). In Egypt also the ideal was that of the quiet, imperturbable man.

15:3. God's Omniscience. This ch. has far more to say about God (vss. 8, 9, 11, 16, 25, 26, 29, 33) than those preceding it in this collection (chs. 10-15; but cf. 16:1-9, 33). One dare not disobey the moral law, since God, who presides over it, knows all that happens—not only **in every** earthly **place** (vs. 3) but even in **Sheol** (vs. 11a; cf. Ps. 139:8; **Abaddon,** like Sheol, is a name for the underworld where all the dead go) and in **the hearts of men** (vs. 11b).

15:4. See above on vs. 1.

15:8, 9. God's Justice. Ritualistic religion, practiced without regard to ethical principles, is obnoxious to God, although he gladly hears the prayers of honest,

straightforward men (cf. vs. 29; 21:3, 27; 28:9). One might suppose the wise man was here simply echoing one of the prophets (e.g. Isa. 1:11-17) if it were not for the fact that such sentiments are also found in foreign wisdom literature—e.g. Egyptian: "More acceptable is the character of one upright of heart than the ox of the evildoer" (The Instruction for King Meri-ka-Re, trans. J. A. Wilson in J. B. Pritchard, ed., *Ancient Near Eastern Texts*, p. 417).

15:11. See above on vs. 3.

15:13, 15. More Psychosomatic Proverbs. Cheerfulness produces health (see above on 14:30). The mood of these proverbs is much more characteristic than that of 14:13.

15:16, 17. Poverty Sometimes Above Wealth. Poverty with the assurance of God's presence and favor is better than riches (vs. 16). A vegetable dinner where there is **love** and harmony is better than a sirloin steak with quarrelsome people (vs. 17; cf. 16:8; 19; 17:1; 19:1). "Better is poverty in the hand of the god than riches in a storehouse; better is bread, when the heart is happy, than riches with sorrow" (Instruction of Amen-em-Opet ch. 6, trans. J. A. Wilson in J. B. Pritchard, ed., *Ancient Near Eastern Texts*, p. 422).

15:18. See above on vs. 1.

15:23. The Pleasure of Speaking Well. The wise men delighted in the well-chosen word, the well-shaped and graceful speech (cf. 25:11).

15:25. See above on 14:31.

15:26. See above on vss. 8, 9.

15:28. The Thoughtful Answer. The good man does not speak before he thinks; the bad has instant answers to every question (cf. 29:20).

15:29. See above on vss. 8, 9.

15:30. Another Psychosomatic Proverb. See above on 14:30. **The light of the eyes** means the cheerful expression of one who brings **good news.**

B. PART II OF THE FIRST SOLOMONIC COLLECTION (16:1-22:16)

The 2nd of the 2 collections included under the title "The proverbs of Solomon" (10:1a) contains a nearly equal mixture of synonymous, antithetic, and synthetic proverbs (see Intro.). They are concerned, more than those in chs. 10-15, with specific acts rather than general attitudes, show more concern for city and court life (e.g. 16:10-15; 17:8, 15; 18:5, 16-18), and were perhaps assembled explicitly for the training of court officials.

16:1-9. Man Proposes but God Disposes. Most of these proverbs have to do with the thought of God's all-powerful guidance of human affairs (cf. 20:24; 21:1, 30, 31; 29:26). Ultimate decisions are not in man's hands but in God's (vss. 1, 3, 7, 9; cf. vs. 33). Although self-justification is natural for man, only God is ultimately in a position to pass judgment (vs. 2; cf. 21:2); the **arrogant** man is headed for disaster (vs. 5; cf. vs. 18). God permits **the wicked** to flourish only to illustrate how wickedness is punished in the long run (vs. 4). Man lives harmoniously and well only as he learns to submit himself to God's **ways** (vss. 6, 7); to lead the right kind of life (i.e. in submission to God) is better than wealth (vs. 8; cf. vs. 19; 15:16). In vs. 6 it is interesting to note how a technical cultic term ("to make atonement for," Lev. 1:4) is given a purely inward and ethical interpretation. Vs. 9 is strikingly illustrated by the Joseph story (Gen. 45:5-8; 50:20).

16:10-15. The King. Cf. 14:28, 35; 25:2-7. Such proverbs are good evidence that this part of the book is to be dated before the fall of the monarchy in 586 B.C. As is to be expected in a book concerned, at least in considerable measure, with training for court life, the monarchy is idealized and regarded as the instrument for God's rule on earth (vs. 10). Such views were common in the ancient Near East. Vs. 11 probably intends to say that part of the king's task is to enforce God's demands for honesty and justice (cf. vs. 13).

16:18-19. Humility. Cf. 11:2; 22:4. Like 15:16, vs. 19 declares there are **better** things than wealth—in this case the humbling of one's **spirit** (cf. Matt. 5:3, 5).

16:25. See above on vss. 1-9.

16:26. Hunger as an Incentive. This vs. is a general observation without any obvious moral content (see above on 13:12).

16:27-30. Four Kinds of Evil Men. Special emphasis is laid on the misuse of speech through unkind gossip (vs. 28), enticement to evil ways (vs. 29), and hypocrisy (vs. 30).

16:31. The Blessing of Old Age. Since a long life was one of the chief rewards promised by the wise men (e.g. 3:2, 16), gray hair was in itself a sign of wisdom and therefore a badge of pride (cf. 20:29).

16:32. Calmness of Spirit. This vs. is a classic expression of the wise men's ideal of the quietness and self-control of the righteous (cf. 15:1, 4, 18; 25:28; 29: 11, 22; see above on 10:12).

16:33. See above on vss. 1-9.

17:1. See above on 15:16, 17.

17:3. God's Judgment of Men. Refiners separated precious metals from lead, iron, and other impurities by melting them in the **crucible** of a **furnace.** The purity of a sample could be assayed by attempting further refinement of it. In view of the general outlook of the wise men, as well as the use of the same metaphor regarding reputation in 27:21, this proverb evidently refers simply to God's knowledge of character, without involving the prophetic idea of purification of the individual or the nation through suffering found in Isa. 1:25-26; Zech. 13:9; Mal. 3:3.

17:5. Care of the Poor. See above on 14:20, 21, 31. The 2nd line adds a warning against rejoicing at the misfortunes of others (cf. 24:17).

17:6. Grandchildren a Blessing. Another reward promised those who sought wisdom (see above on 16:31) was children and grandchildren (cf. Ps. 128:3-6). Thus a man may legitimately take pride in them; they in turn should be proud of him.

17:8. Taking Bribes. Like vs. 7, which warns nobles to behave nobly, this vs. is addressed to officials (cf. vss. 15, 23, 26; 18:5, 16-18; 28:16, 21). Those charged with the administration of **justice** have an obligation to be just. A **bribe** seems to have almost **magic** powers but it is abhorrent to God, for whatever purpose it is taken (vs. 15). The judge's aim must be simply to condemn the guilty and acquit the innocent. He should be entirely fair, being swayed neither by the wealth and social standing of the guilty nor by the insignificance of the innocent. That the corruption of justice was a perennial problem in

ancient Israel is shown by the fact that the prophets were also deeply concerned with it (e.g. Isa. 5:23; Amos 2:6; Mic. 7:3).

17:9. See above on 10:12.

17:10. The Teachable and the Unteachable. An intelligent person learns sufficiently from verbal **rebuke.** The **fool** fails to learn even from **blows** (cf. vs. 16; 26:11; 27:22).

17:15. See above on vs. 8.

17:16. Tuition for Wisdom. It is evident from this vs. that the wise men normally received fees for their instruction (but contrast Ecclus. 51:25).

17:17. Friendship. The wise men accounted friendship one of life's highest values (cf. 18:24; 27:10; Eccl. 4:9-12; Ecclus. 9:10).

17:18. See above on 6:1-5.

17:22. See above on 14:30.

17:23. See above on vs. 8.

17:24. Concentrating on the Present Task. The **fool** is always dreaming of things far away and of possibilities yet to be realized; the wise man knows that **wisdom** is to be found and practiced in the situation where he finds himself at the moment.

17:26. See above on vs. 8.

17:27-18:8. Control and Economy of Speech. The first of these proverbs (17:27) advises one to speak calmly, the 2nd (17:28) to speak rarely, adding—somewhat cynically, it might seem—that this is a good way to acquire a reputation for wisdom (see above on 10:18-21).

But the **fool** has no desire to be educated (18:2); his **opinion** is already formed, and he wishes only to express it (cf. 18:13; 29:9). His loquacity causes trouble for himself and others (18:6, 7). The words of some are like sugar-coated poison, contaminating the springs of individual and social life (vs. 8). Wise speech is like a deep, refreshing stream in an arid land (18:8). On 18:5 see above on 17:8.

18:11. See above on 10:15.

18:13. See above on 17:27–18:8.

18:14. See above on 13:12; 14:30.

18:16-18. The Wise Administration of Justice. It is unfortunately true that a bribe has great power (see above on 17:8) and often gains a man entrance where the pure merits of his case would not bring him (vs. 16). The wise men apparently thought a mere description of the possibility of the situation should be sufficient warning to an honest official. A conscientious judge will not pass judgment until he has heard both sides of the question (vs. 17). Under Hebrew law it was permissible to make certain difficult decisions by the casting of **lots** (cf. Josh. 7:16-18; I Sam. 14:40-42; Acts 1:26); the proverb (vs. 18) suggests that sometimes this is the safest and fairest thing to do.

18:20-21. See above on 10:18-21; 17:27–18:8.

18:22. Marriage a Divine Blessing. Marriage is the proper state for a young man to aim at, although the choice of the right **wife** presents many problems (cf. 11:22; 12:4; 19:14; 21:9; 31:10-31).

18:23. See above on 10:15.

18:24. Friendship. One close friend is better than a multitude of casual and uncertain acquaintances (cf. 17:17).

19:1. See above on 15:16, 17. The sense of this vs. is better given in 28:6.

19:3. Accepting Responsibility for Failure. One

should not blame God for disasters occasioned by one's own **folly.**

19:4. *The Advantages of Wealth.* This and vss. 6, 7 are more proverbs intended to encourage the young man to acquire thrifty habits and preserve his inheritance (see above on 10:15). Vs. 1 shows clearly enough, however, that the wise men did not intend to represent wealth as the *summum bonum* (see above on 15:16, 17). Vs. 6 shows how wealth can be used to gain influence. Generosity is a favorite virtue of the wise men, although here it has a practical rather than a philanthropic motive (cf. 11:24-26; 21:26; 22:9).

19:5. *False Witnesses.* This is another aspect of integrity in the law courts (cf. vs. 28; see above on 17:8; 18:16-18). This and vs. 9 are nearly identical proverbs, illustrating the fact that the individual proverbs had a long history as independent units and as parts of other collections before being assembled in their present form (cf. vs. 1; 28:6).

19:10. See above on 16:10-15.

19:11. See above on 15:1.

19:12. See above on 16:10-15.

19:13, 14. *Family Relations.* A man's life can be made miserable by a bad son (cf. vs. 26; presumably he has not been properly educated; cf. vs. 18; 13:24; 23:13-14) or an unsuitable wife (cf. 21:9; 27:15-16); but a good wife is a gift **from the LORD** (see above on 18:22). Vs. 14*a* is an example of the emphasis throughout the book on the preservation of an **inherited** fortune rather than the acquisition of a new one (see above on 10:15).

19:15. See above on 6:6-11.

19:17. See above on 14:31.

19:21. See above on 16:1-9.

19:22. See above on 15:16, 17.

19:24. Almost a doublet of 26:15; see below on 26:13-16.

19:28. See above on vs. 5.

20:1. *Danger in Wine.* Young men needed then, as today, to be warned against the dangers of overindulgence in wine as well as against the temptations of immoral women. The longest passage on this subject is 23:29-35, where it is combined with the warning against women (23:27-28; cf. also 31:3-7). The wise man's disapproval of strong drink was not moral but prudential. Wine used in excess is likely to lead to carousing and brawling, which are inimical to a successful career.

20:2. See above on 16:10-15.

20:5, 6. *Understanding Others.* Although the deepest thoughts of men are concealed from their fellows, a patient, intelligent person will be able to discover them (vs. 5). One must be cautious in trusting others, however, because their professions of trustworthiness rarely match their real character (vs. 6).

20:8. See above on 16:10-15.

20:9, 10. *God and Man.* An unusually large group of proverbs deals with profound theological-moral issues. Vs. 9 is unique in Prov. in expressing the thought of man's universal sinfulness (but cf. Job 4:17-19; Eccl. 7:20). Vs. 10 speaks of God's concern for justice and common honesty (cf. vs. 23; see above on 11:1). Vs. 12 implies that God, who made the **ear** and **eye,** is certainly able himself to hear and see (see above on 15:3). Vs. 22 enjoins the pupil of the wise men not to practice revenge; God can be

trusted to punish **evil** (cf. 24:29; 25:21-22; Deut. 32:35; Rom. 12:19). Vs. 24 asserts God's ultimate sovereignty over the created order and the will of men (cf. 16:1-9, 33). Vs. 25 warns against the dangerous and superstitious habit of making **vows** without due consideration—and then being sorry afterward (cf. Eccl. 5:4-5). Vs. 27 seems to identify **the spirit of man** as a divine element that makes it possible for him to understand and judge himself. If this is the correct interpretation, it comes very close to the idea of conscience (cf. Wisd. Sol. 17:11).

20:11. *A Child's Behavior.* The wise men recognized that "the child is father to the man"—that his **acts** give indication of what his adult character will be like. This proverb has obvious implications for child training (cf. 22:6).

20:12. See above on vss. 9, 10.

20:13. See above on 6:6-11; 19:24.

20:14. *Business Ethics.* This proverb pictures the hypocrisy that is almost universally bound up with commercial enterprise. The **buyer,** when bargaining, pretends to be dissatisfied with the thing he is bidding for, but his later **boasts** show what he really was thinking.

20:16. *Against Suretyship.* Cf. 27:13, which is almost a doublet. See above on 6:1-5. The words are supposedly addressed to the creditor. "If a man has been foolish enough to guarantee another's debt, exact everything you're entitled to!" Deut. 24:10-13 authorizes the taking of a **garment . . . in pledge,** though under strict limitations (cf. Amos 2:8).

20:18. *The Need for Deliberation.* Important enterprises can be carried out successfully only by consultation and careful planning.

20:22-25. See above on vss. 9, 10.

20:26. *Advice to the King.* In contrast to many warnings to the would-be courtier to show proper respect for the throne (e.g. vss. 2, 8; see above on 16:10-15) this proverb and vs. 28 are for the guidance of the king himself. On **loyalty and faithfulness** see above on 3:1-12.

20:27. See above on vss. 9, 10.

20:28. See above on vs. 26.

20:29. See above on 16:31.

20:30. See above on 13:24.

21:1-3. *God's Omnipotence and Justice.* Like numerous other proverbs in this collection (e.g. 16:1-9, 33; 20:24) vss. 1, 30, 31 express God's absolute sovereignty over his creation. While the idea of God's mysterious guidance of the course of events is common to much oriental wisdom literature, the Hebrew wise men's conception of his absolute independence of—and control over—the created order is quite without parallel. Vs. 1 says that God controls the decisions of kings as easily as a farmer directs the **water** in an irrigation ditch. Vss. 30, 31 sound like the prophetic literature in declaring that **victory** is from God alone (cf. Isa. 8:9-10; 31:1-3). Vs. 2 denies that a man is really capable of judging his own conduct; ultimately this is in God's hands (cf. 16:2). Vs. 3 agrees with the prophets (Hos. 6:6; Amos 5:21-24) in teaching that God prefers ethical conduct to mere ritual exercises (cf. 15:8, 9). The same thought is expressed in vs. 27, without explicit mention of God.

21:5. See above on 6:6-11; 13:11.

21:9. Repeated in 25:24 (cf. 27:15-16). See above on 11:16, 22; 19:13.

21:13. *Care of the Poor.* See above on 14:20, 21, 31; cf. 17:5; 22:9, 16. Those who fail in charity toward the poor will be treated in kind (cf. Matt. 18:28-34; Gal. 6:7).

21:14. *Gifts to Pacify.* It is well for a young man to know that a judiciously chosen gift, offered at the right moment, can often avert even justified anger. Only a thin line, of course, separates this kind of gift from an outright **bribe** (see above on 17:8; 18: 16-18).

21:19. Cf. vs. 9. See above on 11:16, 22; 19:13.

21:22. Cf. 24:5; Eccl. 7:19; 9:15-16.

21:23. See above on 10:18-21; 17:27-18:8.

21:25. See above on 6:6-11.

21:26. Cf. 11:24-26; 22:9.

22:1. *The Value of Reputation.* A man with a reputation for wise and honest dealing will often be able to accomplish more than a rich man. Therefore one should cultivate the good opinion of others.

22:2. *Rich and Poor.* In the view of the wise men God has created social distinctions, but the poor must be helped. This proverb (cf. 29:13) well illustrates their conservative political philosophy. The conclusion intended to be drawn is that God cares for **rich and . . . poor** alike and that each has responsibilities toward the other. Vs. 7 says it is a simple fact that the rich have certain advantages over the poor (see above on 10:15). In vs. 9 generosity toward the poor is declared to be a source of blessing (see above on 14:31; 17:5; cf. 21:26).

22:6. *Training Children.* Education produces character, according to this oft-quoted proverb (see above on 20:11). To be effective the **discipline** must be severe (vs. 15; see above on 13:24; cf. 23:13-14).

22:7, 9. See above on vs. 2.

22:13. See below on 26:13-16.

22:14. See above on chs. 5; 7.

22:15. See above on vs. 6.

22:16. See above on vs. 2.

III. The "Thirty Sayings" (22:17–24:22)

This collection is in some way directly dependent on the Egyptian Instruction of Amen-em-Opet. The translation of an obscure Hebrew phrase as **thirty sayings** in 22:20 (KJV "excellent things") is based on the fact that Amen-em-Opet's book contains 30 chs. In 22:17–23:11 every proverb but one (22:26-27; most of these proverbs consist of 2 vss. each) has a more or less close parallel in the Egyptian book, though the order is different. The quotations below from this work are from the trans. by J. A. Wilson in J. B. Pritchard, ed., *Ancient Near Eastern Texts,* pp. 421-25.

22:17-21. *Title and Preface.* Cf. 1:1-6.

22:22-23. *Care of the Poor.* See above on 14:31; cf. Amen-em-Opet ch. 2: "Guard thyself against robbing the oppressed and against overbearing the disabled." The Hebrew proverb adds the theological motive.

22:24-25. *Avoid Irascible Companions.* See above on 13:20; cf. Amen-em-Opet ch. 9: "Do not associate to thyself the heated man, nor visit him for conversation."

22:26-27. *Against Suretyship.* See above on 6:1-5; 20:16. As noted above, this proverb alone in 22:17–23:11 has no parallel in the Egyptian book.

22:28. See below on 23:10.

22:29. *The Result of Good Training.* Cf. Amen-em-Opet ch. 30: "As for the scribe who is experienced in his office, he will find himself worthy (to be) a courtier." The rare Hebrew word translated **skilful** is also used of scribes in Ps. 45:1 (RSV "ready") and Ezra 7:6. The Egyptian parallel makes clear the precise sense of the proverb.

23:1-3. *Greed at the King's Table.* Cf. 25:6-7; Amen-em-Opet ch. 23: "Do not eat bread before a noble, nor lay on thy mouth at first. . . Look at the cup which is before thee, and let it serve thy needs." The parallel is not as close as in some other instances, but both documents are concerned with discouraging greedy and disgusting habits at table, as are the books of other Egyptian wise men.

23:4-5. *The Deceitfulness of Riches.* Cf. Amen-em-Opet ch. 7: "Cast not thy heart in pursuit of riches. . . . If riches are brought to thee by robbery, they will not spend the night with thee; at daybreak . . . they have made themselves wings like geese and are flown away to the heavens." The substitution of the Palestinian **eagle** for the Egyptian "goose" is characteristic of the freedom with which the original was used.

23:6-8. *The Niggardly Host.* In this instance the parallel with Amen-em-Opet, though clear, is merely verbal, the content having to do with quite different situations.

23:9. *Talking with Fools.* Cf. 20:19; Amen-em-Opet ch. 21: "Spread not thy words to the common people, nor associate to thyself one (too) outgoing of heart."

23:10-11. *Respect for Boundary Markers.* Cf. 22:28; Deut. 19:14. There was always a temptation for the powerful and unscrupulous to move boundary markers to their own advantage. Cf. Amen-em-Opet ch. 6. "Do not carry off the landmark at the boundaries of the arable land, . . . nor encroach upon the boundaries of a widow, . . . lest a terror carry thee off." The Hebrew text introduces the characteristic OT conception of God as the **Redeemer** (lit. "legally appointed vindicator") of the nation and its individual members (cf. Job 19:25; Ps. 103:4; Isa. 44:6).

23:12. *Introduction and Subtitle.* This vs. introduces the collection 23:12-24:22, which completes the "words of the wise" (22:17) but contains no parallels to Amen-em-Opet (see above on 22:17-24:22).

23:13-14. *The Education of Children.* See above on 13:24. Cf. 20:30; 22:6, 15; also the maxim from the Mesopotamian book of Ahikar: "Withhold not thy son from the rod, else thou wilt not be able to save [him from *wickedness*]. If I smite thee, my son, thou wilt not die, but if I leave thee to thine own heart [thou wilt not live]" (trans. H. L. Ginsberg in J. B. Pritchard, ed., *Ancient Near Eastern Texts,* p. 428).

23:17-18. *Envy of the Wicked.* The success of **sinners** was a growing problem with the wise. As in 3:31-35; 24:19-20; Ps. 37 the answer given here is overly simple: "Wait long enough and you will see the law of retribution working out!"

23:19-21. *Avoiding Wine and Gluttony.* See above on 20:1. Here the young man is warned against carousing, since it can lead only to poverty.

23:26-28. See above on chs. 5; 7.

23:29-35. *The Folly of Drunkenness.* See above on vss. 19-21; 20:1. This is a good example of the wise men's use of vivid description, mixed with humor, to convey their lessons (cf. ch. 7; 11:22; 26:13-15). Vs. 35 pictures both the anesthetic properties of alcohol and the incorrigibility of the confirmed **drunkard.**

24:1-2. See above on 23:17-18.

24:3-7. *The Praise of Wisdom.* Over **strength** wisdom has the advantage (cf. 21:22). The **fool** is incapable of getting it (vs. 7; cf. 17:16; 26:7; 27:22). Wisdom is sweeter than **honey** (vss. 13-14; cf. Ps. 19:10).

24:10-12. *Rescue of the Innocent.* While vs. 10 appears to be corrupt, the purpose of vss. 11-12 is to encourage an active concern for the rights of the oppressed. Lazily to plead ignorance of the facts is no excuse, for God the All-knowing will hold one strictly to account both for his sins and for his failure to respond to human need (cf. Luke 10:25-37; Jas. 4:17).

24:13-14. See above on vss. 3-7.

24:17-18. *How to Treat Enemies.* The fine sentiment of vs. 17 is somewhat spoiled by vs. 18 (but cf. Rom. 12:19). The utilitarian motive is introduced for pedagogical reasons. Vss. 28-29, which offer a similar injunction as an absolute ethical principle, are more congenial to modern and Christian taste. Cf. 25: 21-22.

24:19-20. See above on 23:17-18.

24:21-22. See above on 16:1-9, 10-15; cf. I Pet. 2:17.

24:23-34. *Appendix to the "Thirty Sayings."* This brief section is apparently an appendix to 22:17-24:22, as indicated by the title (vs. 23*a;* cf. 22:17*a*). In the LXX 30:1-14 appears between vss. 22, 23.

24:23*b*-26. See above on 17:8; 18:16-18.

24:28-29. See above on vss. 17-18.

24:30-34. See on 6:6-11; 26:13-16.

IV. The 2nd Solomonic, or "Hezekiah," Collection (25:1–29:27)

A new title (25:1) separates chs. 25–29 from the rest of the book. But, as in the case of the first "Solomon" collection (10:1–22:16), internal evidence shows that these chs. consist of 2 smaller collections, chs. 25–27; 28–29. In the LXX 30:15–31:9 is inserted between chs. 24; 25.

A. Part I of the 2nd Solomonic Collection (25:1–27:27)

More than half the proverbs in chs. 25–27 show no real parallelism in construction. They have a greater concern with the life of simple people, especially peasants, than with that of the court. A theological motivation appears only in 25:21-22. The secular character of this collection has led most commentators to consider it probably the oldest in the book. In contrast, however, a recent thorough study (see Intro.) presents evidence for viewing it as the latest of the 4 "Solomonic" collections. The greater length of many of the sections (e.g. 26:1-12, 13-16; 27:23-27) is cited as showing a more developed literary style, while the interest in common life (e.g. 27:23-27) is seen as pointing to a broadening of intellectual horizons.

25:1. *Title.* There is no reason to doubt that the reign of **Hezekiah** (II Kings 18–20) was marked by a surge of literary and cultural activity.

25:2-7*b*. *Preface.* Though the major interest of this collection is with common life, this preface shows that, like the others, it originated at court. Vss. 6-7*b*, which advise the courtier to be modest, are echoed in Luke 14:7-11.

25:7*c*-10. *Lawsuits.* One should avoid going to court if possible and settle disputes privately (cf. Matt. 5:25).

25:11, 12. *The Well-chosen Word.* Cf. 15:23. The proverb of comparison (**is like**) is especially characteristic of this section (e.g. vss. 13, 14, 25, 26; 26:1, 2, 7).

25:13. Cf. 13:17.

25:16, 17. *Moderation.* As too much sweet is sickening, so is too effusive a friendship. Cf. vs. 27; 30: 7-9.

25:20. *Suitability to the Occasion.* Even **songs** are sometimes out of place. The vs. is corrupt, but the translation probably comes close to the thought.

25:21-22. *Feed Your Enemy.* The motive, though utilitarian, is higher than in 24:18: "you will make him ashamed of himself." This proverb is quoted verbatim in Rom. 12:20. In an Akkadian collection of proverbs, possibly from the Kassite period (1500–1200 B.C.), appears: "Unto your opponent do no evil; your evildoer recompense with good; unto your enemy let justice [be done]" (trans. R. H. Pfeiffer in J. B. Pritchard, ed., *Ancient Near Eastern Texts,* p. 426). In the Akkadian context the motive seems to be that of avoiding a lawsuit at any cost (cf. vss. 8-10) rather than of inspiring shame in the enemy (cf. Exod. 23:4-5). In the OT the great exemplar of the forgiving spirit is Joseph (Gen. 50:15-21); he represents the ethos of ancient Hebrew wisdom at its best. It is noteworthy that the motive for Joseph's attitude is said to be a purely theological one (Gen. 50:20).

25:28. Cf. 16:32.

26:1-12. *The Fool*—what he is like and how to treat him. Vss. 4, 5, which appear contradictory, are probably to be interpreted as complementary. Vs. 4 means "Don't act the way fools act!" Vs. 5 advises to "treat a fool as he deserves!" On vs. 12 cf. 11:2.

26:13-16. *The Lazy Man.* Vss. 13-15 show the ability of the wise men to use humor for pedagogical purposes (cf. 11:22; 23:29-35). Any excuse is sufficient to keep a lazy man at home and away from his work (vs. 13; cf. 22:13, where the form is more complete). He turns **on his bed** like a creaky gate (vs. 14). Some seem too indolent even to feed their own faces (vs. 15; cf. 19:24).

26:17. *Mind Your Own Business.* An Akkadian proverb says: "When you see a quarrel, go away without noticing it" (trans. R. H. Pfeiffer in J. B. Pritchard, ed., *Ancient Near Eastern Texts,* p. 426).

26:18-19. *The Practical Joker* is headed for serious trouble.

26:20-28. *Gossip, Slander, and Hypocrisy.* The translation **glaze** in vs. 23 is based on an ingenious comparison of the Hebrew phrase with a word in the old Canaanite Ras Shamra texts.

27:1. *Don't Count on Tomorrow.* Amen-em-Opet (ch. 18; see above on 22:17–24:22) says in a similar vein, "Do not spend the night fearful of the morrow. At daybreak what is the morrow like? Man knows not what the morrow is like."

27:2. Cf. 25:6-7*b*.

27:4. This proverb may be concerned with the same situation as 6:34-35.

27:5-6. *Frankness in True Love.* Love ought to be expressed, not hidden, even if it takes the form of rebuke. Only hypocrisy is always smooth and effusive (vs. 6; cf. vss. 14; 29:5).

27:7-9. *Observations on Life.* See above on 13:12. Vs. 7 parallels a saying of Ahikar (see above on 23: 13-14): "Hunger makes bitterness sweet." Vs. 8 speaks of the pathos of the homeless man. If the RSV is right in substituting the reading of the LXX for the Hebrew of vs. 9*b* this proverb simply means that external **trouble** is as disquieting to the inner life as luxurious unguents are soothing.

27:10. *Friendship.* Cf. 17:17. It is better to make friends among neighbors, who are close at hand, than depend on relatives who are **far away.** Line *b* is meaningless in the context and probably out of place.

27:13. A doublet of 20:16. See above on 6:1-5.

27:14. See above on vss. 5, 6.

27:15-16. Perhaps an expansion of 19:13*b* (see comment).

27:17-20. *More Observations on Life.* See above on vss. 7-9. Vs. 17 says that social life, not solitude, brings out one's true humanity. Vs. 19 probably means that one learns to understand himself through watching others. Vs. 20 testifies that man's reach is always greater than his grasp. On **Sheol and Abaddon** see above on 15:3.

27:21. *Men Judged by Their Reputations.* Just as refiners separate precious from base metals (see above on 17:3) so most men will be judged in the long run by the opinions of those with whom they associate. The point is probably the same as in 22:1 (see comment).

27:22. See above on 17:10.

27:23-27. *The Value of Country Life.* This paragraph may reflect a pessimistic view of the increasingly luxurious and sophisticated life of the city. Wealth, in the form of gold or silver, whether inherited or earned in trade, quickly vanishes, whereas a good herd of animals will provide dependable **food** and **clothing.** A similarly nostalgic view of country life appears in a fragmentary Babylonian essay: "Mankind and their achievements alike come to an end. . . . Take thought for your livestock, remember the planting." (W. G. Lambert, *Babylonian Wisdom Literature,* p. 109.)

B. Part II of the 2nd Solomonic Collection (28:1–29:27)

Chs. 25–29 stand closer, at least in form, to chs. 10–15 than to other parts of the book. The great majority of the proverbs are antithetical, and there is similar concern with the general contrast between the wise and the foolish. In view of the number of proverbs directly concerned with the office of the king (e.g. 28:2, 15, 16; 29:2, 4, 12, 14), the administration of justice, and the condition of the poor (e.g. 28:5, 6, 17, 21, 27; 29:7, 13), the collection may have been assembled as a "Mirror for Princes"— instructions for those destined to rule or hold official positions in the state (cf. 31:1-9). Probably this collection should be dated soon after chs. 10–15.

28:1. *Righteousness as a Source of Security.* One who is wise and does what is right has nothing to

fear. Vs. 1 vividly contrasts the apprehensiveness of the evil man, who stands in constant fear of well-deserved retribution, with the confident carriage of the **righteous** man, sure of his own integrity. Other proverbs in this ch. express in more conventional ways the thought that religion (vs. 14), straightforwardness (vs. 18), and a wise humility (vs. 26) are the best resources for confident living. See above on 14:26, 27; cf. 29:25; Ps. 91.

28:2. *The Importance of Wise Government.* Vss. 2, 15, 16 contain 3 different Hebrew words for **ruler,** but all are general terms used of various kinds of officials, including kings. Vs. 2 refers to constant changes in government such as occurred in the N kingdom at certain periods. Vs. 5 associates the sound administration of justice with sincere religion. Vs. 15 pictures the unhappy fate of a badly governed people. Vs. 16 promises long life to incorruptible officials. Vs. 21 satirizes the dishonesty of some whose favorable judgment can be won by the smallest of bribes (just **a piece of bread**).

28:3. *Care of the Poor.* The opening phrase of this proverb should probably be corrected to read "A man of position." Cf. vss. 8, 27, which promise prosperity to those who are concerned for **the poor.**

28:4. *The Law.* This does not refer to civil law or the "law of Moses" but to the "instruction" or "teaching" given by wise men, prophets, and priests. Cf. vss. 7, 9.

28:5. See above on vs. 2.

28:6. *Poverty Sometimes Above Wealth.* This is almost identical with 19:1. It is further evidence that the wise men's teaching was not merely utilitarian. Cf. vs. 11. See above on 11:28; 15:16, 17.

28:7. See above on vs. 4.

28:8. *Usury.* This echoes the law which forbids the taking of **interest** on loans (Exod. 22:25; Lev. 25:36). In a simple society loans were acts of charity; to take interest was to capitalize on another's misfortune. See above on vs. 3.

28:9. See above on vs. 4.

28:11. See above on vs. 6.

28:13. *Confession Obtains Mercy.* This proverb is doubly unique in that it is the only one which advises confession (publicly?) and the only one which speaks of God's mercy. Cf. Ps. 32:1-5; I John 1:9.

28:14. See above on vs. 1.

28:15, 16. See above on vs. 2.

28:17. *Don't Help a Murderer.* The sense of this is not entirely clear, nor is the reason for its inclusion in the book.

28:18. See above on vs. 1.

28:19-25. *Avarice.* Vs. 19*a* commends farming as an honest way to achieve security; vss. 19*b*, 20, 22, 25 condemn all schemes to get rich quickly. They probably represent a reaction against the rise of a mercantile society. See above on 27:23-27; also 13:11. On vs. 21 see above on vs. 2. The situation envisaged in vs. 24 may be that of a son who claims that what belongs to the family belongs to him and to take it is therefore no robbery.

28:26. See above on vs. 1.

28:27. See above on vss. 3; 14:20.

29:2, 4. *The Importance of Wise Government.* Vs. 2 speaks of the happiness of a people whose officials are upright. Vs. 4 advises against the imposition of heavy burdens on the nation (cf. I Kings 12:4, 9-11).

Vs. 12 suggests that the head of state, by his example, sets the moral tone of his whole administration. Vs. 16 adds that the doom of a wicked administration is sure. Though the power of a king is evident to everyone, vs. 26 declares the final decision is really in the hand of God (cf. 16:1-9).

29:7. Care of the Poor. Genuine concern for the needs of the poor is a sign of wisdom; the absence of it is equally a sign of folly. These words are probably directed to officials, as vss. 13, 14 certainly are. Frequently in the course of a lawsuit rich and poor will appear together before the same judge. He must remember that both are God's creatures (see above on 22:2) and that God is concerned for them both (vs. 13). An administration in which the poor are treated fairly is in a sound condition and will endure (vs. 14).

29:8, 9. Scoffers and Fools. The scoffers (vs. 8) are the intellectually perverse who deny the validity of the law of retribution (cf. 14:6; Ps. 10:4, 11). The fool (vs. 9) is more interested in loudly expressing his opinion than in learning (see above on 17:27–18:8). Unlike the wise man he cannot control his passions (vs. 11; cf. vs. 22; see above on 10:12; 15:1; 16:32). One who speaks before he has time to think is even worse than a fool (vs. 20; cf. 15:28).

29:10. The Wicked Hate the Righteous. If the conjectural translation of the RSV is correct, as it probably is, both lines of this vs. declare that the life of a righteous man is imperiled by the wicked. The thought is unique in Prov., which tends to picture only the blessings of the righteous. It is perhaps intended as a word of caution to officials who are determined to perform their duties without fear or favor. Cf. vss. 25, 27.

29:11. See above on vss. 8, 9.

29:12. See above on vss. 2, 4.

29:13, 14. See above on vs. 7.

29:15. See above on 13:24.

29:16. See above on vss. 2, 4.

29:17. Cf. vs. 15; see above on 13:24.

29:18. Importance of Religious Teaching. A nation needs rulers who are not only wise but also willing to listen to prophets and wise men. On **the law** see above on 28:4.

29:19. Discipline of Servants. Even more than children (cf. vss. 15, 17) slaves require stern correction. Scolding is not enough; beating is needed (cf. Exod. 21:20-21).

29:20. See above on vss. 8, 9.

29:21. See above on vs. 19.

29:23. See above on 11:2.

29:24. Partners in Crime. One who accepts stolen property is putting his own life in danger (cf. 1:10-19). When **the curse** (cf. 30:10) is spoken against the **thief,** it will operate effectively to destroy his **partner** also, even though he is only a passive accomplice (cf. Lev. 5:1; Judg. 17:2).

29:25. Don't Fear Men. Security comes from putting one's trust in God (see above on 28:1; cf. Ps. 56:11). The Hebrew word used here for **fear** means lit. "trembling, animal terror." It is something quite different from the "fear of the LORD" (1:7)—a different word with the connotation of awe and reverence. "Fear of the LORD" includes trusting him.

29:26. See above on vss. 2, 4.

29:27. See above on vs. 10.

V. MISCELLANEOUS APPENDIX (30:1–31:31)

The material in these last 2 chapters is quite different from that in the rest of the book and is of miscellaneous character. In the LXX only 31:10-31 is found here; 30:1-14 follows 24:22, and 30:15–31:9 follows 24:34.

A. THE WORDS OF AGUR (30:1-9)

We cannot be sure just how far **The words of Agur** are supposed to extend. They may include vss. 1-9 or possibly only vss. 1-4. On the basis of the division in the LXX (where, however, the proper name does not occur) many assume the title covers vss. 1-14. The most extensive modern study of this material takes the whole ch. to be the intended unit, stressing on the basis of form its Canaanite-Phoenician rather than N Arabian affinities.

30:1. Title and Beginning. Only the phrase **The words of Agur son of Jakeh** is clear. The Hebrew word *massa* here and in 31:1 might be a common noun meaning "oracles" or "prophecy" (KJV) or a place name, **of Massa.** The latter is more likely, since such a name (referring either to a tribe or a place) is mentioned among "the descendants of Ishmael" (Gen. 25:14). Nothing further is known of Agur, Jakeh, or Lemuel (31:1); but they are to be numbered among the wise men of the non-Israelite "people of the east" who were already famous in Solomon's day (I Kings 4:30) and provided the dramatis personae of Job (1:3).

30:1b. The words following the title certainly do not include the proper names **Ithiel** and **Ucal,** as in most English versions, but are a corruption of some such sentence as "The inspired utterance of the man who struggled with God, struggled with God, and prevailed." The precise translation is uncertain, but the sentence apparently describes some visionary experience which led to the revelation that follows in vss. 2-4 (cf. Job 33:14-16; Ps. 73:16-17, 21-26).

30:2-4. The Mystery of the Divine Nature. As in Eccl. and Job (but not the rest of Prov.) God is represented here as inaccessible to human wisdom. He can be known only as he chooses to reveal himself (cf. Job 28:20-27; Eccl. 9:1).

30:5-6. The Value of Revelation. These lines are probably an addition by an orthodox Hebrew wise man who wished to correct what seemed to him the foreign, skeptical tone of vss. 1-4. Vs. 5 is apparently borrowed from Pss. 12:6; 18:30.

30:7-9. Two Petitions. Like much of the rest of the ch. this is a numerical proverb (see Intro.). It is in the form of a prayer asking for **two** favors: a trustful spirit and a happy mean between being either excessively poor or disgustingly rich. The similarity between vs. 8c and Matt. 6:11 is striking.

B. VARIOUS PROVERBS: NUMERICAL AND OTHERWISE (30:10-33)

This section consists mostly of numerical proverbs (see Intro.). Interspersed are several proverbs of simpler form, none of which has any clear relation to its context: Vs. 10 warns about the effectiveness of curses (cf. 29:24). Vs. 17 threatens those who fail to honor their parents. Vs. 20 presents a fascinating vignette of a shameless woman. Vss. 32-33 warn that it is better to be quiet than arrogant, for arrogant and angry speech will lead to trouble.

30:11-14. *Four Objectionable Persons.* On the analogy of 6:16-19 this may originally have been a more explicit numerical proverb, listing 4 types hateful to God: the unfilial, the self-righteous, the proud, and the greedy.

30:15-31. *Nature and Human Nature.* None of these 5 numerical proverbs has any moral or theological content. They represent another activity of the wise men—careful, systematic observation of the world (see above on 13:12)—and illustrate the beginnings of the scientific spirit. Vss. 21-23 picture **four** situations in which people become intolerable. The others consist of observations of animals and natural objects (cf. I Kings 4:33; Job 38-41) and show a rudimentary interest in classification. Similar lists were produced by Egyptian wise men. Vss. 15-16 speak of **four** objects which cannot be **satisfied.** Vss. 24-28 describe **four** little things which nevertheless arouse wonder because of their cleverness. Vss. 29-31 picture **four** things which have stately movements; what the author intended by the last 2 is uncertain (cf. RSV footnote). Vss. 18-19 humorously compare aspects of nature with the mystery of human courtship.

C. The Words of Lemuel (31:1-9)

31:1. *Title.* See above on 30:1. The vs. illustrates the role that parents played in the early education of youth (cf. 1:8-9).

31:2-9. *The Duties of Kings.* Kings must avoid the corruptions of luxury. Sexual indulgence saps their vitality (vs. 3), while alcohol makes them indifferent to responsibilities (vss. 4-5), drink being useful only to the miserable (vss. 6-7). A king's primary duty is to those who cannot take care of themselves (vss. 8-9; see above on 29:7; cf. Jer. 22:16).

D. The Good Wife (31:10-31)

In Hebrew this poem is an alphabetical acrostic; i.e. each line begins with a successive letter of the alphabet. Far from being mere chattel of the husband, the Hebrew wife here appears as the responsible head of the household (cf. 11:16, 22; 12:4; 18:22; 21:9, 19). She provides for food and clothing (vss. 13-15, 19, 21-22), purchases property (vs. 16), engages in trade (vss. 18, 24), and exercises charity (vs. 20). Physical beauty is a matter of indifference (vs. 30); what is important is intelligence, kindness (vss. 25-26), industry (vss. 15, 17, 27), and above all a religious spirit (vs. 30).

THE BOOK OF ECCLESIASTES

Harvey H. Guthrie, Jr.

Name and Place in Canon. The Hebrew title of the book is "Koheleth" ("Preacher"; see below in 1:1), and Ecclesiastes is the LXX translation of it. After a good deal of controversy, Eccl. was included in the Writings, the final section of the Hebrew Bible. It is one of the 5 Scrolls and is read in the synagogue on the 3rd day of the feast of booths.

Date and Authorship. Although the book is attributed to Solomon (see below on 1:1), language and style indicate a 3rd-cent. B.C. origin. In spite of some opinion to the contrary, it is probably basically the work of one author, his disciples being responsible for certain additions, including the 2 epilogues (12: 9-11, 12-14).

Relation to Wisdom Literature. The background of Eccl., as of Prov., Ecclus., and Wisd. Sol., is the wisdom of the ancient Near East. Cultivated by the common man and the professional wise man of the royal courts alike, wisdom sought to express in terse, polished sayings or parables the nature and meaning of life's realities. Its aim was wise conduct based on accurate observation and mature reflection. It rested on the conviction that a basic order underlay the phenomena of life.

Although present from the beginning as a part of the surrounding culture, wisdom did not become theologically important in Israel until exilic and postexilic times. Then, when the national fall of 586 B.C. had shut off ongoing communal history as the locus of God's revelation of himself, theological interest moved more toward nature and individual morality, and wisdom became increasingly important. The doctrine of reward and punishment for individual action arose, and the wise behavior always cultivated by wise men became theologically significant in more specifically Israelite terms. Wisdom came to be thought of as a personified agent of God (cf. Prov. 8-9), and the scriptural law and prophets came to be seen more as the revelation of wisdom than as a record of God's historical activity (cf. Ps. 119; Ecclus. 24). All this led to a rather rigid orthodoxy, characterized by extreme confidence in its own grasp of the meaning of life and the purposes of God and by a rather narrow, prudential moralism. Against the imposition of such doctrine on the reality of existence Job and Eccl. are, in different ways, protests.

Its Message. Eccl. represents a reaffirmation of the central thing in ancient wisdom—an acknowledgment of the limits of human understanding (cf. the oft-repeated motto "The fear of the Lord is the begin-

ning of wisdom"). Thus it is not necessary to assert Greek influence in the book. The author never denies the sovereignty of God. What he does deny is the ability of finite man to grasp the meaning of life. His assertion is that man's perspective is too limited (see below on 1:3-11) to permit any pronouncement on the meaning of things, too partial to formulate any theory in regard to the individual occurrences of life, but that they are repetitive (see below on 3:1-8, 9-15). His counsel, therefore, is that the ambiguity of life is to be accepted for what it is, not evaded by pompous orthodoxy (cf. 5:18-20; 7:15-22; 8:1-9).

Eccl. thus represents, in terms of a specific time and culture, a protest against the ever-present temptation of faith to shore up its own uncertainty with dogmatism and against the constant tendency of human understanding to overrate its potentiality. The inclusion of Eccl. in a canon that also contains writings against which it protests is a witness to the Bible's location of divine revelation in the givenness of an empirical, conditioned, human history.

For Further Study: G. A. Barton, *The Book of Ecclesiastes,* 1908. A. L. Williams, *Ecclesiastes,* 1922. R. Gordis, *Koheleth: the Man and His World,* 1951.

I. The Heading of the Book (1:1-2)

1:1. *The Superscription.* Solomon is identified as author of the book in the phrase **the son of David, king in Jerusalem.** Prov. and Wisd. Sol. also claim him as the author of wisdom writings. This tradition arose because wise men became official participants in Israel's life in the court of Solomon. Thus he was considered the originator of the literature that came from the wise men in the same kind of way that Moses was considered originator of all the law and David of the psalms (on Solomon's wisdom cf. I Kings 3:16-28; 10). Eccl. must come from a later time than Solomon's (see intro.).

The Preacher is the English translation of the Greek "Ecclesiastes." The Hebrew word is *koheleth,* whose root has to do with gathering an assembly or performing some function in it (cf. the verbal form in I Kings 8:1). Whether it is a proper name or the designation of an office, and whether the writer uses it of himself or for some other reason are questions on which there is no agreed answer.

1:2. *The Theme of the Book.* The word translated **vanity** denotes a breath, exhaled air that disappears. Over half its occurrences are in Eccl. It is the equivalent of the name of the first man in the Bible to die, Abel; and this may be no accident. The author restates his theme in 12:8. It is that, *so far as man can observe,* all that makes up life soon vanishes and loses significance.

II. The Vanity of Life (1:3–6:12)

1:3-11. *A Poem: Nature's Cycle Is Pointless.* The various major subdivisions of the book seem to begin with poetic, or semipoetic, passages (cf. 3:1-8; 7:1-14; 9:17–11:8). This poem turns quickly from human **toil** (the word connotes suffering, trouble, strained labor) and the succession of generations (vss. 3-4) to the earth which is their setting. It too is characterized by monotonous movement to which nothing man can say (a possible translation of vs. 8a is all "words" **are full of weariness**) can impart significance. Here is implied a criticism of the endeavor of the wise men to frame sayings catching the meaning of life (cf. e.g. 1:13 ff.; 7:23 ff.).

1:9. The phrase **under the sun** is recurrent in the book. It sets limits around the author's claim to truth (cf. vs. 13). His is no attempt to overthrow the wisdom tradition. He stands in that tradition in his claim merely to observe accurately what life offers, not to go beyond the outer limits of human wisdom. On that basis he implies that orthodox wisdom has imposed a false order on life. But his own position is no absolute denial of significance. **Under the sun,** or **under heaven** (vs. 13), strictly limits the area of which he speaks. The repetition of the phrase is a clue to its significance for the author, whose skepticism is proximate, not final.

1:12–2:26. *Reflections on Pointlessness.* The author proceeds to recount how all that even a Solomon had been and possessed could lead only to the conclusion reached in the preceding poem. Neither faithful following of the methods of the wise men (1:13-18), nor sheer physical pleasure, nor the things money can buy make of life anything more than vanity (2:1-11). All man's **business** (1:13; the word has to do with that to which men direct thought, emotion, and energy) is pointless—at least so far as can be observed under the sun.

2:18-26 is devoted to human toil (see above on 1:3). Everything gained by toil is left behind at death, the only reward for gain being the exhaustion it produces (vss. 18-23). Yet in the devotion of attention and energy to what each moment brings some enjoyment is to be found, and that enjoyment **is from the hand of God** (vs. 24). God has given the toil, and has given man the ability to see the meaninglessness of it. The wonder of this uncomforting mystery must be recognized and can impart to life a thrill (2:24-26).

3:1-8. *A Poem on "Times."* Again (see above on 1:3) a poem begins a major section. The author here turns from life's setting and content to the times marking its movement. Two words in vs. 1 are central to the poem. **Season** has connotations of "being determined," "fixed," "appointed" (cf. Ezra 10:14; Neh. 10:34). **Time** basically means "occurrence"; it refers to the given moments of existence, definable in terms of their content. The use of **season** at the beginning implies that, for the author, the moments of life enumerated in the poem with

concise beauty are fixed in an unchangeable way. Given vss. 9-15, the implication is that God is responsible for this.

3:9-15. *The Author's Basic Conclusion.* The answer to the question of vs. 9 is central to the author's philosophy. The stuff of life described in the poem, men's **business** (vs. 10), is not something about which the author is utterly skeptical. He asserts that **everything** is **beautiful** (the word denotes fittingness of arrangement) **in its** own **time,** and that God has made it so (vs. 11a).

3:11b is the most controversial sentence in the book. The crucial word is **eternity.** Some have tried to defend the KJV translation "world" (cf. the KJV and RSV translations of the Greek equivalent *aion,* source of English "eon," in Matt. 28:20). Others have suggested various emendations (e.g. "toil," "mystery," "forgetfulness"). But it is best to take the text as it stands. God has put eternity, an intimation of the wholeness of which the recurrent times are parts, into man's mind. Yet it is only intimation, and man is unable to corroborate it on the basis of honest observation of the succession of times he knows here under the sun. Thus the author is not absolutely skeptical. He has faith in the meaning of the totality of things under God. But he is rigorously skeptical of any human claim to state that meaning. Man's wisdom can neither add nor subtract anything from the totality of what God has ordained (vs. 14).

3:15b is difficult to translate—lit. "God searches out what is pursued." In the light of what precedes, the 2 halves of the verse may summarize the 2 sides of the author's thought. From the human vantage point **that which is, already has been** and **that which is to be, already has been.** Human wisdom can discern no order or pattern. But **God seeks what has been driven away**—i.e. in the totality of the eternity of which man has only an intimation, what seems recurrently pointless is pursued, brought back, and given meaning. Precisely God's unfathomable eternity both gives life its meaning and makes life, to the limited view of man, tragic.

Thus the counsel to enjoy each time (vs. 12) is not entirely hedonistic. Undiscernible as it is, there is significance in that with which man occupies himself (vs. 13). Meaningless as the verdict of human wisdom on things has to be, the ultimate issues are in God's hand (vss. 14-15).

3:16–5:9. *Miscellaneous Thoughts on Life's Content.* Following the statement of the author's central thesis come various loosely organized observations on how life bears out what has been said.

3:16–4:3 insists that observation of life reveals no moral order. Contrary both to the earlier Israelite conviction that communal history consists of moments revelatory of the righteousness of God and to the later emphasis on individual rewards and punishments, the author can find no time of righteousness among those times of which life is made up (3:16-17). Not only is human life no different from that of the beasts in its meaningless movement toward death (3:18-21), but what takes place in it makes death desirable (4:1-3).

4:4-12 is basically variations on the theme of the meaninglessness of toil already advanced, vss. 9-12 revealing the author's honesty of observation in their insistence that companionship lightens the oppressive human load.

4:13-16 stands a quoted or invented proverb on its head, the final sentences saying that what is extolled at the opening passes away like everything else. Terse and allusive language makes this section difficult to translate, but the point is clear.

5:1-7 indicates that the author takes the Israelite worshiping community for granted, but holds that what religion provides warrants no more enthusiasm or confidence than anything else under the sun. Religion is the means by which man acknowledges the reality of the God of eternity, but its word here under the sun is not more final than the word describing the vanity of life. Four pieces of advice are given: (*a*) Because of the distance of God above the human sphere, religion should not be attended by the busy activity that takes it too seriously (vs. 1). (*b*) Because there is no possibility of direct correspondence between the utterance of man's mouth and the reality of God, not too many words should be uttered in prayer (vss. 2-3). (*c*) Because of the realism the author always values, a man must not be rash in the making of sacred vows (vss. 4-5). (*d*) In no event should a man put himself in the position of having to excuse himself before God's representative (vss. 6-7; **messenger** probably refers to a priest; cf. Mal. 2:7).

5:8-9 counsels the reader not to be surprised at political oppression. The final part of vs. 8 probably means that each official has to oppress those beneath him in order to satisfy the demands of his superior. Given vs. 8, the difficult vs. 9 probably means that the profit of the land is taken over by the officials mentioned and that no cultivated field is exempt from royal taxes (cf. the RSV footnote).

5:1-6:12. *Maxims on the Possibility of Enjoying Life.* The first half of the book concludes with a series of proverbs, some terse, some more extended, on paths to enjoyment. The first 4 of these (5:10, 11, 12, 13-17) have to do with wealth and goods and are negative.

5:18-20 is positive, insisting that the only enjoyment there is must be found in taking life honestly as it comes, not asking for more and not investing a given time with more significance than man can honestly say it has. The ability to do this is not something man can instill in himself, but is the gift of God (vs. 19). Again, the author does not advocate a sheer hedonism. The point is that enjoyment of life comes, not by what man can attain, but by a power over which he has no control (cf. above on 3:1).

6:1-9 develops the above from the negative side, leading to the 6th proverb in the series in vs. 9. Meditation on the mystery of why some men do not have the gift spoken of in 5:18-20 leads to the conclusion that the man who does not have it, though he **has no burial** (never dies), would have done better to have been born dead (vss. 3-6). The proverb at the conclusion holds that satisfaction is better than perpetual longing (vs. 9).

6:10-12 concludes by repeating the themes of 1:3-11 and 3:1-8. Life is endless repetition (vs. 10). No word uttered even by the wise can give it meaning (vs. 11). The meaning of the totality of life is beyond the ken of man who dies so soon (vs. 12).

III. ADVICE BASED ON REALITY (7:1–9:16)

Though the book is loosely organized and the outline used here is arbitrary, ch. 7 does seem to mark a turn from the author's presentation of his philosophy to more practical advice on the basis of that philosophy. Again a major subdivision begins with poetry.

7:1-14. *6 Poetic Pieces of Advice.* The author may very well here be employing proverbs from wisdom circles, not of his own composition. His opening chs., however, put them in a new framework and make it clear that the good to which traditional wisdom directs men is really only relative good. Thus the author is rooted in his background, but is critical of it.

7:1a bespeaks the value of a good reputation, playing on the Hebrew words for **name** (*shem*) and **ointment** (*shemen*). Vs. 7b fits with what the author has said in chs. 1-6.

7:2-4 holds that wisdom lies in acting in accord with the tragic nature of life as outlined in chs. 1-6 (see above on 3:9-15).

7:5-7 extolls wise censure over foolish pleasure, foolish laughter being likened to the **crackling of** a fire of **thorns** that generates no heat. But, characteristic of the author's realism, the conclusion is that even wisdom can be bought (**oppression** in vs. 7 probably denotes ill-gotten gain).

7:8-10 is based on 1:3-11 and 3:1-8, the point being that each event should be accepted for what it is; heated comparison with its predecessors is foolish.

7:11-12 acknowledges the practical, proximate value of both wisdom and wealth as defenses against life's difficulty and perplexity.

7:13-14 concludes this series on the note so often struck by the author: No one can change what God has ordained. Take the good for what it is when it comes, and when evil comes accept the fact that man's limited perspective does not permit him to see how it fits into the totality of things (cf. 3:9-15).

7:15-22. *Be Satisfied with Relative Good.* What, outside its context, would be the crassest kind of cynically prudential advice must be read in the light of the author's philosophy. The heart of the section is the poetic proverb of vs. 19. The wisdom the author praises there has been defined in chs. 1-6 as recognition of the limited nature of the human perspective. In the light of this, it has to be recognized that reserve is necessary in imputing unqualified righteousness to any one act or position. Furthermore, action should be taken in this light without regard to what others may think (vss. 21-22).

7:23-29. *The Limitations of Wisdom.* In spite of his reservations, the author never denies the value of wisdom. Here he acknowledges his own verification of one theme stressed by the wise men—the dangers of the wicked woman (cf. Prov. 2:16-19; 5; 6:20-7:27). But wisdom is able only to deal with the individual times, not eternity (cf. 3:9-15), with the parts but not **the sum of things** (vss. 25, 27-28a).

8:1-9. *Wisdom Recognizes the Necessity of Compromise.* While some details of translation and interpretation in this section are debated, its point is clear: compromise is the characteristic of wise conduct. As an example the author pictures a wise man in the service of an arbitrary king and holds that the wise man is absolved from responsibility for actions of which he himself might not approve. His wisdom makes him master of the situation, for he recognizes reality for what it is.

8:10-15. *Seek Enjoyment in the Midst of Aimless Order*. The text of vs. 10 is difficult and the subject of debate, and vss. 11-13 are probably an addition by some later, more orthodox annotator. The main thrust of the section is in line with what precedes it: wisdom cannot discern any absolute moral order in the way things work out; so the wise thing is to enjoy what there is to enjoy. The end of vs. 15 again makes clear that the author is no absolute nihilist.

8:16-9:12. *God's Ways Are Inscrutable*. The central thesis of the book, already advanced in 3:9-15, is repeated in 8:16-17: man's study of **the work of God** cannot lead to a knowledge of the purpose of life. Honest observation shows that fortune does not necessarily come to the good (9:1-6) and that life's prizes are not necessarily gained by ability (9:11-12). Death's overtaking of all is the only sure thing (9:3-6, 10*b*), and wisdom dictates making the best of things (9:7-8). Again the author does not categorically deny meaning (vs. 7*b*), but demands honesty on the basis of observation.

9:13-16. *Wisdom Is Nevertheless Worth It*. A realistic parable (vss. 13-15) is followed by a dictum on the value of wisdom (vs. 16). The point here, as elsewhere, is that the wisdom which honestly discerns the aimlessness of life (at least to man's perspective) is more to be desired for the freedom it brings than is the power in which man may delude himself.

IV. Concluding Dicta (9:17–12:8)

9:17-10:20. *A Series of Poetic Proverbs*. This section (again a subdivision is marked by poetry) consists of a collection of maxims, very much like those found in Prov. The author may not have created them all himself, and some may have been added as the content of the text brought others to the minds of copyists. In the context of the whole book, what is said reflects the philosophy of the writer: life is aimless (10:5-7); though wisdom's value may not be apparent, **foolishness** is manifestly worthless (10:1-3, 12-15); prudence characterizes the wise man's behavior (10:4, 20). And there is conviction about the value of **wisdom** (9:17-18).

11:1-8. *Life Must Be Lived*. Like the one following it (11:9–12:7), this section has the flavor of the author's own advice. Though interpreters have debated the meaning of some of its figures (e.g. in vs. 1), the import of this striking poem is clear. Man's limited purview here under the sun, his inability to see enough to find meaning in the totality of life (vs. 5) must not paralyze him. He cannot control the forces by which life is shaped (vss. 3-4); so let him act (vss. 1-2, 6), and enjoy things as they come (vs. 8).

11:9-12:7. *Enjoy Youth While You Have It*. The substance of this passage is a pathetically beautiful description of old age and the inexorable approach of death (12:2-7). The point of it all is advice to enjoy the vitality and optimism of youth while it is possible (11:9–12:2). This is all the counsel with which the author can honestly leave his readers. Many interpreters have found 12:1*a* hard to reconcile with the author's viewpoint. Some have tried to emend **Creator** (e.g. to "wife" or "grave"); others have taken the clause to be a pious interpolation. But such theories are unnecessary. In the light of the author's philosophy, 12:1 is the most pathetic statement in this section. It is saying, "Affirm meaning in life while you can, before age and experience, if you are honest, lead you to my position" (again cf. 3:9-15).

12:8. *The Theme of the Book Repeated*. See above on 1:2.

V. Postscripts on the Author and His Teaching (12:9-14)

12:9-11 is praise of the author by a disciple probably responsible for the "publication" of the book. He has forgotten the ascription to Solomon in 1:1. Vs. 10 indicates that the disciple truly appreciated the master, **uprightly** being the central word. It recalls that the author never compromised the truth as he saw it in order to say what was pleasing.

12:12-14 seems to be a 2nd epilogue by a more pious person, possibly the editor responsible for tempering the sharp words of the writer at some points in the book.

THE SONG OF SOLOMON

ROBERT C. DENTAN

Author and Date. The title of this book in Hebrew is "The Song of Songs [i.e. "the most beautiful song"] which is Solomon's." The beauty of the song is undeniable, filled as it is with rapturous expressions of basic and tender human emotion and of delight in the loveliness of nature; but its attribution to Solomon is no longer taken seriously. Apart from the title vs. (which is certainly much later than the book itself) the claim that Solomon wrote it is based on the fact that his name occurs—in the 3rd person—in certain passages (1:5; 3:7-11; 8:11-12). There is also an ancient tradition that makes him the author of many songs (I Kings 4:32), some of which presumably might be of this character. The way Solomon's name occurs in the text of the song, however, in no way supports the contention that he wrote it; on the contrary it would more naturally be interpreted to imply that he did not. The almost universal consensus of modern scholars, therefore, is that the book is anonymous.

The variety of form the song exhibits and the lack of any progress of thought or clear plan of composition make it likely that different parts come from different hands. When compared with the rest of the OT the book has a certain unity, seen particularly in the use of uncommon words and rare grammatical forms. These, however, may be best explained as deriving from a common geographical background and the use of a particular Hebrew dialect—probably that of N Israel, though as we have it now the book obviously comes from the vicinity of Jerusalem (cf. e.g. 2:7; 3:5).

The date of the book is almost as uncertain as its authorship, with indicators seeming to point in different directions. Since it contains a Persian word ("orchard," 4:13) and one possibly Greek ("palanquin," 3:9), it is impossible to date the text in its present form earlier than the late Persian or Greek periods. On the other hand the use of Tirzah in parallelism with Jerusalem (6:4), apparently as a capital city, suggests the early period of the divided monarchy (cf. I Kings 16:23). Such apparently contradictory data lead many scholars to believe that the book contains material from various periods of Israel's life and that its text has undergone considerable transformation in the course of its history.

Place in the Canon. Because the book nowhere makes mention of God or contains any religious or ethical ideas, its position in the Jewish canon of scripture was long a precarious one (see "The Making of the OT Canon," pp. 1209-15). According to a famous passage in the Mishnah its canonicity was one of the points disputed between the schools of Shammai and Hillel near the beginning of the Christian era; but Rabbi Akiba in the second cent. A.D. could declare that "all the ages are not worth the day on which the Song of Songs was given to Israel." Between the 2 dates the question of canonicity had been settled, probably on the basis of its alleged Solomonic origin, by a rabbinical council at Jamnia *ca.* A.D. 90, when Judaism was being consolidated and reorganized after the fall of Jerusalem.

Apparently a secular interpretation of the song was common up until the date of its final acceptance into the canon, since portions of it were frequently sung at wedding feasts. After it was formally and generally recognized as scripture, however, a religious interpretation prevailed. Its contents were allegorized; and it was understood to be an account of the relation between God, the husband and lover of Israel, his people, who were the bride. It came to be associated liturgically with the Passover, perhaps because of its obvious connection with spring (2:11-13; 6:11; 7:12), and was at one time read during the public services of the festival.

The allegorical interpretation was accepted by Christians, but the figures of Christ and the church were substituted for God and Israel (cf. the ch. headings in the KJV). Sometimes the book was interpreted as a dialogue between Christ and the soul. Theodore of Mopsuestia (5th cent. A.D.), whose opinion was later declared heretical, revived the view that the poem was purely secular, being, as he thought, a love song written by Solomon for Pharaoh's daughter. In modern times the allegorical interpretation has largely fallen into disfavor, and it is usually assumed that the subject of the song is sexual, not spiritual, love.

Original Character. Four views of the original form and purpose of the song are still current: (*a*) it was written as *a drama,* with either 2 characters or 3; (*b*) it was a *collection of wedding songs,* intended to be used at various stages in a marriage ceremony; (*c*) it was *a fertility-cult liturgy;* (*d*) it was assembled as *an anthology of separate love songs* without inner coherence or external organization.

On quick reading the drama theory is appealing, since the poem has a certain dramatic atmosphere and is composed of speeches delivered by various characters, including at least a maiden (1:5-6), a lover (1:9-11), and a chorus (5:9; 6:1). Some think there are 2 lovers, a king (1:12) and a shepherd (2:

324

16). The chief argument against the dramatic interpretation is the impossibility of securing any agreement on what story it is supposed to tell. There are as many plots as interpreters. Further objections are that there is no external indication of the speakers and no dialogue in the strict sense (since each speech is an independent unit) and that the ancient Hebrews were unfamiliar with the drama as a literary form.

During the latter part of the 19th cent. the view that the book was originally a collection of wedding songs gained great popularity as the result of observations by J. G. Wetzstein, who, during many years as Prussian consul in Damascus, noted that Syrian wedding festivities, lasting for over a week, were marked by dances and songs, by saluting the bridegroom and his bride as king and queen, and by elaborate descriptions of their physical beauty. Unfortunately, however, it is not clear that 19th-cent. Syrian ceremonies (which are without parallel, it is said, in Palestine proper) have any bearing on the wedding rites of ancient Hebrews. This interpretation of the song is therefore less widely accepted than it used to be.

An interpretation that has gained increasing popularity in recent years sees in the song the fragmentary, disarranged, and distorted elements of an ancient fertility-cult liturgy, celebrating the sexual union of a god and a goddess. From this standpoint the book's acceptance in the canon would present no problem, since it would have been a religious book from the very beginning; the only problem would have been that of eliminating the pagan elements so as to make it acceptable in Israelite circles. According to one theory representative of this view the book portrays the sacred marriage between Ishtar and Tammuz. It is argued that the aggressive (3:1-4) and warlike (6:10) character of the woman, the boldness of her apparent references to premarital relations (2:4-6 KJV; cf. 1:6), and the strange mythological-geographical references (4:8; 8:5)—among other striking features of the book—are far more suitable for a goddess seeking to renew her marriage to a dead-and-risen deity than for a simple village peasant girl pursuing a rustic lover. Though the fertility-cult interpretation has been ably defended by several capable scholars, their views have failed to win general acceptance. For one thing, it seems difficult to explain how such a liturgy could have found entrance into the circles of normative Yahwism or why anyone would have thought it worth while to expurgate and preserve it.

The view most widely held by scholars today is that the book is simply a loose collection of lyrics—an anthology of songs—united by no special theme other than that of love between the sexes. It is this view that forms the basis of the following commentary. It must be acknowledged, however, that other interpretations may have elements of truth in them. Quite possibly the collection was preserved because many of the songs were popularly used at weddings (e.g. see below on 5:1), though not necessarily in accordance with any fixed pattern. Possibly also some of the songs, which are admittedly difficult to understand as expressions of simple peasant boy-and-girl emotions, originated in the pre-Israelite fertility cult, or at least in a pagan mythological context. Preserved among the common people because of their antiquity and intrinsic beauty, they would gradually lose their original associations and be given a harmless secular meaning. The history of the individual lyrics, as well as of the book as a whole, is undoubtedly far more complex than is usually realized.

Value. The religious significance of the song is 2-fold. First, its inclusion in the canon is a symbol of the church's blessing on marriage and sexual love, a continual reminder that simple human joys, the pleasures of love, and the delights of the natural world have their honored place among the people of God. In the 2nd place it must be recognized that the tradition of allegorical interpretation was not entirely wrong, that there is a real analogy between such love as the song describes and the love of the spirit. It is only from a profound knowledge of human love, in all its manifestations, that men can rise to an understanding of the love that unites God with his children.

For Further Study: W. H. Schoff, ed., *The Song of Songs: A Symposium,* 1924. M. Jastrow, *The Song of Songs,* 1954. H. H. Rowley, "The Interpretation of the Song of Songs" in *The Servant of the Lord,* 1952. T. J. Meek in *IB,* 1956. N. K. Gottwald, "Song of Songs" in *IDB,* 1962. W. F. Albright, "Archaic Survivals in the Text of Canticles" in D. W. Thomas and W. D. McHardy, eds., *Hebrew and Semitic Studies,* 1963.

COMMENTARY

1:1. Title. On the name of the book and the attribution of authorship see Intro.

1:2-4. *A Girl's Invitation to Her Lover.* The girl speaks, perhaps only in imagination, to her beloved and longs to be united with him in marriage. **Wine** and perfumed **oils** are connected with feasting (cf. Luke 7:37-38, 46) and joy. The love of her lover brings to the girl an even greater joy. The Hebrew word translated **love** in vs. 2 is one reserved for sexual love alone; the verb **love** in vs. 3 is from a more common root. **Name** in common Semitic usage connotes the reputation of a man, also his essential nature, his personality. Vs. 4b should probably be translated "Bring me, O king, into thy chambers." The practice of treating the bridegroom as a king is fairly widespread. Advocates of the fertility-cult interpretation see here a real **king,** who enacts the role of the god in the sacred marriage.

1:5-6. *A Girl's Defense of Her Beauty.* Speaking to girls of the city, who despise her, a peasant girl insists that her attractions have not been diminished by her daily exposure to **the sun** and the darkening of her complexion. **The tents of Kedar** are the black goat's-hair tents of the bedouins. **The curtains of Solomon** are unknown. Parallelism suggests that "Solomon" might be a deliberate substitution for the similar-sounding name of some bedouin tribe. The girl's job was to guard the vineyard when the grapes were ripening. While doing so she lost her heart (her **vineyard**) to a man. Her brothers, who—as in oriental society today—would have great authority, are **angry** (vs. 6).

1:7-8. *A Shepherd Girl's Search for Her Lover.* In her imagination the girl begs her shepherd lover to **tell** her where he has gone. Apparently others advise her just to take care of her **flocks** and not bother with him if she does **not know** where he is.

Courtesy of John C. Trever

The oasis of Engedi looking E down to the lower spring and out across the Dead Sea toward Moab

1:9–2:7. A Colloquy of Lovers. The speeches here alternate in a formal way, but there is no real conversation. Several brief dialogue songs have perhaps been joined. In vss. 9-11 the lover praises his beloved's beauty; in vss. 12-14 she praises him in return. The description is full of the imagery of pleasant odors. **Engedi** is an oasis on the W shore of the Dead Sea. In vs. 15 the lover speaks, in vs. 16ab his **beloved.** In vss. 16c-17 they speak together of their nuptial **couch,** decorated with **green** branches.

2:1-7. The lovers' dialogue continues. In vss. 1-3 they compare their beauty to various spring flowers and blossoms. She likens herself to one of the little flowers of the coastal Plain of **Sharon** (see color map 1) or to a **lily** (just what flowers are meant can no longer be certain). In vs. 2 he echoes the comparison; and in vs. 3 she compares him, in his strength and beauty, to a blossoming **apple tree** whose **fruit** she has already tasted. **Banqueting house** means probably the bridal chamber. **Raisins** (cf. Hos. 3:1) and **apples** were in antiquity regarded as exciting sexual desire. The intense eroticism of vss. 6-7 is unmistakable. Advocates of the fertility-cult interpretation see in these vss. the consummation of the sacred marriage of 2 deities such as Ishtar and Tammuz.

2:8-17. The Joy of Love in the Spring. The appreciation of nature exhibited in this book, unparalleled elsewhere in the OT, reaches a climax in this famous passage. The girl speaks of her lover's coming to her, **bounding** with joy, calling to her through the **windows,** asking her to come into the lovely countryside. Vs. 15 appears to be a fragment without context. It is one of 2 passages (the other being 8:8-10) which cannot by any stretch of imagination be given a fertility-cult interpretation, as has been acknowledged even by proponents of the theory. Its meaning is uncertain, but it may be a plea from young girls for

protection from **foxes** (cf. our term "wolves") who would take advantage of their innocence. Vss. 16-17 contain the girl's response to her lover's plea; she will gladly spend the night with him among the fields and hills. With vs. 16 cf. 6:3; 7:10.

3:1-5. The Girl Dreams of Her Lover. In her dream the girl wanders through the narrow **streets** of the town and passes a band of **watchmen** on the way (cf. 5:7) while seeking for her lover. When she finds him she brings him back to her home. Some scholars find in this passage a typical theme of the fertility cult: the goddess seeking for her dead, yet-to-be-resurrected lover. Vs. 5 is identical with 2:7 and similar to 8:4.

3:6-11. A Solemn Procession. This song is entirely unique. It is only here that **Solomon** (if the name is original) appears in his own person; in 1:5; 8:11-12 he is mentioned only incidentally and for purposes of comparison. Some scholars think this is a processional ode actually composed for the marriage of Solomon to some princess. Others believe that the name of Solomon has been substituted for the name of a god who was carried in procession, perhaps a god with a name (such as Shelem or Shulman) which might easily be altered to Solomon. The **column of smoke,** it has often been noted, suggests the coming of Yahweh from Sinai (cf. Ps. 18:8). The strange Hebrew word translated **palanquin** (vs. 9) seems actually to be Greek (though some scholars regard it as Iranian); but this word may, of course, have been introduced only in the latest version of the text. Not until the last vs. does it become evident that the procession is connected with a **wedding.** Defenders of the fertility-cult interpretation naturally find here a god being borne to the temple for the sacred marriage.

4:1-7. Description of the Girl. Descriptive love songs of this type are characteristic of the modern Arabic-speaking Orient as well as the ancient Near East. From antiquity there are numerous examples from both cultic and secular sources.

Some of the similes seem merely grotesque to the modern W reader because to make a comparison with only one point an extended description is given of the object to be compared. E.g. in vs. 1 the only point of comparison between the girl's **hair** and a **flock of goats** is that both are black; in vs. 2 her **teeth** and the freshly washed **ewes** are both white. The fact that the goats are walking down a mountainside E of the Jordan is included only to bring the picture of the flock more vividly to the mind of the reader; the observation that the ewes **bear twins** and **not one among them is bereaved** marks them merely as healthy specimens. In vs. 4 the girl's **neck is like the tower of David** only with respect to its height and delicacy; the **arsenal** with its **bucklers** and **shields** is wholly irrelevant to the image. Vs. 6 is similar to 2:17 and, if original here, expresses the lover's desire for the physical consummation of his love.

4:8–5:1. A Colloquy of Love. It is probable that this section contains 3 originally independent poems, or fragments of poems, which have been brought together to form an artificial unit. Note the 5-times repeated words **my bride** or **my sister, my bride** (4:8, 9-12; 5:1) and the 3 references to **Lebanon** (4:8, 11, 15).

4:8. This is the most clearly mythological passage in the book. The Canaanite-Phoenician setting is unmistakable (**Lebanon . . . Amana . . . Senir . . . Hermon** are all mountains in Syria). It has been suggested that the original speaker was Adonis, inviting his beloved to join him in the hunt which according to legend resulted in his death.

4:9-11. The lover praises the kisses and other charms of his beloved. The curious reference to the beloved as **my sister** can be paralleled from other ancient oriental sources, especially the Egyptian.

4:12-15. The lover declares his beloved is a **locked** garden—inaccessible, a virgin. The comparison of a wife to **a fountain** is also found in Prov. 5:15-18. **Orchard** in vs. 13 is a Persian word (source of the Greek "paradise") and shows that in its present form the book cannot be older than the Babylonian exile.

4:16. The girl begs the winds to entice her lover into the garden.

5:1. He accepts her invitation. The concluding words, **Eat, O friends . . . ,** are presumably addressed to guests at a wedding, although in their original pagan form they may have been an invitation to worshipers to join in the fertility cult.

5:2–6:3. *A Nocturnal Search for the Lover.* Vss. 2-8 have a dreamlike quality and may indeed be intended only as the description of a dream (cf. 3:1-5). The lover knocks on the girl's door after she is asleep (vss. 2-4). When she rises to admit him he is **gone** (vs. 6). As she seeks him through the dark streets the night watch find and beat her (vs. 7), perhaps because they take her for a prostitute. The search theme is so characteristic of the fertility cult that the proponents of that interpretation think of the watchmen as the guardians of the underworld, where the fertility god is held a prisoner.

5:9-16. In response to a query by the **daughters of Jerusalem** (vs. 16; cf. vs. 8) the girl enumerates the charms of her lover. Advocates of the fertility-cult interpretation point out how easily vss. 14-15 might be taken as describing the statue of a god.

6:1-3. In answer to a 2nd query (vs. 1) the girl announces that she knows where her lover may be found (vss. 2-3). Whether her reply is to be understood metaphorically (as referring to the delights of physical love) or literally (as a picturesque account of the present whereabouts of her shepherd lover) is uncertain. With vs. 3 cf. 2:16; 7:10.

6:4–7:9. *Praise of the Girl's Beauty.* This section may well include several originally independent songs, but all except 6:11-12 are unified in their present context by being addressed to the girl in praise of her loveliness.

6:4-10. The use of **Tirzah** in parallelism with **Jerusalem** suggests that it is regarded as capital of the N kingdom of Israel. Because the city had this position only in the period up to Omri (I Kings 16:23-24) many commentators assume the poem must be very early. This may be true, but one must not overlook the possibility of deliberate archaizing (especially since Jews of the postexilic period abhorred Samaria, and the possible symbolic meaning of Tirzah ("delight"). Vss. 5c-6 repeat 4:1e-2. Vss. 8-9 mean that among any number of women—even **queens** and ladies of the court—the beloved would be the most beautiful. The strange combination of **fair** with **terrible as an army** in vs. 10 suggests to

the adherents of a fertility-cult interpretation the common ancient view that certain goddesses (e.g. Ishtar) were patrons of both love and war (cf. vs. 13). Whether this vs. belongs with what precedes (RSV) or with what follows is uncertain.

6:11-12. The RSV assumes the girl to be speaking in both these vss.; some commentators believe vs. 11 is a speech of the lover. The Hebrew of vs. 12 is almost untranslatable. The LXX reads instead of **my prince** a proper name, "Aminadab."

6:13. The girl is invited to perform a **dance.** Since a dance by the bride is a common feature of oriental weddings, it is often assumed that this is its function here. Some doubt is thrown on this interpretation by the fact that she evidently dances naked or nearly so and that the dance is apparently described as a war dance (**before two armies**). Though the term **Shulammite** is often associated by commentators with Abishag the Shunammite (I Kings 1:3), David's concubine, it is perhaps more natural to connect it with Shulmanitu, a Semitic goddess of war and love (counterpart of Shulman; see above on 3:6-11).

7:1-5. The similes are in the style of those in 4:1-7 (see comment). In this instance it is the dancing **feet** that first attract attention; the description then moves upward. **Heshbon** is a city in Transjordan (cf. Num. 21:25-30); **the gate of Bath-rabbim** is unknown; **Lebanon** is a mountain in Syria, of which **Damascus** was the capital; Mt. **Carmel** is on the seacoast of Palestine (cf. I Kings 18:17-40; see color map 8). On the use of **king** for the lover see above on 1:2-4.

7:6-9. The lover, longing for fulfillment, compares his beloved to the stately and nourishing palm tree.

7:10-13. *The Invitation of the Girl.* Although this may originally have been an independent lyric, its position here gives the passage the effect of an answer to vss. 6-9. Vs. 10 is similar to 2:16; 6:3; line *b* resembles Gen. 3:16*d*. The girl invites her lover to taste the full delights of love in the spring-filled countryside (cf. 2:10-14). **Mandrakes** were used to arouse sexual desire (cf. Gen. 30:14-16).

8:1-4. *The Girl's Longing for Her Lover.* The girl wishes that she could always have her lover near her, **like a brother,** so that she could freely express her affection. The emotion she feels, however, is not sisterly but passionately sensual (vs. 3; cf. 2:6). Vs. 4 appears to be some kind of refrain (cf. 2:7; 3:5); its relation to the context is not clear.

8:5. *A Mythological Fragment.* The meaning of this vs. is obscure. There may be some allusion originally to the birth of a god or other mythological figure. The first line is reminiscent of 3:6.

8:6-7. *The Power of Love.* The girl is the speaker. She affirms in general language that nothing is stronger or to be more highly valued than love. The **seal** is a signet, a carved stone cylinder for impressing in clay the equivalent of a modern signature (cf. I Kings 21:8). It was usually carried on a cord about the neck (cf. Gen. 38:18) and thus hung over the **heart.** The seal on the **arm** may refer to a signet ring (cf. Jer. 22:24)—or possibly to an armlet, though no example of this type has been found. **Jealousy** might better be translated "passion." **Death . . . grave . . . flashes . . . many waters** have mythological associations in ancient Semitic thought (see comment on Pss. 18:7-19; 65:5-8).

8:8-10. *The Walls of Innocence.* All recent commentators agree that this passage, at least, has no mythological or fertility-cult significance (see above on 2:8-17). They are not agreed, though, as to whether the speakers in vss. 8-9 are the girl's suitors (for **sister** in this sense see above on 4:9-11) playfully threatening to lay siege to her, or her brothers determined to protect her from all who would take advantage of her innocence. Vs. 10 indicates that she has a mind of her own! The **peace** which she would bring to her lover here means "satisfaction"; the Hebrew word (*shalom*) suggests a play on the name **Solomon** (*Shelomo*) in the following line and Shulammite in 6:13.

8:11-14. *Three Fragments.* In the first fragment (vss. 11-12) the lover says that, valuable as is the **vineyard** of **Solomon,** his own **vineyard** (i.e. his beloved) is far more valuable to him. Nothing is known of **Baal-hamon.** In vs. 13 apparently a lover is speaking to his beloved, but the context of the speech is unclear. Vs. 14 seems to be a fragmentary variant of 2:17*cd*. Some commentators think of these as the girl's words for which the lover of vs. 13 is waiting, but the interpretation is hardly a natural one.

THE BOOK OF ISAIAH

PETER R. ACKROYD

INTRODUCTION

Unity and Disunity. It has for long been recognized that only part of the book of Isaiah can actually belong to the period of the prophet Isaiah ben Amoz, who lived in the latter half of the 8th cent. B.C. and presumably died early in the 7th. Quite clearly it is only in the first half of the book, chs. 1–39, that material from that period may be found. Even here there is much that can hardly belong to so early a date. From ch. 40 onward the historical background is that of the 6th cent., and some parts of chs. 56–66 possibly belong to an even later date. Thus the material of the book extends, so far as its origin is concerned, over a period of at least 200 years, and probably 300 or even more. Consideration of the individual sections reveals sharp divisions of content and background, and a full understanding can be reached only if account is taken of these.

With all the differences of historical background and content there is nevertheless an important sense in which the book is a unity. Its present form cannot be regarded as mere accident. At some stage in its formation it may have consisted of only part of the present work; possibly chs. 36–39—a historical insertion extracted from II Kings, with some differences of text which are important—were appended to a collection already existing before chs. 40–66 were added. But the idea that chs. 40–66 formed a collection of prophecy on their own, entirely unrelated to the Isa. material, and were written into their present position because there happened to be a space on the scroll does less than justice to the facts. It fails to account for points of contact among the various parts of the book—points which, while insufficient to prove unity of authorship, nevertheless suggest a continuity of tradition.

The belief that Isa. wrote the whole book is not, in fact, the only ancient tradition concerning its composition. There is a late Jewish tradition that the book was written by the "Men of Hezekiah," a group said in Prov. 25:1 to have been responsible for the copying of a collection of proverbs of Solomon. We may wonder whether there is preserved here some recollection of a circle of handers-on of the words of the prophet which existed not simply in the time of Hezekiah but on through the succeeding years. Hezekiah has a reputation in some of the records as a reforming king (cf. II Kings 18:3-6; Jer. 26:19, where his pious activities are associated with the influence of the prophet Micah, a contemporary of Isa.). It would not be impossible to suppose that the words of Isa. were handed down by disciples,

associates, followers—whatever term may seem most appropriate—and that this process continued in a group which considered itself in some way linked with the reforming activities of Hezekiah.

There is evidence to show how the words of Isa. were reapplied to later situations, esp. to the problems of the exilic age. It would seem not improbable that it was in association with the circles in which this was done that the unknown author of chs. 40–55 —commonly called 2nd Isa.—gave what could be regarded as a further reapplication of the message of Isa., though it is clear that at the same time it represents a great new prophetic message. Subsequently other prophetic material came to be associated with this tradition, and the eventual formation of the book is the result of a long and complex process in which we can never hope to know fully all that was involved.

But it is not sufficient to take each small section of the book and look at it by itself; we must also try to visualize the whole picture. Nor indeed when we consider individual sections can we get away from the fact that they derive their meaning not simply from the original utterances which they contain but also from the way in which the whole passage is set in a larger context. The interpretation in which we engage when we try to understand the meaning of a passage today is a continuation of a process whose early stages go back virtually to the time of the original Isa. himself. He was, as we can sometimes see, his own first interpreter.

The Historical Setting. It should be clear that there is no one historical moment to which the material of the book is to be attached. For its full interpretation we need a knowledge of the period from *ca.* 740 onward, as far down as the period after the Exile, *ca.* 500, to which the later sections are probably to be assigned, and even beyond this until the final shaping of the book, which is attested by *ca.* 200. Even if no substantial additions were made in the later years, the process by which the book came to be regarded as canonical, i.e. belonging to a recognized collection of sacred books, involves the assumption that it was seen to be continually relevant. The reapplication of the older material to new situations, so vividly seen in the Qumran commentaries (see "The Dead Sea Scrolls," pp. 1063-71) and in a different way in the NT, shows that the preservation of the text is more than a matter of copying; it involves active interpretation.

The clearly datable material belongs to 2 main

periods (see "The History of Israel," pp. 1018-31). The first period is that of the prophet Isa., embracing 2 great crises in the history of Judah: the Syro-Ephraimitic War of *ca.* 734-732 during the reign of Ahaz and the invasion of Judah by Sennacherib in 701 during the reign of Hezekiah. The political and religious aspects of these crises are important factors in the understanding of the prophet.

The 2nd period is that of the 2nd Isa., the great unknown prophet of the Exile, author of chs. 40-55, whose activity is to be placed in all probability within the reign of Nabonidus, the last Babylonian ruler (*ca.* 555-539). At this time the rise of Cyrus the Persian and his rapid series of victories brought the Babylonian Empire to collapse and led to high hopes of restoration among the Jewish exiles. The period overlaps naturally into the years that followed —reflected perhaps in the prophecies in chs. 56-66 —when in various stages attempts were made at reestablishing the life of the Jewish community in and around Jerusalem. During this time the temple was rebuilt and adjustments had to be made to a situation in which, instead of being a more or less independent nation ruled by a king, the community found itself a subject district of a great empire with its main center in Jerusalem, but with many of those who owed allegiance to it scattered in Babylonia, in Egypt, and elsewhere. The gathering of scattered members of the community and the significance of this "dispersion" are factors reflected in some prophecies of the book.

The Prophet and His Successors.

Isa. himself is portrayed for us in narratives and prophecies in the opening chs. of the book. We see him in his conflict with the politically minded Ahaz, in his encouragement of the timorous Hezekiah, in the shattering experience of finding himself in the very presence of God, in the stark and brutal words of judgment against his own people and their leaders. The portrait is an incomplete one, and it is not entirely unified. As with other OT characters, differing traditions have come down to us, and to smooth over the inconsistencies is to do less than justice to the material. In some parts Isa.'s message is of uncompromising judgment; in others, esp. chs. 36-39, found also in II Kings 18-20, he appears as one utterly confident that God will protect his city and people. This confidence bears the marks of the more popular tradition, but it contains within it a true expression of the tremendous faith of the prophet. For here was a man who could face the worst disasters and the prospect of utter devastation and still maintain faith, and who could see that for his people the way to life lay, not through easy maneuvering for security, but in the discipline of obedience and trust.

It is this faith, so characteristic of the prophet, which provides the link to the unknown figures of the later parts of the book. Here and there (e.g. in chs. 40; 49; 61) we seem to get glimpses of one or another of these figures, impressions of the impact on them of the power of God's presence, the relentless control of his spirit. But there is no description of their lives or persons. The 2nd Isa. was almost certainly among the exiles in Babylonia; some of his later successors may well have been active in Palestine. Greater precision is impossible to attain.

But these are not all the successors of Isa. Among his immediate associates there must have been those who appropriated his word and, in handing it on, added their own insights into the nature and purpose of God. The later elaborators of the material, its editors or glossators, were not mechanical manipulators of what had come down to them; they were creative handlers of it, and through them it retained the vividness of its message. The book witnesses not only to great men of crisis moments in Israel's history; it reveals also how rich was the continuity of faith of those who, though "quiet in the land," were the bearers of the tradition and the maintainers of its truth.

Structure. For the purposes of this commentary the book has been divided into 7 sections: chs. 1-12; 13-23; 24-27; 28-35; 36-39; 40-55 (subdivided into chs. 40-48; 49-55); 56-66. The major division, after ch. 39, is justified on the ground that no material in chs. 40-66 belongs to Isa., whereas in chs. 1-39 there is a considerable amount which must be associated directly with him, and there is other material which may be his or based on his original utterances. The first part of the book also contains the narrative material concerned with Isa.

The further subdivisions are dictated by considerations of content. Chs. 36-39 are immediately marked off by the fact that they are found in II Kings also. In chs. 1-35 the section chs. 13-23 contains almost exclusively oracles on foreign nations, and its component parts are marked by the distinctive use of the title "oracle" (lit. "burden"). This section is closely followed by chs. 24-27, in which the judgment on the nations is elaborated into a picture of the final age of both judgment and promise. Chs. 13-27 divide the 2 collections (chs. 1-12; 28-35) in which are found the main oracles of Isa. concerned almost exclusively with Judah and to a limited extent with the N kingdom of Israel. But there are no hard and fast lines to be drawn here. The handing down of the oracles of Isa. carried with it considerable reinterpretation; e.g. the element of promise within judgment, so bound up with Isa.'s message, has been elaborated with oracles of hope, some of which clearly reflect a later period. This is esp. evident in the concluding sections of both the collections of Isa.'s oracles (chs. 1-12; 28-35), and this feature is to be found also in other prophetic collections (e.g. Amos, Mic.).

Analysis of the 2nd part of the book (chs. 40-66) is not so readily made. It is common practice now to divide the book after ch. 55 and to denote chs. 40-55 as the oracles of 2nd Isa. and chs. 56-66 as those of 3rd Isa. This is convenient and has been followed here. So too has the subdividing of chs. 40-55 into 2 sections—chs. 40-48; 49-55. But the divisions are less clear than in the first part of the book. No titles appear to assist the reader. The differences between the sections of 2nd Isa. are partly of content: chs. 40-48 are rather more concerned with the political situation and have direct reference to Cyrus the Persian, whereas chs. 49-55 are more concentrated on the place of Israel in the purposes of God. Attempts have been made to trace direct historical connections for the various passages in chs. 40-48 and to show that they are in chronological order. But their overlaps in content and the extreme difficulty of deciding at what precise points they should be divided make such interpretations very uncertain.

Chs. 56–66 are even more problematic since the material is very difficult to date at all. A reasonable case can be made for allocating most if not all of it to the period ca. 540-500, but there may well be some earlier material, and quite possibly some that is later. Arguments for a single prophet 3rd Isa. are not very convincing; in all probability the collection is made up of material from various dates and from various personalities or groups. Nor is the division between chs. 40–55 and chs. 56–66 quite so clear as has sometimes been suggested; there are overlaps of thought and style (e.g. in chs. 60–62) which strongly suggest a close connection between the 2. The more the process of formation of the book is described in terms of an organic growth within circles closely linked with the tradition of the original Isa., the more it becomes unnecessary to try to make hard and fast divisions among the so-called 3 Isas.

This interconnection in fact cuts right across all the dividing lines. Ch. 35, with its strongly expressed hopes of restoration and a way through the desert, is so obviously connected with ch. 40 that it is difficult to avoid the impression that here we are dealing with poems from the same school if not actually from the same prophet. The poems on the downfall of Babylon in chs. 13–14 are not entirely out of contact with the pronouncements of chs. 46–47, though language and style suggest that these cannot be from the same author. The interpretation of the vineyard theme of 5:1-7 in 27:2-6 and the relationship between 11:1-9; 65:17-25 indicate connections between different parts of the book which must be taken into account in any description of its formation and structure.

Interpretative activity is indeed one of the characteristics of the evolution of the prophetic material which may be most fully illustrated within Isa. The structure is in part at least due to such activity. Isa. himself, as we may see in ch. 28, reapplied his own oracles to new situations; probably there are many such examples less obvious to us. Those who followed him gave new shape to his teaching by their explanation of it. Chs. 24–27 offer an explanation of chs. 13–23 by providing those foreign-nation oracles with a wider setting. Chs. 56–66 may be regarded as providing in some measure an interpretation of the teaching of 2nd Isa. for the generation immediately after the Exile. The history of the formation of the book and the study of its present structure involve considerations of interpretative activity. This means that no purely literary description is adequate to the understanding of a work which, however exalted its poetry and however important the study of literary forms for the analysis of its separate units, is not a work of literature but the deposit of a long process of theological interpretation of the experience of a community.

Interpretation and Significance. The very familiarity of certain well-known phrases from Isa. makes the discussion of interpretation difficult. The NT use of 7:14 or of the so-called "servant" passages in 2nd Isa.; the associations gathered around such passages as 40:1-11, esp. because of their use in Handel's *Messiah;* the precise interpretation of royal oracles such as 9:2-7; 11:1-9—all these give an ini-

tial bias to the understanding of the book which can easily result in missing its full significance. It is in this respect not unlike *Hamlet*—"full of quotations." Nor has this sense of its relevance to later events been restricted to Christian interpretation; to the Jewish community too its promises have been a rich source of encouragement and faith.

The larger questions of biblical interpretation are discussed more fully elsewhere (see "The History of Biblical Interpretation," pp. 971-77). Here the point must simply be made that any narrow understanding of the relationship between the contents of Isa. and later Jewish and Christian experience must inevitably lead to a too limited appreciation of its full significance. To isolate particular passages and concentrate on them without full appreciation of their context leads to a failure to see what the book has to reveal about the nature and purpose of God in the broadest sense. To limit our assessment of it by some artificial scheme of prophecy and fulfillment means that many things in the book either must be twisted from their proper sense to fit the scheme or must be left on one side as belonging only to the past and irrelevant to our present situation.

Isa. belongs to the period in which it was formed. The defining of this period and the dating of the elements of the book are not easy matters. Sometimes a clear historical situation is indicated, as in the vitally important experience of Isa. described in ch. 6. At other points only the most general indications of date can be given. Ideally discovery of the original situation is essential for full understanding; in practice such a discovery is rarely possible. Ideally we should endeavor to say of each passage not only where and when it originated but also how and when and in what ways it has been modified and reinterpreted; in practice such a description can be given only tentatively and in the light of knowledge of the whole range of the OT and of the life of the world to which the OT belongs.

If in reading a given passage we are concerned to discover its meaning in the fullest sense, we need to know these background details. E.g. judgment of what ch. 6 tells us about Isa. and about God must be made in the light of the fuller picture of the prophet derived not only from the book but also from an understanding of OT prophecy as a whole. It must also be made, with due consideration for the principles of historical assessment, in the light of other affirmations about God. To pick out what we might regard as highlights and misinterpret these by looking at them out of context, as if they were statements immediately comparable with NT affirmations about God, not only affords us less than the true meaning of these passages; it also inevitably leads to the tacit assumption that the rest of the book is less important because apparently at a lower standard theologically.

This problem of interpretation is particularly acute in regard to the so-called "servant songs" of 2nd Isa. There has come to be a general agreement among scholars that 4 passages in chs. 40–55 should be so described; they are usually given as 42:1-4 (or 1-8 or 9); 49:1-6 (or 7); 50:4-9; 52:13–53:12. It may be noted that these are not the only passages in chs. 40–55 in which "servant" is used, and also that in 50:4-9 the term itself does not occur.

The isolating of these passages is based on the assumption—which may or may not be justified—that chs. 40–55 consist of small separate units, and on the subjective impression that what is said in these passages differs sufficiently from the remainder of the prophecies for them to be separate, whether because they are by a different author, as some have maintained, or because they represent particular stages in the prophet's thought, perhaps even standing in chronological order. The varieties of interpretation arising from this approach have been so great as to raise questions concerning its validity. Opinion in recent years has moved toward recognition that there is no good ground for regarding these passages as of different authorship and that to study them in isolation from the remainder of the prophecies is to miss their full significance. Jewish interpreters—not being influenced as Christian interpreters are, consciously or unconsciously, by the discovery of points of apparently direct contact between these passages and the NT—have always been more able to see the interrelationship of these servant songs, the other "servant" passages, and the prophecies in which the term is not used even though the same or similar thoughts are present. It is perhaps not too much to say that, in spite of the illumination that has resulted from the detailed studies of these passages, the isolation of the servant songs has been one of the blind alleys of modern OT criticism.

Only a full assessment of the teaching of 2nd Isa. can do justice to the real meaning of the servant songs in context. Only then does the depth of the prophet's insight into the nature and purpose of God, gained as it was in the experience of exile in Babylonia, come out clearly. The significance of what is said about the "servant of God" becomes clearer as it is seen to be bound up in the prophet's appreciation of the meaning of the divine judgment on his people. This judgment, acknowledged to be the rightful outcome of the people's failure, is shown to be the moment both of divine promise and of divine action. It is through a people which has apparently failed that God's promise is revealed to the world; and thus, alongside other interpreters of the same moment, the prophet of the Exile stands out as one who most fully appreciated what the OT repeatedly emphasizes, viz. that "man's extremity is God's opportunity." Such an understanding of God is one of the factors which made possible, humanly speaking, the kind of entry into man's condition which the NT describes and made possible the presentation and appropriation of the understanding of God which is to be seen in the cross of Christ. The relationship between the prophecies of 2nd Isa. and the NT is at a much fuller and deeper level than mere correspondence. It is at the level of insight into the nature of God, the revelation of God through the personality of a man who stands in so many ways head and shoulders above his associates in the OT.

This example only pinpoints the general principle. In every passage what the book says about God must be seen through as sound an understanding of the text as we can reach, with as adequate an assessment of the situation as we can make. If we let its words point us to God, we shall certainly be aware that in the light of the revelation of God in Christ it is never an unshadowed picture of God that we obtain. But we shall also be aware of some of the richness of that revelation of God which was granted to the men of faith who gave us this book, and in the process our own limited understanding of God as he is revealed in Christ may be enlarged.

For Further Study: G. A. Smith, *The Book of Isa.*, 2 vols., rev. ed., 1927. C. R. North, *The Suffering Servant in Deutero-Isa.*, rev. ed., 1956; in *IDB*, 1962; *Isa. 40–55*, rev. ed., 1964. R. B. Y. Scott and James Muilenburg, in *IB*, 1956. E. J. Kissane, *The Book of Isa.*, 2 vols., rev. ed., 1960. John Mauchline, *Isa. 1–39*, 1962. D. R. Jones, *Isa. 56–66 and Joel*, 1964.

I. The First Collection (1:1–12:6)

A. The Title (1:1)

The opening vs. sets the prophet in historical context by listing the **kings of Judah** of his lifetime (see the Chronology, pp. 1271–82). **Vision** (cf. Obad. 1:1; Nah. 1:1) is a general term which emphasizes the prophet's insight into the divine purpose—an insight which is made clear in the description of his experience of divine commission in ch. 6. Perhaps the title originally referred only to chs. 1–12, but it appropriately heads the first part of the book (chs. 1–39), which is closely linked with the 8th cent. prophet. It may also serve to remind the reader that the whole book is associated with the prophetic tradition initiated by Isa. (see Intro.).

B. Faithless and Faithful Jerusalem (1:2–2:5)

1:2-6. Indictment of the City. The failure of the people and the expression of hope and confidence for the future are concentrated in the picture of the city of Jerusalem. In her present state she is faithless, having lost the rightness of life which should be hers. The prospect is of judgment, but a judgment linked with the divine purpose to restore, and her future glory is far to outshine anything she has known. Jerusalem's condition epitomizes that of the whole people, and it is thus appropriate that the passage opens with an invocation to **heavens** and **earth** to act as witnesses, as often in prophetic judgment sayings (cf. Mic. 6:1-2). They are to attest the divine care lavished on Israel and the unnaturalness of her disobedience. The fatherly care which has watched over the people from her beginnings is met with a failure to acknowledge the activity of God (vss. 2-3).

1:4-6. The life of the people is wholly corrupt and is depicted as a body wounded from **head** to **foot** with no alleviation offered to her. Characteristically the corruptness of men's action is linked with the spurning of **the Holy One of Israel**—a title which is frequent in this book but little used elsewhere in the OT, and which expresses the deep sense of both the separation of God from man by reason of the divine nature and also the mystery of the divine action in regard to Israel.

1:7-9. The Devastation of Judah. The general failure infects the whole land as is shown by a detailed picture of Judah (vss. 7-8). This probably refers to the devastation wrought by the armies of Sennacherib in 701, when he claims to have captured 46 cities of Judah and to have shut up Hezekiah like a bird in a cage. Jerusalem is left isolated in the center of the devastated land, and the prophet makes the people acknowledge divine grace: **If the LORD of hosts had not left us a few survivors, we should have been like Sodom** (vs. 9, perhaps better "we should almost have been like Sodom"). The people's failure could have brought about a total collapse, and such dire judgment is not infrequent in the prophet's message. The remnant here is all that is left, and it exists not by right but only as an act of mercy, totally unexpected and totally unmerited (cf. 37:33-37). The prophet recalls the ancient tradition of the destruction of the cities of the plain (Gen. 19) to indicate vividly again what Judah and her capital have deserved. Possibly vs. 7 also contains an allusion to this, since the word for **overthrown** is used most often of this disaster; it has been proposed that the phrase should read "as the overthrow of Sodom."

1:10-17. *Perverse Worship*. So terrible is Jerusalem's failure that her rulers can be described as **rulers of Sodom,** her people as **people of Gomorrah** (vs. 10). They are exhorted to **hear** the divine **word,** the term so often used for the prophetic message, and the **teaching** (*torah*), the law or directive which is often associated, though not exclusively, with the priests. It is in this context that the nature of the failure is more closely defined and again, as in vs. 4, the relationship with God is linked with the need for right dealings.

When a people comes to worship with its hands **full of blood** (vs. 15) the performance of ritual becomes an utter weariness to God. This point is emphasized by several of the prophets (cf. Jer. 7:21-26; Hos. 6:6; Amos 5:21-26), though various interpretations have been placed on their words. It has sometimes been thought that in such pronouncements the prophets rejected all the forms of sacrificial worship, or even all external forms. Though in some cases the interpretation is open to question there can be no doubt of the meaning here. God indicates his unwillingness to listen even to their **many prayers** (vs. 15). The whole of their present worship is unacceptable—the text lists a great variety of observances (perhaps **iniquity,** vs. 13, should be "fasting"). Cf. Ps. 15, where the conditions on which the worshiper may be in the shrine are laid down.

Those who are disobedient to the basic requirements of God's law are unfit to engage in worship; far from receiving blessing and favor when they appear before him, they inevitably call down judgment on themselves. The people's condition is unforgivable because their understanding of worship is so totally wrong. They conceive it as a way of winning, indeed earning the right to, divine favor. They find themselves faced by the inexorable demand that they show their obedience by abandoning those things which deny their professions. Above all they are to protect the **fatherless** and the **widow** and insure the maintenance of right (vs. 17).

1:18-20. *Promise of Forgiveness*. The gloomy picture of alienation between man and God is followed by an exhortation and promise, combined with a further warning. The interpretation of vs. 18 has indeed been variously made. Is it an ironic question: Can your sins be forgiven? Is it a concession for the sake of argument: Let us for the moment ignore

their reality? The context strongly suggests that it is a word of promise and thus provides an answer to what otherwise might seem an insoluble problem. Men have no right to stand in the presence of God with guilt on them. But how can they be released from the sin which besets their lives? Up to a point the OT prophets, like the great Deuteronomic lawgivers, seem to present an optimistic view, suggesting that men have only to be **willing and obedient** for all to be well. They do not always see the depths of human failure as these are seen e.g. by the lawyers of the Priestly school, represented above all in Lev., or by the Chronicler. But, without precisely explaining the relationship, they set the problem of man's willingness or unwillingness to respond in the context of divine promise, and here the promise is of forgiveness.

1:21-31. *Restoration to Former Faithfulness*. The theme of the failure of Jerusalem returns in vss. 21-23, contrasting her present condition with a time when **righteousness lodged in her.** For this, judgment must come, but it will be like the refining of **silver** (vss. 22, 25). It will lead to a restoration of justice as in an ideal past—perhaps with an allusion to the growing tradition of the idyllic reigns of David and Solomon (cf. esp. I-II Chr.). The city will be renamed **city of righteousness, the faithful city** (vs. 26).

1:27-31. A further series of sayings speaks of the purity of the new population of the city—those who **repent** (lit. "return," perhaps meaning from captivity, vs. 27)—and the destruction of the **rebels** against the divine will. The theme of those who **forsake the LORD** (vs. 28) is elaborated in words of judgment which seem to refer to alien cult practices (vs. 29) and in more general words about the powerlessness of the idolaters (vs. 30; cf. Ps. 1:3; Jer. 17:8). Vs. 31 is not altogether clear, but perhaps refers to the destruction of the idolater and his image. The Dead Sea Isa. scroll has plural forms, "your strength, your work," and thereby gives a more general application to the saying.

2:1-5. *Jerusalem, a Blessing for the World*. Since ch. 2 begins with a new heading, not unlike 1:1, it is usually thought that the following vss. form the intro. to a new section. These vss. are found also in a slightly different textual form in Mic. 4:1-5, where they give a contrasting climax to the judgment of Jerusalem depicted in the final vss. of Mic. 3. It seems likely that in Isa. too the oracle is designed to provide a concluding comment to the opening ch. with its theme of faithless and faithful Jerusalem. The full promise is only now reached. Perhaps, since this oracle appears in 2 prophetic books, the words in 2:1 were originally a marginal note suggesting that the saying really is Isa.'s—a first scholarly attempt to deal with the problem of authorship of a passage which probably should be regarded as an independent word of promise.

The place of Jerusalem in the OT tradition is here richly illustrated. As the capital of the Davidic kingdom it had its political significance. As the city in which the royal shrine for Yahweh was built by Solomon, and where the ancient religious symbol, the ark, was to be found, it gathered devotion, as many of the pss. reveal. But still more as the place which God chose, over which his name was called (cf.

e.g. Deut. 12:5; Jer. 7:10), it must become the very center of the world's life—supernaturally the **highest of the mountains,** to which the **nations** will come, the source of the divine **law** and of the divine blessing of peace for the whole world. Here is expressed in vivid symbol the reality of God's presence and his judgment of the world (cf. Ps. 82) and the hope of new life which is his promise (cf. Ezek. 47). The section closes (vs. 5), echoing its beginning (1:2-3), with an appeal to Israel to respond and find her true way of life.

The whole passage, linking together oracles of the prophet and other sayings, some of which may be of later origin, presents a unified picture. It carries a powerful message of warning and promise.

C. THE DAY OF THE LORD (2:6–4:6)

2:6-22. *A Time to Hide.* This section is marked off by the recurrence of a sort of refrain (vss. 10, 19, 21). Each part of the poem is punctuated by a return to the theme of the humiliation of man, of hiding like **moles** and **bats** (vs. 20) in the **caves** and rock clefts before the terror of God in the **glory of his majesty,** as if it were possible to escape as from an enemy invader. The means of judgment is not described here, only the sense of awe at the presence of God. It may be doubted whether these 3 parts originally belonged together, but the common theme of the refrain and the close interlinkage of thought makes understandable their combining, whether by Isa. himself or by his followers. This passage is not inappropriately placed after the opening section of the book. It reechoes the theme of absolute allegiance to God and of obedience to his laws and shows the consequences of failure.

2:6-11. The first part portrays a people involved in alien practices (vs. 6), priding itself in the wealth of its possessions (vs. 7; the period leading up to the time of Isa. was one of prosperity in both N and S kingdoms), and engaged in idolatry (vs. 8); but humiliation must come (vss. 9-11). Vs. 6 presents considerable difficulty. Since it appears to begin in the middle of a condemnation, perhaps the opening of the poem is missing. Possibly vs. 6a should be linked with vs. 5 and read: "For you have rejected your strength [so the Targum; or "your kinsman," i.e. God], O house of Jacob." Despite the uncertain text it seems clear that vs. 6b refers to magical practices, but **from the east** might be amended to "from of old" or "with sorcery." In vs. 6c a small change would give "traders like the Philistines," a good parallel to the bargaining suggested by **strike hands with foreigners** in vs. 6d. On the other hand this last might be rendered "abound in foreign children," pointing to idolatrous practices or foreign marriages.

2:12-19. The 2nd part speaks in highly poetic language of the coming of Yahweh's own **day** of judgment, and depicts the disaster in terms of the overthrow of glorious trees, mountains, towers, and ships (vss. 12-16). Again the picture of humiliation and hiding follows (vss. 17-19). The day of Yahweh is a concept found earlier, clearly in Amos (cf. e.g. Amos 5:18-20). Popular thought seems to have seen it as a day of victory for Israel, but to Isa., as to Amos, it is a day of divine intervention. For those whose unfitness to be God's people is shown by their failure to trust in God, their indulgence in pride and self-sufficiency, and their involvement in social evil, this is to be the day of judgment. The Holy One of Israel will be found to be holy in judgment.

2:20-22. The 3rd part returns briefly to the theme of the futility of idolatry and, after again speaking of humiliation, ends with a warning note—perhaps a scribal comment—against any kind of trust in man.

3:1-15. *Collapse of Civil Order.* The coming of the divine judgment is here described more precisely. All support is to be removed from **Jerusalem** and **Judah,** and the civil order which should prevail will come to an end. The leadership will be lost, military, civil, and religious authority undermined. The inexperienced will rule, and social disorder will follow (vss. 1-5). **Magician** and **expert in charms** (vs. 3) may indicate that all those on whom the people rely for counsel will be removed, but it is possible that these refer to the skilled "craftsmen" taken into exile in 597 (cf. II Kings 24:14). The theme is continued with emphasis on the hopeless situation, in which no one is willing to take responsibility. The disaster appears to be in the future no longer; Jerusalem and Judah have already come to disaster for their defying of the holy majesty of God (vss. 6-8). The combination of phrases suggests a coming day of judgment, envisaged not unnaturally in terms of removal of leaders and chaos in government, for it was in the period of Isa. that such occurred in the N kingdom. The prophet may be looking back on the fall of Samaria in 722 and seeing the disaster coming on Jerusalem in the same form. But interwoven into this is an interpretation of it in terms of siege and famine (vs. 1); and the indication that **Jerusalem has stumbled and Judah has fallen** (vs. 8) and that the city has become a **heap of ruins** (perhaps better "fallen one," vs. 6) suggests that the words of Isa. against Jerusalem have been seen as meaningful again in the time of the disaster of exile in 586. The significance of the prophetic word is not exhausted in its original situation.

3:9-12. The theme of civil chaos continues in vss. 9, 12, with the added point of bringing home the nature of Judah's failure in justice and her insolent sin (vs. 9). On **Sodom** see above on 1:9-10. Vs. 12 should perhaps open: "As for my people, his rulers are wrongdoers, and exactors [or "creditors"] rule over him." Between these 2 vss. stands a wisdom saying (vss. 10-11), moralistic in tone, which should probably be emended to read: "Happy are the righteous, for it shall be well . . ." The blessing of the righteous at the coming of God is contrasted with the inevitable judgment which falls on the wicked (cf. Hos. 14:9).

3:13-15. The judge, God himself, is ready to pass sentence (cf. Ps. 82); he is in the law court to condemn the leaders who have oppressed. The oracle links with the opening proclamation of judgment on the ruling groups.

3:16-4:1. *Judgment on Women.* With the foregoing is placed a further saying concerned with the women —evidently the wealthy women, perhaps the wives of the rulers who are condemned (cf. Amos 4:1-3). Their pride, their love of finery, will be destroyed and their fashionable hair styles and their rich clothing will become **baldness** and **sackcloth,** the signs of mourning and perhaps also of exile (vss. 16-17, 24).

A long list of **finery** is included (vss. 18-23); not every item is clear, but it reveals the kind of rich attire and jewelry which a wealthy Judean woman might possess. Vs. 17c might better be rendered: "the Lord will lay bare their foreheads." In vs. 24e **shame** appears in the famous Dead Sea scroll of Isa.; without this word the text may be translated "branding for beauty."

3:25-4:1. This judgment on the women of Jerusalem suggests—perhaps to Isa. but more probably to a later interpreter in the exilic period—the picture of Jerusalem as the mother of her sons (cf. Lam. 1:1, 18). The **men** have fallen **in battle** and the city is taken. The situation of the surviving women is so desperate that they seek the protection of the few men remaining, asking only the protection of a **name,** not the full care of the marriage relationship.

4:2-6. *Hope in Judgment.* But this terrible series of pictures is not the last word of God, who enters the human sphere in his holiness to judge and to save. The day of the Lord, which is gloom and terror to those who merit it, will also bring blessing and hope. There will be a new sprouting up of life in the final age for the remnant of Israel. The term **branch** (vs. 2) is sometimes used to denote the leader of the new age (cf. Jer. 23:5; 33:15; Zech. 3:8; 6:12), but here it seems to have a more general sense. The survivors will be sanctified, for Jerusalem will be a **holy** city, a place of **life** (cf. Zech. 14:20-21). The wind of divine judgment, as a **burning** fire, will purify the people and remove their defilement. The very presence of God will protect his holy mountain, and it will be a **refuge** and **shelter.**

Just as the opening ch., picturing the faithlessness of the city, issues in the vision of Jerusalem as the center of the world's life (2:2-5), so here the proclamation of judgment—as the coming day of the Lord, the day of siege and exile, the time of total downfall—issues in a further vision of hope. Such visions as these seem to point to a background of disaster and perhaps of exile such as finally overtook Judah in the 6th cent. Set in the context of judgment, they provide a fitting interpretation of the nature of divine promise, placed against the background of human failure and sin.

D. The Lord and His Vineyard (5:1-30)

Though the vineyard song covers only the opening 7 vss., it has been appropriately linked with 2 further elements: a long series of woes (vss. 8-23) exemplifying the failure of Judah indicated in the song, and a culminating word of disaster (vss. 24-30).

5:1-7. *The Vineyard Song.* This song is reminiscent of the marriage poetry of the Song of S., where "vineyard" may actually be used to signify the bride (Song of S. 8:11-12). The poem may thus be based on a love song, highly poetic in its imagery and with a twist imparted at the end of vs. 2. The carefully tended vineyard, provided with everything needful, produces **wild grapes** (lit. "stinking things," perhaps meaning putrid fruit). The plaintiff establishes the relationship of obligation. He has fulfilled his part; the community is summoned to give judgment. As in the parables of Nathan (II Sam. 12) and of Jesus, the hearers are invited to pass judgment, to concur in the sentence passed on the vineyard.

It is to be condemned to destruction, deprived of fertility. But, as in the parables, the judges are in reality judging themselves. They cannot help concurring in the sentence, but it is on the Judah which they themselves are. The care of God for his people has brought from them in response not **justice** but **bloodshed,** not **righteousness** but a **cry**—pairs of words that have similar sound, suggesting the travesty of right life in the people's conduct.

Was the word of judgment intended to come as a surprise to Judah? We cannot be sure, but it seems not unlikely that the symbol of the vineyard for the land and people was of older origin than the time of Isa. It is found in Ps. 80:14-15, and Hosea possibly knew the analogy (cf. Hos. 2:3-6). Later it is used by Ezekiel (Ezek. 19:10-14) and by Jesus (Mark 12:1-9 and parallels).

5:8-23. *Woes of Judah.* This series of woes depicts in detail the people's failure. The first 2 concern matters of social failure and thus link closely to the judgment in the preceding vs. There are those who make wrong use of the **land** (vss. 8-10), which is given by God to his people, an inheritance of his, not theirs (cf. Lev. 25:23). The result is loss of true status for those deprived of their family inheritance (cf. I Kings 21). The luxury **houses** become **desolate** and their fields unproductive—an **ephah** was only a 10th of a **homer** (see table, p. 1285). Similarly concern with feasting and drinking (vss. 11-13) leads men away from a true regard for what God does (cf. Amos 6:4-6). The judgment takes the form of deprivation of true leadership and true knowledge of God.

5:14-17. The pattern here is **Woe to those . . .** followed by **therefore**—or the stronger oath formula **surely** (vs. 9)—introducing the word of judgment. Since vs. 14 begins again with **therefore** and includes another judgment closely similar to that of vs. 13 (on Sheol see comment on Ps. 6:4-5), we may suppose that either a "woe" has been accidentally omitted or, in view of the similarity, 2 alternative forms of the judgment pronouncement have been preserved. Not inappropriately, the essential part of the refrain from the day of Yahweh poem in ch. 2 is introduced in vss. 15-16, perhaps indicating the close of one small collection of woes and emphasizing the absolute supremacy and holiness of God. Vs. 17 is obscure; we expect a continuance of the judgment idea, and it has been suggested that this may be seen more clearly by rendering the 2nd part: "and the ruins of those who have been wiped out young beasts shall eat up" (cf. Lam. 5:17-18).

5:18-23. This new series of woes overlaps the first series with its mention of drunkenness. Vss. 18-21 are concerned with the wrongheadedness of those who fail to see the true nature of God's action, who set right standards at nought, whose trust is in their own cleverness. Vss. 22-23 return to the theme of social evils.

5:24-30. *Culminating Disaster.* The series of woes in vss. 18-23 has no judgment pronouncement corresponding to each woe, but the omission is remedied and the whole section drawn together in this concluding passage. The gloomy refrain at the end of vs. 25 shows that this conclusion—or at least vss. 25-30, in which case vs. 24 should be taken as the judgment word to the woes—is in reality the final stanza of the long poem in 9:8-10:4. Its placement here may be due to accidental dislocation, since 6:1-9:7 could have been inserted into the poem after its stanzas had got out of order; but it seems more probable that the stanza has been used deliberately here to provide the necessary final judgment on the people.

The poem as found in 9:8-10:4 consists of a series of judgments, each culminating in the warning that this is not the last, that the divine anger still blazes. But here, in what appears to be the last stanza, there is no indication of further future judgment. The picture is of a foreign power summoned by God. The strength of its soldiery appears almost supernatural; there is no escape from its relentless onslaught. The final note is of utter **darkness.**

5:26. The singular **nation** may well be the original form of the text, referring to the coming of Assyria. But the Hebrew has the plural "nations," which we should probably understand as due to a reinterpretation of the phrase. The judgment of God, as the OT prophets frequently describe it, is expressed not just in terms of this or that historical moment; it has a finality brought out in the picture of the nations of the world engaging in a final catastrophic battle against Jerusalem (cf. e.g. Zech. 14).

E. The Vision in the Temple (6:1-13)

The events described in this ch. are often said to represent Isa.'s call to be a prophet, but there is no precise indication that it is an initial experience, and it is possible that some of Isa.'s prophecies should be dated before it. What is significant is rather the strength of the prophet's sense of being commissioned by God, with an uncongenial message laid on him by divine compulsion. Here is no casual encounter between man and God, nor is there a voluntary response to a divine call. The hand of God rests heavily on Isa.; finding himself in the presence of Yahweh of hosts in judgment, he can do no other than accept what is laid on him.

6:1-3. The Setting. On the date when **Uzziah** (Azariah) **died** see Chronology, pp. 1271-82. The experience is set in the Jerusalem **temple,** perhaps on some notable occasion, some great annual feast. The stress on the divine kingship suggests the great autumnal festival which many scholars think particularly celebrated this idea and ushered in the new year with a renewal of covenant and a recommittal of king and people to their God (see comment on Deut. 27:9-10; Intro. to Pss.). In the earthly temple—the chosen place of the divine dwelling—Isa. sees the heavenly court, for heavenly and earthly dwelling are intimately bound up together. He becomes aware of the dread holiness of God, conscious of the acclamation of that holiness by the attendant beings; and this sense of God's holiness is clearly a marked characteristic of Isa.'s understanding of him.

6:2-3. The **seraphim** (Hebrew plural of "seraph"; no indication is given of their number) are here members of the heavenly court, uttering praise and carrying out the divine command. If, like the cherubim (see comment on I Kings 6:23-28), they were thought of as human-animal creatures—perhaps winged snakes with human hands and faces, betraying an ancient and alien origin—they are here

subordinated to Yahweh of hosts, the Lord of the heavenly beings as also ruler of the whole earth.

6:4-7. The Divine Presence. The presence of God is expressed, as often, by the earthquake which shakes the earthly building. A great earthquake was remembered from the reign of Uzziah (cf. Amos 1:1; Zech. 14:5), but smaller tremors were not uncommon and became a natural symbol for the divine approach. The effect on the prophet of discovering himself thus in the presence is shattering. He is conscious of the condition both of himself and of his people, of an uncleanness—including but not to be equated with sinfulness—which cannot stand in the face of that holiness. To see God is to die (cf. Exod. 33:20) unless God himself offers protection. Here the heavenly being mediates cleansing, and the way is opened for that hearing of the heavenly deliberations which reveals the reason for the vision.

6:8-13. The Prophet's Commission. The experience as described closely parallels Micaiah's vision in I Kings 22. But Isa. is more involved in his experience. He not only speaks of what he sees taking place but finds himself caught up into it. As the deliberation of the heavenly court proceeds (cf. I Kings 22:20-23) he knows that he is being commissioned, that it is for this that he is being shown the secret purposes of God (cf. Amos 3:7). There is laid on him the commission to proclaim disaster, to speak a message which will fall on deaf ears, a message which will reveal more clearly the disobedience of Judah. The detail is unspoken, but when its grimness calls out from the heart of the prophet the lamentation, so often the cry of the psalmists, **How long, O Lord?** (vs. 11), he is shown a picture of a desolated land, of exile and destruction, of further ruthless judgment even on those who survive.

6:13. The text as it stands pictures total judgment. Perhaps the **tenth** is intended to refer to the sparing of Judah in the first cataclysm, the destruction of the N kingdom in 722, and to point to a further catastrophe which will overtake the S kingdom. But the last words are problematic, and the complete Dead Sea manuscript of Isa. has a different reading, perhaps meaning: "as the oak and the terebinth when the sacred pillar of a high place is overthrown." The total judgment is, however, modified by the last phrase: **The holy seed is its stump** (lit. "pillar," perhaps meaning "sacred pillar"). There has been much discussion whether this is original to the ch. That Isa. thought in terms of a remnant which would survive disaster is clear, though it is also clear that he saw this as an act of divine grace (cf. 1:9). It is not impossible that he himself offered this reinterpretation of his own message, but it seems more probable that it is a later gloss. The Greek translators reveal another stage in the interpretation of the material, for they present a modified text of vs. 12 which introduces the idea of divine mercy even there. Both these later interpretations are still to be seen as part of the tradition, the exegesis of the text in the light of later needs, the discovery within it of a word of God which was perhaps esp. relevant to the generation which saw the ultimate disaster to Judah and Jerusalem at the hands of Babylon, and was also able to see in that disaster the working out of a divine purpose of grace for God's people which could lead to their reestablishment in a new and better relationship.

F. Faith and Power Politics (7:1-25)

The threat of Assyria produced many shifts in policy and changes in alliance during the 2nd half of the 8th cent. The problem for the politicians—in this case Ahaz and his advisers—is to maneuver into security by whatever means offered. The prophet sees each situation as an occasion for divine judgment and promise. So faith and politics are set alongside one another.

7:1-9. The Meeting at the Conduit. As II Kings 16:5 shows, the attempt is being made by the 2 kingdoms of **Syria** and **Israel** to coerce Judah into an alliance against Assyria. Ahaz, being alarmed, appeals to Assyria, and not without good reason. His enemies both outside and within the state may depose him and replace him by a willing rebel. To the panic of king and court, gathered significantly

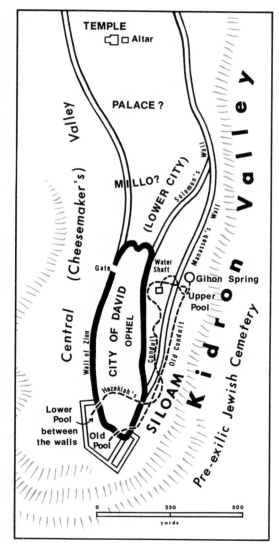

at the water conduit, the prophet speaks the assurance that the divine judgment is on Syria and Israel, that they are frail rather than powerful, and that security in the deepest sense lies in faith in God.

7:3-4. Isa. is accompanied by his son **Shear-jashub**—a name which would appear to be deliberately symbolic, though its interpretation can be variously given. Is it "a remnant shall return" (as in the RSV footnote) or "only a remnant will return"? In any case the name is one of judgment—and of promise only in so far as judgment comes first. Possibly the naming of the child belongs to a lost incident in Isa.'s contact with Ahaz and the king is being reminded of what has earlier been said. No clue is available, for the child is not mentioned again, though the name is reinterpreted in 10:21.

7:5-6. The opponents of Ahaz threaten to put on the throne the **son of Tabeel.** In the vocalized Hebrew text the name is spelled with a wrong vowel point, probably deliberate, that changes its meaning from "God is good" to "no good." The reference to the man by his father's name suggests a dignitary who has succeeded to his father's office and is therefore an influential person. The danger is obviously great that anti-Assyrian groups within the kingdom will see here their opportunity and assist in the overthrow of Ahaz.

7:8-9. These vss. are not altogether clear, but perhaps **the head of** was a proverbial phrase suggesting that destruction would begin with the leaders. The threat in vs. 8c—put in parentheses in the RSV because it clearly interrupts the context—is probably an addition, but it is very obscure, since a threat of disaster **sixty-five years** later would seem to have no precise relevance. An ingenious suggestion is to read "yet 6, yea 5 years more"; this would indicate the imminence of the disaster vividly, but it must remain very uncertain since numerical phrases of this kind are normally in the reverse order (cf. Amos 1:3). The pun in vs. 9cd might be rendered "If you are not firm in faith you will not be firm."

7:10-17. The Sign of Immanuel. In a new situation, perhaps in the court since the address is to the whole **house of David,** Ahaz is offered any **sign** from **heaven** above to **Sheol** beneath the earth (see comment on Ps. 6:4-5) to confirm his faith. His show of spurious piety conceals his lack of faith, but the prophet answers with his own sign, that of the child to be named **Immanuel** ("God is with us"). Without knowing who the child was we cannot be certain of the meaning of the sign, but it seems probable that it represents an act of faith by some unknown woman, perhaps the prophet's wife, who appears in the next ch. But, as in ch. 6, the assurance of divine presence does not bring simple blessing. To those who have faith it is assurance, but to those like Ahaz who do not have faith it is the token of a judgment at the hands of the Assyrians which will overtake the whole land. This theme of faith is echoed again in 8:8, 10.

7:18-25. Judgment at the Hands of the Assyrians. The day of judgment, which is described in terms suggestive of the day of the Lord of ch. 2, is relentless; there is no escape, and the devastation of the land will be complete (cf. 6:11-13). The day, described in 2:12-22 in general terms, is here precisely identified in the Assyrian invasions which were to devastate the land in the time of Ahaz' successor Hezekiah (cf. 1:7-8; chs. 36-37).

G. Judgment and Promise (8:1-9:7)

Many different elements make up this passage, yet there can be seen certain linkages of thought which suggest that they may appropriately be treated together. The theme of judgment is interwoven with the expression of confidence in the saving power of God. The failure of his people finds the prophet confessing his faith, with the assurance that his message and indeed his life bear witness to the purposes of God. The darkness of ignorance and superstition will be answered by the light and rejoicing of a new age—sure because decreed by God—when a true Davidic king will reign in justice and righteousness.

8:1-4. The Birth of a Son. A renewed message of the overthrow of Syria and Israel is centered on the birth of a son to the prophet and the **prophetess,** a sign of the imminent disaster, for his name **Maher-shalal-hash-baz** (lit. "speed spoil haste booty") confidently announces the judgment of God at the hands of Assyria. The name is written on a placard and attested—possibly instead of in **common characters** we should interpret "indelibly"—and the birth of the child, like the birth of Immanuel in 7:14, proclaims the truth of the message.

8:5-10. A Warning to Judah. Judah's lack of faith provides the counterpart to this, so that what might appear to be a message of pure hope becomes a warning of disaster. The rejection of the **waters of Shiloah,** perhaps to be linked not simply with the ordinary water supply of Jerusalem but rather with the hidden river of God (cf. Ps. 46:4), brings on Judah the flood waters of the **River** (i.e. the Euphrates), which is identified as the power of **Assyria.** In vss. 9-10 the **Immanuel** theme is picked up again, and the planned onslaught of the nations —seen now in virtually eschatological vision—is brought to nothing (cf. Pss. 2; 46).

8:11-18. A Warning to the Prophet. The **strong hand** of God rests on his prophet to warn him against accepting the **way of this people.** Their values are wrong, and their awe is misplaced. So God in his holiness becomes to his people, not a source of strength and refuge, but a stumbling block and a snare. The word which should be a word of life becomes to the disobedient a word of death, falling on deaf ears. But for the prophet the assurance of the divine purpose is there, preserved in the teaching which acts as an enduring witness to the divine will. Using the metaphor of a tied and sealed document (vs. 16) he confidently proclaims that what has been said by God through him will be preserved safely, and so too his **children** and **disciples** will be a sign to his people. It has sometimes been thought that these vss. indicate a withdrawal of Isa. from public activity, but there is no real suggestion of this. What is significant is the enduring testimony of his message, preserved **among** his **disciples**— or perhaps, if the Greek translators were right, preserved "so that it should not be understood," making the minds of the hearers dull (cf. 6:9-10) because their lack of faith prevents their acceptance of the divine word.

8:19-22. Apostasy of the People. In sharp contrast to the prophet's faith and his willingness to wait on God (vs. 17) is the panicky search for security of the people who resort to magic and necromancy, turning to **consult the dead** for what they cannot find elsewhere (cf. I Sam. 28:7-19). The obscurity of these vss. prevents precise indication of what is involved, but it is clear enough that here is a people so distressed that they turn against both king and God in the uncertainty of their position.

9:1-7. Restoration of the Davidic Kingdom. The darkness finds its answer in a word of hope. The outlying parts of the ancient kingdom of David which have been lost to it ("the circuit of the nations" is perhaps more correct than **Galilee of the nations**) will be restored, and **joy** (vs. 3) will prevail at the overthrow of the oppressors. Over this reestablished Davidic kingdom there will rule an ideal king, who is acclaimed as a "wonder of a counselor," one whose counsel will be effective for his people's wellbeing; a "divine [i.e. hero] warrior"; a "father [of his people] from of old" (or perhaps "father of plunder," who by his conquests brings benefit to them); and a "prince who brings prosperity." His rule is to be established **for evermore,** and its character will be **justice** for all.

The picture of such a reign of justice is an important element in the kingship conceptions of the OT (cf. 11:2-5; II Sam. 23:3-7). It is expressed in the stories of the foundation of the monarchy and particularly in the figure of **David.** This element becomes embodied in the hopes for the future, for an ideal king. But it would be wrong to think of this only in terms of the future. Insofar as each king enshrines the Davidic promises in himself (cf. II Sam. 7) he can be described in such exalted terms. Though the form in which the promises are here expressed and their setting as an answer to the judgment oracles of the prophet suggest that they may, like ch. 11, be later than Isa., they nevertheless form an important part of the tradition which has come to be associated with him, with their assurance of divine mercy mediated through the Davidic monarchy.

H. Relentless Doom (9:8-10:4)

This section is closely unified by the occurrence in 9:12, 17, 21; 10:4 of the refrain:

**For all this his anger is not turned away
and his hand is stretched out still.**

This refrain also appears in 5:25. It appears likely that the 3 stanzas thus marked off in ch. 9 form the earlier part of a long poem of which 5:24 (or 25)-30 is the conclusion. It proclaims the judgment of God, in its relentlessness, pictured as successive stages in each of which an opportunity of repentance is possible. But Israel proves recalcitrant, and the warnings are unavailing. The structure, and indeed the wording, of the refrain resemble closely the poem in Amos 4:6-12. In the present form of the book the concluding stanza has been utilized to provide a final word of judgment to the woes of ch. 5. The remaining stanzas here have been linked with another woe (10:1-4) which provides a final note.

Many suggestions have been made to explain this arrangement, but nothing can be established with any certainty (see above on 5:24-30).

9:8-21. Judgment on the N Kingdom. The 3 stanzas of the poem speak of different aspects of the people's life. In the first stanza (vss. 8-12) the beginning of the moment of judgment is shown in relation to the confidence of those who regard their present setbacks as only temporary; what has **fallen** they **will build** again and better (vs. 10). The exact historical situation is not evident, but the sense of overconfidence of the people of **Samaria** is a theme fully elaborated in ch. 28. In vs. 9 **will know** should be rendered "will be brought low."

9:13-17. Vs. 13 here could be the opening of the 2nd stanza, but it is possible to read it as a comment, perhaps a marginal note of warning, designed to round off the first stanza. The fate of the leaders and the total failure of the people are indicated in the 2nd stanza. The metaphors of **head** and **tail** in vs. 14, meaning rulers and subjects and expressing total overthrow, have been explained in vs. 15 by precise reference to political leaders and false prophets. The **honored man** is perhaps to be taken as the courtier.

9:18-21. In the 3rd stanza is described the disaster of civil war that has brought utter chaos to the land. In vs. 19 an alternative textual form suggests "is in confusion" for **is burned,** and this is certainly appropriate to the context.

These 3 pictures, reflecting aspects of the life of the truncated N kingdom in the last years of its existence, are terrible indictments of Israel's failure. Their place in the prophecy of Isa. is linked to his concern that the fate which overtook that kingdom should be a warning to Judah. Reading the will of God in history can be dangerous, but learning from the experience of the past and seeing that past in the light of the divine will are ways in which the OT often points to the nature of hope.

10:1-4. The Fate of Oppressors. Here is a **woe** dealing esp. with the falsity of judgment, the manipulation of law to oppress so that it no longer offers protection to the unprotected. The coming **day** of the Lord will find those whose gains are thus ill-gotten entirely without protection, among the prisoners waiting for exile or judgment, or among **the slain.**

The whole passage is dark, almost without relief. It needs to be read in the context not only of the prophet's whole message but also of the use and reuse of his message over the succeeding years. It was such declarations of God's patience in judgment and of his absoluteness of demand which made possible the understanding of disaster and the appropriation of it in such a way that there could survive a community after the Exile which was conscious of being heir to the past and recipient of the promises of divine grace.

I. GOD AND HIS INSTRUMENT OF JUDGMENT (10:5-34)

The concept of an instrument of divine judgment —a nation chosen by God to bring on his own people and on others the disaster which is interpreted as the outcome of their failure—is one which Isa. and others of the prophets employ with some frequency. It is one which it is dangerous to apply indiscriminately, for, as the OT often indicates, and as the NT makes even more clear, there is not always a direct correlation between behavior and fortune. Israel was to learn a deeper significance in her own misfortunes.

The anticipation and experience of invasion by the Assyrians, even the thought that Judah would be totally overthrown, play an important part in Isa.'s interpretation of his own times to his compatriots and in his warnings to them to rediscover their true way of life. At the same time he could not be unaware that Assyrian policy was ruthless in the extreme and that Assyrian rulers spoke in sheer self-confidence of their own achievements. An instrument of God the Assyrian might be in the sense that the will of God could be discerned in what was done; but that he was an unwitting instrument, and was himself under judgment, was also important to recognize.

The poetic and prose passages which make up this section are all concerned with aspects of this theme of the relationship between God's use of Assyria and Assyria's place in the larger working out of his purpose.

10:5-19. Assyria in God's Purpose. With the declaration of God's purpose in using Assyria is contrasted the Assyrian boast of the **nations** which have been overthrown—the cities mentioned in vs. 9 were all taken within *ca.* 20 years. The overthrow of these represents the overthrow of their gods, and now the overthrow of **Jerusalem** seems imminent.

10:12-19. The theme is reiterated but with a new element. The completion of God's **work** at Jerusalem—perhaps in terms of his judging of his people, perhaps in terms of his delivering of the city from the worst disasters of siege and destruction (cf. 1:8; 29:1-4; chs. 36-37)—will find him ready to deal with the **arrogant** boaster. As in 37:24-25, the prophet quotes the Assyrian boasts in language very much like the courtly style of the Assyrian royal inscriptions describing the conquests. But this boasting is out of place. The Assyrian is the instrument of divine action and must be obedient to the divine will; thus judgment will come. God himself will go forth like a **fire** and the Assyrian power like a **forest** will be burned away, leaving only a handful of **trees** standing. Vs. 18c is perhaps to be regarded as an explanatory note, applying the figure of the forest to the people.

10:20-27b. Hope in Judgment. This judgment of Assyria provides a setting for 2 short statements indicating the way of hope for Israel (vss. 20-23, 24-27b). It is only a **remnant** which will remain. The word "remnant" picks up the comment on the greatness of the Assyrian disaster in vs. 19, and also (vs. 21) links to the name of Isa.'s son in 7:3. The first word (vss. 20-23) is thus of judgment, but with it is linked a reassurance (vss. 24-27b) comparing the threat of Assyria with that of **Egypt.** The events of the exodus period are a message of hope, and the point is reinforced with a reference to the overthrow of **Midian** (cf. 9:4) at the hands of Gideon (Judg. 7-8). Vs. 25b should be rendered "my anger will come completely to an end." This exhortation to Jerusalem not to fear the Assyrians may be compared with Isa.'s assurances to Hezekiah in ch. 37.

10:27c-34. The March of Assyria. This poem, probably fragmentary, vividly depicts the Assyrian advance. Its opening line is in a badly corrupted state (see RSV footnote). A slightly superior alternative suggestion is "He went up from before Samaria." The place names provide occasion for some play on words—a device more elaborately used in Mic. 1:10-16. The very sound of some of the names suggests the events in which they are involved. The advance is traced until the enemy is within sight of **Jerusalem.** Vss. 33-34 provide an answer, in which again the Assyrian is depicted as a **forest,** to be **cut down** in judgment by God.

The interpretation of the section is not without its difficulties. It is clear that various elements have been combined because of their relation to the main theme of God and Assyria. What is less certain is which of these materials had a different reference before being applied to this theme. Thus the oracle in vss. 33-34 is sometimes seen as an intro. to the next ch., and if this interpretation is correct the cutting down of the forest indicates judgment on Judah and the fall of its monarchy—a theme taken up in 11:1. It is not unlikely that an oracle originally proclaiming judgment on Judah has been reapplied to Assyria (cf. Jer. 6:22-23; 50:41-42), and the same may be true of vss. 15-19. Such a development in interpretation would show how the message spoken by the prophet to one situation is not limited to that one meaning, but may be seen, by the prophet himself or by his followers, to speak afresh to new moments of experience. Insofar as the prophet mediates the true word of God its truth remains. Its continued significance rests, not in its being a prediction of the future, but in its revealing of truth about God. Like the whole OT, it is Godward looking rather than only forward looking.

J. The Time of Promise (11:1–12:6)

The separate elements which make up this section may well be of very different date, but as they now stand they not only form a unit presenting the theme of hope, partly in terms of the restoration of the Davidic monarchy and partly in terms of a gathering of the scattered members of the community, but also provide a fitting climax to the collection of oracles making up the opening part of the book (chs. 1–12).

11:1-9. Restoration of the Davidic Kingdom. The opening links closely in thought to the end of ch. 10, for whatever the precise application of 10:33-34, the theme of a tree cut down provides the start for an oracle concerning the now fallen house of David. The theme of Davidic restoration is central here, and the significance of the monarchy is seen in the breadth of conception found here. It is likely that both this utterance and that of 9:2-7 owe much of their language and imagery to royal oracles which may be regarded as properly associated with every Davidic ruler, and which may reasonably be traced, so far as form is concerned, back into pre-Israelite royal material. But it seems probable that, relevant as such statements would be at the outset of the reign of any new Davidic king, their present form envisages the situation of the exilic age when the monarchy had come to an end.

11:2-5. The hopes focused on the kings were not lost; they became concentrated on a new and future figure who would restore the kingdom and completely fulfill the requirements of the true king. This is seen in the stress laid on the activity of the divine **Spirit** in the ideal king. Judgment **with righteousness** and the overthrow of evil are vital to this (in vs. 4c we should probably read "violent" for **earth**). But there is a deeper aspect too, for the divine Spirit is to operate in and through this ideal king not only to exercise wisdom and discernment (cf. I Kings 3:3-14) but also to maintain true religion.

11:6-9. The right order to be established extends beyond man into the natural world. In the ideal age to which the oracle points there will be a cessation of enmity between the animals. Peace and the true religion, here expressed as **knowledge of the LORD,** will be found in his **holy mountain** of Jerusalem and hence in the whole land, and indeed in the whole earth. In vs. 6 a good suggested rendering is "calf and lion shall feed together" and in vs. 7 "cow and bear shall be in amity."

11:10-16. The Gathering of the Remnant. The theme of the ideal Davidic king is taken further, portraying him as central to the life of all the **nations** (vs. 10; cf. 2:2-4); and this provides a link to the statement of restoration of scattered members **of his people** (vs. 11), which in turn introduces a poetic utterance developing that theme. The concept of a gathering of the scattered is interwoven with that of the extending of the Davidic kingdom into Edom, Moab, and Ammon, and it is from Assyrian exile in particular that the **remnant** will return. This theme, relevant as it is to the period of Isa., when Samaria fell, is much more significant for the period after the Babylonian exile; and the language, reminiscent of later parts of the book, suggests that this is a later poem. This would fit well too with the theme of reconciliation between **Judah** and **Ephraim,** an idea which can be seen in the exilic period (cf. Ezek. 37:15-28), and which became esp. important in the time of the Samaritan schism in the 4th cent. and later. Here again can be seen the way the material of the Isa. tradition has been welded with later elements so that it continued to speak a message of warning and hope.

12:1-6. A Psalm of Praise. The prospect of a reunited people, a new Davidic kingdom, and a restored world order finds its climax here. Two short ps. passages provide a fitting conclusion to this section and also to the whole complex of chs. 1–12. In vss. 1-2 the saving power of God is stressed, and though the singular form (e.g. **my salvation**) is used the ps. probably refers to the fortunes of the whole people. Vs. 1 points to the experience of exile as that which provokes the reaction, acknowledging judgment and salvation. The obscure opening of vs. 3 perhaps refers to the **water** ritual of the feast of tabernacles (booths; cf. Zech. 14:17), a feast closely linked with the celebrating of the deliverance of the Exodus (cf. Lev. 23:43). The praise of God which follows fittingly concentrates on the greatness of divine salvation—a testimony to all **nations** of God's nature and an invitation for all to acknowledge him. Vs. 6b makes a verbal link back to the realization of the presence of the **Holy One** in the **midst** of Israel experienced by Isa. (6:3); that holiness induces awe, for it is operative both for judgment and for salvation.

II. Isa. and the Nations (13:1–23:18)

A. The Day of Yahweh for Babylon (13:1–14:2)

Chs. 13–14 clearly belong closely together; and the heading in 13:1, **oracle concerning Babylon,** covers them both, as may be seen from the use of the same word for oracle at the beginning of succeeding sections in this collection of foreign nation utterances. But it is convenient to divide the passage into 2 and to make the division after 14:2 rather than at the end of ch. 13, since the words of blessing to Israel in 14:1-2, though quite separate from the preceding material, form a climax, just as 14:32 forms a climax to the succeeding passage. The words of judgment, directed specifically at Babylon as the text now stands, are answered by the assurance of divine promise.

13:1-16. *The Day of Destruction.* Though ch. 13 clearly refers to Babylon (cf. vs. 19), it is less certain that this was the original purpose of vss. 2-16. It has been suggested that **gates of the nobles** (vs. 2) is intended as a play on the name Babylon ("gate of God") but this does not seem very probable. While the imagery of these vss. may be related to the day of Yahweh descriptions of Zeph. 1 the passage is not necessarily late, for there is close connection with the poem in ch. 2 on this theme and with the words of Amos 5. We may reasonably assume that an Isa. utterance on the day of Yahweh has been elaborated and used to give to the judgment on Babylon in vss. 17-22 a universal setting. It is not just Babylon which will fall—though to the community of the exilic period this was of immediate importance. The hostile world, indeed the whole created order, comes under the judgment of God (cf. chs. 24–27).

13:2-10. The day of Yahweh comes as God himself summons his consecrated agents of destruction (vss. 2-3), and he, with his instruments of wrath, prepares for the overthrow of all the **nations,** the destruction of the **whole earth** (vss. 4-5). It is a picture not unlike those of later apocalyptic (see "The Apocalyptic Literature," pp. 1106-09), and it proclaims the absolute sovereignty of God. The poem continues with a vivid portrayal of the terror which his coming brings (vss. 6-8), and the destruction of sinners is accompanied by cosmic evidence of his power (vss. 9-10).

13:11-16. The theme of the high ones brought low, so emphasized in ch. 2, is again brought out in a series of pictures which depict the utter disaster. **Men** will become scarcer than the most precious **gold.** As the **heavens** and **earth** shake (cf. Hag. 2:6, 21) all **will flee** in the hope of finding safety but will be **caught** and destroyed. Knowledge of the actual conditions of warfare and of the devastation of the land such as Judah experienced in the time of Isa. lends vividness to the pictures of this grim day.

13:17–14:2. *God's Purpose in History.* The summons to the **Medes** to bring judgment to Babylon is provided with a wider setting. The overthrow of the power which has brought Judah low is seen not just as a historic moment but as an element within God's total purpose. The relentlessness of the enemy, the shattering of **Babylon, the glory of kingdoms** (vs. 19), the pictures of perpetual desolation (cf. ch. 34)—all express the kind of hostility which Babylonian power evoked. The indication of the

Medes as the agent of judgment points to the exilic age, for it was in fact to the Medo-Persian power under the rule of Cyrus the Persian that Babylon actually fell.

14:1-2. But the meaning of the fall of Babylon is not limited to seeing it as part of a cosmic disaster; it is seen as ushering in the blessing of **Israel.** Though the emphasis is on a reversal of fortunes, with the subordination of Israel's oppressors, there is nevertheless a pointer to the entry of **aliens** into Israel's community which cuts across this otherwise narrow interpretation of God's saving purpose.

B. The Tyrant's Fall (14:3-32)

The prose intro. in vss. 3-4a indicates that the setting of the material which follows is the period of the exile in Babylon and that there is the prospect of a release from servitude when Babylon falls. Together with the interpretative comment of vss. 22-23 it makes the application of the intervening poem seemingly clear as referring to the fall of Babylon. The remainder of the ch. is concerned with an earlier situation, that of the fall of Assyria and a judgment on Philistia (vss. 24-31), culminating in a final hopeful word for Zion.

14:4b-21. *Oracle Against a Tyrant.* An examination of this poem reveals no mention of Babylon, and there are features which suggest that it may have had a general reference, or alternatively have applied originally to Assyria. Whether it derives from Isa. is difficult to say since it contains so much that is unlike other sayings and poems of the prophet, but its subject matter might account for this. The poem is a taunt song or mocking song concerning the downfall of a tyrant. At his fall the nations rejoice and the world is released from servitude. The reference to the **cedars** in vs. 8 is closely paralleled in the Assyrian boasting in 37:24. **Sheol** (see comment on Ps. 6:4-5) greets the tyrant; the **kings**—perhaps those subdued by the tyrant—deride him for being brought as low as they (vss. 9-11).

14:12-15. The theme of downfall is vividly elaborated in a mythological picture. The tyrant is likened to the **Day Star** (vs. 12), pictured as rebelling and seeking to find a place enthroned in the **assembly** of the gods on the far N mountain, to ride the **clouds,** and to be **like the Most High.** The language and allusions of this point to Canaanite mythology, and a comparison may be made with similar material in Ezek. 28. The dwelling of the gods and the riding of the clouds are both known to us from the Ras Shamra texts found at Ugarit in N Syria, and so too is **Dawn** as a deity, of whom this figure is described as **son.** The **Most High** is Elyon, the title so often used of God in his association with Jerusalem. All these elements may be paralleled in the OT, suggesting how richly Canaanite religion and mythology have influenced OT thought.

14:16-21. The picture changes to that of the unburied tyrant, and it has been suggested that this is a scene at his death; but more probably the degradation is simply elaborated with this feature frequent in such taunting and judgment poems. The poem reveals a rich series of pictures concerning **Sheol,** indicating a much more varied pattern of thought than is found in the OT generally. The poem closes with a general reflection on the downfall of **evildoers** (vss. 20*b*-21).

It is clear that this poem would fit many situations. Mythological statement becomes metaphor and can be applied both to wider political issues—e.g. the fall of **Babylon** (so in vss. 22-23, where we should find a bird, probably a bustard, instead of the **hedgehog**)—and to more local and individual needs. In context with the preceding ch., where the fall of Babylon is seen as bound up with the day of Yahweh, the present immediate application can be seen as only one part of its meaning; it carries with it the sense of a world judgment on evil. This may be seen also in the way the ancient rendering of **Day Star** as Lucifer (vs. 12) links it to ideas of a premundane fall and so to the overthrow of the whole power of evil.

14:24-27. Oracle Against Assyria. The application of the poem to Babylon makes for some disunity in the present form of the ch. This judgment oracle on Assyria is not unlike that of ch. 10 and depicts the appropriateness of the breaking of its power in God's own land (cf. Dan. 11:45). The oracle recalls the saving power of God expressed, as in the Exodus, in his stretched-out hand.

14:28-32. Oracle Against Philistia. The final section is dated **in the year that King Ahaz died,** but it is clear that it is not Ahaz' death which has caused rejoicing in **Philistia,** for he was not its overlord. A small emendation of the text would give "In the year that the king died, I saw," and in this context it would be reasonable to assume an allusion to the death of Sargon II of Assyria in 705. The message constitutes a warning against premature rejoicing, and so against rebellion (cf. ch. 20); dire judgment will come from the **north,** i.e. from Assyria.

14:32. This final vs. has been understood as a warning to Judah not to respond to Philistine invitations to rebel, but it can also be understood, like vss. 1-2, as a climax of promise, addressed perhaps to the **messengers** (i.e. ambassadors) of more than one **nation** (the singular being then due to reinterpretation). The downfall of the tyrant, whether Assyria or Babylon, and still more the overthrow of evil by the saving power of God, finds its counterpart in his establishing of Zion as a **refuge** for the **afflicted.**

C. Oracle Concerning Moab (15:1-16:14)

It is difficult to reach any very satisfying conclusions about these 2 chs., both concerned with the fate of Moab, that near and often hated neighbor of Israel E of the Dead Sea. The fact that a large part of the text reappears in Jer. 48:29-38 in another collection of foreign-nation oracles makes genuine Isa. material here seem improbable. The textual problems are great (cf. the RSV footnotes), and it is by no means clear whether this is a reasonably unified poem or, as is more probable, a combination of 2 or possibly 3 poetic utterances drawn together by the prose comment and application at the end (16:13-14).

15:1-9. Lament for Moab. This poem seems to be continued in 16:6-11 (or 12) and perhaps should include 16:2. What is in many ways most remarkable is that it contains a lament at the distressed state of Moab (15:5; 16:9). It is true that 16:6 lays the blame for Moab's downfall on her people's **pride** —a reminder of Isa.'s judgments on the proud (ch. 2). But it vividly portrays the disaster, echoing the place names within the country—in this also resembling oracles of Isa. (10:27-32) and Micah (1:10-16). The chief places named have been identified (see color maps 8, 3). **Kir** (15:1) and **Kir-heres** (16:11) mean **Kir-hareseth** (16:7). The **Brook of the Willows** (15:7) was the Zered, boundary between Moab and Edom to the S. **Dibon** in 15:9, from the Dead Sea manuscript, seems a doubtful correction for the unknown "Dimon" in other manuscripts, since Dibon was not on a river. **Sibmah** (16:8-9) was a few miles SW of **Heshbon.**

16:1-5. A Plea for Refugees. This poem appears to depict ambassadors coming from Moab to Judah seeking refuge for fleeing Moabites. Vs. 2 seems to be an intrusion and may be misplaced from ch. 15. On **lambs** cf. II Kings 3:4. Since a **Sela** in Moab is otherwise unknown, some who view chs. 15-16 as a single poem take it to mean the fortress in Edom (cf. II Kings 14:7; see color map 7) and understand a situation in which Moabites have fled S into Edom (cf. 15:7) and must seek permission from Judah to remain there because Edom is at the time subject to Judah—as e.g. in the reigns of Uzziah and Jotham. The plea ends with the confidence that a rule of **righteousness** and **justice** will be established under a Davidic king. The implication would seem to be that even Moab will share in the final day of blessing. Perhaps such hope is to be linked with the view of Moab implied in Ruth, where David's ancestry is traced to a pious Moabite woman.

16:6-11. Further Lament for Moab. See above on 15:1-9.

16:12-14. Prose Conclusion. Vs. 12, which says that Moab finds no comfort in appeal to her own gods, may be a corruption of the concluding lines of the poem. The comment in vss. 13-14 indicates that the messages spoken concerning Moab refer to the past but now shortly doom will fall relentlessly on her people.

We cannot hope, with these uncertainties, to discover a historical situation. The Assyrians may well have campaigned in Moab. Later disasters also undoubtedly affected that area. Even earlier events could have provoked such words. But what is most significant is the presence here in the OT of such poems as these. Moab, like other nations, is under the judgment of God, but that judgment is not pronounced without an expression of distress at the fate of its people. Such concern with other nations may be seen in Amos 1-2, where the unrighteousness of one nation to another brings down divine condemnation. If, as some scholars have thought, we have here pieces of Moabite poetry, then their inclusion reveals a sympathetic understanding of the fate of a neighboring land. There must have been those in Israel who could not view with equanimity the effects of warfare, and who expressed in poetic form the anguish which they felt and the hope which they cherished for those who were so closely bound up with their own history.

D. The Work of God in History (17:1-18:7)

There is no unity in this section, but it may be helpful to see in it 2 climaxes of thought: 17:7-8, where the first subsection is brought to a close with a recognition of the hope that Israel will learn to trust fully in her holy God; and 18:7, where the hope is extended to point to a day when the envoys of distant peoples will come to Zion. The remaining passages are words of judgment. They concern various peoples and belong in all probability to various situations. In the present form of the material they are subordinated to the prospect of true obedience.

17:1-11. *Oracle Concerning Damascus.* A heading, like those elsewhere in this part of the book, introduces a short oracle (vss. 1-3) proclaiming doom to the Aramean kingdom of **Syria** with its capital at **Damascus,** to which is linked a word of judgment on **Israel** also. This saying belongs to the period of the Syro-Ephraimitic war, indicated more fully in chs. 7-8. Vs. 3*cd* means that what is left of Syria will be no better than what is left of Israel. Vss. 4-6 provide a comment on this: **the glory of Jacob will be brought low,** and in a harvest of disaster nothing will be left but the merest remnant. The **Valley of Rephaim** was near Jerusalem on the SW. The plea for right trust in God in vss. 7-8 thus fits well with oracles which suggest the need for faith so stressed in ch. 7; perhaps here a later exegete has picked up various other sayings from Isa. to make the point clear (cf. 2:20; 22:8*b*-11; on **Asherim** see comment on I Kings 14:15). Vss. 9-11 provide a further comment, stressing both the doom which is to come and the reason for it. God has been **forgotten,** and trust has been placed in **alien** religious practices. The allusion is probably to potted **plants** representing gardens of Adonis.

17:12-18:7. *Judgment on Assyria and Egypt.* As so often in Isa., a specific word of judgment is linked with a more general statement. It is possible that the original reference of 17:12-14 was to the Assyrians, rebuked by God (as in 10:5-11) and suddenly brought to disaster (as in 37:33-38). Similarly 18:1-2 alludes to the activities of Egypt, so closely involved in the political troubles of the reign of Hezekiah. **Whirring wings** probably should read "winged ships," i.e. sailboats. Egypt's Ethiopian rulers are depicted as sending **ambassadors,** and perhaps this was originally intended as a reference to attempts at raising general rebellion against Assyria. But this particular political situation is now given a wider significance. The terms used in 17:12-14 are strongly suggestive of the great final overthrow of the nations (depicted e.g. in Ps. 46) and in 18:3 the whole **world** is invited to pay heed to what God is doing. He looks down from his **dwelling** and doom will fall on the nations (18:4-6). Again it may be that a saying is here used which originally referred to Assyria and to Isa.'s immediate situation, but it is given a wider meaning, not unlike that of the Gog of Magog passage of Ezek. 38-39. The great moment of judgment brings the ambassadors to **Zion,** now not for political intrigue, but because it is where the **name** of God is revealed, where he himself is to be worshiped (18:7; cf. 2:2-4).

E. ORACLE CONCERNING EGYPT (19:1-25)

Three sections make up the poetic part (vss. 1-15) of this ch., which has a heading like other chs. in this part of the book.

19:1-4. *Civil Disruption.* In the first section Yahweh is pictured as **riding on a swift cloud**—a portrayal derived from Canaanite thought—to the dismay of the **Egyptians** and their gods. It is as if he were again engaged in battle with Egypt as at the time of the Exodus. Indeed such a parallelism appears to underlie much of the ch. Disaster is proclaimed in a variety of terms—there is to be civil strife, intercity warfare, and division between the 2 kingdoms of Egypt. There is also dismay which leads Egypt to consult her magicians (as in the plague stories of Exod.). Finally there is conquest at the hands of a **fierce** alien ruler.

19:5-10. *Natural Disaster.* In this 2nd section the picture changes to disaster of a natural kind. The **Nile,** on which the land depends, dries up; gone is the sustenance of **fishermen** and of those whose crafts need good crops for raw materials. **Pillars of the land** (vs. 10) probably should read "craftsmen."

19:11-15. *Failure of Wisdom.* The emphasis in this 3rd section rests on the failure of Egypt's wisdom—again suggesting the plague stories as well as reminding that from Egypt came much of ancient Near Eastern wisdom literature. The vaunted skill of her **wise counselors** and statesmanship of her **princes** has come to nothing. **Zoan** is believed to be a later name for the city called Rameses at the time of the Exodus (cf. Exod. 12:37; see color map 4).

It is difficult to decide whether these judgments on Egypt belong to the period of Isa. Certainly he was much concerned with the unreliability of Egypt and with the danger to Judah of alliance with her (cf. chs. 20; 30-31). The language, however, is not characteristic of Isa. and is closely linked with that in chs. 40-66 and in Ezek.

19:16-25. *Conquest by Judah.* The theme of battle with Egypt is continued in this series of prose oracles. That a number of them speak of what will happen **in that day** indicates that we are dealing, not with precise historical moments, but with a prospect of the final age. It has been well suggested that these sayings are to be linked with the theme of conquest—the exodus ideas of conflict (vss. 11-15) being then appropriately followed by this series about a conquest of Egypt by **Judah** which will bring Egypt to salvation.

19:16-17. Egypt is in **terror** before Judah, just as the inhabitants of Canaan were in fear (cf. Josh. 2:9; 24:12). This judgment theme provides the link with the preceding poetry.

19:18. We are told of **five cities** in Egypt where Hebrew is spoken. It is often suggested that these were places where Jews had settled during the dispersion following 586. From the exilic period onward increasing numbers of Jews were to be found in Egypt. For the earlier period this is attested by the Elephantine Papyri from the 5th cent., which reveal the life of a small Jewish military force living on an island opposite Assuan (see color map 10). After Alexander the Great's conquest there were substantial settlements esp. in Alexandria.

Here one of the cities is given a name, but the text is problematic. If the theme is conquest, then it may be appropriate to recall the conquest of 5 cities of Canaan, including Jerusalem (Josh. 10), and see here a promise that all Egypt will **swear allegiance** to Yahweh. Perhaps this also explains the obscure name **City of the Sun,** a form attested by some manuscripts. An alternative is "City of Righteousness," a designation of Jerusalem (cf. 1:26). If this is the original, it may mean that one of the 5 Egyptian cities will become the Jerusalem of Egypt. On this hypothesis the text was subsequently modified to "City of the Sun," perhaps with an intended reference to Heliopolis, where a temple was built by a refugee high priest during the Maccabean period in the 2nd cent. B.C. An even later alteration designed to deny the propriety of this shrine might then produce the 3rd reading, "City of Destruction." But the whole question is obscure.

19:19-25. In the 3rd saying (vss. 19-22) Egypt turns to God and learns, like Israel in Canaan, by discipline and restoration the way of obedience and life. In the 4th (vs. 23) a still wider prospect is opened with the joining of Assyria to Egypt in the worship of God. In the 5th (vss. 24-25) the "conquest" is complete. Egypt is **my people** and Assyria is **the work of my hands,** while Israel retains a special place as **my heritage.**

To look for a specific situation for such words would be inappropriate; but it may well be that in the Greek period, when Jews found themselves between the power of the Ptolemies in Egypt and the Seleucids in Syria, an exegete of the "school of Isa." saw this rich promise extended even to the enemies of his people. Whatever the situation, the sayings testify to the deep concern for the outside world which can frequently be discerned in this book.

F. The Prophetic Sign of Egypt's Doom (20:1-6)

It is clear that this little narrative of a symbolic action performed by Isa. belongs, with such passages as ch. 7, to the biography of the prophet. But it has been placed here because of its concern with **Egypt,** and thus it provides a further comment on the material in chs. 18-19. It is set in the reign of the Assyrian **Sargon** II (722-705), who took **Ashdod** in 711, though rebellion had broken out in 713. The ruler placed on the throne of Ashdod by the Assyrians was deposed and a rebel put in his place. When the city fell this rebel escaped to **Ethiopia** but was extradited and returned to Sargon for punishment. The prophet, **naked and barefoot**—i.e. wearing only an undergarment or loincloth—portrays himself as a captive to show that the captivity of Egypt is decreed by God. Those who have relied on her help are put to shame. The people of the **coastland** of Philistia are left without hope of deliverance from Assyria.

G. The Prophet as Watchman (21:1-17)

The 3 sections of this ch. are all somewhat obscure, containing textual difficulties and problems of historical interpretation. The first 2 (vss. 1-10, 11-12) have probably been linked together because of the prophet's function as a **watchman,** waiting on God and ready to give men the message which is revealed to him (cf. Hab. 2:1). The 3rd passage too, as it now stands (vss. 13-17), emphasizes the prophet's role as spokesman of God, and it is therefore convenient to treat all 3 together while recognizing that they were originally separate and that

to make a sharp division at the end of the ch. is probably not entirely satisfactory.

21:1-10. The Fall of Babylon. The heading in vs. 1 is obscure, possibly because the text is corrupt, though it may be that the **wilderness of the sea** refers to the area to which Babylon belongs. What is most remarkable is the expression of the prophetic experience in these vss. Just as Micah agonizes at the fate of his people (Mic. 1:8), so this unknown prophet vividly expresses his **anguish** at the disaster he foresees. He portrays the complacency of those who are doomed and yet **eat** and **drink** when they should be alert (vs. 5)—a picture which strongly suggests a connection with the elaborate description of Belshazzar's feast in Dan. 5. The prophet, apparently in Jerusalem, foresees the coming of the message of Babylon's downfall and is able to **announce** to his people the word which has come from God.

The most probable occasion for this prophecy is the fall of Babylon to Cyrus of Persia in 539, though some could have argued that it could refer to the Assyrian conquest of Babylon in Isa.'s own time. But the situation of the prophet's own people (cf. vs. 10a) suggests rather the hope of release from the burden of Babylonian rule. That the prophet should be in a state of anguish at such an event is perhaps to be understood as an expression of the overpowering nature of the divine word, together with the uncertainty which must attend the overthrow of one great power by another.

21:11-17. Oracles Concerning Edom and Arabia. The brief, probably fragmentary, oracle on **Dumah** (vss. 11-12) evidently refers to Edom (see color map 7). Its brevity makes interpretation very uncertain, though it may be an expression of the prophet's concern at the darkness of disaster in Edom and a hope that the **morning** light of deliverance will soon come. The oracle on **Arabia** (vss. 13-17) consists of a poetic saying apparently expressing concern for **Dedanites** who have fled to **Tema** (see color map 7) after a defeat and a prose saying which applies the oracle to a disaster to come upon **Kedar.** In both of these oracles there appears an element of sympathy for non-Judean sufferers.

H. Judah in the Time of Hezekiah (22:1-25)

It is not unreasonable to suppose that all the different elements of this ch. are related to the situation in Judah when Sennacherib invaded the country and for a time Jerusalem was threatened (cf. chs. 36-37); but this is clearer for some parts than for others, which seem to fit a later time better. The obscure title, **valley of vision,** is derived presumably from vs. 5.

22:1b-4. Unjustified Rejoicing. This first part can be understood as referring to Sennacherib's withdrawal, but it must be recognized that the detail does not altogether fit. Rejoicing at deliverance would seem appropriate to that occasion, but the loss of the **rulers** of the city appears out of place. This may be an oracle relevant to the capture of Jerusalem in 597, when those who remained might rejoice but had lost king and leaders. The prophet sees more deeply the nature of the disaster to his people.

22:5-8a. A Day of Confusion. Appropriate to 597 too is this 2nd section, where the description of the disaster in terms of the day of Yahweh fits well with the understanding of that later period, when the words of Isa. were reapplied (see above on 2:6–4:6). The oracle could be of earlier origin and could have been reused in this new context. **Elam,** E of Babylonia (see color map 9), was allied with Merodach-baladan (cf. 39:1) in revolt against Assyria in the time of Hezekiah but may have supplied troops to Nebuchadnezzar in 597. "Aram rode on horses" may be suggested for **with chariots and horsemen,** perhaps referring to Arameans from the region of **Kir,** which was probably in Mesopotamia (cf. II Kings 16:9; Amos 1:5; 9:7).

22:8b-11. *Defenses of the City.* The interpretation of the preceding passages as coming from the period of Hezekiah is really due to this portion, apparently in prose. It describes the lack of faith of those in Isa.'s own time who pay heed to the city's material defenses but not to the purposes of the God who decreed the events now taking place. Such a comment could apply to Ahaz as well as to Hezekiah, but the reference to the **reservoir** seems to point to the latter (cf. II Kings 20:20).

22:12-14. *Revelry in the Face of Doom.* Closely connected is this oracle, which seems to indicate the same kind of situation as in vss. 1-4. The people should see in their present position a summons to **mourning,** but their reaction is superficial. This would fit the period of Hezekiah, but also the days after the capture of Jerusalem in 597.

22:15-25. *Pronouncement Against Shebna.* This utterance provides the clear indication of a historical setting, and is perhaps the basis for the interpretation of the whole ch. The section should be headed "Concerning Shebna," words which have now been wrongly inserted in the middle of vs. 15. The officer **over the household** (lit. "house," i.e. "palace"; cf. I Kings 4:6) was one of the important royal officers. He is condemned here for wrong ambition, building himself a **tomb,** possibly on Zion, and evidently having his own **chariots.** He is condemned to exile in a **wide land,** i.e. flat open country, and is to be deposed from his office.

22:20-23. Shebna's replacement by **Eliakim** seems to be borne out by 36:3, 22; 37:2, where we find Eliakim "over the household" and Shebna "secretary." Was Shebna then simply demoted, or are there other events of which we know nothing? Perhaps behind these events there lie the complex political rivalries of a period when appeal to Egypt was in the air; the sharpness of Isa.'s attack suggests direct opposition to what he believed to be right.

22:24-25. These last vss. contain yet another element, an obscure reference to the danger which threatens Eliakim. The whole section gives insight into Isa.'s intimate concern with the political problems of his day and his judgment on the politicians who lead his people astray (cf. chs. 30–31).

III. Oracle Against Phoenicia (23:1-18)

The poem in vss. 1-12 is headed **oracle concerning Tyre,** but it is clear that it refers to the whole area. Since in the Hebrew **Tyre** does not appear in vs. 1c, we may see a structure in which vss. 1-4 speak of **Sidon,** vss. 6-9 of **Tyre,** and vss. 10-12 of

Canaan (i.e. Phoenicia). The application to Tyre alone may well be due to later reinterpretation.

23:1-14. *Ruin of the Sea Trade.* The text is difficult at many points, but the judgment of Phoenicia and the lament over it are clear. The whole area is pictured as **laid waste,** the lament being attributed esp. to the merchant **ships** on which Phoenicia depends. Vs. 4 perhaps suggests the idea of the **sea** as mother of the people, and vs. 10 may be emended to read: "Cultivate your land (as is done by the Nile)," suggesting the total loss of seafaring activities. The disaster is seen as resulting from God's decree; the wealth of the **merchants** avails nothing (cf. Ezek. 27). On **Tarshish** see comment on Jonah 1:3. News of the disaster reaches the seamen when they stop at **Cyprus** (see color map 10) on the homeward voyage. The **Shihor** was in NE Egypt, perhaps the E arm of the Nile delta.

23:13. It is likely that the poem originally referred to some event in the Assyrian period, for the obscure wording of this verse most probably indicates a reinterpretation to the 13-year siege of Tyre by Nebuchadnezzar in the 6th cent.—the **Chaldeans,** i.e. Babylonians, **not Assyria,** did it. The detail of the vs. makes the description more precise.

23:15-18. *The Recovery of Tyre.* Perhaps at a still later stage the poem was again reapplied, this time to Alexander the Great's destruction of Tyre and its revival in the 3rd cent. Like a forgotten **harlot** the city seeks to win back her lovers. After **seventy years** of judgment—like the period foretold by Jeremiah for Judah (Jer. 25:12; 29:10)—Tyre will recover. But the final word is of the dedication of her wealth to God, part of the tribute of the nations (cf. 61:6). Tyre too will have her place in God's ordering of the world; her merchandise will be a blessing to God's people.

IV. The Last Days (24:1–27:13)

Appropriately enough, the foreign-nation oracles of chs. 13–23 are followed by a section which pictures the final age, the moment of judgment of the whole world and of the fulfillment of promise. Here is expressed more fully an element not infrequently found in judgment oracles on the nations: the setting of what is said about a particular people in the context of the expectation of total judgment and often also of final promise. The whole world is to be brought fully under the divine will, and this involves both the condemnation of failure and the expression of saving power. The establishment of Zion as central to a newly ordered world is the expression of confidence that it is God alone who will reign supreme.

Here are many of the elements subsequently developed in the apocalyptic writings of the last 2 cents. B.C. and the first cent. A.D., of which parts of Dan. and Rev. provide clear examples (see "The Apocalyptic Literature," pp. 1106-09). But these chs. are not apocalyptic; they contain a combination of prophetic and hymnic elements in which the final age is spoken of and the victory of God is acclaimed. These themes run through the whole section, and it is impossible to be certain of the right method of division. One passage links to another as the unknown prophet or prophets and the psalmists combine to express the awe and the joy of anticipating the ultimate purposes of God.

A. The World Judgment (24:1-20)

This passage begins and ends with the total overthrow of the earth. It is completely devastated, and vs. 2 indicates that there will be no escape; no privilege or position will avail to deliver any from the disaster.

24:4-13. Desolation of the Earth. The disaster is portrayed in more detail, and the reason for the judgment is brought out as man's failure. The breaking of the **everlasting covenant**—not here the one with Israel, but in a broader sense the covenant of right relationship between all men and God—(cf. Gen. 9:17) leads to the pronouncing of a **curse,** or rather an oath which is effectual in judgment when it meets with disobedience (cf. Zech. 5:1-4). **Mirth** and festival come to an end, **city** and land are desolate, and the desolation is as complete and final as a harvest (vs. 13, cf. 17:6). There are some obscurities in the text. In vs. 4 the last clause means lit. "the exalted of earth's people languish" and this may be correct; alternatively, omitting "people," we may render "the heights of the earth." In vs. 6 "are appalled" is possible as an alternative to **suffer for their guilt,** and for **scorched** we may substitute "weak." The reference to the **city of chaos** in vs. 10 is obscure. Attempts have been made to identify the city, but perhaps it is not intended to denote a particular place, but rather to give a general picture of the overthrow of city life, a return to anarchy and chaos. The phrase **reached its eventide** in vs. 11 is very improbable; "passed away" is a likely correction.

24:14-20. Joy and Anguish of Final Judgment. The moment of final judgment is one of **praise** at the **majesty** of God (vss. 14-16b). Throughout the earth the faithful welcome his glorious activity. The capital letters for **Righteous One** in vs. 16 are not necessarily correct; the phrase may refer to the righteous ones who share in the new age. For the prophet, however, the moment of judgment is a moment of anguish (vs. 16c-f), and this ushers in a new and even more cataclysmic picture of the disaster. Three alliterative words (vs. 17a)—a possible equivalent would be "panic, pit, petard"—suggest the inescapable doom. The whole universe is **shaken.** The **windows of heaven** and the **foundations of the earth,** i.e. the pillars on which it was thought to stand, refer to ancient mythological notions about the created order. The picture ends in utter ruin (vss. 16c-20).

B. Yahweh's Feast for the Nations (24:21–26:6)

Though the various elements in this section are not all precisely linked to the theme of the feast for the nations, this seems to be the central moment.

24:21-23. Judgment of the Host of Heaven. The expected judgment is extended to the heavenly sphere. The **host of heaven** itself is doomed along with the **kings of the earth.** A comparison might be made with Ps. 82 (see comment), esp. if here, as there, the thought is present of the heavenly beings as rulers of the nations (cf. also Dan. 10:13-14; see comment; see also Intro. to Deut.). **They will be gathered** with the kings who should maintain justice and held **in a prison** until the day of punishment arrives, just as the monsters subdued by Marduk in the Babylonian creation story were kept under guard. This theme was later taken up by the apocalyptists (cf. Jude 6). God is established as supreme ruler on **Mount Zion.**

25:1-5. A Ps. of Praise. The prospect of God's victory evokes a ps. of praise in which the references are not to particular cities or powers but to the hostile forces of the world. In vs. 1 a different division improves the sense: "thou hast made wonderful counsels, faithful and sure from afar [or "of old"]." **The aliens** (vs. 2) should probably be read as "the presumptuous." It is they who are brought low, and the **poor** and **needy,** the afflicted people of God, are raised and protected (cf. Luke 1:46-55). In vs. 4 "winter storm" is to be preferred to **storm against a wall.**

25:6-9. The Feast. Like a king holding his coronation feast, **the LORD of hosts** gathers the nations on Mt. Zion for a rich feast, with the **wine** fully matured. The **veil** of mourning is removed, the hostile power is overthrown (**death** here, perhaps reminiscent of the Canaanite deity Mot—the word which in Hebrew means "death"—is to be understood as the power which works for weakness and destruction), **tears** are wiped away, and the hostility expressed toward God's people is removed. To this prospect the answer **on that day** will be a confession of faith and of rejoicing at God's saving power.

25:10-12. Doom for Moab. Rather strangely the rejoicing is interrupted here by a word of doom for Moab, though vs. 10a may belong with vs. 9, and it has been suggested that "enemy" should be read for **Moab,** thus continuing the theme of general judgment. But the passage appears to contain some allusions to the Moab oracles of chs. 15–16, and perhaps here Moab is to be taken as a typical enemy. The text is not altogether clear. Vs. 10c could be read "in the waters [slime] of the dung-pit," so that the same picture is continued in vs. 11, but there is no reason why 2 entirely different pictures should not be used, that of **straw** being trampled down and that of a man struggling **to swim.** The last phrase of vs. 11 is difficult; perhaps "the arrogance of his boasts" might be read with an allusion to 16:6.

26:1-6. A Ps. of Confidence. The section ends with another **song,** expressing like Ps. 46 confidence in the strength of Zion, established by God, and like Ps. 24 proclaiming the opening of the **gates,** here for the **righteous nation.** The **peace** of the **righteous** who **trust** in God is contrasted with the downfall of the proud. Here as in 25:1-5 the lowly are raised in the reversal of fortunes in the final age. The confidence of the people of God is in him who is their eternal **rock,** and this assurance is significant in a passage which describes world-shattering events. To the one who trusts in God there is no eventuality, not even the overthrow of the world order in which he lives, which will find him lacking in the deepest security of faith.

C. The Prayer of Confidence in God (26:7–27:1)

26:7-10. The Rewards of Obedience. The prayer, close in form to the pss. of lamentation, begins with reflection in the wisdom style on obedience and its reward, the counterpart of the confidence which waits for God's action, confident that the **name** of God (vs. 8), his very nature, is the sure promise of his saving action. The theme of obedience and disobedience continues (vss. 9-10; for **within me** read "in the morning") with the reflection that even when God reveals his **judgments** "like light" (so rather than **for when**) men may **learn** but the **wicked** do not see.

26:11-15. *An Appeal for God's Action.* The reflection is broken across by an appeal for action, for the revealing of God's will toward his people so that the wicked may now **see** (vss. 11-12). The basis of this confidence in God's action is the experience of Israel's history. It is in God **alone** that Israel rests, though **other lords** have **ruled** over her (vs. 13). The reference may be to alien rulers, but more probably it is to evil supernatural powers, which now are seen to be **dead** with no hope of restoration to life (vs. 14; cf. 24:21-23; Ps. 82). Furthermore it is God who has shown protection to his people, giving them increase of numbers and enlargement of territory (vs. 15).

26:16-19. *Hope for the Future.* The theme of **distress** and the petition for help return. The text of vs. 16 is probably corrupt, and perhaps should be emended to read: "O Lord, in distress we sought thee; we were distressed at the oppression of thy chastening." God's protection seems to have been of no avail, for the state of depression remains long with his people (vss. 17-18). But God will act to give life. Unlike the alien powers which have died and will not return to life, God's people **shall live.** The imperative forms of vs. 19*b* should be read as indicatives, "shall awake and sing," with the Dead Sea manuscript and the LXX. Just as Ezek. 37:1-14 depicts the restoration to life of the people, dead in exile, so here the hope of the future is proclaimed. It is less likely that there is here the idea of actual resurrection for members of the community.

26:20–27:1. *The Final Battle.* These vss. point again to the period of waiting for the great deliverance. The day of divine judgment is at hand and the people are exhorted to wait in patience, to **hide** until the moment of **wrath** is over. Judgment will be on all the **earth,** and all **blood** will be avenged. **In that day** the whole power of evil will be overthrown, and this upheaval is depicted in a final battle between God and the power of chaos, described as **Leviathan—fleeing serpent, . . . twisting serpent**—and as the sea **dragon** (see comment on Ps. 74:12-14), all terms which are used similarly in the Canaanite Ras Shamra texts. Thus the prayer of confidence is justified, and the prospect of the final victory of God over evil assured.

D. God's People in the New Age (27:2-13)

Three separate elements make up this passage, but though unrelated they form a pattern.

27:2-6. *The Vineyard Song.* The first may be regarded as an exposition of the vineyard song of 5:1-5. God appears as the **keeper** of his people, warding off all dangers. The **thorns and briers,** which in ch. 5 were expressions of judgment on Judah, are here symbols of the hostile forces from

which the people are now protected. Vs. 4 would read better as: "If there were thorns and briers, in battle I would set out," and vs. 5: "Or they should seek protection with me"—the enemies must acknowledge God's power. The new people of God spreads out into all the world.

27:7-11. *Words of Judgment.* The hopeful prospect is interrupted by sayings speaking again of judgment. Vs. 7 suggests that Israel has not been judged as harshly as might be expected. Vs. 8 should perhaps begin: "By scaring away, by exile." **Guilt** must be removed by the repudiation of all idolatrous practice (on **Asherim** see I Kings 14:15). The **city**—presumably Jerusalem—is judged, and the maker of Israel will show no **compassion.** Perhaps such words of gloom, which contrast sadly with the passages before and after, were inserted later from some other context. But they have an appropriate place here, for they provide a warning such as is to be found e.g. in Zech. 7–8. The coming of the final age is sure, since God has decreed it; but its coming may be delayed by man's failure, and the **people** of God are here in effect warned not to delay the hoped-for day of salvation.

27:12-13. *The Gathering of Israel.* The passage culminates in 2 short sayings concentrating on the

Courtesy of Herbert G. May

Threshing grain, a scene recalling the words of Isa. 27:12: ". . . the Lord will thresh out the grain, and you will be gathered one by one . . ."

gathering of Israel. The first (vs. 12) speaks of the ideal extent of Israel's territory, from the **Euphrates River** in the N to the **Brook of Egypt,** a seasonal stream *ca.* 50 miles SW of Gaza (see color map 4). One might compare the commission of Ezra to impose the law on all those in the province Beyond the River who regard themselves as belonging to the community (Ezra 7:25). In the 2nd saying (vs. 13) **Assyria** and **Egypt** are conventional expressions for the place of exile. All who belong are gathered to the **holy mountain at Jerusalem,** and thus the whole section chs. 24–27 ends with the vision of a renewed and united people in the place where God himself reigns as supreme Lord (cf. 24:23).

V. THE 2ND COLLECTION (28:1–35:10)

A. THE WORD OF LIFE AND THE WORD OF DEATH (28:1-29)

As this ch. now stands, various elements—some earlier and some later—are woven together into a complex whole.

28:1-6. *Judgment of Samaria.* At the outset there is a reminder of the fate which overtook the leaders of Samaria, drunken and arrogant, in the disaster of 722. The remnant of the old N kingdom, consisting of little more than the city of Samaria itself, was brought low by the coming of the Assyrians as the instrument of divine justice. The garlanded **drunkards,** like the **glorious** city, must fall. **Of the rich valley** in vs. 1c probably should be omitted as an intrusion from vs. 4b, though an alternate suggestion is that **of those overcome with wine** should follow vs. 1a. In vss. 5-6 a later exegetical comment speaks of the true **crown of glory** which rests in the **justice** and **strength** that God himself establishes. The word of judgment points to the promise of the **remnant.**

28:7-13. *Oracle Against Judah's Religious Leaders.* But just as the leaders of Samaria failed, so too do the leaders of Judah. First we are shown **priest** and **prophet** drunkenly engaged in a religious celebration, unable to deliver the true message to the people. They mock at the prophet who proclaims their doom, likening him to one who teaches the alphabet to children—the words translated **precept** and **line** (vs. 10) are perhaps best understood as representing such sounds, *tsawletsaw tsawletsaw qawleqaw qawleqaw.* But what to these leaders is unintelligible is the decree of God, and it will be an **alien tongue** that will tell it to them, i.e. a foreign conqueror. They have refused to **hear** the message of well-being, and this refusal turns the **word of the LORD** from blessing to doom. The word of life becomes a word of death.

28:14-22. *Failure of Political Leaders.* Next their rulers are described as mockers, and it may be that this verbal link has led to the placing of this utterance here. The rulers in Jerusalem live in false security, unafraid of the threatened disaster. The prophet mockingly puts into their mouths words descriptive of their real position. They think themselves secure, but their **covenant** is **with death** (on **Sheol** see comment on Ps. 6:4-5). It is with **falsehood,** and their place of **refuge** is in **lies.** We cannot be sure whether this reference is to alien religious practice and trust in alien gods—esp., as has been suggested, a god of the underworld—or to political intrigue, which links more closely with the content of the succeeding chs. concerning false trust in Egypt. The **overwhelming scourge,** or "flood," i.e. Assyria (cf. 8:7-8), will sweep them away. But again their false position is contrasted with true security. God himself offers freedom from fear, for the **cornerstone** laid by him on **Zion** means—perhaps was actually inscribed—that the man of faith will not be "alarmed" (rather than **in haste,** vs. 16; cf. 7:9). God will test men's response by the

standard of **justice** and **righteousness.** The **decree of destruction** (vs. 22) is relentless and inescapable. The series of pictures, a proverbial expression (vs. 20), an allusion to past personal intervention of God. (vs. 21; cf. II Sam. 5:20, 25), the emphasis on the strangeness of **his deed,** the reversal of his saving activity—all point to the absoluteness of his decision.

28:23-29. *Proverbs of the Farmer.* Two concluding passages (vss. 23-26, 27-29) use proverbial material to make the whole point again. The farmer carries through his annual cycle of work, for it is God who **teaches him;** he deals rightly with the crops when they come, for it is God whose **wisdom** is **wonderful.** It may be that the prophet is here justifying the divine action; God orders the affairs of the whole world with the same wisdom as is shown in these natural procedures. Or more probably the prophet is here showing the nature of his own position; the problem of prophetic authority is raised by the mockery of his words (vss. 9-10), but the wisdom which guides the farmer is also that which guides the prophet and directs his message.

B. DISASTER AND DELIVERANCE FOR JERUSALEM (29:1-24)

The various elements of this ch. are linked together by the concern for the fate of Jerusalem, both immediate and more remote.

29:1-4. *Jerusalem Brought Low.* The city of **David** is here described by the title **Ariel,** which possibly has original connections with the idea of the sacred mountain of God, but which subsequently came to mean an altar hearth. The title emphasizes the sacred character of this place where the cycle of religious celebrations continues (vs. 1), perhaps with the implication that it has become nothing but empty observance (cf. vs. 13). Disaster is impending; Ariel will be the altar hearth on which the victims will be her own inhabitants. The city will be besieged and brought low so that the **whisper** from her will be as from the grave.

29:5-8. *Overthrow and Deliverance of the City.* The exact relationship between the opening vss. and this passage is difficult to determine, and in part depends on the interpretation of vs. 5ab. The Hebrew text refers here to "strangers," and this is most often emended to **foes**—a very small change. But the Dead Sea manuscript and the LXX read "proud ones," which makes a good parallel to **ruthless.** This suggests that the picture of the overthrow of Jerusalem is being continued, her leaders and then immediately her whole life being shattered by the onslaught of God. It is also possible, however, that vss. 5-8 form a unit and are concerned with a coming miraculous deliverance. The theme of the onslaught of the nations on Jerusalem is one that appears not infrequently in prophecy (cf. Zech. 14) and in psalmody (cf. Ps. 2); the picture is esp. associated with the last days (cf. Ezek. 38–39), and the expectation of a miraculous deliverance is bound up with it. Though it is possible that there is here some allusion to the events of 701 (cf. chs. 36–37), it is most likely that the prophecy is to be taken as an elaboration of the day of Yahweh providing a counter to the doom oracle of the opening vss.

29:9-12. Blindness of the People. The theme of failure returns with an emphasis on the blindness of the people (cf. 6:9-10). The **eyes** are interpreted in a gloss as **prophets,** and the **heads** as **seers** (vs. 10). The theme is further elaborated in vss. 11-12 with a passage of prose exegesis indicating the futility of those who profess to be able to discern what is to happen.

29:13-16. Perfunctory Worship and Presumption. Two further indications of failure follow. In vss. 13-14 the disobedience is seen in the formality of a worship which is lacking in real feeling, a reverence for God which is without sincerity. Such is the people's insensitivity that when God again acts marvelously, as he acted in the Exodus (cf. Exod. 15:11), his people will not be able to understand and his marvel will be to them strange (cf. 28:21). **Woe** is invoked (vss. 15-16; cf. 5:18-20) on those who plan evil in secret, thinking that God does not see (cf. Ps. 14:1). Such is the disorder that the **clay** criticizes the **potter,** the artifact the one who made it.

29:17-24. Restoration of Israel. As so often in the prophetic books, the failure is answered by an assurance of divine action and an opening of eyes and ears to the reality of what takes place. In what may be a proverbial saying (vs. 17) the change of fortune is stressed, with allusion perhaps to the devastation which will precede restoration, or perhaps to the fall of Assyria and restoration of Israel, with the **Lebanon** image used as in 10:18, 33-34. The change of fortune brings the lowly to their rightful place, and the wicked are **cut off** (vss. 18-21). The theme is reiterated (vss. 22-24) with an allusion to the redemption of **Abraham**—which appears as a motif in late, postbiblical literature—and there is assurance of a restoring of the right relationship between people and God, with the erring brought to a proper **understanding** of his ways.

The variegated pattern within the ch. turns attention again and again to the historical situation in which Isa. was at work and the realities of his people's failure. But in its elaboration within the prophetic tradition it points beyond that situation to show the continued relevance of his message in relation both to subsequent failures and to the final triumph of the purposes of God.

C. Mistrust and Trust (30:1-33)

It is clear that the various oracles gathered in this ch. are not all of one period, nor is it likely that they all derive from Isa. Yet from different points they converge on the one theme: there are certain ways of behaving which deny faith in God, but God is not only waiting to be gracious (vs. 18); he brings into being the conditions for obedience and trust.

30:1-7. Judah's Lack of Trust. The theme begins within the political situation of Hezekiah's reign, esp. in the period 705-701, when appeal to Egypt for help was a characteristic element in Judean policy. The rebellion of Judah is seen as lack of trust. The leaders make a **plan** and "weave a web of intrigue" (so perhaps instead of **make a league,** vs. 1). They turn to Egypt for **refuge** and **shelter**—terms often used by the psalmists as expressions of the intimacy of relationship to God (cf. e.g. Pss. 46; 121).

Vs. 4 is not clear, but a reasonable interpretation seems to be that the Ethiopian pharaoh who united Egypt *ca.* 710 welcomes the Judean representatives through his **officials** at **Zoan** in the Delta area (see above on 19:11-15) and send special **envoys** from his S capital to meet them at **Hanes** on the border between upper and lower Egypt. Nevertheless this false trust results in **shame** rather than **help.**

30:6-7. The thought is amplified in these vss. headed **oracle on the beasts of the Negeb**—the arid, sparsely settled S part of Judah (see color map 1). The curious title is perhaps imitated from chs. 13-23 but may be a textual corruption; "They carry through the heat of the Negeb" has been suggested. The Judean negotiators are pictured transporting gifts to Egypt through this desolate region. But the real point comes in vs. 7 with its description of Egypt as **Rahab**—one of the names given to the chaos monster of Near Eastern mythology that was overcome by God in Creation (cf. 51:9; Ps. 87:4). The text as it stands suggests the impotence of this monster, but it is probable that the original read "Rahab that is subdued." The metaphor of the overthrow of chaos to indicate the overthrow of hostile powers and esp. Egypt is appropriate, but here it is given a twist to indicate that this power of Egypt is useless. She cannot resist God's power, nor can she help those who so foolishly trust in her.

30:8-17. Vindication of the Prophet. This oracle appears to deal with a different aspect of Judah's failure. The rebellion is described as involving **oppression** (vs. 12) and the downfall is indicated as inevitable. It will be an utter destruction, leaving **fragments** so small as to be useless (vs. 14). But there is a relationship of thought in 2 features. (*a*) The prophet is commanded to **write** a message (see "Writing in Biblical Times," pp. 1201-08) which will **witness** against the disobedient (vs. 8). It is not clear what he is to write, and the change of content suggests that we should not look back to the preceding vss. to find the answer. The thought is close to that of 8:1-4, 16; the prophet's word will prevail, and then his people will know. (*b*) The prophet's position is made clear, for his contemporaries are unwilling to hear. Isa. and those who, like him, proclaim the will of the **Holy One** (vs. 11) are unable to gain a hearing, but this will not prevent the carrying through of the divine purpose. There is a reminder here that Isa. is not alone in his interpretation of the events of his time.

30:15-17. These vss. return to the theme of political folly and lack of trust. Such mistrust leads to total disaster, for there is little to suggest real survival here. It is possible that the saying of vs. 15*b* should be emended so as to make even clearer the political aspects of the matter: "In turning back [i.e. avoiding warfare] and keeping the treaty [i.e. of subservience to Assyria; the same word as "league" in 7:2] you will be saved." The obverse of this is true **trust** in God.

30:18-33. The Graciousness of God. The insistence on trust leads appropriately to the recognition of God's continued willingness **to be gracious,** and it is this theme that is elaborated in this series of sayings from a later time, in poetry and prose. To the depressed community of Jerusalem—probably in the exilic period—the confidence of the prophet speaks afresh of the way in which God as **Teacher** of his people will reveal himself. They will not be permitted to **turn** aside from their true **way.** The direct contact with him will be accompanied by the complete repudiation of all idolatrous practice.

30:23-26. The whole land will be blessed, in renewed prosperity, in the blessings of plenty so that the best fodder is there for the domestic animals, and in abundant **water** when judgment is brought on the nations. Miraculously there will come a day of brightness, a day of healing after the moment of judgment.

30:27-28. The theme of judgment of the nations, which is the other side to God's deliverance and blessing of his people, is reintroduced in a vivid picture of the **name,** i.e. the person, of God coming from his secret place to bring about his purpose.

30:29-33. The theme of judgment is applied specifically to the overthrow of the **Assyrians,** suggesting the possibility that an oracle of Isa., like those in ch. 10, has been elaborated into a more general statement of the fulfilling of the divine purpose among the nations. The coming of that day will be as the preparation for a great and **holy feast** (vs. 29), and those who are opposed to the divine will are to be destroyed in a fire like that which burns in the valley of Topheth on the S side of Jerusalem (cf. Jer. 7:32; see comment on Jer. 19:1-5).

The theme of trust issues in this confidence of the ultimate fulfilling of the divine will. As often in the prophetic books, it is in terms of destruction of the hostile nations, yet it is clear from the use of the name Rahab for Egypt that the passage looks beyond immediate historical situations to the overthrow of all evil at the hand of God. There is here material of the kind of which later apocalyptic (see above on 24:1–27:13) was to be made, with its absolute confidence in the midst of situations of despair that the final victory of God is assured.

D. THE WAY OF DEATH AND THE WAY OF LIFE (31:1–32:20)

Another oracle, like 30:1-5, dealing with the folly of relying on Egyptian help in the period of Hezekiah (705-701) provides, as in ch. 30, an intro. to a series of interrelated oracles of judgment, warning, and promise, not all of one period. The series provides a 2-fold presentation of the message that faith leads to life but lack of faith leads to disaster.

31:1-3. *Impotence of Egypt.* The outlook of those who turn to Egypt is ridiculed. They do not recognize where real help lies because they fail to see that no substantial help can come from Egypt. It is God who is the truly **wise** (vs. 2), and he will bring judgment. Those who fail to look to him but turn elsewhere for assurance will soon discover that those in whom they trust are nothing but **men.** The overtones of vs. 3 seem to point to the folly of political alliance with Egypt as just like the folly of trusting in other gods which have no reality, a theme taken up in vss. 6-7. The false trust in **chariots** and **horses** (vs. 1) is also reminiscent of the Assyrian taunt in 36:8 which ridicules Judah for having no riders even if horses should be given them. The whole basis of Isa.'s argument is his conviction that it is faith which counts; without faith there is **disaster.**

31:4-5. *God's Protection of Jerusalem.* The counter to this is provided here. Though the picture of God as a **lion** undeterred by the shouting of the **shepherds** is a strange way of expressing the idea of divine protection, clearly this must be the meaning of both this simile and that of the **hovering** bird. It is conceivable that the lion picture originally referred to the futility of expecting Egyptian power to frighten away the ravaging Assyrian lion. The stress is clear now: it is God and God alone who can save Jerusalem.

31:6-9. *Jerusalem's Special Significance.* The emphasis above leads into this appeal and statement of assurance. Judah must repudiate her idolatry; this is the prerequisite of real trust. The judgment of God will fall on Assyria. It is not by human agency but by the very presence of God himself, who is as **fire** in Jerusalem, that the Assyrian will be overthrown. The thought of judgment on Assyria, which appears in ch. 10 and elsewhere, is here given a larger setting as it is recognized that Jerusalem has a special significance in God's work; it is the center of his activity in judgment.

32:1-8. *Establishment of Righteous Rule.* Though this ch. begins a new theme, there is a link in this thought of judgment from Jerusalem. The presence of God means judgment for the nations; it means the establishment of **righteousness.** In language which is more reminiscent of the wisdom literature (esp. vss. 6-8) than of the royal oracles of chs. 9; 11, the possibility of a new and right ordering of society is set forth in terms of just rulers and judges. In vs. 1 we might render: "If a king reigns . . . , if princes rule" (cf. Eccl. 10:16-17). The condition of the people as Isa. saw them can be changed (cf. vs. 3 with 6:10—there appears to be an element of reinterpretation of the Isa. saying). Right standards and a right ordering of society will follow from wise rule and the establishment of **justice.**

32:9-14. *Judgment of Women.* By contrast these vss. take us back to the picture of judgment. The women of the land (cf. 3:16–4:1) may rejoice now in the **harvest** but soon there will be deprivation. Complacency will give place to lament as the land is desolate. **City** and land are destroyed, and the ultimate end is a gloom as deep as that of Isa.'s temple vision (6:11).

32:15-20. *Promise of a New Age.* The section is rounded off here with a renewal of the promise that in a new age, when the divine **Spirit** is **poured** out on men, there will be renewal of the land. **Righteousness** will bring prosperity, and there will be security. Vs. 19 appears to be an odd line wrongly inserted at this point; its text is corrupt and it may well be a fragment. It is possible that the section should end at vs. 18, and that vs. 20 should be regarded as the beginning of a new section.

Thus again the interaction of 2 aspects of the prophetic message may be seen. The words of Isa., elaborated and reinterpreted by his successors, point to the reality of divine power and the rightness of true faith. It is here that there is a way to life, and the warnings given by Isa. to his contemporaries serve as a continuing reminder that life is to be found where **justice** is established and that the source of that justice is in the working of the Spirit of God.

E. Distress and Deliverance (33:1-24)

The often problematic text of this ch. leaves us in uncertainty about its precise meaning at many points and also makes difficult any entirely satisfactory decision as to how it is to be divided into sections. But just as the first Isa. collection is concluded with a series of ps. passages (cf. chs. 11–12), so here the collection covering chs. 28–32 is followed by what may be a group of passages linked together in a liturgical structure. Its theme is lamentation and appeal on the one hand and confidence in divine deliverance on the other.

33:1-6. *Woe to the Destroyer.* The opening pronouncement of woe on a destroying power (vs. 1) consists of a series of repetitive and punning phrases in which the themes of destruction and treachery are interwoven. It may perhaps be viewed as a counterpart to the blessing in 32:20 (see comment), but it may simply be that the attaching of the woe was occasioned by the previous blessing (cf. Luke 6:20-26). If the woe is Isa.'s it may refer to Assyria, but there is no clue to such an identity in the pronouncement.

33:2-6. Vs. 2 begins like a ps., appealing to God in assurance of his power, and vss. 3-4 describe the terrors occasioned by his presence. This in turn leads into a confident confession of faith in the establishment of **Zion** as center of **justice** and right (vss. 5-6). Though the details of the text are not at every point clear, there is a significant recognition of the place of Jerusalem in God's purpose. It is possible that this short section is a "liturgy" in itself.

33:7-16. *A Lament and an Assurance.* Vss. 7-9 present a new theme of lamentation, describing the condition of the land in terms sometimes reminiscent of the Song of Deborah (Judg. 5) and sometimes of other prophetic passages. These may well be metaphors for general distress, and it would probably be wrong to look here for precise historical conditions. Vs. 7 is difficult to translate: "men of Ariel" (i.e. Jerusalem, see above on 29:1-4) has been suggested for **valiant ones,** and **envoys of peace** might mean "envoys of Salem" (i.e. Jerusalem). The places named in vs. 9 (see color map 8) were noted for their woodlands (cf. 35:2).

33:10-12. Assurance is given by God himself that he will take action. Perhaps addressing the hostile nations, he speaks of the disaster to them; he himself will bring **fire** on them (reading "my breath" in vs. 11).

33:13-16. A new element is found here, emphasizing the purification of Zion, a necessary preliminary to the establishment of a new and purified city (cf. ch. 1). The presence of God in judgment, a theme beloved by Isa. and perhaps here being elaborated by his successors, brings awe to the sinners. As in Pss. 15; 24 the conditions for dwelling with God are laid down in terms of right social action. The righteous will be established, their needs met.

33:17-24. *Restoration of Zion.* It is the purified Zion which is here portrayed. Its people look back on the **terror** of the past, the times of attack by hostile powers and alien nations (vss. 18-19, where the meaning is not so clear as the translation suggests). Jerusalem is portrayed as a place of security (cf. Ps. 46), but clearly there is no suggestion here

of a false trust in its very existence such as seems to have existed in the time of Jeremiah (cf. Jer. 7; 26). Jerusalem's security rests in the presence of God himself, and the picture of God as **judge** and **king** and savior (vs. 22) is carried further in vss. 23-24 with the assurance of well-being for all the people and the overcoming of all enemies (though here again the text is not altogether clear). The theme of the **rivers** of Jerusalem (cf. ch. 8; Ps. 46; Ezek. 47) is elaborated in vs. 21*cd* with what appears to be a rather literalistic statement about its invulnerability to attack by water; and in vs. 23 the same theme recurs, though here the picture of the ship becalmed, which presumably should refer to Jerusalem's enemies, is very loosely attached to the context.

The distresses of Isa.'s period may well provide the starting point for these oracles and psalmlike sayings. But the whole structure, like other liturgical passages in the prophets, points rather to a reinterpretation of Isa.'s message, a recognition of the wider significance of that saving power in which Isa.'s confidence always rested.

F. Judgment of the Nations (34:1-17)

Though there are precise references to **Edom** and to its city of **Bozrah** S of the Dead Sea (see color map 4) in vss. 5-6 (on vs. 9 see RSV footnote) the opening vss. are directed against **all the nations** and also against the **host of heaven** and the latter part of the ch. depicts a world returning to chaos (cf. Jer. 4:23-28). This suggests that an oracle against Edom has been elaborated into a message of total judgment on the nations of the world. Since in chs. 13–14 there is evidence to suggest that oracles against Assyria have been reapplied to Babylon, here too there may be material which originally had a different reference. Thus the phrases of vss. 9-17 need not refer to Edom but could be part of a poetic passage dealing with some other land. The whole ch. now forms a poem of vivid imagery, expressing the dire aspects of the day of Yahweh, but the variety of its references and of its metaphors suggests that it was not originally all of one piece.

The opposition of the world to God's will is here met with the outpouring of divine wrath; the attempt at frustrating his purposes in Zion makes it necessary to reaffirm that God will act **for the cause of Zion** (vs. 8). From the tone of the ch. it is not improper to see its deeper meaning in the conviction of the ultimate triumph of God in his righteousness, the overthrow of the powers of evil being decreed by him. There is in such a message a note of confidence which the great apocalyptists (see above on 24:1–27:13) were to share so intensely.

Thus Edom becomes a symbol of the hostile world (cf. 63:1-6), a symbol to which no doubt the historical conditions of the exilic period contributed, but which was based on a much earlier sense of opposition expressed in the ancient patriarchal traditions of Jacob and Esau.

34:1-8. *Call of the Nations to Judgment.* The symbolic nature of the references is made clear by the invocation to all **nations** to accept their judgment at the hand of God. With them are destroyed the heavens and their **host** (vs. 4), symbols of forces which so often in the OT came to be associated with idolatrous practice.

34:5-8. The vivid and gruesome pictures of vss. 5-7 introduce a quite different element. There is no longer the thought simply of a great battleground, with the slain left unburied. Now it is judgment in a ritual of **sacrifice,** the **sword** of God **sated with blood** and **fat.** Probably vs. 8 should be linked with this, indicating the setting of the Edom oracle in the larger context of the **day** of Yahweh.

34:9-17. Chaos and Desolation. A new series of pictures describes the overthrow of a land, which may or may not be Edom (vss. 9-12). It will return to **chaos,** the dwelling of wild birds—their identification is not certain, but the term translated **porcupine** (vs. 11) must denote some kind of bird. The land will lose its identity as a kingdom (vss. 11-12; **its nobles,** vs. 11*d,* actually the first word of vs. 12 in the Hebrew, is perhaps corrupt, the next phrase might mean "no kingdom shall be acclaimed there").

34:13-14. A different picture of chaos emerges here, referring to a number of **wild beasts,** including the **satyr,** perhaps simply the he-goat, and the **night hag,** a creature known as a storm demon but associated with the night because her name "Lilith" suggests the Hebrew word for night. It is not possible to tell where these terms are intended to describe actual creatures and where evil forces.

34:15-17. These vss. return to the pictures of wild birds occupying deserted buildings. Their occupation of the land is decreed **in the book of the LORD;** we need not ask what book is meant, for the real point is that **not one** of these wild creatures is **missing** because God has brought them in and apportioned the land. It is as if the allocation of the land of Canaan to Israel were here in reverse, and we may in fact wonder whether this last passage was not originally an oracle directed against Israel and its evils.

G. The Holy Road to Zion (35:1-10)

In striking contrast to the gloom of the preceding ch. there opens out here a vision of a new and restored land and a revived people. All that is evil is cast out, and the pilgrim exiles, redeemed from disaster, return in safety to Zion.

35:1-7. Israel Restored and Renewed. The land of Israel is transformed (vss. 1-2) and receives all the blessings which belong to **Lebanon** and to **Carmel and Sharon**—symbols of fertility (cf. 33:9). More still, it is the **glory** of God which is to be seen in the land. To those who lack faith (vss. 3-4) there is the reassurance of God's intervention. This theme is to be seen not only in the major part of chs. 40-55 but also e.g. in Hag. and Zech. Changed fortunes for all the distressed and still more complete change in the character of the land follow on this (vss. 6-7). The allocation of the land to wild beasts in 34:13-17 is here answered by the breaking forth of water and the wild land's becoming pasture. In vs. 6 we may add "shall flow" in the last phrase, following the Dead Sea manuscript. In vs. 7 **swamp** should probably read "cattle range," i.e. a pasture containing (so lit.) "grass with reeds and rushes."

35:8-10. The Holy Way. Most of all, this is the moment for the **return** of those who are scattered

abroad. Plainly this refers to the exilic situation, but it is a theme capable of wider interpretation, for the thought of coming back to Zion formed a strong binding force in the later Jewish community. The way to the sanctuary is open, and it is protected. They will come rejoicing to the worship of God, as in so many of the pss. (e.g. Ps. 122). The text of vs. 8*cd* is difficult; the RSV simply omits 4 words (see footnote), which perhaps should read "it shall be for his people as they journey."

The ch. provides a fitting conclusion to this collection of oracles. It belongs to a later date than Isa., and indeed its language and thought show such close linkages with chs. 40-55 that it may well belong to the same circle. Yet in the context in which it stands the ch. serves to draw together the various oracles of the preceding chs. which look forward to a great day of deliverance, a future of hope and blessing. If much, perhaps most, of this material is later than Isa., it nevertheless stands in his tradition, for it was his to see that true life depends on faith, and that the blessings which God intends for his people are real if only they will turn to him in trust and singleness of mind. At the same time this ch. points forward, beyond the historical chs. 36-39, into the next part of the book, to a people in exile and a prophet in the succession of Isa. who could speak to them with confidence of the divine power to save.

VI. Hezekiah and Assyria (36:1-39:8)

The text of these chs. is almost identical with that of II Kings 18:13-20:19 (see comment). The following points of difference and of special importance to the study of Isa. may be noted:

36:1-37:38. The Deliverance from Sennacherib. This section follows closely II Kings 18:13, 17-19:37, containing textual variants of some interest but not affecting the general sense. The omission of II Kings 18:14-16, which tells of Hezekiah's submission and payment of tribute is significant, for it gives the impression, even more than does Kings, that Judah at this time was released from the Assyrian yoke. The omission serves to emphasize the miraculous and complete deliverance of Judah. The picture of Isa. proclaiming this and condemning Assyrian pride has points in common with what may be seen in the previous chs.; but it is not identical, and we have to recognize here an alternative tradition which emphasizes one aspect of his teaching out of its overall context of divine judgment.

38:1-39:8. Hezekiah's Illness and Envoys from Babylon. The narrative of the king's illness cannot be precisely dated, but the visit of the ambassadors linked with it most probably belongs to the beginning of the reign of Sennacherib, i.e. shortly after 705.

38:7-8. The story of the sign of the sun's **shadow** (cf. II Kings 20:8-11) is shortened and in some confusion, its intro. being misplaced in vss. 21-22 and perhaps added later. It is significant that this narrative portrays Isa. as a messenger of healing, even prescribing the treatment (vs. 21); and some have suggested that he may have been a physician (cf. 1:5-6).

38:9-20. Added here is this ps. of thanksgiving for recovery (see intro. to Pss.), which incorporates

Clay tablet (prism) of the Assyrian King, Sennacherib, relating an account of his siege of Jerusalem

words of lamentation closely resembling those in the Psalter and in the speeches of Job. It shows how such psalmody was understood and used. The title (vs. 9) is similar to those of many pss.; **writing** (*miktab*) may be a miscopying of "Miktam," found in the titles of Pss. 56-60. The text is at many points difficult and uncertain (see RSV footnotes). On **Sheol** see comment on Ps. 6:4-5.

38:21-22. See above on vss. 7-8.

39:1-8. The story of the Babylonian ambassadors forms here an intro. to the 2nd part of the book, containing prophecies from the exilic age, and thus makes an important link between the 2 major divisions of a book which is nevertheless one.

VII. THE PROPHECIES OF 2ND ISA. (40:1–55:13)

The prophecy of exile in Babylon which brings to an end the first half of the book (39:6-7) provides a transition point to the contrasting message of 2nd Isa. (see Intro.) who stood in the succession

of Isa. and during the later years of the Babylonian exile set out his interpretation of the disaster and his understanding of restoration. It is convenient to divide his prophecies into 2 sections, chs. 40–48; 49–55, though the differences between the 2 parts are more apparent than real. The division between 2nd Isa. and what follows in chs. 56–66 is again not always quite so clear as has sometimes been claimed, for there are considerable parts of the latter section closely related to chs. 40–55. But the convention is reasonable, and the following commentary will show the recurrence of themes which bind the sections together.

A. FIRST COLLECTION OF 2ND ISA. (40:1–48:22)

40:1-11. *The Announcement of Salvation.* In sharp contrast to the main part of the message of Isa. the initial note of this opening passage of 2nd Isa. is of **comfort** and deliverance. In this he picks up the faith and confidence of Isa. in the power of the holy God of Israel, and in his situation of national distress it is this element which appears most clearly. The recognition of Israel's failure, however, is never far from his mind.

40:1-5. The opening words (vss. 1-2) transport us, though without any description, into the heavenly council (see comment on 6:1-3) and constitute the equivalent of a prophetic call narrative. The prophet overhears the word spoken by God, the reiteration of the covenant promise—**my people . . . your God** —the assurance that the "hard service" (rather than **warfare,** vs. 2; cf. RSV footnote) is over, **double** punishment for sin received. The Exile is God's judgment, and it is significant for the understanding of the prophet that his message should begin with the affirmation of this alongside his confidence in God's readiness to restore. The proceedings of the council continue as the command is given (vss. 3-5) to **prepare** a processional road through the **desert** for the appearing of God himself. The opening words of vs. 3 may also be rendered "Hark, one cries," but the effect is the same. The **glory** of God will be visible to **all flesh.** The nature of that appearing becomes plain in vss. 9-11.

40:6-8. This is as near as these prophecies come to a statement of prophetic call, though the matter is complicated by the divergence in the evidence for the text. **I said** (vs. 6*b*) has good textual grounds in the Dead Sea manuscript and the LXX, but the standard Hebrew text reads "he said." The absence of any other direct first-person statement in the prophecy appears to be sound reason for preferring the 3rd-person form here; but the argument is not entirely satisfying, for in other prophetic books first-person use is limited or absent. Prophetic experience may be expressed in both first- and 3rd-person forms (cf. Hos. 1; 3); whichever reading is preferred here, this may be regarded as the prophet's own reaction. Nor is it certain whether his response to the heavenly summons to proclaim a message is restricted to **What shall I cry?** Part or all of the next vss. may be included, for the material here is a kind of interpretation of **all flesh** in vs. 5. The revelation of the purpose of God meets with the established knowledge of the frailty of all men. Only the **word of our God** endures.

Courtesy of John C. Trever

The Isaiah Scroll, found in Cave I in the vicinity of Khirbet Qumran (Dead Sea Sect), opened to reveal Isa. 40; on the 2nd line of the column entirely visible are the words: "a voice cries: 'In the wilderness prepare the way of the Lord' "; three insertions by later scribes can be seen on the two cols.

40:9-11. Against this background the nature of the message is made clear. **Zion** herself is summoned to be the **herald** of good news to the surrounding **cities of Judah,** hailing the coming of God, who with his mighty **arm,** as in the exodus events, brings with him his rescued people, caring for them as a **shepherd** cares for **his flock.** All Judah, devastated through the years of exile—the archaeological evidence has made clear that for many of her cities the recovery from destruction was desperately slow—will now see God as he comes. **Reward** and **recompense** (vs. 10) may be variously interpreted, perhaps best as a reference to the people redeemed, but possibly in terms of the offering of compensation for the disasters of exile to those who have suffered.

All the essential elements of the prophet's message are here—his confidence in the presence and power of God to save, his recognition of the dependence of man on God and of the justice of the judgment which has fallen on God's people, his vision of the declaration of God's victory to all the world. Though the highly poetic and rhetorical language often makes it difficult to discern the man behind the poetry, there is a clear sense of his involvement both in the fortunes of his people and also in the message which he is required to give. He stands clearly in the prophetic line in this double sympathy.

40:12-31. *Creator and Sustainer.* Whether this passage is to be regarded as a unified poem or as various units originally separate, it is clear that there is a profound unity of thought. The idea of God as creator dominates. It is he alone who controls and sustains. Only he can order the life of the world, both of nature and of men, and there is none like him. The absoluteness of Israel's allegiance to the

one God which forms the basis of her relationship to him (cf. Exod. 20:2-3) is here reiterated as the basis for understanding her present position and the ground of her hope.

40:12-17. As in Job 38-41 questions are put by God to Job concerning his understanding of God's creative power, so here the absoluteness of his creating is stressed (vss. 12-14). Only he can order the world, and none can regulate his activities. The conception of divine counsel, which issues from God alone, is found further elaborated in Prov. 8; but there is no real contrast between the denial of any associate with God here and the expression of God's own activity in creating wisdom as the agent of his creation, for spirit and counsel and wisdom are expressions of God's action. By contrast the world and its peoples **are as nothing** (vss. 15-17); the absoluteness of his rule extends over all.

40:18-20. The OT often mocks at the absurdity of images, and stress is laid on the repudiation of any kind of portrayal of God. It is the counterpart of the absoluteness of allegiance, but it is also a significant theological statement, for the image as symbol very easily becomes the image as representation and as reality. Briefly here the activity of the image maker is mocked, for the image is nothing but a wooden core with a **gold** overlay. In ch. 44 an elaborate mocking passage is built on this basic thought. Vs. 20*a* is very obscure; most probably the 2 opening words of the Hebrew are glosses indicating the kind of wood commonly used and vs. 20*ab* originally was one line: "He chooses wood that will not rot."

40:21-26. By contrast God is enthroned **above . . . the earth.** From the earth's "founding"—so perhaps rather than **foundations** (vs. 21*c*)—he has been known as creator and overruler of the powers of the nations. In hymnic style the attributes of God are listed in terms of his activity and lead again into the question how God can possibly be described (vs. 25). He is recognizable in his creative and sustaining activity in relation to the whole world.

40:27-31. It is this last point, God as sustainer, which forms the natural bridge to the position of Israel. Oppressed by the experience of exile, thinking herself forgotten by God, aware of the pressures of Babylonian power and religion, she is fearful and lacking in trust (cf. Ezek. 37). But the God who is the creator and who is never weary in his creative activity is also the God whose power for men is inexhaustible. Those who look to him (cf. 25:9) will never be lacking in **strength.**

Israel as the people of God is set in the context of God's power. Her position of distress—a source of dismay to herself and of mockery to others who ask where the God is in whom she trusted—is seen now against the background of the promise of divine action. The movement of political events is the token of the new moment which is about to come.

41:1-29. The Nations in Court. It seems not unreasonable to treat the whole of this ch. together, though it contains a number of readily distinguishable units. It is also closely linked in thought with the chs. preceding and following by its general theme of God's action and the assurances which enable men to recognize what he is doing. At the beginning and end the historical situation is made plain, for though the name of Cyrus the Persian is not mentioned (cf. 44:28; 45:1) there is clear reference to the victorious and speedy campaigns in which he engaged. The nations and their gods are invited to speak; Israel is encouraged to have faith and hope.

41:1-4. The nations are summoned to the **judgment** seat and invited to comment on the events and to indicate who is responsible for them. The court scene is clear in vs. 1, though **renew their strength** appears to have the wrong sense; perhaps some such phrase as "wait for my rebuke" should be read. Vss. 2-3 allude to events well known to the exiles; they belong within a purpose declared from ancient times. Cyrus' tremendous victories are clear (for **tramples kings under foot,** vs. 2d, perhaps read "brings kings low") and the underlying purpose should be plain. This leads up to God's own affirmation of his place. It is alone who acts. The last phrase, **I am He,** frequent in 2nd Isa., strongly suggests an interpretation of the name Yahweh similar to that in Exod. 3:14.

41:5-7. But the events find the nations at a loss. All they can do is consult their idols and encourage one another in the belief that here the answer will be found. Vs. 5c should be taken with vs. 6; it thus further stresses the panic-stricken gathering. The passage anticipates vss. 21-24, where the gods of the nations are directly challenged.

41:8-10. For Israel, however, the situation is to be different. The assurance that it is God himself who acts and who is with Israel removes all cause for fear. This is demonstrated in the historic experience of Israel, from the call of **Abraham,** whom God loved, to the choosing of **Jacob.** The relationship is that of **servant** to master, but it is deeper than that since it is the result of divine choice, and

Courtesy of Herbert G. May

Threshing sledge (see comment 41:11-20)

it is upheld by the assurance that God will not reject. There may be a linkage of thought to the description of Abraham as servant in Gen. 26:24. More important is the recognition that in this term we begin to see something of what 2nd Isa. will be saying about the place of Israel in the divine purpose.

41:11-20. The assurance is continued in a series of 3 pictures: (a) The reversal of fortune (vss. 11-13). Israel, oppressed in exile, becomes the conqueror and her enemies vanish away. (b) The harvest (vss. 14-16). Israel threshes and winnows the **mountains,** herself the **threshing sledge** dragged with its sharp **teeth** across the grain. There is sharp contrast between **Jacob** the **worm** (for **men** in vs. 14b we should probably read "maggot" or "louse") and the strength of the mountains set against her. But the source of her new strength rests in God, **the Holy One,** who is **Redeemer,** i.e. the kinsman who protects and recovers the inheritance, as God did for Israel in the Exodus. (c) The change from barrenness to fertility (vss. 17-20; cf. ch. 35). The oppressed, seen as the **poor** looking for **water,** are promised deliverance and the barren lands are made fertile, so that it may become known to the world what God is like. It is noteworthy that each of these pictures culminates in the affirmation that it is God himself who acts, for all these are illustrations, side by side with the summons to Cyrus, by which Israel may know, and so too can the nations if they will pay heed.

41:21-24. The court scene is recalled with a more specific summons to the **gods** of the nations to **set forth your case,** to show understanding both of what has been and of **what is to come.** The test of a god's validity is his knowledge of events (cf. the test of a prophet in Deut. 18:21-22). The ruler of **Jacob** is the controller of history and hence he knows; the gods are **nothing** and bring disaster on those who look to them. For **be dismayed and terrified** (vs. 23d) the reading "hear and see" of the Dead Sea manuscript seems preferable. It seems clear that the prophet here looks to the coming of Cyrus and to the redemptive action of God as near at hand, representing the things to come, the new things (cf. 42:9). He looks back to the past and, standing as he does in the prophetic tradition, sees how the historic experience of Israel, recent and more remote, makes sense in the light of the revealed will of God.

41:25-29. As evidence for the reality of God and his controlling of history the summons to Cyrus is reiterated. It is God who **proclaimed** it, while the other gods could do nothing. He announced it first to **Zion** (vs. 27) for she could recognize what it meant. The Hebrew of vs. 27a (RSV footnote) is clearly corrupt. Perhaps it might better be emended to "First to Zion I give comfort." Cyrus is described here as one who **shall call on my name** (vs. 25b). The Cyrus cylinder, no doubt describing the campaigns of Cyrus for the benefit of Babylonians, depicts him as acknowledging Marduk as the god who summoned him. Ezra 1:2 (II Chr. 36:23) depicts him as acknowledging the God of the Jews as having charged him to build the Jerusalem temple. Both are propaganda statements, but the prophet here sees the whole context of the historical events as being the purpose of God. They witness to the reality of his purpose, and first Israel and then the nations must learn to read them aright so that they may come to the full understanding of what he is doing and to the acknowledgment of him as Lord.

42:1-18. God's Justice for the World. The previous ch. has appealed to the nations to recognize God. This passage goes on to show the way by which, through his people, his will is to be declared, his justice is to be established, and his light is to come to all nations.

42:1-4. This declaration of the agent by whom God's justice is to be established is closely similar to 41:8-10, and the parallel makes clear that the identifying of the **servant** with Israel by the LXX translators is the right one. **Uphold** (vs. 1a) should rather be "take hold" of Israel—to act, as was said of the true king in ch. 9, to establish justice. Though **justice** here, paralleled by **law** in vs. 4, is wider than any narrow legalistic conception, it is nevertheless not satisfactory to make it mean "religion," as is sometimes done, for it is clear from the following vss. that the establishing of the true rights of all men is envisaged. In fact vs. 2 may mean that because there will be no injustice "one will not cry" in distress. It has been suggested that vs. 3 refers to symbolic legal practices, but in any case it seems clear that the protection of the weak is in mind.

42:5-9. The initial statement of call is followed by this elaboration, where the creator God is shown stressing the nature and purpose of that calling. The message and saving action is to all **nations.** For **covenant to the people** (vs. 6) it may well be right to read "everlasting covenant" (cf. 55:3), the establishing of a new and permanent relationship between God and all men like that which exists between him and Israel. Vss. 8-9 remind the nations, as also Israel, that it is God alone who is to be praised (cf. 41:4); the gods of the nations have no power to **declare** the saving acts which are about to take place.

42:10-13. Fittingly enough, the declaration of God's sole right to be praised leads into this ps. of praise, where the remotest and most hostile places (see comment on 21:11-17; **Sela** was the chief stronghold of Edom) are shown acknowledging his glory. The passage is much like Pss. 47; 93; 96-97. In vs. 10c the Hebrew text (RSV footnote) certainly seems as good as the emendation; it expresses the range of those who offer praise. In vs. 11a "rejoice" (LXX) may be preferred to **lift up their voice.** As in the exodus events (cf. Exod. 15:3) God goes to battle like a great warrior (vs. 13).

42:14-18. The theme of battle is continued in vss. 14-15, where God is vividly depicted as rousing himself (cf. Ps. 78:65). He brings shattering action to the world, transforming it by the intensity of his wrath. In vs. 15c "dry places" has been suggested for **islands.** But God's action in battle is not negative. He leads the **blind**—the nations which have not known him—whereas those who turn to idols will be **put to shame** (vss. 16-17). That **they know not** and **that they have not known** (vs. 16bc) should probably be omitted, for the emphasis is on divine guidance rather than on the newness of the **way.** Vs. 18, usually regarded as the beginning of the next section, may be better linked to this. It closes the passage on a note of appeal that the nations may turn to God and find life.

42:19-43:7. God and His Servant People. The link between this passage and the preceding is perhaps to be seen in the verbal contact of vs. 19 with vs. 18. Here the theme of God's servant returns, but with a difference. The people called to proclaim his word to the nations are in fact in exile, depressed and lacking in faith, apparently unready for the task laid on them. The whole of this passage provides comment on this situation, and a confident statement of the action of God which affects the transformation of Israel.

42:19-25. The **servant** of God lacks insight into God's purpose. He is called and **dedicated**—one of many proposed renderings, including the proper name Meshullam, of which the best is perhaps "set at peace" or "in a covenant of peace." Nevertheless he is **blind.** Vs. 20, which should all be in the 2nd person (cf. RSV margin), suggests a link with 6:9b-10. God has acted to save—**righteousness** (vs. 21) carries the sense of victory or salvation—but his people are in a sorry state, lacking messengers to speak the word of renewal to them. Their lack of faith is due to their failure to **understand** that it is God himself—the God **against whom** Israel has **sinned**—who has brought them into this condition. The prophet in the assurance of salvation never loses sight of this background to the people's position (cf. 40:2).

43:1-7. Now the new act of salvation takes place, and in great poetic sweep the prophet depicts the redemptive activity of God. With perhaps some reminiscence of the exodus events, and with marked emphasis on the presence of God with his people (cf. 7:14), vss. 1-3b describe the people's triumphal progress, culminating in the renewed declaration of God's relationship to them. Israel is to be ransomed and restored (vss. 3c-7). **Seba** was probably S of **Ethiopia** (vs. 3d; see below on 45:14-17); some interpreters have seen here an allusion to Cyrus' conquests as expected to extend this far. **Men** (vs. 4c) should probably be emended to "lands." Because of God's care for Israel he will give nations **in exchange** for her and will summon the remote places of the earth to restore her scattered members to their home. They will all be restored, for they belong to God and were **created** for him (vs. 7).

The contrast between the 2 parts of this section is striking, but it is a contrast not infrequently drawn in 2nd Isa. He sees the present condition of the people in its true perspective, and he sees the coming victory of God without ever losing sight of the need for Israel to learn from that condition what her true place is to be in God's purpose.

43:8–44:5. The Chosen Witness of God. This section follows very much the same pattern as the previous one. God's purpose for the world is declared through his chosen people, called to be his witnesses. He has acted in the past, and now acts again to save. The people have shown themselves to be disobedient and have come under judgment, but God nevertheless makes them into a new people, and through this there will come hope for the world.

43:8-13. The opening appears to describe a court scene, as in ch. 41, with the **nations** assembled and again challenged to produce from among their gods any who can speak rightly of the meaning of history. But God has his own **witnesses.** If vs. 8 refers to Israel, then the sense is that though her **people** are **deaf** and **blind,** yet it is now possible for them to hear and see. It is possible, however, that this vs. refers to the nations brought into court (cf. 42:18). The summons to Israel (vss. 10-13) is based on God's self-declaration. He is the only God; no other exists at all or ever could exist. Vs. 12 appears to stress the establishment of relationship with Israel in her time of purity (cf. Jer. 2:2-3) when no alien gods were worshiped. In vs. 13a **and also henceforth** should perhaps be emended to "even from everlasting."

43:14-21. Again the prophet turns to the theme of the new Exodus, which links to the overthrow of **Babylon.** As in the past, God **makes a way in the sea** and brings to nought the powers ranged against him. Vs. 14c-e is obscure. The traditional Hebrew text of the last line contains the word "ships," which might be a reference to the importance of the river for Babylon; but, as written in biblical times with consonants only, the same letters pronounced with different vowels would mean **lamentations.** The RSV follows generally favored emendations. The old confessions of faith spoke of the deliverance from Egypt, but now (vs. 18) this is to be forgotten in the light of the new saving act of God (cf. Jer. 16:14-15). As then, so now God will lead his people through the **wilderness** to be truly his people, offering him worship. In the Dead Sea manuscript vs. 19d is unclear but seems to read "paths" for **rivers.**

43:22-28. The duty of worship provides the occasion for pointing to Israel's failure (vss. 22-24). The precise meaning is not at every point clear, but the implication seems to be that (a) in the past Israel was not really worshiping her true God but some other and (b) instead of offering worship she **wearied** God with **sins.** The recognition of God's prerogative of forgiveness (vs. 25) leads into a new court scene (vss. 26-28) in which the rightness of

God's judgment of Israel is justified in that, from Jacob onward, those who were spokesmen to Israel and her religious leaders were all guilty, and condemnation had to come. The disasters which have brought her to her present state were entirely right and within the divine purpose.

44:1-5. But, as in 43:1-7, God speaks further words of consolation. The chosen **servant** of God, **Jeshurun** (vs. 2), the true, the upright Israel (cf. e.g. Deut. 32:15), is to be renewed and her descendants blessed. In vs. 4 "like the green poplar" may be read for **like grass amid waters.** The outcome is seen in vs. 5, which may be interpreted in 2 ways. It could mean that the renewed people is now found to be totally obedient, every member of the community acknowledging that he belongs to God. Or—and perhaps this accords better with the place of Israel as the witness to God's saving action—it may be that here are the men of all nations coming and acknowledging God and taking on themselves the words which show their true allegiance. Both thoughts are entirely appropriate to the prophet.

44:6-23. The Folly of Idolatry. The sole reality of the one God is the theme of the opening lines (vss. 6-8). Israel's **King** and **Redeemer**—terms already familiar in these prophecies—declares his uniqueness and challenges any other who makes the claim to divinity to appear and prove his claim by foretelling the things to come. It is a court scene again, as in 41:1-29; 43:8-13. Israel provides the **witnesses** of what God has already made known; he is known to them as the only **Rock,** the one sure foundation. Vs. 7c is corrupt (see RSV footnote) and the RSV rendering represents a simple emendation.

44:9-20. Some interpreters arrange this middle section in lines of poetry, and certainly at many points there is clear evidence of poetic parallelism. If it is not strictly poetry, it is nevertheless highly poetic prose, like e.g. Gen. 1. Perhaps this is the most suitable description of a passage which may best be understood as a sermon, a mocking homily, linked with the emphatically monotheistic passages which precede and follow (vss. 6-8, 21-23) and based perhaps on 40:18-20; 41:6-7. It may be by the prophet himself or by a disciple, but either way it is well placed in its present context, where its sharply ironical statements provide a foil to the hymnic framework. It is repetitive and not clear in every detail, but the overall effect is devastating.

44:9-11. These general statements emphasize the position of embarrassment into which the idol makers and their associates are put.

44:12-17. In this elaborate picture of idol manufacture the order is not logical but moves from one part to another, as if we were looking at a composite painting in which each stage of the process may be seen simultaneously. The fashioning of metal, the marking out of wood, the cutting of a tree all run on from one to another; the workmen are weary from making a god—a curious reversal of what is right, echoed again in 46:1-2. Still more absurd, a man takes a tree and burns a part for warmth and a part to cook his food, then falls prostrate to worship an image made from the remainder.

44:18-20. The final emphasis is on the folly of a man who does this. Surely he can see the foolishness for himself, yet he goes on doing it. He is forced in the end to say **Is there not a lie in my right hand?** and yet is unable to break away because his **mind** is so **deluded.**

44:21-23. The theme of the redemptive power of God is resumed, with **these things** (vs. 21) looking back to vss. 6-8. The hope of Israel lies here; sin is forgiven; restoration invites the people to **return** to their God; at the news the **heavens** and **earth** are summoned to join in the song of praise. In vs. 21d for **you will not be forgotten by me,** an unusual construction, we may read with the Dead Sea manuscript "you will not disappoint me."

44:24-45:13. God's Summons to Cyrus. This passage is remarkable because it actually names Cyrus the Persian. Elsewhere in the prophecies there is clear allusion to his rise to power and anticipation of his conquest of the Babylonian Empire, but he is not identified. It has sometimes been thought that in 45:1 the name was added later, but there appears to be no doubt about its place in 44:28 and **his anointed** in 45:1 cannot be other than he. The God who is creator of all things, controller of the whole universe, the Lord of history, has summoned Cyrus as his instrument—just as he has called Assyria (10:5) and just as Nebuchadrezzar could be called "my servant" (Jer. 43:10). The reestablishment of Jerusalem and the return of the exiles will be the sign to the world that it is God alone who acts.

44:24-28. These vss. take up a theme already frequent in 2nd Isa., the creator and redeemer God. The other gods have already been shown to be worthless (cf. 44:6-23); so too their servants, the **diviners** (vs. 25) and **liars** (perhaps to be rendered "augurs" or "babblers"). But God confirms the word which is proclaimed through his **servant** Israel, and what his prophets reveal is carried through. Thus the promise of restoration is confirmed, for the God who can **dry up** the waters of **the deep**—an allusion to the great events of the Exodus—is he who brings renewal. Vs. 26d may be a later addition; for **their ruins** in the next line the Hebrew text has "its ruins." Cyrus is God's **shepherd,** a common ancient term for "ruler" (cf. Ezek. 34), who will carry through his purposes. Vs. 28cd may represent later expansion of the text, perhaps in the light of Cyrus' decree related in Ezra 1; for the reference to the **temple** is a new element not found in the parallel phrases of 45:13, and in any case the words introduced by **saying** are awkwardly attached. But the addition represents a not inappropriate understanding of the prophet's message.

45:1-7. The summons to Cyrus is described in more detail, in terms not unlike those of royal annals. He is God's **anointed**—the term which in its form "messiah" eventually became a technical term for the future ideal ruler. The line division might better come after this word, with **to Cyrus** beginning the next line. He is to be victorious, and the way is open to total conquest. In vs. 2b **mountains,** from the Dead Sea manuscript, is probably correct, but "ways" has also been suggested. The **treasures** of Babylon are to belong to Cyrus, but it is not for his own sake. It is for God's **servant Israel.** Cyrus, unaware of who is calling him, is under divine compulsion, for it is God alone who acts, and everything is within his grasp. There is no room for any dualistic thought about the ordering of the universe.

The characteristic hymnic outburst of vs. 8 emphasizes the divine victory, for the word **righteousness** carries that overtone.

45:9-13. The same declaration is reaffirmed by being set against the doubts of those who see something strange in the activities of God. As the passage stands it clearly answers the objections of those who think that God should not use the foreigner Cyrus, but it is possible that there is a more general reference to the strangeness of God's ways. The series of images for the impropriety of questioning God in vss. 9-10 is clear enough despite the textual uncertainty in vs. 9b, which might be rendered "a vessel with [i.e. nothing more than] the vessels of earth," though the RSV is probably better. But there is more serious difficulty in vs. 11c. The RSV emendation in effect omits a Hebrew word meaning "things to come"; probably it should be joined to the preceding phrase, as in the Dead Sea manuscript, to mean "the maker of things to come." Even so it is not clear in what sense God is being questioned about his **children.** The creative and restoring activity of God is again brought out in vss. 12-13. Cyrus acts, not as a paid mercenary, but under the authority of God; he can do no other.

45:14-25. God the Only Savior. The theme that there is no other God, already clear in the repeated statements of his creative and saving work, is here taken further in sayings which concentrate on the acceptance of this truth by the nations of the world.

45:14-17. In vs. 14b **wealth** possibly should be "toilers" and **merchandise** "merchants." The tall **Sabeans** of vs. 14c may be inhabitants of Seba, probably S of Ethiopia in Africa (cf. 43:3), rather than the possibly related people of Saba or Sheba in SW Arabia mentioned in Job 1:15 (cf. Ps. 72:10). Represented by these, the world is portrayed as coming to Israel, as captives, as suppliants—not for Israel's own sake but because **God is with you only.** The theme of acceptance (vss. 14-15) is countered by the theme of the absolute saving power of God, while the **makers of idols** are in dismay (vss. 16-17). It is uncertain whether vs. 15 should be regarded as a comment (so RSV) or taken as the continuation of the confession made by the nations. The latter seems more likely, for it suggests that the nature of God has now been revealed in the historic events—the rise of Cyrus, the deliverance of Israel—and hence the hidden God of Israel now comes to be known to all the world. Vs. 16a may be emended to "All who rage at him are put to shame."

45:18-19. This thought of God's self-revelation is taken further in these vss., which provide a reflection on Israel's own understanding of God. The revelation is effective in God's ordered creation. The emphasis here on order rather than **chaos,** on revelation open rather than in **secret** or in **darkness,** leads to the affirmation that God is to be found in order. Israel is not to look for him in a world left in a state of chaos but to see him as he declares himself in victorious and right action.

45:20-25. This too the **nations** can learn. The court scene, with the **idols** held up to scorn because they cannot reveal the secrets of history, is pictured again. Its sequel is the positive appeal that the nations may find salvation. God has **sworn** by his very self—it is the clearest expression of his true nature and purpose—that he is to be acknowledged by all men. Only in him is victory and **strength;** so Israel's descendants shall rejoice. Vs. 24 is not entirely clear, since **it shall be said of me** is an uncertain translation. We might emend to "Only in the Lord is there for man righteousness and strength."

46:1-13. *The Gods of Babylon.* The attacks on the impotent deities are here sharpened into a direct ridicule of the great gods of Babylon. **Bel** ("lord") a title or synonym for Marduk, and **Nebo** ("speaker") the god of wisdom, whose name appears in those of the kings Nebuchadrezzar and Nabonidus, are shown to be so powerless that instead of acting as gods they are carried on the backs of **weary beasts** (vss. 1-2), unable to stop themselves from being borne away to **captivity.** In sharp contrast (vss. 3-4) is Israel, whose God has carried her **from birth** and will care for her to **old age.** The last phrases may be rendered "I will support, I will carry, and save."

46:5-7. Appropriately the theme of the incomparability of God is echoed again, and the impotence of deities which are nothing but immovable objects, **set** in a **place** (vs. 7b; the word might equally well be rendered "shrine"), unable to **answer** prayer or to **save.**

46:8-13. Again the contrast is drawn out in the picture of God who has declared his will to his disobedient people. For **consider** (vs. 8a) we may suggest "be attentive," or "obedient." **From the beginning** his **purpose** has been declared, and now the man he has chosen—**the man of my counsel** (i.e. plan, vs. 11b)—has come, summoned like a vulture to the **prey** (cf. Matt. 24:28). What God has decreed will surely come. Those who lack faith in him will find that his **salvation** is near; he will set it **in Zion,** will set in Israel his splendor (vss. 12-13).

47:1-15. *The Downfall of Babylon.* In a vivid series of pictures the prophet speaks of the coming disaster to Babylon. Confident in her power and security, she imagines that she cannot be touched, but now she is to discover that the resources on which she relies are futile and that the position of privilege which she enjoys is under the control of God, who hands his people over to judgment for a time only. As so often in Hebrew poetry, there are frequent changes of metaphor; but the whole is linked together by the use of repeated phrases. There is no precise strophic pattern, nor are there refrains, but the same phrases appear in different contexts and thus link up the various pictures. E.g. **you shall no more be called tender and delicate** (vs. 1) is echoed in **you shall no more be called the mistress** (lit. "great lady," the title in Israel of the queen mother) **of kingdoms** (vs. 5); vs. 8 is echoed in vss. 10, vs. 9 in vs. 12.

47:1-7. The opening pictures the hitherto untouched city degraded from finery to slavery, working at the **millstones**—a menial task—deprived of rich garments. **Put off your veil** (vs. 2b) probably should be rendered "uncover your tresses." But the picture changes to that of the stripped captive, and again in vs. 3 to the exposure of the adulteress, or perhaps to the woman violently raped. Vs. 3d and the opening words of vs. 4a may be emended to "and I will not be entreated, says our Redeemer." Babylon is degraded for having shown **no mercy** to the people of God committed to her in punishment

for their failure (vs. 6) and for having imagined that her exaltation was to be **for ever** (vs. 7).

47:8-11. The theme of self-confidence continues. Babylon has dared to take on her own lips the words which belong to God alone: **I am, and there is no one besides me** (vss. 8, 10). The **disaster** will be sudden and shattering, and Babylon's love of magical practice will be of no avail to her. This stress on false security and on the suddenness of disaster is repeated, and if we more correctly render "charm away" instead of **atone** in vs. 11, it becomes clear that the false trust in magic is also repeated.

47:12-15. This false trust is now elaborated. Elsewhere in 2nd Isa. there is frequent stress on the total incompetence of the Babylonian gods; here the related realm of **sorceries,** magical practice, and astrology is also shown to be of no avail. Presumably the **they** of vs. 14 refers to the astrologers who, so far from being able to offer protection, are themselves consumed by **fire.** This is no fire which offers comfort; it is the fire of judgment. Nor will Babylon's trading ventures assist her (vs. 15). Probably this is an allusion to attempts at winning support from allies, who wander about at random and cannot help.

The ch. is the natural consequence of what has been said in the previous sections. The gods of Babylon are useless; they cannot protect. The purpose of God is declared; it is to save his people so that the world may know who he is. So Babylon, the instrument of divine judgment, must herself fall under sentence.

48:1-22. *The Word of Salvation to Israel.* Opinions differ as to whether this ch. is to be taken as a unit —an address delivered by the prophet to his people on some religious occasion, a day of penitence or fasting perhaps—or as a combination of various elements built around the theme of the urgency for Israel to respond, to cast off her former disobedience which even now prevents the full appropriation of the divine promise. The repeated stress on hearing, and by implication on obedience, may be the reason for the linking of separate elements. But whatever the true explanation, the passage now presents in a new form some of the elements of the prophet's teaching which have already appeared and, culminating in the summons to escape from Babylon, provides a fitting climax to the first group of the prophecies covering chs. 40-48.

48:1-2. There is a very evident sense of relatedness, indeed of identity, between the Israel of the past and the community now addressed. Some commentators make more of a distinction, e.g. by translating the verbs in these vss. as past tenses and thus contrasting the failure of the past with the hoped-for obedience of the present. But Israel is one. The covenant with the people of the exodus period is the covenant with Israel as she stands now before God to worship him (cf. Deut. 5:3); the Israel of the Exile is still the disobedient people, but a people called to new life in the promise of a new act of salvation. Thus these opening vss. are best understood as a recognition of the continuing duplicity of the people; they gather before God to worship him, invoking his **name,** but they are not wholeheartedly his. Vs. 1f may perhaps better be linked with vs. 2a: "It is not in complete sincerity that they are called by the name of the holy city." Even now Israel has not learned true faith; the polemic against idolatry is directed at her.

48:3-8. This point is reemphasized, for here the already familiar theme of the declaration of saving events by God is taken further in relation to Israel's stubbornness. The declaration was made so that Israel would be in no doubt of the source of these things; the temptation would be to ascribe them to the "not-gods" which are her idols (cf. Jer. 44). This is repeated in a different form in vss. 6-8. The **new things,** i.e. saving events, are only now declared. The people have always failed to hear, and God **knew** only too well from the beginning what his people would be like.

48:9-13. Yet underlying this concern with Israel's disobedience there is the conviction of God's continuing action. The action of God stems from his very nature, his **name** (cf. the stress on this in Ezek. 20:9, 14, 22, 39; 36:21-23). What he has done to his people, disciplining them, has been so that his true nature will be shown to the world. Vs. 10 is not altogether clear; perhaps the negative is out of place in the first clause and we should read: "I have refined you like silver." The declaration issues in a hymnic statement of the glory of the creator God (vss. 12-13).

48:14-16. In its present context, the opening of vs. 14 must refer to Israel, now summoned to recognize that in the work of Cyrus, the chosen instrument, God himself is fulfilling his promise. But it is possible that the original reference was to the nations, called to see what God has done and so to learn of him for themselves (cf. 45:14). But in whichever sense the phrase is interpreted, the work of Cyrus is here put in the context of a divine purpose, declared quite openly from the beginning. The passage is not altogether clear in its phraseology. The phrase in vs. 14: **The LORD loves him; he shall perform his purpose** (vs. 14*cd*) cuts oddly across the first-person forms. Omitting "the LORD" (following the LXX) we may emend to "He whom I love will perform my purpose"; or the phrase "the LORD loves him" might be taken as a title given to Cyrus: " 'The LORD-loves-him' will perform my purpose." Vs. 16*d* is also strange. Perhaps it should be taken as a declaration of the prophet's sense of his commission, and this might be linked to the opening of ch. 49, where the conviction of prophetic call again seems to be strongly expressed.

48:17-19. The **way** of obedience is now drawn out. The promises of God to his people were always promises for life (cf. Deut. 30:15-20) and the whole history could have been different if only the people had responded. As throughout the D history (Josh.–II Kings), the stress on the disobedience of the people is really the occasion for urgent appeal that Israel may be the true and obedient servant which she was always intended to be.

48:20-21. The way to this new hope lies in escape from Babylon. It is to be the declaration of the new act of salvation of God just as the experiences of the exodus and wilderness periods testify to his work in the past. God's **servant Jacob** is again **redeemed.**

48:22. This colophon appears again in 57:21, and the conclusion of the whole book in 66:24 is not dissimilar. The words come like a refrain and

help to bind together the separate elements in this 2nd part of the book. They are the solemn reminder (cf. Hos. 14:9) that the ways of God are blessing indeed to those who accept them but that his word is a word of judgment to those who turn away (cf. John 3:18).

B. THE 2ND COLLECTION (49:1–55:13)

49:1-26. *Israel's Restoration and Mission.* While a suitable break may be made at the end of ch. 48, it is clear that much of the phraseology of this ch. has close links with the preceding sections, as well as with the passages which follow. The theme of restoration and comfort echoes ch. 40; the interpretation of Israel's experience and mission to the nations echoes earlier passages and points to chs. 52–53. The whole ch. is made up of units which may or may not originally have stood together; there is relatedness of theme, but some difficulties in the order have suggested rearrangement. Yet to try to produce logical order does not do justice to the continual movement in 2nd Isa. from one theme to another. The total impression is cumulative rather than the result of ordered argument.

49:1-4. This section begins with a reaffirmation of the **servant** Israel's call, a description so like that of prophetic-call experiences as to suggest that underlying it there may also be the prophet's own strong sense of vocation. From the very beginning God has chosen his people, a firm instrument of his purpose, the mediator of the powerful divine word; and through this people God's glory is to be declared. Yet it appears that Israel's call has been **in vain** (vs. 4); and again in the expression of frustration, indicative of the people's experience of failure and exile, we may sense the prophet's own insight into his people's position in the light of what he has known.

49:5-7. As so often in the prophets, esp. in Jer., we detect close interaction between the prophet's personal experience and his understanding of what is happening to the people with whose life his is so intimately bound up. The answer to this is a double assurance. The forming of the servant was to insure that there would be a people **gathered** to God, a people **honored** and strong in God. But this is not enough. The moment of exile, the experience of failure which seems to suggest the frustration of God's purpose, in fact ushers in a still greater hope. The **nations** are to be given the **light** (cf. 42:6), and this leads to the fullest statement of reassurance in vs. 7, where it is promised that the **Redeemer** will bring the rulers of the nations to acknowledge Israel because of God's own choice of her. The very humiliation of God's people will work the greater glory.

The passage does, however, abound in difficulties —not least because the servant, here so clearly identified as Israel, appears also to have a mission to Israel. Various suggestions have been made for reordering the material, esp. in vs. 5, but we may doubt whether any can carry conviction; there is so great a danger of proving a case by suiting the evidence to it. The answer to the dilemma must be sought first in the recognition of the sense of Israel as a corporate entity which can nevertheless be symbolized by the servant concept. Israel is both the called people of God and also herself called to be the agent of creating the people of God. To the exilic age the conviction of God's choice of his people must be overlaid with the recognition of her failure. At the same time we may perhaps see in the convictions of vss. 5-6 something of the prophet's own experience of a call to bring a message of hope and life to his own people and his realization that this is not all that God seeks of him or of his people. The salvation of Israel is bound up with his own experience and at the same time, as in 52:13-15, with the hope of the world.

The remainder of the ch. develops these themes in various ways.

49:8-13. To the people in exile these vss. speak of the new establishment of a **covenant**—perhaps again an "everlasting covenant" (see above on 42:5-9). The message of comfort, greeted in the shout of praise of vs. 13, echoes 40:1; and the preceding vss. point again to the idea of a **way** through the wilderness, of a restored people delivered from the bondage of exile, of a new series of events like those of the former wilderness wanderings in the exodus period, of the reallocation of **the land** (vs. 8) and the gathering into it of the scattered members of the community (cf. chs. 35; 40). In vs. 12 **Syene** (modern Aswan), a reading probably confirmed by the Dead Sea manuscript, is known from the 5th cent. because of the nearby Jewish military colony reflected in the Elephantine Papyri (see above on 19:18).

49:14-21. The lack of faith of **Zion** (cf. 40:27-31) is answered by the assurance (vss. 14-18) that God cannot forget the city which is engraved on his **hands** and so is ever **before** him. Jerusalem is to be rebuilt and her population will be like the jewels of a bridal diadem. Vs. 15*b* may be rendered "a compassionate mother the son of her womb." The theme of a new population is taken up in vss. 19-21, where the contrast is drawn (cf. Zech. 2:1-5) between present desolation and the future overflow of population. Zion is pictured as a mother contemplating her distress, bereaved of her **children,** and now discovering miraculously that she has new children to take their place.

49:22-26. The hope for the **nations** is echoed in the acceptance by them of Judah's overlordship. The reversal of fortune shows the oppressor nations bringing back God's people to their own place and prostrating themselves to Israel because it is Israel's God who is their hope. Through the metaphors of humiliation and servitude of the nations we are to see the acceptance by them of the worship of the true God. As in the oracles of judgment on the nations—esp. where, as in chs. 24–27, there is an extension into the pictures of the final age—the metaphor of God's great battle with evil is used. It is important to recognize that, however much of nationalistic thought remains, the primary emphasis is on the victory of God and so on the saving of **all flesh** in the knowledge of him. The miracle lies in the release of the **captives of a tyrant,** for here is the assurance that the stronger one, even God himself, comes to deliver (cf. Mark 3:23-27 and parallels).

50:1-11. *Faithless and Faithful.* The interrelated parts of this ch. turn on the contrast between the failure of God's people and those who remain obdurate on the one hand and, on the other, the faithful, the obedient, the true servant of God.

50:1-3. The beginning refers to doubt whether God really cares for his people (cf. 40:27; 49:14). It looks to some as if he has totally repudiated them by irrevocable **divorce,** or has **sold** them to pay his debts. But clearly the questions here expect the negative answer; no such formal divorce has been made, and the idea of God's having **creditors** is absurd. Yet, lest there should be any too easy notion of God's continuing relationship with his people, it is made clear that the selling of Israel, the divorce, are realities because of the people's **iniquities.** As so often in these prophecies, the balance is maintained between confidence in the absolute power and will of God to save and the recognition of justice of Israel's present condition. The theme is elaborated (vss. 2-3) in terms of God's failure to find response and in the doubt of men as to his power to save. With echoes of the plagues of Egypt and the exodus experiences the power of God is proclaimed.

50:4-6. In contrast to this doubt and failure stands the figure in these vss., which together with vss. 7-9 are often taken to be a "servant song." The language is that of pss. of lamentation (cf. Ps. 129:3; Lam. 3:30), making clear that the description is metaphorical. The one who is called into God's service, through whom his **word** is mediated (**the tongue of those who are taught** perhaps means "a disciple's tongue" or "an expert tongue"), is continually summoned to give the message; but he finds himself faced with recalcitrance (in vs. 6*bc* the Dead Sea manuscript has "my cheeks to the iron rods" and "turned" for **hid**). The most natural interpretation here is to understand these words as the prophet's own confession of call, in language much like that of Jeremiah. At the same time the overlap between the prophet's experience and that of his people (see above on 49:1-4) is such that no sharp line should be drawn. As with other prophets (esp. Jeremiah) there is a close sense of unity between prophet and faithful people.

50:7-9. Again like Jeremiah, the prophet finds himself vindicated. The legal terminology of these vss. is strongly reminiscent of the style of some of the speeches of Job. The conviction that he will be protected and his opponents overthrown is one which he shares with both Jeremiah and Job.

50:10-11. In these final vss. there is appeal first to those who are loyal, an exhortation to hear the words of God's messenger to them. The meaning would seem to be that the faithful can share in that vindication which has just been described. By contrast those who trust in their own strength will be brought to disaster. The precise meaning is not clear; yet if a link is seen to the opening vss. of the ch., we may see in this an allusion to the apostasy of those who, thinking that God has divorced Israel, regard themselves as free to look for other gods to protect them. Inevitably they find disappointment.

51:1–52:12. *Summons to the New Redemption.* Though this long section cannot be regarded as a unity, since it is clearly made up of various shorter sections, at least one of which (52:3-6) appears to be in prose, there is an interconnection of thought and language which makes subdivision less satisfactory. The repeated exhortation to hear (51:1, 4, 7, 21), the echoing of the promise of comfort (51:3, 12, 19; 52:9), the summons to awake, addressed to God (51:9) and to Jerusalem (51:17; 52:1), and the many points at which the themes of creation and redemption are drawn out show that here has been gathered a series of statements, exhortations, psalm-like passages—all concentrated on the confident note of the nearness of God's great new act of redemption. It is the answer to those who lack faith; it sets the sufferings of the Exile in their true perspective and provides the most effective foil to the passage which follows in 52:13–53:12, where the full meaning of the sufferings is drawn out.

51:1-3. The section opens with the reiteration of the promise to the people's ancestor. In a right understanding of her past and of the meaning of what God did for **Abraham** and **Sarah** (cf. Gen. 17) there is seen the token of the **comfort** for **Zion,** the restoration of life in its fullness, the desolations made into a place comparable only to the **garden of the Lord.** This confidence in the promise to Abraham was evidently a familiar thought in the exilic period, but it could be rightly or wrongly understood. Ezek. 33:24 addresses those who put a false trust in the knowledge that Abraham, who was **one,** has become **many;** in the context of Ezekiel's emphasis on the absolute primacy of divine action such a trust would be improper. Second Isa. sees a right understanding of the past as a proper element in true faith. The comparison of the restored Zion with **Eden** is a pointer to understanding the nature of the Jerusalem temple. Gen. 2 indicates that Eden is the dwelling of God, committed to man as its guardian; Ezek. 28 shows a similar mythological concept in relation to the king of Tyre. In the OT the temple has a cosmological significance as the chosen dwelling of God from which life and blessing will flow forth (cf. Gen. 2:10; Ezek. 47). In vs. 3 the first 3 verbs are in the perfect tense and are better so rendered, for God has already acted and the issue is not in doubt.

51:4-6. The interpretation of these vss. depends on the opening words. The standard Hebrew text makes the reference to Israel, but the context and some textual witnesses favor the plural "peoples," "nations," and this form seems preferable. As so often elsewhere in 2nd Isa., the hope expressed for Israel is seen to be extended to all nations. God will **rule** over them in power (**my arms,** vs. 5c). The present world order will pass away (for **will vanish,** vs. 6c perhaps render "become murky"), but the saving power of God remains unchanging. The thought of new **heavens** and a new **earth,** fully expressed in the apocalyptic writings, is not here stated; but it is clearly implied (cf. vs. 16).

51:7-8. This short poetic passage forms a bridge to the next section; it is attached probably because of the similarity of the thought of the previous vss., but it makes its point in reference to Israel as the people who understand God's ways.

51:9-11. This is one of the greatest of all OT statements of the meaning of redemption. In rich ps. language—connected with the pss. of lamentation, in which the appeal to God to bestir himself is common (cf. e.g. Ps. 44:23)—it confidently affirms that the God who was the victor in the creation conflict, the victor over the power of Egypt, is here and now acting to deliver his people and to restore them in **joy** to **Zion.** In the primeval days (vs. 9) it was God who by his **arm** (i.e. strength) overthrew **Rahab** and the **dragon** (see above on 26:20–27:1), 2 names to suggest the power of chaos which features in other ancient Near Eastern cosmologies. But for Israel this victory is not a piece of mythology; it is embodied in history. The title Rahab may be used of Egypt (see above on 30:6-7), and the thought of victory over **the great deep** (i.e. chaos, vs. 10) is intimately bound up with the drying up of the **sea** in the exodus events. Creation mythology and past historic experience are together the ground for the confidence in God's present redemptive activity, and in words which echo 35:10 (see comment) the prospect of deliverance is declared.

51:12-16. Perhaps these vss. should be treated as another bridge passage, not all of which appears to be clearly poetic. Vs. 13g looks like a gloss and so too may be the oddly connected vs. 16c-e. There are reminders of the themes of comfort, of lack of faith, of divine creation, of the overthrow of the **oppressor,** which suggest the hand of the later interpreter, providing a brief commentary on the central ideas of the prophet's teaching and showing how closely his various lines of thought are bound together. On **the Pit** (vs. 14b) see above on 14:16-21.

51:17-23. The summons to awake is now addressed to Jerusalem, and in vss. 17-20 the experiences of the disaster to Judah and its capital are recalled. The **wrath** of God is pictured as a **cup** of wine (cf. Jer. 25:15-16) reducing the judged people to impotence. They have **none** to **comfort** (cf. e.g. Lam. 1:2) and no escape from the total **devastation** which comes upon them (vs. 19; cf. Ezek. 14:21). The experience of siege is theirs again (vs. 20; cf. Lam. 2:19). To this recalling and reliving of the experience of the past the answer comes in a reversal of judgment (vss. 21-23). It is upon those who brought the disaster to the people that the judgment will now come, and God's cup of wrath will be theirs, for it is God himself who acts to vindicate.

52:1-6. Again the summons to **awake** is addressed to Zion; in contrast to the degradation of Babylon (47:1-15) Jerusalem is to be cleansed and released. A new and purified people (cf. 35:8) will be there, having put on the **garments** which symbolize the new condition (cf. Zech. 3:4). The **captive** stands up and is freed from the ropes which tie together those taken away into exile. The promised release is commented on in vss. 3-6, a passage which is almost certainly in prose and is probably a later expansion. It explains the nature of Israel's position and compares the present situation with the past—Egyptian sojourn and Assyrian oppression. Perhaps **for nothing** (vs. 4) might be emended to "in my wrath" (cf. 10:5). **Their rulers wail** (vs. 5) appears to refer to the rulers of Israel, but perhaps it should be read "their rulers [i.e. the oppressors] boast," which fits the context better. As in pss. of lamentation, there is an appeal to the honor of God, for while he remains inactive his **name is despised** (see above on 48:9-13). In vs. 6 the 2nd **therefore** should be omitted, as in the Dead Sea manuscript and the LXX.

52:7-10. The theme of good news (cf. 40:9) is resumed with the picture of the **watchmen** standing on the walls and announcing the coming of the messenger of salvation (cf. II Sam. 18:24; Nah. 1:15). The devastated city is restored, Jerusalem is **redeemed,** and **all the nations** see the power of God's saving act. Now God is proclaimed as King in Zion, the place where he has chosen to reveal himself in his royal power (cf. e.g. Pss. 93; 95–99). The kingship of God is supreme, and it will be for the world to acknowledge it. **Hark** (vs. 8a) should probably be omitted as an accidental duplication.

52:11-12. For the full acceptance of God as King in Zion it is necessary that the people march in holy procession from their place of exile to the chosen center. The priests **who bear the vessels** are sanctified. This suggests the ceremonial procession of the ark described in II Sam. 6; I Chron. 13; 15–16 and implied in Pss. 24; 132. It is like the first Exodus, yet it is unlike, for this time there will be no question of **flight** or fear. God himself, like the pillar of cloud and fire, goes before and behind. It is a magnificent climax to the prospect of redemption; the holy people, restored and purified, process again to Jerusalem in acknowledgment of the kingship of the God who has redeemed.

52:13–53:12. *God's Servant—Humiliated and Exalted.* It will be best with this difficult and important passage to consider first its contents and their meaning before making any general comment on the problems of interpretation. So far as possible the attempt must be made to consider the question of meaning without prejudging any of the issues.

52:13-15. The opening statement is in the form of a divine utterance pointing to the **servant** who **shall prosper,** or perhaps better "act wisely," suggesting action which leads to well-being. The prospect is of exaltation in contrast to the humiliated state described in the next vss. The horror of the nations is expressed in the actions of their rulers. In the face of the servant's condition, unrecognizable as that of a man, the kings respond—they **shut their mouths.**

The interpretation is uncertain because of the difficult verb translated **startle** (vs. 15a), which appears to mean "sprinkle." "He shall sprinkle" has been held to mean "he will act to atone," or "to purify" (cf. Lev. 4:6). But the construction is strange, and perhaps **nations** is the subject: "many nations shall carry out a purification ritual." If this is correct, vs. 15ab suggests the horror of the nations expressed in rituals designed to avoid contamination, and vs. 15cd, in which the verbs are perfect tenses ("have seen," "have considered") describe the unheard-of disasters which have been brought to their notice. This recalls statements of the horror produced by Judah's downfall (cf. Deut. 28:37; Lev. 26:32). The alternative would be to regard vs. 15cd as alluding to the new and coming event of deliverance, of exaltation; but this seems to anticipate too soon what is to be said subsequently.

53:1. Just as 52:13 provides the intro. to 52:14-15, inviting attention to the exaltation of the servant in contrast to his degradation, so this vs. provides the intro. to vss. 2-3. There, and again in the following vss., the theme of degradation is elaborated and its meaning made clear. But first there is a reminder

that this is not all; there is a great act of God proclaimed. Just as elsewhere in 2nd Isa. the nations are invited to come to court and consider the realities of the case (e.g. ch. 41) so here there is an implicit invitation. Whether the address is to the nations or possibly to those who have as yet failed to understand the meaning of the Exile cannot be said with certainty. These are not mutually exclusive, since the revealing of the power of God is relevant to all the world and not to Israel only. The Hebrew text has "on whom" rather than **to whom,** perhaps suggesting the revealing of God's power against the oppressors; if so, the first clause, with its emphasis on belief (cf. 7:9), invites trust in God's action. But the point is not clear since the 2 prepositions are often interchanged in the OT, and there is evidence to support the rendering "to whom."

53:2-3. These descriptive vss. imply in this context that the present condition of God's servant conceals his true nature and function. The language is highly poetic. There is the picture of a **plant** growing "straight up" (rather than **before him**) in a **dry** place (contrast Ps. 1:3). **Form . . . comeliness . . . beauty** are suggestive of presence (cf. I Sam. 16:18) or dignity; there is nothing here to suggest one who should be honored. A group of phrases in vs. 3, carried further by the language of vs. 4, suggests the metaphor of leprosy. For **rejected by men** it is possible to render "withdrawing," or "aloof from men"—followed by "a man involved in pain and humiliated by sickness [see RSV footnotes], hiding his face from us; we despised him [a rendering confirmed by the Dead Sea manuscript] and did not esteem him." To some extent the same kind of language is used of Job. In neither case should the metaphor be taken as prosaic description—neither the servant of God nor Job was a leper—but it is difficult to imagine a more apt way to suggest the isolation, the sense of being outcast, than the language applied to such a disease (cf. the action of the kings in 52:15). Leprosy in the OT—probably not the disease now so named—involved such isolation (cf. Lev. 13–14).

53:4-6. The theme of degradation is carried further in a rich series of metaphors. These vss. elaborate the ideas already suggested in vss. 2-3. Thus **stricken** is an appropriate word for continuing the leprosy metaphor, though also suitable to other diseases. The earlier mention of pain and sickness is taken up again and developed into the statement that the servant's suffering is on account of the sin of others. The well-being which comes to them is brought about by what he has suffered. In vs. 5a "pierced through" is better than **wounded.** The humiliation is willed by God (vs. 6; cf. vs. 10) and, if we recall the idea "double punishment" in 40:2, we may recognize here the realization that what came to the people in exile was not merely punishment but a means of bringing well-being.

53:7-9. The picture of straying **sheep** in vs. 6 provides a link to a further elaboration of metaphor in vs. 7, strongly reminiscent of Jer. 11:19; both passages in fact use the kind of phraseology very familiar in pss. of lamentation. The pictures of the **lamb** (lit. "sheep," though a less common word than that in vs. 6) **led to the slaughter** and of the **sheep** (lit. "ewe") being sheared provide a further link to the legal language of vs. 8a. This line is somewhat obscure because the meaning of the word translated **oppression** is not altogether clear; perhaps we should render it "he was taken from authority and right"—i.e. he was given no just trial. For **generation** (vs. 8b) "fate" would be better. The images follow one another with great rapidity—trial, sentence, death, burial. Vs. 8d is again difficult; perhaps it should be rendered "for the transgression of peoples who deserved to be stricken," or perhaps "with transgressors he was stricken to death." Clearly the picture is of **death,** as vs. 9 introduces burial; but **rich man** is odd, and perhaps the word should be rendered "rabble" or emended to "evildoers." **In his death** should perhaps be "in his tomb," as suggested by the Dead Sea manuscript.

The obscurities of detail, however, do not prevent appreciation of the series of pictures. Perhaps most misunderstanding of the passage has occurred through failure to appreciate the presence of metaphor. If any one of these phrases is to be taken lit. there is no good reason why they should not all be; but if all are so taken, the whole becomes absurd. As so often in Hebrew poetry (cf. e.g. Ps. 23) the metaphors change rapidly, without explanation, and we are given an impressionistic picture rather than an exact description. The application of similar metaphors to the king in Ps. 89:38-45, and perhaps also in Ps. 22, may be significant for our appreciation of the prophet's intention. Is he perhaps here understanding the fortunes of his people partly in terms of the figure of their king, Jehoiachin, who suffered 36 years of captivity before being released from prison and restored to some measure of honor (cf. II Kings 25:27-30)? It would be false to identify servant and king; yet a recognition of the intimacy between the experience of people and of king may have led to the use of this kind of metaphorical language.

53:10-12. The final vss. of the passage have many obscurities, but it is clear that the series of pictures leading up to death and burial (vss. 8-9) finds its climax in a picture of renewed life. This is most apparent if on the basis of the Dead Sea manuscript and the LXX vs. 11a is rendered "after his travail he shall see light"; for this phrase indicates the idea of a new coming to life (cf. 26:19; Job 3:20; Ezek. 37:1-14). The outcome includes descendants and prosperity (vs. 10de). This is all set in the context of suffering and humiliation. It was God's **will**—i.e. his pleasure, his purpose—"to crush him with sickness [so more satisfactorily in vs. 10ab], he himself making a sin offering." **By his knowledge** (vs. 11b) probably belongs with **be satisfied**—possibly a parallel to "see light" if the Dead Sea manuscript is correct for vs. 11a. But another meaning of the words may be "he shall have his fill of humiliation," and the larger context favors this (cf. vs. 3). Following this, vs. 11bc may be translated "my servant, himself righteous, will pronounce the righteousness of many" —i.e. will acquit them.

53:12. It is probable that **the great** (the same Hebrew word translated **many** in vss. 11d, 12e) and **the strong** (which can also refer to numbers) should be taken as direct objects of **divide.** Thus God "will divide to him the many as a portion," i.e. as booty for his servant in recompense because he hu-

miliated himself and **bore** their **sin.** The references to **the many** and **the strong** suggest the nations. A theme expressed elsewhere in 2nd Isa. (e.g. 49:22-26), perhaps not very congenial to a modern way of thinking, here returns: the nations are as **spoil** for God's people. Yet to leave that statement without qualification would be to miss the real meaning. It is the hope and confidence that through Israel's humiliation—seen within the context of God's purpose as no longer punishment only but the effecting of his will for men—the nations are brought to God, and for this to be possible they must be brought to Israel, for "God is with you" (Zech. 8:23).

The interpretation of this passage inevitably leaves many problems unresolved. The vocabulary and construction are often obscure and capable of more than one interpretation. It is difficult to avoid favoring the interpretation which fits one's general approach to the problem of understanding 2nd Isa.'s statements about the servant of God. Yet unless good grounds can be shown for separating out this passage and treating it quite independently, it is more natural to relate the thought here to other passages in 2nd Isa. The prophet uses the language of the pss. at many points. He has a familiarity with liturgical language that may be compared with the best in those traditions of preaching and extempore prayer which are dependent on the use of biblical phrase and allusion. He uses hymnic phrases, ideas connected with the kingship of God, statements of the uniqueness of God. Here, though not only here, he reveals his knowledge of that more somber aspect of psalmody which finds its place also in the "confessions" of Jeremiah, and of which the supreme example in the Psalter is perhaps Ps. 22.

This point needs to be in mind when we consider the significance this passage has had for Christian theology and interpretation. Too literal reading of it has sometimes led to extravagant statements about the nature of its relationship to NT material. The claim that the relationship is one of prophecy to fulfillment needs to be carefully defined before it can be acceptable. Insofar as the great truths of OT faith are embodied in such passages as this and Ps. 22 it is not surprising that Jesus and his disciples and the early church should have found in them fit vehicles of expression for what they were saying. In so doing they were carrying further the interpretative tradition already observable in the OT, enriching the faith of the community by the reapplication of passages rich in allusion.

54:1-17. *New Life for the Desolate City.* The theme of restoration in this ch. has 2 main parts. In vss. 1-8 it is mainly concentrated on the renewal of Zion, pictured as a woman; vss. 11-17 turn also to the idea of the rebuilding of the city and its future safety. The 2 are linked by a promise (vss. 9-10) like that made to Noah that there will be no further disaster.

54:1-3. These opening vss. link back naturally to the promise of descendants to God's servant (53:10), but here the figure is of Zion as mother of her **children** (cf. 3:25-26; 49:14). It is elaborated with detail suggestive of the Abraham-Sarah tradition (cf. 51:2; Gen. 11:30), though the theme of the barren woman is common both in the patriarchal narratives and elsewhere in the Bible. The enlarging of the **tent,** joined to the promise of many children, provides a further comment on 49:19-21. It is extended into the promise of a new possessing of the land, a new conquest (vs. 3), and suggests the wide extent of the Davidic kingdom (cf. 9:1).

54:4-8. The same point is made in a different form, with concentration on the idea of God's forsaking his people **for a brief moment,** the moment of exile when his **overflowing wrath** engulfed them. Now the shame of the **wife forsaken** is to be answered in the assurance of a permanent relationship. There are allusions in vs. 4 to the past life of Israel (**the shame of your youth**) and to the Exile (**the reproach of your widowhood;** cf. Lam. 1:1) which invite comparison with the more elaborate use of this type of imagery in Ezek. 16; 23. Confidence rests in the nature of God, described with a rich series of titles in vs. 5. The use of **Redeemer** may be illustrated in Ruth, where Boaz is just such a redeemer, bringing new life to a family otherwise cut off. Vs. 6 is not entirely clear; a suggested rendering is "when he called you, you were a woman forsaken . . . ; but who can cast off the wife of his youth?" The enduring faithfulness of God would be thus even more strongly emphasized.

54:9-10. The oath to **Noah** (cf. Gen. 8:21-22; 9:11-17) reaffirms the absolute faithfulness of God. The continuance of his **love** and his **covenant** even if the **mountains** move recalls Ps. 46. It is significant to find this use of the flood narrative, showing how its tradition is being understood not just in terms of primeval history but also in terms of contemporary experience. The flood as divine judgment has been experienced by Israel in the Exile; the promise of the future includes the assurance that such judgment will not again overtake her. Historically, of course, such an assurance did not prove to be warranted, as events in both the biblical period and after have shown. But that the confidence in God's enduring love and covenant has not been shaken is clear both in the faithfulness of the Jewish people and in the assimilation of this promise into Christian thinking.

54:11-17. The desolate city is addressed, and a new city is promised, built with precious stones. **Set your stones in antimony** perhaps suggests the use of mosaic. Some of the stones are difficult to identify (cf. Rev. 21:18-21). Many scholars read that "your builders" rather than **your sons** will be instructed by God (vs. 13a; cf. the rebuilt temple and city in Ezek. 40–46). The new city will be secure, and any attempt at overthrowing it will be frustrated by divine action. Vss. 15-16 are in part obscure and, in view of their apparent intrusiveness, may represent later elaborations of the text. Vs. 17cd provides a link back to vs. 3, the new possessing of the land and of the city by the servants of God. Thus the promise to exiled Israel is reaffirmed and the future of her life is assured.

55:1-13. *The Assurance of the Promise.* In a series of utterances the climax of the prophet's declaration of promise is reached in this ch., culminating in a renewed vision of the return of the exiles and of the restoration of fertility to the land. The praise offered by the mountains and hills crowns the realization of this new life.

55:1-5. The people are summoned to return to their God, for with him is life in all its fullness. They will here find the blessings of a new promised land, the **wine and milk** which belong to the new age. The promise declared to **David** still stands; through him, as representative of the people, there is a summons to the **nations** who will come to God. The Davidic promise here echoes esp. Ps. 18:43 (cf. II Sam. 22:44); beginning in terms of conquest, it is now understood in terms of the offer of salvation to all the world.

55:6-9. The proclaiming of the day of salvation is not, however, without its warning note. There is promise for men, but it demands their response; they must take advantage of the moment of opportunity. Vs. 6a can be interpreted "while he lets himself be found," an idea which, with **while he is near,** may imply that there can be no deferring of response in the expectation that God will always be there. The appeal is based on the declared will of God to forgive, and man must not presume on this.

55:10-13. The theme of reassurance returns in a declaration of the absolute certainty that God will fulfill his purposes (vss. 10-11), and the promise issues in the vision of returning exiles and renewed land (vss. 12-13). Here is the culmination of promise. A new and restored world offers its praises to God. It is a perpetual witness to the enduring purpose of God and a token of that mercy and comfort and blessing which form so large a part of the message of 2nd Isa.

VIII. The Oracles of 3rd Isa. (56:1–66:24)

The content and style of the opening vss. of this last major section of the book immediately mark a division from what precedes, and yet the division is not absolute. E.g. 56:1-2 echoes the sentiment of 55:6-7, and in 56:5 there is a clear verbal link with 55:13. The Dead Sea manuscript makes the connection by adding "for" at the beginning of 56:1. The view that a new collection begins here, belonging to the Isa. tradition and conveniently ascribed to 3rd Isa., has much to commend it (see Intro.) Yet the recognition that these oracles provide in some measure an interpretation of 2nd Isa. often lights up the relationship. At many points there is closeness in the thought, though often variation in the use of words. There is application of the message to the new and difficult situation of a community reestablishing itself in Judah, though it is not always possible to be certain of dating even in relation to the rebuilding of the temple at Jerusalem.

A. The Blessings of Obedience (56:1-8)

56:1-2. *A Call to Obedience.* The nearness of divine salvation demands the response of right action (cf. Zech. 7–8)—specifically observance of the **sabbath** and avoidance of **evil** in general (cf. Ps. 15). The reference to the sabbath may point to a development of its significance in the exilic period—an ancient custom come to life because of the feasibility of observing it. It was to become one of the fundamental marks of Judaism.

56:3-8. *On Eunuchs and Foreigners.* The general injunction is the occasion for 2 directives, perhaps in answer to a special inquiry (cf. Hag. 2:10-14; Zech. 7:1-3). The **foreigner** and the **eunuch,** whose place in the community is in doubt, are given reassurance. In obedience, in the keeping of the sabbath, and in the maintenance of the **covenant** there is life and blessing and the assurance of **an everlasting name** to take the place of descendants denied the eunuch (cf. Wisd. Sol. 3:14). There is no clear information concerning the status of eunuchs in Israel; Deut. 23:1, often quoted as evidence, does not necessarily refer to the same problem. It has sometimes been supposed that Nehemiah was a eunuch and that his "memoir" was designed to be just such a memorial and name (cf. Neh. 13:31). The status of foreigners was also at times in doubt (cf. the cases in Deut. 23). Here the same basic conditions apply—obedience and service (**minister**, vs. 6b, a term used most often as a technical expression for priestly duty but perhaps here intended more generally).

56:7-8. As in 2:2-4, the temple is a gathering place for all nations, and the God who gathers his scattered people will bring in also those from outside. Here is the application of 2nd Isa.'s proclamation of salvation to the realities of a new situation—perhaps that of the small subject community of returned exiles, with their temple rebuilt (after 516), but faced with many uncertainties. The centrality of Zion, the nearness of salvation, the gathering of the scattered are all themes of hope for such a people.

B. Apostasy, Judgment, and Deliverance (56:9–57:21)

The section begins with sayings concerned with the disobedient but ends with reassurance to the humble. In it a number of passages, probably unconnected originally, are drawn together.

56:9-12. Corrupt Leaders. The failure is at the outset connected with the inability of the people's leaders—perhaps esp. prophets—to provide right guidance. Disaster is coming (vs. 9), though this should not be interpreted lit. or applied to a particular political situation. It is invited because the **watchmen are blind** (cf. Ezek. 3:16-21), the people's **shepherds** have no concern but their own profit and pleasure. The word rendered **dreaming** in vs. 10e is uncertain; perhaps it means "panting," or perhaps "seers."

57:1-13c. Corrupt Worship. Vss. 1-2 are perhaps a fragment, providing a comment on the state of disorder just described. Vss. 1e-2 are obscure; do they perhaps refer to the **righteous** as dead and so out of reach of danger, or are they a wisdom saying used as a comment and offering reassurance?

57:3-10. These vss. describe a judgment scene (**draw near**, vs. 3) and set out in detail the apostasies of the people. The passage is bitter in its condemnation and gathers together every variety of idolatrous practice, with allusions to the evil ways of Canaan and to undesirable sexual practices which are not always clear. Vs. 6 emphasizes that the people's gods are to be found in the **valley**, for **portion** and **lot** here both imply "object of worship," and are so used of Israel's God in Ps. 16:5 (cf. Num. 18:20). Vs. 8h is obscure; the context suggests some kind of religious prostitution or the like, and perhaps the word translated **nakedness** indicates a phallic symbol. **Molech** (or "Melek," lit. "king,"

vs. 9a) probably is to be taken here as a divine title, perhaps referring to the ruler of **Sheol** (see above on 5:14-17). The line might be rendered "You drenched yourselves with oil for Melek."

57:11-13c. The idolatry is answered by words of condemnation. The people have neglected their God, and so nothing that they do will be of any avail. Vs. 12 should perhaps be read as a conditional sentence: "If I tell . . . ." Their **idols** cannot help, for the **wind** will bear them **away**.

57:13d-21. God's Promise of Restoration. Though vs. 13de is usually taken as belonging to the previous section, a contrast begins here. It invites response, and vss. 14-21 contain the assurance. There are allusions to the thought of 2nd Isa., esp. in vs. 14, which reads almost like a quotation (perhaps vs. 14a is intended to indicate this). The assurance is given, as in 66:1-2, that the holy God is ready to help the **humble,** the righteous of 57:1 who are perishing. Vss. 16-19 echo the assurance of 2nd Isa. to Israel that the judgment of the Exile is over and that the people will be restored. Vs. 16 also echoes the opening of the flood narrative in Gen. 6:3 and the creation stories, though the text is not entirely clear. God is apparently affirming that he will not destroy what he has himself created. The passage ends, however, with a look back at the words of judgment and a concluding phrase like that in 48:22. This marks off the section from what follows.

If we try to discover a suitable situation for such sayings as these we can only suggest that such political and religious ills may have occurred in the exilic period, though equally well immediately after. The final vss. seem to reflect the Exile, but they could quite properly be applied to words of judgment from a later date. The passage serves as a reminder that Israel did not abandon all her older ways with the Exile; apostasy and social injustice were perpetually recurrent so that the warnings and the assurances to those who remained faithful did not lose their relevance.

C. True Obedience (58:1-14)

That formal worship, no matter how correctly performed, is of no avail if it is accompanied by wrong conduct is a theme often sounded by earlier prophets and still emphasized in the NT (cf. Mark 7). The approach here is in many ways like that of Mal. with its rhetorical questions; it has less of the direct condemnation of the older prophets and more of the hortatory tone of the preacher. Yet it makes its points incisively enough and points to the source of true blessing in the God who seeks from his people not the mere formalities of worship but the full obedience of the heart.

58:1-9b. True Fasting. The people imagine themselves to be making the right approach to God (vss. 1-2), as if they were entirely righteous in their conduct. They claim (vs. 3ab) to be offering a true fast, and so expect God to heed their prayers, for fasting is regarded as an aid to prayer, a making acceptable of the worshiper (cf. vs. 4cd). But their worship is denied by the outrageous conduct that goes with it (vss. 3c-4). Vs. 3cd is not entirely clear; the RSV footnote indicates a possible alternative translation of vs. 3c that emphasizes the parallel with the following line, which, however, is also uncertain. True fasting is not to be found in the outward forms (vs. 5); it is to be found in the positive pursuit of good in the area of social concern (vss. 6-7)—a text for the portrayal of judgment in Matt. 25:31-46. To an acceptable people the day of salvation will come (vss. 8-9*b*). God himself will respond and reveal himself because the barrier which prevents contact is removed (cf. 59:2; Ps. 15).

58:9c-12. Rewards of Right Action. This appears to be a separate passage brought together with the preceding by reason of similarity of content. **The pointing of the finger, and speaking wickedness** —i.e. contempt and slander, or perhaps, more strongly, engaging in violent attack and promoting trouble—are to be set aside and replaced by positive acts of good will. **Pour yourself out** (vs. 10*a*) perhaps should be "furnish bread," as in the LXX. Such right ways lead into the promise of newness of life for the whole people—not only the **light** of the divine presence (vs. 10*c*; cf. vs. 8*a*) and guidance but the rebuilding of the ruined cities (vs. 12). This may point to the period of the Exile or the years immediately after, when such rebuilding was a problem and life remained economically insecure.

58:13-14. True Sabbath Observance. This 3rd passage presents a similar view of false and true sabbath observance. The promise is that by right action the people will recover their full **heritage.** The allusion to patriarchal promise and the use of the language of Deut. 32:13—**ride upon the heights**—point to a new interpretation of the ancient giving of the land and so the restoration of full life.

D. Confession and Judgment (59:1-21)

The form of a lament ps. (see Intro. to Pss.), with its confession of sin and its culmination in a prophetic word of assurance, is here used as the basis for a prophetic statement of the present condition of the people and the reasons for their distresses. Basically the trouble lies in their **iniquities.** The anticipation of divine deliverance—so much the theme of 2nd Isa.—is disappointed because of the sins of the people, which hinder the effectiveness of God's action. There is no suggestion that God cannot act; it is man who delays the coming of the new age by what he is (cf. Zech. 7-8). The passage is perhaps also concerned with the problem for the righteous of the successes of the wicked, but there is a much more general sense of the whole community's responsibility for its present condition. No too simple division into good and bad, with consequent placing of the blame on other people, is permitted here.

59:1-8. General Indictment. A classic expression of the problem of sin as a barrier between man and God (vss. 1-2) is followed by a series of more specific accusations (vss. 3-8). As so often in earlier prophecy, the emphasis rests on injustice and failure to **know** the right **way** of life. In a series of vivid metaphors (vss. 5-6) the consequences of evil are drawn out.

59:9-15b. Confession. This begins in general terms, with language reminiscent of the passages in Amos 5 descriptive of the day of Yahweh. In vs. 12 direct acknowledgment of sin is made as an expression of the community's total failure. Like a refrain runs the thought that **justice** and **righteousness** are far

away (vss. 9, 11, 14). The meaning of **in full vigor** (vs. 10*d*) is very uncertain. Transposing 2 letters of the Hebrew word for **oppression** (vs. 13*c*) gives "deceit," which fits the context better.

59:15c-21. God's Saving Action. The failure of his people provokes God to action, for it is clear that there is no other source of salvation and right. The point of vs. 16 is not that God might have expected some other to **intervene** in his place but that salvation is his and his alone. Thus he is pictured as the mighty warrior going to battle and with **his own arm** bringing judgment on all who set themselves against him (vss. 17-18). The outcome of judgment is salvation, the acknowledgment of the **name** of God by the nations (vs. 19). Vs. 20 adds to this hope the assurance of God as **Redeemer** of his own people, and vs. 21 represents an elaboration of this point, an interpretative note which brings out the full significance of God's action in the establishment of a perpetual **covenant** from which there is to be no departure. The answer to man's desperate condition, cut off from God by reason of his sin, is found in the assurance both of divine action and of the indwelling of his word in his people.

E. The Glory of the New Zion (60:1-22)

The somewhat somber tone of chs. 56–59 gives way in chs. 60–62 to a sound of triumph and rejoicing. The last vss. of ch. 59 point forward to this, picturing God coming as a warrior in triumph and assuring his people of deliverance. Now the call goes out to rejoice at the appearance of God in his **glory,** bringing **light** to his people and drawing the **nations** to **Zion,** which is to be restored and beautified beyond measure. Much of the language and thought of chs. 60–62 provide so close a recollection of 2nd Isa. as to raise the question whether they may be in reality a further part of his message.

60:1-3. The Dawn of God's Glory. Zion is called to reflect the glory of God, who comes as the **light** of the world and draws the **nations** to this new dawn. The contrast between the **darkness** of the world and the light which God's people enjoy recalls the plague of darkness in Egypt (Exod. 10:22-23); such an echo of the Exodus is characteristic of 2nd Isa.

60:4-9. The Gathering of the Nations. The nations will throng to Jerusalem, bringing back scattered Israel. They will offer their **wealth** for the beautifying of Zion, and their **flocks** will be an acceptable sacrifice in a **glorious** temple. **Thrill** (vs. 5*b*) is lit. "feel awe" or "fear"—suggesting the mixture of strong emotions evoked by such an experience (cf. Jer. 33:9; Hos. 3:5). The peoples named in vss. 6-7 come from various parts of Arabia (see color map 7). **Ephah** was a Midianite tribe (cf. Gen. 25:4). **Nebaioth,** a tribe of Ishmaelites (cf. Gen. 25:13), may be the people later known as Nabateans, whose kingdom during Maccabean and NT times covered most of the territory E and S of Judea (see color map 14). **With acceptance** (vs. 7*c*) should read "for acceptance." Peoples come also from the W, across the sea (vss. 8-9), bringing scattered Israel and treasures. Vs. 9*a* should probably be emended to "For vessels shall gather to me." On **Tarshish** (vs. 9*b*) see comment on Jonah 1:1-3.

60:10-18. Restoration of Jerusalem. The contributions of the nations serve for the rebuilding of the city, which was judged in God's **wrath** at the Exile but is now blessed by his **favor** (vs. 10). A series of pictures portrays the reversal of fortune; the wealth of the nations brings beauty of a new kind to the shrine (vs. 13; cf. 35:2; I Kings 5:8-10; Hag. 2:7), and the city is renamed (vs. 14ef; cf. vs. 18cd; 1:26; 62:2-5; Ezek. 48:35). It is God the **Redeemer** who brings all this about.

60:19-22. God as the Light of His People. No longer will **sun** and **moon** be needed, for God himself is to be an eternal light for his people (cf. Rev. 21:23-26), a sun that never sets. The new age means a new possessing of **the land,** the whole people sharing in the salvation which God brings to them—the meaning of **righteous** in vs. 21a. A new and purified people will increase in number under the blessing he gives.

Whether the whole ch. represents a unified poem or not is of no great moment; it reveals a unity in its stating and developing of the themes which are connected with the new act of divine salvation—a glorified temple, a rebuilt and open city, a gathered people, the drawing in of the nations. The breadth of vision is certainly like that of 2nd Isa.; if it belongs, as is quite possible, to the early years of Persian rule, whether before or after the actual rebuilding of the temple, it is an eloquent witness to the strength of faith which moved men of vision in days which were politically and economically difficult. The return from exile may not have been all that men hoped, but there were those who could see in it the reality of God's saving power (cf. Hag.; Zech. 1-8).

F. The Prophetic Commission (61:1-11)

61:1-3. A Call to Preach Good News. The opening words echo the commission of 2nd Isa. in 40:9, where the summons to give **good tidings** is addressed to Zion. Conscious of the power of the **Spirit** and **anointed** (the term is probably used metaphorically to express the sense of being called) by God himself, the prophet knows his commission to be that of release and hope for his people. **Liberty to the captives** suggests the law governing the release of slaves at the end of a 6-year period (Exod. 21:1-6) rather than the more elaborate jubilee (Lev. 25); **proclaim the year of . . . favor** perhaps suggests a proclamation made at the beginning of such a year of release. But the terminology may well be metaphorical, and shows a particular type of interpretation of the Exile, not altogether unlike that in Lev. 26:34; II Chr. 36:21. It is a period of slavery from which release is offered; now the **day** of hope dawns, the day of divine "rescue" or "requital," rather than **vengeance** (vs. 2b). The reversal of fortune is described in vs. 3 in words which suggest links to ch. 60, esp. 60:21.

61:4-11. Promise of Restoration and Renewal. The general statement of promise is followed by elaboration of the themes. The **ruins** will be rebuilt (vs. 4), perhaps by the nations, though this is not clearly stated. The people of God will be established as the priesthood, with the nations undertaking the other activities of normal life and contributing as is proper to the upkeep of their priests (vss. 5-7; cf. Exod. 19:6; I Pet. 2:9). The Hebrew of vs. 7 is obscure, but evidently the idea of change of fortune is present. The theme of renewed **covenant** (cf. 59:21) is taken up in vss. 8-9, with the characteristically prophetic emphasis on right; the new people, **blessed** by God, will be established and acknowledged by the world. The prospect evokes a ps. of praise (vss. 10-11), in which Zion seems to be the speaker, acknowledging that it is God who has adorned her, as **bride** and **bridegroom** deck themselves. **Righteousness,** i.e. salvation, will **spring forth** before the world by the action of God.

The reading of the opening of this ch. by Jesus in the synagogue at Nazareth at the beginning of his ministry (cf. Luke 4:16-21; it was probably the set portion from the Prophets for that sabbath) shows how appropriately the prospect of release from the Exile could be a picture of the salvation declared in Christ. The presentation of the NT understanding of deliverance is linked not only to the exodus events, themselves so much in the mind of the prophets and esp. those of the exilic period, but also to the experience of exile itself and to the confidence in the power of God to bring release. "Babylonian captivity" becomes a symbolic phrase to express the rule of evil, and such interpretation is found in the prophets of the Exile and after, to whom the experience of disaster was so much a reality. They maintained their confidence in God's power to save even when outward circumstances seemed discouraging.

G. The New Jerusalem (62:1-12)

62:1-5. Zion's Vindication. The function of the prophet in the OT includes intercession (cf. Gen. 20:7; Jer. 14:11), and here the prophet expresses his confidence in God's saving action by pledging himself to ceaseless prayer. The victory for Zion is at hand (vs. 1), and the **nations** will see what God has done. The new city will be like a **crown,** for God himself—probably an allusion to ancient representations of deities crowned with the walls of a city. The theme of a **new name** (cf. 60:14) is taken up, but more elaborately, and linked with the metaphor of the marriage relationship between God and his people used in Hos., Jer., and Ezek. The picture is extended in vs. 5, with the text suggesting the blessing of a marriage between the city and her **sons.** The idea of the city as mother is found elsewhere (cf. 3:25), but perhaps we should emend to read "your builder," i.e. God.

62:6-9. The Security of Zion. It is possible that the prophet continues speaking in these vss. but more probable that they are intended as a divine declaration; for the **watchmen** are best understood as the prophets, intercessors, those **who put the LORD in remembrance,** who bring before him the promises he has made. This is a function often expressed in the worship of the OT. The new establishment of the city brings a confirmation of the promise of enduring peace and well-being. No further disaster will overtake God's people (cf. 54:9-10), nor will the neighboring peoples be permitted to raid the insecure land and benefit by Israel's weakness.

62:10-12. The Way to Zion. In a climax the summons is issued for the preparing of the processional way to Zion (cf. 40:3-5; 57:14-15). God himself comes to his holy place and brings with him victory and holiness for his people. Vs. 11*ef* is a quotation of 40:10*cd*. Again at the end the theme of the renaming of the city is developed, with phrases which are reminiscent both of 2nd Isa. and of other OT promises.

For the generation of the Exile there was great concern with the reestablishment of Zion (cf. Ezek. 40–48). The promises of 2nd Isa. point to the act of salvation by which it is to be accomplished. Perhaps we should see here a reflection of the way in which this concern expressed itself in the difficult years as the temple was rebuilt and life was being reorganized. Like Haggai and Zechariah the prophet of this passage is one who sees the essential place which Zion occupies in his people's understanding of their relationship to God. God chooses to come to them in blessing there, and for the members of the community, near or far, it is the focal point.

H. THE VICTORIOUS GOD (63:1-6)

This vivid poem picks up the proclamation of 61:2 that the **day of vengeance** is at hand (vs. 4), describing the moment also as the **year of redemption** (cf. "year of the LORD's favor," 61:2). It is the moment of God's triumph over his enemies, here symbolized in the reference to **Edom** (see above on 34:1-17; cf. Mal. 1:2-5; Rom. 9:13). In question and answer the prophet—pictured perhaps as a watchman on the city wall (vs. 1)—portrays the coming of the victorious God, like a mighty warrior returning from the **wine press** of wrath (cf. Rev. 14:19-20), from the overthrow of his opponents. God has been provoked to action because there is **no one** else **to help** (vs. 5; cf. 59:16). In vs. 3*b* for **the peoples** the Dead Sea manuscript has "my people," which appropriately suggests God's saving action on behalf of his own. In vs. 6*b* for **made them drunk** (cf. 49:26; 51:17, 21-22) some Hebrew manuscripts read "shattered them" (cf. vs. 3*d*).

The picture of God as a warrior with clothing **stained** with the **lifeblood** of his enemies clearly needs careful interpretation. As an image it has certain obvious disadvantages, yet the apocalyptic writers reveal how effectively such pictures may be used to proclaim the salvation which God brings about. That such pictures have sometimes been interpreted lit. reveals a failure to understand the nature of biblical poetry.

I. THE PEOPLE'S LAMENT AND PRAYER (63:7–64:12)

This passage contains the elements characteristic of the pss. of lamentation (see Intro. to Pss.); many of its motifs and phrases appear e.g. in Ps. 74. Insofar as such laments were spoken on the people's behalf by a religious official—priest, prophet, singer, or possibly at an earlier date the king—this intercession may well be offered by the prophet himself (cf. 62:1). But its form suggests that it represents the lament and prayer of the whole community presented by its spokesman.

63:7-14. *God's Love for His People.* The spokesman begins with hymnic statements calling to remembrance the acts of **great goodness** shown by God to his people, the reiterated expressions of vs. 7 emphasizing their dependence on him. There is recall (vss. 8-9) of the moment of being chosen by God to be a faithful people. He was their deliverer and himself brought them out, continually caring for them and sustaining them. The personal protection is probably indicated in vs. 9*ab*, where the text is uncertain; a preferable rendering, based on the LXX, is "In all their affliction neither envoy nor messenger but his own presence saved them." Alternatively **he was afflicted and** may be omitted as a dittograph.

63:10-14. The divine choice did not, however, find the true response of obedience, for the people **rebelled** and found in their God one who judged them (vs. 10). The reference may be to any or all the occasions of failure after the settlement in Canaan (cf. Ps. 78). The disobedience was at each stage followed by divine mercy as God called to mind the great acts of deliverance which he wrought for them through his **shepherds** (cf. Ps. 77:20). The continuing deliverance and guidance became, as it were, a constant reminder to God of his gracious nature, so that his people were brought again through repeated disasters to their rest in the promised land (cf. Ps. 95:11). That vs. 10 suggests the disaster of 586 is clear enough, yet it contains wider allusions to the long history of Israel. The divine actions are again described in hymnic style. Vs. 11*b* is problematic, since the Hebrew reads "Moses his people" —perhaps a gloss which led to various readings and renderings, of which **Moses his servant** seems a probable one.

63:15–64:5b. *Prayer for Pity.* The people in disaster turn to God, appealing for him to look in **compassion** from his heavenly dwelling (cf. I Kings 8:49) and show the jealousy for his people and the strength which are his. Vs. 16 is not entirely clear; probably it is intended to suggest the concept of **Abraham** and **Israel,** the ancestors of the people, as their guardians. But it is God alone who is **Father** to his people, a relationship expressed by the king in his appeal to God (cf. Ps. 89:26) and here appropriately extended to the whole community. The present distress is judgment (vs. 17), and it is as if God has entirely rejected the people which belong to him. Vs. 18*a* appears to call the period of Solomon's temple, *ca.* 375 years, **a little while;** perhaps it should be emended to read "only a little while ago they dispossessed thy holy people"—an allusion presumably to the still recent disaster of 586.

64:1-5b. A different kind of appeal recalls the greatness of ancient manifestations of God's power, the terrors and earthquakes evoked by his **presence.** As in 2nd Isa., the appeal is to him as the only God who alone will act **for those who wait for him** (vs. 4). He will proclaim himself to the nations as to those who look to him for salvation. Vs. 5*a* may perhaps be emended to read "O that thou wouldst meet him who repents in righteousness."

64:5c-12. *Confession and Final Appeal.* The preceding appeal is supported by an acknowledgment (vss. 5*c*-7) of the uncleanness of the whole people and their consequent separation from God. **There is no one** to intercede, to impress on God the distress of the people (vs. 7); there is nothing but total judgment. Vs. 5*d* is obscure; **in our sins we have been**

a long time represents an attempt at interpreting the lit. "in them of old" rather than hazarding unsupported emendation.

64:8-12. A final appeal points to the people's absolute dependence on God, using the image of the **potter** and the **clay** as in 45:9. City and temple are desolated (vss. 10-11). But Israel is God's people; how can he **restrain** himself from restoration?

If an attempt is made to fit this lament into a precise historical situation, 63:18; 64:10-11 support the conclusion that the fall of the city and the destruction of the temple in 586 do not lie far in the past. The situation is not unlike that revealed in Lam., though conceivably there is allusion to some other event not so clearly known to us. But we should also recognize that the language of such laments is in some degree stereotyped (cf. e.g. Pss. 44; 74; 79). Perhaps this should be considered an elaboration of older forms, a reapplication of words which originally had specific relevance, so that the distress of other and different situations might also be expressed. To those who returned to Palestine to rebuild the temple such language would be deeply expressive; in other moments of need, national and personal, the recall of God's mighty acts and the acknowledgment of his people's dependence would continue to be apt.

J. The Hope of a New Age (65:1-25)

65:1-7. Rebellion of the People. As if in answer to the prayer of the previous section, this passage opens with the affirmation that it is not God who is unwilling to hear (cf. 55:6, "he lets himself be found"; see comment) but his **people** who are rebellious. The passage comes in fact from a situation different from that of 63:7–64:12, but its position here is explained by the link of thought. The condemnation of idolatrous practices and of the unwillingness of men to hear God is a reminder that the people's condition arises from their own failure. Repeatedly it is emphasized (vss. 1-2) that God is more willing to speak than his people to hear. Vs. 1d actually reads "a nation not called by my name," as if repudiated by reason of disobedience, but the context seems to call for the RSV emendation.

65:3-7. The idolatrous practices include the making of **gardens** (cf. 1:29; 17:10) to alien deities, an unknown rite with **incense,** and necromantic practices involving sacrificial meals of unclean food in which the worshipers engage in rituals designed apparently to purify them (cf. 66:17) but not so as to approach God. These are a continual provocation, and God's answer is in total judgment on them (vss. 6-7) just as there was judgment on their **fathers** for similar evils. Vs. 7e is probably corrupt; perhaps **for their former doings** is a gloss.

65:8-16. The Faithful and the Faithless. Yet the people are not wholly depraved, and for the sake of his faithful **servants** God will act to bless and to restore. The faithful are like a **cluster** of good grapes holding the promise of **wine.** Some have taken the saying of vs. 8b to be the beginning of a popular song of which the tune is mentioned in the titles of Pss. 57–59; 75. From the faithful a new people will be established (vs. 9), and the land will be a place of blessing and safety (vs. 10) from the Plain of **Sharon** on the W seacoast (see color map 1) to the

Valley of Achor near the Dead Sea, the latter suggesting a new entry to the Promised Land (cf. Josh. 7:24; Hos. 2:15).

65:11-12. But again there is judgment for the apostates, those who engage in alien cults directed to Gad (**Fortune**) and Meni (**Destiny**), apparently deities of the Syrian and Phoenician area. With a pun on the 2nd name God "destines" the faithless to disaster for their failure to respond, their evil action, and their choice of an obnoxious cult.

65:13-16. The distinction between the faithful and the faithless becomes clearer in a series of sharp contrasts (vss. 13-14) between those who are God's **servants** (cf. **my chosen,** vs. 9, with 2nd Isa.'s use of "servant" and "chosen" for Israel, e.g. 41:8-9; 42:1; 43:10; 44:1-2; 45:4) and those addressed, who will become nothing but a **curse** (vs. 15), an object of warning to the faithful. The thought is that whereas in Abraham the nations would bless themselves (Gen. 12:3), invoking on themselves his good fortune, the **name** of these apostates will be as a curse formula to the faithful, who by contrast will be called by a new name in token of their new nature. The somewhat obscure vs. 16 pictures the faithful as blessing themselves by the God whose word and purpose are sure; he is the **God of truth** (lit. "God of Amen"; cf. II Cor. 1:20; Rev. 3:14) and so the former disasters are set aside.

65:17-25. *New Heavens and a New Earth.* The setting aside of the past and the condemnation of the apostates imply the purification of God's people. The setting for such a promise is a new created order, a new creation like that described in Gen. 1, and a new **Jerusalem,** which will no longer lament (cf. 63:18; 64:10-11) but **rejoice.** Here will be true peace and security (cf. Zech. 8). None will die prematurely, but all will enjoy full life (vs. 20). Probably vs. 20e should be rendered "and he who falls short of being a hundred shall be held in light esteem." They will enjoy the fruits of their labors (vss. 21-23) and not come to an evil end, enjoying the closest of contact with God, whose readiness to **answer** is even more vividly affirmed (vs. 24). Echoing 11:6-9, the prophet speaks of the restoration of peace as at the beginning (vs. 25), with the **serpent** as symbol of evil kept subdued (cf. Gen. 3:14), and with no **hurt** done in God's **holy mountain,** which as the center of the world's life (cf. 2:2-4) is the token of well-being for land and world.

The ch. thus offers a first climax to the whole book. It picks up the themes of disobedience and judgment, with particular reference to Israel's proneness to forsake her God; it affirms the hope that God will not totally destroy, but will save and create a new people for himself; it reveals the promise of blessing to the faithful and holds out the prospect of a new world order, a new age. There is here both warning and hope, encouragement to those who seek God and the consequence of disaster to those who turn from him. Thus the impact of the divine promise is seen as bringing both judgment and salvation.

K. The Final Word of Judgment and Promise (66:1-24)

The summarizing message here is a collection of loosely linked passages elaborating the themes of ch. 65 and, like that ch., providing a reminder of the essential content of the preceding prophecies. Echoes of earlier themes draw together the whole range of the thought of the book and present the reader with a last message of warning and promise.

66:1-2. God's Dwelling Place. An echo of I Kings 8:27 reminds us that no earthly temple can contain the God whose **throne** is **heaven** and whose **footstool** is the **earth.** Yet such is the condescension of God that he chooses to reveal himself to the worshiper who comes in reverence and trust. This is no polemic against the building of a temple; indeed we cannot tell whether the words belong before or after its rebuilding. It is a reminder of the freedom of God, who chooses to reveal himself and to speak from his shrine (cf. vs. 6). The temple is never to be a limiting conception, yet like other elements of institutional religion it is a mechanism through which God in his graciousness chooses to make himself known.

66:3-5. Condemnation of Idolatry. As if echoing the idea of false trust—often emphasized in earlier prophecy (cf. e.g. Jer. 7)—a series of declarations condemns idolatrous worshipers and proclaims judgment on them. Such men pay no heed to God; they do as they please. The precise meaning of vs. 3 is not clear since the Hebrew contains no equivalent for the **like** introduced into each phrase. But comparison is the most likely sense, making the point, as in 1:12-17, that the worship of an unacceptable people, who have **chosen their own ways** is as useless and indeed as dangerous as engaging in the worst of alien religious practices. **Kills a man** in this context may imply human sacrifice rather than simply murder, though the fact that murder automatically disqualifies a man from worship (cf. "your hands are full of blood," 1:15) makes this meaning also possible. Contrasted with such worshipers are the reverent hearers of God's word (vs. 5). They are treated with hostility by reason of their faithfulness and mocked for their allegiance, but **shame** will be on their opponents.

66:6-14. God's Multiple Blessings. God himself makes his intention known not only by declaring judgment from Zion on his enemies (vs. 6; cf. Joel 3:16; Amos 1:2) but also by expressing his purpose in bringing a new people into being by miraculous and speedy **birth** (vss. 7-9). To any who might doubt the reality of this promise and the assurance of its fulfillment the series of questions in vss. 8-9 offers complete confidence. What God has decreed will surely come to pass and that speedily. So in linked oracles an invitation is issued to **rejoice** (vss. 10-11) because of the new life which has come for Jerusalem, a fullness of life and of delight which is expressed in the metaphor of the life-giving **breasts** (vs. 11; the last phrase should be translated "from her bountiful breast").

66:12-14. The same theme is continued with a picture of new prosperity incorporating the image of the **river** as a source of life (cf. 8:6; Ps. 46:4) and the coming of the **nations** with their **wealth** (cf. 61:6; Hag. 2:7), so that the security and bliss of God's people is like that of a child protected (cf. the image of 49:22-23; also 40:11). There is also an echo of the message of **comfort** in ch. 40. God's work for his people offers protection for his **servants** but **indignation** for **his enemies.**

66:15-17. Destruction of God's Enemies. The image of indignation is elaborated (vss. 15-16) in the picture of judgment in fire and storm, a great action against the hostile forces. An added note (vs. 17) makes more specific reference to the enemies as idolaters, indicating similar practices to those mentioned in 65:3-4. In the obscure expression **following one in the midst** the "one" may be feminine and perhaps indicates a goddess. It is possible that **their works and their thoughts** in vs. 18 should be connected with **come to an end** in vs. 17.

66:18-23. The Gathering of the Nations. Thus we are brought to the final picture—perhaps originally poetry rather than prose—of the glory of God revealed to the nations (cf. 40:5), who themselves bring in the scattered members of Israel as a holy **offering** to God, a sign of the faithful worship to be offered. The main part of vs. 19, repetitive of vs. 18, is perhaps a gloss designed to indicate more precisely the distant places involved. **Tarshish** indicates remote Spain (see comment on Jonah 1:1-3). **Put** was evidently in N Africa. Some scholars locate **Lud** also in N Africa (cf. Gen. 10:13; Jer. 46:9; Ezek. 30:5); others, on the basis of Assyrian records which mention "Luddu" in Asia Minor as giving military aid to Egypt, identify it with Lydia. **Who draw the bow** should be read as Meshech, which with **Tubal** and **Javan** (Ionia) was in Asia Minor (see color map 9). The list traces the faraway lands from which the nations will come, places in which God's name and glory are not yet known. The appointment of **priests** and **Levites** (vs. 21) almost certainly refers to the returning members of the community (cf. 61:6), an enlarged priesthood to meet the needs of a larger worshiping people; for with the new creation (vss. 22-23; cf. 65:17) the round of worship from sacred time to sacred time will draw in all mankind.

66:24. A Final Warning. The final vs. introduces a last note of warning concerning the downfall of those who **have rebelled against** God, apostates who come under his wrath. The picture of perpetual **fire** is probably taken from the burning of refuse in the Valley of Hinnom outside Jerusalem (see comment on Jer. 19:1-5; cf. Mark 9:47-49), though perhaps there is also an overtone of the final cosmic battle of the nations against God's people, in which God wins his last victory at the ushering in of the new age (cf. Ezek. 38–39, Zech. 14).

So at the end, with all the prospect of a glorious future in the saving power of God, there is the warning note, the reminder (cf. 48:22; 57:21; Hos. 14:9) that the word which is a word of life is also a word of judgment. The note on which the book began is the note on which it ends; but it is a message lit up by the confidence of a great succession of prophets that salvation belongs to God and that in him men may place absolute trust.

THE BOOK OF JEREMIAH

Stanley Brice Frost

Introduction

Jeremiah's Life and Times. The 60 years 640-580 B.C. are perhaps the most important and certainly the best documented in all Israel's long history (see comments on II Kings 22–25; II Chr. 34–36; "The History of Israel," pp. 1018-31; and Chronology, pp. 1271-82).

In 641/40 Josiah came to Judah's throne just when Assyria's imperial power was beginning to falter. By his 13th year (627) the independence of Judah began to appear a practical proposition, and at this time of political speculation a youth named Jeremiah passed through an experience which convinced him of his call to be a prophet of Yahweh (1:1-2). Instead of joining in the popular chorus of optimism about the nation's future, however, Jer. created something of a stir by speaking repeatedly of an invasion from the N and by insisting that Judah was very far from having Yahweh's good will. Five years later (623/22) the original edition of Deut. (see Intro.) was discovered in the temple and a national reformation was instituted based on its principles (see comment on II Kings 22–23). This new zeal for the covenant and the increasingly favorable political climate made Jer.'s warning of imminent judgment appear irrelevant. His own attitude to the reformation was ambivalent. He seems to have undertaken a preaching mission to help popularize it (cf. 11:1-8) but was not wholly persuaded that this was the answer to Judah's spiritual situation (cf. 8:8-10). There were many prophets in Israel, however, and Jer. was dismissed by those who knew him as unimportant.

During this period of obscurity Jer. even had his own doubts about himself (15:15-18; 20:7-10). So things continued until 612, when Nineveh fell and the Assyrian Empire became a thing of the past. This seemed to show still more clearly that Jer. was wrong in his interpretation of Judah's situation. This period of the prophet's life lasted so long and we know so little about it that it has been suggested that Josiah's 13th year was actually the date of his birth and that he did not begin to prophesy till Jehoiakim's accession *ca.* 18 years later. There is good reason, however, to accept the dates given in the book and to recognize that from the age of 15 or so until he was well over 30 Jer. was an obscure and unregarded prophet.

In 609 Pharaoh Neco marched N through Palestine to salvage what he could out of the wreck of the Assyrian Empire. Josiah tried to stop him at Megiddo, probably relying on divine aid as promised by optimistic prophets; but this was not given and he lost his life in ignominious defeat. While Neco marched on to the Euphrates the people crowned Josiah's son Jehoahaz; but 3 months later Neco on his return journey took the young king captive and placed another son of Josiah, Jehoiakim, on the throne as his vassal, imposing a heavy tribute on the land.

Overnight the outlook for Judah changed dramatically. It was suddenly clear that she had been living in a fool's paradise and that Yahweh either would not or could not save her from the political realities of the times. Jer.'s message, from being irrelevant, became a highly pertinent interpretation of Judah's situation; and the prophet himself became a figure of importance. Since under the new king the reform movement ground quickly to a halt, his strictures on Judah's religious practices and moral standards were no longer so easily to be dismissed.

At the time of Jehoiakim's coronation, or soon afterward, Jer. declared in the temple court that unless Judah changed her ways the very temple itself would be destroyed (7:1-15; 26:1-6). This prophecy caused a riot, and only the intervention of some nobles prevented his being killed by an angry mob (26:7-24). Jer. continued stubbornly in the same vein, however, and in 605/4 after an esp. provocative outburst (19:1-15) the temple authorities tried to silence him with a flogging and a night in the stocks (20:1-2). Since this had no effect, they refused to allow him to frequent the temple. Jer.'s response was to resort to what was quite a new idea: he reproduced his major pieces by dictating to a friend called Baruch and sent him into the temple to read them to the pilgrims. This was an extremely important development, since it meant that Jer.'s book originated by authority of the prophet himself whereas earlier prophetic anthologies apparently were compiled posthumously by disciples.

The abortive rebellion of Jehoiakim against the Babylonians in 598 further defined Jer.'s position. He insisted that Babylon was intended to be world ruler, that she was Yahweh's instrument of punishment in his dealings with Israel—here he was treading in the footsteps of Isaiah, who thought similarly of Assyria—and that Judah must submit meekly to her rule. When in 593 a group of ambassadors met in syria—and that Judah must submit meekly to her rule. When in 593 a group of ambassadors met in Jerusalem to plot further rebellion, Jer. publicly opposed Hananiah ben Azzur, who was prophesying success to the enterprise (27:1–28:16). (In the same year he is said to have arranged for a symbolic act in Babylon, prophesying its ultimate downfall, but such an ambivalence is difficult to credit [see below on 51:59-60].) The rebellion did not take place, and probably Jer.'s determined opposition was, at least in part, responsible. But revolt, bolstered by Egyptian promises, did break out in 589; and by Jan. 588 the Babylonians and their allies had overrun the country and were settling down to besiege Jerusalem.

Jer. stayed in Jerusalem throughout the siege. In its early months Zedekiah sought counsel from him (21:1-14), and he told the king that surrender to the Babylonians was the only way to save himself and the city; but Zedekiah could not hope to carry such a plan with his nobles.

The Egyptian army moved up into Palestine, and the Babylonians turned from besieging Jerusalem to meet it. When Jer. attempted to leave the city at this time to visit his family property he was accused of deserting to the Babylonians and imprisoned (37: 11-15). The Egyptian army faded away again, and the Babylonians resumed the siege. Prisoner though he was, Jer. still urged surrender on all in the barracks where he was held. The exasperated military leaders threw him into an empty cistern to die, but an Ethiopian, probably a slave in the king's household, rescued him. He was returned to the barracks, where he remained for the rest of the siege. As it dragged on, a kinsman offered to sell Jer. a plot of family land in Anathoth, an unattractive proposition, since the future was so uncertain. Yet the prophet bought it and insisted on paying the regular market price as a testimony to his faith that Judah had a future in the purposes of God (32:1-25). This incident is particularly significant in that it shows that the message of hope was truly part of Jer.'s message: after punishment would come restoration.

The city fell in 586. Babylonian intelligence had evidently taken note of Jer.'s advocacy of their cause, for the local commander received orders to allow him his freedom. He chose to remain with the new governor, Gedaliah, and the remnant seeking to rebuild the national life, though he had several times said that Judah's future lay with the exiles in Babylon. When Gedaliah was assassinated and the survivors fled to Egypt, Jer. and Baruch went along also. The last we hear of the prophet is in that country, where he protested vigorously against any belief that Egypt could provide a satisfactory home for Jewry and asserted that Nebuchadrezzar would in fact conquer that country as he had the rest of the Fertile Crescent. It is probable that he died in the companionship of his faithful Baruch in the country he so heartily despised.

Such is the bare outline of his life. But what kind of man was he? Here there is room for a wide variety of interpretations but since all we know of him comes from the book bearing his name, a knowledge of its character and style is necessary.

Origin and Character. As mentioned above, Jer. himself took the initiative in gathering the first collection of his oracles; and when this manuscript was destroyed, he encouraged his friend and adherent Baruch to produce an enlarged collection. It is im-

portant, however, to remember that the individual pieces which went into these manuscripts were not produced for posterity but arose out of particular situations. Thus the book does not have a coherent, sequential text. Rather it consists of a collection of sayings, poems, prayers, oracles, hymns, proverbs, visions, and stories, at first sight brought together quite irrationally, but in fact often grouped in smaller collections having a rationale of their own. The book may be divided into 4 major sections: (*a*) the words of Jer. (1:4–25:14; 25:15-38 forms an independent collection of Jer.'s sayings concerning the nations); (*b*) Jer.'s ministry (26:1–45:5); (*c*) oracles against the nations (46:1–51:64); and (*d*) a historical appendix (52:1-34).

The temple had 2 foci, the life of the inner court where the priests celebrated the cultus, and the life of the outer court where men congregated in "gatherings" (cf. 6:11), i.e. discussion circles or groups (Hebrew *sodh;* cf. e.g. "my intimate friends," lit. "men of my *sodh*," Job 19:19; "hold sweet converse," lit. "relish a *sodh*," Ps. 55:14). Some probably met every evening, thereby serving the purposes of a club, literary association, and newsstand. Others, congregating around a teacher, probably met in the mornings for study and instruction, thus serving the purposes of a school. Others again met on the sabbath and other days of religious observance and were in fact the embryo of the synagogue. Membership was fluid and merely associative. Jer. was closely attached to the life of the temple, but not to that of the inner court of the cultus and the priest. His whole manner of existence was intimately bound up with the discussions, debates, pedagogy, and public life of the outer court.

A man could rely on his gathering to provide him with an audience. Sometimes he had only gossip to relate, at other times solid news; sometimes he had a poem to recite, a ps. expressing his feelings of joy or sorrow or hate in some particular circumstance (see Intro. to Pss.). A prophet might produce an "oracle," i.e. a message from Yahweh, given him to communicate to Israel. A "wise man" might produce a wisdom saying, which could be as short as a 2-line proverb or as long as a didactic ps. A poet might produce a love song, a wit might come up with a riddle (see "The Literary Forms of the OT," pp. 1077-81). At times the current political situation would be discussed heatedly and anxiously. The outer court of the temple provided a home for the intellectual life of Jerusalem and Judah, and Jer. inevitably gravitated there.

The life of such a gathering was ephemeral. Things were said, discussed, admired, and then— as further conversation flowed—forgotten. But some items were too striking to forget and were repeated and remembered. When Jer. wanted to produce a written record of what he had said, he had in addition to his own well-stored memory that of his friend and amanuensis Baruch, who no doubt was a companion in the same group. When, however, he set out to write a new expression of his thoughts or to recount an event which in retrospect seemed significant—i.e. when he was faced with the task of written composition as distinct from oral recollection —he naturally used the common literary style of the day, usually termed Deuteronomic (D) because it was first distinguished by scholars in Deut. These efforts at written composition lie behind the remarkable prose passages in the earlier part of the book (e.g. 1:4-2:3; 7:1-15; 11:1-17) and are paralleled by Baruch's similar production of the later prose narratives.

Compilation. Jer. first produced a written record of his message in 605/4 (36:1-4). It is a reasonable guess that this consisted of 1:4-8:3—the prophet's credentials, indictment of Israel, threat from the N, temple sermon—plus a summary and conclusion in 25:1-14, which also dates itself 605/4. When the scroll was destroyed by the king (36:9-26) it was rewritten with additions (36:27-32), probably 8:4-10:16. Having thus begun to keep a record of his sayings, Jer. continued the practice over the next 20 years, and this accounts for the little collections in 11:1-24:10. Each time the summary and conclusion (25:1-14) was pushed further back by the new material. The anthology 1:1-25:14 thus includes pieces dating from 626 to 586 and may well be called "Jer. his book."

After Jer.'s death in Egypt, Baruch wished to vindicate his friend and his message. He therefore wrote his own account of Jer.'s ministry, esp. the later years. He starts with the famous temple sermon (ch. 26), which he dates 609/8, tells how the prophet further clashed with temple personnel in 593 (chs. 27-29), and then goes straight into the events of the siege, 588-586 (chs. 32-35; 37-39). He tells further of the tragedy of Gedaliah (chs. 40-41) and explains how he and Jer. came to be in Egypt (chs. 42-44) and finally how he came to be writing this book (chs. 36; 45). There has been some disturbance of Baruch's narrative, and a significant interpolation, the "Book of Comfort" (chs. 30-31). But chs. 26-45 as a whole are "Baruch his book."

The 3rd section of the book consists of oracles against the nations (chs. 46-51 plus 25:15-38; cf. e.g. Isa. 13-23; Ezek. 25-32). Not much of this material is Jer.'s, but each piece must be judged separately. The bulk of the collection comes from the 2nd half of the 6th cent.

The 4th section (52:1-34) was added by an editor as a historical summary to the whole Jer. anthology. It reminds us that, in addition to Jer. and Baruch, other hands have been at work and that the original productions have received considerable expansions. Some scholars have in fact identified a D editor, who worked during or after the Exile. He is thought to have compiled the book from 3 major sources of material and also composed a number of passages; but recognition that the common literary style of the period had D characteristics seems to make such a hypothesis unnecessary.

The English versions follow the traditional Hebrew text. The LXX omits *ca.* an 8th of the book and inserts the oracles against the nations (ch. 46-51) after 25:13 in a different order. Dead Sea scroll fragments have shown that this version was based on a variant Hebrew recension at a time when the text of Jer. was fairly fluid.

The Thought of Jer. Jer.'s thinking starts from the conviction that he was a prophet. He has told us what this meant to him. It meant that God's word was given him to proclaim (1:4-10) and that he had

no other commitments. It made him a man apart who must forgo family relationships (11:18-23; 16:1-4). Even though he spent his days in the gatherings of the outer court of the temple and was gregarious by nature, he knew what it was to be withdrawn in the midst of a crowd, a dedicated soul (15:15-18). As a prophet he was prepared to stand alone. Fellow prophets, priests, relatives, people, nobles, king—they all turned against him, one after the other; but he knew that with Yahweh's help he could withstand them all (1:18-19).

Jer. conveys the nature of the prophetic experience. He was seized with trembling and was befuddled like a drunken man by the violence of the divine word coming on him (23:9). But when the pressure lifted, the message he had received had to be passed on to those to whom it was addressed. There may be medical or psychological descriptions of such a state of mind, but for Jer. it was the experience of divine inspiration. We may think that at such moments his subconscious thought welled to the surface of his mind, but that too may be another way of referring to inspiration. Jer. was certainly in no doubt about the fact that Yahweh gave him his word and that he must declare it (20:9). To be a true prophet in Jer.'s mind was to be a member of Yahweh's council (*sodh,* 23:18-22; cf. Amos 3:7); and his one gripping fear, at least in the early days, was that he might be just another deluded fool (15:18*b;* 20:7-18; cf. I Kings 22:19-23). But with fine humility he was prepared to rest his case in the hands of God (10:23-24).

Formally Jer.'s thought about God was not esp. original. He accepted the current covenant theology, which we associate with the D school; and like them he saw Yahweh as a deity who demanded total obedience (3:1-5) to the covenant established between him and Israel at Sinai. Jer. recognized Yahweh as a moral being, requiring righteousness from his people (5:1-2; 9:7-9), and also as creator of all things (10:12-16) and able even to revoke creation (4:23-26). Theologically, if not philosophically, Jer. was a monotheist, i.e. he lived as if Yahweh was the only God in the universe, even though he would not have denied in theory the existence of other gods.

His major interest, however, was in the religious interpretation of political events, and this gave a particular tone to his theology (1:10). He early realized that Assyria was doomed but could not believe that Egypt had the stamina to be her heir. The potent forces were still, he believed, those of the mysterious N—the Medes, the Scythians, the Elamites, and above all the Chaldeans. As the Chaldeans seized power in Babylon and then led the revolt against Assyria, Jer. became more and more convinced that the future lay with Chaldean Babylon. Following in Isaiah's footsteps (cf. Isa. 30:1-7; 31:1-3), he consistently discounted Egypt and saw in the N power the chosen instrument of Yahweh's anger (27:4-7).

Basically Jer.'s interpretation was sound. True, it led him to prophesy that Nebuchadrezzar would conquer Egypt (43:8-13), a feat which Neb. never accomplished, and to write Egypt off as a refuge for Jewry, a view which was belied by the very lively Jewish colonies there for the next 5 cents. But his main policy for Judah was undoubtedly right: loyalty to her own institutions, esp. her own religion, and political submission to imperial powers she could not hope to resist. It was a lesson Jewry learned painfully in the Exile, unlearned in the time of the Maccabees, learned afresh in the Roman disasters, and is once more challenging in our day.

The most influential aspect of Jer.'s thinking, however, and that which was to prove of most moment to the generations that followed, was his experience of personal religion. A man of the outer court of the temple, he was little attracted to the cultic aspect of religion. At one time or another he questioned critically the place in the nation's life of sacrifice (6:20; 7:21-22), circumcision (4:4; 9:25-26), the written law (8:8), the temple (7:1-15), and the institutions of prophetism and priesthood (5:30-31; 23:11-15). For Jer. religious reality centered in his personal communion with Yahweh, and though this experience was never theologically formulated, it irradiated all his thought about God.

Thus, paradoxically, though we are very doubtful that the words are Jer.'s own, the thought of 31:31-34 sums up the positive contribution of his message more fully and richly than any other passage in the book. The effect of his life and teaching was to give men a new understanding of the possibility of a personal relationship with God and a new estimate of the primacy of that relationship. To use his own vivid phrase from another context (32:4), Jer. taught the world that it is possible for a man to know God for himself and to "speak with him face to face and see him eye to eye." The thought of Jer. may need the balance of a healthy doctrine of the church, but his own experience of the reality of God was so genuine that he stands witness over the cents. to this central fact of religion. He still recalls us to the heart of the matter.

For Further Study. J. P. Hyatt in *IB*, 1956. James Muilenburg in *IDB*, 1962. A. S. Peake (Cent. Bible) 1910-12. J. Skinner, *Prophecy and Religion*, 1922. E. A. Leslie, *Jeremiah*, 1954. H. H. Rowley, *Men of God*, 1963. John Bright (Anchor Bible), 1965.

I. Jer.'s Book (1:1–25:14)

A. Jer.'s First Manuscript (1:1–8:3)

1:1-3. Intro. This passage is composite. Vss. 1-2 may have introduced the original first manuscript, which must have had some such identification, and vs. 3 may have been added for one of the later expansions. Even so, it does not cover the whole content of the present book, which includes considerable material relating to the period after the fall of Jerusalem and much narrative apart from actual **words,** i.e. oracles, of Jer.

1:1. The old Hebrew priesthood in premonarchical times was centered in Shiloh (cf. 7:14; I Sam. 1:3) and its best-known leader was Eli. After Shiloh was destroyed the priesthood settled apparently at Nob, near **Anathoth,** 2½ miles NE of Jerusalem (see color map 8). Here they incurred Saul's wrath, and he massacred the whole clan except Abiathar (I Sam. 21:1-9; 22:6-23). Abiathar became David's priest and rose to power in newly captured Jerusalem (II Sam. 20:25). In the succession struggle Abiathar supported Adonijah, however, and when

Solomon won out he was banished to Anathoth (I Kings 2:26-27). Jeremiah was *born* a priest but *called* to be a prophet. He seems never to have served as a priest, and it is one of the marks of prophetism that it was given by its adherents an absolute priority over all other considerations (cf. Amos 3:7-8).

1:2-3. On the dates here indicated see Intro.

1:4–2:3. The Prophet's Credentials. The section forms a unit consisting of a number of oracles recalled in their original poetic form (e.g. vs. 5) together with prose "transcriptions" of others (e.g. vss. 13-19) set in a brief explanatory narrative. It is intended to set out Jer.'s credentials as a prophet. When he composed his first anthology he was debarred from the temple (36:5) because of the kind of thing he had been saying, and it was implied that he was not a true prophet. Hence the need for Jer. to produce impeccable credentials. He cites 4 experiences, the original call and 3 other moments of inspiration whereby it was clarified and made more precise.

1:4-10. The Call. Of the initial experience we are given only the interior account. What exterior circumstance touched off the youth's developing consciousness of the divine to explode in this searing conviction of vocation we are not told, though we may be sure there was one. The boy feels from the very start that this is what God wants him to do. He recognizes his **youth**—he was probably *ca.* 14-15—but feels equal to the call because of the divine resources at his disposal. Much too much has been made of Jer.'s reticence and sensitiveness; from the beginning he was a very tough and determined young man. Yahweh is near; he—not an intermediary (cf. Isa. 6:6)—has put his **words** in Jer.'s **mouth,** and therefore the prophet need be abashed before no one. The word was thought to be very powerful. As Jer. pronounces doom on **nations,** so the divine judgment will fall on them. Where he speaks peace, there peace will follow. But we notice that he expects to have little opportunity for this (cf. 28:5-9). He would not have to travel to be a **prophet to the nations;** his word of judgment spoken in Jerusalem will determine the fate of neighboring tribes and distant empires alike.

1:11-12. The Waker Tree. The **almond** tree was known as the "waker" because its blossom breaks into beauty even before it has unfolded its leaves. Just as through the long years of Manasseh's reign and the 15 years of his successors, when Assyria was everywhere dominant, Yahweh has appeared to be doing nothing, so too in the long months of winter it seems as if, as far as the tree is concerned, God has entirely ceased to operate. But now, in due season, the waker tree is being quickened into beauty once more. So too in world affairs the time is right, and Yahweh will commence his political activity again. Assyria is beginning to falter, and this is a sign that Yahweh is about to act. The pun (see RSV footnotes) on "waker" and **watching,** lit. "waking," is the kind that appealed strongly to the Hebrews' love of word play.

1:13-19. The Blown Pot. Jer. sees a **boiling pot, facing away from the north.** Probably he means a pot set over a fire arranged to receive a draft from the N wind. Smelters who needed intense heat arranged their furnaces thus. The N was in OT times usually the direction from which disaster threatened. Yahweh is going to bring **Jerusalem** to the boil—for refining purposes? (cf. 6:29-30; Isa. 1:24-25; Ezek. 22:18)—by bringing down invasion from the N. The sin mentioned (vs. 16) is idolatry, which covers a very great deal, but esp. a failure to recog-

Courtesy of Harry Thomas Frank

Tilted cooking ("boiling") pot

nize Yahweh's unique character on the one hand and Israel's unique vocation on the other.

1:17-19. This message of doom will not make Jer. popular, but he is to understand that he has the strength to stand alone. In due course the royal house, the nobility, the priesthood, his own family, and the common people—all will turn against him. Though Jer. stood unbending to the end, he felt his loneliness deeply, as later oracles testify (e.g. 15:15-21).

2:1-3. Israel's Original Devotion. This is the 3rd of the messages from Yahweh with which Jer. illustrates and clarifies his mission. The prophetic tradition looked back on Israel's desert period as the golden age of religion—it was the priestly tradition which thought of the desert generation as apostate (cf. Ps. 95:8-11)—and Jer. pictures the Israel of that time as Yahweh's wholly devoted young **bride.** In those days no one dared lay a finger on Israel! Anyone eating **first fruits** instead of offering them in sacrifice was guilty of sacrilege; similarly anyone attacking Israel in those golden days was despoiling Yahweh's sacred preserve and woe betide him! Now, however, Israel is disloyal and no longer **holy to the LORD;** therefore anyone may attack her with impunity. This is the grim message which Jer. has been called to proclaim.

2:4-4:4. The Indictment of Israel. 2:4 is an intro. to the section. As a man with strong N ties—Benjamin (cf. 1:1) was originally allied to the Joseph tribes, as indicated by the tradition that Joseph and Benjamin were Rachel's sons—Jer. often thinks of the nation under the N terms of **Jacob** and **Israel,** and sometimes even addresses Judah thus (cf. e.g.

2:26-28). At other times he uses Israel esp. for the N kingdom (cf. e.g. 3:6-14). Here he mostly has Judah in mind.

2:5-13. A Contention Oracle. This oracle is modeled on law-court practice. Jer. makes his point by presenting the plaintiff's contention in the case "Yahweh vs. Israel." The defendant is challenged to say why he has deserted Yahweh for other **gods** —in the full confidence that no sound reason can be produced. On vs. 5d cf. Ps. 115:8.

2:7-8. Israel is perversely unmindful of her salvation history (cf. Mic. 6:4-5) and has **defiled** her inheritance. The **priests** do not understand their own **law** tradition. The **rulers,** i.e. the aristocracy, have **transgressed,** lit. "rebelled," against Yahweh's guidance. The **prophets** allow themselves to be inspired by **Baal** rather than Yahweh.

2:9-13. What other **nation** has ever deserted its own **gods,** however worthless, to adopt those of another people? **Cyprus** represents the far W, while **Kedar** refers to NE desert tribes (cf. 49:28; see color map 9), and the 2 probably represent the prophet's geographical horizon. Vs. 13 is an esp. forceful image in a city where spring water was at a premium and the population must rely on **cisterns** and reservoirs.

2:14-25. Israel's Apostasy. A man enslaved had few rights, and one born a **slave** could not hope for redemption; but at least he was protected as property by his owner. Israel is Yahweh's servant, as close to him as a **homeborn servant** (cf. Gen. 15:3; Ps. 116:16); and yet Yahweh is allowing her to be despoiled. This would not have happened if she had remained loyal to Yahweh as a servant should. But Israel has to learn that apostasy is **evil** in itself and **bitter** in its results (vs. 19).

2:16-19. This oracle must be dated soon after the summer of 609, when Pharaoh Neco's army invaded Palestine and slew King Josiah, to whom **crown**—i.e. scalp, not royal headdress—**of your head** may refer. **Memphis** was the Egyptian capital and **Tahpanhes** the frontier town through which communication with Egypt flowed (see color map 9). Vs. 18 refers to the futility of relying on political alliances with **Egypt** and the declining power of **Assyria,** which Neco was trying to bolster against the Babylonians. Here Jer. is fulfilling his role as prophet to the nations—he can assess their motives and dependability—but his main concern is Israel's wanton behavior.

2:20-25. Israel refuses Yahweh's service and worships the local divinities. Canaanite worship was sexual in character—hence the frequent use of the metaphor of adultery and prostitution. This image leads Jer. to a vivid interpretation of Israel's character. After describing her as a cultivated **vine** which has reverted to the **wild** strain and saying that her guilty **stain** is indelible, he returns to the sexual metaphor; like an animal in **heat** (vs. 24) she is in the grip of forces she cannot control—she is revolted by her own promiscuity but cannot break free from her degraded way of life.

2:26-28. Reliance on False Gods. Sarcasm and indignation combine to give intensity to this outburst. In the troubled political situation men are turning to Yahweh for help as a drowning man clutches at a straw; but if they have found what they were looking for in other **gods,** why not ask them for help? Cf. Isa. 44:9-20; Ps. 115:3-8.

2:29-32. *Israel's Ingratitude.* This oracle is composed of several expressions of a common theme: Israel is behaving most unfairly. The people rebel and then **complain** that they do not get help. Yahweh chastens them but they respond by slaying his **prophets** (cf. II Kings 21:16); Yahweh has been careful for Israel yet she declares herself **free** of him. A **bride** treasures her **ornaments** and **attire** as tokens of her wifely status, but Israel has been oblivious of Yahweh for long periods. The metaphors reveal not only Israel's perversity but also the prophet's angry indignation on Yahweh's behalf.

2:33-37. *Political Infidelity.* Jer. is against Judah's becoming entangled in foreign alliances because as junior partner she always has to accept the religious domination of her ally. He uses the sexual metaphor to describe Judah's attempts to build such alliances and denounces the shifts in her policy as the wantonness of a prostitute. Judah is such a born harlot that she can teach even the established practitioners! But the result is inevitable: she will be led into captivity (vs. 37) in the posture which soldiers for security reasons force on their prisoners to this day.

3:1-5. *An Irretrievable Situation.* Cf. Deut. 24:1-4. Probably this law was a further definition of the Hebrew marriage code, and Jer. uses the new strictness of interpretation to emphasize the perversity of Israel's behavior toward Yahweh. She is making their ruptured relationship irreparable. **Rain** was believed to be given or **withheld** by God as he was pleased or displeased with Israel, but not even drought has been effective in breaking down Israel's shamelessness. Israel talks to God and about God in aggrieved tones (vs. 4) as if she were the injured party—but she has **done all the evil** possible.

3:6-20. *Faithless Israel, False Judah.* The original oracle is in the poetical material (vss. 12*b*-14, 19-20) and was composed in Josiah's reign. But in order to make it serve his purpose at the time of dictating his book to Baruch in the reign of Jehoiakim, Jer. composed vss. 6-10 as a prose intro. Later an editor inserted the prose in vss. 15-18.

3:6-10. The contemporary explanation of the disappearance of **Israel**—i.e. in this passage the former N kingdom—was that the N tribes were disloyal to the covenant while Judah, at least by comparison, was faithful. But Jer. denies this. Judah should have learned her lesson from the severity of the punishment which fell on Israel. The dissolution of that kingdom and the subsequent disappearance of the 10 tribes is expressed as a **divorce** (vs. 8)—but Yahweh's other "wife" has not taken the lesson to heart. To continue after such a warning is to compound the crime: Judah as yet unpunished is more guilty than Israel, who paid the price dearly for her folly. How great a punishment must therefore be impending over Judah!

3:11-14. The oracle itself is a feeling comment on the fortunes of the N kingdom. Yahweh's pity will yet lead him to **gather** the scattered **one** and **two** at a time and restore them to what is left of Israel, i.e. to Judah with its central shrine on Mt. **Zion.**

3:15-18. This is a prose insertion by a postexilic editor. He picks up the reference to Zion and hangs thereon a general prophecy of the recovery of Israel as a nation under good rulers. Interestingly he does not specify the Davidic line—royal messianism is only sporadic in the OT. At his time of writing the loss of the **ark** in the general destruction of Jerusalem was still keenly felt, but this is to be compensated to Israel by the **presence of the LORD** himself—a perceptive thought—so that the symbol will not need to be replaced. The note of universalism is sounded in vs. 17—a persistent characteristic of the postexilic period (cf. e.g. Zech. 8:23)—and the reunion of Israel and Judah is foretold. The insertion is a valuable witness to the hopes which upheld faith in a desperate period.

3:19-20. Yahweh has been sadly disillusioned. It is the anthropomorphism which gives the poetry its imaginative appeal. Note that both the intimate relationships of the family are employed, marriage and fatherhood.

3:21-4:4. *True Circumcision.* This appeal for repentance serves fittingly to close the indictment of Israel (2:4-4:4). In vss. 21-23 Jer. imagines men gathered **on the mountains** to weep, not for the dead god Tammuz, as was the pagan practice, but for their own wrongdoing. Vs. 22*ab*, the divine call for a change of purpose, is a word play on the idea of turning, lit.: "Return, sons, from your backturnings and I will correct your mis-turnings!"

3:22c-23. Jer. imagines that this appeal meets with the right response, so that Israel replies: "We are disillusioned. The pagan rituals on the hilltops are an evil snare. **Salvation** is to be found in Yahweh alone; we do indeed return to him!" True penitence comes, not from fear of consequences, but from recognition of the fraudulent character of temptation.

3:24-25. Someone has added these vss. as a further comment. The **shameful thing** means the pagan cult, indulging in which has cost Israel her promised land and all that she has put into it and built up within it. On prostration in lament cf. Josh. 7:6.

4:1-4. The word play on "turning" is resumed in vss. 1-2: "If you want to turn, then turn to me." The promise is held out that true repentance will bring true peace—to other nations as well as to Israel. The final piece (vss. 3-4) is a call for inward renewal: circumcision, a survival of tribal marks, which serves to distinguish the Jew from his neighbors, is meaningless except as indicative of an inner loyalty.

4:5-6:30. *Punishment from the N.* Jer. in this section has gathered together a number of pieces which have a common theme—the punishment which will befall Judah if she does not respond to Yahweh's call for penitence and obedience. Much speculation has centered on the identity of the **evil from the north** (4:6; cf. 6:1, 22), but it is probable that the descriptions given in the oracles are not representational so much as impressionistic. Since they were composed over the period 627-605 they may have had several models—Assyrians, Egyptians, Chaldeans, possibly Scythians, and undoubtedly nomadic raiders. The identity of the attacking forces is therefore neither a very practical nor an important matter. The central significance is the inexorable character of the punishment which will befall Israel unless she repents. The section, a series of vivid anticipations of the coming disaster, contains some of Jer.'s most striking poetry, with regard both to language and to emotional intensity.

4:5-8. A Warning. In times of danger peasantry from the countryside took refuge in **fortified,** i.e. walled, **cities.** The oracle declares that such a time is now imminent. The **north** was for the Hebrews always mysterious and ominous, partly because most invasions of Palestine were by N powers, partly because in comparison with the comparatively well-known and defined S it was unknown and illimitable, and partly because it was the numinous quarter in Canaanite thought, which located the mountain of the gods in the N ranges. The oracle is not only a call to flight but also a summons to a penitence which recognizes that the evil which is to befall is not just bad luck but Yahweh's judgment.

4:9-12. The Great Deception. Jer. here includes 3 thoughts which he has no doubt expressed at various times in the discussion of the temple court, but which he has either never put into poetic form or, having done so, has forgotten it. Two are very plain and direct. The first (vs. 9) foretells universal dismay when the disaster strikes; it will not be the kind of thing with which an efficient administration may hope to cope. The 3rd (vss. 11-12) describes the disaster as being like the sirocco—the burning **wind** from the desert, too strong to be used for agriculture or to **cleanse** fetid cities and only destructive in its violence.

4:10. The 2nd idea is more involved. In ancient thought men envisaged God as having to "set up" those situations he desired to bring about; and one of his methods, it was thought, was to entice guilty men or nations into a place or activity or attitude of mind that would result in their punishment (cf. I Kings 22:20). Here Jer. is grudgingly congratulating Yahweh: "You have done a fine job of deception this time! Your prophets are going round saying, **It shall be well with you,** and this complacency is leaving the Jerusalemites uncomprehending in the path of the most terrible danger." But why does Jer. say this to Yahweh? In order that the Jerusalemites may "overhear" and wake up to the fact that prophets who allay fears and foretell prosperity are false prophets, and that Jer. who announces the coming disaster is a true prophet. The whole idea of the false prophet is an anthropomorphism which we cannot accept, but it gives us a deep insight into Jer.'s mental processes (cf. 20:7-12).

4:13-18. Approach of the Invader. Jer. foretells the kind of rumor which will run through the bazaars (vs. 13) and adds an appeal for a realistic assessment of the situation (vs. 14). The announcement will be made in far-N **Dan** and taken up in the hill country of **Ephraim** (see color map 1) and passed on **to Jerusalem:** "The enemy is coming" (vs. 16, assuming that it should end with closing quotation marks). Vss. 17-18 are Yahweh's comment that this bitter doom is his punishment on Israel. **Keepers of the field** (vs. 17) are men who surround it to guard the grain as it ripens, before they move in to reap—Jerusalem is ripe for reaping!

4:19-22. Alarm in Jerusalem. Jer. imagines vividly the panic which will grip Jerusalem when the invasion comes. **Anguish** is lit. "bowels." Men will know what it is to have their bowels **writhe,** their hearts beat **wildly,** their voices scream in terror. When in desperation they ask, "How long will this go on?" they will hear Yahweh's stern reply: "It is all happening because my people are morally **stupid!**"

4:23-28. Utter Desolation. The poet thinks of Yahweh as looking down on the land after the great disaster has occurred. Nature itself has turned against Israel with earthquake and the cessation of all life. As he surveys the land turned back to primeval chaos, Yahweh comments (vs. 28) sadly but unrelentingly: "The very heavens mourn, but as judge of all the earth [cf. Gen. 18:25] I am unable to do otherwise!" Vs. 27 is an editor's valuable comment that, powerful as the prophet's thought is, it needs balancing; God's judgments are never wholly negative, but he always brings something new and creative out of every situation.

4:29-31. The Desperate Harlot. As the invading troops approach, all resistance melts in panic and the whole population streams out of the **city** to try to find hiding places in the hills. Jerusalem is pictured as a harlot who stays behind relying on her power to seduce. But old and tawdry she has no charms; her attempts at decoration are pitiful. The prophet can already hear her catch her breath as she wakes up to reality when it is too late.

5:1-6. Poor and Rich Alike. At this time men are deriving comfort from the thought that since there are some good Israelites left Yahweh cannot let the nation be destroyed—it would be unjust to the righteous! Even if there are only 10 such men left, they will be sufficient (cf. Gen. 18:22-32). Jer. replies: "As in the case of Sodom, you will not find one righteous man, let alone 10!" As he reviews the perversity of the inhabitants of Jerusalem he thinks: "Perhaps this is only so with the common people. Perhaps the aristocracy are better" (vss. 4-5). But he finds them just as bad. Therefore the disaster, pictured as the preying beast (vs. 6), will inevitably fall on them.

5:7-9. A Snatch of Debate. Jer. imagines the kind of reply Yahweh will make when Israel pleads for mercy. How can any righteous judge overlook crimes of such perversity?

5:10-17. Destruction of the Vineyard. Israel was only too familiar with invaders who destroyed vineyards, olive trees, and other long-term producers of food. The vine or vineyard was often a symbol of Israel herself (e.g. Isa. 5:1-7; Ezek. 17:1-6). In this oracle the vineyard is Israel and the command to destroy issues from Yahweh himself. People have tried to shrug off the prophetic warnings: "Nothing will happen. The prophets are just windbags" (vss. 12-13). But the uprooted vines will be for kindling and it will be the prophetic word which will set them ablaze (vs. 14; cf. Ezek. 15:1-8). The metaphor is dropped and the reality described in vss. 15-17. The description does not permit close identification, but probably Jer. is thinking of the Chaldeans. **But make not a full end** (vs. 10*b*)—or at least the word **not**—is probably a gloss, added by a later hand to soften the harshness of the oracle (cf. vs. 18; 4:27).

5:18-19. *A Later Comment.* An editor must have added this passage, which modifies the unconditional threats of Jer. by reminding us that it never was—it never is—God's purpose only to destroy; his punishment of Israel is just and rational, but it is not final (cf. vs. 10*b;* Isa. 28:23-29).

5:20-29. *Creator and Judge.* Because of her history Israel was always in danger of thinking of Yahweh as a national god and a war god but not as the god of the natural order. Weather and harvests were the business of the baals, the local deities. Here Yahweh, in terms which echo the primeval conflict-creation myth (see Intro. to Pss.), insists that he is the creator of the universe and as such commands the **rain** and thus controls Israel's **harvest.** The fact that the rains have been withheld is due to Israel's sinfulness, as exemplified by a greedy and dissolute aristocracy. Jer. here echoes his 8th-cent. predecessors (cf. e.g. Isa. 3:13-15).

5:30-31. *Acceptance of Corruption.* The average run of the **prophets** are saying what the people want them to say, and the **priests** acquiesce because it leaves them in positions of authority and wealth. The common **people** know full well what is going on and like it that way. But when the moment of truth comes, as—Yahweh being Yahweh—it most certainly will, what will these people do then?

6:1-8. *Invading Nomads.* Picturing the time of judgment, Jer. envisages Jerusalem surrounded by a horde of nomads, who settle with **their flocks** around the city to starve it out. Instead of seeking **safety** in the city his fellow Benjaminites would be better advised to get out while they can. He imagines the warning being spread S of Jerusalem. **Tekoa** was probably chosen to pun on the Hebrew word for **blow**—something like "in Bloton blow a trumpet" and **Beth-haccherem,** "house of vineyards," as a commanding height for a **signal** (3,000 feet, if at the most probable site; see color map 11). On the metaphor of a **delicately bred** lady meeting with brutal disaster cf. Isa. 47:1-9.

6:4-5. In this snatch of conversation the nomads plan an **attack at noon,** the hour of siesta, but they are so disorganized that it is **evening** before they realize it. It doesn't matter; they can attack at midnight instead. This detail of incompetent but irresistible power reveals the invading force as naïve, brutal, elemental, horrible.

6:6-8. But there is behind the enemy an organizing mind, coordinating and planning—Yahweh himself. Jerusalem pumps out **wickedness** as a spring pours out **water,** endlessly. The oracle ends with an appeal for Jerusalem to repent; the invasion is yet in the future and Jerusalem can prevent its happening if she will.

6:9-15. *Scornful Hearers.* This summary of the divine message, as Jer. has received it, speaks of the rigor of the punishment to come. Even when only a **remnant** is left Israel's enemies will go over the land again, as a gleaner searches for the very last grape on a vine. This is what Jer. must proclaim, but his hearers are impervious to reason or threats (cf. Isa. 6:10). He has reached the point where his moral indignation cannot be contained, and his **word** will become a terrible doom laid on

young and **old** alike (on **gatherings** see Intro.). For all classes of society are corrupt, esp. the religious leaders. They have encouraged the complacency of Jer.'s hearers with false messages of **peace** —the Hebrew word means well-being in general as well as freedom from war—glossing over the seriousness of the situation. The oracle betrays the strained relations of Jer. with his colleagues and also his lack of popular support. Jehoiakim could not have banished him from the temple unless he had already become a solitary figure.

6:16-21. *Futile Sacrifices.* The oracle gives 2 examples of Israel's perversity. Called to walk in the good old paths of righteousness she refuses. Bid to listen for the warning note she refuses again. Yahweh calls on disinterested parties, the **nations,** the **earth** itself, to witness the justice of his decision to punish her. Israel thinks she can cover up her perversity with incense from **Sheba** in SW Arabia (see color map 7) and lavish **sacrifices,** but worship is no substitute for obedience and morality (cf. I Sam. 15:22-23). Jer. like other prophets (cf. e.g. Isa. 1:12-17; Amos 5:21-24), though probably not against the cult as such, certainly relegated it to a very secondary place (cf. 7:21-23).

6:22-26. *Utter Panic.* Jer. returns to the threat of invasion and draws a vivid picture of the enemy. **Farthest parts of the earth** is poetic hyperbole and probably reflects rumors of the Chaldeans' more distant allies, the Elamites or Medes (see color map 9). Jer. pictures the news of the invasion as bringing paralyzing fear. All escape is cut off, neither **field** nor **road** being safe. Judah will be left to indulge in futile regrets—"If only we had hearkened!"

6:27-30. *The Prophet's Function.* Jer. tells how he conceives of his role. He feels that Yahweh has called him to be an **assayer** of Israel. By his fierce oracles of warning and threat he is to separate out the true Israel from the larger mass of the nation. But in vss. 28-30 he tells of his experience: the hotter he makes the **fire,** the more the base alloys run off, but no residue of true metal appears. There is no true Israel.

At the time he dictated his first manuscript to Baruch (605/4) this was Jer.'s estimate of the people to whom he had been preaching for 20 years. Whether this strong expression of despair (cf. I Kings 19:14; Isa. 22:12-14) represented the totality of his prophetic thought is doubtful; possibly at the back of his mind a hope of renewal always lingered, for later on he undoubtedly expressed such a hope. His words are, however, so negative that editors felt the need to gloss his oracles from time to time with words of hope.

7:1-8:3. *Israel Rejected.* This section of Jer. scroll (see Intro.) emphasizes that Israel's sufferings are not fortuitous but are the consequences of Yahweh's condemnation of her attitudes and behavior.

7:1-15. *The Temple Sermon.* We have 2 accounts of the occasion to which this piece relates (cf. 26:1-6). Here the narrative is set in the interior context of a divine revelation (vs. 1; cf. vss. 16, 27-28), from Jer.'s first-person viewpoint, whereas the other version is an exterior account, from Baruch's 3rd-person viewpoint. Baruch tells us that the prophet nearly lost his life as a result of the sermon, but

Jer. ignores this to concentrate on the message. He does not recall the actual words he used but gives a prose summary. Note that he lacks any sense of the thoughts being his own—he believes they came directly from Yahweh.

7:1-4. The occasion is one which brings **all . . . men of Judah** (cf. 26:2) to the temple "in the beginning of the reign of Jehoiakim" (26:1; see comment), when the future is very unclear. The nation is numb from the shock of Josiah's death in battle, the deposition of his son Jehoahaz, and the imposition of Jehoiakim (see Intro.). At such a disastrous time, when the very existence of Judah is in Pharaoh Neco's disposition, men are comforting themselves with the reflection that Yahweh cannot allow Jerusalem to be destroyed, since it contains the very temple itself. Jer. avails himself of the public forum of the temple's **gate,** i.e. outer court (cf. 26:2), to attack and destroy this false confidence. Men are sheltering themselves from the thrust of events in a pseudo-religious faith. They are piously affirming that the holiness of the Lord's shrine will safeguard the temple and the city along with it. The repetition of **the temple of the LORD** (vs. 4) is a Hebrew idiom for a superlative (cf. Isa. 6:3), i.e. "These buildings are the very temple of Yahweh."

7:5-11. On the contrary, says Jer., only good living can secure Yahweh's protection. The moral defections and religious aberrations of Judah have made the temple not a place of holiness but a **den of robbers,** i.e. a cave where criminals hide and suppose themselves safe from capture.

7:12-15. If men think that Yahweh does not allow his shrines to be destroyed, let them visit the ruins of **Shiloh.** The central shrine of the old Israelite 12-tribe confederacy was at Shiloh (see color map 5), the last of its priests being Eli (I Sam. 1-4). For Jer., a descendant of that family (see above on 1:1-3), the fate of Shiloh would have particular meaning. There is no biblical narrative of its destruction (cf. Ps. 78:60-64), but the shrine drops out of the story at the time of the Philistines' capture of the ark (I Sam. 4), and excavation at modern Seilun has revealed a settlement there destroyed in the 11th cent. Jer.'s point is that what Yahweh has done once he can very well do again!

7:16-20. *Family Apostasy.* Probably this is not a part of the temple sermon but the prose summary of another oracle from the same general period. The corruption has eaten so deeply into the nation's life that it has perverted the very togetherness of the family (cf. 44:15-19). Even man's physical environment is corrupted (vs. 20). The **cakes** were crescent-shaped cookies in honor of the **queen of heaven,** i.e. the moon goddess "Ashtoreth." Her name was really Ashtarath but was written "Ashtoreth" by later Heb. editors (i.e. with the vowels of the word *boseth*, "shame") to indicate that word should be substituted in reading. Cf. comments at 11:9-13; 19:1-13; 44:15-19. Ashtarath was known to the Babylonians as Ishtar and to the Greeks as Astarte. In S. Palestine she tended to merge with Asherah, the great Mother-goddess, who in the OT is prominent as the consort of Baal. Ashtarath was a very popular sex and fertility symbol. Jer. is told not to **intercede** for these people (vs. 16; cf. 11:14; 14:11-12); Yahweh is now resolved on their total

destruction. We need to distinguish here between the divine message of judgment and the prophet's expression of it, to which the apparent mercilessness of God is due. God does punish, but his mercy always responds to genuine repentance. The prophet contributed more to the message than he himself recognized.

7:21-26. *Obedience Rather than Sacrifice.* These vss. are an amplification of the theme "the value of ritual." They may have been said at any time but were felt to be appropriate to this temple sermon section. **Burnt offerings** were esp. holy and could be eaten only by priests, but **sacrifices** were feasts which could be shared by all (cf. Lev. 7:1-21). Jer. contemptuously urges the people to **eat the flesh** in disregard of these trifling taboos. What God commands is not rituals but moral obedience. Hebrew idiom allows the denial of one thing in order to assert another, and the intention here is not wholly to deny but only to relegate to 2nd place. It is doubtful whether Jer. meant to allow sacrifice no place in Israel's original Mosaic religious pattern (cf. 6:20). The picture of Yahweh rising early every day to send his messengers to Israel is an imaginative expression of the continued concern of God at Israel's stubbornness.

An Unresponsive People. Jer. tells how he has been warned by God that he will meet with no response, for **they will not listen.** Isaiah testifies to the same conviction (Isa. 6:9-10).

7:29. *A Call to Lament.* Whether by reason of bereavement, defeat in battle, or a sense of divine displeasure, **lamentation** was accompanied by such manifestations of grief as lying prostrate, pouring dust on the head, beating the breast, rending garments, and cutting off the **hair.** This last was still a sign of fasting in Paul's day (cf. Acts 21:24).

7:30-34. *Topheth.* Here is a compressed version of the oracle given at length in 19:1-13 (see comment). It was included here by an editor as a further oracle of rejection.

8:1-3. *A Desecrated People.* The Hebrews never conceived of man's existing apart from his body. As long as at least the skeleton remained, he remained. To revere the **bones** of the deceased was to revere the deceased; to treat a man's bones with irreverence was the ultimate insult (cf. Amos 2:1). But so complete is Israel's rejection to be that Jer. sees all the bones of deceased generations being emptied **out of their tombs** for mockery and desecration—and yet those still alive will be so wretched that they will long for **death.**

This probably ends Jer.'s first manuscript, apart from the coda now found in 25:1-14. What follows between 8:3 and 25:1 is expansive material, and no doubt includes the "similar words" referred to in 36:32 (see Intro.).

B. FIRST EXPANSION: INDICTMENT AND THREAT (8:4–10:16)

8:4-7. *Intelligence and Instinct.* It is expected that if a man falls he will get up again, or if he wanders inadvertently from the road he will turn back and find his way. But Israel has no such corrective sense. Indeed, like a **horse** with the bit between its teeth, she is running madly out of her true course. Migratory birds have the guidance of instinct to bring them back from their wanderings, but Israel's homing instinct has faded out. She has lost the instinctive patterns of the animal world, and yet she does not conform to intelligent human behavior.

8:8-13. *No Grapes on the Vine.* Barren cupboards, wells that run dry, ore lodes that have petered out—these are the modern equivalents for the metaphors of vs. 13. Jer. is hitting hard at Israel's leadership, esp. her intelligentsia. They are pinning their faith to the fact that they now have the traditional **law** (vs. 8) in written form, i.e. Deut. (see Intro.). How can people be respected as mature who think that a written document, so easily tampered with, or ingeniously interpreted, can really determine matters of religious truth? The oracle documents Jer.'s disillusionment with Josiah's reform and its leadership. Note Jesus' use of this indictment for the leadership of his own day, Mk. 11:13. With vss. 11-12 cf. 6:14-15; Jer. was not above reusing lines from earlier oracles.

8:14-15. *Futile Flight.* With bitter sarcasm Jer. imagines a group planning to leave their village and its stagnant, dried-up well in order to go to the **cities,** where the problem will be worse. The result will be to **perish** there rather than here! The oracle must come from some time of drought which Jer. interprets as a sign of Yahweh's displeasure (cf. 3:3; 14:1-6). He is calling for a more realistic attitude: "Don't run away from the effect; face up to the cause—your sinfulness toward Yahweh."

8:16-17. *An Invasion Threat.* This oracle warns of Yahweh's punishment to come. The enemy is already at **Dan,** the most N area of Israel. The **snorting** of the war horse was to the ancient world what the rumble of the tank is to ours. The foe is an implacable one, as impossible to treat with as an **adder** is impervious to the snake charmer's wiles. It was thought impossible to charm adders because they were deaf.

8:18-21. *Disaster Dialogue.* The prophet laments his distress at Israel's suffering. He imagines the desperate cry: "Where is Yahweh? Will he not help us?" **King** refers to Yahweh, not the Davidic ruler. Yahweh's only reply is to ask why the people provoke him by their disloyalty? They are left to face a stark future—the time of **harvest** is over, and they have no food for the year ahead.

8:22-9:1. *Balm in Gilead.* Gilead, E of Jordan, produced a resinous gum from its trees, and this was much used as an ointment for wounds. But Israel is seriously wounded, and it is no good calling for all the balm Gilead ever produced—no salve can cure this wound.

9:2-9. *Social Comment.* These vss. should probably be regarded as a unit. Because of the corruption of morals Jer. longs to get away from the city to the clean loneliness of the **desert.** Here **neighbor** can no longer trust neighbor. **"What else can I do,"** asks Yahweh, "but punish them?" Men live in cities for mutual support and encouragement, but a city where everyone is trying to cheat his neighbor defeats its own purpose. A wise man will leave, and a moral God will destroy, such a travesty of a city.

9:10-11. *Lament for a Forsaken Land.* This is another oracle of warning. If Israel will not repent, the land will be so devastated by war that it will

be forsaken even by the **birds,** and in the **ruins** of Jerusalem only the **jackals** will remain.

9:12-16. *Question and Answer.* Probably vs. 12 is an original saying of Jer., a rhetorical question implying the same ideas as the foregoing oracle. But a later editor did not like leaving the question unanswered and supplied the appropriate response in vss. 13-16 along very orthodox lines.

9:17-22. *Two Oracles of Lament.* The first oracle (vss. 17-19) calls for the professional **mourning women** to come and lead a lament over fallen Jerusalem, and the 2nd urges these women to make sure their guild is well supplied with practitioners because their services are going to be much in demand.

9:23-26. *True Worth.* Two editorial comments are found here. The first is a somewhat sententious but thoroughly sound statement of what is really worthwhile—not shrewdness in affairs, or physical strength, or wealth, but a true understanding of the nature of God—of which the editor gives a very attractive summary. Paul found these vss. very significant (cf. I Cor. 1:26-31; II Cor. 10:17). The 2nd is directed at some of Israel's neighbors who, like her, practice circumcision but without the meaning it should have. That they also use other distinguishing marks shows them up for the aliens they are (cf. 25:23; 49:32; Lev. 19:27-28). This comment reflects an attempt to claim circumcision as a peculiarly Jewish custom. But another editor who had read 4:4 added his own comment (vs. 26*d*) that Israel also was not properly circumcised. This thought was much in the air in the 7th cent. (cf. Deut. 10:16; 30:6). Israel was learning to distinguish between symbol and reality.

10:1-16. *Ps. on the True God.* It was common to conclude a small prophetic collection with an appropriate ps. (cf. Isa. 6-12; Hab.). The collection 8:4-9:26 is rounded off with this ps. The ideas are fairly commonplace (cf. Isa. 40:18-20; 44:9-20; Ps. 115:3-8). Probably it is not Jer.'s work but comes from about the 5th cent. Vs. 1 is an editorial intro., and vss. 2-5 form a cultic oracle (see Intro. to Pss.). The sentiments are the usual Jewish polemic against idol worship expressed with biting sarcasm. In vss. 12-16 the relationship to Ps. 135 is so close that there must have been borrowing one way or the other. Since Ps. 135 has a more liturgical structure, the chances are that the product of the outer court of the temple was borrowed and polished for use in worship of the inner court (cf. also 51:15-19; Letter of Jer.). Vs. 11 is an editorial comment jotted down in Aramaic by a reader and inadvertently taken into the text by a later copyist.

C. Editorial Insertion: Prophetic Fragments (10:17-25)

These are a number of separate pieces, most of them probably from Jer., which have survived in the collective memory of the prophetic traditionists of the postexilic period. Vss. 17-18 are a warning of judgment to come expressed in the form of an admonition: "Get packed—you're going to be deported!" Vs. 19 is a lament fragment (cf. 8:18) which says that Israel must recognize her woes as divine punishment. Vss. 20-21 are another lament fragment, depicting Israel as a Bedouin widow whose camp has been ravaged and who has no one to help her reconstruct her **tent** or her life. Vs. 22 is a vivid forecast of the threatened invasion as the punishment from Yahweh. Vss. 23, 24 are 2 wisdom sayings (cf. Prov. 20:24; Isa. 28:23-29; I Cor. 10:13). Vs. 25 (cf. Ob. 15-16) is a nationalistic call for vengeance on the **nations,** a frequent element in postexilic prophecy.

D. SECOND EXPANSION: JER.'S WORDS AND DEEDS (11:1-24:1)

This collection of Jer.'s sayings was probably gathered by him with Baruch's assistance (see Intro.) sometime between the burning of his first manuscript (604) and the Babylonians' first capture of Jerusalem (597). It is a heterogeneous anthology and lacks the planned structure of the earlier collection (1:4-8:3).

11:1-17. _Jer. and the Reformation._ After an initial enthusiasm for the D reformation Jer. became disillusioned with it (cf. 8:8-13). It seemed to him that it led men to place faith in external authorities, whereas he believed that nothing short of a changed heart would be adequate to meet the demands of a moral God. In this passage he tells of his initial conviction that he should **proclaim all these words** on a preaching tour in support of the reform. The key words and ideas of Deut.—the **covenant,** the centrality of the deliverance from Egypt, the ideal of God and people as one sacral society, the promise of material prosperity in return for spiritual obedience—these are the theme of his message.

11:7-8. The covenant as the D school understood it was a 2-edged sword: it brought prosperity to the faithful, but it also brought fearful punishments on those who were disloyal. Israel's troubles—the divided kingdom, the loss of the 10 tribes, and more recently Josiah's death and the Babylonian oppression—are interpreted as Yahweh's punishments for her faithlessness.

11:9-13. The charge of disloyalty to the covenant is formulated more clearly. With vs. 13a cf. 2:28. **Shame** (vs. 13b) probably hides the name of a god or goddess—most likely Ashtarath (see above on 7:16-20)—so abhorrent that scribes were unwilling to copy it.

11:14-17. So strong is Jer.'s indignation over Judah's idolatry that it blots out (vs. 14; cf. 7:16) his sense of the infinite patience of God (cf. Ps. 100:5). In vs. 15 we should probably retain the words of both the Hebrew text and the LXX (see RSV footnote) and translate: "Can many vows and sacrificial flesh . . ." Jer. was as convinced of the secondary nature of ritual in religion as he was of that of law (cf. 6:20; 7:22).

11:18-23. _Assassination Plot._ This passage is an oracle in poetry called forth by the profound shock of Jer.'s discovery that his relatives were plotting to murder him, plus an explanatory comment in prose. At the time of original delivery the circle of hearers no doubt knew the circumstances and understood the poem, but when it came to be written down years later some explanation was needed. What roused the relatives' anger we can only guess, but the inclusion of this oracle immedi-

ately after the account of Jer.'s reformation activities may give the clue. The law of the single sanctuary urged by the D reformers must have aroused the bitterest opposition of the priests of Anathoth. When they heard that one of their own clan members was actually advocating the reform, perhaps even had come to Anathoth in his youthful innocence and preached on the virtues of closing the family shrine, their resentment against him may well have flared up to the point of murder. Jer. narrowly evaded death, and a wave of revulsion swept him into an intense cry for **vengeance** (see below on 12:1-4). Years afterward, in reiteration, the curse is in no way weakened—the **men of Anathoth** must bear a fearful **punishment.** Jer. was a man of fierce and intense emotions (cf. 12:5-6; 20:10-12).

12:1-4. _A Ps. of Perturbation._ Why do the **wicked prosper?** Jer. sets the problem out in a wisdom psalm (cf. Ps. 73) but leaves it unanswered; all he can do is say "How long, Yahweh, how long?" (cf. Pss. 6:3; 74:9). In the final analysis we have to recognize that there is no answer except that of faith (cf. Ps. 37:9). Vs. 3 seems misplaced and probably belongs after 11:19. Vs. 4 envisages the **land,** aghast at the **wickedness** within it, refusing to nurture such evildoers and preferring rather to become a sterile wilderness. The ultimate wickedness, however, is the notion that Yahweh is morally indifferent.

12:5-6. _Stark Realities._ The debate going on in Jer.'s mind is turned by him into an interrogation by God. The experience of his brush with the men of Anathoth has jolted him out of an unrealistic assessment of his situation. He now realizes that he has taken on far more than he previously understood. He thought he had to race only **with men;** he now finds he must run against **horses.** He thought he had only to traverse open country; he now finds he must plunge through the **jungle** on the banks of the **Jordan.** Yet he is already feeling exhausted by his previous efforts. Moreover he cannot turn to anyone for help, least of all to his own family, his **brothers** and the **house** of his **father.** What will he do now? Yahweh asks challengingly. Will he weakly give up? No answer is given, but in fact Jer. never failed to conquer his fears and continue in his vocation.

12:7-13. _Abandoned Heritage._ Farming in most of Palestine is precarious, and what one generation sweats to bring into production another will in disgust allow to go back to bush. Yahweh, says the prophet, has reached that point with Israel. He invites **wild beasts** to infest it; the vineyards have already been well **trampled** by nomads and their flocks anyway—possibly a reference to the marauding bands noted in II Kings 24:2. **Harvests** are so miserable that farmers blush for them and let the land go back to nature. The hurtful thing is that no man **lays it to heart.** Yahweh's **house** (vs. 7a), though usually the temple, is here synonymous with **heritage.** In vs. 8 the figure changes and the land becomes an attacking **lion;** in vs. 9a **bird of prey** is probably a mistaken repetition of the same word in the next line. Restore in its place the normal Heb. word for "bird" and read vs. 9ab as: "Is my heritage to me like a speckled bird, with the birds of prey against her round-a-bout?" Discovery of seals inscribed with roosters proves that chickens were known in Jer.'s day, though never clearly mentioned in the OT; and the picture here may be of a hen with hawks wheeling above her. Possibly vss. 8, 9*ab* are misplaced fragments.

12:14-17. *Universal Repatriation.* This is a postexilic neutralizing of the foregoing threat oracle. It promises that not only Judah will be restored but also every other **nation** which learns Yahwism from the Jews, as previously the Jews learned Baalism from them. The editor glimpses the truth that a negative is never God's last word and that the word must be to all mankind.

13:1-11. *A Dramatized Threat of Exile.* Probably it was not long after Babylon became the suzerain power—as a result of the victory at Carchemish in 605 (cf. 46:2)—that Jer. recognized the likelihood that Judah would eventually provoke the Chaldeans and would be driven off into exile as a result. This disaster could be averted only by God; but if Judah continued to be disloyal to him, he would actively procure it. To bring this understanding home to his compatriots Jer. here engages in an "acted oracle," i.e. a symbolic action whereby Yahweh's word is expressed. He attracts a crowd—the nucleus no doubt is his own circle in the temple court—designates some nearby spot the **Euphrates** for the purpose of his mime, and then carries out the sequence of actions. Judah is intended to **cling** to Yahweh as closely as a **waistcloth** to a **man;** but if she becomes estranged from Yahweh and is driven into exile on the Euphrates, she will be a **spoiled** nation and **good for nothing.** The somewhat grotesque imagery should not distract us from the earnestness and urgency of Jer.'s intention. **Israel** (vs. 11) was probably substituted for "Jerusalem" (cf. vs. 9) to suit the pan-Hebraism of the postexilic period.

13:12-14. *A Riddle.* A favorite pastime in Hebrew society was posing riddles (cf. Judg. 14:10-20). Jer.'s proposition is on the surface so trite as to be meaningless; the pottery **jar,** *ca.* 2 feet high and holding *ca.* 10 gallons, was specifically made for storage of **wine.** "Of course jars get filled with wine," his listeners reply. Then the prophet discloses the hidden meaning: the wine is going to be the divine intoxication which blinds men to danger and lures them on to their fate (cf. 25:15; Isa. 29:9; 63:6 and the Greek saying "Whom the gods would destroy they first make mad").

13:15-17. *A Warning Against Pride.* The imagery of disaster here employed is that of a man caught on the **mountains** by nightfall.

13:18-19. *Political Comment.* This oracle concerns an attack on the **Negeb,** the arid S region of Judah (see color map 1). Presumably the attack is envisioned as from the S and therefore probably refers to the threat posed by Pharaoh Neco's N march in 609 at the beginning of the expedition which resulted in the death of Josiah (see Intro.). Jer. was more critical of Josiah than were most of his contemporaries, with whom the king was generally popular. Here he evidently holds Josiah and Jedidah (II Kings 22:1) the **queen mother**—the "first lady" in polygamous society—in some degree responsible. Jer.'s attitude is: "You asked for trouble, and now you have it!" Some interpreters see this oracle as coming instead from the 3-month reign of Jehoiachin (Jeconiah, 598-597), which ended in deportation of the young king

and his mother Nehushta to Babylon (29:2; cf. II Kings 24:8-15). On this assumption vs. 19 would predict Babylonian conquest of **all Judah,** even the S-most region. But the oracle would then be very intrusive chronologically.

13:20-27. *Violation of Judah.* Here is another political comment, this time on invasion **from the north**—probably by Nebuchadrezzar following his victory over Neco in 605 (see above on vss. 1-11). Again it is directed in part against the king, now Jehoiakim. Vs. 21 is obscure but probably means that Jehoiakim's foreign policy is going to boomerang: the very Babylonians he has secretly courted while a vassal of Neco will be the commanders of the new occupying forces.

13:22-27. The violation of Judah is likened to the raping of a woman—a feature of invasion sufficiently common to suggest the metaphor. It accords with the frequent use of the image of adultery to describe Judah's participation in pagan cults—e.g. in vs. 27, where **neighings** compares her to a mare in heat—and thus presents her punishment as "poetic justice." Vs. 23*ab* has become a proverb in the English language. Vs. 23*cd* shows how concerned Jer. was with his countrymen's propensity for evil.

14:1-15:21. *A Little Psalter.* Here are 3 corporate laments (see Intro. to Pss.) with later comments attached, suggesting that when Jer. first produced them they provoked such unfavorable criticism that he came back later with rejoinders. We cannot date the drought which gave rise to the first 2 pss. (14:2-9, 17-22), but presumably it was between 604 and 586. The 3rd piece (15:5-9) deals with invasion and might come out of any of those troubled years. A 4th ps. (15:15-21) is an individual lament, appealing for God's help in the prophet's increasingly difficult vocation. The appeal suggests that Jer. included this little annotated psalter in his anthology as an *apologia pro vita sua.*

14:1-16. *In Time of Drought.* The ps. in vss. 2-9 is a genuine cry for help. The imagery shows Jer. at his poetical best. The confused **servants,** the dumbfounded **farmers,** the wretched **hind** forsaking her fawn, the **wild asses,** panting as they wait for death to come—these (vss. 3-6) are unforgettable pictures.

14:7-9. The appeal to Yahweh is in equally vivid terms. Does he care for the people no more than does a **stranger,** a passing tourist? Or has he in fact lost control of nature, so that he is himself as **confused** as his people? This last piece of rhetoric shows that the appeal to Yahweh is genuine and sincere—only later did the conviction come to Jer. that there would indeed be no merciful intervention.

14:10-16. To the ps. Jer. later attached an oracle (vs. 10), which represents Yahweh as replying that the drought is a thoroughly deserved punishment. Did Jer. represent truly the mind of God in this matter? This question also arose in the mind of his contemporaries. Other **prophets** were interpreting Yahweh's will quite differently. As justification Jer. attached to his ps. and oracle an assertion that his attitude toward the people of Judah was dictated by Yahweh himself (vss. 11-12) and that Yahweh had pronounced violently against the false prophets (vss. 13-16; cf. I Kings 22:1-28; Isa. 30:8-11). The structure of the passage thus enables us to see Jer. at work in the cut and thrust of the violent debate which he incessantly provoked.

14:17–15:4. Appeal and Rejection. The ps. of corporate lament (14:17-22) contains a description of the disaster (vss. 17-18) and an appeal to Yahweh for help (vss. 19-22). That he can help is shown by the fact that in the past he has given his people **rain** —a reminder of the prime importance of rainfall in the lives of Jer.'s fellow countrymen.

15:1-4. As in the preceding passage (14:1-16) there is an added oracle: "Yahweh will not save you" (15:1-3). Even if **Moses and Samuel**—famed as interceders (cf. Exod. 32:11-14, 30-32; Num. 14: 13-19; I Sam. 7:5-9; 12:19-23; Ps. 99:6) and perhaps personal heroes of Jer.—pleaded for them, it would make no difference; they are consigned to various destinies of destruction. In the symbolism of the **four kinds of destroyers** (vs. 3) an image was born which was later to come to maturity as the 4 horsemen of Rev. 6:1-8. Vs. 4 is an editorial gloss laying the blame for Judah's misfortunes on **Manasseh**— a D dogma (cf. II Kings 21:10-15; 23:26-27; 24:3-4) to which Jer. would not subscribe (cf. 31:29).

15:5-14. Yahweh's Lament for Jerusalem. The 3rd ps. (see above on 14:1–15:21) is vss. 5-9. It is a lament ascribed for poetical effect to Yahweh, who is depicted as having run out of patience. He describes Israel's sufferings but because there is no penitence warns that the disaster will run its full course.

15:10-11. Such a message to a city struggling to survive could—if it did not bring forth penitence— only result in anger and enmity. Jer. therefore follows the ps. with a half-humorous apostrophe to his **mother,** by way of comment. Why was he ever born to be such a contentious fellow? But—and here he becomes fully serious—God knows how he has prayed for these people! Clearly 14:11; 15:1-3 do not represent the prophet's own mood. Vs. 11 presents textual difficulties; probably **on behalf of the enemy** should read "with respect to the enemy."

15:12-14. Vs. 12 is obscure. Possibly it is part of Jer.'s prayer, as paragraphed in the RSV, and refers to the obduracy of the Judeans. More probably, however, it is the beginning of the grim divine answer: you cannot **break iron, iron from the north,** and that is what the invasion will be—an iron weapon stabbing deep into Judah's entrails. It will result in Judah's despoliation and exile, for Yahweh's anger is unrelenting. With vss. 13-14 cf. 17:3-4.

15:15-21. The Prophet's Lament. The 4th ps. (see above on 14:1–15:21) is an individual lament. The prophet is the butt of ridicule and the object of hatred. He has found great **joy** and **delight** in attending to the concerns of his ministry, though it has often led to self-imposed ostracism. But is there no answer to his deepest questioning, except the one he cannot contemplate—the utter rejection of Israel? Is Yahweh going to let him down, becoming to him **like waters that fail?**

15:19-21. The answer comes straightway: Jer. must be faithful to his message, whether it pleases him or displeases him, whether it brings him honor or persecution. If he is true to his message, he will prevail in the face of all opposition. It may be at fearful cost but he will prevail, as God will prevail.

We have to recognize that Jer. had limited horizons: he had no hope of an afterlife, nor could he see hope in the historical future. The one thing he could clearly see was that he must cling to his intellectual integrity and speak the truth as he knew it; only so could he hope to emerge—in ways unknowable to him—intact. We ourselves know at least the human sequel: Jer. has stood at the bar of history and has emerged honorably acquitted and has indeed won the highest esteem, while his detractors have long since been forgotten.

16:1-21. Impending Doom and Undying Hope. Looking back, perhaps soon after Nebuchadrezzar first deported part of the population in 597, Jer. sees his own unmarried state as a sign from Yahweh (vs. 2) which points to the impending disaster. The literary development of this thought is a written composition, as distinct from an oral recollection (see Intro.), and thus is in the D prose style which was the characteristic literary style of the period. This, however, is an elevated example which verges at times on the poetic (e.g. vss. 3-4).

16:1-4. Jer.'s Single State. Jer. moved from Anathoth to Jerusalem, and thereby out of the close orbit of his family, while still a youth (cf. 1:6). No doubt one result was that the family was not able, or perhaps was not concerned, to arrange a marriage for him; and since he was never sufficiently driven to seek a wife for himself, he remained single. He now sees in his bachelorhood—a quite unusual status in the ancient Near East—a hitherto unrecognized divine warning that the family life of the nation is going to be cruelly disrupted. Yahweh, knowing what disasters are to befall the population, disasters which derive their poignance from their destruction of family life, has prevented him from becoming involved.

16:5-9. Futility of Mourning. At a time of death the rituals, the visits of sympathetic friends, and the family affairs that must be attended to act as an analgesic. But in the coming disaster these consolatory patterns will be disrupted—as will also the joys of family life.

16:10-13. The Disaster Questioned. Men will ask desperately: "But why has **all this great evil** happened?" Jer. can only give the traditional answer: "It is punishment for your sins." Because Israel was forearmed with this explanation, however, her faith in Yahweh survived the overwhelming shock of the disappearance of the Judean kingdom.

16:14-15. An Editorial Comment. This later insertion, largely repeated in 23:7-8, is a reminder that doom is never God's last word. Even though Judah faced in Jer.'s day the horror of the Exile, the day was to come when return from it would rank with the Exodus itself as a signal evidence of Yahweh's care and concern for his chosen people.

16:16-21. No Refuge. When Yahweh brings down his doom, there will be no place to hide—the **hunters** will quarter the land, their trained falcons the air, their **fishers** the rivers and lakes. If Israel has not realized before the serious purpose of Yahweh (vs. 21), she will certainly learn it then! Into this sequence of thought the later editor has inserted an interesting scrap of poetry (vss. 19-20), which, however, is not as a propos as he presumably thought. The promise is that the **nations** themselves will awake to the worthlessness of their own religious traditions and turn to Yahweh as the one true God (cf. Isa. 45:14; Zech. 8:20-23).

17:1-4. Indelible Evil. The reference to the **horns** of the **altar** derives its force from the fact that in the temple expiation rituals the sacrificial blood was daubed on the 4 corner projections of the altar (cf. e.g. Lev. 16:18). Thus the horns of the altar were the very locus of expiation—and just there Judah's **sin** is indelibly **engraved!** But while this metaphor is telling and vivid, the other thought is even more pregnant: it is written **on the tablet of their heart.** The time will come when the prophetic insight will look for this indelible writing nevertheless to be erased and for a new message to be written there (cf. 31:33). **Asherim** (vs. 2) were wooden poles or images of the fertility goddess Asherah. With vss. 3-4 cf. 15:13-14.

17:5-18. Four Words and a Ps. This section is a little collection of Jer.'s incidental remarks in the wisdom tradition of Israel. In the discussions in the temple court he often produced notable sayings, many no doubt extemporaneously as the conversation flowed, and some he believed worthy of preservation. There seems to be an underlying common theme—permanence.

17:5-8. The Humanist and the Religious. There is a profound difference between the man **who trusts in man,** i.e. whose resources are wholly humanistic, and the man **who trusts in the LORD.** The one has an ephemeral character, the other an enduring. This thought has often been expressed (cf. e.g. Pss. 37, esp. vss. 35-38; 146:3-4), and Ps. 1 is closely related to this passage.

17:9-10. Proverb and Comment. Vs. 9 is a version of the proverb "There's no accounting for human nature." Jer. has capped it with the rejoinder that Yahweh audits every life and the balance he strikes has to be settled.

17:11. Fugitive Wealth. This is a vivid picture of a sterile **partridge** hen enticing other birds' chicks— but there is no natural tie, and they do not stay. Easy wealth is as quick to go as to come.

17:12-13. Permanence of True Religion. Yahweh is abiding reality, and the temple is the visible expression of that reality. The man who has his roots in its worship is a solid character; the man who neglects it is as transient as a message **written in the earth,** i.e. the dust.

17:14-18. Yahweh, Jer.'s Trust. This is an individual lament ps. (see Intro. to Pss.). It begins with the assertion that Jer. has looked up to Yahweh— one can tell the worth of a man by what he praises. Jer. is presently under criticism as a false prophet. People are saying he is a Cassandra whose warnings are never justified by events (vs. 15). But God knows he never wanted these disasters to happen (vs. 16*a-c*). It is just that in the fierce light of Yahweh's truth he knows they must happen (vs. 16*de*). "Yahweh, don't go back on me. Don't let me down. Don't turn out to have been an illusion. Let my critics find the falsity of what they trusted in, but let not me." The little ps. deeply reveals Jer.'s innermost thought: he is so sure he is right about God and the truth of his vocation, but then the abyss appears at his very feet.

Suppose he *is* mistaken? It is a cry of horror we

are hearing: "O God, let it not be so!" True religious faith is balanced precariously on doubt, and Jer. has the spiritual insight to recognize this and go on believing. Cf. 20:7-13.

17:19-27. Sabbath Observance. This is the kind of thing Jer. said when he went on his preaching mission on behalf of the reform party (cf. 11:1-8). The oracle promises prosperity and a stable monarchy if the **sabbath day** is respected. Probably until Josiah's reform the sabbath was little observed. It was Deut. which made the sabbath a meaningful institution. The passage shows a respect for the ordered patterns of life and a readiness to find significance in the cult (vs. 26) which many scholars find foreign to Jer.'s thought. But his mind was characterized by remarkable breadth, and while elsewhere he contemptuously dismisses insincere worship, he might well in another mood recognize the very real value of sincere practices. Vs. 26 names the several regions of Judah (see color map 1): the **land of Benjamin,** the territory N of Jerusalem; the **Shephelah,** the W foothills bordering on the Philistine coastland; the **hill country,** the central backbone from Jerusalem to Hebron; the **Negeb,** the arid region to the S.

18:1-12. Parable of the Potter. Jer. wanders through Potters Street and there the thought strikes him that as the potter shapes and reshapes the **clay** so Yahweh, who made **Israel,** can unmake her and remake her. If Israel will not cooperate with him, he will bring about the collapse of the nation. Jer. does not add "in order to remake her," but that is going to emerge in his preaching a little later. Vs. 12 is probably an editorial comment. Like the addict, Israel knows her plight, but also knows she cannot reform. The comment puts its finger on the weakness of the prophetic preaching—it lacked a gospel. That was to come later.

18:13-17. Israel's Perversity. This is a typical threat oracle. The point of the comparisons was not clear to early editors, and the passage has suffered in transmission. The emendations of the RSV make good sense. For Israel to forsake Yahweh is as contrary to nature as that **snow** should forsake **Sirion,** a peak in the perennially snow-clad Hermon range (see color map 3), or that the snow-fed streams should **run dry.** Therefore Yahweh will punish Israel to the degree that those who behold it will be profoundly shocked.

18:18-23. Opposition. Jer. is no longer blind to the extent of the resentment he is arousing (cf. 11:18-20). He has been attacking priests, prophets, and wise men, Israel's traditional teachers, and they naturally hit back. In gathering his pieces to preserve them Jer. tells us (vs. 18) in order to introduce a ps. of cursing (vss. 19-23; cf. Ps. 109). In the battle of words bitter things are said because both sides feel keenly, as has generally been the case in religious disputes.

19:1-13. The Smashed Flask. The 3rd-person narrative in vss. 1-2, 10-20:6 appears to be a prose contribution by Baruch to the Jer. anthology, but probably he was writing under Jer.'s close guidance and so reporting faithfully.

Because of its nearness to Potters Street (cf. 18:1) and the consequent dumping of a lot of potters' rubbish just outside it, one gate of Jerusalem was known as **Potsherd Gate.** This gate led to a valley known either as the **valley of the son of Hinnom,** after a previous owner, or as **Topheth.** This 2nd name may originally have had other vowels, e.g. Tephath (see above on 7:16-20). "Tephath" may have had a particular significance which is now lost, or it may have been just a place name. Because of its previous association with child-sacrifice cults, Josiah made this valley into a garbage dump for the city (II Kings 23:10) and it smoldered continually with rubbish fires. When the doctrine of an afterlife with rewards and punishments became widespread among the Jews—during the 2nd and 1st cents. B.C.—Ge ("valley of") Hinnom was corrupted into Gehenna, the NT term for hell.

These facts led Jer. to perform another acted oracle (see above on 13:1-11). He gathered a very respectable group, no doubt from the outer court of the temple, and led them to the Potsherd Gate, buying on the way an **earthen flask.** In that place of shards he asserted that Yahweh would **break** Jerusalem irreparably, and then he threw the **vessel** on the ground. The seriousness of this lay in the fact that such symbolic actions by the prophets were held not merely to illustrate the divine activity but indeed to set it in motion, to trigger it, as it were. Hence Pashhur's strong reaction in 20:1-6.

19:3-9. Into the story an editor has inserted this comment. In the catastrophe of the Exile Israel's faith in God was preserved by strenuous insistence that the disaster was his judgment on guilty Israel, who had indeed often been warned. Vs. 2 provided an opening into which a typically D summary of the divine indictment and judgment could be inserted, and it was of this the editor took advantage.

19:14-20:6. *Official Intervention.* Jer. repeats in the outer court of the temple his message of doom against the city. As a result **Pashhur,** the executive priest—the dean of the temple, as it were—tries to silence him by having him flogged and put in the stocks. When he is released the next day Jer. lets loose a mighty curse on Pashhur. Whether it was fulfilled is not specifically recorded, but the mention of another man in the same position in 29:25-26 suggests that Pashhur was one of the officials taken into captivity to Babylon in 597 (cf. II Kings 24:15). Though no date is given for this incident, it seems probable that Jer.'s acted prophecy was inspired by the Babylonian victory over the Egyptians at Carchemish in the late summer of 605 (cf. 46:2) and resulted in his being debarred from the temple, which in turn caused him to begin dictating his first manuscript to Baruch (36:1-3; see Intro.).

20:7-13. *Self-Questioning.* This ps. ranks with the next piece (vss. 14-18) and 15:15-21; 17:14-18 as the best of Jer.'s self-disclosures. The clash with Pashhur which precedes it is useful only as supplying the general circumstances. The ps. was not necessarily provoked by that incident but arose out of Jer.'s situation as a prophet of doom to his generation. He loved people and was a sociable man. No doubt he spent his whole time in the temple court—talking, arguing, withdrawing to be silent and to compose, breaking back into the conversation with his latest piece. But his participation in the group and the general tenor of his pieces were by no means always well received. Prophets of doom are not popular.

Yet Jer. needed encouragement, response, praise. It was this tension which set up the conflict within him (cf. 17:14-18).

At the beginning of this ps. the mood is on him that he may possibly be one of those poor fools whom Yahweh for his own inscrutable purposes lures on to be a false prophet (cf. I Kings 22:19-23). Yahweh has **deceived** him, and how readily he was taken in! He has gone around proclaiming **Violence and destruction!** which have not come, until he is reduced to a **laughingstock.** And yet there is the divine compulsion; if he resolves to be silent, there is **burning fire** in his **heart,** and the urge to communicate becomes uncontrollable. On the other hand—his mind is swinging from one side of the interior debate to the other—he is in very real danger. There are men in the outer court of the temple who are only waiting for one clear instance of false prophecy to get rid of him. But it won't happen! He is not a false prophet; Yahweh is on his side and will soon intervene on his behalf. His enemies will be thoroughly discredited while he will be vindicated. Vs. 13 is an anticipatory thanksgiving for this vindication. Laments were generally brought to such a close in order to assert in the strongest possible manner that the longed-for salvation would indeed come (cf. e.g. Ps. 22:22-31). Thus the ps. ends with Jer.'s confidence in himself and his mission thoroughly renewed, at least for the present. He was a man of faith who had to wrestle with doubt daily.

20:14-18. *A Birthday Curse.* The mood of this 2nd complaint is despondent. Jer. is convinced that he will not be vindicated (vs. 18) and wishes he had never come into existence. He expresses this thought in the form of a curse on the **day** of his birth, and it is a fine example of what was a widely esteemed art form. Cf. Ps. 109:6-19 and Job 3:1-26, which have the same theme; the birthday curse was probably in the common stock of contemporary poets. This is the last of the self-revelations or "confessions" of Jer. After this we have only his comments on public affairs and narratives about him. It is fitting that the last of them should show him despondent, bitter, self-distrustful. This was his inner burden. Outwardly he never faltered in his vocation. Jer. fulfilled his mission at a total cost of himself.

21:1-23:8. *Comments on Kings.* This small collection brings together some of Jer.'s comments on the kings through whose reigns he lived: Josiah, Jehoahaz, Jehoiakim, Jehoiachin, and Zedekiah (see Intro.). The items are arranged in no discernible order.

21:1-10. *Counsel for Zedekiah.* The first piece was inserted by an editor to summarize Jer.'s attitude to the Babylonian siege of Jerusalem in 588-586. It is unlikely that Jer. said in effect: "Whether you surrender or do not surrender, you yourself will die" (vs. 7). It would have weakened his case, and it contrasts with 38:17-18, which comes from Baruch. This story was one more contribution to the massive effort by Israel's teachers during the Exile to show that the catastrophe had been long planned by Yahweh and long merited by Israel. **Pashhur the son of Malchiah** (vs. 1) is not the priest of 20:1-6 but a courtier opposed to Jer.'s policies (cf. 38:1-6). **Zephaniah** was "second priest" (52:24; cf. II Kings

25:18) at the fall of Jerusalem, having apparently succeeded to Pashhur the son of Immer's position (cf. 29:25-26; see above on 19:14–20:6). The names may have been inserted by the editor-author as a touch of verisimilitude.

21:11-12. Warning to a King. The king should not neglect his highest function, the dispensing of **justice.** The first part of the royal day was regularly given over to this (cf. II Sam. 15:1-3; Ps. 101:8). Probably the king addressed is Jehoiakim, who preferred the fruits to the labors of kingship (cf. 22:15-17).

21:13-14. Rebuke to Royal Arrogance. Vs. 13a may be translated: "Behold I am against you who reign over the valley, perched on the projecting cliff." Jehoiakim had built a new palace (cf. 22:13-14) and, since Jerusalem had been spared capture for nearly 200 years, felt very secure. Jer. warns that the blaze of Yahweh's anger will set **fire** to the **forest,** i.e. wooden pillars (cf. 22:7; I Kings 7:2-8) of the palaces, and destroy **all** the city.

22:1-9. Call for Good Government. If the king performs faithfully he will continue in power undisturbed, but vss. 6-7 show the other side of the coin (cf. Isa. 1:19-20). The royal **house**—i.e. the palace, but the word means also "dynasty"—is prized as if it were **Gilead,** the forest-rich district across the Jordan, or the **summit of Lebanon,** famed for its **cedars.** Even so, if the king and his subjects are disobedient, it will be utterly destroyed.

22:10-12. Lament for Jehoahaz. This little oracle is almost unique in the OT, being contemporary comment on the event which proved the turning point of Hebrew history—the death of King Josiah at Megiddo. This disaster was such a profound contradiction of the thesis that the good prosper and the wicked are cut off in the midst of their days (cf. Ps. 37) that no one knew what to say; it is for the most part shrouded in an embarrassed silence. Even Jer., neutral as he was toward the king, refers only here to the incomprehensible occurrence. II Chr. 35:25 mentions a lament for Josiah by Jer. and other elegies, but if they ever existed none have survived. The Chronicler often records what ought to have been rather than what was.

Even here Jer.'s allusion to the tragedy is very much in passing: "Don't weep for Josiah! He is dead and out of it all, happy man! But weep for his successor Jehoahaz [**Shallum** was his pregnal name], who has been carried off to Egypt and will never come back." There will be no divine intervention, no miraculous salvation. Judah will be swept inescapably forward to the political doom and spiritual anguish which her way of life has earned for her. This oracle was no doubt uttered in the year 609, immediately after the event, and to the conviction it implies Jer. was faithful to the end of his ministry.

22:13-19. Jehoiakim's Luxury. Neutral to Josiah, contemptuous of Zedekiah, Jer. harbored only constant enmity for Jehoiakim. Throughout his reign of 11 years this king refused to recognize the new facts of the political situation—that Judah's independence had died at Megiddo with Josiah and that he himself was only a vassal, first of Egypt and then of Babylonia. So insensitive to the urgency of the times was he that he spent most of his reign building for himself a **great house** of remarkable richness (vs.

14; see above on 21:13-14). Required by his overlords to tax his subjects to the utmost to raise a huge annual tribute (II Kings 23:33-35), he carried out his building project by reviving the practice of forced labor which had led to the division of the kingdom at the death of Solomon (vs. 13).

22:15-19. Jer. contrasts Jehoiakim's profligacy with Josiah's conscientious and prosperous rule and prophesies a catastrophic end to the reign. Jehoiakim may live luxuriously, but he will die disastrously, and his burial will be like that of a dead donkey tossed on a rubbish heap. As far as we know, he died and was buried normally (cf. II Kings 24:6; see below on 36:30), though some scholars have conjectured that he may have been assassinated by courtiers who recognized the folly of his rebellion against Nebuchadrezzar. In any case he certainly died facing disaster, for the Chaldeans were at the gates of the city in irresistible force.

22:20-23. A Call to Lament. Since Jehoiakim's reign is to end so disastrously, Jer. calls Jerusalem to bewail her fate. **Lebanon** is N, **Bashan** NE, and the **Abarim** mountains E (see color map 1); at all these points of the compass she will seek her military allies—her **lovers** in the metaphor of the times—and find no help. What good then will it be that Jerusalem has been enriched with cedar-paneled palaces (cf. vs. 14)?

22:24-30. Jehoiachin, the Last of the Line. Jehoiakim's son Jehoiachin—called here by his pregnal name **Coniah,** a shortening of Jeconiah—reigned 3 months only and was deposed by **Nebuchadrezzar** and imprisoned in Babylon for 37 years before the turning wheel of political fortune gave him an easier old age (52:31-34). But he never returned to Palestine. Though his uncle, Zedekiah, did in fact occupy the throne for another 11 years, Jehoiachin was the last generation of the royal line to rule in Jerusalem —from David to Jehoiachin 4 cents. and 20 generations. On the king's **mother** see above on 13:18-19.

22:28-30. While Jer. announces the inevitability of Jehoiachin's captivity, he expresses also in this 2nd oracle its tragedy. The royal house is like a great, fine vase which has held noble wines; but now, cracked and useless, **a vessel no one cares for,** it is fit only to be smashed. The 3-fold **land** (vs. 29) is an idiom of intensity (cf. 7:4; Isa. 6:3) underlining the seriousness of the proclamation. Though the 18-year-old king probably already has **children** (cf. I Chr. 3:17, which lists 7 sons) he will be **childless** in that none of them will occupy the **throne of David.**

23:1-8. Messiah Promised. A promise of a future scion of the old stock who will reascend the throne of David and restore to Judah peace and prosperity is found in this oracle. He is no heavenly being, nor is there any promise of the age to come. These are later concepts, as yet unthought of. The promise here is simply of a "good time" under an ideal king. The last king's name is Zedekiah, meaning "Yahweh is my righteousness," and correspondingly the new king's name will be **The LORD is our righteousness** —which should be taken here as "vindication," with the emphasis on vindication for the nation as a whole. This word play on the name makes it probable that at least this part of the oracle was nearly contemporary with Zedekiah's reign. Jer.—if the oracle is his—was thus one of the earliest exponents of messianism. It was at that time a very simple and undeveloped idea, and the future prince is called simply the **Branch,** as he is often in the OT (cf. e.g. Isa. 11:1; Zech. 6:12). Since vss. 3-4, 7-8 (cf. 16:14-15) view the Jews as dispersed in **all the countries,** they are probably editorial insertions from a later time.

23:9-40. Comments on Prophets. Parallel to the collection of sayings about kings, this collection of sayings about prophets is significant in that it tells us much about Jer.'s understanding of prophecy as a phenomenon and also of his relations with his fellow prophets. Unknown to himself, Jer. was in fact preparing the way for the end of prophecy as a functioning institution in Israel, and indeed in all mature religion. The essence of prophecy was ecstatic intuition—i.e. the message "given" in a parapsychological experience, not arrived at as the result of rational thought processes. When, however, the great crisis of Israel's life arrived, the prophets were fiercely divided, each side condemning the other's interpretation and advice (cf. 28:1-16; 29:8-9, 29-32). Thus the undependability of the institution was revealed for all to see. Other prophets had differed sharply with their colleagues (cf. e.g. Isa. 28:7-8), but never before had the issue been so critical. Deut. 18:21-22 was an honest but naïve attempt to deal with the general problem, but when a generation later 2nd Isaiah's glowing prophecies were not fulfilled, prophecy as an institution was finished (cf. Zech. 13:2-6). Jer. by his controversies undoubtedly contributed largely to its decease.

23:9-12. Ungodly Prophet and Priest. The title for the whole little collection is **Concerning the prophets.** The first oracle begins with a description of the effect of Yahweh's word on the prophet—he is cast into a disordered state of mind whereby he appears befuddled and **drunken.** This reference is intended to authenticate the message which follows: the whole **land** wilts because of the **wickedness** of the spiritual leaders, **priest** and **prophet** together—it is apparent in the temple itself. Jer. does not specify the charges (cf. 5:30-31) but declares that such wickedness will be specifically and discriminatorily punished.

23:13-15. Comparison with Samaritan Prophets. Yahweh says that the prophets of Samaria were bad enough—they worshiped **Baal** and **led . . . Israel astray,** and everybody knows their punishment—but the **prophets of Jerusalem** are worse. They are as bad as the men of **Sodom** and **Gomorrah** (cf. Gen. 18:20; 19:24-25). Yahweh therefore announces his intention to punish them with bitter and deadly experiences.

23:16-20. The Issue. Here the fundamental issue is made clear: The other prophets are optimistic regarding the future and reassure the people as to Yahweh's intentions. Jer. sees that disaster lies ahead, and that this is Yahweh's punitive, purgative purpose. He hates his own message but nevertheless has to proclaim it. His indignation against those who give way to the inner temptation to please the people rather than to declare the truth is all the more intense because his own inner battles are won only at great cost. These others have never been in Yahweh's **council** (sodh; see Intro.); they do not know his purpose—one of **wrath** and destruction. When the time comes they will **understand it clearly** enough!

23:21-22. Uncalled Prophets. Jer.'s opponents have no true vocation and no authentic message. If they had been present at Yahweh's decision-making sessions, they would turn Israel back from her present evil course. That they encourage her in her present evil ways reveals their lack of true insight. This and the preceding oracle imply Jer.'s claim that he has been a member of Yahweh's council; he is privy to Yahweh's secrets (cf. Amos 3:7; Acts 15:28; see "The Prophetic Literature," pp. 1095-1100).

23:23-32. Lying Dreams and the Word. In this important passage Jer. has composed as written prose (see Intro.) a warning against counterfeit revelation. Some prophets evidently rely on their dreams as their source of inspiration. The possibilities for self-deceit are too obvious, and Jer. dismisses their ramblings scornfully—mere **straw** in comparison with the **wheat** (vs. 29) of the authentic word, which is like a **fire** to burn, a **hammer** to smash. Evidently (vs. 30) there is also a good deal of borrowing of ideas, but Jer. rejects such secondhand revelation contemptuously.

23:33-40. Rebuke for a Cant Phrase. In English the word "burden" used to mean the chorus of a song and still can refer to the gist of a message, but its basic sense is something carried physically. This extension of meaning parallels a similar extension of the corresponding Hebrew word (cf. e.g. Isa. 13:1; 15:1, where "oracle" is lit. "burden"). The prophets' use of this double meaning in the phrase **the burden of the LORD** has become, at least in Jer.'s view, a thoroughly undesirable piece of cant—a "burden" which Yahweh will **cast . . . off.**

24:1-10. Parable of the Figs. This account of an oracle concerning the Jews deported to Babylon in 597 with **Jeconiah,** i.e. Jehoiachin (see above on 22:24-30), obviously must come from Zedekiah's reign. It is thus one of the last pieces to get into "Jer.'s book" (see Intro.). It illustrates the way everyday incidents could supply the metaphor in which the divine word expressed itself. Two worshipers have placed in the temple "first fruits" consisting of **baskets of figs.** One man has had a **good** crop, the other a **very bad** one—or has chosen a poor selection for his offering. The contrast strikes Jer. forcibly; and because he has been brooding over the poor quality of leadership remaining in Judah and remembering the worthy men now in Babylon, the 2 baskets immediately become for him a parable, an expression of the divine word. By it he states a value judgment which history has thoroughly substantiated: the future of Israel lies with the exiles in Babylon.

E. CONCLUDING WORDS (25:1-14)

This is probably the endpiece of Jer.'s original anthology (1:4–8:3; see Intro.) but has been worked over by postexilic hands.

25:1-10. Summary of a Ministry. Dating in the OT is by the regnal year of the king, counted in Jer.'s time from the first new year following his accession. Scholars are not agreed on whether Judah observed the new year in the autumn or the spring during this period. If we assume an autumnal new year was continued until the Exile (see Chronology, pp. 1271-82), Jehoiakim's first regnal year began in the fall of 608, nearly a full year after Pharaoh Neco placed him on the throne, and his **fourth year** extended from the fall of 605 to the fall of 604. The Babylonian new year, on the other hand, came in the spring; and the **first year of Nebuchadrezzar,** who succeeded his father in Sep. 605, began in the spring of 604. Thus if the synchronism in vs. 1 is correct —the words in parentheses are missing from the LXX and may be a gloss—the date indicated, which is probably that of the dictation of Jer.'s first manuscript (cf. 36:1), is narrowed to the 6 months between the Babylonian spring and Judean fall new years of 604. Counting back **twenty-three years** (vs. 3), Jer.'s ministry began in 627, which until Sep. was the **thirteenth year of Josiah.**

25:5-10. This is the heart of Jer.'s message—an appeal to repent and be saved. The Christian gospel stands essentially in the prophetic tradition.

25:11-14. *Punishment of Babylon.* Jer. looked forward to a final restoration of Israel (cf. 32:9-15), and he believed the time of her captivity would be *ca.* **seventy years** (cf. 29:10). But these vss. dwell on the punishment which Babylon is to receive after 70 years, and it is probable that they owe much to someone directly interested in seeing Babylon suffer, i.e. to someone writing in the later years of the Exile. Probably the collection for which Jer. himself was responsible (see Intro.) ended with the words **this book** (vs. 13).

F. Universal Judgment (25:15-38)

In the LXX the collection of oracles against the nations (46:1–51:64) is inserted after **book** in 25:13 and this passage is used as the closing summary of that collection. The passage is itself composite. Vss. 15-16, 27-29 record in prose an oracle of Jer. against the **nations** generally, and into this there has been inserted a roll call of the nations (vss. 17-26) to show that none has been overlooked or can hope to escape. Then follow 3 small oracles (vss. 30-31, 32-33, 34-38) on the same general theme. Thus the passage as a whole must be regarded as a little collection of Jer.'s sayings against the nations which was later overshadowed by the larger collection in 46:1–51:46. In one tradition, represented by the standard Hebrew text, it remained independent as it appears here; in the other tradition, represented by the LXX and some Dead Sea scroll fragments, it came to be attached to the larger collection by way of summary (see Intro.).

25:15-16. *The Cup of Wrath.* Jer. has already employed this metaphor of drunkenness against Israel (13:12-14). Now he uses it against **all the nations** to foretell universal war as universal judgment. The passage is continued in vss. 27-29.

25:17-26. *Roll Call for Judgment.* This list of the nations to be punished comes from the period after the fall of Jerusalem, but could be from Jer. himself. **Jerusalem** lies **waste** (vs. 18), and the dominant power is **Babylon** (vs. 26). **Uz** (vs. 20) was probably in the desert to the E or SE, beyond Edom (cf. Job 1:1-3). **Dedan, Tema, Buz** (see color map 7) were Arab desert tribes whose foreign customs aroused strong Israelite dislike (cf. 9:26; Lev. 19:27). The list reveals considerable geographic knowledge in that it places in order the lands and peoples from Egypt

through to Persia. Finally the judgment is to fall on **Babylon also** (vs. 26). This may be a later addition, for it uses the "athbash" cipher for "Babylon," a device popular late in the Exile (cf. 51:1). The cipher substituted the first letter of the Hebrew alphabet for the last, the 2nd letter for the next to last, etc., and with only consonants involved always produced an apparent result. Thus BBL, "Babylon," became SSK, "Sheshach."

25:27-29. See above on vss. 15-16.

25:30-31. *The Lion of Judgment.* This metaphor is used also in Amos 1:2. There is no argument about monotheism, but it is assumed. All men are within Yahweh's **fold**—only now he has become himself the lion which attacks it.

25:32-33. *Universal Plight.* Disaster will move from one **nation** to another like a storm sweeping across the weather-map. Someone has added the gruesome detail that the dead will be too many to bury.

25:34-38. *No Escape for Shepherds or Sheep.* These vss. gather together many of the preceding ideas and metaphors. To refer to rulers as **shepherds** was quite usual (cf. e.g. Ezek. 34:7-10). Jer. uses the image to emphasize the dismay—not only the **flock** but also its keepers are being butchered. The **lion** metaphor is also resumed (vs. 38). The whole piece is a vigorous warning of the divine judgment to come.

II. Baruch's Book (26:1–45:5)

Baruch's book has more structure than at first appears. Omitting chs. 30-31, the "Book of Comfort," which requires separate consideration (see below on 30:1–31:40), the narratives and the probable dates to which they refer are as follows:

Jer. 26	Temple Sermon	Acc. Jehoiakim	609-8
27-28	Clash with Hananiah	4 Zedekiah	593
29	Correspondence with Babylon	Mid-period Zedekiah	593?
32	Purchase of Field	10 Zedekiah	587
33	Further Prophesying	10 Zedekiah	587
34	Freeing of slaves	10 Zedekiah	588
35	Rechabites	10 Jehoiakim	598
36	Writing of scroll	4 Jehoiakim	604
37-38	The siege	10-11 Zedekiah	588-6
40-43	The aftermath	Post fall of Jerusalem	583?
44	Ministry in Egypt	Early Exile	582?
45	Oracle to Baruch	4 Jehoiakim	604

It will be seen that some of the narratives are not in chronological order. Moreover each one has its own little introduction, often of a repetitive nature, giving the strong impression that at one time it circulated separately. A possible explanation is that Baruch, after the death of Jer., felt that he should continue to exert his master's influence on the current situation. The question of the day was whether Israel's faith in Yahweh and in her own distinctive future had been shown by the destruction of the Judean state to be a delusion, or whether it was possible to interpret that disaster in such a way that it could be recognized as Yahweh's deed, a severe disciplining in order to purify Israel for her renewed role in the days to come. This last was the prophetic interpretation of Israel's experience. Baruch wanted to impress this prophetic interpretation upon the exiles in Egypt, many of whom were surrendering both their faith and their national identity (cf. 44:1-30). He therefore wrote up a number of incidents in the life of his master to show that he not only foretold the disaster, but also persisted consistently in the prophetic interpretation of it, before, during, and after the event. These narratives Baruch at first circulated separately among the scattered groups of exiles and later he gathered them together to produce what is here called "Baruch's Book."

The order in which Baruch assembled his narratives was roughly chronological, if we may attribute to later disturbance the only 2 dates (chs. 35; 36) which are seriously out of line. The incident concerning the Rechabites is dated in the text as taking place during the 10th year of Jehoiakim, i.e. 599/98. If this date is correct it was probably intended to relate the incident to the first capture of Jerusalem by Nebuchadrezzar in 597. If, however, Jehoiakim should be viewed as an error for Zedekiah (see below on 35:1-19) the narrative would be in place in the sequential order.

The other misplaced story is that of the writing of the scroll. This should be either at the 2nd place, following ch. 26 or at the end preceding the personal story of Baruch (ch. 45). In this latter position it would authenticate what has gone before, and it may have been written especially to round off the series when the pieces were collected into a book. A later scribe, realizing that it was not in its chronological position, moved it to follow the other "Jehoiakim" story (which was already wrongly assigned to that reign) and so the present disorder was reached.

It should be noticed, of course, that Baruch did not put the events during the siege in the reign of Zedekiah in strict order. The purchase of the field (chs. 32-33) took place after Jer.'s imprisonment; the incidents relating to the freeing of the slaves (ch. 34) and to the Rechabites (ch. 35) took place while he was still free to come and go. But Hebrew writers frequently put the important incident first, even though it was chronologically later (cf. the order of events in the account of the reign of Hezekiah, 2 Kings 18-20). Chs. 32-33 should thus in strict chronology follow ch. 37 or perhaps ch. 38.

A. Events Before the Siege (26:1-29:32)

26:1-24. The Temple Sermon. The phrase translated **beginning of the reign** was apparently a technical term for "accession year," i.e. the part of a year between a new king's actual accession and the following new year, which began his first regnal year (see above on 25:1-10 and Chronology, pp. 1271-82). Thus Baruch's account dates the temple sermon in 609/8. It is instructive to compare his version with that of Jer. in 7:1-15. There Jer. is intent on the message and gives it with some fullness; here Baruch conveys its main thrust and then hurries on to tell what the consequences were—a part of the story

which Jer. ignores. The prophet disregards himself in his message; the disciple conveys the message only to explain how his master was in danger for his life.

26:7-9. The message is so unpalatable that it causes something of a riot, but clearly the inflammatory spark comes from Jer.'s colleagues, the **priests and prophets.** Jer. is in a minority—though not wholly alone (cf. vss. 20-24)—and his message is so contrary to the popular line that he appears to be an "enemy of the people." The nation, it is recalled, is in a state of shock following the death of Josiah and the imposition of vassalage by Pharaoh Neco.

26:10-15. The **princes,** i.e. civic rulers, intervene to stop the riot and hear a formulated charge. Jer.'s defense is that his message is a true word of Yahweh, which if need be he must die rather than withhold. If they condemn him, the magistrates will be guilty of **innocent blood.**

26:16-19. The magistrates wish to avoid decisive action and cite the parallel case of **Micah** (cf. Mic. 3:9-12). They urge on the people a general reformation of behavior—this would make their task easier and ought to satisfy the prophet. The magistrates see the riot as an "incident," to be administered skillfully away.

26:20-24. Baruch shows how the situation might have developed quite differently. Prophets did sometimes lose their lives for their plain speech, and he draws attention to the instance of **Uriah,** who was even brought back—by kidnaping? by deportation? —**from Egypt** to be put to death by **Jehoiakim.** Presumably this took place later in Jehoiakim's reign, and Baruch cites it as an example of what might have happened to Jer. **Ahikam** (vs. 24) and his father, **Shaphan,** were prominent under Josiah (cf. II Kings 22:3, 12) and Ahikam's son Gedaliah was appointed governor of Judah after the fall of Jerusalem (cf. 40:5-41:3). He is therefore an important person, whose protection counts for much.

27:1-28:17. Clash with Hananiah. The story is dated **in the beginning of the reign of Zedekiah** (27:1) and some manuscripts read "Jehoiakim." The phrase has been mechanically copied from 26:1. The date is actually the 4th year of Zedekiah (593), as in 28:1b. Baruch did not find anything in the intervening period to distract him from his main purpose of expounding Jer.'s interpretation of Babylon's role.

27:2-7. During Zedekiah's reign there is an attempt to form an anti-Babylonian alliance. **Envoys** come to Jerusalem from **Edom . . . Moab . . . Ammon . . . Tyre . . . Sidon.** As an acted oracle (see above on 13:1-11) Jer. puts on a porter's **thongs and yokebars** to urge submission to **Nebuchadnezzar**—so spelled by mistake in chs. 27-28 as elsewhere in OT—as world ruler by divine decision (cf. Isa. 20). Babylon's day of punishment will come, he says, but until then all peoples should **serve** him. **My servant** (vs. 6) means "my instrument." The unequivocal statement of monotheism (vs. 5) together with the determination of Chaldean power as limited to 3 generations (vs. 7)—Babylon fell in 539—suggests that the wording has been touched up by a later hand. But the general policy is quite in line with Isaiah's warnings against such alliances (cf. e.g. Isa. 30:1-7) and the attribution of this attitude to Jer. is undoubtedly correct.

27:8-15. Each king represented at the conference has his own spiritual advisers, ranging from magicians to **prophets,** and they are unanimous in support of the alliance. But Jer. dismisses them as dishonest time servers (cf. I Kings 22:1-28 for a close parallel). He esp. includes prophets of Yahweh —they too can be false (cf. 23:21-32).

27:16-22. Jer. carries his message to the **people.** Some popularity-seeking prophets have been telling them that a quick reversal of fortunes may be expected, and esp. that the sacred **vessels** looted from the temple when **Jeconiah,** i.e. Jehoiachin (see above on 22:24-30), was deported will speedily be returned. Jer. says that if they are true prophets they will worry about preventing the rest of the temple treasure from going the same way. For himself he is convinced that the point of no return has already been reached; Judah will now go forward steadily to disaster.

28:1-4. Jer.'s attitude arouses direct contradiction by one particular prophet, **Hananiah the son of Azzur,** who promises a return of both captives and temple paraphernalia **within two years.** The erroneous date **at the beginning of the reign** is repeated from 27:1 (see above on 27:1-28:17), but now the correct date also appears, viz. the **fifth month of the fourth year** of Zedekiah (Jul.-Aug. 593; see below on vs. 17).

28:5-9. Jer.'s reaction is not swift denial. He replies that he hopes Hananiah's prophecy will **come true** but that the tradition of Yahweh's prophets has always been one of punishment and doom.

28:10-11. Hananiah is so sure he is right that he counters Jer.'s acted oracle (see above on vss. 2-7) with one of his own. He steps up to Jer., takes the yoke-bars from him, and smashes them. So will Yahweh break Babylon's power. Jer. does not protest, but goes off quietly to think about it.

28:12-16. The conviction strengthens in Jer. that he is right and Hananiah wrong, and he later reappears with an oracle reasserting the divine intention to sustain Nebuchadrezzar as world ruler. A **wooden** yoke can be broken, but this is one of **iron.** As for Hananiah, Jer. is now convinced that he is a false prophet, and that Yahweh will remove him speedily.

28:17. Two months later Hananiah dies; Jer. naturally sees in this fact divine authentication of his message. Throughout the period of the divided monarchy months seem to have been identified by numbers, rather than names, beginning in the spring. The usage no doubt grew out of international commerce and apparently did not affect the Judean religious and regnal new year observance, which occurred in the fall, and those at the beginning of the **seventh month** (Sep.-Oct.). If by **same year** Baruch means Zedekiah's 4th year (cf. vs. 1), it would indicate that this and other dates in his book are based on regnal years beginning in the spring. On the other hand he may well mean merely the next 7th month without regard to the fact that technically it began Zedekiah's 5th year. His usage in 25:1-3; 36:1, 9 (see comments) seems to support the latter interpretation, but the evidence is inconclusive and exact equivalents of his dates cannot be determined.

29:1-32. Jer.'s Letter. Zedekiah has reason to send envoys to Babylon, and Jer. asks them to carry a **letter** to the Jews now living there in **exile** as a result of the first deportation in 597 (see above on 22:24-30). In the letter he urges the exiles to settle down and build a new life for themselves, for they are to be there for a long time. They are to play the part of good citizens of their new country, for in its **welfare** lies their own. But they are not to cease to be Yahweh's people, even in a strange land. This Jer. can say because his religion is free of all limitation, either geographical or cultic.

29:10-14. This passage is probably a later insertion, coming from an editor who knew that from the battle of Carchemish in 605 (cf. 46:2) to the Persian capture of Babylon in 539 was roughly **seventy years.** The intention is to encourage restoration hopes.

29:15-19. Similarly the postexilic editor has inserted after vs. 15 threats to the royal house (vss. 16-19) to show that the disaster was foretold. Read vs. 15 with vss. 20-23.

29:20-23. There are **prophets** among the exiles (vs. 15)—including some true prophets, e.g. Ezekiel and 2nd Isaiah—but **Ahab** and **Zedekiah** are according to Jer. false prophets. No doubt a great deal of what they said was, from the Babylonian point of view, subversive. Death by burning (vs. 22) was a regular Babylonian method of execution (cf. Dan. 3), and Jer. warns that these foolish men will surely end in the **fire.** Whether the charge of immorality (vs. 23) is seriously leveled we cannot be sure, but Jer. is clearly quite well informed on affairs in Babylon.

29:24-32. A prophet in Babylon called **Shemaiah** objects to the letter and writes angrily to the priest **Zephaniah** in Jerusalem—successor to Pashhur, who earlier put Jer. in the **stocks** (cf. 20:1-6; 52:24)—telling him to use his authority to silence Jer. The priest, however, reads the letter to Jer.—from what motive we cannot be sure, whether by way of admonition or by way of friendship and warning. Jer.'s reaction is characteristically violent, and he sends back the rejoinder that what good is coming for Yahweh's people neither Shemaiah nor **his descendants** will live to see. The quarrel between Jer. and those who differed from him was bitter and intense (cf. 23:16-20). Both sides felt that the future of the nation depended on the prevalence of their point of view.

B. The Book of Comfort (30:1-31:40)

In the early postexilic period the urgent need was to restore Israel's hope in her future. Therefore the fact that many of the great prophets had left behind them oracles of doom, prophesying Israel's utter destruction, was a very real embarrassment. Jer. did not intend to say that Israel would be completely eradicated and did in fact utter oracles of hope and restoration (cf. e.g. ch. 32), but many of his most memorable pieces were oracles of doom. An adherent of the prophetic tradition, perhaps himself of prophetic tendencies, undertook to put the matter in the right light. He took some characteristic sayings of Jer. and counterbalanced them—almost, one might say, reversed them—by words of promise in order to produce a little collection of "Jer.'s" teaching which would be encouraging and stimulating to the battered nation. The result is this little "Book of Comfort." The amount of material in it coming directly from Jer. is probably fairly small. The group to which the editor belonged was profoundly influenced by 2nd Isaiah and many of the pieces are reminiscent of his teaching.

30:1-3. Intro. The editor knows of Jer.'s writing activity (ch. 36) and uses that knowledge to gain an air of authenticity for his own **book.**

30:4-8. Reversal of Doom. Vss. 5-7 are probably an oracle from Jer. himself, typically an oracle of doom. Whether vs. 7d is original is difficult to decide, but it provides the transition to the comforting promise of vss. 8-9. National independence and the restoration of the Davidic monarchy are the 2 promises made. In the early postexilic period the restoration of the Davidic line was often more stressed than the hope of the emergence of a particular prince of that house, i.e. the coming of the "Branch" (23:5).

30:10-11. The Return of Jacob. The compiler has an encouraging little fragment which is more in the tradition of 2nd Isaiah than of Jer.—noticeably in its use of **Jacob** for the whole Hebrew people (cf. e.g. Isa. 41:8, 43:1, 44:1) but also in its general ideas. The last line perhaps should be read "but I will not punish you utterly" (lit. "exact utter vengeance"). This piece is used again for a similar purpose in 46:27-28.

30:12-17. The Healing of Israel's Wounds. Vss. 12-15 look very much like a genuine Jer. oracle. Judah has suffered terrible **punishment** (cf. Isa. 1:5-9 for the same metaphor) and has deserved it. The compiler adds to this oracle of doom a "happy ending," (vss. 16-17) again from the 2nd Isaiah tradition.

30:18-22. The New Jerusalem. This oracle envisages Jerusalem rebuilt, thronged by a numerous citizenry, ruled over by a Jewish **prince** genuinely respectful of Yahweh, with the covenant of God and people firmly renewed. On **rebuilt upon its mound** see "Archaeology," pp. 1054-62).

30:23-31:1. Yahweh's Storm. Again a little saying of Jer.'s, threatening the approach of Yahweh's relentless anger. The compiler has seized on the last line and added his own remark: "Yes, what men will understand is that Yahweh is their God and Israel is his people." He has cleverly made his point: after punishment, forgiveness and restoration.

31:2-6. Yahweh's Everlasting Love. This beautiful little oracle is very much in the style of 2nd Isaiah. The patience of God is inexhaustible (vs. 3). As a result N Israel and Judah will be restored and **Zion** will be the happy center of Yahweh's worship.

31:7-9. The Exiles' Return. This oracle offers a picture of all the scattered Israelites coming back amid universal joy (cf. Isa. 49:8-13).

31:10-14. A Watered Garden. The restored nation is pictured in idyllic terms, again strongly in the style of 2nd Isaiah.

31:15-17. No More Weeping. A fragment of Jer. (vs. 15) provides the text for this piece. He imagines **Rachel,** the mother of the Joseph (i.e. Ephraim and Manasseh) and Benjamin tribes weeping from her tomb in **Ramah** (see comment on Gen. 35:16-20) over her slaughtered **children.** Jer. was himself in a camp for deportees in Ramah (40:1). But the editor takes the imagery further and pictures Yah-

weh as bidding her weep no more. **There is hope for your future,** he says, an expression of the editor's grand theme.

31:18-20. The Prodigal's Awakening. Here **Ephraim,** a common name for N Israel, is envisaged as coming to repentance (cf. Luke 15:17-19). Smiting on the **thigh** (vs. 19) appears to be a gesture of grief (cf. Ezek. 21:12). This time the editor adds his fragment from Jer. at the end: a proclamation of Yahweh's undying love for Ephraim. He thus makes his point that man's penitence will always be met by God's love.

31:21-22. The New Development. Israel is bidden to establish **waymarks** in the desert so that her people may find their way back. She is not to hesitate and think this may be dangerous, for Yahweh has introduced a new factor into the situation which has transformed Israel's whole position. The enigma is in the last line. What is the new move of Yahweh which has so radically changed the whole picture? The translation **a woman protects a man** would seem to mean that **virgin Israel** protects Yahweh, which does not seem appropriate, if only because the new move is of Yahweh's making. Several emendations have been suggested—e.g. "a woman becomes a man," but this does not link with any other biblical, or indeed ancient Near Eastern, cultic or mythological idea. The verb is a form of the root "go around" and thus can mean "encompass." This suggests a woman carrying a man-child in her womb. If this is the meaning, the promised **new thing** is the birth of the Messiah, and the enigmatic character of the oracle is due to its dangerous political implications—Haggai, Zechariah, and Zerubbabel probably all fell foul of the Persian authorities because of messianism. The oracle then ranks with Isa. 9:2-7 as a prophecy of hope based on an expectation of a deliverer to be born to the royal house.

31:23-25. Zion a Blessing. In the day of its restoration Zion will be so pleasant and lovely that men will confidently call down a blessing on it.

31:26. Apocalyptic Framework. Some of the material the editor is using may have come from a work of apocalyptic character in which revelations were represented as being received in dreams (see "The Apocalyptic Literature," pp. 1106-09). Part of the apocalyptic framework seems to have been inadvertently retained.

31:27-28. Yahweh the Farmer. Yahweh's **seed** is Israel, and he will cultivate his holding with very great care. The passage echoes Jer.'s own words in 1:10.

31:29-30. Individual Responsibility. The proverb means: "The generation of Manasseh sinned, but we are bearing the punishment," and implies that Yahweh is unjust. The reply says nothing about the past but promises that in the golden age to come each man will bear the responsibility **for his own sin** only. The oracle testifies to the emerging importance of the individual (cf. Ezek. 18; see comment).

31:31-34. The New Covenant. This oracle is of such importance in the Bible as a whole that scholars have been reluctant to admit that it may not be Jer.'s. It certainly complements his somewhat negative teaching. Circumcision, the ark, the temple, the city, the state, prophet, priest, king can all go, he says, since they are not essential. But what *is* essential? This great oracle declares it: **I will put my law within them, and I will write it upon their hearts.** When the time of restoration comes, men will do what is right from inner conviction and desire. In this way the **covenant** of Yahweh and Israel will be finally and permanently renewed. Ezekiel sets the same idea in different imagery (cf. Ezek. 36:24-28).

Jesus made the phrase **a new covenant** his own at the Last Supper, and the organization of scripture into 2 covenants, i.e. testaments, follows from this. Here the talk is of an old covenant renewed—the covenant of Yahweh and Israel. It is not accompanied by any new obligations, for the old are well known. Jesus used the phrase to speak of a truly new covenant, with mankind rather than Israel, and with new obligations, i.e. those of the law of love. Whether Jer. voiced this prophecy or not, it certainly is in keeping with his teaching, and the profound insight it displays is fully worthy of the prophetic tradition at its best (cf. Num. 11:26-29; Joel 2:28-29).

31:35-37. *The Immutable Covenant.* The Hebrews early grasped the notion of the patterned and stable functioning of nature, a notion on which all modern science is based. Here that idea of imperturbable nature is used to illustrate somewhat grandiosely the immutable character of Yahweh's covenant with Israel—it is as unshakable as a natural law.

31:38-40. *The New City Plan.* This oracle foresees Jerusalem as not merely restored but enlarged. Beginning in the NE at the tower of **Hananel** (cf. Neh. 3:1; Zech. 14:10) the new boundary is traced to the **Corner Gate** (cf. II Kings 14:13), probably on the NW, and on around through the unknown **Gareb** and **Goah** to the **Horse Gate** (cf. Neh. 3:28) so as to take in the Hinnom (vs. 40*a;* see above on 19:1-13) and **Kidron** valleys (see color map 13). All this territory, though now polluted, is to become part of the city **sacred to the LORD.** The idea of the renewed covenant is to be embodied in a renewed Jerusalem. So ends a little work which is one of the most striking in all scripture.

C. Events During the Siege (32:1–35:19)

32:1-25. *The Field at Anathoth.* If the **tenth year of Zedekiah** may be assumed to have ended in the fall of 587 (see above on 25:1-10; 28:17) the synchronism with the **eighteenth year of Nebuchadrezzar,** which began in the spring of that year, dates this incident within the 6-month period between the equinoxes. Jer.'s arrest, confinement in a prison, and transfer, after an appeal to Zedekiah, to the **court of the guard** are related in 37:11-21. Chronologically, therefore, this ch. should come after ch. 37, possibly after ch. 38. The introductory recapitulation of vss. 2-5 suggests that the various narratives in Baruch's book originally circulated independently. **Until I visit** him (vs. 5) means here "until I punish him," i.e. with death.

32:6-8. When a man was forced by need for money to sell part of his land, he was required to offer it first to the members of the family, who had the **right of redemption** (cf. Ruth 4:1-6). **Hanamel** wants to sell a field at **Anathoth,** but it is a highly speculative proposition in which he is trying to interest Jer. since the city is under siege and the future

is very insecure. Money is easily portable by escaping refugees, but it would be foolish to acquire land at such a time. Notice that prophets firmly believed that they received premonitions; Elisha could even be disconcerted by not having had a premonition of a significant event (II Kings 4:27).

32:9-14. Jer. buys the land and we have an interesting description of the attendant formalities. **Silver** money in Jer.'s day consisted of bars or rings which had to be **weighed** at each transaction (on **shekels** see table, p. 1285). Many deeds of sale dated in the next 2 cents. have come down to us from the Jewish colony on the Nile island of Elephantine (see "The History of Israel," pp. 1026-31). To guard against alteration this deed is prepared in duplicate and one copy is **sealed;** i.e. it is rolled and tied and the ties are fastened with clay into which is impressed a signet ring or stamp. The documents are placed for safekeeping in an **earthenware vessel**—cf. the jars in which the Qumran community stored their treasured manuscripts as late as the first cent. A.D. (see ill., p. 1067). **Baruch** (vs. 12) naturally draws attention to his role as Jer.'s confidant.

32:15. Jer. discloses that his actions are symbolic, that the purchase of the field is an acted oracle intended to foretell that Israel will one day be restored. There is little reason to doubt that this message of hope after doom was part of Jer.'s thought, but before the blow fell it attracted little attention. Men were more concerned with the possibility that the disaster could be averted. When Jerusalem had fallen, it became all-important that men should accept and live by this hope.

32:16-25. Baruch recalls that Jer. prayed aloud after the ceremony; and here he gives us his version of that prayer, a version which owes probably more to him than to Jer. The theological standpoint is thoroughly in accord with D orthodoxy. The prayer ends abruptly; perhaps the expansions which follow are substitutes for some phrase like "for thou wilt yet show favor to Jerusalem."

32:26-44. *D Expansions.* Later editors saw at this point in Baruch's narrative an opportunity to reinforce their all-important interpretation of the great disaster. In vss. 26-35 they show why Yahweh punished Judah so severely, and then in vss. 36-44 they stress the message of restoration. On vs. 35 see above on 19:1-13. On vs. 44 see on 17:19-27. Everything is contained within the bounds of D thought, but the notion of the renewed heart is very much to the fore. This passage, esp. vss. 38-40, ranks with 31:33; Ezek. 36:26 as the great OT anticipations of the first summary of Jesus' teaching: "Repent, and believe in the gospel" (Mark 1:15)—i.e. "Change your mind and believe the good news!"

33:1-9. The expansions of Jer.'s message of hope (cf. 32:15) are continued. Vs. 4, which is textually obscure, seems to refer to desperate but not uncommon practices for the defense of a besieged city. Cf. Isa. 22:8*b*-10. But Jerusalem's lot is going to be so changed that her **prosperity** under very evident divine favor will win the respect of her neighbors. Indeed her present persecutors will have reason to **fear** her renewed strength and vitality. But this last thought is not followed up. In later, apocalyptic works it was to become a dominating theme.

33:10-13. The social merriment of a happy people, and the liturgical joy of a worshiping people (cf. Zech. 8:19; Ps. 136:1; II Chr. 5:13; 7:3), both find their place in the renewed city. On vs. 13 see above on 17:19-27.

33:14-26. This expansion is very late and did not secure inclusion in the LXX textual tradition (see Intro.). It is of special interest because it is a messianic prophecy, looking for the divinely chosen descendant of **David** to come and restore the Judean kingdom. His reign is to be characterized by **justice** (cf. Isa. 11:3-4). Not everyone longed for the Messiah, the **Branch** of the old tree of David. The priesthood was generally neutral or even hostile to the idea, and in this passage the references to the priesthood alongside the Messiah may well be placatory in character. The claim that the divine **covenant** with the house of David and with the **Levitical priests** is as immutable as the physical laws of the universe must be recognized as hyperbole; for while Davidic messianism may be held to have come to fulfillment in Jesus, the Zadokite priesthood came to an end in the first cent. A.D. The men behind these additions were thus wrong in some of their prognostications, but they were right in their optimism and their faith.

34:1-7. *A Warning and a Promise.* Baruch's narrative, interrupted since 32:26, continues with this message to **Zedekiah.** It testifies to his accuracy, for vss. 4-5 record an oracle personally reassuring to the king which was not fulfilled (cf. 52:9-11), yet Baruch honestly includes it (see below on vss. 21-22). The fear which a tyrant like Nebuchadrezzar could instill in the little princedoms of Palestine is well caught in **you shall see the king of Babylon eye to eye and speak with him face to face** (vs. 3). Baruch's purpose is to place on record the consistency of Jer.'s message: "This is Yahweh's will; surrender to it." The incident took place in the early months of the siege; and the reference to **Lachish and Azekah,** cities in the foothill region SW of Jerusalem (see color map 8), has received much illumination from the discovery at the site of Lachish of a number of letters written on potsherds during the reign of Zedekiah. One of them, dated in his 9th year

(589/88), is the report of a Judean captain to his superior: "We are watching for the smoke signals of Lachish, . . . because we do not see Azekah." No doubt Azekah was already overrun, and Lachish must have fallen soon after. Jerusalem was left to stand the siege alone.

34:8-22. *Treachery to Freed Slaves.* When the Babylonians first approached Jerusalem there was a great need for national unity; so it was proposed that all **Hebrew slaves** be given their freedom. Jer. refers to the old law that a fellow Hebrew could be enslaved for only **six years** and must then be released (Exod. 21:2; Deut. 15:12). This custom had fallen into disuse, but with the Babylonian threat it was revived. Now the Egyptians have made a show of strength and the Babylonians have had to raise the siege (vs. 21; cf. 37:6-15). Thinking that this is permanent relief, the slaveowners have promptly reenslaved those recently liberated.

34:17-20. Evidently the ceremony of liberation was a solemn and public one, attended by an ancient **covenant** ritual (vss. 18-19) in which the sacrificial beast was cut into **two . . . parts** and the parties to the covenant **passed between** them (cf. Gen. 15:7-10, 17-18). By some legal device the rich have found a way around this covenant, and are reenslaving poverty-stricken Hebrews. This cynicism shocks Jer. deeply. Yahweh, he says, will give the Jewish leaders freedom—freedom from his service and freedom to die by war, hunger, and disease!

34:21-22. Vs. 21 may be meant specifically to revoke the oracle of personal reassurance to **Zedekiah** recorded in vs. 4. The Egyptians soon pulled back and the siege was resumed without further interruption to the tragic end. This incident of the slaves evidently impressed Jer. deeply. It revealed how far-reaching was the decay of Judean public and private morality. Only **fire** could purge such corruption!

35:1-19. *The Rechabites.* This incident is dated in the days of **Jehoiakim** (vs. 1) at a time when the Rechabites have come into Jerusalem for safety because of attack by **Nebuchadrezzar** (vs. 11), but Nebuchadrezzar did not bring his army against Judah until the time of Jehoiakim's death in Dec. 598. The occasion has therefore been taken by some to be the earlier attack by marauding bands of **Chaldeans** and **Syrians** (cf. II Kings 24:2). But in view of the aversion of the Rechabites to city life (see below on vss. 2-11) it seems doubtful that the situation ever became desperate enough to drive them into Jerusalem during the reign of Jehoiakim. If instead we recognize Jehoiakim as a mistake for Zedekiah and the time as the siege, this narrative falls into place chronologically in the series as a whole.

35:2-11. The **Rechabites** were a clan, probably related to the Kenites, who in protest against civilization maintained a seminomadic existence despite the progressive urbanization of Israel. Rather like the modern gypsies, they avoided houses, agriculture, or anything that would tie them to one locality. Since viniculture is a long and restrictive process, a prohibition against **wine** was outstanding among their taboos. Jer. gathers a group of Rechabites in one of the cloister alcoves of the temple and publicly offers them wine, which they refuse as anticipated.

35:12-19. The loyalty of the Rechabites to their

principles provides Jer. with the basis for his prophetic declaration: The members of this clan have an abnormal way of life in which they persist wholeheartedly; Israel has a wholesome way of life and a more pervasive obligation, arising out of a covenant with Yahweh himself, and yet cannot keep to it. There is a future for a disciplined group such as the Rechabites, but for the Israelites there can be only the punishment they have brought on their own heads.

D. The Writing of the Scroll (36:1-32)

The mistaken attribution of the foregoing piece (35:1-19; see comment) to Jehoiakim's reign suggested to an editor bringing this other Jehoiakim story to stand with it. Its proper place is instead probably at the end of Baruch's book, just before the oracle to Baruch in 45:1-4, which is indeed a pendant to this narrative (see above on 26:1–45:55). Chronologically, however, the events belong following ch. 26. See also comment on 19:14–20:6. The dictation of the scroll is dated the **fourth year of Jehoiakim** (vs. 1) and its public reading the **fifth year . . . ninth month** (vs. 9), i.e. Dec. 604. If Baruch counted the 5th year as beginning in the fall (see above on 25:1-10) the writing may have occurred as late as Sep. 604, *ca.* 3 months before the reading, but if he reckoned on a spring new year (see above on 28:17) the interval was at least 9 months and the scroll was prepared in the winter of 605/4.

36:2-8. Jer.'s Exclusion from the Temple. Jer. was a man of the outer courts of the temple, where he warned for many years of a foe from the N, an idea which seemed irrelevant and harmless. When, however, Egypt fell back in 605 before Nebuchadrezzar's advance Jer.'s preaching suddenly became relevant and dangerous. He was meddling in high affairs of state and must be stopped. The way to do this, it appeared, was to deny him the forum of the outer courts. But if Jer. could not speak one way he would find another, and he took the revolutionary step of writing out some of his most striking pieces. Jer. was not thinking of his teaching's survival—Jesus never wrote a book—but was intent solely on its communication.

36:9-10. The Cloister Reading. On a **fast** day, an occasion which Jer. hopes will put the crowds in a mood to accept his message, he sends Baruch into the temple with his scroll. If it consisted of 1:1–8:3 plus 25:1-14 (see Intro.) it could easily be read 3 times in one day. The circle (*sodh;* see Intro.) which customarily gathered in the cloister of **Gemariah** was one with access to officialdom and was doubtless chosen with this in mind. **Shaphan** was secretary under Josiah (cf. II Kings 22:3-10; see above on 26:20-24).

36:11-19. The Secretarial Office Reading. Gemariah's son, probably a youth, hears the cloister reading and hurries to tell his father, whom he finds in the palace in the office of the present **secretary.** With them are the other **princes,** i.e. officials of the government, including **Elnathan,** who brought back the prophet Uriah from Egypt (cf. 26:22). After summoning Baruch and hearing the scroll, they particularly inquire if the sayings were actually dictated by Jer.—lit. "Were these words from his mouth?" Why

Baruch should add the detail **with ink** is not clear, esp. as the word occurs only here; possibly it is an error for a phrase like "on his behalf" or "as much as he would." The fact that this document comes directly from a prophet gives its contents an authority which otherwise they would not have. But the officials recall the king's character and warn Baruch and Jer. to **hide.** The case of Uriah (26:20-23) shows this to be a wise precaution.

36:20-26. The Palace Reading. When the officials report to the king he insists on hearing the scroll read, but the oracles of doom leave him unmoved. Even though 2 or 3 of those present risk the royal displeasure by protesting, he shows his disdain by burning the scroll piecemeal. It is sometimes suggested that the scroll must have been made of papyrus imported from Egypt because the burning of one made of skin would have created a stench. The evidence of the Dead Sea scrolls suggests that leather was the usual material for the Palestinian scribe. The sheets of a scroll were stuck or stitched together, and Jehoiakim evidently cuts them off one after another. After the last one he orders the arrest of Jer. and Baruch, but they have already disappeared. Baruch feels their survival is providential: **the LORD hid them.**

36:27-32. The New Scroll. Jer. and Baruch use their enforced leisure to prepare a 2nd scroll—the former one with additions. This 2nd scroll is probably the groundwork of 1:1–25:14 (see Intro.). Jer. pronounces a curse on Jehoiakim (cf. 22:19), which was not fulfilled (cf. II Kings 24:6). It seems that Baruch was not disturbed by unfulfilled details so long as events bore out the main thrust of his master's prophecy. This he could fully claim.

E. Further Events During the Siege (37:1–39:18)

This narrative is concerned to relate the part played by Jer. during the siege. Baruch refers to other matters only as they are necessary to this purpose.

37:1-2. A Recapitulation. That Baruch's book was issued in separate parts is well indicated by this recapitulation. On **Coniah** see above on 22:24-30.

37:3-5. A Royal Plea. Prayer under these circumstances is considered a sufficiently weighty matter for the employment of the **priest** who is "dean" of the temple (cf. 29:25-26; 52:24) and another important courtier, who are to seek out Jer. and ask him to **pray** for the city. **Jehucal** appears again in a slightly different spelling in 38:1, where he is one of those who take the lead against Jer. The occasion is the brief period during the siege when an Egyptian show of strength temporarily draws off the attacking Babylonian forces. Jer. at this time is still at liberty. Up to this point the narrative is not very coherent because Baruch is still linking this particular story with the general course of events.

37:6-10. Consistent Warning. Amid the general rejoicing at the Babylonian withdrawal Jer. remains unimpressed. He is sure they will return.

37:11-15. Jer.'s Arrest. As the refugees stream out of the city to return to their own homes Jer. is among them. Probably he wants to reestablish connection with his family lands, from which he may have drawn some small remittance enabling him to live in Jerusalem these many years without, so far as we know, secular occupation. Following the Babylonian reverse there is no doubt a general move against known sympathizers with their cause. Jer. is not such a one, but that is what he appears to be, and he is arrested, flogged, and imprisoned.

37:16-21. Royal Inquiry Renewed. After some time in the cellars of Jonathan's house Jer. is brought out to appear before Zedekiah. The return of the Babylonians and the resumption of the siege make it seem possible that he is right after all, and Zedekiah wants to know his version of Yahweh's intentions. Jer. gives the answer sternly and uncompromisingly: the Babylonians will take the city. The king is sufficiently impressed to make things a little easier for the prophet but not to accept his advice and surrender the city.

38:1-6. Jer. in the Pit. Jer. continues to expound his view of the political situation to the anger of the Jewish leaders. In their view he is destroying the morale of their **soldiers,** with whom he is in direct contact in the guardhouse. The king bitterly stigmatizes his own weakness and his complete loss of control of events: he cannot prevent his courtiers from doing what they want. Yet they are not prepared to execute Jer. out of hand. He has the aura of divine protection sufficiently to make them hesitate. They throw him into an old **cistern,** now devoid of **water** but feet deep in mud and debris. Jer. cannot last long there.

38:7-13. The Rescue. An **Ethiopian** slave, **Ebedmelech,** proves indeed a "good Samaritan," a man who acts generously under no obligation when others who have that obligation fail to act. Baruch gives us remarkable detail at this point, as if perhaps he was himself involved.

38:14-23. A Question Repeated. The king makes a pitiable figure, constantly asking for the truth and yet, when he finds it unpalatable, seeking to evade it. Jer. has consistently urged **surrender** in the past, and does so now. Even at this time the king can save the **city** from utter destruction and his own miserable **life** if he will surrender to the Babylonians. Otherwise what Jer. has already seen in **vision** will become a reality: the harem **women** being **led out** to the conquerors wailing a proverb, "You trusted in false friends." The reference is to Egypt, against whom the prophets have warned for so long (cf. Isa. 20:1-6; 30:1-7; 31:1-3), and on whom the resistance party still pins its last hopes. Zedekiah's reply shows how tragic is Judah's position: there are already such animosities among the Jews that he fears, not the attacking enemy, but his own people who have gone over to that enemy. Judah is indeed a sick nation.

39:24-28. A Miserable Subterfuge. To finish this unhappy scene the king begs his prisoner to tell a lie, a request to which Jer. agrees. He will not compromise on the divine word, but in lesser matters he is more accommodating.

39:1-10. The Fall of the City. After a lengthy siege (see Chronology, pp. 1271-82) a **breach** is made in the wall and Jerusalem is taken. The names in vs. 3 have become muddled; probably only 2 junior generals are intended, **Sarsechim the Rabsaris** (lord high chamberlain?) and **Nergal-sharezer the Rabmag** (head of the cabinet?). It is probable that the whole of this paragraph was adapted from II Kings 25:1-

12 by an editor who felt that some account of the fall of Jerusalem should be included. If it is omitted the story of Jer. flows smoothly from 38:28 to vs. 11.

39:11-14. Jer.'s Release. The Babylonian intelligence has evidently sent back favorable reports on Jer., who appears to them as a sympathizer and a 5th-columnist on their behalf. They therefore free him from prison and turn him over to the new governor, **Gedaliah** (see below on 40:7-12).

39:15-18. A Belated Oracle. Baruch now remembers **Ebed-melech,** and somewhat belatedly he tells us that Jer. sent a message of personal reassurance to his rescuer. Since Baruch records the same phrase used of himself (45:5; cf. 21:9), he probably intends us to understand that Ebed-melech was also one of those who survived the indiscriminate butchery and the subsequent fire.

F. THE AFTERMATH (40:1-43:44)

40:1-6. Jer.'s Decision. Here is another intro., suggesting a unit designed for independent circulation. It picks up the incident told already in 39:11-14 and retells it in greater detail. At first Jer. is included in the group of survivors who are to be marched off to Babylon, and he is already at **Ramah,** 5 miles N of Jerusalem (see color map 8), where the exiles are being gathered (cf. 31:15-17). Baruch puts into the mouth of **Nebuzaradan** a speech of quite remarkable orthodoxy, but the outcome is the same as in the previous ch.: Jer. chooses to stay in his beloved homeland. He can tell the exiles in Mesopotamia that Israel's future lies with them (24:4), but he is not himself the stuff of which emigrants are made. Archaeologists are divided between 2 proposed locations of **Mizpah** (vs. 6), where the new governor has his headquarters. One ca. 2 miles N of Ramah is favored by many (see color map 8); but the other, ca. 4 miles SW of Ramah and 1½ miles S of Gibeon, fits the account in 41:10-12 better (see below on 41:11-18).

40:7-12. Gedaliah's Attempts at Salvage. The Babylonians decide to incorporate Judah into their imperial system and appoint Gedaliah, a member of a prominent family (see above on 26:20-24), as **governor.** Gedaliah tries to rally the remaining Jews and succeeds in attracting some who have escaped to other lands to return to Judah.

40:13-16. Gedaliah's Danger. In the disorganized countryside there is still much unrest. To some Gedaliah looks simply like a collaborationist; to others, e.g. the Ammonite sheikh in the desert, he looks disturbingly like a man who may yet put Judah on its feet again; to yet others he is someone of whom to be jealous. Into this last category falls **Ishmael,** himself a member of the royal house (41:1). **Johanan** warns Gedaliah of his danger, but he misreads the situation and is overconfident.

41:1-3. The Murder of Gedaliah. Ishmael kills Gedaliah and many of his supporters, together with the few Babylonian **soldiers** left to represent the imperial power. He also kills a number of **Jews**—though **all** is an exaggeration (cf. vs. 10)—who have accepted Gedaliah's leadership.

41:4-10. Murder of the Pilgrims. Whether these men were normally resident in the towns mentioned we do not know, but the time of the feast has arrived and, though the shrine has been destroyed, they value the act of worship so greatly that they undertake the journey even in such perilous times. Religious patterns of behavior are hard to eradicate. Jer. is being proved right: the temple may be destroyed, but the religion of Yahweh goes on. The disheveled state of dress of these pilgrims (vs. 5) and their somewhat pagan demonstration of grief by inflicting on themselves superficial wounds (cf. Lev. 19:27-28) point to their sincerity. Why Ishmael murders them is not clear, unless it is to keep secret his murder of Gedaliah. Yet he spares **ten** who bribe their way to survival.

41:9-10. As a fortress **Mizpah** has a large **cistern** for water supplies in time of siege, which is traced back to the time of **King Asa** in the 9th cent. This serves as a common grave. Ishmael rounds up the rest of the Mizpah community, mostly women, but including Jer., and presumably Baruch—this story surely comes from an eyewitness—and sets off to hide in the desert among the **Ammonites.** The women and children are marketable as slaves. The **king's daughters** can hardly be daughters of Zedekiah, for the Babylonians would not leave persons so politically valuable behind—usurpers often legitimatized their claims by marrying into the family they were displacing. Perhaps they are Gedaliah's daughters.

41:11-18. *Johanan's Retaliation.* Ishmael doubtless goes to **Gibeon** for water from the **great pool,** i.e. cistern, which was rediscovered in 1956-57 and excavated. If Mizpah lay N of Ramah (see above on 40:1-6 and color map 5) Gibeon would be to the SW and therefore the opposite direction from Ammon. This account therefore favors the location of Mizpah SW of Ramah and *ca.* 1½ miles S of Gibeon. Johanan's attack frees the captives, though Ishmael and some of his men escape. Johanan and the survivors camp near **Bethlehem.** They know the Babylonians will seek to punish someone for this outrage and fear that they will not be too careful in their choice.

42:1-22. *The Oracle of Jer.* The men are seeking, not Jer.'s opinion, but a direct communication from Yahweh through him. **Good or evil** (vs. 6) means simply "pleasing or displeasing." The prophets' ecstatic states could not be brought on at will, though they could be encouraged (cf. II Kings 3:15). On this occasion they have to wait **ten days** before Jer. can deliver the oracle. **Repent of the evil** (vs. 10) is a phrase used very much from the sufferer's point of view and implies only that Yahweh's purpose is now changing.

As it turned out, **Egypt** was to provide a home for generations of Jews, esp. at Alexandria, right on into the 2nd cent. A.D. Some of the best Jewish literature and the best Jewish scholarship was to come from Egypt—e.g. the LXX, Wisd. Sol., and the writings of Philo. But Jer. and Baruch can see no good thing in Egypt. At the end of the ch. Baruch allows his knowledge of subsequent events to appear in the oracle, and the people are berated for a choice they have not yet made.

43:1-7. *Counsel Refused.* The refugees do not trust the counsel of Jer. and say that it is colored by his own prejudices and those of Baruch. This last addi-

tion (vs. 3) suggests that **Baruch** had more influence with the prophet than the rest of the book would lead us to believe. Jer. and Baruch apparently have no choice but to go along with the general decision. **Tahpanhes** (see color map 9) was the first town in Egypt which a refugee from Palestine would reach.

43:8-13. *Babylonian Conquest Foretold.* Probably **Pharaoh's palace** means simply a government building rather than a royal residence, and the symbolic act of hiding the stones **in the mortar in the pavement** may have taken place in the roadway outside. A little knot of men busy with a small hole would not arouse much curiosity. The oracle, if understood by the Egyptians, would most certainly interest them. The Hebrew text of vs. 12*c* reads: "He shall array himself with the land of Egypt as a shepherd putteth on his garment" (KJV), which suggests Nebuchadrezzar carelessly walking off with the country's wealth. The RSV, following the LXX, has a grimmer thought: as a **shepherd** periodically delouses his **cloak,** so Nebuchadrezzar will systematically eradicate all life from Egypt. Nebuchadrezzar may have raided Egypt—an inscription claims a victory over Pharaoh Amasis in his 37th year—but there was never any such sweeping conquest as Jer. foretells. **Heliopolis** (see color map 9) was a center of worship of the sun god.

G. MINISTRY IN EGYPT (44:1-30)

In this narrative Baruch gives an account of the general message of Jer. during his Egyptian exile and of one particular incident wherein he clashes with his fellow refugees.

44:1-14. *Appeal and Warning.* Jer. has settled in **Tahpanhes** on the frontier (43:7). **Migdol** was fairly close by (see color map 9). **Memphis** was the ancient capital of Lower Egypt and **Pathros** was an old name for Upper Egypt. The Jews were already widely dispersed. Vss. 2-10 are an appeal to learn the lesson of their experience. Vss. 11-14 warn that if the sin of disloyalty to Yahweh characterizes them in Egypt as it did in Palestine the same punishment will befall them.

44:15-19. *A Different Reading.* The disloyal Jews to whom Jer. is talking (omit **Pathros** in vs. 15 as a gloss) have observed the same phenomena as he, but they draw very different conclusions. As they see it, during Manasseh's reign their **fathers** worshiped the **queen of heaven** (vs. 17) and all went well with them. Then Jer. and his friends carried through the D reformation, and since then nothing has gone right. Thus they are now returning to Asherah-Ashtarath, the Great Mother (see 7:16-20) —and all will be well. It was a justifiable alternative interpretation of the facts, and yet those who accepted it had no future. The future lay, as events have shown, with the prophetic interpretation of Israel's history, and therein was Jer.'s genuine inspiration from God.

44:20-30. *Reiterated Warning.* Jer. repeats his warning at length and ends by declaring that punishment will befall **Pharaoh Hophra.** His eyes are not on distant cents., but on the immediate future. Hophra was in fact dethroned and murdered, but as a result of internal rebellion, not foreign invasion.

H. Consolation to Baruch (45:1-5)

Baruch, who has so far remained very much in the background, here allows himself to take, as it were, a small bow at the close. The oracle to Baruch is sometimes read as a rebuke to him, but it is a sincerely meant "well done, thou good and faithful servant." In the general disaster he cannot but be involved, but at least his own **life** will be preserved as a **prize of war,** something snatched thankfully out of the conflict. Baruch introduces the oracle here simply to say: "This is who I am, and this is what authenticates for you the foregoing manuscript." He leaves us with the impression that he is a very modest, a very reliable, and indeed a very remarkable person.

III. Oracles Against the Nations (46:1-51:64)

One of the staple subjects of a prophetic ministry was Yahweh's judgment on foreign **nations.** This was especially true of Jer. (1:10). Often the disciples of a prophet gathered together the things he had said about other peoples, and such collections now appear in various places in the prophetic anthologies, e.g. Isa. 13-23. In Jer. the collection is found here in the Hebrew text but after 25:13 in the LXX, which also has the contents in a different order.

A. Concerning Egypt (46:2-28)

46:2-12. The Battle of Carchemish. After the intro. (vs. 2) we have 2 pieces (vss. 3-6, 7-12) which relate to the battle between the forces of Egypt, pushing N in an attempt to gain Syria-Palestine, and those of the Babylonians, pushing S in an attempt to over-

Babylonian Chronicle tablets recording the battle of Carchemish in 605 B.C. and the fall of Jerusalem to Nebuchadrezzar in 597 B.C.

run all the W provinces of the former Assyrian Empire.

46:2. The 2 armies met at **Carchemish** on the upper **Euphrates** (see color map 9). Jer. consistently sees **Nebuchadrezzar** as the instrument of Yahweh's purpose. Babylonian records show that the battle occurred in the summer of 605. The dating **in the fourth year of Jehoiakim** is correct only if his regnal years are counted from a spring new year (see above on 25:1-10; 28:17; 36:1-32), but this vs. may well have been inserted by an editor at a time when the Babylonian calendar was universally observed.

46:3-6. This first piece is decidedly satirical. It describes the Egyptians' careful preparation for the battle as if these are the actions of determined men, ready to do or die. But what's this? They're running away! The moment of revelation comes in the line **terror on every side!** The panic is supernaturally inspired. The Egyptians discover that they are fighting, not against men, but against Yahweh.

46:7-9. Similarly these vss. picture the Egyptian army rising as irresistibly as the **Nile** and spreading relentlessly over the land. The **warriors** of vs. 9 may be mercenaries (cf. vs. 21; on **Put** and **Lud** see comment on Isa. 66:18-23). Again (vs. 10) there is the moment of dreadful revelation. The Egyptians discover that the set purpose of Yahweh is to hold a holocaust **in the north country** and that they are the destined victims.

46:11-12. The tone changes to that of a taunt song: **Go up to Gilead** and see if you can get anything to cure a wound such as this! On Gilead's medical reputation see above on 8:22-9:1.

Whether Jer. produced these pieces before or after the battle, they are by way of comment on current affairs, and their effect is to warn Judah against throwing in her lot with Egypt.

46:13-26. Conquest Foretold. There are here 5 separate pieces with a common theme. They have often been assumed to come from the period immediately following Nebuchadrezzar's victory at Carchemish, but the time of Jer.'s final years in Egypt (cf. chs. 43-44) seems more likely.

46:14-17. The E border towns, and even **Memphis,** the capital (see above on 44:1-14), are warned to **stand ready** for attack. **Apis** was the **bull** worshiped at Memphis as a reincarnation of the god Ptah, later called Osiris. The question is, "Why did your god flee and leave you defenseless?" and the answer, "because Yahweh butted him"—the word is used in Ezek. 34:21 of animals shoving weaker ones aside. Vs. 16 may refer to deserting mercenaries (cf. vss. 9, 21), or it may refer to Jewish refugees. If the latter, Jer.'s point is to say to the Jews that Egypt will be overrun and then in dismay they will ask why they ever went there for protection (see above on 42:1-22; 43:8-13). He finishes (vs. 17) with a piece of telling invective against **Pharaoh** as the braggart who never acts (cf. Isa. 30:7), possibly involving a word play which can no longer be recognized.

46:18-19. Egypt is warned that "a mountain of a man" will invade her and she must get ready **for exile.** But the oracle is of course really directed to Jews—either the pro-Egyptian party in Jerusalem or, more probably, the exiles who fled to Egypt with Jer.—as shown by the comparison with **Tabor** and **Carmel,** mountains in N Palestine (see color map

1), which would mean nothing to the Egyptians.

46:20-21. Egypt's coming distress is foretold. The **beautiful heifer** will run amuck, tormented by a **gadfly from the north,** i.e. Nebuchadrezzar. Her **hired soldiers** (cf. vs. 9), on the other hand, will become as docile as **fatted calves.**

46:22-24. Egypt is pictured as slithering away like a snake through her riverside scrub, while her attackers are like the peasants who swarm to cut the brush down and so deprive her of her last hiding place. Again the enemy is **from the north.**

46:25-26. The theme is repeated in plainest terms in prose. **Thebes** was the chief center of worship of the god **Amon.** The closing promise of restoration is probably a later insertion by a Jew living in Egypt and solicitous for her welfare.

46:27-28. *Editorial Addition.* An editor, wanting to round off this Egypt collection, found a small, reassuring piece in the style of 2nd Isaiah and added it here. It has been used for the same purpose in 30:10-11 (see comment).

B. Concerning Philistia (47:1-7)

This oracle envisages the destruction of the coastal cities of Palestine, both Phoenician (vs. 4*c*) and Philistine. Since the **waters are rising out of the north** (vs. 2) the oracle is clearly of a piece with the foe-from-the-N oracles of 4:5–6:30 and dates from the same general period of Josiah's reign. It is part of the general warning to Judah to repent before the disaster falls. An editor, however, knowing that Philistia succumbed first, not to the Babylonians, but to the Egyptians when Pharaoh Neco captured **Gaza** on his return from his N march in 609, has added an intro. (vs. 1) erroneously linking the oracle to the Egyptian attack.

47:4-7. The **Philistines** are recognized as remnants of the old Aegean civilization which was dominated by **Caphtor,** i.e. Crete (cf. Amos 9:7), and as the descendants by intermarriage of the **Anakim,** the legendary mighty men of pre-Hebrew Palestine (see comment on Num. 13:32-33). Both references emphasize the present disaster by contrasting it with past glories. **Tyre and Sidon,** Phoenician cities, are considered along with Philistine **Gaza** and **Ashkelon** (see color map 8) because they are coastal cities lying in the path of a N invader. How can Yahweh's **sword** hold back when Yahweh has given it a commission against all that **seacoast?**

C. Concerning Moab (48:1-47)

Here are some 12 pieces concerned with Moab. The first 2 (vss. 1*b*-2, 3-8) probably and the 3rd (vs. 9) possibly are Jer.'s own work. They envisage Moab as invaded and exhort her to **flee.** This is in line with Jer.'s general message that Palestine will be overrun by the foe from the N, and that all the little kingdoms must be warned beforehand of the disaster in order that at least the Jews will know that it is Yahweh's doing.

The other pieces reflect the age-old rivalry of Israel and Moab and are jingoistic saber-rattlings in which Moab is told that Yahweh is now going to punish her so that she will never recover. These pieces rely heavily on 2 literary forms, the lament and the taunt song. In the lament the prophet presages the death of his enemy by uttering a dirge over him as already dead; though in reality he will rejoice over it he expresses himself as if the enemy's downfall has broken his heart. This air of authenticity gives his composition the desired potency to unnerve the enemy and convince him of defeat before the battle begins. In the taunt song the psychology is less complicated in that the prophet simply hurls taunts at his enemy and exults over his downfall.

A marked characteristic in both these forms is the use of geographical names to achieve parallelism and poetic intensity. Some place names in this passage are known from other contexts, but some are now unidentifiable. It should also be noticed that some of these oracles make puns on the place names and that some of the phrases were in fairly common use and occur elsewhere in similar collections (e.g. cf. vss. 4-5 with Isa. 15:5).

48:1*b*-2. *Moab Silenced.* The names **Nebo . . . Kiriathaim . . . Heshbon** refer to known Moabite towns (see color map 8). **Madmen** may be a name distorted to make a pun. The victim of the planning in vs. 2 is presumably Israel, and Jer. is saying that the forthcoming destruction of Moab is only, after all, poetic justice.

48:3-8. *Moab's Destruction.* This oracle has suffered in transmission (see RSV footnotes) but the RSV is probably not far from the original intent. The 3 places named were probably all near the S end of the Dead Sea; on **Zoar** cf. Gen. 19:20-22. The **wild ass** (vs. 6) typifies the unapproachable desert dweller. **Chemosh,** the national god of Moab, must bow to Yahweh's plan for history. The implied monotheism is getting to be almost explicit.

48:9. *A Fragment.* This vs. is a victory chant to be sung over and over again by the girls who greet the returning Hebrew warriors as they enter the city with their booty (cf. Exod. 15:20-21; I Sam. 18:6).

48:10. *A Slogan.* This is probably a recruiting slogan, brought out every time a raid on Moab was planned.

48:11-13. *The Decanting of Moab.* This jingoistic piece is redeemed only by the interesting metaphor. Moab's time for being poured **from vessel to vessel** has come, and indeed his very **jars** will be broken. It is also interesting to see that the worship of Yahweh at **Bethel** (cf. I Kings 12:26-33) is reckoned as pagan and false as the worship of **Chemosh** himself.

48:14-20. *The Destroyer of Moab.* Here are 2 pieces, vss. 14-17, 18-20, which both "lament" the approaching downfall of Moab. **Dibon** and **Aroer** were Moabite cities near the **Arnon** River (see color map 8).

48:21-27. *Recital of Cities.* This list of cities aims to say comprehensively that all Moab will be destroyed. Most of the places are unknown. On the image of drunkenness see above on 13:12-14. Vs. 27 means "Did you deride Israel, as helpless as a man fallen into the hands of bandits? But now it is your turn to be derided." On **wagged your head**—a sign of scorn—cf. Ps. 22:7.

48:28-33. *Shouts of Mourning.* Isa. 15:4, 8-10 uses many of the same phrases as appear here. **Kir-heres** is a variant of Kir-haresheth (cf. II Kings 3:25-27).

Sibmah, between Nebo and Heshbon, was in a vine-growing area. **Jazer,** in Ammonite territory N of Moab (see color map 6), may have been a center for the Tammuz cult, in which weeping for the dead god was a prominent feature. The author declares (vs. 32*ab*) that the weeping for Sibmah will exceed even that at Jazer. The original text of vs. 32*d* may have read simply "reached as far as the sea" (see RSV footnote). If so, the meaning may be that Sibmah's wine crosses the Dead Sea (vs. 32*c*) and even has markets on the Mediterranean Sea.

48:34-39. Lament for Moab. The places named in vs. 34 are at the N and S borders of Moab. Discovery of what is believed to be a mouthpiece of the musi-

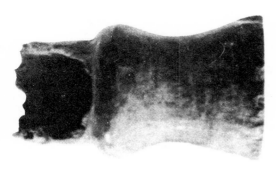

Courtesy of Nelson Glueck

Bone mouthpiece of a flute found at Tell el-Kheleifeh

cal instrument translated **flute** (vs. 36) indicates that it was actually a primitive clarinet (see ill., above). Its reed tone would be esp. suited to mourning. Vss. 37-38 give a vivid picture of an ancient Near Eastern population at a time of public lament. Cf. Isa. 15:2-3.

48:40-44. Threefold Terror. With vss. 40-41 cf. 49:22. The image of the triple peril in vss. 43-44 occurs in Amos 5:19-20 and even more closely in Isa. 24:17-18.

48:45-47. Woe and Hope for Moab. Vss. 45-46 (cf. Num. 21:28-29; 24:17) are very much what we have now become accustomed to, but vs. 47*ab* is something new. When the golden age comes, Moab will be there, like Israel, chastened and pardoned. This promise and those in 49:6, 39 suggest that an editor has worked through the collection marking those nations who may be restored. Such promises do much to redeem otherwise unattractive material. Vs. 47*c* comes from the compiler of the little collection.

D. Concerning Ammon (49:1-6)

Ammon was a seminomadic people on Israel's E border, where the high plateau of Transjordan slopes gently into the Arabian Desert (see color map 8). The first piece (vss. 1-2) comments that the Gadites have lost their territory but even so there are other Israelite tribes ready to inherit it. **Milcom,** the Ammonite god, has certainly no right to possess it. **Rabbah,** modern Amman, was the Ammonite capital. In vss. 3-5 we have the lament-

style invective employing stock phrases (e.g. cf. vs. 3*ef* with 48:7*cd*). On vs. 6 see above on 48:45-47.

E. Concerning Edom (49:7-22)

This is a literary unit put together out of a number of oral pieces. Because the Edomites took advantage of Judah's plight in 586 (see Intro. to Obad.) they became the most hated of all Israel's neighbors (cf. e.g. Ps. 137:7; Isa. 63:1-6; Mal. 1:2-5). Much of what is here is not Jer.'s (e.g. with vs. 9 cf. Obad. 5; with vss. 14-16 cf. Obad. 1-4; see comment) and reflects this later feeling.

49:7-11. Edom Stripped Bare. The inquiry as to whether Edom has run out of wise advice, for which she earlier had a reputation, is sarcastic (cf. Obad. 8; Baruch 3:22). Eliphaz the friend of Job came from **Teman,** a city and district of Edom (see color map 4). **Dedan** was an Arab people living SE of Edom (see color map 7). Beginning in the 6th cent. invasions by Arab tribes drove the Edomites out of their homeland and into S Judah. The reference here may be to a colony of Dedanites already settled in Edom. **Esau** was considered the ancestor of the Edomites (cf. Gen. 36). Vs. 11 is probably more ironical than kindly.

49:12-13. Yahweh's Cup. The metaphor is Jer.'s (cf. 25:15-29) but the suggestion that guilty Edom should be made to **drink** because guiltless Israel has been forced to is foreign to his thought. **Bozrah** was one of the most important of the Edomite cities (see color map 4).

49:14-16. Mountain Aerie No Refuge. Edom was noted for its cliffs, its rock dwellings, and its mountain forts, but even though her refuge is built as high as an **eagle's** nest, Yahweh will bring it down. **Rock,** Hebrew *sela,* may allude to the Edomite cliff fortress Sela (cf. II Kings 14:7; see color map 4).

49:17-22. Edom a Horror. Edom will become a complete ruin like **Sodom and Gomorrah** (cf. Gen. 19:24-25), so that passers-by will **hiss,** the biblical gesture of astonishment. Vss. 19-21 are used again in 50:44-46 (see comment). Vs. 22 uses phrases from 48:40 and is reminiscent of 30:6. It is significant that there is no prophecy that Edom will ever be restored (see above on 48:45-47).

F. Concerning Damascus (49:23-27)

The sentiments and often the phrases are such as we have several times encountered. **Hamath and Arpad** were 2 towns well to the N of the city (see color map 9). If they have fallen there is nothing left to protect Damascus from a N enemy. Vs. 26 is repeated in 50:30. Vs. 27 is adapted from Amos 1:4.

G. Concerning Kedar (49:28-33)

Hazor was a center for the nomadic or semi-nomadic Arabian tribes known rather vaguely as **Kedar** the "dwellers in black tents" (cf. e.g. Song of S. 1:5; Isa. 42:11; 60:7). It is not the famous Hazor of N Galilee but probably an unidentified settlement E of Palestine. There are 2 pieces, vss. 28-30, 31-33; both are probably from Jer. The oracles further emphasize the futility of Judah's attempting to resist the Babylonian manifest destiny.

The nomads were esp. known by, and despised for, their tonsorial habits (cf. 9:26; Lev. 19:27).

H. CONCERNING ELAM (49:34-39)

Elam was renowned for its archers (cf. Isa. 22:6). To set up one's **throne** in a territory is formally to annex it (cf. 1:15; 43:10). The Elamites were a people to the E of Mesopotamia (see color map 9) and probably were first known to the Judeans as part of Nebuchadrezzar's forces in 597, the time of the first deportation. Thus the oracle is probably correctly dated (on **beginning of the reign** see above on 26:1-24) and could come from Jer., though why he should have singled out the Elamites from the rest of the Babylonian soldiery is not clear. A comment adds that after the day of Yahweh the Elamites will be restored to their former affluence (see above on 48:45-47).

I. CONCERNING BABYLON (50:1-51:64)

The oracles devoted to Babylon display a bitter animosity toward that city which is not characteristic of Jer. and rejoice in the fall of Babylon as something which is soon to take place. They borrow pieces from other collections, adapting them perfunctorily to Babylon. This collection was probably compiled during the Exile since it predicts the violent destruction of Babylon, whereas actually its fall to the Persian Cyrus in 539 occurred without a battle and with no damage to the city.

50:2-5. Bel Dismayed. The original saying is in vs. 2 and comments on the falsity of Mesopotamian religion as revealed by the fall of Babylon. **Bel** and **Merodach,** i.e. Marduk, were alternate names of the great Babylonian deity. To this vs. 3, with the characteristic phrase **out of the north,** has been attached to make it conformable to Jer.'s teaching. Vss. 4-5 depict the national repentance for which the compiler fervently longed.

50:6-7. Israel's Plight. The theological interpretation of the fall of Jerusalem as due to sin saved Israel's faith in God and her own future; but it deprived her, at least in part, of the opportunity to blame her enemies. This thought is used here to underline Israel's plight—her enemies can destroy her and justify their actions. We can detect an unspoken indignation: "This is not just!"

50:8-10. Flight from Babylon. As the threat to Babylon grows more ominous, a Jewish prophet calls on his people to lead the flight from the doomed nation.

50:11-16. Yahweh's Vengeance. Though Babylon is the instrument of Yahweh's anger, nevertheless in due time he will punish her for her arrogance. Cf. Isa. 10:5-12. That time has now come, and a Jewish prophet rejoices in the thought.

50:17-20. Israel's Story. This remarkable little piece puts the whole biblical interpretation of Israel's history in 4 vss. But before the blessed golden age should come many more conquerors and epochs were to intervene. Prophets always tend to foreshorten their perspectives. The places named in vs. 19 (see color map 1) were all in the territory of the former N kingdom.

50:21-27. Invitation to Plunder. A prophet in Yahweh's name invites all who will to join in the plundering of Babylon, who richly deserves what she will get. **Merathaim,** which means "double rebellion" in Hebrew, is a word play on a name for S Babylonia; **Pekod,** Hebrew for "punishment," is a similar word play on the name of an E Babylonian tribe. "Double rebellion" will get its deserts and "Punishment" will live up to its name.

50:28. Jewish Escape. A prophet envisages the exiles set free at last, getting back to **Zion** to announce there with great satisfaction that Yahweh has exacted **vengeance** on the Babylonians for the destruction of **his temple.**

50:29-30. Further Invitation. Yahweh is thought of as inviting Babylon's enemies to attack her. Vs. 30 repeats 49:26.

50:31-32. Day of Reckoning. Yahweh announces that Babylon's **time** of punishment has come.

50:33-34. Israel's Redeemer. Because Yahweh is **strong,** he is going to reverse the present situation —**rest** for Israel, but **unrest** for Babylon.

50:35-38. Incantation. This example of solemn cursing is lifted by its literary quality out of the secondariness of this chapter. The sentiment may be regrettable but the style is splendid, esp. in the last scornful phrase.

50:39-46. Borrowed Pieces. Vs. 39 is composed of stock phrases (cf. Isa. 13:19-20). Vs. 40 repeats 49:18. Vss. 41-43 are taken from 6:22-24, except that the original "O daughter of Zion" has been unblushingly altered to **O daughter of Babylon** (vs. 42). Vss. 44-46 are applied to Edom in 49:19-21.

51:1-5. Chaldea's Guilt. This is probably typical of the oracles which circulated widely among the exiles as the Medo-Persian threat to Babylon grew ever more ominous. It is characterized by a spirit of revenge toward Babylon and of reassurance to Israel. **Chaldea** (vs. 1) is written in the athbash cipher (see above on 25:17-26) as LBQMY (see RSV footnote) for KSDYM, Chasdim, Hebrew name for the Chaldeans; but since **Babylon** is written plain the use of the cipher is just an affectation.

51:6-10. Flight from Babylon. Here is another oracle reflecting the growing threat to Babylon. On vs. 7 cf. 25:15-29. Vs. 8 adopts the lament technique for gloating over a foe (see above on 48:1-47) and vs. 9 with artificial hypocrisy says that the speakers wanted to heal Babylon but her wound was too grievous (cf. the same gibe at Egypt, 46:11). The note of patriotic reassurance comes in at the end (vs. 10).

51:11-14. A Siege of Babylon. This is another oracle from the period of Babylonian decline. The **Medes** to the NE (see color map 9) presented the first threat to the Babylonian Empire and became part of the Medo-Persian coalition headed by Cyrus which was eventually to bring Babylon down.

51:15-19. The Creator. Here is a very different type of production. These vss. are quoted from 10:12-16 (for their relation to Ps. 135 see comment there), but in this context they have a particular significance. Vengeance and patriotism have been left far behind, and the question is the contrast between the Hebrew concept of God the Creator and the Mesopotamian notion of an image. The dignity of Israel as the people of God is expressed at the close (vs. 19), a very different sentiment from the rather tawdry chauvinism of the earlier pieces.

51:20-23. The Hammer of Yahweh. This is in the style of 50:35-38, though the repetitions are considerably less effective. The question is, who is being addressed? Formally it is no doubt Cyrus (cf. Isa. 45:1-7), but the real audience is the exiled Jews, who are being encouraged by the news that Cyrus will **break** Babylon and free them from oppression.

51:24-26. The Burnt Mountain. These assorted threats against Babylon reflect the years prior to Cyrus' capture of the city. **Destroying mountain** for the flat plain of Babylon refers probably to the city's artificial religious mountain, the ziggurat, a huge many-storied temple. In the future it will be known as **burnt mountain** because of the fierce fire which will pass over it. Babylon is not even to be a source of reusable building materials. This very ancient practice, deprecated by Kheti III of Egypt as early as 2070 B.C. and deplored to this day by archaeologists, is still current in lands where building materials are scarce.

51:27-33. Babylon Ripe for Harvest. Roughly **Ararat** was modern Armenia and the **Minni** were a people living S of Lake Urmiah on the borders of Media (see color map 9). **Ashkenaz** probably refers to a Scythian tribe. The Jews of the Middle Ages identified Ashkenaz with Germany; hence today Central European Jews are Ashkenazim whereas Spanish Jews are Sephardim (cf. Obad. 20). The oracle pictures the Babylonian soldiery as completely unnerved, while the **king** receives one message after another telling of positions lost, **fords . . . seized,** and **bulwarks . . . burned.** Though unfulfilled since Babylon fell without a fight, this is a fine piece of imaginative composition.

51:34-37. Yahweh's Vengeance. Jerusalem pleads her plight before Yahweh, pointing out what Babylon has done to her. Yahweh promises vengeance.

51:38-44. Babylon's Overthrow. Though the Babylonian soldiers **roar . . . like lions,** Yahweh will send a drunken stupor (cf. 25:15-29) on them, so that they will be led **like lambs to the slaughter.** Babylon will thus be captured, engulfed by the **sea,** and left an utter **desert.** The prophet is mixing his images somewhat violently, but his purpose is to say that the forces of nature will also be ranged against the city. The sea is a constant image of the forces of evil in the OT even where geography would militate against its use (cf. Ps. 42:6-7). It is an echo of the myth in which the Creator battled with the primeval sea monster of chaos. **Bel,** the great god of the Mesopotamian pantheon, here representing Babylon, will be forced to disgorge **what he has swallowed,** i.e. Israel. Babylon in vs. 41*a* is again written in athbash cipher (see above on 25:17-26).

51:45-46. A Warning. This is an admonition to the Jews to get out of doomed Babylon while they can.

51:47-53. Judgment on Images. The downfall of Babylon is prophesied. She is to pay for Israel's dead, as multitudes have died for Babylon. The exiles are to recall Jerusalem (cf. Ps. 137:5-6) and rejoice that the evil powers which the images of Babylon typify are to be utterly overthrown.

51:54-57. Destruction of Babylon. The attacking army is again likened in vs. 55 to the sea, and the metaphor of divinely inspired drunkenness is also employed (cf. 25:15-29).

51:58. Summary. This little oracle sums up all that has gone before. The last 2 lines occur again in Hab. 2:13 and probably were fairly common currency. The meaning is that all the effort which has gone into building Babylon has only been preparing what is to go up in flames.

51:59-64. Symbolic Action. It is unlikely that this is a historical incident, yet it is an action which Jer. might well have conceived. All the foregoing words, i.e. 50:1-51:58, are to be written out in a little collection—an instruction which shows incidentally that written collections of prophetic words were being made at this time—and **Seraiah** is to remind Yahweh of his determination to destroy Babylon and then cast the weighted scroll into the **Euphrates.** Its sinking will symbolize the sinking of Babylon. This is a good instance of an acted oracle (see above on 13:1-11).

We have no other evidence that **Zedekiah** made such a journey in his **fourth year,** i.e. 594/93, but there is nothing improbable in the idea. Since the strong anti-Babylonian sentiments of chs. 50-51 are not characteristic of Jer., however, it is unlikely that he would have set in train the symbolic actions here narrated. The story probably grew up among the Jews of the Exile who hated their Babylonian masters. In vs. 64*b* the editor of this little collection marks its end.

IV. Historical Appendix (52:1-34)

A final editor wanted to equip the whole Jer. complex with a suitable historical reference. He therefore took from the great "History of the Kingdoms" the portion which told of Zedekiah's reign, the capture of Jerusalem, the destruction of the temple, and the deportation of the Jewish population (II Kings 24:18-25:30; see comment). Because the story of Gedaliah is told at length by Baruch in 40:1-16, however, he omitted the shorter account of it found in II Kings 25:22-26. The fact that certain details appearing in vss. 10-11, 18-23 are omitted from II Kings is probably to be explained by later editing of II Kings. The **tenth day of the month** (vs. 12) is given as the 7th day in II Kings 25:8; there is no way to tell which is correct.

52:28-30. Statistics of the Captivity. These vss., which do not appear in the LXX, come not from II Kings but from an entirely different source, perhaps a Babylonian record. The date in Nebuchadrezzar's **seventh year** (vs. 28) is borne out by the Babylonian Chronicle, which records that he captured Jerusalem on the 2nd of Adar, i.e. the 12th month, of his 7th year (Mar. 16, 597). The date of the 2nd deportation, the **eighteenth year,** in vs. 29 conflicts with the **nineteenth year** in vs. 12 (cf. II Kings 25:8) and no satisfactory explanation for the discrepancy has been found. Vs. 29 presents a chief reason that many scholars date the destruction of Jerusalem 587 rather than 586 (see Chronology, pp. 1271-82). The **twenty-third year** (582/81, vs. 30) probably refers to the time of the troubles following Gedaliah's assassination.

The figures for the number of captives are so sober that they sound genuine. What then became of the rest of the population? The answer is that most of them were the **poorest of the land** (vs. 16)

Reconstructed view of Babylon (*ca.* 604-561 B.C.) and the Processional Way as seen from the Ishtar Gate; the tower of Babel is in the right background; reconstruction by Prof. E. Unger, drawn by H. Unger

left to till their little plots and struggle as best they could. Many chose to emigrate—to Egypt and other nearby lands or to Mesopotamia as voluntary exiles. The idea of forced mass deportation (cf. e.g. II Kings 24:14) is historically as well as practically unsound.

52:31-34. *A Concluding Hopeful Note.* The value of the appendix was that it not only substantiated the main thrust of Jer.'s interpretation of Judah's situation but also allowed the book to end, as all scripture must, on a positive and hopeful note. These last vss. record how, even in Jehoiachin's lifetime, the tide began to turn. The changed political situation after the death of Nebuchadrezzar in 562, when Babylon began to feel the need of friends, saw Jehoiachin's status transformed the following year from that of prisoner to royal guest, and this was the first faint light of dawn. Sunrise was to be delayed 23 years; but in 538 a return to Jerusalem was to be permitted, and after another 23 years the temple would stand once more as the house of God.

LAMENTATIONS

Harvey H. Guthrie, Jr.

Introduction

Name and Place in Canon. In the Hebrew Bible the book of Lamentations takes its name from its opening word, **How,** the characteristic beginning of a funeral dirge. The Talmud and rabbinic tradition designate it "Lamentations," and this title is employed in the LXX, Latin, and English. In the Hebrew canon Lam. is included in the Writings as one of the 5 Scrolls and is read in the synagogue on the 9th of Ab (Jul.-Aug.), the day on which the destruction of the temple in A.D. 70 is bewailed. The LXX is responsible for Lam.'s position after Jer. in the Christian canon. The rationale for this move was provided by the tradition of Jeremianic authorship (see below).

Form. The book consists of 5 poems, each of which constitutes a ch. The first 4 are acrostics, whose 22 short stanzas begin successively with the letters of the Hebrew alphabet in order—except that in ch. 3 each couplet within a stanza begins with that stanza's letter, and in chs. 2-4 for some unknown reason the order of the letters *ayin* and *pe* is reversed. Although ch. 5 is not an acrostic, it conforms to the pattern by consisting of 22 couplets. The purpose of the acrostic form may be to provide a memory aid as well as to achieve completeness by running the course of the entire alphabet.

The poems employ literary forms known elsewhere in the OT as well as in the ancient Near Eastern culture of which Israel was a part. Chs. 1; 2; 4 are basically funeral dirges. Ch. 3 is an individual lament, combined with expressions of thanksgiving and trust. Ch. 5 is a communal lament. (For information on these forms see Intro. to Pss. pp. 253-61.)

Origin. The poems all address themselves to what happened to Jerusalem and Judah in the Babylonian invasions of the early 6th cent. B.C. A misreading of II Chr. 35:25 and the LXX preface to Lam. are the basis of the very ancient tradition that the author of the poems was Jeremiah. There is no concrete evidence for the validity of this tradition, and the Hebrew canon (see above) does not associate the book with the prophet.

The consensus of scholarly opinion is that the poems originated in Palestine itself among those remaining after Jerusalem's fall in 586 B.C. Some have held chs. 3; 5 to be much later than the other poems, but the present tendency is to doubt this. Indeed, the order of the poems may reflect the order of their composition, ch. 1 possibly originating after the first Babylonian siege of 597 and ch. 5 at a time somewhat removed from the disaster of 586. The poems

may very well come from one author, although there is no way of knowing. They certainly were written on different occasions. Some have opined that they had a cultic usage at an annual day of mourning over the destruction of Jerusalem and the temple (cf. II Kings 25:8; Jer. 52:12; Zech. 7:3-5; 8:18).

Significance. Lam. is an eloquent statement of Israel's response to her downfall. Into this response has been taken up the prophetic insistence that the purpose of God is the ultimate source of meaning for that disaster just as it was for Israel's origins. Ch. 3 explicitly seeks to invest catastrophe with meaning, and prefigures the servant songs in Isa. 40-55. Thus the book has had significance for Christians as well as Jews, and is traditionally used in many churches during Holy Week.

For Further Study: Israel Bettan, *The Five Scrolls,* 1950. N. K. Gottwald, *Studies in the Book of Lam.,* 1954.

I. A Lonely City (1:1-22)

Hermann Gunkel, whose work on Hebrew poetry was epochal, characterized this poem, as well as those in chs. 2; 4, as a "political funeral dirge," a form for mourning being utilized to bewail Jerusalem's fall. While the poet may not be strictly bound by forms (the latter part of this poem is individual lament), this points to something important. In Lam., as in other Hebrew poetry, modern questions of authorship and of the individual experience of the poet can miss the point. Israel's poetry is based on forms arising out of the life of a worshiping community. This is more important for an understanding of that poetry than modern conjecture about the poet's sentiments. So here ancient forms are used to express a people's reaction to the fall of their holy city, the place that had signified the empirical presence of their God.

1:1-11. *Jerusalem's Widowhood Described.* Alliteratively expressive, **How** is a formal characteristic of the funeral dirge (cf. 2:1; 4:1, 2; Isa. 1:21; Jer. 48:17; a similar word is found in II Sam. 1:19, 25). Jerusalem is pictured as a widow (cf. Jer. 48:17) bereft of any companion to accompany her, as was the custom, in her lament over her loss. This uncomforted aloneness is a theme of ch. 1 (cf. vss. 9, 16, 17, 21). It is theologically important, for the real situation of Jerusalem is thoroughly faced, and this must come before anything else.

1:3. The reference could be to the deportation of

597 or of 586. **Resting place** denotes Yahweh's gift to Israel of the land that was the sign of his presence with her. **Her distress** can also be translated "her narrow defiles."

1:4. The reference is to the cessation of the worship of Yahweh. **Maidens** in this context refers to cultic functionaries (cf. Ps. 68:25; Jer. 31:13).

1:5-7. The funeral dirge here gives way to an element common in laments over individual distress—concentration on **enemies**. Vs. 5 implies a question of whether the gods of the enemies may have prevailed, but then goes on to make the point of the classic prophets: it is precisely the sovereignty of Israel's righteous God that has brought her disaster. Vs. 6 refers to Jerusalem's rulers, Yahweh's surrogates. Thus the problem posed for a faith such as Israel's, based on concrete events and situations, by the catastrophe of 597-586 is expressed. Vs. 7 has too many lines; either the 2nd or 3rd couplet must be an addition.

1:8-9, in terms reminiscent of Hos., Jer., and Ezek., appropriates the prophetic interpretation of Jerusalem's fall. Vs. 9c is a lament cry, presupposing that God's reputation is bound up with the fortunes of his people.

1:10-11 carries out the theme of the last lines of vs. 9. Since the talk is not of the actual destruction of the sanctuary, some cite these verses as evidence that ch. 1 comes from the period between 597 and 586.

1:12-16. *Jerusalem's First Lament.* The viewpoint changes from a lament *over* Zion to a lament *by* Zion. This could indicate that the poem had a cultic usage with different voices taking different parts. **Is it nothing to you** is only a guess at what an obscure text means. One scholar translates, "Now then!" Vss. 12-16 explicitly state that Yahweh is responsible for Jerusalem's affliction, and vs. 12 calls the world outside Israel to look upon this as a manifestation of Yahweh's righteous sovereignty. Vs. 13a then uses language traditionally associated with a deity's visit to earth (cf. Ps. 18:1) to picture Yahweh's activity in Jerusalem's fall. The picture of the hunter (vs. 13b) is often used of enemies, and thus is a strong one to use of Israel's God.

1:14 indicates once again that lamenting Israel has appropriated the prophetic message.

1:15 contains 2 colorful pictures: Yahweh commanding the forces that ruin Jerusalem's finest men and Yahweh treading on Jerusalem as in a winepress (cf. Isa. 63:1; Joel 3:13). **Assembly** has sacral overtones, and may imply more than earthly powers.

1:16 with its picture of weeping Zion reverts to the theme of there being no comforter for her.

1:17-22. *Jerusalem's 2nd Lament.* Vs. 17 is a transition, taking up themes present in the earlier stanzas.

1:18-20 begins like Jer. 12:1. There the words may be sarcastic, but not here. Underlying them may be a custom mirrored in Josh. 7:19-21 according to which one in the wrong praised the righteousness of God. At any rate, the lament of Jerusalem, unlike other laments from the same culture, locates her problem in the facts of divine righteousness and human sin. The prophetic lesson has been learned. Vss. 19-20 recount, as laments always do, the items in the distress.

1:21-22 closes the poem on a note hard for modern men to understand, the imprecation of enemies. Two things lie behind this recurrent element in laments: the empirical, this-worldly theology of Israel and her conviction of the involvement of God's own reputation in the fortunes of his people.

II. THE LORD HAS DESTROYED (2:1-22)

Like the first poem, this is based on a funeral dirge, with the characteristic **How** at its beginning. Attention here, however, is focused on the terrible wrath of God manifested in the unprecedented catastrophe which has overtaken Jerusalem. The poem falls into 2 parts: the poet's own lament in vss. 1-19 and a lament by Jerusalem herself in vss. 20-22. So vivid is the description of what has happened that many have taken this poem to be an eyewitness account of the destruction wrought in Jerusalem by the Babylonians in 586. Some hold that transitions such as those at vss. 11 and 18-20 are due to liturgical use of the poem.

2:1-19. *The Poet's Lament.* The theme of the poem is set down in vs. 1. The cloud imagery comes from the cult, and is connected with manifestations of deity (cf. Pss. 18:11-12; 68:4; 97:2; 104:3; I Kings 8:10-11). It turns a lament into a hymn celebrating God's sacral act, now an act of wrath in which the previous blessing of Zion is reversed. The holy city's divine election holds even in her sin. She remains a witness to the righteousness of God now, given Israel's condition, manifesting itself as wrath. Thus what might merit sheer wailing is here celebrated in hymnic language. Again the prophetic interpretation of Jerusalem's fall has been understood. Couplet 1b applies an astral image, used elsewhere of foreign rulers (Isa. 14:12; Ezek. 28:17), to the sacred city itself; and couplet 1c asserts that Yahweh has deserted his temple. So the **day** (cf. Amos 5:18) is a **day of his anger.** To see how radical this is, cf. what Pss. 46; 48; 132 claim for Jerusalem.

2:2-10 describes, just as a hymn to God's majesty recounts his mighty deeds, what has happened in **the day of his anger.** Vss. 2-5 recall the devastation of the land that led to the siege of Jerusalem herself, first by the Assyrians (*ca.* 730-680) and then by the Babylonians (600-586). In this Yahweh, taken by cheap piety to be an ally, is himself the real **enemy** (vss. 4-5). What vss. 6-7 assert about God's destruction of sacred things and places verges on blasphemy, or would to a faith that did not locate God's activity in empirical events—even tragic events. Vss. 8-9 insist that what has happened is the result not of meaningless fate but of the righteous purpose of a righteous God. He himself is the destroyer of all the institutions through which he was sought (vs. 9). So the conclusion to this section in vs. 10 describes the only reaction now appropriate to the reality of how God's righteous sovereignty has manifested itself.

2:11-12 is a transition in which the poet himself reacts to the situation by lamenting. These vss. give a graphic description of the effect of famine on children in the besieged and fallen city (cf. II Kings 25:3; Jer. 37:21).

2:13-17 takes up a central theme of this poem. The disaster by which Jerusalem has been overtaken is, as the day of Yahweh's wrath, incomparable, **vast as the sea.** There is no parallel to it; therefore no one is qualified to comfort Zion. In the light of this theme, vss. 14-17 look to possible comforters. In vs. 14 the poet explicitly sides with the minority prophets against those in the majority who maintained themselves by prophesying the peace and security Israel wanted to hear (cf. Jer. 14:13 ff.; 23:13 ff.; 26:7 ff.; Ezek. 13:1 ff.). Such prophets have been disqualified by events. Reality has voided their credentials, and they can say nothing to comfort Jerusalem now. The poet makes explicit what has been implicit all along: his acceptance of the interpretation given to Jerusalem's downfall by prophets such as Jeremiah and Ezekiel.

2:15-17. Given what vs. 14 has said, is there any possibility of help from outside Israel? Not at all. Both neutral passers-by (vs. 15) and Israel's enemies (vs. 16) rejoice in Jerusalem's catastrophe, see it as what she deserved. So, can God be Jerusalem's comforter (vs. 17)? No, for the point of the whole poem is that the disaster is precisely God's doing, that, given what Israel had become, his day for her had to be a day of wrath.

2:18-19 moves from the lament of the poet to introduce that of Jerusalem herself. With no comforter (vss. 14-17), Zion can only pour out her grief constantly to God. In hymns praising God's activity the characteristic beginning is an imperative "call to worship" (cf. Pss. 29:1; 47:1; 103:1). Here, in the manner of the poet himself (see above on vs. 1), Jerusalem is called on to recite the deeds of Yahweh in the only way she now can, to be a witness to him even in her present condition.

2:20-22. *Jerusalem's Lament.* The poet has the city speak as a grief-stricken mother, and the horrors catalogued speak for themselves. The pervading theme is stated at the beginning, **"Look, O LORD, and see! With whom hast thou dealt thus?"** This is a central thesis of the poem: no precedent exists anywhere for what has happened to Jerusalem. Thus the siege and fall of city and temple are not just tragic disaster. They plunge Israel into a crisis of faith. God seems to have acted in this day of his wrath in a way contrary to his character and purpose. Though the poems of Lam. probably originated separately, even if from a common author, the crisis of faith enunciated at the end of this poem leads naturally into the one in the following chapter.

III. AN INDIVIDUAL LAMENT AND SONG OF CONFIDENCE (3:1-66)

This poem, unlike chs. 1; 2, is not modeled on a funeral dirge, and its problems have resulted in much debate. Puzzling changes in pronouns occur: an "I" speaks in vss. 1-20, 48-66, while in vss. 40-47 "we" is the subject. Also baffling are the various elements present. Vss. 1-20 are an individual lament, while vss. 21-24 combine elements of the individual thanksgiving and song of trust. Vss. 43-47, where the subject is "we," are a communal lament. (On these forms see Intro. to Pss., pp. 253-61.) Vss. 25-42 combine didactic and hortatory moods, reminiscent of the wisdom literature.

To the problem of finding an interpretation accounting for all this must be added the question of the poem's relation to the rest of Lam. Solutions have varied widely. Noting its differences from the rest of the book and its mixtures of pronouns and forms, many have held this poem to be a composite

and the latest part of the book. More recently others have accounted for the various voices and elements with the theory that behind it lies cultic usage in which different persons and groups played their parts. It has also been held that the alternation between "I" and "we" is no problem, the "I" being collective.

Recent interpreters have tended to date the poem close to the disaster of 586 or in the exilic period. They have seen the author as a comforter of Israel on the basis of tragic experience, who brings meaning to Israel's suffering by a figure not unlike the suffering servant of Isa. 53. There are diverse elements in the poem, but its acrostic form indicates a unity of authorship. The following interpretation seeks to do justice to both.

Not itself a lament over Jerusalem's fall, the poem addresses itself to the tragic problem posed for Israel by the situation so eloquently described in the poem in ch. 2. This argues for common authorship. The poem bases the comfort it offers to Israel on the experience of tragedy and deliverance described in many psalms in which lament, confession of confidence, and thanksgiving are combined (e.g. Ps. 27). Thus vss. 1-24 are the poet's presentation of what will speak to Jerusalem in her disaster. Vss. 25-39 then point to the lesson the poet believes to come from what is presented in vss. 1-24. Vss. 40-51 exhort Israel to act on the basis of the lesson, giving voice to the lament of Israel and of the poet himself. Finally vss. 52-66 are the poet's song of confidence (firm enough that he can use the perfect tense) that Yahweh will act in redemption as he has acted in judgment.

To assign to the poem a definite time of composition or author is very difficult. It could come from almost any time after 586, and, if the other poems originated in Palestine itself, would come from there too.

3:1-24. *The Basis of Hope.* The question of ch. 2 was, Who can comfort Jerusalem in her unprecedented disaster? The answer here is concrete: an appropriation of the tragic cry of true lament. Whatever the particular tragedy presented in a lament might be, the basic point was always that in it chaos was threatening order, death swallowing up life (cf. Ps. 88). This poem holds that in the suffering and disaster that call forth the lament there is a basis for speaking to the Jerusalem which has known the bitter wrath of God.

3:4-18. The heart of a lament is always a compelling and graphic recitation of the suffering being undergone. Three things occupy attention: the lamenter's own suffering, the enemies who plague him (vs. 14), and God, who is withholding his life-giving and saving presence. Here, while everything is permeated with the sufferer's plight, there is remarkable concentration on God's responsibility for the situation—**He has . . . He has . . . He has. . . .** Indeed, as in Job, the utter despair of the sufferer is bespoken as the figures usually used for evil and demonic enemies are applied to God himself (vss. 10-12). The point is that things have come to where it is possible to cry out to God only that order has been overwhelmed by chaos, life by death (cf. such classic laments as Pss. 22; 88; 143).

3:19-23. But all this is cried out *to God*. Implied in every lament, just by virtue of its being expressed, is what is called "the certainty of a hearing." This certainty is itself the subject of OT poetry (cf. Pss. 27: 1-3; 23). So here, after vss. 19-21 have turned from description of distress to direct calling on God, vss. 22-24 express the confidence that God will hear. The basis of the certainty is the important OT concept of *hesed*, usually rendered in the RSV **steadfast love** (vs. 22). The basic connotations of the word have to do with committed, loving loyalty to a covenant obligation. The concrete character of Hebrew thinking is shown by the word's being used here in the plural; it refers to specific events and actions, not an abstract concept. Its meaning is indicated by its being parallel to **faithfulness** (vs. 23).

3:24. The phrase **says my soul** means "I say to myself." The Israelite who takes the covenant seriously can remind himself that Yahweh is his **portion**—the possession measured out to him in life. And Yahweh's record is such that even in deepest distress hopeful waiting is justified. When a lament was recited in a time of distress in the sanctuary, it was answered after a time of vigil by an oracle pronouncing salvation. Thus **I will hope in him** has very concrete overtones.

3:25-39. *The Lesson to Be Appropriated.* Vss. 25-26 provide a transition to the next section of the poem by alluding to the cultic setting of a lament. To seek Yahweh originally meant to go to the sanctuary. The word for **wait** may originally have referred to the period of vigil preceding the oracle of salvation (cf. Ps. 27:14; Isa. 40:31). But the sanctuary is now gone; and, in the style of the wise men, the poet begins to insist that its procedures provide a lesson in the principles by which God works at any time. So vs. 27 is a typical wisdom maxim. It may indicate that the poet is chiefly concerned with the younger generation with whom Israel's future lies.

3:28-30. In line with what has been implied in the preceding laments, particularly ch. 2, the poet insists that the first step to salvation is an acceptance of the situation for what it is (note the reticent realism of vs. 29*b*). Vs. 30 is certainly support for the contention that Isa. 53 betrays a kinship with Lam.

3:31-33. Out of acceptance of judgment can come knowledge of the basically good purpose of God which undergirds his judgment. What to men look, according to the condition in which men are found, like 2 opposing things are to God one thing. His **steadfast love** (see above on vs. 22) is always the same and is the source of what to sinful man has to be described as wrath. But to accepting, repentant man (vss. 28-30) it is the basis of hope.

3:34-37 develops explicitly what underlies the confidence of vss. 31-33. Not meaningless injustice but righteousness is the will of Israel's God (vss. 34-36). And Israel's God is the sovereign Lord. Thus even the tragic disaster through which Israel has passed is something filled with meaning. This is the prophetic insight which redeemed catastrophe from meaninglessness for Israelites who, like this poet, were able to appropriate the prophetic message. This lesson, proclaimed by the prophets and typically enunciated in Israel's ancient faith, is that to which the poet now points Israel. The rhetorical questions of vss. 37-39 provide a transition to the 2 final parts of the poem.

3:40-51. *The People's and the Poet's Lament.* Given the theology underlying vss. 34-39, the cause for lament inevitably shifted in Israel from what it was elsewhere. For Israel, God being what he had shown himself to be, the fundamental human problem was not that creaturely finitude was assailed by meaningless and amoral forces from which salvation was desperately sought. For Israel the fundamental problem was human unrighteousness, creaturely rebellion against the sovereign righteousness of God. Of this basic problem disaster such as that by which Jerusalem had been overtaken was a secondary and understandable by-product. Meaning was to be found for those who would, in ruthless honesty about themselves, seek it (vss. 40-41). And the search would lead to fruitful lament, lament over what was really askew in life (vs. 42).

3:43-51. Though the description in vss. 43-45 of Israel's present condition is as graphic as anything in chs. 1; 2, the communal lament to which the poet calls the survivors of Jerusalem moves in hopeful trust to its conclusion in vss. 49-51. If this whole ch. is understood as a unity, and this section as the poet's rhetorical summons to Israel (with which he identifies himself) to lament, then the switch from plural to singular pronouns in vss. 48-51 is no problem. It is only a sign of the extent to which the poet is himself involved in the situation to which he addresses himself.

3:52-66. *The Poet's Song of Confidence.* In Israel's sacred poetry the counterpart of the lament was the song of thanksgiving, in which, after the deliverance cried for, a man recited how God had saved him (see Intro. to Pss., pp. 253-61). This form underlies the conclusion to the present poem. Having described in traditional lament language a desperate situation (vss. 52-54), the poet uses prolepsis, the figure in which one anticipates coming events as if they have already occurred, to describe how God will answer the cry of Israel (vss. 55-66). The **Do not fear!** of vs. 57 may be a direct quotation of what was said in the oracle of reassurance that followed a lament in the sanctuary. Emphasis on **enemies** not only arises out of the derision to which Israel was subjected following her downfall (cf. Ps. 137) but is in line with the concrete character of Israel's faith, in which God's purposes and the forces opposing them were seen in terms of empirical events and persons in real life. If the sentiments of vss. 64-66 are neither understandable nor acceptable to modern man, they arise from the point of view just described, and are paralleled many times in the psalms. They come from a faith which could not conceive of God's salvation and blessing in other than visible, historical terms.

IV. THROUGH TRAGEDY TO VINDICATION (4:1-22)

Here there is a return to the funeral lament form of chs. 1; 2. The typical **How** (see above on 1:1) is the beginning. In this poem, again an acrostic, the 3-couplet stanzas of chs. 1-3 give way to stanzas of 2 couplets.

In content this poem returns from the themes of ch. 3 to the kind of thing found in chs. 1; 2. It vividly describes the results of the Babylonian siege and destruction of Jerusalem, although at its conclusion it looks through tragedy to vindication. The realism of its reference to the trials of the city has caused some to assert that the poem is the product of an eye-witness of the siege, but the denunciation of Edom at the end may indicate a later time in the exilic period when Edom's encroachment on former Judean territory resulted in a good deal of animosity (cf. Obad. and probably late passages in Jer. and Ezek.).

4:1-2 refers to the destruction of the temple, the chief tragedy of Jerusalem's downfall for the pious Israelite. Vs. 2 leads into what is to occupy attention in most of this lament, the suffering of the people in Jerusalem at its destruction. **The precious sons of Zion** is evidence of the meaning to Israel of her election as God's people.

4:3-5 describes the famine that accompanied the siege, concentrating on the terrible results of it for the children of the city. On the ostrich and its treatment of its young cf. Job 39:13-18.

4:6 is one of a series of stanzas coming at regular intervals in this poem (vss. 6, 11, 16) by which the recitation of the disaster is punctuated with proclamations of it as God's wrath on a rebellious people. Here the proverbial wickedness of Sodom (cf. Gen. 19) serves as a model of the condition of Jerusalem. An insight into the Hebrew view of life is provided in the double meaning of **chastisement** and **punishment.** Each word can denote both evil and the consequences of it in a world ruled by a righteous God. This poem, unlike chs. 2; 3, simply alludes to Israel's sin in a vivid description of the siege and destruction of Jerusalem. It does not dwell on the point, but takes the prophetic interpretation of the dreadful events for granted.

4:7-8 describes in vivid terms the transformation produced in even the most handsome and healthy of Jerusalem's youth (**princes** may not be correct) by the famine.

4:9-10 continues, asserting that death in the famine was worse than falling in battle, and that hunger drove even the most compassionate of mothers to kill and eat their children.

4:11 again explicitly connects what the poem laments with God's judgmental wrath (cf. vss. 6, 16). Unlike 2:20, in which vs. 10 is paralleled, vs. 11 does not question Yahweh's involvement in the disaster.

4:12 provides a transition to a new section by underlining vs. 11. What Yahweh has done in judgment was beyond the imagination even of those not themselves involved in feeling for Jerusalem. This verse brings to mind the advantageous location of Jerusalem (II Sam. 5:6), and also Israel's convictions about her invulnerability (cf. Pss. 46; 48; 87) against which Jeremiah had to inveigh (Jer. 7; 26).

4:13-15 locates the cause of the judgment of Jerusalem in the sin of prophets and priests. Though some have interpreted **The blood of the righteous** as an allusion to some specific wrong of the religious leaders, it more probably refers to their responsibility for what has happened to the innocent in the siege and destruction. Vss. 14-15 probably describe the prophets and priests (cf. vs. 16), though a number of interpreters have applied them to the **righteous** of vs. 13. In line with what all the classic prophets had insisted, this poem asserts that those whose responsibility it was to declare God's way and will

to his people had not done so (cf. Amos 7:14-17; Hos. 6:9; 9:7-8; Isa. 28:7-22; Jer. 6:13-15; 23:11-22; Ezek. 22:23-31). So distorted had Israel's view of her God become, because of the perversions of prophet and priest, that God, without compromising his character, could act toward her only in judgment. So the blood of the righteous is on their hands.

4:16, a counterpart to vss. 6, 11, makes it explicit that the defiling of the sacral persons from their ritual cleanness and their exile into lands not Yahweh's is the work of Yahweh himself as he acts in his wrath.

4:17-20 concludes the lament's account of Jerusalem's terrible fall by describing how nothing could be relied on to avert the disaster. Vss. 17-18 indicate that the poet understood what the prophets had continually insisted—that no foreign alliance could thwart Yahweh's judgment on his people (cf. Isa. 30-31; Jer. 2:18, 36). Vs. 20, contrary to the claims so often made for the Davidic monarchy (II Sam. 7; Pss. 2; 110), recounts how Yahweh's own king could not stop the fall of Jerusalem, but experienced its consequences himself.

4:21-22. Unlike those in chs. 2; 3, this poem does not question the ultimately redemptive purpose of Yahweh even in his wrathful judgment. Thus it ends with words of comfort to Israel. Some have conjectured that cultic usage underlies the poem, and that these final vss. were an oracle of reassurance addressed to the community that had lamented. In line with Israel's concrete view of things (see above on 3:58-66), God's comforting of Israel is pictured as a very visible punishment of her enemy Edom, who had apparently taken advantage of Israel after the Babylonian invasion and therefore came in for much castigation during the exilic and postexilic periods (cf. Obad.; Isa. 34:5-7; Jer. 49:7-22; Ezek. 25:12-14).

V. A Communal Lament and Prayer (5:1-22)

This poem differs from the others in 2 ways. First, although the number of couplets is the same as the 22 letters in the Hebrew alphabet, it is not an acrostic. On the one hand, this fact has been used to argue for its basic unity and for its having come from the same writer as the other poems. On the other hand, some have held this to be artificial and the result of secondary reaction. Current critical opinion tends toward the former view.

Second, this poem is a pure example of the communal lament (cf. Pss. 44; 74; 79; 80; 83; on this form see Intro. to Pss., pp. 253-61). It begins with a cry to God in the imperative, recites the causes of the lament in the first person plural, and concludes with a petition to God for relief. Various hints about the use of such poems (Josh. 7:6-9; Judg. 20:23, 26; I Kings 8:33-34; Jer. 14:2; Joel 1:13-14) make it seem possible that this one was written for some public occasion of lamentation after the fall of Jerusalem in 586 B.C.

5:1-18. The Lament. Vs. 1 begins in the manner of the lament, either communal or individual, with a direct call on God and an imperative request that God **remember** (better, "direct his attention to") the condition of the lamenter or act on his behalf.

5:2 is descriptive of more than a political and economic disaster. The word for **inheritance** is central to Israel's theology. The concrete sign of her relation to God was his provision for Israel of a land of her own. The loss of that land to other peoples presented, therefore, a crisis for faith, and that crisis is the central subject of Lam.

5:3-5. Vs. 3 can be interpreted as a description of the situation when many men had been killed, or, more likely, in line with vs. 2, as a tragic assertion that Israel has been abandoned by her God. Vs. 4 carries on the same line of thought, the point being that the rights to the resources of the land now belong to others. Vs. 5 provides a climax with its declaration of the loss of personal freedom.

5:6-8 forms a unit and refers to pacts made in the 2 centuries before Jerusalem's fall as expansion of various imperial powers began to spell Israel's doom. As the prophets had consistently insisted, the compromise involved in such pacts was apostasy from Yahweh's claim to absolute sovereignty and so has to be characterized as sin and iniquity. Vs. 7 must precede the doctrine advanced in Ezek. 18. Vs. 8 asserts the bitter irony that a people whose relation to their God originated in emancipation from slavery are now subject to peoples whose gods are oppressors rather than redeemers (cf. the view of man in Gen. 1 with that in the Babylonian creation epic).

5:9-15, typical of the lament form, recounts the difficulties being undergone by those who have survived the fall of Jerusalem. Harvesting of crops is made dangerous by bedouin marauders from the desert (vs. 9), famine has produced illness (vs. 10), all elements of society suffer the results of chaotic lawlessness (vss. 11-14), and joy is entirely turned to sadness (vs. 15).

5:16. The hardest fact of all is the voiding of Israel's choice as God's blessed people. The lamenting community accepts the prophetic assessment of the reason for the catastrophe.

5:17-18 provides both the climax of the lament proper and the transition to the petition. The central tragedy of it all for the Israel of God is the cessation of her life as the community whose worship on Zion is the earthly, visible locus of the sovereignty of God. In the most profound sense chaos has replaced order —yet not entirely for the people whose prophets have made possible the confession of vs. 16*b*. If tragedy has meaning, God can still be turned to in prayer for the future.

5:19-22. *The Petition.* What was implied in the above is made explicit in the hymnic introduction (vs. 19). It is not Yahweh's sovereignty but Israel's previous status that has collapsed. So the lamenting **Why** (vs. 20) and a petition for restoration (vs. 21) can be addressed to him. And, if the central fact of life is his sovereignty, then the tragic situation of Israel may even be faced as unalterable (vs. 22). The last verse of Lam. sums up the evidence of all its poetry that there were those in Israel who could accept the prophetic interpretation of her downfall.

THE BOOK OF EZEKIEL

William Hugh Brownlee

Introduction

According to the superscription (1:1-3) and scattered notes (3:15; 11:24-25; 40:1-2) Ezekiel was among the first body of exiles taken to Babylon along with King Jehoiachin in the spring of 597 (cf. II Kings 24:10-17; on the historical background see Intro. to Jer.; "The History of Israel," pp. 1026-31, Chronology, pp. 1271-82). It is thus from "Chaldea," i.e. Babylonia, that he is represented as predicting ruin for Judah until the fall of Jerusalem in 586 (chs. 1–24) and thereafter the doom of Judah's neighbors (chs. 25–32) and the restoration of Israel (chs. 34–48).

Problems of Locale and Unity. Though superficially the book appears more homogeneous than most other prophetic books, the traditional assumption that it is the work of a prophet living among the Babylonian exiles offers a number of difficulties:

a) Ezek.'s prophetic mission is to warn the "house of Israel" of coming ruin (3:16-21). This term as used in the book refers to Judah—except where it means the N kingdom as distinguished from the S (e.g. 4:4-5)—and is limited to the people in Palestine (cf. esp. 22:17-22). When the exiles are included it is charged to the "whole house of Israel" (11:15; 37:11).

b) Ezek.'s sermons are addressed to Judah and Jerusalem. Repeatedly he is told to "make known to Jerusalem her abominations" (16:2; 22:2). Such addresses pervade chs. 1–24 and are usually couched in the 2nd person. He is said to "dwell in the midst of a rebellious house" (12:2), to which he acts out warnings of exile and captivity. His appeals for repentance are motivated by the plea to avoid ruin and death, and the only judgment predicted is that which will befall Judah. In contrast, after the fall of Jerusalem and Judah the messages of comfort in chs. 34–48 are addressed to Jews scattered all over the world rather than specifically to those newly exiled in Babylonia.

c) A number of passages (5:5; chs. 8–11; 21:2-7; 24:25-27; 33:24; see comments) are most naturally understood as involving Ezek.'s presence in Palestine; to fit the traditional assumption that he was in Babylonia they must be interpreted as visions or the like. Esp. the account of Pelatiah's death while Ezek. is prophesying (11:1-13) seems to require an actual confrontation at the gate to the temple (see below on 11:13). Elsewhere he is told to face in certain directions and see different parts of Palestine (6:1-7; 20:45–21:5; see comments).

d) Ezek. shows intimate acquaintance with conditions in Palestine but tells us nothing of conditions among the exiles. Aside from the unique fact that there was a Jewish colony near the river Chebar at a place called Tel-abib (1:1-3; 3:15, 23)—a tradition that could have been known to a late editor—one can gain information about the exiles from the book only by deducing it from an assumption that the prophet resided with them. Contrast Jer. 29:4-23, a letter written to the exiles from Jerusalem, which gives more information about them than this entire book; also Isa. 40–55, written among the exiles at a later time.

e) The statements which place Ezek. among the exiles appear to be editorial. No sermon is concerned explicitly with the Jews in Babylonia; rather such references occur mainly in headings and brief notations. The materials written from an exilic point of view in the visions may also be suspected of being later embellishments designed to identify Ezek. with the exiles.

f) Materials in the book supporting the exilic locale tend to distort Ezek.'s personality. The portrayal of the prophet as situated in Babylonia yet completely absorbed in the affairs of Judah makes him appear given to semimystical daydreaming, as if suffering from a split personality or similar psychopathic condition. Certain exilic passages suggest other abnormal traits. E.g. the stupor in which he is said to remain after going to the exiles (3:10-15) seems cataleptic (cf. 4:4-8). Before he has even started to preach he is allegedly told to go home and keep quiet, his powers of speech paralyzed (3:22-27), and there he supposedly stays till Jerusalem's fall (33:21-22). According to these passages he never carries out his mission of summoning the nation to repentance or obeys the continual commands to speak.

In facing these and other problems of the book scholars convinced of its essential unity and Babylonian locale have generally taken for granted the prophet's psychic abnormality and offered it in explanation of many of the difficulties. But such an approach is superficial and does not deal adequately with all the problems. Hence some have followed the lead of the ancient Jewish historian Josephus (first cent. A.D.), who theorized that Ezek. wrote letters to the Judeans from Babylonia. Since there is no evidence for written correspondence by Ezek. himself the scholars place the burden of it on disciples and others who communicated with Judea. Travelers

411

between the countries, it is assumed, would carry oral reports. Thus the book's sermons calling Judah to repentance would be apostrophes spoken in Babylonia in the hope that report of them would reach the intended audience. While recognizing that there was communication between the exiles and the homeland (cf. Jer. 29), we may question whether reliance on such means would be adequate for a prophet called to confront the Judeans with the threat of ruin.

A number of scholars have proposed a double ministry for Ezek., partly in Palestine and partly in Babylonia, and have suggested rearrangements of the materials to fit the 2 stages. Some see him as going into exile in 597 but returning to Jerusalem after his call and preaching doom until the destruction of the city in 586, after which he was again taken captive to Babylonia and became a herald of hope to his fellow exiles. Others place him in Palestine throughout the first part of his career and assume he was exiled in 586—or probably a few years later (cf. Jer. 52:30) since 33:23-29 implies his being in Judah after its devastation. In either form this theory is attractive as a solution to the book's problems. Once we recognize, however, that Ezek.'s oracles of doom were spoken in person to the Judeans for whom they were intended and reflect fully life in the homeland, we come to expect the same intimacy concerning life in the exile supposing him to be there. Failing to find this, one cannot attribute with confidence any oracles to the prophet himself in an exilic setting. In recent decades, therefore, some perceptive scholars have concluded that Ezek.'s ministry was entirely Palestinian and that all the exilic material comes from editors of later times. This view seems to solve more of the book's problems than any other.

The Prophet and His Message. The reform introduced by King Josiah (II Kings 23) called for the centralization of worship in the Jerusalem temple and the outlawing of worship at the "high places." After Josiah's death worship at these hilltop shrines came into vogue again. Ezek. condemned the rulers of the nation for letting this happen (cf. 6:1-7; see below on 34:1-10). The D law (Deut. 12-26), on which Josiah's reform was based, included new formulations of old laws that were distinctive of Israel. Ezek. upheld these as a safeguard against religious syncretism (11:12; 20:32).

As a priest (1:3) Ezek. revered the temple (7:22; 24:19-21) and was concerned for the "holy things" of the sanctuary (22:8, 26). He insisted that offerings should be presented to Yahweh alone (16:18-19; cf. 24:1-14) and urged obedience to the priestly traditions. Yet much of the priestly material in the book is from later hands; most of the sins which he himself condemns are ethical. He gives the fullest of the prophetic formulations of what constitutes righteous living (18:5-9; cf. Isa. 33:15; Mic. 6:8). His primary interest was in the ethical principles expressed in the D law. His invectives against idolatry were quite as much for ethical as for cultic reasons. His equating of idolatry with adultery was not wholly allegorical (16:24-25; 18:15; 22:9). He esp. condemned crimes against children (16:20-21, 44-45; 20:25-27).

Ezek. is well known as a prophet of individualism (see below on 9:4-6; 14:12-23; 18:1-32; 33:1-20). He was also a herald of divine love for each person. His message was that God loves the sinner and for this reason warns him through the prophet. It is God's displeasure at the prospect of death for the wicked that moves him to throw open the door of repentance and life to all who will enter (18:23, 31-32; 33:10-11).

Ezek. was a younger contemporary of Jeremiah and lived and preached for a time in the same city, Jerusalem. It is evident that he at least heard Jeremiah preach and was influenced by the older prophet's thought. Cf. e.g.:

EZEK.	JER.
7:26	18:18
12:2	5:21
13:16	6:14
20:4-31	7:21-26; 11:1-8; 16:10-13
22:17-22	6:27-30
33:1-9	6:17

The ancient rabbis recorded the tradition that Ezek. was the "son of Jeremiah," i.e. a disciple.

Most of Ezek.'s own material in the book is poetry, though some of his writing is prose (e.g. 2:9–3:3; chs. 8–9). Though some of the poetry has been preserved in essentially its original form (e.g. ch. 19) much has been masked by later editing (e.g. 34:1-10) and interpolating (e.g. ch. 1). Translations of a number of the oracles as restored to their presumed original poetic form are included in the following commentary.

Like all great poets Ezek. excelled in a vivid and colorful imagination. This is esp. characteristic of his allegories (chs. 15; 16; 17; 23). His symbolic imagery is developed most beautifully in his dirges (chs. 19; 27). People listened to him out of appreciation for aesthetic beauty, even though their minds were too engrossed with selfish passions to heed his teaching (33:30-32). Rarely have truth and beauty been combined more effectively in Hebrew literature.

Far from being a recluse living in a remote, imaginary world, Ezek. was a man who mingled freely with the people and felt their every mood. He is constantly addressed as "son of man," i.e. a man among men, an ordinary man despite his priestly descent. His intimacy with the social, economic, political, and religious aspects of Judah's life is continuously manifest. This knowledge was not gained by telepathy, even as a divine gift, but by living among the people of Judah. His divine inspiration lay in his addressing their situation with a word of God.

The genuine text contains 4 visions: (*a*) the glory in the storm cloud (reconstructed from chs. 1-3); (*b*) the eating of a scroll (2:8-3:3) held in Yahweh's hand, who appeared to him as in 8:1*b*-2; (*c*) the coming destruction of Jerusalem (ch. 9); and (*d*) the resurrection of the nation (37:7-10). In none of these is it stated that he was transported miraculously from Babylonia to Palestine, or that he saw events from afar. He does speak, however, of making ecstatic trips to various spots in terms of being *"lifted up" and "brought"* by Yahweh or his Spirit—like Elijah (I Kings 18:12, 46; cf. Acts 8:39-40). Such language was later construed as describing miraculous transport and was used to explain his physical presence in Jerusalem in chs. 8–11.

The Editors and Revisers. The earliest of the additions to Ezek.'s work are no doubt those which promise return of the Jews from the many lands to which they were scattered. The principal themes of these hopeful passages are: (*a*) the dispersion will bring the Jews to repentance (6:8-10; 12:15-16) and (*b*) will purify the nation (13:9; 20:37-38); (*c*) Yahweh will gather them home (34:12-16) and (*d*) this will lead them to know him (20:38, 42; 34:27) and (*e*) move them to repentance (20:42-43) because of his unmerited kindness (16:54, 61; 20:44; 36:31-32), (*f*) which will be solely for the sake of his own holiness and glory (36:17-23); (*g*) restoration will involve the spiritual gifts of cleansing and regeneration (36:24-26) and (*h*) the material gifts of productivity (34:25-31) and security (36:8-13, 28-30); (*i*) the Davidic kingdom will be restored (17:22-24; 34:16, 23-24) and (*j*) the temple will be rebuilt (37:26-28) and once more Yahweh will accept their worship there (20:40); (*k*) thus his name will be vindicated before the nations (36:36). The fact that these passages sometimes misinterpret the earlier passages to which they are attached is evidence that they do not come from Ezek. himself.

The description of the new temple, the new law, and the new land in chs. 40–48 involves a priestly program in which late editors of the book were much interested, and their hand is evident in this section. Yet it is clear that not all this material is from the same stratum. The late editors probably identified the new temple for apologetic purposes with that standing in Jerusalem in their day, which had been built by the returning exiles under Zerubbabel in 520-515 (Ezra 5:1-2; 6:13-15); but underlying their material is an earlier prose work which antedates the rebuilding. Some of this may have been written by an exiled disciple of Ezek., and may have inspired the first unsuccessful efforts at rebuilding in 537 (Ezra 3:8–4:5; 5:13-16).

Two passages (23:36-49; 34:17-22; see comments) seem to reflect the situation described by Nehemiah at the beginning of his governorship and therefore probably date from his time or shortly before.

The oracles against foreign nations (21:28-32; chs. 25-32; 35) contain some supplements from later hands. E.g. some of the additions to the 3 oracles against Tyre (chs. 26–28) may have been inspired by the conquest of the city by Alexander the Great in 332.

That the apocalyptic description of the invasion of Gog (chs. 38–39) is a late addition is shown by its presupposition that a long time has elapsed since the recognized prophets lived (38:17; 39:8). Possibly this material reflects the conquest of Palestine by Alexander the Great.

The latest major editing of the book subjected it to radical rearrangements—including the assembling into 2 parts, chs. 1–24 threatening and chs. 25–48 promising—and to rich and tedious elaborations which intensified its priestly concerns and focused on its assumed origin in the Exile.

The idea that Ezek. was an exilic prophet may have arisen as a misunderstanding of the method of dating certain of his oracles, which may be his own or may have come from a disciple. All the dates, except probably the 30th year in 1:1, are in years of the "exile of King Jehoiachin" (1:2; cf. II Kings 25:27)—apparently calculated from the spring of 597 (see below on 1:1-3 and Chronology, pp. 1271-82)—rather than in regnal years of Zedekiah. This dating rests on the authentic legal fact that Jehoiachin remained king of Judah while in exile (cf. II Kings 25:27-30) and Zedekiah was merely appointed regent or acting ruler. In the ruins of ancient Babylon tablets have been found which refer to Jehiachin as king, and seals and seal impressions on jars found in Palestine show that crown property in Judah was still kept in his name. No doubt many in Jerusalem preferred to ignore this fact, wanting to write off Jehoiachin and seek freedom under Zedekiah—a view reflected in the references to Zedekiah as king and the dating by his regnal years in II Kings 24:17–25:2 and in Jer. Thus it would be easy for those of a later time to misinterpret the dating by Jehoiachin as evidence that Ezek. accompanied the exiled king to Babylonia. Ezek.'s peculiar method of referring to the divine motivation of his travels in the environs of Jerusalem would then contribute to the misunderstanding by suggesting that he was supernaturally transported back to Palestine to deliver his sermons.

Once Ezek. was taken to be an exilic prophet, later editors seized on this assumption and emphasized it as an important basis for the apologetic arguments implicit in their work. In their hands the book was shaped into an effective weapon with which to counter attacks on the legitimacy of the Jewish temple and its priesthood. To certain minds the fact that the temple in Jerusalem was destroyed by the Babylonians proved that it had not been built at the one place which Yahweh had chosen as the site where alone he was to be worshiped with sacrifices (Deut. 12:1-14). The fact that its most prominent priests were exiled (II Kings 24:14; 25:18) seemed to show that Yahweh had repudiated the Zadokite priesthood of Jerusalem. Those advancing such arguments were probably the Samaritans supporting a rival temple on Mt. Gerizim, near the ancient city of Shechem (cf. Deut. 11:29; see color map 11).

The interpretation of Ezek. as a prophet among the exiles provided an effective answer to such challenges. Yahweh's manifesting himself in such overwhelming fashion by the river Chebar (ch. 1) proved that he did not abandon the exiles. His calling of the exiled priest Ezek. to be his prophet proved that he did not reject the exiled priests of Jerusalem. The theme of divine glory provided an argument for continuity between the destroyed temple of Solomon and the rebuilt temple of Zerubbabel. It was only because of sin that the glory departed from the first temple—an event which Ezek. witnessed some years before the fall of the city (8:4; 9:3; 10:1-22; 11:22-23), and which made possible the destruction of the building (43:3). Meanwhile the glory that had resided in the temple from the time of the dedication by Solomon took up its abode among the exiles, where it was seen by Ezek., and where it constituted "for a while" a sanctuary there (11:16). The vision of the restored temple at Jerusalem (chs. 40–48), attributed to Ezek., gave his authority to the rebuilding under Zerubbabel and authenticated the new temple's priesthood and rites. Thus the promise in this vision that the glory which had taken up its abode with the exiles would return to Jerusalem (43:1-7; 44:1-4) gave assurance of the divine presence in the temple of the editors' day. Later Jews referred to God's luminous presence as the "glory of the *shekinah*," lit. "[divine] abode," or simply as the shekinah. Ezek.'s work as edited made possible the tracing of the shekinah succession through the Exile.

The Samaritan rivalry seems to have reached its height in the period following the conquest of Alexander the Great, who according to Josephus gave the Samaritans permission to build their temple on Mt. Gerizim. Thus a reasonable estimate for the date of this editing is *ca.* 300.

The late editors did such a thorough job both of rearranging and of elaborating that a superficial study of the book gives a false sense of literary unity. Fortunately they left some traces of their methods, esp. in chs. 1-3; 8-11; 43:1-5, by which much of their work can be recognized.

For Further Study. C. C. Torrey, *Pseudo-Ezek. and the Original Prophecy*, 1930; a pioneer analysis of the evidence for a Palestinian locale, widely influential despite its unconvincing view of the book as fiction. I. G. Matthews, *Ezek.*, 1939. W. A. Irwin, *The Problem of Ezek.*, 1943; a pioneer restoration of Ezek.'s original poetry. C. G. Howie, *The Date and Composition of Ezek.*, 1950; "Ezek." in *IDB*, 1962; able defenses of the Babylonian locale. H. G. May in *IB*, 1956.

I. Judah's Doom (1:1-24:27)

A. Ezek.'s Prophetic Call (1:1-3:27)

1:1-3. The Dates and Place. The reference of the **thirtieth year** has been the subject of much debate. Some scholars have taken it to be based, like the other dates of the book, on the **exile of King Jehoiachin**—on the significance of this basis see Intro.—and therefore conjectured that it identifies the year, 568, when the book was compiled and published. Poetic criteria, however, indicate that this date in vs. 1*a* was a part of the original poem that underlies the vision of vss. 4-28*b* and therefore refers to the beginning of Ezek.'s prophetic ministry. The date of vs. 2 does not fit these criteria and thus probably belongs to a prose superscription which an early editor prefixed to the poem (cf. Amos 1:1; Mic. 1:1; Zeph. 1:1). It may have read: "The word of Yahweh which came to Ezekiel the son of Buzi, the priest, on the fifth day of the (fourth?) month. It was the fifth year of the exile of King Jehoiachin." If so, the date of vs. 2 was intended to refer to the same event as that of vs. 1*a* and to locate it in time on a more commonly used basis.

Scholars generally reckon the numbering of months in the OT as counted from the spring equinox, in accordance with the Babylonian system; and in this book the years also seem to be counted from a spring new year. Hence the date denoted is Jul. 31, 593. The Targum, i.e. the Aramaic version, explains the 30th year as counted from King Josiah's reform. Starting from the passover of Josiah's 18th year which climaxed the reform (II Kings 23:21-23) Jul. 31, 593, falls in the 30th year, and some scholars today accept this explanation.

In view of the importance of the 30th birthday to one of priestly descent (cf. Num. 4:2-3, 46-47) a number of scholars believe that the reference is to Ezek.'s age at the time of his call. Having become old enough to serve in the temple as a **priest,** Ezek. contemplates his future and goes forth into the plain (see below on 3:22-27), perhaps to pray. The relapse of Josiah's reform looms as very serious in his thinking. The time seems to be drawing near when the curses of the covenant must be fulfilled (cf. Deut. 27:14-26; 28:15-68). When a sudden electrical storm comes up—an unusual occurrence at this season—Ezek. is ready to see in it a vision of Yahweh's glory and to hear a call to become a prophet.

The **river Chebar** was a navigable canal connected to the Euphrates SE of Babylon in the **land of the Chaldeans,** i.e. Babylonia. **King Jehoiachin** (cf. II Kings 24:8-17) and his retinue were kept in the capital, as Babylonian records show (cf. II Kings 25:27-30), but the other Judean exiles are here said to have been resettled by the Chebar.

1:4-28*b*. The Vision in the Storm. Yahweh's **glory** (vs. 28*b*) rides on a **throne** (vs. 26), which surmounts a most intricate chariot, whose locomotive power consists of **four living creatures,** i.e. cherubs (cf. 10:15; see comment on I Kings 6:23-28). Each of these has **four faces**—contrast the cherubs of 41:18-19 with only 2—which may be symbols of the 4 leading deities of Babylon: Nabu, the human-faced revealer; Nergal, the lion-faced god of the netherworld and of plague; Marduk, the leading Babylonian deity, who was represented by a winged bull colossus; and Ninib, the eagle-faced god of hunting and war. Pagan deities were essentially personifications of the powers of nature. Only Yahweh was conceived of as a power distinct from and yet over nature. His throne is only the **likeness of a throne** and his figure is only a **likeness as it were of a human form** (vs. 26) because he is spirit and appears otherwise only in vision. His description in vs. 27 is probably adapted from 8:2.

The chariot's perfect mobility is indicated by the 3-fold means of locomotion: **feet** (vs. 7), **wings** (vss. 11-12, 24), and **wheels** (vss. 15-21). The wheels are **full of eyes** (vs. 18; cf. 10:12) by ways of suggesting omniscience (cf. II Chr. 16:9; Zech. 4:10).

Underlying this vision as we now have it was undoubtedly a simpler original in which Ezek. told of seeing Yahweh's glory in a storm cloud. Fortunately the priestly editors have left many tracks behind where they went about enlarging on it. One of their traits is to insert literary echoes of passages which they have separated from their earlier connections. Thus the original setting of Ezek.'s vision in a plain (3:22-23) can be recognized by the duplication in 3:22*a* of **the hand of the LORD was upon him there** (vs. 3*b*), which in the LXX reads "upon me," and by the duplication in 3:23*b* of *behold* (vs. 4*a*), there translated "and lo," which is followed by a summary reference to the vision in its expanded form.

Ezek.'s vision involves a storm **cloud** (vs. 4), which contains the **likeness of . . . living creatures** (vs. 5*a*). After an interpolated description of them (vss. 5*b*-12) they are introduced again in vs. 13, which gives the original description of them in terms of the storm. Vss. 14-28a are further late elaboration.

If we apply poetic criteria to the vision, on the basis that Ezek. was a poet, as demonstrated elsewhere (e.g. 4:1-2; 19:2-14d; 34:2-10), we may obtain a further refining of his message by deleting small portions of the text which mar the rhythm. In Hebrew poetry the rhythmic pattern consists, not of alternating stressed and unstressed syllables, as in English, but of regular numbers of emphasized syllables per line, with occasional variations to reflect various moods. Following is a restoration and translation of the original poem describing the vision, with its continuation in vs. 28c-2:5; 3:12-14, in which some indication of the Hebrew rhythm is given by the English phrasing and by the indention of lines with only 2 accents. Others have 3, except for 2:1b-2, where three lines (or stichs) take four stresses each.

1:1	It happened in the thirtieth year, in the fourth month, on the fifth of the month,
3b	the hand of Yahweh was upon me.
3:22	Then he said to me, [Ezekiel,] "Arise, go forth into the plain, and there will I speak with you."
23	So I arose and went forth into the plain. And behold!
1:4	A wind of a storm was coming; Out of the north, an enormous cloud! Around it appeared a radiance,
5a	and within it a semblance of beasts! Thus their appearance:
13	as coals of fire aglow. The fire had a radiance, and from the fire came forth lightning!
28	This was a view of Yahweh's glory. When I saw it, I fell on my face, and I heard the voice of one speaking.
2:1	And he said to me: "Son of man, Stand on your feet that I may speak with you."
2	The Spirit then entered me and set me on my feet, and I heard him again speaking to me:
3	"You I now send forth to the house of Israel. who have engaged in rebellion against me, both they and their fathers!
4b	So say to them, 'Thus says Yahweh'—
5a	whether they will listen, or whether they will forbear."
3:12a,	Then the wind caught me up and took me away;
14	and I went in the wrath of my spirit; and with power was Yahweh's hand upon me.

As Ezek. described his experience, then, he felt a divine impulse to go forth into the plain. There he saw, not an imaginary scene, but a real storm approaching. Its dark cloud flashed with lightning and perhaps glowed on the edges from the setting sun. Amid the turbulence Ezek. made out the shapes of animals that suggested to him the cherubs thought to bear up Yahweh (cf. Ps. 18:9-12). Others who saw the storm may have been simply frightened; only Ezek. was aware of the glory of Yahweh in it.

1:28c-2:5. The Prophetic Commission. Overawed, Ezek. falls down and hears the divine voice commanding him to **stand upon** his **feet.** When Yahweh commands, he also empowers, therefore **the Spirit . . . set** him **upon** his feet (cf. 37:10). Then again he **heard** Yahweh **speaking,** to **send** him on his mission. In the

power of the wind he feels the might of Yahweh's hand, which is to sustain him in his whole ministry in the face of the opposition he will meet. As the text now stands his message is to be the word of Yahweh (2:4b) but its content is not specified. A change of person in 2:5a would yield "If only you will listen, if only you will stop," which would become the message introduced by **Thus says the Lord GOD.**

2:6-7. Sitting upon Scorpions. Vs. 6 is a self-contained unit not a part of the visions which precede and follow. After Ezek. begins his ministry he finds that his fears of those to whom he must preach are justified. To sit and talk with them is to **sit upon scorpions.** The hostility suggests actual confrontation of the Judeans whom Ezek. is condemning (see Intro.); preachers who talk about the sins of those at a distance are not generally unpopular. In vs. 7 an editor has repeated parts of vss. 4-5 to tie vs. 6 into the context.

2:8-3:3. The Scroll. What was only metaphor for Jeremiah (Jer. 15:16) becomes vision to Ezek. To **eat** symbolizes acceptance of the divine commission; the filling of the **stomach** means that it has been fully assimilated into his own person; the sweetness like **honey** betokens the satisfaction that comes from proclaiming the word of Yahweh (cf. Rev. 10:8-11). This is not a sequel to the vision of 1:4-28, for in the storm there was no human figure with a **hand,** and even in the expanded version the human figure mounted on the celestial chariot is too remote to extend a hand. Perhaps the original setting is to be found in 8:1b-2. If so, 2:9 is the continuation of 8:2, vs. 8 being an editorial transition.

3:4-9. Courage for the Task. This is the continuation of the preceding scroll vision. Ezek. is not sent out as a missionary to foreigners—such people **would listen** and repent (cf. Jonah 3)—but he must preach to the **house of Israel,** who **will not listen.** Yet this is no time for him to sit in his house and dread a hostile public. He must go out and face his opponents. No matter how grim they may be, Yahweh will make him even more hardheaded and bravehearted. **Hard** here plays upon the name Ezekiel, which means "Yahweh makes **hard,**" i.e. gives strength and courage.

3:10-15. Commission to the Exiles. In contrast to the preceding instruction to preach to the house of Israel, this later addition now sends the prophet to the **exiles** in Babylonia at **Telabib** on the **river Chebar** (see above on 1:1-3). Vss. 12a, 14 were probably adapted from the original conclusion of the storm vision (see above on 1:4-28b). Ezek.'s saying that the wind or the divine **Spirit**—the same word in Hebrew—**lifted** him and **took** him to another place was no doubt mere metaphor, but the late reviser interpreted it as a miraculous mode of transport (cf. 8:3). On **overwhelmed** cf. Dan. 8:27.

3:16-21. Appointment as a Watchman. See below on 33:1-9, where this passage is more fully preserved.

3:22-27. Vision and Dumbness. On vss. 22-23 as the probable original setting of the storm vision see above on 1:4-28b. The **plain** of the vision has often been equated with the "plain in the land of Shinar" (Gen. 11:2; cf. Dan. 3:1), i.e. Babylonia, because the same Hebrew word, *biqah*, is used. But the word means either valley or plain, in either case suitable to Palestine (cf. e.g. Deut. 8:7; 34:3; Josh. 11:8; II

Chr. 35:22; Neh. 6:2). The Gen. Apocryphon among the Dead Sea scrolls identifies the Valley of Shaveh or King's Valley (Gen. 14:17) as the *biqah* of Beth-haccherem and locates it in the vicinity of Jerusalem. Such a place is also mentioned in the Mishnah (3rd cent. A.D.). An area of modern Jerusalem S of the old city known in Arabic as el-Baqa, "The Plain," may be this site. Since Beth-haccherem means "house of the vineyard" the conjecture that Ezek.'s home and vineyard (see below on 19:10-14) were near this "plain" is appealing. Another suitable location, however, is the Valley of Gibeon (cf. Isa. 28:21), for excavations have disclosed a considerable wine industry at Gibeon. Both these valleys as military approaches to Jerusalem would be suitable locations for the vision of 37:1-14, and near each are lookout points from which different parts of the country could be viewed (cf. 6:2; 20:46; 21:2).

3:24-27. These vss. are likewise editorially displaced. Obviously Ezek. was not **shut** in his **house,** stricken **dumb,** and **bound** perhaps with paralysis or catalepsy (cf. 4:8) from the beginning of his ministry till the promised release came with the fall of Jerusalem (33:21-22). For the probable original context and form of this passage see below on 24:25-27.

B. SYMBOLIC PANTOMIMES (4:1–5:17)

4:1-3. *Mimic Siege of Jerusalem.* Vss. 1-2 are in poetic rhythm:

> Now you,
> O son of man, take a soft brick
> and lay it down before you.
> Then engrave upon it a city,
> and place against it a siege wall.
> Then build against it a tower,
> and heap up against it a mound;
> and set armed camps against it,
> and with battering rams invest it.

The words "Now you" are introductory and stand outside the rhythm. Only 2 omissions are needed: the explanation **even Jerusalem** and **against it** after **battering rams.** The fact that even the instructions for a symbolic pantomime should come in poetic form justifies a probing for possible underlying poetry in presumably prose passages.

4:3. This vs. adds further details concerning the siege. It contains no poetry, however, and is probably a later embellishment. The **iron wall** is not the wall of Jerusalem, for the engraving of a city must have included the wall. It probably represents the barrier of the Exile which supposedly separates the prophet from Jerusalem.

4:4-8. *Exile Symbolized.* Here the **house of Israel** and the **house of Judah** distinguish the former N and the still existing S kingdoms of Israel. On **days** standing for **years** cf. Num. 14:34.

The LXX reads only 190 years (vs. 5) for the duration of Israel's exile. This figure subtracted from the date of the first deportations, 734-732 (II Kings 15:29), gives 544-542 for the expected return of the N kingdom. **Forty** years (vs. 6) from the 2nd exile of Judah, 586, brings us down to 546. Thus the 2 exiles would end *ca.* the same time. It is questionable, however, whether they are to be understood as concurrent.

The number **three hundred and ninety** is more difficult to interpret but probably correct. Its explanation may be that 390 + 40=430, the duration of the Egyptian sojourn (Exod. 12:40). If the intent was to depict the combined exiles as being 430 years, then Judah must remain in exile 40 years after the return of Israel. Counting 390 years from the fall of Samaria (722) brings us to 332, the time of the conquest of Palestine by Alexander the Great. At that time Shechem, the first capital of Israel, was rebuilt. Presumably the author of this late passage wrote during the 40 years following that event and predicted a restoration of Judah in 292. It was probably during this period that the book received its last major editing (see Intro.).

4:9-17. *Food Scarcity and Defilement.* Two quite different concerns are represented here: (*a*) scarce food under siege and (*b*) impure food in exile. Features of the 2 are mixed up in the symbolic interpretations (vss. 13-15, 16-17). Either 2 independent symbolic actions have been telescoped into a single narrative or one has been overlaid with the other. The material about scarcity in vss. 9-11, 16 can be restored to poetic form and is probably Ezek.'s. Originally it may have read somewhat as follows:

> Now you, take barley,
> and put it in a vessel,
> and make bread of it.
> Your food shall you eat by weight;
> from time to time shall you eat it.
> And water by measure shall you drink;
> from time to time shall you drink it.
> And he said to me, "O son of man,
> lo, the staff of bread I am breaking,
> that bread they may eat by weight
> and water they may drink by measure!"

It is not certain which grain was mentioned in the original poem, but **barley** seems most likely. With **staff of bread** cf. our saying that bread is the "staff of life." In vss. 16-17 **with fearfulness** and **in dismay** are echoes (see above on 1:4-28*b*) indicating that 12:17-19*a* at one time followed this poem. Vs. 17 is probably an expansion of the conclusion that originally was part of 12:19 (see below on 12:17-20). **I will do this** was supplied by the RSV to make the present connection of vs. 17 smoother.

The rest of the passage cannot be restored to a poetic form and is probably from another hand. The mixture of grains (vs. 9) signifies impure food (cf. Deut. 22:9-11), as does the use of **human dung** (vs. 12) as fuel for cooking. In the Middle East even today small girls gather animal droppings and pat them into discs, which are then dried on the roof and used for cooking.

5:1-17. *The 3-fold Fate of Jerusalem.* As in Isa. 7:20, shaving symbolizes devastation. The **third** of **hair** to be burned **in the city** (vs. 2) is interpreted as death by pestilence and famine (vs. 12). The 3rd to be struck **round about** (vs. 2) is to suggest the doom of the city's defenders. The final 3rd is to be scattered **to the wind** as a symbol of dispersement. The intro. to the interpretation is to be found in vs. 11, where **I will cut you down** could also be rendered "I too will hold a shearing."

Later interpolations of an early hopeful editor (see Intro.) specify that a **small number** of hairs is to be bound in Ezek.'s **skirts** (vs. 3). They are to come from the last 3rd and the binding represents their preservation. One could hardly recover hair thrown to the wind, but God can recover his scattered people. Reference to them is added to the interpretation in 6:8-10; 12:15-16, which, though partly doublets, probably belong immediately after vs. 12. The **fire** which will **come forth** from some of this preserved hair (vs. 4) may reflect the events after the fall of Jerusalem described in Jer. 40:11–41:10 (cf. 15:7; 19:14).

5:5-10. *Jerusalem in the Midst of the Nations.* This passage is independent of the preceding symbolic pantomimes. The indictment (vss. 5-6) may be restored as follows:

> This is Jerusalem!
> Amid the nations I put her;
> Around her are the lands!
> But she rebelled against my judgments
> more wickedly than the nations,
> and against my laws, than the lands!

This is Jerusalem refers to the place where Ezek. is standing. The same words are often heard today in Hebrew radio broadcasts, identifying the station. The city at the **center of the nations** is still unfit to be their spiritual capital (Isa. 2:2-4). Because she has not kept God's **ordinances,** lit. "judgments," she must know God's punitive **judgments** (vss. 8-10).

5:13-17. These vss. are an editorial expansion on the judgments of vss. 8-10 and a conclusion to chs. 4-5. **You shall be,** vs. 15 (RSV), for KJV *it shall be* is supported by one of the Dead Sea Scrolls.

C. ANNOUNCEMENTS OF DOOM (6:1–7:27)

6:1-14. *A Threat to High Places.* Vss. 1-7, 13-14 form a unit which no doubt originally stood before 20:45. The high places were local sanctuaries on hilltops which in accordance with Deut. 12:1-14 were outlawed by King Josiah (II Kings 23:8, 13-14, 19-20) but were revived after his death. These were not without worship of Yahweh, but the danger of idolatry was greater at such centers. When the attack comes the idolaters will flee to the high places for sanctuary and will be cut down there by the ruthless foe. The destruction will extend throughout the land, from the arid **wilderness** in the S to **Riblah** in Syria (see color map 9), the N-most boundary of David's empire. Vss. 8-10 were added by an early hopeful editor to follow 5:12 but later editing interrupted this connection.

6:11-12. This brief unit describes a dance of doom in which Ezek. beats time with his **hands** and **foot** as he chants the coming destruction. **Far off** and **near** clearly refer to distance from Jerusalem.

7:1-27. *The Coming of the End.* Such language as **Now the end is upon you** (vs. 3) and **Now I will soon pour out my wrath** (vs. 8) strongly suggests that Ezek. may be speaking directly to inhabitants of Jerusalem (see Intro.) at a time of crisis, probably when news of Nebuchadrezzar's approach with his army has been received. Yahweh is a God of justice. Though his mercy has spared the people in the past (cf. 20:17) the **day** of reckoning has come (vss. 4, 9; cf. 8:18; 9:10). According to the LXX it is the

"day of the LORD" (vs. 10a). This idea of a catastrophic day of divine action was older than Amos (5:18-20) and Isaiah (e.g. 2:12-21) and was emphasized by Zephaniah, but it became esp. popular in postexilic times (cf. e.g. Joel 1:15; 2:1-2; 3:14-15; Zech. 14:1; Mal. 4:5). Though the idea is not unknown to Ezek. (cf. 13:5; 30:2-3) it is doubtful that here he means anything more than a day of doom for Judah. Thus we may suspect that the statement that the end involves the **four corners of the land,** i.e. the earth, as the phrase is translated elsewhere (Isa. 11:12), is an interpolation.

7:10b-11. This passage is textually corrupt and obscure. With the LXX we may omit **violence** and translate: "Pride has budded, has grown up into a rod of wickedness." The last phrase may mean either a rod used for wicked purposes, referring to Jerusalem, or a rod for punishing wickedness, referring to Nebuchadrezzar. Perhaps both meanings are intended.

7:12-19. The imminence of war leads to falling prices in real estate; but **let not the buyer rejoice, nor the seller mourn,** for both will suffer loss. When Jerusalem is besieged those who are prospering will soon find nothing to buy. **Silver and gold . . . cannot satisfy their hunger.** At all times there are needs greater than money, but only in times of disaster do we fully realize this.

7:20-27. Such an impasse has come because the people have misused their wealth (vs. 20) and have oppressed their fellows (vs. 23b). Men in all stations will be impotent (vss. 26-27). Those who do not recognize God's lordship over life and wealth in times of peace must learn his lordship in a time of judgment.

D. VISITS TO THE TEMPLE (8:1–11:13)

8:1-3b. *The Journey to the Temple.* Part of this passage may belong elsewhere as the intro. to the scroll vision (see above on 2:8–3:3). The original beginning of the present narrative may be extracted as follows: "In the sixth year, in the sixth month, on the fifth day of the month, the elders of Judah were sitting before me; and the Spirit lifted me up and brought me to Jerusalem." **Elders of Judah** would most naturally refer to those active in Palestine rather than to exiles in Babylonia (see Intro.). Their consulting Ezek. on this date, Sep. 18, 592, a little more than a year since his call (see above on 1:1-3), indicates that in this short time he has achieved considerable reputation as a prophet. On the assumption that Ezek. was in Babylonia editors have inserted 2 alternate explanations for his report of visiting the temple in Jerusalem: (a) a miraculous flight **between earth and heaven** and (b) inspired **visions.** Without these vs. 3b is in line with 11:1; 37:1 as a way of describing what was probably a trip into the city from some outlying village in or near the plain of 3:22. For the idea of miraculous transport of a prophet the editor may have been indebted to Elisha's vision of Elijah's departure into heaven (II Kings 2:11-12, 16; cf. I Kings 18:12, 46). In turn this edited account may have suggested the story of Habakkuk's flight in Bel and the Dragon 33-36, 39.

8:3c-6. *The Image by the N Gate.* The words **of the inner court** are apparently an error for **north,**

for that court is not reached until vs. 16. Read rather: "to the entrance of the **north** gate that faces north." Cf. 11:1. The word translated **image** here is used in II Chr. 33:7 as a substitute for the name Asherah in the parallel text of II Kings 21:7. On the worship of this Canaanite fertility goddess cf. Jer. 7:18; 44:17-19, 25.

8:7-12. The Secret Chamber of Images. This is a gate chamber of the outer court of the temple like that portrayed for the inner court in 40:38 (see diagram, p. 435). The entrance from the vestibule has been closed off but the users of this secret chamber have another way of getting in. In the hastily plastered-over doorway Ezek. notes a hole caused by fallen plaster and proceeds to enlarge it and enter. On the wall are portrayed divine beings in animal form, as was common in Egyptian temples. The presence of **seventy . . . elders** (cf. Exod. 24:1, 9; Num. 11:16-17, 24-25) suggests a meeting of a pro-Egyptian party which sealed its conspiracy with Egypt in occult practices. In 592 such a party would need to hide; later it became strong enough to force the puppet Zedekiah into the revolt against his Babylonian overlord which resulted in the final siege and destruction of Jerusalem.

8:14-15. Women Weeping for Tammuz. This scene takes place at the N entrance to the inner court. Tammuz was an originally Sumerian vegetation deity who in Syria came to be identified with Hadad or Baal as a god who died in the summer at the beginning of the dry season and revived with the coming of the rain in the fall (cf. Zech. 12:11).

8:16-18. The Sun Worshipers. Moving ever deeper into the temple precincts, Ezek. is brought by Yahweh into the inner court, where only priests should enter. Solomon's temple was so oriented by its Phoenician architect that the rising sun on the days of the equinox would penetrate the open doors of the **porch** and pass through the "holy place" to shine into the "most holy place" at the back. To the orthodox this may have served as a practical means of dating spring and fall festivals or as a symbol of Yahweh's entrance into his sanctuary (cf. 43:1-5; I Kings 8:11-12). Others, however, are here finding in this an occasion for religious syncretism. To them Yahweh's being a "sun and a shield" (Ps. 84:11) is more than a poetic metaphor. By facing the rising sun these worshipers turn **their backs to the temple,** the place of God's spiritual presence.

9:1-11. A Vision of Slaughter. Grief and vexation at the sacrilege in the temple now give way to mystic vision. Yahweh summons 7 heavenly messengers. One of them, a scribe with a **writing case,** marks the **foreheads** of those **who sigh and groan over all the abominations** to protect them from the death to be administered by the other 6 angels. The **mark** is lit. a letter tau, which in the older script (see "Writing in Biblical Times," pp. 1201-08) had the form of a cross. As today, such a mark was sometimes used as a signature and is so translated in Job 31:35. Here it represents God's signature (cf. Rev. 7:2-3; 14:1). Judgment begins in the temple, for those closest to God are the most accountable (cf. I Pet. 4:17). The idea of individual responsibility and individual punishment in this vision (cf. ch. 18) is contradicted by the declaration in vss. 9-10 that

none will be spared (cf. 7:4, 9; 8:18). These displaced vss. evidently should follow 11:13 (see comment), as indicated by their poetic form and by their intro. in vs. 8, which is an adaptation of 11:13b—a literary echo characteristic of the late editors responsible for the rearrangement (see above on 1:4-28b).

10:1-22. Yahweh's Departure from the Temple. It is possible that the foregoing vision was originally followed by another which portrayed the burning of the buildings of Jerusalem. If so, all except its beginning has been replaced by an extensive interpolation with a different theme, Yahweh's abandonment of the temple. The divine **glory** must leave the temple and the city to make possible their destruction. Small insertions about the glory (8:4; 9:3) have prepared for this. The description of the departure of the glory (vss. 18-19) is concluded in 11:22-23. The burning is never carried out (cf. vs. 7) and nothing is said of how the righteous escape. On the imagery of the chariot, the **cherubim,** and the **wheels** see above on 1:4-28b.

11:1-12. Another Visit to the Temple. The language of vs. 1a indicates a new beginning (cf. 37:1) and introduces a different visit from that of ch. 8. The concern this time is not with cultic sins but with evil counselors of the king. In the **east gate,** probably that of the inner court, **twenty-five men** who are **princes of the people,** i.e. officials, are gathered to confer. They declare that the people in Jerusalem are like meat in a kettle about to be cooked. Under such circumstances their whole effort should be directed toward defense; they should not try to **build,** i.e. repair, **houses.** It is their **wicked counsel** in the past which has brought the city to its present dilemma. This incident originally must have come later than Ezek.'s allegory of the pot (24:1-5), which is dated at the beginning of the final siege. Thus on this occasion Ezek. must have come to the gate from some place inside the city.

11:7-12. Unfortunately this passage has suffered some editorial supplementation which has confused its original meaning. As it now stands the **caldron** seems to symbolize the city's protecting walls and the **flesh** its most distinguished citizens. The prophet's indictment then denies that they are so distinguished and declares rather that the victims of their assassination are the real meat of the city. These counselors will be removed from the kettle and judged **at the border of Israel,** i.e. Riblah (see above on 6:1-14), where after the destruction of Jerusalem a number of leading citizens were taken before Nebuchadrezzar and executed (II Kings 25:18-21). This was of course far N of the actual limit of Judah at that time but as the point of greatest expansion under David and Solomon it was ideally regarded as the proper border by the later contributors to the book (cf. 48:1).

The original meaning of Ezek.'s reply was probably: "This is indeed a kettle filled with the flesh of men you have killed; therefore many of you will be slain and become flesh in the kettle" (vss. 6-7). **Your slain** (vs. 7) means "those of you who will be slain"; **whom you have laid in the midst of it** is a misleading insertion.

11:13. The Death of Pelatiah. There can be no doubt that this vs., which is in poetic form, comes from Ezek. himself and reports an incident in his experience. It is strong evidence for the view that Ezek. was a Palestinian prophet (see Intro.) and confronted in person the people of Judah and Jerusalem with his sermons, during one of which Pelatiah collapsed and died. Defenders of the Babylonian locale have offered various explanations—e.g. that Ezek. learned of Pelatiah's death later—but these do not provide for the interaction described in the text.

11:13b. In Ezek.'s outcry the **remnant of Israel** may mean either Judah, which was left after the N kingdom was destroyed, or Jerusalem (cf. Isa. 1:8-9). Does the death of Pelatiah presage a destruction of this remnant? The original answer is to be found in 9:9-10, which is also poetic, and which is clearly out of place in its present context (see above on 9:1-11). This answer is an unqualified "yes, the remnant will be destroyed." In place of this the later editors have substituted as a more agreeable answer an originally unrelated passage (vss. 14-20) to indicate that a remnant will be preserved in the Exile.

11:14-25. Dispossession of the Exiles. Vss. 14-16 originally had nothing to do with what now precedes them. Rather they come from a later time, after the destruction of Jerusalem, and deal with the situation that arose when the poor left behind by the Chaldeans were **given** fields vacated by deportees (cf. 33:23-29; Jer. 39:10). This distribution included property belonging to exiled relatives of Ezek. **Your fellow exiles** is a substitution from the LXX for the Hebrew "men of your redemption," i.e. kinsmen whose property one is obligated to redeem when it is lost through debt or otherwise (cf. Lev. 25:25; Ruth 4:3-6; Jer. 32:6-12). The property vacated by Ezek.'s relatives should be held in trust by him until their return. More important, Ezek. insists that they have not **gone far from the Lord,** for he will be with them and be their **sanctuary** in the lands to which they have gone (vs. 16). This declaration became an important building stone for the late editors in the development of their theory of the shekinah-glory succession as an authentication of the rebuilt temple (see Intro.).

11:17-25. An early addition of hopeful material is to be found in vss. 17-20 (on vs. 19 cf. 36:26-27). In substituting vss. 14-20 for 9:9-10 (see above on 9:1-11) the late editors added vs. 21 as a characteristic literary echo of 9:10b (see above on 1:4-28b). Vss. 22-23 are the conclusion of the account of the departure of Yahweh's **glory** from the temple and city (ch. 10); when last seen the glory is atop the Mt. of Olives. Finally vss. 24-25 bring the combined temple vision to a conclusion by taking Ezek. back to **Chaldea,** i.e. Babylonia, by the same method or methods by which he is said to have left (see above on 8:1-3b).

E. Oracles and Allegories (12:1-17:24)

12:1-16. Pantomime of Coming Exile. As Ezek. reflects on his frustration in preaching to those who seem willfully blind and deaf, his thoughts come to him as a **word** from Yahweh. The **rebellious house** is the **house of Israel,** to whom he has been sent as prophet (cf. 2:3-7; 3:17). This passage offers strong evidence that Ezek.'s ministry was in Palestine

to the people of Judah rather than in Babylonia (see Intro.). Acting out the threat of exile would be highly effective for impressing on Judeans the risk of their present course; such dramatization would hardly be needed for those already in exile. That Ezek. **dug through the wall** suggests a structure of sun-dried clay bricks and has been noted as favoring a Babylonian locale because the rarity of stone there made such construction common. On the other hand building with this material in Palestine was not uncommon; e.g. at the site of Shechem excavators have turned up walls of this kind from all periods of its history. Cf. Isa. 9:10.

12:3b-7. One going into exile would be able to rescue only a few valuables as keepsakes in addition to the necessities of the journey to form his **baggage.** This would perhaps be carried in a sack over his shoulder. The **wall** dug through depicts a breached city wall, but in the enactment it was probably the wall of a courtyard, perhaps in Ezek's home village. On vs. 6b see below on vss. 8-16.

12:8-16. An editor has added details to the passage (cf. esp. vss. 6b, 12-13) to make it a prediction of the flight of the **prince,** i.e. Zedekiah, and his capture and blinding at Riblah (cf. II Kings 25:5-7; see above on 11:7-12). On vs. 14 see below on vss. 17-20. On vss. 15-16 see above on 5:1-17.

12:17-20. Pantomime of Eating in Fear. The action of this passage was probably not mere stage acting but rather a real experience of Ezek. to which he attached a symbolic meaning (cf. 21:6-7). The Hebrew of vs. 19a probably means "and say to the people of the land." If, as seems probable, this term means rural citizens whom Ezek. is informing of the coming exile, the passage is evidently to be dated before the siege, since thereafter the people of the surrounding countryside were gathered within the walls (cf. 22:17-22). The poetic form of the oracle in vs. 19 may be restored as follows:

> They shall eat their bread with fearfulness,
> and they shall drink their water in dismay,
> that they may waste away under their punishment,
> and look at one another in dismay.

The result depicted in the last 2 lines comes from 4:17b (cf. 24:23), where this brief pantomime evidently once stood (see above on 4:9-17). In rearranging the material the late editors substituted a result that would not logically follow: "that their land may be stripped . . ."—so the Hebrew should be translated (cf. KJV, ASV)—which must have been the original conclusion of vs. 14.

12:21-28. Skepticism About True Prophecy. The validity of prophetic prediction is questioned by the skeptics of vss. 21-25, who point to the **long** time that has elapsed without the threatened doom. Ezek. has been predicting it for several years, and no doubt the same persons have been hearing Jeremiah even longer, yet the end has not come (cf. II Pet. 3:3-4). On the other hand in vss. 26-28 only the immediate relevance of prophecy is questioned, on the assumption that it concerns **times far off.** The answer to both attitudes is that the **fulfillment** is **at hand** (cf. II Pet. 3:8-10).

13:1-16. False Prophets. Condemned here are those who prophesy **peace**—which in the Hebrew means not merely freedom from attack but also prosperity and general well-being—instead of warning of the coming doom (cf. Jer. 8:11; 14:13; 28-29). They are **like foxes among ruins,** indifferent to the destruction of the nation or, if the reference is to jackals (cf. the same Hebrew word in Ps. 63:10; Lam. 5:18), scavengers looking for gain from it. Instead of standing in the **breaches** as defenders or helping to repair the **wall** (cf. 22:30), i.e. the moral defenses of society, they cover its cracks with **whitewash** and leave it to collapse when a hard rainstorm hits.

13:17-23. *False Prophetesses.* This oracle deals with 2 different subjects and possibly represents a combining of 2 originally separate oracles: (*a*) a condemnation of female practitioners who, like the men of vss. 1-16, prophesy **out of their own minds** for a small fee (vs. 19*a*), telling **lies** (vs. 19*c*) in indifference to moral values (vs. 22); (*b*) a condemnation of sorceresses who claim power to slay their clients' enemies by use of **magic bands** and **veils.** The sin of sorcery lies, not in any supposed effectiveness of black magic, or even in its malice, but rather in its presumption in invading the sphere of the supernatural. Thus white magic is also to be condemned. Nothing in the Scriptures justifies hunting witches to blame for our troubles, but much condemns the attempted exercise of occult powers (cf. e.g. Deut. 18:10-11; I Sam. 15:23; Mic. 5:12; Gal. 5:20; Rev. 21:8).

14:1-11. *Idols in the Heart.* A body of **elders of Israel** come to Ezek. seeking an oracle (cf. 20:1; II Kings 6:32*a*). It is uncertain whether this designation is to be distinguished from "elders of Judah" (8:1; cf. 8:11-12). Possibly it refers to leaders from the territory of the former N kingdom (cf. e.g. 4:4-5). If so, their coming to Ezek. may indicate that he lived N of Jerusalem (see above on 3:22-27). The N people came under King Josiah's rule and reform (II Kings 23:15-20) but after his death were separated from Judah and relapsed into their former syncretistic religion (cf. II Kings 17:41), which included use of idols. Whether from N or S—or even from the exiles in Babylonia, where of course there was great temptation to syncretism—the idolatrous elders are to be given no oracle by the prophet, for Yahweh himself will **answer** them with acts of judgment.

14:12-23. *Survival of the Righteous.* From 4 punishments which might befall a land it is repeated that the **righteousness** of even **Noah, Daniel, and Job** would save only themselves but **neither sons nor daughters** (cf. ch. 18; Gen. 18:22-32). Noah is well known for having saved his sons and their families by his righteousness (cf. Gen. 7:1), and we may conjecture that Ezek. knew a version of the Job story in which the sons and daughters of Job 42:13 were the same as those of Job 1:2 (cf. Job 1:5). **Daniel,** therefore, in this book spelled Danel in the Hebrew, cannot refer to Ezek.'s supposed fellow exile (cf. Dan. 1:1-7). As early as 1900 it was suggested that this Danel must be an ancient sage (cf. 28:3) from the tradition of some neighboring people. Such a figure has since been discovered in the tablets dating back to the 15th cent. dug up at Ras Shamra in N Syria, site of the ancient Canaanite city of Ugarit. According to the story told in the tablets Danel was a good and wise king who beseeched

heaven with sacrifice and prayer for a son. At length Baal was moved to intercede for him before the supreme god El and his petition was granted. When the son, Aqhat, reached young manhood he was presented with a magic bow by Kothar, the god of craftmanship. Anath, the war goddess, tried to buy it from him, and on his refusal to sell she brought about his death. The conclusion of the story is not fully preserved, but there are indications that it told that through the prayers of Danel, the pious father, Aqhat was restored to life.

14:21-23. The repeated insistence that only righteous individuals will be saved, applied specifically to Jerusalem (vs. 21), is contradicted by the statement (vss. 22-23) that the **survivors** of the city's destruction going into exile will be typical Jerusalemites who by their manifest wickedness will prove to those already in exile that Yahweh was justified in his punishment. Poetic criteria show that underlying this editorial conclusion is the original ending of Ezek.'s oracle:

How much more when I send upon Jerusalem my judgments,
to cut off from it both man and beast!
Yet will there be left in it some survivors;
[They by their righteousness will deliver their lives.]

The final line or something similar, presumably suppressed by the editors, is implied by **How much more**—what has been true of lands generally is even more true of Jerusalem. The addressing of the contradiction to the exiles is quite exceptional, but cf. the intrusion of "sons and daughters" in 24:21, 25.

15:1-8. *Parable of the Vine Wood.* This oracle evidently was spoken soon after the fall of Jerusalem and refers to the **fire** by which the city was burned (cf. II Kings 25:8-9). Like vine wood, which is low-grade lumber, was Jerusalem before burning. How much less valuable now! The parable proper (vss. 1-5) is poetic and was followed originally by only vs. 6, in which the last clause probably should be translated "so have I given up the inhabitants of Jerusalem." Vss. 7-8 seem to be a later addition in which the experience of the city is traced down to the debacle which occurred at Mizpah (II Kings 25:25-26; Jer. 40:13–41:18). Thus those who escape from the fire of Jerusalem are to go forth to another fiery doom (cf. 5:4; 19:14*a*).

16:1-43c. *Jerusalem the Unfaithful Wife.* Here is a long poem on the history of Jerusalem, presented in allegorical form. For Jerusalem really to perceive the nature of her sins she must see them against the background of all the wonderful things God has done for her in the past.

16:1-5. Jerusalem was originally a Canaanite city, with **Amorite** and **Hittite** inhabitants. In allegorical terms she is described as born of an Amorite **father** and a Hittite **mother** who, rather than give her the care proper for a newly born infant, abandon her in an **open field.** Unwanted infants in pagan society were usually so exposed in a public place, where someone else might take pity on them—cf. Moses left in the bulrushes, also the story of Romulus and Remus.

16:6-7. Seeing the infant Jerusalem in her helpless and impure state, Yahweh says: **Live, and grow up like a plant of the field.** This refers to the sparing of the city during the conquest under Joshua and its being allowed to survive as a Jebusite enclave in Hebrew territory (cf. Judg. 1:21; 19:10-12). The child's being **naked** signifies the poverty of the city.

16:8-14. Yahweh sees that the young lady is now grown and enters into a marriage **covenant** with her (cf. Prov. 2:17; Mal. 2:14). The marriage stands for David's capture of the city by stratagem to make it the capital of his kingdom (II Sam. 5:6-9). He spared the inhabitants and even married some of the Jebusite girls (II Sam. 5:13-16). The spreading of Yahweh's **skirt** over the lady may allude to the pitching of the sacred tent in Jerusalem to house the ark (II Sam. 6:12-19). The adornment, **beauty,** and **renown** of the city reached a climax in the time of Solomon.

16:15-34. As a wife Jerusalem turns to adultery and becomes a **harlot** (cf. Jer. 3; Hos. 1-3). She uses her God-given wealth for the erection of pagan **shrines** and **images,** idols whose service is infidelity to Yahweh (vss. 15-19). She practices child sacrifice (vss. 20-21) and temple prostitution (vss. 23-25) —for idolatry was adultery in more than metaphor (cf. e.g. II Kings 23:7; Hos. 4:13-14; Amos 2:7-8). Even international alliances are cited as infidelity (vss. 26-29; cf. Jer. 2:18-19; Hos. 8:9). These not only showed lack of trust in Yahweh alone for national security (cf. Isa. 7:1-17) but often involved ceremonies recognizing the gods of other nations (see above on 8:7-12) and in times of weakness opened the way to pagan influences in religion (cf. II Kings 16:10-15). Tucked away here is a reference to a reprimand which went unheeded (vs. 27). In the annals of Sennacherib reference is made to his attack on Judah in 701, in which he **diminished** the territory of Hezekiah, turning over certain towns to the kings of cities of the **Philistines.**

The degeneracy of Jerusalem reaches its worst when she has to hire her lovers (vss. 30-34) by annual payments of tribute.

16:35-43. None of Jerusalem's jealous lovers among the nations can count on her fidelity, for she has played off one against the other. Hence they will at last assemble against her and strip her of her **clothes,** i.e. wealth, and leave her **naked and bare** as she was at first. The first Chaldean invasion (II Kings 24:1-16) may be envisioned in vss. 37-39 and the 2nd (II Kings 25:1-21) in vss. 40-41. In pride Jerusalem has ungratefully forgotten her past, from which Yahweh saved her (vs. 43; cf. vs. 22; Deut. 6:10-12; 8:11-19; 32:15-18). Her execution is to be a lesson to **many women,** i.e. nations (vs. 41). We are among those nations who can benefit from such a lesson.

16:43d-63. *Jerusalem and Her Sisters.* Here is an independent indictment (vss. 44-52) which has been supplemented with a message of hope (vss. 53-63). It is united to the preceding allegory (vss. 1-43c) by a transitional statement (vs. 43d), by the insertions of **her husband and** and **their husbands and** (vs. 45), and by the allusion to the **covenant . . . in the days of your youth** (vss. 59-60). The great sin of the Amorites and Hittites (vs. 45b) was the exposing and sacrifice of their **children** (vss. 3-5, 20-21). It is this sin which makes Jerusalem more wicked than **Samaria** and **Sodom.** Samaria was guilty of **abominations,** i.e. idolatry, but not this! Sodom's sin was

pride, self-sufficiency, and neglect of the **poor.** The story in Gen. 19:4-11 was told to illustrate the degeneracy of the city of Sodom after an "outcry" against it arose (Gen. 18:20). This outcry, like that of Isa. 5:7, came from the throats of the oppressed poor. Ezek. is like Jesus in regarding offenses against children as the gravest (cf. e.g. Matt. 18:6, 10-14). That Jerusalem is judged worse than Samaria (vss. 47, 51; cf. 23:11) may owe something to Jer. 3:11.

16:53-63. The promise of the restoration of Sodom and Samaria is probably from the early hopeful editor (see Intro.). If divine love can restore Jerusalem, how much more Sodom and Samaria, who were less sinful. Restoration will precede repentance and be the ground of shame and penitence (cf. 20:42-43; 36:31-32).

17:1-21. *The Eagles, Cedar, and Vine.* This **allegory** takes the form of a fable in which eagles engage in horticulture. The narrative in vss. 3-10 has received an exilic supplement in vss. 22-24. Intervening (vss. 11-21) is an interpretation which leaves no doubt of the story's meaning.

17:3-6. An **eagle,** the king of Babylon, comes to **Lebanon,** i.e. Jerusalem, whose temple and palaces were built of cedars of Lebanon, and takes the **top of the cedar,** Jehoiachin, along with other **topmost . . . twigs,** high officials, and puts them in the **land of trade,** Babylon. Then he takes the **seed of the land,** Zedekiah, and places it **in fertile soil . . . beside abundant waters,** i.e. in a relationship of dependence on the great power of the Euphrates. There it becomes a **low spreading vine,** a subservient vassal, and directs its **branches,** its international ties, toward this eagle alone.

17:7-10. Then another **eagle,** the king of Egypt, appears in the sky; and the **vine,** Zedekiah, redirects its **branches** toward the new eagle so that he may **water it,** i.e. give it military aid. This eagle moves the vine to **good soil by abundant waters,** i.e. makes it tributary to the Nile. Can the newly transplanted vine **thrive?** To this question 2 negative answers are given: (a) **he,** apparently meaning the first eagle, will root it out (vs. 9) and (b) the **east wind,** Babylonia (cf. 19:12; 27:26), will blast it (vs. 10). Probably vs. 9 with its unclear subject is an interpolation by one concerned that the allegory should indicate precisely that Zedekiah was exiled to Babylon and died there (cf. vss. 16, 20). Ezek.'s original prediction (vs. 10), spoken before the event, foresaw only that when struck by the hot sirocco blowing in from the desert, a Chaldean invasion, the vine should **wither away on the bed where it grew,** i.e. suffer military defeat (cf. vs. 21).

17:11-21. Ezek.'s allegory was propaganda against the policies of Zedekiah which he did not dare express in plain language lest he be accused of treason. Not having the close friends in high station that Jeremiah had, he needed to be more covert in his criticism of the king or he might suffer the fate of the prophet Uriah (Jer. 26). Thus it seems certain that Ezek. did not provide this explanation of his allegory but left it to his listeners to interpret as best they could.

17:22-24. *The Messianic Tree.* According to this supplemental allegory a **sprig from the lofty top of the cedar,** i.e. a descendant of Jehoiachin, will be planted on a **lofty mountain,** Jerusalem. There it will grow into a **noble cedar,** a mighty ruler, whose **branches** will shelter **beasts** and **birds,** other countries. As a consequence **all the trees of the field,** all other kings, will **know** that Yahweh is the Lord of nations (cf. Dan. 4). This early hopeful addition (see Intro.) may have in mind Jehoiachin's grandson Zerubbabel (cf. Hag. 2:20-23; Zech. 3:8-10), who some hoped might restore the Davidic monarchy. Matt. 1:12-13; Luke 3:27 trace the ancestry of Jesus through Zerubbabel, whose name means "sprout of Babylon."

F. INDIVIDUAL RESPONSIBILITY (18:1-32)

Here is a thesis for which Ezek. is justly famous. The occasion must have been one of pessimism, when the predicted doom appeared inevitable, or even under way. Instead of taking personal responsibility for what was happening people were blaming their ancestors. Ezek. himself had preached that the people were guilty of perpetuating the sins of their fathers (2:3; ch. 20) and that Jerusalem had inherited certain sins from her Amorite and Hittite ancestors (16:3, 44-45). This inheritance of sin, however, was only sociological and environmental. Sins of the fathers may be inherited, but only because their sons fail to hear or heed the call to repentance.

The popular **proverb** that Ezek. denies (vs. 2) was known to Jeremiah also (Jer. 31:29). Ezek.'s denial is based on his faith in Yahweh's sovereign claim over every **soul** (vs. 4). Every man must make his own answer to God. If he is **righteous** (vss. 5-9) Yahweh will not surrender him to suffer for the sins of his ancestors. Only **the soul that sins shall die** (vss. 4, 20).

The death of which Ezek. speaks is not a natural demise, which each man must face. Nor is it the death of the soul as we use the term, for the **soul** here means the "person," as often in the Bible (cf. e.g. Gen. 2:7). The threat to life envisaged here is the Chaldean invasion (cf. 33:1-6). The message of Ezek., apart from miracle, could not have received lit. fulfillment. There must have been many examples of the wicked escaping (cf. 14:22-23) and of the righteous being slain (cf. 21:3). Yet back of this ch. is a sound faith that God is **just** and deals with people as persons. Ultimately this faith was to be vindicated, but it called for a doctrine of immortality which had not yet been revealed to the Hebrews. Jeremiah did right in transferring faith's fulfillment to the future (Jer. 31:27-30).

The final plea (vss. 30-32) is for repentance based on the love of God, who will punish the unrepentant but is grieved to do so. Each generation, in the light of new insights, is called on to forsake the sins of its **fathers.** To denounce traditional sin calls for courage, and to renounce it calls for equal courage, for it pits the individual against the rest of society with its inherited way of life. Christ died to save men from unworthy tradition (I Pet. 1:18-19).

G. THE FATE OF JERUSALEM (19:1-24:27)

19:1-9. The Lioness and the Young Lions. The reference of the pronoun **your** (vs. 2), which is singular, is a question to which a number of answers have been given, but the most likely is that the poem is to be understood as spoken by Yahweh to Ezek. (cf. 12:1-3a). Thus his **mother,** who is compared to a **lioness,** represents the nation of Judah (cf. Gen. 49:9). In the Hebrew the poem is in 3/2 rhythm, i.e. with 3 stresses in the first part of each line and only 2 in the 2nd part. In the RSV each Hebrew line is rendered by a full line representing the 3-stress part followed by an indented line representing the 2-stress part. This is the rhythm commonly used in a **lamentation** or dirge, e.g. predominantly in Lam.

In the poem as we have it there are 2 exceptions to the regular dirge rhythm. Vs. 4cd is in 2/2 rather than 3/2 rhythm. It identifies the first **young lion** with King Jehoahaz, the son and immediate successor of Josiah, who after a reign of only 3 months was taken captive to **Egypt** (II Kings 23:31-34). To be parallel with Jehoahaz the 2nd young lion should be Jehoiachin, who also reigned only 3 months before being taken into exile by Nebuchadrezzar (II Kings 24:8-16). The 2nd young lion is identified in vs. 9a-c, the other exception to the rhythm, which has an extra part line, 3/3/2. If we eliminate the 2 irregularities, by omitting vs. 4cd entirely and removing from vs. 9bc the words **to the king of Babylon; they brought him,** the explicit references to both Egypt and Babylon disappear and the usual identifications of the 2 young lions with Jehoahaz and Jehoiachin may be reconsidered.

Without vs. 4cd the first young lion is simply **taken in their pit** but not exiled. Thus he may well represent King Jehoiakim, whose 11-year reign ended with his death late in 598 while Nebuchadrezzar was beginning to lay siege to Jerusalem (cf. II Kings 24:6-10; Jer. 22:18-19). The natural parallel to Jehoiakim is Zedekiah, who also ruled 11 years and also by rebelling against Nebuchadrezzar brought on a Babylonian invasion and exile. Even with the interpolation vs. 9 fits Zedekiah better than Jehoiachin, for Nebuchadrezzar came to Jerusalem and took Jehoiachin (II Kings 24:10-12), but Zedekiah was **brought** to Nebuchadrezzar at Riblah (II Kings 25:6; see above on 6:1-14; 11:7-12). Instead of **into custody** (vs. 9c) the Hebrew text reads lit. "into strongholds," evidently referring to those of Riblah.

Because Jehoiachin ruled only 3 months and inherited a hopeless situation from his father, he could accomplish little and might legitimately be skipped in this poem. A possible reference to him, however, appears in vs. 5a, which in the Hebrew text reads "when she saw that she had waited" (see RSV footnote). This could refer to the brief reign of Jehoiachin, who never had a chance to become a young lion.

Each young lion is said to have met his doom when he **learned to catch prey** and **devoured men.** This is a subtle attack on Judean nationalism. The greatness of Judah was to be obtained in other ways (cf. Rev. 5:5-6).

19:10-14. The Vine and Its Strongest Stem. Here Judah is compared to a grapevine (cf. chs. 15; 17; Gen. 49:11; Ps. 80:8-16; John 15:1-8). This poem does not continue the previous allegory but is another on the same theme. Vs. 10a probably should read: "Your mother was like a vine of your vineyard," as in 2 Hebrew manuscripts. The last phrase in all other manuscripts (see RSV footnote) includes "your." These words are apparently addressed by Yahweh to the prophet (see above on vss. 1-9). This suggests that Ezek. had a vineyard and that an experience with one of his vines underlies this allegory. On the location of his vineyard see above on 3:22-27.

19:10-12. The first 3 pairs of lines (vss. 10-11b) are in the 3/2 dirge rhythm (see above on vss. 1-9) and describe Judah in her prosperity. The **strongest stem** has often been taken to mean Zedekiah but more probably represents not so much a particular ruler as the Davidic dynasty. The ruin of the vine is brought about by the arrogance of this main stem. A translation of the unemended Hebrew text of vss. 11c-12 is as follows:

> Its height towered
> among the clouds.
> It was seen in its height
> with the mass of its branches.
> But plucked up in fury,
> she was cast down to the ground.
> The wind from the east
> dried up her fruit—
> now stripped off and withered.
> Her strong main stem,
> the fire consumed it.

"It" and "its" here refer to the strongest stem, and "she" and "her" refer to the vine, which is also "mother."

In contrast with the rest of the poem this portion is in 2/2 rhythm; i.e. each half line has only 2 stresses. The RSV follows most analysts in repunctuating vs. 12c-f as 3/2. Since vss. 11c-12b can be handled only as 2/2, they are often assumed to be a later addition. Yet it is these very lines that unlock the meaning. From them we may recognize that this allegory makes use of a popular myth in which a plant grew so tall that it reached heaven and because of such arrogance met its downfall (cf. Gen. 11:1-9; Dan. 4:10-37). Thus the word translated **thick boughs** (vs. 11d) should rather be understood to mean "clouds" as in 31:3, 10, 14. In the grape culture of Palestine vines were severely pruned and made to lie close to the ground so that they would not be scorched by the sirocco during the dry summer months. The arrogance of the Davidic dynasty, esp. as represented in Jehoiakim and Zedekiah, has exposed the vine of Judah to the **east wind,** i.e. Chaldea (cf. 17:10; 27:26).

19:13-14. The conclusion concerns the aftermath of Jerusalem's fall. **Transplanted in the wilderness** refers to the impoverished circumstances of those remaining in the land. Since the vine has already suffered from **fire** in vs. 12f, the repetition in vs. 14a apparently refers to Ishmael, who as a scion of the Davidic **stem** brought further suffering to the nation (see above on 5:1-17; 15:1-8).

20:1-3. *An Inquiry from Israel's Elders.* On Aug. 14, 591 Ezek. is visited by elders of Israel (see above on 14:1-11) who have come to **inquire of the LORD,** i.e. to secure an oracle from him (cf. Jer. 21:1-2; 27:3-10). Yahweh's refusal to answer is itself an answer. **Is it to inquire of me that you come?** has a double meaning; the Hebrew could also be translated "Is it to seek me that you come?"

20:4-32. *The History of Israel's Rebellion.* Since

they were in Egypt the people of Israel have repeatedly **rebelled** (cf. Ps. 106:7) and have been spared by Yahweh, but his patience is running out. In each period of history the recurrent pattern is: (*a*) revelation of the covenant, or a plea to obey it, (*b*) violation of the covenant, (*c*) threatened punishment, (*d*) deferred anger. In the 2nd cycle (vss. 10-17) elements *c* and *d* (vss. 13d, 14) are repeated in a sort of poetic parallelism (vss. 15-16, 17). The same repetition was intended in the latter half of the 3rd cycle (vss. 21b-24) but is incomplete. Instead of the expected repetition of element *d* we find Yahweh himself giving **statutes that were not good** and **making them offer** child sacrifices (vss. 25-26). Obviously the text is not intact.

After vs. 24 there originally must have come a variation of vs. 17 as the conclusion of the 3rd cycle. Next should follow the beginning of the 4th cycle in vs. 28, of which the opening words should be translated "So I brought them" (cf. vs. 10). The original intro. to vss. 25-26, now found in vs. 27, identifies the ascription to Yahweh of bad laws and the institution of child sacrifice as a blasphemy uttered by the people. Their accusation ends with **first-born,** the remainder of vs. 26 being editorial. Thus the logical original order is vss. 28-29, 27, 25-26a, 30-32. The joining of vs. 27 to vs. 25 calls for the following translation: "In this, moreover, your fathers blasphemed me, while dealing treacherously with me, [saying that] it was I who had also given them statutes that were not good . . ." The restoration fits with the denunciation of child sacrifice in vs. 31 (cf. 16:20-21, 45; Jer. 7:31; 19:5).

20:33-39. *The Purging of Gathered Israel.* Those dispersed will be gathered once more into the wilderness, but instead of being in the **wilderness of the land of Egypt,** i.e. Sinai, they will be in the **wilderness of the peoples,** possibly meaning the desert region of N Arabia, around which the lands of the Fertile Crescent arch. Hos. 2:14-15 also speaks of a new wilderness experience but in the Judean wilderness (cf. 47:1-12). Only those willing to observe God's covenant will be brought from the wilderness into the land of promise—like sheep entering the fold under the counting shepherd's **rod** (vs. 37; cf. Lev. 27:32; Jer. 33:13). The doctrine of individualism expressed here is in accord with Ezek.'s theology, but the concern with the dispersion is characteristic of early hopeful editors (see Intro.).

20:39-44. *The Accepted Worshipers.* Vs. 39 is probably the resounding conclusion to vss. 4-32. If the people are so obstinate, let them **go ahead and serve** their **idols,** but the impending doom will soon bring this profaning of Yahweh's name to an end! In the new setting, however, vs. 39 is transitional to vss. 40-44, and vs. 39b seems to refer to the abandonment of idolatry on the part of those who were dispersed among the nations as a precondition for their acceptable worship in the Holy Land. Those brought home from the dispersion will again worship on Mt. Zion. There alone will they present sacrifices —in accordance with Deut. 12 as interpreted in Josiah's reform (cf. II Kings 22:8–23:23). When Yahweh shows his acceptance of them by his blessings, they will utterly loathe themselves for their past sins (cf. 16:63; 36:31). This is another evident early hopeful addition (see Intro.).

20:45-21:5. *Doom for the Whole Land.* Three oracles belong in this series but the first is misplaced (see above on 6:1-14). Standing where he can see the different sections of the land, Ezek. threatens first the "mountains of Israel" (6:1-7), i.e. those to the N, then turns to the **south** (20:45-48) and finally to Jerusalem (21:1-5). His vantage point would be some place, e.g. the Mt. of Olives, where the N and S areas could be distinguished from the city. The threat to each area becomes an ill omen for the whole land (6:14; 20:47; 21:4).

20:45-48. The name **Negeb,** lit. "parched," is applied to the desert country S of Beer-sheba, but this was not **forest land** (vs. 46), or even brush land. So frequently was the term used to refer to the S that here apparently Ezek. applies it to the wooded area between Jerusalem and Hebron.

20:49. Some of Ezek.'s listeners are inclined to dismiss his messages as enigmatic **allegories.** No doubt their reaction is to those of chs. 16-17 rather than those of chs. 15; 19, which were spoken after the destruction of Jerusalem.

21:1-5. Climactically Ezek. declares that Jerusalem itself is doomed. **Sanctuaries** is evidently a reverential plural used of the temple (cf. Lev. 21:23; 26:31). The cutting off of **both righteous and wicked** (vs. 3) evidently antedates the developed individualism of chs. 9; 18 and thus dates these oracles fairly early. With vs. 4 cf. I Pet. 4:17-18.

21:6-7. *Sighing with a Broken Heart.* This is no mere symbolic pantomime. As in 12:17-20 (see comment) Ezek. interprets his own emotion as a message from God. The vss. come from before the siege of Jerusalem and an editor not unnaturally linked them to the preceding passage with a **therefore.** In vs. 7 **all knees will be weak as water** may also be translated "all knees will flow with water." The LXX renders "all knees will be defiled with water," i.e. urine; in times of fright one may lose bladder control (cf. 7:17).

21:8-17. *The Song of the Sword.* Here is more than a song, for symbolic actions accompany it. This is sword dancing, a more elaborate version of the dance of doom in 6:11-12. Such a performance must have been rhythmical and poetic (cf. 33:30-33). Vss. 10*b*, 13 contain wisdom interpolations (cf. Prov. 13:24; 15:32; 29:15).

21:18-23. *The Sword at the Crossroads.* Judah has rebelled against the Babylonian overlordship. Its yoke has been felt since 605, when Nebuchadrezzar drove Egyptian power from Syria and Palestine, but has been esp. heavy since 597, when an earlier revolt ended in the exile of King Jehoiachin and the installing of Zedekiah as puppet regent (see Intro.). During that revolt the **Ammonites** of Transjordan (see color map 8) aided Nebuchadrezzar against Judah (II Kings 24:1-2) but now they have revolted. So too has Zedekiah, under pressure from prominent Judeans who prefer a return to Egyptian vassalage (see above on 8:7-12).

Ezek. selects a fork in the road to represent the **parting of the way,** the crossing of the caravan routes—actually probably in Damascus (see color map 7)—where Nebuchadrezzar must decide whether to move first against **Rabbah,** the capital of Ammon, or Jerusalem. Ezek. even sets up a **signpost** to differentiate the ways to the 2 cities. He acts out the

part of Nebuchadrezzar using his triple means of **divination** to determine the will of his gods about which place to attack first. On the **arrows** cf. II Kings 13:14-19. On the **teraphim** cf. e.g. Judg. 17:5; Zech. 10:2. Complex instructions for reading oracles from the **liver** of a sacrificed animal, as well as marked clay models of livers, have been dug up in Mesopotamia.

21:23. This vs. is strong evidence for Ezek.'s presentation of the oracle before an audience in or near Jerusalem rather than in Babylonia (see Intro.). Not only does he perceive the reaction of those present to his acting out the processes of divination, but he is aware that some of them have made **solemn oaths,** evidently with the Egyptians who have been fostering the rebellion against Babylonia.

21:24-27. *Indictment of Zedekiah.* This passage contains no mention of the sword but is attached to the preceding by its **therefore.** The poetic indictment of Zedekiah (vss. 25-27) may be restored as follows:

And you, O prince of Israel,
Unhallowed one, whose day has come,
the time of your final punishment—
Thus says Yahweh:
"Remove the turban, and take off the crown!
Exalt the low, and abase the high.
A ruin, ruin, ruin I will make it,
Till he comes whose right it is and I give it to him."

Zedekiah is only a **prince** (cf. 12:10, 12) since he is the regent for the exiled King Jehoiakim rather than rightful king (see Intro.). Thus he is **unhallowed** because he does not participate in the sacredness of the royal office. This situation was not understood by the later editor who inserted **wicked** in an attempt to explain "unhallowed" and thus upset the rhythm. **Things shall not remain as they are** (vs. 26*c*) is a paraphrase of the lit. Hebrew "this, not this"; and **there shall not be even a trace** (vs. 27*b*) involves an emendation of the Hebrew "this too was not." Evidently these are marginal notes that were copied into the text. "This, not this" may mean that the preceding prediction was fulfilled but not the following; if so, "this too was not" means that the prediction following it was not fulfilled. Alternatively these may be notes of a scribe about the text, indicating that one clause was well attested but others were not found in all manuscripts. The final line would be more intelligible if it could follow vs. 26*b* and thus refer to the crown.

This is the only passage in which Ezek. faces Zedekiah in person. The occasion probably was a public appearance just before or during the siege of Jerusalem. To give morale to the war effort Zedekiah dons royal apparel. The wearing of the **turban** and **crown** is a claim to be king and thus a symbol of his revolt against Babylonia, since the Babylonians reserve the title king for Jehoiachin. Vs. 27*c* rightly maintains that the crown must be saved for Jehoiachin, who is expected to return someday (cf. II Chr. 33:10-13).

21:28-32. *The Doom of Ammon.* The sword which was to fall on Jerusalem (vss. 18-23) will finally assail Ammon as well (cf. 25:1-7). Note the numerous parallels in language with other passages declaring the doom of Jerusalem and Judah: with vs. 28*cd* cf. vss. 9-10; with vs. 29*a* cf. 22:28; with vs.

29b cf. vs. 25; with vs. 31b cf. 22:21a; with vs. 32a cf. 15:4a; with vs. 32b cf. 24:7. If this says anything, it means that Ammon is to suffer the same doom as Judah. There is one exception: instead of being exiled Ammon is to be punished on her own soil (vs. 30b). On the **origin** of Ammon cf. Gen. 19:30-38.

22:1-16. The Defiled City. Here Jerusalem is informed of **all** her crimes. Foremost are murder and idolatry. Oppression of the **sojourner,** i.e. resident alien, and of widows and orphans (vs. 7) goes hand in hand with contempt for the **holy things** of the sanctuary and with disdain for the **sabbaths** (vs. 8). Dishonesty and bloodshed have so corroded the city that her lack of morals will mean also lack of morale (vs. 14) and her end will be dispersion **among the nations.**

22:17-22. The Smelting Furnace. The people are fleeing from the small villages into Jerusalem for safety at the approach of Nebuchadrezzar's army. Ezek. seems to be there, and he greets them with this message comparing them to materials thrown into a smelting furnace. **So I will gather you** (vs. 20b) employs a participle which may be best interpreted here as meaning "so I am gathering you." The analogy implies that there will be a purified product emerging from the flame (cf. vs. 15; Isa. 1:24-26).

22:23-31. The Need for a Deliverer. Here the people are still in their rural villages, where withholding of the rain spells disaster in agriculture. This has come as a punishment for decadence in society, affecting all from top to bottom. **Princes** in vs. 25 probably means the kings of Judah; in vs. 27 it translates a different Hebrew word referring to high officials. Vss. 25-27 expand on Zeph. 3:3-4. On vs. 28 cf. 13:1-16. On **people of the land** (vs. 29) see above on 12:17-20. Into the breached **wall** (vs. 30) some heroic figure must step, not only to repair it, but to ward off a hostile foe (cf. 13:5; Neh. 4:13-23). The broken wall is the moral bulwark of society, the breach is sin, and the enemy who opposes is Yahweh (cf. Ps. 106:19-23).

23:1-35. Oholah and Oholibah. With this allegory of Yahweh's 2 unfaithful wives cf. ch. 16; Hos. 1; 3. Marriage with sisters, both living, was forbidden by the later Priestly legislation (cf. Lev. 18:18). **Oholah** means "her tabernacle" and **Oholibah** means "my tabernacle is in her." The former symbolizes **Samaria,** whose temples are considered illegitimate; the latter is **Jerusalem,** which contains the true temple. Ezek. accepts the D principle of only one legitimate sanctuary (Deut. 12:1-14). Samaria and Jerusalem are here viewed as the nations Israel and Judah, and so their marriage could take place in **Egypt.** Their **harlotry** consists of making alliances with foreign nations instead of relying on Yahweh alone for protection. On Oholah's infidelity and punishment (vss. 5-10) cf. 16:15-43. On Oholibah's infidelity (vss. 11-21) cf. 16:15-29, esp. vss. 26-29. On Jerusalem's being **worse** than Samaria cf. 16:46-47, 51; Jer. 3:11.

23:22-35. Oholibah's imminent punishment is to be administered by Babylonia and her Assyrian subjects. **Pekod** is named in Assyrian records as a Babylonian tribe (cf. Jer. 50:21; see color map 9). Proposed similar identifications of **Shoa and Koa** are doubtful. The cruel deeds mentioned in vss. 25-26 represent indignities suffered by captives. The root meaning of the verb for "go into exile" in Hebrew is "go naked" (cf. Isa. 20). In vss. 32-34 a drinking song has been adapted as a taunt song.

23:36-49. Judgment of Oholah and Oholibah. This passage uses the symbolism of vss. 1-35 but applies it to an entirely different situation, in which the infidelity consists of cultic and moral sins. Since it portrays the doom of both sisters as future, it must refer to the postexilic cities of Samaria and Jerusalem. Since both together have **defiled** the temple at Jerusalem it antedates the Samaritan schism and thus is prior to the final editing (see Intro.). The situation described seems similar to that with which Neh. had to contend—cf. his foes from territory of the former N kingdom (Neh. 2:19-20; 4:7) who had allies in Jerusalem (Neh. 6) and were connected by marriage with the Jerusalem priesthood (Neh. 6:18; 13:28) so that one of them was even allowed to use a chamber of the temple (Neh. 13:4-9). That idolatry and child sacrifice (vss. 37-39) should be problems in postexilic Jerusalem is surprising, but cf. Isa. 57:5, 9.

23:45-49. The judgment is to be administered, not by the Chaldeans, the "wicked of the earth" (cf. 7:21, 24), but by **righteous men,** i.e. faithful Jews. A violent reform like that of Josiah is prescribed (cf. Deut. 13:12-16; II Kings 23:15-20). The reforms of Nehemiah and Ezra saved the country from the upheaval proposed here.

24:1-14. The Corroded Cooking Pot. On the very day that Nebuchadrezzar **laid siege to Jerusalem,** Jan. 15, 588 (see Chronology, pp. 1271-82), Ezek. seized a rusty cooking **pot** and proceeded to cook with it until all its contents were burned to a crisp. While cooking meat, he seems to sing a familiar work song; but he adapts it to portray the imminent disaster of Jerusalem. His action became proverbial (cf. 11:1-12). Ordinary people used pottery cooking vessels. Since Ezek. was a priest (1:3) and the **pot** he used was **copper** (or bronze), as was usual for temple cooking vessels (vs. 11; Exod. 27:3; 38:3; I Kings 7:45; Jer. 52:18), this appears to be a castoff utensil from the temple, which had been declared unfit because of its deeply embedded **rust.** This view seems to be confirmed by the words **without making any choice** (end of vs. 6), which is lit. "for **her** no lot has fallen." The fem. pronoun refers to the fem. noun **pot,** not to the masc. noun **piece** of the preceding clause. The casting of lots was a common priestly practice; but no lot was cast for this vessel because of its ritual impurity. (For cooking in the temple, cf. 46:19-24, and for sacrifices on the eve of battle, cf. Ps. 20.) The original oracle about the pot, its contents, and the fire has been elaborated. Editorial interpretation is introduced prematurely in vs. 6ab. By weaving interpretation into the text earlier, it converts literal details of the cooking into instant allegory. Thus **Take out of it piece after piece** after mention of **the bloody city** (vs. 6) suggests exiles rather than pieces of meat (cf. 11:7-12). The words "for her no lot has fallen" were transferred to the end to refer to these worthless exiles (cf. 14:22; Jer. 24; Ob. 11; Joel 3:2-3). The imperatives of vss. 3-5, 6c-f which belong to the cooking song were probably continued by those of vs. 11. The original sequence of connections may have been somewhat as follows:

5c   Boil its pieces, [boil them,]
  d   yea seethe its bones within it—
6c   in a pot whose rust is in it,
  d   whose rust departs not from it,
  f   for which no lot has fallen.
  e   Take out of it piece after piece,
11a   then set it empty upon the coals . . .

Ezek.'s interpretation (vss. 9-10, 12-14) emphasized the catastrophe of Jerusalem due to her deeply ingrained moral corrosion. Her **filthiness** (vs. 13) refers to all the wrongs that King Josiah's reform (cf. II Kings 23) had vainly **cleansed** away. Jerusalem was too corrupt for reformation, so she must be subjected to the scorching flames of the Babylonian siege.

Vss. 6a-b, 7-8. Jerusalem's inexorable blood-guilt was the subject of an independent oracle, which like 22:1-16 (cf. 24:9) was addressed to **the bloody city.** It was inserted into the cooking song in order to explain the city's **rust as the blood she has shed;** but since Ezek.'s pot was **copper** (vs. 11) rather than iron, it would have green rust. The sole point concerning the blood is that like the blood of righteous Abel (Gen. 4:10-11) it cannot **be covered,** but always open to Yahweh's gaze it invokes his **wrath.**

24:15-24. The Death of Ezek.'s Wife. When it is apparent that his wife is to die, Ezek. is told how to behave so that her death will symbolize the impending destruction of the temple. He is to make no outward show of **mourning,** accepting as just the judgment of God. As she is the **delight** of his **eyes,** so the temple is to the people. An editor has tried to turn the emphasis from the temple to the **sons and daughters** of the exiles (vs. 21c; cf. 14:22-23). This is most obvious in vs. 25b, where the Hebrew contains no **and also.** On the date of this event see below on vss. 25-27.

24:25-27. Ezek.'s Dumbness. This continuation of the preceding narrative seems to have been dismembered by the late editors, who placed its beginning in 3:24b-26 and its ending in 33:21-22. The beginning may be restored and translated:

> And he spoke with me and said:
> "And you, O son of man, behold,
> Cords will they place upon you,
>   and bind you with them.
> Go, shut yourself in your house,
>   and go not out among the people.
> Your tongue I will stick to your palate,
>   that no longer you may be their reprover,
>   for they are a rebellious house.

The editors advanced **Go, shut yourself within your house** (3:24c) to the beginning of the divine speech to have Ezek. return home at the end of his vision, but originally it must have followed the warning that he might be **bound** (3:25)—not by a divinely imposed paralysis as in 4:8 but, as the active verbs in the Hebrew suggest, by human hands. Ezek. is in danger of being imprisoned because of the furor aroused by his prediction that the temple will be destroyed (cf. Jer. 26; Mark 14:57-58; Acts 6:8-7:58). Since he is to know of the destruction only by **report** of a **fugitive** (vs. 26; cf. 33:21-22) the house in which he shuts himself must be outside Jerusalem and presumably is his village home. Early in the siege an Egyptian force drew off the Chaldeans for a time so that it was possible to leave the

city (cf. Jer. 37:11-15) and perhaps Ezek.'s departure occurred during that period. Several oracles against Egypt, however, are dated between that time and the fall of the city (29:1; 30:20; 31:1; 32:17). More probably, therefore, this incident took place soon after the breaching of the city wall and the flight of Zedekiah (II Kings 25:3-5; Jer. 39:1-5). If so, Ezek.'s withdrawal to silence was ended in less than a month by the fulfillment of his prophecy. At the coming of the fugitive, Ezek. will be released from his dumbness. The fulfillment of this expectation is 33:21-22. Hence the present passage probably records the experience of **the evening before the fugitive came** (33:22a).

II. Judah's Restoration (25:1-48:35)

The materials of this book have been arranged, no doubt by the late editors responsible for many transpositions (see Intro.), into 2 parts, with their natural division between chs. 24; 25. Part I speaks primarily of doom for Israel, Part II almost entirely of hope—the doom of neighboring nations being viewed as an element of Israel's hope (see below on 28:24-26). In chs. 25-32, seven nations are doomed: Ammon, Moab, Edom, Philistia, Tyre, Sidon, and Egypt. Since the number seven symbolizes completeness, this result may have been achieved editorially. See below at 28:20-24.

A. The Doom of Neighboring Nations (25:1-32:32)

25:1-17. Oracles Against Closest Neighbors. In 21:28-32 the **Ammonites** are threatened with attack from the Chaldeans. Here a later foe threatens, the **people of the East,** i.e. the tribes of N Arabia E of Transjordan (see color map 7). These people are also to take over **Moab** (vss. 8-11; see color maps 5, 8) and **Edom** (vss. 12-14; see color map 4). On **Teman** and **Dedan**—here apparently an Edomite town rather than the Arabian oasis mentioned in 27:20; 38:13—see comment on Jer. 49:7-11. The Arab encroachments may have been somewhat gradual, beginning perhaps during the Exile and increasing during the following cent. (see Intro. to Obad.). As a result the Edomites were driven entirely out of their ancient homeland and settled in S Judah, where they eventually took over the region so that by the time of Alexander's conquest (332) most of Judah's former territory was called Idumea (see color map 11). Meanwhile the encroaching Arabs founded the Nabatean Kingdom with its capital at Petra, where they hewed out many beautiful tombs in the cliffs (see color map 16). In their heyday their power extended around the S and E sides of Palestine from Egypt to Mesopotamia. The foe who is to subdue the **Philistines** (vss. 15-17) is not specified. Gaza, a chief Philistine city, was conquered by Alexander after a 2-month siege. **Cherethites,** here apparently used as an alternate name for the Philistines (cf. Zeph. 2:5), probably designated specifically a Philistine tribe in the S part of the country (cf. I Sam. 30:14).

26:1-21. The Rock of Tyre Laid Bare. Tyre, whose very name meant "rock," was an important Phoenician port on an island half a mile out in the Mediterranean (see color map 11). On Israel's relations with Tyre see I Kings 5; 7:13-45; 9:11-14, 26-28; 16:31; cf. Isa. 23:1-17; Jer. 25:22; Joel 3:4-8; Amos 1:9-10; Zech. 9:2-4.

26:1-2. The incomplete date in the **eleventh year,** i.e. 587/86, seems to set the oracle before the fall of Jerusalem (see below on 33:21-22) but vs. 2 describes Tyre's reaction to this disaster as the reason for her imminent doom. It is uncertain whether the date has been incorrectly transmitted or vs. 2 is a late addition. Tyre rejoices over the collapse of Jerusalem, the **gate of the peoples,** thinking her own riches will be increased because in her commerce by land she will not need to deal with Judean middlemen or pay for the right of passage.

26:3-14. The doom of Tyre is presented first figuratively (vss. 3-5a), her island city being destroyed by **many nations** like **waves** of the **sea.** Next her fate is explained historically (vss. 7-14), with vss. 5b-6 bridging the 2 sections. Weapons of land siege are to be brought to bear against the city. Her **daughters on the mainland** are her suburbs on the shore.

Nebuchadrezzar had to spend 13 years in his siege of the city according to Josephus (cf. 29:18-19). This must have been largely a naval engagement in which he was at a disadvantage. Alexander the Great, however, in 332 captured the "daughters" of Tyre and used their demolished buildings to construct a mole ca. 200 feet wide extending out to the island. He was then able to apply siege weapons and took Tyre after 7 months. This isthmus was broadened still more with the demolished walls and buildings from the island itself, which he threw into the sea (vs. 12). Thus from then on Tyre was a peninsula rather than an island.

It is possible that vss. 1-5a come from Ezek. and anticipate Nebuchadrezzar's attack, but the rest seems to reflect a knowledge of the siege of Alexander the Great and must derive from a later poet.

26:15-21. The coastal cities lament Tyre's downfall in one supplement (vss. 15-18; cf. 27:28-36). Another (vss. 19-21) foretells Tyre's descent into the **Pit,** i.e. Sheol, the **nether world** of the dead beneath the **deep** (cf. 31:15-18; 32:17-32; see comment on Ps. 18:7-18).

27:1-36. *The Shipwreck of Tyre.* The poem of this ch. is a beautiful dirge over the anticipated fall of Tyre, compared with the wreck of a ship. **O Tyre, you have said, "I am perfect in beauty"** may originally have read "O Tyre, you are a ship, perfect in beauty." Her construction (vss. 4-7) is described as the best that international trade can provide. **Senir** is an alternate name for Mt. Hermon (cf. Deut. 3:9; see color map 3) and **Bashan** was in N Transjordan. **Cyprus,** lit. Kittim, is probably the city-state Citium on the island of **Cyprus,** then known as **Elishah** (cf. Gen. 10:4). The ship's crew are **skilled** seamen from all the chief cities of Phoenicia (vss. 8-9b; see color map 10).

27:9c-25a. This passage, in which Tyre is not a ship but a harbor and center of trade, is an interpolation into the poem. Vss. 9c-11 are transitional to an amazing catalog of Tyre's commerce (vss. 12-25a). On **Lud and Put** see comment on Isa. 66:18-23. **Helech** and **Gamad** may have been in N Syria or Cilicia. On **Tarshish** see comment on Jonah 1:3.

Javan is related to Ionia and designates Greece; **Tubal** and **Meshech** were in Asia Minor (see color map 9) and **Beth-togarmah** probably in Armenia. **Helbon** was near Damascus. The places of vss. 19-22 were in Arabia (see color map 7) and those of vs. 23 probably all in upper Mesopotamia (see color map 9) though **Canneh** and **Eden** may have been in S Arabia (see color map 7).

27:25b-36. The ship poem of vss. 3b-9b is now resumed. The heavy cargo presages a wreck (vss. 25b-26). Tyre's wealth is coveted by Chaldea, symbolized by the **east wind** (cf. 17:10; 19:12). Her **pilots** have brought her into stormy seas by rebelling against the Babylonian overlordship (cf. Jer. 27:1-11). Universal **lamentation** follows the sinking of the ship (vss. 28-36), but the dirge seems to end in taunt.

28:1-10. *The Presumptuous King of Tyre.* The word translated **prince** here is not that which Ezek. uses of Zedekiah (see above on 21:24-27) but an equivalent of "king" (cf. vs. 12). Thinking himself secure on his island **in the heart of the seas,** the ruler smugly acts as if he were a **god**—and may even claim to be so. In prophetic thought this is blasphemous and can lead only to dethronement and descent **into the Pit** (see above on 26:15-21; cf. Isa. 14:12-20). This is a pertinent judgment on all men who seek to be gods. It was the sin in the garden of Eden (Gen. 3:5). Vss. 3-5, which attribute the pride of the Tyrian ruler to his **wisdom,** which made him rich, are a later addition, requiring a resumptive review in vs. 6. They share, however, with the rest of the ch. in mythological colorings. On **Daniel** see above on 14:12-23.

28:11-19. *Expulsion from Eden.* The **king of Tyre,** in Ezek.'s time Ithbaal II, in the traditional Hebrew text is compared with a cherub who sinned in the garden of Eden and was expelled (vss. 14, 16 KJV). Thus the king's self-deification is interpreted as an angelic being grasping after divinity (cf. Phil. 2:5-6). A different vocalization of the same Hebrew consonants yields the interpretation of the LXX adopted in the RSV, that the king was **with the guardian cherub,** who **drove** him **out** (cf. Gen. 3:24).

On the king as a **signet** ring cf. Jer. 22:24; Hag. 2:23. The **perfection** of the king at creation consisted in **wisdom** and **beauty.** This first man was not naked but clothed with precious gems. These represent not only the splendor of paradise (cf. Isa. 54:11-12; Rev. 21:18-21) but his special qualifications as a priest-king (cf. Exod. 28:4, 17-21). The LXX text ascribes to him all 12 precious gems of the high-priestly breastplate (cf. Exod. 39:10-13). This Eden is a **holy mountain of God,** a temple site (cf. 20:40); and the king is accused of profaning his sanctuary (vs. 18). On the plural **sanctuaries** see above on 21:1-5.

Tyre's dishonesty in business breeds **violence** (vs. 16). As a port with worldwide trade relations Tyre could have mediated like a priest great spiritual blessings as well, but preoccupation with the material led to the corruption of her wisdom and to her experience of "paradise lost."

28:20-23. *The Doom of Sidon.* Sidon was another Phoenician city ca. 25 miles N of Tyre (see color map 11). Though it was less important than Tyre in the days of Ezek., there were times both earlier and later when it was more important. This oracle, in which divine **holiness** is the ground of **judgments** on Sidon, is so brief and non-circumstantial that one suspects it was added editorially in order to give a total of seven nations that are doomed. See above, the introduction to 25:1–48:35.

28:24-26. God's Purpose in Judgment. Like the preceding passage, this appears to be a later addition. Here the judgment of other nations is seen as enabling Judah to arise as a nation once more, unmenaced by bad **neighbors** (cf. 29:21). It is this widely held view which explains the placing of the collection of oracles against foreign nations (chs. 25–32) at the beginning of the 2nd half of the book, in which hope for Israel dominates. Thus God's **holiness** will become **manifest** both in judgments on the neighbors (cf. vss. 20-23) and in salvation for Israel (cf. 20:41; 36:23).

29:1-32:32. The Dragon of the Nile. This poem, dated Jan. 7, 587, is directed against **Pharaoh** Hophra (588-569). The **dragon** was a mythological foe, thought to be subdued in the Creation but ever and again threatening to undo the work of God. He is variously called Leviathan (e.g. Job 41; Ps. 74:14; Isa. 27:1) or Rahab (e.g. Job 9:13; Ps. 89:10; Isa. 30:7; 51:9-10). During the Babylonian siege of Jerusalem, evidently sometime in 588, Hophra led an army into Palestine to give assistance to his allies who were in revolt against Nebuchadrezzar, but he was soon driven back into Egypt. **Draw you up out of the midst of your streams** may allude to his expedition and **cast you forth into the wilderness** to his defeat. The **fish** that **stick** to his **scales** may represent his subjects, or perhaps the mercenaries which made up a large part of the Egyptian army (cf. Jer. 46:21).

29:6-16. Like the Tyrian ruler (28:2) the pharaoh is guilty of self-deification. But after having fostered revolt against the Babylonians he has proved to be only a flimsy **reed** on which to lean (cf. Isa. 36:6). His land is to be laid **waste** from **Migdol** in the Delta region to **Syene,** modern Aswan, at the S frontier with **Ethiopia** (see color map 10). A dispersement for **forty years** will be followed by restoration to **Pathros,** i.e. Upper Egypt, the territory upstream from the Delta, the traditional original homeland of the Egyptians. This is a later amplification (cf. 4:6; 16:53-63; Jer. 43:8-13; 46:1-25). Egypt was not subdued until 525, when the Persian army of Cambyses conquered the country. It did not lie waste 40 years, but as a Persian province it was a **lowly kingdom.**

29:17-21. A Prey for Nebuchadrezzar. This passage, dated Apr. 26, 571, indicates that Nebuchadrezzar was not enriched by his siege of **Tyre.** From a Tyrian contract found at the site of Babylon, dated in his 41st year (564/63) and attested by a Babylonian "keeper of the seal," it may be inferred that he accepted a relationship of fealty as a condition for lifting the siege. With no opportunity for looting, his soldiers did not receive the expected reward of their **labor**—for their heads **made bald** by constant wearing of the helmet and their shoulders **rubbed bare** by burdens. With the end of the siege of Tyre, however, they were set free to attack and loot Egypt. A fragmentary Babylonian record indicates that in Nebuchadrezzar's 37th year (568/67) they undertook

this. How far they advanced is unknown. In the situation of **that day** of attack on Egypt the **horn,** i.e. power, of Israel is expected to grow up again, and the prophet's message will be so vindicated that his mouth need not be shut by reason of shame (cf. 16:63).

30:1-19. The Day of Egypt's Doom. This passage portrays Egypt's doom first as the work of Yahweh (vss. 1-9; cf. 26:1-6), then as the work of **Nebuchadrezzar** (vss. 10-12; cf. 26:7-14). Unlike the other Egyptian oracles it is undated. Also unusual is the theme of the **day** of Yahweh (see above on 7:1-27).

30:5-12. The prose interpolation in vs. 5 is of interest as listing among Egypt's supporters some from the **land that is in league,** which may also be translated "covenant land," i.e. Palestine (cf. 20:5-6). Jewish soldiers were serving in the Egyptian army. A colony of these was at the S border on the island of Yeb (see color map 10), where they had a temple (cf. Isa. 19:19), as revealed by the Elephantine Papyri dug up at that site. On **Migdol to Syene** see above on 29:6-16. On the 2nd prose interpolation (vs. 9) cf. Isa. 18.

30:13-19. For locations of the Egyptian cities named see color maps 2, 4, 9, 10. On **Pathros** see above on 29:6-16. **Tehaphnehes** is an alternate spelling of Tahpanhes.

30:20-26. Pharaoh's Broken Arm. On Apr. 29, 587, the people are still hoping that Pharaoh Hophra will bring his army back to intervene and permanently relieve the Babylonian siege. They suppose he has recovered from his **broken . . . arm,** i.e. his defeat the year before (see above on 29:1-16), and is ready to try again, but the next time both his **arms** will be broken.

31:1-18. Pharaoh as a Towering Tree. Dated Jun. 21, 587, less than 2 months after the preceding, this passage heaps scorn on the pro-Egyptian propaganda by picturing Pharaoh Hophra as a tall and beautiful tree, which, however, is nothing but overweening pride that spells doom (cf. 19:11-12; 29:3-5). The tree's extravagant growth exceeds that of other trees in the garden of Eden and so it is cut down (cf. ch. 28; Dan. 4:4-33, where Nebuchadnezzar's arrogance is like that of Hophra). The myth has been amplified with later material (vss. 14c-18) which consigns the tree to the **nether world** (see above on 26:15-21), where it is to be placed among other trees, i.e. kings, which have been similarly felled.

32:1-16. A Dirge for the Dragon. This funeral **lamentation** and prophecy of doom for Egypt is dated Mar. 3, 585, and thus follows the fall of Jerusalem. Pharaoh Hophra is flexing his military muscles. He thinks he is a **lion,** but instead he is a **dragon** who muddies the **rivers,** i.e. the Nile branches of the Delta. He will be caught in a **net** and slain by Yahweh (cf. 29:3-5). A later expansion (vss. 9-15) applies the doom to Egypt's **multitude;** the rivers will be **clear . . . like oil** because no one will be left to muddy them.

32:17-32. Sheol the End of Worldly Glory. The date of this passage is incomplete in the Hebrew. The date given in the LXX, Apr. 27, 586, is earlier than that of vss. 1-16—and, if the fall of Jerusalem occurred in the 12th year (see below on 33:21-22), before that event—but it was placed here by the editors as an appropriate conclusion to the series of oracles against foreign nations (cf. Ps. 9:17). **Sheol** in the OT is simply a **Pit** in the **nether world,** i.e. under the earth, where all the dead go. The idea that it contained a place of punishment, a hell, arose later, under Persian influence. In the OT threats that the wicked will be sent to Sheol mean merely that they will suffer an untimely death. This passage is distinctive in that it implies that there is some sort of differentiation in Sheol for the **uncircumcised** and those **slain by the sword.** It eventually contributed to the idea of Sheol as a prison for the wicked (cf. Isa. 24:21-22), from which they would be resurrected for judgment (cf. II Pet. 2:9).

B. The Revival of Israel (33:1–37:28)

In their arrangement of the materials of the book into 2 divisions, the first pronouncing doom and the 2nd proclaiming hope for Israel, the late editors placed the series of anti-foreign messages (chs. 25–32) at the beginning of the 2nd half. Now they present the messages of comfort for Israel, with ch. 33 skillfully edited not only to provide an intro. to them but to point up the overall parallelism between the 2 halves by a series of passages with parallels in the first half.

33:1-9. The Parable of the Watchman. Here vss. 7-9 repeat 3:17-19. The whole passage really belongs in the earlier context, soon after Ezek.'s call; but vss. 2-6 are essential if we are to see this as a parable showing how Ezek. came to understand his mission. Just as in time of national peril a negligent watchman is court-martialed, so Ezek. will forfeit his right to live if he does not **warn the wicked.** The coming death is that to be inflicted by the Chaldean army. Ezek. does not expect to save the entire nation but he hopes to rescue individuals. His own salvation depends on his being a personal soul winner, one who reclaims sinners for true life in the society of God's people.

33:10-11. A Plea for Repentance. As in ch. 18, the quotation of a saying of the people is answered by a call to repent (cf. 18:23, 30-32). The earlier saying (18:2) was one of shirking responsibility. This saying expresses acceptance of responsibility but with a note of despair—it is too late. The answer is that it is never too late for the **wicked** to **turn from his way and live.** The passage is as suitable for a period after the destruction of Jerusalem as before.

33:12-20. Personal Responsibility. This is largely a repetition of earlier material. With vss. 12-16 cf. 18:1-20; with vss. 17-20 cf. 18:25-29.

33:21-22. Release from Dumbness. Here is the continuation of 3:24b-27; 24:25-27. In the present arrangement Ezek.'s dumbness is traced back to the very beginning of his ministry (3:24b-27), which in the view of the late editors consisted of warning of doom before the destruction of Jerusalem and proclaiming hope afterward. Thus each of these divisions of his ministry is made to start with a relationship to his dumbness: at the beginning of the first he becomes dumb; at the beginning of the 2nd he is released from dumbness. Actually Ezek.'s dumbness involved only a brief period before the destruction of the temple (see above on 24:25-27).

The **fugitive** messenger is to come on the day the temple is destroyed (24:25-27). The date given in vs. 21, Jan. 8, 585, does not fit with the record in II Kings 25:8-10; Jer. 52:12-14. The LXX and Syriac versions and 8 Hebrew manuscripts read "eleventh year," which would be evidence for a date of 587 rather than 586 for the fall of Jerusalem (see Chronology, pp. 1271-82). But at best there is an interval of nearly 5 months, and even according to the traditional view that Ezek. was an exile in Babylonia this is too long for word of the event to reach him. Ezra was able to lead a whole caravan from Babylonia to Jerusalem in only 108 days (Ezra 7:9; 8:31). Clearly there is an error in the date, and the most plausible correction is a reversal of the figures for month and day to read "in the fifth month, on the tenth day of the month," i.e. Aug. 17, 586. The mistake may have been either editorial, to harmonize with the editor's idea that Ezek. was in Babylonia, or accidental, helping to give rise to this story.

The wall of Jerusalem was breached in the 4th month, but the Chaldean army which pursued Zedekiah to the vicinity of Jericho did not return to demolish the temple and the rest of the city until the 5th month. The exact date was the 10th of that month according to Jer. 52:12-14. According to II Kings 25:8-10 it was the 7th, but some manuscripts and versions read the 9th day. This last date fits perfectly with the assumption that vs. 21 originally read 5th month, 10th day. On the **evening before** Ezek. has a premonition (vs. 22), as a result of which his **mouth** is **opened** before the arrival of the fugitive **in the morning** with the verifying news. This premonition is meaningful only if it coincides with the destruction of the temple in Jerusalem. Thus the date in vs. 21 is intended to identify the day after the destruction of the temple. Even if the 7th is correct in II Kings 25:8, we may assume that the process of demolition occupied several days and that the destruction of the temple itself took place on the 9th. Thus the passage may be most logically understood on the basis that Ezek. was not in Babylonia—where one who had **escaped** the Babylonians at Jerusalem would certainly never seek refuge—but at his village home (see above on 3:22-27; 24:25-27), near enough for one who slipped out of the doomed city under cover of darkness to arrive in the morning.

The opening of Ezek.'s mouth sounds like deliverance from real dumbness, brought on by the severe emotional stress of his wife's death and his own narrow escape from being imprisoned. For a possible figurative meaning, however, cf. 29:21; Pss. 22:15; 38:13-14; 39:9; Lam. 4:4.

33:23-29. The Land Grabbers. After the fall of Jerusalem the poor were given vacated estates of the exiles (cf. Jer. 39:10). They are now fighting among themselves for even larger holdings. This is the same situation which prompted 11:14-21, placed earlier to provide a parallel in the first half of the book (see above on 33:1-37:28). It is addressed to the same people before they started fighting. **These waste places** and the use of the 2nd person indicate that Ezek. is preaching directly to the guilty persons and thus create difficulties for the suggestion of some scholars that Ezek. had a preexilic ministry in Palestine but was taken to Babylonia with those exiled at the time of the fall of Jerusalem (see Intro.). It is possible but unnecessary to suppose that Ezek. was exiled later, several years after the fall of Jerusalem (cf. II Kings 25:25-26; Jer. 52:30).

33:30-33. Ezek. as a Singer of Love Songs. Ezek.'s voice is so attractive that people listen to his preaching as if he were a popular singer, yet they give no heed to his message. In a way they were right in being reminded of **love songs**, for it was divine love as well as justice which he preached (cf. vss. 10-11). In the context of the subsequent chs. Ezek.'s songs become also promises of hope in the view of the editors. Vs. 33 harks back to 2:5. The doom of the nation still lies ahead in this passage, which could date from almost any time after Ezek. became known for his eloquence. As placed by the editors with only one oracle intervening since his release from dumbness it suggests a meteoric soaring to popular fame.

34:1-10. Doom for False Shepherds. This beautiful poem (vss. 2-5a, 6a, 8b-10) from early in Ezek.'s ministry condemns the leaders of the nation for their selfishness and their failure to enforce the D reform after King Josiah's death, esp. their allowing the resumption of worship at the "high places" (see above on 6:1-14). Unfortunately several prose interpolations have obscured not only the poetry but also the meaning, interpreting the straying of the sheep on the **mountains**, i.e., to the local hilltop shrines, as wandering over the world in a farflung dispersion (vs. 6b). As a result many analysts have denied any part of the ch. to Ezek. and supposed it to be dependent on the postexilic material in Jer. 23:1-3. A closer parallel to Ezek.'s original idea is found in Jer. 50:6-7, which refers to worship at the high places, but it is later than Ezek.'s poem.

34:11-31. Hope for the Scattered Flock. Ezek.'s idea inspired several supplements, mostly from the early hopeful editors (see Intro.). Vss. 11-16 declare that what the rulers of Judah failed to do as shepherds Yahweh himself will undertake (cf. John 10). Vss. 17-21 seem to reflect the troubled situation of the mid-5th cent. in their portrayal of Yahweh as sternly condemning the selfishness of certain members of his flock (cf. Neh. 5:1-5). Vss. 23-24 speak of **David**, i.e. the future messianic king, who is to be the true **shepherd.** Vss. 25-31 promise that Yahweh will renew his **covenant** and impart every material **blessing.**

35:1-15. Doom for Mt. Seir. This is another oracle against Edom (cf. 25:12-14), evidently a product of the early hopeful editors (see below on 36:1-15). **Mount Seir** refers, not to a single peak, but to the whole highland range S of the Dead Sea (see color map 4), which covered most of the land occupied by the Edomites from the time of the Exodus until the Exile. Some of the Edomites pillaged the ruins of Judean cities left by Nebuchadrezzar's army (vs. 5). They are described as wanting to **take possession** of **two countries** (vs. 10), i.e. the territory of both Israel and Judah in Palestine; but the prediction is that their own homeland will be made **a desolation and a waste.** Archaeological evidence shows that in fact the **cities** and villages of the Seir region were **not . . . inhabited** during the 5th cent.—the Edomites were pushed out of their land by nomadic Arabs, who left few traces till later cents. But any Jewish rejoicing over this was premature, for the Edomites settled in S Palestine and in time took possession of most of the former territory of Judah

(see above on 25:1-7), and eventually an Idumean, i.e. Edomite, Herod the Great, became ruler of all Palestine.

36:1-15. Renewal for Israel's Mountains. As the Seir range is to Edom the mountains of Palestine are to Israel. In this antithetical continuation of ch. 35 (cf. Joel 3:19-21; Isa. 34–35) the early hopeful editors say that the desolation predicted for Seir has already befallen the land of Israel at the hands of neighboring nations, but its fertility will soon support a large population of returned people.

36:16-38. Spiritual and Material Blessings. Yahweh's people have suffered exile and dispersion because of their sins, but he will restore them, say the early hopeful editors, to **vindicate** his **holy name** (cf. 20:9). It is no more materialistic to predict abundance than to predict deprivation, provided the spiritual aspects of life are properly stressed. Here spiritual renewal (vss. 25-28) apparently precedes the bounties of nature. At least the spiritual and material blessings belong together.

37:1-14. The Vision of Dry Bones. The language of vs. 1 refers to a physical journey in a state of spiritual compulsion (see above on 8:1-3b). Ezek. is in the **valley** when he sees the dry bones of soldiers slain in one of the battles against the Chaldeans. This could be the same valley, or plain, where he received his call (see above on 3:22-27) or could be the plain of Jericho (cf. Deut. 34:3; II Kings 25:5). In the bones he sees a symbol of his deceased nation: **Can these bones live?** Contemplation gives way to ecstasy and he hears the divine command: **Prophesy to these bones.** When he does he sees them reassembled. He is then commanded: **Prophesy to the breath,** i.e. wind. Thereupon life comes into the bones.

37:11-14. The original conclusion is vs. 11 alone, which speaks to the mood of the day and identifies the bones as the **whole house of Israel.** For those who heard Ezek. speak no more was needed, for they would find there the meaning. It is through prophetic preaching that the nation is to be reunited and have spiritual life breathed into it once more. This will be a work of new creation (cf. Gen. 2:7). An addition (vss. 12-14) overlooks the 4-fold stress on prophesying and states rather that Yahweh will reassemble Jews residing in foreign lands. Thence they will emerge as from **graves;** in the original vision the bones are only **upon the valley,** i.e. on the surface.

37:15-28. Pantomime of 2 Sticks. This symbolic action is reminiscent of others that portray coming doom (chs. 4–5). Ezek. writes **Judah** on one stick and **Joseph,** ancestor of the 2 largest N tribes, on the other and fits them together in his hands as a single stick. When asked what this means he explains that both the S and the N tribes of Israel will be reunited as **one nation.** This hope of reconciliation is further developed by a later author (vss. 20-28), with the citizens of the 2 former kingdoms being reunited in the homeland under a Davidic king and the temple rebuilt. On the **covenant of peace** (vs. 26), i.e. promise of well-being, cf. 34:25-31.

Ezek.'s theme of reconciliation was shared by some (cf. Isa. 56:3-8) but ignored by many of the returning exiles (cf. Ezra 4:1-3). A complete reversal of his pantomime is found in Zech. 11:7-14, where the "brotherhood between Judah and Israel" is annulled.

C. Oracles Against Gog of Magog (38:1–39:29)

38:1-23. *The Invasion and Doom of Gog.* This is apocalyptic material, concerned with a foe of the last days. The name **Gog** has been variously explained. Some derive it from Gyges, founder *ca.* 670 of a great kingdom in Asia Minor, of which Croesus was the last ruler. Others derive it from the name of the Sumerian god of darkness, Gashga or Gaga. More likely it is simply an invention to go with Magog, which is taken, like all the other geographical names in the chapter except **Persia,** from Gen. 10:2-7 (see above on 27:9c-25a). Though most of the nations represented by these names have been identified, Magog is otherwise unknown, unless Josephus is correct in connecting the name with the Scythians, the foe believed to have been threatening from the N during the early part of Jeremiah's ministry. Gog's forces, however, are drawn from all directions, as these names indicate. Rev. 20:8 rightly locates Gog and Magog "at the four corners of the earth."

The prototype of Gog is Sennacherib; cf. "I will put my hook in your nose, . . . and I will turn you back on the way by which you came" (Isa. 37:29). Whereas Sennacherib is thus to be led away from the Holy Land, however, here (vs. 4) Gog is to be brought into it. Vss. 2-9 represent Gog as directed against Israel by Yahweh, but vss. 10-13 view him as motivated by his own lust for plunder—a different perspective that suggests a different hand (cf. Jas. 1:13-14). In Rev. 20:7-8 it is Satan who raises up the hordes of Gog; cf. the similar revision of II Sam. 24:1 in I Chr. 21:1.

The language of this ch. is full of allusions to other parts of the OT, e.g. Ezek., Isa., Jer. It presupposes a return of the Jews from many lands to which they have been scattered, not simply in the first difficult times of resettlement, but after they have long been settled and have become prosperous (vss. 8, 12-14). Description of the land as consisting of **unwalled villages** (vs. 11) probably applies rather generally to postexilic times before the age of the Maccabees despite the fortification of Jerusalem and a few other places. Another indication of late composition is the idea that the great invasion of Gog will fulfill the words of God's **servants the prophets** (vs. 17). Therefore it seems most likely that the historical figure behind Gog is Alexander the Great, whose homeland, Macedonia, has been identified by the author with the Magog of Gen. 10:2. Having conquered Palestine (332) and moved on to the E, he is here represented as about to return to his doom. Some Jews may have welcomed Alexander as a liberator, but this view did not last (cf. Zech. 9:13). The passage expresses the faith that no matter how powerful the foe that assails God's people, or how successful its invasion of their territory, God's almighty hand can give victory (cf. II Macc. 8:18).

39:1-16. *Another Account of Gog.* This passage is more a parallel to ch. 38 than a continuation. Vss. 1-2 are a condensation of 38:2-9, agreeing that Gog is brought against Israel by Yahweh. The concern for Yahweh's **holy name** (vss. 7-8) is also similar to the reason given in 38:16. On the other hand the

doom of Gog described here (vss. 3-6, 9-16) is quite different from that in 38:17-23. With different vowel points the Hebrew for **Valley of the Travelers** may be read as "valley of the Abarim" (vs. 11; see RSV footnote) and thus refer to a mountainous region **east of the sea,** i.e. the Dead Sea (cf. Deut. 32:49).

39:17-20. *Yahweh's Sacrificial Feast.* This passage is prepared for by vs. 4b and gives an appropriately gory conclusion to the picture of Gog (cf. Isa. 34:6-7; Jer. 46:10; Rev. 19:17-18). On the other hand its literary quality so excels the preceding material that it may have been composed by Ezek. himself for a different setting. If so, it is probably a parody on some cult song inviting the Judeans to sacrifice at the high places, where Ezek. predicts there will be a different sort of slaughter (cf. 6:2-7; Zeph. 1:7-8).

39:21-29. *God's Vindication in History.* This is the conclusion not simply of chs. 38-39 but of chs. 1-39. A theme of which the editors never tire is that men will **know** Yahweh through his acts and that his **holiness** will be manifest to **all the nations.** Vss. 21-22 apply to the judgment of Gog (cf. 38:23; 39:7) but they apply equally to the oracles against foreign nations (cf. e.g. 28:23-24; 30:19). In the perspective of history the nations will see that Yahweh is holy and sovereign and that this explains the judgments they have suffered and also those the Jews have suffered (vss. 23-24). The supreme manifestation of his holiness, however, will be his redemption of Israel (vss. 25-29; cf. 20:44; 36:36; 37:28). On **pour out my Spirit** cf. Joel 2:28-29.

D. Design for the Future (40:1–48:35)

The plans of this section for the future temple, its sacrifices, and the allotment of land are presented in the form of a vision, but worked out with a mathematical precision that is more the product of study than of vision. The probability that the architectural details reflect memories of Solomon's temple—as demonstrated by their values as aids to interpreting its description in I Kings 6-7—points to a mid-6th-cent. date for the basic material. Yet the concern for such technicalities, as well as other differences in outlook and style from the original material in chs. 1-39, makes it safer to suggest a disciple rather than Ezek. himself as author of chs. 40-48.

40:1. *The Date.* Though composition *ca.* the time indicated is not unlikely, the precise date is symbolic rather than actual. The **twenty-fifth year** has begun, a quarter of a cent., and the **fourteenth year** is 2 times 7. By the ancient method of counting, the year in which the **city was conquered** is taken as the first year and therefore the first 10 days of the 25th year have begun the 14th year since that event. The **beginning of the year** suggests new year's day. In rabbinic calculation, which may be that of preexilic Judah, this would be the first day of the 7th month, in the fall. Here, however, the **tenth day** is specified and the phrase may refer rather to the first month. The 10th of the 7th month is the day of atonement (Lev. 16; 23:26-32). Another mode of calculation, apparently followed in the dates of chs. 1-39, puts the new year in the spring. The 10th of the first month was said to be the day on which Israel entered the Promised Land (Josh. 4:19; cf. Exod. 12:1-13).

40:2-4. *Intro. to the Vision.* The author uses some of the language of 8:1-3*b* (see comment) to describe his transportation, but here the situation is quite different in that the temple he visits is entirely visionary. The **very high mountain** is the hill on which the former temple stood, its height being exaggerated (cf. Isa. 2:2), and the building on it is a **structure like a city** because it is surrounded by walls and gates. The angelic guide instructs the author to use his **eyes,** to see the vision, his **ears,** to catch the words, and his **mind,** to understand the whole. The reader wishing to apply this instruction may find the diagram on p. 435 helpful in following the details of the description.

40:5. *The Outside Wall.* The guide's **measuring reed** measures **six long cubits.** The cubit, based on the length of the forearm to the fingertip, was variously calculated. Here the long cubit is defined as containing an extra **handbreadth,** i.e. 7 instead of 6 (see table, p. 1285), and therefore would measure *ca.* 20½ inches. Thus the reed is *ca.* 10 feet 3 inches long. This is the height and thickness of the temple's outer wall.

40:6-47. *The Gates and Courts.* Patterned after the Solomonic gates, of which examples have been found at Megiddo and Gezer, the gates described here are admirably suited to defensive purposes, for guards can occupy the **side rooms.** Their purpose is to keep out the unfit (cf. 44:4-15). There are 3 gates leading from the outside to the **outer court,** on the E (vss. 6-16), N (vss. 20-23), and S (vss. 24-27). Corresponding to each of these is an inner gate leading from the outer court to the **inner court** (vss. 28-37). All 6 are identical except that the inner gates are reversed—i.e. the **vestibule,** the largest room, is toward the outside—and have extra rooms attached (vss. 38-43). The **barrier** before the side rooms (vs. 12) probably refers to their raised level. Apparently the first side rooms, i.e. those farthest from the vestibules, are set back 1½ cubits to give the enlarged **breadth** of **thirteen cubits** (vs. 11) to make room for swinging doors.

40:17-19. The **outer court** is the area 200 cubits wide—a **hundred cubits** between the gates (vs. 19) plus **fifty cubits** for each gate (vs. 15)—between the outer walls and the temple proper with its inner court. Fronting on this court, with their backs to the outer wall, are **thirty chambers** for the use of the laity, as a place to eat the sacrificial feasts (cf. Jer. 35:1-5; see comment on Lev. 3:1-17) and to obtain shelter when coming from a distance as pilgrims. In front of the chambers is a **pavement,** probably mosaic, which extends out as far as the ends of the outer gates on three sides and reaches the priests' chambers on the W side (42:3). In clement weather, the laity could congregate or feast there as well.

40:20-37. The N and S outer gates and the S, E, and N inner gates are repetitiously described as like the E outer gate (vss. 6-16). **Seven steps** lead to the N and S outer gates, and presumably to the E outer gate (cf. vs. 6), and **eight steps** to the inner gates.

40:38-43. The gate referred to in vs. 38 is presumably the N gate to the inner court (cf. vs. 35). If so, **tables** are set up in front of it and inside for use in preparing **sacrifices.** A chamber for washing the sacrifices adjoins the vestibule (cf. 8:7-11; Jer.

36:10). Since the E gate is also used for sacrifices (46:1-8) it presumably has the same equipment, including the chamber off the vestibule.

40:44-47. The **inner court** is the **foursquare** area, a **hundred cubits** each way, in front of the temple with the **altar** in its center. Undoubtedly here is to be understood the "upper pavement," probably mosaic, whose existence is implied by the **lower pavement** in the outer court (vs. 18). Opening off the inner court are **two chambers . . . for the priests** which are built on the sides of the N and S inner gates.

40:48–41:26. *The Temple Proper.* The sanctuary itself faces the W side of the inner court. It rests on a **raised platform,** i.e. foundation, 6 cubits high, which extends 5 cubits beyond the building on each side (41:8). Its entry **pillars** are reached by **ten steps.** Passing between them one enters first the **vestibule,** then the **nave,** and finally the **inner room,** which is the **most holy place.**

41:5-11. Into the exterior walls of the sanctuary are built **three stories** of **side chambers,** which are entered by N and S doors opening on the extended portion of the platform. Access to this is just beyond the entrance pillars. On each side a winding **stairway** leads to the upper stories, which are progressively wider because of the **offset,** i.e. stepped narrowing, in the wall between the chambers and sanctuary.

41:12-15a. The **yard** is the open space **twenty cubits** wide (vs. 10) surrounding the sides and back of the temple proper. Beyond this yard **on the west side,** i.e. in back of the sanctuary, is a **building** of unspecified use but of enormous size, 70 by 90 cubits. This may be what is called the "precincts" in II Kings 23:11 and the "parbar" in I Chr. 26:18. Perhaps it did not have a roof but was simply a walled-off place for disposing of the wastes of the sacrifices. This building with its thick walls extends 100 cubits from N to S, and the distance from the outer wall to the rear of the sanctuary is also 100 cubits, forming a square. The sanctuary stands in a 2nd 100-cubit square and, still farther to the E, the altar in a 3rd (40:47).

41:15b-26. The interior of the sanctuary is paneled and decorated with **cherubim** (see above on 1:4-28*b*) **and palm trees,** reminders of the garden of Eden (cf. Gen. 3:22-24). Nothing is said about restoration of the ark of the covenant with its overshadowing cherubs (cf. I Kings 6:23-28; 8:6-7; Jer. 3:16). The only furniture mentioned is an **altar of wood** placed **in front of the holy place,** doubtless as the **table** for the bread of the Presence or showbread (cf. e.g. Exod. 25:23-30; II Chr. 13:11). The height of the temple is not given, but its **windows** would need to be above the 3 stories which surround it.

42:1-14. *The Chambers for the Priests.* N and S of the **W Building** and of the W end of the **yard** are chambers where the priests eat their sacrificial meals and change from secular to clerical garb and vice versa. The meat is collected at the tables by the gates to the inner court (40:38-43). Some portions are burned on the altar, some eaten by the people (see above on 40:17-19), others—the **most holy offerings** (see comment on Lev. 2:2*b*-3)—by the priests in their chambers. **Three stories** (vs. 3) probably refers to a split-level arrangement descending from the yard to the outer court in 3 terraces of unequal width, since they are not to be enlarged by the erection of platforms supported by **pillars.** This explains how the lower wall can be only 50 cubits long while the upper wall is 100 cubits long. The 100-cubit-long **passage** (vs. 4) may be **inward** in the sense of being at the upper level. The 50-cubit **wall** (vs. 7) may mark a similar passage along the **outer court.** The number of their **chambers** and their connecting corridors are not specified; but the prohibition of going into the outer court without changing clothes (vs. 14) shows the need for direct access to the **temple yard** from the priests' chambers.

42:15-20. *Size of the Whole Temple Area.* As a conclusion to the architectural description the angelic guide measures the dimensions around the outside wall. The whole complex is a perfect square, **five hundred cubits** on each side (cf. Rev. 21:16).

43:1-7a. *The Coming of the Divine Glory.* Since the prophet has last been led out the E gate (42:15) and presumably has been standing there while his guide measures the outer wall, his now being **brought** to the **gate facing east** seems to be evidence of editorial rearrangement or revision. No doubt the gate originally intended here is the inner E gate, from which the prophet with his guide **beside** him (vs. 6) can view the coming of the **glory** through the outer E gate and see it as it passes through the inner court into the sanctuary. The late priestly editors (see Intro.) have inserted vss. 3-5 to associate this scene with their elaborated form of the vision in ch. 1 and esp. with their interpolations in chs. 8-11. Dispensing with the guide, they have the prophet transported bodily through the air by the **Spirit** from the outside gate to the inner court. That the temple is to be authenticated by the coming of Yahweh's glory is to be expected (cf. Exod. 40:34-38; I Kings 8:10-11). The late editors, however, tie this in with the rest of the book in order to develop a theory of shekinah-glory succession between the pre-exilic temple and that of their own time, traced through the Exile. In doing so they tacitly identify this visionary temple with that built by Zerubbabel after the Exile, though this sketch is too extensive and elaborate to be embodied fully in that temple.

43:6-12. *The Sanctity of the Temple.* Here is both the conclusion to the preceding description of the temple and a preface to the legal section which follows. The new cult law is spoken from inside the sanctuary by Yahweh himself (cf. Lev. 1:1).

The temple thus consecrated by the return of Yahweh's glory is to be his only **place** of permanent abode among his people. Since his **throne** is there, he is to rule the people as their king from this place and so he will now set forth the sacred, priestly law of his land (cf. I Sam. 8:7; Ps. 80:1; Zech. 14:17). The temple will be so sacred that not only must **harlotry** be avoided (idolatry and sacred prostitution), but the royal palaces and the royal cemeteries must not adjoin the sacred precincts (cf. I Kings 7:1-12). This regulation agrees with the placement of the royal city at a considerable distance away (48:18-35), but the use of the term **kings** for the future rulers rather than **princes** (as in 44:3; 45:8-9) suggests that vss. 7b-9 may be supplemental. The prophet will give a full description of the temple and its laws to the people, so that awed by the

splendor and sanctity of the whole scene they may **be ashamed of their iniquities.**

43:13-27. *The Altar.* The great altar for burning sacrifices is a stepped pyramid, like a ziggurat (see comment on Gen. 11:1-9), with a staircase on the E side. The lowest stage is the **base,** next the **lower ledge,** then the **smaller ledge,** and finally the **altar hearth.** The last is 12 cubits square. Since each stage has a **ledge** one cubit broad, each of the lower stages is 2 cubits longer on a side than the one above. Thus at the ground level the square is 18 by 18 cubits. The altar, with its **horns** (see comment on Exod. 27:1-8), rises 11 cubits above the **base** which may be a basin one cubit deep (not high) to catch **blood.**

Great theological significance attaches to this altar, which is at the center of the N-S and E-W axes of the temple area and on a platform 8 steps higher than the outer court. If the site itself is a **very high mountain** (40:2) the altar hearth is the highest accessible place in the vicinity. The Hebrew word translated "altar hearth" is spelled 2 ways in this passage. The first spelling (vs. 15a) supports the etymology "mountain of God." It is probably derived ultimately from an Akkadian word meaning both "mountain of the gods" and "nether world." Thus at the center of the whole temple is an altar which links heaven and earth, God and man, in a bond of reconciliation, and the God is also one who reigns over the nether world and will not allow it to triumph.

43:18-27. On the consecration of the altar cf. Exod. 29:36-37; Lev. 8:11; I Kings 8:62-64. On the family of Zadok see below on 44:4-31.

44:1-3. *The Shut East Gate.* One may well infer that this passage is directed against some sort of ritual in which the rising sun on the day of the equinox shone through the E gate into the temple (cf. 8:16; I Kings 8:12). For this purpose it seeks to historicize the entrance of the divine glory into the temple by associating it with the practical disuse of the E approach to the sacred area because of the precipitous side of the Kidron Valley (see color map 13). Whereas the chambers around the outer wall are apparently provided for ordinary lay worshipers to **eat bread**—the same word translated **food** in vs. 7, here meaning the portions of their sacrificial offerings which they are to eat (see above on 40:17-19)—the **vestibule** of the E gate is reserved for the **prince,** i.e. the ruler of the line of David (37:25). Ezek. had political reasons for using the term "prince" rather than "king" for Zedekiah (cf. 21:24-27). The fact, however, that the later editors prefer "prince" even for the future kings (cf. 45:7-9, 16-17, 22; 46:2, 4, 8-18; 48:21-22) suggests theological reasons, such as the theocratic concept of Yahweh alone as king (cf. 43:6-12).

44:4-31. *The True Priesthood.* Those to be **excluded** from the temple are **foreigners,** i.e. non-Jews (cf. the Carites, II Kings 11:4, also Tobiah, Neh. 13:4-9; contrast Isa. 56:3-7). Instead of them as temple servants are to be the **Levites,** the former priests of the now illegitimate high places and their descendants; as **punishment** for their faithlessness they are to be limited to only the most menial of tasks in the temple. Those who minister in the inner court and in the sanctuary must belong to the **sons of Zadok,** who was chief priest in the time of Solomon.

As priests in the preexilic temple they are here said to have remained faithful, but surely Ezek. himself would not have forgotten the apostasy which he saw practiced in the temple itself (cf. ch. 8). On their **linen** garments cf. 9:2; Exod. 28:6, 39-43; Lev. 6:10-11; 16:4, 23-24. The contagion of **holiness** is a power which for ordinary people is as dangerous as uncleanness (cf. 42:13-14; contrast Hag. 2:11-13; see comment on Lev. 6:24-30). On the priests' teaching and judging functions cf. Deut. 1:17; 17:8-13; 33:8-10; Mal. 2:4-7. On the other regulations cf. Lev. 21:1-15. The statement here that the priests are to be supported exclusively by **offerings** and have no inheritance is contradicted in the next section (45:4).

45:1-8. The Holy District. See below on 48:8-22, where this material is repeated in fuller form.

45:9-17. Royal Responsibility. The **princes,** i.e. Davidic rulers, since they are to have special crown property for their support (vss. 7-8; cf. 48:21), must refrain from taxes except those which support the temple cult. The KJV rendering (vs. 9d) "Take away your **exactions** from my people" is better than the RSV **Cease your evictions of my people.** The idea of the latter is supported by 46:18, but a reference here to "exactions" (i.e., taxes) is supported by the Targum, also by the Heb. preposition, lit. "from upon." Religious dues of the people are to be collected by the power of the state for the maintenance of the daily sacrifices. The "prince" as head of the state will contribute from his own estate the **offerings** for **sabbaths** and **feasts** (vs. 16; cf. 46:1-15; II Chron. 35:7). Since contributions by both people and ruler are by specified quantity, it is the obligation of the latter to enforce honesty in weights and measures lest "man rob God" (Mal. 3:8).

45:18-20. Atonement for the Sanctuary. In vs. 20 the reading of the LXX, "in the seventh month on the first of the month," seems much more probable. Thus semiannual sacrifices are to purify the sanctuary from any defilement by contact with men who, no matter how scrupulous, may have unknowingly approached it while in a state of uncleanness. This corresponds to the more elaborate ceremony of the annual day of atonement of the P Code (Lev. 16:11-22). Contrast the date of 40:1.

45:21-25. The Feasts of Passover and Booths. It is strange that only 2 of the 3 great annual festivals are mentioned here, the feast of weeks (Pentecost) being omitted (cf. Exod. 23:14-17; Deut. 16:1-17). The ancient rabbis struggled without success to harmonize the rules given here for the sacrifices with those of the P Code (Num. 28:16-25; 29:12-39). Accordingly at the Council of Jamnia (ca. A.D. 90) some of them wished to exclude Ezek. from the canon. It is reported that though Hananiah ben Hezekiah used 300 barrels of midnight oil to explain many of the difficulties of the book in the end the rabbis decided to await the return of Elijah, who would give the definitive explanations.

46:1-15. The Ruler's Sacrifices. Unlike the outer E gate, which is permanently closed (44:1-3), the E gate leading to the inner court is to be open on the **sabbath** and the day of the **new moon,** and also whenever the prince wishes to present a **free-will offering** (vs. 12). He has special privilege inside this gate, being permitted to watch the sacrifices from the **threshold,** i.e. from just outside the inner

court. Nevertheless he is a layman and must return to the outer court by the way he entered. He leads the laity in religious processions at times of festival. To avoid confusion those entering by the S gate must exit by way of the N gate and vice versa. Since the inner court lies in the way, the people must of course go around the E side of it. The prince is to provide the **daily** whole **burnt offering** sacrificed each **morning.** The P Code calls for an evening sacrifice also (Exod. 29:38-42; Num. 28:3-8).

46:16-18. Property Held in Perpetuity. Gifts from the king to his sons, if from his own inheritance, may be held by their heirs in perpetuity. Gifts to a servant, however, must be returned to the royal family in the **year of liberty,** i.e. the jubilee (cf. Lev. 25:8-55). Confiscation of property belonging to the people is forbidden (cf. I Kings 21).

46:19-24. The Kitchen Areas. This is a return to the tour of the temple area and may be displaced from an original position in chs. 40-42, perhaps after 42:14. The place for preparing the holy meals of the priests is at the W end of the N priestly chambers. Likewise, a kitchen would be needed by the S chambers. Since it is forbidden to carry the holy food into the outer court—on **communicate holiness to the people** see above on 44:4-31—passageways giving access to the yard are required. Restriction of the lowest row of chambers to 50 cubits (see above on 42:1-14) left room for this kitchen. Kitchens for cooking the people's food (see above on 40:17-19) are located in small **courts** in the **four corners** of the outer court. The ministers who cook for the laity are Levites (cf. 44:10-11; II Chron. 35:10-14).

47:1-12. The Stream from the Temple. From the temple flows a stream which for the Judean wilderness and the Dead Sea will be a source of "paradise regained" (cf. Gen. 13:10; Josh. 7:24-26; Hos. 2:14; Joel 3:18; Zech. 14:8). The farther this miraculous river flows the deeper it becomes. The idea of additional springs or tributaries would spoil the picture, for this is life-giving water from the temple. The **trees** growing beside it are the trees of life (cf. Gen. 2:9; 3:22; Rev. 22:1-2). It sweetens the water of the Dead Sea—which is 26% mineral salts—so that it becomes good fishing territory. A few **marshes** are to be kept, however, since **salt** is important for the sacrifices (cf. 43:24; Lev. 2:13).

47:13-20. Boundaries of the Holy Land. The N boundary cuts from the Great Sea, i.e. the Mediterranean, at a point near Tripolis (see color map 12) across the Lebanon Mts. to the **entrance of Hamath,** i.e. Riblah (see color map 9), and into Syria. Though at the height of its power Israel extended its sway into Syria (cf. e.g. Num. 34:7-9; II Sam. 8:5-12; II Kings 14:25; Amos 6:14) Phoenicia along the coast was never a part of Israel. From **Hazar-enon,** ca. 75 miles N of **Damascus,** the E boundary angles SW to the **Jordan** S of the Sea of Galilee. Thus Transjordan is excluded as unclean (cf. Josh. 22:19). The S border runs SW from the S end of the **eastern sea,** i.e. the Dead Sea, at **Tamar** (see color map 6) to **Meribath-kadesh,** i.e. Kadesh-barnea (see color map 4). Not far W from there it follows the **Brook of Egypt** NW to the Mediterranean, which is the W border.

47:21-48:29. Tribal Allotments. Resident **aliens** are to be reckoned to the tribes among whom they dwell. There is to be no brutal conquest in which non-Jews are slain or expelled. The tribes are to be settled in horizontal strips, 7 N of the holy portion and 5 S of it (cf. color map 5). The tribes descended from Jacob's concubines are placed farthest from the sanctuary, being allowed no closer than 5th position. Probably reasons for the exchanged places of Judah and Benjamin are that Judah after Jerusalem's fall moved farther N, with its capital at Mizpah, and that the name Benjamin means "son of the right hand," i.e. "southerner," and is hence put S of the temple.

48:8-22. The **holy portion** (cf. 45:1-8) is **twenty-five thousand cubits**—*ca.* 8 miles, 90 yards (see above on 40:5)—square and is divided into 3 strips. **Priests** and **Levites** each have strips 10,000 cubits wide and S of these lies the capital **city** in a strip 5,000 cubits wide. E and W of the holy portion lies the property of the **prince,** the crown property.

The **sanctuary** is **in the midst of** both the priests' portion (vs. 10) and the holy portion generally (vs. 8). This suggests a central location for the priestly strip. The context, however, proceeds from N to S. The fact that the priests are mentioned before the Levites seems to put them and the sanctuary in the N strip. In either arrangement the one fixed point is surely the site of the former temple. With the temple in the N position the capital city would lie 15,000 cubits, *ca.* 4.8 miles, S, at Bethlehem! With the sanctuary in the central location the city would lie 5,000 cubits, *ca.* 1.6 miles, S. With the width of the city included it would reach beyond Beth-haccherem (Ramet Rahel), where royal buildings have been found by archaeologists.

48:30-35. This city has no temple in it and yet its name is "Yahweh Shamah," **The LORD is There** (vs. 35). Like the temple it is square, but it is 9 times as long, *ca.* 1.44 miles, on each side. Like the temple also it has a free area around it in which nothing can be built, and this is 5 times as broad as that of the temple. This whole description has a more elaborate parallel—in which city planning is to be undertaken—in the New Jerusalem Scroll, of which several fragmentary copies have been found among the Dead Sea scrolls. Perhaps both this scroll and Ezek. lie in the background of Rev. 21:9-22:5. Another Dead Sea ms, the Temple Scroll, may also prove important here.

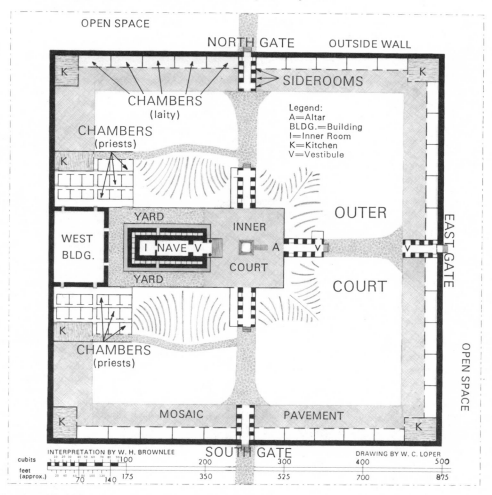

Floor plan of Ezekiel's envisioned ideal temple and surrounding temple area; cf. Steven's reconstruction of Solomon's Temple, p. 185; see comment on I Kings 5:1-7:51

THE BOOK OF DANIEL

George A. F. Knight

Introduction

The book of Daniel is named for its chief character, about whom most of the stories of chs. 1–6 are told, and who describes in the first person the visions of chs. 7–11. He is identified as one of the exiled Jews in Babylon who rose to a high position in the government of Nebuchadrezzar (RSV Nebuchadnezzar) and his successors.

In the English Bible the book appears to head the "minor" prophets or, as often popularly classified in spite of its relative brevity, conclude the "major" prophets. But in the Hebrew the book is not found among the Prophets but is placed among the Writings, the 3rd and latest division of the Hebrew Scriptures to be canonized.

A large section of the book (2:4b–7:28) has come down to us, not in Hebrew, but in a related Semitic language, Aramaic (see "The Languages of the Bible," pp. 1194-1200). The exiles learned to speak Aramaic in Babylon; it then became the people's tongue in the postexilic period, continuing through NT times, while Hebrew was used only in worship and as a literary and scholarly language. The Aramaic section begins within one of the stories and goes through the first vision; it appears to be unrelated to any structural distinction. A number of theories have been put forward to explain the change —some on the assumption that the author composed the material in 2 languages, others on the assumption that one of the languages is a translation. A combination theory conjectures that the author composed the stories and first vision in Aramaic for popular reading but used Hebrew for the remaining visions to appeal to the more learned, and that later someone started to translate the Aramaic into Hebrew but got only as far as 2:4a. None of these proposed explanations is completely satisfactory.

The Contents. Ch. 1 begins with a reference to the first capture of Jerusalem by the Babylonian army under Nebuchadrezzar. Among the exiles removed to Babylon is a fair young man named Dan., meaning "God is judge." In the stories of chs. 1–6 Dan. acts as God's wise judge of events, able not only to declare the meaning of dreams but also what those dreams are themselves. Introduced also are 3 companions of Dan., and the story of ch. 3 focuses on them. They display complete courage and loyalty to God when threatened with death, as does Dan. also in the familiar story of the lions' den (ch. 6).

Chs. 7–12 report 4 visions of Dan. Ch. 7 portrays the ultimate triumph of God over the cruel nations of men and the giving of the kingdom to "one like

a son of man." This passage has had great theological influence, and the gospels record Jesus as referring to it (Mark 13:26; 14:62 and parallels). The vision of ch. 8 forecasts the history of the Near East following the Exile, with the emphasis always on the transcendent rule of Almighty God. Ch. 9 contains a magnificent prayer of confession and trust in God in the face of calamity, followed by a divine promise of eventual vindication. Chs. 10–12 form a unit describing a single vision. After a lengthy setting forth of the revelation to follow, an outline of ca. 400 years of coming events passes before Daniel's eyes, with greater detail of those to occur near the end of that time involving a great struggle and an evil king. The final ch. declares that the outcome of this struggle will be the "end" of the present age, affecting both heaven and earth, time and eternity.

In the Greek versions there are several additions not found in the Hebrew-Aramaic text: the Prayer of Azariah, the Song of the Three Young Men, Susanna, and Bel and the Dragon. According to Protestant usage these are included in the Apoc.; in Roman Catholic editions the first 2 are inserted in the book itself following 3:23 and the last 2 appear at the end as chs. 13; 14. Much of the LXX of Daniel is paraphrased rather than translated, and quite early it was largely replaced in Christian usage by the translation of Theodotion.

Authorship and Date. Since the visions are told in the first person Dan. has traditionally been taken to be the author of the whole book, which is accordingly dated during the Exile in the 6th cent. There are many evidences, however, that it was written at a later time and is pseudepigraphic, i.e. issued under the name of Dan. by another person. There are a number of Persian and Greek words in the text. E.g. the name of one of the musical instruments in 3:5 transcribes a word that is not only Greek but found with this meaning nowhere in Greek literature before the 2nd cent. B.C. The name "Chaldeans" is also used in a special sense it did not acquire till long after the Exile (see below on 1:3-5). The fact that the book in the Hebrew Bible is placed among the Writings rather than the Prophets indicates a late date; if it had been in existence before ca. 200 B.C. it probably would have been included rather among the Prophets, as it now stands in the English Bible. Writing ca. 180 Jeshua ben Sira lists the heroes of the faith from Enoch, Noah, and Abraham through Nehemiah (Ecclus. 44–49) but makes no mention of Dan., evidently because he does not know of the book about him. On the other hand Dan. and his 3 companions are mentioned in I Macc. 2:59-60, probably composed late in the 2nd cent., and fragments of the book apparently produced *ca.* the same time have been found among the Dead Sea scrolls.

These data support evidence in the visions pointing to almost the precise year in which the book was composed. We read in I, II Macc. of a terrible period in Israel's history. Antiochus IV Epiphanes (175-163), Seleucid king of Syria, whose empire included Palestine and the little "city-state" of Judea —consisting of little more than Jerusalem and the villages in the hills round about—had the ideal of uniting all his realm culturally and religiously. He planned to do away with local beliefs and customs and force all his subjects to become devotees of the "new" Greek civilization. Many of the Jews resisted, and the king took stern measures to repress the practice of their faith. It was probably on Dec. 6, 167 (see Chronology, pp. 1271-82) that the temple was desecrated by the erection of an altar to Zeus Olympius (I Macc. 1:54; II Macc. 6:2-5). In Dan. this event is referred to specifically as the "abomination that makes desolate" (11:31; 12:11) and alluded to a number of times. On the other hand, though the early reconsecration of the temple and resumption of worship is foretold, the prediction is too vague to have been written after the actual rededication under Judas Maccabeus, which occurred 3 years later (I Macc. 4:36-58; cf. II Macc. 10:1-8; see below on 8:13-14; 9:27). Thus the book must have been written within this 3-year period, probably near the end of it (see below on 8:9-14).

There has been much discussion of whether the book is of composite authorship. The difference between narrative and vision, 3rd person and first, Hebrew and Aramaic, have been cited as evidence for 2 or more authors; but none of these differences can be related to differences in either viewpoint or literary style. These are so homogeneous that it is simpler to suppose that one man is responsible for the book as a whole. Thus the theory of some scholars that the stories should be dated a cent. earlier than the visions has not been widely accepted.

This is not to say that the stories are entirely the author's creation. Basically they no doubt came down to him from the days of Nebuchadrezzar and Cyrus, but in the form of oral tradition, like the stories in the Arabian Nights. They may well have been cherished among the Jews scattered in Mesopotamia and elsewhere in the intervening years. By the author's time their Babylonian setting had become blurred, with accuracy of historical detail lost. This same kind of thing happened later when medieval painters depicted on canvas biblical stories in an Italian setting. The author was naturally unable to check on 4-cent.-old tales. The important thing he did was to make these old folktales into vehicles that God could use to reveal his saving love for Israel in her darkest hour.

Type of Literature. The visions of Dan. belong to the class of writings known as apocalyptic, and in fact provided the pattern for most of the many apocalypses produced during the following 3 cents. (see "The Apocalyptic Literature," pp. 1106-09). Characteristically such works present in visionary form with much symbolism the promise of early catastrophic divine action to end the evils of the present age and inaugurate a new age of justice and vindication for the people of God. Amid the most difficult times—e.g. persecutions such as gave birth to both Dan. and its NT counterpart, Rev.—they sound a clarion call to the faithful to stand fast in the assurance that even though humanly speaking the situation seems hopeless God is in control of events.

In such circumstances it was dangerous to be specific with one's references. Instead of naming Antiochus Epiphanes, therefore, the author speaks of a "little horn" (8:9) and a "king of the north" (11:40). It was dangerous also to identify oneself. Hence he takes the name and guise of a hero of the past. Dan. is a name handed down from the 2nd millennium as the type of the wise and good man (see comment on Ezek. 14:12-23). In the Ugaritic legends of those early days a man named Daniel dispenses justice and protects the widow and orphan. Perhaps a namesake of somewhat the same character lived among the Jewish exiles in Babylon (cf. Ezra 8:2; Neh. 10:6) and became the hero of traditions passed down to the author of this book. On the other hand he may have chosen a respected and appropriate name around which to gather various traditions about unknown exiles.

In any case the author's concern, shared by his ancient readers, was with the meaning of the events he was recounting rather than with their historicity. His purpose was like that of Jesus in teaching by parables. When one asked "Who is my neighbor?" Jesus replied, not with a discussion of brotherhood in the abstract, but with a story of a Samaritan who demonstrated brotherhood in action (Luke 10:29-37). Perhaps he was telling of an actual happening, but if so factual accuracy in the details would be of no significance—e.g. whether the traveler was going from Jerusalem to Jericho or from Nazareth to Capernaum. More likely Jesus made up the parable out of whole cloth, yet the reality he teaches by it remains just as true and significant.

This kind of story, told to teach a truth, was called a *midrash* in ancient Jewish circles. Midrashic teaching is found throughout all rabbinical literature as well as in the gospels. The story in a midrash may of course be historical fact, or it may be a tale based on history, as in Dan., or it may be wholly fabricated, as some of Jesus' parables obviously are. It is the truth conveyed by a midrash that is all-important. We may note that the story of Dan. in the lions' den (ch. 6) is understood in this light in II Tim. 4:17. Clearly the author's purpose is midrashic in the stories as well as the visions of his book —to preach the power and love and providence of God.

Teachings of Permanent Value. Dan. is highly important for its revelation of God's loving purpose for his people. The Maccabean persecution presented a profound challenge to the faith of Israel. The question was: Can the distinctive ideas that a handful of peculiar people in the hills of Judea hold about the nature and purpose of the divine Being remain any longer relevant in a new age of reason? The dominant international Hellenistic culture was about to envelop and seemingly submerge the Jewish people. "In those days lawless men came forth from Israel, and misled many, saying, 'Let us go and make a covenant with the Gentiles round about us.' " (I Macc. 1:11; see comment).

But there were loyalists in Israel, known as the Hasidim or Hasideans. They remained true to God's *hesed*, the loyal love—or "steadfast love," as the RSV usually translates it—he had bestowed on his chosen people as the content to the covenant he had made with them at Sinai. This book now seeks to support them in their difficult decision to continue to be loyal to him. Israel's calling is thus to be instant in prayer and constant in observance of God's law.

The book expounds what loyalty should mean now by referring to past events in Israel's story which demonstrate God's completely reliable *hesed* in days that were equally painful and challenging. The God of Israel does not change; if he was faithful to Daniel in the lions' den he will remain faithful now. He is Lord of all; if arrogant kings seek to dominate the earth without heeding his purpose their fall is sure. People matter to him; even in the rise and fall of great nations the individual remains in his care. His covenant with Israel still stood when Jerusalem fell to a heathen monarch; it will continue to stand if the holy city falls again. His kingdom is going to embrace not only all men but all creation, and it will endure forever. It will be established when he raises up Israel through her representative head, the "son of man," i.e. the real man. Thus even the dead in Israel will share in his kingdom; for though the "end" will be preceded by a time of trouble, he has promised that all who are written in his book of life, even those now sleeping in the dust of the earth, will enter into everlasting life.

For Further Study. J. A. Montgomery, *Dan.*, 1927. R. H. Charles, *Dan.*, 1929. Arthur Jeffery in *IB*, 1956. S. B. Frost in *IDB*, 1962. H. H. Rowley, *The Relevance of Apocalyptic,* rev. ed., 1964.

I. STORIES OF DAN. AND HIS COMPANIONS (1:1–6:28)

A. OBEDIENCE TO THE FOOD LAWS (1:1-21)

1:1-2. Beginning of the Exile. The record in II Kings 23:34–24:17, confirmed and supplemented by Babylonian annals, shows that **Jehoiakim** became **king of Judah** as a vassal of Pharaoh Neco of Egypt in 609. In 605 **Nebuchadnezzar** defeated Neco at Carchemish (cf. Jer. 46:2), then hurried home to succeed his father as **king of Babylon.** Thereafter he proceeded to take over from Egypt the domination of Syria and Palestine, and Jehoiakim became his vassal for 3 years (II Kings 24:1) before rebelling *ca.* 600. Being occupied elsewhere, Nebuchadrezzar did not bring his own army against Jerusalem till 598. At that time Jehoiakim died, and after 3 months his young son Jehoiachin surrendered on Mar. 16, 597. A Babylonian capture of Jerusalem in Jehoiakim's **third year,** i.e. before Carchemish, can scarcely be fitted into this record. No doubt the author misinterpreted the 3 years of Jehoiakim's vassalage. On the other hand II Chr. 36:5-7, if historical—for the Chronicler was also more interested in theology than in precise history—may indicate that the establishment of Babylonian control over Judah after Carchemish involved some military action, which may have resulted in the taking of a few hostages

Cylinder of Nebuchadrezzar inscribed with three columns of text *ca.* 586 B.C., found buried in the foundation of a temple in Babylon

to Babylon. More probably, however, the tradition followed by the author refers to the first body of exiles deported with Jehoiachin in 597.

Nebuchadnezzar represents the Babylonian name Nabu-kudurri-usur, "Nabu [i.e. the god Nebo (cf. Isa. 46:1)] has protected the succession rights." The form Nebuchadrezzar found in Jer. and Ezek. is thus slightly closer to the original. **Shinar,** an old name for S Mesopotamia, gives a touch of antiquity as an allusion to the tower of Babel (cf. Gen. 11:2), where man's pride and egotism met with God's judgment.

1:3-5. The Wisdom of Babylon. The first deportation in 597 took most of Jerusalem's "intelligentsia." Here it is related that some of the younger of these were chosen for higher education in the rich lore of Babylonia. The selection is obviously a great honor for foreigners and demands that the young men be physically and mentally superior. The **Chaldeans** were a Babylonian tribe that in the 7th cent. became dominant in overthrowing the Assyrian Empire and establishing the Neo-Babylonian Empire. In writings before and during the Exile the name is practically synonymous with "Babylonians" (cf. e.g. II Kings 25:4; Isa. 13:19; 43:14; Jer. 21:4; Ezek. 1:3). In this book it has a meaning acquired later (see Intro.), describing the priestly caste, the intellectual elite of Babylon, who studied and taught the astrology, mathematics, and magic for which the city was famous (cf. Isa. 47:9, 12). To **stand before the king** was to be available to give him advice on demand.

1:6-7. The Names of the Young Men. The Hebrew names of all 4 youths contain syllables meaning

God (el) or Yahweh (iah). But the chief of the royal household gives them Babylonian names. In the ancient world a man's name was meaningful. If he entered into a new relationship he might receive a new name (cf. e.g. II Kings 23:34). **Belteshazzar** is understood by the author to contain the name of the Babylonian god Bel (4:8), but probably it represents a Babylonian name meaning rather "protect his life." **Abednego** is no doubt a corruption of "servant of Nebo" (cf. Isa. 46:1), but the tradition has so far altered **Shadrach** and **Meshach** that their meanings cannot be determined.

1:8-16. *A Test of the Food Laws.* Between the days of the Exile and the 2nd cent. B.C. the Jews had become increasingly impressed with the importance of keeping in detail the ordinances of the Mosaic law. Notable among them were the regulations about "clean" and "unclean" meats (Lev. 11; Deut. 14:3-21). Their observance became a mark not only of obedience to the law but also of separation from the Gentiles. Antiochus Epiphanes' program of forced hellenization seems to have included attempts to require abandonment of this source of difference (cf. I Macc. 1:62-63; II Macc. 6:18; 7:1). In this story Dan. challenges the royal officer to prove by a **test** that the will of God revealed in the food laws will effect more practical good than the **rich food** prepared in violation of them. Rather than eat "unclean" meats, he and his companions will restrict themselves to **vegetables,** none of which are forbidden in the food laws. **Ten days** is too short a time for any natural effects of a difference in diet; the noticeably healthier **appearance** of the 4 youths must be attributed to divine approval of their loyalty. This story must have bolstered the resolve of readers who faced hardship and even persecution in their adherence to Jewish customs.

1:17-21. *The Young Men's Reward.* Because of their obedience to the food laws under difficult circumstances God blesses Dan. and his companions with superior development not only physically but mentally, so that they become **ten times better** than the pagan wise men. Even so, if Israel remains loyal to God, there can be no end to his blessings. The **first year of King Cyrus** (vs. 21) marked the end of the Exile and the call to return to Jerusalem (Ezra 1:1). Thus Dan.'s career is noted as spanning the whole period of the Exile. The reference is apparently to the length of his service in public office rather than of his lifetime (cf. 6:28; 10:1). Some have thought this vs. to be displaced, but at this point it serves as a reminder that God's judgment in the Exile was temporary and thus virtually was a promise to the suffering patriots in 165 B.C. that the days of their trial are numbered.

B. NEBUCHADNEZZAR'S DREAM (2:1-49)

Israel shared with her ancient Near Eastern neighbors the belief that dreams were vehicles for divine communication to men (cf. e.g. Num. 12:6; Job 33:14-18). A dream in a holy place would most likely be god-given (cf. Gen. 28:10-17; I Kings 3:4-15), and therefore it was not uncommon for a king facing a difficult decision to sleep in a temple in hope of receiving guidance. The interpretation of dreams was a profession involving considerable lore, as

borne out by instruction books discovered in both Egypt and Mesopotamia. Persons skilled in this art were maintained as members of royal courts for frequent consultation. To ancient readers it would not seem at all strange that a king should reward superiority in dream interpretation with high public office (cf. Gen. 41).

2:1-13. *The King's Insecurity.* The date **in the second year** is inconsistent with the 3-year training period of 1:5, 18 and seems to be evidence of the original independence of the stories. The unusual element in this account is Nebuchadnezzar's demand that his wise men tell him not merely the interpretation of his dream but the dream itself. It is often said that he is purposely withholding information to test the occult powers claimed by his courtiers, but the ancient story may reflect practical experience of what psychologists have now proved scientifically—that most dreams cannot be recalled; only if one partially wakens during a dream will his memory function. On **Chaldeans** see above on 1:3-5. Their response in vs. 4b begins the Aramaic section of the book (see Intro.). It is preceded in the text by the expression "in Aramaic," which may be a part of the intro. (vs. 4a), meaning that the Chaldeans spoke in that language, but more likely is a parenthetical note of the change of language (see RSV footnote).

2:5-13. Nebuchadnezzar's extremes of threat and promise (vss. 5-6) are not too exaggerated a caricature of the behavior of dictators in both ancient and modern times. Many of them have ruthlessly punished those who aroused their displeasure over trifles and conversely have rewarded their favorites out of all proportion to services rendered. Though seemingly all-powerful, Nebuchadnezzar feels so insecure that he orders the destruction of all his advisers rather than admit that he demanded too much of them. Dan. and his friends were not among the Babylonian **wise men** consulted, but the order includes them.

2:14-23. *The Wisdom of God.* Vs. 16 raises questions: (a) Would Dan., though one of the royal advisers (cf. 1:19-20), at this stage be able to approach the king directly? (b) If Dan. has already made an appointment as stated here, why must he later (vss. 24-25) be introduced by Arioch? Possibly the author has combined variant traditions without bothering to resolve their differences, or possibly the text has been corrupted—e.g. it has been conjectured that vs. 16a may originally have read: "And Dan. besought him [i.e. Arioch] to appoint him a time." In any case Dan. is confident of God's help in meeting the situation. The lore of the most learned class of wise men the world has yet known has found no solution to the problem of political despotism—that faced by the readers of the book under Antiochus Epiphanes—but one devoted to the God of Israel can trust in him.

2:17-23. Dan. is confronted with a **mystery,** i.e. a secret—a favorite word of the Qumran community (see article "The Dead Sea Scrolls," pp. 1063-71)—which is divinely **revealed** to him. His hymn of thanksgiving, which was probably composed by the author of the book as a theological comment on the tradition, deals with a greater mystery, the **wisdom and might** of God. No Babylonian could suppose that one of his gods **removes kings and sets up kings** or **changes times and seasons.** For pagan religion taught men how to change times themselves by magic which manipulated their gods. E.g. in Canaanite Baal worship, closely allied to Babylonian religion, men learned to control, as they thought, the natural processes of autumn rains and spring growth, for their gods were ultimately the deification of nature. But the God of Israel is absolutely other than the creation which he himself has brought into being. Behind the mystery of life his loving purpose is unfolding. He who knows the mind of God therefore learns something of that purpose and thus is given **wisdom and strength.**

2:24-30. *Intro. to the King.* Dan.'s first thought is not for himself but for the **wise men of Babylon** with whom he has been condemned. Part of the secret that God has revealed to him is pity for his fellowmen. This quality was unknown to pagan religion, though it might be possessed by individuals, such as Arioch, who seems glad of an opportunity to be relieved of his duty as executioner. As evidence of the original independence of the stories, contrast the need for Arioch to introduce Dan. here with Nebuchadnezzar's recognition of the superior wisdom of the 4 Jewish youths in 1:18-20 (see also above on vss. 14-23). Not using God's revelation for his own glory, Dan. immediately disclaims that he or any man can unravel the king's **mystery;** rather **there is a God in heaven who reveals mysteries** (vs. 28), and his purpose is to show **what is to be** (vs. 29). The phrase **the latter days** (vs. 28) appears in the prophetic books (e.g. Isa. 2:2; Jer. 23:20; 48:47; Ezek. 38:16; Hos. 3:5) as a designation of the time when God would act in a new and decisive manner for the redemption of the world. Here (cf. 10:14) it refers to the establishment of the kingdom of God (vs. 44).

2:31-45. *The Image and Stone.* Dan. first describes the king's dream (vss. 31-35) and then gives its interpretation (vss. 36-45). The 4 metals of the statue represent 4 successive kingdoms, i.e. empires. The 1st is the Neo-Babylonian Empire of Nebuchadnezzar himself, to whom, Dan. says, God has entrusted rule over not only all humanity but also the **beasts** and the **birds** (vs. 38; cf. Gen. 1:28; Ps. 8:5-8). The 2nd is evidently that of the Medes, which was actually contemporary with the Neo-Babylonian Empire rather than a successor to it (see below on 5:30-31). The 3rd is the Persian Empire, which claimed **rule over all the earth.**

2:40-43. The **fourth kingdom** is the Macedonian-Greek empire of Alexander the Great. After his death (323) it was split among 4 of his generals. The Jews came under the rule of the dynasty of Ptolemies in Egypt until 198, when Palestine was seized by the Seleucid dynasty of Syria, to which Antiochus Epiphanes belonged. That the 4th kingdom is **divided** (vs. 41) apparently alludes to this division. Since in the context this word seems to refer to the composition of **iron** and **clay,** some scholars have taken these 2 substances to symbolize respectively the Seleucid and Ptolemaic empires. **Marriage** (vs. 43)—if this is what the Aramaic phrase means (see RSV footnote)—seemingly alludes to the unsuccessful attempts of the 2 dynasties to gain peace through intermarriage of the royal lines (see below on 11:5-9,

10-19). In the context this refers to an effort to **mix** iron with clay and thus would support the idea that the substances represent the 2 dynasties. On the other hand vs. 42 clearly equates the 2 substances with elements of strength and weakness in a single **kingdom.** This symbolism is probably intended to apply throughout the passage, which therefore presumably describes the Seleucid kingdom, the empire that in the author's day would most naturally be viewed as a successor to Nebuchadnezzar's empire.

2:44-45. To the first readers of the book the reminder that 3 empires under which their fathers suffered had come and gone would give reason to trust that soon God would act to **bring . . . to an end** the whole succession of despotisms with the downfall of the 4th. He is to accomplish this by a **stone . . . cut . . . by no human hand,** i.e. divine power without need of man's aid. In place of these human kingdoms he will establish his own **kingdom,** which will **stand for ever.**

2:46-49. *Nebuchadnezzar's Submission.* Awed by the revelation, Nebuchadnezzar humbles himself before Dan.'s God, to whom rather than himself he attributes the title **Lord of kings** (cf. vs. 37). In reporting without disapproval the command to accord Dan. an **offering,** i.e. sacrifice, and **incense,** as if he were a god, the author no doubt thinks of Dan. as the type of all Israel, in whom is God's glory (cf. Isa. 46:13). When the kings of the Gentiles bow down and "lick the dust of your feet" (Isa. 49:23), they will really be worshiping, not Israel, but Israel's God. So too Nebuchadnezzar is thus worshiping Dan.'s God.

C. The Fiery Furnace (3:1-30)

3:1-12. *The Golden Image.* This story involves only the 3 companions, without even mentioning Dan. Perhaps it represents an entirely separate tradition which the author has combined with the Dan. stories. Being a didactic story, or midrash (see Intro.), it need not require Nebuchadnezzar to remember his humble submission to the God of heaven (2:47) or the **Chaldeans** (vs. 8; see above on 1:3-5) to recall Dan.'s concern to save their lives (2:24). Ancient statues were sometimes huge, as their remains testify; but **sixty cubits,** *ca.* 90 feet, is a great exaggeration, no doubt intended to suggest the colossal absurdity of Antiochus' claims to divinity. Informers always flourish in dictatorial regimes, and thus the envious are quick to report the refusal of the 3 Jewish officials to worship the image. **Satraps,** a Persian term (see below on 6:1-9), is an anachronism applied to Neo-Babylonian officials.

3:13-18. *The Courage of Faith.* To the Jews suffering under Antiochus Epiphanes the **furious rage** of Nebuchadnezzar would seem an apt description of the motivation of their persecutor, and a **burning fiery furnace** a fit symbol of the trial they were undergoing. Thus the response of the 3 young Jews to this threat would suggest the faith in the saving love of God that should inspire their own loyalty. Should God deem it best for them to die, they are ready (cf. II Macc. 6-7). If not, then he is fully **able to deliver** them even when the mind of man can see no way of escape. It is only the God of the Bible who can evoke such absolute trust.

3:19-23. *The Furnace.* The prototype of the furnace of the story would be, as archaeology has shown us, a kiln of the type used for smelting metals. Some have been found *ca.* 9 feet in diameter. **Seven times** is of course the perfect number and meant what we might express as "to the *n*th degree." The victims are bound and thrown into the furnace from above through the flue, from which issue flames and gases so hot that they kill the unfortunate **mighty** men assigned to the detail. Following vs. 23 the Greek versions include a lengthy passage which in Protestant usage is included in the Apoc.—in the RSV under the title the Prayer of Azariah and the Song of the 3 Young Men.

3:24-30. *The Deliverance.* Apparently a sentence of the text has been lost before vs. 24, a statement that Nebuchadnezzar stooped down and peered into the draft opening of the furnace to watch the young men being consumed. Vss. 24-25 then tell how he **rose up** to report what he saw—not 3 men but **four . . . walking** amid the flames.

During the Exile 2nd Isaiah promised in vivid metaphor:

> When you walk through fire you shall not be burned,
> and the flame shall not consume you.
> For I am the LORD your God,
> the Holy One of Israel, your Savior. (Isa. 43:2*b*-3*a*.)

When Dan. was written it was a fact of history that Israel had not been consumed in the Exile. What Israel's Savior had done before, he could do again. Yet God had not saved Israel at arm's length, as it were. He had been with his people in their sufferings and had shared the pain of the Exile with them. Many cents. earlier he had revealed himself to Moses as one who suffered such burning pain as his people experienced, such hurt as Israel went through in Egypt, yet was not consumed (Exod. 3:1-9). So those who trust in him will not be consumed either. In fact, as Isaiah of Jerusalem knew even in the 8th cent., God himself is the fire, the fire of judgment, of wrath, of redemption and purification all in one (Isa. 6:6-7; 31:9; cf. Deut. 4:24). Thus just as Moses was promised that God himself would be with him if he ventured into the flames, and just as Israel heard the same promise in her fiery trial in the Exile, so too Israel could be assured again that God himself was with her still as the very fire of wrath and redemption. If Antiochus had thrown her into the furnace, he had but thrown her into the suffering, redemptive love of God.

3:28-30. Nebuchadnezzar in this ch. does not turn to sing praises to God. Rather he acknowledges the significance of the witness of 3 men who **trusted** in their God (cf. Heb. 11:33-38). It was the faithful witness of a small remnant of the covenant people that preserved Judaism to become the seedbed of the Christian church.

D. NEBUCHADNEZZAR'S INSANITY (4:1-37)

This story develops in detail the theme that there is no such thing as a "divine right of kings," but it also suggests that no human society, whether kingdom or republic, should imagine that rule is vested in it except by God alone. It offers an exposition of such prophetic oracles on the Neo-Babylonian Empire as Isa. 14-15; 47; Jer. 50-51. Probably the underlying tradition originally concerned, not Nebuchadnezzar, but the last of his successors, Nabonidus (556-539), who during most of his reign lived away from his capital and spent a number of years at Tema in Arabia (see color map 10). A biased political poem about Nabonidus, written by certain priests to justify the action of the gods in handing his realm over to Cyrus the Persian, declares in one line: "The king is mad."

4:1-3. *A King's Confession.* The story of this ch. is put into the form of a letter from **King Nebuchadnezzar,** addressed according to the conventions of the Hellenistic period (vs. 1; cf. e.g. I Macc. 10:25; II Macc. 11:27) to his subjects, who are boastfully described as the inhabitants of **all the earth.** Most of what follows carries out the letter idea by being related in the first person by Nebuchadnezzar, but 3rd-person narrative is introduced in vss. 19, 28-33. Nebuchadnezzar announces that he is telling about his experience with the **Most High God;** and his hymn of praise (vs. 3), the thought of which is repeated and expanded in vss. 34-35, represents his viewpoint after the experience.

4:4-9. *An Interruption to Complacency.* Before the experience, Nebuchadnezzar declares, he thought he was **prospering** as master of the known world, but he was not master of his own thoughts and fears. The goodness of God is his very severity. In his love he may need to send the self-satisfied man a bad dream, or a disease germ, or a national enemy (cf. Isa. 5:24-30). Nebuchadnezzar's procedure in consulting first the Babylonian **wise men** and then, after their failure, Dan. parallels that in ch. 2 but shows no recollection of what happened then—unless his recognition of Dan.'s inspiration is to be so understood. The Aramaic plural **gods** may be intended to represent the Hebrew word for God, *elohim,* which is plural in form (see RSV footnote). The assumption that the first syllable of **Belteshazzar** represents the name of a **god**— viz. Bel, title of the god Marduk— is probably incorrect according to the Babylonian etymology (see above on 1:6-7), but the error would not be a problem to the original Jewish readers.

4:10-12. *The Great Tree.* The author builds his symbolism in this passage on the comparison of the pharaoh to a towering cedar in Ezek. 31:3-14, which his readers would know well as a prediction from the Exile of Egypt's downfall. The figure of a tree whose **top reached to heaven** would also remind them of the tower of Babel (Gen. 11:1-9) and the men who learned they could not build a city and a civilization without God. From a material standpoint Nebuchadnezzar's empire seemed a success; his building projects provided work and food for all and produced a capital of unrivaled magnificence. Yet to knowing readers the very description of the tree's greatness would forecast its fall.

4:13-18. *A Decree of Judgment.* The tree's destruction is ordered by a **watcher,** a "wakeful one," who is a **holy one,** an emissary from the holy God. Yet the **stump** is to be left and **bound** with a metal ring, apparently to protect it (cf. vs. 26). The angel's abrupt shift from the tree symbolism to a direct order that a person suffer a mental breakdown suggests that the author combined differing traditions. A

beast's mind, i.e. the delusion of being an animal, is a not uncommon psychopathic manifestation known as zoanthropy. Such a derangement, though often permanent, might end after **seven times,** i.e. years (cf. 7:25e). When Antiochus IV took the surname Epiphanes, meaning "manifested one," i.e. a revealed god, some of his enemies called him instead Epimanes, "madman"—a nickname the Jews esp. had reason to believe justified. In view of the obvious meaning of what Nebuchadnezzar has just related the author might well intimate that the failure of the **wise men** to interpret it was due to discretion rather than inability, but he chooses instead to reemphasize Dan.'s superior inspiration (cf. vss. 8-9).

4:19-27. *Courage to Declare God's Word.* The narrative here shifts from first to 3rd person (see above on vss. 1-3). That Dan. is **dismayed** at the unwelcome interpretation with which he must confront the proud monarch is understandable. As one educated in the court of the most cultured nation of the time, Nebuchadnezzar has a veneer of courtesy (vss. 19b), but Dan. is well aware of the despot's ruthless temper (cf. 2:12; 3:13, 19). His opening words (vss. 19c) are a vestige of what in earlier times was an attempt to avert the ill effect of bad news and transform it into a curse against **enemies,** but he uses the ancient formula as a way of expressing regret for what he must say (cf. II Sam. 18:32).

4:20-25. The great prophets speak of God's "strange . . . work" (Isa. 28:21) when in his saving love he has to act in judgment with seeming cruelty (cf. e.g. Hos. 13:4-8). For in his wisdom he sees that some men cannot be saved until their pride is broken. Only then can they recognize the truth about themselves and experience the love of God. Thus Nebuchadnezzar must learn that, though he is absolute master of a vast empire, in the sight of God, who sees the heart, i.e. the subconscious mind, the real man, he is only a **beast** (cf. Ps. 73:22), and in fact may be reduced through mental illness to living like one.

4:26-27. It is not inevitable fate that rules on high but a loving God. There is opportunity for restoration (vs. 26) when Nebuchadnezzar learns that he reigns under God. Moreover Dan. begs his king to repent at once (vs. 27) and acknowledge his submission to God by concern for the **oppressed** under his sway. With such a reformation the threatened blow may prove unnecessary.

4:28-33. *The Fulfillment.* God gives man time to repent. In this case Nebuchadnezzar is given **twelve months,** yet in spite of the clear warning he remains obsessed with his own **mighty power.** Therefore God must act to destroy his pride (cf. Isa. 47:8-11), and the predicted doom falls.

4:34-37. *The Mercy of God.* For the conclusion the letter form with which the story began is resumed, and Nebuchadnezzar tells in the first person how he recovered his **reason** when he **lifted** his **eyes to heaven** in acknowledgment of God's rule. In a hymn of praise (cf. vs. 3) he confesses that not man but the **Most High** is Lord of all and that none may question him—**none can . . . say to him, "What doest thou?"** (cf. Job 9:12; Isa. 45:9). Having submitted to God's **kingdom,** he is restored to his own and finds **more greatness** in ruling under the divine rule. Is the author perhaps suggesting that there is hope yet in God's love for even Antiochus Epiphanes?

E. BELSHAZZAR'S FEAST (5:1-31)

Contemporary Babylonian records show that Belshazzar was the son, not of Nebuchadnezzar (vs. 2), but of Nabonidus (see above on 4:1-37). Some have supposed he was Nebuchadnezzar's grandson, since Nabonidus seems to have married a daughter of Nebuchadnezzar; but this marriage occurred, if at all, only after Nabonidus became king (556), when the records indicate Belshazzar was already an adult. Belshazzar was never **king** but was made coregent by his father and no doubt was virtual ruler during his father's residence in Arabia. Babylon was taken in 539 by the amy of Cyrus the Persian (see below on vss. 30-31) without a battle, and Greek historians report a tradition that its capture followed a night of feasting. The name Belshazzar means "Bel protect the king" and thus actually includes the designation of the god which the author erroneously assumed to be an element in Dan.'s Babylonian name Belteshazzar (see above on 1:6-7; 4:4-9).

5:1-4. *Belshazzar's Sacrilege.* At a state banquet Belshazzar unashamedly drinks **in front of the thousand** guests, the officials and leading citizens of his empire. In his drunken state he deliberately commits a sacrilegious act by calling for the holy **vessels** pillaged from the **house of God,** the Jerusalem temple (cf. 1:1-2; II Kings 24:13; 25:14-15; Ezra 1:7-11), so that his guests may drink and pour libations from them to their pagan gods. The account would of course remind the original readers immediately of Antiochus Epiphanes' desecrations of the temple and its altar (see Intro.).

5:5-12. *The Writing on the Wall.* The walls of ancient palaces were often finished with white **plaster,** on which writing would show clearly in the light from a **lampstand,** which might hold a number of oil lamps. Belshazzar's terror at the sight of the **hand** is to be understood as due to guilt, a belated realization of the enormity of his sacrilege. The godless man is always horror-stricken at any invasion of his secure little world from the mysterious beyond whose existence he has denied. The consultation of the Babylonian **wise men** and their failure follows the same pattern as in chs. 2, 4 except that here the eventual calling of Dan. is based on his earlier success.

5:8-9. Why the Babylonians are unable even to **read the writing,** which consists of common words in Aramaic (vs. 25), a language known to educated persons throughout the ancient Near East, is a question on which there has been much speculation. Some interpreters suppose the reason is a strange script. E.g. the old Hebrew script in which most of the OT was written would be well known to Dan. but presumably unfamiliar to Babylonians. In the author's day the use of this old script for writing Hebrew was giving way to use of the Aramaic script, from which the Hebrew letters we know today developed (see "Writing in Biblical Times," pp. 1201-08). On the other hand the wise men's failure may be due to the fact that Aramaic, like Hebrew and other Semitic languages, was written in a consonantal alphabet. Being unable to make sense of the writing as a whole, they would be uncertain which vowel sounds to insert and thus, even though recognizing the letters, be unable to pronounce them as words.

5:10-12. Probably the **queen** is to be understood

as Belshazzar's mother rather than one of his **wives** (vss. 2-3; see comment on Jer. 13:18-19). Having just entered the hall without having participated in the drunken sacrilege, she can assess the situation dispassionately. She remembers Dan.'s service to Belshazzar's **father** when he faced similar problems. She ascribes to Dan. even greater abilities than stated heretofore. According to her estimate he is the supreme type of the wise man who knows the mind of God.

5:13-29. *Interpretation of the Writing.* As a true man of God Dan. rejects flattery and promised **rewards** and fearlessly tells the ruler the truth about himself. He cites as a warning the experience attributed to Nebuchadnezzar in ch. 4 but perhaps originally told of Nabonidus, historically Belshazzar's **father** (see above on 4:1-37). Each generation has to learn from experience for itself (vs. 22). Dan.'s reference to **the God in whose hand is your breath** (vs. 23) is striking; even the most powerful man on earth lives only by the grace of God.

5:24-28. The words written on the wall as read by Dan. mean respectively **numbered . . . weighed . . . divided.** Read with different vowels as other derivatives of the same roots (see above on vss. 8-9), the words are a series of weights: mina, shekel, and half shekels (see table, p. 1285). **Parsin,** lit. "halves," sometimes was used of half minas but here more likely indicates half shekels, to form a series in order of descending value. Probably the series was a proverbial expression comparing the abilities of successive rulers—possibly Babylonian kings during the Exile, with the coregents Nabonidus and Belshazzar as the half shekels. There is a further word play in **peres,** which may mean not only "divided" and "half," i.e. the singular of **parsin,** but also **Persians.**

5:30-31. *The Fall of Babylon.* The Babylonian records tell nothing of Belshazzar's death, but mention by the Greek historian Xenophon that the "king" was killed when the Persians took Babylon may refer to him, for the records indicate Nabonidus was captured at a later time. The author's idea that Babylon fell to **Darius the Mede,** who in turn was succeeded by Cyrus the Persian (6:28), accords with his idea of 4 successive kingdoms (see above on 2:31-45), of which the 2nd was the Median Empire, supposedly coming between the Neo-Babylonian and Persian empires. No doubt this idea stemmed from prophetic oracles against Babylon predicting its destruction by the Medes (Isa. 13:17-18; 21:2; Jer. 51:11, 28). Actually the Median and Neo-Babylonian empires, which arose together after the downfall of the Assyrian Empire, coexisted until both were conquered by Cyrus, first the Median Empire *ca.* 550 and afterwards the Neo-Babylonian in 539. The name Darius is not found in the list of Median kings, which is known from historical records; evidently it comes from confused traditions of the later Persian king Darius the Great (522-486), who aided the rebuilding of the temple in Jerusalem (Ezra 5-6), and is mistakenly applied to Astyages, the last ruler of the Median Empire (see below on 9:1-2).

F. The Lions' Den (6:1-28)

This story, one of the most familiar in the Bible, is closely parallel in many details to the story of Dan.'s 3 companions in ch. 3 and proclaims the same message, that God will sustain those who remain loyal to him in the face of persecution. For the Jews threatened with suffering and even death for persisting in the practice of their faith in defiance of the hellenizing decrees of Antiochus Epiphanes its application was clear, and in succeeding cents. it has given courage to many struggling against overwhelming oppression from without or temptation from within.

6:1-9. *Envy of Dan.'s Authority.* Darius the Great (see above on 5:30-31) organized the Persian Empire into provinces under the governance of **satraps,** and his inscriptions indicate that when his conquests brought the empire to its greatest extent the number totaled 29. Possibly later kings extended the title to subordinates (cf. Ezra 8:36) so that there came to be as many as **a hundred and twenty,** but more probably traditions about the size of the empire exaggerated the number of provinces (cf. 127 in Esth. 1:1; I Esdras 3:2). Historical records do not mention the **three presidents,** but such a cabinet of top military and civilian officials is not improbable. No reason for Dan.'s appointment to such responsibility by a new king to whom he was presumably unknown is given in this case (contrast 1:19; 2:48-49; 5:29), but his integrity and efficiency in office are noted as the basis for Darius' intention to elevate him still further to the post of prime minister.

6:4-5. Anyone who advances above his fellows, however great his merit, is likely to arouse jealousy. To this may be added the hatred which sheer goodness provokes in those who prefer darkness rather than light. Dan.'s being a foreigner would of course aggravate the resentment, though the author refrains from mentioning such prejudice. Thus the presidents and satraps submerge their individual rivalries in an alliance to destroy the common object of their envy. Having searched in vain for any **fault** in his administration that might be magnified and distorted into a **ground for complaint,** they conclude that his belonging to a religious minority is the one chink in his armor.

6:6-7. The Aramaic word translated **came by agreement** (vss. 6, 11, 15) and its related Hebrew forms (Pss. 2:1*a*; 55:14*b*; 64:2*b*) are of uncertain meaning. That even high officials would dare throng tumultuously (see RSV footnote) into the royal court seems unlikely. The RSV translators' interpretation of collusion or conspiracy is based on comparison of the several contexts. Thus the envious officers scheme to approach the king together and play on his vanity to obtain his thoughtless assent to an absurd **interdict** they are certain Dan. will violate. Their proposal has the effect of elevating the king to the status of a god to whom all his subjects must pray, and to the book's original readers it would suggest at once the pretensions to divinity of Antiochus Epiphanes.

6:8-9. The phrase **law of the Medes and the Persians** suggests that the author may have supposed that the Persians were included in the Median Empire (cf. 5:28; 8:20), which historically took in Elam to the S and extended N and W into Armenia and Asia Minor but never established rule over the Persians to the E. On the other hand the meaning may be that these neighboring peoples independently followed a legal code that was a common heritage. The idea that a decree issued under this law could not be **revoked** is found also in Esth. 1:19; 8:8 (see comments), where, as here, it is an essential element in the story. Historical records of the 2 empires reveal no evidence of unusual legal practice on which such a tradition might be based.

6:10-13. Faithfulness in Prayer. As Dan. the exile prays in his **upper chamber** (cf. Judg. 3:20; Acts 1:13) he looks in the direction of **Jerusalem,** that spot on earth where God chose "to make his name dwell" (Deut. 12:11; cf. I Kings 8:29). Yet it was in exile that Israel perforce learned that God can be addressed in prayer anywhere and at any time. Paradoxically, man can meet God anywhere only when he has learned to meet him somewhere, and can talk to him at any time because he has learned to do so at specific times. Dan. finds strength in God in this emergency because he has learned to pray to him regularly **three times a day** (cf. Ps. 55:17). But it is his very faithfulness in prayer that provides the plotters with an accusation against him.

6:14-18. The Sentence of Death. Darius genuinely admires Dan. (cf. vs. 3) and spends the rest of the day trying to **deliver** him, presumably by consulting with his legal advisers. But he has been trapped by his vanity and must give the order for Dan.'s execution. Apparently the author visualizes the **den of lions** as a pit somewhat like a cistern (cf. Gen. 37:24; Jer. 38:6), with only a single opening at the top. Over this a **stone** is placed and **sealed** so that its position cannot be **changed** without disturbing a lump of moist clay into which the king's carved **signet** ring has been impressed. Probably the procedure is to tie the stone in place with a rope and enclose the knot in the clay (cf. Matt. 27:64-66). The king is so distressed that he spends a sleepless night.

6:19-27. Dan.'s Vindication. As the pagan king hurries at dawn to the mouth of the den, his hope to find Dan. alive is based, not on any expectation that the lions may have lacked appetite, but on the realization that Dan. serves a **living God,** i.e. one able to take direct action to save (cf. e.g. Deut. 5:26; Josh. 3:10; I Sam. 17:26; II Kings 19:4). His hope proves justified; just as God through his **angel,** lit. "messenger," could keep the flames of the furnace from harming the 3 young men who were similarly faithful (ch. 3), so now he has **shut the lions' mouths** and kept them from harming Dan. (cf. Ps. 91:13). God has so acted because Dan. is **blameless,** i.e. not sinless but constant in his observance of the Mosaic law. To the loyal Jews suffering agonies of mind and body for their continued observance of that law in the face of the hellenizing policies of Antiochus Epiphanes this story was calculated to bring fresh hope, the assurance that God had been and still was powerful to save those who **trusted** in him.

6:24. Lest any reader question whether the lions' sparing of Dan. was due to deficient ferocity rather than divine prohibition, the author quickly goes on to describe their immediate destruction of Dan.'s accusers. The sentencing of the plotters to the same fate they sought for Dan. is in accordance with the Mosaic law (Deut. 19:16-19), but the inclusion of their **children** and **wives** is contrary to that law (Deut. 24:16).

6:25-27. Darius' decree follows the form of Nebuchadnezzar's letter and uses some of the same phrases (see above on 4:1-3), and his hymn of praise is sim-

ilar in language and thought to that of Nebuchadnezzar (cf. 4:3, 34-35). In ending his series of stories of Dan. with the report that this one man's courageous devotion resulted in the commendation of reverence for Israel's God to countless pagans, the author may be meaning to say that an individual's faith is no mere private affair but has a missionary outcome. The loyalty of persecuted Jews in his own day may not only achieve their own salvation but be instrumental in establishing God's kingdom **in all the earth** —as in fact it was.

6:28. The Beginning of the Persian Empire. In a concluding note to the stories the author mentions the accession of **Cyrus the Persian,** which he evidently understands as bringing to an end the Median Empire and inaugurating the Persian Empire. No hint is given of the means by which Cyrus gained the power, no doubt because, having attributed to Darius the Mede the capture of Babylon which historically occurred under Cyrus (see above on 5:30-31), he knows no other tradition of Cyrus' conquest.

II. DAN.'S VISIONS (7:1–12:13)

Chs. 1–6 are intended to interpret the faithfulness of God to Jews suffering sorely from persecution. They do so by presenting traditional stories of the past experience of the Babylonian exile. In contrast, chs. 7–12 look forward to the future. Though most of what they purport to predict has already happened, their emphasis is on the divine action that is soon to occur. They declare that just as God has been faithful in the past, so is he to be relied on now and in the unknown days to come. No matter how strong the forces of evil may become, they cannot prevent the living God from bringing his plans for mankind to fruition. This message is presented in symbolic language and apocalyptic imagery that are in striking contrast to the parabolic narrative style of chs. 1–6, but similarities of expression as well as thought are frequent enough to convince most scholars that the same author is responsible.

A. A DREAM OF 4 BEASTS (7:1-28)

This is one of the most far-reaching passages in the Bible in its influence. Most of the apocalyptic works produced during the next 3 cents. use some of its language and imagery (see "The Apocalyptic Literature," pp. 1106-09; "The Intertestamental Literature," pp. 1110-15). It provided a background for much of Jesus' thought about his vocation, as well as a source for many of the symbols with which the NT authors speak of God's ultimate triumph.

7:1-8. The 4 Empires. The dating of the visions (cf. 8:1; 9:1; 10:1) imitates the dates in some of the prophetic books (e.g. Jer. 26:1; Ezek. 8:1; Hag. 2:1; Zech. 7:1). **In the first year of Belshazzar** locates this dream earlier in time than the story of that ruler's last night (ch. 5), but since the content shows no connection with his reign (cf. vs. 17), the present position as the first of the visions is more appropriate than a chronological placement among the stories. This dream is closely related, however, to the story of ch. 2 containing Nebuchadnezzar's dream of an image made of 4 metals, and it seems to refer to the same 4 kingdoms (see above on 2:31-45).

7:2-3. The **great sea** here is not the Mediterranean, as elsewhere in the OT, but the chaotic waters over and under the earth (cf. e.g. Gen. 1:7; Exod. 20:4). This chaos is sometimes called the "deep" (e.g. Gen. 1:2; 7:11; Ps. 104:6), the Hebrew word being akin to the name Tiamat of the female dragon of chaos in Mesopotamian mythology, to which there are a number of allusions in the OT under the name Rahab. But the God of the Bible is always Lord of chaos, whether conceived in terms of a watery deep (e.g. Job 26:12; Pss. 46:2; 74:13; Isa. 51:10) or of an evil personality (e.g. Jer. 51:34-37; Ezek. 29:3-5). From this sea of chaos and opposition to the God of order rise the **four great beasts** symbolizing human empires that tried to dominate the earth without acknowledging the rule of the living God.

7:4-6. The first beast, resembling a **lion** with **eagles' wings,** represents the Neo-Babylonian Empire (cf. 2:38). The author probably based this symbolism on prophetic metaphors likening Nebuchadnezzar to a lion (Jer. 4:7; 50:17) and an eagle (Ezek. 17:3). Perhaps also he wished to imply a descending order as in the metals of 2:31-45 and thus chose as a parallel to gold the most powerful mammal and bird. The beast's being **made to stand upon two feet like a man** and being given the **mind of a man** is apparently an allusion to the story of the restoration of Nebuchadnezzar's reason (4:34) after he was given a "beast's mind" (4:16). The 2nd beast, **like a bear,** represents the Median Empire, which the author mistakenly believed had savagely torn at Babylon (see above on 5:30-31). The 3rd, **like** a **leopard,** known for its swiftness (cf. Hab. 1:8), represents the Persian Empire. Its **four wings** and **four heads** may symbolize the 4 corners of the earth to which its **dominion** extended (cf. 2:39b) or possibly the 4 Persian kings of whom the author knew (see below on 11:2-39).

7:7-8. The 4th beast, whose **terrible** appearance is left largely to the reader's imagination (cf. vs. 19), represents the Seleucid Empire, which resulted from division of the territory conquered by Alexander the Great and in the author's day controlled Palestine (see Intro. and above on 2:31-45). **Horns** like those of a bull are a common symbol of power in the OT (cf. e.g. "strength," I Sam. 2:1c, "might," Lam. 2:3b, both lit. "horn"). In this book they are used to symbolize rulers (cf. vs. 24), the **little one** here being Antiochus Epiphanes. During most of the reign of his brother, Seleucus IV (189-175), Antiochus was a hostage in Rome. At length Seleucus' son and heir, Demetrius (cf. I Macc. 7:1-4; II Macc. 14:1-2), was sent to Rome to replace him. While Antiochus was on the way home, Seleucus was killed in a conspiracy of Heliodorus (cf. II Macc 3:7-40) to set a younger son on the throne with himself as regent. On hearing the news, Antiochus obtained outside help in Asia Minor, eliminated Heliodorus, and secured the crown for himself. The author, and perhaps many other Jews, considered Antiochus a usurper who had contrived all the events that led to his accession (cf. 11:21) and thus counted Seleucus and Demetrius among the **three of the first horns** uprooted by the little horn, the 3rd being probably the younger son or possibly Heliodorus. To these 3 he may have added Seleucus' 6 predecessors in the Seleucid dynasty and Alexander to get the total

of **ten.** Other lists of 10 have been proposed, however, as well as the possibility that 10 is simply a conventional or symbolic number. On the **mouth speaking great things** cf. vs. 25; 11:36.

7:9-12. *The Divine Judgment.* The poetic imagery of vss. 9-10 is drawn from the psalmists and prophets. On **ancient of days** cf. Ps. 90:2. On the whiteness of his **raiment** and **hair** cf. Isa. 1:18. On his **throne** cf. Ezek. 1:15-26. On **fire** as a symbol of his holiness, wrath, and justice cf. e.g. Pss. 50:3; 97:3-5; 104:4; Isa. 10:17; 33:14. On his council of **ten thousand times ten thousand**—the square of the highest number for which ancient peoples had a word—cf. I Kings 22:19; Ps. 82. On his record **books** cf. Pss. 56:8; 69:28; Isa. 65:6; Mal. 3:16.

7:11-12. The arrogance of the blasphemous **horn** brings the whole beast, i.e. the Seleucid Empire, to destruction in the **fire** of God's judgment. But the other 3 beasts, i.e. Babylonia, Media, and Persia, which in the author's day were provinces of the Seleucid Empire, are permitted to survive **for a season**—apparently an interval which is envisioned between the fall of the Seleucid Empire and the establishment of the divine kingdom. Contrast 2:44, where the divine kingdom is to be established "in the days of those [Seleucid] kings" and cause the simultaneous breaking of all 4 kingdoms. Perhaps the taking of **dominion** from the 3 beasts is to be equated with the breaking of the image as symbolizing an end to the kingdoms' rule over others. Thus the author may be thinking here esp. of the peoples of these lands, who will live on and come under the sway of God's kingdom.

7:13-14. *The Son of Man.* In place of the beasts now **came,** i.e. will come, **one like a son of man.** This term as generally used in the OT is simply a poetic synonym of "man" (e.g. Num. 23:19; Job 25:6; Ps. 8:4; Isa. 51:12). Possibly this is all the author means by it here—a symbol for the coming kingdom that is like a man (cf. 8:15) in contrast to the beasts representing past kingdoms. In Ezek., however, this phrase is used repeatedly as God's way of addressing the prophet (cf. e.g. Ezek. 2:1), and in Hebrew figurative usage "son" suggests likeness in mind and spirit (cf. e.g. Mark 3:17). Thus the author may mean "son of mankind," one who represents God's intention for humanity, who is truly made in the image of God (Gen. 1:26) and is worthy to have **dominion** over all creation (cf. Gen. 1:28; Ps. 8:6-8).

Since the dominion over **all peoples** given to this son of man by God, in contrast to that seized by the beastly rulers, is to be **everlasting,** the implication is that he is in some sense divine. This is suggested at once by his coming **with the clouds of heaven.** In Canaanite mythological texts from the middle of the 2nd millennium the gods are said to ride on the clouds, and such language is used of Yahweh in a number of poetic passages of the OT (e.g. Pss. 18:10-11; 68:4; 104:3; Isa. 19:1). In the LXX the phrase here is "on the clouds," and some have taken it to be original; but the "with" of the Aramaic text perhaps is to be understood as indicating emphasis, not on the mode of transportation, but on the origin of the symbolic human figure in contrast to the sea of chaos from which the beasts arise.

7:15-28. *The Rule of the Saints.* This **interpreta-**

tion is largely repetition of what has been said or clearly implied in the preceding description of the dream. Significant, however, is the fact that nothing further is said of the son of man and instead the kingdom is promised to the saints of the Most High. "Saint" is lit. "holy one," translating the same Aramaic word used earlier of angelic beings (4:13, 17, 23; cf. 8:13 in Hebrew); but the reference here is evidently to Israel, called to be a "holy nation" (Exod. 19:6). In ancient Hebrew thought the people of Israel as a whole could be summed up in one representative figure, such as their king, and yet all together they could be called a "son of man" (Ps. 80:17). Thus the meaning here may be that the saints are to receive the kingdom through one who is their representative head, yet in whom they are all included as a kind of corporate personality. He is to be the first real man, in contrast to the past rulers who have been like beasts in spirit (cf. 4:16), and as such institute a kingdom of real men. This expectation that all dominions shall serve and obey Israel (vs. 27) repeats the promise of 2nd Isaiah (cf. e.g. Isa. 45:14; 49:7, 23; see above on 2:46-49).

7:19-27. The special concern about the fourth beast is to be attributed, not to Dan., who is to live only under the empires symbolized by the first 3 beasts, but to the intended readers, Jews suffering under the Seleucid Empire and its last horn, Antiochus Epiphanes. By his measures to stamp out Judaism and replace it by Greek religion and culture he has made war with the saints and seemingly prevailed over them. His banning of Jewish religious practices has attempted to change the times, i.e. the festival calendar, and the law, i.e. of Moses. But the prediction is that God will permit his oppression to last for only a time, two times, and half a time, i.e. 3½ years (see below on 9:27). The promised divine action is therefore not something far off but only a matter of months away. Surely the loyal sufferers can hold out a little longer!

7:28. Possibly here is the end of the matter marked the conclusion of an early edition of the book which included only some or all of the stories and this one vision. If so, the author no doubt inserted in his enlarged edition the sentence about Dan.'s being alarmed (cf. 4:5; 5:6) in order to suggest his need for the reassurance of the visions being added. The Aramaic section of the book (see Intro.) ends with this vs.

B. A Vision of a Ram and a Goat (8:1-27)

8:1-4. The Ram. The date (vs. 1) indicates that this vision follows the preceding by ca. 2 years (see above on 7:1-8). Susa the capital probably should be translated rather "the citadel of Susa," referring to a large fortified area separated from the rest of the city, as confirmed by excavations (see comment on Esth. 1:2-8 and color map 10). In this area Darius the Great built a magnificent winter palace, which was used by his successors. No doubt the author thought of Susa as the capital of the Persian Empire (cf. Neh. 1:1; Esth. 1:2). Possibly he knew that the Ulai was like the Chebar (cf. Ezek. 1:1; 10:20-22) in being a canal and thus considered it an appropriate place for Dan. to be transported in his vision. Some scholars, however, believe the unusual word

translated river means instead "gate," as in the LXX, so that Dan. in his vision is standing at the entrance to Susa that faces N or NE toward the Ulai Canal, which was near rather than adjacent to the city. The ram he sees represents the Persian Empire. Its two horns symbolize double power (see above on 7:7-8) because of its incorporating the Median Empire (vs. 20; cf. 5:28; 6:8) but the later, i.e. Persian, power is higher. The LXX lists all 4 directions in vs. 4, recognizing that the empire extended all the way to India, but the author probably visualizes the ram as coming from the E.

8:5-8. The He-goat. The rival animal advances from the west with such speed that it seems to move without touching the ground. It represents the Macedonian force that so quickly (334-326) conquered the entire Persian Empire, and its single conspicuous horn symbolizes Alexander the Great (vs. 21), who died soon afterward (323) and was replaced by four conspicuous horns, his generals. They divided his newly won domain toward the four winds, i.e. into 4 major kingdoms in Greece, Asia Minor, Egypt, and Mesopotamia, the last of which soon established itself in Syria and later (198) seized Palestine from Egypt.

8:9-14. Interruption of Sacrifices. From one of them, Seleucus, the general who took over Syria, was descended the little horn (cf. 7:8), Antiochus Epiphanes. His growing great toward the south refers to his campaigns in Egypt (see below on 11:25-28). Since there is no record of his campaigning toward the east until the 2-year expedition during which he died (cf. I Macc. 3:31-37; 6:1-17), this reference seems to date the book within very narrow limits (see Intro.). The glorious land is of course Palestine (cf. 11:16, 41; Jer. 3:19; Ezek. 20:6).

8:10-12. Not content with earthly conquest, Antiochus assaults the host of heaven, i.e. the angelic army, by his claims to divinity and his decrees banning the practice of any religion except his own. The Hebrew text of vss. 11-12 is obscure and corrupt, but the main reference is clear—Antiochus' suppression of the continual burnt offering (the twice-daily sacrifices on the altar of the temple in Jerusalem (cf. Exod. 29:38-42; Num. 28:3-8). Overthrown probably refers, not to physical destruction, but to desecration of the altar by diverting it to the worship of Zeus (cf. I Macc. 1:54, 59; II Macc. 6:2, 5).

8:13. In using the term holy one the author draws no line between the heavenly host and the people of Israel (see above on 7:15-28). Here it evidently refers to 2 angelic beings. Transgression, or "abomination" (11:31; 12:11; cf. 9:27), that makes desolate is a word play on the Semitic title of Zeus, "Baal of Heaven." In reading the Scriptures it was a common practice to substitute such words as "shame," "abomination," and "transgression" in references to the old Canaanite god Baal; and a mere vowel change transformed "heavenly" into "desolating."

8:14. The cessation of worship is to last two thousand and three hundred evenings and mornings, i.e. 1,150 days, or 3 years and ca. 2 months (cf. 3½ years, 7:25; 9:27; 12:7). According to I Macc. (1:54, 59; 4:52-54) Judas Maccabeus and his followers rededicated the altar and resumed sacrifices 3 years to the day after the desecration. Some scholars point out that Antiochus' prohibition of sacrifices (cf. I Macc. 1:45) may have been enforced some weeks before the altar was desecrated and thus that 1,150 days may be the actual period during which the daily offerings were suspended. On this basis they maintain that the author knew of Judas' rededication and therefore must have written the book in the short period between this event and the receipt of news of Antiochus' death. The doubtful evidence of this passage seems to be overweighed, however, not only by the lack of any sign of such knowledge in 9:27; 11:31 but also by the expectation throughout the book of deliverance by God's action rather than by any **human hand** (vs. 25).

8:15-27. The Interpretation. Again (cf. 7:16) Dan. seeks an explanation of his vision, and this time **Gabriel,** meaning "man of God," is instructed to supply it. The naming of angels is a late development which in the canonical OT is found only in this book (in the Apoc. cf. II Esdras 4:1, 36; Tobit 3:17). Both Gabriel and Michael (10:13, 21; 12:1) are among the 7 archangels named in intertestamental works, and both are mentioned in the NT (Luke 1:19, 26; Jude 9; Rev. 12:7). Gabriel has to waken Dan. from an unnatural **sleep,** such as God imposed on the patriarchs before revealing to them his mind (cf. Gen. 15:12). He explains that the vision has to do with the **end,** the time of God's **indignation** and intervention on behalf of his people. The implication is that the destruction of Antiochus Epiphanes will be the beginning of this, for it will be accomplished **by no human hand,** i.e. by God's own action. The instruction to **seal up** the scroll on which the vision is reported is a common convention of apocalyptic works, as an explanation of why a book purporting to have been written so long ago has just been published. On the method of sealing ancient documents see comment on Jer. 32:9-15. Dan.'s return to the **king's,** i.e. Belshazzar's (vs. 1), **business** is inconsistent with 5:10-16, where he appears to be retired from public office and unknown to Belshazzar before the queen's recommendation.

C. AN INTERPRETATION OF PROPHECY (9:1-27)

This ch. is dominated by a sense of urgency. The day of God's intervention (cf. 8:19), a day of both judgment and mercy, as the great prophets taught, is at hand. His people are now living at the time of the end. Its imminence is here demonstrated by a new understanding of a well-known prophecy.

9:1-2. The Prophecy of 70 Years. Unlike the preceding dates (see above on 7:1-8) the **first year of Darius** is esp. appropriate. Darius' supposed conquest (see above on 5:30-31) of the **realm of the Chaldeans,** who destroyed Jerusalem and carried her people into exile, might well cause Dan. to ponder the application of the prophecies in Jer. 25:11-12; 29:10 about God's visiting his people after 70 years. **Ahasuerus** represents the Hebrew equivalent of the name of the Persian king known through Greek transcription as Xerxes, who was the son of Darius the Great (see comment on Esth. 1:1). No doubt the author knew about this Persian king (cf. Ezra 4:6; see below on 11:2-4) but is here referring to a different man, a **Mede** of an earlier time, whom he believed to have borne the same name. Thus like

the author of Tobit (cf. Tobit 14:15) he probably knew by this Hebrew name the Median king known through Greek transcription as Cyaxares (*ca.* 625–*ca.* 585), who conquered Nineveh (see Intro. to Nah.) and largely created the Median Empire. Cyaxares' **son** was Astyages, who was ruler of this empire when it fell to Cyrus the Persian. Perhaps confused traditions linking the later Ahasuerus (Xerxes) to Darius the Great came to be mistakenly associated also with the earlier Ahasuerus (Cyaxares) and resulted in the misnaming of his son.

9:3-19. Dan.'s Prayer. The distinctive style of this prayer and its use of the divine name Yahweh, not found elsewhere in the book, indicate that it is an earlier composition which has been incorporated at this place. The fact that with vss. 4-20 omitted vs. 21 would connect well with vs. 3 has suggested to some that the prayer is a later addition, like the Prayer of Azariah added in the Greek versions after 3:23. Its appropriateness to the context, however, and esp. to the situation for which the book was written favors the more general view that the author thoughtfully chose it to quote at this point. Possibly tradition had already attributed it to Dan., but the content suggests rather that it was composed in or near **Jerusalem** (cf. vss. 7, 12, 16, 19) at a time when the Jews had become scattered in **all the lands** (vs. 7), i.e. late in the Persian period or in Hellenistic times.

The language is comparable with that of the prayers in Neh. 1:5-11; 9:6-37. Each of these prayers places contemporary sinful Israel in focus over against the long history of God's redemptive acts and thus claims his redeeming love for the present generation. The hoped-for restoration of communion between God and Israel requires confession of sins which the **prophets** (vs. 6) declared to be the cause of the Exile, and which must be regarded as the reason God has permitted Aniochus to prevail over his people for a time. The resulting **calamity** (vss. 12-14) may be either the destruction of God's temple during Dan.'s youth or its desecration 4 cents. later. For all who may be yielding to self-pity because of their hardships or to self-satisfaction because of their guerrilla victories or to self-righteousness because of the wickedness of their enemies the plea is that God may **forgive** and may **act** without further **delay.**

9:20-27. The 70 Weeks of Years. In response to his prayer Dan. is given another vision of the angel **Gabriel** (see above on 8:15-27), called a **man** because appearing in human form (cf. 8:15), who is sent as an interpreter. Unfortunately the text of his interpretation is not only complicated but corrupt. The main point is clear, however, that the 70 years of the prophecy (vs. 2), long past at the time of writing, must be multiplied by 7 so that the end of the period, bringing God's visitation of his people in Jerusalem and the dawning of the promised new era, will according to the author's calculation be only a matter of months in the future. The idea of thus multiplying the years of punishment may have been suggested to the author by the 7-fold penalties threatened in Lev. 26:14-39. At any rate **weeks of years** were familiar to him and his readers from the sabbath year of "rest for the land" (Lev. 25:2-7), i.e. leaving it fallow, observed by all loyal Jews (cf. Neh. 10:31; I Macc. 6:49-54) as the last of each cycle of 7 years.

9:25. The end of the first group of **seven weeks,** i.e. 49 years, brings **an anointed one, a prince.** The reference is probably to Cyrus, whom prophecy declared to have been anointed by God to effect the return of the exiles to Jerusalem (Isa. 45:1). Some, however, assuming intended parallelism with the anointed one of vs. 26, believe this reference is to the high priest Joshua (cf. e.g. Hag. 1:1; Zech. 3:1; 4:14), the first anointed after the Exile. A 2nd group of **sixty-two weeks,** i.e. 434 years, a **troubled time** of rebuilding the city, is inaccurately thought by the author to fit the interval between Cyrus or Joshua and the beginning of the final 7-year period, within which he is writing.

9:26. At the start of the 70th week an **anointed one,** i.e. a high priest, is **cut off.** The allusion is probably to the murder of Onias III ca. 3 years after he was deposed in favor of his hellenizing brother by Antiochus Epiphanes (II Macc. 3:1; 4:7-10, 33-35). There is evidence that Onias may instead have escaped to Egypt, but in either case a report of his murder spread among the Jews of Palestine. Soon afterward Antiochus invaded Jerusalem and seized treasures in the temple (I Macc. 1:20-24; II Macc. 5:11-21).

9:27. During this final **one week** of years Antiochus is successful in making a **strong covenant** with those of the Jews who are willing to compromise with his hellenization policy (cf. 11:30, 32; I Macc. 1:11-15). The climax of his persecution is the halting of **sacrifice** in the temple and the desecration of its altar (see above on 8:13, 14). The author dates this event at the midpoint of the final week of years and thus predicts that **half of the week** of years later the **decreed end** will occur. Though in practice the observance of a fallow year in Palestine would have to begin and end in the fall, it seems more probable that the author has counted his final sabbath year according to the spring calendar followed by the Jews at this time and thus looks forward to its end in the spring of 163. The occurrence of a sabbath year at this time is confirmed in I Macc. 6:49-54, which tells of food shortages suffered in 162 as stores ran out before the new crop came to maturity. The interval from the desecration on Dec. 16, 167, till the anticipated divine intervention in 163 might be calculated as 1,150 days (see above on 8:14) or less precisely as 3½ years (7:25; 12:7) or half a week of years.

D. A SYNOPSIS OF HISTORY AND ITS END (10:1–12:13)

Chs. 10–12 form a single whole; the ch. divisions are unfortunate. The section begins with a prologue in which an angel appears to Dan. (10:1–11:1) and ends with an epilogue which deals once again with the time of the end (12:5-13). In between is an outline of history leading up to the time of writing.

10:1-12. *The Setting of the Vision.* On the date see above on 1:17-21. This vision begins like that in ch. 8. The **word** is **true,** i.e. from God, yet it produces a **great conflict** in Dan.'s mind. He is again beside a **river** (cf. 8:2). His angelic visitor, presumably Gabriel (see above on 8:15-27), is again in the form of a **man** (cf. 8:16) yet with otherworldly qualities (cf. e.g. Jer. 10:9; Ezek. 1:27; Rev. 1:14-16). The visitation overwhelms Dan. (cf. Acts 9:7-9). His **deep sleep** (vs. 9) is typical of the ecstatic experience of vision (see above on 8:15-27), but the angel reassures him.

10:13-14. *The War in Heaven.* By the 2nd cent. B.C. the Jews had come to believe that each nation had its heavenly **prince,** i.e. guardian angel, their own being **Michael** (cf. vs. 21; 12:1; Exod. 23:20; see above on 8:15-27). The concept was no doubt rooted in Israel's ancient heritage (cf. Deut. 32:8-9), but much of the later development came from Persian influence. That there should be conflict among these heavenly beings against God, an idea found in the myth alluded to in Gen. 6:1-4; Isa. 14:12; and perhaps Isa. 24:21. Here then is a mythological presentation of the truth that God has given to his whole creation, not just to man, the freedom to be for or against him and his redemptive plan for the world. Thus the author here portrays some angels as opposed to the interpretation of God's truth to Dan.

10:15–11:1. *The Pain of Revelation.* Dan. finds that to be gripped by the truth of God is a painful thing (cf. Jer. 4:19). But another angel brings him the healing of the great Physician (cf. Exod. 15:26; Ps. 103:3). The angel too feels the urgency of God's calling; he has still to **fight** the guardian angels of both Persia and Greece, with only Michael to help him. This heavenly struggle has been going on since the Jewish exiles first came under the dominion of the Median Empire (see above on 5:30-31), but the author gives no hint of how long he supposed this to be.

11:2-39. *A Synopsis of Past Events.* Though exaggerating the length of the Persian Empire's sway (9:25), the author reduces the number of its rulers to only **three more kings** after Cyrus, during whose reign the revelation is purportedly being spoken (10:1). Presumably he supposed that those mentioned in the OT (by Ezra, Neh., Hag., Zech.) were the only ones, viz. Darius I, Ahasuerus (Xerxes I), and Artaxerxes (perhaps both I and II). That the **fourth,** i.e. the last of the 3, should be **richer** and should **stir up all against the kingdom of Greece** would historically fit Xerxes instead; but the author had very scanty sources of information about Persian history, and no doubt he made these assumptions about the supposed last king of the line to explain the counterattack of the **mighty king** (vs. 3), Alexander the Great. On the division of his kingdom (vs. 4) see above on 8:5-8.

11:5-9. In the sketching of *ca.* 150 years of history **king of the south** denotes successive rulers of the Ptolemaic dynasty of Egypt and **king of the north** those of the Seleucid dynasty of Syria. Judea lay as a prize between their 2 kingdoms. Vs. 5 describes the 2 founders of these lines, Ptolemy I and Seleucus I. The latter became for a time one of Ptolemy's **princes,** i.e. generals, when driven from his own domain by another of Alexander's successors. **After some years,** viz. *ca.* 250 (vs. 6), the Seleucid Antiochus II divorced Laodice to marry Berenice, daughter of Ptolemy II, in an effort to **make peace** (cf. 2:43). But Laodice contrived the assassination of Antiochus, Berenice, and their infant son; and for vengeance (vs. 7) a **branch from her roots,** Berenice's brother, Ptolemy III, made war on Laodice's son, Seleucus II. He captured the **fortress** of Seleucia, the port of the Seleucid capital Antioch, and seized great booty (vs. 8) but then had to **refrain from attacking** further because of trouble at home. Seleucus hit back (vs. 9) but was defeated and had to **return into his own land.**

11:10-19. Seleucus II was succeeded by 2 **sons** in turn, Seleucus III (227-223) and Antiochus III the Great (223-187), the latter esp. prone to **wage war.** After some successes he suffered a major defeat by Ptolemy IV in 217 (vss. 11-12) but later came back (vs. 13) against the forces of the infant Ptolemy V, whose regency was plagued with rebellions (vs. 14), which involved some of **your own people,** i.e. the Jews. Antiochus succeeded (vss. 15-16) in capturing a **well-fortified city,** Sidon, and winning other victories by which in 198 he wrested the **glorious land,** i.e. Palestine (see above on 8:9-14), from Egyptian control and incorporated it into the Seleucid Empire. Thereafter (vs. 17) he made **peace** with Egypt by marrying his **daughter** Cleopatra to Ptolemy V. Turning to the W (vs. 18), he attempted conquests in the **coastlands** of Asia Minor and Greece but met with a humiliating defeat (190) by the Roman **commander** Lucius Cornelius Scipio which cost him all his territory in these regions and also a huge tribute. He returned to **his own land** (vs. 19) and lost his life trying to loot a temple in Elam. He was succeeded (vs. 20) by his elder son, Seleucus IV (187-175), who sent an **exactor of tribute,** Heliodorus, to confiscate funds deposited in the Jerusalem temple (cf. II Macc. 3) and later fell victim to a conspiracy of this same Heliodorus.

11:21-24. The author regarded Antiochus the Great's younger son, Antiochus IV Epiphanes, as not only a **contemptible person** but a usurper (see above on 7:7-8). In his view Antiochus was not above contriving the assassination of a **prince of the covenant,** the high priest Onias III (see above on 9:26), whom he had previously deposed in order to make an alliance with Jewish leaders more willing to cooperate with his program of hellenization. Vs. 24 is ambiguous (see RSV footnote); it may refer to using **plunder** taken from Egypt to bribe his Jewish allies, or it may refer to taking plunder from wealthy Jews. At any rate his largesse to those he favored was unprecedented.

11:25-28. These vss. concern Antiochus' intervention in Egypt (cf. I Macc. 1:16-19), where rival factions were supporting the claims of 2 minor sons of his sister Cleopatra (see above on vss. 10-19). He took the side of Ptolemy VI Philometor, and the **two kings** conquered much of Egypt but were unable to dislodge the forces of Ptolemy VII Physcon in Alexandria. Returning with **great substance** (vs. 28), booty secured in Egypt, Antiochus stopped off in Jerusalem to put down a revolt by Onias' brother Jason, whom he had also deposed from the high priesthood (cf. I Macc. 1:20-24a; II Macc. 5:5-21). In this he acted **against the holy covenant,** esp. in entering the temple and seizing some of its treasures.

11:29-31. The name **Kittim** originally meant Cyprus (cf. e.g. Num. 24:24; Isa. 23:1) but came to be used of the Mediterranean coastlands generally and esp. of Greece (cf. e.g. I Macc. 1:1) and, as here and in some of the Dead Sea Scrolls, Rome. On a return campaign in Egypt Antiochus was halted by a Roman emissary, Popilius Laenas, and ordered to **withdraw.** No doubt he was indeed **enraged,** and perhaps his initiating his most drastic **action against the holy covenant** at this time was motivated by the frustration, as the author implies. On this action (vs. 31) see above on 8:10-12, 13.

11:32-39. Having outlined the chief events up to the time of writing, the author here summarizes the situation. Antiochus has been able to **seduce with flattery** a considerable number of Jews who are willing to **violate the covenant.** Yet there are still many **who know their God** and remain **firm** in their loyalty in the face of **sword** and **flame.** To these Judas Maccabeus and his guerrillas are only **a little help;** Israel's true help is in God alone. Meanwhile the **king** continues his blasphemy by claiming divinity for himself and repressing the worship of the traditional gods of his realm—including the **one beloved by women,** called alternatively Tammuz or Adonis—to promote that of a **foreign god,** probably meaning the Olympian Zeus.

11:40-45. *A Prediction of Coming Events.* At this point the author must leave the known past and present and launch into the unknown future. The failure of his guesses to accord with what actually happened next reveals the time of writing within narrow limits (see Intro.). He imagines that a **king of the south**—which Ptolemy he means is uncertain—will begin a new war and make Palestine the battlefield, though the Transjordan territories will be spared. Forgetting the Roman ban (see above on vss. 29-31), he supposes that Antiochus will win and despoil all NE Africa. Then an alarming report will call him back, so that he will be encamped in Palestine **between the sea and the glorious holy mountain,** i.e. W of Jerusalem, when God acts to bring the end. Historically Antiochus' death occurred at about the time the author predicted (see above on 9:27), but the place was in Persia (cf. I Macc. 6:1-16; II Macc. 9).

12:1-4. *The Resurrection.* The OT looks forward, not merely to a day of redemption for God's people, but to the consummation of his mighty plan for his whole creation in which individual men will take their place. This great end, being beyond space and time and the experience of men, can naturally be expressed only in symbols and pictures. The author's vision of what God's intervention will mean is not entirely clear, but he does perceive that God is able to bring good out of evil and so life out of death. The rabbis speak of the "birth pangs of the Messiah" to describe the **time of trouble** that will precede the dawn of the kingdom (cf. Isa. 66:7-9). Other interpreters have regarded vs. 1b as referring to the rise of the Antichrist and the outbreak of a great war before the final victory. That day will not dawn, however, just when we expect it. The end of one tyrant such as Antiochus Epiphanes does not preclude the rise of another. But **Michael,** whom God has set over Israel (see above on 10:13-14), is mediating his care for all those whose names he has written in his **book** of life.

12:2-4. The outcome of God's ultimate victory will be the resurrection of **many.** The **wise** who stood firm, did what they knew to be God's will (cf. 11:33), and actively created **righteousness** in other men will enter into the **brightness,** i.e. glory, of God. But some will awake to **contempt.** This word, translated "abhorrence" in the last line of Isa. (66: 24), means the opposite of life. In both cases the resurrection is probably of Israel only, in that it is to be effected by Michael, whose special charge is the covenant people. On **seal the book** see above on 8:15-27.

12:5-13. *The Time of the End.* In answer to his question of when the things he has just been told about will occur Dan. is told again the cryptic expression **a time, two times, and half a time** (cf. 7:25; see above on 9:27). His further question about what will happen then is turned away unanswered. But Dan. learns he is to rest quietly in his grave until **the end of the days** which is in the hands of God. To the original ending of the book have apparently been added later 2 notes that may be attempts to harmonize the period of suspension of sacrifices in 8:14 with the 3½ years denoted in vs. 7.

THE BOOK OF HOSEA

Charles F. Kraft

Hosea is the first in the Book of the 12 Prophets in the OT canon. It is the collection of writings of the 2nd great prophet of the 8th cent. B.C., probably a younger contemporary of Amos. It is unique among the prophetic books in its clear division into 2 unequal parts: the first (chs. 1-3) mostly biographical (ch. 1) or autobiographical (ch. 3), the 2nd (chs. 4-14) the collected sayings of the prophet with no evident biographical information whatever.

Authenticity. Most of the book is regarded as the authentic experiences or words of the prophet, whether recorded by himself or by disciples. While there is wide diversity of scholarly opinion on the meaning of the biographical and autobiographical sections and their relation to each other, the prevailing view is that they are accurate accounts of the prophet's personal family experiences. As Hos.'s message consists primarily of warning with only a hint of promise, some scholars doubt the authenticity of the apparently sudden reversals of doom to hope (e.g. 1:10-2:1; 2:14-23; 14:1-9). The oracles complimentary to Judah (e.g. 1:7; 11:12c) are also thought to be later additions. The Hebrew text has in many places been so badly preserved that it scarcely makes sense (see RSV footnotes). Hence the reader who compares English versions will note many differences in translation.

Hos.'s Life and Times. Surprisingly little is clearly revealed in the book about the prophet himself. His primary concern with the N kingdom of Israel indicates that his ministry took place there, and his frequent (36 times) use of Ephraim as a synonym for Israel suggests that he may have lived in the S part of the kingdom (see color map 8). The most obvious biographical fact is his marriage to Gomer and fathering of her children. There is no consensus of opinion among interpreters, however, on whether she was a priestess, i.e. cult prostitute, from a Baal fertility shrine or simply a young wife who turned out to be unfaithful. That Hos.'s marriage to Gomer and his love for the unnamed woman of ch. 3, whether Gomer or not, were very important for his message is indubitable. But it seems more likely that both were God-commanded demonstrations of his message—not unlike Isaiah's naming of his sons and marriage to the prophetess (Isa. 7:3; 8:1-4)—rather than that his message grew out of meditation on his family experiences.

According to 1:1 (see comment) Hos.'s prophetic ministry took place during the reign of Jeroboam II

(782/81-753). No doubt it began during the final years of that prosperous reign (see below on 1:4-5); but the background reflected in the oracles is rather the following turbulent period of political and social upheaval in Israel, when king after king gained the throne by assassinating his predecessor.

Jeroboam's son Zechariah reigned only 6 months (753-752) before being murdered by Shallum, who fell after one month to a 2nd usurper, Menahem (752-742/41). Soon Tiglath-pileser III (Pul, 745-727) renewed the Assyrian expansion to the W and attacked Israel. In danger from dissident elements in his kingdom, Menahem quickly came to terms with the invader and agreed to a huge tribute "that he might help him to confirm his hold of the royal power" (II Kings 15:19). With this help he was able to die in his bed, but his son Pekahiah after ruling ca. 2 years (742/41-740/39) was killed and replaced by Pekah (740/39-732/31; see "Chronology," pp. 1271-82). In alliance with Rezin of Syria, Pekah engaged in the Syro-Ephraimitic War (735-734) in an effort to depose Ahaz of Judah and gain Judean aid in opposing Assyria. At the invitation of Ahaz (cf. II Kings 16:5-7) Tiglath-pileser intervened and seized most of Galilee and Transjordan, exiling many of the inhabitants (cf. II Kings 15:29). With his blessing, and perhaps connivance, Hoshea slew Pekah and became the last ruler of the remainder of the N kingdom (732/31-723/22).

The Syro-Ephraimitic War seems to provide the background for 5:8-14 (see comment), but amid the many predictions of destruction and exile at the hands of Assyria there is none showing specific knowledge of the final catastrophe in 722 or of the 3-year siege of the capital by Tiglath-pileser's son Shalmaneser V which preceded it. Therefore it appears that Hos.'s career ended sometime between the Syro-Ephraimitic War and the beginning of the siege of Samaria and thus that his prophetic ministry should be dated ca. 755-730.

Hos.'s Message. In such a time a prime concern of Hos. was the failure of leadership. Priests and cult prophets were worse than useless, and the monarchy itself was an affront to the real kingship of Yahweh. But the basic problem was the cultural and religious sellout of the national life to Baalism, both by Baal worship and by paganization of the worship of Yahweh until the 2 were indistinguishable.

Hos. was profoundly concerned about the covenant history of God's people. He believed that the lack of basic faithfulness, covenant loyalty, and actual intimate knowledge of God was leading the nation to imminent destruction at the hands of Assyria. He saw in the impending calamity Yahweh's intention to take his people back to start over again from a new Egyptian slavery. Baalism is shortly to be smashed, and his people are to be disciplined by exile. Yet basically this act of wrath and judgment will result from Yahweh's suffering and redemptive love for his people. They are his bride of the exodus period (cf. 2:15), his once elect but now wayward son (cf. 11:1-4). His father love calls to repentance, rebirth, and resurrection to new life. Of the immediate response of Israel to Hos.'s new and unique revelation of the nature of God the Father there is no record, but we know that it profoundly influenced later prophets (cf. e.g. Jer. 1-2) as well as all subsequent cents.

For Further Study: W. R. Harper, *Amos and Hos.*, 1905. S. L. Brown, *Hos.*, 1932. H. W. Robinson, *The Cross of Hos.*, 1949. Norman Snaith, *Mercy and Sacrifice*, 1953. John Mauchline in *IB*, 1956. Gunnar Östborn, *Yahweh and Baal*, 1956. G. A. F. Knight, *Hos.*, 1960. J. D. Smart in *IDB*, 1962. J. M. Ward, *Hos.: A Theological Commentary*, 1966.

I. SUPERSCRIPTION (1:1)

This prose title for the book was supplied by an editor to introduce the accounts of the prophet's experiences and his poetic messages. The heading marks Hos. as a true prophet, for it is **the word of the LORD that came** to him, not his own words, which he must proclaim (cf. Joel 1:1; Mic. 1:1; Zeph. 1:1).

Hosea, in Hebrew the same as Hoshea (cf. Num. 13:8, 16; II Kings 15:30; 17:1-6; I Chr. 27:20), is a shortened form of Jehoshua, anglicized in the OT as Joshua and in the NT as Jesus, which means "Yahweh saves" (cf. Matt. 1:21). Of Hos.'s father, **Beeri** ("well"), nothing further is known.

Perhaps because the editor was a Judean he dates Hos.'s ministry first by the Judean kings **Uzziah, Jotham, Ahaz,** and **Hezekiah** (cf. Isa. 1:1; see "Chronology," pp. 1271-82). Of the kings of Israel, where Hos.'s ministry was primarily directed, he mentions only **Jeroboam** II. Though Hos. probably began to prophesy during Jeroboam's reign (see below on vss. 4-5) the background of most of his message is obviously not the prosperity of that reign, which is reflected in the oracles of Amos, but the following descent toward disaster (see Intro.).

II. GOD'S WORD THROUGH HOS.'S FAMILY EXPERIENCE (1:2-3:5)

In this section the word of Yahweh is declared through dramatic accounts of the prophet's family life—one told in the 3rd person (ch. 1), another in the first person (ch. 3). Interpreters' judgments vary widely on the meaning and relation of these accounts, on the identity of the unnamed woman in the 2nd, on the chronological order of the incidents described, on the legitimacy of the 2nd and 3rd children, on whether the experiences are actual or allegorical, and on the authenticity of the hopeful passages. Many of these problems are unsolved and perhaps unsolvable.

The main theme is Israel's unfaithfulness to her God and what he proposes to do about it. This theme is presented in 3 successive family metaphors. The first and 3rd are doubtless parables acted out by the prophet in his family life at God's command. The 2nd may be an allegory based on the figure which seems to underlie all 3, viz. that idolatrous and apostate Israel has forsaken her true God to join in the sexual fertility rites of the nature god Baal. She has done so through appalling ignorance and must be punished, disciplined, reeducated, and redeemed. Thus there are 3 family analogies: (*a*) God's people are children of harlotry (1:2-2:1); (*b*) Israel is a mother of harlotry (2:2-23); (*c*) despite all this God loves Israel and will reeducate her through discipline (3:1-5).

A. THE CHILDREN OF HARLOTRY (1:2-2:1)

When the LORD first spoke through Hosea may lit. be translated "the beginning of the word of Yahweh through Hosea." This is apparently a title for the account of Hos.'s wife and children in vss. 2-9. **The LORD said** introduces each of the 4 stages in the narrative: God's command to Hos. to marry (vs. 2) and God's naming of the 3 children (vss. 4, 6, 9). Hos. obeys the command and the children are born. Presumably all this occupies *ca.* 6-9 years, as ordinarily a child was **weaned** (vs. 8) at the age of perhaps 2 or 3 (cf. II Macc. 7:27).

1:2b. God's Command. Traditional interpretations of Hos.'s experience have been strongly influenced both by W marriage ideals and customs and by the desire for an appropriate analogy between the relation of Hos. to Gomer and that of Yahweh to Israel. Thus, except for the minority view that the account is only allegorical, most commentators through the cents. have understood **wife of harlotry** to mean that Gomer either had or developed harlotrous tendencies unsuspected by the young prophet when he fell in love with her. As a result of his bitter experience and the discovery that he still loved her (cf. 3:1), it has been supposed, Hos. came to realize that his own human love was but dimly comparable to that of God for his faithless bride Israel (cf. Jer. 2:2-8, 32-37).

The love of God for his wayward people is an essential message of Hos., which is later expressed in such terms (3:1) and is also exemplified by father-son love (11:1-9). But the clearly stated point of this opening biographical narrative is to demonstrate that **the land commits great harlotry by forsaking the LORD.** It is to convey this meaning that God commands the marriage and, even more important, the naming of the children. The passage is not primarily an account of Hos.'s family experience; rather it is God's speaking **through Hosea.** Hence Hos.'s marriage to Gomer is not a love marriage. In the custom of the ancient Near East it is an arranged marriage, and God does the arranging.

1:3. The Wife. The name **Gomer** may mean "complete" or "perfection." At any rate **Diblaim** means "lumps" of figs or raisins. Though no point is made of the meaning, as is done with the names of the children, the father's name may connect Gomer with the raisin cakes which were part of the food in the Baal fertility rites (cf. 3:1).

God's demand on the prophet is to demonstrate

Israel's **harlotry.** Surely the analogy here is with the Canaanite theology in which the dying-and-rising fertility god Baal was seen as essentially the husband of mother earth. Popular mourning rites marked the god's death and descent into the underworld at the onset of the summer dry season, and his return from the underworld and marriage with the earth goddess were celebrated when vegetation revived with the autumnal rains. "Cult prostitutes," lit. "holy women" (cf. 4:14), were the celebrants; and presumably Gomer was one of these sacred persons dedicated to magical assistance in the rites providing "the grain, the wine, and the oil" (2:8) for her people.

Hos. must proclaim that true fertility comes, not from the marriage of Baal with mother earth, but from the rain-bringing God of Israel, whom Elijah knew (cf. I Kings 18:1, 41-45). He therefore feels commanded, whether he likes it or not, to marry one of these supposedly holy cult women. In terming her a **wife of harlotry** he brands this popular holiness of Baalism as no more than common prostitution (cf. 4:14, where by synonymous parallelism he equates "harlots" and "cult prostitutes"). By this act Hos. may be declaring Gomer's marriage and motherhood to be superior to the supposedly higher calling of a cult priestess.

1:4-9. The Children. The same idea is probably reinforced in the names of the 3 children, which seem to be parodies on names of Baal cult children. It has been suggested that the children were not simply walking prophetic messages but may have appeared in some dramatic representation before the public at the sanctuary where their mother had been employed. Their names seem to refer in climactic order to the ruling dynasty, the nation as a state, and finally the whole people.

1:4-5. The name **Jezreel** may have a double meaning. Historically it announces the end of the dynasty begun by the bloody purge of **Jehu,** who in 841 toppled the Omri dynasty by murdering Israel's King Joram and Judah's King Ahaziah near Jezreel (II Kings 9:14-29). Jehu's subsequent massacre of the Baal prophets (II Kings 10:18-29), though done in the name of Yahweh, apparently increased his guilt in the eyes of Hos. God will punish this evil dynasty by breaking the **bow,** i.e. power, **of Israel,** evident in Hos.'s day in the reign of Jeroboam II, Jehu's great-grandson. The prediction was fulfilled in 752 when Jehu's dynasty was ended by the murder of Jeroboam's son Zechariah at the hand of the usurper Shallum (II Kings 15:10).

Jezreel means "El sows." El, originally the name of the high god of the Canaanite pantheon, became the Semitic word for "god," meaning "power." Thus presumably a most appropriate name for a child born to a Canaanite fertility-rite priestess would be Jezreel—suggesting that the god sows seed, fertility, and agricultural prosperity. But by a reversal Hos. may mean to say that God sows destruction for an evil dynasty.

1:6. The name of the daughter **Not pitied** declares that God will no longer **forgive** the **house** of Israel, i.e. the Israelite nation state. The "not" in this name and that of the 3rd child (vs. 9) may be a grim pun on cult children's names. The 2 letters of the Hebrew

word "not" are the reverse of those in "El" or "God." Hence instead of the cult name "God pities" the daughter is called "Not pitied" or "Not loved"— an expression of the rejection of motherly compassion, for the Hebrew word "pitied" is from the same root as "womb." God's patience is at an end (cf. Amos 7:1-9; 8:1-3); the death of the nation is at hand.

1:7. Apparently some later Judean editor added this note concerning God's protection of the S kingdom. Its point may be that Judah escaped the fate of Israel in 722, or perhaps it alludes to the deliverance of Jerusalem from Sennacherib's siege in 701.

1:8-9. The cult name which Hosea may be parodying by **Not my people** (see above on vs. 6) presumably would be "God with me" or "God of my people." The shocking announcement in this name that the covenant bond between God and his people is broken means the severing of sacred ties going back to the days of Abraham.

1:10-2:1. The Children Renamed. Perhaps it was the shock of those awful words of divine repudiation (1:6, 9) that brought forth these immediately following words of hope, as well as the later reversal of "Not my people" to "You are my people" (2:23; cf. I Pet. 2:10). Scholarly opinion is divided on whether Hos. himself promised this restoration and renewal. The prediction that **Judah** and **Israel** will be **gathered together** under **one head** and **go up from the land** sounds like an exilic or postexilic promise of the reunion of the scattered Jews under a messianic ruler who will bring them to Jerusalem from the farthest corners of the earth (cf. e.g. Isa. 2:2-4; 11:11-13; Jer. 3:18; Ezek. 37:21-22). This **day of Jezreel** will be a triumphant reversal of the previously predicted day of doom (1:4-5). God will sow, not seeds of destruction, but seeds of posterity; for the promises of numberless descendants of Abraham and Jacob (cf. Gen. 15:5; 22:17; 32:12) will be fulfilled. They will not be devotees of a dying-and-rising fertility deity but will be **sons of the living God.**

2:1. In the exuberance of the hour Not pitied will be commanded to call her brother **My people** instead of Not my people, and he will reciprocate by renaming her **She has obtained pity.** The Hebrew text simply removes the negative signs to form the new names. Its reading "brothers" and "sisters" (see RSV footnotes), if correct, probably recognizes the fact that the children are symbols of the whole people. Thus in his infinite mercy God will reclaim as his own beloved people those who through unfaithfulness have lost all claim to being his.

B. The Mother of Harlotry (2:2-23)

In the language of the law court Hos. now summarizes the case against faithless Israel as Yahweh's ignorant wife, the mother of **children of harlotry.** The imaginary court hearing opens with Yahweh's request to the children to **plead with your mother** and get her to reform before he carries out his threatened action. The action he will take is expressed in 3 subsequent announcements, each beginning **Therefore** (vss. 6, 9, 14).

2:2-5. The Indictment of Israel. In the language of the formula for divorce Yahweh declares: **She is not my wife**—i.e. the marriage bond is broken. Possibly the woman is even wearing the garb and ornaments of the cult prostitute (cf. vs. 13; Gen. 38:13-19). **Harlotry** and **adultery** are Hos.'s figurative terms for false worship, the sexual rites of the Baal cult. According to the law codes the penalty for adultery was death (cf. Lev. 20:10; Deut. 22:22). Here the penalty is nakedness, being stripped of the clothing furnished by her former husband (cf. Exod. 21:10; Ezek. 16:37-39). Her crime is neither adultery nor harlotry in the ordinary sense but ritual prostitution. Hence with consummate irony Hos. declares that these rites which should produce fertile fields will bring only the nakedness of a desert. The **children** must share the divine condemnation as the deluded mother continues to run after her **lovers,** the local Baal gods who she believes provide her food and clothing.

2:6-8. Separation. Yahweh's first announced action will be to protect the mother from her own willful ways. By fencing her in behind a hedge of **thorns** and a **wall** he will stop her cultic search for false gods so that she may come to her senses and realize that life with her **first husband,** i.e. Yahweh, was preferable. The pathos of the situation is Israel's theological ignorance. She does not recognize that it is not the local Baals, but Yahweh, the covenant God of her fathers and her history, who provides both the blessings of the good earth in her own land —**the grain, the wine, and the** olive oil—and the imported **silver and gold** (cf. Gen. 1:29-30; Deut. 7:13).

2:9-13. Deprivation. Yahweh's 2nd announced action will be to cause complete crop failure so that the Baal gods will be proved impotent, for there will not even be enough produce to carry on the customary lavish Baal rituals and festivals. There will be no clothing (vs. 10), no joyous Israelite festivals (vs. 11; cf. Isa. 1:12-14; Amos 5:21-23; 8:10), and no Baal orgies with **incense** and **jewelry** and sexual license (vs. 13). The place of the **vines** and **fig trees** (vs. 12) which were her wages, supposedly given her by her Baal **lovers,** will become a devastated jungle.

2:14-15. A New Courtship. The 3rd of Yahweh's announced actions will complete the reeducation of wayward mother Israel. He will return her to the place of their first honeymoon and woo her back to himself. As at the Exodus (cf. Exod. 19:2; Jer. 2:2-3; Ezek. 20:33-38) he will **allure her . . . into the wilderness** and **speak tenderly to her,** lit. "speak to her heart." The **Valley of Achor,** lit. "trouble," will no longer be a place of setback (cf. Josh. 7:24-26) but will become a **door of hope.**

2:16-23. A New Betrothal. The glorious renewal is now set forth in glowing terms beginning with **in that day** (vss. 16, 21). Whether these expectations come from Hos. himself or from a disciple, they express a true new covenant relation between God and his people (cf. Jer. 31:31-34). Yahweh will truly be Israel's **husband,** not her **Baal,** i.e. "owner" or "master." Indeed the very word "Baal" will no longer be **mentioned** because of its pagan associations.

2:18-20. There will be a universal **covenant** of peace with all creatures of the world, from wild animals to warring nations (cf. Isa. 11:6-9; Ezek. 34:25-31). The new covenant of betrothal will be eternal, and God offers as bride-price or dowry: **righteous-**

ness, right action in relation to him; **justice,** right action in relation to fellow men; **steadfast love,** loyal covenant devotion; **mercy,** motherlike compassion; and **faithfulness,** steady permanence. Thus will his people **know,** i.e. intimately experience, their God.

2:21-23. This new covenant will be evident in the real **Jezreel,** i.e. "God sows" (see above on 1:4-5)—the true fertility cycle of God's rain, responding crops, and abounding harvest. The negative names will become affirmative, and **my people** will in adoration declare: **My God.**

C. The Wife of Harlotry Loved and Reeducated (3:1-5)

The theme of this autobiographical story of Hos.'s marriage is God's love for his people, his discipline of them, and its result. As in the opening account, the action is initiated by God, who commands Hos. to **love** a most unlovable woman, just as God loves his most unlovely people. Traditional interpretation has assumed that this woman is Gomer and that the story is a sequel to the previous narrative. She has left Hos. and become a cheap **adulteress.** He comes upon her being sold as a slave and buys her but refuses marital relations. This may be the meaning. On the other hand the story may recount a 2nd marriage. In either case the point is the same: Hos.'s marriage is to demonstrate God's love and its disciplining and redeeming nature.

3:1-2. In the light of the possible identification of Gomer as a cult prostitute (see above on 1:3) and the allegory of Israel as an ignorant devotee deludedly worshiping her Baal lovers instead of her first husband Yahweh (ch. 2) it may be that this woman is also a Baal cult priestess, described figuratively as **beloved of a paramour** and an **adulteress** (cf. 2:2; 4:14). The **cakes of raisins** were the cult food of worshipers of Baal idols (see above on 1:3). The price for the woman (vs. 2) is perhaps equal to the value of a slave specified in Exod. 21:32; if so, it is paid half in **silver,** half in **barley** (see pp. 1283-85). Hos. pays it either as a bride-price or as the cost of releasing a sacred prostitute from her cult obligations.

3:3-5. The basic import of the story is the necessity and the cost of redemptive love. God's prophet must love one whom his natural inclination might be to abhor—not for erotic indulgence but for discipline. It has been suggested that **many days** refers to the time required to take away the supposed sanctity of the woman's profession as cult priestess. By analogy Israel in exile will be deprived of political leadership and the customary ceremonial accouterments. **Prince** refers, not to a king's son, but to any person with governmental authority (cf. e.g. 5:10; 7:3-5). A **pillar** was a large stone set upright as a memorial or as a Canaanite fertility symbol (cf. e.g. Gen. 28:18-22; 31:45; 35:20; Exod. 34:13; Deut. 7:5). The word **ephod** seems to have been used both for a priestly garment (cf. e.g. Exod. 28; I Sam. 22:18; II Sam. 6:14) and an image of some kind (cf. e.g. Judg. 8:27; 17:5; I Sam. 21:9). **Teraphim** were household gods (cf. e.g. Gen. 31:19, 34-35; Judg. 17:5; I Sam. 19:13, 16).

Presumably Hosea's vow to remain physically faithful to his wife during the **many days** of her discipline implies a promise of Yahweh that he will not forsake Israel and adopt another people during their discipline of exile. And the outcome will be worth all the effort: Israel will return to her God in **fear,** i.e. trembling awe, before his amazing and undeserved **goodness.**

III. God's Word Through Hos.'s Oracles (4:1–14:8)

The bulk of the book is a series of originally spoken oracles which were probably collected and written down by a disciple. Some scholars hold that they circulated orally for many years before being put into written form. There is little discernible organization; but perhaps the following grouping into sections, in part on the basis of form as indicated by the opening words of series and in part on the basis of similarity of content, may be reasonable.

A. Corrupt Leaders, Corrupt People (4:1–19)

4:1-3. *Yahweh's Controversy with Israel.* The **word of the LORD** which Hos. speaks begins in the language of the law court with God's direct indictment, stating his case against all his people (cf. Isa. 3:13; Jer. 2:9; Mic. 1:2; 6:2). The historical background is doubtless that turbulent period of rapid political and social decline which followed the reign of Jeroboam II in Israel (see Intro.). But in Hos.'s view the problem is primarily theological. The language is that of covenant relationship with God, even though the word "covenant" is used only twice in the oracles (6:7; 8:1). There is no **faithfulness,** i.e. no firm stability in keeping the covenant. There is no **kindness,** lit. "loyal covenant love," i.e. no response to God's outpouring love through the covenant. There is no **knowledge of God,** i.e. no real understanding of the divine—perhaps referring to the nature of deity in general, in a wider sense than "knowledge of Yahweh," Israel's historically experienced covenant deity (cf. 2:20; 6:6; 10:12).

4:2-3. This theological failure in relationship to God results in moral chaos, failure in the area of human relations. Vs. 2a may be a specific allusion to the 10 Commandments as the summary of Israel's obligations under the covenant (cf. Exod. 20:13-16), though commandments against the sins mentioned would be basic in any moral code. Man's moral failure even affects nature: ironically **the land mourns** rather than revives under the sinful nature-cult practices, which though aimed at giving nature life actually produce death (cf. Amos 1:2; 8:8).

4:4-9. *Corrupt Religious Leaders.* The blame for Israel's corrupt state rests on the people's religious leaders. The **priest,** who **by day** should declare God's **law,** i.e. his instruction handed down from Moses' day, has **forgotten** (cf. Mal. 2:1-9). The cult **prophet,** who should have visions **by night,** is evidently blind. So God will **destroy** the priestly line, if not the whole family of Israel. On **mother** (vs. 5c) and **children** (vs. 6e) cf. 2:2-4. The **glory** of being God's priests will become **shame** because they are **greedy** profiteers from the sacrificial system. The special privilege of priesthood brings no divine favors, no rescue from punishment which the **people** face.

4:10-19. *The Absurdity of Baal Worship.* The whole harlotrous system of Baal fertility rites is utterly ineffectual as well as degrading. Its purpose is to provide fertility for human beings, flocks, and crops; but though the people **play the harlot,** i.e. carry on the sexual fertility acts at the shrine, they do not **multiply.** The accompanying drunken revelry, the tree worship and divination by dead wooden rods, and the sensual sacrifices in the secrecy of shady groves— all are meaningless magical rites.

4:13e-14. Despite woman's usual secondary place in ancient society, there will be no double standard, for the **men** are responsible for the shame of cult prostitution. It is they who require their **daughters** to become **cult prostitutes,** lit. "holy women," at the shrines, to be used by male worshipers to provide fertility (see above on 1:3). This deluded practice is not holiness but harlotry, and **a people without understanding shall come to ruin.**

4:15-16. Let **Judah** avoid the false swearing of Israel's known sanctuaries at **Gilgal** (cf. 9:15; 12:11) and **Beth-aven**—"house of evil," a sarcastic substitute for Bethel, "house of God" (cf. 5:8; 10:5; Amos 4:4; 5:5; see color map 8). God can hardly treat that **stubborn heifer** Israel as though she were a docile **lamb.**

4:17-19. Israel—here for the first time called **Ephraim,** Hos.'s affectionate term for the people of the N kingdom (see Intro.)—may as well be left undisturbed in her hopeless idolatry. But these harlotrous **drunkards** will be truly ashamed when God's **wind** of destruction blows.

B. Israel's Absent God (5:1-7)

5:1-2. *Summons to Officials.* God calls to task 3 groups of leaders—the **priests;** the **house of Israel,** i.e. probably government officials; and the royal **house**—for having led the people astray; and he promises **chastisement.** Three widely separated cult centers are named as places where the leaders have trapped the people: **Mizpah,** the shrine in Gilead associated with Jacob and Jephthah (cf. Gen 31:49; Judg. 11:11), or possibly the Benjaminite town (cf. I Sam. 7:5-6; see comment on Jer. 40:1-6) if it belonged to Israel at this time; Mt. **Tabor** in S Galilee (cf. Deut. 33:19; see color map 1); and **Shittim** NE of the Jordan mouth, where their fathers sinned with Baal of Peor (cf. Num. 25:1-5; see color map 5).

5:3-7. *Israel's Harlotry.* Though God knows his people, their **spirit of harlotry** prevents their knowing him. Their **deeds** of Baal worship (vs. 4) have so corrupted them that they have lost the power of repentance, the ability to **return to their God.** Their human **pride** (vs. 5) is their own condemnation. When, as in the frenzied ritual searching for the dead Baal god, they come with sacrifices to **seek the LORD** (vs. 6) they will find that he is deliberately absent (cf. Amos 8:11-12; Mic. 3:4). In their Baal worship they give birth to **alien children** (vs. 7), the offspring of sexual cult rites, who do not know their sacred covenantal heritage. Therefore the expected joy of the **new moon** festival will become a day of destruction (cf. Amos 5:18-20; 8:10).

C. Israel's Deathly Sickness (5:8–7:16)

Israel's political, social, and spiritual disease is deplored in a seemingly conglomerate series of oracles.

5:8-14. War's Alarm. The occasion for sounding the alarm (on **horn** and **trumpet** see comment on Ps. 98:4-9) is apparently the Syro-Ephraimitic War of 735-734, when Rezin of Syria and Pekah of Israel unsuccessfully attempted by military power to force Judah into an alliance against the returning might of Assyria (cf. II Kings 15:27-30; 16:5-9; Isa. 7:1-17; see Intro.). Vs. 8 seems to allude to a counterattack by Judean forces, moving N from Jerusalem past the nearby strongholds of **Gibeah** and **Ramah** in their own territory of **Benjamin** (see color map 8) into the Israelite territory at Bethel, here again sarcastically called **Beth-aven** (see above on 4:15-16).

5:9-14. The **princes of Judah** (vs. 10; see above on 3:3-5) are violating the Israelite border (see comment on Deut. 19:14). But, says Hos., their call for the Assyrian Tiglath-pileser III to attack the N kingdom and thereby rescue them from the immediate crisis is folly, for Ephraim and Judah alike will suffer crushing defeat by Assyria (vss. 9, 11-12, 14; cf. Isa. 7:18-23; 8:5-8). Indeed (vs. 13) neither the sending of tribute to the **great king,** i.e. Tiglath-pileser according to his Assyrian title, by Ahaz of Judah (cf. II Kings 16:8-10)—assuming that, as the parallelism suggests, "Judah" was originally included as subject in vs. 13*d*—nor a renewal of the alliance with Assyria which Menahem of Israel made (vs. 13*c*; see Intro.) can be a **cure.** For the sickness is much deeper than mere human warfare. It is God's judgment now eating away the social fabric like **moth** and **dry rot** (vs. 12) and soon to bring sudden destruction **like a lion** (vs. 14; cf. 13:7-8).

5:15-6:6. Complacency and Instability. Yahweh now vows that he will return to his **place,** probably his heavenly temple, until his people repent (5:15). The insertion here of **saying,** which is not in the Hebrew, gives the misleading impression that Yahweh goes on to quote the expression of repentance he desires. Instead Hos. is portraying with subtle irony the people's presumptuous confessional liturgy (6:1-3). It may be based on figures of speech from the dying-and-rising-god cult (see above on 1:3). In some forms of the myth Baal was **torn** as by wild beasts when with the dry summer season he suffered death and went into the underworld, and he was revived by the **showers** of Nov.-Dec. and completely restored to life by the crop-maturing **spring rains** of Apr. **After two days . . . on the third day** (cf. Prov. 30:15-31; Amos 1:3-2:6) may be a way of saying "after only a short time"—that the repentance need not be real, for God's punishment will soon be over. Or possibly it expresses a customary expectation that renewal will take place on the 3rd day of a sacred occasion (cf. Exod. 3:18; 19:11; II Kings 20:5).

6:4-5. Yahweh's response to the people's confession sounds like utter exasperation. His people are as unstable as the mist driven away by the rising sun. The prophets' lethal word of **judgment,** as obvious as **light,** may hammer to pieces those who resist; as God's word it has a power all its own. Its purpose, however, is not to destroy but to redeem.

6:6. This is Hos.'s keynote verse (cf. 2:19-20; 4:1, 6; Matt. 9:13; 12:7). God longs to find in his people **steadfast love,** i.e. constantly loyal devotion responding to his own outpoured covenant love, and true **knowledge of God,** i.e. intimate experience of com-

munion with him, not mere information about him. Whether Hos. believed the sacrificial system to be totally evil or simply irrelevant is debatable (cf. I Sam. 15:22; Isa. 1:11-17; Amos 5:21-24; Mic. 6:6-8), but his emphasis on the prime importance of total inner commitment to God in understanding and loyal obedience to his will is clear.

6:7-7:7. Examples of Israel's Sins. The tragedy of Israel is that instead of steadfast love and the knowledge of God her record shows only a catalog of crimes. Perhaps with a deliberate play on words the list begins with the note that **at Adam,** the place where the waters of the Jordan were dammed up so that their forefathers could cross over (Josh. 3:9-17), they have faithlessly **transgressed,** lit. "crossed over" **the covenant** made at Mt. Sinai (cf. Exod. 24:3-8; Deut. 5:1-3)—no doubt by a recent scandal otherwise unrecorded. The allusion in 6:8 may be to Pekah's seizing the throne of Israel by his treacherous conspiracy with 50 Gileadites to assassinate King Pekahiah in 740/39 (II Kings 15:25). That bands of priests **murder on the way to Shechem,** famous for its ancient temple of Baal-berith but also ironically a city of refuge (6:9; cf. Josh. 20:7, 9; 21:21; Judg. 9:4-6), may be figurative for religious murder in the Baal cult rites (cf. 13:1) or may be an allusion to a contemporary incident.

6:10-7:2. The utter depravity of the **harlotry** of Baalism can result only in a **harvest** of evil. When God tries to **heal** Israel the cancerous illness of her society becomes evident in open thievery and banditry—probably a reflection of the sad deterioration of social conditions in the last days of the N kingdom. Past **evil works** cannot be wiped out; they are inevitably **before God's face.**

7:3-7. Comparable to evil social conditions is the pattern of debauchery and intrigue in the palace (on **princes** see above on 3:3-5). Inflamed by passion, conspirators **devour their rulers** (vs. 7)—a reference to the series of assassinations and dynastic changes in Israel's last 3 decades (see Intro.). During the drunken revelries at each coronation festival plotters deceive the new ruler (vss. 5-6) until **all their kings have fallen,** for **none of them calls upon** Yahweh (vs. 7). The **baker** banks the embers of his **oven** while he prepares the **dough** (vs. 4); then **in the morning** he builds up the **fire** again red hot (vs. 6). There is no security in the palace, for **all** the plotters are **hot as an oven.**

7:8-12. Foreign Intrigues. Internal conditions in Israel are bad enough, but the attempts at international dealings prove her to be a half-baked **cake,** burned on one side and sticky dough on the other. Alien alliances weaken the nation to senility by draining its resources—perhaps a reference to the heavy tribute paid to Assyria. Yet Israel does not recognize her sad condition, and **pride** prevents her **return** to her one source of strength. Torn internally by 2 parties, one pro-Egyptian, the other pro-Assyrian, she will continue to flit between the 2 foreign powers until Yahweh snares her in his **net.**

7:13-16. Rebellion Against God. Yahweh desires to redeem his people but cannot do so when they **cry** only in cult ritual, lacerating themselves in the wailing rites for the dead god of vegetation (cf. Deut. 14:1; I Kings 18:26-28). They treacherously appear to be warriors for Yahweh, who **trained** them, but their unfaithfulness will bring them again into Egyptian slavery. Interpreters differ on whether **Egypt** in this and other passages (esp. 8:13; 9:3; 11:5) should be understood lit. as a threat to Israel or figuratively as a symbol of foreign domination. In Hos.'s day Egypt was militarily at low ebb; but before Tiglath-pileser's W campaigns (see Intro.) she may have seemed the major power on the horizon, and thereafter apparently some Israelites viewed her as the counterbalance to Assyrian might (cf. vs. 11; II Kings 17:4).

D. National Death Ahead (8:1-14)

8:1-3. *A Call to Arms.* The **trumpet** (see comment on Ps. 81:1-5*b*) calling to battle is again sounded, because the **vulture,** i.e. Assyria, is wheeling above Yahweh's **house**—referring perhaps to the Bethel sanctuary but more probably to Israel as his earthly dwelling place. Though the people delude themselves by their ritual cries to God and claim intimate knowledge of him (vs. 2) they really have violated his **covenant** and rebelled against his **law** (vs. 1). Hence the divine sentence is death (vs. 3).

8:4-6. *Causes of National Death.* The nation is doomed for 2 reasons: the selection of rulers without divine approval (cf. 7:3-7; see Intro.) and idolatry. The **calf of Samaria** (vss. 5-6) refers to a bull image such as Jeroboam I set up at Bethel and Dan, to create religious centers for the new N kingdom as rivals to the Jerusalem temple (I Kings 12:26-33). Doubtless the original intent was not apostasy; for the image was probably understood to be a pedestal on which Yahweh was invisibly enthroned (see comment on I Kings 6:23-28). But long since the days of Jeroboam I the Canaanite Baal cult with its sexual fertility worship had baalized the original Yahwism —hence Hos.'s vehement attacks on these manmade constructions (cf. 10:5-6; 13:2).

8:7-10. *The Approaching Whirlwind.* The quotation of a familiar proverb underlines the disastrous result of sowing mere **wind,** i.e. the nothingness of futile idolatry. Such seed brings forth sterile **grain** with no wheat in the **heads.** By her idolatry, which is foreign in origin and thus indicates no trust in her own God, Israel is already **swallowed up** and is **among the nations as a useless vessel.** A **wild ass**—a pun on the name **Ephraim** in the Hebrew—**wandering alone,** contrary to the natural herd instinct, she is forsaken by her **hired lovers,** both Baal consorts and international allies. The death of the nation will soon end the rapid succession of accessions to the throne.

8:11-14. *Cult Without Obedience.* The people **love sacrifice;** they have **multiplied altars** in deluded devotion. But God's teaching—perhaps known in written form at this time in such collections of laws as the Covenant Code (Exod. 20:23–23:19), the Ritual Decalogue (Exod. 34:17-28), and the 10 Commandments (Exod. 20:1-17; Deut. 5:6-21)—they regard as a **strange thing.** A true colleague of his contemporary Amos, in language as well as in message, Hos. pronounces judgment on both iniquitous concentration on the sacrificial system and dependence on material strongholds (cf. Amos 1:4, 7, 10, 12, 14; 2:2, 5; 5:21-24). But, unlike Amos, he predicts at least figurative return to Egyptian slavery as Israel's penalty for forgetting **his Maker** (see above on 7:13-16).

E. Fertility's Failure (9:1–10:15)

The appeal to **rejoice not . . . like the peoples** (9:1) perhaps marks the beginning of a new series of oracles delivered at the autumn harvest festival at Bethel (cf. Exod. 23:16; 34:22). If so, this section of the book may picture most clearly Hos.'s public encounter as he defines the role and the plight of the prophet (9:7-8) and cries out to God for recompense to his faithless children (9:14).

9:1-7c. *The Food of Exile.* Paganized Israel is rejoicing in the ritual Baal marriage rites **upon all threshing floors** (vs. 1). These sexual ceremonies, for which the worshiper must pay the **harlot's hire,** i.e. the fee to the cult prostitute for the privilege of baalized worship with her, are not only a form of **forsaking** Yahweh. Expected to produce crop renewal for the new season, they utterly fail to provide grain and wine (vs. 2). God's punishment will be exile to **Egypt** or **Assyria** (see above on 7:13-16) to live on a starvation diet. The food, like that ceremonially contaminated by a death in the house (cf. Num. 19:14-15; Deut. 26:14), will be **unclean** because devoted to a foreign god (vs. 4; cf. Amos 7:17). With such food Israel cannot keep an **appointed festival** of Yahweh (cf. 2:11) when away in Assyria or in Egypt at the burial ground of the pyramids near **Memphis,** capital of Lower Egypt. Her own land, where once there were jewelry of **silver** and bedouin **tents,** will become a brier patch; for she will **know** the terrible **days** of God's **recompense.**

9:7d-9. *The Prophet's Role.* Though vss. 7*de* may mean that other prophets are **mad** (cf. 4:5), more likely Hos. is quoting the disparaging words of his hearers. They declare him to be crazed (cf. Isa. 28:7-13) because their **iniquity,** i.e. guilt, drives them to such **hatred.** The true prophet, however, filled with God's **spirit** (cf. Isa. 11:2; 61:1; Ezek. 2:2; Mic. 3:8), is a **watchman** over the **people of . . . God** (cf. Ezek 3:16-17; 33:1-20; Hab. 2:1). But he is despised in the **house of his God** when he declares his unpopular word—possibly an allusion to the banishment of Amos (Amos 7:10-13), though Hos. himself no doubt experienced similar rejection. Sinful Israel is as corrupt as the depraved men of the Benjaminite city of **Gibeah** (cf. 10:9; see color map 8), who abused the Levite's concubine until she died (Judg. 19:16-30). From the days of Saul's establishment of his capital there (I Sam. 10:17-26) they have rejected God's kingship by setting up their own manmade kings one after another.

9:10-17. *Loss of Posterity.* This oracle is probably a continuation of Hos.'s words at the harvest festival (see above on 9:1–10:15).

9:10. What more delightful sight to the weary traveler in the desert than an oasis with ripe **grapes,** or to a patient farmer than the **first fruit on the fig tree** (cf. 2:14-15; 10:1; 13:5). But God's delight at his discovery of Israel came to a disillusioned end when he discovered that the **fathers** who had covenanted to be his alone had **consecrated themselves to Baal.** The story of their yielding to the nature cult at Baalpeor (Num. 25:1-5) was well known (cf. 5:2) and illustrated that one becomes what he loves.

9:11-14. The **glory** that will **fly away** is every Israelite's pride in an ongoing family. God will shut up the wombs (vs. 11) and famine, pestilence, and war will destroy the nation's sons (vss. 12-13). Like Jeremiah, Hos. starts to pray for his people (vs. 14), but his prayer ends in the bitter plea that miscarriages will prove to them that their dependence on Baal is folly.

9:15-17. From the time of their entrance into the W Jordan territory at **Gilgal** (vs. 15; cf. 4:15; 12:11; Josh. 4; Amos 4:4; 5:5) the people's conduct has merited God's hatred. He will now **slay their beloved children**—perhaps a reference to the inevitable toll of war (vs. 16). Driven like a faithless wife out of God's house (vs. 15; cf. Gen. 3:24) they will become **wanderers among the nations** (vs. 17; cf. Gen. 4:12-16).

10:1-8. *Loss of King and Image.* The prosperity of the **luxuriant vine** Israel, as in the days of Jeroboam II, meant multiplied **altars** and **pillars** (cf. 3:4; 8:11). Because the guilty people's **heart is false** God will destroy the equipment of this flourishing cult.

10:3-8. Hos. predicts that the petty king of Israel will prove to be helpless, **like a chip on the face of the waters** (vs. 7). The dwellers in the capital city will **tremble for the calf of Beth-aven** (see above on 4:15-16; 8:4-6), whose **glory** will be lost as it is carried off **as tribute to the great king** (see above on 5:9-14). This may be a historical reference to inclusion of the image in the enormous tribute paid to Assyria in the reign of Menahem (cf. II Kings 15:19-20) or, more likely, a prediction that it will be carried off when the nation finally collapses. In any case the problem is blasphemous lack of confidence in the divine king Yahweh or any earthly representative of his (vs. 3) and meaningless **oaths** of allegiance (vs. 4). Therefore God's judgment will spring up like **weeds** over the abandoned cult centers, and the people will wish to be hidden by the **mountains** from the day of judgment or be crushed by falling rocks in order to avoid a worse fate (vs. 8).

10:9-15. *The Storm of War.* As Hos. has previously proclaimed (9:9), Israel's sin is of long standing. **Double iniquity** may refer to 2 crimes of **Gibeah**—the rape and murder of the Levite's concubine (Judg. 19:22-28) and the rebellion against God in setting up the kingship (I Sam. 10:17-26)—or it may simply mean the compounded guilt of the centuries.

10:11-12. In a farming metaphor Hos. indicates that the **trained heifer** Ephraim, perhaps in the earlier wilderness period, **loved to thresh,** docilely and leisurely treading out the grain, free to eat as she wished (cf. Deut. 25:4). But because of her sin she will now be forced to bear a heavy **yoke** and to **plow** and **harrow.** Changing the figure, Hos. pleads for a changed national life, sowing **righteousness** so that the **fruit of steadfast love,** i.e. covenant loyalty, may be reaped. If the people **seek the LORD** instead of Baal, he will **come and rain salvation** on them.

10:13-15. The hope is only momentary, however, for the trust in **chariots** and **warriors** will bring final destruction, a **storm** in which Israel's **house** will be ended. The example of the destruction of **Beth-arbel** and its accompanying atrocities (vs. 14*cd*) is not known. The city may have been located in Gilead (see color map 8). **Shalman** may be the Moabite king Salamanu mentioned in Tiglath-pileser's annals, or possibly Shalmaneser V of Assyria, who dealt the final blow to Israel.

F. God's Unrequited Love (11:1–13:16)

From description of the death blow to Israel as punishment for her unfaithfulness, which has occupied much of God's word to Israel thus far in the book, attention now turns chiefly to divine reminiscence and appeal based on the lessons of covenant history.

11:1-11. *The Love of God the Father.* There now begins one of the greatest passages in the Bible, Hos.'s portrayal of the depth and nature of God's love. It is notable that not husband-wife love but father-son love is described.

11:1-2. According to honored tradition God's election of Israel as his people when they left Egyptian slavery was figuratively the birth of his "first-born son" (Exod. 4:22). Hos. spells out the meaning of that loving fatherhood. God **called** his son, presumably to be the agent of his divine purpose for the world, though Hos. says nothing of fulfillment of the covenant with Abraham (cf. Gen. 12:2-3). Yet despite God's persistent and loving call the son almost at once succumbed to the appeals of the **Baals.**

11:3-4. The marvel of divine love is God's care and patience. He **taught Ephraim to walk,** lovingly carried him in his **arms,** and **healed** him when ill, though the infant did not know it (cf. Deut. 1:31). In vs. 4 the figure seems to change to what has been appropriately called "God's harness of love," by which he would impel rather than compel his people as the farmer does his favorite donkey or yoke of oxen. He **led them with cords of compassion,** lit. "cords of a man," perhaps meaning "human cords." He made their **yoke** light and tenderly **fed them.** On the other hand some scholars believe the shift in the figure is due to textual error and suggest various emendations of vs. 4*cd*, e.g.: "And I was to them as one who lifts a baby to his cheek."

11:5-7. As the nation grows through childhood to adolescence and still has **refused to return** to its father, God must use stern disciplinary measures. He will take his people back to their starting point of slavery in **Egypt** (see above on 7:13-16) or into exile with **Assyria** as their ruler. Devouring destruction will come upon them, and they will be under a severe yoke.

11:8-9. Here Hos. gives the climactic expression of God's love, his divine suffering as he ponders the decision concerning his wayward son. Will he treat his son like **Admah** and **Zeboiim?**—cities destroyed with Sodom and Gomorrah (cf. Deut. 29:23; see color map 3). No, **his compassion grows warm and tender.** Ephraim has felt some destroying anger, but he will be subject to no more. God's apparent inner struggle between wrath and love is over. What marks him as divine is his holiness, his unlikeness to vengeful man; for his holiness is redemptive love. As God and not man he can be depended on as one who will not come to destroy.

11:10-11. Therefore God will bring his people back from their Egyptian-Assyrian discipline **to their homes.** They will quickly come like cubs running to the **roar** of a **lion** or like **doves,** i.e. homing pigeons. Here Hos. may deliberately be using previous warning analogies (cf. 5:14; 7:11; 9:3) to say that God makes good come out of what man deems to be evil.

11:12–13:16. Rejected Rebirth and Revival. Further lessons from covenant history remind Israel of her continual opportunities for a right relationship with her God and of the consequences of her repeated refusals.

11:12–12:1. In contrast to Israel's **lies** and **deceit,** Judah seems to be praised for remaining **faithful** to God. Since elsewhere Hos. views Judah as sharing Israel's guilt (cf. 5:12-14; 6:4; 8:14) many scholars have assumed here some alteration by a Judean editor and have suggested various emendations. But perhaps the present text can be understood unfavorably as referring to Judah's allegiance to the Canaanite god El (see above on 1:4-5) and the "holy ones," i.e. cult prostitutes. Ephraim's foreign alliances—including perhaps Menahem's **bargain** with Tiglath-pileser (see Intro.) and such commercial ventures as exporting olive **oil** to Egypt—exhibit disloyalty to Israel's God and so are like the blighting **east wind** from the desert (cf. 13:15; Ps. 103:16; Jonah 4:8).

12:2-6. Since **Jacob** in this passage clearly means the N kingdom it has been suggested that **Judah** (v. 2a) originally read "Israel." From the story of this ancestor 3 events are singled out: his natal heel-grabbing, a pun on his name (Gen. 25:26); his wrestling with God at the river Jabbok (Gen. 32:22-30); and his encounter with God at Bethel (Gen. 28:11-17). These all seem to recommend Jacob's perseverance in his struggles with God. But the all-important concluding word is that similarly by divine help his people should **return,** i.e. repent, and then keep **love,** i.e. covenant loyalty, and **justice** and **wait continually** for God (cf. Mic. 6:8). Some commentators, however, view vss. 4-6 as an interpolation.

12:7-9. Ephraim is a wealthy **trader,** lit. "Canaanite," but **all his riches can never offset the guilt he has incurred** through unscrupulous, dishonest dealings. Therefore as punishment Israel must again **dwell in tents** as in the period of the Exodus and desert wandering (cf. 2:14-15; 3:4), commemorated in the autumn **feast** of booths.

12:10-14. Israel really has no excuse for waywardness, for God has always provided guidance through his **prophets** with their **visions** and **parables.** The centers of cult iniquity in **Gilead** and **Gilgal** will be destroyed and their **altars** become mere **stone heaps,** Hebrew *gallim,* a word play on the place names. The RSV parentheses around vs. 12 accord with the view of many scholars that it is an interpolation, perhaps displaced from vss. 2-6. It should be noted, however, that Jacob's return from **Aram** involved the building of a stone heap (cf. Gen. 31:43-54) and that the word translated **herded sheep** is from the same root as **preserved** (vs. 13). Moses is the **prophet** by whom Yahweh **brought Israel up from Egypt** and probably that by whom Israel was **preserved,** though some scholars believe the latter reference is to Samuel. By rejecting the prophets Israel has **given bitter provocation** to Yahweh to hold her responsible for her **bloodguilt.**

13:1-3. Ephraim as the chosen son of Joseph was the chief of the 10 tribes of Israel (cf. Gen. 37:5-11; 48:14-20; 49:22-26), but ironically through worship of the supposed god of renewed life and vegetation he **died** spiritually. Hos. heaps scorn on the piling up of **sin** as the people make **molten images** and

idols and in the rites at Dan and Bethel **kiss calves.** Such a society is as ephemeral as **mist . . . dew . . . chaff . . . smoke.**

13:4-11. In appealing tones Yahweh reminds his people that he has been their one and only God from the days of the Exodus. He pleads the intimacy of his relationship with his people: **You know no God but me, and besides me there is no savior.** This they remembered in the adversity of the **wilderness,** but with prosperity in the Promised Land they proudly and thanklessly **forgot** their God (vss. 5-6; cf. Deut. 8:11-20; 32:15, 18). Therefore **like a lion** or a **leopard** or a **bear robbed of her cubs** Yahweh will pounce on them in devouring fury (vss. 7-8; cf. 5:14). When God destroys no earthly thing can save (vss. 9-11). Indeed, as the rapid dynastic changes of the last days of Israel testify (see Intro.), he has both **given** and **taken . . . away** kings in his **anger** (cf. 8:4).

13:12-14. What is to be done with the huge accumulation of God's people's **iniquity?** This dirty pile of evil is to be bagged and **kept in store** to await a final day of reckoning. Its final disposal depends on Ephraim's own decision. Hos. sadly announces that his people have rejected God's offer of rebirth and revival. The **unwise,** Baal-deluded **son** is not willing to be born again into right relationship with God. The people think themselves alive in Baalism but are actually in the clutches of **Death** in **Sheol,** the underworld cavern of the departed (see comment on Ps. 6:4-5). God would **redeem** his people, but they do not wish it. Hence **compassion is hid** from his loving **eyes.**

13:15-16. The nation with its capital, **Samaria,** has sealed its own doom. It began by baalizing Yahwism and it will end in the atrocities of war (cf. 9:16). The dreaded **east wind** (cf. 12:1) from the **wilderness,** i.e. desert, which dries up everything in the hot summer, is Assyria, which will **strip his treasury of every precious thing.**

G. PROMISE OF RENEWAL (14:1-8)

The climax of God's word through Hos.'s oracles is Yahweh's plea for his people's repentance followed by his gracious promise of healing and freely given love. This magnificent conclusion—whether the product of Hos. himself or of a thoroughly understanding disciple—is in the form of a liturgy of penitence (cf. 6:1-3) composed of the customary 3 parts: a call to repentance (vss. 1-2b), a penitential prayer of confession (vss. 2c-3), and Yahweh's response (vss. 4-8).

14:1-2b. Call to Repentance. The urgent plea is to **return** to Yahweh, i.e. turn away from Baalism or baalized Yahwism. False worship is the reason for their inner guilt and outright disobedience. Not sacrifices but **words,** the sincere utterances of a contrite heart, will permit **return to the LORD.**

14:2c-3. Confession. The prayer acknowledges and pleads for the removal of **all iniquity,** i.e. all inner tendency to wrongdoing, therefore all consequent punishment, therefore all guilt feelings. In place of sacrifices it offers the words called for (vs. 2a), the **fruit of our lips,** lit. "bulls of our lips"—perhaps implying not merely the animals used in sacrifice but Baalism's symbols of power and fertility, now acknowledged as belonging to Yahweh. The 2 major sins, international intrigue and idolatry, are renounced. **Assyria,** or perhaps her god Asshur (the same word in Hebrew), and the **horses** of Egypt (cf. I Kings 10:28; Isa. 31:1) cannot **save.**

14:3*e*. One interpreter points out that in the recognition of its self-willed orphanhood Israel discovered the divine fatherhood. Of course the punishment cannot be escaped. The nation, already an orphan, is on the way to war and exile. But there is hope that, having confessed, the onetime wayward child will again be accepted with motherly **mercy,** i.e. compassion of the mother's womb implied in the Hebrew word (see above on 1:6).

14:4-8. *Yahweh's Response.* If his wayward son will now become completely converted away from Baalism and back to him, Yahweh will absolve him of his guilt and reverse the sin-caused disasters. Instead of disease there will be healing, instead of wrath a free outpouring of gracious love, instead of failing fertility the fruitfulness that the name Ephraim implies. Through Yahweh's control of all nature relatively arid, mountainous Israel will have the **fragrance** and the **wine of Lebanon,** famed for its fertile valley. When Israel will **return and dwell beneath** God's **shadow,** she will find that it is Yahweh who answers and looks after her like a protective, stalwart, and fruitful **evergreen cypress.** Her **fruit** is not from Baal but from the God of her fathers. At last she will have learned true knowledge of God.

IV. POSTSCRIPT (14:9)

An ancient reader of the scroll of Hos. adds his word of approval to the prophet's words. As a member of the wisdom school he counsels all future readers to **understand these things.**

THE BOOK OF JOEL

Roland E. Murphy, O. Carm.

Introduction

Author and Date. A dozen men named Joel are mentioned in the OT (e.g. I Sam. 8:2; I Chr. 11:38; Ezra 10:43; Neh. 11:9) but none can be identified with the author of the book, of whose person we are given no information except that he was the "son of Pethuel" (1:1). The familiarity with the temple liturgy shown in the book suggests that he may have been a priest, or perhaps a cultic prophet, though some interpret the references to priests (1:9, 13; 2:17) as evidence that the author did not include himself among them. The interest in Jerusalem suggests that he lived in or near this city.

A date in the postexilic period is suggested by the role of the elders as community leaders (1:2, 14; 2:16), the concern with ritual and sacrifice (1:13; 2:12, 14), the relatively small size of the community, which can be assembled in the temple area (2:16), the reference to Israel as scattered among the nations (3:2), and the acquaintance with the Greeks as a remote people (3:6). In the 20th cent. the only serious challenge to postexilic dating has been a study citing ancient Canaanite cultic practices from Ugarit as evidence for associating the work with a preexilic new year enthronement celebration. This study dates the book as contemporary with Jer., *ca.* 600. But in view of the absence of any reference to the king, who would be at the center of such a celebration, this theory has not won the assent of many scholars.

In the postexilic period references to the temple place the writing after 515, and dependence on later prophets (e.g. 2:32 quotes Obad. 17*a* and 2:11, 31 reflect Mal. 3:2; 4:5) indicates an even later date. The rebuilding of the wall (cf. 2:7) and other problems challenging Nehemiah and Ezra seem to be already settled. On the other hand the reference to Sidon (3:4), in a passage that may be an addition, indicates that the book was completed before *ca.* 345, when this city was destroyed by the Persians under Artaxerxes III. Thus the likely date is the first half of the 4th cent.

Unity. The recent trend among scholars is to accept the general unity of the book—with the possible exception of 3:4-8 and maybe 3:18-21—rather than an earlier theory of dual authorship still favored by some. All would admit that the work divides easily into 1:1–2:27 (a locust invasion) and 2:28–3:21 (judgment on the nations), but the arguments that they must be from different hands are much less obvious. There is no reason that the same author

could not have interpreted a locust plague as an omen and symbol of the coming day of Yahweh.

Occasion and Message. The event prompting Joel's activity is a locust plague that has devastated the land. In the prophetic tradition he interprets this as a visitation from Yahweh, and he urges the Israelites to assemble and mourn. He comes to see the invasion of the locusts as a sign that the day of Yahweh is near and as a symbol of the divine invasion that will characterize that day (see below on 1:15-20). He holds out the hope of deliverance if Israel turns to Yahweh wholeheartedly (2:12-14). He narrates the turning point in 2:18, how Yahweh "became jealous" for his people; and there follows a series of oracles which assure the people of prosperity, an outpouring of the spirit, and victory over the nations in the final battle, when Yahweh will be a refuge and a stronghold to his people.

Literary Style. The dominant literary motif is a liturgy of lamentation, but the 3 chs. present a great variety of literary types: admonition (1:2-3), summons to lament (e.g. 1:5-7, 11-12, 13), complaints (1:16, 19; 2:17), alarms (2:1; 3:9), oracles of assurance (2:19-27), and theological conclusions (2:27; 3:17). These reflect a varied life setting, and the references to priests and sacrifice reveal a cultic background for Joel's activity. However, they lose their individuality in the work as it stands. The book is a *literary* composition which combines these various types into a theological interpretation and message. The literary character is esp. seen in the book's so-called "anthological composition," i.e. the adaptation of earlier biblical language in expressing its ideas. E.g. the paleness of faces (2:6) is from Nah. 2:10, the trembling of heavens and earth (2:10) from Isa. 13:13, the possibility of Yahweh's repentance (2:14) from Jonah 3:9. Joel also draws largely on earlier themes of the day of Yahweh (cf. Zeph. 1; Isa. 13; Ezek. 30; Obad.), the oracles against the nations (cf. Jer. 46–51; Ezek. 29–32), and the threat of an enemy from the N (Jer. 4–6; Ezek. 38–39).

For Further Study: J. A. Bewer, *The Book of Joel,* 1911. H. C. Lanchester, *Joel and Amos,* 1915. G. W. Wade, *The Books of the Prophets Mic., Obad., Joel and Jonah,* 1925. G. A. Smith, *The Book of the 12 Prophets,* vol. I, rev. ed., 1928. A. S. Kapelrud, *Joel Studies,* 1948; an attempt to connect the book with a preexilic enthronement festival. J. A. Thompson in *IB,* 1956. Jacob M. Myers, *Hos., Joel, Amos, Obad., Jonah,* 1959. William Neil in *IDB,* 1962.

I. The Locust Plague (1:1–2:17)

1:1. Title. The name **Joel** means "Yah(weh) is (my) God" or "Yah(weh) is El." Perhaps his father's name, **Pethuel,** means "the young man of God."

1:2-4. A General Summons. The call to **give ear** is reminiscent of the style of the sages (e.g. Prov. 4:1) and the Deuteronomic preaching (e.g. Deut. 4:9). The **aged men,** elsewhere translated "elders" (e.g. vs. 14), the leaders of the Jerusalem community, are addressed. The appalling event is an invasion by locusts which devastates the land. The 4 kinds of locust—**cutting . . . swarming . . . hopping . . . destroying**—probably designate the 4 stages through which the insect evolves. Even in modern times (1915 and 1930) Palestine has been ravaged by such plagues.

1:5-14. A Summons to Several Classes. The **drinkers of wine** are invited to lament because the vines have been destroyed by the locusts and they will be the first to feel the effects of the plague. **Sweet wine**

Courtesy of the American Colony, Jerusalem, Israel

Locusts denuding a fig tree

means juice from newly pressed grapes. Both **vines** and **fig trees** are **stripped** by the **nation** of devouring insects.

1:8-10. The entire community, esp. the **priests,** is invited to **lament** because of the cessation of sacrificial offerings in the temple. The comparison of Jerusalem to a widowed **virgin** is quite poignant; Jerusalem is often called the "virgin daughter" of Judah (cf. e.g. Jer. 14:17; Lam. 1:15). **Grain** and **wine** and olive **oil** (cf. Deut. 7:13) were the chief products of Palestine.

1:11-12. The farmers and **vinedressers** are addressed because they are vitally affected by the destruction of crops and vines and **trees.**

1:13-14. The climax in the series comes with the command that the **priests,** now bereft of their offerings, mourn with the people in the temple on a solemn day of **fast.** The wearing of **sackcloth,** a garment of camel's or goat's hair wrapped about the loins, is a typical sign of mourning in the OT (cf. e.g. I Kings 21:27).

1:15-20. A Ritual Prayer. These lines present snatches of the laments which would characterize the **solemn assembly** (vs. 14) called by the priests.

1:15-16. The great theme of the book, **the day of the LORD,** is now introduced (cf. Ezek. 30:2). The term indicates a specific intervention of Yahweh in history, for weal and/or for woe. Analysis of the important "day of Yahweh" texts (e.g. Isa. 2:12; 13:6, 9; Jer. 46:10; Amos 5:18-20) shows that the phrase has a rich history and imagery associated with it. The day is a day of battle, and Yahweh is at war with his enemies. The imagery probably derives from the wars of the Conquest, when Yahweh intervened to fight for Israel (cf. e.g. Judg. 5:4-31; 7:1-25). Here the day is a day *against* Israel, and the locust plague is its prelude and symbol. In the Hebrew there is a play—as often in Joel—on the word for **Almighty:** "as mighty destruction from the Almighty."

1:17-20. The ancient versions vary in rendering the difficult vs. 17a. The RSV presupposes a plowing under or a rotting due to lack of water. At least it is clear that **there is no pasture** for the animals. Though the "I" in vs. 19 can be understood of the prophet, it is really the community (which was invited to "cry to the LORD" in vs. 14) that speaks. The complaint describes a drought, symbolized by **fire** and **flame.**

2:1-11. Invasion of Yahweh's Army. Unlike the summons in ch. 1, this alarm is sounded by Yahweh himself, and it is in view of an invasion of a **great and powerful people** on the day of Yahweh. Most commentators interpret this invasion as a continuation of the locust plague; the locusts are Yahweh's **army** or **host** (vs. 11) and they are described as advancing **like soldiers** (vs. 7) on the terrible day. Some, however, point out that the invading army is described in terms similar to the divine army which levels Babylon in Isa. 13 and therefore suggest that Joel is here describing the army which is to attack Israel on the day of Yahweh as in ch. 3.

2:2. The description of the day as **darkness** is similar to Zeph. 1:15 (cf. Deut. 4:11; Amos 5:18-20). **Blackness** (vs. 2c) in the traditional Hebrew text reads "dawn," but in the original script consisting of consonants only the 2 words would have been identical. "Like dawn" gives good sense as a description of the suddenness of the invasion.

2:3-9. The military metaphor is continued in the dramatic description of **warriors** and **soldiers** that swarm over the land, devastating **the garden of Eden,** as Palestine is here called (cf. Isa. 51:3).

2:10-11. The quaking and trembling of the **heavens** and **earth** are the usual accompaniment of a divine visitation (cf. Isa. 13:10, 13). The **voice** (vs. 11) of Yahweh is his command for his army to attack. The final question, **who can endure it?** (cf. Mal. 3:2), suggests the totally desperate situation on this day, before a ray of hope is offered in the following vss. 12-14.

2:12-14. Deliverance Dependent on Conversion. Yahweh's invitation to the people to convert is a turning point; their response is to be a conversion in the style of the Deuteronomic ideal—**with all your heart** (cf. Deut. 30:10). The rending of **garments** is a customary OT ritual of mourning, but it must be sincere. Since vs. 12 urges **fasting** in particular, there is no opposition to ritual in itself. However, the prophet strikes out at empty formalism. The motivation for the change of heart is the confession formula of Exod. 34:6, **gracious and merciful,** which is a time-honored characterization of Yahweh (cf. Neh. 9:17; Pss. 86:15; 145:8; Jonah 4:2). The question **who knows** (vs. 14) is idiomatic for "perhaps he will" (cf. Jonah 3:9). God is free to grant mercy and to allow Israel to worship him in sacrifice; unlike the preexilic prophets, Joel manifests great concern about temple worship (cf. 1:9, 13).

2:15-17. *A Summons to National Repentance.* All classes—even the **bridegroom,** who was usually exempted from military service (cf. Deut. 20:7; 24:5)—are summoned on a **fast** day to appeal for deliverance. The **priests** are stationed between the **altar** of burnt offerings and the entrance to the temple, and their prayer indicates the reasons Yahweh should intervene: his heritage, Israel, is a reproach; the nations blaspheme him by questioning, **Where is their God?** Such motifs are frequent in the pss. of lament (cf. e.g. Ps. 79:4, 10).

II. THE DAY OF THE LORD (2:18–3:21)

2:18-27. *The Promise of Deliverance.* Though most interpreters place the major division point of the book between vss. 27, 28, vs. 18 actually marks the decisive transition; from this point on there are only words of consolation for Israel. Yahweh's becoming **jealous** for Israel is a turning in their favor, as the following lines indicate.

2:20-22. The **northerner** is the army of invasion, which is here interpreted in the light of the traditional terminology for invaders (cf. Jer. 1:14; 6:1; Ezek. 38–39). This enemy will be driven into the wasteland, spanning the desert from the Dead Sea (or perhaps the Persian Gulf) to the Mediterranean. The land is given the assurance (vs. 21), expressed in the style of the priestly oracle **fear not,** that Yahweh **has done great things**—in direct contrast to the **great things** ascribed to the invader in vs. 20.

2:23. Zion is assured of **rain** and the attendant material prosperity. The Hebrew of this vs. is obscure. **The early rain for your vindication** is doubtful because this is not the normal meaning for the 2 Hebrew words, which can be lit. translated either as "teacher for justice" or "early rain in due measure." There seems to be a play on the words *moreh* (teacher) and *yoreh* (early rain); perhaps the blessing of rain will point Israel toward a proper relationship to Yahweh. It is not necessarily from this text (cf. the Vulg. messianic rendering "teacher of justice") that the Essenes of Qumran derived their title for their great leader, the "Teacher of Righteousness" (see "The Dead Sea Scrolls," pp. 1063-71). It could have been derived from Deut. 18:15-18; 33:9-10 (cf. Hos. 10:12; Isa. 30:20). In any case the promise of the seasonal rains is clear: the **early rain** in the fall and the **latter rain** in the spring.

2:24-27. The promises of blessings on the land are continued: **grain . . . wine . . . oil**—in contrast to the devastation wrought by the locusts, who are here called **my great army** (vs. 25; cf. 2:11). The climax of the promises is to be found in the "proof" formula of vs. 27, **You shall know that I am in the midst of Israel.** Israel will arrive at a deeper realiza-

tion that Yahweh, the God of the covenant, is present and active in her behalf. This conviction of the divine purpose is derived from the tradition of 2nd Isa. (45:2-6) and Ezek. (e.g. 39:28). Israel can rely on Yahweh's action in her favor, for it will show that he is her God, in her midst (cf. 4:17).

2:28-32. *The Outpouring of the Spirit.* The traditional Hebrew text since 1524 has marked these vss. as ch. 3 and the rest of the book as ch. 4. The wondrous dealing of God (vs. 26) is continued with an outpouring of his **spirit**—a new life and power for weak man. The prophet takes up a traditional theme, the giving of the divine spirit (cf. Isa. 32:15; Ezek. 39:29), to indicate that Israel will be a people of prophets (**dream dreams . . . see visions**). There will be directness and spontaneity in man's relationship to God. Everyone will experience the spirit, as once Moses asked this blessing for all of Yahweh's people (Num. 11:29).

2:30-32. Accompanying the outpouring are cosmic portents (vss. 30-31), the usual signs associated with the day of Yahweh (cf. 2:10). To **call on the name of the LORD** (vs. 32) is to serve him in the temple liturgy. **Jerusalem** will be the haven for those who **escape** the catastrophic events; here the prophet consciously refers to the word of Yahweh spoken by Obadiah (Obad. 17). Those **whom the LORD calls** are the chosen in Jerusalem.

In Acts 2:17-21, the Pentecost speech of Peter, vss. 28-32 are quoted as found in the LXX. The events of Pentecost were seen as part of the pattern proclaimed by the prophet. Vs. 28 announces the outpouring for **afterward.** While this is only a vague indication, it appears to follow on the people's conversion. In Rom. 10:13 Paul quotes vs. 32*a*, **all who call upon the name of the LORD shall be delivered;** hence, Paul says, there can be no distinction between Jew and Greek.

3:1-15. *Judgment on the Nations.* The perspective now broadens to include the nations, who are to be gathered in the **valley of Jehoshaphat** to be judged because of their treatment of Israel. The presupposition is that Judah has been exiled, her **land divided up**—as actually occurred after 586 (cf. Obad. 11-14)—and the people enslaved. The valley of Jehoshaphat has traditionally been located in the Kidron Valley, but it is probably merely symbolic ("Yah shall judge") and a play on the word for "judge." The judgment on the nations is due to their treatment of exiled Israel. **Lots** would have been **cast** for prisoners, with no sense of human dignity (vs. 3).

3:4-8. This section has the earmarks of an insertion into the original text, building on the idea of trafficking in human beings in vs. 3. The context there was the nations, but now a Phoenician-Philistine league is addressed. These peoples are accused of having plundered Judah and of having **sold** Judean slaves **to the Greeks.** The meaning of the questions in vs. 4 becomes clear from the plundering and enslavement of the Judeans which these peoples perpetrated. Fittingly they in turn will suffer by being sold by the Judeans **to the Sabeans** of the Arabian desert (vs. 8). On the bearing of this passage on the date of the book see Intro.

3:9-12. After the digression of vss. 4-8 the nations are issued a call to arms; they are to assemble at the **valley of Jehoshaphat.** Isa. 2:4; Mic. 4:3 is quoted in vs. 10 in a reverse sense with irony: the journey to Jerusalem has become a military advance—to destruction, not peace—so let them **beat their plowshares into swords.** In the enthusiasm of military preparations even the unsoldierly boast of their exploits (vs. 10c). The invitation to assemble is repeated in vs. 11, but the last line about Yahweh's **warriors,** i.e. the members of the heavenly court, may be a gloss (cf. Zech. 14:5). When all the nations are gathered in the valley of Jehoshaphat, Yahweh will be their **judge** (as in vs. 2).

3:13-15. The destruction of the nations, who are **ripe** for the **harvest,** is described in terms of cutting down the harvest and treading the grapes. As in vs. 9 there is no indication to whom the commands of vs. 13 are given—to the people of Jerusalem? to Yahweh's warriors of vs. 11? The valley of Jehoshaphat is also called **the valley of decision,** for here Yahweh will decide for Jerusalem against her enemies. As in 2:10 the decision will be accompanied by cataclysms in the world of nature (vs. 15).

3:16-21. *Blessings for Judah and Jerusalem.* The proclamation of the blessings is introduced by a well-known metaphor from Amos 1:2 (cf. Jer. 25:30): **The LORD roars from Zion.** Now Yahweh's **voice** is against the enemy, and he himself is **a refuge to his people.** His deliverance of Israel will be a proof (as in 2:17) that he is the God of Israel, and in Israel. He acts that Israel may know him as her God, and his dwelling **in Zion** (cf. Isa. 8:18) makes Jerusalem **holy,** separate from **strangers.**

3:18-21. These vss., which are possibly a later addition, describe the paradisiacal blessings of the judgment and deliverance. Yahweh **dwells in Zion** (vs. 21) and brings about the fertility of paradise (vs. 18) and the independence of his people over **Egypt** and **Edom,** who are the classical types of Israel's enemies (vss. 19-20). The fountain that flows **from the house of the LORD** has its model in Ezek. 47:1-12, the stream that flows from the temple. This shall **water the valley of Shittim** (i.e. Acacia Valley), which is probably the Wadi en-Nar, the continuation of the Kidron Valley in the direction of the Dead Sea. The book ends on the theme of Yahweh's dwelling **in Zion**—an important point emphasized by Joel in his view of the age to come (cf. 2:27, 32; 3:17).

THE BOOK OF AMOS

CHARLES F. KRAFT

INTRODUCTION

The book of Amos is a record of the prophetic messages, mostly in poetic form, of the first OT prophet whose collected words are preserved as a book of the Bible. Probably this was the first biblical book to be completed in substantially its present form. Prophetic poetry, understood to be God's revelation in the form of spoken and then written oracles, was a unique literary genre in the history of the world's literature which was first given us by Amos in Israel in the 8th cent. B.C.

Most of the book is commonly regarded as composed of the authentic sayings of the prophet Amos, whether recorded by himself or by disciples. Only the appendix of hope (9:8c-15), coming as it does in stark contrast to the prevailing pronouncements of doom, is regarded by many scholars as added later. Some interpreters also view as additions certain of the oracles against the nations, esp. that against Judah (2:4-5), and the "doxologies" (4:13; 5:8-9; 9:5-6), though others consider the latter to be fragments of an ancient hymn quoted by Amos.

The Prophet and His Times. The career of Amos was of epoch-making importance as the pioneer of a long succession of prophets. His dramatic appearance on the stage of world history is indicated in his conflict with Israelite officialdom at the royal sanctuary of Bethel as told in the one biographical section of the book (7:10-17). That this herdsman and sycamore-fig pruner did not regard himself to be a professional prophet seems clear, but it is equally clear that he felt under divine compulsion to speak (see below on 1:1; 7:14-15). His opening oracles of judgment against the nations (1:3–2:3) show a remarkable grasp of the history of his world. Hence he was no country bumpkin suddenly startled into sermons of warning when he discovered urban wickedness. On the contrary, as the visions in his book confirm (7:1-9; 8:1-3; 9:1-4), he deliberately declared his unpopular warnings at the centers of religious and political life in Israel.

Amos' message was to an age of unprecedented postwar prosperity in the middle of the 8th cent. Assyrian invasions of the preceding cent. had ceased because of that empire's internal struggles. In the midst of his long reign (793/92-753; see "Chronology," pp. 1271-82) Jeroboam II of Israel had brought to a victorious end the cent. and a half of war with nearby Syria. By the time Amos began his public career, evidently very late in Jeroboam's reign, Israel was enlarged to her most extensive boundaries

(II Kings 14:23-29) and Judah was similarly prosperous under Uzziah (or Azariah, 792/91-740/39; see below on 1:1). An era of luxury like that of Solomon seemed to have returned. It was to speak to the false presumptions and vile practices of this heyday that Amos heard God call him from his pastoral and agricultural occupation.

Amos' Message. Amos' purpose was to penetrate the veneer of self-satisfied complacency to the rotten core of the religious and social life of the leaders of Israel who proudly assumed their prosperity to be evidence of the effectiveness of their cultic observances. They had been ungratefully false to the faith of their fathers by syncretistic, if not pagan, Baalized ritual practices. They had repudiated their fathers' obedience to Yahweh's commands by heartless exploitation in cult center, marketplace, and law court. Amos foresaw that their rude awakening, if there could be such, was at hand in a worldwide movement of punishing judgment, a deadly "day of Yahweh" which would mean the death of the nation at the hands of a God-empowered invading enemy. The situation looked almost hopeless to Amos, though possibly, if they turned to "seek the LORD," and if they "let justice roll down like waters," a "remnant" of the nation might avoid the coming death or exile to a foreign land (5:6, 15, 24). It was this God-impelled urgency to proclaim that "the lion has roared" in the hope that at least a few might escape his death-dealing leap which caused the layman-prophet to speak (3:8).

For Further Study: W. R. Harper, *Amos and Hos.*, 1910. J. M. P. Smith, *Amos, Hos., and Mic.*, 1914. N. H. Snaith, *The Book of Amos*, Pts. I-II, 1945-46. R. S. Cripps, *Amos*, 2nd ed., 1955. H. E. W. Fosbroke in *IB*, 1956. A. S. Kapelrud, *Central Ideas in Amos*, 1956. J. D. W. Watts, *Vision and Prophecy in Amos*, 1958. J. D. Smart in *IDB*, 1962. R. L. Honeycutt, *Amos and His Message*, 1963.

I. INTRO.: AMOS AND GOD'S WORD (1:1-2)

1:1. Title. This prose superscription was written by an editor to introduce Amos' prophetic poetry. More complete than the headings of most prophetic books, it locates the prophet in biblical history. The name **Amos** may mean "burden," i.e. of Yahweh concerning his people Israel.

Among the shepherds may not describe Amos as a typical keeper of a small flock. The Hebrew word used here appears elsewhere only in reference to Mesha king of Moab, a "sheep breeder" who delivered a huge annual tribute of sheep and wool to the king of Israel (II Kings 3:4). A similar Arabic term denotes a breed of sheep, but in early Canaanite (Ugaritic) literature the word is used of a temple official responsible for as many as 2,000 sheep and goats belonging to the shrine. Possibly, therefore, Amos was one of several keepers of Jerusalem or Bethel temple flocks. His home base was **Tekoa,**

Courtesy of Herbert G. May
On the ruins of Tekoa

a rather prominent Judean highland city 10 miles S of Jerusalem, *ca.* 2,800 feet above sea level, which overlooked the desolate hills of Judah E toward the Dead Sea (see color map 8). But no doubt the requirements of his occupation—for pasturage and for delivery of its produce—led him along the main routes to the urban centers of the day. At any rate the **words . . . which he saw**—i.e. revelations, not heard, but seen with the inner eye of prophetic perception—were chiefly **concerning Israel,** i.e. the N kingdom, rather than his homeland of Judah.

Amos' prophetic ministry is dated not only by the reigning monarchs (see Intro.) but more specifically in relation to an **earthquake** of such severity as to be long remembered (cf. Zech. 14:5). Archaeologists have found evidence that Hazor in N Galilee was destroyed by an earthquake at about this time, but its exact date cannot be determined. In the Hebrew

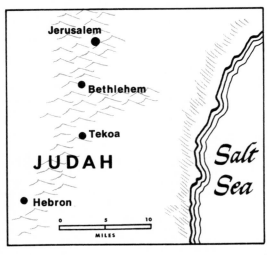

two years is ambiguous and may refer either to the duration of Amos' prophetic work or to its date.

1:2. *God's Voice of Judgment.* This opening word, cast perhaps in the form of a brief liturgy, with excellent Hebrew poetic structure, sounds the keynote of the book. Yahweh, with the panic-producing roar of a lion pouncing on his prey (cf. 3:4, 8), is speaking from **Zion,** his holy hill in **Jerusalem,** the center of worship for Judah. His voice announces immediate doom, the end of prosperity. As in the drought of Elijah's day (I Kings 17:1), the **pastures** will cry out for rain and the **Carmel** ridge, a 12-mile-long mountain headland on the coast near modern Haifa famous for luxuriant plant life, will lose its fertility. Dread divine judgment strikes at agricultural prosperity, the means of livelihood, and with only one outcome—death. Some commentators, assuming that Amos' ministry was confined to the N kingdom, consider this vs. a summarizing couplet by an editor.

II. GOD'S JUDGMENT ON THE NATIONS AND ON ISRAEL (1:3–2:16)

The opening prophetic oracles are a series of pronouncements of doom on neighboring nations (1:3–2:3). They begin with Syria, the nation immediately to the NE. Amos' hearers, only recently recovered from the serious blows of this foe, must gleefully have greeted announcement of its imminent destruction. Next, to the SW, the Philistines, an earlier greatest enemy, are to experience Yahweh's punishing fire. To the NW Tyre, then to the S Edom and to the E the Ammonites and Moab—the order forms a crisscross pattern of divine judgment. Its climax is doom on Israel itself (2:6-16). The grim delight of the hearers over just judgment on enemies turns to terror at learning the fate of their own land.

The very regular form of all these oracles may have been drawn from cultic formulas, as in Phoenician usage, or in Egyptian texts where curses are first pronounced on surrounding peoples and then on individuals within Egypt. Each oracle begins with the typical prophetic perfect tense, lit. "thus has the LORD said," but God's spoken word has continuing effect and thus is properly translated **thus says the LORD.** The repeated expression **for three . . . , and for four,"** perhaps taken from wisdom literature (cf. Job 5:19; 33:14; Prov. 6:16; 30:15, 18, 21, 29), suggests multiplied **transgressions,** lit. "rebellions," against divine authority.

I will not revoke the punishment is lit. "I will not turn it back" or "I will not cause it to return." Most interpreters understand the antecedent of "it" to be the mysterious God-directed punishment which is the inevitable consequence of sin. But if the antecedent is the nation, as seems more natural, then the prophet may be using a figure of speech drawn from a myth of his day about the vegetation god Baal, who was killed and went to the underworld and then returned with the autumn rains. The meaning would then be that Yahweh, the divine power over nature and nations, will never cause the guilty nation to return from its underworld of deserved punishment. Another possibility is that "return" here means "repent,"—i.e. Yahweh will not let the guilty nation repent and be forgiven. Still another is that the word means "restore"—i.e. he will not restore the nation to his favor (cf. Jer. 15:19; 31:18).

Says the LORD not merely marks the end of each oracle; it is a resounding prophetic "Amen." Its omission from the oracles on Tyre, Edom, and Judah has been taken by some as evidence that these oracles are additions to the original words of Amos.

A. ORACLES ON NEIGHBORING NATIONS (1:3–2:5)

1:3-5. On Syria. Famed as the oldest city of the world, **Damascus** was the capital of Syria. The devastating wars of Syria against Israel, doubtless vividly remembered by Amos' oldest hearers, had been waged by King **Hazael** and by his son **Benhadad** (cf. II Kings 8:7-15, 28-29; 10:32-33; 13:3-7, 22-25). **Gilead**, E of the Jordan River and S of Syria, had been the scene of wartime atrocities such as running over prisoners of war with iron-toothed instruments of torture (vs. 3*de;* cf. II Kings 13:7).

1:4-5. The punishment for such cruelty will be (*a*) **fire** destroying the royal citadel, (*b*) ruined defenses as the **bar** of the city gate is destroyed, (*c*) the death of the royal house or provincial governors (in the Hebrew **inhabitants** is singular, lit. "sitter" or perhaps "enthroned one"), and (*d*) return of the Syrians to **Kir,** the E Mesopotamian territory, perhaps near Elam, from which God brought them (cf. 9:7)—a fate as horrible as for the Israelites to be returned to Egyptian slavery. **Valley of Aven,** lit. "valley of vanity" or "wealth" or "idolatry," and **Beth-eden,** lit. "house of delight," may be Amos' ironic play on words. On the other hand the Hebrew consonants of Aven can be read as "On," the name of the Egyptian center of sun worship, which was later applied to Baalbek in the valley between the Lebanon mountain ranges, and Betheden may refer to a NE Syrian city-state on the upper Euphrates River mentioned in Assyrian records.

Amos' prediction was strikingly fulfilled when in 733/32 the Assyrian king Tiglath-pileser III reduced Damascus to a subservience from which she never recovered (cf. II Kings 16:9; Isa. 22:5-6).

1:6-8. On the Philistines. Turning from NE to SW, Amos lays the 2nd curse on Israel's perennial enemy, the Philistines. Perhaps **Gaza** is singled out as the S-most of the 5 principal cities lying at the gateway between Egypt and Asia. **Ashdod . . . Ashkelon . . . Ekron** are mentioned; Gath may have been omitted by Amos either because of the limits of poetic structure or because it had not yet recovered from its subjugation by Hazael decades before (cf. II Kings 12:17). On the other hand a few scholars have suggested a later date for this oracle because Gath was destroyed by the Assyrians in 711 (see below on 6:2). The cruelty of mass slave trade, in which not just individuals but whole nations are involved, is the reason for God's curse (vs. 6*de*). Perhaps the reference is to collaboration in slave trade between Philistines and "Arabs" in the days of King Jehoram of Judah nearly a cent. earlier (II Chr. 21:16-17), but more probably it is to a more recent event not recorded in the OT. Amos' prediction was partially fulfilled in the overthrow of Gaza by the Assyrians in 734.

1:9-10. On Tyre. The object of the 3rd curse, Tyre, chief city of the NW coastland, Phoenicia, was fabulously proud and wealthy because of its maritime world trade. The close similarity of this oracle to the preceding and its brevity (there is no parallel to vs. 8) have caused a number of scholars to question its coming from Amos.

1:9e. What was the unremembered **covenant of brotherhood?** King Hiram of Tyre "loved David" (I Kings 5:1) and once, though disappointed, called Solomon "my brother" (I Kings 9:13; cf. II Sam. 5:11; I Kings 5:1-12; 9:10-14). But in the 9th cent. the political marriage of King Ahab of Israel with Jezebel, daughter of a Phoenician king (I Kings 16:31), had results that hardly cemented fraternal relations. Some regard this reference as not to a broken pact between Phoenicia and Israel or some other nation but to internal conflict in the 7th cent., when Tyre twice sided with the Assyrians against other Phoenician cities. If so, this oracle is of course later than Amos. Possibly the phrase is a general reference to man's inhumanity to man.

Tyre was seriously weakened by Nebuchadrezzar's 13-year siege in the 6th cent. and was finally subdued by Alexander the Great in the 4th.

1:11-12. On Edom. In the 4th oracle God's judgment is on Edom, lying S of the Dead Sea. Here is hatred between blood brothers, for Israel and Edom were traditionally descended from the twins Jacob and Esau, whose rivalry was prenatal and perpetual (cf. Gen. 25:19-34; 27:1–28:9; 33:15-17). Tradition also traced the enmity in part to the Edomites' refusal to let Israel pass through their territory on the way from Egypt to the Promised Land (cf. Num. 20:14-21), but the anger became fiercest over Edom's plundering of Judah after the destruction of Jerusalem in 586 (cf. Ps. 137:7; Obad. 10-14). The breach against brotherhood is emphasized in a word play, for the root of the Hebrew word translated **pity** refers to the womb, the place where Jacob and Esau first struggled (cf. Gen. 25:22). The unceasing fierceness of Edom's wrath is like that of a wild beast tearing its prey. **Teman** was probably the largest and most important city in central Edom, and Bozrah, *ca.* 20 miles SE of the Dead Sea, was the strongest city in N Edom (see color map 4). Because of this oracle's brevity, its generality, and its particular appropriateness after 586, a number of scholars date it later than Amos.

1:13. On the Ammonites. The 5th oracle most resembles the first (vss. 3-5). Perhaps the atrocities in **Gilead** of both the Syrians from the N and the Ammonites from the E were connected, though no specific occasion is known when the Ammonites disemboweled pregnant women in gaining Gilead territory. Traditionally related to Israel (cf. Gen. 19:30-38), the Ammonites apparently began their wars of aggressive expansion to the W and N in the days of Jephthah in the 11th cent. (cf. Judg. 11:4-33). Saul's first military exploit was inspired by their threat of gouging out eyes (I Sam. 11:1-11), and they were later subjugated by David (II Sam. 8:11-12; 12:26-31; I Chr. 18:11; 19:1–20:3). In the 9th cent. they attacked the Judean king Jehoshaphat (II Chr. 20:1-23). They paid tribute, perhaps in Amos' day, to King Uzziah of Judah (II Chr. 26:8) and later to his son Jotham (II Chr. 27:5).

1:14-15. The Ammonites' capital city, **Rabbah,** or Rabbath-Ammon, is the only Ammonite city named in the OT. Now modern Amman, capital of the Hashemite Kingdom of Jordan, it is located on the upper Jabbok River *ca.* 23 miles E of the Jordan. Amos' predicted doom of **exile** for Ammonite leaders—the LXX reads "her kings . . . , their priests and their princes together" (cf. Jer. 49:3)—may have occurred at the command of Nebuchadrezzar after Jerusalem's fall in 586.

2:1-3. On Moab. The last oracle against a foreign nation, Moab, rises to a unique climax in condemning the desecration of the **bones** of the king of another of Israel's enemies, **Edom.** Thus Amos is not a nationalist cursing his country's traditional enemies. Rather he is asserting Yahweh's judgment on any nation's manifestation of cruelty, even including sacrilege toward the dead.

Defilement of any tomb or corpse was looked on with horror in the ancient Near East, as may be seen in tomb and coffin inscriptions pronouncing terrible curses on anyone disturbing their contents (cf. II Kings 23:16-20). Hence deliberately to burn royal bones for the purpose of making lime or plaster (cf. Deut. 27:2, 4) was unthinkable sacrilege. The occasion for this act may have been the 9th-cent. war of Mesha king of Moab against the coalition of Israel, Judah, and Edom (II Kings 3:5-27), but a more recent incident is more probable.

Moab was the fertile tableland E of the Dead Sea lying between Ammon on the N and Edom on the S. The Moabites were traditional relatives of Israel (cf. Gen. 19:30-38), but poor relations between Israelites and Moabites continuing from the days of the Israelite conquest (cf. Num. 21:10-25:5) resulted in a lack of close relations between these peoples (Deut. 23:3-6). **Kerioth** was a fortified city of Moab, perhaps the capital in Amos' day. According to archaeological evidence Moab was already being depopulated in this period. It was taken captive by Tiglath-pileser III in 733, and from the 6th cent. on it was practically no more.

2:4-5. On Judah. The 7th oracle of judgment, against Amos' own homeland, has been regarded by most scholars as a later addition to the book. Its brief form is exactly that of the questionable oracles on Tyre and Edom (1:9-12); its condemnation is in generalities; and its language is akin to that of Deut. and later prophets. Perhaps Amos' climactic denunciation of Israel in the following oracle (vss. 6-16) and the rest of the book includes both N and S kingdoms, **the whole family** of Yahweh's chosen people (3:1). Judah is specifically referred to only here and four other times (1:1-2; 6:1; 7:12; 9:11). If the passage comes from Amos the **law of the LORD** probably means the instruction or teaching of God's word spoken by his prophets (cf. vss. 11-12) rather than any written law, though the Covenant Code (Exod. 20:23–23:19) may have been in written form long before Amos' day. The perverting **lies** are probably the deceitful ways of idols or false gods.

B. Oracle on Israel (2:6-16)

If Amos' hearers received his first oracles with either self-righteous gloating over enemies or belief that at last divine retribution was to come upon those who deserved it, they must have become increasingly uncomfortable as his denunciations completely surrounded them. Now the thunder of God's judgment falls on them.

This lengthened oracle begins with the familiar pattern. Then in 3 successive stanzas Amos declares that (*a*) God's judgment will come upon his own people because of their cruel exploitation of their fellows and their profanation of true worship (vss. 6-8); (*b*) with base ingratitude for what God has done for them they corrupt his spiritual guides (vss. 9-12); (*c*) therefore none can escape the imminent doom of the nation of Israel (vss. 13-16).

2:6-8. Exploitation and Profanation. As in the previous indictments of neighboring nations, cruelty is the chief sin. But with Israel it is not national-crimes against other peoples but exploitation of the underprivileged by the privileged within society. The victims are the **righteous,** i.e. the innocent and honest subjects whose rights have been taken away either in lawsuits or in economic deals. They are the **poor,** the **needy,** the **afflicted,** or "meek," i.e. those helpless before their unscrupulous exploiters. Though the poor man owes no more than the price of a pair of cheap sandals, **they,** i.e. the exploiters, foreclose his mortgage or sell him into slavery (cf. 8:6). Figuratively—or perhaps lit.—they brutally grind the poor man's head down into the ground (vs. 7*a*) or, according to another reading of the difficult text, are so greedy that they pant after the dust which the poor throw on their heads in their mourning rites.

2:7cd. The charge that son and father resort to **the same maiden,** lit. "the girl," has been explained as referring either to secular prostitution or to mistreatment of a slave girl in the household. Most likely, however, it is Amos' way of castigating the practice of cult prostitution. In the nature cult of Baalism the reviving of vegetation after the autumnal rains accompanied the marriage of Baal, the resurrected god of vegetation, with his consort Asherah (cf. Judg. 3:7; I Kings 15:13; 18:19), who had rescued him from his temporary death in the underworld. Worshipers celebrated this season of hope by orgiastic relations with young men and women employees of the shrine (cf. Deut. 23:17; I Kings 14:24; 15:12; 22:46; II Kings 23:7). The female devotees were called lit. "holy women." In bitterest sarcasm Amos declares that this supposed holiness of harlotry purposefully profanes God's holy name. The **house of their God** may mean a Baal shrine, or it may mean a syncretized shrine where misguided Israelites worship Yahweh with the pagan rites of Baalism.

2:8. Amos goes on to declare that exploitation not only is in the places of business and law but is a rot at the core of the religious life. In their shrine revelries **beside every altar** (cf. 3:14; Hos. 8:11) they recline on **garments** the poor have had to pawn (cf. Exod. 22:26-27); and the wine they imbibe has been paid for by levies, perhaps shrine taxes, laid on the underprivileged.

2:9-12. God's Revelation Ungratefully Corrupted. In sharp contrast to what Israel is doing in profanation of God's name is what God has done to guard and guide his people. In the past he cleared the holy land for them. The **Amorite** was the pre-Israelite population of Canaan traditionally regarded as giant in stature and strength (cf. Gen. 15:16; Num. 13:32-33; Deut. 1:28). Yet not just the hearers' fortunate ancestors, but they themselves—**you** (vs. 10; cf. Deut. 5:3)—receive God's redemption from Egyptian slavery and his wilderness guidance.

2:11-12. The **prophets** and **Nazirites** have been and are God's gifts as continuing spiritual guides. From the days of Moses on prophets had been God's spokesmen to reveal his divine instructions (cf. Deut. 18:15-22). Nazirites were sacred persons, either consecrated by their parents or self-dedicated, whose exemplary loyalty to vows of the simple life—letting their hair grow and abstaining from wine, strong drink, unclean food, and contact with the dead (Num. 6:1-21; Judg. 13:2-7)—contrasted sharply with the indulgence of paganized Israelite religious life. Instead of being grateful for God's provisions for his people's welfare, Israel corrupts the very means for spiritual preservation by making Nazirites forget their vows and by silencing the prophets (cf. 7:12-16).

2:13-16. *The Judgment of Inescapable Disaster.* The deep hurt in the heart of God at the rebellion of his people, for whom he has done so much, may be the point of vs. 13*a*, in which the difficult Hebrew seems to say lit., "I am pressed under you." Most commentators, however, see the figure as the inescapable pressure of God's awful judgment on Israel. Not only will the nation as a whole perish, but its skilled defenders—the **mighty** and **swift** infantry and cavalry—will be unable to save even themselves as they strip for fast flight. **In that day** refers to the "day of Yahweh" (cf. 5:18-20). The concluding expression, **says the LORD,** lit. "the utterance [or oracle] of Yahweh," is the solemn prophetic declaration from God.

III. GOD'S TESTIMONIES AGAINST AND WOES UPON HIS PEOPLE (3:1-6:14)

The bulk of the book seems to be composed of 2 series of prophetic oracles. The first and longest series (3:1-5:17) proclaims God's thrice repeated testimony against his people: **Hear this word . . .** (3:1; 4:1; 5:1). The second (5:18-6:14), much shorter, is a series of "woes" upon his people (5:18; 6:1; perhaps 6:4). While such is apparently the general structure of these chs., it is difficult to find either chronological or logical thought structure running through the book. Perhaps an editor has collected Amos' oracles in this general fashion.

A. FIRST TESTIMONY (3:1-15)

Amos' shocking prediction of Israel's imminent doom at once raises inevitable questions in the face of the country's unprecedented prosperity under Jeroboam II. Contrary to the prophet's dour pessimism, are not God's people reaping the material rewards of their favored position as his chosen ones? In a series of testimonies spoken in the name of Yahweh Amos deals with the meaning of Israel's unique relationship to God and the reasons for discerning the signs of disaster.

3:1-2. *Privilege and Responsibility.* The doctrine of Israel's election as God's own people stems from the tradition of his miraculous deliverance of the whole people from Egypt (vs. 1; cf. 2:10; 9:7). While Yahweh directs the course of history of all earth's **families** (cf. 9:7) to Israel God says, **You only have I known.** The word "know" here carries any or all of the following meanings: "recognize as covenant people" (cf. Deut. 9:24; Hos. 13:4-5); "experience intimately" as in the sacredness and closeness of married love (cf. Gen. 4:1); "care for" or "be concerned about" (cf. Isa. 1:3); and "choose" or "elect" (cf. Gen. 18:19).

Yahweh's choice of his covenant people at Mt. Sinai (cf. Exod. 19:4-6; 24:3-8; Deut. 7:6-11) and his subsequent favors have led to the sadly erroneous popular conclusion that as God's darling nation they are enjoying the rewards of his favoritism. Amos starts with the same premise, that Israel is God's elect nation. But his conclusion is radically different: such high privilege carries proportionate responsibility for obedience, and Israel's multiplied **iniquities,** i.e., her guilty and intentional acts of perversity, mark her for the severe punishment which such sin entails.

3:3-8. *Prophetic Certainty, Authority, and Warning.* How does Amos know that punishment is near? By what authority does he speak? To such implied questions Amos replies in the poetic form of wisdom writers' rhetorical questions (vss. 3-6, 8; vs. 7 seems to be prose; cf. Prov. 6:27-28).

3:3-6. Amos' argument begins with a transitional question (vs. 3) perhaps carrying a double meaning: Do not 2 people seen walking together have at least something in common; have not Israel and her God had a close relationship through the years? The following questions (vss. 4-6) imply both disaster and the fact that an effect has its cause: the lion's roar on sensing the nearness of prey, followed by the cub's growl of satisfaction in eating the kill; the bird's swooping down to the lure of bait, followed by the snap of the trap; the chill of terror of the city dweller at the blast announcing the approach of an invading enemy. Amos has cast these questions in the meter of a funeral dirge (see below on 5:1-3). The catastrophe they portend comes, not by chance, but as divine discipline and judgment which is the inescapable result of sin.

3:7-8. It may be a later commentator who adds the prose statement (vs. 7) that Amos' message is an example of God's unfailing procedure of revelation: as his chosen spokesmen the **prophets** can listen in on his **secret** heavenly council planning sessions (cf. 2:11; see "The Prophetic Literature," pp. 1095-1100). The true prophet hears God's lion roar (vs. 8; cf. 1:2) and, even though he may be unwilling, by irresistible divine compulsion he must speak (cf. 7:15; Jer. 1:6-10; 20:9). This is Amos' authority for warning his people before it is too late.

3:9-12. *Witnesses to Confusion and Destruction.* In figurative speech Amos calls on the **strongholds,** i.e. citadel fortresses, of Israel's enemies to gather round her capital to witness her utter confusion (vss. 9d-10) and destruction (vs. 11). The LXX has **Assyria** as the normal parallel to **Egypt,** but the Hebrew text reads "Ashdod," a Philistine city. Amos nowhere else mentions Assyria by name, and it would seem strange that an original "Assyria" would have been erroneously changed to "Ashdod." Perhaps here in bitter irony Amos is calling on Israel's past traditional enemies, Philistia and Egypt, neither of whom has intimate knowledge of God's will, to be public observers of God's privileged people's confusion.

3:9c-10. Israel's capital, **Samaria,** the strong-walled hilltop political center originally established by Omri in the 9th cent., was readily observable from surrounding mountaintops. The **tumults** in her life are the **oppressions** of the poor by unscrupulous exploiters who have gained their wealth by **violence and robbery.** Conscience has been killed; they simply **do not know how to do right,** i.e. what is straightforward and honest.

3:11-12. The resultant doom will be siege and conquest by an invading foreign army (vs. 11). Amos is probably speaking before Assyria's first march W under Tiglath-pileser III in 743, but he anticipates the final blow felling proud Samaria in 722. Using probably a typical shepherd's proverb he describes the scraps left from the invading lion's meal (vs. 12)—bits such as a hired shepherd shows to his employer to prove that he is not legally liable for what has been killed by a wild beast (cf. Exod. 22:10-13). Amos predicts total destruction (cf. 9:1), for what will be left will be but the shreds of former finery, a **corner** of a broken **couch** and **part** of a ruined **bed.** The Hebrew word translated "part," apparently related to "Damascus," may refer to inlay work or damask silk cushions.

3:13-15. Punishment on Sanctuary and Mansion. The climactic oracle of this first testimony predicts destruction of the religious sanctuaries which presumably provide national security, together with the symbols of material prosperity.

3:13-14. The Lord Yahweh, the **God of hosts,** i.e. armies, is speaking. Amos never speaks of him as "God of Israel" but rather as universal sovereign. He is Lord not merely of the armies of Israel but of the heavenly armies governing the whole world and composing the divine council (cf. vs. 7), which perhaps is addressed in this oracle detailing events of the judgment on Israel announced previously (2:6-8, 13-16). Israel is spoken of as the **house of Jacob** because of the patriarch's sacred association with **Bethel** (cf. Gen. 28:10-22; 32:27-28; 35:10), the N kingdom's rival sanctuary to Jerusalem (cf. 7:13). **The horns of the altar** may obliquely refer to the bull images set up at Bethel by Jeroboam I. The equipping of altars with corner projections in the shape of the horns of the bull, symbol of fertility and power, is attested by archaeology. These could be grasped for refuge by a fugitive from revenge (cf. Exod. 27:2; Lev. 4:7; I Kings 1:50-51; 2:28). Amos' indelible point is that the symbols of sacred security will provide no refuge from God's awful punishment (cf. 9:1).

3:15. Nor will wealthy material comforts be of any avail. The **winter house** was occasionally heated in the cold rainy season of late autumn and winter (cf. Jer. 36:22). The **summer house** was either an upper story open to cool breezes in the hot, dry harvest season (cf. Judg 3:20) or a separate dwelling high on a hill. As verified by beautifully carved ivories found by archaeologists at Megiddo and Samaria, **houses of ivory** refers to ivory inlays

used in furniture and decorated paneling in the homes of the wealthy (cf. 6:4; I Kings 10:18, 22; 22:39; Ps. 45:8).

B. Second Testimony (4:1-13)

4:1-3. Punishment of Corrupt Womanhood. The 2nd series of oracles beginning **Hear this word** (cf. 3:1; 5:1) opens with a summons to Israel's women, sarcastically termed **cows of Bashan**—perhaps a proverbial term for the sleek, fat cattle of this fertile tableland E of the Sea of Galilee (cf. Deut. 32:14; Ps. 22:12; Ezek. 39:18; Mic. 7:14). While women were occasionally involved in business dealings and thus could be heartless exploiters, Amos pictures fine ladies of **Samaria** as continuously nagging their **husbands,** lit. "lords," into ceaseless exploitation to keep the endless round of feasts going.

4:2-3. With evident play on the word Amos declares to these ladies with their "lords" that the real "Lord" Yahweh has vowed the most awful vow possible, by his own nature as God, that they will find themselves in a procession of captives going out through the breached wall of the city, caught like helpless fish, with **hooks** piercing their lips. The Hebrew expression translated **into Harmon** appears nowhere else. It may be a misspelling of "naked" or "onto the dung heap" or "to Rimmon," a hill E of Bethel where there were many caves (cf. Judg. 20:45-47; 21:13) and also one of the names for the god Baal (cf. II Kings 5:18; Zech. 12:11).

4:4-5. The Rebellion of Worship. In lyrical poetry and with biting sarcasm Amos invites whoever hears—probably not just the pampered women of the previous oracle—to come to the 2 chief sanctuaries of Israel and carry on their accustomed and beloved sacrificial rituals. But to do so, says he, is not to worship God; it is rather to **multiply** rebellion against him.

On **Bethel** see above on 3:13-14. **Gilgal,** meaning "circle of stones," was possibly a site in the highland N of Bethel (cf. Deut. 11:30; II Kings 2:1; 4:38) but more likely the community near Jericho, famous as first encampment of the incoming Israelites under Joshua and important site in the era of Saul (cf. Josh. 4:19-20; I Sam. 11:14-15). It was denounced by 8th-cent. prophets as a onetime holy sanctuary which had become a center of paganized sacrificial cult rites (cf. 5:5; Hos. 4:15; 9:15; 12:11).

In this, his first condemnation of the sacrificial system (cf. 5:21-25; Isa. 1:10-17), Amos satirizes the elaborate piling up of sacrifices as merely public show and as gratification of selfish pleasures in festival merriment—**for so they love to do.** His detailed references to the types and frequency of the sacrifices, while not absolutely certain in meaning, may ironically exaggerate popular overzealousness.

Sacrifices were animals slaughtered and eaten in a festival meal with God, priests, and worshipers all participating; such an occasion would take place no more than 3 times a year for any worshiper, as it involved making a pilgrimage to the sanctuary.

Tithes, according to the Deuteronomic legislation (cf. Deut. 14:22-29), were the required annual offering of a 10th of the yield of agricultural products, each year involving a shared festival meal, and every 3rd year to be shared with the landless Levite, sojourner, fatherless, and widow.

Leaven, which produces fermentation, was prescribed in certain late laws for "peace offerings for thanksgiving" to be eaten in convivial meals (Lev. 7:13; cf. 23:17); but leaven was clearly prohibited in the older laws for any sacrifice to Yahweh (Exod. 23:18; 34:25; cf. Lev. 2:11; 6:17). Amos may mean that the **sacrifice of thanksgiving of that which is leavened** is typical of the participants' concentration on their festival enjoyment even when supposedly engaged primarily in thanksgiving to God.

Freewill offerings, never required by any law, should be the voluntary expression of the worshipers' response to God. But what is the motivation of those who **proclaim** and **publish** such gifts? Cf. Matt. 6:1-16.

4:6-12. *Chastising Experience Unheeded.* Each strophe of this poem—perhaps a ritual utterance at the Bethel sanctuary—begins with a declaration of what God has done or will do **to you, O Israel** and ends with the refrain **yet you did not return to me,** expressing God's mingled sorrow and judgment that his chosen people have paid no attention to his repeated chastisements, which should have caused them to repent. **Therefore,** the conclusion is, ... **prepare to meet your God, O Israel!** The very indefiniteness is frighteningly vivid. The 5 specific disasters are not identifiable with any known historical calamities.

4:6. The phrase **cleanness of teeth**—because of no **bread** to put between them—is a striking figure of speech for famine.

4:7-8. Contrary to much popular belief that the Canaanite god Baal is the fertility deity responsible for rain and hence abundant crops, it is really Yahweh, the controller of nature, who on occasion has delayed the heavy Nov. rains until Feb. so that the farmer has had no Apr.-Jun. harvest, or who has sent sporadic rains so that some communities have gone staggering to others' cisterns to get a bit of precious water.

4:9. Complete agricultural failures have been due to **blight** caused by the scorching E wind (cf. Gen. 41:6), the yellowing of crops from **mildew,** and a **locust** plague (cf. Joel 1:4-18).

4:10. The expression **pestilence after the manner of Egypt** may be proverbial for diseases as terrible as the famous plagues before the Exodus (Exod. 7:14-11:10); but the scene here is the tragedy of war, with the youth of the nation slain, the **stench** of unburied corpses, and the capture of cavalry, often in the prophets a symbol of pride (cf. 2:15).

4:11. The **brand plucked out of the burning** when God **overthrew some of you** expresses the miracle of anything's having been saved in a disaster compared to the traditional destruction of **Sodom and Gomorrah,** presumably by earthquake and resultant ignition of released sulphurous gases, asphalt, and petroleum (Gen. 19:24-25).

4:13. *First Doxology.* Concluding the oracle is an exalted description of the God whom Israel is to encounter, the first of 3 "doxologies" (cf. 5:8-9; 9:5-6). Most commentators regard these as additions to Amos, written in the language and thought forms of later prophets or wisdom writers (cf. Job 38:4-

21; Prov. 8:22-26; Isa. 40:28; 45:7-8; 58:14), though some think they may be fragments of an earlier hymn adapted for use in prophetic liturgy. They eloquently characterize the majesty of God: He is the creator of all the universe, who yet reveals to man his **thought,** perhaps through the prophets (cf. 3:7) or through his created world (cf. Ps. 19:1-4). He turns **morning** light into the **darkness** of eclipse or storm. There may be double meaning in his treading **on the heights of the earth** (cf. Mic. 1:3-4), for he whose mighty steps stride over the mountaintops can also trample into the ground the "high places," i.e. sanctuaries, of the nature god Baal. He is **God of hosts,** i.e. of all heavenly powers (see above on 3:13-14); this is his **name,** i.e. his nature and being.

C. Third Testimony (5:1-17)

5:1-3. *Virgin Israel's Death.* The 3rd of God's testimonies against his people opens with a funeral dirge over the death of the nation. Perhaps Amos appears in mourning clothes and, accompanied by a musical instrument, sings (cf. Isa. 5:1) in the limping dirge meter of three beats followed by two his elegy (vs. 2). Cast in the Hebrew prophetic perfect tense, the imminent future event of the nation's death is portrayed as already happened as the prophet figuratively gazes on the **virgin** corpse lying **on her land,** lit. "ground." Realistically (vs. 3), in the coming invasion which is God's judgment 90% of the Israelite warriors who go into battle from **city** or village (**hundred**) will come out corpses.

5:4-7. *Two Calls to Seek and Live.* Death and life —these are the choice which Israel yet has. Convinced that Israel is practically dead because of her sins, yet 3 times (vss. 4, 6, 14) Amos holds out hope for life, a survival possible only if Israel will "seek" the right object.

5:4-5. First, **seek me and live,** God calls; **do not seek** the traditional sanctuaries, which are doomed. To "seek" God usually means to come to worship at one of his shrines, but Amos seems instead to counsel direct encounter with God, getting into right relationship with him through obedience. Here he uses ironic play on words. The name **Bethel** (see above on 3:13-14) was also that of a Semitic deity well attested through archaeology (cf. Gen. 31:13; Jer. 48:13). Beth-el, "house of God," will become Beth-aven, "house of **nought,**" i.e. idolatry or wickedness (cf. Hos. 4:15; 5:8; 10:5, 8). Playing on the sound of the name of the other famous N sanctuary, **Gilgal** (see above on 4:4-5), Amos declares that "Gilgal shall go into galling captivity" (Amer. Trans.). To **cross over to Beer-sheba,** a sanctuary 28 miles SW of Hebron associated with the patriarchs Abraham and Isaac (cf. Gen. 21:25-33; 26:23-33), would be to travel to the traditional S boundary of the entire land of God's people (cf. 8:14).

5:6. The 2nd summons warns that God's judgment—as on the neighboring nations (1:4, 7, 10, 12, 14; 2:2, 5) and in the 2nd of Amos' visions (7:4)—will be a miraculous **fire** which no rain magic of the cult at **Bethel** can **quench.** The N kingdom is called the **house of Joseph** because of the importance of the traditional tribal territory of Joseph's sons Manasseh and Ephraim.

5:7. Perhaps the preceding call to seek Yahweh is addressed to **you who turn justice to wormwood.** But the Hebrew is not in the 2nd person, and some interpreters emend it to read "Woe to those who turn . . ." (cf. vs. 18; 6:1) and transpose it to form the beginning of vs. 10. Amos never defines **justice** and **righteousness,** which he normally uses in parallel (cf. vss. 15, 24; 6:12), for he speaks only of their perversion or absence. He seems to use these terms in the forensic sense of the law court and the right or rights of the Israelite citizen. Such righteousness is based on the covenant relationship between the chosen people Israel and their God, though Amos never uses the word "covenant." He does not need to define this well-known duty at the center of Israelite life. He simply deplores its being turned to **wormwood,** an exceptionally bitter-tasting plant (cf. 6:12).

5:8-9. *Second Doxology.* See above on 4:13. As creator and constant sustainer of all nature God set in the heavens the constellations, **the Pleiades** and **Orion** (cf. Job 9:9; 38:31); he provides dawn and dusk and the rain cycle (cf. Job 36:27-30). He who controls all nature also controls human destiny, and so he may destroy mere human strength. Some have emended certain difficult Hebrew words in vs. 9 to names of other constellations.

5:10-13. *Exploitation of the Poor.* The beginning of vs. 10 may be in vs. 7 (see above). Exploiters despise those who protest against their injustices **in the gate**—the civic center where the elders and judges held court (cf. e.g. Deut. 21:19; 22:15; Ruth 4:1, 11; Isa. 29:21)—though they know that these defenders of the exploited speak the **truth.** The shift to 2nd person in vs. 11 may indicate the beginning of a separate oracle. To the specific charges of exploitation previously leveled (2:6-7) Amos here adds **exactions,** i.e. extortions, in the grain market and the **bribe** in the law court. He warns that the profiteers will never enjoy the security and luxury of their houses built of expensive **hewn stone.**

5:13. Many interpreters have taken this to be a reader's marginal comment copied into the text. However, the meaning is probably that in the **evil time** of God's judgment to come the man who thinks that in manipulating God and fellow man to his own advantage he has been "successful" (rather than **prudent;** cf. I Sam. 18:30) will be shocked into stunned silence.

5:14-15. *Third Call to Seek and Live.* In his final plea that his people seek aright Amos by implication defines what it means to seek Yahweh (vss. 4*b*, 6*a*); it is to **seek good,** to respond in ethical obedience to him. In his dealings with his people God has shown his goodness (cf. 2:9-10) and his care for the poor and the afflicted (cf. vss. 11-12; 2:7; 4:1). His people's primary concern must therefore be to search for **good** rather than evil. These general Hebrew terms refer to the whole range of moral and spiritual possibilities. Here good is pinned down to specific acts of **justice in the gate,** i.e. fair dealings in the law court. But it must go deeper; it must be the inner motivation of life. God's people must not simply do good acts and refrain from evil ones; they must **hate evil, and love good.**

Only by such transformation of inner character will it be possible that in the coming judgment by God's grace a **remnant** will be left. This is no doctrine of a righteous remnant, only the slight chance that there will be some survivors (cf. vs. 3) in the coming holocaust. Possibly, however, **remnant of Joseph** here means all Israel, viewed as relatively small and unimpressive even in these prosperous days (cf. "he is so small," 7:2, 5). Thus does Amos deny the false illusions of those who proclaim that Israel's present prosperity is prima facie evidence of God's presence with them (vs. 14*cd*).

5:16-17. *Mourning Rites at Israel's Death.* In this climax of his 3rd series of oracles of God's testimony against his people Amos returns to the funeral dirge meter with which he began it (vss. 2-3). In the doom to come mourning will be complete among all classes of society, both city dwellers in their **squares,** i.e. open places for public gatherings, and **farmers** in their fields and usually joyful **vineyards** (cf. Isa. 16:10). Those **skilled in lamentation** means professional mourners hired for the funeral of any citizen of rank, or possibly Baal cult weepers whose wails now fail to bring the dead god of vegetation back to life (cf. I Kings 18:26-29). As in the covenant ritual of passing between the pieces of the sacrificial animals symbolizing the death of those who fail to keep the covenant (cf. Gen. 15:7-17; Jer. 34:18-20), and as in the final plague in Egypt (cf. Exod. 12:12-30), Yahweh will now **pass through the midst of you,** in deadly pestilence or in devastating war.

D. FIRST WOE (5:18-27)

As the book is now organized Amos' series of testimonies against God's people (3:1–5:17) is followed by a consequent and climactic pronouncement of woes (5:18–6:14), in which God's imminent coming is seen as a day of destroying judgment.

5:18-20. *The Day of Yahweh.* In the first woe Amos turns expected joy into lamentation—**light** into **darkness**—in one of his most important contributions to Israelite prophecy, his reversal of the popular conception of the coming day of Yahweh. That he never defines this term shows that he is referring to a widely understood concept current in his time. Perhaps it was originally used for an annual celebration of the new year. If such a festival in Israel at all resembled the well-known Babylonian new year ceremonies, the ritual included re-enthronement of the king, ceremonial victory over all enemies, renewal of the promise of prosperity, and the setting of fates for the year to come (see Intro. to Pss.). This day of the glorious coming of Yahweh to bless his people for another year may have suggested the idea of a great day of his coming to inaugurate a permanent era of bliss.

It is this pious expectation, supposedly assured by multiplied cultic sacrifices, on which Amos pronounces his first resounding **Woe!** Far from security for a fugitive from a **lion** and a **bear,** this **house** of Israel's improper piety contains a hidden venomous **serpent.** There will be no shred of **brightness** in that day when Yahweh comes, not in reward, but in punishing judgment (cf. 8:9-14; Isa. 2:9-21; Zeph. 1:7-18).

5:21-27. *The Sacrilege of Sacrifice.* In the most vigorous passage in his book Amos hears Yahweh himself condemn a flourishing cult which assumes that rites without righteousness will continue to buy divine favor (cf. 4:4-5). God despises the **feasts,** i.e. the 3 annual pilgrimage festivals hallowed by law and custom (cf. Exod. 23:14-17; I Kings 12:32-33). He will **take no delight in** (lit. "refuse to smell") the clouds of incense from the **solemn assemblies,** really convivial ceremonies. **Burnt offerings** were the most expensive type, for the whole animal was consumed on the altar, leaving nothing as food for the worshiper or payment for the priest; since vs. 22*a* is metrically overlong, this type of sacrifice may be a later insertion. **Cereal offerings** of grain and **peace offerings** of specially fattened animals, the latter to keep amicable relations with the deity, were samples of the food eaten by the worshipers in the communion meals. The accompanying **noise of your songs** and **melody of your harps** were the ancient equivalents of our choral anthems, congregational hymns, and organ voluntaries. Surely God does not refuse to **listen** to the sacred worship of his pious people! Indeed yes, declares Amos, because even the most elaborate and devout ritual has no worth in itself (cf. Matt. 6:7). It may be mere religiosity which, however fervent, misinterprets the nature of both God and his covenant relation with man.

5:24. Some interpreters see the **justice** and **righteousness** of this key verse as God's deliverance, his eventual sending down of his saving powers, now delayed by the people's unresponsive preoccupation with their selfishly noisy festivities. Others take them to mean his awful destroying judgment, not simply in one day of wrath, but in continuing divine "righting" or "righteous" acts, as powerful and relentless as a **stream** which flows even through the dry season. Perhaps the traditional interpretation is correct: Amos here affirms that God's people's loyalty is shown, not in elaborate and expressive ceremony, but in steady rather than sporadic justice in human relationships and righteousness in obedience to God's will (cf. Isa. 1:10-17).

5:25. It is no new commandment, no new ethical standard that Amos is lifting up. Rather it is a recall to the heart of the covenant, the faith of the fathers in the period of the desert wandering under Moses. Whether or not Amos, along with other prophets (cf. Jer. 7:21-23), believed that the period under Moses was really a cultless age, he was convinced that ritual was not necessary, perhaps not really commanded, in that unique time of God's gracious care for his people.

5:26-27. But now, says Amos—if these vss. are not a later addition to his book—in syncretistic cult festivals manufactured idols of **Sakkuth** and **Kaiwan,** Mesopotamian star deities associated with the planet Saturn, are carried along in sacred procession, doubtless as lesser gods in Yahweh's train (cf. 8:14). Yet another sort of procession is forming, to go into **exile beyond Damascus.** If this is Amos' word and the Hebrew text of 3:9 is correct (see comment) this is the closest he comes to identifying Assyria as the conqueror he foresees (cf. 3:11-12; 4:2-3; 6:7, 14; 7:11, 17).

E. SECOND WOE (6:1-14)

This 2nd and final woe castigates the proud leaders of all Israel for their false sense of security (vss.

1-3) and callous self-indulgence (vss. 4-6) and declares that these "first citizens" will become the first of the many to suffer and be carried off into exile (vss. 7-14).

6:1-3. *Illusory Security.* Amos here apparently pronounces woe on the leaders of both Israel and Judah, though many have suspected **Zion,** i.e. Jerusalem, of being a later insertion. To these **notable men** in their role as judges all the house of Israel naturally **come.** In their eyes Israel as God's chosen is **first of the nations.**

6:2. But how does Israel compare with neighboring **kingdoms?** Probably **Calneh** here refers to a N Syrian city-state called Calno in Isa. 10:9 (see color map 9). **Hamath the great,** an important city located on the Orontes River, was in Amos' day the capital of a Syrian kingdom bordering on Israel's N frontier (cf. vs. 14; II Kings 14:25). **Gath** was one of the 5 Philistine city-states W of Judah. Though the Hebrew text is somewhat ambiguous, the expected answer to the question seems to be that none of the nations named compares with Israel in the size of its **territory.** The meaning therefore may be that since Israel is the largest and most prosperous of the states of Syria-Palestine her leaders have so much the more obligation to be responsible. The more common critical interpretation, however, is that these 3 are cited as examples of kingdoms already destroyed by Assyria and accordingly that the vs. is a warning addressed to Judah by a later prophet which was erroneously inserted in Amos' work. Assyrian records indicate that Calneh was captured *ca.* 738 and Hamath and Gath in 711. In Amos' day they had been free from Assyrian attack for nearly a cent.

6:3. The address of this vs. is to the complacent leaders of vs. 1, who refuse to acknowledge the coming of the **evil day** of God's wrath and in their law courts render judgments of **violence** rather than justice.

6:4-6. *Irresponsible Indulgence.* The prophet's curse on these leaders continues (**woe** in vs. 4 is implied rather than expressed in the Hebrew text) with an unforgettable picture of self-indulgence. These who should be Israel's leaders show no concern over the imminent disaster about to befall their land; they **are not grieved over the ruin of Joseph** (vs. 6). Instead they sprawl on luxurious **couches** inlaid with **ivory** (see above on 3:15); they feast on specially fattened lamb and veal (cf. 5:22); they babble drinking songs as they quaff their wine from large sacrificial bowls rather than ordinary cups; and they apply expensive oil cosmetics to their bodies. **Like David** is not in the LXX and makes the line metrically too long; it may be a marginal comment copied into the text.

6:7-14. *The Final Doom.* These irresponsible leaders will indeed lead when, their **revelry** suddenly ended, they head the line of those going into **exile.** The oath of Yahweh (vs. 8)—**sworn by himself,** for nothing is more powerful in the universe—expresses his abhorrence of his deceitful people's **pride** (cf. 8:7) and their human achievements such as their military **strongholds.** But no human power can now avert his destruction of their **city,** viz. probably Samaria.

6:9-10. Destroying pestilence will follow devastating war and wipe out all of a household together. If one survivor huddled in the corner of an inner room of a large house sees the nearest kin come in to find the corpses, to **burn** them in hope of stopping the plague—or, less likely, to burn spices in funeral rites (cf. II Chr. 16:14; 21:19; Jer. 34:5)—the terror-stricken survivor will beg that the name of Yahweh not even be whispered lest his fury break forth anew.

6:11. The destruction of palace and hovel described in this vs. may be from earthquake or from the razing which archaeology has shown to have been common in ancient warfare.

6:12-13. Israel's tragic conduct is unnatural. Her poisonous pattern of injustice (cf. 5:7) is as futile as trying to race **horses** on a stony cliff or **plow the sea** like farmland. Israel's pride is silly. As examples Amos refers sarcastically to the boasting over Jeroboam II's recapture from Syria of 2 small cities in Gilead: **Lo-debar** (actually Debir), meaning a "thing of nought," and **Karnaim** (actually Ashteroth-karnaim), meaning "two horns," symbols of **strength** and also of the Canaanite fertility goddess Ashteroth.

6:14. In contrast to such unnatural human pride let Israel look up, for she will see Yahweh himself coming—this is the emphasis of the Hebrew text—as he causes oppression by a foreign conqueror which will spread to the farthest ideal boundaries of his chosen people's land. The **entrance of Hamath** was a pass in the valley between the Lebanon and Antilebanon ranges which marked the S boundary of the territory controlled by Hamath (cf. vs. 2). The **Arabah** was the deep Galilee-Jordan–Dead Sea valley and its continuation S to the Gulf of Aqaba, but the meaning of **brook of the Arabah** is uncertain. Perhaps "brook" should read "Sea," as in II Kings 14:25—i.e. Amos is ironically quoting Jeroboam II's boast of having enlarged the border of his kingdom to the Dead Sea in the S. On the other hand perhaps II Kings 14:25 should read "brook," meaning the Zered, which flows into the Dead Sea at the SE corner and marked the S boundary of Moab, which Jeroboam may have reconquered for Israel. Other interpreters, however, understand this vs. as describing the ideal boundaries of all Israel, i.e. Israel and Judah together, and therefore make "brook of the Arabah" equivalent to "brook of Egypt" in I Kings 8:65 (see comment).

IV. Visions and Final Dialogues (7:1-9:8b)

The 3rd section of the book contains a remarkable series of 5 visions (7:1-9; 8:1-3; 9:1-4) with interspersed biography (7:10-17) and the concluding oracles of the prophet (8:4-14; 9:5-8). Many interpreters regard the visions as Amos' account of the experiences which constituted his call to become a prophet (cf. Isa. 6; Jer. 1; Ezek. 1-3). They therefore assume that these should be read as prelude to the oracles of the preceding sections of the book. However, in the one clearly biographical section of the book (7:10-17) Amos indicates that he does not regard himself as officially a prophet despite the fact that God has called him from his daily work to prophesy. It is impossible to say definitively whether the visions describe Amos' call or a succession of experiences during his prophetic ministry.

A. Three Visions and a Biographical Episode (7:1-17)

When God causes Amos to see first the locusts and then the fire, his immediate plea is heeded, and God does not let his people be destroyed (7:1-6). But when Amos is shown the plumb line of judgment against the wall of his nation (7:7-9), he makes no reply; and there follows the account of his encounter with Amaziah, the priest of King Jeroboam's sanctuary at Bethel (7:10-17). It cannot be determined whether the 3rd vision was actually closely followed by Amos' encounter and expulsion from Bethel, or whether the sequence in the book is simply editorial, based on the successive references to calamity to befall Jeroboam (vss. 9, 11).

7:1-3. First Vision: Locust Plague. While a scourge of locusts (cf. Joel 1–2) may seem but a natural plague occasionally suffered in the Near East, Amos sees it as God's own warning (cf. 4:9). Possibly the **king's mowings** were the harvesting of the first crop of grass after the autumnal rains, much of which went for taxes. Thus before the spring crop can develop the locusts are devouring everything, so that the poor common man will have nothing. Vs. 2a probably should be emended to read "When they were about to finish . . . ." Amos' plea is not that the locust plague is unjust but simply that God **forgive** his people. The **LORD repented** is the Hebrew way of saying that God's mercy exceeds his justice, so that his mind may be changed by his prophet's intercession (cf. e.g. Gen. 20:7; Exod. 32:11-14; Joel 2:12-14).

7:4-6. Second Vision: Supernatural Fire. Probably the occasion in nature of this judgment is drought caused by the scorching summer sun (cf. 4:7; Joel 1:19-20). But this is no ordinary burning heat. Rather it is supernatural fire which devours even the subterranean **deep**, on which the earth rests, and which flows forth in springs and rivers (see comment on Ps. 18:7-18). Hence Amos blurts out, not "Forgive!" but **Cease!** And, marvelous to relate, God does.

7:7-9. Third Vision: The Plumb Line. Amos now sees the Lord himself **standing beside a wall,** but Amos' eye is not on God but on the plumb line he holds. Seen against this cord with its weight at the end, Israel, God's wall, is obviously so out of perpendicular that it must fall. God's patience is now at an end. There is no chance that he will **again pass by** in forgiveness. Doom will fall on the **high places,** i.e. hilltop shrines, **of Isaac**—possibly a reference to long-esteemed patriarchal centers such as Beer-sheba, traditionally associated with Isaac (cf. 5:5). The proud nation will die with the death of the royal dynasty (cf. vss. 11, 17; Hos. 1:4).

7:10-17. Encounter with the Priest of Bethel. The high priest at the royal religious center reports to King Jeroboam II that Amos is a traitor. Perhaps **Amaziah,** mentioned only here in the biblical text, fears that Amos has magical power by which his prediction (vs. 11) will actually be effected (cf. Jer. 19:1–20:6). Hence **the land is not able to bear all his words,** and Amos must be banished. Whether or not in calling him **seer** the priest derides Amos as a mere dreamer, in his order of expulsion Amaziah declares that Amos may **eat bread,** i.e. earn his living, in rival Judah, perhaps at a sanctuary there, but certainly no longer may speak at Israel's holy **temple** at **Bethel** (see above on 3:13-14).

7:14-15. Amos' reply makes this scene one of the most vivid and important in all OT prophetic books. But the interpretation of Amos' statement about himself varies widely among the scholars. Since Hebrew regularly omits the copulative verb, one can read here either **I am** or "I was." Accordingly some hold that Amos refers to the past, stating that he was not a prophet until called by Yahweh. But the more normal reading is a reference to the present. Probably recognizing that by **seer** Amaziah refers contemptuously to the well-known court or temple prophet who may profiteer from his profession (cf. e.g. Mic. 3:5, 11), Amos declares that he is neither such nor a member of one of the organized prophetic orders (cf. e.g. I Sam 10:5; I Kings 22:6; II Kings 2:3, 5). With high regard for the function of being Yahweh's prophet (cf. 2:11-12; 3:7-8), Amos simply testifies to God's inescapable call. It came to him when as a shepherd he was watching his flocks and herds. His 2nd occupation was in the lowlands where the sycamore-fig trees grow, and his job was to puncture the unripe fruit to make it edible and therefore salable.

7:16-17. Far from recanting, Amos repeats his refusal to be silenced either by officialdom or by popular demand (cf. 2:12), and he predicts details of the imminent disaster. The high priest's own **wife** will be openly ravished by invading soldiers, or perhaps become a prostitute for economic survival. The holy **land** of Yahweh's presence will be sold in **parceled** lots rather than be inherited as a united trust. Yahweh's people will be exiled in a land **unclean** because under the sovereignty of a foreign god.

B. Fourth Vision and Another Testimony (8:1-14)

8:1-3. Fourth Vision: Summer Fruit. This vision brings to a conclusion the movements seen in the preceding 3. A springtime locust plague and midsummer drought are now followed by late summer's ripened fruit, perhaps figs. The announcement of the exhausted patience of God in the plumb-line vision has now resulted in the sentence of doom: **the end has come.** In a play on words of similar sound (indicated in the RSV footnote; cf. Jer. 1:11-12) and, more deeply, in the meaning of **summer fruit** as the last of the harvest Amos sees the end at hand. The irony is that in the popular view the harvest of summer fruit at the end of the long dry season is the moment when God's people anticipate the immediately coming autumn rains with their promise of renewal. Not so, declares Amos. This is not the end of a season but the end of Israel. **In that day** of God's awful judgment now at hand the **temple** or palace (see RSV footnote) **songs** of joy will become howls of lamentation. The mass of corpses will be so stunning that all Israel will fall into a terrified hush (cf. 6:9-10).

8:4-14. The Final Judgment Day. In the language of God's previous testimonies against his people—**Hear this** (cf. 3:1; 4:1; 5:1)—Amos now announces details of the awful judgment day ahead. But first he spells out in further detail (vss. 4-6) the exploitation of fellow man which is Israel's rebellion against

God and the reason for the coming doom (cf. 2:6-8).

8:4-6. The monthly religious festival of the **new moon** and the weekly **sabbath** require holy celebration and stoppage of daily employment. Ironically, the greedy exploiters reluctantly keep holy days and then hurry to cheat their customers. They do so by using an undersize **ephah** to measure the product they are selling and an overweight **shekel** to balance the customer's silver (see table, p. 1285), or by using untrue scales; and they sell the sweepings of the **wheat** as good grain.

8:7-9. Yahweh **has sworn by the pride of Jacob,** i.e. himself (cf. 4:2; 6:8), that the very land producing the grain will suffer earthquake shock as evident and as irresistible as the well-known annual flooding of the **Nile** (cf. 9:5). Amos may be speaking figuratively here, or he may mean a real earthquake (vs. 8; cf. 1:1) and an eclipse of the sun (vs. 9) such as took place in mid-Jun. 763—a most frightening experience to ancient peoples.

8:10-14. In the language of the mourning rites for Baal, the dead god of vegetation, the coming awful day of Yahweh is described. The expected joyous festival period will turn into bitterest **lamentation,** with the mourning customs of wearing garments of goat's or camel's hair and of shaving the head to produce artificial baldness (cf. Deut. 14:1). Frenzied ritual searching, as in the cult rites for the dead vegetation deity, will be carried on to the very bounds of the earth (cf. Ps. 72:8; Zech. 9:10). But the God of their fathers will be absent; he will send his **word** no more to his faithless people. From **Dan** to **Beer-sheba** they have turned to false worship. In Dan, as in Bethel, stands an idolatrous bull image (cf. I Kings 12:28-30; Hos. 10:8). Swearing by the **way** or pilgrimage to the S sanctuary of Beer-sheba may have been customary, but more likely the patron deity of Beer-sheba is meant —a reading suggested by the LXX and a word with this meaning in the Moabite Stone. Even the capital city Samaria has its patron deity **Ashimah,** later described as imported by Assyrian colonists from Hamath (II Kings 17:30). In the face of such idolatry Yahweh now hides himself and his word from his people so that **they shall fall, and never rise again** (cf. 5:2).

C. The Fifth Vision (9:1-8b)

9:1. Destruction of the Temple. In the previous 4 visions Amos says, "God showed me"; in this climactic one, **I saw the LORD.** But there is no description of God. Perhaps as a mysterious huge human figure (cf. Exod. 33:21-23) God is now at the Bethel temple standing "upon"—more likely than **beside** —its holy **altar.** He commands one of his heavenly host to ruin the temple, from its column **capitals** holding up the roof to its foundations, until it comes crashing down on the heads of the worshipers (cf. Judg. 16:23-30). Thus the coming new year festival day of Yahweh ends in doom.

9:2-4. The Fugitives. What has been called the practical or dynamic monotheism of Amos is seen here. Though the fugitives from the final doom may flee to the remotest parts of the universe, there is no place where they can escape Yahweh's **hand** or his **eyes.** The lower limit of the world is **Sheol,** the subterranean abode of the dead (see comment on Pss. 6:4-5; 18:7-18). Its upper limit is the overarching bowl of **heaven,** i.e. the sky. Mt. **Carmel** is the wooded, cave-honeycombed promontory jutting out into the Mediterranean. On the floor of the **sea** is the chained **serpent,** i.e. dragon, of creation, Leviathan, or Rahab, the lashing of whose tail in her struggle to be free produces monstrous waves (cf. Job 26:13; 38:11; Ps. 74:13-14; Isa. 27:1). Even as captives in a foreign land (cf. 7:17) the fugitives can expect no protection from the local patron deity.

9:5-6. Third Doxology. The inescapable power of the God of the universe, so clearly expressed in this last vision and audition of Amos, is now underlined by this doxology (see above on 4:13). The mere touch of the Lord Yahweh's almighty hand causes the earth to undulate in earthquake waves like the annual Nile inundation (cf. 8:8). By the sound of his voice the waters of the sea are drawn up and rained down on the land (cf. 5:8).

9:7-8b. The Destroying Gaze of Yahweh. The clearly genuine words of Amos come to a startling conclusion with 2 searching questions and a final assertion. Amos' hearers must have been pierced to the quick by his questions. Is their chosen status of no significance in Yahweh's eyes? Amos is not necessarily referring to the **Ethiopians** because of the color of their skin (cf. Jer. 13:23). He may be affirming that Israel's failure to be loyal to Yahweh (cf. 3:2) means that they are no better than a distant heathen nation. As master of the destinies of all peoples (cf. 1:3–2:3) Yahweh brought Israel's enemies from their original homelands—the **Philistines** from their home in the sea, Crete and the Aegean area, and the **Syrians** from their former home in N Mesopotamia (see above on 1:4-5). Does Amos' mention of God's care and control of these peoples dare to suggest, as some interpreters hold, that at last, his patience exhausted, Yahweh is about to choose a new people as his own, even Israel's enemies, to replace faithless Israel? At least Amos means that Yahweh's peculiar people by their faithlessness are now deprived of their privilege in his sight. Hence the **sinful kingdom,** the object of God's devastating gaze, is now to be wiped off the face of the earth.

V. APPENDIX OF HOPE (9:8c-15)

Most scholars hesitate to assign the rest of the book (esp. vss. 11-15) to Amos himself, because the contents are almost diametrically opposite to his clear message of impending doom with no hope (cf. esp. 5:2; 8:14). Both in thought content and in language this section seems much more likely to be from exilic or postexilic prophets than from Amos in mellowed maturity. The successive themes seem clear: a righteous remnant will survive exile (vss. 9-10), David's empire will be restored (vss. 11-12), and overflowing material blessings will follow (vss. 13-15). The language occasionally turns Amos' own doom predictions to hope.

9:8c. An Exception to Doom. This clause seems to be a deliberate prose addition to the preceding dirge meter to soften the terrible blow, or to state that the S kingdom, Judah, did survive Israel's fall in 722.

9:9-10. The Righteous Remnant. The figure of the **sieve** in which the Israel **among all the nations,** i.e. in exile, is shaken apparently expresses the turbulence of the experience of captivity in which the sifting of the good from the bad takes place. Though violently tumbled about in God's sieve every **pebble** ("kernel" of grain is a less likely reading), every faithful one of the righteous remnant of Israel, will by God's grace be kept from falling to the ground and perishing, but not so, of course, the **sinners of my people.** Some interpreters, however, take the pebbles to represent the sinners.

9:11-12. Restoration of David's Empire. With the destruction of Jerusalem in 586 David's once glorious "house" (cf. II Sam. 7) became a ruined **booth,** a mere cattleshed or vineyard watcher's hut. But now his empire will be restored to its ancient boundaries, embracing all nations **called by my name,** i.e. "over whom my name is called" and so designated as "my property" (cf. Deut. 28:10; II Sam. 12:28). Among these nations is **Edom,** now a mere **remnant,** perhaps because of Arab or Nabatean invasions.

9:13-15. Blessings of a New Day. In the golden age to come the famines and disasters of Amos' warnings (4:6-9; 5:11; 8:11) will be replaced by miraculous fertility. The abundance of the crop of grain in May will be such that harvesting will be incomplete at Oct. plowing time. Grape gathering, always completed by Oct., will still be going on at Nov. grain-planting time. The hills will seem to be melting with flowing **wine.** The final picture of the rebuilt cities, the fruitful vineyards and gardens, and the security of being firmly planted in the land— **never again** to be **plucked up** and taken off to exile —is the exact reversal of the fortunes predicted by Amos (cf. 4:6-9; 5:16-17; 7:17; 8:11-12).

THE BOOK OF OBADIAH

Roland E. Murphy, O. Carm.

Authorship and Date. The OT mentions a number of men named Obadiah ("servant of Yahweh"; e.g. I Kings 18:3-16; II Chr. 17:7-9; 34:12; Ezra 8:9) but none can be considered even a probable author of this book. Accordingly we must derive our knowledge of the prophet entirely from his composition.

The book is primarily a denunciation of Edom, the land S of the Dead Sea (see below on vss. 2-4 and color map 4). The Edomites were subjugated by Israel under David (II Sam. 8:13-14; I Kings 11:15-17) and continued under the dominion of Judah. They are said to have been ruled by a governor under Jehoshaphat (I Kings 22:47), though a story told of this same period refers to a "king of Edom" (II Kings 3:9, 26). Under the next king, Joram, they revolted (II Kings 8:20-22) and gained their independence for *ca.* half a cent. but were reconquered by Judah under Amaziah and Azariah (II Kings 14:7, 22). When they succeeded in another revolt against Ahaz (II Kings 16:6) it was merely to exchange masters, for Edom soon became a vassal of Assyria and later of Babylonia. At the destruction of Jerusalem in 586 the Edomites aided the Babylonians and took advantage of the opportunity to loot Judah (Ps. 137:7; Ezek. 25:12; 35:5, 10-15; 36:5). Under Arab pressure in their own land, they now found the way open to settle in S Judah and seem to have occupied the area that later came to be known as Idumea, with Hebron the chief city (see color map 11). Archaeological exploration of Edom itself has revealed no evidence of sedentary occupation during the Persian period. During the 4th cent. this territory came under the domination of an Arab people, the Nabateans, who built there a great trading empire that lasted through NT times.

Most scholars interpret vss. 10-14 as referring to the conduct of the Edomites at the fall of Jerusalem in 586 rather than to any event in the preexilic relations between Judah and Edom. The date of the book, then falls in the period between 586 and the occupation of Edom by the Nabateans in the 4th cent. Because it locates the Edomites in their homeland and expresses a memory of their actions fresh enough for deep feeling, it is likely that the writing comes from early in this period—during the Exile or at the beginning of the postexilic era.

Structure and Relation to Other Books. The 21 vss. make Obad. the shortest book in the OT. Nevertheless its unity is questioned. The denunciation of Edom is found in vss. 1*b*-14, 15*bc*. Vss. 15*a*, 16-21 are a supplement, dealing with the day of Yahweh as a judgment on all the nations and with Israel's concomitant restoration, which some think to be an addition by a later author.

The book appears in the 4th place in the Book of the Twelve (the "Minor Prophets"), immediately after Amos; perhaps it was placed there because of the mention of Edom at the end of Amos (9:12). Vss. 1*c*-9 are paralleled in a variant form and different order in Jer. 49:7-22 (see comment) and the relationship between the 2 passages has been much discussed. The present form of the text seems to show mutual influence of one on the other. Perhaps Obad. is the prior work, but both may have drawn on a 3rd source—possibly preexilic—which contained oracles against Edom. The similarity of Obad. to Joel is less striking but worthy of note: both exploit the theme of the day of Yahweh, and vs. 17*a* is quoted explicitly in Joel 2:32.

Theological Viewpoint. It would be shortsighted to write off books like Obad. and Nah. as the outpourings of a fanatic nationalism. There is no denying the vengeance which pervades these books, but vengeance was understood as belonging to Yahweh (Nah. 1:2; Deut. 32:41). It is the justice of Yahweh which is described here, and it is described as motivated by the crimes of which Edom was guilty. Yahweh's dominion over all peoples demands a reckoning and requital (cf. Amos 1:3–2:3). This notion is deeply embedded in the traditions concerning the day of Yahweh. Indeed Edom comes to symbolize any power hostile to Yahweh (vss. 17-21). On the other hand it has been justly remarked that Obad. is no "servant of Yahweh" after the pattern of Isa. 53. Any sense of a mission on behalf of the nations is totally absent.

For Further Study: J. A. Bewer, *The Book of Obad.*, 1911. H. C. Lanchester, *Obad. and Jonah*, 1915. G. W. Wade, *The Books of the Prophets Mic., Obad., Joel and Jonah*, 1925. G. A. Smith, *The Book of the 12 Prophets*, vol. I, rev. ed., 1928. Nelson Glueck, *The Other Side of the Jordan*, 1940. S. Bullough, *Obad., Mic., Zeph., Hag. and Zech.*, 1953. J. A. Thompson in *IB*, 1956. Jacob M. Myers, *Hos., Joel, Amos, Obad., Jonah*, 1959. James Muilenburg in *IDB*, 1962.

I. Judgment on Edom (vss. 1-14)

Vs. 1a. Title. The title of the book is succinct—the 2 words "Obadiah's vision"—without the usual identification of the prophet's family and date.

Courtesy of Herbert G. May

Looking toward "The Rock" towering over the Roman period forum of the Nabatean city of Petra; the Edomite fortress of Sela was on top of the eminence and was taken by storm by Amaziah

Vss. 1b-9. *The Doom of Edom.* Yahweh's messenger summons the **nations** to war against Edom. Vs. 1b does not fit before vs. 1c; perhaps it is misplaced (cf. Jer. 49:7) or a later addition. **We have heard** perhaps should read "I have heard" as in the LXX and Jer. 49:14.

Vss. 2-4. Yahweh himself announces Edom's doom. Despite her lofty and supposedly secure position she shall be brought down and made **small.** The description of the Edomites as living **in the clefts of the rock** is a genuine geographical reference to the rocky wastes of their territory. **Rock** (Hebrew *sela*) may be an allusion to the Edomite fortress of Sela (cf. II Kings 14:7; see color map 4), around which as an acropolis the Nabateans later built their capital city of Petra. The Edomites occupied the rocky highland of Seir, which lay S of Moab, from which it was cut off by the valley of the Brook Zered (see color map 5), and E of the Arabah, the deep valley including the Dead Sea and extending S to the Gulf of Aqaba. A large part of the plateau edge is between 5,000 and 5,600 feet high. The whole surface is tilted E from the Arabah side toward the desert. Across the plateau from N to S ran the King's Highway, an ancient caravan route which was the lifeline of Edomite trade.

Vss. 5-6. In an ironic lament the prophet contrasts the minor damage that **plunderers** or **grape gatherers** inflict with the complete pillaging to be visited on **Esau,** i.e. his descendants, the Edomites (cf. Gen. 36:9). The disaster is described as already having occurred—a vivid way of declaring that it is sure to come. The **treasures** of Edom were not inconsiderable because of the caravan trade.

Vss. 7-9. Continuing the ironic tone, if even the

very **allies** of Edom—Moabites, Ammonites, and desert bedouins—are playing her false, will not Yahweh **destroy** her with all her wise and mighty? Vs. 7 may refer to the Arab pressure during the 6th and 5th cents. that drove many of the Edomites to settle in S Judah (see Intro.); or, if this part is adapted from a preexilic source, it may refer to some threat at an earlier time (cf. Amos 2:1). Edom was famous for her **wise men** (cf. Jer. 49:7; Baruch 3:23; see Intro. to Job), though we know practically nothing about Edomite wisdom. Eliphaz the Temanite (Job 1:11) was probably from **Teman,** a chief city of Edom, ca. 5 miles E of Sela. **Mount Esau** means the Seir mountain range of Edom (cf. e.g. Deut. 2:5).

Vss. 10-14. *The Reason for Judgment.* The crime of Edom against his **brother Jacob,** i.e. Israel, is specified in this dramatic passage. Eight times the **day**—of **calamity,** of **distress,** etc.—is mentioned. The day of Yahweh against **Jerusalem,** when the city was destroyed by **foreigners,** i.e. the Babylonians, was the day of Edom's violence and gloating and looting. Many OT passages (e.g. Isa. 63:1-6; Ezek. 25:12-14; 35:1-15; Joel 3:19) testify to the bitter memory of the Edomites' action on that occasion. The feeling of the indictment is heightened by recalling the brotherly relationship which according to early tradition existed between Jacob and Esau, i.e. Israel and Edom (cf. Gen. 25:24-26). Besides looting, the Edomites actively helped the enemy by capturing **fugitives** from Judah and handing them over to the Babylonians.

Vss. 12-14. The series **You should not have gloated,** etc., is lit. "Do not gloat," etc. Yahweh is forbidding Edom to do what she has already done— a striking way to intensify the enormity of her sin.

The conclusion of the poem is found in vs. 15*bc*, where Yahweh declares that the result will be an exercise of the law of retaliation. The Edomites will be requited with **deeds** such as they themselves performed.

II. THE DAY OF YAHWEH (vss. 15-21)

Vss. 15-16. *Judgment on the Nations.* The prophet announces the approach of Yahweh's day of vengeance on **all the nations** (vs. 15*a;* on vs. 15*bc* see above on vss. 12-14). **You** in vs. 16*a* is plural and means the Israelites, in contrast with the singular referring to Edom throughout vss. 2-15. As the people of Judah have drained the cup of Yahweh's wrath—a frequent metaphor in the prophets (cf. e.g. Isa. 51:17-23; Jer. 25:15-16; Lam. 4:21; Hab. 2:16)—so now the nations shall drink. The ruin of Edom is turned apocalyptically into the day of Yahweh against the nations just as in Joel a locust plague becomes a symbol of judgment on the whole world.

Vss. 17-21. *The Restoration of Judah.* Now **Mount Zion** is pronounced inviolable (vs. 17*a*, quoted in Joel 2:32) and **holy** (cf. Joel 3:17). **Possess their own possessions** is better translated with the LXX "possess those who dispossess them." The **house of Jacob** (i.e. Judah) and the **house of Joseph** (i.e. the N kingdom of Israel) will now unite to **consume** the **house of Esau** (i.e. Edom). The union of Israel and Judah is a feature of the prophetic descriptions of the messianic age (cf. e.g. Ezek. 37:16-22; Hos. 1:11). Edom appears to become a symbol for all of Israel's enemies, all of whom are to be destroyed (cf. Isa. 34:1-17; 63:1-6).

Vss. 19-20. The promise of restoration includes expansion of the boundaries of Judah. The Israelites of the **Negeb** (i.e. S Judah) will take over **Mount Esau** (i.e. Edom) and those living in the **Shephelah** (i.e. the W foothills) will move into the coastal plain of Philistia. The territory of the former N kingdom (**Ephraim** and **Samaria**) and **Gilead** in Transjordan will be occupied. **In Halah**—a place apparently in Assyria where captives of the N kingdom were exiled in 722 (II Kings 17:6)—is an emendation of the Hebrew text, which reads "of this host." In either case the meaning is that descendants of the exiled **people of Israel** will be included in the restoration and will occupy N Palestine as far N as **Zarephath** (cf. I Kings 17:9; see color map 8). **Sepharad** has resisted certain identification but probably refers to Sardis in Asia Minor (see color map 9), where evidence has been found of a Jewish colony existing in the middle of the 5th cent. The ancient rabbis identified it with Spain, so that Spanish Jews came to be called Sephardim.

Vs. 21. This concluding vs. describes the victorious Israelites, who are to **rule** as **saviors**—like the judges (cf. Judg. 3:9, 15, etc.)—from **Mount Zion.** It is the final **kingdom** and reign of Yahweh that is envisioned here.

THE BOOK OF JONAH

Roland E. Murphy, O. Carm.

Authorship and Date. Nothing is known about the author of the book of Jonah, who is not to be identified with the hero of the story, Jonah the son of Amittai. According to II Kings 14:25 this prophet, who was from Gath-hepher in Zebulun (cf. Josh. 19:13; see color map 8), foretold the reestablishment of Israel's boundaries by Jeroboam II. At that time, early in the 8th cent., Nineveh was not the royal residence nor was Assyria the world power it later came to be. It is likely that this man became the subject of the book much as Job (cf. Ezek. 14:14, 20) was chosen to be the hero of the book named after him.

The postexilic period is the likely date for the composition of the book. Only then would one find in Israel such a strong emphasis on universalism and tolerance toward other nations. Some have conjectured that the book was written specifically to oppose the resurgent nationalism and exclusiveness of the Ezra-Nehemiah reform, but its relation to this movement cannot be determined. A postexilic date is borne out by the character of the language and by the evident view of Nineveh and the Assyrian power as belonging to the remote past. The book was already established as one of the "twelve prophets" in the time of Ben Sira (*ca.* 180 B.C.; cf. Ecclus. 49:10) and was known to the author of Tobit (14:4, 8), though he may have confused it with Nah.

Literary Form and Interpretation. The interpretation of the book as history has lost ground in modern times. Were history the intention of the author one would expect names (e.g. of the king of Nineveh) and details, and there would be more concern to explain the implausibilities and the series of remarkable coincidences. The climax of these is the sudden and complete conversion of the Ninevites. There is no opposition, no motivation except Jonah's proclamation of the threat, yet a tremendous conversion of the entire population of a large city takes place —without leaving another trace in the Bible or in history—a conversion which Israel never attained realized by the people who destroyed her. The historicity of the account has been defended primarily because of Jesus' reference to the "sign of Jonah" (Matt. 12:38-42; 16:4; Luke 11:29-32); but the story existed in the OT and this was enough basis for Jesus to refer to it. Interestingly enough, the sign itself was variously interpreted in the NT era, as a comparison of Matt. with Luke shows.

The allegorical interpretation would make Jonah (meaning "dove") out to be Israel. The disobedient nation is swallowed by the fish (Babylon; cf. Jer. 51:34) and then freed from exile to carry its witness to the Gentiles (repentant Nineveh). The anger of Jonah is said to symbolize Israel's impatience at the slowness of the Gentiles to convert. This allegorical interpretation falls of its own weight. For one thing, Jonah does not come from the fish purified and attuned to the divine will—a point to be urged against the psychological allegorizing which sees in the fish a fundamental trial from which Jonah emerges a new man. Allegorical interpretation also lies behind the frequent portrayals of Jonah in early Christian art, esp. in the catacombs. The scenes show Jonah being cast into the sea and being swallowed, his being spewed out on land, and finally his rest under the plant. These were taken to symbolize death, resurrection, and a blessed immortal rest.

It is not enough to characterize the story as legend or folklore. Even if somewhat similar marvels occur in Greek mythology (Hercules and Hesione, Perseus and Andromeda) and elsewhere, there is no question of dependence. At the most there is the folklore motif of a human threatened by a monster, only to be eventually freed. The free and imaginative style of the legend is certainly present, but the whole thrust of the book goes beyond a mere story and takes on the character of parable. Its satirical aspect is exemplified by the very portrait of a dishonest prophet at odds with the God who commissions him. Its didactic intent emerges from its purpose: God's merciful designs are not to be limited; they include all nations, even Israel's traditional enemies.

This purpose is not a casual lesson. It is skillfully drawn out by a meaningful adaptation of Israel's own traditions and by clever literary devices. The traditions involved are the revelation of Yahweh as "gracious . . . and merciful" (4:2; cf. Exod. 34:6) and his willingness to "repent" if one will "turn from his evil way" (3:8, 10; cf. Jer. 18:8). At the risk of oversimplifying one might say that the book is an attempt to interpret these traditions to a later generation. The literary devices are many, some more obvious than others (see "The Literary Forms of the OT," pp. 1077-81). The 4 chs. form a diptych: chs. 1-2, the prophet dealing with foreign sailors who are better than he is; chs. 3-4, the prophet preaching to Ninevites who understand Yahweh better than he does. The sailors are portrayed as men in fear (1:5, 10) who finally offer sacrifice and fear Yahweh (1:16)—a typical wisdom saying, for "the fear of the LORD is the beginning of wisdom" (Prov. 1:7; 9:10). Just so the Ninevites turn to Yahweh in repentance.

The humorous satire of the book will not disguise the fact that this little work is one of the most important in the OT. There is no greater theological mystery than the mercy of God, and the author was brave enough to caricature a narrow-minded Israelite mentality in order to preserve the sovereign freedom of Yahweh. By his insight he anticipated Paul: "Is he not the God of Gentiles also?" (Rom. 3:29).

For Further Study: J. A. Bewer, *The Book of Jonah,* 1912. H. C. Lanchester, *Obad. and Jonah,* 1915. G. W. Wade, *The Books of the Prophets Mic., Obad., Joel and Jonah,* 1925. G. A. Smith, *The Book of the 12 Prophets,* 1928. G. A. F. Knight, *Ruth and Jonah,* 1950. André Parrot, *Nineveh and the Old Testament,* 1955. James D. Smart in *IB,* 1956. William Neil in *IDB,* 1962.

I. JONAH AND THE SAILORS (1:1–2:10)

1:1-3. *A Disobedient Prophet.* The careful reader will not overlook the unusual implications of the very first lines. How could an Israelite prophet be commissioned to preach to the Ninevites? What language would he speak? What authority would he have? Why should there be a mission to the hated Assyrians, the oppressors of Israel? We are in the realm of fiction here. The behavior of the prophet is clearly disobedient; he departs in the opposite direction from Nineveh, boarding a **ship** at **Joppa,** modern Jaffa (see color map 8), bound for **Tarshish.** Many identifications have been proposed for this latter place, which is mentioned often in the OT (e.g. Pss. 48:7; 72:10; Isa. 2:16; 23:1; Ezek. 27:12); but Tartessus, beyond Gilbraltar on the SW coast of Spain, is the most plausible site. Jonah's flight is twice characterized as **from the presence of the LORD.** In ancient Semitic thought there was a close connection between the land and the god of the land (cf. I Sam. 26:19), but as the story develops Jonah will acknowledge Yahweh as the creator of the sea (vs. 9) and discover that one cannot flee from him.

1:4-16. *A Ship in a Storm.* With the typical OT disdain for secondary causality the author attributes the storm directly to Yahweh's intervention. The reaction of the sailors, supposedly inured to the ways of the sea, is somewhat surprising; they turn to their gods in prayer. Thus the sailors at sea become the counterpart to the Ninevites of ch. 4 on land. In contrast Jonah sleeps, and his sleep is interrupted by the "pious" **captain,** who—this is surely not without some irony—urges him to pray.

1:7-12. Misfortune, in the orthodox OT view, points to some sin; and the **lots** single out Jonah as the guilty party. The first question of the sailors in vs. 8 is repetitious (cf. vs. 7) and superfluous after the lots have indicated Jonah, and some scholars have assumed it to be a scribe's accidental duplication. Further, vs. 10b strikes the modern reader as anticlimactic and is viewed by some as a marginal note that came to be copied in the text. But there is no need to omit these. The incoherence stems from the theological interest of the author, who seems less concerned with details than with setting up situations called for by his didactic purpose. The question of the sailors sets up a theological formula as Jonah's answer: his God is the very one who **made the sea** that is now threatening them. The reaction of the sailors—fear of God—is in contrast to the callous disobedience of the prophet. The artificiality of the story is further indicated by Jonah's calm solution to their dilemma: like the cargo, he is to be jettisoned.

1:13-16. Again these sailors betray a surprisingly deep religious feeling. They do not want the responsibility for Jonah's death. Despite their strenuous efforts, Jonah is finally cast overboard—not without a prayer to be acquitted of his **blood**—and the storm is over. Significantly it is now Yahweh whom the sailors fear and to whom they offer sacrifice!

1:17–2:10. *Jonah Returned to Land.* As always in this book, Yahweh is represented as the direct cause of all that happens. It is he who **appointed a great fish to swallow up Jonah,** who is not going to be allowed to escape his commission that easily. The fish has Jonah as his guest for **three days and three nights.** One cannot determine what kind of sea monster the author had in mind.

2:1-9. Inserted here is a thanksgiving psalm (vss. 2-9) which is a classical example of this literary type (see Intro. to Pss.). The reason it has been utilized here and thus preserved is doubtless its references to the sea (vss. 3, 5). The poem begins with a compact description of the psalmist's **distress** and an acknowledgment of Yahweh as his rescuer. **Sheol** (vs. 2) or the **Pit** (vs. 6) was the abode of the dead far beneath the earth amid the waters of the **deep** (cf. Gen. 1:2; see comment on Pss. 6:4-5; 18:7-18). Metaphors like these are used esp. in the pss. to designate human affliction, e.g. sickness or persecution. One cannot specify the precise trouble in which the author of this prayer found himself, but it led to his being separated from Yahweh's **presence** in the **temple** (vs. 4)—the very temple from which Yahweh answered his plea (vs. 7). The prayer concludes with a declaration of loyalty—in contrast to idolaters—as the psalmist vows to offer his **sacrifice** in the temple.

2:10. Again at Yahweh's command the fish spews Jonah out on the **dry land,** presumably that whence he fled. Thus Jonah is back where he started, and Yahweh begins again.

II. JONAH AND THE NINEVITES (3:1–4:11)

3:1-4. *An Obedient Prophet.* Vss. 1-3 are deliberately modeled on 1:1-3; a new moment in the story begins as Jonah now capitulates and obeys the command of Yahweh to go to Nineveh. Excavations at Nineveh have indicated that its **breadth of three days' journey** is not so great an exaggeration, for the Nineveh of old could be envisioned as embracing the so-called "Assyrian triangle," the territory from Khorsabad in the N to Nimrud in the S —a distance of *ca.* 26 miles. In this area the population suggested by 4:11 is conceivable. Appropriately, one of the mounds which mark the site of ancient Nineveh is called Nebi Yunus ("the prophet Jonah"), for here, among many other sites that claim the honor, the prophet is supposedly buried.

3:5-10. The Repentance of the Ninevites. The reaction of the Ninevites is nothing short of astounding; to the possibility (**who knows,** vs. 9; cf. Joel 2:14) of God's forgiveness there is the generous response of the king, the people, and even the beasts. In spite of himself Jonah appears to be the most successful missionary of all time. The proclamation of the unnamed king of Nineveh contains a whole program of Israelite theology based on Jer. 18:7-8, after which it is modeled: repentance and conversion from sin moves God to **repent** of the **evil** he intends to inflict on men. The invitation to the Ninevites that **everyone turn from his evil way** is a Jeremian phrase (e.g. Jer. 25:5; 26:3). There is a noticeable similarity between the situation here and that in Jer. 36; in both the possibility is held out that Yahweh will repent if "every one will turn from his evil way" (Jer. 36:7), but the king of Nineveh is in favorable contrast to the impenitent Jehoiakim.

4:1-4. The Reaction of Jonah. Though no prophet ever experienced such a success as Jonah, he is **displeased** and even **angry.** Now his unspoken narrowness, which reflects a mentality formed by Nah. 3:1-19; Zeph. 2:13-15, begins to reveal itself. He knew Yahweh was "soft," that he would forgive should the Ninevites repent. Indeed he tried to **flee to Tarshish** (1:3) for that very reason—to forestall the eventuality of the Ninevites' conversion.

4:2d. The strong theological flavor of Jonah's reasoning is expressed in this formula, which has a history in the OT going back to Exod. 34:6 (cf. Num. 14:18; Neh. 9:17; Pss. 86:15; 111:4; 112:4; 145:8; Joel 2:13). Jonah is thus rejecting the Yahweh of the covenant, the God of the fathers, who is consistently described in these loving terms. The most adequate commentary on this characterization of Yahweh is the doctrine of Deut. and the prophets, esp. Hosea.

4:3-4. Jonah's request to die—so disgusted is he —is met by Yahweh's question, **Do you do well to be angry?** or, as it might better be translated, "Are you so very angry?" This same question is repeated

in the next scene (vs. 9); the repetition seems to be a literary device to heighten the tension (cf. the delaying tactic in Esther's request in Esth. 5:3-8), as well as a reminiscence of the prophet Elijah in I Kings 19:4. There is no little humor in this exchange: the prophet is ready to die, but Yahweh will not allow him to go without teaching him the lesson that awaits him.

4:5-11. Jonah and the Plant. Jonah does not give up the hope that somehow the doom pronounced against Nineveh will still be fulfilled, and he takes up his residence in a **booth** outside the city. The question has been raised why Yahweh should make a **plant** (probably the castor oil plant) spring up overnight to provide **shade** for Jonah since he already has the booth. Hence some scholars would insert 4:5 between 3:4, 5, immediately after Jonah begins to preach to the Ninevites. But this is not necessary in a fictional narrative where the religious reaction rather than the reality of details determines the course of events.

4:7-9. Jonah's great joy over the plant (deliberately exaggerated in the Hebrew) is of short duration as God sends a **worm** to kill it and an **east wind** (the baleful sirocco) to torment the prophet. An earlier scene now repeats itself: Jonah asks for death (vs. 8; cf. vs. 3) and Yahweh asks if he has reason **to be angry for the plant** (vs. 9; cf. vs. 4).

4:10-11. The whole point of the story comes here, in a sort of *a fortiori* argument. If Jonah pitied the plant, with which he had nothing to do, should not Yahweh **pity** the people of Nineveh? **Who do not know their right hand from their left** may mean that the entire population of the city is religiously ignorant. But in view of the Ninevites' sensitive response to Jonah's preaching, the author is more probably adding to the poignancy of the question by an allusive reminder (cf. Deut. 1:39; Isa. 7:16) that the city contains 120,000 innocent children, not to speak of the **cattle.** There is simply no answer to this touching question. These final vss. constitute the heart of the message: Israel should not presume to limit God's concern only to the people with whom he has covenanted. His mercy spills out beyond even the holy covenant to embrace the Gentiles (cf. Exod. 33:19; Rom. 9:15).

THE BOOK OF MICAH

Bruce T. Dahlberg

Introduction

The name Micah is an abbreviated form of Micaiah, meaning "Who is like Yahweh?" Except for his home and the general period in which he flourished details of Mic.'s life are unknown.

The Judean town Moresheth (1:1), presumably the same as Moresheth-gath (1:14), was probably located *ca.* 20 miles SW of Jerusalem toward the ancient Philistine city of Gath. To assume, however, because Mic. lived in this relatively small town and was concerned for the small landholder (cf. 2:2) that he himself was a peasant takes too much for granted. His sophistication and knowledgeableness in public affairs, which show in his prophetic pronouncements, suggest that he may have been a person of eminence. The fact that Jeremiah's contemporaries over a cent. later compared him to Mic. (cf. Jer. 26:16-19) suggests that Mic. may have had access to the royal court in Jerusalem as Jeremiah did.

Historical Background and Date. The book's introductory heading (1:1) identifies Mic.'s career with the "days of Jotham, Ahaz, and Hezekiah, kings of Judah"—i.e. 742-687/86 B.C., a period much longer than is reflected in Mic.'s own prophecies. Jer. 26:18-19 identifies Mic.'s preaching with the reign of Hezekiah (716/15-687/86) and quotes 3:12 in apparent reference to Sennacherib's siege of Jerusalem (701), though the allusion would fit other Assyrian threats as well. The reference may be merely an inference from tradition, however, and is not necessarily accurate chronologically.

More significant is the reference in 1:6-7 to the destruction of Samaria, capital of the N kingdom of Israel, which fell to Assyria in 722 after a 3-year siege (cf. II Kings 17:5). By the Assyrian Sargon II's own assertion he rebuilt Samaria soon after its fall. Because Mic. appears to know nothing of a rebuilding chs. 1-3 seem to require a date either during the siege or shortly after the destruction of the city, i.e. *ca.* 725-720 (see below on 1:6-9, 10-16). On the other hand chs. 4-7 undoubtedly come from a period after Mic.'s lifetime, probably during or soon after the Babylonian exile (586-539).

Mic. was a contemporary of Isaiah. Like Isaiah he addressed his message primarily to the leaders of the city of Jerusalem in the S kingdom of Judah. Amos and Hosea, who preached in the N kingdom before its collapse, may with Isaiah have been known to Mic., for his message shows affinities with all 3. However, Mic. neither mentions his contemporaries nor is mentioned by them. On the 8th-cent. background of Mic., besides details below, see comments on II Kings 15-17.

Authorship and Literary Divisions. According to both subject matter and style the book falls into 3 divisions: chs. 1-3; 4-5; 6-7. On the basis of the chronological data cited above, including the reference in Jer. 26:18-19, and considering their demonstrable literary unity (see comment), chs. 1-3 certainly are the work of the prophet Mic. In their present form they appear to be a public manifesto of some kind, conceivably a sermon to be preached.

Chs. 4-5, on the other hand, because of their messianic interest, which resembles that of exilic and postexilic literature, and because of the mention of Babylon (4:10), which succeeded Assyria as the imperial power in Mesopotamia after 605, seem with almost equal certainty *not* attributable to Mic. Rather they must come from an anonymous author or authors in the exilic or postexilic years. These 2 chs. appear as a later prophetic commentary on the original work of Mic. (i.e. chs. 1-3).

Chs. 6-7 deal with many of the prophet Mic.'s themes, but in a more reflective way on the whole; and in important respects they go beyond Mic. They seem to be a liturgy of atonement, perhaps born of meditation on the prophecy of Mic. (i.e. chs. 1-3).

For Further Study. J. M. P. Smith, *Mic., etc.,* 1911; a standard scholarly work which, except for certain details from recent research, has not been superseded. S. Goldman in *The 12 Prophets,* ed. A. Cohen, 1948; includes parallel Hebrew and English texts. R. E. Wolf in *IB,* 1956. John Bright, *A History of Israel,* 1959, pp. 252-87; lucid and comprehensive on the historical background of Mic. and his period. John Marsh, *Amos and Mic.,* 1959. Bruce Vawtwer, C.M., *The Conscience of Israel,* 1961, pp. 130-61. E. A. Leslie in *IDB,* 1962. Samuel Sandmel, *The Hebrew Scriptures,* 1963, pp. 98-103.

I. The Crisis of Judah (1:1-3:12)

Except for the introductory heading added later (1:1) chs. 1-3 can be read as a single unified work. They are not merely a collection of separate pronouncements from different episodes in the prophet's career but a prophetic sermon intended for Jerusalem and probably preached there. One sign of their literary unity is the thrice-repeated **Hear!** (1:2; 3:1; 3:9). Further marks of unity appear with a comparison of the beginning and ending lines: the focus of attention shifts with a deliberate sweep from Samaria in the N (1:6-9) to Jerusalem and Judah in the S (3:9-12)—a movement anticipated in the citation of these 2 cities in 1:5. The end answers to the beginning; in both places attention is directed to the temple (1:2; 3:12), and in both the destruction of the city is proclaimed. Such patterns in form and theme suggest that chs. 1–3 indeed form a single composition rather than a loose collection of sayings, even though the prophet may well have incorporated earlier brief pronouncements of his into this longer work.

1:1. *Introductory Heading.* An editor from a later biblical time has supplied this explanatory intro., in form similar to those of other biblical prophetic books. **The word of the LORD** is not merely "words from God" but the total situation about which the prophet will speak. The added expression **which he saw** comes from the terminology of soothsaying, but here it alludes merely to the prophet's inspired insight into the meaning of events around him. Neither Mic. nor any of the classical Hebrew prophets were soothsayers. On the historical references see Intro.

1:2-5. *Prologue: The Advent of God.* Mic. himself begins with a proclamation: God is to appear for a day of judgment. The language, style, and imagery of vss. 2-4 have seemed imitative of 2nd Isaiah to some scholars, who have accordingly taken the vss. as an editor's intro. to the prophecy of Mic. beginning in vs. 5. The language, style, and imagery, however, are classic in the OT (cf. e.g. Ps. 97:1-5; Nah. 1:5) and there seems no compelling reason to date the vss. after the time of Mic. or to separate them from vs. 5.

1:2. The rhetorical effect of the opening summons is to arrest the attention of everyone within hearing, and everyone is meant to **hear.** God will be a **witness against you.** Mic.'s subject involves divine judgment unmistakably. **From his holy temple** God is bestirring himself, breaking out of his ordinary confine, as it were.

1:3-4. The notion of the divine judgment's breaking out is carried forward. This passage has been compared with Isa. 40:3-5; but there the imagery suggests the building of a road for a military conqueror, whereas here it suggests volcanic action, earthquake, or lightning and storm. Natural and supernatural elements seem intentionally blurred, and the language is figurative. The prophet intends to inspire soberness and awe in his listeners in face of the specific circumstances and events he will go on to describe, as the concluding lines (vs. 5) of his intro. make clear.

1:5. Mic. moves now from the poetic and mythological to the concrete and specific. The **transgression of Jacob** and **sins of the house of Israel** remain yet to be detailed and will form the burden of the prophet's message (2:1–3:11). Mic. seems to use the names Jacob, Israel, and Judah interchangeably. The transgression of Jacob is in Mic.'s view first of all **Samaria,** i.e. the corrupt society within her. *Ca.* 40 miles N of Jerusalem, Samaria was the capital of the N kingdom of Israel, politically separated from Judah since the death of King Solomon (931). **What is the sin of the house of Judah?** follows the LXX. The Hebrew, "What are the high places of Judah?" probably should be retained, for Mic. has already

Courtesy of John C. Trever

The site of Samaria (Tell Sebasteyeh) capital city of the N kingdom of Israel; originally built by Omri, the hill was chosen partly for its ease of defense; olive trees are in bloom in the foreground (see also ills. pp. 192, 193)

used **high places** (vs. 3) to describe the focal point of God's judgment, which is precisely what he anticipates for the "high place" that is Jerusalem.

1:6-9. *Samaria an Omen for Jerusalem.* The military destruction of Samaria by the Assyrians, which presumably this passage describes (cf. II Kings 17:1-18), either is imminent or has happened so recently that it can be thought of as in the present tense. The Hebrew forms of the verbs here can refer to either present or future time. In any case Mic. is addressing not Samaria but Jerusalem (vs. 9), using the situation of Samaria as a warning and omen.

1:6. The words here describe lit. the methodical obliteration of a city by an ancient military conqueror. These are the actual circumstances that inspire the figurative description of divine judgment in vss. 3-4.

1:7. Possibly these allusions to idolatry are an interpolation from a time long after Mic. as some scholars think, for the prophet does not elsewhere deal with the subject in these 3 chs. However, King Ahaz of Judah (735-716/15) had imported an Assyrian altar into the Jerusalem temple before this time (II Kings 16:10-16); thus Mic. himself could have spoken these words advisedly. **All her hires** means the wages of a prostitute, here alluding to offerings brought to Samaria's pagan holy places. **To the hire of a harlot they shall return** is Mic.'s way of saying that these sacred objects and gifts will be carried off to Assyrian temples when Samaria falls. The particular terms used here may be at the same time Mic.'s blunt and contemptuous recognition of the practice of ritual prostitution known to the pagan fertility cults that competed with the worship of Yahweh.

1:8. Whether Mic.'s **lament and wail** and his **going stripped and naked** are meant lit. or are rhetorical hyperboles is not clear. Isaiah walked naked—as an exile while being deported was made to walk in humiliation—to signify approaching disaster (Isa. 20:2-4). In any case, given the harsh tenor and controlled fury of Mic.'s speech elsewhere, this vs. scarcely is enough to justify calling him the "wailing prophet," as has been common.

1:9. Samaria is beyond help. The crisis that confronted her, which she failed to meet, now confronts Judah and Jerusalem.

1:10-16. *The Invoking of Disaster.* Mic. now addresses the cities and towns of Judah with a series of taunts and insults as if in fact Samaria's fate were descending on them. Mic. is not so much spreading an alarm here as himself calling down the Assyrian threat on Judah. So far as we know, it did not materialize at this time, but the presence of Sargon's armies in S Palestine to put down a rebellion in the Philistine state of Gaza on the Mediterranean coast (*ca.* 720/19) following the conquest of Samaria must have made these prophetic curses seem no empty threat to the uneasy inhabitants of Judah and Jerusalem.

1:10-15. The saying **Tell it not in Gath** was proverbial (cf. II Sam. 1:20), signifying disaster. Gath, a Philistine city, was in the line of Assyrian attack should it come. In the Hebrew there is a play on the phonetic assonance between "tell" and "Gath." Apparently this caught the prophet's imagination, for all the subsequent taunts in these vss. attempt some sort of play on word sounds—e.g. "-aphrah" (vs. 10) sounds like "dust," and "Achzib" (vs. 14) like "deceitful thing." So far as they can be located the places named were all in the foothills of W Judah (see color map 8).

1:16. Mic. summons the inhabitants of Judah to lament the deportation into exile that would be the inevitable consequence of Assyrian occupation (cf. vs. 8).

2:1-13. *The Inner Sickness of Judah.* Thus far Mic. has spoken of the threat to Judah from without. Now he addresses himself to the threat from within. He documents the subordination of human rights in 8th-cent. Judah to the pursuit of inordinate wealth and power. A political and mercantile aristocracy appears incapable of appreciating Judah's precarious position. For Mic. the collapse of the state is inevitable.

2:1-5. Men with vested commercial and political interests lie awake nights to devise schemes to add to their wealth at the expense of their fellows. Their cleverness enables them to deprive the "little man" of his few real possessions. Mic. sees a day of reckoning when their easy life will be ended abruptly by the invader and their wealth, even their place in the **assembly of the LORD,** will be taken away.

2:6. Judah's affluent aristocracy is incapable of self-criticism and wishes to hear preached, not criticism, but only what is pleasant. Such warnings as were spoken in 1:10-16 are laughed off. The prophet is without honor in his own country.

2:7. Mic. responds with shock and amazement to the rejection and dismissal of his words. **Is the Spirit of the LORD impatient?** he asks. His words are lit.: "Is the Spirit of the LORD shortened?" i.e. is it possible that Mic.'s preaching can have so little effect? In **Are these his doings?** the emphasis in the Hebrew is on "these"—i.e. the sense of the preceding line is reiterated: Can *this* be the consequence of Mic.'s preaching? **Do not my words do good to him who walks uprightly?** i.e. would not a just man recognize the truth of what has been said? The indifference of Mic.'s audience is the measure of their moral insensitivity.

2:8. The Hebrew text is obscure in this vs. **With no thought of war** is a plausible rendition, but the phrase can possibly be translated more exactly as "returning from war." The sense is that, notwithstanding the Assyrian threat from without, the true enemies of the community are these exploiters of the people. The returning soldier confronts worse hardships at home than on the battlefield.

2:9. Even **women** and **children** are evicted from their homes. The picture of the suffering of those who lack economic or social status or any resource for self-defense is a poignant one. Mic.'s righteous and rightful indignation is inspired against a social deterioration in 8th-cent. Judah that was also documented by his contemporary, Isaiah (cf. e.g. Isa. 1:23; 3:14-15; 5:7-8, 23).

2:10. This advice appears to be Mic.'s ironic consolation proffered to the women and children of vs. 9. They are better off to leave this unclean place that is doomed for destruction.

2:11. Mic. returns contemptuously to an earlier theme (vs. 6), the complacent man's contentment with whatever preaching will not disturb him. For this people, Mic. says, a drunken man would be about as good a preacher as any.

2:12-13. The apparent optimism of this section, intruding abruptly into the context of Mic.'s judgment and threat, has led most commentators to think that it is an interpolation by a pious scribe or editor who found Mic.'s preaching too harsh. However, the picture given here of **sheep in a fold** and a **noisy multitude of men** is undignified and is not in fact complimentary. Indeed it is reminiscent of the intoxication suggested in vs. 11. Further, its expectation that this throng, led by its **king** and with God on its side, would break out of a surrounding siege is facile and naïve. Therefore one must agree with the 11th-cent. rabbinical commentator Ibn Ezra, who read these lines as Mic.'s sarcastic ridicule by mimicry of the sort of false preaching for which he shows such contempt in vss. 6, 11. That the words are introduced without any verb of speaking to mark them as a quotation is a practice common in ancient Hebrew.

3:1-12. *God's Departure from His People.* The prophet has finished his case. The divine word has not been heeded. Therefore the people who will have their own way are now to have it altogether. Mic. proceeds to expound the verdict.

3:1-4. The thought of this passage parallels antithetically what has gone immediately before. As in 2:12-13 the figure is again that of the sheepfold, but rather than being led to safety by their leader the people are as if ravaged by wild beasts. The **heads of Jacob** and the **rulers of the house of Israel** in fact consume the people they are supposed to guide and protect. The portrayal of the helpless creature torn limb from limb draws on language reminiscent of the atrocities known to have been perpetrated by the Assyrians on their conquered enemies. As in 2:8 Mic. suggests again that the destroyer from without is scarcely distinguishable from the destroyers within.

Judah's rulers have altogether passed the point of return; repentance can no longer avail them. Should the Assyrian threat become a reality for them, they will discover that they are beyond help (vs. 4). This is Mic.'s explicit rejoinder to those who flatter themselves that **their king will pass on before them, the LORD at their head** (2:13).

3:5-7. Mic. spells out the judgment further, now excoriating those **prophets** who have been willing to underwrite corruption in Judah with their easy promises of divine approval. So long as they are fed they never challenge the status quo. The day of Judah's extremity will discredit them, for they have done nothing to forestall evil. Then they will hold their tongues (vs. 7). Mic. repeats the judgment pronounced in vs. 4. Yahweh will have departed from his people. Judah will discover the eclipse of God. The coming **night** and **darkness** recall the preaching of Amos some years earlier (cf. Amos 5:18).

3:8. The question that has troubled Mic.—that his preaching was of so little effect (see above on 2:7)—is now answered. Judah's devastation will be the vindication of his message. The divine **Spirit** has indeed operated through him **with justice and might** through the judgment that has resulted from his message. Isaiah, Mic.'s contemporary, came to a similar conclusion about his own ministry (cf. Isa. 6:9-13).

3:9-12. Mic. has delivered the burden of his message; now he swiftly brings it to a conclusion. His peroration sums up everything. The **heads of the house of Jacob** and the **rulers of the house of Israel,** the **priests** and the **prophets,** are presented with the final bill of particulars against them, and it needs no explanatory comment. Yet all these have still the audacity to claim: **Is not the LORD in the midst of us? No evil shall come upon us.** This is the last outrage.

3:12. Mic.'s closing words echo the theme with which he began his message (1:2-4, 6-7). The destruction of **Jerusalem** by Assyria, which Mic. saw as inevitable, never happened. When the armies of Sennacherib did in fact approach its gates in 701, the Judean king, Hezekiah, bought them off with tribute as a vassal state (II Kings 18:13-16). Nevertheless a cent. later Mic.'s words were preserved and remembered. They were recalled with effect as Jerusalem was about to fall to the Babylonian onslaught. At that time Jeremiah was called to take a stand not unlike that of his predecessor, and Mic.'s words were appealed to in his defense (cf. Jer. 26:18-19). Thus these words of Mic. spoke to a generation he never knew—a generation that came to understand him better than his own.

II. THE FUTURE RESTORATION (4:1–5:15)

Chs. 4–5 are eschatologically oriented, i.e. concerned with the "last things," the ultimate outcome of history or at least of the era of history with which the author is concerned. Not until later did biblical eschatology look to the final end of history or beyond history. The expectation here, messianic in the literal sense of expectation of a revived political kingdom, anticipates the restoration of the Davidic monarchy and the temple in Jerusalem, both of which seem here to be known to have previously met their end.

These 2 chs. must be a later addition to the record of Mic.'s preaching (chs. 1–3), appended probably in the exilic or early postexilic period, i.e. later than 586, when Jerusalem fell to Babylon. The messianic hope expressed here is quite unlike anything anticipated in chs. 1–3. Indeed it contradicts Mic.'s preaching altogether. To be sure Mic. could have reversed himself at a later time in his life. Nevertheless the language, imagery, and thought of chs. 4–5 resemble closely other prophetic writings known to be from the Exile or after.

The decisive clue to the later composition of this material is that Babylon rather than Assyria is known as the place of exile (4:10). Though Assyria is referred to (5:5-6) what is said cannot possibly allude to that empire as Mic. knew it. Here it is simply the geographical region NE of Palestine which was known to have been territory of the Assyrian Empire earlier. Such use of the term appears in other late OT writing (cf. Lam. 5:6; Zech. 10:10-11).

However, chs. 4–5 were not appended to Mic.'s work arbitrarily. At a number of points they echo the language and imagery of chs. 1–3. They appear to have been inspired by Mic.'s thought and to form a later cent.'s response to him, born of study and reflection on his work.

4:1-5. *The Universal Reign of God.* Except for vss. 4-5*b* this entire passage occurs also in Isa. 2:2-5 (see comment). Its use to begin an appendix to the prophecy of Mic. is quite pertinent in a literary sense. Mic.'s original address concluded with an allusion to the **mountain of the house,** i.e. the hill in Jerusalem on which the temple stood, which would become a **wooded height** (3:12). Vs. 1 now begins in a different vein but with a like reference to the **mountain of the house of the LORD.** The promise that figuratively this mountain will be the **highest of the mountains, . . . raised up above the hills** corresponds antithetically to Mic.'s own prologue (1:4). Thus it is possible that this poem was composed expressly for this addition to Mic. and came to be inserted later into Isaiah's prophecy.

4:4-5. These lines fill out the picture of peace and general felicity which will characterize the ideal future. The sense of vs. 5 seems to be that, whatever the pagan leanings of the surrounding peoples, Judah's fidelity to the one God will abide forever. In 1964, on the occasion of the first visit of a Roman Catholic pope to the Holy Land, the president of the state of Israel greeted Pope Paul VI with the words of vs. 5.

4:6-10. *The Return of the Exiles.* Whether these lines are from the Babylonian exile (586-539) or later cannot be determined. In any case they presuppose a scattered community, and their intro. at this point is doubtless prompted by the desire to comment on Mic.'s earlier prediction of deportation and exile (1:16), ill fortune that is now to be reversed.

4:6-7. The terminology here suggests the forced march of exiles into a distant land (cf. Zeph. 3:19). The contrast between their present condition and what God will make of them, **a strong nation,** dramatically testifies to Israel's faith in the divine sovereignty over history.

4:8. Using poetic allusions to Jerusalem, the author declares that Judah's lost place among the nations will be restored.

4:9-10. The rhetorical question **Is there no king in you?** looks forward to a time when Israel will again have a king. Some interpreters have supposed that these lines refer to political straits later in the postexilic period and accordingly have tried to find

2 or more sources combined in chs. 4–5. There seems little evidence for this hypothesis. In a literary sense, at least, these vss. owe their present place in the text to the fact that for a prophetic commentator on Mic.'s preaching they supply an answer to his prophecy of doom (cf. esp. 1:16; 2:3-5, 12-13).

4:11–5:9. *The New Davidic Kingdom.* At least 2 occasions are documented in the OT literature relating to the exilic and postexilic periods when the people of Judah had reason to think that possibly the Davidic throne might soon be restored: (*a*) the dispensation accorded to the exiled King Jehoiachin in Babylon (*ca.* 561; II Kings 25:27-30); (*b*) the appointment as postexilic governor of Judah under Persian rule of Zerubbabel, a descendant of David, who seems to have entertained such aspirations for himself, being encouraged in this ambition by the prophet Haggai (*ca.* 520; Hag. 2:20-23). A lit. restoration of the Davidic royal house never happened, but the expectation reappears in biblical history (cf. e.g. Zech. 12:1-14; Acts 1:6). This passage illustrates this hope. Indeed, if it is an exilic prophecy, it may have been one of the early sources that fed this hope.

4:11-13. Presumably the situation is that of Jerusalem **(Zion)** either on or after the occasion of her destruction by the Babylonians in 586. The nations surrounding her to gloat over her fate will prove to be like **sheaves** of grain threshed by an ox, i.e. by Jerusalem (cf. Deut. 25:4; Hos. 10:11). The prophet thus expects a reversal of the present distress through divine intervention. Judah **shall beat in pieces many peoples.** War as an instrument of God's judgment is more or less taken for granted in biblical eschatology. The peace and felicity described in vss. 3-4 is thought of as an aftermath, rather than an alternative, to conflict. The historical experience of Judah allows her little occasion to think how else this promise might be implemented except by victory over her former conquerors. The expression **devote their gain to the LORD** is from the language of ancient holy war, in which the possessions of the enemy were utterly destroyed— lit. "devoted" to God (cf. Josh. 6:17-19).

5:1. Judah's fortunes are at their lowest before the expected deliverance. The figure of striking her **ruler** signifies her ultimate humiliation. Possibly there is a reference to the exiled King Jehoiachin (II Kings 24:12) or to the last Davidic king in Jerusalem, Zedekiah, who was tortured by the Babylonians and presumably perished in exile (II Kings 25:7). Possibly it is a proverbial saying, for **ruler** (*shophet*), lit. "judge," plays on the word **rod** (*shebhet*). In view of the following allusions to the rise of David in ancient times (vss. 2-9) the smitten ruler may have originally meant Saul, whose defeat by the Philistines was ultimately reversed for Judah by David (cf. I Sam. 31:1-13; also cf. vs. 10 with II Sam. 1:20). This same symbolism of the ruler being struck, taken as a sign of the approach of the messianic age, appears in Zech. 13:7, where the context is also Davidic messianism (cf. Zech. 12:1–13:6), and it is taken up into the NT interpretation of the passion of Jesus Christ (Matt. 26:31; Mark 14:27).

5:2. The renewal of Judah will be a reenactment of the events of the golden era of David. Though he is not named, the reference to his birthplace, **Beth-**

lehem Ephrathah, as well as other details of the vs. points unmistakably to him (cf. I Sam. 16:1; 17:12). The Christian tradition saw in this passage a prophecy of the birth of Jesus (Matt. 2:6).

5:3. The deliverance of Judah must wait on the birth of the expected heir to David's throne. The connotations of this passage look both backward and forward. It remembers that of 8 **brethren** David was the last to be born. But also the present and coming **travail** of Judah, i.e. her exile, is in the prophet's mind. It must continue until the deliverer appears; indeed he seems to think of it as necessary in order that the deliverer appear.

5:4. These lines compose one of the most beautiful and poignant pictures in OT and NT scripture of the awaited Messiah.

5:5a. The line **And this shall be peace** belongs with the foregoing passage concerning the ruler to come. It may be meant as comment on Mic.'s indictment of the false prophets who cried "Peace!" (3:5).

5:5b-9. The **seven shepherds and eight princes of men** have been interpreted in various ways, but it is unnecessary to look beyond the Davidic tradition which has been seen to dominate this ch. The meaning is doubtless proverbial in the tradition. David had 7 brothers, who, apart from him, were merely shepherds; but all 8, because of him, became "princes of men." The saying expresses the belief that Judah, though presently of little account, will at the coming of the ruler like David reign with him in the messianic kingdom. The theme is developed further in vss. 7-9 (see above on 4:11-13).

5:10-15. *Purification of the Land.* This passage must be compared with Isa. 2:6-11, with which it has an obvious affinity, though the circumstances described there are directly reversed here. The author seems to have drawn on the Isa. material at this point to portray the coming new age.

5:10-11. In the coming age, when the messianic conflicts have passed, Judah will no longer need to trust in military resources. The words may be meant as a response to Mic.'s earlier condemnation of this aspect of Judah's sin (1:13). The parallelism between the 2 lines of vs. 11 suggests that **cities** means fortified cities, continuing the thought of vs. 10 that the machinery of war will be abolished.

5:12-14. All the references are to pagan cult practices. **Pillars** here means stone pillars symbolizing the presence of pagan deities; but all 3. The **Asherim** were sacred objects or images representing the Canaanite fertility goddess Asherah. The occurrence of **cities** in vs. 14 seems quite out of context and may be a scribal error for "idols." The whole passage envisions the uprooting of those evils which the earlier prophet Mic. condemned (cf. 1:7).

5:15. The thought of this concluding vs. returns to the theme of judgment on the **nations afar off** (4:2-3) with which the prophecy began. The way the end completes the beginning is a mark of the unity of chs. 4–5.

III. A Liturgy of Atonement (6:1–7:20)

Biblical scholarship is divided on whether chs. 6–7 are at least in part the words of the 8th-cent. prophet Mic. Certainly it reflects nothing on Mic. or on the value of these chs. to say that they probably are the

Courtesy of Herbert G. May

Canaanite high-place at Gezer with cult pillars (Mic. 5:13); see also ills. pp. 22, 130

work of a later anonymous psalmist. To be sure much in them is consistent with Mic.'s thought as represented in chs. 1–3, but without more evidence than is at hand there is no way to settle the question.

Regardless of initial authorship, these 2 chs. together in their present form constitute a liturgy of worship, in particular a liturgy of atonement. Prophetic language and teaching have certainly been incorporated here. Moreover the similarity of 6:1-2 to 1:2-4 and the allusion in 6:16 to Omri, who built Samaria (cf. 1:6-7), suggest that Mic.'s prophecy (chs. 1–3) has to some degree provided the inspiration for the liturgy. But in their present form, in any case, the character of these chs. is on the whole psalmlike and penitential. There is an orderly alternation throughout between the speeches of God (6:3-5, 9-16; 7:11-17) and a penitential response of the worshiper spoken in the first person singular (6:6-8; 7:1-10, 18-20). The elements which comprise the speeches of God, together with the poetic summons to judgment (6:1-2), show marked affinities in style and content to Ps. 50, and in a lesser degree the responses of the worshiper show some affinity with Ps. 49. Cf. Hab. 3, which is similarly a psalmlike conclusion from a source other than the prophet Habakkuk.

6:1-2. The Summons to Judgment. The motif of **mountains** and **hills,** paralleling that in the opening lines (1:2-4; 4:1) of each of the 2 other divisions of the book, may have something to do with the addition to it of this liturgical piece (chs. 6–7). This formal opening illustrates a rhetorical declamatory style seen elsewhere in the psalms and the prophets (cf. e.g. Ps. 49:1; Isa. 1:2; Jer. 6:18-19).

6:2. A phrase typical of biblical prophetic language, **controversy of the LORD,** draws on the technical vocabulary of forensic debate before a judge in a court of law. Much prophetic dialogue in the Bible shows a "controversy" pattern in its style, vocabulary, and choice of metaphor (cf. e.g. 1:2; Pss. 50:4, 7; 74:22; Isa. 41:1; 51:22; Jer. 2:9; 12:1; Hos. 4:1, 4; Amos 3:1; Mal. 3:5).

6:3-5. God's Saving Acts. That God addresses Israel as **my people** evokes one of the most profound conceptions of biblical religion: God chose Israel to be his "own possession among all peoples, . . . a kingdom of priests and a holy nation" (Exod. 19:5-6). Allusion to the covenant between God and Israel gives tone and urgency to the ensuing dialogue. In the collective expression **my people** each individual worshiper would understand himself to be addressed. The question of whether God has somehow injured or wronged his people is a rhetorical one, capable of only one kind of answer.

6:4. The priestly and prophetic admonition to the worshiper is to **remember** what God has done. The deliverance from **Egypt** was and remains for Israel the pivotal point in her religion. It provides the criterion and norm for understanding the power and goodness of God. Israel's "creed" consists not of doctrinal statement so much as of this "sacred story," which is the presupposition of her worship (cf. Exod. 4:31; see "The Religion of Israel," pp. 1150-58). In vss. 4-5 the history of God's dealing with Israel is skillfully recalled.

6:5. The first 2 lines allude to a memorable attempt by the Moabite king **Balak** to prevent the Israelites at the end of their wilderness wandering from entering the promised land (Num. 22–24). **Balaam,** the prophet hired by Balak to invoke a curse on Israel, **answered** instead with a series of blessings, saying: "The word that God puts in my mouth, that must I speak" (Num. 22:38). **From Shittim to Gilgal** evokes the memory of Israel's crossing of the Jordan to enter the promised land after the episode of Balaam. Shittim was the point of departure and Gilgal the point of arrival (Josh. 3:1; 4:19). Shittim was also the location of Israel's encampment during the episode of Balak and Balaam (Num. 25:1).

6:6-8. God's Requirements. Following the liturgical pattern, the worshiper responds to the summons of vss. 1-2 and to the recital of God's saving acts in vss. 3-5. His question is asked in all solemnity and reverence: **With what shall I come before the LORD?** (cf. Ps. 24:3-6). This passage is often misinterpreted to mean that the possible offerings named in vss. 6-7 are dismissed as without value or meaning. On the contrary they are considered according to an ascending scale of value, and the rhetorical effect is to enhance what is prescribed in vs. 8 as the complete offering.

6:6-7. Animals could be sacrificed from the age of 8 days on (cf. Lev. 22:27) but **calves a year old** were of greatest value (cf. Lev. 9:3). **Thousands of rams, . . . ten thousands of rivers of oil** describes the offering of royalty. King Solomon's dedication of the temple involved such large-scale sacrifice (cf. I Kings 8:5, 63). Oil was used as a libation (cf. Gen. 28:18; 35:14; Lev. 14:10). **My first-born** does not necessarily refer lit. to child sacrifice, as many commentators have thought, though this may have been a problem in Israel at certain times (see comment on Deut. 18:10-11). In the present context, which deals with worthy gifts, it is better to construe this line according to the "law of the first-born" (Exod. 13:2, 11-13) and in the tradition of the boy Samuel (I Sam. 1:27-28) and the boy Jesus (Luke 2:22-23). The explicit consideration of a human life totally dedicated to God leads directly to what follows in vs. 8.

6:8. These words are among the loftiest in scripture. They give classic statement not only to the prophetic but, be it noted, also to the priestly understanding in the OT of the "whole duty of man" (cf. Pss. 24:3-6; 40:6-8; 50:7-15; 51:16-17; Isa. 1:11-17; Jer. 7:22; Hos. 6:6). They also anticipate the teaching of Jesus relating to right worship (John 4:24).

The liturgical nature of this passage and its context suggest strongly that it is an error to construe these words as a rejection of liturgical rite and ritual in favor of intangible virtues of character. What the passage does say rather clearly is that no particular act of commitment or sacrifice, however magnificent or however great the cost in life or living, can fulfill God's total claim over the whole of man's life (cf. I Cor. 13:3). The passage does not reject man's offering (vss. 6-7) but recognizes that every offering, however splendid, even to the point of giving oneself, is humble and imperfect.

Justice represents here a Hebrew noun which signifies not only the task of the judge but also the right and duty of everyone according to his particular station and responsibility in life. The king has his justice to perform; the priest, the public official, the teacher, or the parent each has his justice. This understanding of the word is nicely illustrated in the dialogue between John the Baptist and his listeners in Luke 3:10-14. In short the term "justice" does not define particular duties but challenges one to learn what is his particular duty and obligation and to perform it.

Kindness here translates the Hebrew word which the RSV in most places renders "steadfast love." It has for its chief connotation loyalty in all human relationships, fidelity to man and God.

To walk humbly with your God signifies, not personal piety in any narrow sense, but obedience to whatever God requires or commands. This certainly takes in, even though it is not limited to, worthy worship, including rite and ritual.

Should one ask what is the criterion or norm for such a life as is here described, the vs. has already pointed to it with the reminder that **he has showed you, O man, what is good;** i.e. God's saving acts, recited previously, are precisely the standard for the worshiper in this matter. What God himself has done provides the inspiration for human justice, fidelity, and man's whole walk in life. It has been well said with respect to biblical religion that the indicative mood gives rise to the imperative mood; i.e. what God has done suggests what man ought to be and do in faithful response.

6:9-16. The Failure of Justice. To recognize what God requires (vs. 8) is to recognize how far short of it one has fallen. To hear of God's grace is to hear at the same time a judgment on oneself. With this inexorable logic vss. 9-16 develop out of what has preceded. Esp. does vs. 16a-c contrast explicitly with vs. 8.

6:9. The **city** is addressed (cf. 1:6; 3:9-12), but that is only to say that each inhabitant of it is addressed. Initially the worshiper responds with prudence: **It is sound wisdom to fear thy name.** In place of **assembly of the city** the lit. meaning of the Hebrew should be retained, so that the line reads: "Hear, O tribe, for who has appointed it yet?" I.e. the wise response described in the preceding line is premature. Until one's objective guilt is recognized and acknowledged he cannot stand before the altar. Authentic repentance requires that what follows be heard and acknowledged.

6:10-16. The accusations in vss. 10-12 are self-explanatory, and as a naming of wrongs they are illustrative rather than exhaustive. Vss. 13-15 may be an allusion to specific reversals of fortune or to a dawning sense of guilt (cf. 7:1) or to both. King **Omri** of Israel (vs. 16) built the city of Samaria (cf. 1:6-7). His son **Ahab,** whose wife was the notorious Jezebel, was the antagonist of the prophet Elijah in the 9th cent. Omri and Ahab were remembered as the antithesis of what the king faithful to God should be (cf. I Kings 16:21–22:40). In the present context **walked in their counsels** is the antithesis of **walk humbly with your God** (vs. 8). Suffering and humiliation (vs. 16de) are the realities of judgment, which is nothing abstract. The allusion may be to the Exile, or some other disaster may be meant.

7:1-7. Confession and Trust. The worshiper acknowledges the city's destitution and desolation as his own, as once Isaiah did in the temple (Isa. 6:5).

7:2-6. Spiritual cleansing begins in confession. The words of judgment (6:10-12) are reiterated and elaborated in the language of penitence. The mood is not self-righteous judgment of others but a recognition and acknowledgment of the penitent's involvement in the general human condition (cf. vs. 9). Guilt is by nature collective.

7:7. All claim to virtue is laid aside. The worshiper who has inquired, "With what shall I come before the LORD?" declares now with authentic humility and with trust: **I will wait for the God of my salvation.** Measured by his understanding of what God requires (cf. 6:8) he comes before him with nothing at all.

7:8-10. _Confidence in God's Grace._ Dependent on his own resources the inhabitant of the city could say only **Woe is me!** (vs. 1). Dependent now on God he can begin to hope: **When I fall, I shall rise.** Vs. 9 articulates an explicit and unequivocal confession: God's **indignation,** the present distress being its mark, is just **because I have sinned against him** (cf. Dan. 9:4-19). The radical reversal from self-approbation to trust in God is apparent in the contrast between the earlier summons to **plead your case** (6:1) and the contentment here to wait on God **until he pleads my cause.**

7:10. As humiliation by the **enemy**—possibly Babylon is meant—was a mark of God's judgment (6:16) so defeat of the enemy will signal salvation. The enemy here, though real, is impersonal. In these words one confronts not moral self-righteousness so much as the psychology of suffering and enslavement (cf. Ps. 137:7-9), which demands of the interpreter not moralizing but understanding.

7:11-17. _The Promise of Restoration._ Hope and expectation have displaced despair. Confession and trust inspire a new vision. Here the psalmist does not dwell on the humiliation of the enemy, as in vs. 10, but dwells positively and with enthusiasm on the restoration of the forsaken city (cf. Ps. 51:18-19). **In that day they will come to you** pictures the risen city presiding over the new order in peace and prosperity. The **River** means the Euphrates. **But the earth will be desolate** recalls the defeat of the surrounding nations that have oppressed

Israel (cf. vs. 10). On a small scale Jer. 40:7-12 portrays such a revived community at Mizpah following the destruction of Jerusalem in 586. But in general the theme typifies the exilic and postexilic messianic expectation in Israel (cf. e.g. Jer. 30:18-21; Zech. 8:1-23).

7:14. The language suggests the ideal king in the messianic age (cf. Ps. 78:70-72). **Bashan and Gilead** were former Israelite territory in Transjordan (see color map 8).

7:15-17. Reference to the deliverance from Egypt reiterates the theme struck in 6:4-5, God's saving acts. What God in ancient times began to do, says the psalmist, he will one day complete. The extravagant language of vss. 16-17 is highly stylized. It intends to recall and to celebrate anew the awesomeness and majesty of the God who delivers his people, and it is to be understood in the tradition of the Song of Moses (Exod. 15:1-18), as vs. 15 makes clear and as vs. 18a confirms (cf. Exod. 15:11).

7:18-20. _Adoration and Praise._ Charged with emotion and deeply moving, this concluding hymn pours out thanks for the forgiveness of sins and the lifting of the burden of guilt. The past is redeemed. Over against the divine judgment proclaimed by Mic. (cf. 1:5-6) there appears the overwhelming **love** of the forgiving God. Indeed the jubilant words **Who is a God like thee?** in the Hebrew play on the meaning of the very name of the prophet Mic., which means "Who is like Yahweh?" That the **enemy** has been **trodden down** (vs. 10) is nothing compared to the knowledge that God will **tread our iniquities under foot.**

7:19cd. Among orthodox Jews the custom has been practiced since the Middle Ages to visit the bank of a river or other body of water following the synagogue service on the afternoon of Rosh Hashanah (the Jewish New Year) and to repeat this sentence 3 times while casting crumbs of bread on the water's surface. The ceremony is called _Tashlik,_ Hebrew for the opening phrase **Thou wilt cast.** The celebration of God's forgiveness is eminently appropriate for the beginning of a new year and the beginning of a new life. Having offered his adoration and praise, the worshiper can depart in peace.

THE BOOK OF NAHUM

Simon J. De Vries

Introduction

Historical Background. Characteristic oriental reluctance to record their military defeats caused the last 3 Assyrian kings to leave no record of their empire's decline. The fall of Assyria's capital, Nineveh, however, is the sole preoccupation of the book of Nahum.

The Hebrew kingdoms, N and S, had suffered more from the harsh and relentless Assyrians than from any other oppressor. For 2½ centuries Assyria had harassed them, driving the N kingdom into cruel captivity and virtually demolishing Judah while forcing her kings into rigorously enforced subservience. Now at last Assyria's end was near. As Nah. proclaimed her defeat, he seemed to speak for all Israel and for Yahweh.

Certain vss. added to the book after Nineveh's capture turned Nah.'s prophecy into a hymn of rejoicing. It is probable that the book became a liturgy for the Jerusalem temple and was first employed in an official celebration ceremony between 612 and 609. The latter is the date of Josiah's death, after which the Egyptians, to whom Judah was forced to submit, would surely have suppressed any open exulting over their expiring ally.

Authorship. Who Nah. was we do not know, nor is it possible to locate his home, Elkosh. We can say with assurance only that he was one of Israel's greatest masters of poetic imagery and a thoroughgoing Yahwist with strong nationalistic loyalties. Though his oracles abound in motifs from cult mythology, it is difficult to be certain whether he himself had any direct association with the cult.

Composition. The book consists of disparate materials. Ch. 1 opens with an acrostic hymn proclaiming the awesome might of Yahweh manifesting itself in nature; the ch. continues with alternating threats and promises, while the remaining 2 chs. consist mainly of a dramatic description of Nineveh's fall, so vividly depicted that some have thought the author to be an actual eyewitness of the event. The linguistic evidence, however, makes it quite certain that he was actually predicting the near future, portrayed in the power of his highly inspired imagination and overwhelming passion.

The outstanding problems of the book's interpretation are: (*a*) the extent of the acrostic hymn, (*b*) the identity of the person(s) addressed in the "you" passages, and (*c*) whether the fall of Nineveh is seen as future or as past. Scholars have imposed numerous

alterations or corrections on the Hebrew text in an attempt to resolve these problems. Careful attention to form and style, with observation of grammatical niceties and changes in ideology, produces a reasonably clear picture of the book's meaning and composition without numerous changes.

That the ancient translators often failed to comprehend what was before them is understandable, for it appears that the materials in this book have undergone an unusually complex process of growth and transformation. The most likely theory explaining this may be outlined as follows: (*a*) The prophet or some other person worked out from ancient models a stirring hymn of Yahweh's theophany, or self-revelation (1:2-8), to which a disciple appended a short interpretive application (vss. 9-10). (*b*) Nah. proclaimed 4 denunciatory poems against Nineveh shortly before its fall (2:1, 3-12; 3:1-4; 3:7*b*-15*a;* 3:15*b*-17). (*c*) As the doom of Nineveh approached, another disciple brought the poems together, prefixed the expanded hymn to provide an appropriate intro., transposed the words "an oracle concerning Nineveh" to the beginning of the book, and introduced editorial transitions, perhaps out of Nah.'s own words (1:11, 14; 2:13; 3:5-7*a*). (*d*) Nah. or a disciple spoke words of promise and exultation (1:12-13, 15; 2:2) and a mock lament (3:18-19) after Nineveh's capture; these were inserted into the existing corpus as refrains and as a conclusion, adapting the book to liturgical purposes. (*e*) The final editor of the Book of the 12 Prophets filled out the superscription in 1:1.

For Further Study: Alfred Haldar, *Studies in the Book of Nah.,* 1947. André Parrot, *Nineveh and the OT,* 1956.

I. Interpretive Additions

1:1. *Superscription.* See Intro.

1:2-10. *Acrostic (Alphabetic) Hymn with Expansion.* This hymn originally had nothing to do with Nineveh but may have been written by the prophet. Vss. 1-8 contain a skillfully composed hymn of Yahweh's self-revelation developing the ancient theme of Yahweh's power (**wrath**) in nature (cf. Pss. 18; 29; Hab. 3) and asserting his lordship over mankind, who is reminded that Yahweh is well disposed to all who take refuge in him but unremitting in vengeance on his enemies. Very solemn and ponderous is the beginning (vs. 2), with its stair-like repetition and strong alliteration. A literal translation would be:

A God jealous and avenging is Yahweh,
    avenging is Yahweh and a master of wrath;
  avenging is Yahweh against his adversaries,
    and wrathful is he against his enemies.

The references to **Bashan, Carmel,** and **Lebanon,** as also those to **sea** and **river,** are Yahwistic adaptations of themes found in Canaanite mythology: Yahweh, not Baal, is the God of the holy **mountains,** the God of fertility. Since the thought and structure of these lines seem so perfectly balanced, it is futile to look for the acrostic in the following sections.

1:9-10. This is one of the most difficult passages in the OT, for which numerous alterations or corrections have been proposed. It seems best to take this as a disciple's comment and expansion, holding textual changes to a minimum and translating:

Whatever you may devise against Yahweh
  he will bring to complete destruction,
so that opposition will not arise a second time;
for it will become like interlacing thorns and intertwining brambles
  which are devoured as completely dried-out chaff.

1:11, 14; 2:13; 3:5-7a. Editorial Transitions. Whether or not these vss. originated from Nah.'s own words or any common source, it is clear that a disciple was responsible for placing them where they are in order to bind the Nineveh poems together and provide them with what he considered a proper intro.

1:11, 14. A crucial problem is the identification of the person addressed. Hebrew, unlike English, distinguishes gender and number in all pronouns. The **you** in vs. 9 is anybody; the **you** in vs. 11 (fem. sing.) must be Nineveh since cities are regularly feminine; the **you** in vs. 14 (masc. sing.) has to be the one plotting **evil,** i.e. a certain Assyrian king or the Assyrian kings collectively. Since there seems to be solid reason for observing the text's distinctions in gender wherever possible, vs. 11 is to be understood as the charge and vs. 14 as the verdict against Nineveh and her king, whose end is decreed in formal juridical style.

2:13; 3:5-7a. These are threats against Nineveh in oracular style, with the formal intro.: **Behold I am against you** (fem.), **says the LORD of hosts.** The 1st passage summarizes the motifs of the preceding poem (the siege, the **lions**); the 2nd takes up the theme of 3:1-4, developing the motif of the harlot's public ridicule (cf. Jer. 13:22, 26-27; Ezek. 16:37; Hos. 2:3, 9) as a formal intro. to 3:7b-15a.

1:12-13, 15; 2:2. Liturgical Refrains. These oracles of blessing for Judah, with their formal opening phrases, were probably interspersed in the material to serve as responses in a celebration liturgy. As such they constitute the latest element in the book—apart from the superscription—together with the mock lament at the end. Nineveh has fallen, and though Assyrian armies remain in the field, Judah's complete liberation seems to be at hand. In 1:12 **they** refers to the evil and villainy of the preceding vs.; read "They have been cut off and have passed

away." In vs. 13 **his yoke** refers to the one plotting evil, addressed directly in vs. 14; read "I am breaking . . . am bursting. . . ." Vs. 15 is a summons to a victory feast (cf. Isa. 40:9-11); because **the wicked** is impersonal, we should read "villainy," as in vs. 11. In 2:2 the N kingdom of Israel will be restored along with Judah.

II. POEMS AGAINST NINEVEH (2:1–3:17)

Some scholars consider this passage to be one long poem; others, removing the transitional material in 2:13; 3:5-7a, rearrange the sections in an attempt to make a unified whole of what is left. It is better to view this remaining material as 4 separate poems, delivered at a time when Nineveh had not yet fallen but was so certain to be taken that its capture could be depicted as in progress or even as completed. Here Nah. the poet appears in all his splendor. Strangely, the name of God is not mentioned.

2:1, 3-12. A Taunt: "The Capture of Nineveh." This poem consists of a prelude and 3 strophes, each strophe having 3 couplets of virtually equal length. The meter is artistically variegated and climactic, but the real power of the poem resides in its excited movement and vivid imagery.

2:1. Ringing imperatives in this prelude warn Nineveh's defenders of the impending attack.

2:3-5. The attack begins. The descriptions of the invading warriors and their cavalry are like momentary impressions flashing on the mind. The invaders break through the outer wall into the streets; desperately the confused defenders set up emergency barriers.

2:6-9. The city is taken. Suddenly the river gate is broken open, and the attackers pour through. The **palace** is in consternation; idols and human captives are led forth, streaming out like the **waters** of a broken **pool,** while the conquerors are urged on to the rich **plunder.**

2:10-12. These vss. constitute the taunt proper. Tremendously sonorous and ponderous, 3 nouns in parallelism symbolize the devastation. Proud and mighty Nineveh is taunted as a **lion** who has taken much **prey** but whose **den** has now been destroyed. For other examples of the lion imagery cf. Job 4:10-11; Ezek. 19:1-9.

3:1-4. A Woe: "The End of the Bloody City." This is a poem in 3 short strophes combining the charges of bloodthirstiness, mendacity, deceit, and immorality as reasons for Nineveh's downfall. **Booty** and **plunder** might better be translated "tearing" and "prey" respectively, recalling the imagery of 2:12 rather than of 2:9. Vss. 2-3 return to the rapid and excited style of 2:3-9: short disjointed lines pile up vivid and gory details, combining them in one overpowering, horrifying picture. Vs. 4 is climactic, stating the great sin of Nineveh for which this disaster has come on her: she is a **deadly,** deceitful **harlot.** Elsewhere Judah is taunted as a harlot (Ezek. 16, 23), as are Tyre (Isa. 23:16) and Rome (referred to as "Babylon" in Rev. 17:5, 16). For other examples of the woe form cf. Isa. 5:8-25; 10:1-4; Hab. 2:6-17; Zeph. 2:5-7; 3:1-8.

3:7b-15a. A Taunt with Threat: "Nineveh Is No Safer Than Thebes." That this is intended as a taunt is clear both from the intro. supplied by the editor (vs. 7a) and from the prelude (vs. 7b-c), which rejoices over Nineveh as already fallen. She is taunted for her vain pride in imagining herself safe from divine judgment. Besides the prelude there are 2 divisions (vss. 8-10, 11-15a).

3:8-10. The **strength** of **Thebes** did not protect her. With **the Nile** waters as her **rampart** and strong allies at her side she felt secure (vss. 8-9), **yet** even she came to experience the terrors of **captivity,** with **little ones** murdered and the order of her life shattered (vs. 10). Thebes, lying far up the Nile, was an ancient capital with great prestige; hence its capture by Ashurbanipal's army in 663 was the worst conceivable blow to Egyptian pride and a crowning triumph for Assyria (see color map 9).

3:11-15a. Nineveh's defenses will likewise fail. In direct address her doom is announced (vs. 11). Her warriors are like **women,** her fortresses like **figs** falling from a shaken tree (vss. 12-13a). Her **gates** are thrown **open** to attack. While her defenders frantically rebuild her walls, **the fire** and **the sword . . . devour** (vss. 13b-15a).

3:15b-17. *A Taunt: "Nineveh Is Like a Locust Horde."* This section was directly attached to the preceding because of the catchword **locust,** which, however, elicits quite a different image here than in the previous line. Nineveh's **merchants, princes** (the latter from an Akkadian word perhaps meaning "guardsmen"), and **scribes** (a Sumerian word perhaps meaning "recruiting officials") have descended like a locust horde, stripping every victim bare; but they disappear with the rising of the **sun,** i.e. the destruction of their capital. Though the meter, vocabulary, syntax, and imagery are different from that of the other poems, there is no compelling reason to deny this short poem to Nah.

III. A Mock Lament Concerning the King of Assyria (3:18-19)

This is a form of taunt. Perhaps written by Nah., it was added after Nineveh's fall. That the verbs represent an actual past (not mere projections of the past into the future as in 3:7b) seems likely from the reference to **the news of you**—a report already received. The last words of vs. 17 in Hebrew, which belongs here and is probably to be emended to the usual lament intro. "how," together with the meter used throughout—3 stresses followed by 2 stresses— marks this as a formal lament. It is used, of course, in bitter mockery, for Judah rejoices instead of weeping.

THE BOOK OF HABAKKUK

Simon J. De Vries

INTRODUCTION

Historical Background. Jehoiakim, the 2nd son of Josiah, was a ruler who hastened Judah's day of final disaster. In the Machiavellian game of politics that he played, he first won and then lost everything. When Pharaoh Neco, having killed Jehoiakim's father and deposed his elder brother, offered him the throne at the price of complete subservience, he was willing to comply in order to gain a free hand for pursuing his ruthless internal policies. But in 604 Jehoiakim was forced to submit to Babylonian control as Nebuchadrezzar drove the Egyptians back to their border. For 3 years Jehoiakim served him (II Kings 24:1); then, yielding to the enticements of Egyptian ambassadors as opportunistic as himself, he threw off the Babylonian yoke, precipitating the inevitable retribution. He died while Nebuchadrezzar's army was besieging Jerusalem in Dec., 598.

We gather from the scanty biblical references that Jehoiakim had a character opposite to that of his father Josiah and that he allowed the hard-won gains of the Deuteronomic reform to lapse while a new apostasy seized the religious institutions. II Kings 23:37 records that "he did what was evil in the sight of the LORD, according to all that his fathers had done." Jehoiakim treated the prophets who dared to reprove him with harshness and contempt (cf. Jer. 36). He and his retainers apparently forsook morality based on the covenant, oppressing the poor as cruelly as before, so that Jeremiah was impelled to cry out (Jer. 22:17):

> You have eyes and heart
>   only for your dishonest gain,
> for shedding innocent blood,
>   and for practicing oppression and violence.

This is the setting into which the short prophecy of Hab. is most probably to be placed.

Authorship. One of the crucial questions that must be solved in order to choose among the wide array of possible interpretations is the problem of identifying the "righteous" and the "wicked" appearing in the book. Careful study reveals that in certain passages the wicked one can be none other than a local tyrant, while in other passages he must be a foreign invader. The righteous are correspondingly the oppressed local citizenry in the 1st group of passages and the whole Jewish nation in the 2nd. There is no acceptable solution except to assume that 2 different authors are involved.

In Hab.'s original estimate Jehoiakim seemed a greater threat to the true interests of the covenant people than any invading conqueror could possibly be. For this reason he appears to welcome the vision of 1:5-11, in which Yahweh announces the approach of the Chaldeans (Babylonians), whom he is raising up as the instrument of his judgment against this presumptuous tyrant in his own land. Thus Hab. stands where Josiah would have stood, upholding the terms of the covenant and the now abortive reform; he stands for the simple believer and hence for Yahweh himself. Though he has affinities with Nahum and the "nationalistic" prophets, he is closer to Jeremiah than many have imagined.

The drastic shifts that were constantly occurring in these turbulent times soon led Hab. to see, however, that the delivering Babylonians could indeed be oppressors of God's people (there is little evidence for the theory that the oppressor is Assyria). Soon Nebuchadrezzar loomed as the cruelest tyrant; that Yahweh was using him became a new problem for the prophet's faith. Receiving a new vision of Yahweh's power, Hab. found reassurance that this foreign oppressor would also come under divine judgment (ch. 3). It is this new emphasis that encouraged a disciple of the prophet to refocus the original prophecies against this enemy without, giving the book as a whole a strong nationalistic flavor.

This shift in meaning needs to be kept in mind when attempting to evaluate the book's treatment of the problem of theodicy, i.e. justification of God's ways. In the original form of his complaint, Hab., thinking only of Jehoiakim, asks how God can continue even for a while to tolerate this tyrant's flaunting of his law as he "swallows up" his own pious subjects (1:13). The answer of 2:2-5a is germane to this problem: the vision concerning the Chaldeans will surely come to pass at the appointed time; meanwhile, Hab. is given Yahweh's solemn word that the wicked man does not finally prevail and that the righteous man will live if he only continues faithful. But the disciple gives the question of 1:13 a different dimension: the wicked one becomes the ruthless Babylonian who oppresses the man "more righteous *than he,*" i.e. every Jew suffering at his hand. It is now a question of degree: why does Yahweh allow the more wicked to punish the less wicked?

The Prophet. There is no historical value in the stories about Hab. found in the apocryphal legend of Bel and the Dragon (see comment) or in rabbinic tales. We do not know who Hab. was or where he lived. His name is not found elsewhere in the Bible; it appears to be non-Hebraic, perhaps being derived from an Akkadian word for a garden plant. We are told only that he was a prophet; as a matter of fact, this book is of unusual importance for the phenomenology of prophetic inspiration. We may also infer from Hab.'s use of cultic forms in his prophecies that he had close associations with cult worship.

Composition. In light of the above considerations, the most likely theory of the book's composition would be the following: (*a*) Hab. recites the complaint of 1:2-4, receives the vision of vss. 5-11, recites the renewed complaint of vss. 12-13, then goes to his watch post to await Yahweh's answer (2:1), which comes to him in the words of 2:2-5a. All this he records, perhaps for use in the temple liturgy. He also receives a vision parallel to or as part of the one in 1:5-11, later inserted by his disciple at 1:14-17. (*b*) On other occasions he delivers 4 woes against the local tyrant (2:6*b*-17 in its original form). (*c*) As Hab. later experiences the terrors of invasion, an old hymn of theophany, or divine self-revelation (3:3-15), becomes a new revelation of Yahweh's power. This circulates for a while separate from the rest of Hab.'s writings, receiving liturgical notes for use in the temple. (*d*) The disciple, living perhaps during Zedekiah's reign (597-586), modifies the original material in chs. 1-2, making alterations in the text and adding words of his own. (*e*) An editor binds all the material together, including ch. 3, by supplying a rudimentary superscrpition, an intro. to the woes (2:6*a*), and a derisive poem against idols (2:18-20). (*f*) The final editor of the minor prophets puts the superscription into its present form.

For Further Study: W. F. Albright, "The Ps. of Hab." in H. H. Rowley, ed., *Studies in OT Prophecy*, 1950.

I. SUPERSCRIPTION (1:1)

Oracle is used to describe the entirety of chs. 1-2, including materials not in the oracular style. Cf. the emphasis on the visual aspects of inspiration. The RSV **of God** is not in the Hebrew text.

II. HABAKKUK'S COMPLAINT AND GOD'S REPLY (1:2-2:5)

1:2-4. *A Complaint of Oppression.* Dating from the early years of Jehoiakim's reign, this has the formal marks of a liturgical complaint similar to those found among the pss. The prophet has been burdened by official corruption within the land and by Yahweh's failure to answer his protests. Vs. 2 should probably be translated:

> O Yahweh, for how long have I cried for help,
> but you do not hear!
> I cry out to you of violence,
> but you do not deliver.

As **the wicked** (lit. "guilty") overwhelm **the righteous** (lit. "acquitted, blameless"), covenant law is no longer impartially applied. This lack of justice results in strife, trouble, and violence.

1:5-11. *An Answering Vision: "I Am Raising Up the Chaldeans."* Without formal intro. Yahweh announces the coming of the Babylonians, whom he has appointed to be his instrument of judgment upon

many **nations,** including the wicked oppressor within Judah. The thought is similar to that of Isa. 10:5-11 (cf. Isa. 45:1-8). Textual emendations seem to be required in vs. 7*b,* which may be read as the specific answer to Hab.'s complaint in vss. 2-4: "From him my judgment shall proceed!" One should observe the merging of aural and visual imagery. The poetry falls into 3 approximately equal strophes, the 1st containing the announcement (vss. 5-6), the 2nd a description of the Babylonians' rapidity of movement and **fierce** attack (vss. 7-8), the 3rd a description of the terrifying ease with which they overpower every opponent (vss. 9-11). The RSV **guilty men** in vs. 11*b* is inexplicable except as a tendentious alteration. Following the Qumran *pesher*—a term used to introduce each of the passages in the Hab. commentary of the Dead Sea Scrolls—we may translate:

> Then [like] the wind he sweeps by and passes through;
> and so he makes his might his god.

1:12, 13; 2:1. *The Complaint Renewed.* Ancient scribes changed "thou diest not" to **we shall not die** (so RSV). Because **than he** at the end of vs. 13 makes too long a poetic line, it does not belong to the original text. Hab. is not satisfied with the vision because it seems far from fulfillment. The knowledge that the eternal, undying God has appointed the **wicked** one for judgment, perhaps in the indefinite future, leaves unresolved a vexing contradiction: that so pure and holy a God should tolerate the wicked oppressing the righteous even for a moment. This is the burning question Hab. takes with him to his watch post, which is probably located in the temple rather than on the city wall or in an open field as popularly visualized. Once again aural and visual imagery are mixed: **look forth to see what he will say.** The RSV **what I will answer** should be emended to read "what he will answer."

2:2-5a. *An Answering Oracle.* Considerable confusion has surrounded the interpretation of this crucial passage. Many scholars have thought that the lines containing the famous words, **the righteous shall live by his faith,** are what Hab. is commanded to write, but this is an oracle, not a **vision.** Besides, why would **tablets** be needed for recording so short a message? Actually the vision that Hab. is to write so plainly has already been given: it is the vision of the coming Chaldeans recorded in 1:5-11 (note "look . . . see" in 1:5). Yahweh is now replying to Hab.'s complaint, assuring him that this vision will not tarry but is set for a definite time. Hence he is to wait for it, inscribing it on tablets (metaphorically?) as a permanent reminder and witness.

These words of reassurance are followed by the explanatory oracle of vss. 4-5a. Unfortunately, its contents have been badly garbled, and the versions are of little help in making restorations. Substituting the Qumran *pesher's* (see above on 1:5-11) "wealth" for **wine,** we may translate approximately as in the RSV. The instability of the unrighteous man's wealth and power is underscored while the righteous man is assured that he will live in the surest and highest sense by maintaining his faithfulness (not faith in the NT sense). For the NT adaptation of this passage, so influential on Luther's thinking, cf. Rom. 1:17; Gal. 3:11; Heb. 10:38-39.

The complete Dead Sea Scroll commentary on Habakkuk found in a cave near the ruins of the Dead Sea (Qumran) Sect (see "The Dead Sea Scrolls," pp. 1063-71); the fact that the scroll neither contains nor refers to ch. 3 led some scholars to conclude this ch. was not part of the original book (see comment V, below)

1:14-17; 2:5*b*. *Modifications and Additions*. The passage 1:14-17 may be a separate vision or part of 1:5-11, but in either case it refers to the Babylonians. Its form identifies it as from Hab. himself. References to pagan **sacrifices** to implements of war, though not to fishing equipment (mentioned here only metaphorically), have been found in ancient texts. The disciple who later viewed Babylon as Judah's greatest enemy (see Intro.) placed it here when he added "than he" to vs. 13 and at the same time turned vs. 17 into a question (the original reading was, "Therefore he keeps on emptying his net") and perhaps altering an original "he makes" in vs. 14 to **thou makest**. These changes made Yahweh directly responsible for the enemy's cruelty and intensified the problem for which 2:2-5*a* was supposed to be the answer. Accordingly, the disciple added the interpretive gloss in 2:5*b*—a denunciation of the Babylonians—and also touched up the woes that follow.

III. Woes Against a Tyrant (2:6-17)

Although vss. 18-20 are an editorial addition, there is no reason to doubt that Hab. was the author of the 4 woes of vss. 6*b*-17 in their original form. They all show greater or less evidence of the disciple's rewriting, and it is impossible to recover the original form of vss. 12-14. Each follows the classic woe form (cf. Isa. 5:8-25; 10:1-4; Nah. 3:1-4; Zeph. 3:1-8), containing an invective and a threat.

2:6*a*. *Editorial Intro*. This is a badly confused line, for which the RSV has as good a translation as any. **Taunt** is a technical term for the woe form; **scoffing derision** appropriately applies to vss. 18-20.

2:6*b*-8. *A Merciless Creditor*. One of the cruelest forms of economic oppression was the retaining of **pledges** taken in lieu of unpaid loans or services (cf. Amos 2:8). Here the local tyrant is bitterly denounced and threatened for making himself wealthy with such pledges. The disciple adds words of condemnation for the plundering enemy.

2:9-11. *An Ambitious Builder*. Here the only clear trace of the disciple's rewriting is the line **by cutting off many peoples**. **Forfeited** is lit. "sinned against."

The best commentary on this passage is Jer. 22:13-17. In a time of international crisis Jehoiakim built a pretentious palace with taxes squeezed out of his unfortunate subjects, thereby hastening the day of utter ruin. So flagrant is the wrong that the palace's very beams and stones protest.

2:12-14. *A Cruel Conqueror*. Vs. 12, which seems to recall Mic. 3:10, may have originally referred to Jehoiakim's efforts to glorify Jerusalem at his subjects' expense. Vs. 13*b* is paralleled in Jer. 51:58. Because vs. 14 is obviously borrowed from Isa. 11:9 and reflects a universalistic view of God, it has been taken as postexilic. But probably the disciple is responsible for the entire poem in its present form. Its meaning is that Yahweh's **glory**, filling the whole **earth**, exercises veto power over Nebuchadrezzar's frantic efforts to build **a town** (Babylon?) with the **blood** of his victims, whose labors are **for naught**.

2:15-17. *A Violent Oppressor*. The imagery of drunkenness is probably purely metaphorical, referring to Jehoiakim's cruel and shameless oppression, but sufficiently appropriate to the broader reference to be left unemended by the disciple-redactor. This is the book's most explicit threat against Jehoiakim. The disciple added vs. 17*b*, which is identical to vs. 8*b*.

IV. Ridicule of Idol Worship (2:18-20)

This belongs neither to Hab. nor to his disciple but was supplied by an editor. The catchword **woe**, though not in the proper place at the beginning, made it seem to be an appropriate conclusion to the preceding woes, while the solemn climax, **but the Lord is in his holy temple**, etc., seemed a perfect intro. to ch. 3. It has nothing to do with any oppressor, local or foreign, but is a mocking derision of idolatry similar to Isa. 44:9-20; 46:1-2; Jer. 10:1-4. A better reading for vs. 19*a* would be:

Woe to him who says to a wooden thing, "Awake! Arise!"
    to a dumb stone, "This shall give teaching!"

V. Habakkuk's Prayer (3:1-19)

Because of its striking differences in language and conception, ch. 3 has often been denied to Hab.

Scholars have thought that the liturgical notes and the reference to the **anointed** (vs. 13) clearly mark it as postexilic. When the Qumran *pesher* (see above on 1:5-11) was discovered with no commentary on this ch., such conjectures seemed to be confirmed, but further study has made it seem likely that the composer of the *pesher* simply had no interest in commenting on ch. 3. There can be no doubt that it did circulate separately at one time—the liturgical notes clearly indicate this—but the striking fact is that it did not remain permanently detached from the book bearing its author's name, as did the psalms ascribed to the prophets Haggai and Zechariah (cf. superscriptions to Pss. 146–148 in the LXX). We have observed several features of Hab.'s affinities with cult worship; there is no good reason to suppose that he could not have composed this grand hymn. Recent archaeological and linguistic studies have made it clear that the language of ch. 3 is at least as early as that of the other chs. and that some of its imagery goes back to the time of Israel's origins.

As he witnessed the devastation wrought by the Babylonians, Hab. was evidently driven to prayer. While he waited quietly for an assurance of Yahweh's mercy in the manifestation of his wrath, the words of an ancient theophany, or divine self-revelation, similar to Deut. 33; Judg. 5 became the vehicle of inspiration and assurance, drawing from him the most deeply spiritual utterance of this book and one of the noblest in the entire OT.

3:1, 19b. Liturgical Headings. The intro. contains technical terms similar to those in the headings of the pss. (cf. Ps. 7). Also cf. the word **selah** in vss. 3, 9, 13 and the words at the end.

3:2. A Request for Mercy in the Midst of Wrath. According to its literary form this should be re-garded as an integral and essential part of the hymn.

3:3-15. A Theophany: "Yahweh's Combat." This consists of 2 16-line strophes followed by 5-line refrains.

3:3-8. These vss. constitute strophe I and the refrain. Magnificent language expresses the overwhelming majesty of Israel's God coming from his traditional home in N Arabia (Sinai?). He is like the sun, filling the whole **earth** with **his glory,** shaking **the mountains** in his wrath (cf. Nah. 1:2-8). This is the language of the earliest Yahwistic traditions, set in deliberate opposition to themes from the Canaanite myths. Yahweh, rather than Baal, is engaged in combat with **rivers** and **the sea** (cf. Marduk's struggling with Tiamat, the primordial sea of chaos, in the Babylonian creation myth).

3:9-13. These vss. make up strophe II and its refrain. The actual battle is described in stirring images. All the enemies of Yahweh are vanquished as he goes forth for his people's **salvation.** The **anointed one** in vs. 13 is the Davidic prince.

3:16-19a. The Prophet's Reaction and Response. This is part of the hymn, forming a 12-line 3rd strophe plus a 5-line postlude, but its sources are the prophet's own present experience. Here his inspiration rises to its highest exaltation. The divine manifestation appalls him, leaving him weak and exhausted, but it gives him the calm assurance that however severe the coming trials may be, the almighty Yahweh will surely carry out his purpose against the invaders. These thoughts lead the prophet at the end to rejoice **in the God of** his **salvation.** Whatever he may suffer, whatever may be taken from him, he will continue to be joyful in this great God. Hab. is himself a prime example of the righteous one who lives by his faith.

THE BOOK OF ZEPHANIAH

Simon J. De Vries

Historical Background. Though it has been put at the end of the triad Nah.-Hab.-Zeph., this book belongs chronologically at the beginning. The final editor of the minor prophets, who is responsible for having made this arrangement, probably understood the prophet's great-great-grandfather mentioned in 1:1 to be the famous Judean king and hence concluded that Zeph. needed to be placed after Nah. and Hab., in spite of the specific statement dating him in the reign of Josiah (641-609).

It was characteristic of Israel's prophets that they allowed themselves to recede into the background while placing Yahweh's message foremost, hence most of what we know about Zeph. is drawn by inference from his prophecy. We are provided with the unusually long genealogy in the superscription, however; though it is not from the prophet himself, there is no good reason to reject its statement. Other prophetic genealogies go back only to the father or grandfather; this list goes back to the 5th generation. It is for this reason that many scholars agree that Hezekiah must be the king of that name. This would then put Zeph. within the royal lineage and would lend special weight to his denunciation of the officials and the king's sons in 1:8, which at the very least suggests that he was a familiar figure in the royal court.

The chronological problems are formidable, however, for those who hold this view, since the 5 generations must be squeezed into the period from *ca.* 716 to *ca.* 625. If this is not probable, one cannot say that it is impossible. In any case, various considerations lead us to date Zeph.'s activities not only in Josiah's reign but in the early part of it. Because Baalism and foreign cults are still flourishing (1:4-6), it is clear that the Deuteronomic reform has not yet begun, though Zeph.'s freedom in denouncing them surely indicates that Manasseh and Amon have passed from the scene. The fact that Josiah is nowhere mentioned (except in a dubious passage, 3:15), together with references to the officials and king's sons causing dissension or perhaps plotting insurrection (1:8-9), points specifically to the early years, when Josiah was still a lad. At that time he had not yet come to make a public espousal of the reform program. According to II Chr. 34:3-8, he did not begin to "seek the God of David his father" until the 8th year of his reign and did not undertake reform measures until his 12th regnal year, bringing them to fruition in the 18th year of his rule, 623/22.

One of the most vexing historical problems pertaining to this period is Herodotus' statement that the Scythians, wild and ferocious marauders from the Asian interior, were sweeping over W Asia as far S as Egypt *ca.* the year 626. Both the Medes and the Assyrians were having trouble with them in this period, and later (*ca.* 612) they played an important role in Assyria's downfall. If they did actually approach Egypt, they must have passed through Palestine and Philistia, striking terror into the hearts of peoples living in their path. There is nothing to confirm Herodotus' statement, however, except an apparent preoccupation with an unnamed menace in the book of Zeph. and in Jeremiah's early prophecies (chs. 4-6). Although to identify this foe with the Scythians begs the very question needing to be solved, no better identification lies at hand. In any case, it is clear from reading the book that if the prophet were speaking of them, they did not actually attack Jerusalem, though it is quite likely that they would have raided the Philistine coastlands (cf. 2:4-7). Certainly a deliverance from some definite foreign foe has occasioned the hymn of gratitude found in 3:14-18.

Authorship. With some assurance it may be inferred that Zeph. was a cultic prophet. As such he summoned the pious to a solemn assembly in the temple (2:1-4) and led them in cultic celebration (3:14-18). It is generally agreed, moreover, that he had considerable influence in stimulating the Deuteronomic reform, with its strong cultic motivations and associations.

This book demonstrates as clearly as any within prophetic literature the fact and sometimes the vitality of corporate authorship. Zeph. evidently had a disciple or school of disciples who felt free to adapt his original oracles to new situations. They must have believed that in a real sense they were reincarnating their master, giving his message new life and force. When Josiah died and his reform began to founder, or still later, after Jerusalem had been destroyed (586), these disciples projected the old messages of doom toward a new future.

Composition. We may reconstruct the composition of Zeph. somewhat as follows: (*a*) In the early years of Josiah's reign and probably shortly before the enemy raid, the prophet delivered a series of oracles, proclaiming judgment against all mankind (1:14-18), against various foreign lands (2:5-7, 8-9, 12-14), against all mankind and Jerusalem (1:2-6; 3:1-4, 6-8), and exclusively against Jerusalem itself (1:7-13). (*b*) As the menace approached, Zeph. issued a summons to a solemn assembly at Jerusalem for the purpose of averting destruction (2:1-4). (*c*) After the threat had passed leaving Judah unscathed, Zeph. led the temple worshipers in a joyful hymn of celebration (3:14-18). (*d*) Later, probably during the Babylonian exile, a disciple refocused Zeph.'s oracles of doom and expanded some of them into promises of blessing (glosses, or added interpretations, in 1:9*a*, 10*a*, 12*a;* expansion of 2:5-7; a gloss at 3:5 and additional vss. in 3:9-13; a gloss at 3:16*a* plus 3:19). (*e*) Possibly the same, but probably another, author added taunts against Moab and Ammon (2:10-11) and against Nineveh (2:15) and attached the concluding vss., 3:20. (*f*) An editor rearranged the book into oracles of judgment against Judah (1:1-2:4), oracles against the foreign nations (2:5-15), and oracles of blessing (3:9-20), inserting 3:1-8 after the Nineveh oracle because of the direct address to a city common to both. The same person probably added the superscription.

Literary Quality. For the larger part Zeph.'s prophecy consists of beautiful and dramatic poetry. His disciples generally fail to measure up to him in poetic inspiration but in some respects surpass him in the loftiness of their spiritual understanding.

For Further Study: G. A. Smith, *The Book of the 12 Prophets,* Vol. II, rev. ed., 1928.

I. Superscription (1:1)

Here is the only place where the prophet is named; his name may be doubly theophoric ("Yahweh is Zaphon"—the holy mountain of the N) and hence an explicit polemic against Baalism (cf. current Phoenician names like Baal-Zaphon). **Cushi** ("Ethiopian") may have been a non-Semite.

II. Divine Judgment on Judah and Jerusalem (1:2–2:4)

1:2-6. *An Oracle: "The Overthrow of the Wicked."* The contrast between the 2 strophes of this oracle (vss. 2-3, 4-6) dramatizes its impact upon idolaters in Jerusalem. Moving from the greater to the lesser, from the general to the specific, Yahweh first declares his judgment on all he has made and then pronounces doom upon **Judah** and **Jerusalem.** This contradicts the cherished doctrine of Zion's inviolability (cf. Isa. 37:35), but its force is beyond resisting: if Yahweh is sovereign judge of the whole earth, he is judge of Jerusalem too. **This place** in vs. 4 means "this shrine," i.e. the temple. Fertility rites associated with Baalism were secretly practiced there, along with worship of the Mesopotamian astral deities and human sacrifices to the Ammonite god Malkam (RSV **Milcom;** ="Molech" I Kings 11:7).

1:7-13. *An Oracle: "The Day of Yahweh on Jerusalem."* For the imagery of this poem cf. Isa. 2:12-22; Amos 5:18-20. Zeph. associates the day of divine judgment with the enemy's approach, announcing that it is very near. **On that day** (vss. 9, 10) and **at that time** (vs. 12) are from a disciple, who inserted them in order to redirect the prophet's words to a still-distant future.

1:7-9. Strophe I concerns Yahweh's sacrifice and inspection. Regarding **be silent** cf. Amos 6:10; Hab. 2:20; Zech. 2:13. The **sacrifice** provides an image of blood and slaughter (cf. Isa. 34:6-7; Jer. 46:10; Ezek. 39:17-20). In **I will punish** the sudden change to the first person demonstrates the prophet's complete identification with Yahweh; the verb may have a wider meaning, however, such as "inspect, call to

account" (so also in 1:12; 2:7; 3:7). The officials are indicted for violence and fraud. **Threshold** perhaps designates the pedestal for the royal throne.

1:10-11. Strophe II describes the sound of destruction. The excitement and terror of the approaching invasion are expressed in the form as well as in the dramatic imagery. The foe first comes to Jerusalem's N and least-protected quarter, where live **the traders** and merchants who deserve to be the first victims of the onslaught.

1:12-13. Strophe III is a judgment on the greedy and complacent. These are the groups living according to the ultimate blasphemy: **the Lord will not do good, nor will he do ill**—a blatant contradiction of Gen. 18:25. Words from Amos 5:11 are borrowed for the picture of devastation. Zeph. is depicted in Christian art as holding a lamp in his hand.

1:14-18. *An Oracle: "The Day of Yahweh on Mankind."* This is the source of inspiration for the famous medieval hymn "Dies Irae, Dies Illa" ("Day of Wrath, Day of Mourning"). Because of the striking resemblance between vss. 7, 14, many have held that the former should be transferred to the beginning of this poem, but considerations of form and syntax argue against it. There is nothing in this poem to suggest that it refers solely to Judah, though the general judgment it announces is clearly intended to apply to Judah along with the rest of mankind (cf. 1:2-6).

1:14. In strophe I the **day of the Lord is near.** The RSV makes little sense in its literal translation of the 2nd line, where the text should probably be emended to read: "Swifter is the day of Yahweh than a runner, it hastens faster than a champion."

1:15-17. In strophe II the day is dreadful. A double triad of 3-foot lines produces an overwhelming feeling of doom and desolation. The strong alliteration that is characteristic of Zeph.'s genuine poems is esp. striking here. The concluding words make clear that all men are judged **because** all **have sinned.**

1:18. Strophe III pronounces **the day of the wrath of the Lord** unavoidable. No ransom or bribe can buy escape. There is no 2nd chance or appeal, no exception or exemption.

2:1-4. *A Summons to Solemn Assembly.* Sonorous alliteration, ringing imperatives, and urgent repetitions express the earnestness of this appeal.

2:1-2. Strophe I is a call to the nation. The **shameless nation** is called to show its repentance in a public assembly before the day of wrath breaks on it.

2:3-4. Strophe II summons the humble. In particular, the **humble of the land** are to **seek the Lord,** i.e. come to a fast and service of supplication (cf. Joel 1:14) and live a humble and righteous life. The prophet holds out the hope that they at least may be saved from the coming storm, which is about to sweep over the neighboring territory of Philistia. Some scholars have joined vs. 4 to vss. 5-7; this ignores not only the poem's form but also the point of Zeph.'s appeal, viz. that with the enemy so close by, Judah's leaders had *better* get scared.

III. Divine Judgment on the Nations (2:5-15)

2:5-7. *A Woe Against Philistia.* Cf. this short poem with the woe in 3:1-8; observe that it lacks the invective so prominent there. It is indeed striking and significant that though Zeph. proclaims Philistia's imminent destruction, he does not denounce her for any crime (also the original oracle against Nineveh in vss. 13-14, but cf. his denunciation of Moab and Ammon in vs. 8). Here as elsewhere, the oracular form represents Yahweh as bringing the judgment, though an earthly foe is his agent. In this poem the disciple's adaptations are particularly apparent; he turned the picture of Philistia as a desolate pastureland into an image of bliss and contentment for **the remnant of the house of Judah,** whose **fortunes** Yahweh promises to **restore** (lit. "return their captivity"). Zeph.'s original poem probably read as follows:

> Woe to you, inhabitants of the seacoast,
>   you nation of the Cherethites!
> The word of Yahweh is against you, O Canaan,
>   you land of the Philistines!
> So I will destroy you till no inhabitant is left,
>   and the seacoast shall become pastures,
>   meadows for shepherds and folds for flocks;
> they shall pasture among the houses of Ashkelon,
>   and shall lie down in Ekron.

2:8-9. A Threat Against Moab and Ammon. Judah's E neighbors, Moab and Ammon, were her traditional enemies; hence it is not necessary to date this oracle after 605 (cf. II Kings 24:2). One should cf. this passage with Israel's taunt in Num. 21:27-30 and Isaiah's oracle in chs. 15-16. Here Yahweh swears a solemn oath to make their land as empty and desolate as **Sodom** and **Gomorrah**—surely a more severe judgment than that inflicted on the Philistines. The poem's structure identifies vs. 9d as a genuine conclusion; its reference to a plundering remnant completes the picture of destruction.

2:12-14. A Threat Against Ethiopia and Assyria. This poem expresses the scope of Yahweh's judgment, which reaches from the distant S to the remote **north.** Though the major emphasis falls on Assyria's desolation, her specific sin is not stated. **Nineveh** will become more desolate than Philistia (2:5-7), inasmuch as the **beasts** that are to inhabit her are wild animals rather than sheep; yet she is to be less forbidding than Moab and Ammon (vss. 8-9), where nothing is to dwell.

2:10-11, 15. Taunts Against Moab, Ammon, and Nineveh. These have been added by a disciple and appear to date from a time when these enemies had been destroyed. Both begin with the emphatic word **this,** i.e. the aforementioned desolations. Vs. 15 employs the past tense; hence Nineveh is already fallen; this is then a taunt similar to Nah. 3:18-19 (cf. 3:7). We may suppose that vss. 10-11 likewise refer to the past and are intended to turn vss. 8-9 into a taunt. In any case, the universal rule of Yahweh depicted in vs. 11 lies in the future.

IV. A WOE AGAINST JERUSALEM (3:1-8)

See in Intro. the reasons for this poem's present position between the oracles against the nations and the oracles of blessing. Vs. 5 is a theologizing interpretive addition. After the introductory denunciation (vs. 1), the charges and specifications are set forth in 2 6-line strophes, followed by the verdict or threat in a final strophe of 4 lines. All is artfully balanced and dynamically powerful.

3:2-4. Charges Against Jerusalem. Vs. 2b in this first strophe is emphatic. In effect it says, "In Yahweh she has not trusted, unto her God she has not drawn near"—implying that she has followed other gods. Each group among her leaders is indicted. Since the word here translated **leave nothing** (vs. 3) means "gnaw," possibly interpreted as a description of the gnawing of cubs in contrast to the biting of **wolves;** it means that the rapacious **judges** become ineffectual in administering justice in their proper posts, which they assume in **the morning.**

3:6-7. Yahweh's Warning Scorned. In strophe II Yahweh has judged other **nations** in order to teach Judah to repent, but his patience has only made her leaders more eager for corruption.

3:8. Future Judgment of Judah. Strophe III warns that Judah will surely be included in the general judgment and consumed in the general destruction. **Wait for me** has the same word as is found in Hab. 2:3. For the image of Yahweh as **witness** cf. Mic. 1:2; Mal. 3:13-15, and for the idea of gathering the **nations** for judgment cf. Joel 3.

V. DIVINE BLESSING FOR JUDAH (3:9-20)

3:9-13. An Oracle: "Israel's Return and Renewal." We must refrain from dogmatically denying eschatological dreams to Zeph.; language and form identify this section as an expansion of the woe against Jerusalem, but it has a definite strophic structure.

3:9-10. Strophe I concerns the purification of the nations. Here is a universalism worthy of 2nd Isaiah. The nations will learn Hebrew in order to serve Yahweh. For the RSV **my suppliants, the daughter of my dispersed ones** perhaps a clearer reading is, "those invoking me among the dispersion."

3:11. Strophe II, concerning the purging of pride from Israel, is an echo of 3:1-7.

3:12-13. Strophe III speaks of the holy remnant. The **humble and lowly** are the holy remnant, by whose righteous living the nation is to be saved from judgment. Theirs is a vicarious repentance; to them is accordingly promised peace and bliss.

3:14-18. A Celebration Hymn: "Yahweh Is in Your Midst." Apart from a probable addition from an editor's hand in vs. 16a, there can be little doubt that this is Zeph.'s hymn for a service of deliverance.

3:14-15. Strophe I is exultant—let **Zion . . . rejoice!** As Yahweh brought the menacing enemy as the agent of his judgment, he is responsible for having removed that same menace. In vs. 15b read, "Yahweh rules in your midst." He is the true **King** in the midst of his people and has heard the prayer of the humble.

3:16-18. In this 2nd strophe Yahweh rejoices in his victory. The RSV makes necessary emendations. In vs. 18b, however, one should read, "I have removed disaster from you."

3:19-20. Expansions. Once again the promises to a dispersed remnant and the words **at that time** indicate the work of a disciple. In vs. 19c the sentence structure requires us to read, "even those whose shame was in all the earth." Vs. 20 is a prose-poetry repetition of vs. 19; it may be from the same person who wrote 2:10-11, 15.

THE BOOK OF HAGGAI

ROGER N. CARSTENSEN

INTRODUCTION

The Prophet. Of the prophet Haggai little is known except that 4 oracles are attributed to him and that along with Zechariah he is reported in the book of Ezra to have helped the Jews rebuild their temple (Ezra 5:1-2). Presumably his oracles provided this "help" (Ezra 6:14). The name Hag. means "festal," which may indicate that he was born on a feast day. His reference to the previous temple (2:3) does not necessarily mean he saw it himself, though he may have been an old man at the time of the oracles. The tradition that he was a member of the "Great Synagogue," the traditional first college of learned scribes, which the Jews believed carried the interpretation of the law forward to the later rabbis, suggests he may have been influential in the community.

His Times. The book of Haggai is clearly dated in 1:1 to the reign of Darius I, i.e. 520 B.C. The return from Babylon led by Sheshbazzar had occurred about 18 years earlier (538), soon after Cyrus' conquest. The people to whom Hag. preached were poor but not actually destitute. The future of their province under the insensitive rule of the distant Persian government showed no prospect of improvement. Drought and disease struck the crops, and evidence of the care of the God who softened the heart of Cyrus was nowhere to be seen. The practices of religion were not taken seriously. Since they had made no provision for God to live among them, since his ancient house lay in ruins, the concept of his active and relevant presence in their community had faded.

In the midst of their discouragement, winds of revolution stirred the air. Cambyses by his campaigns (529-522) had hardened the generous policies of Cyrus. When he died on his way back from a campaign in Egypt, the Persian throne was in jeopardy and the affairs of government in chaos. Darius succeeded to the throne in 522, and while he proceeded with energy and courage to consolidate his rule, it was several years before it became clear that the empire would survive.

In 520 the issue was still most uncertain, and hopes for national freedom rose throughout the provinces. The building of the temple plus the attempt to put Zerubbabel of the seed of David on the throne was apparently the direction the revolution took in Judah. It would appear that Darius simply carried out the policy of Cyrus, as Ezra 6:1-15 suggests, for the first project was allowed to proceed while the crowning of a king, never authorized by Cyrus, was frustrated by means that are unknown (see article, "The History of Israel," pp. 1026-31).

His Message and Purpose. The central message of Hag. is, "Build the temple!" That the house of God has been in ruins while men have comfortable homes explains, according to the prophet, the economic and spiritual depression of the struggling community. He holds that a functioning temple will usher in happiness and fulfillment. Hag. emphasis differs from that of preexilic prophets such as Amos, Micah, and Isaiah, who believed that God's kingdom waits upon justice and righteousness. He insists instead that fulfillment depends upon the proper performance of religious rites. To suppose he was indifferent to the moral and social responsibility of the Jew hardly follows; rather he saw the primacy of God's demands for *God* over all else.

Hag. was indeed a practical man, but the motive which moved him was hope. No one can understand the excitement that the project of rebuilding the temple would create unless he is able to sense the great world events which the presence of God would set in motion (2:20-23). The rising of the walls of the sanctuary from the pits of the Jews' despair was the first evidence since Cyrus' decree that God was acting mightily again.

For Further Study: G. A. Smith, *The Book of the 12 Prophets*, Vol. II, rev. ed., 1928. Raymond Calkins, *The Modern Message of the Minor Prophets*, 1947.

I. SUMMONS TO REBUILD THE TEMPLE (1:1-15a)

1:1-11. The Summons. The opening proclamation carries the principal force of the whole book. In practical, concrete terms he outlines the nature, cause, and cure of the Jews' predicament. Hag. indicates no suspicion of religious formalism, nor does he attack immorality and injustice as did most preexilic prophets. It is easy, however, to overdraw the contrast between the earlier and later prophets. The need for the temple was immediate and pressing; for that day, the return to religious responsibility demanded it. Not for 600 years would the Jews be able to dispense with the sanctuary, and even then much of the life and thought of Judaism would still revolve around memories of the ancient altar.

1:1. Hag. began to prophesy in Sept., 520. A brief message comes first of all to **Zerubbabel** (lit. "seed

501

of Babylon") the governor, who was a grandson of King Jehoiachin taken by Nebuchadrezzar (RSV Nebuchadnezzar) to Babylon, and to **Joshua** the high priest, a descendant of the high priest at Jerusalem when it fell in 586. The 2 leaders were political and spiritual heads of the community.

1:2. The people's unwillingness to rebuild was probably rooted in their poverty; however, they take refuge in the memory that Jeremiah prophesied a 70-year interval before the Jews' punishment would be complete, saying **the time has not yet come** (cf. Jer. 25:11-12; 29:10). There is no evidence that the rebuilding had been started and interrupted years before, as suggested in Ezra, or that Hag. knew of an earlier building ban issued from the royal court (cf. Ezra 3:10; 4:23-24; 5:16). The subsequent message to the people (vss. 4-11) insists that putting one's own business above the demands of God is ruinous.

1:4-11. Paneled may be read "roofed," an idea which would better fit the acknowledged destitution of the people than houses ornately decorated. Neglect of the house of God has brought on a depression evidenced in **drought** (vs. 11) and inflation (vs. 6). People have enough to stay alive, but not to enjoy living. Hag. distinctly teaches that the drought is God's doing (vs. 11). Men's hopes have been blasted year after year, but the erosion of spirit has been even more severe than the shriveling of crops. Whether the people's misery was due basically to actual poverty or to the deeper dissatisfaction of the spirit that can make the rich seem to be the noisiest paupers in the community is not clear. Hag.'s temple is not simply a place for God's honor and comfort, but one that looks toward the coming of the Messianic Age, to which the LORD's word, **that I may appear in my glory** (vs. 8), doubtless refers.

Rebuilding the temple is a basic religious duty. However, each man has first to suspend, at least for a time, his private preoccupation—so reasonable and so dangerous—**with his own house** (vs. 9). Success depended on community effort; brotherhood, the fruit of the companionship of labor, would form an invisible sanctuary for the divine Presence.

1:12-15a. The Response. The effectiveness of Hag.'s preaching is witnessed by a general response. **The remnant of the people** refers to the returned exiles. That the people **feared before the LORD** (vs. 12) is evidence that the prophet was genuine, indeed **the messenger of the LORD** (cf. Mal. 3:1). In the tradition of the world's great preachers, Hag. awakens in the people the realization of the presence of God among them. Not all the prophets met with such response, e.g. Ezekiel and Jeremiah (cf. Ezek. 20:49; 33:30-33; Jer. 5:30-31; 18:12; 26:7-9).

II. AN ENCOURAGEMENT (1:15b–2:23)

1:15b-2:9. The Glory of the New Temple. Seeing the discouragement of the people at the modest beginnings of their temple (cf. Ezra 3:12), Hag. characteristically speaks to the situation when he asks, **Who is left among you that saw this house in its former glory** (vs. 3)? Doubtless there were a few who had seen Solomon's temple before it was destroyed. The new building itself may be small—we do not know the dimensions—but the **splendor of this house shall be greater** even than before (vs. 9).

Hag. reminds the people of the covenant faith of Israel by referring to the LORD who brought them **out of Egypt** (vs. 5) and who is about to perform a new work of great scope for his people. The idea of "shaking" **the heavens** and **the earth** (vss. 6-7) is often used to portray God's judgment in political turmoil (cf. Judg. 5:4-5; Nah. 1:2-5; Heb. 12:25-29). Hag. undoubtedly refers to the confusion and disorder of the accession of King Darius, which he interprets to be preparatory to the restoration of Israel to its former glory under David (2:21-23). In a political sense, Israel has always been strongest in a period when the great nations of the Near East have been weak.

The immediate promise Hag. holds out is that **the treasures of all nations shall come in** to the temple (vs. 7). The God who made all **silver** and **gold** will claim it as his own (vs. 8). God is the chief actor in this view of history. Man's function is not to arm himself and fight but to create in the holy community a throne suitable for a victorious God, a chest appropriate to the spoils of triumph.

The victory of the coming of the kingdom is to take place **in a little while** (vs. 6). That Hag. does not intend these words to mean a long time is clear from his subsequent association of the new day with the rise of Zerubbabel (2:20-23). The **prosperity** of vs. 9 is often translated "peace" and should therefore not be limited to affluence. This is the profound and inclusive happiness of God's approval.

2:10-14. The Holy and the Unclean. This passage in itself is easy to understand. Hag. simply calls on the priests to witness that it is the unclean, rather than the clean, which is contagious (cf. Num. 9:6-7). No one knows, however, just why the lesson is included. Many scholars interpret **this people** (vs. 14) as the Samaritans who attempted to participate in the building, in which case the infectious uncleanness might come from them. They are reported, however, to have been previously rebuffed (cf. Ezra 5:1-5) and would probably have been more directly attacked.

Apparently the problem is a delicate one: instead of attacking it head on, Hag. moves by analogy, citing the established sacrificial systems as the rationale of his claim. Perhaps the Jews, who were making the **unclean** offerings, are intended. It may have been that those who never went to Babylon were in some sense unacceptable to God and might compromise the whole enterprise. Since the **priests** themselves are cited as authorities (vs. 11), could it be that Gentiles had at this time already infiltrated the priesthood, as Tobiah the Ammonite, who was probably only partly of Israelite descent, did later (Neh. 13:4-5)? Thus the priests would be cleverly impaled on their own rules. It is also possible that the priests as well as the people had already become involved with foreign women (see comment on Mal. 2:10-16).

2:15-19. Impending Change. It appears that this passage is misplaced and should follow the phrase in 1:15a, "on the twenty-fourth day of the month, in the sixth month." Some of the reasons are: (a) There is no apparent connection between these vss. and the homily on uncleanness (vss. 10, 14). (b) The frame of reference is properly the drought and poverty of ch. 1. (c) The dating in vs. 18, **the twenty-fourth day of**

the ninth month, is probably an explanatory addition, based on 2:10 rather than 1:15a. Moreover, it would seem strange that the blessing should not be operative until 3 months after the work began.

Is the seed yet in the barn? (vs. 19) may be intended to read, "Is the seed still diminishing in the barn?" Otherwise one would suppose that failure to plant was the trouble. But the melting away of their store was the principal problem (vs. 16). The prophet declares that the harvest of the **vine, fig, pomegranate,** and **olive** will be prosperous once the temple is begun in earnest (vs. 19).

2:20-23. *Zerubbabel the Messianic King.* The promise that the LORD will soon **shake the heavens and the earth** (vs. 21), essentially the same as that made in vs. 6, closes this book. The previous promise emphasizes the wealth to be received (vs. 7), while this one emphasizes the overthrow of Gentile power (vs. 22). That soldiers should destroy one another, **every one by the sword of his fellow** (vs. 22), is reminiscent of the victory of Gideon and his 300, whose surprise attack threw the proud Midianites into such a panic that they butchered one another and left the Israelites unscathed (Judg. 7:22).

Joshua the priest is not mentioned. Zerubbabel occupies the center of the stage (vs. 23). Hag. foresees that the relaxed power of Persia will permit a descendant of David once more to occupy the throne as servant of God (cf. Isa. 42:1-4) to bring the authority of the divine signature (vs. 23) into the affairs of men.

The silence of history in regard to Zerubbabel, plus the apparent substitution of Joshua for him in a parallel text in Zech. 6:11, indicates that he failed to fulfill the prophecy. It is quite possible that he was martyred by the servants of Darius upon the reestablishment of Persian authority and of order in all the provinces. Nonetheless, this emergence of the messianic hope, while unfulfilled in immediate history, makes its own contribution to the gathering obsession with the fulfillment of the purpose of God's people.

THE BOOK OF ZECHARIAH

ROGER N. CARSTENSEN

Since, for reasons subsequently to be given, it appears that the material in chs. 9–14 is from a writer other than Zechariah, the 2 sections will be treated separately.

INTRODUCTION TO CHS. 1–8

The Prophet and His Times. Very little is known of the man Zech. He was a contemporary of Haggai and similarly concerned with the building of the 2nd temple (cf. Ezra 5:1; 6:14). He may formerly have been a priest, for he was sympathetic to the priesthood, esp. that of Joshua (3:1-5; 6:13). He prophesied for at least one month concurrently with Haggai (cf. 1:1; Hag. 2:10, which dates Haggai's last prophecy) and continued for 2 more years (520-518 B.C.). The emphasis of Haggai on the reversal of material fortune which the completion of the temple will bring is broadened in Zech; the glories of the messianic age and the wonders of the God of Spirit (cf. e.g. 2:4-5; 3:9; 4:6; 8:20-23) are to him much more important. Zech. was a prophet of hope and joy. God was indeed far beyond man in glory and majesty, but by the same token he was irresistible, and his victory was the central fact of the prophet's universe.

For the period in which Zech. lived and the situation to which he spoke, see the Intro. to Hag.

Visions and Angels. The 8 visions which constitute the greater part of the material in Zech. are strikingly different from most prophetic utterances. The prophet sees extravagant sights almost impossible to understand unless interpreted—and then often obscure. The figures include animals, men, and angels; they deal with a variety of objects strange to the vocabulary of prophecy. Here in a series of glimpses of the world under God's control the reader sees apocalyptic in a partly developed stage (see "The Apocalyptic Literature," pp. 1106-09). Speaking in cryptic and figurative language, the prophet shows how God's purpose, hidden in the maze of human history, will be manifested and fulfilled.

God did not speak directly to Zech. He revealed designs too elaborate and sweeping for ordinary minds to grasp, sending angels to explain their meanings. The presence of angels emphasizes the transcendence of God. Along with angelic ministry—most prominent in Zech. of all OT books—there is a brief but significant appearance of Satan (3:1-2), who as the accuser of Joshua the high priest plays approximately the same role as in the book of Job (Job 1–2). In these instances he is a servant of God, but in I Chr. 21:1, which is later, he apparently operates as an independent demonic force.

Message. The colorfulness and strangeness of Zech.'s visions make it easy to overlook his absorption with moral issues. The introductory pronouncement, "Thus says the LORD of hosts. Return from your evil ways and from your evil deeds" (1:4b), must be taken seriously as an underlying theme in the total message.

Zech.'s approach to the building of the temple was not as direct as Haggai's. Zerubbabel, who began the work, shall finish it (see below on 4:9; 6:12, 13) through the assistance rendered by returned Jews, providing they "will diligently obey the voice of the LORD" their God (6:15).

The role of the Messiah seems largely to have been identified by Zech. with the leadership of Zerubbabel. Here the Messiah seems to be more a sign of the coming of the new age than the medium through which it comes (cf. 9:9-10). The hopes reposing on Zerubbabel as the Messiah, however, were dashed through circumstances no longer known to us. On the other hand, the rising prominence of the high priest Joshua in Zech.'s predictions (3:1-5; 4:11-14) paved the way for the prominence of the priesthood in postexilic Judaism.

Zech. proclaims the unchanging grace of God. The same inflexibility with which he has punished he will now bless: "As I purposed to do evil to you . . . and I did not relent . . . so again have I purposed . . . to do good" (8:14-15). The horrors of the past prophesy the joys of the future: a God great in punishment is also great in blessing (1:14-17).

For Further Study: H. G. Mitchell in *ICC*, 1912. G. A. Smith, *The Book of the 12 Prophets*, rev. ed., 1928. Raymond Calkins, *The Modern Message of the Minor Prophets*, 1947. N. H. Snaith, *The Jews from Cyrus to Herod*, 1956. D. W. Thomas in *IB*, 1956. H. H. Rowley, *The Relevance of the Apocalyptic*, rev. ed., 1964.

I. INTRODUCTORY STATEMENT (1:1-6)

1:1. Date and Author. The prophecies of Zech., like those of Haggai, are carefully dated. Though no day is mentioned here at the beginning, contrary to Zech.'s custom (1:7; 7:1), we gather that the 1st utterance comes 2 months after Haggai began to preach in the year 520 B.C. It is likely that Zech. (the name means "the LORD remembers") was the **son of Iddo,** as claimed in Ezra 5:1; 6:14; Neh. 12:16, instead of his grandson. The appearance of **Berechiah** as his father can be explained as a scribe's misunderstanding of Isa. 8:2, which notes Jeberechiah as the father of another priestly Zech.

1:2-6. Call to Repentance. Zech. draws his text

504

from the past. Those who did not obey the **former prophets** paid the full penalty of their **ways.** But the God who is dependable in punishment is dependable in reward.

In the visions which follow, God is the supreme actor in history. This is the basis of Zech.'s call to repentance: prophets and kings pass away, but the purposes of God are inescapable. History shall not escape his judgment.

II. Eight Visions of Hope (1:7–6:8)

A. First Vision: Report of the Celestial Horsemen (1:7-17)

The date of the 1st vision, and by implication the following 7, is sometime in late Jan. or Feb., 519. Swift angels, whose speed is symbolized by **horses,** ascertain that the world is **at rest,** except for the unsettled spirits of the people of God. God's anger hovers over Israel's contented oppressors; he shall cause his temple to be rebuilt in **Jerusalem** as a seal of the vindication of his people.

The appearance of many angels in Zech.'s visions serves to emphasize the increasing sense of distance between man and God.

1:8. The account of the **horses** seems confused. They probably should appear, as in the LXX, in 4 colors, making their number equal the 4 horns (1:18), 4 winds of the heavens (2:6), and 4 colors of horses in the final vision (6:2-3). The number 4 probably suggests the completeness of the patrol (cf. 2:6).

1:11. While the time of universal peace reported by the scouts is generally supposed to indicate the success of the Persian king Darius in quieting his rebellious provinces (*ca.* 520), some think it is the peace of Babylon before the rise of Cyrus (*ca.* 550). It may be that Zech. begins with visions of the past wonders of God, which resulted when the fathers repented (1:6). On the other hand, it seems unlikely that Zech. would portray the immediacy of God's action for his people by reference to the past **rest.** The appeal to return from Babylon in 2:6-13 sounds as though exiles in Persia are still returning and will help in the building (cf. 6:15).

1:11-13. The principal intermediary angel is the **angel of the Lord.** Some suppose that this is the same **angel who talked with** Zech., but it seems more likely that the 2 are separate. The angel of the Lord never speaks to Zech.; the prophet is a spectator.

1:14-17. Though the patrol reports universal peace, God himself is filled with unrest. God had been **angry** with the Jews, but now his wrath burns toward those who have exceeded their commission to punish his people (cf. Isa. 40:2). The **nations . . . are** indeed **at ease,** but at ease under the anger of God. The **measuring line** (vs. 16*b*) appears to refer either to the building of the temple or to building generally.

B. Second Vision: The 4 Horns and the 4 Smiths (1:18-21)

The 1st vision made clear that the compassion of God for his people and his punishment of their enemies were part of the same great episode of history.

This vision emphasizes the destruction by the agents of God of what once seemed indestructible. Perhaps the fall of Babylon is meant, but the prophet may not have been this specific in his meanings. Those who were the agents of terror are themselves to be terrified. The **four horns** are probably symbolic of the powerful nations hostile to **Judah.** The **four smiths** (vs. 20) are perhaps supernatural agents intended to protect the Jews from further terror (cf. Isa. 54:16-17).

C. Third Vision: The Holy City (2:1-5)

The **measuring line** which the man (some think Zerubbabel) intends to use is not for building but for limitation, to mark the city's boundaries so that walls can be built (vs. 2). The unidentified **angel** who gives the interpreter news for the **young man** with the line is the angel of the Lord (cf. vs. 5). The Holy City will have no walls because of the greatness of its population and the adequate protection provided by God's presence. The city **without walls** (vs. 4), wherein men of faith can be content, will be safer and more glorious than a city with impregnable fortifications. Its strength is not in impressive numbers (vs. 4*b*) but in the presence of the Lord, who as **glory** and **wall** (vs. 5) will be the essential temple and its essential defense.

D. Invitation to Zion (2:6-13)

The description of the glorious city is followed by 2 oracles of intense character. The 1st (vss. 6-9), which is a sequel to the 2nd vision, invites the captives to **flee** from **Babylon** and share in **Zion** the **plunder** (vs. 9) to follow the downfall of their enemies, as prophesied in the vision of the horns (see above on 1:18-21). The 2nd (vss. 10-13), a sequel to the 3rd vision, celebrates the presence of God **in the midst of** his **people** and the reconciliation of the **nations** as a consequence.

2:6. The **land of the north** generally refers to **Babylon.** The LXX reads "will gather you in" instead of **have spread you abroad.** The **four winds** is a conventional phrase for the 4 points of the compass (cf. 6:5).

2:8. Some difficulty arises with **his glory sent me.** Most suppose the prophet is meant, but Zech. himself was not sent to the plundering nations, nor does he ever seem to see himself as an actor in history.

2:10-12. That God shall dwell **in the midst of** men is the essence of bliss, not only because of the joy of the Presence, but because of the environment with which God surrounds himself—in Hebrew thought, the happiness and prosperity of men (cf. 1:17). The **holy land** is thus designated only here in the Bible.

E. Fourth Vision: The Installation of Joshua (3:1-10)

The 4th vision clearly supports the priesthood of **Joshua,** who for a time shared the leadership of the little community with Zerubbabel. The priest's authority had been under fire for reasons we may never know. Cf. the cleansing of Joshua with Isaiah's experience (Isa. 6:1-8). It is the ceremonial cleanness of garments that is emphasized here.

3:1-4. The language of vs. 1 illustrates how awkward it is to identify the interpreting angel as the angel of the LORD (cf. 1:11). **Satan**—more properly here "the adversary"—has not yet been assigned the character of the devil of the NT. Still one of the servants of God, he performs the function of uncovering the weaknesses of men who are highly regarded by God (cf. Job 1:6-12). The angel of the LORD (identified here, perhaps accidentally, as **the LORD,** vs. 2a) gives the rebuke in the 3rd person, **the LORD rebuke you** (cf. Jude 9). That he identifies this authority in an interesting restatement as **the LORD who has chosen Jerusalem** may mean that he is citing the LORD of hosts mentioned in 2:11-12. Thus the angel of the LORD may be speaking of a supreme authority, superior to both himself and Satan. **Those . . . standing before him** (vs. 4a) are angels.

3:5. On the **turban,** which was part of the high priest's vesture, cf. Exod. 28:4.

3:6-9. The commission of Joshua enjoins the priest to **walk in my ways** (moral responsibility) and **keep my charge** (official responsibility) in order that he might have the **right of access** ordinarily attributed to angels. The **Branch** (vs. 8b) no doubt refers to Zerubbabel, but since he is already on the scene, some suppose the phrase may have been added. The **stone . . . set before Joshua** probably is a jewel worn by the high priest symbolic of the removal of **guilt** by intercession (vs. 9).

F. FIFTH VISION: THE GOLDEN LAMPSTAND (4:1-6a, 10b-14)

Joshua and **Zerubbabel** as priest and prince of the revived community share side by side the power of the presence of God. In the vision they are symbolized by **two olive** trees on either side of the **lampstand,** with **seven lamps** which are the **eyes of the LORD** (vs. 10b). This light does not simply illuminate; it sees (vs. 10b). It is not limited to the sanctuary; it covers the face of the **earth** (vs. 10b).

The omission of vss. 6b-10a from the vision is prompted on the one hand by clear indications of interruption—the question of vss. 4-5 is answered in vs. 10b—and by the shift in content. Possibly it is inserted here because the oil used in the lamp, representative of spirit, coincides with the opening of the oracle to Zerubbabel: "Not by might, nor by power, but by my Spirit" (vs. 6b).

4:2-4. Precisely how the **lampstand** appeared is impossible to determine. The **lamps** are containers with spouts or **lips** to hold the wick; the large **bowl on the top** contains a supply of oil for all 7 lamps and probably is connected to them by 7 pipes (vs. 2). The **two olive trees** are on either side of the lampstand. Apparently **these** (vs. 4) refers to the lamps, for Zech. asks about the trees subsequently (vs. 11).

4:6a, 10b-14. Omitting the insertion (6b-10a; see below), we read **then he said to me** (6a) **These seven . . .** (vs. 10b). Note that the lamps **are the eyes of the LORD, which range through the whole earth.** In Hebrew thought, for God to see was to control and provide (cf. Pss. 73:11; 139:1-12). The question regarding the **olive trees** (vs. 11) is, strangely, asked again (vs. 12), including informa-

tion not given in the earlier description. This is the only time a question by the prophet is not acknowledged; the vs. may be an addition. The **two anointed** (lit. "sons of oil") are generally thought to be Joshua and Zerubbabel (cf. Rev. 11:1-13).

G. ORACLE TO ZERUBBABEL (4:6b-10a)

The purpose of this oracle is to encourage **Zerubbabel** to complete the temple. Success in spite of overwhelming odds demonstrates the enabling Presence (vs. 9b). Having overcome mountainous obstacles, Zerubbabel brings forward the capstone **amid shouts** of joy (vs. 7). The **me** in vs. 9b is used as in 2:9, 12 to refer to the angel of the LORD **sent** by the **LORD of hosts,** rather than to Zech. himself. **The day of small things** probably refers to the insignificant beginnings of the building (cf. Ezra 3: 12; Hag. 2:3).

H. SIXTH VISION: THE FLYING SCROLL (5:1-4)

Zech. in this vision sees a large **scroll** representing God's **curse** on thieves and perjurers. How the curse would operate is not clear, but the idea of cleansing is present. The consuming of the **house** of the wicked (vs. 4b) portrays the finality of punishment (cf. Job 18:15-21; 21:28). Stealing and bearing false witness may simply be representative of a much broader list of social sins, but it seems more likely that they were special problem areas in Zech.'s day.

I. SEVENTH VISION: THE WOMAN IN THE EPHAH (5:5-11)

The vision of the woman called **Wickedness** imprisoned in an **ephah,** or cask, is reminiscent of the scapegoat that is sent into the wilderness bearing the sins of the people (Lev. 16:6-10). By sending the woman away in the cask the guilt of **all the land** will be removed at once (cf. 3:4, 9) and taken to the **land of Shinar** (vs. 11), i.e. Babylon. There the abomination of Judah will be worshiped in its own temple.

The ephah was a vessel with a capacity of about 6 gallons. Apparently the woman **lifted** the **leaden cover** (vs. 7) but was **thrust . . . back** by the angel. The **base** (vs. 11) on which the vessel would be set was the pedestal on which idols were placed.

J. EIGHTH VISION: THE 4 CHARIOTS (6:1-8)

Zech.'s 1st vision is of the reconnoitering of the horsemen bringing news that the world is quiet but God is disturbed (1:11-13); his final vision likewise contains the sweep of **chariots**—this time bringing the news that God is satisfied (vs. 8), and so presumably will be his people. Though the horses represent the **four winds of heaven** (vs. 5), they are assigned only 3 directions: N, W, and S—E is not mentioned. The **north country** (vs. 8) refers to Babylonia.

III. ORACLE OF THE THEOCRATIC STATE (6:9-15)

This passage is separate from the series of apocalyptic visions. The oracle as it stands celebrates the crowning of **Joshua** the **high priest** as prince and builder of the **temple.** This makes him in fact a priest-king, which actually was the case later on. There is little doubt, however, that vs. 11 originally designated Zerubbabel for the crowning, as vss. 12-13 indicate. The absence of Zerubbabel's name from the passage suggests that he never actually ruled. A later editor, aware of the subsequent elevation of the priesthood, may have assigned the promises once intended for the prince to Joshua the priest, thus bringing the prophecy into harmony with later history.

In brief the evidences that the passage has been altered are: (*a*) Zech. has already indicated that Zerubbabel, not Joshua, will complete the temple (cf. 4:6-10*a;* Hag. 2:20-23). (*b*) The designation **Branch,** or "Shoot," is never used for a priest but for a messianic king (cf. 3:8; Jer. 23:5). (*c*) The **priest by his throne** (vs. 13*b*) is obviously Joshua; one would hardly expect Joshua as priest-king to have another priest beside him.

6:9-10. Vs. 9—**And the word of the LORD came to me**—formally opens a new series of oracles. We know nothing beyond this passage of the 3 men selected as witnesses to the symbolic crowning or of the **Josiah** to whose **house** they were taken.

6:11-14. While **crown** in vss. 11, 14 is plural in Hebrew, the pronoun **it** in vs. 11 and the singular verb form translated **shall be** in vs. 14 indicate that only 1 crown was the original intention. "Zerubbabel" was probably the original reading for what is now **Joshua** in vs. 11*b* (cf. 4:6-10*a;* Hag. 2:20-23; see comment above on 6:9-15). The close working relationship between priest and king is reflected in vs. 13; 3:8-9; 4:11-14; Hag. 1:12-15.

6:14-15. The **crown . . . in the temple** suggests the dependence of temporal power on the spiritual (cf. 4:6). **Those who are far off** refers to Jews returning from their colonies among the Gentiles.

IV. FROM FASTING TO FEASTING (7:1–8:23)

The 1st vision contained God's message that the time had come for his anger to be suspended and for his people to know once again the happiness he had desired for them from the beginning (1:13-17). Just as God has moved from wrath to pity, the mood of the people will change from sorrow to joy. The temple is being rebuilt, and God is at work. To mourn in this context is to blaspheme.

7:1-3. *The Deputation from Bethel.* The building has been in process *ca.* 2 years when the deputation arrives in the month of **Chislev,** i.e. from mid-Nov. to mid-Dec., 518. The sanctuary at **Bethel** was a center of opposition to Jerusalem. The question the deputation poses regards the limited issue of mourning the destruction of a temple now being rebuilt: Should not the **fast** regularly observed in the 5th and 7th months (vs. 5) over the destruction of Jerusalem and the temple be continued?

7:4-14. *Ineffectiveness of Fasting.* Zech. deals with the question on a broad scale. Fasting is not a substitute for righteous living in good times or bad (vs. 7). The **former prophets** (probably quoted in vs. 9, omitting vs. 8) made it clear that religious responsibilities should be socially expressed (vss. 9-10), but the people **refused** to **hear** (vss. 11-12). Therefore God would not hear them and **scattered them** and made their **pleasant land . . . desolate** (vs. 14).

8:1-17. *Restoration of the Whole Order.* Once again **jealous** for his people, the **LORD of hosts** will restore **Jerusalem** as a peaceful, prosperous city, where the aged meditate in peace and children play unmolested (vss. 1-5). God will gather exiles from **east** and **west** to dwell in Jerusalem (vss. 6-8). Zech. encourages the fainting laborers by assuring them the depression is over; wages and harvests will now be their lot (vss. 9-13).

8:18-23. *Jerusalem Transformed Is Inviting to Others.* The delegation asked simply about the fast of the 5th month, which marked the destruction of the temple, but to Zech. all past catastrophes, in their completeness, become prophecies of wondrous good (vss. 18-19). The **joy** of good hearts will draw people from all **nations** to the house of God. The watchword is not, "Go there," but, "Come with me" (vss. 20-22). Where there is evidence that God is working, people are drawn to the scene: **Let us go with you, for we have heard that God is with you** (vs. 23).

INTRODUCTION TO CHS. 9–14

Authorship. It is now commonplace among students of the OT to recognize that chs. 9–14 are not the work of Zech. Chs. 9 and 12 each begin with the word "oracle," as does the book of Mal. Since Mal. is anonymous (see Intro. to Mal.) it is possible that Mal., the last of three similar oracles, was later detached for the purpose of bringing a collection of the prophets up to the significant number 12.

As for differences in the 2 sections, the following may be noted: (*a*) Chs. 9–14 are largely poetry while the first 8 chs. are prose. (*b*) Zech. uses visions extensively; the last section does not. (*c*) Zech.'s name does not appear in the last 6 chs., contrary to the practice in the former section. (*d*) There is also strong emphasis on the possibility of salvaging Israel, a matter of little interest to Zech. (*e*) The prophets are scorned; violence and bloodshed are highlighted. (*f*) Chs. 9–14 contain no reference to the central theme of Zech.—building the temple—nor to the leadership of Zerubbabel and Joshua. (*g*) That the Messiah is a humble king suggests the motif of the Suffering Servant of Isa. 53, which is absent from chs. 1–8. (*h*) Chs. 9–14 have their own apocalyptic overtones. Much is made of the depravity of man and of great battles leading to the subjugation of the world.

This last section, therefore, seems clearly distinct from the first in style and subject matter, but its background, while indeed difficult to identify precisely, certainly does not reflect the day of Haggai and Zech.

Message. Since the materials in this section are linked together only in a general way and for that matter may be from several authors, there is little value in a summary at this point. The general theme is the victory of God over all the nations, leading the world to universal peace. His own people, though capable of heroism, are largely wicked and misguided. The sheep deserve cruel shepherds (11:7-17) and apparently slay their noblest leader (12:10–13:1).

One God demands ultimately one world. He will not rest until all things are under his feet. "On that day the LORD will be one and his name one" (14:9*b*). The inevitability of this victory—as yet unrealized—becomes for the stormy and perilous days of developing Judaism a fact towering above all the contradictory appearances of history. God is going to win!

For Further Study: See the listings on p. 504.

I. THE ORACLE OF THE COMING OF THE MESSIAH (9:1–11:17)

A. THE WORLDWIDE KINGDOM (9:1-17)

Ch. 9 appears to consist of 3 separate oracles (vss. 1-8, 9-10, 11-17) which have been gathered together without clear connections. The 1st (vss. 1-8) seems to be a judgment on Syria, **Tyre,** and **Philisitia** culminating in the deliverance of Jerusalem and Judah. The Messiah suddenly appears (vss. 9-10) as the agent of universal peace; **his dominion** is worldwide. The next oracle speaks of **prisoners** (vss. 11-12) returning to Judah as the Greeks succumb to the arms of the Jews in bloody warfare (vss. 13-15) and prosperity reigns over the **flock** of God (vss. 16-17).

To interpret these vss. consecutively one would conclude that Syria, Phoenicia, and Philistia will be crushed (presumably by Alexander the Great), and as a result Jerusalem will rise again under her Messiah, crush the Greeks in turn, and, drawing her exiles back from their dispersion, will set up the universal messianic kingdom. Each of the sections shows a certain unity in itself and should be read first of all for its own meanings.

9:1-8. The Downfall of Proud Nations. God himself will conquer the cities of Syria and Phoenicia, notably **Tyre,** the impregnable fortress in the sea (vss. 2-4). The Philistine cities will be demoralized at their neighbor's fate and similarly fall (vss. 5-6). However, the Philistines will be converted to God and observe Jewish food regulations (vs. 7). The people of God shall never again be **overrun** by an invader (vs. 8).

9:1. The RSV translation of vs. 1 rests on shaky foundations. The Hebrew text reads as though God possessed the land of Syria in a benevolent sense and rests in **Damascus!** Though it seems unlikely that the Jews would accept and place other than Jerusalem as a dwelling place for God, other nations also **belong** to him. Tyre is obviously under attack (vs. 4); however, **even as all the tribes of Israel** suggests that Syria now belongs to God just as does Israel. The later reference to the acceptance of the Philistines as one of the clans of Judah (vs. 7*b*) compares them to the Jebusites, in whose city (Jerusalem) God does indeed dwell.

9:1-2. Apparently **Hadrach** was N of Damascus. Where the RSV reads the **cities of Aram** the Hebrew has "eye of Adam," which makes no sense; the change of one easily mistaken consonant changes Adam to Aram (Syria). Perhaps Damascus was known as "the eye of Aram." **Hamath** is also N of Damascus. The fact that Alexander was the only conqueror up to his time to take the city is a principal reason for supposing that this oracle refers to the advance of the Greeks.

9:5-6. Four of the 5 traditional Philistine cities are mentioned, with Gath omitted.

9:7. The **blood** of Philistine mouths refers to eating food either unclean in itself or improperly prepared (cf. Lev. 11:2-23; Deut. 14:3-21). The **Jebusites** were Jerusalem Canaanites whose survivors after David's conquest of the city were apparently absorbed by the people of Israel (cf. II Sam. 5:6-9).

9:8. God, standing **guard** in his temple watchtower, will forever guard Judah from invasion. Strictly speaking, the events in chs. 12; 14 cannot happen subsequent to this, for in both cases invaders are described.

9:9-10. The Humble Messiah. The Messiah who rides into Jerusalem combines majesty and meekness; he fulfills the requirements of the Davidic king who "shall smite the earth with the rod of his mouth" (Isa. 11:4*b*) as well as the Suffering Servant, who when he was afflicted "opened not his mouth" (Isa. 53:7*a*). David, curiously, is not mentioned at all in chs. 9–11.

That the Messiah comes **riding on . . . a colt** is of particular interest to the Christian world (cf. Matt. 21:1-6, where 2 beasts are cited, with John 12:14-15). It is possible that Jesus, knowing what had been written, purposely sought a young **ass** on which to ride when he made his final claim to the allegiance of Jerusalem.

9:11-17. Salvation of the Prisoners of Hope. As it stands, this warlike section has to deal with a time considerably subsequent to Alexander's conquest, for the Jews did not much feel the sting of persecution under Hellenic rule until over a cent. had passed. The key is vs. 13, where **Greece** is mentioned as the destined victim of God's armies. This was probably not Greece itself but the Seleucid dynasty in Syria, 1 of the 4 Hellenic subkingdoms emerging from the empire of Alexander.

9:11-13. The antecedent of **you** (vs. 11*a*) is apparently Zion (vs. 9); her exiles are to be returned. **Prisoners of hope** (vs. 12) is a provocative term esp. applicable to Jews. Some think the reference to **Greece** (vs. 13) is an interpolation, a distant possibility (see above on 9:11-17).

9:15. This vs. is extremely difficult to translate; it is safe to assume a devastating battle is being described.

B. MILITARY EXPLOITS OF THE JEWS (10:1–11:3)

This section consists principally of a passage dealing with the military exploits of the Jews under their own leaders (10:3-12), preceded and followed by brief and apparently unrelated passages (10:1-2; 11:1-3). Of special interest is the return of the 10 tribes (vss. 6-7) not simply to Jerusalem but as far as the border of ancient Israel (vs. 10).

10:1-2. Praying for Rain. The situation here diverges sharply from that in 9:17, where there is an abundance of **rain.** It may be placed directly after 9:17 simply because of a common reference to agriculture. The point is simple: since God alone controls rain, seek it from no other source.

10:3-12. The Rise of the Soldier. This passage has been characterized above (see comment on 10:1–11:3). That the **shepherds** are foreign rulers, probably the Ptolemies of Egypt or the Seleucids of Syria, seems indicated by the phrase in vs. 4, **out of them;** i.e. in the future the leaders of the **house of Judah** will be natives instead of foreigners—they will come out of the flock of the LORD. The transformation of a sheep (**flock**) to a war-horse (**steed in battle**) is one of the boldest figures of speech in the OT (vs. 3*b*). Who their own rulers will be—**cornerstone, ... tent peg**, or **battle bow** (vs. 4)—cannot now be known. God continues to be the real combatant (vs. 5*b*). **Joseph** refers to Israel (vs. 6*a*) as does **Ephraim** (vs. 7*a*). The dominant mood is one of rejoicing.

10:8-11. God **will signal for** his people **and gather them in** (vs. 8) by such a whistle ("whistle" being a variant translation of the word rendered **signal**) as shepherds use to call their sheep together. The 2 nations esp. noted from which they will return are **Egypt** and Syria, here called **Assyria** according to the habit of later writers (vs. 10*a*). They will come to **the land of Gilead** in the NE and to **Lebanon** on the N border of old Israel. The territories of David's kingdom will not hold the new population (vs. 10). Harking back to the past, the prophet predicts a miraculous crossing of the **Nile** and probably the Sea of Reeds (vs. 11).

11:1-3. *The Lament of Fallen Leaders.* This passage may stand here simply because **Lebanon** is mentioned in vs. 1 and, in a different context, in 10:10*b*. However, it is possible that the false shepherds of 10:3 are here ironically mourned under the figures of **fallen** trees, **shepherds** minus sheep, and **lions** without a **jungle.**

C. The Doomed Flock and Its Shepherds (11:4-17)

It is exceedingly difficult to make sense out of this section. Attempts to identify events and characters in history have been many and desperate. The correct solution may have been reached, but it cannot be verified. One point is clear: the flock itself, while victimized, is at fault. God's judgments on such people are just and frightening; the sheep shall fall into the hands of their own shepherds.

How this passage related to the foregoing is not clear. The anticipated union of Ephraim and Judah, it would seem, is temporary, to be broken after the coming of the Messiah and the establishment of the worldwide kingdom (cf. 9:9-10, 13; 10:6-7). The earlier passages, however, give the distinct impression that the reunion of broken Israel is the climactic event to come at the end of the age (10:6-7). Therefore it may be best to read the main sections of chs. 9–11 as separate accounts of events to occur around the end time—accounts not intended to be put together consecutively.

11:4-7. The **shepherd** is really the LORD, manifesting his will through the prophet and receiving payment in the temple (vss. 12-13). The **staffs** (vs. 7), symbols of shepherd and king, represent respectively protection from those who exploited the sheep (**Grace**) and that which prevented the sheep from destroying one another (**Union**).

11:8-12. The **three shepherds** who are **destroyed** cannot be identified. Vs. 8*b* indicates that the victimized people rebuff God's shepherd and are therefore abandoned to **the traffickers in the sheep**, probably foreign rulers or tax collectors who **knew that it was the word of the LORD** (vs. 11). The Hebrew word for **treasury** (vs. 13) is quite similar to that for "potter," which stands in the original; the RSV

is probably correct. God as the shepherd receives his hire (vs. 12).

II. The Oracle of Triumph for Jerusalem (12:1–14:21)

The last chs. of Zech., just as difficult to interpret as the preceding, have as their central theme the triumph of Jerusalem in the coming **day of the LORD.** God does not rescue man *through* the crisis but *from* it. A great leader has been stupidly slain; God ends the tragedy of errors by invading the earth with the forces of heaven. The mountain ridges of Palestine are leveled, leaving Jerusalem on a lofty pinnacle. The perils of night and winter cease. Putting an end to the nonsensical pretensions of man, God rearranges the face of the earth and causes men to acknowledge him in worship. The very horses shall be consecrate; the sacrament may be prepared in a housewife's pots and pans in a time when all things are holy and all things bright.

A. Wounds and a Cleansing Fountain (12:1–13:9)

12:1-9. *Where Ignorant Armies Clash.* Here Jerusalem serves principally as an instrument for God's judgment on all nations. Her powers in war will impress the hostile men of the countryside of Judah. The victory of Jerusalem is attributed in vs. 4*a* to supernaturally induced diseases and consequent panic, a theme expanded in 14:12-15. The **clans of Judah** (vss. 5-6) are the Jews outside the city. The victory of these rural Jews is a reminder to proud Jerusalem that God's people are outside as well as inside her walls (vs. 7).

12:10–13:1. Fast on the heels of the triumph over the slaughtered aliens **wails** of grief are heard over the Holy City; her fairest son lies dead, slain by the hands of his brothers. Why was the victim killed? We cannot tell. The guilty are strangely moved. Enabled at last to weep for someone other than self, they open up an unsuspected fountain for their own cleansing. Their weeping is reminiscent of the **mourning for Hadadrimmon,** a deity; cf. the wailing for the dead god Tammuz (Ezek. 8:14). The **mourning** includes all classes of men (vs. 14). In some sense each in his aloneness said, "This is what I have done." **A fountain is opened ... to cleanse them from sin and uncleanness.** 13:1 clearly belongs with ch. 12 for **the house of David and the inhabitants of Jerusalem** (13:1) were guilty of the murder (12:10) and needed to be cleansed.

13:2-6. *The Status of Prophecy.* Here is pictured the darkest hour of prophecy. Because prophecy was supposed to have ceased, being supplanted by temple oracle and the law of Moses, to prophesy is to lie (vs. 3). To prophesy **in the name of the LORD** is to blaspheme (vs. 3).

13:2-3. To **cut off the names of the idols** means final destruction; prophecy had become idolatry, and the idols will not be remembered. Thus prophecy cannot be re-created. The prophet is equated with the **unclean spirit.** Prophecy has become such an abomination that a man will be killed by his own parents for returning to the ancient practice.

13:4-6. A certain kind of wound distinguished the prophet in those days, probably self-mutilation produced in times of ecstasy. Claiming to be a simple farmer, the prophet is questioned about the scars on his back. He improvises a desperate explanation: a drunken brawl with his comrades culminated in a few friendly knife fights (vs. 6b).

13:7-9. *The Purified Survivors.* A good case can be made for removing this oracle and associating it with ch. 11, where so much is said about shepherds. In 11:17 a smitten **shepherd** is mentioned, as in vs. 7. But the shepherd in the former passage deserves his fate and is punished for deserting the flock, while it appears in the latter passage that the shepherd is wounded for no fault of his own (vs. 7b).

Two themes emerge from this isolated little section: the smitten shepherd and the reclaimed flock. The shepherd who stands next to God (vs. 7a) is a priest or king. He suffers for his faithfulness, for the sheep (as is the case in 11:8) do not deserve the care they receive (cf. Matt. 26:31; Mark 14:27).

B. Triumph of the Lord of Battles (14:1-21)

The last ch. of Zech. is typical of the most fully developed apocalyptic in the OT (cf. Ezek. 38–39; 47). In apocalyptic a final struggle involving all the world may be expected before the last age of peace begins. In such battles God is the real victor.

14:1-5. *The Great Battle and Rescue.* The **spoil taken from you** (vs. 1) was gathered in the early defeat, when half of Jerusalem was lost (vs. 2). The LORD is described as a giant whose **feet stand upon the Mount of Olives,** which is **split in two** and becomes a mighty plain (vss. 4-5; cf. vs. 10). **You shall flee** (vs. 5b) is probably an editorial footnote based on a scribe's misunderstanding. He must have regarded the verb form **be stopped up** to mean **you shall flee.** The central idea is simply that God shall change the face of the earth for his own people (cf. Job 18:4).

14:6-11. *The Order of Things.* Jerusalem stands now on a lonely eminence; she is the central jewel of a new setting. Inaccessible to all but her friends, she is a haven of perpetual **security.**

14:6-8. The Hebrew of vs. 6 is difficult; **cold nor frost** is the Greek reading. **It is known to the LORD** (vs. 7a) is probably inserted to refer to the actual day when God will come. The **living waters** (vs. 8) make rain no longer necessary and purify the waters of the Dead Sea (cf. Ezek. 47:1-12; Joel 3:18).

14:9-10. Vs. 9 is the central theme: the LORD will be one **king** over one people, known by one **name.** **Geba** is 10 miles N of Jerusalem, **Rimmon** about the same distance N of Beersheba. This is about the extent of ancient Judah. Apparently the author describes **Jerusalem** by giving the principal corners of the walls, so that the city occupies roughly the area of its early dimensions.

14:12-15. *How the City Is Delivered.* The enemies of Jerusalem will be struck by a horrible **plague** and in **panic** will slaughter one another (cf. 12:4). Some suppose that Judah's **fight against Jerusalem** (vs. 14a)—odd indeed to account for under these circumstances—means she conquered Jerusalem; this would fit much better with the encouragement of Judah mentioned in connection with the previous panic of 12:4.

14:16-19. *The LORD Is King.* The ultimate subjection of all the Gentile world to the God of the Jews is here attributed to religious observances. The **feast of booths** (which included a water libation) was the new-year festival at which time the LORD had traditionally been declared king (cf. Pss. 47; 68; 93). While **rain** would be denied the nations not making the pilgrimage (vs. 17b), **Egypt,** who needed no rain, would be afflicted with a **plague** (vs. 18).

14:20-21. *Everything Holy.* While it is true that these last vss. exalt ceremonial over moral holiness, there is something about the expression of holiness in every detail of life that catches the imagination. At last Israel is a kingdom of priests. In every home sacramental bread is broken; the family hearth is familiar to the presence of God, and even the **bells of the horses,** freed from battle, ring to the glory of heaven.

THE BOOK OF MALACHI

Roger N. Carstensen

Date. Several clues in the book of Malachi point to the time of its writing. The restored temple, completed in 515 B.C., has been in use long enough for the priesthood to become lax and corrupt (1:6). Judah is under the rule of a "governor" (1:8), i.e. a Persian administrator (cf. Neh. 5:14). The high rate of divorce and remarriage to foreign women (2:11-16) suggests a time before the governorship of Nehemiah, whose reform attacking this very problem would otherwise surely be mentioned. The designation of the priests as descendants of Levi (2:4) rather than of Aaron supports the view that the Jewish community is under the Deuteronomic (D) Code rather than the Priestly (P) Code introduced *ca.* the time of Ezra, who probably followed Nehemiah (see Intro. to Ezra). Since Nehemiah first arrived in 445 it may be assumed that the prophecies of this book were composed shortly before this date, i.e. *ca.* 450.

Author. "Malachi," meaning "my messenger," was evidently placed in the title (1:1) by an editor who took its occurrence in 3:1 to be the author's name. Though for convenience we may use this name, the oracles are actually anonymous and reveal all that is known of their author. That he was associated with the temple and its cult is evident. If he was not a priest—as his attack on the priests as a class suggests—he was at least a cultic prophet, one whose oracles served the cause of the temple and its services.

In his attitude toward the cult Mal. differs from most of the preexilic prophets. They indicted many of the cult activities of their times, not because they were improperly performed, but because their correctness seemed intended as a substitute for morality and justice. But Mal. believes the ceremonies of the cult must be properly performed as reverence proper to God's majesty (1:14). From such reverence will proceed incorruptible justice (3:5). The ideal priest takes God seriously—**he feared me, he stood in awe of my name** (2:5*b*). Isaiah said, "I cannot endure iniquity and solemn assembly" (1:13*c*); Mal. would say, "If you really kept your solemn assembly, you could not perform iniquity."

The prophet uses the method of dialogue to present his message. He anticipates and deals with objections by presenting reasons as authority for his pronouncements. The demands of God can stand the test of rational judgment. Mal.'s arguments illustrate that the later prophets no longer relied simply on the authority of God as he revealed himself to them; they appealed primarily to what their hearers already knew.

Setting. In the middle of the 5th cent. the morale of the small Jewish settlement in and around Jerusalem was at a low ebb. The excitement of the return from exile and of constructing the temple had long since died away. A struggling and poor community, the Jews were losing their identity (2:11). Drought and locusts continually struck the farmers, who were the backbone of the economy (3:10-11).

The worst ills, however, were social. Disintegration of Jewish family life was manifest in divorce (2:16) and adultery (3:5). The rich oppressed the poor and victimized the helpless with impunity (3:5). Dishonesty was a key to business success (3:15), and the sacred principle of covenant, essential to a responsible society, was constantly disregarded (2:4, 10, 14). It was bad enough for the country to be overrun by lawless men, but it appeared that God favored them (2:17)! To be cynical, godless, and corrupt was seemingly to enjoy every practical evidence of God's favor. The mood of the hour was "What's the use of trying!" (1:13). The heart of the Jew's predicament was not hard times as such but the loss of the presence of God (3:1).

The perfunctory performance by priests and people alike of their sacred duty—notably sacrifice (1:8) and tithe (3:8)—was obvious evidence that something was wrong with Judah's religion. Ever-increasing latitude in the interpretation of the demands of God expressed doubt rather than trust in his mercy. Disobedience derived from uncertainty. Irresponsibility at the altar was paralleled by irresponsibility at the lectern and judgment seat (2:7). The priests' teaching function, in part the exposition of the traditions of the past and in part the consultation of sacred omens (see below on 2:6-9), was cynically abused. Thus they forfeited the moral leadership that should have proceeded from the temple (2:9). The failure of the priests in a time of undependable secular authority was a principal cause of the corruption of society.

Message: True Religion Produces Morality. All that the prophet has to say hinges on his conviction that the day is coming when God will act for his people (3:17; 4:3). The day of Yahweh will include his return to his temple (3:1), the swift execution of judgment on wrongdoers (3:5), and reward to the righteous (3:17). Evidence for God's justice is already to be seen in judgments outside Israel (1:1-5) where the nations, whether they know it or not, are honoring God in their sacrifices (1:11).

The failure of the Levitical priests to keep their sacred covenant of responsibility (2:8) has caused God to withdraw from his people both the prosperity which is the seal of his blessing (2:2) and the divinely supported standards of justice which guarantee a sound social order (cf. 2:9; 3:5, 18). The people have been equally guilty. In the broader context of their responsibility they have taken advantage of the laxity of their leaders by bringing maimed offerings (1:13), by divorce (2:14), by failing to tithe (3:8), and by oppressing the helpless (3:5).

The message of the prophet is: return to God, and he will return to you (3:7). More than this, if man meets his responsibilities to God, the windows of heaven will be opened, and multiple blessings will come (3:10).

Since the priests are custodians of temple and oracle, Mal. calls on them to lead in a return to God (1:5; 2:1, 7). They are challenged: Do they really believe God is there (cf. 1:13; 2:2; 3:1)? Those who do not respect the worship of God will not respect his commands (1:13; 2:8).

Mal.'s belief in the priest as messenger of God (2:7) points toward the end of the institution of prophecy. The prophet will cease to function, not because God no longer speaks, but because he will provide access to his word through a cleansed and active priesthood. The instruction of Mal.'s Levites is superior in force to his own oracles. Once God speaks from his temple, there need be no prophet, and the dark saying and obscure visions of spirit-seized men will vanish in the light of perfect law (cf. Num. 12:6-8).

It is not surprising that the next move from the emphasis on a teaching priesthood was a codification of laws to stabilize justice. A half cent. later Ezra would be a priestly scribe, his authority the law of Moses. Interpreters of the law, not prophets, would become key personnel in Judaism; inspiration must cease with Ezra. The first of 2 editorial postscripts added to the book (4:4) expresses this reliance on the law of Moses and points the finger to future developments.

For Further Study. J. M. P. Smith, *Mal.*, 1912. L. E. Browne, *Early Judaism*, 1920. G. A. Smith, *The Book of the 12 Prophets*, rev. ed., vol. 2, 1928. Raymond Calkins, *The Modern Message of the Minor Prophets*, 1947. R. C. Dentan in *IB*, 1956. N. H. Snaith, *The Jews from Cyrus to Herod*, 1956. William Neil in *IDB*, 1962.

I. Superscription (1:1)

Oracle is lit. "burden." A man is a messenger because he carries a message from beyond himself, something of more value than anything he could contrive himself. On the name **Malachi** see Intro.

II. God's Love for Israel (1:2-5)

In proclaiming the love of God the prophet offers supporting arguments. To the ancient Jew divine favor was not an abstract proposition or doctrine so much as it was simply the good life. Had times been prosperous, the announcement—in this sense—would have been unnecessary. But times were bad (see Intro.), and men were doubting the love of God. Mal. believes their troubles are magnified by self-pity. After all, closely related neighbors, the Edomites, are worse off than they are!

1:2c-4. Of the twin sons of Isaac (Gen. 25:23-26) God chose **Jacob**, i.e. Israel, and rejected **Esau**, i.e. Edom. Thus Edom at last is tasting the bitter fruit of the judgment of God. The misfortune of the Edomites was probably an invasion by the Nabateans (see Intro. to Obad.). For them there will be no rebuilding.

1:5. Much as we might like to interpret **Great is the Lord, beyond the border of Israel!** as expressive of the tolerance of other peoples which begins to appear in this period (cf. e.g. Ruth, Jonah), the context shows that it refers to their rejection rather than their acceptance; i.e. God's power to smite Israel's enemies is not limited. This concept of his universal power, however, points the way to a recognition of his universal love.

III. Failure of the Priesthood (1:6-2:9)

In the postexilic period, when the Persian government permitted the Jews no king and the springs of prophecy were drying up, the priest came into his own. Mal.'s attack is not on the priesthood as an institution but on the faithless and cynical priests who betray it. They have failed in 2 respects: prescriptions for sacrifice and public instruction.

1:6-14. *Shoddy Sacrifices.* The basic point of this passage is that one must not give to God that which does not **honor** him. The priests have failed at the point of their assumed expertness, the prescriptions of sacrificial law (cf. Deut. 15:21). God is holy; he will accept only the unblemished.

1:6-10. In his argumentative fashion Mal. sets out to show that the offering of defective sacrifices not only violates cultic law but is an affront to sound sense and decency. Since God is a **father** and **master,** he must be treated with respect. For priests to **despise** his **name** in this way is blasphemy. No one seeking to win the **favor** of the **governor**—a satrap of Persia—would dream of offering him less than the best (vs. 8). Closing the **doors** of the temple (vs. 10) and extinguishing the holy **fire** on the **altar** would be far more acceptable than the insult of cheap offerings.

1:11. This claim of worldwide **incense** and **pure offering,** i.e. sacrifice, to Yahweh, whose **name is great among the nations,** is extraordinary in the OT (though cf. Balaam of Pethor on the Euphrates as a prophet of Yahweh, Num. 22:8; 24:13, and Cyrus king of Persia as his anointed, Isa. 45:1). Some interpreters take this vs. to refer to the worship of dispersed Jews; but this seems improbable both because in Mal.'s time they were not yet scattered **from the rising of the sun to its setting** and because the Jerusalem temple was the only legitimate place for Jews to sacrifice. Rather the meaning must be that the worship which the nations accord to their gods is actually directed to Yahweh. However, Mal. is not primarily interested in asserting the favorable status of sincere Gentiles before God. He is simply shaming Jews and in doing so he seems to be commending aliens. He may not intend the inclusiveness and breadth of vision we recognize in his comparison, but it is there all the same.

1:12-14. The cynical boredom of the priests is their own judgment on their travesty of ritual (vss. 12-13). The layman voluntarily **vows** to give the best of his flock (vs. 14) and then breaks his promise by bringing a **blemished** animal. God is a **great King**; the conscience of even the heathen **nations** would not countenance such flouting of his majesty.

2:1-9. *Irresponsible Instruction.* The faults just described are now laid specifically on the priests, who insult God's **name** (cf. 1:6-7, 11) by their negligence. The **blessings** which God will **curse** are taken by many to mean the benedictions pronounced by the priests over the worshipers (cf. Num. 6:22-27), which as a result will instead cause misfortune. The more probable meaning, however, is the benefits the priests receive for their services, the Levitical tithes and offerings, which will not merely be diminished by the general blight but bring ill when they are received. **Dung of your offerings** (vs. 3) probably refers to the discarded entrails of sacrificed animals.

2:4-5. That the **covenant** is said to have been with **Levi** indicates that at this time the priests, as well as the whole community, are following the D Code adopted in 622 (cf. II Kings 22–23), according to which all Levites were eligible to be priests. This seems to date the writing (see Intro.) before the time of Ezra, when apparently there was a change to the more complex P Code, in which the priesthood was limited to the supposed descendants of Aaron and other Levites were permitted to serve only in subordinate positions in the temple. No **covenant with Levi** is mentioned elsewhere in the OT; perhaps Mal. means simply the special provision for support of the tribe of Levi (cf. Deut. 18:1-8). "The fear of Yahweh" was the conventional term for "religion" in ancient Israel. Thus **fear** and **awe** here mean, not dread or terror, but reverence and a sense of responsibility for obedience and even love and joy in God's service.

2:6-9. The word **instruction** here is *torah*, which is usually translated "law," e.g. in "law of Moses," and which is the name of the Pentateuch in the Hebrew Bible. It is thus commonly assumed that Mal. is referring simply to the duty of the priests to teach the people the various ordinances of the Mosaic law. This was of course a responsibility of the priests (cf. e.g. Lev. 10:11; Ezra 7:10, 25), who were probably the custodians of the few existing copies of the written code. But the language of the passage indicates that it deals primarily with a further duty of the priests—that of securing oracles by means of the sacred lots, the Urim and Thummim (see comment on I Sam. 14:36-46). In the D Code the priests are made the court of final appeal, from whose verdict no one can deviate (Deut. 17:10-13), and in a case where there are not the required number of witnesses the accused and accuser are to be brought to the priests and judges "before the LORD" (Deut. 19:15-19)—i.e. to let Yahweh render the judgment through the sacred lots. That this practice continued after the Exile is shown by the record of a difficult decision in the time of Zerubbabel—or

possibly later (see comment on Ezra 2:1-70)—which was postponed "until there should be a priest to consult Urim and Thummim" (Ezra 2:63; cf. Neh. 7:65; I Esd. 5:40) and by the references to this priestly duty in the P Code (Exod. 28:30; Lev. 8:8; Num. 27:18-21).

That Mal. has in mind this function of rendering oracular judgments is suggested by his calling the priest Yahweh's **messenger** (the same word as in 3:1), whose **mouth** and **lips**, rather than the written word, are the source of **true** *torah*. Thus he speaks of **your** *torah*—hardly a designation of the Mosaic law—and charges the priests with showing **partiality in your** *torah;* i.e. they have mishandled justice. In this light we may understand the relation of the integrity of the priesthood to social conditions in the community. The complaints of injustice in vs. 17 may in large part stem from a breakdown in the system of priestly jurisprudence. It is only as the due process of law is corrupted that men are able to oppress their neighbors. Thus the irreverence of the priests is accompanied by social irresponsibility.

IV. Corruption of Marriage (2:10-16)

When both Nehemiah and Ezra arrived in Jerusalem, the principal social problem they faced was that of "mixed" marriages (Ezra 9:1-2; Neh. 13:23-24). The leaders themselves, including one of the principal priests, were guilty of marrying foreign wives (Ezra 9:2; Neh. 13:28). According to Mal. the Jews' guilt is 2-fold: a religious compromise in marrying a **daughter of a foreign god** (vs. 11) and the moral offense of divorcing a Jewish wife to make such a marriage possible (vss. 14-16).

2:10-12. Mal. cites the fatherhood of God the creator—though some have questioned whether **father** may mean Jacob or Abraham as ancestor of the Jews—as the reason to avoid foreign wives. Vs. 10 is often quoted as a statement of the brotherhood of all men, but it is clear that Mal. is thinking simply of God's fatherhood of the Jews, who accordingly must marry within the family. There are obscurities in the Hebrew of vs. 12, but the idea seems to be that one guilty of this sin will find none to aid him in a lawsuit or in offerings in the temple, without which he cannot prosper.

2:13-17. *Divorce.* Here follows an exposition of the rationale of marriage. Marriage is a solemn agreement before God; hence those who divorce their wives are guilty not merely of **covenant** breaking but of blasphemy (vs. 14). Natural ties enforce the relationship, for the **wife** was her husband's first love and has since been his constant **companion.** The Hebrew of vs. 15 is difficult, but it may refer to the story of woman's creation from the rib of man (Gen. 2:21-24), which gives them one inbreathed **spirit** (cf. Matt. 19:6). This interpretation would seem to apply to marriage among all men, since all descend from Adam. The purpose of a union within God's chosen people is not arbitrary, for God desires **godly offspring** (vs. 15*b*), best nurtured by wives of the covenant people. However, if the universal demands of marriage are meant, then marital faithfulness in itself, rather than marriage within Judaism, produces godly children (cf. I Cor. 7:12-

16). That God **hates divorce** (vs. 16a) suggests that divorce to marry another Jewish wife would be abhorrent to him and raises the question whether the divorce of a Gentile wife, later demanded by Ezra (Ezra 10:11), would have been required by Mal.

V. THE COMING JUDGMENT (2:17–3:5)

2:17. The Justice of God. The prophet turns from the specific charges he has made to the fundamental attitude underlying the sins of the community. God's justice is being brought into question, and obedience to his law, in regard to both ceremonial and moral matters, has suffered as a consequence. This question, emerging by the time of the fall of Jerusalem (cf. Hab. 1:13-17), came to preoccupy not so much the irreligious as the thoughtful and reverent inquirers. It is the question of theodicy: How can God be just and still permit injustice?

3:1-5. The Coming Messenger. Though an ancient editor supposed him to be the author of the book (see Intro.) the **messenger,** or "angel," of this passage seems to represent an agent sent by God to **prepare** for his coming in judgment and grace. Who is he? Will he be supernatural or human? Following what appears to be his identification as Elijah the prophet (4:5) the Christian interpretation has generally identified the messenger as John the Baptist, forerunner to Christ. Mal., however, may have in mind a reforming or messianic priest (cf. 2:7; Job. 33:23; Eccl. 5:6). If so, the **covenant** may be that with Levi (2:4, 8).

3:2-4. The function of the messenger is to make possible God's return to his temple on a **day** of terrible judgment (vs. 2), when the priests will be cleansed in the crucible of suffering (vs. 3), so that acceptable offerings may be made and God may again bless his people (vs. 4). Since this day is not viewed as an end to history (vs. 4; cf. vss. 12, 18; 4:3) the unendurable **fire** (vss. 2-3; cf. 4:1) is probably a poetic exaggeration of the effects of real justice in a kingdom where God rules.

3:5. The meaning may be that God himself will deal with the wicked, but it seems more likely that the cleansed priesthood is again to carry out the mandate of oracular **judgment** (see above on 2:6-9). If God is not in his temple oracular judgment will of course be unreliable, in that either the sacred omens will not function or an irreverent priesthood will disregard them. The cleansing of the priesthood and restoration of right sacrifices on the day of God's return will guarantee temple justice. The stroke of divine judgment will at last fall on those guilty of oppressing the innocent: **sorcerers** who victimize by witchcraft, **adulterers** who steal marriage partners, false witnesses, and the oppressors who exploit the **hireling,** the **widow,** and the **orphan,** who cannot defend themselves, and the **sojourner,** whose human rights are often discounted. Mal. is here in the tradition of the classical prophetic absorption with social justice. He simply puts the temple and its ritual at the center of a just moral order; when God is in his house, his household is in order!

VI. NEGLECT OF TITHES (3:6-12)

This treatment of the obligation and opportunity of the tithe is the most familiar reference to the subject in the OT. The tithe belongs to God, Mal. declares; to withhold it is to rob him. Give God his due and the nation's prosperity will be a worldwide testimony. That Mal.'s argument was not entirely successful is shown by Nehemiah's measures to collect and distribute tithes (Neh. 13:10-14).

3:6-7. As it stands vs. 6 is almost impossible to fit into the context. One may suppose its sense is that the irresistible grace of God alone accounts for the people's survival. Though men act as if God no longer cares whether they obey his **statutes,** he is as ready as ever to **return** and dwell among them (vs. 7).

3:8-11. The word **nation** (vs. 9) is the term ordinarily used of foreigners (cf. vs. 12; 1:11, 14) and therefore implies that by **robbing** God the Jews are forfeiting their privilege as his chosen people. The **tithes** and **offerings** to be brought into the temple **storehouse** seem to reflect the laws of the P Code (cf. Lev. 27:30-33; Num. 18:21-32), by which all of the tithes provide support for the priests and Levites, rather than those of the D Code (cf. Deut. 14:22-29), which specify a triennial cycle with the people consuming the tithe themselves in a ritual meal at the sanctuary for 2 years and in the 3rd year giving it to the Levites and others deserving charitable aid. This fact does not contradict the other evidence that the book was written before adoption of the P Code (see Intro.); it simply shows that the P Code incorporated customs that had already been developed in practice.

3:10b-12. God asks the people as an act of faith to **test** his promises that their obedience will be rewarded. He will **open the windows of heaven,** i.e. send abundant rainfall (see comment on Gen. 7:11-16), and **rebuke the devourer,** i.e. prevent the coming of locusts (cf. Joel 1:4), so that surplus crops will result. The prosperity of the Jewish community will be a witness to **all nations** of the blessing of obedience to Yahweh. It may be noted that the promises here, as usually in the OT, apply to the people as a whole rather than individually. Presumably if enough of them bring their tithes the rains will fall and benefit everyone, even the man who still withholds his contribution (cf. Matt. 5:45).

VII. JUSTIFICATION OF THE RIGHTEOUS (3:13–4:3)

This last of Mal.'s oracles deals further with the question raised in 2:17 about God's justice in relation to the individual rather than the community as a group.

3:13-15. Those who argue with the prophet in his pretended dialogue are asking: "What's the use of serving God?" People who do so seem no better off than their neighbors. In fact the **evildoers** seem to **prosper** more. Even those who defiantly **put God to the test** by flagrant disobedience appear to **escape** punishment. **Walking as in mourning** probably refers to an attitude of penitence, possibly when appearing before the Levitical court. On the other hand **arrogant** may describe the assurance with which influential men come before the priests, knowing that a fraudulent oracle will declare them innocent and condemn their victims.

3:16-18. Those who have been expressing doubt about God's justice in vss. 14-15 are not the wicked but the pious, for it seems almost certain that the LXX is correct in reading not **Then** but "Thus" at the beginning of vs. 16. I.e. Yahweh's response is to the doubt of his justice by those who have been faithful to him but are losing heart. The several OT references (e.g. Exod. 32:32; Ps. 56:8; Neh. 13:14) to God's keeping a **book,** a written record like an earthly king, are a figure of speech expressing confidence that no one of his worshipers will be overlooked rather than a lit. idea that his memory needs such an aid. Thus the **righteous** may be assured that there is coming a **day** of judgment when God will **spare** them and **distinguish** them individually from the **wicked.**

4:1-3. Here as in 3:2-3 the catastrophe of the coming **day** of reward for the righteous and destruction for the wicked is expressed symbolically in terms of fire. It is likely that this sort of language was originally figurative as a way of describing an event which, while it would transform history, would not terminate it (cf. e.g. Isa. 35); but later it came to be taken more and more seriously as descriptive rather than symbolic. It is not certain how far this process has developed with Mal.—whether he thinks of the day as some decisive action by which God will effect the return of simple justice to a depraved society or as a lit. fire that will destroy all the wicked and leave the righteous to live in happiness. **Stubble** or dry grass (cf. Matt. 6:30) was a common fuel for

the peasant's baking **oven.** The idea of the **sun** with **wings** no doubt comes from artistic representation common in the Near East, esp. Egypt, of the sun or a sun god with wings by which he flies across the sky.

VIII. Epilogue (4:4-6)

4:4. This postscript appears to be an addition by the compiler of the Book of the 12 or a later editor intended to tie the whole collection to the **law of . . . Moses,** i.e. the Pentateuch, which by his time was long established as the canonical scripture of Judaism.

4:5-6. This 2nd postscript is apparently another addition by one who wished to identify the messenger of 3:1 as a **prophet,** rather than a priest as in Mal.'s thought (cf. 2:7). Probably he considered **Elijah** as available for the assignment because of the record of his being translated (II Kings 2:11) rather than dying. His idea caught on, so that in later noncanonical literature, as well as in the NT (cf. e.g. Matt. 11:14), Elijah is thought of as returning to prepare the way for the Messiah. The meaning of the reconciliation of **fathers** and **children** is uncertain. Perhaps family breaches symbolize all the social ills for which the forerunner will offer a last chance of healing before the **great and terrible day.**

COMMENTARY on the BOOKS of the APOCRYPHA

THE FIRST BOOK OF ESDRAS

CHARLES T. FRITSCH

INTRODUCTION

This first book of the Apoc. is known to Protestants as I Esdras, from the Greek form of the name Ezra; but to those who follow the tradition of the Vulg., where Ezra is called "Esdras I" and Neh. "Esdras II," this book is distinguished as III Esdras or "Greek Ezra." Unlike most books of the Apoc. it is not included in the Roman Catholic OT.

Contents. I Esdras is a Greek version of a portion of the historical work of the Chronicler (see Intros. to I Chr. and Ezra) which is represented in the canonical books of Chr., Ezra, and Neh. It contains material corresponding to II Chr. 35–36, almost all of Ezra, and Neh. 7:73–8:13a, together with a story about a contest of 3 guards in the court of King Darius I of Persia which is not found in the OT and clearly is a later insertion into the Chronicler's work. With variations from the Hebrew-Aramaic text consisting partly of interpolation and partly of re-arrangement it tells the story of the last days of the Judean kingdom, the fall of Jerusalem, the Babylonian exile, the returns under Sheshbazzar and Zerubbabel, and the reorganization of the Jewish state under Ezra. No mention is made of Nehemiah and his work (see below on 5:7-46). The abrupt beginning with the account of Josiah's passover and the ending with an unfinished sentence (cf. Neh. 8:13) show that this is a fragment of a larger work. The differences in order from the Hebrew-Aramaic text (e.g. see below on 2:16-30) complicate rather than elucidate the chronological problems of these books.

Text and Date. The Greek text of I Esdras evidently represents the original LXX translation of Chr.-Ezra-Neh. made at Alexandria in the 2nd cent. B.C. Scholars are disagreed on whether its variations from these books should be attributed to the translator or to his use of a Hebrew-Aramaic text differing from that later canonized by the Palestinian Jews, and also on the related question of whether the added story of the 3 guards was composed in Greek or in Aramaic. As a translation I Esdras is far superior to the literalistic, wooden Greek version of Chr.-Ezra-Neh., generally attributed to Theodotion (2nd cent. A.D.), which is found in our present LXX. The Jewish historian Flavius Josephus in the last decade of the first cent. A.D. used I Esdras in preference to the canonical Ezra-Neh. as his source for the Persian period in his Antiquities of the Jews. The date of I Esdras therefore must fall somewhere between 200 B.C. and A.D. 90. Since it is definitely related to the early Alexandrian translation in style and vocabulary most scholars date it *ca.* 150 B.C.

For Further Study. S. A. Cook, in R. H. Charles, ed., *The Apoc. and Pseudepigrapha of the OT*, 1913. Nigel Turner in *IDB*, 1962.

I. THE LAST DAYS OF THE KINGDOM (1:1-58)

This ch. corresponds closely to II Chr. 35:1–36:21 (see comment) except that vss. 23-24 are without parallel there. In vs. 34 **Jeconiah** should be Jehoahaz (cf. II Chr. 36:1).

II. THE RETURN UNDER SHESHBAZZAR (2:1-30)

Vss. 1-15 correspond closely to Ezra 1:1-11 (see comment).

2:16-30. Samaritan Opposition. This section—corresponding to Ezra 4:7-24 (see comment) except that Ezra 4:8-10 is missing here—is even more displaced chronologically than in Ezra, probably because of the insertion of the following story of the 3 guards. In Ezra the correspondence with the Persian king concerns only the rebuilding of the city and its walls (cf. Ezra 4:12-13, 21) but in vss. 18, 20 here references to rebuilding the **temple** have been inserted to harmonize with the context. **Coele-syria and Phoenicia** (vss. 17, 24, 27) was the province in the Seleucid Empire which included Palestine, as was "Beyond the River" (Ezra 4:10, etc.) in the Persian Empire.

III. THE STORY OF THE 3 GUARDS (3:1-5:3)

This section is unique to I Esdras and obviously is a late addition to the Chronicler's history (e.g. see below on 4:42-63). It is a fine piece of oriental wisdom literature, describing an oratorical contest among 3 guards in the court of **King Darius** I, who rewards the one he judges to be the winner. It has been adapted to the history of **Zerubbabel** (named in the story itself only in 4:13), **who spoke wise words before Darius the king of the Persians** (5:6).

3:17b-4:41. The Oratorical Contest. The **three young men** lay plans for a debate before the king and each one selects his topic. The first contestant debates on the subject that **wine is the strongest** (3:18-24) and the 2nd that the **king is the strongest** (4:1-12). The 3rd, **Zerubbabel**, debates on 2 subjects, **that women are strongest, but truth is victor**

519

over all things (4:13-40). All the people shout: **Great is truth, and strongest of all!** (vs. 41). Of **Apame** and **Bartacus** (vs. 29) nothing is known.

4:42-57. *Zerubbabel's Reward*. Besides being given a seat next to Darius and being made a **kinsman** of the king, Zerubbabel is granted his request to go to Jerusalem to rebuild the city and **temple.** The king writes **letters** to officials to give safe conduct to the caravan along the way and to supply materials and funds for the construction (contrast 6:23-26, where after the work has started he knows nothing of the authority for it till the decree of Cyrus is located in the archives). Darius also returns to Zerubbabel the temple **vessels** taken from Jerusalem by Nebuchadnezzar. All this is done in accordance with the vow made by **Cyrus,** which evidently, according to this story, has never been carried out (vss. 44, 57; contrast 2:12-15). There is no hint here of a return to Jerusalem in the days of Cyrus (contrast 2:15).

4:58-5:3. *The Conclusion of the Story*. After a prayer of thanksgiving Zerubbabel informs his fellow exiles, who rejoice and join him in the return.

IV. The Return Under Zerubbabel (5:4-7:15)

5:4-6. *A Group of Returning Exiles*. This is an independent fragment which may have been inserted here as a transition between the preceding story and the list of returnees which follows (vss. 7-46). Notice the difficult expression **Joakim the son of Zerubbabel** (vs. 5), for which there is no explanation (cf. I Chr. 3:19-20; also Neh. 12:10, where **Jeshua** is the father of Joakim).

5:7-46. *The List of Returning Exiles*. This passage corresponds closely to Ezra 2:1-70; Neh. 7:6-73a (see comments) except for variations in the names (in the RSV names based on the Hebrew of Ezra and Neh. have been substituted in many cases for the Greek forms of I Esdras, which are shown in footnotes). **Attharias** (vs. 40) is a Greek transliteration of *tirshatha* ("governor"), found in the parallel vss., Ezra 2:63; Neh. 7:65. **Nehemiah and** probably slipped in here because Nehemiah is called *tirshatha* in Neh. 8:9; 10:1.

5:47-73. *The Beginning of Restoration*. Vss. 47-73a correspond closely to Ezra 3:1-4:5 (see comment). Vs. 73b is probably a variant of Ezra 4:24; **two years** is an error, since 8 years elapsed between the death of Cyrus (530) and the beginning of the reign of Darius I (522).

6:1-7:15. *The Completion of the Temple*. This pas-

sage corresponds closely to Ezra 5-6 (see comment). On 6:23-26 see above on 4:42-63. In 7:5 completion of the temple is dated **the twenty-third day of the month of Adar** whereas Ezra 6:55 has the 3rd day. There is no clue for determining which figure is original.

V. The Return Under Ezra (8:1-9:55)

This passage corresponds closely to Ezra 7-10; Neh. 7:73b-8:13a (see comments) except for variations in the names in 9:18-36, 43, 48 (see above on 5:7-46). It is significant that here appear together the Ezra materials which in Ezra-Neh. are separated by the major section of the Nehemiah memoirs. Some scholars believe that the order here—8:1-9:36 (cf. Ezra 7-10); 9:37-55 (cf. Neh. 7:73b-8:13a)—is the original order of the Ezra narrative and that the part of the Nehemiah memoirs in Neh. 1:1-7:73a was inserted into it, either by the Chronicler or by a later reviser. Other scholars, however, think the reading of the law (9:37-55) originally followed Ezra's arrival in Jerusalem (8:1-67; cf. Ezra 7-8) and preceded the action on mixed marriages (8:68-9:36; cf. Ezra 9-10 and see comment).

According to either view 9:37a offers a problem, since it appears to be a variant of Neh. 7:73a (cf. 5:46; Ezra 2:70) and thus to come from the end of the census list of 5:7-46; Ezra 2:1-70; Neh. 7:6-73a. Those who believe I Esdras to be derived from Ezra-Neh. cite 9:37a as evidence that the translator or other editor arrived at the order in ch. 9 by simply omitting Neh. 1:1-7:72 from his copy of Ezra-Neh. Other evidences, however, make it more likely that I Esdras and Ezra-Neh. represent independent versions of the original work of the Chronicler, and so scholars have suggested various other explanations for 9:37a. E.g. if it was originally the link between the arrival of Ezra in Jerusalem (8:1-67) and the reading of the law (9:37-55), the editor who placed the latter story in Neh. 7:73b-8:18 may have omitted this sentence because it so nearly duplicated Neh. 7:73a.

9:49-55. On **Attharates** cf. Attharias in 5:40 and see comment on 5:7-46. The incomplete sentence ending the book (vs. 55b; cf. Neh. 8:13a) shows that we have only a fragment of this version of the Chronicler's history. Possibly the remaining portion included Nehemiah's memoirs, which the Chronicler probably appended at the end of his work (see Intro. to Ezra).

THE SECOND BOOK OF ESDRAS

ROBERT C. DENTAN

INTRODUCTION

II Esdras is not a continuation or parallel of I Esdras but an important apocalyptic work (see "The Apocalyptic Literature," pp. 1106-09). It is comparable in many respects to Dan., Rev., and such noncanonical apocalypses as Enoch and the Assumption of Moses; but it makes less use of fantastic imagery than those books and is sharply distinguished from them by its dominant concern with the problem of human suffering. No other book outside of Job exhibits so profound and intensely personal an interest in this subject. Unlike Dan. and Rev. the book seems not to have been written in a time of persecution but looks back in anguished contemplation on a disaster that has already run its course.

Authorship, Composition, and Date. As it now stands the book purports to be the work of Ezra (Esdras in Greek)—a pseudonym such as is conventional in apocalyptic writing. In 3:1, however, Ezra is strangely and impossibly identified with "Salathiel," i.e. Shealtiel, scion of the Davidic line during the Babylonian exile (see below on 3:1-2); and the date in this vs. and succeeding references to the purported historical situation fit Shealtiel rather than Ezra. Accordingly some scholars believe, with considerable reason, that the nucleus of the book (chs. 3-10 or possibly 3-13) was originally published in the name of Shealtiel. Only in ch. 14 does Ezra appear in his own character, and it is therefore supposed that the addition of this ch. occasioned the attribution of the whole book to Ezra.

The structure of the book is obscured by the presence of chs. 1-2; 15-16, which are of later Christian origin and are found only in the Latin version. They are independent compositions and of slight interest. The main part of the book (chs. 3-14), purely Jewish in character, consists of 7 "visions." The first 3 of these (3:1-5:20; 5:21-6:34; 6:35-9:25) are not so much visions as extended colloquies of a philosophical character between "Ezra" and the angel Uriel or God himself. The next 3 are visions in the strict sense: of the woman who is Zion (9:26-10:59), of the eagle (11:1-12:38), and of the man from the sea (ch. 13). The final "vision," relating the commission of Ezra (ch. 14), is so different from all the others that it is most naturally thought of as a later addition to the series. Differences also apparent in the eagle and man-from-the-sea visions may be due to the author's adaptation of varying sources but more probably indicate that these sections likewise were editorially joined to the preceding visions.

The ostensible date of the basic Shealtiel apocalypse is given as the "thirtieth year after the destruction of our city," i.e. Jerusalem, by the Babylonians in 586 B.C. (3:1); but this is only a dramatic device, for the author's real concern is with the destruction by the Romans in A.D. 70. The 30th year, imitated from Ezek. 1:1, is not to be taken as a precise date, but it points to a time near the end of the first cent. The eagle vision was probably written during the reign of Domitian (81-96; see below on 12:22-30); those who believe it was composed as a part of the Shealtiel apocalypse therefore date this work *ca.* 95. The vision of the man from the sea, or its source, seems to come from a time before the destruction of Jerusalem (see below on 13:1-58). The assumption of 24 canonical books in ch. 14 seems to place this unit after the fixing of the Hebrew canon at Jamnia *ca.* 85-90. Since the finished Jewish work (chs. 3-14) would hardly have been borrowed for Christian use after the Jewish revolt of 132-35, which appears finally to have disrupted communication between the 2 groups, a date of *ca.* 120 seems a reasonable limit for the final editing. Chs. 1-2 are probably to be dated in the 2nd cent. and chs. 15-16 in the 3rd (see below on 15:1-16:78).

The Name and the Text. The present name of the book is derived from 1:1, which was no part of the original apocalypse. Because the book was not included in the LXX and therefore not accounted canonical in the Roman Catholic Church, the Vulg. contains it only as part of an appendix printed after the NT, where it is called IV Esdras—distinguished from I, II Esdras, which represent the canonical Ezra, Neh. of Protestants, and from III Esdras, which is the Vulg. name for I Esdras of the Protestant Apoc. Chs. 1-2 have sometimes been known separately as II Esdras, and chs. 15-16 as V Esdras. The Jewish work (chs. 3-14), or sometimes the whole book, is frequently referred to as IV Ezra or, to avoid confusion, simply the Ezra Apocalypse.

Chs. 3-14 were originally written in Hebrew—less likely Aramaic—and subsequently translated into Greek. Both the Hebrew original and the Greek translation are lost, except for a couple of Greek passages quoted in early Christian writers. The entire book exists only in Latin, but chs. 3-14 are also preserved in Syriac, Ethiopic, Armenian, and 2 Arabic versions, while fragments are extant in Sahidic and Georgian—evidence of the work's onetime great popularity.

521

Latin manuscripts of the book are numerous, but contain many variants and errors. Almost all those now existing are descended from a manuscript of the 9th cent. from which a leaf was cut out, possibly for doctrinal reasons (see below on 7:[75]-45[115]); and ch. and vs. numbers came to be established for this defective text. In 1875 R. L. Bensly published the missing section, which he found in a hitherto unstudied manuscript, and which harmonized with a corresponding section in the oriental versions. Translations since then have included this material following 7:35, with bracketed vs. numbers [36]-[105]. This necessitates an awkward double numeration for the remaining vss. of the ch., 36[106]-70[140].

Religious Interest. Even though the author of the original apocalypse was a fervent, orthodox Jew who believed the world to have been created for the sake of Israel (6:55; 7:11), he is remarkable for his broad concern with the whole of suffering humanity (7:[62]-[69]). His immediate problem is the fact that God's chosen people have been subjugated by the impious Romans (4:23), but his mind can never completely separate this from the broader problem presented by the existence of human misery in any form. A partial answer is found in the universality of sin, caused by the transgression of Adam, who transmitted the disease to all his descendants (3:21-22; 7:48[118]). Even though the power of free choice remains (8:56), most men elect to do evil and therefore deserve to perish (7:57[127]-61[131]; 8:3). But the author sympathizes even with sinners (7:18, 46[116]-56[126]), partly because he knows himself to be one (8:35). His pessimistic view of human nature, corrupted by an evil heart (3:26), has striking affinities with the teaching of Paul, as does his lament that even possession of the divine law does not suffice to save Israel (3:22; 9:36). The continual return to these themes in the first 3 visions shows the extent of the author's emotional involvement in them. His only comfort comes from the apocalyptic truth that "the Most High has made not one world but two" (7:[50]); thus the injustices evident in the present age can be corrected in the age to come.

For Further Study. G. H. Box, *The Ezra Apocalypse,* 1912; "IV Ezra," in R. H. Charles, ed., *The Apoc. and Pseudepigrapha of the OT,* 1913, II, 542-624. W. O. E. Oesterley, *II Esdras,* 1933. Nigel Turner, "Esdras, Books of," in *IDB,* 1962.

I. THE CHRISTIAN PREFIX (1:1–2:48)

Chs. 1-2, originally a separate book (see Intro.), describe the rejection of the old Israel for her faithlessness (1:1-32; 2:1-9) and the choice of a new people, the Christian church, to take her place (1:33-40; 2:10-14). The church is exhorted to joy, good works, and hope of a glorious new age (2:15-32). Ezra has a vision of the redeemed in heaven (2:33-48).

1:1-3. Ezra, whom the canonical OT introduces as a priest and scribe (Ezra 7:1-6, 11; cf. I Esdras 8:1-3, 8), is here represented as a **prophet.** On the date of the **reign of Artaxerxes** see Intro. to Ezra.

1:4-11. The formula **The word of the Lord came to me** is typical of the prophetic books. Ezra is told to denounce the sins of his people. On **pull out the hair** cf. Ezra 9:3.

1:12-23. God reviews the many blessings he bestowed on his chosen people.

1:24-32. Because of Israel's rejection of God he is going to reject them. Vs. 30 reflects Matt. 23:37; vs. 32 Matt. 23:34-35.

1:33-40. Ezra is represented as predicting that the place of Israel will be taken by a **people that will come** (vss. 35, 37), i.e. the Christian church, which will then be accounted as heir to the teaching and leadership of Israel's patriarchs and prophets.

2:1-9. These vss., which reflect the Roman destruction of Jerusalem in A.D. 70, exhibit an unattractive anti-Jewish spirit (esp. vs. 7). The fall of the city—the **mother** and **widow** of vss. 2-6—and the subsequent dispersion of the Jews are said to be God's punishment for their sins. **Assyria** (vs. 8) means Rome.

2:10-14. God now addresses the church as **my people.** She is promised the blessings of the **kingdom** in the coming age. Vs. 13 combines Matt. 7:7; 24:22. Vs. 14 is an oblique reflection of Isa. 45:7.

2:15-32. The church, now addressed as **mother,** is exhorted to engage in good works (vss. 20-25) and to face the future with joyful anticipation (vss. 26-32).

2:33-48. In obvious imitation of such passages as Rev. 4; 7; 14:1-5 Ezra sees a vision of the church's risen martyrs receiving crowns from the **Son of God.**

II. THE EZRA APOCALYPSE: 7 VISIONS (3:1–14:48)

The Jewish apocalypse includes chs. 3-14. The first part of it (chs. 3-10) has a philosophical tone quite different from the rest (see Intro.).

3:1–5:20. *Vision 1: The Problem of Israel's Suffering.* The ostensible occasion of the visions is the **destruction** of Jerusalem by the Babylonians in 586 B.C. (3:1-2). Actually the author is thinking of the destruction by the Romans in A.D. 70. The situation gives rise to the whole question of the meaning of Israel's suffering and of human suffering in general.

3:1-2. The date **in the thirtieth year** imitates the opening phrase of Ezekiel, the first great book of the Babylonian exile. **Salathiel** is the Greek form of Shealtiel, oldest son of King Jehoiachin (Jeconiah, I Chr. 3:17; cf. Matt. 1:12), who was taken captive to Babylon in 597 B.C., and father of Zerubbabel (Ezra 5:2), whom some hoped would be enthroned after the Exile (cf. Hag. 2:23; Zech. 4:6-10). As exiled claimant to the throne of David (cf. 5:17-18) Shealtiel thus symbolizes Israel. Since the situation is clearly that of Shealtiel and not that of **Ezra,** who lived after the Exile (see Intro. to Ezra), when Jerusalem had been rebuilt, it seems probable that only the name Shealtiel stood here in the original text. The name Ezra was then introduced, awkwardly, here and at 5 other places (6:10; 7:2, 25, [49?]; 8:2) when ch. 14 was added.

3:3-11. The doctrine of "original" sin, viz. that Adam's transgression infected the whole race with a sinful tendency, appears here in Jewish literature for the first time (cf. vss. 21-22, 26; 4:30; 7:48[118]).

3:12-27. Even God's everlasting covenant with Abraham (vs. 15) left Israel burdened with the **evil heart** (vss. 20, 22, 26), inherited from Adam. The evil heart is the rabbinical "evil impulse," which along with the "good impulse" was regarded as a normal constituent of man's nature (cf. 4:30; 7:[48], [92]).

3:28-36. Why did God allow the wicked Babylonians, i.e. Romans, to conquer the relatively more righteous Jews?

4:1-12. The angel **Uriel** ("God is my light"), sent to answer the seer's questions, argues that, since man cannot understand even ordinary terrestrial phenomena (vs. 9), he can hardly expect to understand the plans of God (vs. 11). The seer answers that it would be better not to have been created than to be left thus ignorant (vs. 12).

4:13-25. Uriel argues that every creature must learn to live and operate within his own appointed sphere and not try to comprehend things which lie beyond it (vs. 21). The seer complains that it was senseless then to give man the **power of understanding** (vs. 22). And in any event, he declares, he was not asking information about ineffable realities but only about a plain historical fact, that Israel has been conquered by the Gentiles.

4:26-32. Uriel goes on to give the final answer, that indeed **this age is full of sadness** but it will soon pass away to make room for a better.

4:33-52. When the seer asks how soon this will happen, the angel replies that the end is predetermined—it will come when the allotted **number** of the righteous **is completed**, as **Jeremiel the archangel** is reported to have said (vs. 36). The analogy of childbirth shows that the consummation cannot be held back (vss. 40-42). **Hades** in the original Hebrew text no doubt read "Sheol" (see comment on Ps. 6:4-5). Further parables are used to illustrate the truth that the greater part of the present age is past (vss. 44-50).

5:1-13. The imminence of the end will be marked by prodigies, and by the growth of iniquity and misery. The **signs** of the end are traditional (cf. e.g. Mark 13:4-25). Because of differences in style and outlook some scholars think this passage, except vs. 13b, has been interpolated from a different source (see below on 7:26-[44]). If so, 4:52 is probably an editorial intro. to it.

5:14-20. After awaking from the first vision the seer prepares for the 2nd by a 7-day fast. **Phaltiel** (vs. 16) is otherwise unknown.

5:21-6:34. *Vision 2: The Coming of the New Age.* His fast completed, the seer prays, complaining at God's unjust treatment of his chosen people (5:21-30). Uriel comes again and once more warns that human understanding is incapable of discovering the divine plan (5:31-37). Beginning in 5:38 God himself seems to take the place of Uriel for the remainder of this vision.

5:41-55. The seer now introduces a new question: What will be the fate of those who do not live until the new age arrives? God answers that all will be saved simultaneously, for with him there is no past, present, or future (vs. 42). It would, however, have been as unnatural for all men to have been **created at one time** as for a woman to **bear ten children** all at once (vss. 43-49). The reduced stature of the present human race shows that **creation . . . is aging** and hastening toward its end (vss. 50-55).

5:56-6:6. When the seer asks who will be charged with bringing creation to an end, God answers that just as he planned the world by himself (cf. 3:4)

he himself will end it—without assistance (6:6). This seems to be a polemic against certain Jewish, and possibly Christian, ideas attributing creation to intermediaries (cf. Prov. 8:22-31; Wisd. Sol. 7:22a; John 1:3) and seems also to reject the idea of a coming Messiah (see below on 7:26-[44]).

6:7-10. In answer to another question of the seer God declares that the ideal future age will follow immediately on the present age, without an intervening messianic time, just as **Jacob's hand** attached itself immediately to **Esau's heel** (see below on 7:26-[44]). **Ezra** (vs. 10) is probably an interpolation (see above on 3:1-2).

6:11-28. The seer begs to know further **signs** of the end (cf. 4:52-5:13) and is told of additional prodigies to come (vss. 21-24). Afterward the day of salvation will arrive, Enoch and Elijah will appear (vs. 26; cf. Gen. 5:24; II Kings 2:11; Mal. 4:5), and universal righteousness will prevail. On the **trumpet** (vs. 23) cf. I Cor. 15:52. Some scholars regard vss. 13-28, like 5:1-13a, as an interpolation, with vss. 11-12, 29 (cf. vs. 14) as editorial transitions (see below on 7:26-[44]).

6:29-34. In an interlude the seer is told to prepare by fasting for further visions.

6:35-9:25. *Vision 3: The Fate of Righteous and Wicked.* In this, the longest and most complex of the visions, the seer returns repeatedly to his main argument and is, incidentally, provided with a more elaborate program of things to come (7:26-[44], [75]-45[115]; 8:63-9:12).

6:38-59. The seer asks, in view of God's purpose in creation (vss. 38-56), why Israel is subjugated to the heathen (vss. 57-59). **Behemoth** and **Leviathan** were mythical primeval monsters (vss. 49-52; see comment on Job 3:4-10; Ps. 74:12-14). The idea that God created the world only for the sake of Israel (vs. 55; cf. 7:11) is not to be found in the canonical OT.

7:1-25. The seer is told to concentrate on the glories of the coming age rather than the miseries of the present, which are due to Adam's sin (vss. 1-16). When he continues to express sympathy for suffering sinners (vss. 17-18) he is admonished to realize that God is just, for sinners have rejected his law in full knowledge of the consequences (vss. 19-25).

7:26-[44]. On the bracketed vs. numbers see Intro. Some scholars regard this section, along with 5:1-13a; 6:11-28; 8:63-9:12, as an interpolation from another document. The ideas are different from those found elsewhere in the book (cf. e.g. 6:6, 7-10; see comment). The seer is told of the coming of the heavenly city and the temporary messianic age (vss. 26-29), the resurrection (vs. 32), the judgment, hell, and heaven (vss. 33-[44]). The conception of a 400-year messianic kingdom intervening between this age and the one to come (vs. 28) is known from rabbinic sources, but the assertion that the Messiah will die at the end of the period (vs. 29) is without parallel. The Latin version, but not the others, interpolates the name "Jesus" in vs. 28.

7:[45]-[74]. To the seer's renewed complaint at man's tragic lot (vss. [45]-[48]) the divine answer is that sinful souls, being worthless, deserve their fate and should not be lamented (vss. [49]-[61]). When he argues that animals are then better off than men (vss. [62]-[69]) the answer is that sinful men freely chose their course and finally exhausted God's patience which they had so long enjoyed (vss. [70]-[74]).

7:[75]-45[115]. In answer to his question the seer is told of the fate of the wicked and righteous immediately after death. The ideas found in this passage seem inconsistent with the conception of a final judgment at the end of the age, found e.g. in vss. 32-[44]. The long-lost portion of the Latin text (vss. [36]-[105]; see Intro.) may have been deliberately cut out because vs. [105] seems to forbid prayers for the dead.

7:46[116]-61[131]. When the seer says it would be better if man had never been created, or at least had been prevented from sinning, the reply is that free choice is of the very essence of human existence.

7:62[132]-8:3. The seer appeals to the mercy of God, but the only answer is the inexorable dictum **Many have been created, but few shall be saved** (8:3; cf. Matt. 22:14).

8:4-62a. The seer meditates further on the paradox that men, created with such care, must simply perish (vss. 4-19a) and prays, with undiminished persistence, for God's mercy on those **who have no works of righteousness** (vss. 20-36). But God, continuing to affirm both the justice of his ways and the depth of his love (vs. 47), declares (vss. 37-62a) he has no alernative but to accept the decisions men make for themselves, however much the result may contradict his original purpose (vs. 59). The separate title in vs. 19b points to the fact that the following prayer (vss. 20-36), under the name *Confessio Esdrae*, was often printed separately in the Latin Bible and elsewhere. On **before he was taken up** cf. 14:9, 48 RSV footnote. The author's skepticism about average men's being saved by **works of righteousness** (vss. 32, 36) approaches the mood of Paul rather than of normative Judaism.

8:62b-9:12. Rather curiously, the seer again asks when the end of the age will come (8:63) and is given a general résumé of things previously said. The passage may be an interpolation (see above on 7:26-[44]).

9:13-25. The seer tacitly rejects the warning to concern himself only with the glories in store for the righteous (vs. 13) and continues to lament that more will perish than be saved (vss. 14-16). God says it has been difficult to save even the righteous few (vss. 17-22). He instructs the seer to prepare for another vision by eating **flowers** rather than by fasting (vss. 23-25).

9:26-10:59. *Vision 4: Zion, Mourning and Transfigured.* The seer has a vision of a woman mourning for her son (9:26-10:4). After he upbraids her for indulging in selfish grief while Jerusalem lies waste (10:5-24) she is suddenly transfigured (10:25-27a) and it is revealed that she herself is the Zion who mourns but still is glorious (10:27b-57). The idea that Israel's possession of the law brings no assurance of salvation (9:36) again suggests the thought of Paul. The parable of the woman (9:38-10:4) was probably not invented by the author but adapted from a popular tale, similar to Tobit. This would account for a certain lack of coherence between story and interpretation. **Zion** (10:44) is the heavenly

prototype rather than the earthly city (cf. Gal. 4:26). Her **son** (10:46, 49) probably represents the earthly city, now in ruins. The ideal Jerusalem is revealed as still glorious (10:50) despite the destruction of her earthly counterpart.

10:58-59. These 2 vss. are considered by some scholars an editorial transition to the following vision (see below on 11:1-12:51). If so, the original continuation of vs. 57 is perhaps to be found in 12:40-50 or 13:57-58 (see comments).

11:1-12:51. *Vision 5: The Eagle.* This vision, with its fantastic animals and mysterious details, resembles such familiar apocalyptic works as Dan. 7-12 and Rev. much more closely than the earlier part of the book. Probably it stems originally from a different source and was incorporated by the author of the Shealtiel apocalypse or, more probably, by a later editor (see Intro.).

11:1-12:3a. In a dream the seer sees an eagle with 12 wings and 3 heads rising from the sea to rule the earth (11:1-6). Successively the wings and then the heads rise to power (11:7-35), until finally a lion comes out of the forest to announce the eagle's doom (11:36-46), which shortly follows (12:1-3a). The eagle represents the Roman Empire, which **came up from the sea** (11:1; cf. Dan. 7:3), i.e. from the Mediterranean, as viewed from the orient. Both the vision and the interpretation that follows (12:3b-38) have been reworked at least once, leaving some of the details unclear; but it is obvious that the wings and heads represent successive Roman emperors. The **opposing wings** (11:3) are rebellious army officers. The date of this section depends on the identification of the **three heads** (11:23-35), esp. the 3rd, whose fall in the near future will inaugurate the last days of imperial rule (12:2-3a; see below on 12:22-30).

12:3b-38. When the seer asks for an explanation of the vision (vss. 3b-9) he is informed the eagle is the 4th kingdom of Daniel's vision, the wings and heads are kings, and the lion is the Messiah (vss. 10-35); the vision is to be preserved in a secret book (vss. 36-38). In Dan. 7:2-8 the **fourth kingdom,** symbolized by the last of 4 terrible beasts who rise to dominate the earth, is undoubtedly the empire of Alexander the Great and his successors; but here (vss. 11-13) it is taken to refer to Rome, the 3 preceding kingdoms being then understood as the Babylonian, Persian, and Greek instead of the Babylonian, Median, and Persian. The **twelve kings** (vs. 14) are 12 Roman emperors, beginning with Julius Caesar. The **second** (vs. 15), who is to **hold sway for a longer time than any other of the twelve** (cf. 11:13b-17), is obviously Augustus.

12:22-30. The **three heads** are the Flavian emperors, Vespasian (69-79) and his two sons, Titus (79-81) and Domitian (81-96). Vespasian was the first commander in the war against the Jews (67-69); under Titus, Jerusalem was captured and destroyed (70). These facts explain the peculiar importance of these kings (vs. 25). Since Domitian is apparently still ruling (cf. 11:23-35) this part of the book, at any rate, can be plausibly dated in his reign—probably toward the end (*ca.* 95?), when he became increasingly despotic. Rev. is usually dated in the same period. On the other hand, since Titus did not die violently, some scholars have dated the original in the days of Vespasian and assumed later reworking.

12:31-38. The **Messiah** (vs. 32) is strangely represented as both pre-existent and **from the posterity of David.** The **book** to be hidden from common view (vs. 37) is a common apocalyptic idea (cf. 14:26, 46; Dan. 8:26; 12:4, 9; see "The Apocalyptic Literature," pp. 1106-09).

12:39-51. In a curious transitional interlude the seer promises not to forsake his fellow exiles but to return to the city when he finishes his prayers for Zion. These vss. bear no relationship to their present context and probably belong to the original source preserved in chs. 3-10. It has been suggested that originally vss. 40-48 followed 13:57-58, which in turn followed 10:57. If so, **seven days** (vs. 40) refers to the period mentioned in 9:23, now **past** and exceeded by the **three days** of 13:58. Possibly the transition led to a concluding vision (cf. 10:56) which was omitted when chs. 11-13 were added.

13:1-58. *Vision 6: The Man from the Sea.* The seer dreams of a man who arises from the sea and is met by a great hostile army, which he destroys by a flaming breath from his mouth, after which he gathers to himself a large company of peaceful men (vss. 1-13*a*). On awaking the seer asks for an explanation (vss. 13*b*-20) and is told that the man is the Messiah, his flaming breath is the law, and the peaceful company is the 10 lost tribes of Israel (vss. 21-53*a*). This is followed by the usual transition to the next vision (vss. 53*b*-58; see above on 12:39-51).

The conceptions in this vision are so different from those of any of the preceding sections that it almost certainly comes from a different source. Probably it is to be dated before A.D. 70, since the Jews seem to be still living in Palestine, there is no allusion to the destruction of the temple, and there is no single great enemy such as Rome.

Something like the figure of a man (vs. 3) belongs to the same tradition as the "one like a son of man" in Dan. 7:13. The final battle against God's rule (vs. 5) is a common feature of the apocalyptic tradition (cf. e.g. Ezek. 38-39; Zech. 14:2; Rev. 20:8-9). The **great mountain** (vs. 6) is interpreted (vs. 36) as the heavenly **Zion.** On the Messiah's **flaming breath** cf. Isa. 11:4; II Thess. 2:8. In the original form of the story this certainly was not understood to be a symbol of the **law,** as it is here interpreted (vs. 38). The story of the exile of the **ten tribes** (vs. 40) is told in II Kings 17; the remainder of the story told here is entirely legendary.

14:1-48. *Vision 7: Restoration of the Holy Books.* Only in this section does Ezra, the "scribe skilled in the law of Moses" (Ezra 7:6), appear in something like his historical role (see Intro.). God appears to Ezra and warns him, before he is translated, to prepare himself and his people for the evils of the final time that is near at hand (vss. 1-18). When Ezra asks for inspiration to rewrite the sacred books that were destroyed in the burning of the temple (vss. 19-22) God instructs him to prepare for the task by providing writing materials and choosing

scribes (vss. 23-26). Then after a general exhortation to the people (vss. 27-36) Ezra drinks a cup of fiery-colored liquid and during 40 days dictates to 5 secretaries the 94 canonical and apocalyptic books of scripture (vss. 37-48). The obvious purpose of this story is to vindicate the divine authority of the apocalyptic books, which the rabbis tended to view with suspicion.

Like Enoch and Elijah, Ezra is to be translated to heaven, where he will hold converse with the Messiah (vs. 9; cf. RSV footnote to vs. 48). **Thy law** (vs. 21) means here the whole of canonical scripture. The **characters which they did not know** (vs. 42) are those of the Aramaic, or "square" Hebrew, alphabet, traditionally supposed to have been introduced by Ezra (see "Writing in Biblical Times," pp. 1201-08). The **twenty-four books** (vs. 45) are those of the Hebrew canon as fixed by a group of rabbis at Jamnia *ca.* A.D. 85-90—Sam., Kings, Chr., Ezra-Neh., and the 12 minor prophets each being counted as a single book. The **seventy** are apocalyptic works such as this book, which are here clothed with the full authority of Moses (vs. 5) and Ezra. The term "apocrypha" (hidden away) is probably derived from this story (cf. 12:37).

III. THE CHRISTIAN APPENDIX (15:1-16:78)

Though the historical allusions in this section are vague, they refer most naturally to events in the middle of the 3rd cent. A.D. Unlike chs. 1-2 these chs. contain no distinctive Christian ideas, but at so late a date they are unlikely to have been taken over from Jewish sources.

15:1-19. The seer, whom ecclesiastical tradition identifies with Ezra, though he is nowhere named, is told of evils the Lord is about to inflict on the earth for its wickedness, esp. the persecution of God's people (vss. 1-11). **Egypt** is threatened with famine and other disasters (vss. 12-19)—very likely referring to a famine that destroyed ⅔ of the population of Alexandria in the time of Gallienus (260-68).

15:20-33. After another denunciation of doom in general terms (vss. 20-27) there is another historical allusion (vss. 28-33), apparently to a Persian attack on the **land of the Assyrians,** i.e. the Roman province of Syria, which resulted in devastation of a **portion,** viz. Antioch. The **dragons of Arabia** (vs. 29) are the armies of the Palmyrene empire of Odenathus and Zenobia, which acted as a buffer between Rome and Persia. The **Carmonians** (vs. 30) are the Sassanid Persians, Carmania (modern Kerman) being one of the ancient Persian provinces.

15:34-63. This is a vague prediction that **Babylon,** i.e. Rome (cf. e.g. Rev. 18:10), will be destroyed by attacks from various directions. **Asia,** probably meaning the Arabs of Palmyra, will suffer the same fate.

16:1-78. This ch. is in large part merely a pastiche of apocalyptic ideas and biblical phrases. Only in vss. 68-78 does it seem possible to propose a definite historical situation, viz. the Decian persecution of the church (249-51).

THE BOOK OF TOBIT

H. Neil Richardson

Introduction

Tobit is a delightful story of the afflictions of a pious Israelite and the adventures of his dutiful son, who makes a journey in the company of a disguised angel and returns with a bride and the means to restore the father's health and wealth. In addition to its portrayal of ancient Jewish family life the book is important for its religious teachings, which are characteristic of a stage in the development of post-exilic Judaism.

Contents and Literary Affinities. At the beginning of the story Tobit, an exiled member of the tribe of Naphtali living in Nineveh following the Assyrian conquest of Israel, is appointed to a responsible position in the Assyrian government. As a result of his charities for his fellow Israelites, however, esp. his concern to bury the bodies of those executed and left exposed, he loses both position and property and eventually his eyesight. After a quarrel with his wife he prays to God to let him die. At the same time Sarah, daughter of Tobit's kinsman Raguel, who lives at Ecbatana in Media, makes a similar prayer because a demon has killed her 7 successive husbands on their wedding nights. To respond to the simultaneous prayers God assigns the angel Raphael.

Remembering a large sum of money which he placed in the care of another relative at Rages in Media some time before, Tobit gives his son Tobias long fatherly counsel about good conduct and asks him to go for the money. They employ Raphael in the guise of a fellow Israelite as a guide. After a day's journey the 2 reach the Tigris River, where the angel advises Tobias to catch a large fish and keep 3 of its internal organs. On arrival in Ecbatana he directs Tobias to the home of Raguel and suggests marrying Sarah. By use of 2 of the fish's organs Tobias exorcises the demon and then sends Raphael on to Rages for the money while he enjoys a 14-day wedding celebration. Raphael, Tobias, and Sarah return to Nineveh with the money and the 3rd fish organ, which Tobias uses to heal Tobit's blindness. When they offer to divide the money with Raphael he gives them some ethical counsels and then reveals his identity. Tobit is inspired to compose a lengthy ps. of praise. After a long life of charitable deeds he calls Tobias to his deathbed and makes a prediction of the future, including the destruction of Nineveh. Tobias therefore moves to Ecbatana and before his death at a ripe old age hears of the fall of Nineveh.

The dependence of the author on a variety of literature is evident. In the first place he shows acquaintance with books of the OT, including some from all 3 divisions, Law, Prophets, and Writings. As might be expected, he is thoroughly familiar with the commandments of the Law, esp. those in Deut., but those in Lev. and Num. as well. His account of the meeting and wedding of Tobias and Sarah draws on even the phraseology of the stories of Rebecca and Rachel in Gen. 24; 29. His historical setting is of course drawn from II Kings in the Former Prophets, and there are several evidences of knowledge of the Latter Prophets, including a quotation from Amos 8:10, probably from memory, and the naming of either Nahum or Jonah—according to the manuscript being read. Among the Writings, Job has no doubt suggested the general theme of a righteous man suffering affliction, and Pss. has furnished a model for Tobit's ps. (ch. 13). A number of the sayings in the didactic speeches of Tobit and Raphael are obviously adapted from Prov. Readers familiar with the NT will also recognize certain parallels; but these may be attributed, not to literary influence, but to a common background in the life and thought of Judaism.

The author has also drawn to considerable extent on the book of Ahikar, an Aramaic romance of the 5th (or 6th) cent., possibly based on an Assyrian original, about an official in the court of Sennacherib who because of a false accusation suffers various hardships and at length is restored under Esarhaddon. He mentions Ahikar several times (1:21-22; 2:10; 11:18; 14:10) and brings him into the story as an Israelite who is Tobit's nephew. Both in features of the narrative and in moral teachings there are parallels to the book of Ahikar.

The book also draws on several themes from folklore: (*a*) the story of the grateful dead, in which the hero buries a corpse at considerable cost and is later helped to secure a treasure by the ghost of the dead man; (*b*) the story of the dangerous bride, in which all the bridegrooms of a princess die on their wedding nights until the hero with the help of a companion slays the dragon who has killed them; (*c*) another dragon story, in which parts of a fish have magic powers and a dog helps the hero slay the dragon. Versions of these folk tales were probably known to the author of Tobit through oral tradition rather than written sources. He has skillfully combined these folk themes with the religious ideas and practices of Judaism to produce an interesting story designed to win readers for his worthy admonitions.

Original Language. The problem of the text of Tobit is very complex. The oldest complete copies of the book are in Greek, in 3 rather widely differing recensions: (*a*) a long form found in the Codex Sinaiticus (4th cent.); (*b*) a short form found in the Codex Vaticanus (4th cent.) and with minor variants in the Codex Alexandrinus (5th cent.) and most later manuscripts; and (*c*) a mixed form, found in a few later manuscripts, in which some chs. follow the short form and the others (chs. 6–13) are apparently a revision of the long form. The 2nd of these textual forms appeared in the manuscripts available to the first English translators in the 16th cent. and thus has been used in most subsequent translations, including the RSV.

The Old Latin translation is related to the longer Sinaiticus recension, as is also the Vul., which is a rather free adaptation, though Jerome claims he followed an Aramaic manuscript which a Jew translated into Hebrew for him. The Syriac version is based on the Vaticanus recension of the Greek through 7:9 but thereafter resembles the 3rd Greek recension. The Ethiopic, Coptic, and Armenian versions follow the Vaticanus recension. There exist an Aramaic text, not earlier than the 4th cent. A.D., and 3 Hebrew texts which are even later; but none of these can be regarded as witnesses to the original text. Among the Dead Sea scrolls found in the Qumran caves are 4 fragments from Tobit copied in the first cent. B.C.—3 in Aramaic, of which one is on papyrus and the other 2 on leather, and one in Hebrew on leather. All of these are in general agreement with the long recension in Greek.

The Qumran fragments have provided assured answers to 2 questions about the text of Tobit which have been long debated: (*a*) that the longer recension represented by the Codex Sinaiticus is the oldest and (*b*) that the original language of the book was either Hebrew or Aramaic rather than Greek. The choice between the Semitic languages is still difficult. Characteristic syntax, certain mistranslations, and the Aramaic Qumran fragments point to Aramaic; but a number of exclusively Hebrew idioms and the Hebrew Qumran fragment point to Hebrew. The situation is complicated by the presence of Greek idioms which could scarcely have been suggested by a Semitic original. The most plausible reconstruction of the process is that the book was composed originally in Aramaic, was soon translated into Hebrew, and circulated in both languages; the Greek translation was made from the Hebrew; later it was compared with the Aramaic and corrected at some points and was also revised to improve the Greek style.

Since the extant text is a result of 2 stages of translation and is of a character to invite various kinds of editorial revisions—as exemplified by the condensation and revision of the long recension—judgment of its integrity is difficult. Some earlier elaborate theories of stages by which the book grew in size have been discarded, and so has the view that the references to Ahikar are interpolations. A more recent theory that chs. 13–14 were added after the Roman destruction of the temple in A.D. 70 is disproved by the fact that one of the Qumran fragments

contains a part of ch. 14, though the possibility remains that these chs. are an early addition. From the limited evidence at hand it seems more probable that the book as represented in the longer Greek recension is substantially the work of one author. Its textual history is thus one of abridgment rather than addition.

Place and Date of Composition. Most believers in Greek as the original language of Tobit assumed as a corollary its origin in Alexandria, the major center of Greek-speaking Judaism. No doubt the Greek version was indeed produced in Alexandria, but the author of the Aramaic or Hebrew original thought of Egypt as away on the very edge of the world (cf. 8:3).

A few scholars have maintained the book was written in Palestine because of its emphasis on Jerusalem and the temple (1:6-8; 5:13; 13:9-18; 14:5) and on punctilious observance of details of the law. But its atmosphere is rather that of the Diaspora, the large proportion of the Jews who in postexilic times lived in many parts of the Near Eastern world outside Palestine (cf. 3:4; 13:3). Jerusalem is simply a conventional symbol rather than a place where Tobit and his family think of living. That many Jews of the Diaspora tended to become lax in their observance of the law is no doubt the very reason the author composed his story and explains his exhortation to orthodox Jewish practices.

The most likely places are therefore Syria and Mesopotamia. Antioch in Syria became the capital of the Seleucid Empire *ca.* 300 and soon grew to be one of the largest cities of the Near East, with commercial as well as political relations with the region to the E where the setting of the book lies. Many Jews settled in Antioch and were close enough to keep in touch with Jerusalem. Thus an Antiochian Jew might well write from the standpoint of the Diaspora yet strongly support orthodox Palestinian Judaism.

On the other hand the interest of the book in the locale of ancient Assyria and Media strongly suggests that it was written at some center of Jewish population in Mesopotamia, e.g. Babylon. The relatively advanced angelology points to an E origin, since this development in Judaism was largely influenced by Persian concepts—e.g. 7 angels (12:15). The author's errors in locating Nineveh somewhere W of the Tigris River (see below on 6:1-8) and Rages too close to Ecbatana (see below on 9:1-6) should not be overrated as evidence against his living in the same region. Such misconceptions were common in ancient times, when there was little opportunity to learn geography except by personal travel.

The author's historical errors (see below on 1:1-2, 3-9, 10-20; 14:12*b*-15) are much more significant, since they show that his information about the historical setting comes almost entirely from a not too thorough reading of II Kings. Though the use of the first person in the opening section (1:3–3:6) and the angel's instruction to write a book (12:20) no doubt are intended to represent the story as autobiographical, it was clearly written from the perspective of a much later time. Sennacherib's oppression in killing exiled Israelites and refugee Judeans and confiscating Tobit's property (1:15-20) is a necessary element of the plot—no doubt suggested by the story of his attack on Jerusalem in II Kings 18-19 (with 1:21 cf. II Kings 19:36-37)—rather than a reflection of the situation at the time of writing. Since otherwise the book gives no hint of persecution of the Jews most scholars believe it must have been composed before the attempt of the Seleucid king Antiochus IV Epiphanes (175-163) to stamp out Judaism, which struck at the Jews throughout his empire even though the Maccabean revolt against it was confined to Palestine. More specifically, Tobit's prediction about the temple (14:4-5), which mentions no event between its historical rebuilding immediately after the Exile and its promised glorious rebuilding at the end of the age, seems to antedate Antiochus' desecration of the temple. A pre-Maccabean date is borne out by the absence of theological ideas, e.g. resurrection of the dead, characteristic of the Maccabean period.

On the other hand many scholars have dated Tobit only a short time before Antiochus' persecution, viz. during the first quarter of the 2nd cent. This dating is based partly on the similarity of the author's theological and ethical ideas to those of Jeshua ben Sira, author of Ecclus. (ca. 180). Even more it is based on the assumption that the acquaintance with the books of the Prophets, and some of the Writings, which this book expects of its readers was limited to a small group of priests and scribes in Jerusalem until these books began to be read publicly along with the Law in the synagogues. Since Ecclus. is the first clear witness to it, this development has generally been placed at ca. 200. Now, however, the discovery that the Aramaic language of the 3 Qumran fragments of Tobit resembles that of Ezra (ca. 4th cent.) more than that of Dan. (ca. 165) seems to point to a much earlier date for the book—either late in the Persian period (ca. 350) or early in the Greek period (ca. 300). Thus Tobit may evidence general circulation of many OT books a cent. or more earlier than heretofore supposed.

The Qumran fragments show that Tobit was known and used by Palestinian Jews of the first cent. B.C., but it failed to make a place for itself in Jewish regard and by the end of the first cent. A.D. seems to have been completely neglected. Its preservation was due to its inclusion in the LXX, which became the Christian OT. Thus it was known and quoted by Christian writers beginning with II Clement. In later times it became quite popular and influenced liturgy, literature, and art—cf. e.g. the paintings of scenes from the story by such masters as Botticelli, Titian, and Rembrandt. Though placed by the Protestant reformers in the Apoc. it remains a part of the Roman Catholic OT.

Religious Value. In telling his entertaining story the author seeks to inculcate the noblest teachings of Judaism. God is both just and merciful. He judges men rightly (3:2) even though this involves punishing them for their sins (3:3-5). He is merciful and compassionate (3:2; 13:2; 14:5). He has perfect knowledge (3:14) and is a God of power, as indicated by his appellations, who intervenes in human affairs (4:19). He dwells both in heaven (5:16) and in the temple (1:4). He is King (13:6, 7, 15) and Lord (13:4).

In this book Judaism is a personal religion which finds its highest expression in piety, integrity, honesty,

and charity. At all times the good Jew prays and observes the Mosaic law with patience and fidelity. He guards against assimilation with non-Jews by observing the dietary laws (1:10-12) and by marrying within his own family (1:9; 3:15; 4:12-13). He displays proper reverence toward Jerusalem and the temple and its worship (1:6-8; 13:9-18; 14:5). He fasts (12:8) and gives alms (1:16-17; 4:7-11, 16; 12:8-9; 14:11), for these good deeds are pleasing to God and bring their own rewards.

"What you hate, do not do to any one" (4:15) sums up well the morality of the book. One should honor his parents (4:3), shun sexual immorality (4:12), and avoid drinking wine to excess (4:15). Among good deeds the proper burial of the dead occupies an important place (1:17-19; 2:4-8; 4:3-4; 14:11-13). In these and many other ways the book reflects the conventional theology and ethics of such later groups as the Hasideans and the Pharisees.

For Further Study. D. C. Simpson in R. H. Charles, ed., *The Apoc. and Pseudepigrapha of the OT,* 1913; a trans. of the longer Sinaiticus text with intro. and commentary. W. O. E. Oesterley, *An Intro. to the Books of the Apoc.,* 1935. R. H. Pfeiffer, *History of NT Times, with an Intro. to the Apoc.,* 1949. Frank Zimmermann, *The Book of Tobit,* 1958; a trans. of the longer Sinaiticus text with intro. and commentary. Allen Wikgren in *IDB,* 1962.

I. THE TROUBLES OF TOBIT AND SARAH (1:1-3:17)

1:1-2. *Tobit's Genealogy.* Though **acts** is lit. "words" in the Greek, it probably represents a Hebrew or Aramaic word meaning both "words" and "acts." **Tobit** is variously spelled in different versions but in the Qumran fragments is "Tobi," a form of the Semitic word for "good." Identification of an important person by the naming of several ancestors is found occasionally in earlier parts of the OT (cf. e.g. Josh. 7:1; I Sam. 1:1; 9:1; Zeph. 1:1) but seems to have become esp. popular in postexilic times (cf. Ezra 7:1-5; Esth. 2:5; Judith 8:1; Baruch 1:1). None of the persons named is otherwise known. The author attributes the **captivity** of the **tribe of Naphtali** to **Shalmaneser** V (727-722), generally known as the conquerer of the N kingdom (722; cf. II Kings 17:3-6), and overlooks or ignores the record that the tribes of **Galilee** and Transjordan were deported earlier (734) by Shalmaneser's father, Tiglath-pileser III (745-729; II Kings 15:29). A **Thisbe** in Galilee is otherwise unknown. **Kedesh,** NW of Lake Huleh, was an important city in the territory of **Naphtali** (cf. Josh. 19:37; 20:7; Judg. 4:6; see color map 8).

1:3-9. *Tobit's Piety in Palestine.* Tobit's **righteousness** and **acts of charity** are emphasized throughout the story. Here his scrupulous observance of the ritual prescriptions of the Mosaic law while still in his native Galilee is described. On **Nineveh** see below on vss. 10-20. The representation of Tobit as a **young man** when his tribe **deserted the house of Jerusalem,** i.e. the Davidic dynasty, at the division of the kingdoms (931) yet in his prime when the N kingdom fell (722) is so glaringly inconsistent with the series of regnal statistics in I, II Kings that it can hardly be an inadvertent error. Perhaps the author intends it as a hint at the beginning, matched by the exaggeration of Tobit's longevity at the end (14:11), that the story is to be understood as fiction rather than history. The reference to the **temple** in **Jerusalem** as the only legitimate place of worship for **all the tribes** reflects the Judean viewpoint after discovery of the major part of Deut. in 622 (cf. Deut. 12:5-14; 14:23-26; II Kings 22–23). The use of **Most High** and other descriptive designations instead of a divine name is common in Aramaic from at least the 4th cent. on.

1:5-9. *Sacrifice to the Calf.* This is undoubtedly an allusion to the calf cult introduced by Jeroboam I when he became king of Israel (see comment on I Kings 12:28-33). According to Deut. 16:1-16 every male Jew must come to the Jerusalem temple 3 times a year and bring his offerings for the **feasts** of unleavened bread, weeks (Pentecost; cf. 2:1), and booths. Marriage within the family, understood in its broad sense, e.g. with a cousin, is both an ancient and a continuing custom among Semites, reflecting the importance of kinship (cf. e.g. Gen. 24:1-4; see below on 6:9-12). **Deborah** (cf. Judg. 4:4-16) and **Anna** (Hannah; cf. I Sam. 1:1–2:21) were no doubt chosen by the author with the expectation that his readers would be quite familiar with the stories of famous women with these names in the books of the Former Prophets. **Tobias** in the Qumran fragments is "Tobiah" (cf. e.g. Neh. 2:10), meaning "Yahweh is good."

1:10-20. *Tobit's Piety in Exile.* The author apparently assumes that **Nineveh** (see color map 9) was the capital of Assyria when Tobit was first taken there; actually it became so only under **Sennacherib** (705-681) and his successors. After his deportation Tobit continues his observance of the Mosaic law, esp. the dietary rules (vss. 10-12; cf. Dan. 1:8), except for pilgrimages to the temple in Jerusalem, which now presumably are forbidden to him.

1:13-15. Historically the "captives" of both Israel and Judah were not enslaved but simply resettled, so that they were free to prosper according to their abilities in their new homes. A few achieved wealth and positions of influence, e.g. Nehemiah; and stories that some rose to high governmental status, e.g. Daniel, Esther—perhaps suggested by the story of Joseph in Egypt—were popular among the Jews. Thus Tobit is appointed to a responsible office in the Assyrian government, and becomes wealthy enough to deposit a very large sum (on **talents** see table, p. 1285) in **Rages** (Ragae, Rhagae; cf. Judith 1:5), an important city *ca.* 5 miles SE of modern Teheran, the capital of Iran (see color map 10). **Media** was the region E of Assyria. In naming Tobit's employer **Shalmaneser** the author was misled by II Kings, which fails to mention that king's death soon after —or perhaps even before (see "Chronology," pp. 1271-82)—his capture of Samaria. His successor, who carried out the deportation, was Sargon II (722-705), named in the OT only in Isa. 20:1, who was the father of **Sennacherib.**

1:16-18. Sennacherib's **anger** toward Israel was perhaps suggested to the author by the vivid stories in II Kings 18–19 of his representatives' brutal arrogance while besieging Jerusalem during the reign of Hezekiah, but why those **fleeing from Judea** should come to Nineveh of all places is a mystery. Among many ancient peoples the bodies of executed

criminals were left exposed to public gaze—e.g. **thrown out behind,** or "over," **the wall**—both as an example and as an added disgrace (cf. e.g. II Sam. 21:7-14). Later parts of the OT, however, reflect an abhorrence of unburied bodies, left to the wild beasts and birds of prey (cf. e.g. Deut. 28:26; I Kings 14:11; Jer. 7:33); and Deut. 21:22-23 commands that exposure of a criminal's body be limited to the day of execution and be followed by burial. Thus Tobit's burying of exposed bodies is a religious duty like feeding the **hungry** and clothing the **naked** (cf. Isa. 58:7; Ezek. 18:7; Matt. 25:35-36). A few scholars have tried to connect the book's repeated emphasis on proper burial (cf. 2:3-9; 4:3-4, 17; 14:11-13) with some historical situation as a clue to its date, but no proposal has proved convincing. Whether its emphasis on this charity exceeds that of its sources is uncertain.

1:19-20. As in the folklore source (see Intro.) Tobit's good deeds of burying the dead bring him undeserved suffering, which reaches a climax in the following specific incident (2:1-10). The rest of the story then describes the working out of the reward for the burial (cf. 12:12-13), here split between father and son, whose related names symbolize their joint representation of the single folklore hero. Since Tobit's wife and son are later said to be **restored** to him (2:1), **except** (vs. 20) may be a mistranslation of an Aramaic word that in the author's day meant "also"; i.e. Anna and Tobias are taken along with the **property** and presumably enslaved.

1:21-22. *Relationship to Ahikar.* The record of Sennacherib's assassination (vs. 21*ab*) is all but quoted from II Kings 19:37. The story of Ahikar (see Intro.) was quite popular throughout the Near East, not merely in its literary form but as told by the storytellers with many variants. Thus the author could count on his Jewish readers to know about Ahikar yet not question too much his incorporation into the tribe of Naphtali as another Israelite, like Joseph, who made good in a foreign government (see above on 1:13-15). Though there is question about the translation **second to himself** (see RSV footnote), as **keeper of the signet** (cf. Gen. 41:42; see comment on Esth. 3:8-11), able to set the king's seal to any document, Ahikar can exert the royal power over the entire **administration** of the Assyrian Empire.

2:1-6. *Another Unburied Body.* On **restored** see above on 1:19-20. **Pentecost,** from the Greek for "fifty," is the OT feast of weeks (Lev. 23:15-21; Deut. 16:9-11) 50 days or **seven weeks** after passover. This was one of the 3 pilgrimage festivals (Deut. 16:16-17), and according to the Mosaic law Tobit should be celebrating it at the temple in Jerusalem. The lack of any hint that he should be there is probably evidence that the author belonged to the Diaspora rather than Palestinian Judaism. Hospitality was one of the primary virtues of the ancient Near East (cf. e.g. Gen. 18:1-8; Job 31:31-32) and was esp. enjoined at a feast (cf. Deut. 16:11; Neh. 8:10). Tobit demonstrates his piety by sending his son to find a **poor man** as a guest.

2:3-6. So important to Tobit is the religious duty of giving proper burial (see above on 1:16-18, 19-20) that he cannot eat until he has saved the body of an unknown fellow Israelite from possible desecration. **Place of shelter** is lit. "room" and probably refers to Tobit's own house. He must wait until the feast ends at **sunset** because it is a day of rest, like the sabbath. According to the Mosaic law (Num. 5:2; 19:11-13) touching a corpse renders one ritually unclean for a full week, during which he must wash himself on the 3rd and 7th days. That Tobit **washed** himself without such a delay suggests that Jews of the Dispora relaxed the requirement; possibly they had a less stringent rule, like that prescribed for touching the carcass of an animal (Lev. 11:39-40), by which one would wash immediately and remain unclean only until evening. The **food** which Tobit eats after moving the body is not that prepared for the feast, which would be holy and could not be touched by an unclean person (cf. Lev. 7:19-21). The quotation from **Amos** (8:10) has been changed from active to passive, perhaps to avoid ascribing an evil act to God.

2:7-10. *Tobit's Blindness.* Immediately after sunset, which marks the end of the holy day and the beginning of the next day, Tobit hurries to bury the corpse. **Laughed** in the Greek has the sense "derided," which does not fit the context. Probably it represents a Hebrew word which in OT usage had that sense but later under Aramaic influence came to mean "praised." Here it might better be translated "were amazed." In the Sinaiticus recension, which probably represents the original (see Intro.), vs. 9 states that Tobit washed himself again after the burial. He is again **defiled** because of touching the corpse, and presumably will remain so at least until the next sunset (see above on vss. 3-6). Thus he sleeps outdoors to avoid passing his uncleanness on to anything he touches in the house. Vs. 10 is a fantastic explanation for the **films**, i.e. cataracts, on Tobit's **eyes.** According to the Sinaiticus recension they make Tobit completely blind for 4 years and he is supported by **Ahikar** (see above on 1:21-22) for 2 years. **Elymais** is probably a Greek form of Elam, the province E of Babylonia (see color map 10).

2:11-14. *A Family Quarrel.* The Sinaiticus recension indicates that Anna's **women's work** is weaving. In his blindness Tobit is suspicious of what goes on around him without his knowledge and, in spite of his own **charities,** cannot believe the **kid** is a gift. His honesty will not let him eat what he fears has been stolen, even in their dire straits. Anna's natural reaction is all that is needed to bring Tobit to the depths of despair.

3:1-6. *Tobit's Prayer.* In asking God to let death end his **distress** Tobit prays in a typical Jewish pattern; he begins with praise of God's justice and **mercy** and then acknowledges his own **sins** and those of his **fathers,** which have brought deserved punishment (cf. e.g. Ezra 9:6-15; Neh. 1:5-11; 9:6-37; Dan. 9:4-19). The phraseology of vs. 4b is a familiar description of the Exile (cf. e.g. Deut. 4:27; Ps. 44:11; Jer. 9:16; Ezek. 12:15) which might occur to a Palestinian author (cf. e.g. Joel 3:2; Zech. 10:9) as fitting Tobit's situation, but it more probably reflects the viewpoint of an author who is himself among the **dispersed** (cf. Neh. 1:8-9; see Intro.). **For it is better for me to die than to live** (vs. 6b) is an exact quotation from Jonah 4:3, 8, which the author must have expected his readers to recognize.

3:7-15. *Sarah's Prayer.* The parallel prayers of Tobit and Sarah, who **on the same day** are brought to such depths of misery that they ask for death simultaneously (cf. vss. 16-17) and are both saved and brought together by the same train of events, are a skillful bit of literary artistry that helps to explain the popularity of the book. **Ecbatana** (cf. Ezra 6:2; Judith 1:2), the capital of **Media** (see above on 1:13-15), is modern Hamadan, at the N foot of Mt. Elvend in W Iran (see color map 9). The **demon** is in love with Sarah (cf. 6:14) and therefore kills any husband who attempts to consummate his marriage with her. The name **Asmodeus** is thought by some scholars to be derived from that of a Persian evil spirit but is more probably the Greek representation of a Hebrew word meaning "destroyer." Even the **maids,** i.e. slaves, openly accuse Sarah of murdering the husbands herself.

3:10-15. Sarah is reduced to the point of suicide but holds back out of consideration for her family (vs. 10; cf. Gen. 42:38; 44:29, 31). Instead she prays, like Tobit and at the same time, that she may be granted an immediate natural death. Being younger and more hopeful, however, she suggests the alternative of being restored to **respect.** Her reference to marrying a **kinsman or kinsman's son** reflects the author's emphasis on marriage within the family (see comments on 1:5-9; 6:9-12).

3:16-17. *God's Intervention.* In postexilic times the growing sense of God's transcendence inspired frequent use of such expressions as **presence of the glory of the great God** as a means to avoid portraying God in too human terms. The mission of **Raphael . . . to heal** involves a word play in Aramaic or Hebrew, since the name itself means "God heals." In view of the author's literary skill it is somewhat surprising that he detracts from the suspense of his story by summarizing here what is to happen.

II. TOBIAS' JOURNEY TO MEDIA (4:1-6:17)

4:1-21. *Fatherly Counsel.* Taking for granted that his prayer for death will be speedily answered, Tobit is concerned about the support of his widow and son, evidently still in his teens, and recalls his money on deposit in Rages (see above on 1:13-15). Before telling about it, however, he gives his son what may be his final instruction in ethics and morality—the first and longest of the didactic passages in the book. The author uses the occasion as an opportunity to inculcate certain basic principles of Judaism which he holds to be important. In view of Tobit's expectation of death he starts by reemphasizing proper burial. Tobias' **honor** for his mother (cf. 10:12; Exod. 20:12; Prov. 23:22) must include proper burial for her also.

4:5-11. Giving alms to the poor is strongly enjoined in the laws of Deut. (esp. 15:7-11) and in postexilic times grew in esteem as a very meritorious act (cf. Ecclus. 17:22; 29:11-13; 35:2; Matt. 6:2-4) —as it is to this day in Judaism and also Islam. Indeed the word generally translated "righteousness" in the OT came to have the specific meaning "almsgiving." Thus **charity delivers from death** (vs. 10) in the Hebrew was no doubt a verbatim quotation from the similar saying about righteousness in Prov. 10:2b; 11:4b. Other parts of this ch. are reminiscent of sayings in Prov.

4:12-21. The warning against sexual **immorality** sums up a number of passages in Prov. (e.g. 2:16-19; 6:23-29). Vss. 12b-13a reemphasize the importance of marriage within the family (see comments on 1:5-9; 6:9-12). The inclusion of **Noah** as an example is evidently based on one of the legends that were developing about this patriarch in the author's time, for no information about his marriage is given in Gen. On vs. 13b cf. Prov. 16:18; 24:30-34. On vs. 14 cf. Lev. 19:13; Deut. 24:15. Vs. 15a is a negative form of the Golden Rule (cf. Matt. 7:12a; Luke 6:31). A similar saying is attributed to Rabbi Hillel (late first cent. B.C.) and earlier versions are found in the teachings of Confucius and Aristotle. **Place** (vs. 17) is lit. "pour" and in the process of translation into Hebrew an original Aramaic word "wine" in this construction could easily be confused with **bread.** "Pour your wine on the graves of the righteous" is found in Ahikar 2:10. Having concluded his instruction Tobit at last tells his son about the money (vss. 20-21).

5:1-15. *The Employment of Raphael.* The longer Sinaiticus recension (see Intro.) gives fuller details which make this episode somewhat more coherent. Tobias asks (vs. 2) how he can identify himself to the trustee and thus be given the money and also points out that he does not know the way to Media. In his reply (vs. 3) Tobit describes the **receipt,** made 20 years earlier, presumably before Tobias' birth. From legal documents of ca. the same period that have come to light (see comment on Jer. 32:9-14) the description can probably be understood to mean that Tobit and Gabael wrote a statement of the deposit in duplicate on a single sheet, with the signatures of both parties, and then tore it in 2. One half was sealed in the money bags (cf. 9:5) and Tobit took the other, which Tobias can now match with the sealed half to prove it is genuine.

5:4-8. Instead of accosting a stranger with an immediate invitation to accompany him to Rages, Tobias in the Sinaiticus recension strikes up a conversation by inquiring where the stranger comes from and then asks if he knows the way to Media. In reply Raphael speaks of many trips there and mentions, as a credible coincidence, having visited Gabael in Rages. At the end of his speech the Codex Sinaiticus includes a sentence stating the misinformation that Rages is "two days' journey" from Ecbatana (see below on 9:1-6), which lies "in the midst of a plain" (see above on 3:7-15). Since this sentence is not represented in the Old Latin manuscripts, which follow the longer recension (see Intro.), it is probably an interpolation and its geographical errors should not be attributed to the original author. Only after learning this much of the man's qualifications does Tobias propose his acting as a guide.

5:9-15. In the Sinaiticus recension the greetings (vs. 9) include a moving lament by Tobit about his blindness and a reply by Raphael to take courage because his healing is "near to God"—an apparent mere courtesy with deeper meaning for knowing readers. In response to Tobit's question about his **tribe** Raphael in this usually longer recension simply asks why Tobit needs to know. The rebuke (vs. 11a) found in the Vaticanus recension agrees with modern ideas about fair employment practices but not with the author's emphasis on kinship or his por-

trayal of Tobit as the perfect Israelite. The ancient reader would appreciate the name adopted by Raphael—**Azarias,** the Greek form of Azariah (cf. e.g. II Kings 15:1-3; Dan. 1:6-7), meaning "Yahweh helps." **Ananias,** i.e. Hananiah (cf. Dan. 1:6-7), means "Yahweh favors." The **drachma** was the standard monetary unit of the Greek period. It contained ca. the same amount of silver as a Roman denarius, said to be a day's wage for a laborer in NT times (Matt. 20:2). Mention of this coin, if original, would be strong evidence for dating the book in the Greek period, but the translators may have substituted it for some Semitic designation.

5:16-21. *The Departure.* As Tobias and the disguised Raphael prepare to leave, Tobit prays **May his angel attend you**—a pleasing reminder to readers that they know more than he does about the son's companion. The **dog,** though barely mentioned (cf. 11:4), in later times came to be one of the most popular features of the story and was always pictured with Tobias in religious art. Since other biblical references to dogs are all derogatory it has often been said that the ancient Jews did not keep dogs as pets. On the other hand the fact that the dog was unclean for food (Lev. 11:1-8; Deut. 14:3-8) did not prevent, as has sometimes been supposed, its use as a domestic animal, to tend the flocks (cf. Job 30:1) or serve other purposes—cf. e.g. the camel. With dogs around the possibility that a boy like Tobias would make a pet of one can scarcely be ruled out. Nevertheless the dog is probably not a "human touch" but a vestige from a folklore source (see Intro.) where a dog helped the hero slay a dragon. With **goes in and out** (vs. 17) cf. I Sam. 18:16. **Sister** (vs. 20; cf. 7:16; 8:4, 7) is a term of endearment (cf. Song of S. 4:9-12; 5:1).

6:1-17. *The Fish.* Since Nineveh was on the E bank of the **Tigris river** the 2 travelers to Media would not cross the river. Possibly the author thought of their route as along its E side throughout the first day, or had in mind a tributary (see color map 9); but more likely he did not know the exact location of Nineveh, which was not rebuilt after its destruction in 612. The use of 3 organs from the magic fish to accomplish only 2 purposes may be a condensation from a folklore source (see Intro.) where 3 things were accomplished, or perhaps where overcoming the demon required 2 stages. Since **liver** was thought in ancient times to cure night blindness **gall** may have been substituted for an original liver to remove **white films.**

6:9-12. The **law of Moses** which according to Raphael requires the marriage of Tobias and Sarah may be the ruling about the daughters of Zelophehad (Num. 36:6-9) that a woman who will inherit land because she has no brother must marry within her tribe to avoid any intertribal transfer of land. In the Diaspora, where except in large centers the members of a Jewish community would usually be interrelated, this law may have been interpreted as requiring marriage within the kinship group. Possibly the author has in mind also the law of levirate marriage (Deut. 25:5-10; see comment), by which the brother of a man who died childless was obligated to marry the widow and beget a son to be the deceased man's heir. This obligation was extended to other kinsmen in the absence of a brother (cf. Gen. 38; Ruth 4), and in the ancient Jewish view Sarah would be a widow, even though her marriages were not consummated. But the levirate law actually does not fit this case, for it would obligate Tobias as a kinsman of the 7 dead husbands, whereas here it is Raguel who is obligated because of Sarah's relationship to Tobias. There is no law in the OT that would narrow Raguel's choice of a son-in-law to one person, let alone set a **penalty of death** on it. It is not certain that the author is referring to a law known and observed in his own time; he may be hoping his lax Diaspora readers will accept the idea that their ancestors in Tobit's day still followed the example of the patriarchs (cf. 4:12).

6:13-17. Despite the distance the kin in Nineveh and Ecbatana keep in touch, and Tobias has heard of Sarah's jealous demon admirer. Yet Raphael has so won his confidence that he accepts without question the instructions for driving off the demon and is eager to risk becoming his cousin's 8th husband. **Live ashes** no doubt means glowing coals which would cause the fish organs to emit an immediate stench. Along with this procedure derived from a folklore source (see Intro.) Raphael strongly recommends prayer.

III. THE WEDDING OF TOBIAS AND SARAH (7:1-9:6)

7:1-8b. *Arrival at Raguel's House.* Sarah's being the first to meet the visitors is a reminder of the romantic stories of Rebekah, Rachel, and Zipporah (Gen. 24:15-21; 29:9-12; Exod. 2:16-21). **Edna** is a feminine form of Eden, meaning "delight." That Tobias **resembles** his father in appearance as well as in name fits with the joint father-son representation of the folklore hero (see above on 1:19-20). Some of the phraseology in vss. 3-5 is adapted from the story of Rachel (Gen. 29:4-6). **Brother** (vs. 4) is probably not lit. but a term of affection (cf. vs. 8c); presumably Tobit and Raguel are cousins in some degree. Though Tobias has heard of Sarah (6:13-14) Raguel seems to be learning for the first time of Tobias' existence.

7:8c-15. *The Wedding Ceremony.* In ancient Judaism marriage was arranged by the parents; therefore Tobias asks Raphael to act in place of his father in proposing for him. On **in accordance with the law** (vs. 12) see above on 6:9-12. The wedding ceremony consists of Raguel's **taking** Sarah **by the hand** and giving her to Tobias and then blessing the couple. It is accompanied by the writing of a legal **contract** stating the agreed rights of the husband and esp. the wife as well as arrangements about property. Examples of such marriage contracts have been found among Aramaic papyri of the 5th cent. and later. The **seals** were pieces of moist clay attached to the contract, impressed with the respective parties' signets bearing their identifying designs, and allowed to harden. As is abundantly evidenced by archaeological discoveries such seals were commonly used on legal documents and in many kinds of business transactions (e.g. see above on 5:1-15). The verb referring to the sealing is missing from the Codex Sinaiticus and is singular in the Codex Alexandrinus, meaning that only Raguel recorded his assent to the agreement. The plural of the Codex Vaticanus is more likely correct but does not identify

the parties. Normally a marriage contract was sealed or signed by the 2 fathers. Here it is perhaps to be understood that Raphael seals it in place of Tobit (cf. vs. 8c).

7:16-8:4a. *Victory Over the Demon.* The distress of Sarah on entering the bridal chamber, anticipating that Tobias will meet the same fate as her 7 previous husbands, and the comforting by her mother provide a skillful buildup toward the encounter with the demon. The climactic scene, however, in the available versions is rather a letdown, for the action is not described clearly. Obviously 8:4a is displaced, for Tobias must have waited until the **two were alone** before placing the fish organs on the glowing coals. The implication in 8:3 that the demon is already in the room suggests that originally there was a sentence telling of his arrival—perhaps expurgated because it told of his appearing as soon as the couple began to consummate the marriage.

8:3. Defenders of Alexandria as the place where the book was written (see Intro.) have claimed the reference to **Egypt** as evidence supporting their view, on the basis that the author was ridiculing his pagan neighbors for their devotion to magic and divination. To the contrary, however, the specification of the **remotest,** lit. "upper," **parts** shows that the author is thinking of a faraway place near the rim of the world. Because of Egypt's traditional reputation as a land of witchcraft (cf. e.g. Exod. 7:11), as well as a rival at the other end of the Fertile Crescent, he chooses it rather than more recently known E and W extremities. The implication that Raphael can bind the demon only after the **odor** of the scorching fish organs has rendered him impotent reflects the influence of Persian dualism, i.e. the concept of good and evil spiritual powers engaged in cosmic warfare.

8:4b-18. *Prayers of Gratitude.* As Raphael has instructed (6:17), Tobias calls on his bride to join him in prayer. The opening blessing (vs. 5) is the usual invocation in Jewish prayers. Though the Greek of **blessed be thy . . . name** is not identical, it is similar in thought to the opening of the Lord's Prayer (Matt. 6:9). **Like himself** (vs. 6e), instead of "fit for him," in the quotation from Gen. 2:18 (see comment) reflects an interpretation of the same Hebrew phrase found in Gen. 2:20 in the LXX. Whereas Sarah's anticipation that Tobias would be killed aroused sympathy (7:17), now that the demon has been driven away Raguel's spending the night in digging a grave is a delightful touch of comedy. His prayer on discovering the good news, however, is a beautifully characteristic Jewish expression of thanksgiving.

8:19-9:6. *The Wedding Feast.* So joyous is Raguel that his daughter is at length happily married that he plans a feast of **fourteen days,** twice the traditional length for such a celebration (cf. Gen. 29:27; Judg. 14:10-18). No doubt he also shares the desire of Rebekah's family (Gen. 24:55-56; see below on 10:7c-11:1b) to prolong the last days with a daughter leaving for a distant home. His taking an **oath** indicates the seriousness of his insistence on the lengthy feast. Though Tobias would not necessarily be bound by what another man has sworn, the **property** promised him in the oath naturally makes him loath to violate it. Yet as a dutiful son he is much concerned about the effect of the delay on his own parents. In this dilemma he sends Raphael to complete his mission of securing the money at Rages.

9:5-6. According to varying reports of Greek historians Alexander's army took 10 or 11 days of forced marches for the rugged mountain journey from Ecbatana to Rages (see above on 5:4-8 and color map 10). Here the implication is that Raphael, who must travel by human means since he has companionship in both directions, makes the trip each way in a single day. It is evident that the author was unacquainted with the distance and terrain (see Intro.). On the **seals**—presumably lumps of hardened clay enclosing the knots of the cords that tie the **bags** shut—see above on 7:8c-15.

IV. THE RETURN TO NINEVEH (10:1–12:22)

10:1-7b. The Anxious Parents. The poignancy of this scene displays the author's skill in bringing his characters to life. The worried father is **counting each day** and weighing possible explanations for the delay, but the mother dismisses all such calculations and jumps at once to one conclusion, the worst. Yet illogically she keeps watching the **road** for her boy's return. The distress of both is most strikingly revealed in their irritability toward each other (cf. 2:11-14). **Had expired** is lit. "were filled," i.e. "fulfilled" —a Semitic idiom (cf. e.g. Gen. 25:24; II Sam. 7:12). **Detained** (see RSV footnote) is based on the Codex Sinaiticus, which is confirmed by the Old Latin. It fits the context better than "put to shame" of the Codex Vaticanus. The 2 words are similar in Hebrew and might easily be confused.

10:7c-11:1b. Departure from Ecbatana. The action and some of the phrases of this episode follow very closely the account of Rebekah's parting with her family (Gen. 24:54b-60). In accordance with his oath (8:20-21) Raguel gives Tobias, along with his daughter, who is his sole heir (cf. 3:10; 8:17a), **half of his property.** Along with his blessing for both he gives Sarah a final fatherly counsel, extending the injunction of the Decalogue (Exod. 20:12) to her new parents-in-law, who in her new home will become her **parents.** With deeper emotion Edna expresses to Tobias what every mother wants to say to a new son-in-law. On **brother** see above on 5:16-21; 7:1-8b.

11:1c-19. The Healing of Tobit's Blindness. Though passed over quickly, the return journey with wife, slaves, and cattle is necessarily slow (cf. Gen. 33:14). Thus Raphael suggests that he and Tobias **run ahead** to tell the parents of their new daughter-in-law and make preparations. **How you left your father** no doubt refers to Tobit's blindness, for which Raphael has already told Tobias the gall of the fish is efficacious (6:8). The **dog,** said to have left with them (see above on 5:16-21), is now mentioned again at their return (vs. 4) but still plays no part in the story. In the latest Greek recension (see Intro.), however, vs. 6 says that Anna (cf. 10:7) saw the dog running ahead and thus recognized the return of her son—a true "human touch" that would justify the inclusion if it can be considered an original reading that was lost in the other 2 recensions.

11:7-19. Tobias receives hurried instructions about the **gall** from Raphael while his mother is running to him. Having feared her son was dead, the mother

is **ready to die** herself for joy. Tobias then goes on to his blind father and applies the gall to his eyes, whereupon the **white films** are quickly **rubbed** off. When Tobit sees his son again after so many years he characteristically blesses God for his **mercy.** He then goes forth, to the amazement of his neighbors and kinsmen, to greet Sarah at the city **gate.** His acceptance of her is important, for Tobias' marriage to her without his having arranged it was a serious breach of custom. Since he and Anna and his brethren in Nineveh could not participate in the wedding feast in Ecbatana, they hold another feast of the usual **seven days.** On **Ahikar** see Intro. and comment on 1:21-22; on **Nadab** see below on 14:8-12.

12:1-22. Raphael's Departure. In the folklore source (see Intro.) the grateful ghost offers to help the hero who has buried his corpse for a promise of half the treasure they are to gain. In this story the author has told of Tobit's hiring the angel for modest **wages** and an unspecified bonus for a safe journey (5:14-15), but now he lets the father heartily accept Tobias' suggestion that the bonus be **half of what has been brought back.** By the change from his source he emphasizes not only the generosity of father and son but esp. their spirit of gratitude—a virtue he no doubt wishes to teach by the example. He further takes advantage of the narrative situation to put into Raphael's mouth a series of moral and ethical teachings. The passage contains a number of parallels with Prov. and also with the NT.

12:6-10. Before revealing his identity Raphael offers some good counsel. It is right, he says, to **praise God** for his good works **in the presence of all the living,** i.e. publicly, so that others will learn of his goodness. With the practical caution about keeping the **secret of a king** (vs. 7a) cf. sayings in the book of Ahikar: "Cover up the word of a king with the veil of the heart" and "A good vessel covers a word in its heart, but a broken one lets it out." With vs. 7b cf. Prov. 11:27 and contrast Rom. 3:8. The combining of **prayer** with **fasting** and **almsgiving** (vs. 8a) is paralleled in Matt. 6:2-18. **Righteousness** seems out of place in this series and may be a duplication caused by the change of meaning of the Hebrew word to have the specific sense "almsgiving" (see above on 4:5-11). With vs. 8b cf. Prov. 16:8 and with vs. 8c cf. Matt. 6:19-21; Luke 12:33-34; Jas. 5:3. On vs. 9a see above on 4:5-11. With vs. 10 cf. Prov. 8:35-36; Wisd. Sol. 1:12.

12:11-22. With the development in Judaism of the concept of the extreme "otherness" of God came the idea that one of the angelic functions was to bring the prayers of the devout to God's attention. This function was usually esp. attributed to the angel Michael but is here claimed by Raphael also. On Tobit's burials (vss. 12b-13) see above on 1:16-18. The **seven holy angels** (vs. 15) according to Enoch 20:1-8 are Uriel (cf. II Esd. 4:1), Raphael, Raguel, Michael (cf. Dan. 10:13; Jude 9; Rev. 12:7), Sarakael, Gabriel (cf. Dan. 8:16; 9:21; Luke 1:19-26), and Remiel (cf. II Esd. 4:36). With vss. 16, 21 cf. Matt. 17:6, 8. With vs. 19 cf. Luke 24:42-43; John 21:13. With vs. 20a cf. John 20:17. The command to **write in a book** the events of the story reflects the growing tendency in Judaism to emphasize the written word as the revelation of God's will.

V. Epilogue (13:1–14:15)

To modern taste the revelation and disappearance of Raphael bring the story to a satisfying conclusion and the following 2 chs. seem superfluous. Some scholars have therefore viewed them as a later addition. It is true that the ps. of ch. 13 has no relevance to the story and thus may be an interpolation. But to the ancient reader the ending in ch. 14 was a desired assurance that the piety of Tobit and Tobias was duly rewarded by prosperity and long life.

13:1-18. Tobit's Ps. This poem expresses the conventional view that Israel's exile and dispersion are the punishment for her iniquities and that when she turns to God he will gather his scattered people to a gloriously rebuilt Jerusalem to which all nations will come to worship. Jewish theology of the author's time laid considerable stress on the idea that all things come from God—**he afflicts, and he shows mercy** (vs. 2; cf. I Sam. 2:6-8; Wisd. Sol. 16:13). This view is prominent in the literature of the Qumran sect found among the Dead Sea scrolls. The author of the ps., whether or not the author of the book, identifies himself (vss. 3, 6*i*) as one of those scattered in the Diaspora (see Intro.). He addresses readers in like situation (vs. 5; cf. Jer. 29:14) and urges them to **turn** to God (vs. 6*a-d;* cf. Deut. 6:5; 30:2-3). **Turn back** (vs. 6*k*) translates lit. a Semitic verb which may also be translated "repent." The Semitic word underlying **ages** (vs. 10*b*) embodies both temporal and spatial concepts—"ages" and "world." **Tent** (vs. 10*c*) may allude to the tabernacle of the wilderness but more probably refers to the temple. The hope that the **nations** (vs. 11) would come to Jerusalem to worship the God of Israel became a central feature of the thought of Judaism in the postexilic period (cf. e.g. Isa. 2:2-3; 56:6-7; Zech. 14:16-17). On the glory of the rebuilt city (vss. 16-17) cf. Isa. 54:11-12; Rev. 21:18-21.

14:1-15. Tobit's Deathbed Counsel. The statistics in this ch. vary greatly in the different recensions and versions and in any case are not to be taken seriously (see above on 1:3-9). When Tobit is ready to die he calls in Tobias and his grandsons for some final words of advice and a prediction of the future. In place of **Jonah** (vs. 4) the Codex Sinaiticus reads "Nahum," which is more appropriate, since Nah. is vehement in its description of the destruction of Nineveh whereas in Jonah the prophecy of the city's destruction is conditional and is averted by repentance of its citizens. The predicted desolation of **Jerusalem** is its conquest by the Babylonians in 586. The rebuilding of the **house of God,** i.e. the temple, **not . . . like the former one** refers to the 2nd temple completed in 515. The **glorious building** is to be in the age to come, when the **Gentiles** will worship the God of Israel (cf. 13:11).

14:8-15. Along with the advice to **leave Nineveh** in anticipation of its destruction Tobit gives some moral counsel illustrated by the examples of **Ahikar** (see Intro. and comment on 1:21-22) and **Nadab,** probably a scribal error for Nadin. In the book of Ahikar the hero adopts his nephew Nadin and persuades the king to appoint the young man in his own place. Nadin plots against his foster father and gets him banished but later is duly punished while Ahikar is restored to favor. The **destruction of Nineveh** was accomplished by Nabopolassar, the father of **Nebuchadnezzar,** and Cyaxares the Mede in 612. **Ahasuerus,** i.e. Xerxes I (see comment on Esth. 1:1), came to the throne of Persia in 486.

THE BOOK OF JUDITH

H. Neil Richardson

INTRODUCTION

This book of the OT Apoc. is a fictional account of a victory of the Jews thanks to the intervention of a woman named Judith who slays the leader of the opposing army. In some respects it resembles Esth., in that both glory in the ruthless destruction of an enemy accomplished by the hand of a beautiful woman.

The Story and Its Literary Character. Having won a great victory in the E, Nebuchadnezzar sends his general Holofernes to punish the W nations that refused to join him in the war. Holofernes and his formidable army conquer one after another and at length begin the attack on the Jews by besieging a fortified city called Bethulia. After more than a month the citizens are in such dire straits from hunger and thirst that they demand that their leader surrender.

At this point (ch. 8) Judith, a beautiful, wealthy, and pious widow, enters the story. She upbraids the people for not trusting in God and promises that with his help she will deliver Bethulia. Making "herself very beautiful, to entice the eyes of all men who might see her" (10:4), she takes a servant girl with her and goes out to the enemy camp. Holofernes is immediately overwhelmed by her beauty and accepts her promise to inform him when the besieged Bethulians forfeit their divine protection by eating the first fruits and tithes set aside for the temple. He invites her to an intimate banquet, at which he drinks too much wine and falls into a drunken sleep. Judith then beheads him with his own sword.

Putting the head in a bag Judith and her maid leave the camp, ostensibly for prayer, and go to Bethulia with the announcement that God has struck down Holofernes by the hand of a woman. When the enemy soldiers discover that their general is dead they rush off in disorganized flight with the Jews in hot pursuit. Thus Israel wins the victory. The book closes with Judith's song of thanksgiving and the report that throughout her long life and for many years thereafter Israel had peace.

The book is an excellent example of an ancient short story. The characters are well drawn and the plot moves forward with originality and imagination. In spite of the bombastic style, which is typical of Jewish and also Greek literature of the period, and the late introduction of the heroine, nearly halfway through the story, those who come to the book for the first time find it a fascinating story.

Historicity. Few scholars today doubt the fictional character of Judith. Its distortions of history and geography are so many and glaring that they cannot be mere incidental errors in a report of actual events. E.g. the opening verse declares that Nebuchadnezzar "ruled over the Assyrians" whereas he was well known as a Babylonian ruler in power after the Assyrian Empire came to an end. His rival in the E, "Arphaxad," is said to have ruled from the fortification of Ecbatana as capital of Media (*ca.* 700; 1:1-4) till its capture (550; 1:14). Holofernes moves his huge army from Nineveh to "Upper Cilicia" in Asia Minor, *ca.* 400 miles, in 3 days (2:21). Much of the book's Palestinian geography comes from the mind of the author. Many of the localities have fictitious names and cannot be identified; even Bethulia is unknown, though its description suggests Shechem (see below on 6:10-21; 7:1-32). So incredible are some of the "errors"—so contradictory to OT records which were well known to the ancient readers—that it is evident the author never intended his book should be viewed as history.

It is not impossible that the story has some historical basis. With different names and elimination of exaggerations chs. 1–3 might describe an actual invasion of Syria and Palestine by an E army. Of the several possibilities that have been proposed the most likely is a campaign of Artaxerxes III Ochus (358-338) in which a general named Orophernes and a subordinate named Bagoas (cf. 12:11) participated. The poem in 16:2-17 may well be older than the rest of the book and commemorate an actual deed of valor by a Jewish woman (cf. Judg. 4:17-22; 5:24-27). Whatever historical sources the author used, however, most of his book is obviously pure invention.

Date of Composition. Theories about the date of the book have ranged all the way from the 7th cent. B.C. to the 2nd cent. A.D., with proponents for nearly every cent. in between. The period on which most scholars now agree is the 2nd cent. B.C.—specifically *ca.* 150, during the latter part of the struggle for religious and political freedom described in I Macc. The statement that Holofernes "demolished all their shrines and cut down their sacred groves" (3:8) can hardly allude to anything except the attempt of the Seleucid monarch Antiochus IV (175-163; cf. I Macc. 1:10–6:17; II Macc. 4:7–10:9) to force the Jews to adapt their religion to Greek culture; and the reference to Nebuchadnezzar as "god" (cf. 6:2) must reflect the claim to divinity in his surname

"Epiphanes," meaning "manifested one." The pietism of Judith is clearly that of the 2nd-cent. Hasidean movement with its strict observance of the law. The avoidance of fasting on the eve of the festivals (8:6) is an example of the developing Pharisaic oral law during this period.

Language and Place of Origin. Though the earliest extant text is in Greek there is wide agreement that the book was composed originally in Hebrew. The Greek text regularly reproduces Hebrew syntax and idiomatic expressions, and some difficult expressions are best explained by assuming an erroneous translation of the Hebrew. Use of the LXX in the OT quotations in the extant text may be attributed to the translator's familiarity with that version. Jerome refers to an Aramaic text, but this was undoubtedly a translation from the Greek, as are later Hebrew versions.

The use of Hebrew points strongly to Palestine as the place where the book was written, and other evidence supports this locale. The references to political administration both of the Jews as a whole and of the citizens of Bethulia reflect intimate knowledge of the governmental structure of Judea in Maccabean times. The precise observance of the Mosaic law and of its extensions in the oral law which the book demands was practicable only within the range of frequent pilgrimages to Jerusalem.

Purpose and Value. Amid the difficult times of the continuing Maccabean struggle for religious and political independence from the Seleucid Empire many Jews yielded to the pressure to compromise and adopt Greek ways. Others reacted by a stricter dedication to the institutions and practices of Judaism. To this latter group belonged the author of Judith. By his book he sought to encourage his countrymen to stand fast against the onslaught of Greek culture and pagan religion and remain loyal in the practice of God's ritual ordinances. He may well have been a member of the Hasideans (cf. I Macc. 2:42; 7:13; II Macc. 14:6), a party zealous for the law that supported Judas Maccabeus in the revolt but later broke with his successors when they showed more concern for political than for religious goals. The Hasideans were probably the forerunners of both the Essenes and the Pharisees, but the author of Judith shared neither the Essene philosophy of retreat to the wilderness nor the pacificism of some of the Pharisees. Rather he believed in fighting the enemy with every available means and expecting God to give the victory.

Though not accepted as scripture by the Jews, the book found a place in the LXX, which became the Christian OT. There it remains in the Roman Catholic Bible, though placed by the Protestant reformers in the Apoc. Over the cents. it has been quite popular with many, and its heroine is often pictured in religious art. On the other hand many, even in early times, have criticized its underlying moral principle that the end justifies the means. Though Judith is motivated by the noble aim of saving her people, she uses deceit, enticement to lust, and murder to accomplish it, praying all the while for God's blessing on her acts. The moral dilemma posed by her story has provoked much discussion.

In addition to its main point the book in numerous didactic passages seeks to inculcate the essentials of ritualistic Judaism. It stresses the power and justice of God and his concern with the affairs of men. Though it is not certain whether the author believed in an afterlife of reward or punishment (see below on 16:17) he was strongly convinced of the urgency of obedience to God's will.

For Further Study. A. E. Cowley in R. H. Charles, ed., *The Apoc. and Pseudepigrapha of the OT*, 1913. R. H. Pfeiffer, *History of NT Times, with an Intro. to the Apoc.*, 1949, pp. 285-303. Paul Winter in *IDB*, 1962.

I. Holofernes' Conquest of the W Nations (1:1–3:8)

1:1-6. Nebuchadnezzar's War on Arphaxad. The Jews for whom this book was written regularly heard the oft-repeated phrase "Nebuchadnezzar king of Babylon" from II Kings, Jer., and Ezek. read in their synagogues. Thus an opening sentence calling Nebuchadnezzar (605-562) the ruler of the **Assyrians** in **Nineveh**—destroyed in 612 by his father in alliance with Cyaxares, king of the **Medes**—would give them immediate notice that what follows is not sober history but an amusing tale, possibly disguising commentary on contemporary events (see Intro.). Insofar as Nebuchadnezzar is intended to symbolize a contemporary persecutor of the Jews, he may represent both Antiochus Epiphanes as initiator of the effort to stamp out Judaism and his nephew Demetrius I (162-150; cf. I Macc. 7:1–10:50; II Macc. 14:1–15:36), who may have been the Seleucid overlord when the author wrote.

1:1b-4. The homeland of the **Medes** was the mountainous region E of Assyria (see color map 12).

Courtesy of the Oriental Institute, University of Chicago

Median nobles from the ruins of a stairway at Persepolis (see ills., p. 603)

The list of their kings known from historical sources includes no **Arphaxad.** The name is the LXX form of Arpachshad, which the author probably derived from Gen. 10:22, 24; 11:10-13 simply because it struck his fancy—cf. **Arioch** (vs. 6). **Ecbatana,** modern Hamadan, Iran (see comment on Tobit 3:7-15), according to the Greek historian Herodotus was built and made the capital of Media by Deioces *ca.* 700. Since **cubits** were *ca.* 1½ feet the dimensions of the fortifications here are greatly exaggerated.

1:5-6. OT predictions of **war** between Nebuchadnezzar and the Medes (Isa. 13:17-22; Jer. 51:11, 28,

34) were never fulfilled. **Ragae** (Rages; see comment on Tobit 1:13-15) was in the E part of Media, the far side from Nebuchadnezzar's empire. **Hydaspes,** Greek name of the Jhelum River in W Pakistan, may be a scribal error for Choaspes, i.e. the Karkheh, chief river of Elam, the region E of Babylonia, which was mountainous rather than a **plain.** There is no mention elsewhere of a king of the **Elymaeans,** i.e. Elamites, named **Arioch** (cf. Gen. 14:1, 9; see above on vss. 1b-4). The **Chaldeans,** originally from S Babylonia, were the people of Nebuchadnezzar; here they seem to be an "error" for the "Assyrians."

1:7-11. *The Call for Allies.* The W nations summoned to aid in the attack on Media include all those around the E end of the Mediterranean, from **Cilicia** in SE Asia Minor to **Egypt** and **Ethiopia** in NE Africa. **Lebanon** and **Antilebanon** are mountain ranges W of **Damascus.** The **Plain of Esdraelon** is the wide valley of the Kishon River N of Mt. **Carmel** between **Galilee** and **Samaria,** and **Gilead** is N Transjordan. **Chelous** (cf. 2:23), not mentioned elsewhere in scripture, was probably a town in S Palestine. **Kadesh** is the oasis of Kadesh-barnea farther S; and **river of Egypt** probably refers, not to the Nile, but to the Brook of Egypt in N Sinai (see color map 4). Scripture rather than current usage evidently supplied the Egyptian place names: **Tahpanhes** (cf. e.g. Jer. 43:5-13), **Raamses** (see comment on Exod. 1:11), **Goshen** (cf. e.g. Gen. 47:27), **Tanis,** LXX equivalent of Zoan, probably the later name for Raamses (cf. e.g. Isa. 30:11), and **Memphis** (cf. e.g. Hos. 9:6). As an adversary of the people of God, Nebuchadnezzar is "only a man" (see RSV footnote)—a denial perhaps aimed specifically at claims to divinity by the Seleucid rulers (see Intro.).

1:12-16. *The Victory over Arphaxad.* Vs. 12 describes again the **territory** of the W nations in somewhat different terms. **Moab** was the land E of the Dead Sea, and **Ammon** was just across the Jordan from Judea (see color map 11). Historically the Median kings Cyaxares (*ca.* 625-585) and his son Astyages (*ca.* 585-550) conquered an extensive empire extending W into Asia Minor along the N border of Nebuchadnezzar's Babylonian Empire. **Ecbatana** was **captured** only after Nebuchadnezzar's death, by Cyrus the Persian (550), who took control of the Median Empire and later took Babylon (539) and the Babylonian Empire to create the huge Persian Empire. **To this day** (vs. 15) is a common OT phrase applied to evidence surviving from the past, but it scarcely fits a person's death; perhaps it originally read "on that day." Though **one hundred and twenty days** is an obvious exaggeration (cf. Esth. 1:3-4), prolonged and lavish feasts are known to have occurred among ancient peoples.

2:1-20. *The Commissioning of Holofernes.* Nebuchadnezzar now turns to fulfilling his vow of revenge on the W nations that refused his summons to aid in the fight against the Medes (cf. 1:12). Vs. 2b in the Greek reads lit.: "and he finished the afflicting of all the earth out of his mouth." The RSV reconstruction is based on the assumption that the Greek translator confused 2 similar Hebrew verbs, "finished" and "revealed," and thus misunderstood the entire clause. The name **Holofernes** is Persian in form and may be a corruption of Orophernes, a

general sent against Egypt by Artaxerxes III *ca.* 350 (see Intro.).

2:5-13. This grandiose speech is typical of the author's baroque style (cf. 6:2-9; 8:11-27). The **number** of troops is probably an exaggeration in keeping with the fictional character of the work. But **thousand** may translate a Hebrew technical term designating a division of the army rather than a number. The Persian kings required gifts of **earth and water** as symbols of surrender. **Your eye** as a figure for "you" is a Hebrew idiom.

2:14-20. The logistical details serve to emphasize the might of Holofernes' army. At the same time they call attention to the impracticability of moving such a large force without modern facilities. The **mixed crowd** (vs. 20) refers to the camp followers who have always accompanied armies wherever they went.

2:21-3:8. *Holofernes' Conquests.* On the march **from Nineveh to . . . Cilicia** in **three days** see Intro. The geography of Holofernes' movements seems confused. **Bectileth,** otherwise unknown, is described as in the interior of Asia Minor. There too the author seems to locate **Put and Lud.** In the OT they are generally associated with Egypt (cf. e.g. Jer. 46:9) and therefore were probably in N Africa, though some scholars take Lud to mean Lydia in Asia Minor and attribute the association to the use of Lydian mercenaries in the Egyptian army at the battle of Carchemish in 605. **Rassis** is unknown, but the **Ishmaelites** were well known from olden times as living **south** of Palestine (on **Chelleans** see above on 1:7-11). **Mesopotamia** here refers to the NW part, along the upper **Euphrates.** The brook **Abron** is unknown. The reference to **Japheth** (cf. Gen. 10:1-5) is uncertain, and the **Midianites** are another archaism (cf. Judg. 6-8). In spite of these contradictory details, however, the general picture is one of conquest and pillage from Cilicia as far S as **Damascus.** Possibly the "errors" reveal, not the author's geographical ignorance, but his cleverness in combining OT allusions with hints his original readers would recognize and chortle over—Syrian enemies described as victims of aggression. The **wheat harvest,** in early June, dates the sack of the Damascus area *ca.* 6 weeks after Nebuchadnezzar's order (vs. 1)—truly a lightning campaign (cf. vs. 21).

2:28-3:8. On hearing of the S-ward advance of Holofernes' army the non-Jewish peoples on the **seacoast** (see color map 11) hurry to surrender unconditionally. In the N **Sidon and Tyre** were famous Phoenician cities. **Sur and Ocina** are unknown but may be corruptions of Dor and Acco. **Jamnia** was W of Jerusalem. **Azotus and Ascalon** are the Greek forms of Ashdod and Ashkelon, Philistine cities further S.

3:8. Though there was no mention of religion in Holofernes' commission (2:5-13) he is now described as attacking the **gods** of the various peoples and demanding that they **worship Nebuchadnezzar only** (cf. Dan. 3; 6). On the possibility that this may be a veiled allusion to the religious persecution and claim to divinity of Antiochus Epiphanes see Intro.

II. THE ATTACK ON THE JEWS (3:9-7:32)

3:9-4:15. *Judean Preparations for Defense.* In contrast to the speed with which Holofernes has subjugated all the other W nations he now pauses for **a whole month** to prepare for the invasion of Judea. The wait not only allows time for the Jews to prepare to resist but also serves the literary purpose of building up suspense. Strangely the author views the N boundary of Judea as the **edge of Esdraelon** (see above on 1:7-11), thus including most of **Samaria** (4:4), an area not ruled from Jerusalem since the time of Solomon—unless perhaps briefly under Josiah (cf. II Kings 23:15-20)—until it was conquered by John Hyrcanus *ca.* 109. That the book was not written so late as that, however, is shown by the reference to the coastal cities as outside Judea (2:28). This area is assumed to be inhabited entirely by Jews, with no mention of the Samaritans. No satisfactory explanation has yet been found.

Dothan was an ancient city a short distance S of Esdraelon (cf. Gen. 37:17; II Kings 6:13; see color map 8). **Ridge** in the Greek means lit. a "saw"; per-

Courtesy of Herbert G. May

Site of Dothan (Tell Dotha); the mound stands *ca.* 175 feet above the Dothan Plain (see ill., p. 26)

haps it refers to the central highland beginning just S of Dothan, or perhaps it is a textual corruption. **Geba** is probably not the OT city *ca.* 6 miles N of Jerusalem but a town near Dothan. **Scythopolis** was the Greek name of Bethshan (cf. I Sam. 31:10-12) in the Jordan Valley *ca.* 16 miles S of the Sea of Galilee.

4:3. Perhaps the most flagrant historical distortion in the book is the statement that the Jews **had only recently returned from the captivity,** whereas at the date specified (cf. 2:1, 27; 3:10) Nebuchadnezzar was about to exile more of them (cf. II Kings 25:8; Jer. 52:12, 29; see "Chronology," pp. 1271-82). On the other hand the reference to the **temple** and its equipment as being **consecrated after their profanation** clearly alludes to the reconsecration of the temple by Judas Maccabeus 3 years after its desecration by Antiochus Epiphanes (cf. I Macc. 4:36-58; II Macc. 10:1-8). Though Antiochus died soon after (cf. I Macc. 6:1-16), if not before (cf. II Macc. 9:1-29), this event, his successors continued the effort to stamp out Judaism until the time when the book was presumably written.

4:4-7. Of the towns named in vss. 4, 6, all of which are apparently expected to defend the **passes up into the hills,** only **Beth-horon** on the W and **Jericho** on the E can be definitely identified. There is no hint as yet that **Bethulia** (see below on 7:10-21) is to be the scene of much of the story. **Joakim,**

in the Hebrew probably Joiakim, is no doubt to be understood as the son and successor of Jeshua, or Joshua, the high priest under whom the temple was rebuilt after the return from the Babylonian exile (cf. Ezra 3; Neh. 12:10, 12, 26; Hag. 1:1-2). Under the successive empires in postexilic times Judea was ruled by governors who were usually foreigners, and the high priest came to be the political as well as religious leader among the Jews themselves. Thus when Jonathan the Maccabee as leader of the struggle for independence became high priest (152) he virtually became a claimant to kingship of Judea, and in fact some of his successors in the high priesthood took the title of king. The portrayal here as chief military commander of the nation may reflect Jonathan's status.

4:8. The word **senate,** derived from the Latin, translates a Greek word of corresponding meaning, viz. a body of elders. Here it refers to the supreme council of the Jews, later known as the sanhedrin, with judicial and legislative functions, which was composed of priests, scribes, and heads of aristocratic families. There is no evidence that such a body existed before the middle of the 3rd cent., and certainly it did not play such an important role as it does here until Maccabean times.

4:9-15. The practices here described were the regular mourning rites of Judaism and indeed of the entire ancient Near East from very early times, as evidenced by Egyptian tomb paintings. Such rites would be observed not only for the death of an individual but in time of national calamity to support prayers for divine pity. On the participation of the **cattle** (vs. 10) cf. Jonah 3:8. Worshipers of Baal annually observed mourning rites for the death of their deity at the beginning of the dry season. No doubt it was in reaction to such pagan practices that Lev. 21:1-12 greatly restricts mourning by priests and absolutely forbids any show of mourning by the high priest, even for his closest relatives. It seems doubtful, therefore, that Jewish priests would ever approach the **altar** with **sackcloth** and **ashes** as here described.

5:1-21. Achior's History of the Jews. Though neither conquest nor surrender of **Moab** and **Ammon** (see above on 1:12-16) has been reported, presumably they are to be understood as having come over to Holofernes along with the people of the **coastland** (cf. 2:28-3:7). Foreign to the area, Holofernes thinks of them all as **Canaanites,** i.e. dwellers in the land of Canaan. His lumping them together is to some extent justified, for the Moabites and Ammonites, like the Israelites, shared in some aspects of Canaanite culture. Esp. their languages, like Hebrew, were dialects of the Canaanite language. Historically Moabites and Ammonites aided Nebuchadnezzar by attacks on the Jews (II Kings 24:2).

5:5-21. Since the Hebrew letters *d* and *r* are easily confused, it has been suggested that the original of the name **Achior** may have been Ahiud, meaning "brother [or "friend"] of Judah." Vss. 6-9*a* refer to the migration of Abraham and reflect the tradition that he came originally from Ur of the **Chaldeans** on the lower Euphrates River (cf. e.g. Gen. 11:27-28). Another tradition connects him with Haran in NW **Mesopotamia** (cf. e.g. Gen. 11:31-32). Vss. 10-14 summarize the descent of Joseph and his brothers into **Egypt,** the exodus under Moses, and the wanderings in the **wilderness.** Vs. 15*a* refers to the conquest of Transjordan (cf. Num. 21:21-35) and vss. 15*b*-16 to the conquest of W Palestine. To the conventional list of peoples driven out by Israel (cf. e.g. Josh. 3:10) are here added the **Shechemites** —probably an allusion to the Samaritans (see above on 3:9-4:15). Vs. 17 is a succinct statement of the Deuteronomic view of history—expressed throughout not only Deut. but also the editorial comments of Josh., Judg., Sam., Kings—which explained the Babylonian exile as punishment for sin (vs. 18) and the return as a result of repentance (vs. 19). The success of the Jews in their resistance to Holofernes and, as the author no doubt wishes to imply, in the Maccabean struggle will depend on whether or not they **sin against their God.**

5:22-6:21. Achior's Punishment. In portraying the reaction to Achior's speech the author shows considerable literary craftsmanship. All the Assyrian **officers** and the allies present except Achior's own countrymen demand his **death.** Holofernes himself angrily denounces him and his fellow Ammonites as **hirelings of Ephraim**—the name of the chief N tribe, sometimes used for Israel as a whole (cf. e.g. Hos. 11:3)—implying that they have been bribed by the Jews. Yet the general is astute enough to see that merely executing the speaker will not refute the speech and restore the morale of his troops, esp. that of the new allies, whose only motivation is fear of the divine invincibility of **Nebuchadnezzar** (see above on 3:8). Therefore he devises a way to show his disdain for the warning and counteract whatever doubts it has raised—delivery of Achior to the Jews so that he may **perish along with them** and thus discover the falsity of his claim. At the same time the very vehemence of the commander's denunciation suggests that he himself has been impressed. Thus the author prepares us to be convinced when later (ch. 11) Holofernes takes seriously Judith's promise to tell him when the Jews forfeit their divine protection.

6:10-21. The place chosen for Achior to be taken is **Bethulia.** The description of its situation (vss. 11-13) and the mention that **Uzziah,** the chief of its 3 **magistrates,** is **of the tribe of Simeon** (see below on 9:2-4), as well as some further clues (see below on 7:1-32), suggest that Bethulia is a pseudonym for Shechem (see color map 11), which in the author's day was the principal city of the Samaritans rather than a home of Jews (see above on 3:9-4:15). The Bethulians bring Achior before their local **assembly** for a report. After he tells his story he is **praised** and feasted while the people renew their prayers for God's **help.**

7:1-32. The Siege of Bethulia. As Holofernes brings his troops toward Bethulia their number seems to have grown by 50,000 (cf. 2:5, 15); if the increase is not a textual error, as suggested by 120,000 in the Vulg., it may be that the allies from Moab, Ammon, and the coastland (cf. 3:6; 5:2) make up the difference. Whether **Balbaim** and **Cyamon** represent real places or not, they point up the immense size of the army. The **people of Esau** (vs. 8) are the Idumeans, descendants of the ancient Edomites (cf. Gen. 36:1), who in postexilic times inhabited the territory immediately S of Judea. The advice they and others

offer to Holofernes would be unnecessary to an experienced general since cutting off the source of **water** was the usual method of attacking a walled city. It was in precisely this manner that Samaria was captured by the Assyrians in 722. There is some evidence for identifying the places named in vs. 18*b* with sites near Shechem (see above on 6:10-21).

7:19-32. The suffering from lack of water, described in vss. 20-22, causes the citizens to urge surrender. Vs. 28 states the ancient belief of Israel, reflected often in the OT, that punishment of individual faults results in collective punishment. Uzziah promises to capitulate if God has not given them help in **five more days.**

III. JUDITH'S PREPARATIONS (8:1-10:10)

8:1-8. Intro. of Judith. The heroine of the story now makes her belated entrance. Her name **Judith** is the feminine form of Judah or Judas and may be intended to suggest a counterpart to Judas Maccabeus. Though the only Judith mentioned in the OT was a foreign woman (Gen. 26:34) the name in the author's day meant "Jewess" and thus would symbolize the nation personified (cf. ch. 16, esp. vss. 2-5). Perhaps Judith was a well-known legendary figure before this book was written.

8:1b. Most of the names in Judith's fictional genealogy are taken from the OT, and probably in the original Hebrew all of them were so derived. Only the last 3, however, represent the OT personages named; **Salamiel, son of Sarasadai** is the Greek form of "Shelumiel the son of Zurishaddai" (Num. 1:6), leader of the tribe of Simeon during the wilderness wandering, and **Israel** is of course Jacob. Simeon belongs in the list as Judith's tribal ancestor (cf. 9:2) and may have been originally included; on the other hand the author may have chosen to omit him because the OT nowhere reveals from which of his sons (Gen. 46:10; I Chr. 4:24) Zurishaddai was descended. The naming of some of the ancestors after such famous persons as **Joseph . . . Gideon . . . Elijah** suggests that Judith has some of the characteristics of these heroes.

8:2-4. Judith is a **widow.** The account of her husband's **overseeing** workers in the **barley harvest** likens him to Boaz (cf. Ruth 2; II Kings 4:18-20). His name **Manasseh,** that of the largest of the N tribes, may be intended to symbolize Judah's widowhood since the fall of the N kingdom, or possibly it alludes to the location of Bethulia in Manassite territory (see above on 3:9-4:15). **Balamon** has the same consonants as Belmain (4:4) and thus may represent the same Hebrew name, but the place it designates is uncertain.

8:5-8. The description of Judith's punctilious and prolonged observance of mourning rites serves to establish her pious character. This account provides authentic insights into such practices as they were promulgated at the beginning of the Pharisaic movement. The observance of the **day before the sabbath** and before other special days is not mentioned in the written law and shows the development of the oral law of which the Pharisees were such strong proponents. Judith's beauty and wealth make her an appealing romantic figure capable of promoting the author's ideals of piety.

8:9-36. *Rebuke of the Elders.* The reader should not jump to the conclusion that it is Judith's wealth that enables her to **summon** Bethulia's 3 **elders**—obviously **Uzziah** was originally included in vs. 10 (see RSV footnote) since he is later the spokesman (vss. 28-31, 35)—and upbraid them for their governance in the crisis while they meekly listen and then apologize. Apparently the author has in mind rather her reputation for **wisdom** (vs. 29) as the basis for her privilege. Since he puts into her mouth the chief lesson he wants to teach, her criticisms of the **ruler** must be accepted as right and undeniable whereas those of her fellow citizens are **wicked words.**

8:11*b*-27. Judith's view is that by their promise to **surrender** unless God acts **within so many days** the elders are trying to **put God to the test** (cf. Deut. 6:16), to hand him an ultimatum. But **God is not like man** (vs. 16; cf. Num. 23:19) and cannot be **threatened** into changing his plans. Unlike their ancestors, who suffered a **catastrophe,** i.e. the Babylonian exile, because of their apostasy (see above on 5:5-21), the Jews now are free from idolatry and can have confidence that God will not forsake them —a relevant and important message during the Maccabean conflict. All Judea is depending on the Bethulians to ward off the attack and save the **temple.** God is thus **putting** them **to the test,** as he did the patriarchs (cf. Gen. 22:1-14; 29:15-30)— **Mesopotamia in Syria** means the NW part of Mesopotamia, inhabited by Syrians, i.e. Arameans. His purpose is not **revenge** but education.

8:28-36. Uzziah admits the truth of Judith's statement but explains that he was **compelled** by the people and that he must keep his promise. The only hope he can see is a **rain** to relieve the water shortage. Judith, however, declares she will take action herself, and the **rulers** humbly give her their blessing without knowing what she will do.

9:1-14. *Judith's Prayer.* The mourning rites are intended to reinforce Judith's plea for divine aid in her undertaking. It is a typical prayer of the time, appealing to God by recalling his past deeds and by extolling his virtues (cf. esp. vs. 11). The tribe of **Simeon** was allotted territory in the S within that of Judah (Josh. 19:1-9), and apparently it was absorbed into Judah in early times. Here, however, Judith and Uzziah (6:15), and perhaps the whole population of Bethulia, are Simeonites living in the N. The explanation may lie in the allusion to the sack of Shechem by Simeon and Levi to avenge the rape of Dinah (vss. 2-4; cf. Gen. 34). Whereas in the ancient story Jacob criticized their action (Gen. 34: 30) Judith praises it in all its ruthlessness. If Bethulia represents Shechem an aspect of the relation between Jews and Samaritans is undoubtedly symbolized here, but the meaning is uncertain (see above on 3:9-4:15).

9:5-14. God determines the course of all events, and so Judith implores his aid against the attackers whose ultimate aim is to **defile** his **sanctuary**—no doubt an allusion to Antiochus Epiphanes' setting up a pagan altar in the temple in Jerusalem (I Macc. 1:54, 59; II Macc. 6:1-5; cf. Dan. 9:27; 11:31; 12:11). **Deceit of my lips,** lit. "my lips of deceit," is a typical Hebrew expression. Many have decried the morality of Judith's prayer for blessing on a deceit, but others have justified her course as the only

means of defense for herself and her people against a pitiless aggressor and claimed that in such a situation she is acting as God's agent and has his blessing. Certainly her invocation of God as the **helper of the oppressed** is in line with prophetic theology, and his doing so by means of war and violence is the usual OT portrayal. So here as elsewhere the author follows the principle that the end justifies the means.

10:1-10. *Judith's Departure from the City.* Lying **prostrate** full length on the ground is a characteristic posture for prayer among both ancient and modern Semites. Though if the people of Bethulia could have foreseen the outcome they would no doubt have gladly contributed their scanty supply of drinking **water** to provide a bath for Judith, the author's mentioning it without explanation suggests that he forgot this detail of the situation. Vss. 3-4 provide an interesting picture of how ancient Jewish women adorned themselves (cf. Isa. 3:16-23). Judith is also concerned about taking along food and esp. **vessels**—bowls, plates, cups, and other utensils for cooking and eating—so that she may continue her pious observance of the law by eating only "clean" (*kosher*) food while in the enemy camp. Thus prepared she and her servant girl go to the **gate** and are let out with the blessing of the 3 **elders.**

10:11-23. *Into Enemy Custody.* Judith and her maid are soon found by an **Assyrian patrol** and identify themselves as **Hebrews**—the term for Israelites generally used by outsiders in the early books of the OT (see comment on Gen. 14:13). Fugitives volunteering information would in any case be given careful treatment and interrogation, but such is Judith's beauty that she is accorded an escort of a **hundred men** and taken directly to the commander's **tent.** Its **bed,** with posts (cf. 13:6-9) supporting a richly ornamented **canopy,** i.e. net to keep out insects, is true to life, as confirmed by other literature and contemporary art.

11:1-12:9. *The Meeting with Holofernes.* The general greets his beautiful captive with courteous assurance of her **safety,** to which Judith replies with conventional flattery. Then she reminds him of what **Achior** said and confirms it as **true,** that the Jews can be overcome only if they **sin.** Now, she says, they are about to do so, and for this reason she has **fled** from them. In her explanation of the laws of Judaism which are about to be broken the author emphasizes the importance of their strict observance, esp. the **first fruits** (cf. e.g. Exod. 23:16; Lev. 23:15-22; Deut. 16:9-12) and **tithes** (cf. e.g. Lev. 27:30-31; Deut. 14:22-29) due the **priests . . . at Jerusalem.** Judith promises to tell when the Bethulians break these laws and thus become powerless to oppose an advance on Jerusalem. To do so she must leave the camp **every night** for prayer—a practice she must establish to make possible her later escape. Beguiled by her **beauty,** Holofernes is too easily convinced of her **wisdom** on his behalf. When he offers her **some of his own food** she insists that she must eat only what she has brought and promises with double meaning that God will act before her **supply runs out.** The need for her food bag, like her habit of going out each night for prayer and bathing—i.e. ritual ablution to remove the defilement of her contacts in the pagan camp—prepares the way for her escape and at the same time emphasizes her piety.

12:10-13:10a. Holofernes' Banquet. The wait till the **fourth day** for further meeting with Holofernes provides Judith and her maid the needed time to accustom the Assyrian **guards** to their pattern of religious rites involving nightly trips outside the camp carrying their food bag. No doubt the author intends that Holofernes' delay is to be understood as not merely fortuitous but an answer to Judith's prayer, to protect her virtue if not her life. Now that the stage is set she can accept with **joy**—in which the reader of course sees the deeper meaning—the invitation to an intimate dinner with Holofernes brought by **Bagoas** (see Intro.).

12:16-20. Holofernes is quite overwhelmed by both Judith's charms and her elation over being in his company, which of course has a different basis than he supposes. So smitten is he that he is not bothered by her refraining from all except her own food and drink; in fact the effect is to make him drink the more. **Since I was born . . . since he was born** points up the contrast of the 2 characters.

13:1-10a. Perhaps the author might have achieved more suspense in his climactic scene if Holofernes were not already **overcome with wine** by the time the **attendants** leave the 2 **alone.** His emphasis, however, is less on an exciting story than on Judith's trust in God, to whom she dramatically prays for **strength** to perform the assassination—a plea that strongly points up the moral problem of the book (see above on 9:5-14). After the decapitation Judith takes the **canopy** (see above on 10:11-23) to prove the identity of the **head** (cf. vs. 15), which she hands to the **maid** to put into the **food bag.** This scene was popular with medieval and renaissance artists— e.g. the painting by Lucas Cranach, friend of Martin Luther, in which the guileless, prim expression of Judith is in striking contrast to the gory head of Holofernes.

V. Victory for the Jews (13:10b-16:25)

13:10b-20. The Return to Bethulia. The regular practice of Judith and her maid to leave the camp every night for prayer and the appearance of their food bag have become familiar enough to the guards that the 2 are now able to escape without challenge and make their way back to Bethulia. There Judith's **voice** is recognized in the dark, and the gates are opened to let the women in. A crowd quickly gathers, including the **elders.** All are suitably **astonished** and grateful at the sight of the enemy general's head. **Blessed art thou, our God** is a common formula with which many Jewish prayers begin. With Uzziah's address to Judith cf. Gen. 14:19-20; Judg. 5:24. Since in Hebrew the words "head" and "leader" would probably be the same, the phrase **strike the head of the leader of our enemies** may represent an early textual error of duplication; i.e. the original may have read "strike the leader of our enemies."

14:1-10. Achior's Confirmation. The order in this section seems to be disarranged. Logically Achior should verify the head's identity (vs. 6) and Judith should tell the full story of her exploit to the people (vs. 8b) before she proposes a military venture based on it (vss. 1-4), since her plan calls for immediate action (vs. 11). This order is found in the Vulg., where vss. 6-9 precede vss. 1-4, and may represent the original. Vs. 5, not found in the Latin, is probably an editorial attempt to connect the disordered parts. Vs. 10, which even in the Latin remains as an interruption between the military plan (vss. 1-4) and its execution (vs. 11), may also be an interpolation; it contravenes the law against an Ammonite's joining the **house of Israel** (Deut. 23:3). The **parapet** (vs. 1) was a small wall built on top of the main defense wall, behind which the soldiers could stand. Judith's prediction that the enemy will **flee** in panic on discovering the leader's death may be based on the demoralization of the Moabites when Ehud assassinated their king (Judg. 3:15-30), but OT accounts of such panic among Israel's enemies are common enough (cf. e.g. Judg. 7:19-23; I Sam. 14:13-23; 17:50-52) that the original readers would scarcely question her confidence.

14:11-15:7. Rout of the Enemy. Just as Judith has foreseen, the Jewish sortie at **dawn** precipitates discovery of the headless body of Holofernes, and the resulting turmoil while the men are still **in the tents** half awake sends the huge army into terrified flight. The allies **camped in the hills,** i.e. the Edomites and Ammonites (7:18), also flee. The Bethulian soldiers hurry in pursuit, while messengers are sent to the other fortified cities on the **frontiers** to rally all the Jewish forces to join in. Probably in the original Hebrew all the places named were from the list in 4:4, 6. **Those in Gilead,** i.e. E of the Sea of Galilee, **and in Galilee,** i.e. W of the lake, are Jews living in these Gentile regions (cf. I Macc. 5:9-17) who take up arms against the fugitives passing by on the way to their homeland.

15:8-13. Blessing of Judith. The mighty victory brings the **high priest** and the members of the **senate** from **Jerusalem** to congratulate Judith and bless her for her **singlehanded** achievement for the nation. In the extended plundering of the enemy camp Judith is given the **tent of Holofernes,** where her great deed was done, and all its **furniture.** Victory dances such as described in vss. 12-13 are well known both in the OT (cf. e.g. Exod. 15:20-21; I Sam. 18:6-7; Ps. 149) and in other ancient literature. **Branches** is lit. "thyrsi," the wands tipped with pine cones and ivy leaves carried by worshipers of Dionysus. They are said to have been used by Judas Maccabeus' followers in celebrating the rededication of the temple (II Macc. 10:7), but the original Hebrew may have referred to the branches traditional in Jewish celebrations (cf. e.g. Lev. 23:40; Ps. 118:27; I Macc. 13:51; John 12:13). The use of **olive wreaths,** however, is a Greek custom without OT parallel.

16:1-17. A Song of Thanksgiving. This hymn of praise summarizing the whole story in typical Hebrew poetry is introduced as composed by Judith but is more appropriately sung by **all the people** since it refers to her in the 3rd person. Many have pointed out that the literary style of the poem is superior to that of the prose story. This difference and the reference to the **Medes** as allies of the invader (vs. 10b; contrast ch. 1) suggest another author. It is possible that an independent story and poem were combined by an editor but more likely that the story is based on the poem, the author having filled in details out of his imagination. The poet shows his acquaintance with OT poetry, esp. the Pss.; but the introductory and concluding expressions of praise (vss. 2-3, 13-17) are appropriate even if not distinctively original, and the narrative section (vss. 4-12) is imaginative and vivid.

16:4-12. If the poem antedates the rest of the book, the enemy may not have been identified in it as **Assyrian,** since this pseudonym was probably the invention of the prose author. **Titans** and **giants** (vs. 7*bc*) are of course terms from Greek mythology, but no doubt they are merely the translator's rendering of such Hebrew terms as Nephilim, Anakim, and Rephaim (cf. e.g. Gen. 6:4; Num. 13:33; Deut. 2:20-21). **Sons of maidservants** (vs. 12*a*) probably refers to slaves but might have the lit. sense "sons of young women," i.e. mere boys.

16:13-17. With vs. 14 cf. Pss. 33:6-9; 104:30. With vs. 15 cf. Ps. 97:4-5. Vs. 16 might seem to reveal the poet as a subscriber to such prophetic denunciations of the sacrificial cult as Amos 5:21-24; Hos. 6:6; Isa. 1:11-17; Mic. 6:6-8—a view quite at odds with the prose author's concern for precise observance of the ritual law (cf. e.g. 11:11-15). But as conventionally stated here, and understood by the pious in Maccabean times, the thought is merely that **sacrifice** is but a **small** part of the observances required of **one who fears the Lord,** i.e. who obeys his law. That the author of the book should include such a statement is therefore not incredible. Vs. 17 has aroused much discussion of whether it refers to an apocalyptic **day of judgment** (cf. e.g. Isa. 34:8-12; Joel 2:1-11; Obad. 15-18) on which the bodies of Israel's enemies will be consumed by **fire and worms** (cf. Isa. 66:24) or a judgment after death with punishment lit. lasting **for ever**—a concept that began to develop during the 2nd cent. (cf. Dan. 12:2). A definitive solution seems impossible.

16:18-25. *Conclusion of the Story.* On reaching Jerusalem all engage in the proper purificatory rituals and then offer sacrifices, and Judith donates the booty secured from Holofernes. The celebration lasts **three months** (cf. 1:16). In earlier times Judith's reward would have been remarriage and a number of children (cf. Job 42:12-17), but the author considers an extended widowhood more appropriate (cf. Luke 2:36-37). He notes her distribution of **property** in accordance with the law (Num. 27:11) as a final example of her piety. With vs. 25 cf. Judg. 5:31*c*.

THE ADDITIONS
TO THE BOOK OF ESTHER

H. Neil Richardson

Introduction

The LXX of Esth. contains 6 passages, ranging in length from 7 to 30 vss., which are not found in the Hebrew text. These expand the narrative at the beginning and end and at 3 intermediate points. In his Latin translation Jerome worked from the Hebrew text, but he added as an appendix these extra passages from the LXX, with notes of their places in the story. In so doing he put the ending from the LXX in its proper place following that from the Hebrew and then went back to pick up the other passages in their LXX order. By the time ch. divisions —and later vss.—were added to the Vulg. Jerome's notes had dropped out. The numbers were applied to the whole book in this confusing order—and were retained when the Protestant reformers relegated to the Apoc. the part not in the Hebrew. Thus in the RSV Apoc., where these 6 passages comprising the Additions to Esth. are restored to their LXX order, with notes of their relation to Esth., the "book" begins with 11:2 and the numbers 10:4–11:1 come at the end following 16:24. Late in the 19th cent. a scholar preparing an edition of the LXX devised an alternate plan of identifying the 6 passages by the letters A–F. These letter designations, which are not noted in the RSV, have been used by many scholars in writing about the material and therefore are included in parentheses following the boldface references in the commentary below.

Like most of the Apoc. the Additions to Esth. are included in the Roman Catholic OT. Defenders of its inclusion have received some support from a few Protestant scholars who maintain that the extant Hebrew text of Esth. is an abridgment of a longer Hebrew or Aramaic original which is better represented by all or most of the LXX. But this theory has not proved convincing to most scholars because of inconsistencies in story details and differences in general viewpoint and in literary style, which make it hard to believe that any of the additions can be the work of the author of Esth. Authorship by the LXX translator, though sometimes assumed, also seems unlikely since the colophon (11:1) by attesting to the genuineness of the work as translated implicitly denies any supplementation in the process. Thus the additions are best attributed to otherwise unknown authors—perhaps 6 or more different persons, as suggested by the inconsistencies and stylistic differences among them.

There is no clear historical allusion by which any of the additions can be dated. The earliest evidence of acquaintance with them is *ca.* A.D. 90 in the retelling of the story of Esth. by the Jewish historian Josephus, who paraphrases or even quotes all except the first and last, which probably were not congenial to his purpose. The 2 purported royal decrees (13:1-7; 16:1-24) were clearly composed in Greek and therefore must date from after the LXX translation, which probably was made a short time before 77/76 B.C. (see below on 11:1). On the other hand Semitic idioms in the other 4 suggest that they are translations from Hebrew or Aramaic and thus may have been added to Esth. before the LXX translation was made.

The purpose of the additions is 2-fold: (*a*) to add interest to the story by supplying more details at selected spots and (*b*) to provide the religious element so strangely lacking in the Hebrew text (see Intro. to Esth. and comments on Esth. 4:13-14, 15-17). In neither respect are they very successful. The narrative details are mostly unrealistic and contribute little to the understanding of either plot or character. The religious references, it is true, name God, call on him in prayer, and attribute favorable events to his action. But since they are used to express the same vindictive spirit toward Gentiles found in the Hebrew text, they do little to raise the religious level of the book.

For Further Study. J. A. F. Gregg in R. H. Charles, ed., *The Apoc. and Pseudepigrapha of the OT*, 1913, I, 665-84. R. H. Pfeiffer, *History of NT Times, with an Intro. to the Apoc.*, 1949, pp. 304-12. E. W. Saunders in *IDB*, 1962.

Commentary

11:2-12:6 (A). *Mordecai's Dream.* The 2 parts of this addition—the description of Mordecai's dream (11:2-12) and the narrative of his saving the king's life (ch. 12)—may be separate units which happen to have been placed together. The intro. (vss. 2-4) duplicates Esth. 2:5-6 (see comment). **Second year** is inconsistent with the 3rd year in Esth. 1:3. **Artaxerxes** is the LXX translator's interpretation of the Hebrew name now known to represent rather Xerxes (see comment on Esth. 1:1). Probably he had in mind Xerxes' son Artaxerxes I (465-424), whose 2nd year was 134 years after **Nebuchadnezzar** took away the Jewish **captives** in 597.

11:5-12. The dream and its features—**tumult upon the earth,** the **two dragons,** and the conflict between the forces of good and evil—are characteristic of the apocalyptic writing during the Maccabean and Roman periods (see "The Apocalyptic Literature," pp. 1106-09). An interpretation of this dream, perhaps by another author, appears in the final addition (10:4-9). There the **two dragons** are said to symbolize Mordecai and Haman, and the **river** Esth.; but it is not certain that these meanings are intended here. It is clear, however, that the **righteous nation** is the Jews, who are **ready to perish** but having **cried to God** will be saved by him—a contrast with the Hebrew text, where they win the victory by their own strength and the favor of the king.

12:1-6. This episode duplicates Esth. 2:21-23 with some variations. Here Mordecai himself hears the plotters, informs the king directly, is rewarded, and incurs the enmity of Haman for this deed. **Gabatha** and **Tharra** are Greek versions of variant Hebrew forms of Bigthan and Teresh. **Bougaean** is also a Greek representation of a Hebrew corruption of the word meaning Agagite (cf. Esth. 3:1).

13:1-7 (B). The First Edict. This purports to be the text of a letter sent out by the king to order the destruction of an unnamed people who will be identified in **letters of Haman** (vs. 6). It contradicts the account in Esth. 3:10-12, where Haman uses the king's signet ring to send out a single letter in the king's name, which of course specifies the Jews (cf. Esth. 4:3). The erroneous date for the massacre, the **fourteenth** of **Adar** instead of the 13th (cf. Esth. 3:13; 8:12; 9:1, 17), suggests that this edict may have a different author from the 2nd edict (ch. 16), in which the correct date is given (16:20).

13:8-14:19 (C). Prayers of Mordecai and Esth. These are typical Jewish prayers of the first cent. B.C., in which God is extolled as creator and ruler of the universe and savior of Israel. Mordecai's mention of Abraham and the Exodus refers to the 2 early events in the life of Israel in which God entered into significant covenantal relationship with his people. His explanation of his refusal to **bow down** to Haman (13:12-14) indicates that he would not bow to any human being—a position he must have abandoned on being presented by Esth. to the king (Esth. 8:1-2). There is nothing in the OT to prohibit a Jew from making the customary obeisance to a ruler or other superior.

14:1-19. Vs. 2 describes well-known **mourning** practices of ancient times which were the customary reinforcement of prayer for divine mercy in time of great affliction. Esth.'s references in her prayer to the history of Israel as the scene of God's activity (vs. 5) and to the people's sin as the cause of their captivity (vss. 6-10) are good OT doctrine. On the Jews as God's **scepter** (vs. 11) cf. Pss. 60:7; 108:8. Her declaration that she detests being married to a Gentile and even wearing the crown which symbolizes her **proud position** (vss. 15-16) accords with strictly orthodox Maccabean Judaism. So also does her claimed refusal to eat with Gentiles, including even her royal husband (vs. 17); but the evidence of the Hebrew text is against the truth of this claim (cf. Esth. 2:9, 18; 5:5; 7:1).

15:1-16 (D). Esther's Approach to the King. This passage follows the preceding prayers in the LXX but is generally regarded as a separate composition. It takes the place of Esth. 5:1-2, which briefly describes Esth.'s coming to the royal hall and being received at once by the king. This expanded account builds on the fear previously expressed by Esth. because of the alleged law making an unsummoned approach to the throne a capital offense (Esth. 4:11). In highly exaggerated style it portrays the king's initial **anger,** which turns to solicitude when Esth. faints from fright. The 3 references to God are conventional and reveal no religious outlook rising above the secularity of the Hebrew text.

16:1-24 (E). The Counter Edict. This is a purported copy of the decree issued in the king's name by Mordecai to counteract the allegedly irrevocable (cf. Esth. 8:8) decree of Haman calling for destruction of the Jews. Actually it does revoke the previous order (cf. esp. vs. 17). Here Haman is identified as a **Macedonian** (vs. 10) rather than an Agagite (Esth. 3:1), who has attempted to turn the Persian Empire over to the Macedonians (vs. 14)—an anachronistic allusion to the conquest of Alexander the Great, since in the time of Xerxes and Artaxerxes the Macedonians were not militarily significant. The Jews are here pictured as great defenders of the Persian Empire. God is referred to as the ruler of human history who is responsible for the turn in events that has thwarted Haman and destined the appointed **thirteenth day of . . . Adar** (see above on 13:1-7) to be a **joy to his chosen people.** Even the Persians are enjoined to observe Purim (vss. 22-23).

10:4-11:1 (F). Interpretation of Mordecai's Dream. This explanation of the vision described at the beginning of the LXX (11:5-11) is an allegorical treatment of a type most at home in Egypt. Whether it precisely represents the meaning intended in the previous description of the dream is questionable. The fact that the name Purim is plural, though described in the Hebrew text as based on the use of only the singular Pur (cf. Esth. 3:7; 9:24, 26), may have suggested to the author the idea of **two lots.** He here plays on the word "lot," which means not only the object cast to determine a course of action but also destiny—a sense which appears often in the Dead Sea scrolls.

11:1. This colophon dates the arrival in **Egypt,** i.e. Alexandria, of the LXX translation of Esth. The year intended is doubtful because all the kings of Egypt for *ca.* 300 years were named **Ptolemy** and were married to their own sisters, most of whom were named **Cleopatra.** The probable date is the **fourth year** of either Ptolemy VIII Soter II Lathyrus, i.e. 114/13, or Ptolemy XI Auletes, i.e. 77/76, the latter being the more likely. Possibly the translation was made only a short time earlier. It is attributed to **Lysimachus,** a resident of **Jerusalem** but not improbably educated in Alexandria. The declaration that the book, here called the **Letter of Purim,** is **genuine** implies that Lysimachus translated precisely the Hebrew or Aramaic text lying before him, which may have included all the additions except the 2 edicts (13:1-7; 16:1-24; see Intro.).

THE WISDOM OF SOLOMON
Robert C. Dentan

Name and Character. Without dispute the Wisdom of Solomon is the most appealing and important of the OT apocryphal books. Belonging to the general category of wisdom literature (see "The Wisdom Literature," pp. 1101-05), it differs from the older wisdom books, particularly Prov. and Ecclus., in that it forsakes entirely the use of the brief, pithy, didactic epigram in favor of long, sweeping arguments more in the style of the literary essay. In this it betrays both its different purpose and the different cultural environment in which it arose. The purpose is no longer to prepare young men for service in an ancient and stable society based on a homogeneous culture and sure of its inherited mores; instead Wisd. Sol. attempts to preserve a transplanted way of life and thought in an alien environment. The new cultural milieu was plainly that of Hellenistic Egypt, where the Jewish community, though large in numbers, was in danger of losing its identity because of the rivalry of Greek philosophy and the attractions of a relaxed morality.

Eccl. in the canonical OT illustrates the kind of erosion to which ancient Hebrew faith was subject in this period. It can hardly be an accident that 2:1-5 provides so accurate a summary of the argument of that curious book. It was just this kind of argument—that life is short, meaningless, and without hope, with the corollary that God is indifferent to justice and sound morals—that Wisd. Sol. was written to confute. If the author specifically meant to combat the destructive thesis of Eccl. (which had not yet attained definitive canonical status), this aim would largely explain his use of the transparent pseudonym "Solomon." Since Eccl. had been composed in Sol.'s name, it was only fitting that its rebuttal should be launched with the same authority. In view of the fact that the book was written in Greek and is suffused with the atmosphere of the Hellenistic world, the alleged Solomonic authorship can hardly have been taken very seriously even by its original readers.

Contents. The book falls into 3 main parts, each unified within itself, though their relationship to each other is not entirely clear:

a) Chs. 1-5, addressed to Jews, depict the contrasting life and final destiny of the righteous and the wicked.

b) Chs. 6-9, addressed at least rhetorically to the kings of the Gentiles, are a panegyric on wisdom as the unifying principle of the cosmos as well as the guide of individual life.

c) Chs. 10-19 survey God's direction of the course of Israel's history. Strangely, in this part the figure of wisdom plays an explicit role and is scarcely mentioned again (the word occurs casually in 14:2, 5). The continuity is interrupted by 2 important digressions: 11:15-12:27, which tells how God punishes the wicked in ways appropriate to their sins (although he is also merciful, 11:24-26;12:19-22); and chs. 13-15, in which the author discusses the origin of idolatry and its moral consequences. This last division, though occasionally reaching a high level, is on the whole vastly inferior in matter and tone to chs. 1-9.

Unity and Language. The differences in style and tone of the various parts of the book have caused some scholars to suppose that more than one hand was involved in its composition. Since the style of chs. 1-5 is definitely more Hebraic than the rest of the book, it has been sometimes thought that this section (or alternatively chs. 1-10) was originally written in Hebrew (possibly in Palestine). According to this theory, these chs. were translated into Greek by another author, who then composed the rest of the book in the same language.

In spite of the undeniable differences between the sections, however, the similarities in style, vocabulary, and ideas still seem to most scholars at least as impressive as the differences. In the absence of decisive proof to the contrary it would appear best to treat the work as the product of a single author writing in Greek. While the initial impulse to his work, as seen in chs. 1-5, is unmistakable, it is quite possible that other sections of the book were added by him at later times and in somewhat different circumstances. This would sufficiently account for the apparent inconsistencies in form and style.

The abrupt ending of the book has led some to suspect that either its conclusion has been lost or the author left his work unfinished because of death or failure of inspiration. It is more likely, however, that the book is complete, even though it ends somewhat lamely for modern taste.

Place and Date of Composition. It is hard to imagine that this work was written in any other place than Alexandria in Egypt, the greatest center of Jewish life in the Hellenistic world, the city where the tension between traditional Judaism and Greek culture was both most acute and most intellectually productive.

As to date, the book clearly represents a later development in wisdom literature than Ecclus., which is usually dated *ca.* 180 B.C. On the other hand

Philo Judaeus, another Alexandrian writer whose career roughly spanned the first half of the. first cent. A.D., attempted a Hellenistic-Jewish synthesis in ways far more complex and subtle than those of Wisd. Sol. A date of *ca.* 50 B.C. would thus seem most suitable.

Importance. The author of Wisd. Sol. was at least in a general way acquainted with the art, literature, and philosophy of the Greek world and obviously much attracted to it (e.g. 1:7; 7:22-26; 8:7, 19-20; 9:15; 11:17; 13:3-5; 14:15; 17:12; 19:18; see comments). He was also a loyal son of Israel and, in intention at least, thoroughly orthodox. His purpose was not to denature Judaism but to defend it. What is remarkable is the freedom with which he uses Greek terms and ideas to express what he conceives to be the essence of OT faith. He thus became the first to achieve some kind of rapprochement between those 2 great cultures, so different from each other and yet both so basic to W civilization—the Greek and the Hebrew. Philo Judaeus would later follow in his footsteps, and so would the Alexandrian Christian fathers Clement and Origen, and to a greater or lesser degree most of the great thinkers of the Christian church.

In the NT itself one can see the movement taking shape, particularly in the letters of Paul and in Heb. It seems probable that Paul was familiar with the book even though he never quotes it as scripture (cf. Rom. 1:19-32 with chs. 13-14; note that Eph. 6:13-17 also seems clearly dependent on 5:17-19). Heb. 1:3 is influenced by the language of 7:26. Many other passages of the NT show either a direct relationship to Wisd. Sol. or a share at least in the intellectual climate which produced it.

But if the book is important as a monument in the general history of apologetics and theology, it is also important for at least 3 doctrines, fundamental to much of later Jewish and Christian thought, which appear in its pages for the first time: (*a*) the natural immortality of the soul, in contrast to the older Hebraic idea of the resurrection of the body (1:15-16; 3:1-4); (*b*) death and all other evils as the work of the devil, who through jealousy tempted man in the garden of Eden (2:24); (*c*) wisdom in a genuinely metaphysical sense (not merely poetically, as in Prov. and perhaps in Ecclus.) as God's agent in creation and the continuing bond between him and his universe. The consequences of these developments for NT Christology can hardly be exaggerated (cf. 7:22-8:1 with John 1:1-4; Col. 1:15-17; Heb. 1:2-3).

For Further Study: J. A. F. Gregg, *The Wisdom of Solomon,* 1909. B. M. Metzger, *An Introduction to the Apocrypha,* 1957, pp. 65-76. J. Reider, *The Book of Wisdom,* 1957. M. Hadas in *IDB,* 1962. J. Geyer, *The Wisdom of Solomon,* 1963.

I. THE REWARDS OF THE RIGHTEOUS AND THE WICKED CONTRASTED (1:1-5:23)

1:1-15. *Invitation to Seek God, Wisdom, and Life.* The address in vs. 1 to the **rulers of the earth** (cf. 6:1) is merely formal; "Solomon" would of course be expected to address his equals. The audience actually in the author's mind consists of wealthy, educated Jews in Alexandria who were in danger of losing their faith. The author states his thesis here in gen-

eral terms. **Righteousness** is advantageous, in spite of the arguments of skeptics. Through the practice of truth and righteousness men can prepare the way for the attainment of wisdom (vs. 4).

1:6-15. In vss. 6-7 wisdom is identified with God's **Spirit** (cf. 7:22-30; 9:17). The content of the conception of the Spirit in vs. 7 seems derived from the Stoic idea of the world soul. Vs. 12 warns that unrighteousness is punished by **death** (i.e. eternal death, as the subsequent argument makes clear). According to vss. 13-15 God is not the author of death; his creation, and all that conforms to his will, is made for life and immortality.

1:16-2:24. *Death Comes From Sin.* God never meant that men should die; death was the result of sin.

2:1-20. An imaginary conversation of apostate Jews describes the philosophy which the author intends to confute. The argument in vss. 1-5 that a life is brief and meaningless is so close to that of Eccl. that one can hardly avoid the conclusion that the author has this book particularly in mind (cf. Eccl. 3:19-22; 4:2-3; 7:2-3; 9:2-6, 11-12). The following vss. draw more far-reaching conclusions from this pessimistic philosophy than Eccl. does (cf. Eccl. 9:7-10); it was, of course, inevitable that the admirers of that book, like the later disciples of Epicurus, should go far beyond the sober opinions of their master.

2:6-20. Vss. 6-9 advocate an unrestrained, pagan type of hedonism; vss. 10-11 express contempt for the helpless and proclaim that **might** is right (cf. 15:12). Vss. 12-20, in language that suggested to the early church the circumstances of the Crucifixion, declare war on **the righteous man,** i.e. the good, law-abiding, traditional Jew. From vss. 16, 18 it is evident that the fatherhood of God was an element in contemporary Jewish orthodoxy (cf. Ecclus. 23:1, 4).

2:21-24. Their argument was based on a faulty premise. They failed to realize that in a future life righteousness will be rewarded. Vs. 23 concludes, from the fact that man was made in God's **image** (Gen. 1:26-27), that he is by nature immortal. Death was **the devil's** work. For the first time in the history of Jewish thought Satan (cf. I Chr. 21:1) is identified with the serpent of Eden (cf. Gen. 3:4, 19).

3:1-5:23. *Judgment After Death.* The death of the righteous is only an illusion. In reality they will possess everlasting felicity, share in the government of God's kingdom (vs. 8), and enjoy his **love** (vs. 9).

3:10-13a. The wicked have nothing to look forward to in this life or a life to come.

3:13b-4:6. There is blessing for the **barren woman** or the **eunuch** who is righteous. The ancient Hebrew view was that many children were the reward of righteousness (cf. Job 5:25; Ps. 127:3-5). It now becomes necessary to refute this view and assert that in some circumstances it is better to remain childless (cf. Isa. 56:3-5; Matt. 19:12). The many children of the wicked will be despised (3:17; 4:3-6) and will have no immortality (3:18). Righteousness is better than many children.

4:7-19. It was also the ancient Hebrew view that righteousness was usually crowned by a long life (cf. Job 5:26; Prov. 3:16). Since the author cannot deny that the righteous often die young, he must redefine old age (vss. 8-9) and demonstrate that the long life of the wicked is profitless (vss. 16-19). Vss. 10-15 refer to the example of Enoch (Gen. 5:24); on the absence of his name see below on 10:1-4.

4:20-5:14. When the last reckoning comes, the wicked will realize the superior wisdom of the righteous man's life. Vss. 4-13 represent the wicked man's sorrowful condemnation of his own way of thinking and living.

5:15-23. In contrast the final Judgment will bring triumph to the righteous. The picture of the Lord battling for the righteous in vss. 17-20 is based on Isa. 59:17; the language is echoed in Eph. 6:11-17. In vivid metaphor vss. 21-23 describe the devastating fury with which God will destroy their enemies, who in effect will have destroyed themselves (vs. 23cd).

II. The Praise of Wisdom (6:1-9:18)

The destruction threatened against evil rulers in 5:23 provides an opportunity for "Solomon," who now appears for the first time clearly speaking in his own person (6:22; 7:1ff.), to appeal to the kings of the earth to learn the true wisdom, which he acquired and is prepared to expound to them. While the author may hope for some Gentile readers (6:1-11), there can be little doubt that, as in chs. 1-5, his audience is still primarily a Jewish one.

6:12-20. The Nature and Function of Wisdom. Wisdom is pictured in language highly reminiscent of Prov. 1:20-33; 8:1-9:6 etc.; Ecclus. 1:1-10; 24:1-34. Vss. 17-20 are in the form of a chain argument. Wisdom brings men to immortality and participation in God's **kingdom** (vs. 20; cf. 3:8; 10:10).

6:21-7:22a. How Sol. Acquired Wisdom. Sol. tells of his own experience. In vss. 1-6 he describes his birth and makes it clear that his wisdom was not due to any unusual native endowments. He obtained her through prayer (vs. 7; cf. I Kings 3:9), realizing how important it was to possess her (vss. 8-14). God (i.e. God's wisdom) was the source not only of Sol.'s good judgment but also of his skill and scientific **knowledge** (vss. 17-22a; cf. I Kings 4:32-33). Wisdom was the artificer of the universe, God's agent in creation (vs. 22a; cf. Prov. 3:19; 8:30).

7:22b-8:1. Detailed Description of Wisdom. The remarkable description of wisdom in vss. 22-23 is made up of terms borrowed in large part from Greek, especially Stoic, philosophy. Obviously the author wishes to show that whatever words might be used to describe such Greek philosophical concepts as the *logos*, or world soul, might also be used to characterize the biblical concept of wisdom. The importance of this entire passage for the development of NT Christology has been noted in the Intro. Wisdom is the source of universal order (8:1).

8:2-21. How Sol. Sought to Win Her. Sol. fell in love with Wisdom and set about obtaining her for his **bride** (vss. 2, 9, 16). The **virtues** she teaches (vs. 7) are the 4 recommended in Platonic and Stoic philosophy. She conveys private knowledge (vs. 8), inspires respect among counselors (vss. 10-12), gives **immortality** (vs. 13) and skill in government (vss. 14-15). Vs. 19 teaches the Platonic doctrine of the preexistence of the **soul** (cf. 15:8). Wisdom cannot be acquired by effort; she can only be given by God (vs. 21). This thought provides the transition to the prayer that occupies the whole of ch. 9.

9:1-18. Sol.'s Prayer. Cf. 7:7. The parallel use of **word** and **wisdom** in vss. 1-2 prepares the way for the identification of the 2 in NT Logos Christology. The idea of the **copy of the holy tent** (vs. 8) is presumably derived from Exod. 25:9, 40. The conception in vs. 15 of the **perishable body** that **weighs down the soul** (cf. II Cor. 5:1, 4) is Platonic, not Hebrew.

III. How God Directed the Destinies of Israel (10:1-19:22)

The rest of the book is an exposition of early OT history, mainly the Exodus, showing how wonderfully God exercised his control over nature and events for the instruction and deliverance of his people.

10:1-11:1. Wisdom the Protector of the Nation's Ancestors. Wisdom makes her last appearance in this section. In the remainder of the book God himself is the director of history. It may be, however, that the author intended the theme stated here to be understood as implicit in the rest of the story as well.

10:1-4. Wisdom played a part in the lives of Adam, Cain, and Noah. The curious omission of names in the stories and allusions in Wisd. Sol. has often been noted (cf. 4:10-15; 12:3-11; 14:6; 15:14; 18:21). The anonymity helps create a sense of mystery and solemnity.

10:5-8. The **nations** were **confounded** at Babel (Gen. 11:9). Wisdom **recognized** Abraham and **rescued** Lot.

10:9-14. The precise phrase **kingdom of God** is said to occur here for the first time in Jewish literature, though the idea of course is much older (vs. 10; cf. 6:20; I Chr. 28:5; see "The Kingdom of God in the OT," pp. 1159-66). The reference is presumably to Jacob's vision at Bethel (Gen. 28:12). Vss. 13-14 refer to Joseph.

10:15-21. Wisdom effected the Exodus. The **servant of the Lord** (vs. 16) is Moses. Wisdom is identified with the pillars of cloud and fire (vs. 17; cf. Exod. 13:21). **They sang hymns;** cf. Exod. 15:1-18, 20-21.

11:1. This is the last significant mention of wisdom; the word occurs later only in 14:2, 5. **A holy prophet** refers to Moses.

11:2-14. Treatment of Israelites and Egyptians Contrasted. A constant theme in the remainder of the book is the comparison between the plagues suffered by the Egyptians and the corresponding blessings (vs. 5) enjoyed by the Israelites (as the friends of wisdom?). In this passage the contrast is between the **water** from the **rock** which quenched the thirst of the Israelites (vss. 4, 7) and the water turned to **blood** which afflicted the Egyptians (vs. 6).

11:15-12:27. God's Punishment and Kindly Correction. This digression explains how God's punishments are fitted to men's sins. A basic theme in this part of the book is that man **is punished by the very things by which he sins** (vs. 16; cf. 12:23, 27; 16:1). The Egyptians worshiped **animals** instead of God and were therefore punished by plagues of animals (frogs, gnats, flies, locusts). Because God is omnipotent, having **created the world out of** preexistent, **formless matter** (vs. 17, a Platonic idea), he could have sent great, terrifying animals instead of little, annoying ones (vss. 17-19).

11:23–12:2. God's punishment is always tempered by mercy; his love is universal (vss. 24, 26; cf. 12:13). His punishments are gradual and intended to lead men to repentance (vs. 2, cf. 12:10, 20).

12:3-27. God treated even the Canaanites, whose wickedness merited the worst punishment (vss. 3-6), with forbearance although he knew them incapable of changing their ways (vss. 10-11). On **wasps** (vs. 8) cf. Josh. 24:12. Vss. 12-18 reaffirm God's omnipotence and justice. Vss. 19-22 declare that his love and patience are examples for men to imitate. Vss. 23-27 are a transition to the next discussion.

13:1–15:19. *The Nature of Idolatry.* The mind of the author nowhere shows itself more understanding than in 13:1-9, where he distinguishes one form of paganism, the worship of the elements or heavenly bodies, from mere idolatry. To worship things which are a part of God's creation and are by nature beautiful and strong is to be moved by a worthy impulse, which, though blameworthy because it stops short of its true object (vss. 3-5), is relatively forgivable (vs. 6). The argument from the **beauty** and **power** of the creation to the beauty and power of the Creator (vss. 1, 3-5, 9) is Platonic. Paul echoes this argument in Rom. 1:19-20.

13:10-19. There is no excuse, however, for those who worship objects made by their own hands. The argument, with its devastatingly accurate account of how images are made, is similar to that in Isa. 44:9-20. It reaches a climax in the highly rhetorical passage, vss. 17-19, which pictures the folly of begging favors from an object that patently knows nothing of them.

14:1-11. What folly it is to pray for safety at sea to the **wood** of an idol (vs. 1), even though one rightly trusts the wood of a **ship,** built and navigated by divinely given wisdom (vss. 2-5)—as illustrated by the example of Noah (vss. 6-7). Those who pretend to manufacture gods from created things deserve to be punished (vss. 8-11).

14:12-21. The author has given considerable thought to the problem of how so irrational a practice as that of idolatry could have originated and has arrived at a rather sophisticated answer. It began innocently enough, he thinks, in the desire for an image of a departed loved one (vs. 15) or a faraway ruler (vs. 17). This explanation is similar to the theory of Euhemerus, according to whom the gods were but deified mortals. In the end, says the author, the image became an idol and received the name of "god" (vs. 21).

14:22-31. From idolatry came immorality. The bad theology of the pagans was the **cause** of their licentious lives (vs. 27 summarizes the thought; cf. vs. 12). Paul's argument in Rom. 1:24-32 is like this and probably dependent on it.

15:1-6. Israel, knowing the **true** God from the beginning, is saved from the temptation to idolatry.

15:7-13. The supreme folly is to worship molded, ceramic gods. How can a man, made out of **clay** himself, suppose he can make a god of clay (vs. 8)! The point of view of the idolater in vs. 12 is identical with that of the apostate Jews in 2:1-11. Such idolatry has no excuse because those who practice it obviously know better (vs. 13).

15:14-19. Of all idolaters the Egyptians are the worst. The author is probably thinking in vss. 14-17

of the Egyptians of his own time, whose culture seemed so attractive to many of the Jews. In vss. 18-19 he prepares to resume the historical comparison from which he was diverted at 11:15.

16:1–19:22. *Resumed Contrast of Israelites and Egyptians.* The rest of the book completes the series of comparisons begun in 11:2-14 of how the Egyptians and Israelites were treated in such different ways, even though in most instances God was making use of the same natural objects or forces. God's control over nature is such that he can use the same things to bring punishment to his foes and blessings to his friends.

16:1-4. The Egyptians, who worshiped **animals** (15:18-19), were **tormented** by them (vs. 1; cf. 11:15-16); the Israelites, on the other hand, were given animals (**quails,** vs. 2) to eat (Exod. 16:13).

16:5-14. While the people of Israel were for a short time punished **by the bites** of poisonous snakes (Num. 21:6), after which healing was provided (vss. 7, 10; Num. 21:8-9), the Egyptians were bitten by other vermin with **no healing** available (vs. 9). The bronze snake, however, had no magic power; the healing was through God's **word** (vs. 12; cf. vs. 26).

16:15-23. The Egyptians were destroyed by a rain of **hail** from heaven (Exod. 9:24-25); the Hebrews were fed by a rain of manna (vs. 20; Exod. 16:14-18). **Snow and ice** in vs. 22 refers to the appearance of the manna (Exod. 16:14).

16:24-29. This is another digression on how the universe supports the moral order. The whole world is a plastic instrument in God's hand for the punishment of the wicked and the protection of the virtuous (cf. vs. 17c; 19:6). Vs. 28 may refer to some sectarian custom of saying prayers before dawn.

17:1-21. The story of how darkness came over Egypt is told. This ch. is an illustration of the author's vivid imagination and also his tendency to let rhetoric obscure the course of his argument. The account is an elaborate paraphrase of Exod. 10:21-23. Unmistakably Greek is the emphasis in vs. 12 on **reason** as the source of courage; this idea is the entire theme of IV Macc., another typical Hellenistic-Jewish work. When the author speaks of the moral darkness of the Egyptian world (vss. 2-3, 21), he is no doubt thinking quite as much of contemporary Alexandria as of the ancient Egypt of the pharaohs.

18:1-4. In contrast **light** was given to Israel. Not only were the Israelites not affected by the darkness which pervaded Egypt (Exod. 10:23), but they were also accompanied on their later journeys by the pillar of fire (Exod. 13:21-22). Occasionally the author uses traditional language that suggests a narrow view of God's attitude toward the Gentiles (e.g. 12:10-11); such passages, however, as vs. 4, which makes Israel merely a mediator of God's truth to the rest of the world, are far more indicative of his real opinions (cf. 11:24).

18:5-25. The children of the Egyptians were killed in punishment for the death of the Hebrew **children** (vss. 5-19; cf. Exod. 1:16; 12:29). Later, when in the desert death threatened the Israelites (Num. 16:44-45), **a blameless man** (Aaron, vs. 21) was able to avert the danger through **prayer** and **incense** (Num. 16:46-48). Jewish tradition believed that the decorations on Aaron's **robe** (Exod. 28) symbolized the divine omnipotence, each part representing a part of the universe (vs. 24). The "destroyer" of Exod. 12:23 is described in vss. 14-16 as God's **all-powerful word . . . , a stern warrior.** This magnificent passage, partly based on I Chr. 21:16, is one of the principal sources of the account of the activity of the divine Word in Rev. 19:11-15.

19:1-12. While the Egyptians met a strange death in the sea, the Israelites had an equally strange journey through the desert (Exod. 14:21-31).

19:13-22. *Concluding Remarks.* The Egyptians' doom was just **punishment** for their inhospitality. They had treated the Israelites, their **guests,** as viciously (vs. 13) as long before the Sodomites had treated the guests of Lot (vss. 14-17; Gen. 19:1-11).

19:18-22. Like a musician playing on the strings of his **harp** God transmutes the elements at will and plays his own tune on the universe (cf. vs. 6; 16:17, 24). Vs. 22 is a concluding doxology.

ECCLESIASTICUS
OR THE
WISDOM OF JESUS THE SON OF SIRACH

Edward Lee Beavin

Introduction

Author and Date. Ecclesiasticus is one of the most highly regarded and widely used books of the Apoc., and the only one in which the author reveals his name (50:27). Jesus the son of Sirach (Greek), or Jeshua ben Sira (Hebrew), was a sage or wisdom teacher who lived in Jerusalem early in the 2nd cent. B.C. From the evidence in 50:1-24 (see comment) the date of his writing can be fixed within narrow limits and is generally believed by scholars to be *ca.* 180 B.C.

The Title. The original title of the book is unknown, since none of the Hebrew copies preserve the opening passage. The Greek manuscripts introduce it as "Wisdom of Jesus the Son of Sirach" or simply as "Wisdom of Sirach." Since the 3rd cent. A.D. it has been known in the Latin versions as "Ecclesiasticus"—generally taken to mean "The Church Book," presumably because it is the longest or most important of the deuterocanonical books— i.e. those which the church accepted though they were not a part of the Hebrew canon (see "The Making of the OT Canon," pp. 1209-15). While some ancient authors refer to a Hebrew version of the book by the name "Parables," or "Proverbs," or "The Proverbs of ben Sira," it is more likely that the original was called "The Wisdom [or "Instruction"] of ben Sira," which is substantially the title in the Syriac version and the one by which the book is known in the Talmud.

Text and Versions. Though Aramaic was the vernacular in the 2nd cent. B.C. in Palestine, ben Sira wrote in Hebrew, the literary language. His grandson made a Greek translation of the book from a Hebrew copy soon after 132 B.C. (see below on the Prologue), and Jerome utilized a Hebrew copy in making his Latin translation for the Vulg. *ca.* A.D. 400. After that the Hebrew versions dropped from sight until the beginning of the 20th cent. Through that long interval the Greek versions multiplied and even now are regarded as the basic texts. These are extant in 2 major groups—one found in the great uncial manuscripts of the LXX from the 4th-5th cents., the other in the many cursive manuscripts from later cents. They differ significantly, and a responsible modern translation cannot woodenly follow any single text. In addition there are 2 Syriac versions extant. One of them was probably translated from a Hebrew copy and is quite useful in places; the other seems to have been translated from a Greek version. Other rather numerous versions of

the book—e.g. Old Latin, Coptic, Arabic—are for the most part paraphrastic translations from Greek or Syriac and are not very helpful.

Our cent. has seen a dramatic and important reintroduction of Hebrew texts of ben Sira's book. In 1896 a genizah (a storeroom for worn-out or discarded manuscripts) was discovered in a synagogue in Old Cairo, and by 1931 the sifting through its many old manuscripts had produced 5 Hebrew fragments of Ecclus., covering about ⅔ of the book. These are medieval copies, dating from *ca.* the 11th cent., and their worth has been widely disputed. Some have held that they preserve the Hebrew original, though with modifications taken from the Greek and Syriac versions and with changes and errors of a type apt to creep into a copy of a noncanonical book. Others believe that they are retranslations from Greek back into Hebrew. More recently the Dead Sea scroll discoveries have contributed to the solving of this problem. Among them are a scroll of Ecclus. containing 39:27–44:17 and 2 fragments (6:20-31; 51:13-20). These early Hebrew copies tend to confirm the authenticity of the Cairo fragments.

The RSV of Ecclus. rests principally on an edition of the LXX which reflects the texts of the earliest Greek manuscripts. But the translators also used later Greek manuscripts which present a somewhat longer version, and in several places they have included the expanded readings in footnotes. They also carefully considered the Hebrew texts from Cairo. The Dead Sea texts were not available to them, of course.

Nature and Content. Ecclus. belongs to the genre of wisdom literature. It consists of moral and religious instruction and of practical counsel, offered for the most part in a number of "essays" or brief discourses. These are not the terse, highly polished aphorisms which fill most of Prov. or the long, involved discourses of Job, but they stand somewhere in between, being more in the nature of Prov. 1–9 or Eccl. In addition the book includes maxims, hymns, prayers, psalms of praise, autobiographical allusions, and eulogies. It may well be a revised and partially structured edition of ben Sira's oral teaching to his students. Its content is so diverse, however, that no brief summary of it can be given. The book naturally divides itself into 2 parts (chs. 1–23; 24– 50), each of which begins with a treatise on wisdom, and there are a few units of some length which are easily distinguishable. But beyond these the work defies all attempts to outline it in any logical or systematic manner.

Wisdom and the Law. Ben Sira was a scholar and teacher whose life, activity, and thought bridged the gap between the earlier wise men who produced Prov. and the later rabbis of the Talmud. Like the more ancient sages he teaches a wisdom which has developed out of practical experience and observation, and which is man-centered, though it reveres God as the source of all wisdom. He makes paramount their dictum that "the fear of the LORD is the beginning of wisdom" (Prov. 9:10; cf. Prov. 1:4) and interprets it as they did. Fundamentally this means an awesome, reverent acknowledgment of God as creator and sovereign, and a commitment to him which involves seeking, trusting, following, and praising him, and which eventuates in a life of personal piety. Like the earlier sages ben Sira stresses the rewards that come to one who possesses such wisdom—joy, well-being, and long life—and holds to the doctrine of retribution, confident that the wicked must suffer punishment. He shares their belief that reward and punishment are allotted in this life, for the grave is man's end. Like the authors of Prov. he personifies wisdom as one who beckons men to follow her, and he adopts the concept of Prov. 8:22-31, which speaks of wisdom as the first product of God's creation.

In other respects, however, ben Sira's thought is very unlike that of the more ancient wise men. His emphasis is on things foreign to Prov.—the law, the election of Israel as the esp. beloved people of the Lord, the Davidic monarchy, and the eternal nature and great importance of the Aaronic priesthood. This difference arises from the fact that, of all those we know, ben Sira is the first to take seriously the identification of wisdom with the law. This is the unique feature of his book and his greatest contribution. Wisdom *is* the law, "the book of the covenant of the Most High God . . . which Moses commanded us" (24:23). To ben Sira this means fundamentally the Pentateuch—and primarily its moral rather than ritual prescriptions—but he uses the word "law" in a broader sense, too, for it includes all written scripture and the interpretations of it which were being evolved by the elders. How does one attain wisdom? he asks. By listening to the wise men and by meditating on the law (6:32-37).

This identification of wisdom with the law contains 2 basic implications which distinguish ben Sira from the OT wisdom writers and at the same time establish his affinity with the later rabbis. (*a*) It makes central *learning*—the study, interpretation, and exposition of scripture and the preservation of traditions. (*b*) It takes seriously the major features of Hebrew religious faith and life as these are presented in scripture.

Any thorough attempt to explain what ben Sira meant by "wisdom" would elicit a many-faceted definition, but he himself reduced the many to 2:

All wisdom is the fear of the Lord,
    and in all wisdom there is the fulfilment of the
    law (19:20).

The one aspect reflects his heritage from the wise men of Prov.; the other anticipates the development of rabbinic Judaism.

For Further Study. G. H. Box and W. O. E. Oesterley, in R. H. Charles, ed., *The Apoc. and Pseudepigrapha of the OT,* vol. I, 1913. W. O. E. Oesterley, *The Wisdom of Jesus the Son of Sirach, or Ecclus.,* 1912. R. H. Pfeiffer, *History of NT Times with an Intro. to the Apoc.,* 1949, pp. 352-408. B. M. Metzger, *An Intro. to the Apoc.,* 1957, pp. 77-88. T. A. Burkill, in *IDB,* 1962.

I. THE PROLOGUE

The Prologue is not, of course, a proper or integral part of ben Sira's own book but a prefatory statement attached to the Greek version. It is important in that (*a*) it introduces the Greek translation, (*b*) it witnesses to the developing of the canon of scripture, and (*c*) it testifies concerning the nature and purpose of ben Sira's efforts.

There is no valid reason for denying that ben Sira's own grandson prepared the Greek translation or for doubting the information relating to its date. The **thirty-eighth year of the reign of Euergetes** can refer only to Ptolemy VII Euergetes II Physcon, who ruled *ca.* 170-117 B.C. Thus the translation from Hebrew into Greek was made in the years following 132 B.C.—a date quite compatible with the conclusion that the original was written *ca.* 180 (see below on 50:1-24). The translation was made **for those living abroad**—the Jews of the Diaspora living in Alexandria, whose natural language was Greek—because the grandson feared that the Hellenistic culture which surrounded them might obscure their appreciation for Hebrew values, i.e. for **living according to the law.**

II. FIRST TREATISE ON WISDOM (1:1-30)

1:1-10. *The Origin of Wisdom.* This poem contains little that is new and in many respects may be regarded as a typical wisdom writing. It has 3 main points:

a) The Lord himself is the ultimate source of wisdom (vss. 1, 4, 8-9*a*). Obviously ben Sira is thinking of Prov. 8:22-31, which speaks of wisdom as the first of God's creations. The 2 lines of vs. 4 are synonymous parallels; no distinction should be pressed here between **wisdom** and **prudent understanding.**

b) The Lord alone knows wisdom fully (vss. 2-3, 6). That God's works are so great as to baffle man is a frequent theme in Ecclus., as in the OT (e.g. Job 28). In the cosmological view of the Hebrews the **abyss** (vs. 3) was the subterranean deep, an esp. mysterious place (see comment on Ps. 18:7-18).

c) Man can know wisdom at all only as it pleases God to bestow her as a **gift** (vss. 9*b*-10). The meaning of vs. 10 parallels that of 24:6-8: wisdom is made available to all men in limited measure, but she is supplied unstintedly to Israel.

1:11-20. *The Nature of Wisdom.* Here ben Sira declares the essential nature of wisdom—**the fear of the Lord.** This phrase was a favorite of OT writers too, and doubtless underwent a long development of meaning. In Ecclus. it is esp. rich and full. Here it carries no connotation of terror or trembling dread but means basically a reverent recognition of God as the Lord of life and a willingness to live under the obligation which this awareness entails.

1:11-13. These vss. could well be a homiletic expansion of Isa. 11:2-3, but what is said here has many counterparts in Prov. 1-9 and in Deut. **Is** (vs. 11) means "brings" or "results in."

1:14-20. Vs. 14*a* recalls such passages as Job 28:28; Ps. 111:10; Prov. 1:7; 9:10. **Beginning** may mean starting point, or chief part; either sense is balanced by **full measure** (vs. 16)—cf. **crown** (vs. 18) and **root** (vs. 20). Vss. 14*b*-15 can be taken to mean that since wisdom's **eternal foundation** rests in Israel (cf. 24:8-9) she is both the inheritance and the legacy of faithful Israelites (cf. 4:16). The rewards listed in vss. 16-20 are frequently specified in wisdom literature (cf. e.g. Prov. 3:13-18).

1:22-30. *The Marks of Wisdom.* The heart of this passage, and the logical transition from the preceding, is vs. 27. Reflecting, doubtless, on Prov. 15:33 ben Sira here defines the **fear of the Lord** as **wisdom and instruction** (cf. 19:20; 21:11) and identifies **fidelity** (vss. 28-30) **and meekness** (vss. 22-26) as traits of the wise man.

1:22-26. The man who is properly humble avoids **unrighteous anger** and exercises self-control (cf. Prov. 14:29; 29:22). By waiting patiently for the **right moment** to speak he wins praise from others (cf. 4:20, 23; 20:7). Such a godly man produces **wise sayings** from the **treasuries of wisdom** which are open to him, but the **sinner** has no appreciation for this. One who desires thus to tap the treasuries of wisdom must **keep the commandments** (cf. 19:20*b;* 24:23; Eccl. 12:13); then wisdom is his as the Lord's gift.

1:28-30. The wise man does not **disobey** (cf. 2: 15), avoids the **divided mind**, is not a **hypocrite** (cf. 32:15; 33:2), and shows no **deceit**. This list of vices, each a denial of steadfast loyalty, seems to reflect Ps. 12:1-4. The **divided mind** (lit. "double heart") is that which is not totally committed to God but seeks to serve two masters (cf. Jas. 1:8; 4:8). With vs. 30*a* cf. Matt. 23:12. On **your secrets** see below on 27:16-21.

III. Expositions on Fidelity and Humility (2:1-4:10)

These passages further illustrate the characteristics of the wise man named in 1:27.

A. The Endurance of Trials (2:1-18)

It is possible, though by no means certain, that this chap. alludes to the 2nd-cent. struggle between those who wished to adopt Hellenistic culture in Israel and the orthodox "pious" who resisted it. If so, the **calamity** (vss. 1-5) is the Hellenistic threat, the **sinner who walks along two ways** (vs. 12) is the man who is Jewish in religion but Greek in cultural preference, and they **who fear the Lord** (vss. 7-11, 15-18) are they who adhere to Jewish values only.

2:1-5. *Testing by Affliction.* The OT offers various answers to the riddle of human suffering. One is that suffering is a form of divine discipline (e.g. Prov. 3: 11-12; Job 5:17; cf. Heb. 12:7-11). A closely related concept is that suffering is a form of testing or trial (e.g. Gen. 22:1-19; Job 1-2; cf. Jas. 1:2-4, 12-15).

Ben Sira employs both interpretations, though here the element of trial predominates. **My son** (vs. 1) is the teacher's normal form of address to the wisdom student in this book, as in Prov. and in ancient Near Eastern wisdom books generally. **Do not be hasty** (vs. 2) means not to be fearful but to respond to the situation with poise (cf. Isa. 52:12). **Men** and **gold** are alike in that neither is acceptable until **tested** (vs. 5; cf. e.g. Prov. 17:3; Zech. 13:9).

2:6-11. *Trust in the Lord.* These vss. reiterate the plea for steadfastness, echoing the thought of Hab. 2:4—"the righteous shall live by his faith"—and adding an assurance of God's help and reward (cf. 34:13-17). Vs. 6 is similar to Prov. 3:5-6, and even more so to Ps. 37:3*a*, 5. The promise of God's **help** recalls Ps. 46:1 and the exhortation to **hope** Ps. 71:5. Vs. 9 defines the **reward** as **good things, . . . everlasting joy and mercy,** perhaps under the influence of Ps. 103:4*b*-5*a*. "Everlasting" means, not eternal, but constant or enduring (cf. Isa. 35:10; 61:7). The **ancient generations** are the fathers of old (cf. Ps. 22:4-5). The last 2 questions of vs. 10 may be based on Ps. 37:25. In essence they affirm that the righteous are inevitably rewarded and the wicked punished. The language and thought of vs. 11 (cf. 17:29; 18:11-14) derive from Exod. 34:6-7*b*.

2:12-14. *Woe to the Faltering.* Ben Sira denounces those who are weak through shallow commitment (**timid hearts . . . slack hands;** cf. 22:18) or through divided loyalties (**walks along two ways;** see above on 1:28-30) and thus cannot endure trials.

2:15-18. *The Response of the Righteous.* In contrast vss. 15-16 describe the response of **those who fear the Lord** (cf. John 14:15, 23-24). Vs. 17 repeats the theme of humility (1:22-27). Vs. 18 fits the context awkwardly. It could more naturally follow vs. 11, but there is no manuscript evidence for that. The first 2 lines are based on David's remarks to Gad in II Sam. 24:14. Apparently the meaning is that it is better to receive punishment from the Lord than from men, for **his mercy,** which is as great as **his majesty,** will temper his punishment (but cf. 16:11-14).

B. Honoring Parents (3:1-16)

This is the first of 3 expositions on proper humility, all of which carry out the theme that meekness (cf. 1:22-27) is one of the Lord's delights. It is a commentary on the 5th commandment (Exod. 20: 12; Deut. 5:16). Vss. 1-9 adopt a positive approach, vss. 10-16 a negative. With the entire passage cf. 7: 27-28. **Kept in safety** is ben Sira's paraphrase of the "promise" of the commandment. It means essentially **long life** (vs. 6*a*) but includes other attendant blessings. Like the commandment itself and other OT passages (e.g. Lev. 19:3; Prov. 1:8; 6:20) ben Sira insists on the mother's **right** along with the father's.

3:3-4. *A Means of Atonement.* These vss., together with vss. 14-15, suggest one of the most interesting and significant features of ben Sira's thought, that the honoring of parents is a means of winning atonement for oneself—i.e. that deeds performed in obedience to this commandment accumulate as credits or merits which may be used, now or in the future, to help "cancel out" one's sins. The same holds true for deeds of almsgiving (see below on vss. 30-31). Perhaps this belief developed out of an interpretation of Prov. 16:6: "By loyalty and faithfulness iniquity is atoned for." At any rate Dan. 4:27 most explicitly teaches the same point of view. In later times the doctrine was highly developed and widely held—so much so that early Christians found it necessary to deny it pointedly (cf. e.g. Luke 17: 10; Gal. 2:16; Eph. 2:8-9). Ben Sira insisted, however, that no means of atonement was efficacious apart from genuine contrition and repentance (cf. 5:5-6; 34:26; 35:3).

3:5-9. *Other Blessings*. The person who honors his parents receives further blessings. A son's obedience to the Lord relieves his mother's anxiety over the quality of his life (vs. 6b). True honor includes both **word and deed** (vs. 8; cf. Matt. 21:28-31). The stability of a son's newly founded household is affected by the approbation or blame of his parents (vs. 9).

3:10-16. *Warning Against Disrespect*. On vss. 10-12 cf. Prov. 15:20; 17:6; 23:22. **Lacking in understanding** (vs. 13) may mean unlearned but probably suggests the mental deterioration of an aging parent. Vss. 14-15 reaffirm vss. 3-4 (see comment); **kindness to a father,** shown in obedience to the commandment, removes one's sins as **fair weather** melts away **frost.** Some manuscripts indicate that vs. 16a may have had "despises" instead of **forsakes** and that vs. 16b may have read "whoever curses his mother angers the Lord" (cf. Exod. 21:17).

C. The Attitude of Humility (3:17-29)

Ben Sira exhorts his students to be humble. The Hebrew text (see Intro.) of vs. 17 reads: "Walk in your wealth humbly [most wisdom students were young aristocrats, people of some means]; then you will be loved more than he who gives gifts." I.e., a humble wealthy man is more loved than a proud one, even though the latter distributes gifts freely. On vs. 18a cf. Matt. 20:26-27; on vs. 18b cf. Prov. 3:4, 34; on vs. 20b cf. I Cor. 1:26-29.

3:21-24. *Humility in Scholarship*. Ben Sira warns his students against the arrogant presumption that they can know more than God pleases to reveal to them. He counsels them to limit their attention to the law (vs. 22a; cf. Deut. 29:29; Ps. 131:1; Jer. 45: 5), which is itself more than they can understand fully (vs. 23b). Speculation about secret, **hidden** things (vs. 22b), which are really beyond their abilities to know (vs. 23a), will only involve them in error as it has other **hasty** (presumptuous, conceited?) questioners (vs. 24). What was this hidden knowledge against which ben Sira warns? Most scholars believe that it was the speculations of Greek philosophy. Another possibility, however, is early esoteric doctrines which the rabbis developed. These doctrines were not to be taught in public; they could be imparted only to one student at a time. They centered on 2 subjects: cosmological speculation, based on Gen. 1, about what was before, behind, above, or beneath the first day of creation; and theosophical speculation based on the visions in Ezek. 1; 10.

3:26-29. *Afflictions of the Proud*. The **stubborn mind** stands in sharp contrast to the humble. The **end** of life brings blessing and honor to one who fears the Lord (cf. 1:13; 2:3), but **affliction** to the **proud** (cf. Rom. 2:5), for he accumulates **troubles** as the **sinner** accumulates sins. There is no deliverance for him such as is available to those who call on the Lord (cf. 2:10d-11).

3:29. This concluding vs. ties the passage together. The **intelligent man** is the antithesis of both the presumptuous (vss. 21-24) and the stubborn man (vss. 26-28). He desires only to listen to wisdom utterances and to reflect on them (cf. 6:32-37; Prov. 2:2).

D. Almsgiving and Empathy (3:30-4:10)

In this last of 3 expositions on humility ben Sira teaches that it properly expresses itself through concern for the poor (cf. 7:32-36; 29:8-13).

3:30-31. Like the honoring of parents **almsgiving atones for sin** (see above on 3:3-4) and is another specific illustration of obedience to the law (kindness to parents, Exod. 20:12; Deut. 5:16; almsgiving, 15:7-11). **Kindness** in vs. 14 and **almsgiving** here are in Hebrew the same word, which elsewhere is most frequently translated "righteousness." In vs. 14 it carries the general sense of attitudes and acts of "rightness," but here it is used in the specific sense of giving alms—a sense consonant with the practice of other authors of the last 2 cents. B.C. (cf. e.g. the quotation from Prov. 10:2b in Tobit 4:10; 12:9).

4:1-6. Cf. Deut. 15:7-11; Prov. 3:27-28. The **poor** man's **living** is defined in 29:21 as food and drink, clothing and shelter. On vs. 1b cf. 29:8; on vs. 4 cf. Matt. 5:42; on vs. 5 cf. Prov. 28:27; on vs. 6 cf. Exod. 22:22-23; Deut. 15:9; Prov. 17:5.

4:7-10. Rabbi Hillel (late first cent. B.C.) used to say, "Separate not thyself from the congregation," meaning to make oneself a part of the community by sharing its joys and sorrows. That is what ben Sira is saying. One should show the appropriate attitude toward both the **great man** and the **poor** (vss. 7b, 8a). It has been suggested that the original Hebrew in vs. 8b may have meant: "Respond to his 'Shalom!' [lit. "peace," the traditional Hebrew greeting] gently"—i.e. do not in pride ignore the poor man, refusing to return his greeting (cf. 41:20a). Vs. 9 means to work for the just acquittal of a man being **wronged** by a false accusation in court (cf. vs. 27b; Ps. 82:3-4) and vs. 10 to show toward **orphans** a father's concern and toward their widowed mothers a husband's (cf. Job 29:12-13; 31:16-18; Pss. 68:5; 82:3; Isa. 1:17; Jas. 1:27).

IV. The Pursuit of Wisdom (4:11-10:5)

A. The Rewards of Wisdom (4:11-19)

The rewards here promised to him who follows wisdom are often mentioned in scattered passages throughout the book (e.g. 1:11-13). On vs. 11 cf. Prov. 4:8a; on vs. 12 cf. Prov. 3:18; 8:17, 35; Wisd. Sol. 8:16-18. **Seek her early** (vs. 12) means to give her first priority. Vss. 13b-14 are very obscure. The language is much like that of 24:8, 10, where **place** means Israel and **minister** refers to the temple service, but these meanings make no clear sense here. Perhaps the idea is simply that God and wisdom are so closely interrelated that his blessing is wherever she is, that whoever serves her serves him and whoever loves her he loves. On vs. 15a cf. Prov. 8:15-16; on vs. 15b cf. Prov. 1:33; on vs. 16b cf. 1:15; 44:10-13. Wisdom's **discipline** (vs. 17) of those who follow her recalls the Lord's testing of his followers in 2:1-5 (cf. 6:20-21). Her **secrets** (vs. 18) are the knowledge and understanding which she has to offer (cf. 14:21; 39:2b-3, 7; Job 11:6; Dan. 2:21-22).

B. Excess and Deficiency of Humility (4:20–6:4)

The truly wise man shows neither too much humility nor too little. Too much leads to self-effacement or self-abasement (4:20-28), too little to pride (4:29–6:4).

4:20-28. *Excessive Humility.* Wisdom involves a sense of timing, the ignoring of which will **bring shame.** Of course not all shame is bad. At some things one ought to feel shame, and this proper sense of it brings **glory** to the person (vs. 21b; cf. 41:17-23). But the shame mentioned in vss. 20b-21a and illustrated in the following vss. is improper and misdirected (cf. 42:1-8).

4:22. Too much shame may lead one to sin in that it makes him afraid to stand up for the right when he should. When one lets wrong go unchallenged because he fears offending the parties involved, he actually harms himself (cf. vss. 9, 27b).

4:23-25. A 2nd example of improper humility is being ashamed to speak out or to share one's counsel when doing so would make a contribution (cf. 20:30-31). Vs. 24 is qualified by vs. 25 (cf. 5:12; 11:7).

4:26. Excessive humility is also exemplified by the person who is **ashamed to confess** his **sins.** He may as well confess, the vs. implies, because he could as easily stop a river's flow as have his sins pass unnoticed by God (cf. 16:17; 17:15, 20; 23:18-20). Elsewhere ben Sira urges confession and repentance (21:1, 6) and assures the penitent of God's willingness to forgive (2:18; 16:11-12; 17:24; 18:11-14).

4:27-28. Vs. 27 is almost a restatement of vs. 22. To defer to a slave and to **show partiality to a ruler** just because he is a man of rank are alike wrong; both are acts of self-abasement which deny the right, or **truth,** for which one should **strive.**

4:29-31. *Arrogance.* In terse statements ben Sira censures **reckless . . . speech** and attitudes of tyranny, carping, and grasping, all of which reveal a lack of humility. Vs. 29 might be paraphrased: "Do not speak more than you perform, but let your deeds match your words" (cf. 23:7-15; Eccl. 5:2-6).

5:1-8. *Self-Reliance.* These vss. treat the sin of misplaced confidence. Neither **wealth** nor personal **strength** can afford security, and whoever relies on these neglects proper humility before God. Thus he incurs punishment. Ben Sira does not deprecate wealth itself (cf. 31:8) but warns against its dangers (14:3-10; 26:29–27:3; 31:1-2, 5-7).

5:4-8. Ben Sira quickly reviews 3 erroneous attitudes: (*a*) Some (vs. 4) do not repent because they see no need to. Because they **sinned** and nothing **happened** they assume that nothing will happen. In reply ben Sira argues (from Exod. 34:6) that punishment is certain but is delayed by the Lord's slowness **to anger.** (*b*) Others (vs. 5) sin continually, but are **confident** that **atonement** can be easily won

(see above on 3:30-31; cf. 34:25-26). (*c*) Still others (vs. 6) find false security in God's abundant **mercy** and his willingness to **forgive.** Ben Sira points out that his **wrath** is as real as his **mercy** (cf. 16:11-14). He urges (vs. 7) immediate repentance instead of delay **from day to day.** On vs. 8 cf. Prov. 10:2; 11:4.

5:9–6:1. *Insincerity of Speech.* Failure to live in the proper attitude of humility causes sins of speech. Sometimes one's pride will not let him keep silent but drives him to speak out at every opportunity (vs. 9). Instead of speaking consistently (vs. 10), deliberately (vs. 11), and thoughtfully (vs. 12), however, he speaks "opportunistically," saying whatever the occasion seems to demand (vs. 9). This is a type of **double-tongued** speech and follows naturally from being double-minded (see above on 1:28-30). On vs. 11 cf. 11:7-8. On vs. 12 cf. 20:6. On vs. 13a cf. 27:4-7; Prov. 18:21; Matt. 12:37. On vs. 13b cf. 14:1; 22:27; 23:8.

5:14–6:1. Slander (vs. 14; cf. 28:13-16) is another type of **double-tongued** speech. The **slanderer** deserves the thief's punishment because, having ambushed his victim, he steals his reputation. In summary (5:15–6:1) one whose pride leads him to speak insincerely becomes an **enemy** to others.

6:2-4. *Sensuality.* The 4th example of prideful man is he who abandons himself to a passionate life. The Greek and Hebrew texts of vs. 2 differ markedly, and the Greek yields no satisfactory sense. It seems better, therefore, to interpret the vs. from the Hebrew text, which may be paraphrased: "Do not let passion rule over you, thinking that it will increase your vigor." It has instead (vss. 3-4) the opposite effect, destroying your virility and making you an object of ridicule (cf. 18:30-31; 23:5-6; Prov. 14:30).

C. Fidelity in Friendship (6:5-17)

6:5-7. *Choosing Friends.* Vs. 5 offers a contrast to 5:15–6:1. Speaking with a double tongue causes enmity but speaking pleasantly **multiplies friends** (cf. 20:13; Prov. 16:21, 23). For **courtesies** the Hebrew reads "those who say peace"—i.e. those who greet you with the traditional salutation (see above on 4:7-10)—which fits well with vs. 6a. While one should seek a peaceful relationship with **many** (cf. Rom. 12:18) his closest confidants should be few indeed (cf. 8:17; 9:14; 37:7-15) and any prospective friend should be tested (cf. 19:4a).

6:8-13. *False Friends.* Some are "fair-weather friends" only, disappearing in time of **trouble** or loss (cf. 37:1-6; Prov. 19:6). Among true friends a **quarrel** remains a private matter, but the false friend publicizes it, seeking to **disgrace** his fellow (vs. 9; cf. 27:16-21; Prov. 25:8-10).

6:14-17. *The True Friend.* In contrast a **faithful friend** is invaluable (cf. 7:18). He is a potion which adds happiness and health to life (cf. 9:10; the Hebrew text reads "a bundle of life," as in I Sam. 25:29, suggesting a protection). He is a gift from the Lord and is to be regarded as oneself.

D. Attaining Wisdom (6:18-37)

Cf. 4:11-19; 14:20–15:10; 39:1-11.

6:18-22. *Toiling for Wisdom.* To obtain wisdom

one should begin in **youth** (vs. 18*a;* cf. 25:3). Then his knowledge will increase through time (vs. 18*b;* cf. 21:13), as did ben Sira's (24:30-31), and flower in old age (cf. 25:4-6). The figure of the farmer (vs. 19) teaches that while one must work for wisdom's **produce,** the labor seems little in comparison with the richness of **her good harvest** (cf. 24:19-21). The simile of wisdom as a weight-lifting **stone** (vss. 20-22; cf. Zech. 12:3) suggests again her severe testing (cf. 4:17). The weak drop her quickly (vs. 21*b*) because the value of carrying her is not immediately clear to them (vs. 22*b*). In the Hebrew vs. 22 seems to play on a word which can be read both as "discipline" (Greek **wisdom**) and as "withdrawn," hence **not manifest.**

6:23-31. Submission to Wisdom. After addressing his student in a familiar pattern (vs. 23) ben Sira counsels submission to wisdom through the figures of a slave and a yoke bearer. The illustration of the slave (vss. 24, 29) seems clearly to have been inspired by Ps. 105:16-22, which recalls how Joseph was sold as a slave (Gen. 37:28). The **fetters** and the **collar** were Joseph's to wear, for the Lord was testing him. Ben Sira's speaking of wisdom as a **yoke** (vss. 25, 30) is a very rich figure in light of the later rabbis' reference to the law as such. Indeed they called the recitation of the Shema (Deut. 6:4-5: **Hear, O Israel . . .**) the receiving of the yoke —i.e. in saying these words one proclaims the sovereignty of God and takes upon himself the obligation of obedience to his law. This is what ben Sira is saying; he even uses words from the Shema in vs. 26. No matter that he says it of wisdom rather than of the law. To him they are the same thing; he identifies them explicitly (cf. 19:20; 24:23).

6:28-30. One who bears the yoke then finds **rest** (vs. 28; cf. Jesus' recasting of the figure in Matt. 11:29-30). **At last** all of wisdom's **fetters** cease to be burdens and become the joy and glory of life (vss. 29-31). The **strong protection,** the **glorious robe,** and the **golden ornament** may have been inspired by recollection of the signet ring, fine linen garments, and gold chain which Pharaoh bestowed on Joseph as the reward for his wisdom (Gen. 41:42). The **cord of blue** again suggests the law, for in Num. 15:38-39 the Israelites are told to wear cords of blue on each tassel of their garments as a reminder of it. The **crown of gladness** (cf. 1:11; 15:6) recalls the crown which wisdom bestows in Prov. 4:9.

6:32-37. The Way to Wisdom. On the practical level how does one attain wisdom? In 2 ways, ben Sira says: by listening to the **wise** (vss. 33-36) and by reflecting on the law (vs. 37; cf. 3:29; Prov. 2:2; 18:15; 22:17). Ben Sira often encourages the youth to attend the **elders** and the sages (vs. 34; cf. 8:8-9; 9:15; 25:3-6). On vs. 35 cf. 18:28-29. Meditating on the law (vs. 37; cf. Josh. 1:8; Ps. 1:2) culminates in the Lord's gift of wisdom (cf. 14:20-21; 15:1; 32:15*a*).

E. Warnings and Precepts (7:1–9:16)

7:1-17. Warning Against Presumptuousness. After a general introduction (vss. 1-3) ben Sira draws illustrations from practical life, warning his students against pride and the inevitable punishment which follows it.

7:4-7. Avoid self-exaltation (vss. 4-5; cf. Prov. 25:6-7; Luke 14:8-11; 18:9-14) and prideful political ambition. One who actively seeks a judgeship (vs. 6) may find that he cannot execute the office, or he may yield to its temptations (cf. 4:9, 27; Lev. 19:15), thus incurring **disgrace.**

7:8-10. A presumptuous person does not hesitate to repeat a sin, for he is confident that he can easily placate God by offering many sacrifices. Ben Sira denounces such repetition of sin (cf. 5:5; 34:25-26) and denies that a sacrifice offered in this spirit could be acceptable to God (cf. 34:19; 35:12; Prov. 21:27; Isa. 1:11-15). Forgiveness necessitates steadfastness in **prayer** (cf. 21:1) and the giving of **alms** (see above on 3:30-31).

7:11-16. In terse statements ben Sira warns against insensitivity to the poverty-stricken (vs. 11; cf. 4:2; 29:8; Prov. 17:5; on **abases and exalts** cf. I Sam. 2:7), lying (vss. 12-13; cf. 15:8; 20:24-26; 25:2; 41:17), verbosity (vs. 14; cf. 20:7-8; Matt. 6:7), hatred of manual **labor** or **farm work** (vs. 15; cf. 38:24-34; Gen. 2:15), and association with **sinners** (vs. 16; cf. 9:11-12; Ps. 1:1, 6), which brings quick punishment from God (cf. 5:7; 16:11).

7:17. In contrast to such pride ben Sira exhorts his students to humility. There is a marked difference between the reading of the Hebrew text (see RSV footnote), which suggests that one should be humble because the fate of all men is death and the dissolution of the body, and the Greek text, which refers, not to the natural end of all men, but to the **punishment of the ungodly.** That the reading of the Hebrew text is to be preferred is supported by the nearly parallel thought in 10:9-11.

7:18-36. Duties Toward Various Persons. Ben Sira greatly values friendship (vs. 18; cf. 6:14-17). The location of **Ophir** is disputed, but its **gold** was of fine quality (cf. e.g. I Kings 9:28; 10:11; Job 22:24). Vs. 19 resembles Prov. 31:10. The Hebrew text of vs. 19*a* reads "reject not," meaning "do not divorce" (cf. vs. 26; 26:1-4, 13-18). The disciplined **servant** is mentioned again in 33:30-31; his **freedom** (vs. 21) is that which is due him by law after six years of labor (cf. Exod. 21:2; Lev. 25:39-43; Deut. 15:12-18).

7:22-25. Vs. 22 mentions the only nonpersonal relationship in the list. As in Prov. 27:23-27 the profit motive underlies one's concern for **cattle,** though the element of kindness to beasts (cf. Prov. 12:10; Deut. 25:4) may not be altogether absent. In all probability vs. 23 alludes to sons (cf. 30:1-13) since **daughters** are the subject of vss. 24-25. Ben Sira regards daughters as esp. troublesome (cf. 22:3-6; 42:9-11). The father's duty is to discipline them most strictly and to arrange **marriage** for them.

7:26-28. Vs. 26 admits of several interpretations; perhaps it simply means to divorce an evil **wife** (cf. 25:26; Deut. 24:1) but not a good one (cf. vs. 19). Here one's duty to his **parents** (vss. 27-28; cf. Exod. 20:12) rests on gratitude, while in 3:1-16 the motivation is almost entirely the selfish desire for blessings.

7:29-31. Ben Sira counsels regard for the Lord's **priests** and commends the practice of giving them certain portions of the sacrifices and offerings (cf. 45:20-22). This is commanded in Exod. 29:27-28; Lev. 7:31-36; Num. 18:8-20 as a concession to the priests, who could not be otherwise gainfully employed. On the whole ritualistic matters do not loom large in ben Sira's thinking, but he has an extraordinary appreciation for the priesthood (cf. 45:6-22; 50:1-21).

7:32-36. At first sight vss. 32a, 33a seem to be a simple repetition of the plea for almsgiving (3:30-31; cf. 29:8-13) but more than that is involved in this passage. The rabbis employed a concept which they called "deeds of kindness" and sharply distinguished such benevolence from almsgiving. It can be seen that in Ecclus. this doctrine of "deeds of kindness" is already beginning to take shape. Such deeds include preparation or burial of a corpse (vs. 33b; cf. 38:16; Tobit 1:17), empathic mourning (vs. 34; cf. 22:11-12; 38:17; Rom. 12:15), and visitation of the sick (vs. 35; cf. Matt. 25:36; Jas. 5:14-15). In 17:22; 35:2; 40:17 ben Sira uses the words "almsgiving" and "kindness" to denote the two principal branches of charity.

8:1–9:16. *Proper Relationships.* The prudent man avoids quarreling with the **powerful,** the **rich,** and the **chatterer,** for he knows that the right is often overshadowed by strength, wealth, and words (on vs. 3b cf. vs. 10; Prov. 26:20-21). He avoids the **ill-bred** (the meaning of vs. 4b is given by 22:3a; cf. 23:14) and shows proper respect to the penitent, the elderly (cf. 3:12-13; Lev. 19:32), and the dead.

8:8-9. One should attend the **sages** and the **aged** (cf. 6:34-36; 25:4-6). It is possible that their **discourse** refers to the "oral law," which circulated alongside the "written law" (the canonical scriptures). In general it was exposition and commentary on the written law, passed along through a chain of tradition (cf. 39:2) until in the early Christian cents. it was reduced to written form, now preserved in the Talmud. By the time of ben Sira the oral law probably had begun to assume a definite form. **Answer** (vs. 9d) means true counsel to one in need.

8:10-19. These precepts treat persons and situations which the wise man should avoid: association with a **sinner** (vs. 10) or an **insolent fellow** (vs. 11; cf. "scoffers," Ps. 1:1), who will use **your words** against you; lending to the strong (vs. 12; cf. 29:4; such a lender will soon learn the meaning of "might makes right"); giving excessive **surety** (vs. 13; cf. 29:20; Prov. 6:1-5); suing a **judge** (vs. 14; cf. vss. 1-3); traveling with a **foolhardy fellow** (vs. 15); association with a **wrathful man** (vs. 16; the **wilderness** is open country, the uninhabited area between towns); sharing confidential matters with a **fool** or a **stranger** (vss. 17-19; cf. 6:6b; 9:14; see below on 27:16-21). **Divulge** (vs. 18) comes from a verb meaning to "bring forth a child"—i.e. you do not know what "offspring" he may produce from your words.

9:1-9. Ben Sira praises the good wife (26:1-4, 13-18); yet for the most part he is suspicious, antagonistic, and even openly hostile toward women (cf. 25:16-26; 26:6-12; 42:14). These vss. concern proper conduct toward them. One should be neither **jealous** of his wife—lest the jealousy itself produce the thing feared (vs. 1)—nor overly submissive (vs. 2). To keep company with the **loose woman** or the **woman singer** is to risk entrapment (vss. 3-4; cf. Prov. 7:22-23; 22:14; 23:27). Gazing at a **virgin** (vs. 5; cf. Job 31:1; Matt. 5:28) invites penalty (cf. Deut. 22:28-

29). Consort with **harlots** can lead to severe monetary loss (vs. 6; cf. Prov. 5:10; 29:3). Vs. 7 recalls Prov. 7:7-12. On vs. 8a cf. 25:21; Prov. 6:25. Vs. 8b refers to the wife of **another** (cf. 41:21c). On vs. 9 cf. 19:2-3; 26:22. **Destruction** as the adulterer's punishment is figurative; the death penalty of Lev. 20:10; Deut. 22:22 was not enforced in ben Sira's time (see below on 23:22-27).

9:10-16. These vss. conclude the rather lengthy section begun in 8:1. On friendship (vs. 10) cf. 6:14-17; 7:18. Vss. 11-12 treat a proper relationship toward the **sinner** (cf. 7:16). Though it is known certainly that the sinner's **end** will be punishment, vs. 11b indicates that no one knows when or in what form it will come. On envying sinners cf. Pss. 37:1-2; 73:3, 17; Prov. 24:1. Vs. 13 counsels caution in the presence of rulers (cf. Prov. 16:14; 20:2); ben Sira may well be speaking from personal experience here (cf. 51:1-7). The **city battlements** were the topmost fortified walls, a place of great danger. Finally he advises one to know which of his **neighbors** are **wise** and **consult** only with them (vss. 14, 15a, 16a; cf. 8:17), limiting **discussion** to the **law** (cf. 2:16b; Ps. 1:2) and **glorying** to the **fear of the Lord** (vs. 16; cf. 10:22; Jer. 9:23-24).

F. Wisdom in Rulers (9:17–10:5)

9:17-18. Just as the finished product witnesses the **skill** of the **craftsmen** so **speech** testifies to the ruler's wisdom or lack of it (cf. 4:24; 5:13; 27:6-7).

10:1-5. The subjects reflect the personality of the **ruler** (vs. 2). The **wise magistrate,** i.e. king, **will educate,** i.e. discipline, **his people** and under his **well ordered** rule the **city will grow;** but an **undisciplined king will ruin** his subjects (vss. 1, 3). All this is strictly controlled by the Lord, however, since no king can be wise and successful apart from the Lord's gift of wisdom (vss. 4-5; cf. Prov. 8:15-18). **Scribe** (vs. 5) reflects the Greek text's misunderstanding of the original Hebrew word "law maker" or "law enforcer," i.e. ruler (see RSV footnote).

V. Reflections on Pride and Wealth (10:6–15:10)

A. Eight Discourses on Pride (10:6–11:28)

At first sight these passages appear to treat widely diverse subjects, and in the past they have not been regarded as a literary unit. It may be, however, that they are a series of homiletic expositions based on the Prayer of Hannah (I Sam. 2:1-10). If so, these passages are surely among the earliest recognized homilies on scripture. In brief the Prayer of Hannah (a) proclaims the uniqueness of God, (b) denounces man's pride, (c) asserts God's knowledge of every man's deeds, and (d) declares that God controls the fortunes of each man's life as he controls life and death itself. Each of ben Sira's discourses elucidates one or more of these points, but the underlying theme of the whole section is the inappropriateness of human pride. Presumably the location of the expositions in the book is due to the content of 10:4-5 immediately preceding, which reminded ben Sira of the closing sentence of the psalm in I Sam.

10:6-18. *Warning Against Pride.* This first discourse teaches that the vicissitudes of private and national life are attributable to the sin of pride. Anger, **insolence, arrogance, injustice,** and greed are all forms of pride, causing nations to rise and fall (vs. 8; cf. vss. 15-17) as do individuals (vss. 13c-14; cf. 7:11b). On the whole these vss. seem to be based on I Sam. 2:3, but the specific content of vs. 6 may derive from Lev. 19:17-18.

10:9-11. These vss., reflecting I Sam. 2:6, stress the impropriety of human pride in the light of man's lowly nature. As a creature of God he is **dust and ashes** (vs. 9a; cf. 17:32). His life at best is brief (vss. 9b-10), and his fate is death (vs. 11, see above on 7:17).

10:12-13b. Vs. 12 teaches that the **beginning,** i.e. the essence (cf. 1:14), of pride is man's refusal to recognize his dependence on God. To **depart from the Lord** is to deny his Creator. Vs. 13ab means that when man begins to feel pride he sins (cf. Deut. 8:11-14), and if he continues in it he piles up sins (cf. 3:27; 5:5).

10:13c-18. Since the Lord controls the government of the earth (vss. 4-5), he debases proud rulers —**them** in vs. 13cd means the **rulers** of vs. 14a— and **nations,** elevating the **humble in their place.** With these vss. cf. I Sam. 2:4, 8, 10. Vss. 14-17 also resemble Isa. 40:15-17, 23-24. Vs. 18 returns to the thought of vss. 9-11.

10:19-25. *The Truly Honorable.* These vss. are inspired by I Sam. 2:7-8. Who deserve **honor?** ben Sira asks. **Those who fear the Lord,** i.e. who keep the **commandments** (cf. 1:26-27; 19:20). Those who do not are **unworthy** of it. Men honor **their leader,** but the Lord honors his followers (vs. 20). Whatever one's station in life, his highest **glory** derives from his fear of the Lord (vss. 22, 24; cf. 1:11; 9:16; 25:10-11; Jer. 9:23-24). Despising the **intelligent poor man** or honoring the sinner is therefore wrong (vs. 23). A wise man, even though a **servant,** should rule over **free men,** and a **man of understanding** will quietly accept this as a proper relationship (vs. 25; cf. Prov. 17:2).

10:26-11:1. *The Exaltation of the Humbly Wise.* In this 3rd discourse, based on I Sam. 2:3, 7-8, ben Sira reminds his students that exaltation or debasement is the Lord's prerogative, not the individual's own. He explains that the proper **humility** which glorifies a man involves honest self-appraisal (vs. 28). Ostentatious **display of . . . wisdom** and boasting in **want** (vs. 26) are prideful forms of self-exaltation which can no more be justified than can self-abasement (vs. 29). Vs. 27 is an elaboration of vs. 26b (cf. Prov. 12:9). The intelligent man accepts his station in life, confident that while he is **honored** though poor (vss. 30-31; cf. vs. 23) he will be even more so when the Lord elevates him to a seat **among the great** (11:1; instead of "great" the Hebrew text reads "princes"; cf. I Sam. 2:8).

11:2-6. *Deceptive Appearances.* Ben Sira warns against the pride which trusts in present **appearance,** oblivious to the fact that the Lord can mysteriously reverse the fortunes of men. This passage expounds I Sam. 2:4-5, 7-8. One should trust neither comeliness, size, nor dress (vss. 2-4). Vs. 2 recalls I Sam. 16:7. Vs. 3 (cf. Prov. 30:24) may have been a popular proverb. **Fine clothes** (vs. 4a) as an illustration of false pride may have been suggested by Isa. 47:1-2. Vs. 4b repeats the theme of 10:26-11:1 that self-

exaltation is improper, for it is the Lord who exalts (cf. I Sam. 2:7). The reversal of fortunes spoken of in vss. 5-6 (cf. 10:4, 14; I Sam. 15:24-28; 16:6-13) is not understandable to man (vs. 4cd), but it results from the Lord's knowledge (I Sam. 2:3c).

11:7-9. *Impudent Speech.* This concise discourse, the 5th in the series on pride, expounds I Sam. 2:3. The contents of vss. 7-8, stressing the need to be considerate in passing judgment, are stated elsewhere (cf. e.g. 5:11-12; 19:13-17). Vs. 9a recalls Prov. 26:17.

11:10-13. *Against the Self-Made Man.* Speaking perhaps from I Sam. 2:7-8, ben Sira decries the false pride by which one seeks to enrich himself by his own efforts. The person who is overanxious in his pursuit of wealth fails to find it but finds instead that he incurs inescapable punishment (vss. 10-11; cf. Prov. 21:5b; 28:20b). Presumably the reason is that his haste leads him to commit ethical crimes, e.g. oppression and dishonesty. Yet in contrast the Lord can elevate from a **low estate** (vs. 12; Hebrew "dust," with I Sam. 2:8a) the **slow** and the poverty-stricken.

11:14-20. *Wealth No Security Against Death.* In the 7th exposition ben Sira warns against prideful reliance on wealth, teaching that the Lord's reward is the only security. In effect vs. 14 combines Deut. 30:15; I Sam. 2:6-7. Vss. 15-16 (see RSV footnote) elaborate vs. 14 and may have been a part of the original text. Only that which the Lord confers on one is enduring (vss. 17, 20; cf. I Sam. 2:9a); the wealth which one attains through his own efforts (vs. 18; cf. I Sam. 2:9c) cannot secure his life (vs. 19; cf. I Sam. 2:9b).

11:21-25. *Wealth No Security Against Loss.* This passage is closely related to the 2 preceding: vss. 10-13 concern the man who tries to attain wealth but cannot, vss. 14-20 the man who attains it but dies with it, these vss. the man who attains it but loses it. Vss. 21-22 repeat the thought of vss. 17, 20, that God's **blessing** is constant and reliable (cf. Prov. 23:17-18). Just as **quickly** as the Lord can **enrich** the poor, however, he can impoverish the wealthy. Some wealthy men look for new sources of wealth (vs. 23); others relax to enjoy their gains (vs. 24; cf. 5:1). In their pride both fail to recognize the nearness of the **adversity** to which the Lord can reduce them. When it comes past **prosperity** is not of much comfort (vs. 25; cf. vs. 27; 18:25-26).

11:26-28. *Conclusion of the Discourses on Pride.* These vss. are really pertinent to the whole series of expositions begun in 10:6. Since ben Sira does not subscribe to the Pharisaic doctrine of resurrection, he believes that God's rewards and punishment must come to the individual in this life. At times, to be sure, retribution is delayed (cf. 5:4), but should it even be delayed to the last day of life it will come then. Thus not until the **day of death** can one be certain of God's final judgment concerning his life. The saying **Call no one happy before his death** (vs. 28a) was apparently a commonplace in the ancient world. The Hebrew text of vs. 28b reads: "A man will be known through his latter end," which in essence repeats vss. 26-27. The Greek suggests that should one chance to escape retribution before death it will be visited on **his children** (cf. 40:15; 41:6-7).

B. WARNINGS AGAINST EXPLOITERS (11:29–13:13)

11:29-34. The Stranger. There is danger in admitting a stranger into the intimacies of the family circle (cf. Prov. 24:15), for his **mind** is set to entrap his host (vs. 30*a;* cf. Jer. 5:27) and to probe his **weakness** (vs. 30*b;* cf. Gen. 42:9, 12). Even one's virtues he turns into faults (vs. 31), and if he finds a **spark,** i.e. minor flaw, he fans it into flame (vs. 32*a*). On vs. 32*b* cf. Prov. 1:11. On vss. 33*a*, 34*b* cf. Prov. 6:18-19.

12:1-7. The Unworthy Recipient of Alms. Elsewhere ben Sira unreservedly praises almsgiving (cf. 3:30–4:6; 29:8-13); only here does he warn against giving to the **ungodly** (cf. Tobit 4:7; Matt. 7:6; contrast Luke 6:27-36; Gal. 6:10). The reason which ben Sira offers is that a gift to such a person will not be rewarded, as would a gift to a righteous man (vs. 2), but will to the contrary be used against one (vs. 5). Furthermore withholding a gift helps God to punish the sinner (vs. 6; contrast Rom. 12:19-21). The general, rather bland statement of vs. 3 may have arisen from a misunderstanding of the Hebrew text, which may be paraphrased: "No good comes to him who helps the wicked, for this is not a valid act of almsgiving." The rabbis also knew that harm could come from indiscriminate giving, but generally they discounted this.

12:8-18. Enemies. When one is prosperous people flock around him so that it is impossible to distinguish a true friend (cf. 6:5-13). In **adversity,** though, an **enemy** is easily identified; he is the one waiting to take advantage of the unfortunate (vs. 8; cf. vs. 17*a;* Prov. 14:20; 19:4-7). The Hebrew text of vs. 9*a* reads: "When one prospers even his enemy is his friend"—a more natural reading in the context. One should guard against the enemy's deceptive appearance (cf. 27:22-23; Prov. 26:23-25), for his wickedness will manifest itself just as surely as corrosion will appear on an unpolished bronze **mirror** (vs. 10*b*). But polishing will keep the corrosion away (vs. 11*cd*) and vigilance will keep his wickedness from beclouding one's life. Should one suffer misfortune, however, the enemy will take advantage of it (vs. 17) and his previously hidden hostility will then be quite apparent in acts of scoffing derision (vs. 18).

13:1-8. The Rich. Vss. 1-3 introduce the discussion of the rich (vss. 4-8) and the powerful (vss. 9-13). **Will become like him** (vs. 1) would better read as in the Hebrew "will learn his way:" It is not that association with a **proud man** makes one proud, any more than touching **pitch** makes one "pitch-like." The point is, as the following vss. show, that touching pitch stains one, and that he who associates with the proud will be **defiled,** i.e. will suffer evil by him. In any such association the poor and the weak get the worst of it (vs. 2). The rich wrongdoer complains as if he had been wronged; the poor victim must apologize as if he had committed the wrong (vs. 3). Vss. 1-2 are much like vss. 15-20; vs. 3 is like vss. 21-23.

13:4-8. There is an interesting comparison between these vss. and 7:22. The **rich man** will treat you like cattle, keeping you only if you are profitable to him. Though he pretends concern for your needs (vs. 6) his only real interest is in what he can get

from you. Should you accept an invitation to dine on his rich foods you will be impoverished by having to return the favor (cf. Prov. 23:1-3, 6-7). Having thus deceived and **humiliated** you (vs. 8) he will openly **deride you** (vs. 7).

13:9-13. The Powerful. Vss. 9-10 stress the need for tact in the presence of the **powerful man.** The chief content of the passage is the warning in vss. 11-13 against the ruler's interrogation by which he seeks to exploit you. The questioner **will not hesitate** to use your information to inflict punishments (vs. 12). The wise man, aware of danger, will be restrained in his answers (vs. 13). Since vss. 9-10 are so similar to Prov. 25:6-7, vs. 11*cd* may have been inspired by Prov. 25:2*b,* "The glory of kings is to search things out." If so, ben Sira gives the line an interesting twist of interpretation.

C. WEALTH (13:15–14:19)

13:15-20. Social Incompatibility of Rich and Poor. This passage expands the thought of vs. 2. In human relationships, as in those among animals, likes attract (cf. 27:9*a*), unlikes repel, and the strong **prey** on the weak. **His neighbor** (vs. 15) is misleading; it means the man who is **like himself** (vs. 16*b*). On vs. 20 cf. Prov. 29:27.

13:21-23. Society's Preference for the Rich. These vss. elaborate the thought of vs. 3. The public measures a man by his economic status; the rich can say or do no wrong, the poor no right. Cf. Prov. 14:20; 19:4, 7; Eccl. 9:16; contrast ben Sira's assertion that it is not right to despise an intelligent poor man (10:23).

13:24–14:2. The Joy of a Clear Conscience. In the passage above ben Sira has spoken as if "rich" and "unrighteous" were synonymous. He knows, however, that wealth is not in itself bad, and in vs. 24*a* he offers the needed corrective (cf. 31:8-11). It is not wealth that makes a person happy, nor **poverty** that makes him sad—contrary to the popular view (vs. 24*b*)—but the condition of his **heart,** i.e. his moral and spiritual life, which reflects in **his countenance** (vss. 25-26; cf. Prov. 15:13). Scholars are the single exception, he explains; they scowl, not because they are sinners, but because thinking is such hard work! The happy man is he who avoids **sin** and the guilty conscience which it causes (14:1-2). To **blunder** with the **lips** is to give expression to the evil of one's mind (cf. Mark 7:18-23).

14:3-10. The Unhappy Rich. Wealth brings no joy to the **stingy man** (vss. 3-8, 10) nor to the **greedy** (vs. 9). His **property** is of no use (vs. 3) because it does not satisfy him (cf. Eccl. 5:10). The folly of the miser who dies and leaves his wealth to others (vs. 4) is a favorite theme in wisdom literature (cf. Luke 12:17-21). The **grudging** in spirit actually harms himself (vss. 5-8; cf. Prov. 11:17), whether he ignores his own needs or those of others. Even if he seizes another's property the **greedy** cannot be happy (vs. 9).

14:11-19. Proper Use of Wealth. The wise man uses whatever wealth he has to make life pleasant for himself and others, realizing that he must die. This passage appears to be a discourse on Ps. 49, even though the general subject matter of the ps. is a rebuke of those who foolishly trust in wealth. Ben Sira reinterprets its major theme.

14:11-16. The wise man knows that **death will not delay** forever (vs. 12*a;* cf. Ps. 49:9) and that at death he will descend to **Hades** (12*b*, 16*b;* cf. Ps. 49:9*b*, 11*a*, 14; Eccl. 9:10) where there is no **luxury.** Hades is not hell but the Hebrew Sheol or the Pit—i.e. the abode of the dead, conceived of as a gloomy, underground chamber which is the common destination of all men, though not a place of punishment or reward (see comment on Ps. 6:4-5). The **decree** or covenant **of Hades** is God's order which consigns a man there (cf. 41:3). While he does not know the exact day of his death (vs. 12*b*) he does know that he is "appointed for Sheol" (Ps. 49:14) and that he must leave his property to others (vs. 15; cf. vs. 4; Ps. 49:17). Therefore the best course while he lives is to give what he can to himself (vs. 11*a*), to the Lord (vs. 11*b*), and to others (vs. 13), receiving in turn what comes to him (vss. 14*b*, 16*a*), all the while practicing a kind of beneficent deceit on himself (vs. 16*a;* cf. Eccl. 5:18-20) by which he avoids both flippancy and morbid brooding concerning his ultimate fate.

14:17-19. Like **all living beings** a man will **become old** (vs. 17*a;* cf. 8:6-7) and **die.** The **decree** or covenant **of death** (vs. 17*b*), stated in Gen. 2:17, applies to all **generations** and to every man (vss. 18-19).

D. INTIMATE ASSOCIATION WITH WISDOM (14:20–15:10)

This passage should be read with Prov. 8:32–9:6.
14:20-27. Ben Sira repeatedly counsels close association with wisdom (cf. 4:11-19; 6:18-37). Here, after vss. 20-21, which are introductory and similar in thought to 6:37, he uses 3 figures of speech to suggest the student's proper approach to her: she is choice game which he as a **hunter** should stalk (vs. 22); she is a woman against whose **house** he should encamp (vss. 23-25); she is a lush tree in whose **boughs** he should nest for **shelter** (vss. 26-28; the Hebrew of vs. 26*a* reads: "He builds his nest in her foliage").
15:1-6. To live intimately with wisdom means objectively to keep the **law** (for this identification cf. e.g. 1:26; 6:37; 19:20; 24:23). He who does this will enjoy her rewards, which are refreshment (vs. 3; cf. 24:19-21), security (vs. 4; cf. 24:22), exaltation (vs. 5; cf. 4:11; 11:1; 21:17), joy (vs. 6*a;* cf. 1:11; 6:31), and an enduring reputation (vs. 6*b;* cf. 39:9). The figure of wisdom as a **mother** is used elsewhere only in a Heb. fragment of 51:13-20 discovered among the Dead Sea scrolls. The figure of **bread** and **water** (vs. 3; cf. 24:21; Prov. 9:5) in later times was frequently applied by the rabbis to the law.
15:7-10. In contrast to him who keeps the law (vs. 1) the **foolish** and the **sinful** cannot find wisdom (vss. 7-8), for her paths are justice and righteousness (cf. Prov. 8:20). Neither can they rightly praise God, who is the source of wisdom (vss. 9-10). Apparently these vss. are ben Sira's interpretation of Prov. 27:21*b*, "a man is judged by his praise." It has been suggested that the men denounced here are hellenizing Jews—those who have neglected the law in their pursuit of Greek culture.

VI. SIN AND WRATH: REPENTANCE AND MERCY (15:11–18:14)

A. MAN'S RESPONSIBILITY FOR SIN (15:11-20)

15:11-13. No man should argue that the Lord caused him to sin. Such a thing would be impossible because (*a*) for no reason could the Lord want a man to be sinful (vs. 12*b*), and (*b*), hating sin, he would never deliberately bring it about. As in vs. 11*b*, so also in vs. 13*b* the Hebrew text is preferable: "and will not bring them upon those who fear him."
15:14-16. If man sins it is his own responsibility, for God **created** him with the **power** of **choice.** Man's **inclination** (vs. 14) or "impulse," Hebrew *yetzer*, here means the free will which each man possesses to govern his own conduct. By it he may choose between **fire and water,** i.e. opposite types of conduct (vs. 16), which are essentially obedience and disobedience to the **commandments** (vs. 15*a;* see above on 10:19-25). Later the rabbis developed an important and intricate theological doctrine in which they distinguished 2 yetzers within each person—the impulse to good and the impulse to evil—each of which they conceived as an innate drive competing for dominance in the person's life. These refinements were not fully known to ben Sira, but in 37:3 he does lament the creation of the "evil imagination," i.e. impulse.
15:17-20. Whether one chooses obedience to the law, which leads to **life,** or disobedience, which leads eventually to **death** (vs. 17; cf. Deut. 30:15-19; Jer. 21:8) is not determined by the Lord (vs. 20) but is carefully observed by him (vss. 18-19).

B. THE CERTAINTY OF RETRIBUTION (16:1-14)

God cannot let wickedness go unpunished. Ben Sira offers 5 illustrations of the inevitability of retribution—one (vss. 1-4) based on his own personal experience (vs. 5*a*), the others (vss. 6-10) drawn from his knowledge of history (vs. 5*b*).
16:1-4. Against the usual view that highly valued numerous **children** ben Sira argues that quality is better than quantity. **Ungodly sons** are no cause for rejoicing (vs. 1; cf. 22:3*a*) and will not survive. **One** righteous son is preferable to a **thousand** godless ones (vs. 3), for he can build a city (vs. 4*a;* cf. 10:1-5; 40:19*a*) whereas the **lawless** will bring on its ruin (cf. 21:3; Prov. 11:30).
16:6-10. As wickedness bursts into flame **in an assembly of sinners** (cf. 21:9), so God's **wrath** breaks out on a sinful **nation,** e.g.: (*a*) **the ancient giants who revolted** were destroyed in the Flood (vs. 7; cf. Gen. 6:1-4; the details of the revolt are unknown, but cf. Wisd. Sol. 14:6; Baruch 3:26-28); (*b*) the city of Sodom perished for its sin (vs. 8; cf. Gen. 19:12-25); (*c*) a nation was **devoted to destruction** (vs. 9; presumably the Canaanites); (*d*) Moses' followers who complained of hardships in the desert (vs. 10; cf. 46:8; Num. 11:21; 14:22-24) died before they could enter the Promised Land.
16:11-16. If retribution was so sure in the past, it is no less so in the present. God's **mercy and wrath** are equally real (see above on 5:4-7) and each man receives **according to his deeds.** Vs. 14 is subject to 2 interpretations. Perhaps it means God will exert every effort to be merciful (cf. 2:11; 17:29) yet in the

last analysis man's deeds determine the issue—a paraphrase of Ps. 62:12. Or it may mean God will not fail to credit a man with every good deed he performs (see above on 3:3-4) just as he will not fail to punish him for his every sin. It is uncertain whether vss. 15-16 (see RSV footnote) were a part of the original text. They recall God's punishment of the Egyptians (cf. Exod. 5:2; 10:21-23; 11:7) as another example of past retribution.

C. THE FOLLY OF EXPECTING TO ESCAPE GOD'S NOTICE (16:17-23)

The fool (vs. 23) thinks that God does not require man according to his deeds because in so vast a universe the individual is too insignificant for God to notice (cf. Isa. 40:27-28). Vss. 18-19 may be ben Sira's reply, or perhaps an orthodox editor's gloss, to the questions in vs. 17; but more probably they continue the fool's statement by declaring that God is involved with the larger forces of nature rather than with individual man. **Highest heaven** is probably a rhetorical superlative, as in OT usage, rather than an expression of the later concept of heaven as having distinct levels or stages (cf. Test. Levi 3; II Cor. 12:2). On **abyss** see above on 1:1-10.

16:20-22. The Greek text suggests that God's **works** are so great that they surpass all human understanding (vss. 20-21); besides no one knows if or when God's **justice** will express itself in retribution, and at any rate his **covenant**, i.e. decree (cf. 14:12, 17), will not be felt for a long time yet. The Hebrew text follows more closely the thought of vs. 17 and may be paraphrased: God does not notice me or observe my ways (vs. 20). If I sin no one sees it; if I deal falsely in secret no one knows it (vs. 21); if I perform righteous works no one declares it. What hope is there? For God's retribution is remote and uncertain (vs. 22). The sharpest difference between the two is that the Hebrew more pointedly denies both God's punishment of sin and his reward of righteousness. That ben Sira specifically addresses himself to each of these points in 17:20, 22 suggests that the Hebrew text is closer to the original here.

D. GOD'S CONCERN AS SHOWN IN CREATION (16:24-17:14)

16:24-30. Creation of the Cosmos. After a brief intro. (vss. 24-25) ben Sira affirms that God created the cosmos, arranging an **eternal order** by which its various parts have their **divisions** and **dominion.** He refers, of course, to light and darkness, the firmament, the waters, the luminaries, etc. (cf. Gen. 1:3-19; Ps. 104:2-9, 19). These **neither hunger nor grow weary** nor **cease from their labors** (cf. 43:10), in contrast to man and the animals (Ps. 104:22-23). God **filled** the **earth** with **good things** (i.e. food for the creatures, Ps. 104:27-28) and with **living beings** (Ps. 104:30), which **return** to the earth at death (Ps. 104:29).

17:1-14. Creation of Man. In this section ben Sira deals more directly with the skeptic's denial that God is concerned for man.

17:1-10. God **created man . . . in his own image** (cf. Gen. 1:26-27; 2:7) so that he has **authority** over the animals (cf. Gen. 1:28; 9:2), though after a

limited lifespan (cf. Gen. 6:3; Ps. 90:10) he dies (cf. Gen. 3:19; Ps. 146:4). God gave him physical attributes—the **five operations** of vs. 5 (RSV footnote) are the 5 senses—and mental capacity (cf. Gen. 2:17; 3:22), so that he can see God's **works** and **praise** him for them (cf. Ps. 104:24a, 31, 33).

17:11-13. Creation of the Covenant. This is the climax of the passage (cf. 45:5). In the revelation at Sinai (vss. 13; cf. Exod. 19:16-20; 24:17) God entered into **covenant** with Israel (cf. Exod. 24) and **showed them his judgments**—in a general sense the law as a whole; in a more specific sense the commandments of Exod. 20-23—thus allotting to them the law which confers on them both **life** (cf. Deut. 4:1) and **knowledge** (cf. Deut. 4:6, which may be the basis of what is often said to be ben Sira's major contribution to wisdom literature, viz. his identification of wisdom with the law; see below on 24:23).

17:14. This is a summary of all the commandments. Perhaps the first line refers to the Decalogue (Exod. 20:1-17) and the 2nd line to Exod. 21-23 or Lev. 19:18b (cf. Jesus' summary in Matt. 22:35-40 and the summary in the form of the Golden Rule in Matt. 7:12; Luke 6:31).

E. THE CERTAINTY OF GOD'S JUDGMENT (17:15-24)

The fool is wrong in assuming that he is hidden from the Lord (vs. 15; cf. 16:17), for God knows man's ways, esp. those of **Israel,** his chosen people (vs. 17; cf. 24:12). The presence of vs. 17, so awkward in the context, is understandable on the assumption that in this passage ben Sira is thinking of Deut. 32:6-10; if so, vs. 17 is a paraphrase of Deut. 32:8-9 (see Intro. to Deut.). Every sin which man commits is known to the Lord (vs. 20) and will be requited when the Lord arises for judgment (vs. 23). Similarly every good work which man does (vss. 19, 22) will be remembered, for the Lord regards **almsgiving** as like a **signet** ring—the rich and beautiful symbol of royalty (cf. 49:11)—and **kindness** as something esp. precious (see above on 7:32-36). After mentioning repentance as a condition of returning to the Lord's favor (vs. 24a) ben Sira closes the subsection (vs. 24b) with an allusion to Isa. 40:29-31, as he began with an allusion to Isa. 40:27-28 (see above on 16:17-23).

F. REPENTANCE AND FORGIVENESS (17:25-18:14)

17:25-28. An Exhortation to Repent. The sinner should **forsake** his sins and **turn to the Lord** (cf. 4:26; 5:7; 21:1, 6), for the man who dies because of his sins can no longer praise God as can the living (on **Hades** see above on 14:11-16). Such praise is one of the primary purposes of life (cf. 17:10).

17:29-18:14. Assurance of Forgiveness. Ben Sira closes this major section (begun in 15:11) with the assurance that the Lord is aware of man's weaknesses and is therefore patient and merciful toward him.

17:29-18:10. The Lord is characterized by **mercy** and **forgiveness** (17:29). He is the eternal creator (18:1; cf. 16:26-17:14; 42:15-43:33), who controls the stars (17:32a), who **alone** is **righteous** (18:2), and whose great **works** and great **mercies** are beyond human comprehension (18:4-6). Man, in contrast, is mortal (17:30, 32b; 18:9-10; weak and unknowing (18:7-8), and inclined to **evil** (17:31b). **His good** and **evil** alike are inconsequential in comparison with God (18:8b). The text of 17:30 is uncertain. The Syriac reads, "But it is not like this in man [i.e. man is not merciful and forgiving, as God is; cf. 18:13ab], nor is God's thought like that of the sons of men." Using this reading cf. 17:25-30 with Isa. 55:6-9.

18:11-14. Because man is weak and the duration of his life short—**their end will be evil** means they are destined to die—the Lord is **patient,** merciful, and forgiving (cf. 17:29). He tries to help men by rebuking, training, and teaching them and is compassionate to all who **accept his discipline** and **his judgments.**

VII. Discretion in Behavior (18:15–23:27)

A. Caution (18:15-29)

18:15-18. *Giving Charity.* Ben Sira greatly values almsgiving (see above on 3:30-31), but here he warns against offending the recipient by ungracious **words** (cf. 41:19d, 22d). Indeed, if a choice must be made, a kindly **word** is preferable to a **gift,** for it can better allay the **heat** of the unfortunate man's humiliation (vss. 16-17a). Of course the ideal response would be **both,** i.e. a kind word and a generous gift (vs. 17b). **Dim** eyes (vs. 18; cf. Job 17:7) expresses grief or pain (contrast I Sam. 14:27).

18:19-29. *Foresight.* The prudent man takes careful precaution against various contingencies. On vs. 19a cf. 5:11-12; 11:7-8; 33:4; on vs. 19b cf. 30:21–31:2; 37:27-31. Self-examination makes one aware of his sins (vs. 20) so that when the Lord comes for **judgment** he can readily confess them and be forgiven. Vs. 21 means: **Humble yourself** lest you fall **ill,** and repent lest you sin.

18:22-24. Ben Sira repeats the demand of Deut. 23:21-23 for prompt payment of a votive offering or gift (cf. Eccl. 5:4). If one promises a gift when he makes a vow, it ought to be paid. Not to pay would be a sin, and while **death** atones for sin—an axiom of rabbinic theology—it is better to avoid the sin altogether. One should make a vow deliberately, not rashly (vss. 23-24; cf. Prov. 20:25; Eccl. 5:5-6).

18:25-29. The wise man is cautious in that he does not let affluence blind him to the imminence of **poverty** (vss. 25-26; cf. 11:24-28), nor does he sin though there be ample opportunity to do so (vs. 27). The original meaning of vss. 28-29 is uncertain. The RSV translation might be paraphrased: The intelligent person recognizes the wisdom of what I have said, will praise me for it, and will be able himself to teach wisdom (cf. 21:15ab).

B. Self-Control (18:30–19:19)

Ben Sira warns against surrendering to the temptations of lust and appetite (18:30-33), wine and women (19:1-3), gossip (19:4-12), and premature judging (19:13-19).

18:30-33. *Lust and Appetite.* On **appetites** cf. 23:6, where "gluttony" is the same Greek word. On **laughingstock** cf. 6:4. Elsewhere ben Sira warns against **luxury** as destructive of health (37:29-31), of

unsure duration (11:19, 24-25), and leading to poverty (13:7). On **beggar** cf. 40:28-30. The Hebrew text of vs. 33 reads: "Be not a squanderer and a drunkard, else there will be nothing in your purse," which, if correct, indicates that the vs. should be read in close conjunction with 19:1.

19:1-3. *Wine and Women.* Ben Sira, with the OT generally, extols the delights of wine drunk in moderation, but he deplores overindulgence (cf. 31:25-30) here, because it leads to poverty (cf. Prov. 21:17; 23:21). Vs. 2 links **wine and women** as twin evils (cf. Prov. 31:3-5). On yielding to the temptation of illicit sex and consequent punishment cf. 9:2-9; 23:16-26.

19:4-12. *Gossip.* Self-control is also needed to avoid the sin of gossip. He who prattles what he knows to just any listener (vs. 4a; cf. 8:17-19) harms himself (vss. 4-5a), for what he says will be used against him (vs. 9; cf. 13:8-13). Except in a case where it would be sinful to withhold information (vs. 8b) one should never repeat another's conversation (cf. 41:23; Prov. 25:9b-10). Inability to restrain one's speech is the mark of a **fool** (vss. 11-12; cf. 20:19-20; 21:26a).

19:13-19. *Premature Judgment.* Vss. 13-17 seem to reflect Prov. 25:8-9a, as vss. 4-12 do Prov. 25:9b-10. Proper self-control prevents the hasty assumption of another's guilt. One should first investigate the case and then if necessary reprove his **friend** or **neighbor** (cf. 11:7). The accused may be innocent or his conduct may be excusable. On the evils of **slander** (vs. 15) cf. 5:14; 28:13-26. On vs. 16 cf. Jas. 3:2. The **law** referred to in vs. 17 is that of Lev. 19:17 (cf. Luke 17:3; Matt. 18:15). Vss. 18-19 (RSV footnotes) occur in a few manuscripts only. Vs. 19 alludes to the doctrine of **immortality,** which ben Sira does not accept.

C. Drawing Proper Distinctions (19:20–20:31)

19:20-30. *Wisdom, Cleverness, and Ignorance.* True wisdom is the **fear of the Lord** and expresses itself in the keeping of the **law** (cf. e.g. 1:26; 6:37; 15:1; 24:23). Other types of **knowledge,** which do not involve the fear of the Lord, cannot rightly be called wisdom—e.g. that possessed by **sinners** (vs. 22) or the **cleverness** used for **abominable** ends (vs. 23a). Indeed a pious ignorant man is better than a shrewd sinner (vss. 23b-24). Some clever men are very exact about minor details yet on the whole are **unjust** (vs. 25a); they keep the letter of the law but violate the spirit of it. Others cleverly use **kindness** for ulterior motives (vs. 25b; cf. 11:29-34; 13:3-7), or adopt a deceitful attitude, using feigned disinterestedness to get the best of you (vss. 26-28; cf. 12:10-12, 16-18). One way to guard against such a person is to pay careful attention to his **appearance** and mannerisms, for these reveal much about his true character (vss. 29-30; cf. 13:25; 27:22). Vs. 21 (RSV footnote; cf. Matt. 21:28-32) is found in only a few manuscripts and interrupts the context.

20:1-8. *Speech and Silence.* These vss. appear to continue 19:13-17. At times it is better to remain **silent** than to **reprove** (vs. 1; cf. e.g. 4:2-3a) but at other times it is better to speak out in reproof than to remain silent and harbor anger. Besides the offender may recognize and confess **his fault** and be kept from punishment. In no case, however, should **judgments** be executed **by violence.**

20:5-8. There are various reasons for silence. Sometimes the fool is silent because he knows nothing, though this silence may be interpreted by others as wisdom (vs. 5*a;* cf. Prov. 17:28). The wise man may be silent because he lacks sure knowledge of the case (vs. 6*a;* cf. 5:12) or because he knows that it is not an appropriate time for speaking (vss. 6*b*-7*a;* cf. 1:23-24; Eccl. 3:7). The **fool** or **braggart** fails to appreciate the virtue of silence (vss. 5*b*, 7*b*, 8; cf. Prov. 10:19).

20:9-17. *Appearance and Reality.* These paradoxes teach that things are not always what they seem and that normal expectations are not always fulfilled (cf. 11:12-13, 23-25). The **gift** (vs. 10) is one which is given, not received. On vs. 11 cf. 10:14; 11:5. The fool's **courtesies** cannot be taken at face value, for he is calculating ways to get the greatest possible return on his investment. Having given **little,** he reproves and complains if he does not receive **much** (vss. 13-17).

20:18-31. *Inappropriate and Proper Speech.* The fool's speech is inappropriate because he neglects the element of proper timing (cf. 19:11-12; 20:7). In the Syriac version vs. 19 reads: "As the fat tail of a sheep [a choice portion; cf. Exod. 29:22] eaten without salt, so is a word not spoken in season." It is possible that the Greek translator misunderstood the original reference.

20:21-23. Some men remain sinless because they lack the means to sin (vs. 21; cf. 19:28). But there are those who sin by refusing to speak; through a sense of false **shame** they remain silent or feign ignorance (vs. 22; cf. 4:20-21). Conversely others sin by speaking out rashly, making **promises** which they cannot realistically expect to keep (vs. 23).

20:24-26. Lying is a form of perverted speech (cf. 7:12-13; 25:2; Prov. 12:22) which, like slander (cf. 5:14), can be compared with thievery. **Shame** and **disgrace** accompany the liar (cf. Prov. 13:5).

20:27-31. In contrast to all these the wise man speaks sensibly, not hiding his wisdom (vss. 30-31, repeated in 41:14-15; cf. 4:23), but cultivating it (vs. 28*a*). Thus he earns advancement (vs. 27) and the opportunity to win pardons for sin (vs. 28*b*). Nonetheless he needs to be warned against bribes that would **blind** him to injustice (vs. 29*a* is a near quotation from Deut. 16:19) and **muzzle** his reproof of it.

D. Warnings Against Sin (21:1-10)

21:1-7. Ben Sira exhorts to repentance (vs. 6*b;* cf. 17:24-25) and confession in prayer (vs. 1; cf. 4:26; 7:10), assuring the humble that he will be heard by God and **speedily** vindicated (vs. 5; cf. 35:13-17). Sin is deadly, he warns (vss. 2-3; on sin as a lion cf. 27:10), and the **proud,** unrepentant sinner will be destroyed (vss. 4, 6*a*). Vs. 7 seems awkward in the context and its original text is uncertain. The Greek text seems to mean that the proud (or boastful) man is famous but the wise man is more sensitive to his need for forgiveness.

21:8-10. These vss. are a 3-fold reaffirmation of the fact that sin leads to death. To amass a fortune unjustly is in effect to prepare one's own grave (vs.

8; cf. 5:8). The **assembly of the wicked** (cf. 16:6) can be ignited to destruction by a mere spark. On the **smoothly paved** road of the sinner (vs. 10) cf. Prov. 14:12; 16:25; Matt. 7:13. On **Hades** see above on 14:11-16.

E. The Wise Man and the Fool (21:11-22:18)

21:11-28. *A Contrast.* The wise man and the fool stand in sharp opposition in their attainment and appreciation of **knowledge** (vss. 11-15, 18-19, 21), in their **speech** (vss. 16-17, 25-28), and in their conduct (vss. 20, 22-24).

21:11-15. The meaning of vss. 11-12 is similar to that of 19:20-23. Instead of **his thoughts** (vs. 11*a*) the Syriac reads "his yetzer" (see above on 15:14-16), which may be correct. There are two kinds of **cleverness.** In a good sense it is the ability to learn (cf. 6:32), or perceptiveness (cf. 34:10); in a bad sense it is shrewdness used for ignoble ends (cf. 19:23, 25). The wise man's knowledge grows through life (vs. 13; cf. 6:18), as did ben Sira's own (cf. 24:30-31). On **flowing spring** and **broken jar** (vss. 13-14) cf. Prov. 10:11*a;* Jer. 2:13. The fool despises a wisdom **saying** but the wise man applauds and develops it (vs. 15; cf. 6:32-37; 18:28-29).

21:16-24. The fool's story—cf. the foolhardy traveling companion (8:15)—is a heavy **burden** to bear, but **intelligent** speech brings delight and respect (vss. 16-17; cf. 15:5; 39:9-11). Wisdom is as nothing to a fool, who regards **education** as heavy **fetters** (vss. 18-19), but to the wise these shackles become an **ornament** (vs. 21; cf. 6:24, 29-31). In vss. 20, 22-24 the boorishness of the fool is contrasted with the cultivated manners of the wise (cf. 19:30; 31:12-32:13).

21:25-28. Here again the contrast is in speech habits. The text of vs. 25*a* is quite uncertain. One manuscript reads: "Babblers declare what is not theirs"—i.e. what they do not really know (cf. 21:18)—which contrasts well with the wise, who weigh their words carefully (vs. 25*b;* cf. 16:25; 28:25). Fools speak before thinking and wise men think before speaking (vs. 26; cf. 4:24; 5:13.) Vss. 27-28 warn against 2 types of foolish speech. He who **curses** another lays a curse on himself, and the **whisperer** (deceiver? slanderer?) actually harms himself (cf. 19:4*b*). **Adversary** (vs. 27) represents the same word as "Satan" (see RSV footnote). Originally the Hebrew word meant a slanderer or accuser, and probably here it means simply a human enemy.

22:1-18. *The Undisciplined and the Foolish.* Ben Sira values work (cf. 7:15; 38:24-34) but except for a section on idle slaves (33:24-28) speaks only in vss. 1-2 of the **indolent.** In Prov., of course, this is a major theme.

22:3-6. The discipline of children is a favorite subject in this book (cf. 7:23-25; 16:1-3; 30:1-13). In the ancient world generally a **daughter** was valued much less than a son. Besides being esp. troublesome (cf. 42:9-11) she could not perpetuate the family, bring income into it, or support her parents in old age. But nowhere else is this attitude expressed more forcibly or succinctly than in vs. 3*b*. On vss. 4-5 cf. 7:22-28; 42:9-11. An **impudent daughter** probably means one who fails to show proper discretion in sexual matters (cf. 26:11).

22:7-15. Teaching a fool is as useless as trying to mend a broken pot (vss. 7-8). Even the **dead** man is better off than the fool (vss. 9-12). The traditional period of **mourning** was **seven days** (cf. Gen. 50:10; I Sam. 31:13; Judith 16:24). One should avoid close association with the foolish (vs. 13; cf. 27:12), for it is like being burdened with a heavy weight (vss. 14-15; cf. 8:15; 21:16; Prov. 27:3).

22:16-18. The wise man has a **mind firmly fixed** but the fool has a **timid heart.** The one follows **reasonable counsel** and stands unafraid; the other follows a **fool's purpose** and yields in **fear** (cf. 2:2, 12-13). The exact connotation of the words in vs. 17b is unknown and the precise point of comparison is unclear.

F. THE PRESERVATION OF FRIENDSHIP (22:19-26)

The value of friendship is extolled in 6:14-17; 7:18; 9:10. True **friendship** will survive many blows —a quarrel, even if it is taken to the point of battle (vs. 21; cf. 27:21a), and open opposition (vs. 22ab)— but it cannot survive the sneaky attacks listed in vs. 22c (cf. 23:8), of which none is worse than the **disclosure of secrets** (cf. 27:16-21; 41:23; Prov. 11:13; 20:19; 25:9). The maintenance of friendship demands fidelity even though the friend suffers **poverty** and **affliction,** or hostility (vss. 23, 25; contrast 6:8-12; 37:1-5). Vs. 24 interrupts the context.

G. SINS OF SPEECH AND LUST (22:27–23:27)

Ben Sira prays that he may be delivered from sins of speech and lust (22:27–23:6), and then warns his students about the former (23:7-15) and denounces those who surrender to the latter (23:16-27).

22:27–23:6. *A Prayer for Deliverance.* The prayer begins with a near quotation of Ps. 141:3 (vs. 27ab) and an allusion to the thought of Prov. 21:23 (vs. 27cd). Elsewhere ben Sira emphasizes the **mouth** as the cause of sin or the instrument by which sin of the mind or heart is given expression (5:13; 14:1; 23:8; cf. Prov. 18:21). He prays that **discipline** may control his unintentional errors and his willfulness to sin, lest they bring about his downfall (23:2-3). Logically vs. 1 should follow vs. 3, for the **mistakes** and **sins** of vs. 3 are the proper antecedents of **their** and **them** in vs. 1.

23:4-6. The conclusion of the prayer is a petition for deliverance from **lust** (cf. 6:2-4). The phrase **haughty eyes** offhandedly suggests pride, but the root expression is "lift up the eyes," which in some other instances clearly connotes sexual desire (cf. 26:9; 41:20b, 21c; Gen. 39:7). Similarly **gluttony** here derives from the expression "appetite of the belly," which could mean sexual passion (cf. 18:30).

23:7-15. *Sins of Speech.* After a general statement (vss. 7-8) in which he mentions reviling and arrogance as sins of speech (cf. 22:22) ben Sira centers his attention on frequent, thoughtless swearing. The **Name** (vss. 9-10) is the personal name of God, Yahweh. From well back in the OT period this sacred name had been held in such reverence that its pronunciation was avoided (cf. Exod. 20:7). The priest was permitted to utter it in giving the benediction (Num. 6:23-27; cf. 50:20), but in most other cases a substitute, most frequently Adonai, "Lord," was

used instead. From this substitution in reading the Scriptures aloud has come the use of "the LORD" for Yahweh (or "the Lord GOD" for Adonai Yahweh) in the RSV and other English versions of the OT. Of course in making an oath "Yahweh" had to be pronounced, because the oath was validated by invoking the deity by name. In the OT the most common oath forms are "As Yahweh lives" and "May Yahweh do so to me and more also if . . ." (for the implication of "do so" cf. Num. 5:21-22; Job 31; Pss. 7:3-5; 137:5-6).

23:12. The **utterance . . . comparable to death** (or "clothed in death" as most manuscripts read) may mean either (a) blasphemy, i.e. the cursing of God or the denial of him, his work, or his name, or (b) lewd, vulgar speech, which is the topic of the following vss.

23:13-15. One who uses obscene language is an undisciplined son, whose speech in the presence of noblemen disgraces his parents, for it reflects his training and education (cf. 3:1-16; 8:4).

23:16-27. *Sins of Lust.* Ben Sira denounces the fornicator (vss. 16-17), the adulterer (vss. 18-21), and the adulteress (vss. 22-27).

23:16-17. Vs. 16 begins with a numerical introduction (cf. 25:1, 7; 26:5, 28; 50:25; Prov. 6:16-19; 30:15-31; Amos 1:3–2:6). This was a stylistic device perhaps originally intended to aid memory. The **fire** of passion consumes the lustful (cf. 6:2-4). **Bread** is a euphemism (cf. Prov. 9:17).

23:18-21. Ben Sira everywhere advocates faithfulness in marriage, though he does not hesitate to counsel divorce if conditions warrant (cf. 7:26; 25:26). It is noteworthy that in his view the adulterer sins because he **breaks his marriage vows** (cf. Mark 10:11) rather than, as in earlier times, because he wrongs the woman's husband or father (cf. Deut. 22:22-29; see comment). The adulterer errs in thinking that he can conceal his sin from man and God (cf. Job 24:15), for God's **eyes** are bright and he perceives **all** of man's **ways** (cf. 16:17-23; 17:15, 20; Ps. 33:13-15; Prov. 15:3, 11).

23:22-27. Ben Sira frequently speaks out against the adulteress and the harlot (cf. e.g. 9:1-9), but here the specific concern is with the woman who bears a child through an adulterous relationship and thus commits a 3-fold wrong (vs. 23; the **law** is that in the Decalogue, Exod. 20:14; Deut. 5:18). Such a child could not be expected to live (cf. the child born to David and Bathsheba, II Sam. 12), or if it did live could not be expected to have a prosperous life (cf. 40:15; Wisd. Sol. 3:16-19; 4:3-6). The woman's punishment involves arraignment before the **assembly** of her town and **disgrace** (vss. 24a, 26). The absence of any reference to death here and in vs. 21 indicates that the harsh penalty for adultery prescribed in the Pentateuch (Lev. 20:10; Deut. 22:22) was not enforced in ben Sira's time. On vs. 27 cf. 25:11; 40:26-27.

VIII. ATTRACTIVE AND HATEFUL THINGS (24:1–36:17)

A. SECOND TREATISE ON WISDOM (24:1-34)

24:1-22. *A Hymn in Praise of Wisdom.* This is the 2nd of 2 principal poems praising wisdom (cf.

1:1-10), each of which stands at the beginning of a major section (see below on vss. 30-34). After the intro. (vss. 1-2) wisdom speaks of herself in the first person.

24:1-2. Personified wisdom praises **herself** on earth and in heaven. In the context **her people** must mean Israel. **The assembly of the Most High** and **his host** refer to the divine council, the ministers of God who surrounded his throne in the heavens (cf. e.g. Pss. 82:1; 89:5-7).

24:3. Wisdom's origin lies in her having been the first of God's created things (cf. vs. 9; 1:4). Obviously ben Sira is thinking of Prov. 8:22-31, where this is taught, but he also seems to have in mind the creation accounts in Gen. In the P account (Gen. 1:1–2:4a) God creates by speaking; thus ben Sira says wisdom **came forth from the mouth of the Most High.** In the J account of creation (Gen. 2:4b-25) a mist covers the earth before other things are created; so wisdom speaks of herself as **like a mist.**

24:4-7. These vss. describe the omnipresence of wisdom. As the Lord's companion (cf. Prov. 8:30) she is present wherever he is present: in the **pillar of cloud** which was with Israel (cf. Exod. 14:19-20; 33:9-10) and in the **vault** (i.e. the firmament, the dome) **of heaven,** the **abyss** (see above on 1:1-10), the **sea,** and the **earth** (these 4 are enumerated in Prov. 8:28-29).

24:8-12. Wisdom now speaks of **Israel** as her peculiar dwelling place. In a sense she is found in other nations too, for they have their wisdom and wise men, but God **assigned** her esp. to Israel. While appropriate to what ben Sira says elsewhere, vs. 9 seems to interrupt the thought here. It is understandable, however, when one sees that in writing these vss. ben Sira is thinking of Jer. 10:11-16 which mentions the Lord as establishing the world by wisdom (Jer. 10:12). **Creator of all things** (vs. 8) and the references to **Jacob** as the **portion of the Lord** and to the Lord as Israel's **inheritance** (vs. 12) are inspired by Jer. 10:16 (cf. Deut. 32:9). Since the whole passage in Jer. contrasts the Lord's eternality with the perishability of idols, ben Sira is led to make brief reference in vs. 9 to the eternality of wisdom. As she was present in the worship of God from the early **tabernacle** (vs. 10; cf. Exod. 33:9-10), so also she became **established** in the later temple service in Jerusalem. It is clear that ben Sira is thinking of wisdom as the law (cf. vs. 23).

24:13-17. Wisdom speaks of how, having taken **root** in Israel (vs. 12), she flourished in its sweet soil. The figures suggest strength, beauty, pleasantness, and fruitfulness.

24:19-22. In these final lines wisdom invites him who will to eat of her **produce** (cf. 15:3). As the opening lines of the poem are inspired by Prov. 8:22-31, these are inspired by Prov. 9:1-6, where wisdom, having established her house, sets out food and drink and issues her invitation. On vs. 20 cf. Ps. 19:10; Prov. 24:13-14. The reference to wisdom's **help** and to her protection from **shame** in vs. 22 may reflect the contrast between the craftsman who works with his idols, only to be shamed by them (Jer. 10:14), and wisdom who works with man so that he cannot **be put to shame.**

24:23-29. *Wisdom and the Law.* That **all this,** i.e.

wisdom and what is said of her in the preceding hymn, is to be equated with the **law which Moses commanded us as an inheritance for the congregation of Jacob** (vs. 23bc, quoted from Deut. 33:4) may be the most important saying in ben Sira's book. Whether he was the first to make explicit the identification of wisdom and the law (see above on 17:11-13), he was the first of those whom we know to take seriously its implications. By "law" he means, not the Pentateuch only—though it is primary—but all scripture. By equating law and wisdom he integrates fully wisdom and wisdom literature with the priestly, prophetic, and historical concerns of Israel as they are expressed in scripture. Later writers were quick to appropriate this identification (cf. e.g. Baruch 4:1; IV Macc. 1:17) and it became a general assumption underlying rabbinic thought. It is almost a commonplace, for example, to find the rabbis quoting a biblical passage which mentions "wisdom" and applying it as if it said "law."

This is not to preclude other definitions of wisdom. For ben Sira wisdom is still "the fear of the Lord" (see Intro. and comment on 1:11-20). But this is a subjective definition; objectively wisdom is the keeping of the law (cf. 19:20; 21:11).

24:25-29. One who knows the law is filled with wisdom as rivers are full at the time of high water. Four of these are the rivers said to flow from Eden (Gen. 2:10-14). To these is added a reference to the **Jordan** (cf. Josh. 3:15) and possibly the Nile— by a slight emendation of the Hebrew text "go forth like the Nile" may be read for **shine forth like light** (vs. 27a). Such is wisdom's depth, however, that no one can know her completely (vss. 28-29; cf. 1:2-3).

24:30-34. *Ben Sira's Wisdom.* Ben Sira continues the figure of wisdom as **a river** to describe his own personal experience. At first his wisdom was but an irrigation ditch, but it grew greatly in volume and depth. In a 2nd figure of speech he compares his instruction to the brightness of the sun at **dawn** (vs. 32). Vs. 33 clearly shows that ben Sira regarded his **teaching** as inspired and expected his book to be added to the still growing canon of Hebrew scripture. Vs. 34 is repeated in 33:17.

This passage admits of several interpretations: (a) At first he studied only for himself, but as his wisdom grew he felt compelled to teach others. (b) Initially he was concerned only with his small circle of students, but later he was led to write for all men. (c) Originally he intended to write little, but as his knowledge increased he found it necessary to add to his earlier writings. Of these interpretations the last is the most appealing, and the suggestion may be correct that **again** in vss. 32-33 indicates that ben Sira found it necessary to add a 2nd vol. (chs. 24-50) to his original book (chs. 1-23).

B. MISCELLANEOUS OBSERVATIONS (25:1-11)

25:1-6. *Pleasant and Hateful Things.* Mention of the **adulterous old man who lacks good sense** (vs. 2) occasions the digression on the beauty of **wisdom in the aged** (vss. 3-6; cf. 8:6-9; Prov. 16:31; 20:29).

25:7-11. *Ten Who Are Blessed.* Vs. 7b seems to promise a list of 10 praiseworthy men, but the Greek text counts only 9, viz. 2 each in vss. 7, 9, 10 and

3 in vs. 8. The Hebrew and Syriac texts add as the 10th (following vs. 8a): "[he who] does not plow with an ox and an ass," i.e. the man wise enough not to mix unnatural things (cf. Deut. 22:10). The inclusion of the **man who lives to see the downfall of his foes** (vs. 7d) admittedly falls short of the highest ethical ideals. But Ecclus., like Prov., simply does not attain great heights of altruism toward enemies.

25:9-11. The list rises to a climax in the mention of the man of **good sense,** the man of **wisdom,** and the man **who fears the Lord** (vss. 9-10). At first sight these appear synonymous, as indeed they usually are in the book. But here the man of wisdom must be one who is prudent or knowledgeable yet is not a God-fearer (cf. 19:24b) and is thus still inferior to him who fears the Lord. The latter alone possesses true wisdom (see above on 19:20-30). Some manuscripts remove the apparent duplication of "good sense" and "wisdom" by reading vs. 9a as "happy is he who has gained a good friend." Whether this represents the original text is uncertain. On vs. 11 cf. 10:24; 23:27.

C. Happiness and Unhappiness in Marriage (25:13–26:27)

25:13-26. The Evil Wife. The list of 4 vicious things in vss. 13-15 introduces the section on the evil wife (vss. 16-26). Clearly **wound** and **wickedness** (vs. 13) relate to her (cf. vss. 19, 23), and the Syriac could be correct in reading "a woman's wrath" in vs. 15b. The confusion between **venom** and "head" (vs. 15; see RSV footnote) is due to the fact that in Hebrew they are the same word.

25:16-26. On vs. 16 cf. Prov. 21:9, 19. Ben Sira elsewhere warns of the dangers of **woman's beauty** (9:8; 42:12) but praises the beauty of the **good wife** (26:16-17; 36:22). His reference to Eve (vs. 24) as the cause of human sin and mortality is the earliest such doctrinal interpretation of Gen. 3. The figure of an **outlet to water** (vs. 25) may be taken from Prov. 17:14. The suggestion of divorce (vs. 26) rests on the law of Deut. 24:1. **Separate her** is lit. "cut her off from your flesh," since in marriage they are one flesh (cf. Gen. 2:24).

26:1-4. The Good Wife. To ben Sira a good wife and a happy marriage are among life's greatest joys (cf. 7:19; 25:1, 8; 36:22-24; 40:19, 23). It is significant that monogamy seems to be assumed in the happy marriage, while his possible allusions to polygamy (see below on vss. 5-6) are always in contexts of tension and trouble. On this section and vss. 13-18 cf. Prov. 31:10-31. A good wife is regarded as a **blessing,** i.e. a gift or favor from the Lord (vs. 3; cf. 26:14, 23; 36:24; Prov. 18:22). **Rejoices** (vs. 2) lit. says "makes fat"; cf. vs. 13.

26:5-6. The Jealous Wife. Of 4 frightful things the worst is a **wife** jealous of another. While conceivably the **rival** could be another woman outside the marriage relationship, she more probably is another wife of the same husband (cf. 37:11a). Doubtless monogamy was the normal pattern of marriage in ben Sira's time, but the old practice of polygamy—motivated by political reasons, or by love, lust, or the desire for sons—may not have been infrequent. The 2nd wife was called by the technical term "rival," which comes from a root meaning "show hostility" (cf. I

Sam. 1:6). Lev. 18:18; Deut. 21:15-17 state laws relevant to the "rival" problem.

26:7-12. More on the Evil Wife. The evil wife irritates and stings (vs. 7) and the **drunken** or harlotrous wife is esp. troublesome (vss. 8-12). On vs. 9 cf. Prov. 6:25. In vs. 10 **daughter** means wife.

26:13-18. More on the Good Wife. Ben Sira celebrates a wife's **charm** and **beauty,** which shine brightly (vss. 16-17) and gladden **her husband** (cf. 36:22). The **holy lampstand** (vs. 17) is the 7-branched menorah which stood in the temple (cf. Exod. 25:31-40; 37:17-24). The text and meaning of vs. 18b are uncertain. Some manuscripts read "so are beautiful feet on firm heels." While there is no manuscript evidence for it, a more natural analogy would be for **pillars of gold** to refer to legs and a **base of silver** to feet (cf. Song of S. 5:15; 7:1).

26:19-27. More on Marriage Relations. These vss. (see RSV footnote) occur only in 2 Greek manuscripts and the Syriac and Arabic versions. Their authenticity is not established, and they contain little that is not said elsewhere. Vss. 19-21 exhort faithfulness to one's wife (cf. Prov. 5:15-19). The meaning of vs. 22b can be seen from the description of such a **tower** in II Macc. 13:5-6.

D. An Isolated Observation (26:28)

This vs., which lists 3 grievous things, is similar in style to 25:1-2, 7-11.

E. Sins and Sinners (26:29–28:26)

26:29–27:3. Dishonesty in Business. In commercial transactions it is easy to seek a petty advantage and to overlook a shady deal. Indeed thorough devotion to the Lord is the merchant's only protection against the temptation to dishonesty and its resultant calamity. Other warnings against dishonest wealth are found in 5:8; 21:8.

27:4-10. A Digression. The surest **test of a man** is to **hear him reason** (vs. 7; cf. 4:24), for what he says reveals what he thinks and what he is (vs. 6; cf. Matt. 7:16-20). Shaking in a **sieve** or firing in a **kiln** reveals any coarseness (vs. 4) or any inner, hidden flaws (vs. 5). Vss. 8-10 affirm in effect that one reaps what he sows. On vs. 8b cf. 6:31; on vs. 10 cf. 21:2.

27:11-15. Sinful Talk. Fools are unworthy associates (vs. 12; cf. 22:13; Prov. 14:7), whose speech is inconsistent (contrast 5:10) and sinful. On vs. 13 cf. 19:30; 21:20; on vs. 14 cf. 23:11. Their **abuse** of the godly is mentioned again in vss. 28-29.

27:16-21. Betrayal of Secrets. Cf. 22:19-22. Ben Sira greatly values friendship and regards the sharing of secrets as the final step in the attainment of intimacy (cf. 4:18; 8:17-19). The violation of a friend's **secrets** is the ultimate breach of fidelity.

27:22-29. Deceit. One who **winks his eye,** i.e. a deceiver—a frequent OT figure (cf. e.g. Prov. 6:12-15)—speaks sweetly but plots to use **your words** against you (cf. 12:16). **Even the Lord will hate him,** however (vs. 24; cf. Prov. 6:18), and his punishment is sure. With the proverbs of vss. 25-27 cf. Pss. 7:15-16; 9:15-16; Prov. 26:27. Vss. 28-29 seem poorly connected with what precedes, but their inclusion can be understood on the assumption that ben Sira is thinking of Ps. 35:15-26. There the psalmist prays for God to take vengeance on those who "wink the eye" and "conceive words of deceit," mocking and rejoicing as they anticipate his downfall.

27:30–28:7. Vengeance. The mention of **anger and wrath,** treated more fully in 28:8-12, serves here only to introduce ben Sira's comments on **vengeance.** The law affirms that vengeance belongs to the Lord and is not the individual's right (Lev. 19:18; Deut. 32:35). Man's part is to **forgive** one who wrongs him (cf. 10:6), so that in turn God will forgive him his own sins. This is a remarkable passage, in that it so clearly anticipates NT teachings (cf. e.g. Matt. 5:7, 23-24; 6:12, 14-15; 18:23-35; Mark 11:25). These vss. are apparently quite genuine, though it is easy to see why some have suspected them as a Christian interpolation. One should **overlook** an unintended offense against himself (vs. 7) and be deterred in his own sinning by remembrance of his coming **death** (vs. 6; cf. 7:36; 14:17-19) and of the **commandments** (cf. Lev. 19:18b; Matt. 19:17-19).

28:8-12. Strife. These vss. are for the most part a reformulation and expansion of ideas expressed in Prov. to the effect that anger produces strife. E.g. cf. vs. 8 with Prov. 15:18; vss. 8b-9 with Prov. 29:22; vs. 10ab with Prov. 26:20-21; vs. 10d with Prov. 18:23. The mouth's ability to inflame or quench anger (vs. 12) is also noted in Prov. 15:1.

28:13-26. Slander and the Evil Tongue. Apparently ben Sira knows the evil consequences of **slander** from personal experience (cf. 51:2, 5-6), and he has spoken of it earlier (5:14). Since vs. 15 seems to refer to noble wives who have been divorced and **driven** from their homes because of slander, it may be correct to regard vs. 16 as a reference to the husband who will never know the **peace** of a well-ordered home (cf. 26:2) until he learns to ignore slander. The evil **tongue** is a vicious instrument, worse than a **whip** or **sword** (vss. 17-18; in Hebrew **edge of the sword** is lit. "mouth of the sword"), which brings heavy, inescapable hardships (vss. 19-20). Indeed the peace of death is **preferable** to the suffering and trouble caused by the evil tongue, and genuine piety is the only defense against its ravages (vss. 21-23). One should therefore guard his **mouth** as carefully as he does his **property** (vss. 24-25; cf. 16:25; 21:25; Ps. 141:3), lest by it he himself should become a sinner (vs. 26a; cf. 14:1; 23:8; 25:8) and thus be subject to the evil tongue of others.

F. Borrowing and Lending (29:1-28)

29:1-7. The law provided for giving financial help to those who need it by loans without interest (Exod. 22:25; Lev. 25:35-37), though in actual practice this provision was frequently disregarded. Ben Sira sanctions such loans and encourages responsible repayment (vss. 1-3; cf. 4:31). He knows, however, that many persons take advantage of a lender (cf. e.g. 8:12; 18:33). Some humbly petition for a **loan** (vs. 5ab) then default in **repayment,** to the creditor's loss (vss. 5c-7).

29:8-13. Nevertheless one should run the risk and help the needy, for 3 reasons: (a) the commandment (Deut. 15:7-11) requires it (vs. 9); (b) unused funds are subject to loss anyway (vs. 10; cf. Matt. 6:19;

Jas. 5:3); and (c) if the debtor does not repay, your act can be regarded as **almsgiving,** for which the Lord will repay you (vss. 11-13; cf. 12:2; Prov. 19:17; Tobit 4:7-11; see above on 3:30-31). Vs. 11a in the Syriac version reads: "Lay up for yourself a treasure of righteousness and love."

29:14-20. Prov. regards suretyship with virtual horror (cf. Prov. 6:1-5; 11:15; 22:26-27), but ben Sira encourages it as an act of kindness (vs. 14), on the condition that one should not assume an obligation beyond his means (vs. 20; cf. 8:13) or participate in the practice professionally for hope of **gain** (vs. 19). Vss. 15-18 warn against letting one's **surety** suffer loss.

29:21-28. Borrowing another's hospitality is as bad as borrowing money. Either may lead to shame (vs. 28). It is better to be self-reliant though **poor** (vss. 21-23; cf. Phil. 4:11-12; I Tim. 6:6-8) than to be an unwanted visitor who has to perform menial tasks, suffer reproach, and yield place to a more **honored** guest (vss. 24-27).

G. Causes of Joy or Sorrow (30:1-31:11)

This section teaches that disciplined children, health, and financial independence are sources of joy in life, while undisciplined sons, sickness, and the love of wealth cause sorrow.

30:1-13. Children. The disciplining of sons is of major importance (cf. 7:23; 22:3-6; 42:5b) and the rod wielded in love has a prominent place in it (vss. 1, 12; cf. Prov. 13:24; 23:13-14; 29:15). Nonetheless ben Sira's concern in this passage is not so much the good of the child as the joy (vss. 1-6; cf. Prov. 29:17) or grief (vss. 7-13; cf. Prov. 17:21, 25) that the child can bring to the father. Cf. 3:1-16, where the son is advised to honor his parents primarily to secure blessings for himself.

30:14-31:2. Health. Ben Sira declares that **health** is better than **wealth,** and **death** than **chronic sickness** (cf. 41:2), for the **afflicted** cannot enjoy the **good things** which wealth provides (vss. 18-20). In vs. 18 some manuscripts read "before an idol" for **upon a grave.** The placing of food on a grave as a sacrifice to the dead was apparently a pagan practice (cf. Ps. 106:28) and seems to have been forbidden by the law (Deut. 26:14; but cf. Tobit 4:17). Bel and the Dragon ridicules the practice of placing food before idols, and the Letter of Jeremiah 6:27 regards gifts to idols and to the dead as equally foolish. Vss. 18-20 recall Ps. 115:5-6.

30:21-31:2. Ben Sira believes that life should be enjoyable (cf. 14:11, 14, 16). He praises **gladness of heart** (cf. Prov. 13:12; 15:13; 17:22) and warns against excessive **sorrow** (cf. 38:18-20) and other responses which would tend toward emotional illness. The text of vs. 25 is quite uncertain; perhaps it originally said something akin to Prov. 15:15b: "a cheerful heart has a continual feast."

31:3-11. Wealth. The effect of wealth, too, can be either positive or negative. It brings sorrow to him who is **devoted to it** (vss. 5-7; cf. Prov. 11:4a, 28a; 28:20; I Tim. 6:9-10) but is a source of blessing to him who uses it well (cf. 13:24a). Some men remain sinless simply because they lack the means to sin (20:21); the clever, deceitful man will sin if given the opportunity (19:28); but this man remains blameless though he has both the means and the opportunity to sin (vss. 8, 10). Instead he uses his wealth for **charity** (vss. 9, 11; see above on 3:30-31).

Vss. 3-4 appear to be popular proverbs which ben Sira cites as an intro. to this passage. Their relation to vss. 5-7 is clearly seen if one supposes a "nevertheless" between vss. 4, 5.

H. TEMPERANCE AND GOOD MANNERS (31:12–32:13)

It was expected that the wisdom student should become a person of culture, and the type of teaching included in this section is characteristic of Near Eastern wisdom. It may well have constituted an important part of the curriculum in the wisdom schools, where presumably most of the students were young aristocrats.

31:12-22. *Against Gluttony.* The similarity of vs. 12 to Prov. 23:1-2 suggests that **a great man** is better than "a great table" and that the figure of the "throat" is well interpreted by **greedy** (see RSV footnotes). **Greedy eye** (vs. 13) is lit. "evil eye," which in the OT has nothing to do with black magic but is a symbol of stinginess, envy, or greed (cf. 14:8-10). Vss. 14-18 are well summarized in 41:19c, "Be ashamed of selfish behavior at meals." On vs. 15a cf. 6:17. On vss. 19-21 cf. 37:29-31. **Industrious** (vs. 22c) seems out of place, for the context appears to demand "modest" or "moderate." Perhaps the meaning is "be industrious in heeding my instruction."

31:23-24. *The Good and Bad Host.* As they stand these vss. are a digression shifting from the guest to the host. Most commentators are agreed, however, that the Greek has missed the point and that originally they concerned the good guest who praises the liberality of his host and the bad guest who complains against his host.

31:25-30. *Temperance in Drinking Wine.* Ben Sira, with the OT generally, praises the delights of wine drunk in **moderation** (vss. 27-28; cf. Ps. 104:15; Prov. 31:6-7) but deplores overindulgence and stresses its evil consequences (cf. 19:1-2; Prov. 20:1; 23:29-35; Isa. 5:22).

31:31–32:13. *Proper Behavior at Banquets.* Banquets are made for laughter and joy, music and wine. Thus inappropriate topics should be avoided (vs. 31); friendliness, kind modesty, and lack of ostentation should be the order of the day for the **master** (32:1-2), the elders (vss. 3-6), and the younger guests alike (vss. 7-9). The true source of all **good gifts** should be remembered (vs. 13). It is possible that this suggests formal grace at meals, based on Deut. 8:10.

I. STABILITY UNDER THE LAW (32:14–33:6)

The law is a firm support to him who trusts it fully, but it is an unsettling influence on the hypocrite.

32:14-17. The serious wisdom student gives the Lord first priority in his life (vs. 14b) and accepts his hard discipline (vs. 14a; cf. 2:1-5, 15-18). Since he **seeks,** i.e. studies, **the law** (vs. 15a), it becomes a part of his very being, producing right thoughts and **deeds** (vs. 16). In contrast the **hypocrite,** i.e. the

man of divided loyalties, finds the law a hindrance (vs. 15b) and shuns its teaching, reinterpreting it to suit himself (vs. 17).

32:18-23. The wise man does not approach life overconfidently (vss. 20-22) but carefully deliberates each act (vs. 19; cf. 37:16), seeking to do what scripture demands (vs. 23). But the **insolent and proud man** is not so deliberate; he does not **fear** that he is about to transgress against the law (vs. 18b).

32:24–33:3. Unlike the hypocrite (vs. 15b) the wise man finds in the **law** a strong protection (32:24–33:2) and a trustworthy resource (33:3). **Urim** and **Thummim** (cf. 45:10) were oracular devices employed in ancient times to determine the Lord's answer to questions (see comment on I Sam. 14:36-46). Their use after the time of David is not clearly indicated (but see comment on Mal. 2:6-9), and indeed ben Sira feels that they are no longer needed —the Lord's will can be confidently known through the law.

33:4-6. Ben Sira exhorts his students to **prepare** carefully and to teach with steadfast consistency (cf. 5:10-11). Vs. 5 suggests the inconstancy of the fool's mind, which is ever changing (cf. 27:11). The point of vs. 6 is that a **stallion** shows no steadfast affection to any one master; similarly the fool is no true, steadfast friend of the law.

J. OPPOSITES (33:7-15)

All days are alike in that they are lighted by the **sun,** and **all men** are alike in that they are **from the ground** (vss. 7, 10; cf. Gen. 2:7). Yet God has **distinguished** the sabbath and the other religious holidays (vss. 8-9) and likewise he has **distinguished** the destinies of men (vs. 11). Some he has **exalted** (i.e. Israel) and among these he has exalted some even further (i.e. the priesthood; to be **brought near** technically means to minister as priest). Others he has debased (i.e. non-Israelites, esp. Canaanites; cf. Gen. 9:25). The figure of the **potter** (vs. 13), suggesting the Lord's power and prerogative over men, is used rather often in scripture (e.g. Isa. 29:16; Jer. 18:4, 6). But vs. 14 does not say and cannot mean that God makes some men sinners (cf. 15:11-20). Men themselves choose different types of life, and their choice makes them as **opposite** as **good** and **evil** or **life** and **death.** On vs. 15 cf. 42:24.

K. A FATHER'S DUTIES (33:16-31)

33:16-18. *An Interlude.* Ben Sira regards himself as the **last** of a great line of teachers (cf. 24:30-34). The Lord's **blessing** (vs. 16) is his gift of wisdom.

33:19-23. *Toward His Estate.* A father should protect his financial independence by not distributing his estate too soon (see comment on Luke 15:11-12). To become dependent on his heirs would be a disgrace.

33:24-31. *Toward His Slaves.* Vs. 24 virtually puts the slave into the same class as a beast, but of course the slave was a chattel, regarded as a thing. On the whole ben Sira's views are quite lenient and merciful (cf. 4:30; 7:20-21). Strict discipline is enjoined for the sake of obedience and industry (vss. 25-28; cf. 42:5c), but nothing excessively cruel or unjust is permitted (vs. 29). The difference between vss. 30-31 and vss. 24-29 perhaps rests on the distinction between the good and the wicked servant, but the Syriac text may be correct in identifying the man of vss. 30-31 as "an only servant." Buying him **with blood** means with money gained at your own hard labor. Cf. the Pentateuchal laws on slavery, esp. Exod. 21:2-6, 20-21, 26-27; Deut. 15:12-18.

L. Grounds of Hope (34:1-17)

34:1-8. False Grounds. The fool is often excited or elated by **dreams** (vs. 1), but in resting his hopes on them he is likely to be disappointed (vs. 7). Dreams are nothing (vs. 2) or are only reflections of the fool's foolishness (vs. 3b; cf. Prov. 27:19), and cannot disclose anything that is **true** (vs. 4; cf. Job 14:4). False or lying dreams are denounced e.g. in Jer. 23:25-32; 27:9; Zech. 10:2, and all forms of divination and sorcery are forbidden in Deut. 18:9-14. Of course ben Sira has to make allowance for God-given dreams (vs. 6; cf. e.g. Gen. 28:11-16; 37:5-7), but he much prefers the truth of the **law** (vs. 8). This entire discussion seems to have been inspired by Deut. 13:1-5.

34:9-17. True Grounds. In a personal comment ben Sira extols the education and maturity which follow on travel and a broad acquaintance with the realities of life (vss. 9-12; cf. 51:1-2; Job 21:29). He affirms on the basis of his own education and experience that the Lord is the surest ground of man's **hope** and his firm **support** (vss. 13-17; cf. 2:6-13).

M. Worship of the Lord (34:18–36:17)

34:18-26. Unacceptable Worship. Following the highest insights of the prophets and the sages of Prov., ben Sira teaches that atonement for sin cannot be won by the mere mechanics of ritual performance. The sacrifices of the **ungodly** are unacceptable (vs. 19a; cf. Prov. 15:8; 21:27), even if offered in great numbers (vs. 19b; cf. 7:9). To sacrifice **from what has been wrongfully obtained** (vs. 18), e.g. from assets which really belong to the **poor** (vss. 20-22), is a heinous crime. On withholding **wages** cf. Lev. 19:13; Deut. 24:14-15; Tobit 4:14. Similarly fasting is not a proper act of worship if repeated sins nullify its good effect (vs. 26; cf. 5:5).

35:1-11. Acceptable Worship. The most meaningful type of **peace offering** (commanded in Lev. 3) is the keeping of the **law** (vs. 1; cf. I Sam. 15:22). The spirit underlying the gift of **fine flour** (Lev. 2) and the **thank offering** (Lev. 7:12) finds more genuine expression in acts of charity (vs. 2; on **kindness** and **alms** as technical terms see above on 7:32-36). There is no **atonement** without repentance (vs. 3; see above on 3:3-4). In essence ben Sira here restates the prophetic interpretation of sacrifice (cf. e.g. Amos 5:21-24; Hos. 6:6; Isa. 1:11-17; Mic. 6:6-8; also Ps. 51:16-17), for the prophets criticized the substitution of the ritual act for the larger concerns of ethics and morality.

35:4-11. Nonetheless ben Sira cannot ignore the institution of sacrifice itself. After all it is commanded in the law and must therefore be observed (vss. 4-5; vs. 4 is quoted from Exod. 23:15; Deut. 16:16, where each Israelite is ordered to sacrifice

3 times a year). Thus he recommends a **cheerful** and generous participation (vss. 6-11; cf. 7:31).

35:12-20. The Lord's Justice and Mercy. As one who is just, the Lord cannot accept a **bribe** or **unrighteous sacrifice** (cf. 34:18-20) or **show partiality** in favor of a man who has wronged the poor (cf. 34:18-22; Deut. 10:17; Job 34:19). Instead he mercifully heeds the afflicted (vss. 13b-15; cf. Exod. 22:21-23), the righteous (vs. 16), and the **humble** (vs. 17; cf. 21:5).

35:18-20. The subject suddenly shifts to Israel, to whom the Lord will be merciful and for whom he will take **vengeance** against the **unrighteous,** i.e. the Greeks, as he did against other **nations** in time past (cf. 10:14-17; 16:6-14).

36:1-17. A Prayer on Behalf of Israel. The prayer follows naturally 35:18-20 and continues its theme. God has shown his holiness in his restoration of Israel after the punishment of the Babylonian exile; thus ben Sira prays that he show to Israel his greatness by punishing the **nations** (vss. 2-4; cf. Ps. 79:6). The thought of vs. 4a is a favorite of Ezekiel (cf. e.g. Ezek. 20:41; 28:25; 36:23). Vs. 6 pleads for God to act **anew** as he acted in Israel's deliverance from Egypt (cf. Deut. 26:8). The present **enemy** (vs. 7) is of course the Greeks. In vs. 8b the Hebrew and Syriac read: "For who may say to thee, 'What doest thou?' "—suggesting that God can avenge Israel at any time he wishes. The words of the proud, self-reliant **enemy** (vs. 10b) are words which the Babylonians used to say (cf. Isa. 47:8, 10).

36:11-17. These vss. repeat the often expressed wish that the scattered **tribes** of Israel might be reassembled and might again control all of Palestine, with **Jerusalem** as a focus of active worship. **In the beginning** (vs. 15) means the same as **first-born** (vs. 12). The **blessing of Aaron** (vs. 17) is found in Num. 6:24-26.

IX. Proper Discrimination (36:18–42:14)

36:18-20. These vss. are an intro. to a series of passages which counsel proper discrimination, or proper discretion, in various areas of life. Each vs. may have been a popular proverb; similar forms of vs. 19 occur in Job 12:11; 34:3.

A. Social Relationships and Behavior (36:21–39:11)

36:21-26. Choosing a Wife. Marriage is better than bachelorhood (vss. 25-26), but one should use careful discrimination in choosing a wife (vs. 21). The best wife is one that is both beautiful and modest (vss. 22-23; cf. 26:1-4, 13-18). **A helper fit for him** (vs. 24) comes from Gen. 2:18.

37:1-6. Choosing a Friend. Vss. 1-4 are much like 6:7-13 and contain little that is new. On **evil imagination,** i.e. impulse to sin, see above on 15:14-20. Vss. 5-6 are close to 22:23-26. The Hebrew text of vs. 6 reads "in war" for **in your heart** and "when you take spoil" for **in your wealth.** This makes the vs. an elaboration of vs. 5b.

37:7-15. Choosing a Counselor. Proper discrimination will help one to avoid a counselor who is motivated by self-interest or prejudice (vss. 7-11). The **rival** (vs. 11a) is probably the 2nd wife in a polygamous marriage (see above on 26:5-6). Rather one should favor a **godly man** who has one's own interest at heart (vs. 12). Better yet is the **counsel** of one's **own** reason or conscience (vss. 13-14). In either case one should also **pray** to God for guidance (vs. 15).

37:16-26. The Speech of Wise Men. Vss. 16-18 are difficult, but they may be paraphrased: Thought precedes action, and the expression of thought in speech determines the fortunes of a man's life, whether for good or evil. The meaning of vs. 18c is more clearly presented in 27:6-7. The Hebrew of vss. 17-18a may be translated: "The roots of the mind's reasoning produce 4 branches"—though the 4 are really only 2: good-life and evil-death (cf. 15:17; 33:14; Deut. 30:15).

37:19-26. The text of these vss. is very confused, but ben Sira is apparently distinguishing 4 types of wise men. The speech of the first 2 types produces evil: (a) he who can guide others by his wisdom, but whose own life is less than a success (vs. 19); (b) he who is a skillful speaker yet does not prosper because the Lord has not favored him with the gift of true wisdom and his thought therefore lacks content (vss. 20-21). The speech of the following 2 types produces good: (c) he whose words accurately reflect his **understanding** and bring him personal reward (vs. 22); (d) the truly wise, who gives **trustworthy** counsel to others and receives the people's **praise,** and who, though his life may be relatively short, will have an enduring reputation in the life of the nation (vss. 23-26; cf. 39:8-11).

37:27-31. Matters of Food. Proper discrimination should guide the choice of foods, and proper discretion the amount (cf. 31:19-22).

38:1-15. Treating Illness. The **physician** is to be honored because **the Lord created him,** i.e. his profession (vss. 1, 12), because his skill is a gift of the Lord (vss. 2a, 14), and because his value is recognized by **great men** (vss. 1, 2b, 3). Vs. 5 is an allusion to the sweetening of the **water** of Marah (Exod. 15:23-25). In vss. 6-8 **he . . . his . . . him** in all cases refer to the Lord and **them** to the **medicines,** i.e. medicinal herbs, of vs. 4.

38:9-15. Careful attention to the subject of illness discloses 4 proper steps in treatment, all of which presuppose the customary interpretation that illness is a result of sin: (a) Prayer (vs. 9). Steadfast prayer is needed (cf. 7:10; 21:1), since the Lord is the true healer (cf. Exod. 15:26). (b) Repentance (vs. 10). This is basic to all forgiveness and healing (cf. 18:21; 21:1, 6). (c) **Sacrifice** (vs. 11). Ritual matters do not loom large in ben Sira's thinking, and this is one of but few places where he stresses sacrifice (cf. 7: 31; 35:4-10; contrast 35:1-3). The reference is to sacrifice as commanded in Lev. 2. (d) Consulting a **physician** (vss. 12-15), who is regarded as the Lord's instrument of **healing.** Vs. 15 seems to speak disparagingly of the **physician,** but this is not the original intent. The Syriac text reads: "He who sins before his Maker shall be delivered into the hands of a physician." This simply reiterates the view that illness is a result of sin, and this is the sense in which the Greek should be taken. A much later rabbinic saying puts it: "The door which is not opened for charity will be opened to the physician." Still and all, the Hebrew text reads: "He who sins before his

Maker is presumptuous before a physician." I.e. only the sinner despises the physician's skill—a sense which fits well what ben Sira says about him in vss. 1-8.

38:16-23. Mourning. The difference between proper and improper **mourning** should be recognized. The **body** should be properly prepared and buried (vs. 16; see above on 7:32-36). Vs. 16d in the Hebrew says: "Do not hide yourself when he becomes a corpse." One should also indulge in the ritual **lament** (vss. 16-17). Ben Sira's mention of **one day, or two** in mourning, when the traditional period was 7 days (cf. 22:12), may indicate that in actual practice the time varied greatly; or perhaps his reference is only to certain required rituals which could be completed in the shorter period, leaving the remaining days for informal expression. Indeed the whole tenor of his advice seems to stress ritual more than actual psychological involvement in grief. His warning against excessive sorrow (vss. 18-20, 23) is much like 30:21-23. On the finality of death (vs. 21) cf. 14:16-19; 41:3-4. Vs. 22 is a word of counsel from the dead.

38:24-39:11. Craftsmen and the Wise Man. For any serious aspirant to the ranks of the wise **leisure** for study is an absolute necessity (vs. 24). The farmers, engravers, smiths, and potters (vss. 25-30) make society possible and maintain its structure (vss. 32, 34); yet they cannot become leaders of the people, judges, or teachers (vs. 33). The portrait of the ideal scribe or wisdom student (39:1-11) makes no mention of gainful employment in a craft or trade, and apparently ben Sira himself pursued none. The later rabbis, however, customarily followed an occupation.

39:1-3. The ideal scribe or wisdom student is a student of scripture. The canon of Hebrew scripture (the OT) includes 3 well-defined sections: the Law, the Prophets, and the Writings. In vs. 1, as 3 times within the Prologue, the first 2 are clearly distinct, but the 3rd section is not yet firmly delimited. Ben Sira calls it **wisdom;** the Prologue refers to "the others" or "the rest." One would expect that what ben Sira knew as "wisdom" included at least Job, Pss., Prov. Vs. 2a may well be an allusion to the developing oral law, which was to be preserved in memory (see above on 8:8-9), though vss. 2-3 refer not so much to legal interpretations as to the type of wisdom found in Prov. (cf. Prov. 1:5-6; 4:21; 22: 17-18).

39:4-5. The wise man will be a person of stature and of broad experience and will be devoutly religious.

39:6-11. Vs. 6 is a reminder that wisdom is a gift of the Lord, a matter of his favor, without which none can be wise (cf. 6:37; 51:17). **Secrets** (vs. 7) means the knowledge of the Lord, revealed in the law and available only to his intimates. Vss. 8-11 are an expanded restatement of 37:23-26. **It is enough** (vs. 11) means his reputation suffices.

B. GOOD AND EVIL THINGS (39:12–42:14)

Of the various topics treated in this section, some are regarded as good and some as evil; others are either good or evil, depending on conditions or circumstances.

39:12-35. The Lord's Good Works. This passage contains a ps. of praise, blessing, and thanksgiving to the Lord for the goodness of all his works; but the exact structure of the passage is unclear. Most commentators regard vss. 12-15 as an intro., vss. 16-31 as the text of the ps., and vss. 32-35 as an epilogue. The RSV punctuation and arrangement, however, suggest that vs. 16 alone is the ps. itself, and vss. 17-35 a series of further expositions on it. A 3rd possibility is to regard vss. 12-17b as the intro., since vss. 12a, 14cd, 16-17b are in essence repeated in the epilogue (vss. 32-35), leaving vss. 17c-31 as the ps. itself.

39:16-31. However the structure is construed, the content of the passage affirms the goodness of all God's **works** (vss. 16, 33; cf. Gen. 1:31). Since he is omnipotent (vss. 16b, 17c-18; Ps. 33:6-7) and omniscient (vss. 19-20; cf. 17:15; 42:18-20) no one can question his works or the good purpose which he has for them (vss. 17ab, 21, 33-34). Some of his works are obviously **good,** though they can be perverted into **evil** by **sinners** (vss. 24-27). Other things which appear to be evil (vss. 28-30; cf. Hos. 13:15; Deut. 32:24-25a) are in reality good, since they are God's willing instruments of just punishment (vs. 31). Both **blessing** (vs. 22) and punishment (vs. 23; cf. Ps. 107:33-34) are well within his power. In vs. 22 instead of **a river** and **a flood** the Hebrew text reads "the Nile" and "the River," i.e. the Euphrates, which are both known for frequent, extensive flooding.

39:32-35. As noted above, these vss. are repetitive: cf. vs. 32 with vs. 12; vss. 33-34 with vss. 16-17b; vs. 35 with vs. 14cd.

40:1-11. Suffering. Ben Sira's acquaintance with the harsh realities of life convinces him that hardship (vs. 1), mental anguish (vss. 2, 5-7), and physical suffering (vs. 9; cf. 39:29-30) are the lot of all men (vss. 3-4, 8a; cf. Job 7:1-2; 14:1; Eccl. 2:22-23). For **purple and a crown** the Hebrew text of vs. 4a reads "a turban and plate" and thus includes high priest as well as king (cf. Exod. 28:36-37). Suffering mars man's life from birth to death (vss. 1, 11). Man's **mother** is of course the earth (cf. Gen. 3:19). Perhaps vs. 11b should read as the Hebrew: "what is from above [returns] on high" (cf. Eccl. 12:7), the reference being to man's breath rather than to any idea of life after death.

Ben Sira is involved here in a rather serious conflict of thought. Customarily he affirms the basic theological stance of Prov. that sinners suffer but the righteous reap rewards. But here he has to admit that life itself seems to ignore the doctrine. How explain the suffering of the righteous? Elsewhere he interprets it as the Lord's testing, or as his disciplining for their good (2:1-5), but that will not suffice here. All he can do is claim that suffering afflicts the evil much more than other men (vs. 8), that in fact it is for them that these **calamities . . . were created** (vs. 10; cf. 39:25).

40:12-17. Enduring and Transitory Things. Dishonesty and ill-gotten gain will soon pass away (vss. 12a, 13, 14b; cf. 5:8) but honesty and wisely used wealth endure (vss. 12b, 14a; cf. 31:8-11). The **children** of sinners (in the Hebrew text the sinner himself) will not be productive, for their rootage is

shallow (vss. 15-16). **Plucked up** in the Hebrew text reads "dried up"; the idea is that as soon as the stream recedes the **reeds** will perish (cf. 41:5-8; Wisd. Sol. 4:3-5). Charity **endures** (vs. 17; on **kindness** and **almsgiving** see above on 7:32-36) and is abundantly fruitful. In the Hebrew vs. 17a reads: "Kindness, like eternity, shall never be cut off."

40:18-27. Joys of Life. These vss. form a list of 18 of life's delights, culminating in the **fear of the Lord** (see above on 1:11-20). Almost all are discussed at greater length elsewhere in the book. The **self-reliant** man (vs. 18) is one who is independent. The Hebrew text in vs. 20b reads "friends" for **wisdom;** in vs. 23 "a prudent wife" for **a wife with her husband;** and in vs. 27.

40:28-30. The Beggar's Life. This is an example of one of life's evil things (cf. 29:21-28).

41:1-4. Death. Death can be either an evil (vs. 1) or a good (vs. 2; cf. 30:17), but it is inevitable and final (vss. 3c-4; cf. Eccl. 6:6) and should be accepted without fear (vs. 3ab). On **Hades** see above on 14:11-19. The Hebrew text of vs. 3 carries the force: "Remember those who have lived before you and those who come after; all alike share the decree . . ."

41:5-13. Memorials. At death sinners are survived by ungodly children whose **posterity** will **suffer reproach** and will ultimately die out (vss. 5-7; cf. 40:15; contrast 26:21; Prov. 14:26). Thus death is truly the end of everything for the sinner (vss. 8-10). Even a **good** man's **life** is short at best (cf. 17:2; 37:25), but a good reputation **endures** (vss. 12-13).

41:14–42:8. Kinds of Shame. The brief intro. (vss. 14-16) repeats vss. 14b-15 from 20:30-31. The distinction between a proper sense of shame (41:17-23) and an improper one (42:1-8) was drawn in 4:20b-21 and illustrated in 4:22-27; 20:22-23.

41:17-23. Almost all the 20 things listed in this passage are discussed elsewhere. "[Be ashamed] of breaking an oath and a covenant."

42:1-8. Vs. 1b completes the intro. to this subsection (cf. 4:22, 27). Specifically the things of which one should not be ashamed fall under 5 heads: (a) The **law** and the **covenant** (vs. 2a, Hebrew "statute"). This may be directed against "hellenizing" Jews. (b) Justice to the innocent party in a case, even if in general he is **ungodly,** i.e. a Gentile (vs. 2b; cf. 4:9). (c) Honesty in business (vss. 3-5a, 7). The Hebrew text of vs. 4a could be rendered "of accuracy with scales and balances, and of testing measures and weights." (d) **Discipline** in the home (vss. 5b-6). (e) Correction of the **foolish** (vs. 8). In some manuscripts vs. 8b refers to the aged man who is accused of sexual impropriety (cf. 25:2).

42:9-14. Woman's Wickedness. These paragraphs conclude the section on good and evil things.

42:9-11. The troubles which a **daughter** brings on **her father** are also noted in 7:24-25; 22:3b-5 (cf. 26:10-12, though there "daughter" probably means "wife"). Quite possibly **hated** (vs. 9) denotes the less liked of 2 wives (cf. Gen. 29:33; Deut. 21:15-17). **Laughingstock to . . . enemies** occurs also in 6:4; 18:31 in contexts denouncing lust.

42:12-13. In the Hebrew text these vss. are closely related to the preceding. Still speaking of the daughter vs. 12 says: "Let her not display her beauty to any man or converse with married women," and vs.

13 means "lest she learn the wickedness of their ways." But in the Greek texts these vss. are sharply set off as a body of advice to men concerning the wickedness of women in general. Vs. 12a repeats the counsel of 9:8; 25:21, which is not applicable, however, to one's own wife (26:16-18; 36:22).

42:14. This vs. is the climax of ben Sira's deprecation of women.

X. PRAISE OF THE LORD OF NATURE (42:15–43:33)

In addition to hymns celebrating God's creation of wisdom (1:1-10; 24:1-22) Ecclus. includes several other creation poems which extol God's greatness (16:26–17:14; 18:1-10; 33:7-15; 39:16-31). This is the most lengthy. It falls quite naturally into 3 parts: an intro. (42:15-25), a catalogue of some natural objects and forces (43:1-26), and a summary conclusion (43:27-33).

A. INTRO. (42:15-25)

After a single prefatory statement (vs. 15ab; cf. Job 15:17b) ben Sira speaks of God's creating by fiat (vs. 15c; cf. 39:17c; Gen. 1) and of the pervasiveness of **his glory,** which is like that of sunlight (vs. 16). Even the angels are unable to declare the fullness of his **works** (vs. 17). He is eternal (vs. 21b) and all-knowing (vss. 18-20) with reference both to nature and to man. On the **abyss** see above on 1:1-10; on God's ability to know man's thoughts cf. 23:19. His **wisdom** is complete (vs. 21; cf. Isa. 40:13-14). His works are enduring (vs. 23a; cf. 16:27), sufficient **for every need** (cf. 39:21, 33-34), and **obedient** to his control (vs. 23b; cf. 16:28; 39: 31). Though they are distinct they work together harmoniously (vss. 24-25; cf. 33:15).

B. A CATALOGUE (43:1-26)

This list of God's natural wonders is similar to several others; cf. e.g. Job 36:24–38:38; Pss. 136:4-9; 148; Song of the Three Young Men 35-60.

43:1. *The Firmament.* In ancient Near Eastern cosmology the firmament was the arch or dome of the skies, conceived of as a solid substance (cf. Job 37:18) which held up the waters above it (cf. Gen. 1:7), and across which the luminaries moved.

43:2-5. *The Sun.* Ben Sira pictures the sun at dawn, heralding the new day (vs. 2), at blazing midday (vss. 3-4), and toward evening as it follows God's **command** (vs. 5; cf. Ps. 19:1-6).

43:6-8. *The Moon.* Vs. 6 is quite difficult, but apparently the RSV makes the best of a confused text. The moon appears at its proper **season,** to mark the **times,** i.e. months (cf. Gen. 1:14); the Jews followed a lunar calendar. As an everlasting **sign** it is a symbol of permanence (cf. Pss. 72:5; 89:37). It marks the time for the observance of the religious festivals (vs. 7a); the major ones, Passover in the spring and Ingathering in the fall, began with the new moon. Num. 28:11-15 specifies offerings for the time of the new moon, and many religious-social gatherings were held at that time. **The month is named for the moon** (vs. 8) in that the same Hebrew word means both "new moon" and "month."

43:9-12. *The Stars (?) and the Rainbow.* On the idea

of the stars standing according to the Lord's **command** cf. 17:32; Ps. 119:91; Isa. 40:26. Gen. 9:13 records the creation of the rainbow.

43:13-15. *Snow (?), Lightning, Clouds, Hail.* The Hebrew text refers to hail rather than **snow** in vs. 13. Lightning is an instrument of God's **judgment** (cf. Deut. 32:41; Hab. 3:11).

43:16-17b. *Thunder and Storm.* The order of these lines in the Hebrew text is 17a, 16, 17b for vs. 16a describes the effect of thunder rather than of earthquake as some have interpreted (cf. Pss. 18:7-15; 29:3-9).

43:17c-20. *Snow, Frost, and Ice.* Cf. Ps. 147:16-17. The fact that in the Palestinian hills snow falls on an average only 3 days a year adds to the sense of wonder which it causes. Its **whiteness** or cleanness is a frequent figure in the Bible. To the ancient mind frost also seemed to fall from heaven (vs. 19a). In the Hebrew text vs. 19b reads "And produces thorn-like blooms"—a reference to sparkling **pointed** ice crystals on the plants.

43:21-22. *Drought and Dew.*

43:23-26. *The Sea.* On vs. 23a cf. Job 26:12a. In writing vss. 24-25 ben Sira seems to have been thinking of Ps. 104:25-26. Vs. 26 is a concluding statement to vss. 1-25, which declares that God orders and sustains his creation (cf. 42:17d; Col. 1:17). **His messenger** is the wind (cf. Ps. 104:4).

C. CONCLUSION (43:27-33)

Designating God as **the all** (vs. 27b) is certainly no suggestion of pantheism. Ben Sira's meaning is that he is indescribable and unfathomable. Even the angels are unable to recount his works (cf. 42:17), and since he himself is **greater than all his works** (vs. 28b), man cannot expect to **praise him** adequately (cf. Ps. 145:3). At best our knowledge of his works is shallow or fragmentary (vs. 32; cf. Job 11:7; 26:14). The creator of **all things** also created **wisdom** (vs. 33; cf. 1:1-10; 24:1-17) and bestowed her as a gift (cf. 1:10) on the **godly.** This vs. is the connective link between the long poem just concluded and that which immediately follows.

XI. IN PRAISE OF FAMOUS MEN (44:1–50:29)

This long section is a natural sequel to the hymn in praise of the Lord of nature (42:15–43:33; cf. the sequence of Pss. 104–105). Just as all God's works testify to his power and praise him through their obedience, so Israel—in a sense the climax of God's creation, as in 16:26–17:14—praises him through her life. Ben Sira reviews Israel's history by offering individual eulogies of the notable succession of worthy persons who punctuated it, but his praise of them is rightly understood as also a praise of the Lord who **apportioned to them great glory** (44:2). Wisdom itself was a part of God's creation (cf. 1:1-10; 24:1-12) and Israel's greatness was possible only because he granted wisdom as a gift to these godly men (43:33).

44:1-15. *Intro.* In vs. 1 **our fathers** is synonymous with **famous men,** Hebrew "men of piety" or "loyalty" (as in vs. 10 where the same phrase is tr. **men of mercy**). **In their generations** means in chronological sequence. Vs. 2 means that their possibility for greatness was itself a gift of God (cf. 33:11-12). Vss. 3-6 list several types of men who lived in the past—e.g. kings, warriors, counselors. They all were **honored** by their contemporaries (vs. 7), but only some are remembered and still praised in later times (vs. 8), while others are completely forgotten (vs. 9). **These** in vs. 10 clearly denotes the men whom ben Sira is about to enumerate in the following chs. Their memory endures and their children still **stand by,** i.e. live within, the covenant promises which were made to them (vss. 10-15).

44:16. *Enoch.* Scholars have long been puzzled by the fact that Enoch is twice mentioned in the list of famous men (see 49:14). It is now apparent, however, that this was not originally the case. The best Hebrew text and the Syriac version do not include vs. 16 at this point, but begin the list of worthies with Noah (vs. 17). It now seems that vs. 16 has been modified and transposed from 49:14 (see comment), perhaps by those who esp. admired Enoch and felt that he deserved to head the list.

44:17-18. *Noah.* Ben Sira recalls that because Noah was **righteous** and blameless (Gen. 6:9) he was spared from the great **flood** (Gen. 6:11–8:19). On the covenant with Noah cf. Gen. 8:20-22; 9:8-17.

44:19-23. *Abraham, Isaac, Jacob.* Vs. 19a is based on Gen. 17:5, where the patriarch's name is changed from Abram to Abraham, explained by a rather fanciful popular etymology as **father of a multitude.** The addition of **great** may have been inspired by Gen. 12:2: "I will . . . make your name great." **The covenant in his flesh** (vs. 20) refers to the rite of circumcision (cf. Gen. 17:10-14, 23-27). **He was tested** (vs. 20) alludes to the proposed sacrifice of Isaac in Gen. 22:1-14, and the promise of vs. 21 to that in Gen. 22:16-18. **From sea to sea and from the River,** i.e. the Euphrates, **to the ends of the earth** is a traditional description of the ideal extent of Israel's territory (cf. Ps. 72:8; Zech. 9:10). **Isaac** (vs. 22) is a particular illustration of the general statement in vss. 11-12 (cf. Gen. 26:3-5, 24). He gave the **blessing** of the firstborn son to **Jacob** (vs. 23; Gen. 27:28-29; 28:3-4), who in turn blessed each of his **twelve** sons (Gen. 49:28).

45:1-5. *Moses.* Vs. 1 seems to be based on Exod. 11:3. Vs. 2a refers to Exod. 4:16; 7:1, in which Moses is told that he will be "as God" to Aaron and Pharaoh. Since the Hebrew *Elohim* can mean "God," "gods," "angels," or "holy ones," depending on the context, the Greek rather timidly rendered the last. Vss. 2b-3b refer to the plagues which Moses brought on Egypt (Exod. 7-10). Vs. 3d is based on the story in Exod. 33:18–34:8, in which in response to Moses' prayer "Show me thy glory" God declines to disclose the fullness of his being but does reveal his character as being gracious and merciful. Ben Sira teaches that **faithfulness** and **meekness** are qualities in which God delights (see above on 1:22-30); it is for these that God chose Moses (vs. 4). This is based on Num. 12:3, 7, where "entrusted" is a form of the verb "be faithful." Vs. 5 recalls the revelation at Sinai (see above on 17:11-13).

45:6-22. *Aaron.* The extraordinary attention given to Aaron in this passage and to Simon in 50:1-24 testifies to the importance which ben Sira attaches to the priesthood. Aaron the Levite was Moses' **brother** (cf. Exod. 4:14). He was the first priest, the founder of the **priesthood;** God vested the institution in him and his descendants (vs. 7ab; cf. Exod. 28:1-4; 29:9).

45:7c-13. This detailed description of the priestly vestments is based on Exod. 28 (see comment). **Splendid vestments** and **superb perfection** (vss. 7c, 8a; cf. 50:11) in Hebrew involve the words "for glory and for beauty" in Exod. 28:2. On the oracular devices **Urim and Thummim** (vs. 10) see above on 32:24–33:3. An **outsider** (vs. 13) is any person not in the Aaronic descent.

45:14-17. Moses' anointing of Aaron is described in Lev. 8:10-13, but in vs. 15 ben Sira is apparently thinking of Exod. 40:13-15, which also mentions that he shall "serve as priest" in a "perpetual priesthood." Deut. 10:8 says that the Levites were "to minister to him and to bless in his name," and the content of the priestly blessing is given in Num. 6:24-26. It has been suggested that vs. 14 refers to the cereal offering which the priest offered daily in his own behalf (cf. Lev. 6:19-24) and vs. 16 to the burnt offering and cereal offering made **for the people** (cf. Lev. 1-2). Vs. 17 lists the rights and responsibilities of the priests in addition to the temple service; they are teachers and expounders of the law (cf. Deut. 31:9-13; 33:10) and theirs is the authority in judging certain difficult cases (cf. Deut. 17:8-12; 21:5).

45:18-22. Vss. 18-19 recall Num. 16 (see comment), which is a conflation of 2 unsuccessful rebellions by **outsiders,** i.e. those not of Aaron's family.

45:20-22. Vss. 20-21 speak of the dues which were the priests' by right, since they could not be gainfully employed otherwise (cf. 7:31; Num. 18:8-19), and since the Levitical priests were not given property in the Promised Land (vs. 22; cf. e.g. Num. 18:20; Deut. 10:9; 12:12).

45:23-26. *Phinehas.* Ben Sira's statement about Phinehas (vss. 23-24) is based directly on Num. 25:6-13 (cf. Ps. 106:30-31; I Macc. 2:26, 54). Vs. 25 interrupts to compare the **covenant** of the kingship (cf. 47:11) with that of the priesthood. Ben Sira's strong insistence that Phinehas was in the true line of descent of the priesthood of Aaron seems to be some type of apologetic, but the details of it are obscure. Perhaps it has to do with the authority of one of Simon's successors (cf. 50:1-24), to whom vs. 26 is addressed.

46:1-10. *Joshua and Caleb.* Deut. 34:9-10 explains that on Moses' death the leadership of the people passed to Joshua, and **successor of Moses in prophesying** reflects Moses' being called a prophet in that passage. As a **great savior** Joshua lived up to **his name,** which means "Yahweh is salvation," for in taking **vengeance** against Israel's **enemies** (cf. Josh. 10:13b) he saved the nation and won for it **its inheritance** (cf. Josh. 11:23). The language of vs. 2 is borrowed from the description of the capture of Ai (Josh. 8, esp. vss. 18-19), but if the Greek text is correct in reading **cities** (the Hebrew has the singular) the reference is also to the series of conquests recorded in Josh. 10:28-39, each of which was won "with the edge of the sword." Vss. 4-6 celebrate Joshua's victory at Gibeon (Josh. 10:6-14).

46:7-10. The background of vss. 7-8 is Num. 13-14. When the congregation murmured Joshua and Caleb alone supported Moses and Aaron (Num. 14:6-10; cf. I Macc. 2:55-56) and thus survived to enter the Promised Land (Num. 14:38; 26:65; cf. Deut. 1:36, 38) while **six hundred thousand** (cf. 16:10; Num. 11:21) died in the wilderness. Later Caleb (vs. 9), aged but strong, requested the **hill country** of Hebron (Josh. 14:6-14) and in turn passed it on to **his children** (Josh. 15:15-19; Judg. 1:11-15). Vs. 10b alludes to the repeated designation of Caleb as one who "wholly followed the LORD" (e.g. Num. 32:12; Deut. 1:36; Josh. 14:8-9).

46:11-12. The Judges. Ben Sira speaks collectively of the heroes of Judg., expressing the hope that their **memory** may continue to live in their descendants —the meaning of **may their bones revive** (cf. 49:10). Vs. 11 seems to exclude from this wish Gideon, who was involved in **idolatry** (Judg. 8:27) and Samson, whom the Lord left because he disclosed his secret to Delilah (cf. Judg. 16:20).

46:13-20. Samuel. Ben Sira recalls that Samuel was known as a **prophet of the Lord** (vs. 13; cf. I Sam. 3:20) who was faithful and **trustworthy** (vs. 15; cf. I Sam. 9:6). That he also functioned as a priest (cf. e.g. I Sam. 2:35; 9:13) is noted in the longer Hebrew form of vs. 13. He was a judge (vs. 14a; cf. I Sam. 7:15-17) whose efforts helped to bring relative peace (vs. 14b; cf. I Sam 7:12-14), and it was he who **established the kingdom,** i.e. the monarchy (vs. 13), by anointing Saul (I Sam. 10:1) and David (I Sam. 16:13) as kings.

46:16-20. Vss. 16-18 relate to Israel's victory over the Philistines at Mizpah (cf. I Sam. 7:7-11). Since the Phoenicians were not involved in that struggle, **people of Tyre** (vs. 18) must be regarded as an error for "enemy." Vs. 19 is a remembrance of Samuel's address to the people in I Sam. 12:1-5, and vs. 20 refers to the story in I Sam. 28:3-19 in which the dead Samuel, having been conjured from Sheol by the medium at En-dor, predicts Saul's death and Israel's defeat by the Philistines.

47:1-11. Nathan and David. Nathan plays a prominent role in the narratives of II Sam. 7:1-17; 12:1-15; I Kings 1:5-48, but ben Sira is esp. interested in him because he helped continue the prophetic succession between Samuel and Elijah.

47:1b-7. David was chosen from Jesse's sons and set apart for the kingship (vs. 2; cf. I Sam. 16:1-13), just as certain choice portions of the **peace offering** are reserved for sacrifice (cf. Lev. 3:3-5). While yet a youth he killed the Philistine **giant** (vss. 3-5; cf. I Sam. 17) and won the people's adulation for his prowess (vs. 6a; cf. I Sam. 18:7). As king (vs. 6c) he defeated many **enemies** (cf. e.g. II Sam. 5:7; 8:2-14), esp. the **Philistines** (vs. 7; II Sam. 5:17-25; 8:1).

47:8-11. But David is remembered for more than his military exploits. It was he who provided for the worship of the Lord in Jerusalem. Vs. 9 recalls I Chr. 16:4-7, and vs. 8 is a brief summation of the song in I Chr. 16:8-36. In vs. 10 ben Sira alludes to David's provision for daily praises, both **morning** and evening, and for the observance of the **feasts** (I Chr. 23:30-31). On David's **sins** (vs. 11a) cf. II Sam. 12:13; 24:10. The **covenant** (vs. 11c; cf. 45:25) is the promise that David's dynasty would continue (cf. II Sam. 7:12-16; I Macc. 2:57).

47:12-22. Solomon. According to I Kings 4:21 Solomon's territories were extensive, but **fared amply,** lit. "lived in a broad place" (vs. 12b), refers rather to prosperity (cf. I Kings 4:22-23, 26-28; Job 36:16). His prosperity, which included **peace** (vs. 13; cf. I Kings 4:24-25) and afforded the opportunity to build the temple in Jerusalem (cf. I Kings 5:4-5), was not a reward for his own righteousness, for he sinned (vss. 19-20), but **because of him,** i.e. David (vs. 12b; cf. vs. 22; II Sam. 7:12-16) —an illustration of how the prosperity of righteous men remains with their descendants (cf. 44:10-13).

47:14-18. Solomon's wisdom was God's gift to the young king (cf. I Kings 3:7-12). Its abundance (vs. 14b; cf. 24:25-26, 31) expressed itself in **parables . . . riddles . . . songs . . . proverbs . . . interpretations** (probably based on I Kings 4:32-33; Prov. 1:6) and won for him an international reputation (vss. 15a, 16a; cf. I Kings 4:31, 34). As translated in the Greek vs. 16 seems to have involved a play on the name Solomon and the similar Hebrew word **your peace;** but the original play may have been between **your name** and "your fame" (cf. I Kings 10:1), suggesting an allusion to the visit of the queen of Sheba (I Kings 10:1-10). The reference to Solomon's wealth (vs. 18) reflects I Kings 10:21-22, 27.

47:19-22. Ben Sira seems to criticize Solomon for being overly submissive to **women** (cf. 9:2; I Kings 11:1), but his words may also imply the criticism of I Kings itself—that these were women of forbidden nationalities (cf. Exod. 34:16; Deut. 7:3-4) whose gods Solomon favored (cf. I Kings 11:4-8). This is given as a reason for the division of the monarchy just following Solomon's death (vs. 21; cf. I Kings 11:9-13). Even so, ben Sira recalls (vs. 22), the covenant with David was kept (cf. vs. 11; II Sam. 7:15-16; Ps. 89:28-37) and his **descendants** were not completely cut off.

47:23-25. Rehoboam and Jeroboam. Ben Sira's reference to Rehoboam is derived directly from I Kings 11:43–12:17, which offers a 2nd interpretation of the cause of the divided monarchy (cf. vss. 19-21). Rehoboam showed **folly** and lack of **understanding** in refusing to follow the advice of the elders (cf. I Kings 12:8, 13) who counseled him to lighten the burden of Solomon's forced-labor **policy.** The **sin** in which Jeroboam involved **Ephraim,** i.e. the N kingdom of Israel, was improper worship as described in I Kings 12:28-33. The **vengeance** which **came upon them** was conquest by the Assyrians in 722 B.C. (cf. 48:15; II Kings 17:6-18, 21-23).

48:1-11. Elijah. Vss. 2-9 are a series of allusions to the Elijah stories in I, II Kings. The **famine** (vs. 2a) is that of I Kings 17:1; 18:1 (cf. Jas. 5:17). Vss. 2b, 7-8 refer to his visit to **Sinai** (synonymous with **Horeb**) in I Kings 19:8-18, where Yahweh commanded him to anoint **kings** over Syria and Israel and Elisha as his prophetic successor. Elijah **shut up the heavens,** i.e. prevented rainfall (vs. 3; cf. I Kings 17:1) and **three times brought down fire** (cf. I Kings 18:30-40; II Kings 1:9-12). Vs. 5 refers to the story in I Kings 17:17-24 (on **Hades** see above on 14:11-16) and vs. 6 to that in II Kings 1:2-17a. Vs. 9 recalls Elijah's translation into heaven (cf. II Kings 2:11; I Macc. 2:58). He and Enoch were remembered as having escaped death, and it is not surprising, therefore, that both later became the subjects of an enormous amount of legendary material. **It is written** (vs. 10) points to the expectation of Elijah's return (Mal. 4:5-6). The texts of vss. 11 are so poorly preserved that it is impossible to be sure of its meaning.

48:12-14. *Elisha.* The account of Elisha's becoming Elijah's successor is given in II Kings 2:9-15. In speaking of his boldness before rulers ben Sira is apparently thinking of his challenge of Jehoram of Israel (II Kings 3:13-14), of a Syrian king (II Kings 6:15-16, 18), and of an unnamed Israelite king (II Kings 6:33-7:1). Vss. 13*a*, 14*a* refer to the collection of remarkable stories of Elisha in II Kings 2-8 (esp. 2:19-24; 4:1-6:7) and vss. 13*b*, 14*b* recall the revival of the dead man at Elisha's grave (II Kings 13:20-21).

48:15-16. *A Historical Interlude.* Ben Sira interrupts his praise of the ancient heroes to note again the fall of the N kingdom, Israel, to the Assyrians in 722 B.C. (see above on 47:23-25; cf. II Kings 18:11-12). Vs. 15*ef* refers to the survival of the S kingdom, Judah, where the Davidic monarchy continued in accordance with the covenant with David (cf. 47:11, 22). Vs. 16 sums up the Deuteronomic appraisals of the Judean kings (e.g. II Kings 18:3; 21:2).

48:17-22*b.* *Hezekiah.* Hezekiah's strengthening of Jerusalem against Assyrian attack is described in II Chr. 32:5-6. **Hezekiah fortified** is a play on words between the king's name, which means "Yahweh strengthens" and the first word of II Chr. 32:5, lit. "he strengthened." Vs. 22 contains a similar play between Hezekiah and **he held strongly.** The rest of vs. 17 refers to the drilling of the Siloam tunnel, an incredible engineering feat by which workmen dug through 1,749 feet of **rock** to bring **water** from the Spring of Gihon to the Pool of Siloam (cf. II Kings 20:20). Vss. 18-21 contain numerous allusions to the account of the Assyrian threat against Jerusalem (**Zion**) as recorded in II Kings 18:13-19:36; Isa. 36:1-37:37. The reading of vs. 18*a* (see RSV footnote) is a capsule summary inspired by the first and last vss. of the story in II Kings. **The Rabshakeh** (vs. 18; cf. II Kings 18:17-37) was an Assyrian court official. Instead of **made great boasts** some mss. read "blasphemed God" (cf. II Kings 18:35; 19:6, 22). On vs. 22*ab* see above on vs. 16.

48:22*c*-25. *Isaiah.* Isaiah is remembered for **his vision** (vs. 22*d;* cf. Isa. 6?) and for the sign which he gave to Hezekiah when **the king** was ill (vs. 23; cf. II Kings 20:8-11). The sign was given in confirmation of the promise that Hezekiah would recover and live 15 additional years and that the Lord would defend Jerusalem against the Assyrians (cf. II Kings 20:6). Still later (vss. 24-25) Isaiah foresaw the coming Babylonian conquest (cf. II Kings 20:16-18; Isa. 39:5-7), but he **comforted** the people by announcing the end of the exile (cf. Isa. 40:1-2; 42:9) and the glory of the rebuilt community (cf. Isa. 61:1-7). Ben Sira of course recognizes no distinction between the 8th-cent. Isaiah of Jerusalem and the 6th-cent. 2nd Isaiah (see Intro. to Isa.); by his time Isa. was regarded as a unit.

49:1-3. *Josiah.* Ben Sira joins with the Deuteronomic historians in praise of Josiah (on vs. 3 cf. II Kings 22:2; 23:3, 25), for under the inspiration of the newly discovered book of the law (cf. II Kings 22:8-20) he instituted widespread reforms in his kingdom. **He was led aright in converting the people** (vs. 2*a*) would refer to II Kings 23:2-3, but the Hebrew text reads: "He was grieved at our backsliding"—a reference to II Kings 22:11-13. Vs. 2*b* highlights a major feature of the reforms—the removal of every trace of improper worship (cf. II Kings 23:4-20, 24).

49:4-6. *Another Historical Interpretation.* The Babylonians captured Judah and burned Jerusalem in 586 B.C. (vs. 6; cf. II Kings 25:8-10; II Chr. 36:17-19) and the Davidic monarchy **came to an end** (vs. 4*c*). Ben Sira's comment on **David and Hezekiah and Josiah** shows that he was influenced by II Kings (see above on 48:15-16; of the Judean rulers after Hezekiah II Kings praises Josiah only), but his interpretation of the fall of the city and the subsequent exile as a fulfillment of the **word of Jeremiah** may also show that he was influenced by the Chronicler's work (cf. II Chr. 36:21).

49:7. *Jeremiah.* When Jeremiah persisted in saying that the city would fall to the Babylonians, he was beaten, imprisoned, and lowered into a cistern to die (vs. 7*a;* cf. Jer. 37:15; 38:6). The rest of vs. 7 reflects Jeremiah's call (cf. Jer. 1:5, 10).

49:8-9. *Ezekiel.* Vs. 8 alludes to Ezekiel's **vision** (cf. Ezek. 1; 10), but the text of vs. 9 is so uncertain that interpretation amounts almost to guesswork. On the basis of a doubtful Hebrew text some scholars believe that the vs. is a reference to Job (in Hebrew "Job" and "enemy" are very similar words) or to Ezekiel's mention of Job in Ezek. 14:14, 20.

49:10. *The Twelve Prophets.* In Hebrew scripture the 12 prophets (Hos.-Mal. in the OT) are regarded as one book and follow Ezek. in order. On the figure of vs. 10*ab* see above on 46:11-12.

49:11-13. *Postexilic Heroes.* Zerubbabel and Jeshua (or Joshua) are remembered for having built the 2nd **temple** in Jerusalem (cf. Ezra 3:2, 8-9; 5:2; Hag. 1:14; Zech. 4:9; 6:12). Though ben Sira also remembers the mention of Zerubbabel as **like a signet** ring (Hag. 2:23), he does not speak of the messianic (monarchal) expectation which that figure suggested in the time of Hag., and which otherwise surrounded Zerubbabel and Jeshua (cf. Zech. 3:8; 4:14; 6:11-13). He makes much of the eternal nature of the Davidic monarchy (cf. e.g. 45:25; 47:11, 22) but never features the hope for the restoration of the monarchy, even in his prayer for Israel (36:1-17).

49:13. Under Nehemiah's direction the **walls** and **gates** and gate **bars** of Jerusalem were rebuilt (cf. Neh. 3:1-7:1). That he also rebuilt the people's **houses** is apparently an interpretation of Neh. 7:4. The absence of any reference to Ezra is the most glaring omission in ben Sira's list of famous men. Elsewhere the priest-scribe Ezra was regarded as the greatest of the postexilic leaders. Some have suggested that perhaps Ezra and Nehemiah have been fused together in ben Sira's memory. Others believe that since Ezra's thought developed into later Pharisaism, while ben Sira shows certain "Sadducean" tendencies, his oversight of Ezra was deliberate. Still others say simply that the lack of any reference to Ezra is a mystery.

49:14-16. *The Antediluvians.* Having enumerated the heroes from Noah (44:17) to Nehemiah, ben Sira now works backward from Enoch to **Adam.** Vs. 14 may well have contained four lines originally, two of which have been modified and transposed to 44:16 (see comment). Perhaps the vs. originally said:

> Few like Enoch have been created on earth,
> An example of knowledge to all generations (cf. 44:16*b*);
> He walked with the Lord,
> And also he was taken up personally (?, or "from the earth," as the Greek says).

The vs. is an interpretative rendering of Gen. 5:24 "Enoch walked with God; and he was not, for God took him" (cf. Heb. 11:5). "Few" (line *a*) represents the Hebrew text and is probably more correct than **no one.** For "knowledge" (line *b*, meaning the knowledge of God) the Greek mistakenly read repentance (see 44:16*b*). **Pleased** (44:16*a*) is based on the Septuagint text of Gen. 5:24, but "walked with" (line *c*) is supported in the Hebrew text. Ben Sira knew the tradition that Enoch's perfection enabled him to escape death. The words "few" (line *a*) and "also" (line *d*) may reflect the remembrance of Elijah's similar experience (cf. 48:9). Enoch and **Joseph** (vs. 15) are likened in that by tradition Enoch's body was translated and Joseph's was esp. **cared for** (cf. Gen. 50:25-26; Exod. 13:19; Josh. 24:32). **Shem** (cf. Gen. 9:26) and **Seth** (cf. Gen. 4:25-26; the Hebrew reads "and Enosh" for **among men**) were **honored**—because, according to the Hebrew text, they were "visited" with the sacred name Yahweh (cf Gen. 4:26; 9:26)—but Adam above all.

50:1-24. *Simon.* The long section in praise of famous men, begun in 44:1, climaxes in a eulogy of the recent **high priest** Simon. Ben Sira remembers Simon for having directed certain repairs and fortifications (vss. 1-4) and for his leadership in an observance of the Day of Atonement (vss. 5-21).

Who was this high priest Simon? Scholars seem now to be approaching a consensus that Simon the **son of Onias** (Johanan in Hebrew) was high priest from *ca.* 225 to shortly after 200 B.C. The late first cent. A.D. Jewish historian Josephus calls him Simon (or Simeon) II, though it is doubtful that there ever was a Simon I. It seems likely also that he is to be identified with Simon the Just (or the Righteous), who in rabbinical literature is said to have been an important link in the transmission of the traditions from the time following Ezra to the later rabbis.

50:1-4. The RSV is probably correct in considering vs. 1*a* a reference to Simon rather than to Joseph (see RSV footnotes to 49:15; 50:1). **In his life** (vs. 1*c*) indicates that Simon is no longer living at the time ben Sira is writing. His repair and fortification of the **temple** and **city** (cf. 49:11-13) fit well into the historical period immediately following 199/98 B.C., when the Seleucid King Antiochus III the Great seized control of Palestine from Ptolemy V of Egypt. It is not unlikely that this work was done soon after Antiochus' victory and with his consent. Indeed Josephus so indicates.

50:5-21. This description of the temple worship on the Day of Atonement is obviously that of an eyewitness, but ben Sira forgoes the details of the ritual acts—he seems to overlook some of them altogether —to concentrate on the radiance of Simon himself (vss. 6-10). He does mention Simon's coming out from the **inner sanctuary** (vs. 5*b*)—lit. "house of the veil," i.e. the Holy of Holies, to which only the high priest had access, and he only on the Day of Atonement—clad doubtless in white linen garments (cf. Lev. 16:4). Simon puts on the regalia normally worn by the high priest (vss. 11*ab;* see above on 45:7*c*-13), goes to the **altar** (vs. 11*cd*), and from his assistants receives the parts of the sacrificial beasts, which he offers for himself and the people (vss. 12-14; cf. Lev. 16:24-25). Then follows the drink offering (vs. 15), specified in Num. 28:7-8 in connection with the daily sacrifices. The **trumpets** sound (vs. 16; cf. Num. 10:2, 10) and the the people prostrate themselves in **worship,** which involves singing and prayers (vss. 17-19). The climax of the service is Simon's pronouncing of the priestly benediction (vss. 20-21; cf. 45:15; Num. 6:24-26). **Glory in his name** involves the fact that the divine name Yahweh was actually pronounced aloud by the high priest in this blessing (see above on 23:7-15).

50:22-24. As they stand in the Greek text these vss. could be a fitting conclusion to the whole section in praise of famous men. But the Hebrew text of vs. 24 reads: "May his love abide on Simon, and may he keep him in the covenant of Phinehas; may one never be cut off from him, and may his offspring be as the days of heaven." Simon's son and successor, Onias III, was deprived of the high priesthood in 175/74 B.C. when his brother Jason bought the favor of King Antiochus IV Epiphanes (cf. II Macc. 4:7-10). Within 3 years, however, Jason himself was outbid by Menelaus (cf. II Macc. 4:23-26). Smoldering resentment over Jason in the Jewish community flared into outraged riot over Menelaus, and this led eventually to the Maccabean revolt.

Ben Sira reveals no knowledge of the loss of the priestly office by Onias III, or of the subsequent events, though his unusual stress on the importance of the true priestly succession as seen in his praise of Aaron and Phinehas in 45:6-26, the last vs. of which seems addressed to Onias III, reveals dire premonitions that the office is threatened. The knowledge of Simon's fortifications and unawareness of the deposition of Onias III indicate terminal dates of 198-174 for ben Sira's writing. Most scholars suggest a date near 180.

50:25-26. *A Fragment.* These 2 vss., in the literary style of 25:2; 26:5, denounce the Idumeans, the Philistines, and the Samaritans. **Mount Seir** is the chief mountain range within the former land of Edom SE of the Dead Sea and in the OT is often used as a synonym for the nation of Edom. The Edomites long before ben Sira's time had been driven from their land by the Arab Nabateans and lived in S Palestine (Idumea), where they encroached on Judah's territory. Ben Sira is probably using traditional terminology to refer to these Idumean neighbors rather than to the Nabateans who in his day actually lived on Mt. Seir. The Philistines, traditional enemies of Israel, had by his time been largely absorbed into Phoenicia and were receptive to Hellenistic influence. The Samaritans existed as a separate **people,** though **no nation,** who worshiped in a rival temple built on Mt. Gerizim near **Shechem.** Ben Sira may have felt that they also were too kindly disposed toward the Seleucid kingdom.

50:27-29. Colophon. The author signs his book, adding a commendation of its content and a blessing on the reader. Of several minor differences between the Greek and Hebrew texts in these vss. perhaps the most important is that the Hebrew of vs. 27ab reads: "Wise instruction and apt [?] proverbs I have written . . ." This may account for the fact that the word "proverbs" or "parables" occurs in some of the ancient titles by which the book was known. On the author's name see Intro.

XII. APPENDIX (51:1-30)

In the Greek text, which the RSV basically follows, this chap. contains a ps. of thanksgiving (vss. 1-12) and an acrostic poem relating to wisdom and instruction (vss. 13-30). The Hebrew text includes additionally a thanksgiving liturgy quite similar in form to Ps. 136 and at the end of the ch. a doxology—present in variant form in a few Greek manuscripts—and a 2nd colophon, similar to 50:27b.

It has been customary to accept as from ben Sira at least the 2 poems which the RSV includes, but discovery among the Dead Sea scrolls of a first-cent. Hebrew text of vss. 13-20a and 2 words of vs. 30 calls this assumption into question. This text clearly shows that at least this portion of the poem has been extensively modified in the Greek version, and even more so in our other Hebrew copies. It contains no reference to prayer, the temple, or to glorifying the Lord who gives wisdom. Instead it is an allegorical, erotic account of a young man's intimacy with wisdom, who is personified as his nursing mother and then as his teacher and mistress.

The Dead Sea text is contained in a collection of psalms which purport to be of Davidic authorship. Since ben Sira's book was known to the members of the Qumran community who copied it, this poem could scarcely have been attributed to David by them had it been at the same time a part of ben Sira's book as they knew it. This evidence suggests, therefore, that the poem was written by some other wisdom teacher and was affixed to ben Sira's book, presumably because it was so similar in content.

If indeed the acrostic poem of vss. 13-30 is a later addition, one is also led to speculate on the origin of the ps. of thanksgiving in vss. 1-12. It would be a natural assumption that the colophon in 50:27-29 marked the end of ben Sira's work. Thus it is possible that the ps. of thanksgiving was also added later from another source, one point of attraction being ben Sira's statement in 34:12 that he has "often been in danger of death."

51:1-12. A Psalm of Thanksgiving. In a ps. filled with the phraseology of the biblical pss. the author sings praise to God for having delivered him from some mortal danger. One can only guess as to the details of his difficulty, but unless the language is figuratively veiled it would seem that enemies maliciously slandered him before a **king** (vss. 2, 6; the Hebrew omits **to the king**) with a charge punishable by **death** (vss. 5-6; on **Hades** see above on 14:11-16). Though he was innocent (vs. 4) he received no human help (vs. 7) but was delivered by the Lord after he had prayed (vss. 9-12). An interesting point is the designation of the Lord in the Greek text of vs. 10 as the **Father of my lord.** What means "my lord"? Suggestions include: (a) an error for "my life," as in 23:1, 4; (b) a reference to the priest-king of Israel, as in Ps. 110:1, "The LORD says to my lord," or by an extension of meaning to the nation itself; (c) a later Christian rephrasing of the vs. to make it refer to Jesus. Admittedly all these are quite tenuous.

51:13-30. An Acrostic Poem. This concluding passage is an alphabetical acrostic, i.e. a poem structured so that the vss. or lines begin with the successive letters of the Hebrew alphabet.

51:13-22. According to the Greek text this first part describes the search for wisdom by a youth—**from blossom to ripening grape** (vs. 15) means from childhood to manhood—who appreciated the necessity for thorough dedication and self-discipline (vss. 15c, 18, 19ab, 20ab), but who knew also that ultimately wisdom comes only as the Lord's gift. Therefore he prayed for her (vss. 13b, 14a) and, having received her, praises God (vss. 17, 22). Much of this is like what ben Sira says elsewhere: the allusion to his travels (cf. 34:11; 39:4); the value of seeking wisdom in youth (cf. 6:18); the need for discipline (cf. 4:17-19); prayer to God and praise for his gift of wisdom (cf. 39:5-6).

51:23-30. In this last half of the poem a wisdom teacher invites prospective students to come to his **school** (vs. 23)—the earliest known occurrence of this term, lit. "house of study," which later became the common name for advanced schools of biblical studies. Vs. 25 indicates that no tuition was charged, and apparently this is to be taken lit., though in later times there was sometimes a charge. Vss. 26-28 are quite similar in thought to 6:18-31—vs. 28 should be taken figuratively, much in the sense of 6:19. Vs. 29 seems clear enough, but in the Hebrew text the vs. reads: "May my soul delight in my circle of students, and may you not be put to shame in praising me," which may have been the original meaning. Vs. 30 urges the students to be diligent in study, so that they will be ready when the Lord visits them for judgment (cf. 18:20a).

BARUCH

Stanley Brice Frost

Introduction

This book—sometimes designated I Baruch in distinction from the Apocalypse of Baruch, which is then II Baruch—consists of 3 parts (1:1–3:8; 3:9–4:4; 4:5–5:9) which can be recognized as originally independent. The book is extant in Greek and in several translations from the Greek, but almost certainly at least the first 2 parts were composed in Hebrew.

The First Part. A letter containing a prayer of confession (1:15–3:8) has a historical intro. (1:1-14) which claims that Baruch, the amanuensis of Jeremiah (cf. Jer. 36), wrote the letter in Babylon at the time of the fall of Jerusalem in 586 and that the exiles sent it to Jerusalem with the request that the prayer be used in the services there. They also, it is said, defrayed the cost of sacrifices to be offered on behalf of Nebuchadnezzar and his "son" Belshazzar (see below on 1:10-14).

This work is clearly not from Baruch, because he was evidently in Jerusalem at the fall of the city (cf. Jer. 32:12-16) and went afterward to Egypt (cf. Jer. 43:5-7). Since it repeats the mistake of the author of Dan. in calling Belshazzar the son of Nebuchadnezzar (cf. Dan. 5), and since the liturgical prayer is strongly dependent on the prayer in Dan. 9:4-19, it must be dated after Dan., which was written *ca.* 165 b.c. Accordingly some scholars assign it to the Maccabean period.

The content, however, suggests rather a time when the Jews were under foreign domination, i.e. after 63 b.c., during the Roman period. Its purpose is to say: "Baruch and his contemporaries saw the need to submit to Gentile conquerors, and to pray for them; we urge you to do the same." More specifically it requests sacrifices and prayers for a ruler and his son who have just destroyed Jerusalem. If we look for a time when such a message would be relevant, it may be found immediately following a.d. 70, when Titus completed the capture and destruction of Jerusalem after his father, Vespasian, had returned to Rome to become emperor. In such a time this piece might well be written by a Jew living in Rome or some other metropolitan center, e.g. Antioch in Syria, in order to promote submission to the empire and to the Emperor Vespasian and his coregent son Titus—"and we shall serve them many days and find favor in their sight" (1:12). Thus this part of the book is probably to be dated during the reign of Vespasian (69-79) or of Titus (79-81). It hoped to heal the breach between Rome and Jewry by

winning adoption into synagogue liturgies, and there is evidence that in some areas it became for a while part of the liturgy of lamentation on the 9th of Ab, the day when the burning of the temple was remembered.

The 2nd Part. This section (3:9–4:4) is a poem on the theme "Where shall wisdom be found?" It is based largely on Job 28 but goes beyond it by equating wisdom with possession of the Torah, i.e. the Pentateuch (4:1-4)—a point of view characteristic of the later wisdom school (cf. Wisd. Sol. 10). This would suggest a date not earlier than the 2nd half of the first cent. b.c., but we cannot be very definite.

The 3rd Part. This poem of reassurance to the Jewish people (4:5–5:9) gives very little indication of date. The lamentation for captivity of Zion's children to a "nation from afar" (4:15) without mention of any specific event suggests a time during the first cent. a.d. before the disaster of 70.

The 2 poems were no doubt added to the first part sometime in the late first cent. a.d. At that time the mood of most Jews was not in tune with the composite work and it was not very influential among them. Among Christians, however, it came to be widely accepted, and in many LXX manuscripts it stands between Jer. and Lam. The passage 3:36-37 was taken to be a prophecy of the Incarnation, and many church fathers quote the book as scripture. The little book is esp. valuable as a testimony to thought and piety among Jews of the Dispersion in the latter part of the first Christian cent., before the loss of Jerusalem and the rise of Christianity destroyed the older ways of thought and gave birth to the more regimented rabbinism of the Talmud.

For Further Study. B. M. Metzger, *An Intro. to the Apoc.,* 1957. Sidney Tedesche in *IDB,* 1962.

I. The Prayer of Confession (1:1–3:8)

1:1-4. Authorship and Date. On Baruch cf. Jer. 36; 43:5-7; 45:1-5. The **seventh day** of the **fifth** "month" probably should be read instead of **year,** for that was the day Nebuzaradan put the torch to the temple and to **Jerusalem** (II Kings 25:8). At that time, however, Baruch was in the city with Jeremiah, not **in Babylon.** The **river Sud** is unknown. This intro. is designed to give the little work an air of authenticity.

1:5-9. Gifts for the Temple. After the destruction

of 586 worship of some kind was continued on the temple site (cf. Jer. 41:4-5), but we do not hear of any priesthood, and this **Jehoiakim** is unknown. Probably he is an invented detail, though the author may possibly be misdating the postexilic high priest Joiakim (Neh. 12:10). In vs. 8 no doubt he is thinking of the **vessels** mentioned in Jer. 28:3, but Baruch would not have had access to them. **Sivan** is the Babylonian name for the 3rd month, and so this would be nearly a year later; perhaps the author has in mind II Chr. 31:7.

1:10-14. *Prayer for the Ruler.* The mistake of calling **Belshazzar** the son of **Nebuchadnezzar** obviously comes from the story in Dan. 5 (see comment). He was actually the son of Nabonidus (556-539). The purpose of this document now emerges: to encourage cooperation with the ruling authorities (see Intro.).

1:15-20. *Prayer of Confession.* The phraseology is biblical, but cf. esp. Dan. 9:7, 10 (see Intro.).

2:1-10. *Warnings Realized.* The terrible **calamities** of which the prophets gave warning have come true. On vs. 3 cf. Lev. 26:29; II Kings 6:25-30.

2:11-26. *Appeal for Mercy.* The argument of vss. 17-18 is that the **dead** cannot praise God in **Hades,** i.e. Sheol (see comment on Ps. 6:4-5), but the living, however **feeble,** can; therefore may God let Israel continue to live. It is based on Isa. 38:18-19 and should not be taken as evidence of the author's own belief concerning life after death; he is simply concerned to echo a biblical passage (see below on 3:1-8). With vss. 21-23 cf. Jer. 25:10-11. Vs. 24 refers to Jer. 8:1-2. The author shows great familiarity with Jer.

2:27-35. *The Pattern of Compassion.* Relying on the general teaching of the OT that punishment is followed by restoration, the author asks God that, now that punishment has taken place, forgiveness may follow. He writes of post 586 but is thinking of his own times. In referring to **Moses** he may have Deut. 28 esp. in mind.

3:1-8. *The End of Iniquity.* The prayer ends on a note of fine intensity. The author avers that he and his fellows have put away the sins of their **fathers,** and that their fathers, who sinned so grievously, are pleading on their behalf. This thought of life after death contradicts 2:17 but probably reflects more truly the author's own conviction. No doubt he has Jer. 31:29 in mind. He accepts the idea of the solidarity of Israel and the nation's need to confess the sins of many generations; but he is beginning to suggest that, as taught by later Judaism, Israel's sufferings are no longer justifiable in terms of punishment for her own sin. The picture of suffering righteous Israel is beginning to emerge. The prayer may well come from the first cent. A.D. (see Intro.).

II. A Commendation of Wisdom (3:9-4:4)

This excellent example of the work of the Hebrew wisdom tradition stands in line with Job 28, on which it is modeled; Prov. 8; Ecclus. 51:13-30; and Wis. Sol. 7:1-30 and esp. 10:1-21.

3:9-14. *The Reason for Weakness.* Israel is wretched because she has **forsaken the fountain of wisdom.** On **Hades** see above on 2:11-26.

3:15-31. *The Way to Wisdom.* Wisdom will not be found with pleasure-loving **princes** (vss. 15-19) or with lusty youth (vss. 20-21) or in the traditional centers of sagacity (vss. 22-23). **Canaan** here probably means Phoenicia. **Teman** was a city and district of Edom. **Merran** is probably a misspelling for Midian. **Sons of Hagar** means Ishmaelites (cf. Gen. 16:15). All were early neighbors of Israel who had a reputation for shrewdness (cf. Job 2:11; Jer. 49:7; Ezek. 28:2-5; Obad. 8-9). Wisdom rests neither with the legandary **giants . . . of old** (cf. Gen. 6:1-6) nor in distant parts (cf. Deut. 30:12-14). No one knows where wisdom abides (cf. Job 28:12-28).

3:32-4:4. *God's Gift to Israel.* God the Creator knows where wisdom is to be found and has given her to Israel—the wisdom which is the **book** containing the **law,** i.e. the Pentateuch. If Israel will observe the law she will not be wretched (cf. 4:10-12) but, knowing **what is pleasing to God,** will be **happy** indeed.

III. Encouragement for Israel (4:5-5:9)

4:5-20. *Zion's Supplication.* The author reminds his fellow Jews that it is for **sins** that they are being punished. But he exhorts them to be of good cheer, for God will **deliver** them (vs. 18) and **Zion,** their mother, will herself plead for them.

4:21-29. *The Return of Joy.* Zion rejoices because she knows that God will soon intervene to restore her **children** from afar. She calls on her children, since they were headstrong in sin, to have a **tenfold zeal** in repentance.

4:30-5:9. *Jerusalem Exhorted.* Whereas previously the city has been exhorting her children, now the author calls on the city to recognize the coming salvation. She is to put off her widow's weeds, to **put on for ever the beauty of the glory from God.** Her children who have gone out **on foot** will come back **carried . . . as on a royal throne.** The **hills** will lie down and **valleys** will rise up; trees will shade their walk. This little exhortation to hope is very dependent on 2nd Isaiah (Isa. 35:1-2; 40:4; 49:22-23) and on the Pss. of Solomon (11:2-7) but nevertheless has a freshness of its own. The piety is akin to that of Luke 1-2.

THE LETTER OF JEREMIAH

Stanley Brice Frost

Introduction

This little document follows Lam. in the earliest manuscripts of the LXX; but in the Vulg., as well as in many later Greek manuscripts, it was attached to Baruch and thus came to be numbered as ch. 6 of that book. The older English versions included it in Baruch, but the RSV and other modern translations recognize it as a separate work, though retaining the established numbering for convenience of reference.

The work is best described as the transcript of a hortatory address rather than a letter. It is a rambling, repetitious attack on idols and idol worship, said to be written by Jeremiah to Jews about to be taken as captives to Babylon. "Jeremiah" is an obvious pseudonym; but the descriptive details point strongly to the probability that "Babylon" means the actual city of Babylon—rather than Rome as it often does in later literature (e.g. II Esd. 15:43–16:1; Baruch 1:10-14; Rev. 18)—and that the letter is an earnest appeal to Jews living in Mesopotamia not to succumb to the worship of the Babylonian deities. It is likely that the author himself lived in Babylon or some other city of the region and had often witnessed what he here describes. He chose to associate his work with Jeremiah because Jer. 29:1-23 tells of a letter sent by Jeremiah to the captives in Babylon and Jer. 10:1-16 expresses the sentiment on which he wanted to expatiate. No doubt it seemed to him very fitting that he should send out his letter in Jeremiah's name in the hope that it would exemplify the spirit and mind of the great prophet.

The prediction that the captives will remain in Babylon "up to seven generations" (6:3), rather than the 70 years of Jer. 25:11; 29:10 (cf. II Chr. 36:21; Dan. 9:24), suggests that the author may thus be designating the interval from 586 (or 597) to his own day. If so, assuming the standard biblical generation of 40 years, the date of writing is *ca.* 306 B.C. Though this is earlier than most other books of the Apoc., there is no evidence against a date late in the 4th cent. or early in the 3rd. Some scholars, however, prefer to place it in the Maccabean period.

The work is extant only in Greek and translations therefrom but probably was written in Hebrew—or in Aramaic, as a few scholars maintain. In some passages the translator into Greek has misunderstood the original text and as a result has produced nonsense. Sometimes retranslation into Hebrew reveals a probable cause for his error and makes possible reconstruction of the original (e.g. see below on 6:59, 72).

The author has given his work a superficial appearance of structure by repetition at intervals of a summarizing statement or question to the effect that the idols "are not gods" (6:16, 23, 29*b*, 40*a*, 44*b*, 52, 56*b*, 65, 69) and on this basis the RSV divides into paragraphs. These divisions do not mark units of thought, however, for the ideas follow no logical order and are often repeated. The main arguments are that the idols are not gods because: (*a*) they cannot look after themselves, let alone anyone else (6:12-13, 22, 26-27, 55-56, etc.); (*b*) they and their worshipers are immoral and unclean (6:11, 28-29, 43); (*c*) they cannot play the saving role of a true god (6:34-38, 41, 53-54, 66); (*d*) not being obedient to the grand design of the universe, they have no place in its unity of purpose (6:60-64). This last is by far the most original thought in the letter, but it is the least developed.

The little work displays the moral earnestness of Judaism *ca.* the 4th–3rd cents. B.C. and stands worthily in the tradition of Pss. 115; 135; Isa. 44:9-20; Jer. 10:1-16. The Apology of Aristides, a defense of Christianity addressed to the Emperor Hadrian *ca.* A.D. 130, reveals its influence; and an attack on dying paganism by Julius Firmicus Maternus *ca.* A.D. 350 borrows extensively from it. Evidently the letter meant much to the Christian church in the pagan atmosphere of the Roman Empire.

For Further Study. C. J. Ball in R. H. Charles, ed., *The Apoc. and Pseudepigrapha of the OT*, 1913. B. M. Metzger, *An Intro. to the Apoc.*, 1957. Sidney Tedesche in *IDB*, 1962.

Commentary

6:4. The author no doubt often saw processions in which idols were **carried on men's shoulders** (cf. vs. 26; Isa. 46:1-2, 7; Jer. 10:5), esp. at the great New Year festival (see Intro. to Pss.).

6:18. The comparison to **gates . . . shut on every side** on a political offender seems to refer to house arrest of a very strict kind, but it is a curious simile.

6:20. The idols, being made of wood with a thin plating of gold or silver (cf. vss. 8, 39, 50, 55, 57, 70-71), are attacked by insects along with the temple woodwork.

6:29-30. In ancient Hebrew thought a woman **in menstruation or at childbirth** was religiously "unclean" (cf. Lev. 12; 15:19-30; see comment) and the idea of her transmitting the uncleanness to **sacrifices** would be esp. shocking to Jewish readers. Similarly, since Jews limited participation in religious rites to males and had a long tradition of opposition to pagan cult prostitution, the fact that a woman should even **serve meals** to the image of a god would be quite offensive.

6:41-43. The **Chaldeans,** i.e. Babylonians, cannot see that their god **Bel** is in the same plight as the **dumb man** he is being asked to heal. If they could, they would forsake such impotent gods. Vs. 43 evidently alludes to a custom, described by the Greek historian Herodotus as prevalent in the Babylon of his day (*ca.* 450 B.C.), whereby a woman had to surrender her virginity before marriage to any passer-by as a tribute to Ishtar.

6:59. The idea of a **king who shows his courage** is a fine one, but a modest concept would be more in keeping with the rest of the vs. It has been suggested very plausibly that the original Hebrew was "better a stick in a man's hand." This fits better with **household utensil**—that it is better to be something lowly and useful than to be idle and useless.

6:60-63. Cf. Ps. 104:1-4. The author's thought is that anything which is not part of Yahweh's harmony of service is self-condemned.

6:70. This **scarecrow** image is borrowed directly from Jer. 10:5, but it is a telling illustration for the subject at hand.

6:72. The same Hebrew word meant both **linen** and "marble" (see RSV footnote). The translator into Greek apparently knew only one meaning—the wrong one for this context.

THE PRAYER OF AZARIAH AND
THE SONG OF THE THREE YOUNG MEN

George A. F. Knight

Introduction

Additions to the book of Dan. The 2 titles, the Prayer of Azariah and the Song of the Three Young Men, now form together 1 book of the Apoc. Along with Susanna and Bel and the Dragon they comprise the 3 so-called principal Additions to the biblical book of Dan. (see "The Intertestamental Literature," pp. 1110-15). These Additions are not found in the original Hebrew and Aramaic of Dan. (see Intro. to Dan.); therefore they do not appear in our English translations. They are, however, included in the LXX, which was the Bible of the early church.

These writings are an integral part of the Bible used by the Roman Catholic Church. We may find them today in a translation from Theodotion, a Jewish convert who sometime in the 2nd cent. A.D. produced what seems to be a free Greek revision of the LXX on the basis of the Hebrew. The Theodotion version displaced the LXX text in the case of the Additions in the early Christian centuries.

In the Greek versions Susanna forms an intro. to the biblical book of Dan.; we note in Susanna (vs. 45) that Daniel is "a young lad." Appropriately, then, this story comes first. Then the double book, the Prayer of Azariah and the Song of the Three Young Men (or "Holy Children," KJV) is found in Dan. 3, between vss. 23 and 24. Bel and the Dragon, really 2 stories, occurs not within the body of the book of Dan. but as a supplement. When Jerome made his important Latin translation of the Bible *ca.* A.D. 400, he drew attention to the fact that these stories did not occur in the Hebrew Bible and that Bel and Susanna at least were merely "fables."

Date and Composition. The Prayer and the Song both originated in the same period as the book of Dan. (see Intro. to Dan.). The Prayer of Azariah was evidently composed independently of Dan. during the period when worship at the temple was impossible, owing to the Jewish war with Antiochus IV Epiphanes. The Song appears to have been written, probably in Hebrew originally, only a matter of months after Dan., for we read in the Song that the faithful in Israel exulted at the restoration of worship at the temple. This historical incident is represented by the sentence that declares how God "has rescued us from Hades . . . from the midst of the fire he has delivered us" (vs. 66).

The Song has been used in the liturgy of the Christian church throughout the centuries. Vss. 35-65 appear as an alternate canticle in the regular morning prayer service of *The Book of Common Prayer* and take their name—the *Benedicite*—from the opening word in Latin.

The Teachings. We have here clear evidence that a prayer- or hymn-writer, provided he bases his language upon scripture, can produce a vehicle of worship which God can bless and use. The great biblical themes of the sovereignty of God, the judgment of God upon the apostasy of his own people, and of God's delight in showing abundance of mercy are all in evidence in the Prayer. The Song is one of the greatest paeans of praise of the Almighty that any man has ever penned.

For Further Study: R. H. Pfeiffer, *History of NT Times with an Intro. to the Apoc.*, 1949. R. C. Dentan, *The Apoc.: Bridge of the Testaments*, 1954. F. V. Filson, *Which Books Belong in the Bible?* 1957. B. M. Metzger, *An Intro. to the Apoc.*, 1957.

I. The Prayer of Azariah (vss. 1-22)

Azariah is the Hebrew name of Abednego (Dan. 1:6-7), 1 of the 3 young Jews whom Nebuchadrezzar thrust into the fiery furnace for refusing to worship the golden image he had set up on the plain of Dura (Dan. 3). The Prayer (vss. 3-22) purports to be what Azariah uttered in the flames. It is a blessing of God, not a thanksgiving. In the OT a blessing was something potent and conveyed something from the speaker to the one blessed. The willingness of the Almighty to receive a blessing from man is itself a revelation of his loving condescension.

Vss. 3-8. In blessing him, Azariah thanks God also for his **just** exercise of judgment. With the great prophets, he knows that God's judgment *is* his saving love in action. He believes that such judgment on Israel is justified (vs. 5), as did the writer(s) of the book of Lam. when Jerusalem fell in 586 B.C. (Lam. 1:5). In both cases the reason was the same. Israel had not obeyed God's commandments and so had not kept her side of the covenant (cf. Exod. 19:5).

Vss. 9-22. The **unjust king** mentioned here (vs. 9) is Antiochus IV Epiphanes (see Intro. to Dan. and Intro. to I Macc.). He sacked Jerusalem and desecrated the temple in 168 B.C. Azariah pleads that while Israel has indeed broken her side of the covenant, God should not break his: **deal with us in thy forbearance and in thy abundant mercy** (vs. 19), i.e. his "steadfast love" (cf. Ps. 136), which is the RSV translation of the original Hebrew word behind "mercy" and is the word selected to represent the content of the covenant relationship. God should remember **Abraham,** his "friend" (Isa. 41:8), and **Isaac,** his **servant,** and that **Israel** is his **holy one** (vs. 12).

It is true that God has every right to break with his faithless people. Yet they are his "holy nation" (Exod. 19:6) only because he himself is the Holy One. Thus for his own **name's sake** (vs. 11) he will not let them go. This tension in the heart of God is well expressed in Hos. 11:8-9. The steadfast love that Israel should show toward God can only reflect his love for Israel.

Vs. 12 refers to God's promise to Abraham (Gen. 15:5; 22:17; Jer. 33:22). Without temple, without high priest, without sacrifices and offerings (vs. 15), Azariah prays as did Samuel (I Sam. 15:22) that a **contrite heart** (vs. 16) may be the true **sacrifice** (vs. 17) that God will accept. Vs. 18 is a declaration of faith out of the depths, possible only because Azariah knows of God's marvelous works in the past—the Exodus, the restoration from Exile, etc., by which he has shown that he is the Lord, the only God. He therefore prays:

Let them [all mankind] know that thou art the Lord, the only God,
 glorious over the whole world. (vs. 22)

This prayer comes out of "the midst of the fire" (vs. 1). Its theological significance therefore rests in the fact that men have learned to praise God wholeheartedly only when they have met with adversity. Adversity is here represented as fire. Thus even in tribulation the faithful 3 young men are still "in" God, or God is still with them. No wonder they want to praise him.

II. THE SONG OF THE THREE YOUNG MEN (VSS. 23-68)

Vss. 23-28. To give this great benediction a setting in the Maccabean Wars, vss. 23-28 describe its as another hymn (cf. vs. 1) that all 3 young men—Shadrach, Meshach, and Abednego—sing in the burning fiery furnace. The fiery furnace represents the painful experiences the faithful had to undergo when they battled against the forces of Antiochus Epiphanes in the hills and in the beleaguered city of Jerusalem (cf. I Macc. 1; Heb. 11:35-38; see Intro. to Dan.).

Vs. 26. The prose intro. refers to the "son of the gods" of Dan. 3:25 as **the angel of the Lord.** In the OT an angel could represent God in his saving acts and speak for God as if God himself dwelt in him (cf. Exod. 23:20-21; Judg. 13:21-22; Isa. 63:9). Moreover, the LXX frequently translates the Hebrew phrase "sons of God" as "angels." The translator of the Song, then, putting the work into Greek, would be influenced by those sections of the LXX which were already in translation.

Vs. 31. From this vs.—**blessed art thou in the temple of thy holy glory**—we may conclude that this Song was written some years later than the Prayer, perhaps for the rededication ceremonies when the temple was consecrated for use again.

Vss. 32-68. The Song employs language that would come naturally to the lips of the faithful who knew the accepted scriptures of their day. The refrain reminds one of that in Ps. 136. Much of the Song is similar to Ps. 104, a poem which amplifies and theologizes upon the story of creation in Gen. 1. But it speaks also of the God who seeks intimate fellowship with his people, the God **who sittest upon cherubim,** i.e. whose mercy seat is between the cherubim that stretch their wings over the ark (vs. 32; cf. Exod. 25:20-22; I Sam. 4:4). Yet he is also the God who **lookest upon the deeps** (vs. 32), the "waters under the firmament" (Gen. 1:7; cf. Exod. 20:4)—a phrase which pictorializes the chaos out of which God brings forth order, salvation, and light.

Thereafter the Song becomes a summons to all creatures in heaven and earth, animate and inanimate, to **bless the Lord.** In OT times to bless another was to convey to him something of one's own soul, to confer upon him something he did not already possess. In God's case, however, that is not possible, for he is all in all and so lacks nothing that man can give him. Yet the biblical view, paradoxically, is that God seeks man's love and blessing, as if he needed them.

The Song ends with the words, **for his mercy endures for ever,** like the refrain of Ps. 136. **Mercy** we are to understand to be the concept of steadfast love found in the RSV.

THE BOOK OF SUSANNA

George A. F. Knight

Introduction

A Moral and Didactic Tale. For the date and composition of Susanna see Intro. to Prayer of Azariah and the Song of the Three Young Men.

It is interesting to recognize to what extent the art of short-story making was mastered by writers within Israel. This little book is an example of the ability of the Jewish mind to produce moral and didactic tales that, far from the usual overdrawn moralism of such works, are literary gems that are a delight to read. The book belongs to the same general class of literature as the story of Joseph in Gen., where we have a similar incident in reverse. Moreover, it demonstrates in narrative form that God is always faithful and loyal even to individuals within Israel, just as he has been loyal to his chosen people as a whole ever since the days of Moses.

There are only a few characters in the story, and they present a vivid contrast to one another. The issues dealt with are vitally important, for the stakes are life or death. We note the buildup of suspense. As in a good detective story we are led to ask: How will the author extricate his heroine from her plight?

That this book is a didactic *story* and not a historical incident is clear from its geographic setting. The setting is more likely that of Judea than that of Babylon. Just as some of the great Italian Masters could naïvely paint biblical scenes on medieval Italian backgrounds, so this Babylonian story is firmly set in Judea.

The Teachings. In the Intro. to Dan. we noted how Daniel was a legendary wise man who was well known for his judgments. In this book he comes to a judgment on the basis of divine inspiration and his understanding of human psychology just as did Solomon of old (cf. I Kings 3:16-28). It is almost as though he knew the methods employed by a modern detective. But the important point to remember is that, like the meaning of his name, i.e. "God is judge," Daniel's judgment is actually the righteous judgment of God himself. Thus this book emphasizes for the 1st cent. B.C. what must be said at all times, that there is an absolute will of God which he has revealed to man and by which man must live.

One aspect of this revealed will of God is that God hates adultery and passes judgment upon those who indulge in it, for adultery represents a fundamental disloyalty within the marriage covenant. True marriage ought to reflect that perfect loyalty and unshakable love of God for his covenant people which God himself has consistently shown to his

"spouse," Israel (cf. Isa. 50:1; 54:5-8; Mal. 2:14-16). The climax of the story is found in vs. 60: "Then all the assembly shouted loudly and blessed God, who saves those who hope in him."

As in the case of Bel and the Dragon, the text whose translation the RSV uses is that of Theodotion, a Jewish convert who during the 2nd cent. A.D. produced what seems to be a free revision of the LXX based on the Hebrew.

For Further Study: R. H. Pfeiffer, *History of NT Times with an Intro. to the Apoc.,* 1949. R. C. Dentan, *The Apoc.: Bridge of the Testaments,* 1954. F. V. Filson, *Which Books Belong in the Bible?* 1957. B. M. Metzger, *An Intro. to the Apoc.,* 1957.

Commentary

Vss. 1-2. Perhaps **Joakim** is meant to represent the captured king of Judah, Jehoiachin (see article "The History of Israel," pp. 1018-25). We read how he was taken to Babylon in II Kings 24. The behavior of his wife Susanna would then have a direct bearing on the messianic line. "Susanna" is the Hebrew word for "lily." The phrase Israel "shall blossom as the lily" (Hos. 14:5) might suggest to the reader that all Israel was represented in this one woman, the mother of the royal line. Thus the manner in which she withstands temptation is all-important for the future of God's people.

Vss. 2-3. When the author states that Susanna **feared the Lord,** he is using the nearest equivalent of the English "to be religious." To be **righteous** (vs. 3) was not to be perfect but to seek to live by the **law of Moses.**

Vs. 5. The Lord is the God of Israel; it is he who gives true insight to faithful judges (cf. Exod. 22:8; I Sam. 2:25a, KJV); only evil judgments, on the other hand, can come forth from **Babylon.**

Vss. 9-12. Men are deliberately free to turn **their eyes from looking to Heaven**—a reverential alternative for the divine name—and to play with lascivious thoughts. The 2 elders keep their desire for Susanna to themselves. It is something about which a man does not speak even to his best friend (vss. 10-11).

Vs. 20. Thinking that **no one sees** them, the 2 elders approach Susanna to seek relations with her. But she would have destroyed her divinely blessed marriage with Joakim if she had succumbed to temptation.

Vs. 23. Adultery is a sin against God. Lev. 20:10;

Deut. 22:22 both consider it therefore worthy of death (cf. Num. 5:11-31; John 8:4-5).

Vs. 34. The 2 elders lay **their hands upon her head** to point out the accused (cf. Lev. 24:14).

Vss. 42-43. Susanna is confident that God is in control of the powers of secrecy and darkness as they manifest themselves in the 2 false witnesses. She knows that all she need do is trust in God.

Vss. 44-46. Although **Daniel** left Jerusalem as a young man either in 597 or 586, here he is still **a young lad.** At this point it is important to remember that this story is not meant to be historical but to teach a great truth. The meaning of Daniel's name, "God is judge," is the important element here. The manner in which Daniel discovers the truth is in line with Solomon's judgment between the 2 mothers (I Kings 3:16-28); there we read that "the wisdom of God was in him, to render justice." Here, then, Daniel exercises judgment and conveys the justice of the living God.

Vss. 54, 55, 58, 59. These vss. employ puns in the Greek that cannot be translated into English.

Vs. 56. The Canaanites did not possess the law of Moses, and so they were addicted to sexual perversion (cf. Lev. 18).

Vss. 60-61. God does indeed save **those who hope in him.** He does so through the instrumentality of a chosen mouthpiece such as Daniel, who takes his stand solely upon the Word of God.

Vs. 62. The people execute the elders **as they had wickedly planned to do to their neighbor.** Deut. 19:16-21 prescribes the treatment to be meted out to a false witness. The execution of the 2 elders is also an example of the *lex talionis,* "an eye for an eye." It was to counter this attitude that Jesus said, "But I say to you, Love your enemies" (Matt. 5:44).

THE BOOK OF BEL AND THE DRAGON

George A. F. Knight

Introduction

Two Separate Stories. For the date and composition of the book see Intro. to Prayer of Azariah and the Song of the Three Young Men.

Like the Prayer and the Song, this book also is in 2 parts, in fact it is composed of 2 separate stories. In the Codex Alexandrinus (see "The Transmission of the Biblical Text," pp. 1225-36) the book occurs at the end of the Psalter, and so also in many Greek and Latin Psalters, and probably in the Old Latin Version. Its design is liturgical; it was meant from the beginning to be sung in worship. In fact it has been used in Christian worship since the 4th cent.

The book has survived in 2 principal forms, both in Greek. One is found in the manuscript of the LXX known as Codex Chisianus (87), and the other is the text of Theodotion. These may be read side by side in R. H. Charles' work, *The Apoc. and Pseudepigrapha of the OT.* Modern English editions use a translation of Theodotion, since it became the accepted text in the early Christian centuries.

I. The Story of Bel (vss. 1-22)

Bel was the chief god of the Babylonians. Originally known as Marduk, he was founder and "patron saint" of the city of Babylon (cf. Isa. 46:1; Jer. 50:2). He was represented there by a colossal statue in a magnificent temple. He was believed to have an enormous appetite. His priests provided him daily with great quantities of delicious foods and wines. Xerxes I plundered and, according to Herodotus, destroyed this magnificent temple in 479 B.C. (Isa. 21:9). The memory of this event in the troublous times of the Maccabean Wars (cf. I Macc. 1; see Intro. to Dan.), illustrating how the God of Israel showed himself to be stronger than mighty Bel, would give heart to those Jews who were loyally fighting against another Bel, or figure of evil, the Syrian king, Antiochus Epiphanes. Our story is told with a light touch, as if to bring a smile to the lips of hard-pressed Israel. And it is told interestingly, almost in the vein of a detective story.

Second Isaiah had vehemently stressed the folly of worshiping idols whe nhe was living in Babylon as an exile himself (Isa. 44:9-20). In sarcastic verse he described also the statue of Bel as it was conveyed to its shrine in the great pilgrimage through the city during the autumn festival—how it was unable to save itself from falling when its carriers stumbled on the cobblestones of the street (Isa. 46:1-2).

Vs. 6. Now in the next decade after 2nd Isaiah's description (Isa. 46:1-2), King Cyrus, who had succeeded to the throne of Babylon (see "The History of Israel," pp. 1026-31), supposedly believed that Bel was a **living God.**

Vss. 8-20. The test by which Daniel shows the king that the food left for Bel has not actually been consumed by the god but by the priests and their families is another example of the wisdom of this man. Note the cleverness of Daniel, who does not reveal the truth to the king until after the monarch has said, **You are great, O Bel; and with you there is no deceit, none at all** (vs. 18). The deceit was in the hearts of the priests. **Then Daniel laughed** (vs. 19); he had made his point.

Vs. 22. This incident is not historical. Daniel did not destroy the **temple** of Bel. Yet the wholesale execution and the "poetic justice" are both consonant with the spirit of an E didactic tale. The point of Cyrus' acknowledgment of Bel's defeat and of the power of the living God, for Maccabean times, was that it was foolish to doubt that Israel's God could gain the victory.

II. The Story of the Dragon (vss. 23-42)

The theme is again, Which God is the living God? The story would be on a level with one from the "Arabian Nights" were it not that it is told in order to press this theme. Dragons normally reject pitch and hair for supper (vs. 27), and it is only in the land of flying carpets that angels carry prophets 700 miles through the air by the hair of the head (vs. 36). So it is this other theme that we must not miss, and it is of timeless interest and value.

In the creation story of how God brought an ordered world out of the waters of chaos, the word for "deep" (Gen. 1:2) is taken from the name of a Babylonian goddess. She was a monster who personified the deeps of chaos. Those deeps remained under the earth (cf. Exod. 20:4) even though Yahweh conquered them in the initial struggle and is now in complete control over them. Throughout Israel's history the monster of the deeps continued to be pictured, sometimes as a sea serpent and sometimes as a dragon. This monster is assigned various names in the OT: Leviathan (Ps. 74:14; Isa. 27:1), Rahab (Pss. 87:4; 89:10; Isa. 51:9), or the Hebrew *tannin* (Ps. 74:13; Jer. 51:34). In Jer. 51:34 Babylon is the monster that swallows up Israel and thus takes the people of God into exile (cf. Jonah 2:1–3:3).

According to Israelite thought, one particular

figurehead could represent the whole people or nation. Thus, if a nation behaved "monstrously," its king was regarded as a monster himself. In this way Pharaoh himself was the dragon of evil to Isaiah, even as the king of Babylon was to Jeremiah. Rev. 12:9 applies the figure of "the great dragon . . . that ancient serpent" to the devil, as the chief figurehead over the powers of evil.

Medieval morality plays usually dressed up King Herod, who massacred the infants in NT times, in a red costume and decked him out with a red beard. This was because dragons were thought to be red (as was the goddess of chaos, red with the blood of her enemies) and in the habit of spitting flames of fire from their mouth. To this day Mephistopheles on the stage must wear a red costume. The Christian hero, St. George, has to slay a red dragon in the old legend, and then must rescue the fair maiden (the church, the bride of Christ) from its fiery mouth.

Vs. 27. Here the story reaches its climax. When the dragon eats the hairy cakes that Daniel made, he bursts open. **See what you have been worshiping!** exclaims Daniel.

Vss. 28-31. The king has become a Jew was, of course, what Israel hoped one day to hear. Some renegade Jews, in Maccabean days, had succumbed to the extreme pressure put upon them and were joining their Gentile neighbors in acknowledging King Antiochus Epiphanes to be divine. The faithful in Israel, however, who had withstood the forces of evil in the shape of the Syrian army, even to shedding of blood, now had to suffer the horrors of **the lions' den.**

Vss. 29-32. Jewish pride in Daniel forces our storyteller to exaggerate (vs. 29). It is hardly likely that the courtiers would threaten their king with death or that he would give in to them when pressed (vs. 30). There is yet another exaggeration. In Dan. 6:18-23 the time spent in the lions' den is 1 night. Here he is not rescued until the 7th day (vs. 40); there are also 7 lions (vs. 32).

Vss. 33-39. The person of **Habakkuk** is now introduced into the story. He is taken to Babylon in an unusual way (vs. 36; but cf. Ezek. 8:3). He had lived in Jerusalem in days of great tension (about 600, as most scholars presume) when the power of the Babylonians had threatened the utter destruction of Israel. His had been the cry: "Why, O Lord? Why do you allow your faithful people to suffer in this way?" In answer there had come to him a great word from God: "The righteous shall live by his faith" (Hab. 2:4*b*). It is this prophet, then, who long since had thus interpreted the place of faith in the presence of suffering who now, in this story, becomes the instrument of help and comfort to stricken Daniel.

Vs. 42. The punishment of Daniel's enemies is not to be understood as mere vindictiveness. It represents the just judgment of a just God. His saving love for sinners, as revealed in Christ, was not yet fully understood.

THE PRAYER OF MANASSEH

Stanley Brice Frost

Introduction

Manasseh (687/86-643/42) was the most evil of all the kings of Judah, and indeed the chief cause for Yahweh's punishment of Israel through the Babylonian conquest, in the view of the Deuteronomic historian writing during the Exile (II Kings 21:1-16; 23:26-27; 24:3-4). But with the passage of time his reputation came to be whitewashed by a story that after a period of wickedness he was taken as a prisoner to Assyria and there repented of his evil ways, prayed for forgiveness, and was allowed by Yahweh to return home and inaugurate a reformation (II Chr. 33:10-17). This amendment to history was clearly designed to explain how such a wicked king could have had such a long and quiet reign.

In telling the story the Chronicler noted esp. that Manasseh's prayer of penitence and entreaty was preserved in 2 sources (II Chr. 33:18-19). After these sources were no longer available—possibly early in the Maccabean period, though some scholars think in the first cent. B.C. or even later—a Jew living probably in Alexandria, or elsewhere outside Palestine, undertook to compose a prayer such as Manasseh might have said at the time of his repentance. Perhaps he intended it to be inserted in II Chr. 33: 13, but it never won a place in the text itself, though it came to be copied following II Chr. in a number of LXX manuscripts. More often, however, it was included among a group of canticles and liturgical pieces, e.g. the Magnificat and Benedictus, appended to the Pss. It is not possible to establish the original language, but probably it was Greek. If so, this would explain in part why it never found a place in II Chr. This book also, along with I, II Esdras, failed to win a place in the OT canon of the Roman Catholic Church, which includes all the rest of the Apoc.

The structure of the prayer is clear: an invocation of God, with exposition of the divine nature (vss. 1-7c); a confession of sin (vss. 7d-13e); anticipatory praise (vss. 13f-15). The little work is a fine testimony to Jewish piety in the last 2 cents. B.C. and is appropriately ranked with the poetry of Luke 1-2.

For Further Study. H. E. Ryle, in R. H. Charles, ed., *The Apoc. and Pseudepigrapha of the OT,* 1913. L. H. Brockington, *A Critical Intro. to the Apoc.,* 1961. Allen Wikgren in *IDB,* 1962.

Commentary

Vss. 1-7c. Wrath and Mercy. The Creator is characterized by wrath and by mercy. The author is following closely Joel 2:12-13. There "repents of evil" means that God rescinds the divine judgments which bring sufferings on men. Here **repentest over the evils of men** (vs. 7c) probably means that when men commit evil God is ready to change his attitude toward them if they will repent.

Vss. 7d-13e. Confession of Sin. The mention of the sinlessness of the patriarchs (vs. 8c) suggests that this is a product of the late postexilic period, when the idea was widespread. **Setting up abominations** (vs. 10f) means lit. "setting up idols," but here probably the thought is of erecting false gods in the mind and heart. **Depths of the earth** (vs. 13e) is a traditional OT expression (cf. e.g. Pss. 63:9; 71:20) for Sheol, the abode of all the dead regardless of their merit (see comment on Ps. 6:4-5). In this OT sense the line means merely "Do not make me die." At the presumed time of writing, however, the doctrine of reward or punishment in an afterlife was beginning to spread widely; and thus the author may be using traditional language to say: "Do not send me when I am dead to hell." Probably he sensed that such a plea from Manasseh would be an anachronism and did not choose to be too explicit.

Vss. 13f-15. Coda of Praise. In confident anticipation of forgiveness the penitent king lifts up his voice in praise, joining the **host of heaven,** i.e. the angelic army, in the universal song.

THE FIRST BOOK OF THE MACCABEES

George A. F. Knight

INTRODUCTION

Nature and Contents. I Maccabees is a history book. It deals with a section of the period "between the Testaments." It is a sober and trustworthy account in chronological order of the "Maccabean Wars," the Jewish wars of resistance against the Syrian power from 175 to 135 B.C. Thus it includes the period during which the book of Dan. was written and circulated (see Intro. to Dan.).

In addition to the narratives of military campaigns, the book contains other significant material. Most interesting are six poems:

1:24-28, a dirge for Judea
1:36-40, a dirge for Jerusalem
2:7-13, a lament over Jerusalem by Mattathias
3:3-9, a song praising Judas
3:45, another dirge for Jerusalem
14:4-15, a song in praise of Simon

The author also quotes letters that are seemingly authentic, e.g. 11:30-37, where King Demetrius writes to Jonathan. In 14:18 we read that bronze tablets were used for letter writing by the Romans to Simon. As is well known, such a practice has been authenticated by the discovery among the Dead Sea Scrolls of 2 copper scrolls, originally parts of 1 roll. This copper scroll was put "in a conspicuous place in the precincts of the sanctuary" (14:48), while copies of it were deposited in the treasury.

The narrative of the bronze tablets inscribed to honor Simon (14:25-49) provides a reliable history of the period. The author, whose name we do not know, made use of every aid available in his search for accuracy. Possibly he paced over the ground where the battles he records had taken place; possibly he figured out the movements of the contending armies as he stood on the spot and sought to reenact in his mind the clash of arms. Almost certainly, if he lived too late to know what happened firsthand, he interrogated eyewitnesses and survivors, thus enabling him to furnish us with graphic pen sketches of those stirring events he records. He must have resided in Jerusalem in the calmer days after the wars were over, for he had access to the temple records and to written material probably preserved only there. W. O. E. Oesterley believes that when the author declares that "the rest of the acts of Judas . . . have not been recorded" (9:22), he means that they have not been recorded in full, but some of his "very many" brave deeds were surely to be found in writing. The last 2 verses of the book, however, explicitly declare that the exploits of John, at least, "are written in the chronicles of his high priesthood."

The book has come down to us in Greek. But that is certainly a translation from the original Hebrew text. The story of a war for the recovery of the sacred things of Yahweh would most likely be written in the sacred language. Moreover, examples of idiomatic Hebrew phrases occur translated literally into Greek. Yet as early as the end of the first Christian cent. Josephus, the Jewish historian, seems to have known only the Greek translation that we possess.

The style of writing is that of a true craftsman—direct, factual, informative. The story is grippingly told. Our author is a true historian in that he does not obtrude his own personal views but seeks to tell his tale as factually as he is able. On the other hand, he follows the method used by ancient historians generally, of putting speeches of his own composition into the mouths of his characters. Again, he evidently exaggerates the numbers of warriors on both sides who go forth to battle, but this is a practice of ancient writers.

Date and Authorship. We have no sure knowledge as to when it was written. Our author must have lived after the close of the period of which he writes (134 B.C.). In 13:30 he mentions a tomb which Simon built for Jonathan his brother and which "remains to this day." The burial took place in 142 B.C. The phrase "to this day" implies a fairly long memory of the event. The last vss. of the book, however, are a more specific guide. The chronicles of John the high priest would be completed and so named only after his death. This took place in 104 B.C. This is probably then the earliest possible date for the writing of the book. On the other hand, the author shows no effect of the advent in Palestine of the Romans, which occurred in 63 B.C. We suppose therefore that he wrote before that time. It is more than likely, then, that he finished his book soon after 104, when the memory of the battles he records was still fresh in the minds of the older generation. But he may well have begun it a decade or so earlier.

The book is anonymous, like the history writing of the OT. In his account of the Maccabean Wars the author shows that his vital sympathies lay with the Jewish warriors. Thus we may think of him as a loyal patriot. But beyond this we cannot be sure. By his day the pure fires of zeal for the law had died down in the royal line descended from Judas Maccabeus, and most of the country's leadership was split into parties, each of which believed that it represented the true Israel. Our knowledge of the Qumran community, derived from the Dead Sea Scrolls, makes us certain that the author did not belong to the party represented by this group. As between the two major parties, the Sadducees and the Pharisees, there is too little evidence to assign him to either. This uncertainty is a compliment to his ability as a historian. That other good Jewish historian, Josephus, later on obviously makes full use of the material in I Macc., though he never acknowledges the fact.

Historical Background. Only a comparative handful of Israelites returned and rebuilt Jerusalem following King Cyrus' edict of 538 B.C. permitting all "displaced persons" in his realm to go home from Babylon if they wished. From that time on, the Jewish nation living in little Judea was only a small part—though still the "mother" element—of all Jewish people everywhere, the majority of whom were now living in the "diaspora" or as we would say, living abroad. Throughout the succeeding centuries Jews were to be found flourishing in Mesopotamia, Egypt, round the Medterranean (as we learn from Acts and Paul's Epistles), and later even in Rome itself.

The Jews in Jerusalem, after Ezra had made his influence felt, were always more "strict" and "orthodox" than those in the diaspora. They had the advantage of possessing the temple. Their numbers were small, and they might well have lost their identity in the great sea of peoples around them had they not clung loyally to their peculiar customs.

In 334 B.C. Alexander the Great of Macedonia, or upper Greece, began his conquest of the E, and soon Palestine was absorbed into the great Greek empire. 1:1-4 gives a résumé of this sweeping campaign and its outcome. It is alluded to also in Dan. 11:2-3 and probably in Zech. 9:13. At Alexander's death in 323 B.C. the vast empire split up into sections, various generals seizing power wherever they could (1:5-8). Ptolemy seized control in Egypt; thus began the Ptolemaic dynasty, which ended only in 30 B.C. when Queen Cleopatra VII chose the wrong Roman on whom to exert her charms. Seleucus set up his throne at Antioch, N of Palestine, and established in 312 B.C. the rule of his dynasty over the area that today we call the Levant. Little Judea lay immediately between those two new powers and became a prize that each sought to seize.

The books of Dan. and Esth. reveal the E flavor of life that the Jews, being orientals themselves, could well appreciate. But the whole tone and atmosphere of the new Greek civilization was very different from the oriental way of life. By 300 B.C. the philosophical thought of Socrates and Plato, not to speak of all the pre-Socratics, was available in any of the centers of culture of the great empire. Soon also Aristotle's passionate interest in what we now call scientific analysis and the classification of phenomena was known to educated men everywhere.

The Greeks had a missionary zeal about their culture. They sought to propagate it from the Mediterranean to the Oxus and the Indus. One means of doing so was to transplant Macedonian war veterans and give them land in one of the many new Greek settlements, there to propagate what they fervently believed to be the highest form of civilization and culture the world had yet seen. Palestine had its share of these Greek cities, with their Greek names, language, culture, and religion.

We know next to nothing of what was happening in Judea in the 3rd cent. B.C. During the years 323-198 the Jews were subject to the Ptolemies of Egypt and seem to have lived in comparative peace. They must have had ready access by land and sea to Egypt, for by this time the Jewish population of the vast city of Alexandria was some two thirds of all the mixed peoples who lived and traded there.

Two intellectual movements of the century may be noted. First, in Jerusalem there must have been great activity in biblical studies. During this unknown century the prophetic material was evidently collected and edited; also the later writings, such as those of the Chronicler (who gives us I and II Chr., Ezra, and Neh.) and the Psalter, were edited for public use. The ritual, daily and seasonal, at the temple, had now become highly elaborate. Again, a new class of *litterati* had come to the fore, the men whom we call the sages, the "wise men" who have given us Job, Prov., and much of our intertestamental literature. Though their kind go back to the days of Solomon and Jeremiah (cf. Jer. 18:18), they flourished especially in the period leading to the Maccabean Wars. One whom we can name, Jesus son of Sirach (i.e. Ben-sirach) completed his important book Ecclesiasticus, now in the Apoc., in 180 B.C. Yet all this theological and biblical ferment was evidently remote from the vast changes taking place in the life of the nations all around.

The 2nd movement was very different. It was the intellectual awakening of Jews in the diaspora, especially in Alexandria, under the impact of the exciting new Greek culture and of a reverse movement in the area of propaganda. Proud of their heritage but aware that knowledge of it was hidden from the world in the strange Hebrew language, Jews in Alexandria took the initiative in having Jerusalem scholars help them translate the OT into Greek. So the LXX gradually came into being. The culmination of this missionary movement was the work of the great Jewish theologian and philosopher Philo, who was a contemporary of Jesus Christ. His importance lies in his successful efforts to expound the revelation of God to Israel in terms that the Greek mind of his day could appreciate.

Our concern, however, is with the Jews of Judea and Jerusalem. For they, following the lead of Ezra in the 4th cent., had sought to "put a fence around the Law." They had sought to keep themselves "unspotted from the world." The inevitable clash of ideologies had to come sooner or later, of course, and it comes now in the period covered by I Macc. This clash is one of the main background issues of the book, and it is more important to recognize its significance than it is to learn the details of the war which was its outcome.

By 198 B.C. the Seleucids had become the stronger kingdom, and Judea had fallen under its sway. This change of master made little difference at first to the Jews in Judea. But such are the ways of God that unless his people meet with challenge and crisis from time to time their distinctive faith may fade away. It is of his goodness, it seems, that troubles must be met and faced. The crisis came suddenly; but the faith of the Jewish people was equal to the occasion, and Israel was roused, for the first time in centuries, to unprecedented heights of valor and faith.

Antiochus IV came to the Syrian (Seleucid) throne in 175 B.C. Dan. 11:21 calls him "a contemptible person." I Macc. 1:10 refers to him as "a sinful root," and II 9:28 calls him a "murderer and blasphemer." He gave himself the special name of Epiphanes, which means "God made manifest." To the Jews that was a blasphemy. So once they had experienced the ferocity of his ways they called him rather Epimanes, meaning "mad man."

The trouble began when a foolish party in Jerusalem revolted against him at the moment when the Romans had become a thorn in his flesh. So Antiochus took it out on the Jews, as he was unable to come to grips with the Romans. Within a matter of 3 days 80,000 men, women, and children were brutally slain by his soldiers (II 5:11-14). He himself stormed into the temple, plundered its riches, tore down the curtain that hid the Holy of holies, and entered where no one except the high priest, and that but once a year, dared go (II 5:15-16).

Then Antiochus sought to do by force what the Jews of Jerusalem had resisted doing for a century and a half. He insisted that they adopt Greek culture. The plan was to do away with the distinctiveness and uniqueness of Judaism and so have all men in his dominion think the same Greek thoughts. To do so he enforced the cessation of Jewish worship. There were 3 outward marks of this which he forbade altogether: (a) the reading of the Law—in accordance he ordered all scrolls to be destroyed, (b) circumcision, (c) the observance of the sabbath. In the temple he ordered an altar set up on which were to be sacrificed swine (unclean beasts according to the Law; cf. Lev. 11:7), not to Yahweh, but to Olympian Zeus (1:41-63). This act later generations remembered as "the abomination of desolation" (Mark 13:14; cf. Dan. 9:27, KJV) or as "the desolating sacrilege" (RSV).

At once resistance clustered round the family of one man. An old priest called Mattathias slew with his own hands first the king's officer who had come to his village of Modein, between Jerusalem and Joppa, to enforce the royal decree, and then a Jewish neighbor of his who was ready to become a quisling. This little group immediately fled to the hills. Mattathias died almost at once, but his 5 famous sons then became the nucleus of resistance. The eldest, Judas, became the leader, and was given the name of Maccabee. The word probably means "hammer," and he was so named for the same reason that Edward I of England was known as the Hammer of the Scots.

A guerrilla war was waged for 3 years until the little army recaptured Jerusalem and rededicated the temple to the glory of Yahweh once again. This ceremony is remembered to the present day in the festival of Hanukkah, which falls about Christmastime. It is mentioned in John 10:22.

The recovery of Jerusalem did not mean, unfortunately, freedom for all Jews. The war went on. Anti-

ochus died the following year, but the struggle was furthered by his successors. When Judas was killed in battle, his brother Jonathan stepped into his shoes. But the nature of the struggle gradually altered. It became less a religious war and ever more nationalistic in intention; in fact it developed into a war for domination of Judea's immediate neighbors.

The first fine rapturous movement of the spirit in loyalty to Yahweh was thus eventually a thing of the past. By the period soon after the book ends the struggle developed to be a sordid, mutually slaughterous strife, evidencing murder and intrigue and the usual horrors of an E court. Yet in the year 142 B.C., as 13:41 puts it, for the first time for centuries "the yoke of the Gentiles was removed from Israel," and Judea became a completely independent nation.

Though what follows is beyond the scope of I Macc., we may say in a word that from 104 B.C. onward the little kingdom suffered desperately at the hands of a number of ferocious rulers. Finally it lost its independence in 63 B.C., for the last time, to the great new rising power of Rome.

An Apocryphal Book. The story of the Apoc. can be found in the article "The Intertestamental Literature." Discussion of the relationship between canonical and noncanonical books is found in the articles "The Making of the OT Canon" and "The Making of the NT Canon," pp. 1209-24. A word or 2 will be sufficient here on the question of why I Macc. is not considered canonical scripture in the Reformed Churches.

The historical reasons for rejecting I Macc. are no longer valid. The Jewish authorities were not willing to canonize a work which, by the end of the 1st Christian cent., they thought was not originally written in the sacred language, Hebrew; at first the church accepted this Jewish criterion. Today, however, we are not so sure that the first draft of the book was not in Hebrew, and in this we follow the great scholar Jerome. Again, the word "apocrypha," which in Greek means "hidden away," may have been chosen to describe certain books for 1 or both of 2 reasons: (a) They were purposely "hidden" from the eyes of ordinary believers, on the ground that they contained esoteric lore understandable only to the initiated. There is nothing of such a nature in I Macc. (b) They were deliberately "hidden" away because they were heretical in their teaching. This may be true of some books in the Apoc., but it could not be said of I Macc. Why have the Reformed Churches, then, persisted in their rejection of this book? Surely it is of value to the Christian faith to know what happened "between the Testaments."

The following answer to this question is my own way of expressing why the book has not been canonized, i.e. regarded as part of Holy Writ. My point of view is expressed fully in *A Christian Theology of the OT*, rev. ed., 1964.

The OT and the NT together form the Word of God, as they witness to him who is the Word made flesh. The early church had no NT. The OT was sufficient as the church sought to answer the fundamental question Christ had put to men who already belonged within the covenant people: "Who do you say I am?" The risen Christ himself, again, in conversation with two unnamed disciples on the road to Emmaus interpreted all Christology ("the things concerning himself") by beginning with the Pentateuch and the Prophets and continuing with the whole of OT scriptures (Luke 24:27). In other words, the OT as the inspired Word of God ultimately tells us the same things as the NT. For the same God is revealed in them both, as the God of Abraham, Isaac, and Jacob, as the God of Moses, Jeremiah, and Paul alike. I Macc. was not part of the scripture Jesus interpreted on the Emmaus road. Therefore anything I Macc. has to say to us—and it *has* something to say—is not part of the basic Christian gospel and is not necessary for its explication. I Macc. is a secondary book, even as John Bunyan's *Pilgrim's Progress* or Karl Barth's *Dogmatics* is secondary.

The heroes of I Macc. were fighting for a faith which was already revealed to them in God's action in their history as the latter was recorded for them in "Moses and all the prophets" (Luke 24:27). We, in our turn, benefit greatly as we read the book, for we see how God was taking care of his chosen servant people throughout a turbulent period of their history and how believing men and women, motivated by the Word of God to which they sought to be loyal, could remain obedient to God even unto death. But then so have other believing people remained loyal in many other situations in succeeding centuries; however, the Hebrews remained loyal to the God of whom they had already learned in "Moses and all the prophets," and who is the God and Father of our Lord Jesus Christ.

We learn nothing new, therefore, about God from I Macc., but we do learn how *man* can respond to the Word of God and give of himself to the uttermost in response to God's initial act of love in entering into covenant fellowship with his chosen people. I Macc. is thus not scripture, but it is evidence of how faith can grow directly out of scripture. Thus the book is undoubtedly of God; it speaks to us of what God would have us understand in this "derived" situation of which we read, even as ours today too is a "derived" situation.

For Further Study: R. H. Charles, *The Apoc. and Pseudepigrapha of the OT in English,* 1913; Tedesche and Zeitlin, *The 1st Book of Macc.,* 1950; J. C. Dancy, *A Commentary on I Macc.,* 1954; F. V. Filson, *Which Books Belong in the Bible?,* 1957; B. M. Metzger, *An Intro. to the Apoc.,* 1957; L. H. Brockington, *A Critical Intro. to the Apoc.,* 1961.

I. POLITICAL CHANGE AND A RELIGIOUS CRISIS (1:1-64)

A. HISTORICAL INTRODUCTION (1:1-9)

See Intro. above. In the fashion of the Chronicler (cf. II Chr. 26:16), the author is concerned to show that Alexander the Great's pride (vs. 3) is under the judgment of God. His dates are: born 356, became king 336, defeated the Persian power 333 (cf. Dan. 8:5), died 323. He came from the **land of Kittim,** a word that the Dead Sea Scrolls also use for Greece, though some scholars believe that there the reference is rather to the Romans. The statement that Alexander **divided his kingdom among** (vs. 6) his generals before his death is not historical. **The evils on the earth** (vs. 9) which they caused refers to the endless wars, between Egypt and Syria in which Judea became involved.

B. ANTIOCHUS IV EPIPHANES (1:10-15)

1:10. The author now leaps to the years immediately preceding the wars he wishes to chronicle. **Antiochus the king** is Antiochus III the Great (223-187 B.C.). His son Epiphanes is therefore Antiochus IV (175-164); he is the villain of the story to follow. The **one hundred thirty-seventh year of the kingdom of the Greeks** refers to the calendar of the Seleucids of Syria (cf. Dan. 8:9).

1:11-15. Vs. 11 introduces us to the tension little Judea now felt in respect to the influence of Greek culture upon the ancient faith and customs of Israel. Certain **lawless men** (cf. Deut. 13:13), i.e. men acting against the law of Moses, sought to make a compromise with **the Gentiles round about** them. To begin with, this was a political **covenant.** One Jason raised an insurrection against his brother, Onias III, the high priest (II 4:7-9). He secured the support of Antiochus, but part of the price was an agreement that he should open a gymnasium in Jerusalem. Such an institution, for Greeks, was as innocent as a country club to us. The Greeks, however, were accustomed to practice their athletics naked. This custom was anathema to the good Jew. Those Jews who joined the "club" to show their repudiation of Judaism and declare their sophistication and up-to-dateness underwent an operation that **removed the marks of circumcision** (vs. 15). Thus they **abandoned the holy covenant,** of which circumcision was the external sign.

1:15. The statues of Greek gods looked down upon the social life of the gymnasium; philosophers presented their speculative notions within its walls; the youth received cultural training in their own clubrooms—a training that was integrated with a pagan view of life. In fact, the gymnasium offered a total view of life that was completely incompatible with the total revelation contained in the law of Moses. There could be no compromise between the 2. It was a case of either-or. From the Jewish point of view, therefore, when **they joined with the Gentiles** they **sold themselves to do evil.** Jason's act was therefore a declaration of war against Israel's God. The fate of the tiny state of Judea was now at stake within the vast sea of Greek culture that covered virtually the whole known world.

C. ANTIOCHUS' CONQUESTS; DESECRATION OF THE TEMPLE (1:16-28)

Once Antiochus had subdued Egypt and the Ptolemaic line (vs. 18), he naturally seized Judea, for it had been a Ptolemaic province. For vss. 20-24a see Intro. Note his use of Indian elephants in war (vs. 17). They must have been like tanks to a modern army. In times of peace, too, elephants had great prestige value. Some Seleucid coins proudly display this great animal. Jerusalem fell an easy prey to Antiochus' soldiers. The **golden altar** is mentioned in Exod. 30:1-6; the **lampstand** in Exod. 25:31-39; **the table for the bread of the Presence** (or "Face"; cf. Isa. 63:9) in Exod. 25:23-30; and cf. Josephus, *Antiquities,* III, VI.6. According to II 5:21, the **hidden treasures** (I 1:23) amounted to 1,800 talents, let us say about 3½ million dollars. The author now introduces a dirge concerning the tragedy (vss. 24b-28). Dan 8:10 represents Antiochus as assaulting the very stars in an **arrogance** (vs. 24) that reaches to heaven, like the king in Babylon in Isa. 14:14:

> I will ascend above the heights of the clouds,
> I will make myself like the Most High.

D. THE 2ND DESTRUCTION OF THE CITY (1:29-40)

The **chief collector of tribute** (vs. 29) gains access by trickery (cf. Dan. 8:25). II 5:24 names him Appollonius. Vss. 31-32 exaggerate somewhat in that Jews remained living in Jerusalem even after this terrible slaughter. **The city** or citadel **of David** was a strong fortification, the Acra, just W of the temple. **Lawless men** (vs. 34), i.e. foreign troops, are stationed in the city, so again the author gives us a lament (vss. 36-40).

E. THE CALL FOR UNITY (1:41-64)

Antiochus orders the unification of all his subject peoples: **all should be one people, and . . . each should give up his customs** (vss. 41-42; see Intro.). The list of royal demands upon all men in the empire spelled death to Judaism—so it was death either way (vs. 50). Yet once again the author shows his natural bias, for this process of Hellenization was not by decree but by force of political circumstances. But undoubtedly the best of the Jewish people recognized that a crisis had arrived and so went **into hiding** (vs. 53). God's people could do no other. The impious acts of Antiochus culminate in the erection of a **desolating sacrilege upon the altar of burnt offering** (vs. 54; see Intro. and Dan. 11:31) and of local pagan shrines in the villages of Judea, Nov. or Dec. 167. Any copies of the Torah they could find were torn up and burned (vs. 56), and death was meted out to anyone found possessing a copy. II 5:22-7:42 should be read at this point, for it gives details of the persecution.

II. THE KING'S ORDER IS DEFIED; WAR RESULTS (2:1-70)

A. MATTATHIAS AND HIS SONS (2:1-14)

Modein lay where passes from the uplands debouched on the plain, halfway to Joppa from Jerusalem. Mattathias was of a priestly family. Josephus calls his great-grandfather Hasamonaios. From that name the term Hasmoneans arose to signify the dynasty of his descendants. Again the author writes a dirge (vss. 7-13) and puts it in his hero's mouth.

B. THE OUTBREAK OF WAR (2:15-41)

2:15-26. The king's officers give Mattathias the opportunity to capitulate like the majority of the Jews (vss. 15-18). But the priest believes that the situation demands no compromise. He bears the mark of a true zealot when he assassinates one of his own fellow villagers for succumbing to the royal decrees (vs. 24). Then he kills the king's officer too, and the die is cast. For the story of **Phinehas** and **Zimri** (vs. 26) see Num. 25:6-15.

2:27-41. Mattathias' action wins over many waverers; a body of them gather in the **wilderness** of Judea, to the SE of Jerusalem, where John the Baptist later lived and where Jesus met with tempta-

tion. The area is wild and desolate with only pockets of green where domestic animals can graze but with many caves to hide in. As before, the authorities give them the opportunity to change their minds (vs. 33). By refusing to fight on the sabbath, the Jews do two things at once: they demonstrate their loyalty to the law of Moses, and they declare their repugnance at a royal decree that would do away with the sabbath as a distinctive God-given day. So **a thousand** die there as martyrs to a cause they believe to be of God. But Mattathias and his friends recognize that such loyalty demonstrates a misplaced zeal (vs. 41).

C. THE HASIDEANS (2:42-70)

2:42-48. Now the struggle becomes clearly a religious war, always more ferocious than one for political or economic ends. Those Jews who do not join them the guerrilla fighters regard as **sinners** and strike them down (vs. 44), so others flee to Gentile villages for safety. The newcomers to the army in the hills are called **Hasideans,** meaning "loyal ones," i.e. loyal to the covenant made at Sinai (cf. 1:62-63; 2:34). The Hasideans were evidently a party that had formed earlier, less extreme than the group in the wilderness, more sincerely religious. They are mentioned cryptically in Dan. 11:33. They recognized the necessity of making common cause with the extremists even though they did not like them. Once the war was over, however, they parted company with the extremists and became the Pharisees, or "separate" ones.

2:49-64. Mattathias' dying speech again reads like the author's own production, yet such must have been the priest's thoughts and sentiments. Note that the author is acquainted with the book of Dan. (vss. 59-60). This means that that book must have gained instant appreciation when it was first "published" (see Intro. to Dan.). The other biblical references are: **Abraham,** Gen. 22; **Joseph,** Gen. 41; **Phinehas,** Num. 25:1-15; **Joshua,** Num. 27:18-23; **Caleb,** Num. 14; **David,** II Sam. 7; **Elijah,** II Kings 2:1-12. The references to **Abraham** and **Joseph** reveal a theological trend of the period. The law of Moses is now ever more highly exalted. It is looked upon as the eternal Word and so in some sense must have been known to the patriarchs before it was revealed to Moses. It is "suprahistorical." Keeping it has become the means whereby Israel can achieve the favor of God and become worthy of his promises, rather than, as with the psalmists, something one keeps gladly to show gratitude for God's mighty acts of redemption.

2:65-70. Finally the old man names his son **Judas** as his successor. The name **Maccabeus** probably was a nickname he received later (see Intro.). **Simeon** (or Simon) was probably a less impulsive and wiser man, but Judas was the man for the hour. Then Mattathias dies in the year 166 B.C.

III. RESISTANCE UNDER JUDAS BEGINS (3:1-60)

A. AN ODE IN HONOR OF JUDAS (3:3-9)

The author probably wrote this poem himself. Let us note its vehemences. **He burned those who troubled his people** (vs. 5). **He destroyed the un-**

godly out of the land (vs. 8). The Letter to the Heb., on the other hand, almost certainly refers to the amazing exploits of Judas and his men in its stirring ch. 11, esp. vss. 33-38. Judas is an example of those who recognize that it is impossible to be neutral in God's war, so that one is either for him or against him. War cannot be waged daintily. The fierce poem in Judg. 5 begins this way: "That the leaders *took the lead* in Israel, that the people offered themselves willingly [for war], bless the Lord!" Judas did succeed in this way in gathering in **those who were perishing** (vs. 9). Redemption is a costly business.

B. Judas' Initial Victories (3:10-26)

Apollonius was the meridarch, or military and civil governor, of Samaria and Judea. He is probably the "chief collector of tribute" mentioned in 1:29. So Judas wins the first round. **Seron,** a much more important officer than Apollonius, thinks it will be easy to crush the Jewish insurrectionists (vss. 13-14). Note in vs. 15 where the author's sympathies lie; the enemy are **ungodly men.** The **ascent of Beth-horon** is a pass that leads from Lydda on the coastal plain to Jerusalem. The road climbs steeply from the village of Lower Beth-horon to Upper Beth-horon. Judas was occupying the upper village. He thus had a tactical advantage. His little force had just to dash down the hill and sweep the larger army backwards; thus he quickly routed them. This battle revealed Judas to be a clever strategist. **The Gentiles talked of the battles of Judas** (vs. 26). It is not possible to know whether the sentiments Judas utters in his speech to his army (vss. 18-22) were his or the author's, probably the latter. He is referring implicitly to the faith of Gideon (Judg. 7) and to the manner in which God won the victory at that time, not Gideon's army. **Heaven** (vss. 18, 19), we recall, is an intertestamental reverential substitute for "God" (cf. Matt. 4:17 with Mark 1:15).

C. The Forces of Evil Rally (3:27-60)

3:27-37. Judas' victory caught the Syrian empire at a bad moment. Its E portion was in revolt, so Judea's rebellion was more than a thorn in Antiochus' flesh. The king's revenues were low because tribute from the E was at a trickle; thus to give his soldiers **a year's pay** (vs. 28) in advance just because he was suddenly panic-stricken at Judas' success was the mark of an unstable and insecure man. So too was his inhuman command to **Lysias** (vss. 35-36). This then was to be nothing less than total war. The boy **Antiochus**—later known as V Eupator —of whom Lysias was to be guardian (vs. 33), was only 7 years old at this time. The **one hundred forty-seventh year** (vs. 37; cf. 1:10) equals our 165 B.C. Antiochus was successful, by the way, in subduing the king of Armenia, the first of the **upper provinces** of vs. 37.

3:38-41. Judas finally killed **Nicanor** (vs. 38) in 161 (7:43). **Forty thousand** is a round number in Semitic expressions; probaby the army was one fourth that size. It encamps this time, not on a hill (vs. 16), but **in the plain.** Vs. 41 reminds us of the outlook of some armament manufacturers today.

3:42-53. The Jews see the struggle to come as a "holy war," for which the law has given them rules and regulations (Deut. 20-21). One of the Dead Sea Scrolls, "The War of the Sons of Light and the Sons of Darkness," shows that the Qumran community also saw the final war against the powers of evil in this light. For the **Nazirites** (vs. 49) see Num. 6. They could not fight unless released from their vows.

3:56-57. Vs. 56 is based on Deut. 20:5-8 and is reminiscent of Gideon's psychological preparation of those who were wholly committed to God's cause (cf. Judg. 7:3-7). Judas does not now possess the advantage he had at Beth-horon (vs. 57).

IV. Continued Fighting (4:1-61)

A. Two Further Victories (4:1-25)

Renegade Jews **from the citadel** are evidently informers against **Judas,** but he has his sources of information too (vs. 3). His greatest source of strength, however, is his faith in the God who saved his people from Pharaoh's chariots so long before (vs. 9). The Jews were fired by loyalty, faith, and trust both in God's covenant and in the rightness of their cause; the **foreigners** (vs. 12)—mercenaries—were concerned only to earn their wages as soldiers. No wonder the latter were no match for the "covenanters." **Gazara** is Gezer, **Azotus** is Ashdod, **Jamnia** is Jabneh; these are all on the Philistine-held coastal strip. **Idumea** at that time reached roughly to today's Negev. Judas' 2nd victory (vss. 19-25) is again a psychological one. II 8:26 suggests (not necessarily correctly; see Intro.) that they ceased plundering because it was the eve of the sabbath. Pss. 118 and 136 both employ the line in vs. 24. It is inspiring to think that we can share in the **great deliverance** (vs. 25) they experienced when we sing these psalms in our turn.

B. A Year Later (4:26-35)

It is now Oct./Nov. 164 B.C. **Beth-zur** (vs. 29) protects Jerusalem from the S. Lysias must have marched from Antioch S down the coast to Philistia, turned E, then N. He was now in the land where **David** had led his freebooters and where **Saul** and **Jonathan** had fought against the Philistines (vs. 30). Primitive peoples used to recite evil spells against an enemy. Judas relies upon God instead to **melt the boldness of their strength** (vs. 32). How different is his blessing of God (vss. 30-33) from an old spell! Note how he historicizes his faith and sees the past as sacred history—to which he now belongs. Again, then, the faith and **boldness** (vs. 35) of Judas' army sweep them to victory.

C. The Climax of the War (4:36-51)

The arrival in Jerusalem (vss. 38-40) must have been a traumatic experience for the little army. They still have to fight their way into the **citadel** (vs. 41). **The defiled stones** (vs. 43) are the altar to Zeus that Antiochus ordered built over the altar of burnt offerings (1:54). The loyalists have before them for guidance the decision of King Josiah in a similar case (II Kings 23:6). The expectation of **a prophet** (vs. 46) is interesting. It is based on the promise in

Deut. 18:18, and in this period men now look for one like Moses who will sum up the work of all the prophets in himself (cf. John 1:21). The command about **unhewn stones** (vs. 47) is in Exod. 20:25.

D. The Dedication of the Temple (4:52-61)

4:52-59. All preparations, copying the regulations to be found in Exod., were completed on the eve of the great day. **The twenty-fifth day of . . . Chislev** (vs. 52) is probably our December 14, 164 B.C., 3 years exactly after the desecration (cf. 1:59). **Dedication** (vs. 56) in Hebrew is *hanukkah*. The *Jewish Encyclopedia,* VI, 223*b,* recounts the Jewish customs that developed on this day Hanukkah, or the feast of lights. It falls near the winter solstice, when the sun, the great light, begins to increase. The loyalists are very conscious that it is God who has given them the victory, and so they praise him in a great 8-day act of worship (cf. II Chron. 7:9). How appropriate Ps. 124 would be for this occasion! In John 10:22-23 we read: "It was the feast of the Dedication at Jerusalem; it was winter, and Jesus was walking in the temple."

4:60-61. Judas wisely realizes that he must consolidate his easy capture of Jerusalem, for the Syrians will not rest content with his victory. But unfortunately, now that the "religious" war has been won, the Maccabeans make the continuing struggle rather a political and patriotic war. It is now the Jewish **people** as a whole (vs. 61) who are at war with the Seleucid empire.

V. Victories in Transjordan and Galilee; Defeat at Jamnia (5:1-68)

A. The War Continues (5:1-54)

5:1-20. The author recalls the religious nature of the struggle by speaking of the Jews as **the descendants of Jacob** (vs. 2) and the Idumeans as **the sons of Esau** (vs. 3; cf. Gen. 25:30; 36:1; Jer. 49:17; Ezek. 25:12; Mal. 1:2-3). **Akrabattene** (vs. 3) of Idumea lay E of the Dead Sea, surely a long way for a sortie from Jerusalem. Some scholars identify it with a village between Judea and Samaria and so regard **in Idumea** to mean "with an Idumean population." **The sons of Baean** (vs. 4) have not been identified (cf. II 10:18-23). Vss. 6-8 show how Judas has now become like any local commander with a lust for conquest. But he becomes the hope of hard-pressed Jews in Transjordan (vs. 9), who send him a letter asking his help. Then **Galilee** in the N sends a similar request (vs. 14). In Jerusalem a **great assembly** (vs. 16) is held to discuss what measures should be taken. The decision is to set their fighting men in 3 groups. **Simon,** Judas' brother, is to take 1 battalion composed of 3,000 men to fight in Galilee. Another brother, **Jonathan,** is to go with **Judas** and 8,000 men to Transjordan. The 3rd battalion stays to defend Jerusalem.

5:21-54. Simon is successful. He rescues the Galilean Jews and brings them S, women, children, goods and all, to the "city-state" of **Judea.** Judas' army meets with some friendly Arabs, here called **Nabateans** (vs. 25), a people who developed into a forceful empire in the next century. Their report is that the Jewish population have been taken as prisoners to a number of cities, though in some cases they have fortified themselves, as in Dathema (cf. vs. 9). The whirlwind campaign of Judas is entirely successful. Timothy's reasoning in vss. 40-41 shows knowledge of human nature. Then Judas rescues the Jewish population and brings them over the Jordan and S to Judea. No wonder they hold a great service of thanksgiving (vs. 54), since the victories

Courtesy of Herbert G. May

Scenes at the ruins of Petra, famous capital of the Nabateans (see comment 5:21-54); right, the Roman period forum area; left, a tomb facade carved in a cliff; the site of this rugged stronghold is reached by ascending the Wadi Musa and passing through a narrow gorge called the Siq (*sēēk*) which opens into a plain surrounded by massive sandstone cliffs; here, there are ruins of temples and houses and a number of rock-hewn structures, including tombs

in both Galilee and Transjordan must have seemed miraculous. The Jewish armies now have been greatly strengthened.

B. The First Setback (5:55-68)

In disobedience to Judas' express command (vs. 19), **Joseph** and **Azariah** attack **Jamnia** and are defeated. Their action may have arisen from jealousy of the highly successful Maccabean family. Here is the beginning of dissension in the Jewish ranks that was to continue for the next 2 centuries. But the author evidently sees Judas in the light of Joshua of old, leading his people, under God, to their promised land; any divergence or disobedience is thus a form of disloyalty. **Some priests** (vs. 67) evidently imagined that since they were fighting a "holy war," God would protect them miraculously.

VI. Death of Antiochus; Peace Offer Accepted (6:1-63)

A. God's Judgment upon Antiochus (6:1-17)

The author relates the defeats of Antiochus in **Elymais in Persia,** the biblical Elam, lying E of Susa, in the manner of the Deuteronomic editor of I and II Kings, who was concerned to show the purposes of God working out in secular history (cf. e.g. I Kings 8:66; 14:7-10; II Kings 21:16). Antiochus has to retreat to Babylon, a city of ill omen to the Jews; he had refounded it himself as a military depot. Vs. 11 reveals a curious sidelight on this harsh king's nature, as the author sees it. The **flood** here is the old prophetic word for the overwhelming of the wrath of God. We wonder to what extent the author gives Antiochus a conscience he did not have. See Dan. 4:34-37 for the suggestion that there was hope in God's sight even for this cruel, pagan king.

B. The Battle Within Jerusalem (6:18-54)

6:18-47. We find it difficult to grasp that an alien element of Jews and others held out in the citadel, the Acra, even though Judas had occupied all Jerusalem. The Acra actually dominated the temple. These are now the enemy within, and they seek help from the new ruler. The fierceness of this civil war is evidenced in vs. 24. Lysias and Eupator assemble a very large army, with 32 elephants that have already been in combat. It is interesting to read how they gave these beasts their head; as they advanced with the brightly colored pillboxes on their backs, driven by their mahouts, they were surely an awesome sight. Yet the fortitude of one man, Judas' brother **Eleazar** (2:5), turned the tide of the battle (vss. 43-46). However, Judas' small army deemed it wise to retreat.

6:48-54. It is interesting to note another aspect of Jewish loyalty to the Word of God, in that they kept the sabbatical year even in such extremity. The year ran from autumn to autumn and so included both sowing and harvesting (vs. 49). It meant they had **no food in storage** (vs. 53) when the king's army besieged Jerusalem; moreover, their numbers had been greatly swollen with the admission of refugees from Galilee and Transjordan.

C. The Lifting of the Siege (6:55-63)

6:55-59. "In everything God works for good with those who love him, who are called according to his purpose" (Rom. 8:28). Lysias refused to acknowledge the will of the dying Antiochus when he offered Philip the succession and bade him be the guardian of his 9-year-old son and bring him up to be king (vss. 14-17); Lysias took on the task himself. **Philip** is now seeking to make himself sole ruler of the empire (vss. 55-56). Lysias obviously rationalizes the situation when he seeks an excuse to lift the siege, since he must know well the food situation in Jerusalem.

6:60-63. The surrender terms are remarkable. The Jews receive all that they have been fighting for. They are permitted to remain the people of the covenant, follow the Law, practice circumcision and the sabbath, and keep distinct from Gentile culture (cf. 1:44-50). In return they evacuate the Acra. On marching in, Lysias realizes how strong it is; and so, breaking the terms of the treaty, and for his own safety, he orders its wall torn down. II 11:12-38 gives more information about this treaty. Philip fled to Egypt before Lysias (II 9:29).

VII. Further Political and Military Developments (7:1-50)

A. Another Claimant for the Throne (7:1-20)

7:1-14. We are now one year later than the above events. **Demetrius** is a 3rd claimant for the Syrian throne. He establishes himself by having his rivals murdered. The dissident party among the Jews, led by **Alcimus,** goes over to him. **Bacchides** is chosen **governor of the province Beyond the River** (vs. 8). The name is from the old Persian point of view (cf. Ezra 4:10-11; etc.) and applies to the area between the Euphrates and Egypt; thus Bacchides has the same responsibility as Lysias before him. Since Alcimus is truly of the Aaronic line of priests, the pious in Jerusalem are ready to trust him. That **a group of scribes** (vs. 12), as well as **the Hasideans,** are prepared to treat with him shows their dissatisfaction with the leadership of Judas and the Maccabeans. As noted above, internal schisms were to be the bane of Jewish history from this time on. In fact the scribes already seem to be a party in themselves.

7:15-20. Alcimus soon reveals that he is prepared to gain the high priesthood by treachery and blood. Vs. 17 is in part built from Ps. 79. Bacchides even massacres those **who had deserted to him!**

B. Further Treachery (7:21-38)

The civil war worsens. It leads to a treacherous peace offer by **Nicanor,** the royal emissary (II 14:18-30 sees this incident in another light, however). Nicanor now has control of Jerusalem (vs. 33), and Judas is again in the hills. His absence leaves the priests in Jerusalem in an equivocal position. The **elders of the people** are mentioned now for the first time (vs. 33); they are the governing body of senior citizens. Cf. vs. 37 with I Kings 8:29, where Solomon declares that God's "name" is to be encountered in the temple, the representation of his very being.

C. A Resounding Victory (7:39-50)

Before the battle Judas reminds God of his intervention by means of the **angel** of death when the **Assyrians** under Sennacherib were camped round the Holy City (II Kings 19:35; Isa. 37:36; cf. II 15:22). Now his army is much reduced in size from the great 3-year guerrilla war. Yet not only does he kill Nicanor and so rout the enemy, he pursues them down to the plain. Many waverers in their villages join him now that he is winning, and together they make it a total victory. But still they do not yet control Jerusalem (vs. 47).

VIII. An Alliance with Rome (8:1-32)

8:1-16. How wondrous the stories of Roman arms must have sounded to Jewish ears—stories of unimaginably far-off countries like **Spain,** the land of **the Gauls,** and the other places at **the ends of the earth** (vss. 2-4). The Romans **were well-disposed toward all who made an alliance with them** (vs. 1). Even the Seleucids, whom Judas knew as *the* world power, Rome had defeated in 190 B.C. at Magnesia (vs. 6). A later revolt had again been crushed (vss. 9-10), though our author may be referring here to an event that took place 15 years later. The Roman policy of permitting kings to rule under them is noted by Judas (vs. 13), and the fact that Rome was ruled by an oligarchy with an annual change of chairmen, and not by a king, is a matter of profound interest (vss. 15-16). Judas did not realize that the **one man** he had to deal with was merely a local consul.

8:17-32. The journey to Rome was a great adventure for provincials like the Jews in their hill country. The reply they brought back from the Roman Senate was written on 2 bronze tablets (see Intro.) one of which was kept for the record in Rome. It outlines a bilateral treaty between the mighty Roman state and the few thousand Jewish insurgents in the hills of Palestine. But it turned Rome into the enemy of Syria (vs. 32).

IX. Judas Slain; Jonathan Succeeds Him; War Ends (9:1-73)

A. Days of Decline (9:1-22)

For **Bacchides** see 7:8, and for **Alcimus** see 7:5. Vs. 3 shows us we are now in May, 160 B.C. After the enemy show their strength, Judas' army loses faith, and many desert. Judas takes a courageous yet militarily wrong course. He will **die bravely** if his **time has come** (vs. 10). The resulting battle is long and fierce and seemingly indecisive. But Judas is killed in action. The lament for him (vs. 21) is an echo of that uttered by David for Saul and Jonathan (II Sam. 1:19), and vs. 22 reads like a quotation from the history writing in Kings (cf. I Kings 22:45). Judas was a great man, one of the military patriots and heroes of all time.

B. Jonathan Succeeds Judas (9:23-53)

9:23-34. Judas' death is the signal for many waverers to defect, urged to do so by a famine that follows the sabbatical year (6:53). All his days Judas was dogged by a readiness to desert on the part of his troops. The **doers of injustice** (vs. 23) may be actual criminals and fugitives from justice who turned outlaws when the fate of Jerusalem was in the balance. Things are now at their lowest (vs. 27), worse than they had been since the days of Malachi (cf. Zech. 13:3-6). The little remnant of the once great fighting force selects Jonathan, Judas' brother, to be the new leader, and then all flee to the wilderness of Judea (cf. 2:29). There cannot be many of them if they can all camp round one waterhole. We are to keep constantly in mind, however, that humanly speaking there would have been no NT story had this valiant group not kept their faith, courage, and loyalty.

9:35-42. Their morale is dealt an even worse blow when they lose all their worldly goods and brother John is killed seeking the help of the Nabateans, their old allies (cf. 5:25). Blood revenge follows, as in the Arab tradition throughout the centuries, and a wedding festival is turned into a mourning for the dead (vss. 37-42). The booty is recovered, and they retreat to the jungle marshlands of the Jordan.

9:43-53. In the next battle Jonathan seems to have a natural advantage of terrain in that his flanks are protected by a loop of the river. Bacchides perhaps supposes the Jews will not fight on the sabbath. They escape from what has developed into a trap by swimming, but by so doing they must have lost their goods once more. So Bacchides, still in full control of Judea, plants strong points wherever he wishes, to keep it in subjection.

C. The End of the War (9:54-73)

9:54-61. In May-June, 159, **Alcimus** gives the order to pull down the wall separating the inner from the outer court of the temple. Gentiles formerly could use the outer court only; now they can mingle with the Jews and worship as equals. On the surface this seems a good idea, but for the faithful it meant the end of the special covenant relationship between Israel and her God which the prophets had upheld in their interpretation of the law of Moses. Second Isaiah saw the covenant with Israel as the means God intended for the redemption of the Gentiles (Isa. 42:1; 49:6). This is very different from saying, "All religions are at base the same; Gentiles, with their peculiar and sometimes bestial notions of the divine, are welcome to worship the Holy One along with us." The author evidently regards the creeping paralysis from which Alcimus suffers as a divine judgment (vs. 55). The obverse side of his painful death is a 2-year respite for the land of Judea, with the patriots lying low in the hills.

9:62-73. But the tide turns at last. The Maccabees fortify a small fortress near Bethlehem to act as a challenge and bring the enemy out. **Jonathan** and his brother **Simon** divide their forces and are able to discomfit **Bacchides'** army to the point that he decides to retire. Jonathan then seizes the psychological moment to suggest a treaty (vs. 70), to which Bacchides agrees. **Thus the sword ceased from Israel** (vs. 73), but only for 5 years. Yet that was sufficient time for the resistance movement to gain control of many of the villages, though not of the towns or garrisons.

X. Resultant Political Moves (10:1-89)

A. The Maccabees Return "Home" (10:1-14)

The author's interest in describing how and why **Demetrius** sought **Jonathan** as an ally centers in the good news that at last, after at least a decade, the resistance fighters have a chance to go "home" to Jerusalem. There Jonathan at once seems to take command and rebuilds the fortifications of the city. Now **Alexander Epiphanes,** son of Antiochus IV Epiphanes (10:1), in his turn seeks alliance with this bold warrior.

B. Jonathan Becomes High Priest; Death of Demetrius I (10:15-50)

But at Alexander's instigation a new situation arose. For the first time in Israel's history religious, political, and military authority was placed in the hands of one man. Thus there was no balance of power as in former centuries. Trouble would surely ensue. The high priest's vestments (vs. 20) are described in Exod. 28. Demetrius' reaction to Alexander's letter reminds us of the manner in which E and W in our day vie for the good will of the emerging nations (vss. 27-28). Provided that 30,000 Jews (vs. 36) serve in Demetrius' forces (the 3,000 of 11:44 is the more likely figure), the nation is to be completely free from all the oppression it has known. The king offers enormous concessions and even proposes that *he* pay for the restoration of the temple and the walls of Jerusalem (vss. 44-45)! The people of Jerusalem cannot believe such promises by Demetrius, whom they know as a treacherous man; any way, Alexander was the first to make them a good offer. It was as well that they accepted the latter offer, for Alexander soon defeated and killed Demetrius in battle (vss. 48-50).

C. Alexander Weds Cleopatra (10:51-66)

Ptolemais (vs. 56) is the biblical Akko, just N of the present-day Haifa. **Ptolemy** is Ptolemy VI Philometor, who has now ruled in Egypt for a generation. The very name Ptolemais shows the influence of Ptolemy along the coast of Syria. Cleopatra is not, of course, the woman made famous by Shakespeare; she lived a century later. Jonathan accepts the invitation to Ptolemais and arrives looking every inch their equal (vss. 59-60). He is rewarded by being clothed in royal purple and by seeing his personal enemies flee (vs. 64). Yet of course he is really a vassal of King Alexander.

D. Jonathan Consolidates His Rule (10:67-89)

Demetrius, the son of Demetrius I, trying to regain the throne of his father, is naturally angry that Jonathan did not accept his offer and so challenges him to battle. This challenge Jonathan accepts, even though they are to meet on the plain, where there are no stones that can be thrown from rocky crags and no caves to hide in (vs. 73). Jonathan first took **Joppa** (now Jaffa) on the coast, a valuable harbor for the Jews. Its capture also cut Apollonius' land route in two. **Azotus** is about 20 miles farther S. The routed enemy sought sanctuary in **Beth-dagon** —the house of Dagon, the god of the Philistines

since before the days of David (cf. Judg. 16:23; I Sam. 5:2-5). But Jonathan turned the temple into an extermination furnace (vss. 84-85). Alexander was pleased at his successes and so gave him the N part of the land of the Philistines as a gift.

XI. Continued Struggles (11:1-74)

A. Ptolemy Pushes N (11:1-19)

This incident is typical of the deceitful manner in which kings in the Near East pursued their selfish ends; it could have been true of 2000 B.C. as it could of A.D. 800. So far as the Jews were affected, Jonathan seems to have acted in good faith. Ptolemy **put on the crown of Asia** (vs. 13), i.e. of the Seleucid empire. One wonders what his daughter thought of her fate and with what zeal, if any, the warriors of both sides faced one another. The author informs us that both kings lost (vss. 16-18); the only one to gain from the whole treacherous episode was Demetrius, the son of the man who had been the tireless enemy of Jonathan (10:67).

B. Jonathan's Bargain (11:20-37)

For Jonathan to besiege the Acra in Jerusalem was tantamount to rebellion. He would have preferred its garrison to be loyal to himself. Young Demetrius II was then only 16 years of age. Finally Jonathan wins over the new king (vss. 24-26) just as he won Alexander. The king puts the new agreement in writing, a copy of which is to be displayed in Jerusalem. The Acra and Beth-zur (6:49) were actually the only 2 remaining centers of Syrian authority left in Judea. Jonathan seems to have made the better bargain (cf. 10:29-45).

C. Demetrius II (11:38-53)

The islands of the nations were Crete and others nearby (10:67). The Antiochus in vs. 39 later becomes VI. Jonathan gets his wish at last; the foreign troops in the Acra are dismissed (cf. the Roman soldiers in the praetorium in Jesus' day, Mark 15:16). The city that rises against Demetrius (vs. 45) is Antioch. Other authorities credit the king's Cretan mercenaries with most of the carnage (vs. 47). The Jewish mercenaries were probably regarded as heroes on returning home.

D. Wars and Rumors of Wars (11:54-74)

The history of events here reads wearisomely. Troops change loyalties; kings offer bribes; cities are burnt; armies are routed. Jonathan comes out of it all a hero—but how many men have died to make him so?

XII. Friendship with Rome and Sparta; Deceit of Trypho (12:1-53)

A. Alliance Making (12:1-23)

In ch. 8 we read of a Jewish committee visiting Rome. Hellenistic diplomacy required the renewal of a treaty if a change had taken place in the condition of one of the signatories, such as an accession, a death, etc. So Jonathan reaffirms his treaty with

Rome. If we look over the events recounted in chs. 9–11, we see how little this treaty had meant to the Jews. Any treaty with Sparta, then, would mean even less. **Arius** I was king of Sparta 309-265 B.C. **Onias** I was high priest 323-300. So the treaty is intended to belong between 309 and 300. Its historicity is doubtful. But the reply is even more so. It is impossible to imagine any kind of Greek claiming to be descended from Abraham (vs. 21). Possibly the author really believed these letters were sent. Possibly they were sent, but it was all a kind of diplomatic game of polite nothings. Possibly the author supposed that letters genuinely interchanged nearly 2 centuries before belonged to the period he was describing.

B. CAPTURE OF JONATHAN BY TREACHERY (12:24-53)

12:24-38. The wearisome war with the Seleucids continues. When the enemy slips from his grasp, Jonathan turns his wrath on a hapless Arab clan. For recent events in **Joppa** (vs. 33) see 10:75; 11:6. The walls of Jerusaem had already been rebuilt by Jonathan (cf. 10:10); the barrier around the fortress is a new thing (vss. 35-36).

12:39-53. Jonathan now has to be ready to fight on a 2nd front (vss. 39-40), but instead **Trypho** makes an ally of him. But Trypho is as deceitful as was expected of a Levantine king. Jonathan is betrayed and taken prisoner by Trypho. His men get home safely by keeping their heads. **The Great Plain** is the Esdraelon in the SW of Galilee.

XIII. THE RISE OF SIMON (13:1-53)

A. SIMON THE NEW LEADER (13:1-30)

13:1-11. Simon is the last remaining member of the Maccabean family. He is now 50 years old, older than Jonathan. He has already shown both wisdom and valor; thus he becomes the inevitable choice as leader. His first speech is both powerful and courageous, and is effective.

13:12-27. Trypho tries the usual deceit to win his ends. **The money that Jonathan your brother owed** (vs. 15) is a polite circumlocution for "ransom." Simon would have been blamed whether he paid up or not. Trypho, as was to be expected, broke his word and began an expedition against Jerusalem from the S. It was not the snow that stopped him but the fact that Simon's army was always on higher ground than his (cf. 3:24). Trypho wreaks his spite on his prisoner, Jonathan, and has him murdered. Jonathan was not as great a man as his brothers, yet he held the rule for 18 years. We recall that he was susceptible to the flattery of kings; he changed sides several times if he could thereby gain an advantage; he did not endear himself to his people.

13:28-30. Simon must have prepared the 7th pyramid for himself (vs. 28). It is interesting that Simon used both oriental and Hellenic motifs together on the columns (vs. 29). Eusebius tells us that part of this great mausoleum was still standing in his day, the 4th cent. A.D.

B. SIMON CONSOLIDATES (13:31-53)

13:31-42. General Trypho of the Seleucid army was not of royal blood. The fact that he could keep control for 4 years of a section of the empire shows how weak the latter had become. We read of another act of treachery by this man, the murder of the teenage successor to the throne. Trypho, then the common enemy, brings Simon and Demetrius together, not as allies, for Simon is still a vassal, but in a pact of nonaggression. The Jews now no longer must pay tribute to Antioch, but their young men are to do military service there. But the Jews are delighted to imagine that they are independent of the Seleucids at last (vss. 41-42). This was now the year 142 B.C.

13:42-53. The conjectural reading **Gazara** in RSV, vs. 43, seems to be entirely correct. It is supported by 14:7 and by Josephus. It was the OT "Gezer," an important place in the Shephelah, the lowlands bordering on Philistia. Simon shows that he is both a good general and a religious zealot. He draws this city into the sphere of the rule of the law of Moses. Simon's final triumph lay in the capitulation of the citadel in Jerusalem. He shows unusual clemency in just dismissing the foreign soldiers who capitulated. This took place about the end of May, 141 B.C. The **great enemy** (vs. 51) was the Acra itself, towering over the temple and the common life of the city for many a long year. With its capitulation Jewish independence had really begun. Like a wise ruler, recognizing his advancing years, Simon decides to educate his son, John Hyrcanus, to take over the rule eventually.

XIV. SIMON IS LAUDED (14:1-49)

A. IN PRAISE OF SIMON (14:1-23)

After a very condensed note on Seleucid affairs, which need not concern us, the author sings the praise of this Maccabee who was perhaps the greatest of all the brothers. The picture of each man sitting **under his vine and his fig tree** (vs. 12) is to be found in I Kings 4:25, Mic. 4:4; Zech. 3:10; and the general picture of peace and quiet is an amalgam of OT texts, especially Zech. 8:4-23. We saw in 12:1 how the custom of the day was to renew a treaty if a change took place in the dynasty (vs. 18). These letters again may be the author's invention, or else he may have accepted in good faith doubtful information about them.

B. SIMON CONFIRMED AS COMMANDER, ETHNARCH, AND HIGH PRIEST (14:24-49)

The Jews may have borrowed the idea of honoring Simon with an inscribed bronze tablet from the Greeks, for the latter were in the habit of thus honoring individual "benefactors" (cf. Luke 22:25). The proclamation was made about mid-Sept. in the year 140 B.C. in the 3rd year of Simon's high priesthood in **Asaramel.** The footnote in the RSV notes the difficulty of this peculiar word. For **sons of Joarib** (vs. 29) see 2:1. The proclamation covers the ground described in the previous chapters. Its nature and tone reveal why the book is called I Macc. and not merely "A History of the Jews in Seleucid Times." For the arising of a **trustworthy prophet** (vs. 41), see 4:46; 9:27. Finally they give Simon copies of this "testimonial" to pass down to his descendants.

XV. War Begins Again (15:1-41)

A. The Background of Seleucid Intrigue (15:1-14)

This **Antiochus** was the brother of Demetrius II and had been living in Pamphylia. He takes the title of Euergetes, or Benefactor. When he hears the news of his brother Demetrius' capture (14:3), he determines to try his luck. His letter reads too smoothly to be acceptable; he could not have said **certain pestilent men** (vs. 3)—this represents a Jewish editing of the original. The nearer Antiochus draws to Judea, for Dor lies near the later town of Caesarea, the more possibility there will be of trouble for Simon.

B. Letter from Rome; War Renewed (15:15-41)

The letter from Rome may be misdated here, but at least it shows how significant little Judea had become in the eyes of the world powers. Annoyance at Rome's favor to Simon, however, weighs more with young Antiochus (perhaps about 21 years old now) than Simon's gift of 2,000 trained soldiers (vs. 26), and he breaks with Simon and rescinds the letter quoted in vss. 2-9. Then he picks a quarrel (vs. 28); the year is now 138. The sum of 1,000 talents (vs. 31) was not unusual as a tribute in such circumstances. Simon gives a dignified reply to **Athenobius,** Antiochus' emissary, and offers 100 talents for the sake of peace. But the Seleucid king **was greatly angered.** And so the weary war begins again.

XVI. Closing Deeds (16:1-24)

A. Simon's Older Sons: Judas and John (16:1-3)

We recall that Simon had sent his son to Gazara to learn the art of commanding troops (13:53). Before he brings his book to a conclusion, the author introduces us to Simon's sons, for we shall want to know who ruled Judea after Simon's death, as far as the writer can take us. So then we meet John, Judas, and Mattathias (vs. 14), called after his grandfather (2:1). Simon does not need to boast to them of the exploits of his father and brothers; all he need do is tell the tale. This family truly belongs among the great heroes of all times. Simon is the last of the brothers left alive, and he is now some 60 years of age, yet he is conscious that the purposes of God transcend the generations (vs. 3).

B. The Exploits of John Hyrcanus (16:4-24)

As both the book and the life of Simon draw to a close, we read about the skill and loyalty of young John and of his great victory over the Seleucid general. A new chapter of violence and intrigue must just be opening with the murder of Simon and of John's 2 brothers (vss. 14-16). In 15:31 the young Seleucid king Antiochus VII threatens, "Otherwise we will come and conquer you." Other writers in later years take up the tale. Antiochus was in fact sympathetic to Ptolemy's **report** (vs. 18), and in the year 134 he did in fact invade Judea, invest Jerusalem and besiege it for a year. When at last John capitulated, only because his people were starving, Antiochus VII broke down the walls of the city and exacted tribute once again. But John Hyrcanus was able to regain the independence of the Jewish nation when, 5 years later, the Seleucid king was killed in battle. Thereafter they remained a free and independent but quarreling people of many parties until Judea was finally swallowed up in the Roman Empire 65 years later.

THE SECOND BOOK OF THE MACCABEES

ROBERT C. DENTAN

INTRODUCTION

II Maccabees is not the sequel to I Macc. but an account of the same historical crisis told from a different point of view and with a different selection of events. Whereas I Macc. is written in a sober Hebraic style and relates the story in relatively straightforward fashion, II Macc. exhibits the typical flamboyant, emotional Greek style of the Hellenistic period and shows a predominant concern for religious edification, with great emphasis on the spectacular, the miraculous, and even the gruesome.

I Macc. is interested in the rise of the Hasmonean house, which continued to rule the independent Judean state that grew out of the Maccabean revolt; and it describes the careers of 4 of its heroes—Mattathias, Judas, Jonathan, and Simon. II Macc. has only one hero—Judas Maccabeus. It ignores completely the role of his father, Mattathias, in starting the revolt; and in order to preserve the heroic image of Judas it ends the story with his victory over Nicanor, ignoring his final defeat and death (cf. I 9:5-18). In this it seems to reflect the viewpoint of the Hasideans (Hebrew *hasidim*, in the OT usually translated "saints" or "faithful"), the party among the Jews most deeply devoted to the Mosaic law and probably the spiritual ancestor of such later sects as the Pharisees and the Essenes. For a time the Hasideans were ardent followers of Judas (14:6; I 2:42) but because their attitude was basically religious rather than political they ceased to support him and his successors when they felt religious freedom had been secured (I 7:13-14).

Authorship and Composition. The author of the book as we now have it is known simply as the "epitomist," since his book is professedly a "condensation" (Greek *epitome*, 2:28) of a 5-vol. work by a certain Jason of Cyrene (2:23). Cyrene is located on the N coast of Africa (see color map 16) but nothing further is known of Jason. Occasionally the epitomist seems merely to have summarized the original (e.g. 13:19-26). More often he appears to have abridged Jason's narrative by including only those incidents that furthered his own purpose and omitting those that did not. Some scholars believe that his concluding formulas in 3:40; 7:42; 10:9; 13:26b; 15:37a mark the respective conclusions of Jason's original 5 vols. Certain passages, e.g. the martyr stories (esp. chs. 6-7), the epitomist may have added from some other source. The 2 letters at the beginning (1:1-2:18) probably have been prefaced by a later hand.

Date and Place of Composition. The epitomist's concluding remark that "from that time the city has been in the possession of the Hebrews" (15:37) places his work before the Roman conquest in 63 B.C. Probably it is to be dated early in the first cent. B.C., with Jason's 5 vols. late in the 2nd cent., though there are no precise indications by which the times can be determined. While the 2 prefatory letters were presumably written in Hebrew or Aramaic, the rest of the book was obviously composed in Greek, probably in Alexandria, though Antioch has also been suggested.

Contents. After 2 letters purporting to be from the Jews in Jerusalem to those in Egypt, urging them to keep the feast of Hanukkah (1:1-2:18), the epitomist introduces his work (2:19-32). Ch. 3 tells of an unsuccessful attempt to plunder the temple treasury in the time of Seleucus IV Philopator (187-175). Ch. 4 describes the unseemly rivalry for the high priesthood following the accession of Antiochus IV Epiphanes (175-163). With ch. 5 begins the story of Epiphanes' persecution of the Jews (167-164); and the rest of the book (chs. 5-15), including the interlude on the martyrs (chs. 6-7), is concerned with Jewish resistance, under the leadership of Judas Maccabeus, to the repressive policies of the Syrian kings. The narrative reaches its first climax with the death of Epiphanes (ch. 9) and the rededication of the temple (10:1-9). Following the account of the Jews' continued resistance to the policies of Epiphanes' successors, Antiochus V Eupator (163-162) and Demetrius I (162-150), which reaches a 2nd climax in the story of Nicanor's defeat (10:10-15:36), the book concludes with an epilogue by the epitomist (15:37-39). Chs. 5-15 roughly parallel I 1-7.

Religious Interest. II Macc. marks an important stage in the development of religious thought in Judaism. It is esp. notable for its emphasis on the ideas of physical resurrection (7:9, 11, 14; 14:46), prayer for the dead (12:43-45), and the intercession of saints (15:12, 14), as also for its vivid pictures of the intervention of angels in human affairs (3:25-26; 5:2-3; 10:29-30; 11:6-8). Later these ideas were characteristically associated with the Pharisaic party (cf. Acts 23:8). The figure of the martyr, which was shortly to play so important a role in Christendom, first appears in this book (chs. 6-7; 14:37-46), as does the doctrine of creation out of nothing (7:28).

For Further Study: James Moffatt in R. H. Charles, ed., *The Apoc. and Pseudepigrapha of the OT*, 1913.

C. C. Torrey, *The Apocryphal Literature,* 1945. R. H. Pfeiffer, *History of NT Times with Intro. to the Apoc.,* 1949. S. Tedesche and S. Zeitlin, *The 2nd Book of Macc.,* 1954. H. M. Orlinsky and W. H. Brownlee in *IDB,* 1962.

I. Prefatory Letters (1:1-2:18)

1:1-9. *A Letter to Egyptian Jews.* The purpose of this letter is to urge the Jews in Egypt to follow the example of those in Judea in observing the **feast** (vs. 9) commemorating the rededication of the temple by Judas Maccabeus (see below on 10:1-9). The Jerusalem Jews wrote a previous letter in 143 (on the Seleucid dating see "Chronology," pp. 1271-82), during the reign of **Demetrius** II (145-139/38; cf. I 10:67-15:22), in which they told of the persecutions by the Seleucid kings, here said to have been occasioned by the revolt of **Jason** (vss. 7-8a; cf. 5:5-7). But now in 124 (vs. 9) all that is past and they can ask others to join with them in keeping the temple feast. The authenticity of both this and the following letter is open to considerable question.

1:10-2:18. *Another Letter to Egyptian Jews.* This letter purports to have been written earlier by **Judas** —presumably Maccabeus—and other officials in Jerusalem to **Aristobulus,** identified by the Christian writers Clement and Eusebius as a famous Alexandrian Jewish philosopher. The occasion is the death of the persecutor **Antiochus** (1:11-17) and the consequent opportunity to **celebrate the purification of the temple** (1:18). Thus the letter apparently is to be understood as written while the temple is being restored (cf. I 4:42-51) in order to urge the Egyptian Jews to join in the feast that is to climax the process (1:18; 2:16; cf. 10:6-7), with past occasions of God's protection of the temple and its appurtenances (1:19-2:15), largely legendary, being cited to reinforce the request.

This apparent order of events, with Antiochus' death preceding the purification of the temple, agrees with that in 9:1-10:9 (see comment on 9:1-29). According to I Macc., however, the temple was rededicated in Dec. 164 (I 4:52) and Antiochus died in 163 (I 6:16). Historically the latter sequence is the more probable. Possibly, therefore, the letter should be understood as referring, not to the purification itself, but to the commemoration of its first anniversary in 163.

1:11-17. This story of Antiochus' death is inconsistent with the accounts in ch. 9; I 6:8-16 and may be the result of confusion of Antiochus IV Epiphanes with his father Antiochus III, who was indeed killed while attempting to plunder a Persian temple.

1:18-36. The festival (see below on 10:1-9) is said to be associated also with a **feast of the fire** commemorating the rebuilding of the temple and rekindling of the sacrificial fire by **Nehemiah** (vs. 18b). Historically Nehemiah had nothing to do with the rebuilding of the temple, which had been standing for over 70 years when he arrived in Jerusalem; and the story of the miraculous hidden fire is pure legend. **Persia** (vs. 19) is an error for Babylonia. Nothing certain is known of the origin and meaning of the word **nephthar** (vss. 36).

2:1-8a. The mention of the hidden fire leads the author to recount the legend, unknown to the OT,

that **Jeremiah** instructed the Jewish exiles to take some of the altar **fire** with them to Babylonia and, irrelevantly, that he hid **the tent and the ark,** as well as **the altar of incense,** in a **cave** on Mt. Sinai (vss. 4-5).

2:8b-12. The author reminds his readers that **Moses** once called down sacrificial fire from heaven (cf. Lev. 9:23-24), as did **Solomon** at the original dedication of the temple (cf. II Chr. 7:1; not in I Kings 8:62-64). Solomon's **eight days** of celebration (cf. II Chr. 7:8-9) are treated as precedent for the 8-day observance of this feast (vs. 12; cf. 10:6).

2:13-15. Just as the author has wished to establish in some way a parallel between Judas' rededication of the temple and Nehemiah's supposed rekindling of the altar fire, he also attempts to find a parallel in the story that both of them **collected** sacred **books.** Nothing is known elsewhere of their connection with this kind of activity.

2:16-18. The letter ends with another appeal to keep the feast.

II. The Epitomist's Preface (2:19-32)

2:19:32. The epitomist (see Intro.) announces his theme (vss. 19-22) and discusses both his source and his manner of writing (vss. 23-32; see Intro.).

III. The Discomfiture of Heliodorus (3:1-40)

What is called the **episode of Heliodorus and the protection of the treasury** (vs. 40) illustrates in miniature one of the principal themes of the book, viz. that God is able to protect his sanctuary from those who attempt to profane it. When the officer of the heathen king tries to appropriate the funds of the temple he is driven off by angelic forces.

3:1-14a. Jerusalem is enjoying **peace** under the pious rule of the **high priest Onias** III and even **Seleucus** IV Philopator (187-175) is supporting the temple. Then a certain temple official, **Simon,** having quarreled with Onias, reports to **Apollonius,** governor of the province of **Coelesyria** (see color map 12), which included Palestine and Transjordan, that vast sums of money are available in the temple treasury to meet the ever-pressing needs of government. Seleucus instructs his chief minister, Heliodorus, to confiscate the temple funds, much of which do not belong to the temple but have been deposited there by private citizens for safekeeping.

3:14b-30. Heliodorus' demands cause passionate prayers for deliverance to be uttered throughout the city (vss. 14b-21). When he arrives at the treasury he is attacked by an angel on horseback, accompanied by 2 others, and reduced to terrified impotence.

3:31-40. Heliodorus, his life saved by the intercession of Onias, offers a **sacrifice** to Israel's God (vs. 35) and reports his failure to the king. On the concluding formula **This was the outcome of the episode** (vs. 40) see Intro.

IV. Rivalry for the High Priesthood (4:1-50)

4:1-6. Onias goes to Antioch to defend himself before the king against the slanders of Simon.

4:7-22. *Jason's Hellenizing Policy.* Before Onias could reach the court Seleucus was assassinated—as is known from other sources—by Heliodorus, whose intention to seize power for himself was frustrated by the proclamation of Seleucus' brother, **Antiochus IV**, as king. His title **Epiphanes** (vs. 7), meaning "(god) manifest," expresses the common oriental belief in the divinity of kings. Onias' brother, **Jason**, purchases the high priesthood for a large sum (see table, p. 1285) and proceeds to introduce Greek customs into Jerusalem, esp. those connected with athletic contests. The choice of a Greek name, Jason, in place of his correct Hebrew name, Joshua, is indicative of his sympathies. If successful his policy would have led to the complete abandonment of Judaism (cf. I 1:14-15). The extremity of the situation is clearly seen in the enthusiastic hellenizing activities of the priests (vss. 14-15) and the sending of contributions to the worship of Hercules (vss. 18-20).

4:23-50. The High Priesthood of Menelaus. According to the Jewish historian Josephus (late first cent. A.D.) Menelaus was not the **brother of . . . Simon** but another brother of Onias and Jason (Antiquities 12:238). When Menelaus succeeds in **outbidding** Jason for the high priesthood, Jason has to flee into exile in **Ammon** (vs. 26; see color map 11).

4:30-38. The murder of **Onias** is presumably the event referred to in Dan. 9:26, "An anointed one shall be cut off," though possibly only his deposition is meant—some scholars believe that this story of his death is either erroneous or fictitious and that it was this Onias who went to Egypt and founded the famous temple at Leontopolis frequently mentioned by Josephus.

4:39-50. Menelaus' brother and deputy, **Lysimachus** (vs. 29), provokes a riot in Jerusalem. As a result Menelaus is brought to trial but secures acquittal by bribing **Ptolemy,** an intimate of the king (cf. 6:8; 8:8; 10:12-13).

V. The Revolt and Victories of Judas Maccabeus (5:1-15:36)

A. The Background of the Revolt (5:1-27)

5:1-26. Antiochus' Attack on Jerusalem. Taking advantage of a **rumor** that Antiochus has died while invading Egypt in 169, Jason attacks Jerusalem in an attempt to regain his former position (vss. 1-6). Though he is repulsed (vss. 7-10), Antiochus assumes that all Judea is aflame and returns from Egypt to attack Jerusalem. He massacres a large part of the population and, led by the traitor Menelaus, plunders the temple (vss. 11-16, 21).

5:17-20. It is explained—whether by Jason of Cyrene or by the epitomist is uncertain (cf. 6:12-17) —that Antiochus succeeded, where Heliodorus had failed, only because of the sins of the people.

5:21-26. The word translated **captain of the Mysians** (vs. 24) is uncertain and may mean "detestable leader." Thus **Apollonius** may be the provincial governor (cf. 3:5; 4:4, 21) and perhaps the general later killed in an early battle of the revolt (I 3:10-12). The massacre on the **sabbath** (see below on 15:1-19) is evidently that described in I 1:29-32 as occurring 2 years after Antiochus' attack, i.e. in 167.

5:27. Intro. of the Hero. Abruptly it is put in that **Judas** and some companions escaped the slaughter

and fled to the **mountains.** The nickname **Maccabeus** seems to be derived from the Aramaic word for "hammer," but it is uncertain whether it refers to a physical peculiarity ("hammer-headed") or to vigorous leadership ("the hammerer"). It is striking that the whole story of the revolt begun by his father, Mattathias (I 2), is omitted. The omission, which is certainly deliberate, is probably due to the Hasidic and Pharisaic sympathies of the epitomist (see Intro.). In order not to glorify the Hasmonean dynasty he mentions Judas' brothers Jonathan and Simon only in passing (8:22; 14:17) and has nothing to say of their subsequent roles as high priests and chief leaders of the nation—the theme of the last half of I Macc.—or even of Mattathias, presumably because he was the progenitor of the house. Judas, the hero of the Hasideans (cf. 14:6), is the epitomist's only hero also. The account of Judas' activities is continued in ch. 8.

B. Interlude: The Martyr Stories (6:1-7:42)

6:1-11. Antiochus' Forced Hellenization. Antiochus now formally proscribes the practice of the Jewish religion and endeavors to compel its adherents to accept paganism. The temple of Israel's God in Jerusalem is converted into a temple of **Zeus,** as is the Samaritan temple on Mt. **Gerizim.** Sexual debauchery, characteristic of certain forms of paganism, is practiced in the temple; and illegal sacrifices—no doubt including pigs, which were especially abhorrent to the Jews (cf. vs. 18; I 1:47)—are offered (vs. 5; cf. I 1:54; Dan. 9:27; 11:31; 12:11). Jews are forced to participate in the worship of **Dionysus** (Bacchus) and to adopt the Greek manner of life under threat of death (vss. 7-9; on **Ptolemy** see above on 4:39-50). Horrible examples are made of some who persisted in the practice of circumcision (vs. 10; cf. I 1:60-61) or the observance of the sabbath (vs. 11; on **Philip** cf. 5:22).

6:12-17. The Epitomist's Comment. Anxious to justify the power, wisdom, and love of his God, the epitomist—as is clear from the style (cf. 2:19-32)— explains that these dreadful events were permitted in order to **discipline** the people of Israel and prevent them from falling into grievous sins. Other nations, who do not enjoy the Lord's favor, he believes, are allowed tolerantly to continue in sin until at the end of their course doom comes without warning. Thus Israel's sufferings are a sign of God's special concern for them, not of his impotence or neglect.

6:18-31. The Aged Eleazar's Martyrdom. Refusing to eat pork (vs. 19), or even pretend to do so (vss. 21-28a), the 90-year-old Eleazar goes heroically to torture and death (vss. 28b-31). This story and the one that follows are the subject of IV Macc., an important book of the Pseudepigrapha, where they are retold at great length to illustrate the principle that the reason is superior to the emotions.

7:1-42. Martyrdom of a Mother and 7 Sons. Confronted with the same temptation as Eleazar, the first of 7 brothers refuses to **transgress the laws of our fathers**—i.e. laws similar to those of Deut. 14:3-21—and is therefore subjected to hideous tortures, personally supervised **by the king,** which are recounted in graphic detail (vss. 1-6). The quotation from the **song** of **Moses** (vs. 6) is from Deut. 32:36.

7:7-14. After the death of the first brother, the 2nd, being treated in similar fashion, announces his belief in an **everlasting renewal of life** (cf. vss. 11, 14, 23, 29, 36)—obviously the source of his courage (vss. 7-9). The 3rd brother makes clear that this involves belief in resurrection of the physical body, not merely immortality of the soul: as he stretches out **his hands** he expresses his **hope to get them back again** (vss. 10-11). The 4th brother completes the statement of doctrine by announcing that **there will be no resurrection** for the wicked (vs. 14). Dan., which arose out of the troubles of the Maccabean revolt (see Intro. to Dan.), affirms in contrast the resurrection of both righteous and wicked (Dan. 12:2). The doctrine of resurrection appears elsewhere in the OT only in Isa. 26:19, where the text is uncertain. The emphasis on it here is therefore the more striking and probably justifies our seeing in the book evidence of a proto-Pharisaic point of view, esp. when it also has so many stories to tell about the intervention of angels (see Intro.).

7:15-42. Both the 5th and the 6th brothers threaten the king with divine punishment (vss. 17, 19). Finally the **mother,** who has witnessed the death of 6 sons, shows her mettle by urging the 7th and youngest to be no less courageous (vss. 20-29). She affirms her own belief in the resurrection, on the ground that the creator of all things **did not make them out of things that existed** and is therefore able to recreate all things, including the life of man (vss. 28-29). This is the earliest statement of the doctrine of creation out of nothing. After a final, climactic denunciation of the king's wickedness, the 7th young man dies, as does his mother also (vss. 30-41). The epitomist then concludes the interlude, perhaps indicating the end of Jason's 2nd vol. (vs. 42; see Intro.).

C. THE BEGINNING OF THE REVOLT (8:1–10:9)

8:1-36. *Judas' First Victory Over Nicanor.* The story interrupted after 5:27 is now resumed. Judas gathers an army and begins guerrilla warfare against the enemy (vss. 1-7). **Philip,** the governor at Jerusalem (cf. 5:22; 6:11), reports Judas' successes to **Ptolemy,** now the provincial governor (see above on 4:39-50; 5:21-26), who dispatches an army under **Nicanor** and **Gorgias** to suppress the revolt (vss. 8-11; cf. I 3:38–4:25, where Gorgias rather than Nicanor is the principal commander).

8:12-23. Before joining battle Judas exhorts his troops to fight with the power of God. On the **time of Sennacherib** (vs. 19) cf. II Kings 18:13–19:37, esp. 19:35. The **battle with the Galatians** (vs. 20; see Intro. to Gal.) is otherwise unknown. Two of Judas' **brothers** (vs. 22), **Jonathan** (cf. I 9:28–12:53) and **Simon** (cf. I 13:1–16:16), later succeeded him as leaders of the nation, and both became high priests (see above on 5:27).

8:24-36. Nicanor's army is put to flight. Whereas I Macc. says the reason the Jewish fighters stopped pursuing the enemy was the presence of another army close by (I 4:16-18), this account, with its typical concern for piety, says it was in order to observe the **sabbath** (vs. 26). Additional victories are won in battles with **Timothy** (cf. I 5:37-44) and **Bacchides** (cf. I 7:8-20). Nicanor goes back in disgrace to Antioch (vss. 30-36) but is to return to Judea to meet defeat a 2nd time, and to die, in chs. 14–15 (see below on 14:11-14).

9:1-29. *The Death of Antiochus Epiphanes.* This ch. confronts the reader with one of the major chronological problems of the book, since it places the death of Antiochus before the rededication of the temple (10:1-8; see above on 1:10–2:18), whereas the sequence in I Macc. is the reverse (I 4:36-59;

Courtesy of the Oriental Institute, University of Chicago

General view of the ruins of Persepolis looking toward the NW; Antiochus IV Epiphanes failed in his attempts to plunder this city shortly before his death in 164 B.C. (II Macc. 9:2); left, the palace of Xerxes, son of Darius the Great; center, the restored harem of Xerxes; right rear, the treasury and hall of a hundred columns built by Xerxes

6:8-16). Scholars differ as to which is correct, but the balance of probability is on the side of I Macc. It has been suggested that ch. 9 originally followed 10:1-8 (cf. 10:9) and was transposed by the editor who added 1:10–2:18, but this theory would solve only one of the chronological problems (e.g. see below on 11:1-15).

9:1-17. While on a campaign in Persia (cf. I 3:31-37) Antiochus Epiphanes is defeated in an attempt to **rob the temples** (vss. 1-2; cf. 1:13-16; I 6:1-4). On his way back to the W to vent his wrath on the Jews he is stricken with a loathsome disease and suffers a fall from his chariot (vss. 3-11). He repents and vows to free Jerusalem and to repay **many times over** the plunder he has taken from the temple, as well as to **become a Jew** himself (vss. 12-17). The style of this section is highly emotional and rhetorical, and the details are not to be taken as serious history (cf. I 6:8-16).

9:18-27. Antiochus Epiphanes writes a letter to the Jews commending to them his **son Antiochus** as his successor. This document is so moderate in tone when contrasted with the rest of the ch. that it may well reflect an authentic communication from the king to his partisans in Jerusalem.

9:28-29. The king dies and his body is brought back to Antioch by **Philip**—probably not the Philip mentioned previously (5:22; 6:11; 8:8). The report of Philip's flight to **Egypt** raises another chronological problem—whether it occurred before or after his seizure of the government in Antioch (13:23). According to I Macc. Antiochus Epiphanes when setting out for Persia appointed Lysias (see below on 10:10-38) regent and guardian of his son (I 3:32-37) but then on his deathbed gave the same assignment to Philip (I 6:14-15). Thus on his return with the army from Persia Philip claimed the regency while Lysias and the new young king were in Judea fighting Judas. Lysias hastily came to terms with Judas and returned to Antioch to overthrow Philip (I 6:55-63). Josephus adds that Lysias had Philip executed but may simply have assumed this.

10:1-9. *The Purification of the Temple.* Judas and his forces seize the temple and the city—though not its citadel (cf. I 4:41; 6:18-27)—and restore the worship of the God of Israel. They purify the sanctuary from the pollutions of paganism in a ceremony which I Macc. (4:36, 59) calls a "dedication" (Hebrew *hanukkah*) **on the twenty-fifth day of . . . Chislev** (Nov.-Dec.) exactly **two years** after the heathen profaned it. I Macc. gives the year dates 167 (I 1:54) and 164 (I 4:52), indicating an interval of 3 years. The 8-day celebration resembles the **feast of booths** (cf. 1:9, 18) because the guerrillas were not able to observe that feast properly 3 months earlier when they were still fighting in the hills (vs. 6). They order that this occasion be celebrated every year at the same time (vs. 8). This event marks the climax of this part of the book; the 2nd climax is reached in 15:36 with the establishment of Nicanor's Day. The epitomist's concluding formula (vs. 9) may mark the end of Jason of Cyrene's 3rd vol. (see Intro.).

D. Continuing Warfare (10:10–13:26)

10:10-38. *Beginning of Eupator's Reign.* Epiphanes' son **Antiochus Eupator**, being a mere child at his ac-cession, has **Lysias** as his guardian and regent (see above on 9:28-29). Lysias also becomes **governor of Coelesyria** (see above on 3:1-14a) following the suicide of **Ptolemy . . . Macron**, whose policy in that office is now said to have been pro-Jewish (contrast 8:8-9).

10:14-23. Probably material omitted by the epitomist made clear that **Gorgias became governor,** not of Coelesyria, but of Idumea, to the S of Judea (cf. 12:32; see color map 11). The **Idumeans**—descendants of the OT Edomites, who moved into S Palestine during the Exile—with their allies, hellenizing Jews **banished from Jerusalem,** pursue the war against the forces of Judas and are severely defeated.

10:24-38. When **Timothy,** whom Judas defeated on a previous occasion (8:30-32), invades Judea he is soundly thrashed a 2nd time, with the aid of angelic forces (vss. 29-30). The story of Judas' capture of **Gazara** (OT Gezer, vss. 32-36) is evidently erroneous since it was actually taken by his brother Simon more than 20 years later (I 13:43-48). This accords with the tendency of this book to increase the honor of Judas at the expense of the rest of his family (see above on 5:27). The story of Timothy's death (vs. 37) shows the epitomist's carelessness in the use of his sources; Timothy reappears, quite alive, in 12:2.

11:1-15. *The Defeat of Lysias.* This account is out of order. In I 4:26-35 this battle with Lysias takes place during the lifetime of Antiochus Epiphanes and the victory makes possible the rededication of the temple. At **Beth-zur** (vs. 5), *ca.* 15 miles S of Jerusalem (see color map 11), Judas meets the army of Lysias and, with angelic help again (vss. 6-8), puts it to flight. Lysias makes peace with the Jews (vss. 13-15).

11:16-38. *Four Letters Concerning the Peace.* Scholars differ as to the authenticity of these letters, but there is nothing in their style and tone to forbid the assumption that they are genuine. They are dated before the purification of the temple—the first probably in Nov. 165, the last 2 in Apr. 164. In the letter of **Lysias to . . . the Jews** he promises his help in return for their cooperation (vss. 16-21). **Antiochus** Eupator in a letter to **Lysias** approves the restoration of the **temple** to the Jews and freedom for them to practice their religion (vss. 22-26). In his letter **to the senate of the Jews** the king permits them to return peacefully to their homes in the countryside (vss. 27-33). Though the hellenizing policy of **Menelaus** (4:23-50; 5:15, 23) has been defeated and he himself is in exile, Antiochus naturally still recognizes him as high priest and leader of the nation (vss. 29, 32). The final letter, from the **Romans,** is evidence of the growing power of Rome in the Near East, which would result 100 years later in the incorporation of Judea into the Roman Empire. Here the Romans ask merely for consultation on the terms of the peace agreement.

12:1-45. *Judas' Wars with Neighboring Peoples.* Though at least a temporary peace has been established with the central government, it is still necessary to deal with some of the local **governors** and with neighbors who are old enemies of the Jewish nation.

12:3-9. Judas attacks **Joppa** (vs. 3, modern Jaffa),

a seaport *ca.* 35 miles NW of Jerusalem, and **Jamnia** (vs. 8, modern Yabneh), near the coast *ca.* 12 miles S of Joppa. In both cities the intention of the local Gentile authorities is to wipe out their helpless Jewish minorities.

12:10-31. The account of an attack by Arab nomads in vss. 10-12 can hardly be the sequel to the battles at Joppa and Jamnia. It belongs most naturally with the campaign E of the Jordan described in the following section (vss. 13-31). The name of the place to which **a mile from there** refers (vs. 10) must have been lost by the awkwardness of the epitomist's shears, but presumably it was some site in the Nabatean country of S Transjordan. This passage is apparently another version of the events recounted in I 5:24-53. **Caspin** (vs. 13) is probably the Caspho of I 5:26, 36 (see color map 11). **Charax** (vs. 17) is unknown. The **Toubiani** are no doubt the Jews of the "land of Tob" (I 5:13), a city and region in N Transjordan (see color map 6). **Carnaim** (vs. 21) and **Ephron** (vs. 27) were also cities in N Transjordan. **Atargatis** was a Syrian goddess. **Scythopolis** (vs. 29) is the OT Bethshan (cf. I 5:52; I Sam. 31:10), on the W side of the Jordan S of the Sea of Galilee. Having made a swinging movement through Transjordan from S to N, Judas and his troops now complete the circle by turning S from Scythopolis toward Jerusalem. On the **feast of weeks,** Greek **Pentecost** (vs. 32), cf. Deut. 16:9-12.

12:32-45. Again there is a battle with **Gorgias, the governor of Idumea** (see above on 10:14-23). **Marisa** (vs. 35), the OT Mareshah (cf. Josh. 15:44), was evidently included in Idumea, whereas **Adullam** (vs. 38) was in Judea. The relation of vss. 36-37 to the context has been obscured by the epitomist's clumsy abridgment. The discovery of pagan cult objects on the bodies of the Jewish soldiers both explains their deaths, according to the orthodox philosophy (vs. 40), and leads Judas to provide expiatory sacrifices for them (vss. 43-45). Vs. 44 has, historically, been the most important prooftext for the practice of praying for the dead.

13:1-26. The 2nd Invasion by Lysias. With many variations in detail, this ch. tells the same story as I 6:18-63. In vss. 19-26 the epitomist has reduced his story to an outline. These verses provide evidence of his veracity in describing the book as an abbreviation of a much larger work (2:26-31).

13:3-8. For selfish reasons **Menelaus** (see above on 11:16-38) urges **Antiochus,** i.e. Lysias, to invade Judea (vs. 3). It may be that the account of his death (vss. 4-8) has been dislocated by the epitomist and should follow vs. 23. **Beroea** (vs. 4) is the modern Aleppo in N Syria (see color map 12).

13:9-22. Judas and his people, when they hear of the invading army, engage in prayer (vss. 10-12) and advance to meet it as it moves S along the coastal plain (vss. 13-14). **Modein,** where the Maccabean revolt began (I 2:1, 15-28), lies in the foothills NW of Jerusalem (see color map 11). According to I 6:43-46 it was Eleazar, Judas' brother, who **stabbed the leading elephant** (vs. 15) and was crushed to death beneath it. The scene shifts SE to **Beth-zur** (vss. 19, 22; see above on 11:1-15) in the mountains, where Eupator and Lysias are defeated (vs. 22).

13:23-26. From the account in I 6:55-63 it is clear that the seizure of the government in Antioch by **Philip** (vs. 23; see above on 9:28-29) not merely made possible the renewal of peace between the boy king and his Jewish subjects but saved Judas and his forces from a disastrous defeat. The area **from Ptolemais,** OT Acco, N of Mt. Carmel **to Gerar** in the Philistine country to the S (see color map 11) means the whole of Palestine. The epitomist's concluding formula in vs. 26*b* may mark the end of Jason of Cyrene's 4th vol. (see Intro.).

E. Victory Over Nicanor (14:1-15:36)

This account, which parallels I 7, provides the 2nd and concluding great climax of the book (see above on 10:1-9).

14:1-2. Demetrius' Seizure of the Throne. On the death of **Seleucus** IV in 175 his son Demetrius would have become king instead of Seleucus' brother Antiochus Epiphanes if he had not been a hostage in Rome. He now escapes from Rome, revolts against his young cousin Antiochus Eupator, and executes both him and Lysias (cf. I 7:1-4). **Three years later** is apparently an error, for most data indicate that Eupator reigned less than 2 years (163-162). **Tripolis** is N of Beirut in modern Lebanon (see color map 12).

14:3-11. Treachery of Alcimus. Possibly the epitomist omitted some record of Alcimus' former service as high priest; but I 7:5 says, with great probability, only that he "wanted to be high priest." On the **Hasideans** (vs. 6) see Intro. Alcimus convinces Demetrius that peace is impossible **as long as Judas lives** (vs. 10).

14:11-36. Appointment of Nicanor. Josephus states that Nicanor was one of the group who escaped from Rome with Demetrius. If he was the same man who fought Judas earlier (8:9-36) he presumably went to Rome sometime after his ignominious defeat with the hope of recouping his fortunes by helping Demetrius gain the crown. On the other hand the reference to Nicanor's having commanded the **elephants** may indicate that Jason of Cyrene included him in Lysias' army (cf. 11:4; 13:2). With **immediately** (vs. 12) contrast I 7:8-25.

14:15-25. After an initial skirmish at **Dessau** (vs. 16; the place is unknown) Nicanor endeavors to make friends with Judas (vss. 18-25). I 7:27-30 expresses a more cynical view of Nicanor's motives: he was planning treachery.

14:26-36. By raising suspicions of Nicanor's loyalty Alcimus succeeds in thwarting his efforts toward securing a peaceful settlement (vss. 26-27). When Judas escapes (vss. 28-30) Nicanor threatens to destroy and desecrate the temple if Judas is not surrendered to him (vss. 31-33). The priests call for divine help (vss. 34-36).

14:37-46. The Martyrdom of Razis. This story of persecution and suicide is told with even more gruesome details than those of chs. 6-7. The rarity of suicide in the OT and among Jews in general gives the account a special pathos.

15:1-36. Nicanor's Defeat and Death. Both sides now prepare for battle. Instead of putting Judas' army vaguely **in the region of Samaria** I 7:40 says he was encamped at Adasa, *ca.* 10 miles NW of Jerusalem. Some Jewish conscripts in Nicanor's army attempt, unsuccessfully, to dissuade him from fighting on the **sabbath** (vss. 1-5).

15:6-16. Judas encourages his troops by general exhortation (vss. 7-11) and by **relating a dream** (vs. 11) in which **Onias,** the martyred high priest (cf. ch. 3; 4:33-34), and **Jeremiah, the prophet,** appeared to him (vss. 12-16). Vs. 9 shows that **the law and the prophets** had been canonized by the date of writing, but apparently not the Writings, the 3rd division of the OT canon. The vision of Onias and Jeremiah provides evidence for belief in the intercession of saints at this period (vs. 12, 14; cf. Tobit 12:12, 15). In view of vss. 1-5 the vision seems intended to give God's approval for resisting Nicanor's attack on the sabbath, but this is not clear in the present text. Possibly the epitomist, unwilling to admit that Judas fought a battle on the sabbath (cf. 8:26-27; conrast I 2:41), has omitted this element from his source.

15:17-36. The battle is won by the Jews as an answer to their prayers (vss. 21-27). Afterward they cut off Nicanor's **head and arm** (vs. 30) and cut out his **tongue** (vs. 33), though they can hardly have hung his head from the **citadel,** which was not at that time in their possession (see above on 10:1-9). The annual celebration of these events is decreed to take place on the **day before Mordecai's day,** i.e. Purim (vs. 36; cf. Esth. 9:20-22, 26). **Adar** is Feb.-Mar.

VI. The Epitomist's Epilogue (15:37-39)

Cf. 2:19-32. In the sense that the religious freedom of its citizens is no longer threatened the city is now firmly **in the possession of the Hebrews,** but the garrison of the citadel would not be removed for 20 years (cf. I 13:49-52). The epitomist's concluding formula (see Intro.) appears for the last time in vs. 37*a*.

COMMENTARY on the BOOKS of the NEW TESTAMENT

THE GOSPEL ACCORDING TO MATTHEW

Howard Clark Kee

Introduction

Authorship. From the early 2nd cent. down to the present, Christians have believed that the first gospel in the NT was also the first to be written and that the author was Matthew the tax collector, a disciple of Jesus (9:9). The source of this persistent belief can be traced back as far as *ca.* A.D. 130, when Papias, a bishop in Hierapolis, a city of Asia Minor, wrote a work titled "Exposition of the Oracles of the Lord." His writing, which is known only from fragments quoted by later Christian writers, reports that Matthew, the disciple, compiled the sayings of the Lord in Hebrew. Those who have quoted Papias seem to have accepted his statement without question as referring to the First Gospel.

There are several difficulties with this assumption, however. (*a*) The gospel consists of a rather full account of Jesus' public ministry, not merely of a series of sayings. (*b*) Detailed analysis of Matt. shows that the author used Mark as one of his sources (see below). (*c*) Mark and therefore Matt., for which Mark was a source, were written in Greek, not Hebrew. In view of these difficulties, it is plausible to assume that Papias is referring, not to Matt. as we know it, but perhaps to a now lost collection of sayings of Jesus.

If we do not accept Papias' theory, then we must acknowledge that we have no evidence for the origin of Matt. and no assurance of its author's name. The gospel itself makes no such claim; indeed all the gospels are anonymous. Later tradition has attached to them the names they now bear. We use these names for convenience, but we should recognize that the authority of the writings rested in the power of their message, not in the personal authority of the author.

Date and Place of Composition. In early 2nd-cent. Christian writings there are a few passages which seem to be quotations from Matt. The clearest such reference comes from Ignatius of Antioch—indicating that Matt. may have originated in Syria, of which Antioch was the chief city. Clues from other early writers suggest that the place of composition was not Antioch itself, but the area to the E, where there were important colonies of Jews among whom Christianity had spread rapidly and effectively. Since Ignatius quoted Matt. *ca.* A.D. 115, and since one of its sources, Mark, was likely written *ca.* A.D. 70, we may conjecturally assign a date about A.D. 80-85.

Sources. In addition to Mark, Matt. used a 2nd source—a collection of sayings of Jesus. We have no copy of this document, but it can be reconstructed with reasonable certainty by comparing those passages in Matt. and Luke where they have nearly identical material. Often this common material appears in Matt. and Luke in the same order, even though it is not found in Mark, which both Matt. and Luke have also used as a source. One might assume that Matt. copied from Luke, or vice versa, but the more likely explanation is that both used a single sayings source which scholars have come to refer to as Q (from the German word *Quelle,* meaning "source"). Since certain features of Matt. and Luke remain unexplained by this hypothesis, there may have been slightly different versions of Q in circulation in the pre-Matthean church. (See "The Literary Relations Among the Gospels," pp. 1129-35, for a further discussion of these points.)

Matt. also has considerable material not found in any of the other gospels. This includes some of the best-known sections of the gospels: much of the Sermon on the Mount, the coming of the Wise Men, the Lord's Prayer (in its more familiar form), the parable of the sheep and the goats, Jesus' addressing Peter as the rock on which the church will be built. There is no way to tell whether Matt. obtained this material from a written source or whether it circulated in the church only orally. In either case, the whole gospel bears the stamp of the author's own special interests and is expressed in his own distinctive vocabulary. He is no neutral reporter of traditional information; he has effectively edited his material so that the gospel that he produced fulfills his own objectives.

Purpose. Matt. shares with the other gospel writers the intention of presenting a portrait of Jesus as the Christ, and, in doing so, of showing how the ministry, death, and resurrection of Jesus are bound up with his role as Messiah. But Matt. is also concerned about the church and its way of life in response to the message of Jesus. Accordingly he has edited the stories and sayings of Jesus in such a way as to point up the claims that: (*a*) the church is the true Israel, replacing the old Israel in the center of God's purpose; (*b*) the church in the present age is a mixed body, including both worthy and unworthy among its members; (*c*) the church is called to live a new and higher way of righteousness that exceeds even the Jewish law in the radical quality of its demands.

In achieving his aims, Matt. has alternated between narrative and discourse material, so that one receives from this gospel the picture of Jesus as one who not only acts the role of Messiah but also care-

609

fully and fully instructs his followers as to the meaning of his ministry. Thus Matt.'s aims are served by the very structure he has given to his gospel.

Structure. The main sections of Matt. are as follows:

I. The Coming of Jesus as God's Messiah (chs. 1-2)
II. The Ministry of the Messiah (chs. 3-25)
III. The Humiliation and Exaltation of the Messiah (chs. 26-28)

It is in the long middle section that Matt.'s skillful structuring best serves his special aims. Here we see an alternation between narrative and discourse:

Narrative: The Ministry Begun in Galilee (3:1-4:25)
  Discourse: Sermon on the Mount (5:1-7:29)
Narrative: The Authority of Jesus' Ministry (8:1-9:35)
  Discourse: Mission Discourse (9:36-10:42)
Narrative: The Kingdom and Its Coming (11:1-12:50)
  Discourse: Parables of the Kingdom (13:1-52)
Narrative: The Life of the New Community (13:53-17:27)
  Discourse: Greatness and Responsibility (18:1-35)
Narrative: Conflict and Consummation (19:1-24:3)
  Discourse: Revelation of the End (24:4-25:46)

The transitions between these 5 sections are carefully marked by a recurrent phrase, "when Jesus had finished . . ." (7:28; 11:1; 13:53; 19:1; 26:1). It has been suggested that the fivefold structure of this section was intended as an imitation of the Pentateuch, the 5 books of the law of Moses.

Whether Matt. consciously copied the structure of the Mosaic law or not, he had a major concern to show that the OT was fulfilled in Jesus Christ. By direct quotation and indirect allusion he keeps pointing his reader to the words of the law and the prophets that have come to fulfillment in the coming of God's Messiah, Jesus. More than 130 different passages from the OT are cited. Some can be readily associated with the events which Matt. claims to be prophetic fulfillment—e.g. the Messiah's birth in Bethlehem (2:5-6; Mic. 5:2). Others do not seem to us today to fit—e.g. 2:15, where the return of Jesus from Egypt is seen as the fulfillment of a prophetic reference (Hos. 11:1) to God's call of the nation Israel out of Egypt at the time of the Exodus. The difficulty with these prophecies is that we think in historical terms and expect precision in associating prediction and fulfillment. The first Christians, like their Jewish contemporaries, considered their Hebrew Scriptures to possess many possibilities of meaning, not all of them by any means self-evident. To discern the multiple meanings of scripture was a tribute to the divine wisdom that inspired the writings as well as an evidence of the ingenuity of the interpreter who saw in any given event the fulfillment of a text that others might not have detected. There is a similarity between certain Matthean interpretations of the OT and those found in the Dead Sea Scrolls, whose writers likewise believed that the community of God's people to which they belonged was the group for and through whom God would bring his prophetic promises to fulfillment.

Equally important for Matt. is the fulfillment of the *moral* requirements of the law of Moses. The major passage on this theme is 5:17-20, where Jesus is reported as telling his disciples that the law is to be fulfilled, that not a letter of it will pass away, that its requirements are not to be in the slightest relaxed,

and that their conformity to the law must exceed in strictness the righteousness observed by the scribes and Pharisees. How radical that demand for righteousness is may be seen in the specifics of the new formulation of the law as set forth in the Sermon on the Mount. But the strictness of moral expectation by the community for which Matt. writes is apparent in his versions of the parables and other sayings of Jesus. Indeed the tone for this emphasis is set in 3:15, where Jesus says: "It is fitting for us to fulfill all righteousness." Even though this is spoken in connection with Jesus' accepting baptism at the hand of John, it is a characteristic factor in the gospel as a whole.

For Further Study: A. H. McNeile, *The Gospel According to St. Matt.*, 1915; older work, but still the best technical commentary in English. G. D. Kilpatrick, *The Origins of . . . Matt.*, 1946; illuminating study of the background. T. W. Manson, *The Sayings of Jesus*, 1949; exposition of the sayings in Q and the special sources of Matt. and Luke, with a discerning treatment of all the discourse material in Matt. K. Stendahl, *The School of St. Matt.*, 1954; technical analysis of the OT quotations in Matt., with special attention to the interpretive method found in the Dead Sea Scrolls. F. V. Filson, *Commentary on . . . Matt.*, 1960; a helpful recent commentary. G. Bornkamm and others, *Tradition and Interpretation in Matt.*, 1963; penetrating study of the distinctive characteristics of the gospel tradition as edited in Matt., with emphasis on the miracles, the church, and the law.

I. The Coming of God's Messiah (1:1-2:23)

1:1-17. The Genealogy of Jesus. The Greek word employed for **genealogy** (vs. 1) is *genesis*, as though the author wanted to stress the continuity between the OT and the new work that God began in Jesus Christ. Mention of **David** and **Abraham** suggests that Jesus is here thought of as in the line of God's people, beginning with Abraham, and in the royal line, for which David is the ideal figure (cf. Pss. 89:3-4; 132:11-12; Acts 2:30).

1:2-17. The descendants are grouped in 3 sets of 14 each. Why the number 14 was chosen is not apparent. Comparison with the OT accounts shows that the lists are not intended to be complete. E.g. there are 3 generations missing after **Uzziah** (vs. 9; cf. I Chr. 3:11-12, where Uzziah = Ahaziah). Furthermore, the genealogy here is not in agreement with that in Luke 3:23-38. Actually the genealogy in Matt. is that of **Joseph,** who is represented as Mary's husband rather than as the actual father of Jesus (vs. 16). The purpose of the genealogy is twofold: (*a*) to show the continuity and order of God's purpose among his people, culminating in the call of Abraham (vs. 2), the establishment of the kingdom (vss. 6-7), the return from exile in Babylon (vs. 11), and now the birth of Jesus Christ (vs. 16); (*b*) to place Jesus in the legal line of the king promised to God's people.

1:18-25. The Birth of Jesus. Unlike Luke, who recounts the advance notice given to Mary concerning the miraculous birth about to occur, Matt. presents only the direct statement that Mary was **with child of the Holy Spirit.** The story is written out of a knowledge of Palestinian customs, such as the binding nature of a betrothal, which was considered as firm an obligation as marriage itself. Joseph decided to deal kindly with Mary, **to divorce her quietly** rather than make a scandal of her seeming breach of the marriage agreement.

1:20-21. Joseph's dream is the first of a series of dreams, revealing each a divine warning or counsel, which occur in Matt.'s own material (1:20; 2:12; 2:13; 2:19; 2:22; 27:19). Joseph is addressed as **son of David,** indicating his connection with the kingly line of Israel's history and her hope. The child is to be called *Yeshua* or, in its more familiar Greek form, **Jesus.** The name means lit. "he shall save." In the OT the name refers, of course, to God's deliverance of his people from their enemies and his vindication of them by the establishment of his kingdom (cf. Pss. 7; 9). By adding the words **save his people from their sins** Matt. pictures Jesus as the one through whom the forgiveness of sins is announced. There had been no tradition in Israel for a messiah who would save from sin.

1:22-25. At this point appears the first of the explicit claims that in Jesus prophecy is being fulfilled. In the birth story of Matt. these prophecies and the incidents which are seen as fulfilling them provide the framework for the entire account: the virgin birth (1:23); the birth in Bethlehem (2:6); the return of the Holy Family from Egypt (2:15); the slaughter of the children by Herod (2:16-17); the transfer of residence from Bethlehem to Nazareth (2:23). That scripture is being fulfilled is evidence that what is occurring in connection with Jesus is the unfolding of God's plan for man's redemption.

1:23. The Hebrew original of the vs. quoted from Isa. 7:14 speaks of an *almah,* i.e. a "young woman," who **shall conceive and bear a son.** It is the period of conception and birth, not her virginity, that is of importance for Isaiah. The Greek version of the OT in wide use among Jews from the first cent. B.C. on (the LXX—see p. ix) had translated *almah* by the Greek word *parthenos*—virgin. Matt. uses this translation, since it suits his purpose of showing that Jesus was divinely conceived in fulfillment of the Hebrew Scriptures. Although Luke has his own version of the extraordinary birth of Jesus, he does not quote or refer to the virgin birth passage from Isa. Neither Mark, nor John, nor Paul has any hint of the virgin birth story; it seems to have become important for the church only in the 2nd cent. as a way of combatting the charge that Jesus was not truly human. These stories insisted that he was truly *born*, although they also served to place Jesus at least on a par with the pagan savior-gods for whom a miraculous birth was claimed. Indeed, the idea of Jesus' virgin birth does not figure at all in the rest of Matt.; it is the conviction that Jesus is **Emmanuel . . . God with us** that is more significant than the circumstances of his birth.

1:14-25. Joseph obeys the instruction of **the angel** in the dream by his treatment of Mary and by his giving to Jesus the appointed **name.**

2:1-12. *The Visit of the Magi.* The evangelist makes no attempt to present a full chronological account of the events of Jesus' birth and infancy. The fact that Herod deems it necessary to order killed all children up to 2 years of age implies that Jesus was himself already about 2 when the wise men, or magi, arrived from the E. The magi were astrologers, although they represented the closest thing to astronomers that the ancient world knew. They seem to have possessed considerable information about the movement of the stars and planets, but to have treated it in magical fashion, tying the heavenly movements in directly with the destiny of men. It is difficult to discern why the movements of the stars would have a direct bearing on the coming of a Jewish king. The visit of the magi is symbolic of the divine preparation for the advent of Jesus. Their gifts point to the kingly rights of the child and to the worldwide acknowledgment that he is ultimately to receive.

Herod the king is Herod the Great, who ruled over the Jewish people in Palestine from 37 B.C. to 4 B.C., although he was of Idumean rather than Jewish stock. His father, Antipater, had aided the Romans effectively in taking over control of Palestine following the Roman invasion in 63 B.C. Herod was able to ride out the storms resulting from the power struggle that left Octavian (Augustus) in control of the empire. His marriage to Mariamne, of the authentic Jewish royal line (the Hasmonean family), gave him a touch of respectability; his political and military skill kept him in undisputed control until his death in 4 B.C. In the course of his reign he arranged for the murder of his sons and relatives, as well as of his enemies. The murder of the children is in keeping with his character, although there is no report of this crime from any source other than Matt.

2:5-6. The birth of the child **in Bethlehem** is seen as the fulfillment of Mic. 5:2. This is the only place in the NT where Jesus' place of birth is viewed as required by prophecy to be Bethlehem.

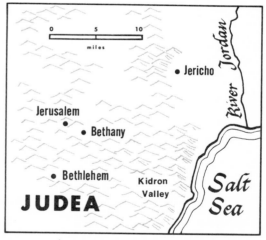

Although the birth is located here in Luke 2, there is no appeal to this prophecy by Luke. The prophecy is probably referred to in John 7:42, but there it is assumed that Jesus is from Nazareth, not Bethlehem. The Davidic origin of Jesus is attested by Paul (Rom. 1:3), but Bethlehem and its royal prophecy are not mentioned by him.

2:9-12. **A dream** warned the magi not to share in Herod's plot to destroy the one **born king of the Jews,** but they did visit the child, **going into the house** where Mary and Joseph were living. Unlike

Luke, Matt. gives no hint that the holy family was merely stopping off in Bethlehem as required by law for census purposes, after which they would return to their permanent home in Nazareth. Rather, Matt. implies that Bethlehem was their home; only in order to escape the vengeance of Herod's son and successor, Archelaus (vs. 22), did they change their residence from Bethlehem to Nazareth, **in the district of Galilee,** which was under the control of another puppet ruler, Herod's son Antipas, tetrarch of Galilee and of Perea, E of the Jordan River.

2:13-23. The Flight into Egypt. Apart from sparing Jesus from the wrath of Herod, the narrative of the flight into Egypt serves Matt.'s purpose by showing that scripture was fulfilled by both the sojourn in Egypt and the return to Nazareth. The great freedom in interpreting scripture that is found among first-cent. Jews is evident in both aspects of this event. The call of God's son **out of Egypt** (vs. 15) is in the OT (Hos. 11:1) a reference to the deliverance of the nation Israel from its period of slavery in Egypt.

2:23. Although we cannot be certain of the scripture referred to here, it is probably an allusion to Isa. 11:1. There the Messiah is described as a *netzer* (Hebrew for "sprout," or "shoot"), implying that, like a tree cut down, the Davidic dynasty will grow up once more and the kingdom be reestablished. Matt. has taken the consonants of *netzer*—since the vowels were not written in the ancient Hebrew text —and has interpreted them as a prophecy referring to Nazareth: **he shall be called a Nazarene.** This method of scriptural interpretation, far-fetched though it may seem, was in common use among the rabbis of Jesus' time, as well as within the community that produced the Dead Sea Scrolls.

The refusal of the magi to cooperate following their "being warned in a dream," coupled with the dream of Joseph, caused the plot of Herod to fail. His death, which in vs. 19 is chronologically linked to the birth of Jesus, gives us our only clue in Matt. as to the date of these events. Since Herod died in 4 B.C., the birth of Jesus would have taken place about 2 years earlier. The attempt to link these events with the mention in Luke 2:2 of the census "when Quirinius was governor of Syria" only complicates the matter of chronology. Matt. gives us the nearest thing to a fixed date for Jesus' birth.

II. THE MINISTRY OF THE MESSIAH (3:1–25:46)

A. THE BAPTISM OF JESUS (3:1-17)

3:1-6. John the Baptist. Both Christian and Jewish traditions gave to John the title **the Baptist,** even though in the earlier account in Mark 1:4 he was known simply as the John who baptizes, or the baptizer. Matt. specifies that he launched his work **in the wilderness of Judea,** the barren territory between the low mountain ridge on which Jerusalem and the cities of Judah lie and the deep cleft where the Jordan River empties into the Dead Sea. His activity is described as fulfilling what **was spoken of by the prophet Isaiah: a voice of one crying in the wilderness** (see on Mark 1:2-3). John's message is identical with that of Jesus in 4:17: **Repent, for the kingdom of heaven is at hand.** The term "kingdom of heaven" (lit. "kingdom of the

heavens") is used here as by pious Jews to mean "the kingdom of God," since it was considered irreverent to pronounce God's name directly.

The garb of John is reminiscent of the prophet Elijah, with whom John is directly identified by Matt. (17:14; cf. Mark 9:13; see also on Mark 1:6), although John's message more nearly resembles that of the later prophets, Zechariah or Daniel. His strange diet of **locusts and wild honey** is an indication of the ascetic life he lived. The response to John may be described by the gospels with some exaggeration—**Jerusalem and all Judea and all the region about the Jordan**—but the Jewish historian Josephus attests the wide appeal that John's ministry had among his contemporaries. They came, however, not to witness a great sight or to hear a consoling message, but to confess **their sins.**

3:7-10. John's Call to Repentance. Matt. singles out for attack the Pharisees and the Sadducees (cf. Luke 3:7), who were the 2 leading groups within Judaism in the first cent. The **Sadducees** were from the priestly families and were conservative in their view of scripture in that they acknowledged only the first 5 books of the OT as authoritative. The **Pharisees** sought to make the ancient faith and the teachings of scripture relevant to their own day by an elaborate interpretive process, but the result of their detailed interpretations was often to make obedience to the law burdensome or even to avoid the clear intent of the laws themselves (see below on ch. 23).

They are to accept **baptism** at the hand of John to prepare themselves for **the wrath to come.** It would appear that John taught that men should purify themselves by baptism now so that they would be cleansed and ready to pass safely through the fires of judgment that were to fall. Hence the contrast in vs. 11 between baptism with water and baptism with fire. What God expects of those who call themselves the people of God is **fruit that befits repentance.** It is not sufficient to repeat the proud claim that they are **children to Abraham;** God is able to create a new people **from these stones.** The judgment is as sure to come as the tree is sure to fall when **the ax is laid to the root.** The fate of the unrepentant sinner in the judgment will be **the fire,** John declares.

3:11-12. John's Announcement of the Messiah. John offers 2 contrasts between himself and him **who is coming:** (*a*) The Coming One is **mightier** than John, and (*b*) he will baptize **with the Holy Spirit and with fire.** As was noted, the baptism with fire points to the judgment that is to fall on mankind, but there is no clear indication here of how the Holy Spirit is related to the fire. It has been suggested that John's original prediction was simply of a baptism with fire and that the early church added the mention of spirit baptism following the Pentecost experience. Whatever the original force of John's words may have been, the early church did not abandon baptism **with water** when it received the Holy Spirit; rather water became the symbol of baptism with the Spirit. John expects the Coming One to carry out the judgment he has been predicting. Like grain at threshing time, the worthy will be separated from the useless, here compared with **chaff** fit only for burning **with unquenchable fire.**

3:13-17. Jesus' Baptism by John. John's initial re-

Flooding Jordan River at the traditional site of the baptism of Jesus; the terebinth trees and shrubs on the bank form part of the "jungle of the Jordan" (Jer. 12:5)

fusal to baptize Jesus calls to the reader's attention the fact that it was not appropriate for Jesus, who had no consciousness of sin, to accept a baptism which was a sign of repentance. Further, Matt.'s version of this incident suggests that John already recognized who Jesus was and was aware of his own inferiority (but see below on 11:1-9). Jesus' reply sounds a theme which pervades the whole of this gospel: **fulfil all righteousness.** This motif is developed especially in the Sermon on the Mount, where Jesus exhorts men to be obedient to the law of God in such a radical way as to exceed the zeal for righteousness of even the Pharisees (5:17-20; see also on Mark 1:9-11).

3:16-17. Unlike Mark, who depicts the coming of the Spirit and the **voice from heaven** as a private experience of Jesus, Matt. implies that the heavenly voice addressed the onlookers, since the words are not addressed to Jesus: **This is my beloved Son, with whom I am well pleased.** The first part of this declaration is reminiscent of Ps. 2:7, where the king of Israel is addressed as the son of God, meaning the one who rules in God's stead. The 2nd half of the statement comes from Isa. 42:1 and was originally spoken to Israel as the servant people of God. Here, then, are combined 2 great streams of Jewish hope: the coming of the ideal king and the acceptance of the servant role, though now by an individual rather than by the nation as a whole.

The descent of the **Spirit** upon Jesus and its appearance **like a dove** are given a somewhat more concrete description in Matt. than in Mark. It is difficult to know what it was about the coming of the Spirit that could be described as "like a dove." The

dove in the OT tradition as interpreted in first-cent. Judaism was the symbol of God's Spirit, hovering over the creation (Gen. 1:2) and caring for his people in the days of their wilderness wanderings (Deut. 32:11).

The whole story of Jesus' baptism has been so overlaid with symbolism that it is no longer possible to separate historical from symbolic elements. The suggestion of some scholars that the entire incident is a legend or a misplaced story of a post-resurrection appearance of Jesus does not help us to understand the incident. Indeed, the fact that Jesus was baptized by John was a source of embarrassment to the early church, since John's followers claimed that Jesus' submission to John showed John's superiority. Thus the account would not have been invented or even recalled if it did not have some basis in fact. Nevertheless, as it stands it symbolizes the entrance of Jesus into his ministry, empowered by God's Spirit and acknowledged by the God-sent forerunner, John the Baptist, as the Coming One.

B. The Temptation of Jesus (4:1-11)

4:1. The temptation of Jesus is not an effort on the part of **the devil** to lure Jesus into committing some immoral act, but rather an attempt to force him to set aside his complete obedience to the will and purpose of God by adopting an easier means to the fulfillment of his mission. In the gospel tradition the devil (called Satan in Mark, in keeping with the Jewish name for God's archenemy) is waging an unsuccessful effort to wrest final control of the creation from God; i.e. the movement of history is

Courtesy of Herbert G. May

Wilderness of Judea between Jericho and Jerusalem; into this type terrain Jesus was "led up by the Spirit" (Matt. 4:1); the sign in the foreground marks sea level

the conflict between the kingdom of God and the kingdom of Satan. By offering him enticing possibilities, the devil is here pictured as trying to trick Jesus into submitting to his ways. Although Luke and Matt. present the details of this story in different order from each other, they agree on the main features.

4:2. The **forty days** that the temptation lasted are a round figure for an extended period of time.

4:3-11. The first suggestion of the **tempter** is that Jesus utilize his extraordinary powers to convert **stones** into **bread.** The Roman rulers found very soon that one way to gain the favor of the masses was to distribute free bread; the tempter's proposal follows this line of reasoning. Jesus' response, quoted from Deut. 8:3, affirms that the **word** of God is more vital to man's existence than the food he eats. Jesus' task is to declare God's message, not to fill stomachs. The 2nd proposal of the tempter is that Jesus demonstrate God's care over him by throwing himself from the **pinnacle of the temple.** But Jesus refuses to put God to the test merely for purposes of public display. The 3rd offer would have eliminated all the humiliation and suffering that Jesus was to undergo in fulfillment of his mission: all that was required was that Jesus **fall down** in acknowledgment of his subservience to the devil. Jesus will offer **worship** to God alone and will **serve** only the coming of his kingdom. God's continuing favor toward and support of Jesus is portrayed in the attendance upon him of the ministering **angels.**

C. Jesus Launches His Ministry (4:12-25)

4:12-17. *Jesus' First Preaching in Galilee.* The indication that Jesus did not begin his public ministry until he **heard that John had been arrested** has suggested to some interpreters that Jesus and John the Baptist at first carried on their work concurrently (cf. John 4:1), but that Jesus—presumably as a result of disagreement with John—resumed his work only after John was off the scene. This view receives some support from the uncertainty about Jesus' mission implied in the questions John sent to Jesus from prison (see below on 11:1-9). It is possible that Jesus' friendship with religious outcasts was abhorrent to John, with his strict and somber message of doom to sinners.

4:15-16. Matt. sees in the beginning of Jesus' ministry in Galilee the fulfillment of scripture. The fact that it is called **Galilee of the Gentiles** gives the reader the clue that in Matt.'s account Jesus' work

will culminate with the launching of the mission to the whole world. For the time being, however, his work will be limited to "the lost sheep of the house of Israel" (10:6).

4:17. Jesus' message is presented by Matt. as identical with that of John: repentance, in light of the inbreaking of the **kingdom of heaven.** The word translated **is at hand** means "has drawn near." Jesus is not declaring, therefore, that the new era in which God's rule will be sovereign over his creation has already come, but rather that it has drawn so near that its signs are already evident in the ministry of Jesus. They may be seen in his triumph over the demons (12:28) as well as in the new fellowship that Jesus is establishing with the poor and with those considered unworthy by the religious standards of his day (11:19). The whole of Jesus' ministry is in a sense a sign that in his person and work the reign of God has drawn near.

4:18-22. *The Call of the Disciples.* The first 4 disciples called to follow Jesus are 2 pairs of brothers: **Simon** (who was given the nickname **Peter,** meaning "rock") and **Andrew** and **James** and **John,** the mention of whose father, **Zebedee,** suggests that he was himself a well-known person in the early church. All are **fishermen** by trade; all are called to be **fishers of men,** i.e. to call men out from their ordinary way of life in order to prepare for the coming of God's kingdom. Although there is no hint here of prior contact between Jesus and the disciples, there is evidence in John 1:35-42 that Jesus had these men as followers during the period of his association with John the Baptist. But now **they followed him immediately.**

4:23-25. *Scope of the Ministry.* At this point Matt. departs from the Markan order of events and inserts a summary statement which gives a capsule picture of what Jesus did and where he ministered. His work comes under 3 headings: **teaching . . . , preaching . . . , healing.** That the teaching was carried on in the Jewish synagogues confirms the impression received from the rest of the gospel that Jesus worked almost entirely within the structures and institutions of Judaism, even as he was seeking to transform it in the light of what he knew to be God's redemptive purpose. The healing activity is as well attested in the gospel tradition as the teaching ministry, so that Jesus' power to heal cannot be dismissed as a late addition. Even from polemical Jewish sources we learn that Jesus was believed to possess the power to heal and to expel demons; the only question in the mind of his detractors was, "Who was the source of his power, God or Satan?" His work attracted the attention of those living outside the bounds of Galilee in such pagan territories as **Syria** and the cities of the **Decapolis.** The latter was a loose confederation of 10 Greek cities built by the successors to Alexander the Great and improved by the Romans. They were located in S Syria and on the E side of the Jordan and were inhabited largely by Gentiles. The summary passage also serves Matt. as a means of transition from narrative to the first and best known of his great discourses.

D. The Sermon on the Mount (5:1-7:29)

5:1-2. *Introduction.* Jesus' going **up on the mountain** was to withdraw from the crowds, not to gain a vantage point from which he might be seen and heard. His words are addressed to **his disciples.** No particular mountain seems to be intended; rather Matt. has likely provided the setting, since it contrasts with the "level place" on which Luke locates the comparable "sermon" (Luke 6:17). Matt. does not call this a sermon, and indeed it is not a sermon, but a bringing together of the teachings of Jesus on the meaning of obedience in such a way as to set forth dramatically his understanding of the radical devotion to God's will that God expects. In compiling this discourse material Matt. has drawn on the Q source, although he considerably rearranges the material. In addition he has utilized a source uniquely his own among the gospels.

5:3-12. *The Beatitudes.* The Beatitudes have been regarded as timeless rules for the good life. Although one can extract from them certain enduring ethical demands, they are not moral laws, but eschatological promises. ("Eschatology" means lit. "the study of the last things," but in relation to the Bible and theology it refers to the events and experiences associated with God's consummation of his purpose in the world, i.e. with the coming of his kingdom.) Matt. has modified the form of the Beatitudes somewhat; originally, as evidenced in Luke's version (Luke 6:20-21), they were addressed directly to the hearer ("Blessed are you poor") and made explicit the contrast between man's response to the will of God now and his fate in the kingdom ("Blessed are you that weep *now*, for you shall laugh"). Now they have been changed to sound more like general principles. Matt. may well have expanded the original set, since several of his beatitudes do not appear in Luke.

5:3. The phrase **poor in spirit** does not mean one who is weak in spirit, but one who, like the psalmist (Ps. 34), looks to God alone to preserve him in the midst of his afflictions. He does not live out of his own resources, nor is he relying on his own achievements to overcome the seemingly overwhelming difficulties that he faces—his trust is in God:

> This poor man cried, and the LORD heard him,
> And saved him out of all his troubles (Ps. 34:6).

It is the poor ones who will receive the kingdom, rather than those who are proud and confident in their moral achievements.

5:4. Possibly **those who mourn** refers to persons who are bereaved, but if this beatitude is a parallel to the preceding, it may describe those who bewail the present state of affairs in God's world and long for the coming of the new age. God will comfort them by establishing his kingdom.

5:5. This saying, which probably originated with Matt. or his special source, reads like a modification of Ps. 37:11. Moses was called the meekest of men (Num. 12:3) not on account of his timidity, but because of his awareness of his own limitations and his consequent dependence on God. It is such persons who will **inherit** the kingdom when it is established in **the earth.**

5:6. Again Matt. has augmented (by adding **and thirst for righteousness**) the simpler form of the saying found in Luke, which pronounces the blessing on those who now "hunger." It is possible that Matt. is using the word "righteousness" in a special eschatological sense to refer to the new situation that will

obtain in the earth when God's kingdom is established. His linking of "kingdom" and "righteousness" in 6:33 may confirm this. But in the light of his heavy stress on obedience to the will of God, it seems more likely that he is using righteousness in the sense of holy living. Only those wholly devoted to obedience will be found worthy to see the new age in which their aspirations for mankind will be **satisfied** by the establishment of God's righteous rule over his obedient people.

5:7-9. Only those who practice **mercy** can expect to receive it from God at the judgment. Only those whose heart is pure can come into God's presence. The **heart** is understood to be far more than the seat of the emotions: it is the center of the inner life, the source of thought and understanding, of will and of decision. A full transformation of the deepest level of man's life is what is demanded. The direction that this change takes is implied in the call to be **peacemakers,** since this is God's own work in the world. To **be called sons of God** means that one has sought to do what God is doing; in this case it is God's reconciling work in the world in which man is called to participate.

5:10-12. Those who will one day share in the kingdom are now expected to accept calmly the persecution and reviling which they will receive as a result of their devotion to Jesus and the work of the gospel. They are to understand their harassment as a sign of God's favor rather than as an indication of his displeasure, and therefore to **rejoice:** God has already laid up for them a **reward in heaven.**

5:13-16. *Words on Salt and Light.* Perhaps these words were originally addressed to Israel, rebuking the nation for its failure to fulfill its mission to the Gentiles, to whom it was intended to bring the light of the knowledge of God (Isa. 42:6). As they stand in the sermon, they are now addressed to the church, which is called to fulfill its mission as **the salt of the earth** and as **the light of the world.** When salt and light are not fulfilling their proper function, they are utterly useless; but when the church discharges its light-giving role, men glorify, not the church, but God. (See also below on 6:22-23.)

5:17-20. *Words on the Law.* All these words about the law are set in an eschatological setting; i.e. they speak of the law's enduring until the end of the age and of the reward that will come in the new age for those who faithfully obey the commandments. The claim attributed here to Jesus that he has **come** (meaning God has sent him) **to fulfil . . . the law and the prophets** means far more than that Jesus is acting out a role laid down for him in the words and prediction of the prophets of Israel. It is rather the declaration that both the purpose of God disclosed through the prophets and the demands of God that his people obey him have found their fulfillment in Jesus. There is to be no relaxation of the strictness of the commandments. For Matt., at least certain aspects of the ceremonial law are as binding as the moral sections (cf. 5:23; 6:17).

5:18. This may have been originally an ironical declaration of Jesus against the Jewish interpreters of the law who, he said, would rather have **heaven and earth pass away** than to have the smallest letter or **dot** of the written law altered (cf. Luke 16:17). But as it stands in Matt., Jesus is portrayed as laying an extremely heavy burden on his followers, since they are to meet the law's demands in full. They are to surpass the scribes in their zeal, because their **righteousness** is to exceed **that of the scribes and Pharisees,** who make demands that they themselves are not able to carry out. Even these requirements the disciples are to fulfill, Matt. declares (cf. 23:3). What this type of righteousness demands is spelled out in the detailed interpretation of the law that follows.

5:21-26. *Words on Murder and Anger.* The focus shifts from the external meaning of the law against murder (Exod. 20:13; Deut. 5:17) to the inner attitude of the heart, concerning which there can be no legislation. Hatred and insult toward one's brother are as serious violations of God's will for his people as the overt act of murder. It is God's intention that men become reconciled. To underscore this truth a brief parable is introduced: if an accused man has the prudence to ingratiate himself with his accuser while they are on the way to court, how much more should a disciple be reconciled with his brother in this time prior to God's judgment of all men!

5:27-30. *Words on Adultery and Lust.* Merely to stop short of the overt act of adultery is not to obey the intention of God which lies behind the law (Exod. 20:14; Deut. 5:18). To desire another man's wife is as much a violation of God's purpose for man as is the act of adultery itself. What is demanded is complete self-control of the members of the body, so that obedience may be complete. (See also below on 18:8-9.)

5:31-32. *Words on Divorce.* That this problem was important for the church of Matt. is evident from the fact that he included both the Q form of the words and that found in Mark. The most radical form appears in Mark 10:11, where Jesus unconditionally denounces divorce and remarriage. Here an exception is made: a man may divorce his wife and marry another if his first wife has been guilty of **unchastity.** But such a position is no different from that of the rabbinic interpreter of the law in Jesus' day, Shammai, who insisted on strict, literal observance of Deut. 24:1, where the phrase "because he has found some indecency in her" was understood to mean that he discovered that she had been unfaithful to him. In Mark 10:2-9 Jesus gives his basis for rejecting divorce: it violates the intention of God in establishing marriage, which is to be an enduring relationship, since it was a part of God's original creative act in fashioning man as male and female. Jesus, therefore, was reminding his hearers of the meaning of marriage; he was not giving a severely strict interpretation of the ancient law on divorce. Matt., with his interest in legal questions, has introduced the condition in the otherwise unconditional word of Jesus. (See also below on 19:3-9.)

5:33-37. *Words on Swearing and Oaths.* The clue to the interpretation of this passage is given in vs. 37: one is always to speak the truth. The man of truth will not need to add force to his words by an appeal to God or anything that God has created; he will not need to swear by anything, since his word can be relied on as it stands. The last phrase in vs. 33, which speaks of performing **to the Lord what you have sworn,** is probably an addition to the word of Jesus, since it deals with a vow (i.e. a promise made to God) rather than with an oath (i.e. a solemn affirmation made to another man). Jesus declares that when men are truthful, oaths are wholly unnecessary.

5:38-42. *Words on Retaliation.* The ancient Hebrew law of retaliation (Exod. 21:23-25) was an advance over the tribal practices which assumed that a single offense against a member of the tribe called for wholesale destruction of the offending tribe. But Jesus rejects the whole notion of retaliation and demands instead a response to a misdeed that is the reverse of what is expected. It is not the recommendation of such a negative factor as nonresistance; it is rather the response of positive good in the face of evil. Several illustrations are given: When one is insulted (i.e. struck **on the right cheek**), he is to offer the other cheek as an act of love. This act, because it is not the "normal" human reaction, is intended to challenge the aggressor by grace rather than by retaliation. When one is sued for his essential clothing, his **coat** (the long garment reaching to the ankles that served as a basic covering for the body), he should offer as well his outer **cloak** (a heavy, more expensive garment which served for protection against sun, cold, or rain, as well as bedding for the night). Again, the act of grace, which contradicts ordinary human reaction to harsh treatment, is intended to overcome the wrongdoer by love instead of by a greater show of coercive force.

5:41-42. The response of grace is to be seen in reaction not only to private individuals who seek to work harm but even to the authorities of the state, when they press one into service. The word translated **forces . . . to go** arose during Persian times, when the success of the mail system established by the Persian Empire depended on the possibility of impressing subjects into service by way of providing assistance for carrying the mail; later it came to mean any form of forced assistance to governmental or military authorities. In a time when Jewish nationalism was urging defiance of Roman rule, it was perilous for a Jew to utter what might sound like a collaborationist appeal. Jesus calls for his followers not only to cooperate with Roman authorities, but also to do twice what is demanded. His aim, of course, is not political collaboration, but shocking one's enemies by an act of grace. The same point is implied by the word to **give** freely to those who beg or borrow. It is the surprising reaction of love that Jesus calls for from his followers.

5:43-48. *Words on Love of Enemies.* The high point of the sermon is reached here: Jesus' moral appeal is grounded in nothing less than the nature of God himself. Those who obey him are to seek to emulate his character, i.e. to become God's **sons.** In Hebrew thinking, to be a son of someone is to resemble him in his manner of life; e.g. the sons of darkness are those whose way of life is that of the Prince of Darkness, Satan. To speak of becoming a son of God does not presuppose some sort of supernatural rebirth; rather it means adopting a new goal and mode of life patterned after the nature of God himself. To adopt this goal, however, is to reverse the ordinary pattern of human behavior, which is to love one's friends and hate one's enemies.

Jewish scholars have pointed out that nowhere in the OT is Israel instructed, "hate your enemies."

Although there are in the Pss. and some of the prophetic writings appeals to God to bring down judgment on Israel's foes, there is no direct command to hate the enemies. This appeal has, however, been found among the Dead Sea Scrolls, so that it may be this Jewish tradition that Matt. has in mind in vs. 43.

That the love which is commanded is more than an emotion is implied both in the parallel command to pray for one's persecutors and in the portrayal of God's love in its active form: sending **rain** and causing the **sun** to **rise** on all men, regardless of their moral worth or their attitude toward God. Even the Gentiles and the tax collectors—both of which groups were despised by pious Jews—observe the rule of treating kindly their own friends. But for the one who would be truly obedient, nothing less than God's own way of working is the ultimate standard. The call to be **perfect** could be an appeal for maturity and completeness, or it could be based on a Hebrew word which connotes peace, wholeness. In this case, to be perfect would be to share in God's reconciling work (cf. II Cor. 5:18-19).

6:1-18. Words on Alms, Prayer, and Fasting. The 3 chief pillars of Jewish piety in the first cent. were alms, fasting, and prayer. Matt. now represents them as established, with significant differences, as a proper part of Christian piety. The chief objection here registered to the Jewish pious practices is that they were done with hypocrisy and ostentation. Almsgiving accompanied by **trumpet** blasts may be an exaggeration of actual practices, but it points to the fact that man's perverse nature may lead him to convert an act of charity into a prideful form of public display. Similarly, prayer and fasting are to be purely private acts, involving only God and the penitent one (vss. 6, 18). Fancy **phrases** and drawing attention to one's self-denial make a mockery of the pious acts.

6:9-13. Matt. has inserted at this point what we know as the Lord's Prayer. Comparison with the older form in Luke 11:2-4 shows that in Matt. the prayer has already been somewhat expanded and modified to serve the worship needs of the church. The direct address to God in Luke 11:2, in contrast with the formal (though to us more familiar) address here in vs. 9, illustrates the fact that Luke has preserved the older version of the prayer.

6:9-10. To pray **Hallowed be thy name** means not merely to ascribe honorific titles to God, but to work as well as pray for the day when God's lordship over the creation will be both universally acknowledged and actualized. "Thy name be hallowed" is but another way of saying **Thy kingdom come,** which is in turn explained by the words **Thy will be done, on earth as it is in heaven.** The coming of the kingdom means the fulfillment in the creation of God's purpose, the realization of his will in the world that he has made. The Jews believed that God's will already prevailed in heaven; in the last day it would be triumphant on earth as well. The whole of the prayer, like the Beatitudes, is eschatological (see above on 5:3-12); but whereas the Beatitudes are eschatological promises, here we have an eschatological prayer.

6:11-12. The petition for **our daily bread** (lit. "our bread for tomorrow") means that we have the right to ask God only for what is essential to our basic day-to-day needs, since our goal is that God will act to fulfill the hope of the kingdom. Meanwhile, we are to pray that God will forgive us for those obligations to him that have gone unfulfilled (i.e. **debts**) while at the same time we are to be forgiving toward those who have failed in their responsibilities toward us. Matt. has inserted in vss. 14-15 the words of Jesus (cf. Mark 11:25-26) which warn that we cannot expect God's forgiveness if we are unwilling to exercise forgiveness toward others.

6:13. The prayer for deliverance from **temptation** and **evil** probably does not refer to temptation to sin, as though God would place us in the position where we would be inclined to immoral actions. Rather it is the notion found in Jewish apocalyptic writings (see pp. 1106-09) that just before the end of the age there would occur a time of trial and testing of God's people. This period of persecution, with the attempt to turn men aside from the way of faith and obedience, was known as the temptation or the tribulation. It is to be delivered from this situation and from the power of the Evil One (Satan) that Jesus tells the disciples to pray.

6:19-24. A Collection of Sayings. The more original form of the word about **treasures** (Luke 12:33-34) is a warning to those preoccupied with the things of this world to divest themselves of such treasures in order to be ready to enter the kingdom. Matt., in keeping with his stress on righteousness, presents this saying of Jesus as an appeal to be mindful of the rewards that God is even now laying up for those who are living and serving in a worthy manner. Since God is storing them up, man has no need for worry that they might be lost or harmed, as is the case with the anxiety that always comes from the effort to hold on to earthly possessions.

6:22-23. The strange saying about **light** seems to presuppose that **the eye** is both light and lens by and through which the image of the world around enters man and is comprehended by him. When the eye is functioning properly, man is **full of light;** otherwise he lives in darkness. Obviously this is not meant physiologically, but raises the question, How do you view the truth? If you see rightly, then your whole life is illuminated thereby; if not, you remain in the dark. These vss. have a parallel in the Gospel of Thomas (see pp. 1225-36) discovered in 1945 in Upper Egypt: "Within a man of light there is light and he lights the whole world. When he does not shine, there is darkness." This version of the saying considers the man of faith to be the "light of the world," and therefore calls on him to shed light, i.e. to spread the truth (cf. 5:14-16).

6:24. Another saying in the Gospel of Thomas adds to the familiar warning against serving 2 masters the comparison that no man can ride 2 horses. The point is not that possessing wealth and serving God are incompatible, but that *serving* one's possessions (mammon, from an Aramaic word meaning "property" or "riches") cannot coexist with the service of God.

6:25-34. Words on Freedom from Anxiety. The KJV of these sayings carries a mistaken implication in current English when it admonishes to "take no thought" about the necessities of life. The real meaning is clear in the RSV: **do not be anxious.** The passage seems to embody elements of Hebrew poetry, in which the lines rhyme in their sense rather than in their sounds:

> Look at the birds of the air:
>   They neither sow nor reap,
>   Nor do they gather into barns;
> And yet your heavenly Father feeds them.
> Are you not of more value than they?
>
> Consider the lilies of the field,
>   How they grow;
>   They neither toil nor spin;
> Yet I tell you, even Solomon in all his glory
>   Was not arrayed like one of these.
> But if God so clothes the grass of the field,
>   Which today is alive
>   And tomorrow is thrown into the oven,
> Will he not much more clothe you, O men of
>   little faith?

Such phrases as **heavenly Father** and **men of little faith** probably originated with Matt., since they are found only in his gospel; but the passage as a whole breathes the atmosphere of Jewish Palestine and in essence must go back to Jesus.

The message of these words is clear: If God has given man his life, he will surely provide the means of sustaining that life. Man is here thought of as consisting of a **body**, i.e. a self or form, and **life,** which means the vital force that enables man to live (vs. 15). The form needs to be clothed; the life needs to be sustained; God who gave both will sustain and preserve both. Man can therefore be free from anxiety when he lives in consciousness of his dependence upon God. Only those outside the people of God (**Gentiles**) would give way to such foolish anxieties, since God **knows** fully man's need. The aim of man's life is to **seek** for the coming **kingdom** (to which Matt. has characteristically added **and his righteousness;** cf. Luke 12:31). God will provide all that man needs, just as he will fulfill the promise of the kingdom in his own way and time.

7:1-23. *Another Cluster of Sayings.* In keeping with the Jewish reluctance to pronounce directly the name of God, vss. 1-2 mean: Take care how you **judge** others since you will **be judged** by God. He will hold you to account for the way you have dealt with others. The same point is made in Mark 4:24, as well as in Luke 6:37-38, although Luke stresses the generosity of God's grace: "good measure . . . running over."

7:3-5. The word about the **speck** and the **log** in one's eye is a vivid picture of the self-appointed censor of the actions of others who cannot see his own glaring faults. It probably was originally addressed to Jesus' opponents, rather than given out as advice to the disciples.

7:6. The saying about giving to **dogs what is holy** and throwing **pearls before swine** is, on the other hand, likely to have been a solemn warning that not all men are ready to receive the mystery of the coming of God's kingdom. Later on the church used this vs. to defend its withholding of the sacraments from those it deemed unworthy. Since the saying is found only in Matt. it may have originated among certain exclusivist Jewish Christians.

7:7-11. This is a group of sayings intended to encourage among the disciples the confidence that

God is ready and eager to answer prayer. The words are phrased so as to avoid direct mention of God, but the implication is clear: "Ask, and God will give . . . ; knock, and God will open to you." The comparison is offered with an earthly father—if he will grant requests that his son's needs might be met, **how much more will your Father who is in heaven** answer your prayers? The passage is more of a comment on what God is like in his providential care than an absolute guarantee that any request will be complied with by God.

7:12. The so-called Golden Rule is found in one form or another not only in Judaism but also in several other religious traditions. There is in this saying an element of enlightened self-interest which does not reach the height of insight of Jesus' appeal to love one's enemies or to respond to abuse by works of love. It is nevertheless an advance over the form of the saying current in Jewish circles of Jesus' day, which called for men to avoid doing to others what they would not like to have done to themselves.

7:13-14. Similarly, the contrast of the **wide** and the **narrow** gates is paralleled in first-cent. Judaism, where there was a highly developed tradition of the 2 ways open to man, one leading to vindication by God and the other to destruction. In one of the rather rare pessimistic notes in the Jesus tradition, it is here declared that those who choose the way that leads to life **are few** in number.

7:15-20. The warning that men display their true worth, not by how they appear, but by what they do, is based on 2 figures: the wolf disguised as a sheep and the tree that produces worthless fruit. The first image is drawn from Ezek. 34, which denounces the leaders of Israel for their exploitation of the people over whom they have been given authority. What is in Matt. a general warning against treachery may have been on the lips of Jesus an attack against the ruthless leaders of the nation. Vs. 19 is reminiscent of the warning uttered by John the Baptist (3:10) that those who failed to produce the fruits of right living would be cast into the fires of judgment. The true nature of man, therefore, is to be seen in what he does, not in what he merely claims to be.

7:21-23. Following through on this theme, Matt. has adapted a saying of Jesus about those who call him **Lord** but do not obey his teachings (Luke 6:46), and has made it into a criterion by which man will be admitted or refused admission to the **kingdom of heaven.** Here the contrast is between doing the **will of my Father** and merely making a profession of faith in Jesus' name.

7:24-29. *Parable of the Wise and Foolish Builders.* This parable is found in Luke 6:47-49 in an altered form that betrays unfamiliarity with terrain and building methods in Palestine, both of which are accurately reflected in Matt.'s version. In Palestine there are many dry stream beds in which a foolish man might more easily build than on the safer slopes. Such a stream bed, called a *"wadi,"* is sandy, so that the foundation could easily be dug and the builder would be saved the effort of carrying stones up the side for the construction of the walls. All would go well until the rainy season came, when the wadi would become a raging torrent. The parable is eschatological (see above on 5:3-12); it raises the

Wadi running through hill country of Judea; note the orchard and buildings located in the wadi (center of picture); modern drainage systems handle seasonal inundations; road runs between Jerusalem and Bethlehem

question, Are you prepared for the day of judgment that is to come upon mankind? Take care how you are building your life, the parable warns, so that you may be able to stand in the testings that will come upon God's people before the kingdom comes in its fullness.

7:28-29. This sentence includes the characteristic words which mark off the divisions of Matt., **when Jesus finished these sayings.** The remainder is an echo of the recurrent words in Mark (e.g. Mark 1: 22), which depict the **authority** that characterized Jesus' ministry and that attracted widespread interest. The **scribes,** the official interpreters of the written and oral law of Judaism, appealed to legal precedent to lend authority to their interpretations. But Jesus did not appeal to authorities; he **had authority.**

E. THE AUTHORITY OF JESUS' MINISTRY (8:1–9:35)

At this point Matt. resumes the order of events from Mark, which he interrupted after 4:23-25 (cf. Mark 1:39) to insert the Sermon on the Mount. Like his first main division Matt.'s 2nd begins with an account of the activity of Jesus drawn mostly from Mark, but with some material from Q as well. All of it has been reworked to suit Matt.'s own special aims. The miracle stories, e.g., are compressed in such a way as to minimize the details of the healing procedures and to emphasize Jesus as the central figure, the Messiah at whose word the healing occurs. Matt. also stresses the power of saving faith on the part of the sick one or of his family.

8:1-4. *The Healing of a Leper.* The OT laws (Lev. 14:2 ff.) made provision for the ceremonial cleansing of a leper who had been healed, although there is no report of anyone's having been healed and then having followed through the prescribed ritual. The disease itself is variously thought to have been anything from a severe skin inflammation to actual leprosy (Hansen's disease), medical terms in antiquity having been so imprecise. How a modern medical observer would describe the disease and its cure in this case there is no way of knowing. But the point of the story is clear: Jesus has the power to heal "every disease" (4:23), and "all who were sick" (8:16). The story also implies that Jesus' ministry is in fulfillment of scripture, since he commands compliance with the Mosaic regulations.

8:5-13. *The Centurion's Servant.* The authority of Jesus is underlined in this story by having the centurion address him as **Lord** (cf. vs. 2; also Luke 7:3, where Jesus is not spoken to directly by the centurion). The Greek word translated "centurion" means lit. "leader of one hundred," indicating that the man was a minor officer in the Roman army and hence a Gentile, since Jews were exempted by the Romans from military service. Matt. does not mention the centurion's assistance to Judaism (Luke 7:4-5), which statement may have originated with Luke, whose gospel stresses the eagerness of Gentiles to obey the will of God. The weight of Matt.'s version falls on the centurion's sense of authority and therefore on his recognition of the authority of Jesus. This awareness of Jesus' power is acclaimed as **faith**—of such kind as Jesus had not seen among Jews.

8:11-13. At this point Matt. has introduced a Q

Ruins of the ancient synagogue at Capernaum; Capernaum is named specifically as the setting of many incidents in Jesus' Galilean ministry; in Capernaum Jesus is reported to have healed a man with an unclean spirit (Mark 1:21-28; Luke 4:31-38); the city was also the setting of the incidents and the sermon which follow the feeding of the five thousand (John 6:16-59); see also ill., p. 683

saying (found also in Luke 13:28-29) which anticipates the response of Gentiles to the gospel and their consequent participation in the kingdom of God, where they replace the **sons of the kingdom,** i.e. the unbelieving Jews. Before giving the conclusion of the centurion story from Q, Matt. inserts his favorite phrases about the fate of the wicked in **outer darkness,** where they **will weep and gnash their teeth.** The story ends with the emphasis on the faith of the centurion: **Be it done for you as you have believed.**

8:14-15. *The Healing of Peter's Mother-in-Law.* The brief account of this healing in Mark 1:29-31 is further abbreviated by Matt. All the references to the other disciples have been omitted, and in spite of the special interest in Peter that we might expect from Matt. (cf. e.g. 16:17-19, found only in Matt.), no details about Peter's house or family are given.

We can infer only that Peter had a **house** in **Capernaum** (vss. 5, 14) and that he was married, although only his mother-in-law is here mentioned. Paul implies that Peter took his wife along with him on his apostolic journeys (I Cor. 9:5).

8:16-17. *Summary View of Jesus' Healing Ministry.* This brief summary of Jesus' healing work has been taken over from Mark 1:32-34, but Matt. has attached to it a quotation from Isa. 53:4, in keeping with his interest to show that Jesus' work is the fulfillment of the OT. The quotation is drawn from the LXX (see p. 1228). The surprising thing is that it focuses on the healing ministry, rather than on the atoning death, for which the early church found predictions in Isa. 53.

8:18-22. *The Cost of Following Jesus.* The first man who volunteers to follow Jesus is warned that to do so will mean giving up the security of his home—Jesus himself has no fixed dwelling place. In his poetic response Jesus is reported as referring to himself as **Son of man.** "One like a son of man" is described in Dan. 7:13, probably referring to the human-appearing people of God through whom the kingdom is to be established, in contrast to the beast-like appearances of the pagan empires soon to be overthrown. The term appears with more developed significance in the non-canonical I Enoch as the title of the redeemer figure sent by God at the end of the age to establish his kingdom. The suffering Son of man is well known from Mark 8:31; 9:31; 10:33; but nowhere in Q, from which Matt. has here drawn, does the Son of man appear as one who suffers. Rather he is pictured either as the coming judge (24:37; Luke 17:26), or simply as a man who came into the world with no special authorization from God (11:19; Luke 7:34). What may be implied in vs. 20 is that, although Jesus possesses the extraordinary powers that the crowds have witnessed in his healings and exorcisms, he comes only as a man. Those attracted to him should be aware that he not only does not have a luxurious way of living to offer but does not even share the certainty of dwelling place that a bird or an animal might have. To follow him is to abandon all earthly security.

8:21-22. Discipleship also may call for neglect of family obligations. Honorable burial of the dead was an important duty for every pious Jew, and especially in behalf of a member of one's family. Now Jesus says that one who is thus preoccupied with domestic duties is not ready for the demands of discipleship.

8:23-27. *Stilling the Storm.* Jesus' role as Lord of the Christian congregation is underscored in Matt.'s version of this miracle, since his title as "Teacher" in Mark 4:38 has been replaced by **Lord.** The act of Jesus in stilling the storm is told in extremely brief form; what is stressed is the **little faith** of the disciples and the implication that Jesus is an extraordinary person: **What sort of man is this?** Rationalistic proposals about the miracle are of little help. E.g. a natural subsidence of the storm at the moment that Jesus spoke would make the disciples out as dupes and Jesus as a fraud. The intent of the story is to show that God's authority at work through Jesus is victorious not only over human disease and disorder but also over the destructive powers of nature as well. Man is called to a life of faith and trust under such authority.

8:28-34. *Two Demoniacs at Gadara.* Told in greatly abbreviated form (cf. Mark 5:1-20), this tale of the demons being driven out of a man—here 2 men, in keeping with Matt.'s tendency to double the figures—and into a herd of swine lays emphasis on 3 factors: (*a*) the demons' recognition of Jesus' power over them; (*b*) the authority of Jesus' word (**Go!**); (*c*) the rejection by the people, who ask him to leave their vicinity. The vivid detail of Mark has been eliminated in order to bring out these points.

Courtesy of Herbert G. May

Newly discovered main gateway to the city of Gerasa (Gadara) in the country where Jesus is said to have driven out the "demons" from two men (Matt. 8:28-34)

9:1-8. *The Healing of the Paralytic.* Here, as in the preceding story, Matt. has eliminated considerable material from the fuller account in Mark. The result is that the authority of Jesus in both healing and forgiving sins is highlighted. This was originally (see on Mark 2:1-12) a story about the healing of a paralytic, but has been combined with a passage claiming the authority of Jesus to forgive sins. Actually Jesus does not forgive sins, but announces that God has forgiven them. To speak in God's name, however, is to invoke his authority, and it is on this ground that he is accused of **blaspheming.** The use by Matt. of the phrase **God who had given such authority to men** in vs. 8 suggests that the title **Son of man** in vs. 6 is meant to imply that Jesus is human. But what a man! To him has been granted this unprecedented power from God himself. As he continues to draw on his

Markan source in the stories that follow, Matt. will emphasize the authority that God has given to Jesus, yet without making specific messianic claims in Jesus' behalf.

9:9-13. The Call of Matthew. Still following the sequence of events in Mark, Matt. adds one interesting detail at this point: he changes the name of the tax collector called by Jesus from Levi to **Matthew** (cf. Mark 2:14). It has been conjectured that the author was intentionally correcting the Markan tradition by supplying his own name. But comparison of the lists of the disciples in 10:2-4 with Mark 3:16-19; Luke 6:14-16 shows that the gospel tradition has not preserved a uniform list of names. The point of this story lies, not in the identity of the man called, but rather in the occupation from which he is called to become a disciple. The men who collected taxes for Rome from among their fellow Jews were doubly despised—as traitors to the nation and as often unscrupulous extortioners.

9:10-13. The tradition linked the story of the call of the tax collector with that of the meal which Jesus ate at his home. Such a person was considered ceremonially unclean by Jewish standards. The disregard of dietary and cleansing regulations is further evident in that there were present at the same meal other undesirables—as adjudged by the official standards of Judaism—with whom Jesus also enjoyed table fellowship. To eat a meal with someone was considered to be a most intimate kind of personal contact, so that a scrupulous Jew would be extremely careful about the company in which he would share a meal. Jesus, however, has no hesitation about such contacts and, under pressure to account for his lax attitude, justifies what he is doing on the ground that this is a part of the mission that God has sent him to fulfill: **I came** (i.e. God sent me) **not to call the righteous, but sinners.** The setting of the story, which pictures **Pharisees** as witnessing the meal, is probably artificial, but the message is doubtless historical: Jesus saw his messianic mission as calling into the fellowship of God's people the religious outcasts, rather than as confirming the pridefully righteous in their sense of moral superiority.

9:14-17. The Question about Fasting. Several sayings have been brought together in this passage. Only one of these deals directly with fasting, which was likly a serious problem for the early church in its relations of tension with Judaism. The 2nd thrust of the passage is a veiled prediction of Jesus' death, which is here pointed to as the time of sorrow which will come when he has been **taken away from them.** It is in that situation of separation from their Lord that the church will be justified in fasting. The remaining sayings about patches and **wineskins** all point up that when something **new** has come, the **old** is bound to be inadequate. Hence, when the new is added, the old cloth tears and the dry wineskins burst. God is doing a new thing through Jesus, and the older Jewish patterns will be shattered as a result.

9:18-26. The Ruler's Daughter and the Woman with the Hemorrhage. This is another in the series of Markan stories that Matt. has reproduced in condensed form (Mark 5:21-43). Much of Mark's vivid detail is accordingly missing, but the now familiar emphasis on the authority of Jesus' word is force-

fully presented. Matt. has somewhat blunted the dramatic point of the story, however, by reporting that the little girl was **dead** when the ruler first came to Jesus. Thus the problem created in Mark's version by Jesus' being delayed to heal the woman with the hemorrhage loses its urgency in Matt. Matt. has reported that the girl was already dead in order to remove any ambiguity as to whether Jesus merely aroused her from sleep, as vs. 24 implies. Jesus, Matt. tells us implicitly, has the power over life and death.

9:27-31. Two Blind Men at Jericho. This is a modified and somewhat shorter version of Mark's story of blind Bartimaeus, who was healed near Jericho. Here there are 2 blind men in an unspecified locale, but otherwise the account differs little from Mark 10:46-52. Matt. has included the Jericho incident in its Markan setting and order as well (20: 29-34). Here he appears to have introduced this incident and the one following it, creating the stories either on the analogy of Markan tradition or on the basis of variant forms preserved in the oral tradition. The stories are of service to him at this point in his gospel, since he is rounding off his account of Jesus' activity before turning to the next great discourse in 9:36-10:42. Once more the point of the story is 2-fold: the authority of Jesus, who is here greeted as **son of David** and **Lord,** and the faith of the men who believe that Jesus is able to heal them.

9:32-34. The Healing of the Dumb Demoniac. This story sounds like a variant of the more familiar incident in which Jesus' opponents accuse him of being in league with the prince of demons (12:25-29). It serves as a fitting conclusion to Matt.'s section on Jesus' healing activity and leads smoothly into the summary statement which follows.

9:35. Summary of Jesus' Public Ministry. Each phrase of this brief summary is important. Matt. stresses the comprehensiveness of the ministry—**all the cities and villages**—to show that all Israel had an opportunity to hear and respond to Jesus. The ministry included both **teaching** and **preaching,** as well as **healing** and exorcisms. It is significant that Matt. says the work was carried on **in their synagogues,** suggesting that there is a consciousness within his community of being over against the Jewish community.

F. The Sending of the 12 Disciples (9:36-10:42)

Although less well knit than the Sermon on the Mount, this mission discourse carries throughout the theme that the disciples are sent out in the name of and with the authority of Jesus. Accordingly they can expect persecution for his sake, and at the same time they can look forward to the benefits of God's providential care upon their ministry. The material Matt. has here brought together is drawn from both Mark and Q, as well as from his own special source. But the whole bears the unmistakable stamp of his peculiar interests.

9:36-38. The Needs of the Crowds. The image of the people of God as a flock **without a shepherd** is a familiar one in the OT (Num. 27:17; I Kings 22: 17; Ezek. 34) and reminds us that Jesus was not concerned merely with the individual, but recognized that the man of faith can live and flourish only within the people of God, whose shepherd God had appointed him to be. But the work of shepherding the flock of God requires co-workers. Or, to change the figure, as Matt. does, the **harvest**, which will bring to a close this age and establish the kingdom of God, requires **laborers.** It is to share in this work of God that the disciples are called.

10:1-15. *Commissioning the Twelve.* The number 12 may be the historical recollection of the actual number of Jesus' intimate followers, but 12 has symbolic significance as well. It is not only the number of the tribes of Israel but also the number of eschatological judges that the tradition reports will judge Israel in the Last Day (19:28). The gospel writers seemed to feel that it was important to preserve the "12-ness" of the group, as can be inferred from the story of the selection of Judas' replacement in Acts 1.

10:2a. The 12 are here designated **apostles.** This term is transliterated from a Greek word which is itself a translation of a Semitic word meaning originally "one commissioned by the king to fulfill a mission in his name and with his authority." The term "apostle" was probably not used until after the Resurrection, but since the early church is here looking back on the sending of the 12 in the light of its own mission, the use of the term is understandable. It seems to have been used in the NT only of those of the first generation of Jesus' followers who were specially commissioned by him when he appeared to them as risen from the dead.

10:2b-4. The variations in the lists of names of the disciples show that the church preserved a firm tradition only in relation to the inner core of Jesus' followers. The variants in relation to Matthew (or Levi) have been noted; some ancient manuscripts list Lebbaeus in place of **Thaddaeus.** The meaning of **Iscariot** in connection with **Judas** is uncertain. Some have tried to associate it with a group of revolutionaries who appeared in Palestine just before the Jewish revolt of A.D. 66-70, and who were known as Sicarii, meaning "dagger-men." But it probably means only "man of Kerioth," especially since the Sicarii are unknown until more than 30 years after the crucifixion of Jesus.

10:5-6. Although many of the details in the charge to the 12 are to be found in Mark 6:7-11 (the commissioning of the disciples) or Luke 10:1-16 (the sending of the 70—presumably symbolizing the 70 Gentile nations into which Jews thought mankind was divided), what is unique here is the limiting of the mission **to the lost sheep of the house of Israel.** Preaching among **Gentiles** and **Samaritans** is specifically forbidden. Some scholars think these words correspond to the historical fact that Jesus restricted his work to his fellow Jews. But apart from lack of clear evidence that he did so limit his ministry, it must be seen that Matt. understands the work of God to be carried on in 2 stages, as did Paul: to the Jew first, and then—when the message has been spurned—to the Gentiles. That this is Matt.'s view is clear from the universal outreach anticipated in 28:19. The phrase "lost sheep of the house of Israel" could refer to those from among Israel who are lost, or it could mean that all Israel is estranged from God. Probably it is an allusion to the Jews who did not observe the laws of separateness and who were considered by the religious officials as outcasts not worth bothering with.

10:7-15. The nature of the ministry of the 12 is in direct continuity with what Jesus has been doing: preaching, healing, raising, cleansing, casting out demons. The saving actions demonstrate the nearness of the kingdom that the preaching proclaims. Matt. goes beyond Mark in further limiting the slim resources that the itinerant messengers of the kingdom are to take with them. Indeed, they appear in Matt. as ascetic figures, with no **sandals** to protect their feet and no **staff** to protect their persons against attackers, human or animal. Unlike Mark, who warns against moving from house to house in a village until the preacher finds the most satisfactory accommodations, Matt. insists that the **house** where the messenger stays must be **worthy.** The disciples are to anticipate rejection, but are to move on to other places in the expectation that **judgment** such as fell on the wicked cities of **Sodom and Gomorrah** will fall on those towns that refuse to receive them and their message.

10:16-25. *The Perils Involved in the Mission.* The sayings included in this section are drawn in large measure from Mark, who has placed them in his apocalyptic discourse (Mark 13), in which Jesus predicts the tribulations that will overtake God's people in the time immediately preceding the coming of the **end** of the age. The situation in which the followers of Jesus experience interrogation and persecution before **councils** and **kings and governors** is more fitting for later apostolic times than for the period of Jesus' own ministry, during which his disciples were in direct association with him. Those who seek faithfully to bear witness to Christ during this time of persecution will be empowered by God's **Spirit** so that they will know what they **are to say.**

10:23. One of the most problematical sayings in the whole of the Synoptic tradition is this explicit statement that the disciples will not have completed their mission tour **before the Son of man comes,** i.e. before the age ends and the kingdom of God arrives in its fullness. The difficulty is that it is nowhere apparent that this event occurred. There seem to be 3 major possibilities for explaining this problem: (a) Jesus was mistaken; (b) the prophecy was fulfilled, but in a manner not publicly observable; (c) the saying is not authentic, but was created by the early church for some special purpose. The first explanation was adopted by Albert Schweitzer, who declared that Jesus was so disappointed when the kingdom did not arrive by the time of the disciples' return that he went up to Jerusalem to force God's hand by acknowledging his messianic role to the authorities. The 2nd explanation is impossible to sustain, since Matt. ends his gospel with the coming of the kingdom and the end of the age still awaited in the future (28:20). The 3rd explanation is likely to be correct, in that it assumes the saying arose within a group which was concentrating on preaching to Israel, and which expected the end to come before its mission was completed.

10:24-25. Just as Jesus was denounced as being in league with the prince of the demons, **Beelzebul,** so can the disciples expect denunciation as they seek to carry out their mission.

10:26-42. *The Cost and Rewards of Discipleship.* The disciples are promised that God's providential care is over the world, both to judge the wicked who oppose his people and to watch over his own as they go about fulfilling their witness. They are advised that they are to **proclaim** openly the mystery of the kingdom, now only **whispered.** Those who now bear faithful witness will be vindicated before God in the day of judgment; conversely, those who now deny Jesus will be denied **before my Father** in the last day.

10:34-39. So great are the demands of discipleship that obedience leads to conflicts within one's family and opposition by one's own parents. Indeed, devotion to Jesus must take precedence over one's family obligations and affections. For Judaism, where the family with its mutual loyalties is the center of existence ("Honor thy father and thy mother"), this was an especially radical view. But the paradox of vs. 39 is still greater: full conformity to God's will can be found only by those willing to give up their lives in order that they may find the authentic life God has intended for them to live.

10:40-42. The response of the world to the follower of Jesus and the response to Jesus himself cannot be separated, Jesus here declares. Even a simple deed of kindness performed for the benefit of one of his disciples will be noted by God and rewarded.

G. THE KINGDOM AND ITS COMING (11:1-12:50)

This is the activity section of the 3rd main division of Matt. It is marked off from the preceding section by the stereotyped words of 11:1. The material is drawn about equally from Mark and Q and in general is presented in the Markan sequence.

11:1-9. *John the Baptist and Jesus.* In response to questioners sent by John the Baptist, Jesus interprets his ministry in terms of the redemptive activity that he is performing rather than by appeal to traditional titles or types of messianic expectation. In the course of drawing attention to the kinds of healing work he is carrying on, Jesus refers indirectly to such OT passages as Isa. 29:18-19; 35:5-6; 61:1, though without expressly claiming that in his work these prophecies are fulfilled. Jesus, therefore, does not fit the judgmental messianic role that the Baptist has expected; it is not surprising that he has grave doubts as to whether Jesus is in fact **he who is to come.** There is something touching in Jesus' expression of hope that, even though he does not conform to John's expectations, the Baptist will not be offended by him.

11:7-11. At the same time Jesus has a high regard for John and scorn for the crowds who at first flocked out to hear John, but who have ignored his solemn warning of judgment. Jesus is now reported as asserting what is a basically Christian understanding of John, although it is possible that the statement includes authentic words of Jesus: John is **more than a prophet;** he is the one who prepares the way for Jesus' coming. Unlike Mark, Matt. explicitly identifies John as **Elijah** (vs. 14). Among all men thus far born there is **no one greater than John,** but those who are even now ready to enter the kingdom of God and are now enjoying its powers in the present are in a relationship to God far superior to that of John.

11:12-19. The period up to John's coming has been filled with violence brought about by the struggle between the power of God and the powers of darkness; men who triumph in the struggle have already entered the kingdom, at least in an anticipatory way. Instead of thus responding with faith and courage, the present generation, Jesus says, is like some peevish **children** who want neither the solemn asceticism of John (**neither eating nor drinking**) nor the joy of Jesus' fellowship (**a glutton and a drunkard**). Both sets of images are drawn from the Jewish picture of the eschatological age as a time of banqueting and revelry. The term **Son of man** by which Jesus here refers to himself may imply simply the contrast between John, who came as God's messenger, the prophet, and Jesus, who came as a man among men. God's **wisdom** in working in this paradoxical way will be **justified** by the outcome, which will see the fulfillment of God's redemptive purpose.

11:20-24. *Woes on the Cities of Galilee.* The judgment that will fall on the unrepentant Jewish cities of Galilee is all the more solemn, since even pagan cities such as **Tyre and Sidon . . . would have repented** had they had such an opportunity to see and hear what God is doing and is about to do for man's redemption. **It shall be more tolerable** for the heathen cities, since they lacked the opportunity which the cities of Palestine have been given, but to which they have responded not with faith but with hostility.

11:25-30. *Jesus as the Revealer of God.* This section is in 3 parts (vss. 25-26, 27-28, 29-30). The first subsection is wholly in keeping with Jesus' declaration elsewhere that the persons ready to receive the message of the kingdom are those who by the standards of official religion are ignorant and unable to grasp the learned truths of the scholars of Judaism. Jesus declares, "It is these **babes,** not the self-styled wise, who have laid hold on the truth of what God is doing."

11:27-28. The 2nd subsection—in contrast with the 1st and 3rd, which are thoroughly Semitic in character and language—sounds more like the Gospel of John than like the rest of the Synoptic tradition. For this reason it has been seen by some interpreters as the product of the Greek-speaking church. It could as well, however, be the utterance of a Christian prophet in the Palestinian church, since it was believed that the risen Lord continued to speak to the church through the prophets (cf. I Cor. 13:2). To accept this subsection as authentic, we would have to assume that the earthly Jesus held a view of himself close to that of the creeds formulated in the church in later centuries. On the other hand, since this passage stood in Q, which is thought to have originated in Palestine by about A.D. 50, it cannot be a late product. It should be viewed as a formulation of the church on the way to the fully developed Christologies of the 2nd and 3rd cents.

11:29-30. The 3rd subsection is an invitation to discipleship, to accept the commandments of God as Jesus has set them forth. It is the biblical equivalent of the phrase from the prayer book, "whose service is perfect freedom."

12:1-14. *Controversy Concerning the Sabbath.* Two stories are here reproduced from Mark 2:23-3:6, both of which have as their point the question of Jesus' violating or condoning violation of the sabbath law, one of the most sacred and distinctive of all Jewish institutions. In neither incident is there a problem that the afflicted persons involved will die if their needs are not met instantly. Rather the hungering disciples could surely survive until later in the day and the crippled man could have waited until the next day to be healed. But Jesus faces the issue. The force of the stories in the form in which Matt. has produced them is the lordship of Jesus over the sabbath, as vs. 8 declares explicitly.

12:5-6. The point is made even more emphatic by Matt.'s. having introduced the reference to the superiority of Jesus to the temple. The Jerusalem temple was more than the central shrine for the Jewish people; it was their chief source of pride as one of the great buildings of the world in its time. It was believed to be the place where God was invisibly present in the midst of his people, so that the nation's continuing acceptability before him depended in large measure on the continuity of the sacrificial system there. It was no small claim, therefore, to assert that Jesus was more important than the temple. The anti-Jewish polemic of Matt. is once more apparent.

12:8. Matt. has omitted the statement in Mark 2:27 that the sabbath was made for man. Although some scholars think that Jesus' original statement was that man was **lord of the sabbath,** it is clear that for Matt. it is Jesus as **the Son of man** who exercises rightful authority over even such a venerable institution as the sabbath.

12:14. The appeal of Jesus to his opponents to be more concerned for compassion toward the ill than for observing the law strictly falls on deaf ears. Not only did the onlookers not see in his action the hand of God; they also **took counsel** together, **how to destroy him.** The miracles of Jesus do not convince unbelievers; they merely arouse deepened hostility.

12:15-21. *Response Among the Gentiles.* Building on a tradition preserved in Mark 3:7-12, Matt. has contrasted the opposition of Jewish officialdom with the receptivity of the Gentiles. Their response is in fulfillment of prophecy (Isa. 42:1-4)—**and in his name will the Gentiles hope.** In what follows Matt. turns back to the antagonism that Jesus encounters among the Jews, even from within his own family.

12:22-50. *Controversy over the Source of Jesus' Authority.* Matt. has drawn on a Q story of the healing of a man who was **blind and dumb** to serve as his introduction to an incident that was apparently in both Mark and Q: the charge that Jesus was in league with **Beelzebul, the prince of demons.** By this introduction Matt. has obscured what is implied in Mark 3:21, 31-35—that Jesus' family came to the conclusion that he was out of his mind or that he was under the control of demonic forces. Perhaps in his interest to present Mary and Jesus' family in a good light he left this incident out.

12:25-26. Jesus' response to the charge of demonic domination is presented in a form that combines what were probably separate statements on the same general theme of Jesus' conflict with the demonic forces. The first argument is that when a **city** or dynasty (**house**) is **divided against itself,** the consequence is its own destruction. Therefore, it is implied, Jesus' success in destroying the control of the **demons** over men cannot be attributed to the prince of demons, who would not aid in diminishing his own power.

12:27-28. The 2nd argument is that not everyone who performs exorcisms is in league with Beelzebul, since that would mean that those able to cast out demons among the Pharisees would themselves be under Beelzebul's control. What is significant in Jesus' exorcisms is not the mere fact that he performs them, but that he discerns in them the power of God at work through the **Spirit.** To the extent that the rule of Satan is being overcome through the exorcisms, to that extent **the kingdom of God has come upon** Jesus' contemporaries.

12:29-30. The figure changes again, and the coming of God's kingdom is compared with plundering another man's possessions. Satan is in control in this present age, but Jesus' work is binding **the strong man** (i.e. stripping him of his power), and the outcome will be the establishment in fullness of God's kingdom.

12:31-37. The question about the **sin** that **will not be forgiven** is really the question about the source of Jesus' authority. His opponents attribute to Satan the power he wields, whereas it should be attributed to its true source, **the Holy Spirit.** Like a fruit **tree,** the worth of Jesus is to be adjudged by what he does; there should be no problem in distinguishing God's power at work through Jesus from evil powers at work through evil men.

12:38-42. Here **the scribes and Pharisees** are depicted as pressing their opposition from another angle; they ask him to perform **a sign** from heaven as a way of providing divine authentication for his work. This request he refuses to honor. The only sign to be granted to this **adulterous generation** is **the sign of the prophet Jonah.** Luke 11:29-32 probably has the more original form of this Q saying, according to which the sign of Jonah was Jonah's message, which carried its own authority without any corroborative miracles or divine attestations. Matt. has added an interpretation which sees in the sign of Jonah a prediction of Jesus' resurrection. If this had been the original intention of the saying, it is difficult to imagine why Luke would have omitted it from his version of the Q saying. The period of **three days and three nights** does not fit the gospel tradition's chronology of the Resurrection—that the interval in the tomb lasted part of 3 days, but not 3 nights as well. The interpretation seems to have arisen from Matt.'s interest in the specific, detailed fulfillment of prophecy. The rest of the passage shows that what was significant about Jonah was not his experience within the whale but his **preaching,** in response to which the people of Nineveh repented. Similarly it was the **wisdom of Solomon** that led the queen of Sheba (I Kings 10:1-13) to journey **from the ends of the earth** in order that she might hear it. One greater in wisdom and with a greater message is here; Israel must not seek for signs, but heed the message.

12:43-45. The implied judgment on the unrepentant nation is carried further by the story of the man who, once cleansed of a demon, in the end is worse off than ever, possessed **by seven other spirits more evil than** the first. The point is obvious: although Israel had her chance to be God's holy people, if now she turns from him she will be many times worse off than before. Probably the original force of the saying, if it is authentic, was simply that it was not sufficient for a man to be liberated from demonic control; unless he submitted himself to the power of God, he would be in a worse condition than before the exorcism was performed.

12:46-50. The concluding challenge to Jesus' authority comes from his own family. Although the direct charge that "he is beside himself" (Mark 3:21) has been omitted by Matt., the sense of hostility is evident in Jesus' response, wherein he redefines what the family relationship is. The bonds that link together those who are seeking to do **the will** of God are not only more enduring but more important than the ties of the family, no matter how deeply venerated they are in Judaism.

H. THE PARABLES OF THE KINGDOM (13:1-52)

13:1-9. *The Parable of the Sower.* Following a somewhat stylized introduction in which Jesus is pictured sitting in **a boat** with **great crowds** gathered along **the beach,** Matt. (following Mark) describes Jesus' teaching **in parables,** launching without explanation into the parable of the sower. Unlike most of the parables subsequently reported by Matt., this one is not introduced by "The kingdom of God is like . . . ," but it is related to the coming of the kingdom nonetheless. The question is how and with what intention.

13:3b-8. If we take the parable as it stands (setting aside for the moment the allegorical interpretation given in vss. 18-23), its point lies in the contrast between the mixed results that the beginning of the work brings forth and the astonishingly fruitful outcome in the harvest. The parable, then, is an encouragement by Jesus to his followers, warning them that much of their work in proclaiming the coming kingdom will be wasted effort, but promising them that God will bring forth results far exceeding their expectations (cf. Eccl. 11:6). The parable is told against the background of what are to us strange farming methods, such as sowing before plowing or before the ground has been cleared.

13:9. The closing sentence, **He who has ears, let him hear,** was probably a free-floating saying of Jesus which was attached by the tradition or by Mark to this parable, even though it is not directly relevant to its point.

13:10-17. *The Purpose of Speaking in Parables.* A parable may be defined as an extended metaphor in which the comparison is based on a brief narrative rather than on a simple likeness to another object. The parable as a mode of communication was in wide use among the rabbis of Jesus' day, although it was not common in the Gentile world. What was widely used there in teaching and literary endeavors was allegory, in which each element of a narrative represents symbolically a reality in another sphere. The Stoic philosophers of Greece, e.g., had allegorized the Homeric myths, so that the tales of the conflicts and schemes of the Olympian deities became symbolic portrayals of the conflicts of natural forces. The Semitic word which lies behind the Greek word "parable" can mean not only the literary form we know as parable, but also an enigma, puzzle, or riddle. When Mark links up these possibilities with the "secret" or "mystery of the kingdom," the result is to suggest that Jesus taught in parables with the purpose that those on the outside of the circle of his followers might not be able to discern his meaning. Matt. has somewhat modified the force of this statement and has done so in 3 directions: (*a*) He has changed the secret to **secrets** (vs. 11), thus implying that what is involved is not merely the clue to the coming of the kingdom, but private information about its nature. (*b*) By introducing vs. 12 (cf. Mark 4:25) at this point, and by quoting (from the LXX, not the Hebrew) the full passage from Isa. 6:9-10 (vss. 14-15), he has stressed that the inability of Israel to comprehend what God is doing in Jesus is a fulfillment of prophecy. (*c*) By changing "so that" (Mark 4:12) to **because** (vs. 13), Matt. quotes Jesus as saying that the *result* of Israel's willful blindness is that they do not discern the mysteries of the kingdom, rather than Mark's flat statement that Jesus' teaching in parables is *intended* to prevent Israel from discerning the secret of the kingdom.

13:16-17. It is fitting, therefore, for Matt. to introduce at this point from Q (cf. Luke 10:23-24) Jesus' pronouncement of the blessedness of the disciples to whom the secrets have been given. They now understand what the **prophets and righteous men** could discern only dimly, if at all.

13:18-23. *The Interpretation of the Parable of the Sower.* The process of allegorization by which the church has tried to understand the parables of Jesus and has accordingly distorted them is apparent within the Synoptic tradition itself, as is seen in the explanation of the parable of the sower that Matt. has reproduced from Mark 4:13-20. Each point of the parable takes on special significance; but, as so often happens in allegory, the explanation cannot be carried through with consistency. At first the soil is the one who **hears,** the seed is **the word,** and the enemy is **the evil one.** But suddenly the hearers are compared with the seed **sown on rocky ground.** The inconsistency continues, with the hearers compared with the soil and then with the seed or the plant. Instead of a message of encouragement addressed to the messengers, the parable has become a word of warning addressed to the church. It no longer says, "Sow with assurance," but, "Receive the word with fruitfulness or fear the outcome."

13:24-30. *The Parable of the Weeds.* The original force of this parable is probably similar in part to that of the parable of the sower: carry on your work faithfully in spite of mixed results. It is a word of encouragement, only in this case based, not on the astonishing results, but on the promise that God will evaluate the results in the judgment. In vss. 36-43, however, Matt. has furnished an allegorical interpretation which radically alters its meaning and enables him to introduce some of the distinctive features of his own theology.

13:31-32. *The Parable of the Mustard Seed.* In abbreviating somewhat from Mark 4:30-32, Matt. has shifted the point of this parable so that the contrast is no longer between the tiny seed and the large shrub that it becomes, but between the seed and its supernatural transformation into **a tree.** In this and the preceding parable the characteristic introductory phrase appears, **The kingdom of heaven is like . . . .** But the comparison is not between the kingdom and the seed or the man who sows the seed, but between some aspect of the kingdom and the whole incident. It might be clearer to translate or paraphrase this introductory formula as: "It is with the kingdom of God as it is with the following incident."

The story would then point to the almost unnoticed beginnings of the work of the kingdom in the ministry of Jesus as contrasted with the surprisingly great results that are promised in the eschatological fulfillment.

13:33. *The Parable of the Leaven.* As it stands, this parable also makes the point of contrasting the small beginnings with the extensive results of the power of the kingdom now at work. The saying comes from the Q source, as would appear from the parallel in Luke 13:20-21 and from its nonappearance in Mark, which Matt. is otherwise following at this point. It is likely, however, that the original import of this saying did not refer to the hidden working of the powers of the kingdom, but to the stealthy operation of the powers of evil. This proposal receives some support from the use of the figure of leaven elsewhere in the Synoptic tradition to refer to evil (16:6; Mark 8:15; Luke 12:1). Similarly, Paul uses leaven as a symbol of evil that is seeking to pervade the Christian community (I Cor. 5:6). The Corinthian Christians are called to purge out this corrupting influence in order that they might be the pure loaf. Matt., however, has clearly understood it as the silent action of the coming kingdom of God.

13:34-35. *Why Jesus Uses Parables.* Matt. has modified Mark's form of these words (Mark 4:33-34), where the meaning is that the parables were Jesus' way of keeping the secret of the kingdom within the inner circle of the disciples. The quotation is not from a **prophet** (some ancient manuscripts read "the prophet Isaiah"), but from Ps. 78:2. The quotation closely approximates the Hebrew text as we know it, but may show some influence from the LXX. What is important for Matt. is that even the form of Jesus' teachings—in this case, **in parables**—is a part of the divine plan laid down in advance in the scriptures.

13:36-43. *The Interpretation of the Parable of the Weeds.* Once more we have an allegorical interpretation of a parable, but this time it is from Matt. rather than from the tradition on which he draws. Vs. 41 gives us a clue to one of the main themes of Matt.'s understanding of the church and its destiny. The kingdom of the **Son of man** is the church (cf. **his kingdom,** vs. 41) in contrast with the **kingdom of their Father** (vs. 43), which is the new age, from which all evil persons have been removed. The church, therefore, is a mixed body, containing both good and bad, and the point of the interpretation is that the task of differentiating worthy from unworthy members is not up to the church, but will be accomplished by the Son of man as judge at **the close of the age.** The **evildoers** will be punished and will **weep and gnash their teeth** in anguish, as Matt. delights to say. His designation for the good is **the righteous,** which, as has been noted, is a pervasive theme in this gospel.

13:44-46. *Parables of the Treasure and the Pearl.* Both these parables point to the supreme importance of sharing in the kingdom of God, in comparison with which every other value should be sacrificed. The covering up and the secrecy about the treasure are not the significant points; it is rather that the man **sells all that he has** in order to gain one thing—the kingdom. The parable of the pearl is found in almost the same form as here in the Gospel of Thomas (see above on 6:22-23).

13:47-50. *The Parable of the Net.* The specific details of this parable are reminiscent of the parable of the weeds as interpreted by Matt. (vss. 40, 42), including the burning of the bad and their anguished weeping and gnashing of teeth. The parable is here used to warn that the good and bad will be separated from within the church at the last judgment, and the unrighteous will be punished. The explanation given in vss. 49-50 is almost certainly not authentic, but it is an extension of Matt.'s own views. The fact that the way of handling inedible fish would not be to burn them demonstrates the artificiality of the parable as it stands.

13:51-52. *The Parable of the Householder.* Here we have the clearest hint as to the way Matt. viewed himself. He is a **scribe,** and therefore one who, through reinterpreting the will of God as embodied in the scriptures, adopted the role of the leaders of Pharisaic Judaism, whose task was to study and transmit the ongoing interpretations of the law. The special training of the Christian scribe, however, enabled him to do more than merely preserve the tradition; he brought out new realities as well from the treasure of scripture and the gospel tradition. This is, of course, precisely what Matt. is engaged in: showing from the law and the prophets how Jesus is the fulfillment of the hopes of Israel and the one through whom God is establishing the true Israel. The passage tells nothing about Jesus' understanding of his mission; it tells a great deal about Matt.'s understanding of his own.

I. The Life of the New Community (13:53–18:35)

Appropriately Matt. begins the action section of the 4th main division of his gospel with the account of Jesus' rejection by official Judaism as typified by the synagogue leaders in Nazareth. At this point he resumes following the Markan sequence of events. The opening vs. 53 marks off the main division with the words **when Jesus had finished** . . . .

13:53-58. *The Rejection at Nazareth.* Once again we see that the opportunity to observe the **mighty works** Jesus performed did not convince his opponents that God was at work through him. Instead **they took offense at him,** denouncing him as one who had come from their own town and whose family was known to them and implying that a man of such humble origins could not possibly be God's agent. It is noteworthy that they regard him as **the carpenter's son,** meaning, of course, Joseph's. There is no hint here of supernatural origin. At this point Matt. has diverged from Mark, who (in the most reliable manuscripts) quotes the townspeople as referring to Jesus as simply "the carpenter" (Mark 6:3). It may be that Matt. considered it undignified to speak of Jesus as a carpenter, but his version of the saying raises more serious questions by suggesting that Joseph was Jesus' father. It should be kept in mind that John likewise speaks of Joseph as the father of Jesus and contains no hint of the supernatural birth of which we read in the infancy stories of Matt. and Luke (cf. John 1:45; John further assumes that Jesus was born in Galilee rather than Bethlehem; John 7:41).

14:1-12. *Herod and John the Baptist.* Whereas in Mark 6:14-29 the story of the death of John the Baptist is told as though the evangelist wants to take up the time while the disciples are out on their mission journey, the incident serves in Matt. as a warning to Jesus of the rejection that he can expect from the governmental officials as well as from the religious leaders. News of John's death leads Jesus to withdraw, at least for the moment, from public activity (vs. 13). The gruesome story of the mode and motive of John's murder is presented in shortened form by Matt. The **Herod** spoken of here is, of course, not Herod the Great of the infancy stories, but his son, Herod Antipas, who was ruler of Galilee and Perea (see color map 15). Judea, in which Jerusalem was situated, was under the direct control of the Roman governors; but when Jesus was in Galilee, the person who had life-and-death control over him was Herod Antipas.

14:13-21. *The Feeding of the 5,000.* This story, which is one of the few incidents to be reported by all 4 of the gospel writers, is filled with symbolic elements arising from the eucharistic practices of the early church. The words of blessing and distribution follow quite precisely the traditional words of ritual of the Lord's Supper. This is not to suggest that there is nothing historical about the event; it is rather to suggest that what is historical is so overlaid with what is symbolic that the 2 can no longer be differentiated sharply.

Many rationalistic explanations have been offered for the miracle of the loaves and the fishes, but none of them is really helpful in understanding the story. Albert Schweitzer suggested that, although in actuality each person received only a tiny fragment of food, the joyous realization that the eschatological situation was breaking in through the ministry of Jesus was so powerful that each felt satisfied. A century ago it was common to propose that the crowd had brought food but kept it concealed until the small boy (mentioned only in John 6:9) offered to share his lunch and shamed the others thereby into offering theirs. But such explanations have missed the point of the story, that Jesus is able to supply men's needs in abundance. John has seen this most clearly in linking the feeding story directly with the discourse on the bread from heaven.

14:17-19. The **loaves** are obviously significant in the early church in connection with the Eucharist. But the **fish** were also important as a Christian symbol. The fact that the letters of the Greek word for "fish," *ichthus,* were the initials of the full title of Jesus as worshiped in the church—*Iesous Christos Theou Uios Soter* (i.e. Jesus Christ God's Son, Savior) —made this symbol especially appealing.

14:20-21. The tradition wants to emphasize that the miracle really did occur by the mention of the many fragments remaining and the note (not mentioned in Mark 6:44) that the number 5,000 did not include the women and children. This comment is in keeping with Matt.'s tendency to heighten the miraculous element.

14:22-33. *Walking on the Water.* Jesus' power over nature in creating bread to feed the multitudes is seen here once more in his walking on the water. The account has many of the characteristics of stories told about other great figures in various religions and cultures. Some have conjectured that it arose in the postresurrection period on the occasion of an appearance of the risen Lord to the disciples, but it is presented here to show that the authority of Jesus ex-

tends not only to sin and sickness but to the forces of nature as well. God's kingdom must be sovereign over the whole of the creation, not merely the world of men. The account is full of vivid detail about **the boat . . . beaten by the waves** and **the disciples, who were terrified.** To the community of faith, as to the distraught disciples, comes Jesus' word: **Take heart, it is I; have no fear.** The intention of the story is made clear in vs. 33, where Jesus is acclaimed as **the Son of God.**

14:28-33. To this Markan story Matt. has appended a brief account concerning Peter, which presents vividly and succinctly Peter's brashness **(bid me come to you),** his lack of courage **(he was afraid),** but also his ultimate faith in Jesus **(Lord, save me).** The presence of Matt.'s favorite phrase **little faith** suggests either that he has created this story or that he has reworked it to suit his purpose.

14:34-36. *Healings at Gennesaret.* This brief narrative is in the nature of a summary of Jesus' ministry of healing. The exact location of Gennesaret is not known, although it was probably an area on the NW shore of the Sea of Galilee.

15:1-20. *How Does Man Become Defiled?* For first-cent. Christianity, especially where there was close contact with Jews, there was a perennial problem as to the extent to which Jewish laws, whether from scripture or tradition, were binding on Christians. There are 2 main issues discussed here: honoring one's parents in keeping with the 5th commandment, and preserving one's ceremonial purity in keeping with the dietary laws and traditions.

15:3-9. Jesus' criticism in relation to the law commanding **honor** to parents is that the oral tradition has invalidated the written law. According to the oral tradition, a man could announce that his possessions had all been **given to God**—understood as freeing him from any obligation to support his parents. The hypocrisy of this action was compounded by the fact that, in the name of piety toward God, a man evaded his direct responsibility to obey the express command of God. By placing the quotation from Isa. after the passage exposing the hypocrisy of the oral tradition, Matt. has rendered the point about **the precepts of men** even more forceful than its Markan form.

15:10-20. The critique of the regulations about ritual cleanliness is even more radical than in the preceding case. Vs. 11, with its claim that man is defiled not by what enters his mouth but by what comes out of his heart, implies the setting aside of the entire dietary and ritual cleansing code, oral and written. The direction of the oral law had been to expand the dietary and cleansing regulations; Jesus now renders them all irrelevant to the question of genuine purity. It is man's **heart** (i.e. will) that needs to be cleansed, not his **hands.** The question about the parable, which in Mark 7:17 refers to Jesus' statement about what constitutes defilement, is linked in Matt. with a veiled denunciation of the leaders of Israel as constituting a group which has no rightful claim to call itself the people of God: they are a **plant which my heavenly Father has not planted . . . ; they are blind guides** (vss. 13-14). Thus Matt. has transformed a critique of Jewish institutions into a repudiation of Judaism itself. Clearly he is writing within a polemical situation in which the church is set over against Judaism.

15:21-31. Mercy for the Outcasts. The first incident in this section takes place in Gentile territory visited by Jesus following his experience of rejection in Galilee. **Tyre and Sidon** lie just to the N of Palestine along the Mediterranean coast in what is now Lebanon (see color map 11). The inhabitants of this area were racially and linguistically connected with the ancient Canaanites, who lived in Palestine at the time of the coming of the Israelites. Matt. prefers **Canaanite** to the term common in his time, "Syrophoenician" (Mark 7:26). It has been conjectured that Matt.'s use of the old name, which was still preferred in the first cent. by the inhabitants themselves, indicates that the church for which Matt. wrote was located in this area of Tyre and Sidon. Yet it is in his gospel that the woman addresses Jesus as **Son of David,** a title which gives expression to the national hopes of Israel for the reestablishment of the Davidic kingship, and which is scarcely appropriate for a Canaanite woman.

15:24-28. The comparison Jesus draws between allowing Gentiles to share in the benefits of the kingdom and throwing **the children's bread . . . to the dogs** does not sound like a charitable response to a gravely concerned mother. Attempts to account for this as spoken in jest do not ease the difficulty at all. We should probably see here either the inner struggle of Jesus when confronted with the request to extend his mission beyond the Jewish limits in which he had begun it or the struggle within the early church as to whether the message and powers of the kingdom of God were open to Gentiles as well as Jews. The reappearance of the phrase **the lost sheep of the house of Israel** (cf. 10:6) strengthens the impression that this story is preserved because of its bearing on the question of the limits of the church's mission. The obvious answer is that the mission is to be extended to wherever it encounters **faith.**

15:29-31. Matt. has omitted the Markan account of the healing of the deaf mute, with its details of the healing process (Mark 7:32-36), limiting himself instead to a general statement of the types of sufferers that Jesus healed: **the lame, the maimed, the blind, the dumb.** The important thing is that he healed them, and in so doing raised the question among the onlookers as to the source of his powers. The reader of this tradition who knew his OT would immediately have called to his mind by these incidents the prophecies of Isa. 29:18; 35:5-6. It is not only as redemptive events in themselves that these healings are important; they are manifestations of God's fulfillment of his purpose of redemption of the world through Jesus.

15:32-39. The Feeding of the 4,000. The oral stage of transmission of the Synoptic stories and sayings seems to have preserved 2 different versions of the feeding incident. Mark recorded them both and Matt. has followed his example (cf. 14:13-21). Presumably this feeding took place on Gentile soil, since the last place-names mentioned (in Mark 7:31) were the cities of the Decapolis (see above on 4:25). It is likely that the number of baskets filled with fragments, **seven,** is symbolic of the mission to the Gentiles, just as the 12 baskets in the earlier account (14:20), symbolize the mission to the Jews. This division of labor and these numbers appear in Acts 6:2-3, where the church assigns different responsi-

bilities to 2 groups: the 12 from among the Hebrews and the 7 from among the Greeks (Gentiles).

16:1-12. Unbelief of the Pharisees. Following Mark, Matt. presents here the brief account of Jesus' refusal to give **a sign** in response to the demand from his opponents. But Matt. has introduced 2 elements not found in Mark 8:12, where there is simply a categorical refusal. First there is a saying from Q (cf. Luke 12:54-56) in which Jesus scoffs at his detractors, since they can predict the next day's weather by reading certain signs in the sky but cannot discern the signs that **the times** are about to change and that God is already performing in their midst signs of the inbreaking of the new age. The 2nd innovation is the combining of Mark's form with the Q form to create a new composite saying, which declares that no sign will be given **except the sign of Jonah** (vs. 4). Here no specification of this sign of Jonah is given, although in 12:38-40 Matt. has linked it with the burial and resurrection of Jesus. Jesus' point here is that the signs of the kingdom are there to be discerned in the works which he is performing, but they will not be performed merely to satisfy the curiosity of his critics.

16:5-12. The story of the feeding of the multitudes is once more recalled. The disciples have forgotten to bring along **bread,** and their negligence becomes the occasion for a curious explanation which is as difficult and enigmatic as the events which it purports to explain. **The leaven of the Pharisees and Sadducees** is interpreted as referring to their **teaching** (vs. 12), which is not according to the truth and therefore works its harmful influence. Jesus warns his followers to **beware of** this teaching. But the reference to the 2 feedings, of 5 and 4 thousand respectively, is presented as though it were self-explanatory, which it is not. Matt.'s implication is that the feeding stories contain some teaching of the truth, which his followers are supposed to grasp. No specific accusation is brought against the teaching of the Pharisees or the Sadducees, except the warning of the error which it contains. Elsewhere in Matt. the Sadducees come under indirect attack for their rejection of the belief in the resurrection (22:23-33), while the Pharisees are repeatedly denounced as hypocrites, whose traditions and burdensome regulations stand in the way of men's obedience to the will of God (see esp. 23:1-36).

16:13-23. Confession of Jesus' Messiahship. In all 3 Synoptic gospels the incident at Caesarea Philippi marks a turning point in the story of Jesus, since from this point on Jesus begins to speak of his destiny in terms of his suffering and death, rather than speaking only of the coming of the kingdom of God. By far the fullest account of this incident is in Matt.

16:13a. The city of **Caesarea Philippi** was located at the sources of the Jordan (see color map 14). It was enlarged and renamed by Herod's son, Philip, in honor of Caesar Augustus (or possibly Tiberius) and of himself. The site of a pagan shrine to Pan, it was a Gentile region outside the bounds of Jewish Palestine. Since the city had no known significance for the early church apart from this event, it can scarcely have been the imagination of the church that located the event here: in short, this appears to be one of the firm topographical references in the gospels.

16:13b. Unlike Mark 8:27, where Jesus simply

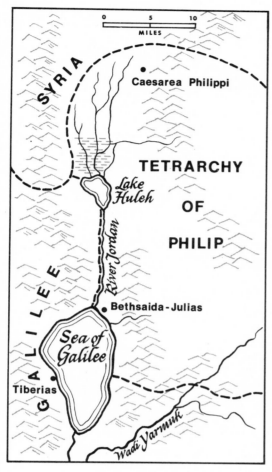

reappear on the earth in the last days to prepare for the coming of the Lord God (Mal. 4:5). It is possible that there were some Christians who identified Jesus with Elijah, but Matt. is quite explicit that John the Baptist is Elijah (17:13), even though in John 1:21 the Baptist flatly rejects this role.

16:14cd. Linking Jesus with **Jeremiah** was understandable, since it was he who had predicted the establishment of the new covenant (Jer. 31:31-40), and the words of Jesus mirrored the language of the new covenant (26:28; cf. I Cor. 11:25). Otherwise there is no tradition of Jeremiah's returning at the end time, such as there is concerning Elijah and Enoch. The answer **one of the prophets** is obviously rather vague. But it may have been originally "the prophet." In that case it would have had great significance, since Deut. 18:15-22 promised that in the days of the restoration of the nation God would send them a greater prophet like Moses, to whom the nation would finally give heedful obedience. That the Qumran community, in which the Dead Sea Scrolls were produced, treasured this prophecy and awaited God's fulfillment of the promise for and through their community has been learned from a list of messianic prophecies preserved in one of their caves.

16:15-16. When Jesus' question is turned directly to the disciples themselves, it is Peter as usual who is the spokesman for the group. Matt. gives his answer in fuller form than in Mark 8:29: **You are the Christ, the Son of the living God.** It is remarkable that the tradition speaks here of *the* Christ, i.e. Messiah, meaning "anointed" by God to perform a prescribed task. The term is used in the OT of a pagan ruler who does God's bidding (Isa. 45:1) as well as of Israel's king (Ps. 45:6-7). Actually there was not a single image of such a redemptive figure that could be designated as "the Christ." Perhaps the closest one could come to this would be the nationalistic hope of the reinstatement of the monarchy, with God's anointed one (Christ) ruling as his vicegerent over his people. Since the king would be spoken of as God's son (Ps. 2:6-7), this may be the implication of the title that Peter ascribes to Jesus.

16:17. The words which follow are found only in Matt. and are among the most controversial in the whole of the NT. There is evidence of Semitic forms of speech behind the Greek text of Matthew here, but that does not prove that these words are authentic. It shows only that they likely originated in a Semitic-speaking community. Peter is addressed by his Semitic name, **Simon Bar-Jona,** which means simply "Simon son of Jonah." He is here given the nickname *Kepha* (Cephas; cf. John 1:42), an Aramaic word meaning "rock," which is translated into Greek as *Petros.* The word for rock would be feminine, *petra,* but it is given a masculine ending (*-os*) in order to make it suitable as a man's name. What Peter has affirmed has not been disclosed to him by any human agency (i.e. by **flesh and blood**), but directly by God himself. Matt.'s use of the phrase **my Father who is in heaven** shows that he has reworked the tradition, adding two of his own favorite phrases (cf. 6:9).

16:18-19. Peter's nickname now becomes the basis for a play on words: Peter (*Kepha*) is to be the rock (*kepha*) on which the church will be built. Only in Matt. (here and at 18:17) among all 4 of the gospels is the church mentioned directly. This suggests that the passage in its present form is the product of the

asks who men say he is, Matt. reports Jesus as designating himself as the **Son of man.** The term "son of man" is used in Dan. 7:13, not as a title, but as a way of contrasting the kingdom of God (which is compared to a human being, lit. a son of man) with the kingdoms of the idolatrous world powers, which are depicted under the forms of horrendous beasts. In I Enoch (see p. 1111) the Son of man is a title for a heavenly personage who comes to earth to judge the enemies of God and establish his rule in the earth. It is not certain whether the section of I Enoch in which the Son of man appears is a pre-Christian document, but it apparently incorporates ideas of God's redemptive agent that were abroad in Judaism before the birth of Jesus. It appears, therefore, that Matt. is placing a Christian witness to Jesus as the Son of man on the lips of Jesus himself; the actual question was perhaps more tentative with regard to Jesus' messianic mission.

16:14ab. The answers to his question are varied. Those who say **John the Baptist** apparently shared with Herod Antipas (14:2) the belief that Jesus was John raised from the dead. Indeed, the fact that both announced the end of the age, the coming judgment, and the establishment of God's kingdom would make the confusion easy to understand. The association of Jesus with **Elijah** was a natural development, since Jewish tradition expected that Elijah would

church rather than an authentic word of Jesus. Attempts have been made to demonstrate the authenticity of the words, but only by assuming that they were spoken by Jesus in the period subsequent to the Resurrection. The designation of Peter as "the rock" does not view him as the first bishop of Rome and the founder of the Roman hierarchy, but as the first witness of the Resurrection and therefore as the prime apostolic witness that God raised Jesus from the dead (I Cor. 15:5).

The word translated **church** (in Greek *ekklesia*) refers to the community of faith, not to an ecclesiastical organization as the church later of necessity came to be. The exercise of authority to **bind** and **loose** has to do with the regulation of the inner life of the community. It has its parallel in the work of the rabbis as interpreters of the law in the necessity of deciding what is permissible for the faithful and what is not. The promise here given is that they are not exercising this authority in independence: rather God's plan is being worked out through what they do. The binding and loosing **on earth** has its counterpart **in heaven.**

16:20. The charge to **tell no one,** if authentic, may have been originally a blanket rejection by Jesus of the title of Messiah. Nowhere is there a record of his assigning this title to himself. Instead, he repeatedly calls attention to the implications of his work for the coming of the kingdom. He regards his mission as messianic without identifying himself as the Messiah. Here, in any case, he enjoins silence on his followers concerning his role as the Messiah.

16:21-23. When, however, Jesus starts to explain to his followers that his mission involves his own suffering and death, Peter rejects this notion vehemently. He in turn is denounced as the spokesman for **Satan,** the enemy of God's purpose through Jesus. It is likely that the specific details of Jesus' prediction of the Passion have been introduced into the tradition after the events occurred. But there is no reason to doubt that Jesus foresaw his death, that he viewed it as a part of the divine purpose, and that he forewarned his disciples concerning it. It is equally likely that they failed to understand the seriousness of his warning or to discern any connection between his death and the coming of the kingdom of God. Only in the light of the Resurrection did this connection begin to become clear.

The prediction is repeated twice (17:22-23; 20:17-19). In all 3 cases Matt. corrects Mark's dating of the Resurrection from "after three days" (Mark 8: 31; 9:31; 10:34) to **on the third day.** What is perhaps more significant is that in all 3 (though not in 27:63-64; 28:6-7) Matt. alters Mark's active voice, "he will rise," to the passive, **he will be raised.** The oldest witnesses to the Resurrection—Paul's letters and the traditions of early preaching in the first half of Acts—say that God raised Jesus rather than that Jesus rose.

16:24-28. Conditions of Discipleship. Just as Jesus called his followers to share in the works of the kingdom, so he began to announce that they must be prepared to share in his sufferings. It has been suggested that **take up his cross** originally referred, not to the instrument of Jesus' death, but to acceptance of the stigma attached to him and his work. But clearly the tradition and the gospel writers understand these sayings to speak of sharing in the

sufferings of Christ in the light of the cross. For one to accept this way of life means to **deny himself,** even to **lose . . . his life** in order that he may find the true way of life that God alone can provide. There is no way to recover the loss resulting from a wasted life—nothing can one **give in return for** it.

16:27.—The seriousness of the situation is heightened by the warning that **the Son of man is to come** as judge to mete out rewards and punishment appropriate to the stewardship that men have performed with their own lives. The term is used in a way familiar in Jewish apocalyptic writings to refer to the coming eschatological judge. It is remarkable that here, as is nearly always the case where the coming Son of man is mentioned in the Synoptic tradition, Jesus speaks of him in the 3rd person, as if it is someone other than himself. The contrast between himself and the Son of man is more evident in Mark 8:38, but it is implied here and also in vs. 28.

16:28. This saying raises another kind of difficulty, since it declares that the coming of the Son of man, whose advent will mark the end of the present age, will take place during the lifetime of some of Jesus' disciples. On this basis, therefore, the end should have occurred sometime between A.D. 70 and 100, depending on how long the last of Jesus' followers lived. Some interpreters try to get around the difficulty by suggesting that the kingdom's coming is to be seen in the transfiguration story which follows immediately (17:1-8). Others think the **coming in his kingdom** refers to the resurrection of Jesus. But if we take the humanity of Jesus with full seriousness, we should perhaps acknowledge that he, in the sense of urgency and power that attended his ministry, actually expected the end to come within that generation. Although his expectation was not fulfilled in that form, the experience of his resurrection and the consequent powerful coming of the Spirit upon the church produced transforming effects in the lives of men of faith. This led the church to conclude that the signs of the kingdom were in fact present in the ministry of Jesus, even though the consummation did not occur at the point in time that Jesus seems to have expected it.

17:1-8. The Transfiguration. Many interpreters have found in this story a kind of advance viewing of the glory of the risen Christ. It is surely so understood by the author of II Pet. 1:17-18, who speaks as though he had been present when the revelation of Christ's glory took place. More likely, however, the story is the product of the early church, which rightly saw in the redemptive significance of Jesus many parallels with the great redemptive act of God in behalf of old Israel—the Exodus and the giving of the law at Sinai. It is in the latter that the analogies are most clearly to be seen: withdrawn on a mountain, God's servant hears the voice of God speaking out of a cloud, as a consequence of which his very appearance is changed. We see these features in the story: a **high mountain** (vs. 1); **apart** (vs. 1); **his face shone** (vs. 2); **a bright cloud overshadowed them** (vs. 5); **a voice from the cloud said, "This is my beloved Son"** (vs. 5). Significantly, the voice from the cloud uses the same words and confirms the message which came from heaven at the baptism of Jesus (3:17).

It is difficult to understand how the disciples could have missed the intention of Jesus so completely—as they in fact did—if they had had such divine communications as these. Even if we assume that there was some historical experience behind this account—such as a corporate vision by the inner group of disciples—we would still have to acknowledge that the account has now been overlaid with OT imagery.

The point of the story in the purpose of the gospel writers is clear and important: God's redemptive purpose through Jesus did not start with the Cross and the Resurrection, but was operative throughout the whole of his earthly life and ministry. Furthermore, those whose eyes were opened in the light of the Resurrection to discern the glory that was present in the earthly life were the disciples, among whom the prime witnesses were **Peter and James and John.** In spite of the idle proposal to build **three booths,** as though this would in some way preserve this moment of glory (Mark 9:6 tells us Peter suggested this for want of anything better to say), the scene quickly fades, **Moses** and **Elijah** vanish, and **Jesus only** remains.

17:9-13. The Coming of Elijah. Frequently in Mark, Jesus commands the disciples to be silent about what they know of him. Matt. has here taken over Jesus' instruction (cf. Mark 9:9), although he has omitted the suggestion that the disciples did not understand what being **raised from the dead** meant. The movement of thought is somewhat awkward in the Markan version, but Matt. has sought to give a unity to the whole by referring in vs. 12 once more to the Son of man and his suffering. It is not known which scribes expected Elijah to come **first** in order to restore all things, nor is it known what "first" implies, whether before the Messiah (Matt. presumably understands it in this way) or before the end. The argument now runs, Elijah has come and has suffered—i.e. **John the Baptist,** as vs. 13 makes explicit—and suffering will also befall the one whose forerunner Elijah was, i.e. the Son of man.

17:14-21. Healing the Epileptic Boy. Matt.'s version of this story is considerably abbreviated, but it is told in such a way as to minimize the miracle itself and to emphasize the inability of the disciples to perform the healing. Stress is laid on the faults of this generation (it is **faithless and perverse**) and on the failings of the disciples (they have **little faith**). To this rebuke Matt. adds the word about **faith as a grain of mustard seed,** by which men of faith are able to accomplish the seemingly **impossible.**

17:22-23. The Passion Predicted Again. The 2nd direct prediction of the Passion is not so detailed as the first (16:21). This time Mark comments that the disciples "did not understand" and were "afraid to ask" for an explanation (Mark 9:32), but Matt. says merely that they were **greatly distressed.**

17:24-27. The Coin in the Fish's Mouth. It is an understatement to say that this story, perhaps more than any other of the Synoptic miracles, stretches the credulity of modern man. Attempts have been made at rationalistic explanations and at allegorical interpretation, but neither approach is really fruitful. It seems rather to be a story that arose, or at least that assumed its present form, in the days when serious questions were beginning to arise as to the

relation of the young church to the Roman state. Following the destruction of the temple in Jerusalem in A.D. 70, the Romans continued to collect the half-shekel tax originally designated for support of the temple (Exod. 30:13), but channeled the funds into support for the pagan temple of Jupiter. The purpose behind the story is to tell inquiring or reluctant Christians that, although their freedom as children of God releases them from a moral obligation to pay such a tax, it is better to avoid **offense** by paying it. The story thus serves to provide the sanction of Jesus' reaction to the problem for Christians who face the difficulty of whether or not to obey the pagan state.

18:1-5. True Greatness. Matt. has changed the immodest discussion among the disciples as to which of them was the greatest (Mark 9:33-34) into a question, **Who is the greatest in the kingdom of heaven?** The older form of Jesus' answer (Mark 10:15) does not specify what it is about a child that prepares one for admission to the kingdom. But for Matt., to become like a child one **humbles himself.** Humility, then, is the guarantee to greatness in the kingdom.

18:5. Mention of the child calls to mind another saying about children, according to which receiving **one such child** is the same as receiving Jesus. This is a recurrent theme in the tradition; the treatment accorded the followers of Jesus or those who come in his name is actually treatment offered to Jesus himself. We shall see that Matt. has the fullest statement on this theme in the parable of the last judgment (25:31-46), which is found in his gospel alone.

18:6-35. Mutual Responsibilities. We now have a series of loosely connected sayings dealing with the general theme of the solemn obligations that fall upon those who share in the life of the Christian community. The sayings were probably addressed originally to Jesus' disciples, but they have been placed here in a setting which makes them a set of regulations for guiding the inner life of the church. The train of thought moves easily from the children spoken of in the previous section to the **little ones.** These are not children in the literal sense, but those who have newly come into the fellowship of community. To cause them to stumble (see below on 18:7) as they begin the life of faith is a grievous sin. The consequences of such action for the guilty person are so grave that Jesus here advises him—using typical Semitic overstatement—to try to flee from the wrath of God's judgment by drowning himself in the **depth of the sea.**

18:7. This saying reiterates the theme of the preceding. The RSV confuses the meaning by translating the word for "stumbling blocks" as **temptations to sin.** There is no suggestion here of a conscious luring of the little one to sin or even of some testing experience that he undergoes in fulfillment of his witness. Rather it is acknowledged that factors will arise in the world which will cause those of weak faith to stumble; the man through whom these occasions for stumbling occur will be held accountable to God.

18:8-9. The man of faith is to exercise control over his own faculties, so that what is handled, what is entered into, and what is seen is not outside the range of his responsibility and therefore not beyond those factors for which God will hold him accountable. In vivid imagery, repeated from 5:29-30, Jesus tells his followers they must be ready to **cut . . . off** the offending **hand** or **foot** or to **pluck . . . out** the offending **eye.** Nothing less than complete self-control is expected of those who would enter the life of the age to come. The alternative is to yield to unworthy motives and urges, and the consequence will be exclusion from the presence of God. The **hell** (Greek *gehenna*) **of fire** is an image taken over from ancient Israel, when the Valley of Hinnom (Gehenna) was the place of refuse for the city of Jerusalem. Its smoldering fires made it an obvious symbol for the fate of the worthless and the useless.

18:10-14. Concern for **these little ones** continues. Matt. has placed here the parable of the lost sheep, which he drew from his Q source (cf. Luke 15:3-7). By referring to the little ones at the beginning and ending of the parable Matt. has given it a new direction. In the original form it speaks of the joy of God at the recovery of one of his own children who repents. Here it is the welfare of the little ones that is stressed. The parable was probably addressed originally to Jesus' critics, who objected to his pervasive interest in the outcasts and the sinners. In Matt.'s setting it is addressed to the church leadership, which is being called to account for the welfare of the weak in faith, the new converts. God's concern for these is to be reflected in the leaders' active concern in behalf of the immature believers within the community. The notion that **their angels always behold the face of my Father** is paralleled in the rabbinic teachings of the time, according to which angels watch over men and have direct access to God. The little ones are therefore under unceasing providential surveillance.

18:15-35. The remainder of this section deals in a variety of ways with the question of resolving disputes within the community. The whole section has been given its present form by Matt. in the interests of lining out procedures for dealing with disputes. Vs. 15 presents the first stage: the one offended is to take the initiative in settling matters privately with the **brother** who has caused the offense. If this does not work, stage 2 (vs. 16) is to be put into effect: **one or two others** are to listen to the dispute as **witnesses,** in accord with the OT method of gathering evidence (Deut. 19:15). If this also proves to be ineffective, the 3rd stage (vs. 17) comes into operation: there is a hearing on the issue before **the church,** i.e. the entire congregation. If no settlement can be reached on this basis, the offending member is to be put out of the community, as Israel would treat a **Gentile and a tax collector.** What is in effect here is the beginning of judicial procedure within the church and the first suggestion of a process of excommunication. It seems certain that such advanced regulations did not come from Jesus, but from the early church itself, operating in keeping with what it understood to be his intention.

18:18-20. The authority exercised in the church is understood to have heavenly sanction, since it is believed that there is an exact correspondence between the will of God in heaven and the functioning of the authorities within the church on earth. As was noted in connection with 16:19, this belief is

paralleled in that of the rabbis. The moral decisions of the community are to be equated with the moral judgments of God. This same element of correspondence is to be seen between the petitions of the church on earth and the will of God in heaven. Prayer is not a purely private matter, but an expression of the will of **two** or more. **Anything they ask** God will do. The safeguard in what may appear to be a blanket promise is the presence of the living Christ in the midst of the community: **There am I in the midst** of the church. This theme will reappear in the closing words of the gospel, 28:20.

18:21-22. Again as spokesman for the group of disciples, **Peter** asks for a ruling as to the number of times one must forgive the person who has committed a wrong. He thinks that he is being most charitable in suggesting that he will forgive a man **seven times.** Note the parallel between this passage and the cry of vengeance in Gen. 4:24:

> If Cain is avenged sevenfold,
> truly Lamech seventy-sevenfold.

In the pre-Israelite period vengeance toward one who had done wrong knew no limits. Jesus is here saying that, among those who await the coming of God's kingdom, mercy can have no limits. **Seventy times seven** is not to be taken literally; it points rather to the limitless grace which is to be displayed by the child of God.

18:23-33. The **therefore** shows that Matt. intends the parable to be a comment on the same theme. **The kingdom of heaven** is being compared, not with the **king** only, but with the whole story that follows. Strictly speaking, the parable tells more about the nature of God than about the nature of the kingdom. The story is vivid, even though the details seem overdrawn. The debtor owes the king the equivalent of $10 million. The aim is to depict the debt as the greatest imaginable to a first-cent. mind—hence we have the highest number in normal usage (**ten thousand**) and the largest monetary unit (**talent**). But **the servant** who owes this enormous debt is himself owed about $20. The king is willing to forgive the huge sum, but the wretched servant will not forgive his debtor, insisting rather that the man be put in debtors' **prison.** When word of this reaches the ears of the king, he reminds the servant of the great debt that has been forgiven and asks why he could not likewise have shown **mercy.**

18:34-35. It is likely that the original parable ended with the question in vs. 33. Matt.'s concern for the punishment of the wicked shows up in the lines which have been added, according to which the king delivers up the servant to the torturers (the RSV has toned this down to read **jailers**). Apparently it is to be assumed that the servant's family would put up the money for his release in order to bring his torment to an end. But this detail blunts the point, which must have been: If God has forgiven us all, how much more should we be ready to forgive those who have done wrong to us! Matt. states it in the negative: God will punish you **if you do not forgive your brother from your heart.**

J. CONFLICT AND CONSUMMATION (19:1-25:46)

This, the last main division of Matt.'s 5-fold structure, begins with a series of controversy stories and ends with the Synoptic apocalypse in Matt.'s expanded version. Throughout there is a sense of mounting hostility between Jesus and the leaders of Judaism. The ground of that hostility and Matt.'s own vengeful attitude toward the Jews is made clear in these chs.

19:1-12. Marriage, Divorce, and Celibacy. This section opens with Matt.'s typical transitional phrase, **now when Jesus had finished . . .**, which is followed by a strange reference to **the region of Judea beyond the Jordan.** Both Mark and John depict Jesus as carrying on a ministry E of the Jordan. An interesting theory that has been proposed is that this ministry was carried on in an interim after Jesus' confrontation with the Jewish authorities at his cleansing of the temple and before the final events in Jerusalem, all of which (the theory runs) have been telescoped into a single week by Mark. Actually the nature of Jesus' activity is such that the location is of little consequence in any case.

19:3-8. The first issue between Jesus and the Jewish leaders is divorce. This theme has already been touched on in the Sermon on the Mount, where it appears in the series of antitheses ("you have heard it was said . . . but I say to you . . ."). Vs. 3 sets the issue in the framework of the controversies that were going on within Judaism: What are the conditions, if any, under which it is **lawful to divorce one's wife?** As already noted (see above on 5:31-32), Jesus refused to take sides on this legal dispute; instead he rejected the practice of divorce and remarriage as contrary to the will of God. The basis for interpreting the will of God is given in greater detail here. By rearranging 2 strands of tradition from Mark 10:2-9 (the denunciation of the practice of divorce and the appeal to Gen. 1:27; 2:24 for the stability of the marriage relationship) Matt. has made the argument more compelling than it is in Mark. Since God has indicated by creating man as a sexual being that he intended for man and woman to be joined and remain joined together, there is no place in his purpose for divorce. Matt. repeats (vss. 4, 8) that God had in mind this intention of indissoluble unity **from the beginning.**

19:9. Repeated from 5:32 is the one condition under which divorce is to be permitted—**unchastity.** Some of the ancient manuscripts add to or modify this qualification, in order to bring it fully into line with the form of Jesus' words in 5:32. No matter how it is read, however, it has the effect of setting aside the unconditional rejection of divorce and remarriage in Mark 10:11, which was surely the teaching of Jesus himself. Matt. shows that the early church was not able to live by the radical demands of Jesus, but had instead to modify them in order to render them—as it thought—practicable.

19:10-12. This paragraph includes material found only in Matt. The disciples' comment in vs. 10 uses terms which sound like Paul when he is speaking (I Cor. 7:25-40) about the advantages of being single. The reply, however, goes beyond anything found in Paul. The rabbis mention only the first 2 of the 3 categories of eunuchs indicated here: (a) those who are congenitally impotent; (b) those who have been castrated; (c) those who voluntarily abstain from sexual relationships. Occasionally the words in which this 3rd type are described by the tradition—**eunuchs who have made themselves**

eunuchs for the sake of the kingdom of heaven—have been taken literally. This was true in the case of Origen, the learned biblical scholar of the church in Alexandria in the early 3rd cent. But the saying likely reflects the growing tendency of the church, even by the end of the first cent., to regard abstinence from the marriage relationship as a sign of holiness. The passage tells us about the early church; it reveals nothing about the attitude of Jesus toward marriage.

19:13-15. Children and the Kingdom of God. These sayings are of a piece with those found in 18:1-4, where becoming like a child is considered a prerequisite for entering the kingdom. It is worth noting that in variant forms of this saying which appear in the Gospel of Thomas (see pp. 1106-09) to become like a child is to renounce one's sexuality rather than to become humble or willing to receive the kingdom as a gift, as the Synoptic tradition interprets this saying. The ascetic tendency which is developed in Thomas is already at work in Matt., even though it is not hinted at in vss. 13-15. It may be that the location of this passage following the word about eunuchs led Thomas to link the 2 ideas of childlikeness and asceticism.

19:16-30. How to Inherit Eternal Life. The refusal of Jesus to accept the epithet "good" in Mark 10:18 is modified in Matt. to read: **Why do you ask me about what is good?** It appears that Matt. has sought to avoid the implication present in Mark that there is a contrast between the goodness of God and that of Jesus. But the original force of the saying of Jesus shows through in the statement, **One there is who is good,** meaning God is the only one who is good in the full sense.

19:17c-22. The thought then turns to the man's question as to **what good deed** he must do **to have eternal life.** The answer of Jesus is simply to recite the commandments, although the commandment about loving God with all one's heart is omitted, as it is in the accounts of the other evangelists. The young man replies with supreme moral confidence: **all these I have observed.** But Jesus' proposal that he sell his possessions and give the money to the poor is utterly discouraging to him, and he leaves sorrowful. The highest good in this man's life is not his exemplary conformity to the moral requirements of his religion, but the possession of wealth. He cannot bring himself to part with the **great possessions** which he holds so dear and fling himself upon God's providential care. He lives, not by faith, but by holding on to what he has. Accordingly he is not ready to **enter the kingdom of heaven.** It should be noted that Matt. treats **eternal life** (vs. 16) and entering the kingdom as virtually synonymous. Eternal life probably means here, not everlasting life, but the life of the age to come, since the Greek word *aionios,* translated "eternal," is related to the word *aion,* meaning "age."

19:23-24. The comment made to the disciples is appropriate, even though it may have been spoken originally in a different circumstance. It is in keeping with the eschatological promise that the poor are those who will possess the kingdom; here the converse is pronounced. Vs. 24 presents a vivid image of the difficulty that the rich man faces in the familiar comparison with the **camel** going **through the eye of a needle.** The attempts to make this figure less grotesque have been ingenious. It has been suggested that a slight shift of Semitic roots will make this read that it is easier for a rope to pass through a needle's eye. A more romantic proposal speaks of a gate left open after the large city gates are closed, so small that the camel must have its burden stripped off before it can pass through. But anyone who has witnessed a camel arising or settling down and has heard its raucous cries of complaint at changing its position will appreciate the superb irony in the notion that a camel could ever make it through the eye of a needle.

19:25-30. The disciples' response is understandable; salvation on these terms is humanly impossible. And Jesus agrees that it is; but it is possible **with God,** whose kingdom it is that man enters, and who gives man the possibility of entering it by his grace, not by man's merits. Man's greed once more asserts itself when **Peter** asks (vs. 27) what Jesus' disciples will gain in exchange for what they have given up to follow him. In giving Jesus' reply Matt. has omitted much of the strange detail about the 2 stages in the reward of the disciples described in Mark (10:29-30), but has added a Q saying (cf. Luke 22:28-30, about the role of the disciples as judges, seated with the Son of man in the age to come. But further, Matt. continues, there will be a **hundredfold** reward for accepting the deprivations that go with discipleship, and beyond the reward is the possibility of entering the **life** of the age to come. The concluding comment is found in many contexts in the Synoptic tradition and adds nothing to the meaning of the section here.

20:1-16. *The Laborers in the Vineyard.* Only Matt. has preserved this, one of the more problematical parables. The whole of the story runs counter to man's sense of fairness. It would be preposterous to look to this parable in defense of unconditionally free enterprise or as a basis for labor-management relationships. The parable presupposes the situation in first-cent. Palestine.

The **householder** does not have a crew of regular workers, but is dependent instead on the occasional help of men from the village. The first group of workers went out to the fields from the village at sunrise (**early in the morning**), the next at 9, the next at noon, the next at 3 in the afternoon, and the last group at 5. At sundown (the 12th hour) all were called together to be paid. When those who had worked only one hour received an amount (**a denarius,** equal to about 20 cents) that was considered generous for a full day's work, the others must have quickly calculated how many times more than a denarius they would receive. To their astonishment and chagrin, all received the same. That **they grumbled** is understandable, especially to anyone who has worked under the hot Palestinian sun. The householder will not yield to their complaints, however, since he insists that he is free to be equally generous with all. He is sovereign over his own lands and household; if he chooses to, he can give freely to all. There is no ground for complaint, he insists, against such action.

20:15. The 2 main points of the story appear in the double question which probably brought the original parable to a close: **Am I not allowed to do what I choose with what belongs to me? Or do you begrudge my generosity?** The householder operates by the standard of grace, not of merit. The laborers are so bound to legalistic thinking that they cannot conceive of anyone motivated by grace rather than by measuring out rewards appropriate to the services rendered. The central actor is the generous householder, not the disgruntled employees. The parable is a defense of Jesus' message of God's grace to all against the attacks of the defenders of a religion of meritorious works.

20:16. The concluding comment, which is nearly identical with 19:30, blunts the point of the parable by drawing attention to the irrelevant fact that those workers who came last are paid first. The saying floated freely in the tradition and has been attached to the parable because of the purely verbal connection with the order in which the workers are paid. This conclusion, however, has led some to interpret the parable as though it were a contrast between the Jews, who came to God's vineyard first, and the Gentiles, who came last.

20:17-19. *Prediction of the Passion.* This is the 3rd and most detailed of the predictions of the Passion, which began following Peter's confession at Caesarea Philippi (see above on 16:21-23). It is spoken here in connection with the movement of Jesus from the area E of the Jordan, through Jericho, and so up to Jerusalem. The consensus of the gospel tradition on the decision of Jesus to leave Galilee and go to Jerusalem, there to confront the religious leaders of the nation, probably rests on historical fact. Identifying himself as the **Son of man,** Jesus reportedly predicts the main outlines of the passion events: seizure by the priests, condemnation, deliverance into Gentile hands, mocking, scourging, and crucifixion, followed by resurrection on the 3rd day. The reader of the gospel is now fully alerted as to what is in store for Jesus in Jerusalem.

20:20-28. *On Becoming a Servant.* The occasion for this statement about becoming a servant is the request for a place of special favor for the **sons of Zebedee,** James and John. Whereas in Mark 10:35 these disciples themselves make the request, according to Matt. the petition is voiced by their **mother.** The change has the effect of softening the seeming audacity of the sons of Zebedee. Jesus' reply, however, is addressed to the 2 disciples: **Are you able to drink the cup that I am to drink?** The fact that Jesus does not here speak of his passion in the specific terms of the previous section (vss. 17-19), added to the report preserved by the early church that John lived to an advanced age rather than that he died as a martyr, has led many scholars to the conclusion that here we have an authentic word of Jesus in which he anticipates his own death and that of his followers. The cup is clearly the cup of suffering—and in this case suffering which leads to death. The response of the disciples is glibly uttered with no awareness of the real consequences: **We are able.**

20:23. The first clause of Jesus' reply is a warning to the sons of Zebedee that they *will* experience martyrdom. But the rest of the vs. returns to the theme of their original request, to which Jesus replies that the awarding of places in the age to come is the work of **my Father** and **not mine to grant.** Some interpreters have found in these 2 parts of Jesus' response a contradiction: on the one hand he suggests that one should not aspire to a place of honor in the age to come since it always involves suffering; on the other hand he declares that it is not his prerogative to award honors. One thing is sure, Jesus would scarcely have taught his followers to accept suffering with the motive of gaining places of honor in the new age. Possibly the original form of this incident dealt only with preference in the new age, and the tradition added the words about suffering (vss. 22-23a, or more accurately Mark 10:38-39, on which Matt.'s version is based). But we cannot determine by current standards of logic what would be the line of reasoning for first-cent. Jews, steeped in apocalyptic ways of thinking.

20:24-28. The climax of the section comes in the contrast between the ordinary way men exercise authority over others when they **lord it over them** and the way God's power is evident through one who accepts the **servant** role. Vs. 28 is perhaps a comment of the early church on the significance of Jesus as servant. The son of man announces that he will **give his life a ransom for many** (the latter phrase reflecting the language of Isa. 53:11). The Son of man was for Judaism a figure of triumph; the servant was a figure of humiliation. Jesus is here seen as one who moves through humiliation to triumph. (See also on Mark 10:42-45.)

20:29-34. The Blind Men at Jericho. Instead of a single blind man, as in the Bartimaeus story (Mark 10:46-52), Matt. reports Jesus as healing **two blind men** on the way out of Jericho. Twice they cry out to Jesus, whom they address as **Son of David,** thereby calling to mind the traditional messianic hope for Israel for the restoration of the Davidic kingship. But the 2nd time they also call Jesus **Lord,** which is clearly a title attributed to Jesus in the earliest Christian communities, following his resurrection. Again they call him **Lord** (vs. 33) when they beseech him to heal their blindness. Emphasizing the compassion of Jesus on their condition, Matt. tells us that they were healed **and followed him.** There is a deep symbolic touch in this story, which informs us that on the way to Jerusalem, where he is to present his claims before the official spokesmen for the Jewish people, only the blind can see who Jesus really is.

21:1-9. The Entry into Jerusalem. The most direct route from Jericho to Jerusalem leads through the wilderness of Judea, over the top of the **Mount of Olives,** and down the slopes into the city of Jerusalem (see color map 1). The Mount of Olives is a part of the ridge that runs N and S throughout central Palestine, sloping off gradually toward the Mediterranean on the W, and on the E dropping abruptly into the Jordan Valley, which at its lower end is more than 1,200 feet below the level of the Mediterranean. The climb from Jericho to the summit of the Mount of Olives is about 3,600 feet. From the crest of the ridge at the Mount of Olives one can see the whole of Jerusalem spread out on the lower hills below. **Bethphage** was a village on the E slope of the Mount of Olives—the last settlement through which one would pass before reaching Jerusalem. **The village opposite,** where the disciples were to find the ass and the colt, may have been Bethany, just to the SE of Bethphage.

21:2-5. There is an element of mystery about

the prearrangement with the owner for making the animals available. The only point in obtaining 2 animals—one would have been quite sufficient for transporting Jesus, as Mark 11:2 makes clear—is that a literal reading of the poetic words of Zech. 9:9 implies that there were both an **ass** and a **colt** on which the eschatological king would ride into the city. Matt., misunderstanding the Hebrew parallelism by which the lines were matched by sense rather than by sound (see pp. 1077-81), considered it essential to add the 2nd animal. If Jesus arranged this in advance, he was obviously intent on enacting this prophetic promise. It is possible, however, that he simply rode into the city, and his followers, recalling the prophecy, interpreted his action in this way.

21:9. The greetings of the crowd, **Hosanna,** and **Blessed be he who comes in the name of the Lord,** are quoted from Ps. 118:25-26. This psalm was originally used as a greeting to the pilgrims who came up to the Jerusalem temple to worship. The phrase "in the name of the Lord" was intended to be linked with "blessed," and "he who enters [comes]" meant "he who comes to worship." Its meaning has been altered, so that now it is an acclamation of the one who comes as the Messiah. Similarly, **Hosanna** (meaning "Save us") **in the highest** meant that the prayer for salvation was addressed to the Highest One, i.e. to God. Here, however, it implies that the prayer is uttered at the highest level or with the utmost earnestness of devotion.

21:10-17. Jesus in the Temple. Matt. alone suggests that **all the city** took notice of Jesus' entry into Jerusalem. The way Jesus was identified by the crowds is noteworthy, since it is in many respects an accurate description of what he must have seemed to even sympathetic observers: **the prophet Jesus from Nazareth of Galilee.** He comes without official standing, authorization, or credentials. His message and actions carry their own authorization. Nowhere is this authority more forcefully seen than in the cleansing of the temple.

21:12-13. By driving out the money-changers and the sellers of small animals for sacrifice Jesus threatened the economic functioning of the temple, which must surely have been one of the largest commercial enterprises in Palestine. All contributions to the temple had to be made in Jewish money, so that Jews from the lands of the Roman Empire and beyond who came to Jerusalem had to exchange their local money for Jerusalem coinage—to the benefit of the money-changers, of course. It is the commercialism of the temple area that Jesus denounces by quoting from Isa. 56:7; Jer. 7:11. The former reads: "My house shall be called a house of prayer for all peoples." Mark 11:17 quotes it in its entirety, but Matt. strangely omits the last phrase. This heightens the denunciation, but misses the point that the Court of the Gentiles, the locale of the commercialization, was intended to be a place where all men of whatever nation could approach God.

21:14-16. The reaction of the priests is understandably hostile and regrettably vindictive. They are not impressed favorably by **the wonderful things that he did.** Men disposed to think ill of Jesus are never persuaded by his extraordinary powers, as is seen from the gospel tradition throughout. Matt., with his feel for paradox, represents the children echoing the cry of the crowds, **Hosanna to the Son of David,** so that once more the simple-minded can perceive what is hidden from the eyes of the learned—that Jesus is the Messiah. This incident also provides Matt. the occasion to see the fulfillment of scripture (Ps. 8:2) in that the **babes** are those who utter **praise** to God's Chosen One.

21:17. Following this display of authority and the resulting determination on the part of the leaders to destroy him, Jesus withdraws from the city to the nearby village of **Bethany.** Jewish custom required all pilgrims to be within the city during the celebration of the Passover, the feast in which Israel celebrated its deliverance from bondage in Egypt. But since the city could not hold the crowds that flocked to it on festival occasions, the city limits were technically expanded to include surrounding towns, such as Bethany.

21:18-22. *Cursing the Fig Tree.* As a straightforward story this account of the cursing of the fig tree is difficult to comprehend. It seems like an act of petulance on the part of Jesus to curse a tree because it cannot provide fruit at the moment that he is hungry. The curse was evidently effective, since **the fig tree withered at once.** It would appear, however, that the story is largely symbolic, at least in its present form. It points to the nation Israel, which has not brought forth the fruits of repentance (in the phrase of John the Baptist) and is therefore depicted by the Synoptic tradition as under God's curse. Whatever historical elements there may have been behind this account have been obscured by the tradition in its eagerness to point out that God's favor no longer rests on the nation that rejected his Messiah.

Courtesy of Herbert G. May

Fig tree in the hill country N of Jerusalem in August (cf. ill., p. 462); in the background are olive trees

21:20-22. The explanation of the cursed fig tree requested by the disciples does not really speak to the problem, but becomes instead an appeal for confidence in prayer. Matt.'s appeal for men to have great faith is introduced here once more.

21:23-27. *The Source of Jesus' Authority.* In a section in which Matt. follows Mark 11:27-33 very closely Jesus is questioned by the leaders of the Jews as to the source of the authority by which he acts and teaches. His response is in turn a question which requires them to take a stand on the role of John the Baptist, whether he was from God or not. The enormous popular following of John is attested

by Josephus, the Jewish historian of the period. The leaders would incriminate themselves if they acknowledged the divine origin of John's ministry, since they had not heeded John. On the other hand they would risk the resentment of the populace if they denied that God had commissioned John. Jesus leaves them with precisely the same dilemma regarding the source of his authority. Jesus seems to see in the work of John more than an analogy to his own work. Rather he sees a continuity between John's ministry and his own—not merely historical, in that they were earlier associated, but also theological, in that God, who began a new thing with the coming of John, is bringing it to completion through Jesus.

21:28-32. *The Two Sons.* Here begins a series of 3 parables, only the 2nd of which is found at this point in Mark's account. The first, which appears in the NT only in Matt., culminates in a question, as indeed many of the parables probably did in their original form. The son who refused to work but changed his mind and did is contrasted with the son who agreed to work but did not actually go. Jesus turns this question to those who are presumably his critics: **Which of the two did the will of his father?** The critics, perhaps unwittingly, condemn themselves in their answer: **the first.** Jesus' response goes to the heart of his gospel message. What God calls for is repentance on the part of those who are in need of his grace and are willing to acknowledge their need. The proud, self-righteous, "religious" people do not know of their own need and refuse the message. The religious leaders have refused to repent, and therefore the outcasts—**the tax collectors and the harlots**—who have repented will enter the kingdom of God first. The cloak of religious respectability means nothing in God's sight, unless the man is genuinely repentant, as these poor sinners are.

21:33-46. *The Wicked Vineyard Workers.* Once more Matt. has provided us with both a parable (from Mark 12:1-12) and his understanding of its meaning. The picture in the parable is of a vineyard, the absentee owner of which is naturally interested in receiving the earnings from the tenants who are working in it in his absence. The brief description of the vineyard fits the conditions in first-cent. Palestine—a crude **tower** for watchmen, a protective **hedge,** or fence, to discourage marauders, human or otherwise, and a **wine press** dug out of the soft limestone of the Palestinian hills. The **fruit** that is sought is not the grapes, but the money earned by the sale of the wine.

The **servants** who come to collect from the tenants are beaten, stoned, and killed. Finally the **son** of the owner is put to death, on the assumption that with the heir of the owner gone, the tenants can claim the property by reason of their occupying it. The owner then comes to destroy the tenants and to turn over the stewardship of his property to others, who will produce for him the results appropriate to their labor in his vineyard.

The background of this image is the allegory of the vine in Isa. 5, where it is explicitly stated that the vineyard is the house of Israel (Isa. 5:7) and the owner is the Lord of Hosts. The implication of Jesus' parable is obvious: Israel's role as the people of God has not been faithfully discharged; indeed, God's servants have been rejected by Israel, which is soon to reject his Son. A slight shift in detail from Mark 12:8, "killed him and cast him out of the vineyard," to Matt.'s vs. 39, **cast him out of the vineyard, and killed him,** shows how the course of events of the Passion influenced this parable, since Jesus was actually taken out of the city first and then killed.

21:41-46. Matt.'s vindictiveness against the Jewish leaders is evident in the details which he adds to the words of judgment. The tenants are for him **wretches,** whose fate is a **miserable death.** The new tenants can be counted on to produce according to expectations. After quoting one of the favorite texts of the early church (Ps. 118:22-23), which speaks of the Messiah as the rejected **stone** now become the cornerstone of God's new building, Matt. returns to the agricultural image and points to the church as the **nation** which will replace Israel in the purpose of God. The point is not lost on the Jewish leaders, who recognize that Jesus **was speaking about them.**

The parable verges on allegory, so that it is difficult to determine how much of it in its present form may be traced back to Jesus and how much has originated in the situation of conflict between the church and Judaism in the later first cent. Its main outlines are present in Mark's version, but it may have assumed that form in the years just before the final break between the church and Judaism, which occurred in the period A.D. 66-70.

22:1-14. *The King's Marriage Feast.* There are many significant differences between Matt.'s version of this parable and that found in Luke 14:16-24. Luke depicts a man giving a banquet; Matt. presents a king giving a wedding feast for his son. The allegorical interest of Matt. is obvious: this passage now has become an allegory of God's preparation for the eschatological time of joy, described under the favorite Semitic image of a wedding. The allegorical factor of the church as the bride of the king's son is surprisingly absent, however.

22:3-6. The invitation was issued, in Palestinian fashion, in 2 stages: a preliminary announcement that the feast was being planned and a final notice that preparations were now completed. Those invited did not take the invitation seriously, but went about the routine business of life, **one to his farm, another to his business.** Others abused the servants sent with the invitation.

22:7. The reaction attributed to the king shows once more the allegorical reworking of the parable in the light of historical developments. The king **sent his troops** and **burned their city,** an unmistakable allusion to the coming of the Roman troops (viewed as the instruments of God's judgment on the nation Israel) and the destruction of the city of Jerusalem in A.D. 70.

22:8-10. The parable now shifts to a 2nd phase. Those originally invited have proved to be **not worthy** (a favorite term of Matt.). Accordingly the invitation is to go forth everywhere, into the wide **thoroughfares** and the narrow **streets,** i.e. to all men. The result is a wide response. That the persons who come are of a mixed nature is characteristic of Matt.'s view of the church (see above on 13:36-43).

22:11-14. Those who have failed to provide themselves with the **wedding garment** of righteousness (another favorite teaching of Matt.) will be **cast . . . into the outer darkness** (Matt.'s typical phrase for the fate of the unrighteous). The concluding saying (vs. 14), which probably was preserved in the oral tradition without a specific context, serves Matt.'s purpose here, since it contrasts the wide sweep of the invitation to accept the gospel and the small number of those actually found worthy.

22:15-22. *Tribute to Caesar.* This is the first of 4 controversy stories which serve to bring out some of the issues not only between Jesus and his critics but between the church and Judaism. The first has to do with the payment of a head tax of one denarius (see above on 20:2) required by Rome from all subject people. The question is raised by representatives of 2 groups: the Pharisees, who objected strenuously to having to pay the tax, and the Herodians, who presumably favored the tax, since they were sympathetic with the family of the Herods, who ruled as Rome's puppets. For Jesus to have sided with the Herodians would have alienated all who longed for Israel's freedom; to have sided with the opponents of the tax would have laid Jesus open to charges of subversion. His answer has the effect of thrusting the decision back on his interrogators, since one must still determine what is rightfully **Caesar's** and what can be claimed by **God** alone.

22:23-33. *The Question Concerning the Resurrection.* The issue here is not the resurrection of Jesus, but whether there is a resurrection of the faithful at all. The **Sadducees** rejected such a teaching, since it could not be documented in the first 5 books of the OT, which they alone recognized as scripture. The form of the question presupposes the Jewish custom of levirate marriage which required the surviving brother of a deceased husband to marry his brother's widow. In this story, which must have been a stock question raised by those skeptical about the possibility of a resurrection, the woman becomes the wife of 7 brothers successively as each dies and the next brother takes her as his wife. Jesus does not deal with the problem on the ridiculous terms in which it was raised, but points instead to the transformation of human existence which is involved in the resurrection life. He describes it only indirectly when he says that marriage has no place in it. His statement that it is like that of the **angels in heaven** is not much help, since we know nothing of the character of angelic or heavenly existence.

22:31-33. The conclusion of the discussion, in which appeal is made to scripture (Exod. 3:6), does not fit neatly with what has gone before, since the quotation says nothing directly about resurrection. The weight of the argument falls on the tense of **I am the God**—i.e. God's relationship to Abraham, Isaac, and Jacob is a continuing one, even though these patriarchs were from successive generations and all have long since died. He was and still is their God; therefore he is the God **of the living.** What is implied in this argument is not resurrection of the dead, but the personal survival of God's people.

22:34-40. *The Great Commandment.* According to Matt., the initiative in questioning Jesus now passes from the Sadducees to the Pharisees. Their question, which seems to have been raised often by the rabbis, is: **Which is the great commandment in the law?** In reply Jesus links together the commandments to love God (Deut. 6:5) and to love one's neighbor (Lev. 19:18*b*), as the pre-Christian Jewish book The Testaments of the Twelve Patriarchs had done and as other rabbinic interpreters of the law seem to have done. What was new was not the content of Jesus' teaching on this subject but his redefinition of what the love of God was—how it manifested itself, and who a man's neighbor is. In this expansion of man's horizons of obligation, as well as in the mode of life that accompanied and exemplified his teachings, lay the revolutionary, new element of Jesus' ministry.

22:41-46. David's Son. The last of the 4 controversies involves a question raised by Jesus rather than by his opponents. It was widely understood that the eschatological king of Israel—the Messiah, i.e. **the Christ**—would be a descendant of the royal line, a **son of David.** When this answer is given, Jesus cites the opening lines of Ps. 110, one of the most notable of the messianic psalms, even though the word "messiah" is not used in it. One would suppose that the son would be subordinate to the father, and yet here David (for Jesus shares with his hearers the assumption of this authorship) speaks of the subject of his psalm as **my Lord.** Jesus offers no solution to this dilemma, and at first glance the implication might seem to be that he is denying his Davidic descent. But Matt., in taking this story from Mark 12:35-37, surely did not so understand it (cf. 1:1; etc.). Rather Matt.'s interpretation must be that Jesus is not merely Son of David but more; he is Lord.

Although some interpreters have assumed that Jesus was here wrestling with questions concerning his own messianic consciousness, it is more likely that a controversy which arose in the early church is here attributed to Jesus. It was the church which acclaimed him as Lord; very early in the church he was also asserted to have been born of David's lineage (Rom. 1:3). It was the attempt to bring these two affirmations together, in a situation of controversy with the Jews over the interpretation of scripture, that seems to lie behind this discussion.

23:1-36. Woes Against the Pharisees. This long discourse, in which the Pharisees are denounced for their hypocrisy rather than for the content of their teaching, appears only in Matt., although parts of the material are found scattered through the other 2 Synoptic gospels. It seems to be the creation of Matt., even though there is no reason to doubt that it includes authentic words of Jesus. The vindictive attitude toward the Pharisees should probably be credited to Matt. or to the church for which he is the spokesman.

23:3-12. The first thrust of Jesus' criticism is against the hypocrisy and ostentation with which the Pharisees go about their religious living. There is no complaint against their teaching—**practice and observe whatever they tell you.** What is objectionable is the way they live; they think up burdensome moral obligations for others which they are unwilling themselves to assume, and they strut their piety in public, taking delight in fancy robes and honorific titles. By contrast the disciples are to be humble.

At this point the terminology of the early church —**one Father . . . in heaven; . . . one master, the Christ**—betrays that we are here dealing with church teaching rather than words of Jesus.

23:13-32. The Pharisees' favorite acts of piety are now enumerated and denounced: making converts to Judaism who are more flagrant violators of the intention of the law than the Pharisees themselves (vs. 15); trying to erect guarantees for their word by means of oaths, while in actuality making pious excuses for telling lies (vss. 16-22); worrying about petty matters of legal observance while ignoring serious trespasses of God's will (vss. 23-24); paying attention to externals while the inner life is corrupt (vss. 25-26); piously honoring the tombs of the prophets while opposing the messengers of God and seeking to have them killed (vss. 27-32).

23:33-36. This last issue, which brings the section to a climax, moves beyond the situation of the time of Jesus to the period of violent hostility between Judaism and the church. It is here claimed that the whole history of the people of Israel as recorded in scripture is uniformly one of rejection and murder of those who have spoken for God. The first book of the Hebrew canon reports near its beginning the murder of a faithful worshiper of God, **Abel** (Gen. 4:8); the last book of that canon records that a faithful priest, **Zechariah,** was murdered within the court of the temple when he tried to call the people to obey the commandments of God (II Chr. 24:20-21; **the son of Barachiah,** not found in Luke 11:51, is apparently an error based on Zech. 1:1). The clear implication is that this pattern of murderous rejection of God's messengers has continued in the response of the Jewish leaders to Jesus and to his messengers now at work among them.

It is interesting to see how those messengers are described: **prophets and wise men and scribes.** That none of these offices except that of prophet is familiar to us from other parts of the NT suggests that in the church for which Matt. was writing there were functions which resembled more closely the Jewish institutions than those in the church in other cultural settings. It is ironic, and yet psychologically quite understandable, that the segment of the church that was in many ways most Jewish should at the same time be most bitterly denunciatory of Judaism and its official leadership.

23:37-24:3. This section consists of 2 parts: (*a*) Jesus' lament over the impending destruction of the city, in the light of his ceaseless yearning for the city (here symbolizing the nation) to repent. The warning is given that the next opportunity to see Jesus will come when he is disclosed in his eschatological glory. The passage has apparently been reworked by the early church and cannot all be traced back to Jesus. (*b*) The announcement that the temple will be destroyed. The source and occasion for great and warranted pride among the Jews of the world in the first cent., the temple must have appeared as though it would stand forever. It seems to be historically certain that Jesus did predict the temple's destruction, since this is the issue that is raised repeatedly and in various forms in connection with his trial. The question raised by the disciples as to the time when this catastrophe will occur becomes the occasion for the apocalyptic discourse which follows in all 3 of the Synoptic gospels.

24:4–25:46. *The Apocalypse.* Writing in language and employing imagery that is characteristic of the apocalyptic writings of Judaism in the period about the time of Jesus' birth, Matt. adopts and expands Mark 13:3-37 in order to describe the conditions that will obtain on the earth in the time immediately preceding the coming of the Son of man, which will mark the end of the age. To Mark's material Matt. has added some extended parables and a group of sayings about the need to be watchful, since no one can predict when the end will come.

24:4-36. *Signs of the End.* The signs which will give warning of the approaching end are rather general in nature: claims of false Christs (vs. 5), international strife (vss. 6-7*a*) and natural disturbances (vs. 7*b*). But these are but **the beginning of the sufferings.** The word used here is almost a technical term for the difficulties that the people of God must pass through before their deliverance comes.

24:9-14. The theme now turns to the way that the time of tribulation will affect the people of God directly. They may expect to be brought to trial before civil authorities, to be universally **hated,** to be victimized by **false prophets.** But if they are able to maintain their witness faithful **to the end,** they can be confident that God will preserve them—i.e. they **will be saved.** But before the end can possibly arrive, the world mission of the church must be carried out **to all nations.** This represents a shift from the strategy that Matt. portrays during the opening of Jesus' ministry, when the mission was to be limited strictly to Israel (10:6).

24:15-22. There is one overt sign by which the community can recognize the approach of the end— **the desolating sacrilege . . . in the holy place.** Dan. 9:27; 11:31, 12:11 were written about the erection in the temple of an image of a pagan god in the time of the Maccabees (I Macc. 1:54; II Macc. 6:2), but are here interpreted as predicting desecration of the temple by the Romans. The fact that in this apocalypse Mark, followed by Matt. and Luke, is reproducing a document is disclosed by the phrase **let the reader understand,** which could not conceivably have been a part of an orally communicated statement by Jesus himself. Some scholars think this is part of a warning sheet distributed among the Christians in Jerusalem just prior to the fall of the city to the Romans in A.D. 70, on the basis of which advice the Jerusalem Christians fled to the city of Pella E of the Jordan. The need for sudden flight could explain the details about not entering the **house,** not stopping to take up one's **mantle,** and the difficulty of flight **in winter,** when the Jordan would be at flood stage.

24:23-31. The warning ends with the announcement of the unprecedented difficulties that will come on the earth before the consummation occurs. The themes of false messianic claimants (vss. 23-25), the impossibility of accurate predicting of the sudden end (vss. 26-28), the natural disturbances that will accompany the coming of the **Son of man** (vss. 29-31) are repeated once more.

24:32-36. The section ends with the analogy of a fig tree: when the first signs are evident, the time of fruition is not far off. But even so, no one, not even **the Son,** can predict the exact time of the end, since this is known to God alone. Drawing as it does on traditional apocalyptic material and, on various strands of the gospel tradition, the apocalypse in its present form reveals more of the situation of the church in the midst of conflict and persecution than it does of the time of Jesus.

24:37-51. *The Need for Watchfulness.* Using material from Q, which is scattered in Luke's version, Matt. heightens the sense of the need for watchfulness by appeal to 3 analogies: (*a*) In **the days of Noah** men were preoccupied with the affairs of life and therefore totally unprepared for the judgment of God that fell on all mankind. Thus in the last days men will be taken away in judgment without warning as the indifferent contemporaries of Noah were. (*b*) A parabolic word concerning a **householder** who is not prepared for the coming of a **thief** points to the need for preparedness in light of the unpredictability of the end. (*c*) Just as the owner of a **household,** when making arrangements for the handling of affairs in his absence, commissions a trusted **servant** to perform his duties and expects him to fulfill these obligations faithfully, so the disciples are charged to be diligent in their work in light of the impossibility of determining when the absent Lord will return. **My master is delayed** may well have originated in the early church at a time when the keenness of expectation of the coming of Christ had begun to wane. Men were growing lax or exploiting for their own ends the authority entrusted to them within the church. This parable serves to warn against such behavior by reminding them that they must be ever ready for the coming of the end.

25:1-30. *The Parables of Watchfulness.* Here are 2 familiar parables, the point of each of which is the need to be ready for the unpredictable coming of the Lord. The first, found only in Matt., involves **ten maidens** following the marriage customs of first-cent. Palestine. That no mention is made of the bride (i.e. of the church) shows that this has not become a full-fledged allegory. The **wise** maidens are prepared, no matter how long the wait may be; the **foolish** are not ready and find themselves excluded. Lest the reader miss the point, Matt. adds: **Watch, therefore, for you know neither the day nor the hour.**

25:14-30. The parable of the **talents,** adapted from Q (cf. Luke 19:12-27), is also intended as a message on the need for faithful stewardship of the responsibilities that have been assigned during the interim before the end—an interim for which no one can predict the terminus. The responsibilities differ widely: **one . . . two . . . five talents** (worth about $1,000 each). The issue is stewardship in light of the unexpected return of the owner. Matt. depicts the fate of the irresponsible servant in his favorite terms: **men will weep and gnash their teeth** (vs. 30).

25:31-46. *The Last Judgment.* Although this final parable of Matt. does not appear elsewhere in the NT, and gives evidence of his own special language and theological interests (e.g. the kingdom of the Father contrasted with the Kingdom of the Son of man), it preserves a theme that is found throughout the gospel tradition: that the decisions made by men now in relation to Jesus are determinative of their destiny in the age to come.

The **Son of man** appears here as the judge, which is his traditional role in the apocalyptic view. All the nations are judged, not merely Israel. They are separated into the **sheep** and the **goats**; i.e. into those who are or are not worthy to enter the Father's kingdom. The criterion for their separation is whether they have performed acts of mercy toward the **least of these my brethren.** Some interpreters think this phrase meant originally the disciples, who were to be received in Christ's name, but it is more likely that the parable now is extended to include all mankind. **My brethren** refers to any human beings who are in need. To receive such a one is to receive Christ; to refuse to aid such a one is to refuse Christ. The surprising element in this parable-like description of the judgment is that those who are welcomed into the kingdom have had no consciousness that the acts of mercy they performed had any relationship to Christ, much less to their eternal destiny. They acted because their fellow man was in need, not in order to earn a reward or to merit admission to the kingdom.

III. The Humiliation and Exaltation of the Son of Man (26:1–28:20)

26:1-16. The Death of Jesus Plotted and Foretold. The familiar words **when Jesus had finished . . .** open this final division of the gospel. Matt. follows Mark's telescoped chronology of Holy Week, so that only **two days** elapse between the launching of the plot by the **chief priests and the elders** to destroy Jesus and the carrying out of their plans on the night of **the Passover.** Commentators have drawn attention to the stated wish of the plotters to take Jesus secretly and **not during the feast** in order to avoid a popular uprising in his support. This would imply that the trial took place at some time other than on the Passover day. But the imagery of the Passover so influenced the Christian understanding of the Last Supper and of the death of Jesus that Passover and Last Supper are interwoven in the present form of the tradition.

26:6-13. The anointing of Jesus by **a woman . . . at Bethany** is an enacted prediction of his death. The incident provides the opportunity to demonstrate the lack of understanding by the disciples, who complain about the waste of such **a large sum.** But it is also the occasion to praise the woman, who shows greater insight and devotion at this moment than any other follower of Jesus. In its present form the story reflects the opinion of the early church, even though it may also reproduce the outlines of an actual historical occurrence.

26:14-16. The final stage in the plot to destroy Jesus takes place when Judas Iscariot agrees to **deliver** Jesus over **to the chief priests** in exchange for a sum of money. The specific amount may have been fixed by the tradition when it saw a connection between Zech. 11:12 and the traitorous act. Why Judas betrayed Jesus cannot be determined. The notion that he was disappointed because Jesus did not lead an uprising against Rome is no more than a romantic guess. What Judas betrayed is not clear, either, though it may be simply that Judas agreed to lead the guards to the place where Jesus spent the night outside the city walls, so that he could be taken by stealth.

26:17-29. The Last Supper. In Jewish practice the **first day of Unleavened Bread** was the occasion for the celebration of the Passover meal, which was eaten during the night by the family. The account in Matt. states that this was the day when preparations were made for the feast. John probably has the historically correct chronology in considering the Friday afternoon on which Jesus was put to death to be the day of Preparation, which according to Jewish thinking began at sundown on Thursday night—hence the reluctance of the Jews to defile themselves by entering Pilate's hall (John 13:1; 18:28; 19:31, 42). It is doubtful that the last meal of Jesus was a Passover meal, especially since most of the characteristic elements of that meal (lamb, bitter herbs, etc.) are missing in the gospel accounts. Probably the Christian understanding of the death of Jesus in the light of the Passover tradition—i.e. as God's new act of deliverance of his people—has influenced the reporting of the Last Supper.

26:18-23. The circumstances surrounding the preparation have an almost miraculous quality about them, although Matt. has omitted some of the detail from his version (cf. Mark 14:12-16). The whole of the account of the supper is so closely linked with OT passages considered to have been fulfilled by Jesus in the passion events that it is difficult to tell where historical recollection leaves off and the influence of scripture begins. One such detail is the saying about the betrayer eating from the common **dish** with Jesus (vs. 23), which recalls Ps. 41:9.

26:24. This vs. is of special interest, since it brings together the elements of human freedom (Judas' intention to betray Jesus) and divine determination (the prediction of the death of the Son of man). In actuality, there is no passage in scripture or known extra-biblical writings where **it is written** that **the Son of man** will go the way of suffering and death. Evidently this saying is based on equating the Son of man with the suffering servant of Isa. 42–53 (see above on 8:18-22; 16:13*b*).

26:25. Judas identifies himself by his very question as the one who will betray Jesus to his enemies. The seemingly noncommittal answer of Jesus, **You have said so,** implies that Judas has spoken the truth. This revelation of the traitor to the other disciples is not found in Matt.'s source (Mark 14:17-21) or in Luke 22:21-23 (cf. John 19:21-30).

26:26-28. The taking of bread and the drinking of the cup are described as occurring during the course of the meal, rather than as a separate ceremony. In all likelihood this was the way the earliest church celebrated the Supper until excesses at the common meal required that the meal and the Eucharist (meaning service of thanksgiving) be separated (cf. I Cor. 11:20-21). The words **took . . . blessed . . . broke . . . gave** all became the technical terms for the celebration of the Lord's Supper in the church. It was God who was blessed, not the bread that was in some way sanctified. The **bread** symbolizes Jesus' total self, which is given for man; the **cup** symbolizes the life of Jesus, which is offered up to seal the new **covenant** by which God is calling into being his new people, the church. Matt.'s special interest in sin and forgiveness is evident in the addition of the phrase **for the forgiveness of sins.**

26:29. The element in the Eucharist which was probably of the greatest importance for Jesus and for the earliest Christian community was the conviction that the meal which Jesus was celebrating with his followers was a foretaste of the full fellowship to be experienced when the kingdom of God has come and all God's people are gathered into one. Then **the fruit of the vine** will be drunk once more in **my Father's kingdom.**

26:30-35. *Jesus in Gethsemane.* Leaving Jerusalem after the meal, Jesus and the disciples go out E of the city across the Kidron Valley, which separates the city from the **Mount of Olives.** Jesus predicts that the disciples will desert him, in fulfillment of scripture (Zech. 13:7), but that they will be restored following his being **raised,** when he will **go before** (or precede) them **to Galilee.** Peter makes the idle boast that he will stand true to Jesus, but his claim is immediately discredited by Jesus' prediction of Peter's threefold denial. The promise of the appearance of the risen Lord in Galilee is one of 2 strands in the gospel tradition, the other of which reports the appearances as occurring in the vicinity of Jerusalem (Luke 24; John 20).

26:36-46. The meaning of the name **Gethsemane,** "olive press," suggests that it may have been a grove of olive trees of the sort still to be seen in this area on the W slope of the Mount of Olives. The vivid

Courtesy of Herbert G. May

View from the Garden of Gethsemane; in the distance the Muslim shrine "Dome of the Rock," completed A.D. 691, can be seen over the top of the wall surrounding the temple area

account of the struggle of Jesus points up the inability of the disciples to grasp the seriousness of the occasion, since they soon are **sleeping** (vs. 43). The possibility of our having here an eyewitness account of the struggle of Jesus is slim, since by definition no one was there to observe except the disciples, who were asleep. It is probably an imaginative account, but it does reflect accurately the issue that would have confronted Jesus under the circumstances: the temptation to avoid by flight the inevitable trial and death that he must have known awaited him. With the advent of the betrayer the movement of events is inexorable.

26:47-75. *The Seizure and Hearing by the Jewish*

Authorities. The group that arrests Jesus is a **crowd** sent by **the chief priests and the elders,** who together provided the membership for the sanhedrin, a kind of senate that was permitted by the Romans to exercise considerable authority. A false show of affection by Judas and a mistaken effort at protection by one of the disciples lead Jesus to declare, according to Matt.'s addition, that he will not invoke the support of **angels** in order to preserve himself from his enemies, since his death is so that **the scriptures** may **be fulfilled.** The entire group of disciples abandon him to his fate.

26:57-68. The sanhedrin is convened in the house of the high priest, **Caiaphas.** The only charge that can be lodged against Jesus is that he is going **to destroy the temple of God and to build it in three days.** To this Jesus offers no reply or defense. To the high priest's question as to whether he is **the Christ,** he responds with the same equivocal answer he had given to Judas: **You have said so** (cf. the unequivocal "I am" in Mark 14:62). And thereupon he turns to the prediction of the coming of **the Son of Man** (cf. 24:30; Ps. 110:1; Dan. 7:13), which is interpreted as a claim that he is the Son of man. The charge of **blasphemy** is brought against him, which was punishable by death at the hands of the Jews, by Roman agreement with the Jewish authorities of the time.

26:69-75. At this time **Peter,** under pressure from various members of the crowd, denies that he has had any acquaintance with Jesus. In adapting Mark 14:66-72 Matt. alters several details of the story—e.g. Peter is recognized by his N **accent.** Matt. emphasizes the bitterness of Peter's remorse (vs. 75).

27:1-26. *The Hearing Before Pilate and the Condemnation.* On the morning following the hearing before the sanhedrin, which would be still the day of Preparation for the Passover by Jewish reckoning, Jesus is turned over to **Pilate,** the provincial governor. Since A.D. 6 Rome had ruled Judea directly by governors, after Archelaus, son of Herod, had proved a hopelessly inefficient administrator.

27:11-18. Pilate's questions concern Jesus' political ambitions: **Are you the King of the Jews?** By this time Pilate had been forced on several occasions to put down incipient messianic revolutionary movements (cf. Luke 13:1). Although there is no record of such a practice from Jewish or Roman sources, the gospels report that Pilate had a custom of granting amnesty to a prisoner on the occasion of the Passover (vs. 15). The tradition hints that Barabbas was himself an insurrectionist (see on Mark 15:7), but Matt. describes him only as a **notorious prisoner.** In a few mss. of Matt. his name appears as Jesus Barabbas, and some scholars have argued for its probability.

27:19. Only in Matthew is there the report of the dream of Pilate's **wife,** which is presented as a divine warning that Jesus is innocent.

27:20-23. The crowd's choice is for the release of Barabbas, and they cry out for the crucifixion of Jesus. This was a mode of execution used by the Romans alone and would be appropriate for one charged with revolutionary aims.

27:24-26. Pilate accedes to their demand, even though no evidence is adduced to support the charge. He publicly discharges himself from responsibility for Jesus' death by washing his hands before the crowd. Matt. emphasizes that the Jews accept the responsibility, even though both the charge and the mode of execution are related to Roman rather than Jewish law. The bitter words he attributes to the Jews have caused endless harm in arousing anti-Jewish emotions: **His blood be on us and on our children.**

27:27-66. The Crucifixion and Burial. The **plaiting** and placing of the **crown of thorns,** as well as **the scarlet robe** and the **reed** as a mock scepter, point to the scorn of Jesus by the Roman soldiers as a kingly pretender. This confirms the impression that the historical basis for the death of Jesus was not ultimately the rejection of him and his message by Israel, but the Roman determination to execute all possible leaders of freedom movements among the Jewish nationalists.

27:32. Concerning the man who was **compelled to carry** Jesus' **cross** see on Mark 15:21.

27:33. The fact that the name **Golgotha** must be interpreted as **the place of a skull** shows that Matt. is writing for non-Semitic-speaking people. The name of the place might imply nothing more than an association of the spot with the dead, but it has been thought to be due to a domelike limestone outcropping that may have resembled a skull. The traditional site of the crucifixion and burial, now enclosed by the Church of the Holy Sepulcher, lay outside the walls of the city in Jesus' time, although included in what is known as the Old City of Jerusalem, the main outlines of which date from the time of the Roman Emperor Hadrian (*ca.* A.D. 135). See color map 13.

27:34-44. The soldiers offer Jesus a sedative in the form of **wine . . . mingled with gall.** Matt. uses "gall" in place of "myrrh" (Mark 15:23), probably under the influence of Ps. 69:21 ("They gave me poison [gall] for food, and . . . vinegar [sour wine] to drink"). The casting of lots for Jesus' garments corresponds to Ps. 22:18, and the derision of the passersby to Ps. 22:7. A taunt added by Matt. (vs. 43) accords with Ps. 22:8. The **two robbers . . . crucified with him** are actually insurrectionists, so that the ironic title **This is Jesus the King of the Jews** completes the picture of the Roman vengeance on those accused of fomenting political revolution. The taunting of the other condemned men follows the lines of Jewish objection to Jesus, however—his claims about destroying and rebuilding the temple and about being the Messiah. **The chief priests, with the scribes and elders,** in their mockery unwittingly bear witness to who Jesus really is—**the King of Israel, . . . the Son of God.**

27:45-50. There is **darkness over all the land** (or the whole earth) from noon until 3 P.M. Jesus' cry to God—which is given by Matt. in a form somewhat imperfectly transliterated from Hebrew (**Eli, Eli, lama sabachthani**) instead of the Aramaic of Mark 15:34—is a quotation from Ps. 22:1. Even in the depths of a sense of abandonment Jesus nevertheless cries out to God. The crowd, misunderstanding, thinks he is calling for **Elijah** to come and deliver him from his agony. The **vinegar** is probably the sedative of vs. 34, though a different Greek word is used. Jesus uttered a loud cry and, Matt. implies, **yielded up his spirit** by an act of will, rather than merely dying of exhaustion, as was the usual case with those who were crucified.

27:51-54. At the moment of Jesus' death, Matt. reports, not only was the temple **curtain . . . torn in two,** but an earthquake shook the city and opened **tombs,** from which there came forth the departed **saints.** This group of incidents is full of symbolic meaning. The torn temple curtain suggests the opening up by Jesus' death of the way into the presence of God, who, according to Jewish beliefs, was invisibly present behind the curtain of the temple and accessible directly only to the high priest. The appearance of the saints is a foretaste of the resurrection, although it is odd to have it occur even before the resurrection of Jesus, who was called by Paul "the first fruits of those who had fallen asleep" (I Cor. 15:20). The pagan centurion acknowledges what the religious leaders cannot see: **Truly this was the Son of God!**

27:55-61. The only witnesses of the crucifixion from among Jesus' followers are the group of **women . . . from Galilee,** who watch **from afar.** But just before sunset, when the feast day would begin, **Joseph,** from the village of **Arimathea** in the hill country NW of Jerusalem, received permission from Pilate to remove the body. This was an act of piety, since the Jews believed that a dead body exposed polluted the sabbath. Hastily, and without adequate preparation of the body, Jesus was placed in a tomb that Joseph owned, recently hewn from the soft limestone of the hills on which Jerusalem stands. The women saw the place and presumably made plans to return at the earliest possible moment to complete the preparation of the body, which could not be carried out on the sabbath just then beginning.

27:62-66. The chronological reference here is problematical, since it would suggest that the Jewish leaders approached Pilate on the sabbath itself with their request for a guard at the tomb. The story, which is found only in Matt., is probably not historical, but arose at a time when Jews were charging that the resurrection claims of the Christians were a hoax and that the disciples had actually stolen the body of Jesus. It was introduced to show that even official action by Pilate could not have prevented the Resurrection from occurring.

28:1-15. The Women at the Tomb. But, Matthew continues, in spite of all precautions, when the women arrived on Sunday morning to complete the preparation of the body, Jesus had already been raised. Vss. 2-4, found only in Matt., describe the miraculous events that followed the Resurrection. Instead of a young man in white at the tomb (Mark 16:5), Matt. reports **an angel** descending **from heaven,** an earthquake, the stone **rolled back,** the swooning of **the guards,** and the understandable astonishment of the women. The stone was shaped like a millstone and placed in a groove in such a way that gravity would cause it to roll down and block the doorlike opening to the tomb. The purpose in rolling back the stone is to allow the women to **see** that Jesus **has risen,** rather than to allow Jesus to come out.

28:7-10. There follows the instruction, recalling 26:32, to return to **Galilee,** to which Jesus is even now **going.** There the appearances of the risen Christ will occur. There is, however, a brief encounter between the risen Christ and the women, but its net effect is to underscore the importance of the disciples' return to Galilee.

28:11-15. The attempt by the Jewish leaders to discredit the story of the Resurrection builds on the earlier report of the guard at the tomb (27:62-66). Since the soldiers were by this testimony asleep when the body was removed, their word could not be credited in any case. Like the earlier part of the guard incident, it arises in a situation of mutual hostility between Jew and Christian.

28:16-20*a*. The Commissioning of the Disciples. Here, more than anywhere else in his gospel, Matt. discloses the main themes of his interest. The disciples have returned to Galilee. That, even when they encounter him risen from the dead, some are still unbelieving (vs. 17) accords with Matt.'s picture of the church as a mixture of faith and unfaith (see also on Mark 16:8). Jesus now appears as a figure of complete **authority in heaven and on earth.** It is he as the authoritative one who sends forth the disciples. Their task is threefold: (*a*) Going among **all nations,** seeking to **make disciples,** i.e. to summon those who will follow Jesus and be the bearers of his word and his authority. (*b*) **Baptizing** the new disciples in the full trinitarian **name** of God: **Father . . . Son . . . Holy Spirit.** This is one of the few places in the NT where the names of the Trinity are explicitly used. (*c*) **Teaching** obedience to Jesus' commandments in their entirety.

28:20*b*. The commission ends with a promise of the unceasing invisible presence of the authoritative Lord with his disciples **to the close of the age.** Then, as Matt. has already informed his readers elsewhere in his gospel, the Son of man will be visibly present to his people in the kingdom of God. Meanwhile, both their responsibilities and their resources have been made available by the risen Lord for the fulfillment of their appointed task.

THE GOSPEL ACCORDING TO MARK

Lindsey P. Pherigo

Introduction

Modern scholarship is in broad agreement with the 2nd-cent. traditions about this gospel: that it was written by a man named Mark, a missionary companion of both Peter and Paul; that it was written in Rome, far away from local traditions about Jesus; that it dates from after the death of Peter (A.D. 64), at least 35 years after the events described. This gospel represents, therefore, a collection of traditions gathered, arranged, and edited by one who did not participate in the events personally.

Relation to Matt. and Luke. Literary analysis of the agreements and differences among the first 3 gospels has established that Mark was the earliest of the 3 and was used independently by both Matt. and Luke as their major source of information about the life of Jesus (see "The Literary Relations Among the Gospels," pp. 1129-35). This 2-fold reliance on Mark verifies its general historical reliability. The fact that the 2 later gospels have incorporated practically all of it in their accounts indicates that they intended to replace Mark rather than simply to supplement it. The changes introduced by Matt. and Luke are noted in the following commentary. They show how this earliest gospel was understood in its own day and help us to grasp its original purpose.

Date and Occasion. The tradition that Mark put together his gospel after the death of Peter on the one hand and the manner of its use by Matt. and Luke on the other limit the date of writing to the period from A.D. 64 to *ca.* 75.

Taking the tradition to imply a time very soon after Peter's death, many have assumed a date during Nero's persecution of the Roman Christians (A.D. 64-68) and accordingly deduced that Mark's chief motive in writing was to encourage his fellow church members facing this crisis. His reporting of Jesus' teaching about the costs of discipleship (e.g. 8:34-38; 9:35; 10:29-31, 35-45) and the large space he devotes to Jesus' own example of martyrdom are cited as confirmation. This emphasis no doubt reflects persecution, in recent memory if not as a present peril, but it is not pervasive enough to explain the whole gospel.

Many also have sought for evidence that Mark knew of the Romans' capture of Jerusalem and destruction of the temple in A.D. 70 and, finding no unmistakable allusions, have assumed that he must have written before this date. It is not certain, however, that Mark would necessarily allude to this event if he knew of it; and in fact there may be allusions to it in 12:9; 13:2, 14 (cf. 9:1; 13:30). Thus the

fact that Mark's work had circulated long enough to survive the attempts of Matt. and Luke to replace it provides the only sure limit to its date.

During the whole period in which this gospel could have been written, Christianity was in transition from its original home in the Semitic culture of Palestinian Judaism to the Gentile culture of the Roman Empire. The older Christianity held tenaciously to the traditional Jewish customs (such as circumcision and the food laws), but the newer (Gentile) version abandoned these entirely. More significantly, the older Christianity understood Jesus mainly under the Jewish concept of the Messiah, whereas the newer found more meaning in him as a divine being, the Son of God, Lord, and Savior. The older view clung to the Semitic concept of religion as obedience to God's will, whereas the newer openly abandoned this as hopeless by man's own effort and espoused a religion which redeemed man from his slavery to sin by an act of God's grace (the Christ event).

Against this transition background Mark presents Jesus from the newer (Gentile Christian) viewpoint (see below on 2:26; 6:14, 17; 7:1-8, 14-23, 31; 8:10; 14:12). Although not strictly Pauline in his terminology, Mark reflects an understanding of the problem of man, the person of Christ, and the nature of salvation quite closely related to that found in the letters of Paul. These letters, therefore, as parallel expressions of early Gentile Christianity, help us more than any other part of the NT to understand the religious message of Mark. Matt. and Luke repeat the story of Jesus from a more conservative position.

All cultural transitions are marked by tension between the conservatives (defending the older) and the liberals (introducing the newer). Since the 12 disciples of Jesus became the leaders of the conservatives, Mark shared Paul's coolness and reserve toward their authority (cf. I Cor. 9:1-18; Gal. 2:1-10). He makes it plain to the reader that the 12 never understood Jesus properly and therefore are not the best guides. This is not a frank and naïve report of their weaknesses in a period before apostolic veneration began; Mark is helping the reader to understand why the view of Jesus among the conservative Jewish Christians is so unsatisfactory to the Gentile Christian church. Matt. and Luke systematically alter this portrayal of the 12 to give readers confidence in their leadership (see below on 4:13, 38, 41; 6:37, 50-51; 8:4, 14-21, 27-30, 31-33; 9:2, 10, 30-32, 34; 10:35-45).

Authorship. Tradition has given the author of this

gospel the name Mark. From early times he has been identified with John Mark, kinsman of Barnabas (Acts 12:12, 25; 13:5, 13; 15:37-39; Col. 4:10; II Tim. 4:11; Philem. 24; I Pet. 5:13); and many scholars today accept this identification, largely on the basis that a gospel would not be attributed to so remote a witness unless he was actually the author. However, if a gospel author named Mark was otherwise unknown, there would be a strong tendency to identify him with any known early Christian of that name, even one with so little authority as John Mark.

Careful study of the book itself makes it difficult to believe that the author was John Mark of Jerusalem, because he seems to treat both Palestine and Palestinian Judaism as an outsider. His attitude toward the 12 and his reflection of the Pauline viewpoint, as noted above, make it probable that he was a prominent member of the Gentile Christian community. His background must have been that of liberal Hellenistic Judaism rather than that of Jerusalem. The strong Semitic coloring of some of his writing can be attributed to the sources he used rather than to his own experience.

There is no reason to doubt a tradition that the author derived much of his information about Jesus from the sermons of Peter, but it must be remembered that he presents this information from a Gentile Christian point of view, and that he also includes much that did not come from apostolic memory at all. In Gentile Christianity a great deal of reliance was placed on learning of Jesus from OT statements believed to be about him.

For Further Study: Benjamin Bacon, *The Beginnings of the Gospel Story*, 1909; somewhat out-of-date, but still very helpful. B. H. Branscomb, *The Gospel of Mark*, 1937; a useful commentary on the Moffatt translation. F. C. Grant, *The Earliest Gospel*, 1943; very helpful on the background of Mark. F. C. Grant in *IB*, 1951. Vincent Taylor, *The Gospel According to St. Mark*, 1952; best modern technical commentary. Sherman Johnson, *The Gospel According to St. Mark*, 1960; best modern nontechnical commentary, with an original translation. C. E. B. Cranfield in *IDB*, 1962.

I. THE BEGINNINGS

A. INTRODUCTION TO THE BOOK (1:1)

Mark begins his book very abruptly with a terse titlelike phrase. It is not a complete sentence. It can be taken as the introduction to the whole book, but more likely it was intended simply to introduce the first part of the story, the work of John the Baptist. Some ancient manuscripts have the descriptive phrase **the Son of God** at the end, and others do not have it; but whatever its origin it expresses well the main viewpoint of Mark about Jesus. In this book Jesus of Nazareth is not merely the Jewish Messiah (translated into Greek as the **Christ**); he is the strong Son of God, able to deliver us from the powers of evil around us that hold us in bondage to them. On **the gospel** see below on vss. 14-15.

B. JOHN THE BAPTIST (1:2-11)

1:2-3. *The Introduction to John.* The story of John is introduced by quoting OT prophecy. The quotation shows that Mark was apparently not a careful scholar of the Hebrew Bible. He was probably writing on the basis of popular quotations already in circulation in Christian communities and did not check his references very carefully. His main point is quite sound, but he has made 2 interesting mistakes in presenting it.

In the first place Mark has put together 2 separate quotations and attributed both to Isaiah. Actually the first quotation seems to be a free version of Mal. 3:1 (although the first part of it is exactly like the LXX version of Exod. 23:20), and the 2nd one is from Isa. 40:3. In Matt. and Luke this error is corrected (cf. Matt. 3:3; Luke 3:4); they use the Exod.-Mal. quotation later on in the story and do not identify it with Isaiah (Matt. 11:10; Luke 7:27).

In the 2nd place the use to which the 2nd quotation is put reflects unfavorably on Mark's understanding of Hebrew poetry. The main trait of this poetry is not sound rhyme, like our poetry, but idea rhyme. Everything is usually said twice; the 2nd line repeats, in different words, the idea of the first line (see the Intro. to Pss.). Thus the OT form of this vs. in Isa. 40:3, as set up in poetical form, reads:

A voice cries:
"'In the wilderness ²prepare ³the way ⁴of the Lord,
¹In the desert ²make straight ³a highway ⁴for our God."

As Mark uses it, however, the phrase **in the wilderness** is taken out of the poem itself and made into a phrase describing **the voice of one crying.** The change makes the prophecy fit John more closely.

This became a standardized treatment of this quotation in the early church, and may already have become part of the tradition before Mark wrote his gospel. The idea behind the original poem is the custom of an oriental monarch traveling over territory where there was no road. Before him went a crew of workers, making the rough places smooth enough for the king's chariot (cf. Isa. 40:4). Everybody should be preparing the way for the coming of the Lord. This is what John did for Jesus and why the early church felt that this scripture fitted John so well. It seemed perfectly justifiable to make it fit a bit better.

1:4-8. *The Ministry of John.* This is the earliest account of John and his work. Josephus, a Jewish historian of the last part of the first cent., wrote of John that he "was a good man, and commanded the Jews to exercise virtue, both as to righteousness towards one another, and piety towards God, and so to come to baptism" (Antiquities of the Jews XVIII.

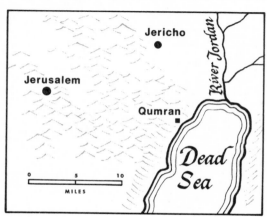

5.2). John's baptism was **a baptism of repentance for the forgiveness of sins.** As such it was very much like the old prophetic message. The exact manner of baptism that John used is nowhere described. Neither is it known how it arose. It seems probable that it was not introduced by John but was already a familiar custom. It probably signified a cleansing or purification, and it was most likely a regular immersion, rather than a pouring or a sprinkling.

1:6. The description of John is that of a simple ascetic. **Camel's hair** may mean either a skin from a camel or a fabric woven from camel's hair. The latter was common and cheap, and so is more probable. The **leather girdle around his waist** reflects the description of Elijah in the LXX of II Kings 1:8, where exactly the same rare phrase used here of John is used of Elijah. In fact this description of Elijah's characteristic appearance so closely parallels Mark's description of John that it must be assumed that Elijah established (or illustrates) a prophetic costume which John accepted as his own. If not, then the Christian view of John as the forerunner of Jesus naturally assumed that he dressed in accord with his role. The link with Elijah is more basic than one of costume, however (see below on 9:13). Eating **locusts and wild honey** is common among the poor bedouin of Palestine and Arabia.

1:7. The teaching of John is given only in the barest outline. All the other gospels give more attention to this. The description could easily be predicted in the light of John's role as the messianic forerunner. **After me comes he who is mightier than I** is simply putting his basic role into proclamation form. The word translated "mightier" is one often associated with great supernatural beings. It is used to describe the power of Satan in 3:27. In Rev. 10:1; 18:21 it is used to describe angelic power, and in Rev. 18:8 to refer to the power of God.

1:8. The words **I have baptized you** certainly make it probable that baptism was something that John did for (or to) the one being baptized, rather than something which they did for themselves. **With water** is more explicit than the underlying Greek text; "in water" would be equally correct and fits baptism by immersion better. The contrast between the baptism in water of John and the baptism in the Holy Spirit of Jesus has some puzzling aspects. Does Mark suggest that Spirit baptism will replace water baptism? Does he mean that Jesus will add the Spirit to the water-baptism ritual? There is some confusion here in the earliest records, and it is not clear whether Jesus himself practiced water baptism (as affirmed in John 3:22; 4:1, but denied in John 4:2), or whether the practice began after the Resurrection with the coming of the Holy Spirit. The origins of Christian baptism, unfortunately, are obscure.

1:9-11. *The Baptism of Jesus.* Jesus' baptism by John marks the real beginning of the gospel story. What Jesus did before that event is of no interest to Mark. The baptism itself is one of those parts of the gospel story that seems most historically sound. It was a source of embarrassment to the early Christians on 2 counts and therefore is not likely to be the result of a development within Christian piety.

One embarrassing aspect stems from the nature of John's baptism. All accounts agree that it was a baptism "of repentance for the forgiveness of sins" (1:4; cf. Matt. 3:6; Luke 3:3). If Jesus was baptized by John, then the inference is that he too had repented and was seeking forgiveness of his sins. Since Christians began very early to believe that Jesus had been sinless (cf. Heb. 4:15; I Pet. 2:22), his coming to John for baptism began to need explanation. Matt. is the only gospel in the NT that attempts to deal directly with this problem (see on Matt. 3:14-15). The Gospel According to the Hebrews, which now exists only in fragments but was an important 2nd-cent. extracanonical gospel, has Jesus say, before going along with his brothers to John, "Wherein have I sinned, that I should go and be baptized of him? unless peradventure this very thing that I have said is a sin of ignorance." Neither attempt—Matt.'s or that of the Gospel According to the Hebrews—is very successful.

The other embarrassing aspect of Jesus' baptism by John is that it puts Jesus in an inferior position to John. John's religious movement and Jesus' continued to exist as separate and even rival groups (see below on 2:18-22). In this situation the disciples of John had the advantage of claiming that their master was the superior one because he had baptized Jesus. The 4th Gospel is especially sensitive to this situation. Not only does it represent John as expressly denying all claims to superiority (1:20; 3:28) and acknowledging his inferiority (3:29), but it even omits any account of the baptism.

1:10. The word translated **immediately** is a common connective in Mark, being used 41 times. It is not to be taken as necessarily suggesting speedy action, or a rapid succession of events. Rather it is primarily a literary device and usually expresses mere sequence. The fact that **he came up out of the water** makes it probable that the baptism took place in the Jordan River itself, rather than on its banks.

He saw (i.e. Jesus saw) by the most natural reading means that in Mark's view no one else shared this experience of Jesus. The voice in vs. 11 is also apparently addressed to him alone. That it was a personal religious experience of Jesus seems to be required by the historical evidence that John was not aware of Jesus' messiahship, according to the views of all the first 3 gospels (cf. Matt. 11:2-6; Luke 7:18-23).

The heavens opened is a fairly mild translation of a rather violent Greek word meaning "split apart." It was commonly believed among Jews of this period that direct communication from heaven was quite rare and involved a rending of the barrier between heaven and earth (cf. John 1:51; 12:27-29; Acts 7:56; Rev. 4:1; 11:19; 19:11). **The Spirit descending upon him like a dove,** the 2nd thing he saw, also reads like a personal experience. The symbolism of the dove as representing the Holy Spirit is obscure. It is interesting to note that both Matt. (3:16) and Luke (3:22), in retelling the story of Jesus' baptismal experience, describe it as an objective event.

1:11. The **voice** that **came from heaven** is a special, but familiar, feature of Jewish piety. Note that the voice is addressed to Jesus himself, not to the bystanders (as in Matt. 3:17). This type of voice is a familiar part of a visionary experience and occurs again on the Mount of Transfiguration (see below on 9:2-8). A striking example of this type of thing is the experience of Paul on the road to Damascus (Acts 9:1-9); it includes both "seeing" and "hearing" and is later described as a "heavenly vision" (Acts

26:19). What the voice said to Jesus recalls Ps. 2:7, which is one of the "enthronement" psalms used during the coronation of a king of Israel. It also recalls Isa. 42:1, the consecration of God's servant. It is not, however, an exact quotation of anything in the OT.

C. The Temptation of Jesus (1:12-13)

The temptation of Jesus is only briefly told in Mark. It is greatly elaborated in both Matt. and Luke, but eliminated entirely in the 4th Gospel. It finds a parallel in the life of many a saint. That the newly baptized convert entered immediately into temptation was certainly true in Mark's time.

1:12. The **wilderness** is not identified and may be a symbolic name for the home of evil spirits.

1:13. The number **forty** is an expression commonly used in the OT to indicate a fairly long period of time. **Tempted by Satan** is the customary late Jewish understanding of temptation. Satan was God's enemy, and God and Satan were engaged in an all-out war, in which Satan tried mightily to increase his forces of rebellion. This ancient view of the temptation process would be explained by most people today in other terms, but the underlying reality is just as much a problem now as it was then. The **wild beasts** and the **angels** are symbolic of the personnel of the opposing armies of Satan and God.

II. The Ministry in Galilee (1:14-8:26)

A. Introduction to the Ministry of Jesus (1:14-15)

1:14. The first 3 gospels make it plain that the ministries of John and Jesus were successive, that Jesus did not begin his preaching and religious work until **after John was arrested.** This is easier to fit in with the Christian interpretation of the work of John as a forerunner of Jesus. The report of the 4th Gospel (John 3:22-24; 4:1) that their ministries overlapped is more difficult, but it is likely to be more historical in the light of subsequent events. **Galilee** was the scene of most of Jesus' ministry.

Preaching the gospel is a favorite Markan expression (cf. 1:1; 8:35; 10:29; 13:10; 14:9) and typical of the viewpoint of early Gentile Christianity. The "gospel" is not a compendium of teachings by Jesus but the proclamation that God has acted in Christ to save mankind. It is a message about Jesus rather than a message by him. Only in the 4th Gospel are these 2 united so that Jesus is represented as preaching a message about himself.

1:15. The proclamation that **the time is fulfilled** refers to the common understanding of the time that God planned to end the present age and begin a new one. The old age of strife and evil and opposition to God would be replaced by **the kingdom of God.** This great event is the theme of all apocalyptic books, such as Rev. (see "The Apocalyptic Literature," pp. 1106-09). Jesus not only shared this eschatological hope (i.e. a hope that the end of this evil age would surely come) but believed that according to God's schedule the time for accomplishing it was in his own day (see below on 9:1). **The time** of waiting **is fulfilled, and the Kingdom of God is at hand.**

Repent is not a characteristic theme in Mark (or in Paul, or in Gentile Christianity in general). Repentance implies real freedom on the part of man, whereas early Gentile Christianity proclaimed Christ as God's rescue act, redeeming lost and helpless mankind from its slavery to sin. Repentance is a major theme in Luke's presentation of Jesus' teachings, but the message of salvation there is more closely related to a Jewish obedience-centered religion. In contrast, Mark proclaims a strong Son of God who overpowers our enemy for us. **Believe in the gospel** lies close to the heart of Mark's message to the reader. The story of Jesus is the gospel; to be a Christian and to know redemption is to believe in this story about God's gracious rescue act.

B. The Call of the First Disciples (1:16-20)

Mark's version of the call of the first disciples is the most popular one. It is repeated without significant change in Matt. Its popularity is due not simply to its use in Matt. but to the fact that from the beginning it has been useful to preachers. It is not only an account of the first disciples but also a picture of the ideal response of every man. When the voice of Jesus calls, we should drop everything and respond. Note the double emphasis: vss. 16-18 make the point first, then vss. 19-20 repeat it (cf. also 2:14). Luke's version (5:1-11) expands the story with other material that appears elsewhere in the other gospels, and John (1:35-51) has an account which is distinctly different from both Mark's and Luke's. The example of instantaneous response is apparently what Mark is emphasizing.

1:16. The generalized reference to **by the Sea of Galilee** is characteristic of Mark's geographical notices. **Simon** is later called Peter (see below on 3:16).

1:17. The **fishers of men** saying is the key to the whole account and was probably better known in the early church than the exact details of the call of the first disciples.

C. First Activities (1:21-2:12)

1:21-28. *The Beginnings in Capernaum.* The very first event of Jesus' ministry, as Mark presents it, is one that expresses his authority. In the introduction to the story Jesus appears as **one who had authority,** in contrast to **the scribes.** The Greek word for "authority" means lit. "out from himself." Jesus did not depend on the authority of some previous expert but was the expert himself. He did not quote the "authorities" but acted like one himself. By this opening event Mark wishes to inform the reader that Jesus was not an ordinary human but a super-human being; he was indeed the Son of God, come to rescue man from the demonic forces which enslave him.

1:21. The city of **Capernaum,** on the NW shore of the Sea of Galilee (see color map 15), was apparently the chosen headquarters of Jesus' mission (see below on 2:1). The gospels all witness to Jesus' loyalty to the **synagogue** of his time. He apparently made no effort to establish a new type of worship but worked only to purify the old.

1:22. The **scribes** were the experts in the laws of the first 5 books of the Bible. As such they were often consulted by the people when the authority of Moses was desired on a question.

1:23. The term **unclean spirit** is common in the NT for a demon. Demon possession was widely held responsible for many of man's ills in Jesus' time. Humans were at the mercy of these demons, unless under the protection of some stronger spiritual power. Jesus' own belief cannot now be recovered, but in any case his effectiveness in healing people who believed in demon possession would require that he seem to believe it also, whether or not he actually did.

1:24. The designation **Jesus of Nazareth** would certainly imply to the ancient reader that Jesus was born in Nazareth. In identifying a man by a place name, like "Saul of Tarsus" or "Joseph of Arimathea," the custom of the times was to use his birthplace, not his present residence. Mark (and John; see esp. John 7:41-42) knew nothing of the Bethlehem tradition found in Matt. and Luke. There is a possibility, however, that "of Nazareth" (lit. "the Nazarene") is not a place name reference at all, but a party name, like "Simon the Zealot."

Have you come to destroy us? is the basic question. Mark's answer is clear: yes, he has. In fact, it probably should be read, not as a question at all, but as an exclamatory declaration, a defiant cry, parallel in form to I Kings 17:18.

The Holy One of God is an excellent and appropriate title for Jesus. It shows again that Jesus is a superhuman person, and the whole reported dialogue is intended by Mark to reveal clearly to the reader what the contemporaries of the event did not recognize at all. All the way through this gospel only the demons recognize Jesus as he really is. By means of the dialogue with demons the reader is kept fully informed.

1:25. The rebuke of Jesus is not intended to be a denial of his title "the Holy One of God," but rather a suppression of it. **Be silent** is Jesus' constant command to the demons who recognize him. This is Mark's answer to the pressing question of his own day: "Why wasn't Jesus recognized as the Son of God during his earthly lifetime?" He was recognized, Mark says, but only by the demons, and he silenced them.

1:28. The vagueness of **the surrounding region of Galilee** is characteristic of Mark's geographical notices.

1:29-31. *Healing Simon Peter's Mother-in-Law.* This healing of Simon's mother-in-law is a 2nd example of Jesus' power. He does not rely on magical formulas that bring some outside supernatural force into the situation, but he himself is the power to heal.

1:29. The natural assumption is that **Simon and Andrew** had their home in Capernaum. The fact that his early disciples lived there may have been a factor in Jesus' apparent decision to make Capernaum his headquarters (see below on 2:1).

1:30. That Simon's mother-in-law lived with him makes it highly probable that his wife did also. Becoming a disciple of Jesus, therefore, did not necessarily mean the repudiation of normal human relationships. Simon Peter's wife seems to have accompanied him on his later apostolic journeys, as did the wives of the other apostles (cf. I Cor. 9:5).

1:32-34. *Other Healings.* These 2 specific healing incidents are followed by a statement of healings in general. Some of these are exorcisms, others are not. In the exorcisms Jesus characteristically **would not permit the demons to speak, because they knew him.**

1:35-39. *Departure from Capernaum.* In general this is an account of the extension of Jesus' ministry into all of Galilee. He was not merely a local healer and teacher in Capernaum.

1:35. The **lonely place** to which Jesus retired was not the wilderness, for the country around ancient Capernaum was probably cultivated.

1:38. The natural effect of this vs., taken alone, would be to suggest that Jesus felt that his ministry to health problems was crowding out his preaching, but the next vs. makes this unlikely. What does Jesus mean when he says, **That is why I came out?** Does he mean to explain why he left (came out of) Capernaum and went to the other towns of Galilee? Luke understands it differently and makes it refer to the basic purpose of Jesus' ministry (Luke 4:43). The former meaning is most harmonious with Mark's overall viewpoint, the latter with Luke's.

1:40-45. *Healing a Leper.* It is noteworthy that Mark's first emphasis is on Jesus' power to heal. Who Jesus was, rather than what he taught, is the main interest of Mark.

1:41. The phrase **moved with pity** is not nearly so simple as it seems. It is probably a substitution for an original "being angry," which is preserved in some of the ancient manuscripts. The phrase is omitted in both the later accounts (Matt. 8:3; Luke 5:13) as is any sign of emotion on the part of Jesus. If it did originally read "being angry," the meaning is obscure. That it was omitted by Matt. and Luke and changed to "moved with pity" in later copies of Mark suggests that it was as difficult for ancient interpreters as for us (see below on 3:5).

1:42. The disease **leprosy** was not diagnosed precisely in ancient times; the term covered a variety of skin diseases and blemishes (cf. Lev. 13-14). It is hopeless to attempt a diagnosis of this man's ailment now.

1:44. The admonition to **say nothing to any one** does not reflect the concern of Jesus (in Mark) to keep secret his true identity, but is intended to put limits on his popularity as a healer. Spiritual healers were relatively common in those days, and the curing of leprosy would not automatically cause the healer to be regarded as a supernatural being.

1:45. Jesus' popularity as a healer becomes so great that he cannot **openly enter a town.**

2:1-12. *Healing a Paralytic.* This is a complex healing story. As literature it seems to be a combination of 2 stories. The first story, a healing miracle, is more complete (vss. 1-5a, 11-12). The 2nd (incomplete; vss. 5b-10) is inserted into the first somewhat after the manner of 5:21-43 (where vss. 25-34 are inserted). The 2nd story here is controlled by a theological interest, i.e. the power of Jesus to forgive sins. It is primarily a dialogue between Jesus and his enemies, the scribes. The first story is set in his Capernaum home, where he is surrounded by his followers and disciples. The original setting of the 2nd story is now lost, but it was probably a public healing of another paralytic, hence the later confusion of the 2 accounts. The combination is repeated in both Matt. (9:1-8) and Luke (5:17-26).

2:1. The idiom **at home** (lit. "in a house") seems to mean that Jesus was in the house where he lived. Scholars are divided in interpreting this as Simon's house (based on 1:29-31) or Jesus' own house (the more natural meaning of the Greek; see below on 2:15 and 2:17).

2:4. The exact meaning of **they removed the roof** is obscure; ancient interpreters were as puzzled as modern scholars. Cf. Luke's view (5:19) and Matt.'s omission of it.

2:5a. The **faith** of the men who brought the paralytic is emphasized, rather than the paralytic's faith. This first story continues at vs. 11.

2:5b. This is the only use in Mark of **my son** (lit. "child") as a term of address. Although the term is used elsewhere in Luke, it is somewhat strange that Luke's parallel (5:20) here changes "child" to the more impersonal "man." This suggests fear that the use of "my son" might be cited to justify the charge of blasphemy which follows, inferring that Jesus was now claiming the role of the heavenly Father.

To say **your sins are forgiven** as a healing formula implies an association between sin and sickness. This was certainly traditional in Judaism (cf. esp. Ps. 38), but it is not Mark's intention to raise this problem. Here it is simply a question of Jesus' authority and his power (vs. 10). Luke reports teachings of Jesus that deny a causal relationship between sin and calamity (Luke 13:1-5). Perhaps in this story the paralytic is under the old view.

2:7. In Mark's theology Jesus is the incarnation of God's Spirit, as described in 1:9-11, and therefore **can forgive sins.** In Jewish eyes this would be regarded as **blasphemy.** As the Son of man coming to judge the world (implied in passages like 8:38; 9:1; 13:26, but plainly stated in Matt. 19:28), he clearly has the authority to forgive sins now.

2:10. The phrase **Son of man** is an old Jewish idiom meaning simply "man," as illustrated best in the poetry of Ps. 8:4 or in Ezek. 11:2. In later Judaism, however, it came to be a special term for a superhuman being coming on the clouds of heaven to deliver the righteous from the hands of their enemies (cf. Dan. 7:13-14; I Enoch 46; 62). It seems to be used in this latter sense here.

D. First Conflicts (2:13-3:6)

2:13-14. *The Call of Levi.* The call of Levi follows the pattern of 1:16-20; Jesus calls and there is immediate and unquestioning response. The identification of this disciple is difficult. He does not appear in any of the official lists of the 12 (see below on 3:13-19). Identified here as **the son of Alphaeus** (lit. "the one belonging to Alphaeus"), he may be related to, or the same as, "James the son of Alphaeus" of 3:18. Luke retains the name "Levi" but not "the son of Alphaeus" (Luke 5:27). Matt. replaces "Levi" by "Matthew" (9:9) and does not mention Alphaeus. Were Levi and James brothers? Are they supposed to be the same? Are Matthew and Levi the same? Are all 3 the same? There is also a possible connection between Levi and Thaddaeus (3:18). That there is considerable confusion in the manuscripts where these names occur shows that it has been a problem from the earliest times.

2:15-17. *Association with Sinners.* The calling of a tax collector into the disciple group is here naturally coupled with a popular story about Jesus' reply to those who criticized his association with **tax collectors and sinners.** The story seems to belong later in his ministry than Mark has placed it, because it refers to his **disciples** as **many** (only 5 have been mentioned to this point).

2:15. The Greek for **sat** is "reclined," in the Gentile eating style familiar to Mark. **In his house** may mean Jesus' house (see above on 2:1) or Levi's house; the Greek is as ambiguous as the English. Luke 5:29 interprets Mark to mean Levi's house, but the presence of scribes there is not likely. **Sinners** here are Jews who are not scrupulous in observance of the details of the ritual law, rather than criminals or moral degenerates. The RSV punctuation is possible, but more natural is the reading "and his disciples, for they were many, and they followed him." The awkwardness here is a trait of Mark's style.

2:16. The phrase **the scribes of the Pharisees** is used only here; "scribes of the Pharisees' party" (Acts 23:9) expresses the idea more accurately. They would not necessarily have to be present at the dinner and probably should be thought of as criticizing him among themselves. The whole matter of table fellowship was a problem in the early church, and the Gentile Christians were most sensitive here (cf. Gal. 2:11-12).

2:17. This saying of Jesus was probably proverbial and is merely applied here to this situation. It fits the call of a sinner into the disciple group (vss. 13-14) but not the question of eating with sinners. Cf. Matt. 9:13; Luke 5:32. **To call** probably does not refer to table fellowship at all; Luke interprets it as a call "to repentance." If "call" does mean "invite to dinner," then Jesus would have to be acting as host, presumably in his own house.

2:18-22. *Jesus and Fasting.* To a short incident about fasting (vss. 18-20) Mark adds 2 sayings that symbolize the relationship between Christianity and Judaism (vss. 21-22). The fasting question reveals that John's disciples and Jesus' are independent groups, following different customs (cf. Matt. 9:14; John 4:1; Acts 19:1-5). It also reflects a tradition that Jesus and his disciples were not ascetic (cf. Matt. 11:18-19; Luke 7:33-34).

2:18. The words **and people came** (lit. "and they came") are typically ambiguous. Matt. (9:14) interprets the questioners to be John's disciples and rewords accordingly. Luke (5:33) associates them with "the Pharisees and their scribes" (5:30) of the previous incident, thus welding the 2 units into one. **Fasting** may refer to a general ascetic practice, but likely it refers to one of the special periods of fasting in the Jewish calendar, abandoned by Gentile Christianity.

2:19-20. This answer is expressed in the language of the early Christian community and from the viewpoint of this community, which now has some established fast days of its own. The problem being faced is: Why does the church have fast days if Jesus and his disciples did not observe them? The answer is that Christian fasting is a memorial of his death and therefore was inappropriate in the days before his death.

2:21-22. In these 2 parallel analogies there is a recognition that Christianity and Judaism are incompatible. This is the typical Gentile Christian view (cf. e.g. Rom. 7:4-6; Gal. 3:10-14). It is too radical for Matt. and Luke; see their independent additions (Matt. 9:17; Luke 5:39). Mark's use of these sayings, however, is probably not the way Jesus used them, for Jesus was not this radical either (cf. Rom. 15:8). The original purpose is now lost.

2:23-28. *Sabbath Violation.* This story intends to

show in another way the difference between the religion of Jesus and Jewish legalism (a major interest of Gentile Christianity). It is officially a sabbath violation story, although the unlawfulness of the action described is not clear. The historical inaccuracies (see below on vs. 26) show further the Gentile Christian background of Mark. The story seems to culminate in the strongest anti-sabbath statement in the gospels, omitted in both the parallel versions.

2:23. The action is not clear (in the Greek); the manuscripts have many different scribal "corrections," or "improvements." Matt. (12:1) makes the offense plucking and eating; Luke (6:1) makes it a kind of crude threshing ("rubbing them in their hands"). The Pharisees permitted "plucking and eating" in case of need, but not harvesting or threshing. Perhaps Mark is caricaturing Pharisaic legalism.

2:26. The reference **when Abiathar was high priest** has 2 inaccuracies: (*a*) There was no high priest in David's time; this office developed much later. (*b*) The OT account (I Sam. 21:1-6) gives the name of the priest as Ahimelech. Matt. 12:4; Luke 6:4 correct these errors. Mark characteristically reflects less accurate knowledge of Palestine, the OT, and Jewish affairs in general than Matt. and Luke.

2:27. This is a most remarkable statement, omitted from both parallel versions, that was certainly understood in early Gentile Christianity as laying the foundation for abandoning the sabbath entirely. The changeover from sabbath (Saturday in the Gentile calendar) to Sunday as the day of worship was accomplished by the early 2nd cent.

2:28. This seems to justify the action of Jesus on the special ground that he was privileged to do things on the sabbath that ordinary men should not.

3:1-6. *Healing the Withered Hand.* This is another sabbath violation story. There is no faith element but simply a deliberate healing to prove a point, somewhat after the manner of the Fourth Gospel. The stricter Pharisees permitted medical attention on the sabbath only when life was in danger.

3:4. The question of Jesus (preserved in Luke 6:9) becomes actual legislation in Matt. 12:12.

3:5. The phrase **with anger** is a sign of the emotional involvement of Jesus in this cause, and is omitted in Matt. 12:12; Luke 6:10 (see above on 1:41).

3:6. The name **Herodians** implies that they were partisans of Herod Antipas (see below on 6:14) and friends of the Herodian dynasty.

E. Editorial Summary (3:7-12)

This paragraph is a general statement of the popularity of Jesus at the height of his Galilean ministry.

3:7-8. These vss. list in succession the peoples attracted to Jesus. Not only Galileans but many from faraway places come to him. This is the first mention of Judeans as followers of Jesus. The text of vs. 7 is uncertain, but the most probable form of it does not have **followed** after **Galilee** and should be read "a great multitude from Galilee and from Judea and . . . came to him."

3:9. This vs. prepares the reader for the incident to be described in 4:1. The word behind **crush** is one that means "squeeze," or "compress."

3:10. In both Matt.'s version (12:15, much abbreviated and put later in the story of Jesus) and

Courtesy of Herbert G. May

Southern end of the Sea of Galilee looking eastward across part of the Jordan Valley

Luke's (6:17-19) Jesus "healed them all," rather than **healed many.** The word **diseases** ("plagues" in the KJV) is not a medical but a disciplinary term. It means lit. a whipping or a scourging and is translated that way in Acts 22:24; Heb. 11:36. The idea behind this usage is that some illnesses or diseases are sent by God as punishment.

3:11. The testimony of **the unclean spirits** is a clear revelation of the theology of Mark. How would the author have learned of this if no one except Jesus was aware of it? This is communication between the author and the reader to remind the reader of the true understanding of Jesus. **The Son of God** is not a messianic title; it is the title of a supernatural being, a divine being. It expresses Mark's convictions about Jesus as a guide to the reader.

3:12. As earlier (1:24-25), and consistently throughout the gospel, Jesus' true identity as a divine being (Son of God rather than Jewish Messiah) is not revealed to his associates. The demons know it, but are forbidden to reveal it. (See below on 8:27-30.)

F. The 12 Disciples (3:13-19a)

The appointment of the 12 looks far more simple than it actually is. Its unsystematic use of different kinds of names, its omission of Levi, whose call has already been described, and its use of strange terms like **Iscariot** make it highly likely that Mark is here simply handing on a traditional list. Since the setting of the appointment is very vague and general, it should be assumed that the evangelist has provided this setting himself, as a good author would.

The idea of **twelve** chief disciples is deeply rooted in early Christian tradition. The earliest extant reference is in I Cor. 15:5. It occurs in all the gospels, but with interesting differences in details. It is possible that the idea of the 12 is a later development which was mistakenly believed to have been established by Jesus. There were 12 tribes of Israel; so 12 missionary aides is a convenient number. Since, moreover, most of the names in the list do not emerge in early Christian tradition as real actors on the stage of history, it can be suspected that a small handful of actual leaders were added others not so important to bring the number up to the desired 12. Discrepancies in the 2 extant lists (Mark's and Luke's) seem to support this.

The problem, however, cannot be solved on the

basis of surviving evidence. It may be sufficient to note that Mark's list is followed by Matt. (10:1-4) and that Luke's changes (6:12-16) are repeated in Acts 1:13. The 4th Gospel mentions the 12 (John 6:70; 20:24) but nowhere gives a list. It does not even mention by name James and John and includes disciples, like Nathanael, Nicodemus, and Lazarus, who do not appear in either of the lists of the 12.

3:13. It is implied that there was a larger group with Jesus and that out of these he chose 12. Luke 6:13 makes this explicit.

3:14-15. The expressed purpose of the appointment of the 12 is **to preach and have authority to cast out demons.** There does not seem to be here envisioned their future role as general overseers of the church, as described in Acts. Mark, as a spokesman for Gentile Christianity in general, may be reflecting the resistance of Gentile Christianity to the administrative leadership of the 12. It is probably significant that Luke leaves this statement of purpose out entirely.

3:16. It is strange that Simon Peter is separated from his brother Andrew in this list. Both Matt. and Luke rearrange the order to bring the brothers together. Mark may have chosen his arrangement to give precedence to the ones who seem to have been the actual leaders, i.e. Peter, James, and John. This trio is customary in Mark (e.g. 9:2; 14:33; also Gal. 2:9, where, however, James is evidently "the Lord's brother," as in Gal. 1:19). Andrew simply was not as important; so Mark puts him in the group of those who are only names to us. The list in Acts 1:13 follows Mark in this, as over against Matt. and Luke. The surnaming of Simon with the name "rock" (**Peter** in Greek; "Cephas" in Aramaic) is not reported as a special event in Mark, as it is in Matt. 16:17-18; John 1:42. This, however, is a transitional vs. in Mark; before this the disciple is called Simon; after this (except in 14:37) he is called Peter.

3:17. The surname **Boanerges** seems to be a corrupt transliteration of an original Hebrew or Aramaic title that is difficult to recover. Even the early explanation, **sons of thunder,** has an uncertain meaning—possibly related to Luke 9:54. "Boanerges" might mean that they were twins. It probably refers to a personality trait in the 2 brothers.

3:18. Though mentioned several times in John, **Philip** does not appear in the first 3 gospels, or in Acts, except in the lists of the 12. The deacon Philip of Acts is a different person.

Bartholomew appears not to be a personal name, but an identification based on the father. Translated back into Aramaic it would be "son of Talmai." Since all the gospel lists of the 12 name Bartholomew following Philip (though Thomas intervenes in Acts 1:13) whereas a disciple named Nathanael is linked with Philip in John 1:45, and since Bartholomew appears in all the lists but never in John whereas Nathanael is a disciple in John but is not included in the lists, it is possible that these names refer to the same man, Nathanael son of Talmai.

Matthew has somehow replaced Levi, who was called earlier (2:14) but is not included in the list. Matt. identifies Matthew as "the tax collector" and substitutes this name for Levi in the story of his call (see above on 2:13-17).

Thomas is identified by John (11:16; 20:24; 21:2) as the one "called the Twin" (transliterated as "Didymus" in the KJV), but any more exact meaning is unknown.

James the son of Alphaeus is identified this way to distinguish him from James the son of Zebedee. Since Levi was earlier identified as "the son of Alphaeus" (2:14), some have guessed either that James and Levi are to be identified or that they were brothers. Is he the same person as "James the younger" of 15:40?

Thaddaeus is the most obscure of all. The manuscripts have different readings, some having "Lebbaeus." The lists of the 12 in Luke and Acts substitute "Judas the son of James" for Thaddaeus. All are otherwise unknown.

Simon the Cananaean was a political zealot. "Cananaean" and "zealot" were apparently older and newer terms for members of the extreme nationalist movement in Palestine. Luke's reading, "Simon who was called the Zealot" (6:15), is probably justified.

3:19a. The surname **Iscariot** is obscure in meaning. It has been guessed that it means "man of Kerioth" (either a village 12 miles S of Hebron or one in Moab). Another guess is "assassin." Since Mark offers no explanation, it may have been obscure to him also.

G. THE DEMON-POSSESSION CHARGE (3:19b-35)

This section is a remarkable revelation of the relationship between Jesus and his family. They were blind to his true significance as the Son of God and came to rescue him from the consequences of his "condition," **for they said, "He is beside himself"** (i.e. demon-possessed). Vs. 21 should be followed immediately by vs. 31 to get the force of this section; vss. 22-30 interrupt the natural flow of the family incident and were probably added here because they denounce the demon-possession accusation. For study purposes read vss. 19b-21 with vss. 31-35, and vss. 22-30 separately.

3:19b-21. Note that both Matt. and Luke omit these vss. even though they have parallels to vss. 22-30 (Matt. 12:24-32; Luke 11:15-22; 12:10) and vss. 31-35 (Matt. 12:46-50; Luke 8:19-21). Since, however, the vss. provide the reason for Jesus' refusal to go with his family, they are necessary for the best understanding of vss. 31-35. Matt. and Luke, in harmony with their infancy narratives, carefully eliminate any suggestion that Jesus was not accepted by his own family. Note also the omission of Mark's phrase "among his own kin" (6:4) in the parallels of Matt. 13:57; Luke 4:24. On **home** see above on 2:1.

3:21. The RSV translation **his friends** is misleading; the text simply has "his own," or "those belonging to him." It is an idiomatic way of referring to one's family, as most modern private translations acknowledge. The content of the phrase is supplied by vs. 31. **To seize him** implies concern for his safety and welfare. **Beside himself** means that his spirit was outside his body, which was being directed by a foreign spirit (a demon).

3:22-30. The purpose of this interruption of the family incident of vss. 19b-21, 31-35 is to make plain that Jesus was not demon-possessed. It was the Holy Spirit of God, not a demon, that possessed him. Two originally independent traditions seem to be combined here to make the point: vss. 22-26, the reply to the scribes, and vss. 27-30, a collection of 2 sayings of Jesus.

3:22-26. Though other sources have been suggested, the name **Beelzebul** probably comes from an ancient title of the god Baal (see below on 3:27; also comment on II Kings 1:2). Most interpreters, including Matt. and Luke, have understood Beelzebul and Satan to be alternate names for **the prince of demons.** Mark's 2 clauses quoted from the scribes can be read, however, as 2 entirely separate accusations. Since Jesus' reply answers only the 2nd, it is possible that Mark has used an isolated bit from another tradition, **He is possessed by Beelzebul,** to form a bridge from the family theory of demon possession to the interpolated story of Jesus' decisive refutation of the charge that his power came from **Satan.**

3:27. Here the argument shifts. Jesus' exorcisms prove that **the strong man** (Satan) is bound. The ultimate defeat of Satan and his kingdom is clearly forecast; even now his **house** is being plundered. Some have seen a word play in the fact that the apparent meaning of Beelzebul is "master of the house."

3:28-30. This "unforgivable sin" saying has been a problem to Bible interpreters in every age. In this context it refers to failure to recognize the Holy Spirit—calling it a demon. But vs. 30 is found in Mark only; the heart of the saying is stated in Matt. 12:31 without an explanation and in Luke 12:10 also in an entirely different setting. Mark's interpretation (vs. 30) remains the most satisfactory.

3:31-35. Jesus' family appears only twice in Mark, here and in 6:1-6. Both times the family members appear as outsiders rather than sympathetic members of his group. True brotherhood and true kinship is spiritual, not physical. Cf. John 1:11-13; Rom. 8:14, 29; also the parallel story in Luke 11:27-28.

3:31. Jesus' **mother** is mentioned only twice in Mark, here and in 6:3. His father, or the father in his family, is never mentioned. **His brothers** appear once more in 6:3, where they are named. From the references here and elsewhere in the NT there is no reason to think of them except in the ordinary sense as blood brothers. Roman Catholic teaching, believing in the doctrine of the perpetual virginity of Mary, has traditionally explained the brothers as cousins (children of Mary's sister) or legal stepbrothers (children of Mary's husband by a supposed earlier marriage).

H. Teaching by Parables (4:1-34)

4:1-9. *The Sower.* The parable of the sower introduces a section dealing with parables and their purpose and use. In general a parable as a teaching device is best understood as a story to illustrate a teaching.

4:1. The setting, teaching from a **boat** to a **crowd . . . on the land,** is retained in Matt.'s parallel account (13:1-2), but Luke moves this setting to a different point (5:3) and has this parable taught in an ordinary setting (8:4).

4:2. The use of **parables** was characteristic of the teaching of Jesus.

4:3-8. This parable itself might more accurately be described as the parable of four kinds of soil. Like the other parables in this section, it does not so much contain a positive teaching of Jesus as explain why his teaching was not always immediately successful.

4:9. This formula appears at the end of the parable in all of the first 3 gospels, and appears again in 4:23; 7:16 (RSV footnote). It indicates the need to be careful in interpreting the meaning because it is either difficult or commonly misunderstood. Whether this is intended to be a saying of Jesus or of Mark is not clear, but probably it is Mark's. It prepares the reader, at least, for the explanation to follow (vss. 13-20).

4:10-12. *The Purpose of the Parables.* This explanation that the purpose of parables was to conceal truth from outsiders is rooted in doctrine rather than history (cf. I Cor. 1:18-3:1, esp. 2:7). Such a purpose would be naturally assumed in the environment of early Gentile Christianity, but in the practice of Jesus parables were obviously to make truth plain to all hearers (see vss. 21-25). The difficulty here arises from the fact that Mark added an originally independent saying (vss. 11-12) to this context (note that vs. 10 leads directly into vs. 13). He seems to have felt that this was a proper place for a saying about parables, but he may have misunderstood the meaning of **in parables** in vs. 11. Rather than referring to the story parables of Jesus, it probably here means "in riddles" (the same word in Aramaic or Hebrew), making the sense of the saying: "For those outside everything becomes a riddle" (cf. I Cor. 2:14). The gospel as preached in early Gentile Christianity begins with a faith relationship, and without that the whole message is foolishness.

4:13-20. *The Sower Parable Explained.* Since the explanation of the parable offered here is an allegorical one, most scholars regard it as a later development in the transmission of early traditions about the teachings of Jesus. Mark has in effect brought the parable up to date and made it refer to the apostolic preaching of his own time.

4:13. The comment of Jesus about the failure of the 12 to understand his parable is omitted in the parallel versions of Matt. 13:18; Luke 8:11, in harmony with their respect for the authority of the 12.

4:14. In Mark's time **the sower** is the apostolic preacher. **The word** is the gospel proclamation, the good news about Christ.

4:21-25. *Sayings About Parables.* The general import of these vss. is understood by Mark to shed light on Jesus' use of parables. They are to enlighten, rather than confuse, their hearers. The arrangement is editorial here, as the parallels in Matt. and Luke show clearly. These sayings are found in Matt. in 5 different contexts (5:15; 10:26; 7:2; 13:12; 25:29), and in Luke the arrangement is even more complex. Luke 8:16-18 is the basic parallel, but the saying in vs. 24 is taken out and put earlier (Luke 6:38), and 3 of the sayings that do appear in the official Lukan parallel (8:16-18) are repeated in a different context elsewhere in Luke, with slight variations. A table will show the situation clearly.

MATT.		MARK 4		LUKE
5:15	=	21	=	8:16; 11:33
10:26	=	22	=	8:17; 12:2
13:9, etc.	=	23	=	8:8b, etc.
		24a	=	8:18a
7:2	=	24b	=	6:38
13:12; 25:29	=	25	=	8:18b; 19:26

It is safe to conclude that the sayings contained in these vss. are remnants of much longer original teachings, the context of which is now lost. They are pithy and terse, and should be interpreted simply in terms of their content, without regard to their present context.

4:22-23. Eventually all mysteries will be cleared up (cf. I Cor. 13:12). On vs. 23 see above on vs. 9.

4:24-25. The first part of vs. 24 is connected directly to vs. 25 in one of Luke's parallels (8:18), with a resulting difference in meaning. Mark's coupling of 2 sayings in vs. 24 forms an exhortation to be careful to hear correctly and seems to make understanding conditional on sharing. Vs. 25 has long been a troublesome saying. On the surface it seems unfair, but on deeper thought it is an accurate reflection of the way things actually are. The parable of the talents (or pounds) makes this point in more detail (Matt. 25:14-30; Luke 19:12-27).

4:26-29. *The Seed Growing Secretly.* This parable, omitted from both Matt. and Luke, is rather difficult. It points to the kingdom as a divine act rather than a human accomplishment. It calls on man to be patient with the delay of the kingdom in coming.

4:30-32. *The Mustard Seed.* This parable might illustrate the ways the kingdom **grows,** gradually and naturally instead of suddenly and dramatically. But it is more harmonious with the other teachings to see it as a contrast between the small, insignificant beginnings of the Christian movement and the final tremendous kingdom that is its destiny (cf. Matt. 13:31-32; Luke 13:18-19). Mark has grouped these three "seed parables" together out of some conviction that they teach related truths about the kingdom of God.

I. SPECIAL MIRACLES (4:35–5:43)

4:35-41. *The Storm at Sea.* The stilling of the storm is clearly a demonstration of Jesus' power over nature. It is possible, but beside the point, to try to give it a natural explanation.

4:38. The reaction of the disciples is presented quite unfavorably. They rebuke Jesus for his lack of concern. Matt. 8:25; Luke 8:24 change this rebuke into an appeal for help.

4:39. It is a pathetic kind of rationalization to explain Jesus' command **Peace! Be still!** as originally directed to the disciples rather than to the wind. The intention here is clearly to portray Jesus as Lord of nature.

4:41. The disciples, however, do not grasp the significance of Jesus' action. They are amazed, but left bewildered, as usual in Mark.

5:1-20. *The Demonic Legion.* The story of the Gerasene demoniac teaches the reader the same basic truth about Jesus as the account of the stilling of the storm. Both the howling wind and the howling demon are subject to the Son of God. At his command both the sea and the man find their peace. The history of this story is complex. The setting is clear in general, but not in detail (see below on vs. 1). Luke (8:26-39) uses the full story almost as it appears in Mark, but Matt. (8:28-34) drastically abbreviates it and yet makes it the story of 2 demon-possessed men instead of one. The background of the story is more Gentile than Jewish (Jews did not keep swine, and Palestine is a difficult setting for

Gentiles to have such a large herd). To complicate matters further, there are some other versions of this story, with other exorcists as heroes. The probabilities are that this was a popular story that got attached to Jesus in the traditions of early Gentile Christianity.

5:1. The general location is reported to be the E shore of the Sea of Galilee but the exact location is reported in different ways. The oldest and best manuscripts have Gerasa, but this is too far from the

Courtesy of Herbert G. May

Ruins at Gerasa, one of the cities of the Decapolis (a federation of Greek cities in Palestine); the oldest and best mss. identify this as the "country of the Gerasenes" (Mark 5:1), but see comment

Sea of Galilee to fit well (see color map 15). Matt. changes this to Gadara ("the country of the Gadarenes," 8:28), but this, though nearer, is still too far from the water. Later copyists change both to "Gergesa," which may correspond to some ruins on the E side of the sea. It remains a problem.

5:2. Palestinian burials were often in caves set aside as **tombs.** It was commonly believed that demons lived in them.

5:6. As is usual in Mark, **he ran and worshiped him** means that the demons, not the man, recognized Jesus.

5:7-8. The story is awkwardly told at this point, with the demonic response coming before the command of Jesus.

5:9. The name **Legion** suggests that many demons, rather than one demon, were possessing the man, and this meaning is confirmed by the following phrase, **for we are many.** A Roman legion at full strength numbered 6,000 men.

5:10. The term **out of the country** probably means out of the inhabited area; into the desert, a traditional haunt of evil spirits.

5:11-13. The plight of the poor pigs would scarcely have been of concern to the early Christian. The naturalistic theory that the pigs were stampeded by the antics of an insane man undercuts the main point of the story, viz. Jesus' control over the demons.

5:20. The Decapolis was a group of 10 Gentile

cities in the area between Judea and Galilee on both sides of the Jordan (see color map 14).

5:21-43. *Jairus' Daughter.* This account is an unusual combination of 2 miracle stories, one contained within the other. Matt. 9:18-26 retells Mark's 23-vs. version in only 9 vss. and places it earlier. Luke 8:40-56 parallels Mark.

5:21. The seaside setting of Mark is abandoned by both Matt. and Luke.

5:22. The ancient Palestinian synagogue usually had only one **ruler,** but the author may mean one of the class of synagogue rulers.

5:23. Technically it is difficult to know whether the author intended this account to be a healing **at the point of death,** as this vs. suggests, or a bringing back to life of one who has already died, as vs. 35 suggests. Luke follows Mark closely and retains the same ambiguity, but Matt. resolves the problem by stating clearly at the outset, "My daughter has just died." The point of the story in all 3 versions is to demonstrate the power of Jesus over life and death.

5:25-34. The healing of this woman is a remarkable example of the power of Jesus to heal. Although **faith** must be presupposed to account for her action, and her faith is specifically mentioned at the end of the story as the reason for her cure, nevertheless the actual healing was accomplished by the power of Jesus. It would not be true to the meaning of the story as Mark and Luke tell it, to think of the woman's faith as anything more than that which allowed the power of Jesus to be effective.

5:27. The **garment** of Jesus is not specifically described. Mark does not seem to ascribe any particular significance to it here (but cf. 6:56). Both Matt. and Luke expand the designation to "the fringe of his garment," probably out of a closer orientation to Jewish customs (see comment on Luke 8:44).

5:30. Traditions about Jesus were recorded in different ways. A comparison of this vs. with Luke 8:45-46 illustrates this very effectively. Note that what is a description by the author in Mark, **Jesus, perceiving in himself that power had gone forth from him,** becomes in Luke a saying of Jesus, "I perceive that power has gone forth from me." Each evangelist apparently felt free to write conversational sayings for Jesus as needed in history.

5:36. Faith—**only believe**—is stressed in this healing, or resurrection, but it differs from the faith of the woman with the flow of blood. Here it is not the faith of the one being healed but that of a 3rd party. The faith of the father is somehow related to the restoration of the daughter.

5:37. The recognition that 3 disciples, **Peter and James and John,** had a special relationship to Jesus is characteristic of Mark.

5:39. Those who see this story as a healing rather than a resurrection take Jesus' words here lit.; others take them symbolically. **Sleeping** is commonly used in antiquity to describe death.

5:41. Jesus' **taking her by the hand** is a typical healing method in Mark. Cf. 1:31, where Jesus heals Simon Peter's mother-in-law in this way.

5:42. Mark's description here is awkward. Matt. leaves out both the walking and the age of the girl. Luke is much more skillful, describing the age of the girl at the beginning of his account.

5:43. The strict charge **that no one should know this** is in harmony with Mark's constant explanation to the reader that Jesus did not seek publicity but preferred to remain the unrecognized Son of God.

J. Rejection at Nazareth (6:1-6a)

The belief of virtual strangers, like Jairus and the woman, is now contrasted sharply with the unbelief of those who supposedly knew Jesus well. Behind this arrangement it is not difficult to see the feeling of the early Gentile church that it really understood Jesus better than the Jewish Christians who had known him personally. Mark's version of his rejection at Nazareth is closely paralleled in Matt. 13:53-58 but is replaced in Luke (4:16-30) by a distinctly different account.

6:2. The astonishment of the people at Nazareth is similar to that which Jesus first aroused in Capernaum (1:22). There, however, he was a stranger; in Nazareth, on the other hand, he was well known already in quite another role. Their rejection is understandable.

6:3. This is the only clue to Jesus' occupation prior to his full-time ministry. It is changed in Matt. 13:55; Luke 4:22 and by some of the later copyists as well. The thinking of the townspeople seems to have been just the reverse of the early Christians. Whereas the townspeople asked, "How can **the carpenter** be the Lord?" the Christians asked, "How could the Lord have been a common carpenter?" It is noteworthy that Mark mentions only **Mary** whereas Luke mentions only Joseph. The listing of the names of Jesus' brothers and the mention of his sisters is a very valuable bit of incidental information. On the relation between Jesus and his brothers see above on 3:31.

6:4. This saying of Jesus is proverbial in form and could be a quotation of a well-known truth, here applied to himself; but since ancient examples of its use are missing, it may have begun with Jesus. It makes necessary the assumption that Jesus' immediate family did not honor him as a prophet. Matt. 13:57; Luke 4:24 soften these family implications.

6:5. In place of **he could do no mighty work there** Matt. 13:58 reports simply that "he did not do many mighty works there," and Luke omits any such statement. Mark's version implies that his power to heal was conditioned by the faith of those who desired to be healed.

K. The Mission of the 12 (6:6b-13)

The tradition about Jesus' sending the 12 out by 2's is preserved in a larger complex of materials. It is a feature of the first 3 gospels only, and Mark's account seems to be the basic one. The purpose of the mission was apparently to cast out demons (vs. 7) and to preach repentance (vs. 12). Matt. 10:7; Luke 9:2 specifically describe the preaching mission as a proclamation of the kingdom. Some elements of Mark's account are then repeated, and some of Matt.'s additional material appears in Luke's account (10:1-16) of the sending out of the 70, which does not appear in Mark at all. The historical situation behind these accounts is not clear. The return is described in 6:30.

6:6b. This short sentence actually seems to stand by itself. It is neither the end of the previous story nor the beginning of the next but simply a link. It lit. says that Jesus "went about in a circle."

6:8. The purpose of the **staff** is not clear, and the parallels (Matt. 10:10; Luke 9:3) forbid taking a staff. The **bag** could be a beggar's sack or possibly a money belt.

6:9. The admonition **to wear sandals** seems to imply a long journey, but they are forbidden in Matt. 10:10; Luke 10:4 (for the 70). **Two tunics** are forbidden in all accounts.

6:10. This may mean that one should be satisfied with his first invitation and should not seek a better one.

6:11. For one to **shake off the dust** on his **feet** for **a testimony against them** is a traditional Jewish custom. Cf. Acts 13:51.

6:13. Healing by anointing **with oil,** a regular practice in ancient times, is mentioned in the gospels only this once. Cf. Jas. 5:14.

L. The Death of John the Baptist (6:14-29)

The reputation of Jesus leads some to regard him as a reappearance of **John the baptizer.** At this point Mark, realizing that he has not recorded the death of John, attaches a lengthy description of his execution by Herod. Matt. simply follows Mark's rather awkward procedure; Luke has a brief summary of John's imprisonment earlier in his story (3:19-20) and omits the story of his execution.

6:14. The title **King** did not belong to this **Herod;** he was a "tetrarch." Matt. 14:1; Luke 9:7 make this correction. The reference is to Herod Antipas, one of the sons of King Herod the Great and local ruler of Galilee and Perea. **John . . . has been raised from the dead** should probably be understood figuratively to mean that Jesus was similar to John. If literal, it may be a bit of popular superstition, or may reflect some kind of reincarnation belief. The expression **these powers** refers to miracles. Does this not make it necessary to credit John with miracles also?

. **6:15.** The return of **Elijah** was expected just prior to the coming of the Messiah (cf. Mal. 4:5). **A prophet** was a highly regarded person in Jewish piety, 2nd only in esteem to the Messiah himself.

6:17. The reference to **his brother Philip's wife** is probably a mistake. According to Josephus' account of the Herodian family Herodias was not Philip's wife but the wife of another half brother of Antipas who was also named Herod. Some later copyists have tried to bring the 2 accounts into harmony by reading simply "his brother's wife."

6:20. It is not clear what was intended by **he was much perplexed.** Matt. 14:5 leaves it out, and many manuscripts replace it by "did many things," a phrase which is equally difficult.

6:22. According to Josephus, **Herodias' daughter** was named Salome. It was she who married Herod's half brother Philip.

6:29. John's **disciples** buried him. Christians are likely to regard John simply as the forerunner of Jesus and fail to see him at the center of an important religious movement. He had a group of disciples that continued long after his death, in rivalry to the Christian movement (see above on 2:18-22).

M. Special Group I (6:30–7:37)

6:30-44. *Feeding the 5,000.* The story of the feeding of the 5,000 (and the 4,000 of 8:1-9) is shaped by

2 completely separate influences. One factor is the miracle of Elisha in II Kings 4:42-44. The resemblances are too striking to be simple coincidence. The other is the practice of the love feast in primitive Christian worship. As we have it, the feeding proceeds in the manner of a love feast, giving the sanction of Jesus himself. The miraculous element should not be explained away along rationalistic or naturalistic lines. It was not a great sharing experience, but the demonstration of Jesus as the sustainer of life. John 6:1-14 makes the link with the Elisha miracle closer by specifying "barley loaves" and is much more explicit about the connection between Jesus' miracle and the Lord's Supper.

6:34. The **sheep without a shepherd** image is not used in the accounts of Matt. and Luke. Matt. has already used it earlier in a different setting (9:36). Whereas Mark portrays Jesus as a teacher, Luke (9:11) adds healing activities and Matt. (14:14) mentions only the healing ministry.

6:35-36. The suggestion that the crowd be dispersed to buy food in the nearby villages shows that their needs could have been met without a miracle. Therefore, Mark implies, we should not regard Jesus' miracles as emergency measures when all else failed.

6:37. The question about buying **two hundred denarii worth of bread** is rhetorical and even sarcastic. A denarius was a Roman silver coin approximately worth one day's field labor, according to Matt. 20:2. Obviously the disciples could muster few such coins, and their estimating a specific large number pointedly brands Jesus' instruction as absurd. Thus again Mark shows the reader how little the 12 understood their Master. Matt. omits any suggestion of the disciples' buying food, and Luke removes the barb by leaving out the estimated figure.

6:38. The total of **five . . . and two** is 7, the number of loaves in the feeding of the 4,000 (see below on 8:1-9). All 4 gospels have the 5-2 combination. The elements bread and **fish** appear in some early Christian portrayals of the Lord's Supper, making the connection between this miracle and the sacrament more explicit.

6:39. The orderly arrangement of people prior to the feeding is reminiscent of Paul's protest that in Corinth the Lord's Supper is disorderly (I Cor. 11:20-22) and that Christian worship in general "should be done decently and in order" (I Cor. 14:40).

6:40. The grouping **by hundreds and by fifties** seems to be Mark's personal touch. It is reminiscent of Moses' division of the people in Exod. 18:21. Matt. omits all reference to this; Luke 9:14 has them sitting "in companies, about fifty each."

6:41. It is traditional in Judaism to bless God before breaking bread. Another appearance of this as a practice of Jesus with his disciples can be seen in Luke 24:30-31. All 12 disciples act as servers.

6:43. The **twelve baskets** probably are intended to agree with the 12 disciple-servers. These baskets were traditional Jewish food carriers. The expression **broken pieces** appears in an early Christian writing (Didache 9:3-4) as a description of the bread of the Lord's Supper. Matt., Luke, and John all omit the specific reference to leftover fish.

6:44. Mark's number, **five thousand men,** is repeated in Luke 9:14 exactly and in John 6:10 in a different form, but Matt. 14:21 makes it explicit that this does not include the women and children.

6:45-52. Crossing the Sea. This story is difficult for modern readers. Though the dominant element is the walking on the water, there are still traces of a stilling of a storm (as in 4:35-41) in the phrases about the **wind** in vss. 48, 51. The chief difficulty is understanding the purpose of the action. Jesus' walking was apparently not to rescue, or even to help, the disciples in their distress (vs. 48). What we have is actually a nature miracle that would leave the reader in no doubt about the status of Jesus as a divine being. Since this is a main concern of Mark, it was probably his reason for including the account in his gospel. It is possible that he was influenced by Ps. 77:16-19 or that he was writing an allegorical account of Jesus' triumph over death. It is also possible that the story originally belonged to the group of resurrection appearances. It is not likely that we are here dealing with a natural event which has developed legendary proportions. Matt. has a parallel version (14:22-33) which leaves out the difficult phrase in vs. 48, **he meant to pass them by,** but adds an account about Peter walking on the water also. This detracts from Mark's emphasis on the uniqueness of Jesus as the Son of God. Luke omits the whole story. John's version (6:16-21) is similar in spirit to Mark's.

6:48. The **fourth watch** was the last one, from 3 A.M. to 6 A.M. Mark refers to the daytime by hours (12 beginning at 6 A.M.) and to the nighttime by watches (4 of 3 hours each following Roman custom).

6:49. The explanation that **they thought it was a ghost** suggests the possibility that this experience was originally after the Crucifixion.

6:50-52. As is customary in Mark, demonstrations of the true nature of Jesus as the Son of God are clear only to the reader; the disciples never seem to see it. Mark concludes that **they were utterly astounded** and then tells the reader that they did not understand the feeding of the 5,000 any better, for **their hearts were hardened.** Matt.'s version does not give this impression of the disciples at all, but has them recognize him fully (Matt. 14:33).

6:53-56. On **fringe of his garment** see on 5:27.

7:1-23. Controversy with Pharisees. This is a composite section dealing with 3 issues and directed to 3 different groups. Vss. 1-8 treat the problem of unwashed hands, vss. 9-13 the Corban vow, and vss. 14-23 the problem of kosher food. The first 2 problems are directed to the Pharisees; the 3rd is expressed first to the people (vss. 14-15) and then to the disciples (vss. 17-23). Note that since the most ancient manuscripts do not have vs. 16, it is omitted from modern versions (see RSV footnote). The general unity of this section implies the early church problem of loyalty to Jewish customs. The solution, viz. freedom from them, is here attributed to Jesus himself. It is noteworthy, however, that Paul deals with this problem in I Cor. 8-10; Rom. 14:1-15:13 as though it were a new one and shows no awareness that Jesus had already solved it in principle. Luke leaves this whole section out, probably because in his judgment the problem was solved by Peter in his experience with Cornelius (Acts 10-11).

7:1-8. Mark's description of Jewish customs certainly implies that his intended readers are Gentile and need this kind of explanation. It also exposes the probability that he too is outside the circle which has firsthand knowledge of these customs, for his explanation is partly inaccurate. He attributes, out of poor information or prejudice, to **all the Jews** (vs. 3) what was a custom of the strict Pharisees only.

7:1-5. This seems to be the 2nd official investigation of Jesus (the first being reported in 3:22). The picture of conflict with the authorities is building up. As an actual investigation this is unlikely, for the Jews who did not observe this custom were very numerous and often in high official positions.

7:6-7. The violence of the reply is certainly surprising. It expresses the later hostility between church and synagogue from the Christian point of view.

7:9-13. The criticism of Pharisaism here explains itself. **Corban** was a special gift to God, usually money or property. Jesus is here condemning abuse of this practice as a pious excuse for neglecting obligations to one's parents.

7:14-23. The question of ritually unclean food (not kosher) is clearly declared solved in this section. The viewpoint is that of the Gentile church. Matt. represents a more conservative aspect of early Christianity. In his reworking of this material (Matt. 15:1-20) he removes all reference to the non-kosher food problem and focuses on the problem of kosher food which has been made unclean by unwashed hands.

7:15. This is the key verse; the rest is explanation.

7:19. The translation **and so passes on** is a gentle one for a plain statement in the Greek, "and so passes into the privy." It is possible that the explanation **thus he declared all foods clean** is a later addition, but since the manuscript evidence does not give this theory much support, and since the statement is harmonious with Mark's Gentile Christian background, it may be original. In any case this conclusion is implied in the whole section.

7:21. The Greek word behind **fornication** means any kind of sexual vice. **Envy** is lit. "an evil eye," which may be a reference to the common superstition or may be related to Luke 11:34 (cf. Matt. 6:22-23). **Slander** is lit. "blasphemy," a word used of untrue accusations against God and men.

7:24-30. The Ministry to Gentiles. Mark now relates a story about Jesus and a Gentile woman, which Luke omits and Matt. alters (Matt. 15:21-28). It is a symbolic statement of how Jesus went first to the Jews but finally to the Gentiles. Matt. changes this aspect also, having Jesus go "only to the lost sheep of the house of Israel," and makes it simply another healing story.

7:24. That Jesus **entered a house** (of a Gentile) was contrary to the practice of a pious Jew (and thus omitted in Matt. 15:21).

7:26. The identification of the woman as **Greek** is significant. Matt. calls her a "Canaanite" (see comment on Matt. 15:22).

7:27. The **children** are symbolic of Israel, the children of God. **First** is symbolic of the mission of Jesus to his own people. It was only after they rejected him that full attention was paid to the Gentiles (cf. John 1:11 and the portrayal of Paul's mission in Acts 13:44-48; 28:25-28). The **dogs** are symbolic of the Gentiles (cf. Matt. 7:6). The overtones of Jewish ethnocentrism here are alien to the general spirit of Mark, but the emphasis is related to the general acknowledgment of early Gentile Christianity that "salvation is from the Jews" (John 4:22), or that the actual order of priority is "the Jew first and also the Greek" (Rom. 2:10).

7:28. It is highly significant that this Greek woman is the only person in Mark to call Jesus **Lord.** Jesus also refers to himself (or to God?) as "Lord" (5:19; 11:3), and this is certainly the viewpoint of Mark. The recognition of Jesus as Lord in Mark is credited solely to Gentile devotion and insight. This vs. is closely related to 15:39. It misses Mark's point here to render "Lord" as "sir," as in several modern translations.

7:29. The woman's daughter is healed **for this saying**—that the **dogs** are entitled to **the children's crumbs.** The real meaning should not be sought in the intentions or personality of Jesus but in the message of Mark to the reader. This message is simply the recognition of the accuracy of the claims of the Gentiles to share in the salvation of the gospel. The actual historical scene is obscured by these vital issues.

7:30. Note that this is a striking instance of healing from a distance and on the basis of the intercessory faith (implied in Mark in the confession "Lord") of a 3rd party.

7:31-37. *Healing the Deaf Mute.* This account gives more about the actual mechanics of healing than is usual in the gospels. Neither Matt. nor Luke repeats the story, perhaps because it resembled too closely a common healing account. It is replaced in Matt. 15:29-31 by a general description of healings.

7:31. The route described here is very unlikely, as Sidon is beyond Tyre to the N and **the Decapolis**

Courtesy of Herbert G. May

Ruins of the theater at Philadelphia, one of the cities of the Decapolis (Mark 7:31); see also ill., p. 653

(see above on 5:20) beyond the Sea of Galilee and S (see color map 14). It probably reflects the author's inaccurate knowledge of the geography of Palestine. In his understanding Jesus now works in Gentile territory.

7:37. The astonishment of the people, as is customary in Mark, does not lead to recognition of Jesus as the Son of God; it is the reader of the gospel that is learning this.

N. Special Group II (8:1-26)

This section of Mark is strangely repetitious of the previous section (6:30–7:37). It is not precisely the same, of course, but it has an overall pattern that is not likely to be due simply to coincidence. This may be a reflection of Mark's sources, which in these incidents differed enough so that Mark simply used both of them. It cannot now be determined whether his sources were oral or written; he probably used both kinds. There also may be some connection

between the sequence of events in Isa. 29:13-19 and these incidents. Isa. 29:13-14 lies behind 7:1-23, and it may have been believed that Isa. 29:18 had been fulfilled by the healings of 7:31-37; 8:22-26.

8:1-9. *Feeding the 4,000.* This story parallels the earlier feeding of the 5,000 (see above on 6:30-44). Despite an overall similarity there are some interesting differences. **Seven loaves** replace the earlier "five, and two fish" (6:38). There are, correspondingly, **seven baskets** of leftovers instead of the "twelve baskets" of the earlier version (6:43). This suggests that Jesus was assisted by 7 helpers rather than 12, in striking harmony with the 7 deacons of Acts 6:1-6, appointed "to serve tables." Again the imagery of the love feast of apostolic times appears, this time more in harmony with the organization reported in Acts. Luke, who has an account of the feeding of the 5,000, does not have the feeding of the 4,000 at all. Did Luke recognize the 2 accounts as different versions of the same event and chose between them?

8:4. The failure of the disciples to respond to Jesus' 2nd proposal for feeding the multitudes is simply another instance of Mark's insistence that they never understood. He has already charged that "they did not understand about the loaves" (6:52), and their response to the 2nd situation simply illustrates this theme again.

8:6-7. On **having given thanks** see above on 6:41. The blessing of the fish corresponds to the consecration of the elements in the Lord's Supper. This feature is missing from the earlier version. Note that the "two fish" of the earlier version have here become **a few small fish.**

8:8. It is a theme of both versions that more was left over than they had to begin with. This symbolizes the inexhaustible grace of Christ, who is "the bread of life" (John 6:35; all of John 6 is important for understanding the early Christian meaning of the miraculous feeding story).

8:10. *Crossing the Sea.* The crossing of the Sea of Galilee to **Dalmanutha** parallels 6:45-52. This version is much simpler, with the walking on the water eliminated (see below on vss. 11-13). Matt.'s version has Jesus cross to "the region of Magadan" (15:39; see color map 15), probably because Dalmanutha is obscure. Since the place is quite unknown, early copyists have made a variety of alterations. It probably illustrates again Mark's unfamiliarity with Palestinian geography.

8:11-13. *Controversy with Pharisees.* This conflict parallels the earlier one in 7:1-23, and it is also an interesting contrast to 6:46-56. In the earlier series the crossing of the sea included an account of Jesus' walking on the water, which was certainly intended as a **sign** of Jesus' divinity. To this was added the general description of his healing ministry, also intended in Mark to be a sign of his divinity. But here these spectacular signs are replaced by a short section against performing signs. This forms the content of the controversy with the Pharisees in this 2nd series. Two different points of view may be preserved here.

8:12. Jesus' refusal to give a sign to the Pharisees is consistent with his constant effort to keep his real identity secret. Mark is saying, not that Jesus did no signs, but that he did not advertise himself in this way. The reader is informed by these mighty acts; the disciples should have been, but were not.

8:14-21. *The Disciples' Failure to Understand.* This paragraph has, at first glance, but little relationship to its parallel story in the first series, the healing of the Gentile woman's daughter (7:24-30). The more they are studied, however, the more common themes emerge. Both symbolically deal with the gospel message under the figure of **bread.** Both deal with the general theme of the failure of the Jews to respond and the necessity of turning to the Gentiles, though the emphasis is different. The theme here is the failure of the 12 (representing the Jews in general) to understand. The account is full of cryptic, symbolic phrases, left uninterpreted.

8:15. Matt. in an addition of his own (16:12) explains that **leaven** is symbolic of "teaching." This fits the phrase **the leaven of the Pharisees** nicely, but makes **the leaven of Herod** obscure. Matt. changes "Herod" to "the Sadducees," and some later copyists of Mark change it to the equally difficult "the Herodians." Perhaps leaven represents evil influence.

8:17. It is plain that Jesus is dissatisfied with the 12, presumably for their failure to understand the symbolism of the bread, or his power to supply "bread."

8:18. The expressions in this vs. may be read as questions or exclamations. The general treatment of the 12 in Mark would seem to make the exclamatory version more probable. If so, this vs. is a high point in Mark's condemnation of the 12.

8:19-20. The sufficiency of Jesus is not grasped at all. Almost in despair he recounts the signs of the miraculous feedings. The **twelve** and **seven** baskets have made no impression. Pathetically Jesus asks, **Do you not yet understand?** The reader realizes that they do not. He must rely on the Gentile Christian leaders for a true understanding of Jesus.

8:22-26. *Healing the Blind Man.* This story completes the 2nd series of parallel episodes. Its parallel is the healing of the deaf mute in 7:31-37. In both stories the healing is done privately, the process stresses touching, saliva is used, and secrecy is enjoined. These unusual ties are more than coincidence and show the parallel nature of the stories. Both may be a fulfillment of Isa. 29:18, since this very section of Isa. has been quoted in 7:6-7. Neither Matt. nor Luke uses either story.

This story is open to the possible objection that Jesus' first attempt is only partially successful; a 2nd action is required to complete the healing. If the blind man is symbolic of Israel then the story may be an acknowledgment that the conversion of Israel will be in 2 stages, first the elect and then all Israel (as in Rom. 10–11).

The story is symbolically related to the immediately following description of Peter. Along with the rest of the 12 he has not demonstrated a real grasp of the significance of Jesus. He is blind, so to speak. His "cure" is described as beginning with the confession at Caesarea Philippi and being aided by the transfiguration experience, but even that represents only a partial cure. The story of Peter's full enlightenment is not recorded in Mark.

III. The Ministry Beyond Galilee (8:27–9:29)

8:27-30. *Peter's Confession.* Mark here faces squarely the question of the disciples' view of Jesus.

In one sense it is a record of their insight, even though it is belated. Peter, as spokesman for the others, affirms his faith in Jesus as the Messiah. In another sense, however, it is an indictment of the Christology of the 12, for it reveals a messianic view (see below on vs. 29) that falls far short of Mark's Son of God Christology (that of early Gentile Christianity in general). Sensitive to this negative aspect of Mark's account, both Matt. (16:13-23) and Luke (9:18-22) make additions to Peter's confession to make it more harmonious with what came to be the "orthodox" view of Jesus.

8:27. The setting near **Caesarea Philippi** is in Gentile territory (see color map 14).

8:29. The title **Christ** is the Greek translation of the Hebrew "Messiah." Both words mean "anointed one." The concept of the Messiah in Jewish circles implied, not a divine being, but an appointed human.

8:30. As the demons who recognized Jesus' divinity have always been silenced, so now the 12 are forbidden to reveal his messiahship (see above on 1:25).

8:31-33. *First Prediction of the Passion.* This is the first of 3 predictions which Jesus makes to his disciples to prepare them for his death and resurrection. But all 3 are in vain, for Mark's account portrays the disciples as consistently failing to understand. The point of the 3-fold attack on the understanding of the 12 is to establish firmly in the mind of the reader the defectiveness of their grasp of the significance of Jesus. To leave no excuse for them, Mark (only) stresses in this first prediction that Jesus was no longer talking in parables and figures but **said this plainly** (vs. 32; cf. Matt. 16:21-23; Luke 9:22).

8:31. On **the Son of man** see above on 2:10. The memory of Jesus' own predictions would almost certainly be affected by the tradition of what actually did happen. The prediction and the fulfillment, therefore, would necessarily be in full agreement as we now have them. This first prediction interprets the coming resurrection as the victory of Jesus over death in the phrase **rise again.** Jesus is not the passive instrument of God's action; he will not "be raised" from the dead (as he is in the parallels to this in Matt. 16:21; Luke 9:22), but he himself will rise. This probably anticipates a theology of the atonement which centers in the victory of Jesus over the final demonic enemy of man, death.

8:32. The reaction of Peter illustrates his lack of understanding and makes it necessary to view his confession of faith in Jesus as the Messiah as less than a full comprehension. Luke leaves out this rebuke of Jesus altogether, and Matt. softens it by describing the "rebuke" in such a way that it is no longer a rebuke but a protest.

8:33. Jesus, in turn, gives Peter his most serious personal rebuke, calling him **Satan** and accusing him of being **not on the side of God.** The phrase **get behind me** is a Jewish way of saying "begone." The doctrine of the cross was central in early Gentile Christianity (cf. I Cor. 1:17-25) but not in the Jewish Christianity which the 12 represented.

8:34–9:1. *Standards of Discipleship.* This paragraph is a collection of several short sayings of Jesus, arranged here by Mark to give some standards for true discipleship. Three of them existed also in Q, the other collection of traditions about Jesus used by both Matt. and Luke. They are appropriate here because of Peter's failure to grasp the significance of Jesus' coming crucifixion.

8:34. The **multitude** should be understood as including the reader of the gospel. **Take up his cross** is probably a post-crucifixion phrase among the early Christians, here used to express a basic thought of Jesus. It is possible, however, that it was a proverbial expression in the Roman Empire and was used by Jesus without special reference to his own crucifixion. In a cryptic way it expresses the Christian life as the way of the cross, probably as understood in Gentile Christian preaching. Matt. 16:24 repeats the saying exactly, and Luke 9:23 is almost exact, reading "take up his cross daily." Matt. 10:38; Luke 14:27 use also a Q version of the saying.

8:35. The phrase **and the gospel's** is omitted in Matt. 16:25; Luke 9:24, probably because their other source, Q, had the same saying without it (Matt. 10:39; Luke 17:33). This is obviously symbolic of the Christian way of the cross. It has overtones of death and persecution in it, on both the historical and the symbolic levels.

8:36. This question calls for a true sense of values. Cf. Luke 12:15-21.

8:38. This vs. certainly reflects the situation a Christian faced under official Roman persecution. To deny Christ is to be saved in this world but to be lost in the next. This saying too is found in Q (Matt. 10:33; Luke 12:9). Matt. does not use the Markan version, but Luke does (9:26). This picture of the end of the present evil age, ushered in by the triumphal **Son of man . . . in the glory of his Father with the holy angels,** is described in ch. 13 much more fully.

9:1. This note of time is important. The apparent meaning is that Jesus expected the end of the age within the current generation (cf. 13:30). This expectation was a feature of the earliest Christian community also (cf. I Cor. 7:26-31; I Thess. 4:15-18). The failure of this expectation forced theological interpretation such as is found in John 3:18-19; 11:24-25 in one way and in II Pet. 3:3-10 in another. It is remarkable that the Christian community preserved a saying of Jesus that was not fulfilled, but it was probably established before it could be so recognized. The absence of an explanation or reinterpretation by Mark probably means that none was needed yet, that some of Jesus' generation were still alive at the time he was writing (but see below on 13:32-37). The same conditions seem to prevail in the environment of Matt., who preserves both the sayings without explanation also (16:28; 24:34). Luke preserves them also (9:27; 21:32), but may have understood their fulfillment with the coming of the Holy Spirit at Pentecost. He therefore leaves out Mark's phrase **come with power,** which would tend to make the traditional view necessary. It is interesting that both Mark (13:32) and Matt. (24:36) have one "loophole" explanation, which Luke does not preserve.

9:2-10. The Transfiguration. The Transfiguration represents a special attempt of God to cure the spiritual blindness of the chief disciples, Peter, James, and John. They see Jesus exalted and transfigured; they hear the voice from heaven informing them what it earlier (1:11) has said to Jesus (to inform the reader). But seeing and hearing is not understanding; so they do not perceive, or at best they perceive

Courtesy of Herbert G. May

Mount Tabor; this isolated hill located in the Valley of Jezreel approximately 6 mi. E-SE of Nazareth and 12 mi. W-SW of the S end of the Sea of Galilee is the traditional site of the Transfiguration, though it is not named in the gospel narratives

only dimly. The attempt of some to see this story as the spiritual illumination of Peter, in vision form, runs counter to a main theme in this gospel. To regard it as a misplaced resurrection account, as others do, adds problems, though this is a possibility. Matt. 17:1-8; Luke 9:28-36 have the story.

9:2. The phrase **after six days** is repeated in Matt. but changed to "about eight days after" in Luke. Six days after some general sayings? It is a strange introduction, found nowhere else in Mark, Matt., or Luke. A similar one occurs once in John, to introduce a resurrection story (20:26), but that is hardly proof that this too must be a resurrection story. The "six days" is probably patterned after Exod. 24:16, so that the heavenly voice comes on the 7th day (the sabbath). **Peter and James and John** are later to be pillars of the Jerusalem church, and here they are symbolic of that church's inability to perceive the true nature of Jesus. The high mountain is patterned after the Exod. passage (24:15-18) and is not to be sought for geographically. It is simply a place of revelation (as in Matt. 5:1). The word behind **transfigured** is exactly the same as the one used by Paul in II Cor. 3:18 for "being changed" into his likeness. The true nature of Jesus is being revealed to Peter, James, and John (and to the reader, who alone perceives it). See also Rom. 12:2 and the idea behind I John 3:2-3.

9:3. The fact that the ancient **fuller** (one who bleached cloth) had a low place in society may have led both Matt. and Luke to change the figure of speech to "light" (Matt. 17:2) or "dazzling" (Luke 9:29). The whiteness is symbolic of heavenly things.

9:4. The presence of **Elijah** and **Moses** with Jesus is not explained by Mark. Perhaps they were considered to be the greatest religious figures in Israel's past. There is in Judaism a traditional connection between the Messiah and Elijah but not between the Messiah and Moses. Among the Samaritans, however, the Messiah was expected to be a reappearance of Moses, and there may be here a blending of Jewish and Samaritan messianic hopes. Another, more plausible, possibility is that they represent the 2 official witnesses to the Messiah, mentioned in Rev. 11:3-6, where vs. 6 identifies them figuratively as Elijah (I Kings 17:1) and Moses (Exod. 7:20). These witnesses are reflected (in their literary role) also in Luke 16:29-31, where it must be remembered that Elijah symbolized the prophets.

9:5-6. Peter's response is not supposed to be very intelligible, for Mark comments that **he did not know what to say** (omitted in Matt., of course). His reaction was one of great fright. Jesus is first called "Rabbi" (**Master**) here.

9:7. The **cloud** is a parallel to the cloud of Exod. 24:15-18, and the **voice** is parallel to the voice there. What the voice says is supplied from Ps. 2:7 and represents the Christology of Mark. This is a repetition of the baptismal scene for the benefit of the disciples. Cf. Isa. 42:1.

9:8. The disappearance of Moses and Elijah leaving **Jesus only,** suggests that Jesus replaces them in the new order.

9:9. The meaning of this vs. includes an acknowledgment that this vision (the word actually used in Matt.'s parallel, 17:9) was unknown until after the Resurrection.

9:10. The disciples, as usual, do not understand what **the rising from the dead** means. Matt. and Luke, in harmony with their consistent defense of the disciples, omit this part of Mark.

9:11-13. *The Elijah Prophecy.* This conversation about Elijah may have grown out of the appearance of Elijah in the transfiguration scene. At any rate Mark felt it to be appropriate here. It is based on Mal. 4:5-6.

9:12. The meaning of **to restore all things** is found in the prophecy in Mal. 4:5-6. The problem is that John the Baptist did not accomplish this. Justin Martyr, in the 2nd cent., believed that Elijah (John) would be the forerunner of the Second Coming also and that then he would "restore all things" according to prophecy.

9:13. The claim that **Elijah has come** as John the Baptist answered one of the strong Jewish arguments against the early Christians, that Jesus could not have been the Messiah because Elijah had not come as forerunner. **As it is written of him** is a standard way of referring to scripture, but no such prediction exists in our OT. This might be based on a tradition found in the Biblical Antiquities attributed to Philo, where the reappearance and martyrdom of Elijah are described somewhat like the account in Rev. 11:7-13. Since the Rev. passage assumes a martyrdom, the existence of such a tradition is clear. It is significant that the early church was by no means in agreement on this identification of Elijah and John. It is flatly repudiated in John 1:21. Matt. 17:13 makes the identification explicit (cf. also Matt. 11:14) and adds the reassuring, but anti-Markan, detail that "the disciples understood." Luke omits the whole conversation.

9:9-14. *The Demon-possessed Boy.* The healing of the demon-possessed boy (called an epileptic in Matt. 17:15) seems to be a fusion of 2 originally separate stories. It is easier to follow if these are distinguished. The first is in vss. 14-20 and is a simple exorcism of a dumb spirit. The 2nd, vss. 21-27, is a more complex account of the exorcism of a deaf and dumb spirit. Vss. 28-29 are a poorly adapted conclusion that does not fit either story very well and is left out by Luke and drastically altered by Matt. (17:19-20). The content of Matt.'s alteration is found in another setting entirely in Luke 17:6. Both Matt. and Luke combine the 2 stories into one (Matt. 17:14-21; Luke 9:37-43a). The 2nd story has lost its be-

ginning; the stories probably got confused in tradition because of their striking similarity.

9:14-20. In this first story the inability of the disciples to exorcise the demon is explained as due to the faithlessness of the people. Then Jesus seemingly casts it out in spite of their faithlessness, but the ending is replaced by the introduction of the 2nd story. Note that the crowd is present from the beginning.

9:21-27. In this 2nd story the inability of the disciples is not mentioned. The main concern is the faith of the **father.** The **crowd,** always present in the first story, gathers around Jesus in the middle of the 2nd one (vs. 25).

9:28-29. This returns to the theme of the first story and is believed by some to be the original conclusion of it.

IV. PRIVATE INSTRUCTIONS TO THE DISCIPLES
(9:30-50)

9:30-32. *The 2nd Prediction of the Passion.* In this 2nd prediction of Jesus' death and resurrection (the first was in 8:31-33) Mark leaves no room for doubt as to his intention, telling the reader that the disciples **did not understand . . . and they were afraid to ask him** (vs. 32). Vs. 31 lays special emphasis on Jesus' teaching his disciples. This is omitted in the parallel accounts (Matt. 17:22-23; Luke 9:43b-45), where of course the disciples are defended: Matt. says "they were greatly distressed" (17:23), and Luke says they were providentially kept from understanding (9:45). These are characteristic alterations.

9:33-37. *The Quarrel over Rank.* In the first of 2 similar episodes (the 2nd is in 10:35-45) the disciples are caught discussing among themselves which of them **was the greatest.** Cf. Matt. 18:1-5; Luke 9:46-48.

9:33. This is the last mention of **Capernaum** in Mark. **In the house** (Moffatt: "indoors") is Greek idiom for "at home" (see above on 2:1).

9:34. The disciples **were silent** because they were ashamed of their discussion. This unflattering view of the disciples is well drilled into the reader of Mark. Luke 9:46 preserves Mark's account, but Matt. 18:1 alters it drastically in the interest of the disciples.

9:36-37. Mark adds an episode about receiving a child in Jesus' name that does not seem to fit the dispute about rank. Luke has a similar account (9:47-48), but Matt. greatly strengthens the structure by inserting 2 other separate units within Mark's. The first of these (Matt. 18:3) is found elsewhere in Mark (10:15); the 2nd (Matt. 18:4) is repeated in Matt. (23:12) and appears twice in Luke (14:11; 18:14). Passages like these illustrate well the editorial work required by the gospel writers.

9:38-41. *The Independent Disciple.* This paragraph consists of a short dialogue between Jesus and John, with 2 originally separate sayings vss. 40, 41. The original setting has been affected by the circumstances of the early Christian community. The use of Jesus' name as a formula for casting out demons began after the Resurrection and is here read back into the earlier period. The problem faced here is the legitimacy of Christian workers who are not in fellowship with the 12, i.e. the leaders of the Gentile Christian church in general. What about those (like Paul) who worked independently? The answer is that they are acceptable to Jesus. It is a dialogue story which Matt., quite naturally, prefers not to use, and which Luke abridges (9:49-50). Cf. the reverse of vs. 40 in Matt. 12:30; Luke 11:23.

9:41. This saying really has no relationship to the preceding vss. It seems to commend any favorable treatment accorded to Christians in an era of persecution. Cf. Matt. 10:42.

9:42-48. *Sayings on Temptation.* Collected here are sayings of which the meanings are often obscure. Vs. 42 deals with tempting others, vss. 43-48 with the problem of one's own temptations.

9:42. The central problem here is the original meaning of **little ones.** The context at first suggests children. Since they are further described as ones **who believe in me,** they seem to be Christian children. But since Jesus sometimes referred to his disciples as children (cf. 10:24), it seems at least possible that the original reference was to his followers of any age. Cf. Matt. 18:6; Luke 17:1-2.

9:43-47. Three parallel figures—**hand, foot,** and **eye**—represent the common agents of temptation. They should not be pressed lit., of course, because one eye is hardly more to be blamed than the other for visual temptations, nor one foot more than the other for straying from the path. Behind the word **hell** is the Greek "Gehenna," a transliteration of the Hebrew name of the Hinnom Valley SW of Jerusalem, which at one time was used for infant sacrifices to the Ammonite god Molech (cf. II Kings 23:10; Jer. 32:35) and later, in contempt, was used as the garbage dump for Jerusalem. Before Christian times the name became symbolic for hell. This is not the same word or concept as the Hebrew "Sheol" (see comment on Ps. 6:4-5) or the Greek "Hades." Cf. Matt. 5:29-30; 18:7-9.

9:48. This clause is taken from Isa. 66:24. It is not found in Matt.'s version (18:7-9). Most later manuscripts of Mark have added it as vss. 44, 46 also (hence the KJV), but the early manuscripts have it only at the end (as in the RSV). It symbolizes the finality of God's judgment.

9:49-50. *Sayings on Salt.* Three sayings on salt are here grouped together editorially. They are unrelated to each other in meaning.

9:49. This saying is not found in any other gospel. Some manuscripts add "and every sacrifice will be salted with salt." It apparently teaches the acceptance of suffering as a normal experience. Cf. I Pet. 4:12; Heb. 12:8.

9:50a. Matt. 5:13; Luke 14:34-35 have a more elaborate version of this saying. Luke recognizes its symbolic difficulty by adding the formula "He who has ears to hear, let him hear." Matt. introduces it with "You are the salt of the earth," making the saying easier to interpret. The original intent is elusive.

9:50b. This is another cryptic saying (found in Mark only) that depends for its meaning on the interpreter. The exhortation to **be at peace with one another** is refreshingly plain and clear. Cf. Rom. 14.

V. The Journey to Jerusalem (10:1-52)

10:1-12. *On Marriage and Divorce.* This account represents a Gentile Christian adaptation of Jesus' original teaching. The situation presupposed in vss. 11-12 is not that of a Palestinian Jewish community

(the environment of Jesus) but that of the Greco-Roman world (the environment of the Gentile Christian church). In Jesus' environment adultery was not a crime against the wife (as in vs. 11) but against the other wife's husband. Matt. 19:9 more accurately represents Jesus by omitting the phrase **against her.** Moreover, the wife did not have the opportunity to divorce her husband in Jesus' environment (as in vs. 12), but she did in the customs of the empire. Matt. therefore omits this vs. entirely. Luke omits the whole account.

10:1. This vs. introduces the journey of Jesus from Galilee to Jerusalem. The geographical route is only vaguely suggested—from **there** (i.e. Capernaum, 9:33) to **Judea**—but it seems intended that the reader understand Jesus as avoiding Samaria by coming down the E side of the **Jordan** (see color map 15). Neither Samaria nor the Samaritans are ever mentioned in Mark. **As his custom was, he taught them.** Matt.'s parallel (19:2) stresses healing instead of teaching, and this curiously reverses the main emphasis of both gospels.

10:2-9. The discussion on marriage is related to a widely disputed point in Jesus' time. Followers of the Rabbi Hillel taught and practiced a very lenient interpretation of Deut. 24:1, permitting men to divorce their wives for minor matters. Followers of Rabbi Shammai were much stricter in their interpretation, allowing divorce only on grounds of adultery. Note how Matt.'s version of Jesus' final saying (19:9) adapts it to the views of the stricter party. Mark, however, perhaps not so intimately acquainted with the Jewish discussion, presents a view that is stricter than Shammai's. This view is found also in an earlier Christian writing (I Cor. 7:10-11). It is noteworthy that Mark's account here does not proceed in rabbinic fashion, with its citation of scripture against scripture. Rather it is a matter of scripture against the unwritten will of God, after the fashion of Philo (who found the real truth of scripture in hidden meanings) and Paul (who got his central insights by revelation).

10:4-5. The law of Moses is presented as a concession made necessary by the **hardness of heart** of the people. Actually Deut. 24:1 was a provision of mercy and justice that, in its own time, helped women by requiring divorce rather than mere abandonment. But Jesus probably saw it as an excuse for irresponsible behavior and so adopted a stricter view.

10:6-8. The symbolic meaning apparently intended here is understood as making marriage permanent. The textual basis is Gen. 1:27; 2:24. The interpretation in vs. 8b is based on a type of thinking reflected in more detail in I Cor. 6:15-16. In this popular ancient view it is not love or the marriage ritual that permanently unites, but the sexual act. This is perpetuated in later, more sophisticated versions of this thinking, such as the Roman Catholic teaching that a valid marriage must include consummation in the sexual act. This particular explanation may not go back to Jesus himself, since its native environment is non-Palestinian. It reflects a concern with being, or nature, that is non-Semitic and characteristically Greek. Moreover, it implies the monogamous customs of the Gentile world rather than the polygamous customs of the Semitic world. Judaism did not officially abolish polygamy until a thousand years after Jesus.

10:9. The uniting of the 2 into one is regarded as an act of *God,* i.e. a uniting so mysterious that it cannot be explained in natural terms. The question for us is, How does God unite 2 people with a genuine unity? The answer is not clear; the sex act is too simple a solution.

10:10-12. The representation of the disciples as needing a private explanation is characteristic of Mark and naturally omitted in Matt.'s parallel. On vss. 11-12 see above on 10:1-12.

10:13-16. *Jesus and Children.* The disciples fail here to understand the relation of children to the kingdom. The indignation of Jesus at the disciples (vs. 14) is omitted in Matt. 19:13-15; Luke 18:15-17. The brief setting serves only to put the disciples in a poor light and to introduce a very popular saying of Jesus. This saying, like so many of Jesus' sayings, is not clear. Children have all kinds of qualities, some desirable and others not; the interpreter reads in what he feels to be appropriate. The most probable clue, from vs. 15, suggests that the kingdom is a gift, not an achievement, like the Gentile Christian doctrine of salvation by grace.

10:17-22. *The Rich Man's Question.* The story of the rich man gives us a fine example of the basic traits of Mark and deserves careful study. There are 3 other versions of the story, one of which (Luke 18:18-23) follows Mark's very closely, except that the man becomes "a ruler." The changes in Matt.'s version (19:16-22) illustrate well the differences between Mark and Matt. It requires combining versions to get the popular title "The Rich [all] Young [Matt. only] Ruler [Luke only]." The 4th version is found in the noncanonical Gospel According to the Hebrews, which exists only in fragmentary quotations. In certain respects it has obvious values that lead some to pronounce that it is the best version. This 4th version follows as translated from *Gospel Parallels* (Thomas Nelson & Sons, 1949):

> The second of the rich men said to him, "Teacher, what good thing can I do and live?" He said to him, "Sir, fulfill the law and the prophets." He answered, "I have." Jesus said, "Go, sell all you have and distribute to the poor; and come, follow me." But the rich man began to scratch his head, for it did not please him. And the Lord said to him, "How can you say, I have fulfilled the law and the prophets, when it is written in the law: You shall love your neighbor as yourself; and lo, many of your brothers, sons of Abraham, are clothed in filth, dying of hunger, and your house is full of many good things, none of which goes out to them?" And he turned and said to Simon, his disciple, who was sitting by him, "Simon, son of Jonah, it is easier for a camel to go through the eye of a needle than for a rich man to enter the kingdom of heaven."

10:17-18. The salutation **good Teacher** is rejected by Jesus, who affirms that goodness belongs to **God alone.** In the sense of absolute goodness, in all its perfection, this would represent the traditional Jewish view (e.g. Pss. 100:5; 106:1; 107:1; 145:9). But against the background of Markan theology and the Gentile Christian community this is probably more reflective of the helplessness of man in the power of sin, as expressed in Rom. 7:18. This does not mean that Mark is portraying Jesus as having a sense of his own sinfulness. Mark is simply using this story to reveal the true answer to man's question about

salvation. This true answer does not lie in obedience, for even if that could be done, man still lacks the essential requirement of salvation, viz. complete renunciation of all worldly dependencies and acceptance of salvation as God's gift in trust and faith. From a different theological perspective Matt. changes this opening question and answer, but his version is incompletely changed and clearly a secondary account.

10:19. In Mark's free summary of the Ten Commandments, **do not defraud** is not directly related, and so it is omitted in Matt. 19:18-19; Luke 18:20. **From my youth** suggests that he is no longer a youth and is therefore omitted in Matt. 19:20, which describes the man as "young."

10:21. The note that Jesus **loved him** is in Mark only. His **lack** should not be understood as his special problem, because in Markan theology obedience is not the way to salvation (see above on vss. 10:17-18). Note that in Matt.'s version obedience is the clue to salvation, and the renunciation which is required in Mark is turned into a counsel of perfection, i.e. something beyond the actual requirements.

10:23-31. *On Riches and Discipleship.* These sayings follow appropriately on the story of the rich man. Matt. and Luke follow Mark's plan here, and Luke actually takes the words of Jesus to his disciples and addresses them to the rich ruler (cf. vs. 23 with Luke 18:24).

10:25. This vs. repeats in hyperbole form the teaching of vs. 23. The pious explanation that there was a Needle's Eye Gate into Jerusalem that a camel could enter only on its knees after a medieval sermon unfounded in fact. The plain meaning is that it is impossible for the rich to enter the kingdom. This is confirmed in vss. 26-27.

10:27. The most striking idea in this story is the common Gentile Christian conception of salvation as entirely the work of God, his rescue of helpless man.

10:28-31. This dialogue between Jesus and Peter is related to vss. 17-22, 23-27 but seems to be a unit in itself. Peter claims, for all the disciples, that they have done what the rich man refused to do, viz. **left everything and followed Jesus.** Jesus replies, in general terms, that renunciation of things in this world will bring everything in return, in both this life and the next.

10:29. The phrase **for the gospel** reflects the situation of the early church and is deleted from the parallel versions (Matt. 19:29; Luke 18:29).

10:31. This saying is not part of the preceding dialogue, but has been added by Mark, probably to detract from the prestige of the 12. Luke removes it to an earlier section (13:30). It says that man's values are not necessarily God's and, in particular, that the 12 may not be entitled to any special priority finally.

10:32-34. *The 3rd Prediction of the Passion.* This 3rd prediction, made again privately and personally to the 12, follows the pattern of the first 2 (8:31-33; 9:30-32). There is no hint that the disciples now understand, and Luke clearly recognizes this (18:34).

10:32. It may be that we have here a brief glimpse of Jesus moving at the head of a single file of disciples, which would customarily be arranged strictly according to seniority. This was a formalized procedure in first-cent. Palestine. The amazement and fear of the disciples is a Markan feature omitted from Matt. 20:17; Luke 18:31.

10:34. On **he will rise** see above on 8:31.

10:35-45. *The Ambition of James and John.* Here James and John are represented as selfishly seeking the chief seats in heaven. This gives Jesus occasion to teach the disciples humility. Since it casts a poor light on the disciples, especially James and John, Luke omits the James-John part entirely, and Matt. imperfectly alters the beginning of the story to shift the stigma of selfishness to their mother, transforming it into motherly ambition (Matt. 20:20-28).

10:38. The phrase **drink the cup** is idiomatic for martyrdom. **Baptism** as symbolic for death is found also in Luke 12:50; Rom. 6:3-4.

10:39. This seems to reflect clearly the martyrdoms of James and John. That of James is reported in Acts 12:1-2. The death of John is less certain, with conflicts in tradition. This prediction is itself the best evidence, for had it not been fulfilled it probably would not have been preserved.

10:41. The indignation of **the ten** at James and John makes it difficult to interpret their request in any way that would absolve them from criticism.

10:42-45. The meaning of discipleship is not privilege but service, and Jesus exemplifies this service. His highest service is finally that he gives **his life as a ransom for many.** Being contrary to the mainstream thinking of Matt. and Luke-Acts, the ransom phrase is omitted in Luke 22:27 in favor of service as good deeds and in Matt. 20:28 may be simply a carryover from Mark. The idea of Jesus' death as a ransom is undeveloped in Mark, but it is certainly related to I Cor. 6:19-20; 7:23; Gal. 1:4; 2:20. It is one way that Gentile Christianity expressed its conviction that Christ is God's action to rescue men helpless in the power of sin. This conviction may be a development of Jesus' own attitude, especially if his own view was shaped by Isa. 53. See also below on 14:24 and on Matt. 20:24-28.

10:46-52. *Healing Bartimaeus.* The healing of Bartimaeus reads like other healings in Mark but introduces the title **Son of David** for Jesus. This title emphasizes the descent of the Messiah from David. Paul acknowledges this in Rom. 1:3 but never refers to it elsewhere. The main Gentile Christian view of Jesus as the divine Son of God found the Son of David title more confusing than helpful. It was tolerated only if properly understood; it was eventually easier to describe Christ in other ways, and this even led some to deny his descent from David. Mark's feeling is expressed in 12:35-37, in harmony with John 7:40-43. See below on 12:35-37*a*.

10:46. In Aramaic **Bartimaeus** means **the son of Timaeus.** The name is omitted in Matt. 20:29-34; Luke 18:35-43. Matt. tells the story as a healing of "two blind men."

10:47. On **Jesus of Nazareth** see above on 1:24.

10:52. The healing is by word (as in Luke also); in Matt. Jesus touches "their eyes" and omits Mark's explanation **your faith has made you well.** The words **followed him** imply discipleship, but Bartimaeus is otherwise unknown.

VI. The Ministry in Jerusalem (11:1-13:37)

A. The Entry into Jerusalem (11:1-10)

The account of the entry into Jerusalem is a traditional story of the popularity of Jesus that has been theologically adapted to a messianic announcement after the manner of the prophecy in Zech. 9:9. The Fourth Gospel reports candidly that the disciples were not aware of any messianic significance to the entry at the time, but that later, reflecting on it, they saw its true significance (John 12:16). Mark's account has been shaped by this later understanding, as is illustrated by the unusual use of **the Lord.**

11:2-3. The intent of Mark here is probably to illustrate to the reader the supernatural knowledge of Jesus. It is possible, however, that Jesus is deliberately fulfilling the prophecy of Zech. 9:9 and has planned his entry carefully. At this point Matt. 21:4-5 makes explicit the connection between this event and the prophecy of Zech. **A colt . . . on which no one has ever sat** is based on the Greek translation of the prophecy, which reads "a new [i.e. unbroken] ass."

B. Radical Actions (11:12-25)

11:12-14. *Cursing the Fig Tree.* This story is difficult to understand. As we have it in Mark, the tree is in leaf, but **it was not the season for figs.** Seeking fruit on it nevertheless, and finding none, Jesus lays a curse on it to prevent it from ever bearing fruit again. Then they all go on into Jerusalem, where Jesus drives out the money-changers. The barren fig tree is probably symbolic of Israel and the coming destruction of Jerusalem. Mark records the episode as an example of the power of Jesus. It is probably a variant version of an original symbolic teaching, now preserved in Luke 13:6-9. It is significant that Mark and Matt. have an incident but no parable; Luke has a parable but no incident. Tradition has apparently dramatized the parable. See further below on vss. 20-25.

11:15-19. *The Temple Cleansing.* This incident is reported in all the gospels, but at different points in Jesus' life. Matt., Mark, and Luke put it at the beginning of the last week (Matt. on the first day, Mark on the 2nd, and Luke on an unspecified day). John, however, places it during a Passover 2 years earlier (2:13-22).

11:15. The persons **who sold** were merchants, profiteering on the pilgrims. The **money-changers** were bankers, exchanging various foreign currencies for that which could be used in the temple. These changers charged a commission, of course. **Those who sold pigeons** (or doves) were selling sacrificial offerings to the pilgrims. The priestly families seem to have had control of this business.

11:16. This prohibition is peculiar to Mark's account, and probably reflects the influence of Jer. 17:27. The original prohibition applied only to carrying things on the sabbath, but this was extended eventually to the temple area for all days. The Jewish regulation, as found in the Mishnah (Berakoth 9:5), reads: "A man . . . may not enter the Temple Mount with his staff or his sandal or his wallet, or with the dust on his feet, nor may he make of it a short by-path; still less may he spit there."

11:17. The scripture quotation is a combination of Isa. 56:7; Jer. 7:11. Matt. 25:13; Luke (19:46), out of closer sympathy with a more conservative (Jewish) Christianity, omit the phrase **for all the nations.**

11:20-25. *The Withered Fig Tree.* The effect of the cursing is discovered the next morning. Naturalistic explanations are beside the point if the incident is simply a variant of the parable of Luke 13:6-9.

But since Mark presents it as an incident, further displaying the power of Jesus, he finds some teachings on the power of faith entirely appropriate here. That this was Mark's editorial decision is shown by the appearance of some of these sayings in other settings in Matt. 6:14; 17:20; Luke 17:6.

11:22-24. It is a distortion of the intention of these vss. to take them to mean that a man of faith and prayer can be a powerful magician. God acts through us in accord with his will and not ours. A more carefully phrased expression of the power of faith and prayer is found in I John 5:14.

11:25. This valuable saying on prayer has been placed here by Mark; Matt. has it much earlier in his gospel (6:14) in an abbreviated form.

C. Jesus in Controversy (11:27–12:44)

11:27-33. *The Question About Authority.* The first event of the 3rd day of this last week is a question from the authorities. Since it has already been reported that they are plotting to destroy him (vs. 18), it is safer to assume that these questioners are not genuine students but clever hunters. They are seeking to discredit him with the people so that he can be destroyed without popular reaction. This first question is about Jesus' credentials. His answer is not an answer at all but an evasion. This pattern of evading insincere questions is carried out in the next 2 questions also.

11:27. The mention that **they came again** is the basis for assuming this to be the 3rd day. That Jesus **was walking in the temple** after having purged it of its mercenaries only the day before shows the strength of his popularity at this time.

11:29. Jesus "answers" their question with one of his own, about John's baptism (the environment of the divine commissioning of Jesus, which was the source of his authority).

11:31-33. Because they cannot answer the question without discrediting themselves, they simply reply, **We do not know.** So Jesus refuses to answer their question. It is a bit too sophisticated here to think that Jesus refused because they would not have understood his answer. He simply dealt cleverly with an insincere question.

12:1-12. *The Parable of the Wicked Tenants.* This parable is so appropriate that both Matt. (21:33-46) and Luke 20:9-19) have left it in this place. It is not really a parable but an allegory on the rejection of the Jews by God, reflecting a later Christian setting. Its theme is "the true Israel" (cf. Rom. 9:6-8). The rejection of Jesus by the Jews has caused God to **give the vineyard to others,** viz. the Gentiles. This is a major plank in the platform of early Gentile Christianity. The allegory is similar to Isa. 5:1-7. The **man** represents God. The **vineyard** is Palestine. **Let it out to tenants** refers to God's giving of Canaan (Palestine) to Israel. **To get from them some of the fruit** symbolizes the obedience God expects. The **servant** and the others to follow are the prophets, sent by him to exhort obedience. The tradition that all the prophets were martyred was popularly read in Jesus' time in a late Jewish writing called the Lives of the Prophets. The **beloved son** is of course Jesus himself. Vs. 8 is symbolic of the crucifixion and rejection of Jesus by the Jews. Vs. 9 is symbolic of the fall of Jerusalem and the rise of early Gentile Christianity, claiming to be the true

Israel. The OT "prophecy" to support this (vs. 10) was found in the very popular Ps. 118:22-23.

12:13-17. *The Question about Taxes.* The 2nd question **to entrap him** raised an explosive political issue. What about the offensive taxes that Rome collected, should they be paid? If Jesus replied "no,"

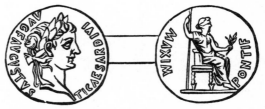

A denarius, showing the head of Tiberius; Jesus used a denarius in his reply to the Pharisees in Mark 12:15; this Roman silver coin, weighing 3.8 grams, was a day's pay for a laborer

he would be even more popular, but subject to immediate arrest and execution. If he replied "yes," he would be in danger of losing his popularity with the people, as a friend of Rome. Jesus, **knowing their hypocrisy,** gave an ambiguous answer and let them interpret it as they wished. **And they were amazed at him.**

12:18-27. *The Question about the Resurrection.* The 3rd question revolves around a disputed religious question. The **Sadducees** did not believe in a resurrection (vs. 18). In ridiculing it they intended to ridicule Jesus, who shared with the Pharisees a belief in the resurrection. After one woman has been the **wife** of **seven brothers** successively, whose wife will she be in the resurrection? Jesus' reply is again enigmatic. In effect he says that the question is inappropriate to life in the resurrection, for then we will be **like angels.** But how are the angels?

12:19. See Deut. 25:5-6.

12:25. The implication of **they neither marry nor are given in marriage** is that life in the resurrection will not have these physical necessities. Angels do not cohabit, for they are immortal beings; conception and birth belong only in the age of mortality. See I Cor. 15:35-57 for the best commentary on Jesus' answer.

12:26-27. This argument for the resurrection turns on the present tense of the verb as God spoke to Moses, saying, **I am** [not "I was"] **the God of Abraham** [who has long been dead]. Hence Abraham, and the others, must not be dead from God's perspective. God is a **God . . . of the living,** not the **dead.** But since it is obvious that Abraham *did* die, then he must be alive in some sense other than the ordinary one. He is alive in the resurrection plans of God; hence the Sadducees **are quite wrong.**

12:28-34. *The Question about the Greatest Law.* After the 3 insincere questions there comes one that seems sincere. The basic function of this paragraph is to present clearly a central doctrine of early Gentile Christianity. Righteousness is not to be understood as strict obedience to a complex code of laws and customs. The one commandment that is central is the principle of **love** (cf. e.g. John 13:34-35; 15:17; I John 3:23; 4:7).

12:29-30. The quotation of Deut. 6:4-5 would be satisfactory to all Jews. These are the most treasured vss. of Judaism.

12:31. The 2nd, from Lev. 19:18*b*, was uniquely expressive of the Christian concern and could hardly be offensive to anyone. The concluding statement in Mark, that **there is no other commandment greater than these,** is the affirmation of early Gentile Christianity. Both Matt. and Luke omit this affirmation. Matt. 22:40 changes it to make all the other laws grow out of these 2. Luke has rewritten the whole episode (10:25-28), having the scribe say what Jesus says in Mark. Note that Luke has the whole conversation earlier in Jesus' ministry. It should be noted that the linking together of love for God and neighbor first appears at the end of the 2nd cent. B.C., in the Testament of the Twelve Patriarchs (Isaachar 5:2; 7:6; Dan. 5:3).

12:35-37a. The Davidic Ancestry of the Messiah. This difficult section seems to be an argument against thinking of the Messiah (Christ) as a descendant of David. The Messiah was David's Lord rather than his son, the argument from Ps. 110:1 seems to say. It would be natural to think that it must have arisen in early Gentile Christianity, which wanted a Lord and Savior more than a Jewish Messiah, or Son of David. The 4th Gospel has a similar section (John 7:40-43). But if this apparent meaning is correct, it is difficult to understand why Matt. 22:41-46; Luke 20:41-44 (see comments) repeat it. Perhaps the original purpose was not to deny Jesus' Davidic sonship but to assert that his greatness is independent of David's prestige and actually prior to David.

12:37b-40. Denouncing the Scribes. This denunciation of hypocrisy and formalism is greatly expanded in Matt. 23:1-36.

12:41-44. The Widow's Gift. Within the temple enclosure, but outside the building proper, there were 13 offering boxes. Apparently Jesus sat for a while watching people come up to these boxes and leave their offerings. The **copper coins** are lit. "leptons," the smallest denomination of the Greek-Syrian system. Mark explains for his readers that the **two** leptons equal the smallest Roman coin, the "quadrans" (**penny**; see table, p. 1285). Perhaps originally the story was told with only one lepton.

D. The Last Days (13:1-37)

13:1-4. The Setting. This dialogue provides the setting for the longest "speech" of Jesus in Mark. The destruction of the temple is associated with the end of this age and the coming of the kingdom of God. The destruction of the temple actually occurred in A.D. 70 at the hands of the Romans, but without the end of the age.

13:3. The secrets of the end of the age were given, according to Mark, only to the 4 senior disciples. Neither Matt. (24:3) nor Luke (21:5-7) follows Mark in this. By restricting the revelation to these 4 Mark indicates that this teaching was not originally a feature of the public teachings of Jesus, nor even of his special instructions to the 12, but rather something shared only with a very few.

13:5-37. The Apocalyptic Prophecies. This complex discourse (the only one in Mark) is often called "The Little Apocalypse." In form and content it resembles Dan. 7-12 and Rev. Technical study of it reveals that it is composite, being made up of some genuine sayings of Jesus that were expanded and adapted to current community needs in written form before being incorporated into Mark. This discourse was probably the result of a special interest group, just as today there are groups who find special satisfaction in Dan. and Rev. Matt. 24-25 and Luke 21 have parallel accounts (cf. also I Thess. 5:1-11).

13:5-6. These vss. parallel vss. 21-23. Do they represent 2 versions of a traditional warning? Cf. I John 2:18.

13:7-8. The expectation of strife and natural disasters at the end is a pattern in apocalyptic thinking. This theme is carried on in vss. 24-25. In this understanding salvation comes in the darkest moment; things get progressively worse until, all at once, they are over. This is fully developed in Rev. The Greek word behind **sufferings** means "birth pangs," i.e. the birth of the new age.

13:9-13. This too is standard theme material. It reflects the problems of persecution and seems to be influenced by the circumstances of Roman persecution of the Christians, but of this we cannot be sure. All apocalyptic literature is "persecution literature," exhorting the faithful to hold on to the end (e.g. Rev. 2:10). Perhaps the experiences of Paul have influenced the present form of vss. 9-10.

13:14-20. The **desolating sacrilege** is apocalyptic code for something. Matt. took it to be the same as referred to in Dan. 9:27; 12:11, but it is now thought that Dan. refers to an event of 167 B.C. (see comment). That the term has a hidden meaning is indicated by the parenthetical note **let the reader understand**—quite out of place in a speech. If it was intended to refer to the desecration of the temple in the war of A.D. 66-70, then that would tell us that Mark was written after that event. Luke 21:20 substitutes for this "sacrilege" a siege of Jerusalem, probably because that is what actually took place. Cf. II Thess. 2:3-4.

13:20. The doctrine reflected in **the elect, whom he chose,** although related to the chosen-people idea in the OT, is a distinctively Gentile Christian concept. It is assumed by Paul (Rom. 9–11) and John (e.g. 6:44, 64-65; 8:42-47). It is a necessary part of a theological system which understands salvation as God's act to rescue helpless men.

13:21-23. See above on vss. 5-6.

13:24-25. These wonders are thematic in apocalyptic literature. Insisting on them has the effect of curbing enthusiasm for radical interpretations of ordinary events as signs of the end. The view of the universe reflected here is of course prescientific.

13:26-27. The **coming** of the **Son of man** in this fashion was the popular early Christian expectation. The belief was shaped by OT passages like Deut. 30:4; Isa. 13:10 LXX; 14:12; Dan. 7:13; Zech. 2:6. It can be seen also in Acts 1:9-11; I Thess. 4:17.

13:28-29. Cf. 4:26-29; Jas. 5:7-8.

13:30-31. These are 2 originally separate sayings. The phrasing of the 2nd (vs. 31) may be influenced by Isa. 51:6. In it Jesus' words are presented as eternal, a position which they share in Matt. and Luke with "the law and the prophets" (Matt. 5:17; Luke 16:17). Here we can see again the more radical nature of Markan Christianity and the more conservative bent of Matt. and Luke.

13:32-37. The lesson in all this is that, since no one knows the exact schedule for the end of this age and the coming of the kingdom, everyone should be ready at all times. The fact that variations of these watchfulness sayings are found elsewhere in Luke (12:38, 40; 19:12-13) and in Matt. (24:42; 25:13, 14-15), shows clearly that they are editorially arranged here. Cf. I Thess. 5:2; Rev. 16:15.

13:32. This saying is particularly significant, for it preserves an early admission that Jesus (as the Son) did not have perfect knowledge of all things. Since this seems to conflict with the later doctrinal conclusions about Jesus, it was a common tendency of the copyists to omit the phrase **nor the Son.** This saying may be connected with the efforts of the later apostolic age to explain why Jesus' prediction of the end did not in fact happen (see above on 9:1). This explanation would admit candidly that he did not actually know the schedule, for that was reserved for **only the Father.** Note that Luke has reworded the explanation and assigned it to the resurrection period rather than the earthly ministry (Acts 1:6-7). It is a mistake to regard Mark as intending to emphasize the inferiority of Jesus to the Father; the intention is just the opposite. The Son is not classified among men, nor even among the angelic beings, but he is superior to both.

VII. THE PASSION STORY (14:1–15:47)

A. EVENTS PREPARATORY TO THE CRUCIFIXION (14:1-42)

14:1-2. *The Conspiracy.* The emphasis is on urgency and secrecy. This is the best explanation for the actual trial and crucifixion schedule as reported in all the gospels. Jesus was to be disposed of before the Passover; hence there was a hasty trial and execution. Note that Mark's comment on the date (**two days before the Passover**) is reported in Matt. as a saying of Jesus (26:2). Luke simply says that the feast was drawing near (22:1).

14:3-9. *The Anointing of Jesus.* The story of the anointing at Bethany appears, with interesting variants, in all 4 gospels (Matt. 26:6-13; Luke 7:36-50; John 12:1-8). The purpose in Mark (closely followed in Matt.) is expressed in vs. 8—to anoint the **body** of Jesus **beforehand for burying.** The story of the women going to the tomb early in the morning after the sabbath (16:1) expresses the same basic concern. In the first 3 gospels the body of Jesus is not properly anointed, and this deficiency is met in piety by this account of the Bethany anointing (in some circles) and by the intentions of the women (in other circles). Mark preserves both traditions. Luke, however, uses the story quite differently. John seems to have an independent version that retains Mark's basic purpose, but also reports an official anointing (John 19:39-40).

14:3. Simon the leper becomes in Luke a "Pharisee" named Simon, and in John the incident is reported as happening in the house of Lazarus. The **woman** is not identified in Mark (or Matt.), but in Luke she is a forgiven sinner, and in John she is Mary, the sister of Lazarus. In Mark (and Matt.) it is Jesus' **head** that is anointed, whereas in Luke and John it is his "feet."

14:5. The value of the ointment is specified in both Mark and John as **three hundred denarii.** Based on the wages indicated in Matt. 20:2, this sum would approach a laborer's total annual income.

14:7. The meaning is simply that the time for do-

ing something for Jesus was running out. There is no reason to think that Jesus believed poverty to be inevitable. This vs. is not a social analysis but simply a statement of present opportunity. Cf. Matt. 26:11; John 12:8.

14:8-9. These vss. probably represent the reflection of the community as it pondered the significance of the original event. It is possible that the anointing originally represented a messianic anointing ceremony (cf. I Sam. 9:15-16; 10:1), replaced in Mark's story by the spiritual anointing at the time of the baptism. The anointing-for-burial interpretation has become the official one, however.

14:10-11. *The Defection of Judas.* Judas' betrayal of Jesus is not completely explained in the gospels. Matt. 26:14-15; John 12:6 assume a motive of financial greed. John 13:2; Luke 22:3 seem to make Judas the agent of Satan. But Mark simply reports Judas' betrayal. Probably Judas failed to understand Jesus and acted in disillusionment. It is possible that he betrayed him in order to force him to reveal his messianic powers and to usher in the kingdom. Mark never reports any repentance from Judas, nor does he tell what happened to him after the Crucifixion.

14:12-16. *Preparation for Passover.* Mark's description of the Last Supper as the Passover meal has been a point of controversy ever since the 2nd cent. John states clearly that everything took place before the Passover began (13:1, 29; 18:28; 19:14, 31). In John the Crucifixion occurs at the time of the sacrificing of the paschal lamb, i.e. on the day before the Passover. Several things combine to make John's dating preferable to Mark's: (*a*) Mark's account itself contains traces of the Johannine view in the expressed plans of the Jewish leaders (see above on vss. 1-2; also on 15:46). (*b*) A Jewish hearing or trial on the first day of Passover is not very likely. (*c*) The presuppositions of the earliest Christian literature, the letters of Paul, favor John's view: in I Cor. 5:7-8 the Crucifixion is the Christian Passover sacrifice; in I Cor. 15:20 the Resurrection corresponds to the "first fruits" of the Passover feast; in Mark's dating both would have come a day late for these associations. Matt. and Luke are both secondary on this question, depending on Mark's version and therefore agreeing with it. Various efforts have been made to harmonize the 2 traditions, but Mark states too clearly that the Last Supper was the Passover meal (vss. 12, 14, 16), and John just as clearly maintains that the Crucifixion was prior to the beginning of the feast (19:14).

14:12. Mark's Gentile Christian background causes him to be technically inaccurate here. The **passover lamb** was not **sacrificed . . . on the first day of Unleavened Bread** but on the day before. Matt. 26:17; Luke 22:7 correct this, in different ways. Probably Mark reckoned the days in Gentile fashion, as we do now, from midnight to midnight. The Jewish reckoning, of course, is from sunset to sunset. To a Gentile the afternoon sacrifice and the evening meal would all be on the same day. To a Jew, however, the afternoon sacrifice is on the day before.

14:13-16. This unusual account is strikingly similar to 11:1-6. There are even more verbal agreements in the underlying Greek text. Both accounts seem to have the same significance—they can be regarded as the working out of providential plans, known to

Jesus, or they can be regarded as Jesus' own pre-arrangements. This 2nd one may also have some connection with the story beginning in I Sam. 10:1.

14:17-21. *Prediction of Betrayal.* In all of the gospels Jesus predicts his betrayal. Matt. (26:25) and John (13:26) are more specific than Mark or Luke (22:21-23). The Christian tradition owes something to Ps. 41:9. Mark's general lack of sympathy with the 12 makes it easy for him to report, matter-of-factly, how one of them betrays him. Matt. involves Judas in remorse, repentance, and suicide. Luke ascribes the betrayal to Satan's influence. Thus both the later evangelists defend the reputation of the 12.

14:21. The NT assumes in many places that the crucifixion of Jesus is according to OT prophecies. If the suffering servant poems of Isa. 42–53 are regarded as messianic prophecies, then the NT assumption is intelligible. Since it is known that the early church did associate Jesus with the suffering servant, this is the best explanation for this vs.

14:22-25. *The Last Supper.* Mark reports as the main event of the Last Supper the institution of the Lord's Supper. This is supported by the earlier account in I Cor. 11:23-25 and may be fairly considered as the "orthodox" version among Gentile Christians of his own day. Paul's account seems to reflect a memorial service; there is little or nothing in the gospel accounts of the supper to justify repeating it ritually; only in John 6:52-58 is full sacramental significance attached to a very indirect discussion of the custom. In the first 3 gospels the supper has eschatological significance; it will be repeated only after the kingdom comes.

14:22. The blessing that accompanied the breaking of bread was traditional in Judaism. Jesus may have had a distinctive way of doing this (cf. 6:41; 8:6; Luke 24:30-31, 35). **This is my body** probably became ritually fixed before the writing of the gospels. It lends itself well to a variety of interpretations, ranging from the "real presence" interpretation (of Roman Catholicism) to purely symbolic views (like that of the Quakers).

14:24. This expresses well the idea of Jesus' death as a ransom (see above on 10:45), inaugurating a new covenant (cf. Exod. 24:8). The thought of drinking blood was very repugnant to Jews and is strictly forbidden in their code of food laws. It is difficult even to imagine an analogy like this arising out of Jewish piety. Luke omits all reference to the wine as blood. Paul claims that his account was received "from the Lord" (I Cor. 11:23), and that probably is sufficient to indicate that the present account arose in Gentile Christianity and is here presented anachronistically.

14:25. The natural meaning here is that the coming of **the kingdom** is expected to take place shortly after the death of Jesus. Matt.'s phrasing (26:29, adding "with you") makes this meaning more explicit.

14:26-31. *Predictions of Jesus.* This section contains Jesus' prediction of the desertion of his followers, especially Peter, and of his resurrection appearance to the disciples in **Galilee.** The desertion is understood as a fulfillment of Zech. 13:7. The resurrection prediction seems to intrude into the desertion discussion; perhaps its meaning is that after **the sheep** have been **scattered** (by desertion) the risen Lord himself will gather them together again. Luke omits this prediction on 2 grounds: (*a*) it con-

flicts with his report that all the resurrection appearances were in the Jerusalem area, and (*b*) in Luke the role of restoring the scattered community is assigned to Peter (22:32).

14:26. The singing of **a hymn** after the supper is most naturally understood as the Hallel (Pss. 113–118 sung in praise to God) of the Passover meal.

14:29-31. Peter's vehement denial of his forthcoming desertion only serves to make it worse when it does happen.

14:32-42. *Jesus in Gethsemane.* This story marks another high point in Mark's denunciation of the 12. In the hour of Jesus' greatest spiritual anguish they all fall **asleep,** oblivious of the real nature of his struggle. The 3 leaders are chosen for special companionship at this crucial hour, but they, like the others, fall asleep. To drive the point home, it happens 3 times. Matt. (26:36-46), very surprisingly, makes no effort to soften this picture, but Luke (22:40-46) characteristically explains that they were sleeping "for sorrow" and omits the 2nd and 3rd occurrences.

The historical problem is acute here. If Jesus was accompanied only by sleeping companions, how did anyone later on learn of what went on? The traditional explanation, that Mark himself was the young man of vs. 51 and therefore witnessed the whole scene from his hiding place, is mostly an ingenious effort to preserve the literal historicity of the story. This explanation borders on the fancies of the historical novel. See below on vss. 51-52.

The Gethsemane story is demonstration in life of the prayer which Jesus taught his disciples, "Thy will be done, on earth as it is in heaven" (Matt. 6:10). Both versions—the teaching and the demonstration—became very popular. Matt. has both, but the 4th Gospel has neither, because in it Jesus always does the will of God without struggle. The agony described in the Gethsemane scene of the first 3 gospels is emphatically denied in John 12:27. It is reflected clearly, however, in Heb. 5:7-10.

14:34. The admonition to **watch** would be more appropriately translated "keep awake." Thus the disciples' conduct is a direct violation of instructions.

B. The Trial (14:43–15:20)

14:43-52. *Betrayal and Arrest.* The story of the arrest appears in its simplest form in this gospel. The later gospels (Matt. 26:47-56; Luke 22:47-53; John 18:1-12) add both conversation and details and introduce a few changes. It appears in Mark's account, which is followed by Matt. and Luke, to be a mob arrest directed by the Jewish leaders, but John reports "a band of soldiers." Judas betrays Jesus with a kiss in Mark and Matt., but contrast Luke 22:48-49. Mark's simple story of the attack on the high priest's slave undergoes interesting developments in the later gospels.

14:43-46. This is the arrest story proper. It seems to describe the nature of Judas' betrayal as affording positive identification of Jesus for a secret (nighttime) arrest. To **lead him away safely** means to hold him so firmly that he cannot escape; it does not mean to do him no harm.

14:47. It is possible that this episode of resistance by a bystander (identified by Matt. as a disciple and by John as Peter) was originally a separate tradition.

All the other gospels elaborate the incident and include some form of rebuke by Jesus.

14:48-49. This protest of Jesus is unique in the gospels; elsewhere he suffers without protest. In Mark he speaks to those who have arrested him. In Matt. 26:55 he is addressing the crowd. In Luke 22:52 he is speaking to "the chief priests and captains of the temple and elders," who are not even present in Mark or Matt. There is no protest at all in John's account. The explanation of Jesus' non-resistance is found in scriptural prophecy, retained in Matt. 26:56, and even introduced 2 vss. earlier, but Luke does not use it. The scripture intended must be a general prophecy of death, such as the Christian interpretation of Isa. 53, rather than some specific prophecy of the arrest. **Day after day** implies a longer ministry in Jerusalem than Mark reports.

14:50. The desertion of the disciples is reported very directly. It is repeated in Matt. 26:56. Luke omits it, but it is implied in his story. The disciples fled back to Galilee, "each one . . . to his own home," according to the apocryphal Gospel of Peter. More likely Mark intends to imply simply that they deserted Jesus in fear of being arrested themselves; his sole point is their cowardice.

14:51-52. This **young man** may be an addition to the story that came originally from a Gentile Christian reading of Amos 2:16. If not, it is obscure. It appears in no other gospel and must have been originally a separate tradition from the arrest story. See above on vss. 32-42.

14:53-65. *The Jewish Trial.* The trial of Jesus before the Jewish authorities is represented in Mark as taking place between midnight and dawn, a most unlikely time. Matt. 26:57-68 follows Mark, but Luke moves the proceedings to the following morning (22:66). The trial itself is based on the accusation of blasphemy (vs. 64), but the charge is never justified.

14:53. The **high priest** is correctly identified in Matt. 26:57 as Caiaphas (the account of John, mentioning both Annas and Caiaphas, needs special study). The assembly appears to be quite a formal and official session, although in all probability the real hearing was hasty and unofficial. The setting is the home of the high priest (see vs. 54 and the explicit statement in Luke 22:54).

14:55-59. Jesus was not judged guilty of blasphemy on the testimony of others, for their **false witness . . . did not agree.** It was on his own testimony that he was condemned.

14:61. The silence of Jesus is a Gentile Christian reading of Isa. 53:7.

14:62. The confession of Jesus is not intended to contradict his silence in the preceding vs., but to document from Jesus himself the faith of the evangelist that Jesus truly was a divine being, the Son of God. This confession is for the reader of the gospel; it did not successfully inform the high priest, or anyone else in the story, of his divinity. The great secret is preserved to the end.

14:63-64. The verdict of the high priest is clearly stated but hardly justified. No one among the Jews would have considered a messianic claim to be blasphemous. The condemnation as **deserving death** suggests that this court either could not or did not pass down an actual sentence of death. John states that

they could not (18:31), but the evidence on this point is not clear. The establishment of official trial procedures for this period is difficult, uncertain, and finally irrelevant if Jesus' trial was illegal.

14:65. The mocking by the Jews parallels the later mocking by the Romans (15:16-20). The theme of the Jewish mocking is religious whereas the theme of the Roman mocking is political.

14:66-72. *The Denial of Peter.* This is foretold in vs. 30. The setting is laid in vs. 54. Matt. 26:69-75 follows Mark closely, but Luke 22:54-65 puts the denial before the Jewish trial, rather than after it, bringing together the setting and the denial itself. In Mark **the cock crows twice,** in both the prediction (vs. 30) and the fulfillment (vs. 72). In all the other gospels there is just one cock-crow. In all 4, however, there is a 3-fold denial (cf. John 18:15-18, 25-27). The 4 accounts are not agreed on the accusers of Peter. His weeping is augmented in both Matt. and Luke. Mark exposes Peter's weakness; Matt. and Luke emphasize his repentance. Peter's reputation is restored, in very different ways, in Matt. (16:18-19), Luke (22:31-32), and John (21:15-19), but not in Mark.

15:1. *The Jewish Consultation.* The Jewish leaders have a consultation **as soon as it was morning** and deliver Jesus to Pilate. **The whole council** implies an official gathering of the sanhedrin. This is the occasion which Luke describes as the Jewish trial. Mark has a night trial, a mocking, and a morning consultation. Luke has a night imprisonment and mocking and a morning trial.

15:2-20. *The Roman Trial.* Mark has the simplest account; all the later gospels (Matt. 27:11-31; Luke 23:2-25; John 18:28–19:16) add details. All accounts assume a political charge of messiahship in the sense of rebellion against Rome. All accounts declare the innocence of Jesus and the sympathy of Pilate. All include the Barabbas incident, and all leave the reader with the impression that the Crucifixion was caused by hostile Jewish pressure on a weak Roman agent. It is historically probable that Pilate exercised a stronger role in the trial than the gospels indicate. He is known to have been severe and prompt in putting down possible rebellions (cf. Luke 13:1-2), and indeed was finally recalled to Rome and replaced because of his excessive cruelty to the Jews.

15:2. The charge of kingship was the only point that would concern Pilate. Jesus' reply is ambiguous.

15:5. Mark's report of Jesus' refusal to reply to the charges, as in the Jewish trial, is probably based on Isa. 53:7.

15:6. This custom is not reported anywhere in ancient literature except in the gospels.

15:7. In Mark **Barabbas** is an insurrectionist. The later gospels tend to transform him into a common criminal. The name itself means "Son of the Father," and was probably a messianic title. The scene actually seems to describe the offering to the people of the release of one of 2 men charged with insurrection plots against Rome. It is even possible that both men were named "Jesus" (in Matt. 27:17 some manuscripts read "Jesus Barabbas or Jesus who is called Christ"). Quite understandably, under these circumstances, the crowd would prefer the experienced revolutionary, Barabbas.

15:15. The scourging was customary in many death sentences. In Luke the scourging is a proposed substitute for crucifixion (23:22). The act itself was a severe lashing, and some men actually died under the lash. This may help explain why Jesus died on the cross sooner than expected.

15:16-20. The mocking by the Roman soldiers emphasizes again the real political element in the charges against Jesus. He was executed as a potential revolutionist. Matt. follows Mark closely; but Luke, in reporting earlier (23:6-12) a trial before Herod that the other gospels do not mention, describes the mocking as done by "Herod with his soldiers."

15:17. The **purple cloak** becomes "a scarlet robe" in Matt. 27:28 and "gorgeous apparel" in Luke 23: 11. The clothing of royalty is thus differently described by a generation which knew few actual details. The **crown of thorns** is also mock royalty.

15:18. The **reed** is identified in Matt. 27:29 a the mock king's staff, or scepter.

C. THE EXECUTION (15:21-47)

15:21. *The Journey to Golgotha.* The short journey to the crucifixion place is not described except for this **Simon of Cyrene** incident. It is full of obscurities. **Cyrene,** on the N coast of Africa opposite Crete (see color map 16), was a Greek city with a large Jewish population (cf. Acts 13:1). **Coming in from the country** seems to mean no more than that Simon was on his way into the city as the execution squad was going out. The detail that he was **the father of Alexander and Rufus** suggests that the original readers of Mark would know the sons and that the incident is included because of this personal knowledge. This forms the strongest reason for regarding it as historical, in spite of the denial in John 19:17. Matt. 27:32; Luke 23:26 preserve Mark's account but reveal lack of acquaintance with Alexander and Rufus by omitting their names. Nothing further is known of Simon, Alexander, or Rufus (but cf. Rom. 16:13).

15:22-37. *The Crucifixion.* The details of the crucifixion story are supplied by OT scripture (mostly Ps. 22; Isa. 53) more than from firsthand testimony. Nothing is known beyond the simple fact that he was crucified. Neither the location nor the circumstances can be recovered.

15:22. The location of **the place called Golgotha** is unknown. As **the place of a skull** it may have been a place that resembled a skull. "Calvary" is the Latin translation of Golgotha. One tradition explained the name as the site of the burial of Adam's skull. That it was outside the walls of the city is the only certainty.

15:23. This detail may be derived from Ps. 69:21. Matt. 27:34 makes the agreement more exact. It seems to appear again in vs. 36.

15:24. The dividing of Jesus' **garments** and the **casting** of **lots** is almost certainly derived from Ps. 22:18.

15:25. The fact that Jesus is crucified at **the third hour** (9 A.M.) emphasizes the hastiness of the trial procedures.

15:26. The inscription is reported, with differences, in all 4 gospels. It stresses the political nature of the charges against Jesus.

15:27. The **two robbers** crucified with Jesus may be an expression of Isa. 53:9, 12, explicitly noted in later copies of the gospel (see RSV footnote).

15:29-31. This detail comes from Ps. 22:7.

15:32. The note that both of the robbers **also reviled him** is modified in Luke 23:39-43.

15:33. The supernatural **darkness** beginning at **the sixth hour** (noon) and lasting for 3 hours is symbolic. There is no report of it elsewhere in ancient literature. Cf. Amos 8:9.

15:34. The cry of Jesus is the opening line of Ps. 22, a psalm which the early Gentile church understood as the words of Jesus (cf. Heb. 2:10-12) and which supplied many details of the crucifixion story. No other saying from the cross is reported in Mark. Matt. follows Mark closely, but both Luke and John are independent—from each other as well as from Mark. Of the "7 last words," one is from Mark, 3 from Luke only, and 3 from John only. In all cases the evangelists themselves seem to be responsible for them. Mark's original tradition probably contained only a **cry** (as in vs. 37), which he then interpreted from Ps. 22:1 (whereas Luke preferred Ps. 31:5; cf. Luke 23:46). The quotation, **My God, my God, why hast thou forsaken me?** is given in Aramaic in Mark and in Hebrew in Matt.

15:35. The confusion with the name **Elijah** would arise more naturally out of the Hebrew form "Eli" used in Matt. 27:46 rather than the Aramaic **Eloi.**

15:36. The offering of **vinegar** to drink may be related to vs. 23, and both may be expressions of Ps. 69:21.

15:37. Jesus' death is placed at **the ninth hour** (vs. 34), only six hours after the beginning of his crucifixion. This is much shorter than usual (cf. vs. 44) and no explanations are offered.

15:38-39. *The Effects.* The effects of the Crucifixion are expressed theologically by Mark. The rending of **the curtain** which protected the Holy of Holies in **the temple** is explained in Heb. 9:11-14; 10:19-22 as the high point of the sacrificial offering of Jesus. The Greek of the centurion's statement could mean either "a son of a god," or "a son of God" (as in early editions of the RSV and in most other modern translations), or **the Son of God.** Whether the centurion himself was expressing a pagan or a Jewish concept, it is clear that Mark thought of his words as a recognition of Jesus' divinity. This reaction climaxes Mark's conviction, systematically stressed throughout the gospel, that Jesus' Jewish friends never truly perceived his divine nature. It was a Gentile centurion who first recognized it, in sharp contrast to the 12, who never advanced beyond a vision of Jesus as the Jewish Messiah (see above on 7:28). It is doubtful that Mark intends to convey the impression that the centurion became a Christian, as later tradition says. The centurion here is representative of Gentile Christianity, which saw the significance of Jesus as the Son of God revealed in the drama of the cross (e.g. I Cor. 1:17-25).

15:40-41. *The Witnesses.* The witnesses to the Crucifixion are briefly described by Mark as **women . . . who, when he was in Galilee, followed him** (see Luke's more skillful version, 23:49). Mark singles out for special mention **Mary Magdalene,** another **Mary, the mother of James the younger and of Joses, and Salome** (cf. Matt. 27:56; Luke 23:49). Note that they were **looking on from afar** (cf. Ps. 38:11).

15:42-47. *The Burial.* Unless someone specifically

requested it, the body of a crucifixion victim was usually left to rot on the cross or simply discarded. Jewish tradition, based on Deut. 21:22-23, requires burial on the same day the death occurs. **Joseph of Arimathea,** a minority leader in the Jewish **council** that condemned Jesus, seems simply to be doing the decent thing for Jesus.

15:46. The purchase of the **shroud** implies that the Passover has not yet begun, for during the feast the shops would all be closed. Tombs **hewn out of the rock** in the Judean hillsides were common at

Courtesy of Herbert G. May

Entrance to underground chambers of a first-cent. tomb of the royal family of Adiabene; note the large stone used to seal the tomb; see also ill., p. 726

this time. Each tomb was used many times over the centuries. See above on 5:2.

15:47. The 2 Marys here are presumably the same as those in vs. 40, but it is unnatural in Greek to use the expression "Mary the one of Joses" (lit. translation) to designate a mother-son relationship. Without vs. 40 it would have to be translated "Mary the wife (or daughter) of Joses."

VIII. THE RESURRECTION (16:1-8, 9-20)

16:1-8. The Empty Tomb. The discovery of the empty tomb is made by the women who were the crucifixion witnesses. The 2 Marys (the 2nd now identified as "Mary the one of James"—see above on 15:47) and Salome go at the first opportunity to anoint the body of Jesus (see above on 14:3-9). The historical center of the story seems to be that there was a tradition that the women visited the tomb and found it empty. The details vary in the other gospels.

16:2. The time is after sunrise (contrast "while it was still dark" in John 20:1).

16:3-4. No further details are known about the size, shape, or position of the stone.

16:5. The **young man** becomes an "angel" in Matt. 28:5, "two men" in Luke 24:4, and "two angels" in John 20:12. The intent of Mark was probably to describe an angelic being.

16:6. On **he has risen** see above on 8:31.

16:7. The expression **his disciples and Peter** is strange and remains unexplained. The reference to a promised appearance in **Galilee** is in accord with 14:28, but quite out of harmony with the whole resurrection tradition in Luke-Acts.

16:8. The reaction of the 2 Marys is one of **trembling and astonishment,** for, like all the personal disciples of Jesus in Mark, they do not comprehend his true significance. Their decision to say **nothing to any one,** out of fear, confirms this. This vs. ends very abruptly, apparently before completion of the sentence (the Greek word for **they were afraid** usually means "afraid of . . ."). The earliest manuscripts of Mark end at this point.

The Problem of the Ending. Since the authentic text of Mark breaks off at vs. 8, the continuations found in many manuscripts being clearly later additions (see below on vss. 9-20), there arises the problem of explaining this abrupt and seemingly incomplete ending. Scholars are divided among 4 possibilities:

a) One theory is that nothing has been lost. A minority of scholars find it possible to accept what we have in vs. 8 as the original and intended ending. Jesus has risen, and the original disciples are uncomprehending and afraid. The grammatically strange final word **they were afraid** (see above on vs. 8) has a parallel or 2 in ancient literature. But most scholars believe that the existence of 2 late additions, felt to be necessary by the church, is *prima facie* evidence that Mark is incomplete. Logically vs. 7 (cf. 14:28) looks forward to a Galilean resurrection appearance that is missing.

b) A more popular theory is that the author was interrupted at this point and never got to complete his gospel. Whatever the occasion for his stopping work in the midst of a sentence, the assumption would be that it was death which prevented him from ever returning to it.

c) Another theory is that the original ending was accidentally lost, before Mark was used as a source by Matt. and Luke. Perhaps, depending on the form of the manuscript, the end of the scroll was damaged or the final page was lost. A majority of scholars favor this theory.

d) A 4th theory, deserving renewed consideration, is that Mark's original ending was deliberately destroyed. It has been suggested in the past that the reason for the suppression was this ending's account of Jesus' resurrection appearance to the disciples in Galilee, which contradicts the tradition represented in Luke that all the appearances occurred near Jerusalem. Not many scholars have found this a convincing reason, because Matt.'s brief ending reports this Galilean appearance, and it survived. Some more drastic cause for dissatisfaction is needed.

A more probable reason for the suppression of Mark's original ending is that it portrayed the disciples as not believing in the Resurrection. Contrary to the usual view, this ending was known to Matt. and Luke. The evidence is found in Matt. 28:17 and Luke 24:41, each of which preserves a modified version of a tradition that the disciples disbelieved. Each modification is typical of its author's distinctive way of modifying Mark in the interest of the disciples' good reputation. Matt. regularly alters Mark's statement about them, whereas Luke, if he includes it at all, adds an explanation. Thus the presumed Markan original that the disciples disbelieved has been altered in Matt. 28:17 to read "but some doubted," and in Luke 24:41 it has been explained—they "disbelieved for joy" (cf. "sleeping" in Mark 14:37 and "sleeping for sorrow" in Luke 22:45).

Neither Matt. nor Luke, loyal to the disciples as each was, would have reported doubt or disbelief if it had not been present in their source. On the other hand, Mark's report that the disciples disbelieved the Resurrection is a fitting climax to the characteristic portrayal of them in his gospel, and can be recognized as another aspect of the early Gentile Christian criticism of the leaders of Jewish Christianity.

16:9-20. *Later Additions.* Two attempts to supply a substitute for the missing ending of Mark have come down to us:

a) The "longer ending" appears in almost all of the later manuscripts and therefore in the KJV, as well as most other versions; in the RSV it is placed in a footnote. Technical study makes clear that it comes from a different author and is based on Luke, John, and some other sources. Since it reports, in typical Markan fashion, the disbelief of the disciples and has the risen Jesus upbraiding them severely **for their unbelief and hardness of heart** (vs. 14), and since it has a typically Markan understanding of the gospel (vss. 15-16), there is good reason for thinking that its principal "other source" was the original ending itself. It may therefore be regarded as a revised version of the original. The best explanation of why the original ending itself was not restored is simply that it was now lost except in the memory of oral tradition. The longer ending, therefore, probably represents a conscientious effort by the church to restore the lost or suppressed ending.

The original and primitive elements of the longer ending now appear alongside influences from the resurrection stories of Luke and John. Vs. 9 reflects John 20:1-18. Vs. 12 reflects Luke 24:13-35. Vs. 14 reflects Luke 24:36-42. Vs. 15 may reflect Matt. 28:19-20, but if so it is altered to represent Gentile Christian theology. Vs. 16 reflects Acts 16:29-33. The emphasis on signs in vss. 17-18 has affinities with Luke-Acts (cf. Acts 2:4; 4:16, 22; 16:16-18; 28:2-6. 8). Vs. 19 reflects Ps. 110:1; Acts 2:29-35. Vs. 20 reflects the whole book of Acts. A special problem arises out of the poor connection between vss. 14 and 15, but it is unsolved. It may reflect different sources, with the memory of the original ending dominating vs. 14 and other material (Matt. 28:19?) dominating vs. 15.

b) The "shorter ending" (see last paragraph of RSV footnote), found only rarely in the later manuscripts, is obviously a late editorial addition to give the gospel a satisfactory conclusion. It is probably based on Matt.

THE GOSPEL ACCORDING TO LUKE

William Baird

Introduction

General Character and Purpose. The Gospel According to Luke is the first half of a 2-volume work —Luke-Acts—which constitutes over a 4th of the NT. As a part of a historical work Luke resembles the historical writings of its time. Unlike many Greek histories, however, Luke is religious history— it is written with a purpose. As a gospel it follows the pattern of a unique kind of Christian literature whose prototype is Mark. A gospel is not primarily biography; it is proclamation. Yet as a historical work Luke makes clear that the gospel is preached through history.

In order to accomplish this purpose the author develops an apology for Christianity. He insists that what God has done in history is according to law and order. Thus Pilate, who represents Rome's legal genius, declares repeatedly (23:4, 14, 22) that Jesus is guilty of no crime. The Crucifixion is the responsibility of the leaders of the Jews (23:25). Indeed these priests and rulers have so perverted their heritage as to have abandoned it. Christianity has become the true Judaism, and the coming of its leader heralds the fulfillment of Israel's hope (2:25-38).

The author is also anxious to explain why the end of the world has not come. Mark imagined that the Son of man would return before the first generation of Christians had passed away (Mark 13:30). Now the time has grown late. Why has he not come? To answer this question the author of Luke develops a theology of history—a view of the course of events which is grounded in his faith. He seems to see history as divided into 3 eras: the time of the Jews, which is finished; the time of Jesus Christ, which is the key to history; and the time of the church, which is now. This last may be extended into the distant future so that the time of the end remains remote.

The time of the church will be the subject of the 2nd volume, but the first is concerned with Jesus Christ. Luke's presentation of Jesus is marked by some unique features. E.g. this gospel has a special interest in the geographical ordering of the story. In 9:51 Jesus sets out on a journey toward Jerusalem —a journey which does not reach its goal until 19:27. Although he immediately enters Samaria, by ch. 10 Jesus is saying things that would make sense only in Galilee. It may be that Luke's knowledge of Palestinian geography is confused, but more likely he intends to present the whole ministry of Jesus as moving toward the Holy City. The purpose of God

in history is to be accomplished in the suffering and death of his Christ.

Jesus is presented as bringing God's salvation to those who need it most—publicans, sinners, Samaritans, and Gentiles. Only in Luke does Jesus dine with Zacchaeus (19:1-10). Only in Luke are we told of the Samaritan whose mercy shames priest and Levites (10:29-37). The Jesus who cares for the poor and the outcasts is portrayed in soft colors. Women play a special role in his ministry (8:2-3), and Jesus is depicted as a man of prayer. Not just the son of Abraham, he belongs to humanity; he is "the son of Adam, the son of God" (3:38).

Authorship. According to tradition this gospel was written by Luke, "the beloved physician" and travel companion of Paul (Col. 4:14; Philem. 24; II Tim. 4:11). Actually the tradition is not very old. It appears first in the writings of Irenaeus, who was a theologian living in Gaul during the latter part of the 2nd cent. The Muratorian fragment (*ca.* A.D. 200), a document which presents an official list of Christian scriptures, supports the same conclusion.

What is the basis for the belief that Luke is the author? It was no doubt early assumed that Luke and Acts were by the same author. This was a valid assumption. Both books reveal similarity of language, style, and thought. Both begin with prefaces which are similar in form and content. As students began to look at the 2nd volume, they discovered that its author in certain passages referred to the participants as "we." These "we sections" (Acts 16:10-17; 20:5-15; 21:1-18; 27:1-28:16) seemed to identify the author of Luke-Acts as accompanying Paul on these occasions. Since the last of them brings him to Rome (Acts 28:16), the author must be none other than Luke, who alone remains with Paul in a Roman prison (II Tim. 4:11).

Although these data could explain the rise of the Lukan tradition, the matter is much more complex. The "we sections" can be explained on other grounds (see Intro. to Acts), and inconsistency with Paul's letters raises the question whether Acts could have been written by any companion of his. Actually the traditional identification of the author is of no great importance. In no case can he be recognized as an eyewitness of events in the career of Jesus. His own account is at best secondhand, depending on the works of those who "were eyewitnesses and ministers of the word" (1:2) before him. We can conclude that the author was a competent historian of broad learning and profound faith.

Date and Place of Composition. The exact date and place of the writing of this gospel cannot be ascertained. Since the author uses Mark as a source and since he seems to have accurate knowledge of the destruction of Jerusalem by the Romans (19:41-44; 21:20-24; see pp. 1029-31) he evidently wrote after A.D. 70. He must have written before 140, when his gospel was included in the canon of the heretic Marcion. Since the situation of the church reflected in the gospel fits well the political situation of the reign of the Emperor Domitian (81-96), a date from about 85 to 95 is most likely.

According to one tradition Luke wrote his histories in Rome. Another locates his writing in Greece. Since there is a correlative tradition that the evangelist died in one of the Greek provinces, this latter tradition has better support. Any of these locations assumes the traditional authorship and bears the same burdens. Perhaps all we can say is that the gospel was written from some locale where Greek was the primary language and where cultured readers like Theophilus (1:3) would be at home.

Sources and Their Arrangement. As Luke acknowledges in the preface, his gospel is based on a variety of sources. Most basic is Mark. Over half of Mark's subject matter is taken over to constitute about a 3rd of Luke's gospel. Although Luke omits large sections of Mark (e.g. Mark 6:45–8:26) and although he inserts into his narrative large blocks of non-Markan material (e.g. Luke 6:20–8:3; 9:51–18:14), the basic outline of his first volume is determined by the structure of Mark.

The material which Luke inserts into this outline comes from several sources. For one, he uses the document which scholars have called "Q" (for the German word *Quelle,* which means "source"). This material, which he shares with Matt. (see Intro. to Matt.), is the basis for about 250 of Luke's total of some 1,100 vss. It consists mainly of teaching material and parables. Besides this, Luke has a source (or sources) exclusively his own. This material, sometimes called "L," is the ground for around 280 vss. It is the source for Luke's understanding of the birth of Jesus, his special collection of parables, and his dramatic account of the Resurrection. L may be composed of oral tradition as well as written documents. Luke is faithful in following his sources, and his adaptation of them to his own narrative is a key to his particular understanding of the gospel.

Language and Style. Luke writes a Greek of high quality. E.g. he occasionally improves on the style of Mark. Foreign words like "rabbi" and "Golgotha," since they might grate on the ear of the Hellenistic reader of the Greco-Roman world, are omitted. A distinctive feature of Luke's style is his fondness for 2-fold constructions. He likes double names (e.g. "Martha, Martha," 10:41), repetitious sentences (e.g. 19:31, 34), and parallel illustrations (e.g. Noah and Lot, 17:26-32). This parallelism probably finds its background in the LXX and may reflect the OT conviction that 2 witnesses are essential for the establishing of evidence (Deut. 19:15). Thus the innocence of Jesus is established not only by the trial before Pontius Pilate (23:1-5) but also by a judgment before Herod Antipas (23:6-12). Luke takes the early Christian concept of witness seriously and understands his own endeavor as literary witness (cf. 24:48; Acts 1:8).

For Further Study: John Martin Creed, *The Gospel According to St. Luke,* 1930. William Manson, *The Gospel of Luke,* 1930. S. MacLean Gilmour in *IB,* 1952. Henry J. Cadbury, *The Making of Luke-Acts,* 2nd ed., 1958. A. R. C. Leaney, *The Gospel According to St. Luke,* 1958. Hans Conzelmann, *The Theology of St. Luke,* 1960. C. K. Barrett, *Luke the Historian in Recent Study,* 1961. Vincent Taylor in *IDB,* 1962. Bo Reicke, *The Gospel of Luke,* 1964.

I. Preface (1:1-4)

1:1-2. In writing a preface to his first volume Luke participates in a literary convention of his day; historians and medical writers often began their work with such an introduction. Luke's preface reveals his dependence on predecessors: **many have undertaken to compile a narrative,** and the results of their work he has used as sources. Ultimately the gospel tradition is dependent on oral reports which go back to those **who from the beginning were eyewitnesses and ministers of the word.**

1:3-4. Although Luke's reference to previous work necessitates no criticism of his sources, his intention to write a new narrative suggests the superiority of his own endeavor. His proposal to write a better account rests on 2 claims: (*a*) the thorough nature of his research, in that he has **followed all things closely for some time past;** and (*b*) his intention **to write an orderly account.** The significance of this latter claim is not entirely clear, since the Greek word for "orderly" simply means "one after another," and the order can be temporal, spatial, or logical. Many have supposed that Luke is proposing a better chronological account or is offering a consecutive narrative. However, in both chronology and sequence Luke offers little which is new; he mainly follows Mark. It may be that the unique feature of Luke's order is geographical—his beginning in Jerusalem, moving from there to Galilee and then back to Jerusalem, ending again in the Holy City.

Who is **Theophilus,** to whom the gospel is addressed? Since the name means "friend of God," some have concluded that it is symbolic—that the book is dedicated to the true Christian. However, since the name has been found in contemporary literary sources, Theophilus is probably a real person. The title applied to him here, **most excellent,** is used in Acts to describe government officials. At least we can conclude that Theophilus is a person of high social rank. Many have debated his relationship to Christianity. Is Theophilus a pagan whom Luke hopes to convert? Is he a Christian who needs more instruction? These questions seem to ignore the fact that a dedication to a prominent person was a device of Hellenistic literature. Theophilus is probably Luke's patron. The gospel is directed to a wider audience—one which needs to be informed concerning **the things which have been accomplished among us.**

II. Preparation for the Acts of Jesus (1:5–4:13)

A. The Beginnings of Jesus and John the Baptist (1:5–2:52)

After the complex literary Greek of his preface Luke changes his style to present the birth narrative. This may reflect sources which are Semitic in character, but mainly illustrates Luke's ability to adapt his writing to the narrative. He wants to give his account the religious quality of the OT; thus he employs poetic and symbolic language. The ultimate source of this material may have been the followers of John the Baptist. They probably believed John to be the long-awaited Messiah and continued their influence as late as the events described in Acts 19:3. Although Matt. has an account of the birth of Jesus, it rests on a tradition independent of that preserved here.

1:5-25. *The Annunciation of the Birth of John.* Luke sets his story into the context of contemporary history. John is born **in the days of Herod, king of Judea.** The Herod mentioned here is Herod the Great, who ruled from 37-4 B.C. By Judea, Luke means the whole area of Palestine (see color map 14). The parents of John represent Jewish piety at its best. **Zechariah,** the father, is a member of one of the 24 divisions of the priesthood. His wife **Elizabeth** is also of priestly descent. Although they are righteous before God, they have not received the blessing of a child (cf. I Sam. 1-2).

1:8-10. Zechariah goes to Jerusalem with his division to officiate at the temple. While there Zechariah is chosen **by lot** to offer incense in the holy place. The casting of lots was believed to guarantee divine approval (cf. Acts 1:26). **Incense** was offered morning and evening. The service was preceded by a call to prayer, and while the priest was in the temple proper, the people remained assembled in the courtyard.

1:11-13. While Zechariah is performing this rare duty, the **angel of the Lord** suddenly appears beside **the altar of incense.** The angel is **Gabriel** (vs. 19) —one of the 7 archangels of Jewish tradition. Zechariah is shocked, although he might have known that the offering of incense provided the proper setting for supernatural revelation. At any rate the angel brings good news: Elizabeth is to bear a son; his **name** is to be **John** (OT Johanan, e.g. Neh. 12:22-23), which means "God is gracious."

1:14-17. Gabriel now bursts into song: The birth of John will bring **joy** to **many** people. The child is to be dedicated to God, and therefore like a Nazirite (cf. Num. 6:1) **he shall drink no wine nor strong drink.** Since Luke stresses the idea that God's work in history is accomplished through the Holy Spirit, it is noted here that John is to be **filled with the Holy Spirit** from birth. He also will come **in the spirit and power of Elijah.** The idea that Elijah would come as herald of the end of the world finds its roots in Mal. 4:5. For the early Christians the returning Elijah is interpreted as the forerunner of the Messiah promised in the OT. Luke, unlike Mark and Matt., does not explicitly identify John as Elijah. However, the one who comes in the spirit of Elijah has an eschatological mission: to prepare the people for the coming of the kingdom of God.

1:18-23. When Zechariah hears this he cannot believe. The evidence is all against it: he is **old** and his **wife is advanced in years** (cf. Gen. 15:8; 17:17). The angel now presents his credentials. He is one who stands **in the presence of God,** so that his predictions are sure. Moreover, Zechariah will be struck dumb because of his unbelief. This traditional experience of dumbness (cf. Dan. 10:15-17) after receiving revelation indicates the overpowering character of

the divine word and the miracle of revelation. Meanwhile **the people** become anxious. According to the ritual they must remain praying until the officiating priest comes out to offer the benediction. When Zechariah belatedly appears, it is evident that some wonder has occurred. The priest can only make **signs;** he cannot speak. After his week of duties is complete, Zechariah goes home to await the work of God.

1:24-25. Elizabeth conceives and praises God for removing her **reproach among men.** Childlessness was blamed on the woman. Elizabeth hides herself **for five months.** Since this was not a customary practice of pregnancy, something symbolic was probably meant. Just as Zechariah's silence awaits the word of God, so Elizabeth's secrecy awaits divine revelation.

1:26-38. *The Annunciation of the Birth of Jesus.* Parallel to the annunciation of the birth of John is the account of the annunciation of the birth of Jesus. The ultimate source of this material may have been the followers of John the Baptist. If so, the annunciation originally came to Elizabeth rather than to Mary. This would afford a parallel to the annunciation to Zechariah as well as explain how Elizabeth knows the name of the child (1:60). Gabriel is again the heavenly actor, while the appearance occurs in **Nazareth,** a town in the hill country of S **Galilee** (see color map 15). As usual Luke shows an interest in dates; the event takes place in the **sixth month** of Elizabeth's pregnancy.

1:26-31. The angel comes to **Mary,** a virgin betrothed to a man named **Joseph.** According to the customs of the day, betrothal was an official relationship; it often involved cohabitation culminating in the legal recognition of marriage. Betrothal usually occurred early, so that Mary was probably quite young. Since the child is to receive **the throne of his father David** (vs. 32), it is important to note that Joseph is **of the house of David.** Until vs. 34 the account seems to assume that Joseph will be the father. The angel's greeting, that Mary will be especially favored of God, comes as a complete surprise. Some manuscripts add the phrase, "Blessed are you among women" (cf. RSV footnote), and this reading has contributed to the formulation of the "Ave Maria." The real mission of Gabriel is to declare that Mary will **bear a son.** He shall be called **Jesus**—the Greek form of the ancient Semitic name Joshua, which means "the Lord is salvation."

1:32-33. The angel now breaks into song. In form and content this psalm reflects the poetry of the OT. Its main theme is the messianic role of the promised child. He will be **called the Son of the Most High,** like the king addressed in Ps. 2:7. For the Hebrew mind divine sonship did not require a supernatural birth. The child will also inherit the kingdom of David; he will fulfill the Jewish hope of the reestablishment of the Davidic reign (cf. II Sam. 7:13-16). The resulting kingdom will be eternal, as prophesied by Ps. 89:29.

1:34-35. The surprise of Mary comes as a surprise to the reader. Since she is betrothed and about to consummate her marriage, why should the news that she will bear a son come as anything unusual? Originally the surprise may have been, not that she was to bear a child, but that the child would be the Messiah. Luke has used this question (vs. 34) to introduce the doctrine of the virgin birth. On Hellenistic soil, where supernatural occurrence was the common feature of the births of kings and heroes, a miraculous origin of the Messiah seemed natural. Although she has not had sexual intercourse with a man (the literal meaning of vs. 34), Mary will bear a child conceived by the power of **the Holy Spirit** (vs. 35). The resulting child will be **the Son of God** in a special sense; he will have a unique nature.

1:36-38. The proof that God can do this is seen in the miracle of Elizabeth. This kinswoman of Mary's has conceived a child in her old age and in spite of her barrenness. With God all things are possible. Since Mary is a relative of Elizabeth, she too may be of priestly descent and thus not of the house of David. In any case she is subservient to the divine election. She accepts the word of God in humble obedience as **the handmaid** (or slave) **of the Lord.**

1:39-56. *Mary's Visit to Elizabeth.* Since Mary has received divine revelation, she demonstrates her faith by immediate action. She goes **with haste** to a town of the **hill country** of Judea. Various efforts to identify this home city of Zechariah and Elizabeth have proved futile. When Elizabeth meets Mary, the child John leaps **in her womb.** This is reminiscent of the struggle in the womb of Rebekah (Gen. 25:22) and signifies that John recognizes the superiority of Jesus before either is born. Elizabeth's exclamation is inspired. She blesses Mary and tells of the action of the fetus within her. Most of all, she calls Mary the **mother of my Lord,** giving to Jesus the title typical of early Christian adoration.

1:46-55. The song which follows is commonly called the "magnificat," from the opening word in Latin. Although it is attributed to Mary, many think it was originally spoken by Elizabeth. Some of the manuscripts actually read "Elizabeth" in vs. 46; and its background is surely the song of Hannah (I Sam. 2:1-10)—a hymn which fits Elizabeth better than Mary. For Luke, however, it surely belongs in the mouth of Mary. She is the model of faith who has believed **what was spoken to her from the Lord;** she is the one who fulfills Jewish expectation. The poem has 2 parts. The first expresses Mary's personal thanksgiving. She is the lowly **handmaiden** who will be called **blessed** by all generations. Though she is lowly, God can work through her for the salvation of many. The 2nd half of the song expresses the thanksgiving of the nation. God is the powerful one who has destroyed the enemies, **scattered the proud,** and reduced the rich. The lowly he **has exalted,** and he will remember his promises to **Israel.** Since the poem calls Israel the **servant** of the Lord, it is evident that the servant psalms of the latter part of Isa. are basic to Luke's understanding of the messianic age.

1:56. After remaining **three months** with Elizabeth, Mary returns to her home. We can assume that, since she came in the sixth month of Elizabeth's pregnancy, Mary stays in Judea until John is born. The **home** to which she returns is probably that which she shares with Joseph in Nazareth.

1:57-80. *The Birth of John.* Elizabeth delivers her child and there is great rejoicing; the promise of the angel (1:14) is fulfilled. The idea that **neighbors and kinsfolk** should join in the naming of the child

is traditional (cf. Ruth 4:17). That the ceremony of circumcision and the giving of the name coincide may represent a later practice. At any rate the account is characterized by 2 miracles. The first has to do with the naming of the child. As was often the custom (cf. Tobit 1:9) the guests assume that the boy should be named **after his father.** Elizabeth insists that his name should be John, even though none of his family is known by that name. **Signs** are made to Zechariah, who now appears to be deaf as well as dumb. Taking up the father's prerogative to name his son, he scratches "John" on the **writing tablet** of wax on wood (see "Writing in Biblical Times," pp. 1201-08). The agreement between father and mother seems divinely inspired. Besides, another wonder occurs at once: Zechariah, who was struck dumb, is able to talk. The news spreads throughout the neighborhood and an expectant question is raised: **What then will this child be?** (vs. 66).

1:67-75. Zechariah, who has received the miraculous gift of speech, prophesies under the guidance of the Spirit. Traditionally his song is called the "Benedictus," from the first word in Latin. In content it appears to be a typical Jewish messianic hymn and resembles the thanksgiving psalms of the Dead Sea Scrolls. In this first part the prophecy stresses the fulfillment of Jewish eschatological hopes. God has visited his people with salvation and redemption. The **horn of salvation** is a symbolic way to refer to the power of God (cf. I Sam. 2:10). All the predictions of the **prophets** shall be fulfilled, and the **covenant** with **Abraham** will be remembered. The **enemies** who are being overthrown would be identified as the Romans by the Jewish interpreter, but for Luke they are the foes of Christ, or the persecutors of the church. Throughout this section of the poem the child John is seen to fulfill the typical expectation of a nationalistic Jewish Messiah.

1:76-79. In this 2nd part John is presented under the Christian interpretation as the forerunner of the Messiah, **the prophet** of the end time who will **prepare** the way of the Lord. Here the Elijah motif of Mal. 4:5 is taken up, and **the Lord** in vs. 76 is no doubt to be identified as Jesus. The main feature of this preparation is to make way for God's saving and redemptive action. Vs. 78 is difficult to translate, but the meaning is clear: with the prophetic activity of John the messianic age has dawned. The idea of God's revelation symbolized by **light** is typical (cf. Isa. 9:2), while the concept of the rising of the sun of righteousness is found in Mal. 4:2.

1:80. John's growth is reminiscent of the development of Samuel (I Sam. 2:26) and of Samson, who like John was dedicated to God as a Nazirite (cf. Judg. 13:24). That John becomes **strong in spirit** points to the inner development of his life. Some have taken the statement that he was **in the wilderness** from his youth to indicate that John was raised by the sectarians of Qumran. If this is true, he certainly broke with them before he embarked on his mission; their message was to a select few while his was to all Israel. The time of John's **manifestation to Israel** is the time of expectation; his appearance heralds the preaching of the kingdom.

2:1-20. *The Birth of Jesus.* Jesus is born in **Bethlehem.** According to Luke this event occurred in the Judean city because of an imperial census. **Augustus,** Roman emperor from 27 B.C. to A.D. 14, decreed that the entire empire **should be enrolled.** The historicity of this census has been debated. There is no other record of a universal census at this time, and an imperial enrollment within the realm of Herod the Great seems unlikely. There actually was a Palestinian census in A.D. 6, which was precisely the time **when Quirinius was governor of Syria,** but this is over 10 years too late.

On the other hand, some recent research into Roman practices has indicated that a census may have involved 2 steps: (*a*) the enrollment in which the data were collected, (*b*) the assessment in which the actual taxation was declared. The enrollment did require that a man appear for census in the area where he owned land, and on some occasions his wife came along. It may be that Caesar maintained control of taxation within Herod's kingdom. Evidence has been found that P. Sulpicius Quirinius, though not yet governor of Syria, was a viceroy in this area after 12 B.C. Thus, although Luke's picture is not entirely accurate, an enrollment could have been held in Palestine during the reign of Herod the Great, perhaps *ca.* 6 B.C.

2:4-7. Actually Luke's purpose here is more theological than historical. He, like Matt., wants to show that Jesus was born in the city of David. Since he is the Son of David and the Messiah, he must be born in a messianic city, in Bethlehem, from whom "shall come forth for me one who is ruler in Israel" (Mic. 5:2). Here Mary gives **birth to her first-born son,** wraps him **in swaddling cloths,** and lays **him in a manger.** The information that **there was no place for them in the inn** is misleading; the word translated "inn" is better rendered by "guestroom." The intention is to contrast a place of human lodging with an area for feeding animals. The **manger** is a feeding trough for stock; it could be located under the house or out in the open. In all of this the birth of Jesus is presented in simplicity and humility.

2:8-12. Whereas Matt. brings wise men from the E, Luke relates the coming of Judean **shepherds.** These humble pastoral folk are **out in the field** at night with their **flock**—a feature of the story which would argue against the birth's occurring on Dec. 25 since the weather would not have permitted it. Suddenly **an angel of the Lord** appears to them accompanied by the radiance of heavenly **glory.** Since light is the typical symbol of divine revelation, the angel's message can be accepted as word from God. In content this message announces **good news . . . to all the people;** the birth of Jesus has universal significance. The one who is born is **Savior,** and he is to be confessed as the Messiah and Lord of all men. The **sign** that all this is true can be seen in the simple surroundings of the birth (cf. Isa. 7:14-15).

2:13. The angel is suddenly accompanied by the **host** of heaven, who join in praises **to God in the highest.** The 2nd part of their hymn is not entirely clear. Some Greek manuscripts read "on earth, peace, good will among men," and the Latin versions have "peace to men of good will." The RSV is to be preferred here; not only is it based on the best text, but the notion that divine peace is dependent on human attitude is totally against the theology of Luke. For him the new situation on earth is due to the grace of God in the gift of Jesus Christ.

2:15-20. The shepherds act immediately on the revelation which they have received. At Bethlehem they see Mary, Joseph, and the child Jesus. This lowly birth is only a sign of the great things which the angel has promised. The shepherds relate their heavenly vision, to the wonder of all. We are given the impression that a large crowd of witnesses is present. Mary, who is again rapt in awe and wonder, treasures all these things **in her heart.** The shepherds return **glorifying and praising God** much as the angels did. They become prototypes of the Christian mission witnessing to all what they have **heard and seen.** Luke's picture of the birth of Jesus is presented in the quiet tones of pastoral life. The people of the flock are depicted, as often in Hellenistic literature, with an aura of beauty and purity. They remind us of the peaceful flocks of the shepherd king whose successor has been **born this day** in Bethlehem.

2:21-40. *The Destiny of Jesus.* Jesus is taken to Jerusalem for the fulfillment of religious duties and the prediction of his destiny. First he is circumcised on the 8th day, according to the ancient custom, and given the name announced by the angel Gabriel. Then he is taken to the temple in Jerusalem. In recounting the events there Luke seems to have combined 2 OT rituals.

The ceremony of **purification** is described in Lev. 12:2 ff. According to this text the mother is considered unclean after the birth of her son for 7 days, and on the 8th he is circumcised. Counting from that day, the mother is to remain separate 33 days longer. At the end of that time, or 40 days from the birth, she is to offer a sacrifice consisting, for a poor woman who could not afford a lamb, of **a pair of turtledoves, or two young pigeons.**

The 2nd ceremony which Luke assumes is the redemption of the firstborn. According to Exod. 13:2, 12-13, which is quoted here, a firstborn child is considered **holy,** or belonging to the Lord. He must be redeemed with an offering of 5 shekels. Luke gives the impression that the purification sacrifice suffices for the redemption offering. Actually the former was performed by the mother while the latter was the duty of the father. Neither had to be offered at the temple. Luke is anxious to have parents and child together in Jerusalem since it is the place of Jesus' destiny.

2:25-32. That destiny is announced by **Simeon,** the aged prophet who has been awaiting **the consolation of Israel;** i.e. he has been looking for the messianic age. Under the inspiration of the Holy Spirit he has been informed that he will not die before the Messiah comes. The Spirit inspires him to go to the temple at just the moment when the parents of Jesus are performing their duties. It is clear to him that in Jesus his hopes are fulfilled. Taking the child in his arms he pronounces a prophetic hymn which in traditional liturgy is called the "Nunc Dimittis," from the opening words in Latin. The main point of the poem is that **salvation** has now come and that this salvation is for all people. Not only will there be **glory to . . . Israel,** but there will be **a light for revelation to the Gentiles.** Since he has seen this salvation, Simeon can **depart;** i.e. he is prepared to die.

2:33-35. Mary and Joseph (who is called **his father**) marvel at what has been said. Then Simeon offers a special blessing to the **mother.** This blessing seems to reflect OT symbols: with **the fall and rising**

cf. the stone of stumbling of Isa. 8:14; with the **sword** cf. Ezek. 14:17. In context these figures make 2 important points, that the coming of the Messiah means (a) decision and judgment and (b) suffering. The suffering pierces the **soul** of the mother of Jesus —a prediction of his passion.

2:36-38. As a parallel witness to Simeon the ancient **prophetess, Anna,** appears. Jewish tradition recognized the validity of 7 prophetesses, among them Hannah of I Sam. 2. Anna's **great age** is emphasized. **Till she was eighty-four** is lit. "till 84 years," which could refer to the period of her widowhood and make her age over 100. She is continually in the temple enclosure praying and **fasting.** Her presence, along with that of Mary, indicates that the events described in vss. 27-38 took place in one of the outer courtyards where women were allowed. Anna, like Simeon, arrives **at that very hour** when Jesus is dedicated. She gives thanks to God and also indicates that the hope of **redemption** is fulfilled in the child.

2:39-40. The parents and child return to **Nazareth,** their home in **Galilee.** Jesus, much like John (1:80), grows in strength and **wisdom.** It is important

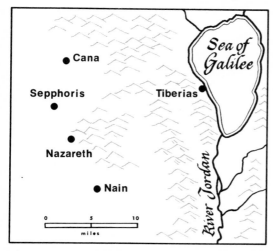

to note that **everything according to the law of the Lord** has been performed. Jesus is presented as "born of woman, born under the law" (Gal. 4:4).

2:41-52. *The Boyhood of Jesus.* The **temple** is again the seat of activity for the young Jesus. This is possible because his parents are pious Jews who annually attend the feast of the **Passover.** The law required every faithful Jewish male to go to Jerusalem 3 times a year (Exod. 23:14-17). On this occasion Jesus is **twelve years old;** he has just become a "son of the Law," and therefore accepts his duty to attend the feast. The Passover festival, joined with the feast of Unleavened Bread, lasts 7 days. When the festival is finished, the parents return toward Nazareth, assuming that Jesus is with relatives or friends. A search at the end of the day's journey, however, indicates that the lad is lost. **After three days** Mary and Joseph find him in the temple **among the teachers.** The "three days" would include the journey from Jerusalem, the return, and one day of searching within the city. Jesus is primarily presented as a learner who listens and asks

questions—in contrast to the paintings which portray him in the attitude of a preacher—but **his answers** indicate a precociousness which amazes his audience.

2:48-50. Mary's reaction contains a mild rebuke: **Son, why have you treated us so?** Joseph is again described as **your father.** Jesus' answer is utterly baffling to his parents—a fact which indicates that this material comes from a tradition other than that which has described the miraculous birth. Jesus expresses surprise that they have been seeking him, but his reason is not entirely clear. The Greek reads lit.: "Did you not know that I must be (in, among) my Father's?" This idiom allows the translation ". . . about my Father's business" (KJV), but the more likely meaning is **in my Father's house.** The important thing for Luke is that Jesus is in the temple.

2:51. Mary again keeps all **these things in her heart.** Parents and child return to the Galilean home, and he is **obedient to them.** This situation is seen to be only temporary, however, for they do not adequately understand the role he is to play, while he— even in his youth—seems to anticipate what his destiny must be.

2:52. Jesus' growth **in wisdom and in stature, and in favor with God and man** reminds us of the development of the prophet Samuel (cf. I Sam. 2:26). In any event Jesus is reared in a home of true Jewish piety; he obeys his parents, he follows the law. Like Moses and the other heroes of his time Jesus is a precocious child. Most important of all, he calls God "Father" and recognizes a unique relationship with the Almighty which will determine his whole life.

B. THE WORDS AND DEEDS OF JOHN THE BAPTIST (3:1-22)

3:1-6. *The Prophet in Historical Perspective.* Considerable time has elapsed since the previous narrative. Again Luke is anxious to set his account in the context of contemporary events. It is **the fifteenth year** of the Emperor **Tiberius;** this would be A.D. 28-29. The rulers of Palestine are listed. Over **Judea** is **Pontius Pilate,** a procurator appointed by Rome; he ruled from A.D. 26 to 36, and his presence in Palestine is confirmed by an inscription found recently at Caesarea, his capital city. Ruler of **Galilee** is **Herod**—a son of Herod the Great known as Herod Antipas, whose realm also included Perea E of the Jordan. The title **tetrarch** originally referred to the ruler of a 4th of a region, but in Hellenistic times it could be used for any ruler of a petty kingdom. Since Luke lists 4 Palestinian rulers here, he may intend the title to carry its original meaning. Over **Ituraea and Trachonitis** rules **Philip.** He too was a son of Herod the Great and half brother of Antipas; his area was to the N and E of the Sea of Galilee (see color map 14). **Lysanias** is tetrarch of **Abilene**—a region still farther to the N. It is known that a certain Lysanias ruled this region in the first cent. B.C., but the man mentioned here is perhaps Lysanias II.

3:2a. Luke also gives the religious setting of his story. It takes place during **the high-priesthood of Annas and Caiaphas.** This statement is confusing, since there could be only one high priest at a time.

According to Jewish custom a man was appointed to the office for life. The Romans, however, prevented this practice and appointed high priests by their own authority. Thus Annas held the office from A.D. 6 to 15, while Caiaphas (his son-in-law) was recognized as high priest from A.D. 18 to 36. Perhaps the Jews still considered Annas to hold the position, or it may have been that Annas was the real power behind the high-priesthood of the younger man.

3:2*b*-3. The important event of this time is the coming of **the word of God** to John the Baptist. This clearly puts John within the tradition of Israel's prophets upon whom, like Jeremiah, "the word of the Lord came" (Jer. 1:2). In contrast to Mark 1:45 and Matt. 3:1, 5, John is presented here as going out into **all the region about the Jordan** to preach. His message has 2 main features: a call to repentance and the demand of baptism. The idea that he preached **a baptism of repentance for the forgiveness of sins** is dependent on Mark 1:4 (see comment). For Luke repentance has become practically synonymous with conversion, while baptism is the action which symbolizes the acceptance of the new faith.

3:4-6. Mark is also Luke's source for the quotation from Isa. Luke modifies his source at 2 points: (*a*) He omits the first part of the quotation which Mark erroneously attributes to Isaiah (actually from Mal. 3:1). (*b*) He lengthens Mark's quotation of Isa. 40:3 to include vss. 4-5. The result of this 2nd change is to stress the universality of the coming salvation: **all flesh shall see the salvation of God.** Luke's understanding of John is similar to the rest of early Christian tradition: he is **the voice . . . crying in the wilderness** to **prepare the way of the Lord.** The **Lord** here is Jesus; John is the forerunner of the Christ.

3:7-20. *The Message of John.* Luke omits the description of John found in Mark 1:6. The presentation of John's message of doom is based on Q; vss. 7-9 are practically identical with Matt. 3:7-10 (see comment). Whereas Matt. presents these words as spoken to the Pharisees and Sadducees, Luke reports that they are directed **to the multitudes.** In content this Q material declares the wrath, or judgment, of God. Before it sheer dependence on descent from **Abraham** is of no avail. Judgment is imminent; **the ax** is already at **the root of the trees.**

3:10-14. John's message of judgment has demanded **fruits that befit repentance.** In a passage which has no parallel Luke describes what this means. The multitudes ask, **What then shall we do?** John answers that those who have abundance should **share** with the needy; this is true for both food and clothing. Representatives of various groups now come to inquire what the fruit of their repentance should be. The tax collectors, or publicans, were notorious on 2 counts: (*a*) they had sold out to the Romans who had farmed the collection of taxes out to them; (*b*) they were constantly tempted to charge a rate as high as the traffic would bear. John's advice is directed to this latter sin: **Collect no more than is appointed you.**

Next **soldiers also** came. Since Jews were exempt from service in the Roman legions, these may have been troops of Herod Antipas. The Baptist demands that they refrain from the typical evils of soldiery—violence, extortion, and discontent. That these social commands are not entirely in harmony with the eschatology of John seems evident. Perhaps Luke is attempting to define repentance in terms meaningful to an ethical Greek. Some of Jesus' teachings from the Sermon on the Plain (6:17-49) are thereby anticipated.

3:15-18. Luke's presentation of the messianic preaching of John is based on Mark and Q. Only Luke, however, records the question of the people **concerning John, whether perhaps he were the Christ.** Luke therefore makes John's denial of his own messiahship and confession of one **who is mightier** than himself more explicit than the other evangelists. The figure of the slave who is not even **worthy to untie** his master's **sandals** is taken from Mark 1:7, while the symbol of the terrible thresher is based on Q (cf. Matt. 3:12). The linking of **Holy Spirit** and **fire,** found also in Matt., has special significance for Luke; it anticipates the events of Pentecost (Acts 2:3-4), when "tongues as of fire" will be distributed upon those who receive the Spirit. Luke adds the editorial note that **with many other exhortations, he preached good news.** John's note of doom has little to commend it as "good news," but by Luke's time the word had become a technical term for preaching in the mission of the church.

3:19-20. Luke adds a final note about the end of John's career. This account reflects John's criticism of Herod's marital relations, but the story of John's death as recorded in Mark 6:17-29 is lacking in Luke. It may be that this historian is intentionally correcting Mark's mistaken notion that Antipas' wife had been married to Philip. In any event Luke is anxious to complete his story of John so that he can go on to Jesus. The Baptist will appear again in ch. 7, but from now on his significance is solely in relationship to Jesus.

3:21-22. *The Baptism of Jesus.* Among those who come for baptism is Jesus. Luke's account of this event is based on Mk. 1:9-11 (see comment) though some traces of Q are discernible. The resulting narrative has 3 unique features: (*a*) Luke makes baptism subordinate to the coming of the Spirit. In fact the actual baptizing of Jesus is not described, but is only a part of a dependent clause which points to the important event: **the Holy Spirit descended upon him.** (*b*) Luke tells us that the coming of the Spirit is preceded by a period of private prayer. Luke, more than any other of the gospel writers, depicts the prayer life of Jesus. The connection between praying and the coming of the Spirit is found also in Acts 8:15. (*c*) Luke says that the Spirit descended on him **in bodily form, as a dove.** The rabbis described the brooding of the Spirit in the creation story (Gen. 1:2) as being like the hovering of a dove, and Luke surely understands his account in a symbolic fashion. The point is to show that the event of the Spirit's coming is not subjective but an actual act of God. This real possession of the Holy Spirit is basic to Luke's whole understanding of the ministry of Jesus; he is the one who has the Spirit; he is the one through whom God acts.

3:22*b*. Revelation by a **voice . . . from heaven** was a traditional feature of rabbinic debate. Perhaps the text should read: "Thou art my Son; today I have begotten thee" (cf. RSV footnote). This quotation of Ps. 2:7 was often employed in the discussions of the nature of Christ among the early Christians. Because of its conflict with the virgin birth doctrine and its possible support of a notion that Jesus was adopted as Son of God at his baptism, the text could have been suppressed and assimilated to the wording of Mark and Matt. At any rate it is clear that Luke understands Jesus to stand in a special relationship to God—a relationship that defies ordinary definition and demands a whole set of symbols which point to the divine.

C. The Genealogy of the Son of God (3:23-38)

Luke's account presents 2 problems: (a) the relation of this genealogy to that of Matt. 1:1-16; (b) the tension between the genealogies and the virgin birth. Since the genealogies of Luke and Matt. differ, they probably rest on different traditions. Both depend to some degree on the OT. Luke's list e.g. makes use of passages like Gen. 5:3-32. The main differences between Matt. and Luke are: (a) Matt. begins with Abraham and traces the descendants down to Jesus, while Luke starts with Jesus and lists the ancestry back through **Abraham** to **Adam** and finally to God. (b) Matt.'s genealogy includes 42 generations, while Luke's total is 77. Even within the same period, from Jesus to Abraham, Luke has 56 names while Matt. has only 42. (c) The names of the 2 lists, though agreeing at many points, differ especially between Joseph and Zerubbabel. Luke lists the father of Joseph as **Heli** while Matt. has Jacob.

Luke is aware of the tension between genealogy and virgin birth. He says that Jesus was **the son (as was supposed) of Joseph.** The fact that he lists Joseph indicates that Luke intends to trace the ancestry of Jesus through his earthly father. The notion of some interpreters that Luke is proposing a genealogy through Mary is without support. It is possible, of course, that Luke wishes to establish the Davidic descent of Jesus by listing the legal father of Jesus. At any rate he is alert to the fact that a genealogy which traces the divine sonship through human ancestors is not entirely consistent with the belief that Jesus is conceived by the Spirit. Most likely Luke is true to the various traditions he has received. Though not entirely harmonious, they point to a confession which transcends biological beliefs. Jesus is both son of David and Son of God.

That symbolic ideas are involved is clear from Luke's total of 77 generations. Apparently the figure is the result of 2 important Hebrew numbers: 7 is the normal holy digit, while 12 is the true number of God's people. Jesus initiates the 12th, or perfect, generation; 7 times 11 equals 77, or the number of generations before Christ. The use of Adam involves another typical Lukan idea—the universal significance of Jesus. He is not simply the Jewish Messiah, son of Abraham and son of David; he is the **son of Adam,** the son of the father of the whole human race.

D. The Temptation of Jesus (4:1-13)

Jesus has received the Spirit at baptism. Now **full of the Holy Spirit,** he is **led by the Spirit** into the **wilderness** to be **tempted by the devil.** The source of this account is Q (cf. Matt. 4:1-11; see comment).

4:2b-4. In introducing the first temptation Luke makes the fasting of Jesus more explicit—**he ate nothing in those days.**

4:5-8. Presenting the temptations as occurring in a different order from that reported in Matt., Luke describes as the 2nd temptation the vision of **all the kingdoms of the world in a moment of time.** It may be that he envisages the temptations moving W from the wilderness of the Jordan to the mountains and finally into Jerusalem. In any case Luke does not say that this temptation occurred on a mountain. Instead **the devil took him up,** as if Jesus is taken up into the air. For Luke the mountain is a place of prayer and revelation, not a location for temptation.

Courtesy of Herbert G. May

Traditional Mount of Temptation (right background) in the wilderness of Judea; but see comment on Luke 4:5-8

4:9-12. The 3rd temptation is practically the same as Matt.'s 2nd. For Luke it is climactic, since important events occur in the Holy City; it is the place of Jesus' destiny.

4:13. The Lukan account of the ending of the temptation narrative differs from that of Matt., who speaks of ministering angels not mentioned by Luke. For him the important thing is that the **devil departed from** Jesus **until an opportune time.** Since the devil does not again appear in this gospel until he comes to enter Judas (22:3), the period of Jesus' life is a time when Satan has been expelled. It is the time when God's purposes are being fulfilled in history. To be sure, Luke understands the temptation in terms consistent with the tradition. After his baptism Jesus must wrestle with the meaning of his divine sonship. He rejects all temptations to be a popular or miracle-working messiah. He interprets his role by means of the OT. That he is the Son of God is confirmed by his defeat of Satan.

III. The Acts of Jesus in Galilee (4:14-9:50)

A. Preaching and Rejection in Nazareth (4:14-31)

4:14-15. A Summary. The source of this summary of Jesus' work in Galilee is Mark 1:14-15 (see comment). Luke makes some interesting changes. For one thing he does not say that Jesus' work began after the arrest of John, but points out that **Jesus returned in the power of the Spirit.** The Holy Spirit which he received at baptism becomes the ruling force in his whole ministry. Luke also fails to say that Jesus was preaching the imminent coming of the kingdom of God. As often, he avoids details which would focus upon the futuristic features of eschatology.

4:16-30. Jesus' Reading from Isaiah. In presenting the mission of Jesus as beginning in **Nazareth,** Luke departs from the order of Mark. Although his account has a few points of contact with Mark's later report of a ministry in Nazareth (Mark 6:1-6), the source of this narrative is basically Luke's special material, L. However, Luke is aware of the fact that Jesus did not really begin his ministry in his home town; in vs. 23 he makes it evident that previous work had been done at Capernaum. Luke's order therefore must have been shaped by some purpose other than the historical. It attempts to present a kind of prefiguring of the whole mission of Jesus. Although accepted by others, Jesus is rejected by his own. Luke's story is a comment on Mark 6:5—a passage omitted by Luke—which says that Jesus "could do no mighty work" in Nazareth. Luke points out that Jesus has done mighty works elsewhere after his own people have rejected him and because this mission to others was of the very purpose of God.

4:16-17. The actual mission to Nazareth took place in **the synagogue.** Since it was his custom to be there on the sabbath, Jesus is presented as a faithful Jew. His behavior in the synagogue is according to regular practice. Any layman could participate, and the posture for reading was to stand, while one sat to expound. The text which Jesus reads was a familiar one—Isa. 61:1-2. It would be found in a scroll from the treasured collection of the synagogue.

4:18-21. The surprising thing is Jesus' interpretation. **Today this scripture has been fulfilled in your hearing** means that Jesus understands his own mission as fulfilling the ancient prophecy. He is the one **anointed . . . to preach good news to the poor;** his baptism was the event of his anointing with the Spirit. Jesus is the one who will **proclaim release to the captives and recovering of sight to the blind.** The latter anticipates Jesus' ministry of physical healing, whereas the former, along with the declaration that he will **set at liberty those who are oppressed,** refers to Jesus' ability to cast out the demons who hold men in bondage. In a deeper sense the entire ministry of Jesus provides a salvation which releases man from the forces which oppress him. Most important, Jesus announces **the acceptable year of the Lord.** It might be better to translate this "the year of the Lord's favor," as in Isa. 61:2, for it means that now is the time of God's fulfillment. Now is the acceptable time; all of the prophetic expectations reach their accomplishment in Jesus Christ.

4:22-24. The reaction to this sermon seems to be double. While **all spoke well of him,** there are some who doubt. **Is not this Joseph's son?** The evidence is against his being the Messiah. To make this division even sharper, Jesus tells 2 proverbs. The first gives voice to his critics: **Physician, heal yourself.** This means that Jesus is being challenged to begin his work at home. Instead Jesus has been performing acts of power in rival **Capernaum.** The 2nd proverb says, **No prophet is acceptable in his own country.** This is Jesus' reply to the first. The reason a prophet cannot perform his works at home is that no one there is ready to accept him. Both proverbs are joined in a striking way in the recently discovered Gospel of Thomas (see pp. 1144-49). "No prophet is acceptable in his village; no physician heals those who know him."

4:25-27. Jesus goes on to alienate his countrymen further. This time he takes up 2 biblical illustrations. In the first **Elijah** provides never-failing meal and oil for a **widow** (I Kings 17:8-24). The point is that she comes from **Zarephath in the land of Sidon.** Though there were many widows in Israel, God sent his prophet to a woman of the Gentiles. Similarly **there were many lepers in Israel at the time of . . . Elisha** (II Kings 5:1-27), but God's healing came to none of them. Instead his power cleansed a Gentile—**Naaman** of Syria. Thus what Jesus is doing is according to the purpose of God: to abandon his own who have rejected him and turn to those who are ready to receive.

4:28-30. The angry crowd puts Jesus out of the synagogue, **out of the city,** and tries to destroy him. This account of an attempt to push Jesus over a cliff is recorded nowhere else in the NT. The traditional place can be viewed by modern visitors to Nazareth —a high bluff overlooking the plain of Esdraelon. Jesus escapes, and his ability to pass **through the midst of them** seems miraculous. This effort to execute Jesus is prophetic; it looks forward to his death in Jerusalem. Just as Jesus is rejected in his home town, so he will be destroyed by the rulers of Israel. His escape, however, makes possible a mission elsewhere, just as his resurrection will make possible a mission to the world.

B. ACTIVITY IN THE VICINITY OF CAPERNAUM (4:31-5:16)

4:31-37. *An Exorcism in the Synagogue.* After describing the ministry in Nazareth, Luke presents Jesus as going **down to Capernaum.** The journey did involve descent; Nazareth is in the hill country, while Capernaum is on the edge of the lake, over 600 feet below sea level. A synagogue on the N shore of Galilee has been excavated which, though dating from about A.D. 200, probably rests on the site of the Capernaum synagogue of Jesus' day. The account here is taken from Mark 1:21-28 (see comment). Luke informs the non-Palestinian readers that Capernaum is **a city of Galilee** and omits Mark's notice that Jesus' authority was acknowledged as superior to that of the scribes.

4:33-37. Luke preserves the main content of the Markan story. The preaching of Jesus evokes a protest from a demoniac. Luke makes it clear that the man is possessed by **the spirit of an unclean demon.** Since Luke's readers believe the world is populated by hosts of demons, good and bad, it is important to point out that this spirit is evil. The demon, as in Mark's version of the story, recognizes the true nature of Jesus—he is **the Holy One of God,** i.e. the Messiah. In describing the exorcism Luke heightens the miracle by saying that the man was **thrown . . . down in the midst** of the synagogue, yet without **harm.** The crowd is amazed at the power of Jesus and asks, **What is this word?** Here Luke employs the Greek *logos,* which had become in his time a technical term for the "word" of Christian preaching (cf. vs. 32; 5:1; 8:11; John 1:1, 14; Col. 3:16). That Jesus had the power to cast out demons is attested by the historical evidence, although demon possession and exorcism reflect a world view foreign to our own.

4:38-44. *Healings at Simon's House.* Although Luke has omitted Mark's account of the call of the first disciples (Mark 1:16-20), he presents the story of a group of healing miracles at the house of Simon (see comment on Mark 1:29-39) but shortens the Markan account. E.g. in his narrative of the healing of **Simon's mother-in-law** he omits the names of Andrew, James, and John. However, Luke does give a fuller description of both the disease and the healing. Only he tells us that the mother-in-law **was ill with a high fever.** Although this has been interpreted as illustrating Luke's clinical interest, his description of the manner of healing belies any evidence that the author was a physician. He says that Jesus **rebuked the fever.** Surely the Hellenistic doctors knew that fever was a symptom rather than a cause of disease, while the method of cure reflects the ancient notion that evil spirits were responsible for human malady.

4:40-41. Since it is the sabbath, large crowds cannot come for healing until the holy day has ended at sunset. Again Luke heightens the miraculous by noting that Jesus healed **every one** that came; Mark merely says he cured "many." The mode of healing is again described, for Jesus is depicted as laying **hands** on his patients. As in the synagogue the **demons** recognize Jesus to be **the Son of God.** This is further clarified by the note that Jesus **would not allow them to speak, because they knew that he was the Christ.** What ordinary men cannot recognize the demons do; Jesus is the Messiah, whose power threatens their very existence.

4:42-44. Since he is in danger of being understood as a miracle worker, Jesus departs to **a lonely place.** Though Luke usually emphasizes Jesus' prayer life, he does not say here that Jesus was praying. Instead of being pursued by the disciples, Jesus is followed by **the people,** who are anxious to retain this powerful practitioner. Jesus insists that he must go on to other cities. His very purpose is to announce **the kingdom of God.** This is the first time this phrase has been introduced into Luke's narrative. For him it means that God's rule has come into history in Jesus himself; his power over the demons is proof of this. Moreover Jesus follows the divine intention; he **was sent** from God **for this** very **purpose.** When Luke concludes that Jesus **was preaching in the synagogues of Judea,** he should not be understood as suggesting a mission to the S; as often, **Judea** to Luke means Palestine (cf. Acts 10:37).

5:1-11. *The Call of Disciples.* As a substitute for Mark's call of the first disciples (Mark 1:16-20) Luke records the account of the miraculous catch of fish. This story has no parallel in the other gospels. The fact that Jesus sometimes **taught the people from a boat** is mentioned in Mark 4:1, but the bulk of Luke's narrative is taken from his special tradition, L. Some think the original was a post-resurrection story, because a kind of parallel is found in John 21 and because the confession of **Simon** would make better sense after his denial. At any rate Luke presents this event as occurring by the lakeside as Jesus is teaching. Typically Luke calls the sea **Gennesaret** and refers to it as a **lake;** the word "sea" would be understood by his readers as describing the Mediterranean. The message of Jesus is again called **the word of God** (see above on 4:33-37).

5:4-9. Jesus gives the command for Simon to **put out into the deep.** That symbolic ideas are involved is seen in the fact that catching fish is a sign of the Christian mission. The deep is the abyss (cf. 8:31) from which men must be saved. When Jesus com-

mands that he should **let down your nets** Simon responds with a title of respect, **"Master,"** but his doubts are evident: **We toiled all night and took nothing!** Nevertheless, he is obedient. The resulting catch is so great that nets are breaking and 2 boats begin to sink. At this point Simon falls down before Jesus and cries, **Depart from me, for I am a sinful man, O Lord.** He recognizes Jesus to be more than master; he is the exalted Lord of all men. Simon's confession of sin indicates that he has doubted Jesus; he has not believed that Jesus is the Christ; he has not realized that the power of God is at work in him.

5:9-11. As well as Simon, **James and John** are astonished. These together make up the inner circle; Andrew is not mentioned. The 3 are called to participate in Jesus' divine mission. **Henceforth** they **will be catching men.** The phrase translated **henceforth** lit. means "from the now," i.e. "from now on." "Now" is a favorite word of Luke's; it means that God's eschatological purposes are at this time being fulfilled in history. The disciples respond, leaving **everything** to follow their Lord. Thus the call of the disciples is given a dramatic setting; the mission of God is grounded in the miracle of divine action.

5:12-16. *Healing a Leper.* The power of Jesus to rescue men is seen in this story, which is based on Mark 1:40-45 (see comment). Although he shortens the account and adds his own introduction, Luke reproduces the Markan narrative faithfully. He tells us that the man was **full of leprosy** so that the seriousness of the disease is certain. The leper addresses Jesus as **Lord,** thus offering a kind of confession. The belief that Jesus healed him out of compassion is missing from Luke's narrative, and the warning **to tell no one** is less severe. Luke also adds his own ending to the story: Jesus **withdrew to the wilderness and prayed.** As well as revealing Luke's interest in Jesus as a man of prayer, this ending serves to correct Mark's notion that "Jesus could no longer openly enter a town" (Mark 1:45); in the very next paragraph Jesus is described as entering Capernaum. In this text Jesus is again presented as faithful to the cultic requirements (Lev. 14:2-32), but the man who goes **to the priest** gains his main importance as a witness to the people of what God has done.

C. CONTROVERSIES WITH THE PHARISEES (5:17-6:11)

5:17-26. *Healing a Paralytic.* Luke begins a series of stories which illustrate the growing conflict between Jesus and his opponents. The healing of the paralyzed man is recorded in Mark 2:1-12 (see comment). Luke's account is shorter and less vivid. E.g. he leaves out the detail that the paralytic is carried by 4 men. Luke's narrative also includes references of special interest to his readers. He explains that scribes are **teachers of the law** and assumes a non-Palestinian architecture in noting that the sick man was let down **through the tiles.** He displays his typical interest in the Christian mission—Jesus' hearers come from **every village of Galilee and Judea and from Jerusalem.** Although the source for this information could be Mark 3:7 it is unlikely that Jesus aroused such an extensive following at this stage of his career. Similarly Luke's notice that the man who had been healed **went home, glorifying God** stresses the importance of Christian witness. Throughout the story Jesus is presented as the exalted Christ, the **Son of man,** who has the power and **authority** to forgive sins—a prerogative which the Jews assigned to God only.

5:27-32. *The Call and Feast of Levi.* The source for this account is Mark 2:13-17 (see comment). Luke shortens the introduction by omitting the information that the event occurred beside the lake. The commitment of Levi is heightened; Luke tells us that **he left everything.** This seems out of harmony with the rest of the story, for if Levi left everything how could he make a **great feast in his house?** Luke has the charge of the opponents directed against the disciples instead of Jesus. It is the church, rather than its Lord, which is being attacked. The mission must go to those who need it most; Jesus came, not **to call the righteous, but sinners.** Only Luke adds that the call is **to repentance,** thus indicating that man is required to respond to the work of God.

5:33-39. *Fasting and Rejoicing.* At the feast of Levi the question is raised concerning the failure of the disciples to fast. The answer shows that Jesus has little interest in cultic ritual and that his message, in contrast to that of John the Baptist, is one of joy. Two illustrations, the patch on a **garment** and **new wine** in **old wineskins,** show that the faith embodied in Jesus is radically new. The source is Mark 2:18-22 (see comment), and Luke offers only minor changes. For one thing he makes the parable of the patch ludicrous. To be sure, no one tears a **new garment** to patch an **old;** the result would be the ruin of both. Luke also adds a unique conclusion to the episode. Since **the old is good** no one wants to drink new wine. This saying, which is lacking in some manuscripts, may represent the irony or humor of Jesus, but more likely it originates in the later life of the church. At a time when Christians are being challenged with a mission to the world some hold to the outmoded ways of Judaism.

6:1-11. *Concerning the Sabbath.* Two incidents illustrate the controversy over keeping the holy day. The story about "harvesting" grain on the sabbath is based on Mark 2:23-28. Some Lukan manuscripts say this event occurred on a 2nd sabbath (cf. RSV footnote), but what this would mean is not clear. The sin of the disciples is not that they ate grain which did not belong to them but that they "worked" on the sabbath day. Luke makes this infraction explicit in his description of the disciples as plucking **ears of grain** and **rubbing** them **in their hands.**

6:3-5. In defending this action Jesus cites an incident from the career of David (I Sam. 21:1-6). Luke omits Mark's mistaken reference to Abiathar as high priest at that time. After vs. 4 some manuscripts add the following saying: "On the same day he saw a man breaking the sabbath by working and said to him, 'If you are doing this deliberately, you are blessed: but if you are acting out of ignorance, you are transgressing the law and are accursed.'" It is unlikely that these words are authentic, but they indicate the early Christian belief that the sabbath should be intentionally broken. Luke omits Mark's word that "the sabbath was made for man, not man for the sabbath"—a statement indicating that Jesus originally said that *man* (the meaning of the Aramaic idiom "son of man") is **lord of the sabbath.** For Luke the meaning is that Jesus Christ, the exalted Lord, is ruler of the sabbath; he has abrogated ritual laws and his followers need not obey Jewish regulations about holy days.

6:12-16. The 2nd incident concerns a man with a serious malady. Luke notes that it is his **right hand** which is **withered** and specifies the **scribes and the Pharisees** as Jesus' opponents on this occasion. With typical supernatural power Jesus knows the **thoughts** of his accusers. He does not, as in Mark, look at them with anger. Instead it is the foes of Jesus who are **filled with fury.** Luke does not list the Herodians among them, since these would have been unknown to his non-Palestinian readers. The healing of the man illustrates Jesus' belief that the sabbath is a time **to do good.** Of course no rabbi imagined that the sabbath was a day **to do harm,** yet for Jesus not to do good was an evil in itself.

D. The Call of the Twelve (6:12-16)

To aid in the mission Jesus enlists 12 disciples. This list of names, with minor variations, is found in Mark 3:13-19; Matt. 10:1-4; Acts 1:13 (see comments). Some scholars do not believe the selection goes back to Jesus himself, since the lists are not entirely consistent. Luke names **Judas the son of James** where Mark and Matt. have Thaddaeus. In his unique introduction to the account Luke says that Jesus **continued all night in prayer;** thus the choice of the 12 is by divine guidance. Luke has Jesus confer on them the title "apostle." For Luke the important thing about the **apostles** is their official position in the early church. Perhaps this explains his omission of their more charismatic functions, "to preach" and "to cast out demons" (Mark 3:14-15). It may be this more refined view of ecclesiastical office which has led Luke to avoid the description of James and John as "sons of thunder" (Mark 3:17).

E. The Sermon on the Plain (6:17-49)

6:17-26. *Setting, Blessings, and Woes.* In order to declare the demands of discipleship Jesus presents a sermon. Most of its contents can be found in Matt.'s Sermon on the Mount. But since Matt. includes much material which is found in other contexts, we can conclude that Luke probably follows Q more faithfully. Luke prefers to preserve the mountain as a place of prayer and vision; he has Jesus come down to **a level place** to deliver the sermon. The account of its setting is based on Mark 3:7-11. Again the mission of Jesus is presented as casting an influence over a wide area. The crowd which comes from distant places is anxious **to touch** Jesus, for a sort of supernatural force emanates from his person.

6:20-23. Luke is usually credited with presenting the Beatitudes in their more original form (see comment on Matt. 5:3-12). He lists only 4 and presents 4 "woes" in parallel. In contrast to Matt. the form of Luke's account is briefer and less interpretative. He has Jesus bless the **poor** and the **hungry** without offering any spiritual interpretation. As well as betraying Luke's interest in the lower classes this formula sounds a religious and eschatological note. The poor symbolize the pious of Israel who await the coming of the Lord. The vivid character of Luke's blessings can be seen in the 3rd beatitude: the contrast between weeping **now** and laughing in the time to come. Throughout this section of the sermon Jesus is presented as speaking directly to his auditors: **Blessed are you.**

6:24-26. The woes, together with the blessings, present the reversal of values in the time of fulfillment (cf. 1:51-55) and also reflect the prophetic condemnation of the oppressors (cf. Isa. 65:13). The woes have no parallel in Matt.

6:27-45. *The Demands of Love.* This section of the sermon is also drawn from Q (cf. Matt. 5:38-48; see comment). First Jesus is presented as requiring love and rejecting retaliation. Luke's reporting here is fuller than Matt.'s. The love which discipleship demands, like the love of God, extends to those who do not deserve it: to **your enemies,** to **those who hate you,** to **those who curse you,** and to **those who abuse you.** Luke then gives concrete examples of this love which are found also in Matt. Luke's form of the **cloak** and **coat** illustration is different from Matt.'s. He assumes that the outer garment, the cloak, is taken first, while Matt. has it the other way around. Where Matt. seems to assume some legal loss of shirt, Luke appears to visualize an act of theft.

6:32-36. Luke's presentation of a love which reaches out to those who do not love you is more explicit than Matt.'s. Vs. 34 has no parallel; it declares that the disciple must **lend** without expecting to be repaid. That no bank could operate on such principles is obvious, but the demand of love conforms to no ordinary standards. Instead one must **be merciful, even as your Father is merciful.** This form of the command is probably more original and more demanding than Matt.'s. To be perfect in the OT is an attainment of man; to be merciful is an attribute of God.

6:37-38. Luke's word forbidding judging is similar to Matt. 7:1-5 (see comment), but his description of giving is fuller. The one who forgives and gives receives in return **good measure, pressed down, shaken together, running over.** This figure of speech is borrowed from the grain trade; it represents filling a container to full and overflowing. The word translated **lap** refers to a fold of cloth gathered over the girdle—a sort of big pocket which could hold a large quantity of one's personal possessions.

6:39-45. Into the discussion of judging Luke inserts the parable of the **blind** leading the **blind** (cf. Matt. 15:14) and the saying that **a disciple is not above his teacher** (cf. Matt. 10:24-25). These words seem out of context here. The connection appears to be with what follows. The saying about the **speck** and **log** in one's **eye** indicates that the leader must have good vision; a blind man is not a good guide for the blind. But if one judges his brother, evidence is given that he does not have good sight; he cannot be a leader or teacher. All of this describes the kind of leadership needed in the church of Luke's day. The word about the **good tree** and the **good fruit** makes the same point (cf. Matt. 7:16-20). There must be a unity between the inner and the outer man. Only the truly **good man out of the good treasure of his heart** can produce **good.** Disciples are men who do not judge, whose vision is clear, whose heart is right.

6:46-49. *The Parable of the Builders.* Luke, like Matt., concludes the sermon with a parable taken from Q (cf. Matt. 7:24-27; see comment). Essentially the same, the parables make clear that Jesus expects his words to be obeyed. Luke's version seems to imagine a non-Palestinian urban setting. Instead of

choosing a place to build, his builder **dug deep, and laid the foundation upon rock.** Rather than the torrential rains of Palestine, Luke depicts the swelling of some important river. In any event the house falls if it is not properly constructed; man falls if he does not the words of his Lord. Perhaps Luke is envisaging the testing which comes upon the church.

F. Acts of Healing (7:1-50)

7:1-10. *The Centurion's Slave.* Although the source is Q, Luke's account is longer than Matt.'s (cf. Matt. 8:5-13). The story recounts the cure of a Gentile's servant and approves this centurion's faith as greater than any Jesus has encountered in Israel.

Model of an ancient synagogue at Capernaum, built in the 3rd century A.D.; the centurion in Luke 7:2 is reported to have "built us our synagogue" (Luke 7:5); cf. ill., p. 619

The unique feature of Luke's narrative is its failure to relate any direct contact between the centurion and Jesus. Instead 2 delegations are sent as intermediaries. The first, composed of the leaders of the Jewish congregation, points out that the foreigner is deserving of help; **he loves our nation, and he built our** place of worship. Thus the centurion is a "God-fearer"—a Gentile sympathetic to the Jewish religion who has not become a proselyte.

7:6-10. The 2nd delegation brings the message that the centurion is **not worthy to have** Jesus **come under my roof.** Luke's form of the story, therefore, heightens the officer's humility, since it also implies that the centurion is unworthy to come into Jesus' presence. At any rate the Gentile is a man who knows both how to exercise and how to accept authority; his submission to the authority of Jesus is a sign of his faith. Luke does not include Matt.'s word that "many will come from east and west," since he uses it elsewhere (13:28-30). Yet its message echoes a Lukan theme: the mission to the ends of the earth is begun by Jesus himself, even though the work is to be accomplished through intermediaries.

7:11-17. *The Widow's Son.* The story of the raising of the widow's son comes from Luke's special material, L; it is without parallel in the gospel tradition. The background of the account is found in I Kings 17:17-24, where Elijah gives life to a widow's son, and in II Kings 4:32-37, where Elisha performs a similar miracle. When Luke concludes his narrative by noting that the people exclaim, **A great prophet has arisen among us,** it is evident that a major purpose of the story is to present Jesus in parallel to the powerful prophets of old.

7:11-12. A town some 6 miles SE of Nazareth has been identified as the ancient site of **Nain** (see color map 15). Outside the E gate a cemetery is located. According to Jewish custom a person was buried late in the afternoon of the day of death. Since giving honor to the dead was considered a meritorious work, the large funeral procession is to be expected.

7:13-17. In introducing Jesus to the story Luke calls him **Lord.** Jesus is the Lord of life with power over death. The motivation for his action is **compassion;** nothing is said of faith. Jesus touches the corpse, contaminating himself with ceremonial uncleanness of death. The Jews carried their dead enshrouded upon a stretcher; the term **bier,** or casket, reflects Luke's familiarity with the customs of the Greek world. At Jesus' command the young man rises from the dead; Jesus is the one who calls the living forth from the dead. Not only is this miracle a sign that Jesus is a **prophet;** it also indicates that **God has visited his people.** This means that God is present in the act of Jesus; little wonder that **fear seized them all.**

Although Luke understands it as a miraculous event, the primary significance of this resurrection is its meaning for faith. It expresses the Christian's conviction that life comes through encounter with Jesus Christ. The story also prepares for the witness to John the Baptist: "the dead are raised up" (vs. 22).

7:18-35. *The Significance of John.* The stage is now set for introducing the messianic question of John the Baptist. Luke's source for the account is Q (cf. Matt. 11:2-19). First John sends representatives to inquire about Jesus' messiahship. They are told **to tell John** that they have seen the messianic prophecies fulfilled in the acts of Jesus. Luke, with his usual fondness for a double witness, suggests that **two** of John's **disciples** are sent. He also gives the messianic question more emphasis through repeating it a 2nd time. In his account the acts of fulfillment are accomplished immediately before the eyes of John's emissaries; **in that hour** Jesus **cured many of diseases and plagues and evil spirits** (cf. Isa. 29: 18-19; 35:5-6; 61:1). Luke's normal stress on eschatological fulfillment in the present moment of Jesus' mission is evident.

7:24-30. Now that John's question about Jesus has been answered the narrative proceeds to relate Jesus' view of John. In essence John is recognized as a **prophet** who plays the role of forerunner of the Messiah. Although **among those born of women none is greater than John** he still belongs to the old age. **He who is least in the kingdom of God is greater than** John, and the new age has started to come in Jesus. Luke inserts a parenthetical sentence which further evaluates John's work. He notes that those who submitted to John's baptism, the ordinary **people** and the sinful **tax collectors, justified God;** i.e. they acknowledged that God's way was just. On the other hand, those who refused the baptism of John, **the Pharisees and the lawyers, rejected the purpose of God.** All of this indicates that Luke accepts the mission of John as determined by the plan and purpose of God.

7:31-35. The parable of the fickle **children** illustrates the vacillation of the hearers of both John and Jesus. John has come as an ascetic and the people suppose him possessed; Jesus has come **eating and drinking** and they charge him with excesses. The final saying of Jesus is perhaps proverbial. It suggests that true **wisdom** is approved **by all her children.** In contrast to the foolish children of the parable these children of wisdom are those who have accepted John and Jesus. In them the wisdom of God—his purposes in history—are manifest.

7:36-50. *The Forgiveness of Sins.* Luke has a fondness for banquet scenes and employs one as the setting for Jesus' forgiveness of a gross sinner. Although there is some relationship to Mark 14:3-9, the source of this narrative is L. The previous story has concluded with a description of Jesus as a friend of sinners; now that description is illustrated with an actual event. Jesus, who is still on relatively good terms with his opposition, is invited to the **house** of **Simon,** a **Pharisee,** for dinner. As the meal proceeds, a sinful **woman** washes Jesus' **feet** with her **tears,** wipes them with her **hair,** kisses his feet, and anoints them with ointment from **an alabaster flask.** Since the position for eating is to recline with feet away from the table, the woman approaches Jesus from **behind.** However, **if he were a prophet,** as his actions seem to indicate, he would know **what sort of woman this is.** To be touched by her is to be contaminated with her sin. Just what kind of sinner she is has not been made clear, but it is implied that her sin is of the lowest sort, perhaps prostitution.

7:40-43. To counter Simon's criticism Jesus tells a parable. His ability to perceive the thoughts of his host, of course, proves him to be truly a prophet. The parable tells of a **creditor** who **had two debtors.** One owed him **five hundred denarii,** while the other's debt was **fifty.** Since one denarius was a day's wage for common labor (cf. Matt. 20:2; see ill., p. 664), it is evident that the first debtor owed a large amount. The creditor forgave them both. **Which,** asks Jesus, **will love him more?** Simon answers, with Jesus' approbation, **The one . . . to whom he forgave more.**

7:44-46. Next Jesus applies the parable to the situation at hand. Simon has failed to offer Jesus the ordinary courtesies of a guest. He has not provided for the washing of Jesus' **feet;** he has not presented Jesus with the **kiss** of greeting; he has not honored Jesus by anointing his **head with oil.** The woman, by way of contrast, has offered all these duties with utmost humility. The failure of Simon to accept the responsibilities of a host gives the story a certain sense of unreality, although it is possible that Simon treats Jesus without respect as an inferior guest.

7:47-48. Jesus concludes his application by saying, **Her sins, which are many, are forgiven, for she loved much.** Actually this conclusion is not supported by the parable, in which we were told that one who was forgiven much loved much; the same point is made in the latter part of vs. 47 when Jesus goes on to say that **he who is forgiven little, loves little.** Luke's reversal could indicate that the woman was previously forgiven by Jesus and now is expressing the love which results. Most likely Luke is not aware of any tension; the love and forgiveness of God is always prior to its appropriation on the part of man.

7:49-50. However, it is still apparent that Luke has combined more than one tradition here. The final words of the passage introduce the debate about the right to forgive sins, which is out of context. Moreover, the expression that the woman's **faith has saved** her introduces ideas which are foreign to the narrative.

G. Teachings of the Kingdom of God (8:1-56)

8:1-18. *The Purpose of Parables.* Luke begins this section with a description of the ministering women. Although reference to their activity is found in Mark 15:40-41, this passage is without exact parallel. It indicates that Jesus' Galilean ministry was supported by a group of well-to-do women who had benefited from his power to cast out **evil spirits** and cure **infirmities.** Specifically, **seven demons** had been exorcised from **Mary . . . Magdalene,** who is not necessarily to be identified with the sinful woman of the preceding passage. To be sure, Magdala had a reputation for prostitution. **Joanna,** the wife of Herod's steward, is mentioned again in 24: 10; **Chuza,** the name of her husband, has been found in Nabatean inscriptions, but about the man and his office nothing is known. **Susanna** is mentioned nowhere else in the biblical record. Luke says that there were **many others.** Although Luke had a special interest in women's place in the kingdom's ministry, his story is probably based on good historical data. The manuscripts which read that the women provided for **them** are to be preferred to those which say "him"; the ministry was to Jesus and the 12, not simply to Jesus alone.

8:4-8. During this preaching mission Jesus delivers the parable of the sower. Here Luke returns to Mark (4:1-25) for the first time since 6:17. In an abbreviated form Luke reproduces the story of the sower who **went out to sow** and whose seed fell on a variety of soils. Luke adds that the seed which **fell along the path . . . was trodden under foot.** Instead of "rocky ground" he says that some fell on **the rock** and **withered away, because it had no moisture.** Apparently Luke envisages a thin layer of soil over a shelf of rock. Luke adopts only Mark's high estimate of the harvest from the good ground; it **yielded a hundredfold.** On vs. 8*b* see comment on Matt. 13:9.

8:9-10. Luke's account of the reason for speaking in parables is much milder than Mark's. For one thing Luke applies this purpose, not to all parables, but only to the parable under discussion. He also omits the Markan word that this explanation is spoken to the 12 "alone" and refrains from describing those who do not understand the parables as "those outside." Most important, Luke drops Mark's idea that the parables are spoken "lest they should turn again, and be forgiven." Mark was attempting to explain how some could hear the parables of Jesus and not understand. He believed that the answer must be found in the very intention of God (cf. Isa. 6:9-10, which Matt. quotes here). Luke, on the other hand, while recognizing that the **secrets,** or mysteries, of the kingdom remain hidden, avoids the conclusion that matters are destined to remain so; his very purpose is to make the message of Jesus clear.

8:11-15. In interpreting the parable of the sower

Luke follows Mark. The parable had been turned into an allegory by the church in an earlier stage of the tradition. This allegory reflects the missionary situation of the early church. At some points Luke's application is clearer than Mark's. He interprets the seed as the **word of God,** thus employing the technical term for the Christian gospel (see above on 4:33-37). He also describes those who **believe** and are **saved,** presenting a system of salvation which is supported by the early chs. of Acts. The allegory is not entirely clear. While the seed is said to be the word, it is soon identified with the variety of hearers.

8:16-18. The concluding sayings of the text are more in harmony with the original purpose of the parables. A **lamp** is put **on a stand** so that **those who enter may see.** That which is hidden shall **be made manifest.** He who hears will be able to understand increasingly. Jesus intended his parables to reveal the purposes of God.

8:19-21. *Jesus and His Relatives.* Whereas Mark located this story just prior to the parable of the sower (Mark 3:31-35), Luke puts it immediately after. Luke shortens the Markan account and presents the clash between Jesus and his family in much milder form. This is partly the result of Luke's failure to present the story in the context of the charge that Jesus is beside himself. Yet since this setting is lacking, what meaning can the account have in the context of Luke? The answer seems to be found in the climax of the story: the true relatives of Jesus are **those who hear the word of God and do it.** I.e. this narrative carries on the activity just announced in the parable; the mission of God creates a new order of relationships.

8:22-25. *Commanding the Winds.* Luke begins a series of powerful miracle stories based on Mark. The stilling of the storm is drawn from Mark 4:35-41. In essence the story tells how Jesus was able to quiet a raging storm. Luke again calls Galilee **the lake.** He does not say that it is evening, although that could be inferred from the fact that Jesus **fell asleep.** The title **Master** is used for Jesus; he is recognized as the one of authority. His rebuke of the disciples is slightly softer than in Mark. Whereas the nature miracles appear to us to involve triumph over natural law, Luke understands them in the setting of a world controlled by supernatural forces. A sudden storm is caused by a demon, and Jesus' rebuke of wind and waves confirms this world view. The point of the story is to reveal to the disciples one of the mysteries of the kingdom—the power of Jesus. Indeed he does the very things which God can do (cf. Ps. 107:25). The disciples raise the expectant question, **Who then is this?**

8:26-39. *Casting Out Demons.* Still following Mark's account of astounding miracles (Mark 5:1-20), Luke records the healing of the Gerasene demoniac. Essentially the story describes the cure of a man possessed of a number of demons. After recognizing Jesus as the Messiah this **Legion** of evil spirits invades a herd of swine, causing them to rush to their destruction at the bottom of the lake. Luke seems to assume that the **country of the Gerasenes** is non-Jewish territory, since it is **opposite Galilee** (on the geographical and textual problems in this see comment on Mark 5:1-20). His concern is to show that the power of God is effective beyond the Palestinian orbit.

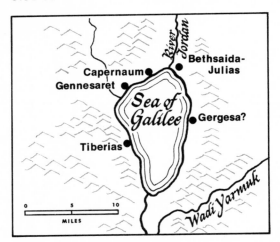

8:31-39. Only Luke tells us that the demons begged not to be sent **into the abyss.** The abyss, here symbolized by the depths of **the lake,** represents hell or the place where evil powers are kept captive for final judgment.

8:34-39. When Luke points out that the man **who had been possessed with demons was healed,** he uses the Greek term which also means to be saved. According to Luke **the people in the surrounding country . . . were seized with great fear.** This probably should not be construed to suggest that they are worried about their economic losses but that they stand in awe of the mighty acts of God. Just as demons have been driven into perdition, so a man has received salvation.

8:40-56. *Healing a Woman and Raising a Girl.* Luke's 3rd great miracle story in this section of his gospel is the raising of Jairus' daughter; into this story is woven the healing of the woman with the hemorrhage. The source is Mark 5:21-43. In relating this restoration of life Luke presents the 2nd witness of Jesus' power to raise the dead (cf. 7:11-17). The cure of the woman illustrates Luke's word from 6:19: "All the crowd sought to touch him, for power came forth from him." According to Luke, Jairus' **daughter,** like the son of the widow of Nain, is an **only** child. The 2 miracles are already joined in the Markan account, but Luke seems to find some connection in the fact that the daughter is **about twelve years of age** and the woman has been ill **for twelve years.**

8:42b-48. Luke abbreviates Mark's account. For one thing he fails to say that the woman had "spent all that she had" on "many physicians" and that she "was no better but rather grew worse." Instead of indicating sympathy with the medical profession this omission probably reflects an effort to remove irrelevant detail. Luke, like Matt. (9:20), says that the woman **touched the fringe of his garment,** thus referring to the tassel on the corner of Jesus' garment which was thrown over his left shoulder—a reminder of Israel's obligation to the law (cf. Deut. 22:12).

8:49-56. Luke adds a promise that the young girl will **be well,** using again the Greek word meaning both "healed" and "saved" (see above on vss. 34-39). The act of raising is related without reference to the Aramaic words of Mark 5:41—a typical Lukan

omission. Luke makes it clear that the mourners know **that she was dead.** The understanding of death and resurrection, however, betrays Greek ideas. In saying that **her spirit returned** Luke illustrates the Hellenistic belief that death involved the departure of the spirit from the body. As in the case of the widow's son the miracle has its meaning for faith. This is seen in the fact that only **Peter and John and James** are taken along to witness the raising; the private character of the miracle is even clearer in Mark. The meaning for faith is obvious: Jesus is the one who gives salvation to the dead now.

H. INSTRUCTIONS TO THE DISCIPLES (9:1-50)

9:1-6. *The Mission of the Twelve.* Luke continues to follow the order of Mark. Mark's account of the rejection at Nazareth has been omitted, but Luke has used this material previously (4:16-30). The report of the sending out of the 12 is based on Mark 6:6b-13 (see comment); there are minor agreements with Matt. 10:1-14. In essence the fact that Jesus called the disciples to share in his mission is recorded. The form of the mission reflects practices of the earliest community rather than those of the time of Jesus or of the time of Luke. The Lukan account suggests that the 12 were given **power** as well as **authority over all demons.** The task is not only **to heal** but **to preach the kingdom of God.** Surprisingly Luke, in spite of his fondness for double witness, omits Mark's detail that they went out "two by two"; he will employ this description of the mission in his account of the sending out of the 70 (10:1-16). The radical dependence on God is seen in the fact that **no staff** is to be allowed. The story shows that the church's mission had its origin in the career of Jesus, that the mighty deeds of Jesus are repeated by the leaders of the church.

9:7-9. *The Reaction of Herod.* The mission has its effect on the highest authority. In describing the reaction of Herod Antipas to Jesus, Luke follows Mark 6:14-16 (see comment). The word here that Herod **beheaded** John is the only Lukan reference to the Baptist's death; Luke has not recorded the story of John's execution (Mark 6:17-29). In general the account reports the popular opinion about Jesus —an opinion confirmed by the record of Peter's confession (vss. 18-22). Luke more accurately refers to Antipas as **the tetrarch** (see above on 3:1). In contrast to Mark's report that Herod identified Jesus with the risen John, Luke insists that the tetrarch raises the expectant question: **Who is this?** Luke also adds the note that Herod **sought to see** Jesus. This desire will be fulfilled at the trial of Jesus (23:8).

9:10-17. *Feeding the Crowd.* On the return of the 12 from their mission Jesus performs the miracle of the feeding of the 5,000. The source is Mark 6:30-44 (see comment); Luke has shortened the story. Basically the tradition reports that Jesus fed a multitude of people by miraculous means. To the early church this act symbolized the Eucharist; the blessing and breaking of bread prefigured the Lord's Supper (cf. 22:19; 24:30). Only Luke notices that the event took place in the vicinity of **Bethsaida**— a title which means "house of the fisher" (see color map 15). Luke also points out that the activity of Jesus on this occasion is twofold: preaching **the**

kingdom of God and curing **those who had need of healing.** In Luke's account the concern is not only with **provisions** but also with a place **to lodge.** The church, which offers teaching and salvation, provides through its central act of worship the basis for all of life.

9:18-27. *The Confession of Peter.* This account is based on Mark 8:27–9:1 and follows Luke's "great omission," i.e. the material of Mark 6:45–8:26 which is lacking in Luke. The skip may be explained either by Luke's intentional abandonment of his Markan source or by his use of an edition of Mark which did not include this material. Luke's account of the confession follows Mark closely, though with variations. E.g. Luke does not locate the event in Caesarea Philippi but leaves the reader to suppose it occurred on Israelite soil. In noting that Jesus **was praying alone** when he raised the question about his popular identity Luke gives a divine setting. The answer confirms the report about Jesus which Herod received (vss. 7-8). The actual confession differs slightly in all 3 Synoptic gospels. Luke's version— **the Christ of God**—is early in form and reflects simple recognition of Jesus' messiahship.

9:23-26. The effort of Peter to dissuade Jesus from his suffering role and the subsequent rebuke from Jesus (Mark 8:32-33) are omitted by Luke. Perhaps he prefers to preserve the reputation of the apostolic leader, but more likely Luke wants nothing to detract from the necessity of the Christ's journey to Jerusalem. Discipleship demands following Jesus on this way of suffering. The call to **take up cross daily** may reflect, as many have claimed, a postresurrection effort to spiritualize the demand of martyrdom and express in terms of Jesus' own crucifixion the realization that suffering is of the essence of the Christian life. On the other hand it is possible that Jesus depicted discipleship under the demand of martyrdom and used as a symbol the cross, which was the common instrument of execution under the Romans. On vs. 24 see comments on Matt. 10:39; Mark 8:35.

9:27. Luke does not suggest that **some standing here** will see the kingdom come "with power" (Mark 9:1). Yet some who have witnessed the confession will see the **kingdom of God** manifest immediately in the transfiguration of Jesus.

9:28-36. *The Transfiguration.* Jesus' suffering has been predicted; now his glory is revealed. Luke's source is Mark 9:2-8 (see comment); his account is slightly longer.

9:28-32. Luke says that this event occurred **eight days after** the confession rather than Mark's "six." Using the Roman method of reckoning time, he seems to assume a date one week later. Again Jesus is presented in the posture of prayer. To the story Luke adds that **Moses and Elijah . . . spoke of his departure;** i.e. they are discussing the ultimate result of Jesus' trip to **Jerusalem**—his death, resurrection, and ascension. Only Luke points out that **Peter and John and James . . . were heavy with sleep.** This suggests that the transfiguration occurred at night—a setting which would magnify the radiance of the **raiment** which **became dazzling white.**

9:33-36. Luke makes it clear that Peter did not know **what he said** and that the fear of the disciples is concurrent with the coming of the **cloud.**

They are afraid of losing their master and in danger of failing to listen to the **Chosen** one of God. This event, which reflects the postresurrection faith, is presented as happening **in those days;** i.e. in the history of Jesus the glory of the risen Christ is revealed.

9:37-50. *The Weakness of the Disciples.* When Jesus comes down from the mountain **on the next day,** he is met by a man whose son is possessed by a demonic spirit. The account of their encounter is based on Mark 9:14-29. Luke abbreviates the story by omitting such details as an argument between the disciples and the scribes and a lengthy description of the history of the disease. He adds that this son is an **only child.** After rebuking the **unclean spirit** Jesus gives the boy **back to his father** much as he did the widow's son (7:15)—an expression reminiscent of I Kings 17:23. Stress is put on the fact that the miracle is accomplished by the **power and majesty of God**—a power which Jesus possesses and which eludes the disciples.

9:43*b*-45. Unlike Mark 9:30-32, Luke connects the following account directly to this incident. Jesus gives another prediction of his passion. More emphatically than Mark, Luke indicates that the disciples do **not understand** and that the meaning of the **saying** is **concealed from them** by their lack of faith. The Passion is taken seriously by Luke, since no prediction of the Resurrection is included here. The point of the story is to indicate that Jesus is to be removed from the disciples; doing the work of God will depend on them and the power of their faith.

9:46-48. Proof of their lack of understanding is seen in the disciples' argument about greatness, which Luke, in contrast to Mark, attaches immediately to these sayings. Jesus' answer to their debate indicates that true greatness is to be found in lowliness; the power of God works through the lowliness of faith.

9:49-50. That power can operate even in those who do not belong to the official group (see comment on Mark 9:38-41). At any rate the ministry in Galilee is now finished. God's acts of power have been performed. Jesus has been recognized as the Messiah. The disciples do not fully understand, yet the destiny of Jesus is determined: he must go to Jerusalem.

III. The Journey to Jerusalem (9:51–19:27)

Throughout these chs. Jesus is presented as a wandering teacher. The source for this section of Luke is mainly Q and L. Actually very little of the material demands the setting of a journey. Although the trip is mentioned on occasion (9:51; 13:22; 17:11), the purpose is not historical but theological. The divine intention of Jesus' mission is to go toward suffering; the demand of discipleship is to follow.

A. The Cost of Discipleship (9:51-62)

9:51-56. The story of Jesus' rejection by a Samaritan village is from Luke's special material, L. Again the evangelist makes it clear that Jesus goes to Jerusalem **to be received up,** i.e. to be crucified, raised, and ascended. Hostility between Samaritans and Galileans is traditional, but the reason for the rejection of Jesus is his purpose to go beyond them;

his face was set toward Jerusalem. Seeing this rejection, **James and John** suggest that he call **fire down from heaven** much as Elijah did (II Kings 1:9-10). Some manuscripts say, Jesus rebukes them because "you do not know what manner of spirit you are of." His mission is not like Elijah's; his intent is to undergo suffering, not cause it. Just as he was rejected at the beginning of his Galilean ministry by Nazarenes, so he is rejected at the beginning of his journey to Jerusalem by Samaritans.

9:57-62. These vss. based largely on Q (cf. Matt. 8:18-22; see comment). Luke presents the person who hopes to follow Jesus simply as a **man** rather than a "scribe," as in Matt. He adds the word about saying **farewell to those at . . . home** and putting **the hand to the plow.** This simply indicates that the demand of the kingdom is absolute; no other duty can detract from following Jesus.

B. The Mission of the 70 (10:1-24)

10:1-12. *The Sending of the 70.* Only Luke relates the mission of the 70 (or 72, as some manuscripts read) disciples. The source of the account, however, is Q's account of the mission of the 12 (cf. Matt. 9: 37–10:15). Apparently Luke has created this narrative to symbolize the later mission of the church to the Gentiles. Traditionally the Jews conceived of 70 or 72 non-Jewish nations. Luke describes the participants as going out **two by two**—a practice illustrated in his description of the Gentile mission in Acts. He adds the advice that the disciples should **salute no one on the road**; the mission is urgent and allows no time for the complexities of oriental greetings. This urgency is also seen in Luke's emphasis on the belief that **the kingdom of God has come near.** The enactment of the Gentile mission prepares for the accomplishment of the rule of God. The journey toward Jerusalem makes possible universal salvation.

10:13-16. *Woes on Palestinian Cities.* Although he is theoretically on a journey through Samaria, Jesus is presented as hurling woes on cities of Galilee. This probably betrays Luke's hand in the construction of the travel narrative more than it indicates an ignorance of Palestinian geography. In any case, the account is from Q (cf. Matt. 11:20-24; see comment). The importance of the sayings in context is their connection with the mission of the 70. They make the point that the preaching of the Gentile mission involves the word and authority of Jesus; **he who hears you hears me.**

10:17-24. *The Return of the 70.* Since only Luke tells of the sending of the 70, his is the exclusive report of the result of their mission. The disciples return confessing Jesus as **Lord** and declaring how the **demons are subject to us in your name;** i.e. the 70 have the power to perform the same sort of exorcisms as Jesus. They exercise this power, however, through their relation to him; the very announcement of the name of Jesus drives the demonic forces into defeat. Next Jesus tells of his vision of **Satan** falling **from heaven.** When this vision was seen is not certain, but it seems to have been coincident with the mission of the 70. The fall of Satan indicates that the prince of demons has been overcome (cf. Isa. 14:12); the mission to the Gentiles defeats the reign of evil.

10:19-22. Jesus says that he has given the disciples **authority to tread upon serpents and scorpions.** This power was predicted by the OT (Ps. 91: 13). Since the rabbis used scorpions and serpents to symbolize demonic forces, the expression is a figurative way to suggest that the **spirits are subject to** the disciples. Yet something is more important than power over the demons—having **your names written in heaven.** This is an OT allusion (cf. Exod. 32: 32-33) which indicates that those whose names are inscribed in the heavenly book are those who share in the kingdom of God.

10:21-24. To these sayings Luke attaches some material from Q (cf. Matt. 11:25-27; 13:16-17). Jesus has just said that the names of the faithful are written in heaven. Now he offers a prayer, thanking God that revelation has been granted to **babes,** i.e. to the humble ones who participate in his mission. Then he turns to the disciples, offering them a blessing; they have seen what **prophets and kings** longed to see—the revelation of **the Father** through **the Son.**

C. The Questions of Men (10:25–11:13)

10:25-37. *Eternal Life and the Neighbor.* Since Jesus has spoken of revelation, an expert in the law tries to **put him to the test.** Luke's source is Mark 12:28-31 (see comment). Whereas Mark has the question raised by a scribe, Luke mentions **a lawyer.** The question for Luke concerns **eternal life** rather than the foremost of the commandments. These changes would make the material relevant to Hellenistic readers, who knew little about scribes and cared less about the Jewish law. That keeping the law was essential to eternal life was an OT concept (cf. Lev. 18:5). Luke has the lawyer, instead of Jesus, answer the question about **what is written in the law.**

10:29-32. In order **to justify himself,** or to find some way to escape the demands of the law, the lawyer raises a question, **Who is my neighbor?** Jesus tells the parable of the good Samaritan in answer. This parable is without parallel in the other gospels. The meaning of the story is clear. A man went down the dangerous road **from Jerusalem to Jericho.** Attacked and beaten by thieves, he was left beside the road to die. First a **priest** and then a **Levite** came along and **passed by on the other side.**

Courtesy of Herbert G. May

The Ascent of Adummin (Josh. 15:7) looking toward the traditional site of the Good Samaritan Inn (Luke 10:30)

These 2 represented the religious leaders of the Jews, and Jericho was noted as a residential center for priestly families. Perhaps they had completed their service in the temple and were anxious to get home. Just why they passed by the needy man is not stated; possibly they feared contamination from the dead or were reluctant to associate with the lowly "people of the land."

10:33-35. The introduction of the **Samaritan** into the story was shocking. In contrast to priest and Levite the listeners might have expected a layman. But the man from Samaria represented both racial impurity and religious heresy. Without fear of contamination or exposure to the robbers, this stranger treated the **wounds,** brought the unfortunate to the nearby **inn,** and left enough money to care for him. **Oil and wine** were believed to have curative and antiseptic value. On **two denarii** see above on 7:40-43.

10:36-37. When Jesus asks the question, **Which of these . . . proved neighbor to the man who fell among the robbers?** some scholars see evidence that the story is out of context. The question of the lawyer was, Who is my neighbor? The question of the parable is, Who acted like a neighbor? Perhaps Jesus changed the question. One must not escape the demand of the law by asking Who, but respond to the divine demand by seeking How. In any case the commandment is clear: show love to those who need it.

10:38-42. *The True Service.* Having illustrated the command to love one's neighbor Luke describes the meaning of the commandment to love God. The story is taken from L. In contrast to the Samaritans, who have rejected Jesus, **Martha** receives him as guest in **her house.** This home, according to John 11:1, is located in Bethany, but Luke does not imagine Jesus to be so near Jerusalem at this time. While Martha is **distracted with much serving,** her sister **Mary** sits **at the Lord's feet** and listens **to his teachings;** she acknowledges him as her Lord.

10:40-41. The amount of distraction may indicate that Martha has a crowd of guests to serve, and according to custom serving honored guests is an important duty. Little wonder that she complains to Jesus about the inefficiency of Mary. His response is a mild rebuke; Martha is **anxious and troubled about many things.**

10:42. The rest of Jesus' answer varies in the different manuscripts. Some read **one thing is needful,** while others say "few things are needful, or only one." It is also not clear whether the one which is needed refers simply to the number of dishes of the meal or has some spiritual significance. Probably both are true. The dishes of food represent devotion to the Lord. Not many things are needed, but only one dish; **Mary has chosen the good portion,** for her "dish" is to hear and obey the word of God.

11:1-13. *Prayer.* One may sit at the Lord's feet through prayer. Luke's account of the Lord's Prayer is based on Q (cf. Matt. 6:9-13; see comment). Since Matt.'s version is longer and betrays liturgical embellishment, Luke's form of the prayer is probably closer to the original.

11:1. Matt. puts the prayer in the context of the Sermon on the Mount, while Luke presents it in the setting of Jesus' own **praying.** That John's **disciples** pray is confirmed by 5:33.

11:2-4. The simple appellation **Father** (found in the best manuscripts) no doubt stands for the Aramaic *Abba*—the term of direct address which a child used for his own father. The force of the eschatological note **thy kingdom come** is not reduced, as in Matt.'s version, by reference to doing the will of God on earth. However, Matt.'s "debts" and "debtors" probably represent a parallelism more primitive than Luke's effort to explain debts as **sins.**

11:5-8. The parable of the **friend . . . at midnight** is found only in Luke. It tells the story of a man who receives a late guest. Since there is no opportunity to buy food he goes to a friend's house and asks to borrow **three loaves**—the amount of bread needed for a man's meal. The friend replies that he does not want to be bothered; the door, barred with a beam through a ring, is difficult to open, and the whole family is in bed on a mat on the floor. Nevertheless he will get up and give the provisions, not out of friendship, but because of the **importunity,** or persistence, of the request. The point of the parable is not that God is like a man who does not want to be bothered and answers prayers only because he is tired of listening. Rather it is the typical rabbinic argument from the lesser to the greater: if even this reluctant man responds to requests, **how much more** will God, who is anxious to meet our needs (vs. 13).

11:9-13. To the parable Luke attaches other sayings from Q (cf. Matt. 7:7-11; see comment) which also indicate the surety of answer to prayer. Here the illustration is from fatherhood rather than friendship. If earthly fathers **know how to give good gifts . . . , how much more will the heavenly Father.** Luke omits Matt.'s word about loaf and stone and adds the illustration that a father will not give a **scorpion** for an **egg.** He also suggests that God's gifts are of a higher category; he will **give the Holy Spirit to those who ask him.**

D. CONTROVERSIES AND CONFLICTS (11:14-54)

11:14-28. *Concerning Exorcisms.* To the activity of the Spirit of God is contrasted the activity of the evil spirits. The source of this account is Q (cf. Matt. 12:22-30), although some relationship to Mark 3:22-27 (see comment) is evident. After Jesus has cast a **demon** out of a **dumb man** (Matt. says that he is blind as well), the charge is made that he exorcises demons by **Beelzebul** (or Beelzebub), **the prince of demons.** Jesus' argument is 2-fold: (*a*) if he were casting out demons by the prince of demons, then **Satan** would be fighting **against himself;** (*b*) if he casts out demons by Beelzebul, the accusers' own exorcists are worthy of the same charge.

11:20. Whereas Matt. says that Jesus' exorcisms are "by the Spirit of God," Luke reads, **it is by the finger of God that I cast out demons.** This form is probably more original; it is a vivid way to point out that the works of Jesus are ultimately the acts of God (cf. Exod. 8:19).

11:23. This saying is not in harmony with 9:50, but here the intention is to enlist men in the battle on the side of God.

11:24-26. The word about the unclean spirit who returns to his former dwelling with **seven other**

spirits more evil than himself is taken from Q and is almost identical with Matt. 12:43-45 (see comment). The saying indicates that in the battle men are constantly threatened with the power of Satan.

11:27-28. The brief word about the woman who cries, **Blessed is the womb that bore you,** is found exclusively in Luke. It means, "How happy the mother of such a son must be!" and is a sort of messianic confession. Jesus' response indicates that in the struggle against evil the important thing is not to give lip service to himself or his mother but **to hear the word of God and keep it.**

11:29-36. *Concerning Signs.* The source for this material is Q (cf. Matt. 12:38-42; see comment). Luke has noted how a woman has missed the point of Jesus' mission; now he indicates that the crowd has done the same. Taking up the request for a sign (vs 16) Jesus replies that **no sign shall be given . . . except the sign of Jonah.** Luke's understanding of the sign is probably more original. Whereas Matt. sees the 3 days and 3 nights of Jonah in the belly of the whale as a symbol of the resurrection of Jesus, Luke presents the sign simply as Jonah's preaching of repentance. The meaning is that someone **greater than Solomon** and Jonah **is here;** men should not ask for a sign but listen to his message.

11:33-36. The sayings about **light** are based on Q (cf. Matt. 5:15; 6:22-23; see comment). In context they indicate that the message of Jesus is clear and perceived **when your eye is sound.** This figure describes the person of integrity and singleness of purpose. If one responds to the light of God's word with his total being, then the **whole body** (or whole person) **is full of light.**

11:37-54. *Woes to Pharisees and Lawyers.* Luke puts these sayings into the setting of a Pharisee's meal. The source is Q (cf. Matt. 23:1-36). The woes to the Pharisees are provoked by the notice that Jesus fails to practice ceremonial hand washing **before dinner.** Within the passage Luke presents 6 woes—3 spoken to the Pharisees and 3 answering the question of a lawyer.

11:39-41. In the saying concerning the **inside** and **outside of the cup** Luke speaks of giving **alms** of **those things which are within.** This could represent a mistranslation of the Aramaic original, which may have said "purify the things within," or it might suggest that true almsgiving has to do with the inner man.

11:44. Luke's form of this saying is different from the parallel in Matt. 23:27-28. He envisages **graves** beneath the ground upon which men unwittingly **walk** and are defiled; the evil of the Pharisees is concealed, but it contaminates Israel.

11:47-51. Luke adds that **apostles** as well as **prophets** are sent by God and killed by men. He thinks of the later leaders of the church and the persecutions which they endure. When he adds that **blood . . . shall be required of this generation** Luke perhaps thinks of the destruction of Jerusalem.

11:53-54. Luke ends his account with an editorial note concerning the attempt of **the scribes and the Pharisees** to find evidence of Jesus' error.

E. THE DEMANDS OF DISCIPLESHIP (12:1-13:9)

12:1-12. *The Necessity of Confession.* In the hearing of a huge **multitude** Jesus cautions his disciples to **beware of the leaven of the Pharisees.** This expression is found in Mark 8:15 without explanation. Luke has Jesus interpret this leaven as Pharisaic **hypocrisy**—a hypocrisy seen in the inner, hidden corruption of the Pharisees.

12:2-9. These vss. are based on Q (cf. Matt. 10:26-33) and describe how hypocrisy can be avoided. Basically one must **fear** only him who controls man's eternal destiny. One must trust God, who cares even for the **sparrows.** Matt.'s version omits reference to the **Son of man.** Here Jesus seems to distinguish himself from that figure. Yet Jesus is the representative of the coming Son of man—the exalted Messiah of the end time—since confession of Jesus guarantees acknowledgment by that transcendent representative of the power of God in the future.

12:10-12. Since Jesus is but a veiled emissary of the Son of man on earth, blasphemies against him can be forgiven (cf. Matt. 12:32). Blasphemy **against the Holy Spirit will not be forgiven,** since it would involve rejection of the very action of God which forgives. Luke seems to understand the unpardonable sin as a failure to listen to the Holy Spirit in the hour of trial (cf. Matt. 10:19; see comment). It is in the mission of the church that the power of the Spirit to save or to condemn is operative.

12:13-21. *The Threat of Covetousness.* The parable of the rich fool, found exclusively in Luke, is told in the setting of a discussion about inheritances. According to Jewish custom the older son in a family of 2 received ⅔ of the father's possessions. The man who asks the question of Jesus is probably the younger brother, and it is implied that the older son has divided nothing of the inheritance with him. Jesus refuses to judge between them, noting that covetousness is a threat to both.

12:16-21. To illustrate his point he tells a parable. A certain man had an abundance of produce. To take care of the excess he built larger **barns.** Then he said to his soul (i.e. to his inner self), **You have ample goods for many years.** While he is enjoying his abundance the rich man is interrupted by the word of God: **Your soul is required of you.** I.e. the man is required to die; his possessions are of no avail. Luke adds the note that **he who lays up treasure for himself . . . is not rich toward God;** the true way to lay up treasures will be explained later (vs. 33). The parable illustrates the fate of the man who loves neither God nor neighbor.

12:22-34. *The Futility of Anxiety.* Although the disciple is not to lay up treasure for himself, he need **not be anxious** about the basic needs of life. Luke's source here is Q—material which Matt. includes in his Sermon on the Mount (Matt. 6:19-33; see comment). Basically the text tells the faithful to put their trust in God; as he cares for **ravens** and **lilies,** so he will provide for the needs of his people. When Luke adds that they should avoid anxiety because they **are not able to do as small a thing as that** (vs. 26), he may indicate that they cannot add a **cubit** (about 18 inches) to their "stature" (one possible meaning of the Greek word); adding to one's **span of life** (another possible meaning of the same word) is hardly a small thing. The RSV footnote might also be preferred when we read with some manuscripts that the lilies "neither spin nor weave"; this variant fits the context better.

12:32-34. Luke's reference to the **little flock** is unique. Taking up a common OT figure (e.g. Pss. 80:1; 95:7; 100:3; Isa. 40:11; Jer. 23:1-4; Ezek. 34), he describes the disciples as the sheep of God. This suggests that they are the humble people who are ready to accept the divine rule. In contrast to Matt., Luke suggests that these faithful ought to play an ascetic role: **Sell your possessions, and give alms.**

12:35-47. *Exhortation to Watchful Waiting.* Rather than concern for possessions the disciples should show readiness for the coming of **their master.** Vss. 35-38, although similar to Matt. 25:1-13, are from Luke's special material, L. Like **faithful servants** the disciples must be ready for their returning Lord. The admonition that their **loins be girded** refers to binding up the loose Palestinian robe, ready for action, ready for service. That their **lamps** should be **burning** indicates that the crisis comes at night. Since Jewish night was divided into 3 watches, readiness at the **second** or **third** denotes wakefulness at the time of one's greatest temptation to sleep. When spoken by Jesus, these words stressed the need of preparedness for the coming kingdom; in the time of Luke they urge readiness for the return of the Christ—a coming which has been delayed.

12:39-46. The same point is made in the following vss. Here the source is Q (cf. Matt. 24:43-51). If a **householder** knew the **hour** that a **thief** would arrive, he would be prepared; so the faithful must be ready for the unexpected **coming** of the **Son of man.** Peter asks if this parable is for the disciples or **for all.** Although no answer is given, it is clear that this Lukan question implies instruction to the leaders of the church. The **wise steward** of the Lord's work will be found active when **the master** comes; the servant who presumes on the master's delay will be severely punished.

12:47-48. Responsibility of leaders is also the theme of Luke's unique conclusion. The view that conscious sins are more severely punished than unwitting errors is common to Jewish theology. Continuing his illustration from the servant-master relationship, Luke suggests that intentional disobedience deserves **a severe beating,** while disobedience out of ignorance results in **a light beating.** The leader of the church, who has been granted special knowledge of the divine will, is required to fulfill a higher standard of responsibility.

12:49-59. *The Certainty of Judgment.* To be sure, the disciples will face judgment. Vss. 49-56 are from L, although minor parallels are found in Matt. 10:34-36; 16:2-3; Mark 10:38.

12:49-50. The judgment is presented under 2 figures. The idea of casting **fire upon the earth** could suggest either punishment or purification. The 2nd figure, **baptism,** may support the latter. In any case the baptism Jesus is **to be baptized** with refers to his martyr's death. This death releases the Spirit, which both judges and purifies the **earth.**

12:51-53. The coming of Jesus brings division within the household. The **five** who are **divided** are probably the **father,** the **son,** the **mother** of the son's bride, her **daughter** (the bride), and the son's mother as the **mother-in-law** of the bride, who is thus **daughter-in-law** as well as daughter. **Three against two and two against three** may indicate a conflict between the older generation (father, mother, and mother-in-law) and the younger (son and his bride). In the context these vss. mean that the encounter with Christ brings a crisis; the response of faith creates a division within the people.

12:54-56. The words about the weather carry on the theme of judgment. Jesus turns to the crowd. When they **see a cloud rising in the west** they know that **a shower is coming.** The sea is to the W and rain storms come from that direction. When they **see the south wind blowing** they know that **there will be scorching heat.** The desert is to the S and torrid winds originate in that area. The point is: the **multitudes** know how to read the signs of the weather; they do not know how **to interpret** the signs of **the present time.** *The* sign of the present is the appearance of Jesus; his preaching heralds the coming of the kingdom of God.

12:57-59. The discussion is carried further in these vss. The source is Q (cf. Matt. 5:25-26). The meaning is clear: just as a prudent man agrees with his **accuser** while they are on the way to the **magistrate,** so a wise man should be reconciled to God before the judgment comes. The way is short and the judgment severe; one does not escape until he pays **the very last copper.** The coin which Luke has in mind (the lepton; see also p. 1285) was scarcely worth anything; it is the widow's "mite" mentioned in 21:2.

13:1-9. *The Need of Repentance.* In view of the coming judgment Israel must repent. This passage is closely connected with the previous one, since Luke speaks of **some** who were **present at that very time.** No parallel is to be found in Mark or Matt. Those present remind Jesus of **the Galileans whose blood Pilate had mingled with their sacrifices.** The historian Josephus reports an occasion when the Roman governor massacred some riotous Jews in Jerusalem and another, evidently after Jesus' crucifixion, when he destroyed some Samaritan worshipers on Mt. Gerizim. Luke's incident seems different from either of these. It must have occurred near the temple in Jerusalem, where Galilean Jews would come to sacrifice. Similarly there is no other account of the fall of the **tower in Siloam** which was fatal to **eighteen** citizens of Jerusalem. In both cases Jesus draws the conclusion that those who perished were not **worse offenders** than those who escaped. He refutes, therefore, the Jewish doctrine of retribution—the doctrine that those who receive special punishment must be guilty of some great sin. Instead Jesus finds **all** men guilty before God, all in need of repentance.

13:6-9. The parable of the **fig tree** indicates that there is still time to repent. It may be Luke's substitute for Mark's account of the cursing of the fig tree (Mark 11:12-14, 20-21; see comments). The use of a **vineyard** as symbol of the people of God is a typical OT figure (cf. Isa. 5:1-7). Although the fig tree has not produced fruit for **three years,** the **vinedresser** requests a **year** for cultivating and fertilizing. If it does not bear fruit then, it will be **cut down.** So also Jesus comes with a call for repentance; Israel is granted a final chance.

F. HEALING AND TEACHING (13:10-35)

13:10-17. *A Crippled Woman.* This narrative is taken from Luke's special tradition, L. The setting is a synagogue where Jesus has been teaching. He encounters a woman who has been ill **for eighteen years**—a fact which indicates the seriousness of her malady. Apparently she is afflicted with a sort of paralysis, since she is **bent over** and cannot **fully straighten herself.** When it is said that she has a **spirit of infirmity** and that **Satan** has **bound** her, it is clear that her contemporaries considered her disease the result of demon possession. The fact that Jesus calls to a woman would seem strange to them; it shows that the call of repentance is given to all, even the lowly and the helpless. Jesus, like the healers of his time, **laid his hands upon her;** he has the power to save. The power, of course, comes from God whose praise the patient proclaims.

13:14-17. Since it is **the sabbath** the **ruler of the synagogue** is **indignant.** His word is an adaptation of Deut. 5:14; man is not to work—or to heal—on the sabbath. Jesus replies that since the law allows one to **lead** his animal **to water** on the holy day it ought to make possible the release of a person from demonic power. He describes the woman as a **daughter of Abraham**—a rare expression which identifies her as one of the faithful people of God. Of course Jesus does not note that care for one's animals was allowed only if certain conditions, such as the distance to the watering place, were met. The ruler of the synagogue might have replied that livestock need water every day; a woman who has been paralyzed for 18 years could wait till tomorrow. Jesus, however, announces another doctrine of the sabbath: it is the time when the work of God should be done, the message of repentance declared, and God's salvation offered.

13:18-21. *Parables of the Kingdom.* Although Luke presents Jesus as still speaking in the synagogue, both of these parables are drawn from Q (cf. Matt. 13:31-33). The **mustard seed** parable is also found in Mark 4:30-32 (see comment). The fact that the recently discovered Gospel of Thomas (see pp. 1144-49) has this parable separated from the parable of the **leaven** suggests that the linking of the 2 is the responsibility of Q. Luke's version of the mustard seed parable is abbreviated; he does not say that the mustard is the "smallest of all seeds" or that its **tree** is the "greatest of shrubs." In essence both parables contrast small beginnings and big endings. Although Jesus' announcement of the kingdom of God awakens only a meager response, the kingdom will come with a power which challenges all Israel and includes people of all the world.

13:22-30. *The Narrow Door.* Those who are included in the kingdom are now described. Although parallels are found in Matt., this passage is based on L. The setting is the journey of Jesus **toward Jerusalem.** The discussion is provoked by a question put to Jesus: **Will those who are saved be few?** The answer by implication is "Yes," since **many . . . will seek to enter and will not be able.**

13:24-29. Whereas Matt. 7:13-14 (see comment) conceives of a "hard way" and a "narrow gate," Luke imagines the **door** of a house. This door is also **narrow** and thus difficult to enter. However, the possibility of entering is now open, so that Jesus can urge his listeners to **strive to enter.** One strives presumably by hearing the words of Jesus and doing them (cf. 6:47). When the door is closed, the time

to enter has passed. Those who **stand outside** knocking will claim acquaintance with the **Lord.** Did he not pass through their village, eating with them and teaching in their **streets?** Jesus, who is now presented as host in the house, will not recognize them; their works are evil. But while the door is ajar those who **weep** and **gnash** their **teeth** catch a glimpse of the messianic banquet. Who is seated there with the patriarchs and **prophets?** Indeed, those who come from the 4 corners of the world (cf. Isa. 49:12). Israel has been rejected, but Gentiles are participants in the **kingdom of God.**

13:30. The saying about the **last** and the **first** finds a parallel in Matt. 19:30; 20:16. The first represent the Jews to whom Jesus has come; the last are the Gentiles with whom the church's mission is effective.

13:31-35. *Jerusalem and the Prophets.* In contrast to Jesus' prediction of the rejection of Israel, Luke records a prophecy of Jerusalem's rejection of Jesus. Vss. 31-33 are without parallel in the other gospels. Since Jesus is presented as being on good terms with the Pharisees and since the encounter with Herod Antipas might better fit the Galilean ministry, it may be that this event originally occurred earlier in the career of Jesus. At any rate the view of Herod seems to have become more negative than that described in 9:9. Then he wanted to see Jesus; now he wants to **kill** him.

13:32-33. In depicting Antipas as **that fox** Jesus could be adopting either OT or Greek usage. For the OT the fox was an animal of destruction; for the Greeks he symbolized craftiness. Jesus' cryptic words about **today and tomorrow, and the third day** indicate that his time of ministry is short. The 3rd day also alludes to his resurrection, when he will **finish my course.** Above all Jesus must do his work. He will be killed, to be sure, but Herod cannot interrupt his destiny. **It cannot be that a prophet should perish away from Jerusalem;** the death of Jesus is according to the plan of God (cf. Acts 2:23).

13:34-35. These vss. are based on Q (cf. Matt. 23:37-39; see comment). In the context of Luke they make it evident that the fate of Jesus and the fate of Jerusalem are related. Jesus will be rejected just as the ancient prophets have been stoned and killed. This rejection will seal the doom of the city; her **house is forsaken.** Only as Israel recognizes the messiahship of Jesus will it be redeemed.

G. At a Pharisee's Table (14:1-24)

Into the narrative of the journey to Jerusalem Luke inserts a pause. Jesus dines at the house of a Pharisee. The wanderer, as at the house of Martha (10:38-42), is received as guest. The banquet was a typical setting for the utterances of Hellenistic teachers, and Luke employs the meal as the site of a collection of Jesus' sayings.

14:1-6. *Healing on the Sabbath.* This passage is found exclusively in Luke. In a sense it is parallel to 13:10-17. The **ruler,** who belongs **to the Pharisees,** could be either a leader of the synagogue or a member of the sanhedrin. Apparently other Pharisees are present to watch Jesus; they hope to trap him. A man appears who is afflicted with **dropsy.** This malady involves an excess of liquid in the tissues of the body; it is a symptom, not a disease. According to the rabbis the condition resulted from sins of unchastity.

14:3-6. Jesus asks the **lawyers and Pharisees**—the experts in the law—whether it is proper **to heal on the sabbath.** When they remain **silent** he takes hold of the man and cures him; the power to heal operates through Jesus. At once he puts another question to the critics: If **an ass or an ox** tumbles into a well, what owner will not work to save it on the sabbath? Some manuscripts suggest that it is a son, not a donkey, who has fallen into danger, but Jesus probably intends to speak of animals. If one will help his ass or ox on the holy day, how much more he should save his brother. Again the sabbath is interpreted as a time to do God's work, but more seriously than in the story of the crippled woman. There the stress was on caring for the normal needs of livestock; here it is a question of life or death.

14:7-17. *Place of Honor.* The situation of the meal makes possible a parable, again from L. When invited to a **wedding feast,** or to any important festival, one should not select the **place of honor.** Palestinian feasts involved an arrangement whereby guests reclined on couches in groups of 3; the center grouping was considered a location of esteem and was awarded on the basis of office, wealth, or power. If **a more eminent man** comes late—a practice not infrequent among the prominent—the man who has chosen the high place may be asked to step down. Instead one should take **the lowest place,** so that he may be requested to **go up higher**—a request which evokes the honor of all. The advice reflects simple social prudence and is reminiscent of ancient Jewish wisdom (cf. Prov. 25:6-7). That this parable is directed to the Pharisees is perhaps hinted by their love of the "best seat" (11:43).

14:11. This vs. has parallels elsewhere in the gospels (18:14; Matt. 18:4; 23:12). It summarizes the meaning of the parable: the **one who exalts himself will be humbled** and vice versa. At the end of time values will be reversed (cf. 1:46-55).

14:12-14. The host is told how guests should be invited. One ought not ask those who can return the invitation, but rather **the poor, the maimed, the lame, the blind.** It may be that Jesus originally stressed only the poor. They would fit the context better; the others may prepare for vs. 21. If they do belong in the original, their inclusion marks a sharp contrast to contemporary religious practice. The lame and the blind were forbidden entrance to the temple and were likewise excluded from the community of Qumran. The invitation of God, however, includes the lowly. In his dealings with his fellows man should display the same sort of mercy. To be sure, no reward for such action can be expected in this age, but in the time to come—**at the resurrection of the just**—God will bless the merciful. It is not necessary to conclude that Jesus is adopting the notion that only the righteous will be raised; he is simply saying that those who obey God will share the blessings of the righteous in the end time.

14:15-24. *Invitations to the Banquet.* The mention of the resurrection suggests a discussion of the future. The remark of one of the guests provides a transition from the earthly meal to the messianic banquet. Although a parallel is found in Matt. 22:1-10 (see comment), Luke's account represents an independent

version of the same tradition. A parallel is also found in the recently discovered Gospel of Thomas (see pp. 1144-49) which is closer to Luke. The declaration that **he who shall eat bread in the kingdom is blessed** offers the opportunity for Jesus to announce a parable which describes the invitations to the messianic feast. The parable rests on Jewish invitation customs. Actually the host sent 2: the first was the primary invitation; the 2nd announced the moment when the banquet was ready. Failure to hearken to the 2nd after accepting the first was considered gross discourtesy.

14:16-22. In Jesus' story a man invites many to a great feast and **at the time for the banquet** sends **his servant.** The response is a variety of excuses—purchase of **a field,** acquiring **five yoke of oxen,** marriage—all considered more important than attendance. In Jesus' application these refusals suggest that all sorts of worldly involvements are considered more important than his invitation to enter the kingdom. Perhaps he too envisages 2 invitations: one at the time of his preaching, the other at the moment when the kingdom comes. In any case another invitation is offered. **The poor and maimed and blind and lame** are asked to attend; i.e. those who are not considered worthy of the Jewish rites—tax collectors and sinners—are invited as replacements for the Pharisees.

14:23-24. There is still room for more. The master sends his servant out into the **highways and hedges,** i.e. into the country. Since Israel has rejected the invitation Gentiles will be brought in. The order to **compel** them could better be translated "urge." Perhaps Luke has in mind the oriental custom whereby the stranger was taken by the arm and drawn into the house. The application is clear: those who do not accept the invitation of Jesus shall not taste the messianic meal; they shall not share the blessings of the end time. That these words are spoken to the listeners of Jesus and not just the servant of the parable is seen in the fact that the **you** of vs. 24 is plural.

H. RENUNCIATION AND DISCIPLESHIP (14:25-35)

14:25-27. *Demands of the Kingdom.* The announcement that the kingdom is open to all leads to the assembling of **great multitudes.** Now it is seen that on those who are invited sharp demands are laid. The source is basically L. First the kingdom demands renunciation of the family. This saying has a parallel in both Matt. 10:37-38 and the Gospel of Thomas (see pp. 1144-49). The latter agrees with Luke in making the demands more stringent; one must **hate his own father and mother.** To Matt.'s list of "son or daughter" Luke adds **wife . . . , brothers and sisters, yes, and even his own life.** This last demand is illustrated by the word about bearing one's **cross,** which comes from Q (cf. Matt. 10:38) and duplicates a similar word previously taken from Mark (see above on 9:23-26). The cross, a symbol of execution, indicates that a man must renounce all to follow Jesus.

14:28-33. *Parables.* The pair of parables about building a **tower** and preparing for **war** has no parallel in the other gospels. The 2 suggest a contrast: the tower is a simple farm building or vineyard watchtower of the ordinary farmer; the battle is the concern of a **king.** In both cases the parables illustrate the cost of the kingdom; one who seeks to enter must be aware of its demands. Actually these 2 parables do not clearly illustrate the idea of renunciation which is stated in vs. 33. Instead they give the idea of careful calculation. Yet Jesus may hope to suggest that calculation will have only one conclusion: the demand of the kingdom is absolute; **all** must be renounced.

14:34. *Preservation of Character.* The word about **salt** is common to the Synoptics (cf. Matt. 5:13; Mark 9:50). Palestinians knew that salt extracted from the Dead Sea or the Mediterranean had to be pure. So the disciple must preserve his true character—absolute obedience to the rule of God.

I. JESUS AND SINNERS (15:1-32)

15:1-10. *The Lost Sheep and the Lost Coin.* Jesus' invitation to the lowly has evoked a response from **tax collectors and sinners.** For this he is rebuked by **the Pharisees and the scribes** and in response declares these parables. Although the story of the lost sheep may be found in Q (cf. Matt. 18:12-14) Luke's special material seems to have the 2 parables already joined.

15:3-7. The lost sheep parable has its background in such OT passages as Ezek. 34:12. The shepherd who has **a hundred sheep** seeks diligently for **one which is lost.** When he finds it **he lays it on his shoulders.** This was a typical way to carry sheep, revealing care and concern (cf. Isa. 49:22). The shepherd rejoices and calls his friends to share his joy. In application Jesus insists that there will be a similar celebration **in heaven** (a circumlocution for God) over one repentant sinner.

15:8-10. The parable of the lost coin is without parallel in the other gospels. It tells of a **woman** who has **ten silver coins**—lit. "drachmas," Greek-Syrian coins of approximately the same silver content as the denarius (see above on 7:40-43 and also p. 1285) but officially discounted by the Roman administration. For the average Palestinian woman 10 drachmas would represent the savings of many months. When the woman of the parable loses one, perhaps hearing it drop on the stone floor, she lights **a lamp** and sweeps **the house** until she finds it. She too celebrates her joy with **friends and neighbors.** The application is similar: the repentance of the individual sinner results in **joy before the angels of God** (i.e. in the court of heaven, meaning that God himself rejoices). Both parables show that God's love persistently seeks the lost and rejoices at their redemption.

15:11-32. *The Two Sons.* To the parables of the lost sheep and lost coin Luke joins the story of the lost son. Traditionally called the parable of the prodigal son, the story displays mastery of this figure of speech. Its omission from the other gospels is striking; but the genius of the story, together with its Semitic terminology, establishes its authenticity.

15:11-12. According to the story the **younger** of 2 sons asks to receive his inheritance, which by Jewish custom (cf. Deut. 21:17) amounted to a 3rd of his father's possessions. According to normal practice the division of a father's property was determined during his lifetime, but his sons did not actually receive their inheritances until his death.

That some heirs, like this younger son, tried to get their portions earlier can be substantiated by Jewish literature (cf. Ecclus. 33:19-23). A son granted such a privilege had to renounce all further claim on the parental estate. The father in the parable, since he has servants (vs. 17), is a well-to-do landowner. Apparently the sons are unmarried—a fact which could establish their ages as under 20.

15:13-16. After the request is granted the young son sets off to a far country. By implication he goes overseas to the Jewish dispersion. He spends his wealth **in loose living,** which could mean either extravagance or immoral spending. After a **famine** strikes the youth is reduced to poverty. He takes employment as a swineherd. To the Jews the pig was an unclean animal and caring for it was the lowliest of occupations. A rabbinic saying declares, "Cursed is the man who rears swine, and cursed is the man who teaches his son Greek philosophy." Symbolically it is suggested that the young man has rejected the law. In this lowly condition he eats the **pods that the swine ate;** these are the foot-long pods of the carob tree, used in Palestine for animal fodder and sometimes eaten by the poor. The rabbis considered eating them to be an act of penance.

15:17-24. The depth of his situation leads the young man to come **to himself.** He thinks of his father's abundance and resolves to return, confessing his sin and offering himself as servant. Sin **against heaven** means sin against God. While the son is still a distance away the father runs out to meet him and embraces and kisses him. The motive of the father's action is **compassion;** it is evident that he has been looking for his son's return all along. When the son repeats his confession, the father makes him, not a servant, but an honored son. Not work clothes, but **the best robe,** is put upon him; not the yoke of slavery, but the **ring** of sonship; not the barefoot service of slaves, but the sandals of a son. A great feast is held with the young man as honored guest.

15:25-30. The **elder son** is in the field working; he anticipates a greater inheritance. The sound of **music and dancing** comes from the house; he has not heard this since his brother left. Inquiring of a household slave, he learns of his brother's return and is angry. The father goes out to the elder son, just as he had to the younger. He is met with reproach from the angry youth: **These many years I have served you** and for this received no reward. Not even a **kid** from the many in the father's flock has been provided for his celebrations. Yet for his younger brother, whom he accuses of infidelity and immorality, there is killed **the fatted** (lit. "grain-fed") **calf.** The father's reply is true to the parable, but not to the actual economy of men: **All that is mine is yours.** In fact the feasting of the younger son has depreciated the possessions of the elder. But it is not so with God; his grace abounds to self-righteous as well as sinner. The final statement of the father repeats the early basis for rejoicing, **Your brother was dead, and is alive; he was lost, and is found.**

Although it is commonly agreed that a parable makes only one point, this story has a double moral: (*a*) God loves the sinner and forgives him on the basis of his repentance; (*b*) the Pharisees ought to respond at the salvation of sinners just as God does. The younger son stands for the sinners and tax collectors; the elder son represents Pharisaic self-righteousness. Perhaps the 2 points are at root one: God's saving love goes out to sinner and self-righteous alike.

J. THE THREAT OF RICHES (16:1-31)

16:1-13. The Crafty Steward. Jesus has just spoken to the Pharisees; now he directs a parable to the disciples. The source is L. A certain **rich man** has received the report that **his goods** are being wasted by his **steward.** The steward is told that he must give an **account of your stewardship**—he must close the books—and give up his position.

16:3-7. Musing within himself, the steward seeks a way to provide for his needs after he is **put out** of his stewardship. He is **not strong enough to dig, and . . . ashamed to beg**—a saying which was proverbial. He decides to help the master's creditors gain reduction of debt, so that they will offer hospitality in his time of need. He tells a man who owes **a hundred measures of oil** to **write fifty** and one who is in debt for **a hundred measures of wheat** to **write eighty.** I.e. he suggests that each falsify his promissory note. The debts are large in both cases, since 100 **measures** (lit. "baths") **of oil** totals about 550 gallons, and 100 **measures** (lit. "cors") **of wheat** is equal to something over 500 bushels (see table, p. 1285).

16:8-9. The conclusion of the parable is probably to be taken as words of Jesus; the term translated **master** really means "Lord" and is one of Luke's typical titles for Jesus. If so, he commends **the dishonest steward for his prudence,** noting that the **sons of this world** (lit. "age") **are wiser . . . than the sons of light**—an expression reminiscent of the "sons of light" of the Dead Sea Scrolls. When Jesus says that the former are wiser **in their own generation** it is thus implied that the wisdom of the righteous has to do with *their* generation—the age to come.

Interpretation of this parable has led to considerable debate. It is suggested, e.g., that Jesus is only commending prudence: just as the unrighteous are prudent in the affairs of this world, so the righteous must be prudent in regard to the matters of the kingdom. Others see a typical argument from the lesser to the greater: if even an unrighteous steward knows how to deal with the matters of the world, how much more the sons of light ought to know how to respond to God. Perhaps the parable is best interpreted in context: just as the steward faces a crisis, so does the disciple; in time of crisis radical decision must be made.

16:10-13. The additional sayings indicate how this decision is to be made. The first contrasts true riches with **the unrighteous mammon.** The disciples must seek the former and reject the latter. Faithfulness in spiritual things begins in the common questions of honesty. The saying about **two masters,** paralleled in Matt. 6:24, attempts to avoid a misunderstanding of the parable. In no way does it suggest that disciples are to emulate the steward in their use of money. Indeed their prudence has to do with true riches; they **cannot serve . . . mammon,** i.e. possessions or wealth acquired by evil means.

16:14-18. The Demands of the Kingdom. Luke inserts here a collection of sayings about money and Pharisees which are taken from L and Q. The Pharisees, who have overheard Jesus' rejection of mammon, scoff at him. Luke's charge that they are **lovers of money** may be confirmed by the fact that the Pharisees were a bourgeois class—urban businessmen who were gaining economic prominence. Their effort to **justify** themselves **before men** probably refers to the Pharisaic effort to attain righteousness by the giving of alms. According to Jesus, God is not impressed by external righteousness but knows the **hearts** of men; there is the true almsgiving (see 11:41). In God's economy values are reversed.

16:16-18. In these vss. taken from Q (cf. Matt. 11:12-13; also 5:18, 32) Luke draws the distinction between the old era and the new sharply; **John** is the dividing line. In this context those who enter the kingdom **violently** are probably the Pharisees who strive for righteousness by their own effort. Nevertheless God's demands remain secure; not **one dot of the law** will **become void.** The will of God is even more demanding than the OT acknowledges, as the prohibition of divorce shows (cf. Mark 10:11-12).

16:19-31. The Rich Man and Lazarus. Still speaking to Pharisees, Jesus relates a parable found exclusively in Luke. It points out that the law, which has just been under discussion, is understood better by the religiously disenfranchised than by the supercilious Pharisees. The parable contrasts 2 men. The **rich man** is **clothed in purple** (the expensive robe of royalty) **and fine linen** (a luxurious undergarment). He **feasted sumptuously every day;** his whole life is a constant feast. The **poor man named Lazarus,** on the other hand, would be happy to eat the crumbs from under the **table.** Since he lies at the **gate,** he may be lame. **Full of sores,** he is tormented by odious **dogs.**

At death the poor man is carried **to Abraham's bosom,** while the rich man finds himself in **Hades.** It is not clear whether these situations constitute an intermediate or a permanent state. Being in Abraham's bosom probably symbolizes companionship with the patriarch at the messianic banquet. **Hades,** the OT Sheol (see comment on Ps. 6:4-5), has become a place of **flame** and **torment.** The rich man asks aid from Lazarus and is reminded that the situation after death is exactly reversed. Abraham points out that **a great chasm has been fixed,** so that communication between the 2 realms of the dead is impossible. Judgment has been final, and the situation beyond the grave cannot be modified.

16:27-31. The rich man then requests that Lazarus be sent to his **brothers,** for **if some one goes to them from the dead, they will repent.** Abraham insists that if they ignore **Moses and the prophets,** even a resurrection will not convince them. This means that the law itself is the word of God which men should obey; texts like Isa. 58:7 demand food and hospitality for the poor. In the context of Luke the resurrection of Christ is implied; even when the risen Lord comes to men many will not have faith.

K. FORGIVENESS AND FAITH ON THE GROUND OF GRACE (17:1-19)

17:1-10. Sin, Forgiveness, and Faith. Luke now includes a collection of sayings spoken to the disciples. He presents Jesus' description of the fate of one who causes an offense to **one of these little ones** and applies this teaching to the life of the church. That the later ecclesiastical situation is reflected is seen in the probability that the disciples of Jesus had no servants (vs. 7). Although there are parallels in Matt., and even Mark, Luke may be using here his special source, L. The word translated **temptations to sin** is sometimes rendered "stumbling blocks" but lit. refers to the trigger of a trap or snare. The point of the saying, as of the parallel in Matt. 18:6-7 (see comment; cf. Mark 9:42), is that he who causes one of God's faithful to be ensnared by evil deserves severe judgment.

17:3-4. However, if one of these little ones sins, he should be forgiven. Jesus suggests that the disciple should first **rebuke him** (i.e. warn him or address him earnestly). Luke's form of the forgiveness teaching is different from that in Matt. 18:21-22; there one is to forgive "seventy times seven," while here the disciple is to forgive **seven times in the day.**

17:5-6. Just as they need the mood of forgiveness, so also the disciples must have faith. Luke portrays them as requesting an **increase** of **faith;** they say, "Bestow on us more faith." That an increase would be fitting is seen from a comparison of their faith with **a grain of mustard seed.** If faith were even that tiny size it could do the impossible—not, as in Matt. 17:20 (cf. Matt. 21:21), move a mountain, but uproot a **sycamine tree** and plant it **in the sea.** The sycamine is apparently the common black mulberry or perhaps the sycamine fig (cf. Matt. 21:21).

17:7-10. The parable of the unworthy **servant,** found only in Luke, describes a servant or slave of a farmer who works all day in the fields and then is required to serve his master in the evening. His eventual right to **eat and drink** is understood as no reward for extra services; he has done only what was his **duty.** Thus the disciple can make no claim on God; he simply obeys the Lord's will. What he receives is by the grace of God. He is one of the little ones who has learned the meaning of faith.

17:11-19. *The Thankful Leper.* He who receives the divine grace ought to be thankful. To illustrate this point Luke records the healing of **ten lepers**—a narrative not found elsewhere in the gospels. Jesus is again described as **on the way to Jerusalem.** The remark that **he was passing along between Samaria and Galilee** has been interpreted to mean that Jesus is moving from W to E, but it is possible that Luke conceives of the border between Galilee and Samaria as running N and S. Although lepers were not allowed in Jerusalem, they could abide in a **village** if they **stood** their **distance.** Apparently they have had some previous encounter with Jesus, since they call him by name and use the title **Master,** which his disciples sometimes employed (cf. 8:24). Instead of crying "Unclean" they ask for **mercy.**

Jesus sends them **to the priests.** Only the cultic officials in Jerusalem could establish their health and assure their restoration to the religious community (cf. 5:14; Lev. 14). The sending is a kind of test; Jesus has spoken no word of healing. On noting his cure **one** of the lepers, **a Samaritan,** returns to give **thanks.** He praises **God,** who is the ultimate source of his salvation, and falls prostrate before Jesus, who has performed it. The Master, who notes that the thankful man is a **foreigner,** makes him an example for Israel (cf. 4:27). As well

as showing the need of gratitude to God the story illustrates the nature of **faith,** about which the disciples have asked (vs. 5); it is the sort of thankful response to God's grace which makes a man well; it is the faith which saves.

L. THE COMING OF THE KINGDOM (17:20–18:34)

17:20-37. *The Days of the Son of Man.* Apparently the healing of the leper is taken as an eschatological sign. The Pharisees ask about the time of the kingdom's coming, and Luke replies with material drawn from his own sources, though with some parallels in Q. The result is an adaptation of Jesus' words to the eschatology of the author. First it is stated that the **kingdom** does not come with dramatic **signs** which can be **observed;** instead the reign of God is "within you" (the more common meaning of the Greek preposition) or **in the midst of you** (an alternate meaning favored by scholars as more consistent with other references to the kingdom in the gospels). Thus on the lips of Jesus this remark could mean that the kingdom is an inward reality, or that it has started to come into history with his own mission. For Luke it could mean that the kingdom is present in the church through the gift of the Spirit.

17:22-37. The **days of the Son of man,** on the other hand, will come in the distant future. One should not be misled by advice which cries, **Lo, there! . . . Lo, here!** since the Son of man will come like a flash of **lightning.** Though there has been some delay, Luke assures his readers that the end of time will come and the triumphant Messiah will be visible to all. Yet before this happens **he must suffer many things and be rejected;** Jesus is identified as the Son of man, and the route to triumph leads through Jerusalem. Because of this hiddenness of the Messiah his triumphant coming will be as a surprise. **As . . . in the days of Noah** and of **Lot** men were going about their ordinary business, so in the days of the Son of man judgment will come unexpectedly. When this happens no man should be distracted by the concerns of this world. Salvation can be lost in the last moment, as it was for **Lot's wife.** The judgment will come as a crisis which divides: of **two men** sleeping side by side or **two women** turning a millstone together only one will be **taken.** Again the question of **where** is raised. The answer is symbolic and likely proverbial: **Where . . . the eagles** (or "vultures") are **gathered.** I.e. wherever men refuse to be alert and ready for the Son of man in faith, there will be the judgment.

18:1-8. *The Vindication of the Elect.* In spite of the delay of the Son of man, Christians should continue to **pray** and not despair. To illustrate the need of persistent prayer Luke introduces a parable which has no parallel in the other gospels; it is similar to the parable of the friend at midnight (11:5-8). The **judge** is reminiscent of Josephus' description of King Jehoiakim, who was "neither religious toward God, nor kind toward men." In short the judge is corrupt. The **widow** is one of the typical needy of the Bible (cf. Exod. 22:21-24). Since her case is brought before an individual, it is probably a litigation concerning money, perhaps an inheritance. She **kept coming** asking vindication, so that finally the judge answers. The root meaning of **wear me out** is "beat me under the eye" (cf. the same verb, translated "pommel" in I Cor. 9:27), but Jesus probably intends the figurative idea.

18:6-8. In the application **the Lord** uses the typical argument from the lesser to the greater. If an **unrighteous judge** hears the pleas of a woman because of her persistence, how much more God will respond to the continual prayers of his people. The translation of vs. 7*b* is uncertain. According to the usual meaning of the verb it reads lit., "and he is [or "is he"] long suffering over them." This might be taken to mean that God will show patience in hearing the cries of **his elect.** In this context, however, the emphasis seems rather on the speedy vindication of God's chosen—**Will he delay long over them?** Luke no doubt sees this applied to the church in time of trial. The important thing is that **faith** will be found **on earth**—that this kind of prayerful hope will persist—when the Son of man finally comes.

18:9-14. *The Pharisee and the Tax Collector.* Instead of having faith in God, some trust **in themselves.** The point is illustrated by another parable found only in Luke. It contrasts **two men** who go to the Jerusalem **temple to pray.** Since they go at the same time, it is probably one of the prescribed hours of prayer—9 A.M. or 3 P.M. **The Pharisee** takes the stance of pride and thanks God that he is not guilty of the sins of many men, e.g. that tax collector. He does more than the law requires. The Pharisaic fondness for Monday and Thursday fasting was not required of all Jews, and tithing was enforced only for produce, not of **all** that one received.

18:13-14. The **tax collector** takes the stance of penitence. To repay fraud, a persistent temptation of his position, the tax collector must return the original amount plus 20%; this he is unable to do. He can simply cast himself on the mercy of God and confess his sinfulness. In commenting on the story Jesus insists that the tax collector is pronounced righteous and the Pharisee not. The worst sort of sin is self-righteousness, and man is **justified** by his trust in God, not in his own efforts. The final vs., which has frequent parallels in the gospels (14:11; Matt. 18:4; 23:12), refers to the reversal of situations in the end time.

18:15-17. *Children and the Kingdom.* Another example of faith is seen in the coming of children. Here Luke returns to his Markan source (Mark 10: 13-16), which he abandoned at 9:50. His mention of **infants** shows that the children are small. Luke omits Jesus' indignation with **the disciples** and his blessing of the children. He stresses the idea that Jesus **called** the children. To **enter** the kingdom one must have a childlike trust.

18:18-30. *The Rich Man and the Kingdom.* Again the question of entering the kingdom is raised. Luke answers with a narrative drawn from Mark 10:17-31 (see comment). His account omits some of Mark's vivid detail; there is no mention of the man's running to Jesus or of the information that Jesus "loved him." However, Luke does not shrink from reproducing the statement that **no one is good but God alone** (cf. Matt. 19:17). For Luke the man is **a ruler,** perhaps a member of the sanhedrin or a leader of the synagogue. Luke also adds that renouncing one's family is **for the sake of the kingdom of God.** The story makes the point that entering the kingdom demands more than obedience to

the law; it requires surrendering possessions and home. The one who makes this decision receives **in this time** spiritual blessings and **in the age to come eternal life.**

18:31-34. *The Fate of the Son of Man.* The decision about the kingdom involves an understanding of the fate of Jesus. Following Mark 10:32-34 Luke presents his 6th prediction of the passion (9:22, 44; 12:50; 13:33; 17:25). He apparently considers Mark's introduction unimportant but finds the mention of **Jerusalem** germane to his theme; the long journey is about to reach its goal. Luke omits reference to the verdict of the chief priests and scribes because it is not entirely in harmony with his own passion narrative. Instead he stresses understanding the rejection of the Son of man as fulfillment of prophetic prediction. This prepares for 21:27 but, more important, indicates that the destiny of Jesus is according to the purposes of God. Luke introduces the failure of the disciples to understand and emphasizes their obtuseness by repeating the remark 3 different ways. Their lack of understanding is of course due, not to a failure of clarity in Jesus' words, but to the inadequacy of their own faith.

M. EVENTS IN JERICHO (18:35–19:27)

18:35-43. *Sight to the Blind.* In order to understand, the disciples' eyes must be opened. Luke illustrates this with a miracle story based on Mark 10:46-52 (see comment), omitting the request of the sons of Zebedee (Mark 10:35-40). Whereas Mark reports that Jesus healed a blind beggar named Bartimaeus as he was leaving Jericho, Luke speaks merely of **a blind man** and locates the cure **as he drew near to Jericho**—perhaps to provide a setting for the Zacchaeus narrative. At any rate, since he agrees that the incident occurred in the vicinity of Jericho, he is describing Jesus as drawing closer to Jerusalem. The main theme of the passage is the recognition of Jesus as the Jewish Messiah—he opens the eyes of the blind (cf. Isa. 35:5). Jesus is called **Son of David** in preparation for his triumphal entry into Jerusalem (19:38). There the disciples will see and believe.

19:1-10. *Salvation to Zacchaeus.* This narrative is found only in Luke. With the blind man Zacchaeus presents a double witness to Jesus as the bringer of salvation. Zacchaeus is described as a **rich**

Courtesy of Herbert G. May

The mound of NT Jericho; this city was the home of Zacchaeus; in the center are the ruins of the palace of Herod the Great, founder of NT Jericho; modern Jericho is in the background

man who has made his wealth through the despicable practice of collecting taxes. The word translated **chief tax collector** has been found nowhere else in Greek literature, but it no doubt describes one who supervised tax collecting activity. Jericho, situated on an important commercial route, was a center of taxation. Since he is **small of stature** Zacchaeus climbs a tree in order to see Jesus. This **sycamore tree** has no relation to the American sycamore; it is a variety of fig which resembles a mulberry tree.

19:5-8. Jesus, displaying prophetic power, addresses Zacchaeus by name. The tax collector receives the Lord into his house as guest. Again the typical murmuring of the crowd occurs, for Jesus enters the home of **a sinner.** Vs. 8 is perhaps an interpolation, since Jesus' remark in the following vs. is directed to the objections of the crowd, not to the tax collector's promise of restitution. The pledge that he would **restore . . . fourfold** is reminiscent of the OT requirement to return 4 sheep for one which was stolen (Exod. 22:1).

19:9-10. The important thing is that **today salvation has come to this house.** The moment of encounter with Jesus is the time of redemption. The salvation of the household anticipates a typical theme of the Acts narrative (e.g. Acts 10:2; 11:14). The tax collector, though viewed as an outcast, is restored to the people of God; **he also is a son of Abraham.** It is to just such sinners that the Messiah is sent (cf. 15:4, 8).

19:11-27. *The Demand of Faithfulness.* Since the Messiah is approaching Jerusalem his followers imagine that the **kingdom** is **to appear immediately.** Luke answers that mistaken notion with a parable of Jesus. Although there is some relation to Matt. 25:14-30, Luke has his own version of this illustration. Apparently an original parable has been allegorized in terms of Luke's historical and eschatological interest. The background of the story is seen in Palestinian history where Herodian princes went to Rome to confirm their **kingly power** and Jewish embassies asked Caesar to deny it.

19:12-19. According to the parable a **nobleman went into a far country to receive kingly power** (or kingdom). Luke sees this as a sign that Jesus will receive his kingly power, not in Jerusalem, but in some distant order; before the kingdom comes with power there will be delay. Before leaving, the nobleman gives an equal sum of money to **ten of his servants.** The amount is a **pound**—lit. "mina," the term in the Greek-Syrian monetary system for 100 drachmas (see above on 15:8-10 and also p. 1285). Though the talent of Matt.'s version was 60 times as much, a mina had enough purchasing power to start a businessman in **trade.** When he returns as king the nobleman asks the servants to give an account of their stewardship. That only 3 of the 10 report indicates a parallel with Matt. and shows that 10 is a round number. The first servant has increased the one pound 10 times, while the 2nd returns 5. These faithful servants are granted **ten** and **five cities,** respectively—a fact incongruous with reality, yet illustrating a huge return from a small investment.

19:20-25. The 3rd servant has hidden his pound **in a napkin**—a neck scarf worn for protection from the sun—and has made no profit at all. At least the **money** could have earned **interest** in the **bank,** but

the return without increase leads to serious judgment. The one pound is taken away and given to the servant who earned 10, while objections (omitted in some manuscripts) are raised by the observers (vs. 25).

19:26-27. The conclusion makes 2 points: (*a*) **to every one who has will more be given; but from him who has not, even what he has will be taken away.** This expression is found elsewhere in the gospels (Mark 4:25 and parallels). It declares that the rule of God calls for fearless venture; he who does not produce the fruits of repentance and faith is not worthy of the kingdom at all. (*b*) The **enemies** of the king will be slain. Those who oppose the kingly power of Jesus (vs. 14) will be destroyed. These are the Jerusalem leaders whose rejection of the Messiah seals the fate of their city.

IV. THE ACTS OF JESUS IN JERUSALEM (19:28–24:53)

A. ENTRY INTO JERUSALEM (19:28-46)

19:28-40. *The King Who Comes in the Name of the Lord.* Although the latter part of Luke's passion narrative is unique (sometimes showing parallels with John), the early sections follow Mark. The major difference is Luke's inclusion of the lament over Jerusalem and the cleansing of the temple as part of the entry itself. The account of the entry is based on Mark 11:1-10 (see comment).

19:28-34. In preparation 2 disciples enter a village and **find a colt.** Luke stresses the idea that the **Lord has need of it**—a phrase repeated a 2nd time. Only Luke notes that the **owners** inquire about the **untying** of the colt, so that they give a tacit approval to the triumph of Jesus. In no sense should this be interpreted as prearranged; Jesus knows of the colt by prophetic power.

19:37-40. Only in Luke do we read of **the descent of the Mount of Olives;** this makes possible a view of the whole city from the E and prepares for the lament which follows. Luke also refers to **the whole multitude of the disciples,** perhaps envisaging a large crowd which has followed all the way from Galilee. The hymn of praise does not mention the Davidic sonship of Jesus (cf. Mark 11:10; that has already been confessed in 18:39. Emphasis instead is placed on his present kingship, and the words of praise are reminiscent of the heavenly choir of 2:14. The attempt of the Pharisees to get Jesus to **rebuke your disciples** (found only in Luke) illustrates the activity of the enemies who oppose his kingship (cf. vs. 27). But if the disciples should be **silent,** cosmic forces would speak; **the very stones would cry out** (cf. Hab. 2:11).

19:41-44. *The Fate of Jerusalem.* At the sight of the city Jesus weeps. The account is based on L. Jesus expresses the wish that the city **knew the things that make for peace.** These things would be those which lead to right relationship with God, including repentance and recognition of Jesus as Lord **today.** But Jerusalem does not know; these things **are hid from** her **eyes.** The multitude has sung of **peace in heaven** (vs. 38), yet in Jerusalem there shall be destruction. Eschatological judgment is to be fulfilled in history. Although Jesus may have predicted the fall of the city, Luke's description reflects knowledge of the events of A.D. 70 (see pp. 1026-31). In particular the **bank** which the

Courtesy of Herbert G. May

Jerusalem from Mount of Olives looking across the Kidron Valley to the walled city; the Muslim shrine "Dome of the Rock" (top right) locates the temple area

enemies will cast up is reminiscent of the wall which the Romans constructed around Jerusalem to facilitate their siege.

19:45-46. *The Cleansing of the Temple.* This record is based on Mark 11:15-19 (see comment), but Luke shortens the account drastically. In linking the cleansing to the entry narrative he destroys Mark's chronology of presenting particular events as occurring on certain days of the passion week. The cleansing prepares the temple for Jesus' Jerusalem ministry—a ministry which seems to have lasted several days (cf. vs. 47). Most important, the structure of Luke's narrative makes the cleansing of the temple the goal of the entry. Indeed the temple is the goal of the trip to Jerusalem. There the old religion is encountered; there the new teaching is given; there the mission of the church is begun (cf. 24:53).

B. Opposition to Jesus (19:47–21:4)

19:47-20:8. *The Question of Authority.* Luke's general statement about the Jerusalem ministry is based on Mark 11:18-19. His major purpose is to present a sharp contrast between the leaders and the people. As well as **chief priests** and **scribes** Luke lists **principal men** (probably lay members of the sanhedrin) among the Jerusalem officials. **The people,** on the other hand, are not called "the multitude," i.e. "crowd" (Mark 11:18); they are potentially the people of God. Luke has no account of the cursing of the fig tree (Mark 11:12-14).

20:2-8. The debate about authority is drawn from Mark 11:27-33 (see comment), which Luke follows faithfully. He does add that Jesus is **preaching the gospel** as well as **teaching;** the question for Luke concerns the authority of the church's message. He also notes that the leaders are afraid **the people** will **stone** them if they fail to acknowledge **John** as **prophet.** Possibly Jesus is to be seen as conspiring a clever evasion of the question (cf. Acts 23:6-10), but more likely the theme is positive: "John's authority is from God; so is mine."

20:9-19. *The Parable of the Evil Tenants.* The one who has been questioned puts his opponents in question. Jesus does this by a parable; the leaders of the Jews perceive that it is spoken **against them** (vs. 19). The source is Mark 12:1-12 (see comment).

20:9-15. Luke makes some interesting modifications. For one, he says that the man who went to **another country** was gone **for a long while.** Until

the time of John the prophetic word had not been heard for generations. Luke also increases the climax of the story by refusing to have the **third** servant killed; the only one destroyed is the **son.** That postcrucifixion motifs are involved here is seen by the fact that he reverses Mark's order so that the son is **cast out of the vineyard** and then **killed** (cf. Matt. 21:39), reflecting the tradition that Jesus was executed outside the city.

20:16-19. When the listeners imagine what judgment might befall these tenants, they cry, **God forbid!** I.e. they fear such condemnation might come upon themselves. To the quotation of Ps. 118:22-23 Luke adds an allusion to Isa. 8:14-15. The cornerstone has become a stone of stumbling. Rejection of Jesus means judgment upon Jerusalem.

20:20-26. *The Question of Tribute.* What relation does the authority of Jesus have to the authority of Rome? This question is answered on the basis of Mark 12:13-17 (see comment). Luke's use of the narrative has one main purpose: to make the political guiltlessness of Jesus absolutely clear. Luke accomplishes this by editorial work at the beginning and end of the account. In the introduction he points out that **spies** are sent to watch Jesus so that evidence may be found **to deliver him up to the authority and jurisdiction of the governor.** At the end of the story Luke shows that no incriminating evidence has been found; **they were not able . . . to catch him by what he said.** On the lips of Jesus the word about rendering **to Caesar . . . and to God** may suggest that the realm of Rome is unimportant in face of the kingdom of God; to it belongs the unrighteous mammon symbolized in the denarius. To Luke the saying implies that obedience to the will of God brings one into no conflict with Caesar.

20:27-40. *The Problem of the Resurrection.* Luke proceeds to give a fuller description of the realm of God. His source is Mark 12:18-27 (see comment), and his changes are primarily stylistic. He presents Jesus as more tolerant of the opposition, omitting the 2 Markan statements that the Sadducees are "wrong." Luke stresses the idea that the life of the resurrection is totally different from the realm of Caesar. Similarly those who share it have a new nature. They become **sons of God** through **being sons of the resurrection.** Perhaps Luke conceives of this new being as present in the life of faith; not only do the faithful worship a living God but they also **all live to him** through their response now to Jesus. Luke ends the story with an editorial note which again shows that no one **dared to ask him any question.** Jesus answers both Pharisees and Sadducees.

20:41-44. *The Christ and the Son of David.* To make it perfectly clear that Jesus is not a political ruler Luke introduced the Markan argument that the Christ is not **David's son** (Mark 12:35-37; see comment). Luke of course does not intend to deny that Jesus is the Davidic Messiah; he has previously argued that Jesus is the son of David (1:32; 3:31). However, he does insist that Jesus is not the typical nationalistic figure of Jewish expectation. Above all the title "son of David" is not fully descriptive of him; he must be called **Lord.**

20:45-21:4. *The Scribes and the Widow.* Jesus now attacks his opponents directly. The source is Mark 12:38-44 (see comment), which is followed carefully, though abbreviated. Luke does add that these words are spoken **to his disciples . . . in the hearing of all people;** those attacked are foes of the church. Jesus warns of the pride and pretense of the **scribes** and contrasts their imaginary piety with the genuine offering of a **widow.** She is a type of the poor who accept the demands of the kingdom, who know that one's whole life is dependent on God.

C. A Discourse on the End of History (21:5-37)

21:5-7. The Fate of the Temple. Luke's apocalyptic section is based on Mark 13. Its major feature is the separation of the destruction of Jerusalem from the eschatological events of the future. This feature results from Luke's doctrine of the end, which is shaped in part by the delay of the Lord's return in triumph. The prediction about the temple has a slightly different setting from that described in Mark 13:1-4 (see comment); here the word is apparently spoken in the temple and to a larger group than just the disciples. Although Jews are inclined to marvel at the **noble stones** of the temple, this center of worship shall be destroyed. The "prophecy," as Luke well knows, is to be fulfilled in A.D. 70 by the siege and destruction of Jerusalem by the Romans.

21:8-11. Signs of the End. This part of the discourse is based on Mark 13:5-8 (see comment). Luke makes some important modifications. For him the threat is not simply that imposters come in the Messiah's name but that these false Christs say, **The time is at hand.** The real heresy is the belief that the end is coming soon. In truth **the end will not be at once.** This is why Luke omits the Markan word that historical and cosmic **signs** are "the beginning of the sufferings"; he wants to avoid the impression that portents on earth and in heaven provide evidence that the messianic travail has already started.

21:12-19. Persecution of the Faithful. Again Luke changes his Markan source. He points out that persecution will take place **before all this,** i.e. before the end comes. In describing the persecutions he mentions those who are delivered up to **prisons;** he probably thinks of the imprisonments which he will describe in Acts (e.g. 4:3; 5:18). The prophecy that the faithful will be **brought before kings and governors** is fulfilled in the life of Paul (Acts 24:10-25:12; 26:1-32). Luke omits the saying which implies that the end will come after the gospel is "preached to all nations" (Mark 13:10). For him the Gentile mission is a historical reality, but the triumphant Lord has not yet returned. The promise that the disciples will be given **a mouth** is a Semitic way of saying that they will be told what to say; in Hebrew anthropology the organ stands for the function which it performs.

21:16-19. Vss. 16 and 18 seem to be in contradiction. In vs. 16 **some** will be **put to death,** but in vs. 18 the faithful are promised that **not a hair of your head will perish** (cf. 12:7; Matt. 10:30). Either Luke is contrasting 2 different groups, or he is suggesting that though the Christians are persecuted, or even executed, they cannot be ultimately destroyed; their salvation is sure.

21:20-24. The Destruction of Jerusalem. This crucial section of Luke's eschatological discourse is based on Mark 13:14-20, but the intention of the Markan passage has been changed. Mark was concerned with happenings of the end of history; Luke is describing an event which has occurred in history—the destruction of the Holy City. In place of Mark's "desolating sacrilege"—an apocalyptic symbol borrowed from Dan. 12:11—Luke has a reference to **Jerusalem surrounded by armies.** Similarly Luke directs the eschatological warnings to **those who are inside the city.** Though what happens in the **days of vengeance** is historical, it fulfills **all that is written.**

21:24. Luke's word that **Jerusalem will be trodden down by the Gentiles** refers to the capture and razing of the city by the Romans. By **the times of the Gentiles** he may mean the era of the Gentile mission. The rejection of Jesus means the destruction of the city, but it is from Jerusalem that the Gentile mission is launched. The time of the Gentiles is the time of the church; it continues until the coming of the Son of man. Although the fate of Jerusalem is sealed already in the rejection of Jesus, Luke does not agree that the days have been "shortened" (Mark 13:20); the coming of the Lord is an event distinct from the destruction of Jerusalem.

21:25-33. The Coming of the Son of Man. Luke now turns to the future—the cataclysmic return of the Son of man. His source is Mark 13:24-32, but he makes interesting changes. To the description of the cosmic signs he adds **the roaring of the sea,** probably from OT passages like Ps. 65:7. It seems strange that after showing such an interest in heavenly messengers in the birth stories, he omits any reference to the sending of angels here. Probably he wants nothing to detract from **the Son of man coming in a cloud.** Only Luke has the word that **when these things begin to take place** the faithful will know their **redemption is drawing near.** The concept is rare in the Synoptics; and Luke's idea here that redemption is granted, not through the death of Christ, but through his return, is striking.

21:29-31. Luke follows Mark's version of the parable of the fig tree closely. Its point is that as one can observe the signs of nature and know **summer** is at hand, so one can see these cosmic portents and know the end **is near.** To be sure, this understanding of signs contradicts Jesus' word that the "kingdom of God is not coming with signs to be observed" (17:20), but this simply shows that the ch. under discussion represents the eschatological tradition of the church more than the teachings of Jesus.

21:32-33. In discussing the time of the end Luke omits the idea that the Son does not know the day or hour (Mark 13:32); his Christology is too high to allow a limitation of the Lord's knowledge. **This generation will not pass away till all has taken place** is open to two interpretations: if it refers to Jesus' generation, it means that all things began to be accomplished in the destruction of Jerusalem; if to Luke's generation, it means that the events of the end are not too distant.

21:34-37. Exhortation to Watchful Waiting. Luke omits Mark's parable of the man who went on a journey and adds his own ending to the discourse. It stresses the need for watchful waiting, since the **day** of the Lord will come **like a snare,** i.e. as a surprise. The effect of this eschatological event will be universal—**upon all who dwell upon . . . the whole**

earth. Luke's own generation is reflected here; it is a time when **hearts** can **be weighed down** with **cares** of this life, i.e. when the vital expectation of the end is waning.

21:37-38. This is Luke's summary of the Jerusalem ministry. **The temple** has been the seat of Jesus' teaching, which apparently has been carried on for several days. At night he has **lodged on the mount called Olivet**—information not necessarily inconsistent with the mention of Bethany in Mark 11:11, since this village is just beyond the crest of the hill. However, Luke probably thinks of the place of lodging as identical with the place of prayer (22:40). He emphasizes the fact that the people assemble **early** to hear Jesus. This indicates the eagerness of their response in contrast to the villainy of the leaders.

D. The Last Supper (22:1-38)

22:1-6. *The Conspiracy Against Jesus.* Luke's account is based on Mark 14:1-11, although the narrative of the anointing at Bethany is omitted. Luke seems to make the mistake of identifying **the feast of Unleavened Bread** with **the Passover;** they are actually 2 different festivals, the former following immediately after the latter and lasting 7 days. Luke's saying that the feast **drew near,** in contrast to Mark's "two days," is another indication that he thinks of a longer ministry in Jerusalem. He omits Mark's report that the Jewish leaders sought to avoid killing Jesus during the feast, probably noting its inconsistency with Mark's dating (which he follows) of the arrest on the evening when the Passover was eaten and the execution during the feast of Unleavened Bread.

22:3-6. The distinctive feature of Luke's narrative is the statement that **Satan entered into Judas.** The last appearance of Satan was in 4:13, where the devil "departed from him until an opportune time." Apparently he has been absent during the whole ministry of Jesus. The opportune time is now —the time of the Crucifixion. Satan has entered Judas, so that this **member of the twelve** and the leaders of the Jews who follow him (vs. 47) have become instruments of Satan's power.

22:7-13. *Preparation for the Passover.* Although he abbreviates the account, Luke follows Mark 14:12-16 faithfully (see comment). By omitting Mark's question by the disciples, however, he implies that the initiative for the supper rested with Jesus. He also identifies the 2 sent to make the preparations as **Peter and John**—heroes of early episodes in Acts. The story of locating the **upper room,** like that of finding the colt (19:30-34), suggests, not prearrangement, but prophetic power. Like Mark and Matt., and in disagreement with John, Luke identifies the supper as a Passover meal (see comments on Matt. 26:17-29; Mark 14:12-16; John 13:1).

22:14-23. *Eating in Anticipation.* The major problem of this passage is the question of the proper text. Most ancient manuscripts include vss. 19*b*-20—words which the RSV relegates to a footnote. If this longer text is genuine, the account contains 2 cups. But since the ceremony of the Passover includes more than one, possibly only the 2nd cup is involved in the institution of the Lord's Supper. The longer text closely resembles I Cor. 11:23-25. It is just this sim-

ilarity that makes most scholars doubt its authenticity. Moreover, it is easy to surmise how the short text found in a few important manuscripts was lengthened to conform to traditional liturgical practice; but an explanation of why the longer text would have been shortened is almost impossible to find.

Accepting the short text as original, we can conclude that Luke presents a special tradition of the supper. The distinctive feature of this tradition is that the cup precedes the bread—a practice which perhaps finds some support in the 2nd-cent. document known as the Didache, or The Teaching of the Twelve Apostles. The result of this arrangement is to stress the bread more than the cup. The references to "breaking of bread" in Acts 2:42; 20:7 may indicate the importance of this emphasis for Luke.

22:14-19. In any event adopting the short text reduces some of the liturgical and theological arguments traditionally associated with the passage. Rather than stressing sacramental elements Luke emphasizes eschatological factors. The supper is primarily an anticipation of the messianic banquet. When Jesus is reported as saying that he has **earnestly desired to eat this passover** it is not clear whether he actually partakes or refrains; in some manuscripts his pledge is that he will **not eat it** "again" until the supper **is fulfilled in the kingdom of God.** Yet whether he eats or not, one thing is clear: the elements of the supper look forward to the coming of the kingdom. The joyous feast of the future cannot take place, however, until Jesus' purpose is accomplished. That will happen at his death —an event dramatically anticipated in the breaking of the bread. To share in this supper will make **the apostles** participants in the fate of Jesus as well as guarantee their presence at the messianic meal.

22:21-23. Still at the **table,** Jesus predicts his betrayal. The account is based on Mark 14:18-21 (see comment). In contrast to Mark, Luke locates this prophecy immediately after the words of institution. The effect of this change is to make it clear that even those who share in the supper are in danger of falling away. The passage also shows that, even though the death of Jesus is accomplished by Satan through the instrumentality of the betrayer, the destiny of Jesus is **determined** by God. The guilty, however, is not absolved but becomes the object of the divine **woe.**

22:24-38. *The Misunderstanding of the Disciples.* Here Luke presents Jesus as offering a discourse at the table—a theme more fully developed in John. The question about the identity of the betrayer leads to a discussion of greatness. Jesus replies that in the kingdom it is not measured by the standards of the world. There **kings . . . exercise lordship** and **authority** and are called **benefactors**—a title actually applied to Hellenistic rulers. In the **kingdom** the **greatest** is the **youngest, and the leader is one who serves.** The youngest may reflect the "young men" who perform duties in the early church (cf. Acts 5:6, 10). The example of service is seen in Jesus himself; he is not **one who sits at table** but **one who serves.**

22:28-30. Those who share this table will participate not only in his **trials** but also in the messianic banquet. The promise that they will **sit on thrones**

judging the twelve tribes of Israel (cf. Matt. 19:28) is simply another symbolic way to say that they will share the blessings of the end time.

22:31-34. According to Luke the prediction of Peter's denial is a part of this discourse rather than a saying spoken on the road (Mark 14:29-31). Luke basically uses his own material. The idea that **Satan demanded to have you** (plural in the Greek; cf. RSV footnote) is reminiscent of Job. Just as he has engineered the betrayal, so the devil puts the disciples to the testing which leads to denial. Although Luke does not say that all the disciples support Peter's pledge of fidelity (cf. Mark 14:31), he does imply that all are involved by his use of the plural of **you** in vs. 31. The figure of sifting **like wheat** is borrowed from Amos 9:9, where it symbolizes judgment of Israel. Peter's promise of faithfulness includes the idea that he is ready to undergo imprisonment; after the Resurrection this pledge will be kept. Indeed the central feature of the saying is the allusion to Peter's experience of the risen Christ. Though he will deny, the resurrection faith will lead Peter to turn **again** and **strengthen** the other disciples (cf. 24:34; I Cor. 15:5).

22:35-38. These vss. are without parallel in the other gospels. In view of the imminent testing the disciples must be prepared. Jesus refers back to the mission of the 12 (9:1-6), when they were sent out without **purse or bag or sandals**—equipment more clearly forbidden for the mission of the 70 (10:4). He then asks, **Did you lack anything?** At their denial he declares that the present time of trial is utterly different; **now** they need everything they can get their hands on, even a **sword.** The testing is serious—a matter of death for Jesus and persecution for the church. Jesus' death has been predicted by the OT (Isa. 53:12), which indicates that he will be executed like a common criminal (cf. 23:32). For Jesus, of course, the testing is a matter of the spirit, and the sword is a symbol of conflict and death. The disciples misunderstand completely: **Look, Lord, here are two swords.** Resigning himself to their blindness, Jesus ironically cries out in despair, **It is enough.**

E. The Arrest (22:39-62)

22:39-46. *Prayer on the Mount.* After the discourse Jesus and the disciples go to the Mount of Olives. Luke's account of Jesus' prayer there is parallel to Mark 14:32-42 (see comment), although it may reflect his special tradition. He abbreviates the story by reporting that Jesus prayed and returned to the disciples only once instead of 3 times.

22:39. That it was Jesus' **custom** to go **to the Mount of Olives** confirms the previous information (21:37) that this hill E of Jerusalem was the place of lodging during the ministry to the city. This customary action may hint too that the wrestling described in the prayer has gone on for some time.

22:40. Luke refers simply to the **place** of prayer, omitting as usual Mark's Aramaic—the name "Gethsemane." He emphasizes the meaning of the event more for the faith of the church than for the experience of Jesus. **Pray that you may not enter into temptation,** which in Mark's version is part of a rebuke to the disciples for their failure to watch, is in Luke's account the instruction to them as they

come to the place and then is repeated when they are aroused from sleep (vs. 46). The stress is on the church's need for preparation to face testing, i.e. persecution.

22:41-42. Luke omits Mark's separation of Peter, James, and John from the rest of the disciples. He adds that Jesus **withdrew . . . about a stone's throw** —a Greek and biblical expression which describes a short distance—and says that he **knelt down** instead of "fell on the ground." The content of Jesus' petition is not precisely the same in any 2 of the Synoptics. Luke omits the Aramaic "Abba" of Mark, although his term **Father** means the same. All 3 accounts agree that Jesus prays that God's **will,** not his own, **be done.**

22:43-44. These vss. have no parallel in the other gospels. Though not found in some ancient manuscripts, they represent Lukan style and probably are original. The **angel** who comes to help in time of trouble is a typical feature of Jewish martyr stories (cf. Dan. 3:25). Misunderstanding of vs. 44*b* has given rise to the common expression "sweat blood," but the meaning is rather that **his sweat** rolled down **like great drops of blood** from a wound—a simile suggesting the anxiety involved in the experience.

22:45-46. Luke excuses the disciples' lack of watchfulness by explaining that they were **sleeping for sorrow,** and Jesus' rebuke is very mild (see above on vs. 40).

22:47-53. *Betrayal and Capture.* This narrative is apparently based on both Mark 14:43-52 (see comment) and L. Luke observes that **Judas** leads the **crowd**—information which indicates that Satan's purposes are being accomplished through **one of the twelve** (cf. vs. 3). The impression is given here that Judas approaches, but does not actually **kiss,** the **Son of man;** Jesus' consciousness of the betrayer's intention is a sign of prophetic power. The question about **the sword** is reminiscent of vss. 35-38. Use of the sword results in the wounding of **the slave of the high priest;** Luke and John 18:10 agree that it is his **right ear** that is **cut off.** It is not clear in the Greek whether Jesus' response is directed to the use of the sword or to the act of capture. I.e. it may be translated either **No more of this,** meaning no more use of the sword, or "Let them have their way" (NEB), forbidding further interference with the arrest.

22:52-53. Jesus' words in rebuke of his captors are directed, not as in Mark to those who are sent out by the Jerusalem leaders, but **to the chief priests and captains of the temple and elders** themselves. The mention of the captains is exclusive with Luke and refers to officers of the temple police (cf. Acts 4:1; 5:24). Jesus' censure gets its force from the setting. Although he is **day after day** teaching **in the temple,** his enemies come to capture him at night. This setting makes possible a symbolic remark: **This is your hour,** i.e. the hour of their triumph. But the character of the hour is signified by the night as evil. It is **the power of darkness.**

22:54-62. *The Denial of Peter.* From this section of the passion narrative Luke has omitted the flight of the disciples (Mark 14:50), the escape of the young man (Mark 14:51-52), and the trial before the sanhedrin at night (Mark 14:57-61). The result of the last omission is to place the denial of Peter prior to the hearing before the sanhedrin in the morning and to put Jesus (as captive) and Peter together in the courtyard of the high priest's house as a setting for the denial. The source is probably Luke's special material L, plus Mark 14:66-72 (see comment).

22:54-60. The account of the 3 denials is slightly different from Mark's. The second charge, e.g., is made by **some one else,** whereas Mark attributes it to the **maid** again. Luke presents only the 2nd charge in direct address to Peter, while Mark has this form of accusation in the first and 3rd encounters. To add to the climactic character of the narrative Luke allows **an hour** to elapse between the 2nd and 3rd denials. He also improves the character of Peter by omitting Mark's report that this future leader of the church invoked a curse upon himself and swore. Perhaps Luke conceives of a progression of denial: in the first Peter denies his association with Jesus; in the 2nd he denies his association with the disciples; in the 3rd he makes an absolute denial, for he does not know what they are talking about.

22:61-62. Mark's idea that the **cock** would crow twice is lacking in Luke. Only one crowing is necessary to give the disciple the sense of guilt. The words that Peter **went out and wept bitterly** are not found in some manuscripts and may be assimilated from Matt. 26:75. Only Luke includes the most dramatic note of the entire narrative: **The Lord turned and looked at Peter.**

F. The Trials (22:63–23:25)

22:63-71. *Before the Council.* Although Luke does not include the trial before the sanhedrin at night, he records a hearing before the council in the morning. The source of the account is probably L edited by use of Mark 14:53-65. Here the mockery takes place before the hearing rather than after it as in Mark. The content of the 2 accounts is similar. Jesus is **blindfolded . . . , struck,** and asked **who** hit him; a prophet should have the power to identify his assailant. Luke omits Mark's information that the mockers, probably to be identified as the temple police, spit on Jesus.

22:66-68. Luke's version of the hearing conforms more closely to Jewish legal practice; it is not held illegally at night as Mark's describes. In the narrative he follows much of the content of Mark's nocturnal trial but omits the report that false witnesses were brought in and the charge that Jesus intended to destroy the temple. Luke's trial is more theological than historical. The questioning is unrealistic, since it is done, not by the high priest, but by the whole assembly in chorus. First they ask if Jesus is **the Christ.** To this he responds that they would **not believe** if he told them; they do not know the nature of the Messiah.

22:69-71. In contrast to Mark's reference to seeing the Son of man in power, Luke has Jesus announce that **the Son of man shall be seated at the right hand of the power of God.** For Luke the moment of rejection of Jesus is the time of his triumph. This occurs **now,** i.e. at the moment of decision about Jesus. The statement about the Son of man leads to the question, **Are you the Son of God?** Thus Luke interprets the title "Son of man" at its highest level —the level of the divine nature of the Christ. Jesus' reply, **You say that I am,** can be taken as either affirmation or denial. Luke's intention is to place

the responsibility of decision on the Jewish leadership. They assume his response to be an affirmation and therefore blasphemy **from his own lips** which seals his condemnation. In a deeper sense these words declare a theological truth: Jesus' own words send him to his death. No official verdict is pronounced; Jesus is sent to another authority.

23:1-5. *Before Pilate.* Although vs. 3 has a parallel in Mark 15:2, Luke's narrative here is based primarily on his special tradition, L. His purpose is to present Jesus as innocent, to confirm the guilt of the Jewish leaders, and to absolve the Romans of any injustice. This is accomplished by Pilate's 3-fold declaration that he finds **no crime** in Jesus (vss. 4, 15, 22). The guilt of the Jews is supported by the information that **the whole company** of the council **brought** Jesus to Pilate and made false charges against him. In essence the charge is that Jesus is a revolutionary; he forbids the people **to give tribute to Caesar**—an accusation which Luke's readers know to be erroneous (20:25)—and he says that **he himself is . . . a king.** Since kingship becomes the dominant motif of Luke's account, it bears a certain similarity to John 18:29–19:22.

23:3-5. Jesus' response to the question is similar to his answer before the council (22:70): **You have said so.** Pilate understands this to be a denial; if Jesus were claiming to be king evidence of insurrection would be sure. When Pilate asserts Jesus' innocence, the accusers give further evidence of his sedition. Their charge that he has been **teaching throughout all Judea, from Galilee even to this place** not only provides the ground for sending Jesus to Herod, the ruler of Galilee, but expresses a summary of the whole mission of Jesus.

23:6-12. *Before Herod.* Discovering that Jesus is **a Galilean,** Pilate sends him to **Herod** Antipas, who is **in Jerusalem,** perhaps to attend the feast. As we were told in 9:9, Herod has been hoping **to see** Jesus. Now we discover that his purpose has been to behold some act of power. Although **questioned . . . at some length** Jesus makes **no answer,** and presumably performs no miracle. His silence adds an aura of mystery to the proceedings, as well as fulfills prophecy (cf. Isa. 53:7).

23:11-12. Herod is no doubt exasperated. He **with his soldiers** treats Jesus **with contempt.** This mockery is a substitute for the mocking by the troops of Pilate in Mark 15:16-20; Luke prefers to present a "Jewish" ruler in the role of persecutor rather than Rome. When he says that the soldiers put **gorgeous apparel** on Jesus, he uses the same term which Josephus employs to describe the royal robe of Solomon. With sarcasm Jesus is being treated as king. After the mockery Herod sends Jesus back to Pilate. It is clear from vs. 15 that his verdict is "not guilty." **Herod and Pilate became friends** apparently because each recognized the other's authority.

Since this hearing is not found elsewhere in the gospels, some doubt its historicity. It seems unlikely that a Roman governor would recognize the rights of a petty tetrarch outside his own jurisdiction. In any case the purpose of the narrative is perhaps revealed in Acts 4:25-28. There Herod and Pilate are explicitly mentioned as fulfilling the prophecy of Ps. 2:2, that "kings . . . set themselves, and the rulers take counsel . . . against the LORD and his anointed." For this prophecy to be fulfilled there must be a king as well as a governor involved in the trial of Jesus. Moreover, Luke's interest in 2 witnesses is again visible; not only Pilate but also Herod finds Jesus innocent.

23:13-25. *Before the Crowd.* After Jesus is returned Pilate assembles **the chief priests and the rulers and the people.** He repeats the charge, reaffirms his own verdict, and announces Herod's concurrence. Since Jesus has done **nothing deserving death** the governor proposes the comparatively mild punishment of chastisement and **release.** These vss. are found exclusively in Luke.

23:18-23. The crowd cries for **release** of **Barabbas** —a man imprisoned **for an insurrection . . . and for murder.** Here Luke turns to Mark 15:6-15 (see comment). Luke states clearly that Pilate wants **to release Jesus.** The mob, swayed by the demonic power of the leaders, demands crucifixion, even though Pilate affirms his belief in innocence for **a third time** and repeats his proposal to **chastise** and **release** Jesus. Nevertheless the crowd is urgent and ultimately prevails.

23:24-25. Luke's presentation of the outcome is ironical. Barabbas, who is apparently guilty of sedition **in the city** and murder, is released; Jesus, who is innocent of insurrection and has come to save Jerusalem, is condemned. Luke makes it clear, however, that the leaders of the Jews are really guilty. He says that Pilate **delivered** Jesus, not "to be crucified," as Mark expresses it, but **up to their will.**

G. THE CRUCIFIXION (23:26-56)

23:26-31. *The Way to the Cross.* Luke, more than the other Synoptic writers, stresses the procession to the Crucifixion. Although vs. 26 finds a parallel in Mark 15:21 the narrative is drawn from Luke's unique tradition. **Simon of Cyrene** symbolizes the true disciple; he takes up the cross and follows Jesus (cf. 9:23; 14:27). The background of the wailing **women** is found in Zech. 12:10. For Jesus the idea is applicable to the present situation; they should not **weep** for him but for themselves. **Jerusalem,** not Jesus, is in serious danger. When its destruction comes—a fate sealed by the rejection of Jesus—the childless will be most fortunate. The call **to the mountains** is a quotation from Hos. 10:8, while the word about **green** and **dry** wood is proverbial. The 2 figures stress the seriousness of the city's future. One will do anything to hide from its horrors, and if Jerusalem can commit a crime like the Crucifixion in a time of tranquility, how great will be her punishment in the crisis of judgment.

23:32-43. *The Place of the Skull.* Luke's account of the crucifying appears to be based on both L and Mark 15:22-32 (see comment). It does not include the Aramaic word "Golgotha," but only its translation, **The Skull.** The saying **Father, forgive them; for they know not what they do** is found exclusively in Luke, and there not in some important manuscripts. It is probably original, however, since it is consistent with Luke's general portrait of Jesus and finds a parallel in Acts 7:60. A major feature of this narrative is the idea that sinners are given another chance, especially those who have acted in ignorance (cf. Acts 3:17). Another emphasis of the account is the sharp distinction drawn in vs. 35 between the **people,** who simply **stood by, watching,** and the **rulers,** who **scoffed** at Jesus. The scoffing involves ridicule of the acknowledgment of Jesus as God's **Chosen One**—a title which presents the Messiah as the Elect of God (cf. 9:35). The **inscription** on the cross is not precisely the same in any 2 of the gospels. Luke places the words **This is the King of the Jews** at the end of his description of the mockery as a climax.

23:39-43. The penitent thief is described only in Luke. In contrast to the other criminal this man confesses his guilt and expresses faith. Although he is without hope, the penitent asks that Jesus **remember** him when he comes in his **kingly power** (or into his kingdom, as the Greek can also mean). Jesus' statement, which has led to considerable debate, is perhaps not intended to stress the time of the thief's entrance into Paradise. As often in Luke, **today** or "now" may refer to the time of salvation which is the time of encounter with Jesus. However, Luke may wish to stress the conviction that Jesus at death comes into his power as king (cf. 22:69)—an event which occurs "today." **Paradise,** which basically means "garden," is used by Jewish authors of this period for the abode of the righteous dead, referring to either the intermediate or the final state. When stripped of its symbolic mode of expression, the narrative simply suggests that the repentant sinner can receive salvation now through faith in Jesus Christ.

23:44-49. *The Death of Jesus.* Here Luke has combined his special material with Mark 15:33-41 (see comment). His explanation of the **darkness**—that **the sun's light failed**—led some early readers to assume an eclipse, and alter the text. Of course at Passover time, when the moon is full, an eclipse of the sun is impossible. This fact forced others to modify the text to read "the sun was darkened." They correctly interpreted Luke as stressing supernatural events, as his inclusion of the rending of the temple **curtain** shows. This curtain separated the holy place from the Holy of Holies. The tearing of the curtain allows 2 possible interpretations: (*a*) the entry to God's dwelling is open; the death of Jesus provides access to God. (*b*) God has made his exit from the temple, splitting the curtain in two; the death of Jesus means judgment on Israel.

23:46. The word "My God, my God, why hast thou forsaken me?" and the discussion about Elijah reported by Mark and Matt. are lacking in Luke. Instead he includes the saying **Father, into thy hands I commit my spirit.** It seems unnatural for Jesus to cry **with a loud voice,** but some have noted that this occurred at the time of the trumpet call to evening prayer. The prayer of Jesus gets its content from Ps. 31:5 and suggests that at his death his spirit returns to God, from whence it came (cf. 3:22).

23:47-49. The **centurion** comes from Mark's narrative, but Luke has him merely confirm Pilate's verdict that Jesus is **innocent.** This Roman officer presents a kind of parallel with the penitent thief, indicating that the chance for repentance is still open. Two other groups observe the cross. The **multitudes,** who have watched silently, return **home** in a mood of penitence. The **acquaintances** probably include the disciples, since Luke has not reported their flight. The **women** are the ministering ladies of 8:1-3. Together these are witnesses of the death of Jesus so that they may become witnesses of his resurrection (cf. Acts 1:22).

23:50-56. *The Burial.* Luke's account modifies Mark 15:42-47 (see comment), perhaps on the basis of his own tradition. **Joseph . . . of Arimathea,** somewhat in parallel with Simeon (2:25), is presented as **a good and righteous man.** Luke says that he **had not consented to** the **purpose and deed** of the sanhedrin even though he was a **member.** Mark's information that Pilate inquired about the death of Jesus is lacking. Luke also omits Mark's explanation that **the day of Preparation** means "the day before the sabbath" (cf. John 19:14). **Was beginning** is lit. "was dawning"—perhaps a reference to the appearance of the evening star, since the sabbath began at sundown. The fact that the women **saw the tomb** makes it possible for them to find it on Easter morning. In contrast to Mark, Luke suggests that these women **prepared spices and ointments** before the sabbath.

H. THE RESURRECTION (24:1-53)

Although he uses Mark, Luke's account of the Resurrection is unique. For one thing he groups all the events into a single day and presents them under the motif of the early church's celebration of Easter. He also depicts all the appearances of the risen Christ as happening in the neighborhood of Jerusalem.

24:1-12. *The Empty Tomb.* The story of the women coming to the tomb is similar to Mark 16:1-8 (see comment). The women are named in vs. 10, but the list is different from Mark's.

24:4-5. At the tomb the women meet, not one, but **two men** dressed in **dazzling apparel.** Luke's fondness for 2 witnesses is again apparent (cf. Acts 1:10). Faced with these heavenly messengers the women are afraid and look **to the ground.** The men offer a mild rebuke and say, **Why do you seek the living among the dead?** A majority of manuscripts add, "He is not here but has risen," but it is usually supposed that this has been assimilated from Mark.

24:6-7. The important difference from Mark is the word about **Galilee.** In Mark's account it is announced that the risen Christ "is going before you to Galilee," but Luke says, **Remember how he told you, while he was still in Galilee.** This of course refers to prediction of the Resurrection **on the third day** presented in Galilee (9:22), but Luke's real intention in this modification is to confine all resurrection narratives to the environs of Jerusalem.

24:8-12. The women do not flee, as in Mark's account, but return **to the eleven** and bear witness. The latter are the leaders of the church—**apostles.** In spite of the witness they do **not believe.** This report of the empty tomb is not adequate for faith. Most ancient texts add vs. 12 (see RSV footnote), in which Peter runs to confirm the women's story. Although this may have been added to Luke under the influence of John 20:3-10, it could be original. Sometime before vs. 34 Simon Peter has an experience of the Resurrection.

24:13-35. *The Pilgrims of Emmaus.* This is the most dramatic resurrection narrative in the NT. It is found only in Luke. He makes it clear that the event took place **on that very day,** i.e. on Easter. The site of **Emmaus** has never been positively identified; 4 modern villages have been considered as possibilities. According to the story **two** disciples

are walking **from Jerusalem** to this town. One of them is called **Cleopas,** who is sometimes identified with Clopas, the father of Simeon, who succeeded James as leader of the Jerusalem church. Luke's intention is to give the story a quality of history; the name of one of the 2 is known.

24:15-18. As they walk along **discussing** the recent happenings in Jerusalem, they are joined by the risen Jesus, who is not recognized. We are told that their **eyes were kept from recognizing him.** This probably means, not that some miracle of blinding has occurred, but that a special opening of the eyes is necessary for seeing the risen Christ. Proof of the inward character of this blindness can be seen in the fact that even when they stand **still** they do not know the identity of the other pilgrim. When Jesus feigns ignorance of the recent events Cleopas is surprised. His response is open to slightly different translations, but its meaning is clear: the event of the Crucifixion is widely known.

24:19-24. To answer Jesus' lack of information the 2 disciples tell the basic elements of the message of Jesus. They have accepted him as a **prophet.** The **chief priests and rulers** of Jerusalem are guilty of his **death.** The disciples hoped he was the Messiah, but now their hopes have been dashed. The reference to the **third day** hints knowledge of Jesus' prediction of his resurrection. To be sure **women** have found no body and claimed a **vision,** while others have tested their report (perhaps a reference to vs. 12). Yet for all the evidence of an empty tomb no one has seen the risen Lord.

24:25-27. Jesus criticizes their lack of faith, using the whole OT to prove that **the Christ should suffer . . . and enter into his glory.** Specific texts which make these points are not easy to find, but Luke believes the total witness of **Moses and all the prophets** is that the Messiah's role involves a suffering which leads to triumph.

24:28-31. Arriving at the home of the travelers, Jesus is invited to share their hospitality. Suddenly the stranger assumes the role of host. Taking **bread,** he blesses and breaks it, and the disciples' **eyes were opened.** The breaking of bread is reminiscent of the feeding of the 5,000 (9:16) and the Last Supper (22:19). This indicates that the miracle of seeing the risen Christ occurs in the celebration of the Lord's Supper. Of course this is not to suggest that his reality is to be found only there or that the fellowship of the church somehow creates the resurrection faith. It is simply observed that in this event of the church's worship the risen Christ is made **known** (vs. 35).

24:32. When the 2 disciples exclaim, **Did not our hearts burn within us while he talked to us on the road?** they confess that the experience of the Resurrection illuminates their whole past. The **scriptures,** once so opaque, now are **opened** through the risen Christ.

24:33-35. When the pilgrims return **to Jerusalem** to witness they find that **the eleven** have already heard the good news. The report that **the Lord . . . has appeared to Simon** confirms Paul's account of the Resurrection (I Cor. 15:5; see above on vss. 8-12).

The Christ who at first is invisible, who then appears at places removed in distance, who appears again and vanishes, is hardly an ordinary person.

Although the following vss. will partially blur this image, it is evident here that Luke, like Paul (I Cor. 15:44, 50), supports belief in a spiritual resurrection.

24:36-49. *The Appearance in Jerusalem.* This narrative is without parallel in the other gospels. It seems to rest on a different tradition from the Emmaus story, since the disciples are **startled and frightened.** If they had already heard the reports of Peter and the 2 from Emmaus about the risen Christ, his appearance would not have been so shocking. As a matter of fact, the purpose of this account is to refute the beliefs of docetism—a heresy which asserted that Jesus only seemed to have a physical body. In announcing that the risen Christ has **flesh and bones** the tradition goes beyond what is implied in the previous narrative and what is suggested by his sudden appearance here. Luke apparently wants to avoid the notion that the risen Lord has no concrete reality. The word rendered **spirit** here would better be translated "ghost." Christ is no vaporous specter. He can eat **a piece of broiled fish.**

24:44-49. Again it is stressed that the death and resurrection of Christ are according to scripture. Christ is not only the fulfillment of the OT but also its interpreter. Most important, his interpretation must be announced to the world. The message of **repentance and forgiveness of sins** granted through Christ must be preached **in his name to all nations.** The punctuation of the passage is not clear, so that it is not certain whether the preaching or the witnessing is to begin **from Jerusalem** (see RSV footnote), but the 2 are essentially the same. Witnessing is not to occur at once, for the disciples must **stay in the city** until they receive **power from on high;** this will take place on Pentecost (Acts 2:1-4). Now it is clear why the events of Jesus' death and resurrection occur near the city: Jerusalem is the traditional messianic center; there the prophets have been executed; there the Christ is raised; there the risen Lord establishes his mission to the world; there the church will begin.

24:50-53. *Departure from Bethany.* This account has no parallel in the other gospels, but its relation to Acts 1:9-11 has created a problem. It seems that both texts describe the ascension of Christ. The words "and was carried up into heaven," added after vs. 51 in most manuscripts (cf. RSV footnote), make this clearer. But while the Acts narrative presents the Ascension as occurring 40 days after the Resurrection, this account includes the departure of Jesus as an event of Easter day. Perhaps Luke, concerned less with chronology than with theology, presents both accounts to make different points. An ascension soon after the death of Jesus seems historically probable, as the promise to the penitent thief implies (23: 43). Of course the Ascension cannot occur until the resurrection appearances of Easter have occurred. The Acts account wishes to stress the importance of the risen Christ for the founding of the church. Thus Christ is the end of the gospel and the beginning of the mission.

24:52-53. After Jesus has departed the disciples return **to Jerusalem with great joy.** They praise God, who has accomplished all these things. Luke's gospel ends as it began—**in the temple.**

THE GOSPEL ACCORDING TO JOHN

Massey H. Shepherd, Jr.

The gospel of John was published in Asia—i.e. the Roman province comprising the W part of Asia Minor (see color map 16)—not later than the early years of the 2nd cent. Its sources and circumstances of origin remain veiled in mystery. Yet no document has influenced so powerfully and imaginatively the minds and sentiments of Christians. Nor has any book of the NT received so many diverse interpretations of its meaning and judgments of its historical value. The very fecundity of critical and devotional commentary which the gospel has evoked is perhaps its strongest claim to an authentic inspiration. The testimony *of* Jesus and *about* Jesus in this gospel meets all sorts of men, of varied religious experience and insight, with manifold discernments of revelation.

The gospel itself encourages an ever-deepening search for meaning. Throughout the work there are explicit notices that Jesus' contemporaries did not understand the true purport of his sayings and actions. His mother and brothers, his disciples and friends, the Jewish rabbis and priests, the Samaritan woman, Pontius Pilate—all of them miss the point of his sayings and are dumbfounded by his behavior. Everything in the gospel is a "sign" that points to a fulfillment—not only in the historic "hour [which] is coming, and now is" when Jesus accomplishes his mission from God, but in a judgment that separates those who believe and those who do not believe in him both now and in the "last day."

Purpose. The author is explicit about his purpose: the work is a gospel—i.e. "written that you may believe that Jesus is the Christ, the Son of God, and that believing you may have life in his name" (20:31). Did he know other written gospels? If so, was his aim to correct, supplement, or displace them? These questions have received diverse answers, in both ancient and modern times. The similarities of basic structure and content with other gospels, canonical and apocryphal, are matched by noticeable differences—in chronology, style, and method of presentation. These internal characteristics of the work have been evaluated by reference to the variant traditions about the author and the circumstances of his writing.

From the early 3rd cent. a tradition was established that John the apostle dictated the gospel in old age, independently but with knowledge of the other gospels, from his reminiscences, supplementing them with accounts of Jesus' ministry before the imprisonment of John the Baptist. This viewpoint finds continued expression in chronological "harmonies" of the gospels that follow the 3-year framework of this gospel—i.e. 3 Passovers (2:13; 6:4; 11:55)—as over against the single-year ministry implicit in the Synoptic gospels. Many modern interpreters, without committing themselves to the chronological problem, are also persuaded that John depended, not on any previous written gospel, but on his own independent traditions. Others, however, believe that he used Mark, and a few find literary relationships with Luke.

Clement of Alexandria, writing *ca.* 190, said that John "last of all, perceiving that external facts had been shown in the gospels [i.e. the Synoptics], and urged by his disciples and inspired by the Spirit, composed a spiritual gospel." I.e. the Synoptics give us history; John gives us theological interpretation. This evaluation has been popular until recent times. But the distinction is overly simplified. Each of the gospels has a theological evaluation of the history it records. This is what makes it gospel and not mere biography. With regard to John specifically the documents discovered at Qumran (see "The Dead Sea Scrolls," pp. 1063-71) have contributed to a fresh appreciation of its roots in a sound historical tradition.

Like all other gospels this book was designed for use by Christians, those "who believed in his name" (1:12)—for witness and preaching to potential converts, for teaching and worship within the church community, and for meditation of those who "dwell" and "abide" in Christ and his life-giving words and sayings. The gospel is universal in scope—for "every man," for "the world"—not only for those who have seen and heard the truth in Jesus through bodily sense perception but for those whose belief is responsive to the testimony and word of eyewitnesses (cf. 17:20; 20:29; I John 1:1-3).

Date, Place, and Situation. The time and locale of publication of the gospel can be approximately determined. Apart from considerations of authorship and its use of other gospels, internal evidence suggests a date after the destruction of the Jewish temple in Jerusalem in 70 (cf. 2:19-20; 4:21) and probably after the expulsion of Jewish Christian believers from the synagogues, which was effective *ca.* 85-90 (cf. 9:22; 16:2).

The earliest citations of the gospel are disputed. Some scholars believe that it was known to the martyr-bishop of Antioch, Ignatius, whose extant letters (ca. 115) to churches in Asia show several phrases of possible allusion. The letter of Bishop Polycarp of Smyrna, whom tradition considered a disciple of the author, does not cite the gospel, but does contain a quotation from I John, which is generally considered later than the gospel. The eminent Gnostic theologian Valentinus certainly knew and used the gospel in his meditation The Gospel of Truth (ca. 140), recently discovered in a Coptic version among Gnostic manuscripts uncovered at Nag Hammadi, Egypt. Circulation of the gospel in Egypt by the 2nd quarter of the 2nd cent. is attested by a papyrus fragment of the text of 18:31-33, 37-38.

All this evidence is concordant with the testimony of Irenaeus, bishop of Lyons (ca. 177-200), a native of Smyrna and in his youth a hearer of Polycarp, that "John" delivered his gospel to the elders in Asia, remaining among them until the time of the Emperor Trajan (98-117). Nor is there good reason to doubt the unanimous tradition of Irenaeus and his contemporaries that the gospel was published in Ephesus, despite the theories of some modern critics that its provenance was possibly Antioch or Alexandria. Christians, with their ideas and writings, shared no less than others the ease of travel and communication of the Roman Empire. A book produced in any urban center would soon find its way to other cities. It would not take several years or a decade for a book published in Asia to circulate in Syria or Egypt or in Rome and the W.

All early Christian writings were written to meet specific needs and situations. This gospel is no exception. Even the casual reader will note throughout an engagement, explicit or implicit, with the "Jews" —so much so that Jesus himself often appears as one separate from and opposite to the Jews. Yet there is no denial of his Jewish identity, whether in contrast to a Samaritan (4:9, 22) or to a Gentile (18:35).

The author's concern with Judaism is not that of the apostolic age, viz. the mission to the Gentiles and acceptance of them by their faith in full fellowship with Jewish Christians who continue to keep the OT law (cf. Acts 15; Gal. 2). His problem is a more subtle one: a Judaizing form of Christianity, open to Jew and Gentile alike, that adheres to Jewish practices and legal demands—e.g. circumcision and sabbath observance—but interprets them in general, universal terms drawn from Hellenistic cosmology and philosophy. In such a scheme the scandal of God the Word-made-flesh in Jesus of Nazareth and his decisive once-for-all act in suffering and dying for the sin of the world are incredible, if not blasphemous. They did not deny the coming of a heavenly "Christ," but their interpretation of scripture did not persuade them that he could be a man from Galilee (see below on 7:40-52).

This Jewish-Hellenistic construction—combining outward observance with spiritualized interpretation —had its roots in the apostolic age. Paul combated it constantly (cf. Col. 2:8-23; Gal. 5:1-18; 6:12-15). But it was esp. virulent in Asia in the latter first and early 2nd cent., being the progenitor of the Gnostic systems that spread throughout the church in the middle of the 2nd cent. The seer of Patmos

identified them as those "who say that they are Jews and are not" (Rev. 3:9). Ignatius' letters to the Asian churches are a persistent attack on the problem of those who preach Christ but continue to observe Judaism. "It is better," he writes to the Philadelphians, "to hear about Christianity from one of the circumcision than Judaism from a Gentile" (6:1, trans. C. C. Richardson).

The argument with the "Jews" in John is admirably summarized by Ignatius:

> When I heard some people saying, "If I don't find it in the original documents [i.e. the OT], I don't believe it in the gospel," I answered them, "But it *is* written there." They retorted, "That's just the question!" To my mind it is Jesus Christ who is the original documents. The inviolable archives are his cross and death and his resurrection and the faith that came by him. (Philadelphians 8:2, trans. C. C. Richardson.)

The same controversy is reflected, though with more speculative opponents, in I John (see Intro.) and in the Pastoral letters (cf. I Tim. 1:3-11; 4:1-5; 6:3-5; II Tim. 3:1-9; Tit. 3:9-11), which also date from this period and were addressed to leaders of the church in Asia and the Aegean islands. The author of the gospel, like Ignatius, sees the crux in a right interpretation of the OT, as fulfilled and perfected in the incarnate Son of God, who is none other than the historical Jesus:

> The law was given through Moses; grace and truth came through Jesus Christ. (1:17.)

> It is Moses who accuses you, on whom you set your hope. If you believed Moses, you would believe me, for he wrote of me. But if you do not believe his writings, how will you believe my words? (5:45-47.)

> You are his disciple, but we are disciples of Moses. We know that God has spoken to Moses, but as for this man, we do not know where he comes from. (9:28-29.)

Author. The acceptance of the gospel in the NT canon in the late 2nd–early 3rd cent. was a seal of acceptance of its authorship by John son of Zebedee, one of the 12 apostles of Jesus. Though contested at that time, this official view held the day without serious challenge until recent times; and it is still stoutly defended by many able scholars, Catholic and Protestant. Its strongest support is the testimony of Irenaeus, who claimed to have received the tradition firsthand, when a youth, from Polycarp.

The tradition would perhaps be stronger if it did not claim too much, for in addition to the gospel it places under John's authorship the three letters and Rev. Distinguished theologians of the ancient church, e.g. Bishop Dionysius of Alexandria (d. ca. 265) and Bishop Eusebius of Caesarea (d. ca. 340), were doubtful that the same hand produced both the gospel and Rev. They were keen enough to note the differences in these writings both of literary style and of doctrinal viewpoint. They resorted therefore to a 2-John hypothesis: (a) the apostle, who wrote the gospel and letters; (b) a "disciple of the Lord," who composed Rev. Support for this thesis was found in a book of Oracles of the Lord by Bishop Papias of Hierapolis, a contemporary of Ignatius and Polycarp, who distinguished 2 Johns: (a) an apostle, one of the 12, and (*b*) a disciple, who lived to his own times. Papias was conversant with all the "Johannine" writings, though he preferred oral to written traditions. But it is not clear from the surviving fragments of his work to what John he ascribed the books under that name. Many modern scholars reverse the judgment of Dionysius and Eusebius by ascribing Rev. to the apostle—as did Justin Martyr, *ca.* 150—and the gospel and letters to the "disciple."

The gospel itself has an appendix (ch. 21), which includes a colophon (vss. 24-25) ascribing the "witness" of the gospel to the unnamed "beloved disciple" who lay close to Jesus' breast at the Last Supper (cf. 13:23-25; 20:2; 21:20-24). No reader of the gospel who was not familiar with the Synoptics and Acts would identify the "beloved disciple" with John, or with either of the "sons of Zebedee," who are mentioned only in the appendix (21:2). But the church in Asia made this identification, as is clear not only from the testimony of Irenaeus but more esp. from a letter of Bishop Polycrates of Ephesus (*ca.* 190) preserved by Eusebius. In listing the "great luminaries" who have "fallen asleep" in Asia, Polycrates mentions first Philip the apostle, whom he confuses with Philip the evangelist of Acts, and his daughters and then John, "who leaned on the Lord's breast, who was a priest, wearing the sacerdotal breastplate, both martyr and teacher." It is notable that he does not call John an apostle, as he does Philip!

The colophon (21:24-25) distinguishes 2 stages in the composition of the book: the "disciple" who bears witness, and "we" who attest to the truth of his testimony. This suggests a posthumous publication by disciples, or an editor, of the eyewitness disciple. Indications of editorial revision have often been noted—e.g. 2:21-22; 4:2 seem obvious, not to speak of the appendix itself. There are abrupt transitions both of geography and of discourse. Ch. 6 would seem to make more sense if it preceded ch. 5. The dangling summons of 14:31, "Rise, let us go hence," intrudes in the middle of a long discourse; and the logic of argument and exposition in chs. 7; 8; 10 is curious. There is no manuscript evidence to support any transpositions of the text; nor is there evidence that the gospel ever circulated without the appendix. Nonetheless editorial work seems plausible.

There is a growing consensus that the author—whether "disciple" or "witness"—had access to good historical traditions stemming from Palestine, no less than the writers of the Synoptic gospels. His facts, as well as his interpretations, must be taken seriously. He knew the geography of Palestine and the customs of the Jews better than Mark, and he may have had Judean associations more immediate than those of the Synoptic writers.

He was undoubtedly a Jew, one whose native tongue was the Aramaic spoken by Jesus. He thinks and writes in a Semitic idiom; and the sayings of Jesus he records, however different in style from those of the Synoptics, betray the same Semitic parallelism of structure. Yet he writes a clear and grammatical Greek. Efforts of some scholars to prove that the gospel was translated from Aramaic have not won general acceptance. His Hellenistic culture has perhaps been exaggerated, but it was not negligible.

He was more than a match for his theological opponents.

Structure. The apparent dislocations of content, combined with a "spiral" method of exposition—i.e. words and phrases once introduced are later taken up and developed in new combinations—make it difficult to outline the gospel in any definitive way. The gospel lacks the continuous flow of narrative in which teachings are inserted, as in Luke, or the topical divisions of narrative plus teaching that characterize the 5-fold arrangement of Matt. It is most commonly analyzed by commentators into (*a*) ch. 1, which introduces all the titles and interpretations of Jesus used throughout the gospel; (*b*) chs. 2-11, consisting of narratives of a series of "signs," each pointing to the death-resurrection theme of the following chs., interspersed with discourses and controversies about the true nature of Jesus' revelation; (*c*) chs. 12-20, which contain the passion and resurrection narrative, including a long discourse to the disciples and final prayer at the Last Supper; (*d*) ch. 21, the appendix. In addition to this conventional analysis there is another illuminating one that views the gospel as presenting the manifestation of the Christ to the world (chs. 1-4), to the Jews (chs. 5-12), and to the disciples (chs. 13-21).

For Further Study. Beginning students would do well to orient themselves by reference to a dictionary article such as the classic one of Baron Friedrich von Hügel in *Encyclopaedia Britannica,* reprinted since 11th ed., 1911, or of J. N. Sanders in *IDB,* 1962, and to critical and thematic surveys such as those of W. F. Howard, *Christianity According to St. John,* 1946, and *The 4th Gospel in Recent Criticism and Interpretation,* 4th ed., 1955. The great commentaries in English are those of J. H. Bernard, 2 vols., 1929; E. C. Hoskyns and F. N. Davey, 1940; C. K. Barrett, 1955; R. H. Lightfoot, posthumous, 1956; and R. E. Brown, S.S., 2 vols., 1966-68. Less extensive commentaries are by W. F. Howard in *IB,* 1952; Alan Richardson, 1960; and A. M. Hunter, 1965. The magisterial commentary in German of Rudolf Bultmann is not yet available in English trans. but one may gain insight into its positions from D. M. Smith, Jr., *The Composition and Order of the 4th Gospel,* 1965. The vols. of C. H. Dodd are fundamental: *The Interpretation of the 4th Gospel,* 1953, and *Historical Tradition in the 4th Gospel,* 1963.

Special studies of influence are: B. W. Bacon, *The Gospel of the Hellenists,* 1933; Percival Gardner-Smith, *St. John and the Synoptic Gospels,* 1938; J. N. Sanders, *The 4th Gospel in the Early Church,* 1943; Oscar Cullmann, *Early Christian Worship,* 1953, Part II; Aileen Guilding, *The 4th Gospel and Jewish Worship,* 1960; J. A. T. Robinson, *12 NT Studies,* 1962, pp. 94-138; André Feuillet, *Johannine Studies,* 1965; R. E. Brown, S.S., *NT Essays,* 1965, pp. 51-213.

I. Intro. of the Messiah (1:1-51)

1:1-18. *The Prologue.* The gospel opens with a hymn that celebrates God's revelation of himself to the world. From all eternity God has existed with his **Word,** who is his mind and purpose and the agent of his self-disclosure. By his Word he created the world, and imparted to it **life** for fellowship with him and **light** for knowledge of him. But his gifts of life and light, ever present and ever active, have been resisted or ignored by his creation, and even rejected among those esp. chosen as **his own people,** viz. the Jews. Finally the Word revealed God's **glory** by becoming himself a man of **flesh** like other men. In the person of Jesus Christ the character of the eternal and invisible God, in all the fullness of his love and truth, has been made known.

The prologue hymn thus summarizes the themes developed in the gospel: Jesus the Christ is the agent of a new creation (chs. 1-2). He is the life of the world (chs. 3-6) and the light of the world (chs. 7-9), rejected by his own people (chs. 10-12), but acknowledged by all who believe in him (chs. 13-20).

The author has inserted in the hymn several prose comments—in modern works they would be footnotes—that anticipate the "witnesses" to God's Word of revelation which he will unfold in his gospel: (a) the testimony of John the Baptist (vss. 6-8, 15), the final prophetic voice to announce the appearance of the Word among men; (b) the belief of the new people of God (vss. 12-13), who are his **children,** not by reason of natural birth or race, but by their faith in his Word; (c) Jesus the Word himself (vs. 17), in whose incarnate life God surpassed even the glory of **grace and truth** which he revealed to Moses when he gave the law on Mt. Sinai (cf. Exod. 34:6-7).

Much learned discussion has been devoted to the sources of this prologue hymn. Its cue is undoubtedly Gen. 1, the OT creation song "in the beginning"—and possibly also Mark 1:1, the "beginning" of the gospel. Cf. the imitation of it in I John 1:1-4. Basic is the OT concept of the word of God. God spoke and it was done—in the act of creation (Gen. 1:3-27; Ps. 33:6, 9; Isa. 55:10-11), in the gift of the law (Exod. 20:1; Deut. 5:22; 6:6; Ps. 119:105), in the mouth of the prophets (e.g. Isa. 1:2; Jer. 1:4; Ezek. 1:3). A ps. of the Qumran community expresses it thus:

> By his knowledge all has come into being,
> and by his thought he directs everything,
> and without him nothing is done.
> (1QS 11:11.)

The Word is also the wisdom of God that is reflected in the reason and moral sense of upright men and in the order and beauty of creation (cf. Prov. 8:22-31; Wisd. Sol. 7:7-22a; Ecclus. 1:1-10). Non-Jewish readers of the gospel would recognize this concept of the Word, in Greek *Logos.* The term came into Greek philosophy with Heraclitus of Ephesus (*ca.* 500 B.C.), whose speculations on the unity in diversity of the cosmos he considered a *"Logos* that is ever true, though men are unable to understand it . . . ; for though all things come to pass in accordance with this *Logos,* men seem as if they had no experience of them" (trans. J. Burnet). Both Stoics and Platonists made much of the *Logos* as the "mind of God" reflected or immanent in the intelligibility, rationality, order, and harmony of the universe—a conception admirably summarized in Wordsworth's lines:

> Whose dwelling is the light of setting suns,
> And the round ocean and the living air,
> And the blue sky, and in the mind of man;
> A motion and a spirit, that impels
> All thinking things, all objects of all thought,
> And rolls through all things.

The Jewish philosopher Philo of Alexandria, a contemporary of Jesus, attempted a synthesis of the Jewish and Greek concepts of the *Logos* as the image of God's mind in creation, in the law, and in man's reason. But none of the philosophers, as Augustine testified, approximated the originality of the gospel in an affirmation that **the Word became flesh.**

1:19-34. *John the Baptist.* The gospel presupposes among its readers a knowledge of the fame of John the Baptist as a prophet of the coming Messiah expected by the Jews. It assumes the early tradition of Christian believers that John's preaching and baptism were the immediate intro. to the public ministry and work of Jesus (cf. Mark 1:2-11; Matt. 3; Luke 3:1-22; Acts 1:5; 10:37; 13:24-25). It knows that John left behind him many admiring disciples, who continued his work, often in conscious rivalry with the disciples of Jesus (cf. 3:22–4:3; Mark 2:18-22; Matt. 11:2-19; Luke 7:18-35; 11:1). To many Jews John was the preeminent **prophet** (vs. 21)— like Moses (Deut. 18:15-18) or **Elijah** (Mal. 4:5; Mark 9:11-13), the expected precursors of the Messiah (cf. II Esdr. 6:26; Rev. 11:3-12), if not indeed the very Messiah (Christ) himself.

1:19-28. In this gospel John the Baptist denies categorically all claim to any special status or authority in Judaism—and that too before the embassies of **priests and Levites** sent by the temple officials, the Sadducees, and **from the Pharisees,** the teachers of the law in the synagogues. Yet he is no less, in all humility, a **voice** of God—**sent from God** (vs. 6)— not merely as a forerunner to the true Messiah, but as the first **witness** to and believer in him. He is indeed a "burning and shining lamp" (5:35), a light that testifies to the true Light now appearing **after** him in time but existing **before** him in all eternity. "He must increase," John says, "but I must decrease" (3:30).

1:29. The title of Christ as **Lamb of God** is peculiar to this gospel and to Rev., in which, however, a different Greek word for "lamb" is used (e.g. Rev. 5:6; 14:1; 15:3; 19:7). There has been much discussion about the proper interpretation of this title. It is but one of many examples of an amazing subtlety in the Johannine writings of using terms and expressions that combine many themes and evoke many images and symbols.

One thinks at once of the Passover lamb (Exod. 12:5), for the gospel is explicit in dating the death of Jesus on the afternoon of the "Preparation" day, when the paschal animals were slaughtered (18:28; 19:14). The chronology of the gospel is built around the three Passover seasons when Jesus performed impressive "signs": the cleansing of the temple (2:13), the gift of the bread of life (6:4), and the raising of Lazarus from the dead (11:55). The gospel shares with Paul an interpretation of Christ as "our Passover" who is sacrificed for us (cf. I Cor. 5:7-8). Yet the Passover sacrifice and festival, though a commemoration of deliverance from bondage, was not in any sense an observance "that takes away sin."

Hence others see here a reference to Isaiah's suffering servant—the lamb slaughtered for the sin of many (Isa. 53:7-12; cf. Acts 8:32; I Pet. 1:18-19), a fulfillment of the most profound and poignant prophecy of the OT regarding God's ultimate redemption of mankind in and through his chosen people.

Another view relates the symbol of the Lamb to the ram figure of Jewish messianic expectation—the militant, victorious ruler and leader of God's flock, who will finally make an end of sin in the world. It is this figure that dominates Rev., the Lamb who stands in heaven as one that was slain, the Lamb who stands on Mt. Sinai with the hosts of his saints, the Lamb who overcomes the armies of the evil beasts, the Lamb who summons the redeemed to the marriage supper with his bride—the King of kings and Lord of lords.

1:30-34. John's baptism **with water** is in the Synoptic gospels an instrument of "repentance for the forgiveness of sins" (Mark 1:4; cf. Matt. 3:11; Luke 3:3; Acts 13:24). In this gospel it is never so described. It only points to him who alone can take away sin, and who **baptizes with the Holy Spirit** (cf. 3:5; 20:22). Hence the author avoids any mention of Jesus' baptism by John, for this would imply that Jesus was himself a sinner needing forgiveness (cf. Matt. 3:14-15). Instead John witnesses to the descent of the Spirit on Jesus, revealing him as the **Son of God** (cf. Mark 1:10-11). Thus "John did no sign, but everything that John said about this man was true" (10:41).

1:35-51. *Call of the Disciples.* As with John the Baptist, so with the gathering of the first community of disciples about Jesus, the gospel author has his own traditions and interpretations that are not altogether in accord with the narratives of the Synoptic gospels (cf. Mark 1:16-20; Matt. 4:18-22; Luke 5:1-11). John the Baptist, not Jesus, takes the initiative in the calling of the disciples; it takes place in Judea, not in Galilee; and the first 4 disciples are Andrew and Peter, Philip and Nathanael, not Peter and Andrew, James and John.

1:35-40. The unnamed disciple of these vss. has often been taken as a reticent reference of the gospel author to himself, viz. John son of Zebedee. But the context suggests that he is Philip (cf. vs. 43). The sons of Zebedee, James and John, are mentioned only in the appendix (21:2). In fact the author never gives us a list of the names of the 12 disciples, as do the Synoptic writers (Mark 3:16-19; Matt. 10:2-4; Luke 6:14-16; Acts 1:13), though he refers to them (6:70-71), and the names which he introduces from time to time in his narratives are the same as those of the Synoptics except for Nathanael.

1:41-45. Andrew and Philip are prominent in the gospel as disciples who lead others to Jesus (cf. 6:5-9; 12:20-22). Both of them bear Greek names; and they are said to come from **Bethsaida,** a large city on the NE bank of the Jordan River's entrance into the Sea of Galilee (see color map 15), where Jews and Gentiles met in daily exchange. The city is a fitting symbol of the universal outreach of the gospel. Andrew and Philip, themselves convinced that Jesus is the **Messiah** (vs. 41) promised in scripture (vs. 45), become the first missionaries: Andrew finds Simon, Philip finds Nathanael.

The gospel does not overlook, however, the eminence of Simon Peter in the early tradition. He receives from Jesus, at the time of his calling, the special nickname "Rock" (vs. 42; see RSV footnote; cf. Mark 3:16); at a critical moment in Jesus' ministry Peter leads the other disciples in loyalty and confession of faith (6:68-69; cf. Matt. 16:16-19); and Peter will assume his prominent role, as in the Synoptics, in the passion and resurrection narratives (chs. 13; 18-21).

1:46-51. The figure of **Nathanael** is enigmatic. He is mentioned only here and in the appendix (21:2), where he is said to come from Cana, a Galilean village *ca.* 9 miles N of Nazareth. Vs. 46 suggests a certain rivalry between the 2 Galilean towns. Efforts have been made, without success, to identify him with one of the 12—with Bartholomew, Matthew, or Simon the Cananean, none of whom are mentioned in this gospel. Others believe him to be the elusive "beloved disciple" of the gospel. Were it not for 21:2 the most likely alternate name for him would be Thomas—a nickname that means "Twin." Thomas has a significant role in the gospel (cf. 11:16; 14:5; 20:24-29); and in the ancient tradition of the church in Asia, preserved by Bishop Papias of Hierapolis, the names of the disciples occur in this order: Andrew, Peter, Philip, Thomas, James, John, Matthew.

Nathanael is certainly portrayed as a very real person—devout, cautious, a bit stubborn, but also curious. Yet the author has subtly made him an ideal disciple, to whom Jesus gives the promise of witness to the final glory of revelation at the end of the ages. His name means "God has given," and so Jesus will describe his disciples in his prayer to the Father (ch. 17). His hometown Cana, not mentioned in the Synoptics, is to be the scene of the 2 first "signs" of Jesus' glory in Galilee (cf. 2:1-11; 4:46-54).

Jesus indicates that Nathanael is a true **Israelite** without **guile**—unlike the dissimulating Jacob, after whom the Jews adopted the name Israel (Gen. 32:28; 35:10). Unlike the "Jews" also, who are the antagonists of Jesus in this gospel, Nathanael confesses Jesus to be the **King of Israel.** Nathanael's abode is **under the fig tree,** an OT symbol of the shelter of the true Israelites in the age to come (cf. Mic. 4:4; Zech. 3:10), dwelling in peace and safety (cf. I Kings 4:25). But the vision of this coming age, promised by Jesus to Nathanael as to all other true disciples, is portrayed in an imagery that recalls at once Jacob's dream of a ladder to **heaven** (Gen. 28:12) and the traditional figure of the **Son of man** coming to judgment in the last day on the clouds with the **angels** (cf. 3:13; 5:25-29; Dan. 7:13-14; Matt. 25:31; Mark 13:26-27; 14:62; Rev. 1:13).

II. The Signs of the Messiah (2:1–11:57)

Like a symphonic overture the intro. (ch. 1) has unfolded a theme: out of the hiddenness of eternity and the obscurity of time there emerges a historical figure bearing titles both heavenly and earthly—the Word, the Son of God, the Lamb, the Teacher, the Messiah-King of Israel, the Son of man. Geographically he moves within a territory bounded by the wilderness of Judea and the N limits of Galilee, with his home village Nazareth. Chronologically he is placed by reference to the prophet who precedes him and the disciples who follow him. His human name is Jesus. He brings the life and light, the grace and truth of God to men; he baptizes with the Holy Spirit; he opens the way to the kingdom of God.

This extraordinary appearance is measured within the compass of a week, which is itself symbolic. A new creation replaces the week of the old creation (Gen. 1). More important, it looks to the final week of this revelation on earth, the Passover week when Jesus is slain (cf. 12:1), when what is foreshadowed will be "finished" (cf. 19:30). The clue to this chronological symbolism—albeit one that will be recognized at once only by a Christian reader—is the phrase that links the intro. to the "book of signs" that follows it without break, viz. **on the third day** (2:1). For the 3rd day is the day after this week, the day of Resurrection, the day that is the sign to which all preceding signs point.

The term "sign" has a peculiar nuance in this gospel. Ordinarily the word refers to a miracle ("signs and wonders") that may or may not induce belief in the miracle worker. In this gospel Jesus himself generally refers to such deeds as his "works." He refuses, as in the Synoptics, to work "signs" on demand of the unbelieving (2:18; 6:30; cf. Mark 8:11-12). That he did many signs not recorded in the gospel is attested several times by the author (2:23; 12:37; 20:30). Certain ones, however, have been selected by the author as significant in revealing the true nature of Jesus' person, and more esp. as pointers to the meaning of his death and resurrection. It is around these "major" signs that the gospel narratives and discourses are unfolded from the miracle at Cana to the raising of Lazarus. Most of them, though not all, are miracles.

A. MANIFESTATION TO THE WORLD (2:1-4:54)

2:1-12. *The Miracle at Cana.* Each of the gospels begins the story of Jesus' ministry in Galilee with incidents and sayings appropriate to its thematic emphasis. John selects the first of Jesus' **signs** which **manifested his glory,** and as a result of which **his disciples** not only followed him but **believed in him** (vs. 11). The scene is laid in **Cana**—possibly as a link with the preceding call of the "true Israelite," Nathanael (see above on 1:46-51). It initiates a cycle of stories and discourses which will return for a 2nd sign in Cana (4:46-54), and which will introduce the manifestation of Christ to the world of Jews, Samaritans, and Gentiles.

The incident is an excellent example of the author's ability to tell an interesting story, with details that are inherently plausible but at the same time full of symbolic meaning. He is a consummate allegorist. It will be noted that in this gospel Jesus never imparts his teaching by parables, though he often uses allegories.

The miracle takes place **on the third day,** an unmistakable pointer to the resurrection and exaltation of Jesus. The village wedding feast is a foretaste—with the **good wine** supplied by Jesus—of the "marriage supper of the Lamb" (Rev. 19:7-9; cf. Matt. 22:2-14; Luke 12:36-37). The water jugs of Jewish purification ceremonies have become empty (cf.

Mark 7:1-4). They are now to be filled with the new wine of the last times (cf. Amos 9:13-14; Enoch 10:19; II Baruch 29:5)—and wine in abundance. In this miracle Jesus produces some 120 gallons (vs. 6), an excessive amount indeed if intended merely as a detail of wine needed for the local feast. Numerous early Christian paintings and sculptures associate the Cana miracle and the feeding of the multitude (ch. 6) with the feasting of the redeemed in the age to come.

Wine is also the symbol of blood. The first miracle and sign of Moses leading to the deliverance of the people of God from bondage in Egypt was the turning of water into blood (cf. Exod. 7:14-24). The gospel author stresses the life-giving water and blood that Jesus will give his disciples to drink (cf. 4:13-15; 6:53-56); and the final sign of this new life in the Spirit is attested in the streams of water and blood that flow from his pierced side when his death is accomplished (cf. 19:34-35; I John 5:6-8). Many interpreters, both ancient and modern, see in this symbolism specific reference to the cleansing and empowering gifts of Christ in the sacraments of baptism and the Lord's Supper.

2:3-4. The conversation of Jesus with his mother is suggestive of latent meaning—at least to the Christian reader. Mary appears only here and at the foot of the cross (19:25-27), where she is committed to the care of the beloved disciple. In both places Jesus addresses her in an unusually formal manner, as **woman.** She is gently rebuked for her trustful attempt to induce Jesus to perform a sign before his proper **hour,** i.e. the time chosen by his Father for his death and glorification (cf. 12:27-28); it cannot be anticipated by any kind of human intervention (cf. 7:30; 8:20). Nonetheless Jesus does perform a sign—a sign that points to the final accomplishment of his "hour." As "woman" Mary symbolizes the believing church (cf. Rev. 12:1-6). But the church cannot bring to pass the "works" of Jesus until he has fulfilled his ministry and mission and returned to his Father (cf. 14:12-13).

2:12. This verse is somewhat awkward, if not an editorial insertion—a summary of Jesus' early Galilean ministry, centered in **Capernaum,** which is treated more fully in the Synoptics (cf. Matt. 4:13; Mark 1:14; Luke 4:31). It differs from the Synoptic tradition in dating this ministry before the arrest of John the Baptist and in associating Jesus' family with his disciples during this period (cf. Mark 3:31-34) though the author notes later (7:5) that Jesus' brothers did not believe in him.

2:13-25. *The Cleansing of the Temple.* The miracle at Cana has suggested that Jesus' revelation fulfills and supersedes the ordinary daily ceremonies of the Jewish cultic system. The cleansing of the temple illustrates the theme with reference to the very heart and center of Jewish sacrificial worship. In the Synoptic gospels (Mark 11:15-18; Matt. 21:12-16; Luke 19:45-48) this bold act of Jesus is placed within the last week of his life and is portrayed in terms of prophetic protest against the profanation of the temple by fraudulent practices in its precincts. It recalls the condemnation of Jer. 7:11. It is a purification of the holy place, making it fit as a "house of prayer for all the nations" in the coming messianic age. Its effect is to solidify the opposition of the

Jewish religious leaders to Jesus and to engage them in a concerted effort to "destroy" him.

The incident as recorded in this gospel bears all these meanings and more. It is placed near the beginning of Jesus' ministry, albeit at Passover time; and though it is not a miracle, it is no less a **sign** (cf. vss. 18, 23) of what will be fulfilled in his death and resurrection. Significantly Jesus drives out not only the wicked **money-changers** but also the innocent animals and thus points to a more drastic "purification" of worship: the end of the old cultus of animal sacrifice and the inauguration of a worship "in spirit and truth" (cf. 4:23-24).

2:19-22. The **temple,** begun in 20/19 B.C., was not finished till *ca.* A.D. 64 and then was destroyed by the Romans in 70. Its destruction was probably predicted by Jesus (cf. Mark 13:2; Luke 19:43-44). The prophecy was used against him at his trial before the Sanhedrin (cf. Mark 14:57-59; 15:29). Possibly the original form of Jesus' prediction is preserved in vs. 19, with reflection on its true meaning and purport. As the true "Lamb of God, who takes away the sin of the world" (cf. 1:29), his sacrificed **body** is the new **temple** in and through whom the disciples and believers will offer a spiritual sacrifice acceptable to God, in a living building not made with hands. The theme is a basic one throughout the NT (cf. Acts 7:48-50; I Cor. 3:16; 6:19; Eph. 2:19-22; Heb. 9:11-14; I Pet. 2:5; Rev. 21:22). Christian insight into this truth, it has been suggested, may have stemmed from the "Hellenist" group in the early church at Jerusalem led by Stephen (cf. Acts 6:12-14).

2:23-25. The author introduces briefly the question of **signs** by way of summary of the preceding narratives. The sign of the cleansing of the temple, not being a miracle, is not immediately obvious even to Jesus' disciples, much less to the populace. Those who believe in him by this time are still overly impressed by the miraculous as such. Jesus consistently rejects this basis for belief. It is too shallow. Jesus himself knows how easily swayed are men's minds by the merely marvelous—"signs and wonders" (cf. 4:48). He does not **trust himself** to human **witness.** Insight into his true signs comes only by revelation from God (cf. 3:31-36; 5:19-24).

3:1-21. *Discourse with Nicodemus.* The author now turns from consideration of Jesus' encounter with the Jewish cultic system to an encounter with its legal system as represented by a distinguished Pharisee, who as a **ruler of the Jews** sits on the supreme council of the Sanhedrin. Nicodemus is known only from this gospel. He was undoubtedly one of the more liberal Pharisees, open to new teachings and interpretations. Though he was attracted by Jesus' signs, there is no clear evidence in the gospel that Nicodemus was a "secret believer" in Jesus. But later he defends Jesus from unjust and prejudiced accusations (7:50-51) and joins with Joseph of Arimathea in providing for him a decent burial (19:39). Nicodemus' fairness and adherence to strict rules of judicial procedure remind one of another great Pharisee, Gamaliel, who protects the rights of the early disciples (Acts 5:34-39).

The interview of Nicodemus with Jesus is marked by mutual courtesy, respect, and concern for issues of utmost importance. Its secrecy, **by night,** is simply a matter of caution on the part of Nicodemus, in view of the hostility of the Jewish leaders toward Jesus. Despite the marked difference in worldly status of the 2 men, each respectfully addresses the other by the title of **Rabbi** or **teacher.** But the conversation leads to no agreement, for Nicodemus really does not comprehend what Jesus is talking about. In fact Nicodemus fades out of the picture after vs. 9 as Jesus' discourse appears to address a wider audience—a stylistic device characteristic of this gospel.

3:3-13. One would expect the conversation to revolve about the problem of whether salvation is possible through keeping of the law. The rabbis taught that when all Israel kept the law the kingdom of God would come. Jesus, however, immediately moves the discussion to a different level. Salvation in the **kingdom of God** requires a new birth, which by an ambiguity of the Greek word is also a birth "from above," from heaven itself—a birth not merely in a baptism of **water,** such as John the Baptist offered, but a birth through the operation of the **Spirit.** Such a birth is possible only by belief in the Son of man and Son of God, viz. Jesus himself.

3:14-15. To illustrate this teaching, so incredible to Nicodemus, Jesus uses a sign—not one of his own, but one of **Moses** the lawgiver. When the people of God sinned **in the wilderness** through disbelief, they were afflicted with serpents, and many of them died; but through Moses' intercession God gave them a sign—the standard of the bronze **serpent**—that whoever looked on it and believed would live (Num. 21:4-9). So it shall be with the Son of man, when he is **lifted up** on the standard of the cross, a cursed thing like the serpent itself (cf. Gen. 3:14-15). Whoever believes in him will have **eternal life** (cf. 8:28; 12:32-34).

3:16-21. Thus the discourse with Nicodemus becomes a pointer to the final sign of Jesus' death and resurrection. At the same time it recapitulates the broad themes of the gospel prologue. **Light** and **life** have come into the world in the person of God's only Son. Those who receive him and believe in his name are reborn, not by fleshly means, but by God. Hence the distinction between those who believe and those who do not is evidence of the arrival of the final **judgment,** lit. "crisis." God himself does not make this judgment but rather ratifies a judgment which men make for themselves by their own decisions (cf. 5:22-30; 12:31; 16:8-11).

3:22-36. *Discourse with John's Disciples.* The discussion with Nicodemus about baptism in **water and the Spirit** leads the author inevitably to a return to the question of the relation of Jesus and John the Baptist and of their respective disciples. In the only passage in all the gospel tradition that intimates that Jesus himself ever **baptized** he locates Jesus in **Judea** while John carries on similar activity in NE Samaria at **Aenon** ("springs"; see color map 15).

In contrast to the priestly and rabbinic traditions of cult and observance, John the Baptist represented the last and greatest figure of the prophetic strain in Judaism with its insistence on spiritual repentance and renewal. Of all Jews he was closest to Jesus, both in the relationship of master and pupil and in teaching about the coming kingdom of God. As we have seen (see above on 1:19-34), John the Baptist is portrayed in this gospel not only as a forerunner but as a first witness to Jesus, and indeed as the figure who directs to Jesus the first disciples. In this passage the testimony of John is reaffirmed and underscored. He makes no claim for himself. He is from the **earth**; Jesus is from **heaven**. His fullest joy is to be accounted the **friend of the bridegroom** (cf. Mark 2:19-20). On Jesus, more than on any other prophet, God has poured out his Spirit beyond measure. Jesus utters the true **words of God**. Belief in him and obedience to him are decisive as to whether a man comes to **life** or to **wrath** in the coming age (cf. Matt. 3:7; Luke 3:7). It is indeed a remarkable testimony. Some scholars believe, however, that vss. 31-36 are words of Jesus, not of John the Baptist, since the style is very similar to Jesus' words to Nicodemus, and that they should be transposed, probably to follow vs. 21—or else that vss. 22-30 should follow 2:12.

The setting of John's witness is the rivalry of John's and Jesus' disciples for adherents to their respective leaders (cf. also 4:1-3), and more esp. the question, raised by an unidentified **Jew**, about the meaning of their baptisms. In the Synoptic gospels the tension between the 2 groups of disciples is not over baptism but concerns customs of fasting and prayer (cf. Mark 2:18-22; Luke 11:1). Many scholars see here a reflection of early Christian polemic against a sect of Baptist disciples. But the attempt to locate such a group in Ephesus, where this gospel was probably written, on the basis of Acts 18:24–19:7 is very problematic.

Several Christian writings of the 2nd cent. refer to Jewish baptist sects in Samaria and Transjordan that may owe something to John the Baptist's teaching and practice, though they have been influenced by other religious currents, e.g. the Qumran traditions and Gnostic speculations. One source, the Clementine Recognitions (1:60), records a controversy with Christians by a disciple of John who claimed for the Baptist the title of Messiah "inasmuch as Jesus himself declared that John was greater than all men and all prophets" (cf. Matt. 11:7-11). In Iraq today there is a small baptist sect known as the Mandeans who assert a direct descent from John the Baptist's ministry and teaching.

The gospel author, more by implicit suggestion than by explicit statement, considers John's baptism as a **purifying** rite comparable to similar Jewish ceremonies. He certainly does not account it a sacramental "new birth" in the Spirit, conveying the forgiveness of sins, like Christian baptism. In this view of John's baptism he is in agreement with the Jewish historian Josephus (ca. 37-100), the only source outside the NT we have for the career of John:

[He] was a good man and commanded the Jews to practice virtue, by exercising justice towards one another and piety towards God, and to come together to baptism. For the baptism would be acceptable to God if they used it, not for the putting away of certain sins, but for the purification of the body, the soul having previously been cleansed by righteousness. (Antiquities 18:116-19, trans. C. K. Barrett.)

4:1-42. Discourse with a Samaritan Woman. The location of John's baptizing in Samaria (3:23) provides the link that leads to Jesus' mission of self-revelation to the Samaritans. The editorial transition

in vss. 1-3, however, is awkward, and vs. 2 contradicts 3:22.

The schism between the Jews and Samaritans was quite as bitter as described in vs. 9, and this is reflected also in the Synoptic gospels (cf. Matt. 10:5; Luke 9:51-56). The origin of their separation and hatred is generally traced to the time of Nehemiah (5th cent. B.C.; cf. Neh. 4). But there is no clear evidence of a religious schism in any formal sense until the Samaritans built a temple of their own on Mt. Gerizim near **Sychar** (vs. 5), i.e. ancient Shechem, probably after their revolt against Alexander the Great in 331 B.C., when Alexander rebuilt the city of Samaria as a Hellenistic colony. The faithful

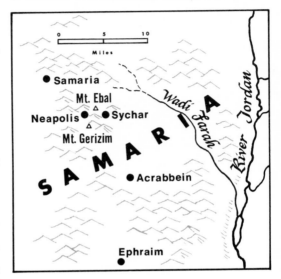

remnant of Samaritans then retired to the site of Shechem, hallowed by traditions of the patriarchs **Jacob** and **Joseph** (cf. Gen. 33:18-20; 48:22; Josh. 24:32) and the establishment of the N kingdom of Israel (cf. I Kings 12:1-25). In 128 B.C. the Jewish Maccabean ruler John Hyrcanus destroyed the Samaritan temple and attempted to suppress the separate Samaritan cult. When the Romans took over control of Palestine in 64-63 B.C., however, the Samaritans were free to restore their independent religious customs.

On the surface the mission of Jesus to the Samaritans appears to have happened, as it were, accidentally through a chance conversation. Yet it is undoubtedly a providential development of revelation of salvation that anticipates the spread of the gospel, first in Jerusalem and Judea, then in Samaria, then to the end of the earth (cf. Acts 1:8). In the Synoptic traditions only Luke exhibits any special appreciation by Jesus of the despised Samaritans (cf. the parable of the good Samaritan, Luke 10:30-37, and the healing of the lepers, Luke 17:11-19). In this gospel the Jewish feeling of superiority to and aloofness from the Samaritan schismatics is expressed by Jesus (vs. 22), but this only heightens the dramatic contrast of his willingness to enter into communication with them, and specifically with a Samaritan woman of disrepute—a circumstance as startling to the woman herself (vs. 9) as it is to Jesus' disciples (vs. 27). It is the author's peculiar way of indicating that the **Savior of the world** (vs. 42) came indeed to "seek and to save the lost" (Luke 19:10).

4:7-15. Jesus' discourse with the woman, like that with Nicodemus (3:1-15), develops on 2 levels of meaning. The woman thinks of **water** in earthly terms of necessity for man and beast, whether it comes from wells or cisterns, fountains or streams. This was a natural concern in Palestine, where water supply is not always sufficient, much less abundant. Jesus, however, speaks of **living,** i.e. flowing, water as a sign of **eternal life,** whose source is God (cf. Isa. 55:1; Jer. 2:13), whose depths are in his wisdom (cf. Prov. 18:4; Ecclus. 24:21), and whose abundance is assured in the wells of God, the city of God of the coming age (cf. Ezek. 47:1-12; Zech. 14:8; Rev. 22:1-2). A similar figure is used in the Manual of Discipline of the Qumran community: "He will cleanse him of all wicked deeds with the spirit of holiness; like purifying waters he will shed upon him the spirit of truth" (1QS 4:21, trans. G. Vermes).

Jesus is himself, of course, this gift of life-giving water. He will later make this more explicit (7:37-39) and identify the living water with the Holy Spirit, who will be given after his glorification. Hence many interpreters see here also a cryptic reference to baptism, such as the reference to water and Spirit in the discourse with Nicodemus (3:5).

4:16-26. The woman only begins to comprehend that a prophetic utterance is being made after Jesus unexpectedly reveals his insight into her personal life. She immediately becomes defensive and shifts the conversation to argument about differences of Jews and Samaritans. Jesus picks this up with the reminder of their common hope in the messianic age, when cultic estrangement will be transcended in unfeigned worship **in spirit and truth.** The discussion closes with Jesus' dramatic revelation: **I . . . am he** (vs. 26)—an anticipation of his remarkable "I am" sayings in later incidents of the gospel.

4:27-42. The universal mission of the Christ is then intimated in 2 ways: (*a*) the disciples are forewarned by Jesus of the imminent **harvest** (cf. Matt. 9:37; Luke 10:2); (*b*) the disreputable woman herself becomes the agent of evangelism among her fellow Samaritans. Salvation has broken through the rigid confines of orthodox Judaism, though the disciples are slow to comprehend this extraordinary fact. **One sows and another reaps** (vs. 37). John the Baptist, Jesus himself, the Samaritan woman, and the Hellenist Philip (Acts 8:4-13) sowed the seed in Samaria. The Jewish-Christian church would have misgivings (cf. Matt. 10:5), but the apostles found there a rich harvest (cf. Acts 8:14-25).

4:43-45. *A Transition.* This transitional passage is even more difficult and contradictory than that in vss. 1-3. Jesus' remark about his Galilean countrymen's rejection recalls Mark 6:4, yet this stands in immediate connection with the author's statement of their welcome (vs. 45). But it may be that their welcome is based on a misunderstanding of his signs (cf. vs. 48; 2:23-25). They judge him outwardly as a wonder worker yet do not believe in him inwardly for his true significance.

4:46-54. *Healing of a Nobleman's Son.* This story brings us again to **Cana** (cf. 2:1) and a **second sign** in **Galilee** (vs. 54). The miracle is a variant tradition

of the healing of the centurion's servant in the Synoptics (Matt. 8:5-13; Luke 7:1-10). The **official** is undoubtedly a Gentile. In all 4 gospels Jesus performs his acts of mercy for Gentiles at a distance and solely in response to their insistent faith. His mission is primarily to Israel, but the incidents of his concern for Gentiles in distress are indicative of his universal mission to all who come to him in trustful belief.

The time of the cure is noted as the **seventh hour** (i.e. 1 P.M., vs. 52). This may be merely a detail of the story without significance. But the author rarely gives details without hidden significance. It is *ca.* the 7th hour that Jesus is crucified (cf. 19:14) and fulfills all signs.

B. Controversy with the "Jews" (5:1-10:42)

Ch. 5 continues without break the cycle of Jesus' signs that point to his death and resurrection. But a new emphasis becomes manifest. In chs. 2-4 his signs have suggested the uniqueness of his person in an all-encompassing circle, beginning with his family, disciples, and friends, then reaching out to his people, the Jews—priests, Pharisees, disciples of John the Baptist—and then with increasing reserve to Samaritans and Gentiles. The arrangement rests on historical tradition, but is no less symbolic: the Christ is the Savior of the world.

With ch. 5, however, and continuing through ch. 12, the attention of the gospel is concentrated on the "Jews," who are not only Jesus' historical antagonists but in the concern of the author symbolic of Judaizing Christians of his own day who thwart the universal mission of Christianity (see Intro.). The narratives and discourses are all related to specific occasions of Jewish festivals—sabbath (5:9*b*-10), Passover (6:4), Tabernacles (7:2), Dedication (10:22), and at the close another Passover (11:55), that of his death and glorification. In this midsection of the gospel Jesus speaks more openly of himself and his relation to God the Father. The discourses become increasingly controversial and embittered. Tension mounts. The "hour" approaches.

5:1-9. *Healing of a Paralytic.* The first incident of this new section occurs in Jerusalem on a **feast of the Jews,** which is identified (vs. 9*b*) as the **sabbath.** The story has parallels in the Synoptics—the healings in Capernaum of a paralytic (Mark 2:1-12) and of a man with a withered hand (Mark 3:1-6). The latter also occurs on the sabbath and is the occasion of a similar controversy with the Pharisees about the lawfulness of such an act on the day of rest from labor. There is a suggestion also, though less prominent here than in the Synoptics, that the healing of the body is accompanied by the forgiveness of sin (vs. 14). The locale of the incident has been confirmed by modern excavation of a **pool**—whether Bethzatha or Bethesda or Bethsaida—N of the temple area, to which the **sheep gate** no doubt gave entrance (see color map 13, and map, p. 228).

The story has several "Johannine" characteristics. Jesus performs his sign on his own initiative and his peculiar knowledge of men (vs. 6). He chooses one of many possible subjects of his saving action, in this case a sick man of little initiative himself and of scant gratitude. The sick man himself is a personification of the impotence of Judaism. The charge against him of breaking the sabbath by carrying his **pallet** is but a foil for the weightier charge against Jesus for **working** on the sabbath. The narrative sets the stage for the discourse.

5:10-47. *Discourse on the Sabbath.* In the Synoptics Jesus' controversy with the Jews over the proper observance of the sabbath revolves about the question of priorities: the need of men versus cultic restrictions (cf. Mark 2:23-3:6). The argument in this gospel goes deeper. Jesus defends his work on the sabbath by appeal to God the Father's work on the sabbath. God's rest on the sabbath (cf. e.g. Gen. 2:2-3; Exod. 20:11) does not mean—as even the rabbis admitted—that God does not continue his providential care of the world during the sabbath. On the sabbath he brings men to birth, and also to death and to judgment. Thus Jesus works on the sabbath, as his Father works still—raising men from spiritual death to eternal life. Indeed the **hour** is at hand, the decisive hour of death and **resurrection** and **judgment**—for the **Son of man** has come (vss. 25-29).

The issue between Jesus and the Jews is thus shifted from sabbath observance to decision about the person of Jesus, who identifies himself with the **Father** (cf. Mark 2:28: "the Son of Man is lord even of the sabbath"). What then is the authority to support Jesus' exalted claim? The testimonies are 3-fold: (*a*) the **witness** of John the Baptist, in whose **light** the Jews rejoiced **for a while** (vss. 33-35); (*b*) the **works** of Jesus himself, who claims only that he does God's will (vss. 36-38); and (*c*) the **scriptures,** indeed **Moses** himself, on whose writings the Jews set all their confidence and hope (vss. 39-47). Moses, like Jesus, did not seek his own glory but only the salvation of God's people (Exod. 32-34); he predicted the coming of a "prophet" like himself who would speak God's words (Deut. 18:15-22); and he foresaw the apostasy of Israel from the covenant (Deut. 31:16-29). These themes are to be continued and developed in later controversies.

6:1-15. *Feeding of the Multitude.* The scene is abruptly shifted to Galilee. Many interpreters would transpose the order of chs. 5; 6. But transitions are always abrupt in this gospel, and there is no certain clue as to editorial rearrangements.

The miracle of the feeding of the multitude is the only incident of Jesus' ministry in Galilee which this gospel shares with the Synoptics (cf. Mark 6:32-44; Matt. 14:13-21; Luke 9:11-17; see comments) as it also shares the sequel: the miracle of Jesus' walking on the water; a discourse on bread, here much developed, however (cf. Mark 8:14-21); and, most significant of all, a decisive separation from Jesus of his popular following in contrast to the continuing loyalty of the 12 disciples (vss. 66-71). Note the prominence in this account of Philip and Andrew (see above on 1:41-45) and the emphasis on Jesus' controlling initiative—**he himself knew what he would do** (vs. 6). The moral of the story is that the disciples do not yet believe that Jesus can satisfy the need of so great a multitude from so small an offering. But the unnamed youth who gives his lunch represents all who give what they have, without reservation, into Jesus' hands, that he may make it expendable for many. More is left over, even so, than

what was offered—**twelve baskets,** one for each of the 12 disciples!

The feeding miracle in all the gospels is a decisive conclusion to Jesus' Galilean ministry. It is a final **sign** of the awaited **prophet** (vs. 14; cf. 1:21; Deut. 18:15), like Moses' feeding the people of God in the wilderness with manna (Exod. 16) or like Elisha's multiplying barley loaves for hungry men (II Kings 4:42-44). The people recognize the sign, but they misinterpret the nature of Jesus' messiahship. They wish to make him a **king,** a temporal ruler to restore their independent sovereignty and give them material plenty (cf. vs. 26). But Jesus' "kingship is not of this world" (18:36). In refusing this role Jesus loses his popular following, including **many of his disciples** (vs. 66; cf. Mark 8:11-21). His enemies among the Jewish leaders are to use this occasion, however, for specious charges about him before Pilate in order to seal his earthly fate as a revolutionary leader against the Roman authority (18:33-37; 19:12-16).

As with all the signs in this gospel, the feeding of the multitude points to the denouement in Jesus' death and resurrection. The incident is dated at **Passover** (vs. 4). Jesus' giving **thanks** over the food (vs. 11; cf. vs. 23) is expressed by the verbal form of *eucharistia* ("thanksgiving" or "Eucharist"), which by the time the gospel was written had probably already become a common term for the commemoration of Jesus' Last Supper. The miraculous crossing of the sea that follows (vss. 16-24), the discourse on the **living bread . . . from heaven** (vss. 25-59), the subtle reference to Jesus' ascension and gift of the Spirit (vss. 60-63), and many other allusions suggest the new redemptive Exodus that Jesus will accomplish. The confession of Peter (vss. 68-69; cf. Mark 8:27-30) anticipates the confession of the church, as of all true believers, in the **Holy One of God.**

6:16-24. *The Walking on the Sea.* The withdrawal of Jesus from the people and the disciples leads to a somewhat complicated and elaborate account of movements to change the scene to a synagogue in Capernaum (vs. 59). There may be some editorial redaction here. The gospel follows, in any case, the tradition recorded in the Synoptics (cf. Mark 6:45-54) of Jesus' miraculous walking on the sea to meet his disciples and calm their fears in a sudden squall which they encounter on the waters. Some interpreters see in this narrative one of the major signs of Jesus; but the evangelist does not develop the story in his customary manner of expounding signs, for the discourse which follows refers exclusively to the miracle of the feeding rather than to the walking on the water. The exodus theme, noted above, is doubtless veiled here: the stormy waters are symbol of passage from bondage and death to freedom and life. The appearance of Jesus suddenly and unexpectedly, with his reassurance **do not be afraid,** reminds one of the situation in which his resurrection appearance takes place (cf. 20:19-23; Matt. 28:10; Luke 24:36-39). His emphatic **It is I**; lit. "I am [he]," is a 2nd indication (cf. 4:26) of his revelation of his person that will be picked up and developed in the discourses and controversies to follow.

6:25-71. *Discourse on Bread of Heaven.* The theme of this discourse, **I am the bread of life** (vs. 35), elaborates the true meaning of the feeding miracle, which the people have misunderstood. The style and manner of its development are already familiar from previous discourses in the gospel. Question and answer, even argument, between Jesus and his audience reveal that Jesus is speaking from a deeper level of spiritual insight than that of his hearers. Dialogue shifts into proclamation, and this in turn produces controversy and division. The spiritually discerning hold on to belief; the materially minded reject Jesus' claims. Yet even the former follow more in faith and hope than in full understanding.

6:27-40. The dialogue has close parallels with the conversation with the Samaritan woman (ch. 4), the symbol of **bread** here being comparable to the symbol of water there. The bread given in the miracle of feeding, no less than the **manna** given to God's people in their wilderness pilgrimage (vs. 31; cf. Ps. 105:40b), supernatural though it is, is perishable, sufficing only for the day. It cannot give **life to the world** much less **eternal life** (cf. Deut. 8:3; Isa. 55:2-3a). The writers of wisdom, the apocalyptic seers, the rabbinic interpreters—all of them used the manna as a type of life in the world to come. Now this true bread, this word of God, this heavenly food, this life raised up **at the last day** is revealed. And faith in him is fulfillment in doing the **will** and the **work** of God. Note that in this gospel faith, truth, etc. are not abstract; they are positive commitment, action, obedience.

6:41-51. The opposition to Jesus now shifts from the **people** (vs. 24) to the **Jews,** i.e. those who oppose the revelation of God in the Word-made-flesh (see Intro.). Such extraordinary claims come from the **son of Joseph, whose father and mother we know** (cf. 7:27, 41-42). They **murmur** against him who is sent from God no less than did the fathers who **died** in the wilderness (cf. I Cor. 10:1-12). No sign, no miracle, no testimony of truth convinces them (cf. Luke 16:31). Vs. 45 quotes Isa. 54:13.

6:52-59. But Jesus presses further. He, the living bread from heaven for the life of the world, is given as **flesh** to eat and **blood** to drink. This is no doubt a reference to his believers' experience of the Eucharist. It comes unexpectedly, since as yet the holy supper of bread and wine has not been instituted. For this reason many scholars consider vss. 52-56 a later editorial insertion. But the evangelist speaks to many levels among his readers. It is not strange that he should in this way anticipate what one would expect him to relate in ch. 13. He is not interested in mere historical sequence. These vss. are his way of pointing to an "institution" of "This is my body; this is my blood." The Christian reader gets the message, as in the veiled allusions of the miracle at Cana or the cleansing of the temple.

6:60-65. Obviously the **disciples** find these words a **hard saying**—just as they do not understand his words and actions at the Last Supper until after his revelation of resurrection in the breaking of the bread (see below on 21:1-14). To eat flesh and to drink blood was naturally offensive to a Jew (cf. e.g. Gen. 9:4; Lev. 3:17; Deut. 12:23; Ezek. 39:17-19; Acts 15:20). The crisis of belief is now upon the disciples: they "murmur" and **take offense.** The scandal of Jesus confronts them also with decision. Can they understand that Jesus speaks of final things —of the Spirit that gives life (cf. II Cor. 3:6)?

6:66-71. Simon Peter makes the leap of faith and speaks for all of the 12 except one. From this point on only Jesus' intimate band, and a few others, keep following—and indeed stronger tests of their faith are yet to come. This is the only passage where the evangelist specifically speaks of the **twelve,** almost casually assuming among his readers a knowledge of the tradition. Here also he first mentions the betrayer **Judas**—as always (cf. 12:4-6; 13:26-30; 18:2-5) with hostility. But the evangelist does not give us any more of a clue than do the Synoptic writers for the motives of Judas' treachery. From this point on in the gospel we continually meet the impending shadow of Jesus' death.

7:1-52. *Discourse at a Feast of Tabernacles.* This long interlude (continued in 8:12-59) of controversy and heightening bitterness of the **Jews** toward Jesus is peculiar to this gospel—developing what is concisely intimated in the Synoptic tradition of Mark 8:11-21. Transitions are abrupt; themes are involved and follow no logical sequence; a general impression is given of confusion, with controversies unresolved, actions frustrated, language increasingly abusive. The overriding theme, if any, is that the **Jews sought to kill him** (vs. 1).

7:2. The background is the celebration of the **feast of Tabernacles** (Booths), one of the major festivals of Judaism, held at the beginning of autumn. It was a pivotal time, combining the feastings of ingathered harvest and hopeful projections of renewed prosperity in the coming year. Its focus was in the temple rather than in the domestic celebrations that characterized Passover. Brilliant illuminations of the temple precincts were characteristic, as were special water libations rooted in ancient rainmaking ceremonies to insure good crops. The people lived in temporary shelters or "booths" reminiscent of harvest and vintage conditions, but reminders, more seriously, of their pilgrimage condition in this world as dependents on God's gracious providence. In this setting Jesus' words about **thirst** (7:37) and **light** (8:12) have their peculiar reference.

7:3-9. The section opens with the taunting challenge of Jesus' **brothers,** whose disbelief in him is matched by their interest, if sincere, in his signs. The contrast with the faith of his disciples (6:68-69) is striking, the more so because of his brothers' sarcasm. The Synoptic tradition on the attitude of Jesus' brothers is more ambiguous (cf. Mark 3:31-35), though Luke places them among the believers after the Resurrection (cf. Acts 1:14). As usual Jesus does not rise to the bait of this challenge (cf. 2:23-25) but keeps his own counsel and control of his actions.

7:10-31. The realism of the evangelist in setting a scene is also evident in his reference to the gossip and argument about Jesus among the people at the festival, followed by the dramatic public appearance of Jesus **about the middle of the feast.** An argument is going on about his authority as a teacher, since he has not **studied** in the manner of rabbinical training. So Jesus breaks in and takes up the question—exactly where he left off at the last festival he attended in Jerusalem (ch. 5). He is to be judged, not by **appearances** or conventional credentials, but by what he says and does. Least of all is he to be judged by his family background or the place of his upbringing.

7:32-39. Another misunderstanding in this controversy arises from Jesus' reference to his going away—a theme to be developed again in his farewell discourse to his disciples (ch. 14). He points of course to the consummation of his mission, his return in glory to his Father, and the pouring out as **rivers of living water** (vs. 38; cf. 4:14) of the Spirit. His opponents see his promise as a plan to carry his message beyond the confines of Judea and the people of God not only to the **Dispersion,** i.e. Jews living outside Palestine, but to the Gentiles, as though he were some sectarian teacher seeking a following wherever he might gather it (cf. Matt. 10:5, 23; 15:24). They cannot see his coming as a fulfillment of God's purpose for his people Israel, that through them God may fulfill their destiny to bring salvation to the whole world. Their pride and exclusiveness blind them to the true mission of Jesus, and hence of themselves in God's plan of salvation for all mankind.

7:40-52. The question of where Jesus comes from (cf. vs. 27) is now taken up again. The evangelist of course knows of Jesus' true pedigree and origin—**descended from David, and comes from Bethlehem** (vs. 42). But even Matt. and Luke, which narrate in detail Jesus' birth in Bethlehem and his human descent from David, represent him in his public ministry as "Jesus of Nazareth," a Galilean (cf. esp. Matt. 2:23). And Jesus himself challenges the purely temporal and material claim to messiahship by Davidic blood descent, so embedded in Jewish expectations (cf. Mark 12:35-37). The truth about the Christ rests on divine not human credentials and authority (cf. Mark 11:27-33). It is no matter if he does come from **Galilee,** or that they cannot find in their **scripture** a clear indication that the **prophet** like Moses (vs. 40; cf. 1:21; 6:14; Deut. 18:15) would **rise from Galilee** (vs. 52, where the reading "the prophet" is attested by a papyrus of the early 3rd cent.). It is always a scandal to human pretensions of judgment that God does not witness to himself through the neat categories of our preconceived calculations.

7:53–8:11. *Jesus and the Adulteress.* This passage is omitted or set off in modern editions of the gospel since it does not appear in the oldest and best manuscripts and is apparently a later interpolation. In some manuscripts it occurs after Luke 21:38. Though not an original part of this gospel, it need not be taken as an unauthentic tradition about Jesus. It conforms to all we know of him as one who came to seek and to save the lost, not to condemn men but to offer them God's forgiveness and acceptance. Its inclusion here in later texts was probably suggested by 8:15, 46. It has interesting parallels with the story of Susanna in the Apoc.; Jesus is the new Daniel come to judgment in truth and equity. The story certainly does not mean that Jesus either condoned sin or did not acknowledge the justice of the law. His clemency and compassion indicate his concern for the motives of the woman's accusers, with regard both to her and to himself (cf. 2:24).

8:12-59. *Continuation of the Tabernacle Discourse.* The discussion of where Jesus comes from and where he is going continues. His opponents, who judge only **according to the flesh** (vs. 15), i.e. think in earthly frames of reference, misunderstand him at every

point. Some absurdly think his reference to going away indicates suicide (8:21-30)—perhaps their own death wish for him in view of the constant frustration of their schemes to kill him. Jesus picks up this suggestion to probe more deeply into the issues of death and life, falsehood and truth, bondage and freedom. But the controversy continues at cross-purposes and ends in insults and name-calling.

8:31-47. The argument comes back again to earthly descent and pride of race and blood. The Jews insist on their status and destiny as **descendants of Abraham.** This is their guarantee of ultimate freedom, and life in the age to come in the final resurrection. Jesus rejects this claim categorically, as in fact John the Baptist did (Matt. 3:7-10; Luke 3:7-9; cf. Rom. 4). Salvation comes only to those who believe the word of God in Jesus, the **truth** that alone delivers men from sin and makes them **free.** The "Jews'" father is not Abraham, who believed God, but the **devil,** the **father of lies,** who from the beginning (cf. Gen. 3) led men into sin and death.

8:48-59. The ultimate blasphemy of Jesus' opponents is reached when they accuse him of demon possession (cf. Mark 3:22-30). His answer is the most absolute and categorical claim of his true person made in this gospel: **Before Abraham was, I am.** For in the OT "I am" is the name of God (cf. Exod. 3:14). So they pick up **stones** to slay the blasphemer. The issue is now decisively drawn, but the proper "hour" is not yet. The judgment of who is the true blasphemer in this altercation is suspended.

9:1-41. *Healing of a Blind Man.* The incurable spiritual blindness of the "Jews" is now dramatically illustrated in the great sign of healing of a man physically **born blind.** The details of the miracle story recall examples in the Synoptics of Jesus' healing of the blind (Mark 8:22-26; 10:46-52)—expected fulfillment of the Messiah's coming role (cf. Isa. 29:18; 35:5; 42:7; Matt. 11:5; Luke 7:21-22).

The parallel with the Synoptics is further indicated by the **sabbath** setting of the miracle (vss. 14-16; cf. Mark 3:1-6; Luke 13:10-17; see above on 5:10-47), for there is no necessity of performing this work on the sabbath; the blind man could easily be healed on another day. But to Jesus the sabbath is a sign of the new age of God's work of re-creation; not a mere day of rest, closed by the **night . . . , when no one can work** (vs. 4).

Another interesting detail, which indicates how the evangelist uses allusive symbolism, is the reference to the **pool of Siloam** (vs. 7), where the healing takes place. This pool, at the SE extremity of Jerusalem (see color map 13), was the source of water used at the Tabernacles ceremonies (cf. 7:37). Isaiah noted how Israel refused these waters and hence would be overwhelmed by waters of another river (Isa. 8:5-8).

Not only the symbolism of water but more esp. that of light is taken up in the story: **I am the light of the world** (vs. 5; cf. 8:12). Jesus is the "true light that enlightens every man . . . coming into the world" (1:9), both physically and spiritually. Yet the sin of man and of his **parents,** i.e. forebears, causes him to love darkness rather than light (cf. 3:19). Men struggle in darkness since the sin of Adam, preferring evil to good, blind to their own condition, until the light comes to open their eyes to God.

Courtesy of Herbert G. May

The Pool of Siloam (cf. ills., p. 218)

Thus the revelation of the true light unfolds to the man—any man—whose eyes Jesus opens. At first he sees Jesus simply as a **man** who helps and heals (vs. 11). Such a man, however, cannot be a **sinner** if he does such a work—**he is a prophet** (vs. 17). With greater confidence the healed man argues with those who deny the fact that such a prophet must come **from God** (vs. 33). Now he is forced to decision: remain secure in the **synagogue,** or reach out to faith yet dim—though now he can see—in the **Son of man** (vs. 35). Thus the story of an earthly healing of a man's sight is a parable of a spiritual pilgrimage to unshakable faith. It is indeed a **marvel** (vs. 30). The blind man comes through to Jesus against every natural obstacle: his own puzzlement, his parents' cowardly fear of getting involved, his religious leaders' unfair advantage of him in argument from authority and precedent, and the threat of excommunication. The moral is clear: only those are blind who will not see.

Those who see in this narrative a sacramental reference, comparable to the Eucharistic allusions of ch. 6, point to many parallels in the ancient church's liturgy of baptism—the anointing, the washing, the confession of faith—and in the doctrinal interpretation of baptism as release from the guilt of original sin and enlightenment by faith in Christ. It may well be that the early church's liturgy of baptism was influenced by the gospel rather than that the gospel reflects an already developed liturgy. It is significant, however, that the oldest Christian paintings in the catacombs show a preference for the

Johannine signs of chs. 2; 4–6; 9; 11 as reminders of the deliverance of the believer from sin and death by sacramental incorporation into Christ. And the ancient liturgies of E and W give preference to the reading of these signs as lessons in the seasons of Lent and Eastertide, when candidates for baptism were prepared and initiated into the new life in Christ.

10:1-42. *Discourse at a Feast of Dedication.* The parable and allegory of vss. 1-18 are a new discourse of Jesus, abruptly inserted, to bridge the controversies with the Jews at the festivals of Tabernacles and Dedication (Hanukkah) respectively. Actually vss. 19-21 appear to pick up the end of ch. 9; vss. 22-30 to develop the new theme of ch. 10; and vss. 31-39 to elaborate the altercation of ch. 8. This apparently illogical sequence has provoked many theories of editorial, or accidental, changes from the evangelist's original order of presentation; but no one rearrangement has gained a general consensus among scholars.

The Hanukkah feast was instituted in 164 B.C. by Judas Maccabeus in solemn rededication of the temple 3 years after its defilement under Antiochus Epiphanes by sacrifices to Zeus on its altar (I Macc. 4:36-59). The festival took place in mid-Dec. and its ceremonies were modeled on those of Tabernacles, esp. the kindling of lights—hence its popular name "Feast of Lights." Some of the high priests of that time had compromised with the Gentile conquerors and oppressors (cf. II Macc. 4:7–5:26). They had been overthrown by a revolt led by the priestly family of the Hasmoneans, nicknamed the Maccabees, who were fanatically devoted to the law. Once having won independence for the Jews in Palestine, the Hasmoneans set themselves up as priest-kings. But the dynasty soon proved to be itself an oppressive tyranny and provoked a new schism of strict observers among the priestly caste—the Essenes, whose monastery and manuscripts came to light at Qumran (see "The Dead Sea Scrolls," pp. 1063-71). These latter withdrew altogether from active participation in the temple services. In Jesus' time the priestly families who controlled the temple were a wealthy, aristocratic coterie, the Sadducees, conservative in religion though liberal in manners of living, politically subservient to the Romans, and generally unpopular with the people. They were hardly exemplary pastors of the Lord's flock according to the OT ideal figure of the shepherd held up to priests and rulers.

Jesus' parable of the good shepherd is thus an apt prelude to a feast celebrating the purifying of the temple. It is based on Ezek. 34, one of the lessons assigned in the synagogues during the feast. The parable has a sharper edge to it than the tender parable of the lost sheep in the Synoptics (Matt. 18:12-13; Luke 15:3-7); it is closer to the saying recorded in Matt. 9:36 (cf. Mark 6:34).

Vss. 1-5 comprise the only parable in this gospel, and they are followed by an allegorical interpretation, vss. 7-18, similar to the development of the parable of the sower in the Synoptics (Mark 4:13-20), by application to specific contemporary situations in the life of God's people. But the **thieves and robbers** should not be exclusively applied to the priests; they include all messianic pretenders and revolutionaries who destroy the flock by their temporal ambitions. Some would see the allegory as a more immediate reference to the situation of the church in the evangelist's own time—esp. the **hireling** representing false teachers and the **wolf** representing the Roman persecutors. Whatever the allegorical interpretation, the evangelist emphasizes esp. the love of the true **shepherd,** viz. Jesus, who is willing to **lay down my life for the sheep.** The death-resurrection theme is accented in vss. 17-18.

C. THE RAISING OF LAZARUS (11:1-57)

11:1-44. The Miracle. The last and climactic sign of death-resurrection in the gospel is the raising of Lazarus. It is more stupendous than the messianic signs of raising the dead recorded in the Synoptics (Mark 5:21-24, 35-43; Luke 7:11-17). Here the miracle is heightened, as it were deliberately, by the delay until Lazarus has been dead **four days** (vss. 17, 39). It was a popular belief that soul and body were finally separated after 3 days—with no hope of resuscitation. Lazarus' resurrection thus points to Jesus' resurrection. The event forces decision on belief or disbelief in Jesus (vss. 45-53); his enemies understand that the die is cast. It is this decisiveness for faith, in a miracle that surpasses any possibility of rational explanation, that gives the incident its primary dramatic tension.

For, one must ask, what is the motive for this sign? It is not compassion, despite the obvious sympathy of Jesus for his close friends, not to speak of his own personal grief; otherwise Jesus would come speedily to heal him before death. It is hardly a compassionate act to bring a man back from the peace of death to the trials and sufferings of this life. Nor are we given any hint that Lazarus, once restored to life on earth, has any special mission to fulfill. The true motive is baldly stated by Jesus: **it is for the glory of God, so that the Son of God may be glorified by means of it** (vs. 4). Thus the theme of glorification of God in the death and resurrection of Jesus is announced, and will be elaborated further in the coming passion narrative—though it has already been hinted in 1:14; 2:11; 7:18.

The raising of Lazarus is also a test, not only of Jesus' disciples and friends, and of the "Jews," but of Jesus himself. Jesus takes a great risk. It is not a risk of proving unable to raise Lazarus, of having his prayer to God unanswered. Jesus never doubts that God will hear him in this crisis. It is rather the risk of disbelief in him, despite the great sign, that will bring about his final rejection. The disciples have intimations of this (vss. 8-16): **Let us also go, that we may die with him.** The sisters, Mary and Martha, believe in him but can project their faith and hope only **at the last day** (vs. 24). Jesus summons to faith and decision *now:* **I am the resurrection and the life; . . . whoever lives and believes in me shall never die"** (vss. 25-26).

Who then is Lazarus? Why should he be singled out by personal name from among all the recipients of Jesus' signs in this gospel? This question cannot be answered definitively. His was a common name among the Jews, i.e. Eleazar ("God helps"). Some scholars believe that the evangelist selected it from the parable of the rich man and Lazarus (Luke 16:

19-31), a story of life after death, but this seems unlikely. Luke does tell us of Jesus' friendship with Mary and Martha (Luke 10:38-42), yet it does not mention a brother or the location of their home at **Bethany** (on vs. 2 see below on 12:1-11).

Courtesy of Herbert G. May

Modern Bethany; this village was the home of Lazarus (John 11:1)

Jesus' **love** of Lazarus (vss. 3, 5, 36) is emphasized. This indication of love for disciples begins here to be intensified (cf. e.g. 13:1; 14:21) and is esp. directed to a particular disciple "whom Jesus loved" throughout the passion and resurrection narratives. Tradition has of course identified this "beloved disciple" with the evangelist, and more specifically with John the son of Zebedee. But many scholars today believe that Lazarus is the beloved disciple—though there is no reason to suppose that he was included among the 12.

We have here an example of the evangelist's subtlety in weaving together historical persons with symbolic types—as he did with Nathanael, or the Samaritan woman. Lazarus represents every believer who loves Jesus and is loved by him—whom the Lord will raise up at the last day. So also Jesus' words **Take away the stone** (vs. 39) and **Unbind him, and let him go** (vs. 44) speak not only to the historical event of Lazarus' resurrection but more deeply to every believer's condition: "Release from the stony heart of sin; let go to life in God."

11:45-57. The Reaction of the "Jews." On hearing of the raising of Lazarus the council of **chief priests** and **Pharisees** meets to decide what must be done. **It is expedient for you that one man should die for the people, and that the whole nation should not perish** (vs. 50). This counsel of the high priest **Caiaphas** is crucial. It is a decision made in hatred, fear, and expediency. By sacrificing an innocent man, however much disliked by them, the council reckons that it can save its own position and prestige—indeed can save the whole country from war and destruction. The people, or at least all too many of them, **believe** this man Jesus to be the Messiah. This means war with the **Romans**—no matter that Jesus has rejected all temporal, revolutionary claims, no matter what he has really said and done. The high priest prophesies without knowing it. So God confounds the evil counsels of men to bring about his own purposes of salvation. The death of Jesus is not for one people alone, much less for their political security. It will be the agency by which God brings into one reconciliation all his children **scattered abroad.**

Caiaphas' supposedly humane policy of course came to nothing, even in the course of historical events. Within a generation (66-70) the Jewish revolt against Rome, in which no Christian disciples took part, ended in the destruction of Jerusalem and of the temple—the latter never to be rebuilt. To the evangelist and his first readers the irony of the high priest's statement had become evident.

11:54-57. The geographical framework of the Lazarus miracle is not without hidden meaning. Jesus has come forth from the wilderness **across the Jordan** (10:40) where his earthly ministry began with the preaching of John the Baptist (cf. "Bethany beyond the Jordan," 1:28). He now retires to a place near the edge of the **wilderness** (vs. 54) before his final return to Passover for the fulfillment of his destiny. Yet so obtuse are many that they engage in the same gossip about Jesus at this climactic time as they did before the feast of Tabernacles (vss. 55-57; cf. 7:11-13).

III. THE PASSION AND RESURRECTION (12:1–20:31)

A. THE PREPARATION (12:1-50)

The incidents and sayings in this ch. are transitional: vss. 1-19, which relate to the coming passion, the anointing of Jesus for burial and the entry into Jerusalem; and vss. 36b-50, which summarize the proclamation of Jesus in his earthly ministry. The bridge between them is vss. 20-36a, in which is again set forth the death-resurrection theme, and the glorification of Jesus thereby that brings judgment and light to the whole world.

The final week of Jesus' earthly life fulfills the promise of the first week of his ministry (see above on 2:1–11:54). As the first week opened with his baptism and consecration to his mission, this last week opens with his anointing and consecration for his fulfilled mission in death. The first week ended in the joyous wedding feast that manifested his glory to the disciples; the last week ends in another Galilean feast that reveals his resurrection glory and seals his disciples' faith and obedience.

12:1-11. *The Anointing.* This scene is comparable to the account in Mark 14:3-9, with details that recall also the incident in Luke 7:36-50. It differs from the Synoptic story in being placed before the Triumphal Entry—as it were, an anointing not only for burial, after the custom of the times, but for his kingship, now to be acclaimed and then rejected in its earthly dimension, though revealed to faith in its eternal glory. It differs further in being located in the home of Lazarus rather than of one Simon the leper—thus being linked to the preceding story—and in highlighting Judas the betrayer as the objector to the costly waste. The variations are undoubtedly due to differences that arise from stories transmitted by oral tradition. Hence the attempts of later interpreters to harmonize Mary of Bethany with the sinful woman of Luke 7:36-50 and the sinful woman with Mary Magdalene (Luke 8:2) are farfetched.

12:4-7. The portrayal of **Judas Iscariot** as an avaricious **thief** is more pronounced than in the Synoptics (cf. Mark 14:11) and may be intended to suggest the reason for Judas' treachery (cf. 13:29). But the real motives of Judas are difficult to ascertain, and the author is possibly nearer the truth in his indication of the devil's taking possession of him (6:70; 13:2, 27).

12:8. This vs. is omitted in the "Western" manuscripts and may well be an interpolation from Matt. 26:11 (cf. Deut. 15:11). The saying, in any case, is a reminder that costly gifts of devotion to Jesus neither preclude nor exclude the obligation of concern for the poor.

12:12-19. *The Triumphal Entry.* Jesus' entry into Jerusalem is narrated also in much the same way as in the Synoptics (cf. Mark 11:1-10; Matt. 21:1-11; Luke 19:29-40), but John uses the story as a link between the sign of Lazarus' raising from the dead and the glorification of Jesus and his true kingship (cf. 1:49; 6:15) as revealed in the impending death and resurrection. The **crowd** who acclaims him represents the **world** which **has gone after him** (vs. 19)—but a world very different from those who desire and seek a temporal dominion, though his enemies do not know this.

12:20-36a. *Jesus' Hour.* The decisive **hour has come** (cf. 2:4). Not only the Judean **crowd** now look to the revelation of the **King of Israel** (vss. 12-13) but the **Greeks** from the wider world appear seeking Jesus, brought to him by that peculiar pair of Johannine disciples, **Philip** and **Andrew,** from the city of Bethsaida, where Jew and Gentile intermingled (cf. 1:44; 6:5-8). These Greeks are representatives of the Hellenistic world—whether Greek-speaking Jews of the Dispersion or Gentiles (cf. 7:35; Acts 6:1; 11:20). For Jesus the Messiah-King, the Son of man, is now to be **lifted up** on the cross that he may **draw all men** to himself (vss. 32-33; cf. 3:14-15).

12:27-36a. It is a moment of portent. While the world of Jews and Greeks watches, Jesus in agony makes his final decision of obedience unto death, in servanthood and sonship. Such obedience is indeed the glorification of God. And God answers: He has **glorified** his **name;** he will **glorify it again.** It is **judgment;** it is the overthrow of Satan; it is salvation. Who comprehends it? Is it merely the sound of thunder or is it the voice of an **angel?** Both material and spiritual perception of revelation are mixed, depending on whether one is in the **light** or in **darkness.** In no instance has the evangelist displayed more remarkably his powers of suggestive symbolism than in these vss. The reverberation contains the whole symphony of sounds associated with the voice of God from the ancient creation ps. (Ps. 29:1-4) to the final paean of the saints in the age to come (Rev. 14:1-2).

12:36b-50. *The End of Public Discourse.* This epilogue concludes Jesus' public ministry—his manifestation to the world and to the Jews. From this point on his teaching is confined entirely to the inner circle of his disciples. These are words of judgment—not that he judges but that men judge themselves by virtue of their response to him. They are also a reflection of Christian judgment on the varying responses to the gospel. The citation from Isa. 53:1 is paralleled, with similar interpretation, by Paul (Rom. 10:16) and that from Isa. 6:10 is quoted also in Matt. 13:14-15; Acts 28:25-27 (note its climactic position). In characteristic Johannine fashion the theme of the **commandment** of God with which the section closes picks up an earlier suggestion (10:18) that will be unfolded in more detail in coming discourses (chs. 13–16). Its basis is Deut., the prophetic book of the law (e.g. Deut. 18:18-19; 32:46-47), the sayings of the prophet like Moses (cf. 6:14).

B. The Last Supper (13:1–17:26)

The most obvious characteristic of this account of the supper is the lack of any formal institution of the Eucharist with the elements of bread and wine (cf. Mark 14:22-24; Matt. 26:26-28; Luke 22:17-19). Many theories have been posited to explain this omission—e.g. (*a*) the author's chronology, according to which this was not a Passover meal (see below on 13:1); (*b*) at the time of writing the Eucharist was a "secret" not to be revealed to an unbaptized reader; (*c*) the evangelist was not interested in sacraments themselves; (*d*) he presupposes among his readers both a knowledge of the Synoptic gospels and of the rites of the church. The fact is, the evangelist chooses his own way of use of, or allusion to, tradition. In no place does he give any hint of an institution of baptism. Yet baptismal and eucharistic themes constantly recur, as often noted above, throughout the gospel. The Eucharist is specifically referred to in 6:51-56.

13:1. The Johannine Chronology. The evangelist dates the supper **before the feast of the Passover** instead of equating it with the Passover meal as do the Synoptics (cf. Mark 14:12; Matt. 26:17; Luke 22:7-8). He places the Crucifixion on the eve of Passover, when the lambs were sacrificed (cf. 18:28; 19:31). It is the slaughter of the true paschal lamb, and by implication the true paschal feast is the meal of the risen Lord with his disciples on the day of the Resurrection (cf. I Cor. 5:7-8; Rev. 19:6-9). This discrepancy in chronology has been occasion for endless debate.

All 4 gospels agree that the Last Supper was held on Thursday evening and that the Crucifixion took place on Friday. But John is explicit that Friday was not the Passover feast day but the day of Preparation (19:31), and that in this year Passover and the sabbath coincided. There is no way to resolve this conflict of dating by astronomical calculation, since we do not know the exact year of Jesus' death— sometime between 29 and 33. In his time the new moon of the month Nisan, in which Passover was celebrated at the full moon, was determined by observation, so that weather conditions might cause a 24-hour delay in proclamation of the beginning of the month. Outside Palestine, in the Jewish Dispersion, the date of the feast was calculated by fixed tables of the moon months. Hence it is possible that the Synoptics represent a memory of the fateful year of Jesus' death based on a fixed calendar, whereas this gospel goes back to Palestinian tradition and a memory that in the year of Jesus' crucifixion the Passover fell a day later than the reckoning of fixed calendars.

13:2-20. The Foot Washing. This has been subject to diverse interpretations. Many see it simply as a final acted parable of humility and love that opens the discourse on the theme of Jesus' relationship to his disciples and theirs in turn to one another. Others see in it a veiled sacrament of the "baptism" or consecration of the apostles. Some Christian groups in the course of history have taken it lit. as a special ceremony instituted by Jesus. Another problem concerns the textual tradition of vs. 10. Many ancient manuscripts of good authority omit the words **except for his feet.**

Jesus' act is certainly an example of that humble, selfless service, even to the most menial deeds of kindness, that characterizes the true disciple-servant who shares with him his master-servant role in his kingdom. This is explicit in Jesus' own interpretation of his act (vss. 12-17). The story is exactly comparable to the words of Jesus at the supper recorded in Luke 22:24-30. His kingdom is not a realm where some are great in authority and privilege and others are slavish in lowly service. In his kingdom the greatest is the least—the servant of all (cf. Mark 10:42-45). This is his final lesson to his disciples; and the Eucharist is, if nothing else, his instrument by which and through which he serves us with his whole life and we serve one another in sharing servanthood of all that we are and possess. The foot washing is a profound exposition of the Eucharist, of that most intimate relationship of Jesus with the members of his body the church.

In this sense Jesus' washing of the disciples' feet is indeed their baptism into his death, their consecration into his priesthood and kingship. As Mary anointed him for his unique fulfillment of his destiny (12:3) with costly ointment poured out on his feet, so he now "anoints" his disciples' feet with the lowly cleansing water, that they may have full **part** in him (vs. 8). They have **bathed** (in the baptism of John?), but they need this final anointing and purification from himself (cf. I John 2:26–3:3). The revelation of Jesus is now completed for his disciples (cf. **I am he**, vs. 19) and their mission is established. In humility and love the Father sent the Son; now the Son in humility and love sends the disciples. Whoever **receives** them receives Christ, just as whoever receives Christ receives the Father (vs. 20). The last discourse will develop the theme.

13:21-30. Identification of the Traitor. This incident has many similarities to the account in Mark 14:17-21, but the evangelist uses it as a foil to introduce the "beloved disciple" (but see above on 11:3). The Christian reader would assume that the disciple **whom Jesus loved** is one of the 12, though this gospel does not limit the number of disciples at the supper to the 12 (contrast Mark 14:17; Matt. 26:20). And though the tradition has identified this disciple with John son of Zebedee (see Intro.), nothing in the gospel itself would lead one to that conclusion. It is certainly possible that the beloved disciple is John; but his role here and in the subsequent narrative of the Crucifixion and Resurrection (cf. 19:26; 20:2; 21:20) suggests a personage whom the evangelist employs as a "type" of the true disciple—a merging of historical and typological witness so characteristic of his method and manner of presentation (cf. e.g. Nathanael, the Samaritan woman, the man born blind, and Lazarus). The beloved disciple lies close to the **bosom** of Jesus (vs. 23). This recalls the Prologue, where it is said that

Jesus is "in the bosom of the Father" (1:18). It is another indication by the evangelist that the intimate union of Jesus with his disciples is image of his intimate union with the Father.

Neither this gospel nor the Synoptics make clear why the disciples do not react more positively to the identification of the traitor. But they are obviously unaware of its implication.

13:31–16:33. *The Farewell Discourse.* This lengthy discourse is a peculiar tradition of the evangelist. Yet it corresponds in many ways to the "apocalyptic" discourse of Jesus before his passion recorded in Mark 13; Matt. 24; Luke 21. For it deals, albeit in a very different style and manner, with the imminent departure of Jesus and the consequent fate of his disciples, and with his return to them in succor and deliverance.

In fact there are 2 discourses here, separated by the strange summons of 14:31, **Rise, let us go hence,** and the allegory of the vine (15:1-9), and concluded with a final question, **Do you now believe?** (16:31). Both discourses treat of the same themes—the impending death, bodily departure, and continued presence of Jesus, and the consequences of these events for the life and mission of the disciples, both in their inner corporate community and in their outward witness to the world.

The parallelism of the 2 discourses is evident, in that the first (13:31–14:31) speaks of the immediate fate of Jesus and his disciples in the impending crisis of his death and the 2nd (15:10–16:33) projects this experience into the future life of his disciples, i.e. the church, and their respective followers in the world. The distinction, however, is not absolute; the evangelist always anticipates themes for further comment. In fact this interweaving of present and future gives the discourse a dramatic tension. In the immediate situation the disciples will falter; Peter will indeed deny him; they do not understand what he is saying, do not know who he truly is; they will be scattered and leave him alone to his fate. Yet they will not really fall away. Only one, Judas, has irrevocably gone out into the **night** (13:30) of the world which has rejected him. They will be valiant in witness even unto death, and in tribulation they will find joy. Though denial and desertion lie immediately ahead, they will **follow**—and **lay down** their lives for him as he is now going to lay down his life for them. The suffering of Jesus will be their suffering; his triumph will be theirs also.

A little while, and you will see me no more; again a little while, and you will see me (16:16; cf. 13:33; 14:19). This prediction is the basis of Jesus' discourse. The "little while" is of course the impending time of his death and departure. But the evangelist uses two Greek words for "see" which cannot easily be distinguished in English translation. In the first clause they are no longer to see him present physically or by means of inward perception. But in the 2nd they will see him in his glorified, exalted life, in a vision that includes but surpasses mere physical sight. This 2nd verb is used of the resurrection appearances in 20:18, 25, 29 (cf. I Cor. 9:1; 15:5-8; I John 1:1-3; 3:2, 6). It is a seeing that is also knowing; for though "no one has ever seen God" (1:18), **he who has seen me has seen the Father** (14:9).

In order that this seeing may take place, Jesus must **go to the Father** (14:28), i.e. ascend into heaven (cf. 3:13; 20:17), to his **Father's house** (14:2), heaven being commonly viewed as God's temple. This departure is not an occasion of **sorrow** but a cause of **joy** (16:20-22). Only thus can Jesus open the **way** to eternal life (14:6). There he is to **prepare a place** (14:2) for those who will **follow** him (13:36). And only by his return to the Father can he send **another,** i.e. his **Spirit,** who will be with the disciples at all times and in all places (14:16-17). So long as he is bound within his fleshly body he is limited by time and space. His ascension assures his omnipresence to his own wherever they may be and forever. It is promise also of **greater works** than even he could do in his earthly life, for then **whatever you ask in my name, I will do it** (14:12-14).

Who then is this "other" whom Jesus will send? The evangelist calls him by a title peculiar to the Johannine writings, *parakletos,* lit. "one called alongside," i.e. to help. The term is variously translated as "advocate" (I John 2:1, where it is applied to Jesus himself), **Counselor,** "Comforter" (KJV), but is better simply transliterated "Paraclete." The discourse makes plain that the Paraclete is the **Spirit of truth,** the **Holy Spirit** (14:17, 26; 15:26; 16:13). He comes from the Father in Jesus' name and **dwells** with the disciples. He is in fact the presence of God in Christ continuing with his faithful servants and witnesses after the ascension of Jesus, fulfilling and perfecting his work. Only the disciples will know him, for the **world cannot receive** him (14:17).

The work of the Paraclete is 2-fold. Within the fellowship of Jesus' disciples he is the guide and teacher of truth, to **bring to . . . remembrance** what Jesus said (14:26) and reveal those **things that are to come** by virtue of what Jesus accomplished (16:13). Thus he is to **declare** all that is of Jesus and about Jesus and so **glorify** him as Jesus has glorified the Father (16:14). The Paraclete is also the bearer of **witness,** through the testimony of the disciples, to the world outside, convicting it **of sin and of righteousness and of judgment** (15:26-27; 16:8-11). He directs the disciples both in their preaching of the gospel and in their steadfast testimony in persecution. The love, the prayer, the obedience of the Christian disciple are the gift of grace of the Paraclete. This Spirit Jesus breathes on his disciples in the Resurrection (20:21-22; cf. 14:27).

The Johannine conception of the Paraclete is of course rooted in the OT witness to the Spirit of God who comes upon the prophets to inspire them to speak God's words. But in the NT teaching the Holy Spirit is poured forth not only on specific chosen witnesses but on all the faithful believers in Christ (cf. Acts 2:33; I Cor. 12:7-13). In the Manual of Discipline of the Qumran community mankind is divided between those who follow the 2 spirits (or angels) of truth and of perversity, of light and of darkness, respectively. Of the spirit of truth it is said that his function is

> to enlighten the heart of man,
> to make straight the paths of true righteousness,
> to set fear in his heart of the judgment of God,
> the spirit of humility and patience,
> of abundant mercy and eternal goodness,
> of understanding and intelligence,

of mighty wisdom that trusts in God's deeds
    and leans on his lovingkindness;
the spirit of discernment in every purpose,
    of zeal for just laws,
    of holy resolution with steadfastness,
    of great love toward the sons of truth,
    and glorious purity that hates unclean idols,
    of humility sprung from understanding,
    and prudence concerning the mysteries of God.
Such are the counsels of the Spirit
    to the sons of truth in this world. (1QS 4:2-6.)

The Farewell Discourse has been a primary source for the development of the ancient church's doctrine of the Godhead as Unity in Trinity, from such pregnant sentences of the relationship of the Father and the Son and the Paraclete as 14:9, 11, 26; 15:26 (cf. 17:21).

The allegory of the vine (15:1-9) that binds together the two parts of the discourse also has its roots in the OT figure of Israel as God's vine (Ps. 80:8-16; Jer. 2:21; Ezek. 15:1-8, 19:10-14; cf. Isa. 5:1-7). A crucial parable of Jesus recorded in the Synoptics (Mark 12:1-12; Matt. 21:33-46; Luke 20:9-19) makes the same comparison. The Johannine use of the figure includes all the OT associations of God's care for and judgment on the vine, but at the same time it goes beyond them by its identification of Jesus as the **true vine.** Thus Jesus is the true Israel, in whose stem are incorporated the **branches** of the people of God, who find their fulfillment and life in him. The allegory is comparable to his discourses on the bread of life (ch. 6) and the good shepherd (ch. 10). It is another revelation of "I am." It is also a Johannine commentary on the "fruit of the vine" (Mark 14:25), the cup of the Eucharist.

17:1-26. The High Priestly Prayer. The few prayers of Jesus recorded in the Synoptics are invariably short and addressed with intimate immediacy to his "Father." The 2 examples hitherto in this gospel—11:41-42 (cf. Matt. 11:25-27) and 12:27 (cf. Mark 14:36)—share these characteristics, and each of them is a "cry" of Jesus at a moment of great tension. The extended prayer of this ch. is more serene and meditative, gathering up the themes of the preceding discourse. It is both a final resolution of Jesus' obedience to the death which will be his glorification and an intercession for the fruits of his accomplished work after his ascension. The literary form no doubt is due to the constructive skill of the evangelist—e.g. vs. 3 is hardly the way one would expect Jesus to address his Father. It is in a sense another discourse.

The popular title of this ch. is "The High Priestly Prayer" of Jesus; i.e. it is his consecration of himself as the mediator of salvation. It expresses exactly what the author of Heb. projected of his eternal intercession: "He is able for all time to save those who draw near to God through him, since he always lives to make intercession for them" (Heb. 7:25). It sums up the Johannine concept of the work of Christ.

The prayer has four focuses of concern: (*a*) Jesus' offering of himself for his Father's purposes (vss. 1-5); (*b*) his concern for the destiny of his disciples after his ascension (vss. 6-19); (*c*) the outreach of intercession to all future believers until the end of time (vss. 20-23); and (*d*) the expectation of final consummation in the age to come (vss. 24-26).

The **glory** of Jesus—**before the world was made, in the fulfillment of his hour . . . on earth,** and in his return eternally to God's **own presence** (vss. 1-5)—this will be manifested to the world in the unity in **truth** (vss. 17-19) and **love** (vs. 26) of all his disciples and believers. Such unity will suffer many strains, not least in their temptations and persecutions (vss. 14-15). Here the evangelist no doubt thinks of the schisms and apostasies of his own generation, which will be repeated in coming generations. But the last and the eternally continuing prayer of Jesus is that the unity of love and purpose he has with his Father will be reflected in the unity of the church in himself, and that the mission he received and fulfilled from his Father will be the same mission of all who find **joy fulfilled** in his discipleship throughout all times and ages.

This consummate prayer of Jesus must be the prayer of all who follow him. Many commentators have seen in it an exposition of the succinct Lord's Prayer of the Synoptics. In both cases there is a curious lack of reference to the Spirit.

C. The Crucifixion (18:1–19:42)

Both in the order of the narrative and in many details the Johannine passion story is closer to the Synoptic tradition than any other extended portion of the gospel. Yet the differences, both in omissions and in additions (on the difference in chronology see above on 13:1), give it a tone and interpretation that is quite distinctive. In general it magnifies the "kingship" of Jesus. He goes to his death, not in weakness and humiliation, but as a hero fulfilling his destiny in triumph.

The physical frailty and anguish of Jesus are not emphasized. They are certainly not omitted—e.g. the cruel and sardonic mockery of the soldiers (19:1-3) and the final agony of thirst (19:28). But there is no wrestling in agony of spirit in Gethsemane (cf. 12:27); he is able to bear his own cross (19:17; contrast Mark 15:21); and he does not suffer the taunting mockery of those who watched him die (contrast Mark 15:29-32).

Here Jesus is in full control of what happens. His arrest is not possible without his voluntary submission. He does not remain silent, for the most part, either at his trial before the chief priests or in the presence of Pilate. He defends himself and his teaching with dignity and forthrightness. He reminds Pilate in no uncertain terms that he is powerless either to crucify or to release him without divine permission. Indeed the trial before Pilate becomes, as it were, a judgment on the governor himself. And in death's last throes Jesus utters, not a cry of despair, but a word of accomplishment: **It is finished** (19:30; contrast Mark 15:34-37, though note the more peaceful ending in Luke 23:46).

18:12-19:22. The Trial. The political overtones are prominent in this account, in ways both paradoxical and ironic. The preliminary hearing before the Jewish high priest (18:19-23) is more in the nature of an investigation than a trial; and no specific charge, whether of blasphemy or of messianic claim, is formulated. The Jewish authorities simply turn him over to Pilate as an **evildoer** (18:30); yet as the trial before Pilate proceeds, the issue be-

Courtesy of the Sisters of Zion, Jerusalem, Israel

The Lithostrotos (stone path); this pavement, located under present-day buildings in Jerusalem, is believed by some to have been Pilate's judgment hall (praetorium); cf. John 18:28, 33; 19:9

comes clear: Jesus' kingship challenges the kingship of Caesar. Neither the Jews nor Pilate really believes that Jesus is the **King of the Jews,** and Jesus positively rejects any claim to be a temporal ruler (18:36; cf. 6:15). The hypocrisy of the Jews is evident to Pilate; so he mocks them when they object to the **title,** i.e. the inscription stating the charge, which he has ordered placed on the cross (19:19-22). It is evident also to Pilate that Jesus is innocent; but he yields to the fear of his own political position when they say, **If you release this man, you are not Caesar's friend** (19:12). Were it not for Jesus' dignity the whole proceeding would be a farce.

There is no doubt that the evangelist himself places the major blame for the tragedy on the "Jews" and attempts, albeit unsuccessfully, to exonerate Pilate by portraying him as yielding to pressure. This slant—evident also in Matt. and Luke—has unfortunately been a source of unwarranted anti-Semitic attitudes among later generations of Christians. But it reflects a situation of the evangelist's own times: the increasing hostility between church and synagogue and on the other hand the desire of Christians in the face of persecution by the Roman government to attest their loyalty to the established order and to minimize the threat posed by their messianic hopes.

19:25-27. At the Cross. A singular scene in this account is the appearance of Jesus' **mother** and the **disciple whom he loved** at the foot of the cross. In the Synoptics the women watch from a distance; the disciples have all fled into hiding. It is of course possible that the evangelist preserves here a true factual reminiscence. Many commentators believe it reflects a later tradition of Ephesus, where they assume the mother of Jesus lived in the care of John the son of Zebedee. But the scene has symbolic meaning. Mary

is the representative type of the church (see above on 2:1-12), the believing community; the disciple is the representative type of every individual believer (see above on 13:21-30). Thus in his final act on earth Jesus entrusts to those who love him and believe in him (cf. 20:8) the care of his church.

19:28-37. The Death of Jesus. The cruel punishment of crucifixion, which the Romans took over from the Carthaginians and Persians, was inflicted only on slaves and "foreigners," usually for robbery or sedition. It might last for several days before death at last occurred from hunger and thirst, exhaustion, or bleeding from wounds—including the wounds of scourging, which usually preceded it. Breaking the **legs** of the crucified added to the agony, though it hastened the end—and was possibly a precaution against escape. Jesus' death within three hours was unusual (cf. Mark 15:44-45), but he had already suffered much abuse. The Jewish law required that the body of an executed criminal displayed as a public example should be buried by nightfall (Deut. 21:22-23); but it is doubtful whether the Romans respected this injunction, even when the following day was a special Jewish holy day. The author's interest, however, in the circumstance that Jesus' legs were not broken has possibly 2 allusions: (a) the Passover lamb that is sacrificed should not have a broken bone (Exod. 12:46; Num. 9:12); (b) the psalmist noted that the Lord keeps all the bones of the righteous so that "not one of them is broken" (Ps. 34:20). In all the gospels much of the passion narrative is considered in detail as fulfillment of OT passages viewed as prophetic of the Christ.

That Jesus' **side** was **pierced** after his death—a fulfillment of Zech. 12:10—is another of the peculiar features of this account, one of great importance to the Johannine authors (cf. 20:25, 27; Rev. 1:7). The

"Garden Tomb" outside Jerusalem's N wall, thought by some to have been the burial place of Jesus (but see comment on 19:41-42); the opening was originally sealed with a large rolling stone

motive behind the soldier's spear thrust is not clear.

More mysterious is the issue of **blood and water** —as there is no adequate medical explanation for such a phenomenon. Yet the author gives to this "miracle" a most solemn attestation, for it undoubtedly served as a final and consummate sign of the meaning of Jesus' death and triumph. That there is a deep symbolic significance to the blood and water is evident; but interpreters, both ancient and modern, have not agreed about its exact connotation. Most obvious perhaps is the sense that in the self-offering of Jesus all the old legal rites of purification and sacrifice are fulfilled and brought to an end. Others, however, see in the sign a hidden reference to the church's sacraments—the more so if one connects with the miracle the giving up of Jesus' **spirit** (vs. 30; cf. the 3 witnesses of I John 5:6-8, "the Spirit, the water, and the blood"). The life of Jesus, now closed on earth, continues to be imparted and to flow into the life of his followers in his Spirit-empowered gifts of baptism and the Eucharist—or what the ancient church significantly called the "paschal mystery."

19:38-42. The Burial. The burial of Jesus is similarly related in all four gospels. It was important testimony to the real fact of his death, in contrast to later Gnostic theories, found in some of the apocryphal gospels, that Jesus, not being a real human being, departed to his Father before his actual death on the cross. The ancient orthodox creeds also emphasize the fact that Jesus was "buried." Without such a fact the tradition of the empty tomb is meaningless.

19:38-40. As one might expect, this account has its own peculiar details. **Joseph of Arimathea,** whom the Synoptics identify as a member of the Jewish "council" (Mark 15:43), is here described as a secret believer. He is associated with **Nicodemus**

(cf. 3:1-10; 7:50-51), who is presumably a similar believer. In contrast to the mean manner of Jesus' death these men provide him with a sumptuous burial, including **linen cloths** wound about the body (cf. 11:44; 20:6-7) and a lavish supply of **spices,** according to Jewish **custom.** Nicodemus provides these spices at the time of burial; and there is no mention of the loving women who in the Synoptics watch to see where the body is laid—though ch. 20 assumes that at least one of them knows where it is—so that they may prepare the spices and apply them as soon as the sabbath is over.

19:41-42. The tomb is a new one, hitherto unused (cf. Luke 23:53), and thus an honorable place for Jesus. This gospel alone locates it in a garden (cf. 20:15) near the place of crucifixion. This close association of place of death and place of burial has been attested at least since the 4th cent. by the traditions of the Church of the Holy Sepulchre in Jerusalem, first erected by the Emperor Constantine on the holy sites. Recent investigations underneath the present church—shrine of so constant a pilgrimage through the cents.—suggest the proximity of the two sites in a quarry area outside the city walls, but do not—and possibly cannot—confirm a garden setting of the tomb. Symbolism is always allusive, if not illusive, in this gospel. The fact that Jesus was betrayed in a garden (18:1) and buried in a garden may be the evangelist's way of emphasizing that what man lost in the Garden of Eden by sin and disobedience is now recovered in a garden by obedience unto death. So Paradise is regained.

D. THE RESURRECTION (20:1-31)

The account of the empty tomb and the appearance of the risen Christ to his disciples has many similarities to the tradition recounted in Luke. But there are Johannine emphases and details that are distinctive.

20:1-18. The Empty Tomb. In each of the Synoptics several women come to the tomb for the purpose of completing preparation of the body for burial (see above on 19:38-40). In this account, however, only one woman is mentioned, **Mary Magdalene,** and her reason for visiting the tomb perhaps should be assumed to be devotion to her buried Lord.

20:2-10. These vss. seem to be an expansion—or correction—of the tradition in Luke 24:11 about the disciples' reaction to the women's report of the empty tomb. Peter and the beloved disciple hasten to verify the testimony. Though they do not see Jesus, they are convinced. In this narrative the evangelist in his subtle way refers to the primary experience by Peter of the Resurrection (cf. Luke 24:34; I Cor. 15:5). The beloved disciple, who actually arrives first at the tomb, becomes a representative of all believers, both among the disciples and among all those who accept the disciples' witness, beginning with Peter. It is interesting to note that Peter is the first to see; the beloved disciple is the first to see and believe (vs. 8).

20:11-18. Vs. 11 takes us back to Mary Magdalene at the tomb, as though vss. 2-10 were an interruption. She now sees the **two angels** (cf. Luke 24:4; only one in Mark 16:5; Matt. 28:2-3), but before they deliver any message Jesus himself appears (cf. Matt. 28:9-10). The vision is real, but she cannot grasp him, for the truth of his resurrection is not yet fully revealed. She can only report that she has seen him and he has spoken to her.

20:19-23. First Appearance to the Disciples. The scene now shifts to the closed room, presumably in Jerusalem (cf. Luke 24:33-49), where the frightened disciples are hiding. Jesus identifies himself by showing the marks of his passion. He bestows on them the full grace of his risen and glorified life: **peace,** the true peace that restores them to inner security and fearlessness (vss. 19-20); mission, the command to take up his work (vs. 21); and power, the gift of the **Holy Spirit,** which is his life, for it is his gift alone by which the disciples can declare the forgiveness of sins (vss. 22-23). The Resurrection thus brings into being the church—its unity, its commission, its endowment. All that Jesus has won is now given to his disciples.

20:24-31. The Response of Thomas. There is, however, a further attestation. In Matt. 28:17 we are told that at the resurrection appearance "some doubted." In view of the stupendous nature of the event this is understandable. Is it only a vision, or possibly a hallucination? Here the doubt is made concrete in the person of Thomas. Jesus must not only be seen; he must be handled—the whole person must be grasped. And Thomas' doubt—representing that of all who come after him—is turned to certainty. Those who have never seen the Christ can believe in him, for they can touch his very body from which his blood outpoured. It is not fanciful to see here a reference to the Eucharist, and also to the very material love of Christian believers one for another and for the whole world, for all men who bear the marks of suffering for whom Christ suffered.

The resurrection narrative thus builds up into a dramatic climax. First there is the immaterial evidence of the empty tomb, then the vision of what this empty tomb signifies: Jesus is risen and alive. The vision becomes concrete in the experience and acceptance of grace and of empowerment for redemptive mission, and finally by incorporation through faith in his glorification through suffering.

The final response, **My Lord and my God!** is the believer's answer to the initial proclamation: "The Word was God. . . . No one has ever seen God; the only Son . . . has made him known" (1:1, 18).

IV. APPENDIX: ATTESTATION OF WITNESSES (21:1-25)

The obvious ending of the gospel in 20:30-31 is followed by 2 narratives and a colophon, which all commentators denote as an "appendix" (see Intro.). The fact that vs. 24 distinguishes the **disciple who is bearing witness** and the **we** who vouch for his witness suggests an editorial compilation—of which evidences have been noted here and there in the gospel text itself. Thus many believe that this ch. is a later addition—though careful studies of its vocabulary and style are inconclusive, and there is no evidence that the gospel ever circulated without it. Both subject matter and style recall esp. ch. 6—a miraculous feeding and a confession of Peter. It is possible that an editorial redaction—whether by the author or others—transferred to this place incidents that in the original plan of the gospel were included in the Galilean ministry. Thus the **third** manifestation of Jesus to his disciples (vs. 14) may have been the 3rd miracle of his revelation in Galilee (cf. 2:11; 4:54). The testing and call of Peter might logically have followed his confession in 6:69.

21:1-14. The Miraculous Catch of Fish. This episode, with its setting at the **Sea of Tiberias** (cf. 6:1), has similarities to the story in Luke 5:2-11—esp. in the initiative of Peter, followed by his call to discipleship; the mention of the sons of Zebedee, only here in this gospel; and the heavy weight of **fish.** The story may well be a completion of the unfinished and unfulfilled promise of Mark 14:28; 16:7 of an appearance to the disciples in Galilee. But the author has given the tradition a Eucharistic allusion, comparable to that in the feeding of the multitude (ch. 6)—i.e. the risen Lord is made known in the breaking of bread (cf. Luke 24:35; Acts 10:41). Note that Jesus has already prepared the breakfast of bread and fish before ever the fish are brought in by the disciples. Note too that it is the beloved disciple who is first to recognize the Lord, as it was he who was first to believe in the Resurrection (20:8). The number of fish, **a hundred and fifty-three** (vs. 11), has inspired many attempts at symbolic interpretation—e.g. Jerome declared it the total of species of fish, and Augustine discovered it is the sum of the numbers 1 to 17, which in turn is the sum of the symbolic numbers 10 and 7.

21:15-19. The Dialogue with Peter. This scene is also allusive in the Johannine manner. The 3-fold question and answer correspond—by way of restoration—to the 3-fold denial of Peter before the Crucifixion (13:38; 18:17-18, 25-27). It is also a reaffirmation of Peter's call, with that of other disciples, to **follow** Jesus (cf. 1:41-43; Mark 1:17), and the Johannine recognition of Peter's leadership in the apostolic band of disciples. He receives his commission, as representative of all the apostles, to shepherd the Lord's flock (cf. 10:1-18), with the promise that he too, like his Lord the Good Shepherd, will lay down his life for the sheep. Vs. 18 has generally been taken as a reference to the tradition that Peter suffered martyrdom, probably by crucifixion in the persecution of Nero, A.D. 64.

21:20-25. *The Future of the Beloved Disciple.* Peter's love is now equated with that of the beloved disciple. His query about the fate of this companion (vs. 21) is both a natural curiosity about the destiny of the man himself and a deeper allusion to those whom the beloved disciple represents figuratively. The colophon (vs. 24) makes clear that the beloved disciple—whoever he was—had died by the time the gospel was published. But in a sense the beloved disciple does not die; he remains until Jesus comes again (vs. 22). In every generation, from the time of Jesus' resurrection until the end of the world, disciples whom Jesus loves and who love Jesus in return shall remain with us. Cf. a similar query and response in Acts 1:6-8. Whether soon or late, the summons of Jesus comes to every disciple, to **follow** him and to bear **witness** to him.

THE ACTS OF THE APOSTLES

WILLIAM BAIRD

Nature and Purpose. Acts is the 2nd volume of the historical work Luke-Acts (see Intro. to Luke). Unlike the gospel, its nature is not predetermined by a Christian type of writing but is shaped after the pattern of Hellenistic historical works. The author is interested in the details of contemporary history (cf. 12:20-23; 18:2, 12) and describes matters of geography and government with accuracy. Like the historians of his day this author attributes speeches to his characters. These speeches constitute about a 5th of the total narrative, but are relatively short in comparison with contemporary models. Thus at best they could only approximate what was said and are in the main compositions of the author, sometimes including authentic material (cf. 13:38-39). He employs these discourses, not to parade his rhetorical ability, but to present his understanding of the Christian message. Throughout his work the author writes history with a religious purpose and is closer to II Macc. than to Thucydides.

The precise purpose of Acts is debatable. It has been argued e.g. that the author is preparing a dossier for use at the trial of Paul or that he is anxious to harmonize the controversy between Jewish and Gentile factions of the church. Most likely the purpose is 2-fold: (*a*) to prove that the church is not in conflict with Rome (25:8); (*b*) to describe the spread of Christianity under the guidance of the Spirit (1:8). The former is directed to Gentiles while the latter is instruction for the Christians. In essence the author is champion of the Gentile mission of the church (10:1 ff.; 11:20; 13:46-48).

Authorship. According to tradition Acts was written by Luke (see Intro. to Luke). This tradition is more important for Acts than for the gospel, since authorship by a companion of Paul would mean that the narrative was written by an eyewitness of some of the events. The discussion of this question usually finds its point of departure in the "we sections," where the narrative switches to the first person plural (16:10-17; 20:5-15; 21:1-18; 27:1–28:16). It is easiest to suppose that these sections were written by the author himself and that in them he envisaged himself as a participant in the events. Of course this could explain the origin of the Lukan tradition, and the phenomenon is open to two other interpretations: (*a*) The "we sections" are a stylistic device whereby the author changes persons to give his narrative vitality. (*b*) The "we sections" represent a source—perhaps a diary or travel itinerary—used by the author.

To solve this problem it is necessary to compare the data of Acts with parallel material from the Pauline letters. If Acts was written by a travel companion of Paul the 2 ought to be consistent. Although the problem is complex, a few illustrations may serve to show that there are discrepancies. In Acts e.g. Paul's attendance at the Jerusalem conference (15:6-29) occurs on his 3rd trip to that city after his conversion; as described in Gal. 2:1-10 the conference visit is only his 2nd. The description of Paul's first visit in Acts 9:26-30 also contradicts that presented by Gal. 1:18-24. Another instance is found in the fact that in the letters Paul's central message is the doctrine of justification by faith (e.g. Rom. 3:21-31; Gal. 2:15-21) whereas the Pauline speeches of Acts scarcely allude to this idea (cf. 17:22-31; 26:2-23). This evidence makes it questionable whether a companion of Paul could have written Acts and suggests that the "we sections" represent a source used by the author. Nevertheless for convenience we may continue to refer to the writer as "Luke," realizing that the identification is questionable.

Date and Place of Composition. It is sometimes supposed that since the narrative ends without relating the death of Paul, Acts must have been composed before that event. This conclusion fails to realize that Acts was not written as a biography of Peter or Paul. Its intention is to describe the preaching of the gospel from Jerusalem "to the end of the earth" (1:8). When the good news is announced in Rome the climax of the story has been reached and the purposes of God have been fulfilled (28:28). Moreover, 20:25; 21:10-14 suggest that the author knew about the death of Paul. In any case the probability that he wrote Acts following his gospel practically rules out so early a date (see Intro. to Luke). The inconsistencies with Paul's letters indicate that he wrote before these letters were collected and given wide distribution sometime near the turn of the century. Probably, therefore, the best estimate for the date of Acts is between A.D. 90 and 100.

The place of composition of Acts remains unknown. The few traditions about it are based entirely on the assumption that the author was Luke, the companion of Paul (see Intro. to Luke).

Sources and Arrangement. Besides the material underlying the "we sections" other sources were no doubt used in the composition of Acts. Efforts have been made e.g. to identify 2 overlapping traditions in the early chs. It is argued that since ch. 3 duplicates some of the narrative of ch. 2 the author had 2 different sources. Although it cannot be proved that these accounts are doublets, it is agreed that a variety of material, written or oral, underlies this section. It is also held that the chs. 6-15—usually accepted as more historical than the earlier material —embody tradition which grew up around important Christian centers such as Jerusalem (8:14-24) and Antioch (11:19-26). Possibly a parallel development around the lives of outstanding church leaders like Peter (9:32-43) or Stephen (6:8–8:1) can be posited.

As in his gospel, Luke builds up his material in blocks. The possibility that he sometimes has more than one source for the same event could explain some of the possible doublets (e.g. 2:4; 4:31). The blocks of source material are joined together by editorial summaries composed by the author (e.g. 2:41-42, 46-47). These summaries may present a key to the arrangement of Acts. It has been suggested, e.g. that the summaries divide periods of 5-year duration. Most likely, however, the order is geographical rather than chronological. Acts 1:8 is not an outline of the book, but it does state the theme and indicate that the order follows the expansion of the church—from Jerusalem to Samaria, Syria, Asia Minor, Greece, and finally Rome.

Acts has been preserved in 2 different types of Greek text (see "The Transmission of the Biblical Text," pp. 1225-36). One of these, supported by manuscripts which became standard in the W, makes many changes and additions to the narrative. E.g. in describing the letter sent out from the Jerusalem council (15:20) this Western text changes the content so that it refers to moral rather than Jewish ritual demands—a modification which indicates an effort to make the narrative conform to later Gentile concepts of the church. We can conclude, therefore, that the shorter text, supported by the majority of manuscripts, is to be preferred in most cases.

Acts is a unique composition. The only book of its kind in the NT, it displays a freedom and grandeur of style superior even to Luke's gospel. As the only source for much of the history of the early church it remains a document of extreme value despite its weaknesses and inaccuracies. Luke understands its story as the unfolding of the divine drama of redemption. The Lord has not yet returned, but in the meantime the word of God is being carried on by the church—the Gentile mission is itself the eschatological action of God.

For Further Study: F. J. Foakes-Jackson and Kirsopp Lake, *The Beginnings of Christianity,* 5 vols., 1920-33. F. J. Foakes-Jackson, *The Acts of the Apostles,* 1931. F. F. Bruce, *Commentary on the Book of Acts,* 1954. G. H. C. Macgregor in *IB,* 1954. Martin Dibelius, *Studies in the Acts of the Apostles,* 1956. Henry J. Cadbury, *The Making of Luke-Acts,* 1958. C. S. C. Williams, *The Acts of the Apostles,* 1958. J. C. O'Neill, *The Theology of Acts,* 1961. H. J. Cadbury in *IDB,* 1962. Floyd V. Filson, *Three Crucial Decades,* 1963.

PREFACE (1:1-5)

Like his **first book** Luke's 2nd volume is dedicated to **Theophilus** (see comment on Luke 1:1-4). The

preface of Acts summarizes that gospel. It began with the ministry of Jesus (no reference is made to the birth stories) and ended with the account of Jesus' ascension; at that time **he had given commandment** that they should witness to these events (Luke 24:48-51). This initial reference to the gospel indicates that the history of Jesus is basic for Acts.

1:3-4a. Only Acts tells us of Jesus' **staying** (or possibly "eating"; the meaning of the Greek word is uncertain) with the disciples for **forty days** after his resurrection. This information conflicts with the view of the Ascension presented in Luke 24:51 (see comment), and the number 40 is a traditional symbol (cf. Exod. 24:18). Apparently Acts intends to connect the risen Christ with the beginning of the church. The charge **not to depart from Jerusalem** seems to acknowledge the contrary tradition of a return to Galilee (cf. Mark 16:7), but this has already been refuted in Luke 24:6. For Luke, Jerusalem is the messianic center; there the resurrection appearances occur, and there the mission of the church is begun.

1:4b-5. Probably **the promise of the Father** (cf. Luke 24:49) is a reference to Joel 2:28-32—a text which will be developed later (2:16-21). The promise has to do with the coming of **the Holy Spirit.** This has been predicted by John (Luke 3:16; cf. Acts 11:16), and fulfillment will take place on Pentecost (2:4). The Spirit is of primary importance for Acts; the whole course of events is moved by its power.

I. THE BEGINNING OF THE CHURCH IN JERUSALEM (1:6–5:42)

A. THE TIME OF PREPARATION (1:6-26)

1:6-11. *The Promise of the Spirit.* Those who **come together** are probably the 11 listed in vs. 13. The place of gathering is apparently the Mount of Olives (vs. 12)—the traditional site of ascension (cf. Zech. 14:4). Since Jesus has mentioned the promise, the apostles suppose that he refers to the coming of **the kingdom.** Jesus, however, insists that the **times** of the end cannot be known, and instead of the kingdom the **Holy Spirit** is coming. Luke's typical interest in the delay of the Lord's return (see comment on Luke 21:5-37) is evidenced; rather than stressing the end he emphasizes the era of the church as the time of God's activity. During this time the leaders are to witness from **Jerusalem . . . to the end of the earth** (cf. Isa. 49:6). This shows that the message of Christ is not limited to **Israel** but is universal in character. The risen Lord is the founder of the Gentile mission.

1:9-11. Suddenly Jesus is **lifted up** into a **cloud,** much as Moses became invisible at his departure from the earth (according to Josephus). **Two men** dressed in the typical garb of heavenly messengers (cf. Luke 24:4) appear. They insist that the apostles must not keep **looking into heaven;** the Lord will return **in the same way** that he left (cf. Dan. 7:13), but the time of his return is in the distant future, after an extensive mission has been accomplished (vs. 8).

1:12-26. *The Restoration of the Twelve.* Returning to Jerusalem, the witnesses of the Ascension enter **the upper room** (cf. Luke 22:12). The list of the 11, except for order, is identical with Luke 6:14-16 (see comment). They pray that the promise will be fulfilled and are joined in **prayer** by the **women** (cf. Luke 8:2; 24:10) and the family of Jesus. **Mary** is important to Luke's gospel, and James, Jesus' brother, will play a significant role in Acts (12:17; 15:13; 21:18). Those closest to Jesus are believed to be involved in the mission of the church.

1:15-20. In the **days** between the Ascension and Pentecost, **Peter** makes a speech to **about a hundred and twenty . . . brethren.** This number may result from the rabbinic notion that leaders of a community should compose a 10th of the total; 10 times 12 equals 120. Into this speech Luke has inserted information about the death of Judas—material not consistent with Matt. 27:3-10. Apparently early tradition devised a variety of stories about the fate of the betrayer. Although **Akeldama** may mean **Field of Blood,** it might be Aramaic for "Field of Sleep," referring to a burial place, or, as Matt. says, a "potter's field." Peter believes Judas' place among the 12 must be filled, since scripture requires it. The first text, Ps. 69:25, predicts the desolation of **his habitation,** i.e. the desolation of the "field" (or farm) which he has purchased, and thus implies Judas' death. The 2nd, Ps. 109:8, insists that his apostolic office be filled.

1:21-26. Two candidates who meet the qualifications are put forth. To be an apostle one must have been a witness of the acts of Jesus from the Baptism until the Ascension. This would include the Resurrection, which is most important, for the apostle's primary task is to **become . . . a witness to his resurrection.** Those nominated are **Joseph . . . Barsabbas,** whose Latin name is **Justus,** and **Matthias,** whose name means "gift of the Lord." Selection is made by casting **lots**—a practice whereby names are inscribed on stones, put into a container, and shaken until one falls out. The method, in the mind of the primitive Christians, gives confidence that ultimately the choice is God's. Matthias is chosen, but never again mentioned in the narrative. The 12 are recognized as the divinely appointed leaders of the church; their number must be preserved. That Peter is their leader is obvious; according to the Western text he is the one who makes the nominations.

B. The Events of Pentecost (2:1-47)

2:1-13. *The Coming of the Spirit.* The disciples are gathered **all together**—whether the 12 or the 120 is not clear. The place is simply identified as **the house.** The feast of Weeks (see Lev. 23:15-21; Deut. 16:9-12) acquired the Greek name **Pentecost** because it was observed 50 days after Passover. Originally an agricultural festival, in Luke's time it commemorated the giving of the law. The occurrence of a miracle is indicated by the **sound . . . of a mighty wind** and the appearance of **tongues** like **fire** which rest on each of the 12 (or 120). The latter is reminiscent of the "voice of the Lord" which "flashes forth flames of fire" (Ps. 29:7), while the term "wind" is another translation for the Greek word "Spirit." John's prediction (Luke 3:16) has been fulfilled.

2:4. Further evidence that the Holy Spirit has been given is seen in the speaking in **tongues.** Although Luke interprets this phenomenon as a miracle of linguistics, the original was probably an outburst of emotional babbling like that discussed in I Cor.

12; 14. This seems to be the meaning of the expression elsewhere in Acts (10:46; 19:6), and the description of the disciples as **filled with new wine** (a wine which was recently produced but intoxicating) fits emotional speech and not proficiency in foreign languages. Actually no miracle was necessary; everybody in the audience spoke either Aramaic or Greek.

2:5-13. Luke has introduced vss. 5-11 to offer a rational explanation of the miracle. Since it is a time of national festival, **Jews . . . from every nation under heaven** are in Jerusalem. That these vss. are not part of the original source is clear from Peter's speech, which addresses primarily the **men of Judea.** Moreover the change of setting is abrupt and unnatural; in vs. 2 the disciples are in the house, but in vs. 6 a huge **multitude** is assembled **at this sound**—whether of the Spirit (vs. 2) or of the speaking is not clear. If one omits the reference in vs. 11 to **Cretans and Arabians** as an editorial addition, the listing of nations moves basically from E to W (on **Asia** see below on 16:6b-8), terminating in Rome. At any rate the point is clear: the gospel announced on Pentecost is universal; it is heard by representatives of the whole world. This is similar to the rabbinic notion that at the giving of the law all the nations of the world were offered an opportunity to accept God's revelation. When one notes that in Philo's description the giving of the law was accompanied by signs of fire and spirit, the parallelism is complete.

2:14-36. *Peter's Sermon.* Peter explains the ecstatic speech. The speakers **are not drunk,** for **it is only the third hour;** it is 9 A.M. and nobody is intoxicated that early. Instead the words of Joel 2:28-32 are being fulfilled: **the Spirit** has been poured out and **the day of the Lord** has come. For Joel the "Lord" was God and the "day" was the end, but for Luke the "Lord" is Jesus and the "day" is the time of preaching. Apocalyptic signs of **blood, and fire, and vapor of smoke** are interpreted to symbolize the importance of the event which has occurred in history. That the speech in its present form is the responsibility of Luke is indicated by the use of the Greek LXX; Peter would have employed an Aramaic version of the prophet.

2:22-36. The main body of the sermon emphasizes the act of God through **Jesus of Nazareth.** The crucial events of his career are his death and resurrection. Although the former was according to the **plan** of God, the Jews (**you**) bear its guilt. It seems unlikely that Luke himself would refer to the Romans, the instruments of Jesus' crucifixion, as **lawless men.** This could be indicative of a genuine reminiscence of Peter's speech, but more likely Luke understands "lawless" to mean "without the law" —a simple reference to Gentiles. The Resurrection is the act of God which **David** predicted. The quotation (Ps. 16:8-11) speaks of one whose **soul** would not be abandoned in **Hades** (the place of death), and who would not **see corruption.** Since David is dead and **buried,** this text must refer to the one who has been raised. Moreover God swore an oath to David that one of his descendants would occupy his throne (Ps. 132:11), and David recognized the Christ as his **Lord** (Ps. 110:1). The conclusion is undeniable: Jesus is the one who was raised, whom God has made **both Lord and Christ.**

2:37-47. *Response to the Proclamation.* The crowd

responds in chorus: **What shall we do?** Peter demands repentance and baptism. These were already linked by John the Baptist, but Luke adds **the gift of the Holy Spirit.** He seems to support a doctrine of baptismal regeneration and to present baptism as a prerequisite for receiving the Spirit. Actually the matter is more complex. Elsewhere he records incidents of conversion without mentioning baptism (9:35; 13:12, 48). Baptism does not always guarantee the Spirit's coming (8:17; 19:6); on one occasion the Spirit precedes it (10:47). Apparently Luke is presenting here an order of admission into the Christian community which is more uniform than the sources warrant.

2:39. The **promise** of forgiveness and the gift of the Spirit is universal; it is granted to those of later generations and distant places.

2:41. In response to this exhortation to salvation **three thousand** are **baptized** and **added** to the church. This number would present difficulties in administering the rite and is no doubt idealized.

2:42-47. Two summaries of life in the community are given: vs. 42 outlines the religious life of the believers; vss. 43-47 present additional information. **The apostles' teaching** would involve instruction in the sort of doctrine contained in Peter's sermon. The term translated **fellowship** means "participation" and stresses the sharing of a common life under the leadership of the 12. The **breaking of bread,** observed **in their homes,** is the distinctive feature of early Christian worship. Although it involved a full meal, the breaking of bread is Luke's terminology for the Lord's Supper (cf. Luke 22:19; 24:35). The supper perhaps took on sacramental ideas in the Pauline churches; the distinctive character of the early Jerusalem practice is a partaking **with glad and generous hearts** and an observance **day by day.** Other acts of worship include **prayers** at home and in **the temple** (cf. 3:1). The fellowship also involves a sharing of **possessions** (cf. 4:32–5:11). At **wonders and signs** an awesome **fear** comes on everyone, and **the Lord** is the one who adds to them **those who were being saved.** Thus the church, like the young Jesus (Luke 2:52), finds **favor** with both God and man.

In many ways the early church resembles the community at Qumran (see pp. 1063-71). As the Dead Sea Scrolls tell us, they too engaged in ritual washings, a common meal, and community of goods.

C. The Acts of Peter and John (3:1–4:31)

3:1-10. *Healing a Lame Man.* Some scholars believe this section of Acts to be another (perhaps older) account of the beginning of the church. The story ends, like the Pentecost narrative, with a description of the receiving of the Spirit (4:31). Luke, however, understands this as a later event, as an illustration of the Spirit's work in empowering the church for its mission.

3:1. As loyal Jews **Peter and John** go **up to the temple at the hour of prayer.** The **ninth hour** is 3 P.M.—the traditional time of evening prayer. Although John Mark is possible, **John** is probably the son of Zebedee. The pair illustrate Luke's fondness for 2 witnesses; earlier they were joined in obeying the Lord's command (Luke 22:8).

3:2. The **gate . . . called Beautiful** cannot be positively identified. One of the E entrances to the temple was decorated with Corinthian bronze and noted for its beauty. If this gate is intended, the disciples, approaching from the E, may still be living in Bethany.

3:3-10. In relating the miracle Luke stresses the seriousness of the illness and the immediacy of the cure. The man has been **lame from birth** (vs. 2), but after the healing he is described as **leaping up and walking.** Luke's reference to **feet and ankles** is hardly medical language, but it does display his interest in details of this sort (cf. Luke 4:38). The actual miracle is performed **in the name of Jesus Christ of Nazareth.** To the ancients the name carried the power and authority of the person. The miracle shows that the leaders of the church possess the power once operating through Jesus. This power has nothing to do with earthly authority, as evidenced by Peter's lack of **silver and gold**—poverty hard to square with 4:35. In any case the power to heal comes ultimately from God; it is he who is praised. The people are amazed and present evidence to support the miracle; they identify the healthy man as the beggar who used to sit at the gate.

3:11-26. *Peter's Address.* The miracle provides the occasion for a sermon. A crowd follows Peter and John to the **portico called Solomon's**—an E section of the great colonnade which surrounded the outer court of the temple. Peter insists that the healing was performed, not by some magical power of the apostles, but by God. He is the God of Israel, **the God of Abraham and of Isaac and of Jacob** (cf. Exod. 3:6, 15). The miracle, however, is but a sign of the power of God which raised Jesus. This Jesus is the one whom the audience delivered to **Pilate** for execution, even though the Roman governor repeatedly found him innocent (cf. Luke 23:4, 14, 22). Here Jesus is interpreted as a fulfillment of the idea of the **servant** of Isa. 53. The servant has been **glorified** (Isa. 52:13), and he is called the **Righteous One** (Isa. 53:11). Jesus is also contrasted with Barabbas (Luke 23:18-25). The latter was **a murderer,** while Jesus was **the Author of life,** i.e. the one whose resurrection heralds the raising of the faithful (26: 23). It is to this death and resurrection of Jesus that the apostles **are witnesses.**

3:16. This vs. is difficult to translate. Its major point is that the lame man was healed by the power of the **name** of Jesus (cf. vs. 6), and it may simply repeat this concept in a parallel statement. In any case the **faith** that is involved is that of the healed man (cf. 14:9), and the RSV's **faith which is through Jesus** is misleading. The NEB is clearer: "And the name of Jesus, by awakening faith, has strengthened this man, whom you see and know, and this faith has made him completely well, as you can all see for yourselves."

3:17-23. Peter now applies this message to the present situation. The crucifixion of Jesus was committed **in ignorance**—a common Lukan theme (e.g. 13:27; Luke 23:34)—yet it was in accord with the plan of God. The idea that **Christ should suffer,** reflecting Isa. 53, is also an emphasis of Luke (cf. 17:3). The sermon calls for repentance and conversion, though no mention of baptism is made. **Times of refreshing** refers to the blessings of the end time, as the parallel reference to the sending of Christ indicates. This could suggest that the raising of the prophet like **Moses** alludes to the resurrection of Jesus, as does vs. 26. At any rate vss. 22-23 are a composite quotation based on Deut. 18:15, 19 and Lev. 23:29. This joining of biblical material may evidence an early collection of OT texts used by early Christian preachers.

3:24-26. The idea of **all the prophets . . . from Samuel** seems strange (cf. 13:20), but Luke probably understands Samuel as the next prophet after Moses and may remember him as the anointer of David, the type of the messianic king. The **covenant** with **Abraham** refers to Gen. 22:18 and is interpreted to suggest that the blessing to **all the families of the earth** is granted through Jesus. The idea of the servant's being sent to Israel first is a typical Lukan theme (cf. 13:46).

4:1-12. *Arrest and Trial.* Peter's speech, like his Pentecost sermon (2:37), is "interrupted" after it is finished. Those who take the apostles into **custody** are **the captain of the temple and the Sadducees.** The former is either the adjutant of the high priest or one of the lesser captains (cf. Luke 22:4) who commands the temple guard. The Sadducees are stereotyped opponents (cf. 23:8) whose introduction into the narrative is not realistic; the concern of the hearing is not with an academic discussion of **the resurrection** but with the question of the authority for healing. Pharisees, who were talking about the resurrection all the time, ran no danger of being imprisoned.

4:3-4. The necessity of delaying the trial **until the morrow** indicates either that the sermon was long —it began shortly after 3 P.M.—or that the hearing is expected to run beyond sundown. At any rate Luke is anxious to show that the trial is legal and thereby presents a parallel to his account of the trial of Jesus (Luke 22:66-71). His summary notes that the preaching has evoked faith and that large numbers are being added to the church.

4:5-7. The hearing of the next day takes place before the council which has recently judged Jesus. The **rulers** hold official positions in the priestly hierarchy, while the **elders** belong to the sanhedrin by ancestry, wealth, and religious prestige. **Caiaphas,** not **Annas,** is the official **high priest** at this time (see comment on Luke 3:2). Some manuscripts read "Jonathan" for **John** and may refer to the Jonathan who became high priest in A.D. 36. The words translated **high-priestly family** can mean either members of the high-priestly clan or men of rank among the priests. Since the charge has to do with the **name** by which the act of power has been accomplished, it is more a matter of Lukan theology (cf. 3:6; 4:16) than of Jewish jurisprudence.

4:8-12. Peter responds under the guidance of the **Spirit.** This reflects the notion that the Spirit comes sporadically for inspiration (cf. I Sam. 19:20). Peter again witnesses to the death and resurrection of Jesus. The Crucifixion is the act of men; the Resurrection is the accomplishment of God. Jesus is described as the **stone which was rejected by you builders**—a reference to Ps. 118:22. Although this stone could be either the capstone or the cornerstone, the latter seems suggested in Luke 20:17-18. This foundation makes possible the superstructure of life. God's power extends beyond healing a lame man

to giving **salvation** to the world. Indeed, **no other** means of salvation is possible.

4:13-22. *The Verdict.* The author presents the sanhedrin's estimate of Peter and John. **Uneducated** lit. means "illiterate," and **common men** classifies the apostles among the "people of the land"—the ordinary folk of Palestine who know not the niceties of Pharisaic piety. **Recognized that they had been with Jesus** may mean that the council has not previously known the identity of Peter and John. More likely, however, Luke stresses the council's recognition of the source of apostolic **boldness,** or courage, as residing in Jesus. The **man that had been healed** is also present. Is it suggested that he too has spent the night in jail, or is he simply evidence introduced into the trial? The notice that the sanhedrin has **nothing to say in opposition** is fulfillment of Luke 21:15.

4:15-20. The council members go into secret session. They admit that a **sign** has been done, but hope to prevent further preaching **in the name of Jesus.** This section of the narrative lacks the ring of reality. How Luke could have received a record of the secret proceedings is problematic, and the picture of Jewish leaders who recognize the power of God yet try to oppose it is artificial. The charge to the apostles is a stage setting for the apostolic declaration of obedience to God. The first part of their response is perhaps proverbial, going back as far as Socrates, who said, "I shall obey God rather than you." The 2nd part is more important to Luke, who hopes to stress the apostles' witness to **what we have seen and heard.** This includes God's acts of power through Jesus, especially his resurrection.

4:21-22. The trial results in release of the prisoners. Since there is **no way to punish** Peter and John it is clear that they are actually innocent. The people sympathize with the disciples as they earlier did with Jesus (Luke 19:48). The magnitude of the cure is again emphasized; the man who was lame from birth is **more than forty years old.**

4:23-31. *Report and Prayer.* After their release Peter and John return **to their friends,** lit. "their own." Though it is sometimes supposed that the friends would include the whole **company of those who believed** (vs. 32), this number seems too large. Perhaps only the apostles, or possibly the 120 (1:15), are intended. The place of meeting is obscure, but it may be the upper room (1:13) or the house of John Mark's mother (12:12).

4:24. At the report of the sanhedrin's warning the disciples **lifted their voices** in prayer. The resulting praise and petition is more an expression of the theology of witness than a prayer which meets the situation. In style the prayer has the quality of Semitic poetry reminiscent of the poems of Luke's birth narrative (Luke 1–2), and its address to God finds a background in passages like Isa. 37:16-20. The title **Sovereign Lord** is based on a Greek term which our word "despot" transliterates; it stresses the mighty power of God and is found also in Luke 2:29.

4:25-30. The prayer quotes Ps. 2:1-2 and finds its fulfillment in the life of Jesus. The **Gentiles** have raged against the Christ, as the crucifixion by the Romans proves. **Herod** has fulfilled the prophecy that **kings of the earth** oppose the **Anointed** of God, and **Pilate** represents the **rulers** who **gathered**

together against him (cf. Luke 23:6-11). Though God's plan has been accomplished through these leaders, Luke here emphasizes the guilt of Pilate and Herod, in contrast to his narrative of Luke 23. The reference to Jesus combines 2 christological ideas: (*a*) he is the **servant** of 2nd Isa.; (*b*) he is the anointed Messiah. The anointing took place at baptism (Luke 3:22; 4:18). For Luke the two ideas are one: Jesus is the Messiah, whose mission demands humble acceptance of the servant's role.

4:31. Just as Pentecost was accompanied by wind and fire, so this event is punctuated with a shaking of the ground (cf. I Kings 19:11-12). The concept of the sporadic coming of the Spirit (cf. vs. 8) is again apparent, and Luke's materializing view of the Spirit is visible in the idea of being **filled** (cf. Luke 3:22). Though the gift of the Spirit followed by a reference to speaking is parallel to the Pentecost events, Luke sees this occurrence as different. Here the Spirit's work becomes actualized in the life of the church; its leaders do not speak in tongues but proclaim the gospel—**the word of God.**

D. Life in the Church (4:32–6:7)

4:32-37. *Community of Goods.* Luke presents a summary of the church's life parallel to 2:42-47 (see comment). The expression **heart and soul** is biblical (cf. Deut. 6:5) and reveals the inner unity of the faithful. The major task of the leaders is to witness **to the resurrection** (cf. 1:22). The sharing of possessions is voluntary (cf. 5:4) rather than required, as at Qumran (see above on 2:42-47). Moreover there is no community of production or notion that a new economic order is being established. The laying of money **at the apostles' feet** is reminiscent of ancient customs in transfer of possessions or of religious dedication of an offering to the gods.

4:36-37. A specific illustration is **Barnabas.** His real name is **Joseph**, but the Aramaic original of his surname is elusive. Some think it is "son of Nebo," the Babylonian god. The name could mean "son of a prophet," as well as "son of exhortation," i.e. **encouragement.** Luke's derivation is based on knowledge of Barnabas' later activity (cf. 11:22). Though he is **a native of Cyprus,** Col. 4:10 says he is a cousin of John Mark—an inhabitant of Jerusalem.

5:1-11. *The Judgment of God.* In contrast to the generosity of Barnabas is the case of **Ananias** and **Sapphira;** judgment as well as grace is operating in the community. The story seems to be a legend which makes this point. Its background is found in OT passages like Josh. 7:1; I Kings 14:1-20. At Qumran one who lied about his wealth was excluded from the common meal for a year and deprived of a 4th of his food ration. The name **Ananias** can be translated "the Lord is gracious," while **Sapphira** means "beautiful."

5:1-3. According to the story Ananias sells **a piece of property** and brings to the apostles a portion of the **proceeds,** holding back the rest for himself. Thus the statement that everything was held "in common" (4:32) is qualified. **Peter,** who seems to be endowed with a kind of prophetic power (cf. Luke 6:8; 19:30), rebukes Ananias for attempting to **lie to the Holy Spirit.** Here the Spirit seems to be a special possession of the church and its leaders, and falsehood

toward the Spirit is the same as toward God (vs. 4).

5:4. This vs. is apparently Luke's expansion to make clear that the sin of Ananias is not his failure to share his goods but his hypocrisy—his effort to appear generous when he is really miserly. The danger of wealth is a Lukan theme (e.g. 1:18; 8:18). The guilt is paradoxical: Ananias is charged with having **contrived this deed in your heart** even though **Satan filled your heart** to do it (vs. 3; cf. Luke 22:3, 22).

5:5-6. It is possible to interpret Ananias' death as coincidental or as the result of emotional shock, but Luke understands the event as a miracle of God's judgment. The punishment seems radical, devoid of the Christian concept of forgiveness (Luke 17:4) and contradicting the divine forbearance in "times of ignorance" (17:30). The **young men** (lit. "youngers") who perform the burial duties (cf. vs. 10) have been thought by some to represent an official body within the church, parallel to the "elders" (e.g. 11:30; 14:23) but mere reference to those of youthful vigor is more probable.

5:7-10. Sapphira serves as a 2nd witness to judgment against dishonesty. The implication that the church is still in session 3 hours after the death of Ananias is another element suggesting the unreality of the narrative. Sapphira repeats the lie of her husband and is charged with conspiring with him to **tempt the Spirit.** Thus the OT motif of testing God (cf. Exod. 17:2) is taken up; here the emphasis is on going as far as possible before retaliation strikes. Sapphira's death could be attributed to the shocking news of her husband's fate, but Luke interprets it as a sign of God's wrath.

5:11. In view of the events, the news that **fear** fell on **all who heard** is not surprising, but the statement sounds a common Lukan theme (e.g. 2:43; 19:17). The term **church** appears here for the first time in Acts. In the LXX the same Greek word is used for the assembly of the people of Israel under the call of God. Usage on the part of the Christians indicates their understanding of themselves as the true people of God, called to do his work. In Acts the term can be used either for the whole body of believers (e.g. 9:31) or for the local manifestation of God's people (e.g. 13:1).

5:12-16. *Acts of Power.* Another Lukan summary, this passage expands the reference to "wonders and signs" of 2:43 and answers the prayer of 4:29-30. It is not clear whether those who are **together in Solomon's Portico** (cf. 3:11) included only the apostles or the whole church. If the latter, **the rest** who **dared** not **join them** would be people who refrained from association with the Christians for lack of courage. This interpretation would be in tension with vs. 14, where enthusiastic uniting with the community is recorded. It is better to understand those gathered as the apostles; they are the real subject of the text. Those who do not join them are ordinary members of the church who lack the power attributed to the leaders.

5:15-16. The carrying of **sick into the streets** for healing is reminiscent of Mark 6:56, and cure by the **shadow** of **Peter** is parallel to healings accomplished by handkerchiefs carried from the body of Paul (19:12). **Fall on** is lit. "overshadow"—the same verb that is used for the cloud at Jesus' transfiguration (Luke 9:34)—and is thus a symbol of the divine power. Here it is suggested that an apostle has this power working in his ministry—a power which emanates from his person without direct physical contact. This ministry draws people from towns beyond Jerusalem and successfully heals **all**.

5:17-26. *Imprisonment and Release.* This section involving a 2nd arrest and trial of the apostles is parallel to 4:1-22; the miraculous release from prison anticipates 12:6-11. Though it is sometimes supposed that vss. 17-22 are a doublet, the account may be historical. Jewish legal practice, at least at a later date, involved 2 steps, warning and legal action. In any case Luke understands this as a 2nd legal encounter which reflects a heightening of the official opposition.

5:17-18. As the story goes, the **high priest** and the **party of the Sadducees** take action against the **apostles,** who, except for Peter (vs. 29), are unidentified. The opponents are **filled with jealousy** apparently because of the growth of the Christian community (vs. 14). The **common prison** is lit. the "public" jail, but the adjective could be an adverb —the apostles were thrown into prison "publicly."

5:19-21*a*. For Luke the **angel of the Lord** is the angel of God (cf. 7:30). The same sort of supernatural being protected Daniel during his imprisonment (Dan. 6:22). It is sometimes supposed that since the angel performs mundane acts the story suggests human complicity. Luke, however, understands the escape as a miracle. It has taken place **at night,** but the apostles do not begin their teaching **in the temple** until **daybreak.** Though the temple is open during the night, worshipers do not come until morning. The message proclaimed is here described as **all the words of this life.** The expression means essentially the same as "the message of this salvation" (13:26).

5:21*b*-26. It is not clear whether Luke understands the **council and all the senate of Israel** as 2 separate bodies or, correctly, as 2 different ways to refer to one group. The report that the doors of the prison are **locked** and the **sentries** still in position indicates the magnitude of the miracle. That an angel could go unnoticed through locked doors is possible, but the escape of the apostles by this means is incomprehensible. Little wonder that a typical Lukan expression of amazement is repeated: What would this **come to?** The **captain of the temple** is the chief of the temple police; the **officers** are his subordinates. Their fear of **being stoned** by the mob is perhaps unrealistic, but the point is clear: though hated by the leaders, the Christians are loved by the people.

5:27-42. *Before the Council.* The apostles are brought before the sanhedrin. The previous prohibition **to teach in this name,** i.e. in the name of Jesus (4:18), has been ignored. In contrast to Matt. 27:25 this text presents the council as resisting responsibility for the **blood** of Jesus.

5:29-32. Peter's response is a sermon in miniature. Stress is placed on the church's witness to the death, resurrection, and exaltation of Jesus, as well as to the opportunity for **repentance . . . and forgiveness of sins** through him. The obligation to **obey God rather than men** is more clearly stated than in 4:19, and the ensuing activity of the apostles has confirmed their obedience. The reference to Jesus'

hanging . . . on a tree is reminiscent of Deut. 21:22; the same terminology appears in a later sermon of Peter (10:39). The word translated **Leader** is rendered "Author" (of life) in 3:15. Though it could carry a military connotation like "captain," the basic meaning is an originator. In this context Luke sees Jesus as the one who leads the way to salvation. The idea that the **Holy Spirit** participates in the witness of the apostles presupposes their reception of the Spirit (2:33), the boldness of their proclamation (4:31), and their acts of power (4:12-16).

5:33-37. The members of the council are **enraged** by the speech—lit. "sawed through," or "cut to the quick." More irenic is the spirit of **Gamaliel.** He belonged to the moderate school of Hillel and as a **Pharisee** would be more sympathetic with the Christian doctrine of the resurrection. Jewish tradition holds him in high esteem, but his tolerance seems to have had little effect on his pupil, Saul of Tarsus (22:3). Luke attributes to Gamaliel 2 historical errors: **Theudas** did not lead his revolt until some 10 years after this speech; and **Judas,** who is said to have led a later insurrection, actually revolted at the time of the census of A.D. 6. Some scholars interpret these errors as an indication that Luke carelessly used Josephus' Antiquities of the Jews as a source.

While it is possible to acknowledge the essential historicity of Gamaliel's speech, clearly its real burden is to support Luke's apologetic (cf. Luke 20:4). The officials of Judaism and Rome should let Christianity run its course; when it has reached its goal, it will be evident that God has been working in it. When Gamaliel is reported as saying, **if it is of God,** the form of his expressions assumes the reality of the condition. His conclusion is Luke's: **You might even be found opposing God** or, as the Greek says in a terse adjective, "God-fighting."

5:40-42. The council takes Gamaliel's advice, but not without reservations; the apostles are beaten with the traditional "forty lashes less one" (II Cor. 11:24) and charged to keep silence. However, the leaders of the church rejoice that they have been found **worthy to suffer dishonor for the name** of Jesus (cf. Luke 6:22); and they continue their daily worship **in the temple and at home,** together with **teaching and preaching** lit. "the Christ Jesus," which as Greek idiom may mean either "Christ Jesus" or **Jesus as the Christ.**

II. The Mission to Israel (6:1-9:31)

A. The Appointment of the 7 (6:1-7)

Here Luke, apparently following a new source, turns to a new subject. Evidence of a change in source material is seen in the abrupt presentation of 2 groups, the **Hellenists** and the **Hebrews,** without explanation. The Christians are called **disciples** for the first time in the Acts narrative, and mention of **Antioch** could indicate the origin of the source (cf. 11:26). As to the identity of the Hellenists, 2 major theories have been proposed: (*a*) They are Greeks; some manuscripts of 11:20 use the term "Hellenist" in this sense. (*b*) They are Greek-speaking Jews who have lived outside of Palestine but have returned. Luke supports the latter; his introduction of Gentile converts into the narrative is later and with considerable emphasis (10:1-11:18).

6:1. The dispute between the Hellenists and the Hebrews ostensibly concerns the administration of the dole. The care of **widows** was inherited from Jewish practice, but the method of **distribution** is not clear. It is not certain whether serving **tables** describes the role of a waiter at the common meal or refers to the money tables of the community's administration. At any rate the widows of the Hellenists seem to be **neglected,** perhaps supposing that they do not receive a fair share.

6:2-6. To solve the problem **the twelve** summon the whole church and propose the selection of **seven men** to supervise the distribution of food. It seems obvious that the apostles should not forgo **preaching the word of God,** i.e. the gospel, in order to wait tables or administer finance. The men who are to be appointed should be filled with the **Spirit** and **wisdom.** That a certain amount of worldly wisdom would be required is clear, but a special endowment with the Spirit does not seem necessary for such a mundane task. This, together with the use of the sacred number 7, suggests a more important sort of leadership. Whereas most texts assume that the selection is made by the church, at least one manuscript implies that the choice was made by the 12. In any case the important action is performed by the apostles—the laying on of **hands.** This ceremony, which elsewhere in Acts is related to the conveying of the Spirit (8:17; 19:6), is understood here in the OT sense of transmitting authority (cf. Num. 27:23). Luke interprets the ritual in terms of ordination practice common to the church of his day.

Considerable debate has raged about the actual function of the **seven** in the early church. It has been urged e.g. that they were the deacons of the Jerusalem community; but the title is lacking in the text, and the duties do not conform to the practices of that office in the later church. Most likely they represent a distinct faction within the Christian community. All their names are Greek; the absence of Hebrews from a rations committee seems difficult to explain. Of the 2 Hellenists about whom we have information (**Stephen** and **Philip**) there is no record of serving tables but reports of their **ministry of the word** (6:7–7:60; 8:4-40; 21:8). It is surprising, too, that the persecution which Stephen provoked did not seriously affect the apostles (8:1). We can conclude that within the Jerusalem church were 2 groups: the Hebrews with the apostles as their leaders and the Hellenists under the guidance of the 7.

6:7. This summary refers again to the increase in the church's membership. It includes the only record of converts from the Jewish priesthood. Apparently the church had little impact on the cultic leaders of the Jews and, in contrast to the sect of the Dead Sea Scrolls, had little interest in the priestly tradition.

B. Acts of Stephen (6:8–8:3)

6:8–7:1. *The Arrest of Stephen.* The activity of one of the 7 is here described. Possible doublets within the narrative have led to a theory of 2 sources. The charge against Stephen is repeated (vss. 11, 13-14), and his stoning is presented as both mob violence (7:54, 57-58a) and legal action (7:1, 58b-59; see below on 7:57-58). The account of the glory of

Stephen's **face** (vs. 15) should probably be joined with the prayer of 7:59-60. Perhaps Luke has adapted sources to his own purpose, inserting Stephen's speech into a narrative which proceeds well without it.

6:8-10. Since Stephen is **full of the Spirit** (vs. 3) acts of **power** are to be expected from him. Though Luke lists no specific miracles, Stephen's **wonders and signs** are probably similar to those attributed to the apostles (5:12). It is apparently his preaching which arouses opposition. Those unable to **withstand** Stephen's **wisdom** cannot be positively identified since the Greek is ambiguous. They certainly include members of a **synagogue** composed of Hellenistic Jews, but it is unclear whether Luke conceives of one synagogue that includes **Freedmen**

The Biblical Archaeologist, Vol. VII, No. 1, Fig. 9, by G. Ernest Wright

Theodotus inscription from the Synagogue of the Freedmen (see comment 6:8-10); the inscription reads: "Theodotus, son of Vettenos, priest and ruler of the synagogue, son of a ruler of the synagogue, grandson of a ruler of the synagogue, built the synagogue for the reading of the law and for the teaching of the commandments; furthermore, the hospice and the chambers, and the water installation for lodging of needy strangers. The foundation stone thereof had been laid by his fathers, and the elders, and Simonides."

... **Cyrenians** ... **Alexandrians** ... **those from Cilicia and Asia** or as many as 5 different groups. Most likely he means 2: the synagogue of the Freedmen, which is composed of Cyrenians and Alexandrians, and a group from Cilicia and Asia. The **Freedmen,** lit. "Libertines," are usually identified as Jews who have been redeemed from slavery—perhaps descendants of those captured by Pompey—but some scholars accept the variant reading "Libyans" as a reference to the area from which the people of Cyrene and Alexandria come. Regardless of the interpretation, the opponents seem to be Hellenistic Jews—representatives of the background from which Stephen comes.

6:11–7:1. This group is able to arouse **the people** (in contrast to 5:26) and bring the case to the sanhedrin. The charge is reminiscent of that made against Jesus (Mark 14:58). **False witnesses** do not seem to be needed, since Stephen's speech confirms his opposition to **this holy place,** i.e. the temple. However, his view of **the law,** according to Luke, is true, so that the witnesses appear guilty of falsehood in this respect. The transformation of Stephen's face has its background in texts like Exod. 34:29-35; it reflects the early Christian trend toward glorification of the martyrs.

7:2-53. *Stephen's Speech.* Though the speeches of Acts often rest on valid tradition, they usually reflect Luke's own understanding of the events. Stephen's, since it goes beyond the idea of serving tables (6:2-3), may contain accurate historical information about the beliefs of the Hellenists. On the other hand it does not directly answer the charges, and it begins with a form of address identical with that of one of Paul's speeches (22:1). It seems to have 3 main points: (*a*) the major events of divine revelation have occurred outside Palestine; (*b*) God's purposes are continually being misunderstood and rejected by Israel; (*c*) true worship of God cannot be confined to the temple of Jerusalem. The last point proves Stephen's opposition to the temple; the whole sermon is based on Luke's understanding of the law.

7:2-8. *The Promise to Abraham.* Though this account is based on Gen., Stephen appears to make 2 errors: (*a*) The call of God is said to have come to the patriarch **when he was in Mesopotamia, before he lived in Haran.** But according to Gen. 11: 27–12:5 God's command to go to the promised land occurred after Abraham was in Haran. This mistake could rest on texts like Gen. 15:7, where the impression is given that the call came in **the land of the Chaldeans.** (*b*) It is said that Abraham did not move to the promised land until **after his father died.** Yet references to the age of Terah in relation to the chronology of Abraham (Gen. 11:26, 32; 12:4) indicate that Terah lived 60 years after his son left Haran. Both of these mistakes are found in Jewish writers, e.g. Philo.

7:5-8. Luke emphasizes the fact that Abraham did not actually possess any of the **inheritance . . . , not even a foot's length** (cf. Deut. 2:5). For **four hundred years** (430, according to Exod. 12:40) the Israelites were **aliens** and slaves in the land of Egypt. God's action in redeeming them was primarily, not to give them a new land, but to provide them with valid worship at Sinai; Gen. 15:13-14 is interpreted in light of Exod. 3:12. Throughout this period the continuity of the people of God was preserved in the **covenant of circumcision,** which had been granted outside Palestine and prior to the temple.

7:9-16. *Salvation in Egypt.* Stephen turns to **Joseph** and his brothers, **the patriarchs.** Some criticism of the fathers is implied in their being jealous, but the main point of the Joseph story is that **God was with him**—the purposes of God are accomplished in spite of the ignorance and opposition of men. Two questions of accuracy can be raised: (*a*) The **kindred** of **Jacob** who **went down into Egypt** are said to number **seventy-five souls,** while the Hebrew text of Gen. 46:27 says "seventy"—evidence that Luke used the LXX, which reads "seventy-five." (*b*) It is said that Jacob (or possibly Joseph) and the patriarchs were buried in **Shechem;** but, whereas Josh. 24:32 records the burial of Joseph there, Gen. 50:13 (cf. Gen. 23:19) says that Jacob was buried at Hebron—the place where the traditional tombs of the patriarchs can be seen today. In any case the main meaning of the text is clear: the salvation of Israel occurred outside the Holy Land through a man who had been rejected.

7:17-34. *The Early Life and Call of Moses.* The account of Moses' career is based on the early chs. of Exod. In vs. 20 the word translated **beautiful** is found in the LXX of Exod. 2:2, but the idea that

as an infant he was particularly pleasing **before God** is not recorded in the OT. While Jewish writers sound this theme, Luke may be suggesting a parallel to texts like Luke 2:52. Similarly vs. 22 has no basis in the Exod. narrative. Though **the wisdom of the Egyptians** was proverbial, the notion that Moses was **mighty in his words** is contradicted by Exod. 4:10. Perhaps Luke is presenting him as a type of Jesus, who was "mighty in deed and word before God" (Luke 24:19).

7:23-29. The information that Moses was **forty years old** when he attempted to deliver his **brethren** is lacking in the OT, but the division of his life of 120 years (Deut. 34:7) into 3 periods of 40 years (cf. vs. 30) is found in Jewish tradition. The content of vs. 25 is also missing from the Exod. account, though Jewish writers sometimes excused Moses for his good intentions. Luke, in presenting the failure of Moses to be understood, is probably following the motif of the prophet who is rejected by his own (cf. Luke 4:24). Though the account of the quarrel between the 2 **sons of Israel** is slightly different from Exod. 2:13, the important feature is the reason for Moses' flight from Egypt. Whereas in Exod. 2:15 Moses flees from Pharaoh, in Acts he retreats into exile because of rejection by his people.

7:30-34. Again, it is on foreign soil that God speaks to Moses. Though Luke refers to the place as **Mount Sinai** in contrast to "Horeb" (Exod. 3:1), the 2 terms are used interchangeably to refer to the same mountain. Luke presents the command for Moses to remove his **shoes** as coming after the words of revelation. By putting the command in climactic position Luke may hope to stress the fact that, as in the case of Abraham, the **holy ground** of God's call is located outside the Holy Land.

7:35-43. *Opposition to Moses.* The one who was repudiated as **a ruler and a judge** (cf. vs. 27) has been chosen by God as **ruler and deliverer;** this both parallels the rejection of Joseph (vs. 9) and anticipates the redemption through Jesus (Luke 24:21). Moses is also a type of the miracle worker, as the plagues of Exod. 7–12 show. The reference to a **prophet** like Moses, based on Deut. 18:15, is a typical Lukan theme (e.g. 3:22). **The congregation in the wilderness** is reminiscent of the assembly of the people to receive the law (e.g. Deut. 9:10; 18:16). Though possibly based on Deut. 33:2, the idea that the law was mediated through angels (cf. vs. 53) developed in Jewish tradition (cf. Gal. 3:19; Heb. 2:2). The description of the law as **living oracles** suggests that its content is divine utterances which give life to the hearer (cf. Deut. 32:47; Ezek. 20:11).

7:39-42a. Even though Moses and the law have been glorified by tradition, his contemporaries **thrust him aside** as the 2 Hebrews had done years before (vs. 27). Almost no blame is placed on **Aaron** for the golden **calf** (cf. Exod. 32:2-4, 25); the burden of guilt must be borne by the people. **The works of their hands** is a typical phrase of the Jewish polemic against idolatry (cf. Ps. 115:4). **The host of heaven** refers to the astral deities of Babylonian and Assyrian religion, whose worship involved the adoration of idols (cf. Deut. 4:19; Jer. 8:2).

7:42b-43. The quotation from **the book of the prophets** is from the LXX of Amos 5:25-27, which varies in some respects from the Hebrew text (see comment). Both the LXX and the Hebrew, however, read "beyond Damascus," referring to Assyria, rather than **Babylon.** Luke understands the Babylonian captivity as the punishment for apostasy in the desert. For Amos the time of wilderness wandering was a golden age, but Luke sees it as a time of idolatry.

7:44-53. Building the Temple. At last the charges against Stephen are taken up. The indictment that he speaks **against this holy place** is confirmed, though his attack on the temple is based on **the law** (6:13). The narrative which makes these points is not without problems. Vs. 44 does not logically follow vs. 42; the approval of the tabernacle contradicts the opposition to the worship in the wilderness. Possibly vss. 38-48 represent another source which has been inserted here, and the only connection between the 2 sections seems to be the repetition of the word **tent.**

7:44-47. Luke's description of the tabernacle as the **tent of witness** employs the typical LXX substitute for the Hebrew "tent of meeting." The information that God presented **Moses** with a **pattern** of the portable sanctuary is found in Exod. 25:40. The tabernacle is thereby contrasted with the temple **made with hands.** From the time of **Joshua** to **David** this tabernacle served as the place of worship. It was David who asked permission to **find** a permanent **habitation** for God (cf. Ps. 132:5). Actually, although the following vss. indicate that "habitation" refers to the temple, the best manuscripts say it was "for the house of Jacob." If this reading is original, it may reflect the reference to the house of David in II Sam. 7:26. Perhaps Luke views the place of worship as a dwelling for both God and the people, or perhaps the substitution of "house of Jacob" for "Mighty One of Jacob" in his allusion to Ps. 132:5 is a subtle criticism of the temple implying the same idea as vs. 48.

7:48-50. The title **Most High** is used in the OT to express the recognition of the true God by foreigners (Gen. 14:17-24); it is a favorite phrase of Luke (Luke 1:32, 35). When Stephen says that God **does not dwell in houses made with hands,** he implies that heathen gods do, but that God cannot be confined to the temple. The idea that neither earth nor heaven can contain God is found in Solomon's prayer of dedication (I Kings 8:27), but the quotation which Stephen uses is the LXX of Isa. 66:1-2.

7:51-53. Stephen's final word is a collection of judgments based on the OT. They are **stiff-necked people** (Exod. 33:3), **uncircumcised in heart** (Lev. 26:41) **and ears** (Jer. 6:10). **The Holy Spirit,** which they have resisted, is the spirit of prophecy which has been speaking to them through **the law;** Israel's failure to understand the law has led to her distortion of worship. The notion that all the prophets were persecuted and **killed** cannot be supported by the OT but had become traditional (cf. Luke 13: 34). According to that tradition it is not surprising that the descendants of the **fathers . . . murdered** Jesus, who is here called **the Righteous One** (see above on 3:14).

7:54-8:3. The Stoning of Stephen. The stern words of Stephen's conclusion provoke a bitter reaction. On **enraged** see above on 5:33-39. The gnashing of **teeth** is a biblical figure describing the hostility of the wicked against the righteous (e.g. Pss. 35:16;

37:12; 112:10). By way of contrast Stephen is presented as possessing the Spirit and seeing **the heavens opened.** Possession of the Spirit was a normal feature of his religious life (cf. 6:5), but here **the Holy Spirit** seems to be a special gift which makes possible this unique experience. The theme of visionary experience preceding martyrdom is found in Jewish literature.

7:56. As to the content of the vision, 2 features are important: (a) Stephen refers to Jesus as the **Son of man**—the only such usage outside the gospels. The prediction of Luke 22:69 is fulfilled, and Jesus is now to be recognized as the supernatural Messiah of Jewish eschatology. (b) The Son of man is portrayed, not as sitting (Luke 22:69), but as **standing at the right hand of God.** Perhaps this symbolizes the one who stands as advocate of the righteous in the time of judgment (Job 16:19), or possibly Luke is depicting Jesus as standing to welcome Stephen into heaven. If so, the Lukan note of ascension immediately after death is again sounded (cf. Luke 23:43).

7:57-58. It is not clear whether Luke imagines a lynching or a legal process (see above on 6:8-7:1). The information that they (the council or the people?) **rushed together upon him** and threw him **out of the city** suggests mob violence; but the reference to stoning by **the witnesses** reflects judicial procedure, since witnesses were customarily the executioners. Moreover stoning was normally performed outside the city and was the regular punishment for blasphemy (Lev. 24:10-23)—a charge perhaps reflected in **stopped their ears.** The victim was usually put in the bottom of a pit and heavy stones were pushed upon him. No record is found of the executioners' removing **their garments,** although the victim was stripped of his clothing.

7:59-60. The death of Stephen reflects motifs from the passion of Jesus: he too committed his spirit to God (Luke 23:46); he too prayed for the forgiveness of his executioners (Luke 23:34).

8:1a. The name **Saul** is used for Paul until 13:9. It is a Hebrew name (cf. I Sam. 9:2 ff.) meaning "asked"; Paul is Latin and means "little." Cf. Jewish "John" and Roman "Mark" (12:12). That Paul **was consenting to** Stephen's **death** has been interpreted as hinting that he participated in the official action of the sanhedrin (cf. 22:20; 26:10).

8:1b-3. The effect of the execution was **persecution . . . against the church.** The idea that **all** were **scattered** is modified by Luke's indication that the persecution did not disturb the **apostles.** As some manuscripts say, these leaders "remained in Jerusalem." The opposition was directed against the Hellenists (see above on 6:1-7) just as the stoning was aimed at one of their number, Stephen. There is abundant evidence that Paul persecuted the church (Gal. 1:13, 23; I Cor. 15:9; Phil. 3:6); since he was from Tarsus of Cilicia, he could have been one of the Cilicians who originally opposed Stephen (6:9).

B. THE ACTS OF PHILIP (8:4-40)

8:4-13. The Mission to Samaria. Perhaps following a new source, Luke presents the extension of the mission beyond Judea. The leader of this movement is **Philip,** one of the Hellenists (see above on 6:1-7). He goes to **a city of Samaria** which is unnamed, but later tradition connects Simon the magician (vss. 9-24) with Gitta, halfway between the Samaritan capital Sebaste (OT Samaria) and Caesarea (see color map 15). Though the narrative finds the impetus for this expansion in the persecution of vs. 1*b*, the Hellenists believed a mission beyond the shadows of the temple to be of the essence of Christianity. To be sure, the Samaritans were similar to the Jews, worshiping the same God and following the first 5 books of the Law; yet they were considered by the Jews to be inferior (cf. John 4:9, which, however, represents an extreme view) and therefore were a step toward the Gentiles. Possibly Luke sees the evangelizing of Samaria as fulfilling the unrealized intention of Jesus (cf. Luke 9:51-56).

8:4-8. Philip's mission is described in general terms. His primary activity is to proclaim Jesus as **the Christ.** I.e. Jesus is the triumphant Messiah through whom God has acted to offer man salvation. This is especially seen in the later reference to preaching **good news about the kingdom of God** (vs. 12); God's rule has broken into history with Jesus and now operates in the church. The power of God so worked in him that healing was done in his **name** (3:6) and now that power is operating in the church's proclamation, **the word of God** (vs. 14). The potency of this message is confirmed by **signs.** Like Stephen (6:8) Philip is able to cast out demons and cure the sick. The mission evokes an enthusiastic response.

8:9-11. In the tradition of the later church **Simon** the magician became the arch heretic—the father of Gnosticism. Soothsayers and astrologers were common in the ancient world, but Simon is unusual in demanding special loyalty to himself (cf. 5:36). Indeed all the people **from the least to the greatest** acclaim him to be the **power of God.** This seems to suggest that his followers worship him as a divine being—the supernatural power which stands between man and the high God as mediator.

8:12-13. The power of Christianity is greater than the power of magic. The Samaritans believe the preaching of Philip and confirm their faith by baptism—a baptism which does not convey the Spirit (vs. 16). Simon too is **baptized,** apparently more impressed by the miracles than by the message; he continues **with Philip,** becoming a kind of disciple.

8:14-25. *Apostolic Confirmation.* This text affirms the authority of the **apostles** in supervising the mission of the church. Such close cooperation between the Hellenists and the Jerusalem leaders seems unlikely, and the power to confer the Spirit does not appear to be the special prerogative of the 12 (cf. 9:17). The account of the sending of **Peter and John** indicates Luke's typical interest in 2 witnesses. Though it is possible that the 2nd man is to be identified as John Mark, more likely the companion of Peter is John the son of Zebedee; the 2 are often associated in Luke (e.g. 22:8) and Acts (e.g. 3:1).

8:14-17. The notion that the Spirit is not conveyed through baptism is also found in 19:1-6. There those who do not receive the Holy Spirit have been baptized in John's baptism, while here the rite has been performed **in the name of the Lord Jesus.** Luke is not describing some practice of baptism which differs from that of 2:38; he is stressing the apostolic leadership of the church. Apparently laying on of hands was a regular feature of early bap-

tismal practice; at Ephesus emphasis is put on re-baptism of the converts, with laying on of hands as a normal conclusion of the ritual (19:5-6). The Christian rite involved a combination of John's baptism and baptism with the Spirit (1:5). Possibly immersion in water symbolized the former, while laying on of hands portrayed the latter. Earlier the laying on of hands depicted the commission to special service (6:6); here it confers to the converts of Samaria the right to be a part of the church.

8:18-24. While the narrative suggests that Simon covets the authority to confirm Christians, he is really interested in gaining the power to perform miracles. Simon's attempt to purchase the right of the apostles has given birth to the term "simony"—the attempt to obtain church office by money. Peter makes it clear that the authority to convey the Spirit is a **gift of God;** he heaps on Simon a stern rebuke, based on OT allusions (cf. Deut. 12:12; Ps. 78:37; Deut. 29:18). It has been debated whether **if possible** means if Simon repents or if God wills—the latter implying that God remains free in his right not to forgive. The remorse of Simon is perhaps a polemic against Simonians of Luke's day, but the addition in some manuscripts that Simon "did not cease from much weeping" is exaggerated.

8:25. The apostles go back **to Jerusalem,** the seat of authority. On their way they preach to Samaritan **villages.** Here **the gospel** is called **the word of the Lord** (cf. vs. 14).

8:26-40. *Mission to a Eunuch.* The narrative returns to the activity of **Philip.** Revelation through an **angel** is a common Lukan motif (e.g. Luke 1:11, 26; 2:9), and here the heavenly messenger performs the same function as **the Spirit** (vs. 29). **Gaza,** the ancient S-most city of the Philistines, is SW of Jerusalem on the route to Egypt (see color map 14). The **Ethiopian** is a Nubian from an area S of Egypt, not an Abyssinian. As a **eunuch** he cannot be admitted to the Jewish congregation (Deut. 23:1), despite the more tolerant attitude found in Isa. 56:3 (cf. Jer. 38:7-13). Luke shares the latter views, since he considers the Ethiopian to be not a Gentile but a proselyte—he has been **to Jerusalem to worship** and is reading one of the prophets. The first Gentile convert, according to Luke, is Cornelius (10:44-48); Philip's mission only prepares the way. In the mind of the Hellenists, however, the eunuch may have represented a non-Jew. At best he is on the fringes of Jewish religion. **Candace** is the title of the **queen,** not her name.

8:29-31. Under the guidance of the Spirit, Philip runs after the Ethiopian's **chariot** (or carriage). He hears the eunuch **reading,** for in the ancient world reading was done aloud.

8:32-33. The text is Isa. 53:7*b*-8*a*. Since this is one of the first clear uses of this important passage in reference to Jesus, the question can be raised whether this usage appeared so early in the life of the church. Of course it is possible that the earliest Christians interpreted the meaning of Christ out of the servant poems of 2nd Isa., and some scholars hold that Jesus understood his own role in light of these passages. However, the term "servant" is not applied to Jesus here and the references to one who has borne our sins (Isa. 53:4-5, 8*b*) are lacking. Luke is simply emphasizing his conviction that OT expectation has been fulfilled in the suffering and resurrection of Jesus (cf. Luke 24:25-27, 44-47). The **lamb** which is **dumb** refers to the silence of Jesus at his trial (Luke 23:9) and the denial of **justice** in his unjust execution (Luke 23:4, 14-15, 22). His **generation** has been destroyed by his crucifixion. The prediction that **his life is taken up from the earth** has been fulfilled in his resurrection, ascension, and exaltation.

8:34-38. Philip preaches **the good news of Jesus.** His sermon apparently includes the demand of 2:38 to repent and be **baptized.** The Western text adds a call to confession by Philip and the eunuch's response (RSV footnote). This addition seeks to moderate the abruptness of baptism without instruction and evidence of faith.

8:39-40. After the baptism, the Spirit sends Philip on his mission. Here some manuscripts say that the Spirit came on the eunuch and the angel caught up Philip. This would indicate that the Ethiopian has received the Holy Spirit at baptism. Philip proceeds to **Azotus** (OT Ashdod), preaching in towns (perhaps Lydda and Joppa; cf. 9:32-43) on the way to **Caesarea** (see color map 15, and below on 10:1-8).

C. The Conversion of Paul (9:1-31)

9:1-9. *The Heavenly Vision.* The account now picks up the narrative of 8:3. The conversion of Saul (Paul) was not without preparation; he had witnessed the stoning of Stephen as well as the persistence of his victims. The actual conversion is described 3 times in Acts (9:3-19; 22:6-16; 26:12-18), all with minor variations.

9:1-2. It is sometimes supposed that I Macc. 15:16-21 establishes the right of the **high priest** to extradite criminals who had fled to another country, but recognition of that right by the authorities of **Damascus** in Syria (see color map 14) in Paul's day seems unlikely (cf. II Cor. 11:32). That a group of unorthodox Jews flourished in Damascus is confirmed by the Damascus Document—a writing composed by a sectarian faction similar to that at Qumran (see pp. 1063-71). Paul plans to persecute those **belonging to the Way**—an early designation for the Christians (19:9, 23; 24:14, 22) which is also used in the Dead Sea Scrolls for the Qumran sect.

9:3-7. Paul's vision is presented in the form of ancient symbolism. The **light from heaven** signifies divine revelation, and the heavenly **voice** is reminiscent of the supernatural word heard in rabbinic debate (cf. Luke 3:22). The charge against Paul makes it evident that persecuting Christ is the same as persecuting Christ (cf. Luke 10:16). In this account Paul seems to hear, but not see, the heavenly spokesman (cf. **when his eyes were opened,** vs. 8); his own writings assert that he has "seen Jesus our Lord" (I Cor. 9:1). The command that he go to **the city** to receive instruction conflicts with his own assertion that he did not receive his commission to preach from men (Gal. 1:11-16), and the information that his companions **stood speechless** is not in harmony with 26:14. Similarly Luke's statement that these companions were hearing **the voice** is contradicted by his later declaration that they "did not hear the voice" (22:9). On the one hand he wants to present witnesses to the event; on the other he is anxious to interpret the vision as an experience of Paul.

9:8-9. Paul's blindness is probably to be viewed, not as punishment, but as a result of the radiance of the vision (cf. 22:11). His failure to eat and drink may be interpreted either as penitent fasting or as the effect of the vision's impact. In general the Acts accounts focus on the externals of the conversion, while Paul himself emphasizes the inward character of the experience. For him the conversion has 2 main elements: Christ appeared to him (I Cor. 15:8); God called him to preach (Gal. 1:16).

9:10-19. *Acceptance into the Church.* The scene shifts to **Ananias;** the traditional site of his house can be visited in Damascus today. The parallel of this narrative is found in 22:12-16. There Luke records that Ananias was respected by the Jewish community and must have been converted to Christianity out of that background. How the gospel came to Damascus is unknown, although Ananias may have been won to the church by the Hellenist mission (8:1; 11:19).

9:10-16. Just as **the Lord** has appeared to Paul on the road, so he speaks to Ananias **in a vision.** The vision instructs him to find Paul, who is residing on **the street called Straight**—a main E-W artery of ancient and modern Damascus. At this very time Paul is praying and seeing a vision which corresponds to that of Ananias (for similarly corresponding visions cf. ch. 10). Ananias resists this instruction, recalling the persecution which Paul has promoted in Jerusalem (8:1) and proposes here (9:2). **Saints** and those **who call upon thy name** are typical biblical terms for the Christians (cf. I Cor. 1:2). Ananias' reluctance, which appears to be an affront to the risen Christ, serves to emphasize the greatness of Paul's conversion. In spite of his past he is to be **a chosen instrument** (lit. "vessel"; cf. II Cor. 4:7) to carry the Lord's name to **the Gentiles and kings and the sons of Israel**—a prediction which will be fulfilled later.

9:17-19. Ananias goes to the place Paul is staying and addresses him as **Brother** (cf. 1:16; 6:3). He lays hands on him (cf. 6:6) so that the power of God can return his sight and convey **the Holy Spirit** (cf. 8:17). The mention of **something like scales** falling from **his eyes** may be simply a symbolic way to describe the miracle. Though the sequence of events is not clear, receiving the Spirit seems to precede baptism (cf. 22:16). The suggestion that Paul has something to eat demonstrates the completeness of his recovery (cf. Luke 8:55).

For Luke this episode incorporates Paul into the church and implicitly commissions him to mission (cf. 13:3). Paul says he made a trip to Arabia at this time (Gal. 1:17), but Luke does not mention it; instead he represents the convert's eagerness to preach as answered in Damascus (vss. 19b-22). According to Paul himself the Gentile mission was of the essence of his conversion, and his commission to preach was not conferred through "flesh and blood" (Gal. 1:16).

9:19b-31. *From Damascus to Jerusalem.* Paul enters the **synagogues** of Damascus as a preacher instead of a persecutor. His message presents Jesus as **the Son of God.** This usage is unique in Acts but typical of Paul (e.g. Rom. 1:4; II Cor. 1:19). For Luke the title presents Jesus as the promised Messiah (cf. Luke 22:70), who stands in special relationship to God (cf. Luke 1:35). The **Jews** of the city can offer no answer to Paul's proof that Jesus is **the Christ.**

9:23-25. Paul's escape from Damascus is described also in II Cor. 11:32-33. There "the governor under King Aretas" is identified as the one who is attempting to seize him. This ruler would be Aretas IV, who ruled Nabatea (an Arabian region SE of Damascus and of Palestine; see color map 14) from 9 B.C. to A.D. 40. Just what authority he had in Syrian Damascus is not clear, but opposition from his officers suggests that Paul's trip to their area (Gal. 1:17) involved more than prayer and meditation. Luke presents the Jews as the stereotyped opponents of the gospel (cf. 13:50; 14:19). The description of Paul's escape **over** (lit. "through") **the wall** is confirmed by his own account of his flight "through a window in the wall" (II Cor. 11:33). The traditional window, a popular tourist attraction in Damascus, has been constructed at a later time, yet windows are still visible in sections of the older wall nearby.

9:26-30. Paul's difficulty in joining the **disciples** in **Jerusalem** is not surprising. The account of Barnabas' mediation, however, is dramatic and possibly reflects knowledge of his later association with Paul. Here they are distinguished from the **apostles,** but later (14:4, 14) that title is applied to them. According to Paul's own account this visit occurred 3 years after his conversion (Gal. 1:18-23). Paul also swears that he saw only Cephas (Peter) and James the Lord's brother during this visit and that he "was still not known by sight to the churches of Christ in Judea." This is difficult to square with Luke's statement that **he went in and out among them . . . preaching boldly.** Apparently Luke is anxious to present Paul as filling the role of Stephen, who also **disputed against the Hellenists** (cf. 6:8-9). Paul's departure to **Tarsus** in Cilicia, his home town, is confirmed by his own reference to going to Syria and Cilicia (Gal. 1:21; see color map 16).

9:31. Again Luke summarizes the mission. He refers to the church **throughout all Judea and Galilee and Samaria** in the singular; the whole church is understood as a unity.

III. The Mission to the Gentiles (9:32–12:25)

A. The Missionary Activity of Peter (9:32–11:18)

9:32-43. *To Lydda and Joppa.* Peter was last mentioned in 8:25. Thus his going **here and there among them all** may refer to his visit to Samaritan villages (see also below on 12:1-19). His purpose is to confirm **the saints** who have been converted, probably by Philip's mission (8:40). At **Lydda,** a town some 25 miles NW from Jerusalem in the coastal plain of **Sharon** (see color map 15), Peter heals **Aeneas.** As is typical of the miracle stories in Acts, the name of the patient (cf. vs. 36) and the duration of the illness (cf. 4:22) are recounted.

9:34-35. The verb translated **make your bed** could also mean "spread your table"; either meaning would stress the completeness of the cure (cf. 9:19). The intention of this narrative is to present Peter in parallel to Jesus, in whose power the healing has been performed (cf. Luke 5:17-26). The notion that **all the residents** of the region **turned to the Lord** (i.e. were converted; cf. 11:21) is exaggerated; according to Luke's own understanding of the course

of events no Gentiles were added to the church at this time.

9:36-42. The port of **Joppa** is on the Mediterranean some 11 miles beyond Lydda (see color map 15). **Tabitha** is an Aramaic name for which Luke gives the Greek equivalent, **Dorcas;** the RSV adds its English translation, **Gazelle.** The lady who bears this name seems to be one of the **widows** of the Joppan church. In later times widows constituted a special ecclesiastical class who directed programs of **charity;** the **coats and garments** are probably evidence of such a project. After her death the body of Dorcas is **washed** according to ancient customs of purification. The summoning of Peter by **two men** reflects Luke's fondness for 2 witnesses (cf. 10:7). The description of the miracle is reminiscent of I Kings 17:17-24; II Kings 4:32-37; and Peter's action is parallel to the raising of Jairus' daughter (Luke 8:49-56; cf. Mark 5:40). In both Lydda and Joppa conversion is accomplished by deed rather than word; God's action participates in the mission of the church.

9:43. Peter stays at Joppa with **Simon, a tanner.** The hosts of the missionaries are frequently mentioned by Luke (e.g. 9:11). As a tanner Simon belongs to a profession despised by the Jews.

10:1–11:18. *To Cornelius.* It is often supposed that this material is out of place. Perhaps it belongs after Peter's escape from prison (12:19); a Roman garrison was not established in Caesarea until after the death of Herod Agrippa I (12:20-23).

The importance of this narrative for Luke cannot be overestimated; it describes the beginning of the Gentile mission and prepares for the Jerusalem conference of ch. 15. However, the historicity of the passage is debatable. If it is taken literally, the conduct of Peter described in Gal. 2:11-12 is difficult to explain, and the significance of Paul as leader of the Gentile mission (Gal. 2:7) is minimized. Apparently Luke has taken a simple conversion story (like that of 8:26-40) and expanded it into a pivotal event. The abundant use of repetition reflects the Semitic style of emphasis.

10:1-8. *Cornelius' Vision.* The city of **Caesarea** (see map, p. 742, and color map 14) was the beautiful seaport rebuilt by Herod the Great in honor of Augustus. After Herod's death it became the official residence of the Roman governor. The ruins of a forum, an aqueduct, and a Greek theater, set on the edge of the azure Mediterranean, are still visible.

Cornelius is a common Roman name. The **Italian Cohort,** a detachment of troops containing theoretically 600 (or perhaps 1,000) men, was stationed in Syria at a later time. Cornelius may be in Caesarea in retirement, as the reference to **his household** could indicate. However, he seems to have soldiers in his command (vs. 7). Luke views him as a "Godfearer" (cf. 13:16, 26; 16:14), i.e. a Gentile who attended the synagogue, accepted Jewish monotheism and ethics, but did not become a proselyte. His piety is demonstrated by generosity in giving **alms liberally to the people** (the Jews).

10:3-8. Like a pious Jew, Cornelius follows the prescribed hours of prayer. **The ninth hour** is 3 P.M. (cf. 3:1). Vision at the time of prayer is not surprising (cf. 22:17-18) and the **angel** is a typical mediator of revelation (e.g. Luke 1:11). The idea that Cornelius' prayers have **ascended as a**

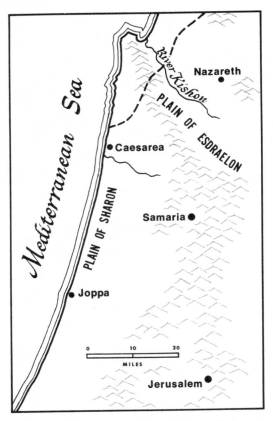

memorial is reminiscent of the meal offering described in Lev. 2 (cf. also Ecclus. 35:7). A memorial before God means that God will remember this offering with action. Cornelius is told to send for Simon . . . Peter; the drama is heightened by the fact that nothing more is hinted concerning his identity (but cf. 11:14). Joppa is some 30 miles distant.

10:9-16. *Peter's Vision.* The next day after Cornelius has sent for him Peter is praying on the housetop. Palestinian houses were flatroofed with an outside stairway (cf. Deut. 22:8). Although noon (the sixth hour) is not one of the regular times of daily prayer, it is recommended by Ps. 55:17. Luke's purpose is to present Peter's hunger at lunchtime. While food is being prepared he falls into a trance—lit. "a trance fell on him," indicating the initiative as God's. A trance, lit. "ecstasy," is common at time of prayer (cf. 22:17) and indicates readiness for divine revelation.

10:11-16. Various efforts have been made to discover psychological stimuli which aroused the vision. It has been conjectured that Peter has been wrestling with the problem of Gentile mission, or that he has seen in the distance a sailboat suggesting the sheet of his vision. More likely we have a religious picture constructed out of OT material. The animals of the sheet are reminiscent of the passengers of the ark (Gen. 6:20), while the protest of Peter is parallel to the words of Ezek. 4:14. A voice, which is later identified with the Spirit (vs. 19), commands Peter to eat unclean beasts (cf. Lev. 11) because God has cleansed them. The message is repeated a 3rd time

for emphasis. It is evident that the point of the vision is not Gentile inclusion in the church but the question of ritual regulations concerning food.

10:17-35. *The Meeting with Cornelius.* As Peter is pondering the vision the men from Cornelius arrive. The coincidence of their arrival makes the meaning of the vision clear to the reader, although Peter does not discover it until vs. 28. Now it is the Spirit that addresses the apostle (cf. vss. 13, 15) and goes on to say, I have sent them; perhaps Luke identifies the Spirit as the risen Christ (cf. 9:5). In any case the Spirit informs Peter of the men who are seeking him. Some manuscripts read "two" rather than three men; this may be an attempted correction by a scribe who failed to count the soldier of vs. 7, or the use of "three" could represent harmonizing of an original "two" with 11:11.

10:22-23a. The visitors describe Cornelius and refer to his vision (vss. 3-6). Receiving Gentiles as guests might have been strange among orthodox Jews, but the Diaspora was more liberal. Peter is already prepared for social intercourse with non-Jews.

10:23b-29. On the next day Peter goes with these emissaries to Caesarea, taking with him brethren from Joppa as witnesses; according to 11:12 there are 6 of them. Cornelius, though knowing nothing about Peter, collects his kinsmen and close friends in great expectation. The way is prepared for the household conversion of 11:14. The Western text adds that a slave ran forward to announce Peter's arrival—an effort to smooth out the narrative and clarify the entry of Peter to the town and to the house. The attempt of Cornelius to worship the apostle is a typical Lukan motif (cf. 14:15). The word unlawful which Peter uses of associating with Gentiles means, not "contrary to the Mosaic law," but "improper" or "taboo." His reference to the vision clarifies its meaning, but a change has been made: in vs. 15 it is things (animals) which are no longer unclean, while here no man is to be called common or unclean.

10:30-33. Cornelius recounts his visionary experience (vss. 3-6). Four days ago means 3 days by our way of reckoning; as the various references to time indicate (vss. 9, 23, 24), Cornelius' speech falls on the 4th day. It is possible to interpret the phrase to suggest that he has been praying constantly since the vision occurred. His conclusion reaches a climax of expectation and focuses on the speech of Peter.

10:34-43. *Peter's Sermon.* In presenting the speech Luke employs Semitic style. It offers a summary of his understanding of early Christian preaching. The belief that God shows no partiality is also found in Rom. 2:11. No notion of salvation apart from Christianity is implied in the statement that the righteous in every nation are acceptable to God; instead the way is cleared for the Gentile mission.

10:36-38. The content of the gospel is Jesus Christ. That the associates of Cornelius really know this word seems unlikely. The comment that Jesus is Lord of all is perhaps an editorial addition by Luke. The expression is used in Hellenistic Judaism to extol the cosmic might of God (Wisd. Sol. 6:7; 8:3), but here it suggests the universality of salvation through Christ. The idea that the ministry of Jesus began after the baptism of John (cf. 1:22) and progressed from Galilee to the Holy City reflects Lukan motifs (cf. Luke 23:5). The presentation of Jesus' ministry as the content of early Christian preaching is not frequent, but Luke understands his gospel as a commentary on this idea. Basic to it is the conviction that the ministry of Jesus resulted from his being **anointed . . . with the Holy Spirit** (cf. Luke 4:18).

10:39-43. The witness of the disciples is essential to the proclamation (cf. 1:21-22). They have observed the crucial events in the career of Jesus—his death and resurrection. Reference to **death by hanging him on a tree** is typically Lukan (cf. 5:30). In contrast to Mark's resurrection "after three days" (Mark 8:31) Luke describes the raising of Jesus as occurring **on the third day** (cf. Luke 9:22). The fact that disciples ate with the risen Christ (Luke 24:42-43) witnesses to the reality of his resurrection. His command **to preach** is being obeyed here, and this proclamation testifies to his position as **judge** of the future. Thus the risen Christ fulfills the role of the triumphant Son of man (Luke 22:69)—the eschatological judge, the vicegerent of God (cf. 17:31).

10:44-48. *The Gift of the Spirit.* Peter's speech results in the Spirit's falling **on all who heard.** This event is described as an interruption—in fact 11:15 asserts that it came at the very beginning of his remarks—but as usual (e.g. 2:37; 4:1) the sermon has been completed. The gift of the Spirit preceding baptism is unique (see above on 2:37-47). The usage here is a special sign to demonstrate God's acceptance of the Gentiles. Proof of this is seen in their **speaking in tongues**—an external display of the Spirit's presence (2:1-13). The companions of Peter, who are Jewish Christians, express amazement that God's gift is conveyed to **Gentiles;** the experience of Cornelius and his household is generalized.

10:47-48. Baptism of course cannot be withheld from those who have received the Spirit. The Christian rite is understood, as in the experience of Jesus (Luke 3:21-22), to involve both water and Spirit. Peter does not perform the baptism himself, but is presented as the apostolic supervisor (cf. 8:14-17). The baptism is **in the name of Jesus Christ** rather than by the trinitarian formula of Matt. 28:19.

11:1-18. *The Report to Jerusalem.* Although Peter's report to Jerusalem is highly repetitious, it is completely clear only to the reader of ch. 10. The Western text somewhat softens the opposition by inserting in vs. 2 the suggestion that Peter went to Jerusalem for the purpose of reporting his activities among the Gentiles. The charge of the **circumcision party**—that he had eaten with **uncircumcised men** —is reminiscent of criticism leveled at Jesus (Luke 15:2).

11:4-17. Peter's response recounts his vision (10: 9-16) with minor variations (e.g. the addition of **beasts of prey**) and summarizes his trip to Caesarea (10:17-24) and the events at Cornelius' house (10:25-48). In vs. 12 the phrase translated **without hesitation** probably means "without distinction," i.e. in regard to the visitors' situation as Gentiles (cf. 15:9). The report that the angel told Cornelius that Peter would **declare . . . a message** of salvation differs from the original narrative (see above on 10:3-8). The reference to **the Holy Spirit** as falling on Peter's hearers **at the beginning**—another variation (see

above on 10:44-48)—no doubt remembers Pentecost (2:1-4). In the gospels the promise **John baptized with water, but you shall be baptized with the Holy Spirit** is attributed, not to Jesus, but to John (Mark 1:8; Matt. 3:11; Luke 3:16); but Luke has already reported the same words as spoken by the risen Christ (1:5).

11:18. Peter's report silences all opposition. The audience gives glory to God, since **repentance unto life** has been **granted** to the **Gentiles.** This conclusion prepares for the Jerusalem council of ch. 15.

B. The Church at Antioch (11:19-30)

At **Antioch** the congregation includes both Jewish and Gentile Christians. The evangelization of the Gentiles is described unobtrusively (vs. 20). Luke seems to be following another source here, which avoids the emphasis of the Cornelius story. Evidence for an earlier use of this source is seen in 8:4, where **those who were scattered because of the persecution** are mentioned. It may have had its origin in Antioch. In the mind of Luke the geographic expansion of Christianity is a slow process moving out from Jerusalem to Samaria, to the Palestinian cities of Joppa and Caesarea, and now to a great center of Greek culture, Antioch on the Orontes (see color map 16). The 3rd city of the empire, Antioch boasted a population of 800,000; it was a prominent commercial city, noted for its blatant paganism.

11:20-21. The **men of Cyprus and Cyrene** are not identified, although they may include those mentioned in 13:1. In 4:36 we have been told that Barnabas was a "native of Cyprus." Some manuscripts read "Hellenists" rather than **Greeks** (cf. 6:1). It is clear, however, that the author is referring to Gentiles, since the action of the Cypriots and Cyrenians is in contrast to **speaking the word to none except Jews.** The content of their message is **the Lord Jesus.** The Greek idiom here, which is the same as in 5:42 (see comment), may mean that they were preaching "Jesus as the Lord" (cf. I Cor. 12:3), i.e. the Lord of their lives in contrast to the lords of the Hellenistic cults. The title "Lord" is employed 3 times in the passage. The notice that **the hand of the Lord was with them** is a typical OT expression which recognizes divine assistance and support (cf. II Sam. 3:12). The Jewish and Gentile converts apparently participate in the common life of the church, at least at this time, without incident (contrast Gal. 2:11-14).

11:22-26*a*. According to Luke, **Barnabas** is sent from Jerusalem to supervise the Antioch church. Thus he plays a role similar to that of Peter and John in Samaria (8:14-24). Elsewhere he is given the title "apostle" (14:14). The reader receives the impression that **Saul** (Paul) has dropped into obscurity, but not that a great amount of time has elasped since 9:30 (contrast Gal. 2:1). Actually Paul has been busy in Syria, Cilicia, and perhaps farther W promoting a mission similar to that of Antioch (Gal. 1:21).

11:26*b*. The observation that **the disciples were . . . first . . . called Christians** in Antioch has led to debate. The name is presented in a variety of forms in the manuscripts, but its ending is the familiar Latin "-ian." This ending suggests that the name describes its bearers as followers of Christ (taken as a proper name) or, in a frequent variant, of Chrestus (a common Greek name meaning "good" or "worthy"). It is not clear, however, whether the Christians devised this name for themselves, or whether outsiders, perhaps the populace of Antioch or the police of Rome, devised it as a nickname.

11:27-30. Even more problematic is the sending of **relief** to Jerusalem **by the hand of Barnabas and Saul.** Though famine did occur in various parts of the empire during the reign of **Claudius** (A.D. 41-54), the possibility of a **famine over all the world** seems excluded by the text; such a famine would affect Antioch too. Moreover a trip to Jerusalem by Paul is contradicted by his own record. If the conference described in ch. 15 is the same as that mentioned in Gal. 2 (which is probable), then Paul's attendance at the conference constitutes his 2nd (Gal. 1:18; 2:1), not his 3rd (9:26; 11:30; 12:25; 15:4), visit to Jerusalem after his conversion.

Among the many possible solutions 2 commend themselves: (*a*) the "famine visit" is a doublet with the "conference visit"; (*b*) the "famine visit" is a doublet with the "offering visit" (21:15; cf. Rom. 15: 25). Both solutions assume that Luke had more than one source for the same event but misunderstood these as representing 2 different events. The 2nd solution is preferable since in 21:10 **Agabus** appears again as prophet.

The passage introduces 2 classes of church official. The **prophets** were not ecclesiastical functionaries but charismatic leaders, i.e. men moved by the Spirit (I Cor. 12:28; 14:5-6). Though associated with Jerusalem and Antioch (cf. 13:1) the prophets, according to the Didache (early 2nd cent.), were not restricted to a local church. The **elders,** on the other hand, seem to have been local officials (cf. 14:23). They find their background in Judaism (cf. 4:5, 8) and may have been appointed by the apostles, as were the 7 (6:3), to administrative duties.

C. Persecution of the Church (12:1-25)

12:1-19. *The Escape of Peter.* Ch. 12 is presented as an interlude between 11:30 and 12:25. Though Paul and Barnabas are supposed to be in Jerusalem during this time, no mention is made of them. Since the Jerusalem visit of 11:30 is possibly a doublet with the offering visit of 21:15 (see above on 11:27-30) displacement of material seems likely. Perhaps Peter's departure **to another place** (vs. 17) refers to his mission to Lydda, Joppa, and Caesarea (9:32-43).

12:1-5. Since the ruler of Palestine is anxious to please the Jews, his policy of opposition to the church is to be expected. **Herod the king** is Agrippa I, grandson of Herod the Great. Reared in Rome, he was given the title "king" and the territory of Philip (cf. Luke 3:1) by Caligula in A.D. 37. By 44, under Claudius, he became the ruler of all Palestine. Herod's first victim was **James the brother of John,** the son of Zebedee, one of the 12. It is sometimes supposed that his brother John was also martyred on this occasion (cf. Mark 10:39).

12:3-5. Peter's imprisonment and miraculous escape find a parallel in 5:18-23. Herod's intention to avoid drastic action during the feast is reminiscent of Mark 14:2. As in Jewish folk tradition, the **Pass-**

over and **Unleavened Bread** are confused (cf. Luke 22:1). A squad was normally composed of 4 soldiers —one for each of the watches of the night. The assignment of **four squads** to Peter implies 4 men for each watch, so that the magnitude of the miracle is emphasized. The description of the **earnest prayer** of the church employs language similar to that describing the prayer of Jesus in Luke 22:44.

12:6-11. Because of the mention of 7 steps in some manuscripts it is sometimes assumed that the place of Peter's confinement was the Tower of Antonia (cf. 21:40; see color map 13). The practice of chaining the prisoner to a guard is attested in Roman literature. The appearance of the **angel** with accompanying **light** is a Lukan theme (Luke 2:9); the opening of doors by their **own accord** is a motif of Hellenistic legend. Four guards, the whole squad, have apparently fallen asleep. The story has a strange mixture of realism (the waking of Peter, the conversation of the angel) and the miraculous (the falling **chains,** the idea of a **vision**).

12:12-16. According to later tradition **the house of Mary, the mother of John . . . Mark** (vs. 25; 13: 5, 13; 15:37-39) is the place of the Last Supper and the headquarters of the Jerusalem church. Peter, knowing this as a gathering place of the Christians, knocks **at the door of the gateway,** i.e. at the door which opens from the street into the courtyard of the house. **Rhoda** (meaning "Rose," a typical name for slave girls) is the doorkeeper. While she is convinced by **Peter's voice,** those inside the house suppose her **mad** or believe that she has heard Peter's **angel.** This refers, not to the angel of the Lord which has accomplished his escape, but to Peter's guardian angel (cf. Tobit 5:21; Matt. 18:10). The picture of Peter continuing to knock at the gate is a dramatic feature of the story.

12:17. In contrast to chs. 1-5, **James** is now clearly the leader of the Jerusalem church (cf. 15:13; 21:18). Perhaps he is so well known that Luke does not think to identify him as "the Lord's brother" (Gal. 1:19; cf. Mark 6:3). James is not present at this gathering. Is he worshiping at some other one of the Jerusalem household churches? Is he in hiding because of the persecution?

12:18-19. Herod is disturbed by Peter's escape. Though the Greek simply says that the **sentries** were "led away," **put to death** is probably an accurate translation (cf. Luke 23:26). The guard, according to Roman law, was responsible for the life of his prisoner. Herod (or possibly Peter) goes to **Caesarea,** so that the events of the following vss. occur there.

12:20-23. *The Death of Herod.* We are not told why Herod is **angry with . . . Tyre and Sidon** or what has persuaded **Blastus** to intercede. The dependence of these Phoenician cities on Galilean grain goes back to OT times (cf. I Kings 5:9).

12:21-23. Another account of Herod's death is found in Josephus' Antiquities of the Jews. There it is said that the occasion for Agrippa's appearance in Caesarea was a celebration in honor of the emperor. Herod's **royal robes,** according to Josephus, were made "wholly of silver," and it was his appearance which led **the people** to acclaim him divine. The **angel** of retribution is a feature of OT religion (cf. II Kings 19:35). Josephus says that the appearance of an owl, taken as an evil omen, signified Herod's death. Failure to give **glory** to God is understood as evidence of sinful pride. To be **eaten by worms** was a typical mode of death for tyrants (cf. II Macc. 9:9). Josephus says that Herod was stricken with a severe pain in the abdomen and died 5 days later.

12:24-25. *Growth of the Church.* These vss. provide a Lukan summary (cf. 6:7). Luke evidently intends that vs. 25 describe Paul and Barnabas' return from the famine visit (11:30). Actually the best manuscripts read **returned to Jerusalem,** implying still another trip to the Holy City. However, the term "return" suggests a coming back to Antioch, and the reference to bringing **John . . . Mark** implies the same.

IV. THE MISSION TO ASIA MINOR (13:1–15:35)

A. CYPRUS (13:1-12)

Here Luke presents the first of Paul's "3 missionary journeys." Though the narrative may rest on adequate sources (possibly a travel itinerary) the concept of 3 journeys is largely a construction of Luke. The first journey introduces problems which are to be solved at the Jerusalem conference (cf. 15). Antioch is understood as the instigator of this mission, since it is both the point of departure and the goal.

13:1-3. Paul and Barnabas are commissioned by **prophets and teachers** of the Antioch church. In

contrast to 11:27, the function of these prophets seems to be localized. Except for Barnabas nothing is known of those listed. Efforts have been made to identify **Symeon . . . Niger** with Simon of Cyrene (Luke 23:26) and **Lucius of Cyrene** with Luke. The Greek word used of **Manaen** means lit. "one reared with" the ruler but had come to be a conventional term for a **member of the court.** His patron **Herod the tetrarch** was Antipas, who governed Galilee during Jesus' ministry (Luke 3:1; 9:7;

23:7). Actually Paul and Barnabas are **set apart** by **the Holy Spirit,** whose action has been awaited by **fasting and praying.** Luke seems to understand the laying on of hands as a kind of ordination (cf. 6:6), since the title "apostle" is applied to Paul and Barnabas only after this event (14:4). Paul refutes this idea in Gal. 1:1.

13:4-5. Departure for the W is from **Seleucia**— the seaport of Antioch, some 15 miles to the W. They sail to **Cyprus,** landing at **Salamis,** an important city on the E coast (see color map 16). According to Luke's pattern (13:14; 14:1) preaching begins in **the synagogues.** It is said that **John** Mark serves as an assistant or helper, but the nature of his service is not described.

13:6-10. The missionaries move across the island to **Paphos,** the provincial capital. The ruler of this senatorial province is **Sergius Paulus,** who is accurately described as **proconsul.** Since Elymas cannot be a translation of **Bar-Jesus,** some have supposed that 2 different individuals, a Hellenistic **magician** and **a Jewish false prophet,** have been combined in the tradition. Others have attempted to show that some form of Elymas may be the Aramaic or Arabic equivalent of Bar-Jesus. Possibly it is simply a nickname. Paul's epithet **son of the devil** is the exact opposite of Bar-Jesus, which means "son of salvation." The change from **Saul** to **Paul** at this point may indicate that as he moves W Paul increasingly employs the Roman version of his name (see above on 8:1*a*). The appearance of Sergius Paulus in the narrative may provide the literary device for its introduction here.

13:11-12. The idea of **mist** falling on the magician is an expression as old as Homer, who used it to describe the darkness which covers a dying man's vision. The miracle of judgment convinces the proconsul that Christianity is superior to magic (cf. 8:14-24).

B. ANTIOCH OF PISIDIA (13:13-52)

13:13-15. *Arrival.* Leaving Cyprus, the missionaries sail to the S coast of what is now Turkey. Though **Perga** is the first stop, **Paul and his company** (he is clearly the leader of the group) go immediately to the inland plateau (see map, p. 746). This may indicate a sudden change of plans, possibly supporting the notion that Paul went to Galatia for his health (cf. II Cor. 12:7; Gal. 4:13). **John** Mark's departure might also be explained by this decision to travel the difficult road to a more remote area. That Paul is displeased with John's defection is clear from 15:38.

13:14-15. The main city of the S part of the province of Galatia was **Antioch of Pisidia** (see map, p. 746). Most scholars believe the churches founded in this area are those addressed by Paul in Gal. (see Intro. to Gal.). The service of the **synagogue** included **reading of the law and the prophets** (the 2 most important sections of the OT), followed by exposition. **The rulers of the synagogue** (cf. Mark 5:22) were charged with the oversight of worship. Perhaps Paul's bearing marked him as a Pharisee, but any visiting teacher might be allowed to address the congregation (cf. Luke 4:16-17).

13:16-41. *Paul's Sermon.* Like other speeches of

Acts this sermon is largely the composition of Luke. It contains reminiscences of the speeches of Peter and Stephen. Though some hints of Pauline doctrine may be discovered (vs. 39), the main elements of Paul's preaching as summarized in Rom. are lacking. Luke understands this sermon as a model of the preaching which was offered to the Hellenistic synagogue. The normal pose of the Jewish speaker was sitting (Luke 4:20); Paul is presented after the order of a Hellenistic rhetorician who stands and gestures. The sermon is addressed to Jews and "God-fearers" (vss. 16, 26; see above on 10:1-8).

13:16-22. The main theme of this sermon is Jesus as the son of **David.** Perhaps this is why the activity of Moses, emphasized in Stephen's speech (7:20-44), is ignored. The Exodus, accomplished by God's **uplifted arm** (cf. Deut. 4:34; 5:15), is a type of the salvation granted through **Jesus.** Because of a variation of one letter in the manuscripts it is not certain whether the translation should say that God **bore with** or "cared for" (cf. Deut. 1:31) Israel during the **forty years** (cf. Num. 14:34) **. . . in the wilderness.** The **seven nations . . . of Canaan** are listed in Deut. 7:1. **After that** (lit. "these") appears to refer to **about four hundred and fifty years** and thus indicate that this period elapsed between the occupation of the land and the judges. But "that" more probably is intended to point back to the occupation at the beginning of the 450 years, in conformity with traditional OT chronology (I Kings 6:1). The Western text has the words transposed to: "And after that he gave unto them judges about the space of four hundred and fifty years" (KJV). As in Peter's speech (3:24), **Samuel** is the first of the prophets. **Saul,** whose reign according to Josephus was **forty years** (cf. I Sam. 13:1 and RSV footnotes), was **removed** from the throne by God's rejection (I Sam. 15:23). God's word about **David** is a composite quotation based on Ps. 89:20; I Sam. 13:14; Isa. 44:28.

13:23-25. Fulfillment of the promises concerning the son of David (II Sam. 22:51; Ps. 132:11, 17) began in **John** the Baptist (1:22). His distinctive act was a **baptism of repentance** (19:4) but he denied any messianic pretensions for himself (cf. Luke 3:15-17 and parallels).

13:26-31. The concept of **salvation** is suggested by the name "Jesus" (cf. Matt. 1:21). Israel's failure to recognize this one prophesied in the **sabbath** readings is another sign of her ignorance (cf. 3:17). As Pilate repeatedly said (Luke 23:4, 14, 22), Jesus did **nothing deserving death.** The actual crucifixion is not described here (except in some manuscript additions), and the cryptic reference to **the tree** (cf. 5:30; 10:39; Gal. 3:13) might not be clear to hearers unfamiliar with Luke's narrative. **Many days** (cf. 1:3) and **those who came . . . from Galilee** (cf. 10:37) represent Lukan motifs. The speaker seems to distinguish himself from the **witnesses** of the Resurrection—a concept foreign to Paul (cf. I Cor. 9:1; 15:8).

13:32-41. The 3 texts cited in vss. 33-35 are taken as proof that David's son was to be raised from the dead and that Jesus is the son of David, heir of the promises. Ps. 2:7 indicates that the son of David is actually the **Son** of God whose eternal nature and divine power is revealed in the Resurrection (cf. Rom. 1:3-4). Isa. 55:3 and Ps. 16:10 are held together by the term **holy;** the former shows that the **blessings of David** are applied to his son, and the latter indicates that the son will **not . . . see corruption.** Since David's activity was confined to **his own generation,** since he **fell asleep** (died) and **saw corruption,** the promise cannot be fulfilled in him. Instead it is fulfilled in David's son, whom **God raised up,** who **saw no corruption,** i.e. Jesus Christ. The idea that **forgiveness of sins is proclaimed** through him is typically Lukan (cf. 2:38; 10:43). Vs. 39 does contain superficial Pauline elements, although the depth of faith and the paradox of **the law** is lacking. A final warning to the anticipated opponents is sounded in vs. 41 from Hab. 1:5—a text understood in the Dead Sea Scrolls as referring to events of the last days.

13:42-52. *Turning to the Gentiles.* Paul's sermon creates a favorable response. According to some manuscripts it is the Gentiles who request a similar sermon for **the next sabbath.** Luke, however, is not anxious to introduce them into his narrative until vs. 46. The mention of **devout converts** is confusing, since the 2 terms describe different groups: the **devout** are the "God-fearers" (vss. 16, 26), while the word translated **converts** is lit. "proselytes." Perhaps Luke is describing the former in an imprecise fashion. **Paul and Barnabas** (who is now mentioned for the first time in the Antioch of Pisidia narrative), in urging those who follow them from the meeting **to continue in the grace of God,** are suggesting that they maintain a relationship with God wherein his favor and help are effective.

13:44-46. The description of **the next sabbath** is exaggerated. The synagogue could hardly accommodate **almost the whole city.** At first Jewish opposition is moved by **jealousy,** but the fact that they contradicted Paul's message implies a dispute over doctrine. The word translated **reviled** means "blasphemed"; Luke may understand opposition to the word as blasphemy against God. The idea that salvation was offered **first** to the Jews is both historical and true to the early Christian understanding of the drama of redemption (cf. Rom. 1:16). The **turn to the Gentiles,** on the other hand, is basically a pattern constructed by Luke (cf. 18:6). That Paul, this late in his career, directed his mission for the first time to the Gentiles is at variance with both Acts (22:21) and his letters (Gal. 1:16).

13:47-52. The text cited to support this action is Isa. 49:6. Originally the words were directed to the servant of the Lord, and in Luke 2:32 Simeon applies them to the child Jesus; here they are addressed to the missionaries. The observation that some were **ordained to eternal life** (i.e. life in the age to come) could imply a concept of predestination (cf. Luke 10:20), but Luke's stress on their belief qualifies his determinism. The phrase **devout women** has been inscribed on the principal seats of the theater at Miletus. **Shook off the dust from their feet** (cf. Luke 9:5; 10:11) symbolizes either scorn or disavowal of responsibility.

C. Iconium (14:1-7)

Iconium was an important commercial center located some 80 miles E of Antioch of Pisidia (see map, p. 746). Though its inhabitants considered themselves Phrygians, the city had been part of **Lycaonia** (vs. 6) and now belonged to the Roman province of Galatia. Luke presents only a generalized picture of the mission. The pattern of entering the synagogue first, seemingly precluded by 13:46, is repeated. The word translated **together** can also mean that they carried on the mission "after the same manner" as in Antioch. The idea that they **remained for a long time** is surprising in view of the action of **the unbelieving** (lit. "disobedient") **Jews.**

14:3-7. Luke presents Paul and Barnabas as doing the **signs and wonders** attributed to the **apostles** (cf. 5:12). In fact he applies that title to them here and in vs. 14. Since Luke normally thinks of the apostles as Jerusalem officials (e.g. 8:14) it may be that his use of the term here depends on the source which underlies 14:14; or possibly he is using the word in a general way, meaning "those who are sent." The proposal to **stone** the missionaries anticipates 14:19.

D. Lystra (14:8-18)

The missionaries flee to **Lystra,** 20 miles S (see map, p. 746). Formerly a part of Lycaonia, this city had been incorporated into the province of Galatia. The narrative of the mission does not follow the Jew-Gentile pattern, and its vividness of detail may suggest solid sources. However, parallels to other sections of Acts betray the hand of Luke. The healing of the **cripple** is similar to Peter's cure of the man at the temple (3:2-10). Both had been lame **from birth** (3:2), the healer looked **intently** at them (3:4), and they **sprang up and walked** (3:8).

14:11-12. The effort to identify the apostles as gods in the **likeness of men** rests on a legend in which Zeus and Hermes once descended to this area. The notion that Paul refers to this incident in Gal. 4:14 is unconvincing. The identification of

Barnabas as **Zeus** could suggest that something about his bearing commends him as leader of the mission. More likely stress is placed on **Paul** as **Hermes,** the patron of oratory, so that Paul can be presented as **the chief speaker**—an emphasis which provides the occasion for his sermon. The use of **Lycaonian**—a dialect employed in this region until the 6th cent. A.D.—makes possible a period of misunderstanding by the missionaries which allows time for the organizing of the **sacrifice.**

14:13-14. The Greek reads lit. "Zeus before the city," but reference to the **temple** is probably intended. Unfortunately no archaeological efforts have been made at Lystra to recover this building at whose **gates** sacrifice was to be made. **Oxen** or bulls were typical victims of pagan sacrifice, symbolizing power and fertility. The **garlands** consisted of wool and sometimes flowers. Tearing of **garments** was the prescribed Jewish reaction to blasphemy (cf. Mark 14:63).

14:15-18. Paul's speech is a preview of his sermon in Athens (17:22-31). The protest that **we also are men** is reminiscent of 10:26. The word translated **of like nature,** lit. "of like feelings," reflects the contemporary pagan belief in the "impassivity," or lack of feelings, of the gods. Paul's answer to these pagan ideas is not philosophical argument but proclamation of OT faith in God as creator. To **turn from these vain things to a living God** has a Pauline ring (cf. I Thess. 1:9), as does the reference to God's providential care as a **witness** to him (cf. Rom. 1:20). More important is the Lukan emphasis on God's allowing **the nations to walk in their own ways** (cf. 17:30).

E. Return to Antioch (14:19-28)

14:19-20. The sudden change of the Lystrans under the persuasion of **Jews** from out of town is difficult to explain. The stoning of Paul, however, is possibly supported by II Cor. 11:25 (cf. II Tim. 3:11). Some manuscripts add that the companions of Paul stayed by him until evening, when he was revived. This would facilitate entry into the hostile town. In any case the persecution was unbelievably brief (vs. 20). **Derbe** is some 30 miles to the SE (see map, p. 746). The mention that they **preached the gospel** picks up the narrative of 14:7; the material about Lystra is perhaps from a separate source.

14:21-24. The **strengthening** of churches already established follows a Lukan pattern (cf. 9:32-43). It is possible that the material following 16:5 belongs here and that Paul goes on from this area to N Galatia and the W. At any rate the concept of **faith** expressed in this text (meaning "Christianity" or "orthodoxy") is not Pauline. The **kingdom of God** here refers to the realm which the faithful will enter after death (cf. Luke 23:42), and the idea that **tribulations** are a prerequisite is typically Lukan (cf. Luke 24:26). The term **elders** (cf. 20:17) never appears in the authentic letters of Paul; Luke understands the church's organization as following the pattern of the synagogue (cf. Luke 7:3).

14:25-28. The city of **Attalia,** near **Perga** (cf. 13:13), was the principal port of **Pamphylia** (see map, p. 746). From there the missionaries could sail directly to Syria. Why they did not return to strengthen the churches of Cyprus is not explained.

On returning to **Antioch** of Syria, Paul and Barnabas report on the mission, which is understood as the work of God. The reference to a **door** which has been **opened** reflects Pauline language (I Cor. 16:9). The object of the mission has been the **Gentiles,** whose role in the church must now be decided.

F. THE CONFERENCE AT JERUSALEM (15:1-35)

The report of this conference constitutes some of the most problematic material of Acts. Two questions should be faced at the outset: What is the relation of this council to that described in Gal. 2:1-10? What was the topic discussed at the conference?

To the first question 2 major solutions have been proposed:

a) That the meeting described in Gal. 2:1-10 occurred during Paul's visit to Jerusalem which Luke mentions in 11:30. This would mean that the conference Luke now describes took place after the writing of Gal., that the beginning of the controversy discussed here is seen in Gal. 2:11-14, and that the men who **came down from Judea** (vs. 1) are to be identified with the men "from James" (Gal. 2:12). This theory has been devised primarily to harmonize Acts and Gal.—a harmonizing which puts the conference of Gal. 2 too early in Paul's career (cf. Gal. 1:18; 2:1).

b) That vss. 1-19 of this ch. and Gal. 2:1-10 represent different accounts of the same event. Antioch and Jerusalem are the places of conflict in both narratives, and in both Paul and Barnabas go to Jerusalem for the discussion of the issues. This would mean that the dispute described in Gal. 2:11-14 occurred after the conference and that Luke's account in vss. 20-29 represents a later attempt to settle this 2nd dispute after Paul has left Jerusalem. It is unlikely that the apostolic letter (vss. 23-29) was composed with Paul's concurrence, since in 21:25 he is told of it as if for the first time, and since his treatment of the question of meat offered to idols (I Cor. 8) belies knowledge of it. The men from James (Gal. 2:12) are perhaps to be identified with the delegation which brings the "letter" to Antioch (vss. 22-29). This 2nd theory is the more widely accepted.

The debate about the topic of discussion is best answered by Paul's own account (Gal. 2:1-10). There it is clear that the real question of the conference is circumcision or, better, the right of the mission to the uncircumcised (Gal. 2:7). The question of social intercourse between Jewish and Gentile Christians arises in Antioch later, after Peter and the men from James come from Jerusalem (Gal. 2:11-14). Though Luke's account here gives the impression that circumcision is the question (vss. 1, 5), the settlement does not explicitly mention this issue (vs. 19), and the concluding apostolic decree (vss. 20-29) deals with the other question. Luke has confused the 2 issues earlier in his narrative (10:1–11:18).

The discrepancies in Acts are perhaps due to dislocation of inadequate sources, although theological motifs are apparent. The council is presented at the midpoint of the narrative; it symbolizes the movement of interest from Jerusalem to the W. The apostles drop out of the story, and the Gentile mission is the central concern. The transition from Jewish to Gentile Christianity, however, occurs without conflict; the decision is made in Jerusalem, the source of the church's mission.

15:1-5. *The Controversy.* The **men . . . from Judea** are converts **who belonged to the party of the Pharisees** (vs. 5). Coming out of a legalistic background they believe **the law of Moses** must be obeyed by Christians. Their program in Antioch does not have authorization from Jerusalem (vs. 24). Whereas vs. 1 presents them as demanding circumcision for salvation, vs. 5 might mean that it is a prerequisite for social participation in the Christian community. Those on whom they lay this requirement could include Titus (Gal. 2:3), who may be one of **the others** accompanying **Paul and Barnabas.**

15:2-5. Our text implies that Paul and Barnabas are **appointed** by the Antioch church, but some manuscripts suggest appointment by the men from Judea—an authority which Paul would not attribute to Jerusalem (Gal. 2:2). Luke understands the officials of Jerusalem as consisting of 2 groups: the **apostles,** i.e. the 12; and the **elders,** who exercise an authority parallel to that of the Jewish sanhedrin (cf. 11:30). The description of visiting churches on the way to Jerusalem follows a Lukan pattern (cf. 8:25). The conversion of **Samaria** has been described in 8:4-25. Though no work in Tyre and Sidon has been recorded, a mission to **Phoenicia** is implied in 11:19.

15:6-21. *Discussion and Decision.* It is sometimes supposed that since Paul implies both a larger and a private hearing (Gal. 2:2) the meeting with the **apostles and the elders** (vs. 6) refers to the private hearing while **the assembly** (vs. 12) describes the larger audience. Though Luke may think of the conference as involving a plenary session of the whole church, the reference to **all** the assembly may mean only the total group of apostles and elders. In any case his narrative does suggest a presentation to the church (vs. 4) and to a group of its leaders (vs. 6).

15:7-11. Peter's role in the conference seems to conflict with the description of him in Gal. 2:7. God's **choice in the early days** (vs. 7) refers to the conversion of Cornelius (10:1–11:18), and the gift of the **Holy Spirit** (vs. 8) is reminiscent of 10:44 and 11:15. **God who knows the heart** is a Lukan expression associated with Peter in 1:24. The idea of **no distinction** (vs. 9) is a cryptic reference to Peter's vision (10:15, 28). To **make trial of God,** an OT expression (cf. Exod. 17:2), means to try his patience after his will has been revealed (I Cor. 10:9). Actually this latter part of the speech is more Pauline than Petrine (cf. 13:38-39). The **yoke** is reminiscent of Gal. 5:1-3, and the idea of salvation through **grace** is a typical Pauline theme (Rom. 3:24).

15:12-18. Paul and Barnabas are presented in a passive role (contrast Gal. 2:2-10). They simply relate the events of their mission, notably **signs and wonders** (cf. 14:3) which confirm God's participation. The decision is rendered by **James** the Lord's brother, who has become the leader of the church (see above on 12:17). He supports the testimony of Peter and becomes a 2nd witness to the validity of the Gentile mission. James's speech has a Jewish quality. He speaks of Peter as **Symeon,** using the Semitic form of his name; in referring to the conversion of Cornelius he uses the OT idea that God **visited** his people (cf. Luke 1:68; 7:16). However, his quotation from **the prophets** (Amos 9:11-12) employs the LXX; his argument is not supported by the Hebrew. It seems unlikely that James himself, a Palestinian Jew, would use the Greek translation, particularly in a text which misrepresents the original.

15:19-20. James's **judgment** embodies the authoritative conclusion of the church. That Jewish Christians **should not trouble** the Gentile converts refers to the yoke (vs. 10) and implies that circumcision is not to be required. The requirements which are made (vs. 20; cf. vs. 29) constitute the "apostolic decree." It presents 2 problems: (a) What is its proper text? Some manuscripts omit **what is strangled** and add a negative form of the Golden Rule. (b) What is its meaning? If we accept the best text (including 4 prohibitions), the meaning is cultic, i.e. the decree contains ritual requirements regarding food (Lev. 17). The **pollutions of idols** means meat which has been "sacrificed to idols" (vs. 29; cf. I Cor. 8). **Unchastity** describes immoral aspects of pagan worship. Eating **what is strangled** or contains **blood** is forbidden to Jews (Gen. 9:4; Lev. 3:17). The manuscripts which omit "what is strangled" and add the Golden Rule have attempted to change cultic requirements into ethical instructions.

15:21. The fact that the law **is read every sabbath** throughout the empire may be taken either to support the Gentile mission (vss. 16-18) or to confirm the decree. In any case the result of the conference (in contrast to Gal. 2:6-10) is a compromise: circumcision is not required for salvation, but Jewish ritual requirements are essential to fellowship.

15:22-29. *The Apostolic Letter.* The decision of the conference is put into the form of a letter, which may be, after the style of Hellenistic historians, a composition of Luke. The emissaries who bring this letter **to Antioch** are **Judas . . . Barsabbas** (possibly some relation to Joseph Barsabbas, 1:23) and **Silas,** later to become a companion of Paul (vs. 40). Luke seems to identify Silas as a Roman citizen (16:37), and the letters prefer the Latin form of his name, Silvanus (I Thess. 1:1; II Cor. 1:19; I Pet. 5:12).

15:23-29. In sending the letter the Jerusalem leaders assume authority over a wide area. Actually it is addressed only to the Christians of **Syria and Cilicia** (cf. Gal. 1:21), but Paul delivers its decisions to the churches founded on his earlier mission (16:4), and James considers it directed to all Gentile Christians (21:25). The letter denounces the Judaizers of vs. 1 and commends its bearers as **men who have risked** (or, as some maintain the word should be translated, "devoted") **their lives** (cf. Rom. 16:4) for the Lord's sake. The decision of the conference is said to have been moved by the **Holy Spirit** (vs. 28). On vs. 29 see above on vss. 19-20.

It is unlikely that Paul would have approved this letter or brought it to Antioch. If it is historical, it must have been composed after Paul and Barnabas left Jerusalem. This is hinted in the fact that James's speech makes no mention of them.

15:30-35. *Return to Antioch.* The Christians at Antioch rejoice at receiving the letter. Apparently they are happy that so few requirements are placed on them. Actually the decree would be a restriction

of their previous practice (11:19-26), and the seriousness of the dispute about table fellowship is obscured (cf. Gal. 2:11-14). **Judas and Silas** are now identified as **prophets** (cf. 11:27), whose essential task is exhortation (I Cor. 14:3). Since their being **sent** back to Jerusalem (vs. 33) contradicts vs. 40, there was added in some manuscripts a decision by Silas to remain in Antioch (vs. 34, RSV footnote).

V. THE MISSION TO GREEK LANDS (15:36-19:41)

A. RETURN TO ASIA MINOR (15:36-16:5)

15:36-40. Here begins the narrative of the "2nd missionary journey" (see above on 13:1-12); new territory is not reached until 16:6-7. In contrast to 13:2 Paul is presented as the instigator of the mission. The **sharp contention** between Paul and Barnabas is attributed to the defection of **John . . . Mark** in Pamphylia (13:13). More likely their dispute concerned the question of table fellowship with Gentile Christians (Gal. 2:13). **Barnabas** is not mentioned again in Acts (but cf. I Cor. 9:6), while Mark seems to have been restored to Paul's good favor (Philem. 24). With Mark, Barnabas sails to **Cyprus**—his native land (4:36), where both have worked (13:4-12). When last mentioned previously in the narrative Mark (13:13) and Silas (15:33) were in Jerusalem.

15:41-16:3. After passing **through Syria and Cilicia** (cf. 15:23) Paul and Silas revisit the churches of the previous mission (14:6-23). I Cor. 4:17 implies that **Timothy** was a convert of Paul. Marriage with Gentiles was contrary to Jewish custom, but the offspring of such a marriage were accepted as Jews (cf. I Cor. 7:12-16). Timothy's association with Paul is well attested in the letters (e.g. I Cor. 16:10-11; Phil. 1:1; I Thess. 1:1), although the Pastoral Epistles addressed to him are probably not authentic Pauline letters (see "The Letters of Paul," pp. 1136-43).

The historicity of the circumcision of Timothy is questionable: (a) The Jerusalem conference (15:1-29; Gal. 2:1-10) decided not to require it. (b) Paul refused to submit Titus to the requirement (Gal. 2:3). (c) Paul was opposed to the demand of circumcision (Gal. 5:2-6). Actually the issue is not circumcision as a prerequisite for church membership; Timothy apparently was a member already (16:2). Luke understands Paul's action according to the pattern of missionary activity. Since the missionaries go first to the synagogue (13:14) Timothy must be prepared for social relations with the Jews (cf. I Cor. 9:20).

16:4-5. In contrast to what is historically probable (see above on 15:1-35) Paul informs the churches of Jerusalem's **decisions** (15:22-29)—a term used for official decrees of the emperor (cf. 17:7; Luke 2:1).

B. THE CALL TO MACEDONIA (16:6-10)

The mission moves W under the guidance of the **Holy Spirit.**

16:6a. The effort to determine Paul's route has resulted in the S and N Galatia theories (see Intro. to Gal.). The S Galatia theory supposes that **the region of Phrygia and Galatia** refers to the Phrygian region of the province of Galatia, i.e. the area visited on the "first missionary journey" (13:13–14:23). The N Galatia theory interprets the phrase as mentioning 2 regions, **Phrygia** and **Galatia,** thus meaning that after Paul passes through Phrygia he proceeds into N Galatia—the original Galatian region. Supporters of this theory explain the lack of detail about the mission to the N by saying that Luke's sources may not have included information about it and that he is anxious to bring the missionaries into Macedonia without delay.

16:6b-8. The Roman province of **Asia** in NT times consisted of the entire W coast of Asia Minor and the hinterland extended to **Galatia** on the E and **Bithynia** on the NE (see color map 16). The region of **Mysia,** in which was located **Troas** (an important port some 10 miles S of the site of ancient Troy; cf. 20:6-12), was the N part of this province. Apparently Luke, however, uses the name "Asia" to mean, not the whole province, but the territory around the capital city, Ephesus (see below on 18:19-21). Thus Paul, being forbidden to preach around Ephesus, moves N toward Bithynia and then, being forbidden again, turns W to go through Mysia (**passing by** evidently means not preaching) to Troas. Is the **Spirit of Jesus** which prevents Paul's entrance into Bithynia to be understood as implying a vision of the risen Lord? Cf. 23:11.

16:9-10. It is sometimes supposed that the **man of Macedonia** is Luke himself, since a "we section" (see Intro.) begins in the next vs. Luke, however, understands this as a **vision** communicated to Paul in a dream (cf. 18:9).

C. Philippi (16:11-40)

16:11-15. *Conversion of Lydia.* From Troas, Paul and his company sail to **Neapolis** (modern Kavalla, see color map 16), stopping overnight on the island of **Samothrace.** Accomplishment of this journey in 2 days required favorable winds (20:6). Taking the Via Egnatia (the Roman road to the W) they travel

inland some 9 miles to **Philippi.** Since Philippi was not **the leading city** of the province of **Macedonia** (see below on 17:1), perhaps the text should read:

"Philippi, a city of the first district of Macedonia." Inhabitants of a **Roman colony** enjoyed self-government and the right of citizenship (cf. vs. 21).

16:13-15. The word translated **place of prayer** is a synonym for "synagogue." However, just W of the Roman arch which may mark the pomerium (the area around the city from which foreign cults were excluded) the river makes a bend providing a small natural amphitheater. Since Paul makes no mention of **Lydia** in Phil. her name may be a title; **Thyatira** was a city of the region of Lydia (see map, p. 950) noted for its industry of **purple** cloth. Lydia has been a "God-fearer" (see above on 10:2), and **the Lord opened her heart** to receive the gospel (cf. Luke 24:45). Her conversion involves the baptism of her relatives and slaves, since the decision of the master is valid for the whole **household.** The church which resulted from this conversion maintained good relations with Paul (Phil. 1:3-5; 4:10, 15-16).

16:16-18. *An Exorcism.* Again the church encounters sorcery (cf. 8:9; 13:6). That Paul could perform signs and wonders is attested by his own writing (II Cor. 12:12; Rom. 15:19). The **spirit of divination** which the **slave girl** possesses is lit. "a python spirit"—a term which originated in the legend of Apollo's slaying the dragon at Delphi and later was applied to ventriloquism and soothsaying in general. To her **owners** she brings economic **gain** (cf. 19:24). The demon's recognition of the **servants of the Most High God** is reminiscent of the exorcisms of Jesus (cf. Luke 8:28). Paul, who seems to act without interest in the girl, is not portrayed in his best light. A miracle performed **in the name of Jesus Christ** is a familiar theme (cf. 3:6).

16:19-34. *Imprisonment and Escape.* Paul and Silas are **dragged . . . into the market place**—an action implying a sizable group of opponents. **Rulers** and **magistrates** are apparently 2 terms used to describe the same leaders. The latter means "praetor"—a title higher than the officials in Philippi deserved (see above on vss. 11-15), though it is attested in inscriptions. The agora of a Greek city, like a Roman forum, was both **market place** and judicial center. The ruins of the agora at Philippi include a platform used for public speeches and trials (see below on 18:12-17). The missionaries are charged with being **Jews** who have disturbed **the city.** Since Judaism was a tolerated religion under Roman law, a charge against Jews would have to be based on an illegal attempt to make proselytes. Perhaps Luke wants to show that the charges are utterly false: the missionaries are not Jews and have done nothing contrary to Roman custom (see above on vss. 11-15).

16:22-24. The victims are stripped as a preparation to **beat them with rods** (cf. II Cor. 11:25). Paul's suffering at Philippi is attested by I Thess. 2:2 (cf. Phil. 1:30). The **jailer** is probably the warden of the prison, holding perhaps the rank of centurion. The inner prison may have been underground; the traditional site can be visited today. The description of **feet** being put in **stocks** (lit. "wood") and the other extreme measures of security serve to enhance the miracle of escape.

16:25-26. There are evidences that legendary material has been inserted into the story of the escape: (*a*) the narrative of vss. 35-40 proceeds as if the **earthquake** and escape have never happened (an omission corrected by the Western manuscripts); (*b*) the other **prisoners** apparently do not escape and are ignored by the jailer (this is also corrected by the Western manuscripts); (*c*) the account has parallels to the escape of Peter (12:6-11); (*d*) typical paraphernalia of Hellenistic escape legends (e.g. the automatic opening of **doors, the singing** of the prisoners) are included.

16:27-31. The jailer's attempt on his own life is an effort to avoid humiliating judgment at the hands of his superiors (cf. 12:19). His question, which historically would be no more than a call for help, becomes the cry of one ready to obey the gospel: **What must I do to be saved?** (cf. 2:37). The answer is a simple confession of the Pauline faith (Rom. 10:9); the prediction that Paul and Silas **proclaim . . . the way of salvation** (vs. 17) is fulfilled. The call for **lights** may be symbolic.

16:32-34. Apparently the jailer takes the prisoners to his **house** for further preaching of the gospel. Then the whole group goes to a place where the **wounds** can be **washed** and the entire **family** can be **baptized** (cf. vs. 15). The setting of food before Paul and Silas is probably not a reference to the Lord's Supper but an act of kindness like the washing of their wounds. Two late manuscripts give the name of the jailer as Stephanas (cf. I Cor. 1:16).

16:35-40. *Apology of the Magistrates.* The **magistrates** send **police** to release the prisoners. The police are "lictors" (lit. "rod bearers") — men who carry the fasces (an ax bound with rods), which symbolizes their power to execute judgments of the magistrates. Paul is told of his release by the jailer, who employs the biblical admonition **Go in peace** (e.g. Exod. 4:18; Luke 8:48). Paul is incensed, insisting that officials who have **beaten . . . publicly . . . Roman citizens** must **come themselves** and release them. His charge that they are **uncondemned** probably means that they have been condemned without adequate investigation.

16:38-40. Since Roman citizens were exempt from scourging, the **magistrates** fear repercussions, perhaps removal from office. To their apology the Western text adds a confession that the missionaries are righteous men. Perhaps Paul had no opportunity to reveal his citizenship earlier (cf. 22:24-25), or possibly Luke has saved this revelation for the climax of his story. Paul is casual about leaving, stopping to visit the church which meets at the house of **Lydia.**

D. THESSALONICA (17:1-9)

17:1. Paul and his companions travel W to **Thessalonica** by way of the Via Egnatia through **Amphipolis** and **Apollonia;** the total trip is over 100 miles (see map, p. 750). Thessalonica is the most important city of Macedonia. Although the seat of the Roman provincial government, it had become a free city with its own administration.

17:2-4. According to Luke's scheme, the mission begins in the **synagogue** (cf. 13:14). A period of more than **three weeks** (lit. "three sabbaths") is suggested by Paul's claim that he worked in the city to support his mission (I Thess. 2:9) and that he received 2 offerings from Philippi while there (Phil. 4:16). The theme of the preaching is Lukan:

the scriptures are used to prove that **the Christ** must **suffer** (cf. 3:18; 26:23); since **Jesus** suffered, he must be the Christ. In I Thess. (1:5; 2:8, 13) Paul describes his message as the powerful word of God. The letter also indicates that the majority of converts were from paganism (I Thess. 1:9). This is supported by Luke's reference to **devout Greeks** (God-fearers; see above on 10:1-8) and **leading women** (cf. vs. 12), implying a mission beyond the synagogue.

17:5. Opposition to the mission is confirmed by I Thess. 1:6; 2:14, although the latter identifies the opponents as "your own countrymen." Luke's picture of the **Jews** as **jealous** (cf. 13:45) may reflect their view of the God-fearers as potential proselytes. **Rabble** from the market place are enlisted to stir up the city; opposition to the church is from the disreputable, not the law-abiding. Apparently the missionaries are staying at the house of **Jason** (vs. 7), who is at least sympathetic to the Christian cause.

17:6-9. Jason and **some of the brethren** (Christians) are **dragged** before the **city authorities** (lit. "politarchs"—a title used exclusively in Thessalonica). The charge is ironic: the rabble rousers have the audacity to accuse the Christians of disturbing the order, of having **turned the world upside down.** Jason is charged with guilt by association, while the Christians are thought to be guilty of insurrection (cf. Luke 23:1-3; John 19:12-16). Taking **security** means demanding bond—a fee which will be forfeited if the Christians cause difficulty again.

E. BEROEA (17:10-15)

17:10-12. With a measure of secrecy the Christians send Paul and Silas to **Beroea** (see map, p. 750). In that day it was an important city, and the success of Paul's mission is attested by the presence of Sopater of Beroea among his companions in 20:4. The mission begins as usual in the **synagogue,** but the Jews are **more noble** (a term which can refer either to status or to character) than those of Thessalonica. They accept **the word with all eagerness,** studying the OT to see if Paul's claims (cf. vss. 2-3) are valid. Again **Greek women** (cf. vs. 4) of high position (or character) are converted in large numbers; the Western text modifies this vs. to put equal stress on the **men.**

17:13-15. As at Thessalonica, converts among the prominent cannot prevent opposition to the church. Jews come 45 miles from Thessalonica to stir up **the crowds** (cf. 19:19), so that Paul is again hurried out of town. Most manuscripts seem to assume a route to **Athens** by **sea,** but the Western text favors an overland trip (see color map 16). The **command** for Silas and Timothy (mentioned for the first time since 16:3) to **come to him as soon as possible** appears to be answered in 18:5 with the arrival of Silas and Timothy in Corinth. However, Paul himself (I Thess. 3:1-6) implies that Timothy has accompanied him to Athens, returned to Macedonia, and rejoined him before the writing of I Thess.

F. ATHENS (17:16-34)

17:16-18. No longer of political importance in NT times (Corinth was the capital of the province of Achaia), **Athens** remained an intellectual center.

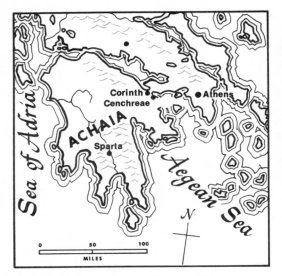

Courtesy of Herbert G. May

View from the Areopagus (Mars Hill, but see comment
on 17:19-21) looking down to the agora (marketplace)
of Athens; modern Athens is in the background

Paul is **provoked** into mission by the city's paganism.
He begins in the **synagogue,** where he encounters
Jews and God-fearers (see above on 10:1-8). The
market place (agora; see ill., col. 2) is located NW
of the Acropolis. The **Epicurean and Stoic philosophers** represent the 2 leading philosophical schools
of the day. Some of their views may be expressed in
Paul's speech. **Babbler** is lit. "seed picker" and was
used to describe birds; perhaps Paul is viewed as
an intellectual scavenger. The assumption that he
is preaching **foreign divinities** could result from his
proclamation of **Jesus and the resurrection;** the
Greek word for "resurrection" is *anastasis,* which
Paul's hearers may have construed as the name of a
goddess. More likely, however, Luke's use of these
terms sounds the major theme of Paul's sermon (cf.
vs. 31).

17:19-21. The identification of the **Areopagus** is
debated; there are 2 theories: (*a*) it is the hill of the

Courtesy of Herbert G. May

The Acropolis at Athens viewed from the W over the
Areopagus (Mars Hill, but see comment on 17:19-21)
in the foreground

god Ares (Mars Hill), a knoll W of the Acropolis;
(*b*) it is a court which originally met on the hill but
in Paul's time may have convened in a building of
the agora. The latter view is supported by the information that Paul stood **in the middle of** it (vs. 22)
and that he **went out from among them** (vs. 33).

Apparently this court supervised educational policies,
possibly investigating the credentials of foreign lecturers. Luke's notion that the Athenians were always
anxious to hear **something new** is confirmed by
Hellenistic authors.

17:22-31. About Paul's sermon much discussion
has raged. Two questions call for consideration:
(*a*) What is the relation of this sermon to the preaching of Paul? Though there may be points of contact
with Rom. 1-2, the main elements of Pauline theology are lacking. Probably the speech is a composition of the author of Acts, expressing his understanding of Christian preaching to pagans (cf. 14:
15-17). (*b*) What is the religious background of the
speech? While some features of Hellenistic philosophy
are found in the sermon, its main background seems
to be Hellenistic Judaism. The speech is a Christian
adaptation (vss. 30-31) of the typical missionary
preaching of the Hellenistic Jews.

17:22b-23. The reference to the Athenians as **very
religious** is probably intended in a positive sense,
although the term can mean "superstitious" (KJV;
cf. vs. 16). While no inscription reading **To an unknown god** has been discovered, inscriptions which
mention unknown gods have been unearthed in the
vicinity of Athens. Perhaps Luke has modified the
reference so as to give a monotheistic basis for Paul's
proclamation of the unknown God. The theme of the
sermon seems to be: knowledge of the one God,
Creator of all, demands the Christian faith.

17:24-29. Such a God **does not live in shrines
made by man** (cf. 7:48) and does not need the service of **human hands.** He has created all men **from
one** (some manuscripts add "blood"), i.e. from Adam,
so that a universal revelation is implied. The
idea of **allotted periods** and **boundaries** reflects
apocalyptic motifs (cf. I Enoch 2:1) and shows that
the Creator is also ruler of history. The belief that
all men **seek** this God, feeling or groping **after him,**
is Stoic. That all men find their being in God—**in
him we live and move and have our being**—may
reflect a Hellenistic poem, although the idea is not
lacking in Judaism (cf. Rom. 11:36). **For we are indeed his offspring** is a quotation from Aratus, a
Cilician, born about 310 B.C. The speech employs
these themes to disqualify pagan religion, specifically
its idolatry. Since men are offspring of a living God,
it is folly to suppose **the Deity is like gold, or silver,
or stone,** shaped by the hand of man.

17:30-31. The specifically Christian material is now introduced. It makes the point that the unknown God, who is creator of heaven and earth, is revealed in Jesus Christ. The idea that **ignorance** is **overlooked** by God is a Lukan theme found also in Paul (Rom. 3:25). The call to **repent** is typical of early Christian preaching (cf. 2:38), and the idea of judgment through a **man** may represent the Son of man Christology of the gospels (cf. Luke 22:69).

17:32-34. In any case the **resurrection** is the main theme of the message (cf. 23:6); that it is not to be identified with the Greek doctrine of immortality is seen in the reaction of the audience, although any concept of life after death was rejected by the Epicureans. While Paul suffers no persecution in Athens, he founds no church. **Dionysius the Areopagite** becomes a fanciful figure in later tradition. About **Damaris** nothing is known. Paul's assertion that "the household of Stephanas were the first converts of Achaia" (I Cor. 16:15) seems to deny any results in Athens. The notion some have advanced, however, that I Cor. 2:1-5 indicates a change in tactics after failure in Athens represents romanticizing.

G. CORINTH (18:1-17)

18:1-4. Located on the isthmus between N Greece and the Peloponnesus, **Corinth** (see map, p. 752) was a teeming commercial center. It had imported a host of pagan cults and was noted for immorality. There Paul met **Aquila** and **Priscilla,** recently driven from **Rome** by the Emperor **Claudius'** decree (mentioned by the historian Suetonius). While Paul makes several references to supporting himself by his work (I Cor. 4:12; 9:1-18; I Thess. 2:9), Luke is the first to identify his **trade.** Some scholars maintain that the word for **tentmakers** in NT times had come to mean "leather workers." Since Paul makes no mention of their conversion (cf. I Cor. 1:14-16), Aquila and Prisca, as he calls her (I Cor. 16:19), were probably Christians when he met them. Later they travel with him to Ephesus (18:18-19), perhaps returning eventually to Rome (Rom. 16:3). The **synagogue** (vs. 4) may have been near the gateway into the Corinthian agora, where an inscription has been found reading "Synagogue of the Hebrews."

18:5-6. The arrival of **Silas and Timothy** (see above on 17:13-15) seems to allow Paul to concentrate on **preaching.** Perhaps those who arrive **from Macedonia** bring a financial contribution (cf. II Cor. 11:9) which alleviates the burden of self-support. Paul's message, **that the Christ was Jesus,** represents Luke's typical understanding of early Christian preaching to **Jews** (cf. 18:28). Since Paul has already turned to the Gentiles (13:46) and since he will return to the synagogue in Ephesus (18:19), Luke seems to see this turning take place at every point of the mission. It illustrates the movement of the history of salvation from the Jews to the Gentiles. Here the rejection of the Jews is graphically portrayed. Shaking out **his garments** is reminiscent of 13:51; it symbolizes casting guilt on those who reject Jesus. The idea of **blood . . . upon your heads** is an OT expression (II Sam. 1:16; cf. Matt. 27:25).

18:7. Some manuscripts suggest that when Paul moves to the house of **Titius Justus** he leaves the shop of Aquila. The reading "Titus" (RSV footnote) in some manuscripts is probably an error; Paul's

host can hardly be identified with the Titus of the Pauline letters (Gal. 2:1; II Cor. 2:13).

18:8-10. Among Paul's **many** converts is **Crispus, the ruler of the synagogue** (13:15), who **with all his household** (cf. 16:15) is **baptized** by Paul (cf. I Cor. 1:14). Paul's **vision** (cf. 16:9) portends trouble **in this city.** He should **not be afraid,** a typical admonition of ancient visions, since God guides the mission.

18:11. Paul's **year and six months** in Corinth can be dated with some accuracy. According to an inscription **Gallio** (vs. 12) became governor of Achaia in A.D. 51 or 52. If Paul's appearance before him occurred at the end of the apostle's stay in Corinth, the mission must have begun in 50 or 51.

18:12-17. Luke accurately identifies **Gallio** as the **proconsul of Achaia.** He was the brother of the philosopher Seneca. The **tribunal** (lit. "step"; cf. English "bench") was probably a large marble platform which has been excavated in the center of the agora at Corinth (see above on 16:19-34). Though the charge may suggest that Paul has violated either

Courtesy of Herbert G. May

Ruins at Corinth with the Acrocorinth, site of a temple of the goddess Aphrodite, in the background; there is little doubt that these ruins locate the area where Paul was brought "before the tribunal" (Acts 18:12-17)

Roman or Jewish law (cf. Gallio's response, vs. 15) Luke probably intends to suggest simply that the Christians are disturbers of good order (cf. 17:6). However, the proconsul declares that the Christians are guilty of no **wrongdoing or vicious crime** (cf. Luke 23:4, 14, 22). **Sosthenes** has been understood by some as a Jew (**ruler of the synagogue**) beaten by the crowd (Western text "the Greeks"), by others as a convert to Christianity (cf. I Cor. 1:1) beaten by the Jews.

H. EPHESUS (18:18–19:41)

18:18-23. *A Trip to the East.* Paul leaves Corinth casually (cf. 16:40) and sails **for Syria.** Perhaps Luke continues to view **Antioch** as Paul's missionary base (cf. 13:1-3; 14:26-27). That **Priscilla and Aquila** cross the Aegean and found a household church at Ephesus is confirmed by I Cor. 16:19. Apparently Paul (not Aquila) has made a Nazirite **vow,** which normally was terminated by shaving the head (Num. 6:5, 18). At **Cenchreae,** the E port of Corinth, a suburban church had been established (cf. Rom. 16:1).

18:19-21. An important port at the terminus of

trade route from the E, **Ephesus** (see map below) was the capital of the Roman province of Asia (see above on 16:6*b*-8). The temple of Artemis, one of the 7 wonders of the world, had been built outside its walls (see below on 19:26-27). Paul's preaching in **the synagogue** probably represents an effort to present the apostle as founder of the Ephesian church (cf. 18:27).

18:22-23. After landing **at Caesarea,** Paul goes up and greets **the church;** the terminology implies a visit to Jerusalem. Since no mention of this visit is made in the Pauline correspondence, 2 theories have been devised: (*a*) It is a doublet with the conference visit (15:1-35; see comment); Paul (Gal. 2:1) seems to date the conference later in his career than Luke places it, and parallels can be found in 16:6; 18:23. (*b*) It is a doublet with the collection visit (21:7 ff.); both are made via Caesarea (21:8), involve a vow (21:23), and predict danger in the city (18:21; 21:14).

18:24-28. *The Mission of Apollos.* The activity of **Apollos** is the only non-Pauline mission described in Acts 16-28. He is said to be an **eloquent** (or learned) man, **well versed** in the OT. Perhaps he is steeped in the philosophy and allegorical method of **Alexandria.** Luke views him as a Christian whose understanding of the faith is incomplete. He is familiar with the life and teachings of **Jesus** but knows **only the baptism of John**—a baptism which does not convey the Spirit (19:1-7). After instruction from **Priscilla and Aquila,** Apollos preaches Jesus as the Messiah—a message identical with Paul's (cf. vs. 5).

18:27-28. Apollos' mission to **Achaia** is supported by a letter of recommendation (cf. II Cor. 3:1-3) from the Ephesian church. His presence in Corinth is attested by I Cor. 1-4. Though Luke records no meeting of Paul and Apollos, their personal contact is affirmed by I Cor. 16:12.

19:1-7. *Paul and the Disciples of John.* Paul re-

turns to **Ephesus** by way of **the upper country,** i.e. overland through the interior of Asia Minor, the **region of Galatia and Phrygia** (18:23). Though Luke's account of Paul's Ephesian ministry is detailed, events known from the letters are lacking. E.g. Paul's difficult relation with the Corinthians involved a hasty trip to Corinth (II Cor. 12:14; 13:1) and the writing of 3 letters (I Cor. 5:9; II Cor. 7:8). Luke nowhere mentions Paul's literary activity. The apostle suffered various difficulties in Ephesus (II Cor. 1:8); some have claimed that he was thrown into the arena (I Cor. 15:32) or imprisoned (see Intro. to Phil.).

19:1*b*-7. Paul encounters **disciples** who have not received the **Holy Spirit.** Luke assumes that these **twelve** (vs. 7) are Christians who, like Apollos (18:26), need fuller instruction. However, Christians who **have never even heard that there is a Holy Spirit** would be an anomaly. These are more likely members of a sect of John the Baptist. Paul characterizes John's baptism as a ritual of **repentance** (cf. 13:24; Luke 3:3) and interprets his message as proclaiming the coming one (cf. Luke 3:16). In contrast to Apollos these disciples are rebaptized **in the name of . . . Jesus** and after the laying on of **hands** receive the Spirit. Luke sees them as similar to the converts of Samaria (cf. 8:14-17) and attributes to Paul the apostolic power to convey the Spirit. Proof of its presence is their speaking in **tongues** (cf. 2:4; 10:46) and prophesying—manifestations of the Spirit which the author considers identical (cf. 2:17).

19:8-22. *Preaching the Word and Acts of Power.* Again Paul preaches in the **synagogue** (cf. 18:19). In Acts the **kingdom of God** seems similar to the church (cf. 8:12), but the idea of God's rule to be consummated in the future is not lacking (cf. 14:22). Paul's withdrawal from the Jews fits the Lucan pattern (cf. 18:6). The **hall** (or school) **of Tyrannus** is a lecture room rented to visiting philosophers; Tyrannus could be either a rhetorician who used the hall or its owner. According to the Western text (RSV footnote) Paul preaches from 11 A.M. to 4 P.M., i.e. during the time of leisure when an audience is available. The **two years** are in addition to the **three months** in the synagogue (cf. 20:31). The reference to **all the residents of Asia** is an exaggeration, but Luke may be suggesting a mission into other cities (see above on 16:6*b*-8; cf. Col. 2:1; 4:13; Rev. 1:11).

19:11-13. Paul's encounter with the Jewish exorcists is probably legendary; the story has parallels to the miracles of Peter (5:12-16). Paul's power to perform signs and wonders is of course claimed in his own writings (Rom. 15:18-19; II Cor. 12:12). However, the notion that **handkerchiefs or aprons** were permeated with a healing power which exuded from Paul's **body** (lit. "skin") borders on magic. The existence of Jewish exorcists is attested by the appearance of Semitic names in Greek magical papyri which have been discovered, and the incantation "I adjure you by Jesus the God of the Hebrews" is also found in this literature.

19:14-20. The story of the **seven sons of . . . Sceva** is humorous. Actually no **Jewish high priest** with this name is known; perhaps these men are impostors. **Seven** heightens the miraculous—one person possessed with a demon can overcome 7 men.

The demon's response, **Jesus I know, and Paul I know; but who are you?** indicates that the name of Jesus is powerful but dangerous; only those who have accepted the name dare use it. This point of view is not entirely consistent with the words of Jesus (Luke 9:49-50). News of this bizarre incident works conversions among the magicians. **Divulging their practices** may mean that they reveal their secret spells and incantations. The **books** (i.e. scrolls) which are **burned** probably record their charms and spells; Ephesus was famous for magical writings, some of which were called "Ephesian scripts." A precedent for burning unfavorable books had been established by Augustus. The total value of the literature is said to be **fifty thousand pieces of silver**—presumably drachmas (see comment on Luke 15:8-10).

19:21-22. Paul's travel plans are disclosed in what is almost an outline of the rest of the book (cf. 1:8). His trip to **Macedonia and Achaia** is realized in 20:1-2 (cf. I Cor. 16:5-9; II Cor. 2:12; 7:5) and his journey to Jerusalem in 21:17. The actual purpose of the latter, taking an offering to the Jerusalem church (Rom. 15:22-29), is barely mentioned by Luke (24:17). **Rome** is the goal of his entire book (28:14). The travels of **Timothy** are confirmed by I Cor. 4:17; 16:10. Is **Erastus** the same as the man mentioned in Rom. 16:23 (cf. II Tim. 4:20)? No mention is made of Titus, who figured prominently in Paul's mission at this time (II Cor. 2:12-13; 7:6; 8:16-24).

19:23-41. *Conflict with Paganism*. This narrative is full of local color; it rests on accurate information. **Demetrius** is presented as **a silversmith, who made silver shrines of Artemis.** An inscription has been found which refers to a certain Demetrius as a "temple maker," i.e. one of the officials of the Artemision, the ruling body of the temple. No silver **shrines,** presumably replicas of the temple, have been found at Ephesus, but small souvenir temples used as amulets have been discovered elsewhere. Possibly, however, Demetrius makes miniature images of the goddess. **Artemis,** while bearing the name of the Greek virgin huntress, is actually a form of the Asian "Great Mother"—a fertility deity widely worshiped in this section of the empire (vs. 27).

19:26-27. Christianity challenges pagan business practices (cf. 16:19)—a fact confirmed by Pliny's letter to the Emperor Trajan (A.D. 112). Demetrius' charge that **Paul has persuaded** many **people** would be understood by the Christian reader as proof of the mission's power. That Paul attacked idolatry is according to Lukan ideas (cf. 17:29), but no pagan believed that **gods made with hands** were really **gods.** The **temple of . . . Artemis** was the sign of Ephesus' greatness (see above on 18:19-21). About 340 by 160 feet in dimension, it displayed over 100 columns some 60 feet high; its marble blocks, according to some reports, were cemented together by gold instead of mortar.

19:28-34. The cry of the rioting populace, **Great is Artemis of the Ephesians,** has been found in inscriptions. Ruins of the **theater** where they gathered are still clearly visible to the modern traveler (see ill., p. 756). On Paul's **companions** who are dragged into the **confusion** see below on 20:4. Paul is pre-vented from entering the theater by **friends** who are among the most prominent people of the province—the **Asiarchs.** Although their exact function is not known, these wealthy officials of Asia were patrons of public events and supervisors of religious festivals. The role of **Alexander** is not clear. He may be a Jew who hopes to distinguish his people from the Christians, or he may be a convert who is attempting to defend Paul. According to the Pastoral Epistles a certain "Alexander the coppersmith" is an opponent of the apostle (II Tim. 4:14; I Tim. 1:20).

19:35. The **town clerk** is the executive officer of the civic assembly—the governing body of this free city. His speech is a composition of Luke. The title **temple keeper** (lit. "temple sweeper") was given to cities which were centers of emperor worship; inscriptions have been discovered which show that Ephesus was noted both for this honor and also as the temple keeper of Artemis. The reference to **the sacred stone that fell from the sky** is obscure. Perhaps the temple contained an image which was supposed to have had a supernatural origin, or possibly the statue of the goddess had been a meteorite. Images of Artemis, standing with high crown and upper body covered with breasts, have been found at Ephesus.

19:36-41. The main point of the speech is that Paul and his companions are guilty of no civil offense; they are not **sacrilegious** or **blasphemers** of the goddess—a point which seems to mollify Paul's normal attack on idolatry (cf. 17:29). If Demetrius and the members of his guild have valid charges let them follow legal procedure (cf. 24:19). Ephesus, as a provincial capital, is the seat of the proconsul and his court. **The courts are open** on stated days. If this is not satisfactory they can appear before one of the 3 **regular** monthly meetings of the municipal **assembly.** The real **danger** (cf. vs. 27) is that the citizens could be charged with rioting—a crime not tolerated by the Romans. Charges against the Christians are made by a riotous mob, but legal process would vindicate them.

VI. The Journey to Rome (20:1–28:31)

A. Return to Jerusalem (20:1–21:14)

20:1-6. *A Visit to Greece*. Paul's trip to **Macedonia** and **Greece** fulfills the plans of 19:21 (cf. I Cor. 16:5). His route is via Troas (II Cor. 2:12-13) to Philippi (II Cor. 7:5-7) and through Macedonia to Corinth. During his stay of **three months** in Achaia he writes Rom.

Paul's original plan seems to have been to sail from Corinth directly to Palestine to take the collection from his churches to the saints of Judea (see above on 19:21-22). Since Macedonia and Achaia have already made their contribution (Rom. 15:25-26) a trip through these provinces is not needed. The nature of the **plot** against Paul is not explained; perhaps the large amount of money offered a temptation. Though Luke seems to assume that the representatives of the churches have gathered at Corinth, it is possible that Paul changes his plans because of difficulties involved in the collection (cf. I Cor. 16:1-5; II Cor. 8-9) and that he gathers the delegation on the way to the E.

20:4. Seven representatives are named; no dele-

Courtesy of Herbert G. May

The theater at Ephesus capable of seating *ca.* 24,000 spectators; it was here that silversmiths stirred up a riot against the disciples of Paul (see comment on 19:28-34)

gation from either Corinth or Philippi is mentioned. Some have wanted to identify **Sopater** with Sosipater of Rom. 16:21, but there is no evidence for a connection. **Aristarchus** appears also in 19:29; 27:2; Col. 4:10; Philem. 24. How is **Gaius of Derbe** in Galatia to be reconciled with "Gaius and Aristachus, Macedonians" in 19:29? Possible solutions are: (*a*) Two different men are intended (cf. others of this name in Rom. 16:23; I Cor. 1:14; III John 1). (*b*) **Of Derbe** (lit. "Derbean") is the identifying surname of a Macedonian who came originally from Derbe. (*c*) **Of Derbe** is a scribal error for "of Doberus," a town near Philippi (more probably this reading in a few manuscripts is an attempt to "correct" the inconsistency). (*d*) **Gaius** belongs with **the Thessalonians,** while (by slight emendation of the Greek text) **of Derbe** goes with **Timothy** (cf. 16:1). (*e*) A whole line of text has been lost between **Gaius** and **of Derbe,** reading "and of the Galatians" followed by one or more names, the last being a Derbean. Probably only **Tychicus** (cf. Col. 4:7) and **Trophimus** (cf. 21:29; II Tim. 4:20) wait for Paul **at Troas.** Either this is the place where they join the group or they have been sent ahead to make travel arrangements.

20:5-6. Here another "we section" begins (see Intro.). Since this usage appeared last in **Philippi** (16:16-17) it is possible that the writer of the "we" source joined the company again at that place. The celebration of **the days of Unleavened Bread** at Philippi is not explained. Is this some early form of an Easter service, or are the Christians observing Jewish ritual? (cf. vs. 16). At this season sailing conditions are not good; the trip from Neapolis to Troas takes **five** days (cf. 16:11).

20:7-12. *Preaching in Troas.* At Troas (see above on 16:6*b*-8) Paul participates in the weekly worship of the church. The **first day of the week** is Sunday; but it is not clear whether the meeting takes place on Sunday or Saturday evening, i.e. whether Luke follows the Greek or Jewish method of reckoning time. Probably the former, since the **morrow** seems to occur at **daybreak** (vs. 11) and not at sundown. The breaking of **bread** (cf. 2:42) is apparently the primary act of worship. Its observance included a whole meal (vs. 11)—an early form of the agape, or love feast—but the breaking of bread seems to have been a distinct part of the meal which had eucharistic meaning.

20:9-12. Like 19:13-17 the story of **Eutychus** is not without comic elements. The reference to **many lights** (Western text "many small windows") could explain the stuffiness of **the upper chamber** or suggest that the **young man** (a lad or boy in vs. 12) fell asleep in spite of the light. After the fall **from the third story** Eutychus is **taken up dead.** Though Paul says that **his life is in him** (cf. Luke 8:55) Luke intends to describe a miracle of resurrection. Its background is found in I Kings 17:21; II Kings 4:34-35; it is parallel to a raising performed by Peter (9:36-41).

20:13-38. *Farewell at Miletus.* Paul's trip from Troas to **Miletus** (see map, p. 754) is sketched in a "we section" (see Intro.). While his companions sail around Cape Lectum to **Assos,** Paul takes the more direct route by land—a distance of about 20 miles. There he joins his company; and together they sail S to **Mitylene,** the chief town of the island of Lesbos, and then between **Chios** and the mainland, coming eventually to Miletus. It is not clear whether they actually stop at **Samos** on the way or simply come near. Some manuscripts add (RSV footnote) that they landed at **Trogyllium**—a port on the mainland opposite Samos. This would have been a more convenient place for Paul's meeting with the Ephesian elders. **Miletus,** however, was an important port in Paul's day. Its impressive ruins, especially the magnificent theater, can still be seen.

20:16. According to Luke, Paul sailed **past Ephesus** because **he was hastening** on to **Jerusalem** in order to arrive by **Pentecost.** No mention is made of this, however, in the narrative of his arrival in Jerusalem (21:15 ff.), and there is time to tarry at both Tyre (21:3-4) and Caesarea (21:10). Moreover, the round trip from Miletus to Ephesus to summon the elders must have required at least 4 or 5 days. Therefore the motive for missing Ephesus was more likely the danger involved in facing the opposition there (cf. II Cor. 1:8-10).

20:17-18a. The speech to the Ephesian **elders** (cf. 14:23) is the only Pauline sermon to Christians recorded by Luke. Since it contains prophecy after the event (vss. 23, 25) and contradicts Paul's own anticipation of this journey (Rom. 15:28, but cf. vs. 31) the speech is essentially a composition of Luke. Its purpose is to present the goal of Paul's entire mission. It is written in the style of a farewell address.

20:18b-21. First the speech recalls Paul's missionary activity in the past. He has served **the Lord with all humility and with tears** (cf. vs. 31; II Cor. 2:4). Although no **plots** have been mentioned in connection with the Asian mission, one was faced at Corinth (vs. 3). The idea that Paul **did not shrink from declaring** his message is a theme of the speech (cf. vss. 27, 31); perhaps Luke has in mind some specific opponents, or heretics who did not proclaim **the whole counsel of God.** The content of the message—**repentance** and **faith**—is typical of Lukan summaries of the gospel (cf. 17:30; 16:31), as is the notion that Paul repeatedly made converts among both **Jews** and **Greeks** (cf. 18:4).

20:22-27. Next Paul's future is revealed. He will **go to Jerusalem, bound in the Spirit,** i.e. under the guidance of God (cf. 19:21). Up to this point the reader has not been told of the Spirit's prediction that **imprisonment and afflictions await** Paul; this will be disclosed in 21:4, 10-14. Although the Greek construction of vs. 24 is confusing, the meaning is basically clear: Paul is ready to lay down his life **to testify to the gospel.** This idea, together with the statement that **they should see his face no more** (vs. 38; cf. vs. 29) betrays the author's knowledge of Paul s death. Only here does Luke report Paul's using the term **gospel** (cf. 15:7), although it is common in his letters. On **the kingdom** see above on 19:8-22. That Paul is **innocent of the blood** of his hearers means that he has faithfully proclaimed the message which offers life.

20:28-31. Next Paul's admonition to the elders is presented (cf. I Pet. 2:25; 5:2-4). The understanding of church organization here is postapostolic. Paul's charismatic leaders (cf. I Cor. 12:27-31) have been replaced by the officials of the Pastoral Epistles; the **Holy Spirit** functions through the institution. The elders are called **guardians**—lit. "overseers" or, according to the English adaptation of this Greek

term, "bishops" (cf. Phil. 1:1). These leaders are presented under the figure of the shepherd and the sheep (cf. John 10:7-18)—a typical representation of the bishop and the church in later Christian literature.

20:28b. This clause is confused by textual variants. While the best manuscripts read **church** "of God" (RSV footnote), Luke would not suggest that the church was **obtained** (or saved; cf. Luke 17:33) by God's **own blood.** Actually the idea of salvation through blood is not a Lukan concept, so that Luke is using (perhaps inadequately) traditional material here. The translation could be "the church of God which he obtained by the blood of his own," i.e. Christ (RSV footnote; cf. Rom. 8:32).

20:29-31. Paul's warning to the church might suggest dangers both from without (persecution) and from within (heresy). However, the use of **wolves** to describe false teachers is common in early Christian authors (cf. Matt. 7:15). That heresy actually arose in Ephesus is attested by I Tim. 1:3-7.

20:32-35. Finally Paul speaks his farewell in the form of a last will and testament (cf. I Sam. 12:2-3). He commends the church to the **grace** (favor) of God. His own self-support (see above on 18:1-4) is an example of how the elders should work to **help the weak** (cf. I Thess. 4:11; also Eph. 4:28). The phrase **remembering the words of the Lord Jesus, how he said** has become a formula (cf. 11:16; Luke 22:61). The words **it is more blessed to give than to receive** may represent an authentic saying of Jesus not preserved in the Synoptic tradition, although the words were proverbial in the Hellenistic world.

20:36-38. The farewell scene is portrayed with affection. After prayer the elders **embraced** Paul, lit. "fell on his neck"—an OT expression (cf. Gen. 33:4; 45:14) used in the parable of the lost son (Luke 15:20).

21:1-14. *The Trip to Palestine.* Though this material is part of a "we section" (see Intro.), only the stations of Paul's journey between Miletus and **Tyre** are mentioned (see color map 16). His course is S to **Cos,** the main city of the island of that name, and then to **Rhodes,** coming finally to **Patara**— a town on the SW corner of what is now Turkey (see color map 16). The Western text (RSV footnote) adds that he goes a short distance E to Myra—a more important port (cf. 27:5-6). From there it may have been easier to find a **ship** sailing directly to **Phoenicia.** The distance to **Tyre** is about 350 miles. **Cyprus** is sighted, but the course is to the W and S of it, supported by the prevailing winds from the NW. Because of commercial red tape **seven days** would not be an inordinate length of time to **unload the cargo.**

21:3-6. No information about the founding of a church in **Tyre** has been recorded (but cf. 11:19; Luke 6:17). Paul seems to know of its existence and seeks out **the disciples.** Probably Luke does not intend to suggest that the **Spirit** warned **Paul not to go on to Jerusalem,** since that journey is according to the will of God (vs. 14). Instead the Christians have received a revelation of the future tragedy and on their own behalf urge Paul not to proceed. The phrase **when our days there were ended** could be interpreted to mean "when the ship was fitted

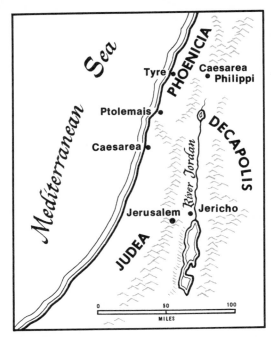

out for the journey" (but see below on vs. 7). The farewell scene parallels that of 20:36-38.

21:7. The meaning of this vs. is not entirely clear; it could read: "After we had completed the voyage, we arrived at Ptolemais from Tyre"—suggesting an overland trip of about 20 miles. At **Ptolemais** (see color map 14) Paul meets the church and presumably says farewell. The distance to **Caesarea** (see above on 10:1-8) is about 40 miles. **Philip** was last mentioned in 8:40 at Caesarea. The title **evangelist** is rare in the NT (only Eph. 4:11; II Tim. 4:5), and here it seems to refer to the preaching activity of Philip—one of the 7 (6:5). Though the content of their prophecy is not related, the **unmarried** (virgin) **daughters** of Philip no doubt confirm the word of the Tyrians (vs. 4) and anticipate the prediction of Agabus (vss. 10-14).

21:10-14. Luke has **Agabus** (11:28) foretelling the famine that occasioned a trip by Paul to carry relief to the Jerusalem church. Since that visit is probably the same as this one (see above on 11:27-30) Agabus plays his only role here. The binding of **his own feet and hands** with **Paul's girdle** represents the symbolic action of the OT prophets (cf. Isa. 20:2; Jer. 13:1-7). Though the Jews themselves will not actually bind Paul (vs. 33), they are, as in the case of Jesus, ultimately responsible for delivering him **into the hands of the Gentiles** (cf. 2:23). While he is moved by the concern of the Christians, Paul is **ready not only to be imprisoned but even to die at Jerusalem for the name** (or "sake"; cf. 5:41) **of the Lord Jesus.** Paul, like Jesus (Luke 22:42), determines to follow the **will** of God. A paradox of the necessity of Paul's journey (20:22) and the freedom of his own decision is maintained.

B. Jerusalem Events (21:15–23:30)

21:15-26. *Church and Temple.* Jerusalem is about 65 miles from Caesarea (see map above). Since the journey cannot be made in a day (cf. 23:31-33) **the house of Mnason** is probably a convenient stop on the way. It is possible, of course, that Mnason lives in the environs of Jerusalem and that Paul considers him more sympathetic to the Gentile mission. Like Barnabas (4:36) Mnason may have been one of the **early** converts from **Cyprus** (cf. 11:20).

21:17-19. In Jerusalem the church receives Paul **gladly.** No mention is made of his delivering the offering (Rom. 15:25-27). On the next day Paul appears before **the elders.** The apostles are not mentioned, and **James** is the leader (see above on 12:17). Paul's report is reminiscent of 15:4, 12; the response suggests Jerusalem's enthusiastic support of his mission.

21:20-25. This is a "collective speech"—the leaders speak in chorus. Their point is that Paul should prove his loyalty to Judaism by participating in Jewish ritual. **Thousands** is lit. "myriads," i.e. "ten thousands"—an exaggeration. These Jewish Christians charge that Paul teaches the Jews of the Dispersion to **forsake Moses,** abandon circumcision, and neglect **the customs.** The reader of Paul's letters knows that these charges are essentially true (cf. Rom. 10:4; Gal. 5:6), but the reader of Acts is confident that they are false—Paul has insisted on the circumcision of Timothy (16:3) and has been scrupulous about ritual (18:18).

21:23-24. The elders advise Paul to support **four men** in fulfilling their **vow.** Since they are going to **shave their heads** a Nazirite ritual is in view (see above on 18:18-23). The **expenses** included the cost of sacrifices which completed the vow (Num. 6:13-20). To pay this for another was considered a meritorious act. What the elders mean by suggesting that Paul **purify** himself (cf. 24:18) is not clear. Since the Nazirite vow required 30 days Paul could not have become involved. Perhaps Luke thinks of some special defilement which required **seven days** (vs. 27) of purification (cf. Num. 19:12), or possibly he has misunderstood the length of the Nazirite vow on the basis of Num. 6:9.

21:25-26. The **letter** to Gentile converts (see above on 15:20-21, 23-29) is mentioned as if Paul has never heard of it. While the apostle is able to make concessions to the Jews (cf. I Cor. 9:20), participation in a ritual to prove his loyalty to the law (cf. Rom. 7:12) would be out of character.

21:27-40. *Paul's Arrest.* The arrest and imprisonment of Paul are narrated in detail; parallels with the passion of Jesus are apparent. The trouble is instigated by **Jews** who have come from **Asia** (i.e. Ephesus; see above on 16:6b-8), perhaps for Pentecost (cf. 20:16). They have seen **Trophimus,** a Greek of their own region (20:4), in Jerusalem with Paul and assume that Paul has taken him **into the temple** (cf. 24:6). Their charge is reminiscent of 6:13. Gentiles were debarred from the temple; as inscriptions which marked the barrier between the court of the Gentiles and the court of Israel show (see ill., p. 759), they entered at the cost of their lives.

21:30-36. Paul is **dragged . . . out of the temple** and the **gates** are **shut,** presumably to prevent rioting within the holy precincts. Report of the commotion comes to the **tribune of the cohort** (cf. 10:1) who commands a garrison of theoretically 1,000 men. Taking with him **centurions** (the plural sug-

Courtesy of the Musées d'Archéologie d'Istanbul

Balustrade inscription from Herod's temple in Jerusalem warning Gentiles not to enter; it reads: "No foreigner is to enter within the balustrade and enclosure around the temple. Whoever is caught will render himself liable to the consequent penalty of death"; see comment on 21:27-40

gests at least 2) and their commands (no less than 200 men), the tribune saves Paul from lynching by the mob. Paul is **arrested** and chained between **two** soldiers (cf. 12:6); the officer considers him the cause of the disturbance (vs. 38).

21:34-36. The confusion of the crowd makes it impossible for the tribune to **learn the facts**—a theme of Luke's imprisonment narrative (cf. 22:30; 25:26). Paul is brought to the **barracks,** which are probably in the Tower of Antonia located in the NW corner of the temple area (see color map 13). The fact that he has to be **carried** to the **steps** which led into the tower may hint that Paul has been beaten into unconsciousness. Luke may have ignored this detail in order to make possible Paul's speech.

21:37-39. The tribune notes that Paul can speak **Greek.** Not only is he a cultured man, he is not to be mistaken as **the Egyptian.** According to Josephus this insurrectionist led a group of people from **the wilderness** to the Mt. of Olives in a revolt. Though they were defeated, their leader disappeared. Josephus also mentions the **Assassins** (the Sicarii, or "dagger bearers"), though not in connection with the Egyptian. Paul's response makes 2 points: (a) He is a Jew and therefore has a right to enter the temple, (b) He is a **citizen** of **Tarsus** and thus not an Egyptian. **No mean city** is a typical Hellenistic expression.

21:40. That a Roman officer would allow a prisoner responsible for a riot to speak to the crowd which has been rioting is unlikely. Paul motions **with his hand** to quiet the crowd and speaks in Aramaic, popularly called **Hebrew.**

22:1-21. *Paul's Defense Before Israel.* This speech is a composition of Luke. Not only is its setting improbable (see above on 21:40); the speech makes no contribution to the progress of the narrative (cf. 21:34 with 22:24). The purpose of this **defense** (apology) is to prove that Paul's mission is motivated by the God of Israel. The address **Brethren and fathers** is identical with that used by Stephen before the sanhedrin (7:2). Although **a great hush** has already come over the crowd (21:40), the auditors become even **more quiet** at hearing Paul's "Hebrew" (see above on 21:40).

22:3. This vs. is subject to a variety of interpretations. Instead of the translation adopted by the RSV, "Paul" may mean, "I was born at Tarsus, brought up in this city, educated at the feet of Gamaliel"; i.e. Luke may accept the tradition that Paul's parents moved to Jerusalem when he was quite young (cf. 23:16; 26:4). It is also not clear whether Paul is supposed to have been educated in a **strict manner** or in the **strict** "interpretation" **of the law** (cf. Phil. 3:4-6). The former would allow as a further alternative that he was **zealous** "for the law" (cf. 21:20) rather than **for God** (cf. Rom. 10:2). Sitting **at the feet** of a rabbi is the typical posture of the Jewish learner (cf. Luke 10:39). On **Gamaliel** see above on 5:34.

22:4-5. Paul's conversion has been discussed in connection with 9:1-22 (see comment). Both accounts set the narrative in the context of Paul's persecuting. Here it seems implied that **the high priest** at that time (in fact probably Caiaphas; see above on 4:5-7) was the same as the current one, Ananias (23:2; some manuscripts add his name here). The **council of elders** is the sanhedrin. The wording of vs. 5 may suggest that those persecuted in **Damascus** had fled there, perhaps from Jerusalem.

22:6-11. In the narration of the conversion experience the major differences in the 2 accounts are: (a) Here mention is made of the time of Paul's vision as **noon** (cf. 26:13). (b) Jesus is called **Jesus of Nazareth.** (c) The companions of Paul are said to have seen **the light** but not heard **the voice** (cf. 9:7).

22:12-16. The account of **Ananias,** though similar to 9:10-19, makes a different emphasis: Ananias is a **devout** Jew, highly regarded **by all the Jews** of Damascus. No mention is made of his vision. The content of his speech has an OT flavor. Christ is described as the **Just** (or "Righteous") **One** (cf. 3:14). The question **Why do you wait?** may represent an early formula used in baptismal liturgy. Stress is placed on Paul's role as a **witness** (cf. 1:22).

22:17-18. The narrative of Paul's first visit to Jerusalem after his conversion differs from 9:26-30 (see comment). For one thing the impression is given that Paul returns to the Holy City immediately after his baptism (contrast Gal. 1:17). The description of this **trance** has no parallel in Acts. Though Paul was not without ecstatic experiences (cf. II Cor. 12:2-4), the notion that his Gentile mission is motivated by a vision in the temple is inconsistent with Gal. 1:16. Luke is anxious to present Paul as a loyal Jew who is found **praying in the temple** and receives his commission from the messianic center (cf. Luke 24:47-48). The narrative also fits Luke's pattern of a Gentile mission following Jewish rejection (cf. 13:46; Luke 14:16-24).

22:19-21. Again reference is made to Paul's career as a persecutor (cf. Phil. 3:4-6; Gal. 1:13-14; I Cor. 15:9) and to his role in the death of **Stephen** (7:58; 8:1, 3). The mention of Stephen's **witness** even to the shedding of **blood** shows the trend toward the early Christian emphasis on martyrdom as the supreme form of witnessing (cf. Rev. 2:13). In contrast to vs. 19 Paul's past probably made him a more effective witness to the Jews.

22:22-29. *Jewish Mob and Roman Citizen.* Paul's

759

speech is "interrupted" after it is finished (cf. 4:1; 7:54). Apparently the mention of **Gentiles** sets the crowd into an uproar. A mission to Gentiles should not have troubled the Jews (cf. Matt. 23:15), but Paul is claiming divine inspiration for a heretical mission. The cry **Away with such a fellow!** is reminiscent of the mob's reaction to Jesus (Luke 23: 18). It is not clear from the Greek verb used whether the **garments** are thrown off or brandished; the typical response would have been tearing their clothing (cf. 14:14). Throwing **dust into the air** has no known ancient parallel, but it evidently symbolizes extreme wrath.

22:24-26. Again the **tribune** commands Paul **to be brought into the barracks** (cf. 21:34). To examine **by scourging** means to exact confession by torture. Vs. 25 can mean either that they **tied him up with the thongs** in preparation for scourging (cf. vs. 30) or that they put him forward to receive the thongs— i.e. the lash, which was made of leather thongs. Paul's failure to reveal himself as a **Roman citizen** (cf. 16:36-39) earlier seems strange, but it probably displays Luke's ability to build a climax. The word **uncondemned** could mean either that Paul is about to be punished without a trial or that he is about to be scourged without legal sentence. Citizenship made one immune from either examination by scourging or from punishment without trial.

22:27-29. The tribune has purchased his **citizenship for a large sum**—a practice common during the reign of Emperor Claudius. This is confirmed by the tribune's name, Claudius Lysias (23:26), since a new citizen normally took the name of his emperor. Perhaps Paul's father received citizenship from Mark Antony, who granted the privilege to whole peoples in the E.

22:30-23:11. *Paul Before the Sanhedrin.* This scene is of doubtful historicity. It is unlikely that a Roman tribune would keep a citizen bound overnight and then bring him before a Jewish court instead of hearing his own explanation as to the **real reason why the Jews accused him.** No progress is made in the narrative; for the 3rd time Paul is ordered brought **into the barracks** (vs. 10; cf. 21:34; 22:24). Paul's claim that he has **lived before God in all good conscience** seems to ignore confessions like I Cor. 15:9. While the term "conscience" is common in Paul (e.g. Rom. 2:15; II Cor. 1:12), this notion of a "clear conscience" (24:16; I Tim. 1:5) represents a different meaning.

23:2-5. According to Josephus, **Ananias** was appointed **high priest** in A.D. 48 and was an insolent man of bad temper. Perhaps he is enraged by Paul's consistent plea of innocence; the striking of Paul is parallel to that of Jesus (John 18:22). Paul's rebuke, that the high priest is a **whitewashed wall,** is reminiscent of Matt. 23:27 and Ezek. 13:10-11. Possibly Luke knows of the assassination of Ananias (A.D. 66). Why Paul is not able to recognize the presiding officer is not explained. Luke's purpose is to present the high priest as acting **contrary to the law,** while Paul, even in criticizing himself, quotes the OT (Exod. 22:28).

23:6-7. That Paul would use his former position as a **Pharisee** (cf. 26:5) to escape the judgment of the council seems out of character and in conflict with texts like Phil. 3:2-11. In spite of 24:21 belief

in **the resurrection of the dead** is not the charge which has been leveled against Paul (cf. 21:28). Moreover, the translation **the hope and the resurrection,** as if Paul were talking about 2 different things, is misleading; the meaning is probably "the hope of the resurrection" (cf. 24:15). Luke is apparently indicating that the bond between Christianity and true Judaism is belief in resurrection.

23:8-10. That the **Sadducees** rejected the idea of **resurrection** is supported by both the Synoptics (Mark 12:18-23) and Josephus; that they did not accept **angels** or **spirits** is attested only here. Luke gives the impression that the Sadducees, rather than rejecting these beliefs because of their adherence to the Pentateuch, are guilty of skepticism. While **the scribes of the Pharisees' party** (cf. Luke 5:30) are presented as the defenders of Paul, Judaism is discredited by its divisiveness. The Pharisees' acknowledgment that Paul may have received revelation implies their assent to either his conversion experience (22:6-11) or his vision in the temple (22: 17-21). Some manuscripts, in the spirit of 5:39, add: "Let us not fight against God."

23:11. At this time of crisis Paul has another vision (cf. 18:9-10). His purpose since 19:21 has been to go to Rome, but now divine sanction is given to this intention in spite of human opposition.

23:12-22. *A Plot Against Paul.* According to Luke, Paul is removed to Caesarea in order to escape a plot; his Roman citizenship would guarantee the transfer anyway. The theme of destroying the apostle by an ambush is repeated in 25:3. Though the Jews had methods to find release from an oath, the reader is left wondering whether the **more than forty** starved to death. Since only **the chief priests and elders,** not the Pharisees, are mentioned, the plotters may be making their request of the Sadducean faction of the sanhedrin (but cf. 4:23). The wording of the proposed request could mean either that the council members wish to know more about the case or that they hope to reach a verdict. The idea of accurate knowledge is thematic (vs. 20; cf. 21:34; 24:22).

23:16. The reference to **the son of Paul's sister** may represent a tradition that Paul grew up in Jerusalem (cf. 22:3; 26:4). How the **young man** learns of the plot is not clear. Perhaps Paul's sister has connections with the hierarchy, or possibly the boy has stumbled onto the information by accident. Prisoners were allowed visitors (cf. Matt. 11:2; 25: 36). The mention of **Paul the prisoner** need not imply that the apostle is still in bonds. The young man's interview with the tribune is related with a relish for artificial personal detail. He repeats the vow of Paul's enemies with unnatural accuracy (cf. vs. 12). Depending on manuscript variants vs. 20 can mean either that **they** (the sanhedrin) or "you" **were going to inquire;** vs. 15 argues for the former.

23:23-35. *Removal to Caesarea.* While it is certain that Paul was taken from Jerusalem to Caesarea, the details of this narrative are questionable. For one thing the number of troops in Paul's escort—a total of 470, or about half the Jerusalem garrison (see above on 21:30-36)—is exaggerated. The meaning of the word translated **spearmen** is uncertain; later it came to mean "light armed soldiers." **The third hour of the night** was about 9 or 10 P.M. Luke seems to have ignored the fact that secrecy would be prevented by the size of the escort.

23:24. Antonius **Felix** was the brother of Pallas, a favorite of the Emperor Claudius. The length of his rule in Palestine is debated; he gained power in A.D. 52 or 53, but the estimates of his recall range from 55 to 60. Ancient historians are agreed in judging him an evil man, guilty of maladministration.

23:25-30. The **letter** from the tribune to the governor is a composition of Luke. The address follows the form of 15:23, and the **accusers** certainly would not have been ordered to bring their charges before the governor until after Paul had been slipped out of town. Felix is addressed as **Excellency,** the same title used for Theophilus (Luke 1:3) and Festus (26:25). The letter presents Lysias' version of the rescue of Paul (21:31-40); no mention is made of his intention to scourge him (22:24-29). Throughout the letter legal terms are used, and its purpose is to prove that the first Roman official to view the evidence finds Paul guilty of no crime **deserving death** (cf. Luke 23:4, 14, 22). Like Gallio (18:15), Lysias concludes that the charges against the Christians are matters of Jewish religion which are of no concern to Roman authority.

23:31-35. The soldiers bring Paul as far as **Antipatris** (see color map 14), a Roman military relay station some 35 miles from Jerusalem; only the cavalry accompany him the final 30 miles to Caesarea. Felix's question tries to determine venue; Paul can be tried in either the **province** where the alleged crime has been committed or in his native province (cf. Luke 23:6-7). The governor can hear the case either as procurator of Judea or as the deputy of the legate of Syria and **Cilicia.** His attempt to delay matters is consistent with his character. **Herod's praetorium** is apparently the palace built by Herod the Great, now used as the governor's residence or administrative headquarters.

C. Paul in Caesarea (24:1-26:32)

24:1-9. *The Case Against Paul.* Luke's narrative of the judicial proceedings against Paul continues. Throughout this passage legal terms are used frequently. After Paul has been in Caesarea **five days** (see below on vss. 10-21), **the high priest** and representatives of the sanhedrin appear **before the governor.** Their charges are presented by **Tertullus,** their **spokesman,** or attorney—a professional counsel for the prosecution. The notice that Paul is **called** suggests that he has received a legal summons.

24:2b-4. Tertullus begins the accusation with the conventional attempt to secure the judge's favor (cf. vs. 10). The use of **we** and **this nation** implies neither that Tertullus (a Latin name) identifies himself with the Jews nor that he distinguishes himself from them; he simply represents his clients. The word **nation** can refer to the Jews (cf. Luke 7:5; 23:2) or possibly to the province of Judea (cf. 26:4). Since this praise is conventional, the references to **much peace** and **reforms** reveal little about the actual conduct of Felix's administration (see above on 23:24). The promise of brevity is typical of speakers ancient and modern.

24:5-9. The charge against Paul is 3-fold: (a) He is guilty of sedition, because he is a **pestilent** (i.e. troublesome) **fellow** who has upset order

throughout the empire (cf. 17:6). To the Romans this would be a significant charge (cf. Luke 23:5). (b) He is the **ringleader** of a heretical **sect** (cf. vs. 14; 28:22). The term **Nazarenes,** used in the plural only here, indicates that the Christians are followers of Jesus of Nazareth (cf. 2:22). Though Luke assumes that this sort of charge means little to the Romans (cf. 18:15; 23:29), he may be presenting Paul's opponents as arguing from Judaism's status as an "approved religion"—a status which Christianity does not enjoy. (c) Paul has **tried to profane the temple** (cf. 21:28). While the Romans are not concerned with the niceties of Jewish religion, they recognize the right of the Jews to regulate their own practices. The Western text adds vss. 6b-8a (RSV footnote), which suggest that Lysias overstepped his authority in interfering with the Jewish right to judge Paul. The Jews are convinced that an examination of Paul will confirm their charges.

24:10-21. *Paul Before Felix.* Like Tertullus (vss. 2-3) Paul begins his speech with an attempt to gain the governor's favor. The reference to **many years** is conventional, so that little is disclosed about the length of Felix's rule (see above on 23:24). Paul's observation that **it is not more than twelve days since I went up to . . . Jerusalem** seems to suggest that the events are recent enough for Felix to conduct a careful investigation. Actually the events which have occurred since Paul's arrival in Jerusalem demand at least 16 or 17 days. Luke's 12 apparently results from adding the 7 of 21:27 and the 5 of 24:1.

Paul's **defense** has 2 parts (vss. 10-16, 17-21); both make essentially the same points.

24:11, 17. First, he went up to Jerusalem **to worship** or, as he says in vs. 17, **to bring to my nation alms and offerings.** Though this may be a reference to Paul's offering at the completion of religious vows (cf. 21:26), it could be a hint of Luke's knowledge of Paul's offering for the Judean Christians (see above on 20:1-6). If so, Luke has misunderstood Paul's collection as intended for the temple.

24:12, 18a. Since Paul has gone to Jerusalem for religious purposes he is not guilty of **stirring up a crowd.** Instead he was found **in the temple, without any crowd or tumult.** In fact, rather than being guilty of profaning the temple (vs. 6), he has participated in a ritual of purification (cf. 21:26).

24:13, 18b-19. His opponents can **prove** none of their charges against him (vs. 13); **some Jews from Asia** (not a large crowd) falsely understood his purpose in the temple, but if they had any valid charges, they should be present to make them.

24:14-15, 21. Rather than being the leader of a heretical sect (vs. 5), Paul is a follower of **the Way** (cf. 9:2)—the culmination of true Judaism. Although actually Paul did not believe **everything** in the **law** and **prophets** (cf. Gal. 3:25; Rom. 10:4), Luke sees Christianity as fulfillment of the OT (cf. Luke 24:44). This is seen in the **hope** of a **resurrection,** which is common to Paul and the best of Judaism (cf. 23:6-9). While both Paul (I Cor. 15) and Luke (Luke 14:14; 20:35) stress the resurrection of the righteous, the belief in a **resurrection of both the just and the unjust** may be implied in Luke 16:19-31.

24:20-21. It is sometimes supposed that Paul

here confesses that his strategy in 23:6-9 involved **wrongdoing.** More likely the statement involves irony: **the resurrection of the dead** is a truth recognized by the Jews which is of no concern to the Romans.

24:22-27. The Indecision of Felix. The governor delays a decision under the excuse that the **tribune** (cf. 21:31 ff.) can bring additional evidence. How Felix has acquired **knowledge of the Way** (cf. 9:2) is not explained—perhaps through his **wife,** who is a **Jewess** (vs. 24). Paul is kept in custody, but not in a public prison; he has **some liberty** and is allowed visitors (cf. 28:16). Luke shows that Roman officials understand Christianity and treat its leaders well.

24:24-25. According to some manuscripts it is **Drusilla** who instigates the interview with Paul. She was the youngest daughter of Herod Agrippa I (ch. 12) and was noted for her beauty. According to Josephus, Felix lured her away from her husband with the help of a pseudo magician. The governor is **alarmed** at Paul's stress on the ethical implications of **faith in Christ Jesus** and the concept of a **future judgment;** for **self-control** is one thing Felix lacks. Paul is dismissed without decision. This story bears a slight resemblance to the account of John the Baptist's execution in Mark 6:17-28—material which Luke has not included in his gospel.

24:26-27. Felix hopes to get **money** from Paul; he has heard of the offering (vs. 17). This avarice, though true to the character of Felix, explains to the reader why Paul is kept in custody though innocent. The reference to **two years** apparently describes the length of Paul's imprisonment, though it could refer to the duration of Felix's rule (see above on 23:24).

25:1-12. Paul Before Festus. Almost nothing is known of **Porcius Festus.** Estimates of the date of his assumption of power range from A.D. 55 to 60. Apparently he was a man of higher character than his predecessor. The Greek word used for Festus' coming **into his province** may mean entering "into his office." In order to create cordial relations with the Jews the new governor goes immediately **to Jerusalem.** Since Festus desires cordiality the Jewish leaders ask a **favor** (cf. vs. 9)—that Paul be sent to Jerusalem. Probably their intention is to have his case commuted to their jurisdiction; the idea of an **ambush** is secondary and thematic (cf. 23:12-15). Festus refuses a change of venue but provides for the reopening of the case in **Caesarea.**

25:6-8. After returning to his capital Festus takes **his seat on the tribunal,** i.e. judgment bench (see above on 18:12-17), and sends for Paul. The **serious charges** are not enumerated, but they are well known to the reader. Paul's **defense** names the major issues: disregard of **the law of the Jews** (21:21), profanation of **the temple** (21:27-28), and offenses **against Caesar** (24:5). In this defense Paul distinguishes himself from Judaism (contrast 24:14-15). The real issue is the charge of offenses against the state.

25:9. In view of the mention of **Caesar** it seems unlikely that Festus would suggest a trial in Jerusalem. Though the governor does not intend to relinquish Roman jurisdiction, it is clear that Paul should resist this suggestion; Festus is anxious to do a **favor** for the Jews. Here Luke affords his most

critical estimate of a Roman official; except for Festus' effort to please the Jews the guiltless apostle could be acquitted.

25:10-11. The Roman practice of **appeal to Caesar** (*provocatio*) is not adequately understood. Apparently a Roman citizen, when charged with a capital crime, could appeal to the imperial court as a sort of supreme tribunal. It is not clear whether this appeal was made before or after a verdict was rendered in the lower courts. While there is no evidence that a defendant could not be released after he had made an appeal (26:32), a matter consigned to the emperor would be modified with reluctance. Paul's reasons for appealing at this point are probably: (*a*) his intention to avoid a trial at Jerusalem; (*b*) his belief that Festus has a negative view of his case—a view more hostile than Luke is willing to admit. Luke does admit, however, that Paul's case is more than a matter of Jewish religious dispute (contrast vs. 19), that it is a case for **Caesar's tribunal**—a somewhat inaccurate way to describe the Roman court at Caesarea.

25:12. Festus' conference **with his council** indicates that the appeal is not automatically granted. His legal advisers probably check Paul's credentials of citizenship and the seriousness of the case.

25:13-26:32. Paul Before Agrippa. This narrative seems historically improbable. Not only are some of the events related in an artificial manner (25:23-26:32), but there is included a private conversation between governor and king (25:14-22) which would not be available to the author. The notion that Festus would need Agrippa's help in formulating charges is out of character with a Roman governor, who would have adequate opportunity for investigation. The purpose of the narrative is to present a parallel to Luke 23:6-12 and to fulfill the prophecy of 9:15.

25:13-27. Festus Presents Paul. Herod **Agrippa II** was the son of Herod Agrippa I (ch. 12). Reared in Rome, he was gradually granted power until he ruled the areas of Philip and Lysanias (cf. Luke 3:1) and controlled some Galilean and Perean towns. He had custody of the temple treasury in Jerusalem and authority to appoint the high priest. According to rumor Agrippa was guilty of incestuous relations with his sister **Bernice**—the oldest daughter of Herod Agrippa I (cf. above on 24:24-25). Though a widow at the moment, Bernice was married a total of 3 times and eventually became the mistress of the Emperor Titus. However, on one occasion she appeared barefoot before the procurator Florus as a penitent interceding for the Jewish people.

25:14-17. Festus' reason for presenting Paul's case to the king is to be explained in vs. 26. While the reader knows that he has been subject to political pressures (see above on vss. 1-12), Festus depicts himself as a champion of Roman justice. The idea that **the accused** has the right to meet his **accusers face to face** was an established principle of Roman law. Unlike Felix (24:22), Festus has heard the case with **no delay.**

25:18-19. The charges, however, are matters of Jewish religion rather than Roman law (cf. 18:15). Most modern translators use "religion" rather than **superstition** (cf. another form of the same word in 17:22) since Festus would not have offended his guest—a nominal adherent of the Jewish faith. If the Greek word actually bore this negative connotation, then **their own** (lit. "the own") perhaps should be understood as "his own," i.e. Paul's, "superstition." It is clear here that the resurrection question has to do with the raising of **Jesus** (contrast 24:15).

25:20-22. Festus admits that Roman officials are not competent to **investigate** such matters. His implication that he proposed a **Jerusalem** trial in order to amass more evidence is at variance with the motive of vs. 9. On Paul's appeal **to the emperor** see above on vss. 10-11. Agrippa's desire to **hear** Paul is reminiscent of Luke 23:8.

25:23. The vivid picture of Paul's appearance before important people portrays Christianity as well known in significant circles (cf. 24:22; 26:26). The **audience hall** is probably a large room of Herod's palace (23:35) used for important judicial proceedings. The **military tribunes** would be the commanders of the 5 cohorts (see above on 10:1-8) stationed at Caesarea. The **prominent men** are the notables **of the city;** some manuscripts say that they are the leaders of the province.

25:24-27. The **whole Jewish people,** of course, have not **petitioned,** but only their leaders (vss. 2, 7, 15). The petitioning has occurred in **Jerusalem** (vss. 2-3) and **here** (vs. 7). The **shouting** of the Jews may echo the mob scene of 22:22. Again Paul is judged guilty of **nothing deserving death** (cf. 23: 29; also Luke 23:22). The recognition of the emperor as **lord** had been employed since the time of Caligula. As a matter of fact the governor was required to send formal **charges** with the prisoner.

26:1-23. *Paul's Defense.* The author understands the speech before Agrippa as the high point in Paul's defense. While it is evident to the historian that the political charges were the primary concern of the Romans (cf. 24:5; 25:8), Luke has been insisting that Paul has committed no crime against the state (18:15; 23:29; 25:25). Christianity is no threat to good order; it is a religion of resurrection, fulfilling the hopes of Jew and Gentile. Now the reader is told that Paul's mission to the Gentiles is the cause of the whole process against him (vs. 21; cf. 22: 21-22).

26:1-3. The style of the speech imitates classical forms. Paul **stretched out his hand** like a Hellenistic rhetorician (cf. 13:16; 21:40). He begins with the conventional attempt to win the hearer's favor (cf. 24:2-3, 10). Like Felix (24:22), Agrippa is said to be **familiar with all customs and controversies** (or questions) **of the Jews.** In the Greek **especially** falls between vss. 2 and 3, so that it may mean either that Paul is especially fortunate to appear before Agrippa or that the king is especially familiar with Jewish customs. While Agrippa was pro-Roman, he considered himself king of the Jews.

26:4-8. As in 22:3 ff. Paul describes his early life. Details told there are not repeated; the earlier material is known to the reader. The main point is that Paul has been a Jew of **the strictest party** (lit. "sect"; cf. 24:5) and that this fact is **known** to the Jews. The RSV seems to suggest a contrast between **nation** and **Jerusalem,** as if the former means "province" and refers to Paul's days in Cilicia. More likely "nation" stands for the Jews (cf. 24:2, 10), without reference to the time of Paul's move to Jerusalem (see above on 22:3). As a former **Pharisee** (cf. 23:6) Paul sees the resurrection **hope** as the fulfill-

ment of ancient **promise** (cf. Luke 24:44-49)—the hope of all Israel (the **twelve tribes**). At vs. 8 the defense is turned into a missionary appeal.

26:9-11. Paul's testimony is confirmed by his earlier role as a persecutor (contrast 22:18). The picture of his opposition to Christianity is sterner here than in 22:3-5. He not only imprisoned the believers but advocated a sentence of **death.** While the phrase **I cast my vote against them** does not prove that Paul was a member of the sanhedrin, since the expression may be metaphorical, Luke seems to suppose that Paul played some official role in the execution of Christians. His effort to **make them blaspheme** may anticipate the persecutions of the 2nd cent. where Christians were compelled to curse Christ.

26:12-14. Paul's conversion has been described in 9:1-9 and 22:6-11 (see comments). While this account is not entirely consistent with the others (cf. vs. 14 with 9:7), it is easier to harmonize with Paul's own description in Gal. 1:12-17. The time of the event, as in 22:6, is **midday.** The address **Saul, Saul** (in all 3 accounts) is explained—the voice speaks **Hebrew** (actually Aramaic; cf. 21:40). Strangely, the voice announces a Greek proverb: **It hurts . . . to kick against the goads** (prods used on unruly animals); the saying was used by the Greeks to depict men who resisted the will of the gods.

26:15-18. Most important, Paul's commission to preach to the **Gentiles** is given in his conversion experience (cf. Gal. 1:16). The material about Ananias and Paul's blindness (9:10-18; 22:12-16) is omitted. The commission of Paul is presented under the motif of the prophetic call (cf. Ezek. 2:1; Isa. 35:5; 42:7, 16). This use of OT allusions makes it clear that Paul's mission is under the direction of the God of Israel. Vs. 16 is opaque; the NEB is clearer: "to appoint you my servant and witness . . . to what you have seen and to what you shall yet see of me." The promise that Paul will be delivered does not imply that Luke believes the trial will end in acquittal (cf. 20:25); Paul is to be "delivered" in the sense that his witness will be accomplished.

26:19-21. The mission involves obedience. The notion that Paul began an extensive mission in **Damascus** and **Jerusalem** immediately after his conversion enlarges on 9:28-29; the idea that he preached **throughout all the country of Judea** contradicts Gal. 1:22. The theory that Paul was sent to both Jews and Gentiles, though not consistent with Gal. 2:7, is a Lukan motif (cf. 9:15). The word translated **to kill** was used in 5:30; lit. it means "to lay hands on violently" and refers to the mob action of 21:30-32.

26:22-23. Paul's gospel is nothing more than **what the prophets and Moses** predicted (cf. 3:22-24). While the Jews did not expect a suffering Messiah, the Christian experience of the Crucifixion and Resurrection led to a messianic interpretation of texts like Isa. 53. The idea that Christ was **the first to rise from the dead** finds parallels in I Cor. 15: 20; Col. 1:18.

26:24-32. *Verdict of Governor and King.* Paul is again "interrupted" after he has finished (cf. 22:22). The cry of Festus accentuates the inability of Romans to prosecute Christians (cf. 25:20, 26) and the greatness of Paul's **learning** (cf. 22:3). The phrase **turning you mad** is a common Hellenistic saying. Paul replies that what he is saying is **the sober truth**—lit. "words of truth and reasonableness."

26:26-27. Agrippa's knowledge (cf. vs. 3) emphasizes the Lukan notion that Christianity is appreciated by important people (cf. 24:22; 25:23). This is also expressed by the claim that **this was not done in a corner**—a Greek proverbial saying which displays the whole program of Acts (cf. 1:8; 2:36; 24:22). Paul's appeal to the king's belief in the **prophets** assumes Agrippa's role as Jewish monarch (cf. vs. 3).

26:28. Agrippa's response involves sarcasm, but its exact meaning is obscure. Using the best manuscripts the sentence reads lit.: "In little [i.e. "time," or perhaps "effort"] you are persuading me to make [i.e. "play" (act)] Christian." The RSV's **think to make me a Christian** rests on a manuscript variant, and another manuscript variant allows the translation "you are persuading me to become a Christian." On **Christian** see above on 11:26.

26:29. Paul's reply plays on Agrippa's words—**whether short or long** (lit. "in little and in big")—and makes a missionary appeal to the whole audience. The **chains** symbolize Paul's status as a prisoner; a literal understanding is not entirely consistent with 24:23.

26:30-32. As in Luke 23:14-15, king and governor agree that the accused deserves neither **death** nor **imprisonment** (cf. 23:29; 25:25; Luke 23:22). On Paul's appeal see above on 25:10-11. It is sometimes supposed that vs. 32 betrays Luke's knowledge of Paul's conviction in the imperial court. Actually Luke may be suggesting that the divine intention of a mission to Rome must be fulfilled (cf. 23:11).

D. Voyage to Rome (27:1-28:16)

27:1-12. To Crete. Along with **other prisoners** Paul is sent to Rome (see color map 16). He is in the custody of **Julius,** a **centurion of the Augustan Cohort** (see above on 10:1-8), which was stationed in Caesarea about this time. Paul is **accompanied by Aristarchus** (19:29; 20:4; Col. 4:10; Philem. 24) and presumably by "Luke," since 27:1-28:16 is the last and longest of the "we sections" (see Intro.).

27:2-4. Ships sailing from Caesarea directly to **Italy** are not available. Instead the prisoners are put on a vessel of **Adramyttium,** a port near Assos (cf. 20:13-14; see color map 16); it is about to embark for important **ports** of the province of **Asia.** The course is N along the coast to **Sidon.** There Paul is permitted to visit **his friends,** lit. "the friends"—perhaps meaning the Christians (cf. III John 15) since no trip to Sidon by Paul has been recorded. Because the prevailing **winds** are from the NW the ship sails on the E and N of **Cyprus.** After hugging for a time the coast of **Cilicia,** it sails **across** the bay which is off the coast of **Pamphylia** (see map, p. 746). Some manuscripts add that this short journey required 15 days.

27:5-8. At **Myra,** a port for grain ships sailing from Egypt to Rome (see above on 21:1-14), the prisoners board an Alexandrian vessel hauling wheat (vs. 38) and passengers (vs. 37) to the capital. Head winds make the trip to **Cnidus** difficult. Turning S, the ship sails around the E point of Crete, Cape **Salmone,** and arrives at **Fair Havens**—a small bay on the S shore of the island (see color map 16).

27:9-11. It is now evident that the trip is being made too late in the year. Travel on the Mediterranean was closed from Nov. 11 to Mar. 10, and any trip after Sep. 14 was considered **dangerous.** The **fast** was probably the Day of Atonement, which would be observed in late Sep. or early Oct. Though Paul has had considerable experience in sailing (II Cor. 11:25) it is unlikely that a prisoner would be consulted about nautical affairs. At any rate the **centurion** accepts the advice of the **captain** and the **owner.** What authority the centurion might have is not clear. The **majority** decision is perhaps that of the leading men on board. Luke is anxious to stress the importance of Paul, his prophetic power, and his right to say "I told you so" (vs. 21).

27:12. The location of **Phoenix** is debated. It is clearly a better harbor, farther W, on the S shore of Crete; but whether it is at the site of Lutro (facing E) or Phineka (facing W) depends on one's interpretation of the Greek phrase describing it (see color map 16).

27:13-44. Shipwreck. This narrative is written in fine literary style. The details are vividly described, and nautical terms are frequently used. The author may be following a written source or duplicating the pattern of Hellenistic sea romances.

27:13-16. When the **south wind** begins to blow **gently,** the crew assume that the voyage around Cape Matala and NW across the Gulf of Messara to Phoenix (vs. 12) can be readily accomplished (see color map 16). They sail W along the S coast of Crete, cautiously hugging the shore. No sooner are they beyond the cape and exposed to the open sea than a mighty **wind** sweeps **down from** the heights of Mt. Ida, 7,000 feet in elevation. The term translated **tempestuous** suggests a typhoon or hurricane. In sailors' jargon this wind is called *Euraquilo*—a combination of Greek and Latin which means **northeaster.** Driven into the open sea, the ship sails south of **Cauda** (or Clauda), a small island some 25 miles S of Phoenix. The **boat** which we (contrast vs. 17) . . . **secure** is the ship's dinghy, used in boarding and escape (vs. 30). It is apparently being towed but, on becoming filled with water, is hoisted on deck.

27:17-20. What it means **to undergird the ship** is debated. Some scholars suggest that the vessel is bound together from side to side, either by ropes which go under the keel, or by chains which are stretched across the beam below deck. Others believe the ship is bound from stem to stern, either around the outside, or by lines which run longitudinally over the deck supported by props. **Took measures** is lit. "used helps," which could mean props. The **Syrtis** is a gulf along the coast of Africa W of Cyrene where shifting sands create a dangerous shallows. Since the direction of the wind could drive the ship S into this hazard, the words **lowered the gear** suggest some maneuver which either assured a more W course or slowed the ship's progress. Thus some suppose that the sails are set to tack, while others believe the main sail is taken down or an anchor lowered. The **cargo** and surplus **tackle** are thrown overboard (an action not completed until vs. 38) in order to ease the storm's strain on the ship (cf. Jonah 1:5). The disappearance of **sun** and **stars** leads to loss of **hope,** since navigation is dependent on them.

27:21-26. Paul comes forward in the time of crisis. As a speech in the midst of a hurricane seems unlikely, vss. 21-26 (as well as vss. 33-36 or 38) may have been inserted into the narrative. Paul points out that his advice (vs. 10) should have been heeded, but no one had actually recommended sailing away **from Crete** (cf. vs. 12). During the night Paul has seen **an angel of . . . God** (cf. 10:3) in a vision and has been told that it is God's will for him to **stand before Caesar** (cf. 23:11). The apostle also predicts what will be described in vss. 40-41.

27:27-28. On **the fourteenth night** after leaving Crete the ship is **drifting across the sea of Adria.** Experts conclude that the rate of a ship's drift in this kind of weather would require about 14 days to reach Malta (28:1). Though the main body of the Adriatic lies between Italy and Dalmatia, the ancients considered its S extent as reaching to North Africa. At **midnight** the **sailors** believe the ship is approaching **land**—lit. "land was drawing near." This is surmised, perhaps, by the drag of the anchor or the sound of breakers; some manuscripts say that the "land was resounding." Soundings of **twenty** and then **fifteen fathoms** (120 and 90 feet) correspond to the E approach to St. Paul's Bay, which is located in the NW part of Malta (28:1).

27:29-32. Throwing out **four anchors** is prompted by the violence of the storm, and anchoring **from the stern** is essential to keep the bow toward the beach in readiness to run aground. It is unlikely that sailors would attempt to **escape** during the night in a fierce storm on a foreign shore; **laying out anchors from the bow** to secure the ship is precisely what the situation demands. Both Paul and the **centurion** misunderstand this maneuver; **the soldiers** in the latter's command **cut away . . . the boat** (vs. 16) which the sailors are preparing to use. Though Paul is presented as the prophet who can announce the salvation of all who remain on board, securing the ship might have prevented the wreck, and the dinghy could have provided the means of escape.

27:33-34. With a captive audience Paul makes another improbable speech. The failure to eat has resulted, not from lack of provisions (cf. vs. 38), but from seasickness or fear. Paul urges taking **food** for **strength** and promises that **not a hair is to perish from the head of any** of his hearers—an OT expression (e.g. I Sam. 14:45; II Sam. 14:11; cf. Luke 21:18).

27:35-38. The **giving** of **thanks** and breaking of **bread** is probably only a picture of Christian conduct at table, although eucharistic language is used (cf. Luke 22:19). Some manuscripts add that Paul "distributed" the food "to us," reflecting an observance of the Lord's Supper. The number of people on board is perhaps mentioned because of the problem of rationing the provisions. A total of **two hundred and seventy-six** passengers and crew is not impossible, but some manuscripts read the more conservative "76"; a slight change in Greek letters could account for the difference. The ship is **lightened** as the last of the cargo (**wheat;** see above on vs. 6) is thrown overboard (cf. vs. 18). A lightened vessel would be able to run aground higher up the beach.

27:39-41. When **day** comes the crew observe that the ship is situated off an unfamiliar **bay.** The **anchors** (vs. 29) are **cast off,** and **the rudders**—normally 2—are loosened; they would have been previously lashed to the stern to help secure the ship. An ancient vessel also had 2 sails: a large mainsail (already removed either at vs. 17 or at vs. 29) and a small **foresail** attached to a mast which slanted forward. The latter, like the rudders, was used in maneuvering the ship. The **shoal** (cf. RSV footnote), sometimes translated "cross currents," is probably a promontory or sand bar extending into the bay. **Stuck** on this shallow ground, the ship breaks in the **surf.**

27:42-44. The soldiers would prefer **to kill the prisoners** rather than have them **escape,** but the **centurion,** recognizing the importance of Paul, intervenes. Passengers who can swim make for the land, while others float to shore **on planks** or **pieces of the ship**—lit. "some of those from the ship," which could refer to members of the crew, possibly providing an ancient picture of lifesaving. Paul's prediction (vs. 34) is fulfilled; **all** make their way to **land.**

28:1-10. *At Malta.* It is generally agreed that Paul's shipwreck occurred at Malta. This small island (18 by 8 miles) is located some 60 miles S of Sicily. The **natives** (lit. "barbarians," i.e. non-Greeks) were descendants of the Phoenicians. They spoke a Punic dialect, but Luke's narrative (vs. 4) presents them as conversant in Greek. The word **welcomed** (lit. "took forward") could mean merely that they brought Paul and his companions (no mention of soldiers or crew) to **the fire.** A variant text reads instead that they "revived" them. In Oct. low temperatures on Malta are in the 50's, while 5 to 12 days of **rain** may be expected.

28:3-6. Paul's encounter with the **viper** has Hellenistic parallels. An epitaph has been discovered which tells of a man who survived shipwreck only to be killed by snakebite. Actually there are no poisonous snakes on Malta, and a viper does not fasten on when it bites. The natives, however, are convinced of the snake's deadly power and assume that Paul will **swell up or . . . fall down dead.** His escape **from the sea** followed by this terrifying fate proves that he is guilty of some serious crime. The word translated **justice** is *Dike*—the goddess of vengeance and justice. When Paul escapes misfortune the observers **changed their minds** completely and suppose him to be **a god.** In contrast to 14:11-15 this conclusion is not rejected, and the recognition of Paul's divine power is made the climax of the story.

28:7-10. Paul arouses interest among important people (cf. 13:7; 24:24). On Malta his host is **Publius,** the **chief man** (lit. "first") of the island. This official title has been found in inscriptions, but it is not clear whether it denotes a native ruler or the representative of Rome. Paul's cure of Publius' **father** is reminiscent of Luke 4:38-40. The word **fever** appears in the plural, perhaps suggesting repeated attacks. Laying on **hands** as a means of miraculous cure finds a parallel in 9:17. The healing of this man leads to the cure of **the rest of the people on the island who had diseases**—an exaggeration. The response of the people is lit. that they "honored us with many honors" (RSV footnote), which probably means that they **presented many gifts** and contributed provisions for the journey to Rome.

28:11-16. *Arrival in Rome.* If he leaves Malta **after three months** Paul apparently sails to Italy in Jan. or Feb. (cf. 27:9, 27). The sailing season did not open until Mar., though travel was sometimes attempted in Feb. The **ship**, probably another grain vessel of **Alexandria**, has also **wintered in the island.** The **Twin Brothers** are Castor and Pollux, sons of Zeus and patrons of sailors, whose images are carved or painted on the prow.

28:12-14. The ship spends **three days** at **Syracuse**, the beautiful port on the E coast of Sicily. To make a **circuit** suggests sailing along the curved shore of Sicily N to **Rhegium** (Reggio di Calabria) on the toe of Italy's boot (see map below). Reaching **Puteoli** in 2 days would require an average speed

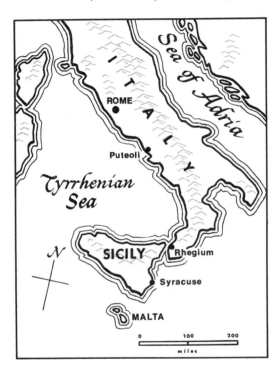

of 5 knots—almost as fast as an ancient sailing vessel could travel. This port on the Bay of Naples was Italy's best harbor and the destination of most grain vessels from Egypt. Paul spends **seven days** there with the **brethren** (Christians) to allow time for the Roman Christians to meet him on the way.

28:15. The Christians of Rome meet Paul **at the Forum of Appius,** a town 43 miles from the city, and at **Three Taverns,** a station at an important crossroad 10 miles nearer the capital; both are on the Appian Way. The church at Rome is not mentioned again in the narrative, and Luke presents Paul almost as if he were the pioneer preacher of Christianity there.

28:16. In Rome, Paul is held under "household arrest" with a single guard and considerable freedom (but cf. vs. 20). The Western text adds that the centurion delivers the prisoners over to a Roman

official. No mention has been made of Paul's military escort since 27:43. The use of "we" drops out of the narrative at this point; Paul has reached his destination (cf. 16:17; 21:18).

E. The Gospel Is Preached in Rome (28:17-31)

Luke's narrative has reached its climax. The Christian message has been proclaimed in Rome, and thus, symbolically, "to the end of the earth" (1:8). Throughout this section the Roman church (vs. 15) is ignored; as always (cf. 13:46; 18:6) the mission begins with preaching to the **Jews.** The turning to the **Gentiles** (vs. 28) reaches its high point: Jewish rejection is fulfillment of prophecy, and Gentile Christianity is the heir of the OT faith.

28:17-19. Shortly after arriving in the city Paul summons the **leaders** (lit. "first"; cf. 13:50; 25:2) of the Roman **Jews.** He addresses them in the same terminology used by Peter in 2:29. Paul argues that, although he has **done nothing against** the Jews or **the customs of our fathers** (cf. 25:8; 26:3), he has **been delivered . . . into the hands of the Romans** —words reminiscent of the passion story (cf. Luke 9:22; 24:7). They found no grounds **for the death penalty** (cf. 23:29; 25:8, 25; 26:31). Paul's **appeal to Caesar,** somewhat in contrast with 25:9-12, has been due to the Jewish objection to his release. In this passage Paul is distinguished from **the Jews** as if they were not his **brethren** at all.

28:20-22. Paul has summoned the Jewish leaders to set the record straight. He has not betrayed the ancient faith but is **bound with this chain** (see above on 26:29) **because of the hope of Israel**—a hope realized in the resurrection of Jesus (cf. 25:19; 26:6). The Jews reply that they have received no negative report about Paul either by **letters** or by visitors from **Judea.** They are anxious to hear Paul's **views,** since **this sect** (cf. 24:5) **. . . is spoken against** everywhere. The impression given—that the Roman Jews know nothing about Christianity—is misleading; the church has been established in Rome for some time and includes among its membership converts from Judaism (Rom. 2:17; 4:1).

28:23-24. On an **appointed . . . day** Jews **in great numbers** come to Paul's **lodging** to hear his proclamation. How a prisoner living **at his own expense** (vs. 30) is able to provide an audience room large enough is not explained. The apostle's message has been summarized throughout Acts: **the kingdom of God** (cf. 8:12) and **Jesus** as the Messiah (cf. 2: 22-24; 13:30-39)—content which fulfills OT expectation (cf. Luke 24:27).

28:25-29. Paul quotes Isa. 6:9-10; the LXX is followed almost verbatim. Luke has used this text in his gospel (8:9-10) to explain the misunderstanding of the parables. Here, however, the point is that Jewish rejection of the gospel is final and according to the will of God; **salvation . . . has been sent to the Gentiles**—a point not entirely consistent with Rom. 9-11. Vs. 29, which describes the departure of the Jews (RSV footnote), is not found in the best manuscripts.

28:30-31. Paul lives on in Rome **at his own expense**—the word is regularly used of money rather than of a house, as in the RSV footnote. The picture of the apostle continuing in the capital city with much freedom (vs. 16) and able to preach the **king-**

dom and **the Lord Jesus Christ** (cf. 11:17; 15:26) **... openly and unhindered** proves that the Romans have nothing against Christianity. Luke hints that after **two whole years** a change in Paul's situation occurs. There has been much debate over why the narrative ends without reporting this event. Efforts to show that Paul was released, or that Luke projected a 3rd volume to complete the story, remain unconvincing. The careful reader will come to the conclusion that Paul was finally executed (cf. 20:25, 38), and that Luke purposely chose not to include this result in his book, quite apart from the fact that it would detract from his apologetic to the Romans. The real interest of Acts is not with the ultimate end of its heroes, but with the triumph of the message they delivered to the world.

THE LETTER OF PAUL TO THE ROMANS

Edwin Cyril Blackman

INTRODUCTION

The letter to the Romans is Paul's most considered writing, and it has influenced subsequent Christian thought probably more than any other NT document. It is difficult to understand because it deals with objections and misunderstandings arising out of Jewish opposition which was part of Paul's situation then but is not part of the situation today. Difficulty also stems from the personal factor of Paul's intellectual vitality. A quick-moving mind like his does not always provide his chain of argument with as many links as his interpreters would like, but wrestling with his work is rewarding because of the majesty and continued relevance of his theme: God's judgment and mercy addressed to man's disobedience. Rom. is a restatement, in the light of Christ, of the biblical insights into God's righteousness applied to the moral failure of man and society both then and now.

Occasion and Purpose. Paul wrote in the first instance to introduce himself to the Rom. church and

Courtesy of the Semitic Museum, Harvard University

Papyrus fragment with the opening of Paul's letter to the Romans

to acquaint its members with his desire to visit them and his plan for apostolic journeying farther W. But self-introduction was no merely personal matter for him; it meant more than explaining his movements and his strategy as a church builder. It meant no less than an exposition of God's good news (1:1) as he understood it, or rather as he had experienced it in the face of Jewish misunderstanding.

Paul was the chief architect of extra-Palestinian Christianity. He was by no means the only missionary, as the very existence of the Rom. Christian community attested. He was himself ready to admit that others had laid foundations which he respected (15:18-21). But he had a conception of one gospel, one church, one empire (1:14-16). The saving righteousness of God which Paul discerned dynamically at work in and since the passion of Christ has the whole of mankind in its purview.

Moreover the time was limited. Such a revelation of righteousness and manifestation of spiritual power as was evident to Paul in the ministry of Christ and its effects signified the imminence of the end of history (see below on 11:26-27; 15:18-21). The uniqueness of Christ meant finality of revelation and this must be the prelude to the climax of God's purpose. To put this in more exclusively Jewish terms: if Jesus was the Messiah, the messianic age was present, the final act of the human drama was being played. When the full objective of the Messiah's coming had been achieved—the gathering in of unbelieving Gentiles as well as recalcitrant Israel, and the triumph of the everlasting mercy of God (11:25-32)—that would be the glorious consummation divine wisdom had planned (11:33-36). The proclamation of this was the special responsibility of the churches, in fact their sole justification, and there was urgency about it. Paul saw his own divine commission as the apostle to the Gentiles (11:13; Gal. 1:16) in relation to this proclamation. It motivated his letter and put a cutting edge on his words.

The New Theology. Paul used the occasion of his anticipated visit to Rome to set forth his conception of what God is doing for mankind, in spite of the insensitivity of both Jews and Greeks (1:16). The mighty act inaugurated in the life of Christ is continuing in its effects. It is primarily a revelation of righteousness, directed to man's age-old need of righteousness. This was evidenced in the corruption of the pagan world and also in the failure of the favored Jews—the churchgoing section of mankind, so to speak—to recognize the presence of their Messiah.

Thus in the 2nd place God's action has reference to human sin. Man is in the grip of sin and cannot free himself; his moral sense—law, conscience, categorical imperative—convicts him of sin but does not liberate him. But liberation is God's gracious gift, and it is available; men can be sure of that if they look into the self-sacrificing love of Christ, which is the love of God. To respond to this love, to open one's mind to it, is what Paul calls faith. It is the essential preliminary, and it is open to all (10:8-12). Once this is done new life begins, a new start in the realization of that righteousness which God demands (8:1-4).

Thirdly, God's power deals with the death that accompanies sin. The new life that Christ makes possible is freed not only from sin but from death (5:12-21; 8:10-11, 37-39). There is inaugurated a new humanity, reconciled with God, emancipated from sin and death, morally empowered and spiritually privileged as no previous generation has been (8:1-39). The era of law and the preeminence of Judaism are over. Man cannot live on moral imperatives alone and no longer needs to try to (10:1-4.) Judaism's position is unusual, and Paul feels obliged to discuss this at length (9-11). He holds to the conviction that the Jews will by divine mercy be delivered from their stubborn resistance and find their place with Gentiles in the final redeemed society (11:1-32).

These convictions were the result of Paul's mature reflection on his experiences as missionary and church builder during the period which occasioned the writing of Gal., I, II Cor., and possibly other letters. His work had been done in the teeth of pagan opposition (1:18-32; I Cor. 5-6; I Thess. 4:1-9; Acts 19:23-41). Equally, Jewish opposition was real and it demanded Paul's subtlest argument. The middle chs. of Rom. reflect not only his own thought but actual debates in the churches and synagogues concerning the Mosaic law and the priority of Jew to Gentile. Rom. shows far deeper reflection on the Jewish problem than is mirrored in I Thess. 2:14-16.

The Church at Rome. Paul addressed a well-established Christian community that was already becoming famous in the Christian world (1:8) and obviously destined by its locale in the metropolis to be an important church. Its founder-preacher and the details of its origin are unknown. Converts from Palestine whose business took them to Rome must have sown the first seeds of the "good news of God."

Conceivably the expulsion of Jews from Rome by Claudius (Acts 18:2) may have been occasioned by disputes in the synagogues over this new teaching about a Messiah. A reference to it by the Rom. historian Suetonius can be understood in this sense. It is thus a good guess that the Rom. church was formed before that time. It was Greek-speaking until the end of the 2nd cent. and probably recruited its membership from Greek freedmen and slaves as well as Jews. Rom. Catholic tradition assumes a visit of Peter, possibly in 42, to found the church in Rome.

Date and Place of Composition. The stage in his career at which Paul is writing and planning his apostolic campaign W of Rome is clear from 15:19-28. He feels that his work in the E regions is complete. He still, however, must deliver at Jerusalem the financial contribution he has raised among his Gentile converts for the relief of the Jerusalem Christians, in fulfillment of the agreement made a few years previously at Jerusalem (Gal. 2:10). In that agreement Paul won recognition of his preaching to Gentiles without requiring circumcision as a condition of membership in the church, but in return he admitted that Gentile converts should be made aware of obligation to the original Jewish members. This was not a mere *quid pro quo* in Paul's understanding of the relationship of Jewish to Gentile Christians; it involved the responsibility of each for unity and mutual edification (15:27). Paul attached much importance to this; II Cor. 8-9 shows how much trouble he took to get the Corinthians to see the point (cf. I Cor. 16:1-4). In addressing the Roms.—a mixed church, in which Gentile members probably outnumbered Jewish—he expects to be understood when he explains that this task must be accomplished before he turns his face W.

For further details we may consult the narrative in Acts 20 of Paul's movements from the end of his Ephesian ministry to his departure from the Aegean area in his journey to Jerusalem. He is said to have traveled from Ephesus through Macedonia to Greece, where he spent 3 months (vss. 1-3). This stay is the most likely time for the writing of Rom., since he was originally planning to set sail from there directly to Syria and Jerusalem (vs. 3). The place was probably Corinth, though nearby Cenchreae (see color map 16) is possible, in which case the reference to Phoebe (16:1) has more point.

Changing his plans, Paul goes back through Macedonia, accompanied by several men (vs. 4), who may well be trustees of the money he is to deliver in Jerusalem (15:25-27; cf. I Cor. 16:3-4). He spends Passover in Philippi and 7 days in Troas (vs. 6) but passes by Ephesus for a brief stop at Miletus in hope of reaching Jerusalem for Pentecost (vss. 16-17). Conceivably Paul could have dictated the letter at one of these places, or even on board a ship (vss. 6, 14-15), though ancient sea travel did not provide much comfort.

For dating this period of Paul's career the only contact with outside historical sources is the statement of Acts 24:27 that after 2 years Felix was relieved by Festus as procurator of Judea. Unfortunately the sources are contradictory, so that the date of this event is uncertain. If we assume that it was 59 (see table, p. 1275) and that the 2 years are counted from Paul's arrest, the date of his 3 months' stay in Greece becomes the winter of 56-57. Other estimates have placed the date as early as 55 and as late as 59.

Rom. thus belongs among the letters of Paul's middle period, I, II Cor. and Gal.—also Phil. and possibly Col. and Philem. if, as some believe, they were written from an imprisonment in Ephesus. Its greatest affinity is with Gal., esp. in relation to the meaning of faith and justification, the subordinate place of law in the divine dealing with sinful man, and the antithesis of spirit and flesh.

Authenticity and Integrity. There has never been any question about the genuineness of Rom. as a writing of Paul's. Even the most radical criticism has taken as axiomatic the authenticity of Rom., I, II Cor., and Gal.

Some peculiarities in the transmission of Rom. in the early church are revealed in the manuscripts, however, which raise questions about certain portions:

a) The doxology, 16:25-27, is found in the majority of manuscripts at the end of ch. 14; in one manuscript, the earliest written and therefore very important, at the end of ch. 15; in some of the most trustworthy at the end of ch. 16. This suggests that copies were in circulation which ended at these points. It has been argued that the doxology is by a later hand than Paul's. That is reasonable on internal evidence, and would partly explain its various positions in the manuscripts. The object of adding it may have been to provide a conclusion for the whole collection of Pauline letters, as there is evidence that Rom. was sometimes placed at the end of the Pauline section of the NT.

b) The above considerations indicate that not all copies of Rom. contained ch. 16. Though a very few scholars have viewed this ch. as an addition by another hand, the vast majority have seen no reason to doubt that it is Paul's work; the question is whether it was originally part of Rom. or part of a letter to another church. The contents are more naturally explained on the latter view, and a plausible case can be made for Ephesus as its destination (see below on ch. 16).

c) One manuscript, with patristic support, lacks "in Rome" in 1:7, 15. This indicates attempts in some areas to remove traces of reference to a particular church and thus make the letter more obviously universal in its range. Such motives would also explain the removal of ch. 16—if it was removed rather than added to an original shorter form. It is not impossible that Paul himself approved a longer and a shorter edition (see below on ch. 16).

For Further Study. C. H. Dodd, *Rom.*, 1932. John Knox, in *IB*, 1954. C. K. Barrett, *Rom.*, 1958; an excellent recent exposition. William Sanday and A. C. Headlam, *Rom.*, 5th ed., 1962; still the best commentary in English on the Greek text. F. W. Beare in *IDB*, 1962.

I. Greeting and Thanksgiving (1:1-17)

1:1-7. Salutation. The opening salutation is different from those of the other letters of Paul. This church was not of his own founding and had not even been visited by him. Paul introduces himself as an emissary esp. appointed to broadcast the good news of what God has done for mankind. A full explanation of what this signifies occupies the first 8 chs., and Paul begins this in earnest in vs. 16. In his introductory words he contents himself with making 3 points:

a) The content of the gospel is Jesus Christ, whom Christians call **Lord** (vs. 4; cf. 10:9-13). Christ is also recognized as God's **Son**, in virtue of his resurrection from the dead. This makes it clear that God's Spirit was operating through him to an unprecedented degree (vs. 4*a*) though he was also a real man, of Jewish descent (vs. 3). Paul has no doubt about the real humanity of Christ.

b) The career of Christ is not inexplicably novel, because it was part of the eternal plan of God. His Jewish descent means that he emerged in the life of the covenant people through whom God was revealing his good will toward men. Jesus is intelligible only within the framework of Judaism (vs. 2; John 4:22*b*).

c) The gospel now made known in Christ has resulted in a new universal mission (vs. 5), which is the impulse behind Paul's activity. He calls it his **apostleship** (vs. 5).

1:1*a*. Paul is accustomed to think of himself as Christ's **servant**, lit. "slave" (cf. e.g. Gal. 1:10; Phil. 1:1), as are all Christians (cf. I Cor. 7:22; Col. 4:12). "Slave" is the proper antithesis of "Lord," i.e. owner, and thus appropriate for the Christian relationship to Christ. When he is stressing the high privileges of Christians (e.g. 8:14-17; Gal. 3:26–4:6) Paul uses other terms (see below on 6:15; cf. John 13:13-16; 15:14-15).

1:1*b*. The participle **called** (cf. I Cor. 1:1) may be understood as having the force of a noun, i.e. a divinely summoned one (cf. vss. 6-7; there is no word for **to be** in the Greek). An **apostle** is lit. "one sent out," a missionary. But the NT usage refers not merely to traveling but to the responsibility of testifying to the gospel—the main point in this passage. There is a corresponding Hebrew word meaning a delegate of a Jewish authority such as the Sanhedrin; that person's significance consisted solely in his representative capacity. Paul speaks of himself and his fellow apostle to Corinth, Apollos, as "stewards," imparting to the Corinthians what has been entrusted to them by God (I Cor. 3:5-6; 4:1-2). The apostle is the custodian of the truth revealed in Christ. In Christian usage the term "apostle" in time became confined to the 12 plus Paul; but there was an earlier, wider usage (see below on 16:7).

1:1*c*. The verb **set apart** is used again in Gal. 1:15 with reference to Paul's destiny to preach the gospel to the Gentiles, and in Acts 13:2 of his being commissioned with Barnabas at Antioch to the W campaign (Acts 13–14). The basic idea may come from the consecration of the Levites in ancient Israel (Num. 8:5-22; esp. vs. 14). Or possibly Paul may be thinking of his separation as a Pharisee from the ordinary, less scrupulous Jews. As a Christian he has come to regard the ideal of consecration, not negatively, as the avoidance of sinful contact, but positively, as the service of the good news of God's saving purpose in Christ.

1:2. The beneficent, divine activity which Paul is set apart to proclaim is no sudden departure. It was already envisaged in the OT.

1:3-4. Christ was a son of **David** by physical descent, a reference which would convey that he was not merely a Jew but in the messianic succession. But there is something more important to assert, of an even higher order, **according to the spirit of holiness:** as a result of the **resurrection** which climaxed his earthly career Christ was **designated Son of God.** These 2 vss. could conceivably be part of a rudimentary creed which Paul is quoting (cf. 4:25; 10:9-10). On Christ's lordship, which expresses his relationship to men, see below on 10:9-11. His relationship to God is expressed by the affirmation of his sonship.

The phrase "son of God" referring to Israel as a whole, or to the king considered as representative of the whole people, was familiar to Jews. It did not signify the Messiah except insofar as the Messiah was regarded as the king. But in reference to Jesus it was a part of the earliest Christian faith, because it went back to the thought of Jesus himself. The matter has been much disputed, but in the light of Matt. 11:27; Mark 12:1-11; 13:32 it cannot be denied that Jesus regarded himself as God's Son in the sense of having a unique mission and a unique relationship to God as his Father. This is the foundation stone of the church's estimate of him (Christology; see "The NT Interpretation of Jesus," pp. 1167-75).

1:8-17. Personal Address. This paragraph begins in a more personal vein, complimenting the readers on their faith. Paul's intention to visit them has often been frustrated (vs. 13). He refers to this more in detail in 15:23-24, where we learn that the visit to Rome is part of a larger project, to preach his gospel as far W as Spain. His activity at Rome will be designed, not to make converts, but for the deepening of their spiritual experience (vs. 11) and for their mutual encouragement (vss. 12-13).

1:13b-15. The last phrase of vs. 13 implies that the Roman community is mainly of Gentile composition. Whether the Jewish-Christian section among them was small or large, the Roman church as Paul now visualizes it symbolizes the turning of the pagan world to God. This is the special concern of his own apostleship. He feels an obligation to preach **to Greeks and to barbarians** (vs. 14), to all men outside Judaism irrespective of mental capacity, culture, or lack of culture. "Barbarian" was the contemptuous term used by Greeks for races who lacked their culture and could not speak their language. This is parallel to Jewish contempt for Gentiles and to the modern white man's sense of superiority to colored races. The gospel knows no such distinctions (cf. Gal. 3:28; Col. 3:11).

1:16. What Paul has to offer is good news that makes him proud: divine **power** for human inability to achieve **salvation.** This is a gracious gift, but it is available wherever there is response, **to every one who has faith.** The logic here would seem to be that all men alike need salvation and that no one, not even the **Jew,** has any advantage; **first** is therefore surprising. But Paul is too much of a Jew to forget that in fact Judaism has had great advantages in relation to God. Yet this power is also for Greeks whose previous experience has not been so markedly religious. It is for human beings of whatever history and culture who need salvation—i.e. for all. Paul will have to demonstrate the need of salvation, and 1:18-3:20 is devoted to this.

1:17. Paul mounts to a climax with this vs., which indicates why so much importance is to be attached to **faith** and introduces the other main key word of this letter, **righteousness.** The classic phrase "justification by faith," which has played such a part in Protestant theology, is based on this vs. and the argument of chs. 5-8. It is helpful to remember that the words "justification" and "justify" represent the same underlying Greek terms as underlie the noun "righteousness" and the verb "pronounce righteous."

The central affirmation of this letter is that a divine righteousness is **revealed** and in some sense communicated to men who have failed to achieve righteousness. This is implied in this vs., though the negative assertion, that human life lacks righteousness, has to be proved in the detailed argument of 1:18-2:29. The force of the present tense of the verb should be expressed more emphatically: **is** *being* **revealed.** Contrast 3:21, where Paul is content (using a different verb) to look back on the revelation as in one sense complete with the passion of Jesus Christ. Here, however, Paul is stressing the process of continuing revelation. In Christ's life and passion, and all that results from it in Christian experience, God's own righteousness is being made available. What has hitherto been regarded in Jewish thought about the end time as a feature of a future life is now, Paul affirms, a matter of present experience. This is the gospel of God, the achievement of Christ, and the new prospect for mankind. It is the continuation and the restatement in Pauline vocabulary of the teaching of Jesus himself about the realization, or inauguration, of the kingdom of God through his own ministry (see "The Kingdom of God in the NT," pp. 1176-86).

The requirement for righteousness on the human side, if the divine offer is to be accepted, is what Paul calls faith. The curious combination of the words **through faith for faith** is probably nothing more than a form of emphasis. Human experience, whether of nation, race, family, or individual, nowhere exhibits perfection. But perfection is God's will, and **the gospel of God ... concerning his Son** (vss. 1, 3) declares that God has taken the initiative in enabling man to attain it. The indispensable requirement on each individual human being is not moral effort but trust in God's purpose and a genuine response to his gracious offer.

This is supported by an OT quotation, which would strengthen the argument in the eyes of a Jewish reader. Paul quotes, with an insignificant omission, the ambiguous LXX rendering of Hab. 2:4b, lit.: "The righteous out of faith shall live." This can mean either **He who through faith is righteous shall live** or "The righteous man shall live as a result of faith." The original Hebrew probably means that the righteous shall live by his faithfulness, i.e. by faithful observance of God's commands—the antithesis of Paul's meaning.

But in terms of the Greek translation Paul gets support for his point. He will make clear what he understands by faith in ch. 4. We must define it briefly here as our initial receptiveness which allows God to begin his salvation within us. It antedates our doing good and even our renouncing sin and sets up a right relationship with God out of which our service to him and our fellow man naturally flows—righteousness *out of* faith.

Righteousness has here, not the abstract sense of moral rectitude usual in English and Greek usage, but a more dynamic sense which derives from the Hebrew. God's righteousness in the OT is his concern that right shall be done, that the good man when wrongly accused shall be vindicated (e.g. Job), that poor Israel, striving to live rightly as God's covenant people but oppressed by foreign powers, shall be set free. This last sense is prominent in 2nd Isa., where God's righteousness means his vindication or salvation of his people, e.g.:

My deliverance [LXX "righteousness"] draws
    near speedily,
my salvation has gone forth.
. . . .
but my salvation will be for ever,
    and my deliverance will never be ended.
                      (Isa. 51:5-6.)

The process of man's spiritual liberation was set in motion by the impact of Jesus on Judaism. The prospect of final deliverance moved nearer. Paul's gospel is that the church is the sphere within which this experience continues to happen. He calls it the power of God for salvation and the revelation of God's righteousness. Later in the letter he refers to it as the fulfilling of the moral law (8:4; 13:10), the new life (5:17-21; 8:9-14), the final triumph (8:37-39), and mercy for all (11:32).

II. THE HUMAN SITUATION (1:18-3:20)

A. PAGANISM (1:18-32)

1:18-20a. *Natural Knowledge of God.* Paul now embarks on his demonstration of mankind's desperate need of the divine intervention referred to in vs. 17.

1:18. The evil is characterized summarily as **ungodliness** (i.e. lack of respect for religion) and the **wickedness** of those who **suppress the truth** (i.e. hostility to moral and intellectual endeavor). This does not go unnoticed by God; his reaction to it is described in parallel terms to the revelation of his righteousness in vs. 17. In this case it is his **wrath** which **is revealed.** The conception of the divine anger roots far back in Hebrew thought. It is primitive but not ignoble, for it means, not the caprice of a vengeful deity, but the reaction of holy love to behavior which contradicts love. Israel experienced God, not as a static ideal, but as an active righteousness revealing itself and punishing unrighteousness among men.

1:19-20a. Sinful men may not claim the excuse of ignorance, for knowledge of God is available. They do not lack truth; they suppress it. Behind the visible world is an invisible Creator. The universe points beyond itself to an Author whom human observers, if they really think, will recognize and reverence. The NEB brings out in vs. 20a a contrast between 2 Greek words: "His invisible attributes . . . have been visible . . . to the eye of reason."

Paul is speaking, not of the full self-disclosure of the Father of our Lord Jesus Christ, but of what is called natural religion. These 2 vss. do not provide sufficient ground for a natural theology, nor are they typical of Paul's total thought about God. But at the present point of his argument he feels that there is a truth in natural theology which needs to be asserted (cf. I Cor. 8:6; Col. 1:15-17).

1:20b-32. *The Evils of Idolatry.* The terminology of this passage is considerably different from Paul's usual. He allows himself to use language similar to that of the Stoics which was current in Jewish writers outside Palestine. He is, after all, contemplating the pagan world. For a typical piece of Jewish polemic against paganism cf. Wisd. Sol. 11-15 (esp. 12:24-27; 13:7-9) and Isa. 44:6-20.

The wisdom which is the fear of the Lord knows instinctively that veneration of the created world is a sin which vitiates the whole of life; only the Creator must be worshiped (vs. 25). Both the common man's deification of specific objects (**the creature rather than the Creator,** vs. 25b) and the philosopher's absolutizing of the whole cosmos (Stoicism in Paul's day and immanentism and pantheism of all periods) are essentially idolatry.

Men are **without excuse** for involvement in idolatry and its degrading associations (cf. Wisd. Sol. 14:8-14). Contemplation of his environment should warn man against this folly and make him sensitive to **truth about God** (vs. 25; cf. vs. 18), which must not be given up in favor of lesser truths. This truth has consequences for philosophy and ethics as well as for religion. It is God's **decree** (vs. 32), or just demand.

1:21-23. These vss. make it clear that idolatry is in Paul's mind. **They became futile** carries this implication (cf. 8:20). Paul refers first to its motivation in mental corruption (vs. 21), then to the outward evidence in **images** of animal as well as human form.

1:24-31. Paul regards the accompanying moral degradation as caused by God. The thrice repeated **God gave them up** (vss. 24, 26, 28; cf. Acts 7:42)—i.e. abandoned them to the consequences of their ungodliness—carries this meaning definitely. It is not enough to say that God simply permits it. That would be, in Paul's opinion, not to relate God sufficiently closely to the human problem—a diluted conception of divine providence and an insufficiently serious estimate of man's degradation.

Paul surveys the evidence of moral delinquency and describes it in terms of the working out of the divine wrath, which is in a continuous process of revelation (vs. 18). In proportion to the intensity of his conviction that God has destined man for righteousness, Paul holds that God's attitude toward rapacity and debauchery may appropriately be described as anger. It is not enough to speak of a kind of impersonal process of retribution whereby men are involved in the consequences of their shameless conduct. That hardly does justice to the prominence of God as subject of the verb "gave them up" (cf. 3:5b).

The facts are frankly stated—perhaps influenced by conventional Jewish descriptions of the "abominations of the heathen." But they were true enough of that ancient Roman world; and they apply also to our modern culture, so that no reader today dare feel superior. Even those who have difficulty with the concept of divine anger must give Paul credit for facing the harsh realities of man's life in society. On the other hand he understands the function of Christ as being to deal with them and provide emancipation (cf. 8:3-4). The gospel of God is great enough to meet a situation as corrupt as that outlined here.

The 3 descriptions of social corruption considered here are the uncontrolled indulgence leading to sexual license that accompanied some idolatrous rites (vss. 24-25), sexual perversion (vss. 26-27), and a **base mind** (NEB "depraved reason"), many specific consequences of which are listed (vss. 28-31).

1:28. The **base mind** is directly connected with

failure to acknowledge God. This is subtly suggested by a play on words which might be freely represented by: "As they *refused* the opportunity of attaining knowledge of God, God gave them over till their mind became like *refuse*."

1:32. The climax of the description of Gentile sinfulness is the remark that it is deliberate and self-congratulatory. Paul cannot believe that sinners act in utter ignorance of the divine sanction of morality and the divine condemnation of sin as self-destroying (cf. 6:23*a*). The connection between sin and death is developed more fully in 5:12-21.

B. JUDAISM (2:1–3:8)

Paul now turns his attention to Judaism. This is not mentioned explicitly until 2:17, though it is clearly implied in 2:12. But from the opening words of ch. 2 he is confronting people who are scandalized by the gross behavior referred to in 1:22-32 and are inclined to sit in judgment on it.

2:1-11. *Spiritual Arrogance.* This attitude of superiority is inexcusable. The sins of the refined and the religious are equally as blameworthy as the crude sins exposed in ch. 1. Hard-heartedness and impenitence (vs. 5) may not express themselves in sexual vice but are no less deserving of God's anger.

This seems to be the main point, but other suggestions in these vss. complicate the interpretation. The critical person Paul has in mind is twice said to be guilty of committing the crimes he condemns in others (vss. 1, 3; cf. vss. 21-24). This is psychologically quite understandable. Jesus himself exposed this often in his condemnations of hypocrisy (cf. e.g. Matt. 23). Are we then to assume that **you, the judge, are doing the very same things** (vs. 1) actually envisages Jews as guilty of the excesses detailed in ch. 1? This is a possible explanation when allowance is made for the corrupting influence of a pagan environment on Jews living outside Palestine.

An alternative explanation of the censorious attitude is that Gentiles are included in it. This is not so likely, however, because the terminology of this paragraph—God's **judgment . . . forbearance . . . wrath**—is Hebrew rather than Greek. The presumption of vs. 4*a* is not the *hubris* (insolence) which figures so largely in Greek tragedy but one of the less happy consequences of the Jewish sense of privilege as recipients of divine favor (cf. 9:4-5).

This idea is expressed in many contemporary Jewish writings, e.g. Wisd. Sol. 15:2: "Even if we sin we are thine, knowing thy power; but we will not sin, because we know that we are accounted thine." (Cf. also Wisd. Sol. 11:9-10; 12:22.) The greatest teachers of Israel reminded their people that privilege implies responsibility (cf. Amos 3:2). The lax type of Jew who imagines he has a right to God's kind forbearance and ignores the opportunity of **repentance** (vs. 4; cf. Wisd. Sol. 11:23) will experience the stern judgment of God ultimately (vss. 5-8). Whatever priority the Jew has (vs. 9) must include priority in requital for evil deeds. God may have elected the Jews to special favor and responsibility, but he **shows no partiality** (vs. 11). In the new dispensation God's offer of righteousness is open to Gentiles as well as Jews, on the basis of faith, which is possible for all alike (cf. 3:29-30; 10:12; 11:30-32).

2:8. In this context **factious** is not so much the sense as "governed by selfish ambition" (NEB).

2:12-16. *Both Jews and Gentiles Sinners.* In vs. 12 Paul speaks in terms of the Mosaic **law** to express the distinction between Jewish and Gentile ways of living. The Gentiles' sins cannot be defined as contraventions of the law, and their consequent perishing cannot be explained by reference to it. This is rather unprecise, but we note that Paul does not say that Gentiles do not sin or that they do not suffer the consequences. Jews, on the other hand, sin in spite of the law and will be judged by its standards. But Paul is moving on to a more positive statement in vss. 14-15. Some Gentiles may be said to have the law **written on their hearts,** and in virtue of this their conduct does in fact conform to the law's demands. On the basis of this they may be reckoned to be **justified** (vs. 13*b;* see below on 3:24).

Paul is here reasoning in line with the more generous Jewish attitude to the decent pagan. The use of the word **conscience** (vs. 15*b*) suggests that he is influenced by Stoic ideas, but this is probably indirect, through Jewish Hellenistic thought. The recognition of this conformity of Gentile moral endeavor with the Jewish law is apparently not to be made known until the final judgment (vs. 16), but again the thought lacks precision. It is an unusual line of argument for Paul, and in fact vs. 13 is contrary to his characteristic understanding of how man attains righteousness before God (cf. 1:17; 3:20-21; Gal. 2:16).

Some take vss. 13-15 as a parenthesis and connect vs. 16 directly with vs. 12, thus lessening the confusion of the thought in the whole passage. We still have the ambiguity as to whether law means Mosaic law, as in vss. 12-13, or moral sense generally, as in vss. 14-15. In these latter vss. Paul is more under the influence of Stoic ethics, with its innate moral sense, than of the rabbis who speak of the law **written on** the **hearts** only of Israelites (cf. Jer. 31:33). Some rabbis would not even allow the law to be taught to Gentiles.

2:17-24. *Jewish Profession and Practice.* Paul's exposure of Jewish guilt, following the exposure of the guilt of paganism in ch. 1, has got sidetracked into a comparison of Jew and Gentile, but he now calls attention to the gap between Jewish pretension and achievement. The law gives instruction not only in ordinary morality but in its finer points, so that the Jews can **approve what is excellent** ("are aware of moral distinctions," NEB). They thus have a missionary responsibility to be a **guide to the blind,** i.e. the Gentiles. But instead of making the religion of Israel attractive to non-Israelites Judaism effects the opposite; it tends to monopolize **truth** (vs. 20). The argument is somewhat rhetorical and mounts to a climax in vs. 24 with a quotation from the LXX of Isa. 52:5, which adds the phrase **among the Gentiles** not found in the Hebrew.

2:25-29. *True Circumcision.* These vss. take up again the contrast of Jew and Gentile, or rather the comparison between the best of Judaism and the best of Gentile moral conduct. This spiritualized conception of circumcision could well have been developed at greater length. Nowhere else does Paul touch on this theme. What Judaism, its rite of circumcision, and the whole conception of an elect people really represent is the primacy of unwavering devotion to God. And it is possible, Paul argues, for those who are not Jews to represent this ideal.

If there is no conformity with the law's demand Jewish profession is meaningless (vs. 25; cf. vs. 12*b*). On the other hand a Gentile may be the moral equal of a professing Jew (vss. 26-27; cf. vss. 14-15), though a Jew might object that no Gentile does actually **keep the law** (cf. 3:20). Circumcision has significance if it is more than a physical mark, if it is a symbol of consecration which is attested by good living (vss. 28-29; cf. vs. 13).

Paul has gone further than most of his contemporaries in this assertion that possessing the law and circumcision do not by themselves mean obedience to the will of God. But he qualifies what he has said in the next paragraph (3:1-8) in attempting to point out the value of circumcision. Nor must we forget that the notion of a spiritual circumcision is familiar to the OT (cf. e.g. Deut. 10:16; 30:6; Jer. 4:4). For the later rabbis, however, any spiritualizing of it was intolerable. The outward mark was essential. It secured God's favor and entry into the age to come. It was God's ordinance, not simply a piece of symbolism.

3:1-8. Has the foregoing discussion left no distinctive place for Judaism? If all alike can know and do God's will, was the special revelation to which Jews appealed—**the oracles of God** (vs. 2) —superfluous?

We have to wait until chs. 9-11 for Paul's full-length answer to these questions, but he realizes that he must say something in reply at this point. He has not given up the traditional belief that his people have a special place in the history of man's salvation. The Jews were the recipients of special revelation through Abraham, Moses, and the prophets. The backsliding of Israel, past and present, which is what he is stressing here, does not erase history or alter its significance. It is part of the continuing problem for God the Lord of history, who has inaugurated a new saving action in Christ (cf. 3:21-26). God's dealing with men also involves **wrath** (vs. 5*b*; cf. 1:18; 2:2-5) and ultimate judgment (vs. 6; cf. 2:5-11). But he is the Lord and Saviour of men, as the past history of Israel rightly understood testifies, and Israel's present disloyalty to its glorious past does not nullify that past. The main factors in it were God's **faithfulness** (vs. 3), **justice** (vs. 5), and **truthfulness** (vs. 7). We should translate "righteousness" rather than "justice" in vs. 5 because it is the same word in Greek as in vs. 21 and 1:17. God's faithfulness, righteousness, and truth mutually implied one another, and all are implied in the main theme of Rom.: the revelation of God's righteousness.

This whole paragraph appears to have been hastily put together, and it is wise not to interpret it too rigorously. The quotation of Ps. 51:4 in vs. 4 is from a classic confession of sin; the point is that there can be no question of the divine justice which condemns human sin. Vs. 7 is best taken as an imaginary objection, or one that Paul has met in debates elsewhere (cf. vs. 5*b*); and this suggests to him a familiar slander on his preaching (vs. 8).

C. THE UNIVERSALITY OF SIN (3:9-20)

Paul breaks off the foregoing development peremptorily and proceeds to the logical inference from his argument in 1:18-2:29: the common sinfulnes of Jews and Greeks. A series of extracts from Pss. and Isa. assert the universal fact of sin, which he has demonstrated from ordinary experience. The appeal to scripture is necessary to make the argument convincing for Jewish readers. The point was admitted both in the OT and in rabbinic writings.

3:9. The Power of Sin. Sin means the inability of man to carry out the will of God. **All men,** even the elect recipients of special revelation, are under its **power.** It is assumed that **Greeks** as well as **Jews** have some conception of the will of God, a moral sense understood as divinely implanted (1:19). Here then is Paul's diagnosis of the human problem: the whole world is **accountable to God** (vs. 19*b*). What is man to do? His claims to moral integrity must be given up (cf. Pss. 7:8; 26:11). The basic problem for Paul is that stated by Job: "How then can man be righteous before God" (Job 25:4)?

The ethical dimension presupposes the religious; sin is a religious, not simply an ethical, term. For Paul the first man was the first sinner, and it is increasingly difficult for successive generations to avoid sin. Since Adam, in whom sin entered the world (5:12), sin is an objective condition of human existence. It has a stranglehold. It is in league with death (5:12-14). The conception becomes personified, even mythical, but it is always related to the facts of moral experience. Man as sinner is in a hopeless plight. But God has broken the entail of sin. Through Christ he has inaugurated the possibility of a sinless humanity (3:21-25; 5:15-21).

3:10-20a. Proof from Scripture. The quotations in vss. 10-18—some rather free—are from the LXX of Pss. 14:1-3 (or 53:1-3); 5:9; 140:3; 10:7; Isa. 59:7-8; Ps. 36:1. As words of the **law**—here used in the sense of scripture in general rather than specifically of the Pentateuch—they are final for **those . . . under the Law,** i.e. Jews (cf. 2:12*b*). The guilt of the pagan world also is presupposed in the light of 1:18-32 and vs. 9. No human being can claim righteousness before God on the basis of his moral conduct, **works of the law.** This is the premise which Paul starts. Righteousness has to be attained on another basis, **apart from law** (vs. 21).

3:20b. The Function of the Law. This clause, though parenthetical, is very important. It answers the implied question in the mind of a Jew: Why do you speak so derogatively about the law? Has it no function in man's attainment of righteousness? In Paul's understanding of it the function of the Mosaic code—and of any moral code—was not that of producing good conduct but the more negative one of creating awareness of sin. This departs from the normative rabbinic view but has solid prophetic teaching behind it. It is more fully stated later (5:20; 7:7-23; 8:3-4; 10:4; 13:8-10; also Gal. 2:19-21; 3:10-25).

The optimistic view that commandments and ideals simply have to be carried out, whether represented by first-cent. Judaism or 19th-cent. liberalism —"We needs must love the highest when we see it," etc.—is radically challenged by this teaching of

Paul's. He is too conscious that ideals are not realized and that when men saw the highest they crucified him.

III. The Divine Offer of Righteousness (3:21-26)

Paul affirms that, however serious the diagnosis of man's moral need as outlined in the previous 2 chs., the situation is not hopeless because God himself has acted. Some German scholars detect a pre-Pauline basis, filled out with Pauline emphasis, in this paragraph. This cannot be proved, but the overloaded sentences make it plausible. That Paul is thinking of the reflection on the meaning of Christ's death which was already developing in the church, esp. in relation to the observance of the Lord's Supper (i.e. liturgically), can hardly be denied. It may be that the key words **redemption** and **expiation** belong to this earlier atonement theology. Such a pre-Pauline core might be: "The righteousness of God has been manifested for all who believe. They are justified by his grace as a gift, through the redemption which is in Christ Jesus, whom God put forward as an expiation by his blood."

3:21. God's Saving Righteousness. God has **manifested** his righteousness. Paul is now thinking of this as already complete in the passion of Christ; hence the verb is in the past tense, not the present, as in 1:17, where he was stressing the continuing effects. There is no contradiction. The divine rescue operation, God's righteousness — his "way of righting wrong," as the NEB translates the word in vs. 22; 1:17 — is evidenced in the life, death, and resurrection of Christ, and in its transformation of men's lives as they respond to the proclamation of this by Christian preachers and grow in moral and spiritual stature in the expanding fellowship of the churches (cf. 6:1-14; 12:1-2).

This happens quite apart from the function of the **law,** but is nevertheless foreseen in **the law and the prophets,** i.e. the OT (cf. 1:2). The gospel is not an innovation in God's dealing with man, nor is it to be put in rigid antithesis to moral codes, though its effectiveness is positive while theirs is negative (cf. 8:3-4). It is rooted in God's **gift** (vs. 24), which is prior to his demand, in his saving act rather than in man's moral endeavor (**works of the law,** vs. 20).

3:22a. The Response of Faith. The benefits of God's saving act are open to any who have faith. This is not an act or effort on man's part, but a response, a reaching out of the hand to accept God's gracious offer (emphasized in vs. 24). It is important to grasp Paul's point here, for otherwise the whole argument of chs. 1-11 will be misunderstood. Faith is essentially a response to divine initiative. Sinfulness being universal (vs. 23), man can do nothing to secure his salvation other than fitting into the conditions created by divine grace made visible in Christ. It is not for man to set his goal and go after it in his own self-generated enthusiasm. Man's business is to recognize his dependence on a gracious controller of his destiny, who is revealed in the self-sacrifice of Christ's death. Responding with gratitude, he can face his moral obligations with what Paul calls the "obedience" of faith (1:5; 6:16-17).

3:22b-24. The Gift of Redemption. Vss. 22b-23 are really a parenthesis explaining **all** in vs. 22a. "**Fall** short of the glory**" presupposes Jewish reflection on the creation of man in the image of God (Gen. 1:26) and the admission that the divine glory which should show in the way man bears himself in fact is lacking. But it was expected to be restored in the age to come.

Justified is a verbal form from the same root as "righteousness." It means not so much "made righteous" in the sense of morally perfect as "pronounced righteous," i.e. "acquitted." The gift is thus freedom to leave court rather than go to prison, freedom to resume life with all its obligations, in grace (5:20-21), in the power of Christ (6:4-11; 8:10), in the Spirit (8:4).

Redemption strictly signifies the emancipation of a slave by the payment of money. There seems to be no thought here of the price. If that question is raised, the answer has to be: Christ's life, or **blood** (vs. 25). This has been featured in some Christian theories of the atonement. But probably Paul is content with the simple sense of liberation. He uses the word again in 8:23 with reference to the final deliverance (so also his adherent who wrote Eph. 1:14; 4:30).

In I Cor. 1:30; Col. 1:14 "redemption" means the present privilege of Christians, including forgiveness of sins. This blessing is here said to be "in" Christ. It is God's gracious gift, and its availability for mankind is due to what Christ was and did. Jews would point to its exemplification in their deliverance from Egypt and from Babylon. Christians point to the new life in Christ as the great example and to Gentiles, not Jews only, as the beneficiaries.

3:25a. Expiation by Christ's Sacrifice. The even more suggestive term **expiation** implies the efficacy of sacrifice, familiar to Paul and to Jews through the daily ritual of the Jerusalem temple, familiar also in the Gentile world. The blood of sacrificial animals was believed to have potency for restoring a right relationship between men and God. Paul's affirmation is that Christ's **blood,** i.e. his self-sacrifice, really does have this efficacy.

An alternative interpretation regards the word "expiation" as meaning the "mercy seat" (Exod. 25:17-22; Lev. 16:13-15), i.e. the place where reconciliation was effected, according to Jewish ritual. In this view the mercy seat for Christians is Calvary.

In all this biblical language about expiation the thought is not that God has somehow to be coaxed into a forgiving mood; that is paganism. In the Bible God is always waiting to forgive the sinner, even though he is said to be angry with him. God hates sin, and the basic problem is to get rid of sin and liquidate its power to cause hostility between man and God (5:10a). This was the task to which Christ's life was directed (8:3-4). God was in Christ reconciling the world to himself (5:10-11; II Cor. 5:19).

This passage has become classic in Christian theories of the atonement. Something necessary for man's achievement of goodness was effected by Christ through his death. The word "expiation" draws a comparison with the death of sacrificial animals which was intelligible enough in Paul's day because this was a familiar feature of ancient religion. But it is difficult, if not meaningless, today. This is only an analogy however. Christ was not an animal, and his death was not sacrifice but self-sacrifice. The positive point here is that as a result of the new insight into the method of divine grace which arises from contemplation of Christ's self-sacrifice a new beginning of moral experience becomes possible. A new spiritual outlook is generated—conversion, enlightenment, reorientation. Theological reflection on this experience sees behind it an initial act of God for man's salvation. That is the significance of the life and death and resurrection of Christ.

3:25b-26. Before Christ God was tolerant, overlooking sins. Positively this is an aspect of his forgiveness, but negatively it might be taken to mean that he let sin go unpunished, thereby allowing doubt to arise concerning his justice. Paul seems to have some sensitivity to this and asserts that what we now learn of God through Christ is all the demonstration and vindication God's justice needs. This is how God deals with sinful man, not only giving him a new start but exhibiting in Christ a creative love which will motivate sinful men afresh and rob sin of its power. In this way God's justice is seen at work. On the objection that Paul's conception of God makes religion too easy cf. 6:1, 15.

IV. The Human Response: Faith (3:27-4:25)

3:27-31. Faith Required of All. Paul briefly draws 2 inferences from his announcement of the manifestation of God's righteousness. First, it leaves no place any more for human merit. The man who begins anew under the inspiration of what God offers in Christ will claim no moral progress as his own achievement. Self-congratulation is ruled out for Christians. The word translated **boasting** in vs. 27 is an aspect of the zeal characteristic of Judaism (cf. 10:2-3) and seems to be a favorite word of Paul's. We see what he means by it in his autobiographical remarks in Gal. 1:13-14; Phil. 3:3-6; II Cor. 11:16–12:10. The basis of the Christian life is not moral striving but trust in God. Instead of "basis" Paul actually uses the word "law" (vs. 27) because it was basic in Judaism, but in this context we must translate it **principle** or "authority."

3:29-30. The 2nd inference is that faith is a great leveler. Jew and Greek alike are dependent on the one God who makes goodness arise out of faith. There is no distinction among those who live by faith, any more than there is in a common sinfulness (vs. 23a). Even Jews owe their salvation, not to **works** (vs. 28), but to faith, as will be pointed out in the case of Abraham in ch. 4.

3:31. We expect Paul to sum up by saying that the Mosaic law, or moral obligation generally, no longer applies to Christians who take their stand on faith. The objection is anticipated from the Jewish side: You are setting up a rival principle to moral authority. What guarantee is there that men will behave morally? Paul is greatly concerned about this. Where he differs from his Jewish critic is in his perception that what is needed is not exhortation but vision and impetus. These can come only out of what he calls faith.

It is somewhat surprising that Paul's answer to the objection is that he does assign a proper place to the law. Vs. 20 gives part of his meaning, but this needs to be developed more fully. Apart from

4:13-15, which subordinates the law to "promise," we have to wait for the arguments of 6:15–8:4. Paul is not yet ready to say Christ means the end of the law (10:4), or that he himself has died to the law (Gal. 2:19), though either of these statements would logically follow vss. 9-26.

4:1-12. Abraham as an Example of Faith. At this point Paul finds it to his purpose to put beyond misunderstanding what he means by faith. Instead of continuing his positive exposition about the effects of receiving God's righteousness he therefore pauses to exemplify faith by reference to a figure recognized by all Jews as of overriding significance in the relationship between man and God. Concerning the precise ground of Abraham's religious importance there was some divergence among Jewish theologians. Some of their thought must have been known to Paul. The majority view was that his status of acceptance with God was due to his **works**, i.e. his good conduct. He could be regarded as having demonstrated perfect obedience to God's commands. Outstanding examples of this were his circumcision (Gen. 17) and his willingness to sacrifice his dear son Isaac (Gen. 22). Some rabbis held that he did in fact fulfill the law, even though it was not revealed until the time of Moses, cents. later.

Paul finds Abraham's significance elsewhere, not in his meritorious deeds (cf. Jas. 2:21-24) or in his temptations (cf. I Macc. 2:52; Ecclus. 44:19-20), but in his trustful attitude to God, his faith. The main text in his interpretation is therefore Gen. 15:6 (vs. 3; cf. Gal. 3:6).

4:4-5. Paul's reasoning in these vss. seems a little strained, but it would not appear so to those accustomed to the subtleties of rabbinic interpretation. "Believing" or "trusting" in Paul's mind implies as its antithesis "doing" or "working." Working cannot be meant in the case of Abraham, Paul suggests (vs. 4), because in that case payment or **due** would be mentioned, not **gift.** It was not a matter of working at all (vs. 5a) but of trusting, of relating himself to God as one who pronounces righteous even the **ungodly** (see above on 3:24).

4:6-8. This idea is supported by a quotation from Ps. 32:1-2a which is useful for Paul's argument because it refers to the blessing of forgiveness, thereby implying something other than meritorious obedience, and also because it uses the same Greek verb that Paul has found in the LXX of Gen. 15:6 with the sense "credit to," "reckon as." The verb basically means "think," "count," "reckon," and in the metaphor of bookkeeping "enter to the credit of." The bookkeeping metaphor is not adequate for the expression of man's relationship with God. Man's progress in goodness is never sufficient to establish a credit balance. God puts us in his credit by his gracious gift (vss. 4-5; cf. 3:24).

4:9-12. Paul takes from Ps. 32:1-2a the idea of blessing and transfers this to the privilege of Abraham mentioned in Gen. 15:6. He then proceeds to point out that at that stage of Abraham's life he was still **uncircumcised**—circumcision is not mentioned until Gen. 17—and draws the inference that Abraham's real significance is as the forerunner of Gentiles, who are men of faith and on that basis recipients of God's offer of righteousness (vs. 11). Abraham is also the ancestor of the Jews, but the relationship between him and them is to be understood as rooting in the faith which he had before he received the outward mark of Judaism, circumcision (vs. 12). This implies a distinction between Jews who have faith and those who are content with the badge of circumcision and strive to please God by their good works. This is not quite the same conception as in 2:25-29 between the merely outward circumcision and that which fulfills the law.

This method of using scripture strikes modern readers as arbitrary. But it conforms to rabbinic standards; and even if Paul's position might seem extreme to his Jewish readers, they could not object to his method of interpretation. We shall have further examples of it in chs. 9–11. The incongruity of the methodology with modern logic and biblical criticism should not blind us to the force of Paul's arguments in general; they are able to stand by their inherent logic. E.g. here the real weight of these vss. is that Abraham's acceptance with God was not effected by the ritual of circumcision. That rite was not the cause of God's approval but the **sign or seal** of it. Baptism, the Christian analogue of circumcision, was also called a "seal" from the 2nd cent. onward. It confirmed what had been effected already by divine grace.

To Paul's reflection on the Gen. stories Abraham was singled out by an awareness of God and sensitiveness to his call which was prior to his outward obedience. This was his "faith"; this was what he "gained" (if such is the correct reading in vs. 1; see RSV footnote). This idea stands out clearly enough, whatever manipulation of texts is used to support it. We miss the reference to Gen. 12:3 which is quoted in Gal. 3:8-9. The argument of Gal. 3 supplements that of this ch. and brings out more clearly that the Christians are the true posterity of Abraham (Gal. 3:29).

4:13-25. The Promise to Abraham. Paul now picks out another episode from the Abraham narratives of Gen., viz. the promise (Gen. 12:1-3; 17:5; 18:18; 22:17-18) that his destiny is to be a source of blessing for all nations. The logic is tortuous because here, as elsewhere, the links of the thought are not all expressed. The promise means God's guarantee of final salvation. For Christians this means all that they experience through Christ, who is the seed of Abraham (Gal. 3:16) and the authenticator of all God's promises (II Cor. 1:20). The correlative of the promise on the human side is trust in God. It is exemplified in Abraham, and is now called **righteousness of faith** (vs. 13*b*) and not living according to the law (**not . . . through the law,** a phrase which very emphatically begins the sentence in the Greek).

4:14-15. These vss. are parenthetical. The law principle is utterly opposed to the principle of the promise, or of faith. Law demands obedience and, if that is not forthcoming, retribution (**wrath**). That is not the way of salvation. To imagine God's way of dealing with men as confined to this method is to nullify both the promise and faith (vs. 14). Vs. 15*b* is obscure. It may mean that God's saving action lifts men to a level above the law, where ultimately transgression does not enter in, i.e. moral failure does not mar the relationship between man and God.

4:16-17. The alternative to the law is faith, promise, grace, and this marks the true succession from Abraham. **All his descendants** includes Gentiles as well as Jews (cf. 3:29-30). Rabbis could speak of Abraham as the first proselyte. Paul illustrates this from Gen. 17:5 (vs. 17*a*). Vs. 17*b* memorably characterizes God as the object of faith: **gives life to the dead** gets point from vs. 19; **calls into existence the things that do not exist** includes the physical universe, man in God's image, and, finally, the perfected society in a perfected universe (8:18-23).

4:18-25. The root of faith is the conviction that God is as described in vss. 17, 21: **able** to put in the place of man's nonexistent righteousness a righteousness of faith, to overcome even death, as evidenced in the resurrection of Christ (vs. 24*b*) and foreshadowed in the birth of Isaac to parents who were near death. Curiously, Paul makes no use of the story of the sacrifice of Isaac (Gen. 22), which might have served his purpose here (cf. Jas. 2:21; Heb. 11:17-19).

In the total setting of chs. 1–8 the nonexistent thing which God causes to exist is the righteousness of sinners. This is his "new creation" (cf. II Cor. 5:17). God is this kind of God; he creates righteousness where there is the receptiveness of faith (vs. 22). The evidence for this is not only the example of Abraham and the words of promise but the death and resurrection of Jesus (vss. 24-25).

V. The Effects of Faith (5:1–8:39)

We are now ready to hear about the consequences of the divine offer of righteousness and man's reception of it by faith. How does it actually work out in the new Christian, i.e. nonpagan and non-Jewish, experience? Ch. 5 explains this new life in terms of a general spiritual release (vss. 1-11) and esp. a release from death (vss. 12-21). The more ethical inferences will be drawn in chs. 6–7; 12–14, though the distinction between religious and ethical is ours rather than Paul's. Christian ethics can be worked out only when obedience to God and gratitude for what he has given in Christ are seen as the preliminary to all moral endeavor and spiritual growth.

A. Reconciliation (5:1-11)

5:1*a*. Justification by Faith. This clause recalls 3:24 (see comment), with the difference that **are justified** is now in that characteristic Greek past tense which implies that the action is complete. The meaning is not that as soon as a man has faith he is morally perfect; that would be a denial of plain facts. Nor do we have to interpret the verb as implying a legal fiction: you are not righteous, but God is prepared to treat you as if you were and be tolerant of any future sins.

Paul has indeed argued, in view of the evidence of human delinquency quoted in chs. 1–2, that the whole of mankind is guilty and no single individual, Jew or Gentile, deserves to be acquitted; everyone should be sent to prison (3:19-20). But his use of the verb "justify" presupposes not only the negative of man's moral failure but the positive of Christ's perfect life and sacrificial death, which constitute a new factor in the moral situation. In terms of the forensic metaphor we may compare this to a judge acquitting an accused person in view of fresh factors brought before the court, or a new counsel for the defense (cf. 8:33-34). Thus freed, the accused leaves the court to resume life among his fellow citizens; he is no more morally perfect than they, but he is not in prison and can make a new start with his life. In describing this new start we can dispense with the metaphor of the law court, as Paul does in vs. 1*b*.

5:1*b*. Peace with God. Surprisingly Paul seems to say "let us have" (so the majority of manuscripts) rather than **we have** peace in relation to God. This word "peace" expresses the new situation simply. It is synonymous with the more formal theological term **reconciliation** in vs. 11. The trouble with sinful living is that it is out of touch with God, which is man's rightful relationship; worse still, it is a relation of enmity or hostility (vs. 10*a*). The sinner refuses to acknowledge God's law and is, as it were, fighting against him. This is not merely a series of defiant acts but a settled disposition (cf. vs. 10*a;* 8:7). The basic human problem was involvement in this broken, vitiated relationship toward God, this state of cold war. God himself has taken the initiative to break the deadlock. His revelation of righteousness through Christ makes a new relationship of peace possible.

5:2-5. New Hope. Christ has given believers **access** to God's presence (cf. Eph. 2:18; 3:12; Heb. 7:25; 9:24) and a new experience of divine **grace** (cf. 3:24), which means essentially God's willingness to have dealings with sinful humanity, and in this sense is the same as his **love** (vs. 5). This causes a new outlook on life (cf. vs. 18*b;* 6:4) and **hope,** i.e. confidence, of ultimate salvation. Paul does not speak of this new experience as being saved but keeps salvation for the future sense (vs. 10*b*). This hope cannot be shaken by anything that may happen in life's hardships, which instead result in **character** (NEB "proof that we have stood the test") that in turn strengthens hope. It is a product of the encounter with God which Paul describes by the vivid metaphor of the pouring out of **God's love.** The NEB "flooded our inmost heart" sounds exaggerated but is not more so than Paul's Greek here. How different this metaphor from the forensic one implied in "righteousness"! Paul connects God's love with the onrush of the **Holy Spirit** (cf. I Cor. 13; Gal. 5:22).

5:6-11. Evidence of God's Love. This talk about God's love is not pious fancy. There is concrete evidence of it in what Christ did, in his devotion to men without scrutinizing their merit. Human experience (vs. 7) provides no parallel to what Christ has done for men, even for the **ungodly** (cf. Mark 2:15-17; Luke 7:44-47; 23:33-34).

5:9. Reference to Christ's death suggests to Paul the thought of justification (cf. vs. 1) by **blood** (cf. 3:25*a*). This has past and present reference, and Paul now adds a future reference, the certainty of not having to experience the final **wrath,** i.e. retribution, here thought of, not as in 1:18, but as connected with the ultimate judgment, as in 2:5.

5:10-11. To be **reconciled** is the same as to be justified (vs. 1). Paul's usage implies always man's need to be reconciled to God, not God's need to be changed at all in his attitude toward man. Justification is not a judge's acquittal so much as a father's welcome, and reconciliation brings in the idea of reunion with the life of the family (cf. II Cor. 5:18-21; Col. 1:19-22).

B. Freedom from Sin and Death (5:12–6:14)

5:12-21. The New Humanity. The new relationship of peace with God is also a new type of life for believers as they live in relation to one another and their nonbelieving fellow men. They have been initiated into a great liberation, viz. from the power of sin, and this also means liberation from death. This is God's **free gift** (vs. 15), but it can be described as sharing the life of Christ (cf. **saved by,** lit. "in," **his life,** vs. 10). Christians are pioneers of a new humanity "in Christ."

This is worked out in terms of a contrast between **Adam** and Christ. Adam is the representative figure of the old humanity, unable to attain righteousness because limited by sin and doomed to die. Christ is the dominant figure of the new humanity, the creator of the possibility of overcoming sin, of becoming righteous and continuing to **reign in life** (vs. 17), **eternal life** (vs. 21), i.e. life of a quality which is not affected by death.

This is Paul's doctrine of Christ as the 2nd Adam. Though it occurs only here and in I Cor. 15:45-57, it presents his main thought about how Christ is effective for man's redemption; i.e. it is the theory of atonement to which he attaches the greatest value. It does not rest on the sacrificial analogy, but it recognizes the need of mankind as dominated by sin and mortality. It affirms that Christ introduces positive energies which are beyond the corrupting influence of sin and death. What Adam failed to achieve is achieved by Christ and made available to all who attach themselves to him, i.e. by faith.

This argument presupposes our ability to think corporately. Adam and Christ are both historic figures, but for Paul they are corporate entities and not isolated individuals. Adam stands for the whole of mankind, understood as in Gen. 3, yielding to temptation and involved in its consequences. Abraham similarly in ch. 4 stands for Israel depending on the great promise of her God. Christ is the conqueror of sin and death, not for his own release from earthly life, but vicariously for those who are to be incorporated in his body, the church, the new Israel.

This kind of thinking was natural enough for the ancient Hebrew; it is not so easy for the modern mind. The tendency now to absorb the individual into larger units like the state or the industrial corporation, dangerous as it may be to personal freedom, may make biblical modes of thought less strange.

5:12-14. The problem is stated in these vss. The **one man** is Adam. He was responsible for the entry of sin into human experience. But the real fact from which Paul starts is not the guilt of Adam but the universality of sin—**all men sinned**—and the universality of death, regarded as the inevitable concomitant. This is questionable to the modern mind, but it was a regular inference in Jewish interpretation. Death for Paul, as in the OT, means more than the end of physical existence; it is a spiritual fact, connected with divine judgment on sin, and a part of the effects of sin. It exerts a sinister control (**reigned,** vs. 14*a*). Sin and death are aspects of the kingdom of Satan, which is to be replaced through Christ by the kingdom of God (cf. Mark 3:23-27). The metaphor of reigning is used again in vss. 17, 21.

Sin vitiated human life from the very beginning. Paul thinks of it objectively, i.e. apart from whether it is deliberate or not, in fact apart from man's moral awareness. It is not synonymous with guilt, which is man's awareness of his sin, with varying degrees of remorse. This awareness depends on moral **law** (vs. 13*b;* cf. vs. 20*a*). But sin is a wider term. It means all that prevents man from realizing God's purpose and, in terms of Gen. 3, obeying the commandment. The more individualized concept of guilt is included in the reference to sin as **counted** (vs. 13*b*)—an allusion to the Jewish picture of heavenly books which recorded all men's sins. The **transgression of Adam** (vs. 14*b*) was deliberate defiance of a divine command. **Type** is lit. "stamp," hence "likeness" or "correspondence."

5:15-19. Vss. 12-14 are really one long subordinate sentence which is not finished because Paul starts afresh in vs. 15 instead of constructing the clause anticipated by **as** in vs. 12. Where Adam failed Christ succeeded. Here begins a series of carefully balanced antitheses drawing out the parallelism between Adam and Christ. Something of precision is sacrificed but the main thought is magnificently clear. **Trespass** (vs. 15) means a particular sinful act, an outcrop, so to speak, of the underlying sin which holds mankind in its grip. Christ makes possible justification (vs. 16), righteous living (vss. 17-18), and the triumph of grace over sin (vs. 19), thus reversing the process which produces their opposites. The old humanity was characterized by the **disobedience** exemplified in Adam; the redeemed humanity reproduces the **obedience** shown in Christ's perfect life. **Made righteous** appears to mean complete moral perfection, a more developed stage than is implied by justification (**acquittal and life,** vs. 18*b*) and this is why the verb is in the future tense.

5:20-21. This sentence goes beyond 3:20 in saying that the function of the **law** is not to solve the moral problem but to show it up in its true dimension, and in a sense aggravate it, **increase the trespass.** This paradox is explained in 7:7-13. It is divine **grace** (cf. 3:24; 5:1) which meets human need and is far more powerful than sin and all its effects, including death.

6:1-14. *New Life in Christ.* The Christian is sure of salvation (ch. 5) but he has to develop in moral stature. Grace does not mean license (vss. 1, 14) but moral power (vs. 11). Moral obligation continues and should be gladly faced in the **newness of life** (vs. 4) on which the Christian embarks.

6:1. The objection envisaged here (cf. vs. 15) may be ironical only, assumed to come from a Jewish critic voicing his impression that Paul's argument since 3:20 has been indifferent to moral issues. On the other hand there have been enthusiasts who from time to time in history have held that Christian freedom means freedom from all restraints. The

term "antinomianism" is used to describe this aberration. It is most noticeable among groups—esp. some in the 2nd and 16th cents. and some modern sects—which claim control by the Spirit. Possibly there were groups of this sort among Paul's converts at Corinth, and also in the church at Rome. His language in chs. 5; 7 exposes him to this objection, whether actually made by his critics or simply rhetorical. It is a travesty of his intention, but he realizes he must make himself clear on the moral issue. His direct answer to it is vss. 6, 11.

6:2-4. Paul is still writing in terms of clear contrasts, not now between Christ and Adam, nor even between Christ and sin, but between the believer's new life and the old life dominated by sin and death from which he has been emancipated. The clean break from that old life is emphasized. It is compared to **death,** and this strong emphasis is part of the interpretation of **baptism** as a sharing of Christ's burial. This is no mere initiatory ceremony but points back to the passion and **resurrection** of Christ, which were the means under God of effecting the new life of freedom from sin. Entering the water is like Christ's entering the grave; coming up out of the water is like Christ's coming out of the tomb. It may have been Paul who first thought of the comparison, though this is not certain; but it was a customary emphasis of his, as we see from its recurrence in Col. 2:12. **Glory** (vs. 4) is equivalent to "power" (cf. Col. 1:11; II Thess. 1:9)—possibly an echo of credal language.

6:5-11. The pre-Christian part of life is finished, even if not forgotten; Paul goes so far as to say it is **crucified** (vs. 6*a*), because he is sure that the continuing life of the believer is dependent utterly on Christ, to such a degree that it can be thought of as a sharing of Christ's risen life after crucifixion (vss. 5, 8). Here is the basis of the idea of the church as the body of Christ, and of believing existence as incorporation into Christ. This is the new solidarity in, or with, Christ, contrasted with the old solidarity in Adam. It is expressed in the word **united** (vs. 5), lit. "grown together," found only here in the NT.

Sinful body (vs. 6) does not mean body as opposed to soul or spirit. Paul can use the word "body" in the sense of "personality" or "self" (NEB). The lit. Greek here is "body of sin," the genitive "of sin" being descriptive, as in the similar phrases "body of humiliation" and "body of glory" in Phil. 3:21. The body or whole person is in the grip of sin, as explained in 5:12-21. "Sinful flesh," lit. "flesh of sin," in 8:3 is not an accurate parallel because there it is implied that the flesh, i.e. the physical part of man, is the location of sin (cf. 7:18*a*).

That the sinful self is to be **destroyed,** lit. "reduced to inactivity," would seem to mean nothing less than inability to sin any more. But sinlessness probably goes beyond Paul's intention here. He does not say Christians *cannot* sin, as is said in I John 3:6-9. He has too shrewd a sense of the realities of experience to dogmatize on this point. He knows that the imperatives of vss. 12-13 are in place (cf. 8:12-13). The moral struggle is still actual for the redeemed man, though the scales are not hopelessly weighted against him, so that defeat is inevitable, as in the old conditions of existence before Christ introduced the prospect of victory. Being **freed from sin** (vs. 7) means for Paul primarily being no longer subject to those conditions (for this objective sense of sin cf. 5:13-14; Ps. 51:5; for a more graphic account of the moral conflict cf. 7:13-23). In spite of the importance Paul attached to baptism, he did not regard it as making moral endeavor meaningless. Then, as now, the notion that sacraments confer immunity from temptation and sin was familiar. Paul's teaching on righteousness is a safeguard against such unethical sacramentalism. The point he is making is that the baptized man has said good-by to his former existence; he is **dead to sin** (vs. 11).

6:12-13. These imperatives follow naturally. They ought not to need stating after the glorious indicatives of the freedom symbolized by baptism, of Christ's triumph in the resurrection made beneficial to all believers, of Christ's headship of a new humanity, and of the privilege of reconciliation with God. But Paul is too shrewd a man, and too faithful a shepherd of souls, not to know that the imperative has to follow the indicative. Even the redeemed man has to be exhorted to "become what you are." Watchfulness and moral endeavor are never superfluous.

6:14. The conclusion mounts to a peak of confidence. Sin's **dominion** is broken. The same word is used in vs. 9 of death, and in 5:14, 17 we read of death's "reign." The reign of sin and death was the condition of humanity before Christ set up among men a new kingdom, drawing on himself all the attacking malice of evil and submitting in the end to death. But because he was the incarnate power of God this was not the end but a new beginning. The kingdom, i.e. supreme authority, is God's; the dominion, or lordship, is Christ's, acknowledged by believers in every mention of his name.

C. God's Holy Service (6:15-23)

6:15-19. Vs. 15 picks up vs. 14b and also vs. 1. It is unthinkable that the Christian's new status should be abused. Though no longer responsible to law, he is dependent on divine grace, which means the gift of righteousness (3:24) and life (5:21). This is developed under the metaphor of a change of ownership of **slaves.** Christian freedom is a new kind of allegiance; sin is the old master who has no further claim. The figure is set out in terms of contrast between **law . . . sin . . . death . . . impurity . . . iniquity** on the one hand and **grace . . . obedience . . . righteousness . . . sanctification . . . God . . . life** on the other. The comparison with slavery is somewhat humiliating—and Paul apologizes for it in vs. 19a—but it makes the point clear. The difference about Christians as slaves is that theirs is a self-imposed slavery. Paul does not explicitly say this, and we must beware of attributing modern notions of free will to him—his discussion of divine control in chs. 9-11 shows that he allowed little or no place to it. Nevertheless we may venture to modify his metaphor in this way as we apply it to ourselves. Paul's thought is mainly of the objective condition of humanity as being under the control of either sin or Christ. Modern individualism needs to

take account of this. The other side of the picture is the Christian's freedom (8:15).

6:19. The meaning of **natural limitations,** lit. "weakness of your flesh," is inability to understand what the new status involves if Paul does not explain it by an analogy drawn from everyday experience, viz. slavery. "Flesh" means our physical constitution as contrasted with mind or spirit (see below on 7:18). **Sanctification** is the opposite of **impurity** (cf. I Thess. 4:3-8). Christians are part of a holy community, like Israel. They are incorporated by baptism into Christ (vss. 3-5, 11). Sanctification is sometimes used in the sense of justification (cf. I Cor. 6:11). Here it means the progressive growth in moral stature which follows on the initial justification or acceptance with God on the basis of faith.

6:20-23. Death as the **end,** i.e. the result, of sin (vs. 21) is comparable to **wages** due, in contrast to a new **life** that is **eternal** (vs. 23)—i.e. not simply everlasting in duration but of higher quality—which God bestows as an unearned gratuity. This life is for those who are **in Christ Jesus** (cf. vs. 11), the holy community.

D. Freedom from Law (7:1-25)

7:1-6. *Dying to the Law.* The thought of slavery to sin (ch. 6) leads Paul to consider the tyranny of the moral law. The changeover of authority which is part of the believer's experience is now considered in terms of law and illustrated by reference to the subordination of wife to husband in the marriage relationship—a feature less prominent in modern marriage than in ancient. The point is that the death of a husband sets a woman free to marry again (vss. 2-3). Thus Gentile Christians are no longer subservient to false gods or pagan customs, and Jewish Christians are freed from dependence on the law of Moses in order to serve Christ, who takes the place of the law (cf. 10:4; Gal. 6:2).

7:4. As Paul develops his metaphor, instead of saying the law is finished as far as Christians are concerned he says they **have died** as far as the law is concerned—repeated with emphatic verbs in vs. 6. The confusion is no doubt due to the thought of 6:4, 8 and to the wish to describe Christian experience on the model of Christ's, in terms of death and resurrection. **Through the body of Christ** is taken by some commentators to imply the thought of Christ's body as the efficacious offering which atones for sin and creates freedom (see above on 3:25a). More probably it refers to the new community into which believers are incorporated, as in the NEB: "by becoming identified with the body of Christ" (cf. 6:4, 11; 12:4-5; I Cor. 12; Eph. 4:4-16). **Bear fruit for God** suggests that the marriage metaphor is still in Paul's mind. The Christian's relation to Christ is not without results; good works are produced! These are never the ground of our acceptance with God—as so strenuously argued in 3:20, 28—but are the outcome of it (cf. 6:22).

7:5-6. On flesh see below on vss. 18-20. **Aroused by the law** means "encouraged" or "occasioned" by it. This effect of the law is explained in vss. 7-11. Vs. 6 merges into the former analogy from slavery (6:16-20). **New life of the Spirit** parallels "newness of life" (6:4).

7:7-12. The Law as the Stimulus of Sin. The Christian has finished with law and now lives under new conditions (vs. 6). In what sense then can Paul speak of upholding the law (3:31)? He can no longer put off explaining what positive value he ascribes to it. His imaginary Jewish objector is now pressing him to say definitely whether or not he equates it with sin (vs. 7). Paul cannot allow this objection to stand for a moment. His reply begins by reaffirming what he has said in 3:20: law makes us aware of what sin is (vs. 7b), in fact of our own actual sinfulness (vs. 8), i.e. our guilt. In the objective sense in which Paul uses the term "sin" (i.e. in 5:12-14) a man may be sinful but not guilty; but here he is talking about guilt, i.e. sin in its subjective and personal sense. This is not possible apart from the law, which confers moral awareness: **Apart from the law sin lies dead** (vs. 8b). This connects with 5:20: "Law came in, to increase the trespass" (cf. Gal. 3:19a).

Paul is clearly going much further than his previous statements. He has said that the law is not intended to be the means of attaining goodness (3:20a) or of effecting the promise (4:13). He now indicates that its function is to be a catalyst of moral struggle and inner tension. There is acute discernment here, even if this cannot be everybody's experience, and even if the descriptive terminology is exaggerated, e.g. the references to death in vss. 9-11. Moral consciousness is not simply the incentive to good behavior—the assumption of optimists and Pharisees in every age. It may equally well produce a fascination with evil. Sin finds **opportunity** (vs. 8) in the commandment. The underlying Greek word here means "starting point" or "base of operations" or, in current war metaphor, "beachhead." This is not nonsense, but serious reckoning with the tragic facts of man's moral experience.

Some writers describe these facts in terms of Satan, or demonic action. Contemporary Jewish teachers sometimes used the notion of an evil impulse located within each human being. Paul ascribes these sinister facts to the operation of sin. This is his doctrine of sin at its most baneful level, making use of a divine gift—the law, acquaintance with which makes man a moral being—to produce an inward conflict which may be spiritually fatal (vss. 9-11; cf. vss. 22-24).

Vs. 9 refers to childhood, before the dawn of knowledge of right and wrong. This period in the individual corresponds to the period from Adam to Moses in the history of mankind (5:13-14). Gen. 3 is at the back of Paul's mind here. He must also have been conscious of the Jewish custom by which a boy at 13 became a "son of the commandment" (*bar mitzvah*), i.e. assumed the responsibility of an adult Jew to live according to the law.

7:13-25. Inner Tension. It is not the law which causes the death described in vss. 9-11. Law as a divine instrument serves the purpose of showing up sin in its blackest possible colors—**sinful beyond measure.** This is one of Paul's ways of referring to guilt, not sin it its objective sense. Sin makes use of the law. Man cannot blame the law; his culpability remains his own, except insofar as he is incapacitated by the power sin has over him.

7:14-17. This power is briefly illustrated by the metaphor of slave and owner—**sold under sin,** "the purchased slave of sin" (NEB, vs. 14; on **carnal** see below on vss. 18-20)—but this metaphor is overshadowed by the more sinister one of an indwelling evil influence corrupting the nobler impulses and causing an intolerable inner conflict (vss. 15-17). This is the moral havoc wrought by **sin which dwells within me** (vss. 17, 20). The picture is unmistakable and morally realistic. Rabbis sometimes explained this by their doctrine of an evil "inclination," or an evil and a good inclination in tension within man. Paul was probably influenced by that doctrine, but the difference would be that, whereas the rabbis recommended the study of the law as the remedy, Paul is convinced that it is the categorical imperative of the law which is made use of by the "inclination," or indwelling sin, to cause the inward conflict. Paul's Christian insight made him more aware of the dimension of that conflict.

7:18-20. The language here reveals another aspect of Paul's thought which seemed to him relevant to this matter of moral failure, but which is difficult for the modern man: his view of the **flesh** (vs. 18; cf. vs. 25; **carnal**, lit. "fleshly," vs. 14, and **members,** vs. 23, mean the same). Flesh for Paul starts with the sense usual in the OT of the physical part of man, body as opposed to soul or mind or spirit. Hence it comes to mean what used to be called our lower nature (cf. NEB "unspiritual nature"). Flesh is not sinful in itself but the apparent association with it of instinctive behavior and **passions** (vs. 5) leads Paul to the view that it is the door through which the indwelling sin gains entry (cf. **sinful flesh,** 8:3). The assumption of some scholars that this is evidence of Greek influence on Paul is not necessary. Hebrew ideas are a sufficient explanation, and we now have cases of similar senses of "flesh" in the Dead Sea scrolls. The absence of reference to Satan's activity in all this discussion is noteworthy.

7:21-25. Paul's use here of the word **law** in the sense of "principle" (cf. 3:27; 8:2) is very confusing. The **law of God** is the Mosaic law. **Another law** means the demand of his **members**—equivalent to flesh (vs. 18) and **body** (vs. 24)—which is antithetic to the law of God and therefore can be called outright the **law of sin.** Finally the **law of my mind** means either the Mosaic law or the moral law generally, with the addition that Paul's reason, his **inmost self,** approves of it. Nevertheless his "members" are a battleground and the winner in the conflict is **sin,** which leads him off as a **captive.** In vs. 25b, which appears to be out of place and to belong after vs. 23, this military metaphor gives way to that of slavery. The meaning of **body of death** is given in vs. 11 (cf. 6:6, 23). But Paul knows of deliverance from his hopeless plight. The sublimity of vs. 25a finds a parallel in the serene confidence of 8:37-39 (cf. Gal. 2:20; Phil. 1:21).

How much are we to read into the first-person pronouns of this ch.? Some interpreters have inferred that it is autobiographical, i.e. that here we have a transcript of Paul's own experience of frustration and freedom. But there is no hint of reference to his conversion (Gal. 1:15; Phil. 3:6-9; Acts

9:1-22). Paul is certainly arguing from what he has himself gone through, but his object is something more than autobiography.

On the other hand, we have here no stylized composition or rhetorical exercise. Paul is really writing about the power of sin—not objectively, as in 5:12-21, or ethically, as in 6:15-23, but in terms of inner conflict so threatening to the personality as to result in utter despair, apart from Christ. This is the true Christian experience interpreted by a man of supernormal intensity who had been disciplined in Judaism to the point of achieving the Jewish ideal ("blameless," Phil. 3:6) but in Christ was schooled to a complete transvaluation (Phil. 3:7-12).

A related question is whether Paul is dealing with the Christian life before or after conversion. This ch. by itself suggests preconversion experience, but the answer should have in view other passages. In the light of ch. 6 it would seem necessary to say that the experience of the believer as well as that of the nonbeliever is under survey. The paradox of Christian experience is that the power of sin is not broken after the first full response to the gospel (faith, conversion). The Christian is at the same time righteous and sinful, as Martin Luther said in a phrase both simple and profound. Righteousness, according to this letter, is real, not fictitious; but it does not amount to moral perfection or immunity from the downdrag of sin. Indwelling sin is not dislodged. There is internal tension so distressing as to be comparable to civil war (vs. 23), and on normal expectation this would be fatal (vs. 24). But the last word is with God, who is imparting his righteousness to man and will in the end reveal his mercy to all (cf. 11:32).

E. NEW SPIRITUAL ENDOWMENT (8:1-17)

Vs. 1 of this ch. is parallel to 5:1. **There is . . . no condemnation** is the negative to the positive "since we are justified" in 5:1. We are now ready to move forward to a fuller comprehension of the effects of what God has done in Christ for sin-ridden humanity. We are in a better position for this move because the intervening chs. 5-7 have shown how the power of Christ has dealt with man's fundamental disharmony with God (5:1-11), the dominance of sin and death (5:12-21), and the continuing challenge of sin (chs. 6-7). The inadequacy of law to meet man's need has also been explained (5:20; 7:7-14); now Paul can refer to it summarily as **the law of sin and death** (vs. 2).

8:1-4. Paul's Gospel. These 4 vss. might be said to have compressed in them the whole of Paul's triumphant theology. As in 7:21-23, **law** is used in vs. 2 in the sense of "authority" or "principle." The new regime is inaugurated by the **Spirit** (see below on vss. 5-11)—or alternatively by Christ as the 2nd Adam (5:12-21)—which is, or creates, **life;** and it cancels out the results of that other regime which disseminated **sin and death.**

8:3. The word **likeness** (cf. Phil. 2:7) might seem to imply a limitation of Christ's real humanity, but the context and Paul's total view of Christ show that no such implication is intended. Christ was fully human and therefore **sinful** in the objective sense of sin (5:12-14) though not in the sense of

being guilty, because his life provided the complete antithesis to Adam's disobedience (5:18-19; cf. II Cor. 5:21*a;* on **sinful flesh,** lit. "flesh of sin," see above on 6:5-11; 7:18-20). Christ's mission on earth was **for sin,** i.e. concerned with sin, or possibly "as a sin offering," in the sense of 3:25.

Condemned sin is a bold expression which stresses the reversal brought about by God's action in Christ. It is now sin, not the sinful man (vs. 1), who is the prisoner being sentenced. Sin's dominance (5:12-21) is broken. It is condemned **in the flesh** by Christ's being himself a man. Apart from full identification with humanity Christ could not be mankind's savior. He had to expose himself to sin and death without any immunity. By so doing he exhausted their power and robbed them of their rights (cf. Gal. 3:13).

8:4*a.* The reasoning on the basis of which the assertions of vss. 3-4 are made has been given in the preceding chs. The new point is the declaration that the **just requirement of the law** is to be met after all. That is what church experience involves. The righteousness of God (1:17), which is a divine gift, is not unrelated in its effects to the law's moral demands. Paul has never denied that the Mosaic law, and all moral codes, have a just requirement. What Immanuel Kant called the categorical imperative is a basic element in human experience, of which psychology and ethics have to take proper account. But this element in the human constitution does not inevitably produce good conduct. This is the plain fact of experience from which Paul's central argument in this letter starts.

Paul is able to announce as his gospel that God offers to men resources over and above their sense of moral obligation. This is the significance of the life of Christ and the life of the church motivated by the Spirit. This divine initiative in Christ and in the church—revealing of divine righteousness (1:17; 3:21), pouring out of divine love (5:5), incorporation into Christ (6:4-5; 8:29), life in the Spirit (vss. 5-17)—is the saving gift which makes all the difference between moral despair (1:18-3:20; 7:24) and moral perfection. Religion does what morality alone cannot do.

8:4*b.* The summary of vss. 1-4 concludes with a characteristic Pauline contrast of **flesh** and **Spirit** (cf. Gal. 5:16-24), which states how the Christian is actually able to live up to the demand of the moral law and gives the final answer to the objection sensed in 6:1, 15. Spirit has been mentioned in vs. 2 and hinted at earlier in 7:6*b.* Paul now introduces it as the subject for development in the rest of the ch.

8:5-17. *Life According to the Spirit.* Spirit means divinely provided equipment and moral power in virtue of which the Christian is proof against the downdrag of fleshly existence (cf. 7:14). It is the Spirit which gives power to **put to death the deeds of the body** (vs. 13), i.e. to the old sinful way of life which Paul has enjoined his readers to finish with in 6:12-14 (cf. Col. 3:5-7).

8:9. The great difference between Christian and non-Christian ways of living is the Christian's endowment of divine guidance and power which Paul, following OT usage, calls the **Spirit of God,** or, alternatively, the **Spirit of Christ.** This vs. is quite explicit about it. No sense of superiority is implied; this is excluded for Christians from the very beginning (3:27). It is simply that the Christian, having learned through Christ what God is like in his concern for man's lack of righteousness, is open to receive God's gift of righteousness and from then on is under God's control. In this ch. this is explained in terms of the Spirit.

8:10-11. In rounding off a neat antithesis vs. 10 drops something of precision. It reads lit.: "If Christ is in you, the body is dead because of sin but the Spirit is life because of righteousness." Some take this to mean that the readers have "died to sin" as in 6:2-11, but it seems more likely that Paul means that their bodies are subject to death because of sin which has all men in its grip apart from Christ (cf. 5:12-14). On **because of righteousness** cf. vs. 4; 5:21; 6:11. Vs. 11 has sometimes been taken to refer to the life after death, but the context indicates that Paul means his readers' present situation. Their **mortal bodies,** even though Spirit-controlled, are still looking forward for final redemption (cf. vs. 23).

8:12-15b. The Spirit is not only new moral energy by which Christians gain release from mortgage to the flesh. It is a new relationship with God, a new high level of privilege. It is what some of the Greek religious groups called deification. Paul, with his Jewish horror of pagan minimizing of the "otherness" of God, cannot use that terminology; but he goes so far as to affirm that Christians become **sons of God.** His doctrine seems to be that though God is the Father of all men, all men are not his sons until they enter on the experience of faith and are **led,** i.e. motivated, **by the Spirit.** Men need to be brought into this relationship. This is suggested by the metaphor in vs. 15, not of birth, but of **sonship,** lit. "adoption" (cf. the same word in vs. 23), referring to a common practice of the Roman world in families where there was no heir to the property.

8:15c-17. Here is a glimpse into the prayers of the earliest churches, still using the original Aramaic **Abba** for **Father.** Prayer is connected with the activity of the Spirit again in vss. 26-27. It is the function of the Spirit to **witness,** i.e. to cause consciousness of the new and unique privilege of relation to God. This has been described as peace and grace (5:1-2) and freedom from condemnation (vs. 1), but the new metaphor is more warm and intimate. Those who are adopted into the family of God are brothers and **fellow heirs with Christ,** who alone could be called a "natural" son of the Father (cf. Gal. 4:4-7). The inheritance for Christians is the final share of the glory of God's presence (cf. vs. 21). It has been implied in the use of "promise" in 4:13-25. One aspect of the finitude of our present earthly life is that it lacks the divine glory (cf. 3:23). **Provided we suffer** really means "if, as is actually true, we suffer." The suffering of the Christian is not an option which he may refuse. The precise sense of suffering with Christ is not made clear, but it must signify that the Christian in this life is exposed not only to sin (7:7-25) but to malice and misfortune as Christ was (cf. 5:3; II Cor. 1:5; Col. 1:24).

F. Certainty of Final Redemption (8:18-39)

Paul proceeds naturally when he is thinking of the Spirit to the theme of the consummation of God's purpose. The outpouring of the Spirit meant for him, as for all the early Christians, the beginning of the end of history, "the last days," as prophesied in Joel 2 and quoted in the first recorded Christian sermon (Acts 2:16-18). That was no occasional piece of prophecy confined to the postexilic prophet Joel. It was a definite prophetic notion that when the Messiah appears all who adhere to him will share the Spirit which he will impart (cf. Isa. 11:2; 61:1; Ezek. 36:26-27). The Spirit is the life principle common to the Messiah and his people. Paul accepts this, and his own special emphasis is that the Spirit is inseparably connected with Christ (cf. vs. 9; II Cor. 3:17). Others partake of it only by their union with him (vss. 29-30; cf. 6:3-5; 12:4-5).

The Christian possession of the Spirit, however, is comparable to the **first fruits** (vs. 23), in contrast to the full harvest which is still in the future and the object of hope (vs. 24). It is described as the **glory that is to be revealed** (vs. 18b), the full development of sonship (vss. 19b, 23b) for which the present experience of the Spirit is the anticipation (vs. 14).

Here Paul is touching on the basic paradox of Christian experience: The believer is saved, justified, even glorified (vs. 30b) and yet is still to be finally redeemed. The kingdom came with Jesus and yet is to come completely at his final glorious appearing. The Christian is sure of victory over sin and death (5:12-21; 6:8-11) and yet the perishable has not yet put on immortality (I Cor. 15:53-56). The Spirit is the guarantee (II Cor. 1:22; Eph. 1:14) of this final victory, the first fruits of a harvesting already begun which will ultimately bring all mankind under the divine mercy (11:32).

8:18-25. *The Redemption of the Universe.* The imaginative and poetic quality of this passage warns us not to treat it as ordinary theological prose. How can **creation** share in the redemption of man (vs. 21) or be said to long for it (vs. 19)? What is the precise meaning of the term here? Some interpreters take it to mean unredeemed humanity as contrasted with Christians. But almost certainly "creation" here means more than this: it includes animals and inanimate nature. Indeed we must assume that Paul is bold enough to conceive of the redeeming purpose of God as including the whole physical universe, considered as not yet perfect, whatever connection there may be between its imperfection and the sin of mankind. It is curious that there is no reference to sin and death as in 5:12-21.

8:20-21. The classic narrative of the Fall (Gen. 3) is presupposed here, and Paul was probably also acquainted with contemporary Jewish speculation about the messianic age as destined to right all the wrongs and imperfections of mankind and the universe. The doctrine of the Fall is that the universe, including man, is not what God created it to be. Because of man's sin it **was subjected** (cf. Gen. 3:17-19) **to futility,** or "frustration" (NEB)—probably referring to the gods of the heathen, or to the elemental spirits of Gal. 4:8-9, or to the principalities and powers of vs. 38. **Him who subjected it** must refer to God rather than Satan or Adam. The thought of such subjection arose from reflection on the fact that man's environment is not ideal and his will not entirely free. But as soon as man becomes persuaded, by faith, that God has prepared redemption for him he affirms that redemption must **set free** his whole environment—provided, of course, he thinks in biblical terms of the universe as God's creation. There have been Christians since the 2nd cent. who do not think this and confine their idea of salvation to mankind alone. These Christians have never been in the mainstream of Christian thought. They tend to reject the OT.

8:22-23. The strong and colorful verbs express the duress of life apart from Christ. Christians' full experience of **adoption** (cf. vs. 15) is future, but they have the **first fruits of the Spirit** to sustain them in their present existence. For **bodies** the Greek has "body" in the singular, and it should be so translated. The meaning is not the physical body in contrast with the soul or spirit but the "person" or "self" (cf. 6:12; 12:1).

8:24-25. The replacement of faith by **hope** is understandable in this context, but they are not synonymous. In view of Paul's understanding of faith we cannot translate "saved by hope" (KJV and even Luther). The full meaning is that **we were saved**—i.e. by Christ's achievement, regarded as complete, hence the past tense—so as to live now **in . . . hope.**

8:26-27. *Intercession of the Spirit.* On the relation of the Spirit to prayer cf. vss. 15c-16. That the Spirit **intercedes for us** distinguishes the Spirit from God. In vs. 34 intercession is the work of Christ. **Sighs** is the same Greek root as "groan" in vss. 22-23. **Too deep for words,** lit. "unutterable," possibly means "inarticulate" (NEB). Some have taken it to be an allusion to the practice of speaking in tongues discussed by Paul in I Cor. 14, but this is hardly likely. Probably it means nothing audible but an inward Spirit-motion which is intelligible to God alone.

8:28-30. *The Divine Plan.* Vs. 28 is often quoted in support of a vague optimism which can hardly be Paul's meaning. The precise sense cannot be certainly established, partly because not all manuscripts contain the word **God** as subject of **works.** Thus it is possible to take as subject **everything** (cf. KJV) or the Spirit, as in vss. 26-27 (NEB), though by the logic of the latter choice the Spirit would also be the subject in vs. 29, where it is out of the question. **Those who love him** refers to the subjective aspect, and **called according to his purpose** to the objective which Paul is more concerned with, as vss. 29-30 make clear.

8:29-30. Quite apart from human understanding or merit there stands the divine plan, in which Paul distinguishes: foreknowledge as the original conception (vs. 29a); likeness to Christ as the object or pattern (vs. 29b); the actual constituting of this new Christlike brotherhood (**called,** vs. 30a) as the purpose taking shape in history; the divine activity within them, conferring the new status of justification (vs. 30b, cf. 3:24; 5:1); and finally glorification (vs. 30c), which is still future, though Paul can refer to it in the past tense of prophetic certainty. Our human distinction of past, present, and future is

not applicable to the divine ordering of history. On vs. 29b cf. vs. 17; 6:3-5; 12:5.

The thought of divine predestination is an encouragement, not a solemn threat. It need not imply the negative of ultimate reprobation. These vss. are the basis of Christian confidence, whatever difficulties life in this world may bring, whether inwardly in the continuing struggle with sin or outwardly from the mockery or malice of pagan neighbors.

8:31-39. *The Divine Love.* This is a paean of triumphant faith rather than a logical argument. The Christian's confidence for the future in this world and the next is based on the Incarnation and the Cross, conceived as an act of God's grace (3:24) or as an act of Christ (vs. 34) or as due to the love of God in Christ (vss. 35-39).

8:33-36. The accuser of **God's elect** is thought of probably as Satan (cf. Job 1:6), possibly the law, or the critic behind 6:1, 15; 7:7. But the question is rhetorical, as is the next question, and the answer to both is "no one." The metaphor is that of the law court; at the final trial the strength of the defense will far outweigh any arguments offered for the prosecution. The relative clauses in vs. 34 suggest that a rudimentary creed is in mind. On the heavenly intercession cf. Matt. 10:33; John 17; Heb. 7:25; I John 2:1, from which it is clear that this is not a peculiarly Pauline idea. **Persecution** was a real possibility (vs. 35; cf. 5:2-4; I Thess. 3:3-4; for Paul's own experience of it cf. Col. 1:24; II Cor. 11:23-33). Vs. 36 is quoted from Ps. 44:22.

8:37-39. But neither the evils that man may cause nor evil influences from more mysterious sources can disturb the Christian's salvation, which is due to the **love** of God. **Angels . . . principalities . . . powers** refer to supernatural powers which were then widely believed to influence human life (cf. I Cor. 15:24; Gal. 4:8; Eph. 1:21). **Height** and **depth** were astronomical terms referring to the position of planets in the sky and their power to affect what happened on earth. This passage rises to an even higher level of confidence than vss. 28-30, using not the theological language of election, but the personal language of love. Love for Paul is that which causes God to justify sinners. For its connection with the Spirit cf. 5:5; I Cor. 13.

VI. THE PROBLEM OF ISRAEL'S UNRESPONSIVENESS (9:1–11:36)

Jewish recalcitrance has been at the back of Paul's mind since 3:1-8, which he left inconclusive because he wanted to get on to the statement of his main theme, the saving righteousness revealed in the Cross for the benefit of all the unrighteous (3:21-26). How poignantly he feels the rejection of the gospel by Judaism is very clear from the opening vss. of ch. 9. It raises the problem of whether God's purpose has been frustrated. This is unthinkable, and yet it has to be faced, so serious to a loyal Jew is it that his own people, privileged as they are in their experience of God's grace in revelation, have been obstructive to the climax of revelation in the Messiah.

Paul eases the problem by making a distinction between the totality of Israel and the true Israel (9:6-13), asserting that God's purpose to which the promises refer is a selective one. He moves on into a general argument concerning divine sovereignty (9:14-21), which is the main premise in the whole discussion in chs. 9–11. The extension of the church to Gentile members is brought in as an illustration of divine mercy (9:22-24). It means that the messianic age has begun and the new messianic people are in existence (cf. Gal. 3:26-29; Col. 3:11).

But what is the implication for Jews? How ultimate is the stern language about hardening (vs. 18), wrath (vs. 22), stumbling (vs. 32) applied to them? The predestinarian type of thought is difficult for us moderns, not only because it is impossible to reconcile with freedom of the will, without which man cannot be held responsible for his wrong choices (vs. 19), but also because its congruity with the Christ presented in the gospels is questionable.

Paul has evidently faced the possibility that Jewish failure to respond must be regarded as final. He certainly has not minimized the element of sheer disobedience and tried to pretend Israel was not really to blame. He is aware that it raises the question: Is God unfair (vs. 14)?

God has been stern in dealing with Israel, but precisely because God, *their* God, is righteous (vs. 14), the Jews have to experience his wrath (vss. 22, 28). For all their profession to do so they have failed to fulfill the law (vs. 31; cf. 2:12-13) or to respond to the prophetic announcement of God's continuing purposes, which for Paul includes the work of Christ (10:16). They have shown themselves to be lacking in that responsiveness to God which is the essential preliminary for a right relationship to him, viz. faith (vs. 32a).

By the end of ch. 9 the argument is getting dissipated and has to be refocused in ch. 11, after the relationship of righteousness to faith has been examined in ch. 10.

Paul's reasoning is strange by modern standards, but not by rabbinic standards. Its effectiveness must be measured by those standards and recognized as the substructure for the great affirmations of 11:22, 29-32 and the climax in 11:33-36.

A. GOD'S SOVEREIGN SELECTIVITY (9:1-29)

9:1-5. *Paul's Love for Israel.* Paul expresses **in Christ**—i.e. as a Christian, with new insight into God's truth—his **anguish** over the unresponsiveness of his Jewish **brethren.** The vehement language in vs. 3 is typical of Paul (cf. Gal. 1:7-9; Phil. 3:2-7). The parallel with Moses in Exod. 32:32 is noteworthy. On **sonship** (vs. 4) see above on 8:12-15b. **Glory** means God's own reality, manifested to Israel in special revelations and supremely in the giving of the law through Moses (cf. Exod. 33:18-23; 40:34-35). The **worship** is the ritual of the temple in Jerusalem (cf. I Kings 8:10-11). Climax of the list is **the Christ,** the Messiah who is the bringer of salvation, and who **according to the flesh,** i.e. by physical descent, was a Jew. There has been much discussion about the interpretation of vs. 5. The word order of the Greek is "the Christ according to the flesh who is over all God blessed for ever." Without punctuation, which was unknown in ancient times, this is quite ambiguous and could mean that Paul equated Christ with God. Since he does

not make this equation elsewhere, however, it is likely that a period belongs after "flesh" and that what follows is a simple doxology.

9:6-13. *God's Choice of Israel.* According to Paul's concept of the reality of God and his **word**—i.e. not only revelation but purpose, including the **promise** (vss. 8-9; cf. 4:13-25)—the suggestion of failure is blasphemy. He believes in divine sovereignty of choice which is both apart from human merit and prior to human existence (vs. 11). The working out of God's purpose involves choosing some and rejecting others even within the posterity of **Abraham,** as shown by the quotations from Gen. 21:12; 18:10; 25:21, 23; Mal. 1:2-3. **Jacob** is serviceable to the divine purpose, not because of his latent capacities, but simply because God decides to make use of him. The argument is God-centered, not man-centered; i.e. it views history from God's point of view rather than from man's (cf. vs. 16). Jacob is not seen as representing obedience and Esau worldliness. It is simply that God made one his instrument and not the other. The verbs **love** and **hate** are here used in their OT sense, quite objectively, for preference and rejection.

9:14-21. *God's Sovereign Power.* Is God unfair? Is his justice called into question? Paul does not allow this for a moment. God's action in choosing this one and not that one, and even "hardening" this man and not another (vs. 18), is really merciful in the light of Exod. 33:19 (vs. 15) and the preceding episode about the worship of the golden calf. When sin has been committed, e.g. the idolatry of Israel, God's mercy will still be in evidence even though the sinners are punished. In the case of the non-Israelite **Pharaoh** (Exod. 9:16) God **hardens the heart,** i.e. causes spiritual insensitivity, so that ultimately God's purpose with Israel may be carried out (cf. Exod. 7–11).

That Pharaoh actually opposed the Israelites' attempt to break free from their slavery is a fact of history. Its explanation is seen in this doctrine of divine hardening, of which Pharaoh personally was unaware. Something similar is said about Israel in 11:7-8. This certainly stresses the sovereign control of God over human destiny, but it is doubtful whether it safeguards the doctrine of God's righteousness as Paul professes to be doing (vs. 14). Absolute authority is terrifying if it is not righteous authority. This is the limitation of the analogy of the **potter** and the **clay** (vss. 20-21; cf. Isa. 45:9). It expresses well the dominance of creator over creature, but it does not allow for the element of free will in man. Man is not simply pliant clay. He does in fact **answer back to God** (vs. 20); in terms of the problem Paul is dealing with he opposes the preaching of the advent of the Messiah.

9:22-29. *Mercy for Gentiles.* The potter metaphor is developed rather unexpectedly, but in a way to serve Paul's main argument. He is interested, not in the contrast between beautiful vases and common pots (vs. 21), but in the contrast between what the potter reduces to mere lumps on his turning wheel, **vessels of wrath made for destruction** (vs. 22), and what he fashions with skillful fingers till they result in shapely pieces fit for a palace, **vessels of mercy which he has prepared beforehand for glory** (vs. 23). These phrases refer to those who resist and those who conform to God's will. Vs. 24 drops the figure and in plain prose states that the redeemed are not to be identified with Israel but include Gentiles.

9:25-29. The inclusion of the Gentiles is supported by quotations from Hos. 2:23; 1:10—not the most obvious passages in the OT advocating God's favor to non-Israelites, and not passages which were taken by Jewish expositors to imply the rejection of Israel. Complementary to the Gentiles as "vessels of mercy" is the thought of Israel, or some from Israel, as "vessels of wrath." This in turn is confirmed by quotations from Isa. 10:22-23; 1:9. The **remnant** idea has been anticipated in vss. 6-7 and will be more positively treated in 11:2-6. The emphasis in this context is more on the punishing judgment of God on those who do not form the remnant.

The disobedience of Israel is not a new factor occasioned by the advent of Christ. It has been in evidence from the beginning. God's sovereign wisdom has known it and even in some sense caused it (9:18, 22). His saving acts always divide men into those who believe and those who take offense (9:33). The new factor balancing Israel's unbelief is Gentile belief (9:30-31). This calls for a fresh consideration of faith in relation to righteousness in ch. 10.

9:30-10:4. Gentile Admission and Jewish Exclusion. The reception of grace by Gentiles is described as **righteousness through faith** (vs. 30; cf. 1:17; 3:21-22; 4:13). Judaism, on the contrary, for all its pursuit of righteousness (vs. 31) failed to attain it. This failure is explained as stumbling, divinely caused in some degree, in the light of 2 OT passages. That these same passages (Isa. 8:14; 28:16) similarly conflated occur in I Pet. 2:6-8 suggests that Paul is drawing on an early collection of proof texts. Other reasons for Judaism's failure are given as ignorance (10:2-3) and hardening (11:7-8). The relevance of vs. 33 becomes clearer in 10:5-8, where Paul explains **he who believes.** The **rock** means Christ.

10:2-3. The Jews have **zeal,** but this leads astray unless governed by knowledge of God's character and purpose. The Jews fall short at this point and also in submission—a serious lack in a religion like Judaism for which God is sovereign and man's duty is unquestioning obedience (cf. 9:20-21; Deut. 6:4-5).

Zeal for God is characteristic of Hebrew religion. The Greek word used here can have a bad sense—fanaticism, exemplified in Paul himself before his conversion (Acts 9:1-2). But in Hebrew the good sense predominates, and this is intended here. For its exemplification in Paul cf. Gal. 1:13-14; Phil. 3:4-6. The Greeks, who regarded excess even in goodness as disproportionate, found this characteristic zeal laughable in Jews. Why take religion so seriously? Why try to relate every circumstance of life to the will of God? Paul experienced Jewish zeal as opposition to the growing church and as a persecution mania against himself (Acts 9:22-29; 18:12-17; 21:27-36). He does not refer to this here, but analyzes the zeal of his fellow Jews as deviation from God rather than loyalty, and as a putting of their own ideals in the place of what God has made known of his will. Their very intensity has blinded them to new truth; the Messiah has come and they have not recognized him. The highest religion of the world is exposed as fighting against its own highest development.

10:4. The tragedy of the Jews, Paul believes, is their inability to see that the Messiah has come and that this outmodes moral endeavor as a way of salvation. The **law** is no longer the highest revelation of God; Christ is its **end.** This is a major affirmation which requires careful interpretation. For Judaism the idea of the law's being dispensed with, even by the Messiah, was intolerable. For Paul the light of Christ made possible a fresh beginning of thought about the law and salvation.

God's purpose in relation to the need of men is to reveal (i.e. impart) righteousness (1:17). The law does not further this purpose, except negatively, for it reveals only man's lack of righteousness (3:20) and occasions inner disharmony (7:7-20). According to the parallel argument of Gal. the law has only temporary usefulness for man's salvation, and with the advent of Christ it becomes out of date (Gal. 2:19-20; 3:19-25). Christ, as it were, takes it over, so that for believers moral obligation can be described as the law of Christ (Gal. 6:2). The Pauline logic then requires "end" here to be understood in the sense of termination rather than of fulfillment or perfection, as is urged by some commentators.

The Messiah's task was to be the instrument of God's redeeming righteousness, and this has been achieved in the life, death, and resurrection of Jesus. Understanding and accepting this is what Paul means by faith, and it is the indispensable starting point for a right relationship to God. Faith is not mere belief as opposed to action—as in Jas. 2:14-26—but belief in the sense of a fundamental attitude which determines conduct. Christ has inaugurated this new possibility and therein replaced the Mosaic law as the basis of true religion. The law itself points forward to this; the true lordship, i.e. authority, belongs to him.

10:5-13. The Lordship of Christ. Paul is aware that vs. 4 will sound blasphemous to the Jews and absurd to the moralist, and he proceeds to explain faith righteousness in terms of a contrast between it and legal righteousness. The latter puts the accent on human activity (vs. 5; cf. Lev. 18:5). The same point is made in Gal. 3:11-12, and was perhaps a favorite argument of Paul's. This new, Christian righteousness is in a sense simpler; it does not begin with the demand for great moral effort (vss. 6-7). It is concerned first with the response of the heart (vs. 8) and an inward conviction about something God has done in Christ. This discernment of divine action issues in a confession of the lordship of Christ (vss. 9-10). On this basis a man can proceed in the direction of good living. This is the new way of believing, rather than doing, as the approach to right conduct.

10:6-7. The references to bringing Christ down from heaven or up from the nether regions is unexpected. It is a Christian application of Deut. 30:11-14, the point of which is that the law was God's gift and Israel did not have to make its own effort to fetch it from heaven. For Christians the supreme gift of God is not the law but Christ. No human effort to scale the heavens or to go to the uttermost bounds of the earth has brought him or made possible either his incarnation (vs. 6b) or his resurrection (vss. 7b, 9b). Paul's substitution of **abyss**—i.e. Hades, the abode of the dead—for the Deuteronomic "beyond the sea" (LXX) may betray acquaintance with the myth of Christ's descent to Hades, which has found a place in I Pet. 3:19.

10:9. Here is possibly a hint of an embryonic creed which mentioned the lordship and resurrection of Christ. The public confession of Christ as Lord was no doubt a part of the earliest baptismal ceremony. The trinitarian confession (Matt. 28:19) must have evolved later. **Jesus is Lord** is the irreducible minimum of Christian faith. It distinguishes it from the monotheistic faith of Judaism and yet relates Jesus intimately with God by ascribing to him the title which in the OT refers to God. Logically this implies bitheism, and this is the standing objection to the Christian faith in the mind of a Jew.

The distinctive feature in the Christian understanding of God is the place of Christ. He is Lord. He is more than man, and worship cannot be withheld from him—in spite of Deut. 6:4-5—for in him the climax of God's saving acts has been reached (3:21-25; 4:24-25; 5:21). The Resurrection is the evidence of this (1:4; 4:24). He is the emancipator from sin, the giver of righteousness, and the pioneer of a new humanity (5:12–6:11). He is the carrier of God's own love (8:39). Converts from paganism would find this difficult, but the term "Lord" would be meaningful to them in the sense of a heavenly benefactor; many cult deities were so addressed. What pagans had to learn was that worship of Christ excluded all other cults (cf. I Cor. 8:6).

10:11-13. The simplicity of faith righteousness is rooted in the mercy of God and knows no limits, as the quotation from Isa. 28:16 (vs. 11) assures. The old **distinction between Jew and Greek** is now outmoded. The "first" of 1:16 refers to the past only. Faith is the great leveler (cf. 3:28-30)! **Lord** in vs. 12 refers to Christ, though in the quotation from Joel 2:32 in vs. 13 it refers to God.

10:14-21. *The Need to Preach the Gospel.* There is urgent need for worldwide proclamation of this free mercy of God, as recognized in the quotation from Isa. 52:7 (vs. 15b). It can now be identified with the Christian **gospel** (vs. 16a) or the **preaching of Christ** (vs. 17). Alternatively it can be called the **word of faith** (vs. 8b). There is urgency because Israel's return to faith depends on the prior conversion of the Gentiles (11:11-12, 25-26). Vs. 16, quoting Isa. 53:1, seems misplaced, for it reintroduces the main theme of chs. 9–11, viz. Jewish obtuseness, and belongs with vss. 18-21, which adduce further OT quotations (Ps. 19:4; Deut. 32:21; Isa. 65:1-2) to prove that this opposition was experienced long before the advent of Christ and, more positively, that the Gentiles are included in God's purpose. The curious notion **make you jealous** (vs. 19) is developed in 11:11-14.

11:1-6. *The Remnant Chosen by Grace.* The negative factor of Israel's disobedience (10:18-21) has been long evident and is not a result of Christian preaching alone. But it cannot be final or total: **God has not rejected his people whom he foreknew** (vs. 2). Their present recalcitrance is a case of stumbling rather than falling; it is not a complete collapse (vs. 11).

Paul is now reminded of the doctrine of the **remnant** in reference to the experience of **Elijah** (I Kings 19:10, 18). This is an illustration of the divine **grace** (vss. 5-6). The argument of 10:5-8 is presupposed. What Paul there calls faith righteousness might equally well be called grace righteousness; for faith is the response on man's side to God's grace, i.e. his gift of righteousness (3:24).

The point Paul is making is the same as in 9:6-13. God's purpose is working out by concentration on a minority who respond to his call. Not all are responsive, but God can always discern some who are. There must be a **remnant** now (vs. 5), Paul believes; he calls them also the **elect** (vs. 7). Is he thinking of Jewish Christians, or of a larger unit of Jews who are to be converted? The ultimate outcome is the saving of **all Israel** (vs. 26), which apparently means both the elect and the **rest** (vs. 7), and all mankind (vs. 32).

11:7-12. *Israel's Temporary Obtuseness.* The problem remains concerning those who have not responded. Israel's stumbling is now examined on its more subjective side and described as due to moral insensibility. The **rest**, in contrast to the **elect** remnant, **were hardened.** This is not the same verb as in 9:18, with reference to Pharaoh, but the meaning is the same, viz. made hard, insensitive. The variety of terms shows how much Paul has reflected on the problem. Jesus was confronted by the same inability to appreciate the working of divine mercy, and it moved him to both grief and indignation (Mark 3:5). Paul explains the meaning by the quotations that follow, a conflation of Isa. 29:10; Deut. 29:4 (vs. 8), and Ps. 69:22-23 (vss. 9-10).

11:11. The contrast between stumbling and falling expresses the difference between Israel's present lack of cooperation with the divine plan and the conceivable loss of her ultimate salvation, which is part of that plan. It is a case of temporary failure rather than final disaster. A good thing has come out of it, the **salvation** of the Gentiles. This is not an afterthought on God's part, making a virtue of necessity—though vs. 30b seems to suggest something like this. God has not been taken by surprise by Israel's defection, and mercy to the Gentiles has always been part of his plan. Paul goes so far as to suggest (vs. 11c) that God will make a positive use of the response of Gentiles in the restoration of Israel; he will cause it to **make Israel jealous.** This is repeated in vs. 14 and has been anticipated by the quotation from Deut. 32:21 in 10:19. The meaning is a fresh stimulation of the Jews' zeal (10:2) so that it is directed again to the knowledge of God and his will, which they have been ignoring. They need to be shocked into realizing the privilege of God's salvation by the sight of others entering upon it.

11:12. This is rhetorical rather than logical, like vs. 15, but it shows that Paul is assuming the eventual restoration of Israel. **Failure** and **full inclusion** (NEB "falling off" and "coming to full strength") are somewhat unprecise, though they make a neat antithesis. "Failure" here might mean "reduction to a remnant." On the restoration of Israel cf. vss. 23b, 24b, 26.

11:13-24. *God's Kindness to Gentiles.* The Gentiles must be warned not to be supercilious. The broken-off **branches,** whose place they have been allowed by God's election to take, are not discarded forever. The original intention of God still has them in view; the consecration is not nullified (vs. 16). That basic consecration now extends to Gentiles, and they should recognize their dependence (vs. 18). They may be "vessels of mercy" in comparison with Jews who are "vessels of wrath" (9:22-23), but both Jews and Gentiles are in the hand of the divine potter (9:21). Therefore no boasting (vs. 18), no pride (vs. 20b). Boasting is excluded where man's relation to God is concerned, i.e. where faith is the decisive factor (vs. 20a; cf. 3:27).

11:16. At the back of Paul's mind is the thought of the holiness of Israel, rooted in the "forefathers" (vs. 28) and primarily in the divine election, which passes from generation to generation and now from Jews to Gentiles.

11:21-24. The Gentiles have so far experienced God's **kindness,** but it is not inconceivable that they, like the Jews, could experience his **severity,** lit. "cutting away." This rare word expresses God's judgment on defiance of his will. Many Jews thought it applied only to God's attitude toward Gentiles. No dualism in the character of God is implied; kindness and severity are both included in the love or mercy of God (vs. 32), which means his saving activity in dealing with mankind.

Paul speaks in terms of mercy when he is dealing with the final outcome. He can also speak of God's wrath in this connection (2:4-9). But his terms "kindness" and "severity" here refer to God's dealings with men during the course of history, and each may be experienced successively. E.g. the Jews may be restored (vss. 23-24) and the Gentiles rebuffed (vs. 21; cf. vss. 30-31).

11:25-32. *The Final Reconciliation.* This closing section deals with the consummation of God's plan in the restoration of Israel and the final salvation of all mankind.

11:25. The word **mystery** refers to a secret concerning the events of the end which is now made known in Christian preaching (cf. I Cor. 15:51). Israel's obtuseness is partial and temporary. The hint has already been offered in vs. 11 that the place of the Gentiles in God's favor will make the Jews realize what they are missing. Paul now supplements this with the notion of the **full number of the Gentiles.** Since the expression is not used elsewhere by Paul we must determine its meaning from the present context. The Greek word, lit. "filling up," has many meanings, e.g. **full inclusion** in vs. 12 (cf. Col. 1:19; 2:9). In the light of the parallel expression **all Israel** in vs. 26 we must take the fullness of the Gentiles to mean every living Gentile. The verb **come in** is unprecise but presumably means entry into the final redeemed society. Nothing short of this does justice to vs. 32b, or to the exalted outburst of vss. 33-36.

11:26-27. The words **and so** must be understood in a temporal sense—the next step after the fullness of the Gentiles has entered. The quotations from Isa. 59:20-21; 27:9 refer to the salvation of Israel after the advent of the Messiah, the **Deliverer.** Christian teaching was that the Messiah had already come; the final process had to that extent been inaugurated. The coming in of the Gentiles is being effected in Paul's missionary activity (cf. 15:15-19).

On its completion the full response of Israel will no longer be delayed. Such is the scheme which Paul has in his mind. **All Israel** must include not only the "elect" within Israel, but also the "rest," i.e. the hitherto unresponsive (cf. vs. 7).

11:28-29. Again the neatness of a parallelism leaves the meaning obscure (vs. 28). Opposition to the gospel reveals the Jews as **enemies of God,** i.e. opposing his will, but the Gentiles gain by this (**for your sake**). The original election of Israel, however, means that they are still beloved (NEB "God's choice stands"). This is emphasized in vs. 29.

11:30-32. The actions of men which have to be described as **disobedience** (vss. 30-31) or even hostility to God (vs. 28) testify to the reality of God's judgment (1:18; 2:5; 3:5; 5:18). But this is temporary. If we are thinking about the final outcome we speak of God's **election** (vss. 28), his **gifts** and **call** (vs. 29), and his **mercy** (vs. 32). And this means the ultimate elimination of man's disobedience, compared to release from prison.

This view that Paul's thought climaxes in a conviction of the ultimate salvation of all mankind is not accepted by all commentators and has not been the majority view during the history of Christian theology. Nor is it suggested here without recognition of the complexity of the issue of man's freedom in relation to God's control or of the baffling alternations of Paul's statements, both in chs. 9–11 and in his letters as a whole—e.g. the contrast between triumphing mercy in 11:22-32 and judgment in 2:2-16; I Cor. 6:9-11; II Cor. 5:10.

That he may have mercy upon all—coming as it does at the end of one of the longest considerations Paul gives to any single theme, and immediately taking wings in the doxology of vss. 33-36 because Paul realizes that he is in a realm beyond human logic—represents a considered climax and deserves to be given priority to other references to the theme of ultimate reward and punishment. The affirmation of mercy for all, therefore, should be given its full weight of meaning. A widely held alternative interpretation is that Paul was thinking in terms of totalities rather than individuals, that both Israel and the Gentiles qualify for salvation but under each heading there may be individual exceptions. Some commentators leave the question open, but this is no interpretation at all.

VII. Gospel Ethics (12:1–15:6)

This section of the letter is often referred to as ethics, the purely theological argument having been brought to a climax at the end of ch. 8 and chs. 9–11 being theological rather than ethical. There is a point in this distinction, and in this regard Rom. exhibits a similar structure to that of Gal., Col., Eph. But it must be remembered that for Paul and the NT generally there is no autonomous ethic; ethical ideal and demand are always related to what is known of God and his purpose for men. The NT ethic is theonomous or "Christonomous."

A. General Principles (12:1-21)

12:1-2. *The Basis of Paul's Ethics.* The theological grounding of Paul's ethics is very clear in the opening vs. The basic principle is response to God, and this is expressed in terms of **worship.** This consisted mainly, according to the custom of the ancient world, both Jewish and pagan, of animal sacrifice; and Paul again makes use of this analogy (cf. 3:25). His appeal is to **present your bodies as a living sacrifice.** The basic meaning is that we are to make a total response to the grace of God, who has acted savingly in Christ. The sacrificial metaphor made this very meaningful for the first readers of the letter. Significant differences from the usual practice of sacrifice are implied, however:

a) Paul is talking of living persons, not dead animals (cf. NEB, "offer your very selves"—a translation of the Greek word for **bodies** which is legitimate in the case of Paul; cf. 6:6; 7:24).

b) The Christian offers himself to God; it is not a case of a priest performing ritual acts with the dead body of an animal. Worship is still corporate, and there is still a place for the guidance of priest or minister, but something is lacking without the personal participation of each individual.

c) Whatever ritual acts may be performed, Christian worship is essentially **spiritual.** The Greek word is not that usually so rendered (e.g. 1:11; 7:14; cf. 8:5-15) but another which is difficult to translate here. "Rational" would be its most direct equivalent (NEB paraphrases "offered by mind and heart"). Since it is related to "word" (cf. John 1:1) some take it to mean "in conformity with God's word," i.e. the Christian revelation. But it suggests Greek rather than Hebrew background and in the main implies the antithesis to "material." On the notion of spiritual sacrifices and all Christians as priests cf. I Pet. 2:5, where "spiritual" is the usual word.

Worship in this sense is the whole of life. It is our adoring response to God, of whose mercies we are aware. We who would otherwise be unable to rise to our duty can do so because God has had compassion on us. A new humanity has been inaugurated.

12:2. For those who are incorporated into Christ life has a new quality (6:3-5); they have made the break from casual secular ways (6:6-14) and are no longer **conformed to this world.** The measure of this change is emphasized by the remarkable expression **renewal of your mind.** Paul is using formal language here to bring out the distinctive character of responsible Christian living, for which perfection is God's will, work is prayer, and duty is privilege. His conception of the Christian's growing likeness to Christ is also in the background here (cf. 8:29; II Cor. 3:18; Phil. 3:21).

12:3-8. *Membership in the Body.* When it comes to particular aspects of Christian character Paul thinks first of sobriety and the need to avoid conceit. The natural tendency to take undue credit for spiritual and moral progress must be watched. Paul warns against it often (vs. 16; Phil. 2:3; Gal. 6:3, 12-15) and expects the man of faith to realize the danger. With **according to the measure of faith** (vs. 3) cf. **in proportion to our faith** (vs. 6; see below). We note again the intimate relation of faith and morals. The Christian community provides the obvious opportunity of rendering "spiritual" service. All have faith, but not all have the same "measure of faith." Some are "weak in faith" (14:1).

12:4-5. Curbing one's pride has in view the relationship with one's fellows, and this leads Paul to his conception of the church and each particular congregation as Christ's **body.** The essential idea was expressed in 6:3-11, but now the metaphor of the body is introduced—a living organism with many functions which, though different, work harmoniously together for the health and growth of the whole. This body is the instrument which Christ uses to carry out his purposes in the world. In the more detailed application of the metaphor Christ is spoken of as the enlivening spirit (I Cor. 12; cf. also Christ as the head of the body, Col. 1:15-18; 2:6-10; Eph. 4:11-16).

12:6. The meaning of **in proportion to our faith** is in right relationship with faith, observing the sobriety which faith requires (cf. vs. 3), not unrestrained utterance, to which a Christian prophet might be tempted.

12:9-21. *Instruction in Christian Virtues.* This section consists of more general exhortation, typical of what many regard as "catechumen virtues," i.e. the instruction given to new converts prior to baptism (cf. I Thess. 5:12-22; I Pet. 3:8-12). It was based on the Pss. and wisdom literature. This material was already taking fixed form when Paul wrote.

This section, together with I Cor. 13, may be called the Pauline analogue to the Sermon on the Mount. Paul's familiarity with the legacy of Christ in this matter of ethical teaching is obvious. The key word here, as in I Cor. 13, is **love.** It is the comprehensive Christian term for obligation to one's fellow. It was exemplified in the Lord himself, and it is the highest fruit of the Spirit in the church (I Cor. 12:31; Gal. 5:22). In the main it is the Christians' relations with one another that Paul has in view (NEB "love for our brotherhood," vs. 10), but the broadening out of concern for non-Christians is clear in vss. 17-21; 13:1-10.

12:9-16. The word **genuine** (vs. 9), lit. "unhypocritical," refers to acting without the parade of insincerity which Jesus denounced unsparingly. In vs. 11 **aglow with the Spirit** is similar to the phrase describing Apollos in Acts 18:25. **Serve the Lord** seems to require the notion of some specific task done with **zeal** and spirit. Alternatively the point may be that all the Christian does for others is service of the Lord (cf. Matt. 25:34-40). An alternative reading, "serve the time," is found in some manuscripts. This would mean "use to the full your opportunities" (cf. Col. 4:5; Eph. 5:16). The Greek of **associate with the lowly** (vs. 16) is ambiguous, for "lowly" can mean either persons or things (see RSV footnote). The gospel parallel in Mark 2:13-17 throws some light on this passage.

12:17-18. A word of Jesus (Matt. 5:38-39; cf. Prov. 20:22) provides a parallel to vs. 17*a*. It is not likely, however, that Paul has this in mind, for in vs. 17*b* he is writing in the manner of the best Jewish and pagan ethical writers of the time. Vs. 18 has in mind the difficulties Christians (and Jews) might have among unsympathetic pagan neighbors. Christians are not to cause trouble, either in the more personal contacts, as here, or in broader socio-political involvement (cf. 13:1-7; on the social environment of the first Christian communities cf. I Cor. 6-10).

12:19-21. "Getting even" is absolutely forbidden for Christians. Jesus' way of saying this is Matt. 5:43-48. Paul is more rabbinical and quotes scripture—apparently a free rendering of Lev. 19:18; Deut. 32:35 (vs. 19) and Prov. 25:21-22 (vs. 20). **Burning coals** has never been fully explained. There is some evidence that it signified not simply punishment but signs of repentance. Christian reaction to ill treatment should be not an equal return but the attempt to make the other man repent. This interpretation holds together the unity of vss. 17-21. Vs. 21 is very general in terms of the opposition of good and evil, which is fundamental for most moralists. This teaching is more concrete in 13:10 and more metaphorical, in terms of the light-darkness dualism, in 13:11-12.

B. THE CHRISTIAN'S CIVIC DUTY (13:1-10)

13:1-7. *Respect for Civil Authorities.* The keynote of Paul's advice is respectful submission on the ground that secular **authorities** would not exist at all apart from divine permission (vs. 1*b*). They are real authorities, though subordinate to the overall sovereignty of God. What they do in promotion of good and restraint of evil is definitely the service of God.

13:1. A significant recent interpretation takes the **authorities** to mean supernatural powers using earthly rulers as their instruments. The idea was familiar to the Hellenistic world, and even Judaism could think of pagan nations as in subjection to angels, as Israel was to Yahweh (cf. Deut. 32:8-9; Dan. 10:13; 12:1). Whether Paul's use here presupposes that conception falls short of being certain. That he accepted the existence of these higher powers is clear in view of 8:38 (cf. I Cor. 2:8; 15:24; Gal. 4:9; Col. 1:16; 2:15; cf. also Eph. 3:10; 6:12). But it is not so clear that he thought of them as controlling the life of nations through their civil rulers as he speaks of it here. It can be plausibly argued that in addressing Rom. Christians on their duty to the state Paul had in mind the widespread notion that the state was part of the whole cosmic system, and the emperor himself, if not actually a god, was under divine control.

13:2. It follows that Christians should not be drawn into movements for the overthrow of properly constituted governments. Did Paul know of this tendency among the Rom. Christians? Not necessarily; but he may have detected some official suspicion of the growing numbers of Christian groups, and he must have known of the precautions taken against secret societies. Acts gives the impression that whenever Rom. officials took cognizance of Christians they did not regard them as betokening any danger to the empire. Jews might be troublemakers, but not Christians! The official Jewish attitude toward the empire was similar to what Paul advocates here. But Jewish zeal did sometimes produce messianic claimants, who from the Rom. point of view would be political agitators. Acts 5:34-39 is informative here. Paul may well have felt the need to warn the churches against allowing such ambitions to develop, and this had extra relevance for the church in Rome itself. Christianity is the agent of society's redemption, not its disruption.

For the similar Jewish attitude to secular authority cf. Dan. 2:20-23, 37-38; 4:28-37; Wisd. Sol. 6:1-11. For NT parallels with Paul's teaching cf. I Pet. 2:13-17; Tit. 3:1. The very different attitude of Rev. is explicable out of the persecution situation which occasioned that writing and forced its author to the conviction that secular power—the Rom. Empire—was in the control of Satan, a possibility not envisaged by Paul.

13:3-7. The Greek word **servant** (vs. 4) was used in a broad sense, esp. of household duties (cf. NEB "agents" here). For the beginning of the ecclesiastical development which applied this term—in this sense transliterated "deacon"—to a church officer subordinate to bishop and apostle cf. Acts 6:1-6. But Paul can use a form of this word of his own "ministry" (11:13). The alternative term **minister** which Paul applies to tax officers in vs. 6 originally signified donors of public benefactions to Greek city-states but tended to pick up religious associations (cf. 15:16) and eventually settled down in Christian usage with reference to worship (liturgy).

Paul does not hesitate to describe the negative aspect of human justice in terms of the divine **wrath** at sin. He presupposes this as a conception familiar to Jews from the OT. For his own understanding of God's wrath and its relation to the revelation of God in Christ, see 1:18-32; 2:5-8. In executing the wrath magistrates are legally justified in doing what the individual Christian is forbidden to do (12:19).

The Christian's conformity with the directions of earthly rulers is motivated not only by fear of punishment, even when such punishment is thought of as willed by God, but also by **conscience.** This conformity is positive, prompted by desire to collaborate with the government in its task of achieving the good which overcomes evil (12:21) and is the will of God for human life (12:2*b*). On vs. 7 cf. Mark 12:13-17.

13:8-10. *The Supremacy of Love.* This passage would naturally follow ch. 12, though there is no need to assume that 13:1-7 is an insertion. We may be inclined to label "personal" and "social" ethics, but these distinctions would seem unnecessary to Paul. Moreover, there is a connection between vss. 7, 8. The Christian is to discharge all his obligations, whether of public duty or of private relationships. Here the keynote is love. Paul's emphasis on the primacy of love for the fellow man accords perfectly with the teaching of Jesus (cf. Matt. 5:44; Mark 12:28-34).

It should be noted here that Paul, in spite of his earlier statements about the tyranny of the **law** (2:12; 3:19-20; 4:13-15; 5:20; 7:1-12; 8:1-3; 9:31–10:4), can speak of its being fulfilled. There is no question of self-contradiction. The Christian is equipped to fulfill the law's demands by his endowment with the Spirit (8:4).

C. IMMINENCE OF THE END TIME (13:11-14)

Here the keynote is watchfulness—the urgency of the Christian's existence underlying his relationships with public officials, fellow men, and fellow Christians. The theme is not peculiar to Paul (cf. I Pet. 4:7; 5:8; Jas. 5:7-8) and it has its root in the teaching of the Lord himself (cf. e.g. Mark 13:33-

37; Matt. 25:1-13). Thus it was a regular feature of the earliest Christian ethical teaching. Some scholars think it was part of the pattern of instruction given to new converts. The point of it was to encourage, not anxious calculation of the date of doomsday, but a moral seriousness which differentiated the Christian from other men.

The Christian has something better to live for than ease and sleep (vs. 12), self-indulgence, sexual pleasure, or the common struggles and ambitions of the world (vs. 13). The life of faith and Christian engagement is like rising eagerly to meet a new day which is the new life Christ makes possible, and the clothing, or **armor,** to be worn that day is Christ himself (vs. 14a).

Life that shows something of the power and quality of Christ is not only secure against temptation; it is true living as contrasted with mere existence. It is the distinctively Christian understanding of success.

On the metaphor of "putting on" cf. Gal. 3:27; Col. 3:10, 12. The metaphor of **night** as the present life and **day** as the life to come has rabbinic parallels. But it was probably a Christian development, as part of baptismal catechism, to present Christian converts as children of light. The conception of their new life also as the putting on of a new garment may belong to the baptismal vocabulary.

D. Patience with Scruples (14:1–15:6)

The subject matter of this long section—abstinence from meat and observance of special days—appears somewhat trivial, even when allowance is made for the greater appeal of these things in the ancient world, esp. among Jews. There seems to be considerable disproportion between the 29 vss. devoted to these matters and the meager 7 vss. devoted to the Christian and the state in ch. 13.

The interest here, however, lies in the way Paul, when giving judgment about a relatively unimportant issue, appeals to fundamental Christian principles—e.g. (a) the example of Christ (14:9; 15:3); (b) charity (14:15), the attitude which regards a fellow Christian, not as weak and unprogressive, but as a brother for whom Christ died; (c) the Christian church as a society for mutual service, not for the private cultivation of wisdom or holiness (15:1). The key word is edification, in a corporate sense (14:19; 15:2). Christians should not criticize one another but labor together in God's work of building the perfect society (cf. I Cor. 3:9-11).

14:1-4. Scruples About Meat. With **weak in faith** cf. the gospel expression "of little faith" (e.g. Matt. 6:30). Here the emphasis is on "weak" in contrast with "strong" (15:1). **Welcome him** (cf. vs. 3; 15:7) is lit. "take him to yourselves," i.e. do not leave him on his own. In the relationships of the community the true Christian aim is **not for disputes** but rather **for peace and for mutual upbuilding** (vs. 19).

14:2. Eating **only vegetables** is not our modern vegetarianism. The motive was not concern about killing animals but horror at eating the flesh of an animal slaughtered in a pagan ceremony. To a sensitive Christian, therefore, meat carried the taint of heathenism. The very place where it was bought might be a corner of a pagan temple! Some have assumed that this problem was esp. urgent at Rome, but it would arise in all towns in the Rom. Empire. Embarrassment would arise if Christians were at dinner with pagan neighbors; one Christian might take the meat course and another refuse. Should Christians decline invitations to dinner, thus shutting themselves off from their pagan neighbors? Paul gives his advice on this in I Cor. 10:25-31. Here he is dealing with the disputes among Christians themselves, between those who like Paul have no scruples (**we who are strong,** 15:1) and those who cannot set scruples aside.

14:3-4. Probably it was Jewish church members who had scruples against meat slaughtered under pagan auspices, as a result of their background of religious dietary restriction. Gentiles would be used to such meat and would be tempted to **despise,** i.e. be scornful of, their Jewish brethren for abstaining from it. On the other hand the abstainers **pass judgment** on those who eat (cf. 2:1-4). But the welcome which God shows (vs. 3c), and which is exemplified in Christ (15:7-9), must not be contradicted by such rivalry between broad-minded and scrupulous members of the church. A judging attitude is unthinkable among Christians (vs. 4). Only the **Master**—in Greek the same word as "Lord"—has a right to judge, i.e. to say the behavior of any of his servants is not in accord with their relationship to him.

14:5-9. Scruples About Special Days. In the same category as the meat question, in Paul's view, is the difference of opinion and practice about special days. Probably the reference is to Jewish Christians who continue to observe the sabbath and perhaps the feasts and fasts specified in the OT whereas Gentiles ignore them. But Paul sees the problem as rather whether there can be more than one expression of Christian faith in outward conduct and social habit. He is patient with both types and his argument moves toward general considerations which both will heed. He is trying to get those on both sides to see that the others may be equally as right as they are. The scrupulous may be just as much acting in accord with Christ's guidance as the libertarians, and vice versa. The question is whether both are **fully convinced** that Christ's claim is paramount. Is their conduct, whether observing or ignoring, eating or abstaining, **in honor of the Lord?**

14:7-9. These vss. imply a restraining principle: Christian liberty is never license but discharge of our responsibility **to the Lord.** In the whole of our experience, including death itself (and beyond), we are related to the Lord. Not all men realize this, but the believer does. He should let it determine his attitude toward his fellow believer and not be harsh and critical toward him.

14:10-23. The True Standard. Paul sounds the warning note of accountability at the judgment day (vss. 10-12, quoting Isa. 45:23) but patient pleading is the dominant tone of the whole discussion. The issue is serious, however, in Paul's judgment, because one man's liberty may become a **stumbling-block** (vs. 13; cf. vs. 21; 9:32-33)—a term that appears to have been stereotyped in the sense of what prevents or destroys faith. It may cause spiritual **ruin** (vs. 15) to the overscrupulous brother—i.e. loss of faith (vs. 23) to him personally and also disruption of a church (vs. 20*a*). The really deplorable thing about this mutual criticism is that it hinders the harmony and growth of the church (vs. 19). Food taboos are substituted for the true demands and privileges of the kingdom (vs. 17). If Paul had been addicted to quoting the sayings of Jesus he might have called this a preference for tithing "mint and dill and cummin" to the neglect of "weightier matters of the law" (Matt. 23:23). It comes down to a question of motivation—no Christian fruit except from a Christian root, i.e. **faith.** Conduct not thus motivated is **sin** (vss. 22-23).

15:1-6. *Christian Responsibility*. Vss. 1-2 express the hallmark of the Christian community as contrasted with the whole of secular society: being **strong** involves responsibility and self-subjection, not doing as you please. Individualism is suspect. Paul is perhaps thinking of the stress ancient Stoicism laid on the independence of the wise man, the Stoic ideal. Not independence but consideration for the weaker brother is the Christian law (cf. Gal. 6:2). **Bear with the failings** makes the meaning more negative than the Greek intends; the NEB paraphrase "accept as our burden the tender scruples" expresses the sense better. The example of Christ (vs. 3, quoting Ps. 69:9) and scripture as a whole (vs. 4) encourage the weak. Ultimately God will bring unanimity about these matters (vss. 5-6) and rivalry will be dissolved in adoration of the God revealed in Christ. Then praise will take the place of argument. Vs. 6 is the climax of the discussion.

E. Welcome for Both Jew and Gentile (15:7-13)

The mutual relationships of Christians are to serve the glory of God, i.e. cause one another—and the outside observer—to praise God. Antipathies must be overcome because Christ overcame the barrier that separated him from sinful men. The reference may be backward to the distinction between "strong" and "weak" in 14:1–15:6 or to the Jew-Greek groupings, as is perhaps more likely in view of vss. 8-9, which make the point that Christ belongs to both groups. On the other hand the use of **welcome** (vs. 7) connects with the same verb in 14:1. The parallelism between vss. 8, 9 is fairly close in spite of the variety of wording. God's **truthfulness** is practically synonymous with his **mercy,** and the OT citations in vss. 9*b*-12 (from the LXX of Ps. 18: 49; Deut. 32:43; Ps. 117:1; Isa. 11:10) might be called **promises** to the Gentiles, thus balancing vs. 8*b*. Christ's coming is service of God and men in that it inaugurates a new order of righteousness based on faith which includes all men and dissolves inveterate divisions. Hence the prospect of **joy and peace** and of **hope** (vs. 13).

VIII. Paul's Own Mission (15:14-33)

15:14-17. *His Mission to Gentiles*. Paul's thought was beginning in vss. 8-9 to move away from church dissensions to the ongoing divine purpose. He now develops this with reference to his own part in the mission to Gentiles (vss. 15-16). It is only by God's grace that he can carry it on and write letters to Christian communities as boldly as he does. He is Christ's **minister**—i.e. "servant," though not his

usual term "slave" for his relationship to Christ, or yet the word transliterated "deacon," but the rarer word used in 13:6 of magistrates. He goes on to describe his function in terms of priesthood. His use of this metaphor in vs. 16 leaves his precise meaning a little ambiguous. Is he thinking of the **gospel** itself, or rather of his proclamation of it, as the **offering,** comparable to the part of the sacrificial animal which the priests placed on the altar, while the Gentile converts are in the place of the worshipers watching the ritual performed? Or are the Gentile converts themselves conceived of as the offering? It would seem that the words **acceptable** and **sanctified,** which are used of the sacrificial victim in the OT, make the 2nd meaning the more probable (cf. Isa. 66:20).

In either case Paul is their ministrant, and his aim is to make men fit for the presence of God—even Gentiles, who according to Jewish ideas were separated from God by their polytheism and disgusting habits. He can even be **proud** of it (vs. 17) though pride is a dangerous emotion for Christians (cf. 3: 27). But this is **in Christ Jesus,** i.e. not only in his "fellowship" (NEB), but arising out of all that he is, has done, and continues by the Spirit to do through the church. Since Paul gives no hint that he is thinking of Calvary (as in 3:25) there is no need to follow those commentators who interpret the priestly metaphor to imply that the Cross is the altar. On the Spirit's sanctification cf. 6:19, 22; I Cor. 6:11.

15:18-21. *His Work Thus Far*. Notice 2 things:

a) The wide area Paul's missionary activity has covered. In this the miraculous factor, the **power of the Holy Spirit,** must not be lost sight of (vs. 19). It was sheer miracle that the church took root in the Greco-Rom. world. We know nothing either from the letters or from Acts of a visit to **Illyricum,** the Rom. province on the E coast of the Adriatic Sea. Some commentators suggest that Paul is not to be taken too lit. here, and that preaching in this territory was done by Christians from Corinth or Thessalonica.

b) Paul's principle of not building on **another man's foundation,** i.e. of avoiding spheres of work already opened up by others. This must be understood, not as unwillingness to cooperate—I Cor. 3:5-11 should rule out that interpretation—but as an expression of his sense of urgency. The time is too short to permit duplication of preachers!

The gospel is on the march W from its place of origin. Around the NE quarter of the Mediterranean Paul has **fully preached,** lit. "filled up," **the gospel.** Apparently this means in the places where no other missionary has taught (vs. 20). He and others between them have covered the area. The suggestion has been made that **as far round as** really means that Paul has in view the complete circle of the Mediterranean from Jerusalem via Illyricum, Rome, Spain (vs. 24), and back through Africa and Egypt. Evidently he thinks that it is God's will for the church to be planted in every region of the Rom. Empire before the final day, which is not in the indefinite future and may be soon (13:11-12). Hence the urgency for the Christian missionary. This may be why he shows no concern for the extension of the church E from Jerusalem. If time is limited the centers of civilization take priority and for Paul, the Rom. citizen, civilization means the Rom. Empire.

Prophetic visions of the conversion of the heathen are coming to fulfillment (vs. 21, quoting Isa. 52:15, the task of the servant of the Lord). Nothing less is meant by what Christ is effecting through Paul (vss. 18-19). The saving righteousness of God is at work (cf. 1:16-17). Paul and his converts have the evidence plainly before them, and it portends that human history has moved into its final phase (cf. Matt. 24:14).

15:22-23. *His Plans for Future Service.* Paul has had to delay visiting Rome till his responsibilities in the E have been discharged. Now he feels ready to move on to the W and tells of his plans.

15:24. With other Christian missionaries presumably covering Italy, Paul looks beyond to **Spain.** This land was an organized Rom. province, connected by trade with the E Mediterranean, and having a number of Jewish synagogues where Paul could make contacts. But he would hardly have been able to use the Greek language, and so would have had to depend on interpreters. Paul wants to be **sped** on his way by the Roms. The precise meaning of the verb remains uncertain, but it seems to have been a regular Christian practice (cf. I Cor. 16:6, 11; II Cor. 1:16; Acts 15:3; III John 6). Nevertheless he looks forward to enjoying the company of the Rom. believers. That will be a spiritual tonic to him (vss. 32b) and he will impart much to them, for the **blessing of Christ** which he believes rests on his whole missionary project will fall on them if they welcome him for the sake of it (vs. 29; cf. 1:11-12).

15:25-29. Paul will be free to begin his W tour as soon as he has taken to Jerusalem a financial gift for the **saints**—his term not only for those at Jerusalem but for all church members (cf. 1:7; I Cor. 1:2), the people of God as distinct from the totality of mankind who are not yet aware of the gospel. He has raised the fund among his Gentile converts in **Macedonia and Achaia**—to which we must add Galatia and Asia (Acts 20:4; I Cor. 16:1). Paul attached much importance to this contribution. It was more than relief of poverty at Jerusalem; it was a bond between Jew and Gentile within the new Christian fellowship. It was a recognition of mutual indebtedness (vs. 27). This view is different from that of Gentile-Jewish relations in 11:25-32, but this serves to show Paul's versatility. Paul the rabbinical theologian and Paul the practical pastor are the same man, who could do all things in Christ's strength (Phil. 4:13). His anxiety about the raising of the money shows in his extended appeal in II Cor. 8-9.

Delivered (vs. 28) is lit. "sealed," a word implying confirmation. Perhaps Paul is thinking of how he will assure the Jewish Christian recipients of the genuineness of this contribution as a real piece of Christian "sharing" (vs. 27).

15:30-33. We do not know what effect the gift had on the Jerusalem recipients, because Paul was arrested soon after arrival there (Acts 21:17-36). As a result his visit to Rome took place in circumstances very different from those he envisages in this letter. That he sensed such sinister possibilities is clear from his request for **prayers.** He was, in the event, not delivered from the **unbelievers in Judea.**

Even the greatest of God's servants do not have all their wishes granted.

IX. An Addendum (16:1-27)

This final ch. is not related to ch. 15. It contains personal messages (vss. 1-16, 21-23), a warning against heresy (vss. 17-20), and a long ascription of praise (vss. 25-27).

How did Paul know so many people in a church which he had never visited—more here than in any other letter? And with all these individual names why no word of greeting to the officers of the church at Rome, either personally or by title? Scrutiny of the names does not suggest a destination in Rome as more probable than any other place. It is not impossible that Paul had met all these people in Asia and that they had since moved to Rome. There was considerable travel in the Mediterranean—e.g. Prisca and Aquila, whom Paul knew in Corinth and Ephesus, may well have returned to their former home at Rome. But it would be more natural if the people named belonged to a church familiar to Paul.

These questions about the content of the ch., added to certain variations in the manuscripts (see Intro.), have inspired much discussion about whether it was an original part of Rom. A good number of scholars today maintain that it was. On the other hand a very few see it as the work of a later writer seeking to give Pauline authority to the warning of vss. 17-20. The majority, however, view it as a short separate Pauline letter, or part of a letter, which at some stage in the collection of Paul's correspondence got attached to Rom. From the greetings in vss. 3-5 the most natural address for such a letter is Ephesus, where Paul spent 3 years (Acts 20:31) and would have many friends (vss. 6-15). This address also makes less surprising Paul's knowledge of dangerous tendencies in the church (vss. 17-20).

A more recent modification of this theory suggests that Paul, having expressed to the Roms. his mature judgment on the issue of Jew and Gentile, law and gospel, decided to publicize it by sending a copy to Ephesus for dissemination in Asia, with personal references appended. The omission of "in Rome" in 1:7, 15 in one manuscript supports the likelihood that one or more copies were sent elsewhere than to Rome.

16:1-2. *Recommendation of Phoebe.* Doubtless the carrier of the letter—whether ch. 16 or all of Rom. —Phoebe is endorsed as **sister,** i.e. a fellow Christian, and a **deaconess,** presumably indicating that in the churches of Paul's day women could be included among the deacons. In chs. 1-15 **church** has been used in the inclusive sense (cf. vs. 23); here it occurs in the sense of a local congregation (cf. vss. 4, 5, 16). **Cenchreae** was the port across the isthmus from Corinth (cf. Acts 18:18; see color map 16). **In the Lord** (vs. 2) means as a fellow Christian (cf. vs. 12; 6:8-11; 12:5). The word translated **helper** may imply high social standing for Phoebe, enabling her to protect a suspected minority.

16:3-16. *Greetings to Friends.* Paul's first greeting is to **Prisca** and her husband **Aquila,** with whom he has worked at his trade of tentmaking (Acts 18: 2-3; cf. Acts 18:18-19, 26; I Cor. 16:19; II Tim. 4:19;

Prisca is called Priscilla in Acts). Possibly they were well-to-do, with a **house** large enough for Christians to meet in (vs. 5; I Cor. 16:19) and enough wealth to be able to migrate from Rome to Corinth, then to Ephesus, and possibly back to Rome on the death of the Emperor Claudius in A.D. 54. We know nothing of the risk they took on Paul's behalf.

16:5*b*-15. The phrase **first convert** is lit. "first fruits." The spread of Christianity is like harvesting. **Andronicus and Junias** are **kinsmen,** i.e. Christians of Jewish origin like Paul—but why are not Prisca and Aquila so called? Another thing they have in common with Paul is that they have known imprisonment for the gospel, as preachers from place to place. We have no information about this, but we note that Paul includes them among the **apostles,** using that word in a sense not confined to the 12 but equivalent to missionary (cf. Barnabas, Acts 14: 14). It is even possible that the 2nd name might be "Junia," i.e. a woman, in which case Andronicus and Junia would probably be man and wife. The contribution of women in those first days of the church's growth should be clear from this ch. (cf. I Cor. 11:3-16; 14:34-35). There are still to be mentioned Tryphaena, Tryphosa, Persis, Rufus' mother, Julia, Nereus' sister (vss. 12-15). They are only names to us, but they hint at the liberating power of Christ's gospel. They, and the menfolk too, may have been slaves or ex-slaves.

16:16. The **holy kiss** as a sign of fraternity is referred to by Paul elsewhere as if customary (I Cor. 16:20; II Cor. 13:12; I Thess. 5:26), and I Pet. 5:14 is evidence for it outside Pauline circles. By the middle of the 2nd cent. it had become a fixed part of the liturgy of the Lord's Supper.

16:17-20. *Warning Against Heresy.* The community has to be prepared to deal with persuasive teachers who propose deviations from the original preaching and cause **dissensions.** Their motives are low (vs. 18) and they are best avoided altogether. But the victory of God over **Satan** is not in doubt (vs. 20). This is something of a set piece (cf. Phil. 3:18-19; Jude 17-25). The short benediction of vs. 20*b* is found in some manuscripts after vs. 23 and in some after vs. 27. This is part of the evidence that the ending of the letter was known in different forms to the early copyists.

16:21-23. *Greetings from Companions.* Paul's entourage at the time of writing joins in sending greetings. **Timothy** is well known from Acts 16:1-3 and references in Paul's other letters. **Gaius** is no doubt the Corinthian convert mentioned in I Cor. 1:14. The identification of **Erastus** with the Erastus of Acts 19:22; II Tim. 4:20 is less certain.

16:25-27. *Doxology.* The closing doxology has its own impressiveness, but the fact that it appears in the manuscripts at various places (see Intro.) raises questions not only about its place but also about its authorship. It may well be the work of a 2nd-cent. copyist making use of Pauline phraseology (cf. e.g. 1:1-2; Gal. 4:4; Eph. 3:9-11).

To declare that the **only wise God** commanded his saving purpose, which had been a **mystery,** to be revealed in Christ is the root of Pauline and Christian orthodoxy. But the stress on **through the prophetic writings** reads a little awkwardly, as if the phrase was deliberately interpolated to meet heresy like that of Marcion (A.D. *ca.* 140), who rejected the OT. On the whole it lacks the full Pauline impact.

THE FIRST LETTER
OF PAUL TO THE CORINTHIANS

JAMES L. PRICE

INTRODUCTION

Corinth. Leadership in resistance to the Roman domination of Greece brought disaster to the principal city in the Achaean League; and in 146 B.C. it was reduced to ruins. The Corinth which Paul knew was rebuilt on the site a cent. later, probably under orders from Julius Caesar, and quickly grew to be an important Roman colony.

From the dawn of Greek civilization the place seems to have been a major maritime center. Its strategic location at the meeting point for the shipping lanes of E and W (see color map 16) assured the rebuilt Roman city a new era of prominence. Seamen persisted in the age-old practice of avoiding the dangerous voyage around the S promontory of Greece, preferring to drag their smaller vessels on rollers across the 4-mile-wide isthmus N of Corinth and to unload capital ships at the Aegean port of Cenchreae and reload them at the W port on the Gulf of Corinth and vice versa. Accordingly by Paul's time Corinth had become a prosperous commercial center with a population estimated at *ca.* 600,000 and many transients.

There were other factors besides commerce which attracted people to Corinth. Near the city the Isthmian Games were held, 2nd only in popularity to the Olympics. On the summit of Acrocorinth, a peak rising 1,800 feet above the city streets, was a famous temple to Aphrodite, the goddess of love. To this site were drawn many visitors, less interested perhaps in the magnificent view of the Peloponnesus Mountains which the climb afforded than in the numerous sacred prostitutes attached to the temple. For Corinth had become a byword in the Greco-Roman world for vice. In the theater a Cor. was the stereotype for a drunkard, and "live like a Cor." was a slang term for debauchery.

Paul's Mission to Corinth. Acts 18:1-18 provides a brief narrative of the founding of the church in Corinth. So far as we know, Paul was the first Christian missionary to Corinth. To many men this city might seem a most unlikely place to preach the gospel, but Paul was challenged by the mighty metropolis. He stayed longer in Corinth than anywhere except Ephesus, and even there he kept in touch with the Cor. community and guided its development.

The reader must draw largely on the Cor. letters, as well as his imagination, to expand the scanty information given in Acts on the 18-month mission of Paul at Corinth. The author of Acts emphasizes the Jews' opposition to him and describes his ar-

raignment before Gallio at their instigation (Acts 18:12-17). An inscription about Gallio found at Delphi has provided an important point in determining Pauline chronology. A calculation of the date of Gallio's arrival at Corinth as the summer of 51 has been accepted by most scholars, and he seems to have been proconsul there for only a year. Relating this clue to Acts, we may conclude that Paul's mission to Corinth began in the winter or spring of 50 and ended late in 51 or early in 52. Aquila and Priscilla, whom Paul calls Prisca (I 16:19), are introduced in Acts 18:1-3, where the note that they have recently come to Corinth because the Emperor Claudius expelled the Jews from Rome provides another point of reference to the general history of the time. This edict is mentioned by the Roman historian Suetonius and probably is to be dated *ca.* 49.

Of more interest to students of the Cor. letters are the references to Apollos (Acts 18:24–19:7). Paul speaks of Apollos with full respect for him and his labors (cf. I 3:5-9; 4:6; 16:12), but it is apparent that some of his followers were troublemakers in the Cor. church (cf. I 1:11-12; 3:4).

After Paul's initial work at Corinth Acts 18:18-22 reports that he made a trip to Judea and Syria, though some scholars question his visiting Jerusalem at this time (see comment on Acts 18:22-23). It is likely that his "3rd missionary journey" (Acts 18:23–20:37) began early in 53. His eventual destination was Ephesus, the capital and chief city of the province of Asia (i.e. W Asia Minor), and he worked there for nearly 3 years (53-56). Both I and II Cor. contain references to Paul's plans and movements following the Ephesian ministry; Acts reports only that he stayed in Achaia—probably at Corinth—for 3 months before leaving the region for Jerusalem (Acts 20:1-3). This last visit to Corinth probably occurred in 56.

Paul's Letters to Corinth. While at Ephesus, probably in 55, Paul heard of the distressing moral laxity in the Cor. church. I 5:9 refers to a letter by Paul in response to this report, obviously written earlier than I Cor. This previous letter is no longer extant, unless the scholars are right who claim that a fragment of it is preserved in II 6:14–7:1 (see comment).

Further reports of disorders at Corinth reached Paul at Ephesus (I 1:11). A delegation from the church came to him (I 16:17), and a letter sought his counsel on certain divisive issues (I 7:1a; 8:1a;

12:1; 16:1a, 12a?). In answer to these disturbing reports, gleaned from several sources, Paul wrote I Cor. Some scholars have questioned the unity of this letter, pointing to seams in its fabric as evidence that it was made up of parts of several writings of Paul to the Cors.; but this evidence is not conclusive.

Paul sent Timothy to follow up the letter in the hope that some of the developments and abuses in the church might be corrected. Reports from Timothy and perhaps other sources led Paul to conclude that the situation had become critical. Apparently he made a hasty visit to Corinth, altering his previous plans. Acts does not record this visit, but notes in II 2:1; 12:14; 13:1-2 which cannot otherwise be explained satisfactorily, indicate that Paul paid a flying and "painful" visit to Corinth.

The crisis at Corinth was worsened by Paul's 2nd visit. II 2:4 refers to a sternly worded letter, composed by Paul "out of much affliction and anguish of heart and with many tears," and 7:8-12 speaks of its effect on the Cors. Scholars call this third letter to Corinth the "severe letter." Some have sought to show that these references must be to I Cor., but description of it is ill suited to the content and mood of that letter.

Many scholars hold rather that II 10-13 contains a substantial fragment of the severe letter. Observing the content and tone of II 1-9, they cannot believe that Paul could have experienced such a radical change of mood that he would put into the same letter the bitter, sarcastic remonstrance and self-defense found in chs. 10-13. Moreover they argue that several statements in chs. 1-9 presuppose or echo statements in chs. 10-13 (e.g. cf. 1:23 with 13:2; 2:3 with 13:10; 2:9 with 10:6).

Since no notice is taken of II Cor. by writers of the church before the middle of the 2nd cent., whereas I Cor. is cited as early as the 90's, some force is added to the view that II Cor. was compiled by an editor from several fragments of Paul's correspondence—including even perhaps some work of another author (see below on II 6:14-7:1). In contrast to those who find the severe letter in chs. 10-13, certain scholars have claimed that these chs. are a fragment of a letter written by Paul to the Cors. later than the letter or letters preserved in chs. 1-9. Still others believe that chs. 8-9 should be separated from chs. 1-7 and assigned to one or more letters of Paul. Of these several partition theories, the case for identifying chs. 10-13 with the severe letter is the strongest.

The evidence for all such theories falls short of proof, however, and there is no compelling reason why II Cor. as it now stands could not have been dispatched by Paul as a single letter to the Cor. church. Dictating a letter in ancient times was a slow process, and for one of this length several interruptions would be quite probable. Such breaks may well explain the abrupt shifts of thought and mood found in II Cor.

Advocates of the theory that chs. 10-13 are the severe letter believe that Paul's last correspondence to the Cors. survives in chs. 1-9—from which most of them omit at the least 6:14-7:1. They have called the remaining Paul's "thankful letter." Unquestionably they are correct in holding that the dominant mood of chs. 1-9 is joyful confidence.

When Paul wrote his last word to the Cor. he was hopeful that a basis had been established for a lasting reconciliation of the differences and distrust which had alienated the church from him. But he was not without misgivings and anxiety, and signs of this disquiet should not be overlooked. He was anticipating a 3rd visit to Corinth in the near future, and the situation in the church which confronted him when he wrote makes it reasonable to believe that he added chs. 10-13 before dispatching the letter and going for the last time to Corinth.

For Further Study. On I Cor.: James Moffatt, 1938; C. T. Craig in *IB*, 1953; S. M. Gilmour in *IDB*, 1962; Jean Héring, 1962. On II Cor.: Allan Menzies, 1912; R. H. Strachan, 1935; F. V. Filson in *IB*, 1953; R. V. G. Tasker, 1958; S. M. Gilmour in *IDB*, 1962.

I. EPISTOLARY INTRO. (1:1-9)

1:1-3. Salutation. Paul's letters begin with conventional modes of address, but his intros. are never mere formalities. They provide clues to his self-understanding and conception of his mission; sometimes they disclose his special purposes in writing. So in this letter the first sentence reveals a man emphatically defending his own authority and reminding his readers who they are. It is a fitting superscription to a letter addressed to a congregation of rugged individualists at cross purposes, apparently spoiling to be independent of Paul and of traditional standards of personal conduct, and shirking their corporate responsibilities.

As we read on it becomes evident why Paul writes as he does: If this young church is to mature, its members must recognize the legitimacy of his authority over them. They must also know themselves to be a congregation of God's people, sharing one Lord and a common life, and helping to shape the future of a community far wider than their own disorderly world.

Sosthenes (cf. Acts 18:17) may be Paul's secretary, or he may be introduced here as one esteemed by the Cors. In any case his views do not intrude. Paul writes in the first person singular, as an apostle who is uniquely related to his readers as their "father in Christ Jesus" (4:15).

1:4-9. Thanksgiving and Assurances. Some have felt that here the polite conventions of letter writing momentarily led Paul to idealize the Christian community at Corinth, that he could not have given thanks for actual conditions there. Others suppose that in view of the distressing reports he resorted to irony: Possessing **all knowledge** indeed! The Cors. were **not lacking in any spiritual gift** (*charisma*, lit. "grace-gift"), yet only in a proper regard for and use of these gifts would the church be **guiltless** in the day of judgment. Indefensible was their present conduct in view of God's faithfulness.

More probable is the view that Paul continues to stress positively the true nature of Christian existence. A new historical situation and community exist for men as a consequence of the coming of Jesus as the Christ. If the Cors. are to rise above their quarreling and callous independence they must acknowledge what God has done for them, what he now offers them, and what they ought to be—in Christ. Paul can sincerely be thankful that such **grace** has become available to the Cors. though he knows that they have so little understood and appropriated the gift. He makes no reference to their progress or good reputation (cf. I Thess. 1:2-8).

II. Serious Disorders Reported in Corinth (1:10–6:20)

A. Dissensions (1:10–4:21)

1:10-12. The Situation. The unity of the church at Corinth is threatened by **dissensions**, lit. "fissures," or "rifts." Perhaps it is too much to speak of the emergence of opposing parties, or even of factions. Paul's words suggest, not that groups have separated and are meeting apart (cf. 11:17-22), but rather that cliques are manifesting themselves within a single congregation. The **quarreling** has been reported to him **by Chloe's people**—presumably slaves of a woman known to the Cors. He condemns the spirit of the schismatics, not their opinions; he exposes their common errors, not their respective claims. It is therefore possible neither to infer the existence at Corinth of heresies, i.e. peculiar doctrines, nor to identify the beliefs distinguishing those who say that they belong to Paul, Apollos, etc. The divergent attitudes on moral issues which Paul discusses in chs. 7–9 have also sometimes been assigned to one or the other of the groups of vs. 12, but such conjecture is unprofitable. The dissensions are here attributed to personal loyalties rather than to theological or ethical causes, and Paul does not refer to them in this way again.

1:12. The eloquent **Apollos**, a Hellenistic Jewish Christian from Alexandria, seems to have worked in Corinth after Paul's first labors there (cf. 3:6; Acts 18:24-28). The reference to **Cephas**, i.e. Simon Peter (see comment on Gal. 1:18-20), may imply a Cor. ministry for this apostle, or it may indicate that the aura of Peter's authority adhered to Jewish Christians baptized by him and now living in Corinth. **I belong to Christ** is puzzling. Some take it, not as the slogan of a 4th party, but as a counter-slogan of Paul (cf. II 10:7), or possibly as the marginal comment of a scribe which came to be copied in the text. But the indignant question **Is Christ divided?** (vs. 13) suggests rather that particular schismatics were exclusively claiming the name of Christ. Some Christians at Corinth were asserting their freedom to the point of disowning all restraints. They called themselves spiritual men and denied all authority apart from the Spirit of Christ and their professed private visions of him. It is not possible, however, to establish their identity as the "Christ party."

1:13-17. The Primacy of Christ. Eager to claim the loyalty of the Cor. Christians, Paul nonetheless deplores the misguided sentiments of those enrolling themselves under his own name. Did some suppose that the authority of an apostle legitimized baptism? Whatever the answer to this question, Paul is glad to recall that he has **baptized** only a few; in this there is no pretext for hailing him as a potential party leader. Paul was not one to disparage baptism (cf. Gal. 3:27; Rom. 6), but he focused his energies on preaching, doubtless leaving baptism to his helpers, as Jesus may have done (cf. John 4:1-2).

His main concern is clear: no clique can own Christ or claim to be his favorite; no apostle's word or action can eclipse Christ's lordship. Ten times already in this letter Paul has named Christ. This name alone (cf. vs. 10) is the rallying point for Christian unity.

1:18–2:5. The Wisdom of Men. Many interpreters hold that Paul here gives special attention to those who unfavorably compare his own lack of sophistication and rhetorical skill (2:1-5; cf. II 10:10) with the learning and eloquence of Apollos. There is no cause for suspicion that Apollos was at fault, or that Paul is critical of his fellow worker (cf. 16:12). That the champions of Apollos were striving for **wisdom** in the way the **Greeks** sought it (vs. 22b) and priding themselves in their intellectual prowess is a reasonable inference. But Paul's words in vss. 18-31 seem to refer to an error common to all the schismatics at Corinth, viz. too exalted an estimate of the words or actions of particular leaders.

Lest the Cors. conclude that the Christian message is after all a form of **wisdom** comparable to some popular Greek philosophy, or that Christian leaders as wisdom teachers are themselves wise, Paul emphasized 2 points:

a) In men's eyes the gospel itself—not men's preaching of it—is both offensive and absurd. To the **Jews** the idea of a crucified Messiah is self-contradictory and blasphemous, a **stumbling block.** Jesus' crucifixion leads **Greeks** to conclude that it is **folly** to make of Jesus a clever teacher or a strong hero; the divine claims of one ignominiously executed cannot be taken seriously. Yet Paul reminds the Cors. that **Christ crucified** has done something for them that all the wisdom and power of men could never accomplish.

b) Paul asks his readers to consider their former lives and to recall the occasion of his initial visit. Nothing in these human circumstances gives them any cause for boasting (1:26; 2:1-5).

It would be erroneous to conclude that Paul here idealizes simplemindedness and countenances anti-intellectualism. He opposes proud man's misplaced confidence in autonomous reason and other powers to transcend ignorance and to save himself. He is not condemning human wisdom, i.e. philosophy, in principle, nor is he scorning the powers of reason to discern truth (cf. Rom. 1:19-20). But to him the pretensions of the Cors., snobbishly following great teachers as though they alone have fathomed all mysteries, and parading their own sophistry in the grandiose rhetoric of Greek orators of the age, appear foolish indeed in comparison with that wisdom manifested in God's love of men in the cross of Christ, a wisdom powerful to save.

Some interpreters suppose that in vss. 24, 30 Paul identifies Christ with wisdom and that his thought is influenced by Jewish wisdom literature in which the wisdom of God is personified (cf. e.g. Wisd. Sol. 7:24-26; 9:9; see below on 2:9-10a; 10:1-4). The quotation in vs. 19 is from Isa. 29:14; that in vs. 31 is from Jer. 9:24.

2:6–3:4. The Wisdom of God. The chief difficulties in this passage are Paul's allusions to certain basic and commonplace features of his world view which are strangely archaic to modern ears. His main points are clear: Man's comprehension of the purposes of God proclaimed in Christ depend on the Spirit's enlightenment. The quarreling Cors. evidently do not possess fully this Spirit and therefore do not possess this wisdom—indeed have proved themselves unready to receive it.

2:7. Commentators do not agree about the reference to the **secret and hidden wisdom of God.** It is unlikely that only the **word of the cross** (1:18) is implied—though some support for this interpretation may be given by those manuscripts which read "mystery" in place of **testimony** in vs. 1—for Paul's proclamation of the cross was received by all his converts. Neither does Paul seem to be speaking here of some esoteric, revealed knowledge as he does in II 12:1-5, for on his own account such disclosures are not communicable. Rather this secret wisdom of God which Paul imparts and some men are able to receive is probably the plenitude of God's purpose of redemption in Christ, which includes, among other things, the incorporation of both Jews and Greeks in the church and man's victory over death (cf. 15:51; Rom. 11:25; Col. 1:26-27). Unlike initiation into the secrets of a pagan mystery religion, baptism does not confer saving knowledge in its fullness. But this does not mean that Paul has 2 gospels, one for "babes"—the word of the cross—and another for the **mature** (vs. 6; cf. II 11:4; Gal. 1:6-9). The preaching of Christ crucified, properly understood, is the wisdom of God for all mankind, but at least some of the Cors. have not grasped its present meaning, to say nothing of its future promise.

2:8. The phrase **rulers of this age** has also been variously interpreted. Some limit it to Pilate and the Jewish rulers of Palestine (cf. Acts 4:27-28; John 7:25-26), but Paul probably has in mind the invisible powers of the spirit world behind these governing authorities, influencing their actions and blinding their eyes to the truth (cf. 6:3; 11:10-12; 15:24; II 4:4; Rom. 8:38; Gal. 4:3; Col. 2:8). Beliefs such as these were shared by many writers of Paul's day, non-Jews as well as Jews. Paul believes that the power of these spirit-rulers, like the present age, is short-lived, doomed by the event of the crucifixion of Christ (cf. Col. 2:15; John 12:31). Unwittingly these rulers have sealed their own fate, yet a final defeat awaits the coming of the **Lord of glory** and the resurrection (cf. 15:24-25; Rom. 8:18-25; Phil. 3:20-21). Christians are able to comprehend this wisdom only insofar as the Spirit of God reveals it to them. But since the Spirit has been given what the future holds in store is in part present knowledge.

2:9-10a. The origin of the "scripture" which Paul cites here is not certain. Some detect a conflation of Isa. 64:4; 65:17; Jer. 3:16. Others discern an allusion to Baruch 3:16, which is dependent on Job 28, and find support in this text for the view that Paul identified Christ with the wisdom of God (cf. 1:24, 30).

2:10b-16. The meaning here is obscured by grammatical difficulties, the most important of which is the ambiguity in vs. 13 reflected in the alternative readings of the RSV footnote. Also Paul's varied use of the word **spirit** is at first sight confusing. He seems to have been influenced here by the Cors.' misappropriation of this and related terms. The word **spiritual** is otherwise infrequently used by Paul, and **spiritually** occurs only here.

Paul's argument seems to run as follows: There are certain things in man of which he alone is conscious; so it is with God. There are **depths** of God's nature which, if known, must be disclosed by him. Yet not all men can receive this knowledge. Only the man who is **spiritual,** i.e. dominated by God's self-revealing Spirit, by being actively receptive and obedient can comprehend God's **gifts** (see above on 1:4-9). The man who is **unspiritual,** i.e. chiefly directed by the impulses and needs of his merely physical existence, is insensitive to these gifts and to their value. Cf. 15:44-50, where the same contrasting terms are employed. Only the spiritual man, therefore, **judges,** or investigates, **all things**—or persons, as the Greek can also mean—even the **depths of God,** and is himself finally independent of all judgments other than God's. In these words Paul sets forth an ideal rather than an established fact. The quotation in vs. 16 is from Isa. 40:13.

3:1-4. The Cors., who are claiming to be truly **spiritual men,** are acting like **ordinary men**—at the most **babes in Christ**—as their **jealousy and strife** prove. Paul holds that the hallmark of the Spirit is love. The absence of this quality mocks the conceit and pretensions of the Cors.

3:5-4:5. _Cooperation Among the Apostles._ In referring again to the personality cults among the schismatics Paul emphasizes the nature of any apostle's work and its value in God's eyes. While it is possible to render vs. 9a "we are God's fellow workers," the context seems to require **fellow workmen for God,** i.e. in God's service (vs. 5).

3:10-17. The same idea is developed in the image of the **foundation** and superstructure of a building. It is just possible that this metaphor was suggested to Paul by the claims of those in Corinth hailing Cephas as their leader, since he may have known of the tradition of Peter as the "rock" on which the church would be built (Matt. 16:18). But again Paul is not thinking of origins so much as of consequences. What matters most is not the primacy but the quality of anyone's **work.** And the Cors. are not warranted in making their comparative judgments. Only the coming **Day,** i.e. of judgment, **will disclose** what sort of work each of the apostles has done. Good workmanship will endure, but the fires of judgment will destroy the worthless products of any man's labor. Any man's salvation depends, not on works—notice Paul's avoidance here of this plural —but on God's grace. Yet the master builder whose work stands the test will be rewarded in proportion to his work (cf. II 1:14; Phil. 2:16).

3:16-17. Paul's architectural metaphors have a theological, not a logical, relation. **God's building** (vs. 9) becomes **God's temple** because the work of God's Spirit is holy. Already Paul may be thinking ahead to those Cor. Christians who desecrate God's temple by the sexual immoralities which he severely censures in chs. 5-6.

3:18-23. It is not obvious why Paul now resumes his attack on a particular type of **wisdom** which is **folly** with God—supported by quotations from Job 5:13; Ps. 94:11. Does he have in mind some particular leader, perhaps claiming to belong to Apollos, who is threatening to destroy God's temple, the Cor. church? We can only conjecture, but it is clear from vs. 21a that the quarreling at Corinth is still the subject for rebuke. The schismatics should not think of themselves as belonging to Apollos or one of the others. As servants of Christ and of his church the apostles belong to them all—notice Paul's inversion of the slogans of 1:12.

4:1-5. Paul now brings to a conclusion his formal arguments against the schismatics at Corinth. The apostles can be judged properly only in terms of their faithfulness **as servants of Christ,** entrusted with the **mysteries of God.** Instead of passing hasty judgments on the apostles the Cors. had better give thought to themselves and to him who will **judge** all men and their motives (cf. II 5:10).

4:6-13. *The Humility of the Apostles.* Paul here makes explicit what the reader may have suspected earlier. In boasting of certain apostles the schismatics, both leaders and followers, have been boasting of their own wisdom and superiority (3:18-23). Paul now says that he has taken himself and Apollos as illustrations of principles which might more obviously be applied to others. In ch. 3 he has put forward the names of persons not really responsible for the divisions at Corinth. Those persons more directly to blame must now recognize that in one important respect their situation is precisely that of the apostles (vs. 7a). All that they now possess as Christians has been given to them. Since all depends on grace, what objective cause does anyone have for boasting, for making invidious comparisons?

4:6-7. The meaning of Paul's rhetorical questions in vs. 7 is somewhat obscured by the puzzling phrase in vs. 6 paraphrased as **to live according to scripture.** The Greek reads lit. "not beyond what is written." An attractive theory is that these words should be omitted as a scribe's marginal comment later copied into the text. If the text as it stands comes from Paul, probably he is here opposing the self-styled "spiritual men" who reject all traditions in favor of private revelations.

4:8-10. Having taken up the attack Paul now scorns the presumed superiority of the offenders. His sarcastic thrusts reveal the interrelatedness of his 2 major indictments: (a) contrary to their arrogant professions the Cors. have not comprehended the wisdom of God and (b) they are not "spiritual." Though they possess the gifts of the Spirit, they have wrongly supposed themselves fully instructed in a "secret and hidden wisdom of God" (2:7). They claim that they are now reigning with Christ, who has risen from the dead, and hence that they are able to stand in judgment on all others, including the apostles. Ironically Paul contrasts the fanciful state of the Cors. with the actual existence of Christ's apostles, who like gladiators condemned to death in the arena have sacrificed rather than glorified themselves.

4:11-13. Since Paul believed tribulations must be endured by all Christians before the consummation of Christ's kingdom (cf. I Thess. 3:3-4; Rom. 5:1-5) it is perhaps unwise to consider these vss. merely autobiographical (cf. II 4:7-11; 6:4-10; Rom. 8:35-37). Only when the legitimacy of his apostleship was seriously questioned did Paul bring himself to record his unique experiences—and then with reluctance, as in II 11:22-23 (cf. Gal. 1-2). In his sufferings Paul held in mind the teaching of Christ concerning nonretaliation (Matt. 5:44-48; cf. Rom.

12:14-21) even though not always able to live up to it. Reviled and slandered at Corinth, Paul did not limit himself to blessing, but he did seek by every means to **conciliate.**

4:14-21. *A Personal Appeal.* Paul's disavowal in vs. 14 is qualified by 6:5; 15:34. He is moved by his feelings of special responsibility and affection to stress his paternal love for the Cors., but there is still irony in his words. They may have **countless guides**—lit. "pedagogues," which in Paul's day meant, not teachers, but slaves who took small boys to school, so that the remark is no compliment—but they have but one **father.** Just as children may be expected to imitate their parents, so the Cors. should see in Paul's humility a rebuke of their arrogant ways.

4:17-21. Because Paul is their father and is expected to exhort his children, **Timothy** is being sent for that purpose—evidently by a roundabout route which will bring him to Corinth after arrival of the letter (cf. 16:10-11). But soon Paul will visit them himself. These notes concerning his future plans reveal his defensiveness. Was it being said that he was inconsistent in teaching, vacillating in decision, a big talker but a timid soul? His question in vs. 21 anticipates events to come: a painful visit to Corinth, followed by his severe letter to the church. Indeed the hints contained in these vss. are explicitly developed in II 12:14-13:13, which provide the best commentary on this passage.

B. Sexual Immorality and Litigation (5:1-6:20)

A new subject is abruptly introduced with this section. Paul still concerns himself with reports of the unruly conduct of Christians at Corinth—disorders symptomatic of the arrogant independence of this church's leadership—but it is probable that he has been presented new evidence. Perhaps the bearers of a letter from the Cors. (cf. 7:1a; 16:17-18) have reported a case of incest in the church (5:1-5) and notorious legal disputes among its members (6:1-6). Paul's consternation may have led him to resume dictation of his letter with these subjects. Moreover since his visit to the Cors. is to be delayed, their questions deserve an immediate reply. It is noteworthy that from this point in the letter his instructions become quite concrete and specific. They are supported by theological principles which are sometimes only implicit.

5:1-5. *A Case of Incest.* Apparently a prominent man in the church has married his stepmother. His father must have died or been divorced, for this sexual union is not termed adultery. Such a marriage was forbidden by the Jewish law (Lev. 18:8; Deut. 22:30; 27:20) and also by a Roman statute. But Paul does not appeal to law. The Jewish law was not binding for Christians, esp. Gentile converts, and the offender was probably a non-Jew. Roman law may have been discounted by social customs at Corinth, as well as by the antinomianism —i.e. belief in complete freedom from law—of some in the church, which provided further reason for the church's indifference to the matter (cf. 6:12). Paul is certain that even pagan sensibilities are being offended, and in this he finds support for his condemnation of the man. Either the woman is not a Christian and therefore not subject to Paul's discipline, or he considers the man the principal offender.

5:2-4. Paul does not limit himself to demanding the severest punishment of this offender; he strongly condemns the complacency of his fellow members. Instead of being undisturbed by the incident they should be grieving as though a death had occurred in their midst! A congregational meeting must be called at once and Paul's decision in the matter ratified as though he were **present.** Reference to the cooperation of Christ's **power** may suggest that the prayers of the congregation will confirm this action.

5:5. Most commentators believe that this vs. commands excommunication and that it implies belief that the man will be left to the unlimited power of **Satan** (cf. Rom. 1:24-32, where Paul speaks of the sexually immoral as given over to the wrath of God). Paul may intend that a curse of death be invoked on the man. Elsewhere he writes that Satan's power causes unceasing pain (II 12:7) and thwarts the purposes of men (I Thess. 2:18). But Satan's power is limited to the **destruction of the flesh;** soon the **day of the Lord Jesus** will bring the resurrection, with a new spiritual body (cf. 15:42-50) and the possibilities of this corrupt man's salvation.

Christian love may seem to demand an unlimited forbearance of evil (cf. 13:7), but in Paul's judgment this situation requires the use of the **rod** instead of the **spirit of gentleness** (4:21). Failure to expel such an unrepentant offender might encourage the sexual license exhibited in this church and seriously impair its witness to outsiders.

5:6-13. *The Purity of the Church.* Paul's repeated reference to the arrogance of the spokesmen for the church (vs. 6; cf. vs. 2) emphasizes the gravity of the situation at Corinth. To condone the sexual immorality of a member is deplorable, but to boast of such freedom as a spiritual privilege is perverse. Moreover the lax attitude of these leaders is like **leaven,** infecting the life of the entire congregation. In Paul's thought the yeast or other leavening organism is associated with the process of putrefaction and corruption. His allegory is based on the Jewish Passover, during which Jewish houses had to be cleansed of any trace of leavened bread, lest ceremonial impurity result (cf. Exod. 12:19). Christians, like loyal Jews, must keep the true Passover by making actual the ideal of moral purity symbolized by unleavened bread; any impurity within the household of faith can only compromise this loyalty and ideal.

Paul's allegory is derived also from convictions associated with the Christian gospel. He recalls the tradition that Jesus was put to death just before the celebration of a Passover in Jerusalem (see comment on John 13:1), becoming for those who believed in him the **paschal lamb,** slain once and for all. This crucified and risen Lord, who himself purifies men from sin, demands of his church moral purity. Thus Paul combines the indicative and the imperative of the gospel: by their conduct the Cors. are to become what they already are by virtue of Christ's sacrifice and their faith union with him.

5:9-13. In vs. 9 Paul speaks of words he has written earlier which have been misunderstood at Corinth. He clearly is referring here to a previous

letter. In this he warned against keeping company with **immoral men**—the translation of a more specific Greek word meaning those who indulge in extramarital sexual relations. Sex offenders stand at the top of Paul's list, here and in 6:9-20, because of their prevalence in the Cor. church. The other offenders listed in vs. 10 may have been suggested by the following progression of thought: the sexually **immoral** sin against themselves (cf. 6:18); the **greedy and robbers** sin against their fellow men; **idolaters** sin against God.

5:11-13. Many scholars today maintain that II 6:14-7:1 reproduces a part of the previous letter to which Paul refers in vs. 9 (see Intro.), but evidence for this conjecture falls short of proof. We are not left to conjecture about the contents of the previous letter, however, for Paul now clarifies the points he made before. He has not urged the physical isolation of the church from non-Christians—which is indeed not possible. Rather he has written that the self-discipline of the church is necessary. The church must judge and expel from its membership the wicked person.

6:1-8. *Court Quarrels Among Christians.* The relation of the church to pagan society and Paul's conviction that the church must judge its own members lead naturally to a consideration of a 3rd example of the disorderliness of the Cors. If church members are not allowed to judge outsiders, then neither should church members expect to be judged by them. Nevertheless this passage is a kind of digression; Paul returns shortly to the subject of the notorious sexual immoralities at Corinth.

6:1. Paul is indignant that Christians should be taking their trivial property disputes into pagan courts. **Unrighteous** simply identifies **unbelievers** (vs. 6), i.e. non-Christians, and should not be taken as disparagement of the Roman tribunals. Paul believes that the state has received from God its mission to maintain peace and justice among men (cf. Rom. 13:1-8) and his letters disclose no disillusionment in this matter.

6:2-3. The rhetorical questions in these vss. are parallel, both having reference to the **world** of the **angels,** i.e. to the domain of the "rulers of this age" (see above on 2:8), elsewhere designated "principalities" (Rom. 8:38) or "elemental spirits" (Gal. 4:3). Some interpreters suppose that Paul speaks here of judgment of the world of men as well as of angelic beings. Yet Paul consistently holds that the **saints,** i.e. Christians, have no authority in this age to **judge** unbelievers, and he nowhere writes of a resurrection of unbelieving men in the age to come which might provide opportunity for the saints to judge them. Always in speaking of the judgment to come Paul writes that it is God alone, through the agency of Jesus Christ, who judges men (cf. Rom. 2:11-16; II Thess. 1:7*b*-12).

6:4-6. The cause of Paul's outrage is that these legal squabbles among Christians are additional evidence of their immaturity, and threaten their Christian witness to outsiders. At the time the Cors. are professing wisdom there appears to be no one of them **wise enough to decide between members of the brotherhood.** Instead Christians are turning to **unbelievers,** i.e. pagans, who count for nothing in the church—the probable meaning of vs. 4.

6:7-8. Do the Cors. speak of sharing now in their Lord's messianic reign? (Cf. 4:8.) Their quarreling reveals their actual **defeat,** not their victory. Indeed victory over all evil is not their destined lot in the present age. As their Lord suffered, they too must be ready to suffer wrong. Instead they are inflicting it—on their own brethren.

6:9-11. *Warning Against Immorality.* Paul sharply warns his readers that there are vices which disqualify men from inheriting the **kingdom of God** —that realm into which the Christian dead enter after their resurrection according to Paul's view (cf. 15:50; Gal. 5:19-21).

6:9b-10. The **greedy,** the **thieves,** and the **robbers** may refer to the Christians who are defrauding one another in their property disputes (vs. 8). References to sex offenders (see above on 5:9-13) recall Paul's outrage as he writes about the case of incest (6:1) as well as point forward to a continuation of his attack on sexual immoralities at Corinth. **Homosexual** renders 2 Greek terms, perhaps referring to potential and to actual homosexuals. In the Greco-Roman world homosexuality was not greatly condemned; but Paul, in company with Jewish teachers and other Jewish-Christians, attacks it as a grave evil (cf. Rom. 1:26-27).

6:11. Paul may refer in vs. 11a only to the former lives of some of the Cors.; but more probably he is implying, on the basis of the reports he has received, the continued existence of all these vices within the church. If so, we may wonder how he can write of such Christians as in vs. 11b. Of course by **justified** he does not mean that they are already made righteous, i.e. morally perfect. Rather they are at peace with God in their relation to Christ, even though they remain sinners (cf. Rom. 5:1-11). **You were washed, you were sanctified** probably recalls that the Cors. have received baptism and the gifts of the Spirit. Certainly Paul is not commending their moral qualities or their professed spirituality.

6:12-20. *Sanctity of the Body.* Some church members at Corinth evidently were claiming that sexual relations outside marriage were not immoral and that as Christians they were free to consort with prostitutes without blame. Probably **all things are lawful for me** was the slogan of these free-thinkers. Paul agrees with them in principle, but he offers 2 serious qualifications. Some actions are definitely not **helpful**—i.e. to others, probably (cf. 10:23-24) —and some by their very nature are enslaving. Paul cannot agree that the sex act, like eating food, is only natural and therefore of no moral or spiritual significance.

Many scholars believe that the views against which Paul contends here spring from an ideology identified by 2nd-cent. Christian apologists as Gnosticism. Gnostics commonly believed that man's body, like all material things, was the creation of an inferior deity and thus destined for destruction. For this reason Christians influenced by Gnosticism were unable to believe in the resurrection of the body (vs. 14; cf. ch. 15). For this reason also some of them believed that no bodily function possessed any importance for man's spiritual life and thus that sexual acts could not really defile the human spirit, which alone could inherit the kingdom of God.

These may be called Gnostic libertines. Others, however, influenced by the same Gnostic view of the body as material and mortal, practiced asceticism, denying the bodily functions their proper expression on the ground that man's immortal spirit had already been redeemed from his mortal body. These may be called Gnostic ascetics.

Prevalence of this ideology in first-cent. Corinth is supported by Paul's letters to this church. Some historians prefer to label such views pre-Gnostic, lest they be confused with the complex Gnostic heresies of the 2nd cent.

6:13-14. Paul can agree with Gnostics that both the stomach and food are to be destroyed (cf. 15:50). But the Christian's body, Paul holds, being created **for the Lord,** is **not meant for immorality.** The mortal body, destined to be raised and freed from corruption, must not now be defiled. It goes without saying that Paul, contrary to the Gnostics, shares the Jewish belief that a man's whole being is a creation of God.

6:15-20. This passage touches on an important aspect of Paul's teaching. The present union of the believer with Christ is described as membership in his body (cf. 12:12-27). The extent to which Paul intends this figure to be taken realistically is a subject for debate, but it is obvious that this union is sufficiently real for him to exclude all other unions not compatible with it. On the basis of OT teaching (e.g. Gen. 2:24, quoted in vs. 16), reaffirmed by Jesus (Mark 10:2-12), he believes that sexual intercourse is not an inconsequential, isolated act but one uniting man and woman in an intimate, complete, and enduring bond. Consequently he is revolted by the thought that a member of Christ's body should ever be united with the body of a prostitute. In Corinth most of the prostitutes were slave women attached to the service of a pagan temple. It was commonly thought that any man having sexual relations with these sacred prostitutes entered into communion with the god whom they served (cf. 10:18-22). This belief may explain Paul's emphasis in vs. 15 and also his claim, otherwise questionable, in vs. 18.

III. ANSWERS TO QUESTIONS FROM CORINTH (7:1-16:12)

Paul's thoughts lead him directly to a matter about which the Cors. have written (7:1a). The appearance of the same formula, **now concerning,** in 8:1; 12:1; 16:1 identifies other questions raised in their letter, delivered perhaps by Stephanas and his companions (16:17). Possibly the church also has raised a question concerning Apollos (16:12).

A. CELIBACY AND MARRIAGE (7:1-40)

7:1-7. *Marital Obligations.* Vs. 1b probably cites a slogan of some Gnostic ascetics in Corinth. Possibly Paul's stern judgments on sexual immorality directly led some Christians to adopt the position that avoidance of all sexual relations provides the best preventive (cf. 5:9-10). Paul contends that this is a valid position for anyone to take provided he has received the **special gift from God** (see above on 1:4-9) of celibacy (cf. Matt. 19:12)—a gift given to Paul (vs. 7). But since all men do not have this gift celibacy cannot become a general principle for Christians or be considered a matter of merit.

Paul unequivocally rejects the view that the sexual relation in marriage should be denied to Christians. Indeed husbands and wives have no right to continence, and mutual consideration in the conjugal relationship is commended. That Paul should advocate this equality of rights for women in marriage is surprising in view of his Jewish heritage and other statements (cf. 11:3, 8-9), but his Christian faith was at cross purposes with his upbringing (cf. Gal. 3:26-28). The exceptive clause in vs. 5 shows that he shared the current belief that sexual intercourse brought cultic impurity, but his main point is that prolonged continence constitutes a strong temptation and may be disastrous. He does not command continence, even temporarily, for those who have not the gift.

7:8-9. The Unmarried and Widows. Since Paul repeats himself and returns to the special cases he has discussed in passing (cf. vss. 8, 25) the subdivisions of ch. 7 are inexact. Here Paul repeats his qualified acceptance of celibacy, perhaps for emphasis, and applies his view to 2 cases. The word translated **unmarried** may mean one separated from a former spouse as well as one never married.

7:8. Since Paul speaks of himself as unmarried some have observed that this vs. is compatible with the view that Paul was a widower. This assumption is based on an inference drawn from Acts 26:10 that Paul was once a member of the Jewish Sanhedrin (council), to which only married men were eligible. The testimony of Paul makes this assumption improbable. His unmarried state was the result of a gift of God, not an "act of God."

7:9. While Paul considers marriage to be proper for all Christians lacking the gift of continence, he only grudgingly approves of it as an antidote to sexual immoralities.

7:10-16. Separation and Divorce. Throughout this discussion Paul is careful to distinguish between the teaching of Jesus and his own opinions (vss. 10, 12; cf. vs. 25). The tradition had brought him commandments of **the Lord** and on the basis of these he charged his congregations (cf. 15:3a). He did not consider that his personal judgments had the same authority, but neither did he think of them as mere opinions. His judgments were responsibly determined under the Spirit's influence, and the word of an apostle was to be taken seriously (cf. vss. 25, 40). A saying of Jesus recorded in 2 of the earliest sources—Mark (10:2-12; cf. Matt. 19:3-9) and Q (Matt. 5:32; Luke 16:18)—condemns divorce and denies remarriage to husband or wife. Paul notes here only the commandment that the wife remain single, but he recognizes the common responsibility of Christian partners in marriage.

7:12-16. In referring to **the rest** Paul has in mind situations in which one partner in marriage remains a pagan—cases of "mixed marriage." In this event the Christian convert must never initiate separation, but if the unbelieving partner desires separation the Christian cannot compel the continuation of a relationship sustained before his conversion. Paul's counsel is based on his belief that sexual union affects the whole personality, a view consistent with what he says in 6:16. In this case, however, Paul thinks

of the positive potentialities for the unbeliever married to a member of Christ's body, and for the **children** of this marriage (vs. 14). Paul emphasizes only the possible effects of the marital relationship on the unbeliever; he cannot speak of certainties (vs. 16).

7:17-35. Maintaining the Status Quo. When Paul wrote to the Cors. he was dominated by a conviction that **the form of this world is passing away** (vs. 31), that the **time has grown very short** (vs. 29; cf. Mark 13:30) before the coming of the Lord in glory. In view of this **impending distress** (vs. 26) he urges his readers to be single-minded, concentrating their interest on the affairs of the Lord, on which their lasting well-being depends rather than on relations which are short-lived and fraught with tribulation (cf. 15:51-52, 58; 16:22; II 4:16-18; Rom. 13:11-14).

7:25-35. Paul's advice to the **unmarried** in the Cor. church is better understood in view of his conviction of the imminent end of the present age. He would secure for his converts their **undivided devotion to the Lord** (vs. 35) and save them from those worldly tribulations which he associates with the last days. His position may be compared to that of the celibate Qumran sectarians domiciled in the desert region near the Dead Sea and living in keen expectation of the end (see "The Dead Sea Scrolls," pp. 1063-71). One may suspect that Paul was rationalizing his personal predilections when he wished that all Christians might follow his example in eschewing marriage and idealizing the superior effectiveness of a celibate Christian's witness. But the interpreter should not overlook Paul's basic affirmation: **each has his own special gift from God** (vs. 7). Most Christians, not having the gift of celibacy, find that the divided interests which attend marriage challenge and sustain a faithful obedience to Christ.

7:36-38. A Special Case. Interpreters have not been able to identify with certainty the situation Paul has in mind here because of question about the precise meaning some of the Greek words had in his day. **Betrothed** here is lit. "virgin," and the verb translated **marries** (vs. 38) apparently should mean "gives in marriage." Thus the counsel has traditionally been assumed to be addressed to a father and to concern whether he should marry off his daughter. But it has always been difficult to make sense of this interpretation in view of Paul's other statements.

If the passage is addressed rather to the potential bridegroom—assuming that the verb could mean simply **marries** at the time the letter was written —2 alternative interpretations are possible: (a) The man may have taken the young woman under his protection to live with him but agreed never to have sexual relations with her because of a common commitment to the ascetic ideal of continence. Later Christian sources describe "spiritual" marriages of this sort, and it is not impossible that this custom had its antecedents in the church at Corinth. (b) More probably Paul is still speaking generally of the **unmarried** (vs. 25), but esp. here of those engaged couples who despite their belief that the end is imminent find it hard to refrain from sexual relations or to reject marriage in favor of the celibate life. Whatever uncertainty must remain concerning the precise situation envisaged, Paul was consistent in his teaching: he expressed his preference for celibacy, recognized the rightness of marriage for persons lacking the gift of continence or self-control, and rejected the ascetic ideal—however strong the arguments in its favor—as being impractical for everyone.

7:39-40. *Remarriage of Widows.* Apparently Paul did not believe that vows of celibacy were permanently binding. He may have recognized that special hardships were also being imposed on some widows in the church at Corinth (cf. I Tim. 5:14). Were the Gnostic ascetics esp. insistent that widows not remarry? This freedom is not to be denied to them, Paul writes. But again he recommends the **happier** state. His word here echoes vss. 28*b*, 35.

B. FOOD OFFERED TO IDOLS (8:1–11:1)

8:1-13. *Knowledge and Love.* In Corinth, as in other cities of Paul's day, the public and private worship of the many deities of the Greco-Roman world included animal sacrifices. Slaughterhouses were often located next to temples. Parts of these slain animals would be consumed by the altar fire but the leftovers might either be given to priests or other worshipers or be sold in the market places. Some persons used portions of this consecrated food to give banquets at home or in the temples in honor of a god, and persons were invited to feast in the name of, or in communion with, the deity.

Courtesy of Herbert G. May

Ruins of the temple of Apollo at Corinth; seven of the 38 monolithic Doric columns, *ca.* 24 ft. high, still stand

As a result of such practices a many-faceted problem arose for converts to Christianity. Some Christians at Corinth had a simple solution. They held that the whole range of questions associated with the idol meats was of no consequence. If one ate or did not eat them he was none the **better** or the **worse** (vs. 8). Paul seems to be voicing his basic agreement with the premises of these persons when he quotes their sayings in vss. 1*a*, 4. But Paul recognizes that this knowledge is being used by Gnostic libertines at Corinth to exalt themselves. On the inconsistency between Paul's counsel on this question and Acts 15:29; 16:4 see comment on Acts 15:1-35.

8:1*b*-3. The brevity of the statements in vss. 1*b*-2 may obscure the thrust of Paul's indictment. As in the case of wisdom he recognizes 2 kinds of knowledge: (*a*) that which some Cors. imagine they possess fully and (*b*) the true knowledge which the Christian does not now possess but will eventually gain as a result of his having been known by God (cf. 13:9, 12; Gal. 4:8-9). Perhaps one may contrast the attitude of a man who knows that he is enlightened, and who proudly defends his actions as justified by this knowledge, with the attitude of another man who acknowledges God as he is self-revealed in Christ, and who therefore recognizes that he does not yet know as he ought. For since a Christian's knowledge is that God is **love,** the criterion that one's knowledge is true is that one is likewise loving (cf. 13:1). It is probable that vs. 3 should read: "But if one loves [i.e. loves others] he is known [i.e. acknowledged] by God." This meaning is supported by the earliest papyrus manuscript and by the context.

8:4-6. These vss. present a more difficult problem for the interpreter. Paul seems both to deny and to concede the existence of many gods. The influence of contemporary theology on Paul explains this apparent paradox. Of course to the Jewish monotheist the gods of the pagans—Artemis, Hermes, and the rest—were idols. Yet a real existence was not denied to certain invisible powers and authorities. These affected the lives of men, and men were tempted to worship them. Numerous passages support the view that Paul acknowledged the existence of these angelic beings. Indeed on one occasion he writes of the "god of this world" (II 4:4), evidently not referring, as he does here, to **one God, the Father from whom are all things.** It is against this background that Paul's somewhat equivocal teaching concerning idol meats must be viewed.

8:7-13. Paul's counsel here is an elaboration of his warning **take care lest this liberty of yours somehow become a stumbling-block to the weak** (vs. 9). It is clear that the weak man to whom Paul refers is the Christian with an uneasy **conscience** about anything associated with idol worship. To the **man of knowledge** this brother appears only to be overscrupulous; adequate knowledge should dispel once and for all his absurd fears. But Paul knows that the emotions of some men are more deeply affected by the popular beliefs which they have so recently renounced. They are not easily emancipated. In principle it is not evil for anyone to purchase this idol meat and eat it in one's home or another's, but in practice some persons by doing so will be led to relapse into paganism. Such a disastrous result cannot be lightly dismissed. To prevent the fall of the weak those who have no doubt about the rightness of their views should be willing to forgo their rights (vs. 13). While Paul is sure that their basic position cannot be gainsaid in this matter of Christian liberty (vs. 8), he certainly does not share their spirit. One may ignore the pagan gods. They do not exist. But one cannot ignore a **brother** and the existence of his tender conscience.

9:1-27. *Renunciation of an Apostle's Privilege.* The sudden defensiveness which appears at the beginning of this ch. seems to some interpreters so unsuited to the context that they assign the entire passage to another, perhaps later, letter to the Cors. But there is no need to resort to such a hypothesis. In the course of speaking of forgoing his rights (8:13) perhaps Paul became conscious that some readers might consider him uncertain of his authority as an apostle and view his readiness to pattern his actions according to the judgments of the weak as a telltale sign of self-doubt. In a series of short rhetorical questions (vs. 1) he reveals the ground for his self-assurance, echoing other apologetic passages in his letters. He rests his defense on an appeal to the motives which have prompted him to renounce the legitimate rights of an apostle. Surely the Cors. know that he might have claimed their financial support. Other apostles have exercised this right, fully justified by custom (vs. 7), scripture (vss. 8-12), cultic practice (vs. 13), and a commandment of the Lord (vs. 14).

9:19-23. Though Paul may have digressed somewhat in self-defense, it now becomes evident that he has not lost sight of the main thread of his argument in appealing to his own example. The Christian is indeed **free** of the judgments of others, free to do what his Christian knowledge dictates. But like a **slave** he is bound to do those things which further the gospel and build up the Christian community. Paul may have acted differently as particular circumstances demanded, but he cannot be fairly charged with personal insecurity or aimless vacillations. Since the church's mission is directed to both Jews and Greeks he has adopted different strategies. And since members of the church hold conscientiously different opinions in matters of conduct, as the idol-meat controversy illustrates, the apostle of Christian unity needs to be flexible in his attitudes, suiting his action to each situation as it arises. For further discussion of this point cf. 10:31–11:1.

9:24-27. The illustration of a foot **race** comes to Paul's mind, suggested perhaps by the Isthmian games held at Corinth. The thought of these various athletic contests may have led him to mix the metaphors of racing and boxing. At any rate these figures of speech reinforce his warning in ch. 8. The **man of knowledge** must recognize his need for self-examination and hard discipline—as Paul has in the course of his work—lest at the end, having taught others to run, he find himself **disqualified.**

10:1–11:1. *Additional Guiding Principles.* Traditions of Israel's exodus from Egypt are now recalled to warn the proud libertines who believe themselves secure in their knowledge and exempt from temptations to idolatry. In drawing this lesson from history Paul assumes that his Gentile readers share the conviction, common in the early church, that as Christians they are the spiritual descendants of the Israelites. By this he means not merely that they hold many beliefs in common but that the Christian church, being the community of the Messiah, is the new Israel of God (cf. Gal. 6:16). Christians at Corinth are a part of the congregation of God's people at the end time, experiencing the fulfillment of his purpose of redemption (cf. 1:2, 4-9) which was partially accomplished by his mighty acts at the time of Israel's exodus. This seems to be the meaning of Paul's curious expression **upon whom the end of the ages has come** (vs. 11). The Christian community has come into existence at the point of intersection between 2 ages—the present age and the age to come—so that the end of the old age coincides with the beginning of the new. Thus Paul can view the Christian's life on the one hand as existing

in the last days of the age that is passing (cf. 7:31) and on the other hand as entering the new and final age soon to be manifest to all, since the kingdom of Christ is a present reality (cf. 7:29; 15:23-28; II 5:17; Col. 1:13).

10:1-4. Paul views from this perspective the important events in Israel's history associated with God's purpose of redemption. He uses a mode of scriptural interpretation, known as "typology," which was as familiar in his day as it is strange in ours. This method sees events described in the OT as "types" or foreshadowings of contemporary experiences which, though generally different, have some suggestive similarity. Thus for Paul each redemptive event in Israel's history foreshadows the final victory of God's righteousness now manifested in Jesus Christ. The crossing of the **sea** (cf. Exod. 14:21-31) and the enveloping **cloud** which protected the Israelites on their wilderness journey (cf. Exod. 13:21-22; 14:19) are types of Christian baptism. The miraculous **food** (cf. Exod. 16) and **drink** (cf. Exod. 17:1-7; Num. 20:2-13) supplied Israel in the desert are types of the Lord's Supper, and the **Rock** from which the water sprang is a type of Christ himself.

Comment on the exodus traditions in Jewish wisdom literature may have provided patterns of thought for Paul here. Or perhaps he and his Hellenistic readers were acquainted with such interpretations as are found in the writings of his older contemporary, Philo of Alexandria, who sought to reconcile Judaism with Greek philosophy. E.g. Philo identified the rock with the wisdom of God; and rabbis, noting its location at 2 different places (Exodus 17:6; Num. 20:1), explained that it **followed** the Israelites in their trek through the wilderness. But Paul's Christian view of the coming new age makes his reading of the exodus traditions unique.

10:5-13. These considerations enable us to appreciate the force of Paul's warning. The libertines in the church at Corinth have neither perished nor disqualified themselves (cf. 9:27). But the OT types warn them of the possibility of such disasters. They must recognize the threatening, seductive nature of the influences surrounding them (vs. 12). Participation in the Christian sacraments provides no final security. All those redeemed by God from Egypt's bondage had undergone a baptism, had partaken of sacramental food and drink. Yet **with most of them God was not pleased.** Many succumbed to evil desires (vs. 6; cf. Num. 11:4-34), idolatry (vs. 7; cf. Exod. 32:1-6), immorality (vs. 8; cf. Num. 25:1-9), testing God (vs. 9; cf. Num. 21:4-9; Ps. 78:18), and grumbling (vs. 10; cf. Num. 16:41-50), which led them to apostasy.

10:14-22. Paul now makes clear the potentially dangerous situation at Corinth. Once again he applies his premise that a Christian's faith prohibits any kind of relationship incompatible with his union with Christ (cf. 6:15-16). But this time he links the reality of this union with the **table of the Lord.** If a Christian partakes of a ceremonial feast in a pagan temple, he severs himself from **participation in the blood of Christ** and the **body of Christ.** Paul recognizes that his readers may draw the false conclusion that despite his previous disclaimer he believes in the existence of the pagan deities after all. And so he appeals to Jewish **practice** and to scripture. One would not find here support for polytheism, but Paul has found support for his view that pagan sacrifices are offered **to demons and not to God** (vs. 20; cf. Deut. 32:17; Ps. 106:37).

At first sight it might seem that Paul's argument is highly artificial. Yet earlier statements in this letter have clearly revealed Paul's belief that angelic powers lay behind the pagan world order. It was a short step to conclude that these powers were active at pagan temples. In tempting Christians to partake of idol meats in these places the "elemental spirits" became, in Paul's thought, demonic powers. And so he writes that the table in an idol's temple is a **table of demons** (cf. 12:2).

10:23-30. Reinforcing his argument, Paul cites again the slogan of the Cor. libertines (vs. 23; cf. 6:12). He reiterates also his major principle that concern for others affects the exercise of Christian liberty (vs. 24; cf. 8:9; Rom. 14:13, 15, 19; 15:1-2). Christians may continue to buy their meat in the **market** and serve it in their homes. They need raise no **question** which their consciences do not raise, for scripture (Ps. 24:1) declares that all on earth belongs to God. Moreover Paul sees no objection to their being dinner guests in the homes of **unbelievers** (vs. 27; cf. 5:9-10). Parenthetically (vss. 28-29a) he thinks of one occasion at such meals when tactful consideration for someone's conscience would impose a voluntary limitation on one's freedom of action. But Paul is chiefly concerned here to defend the right of Christians to eat anything set before them in pagan homes and to express their sincere **thanks** to God for such benefits.

10:31-11:1. At this point did Paul have what he had just dictated read back to him? In appealing to his own example he now gives testimony in words reminiscent of those recorded in 9:19-23. It could be argued that his advice has effectively put an end to Christian liberty, foisting on the people of God a new legalism determined by the scruples of the weaker members of the church. But his last words on the subject show that he has always acted freely, in matters of food and drink as in all things, **to the glory of God.** He has sought, as any Christian must seek, to pattern his actions after the example of Christ.

C. CONDUCT AT CONGREGATIONAL MEETINGS (11:2–14:40)

Paul's attention turns to reports of various disorders in the worship services at Corinth. He can **commend** the church for not forgetting him and the **traditions** he has taught; yet recent local practices exhibit a practical misunderstanding of these traditions and offend Paul's sensibilities.

11:3-16. *The Scandal of Unveiled Women.* First to be noted is the fact that some women are taking part in the worship services with their heads uncovered. Paul's protest is vigorous and emotional, based on theological considerations, social convention, and an argument from nature. From the biblical account of creation (Gen. 2) he adduces the belief common to the Jews that woman is inferior to man (vss. 8-9), and this conviction underlies the whole discussion.

11:3. Paul's statement of the hierarchical orders is somewhat obscure. Perhaps it may be paraphrased: "While every male has Christ for his head [Christ being the agent in his creation; cf. 8:6; Col. 1:16], woman's head is man as Christ's head is God [i.e. one is clearly subordinate to the other; cf. 3:23; 15:28]."

11:4-9. In vss. 4-6 Paul uses **head** in both figurative and literal senses, but his meaning is clarified in vss. 7-9 by words which echo Gen. 1:26-27. Man's uncovered head symbolizes his acceptance of the authority given to one created in the **image . . . of God.** To cover his head with a symbol of inferiority would be dishonorable. But woman was created for subjection and she **dishonors her head,** i.e. man, in uncovering her head, for by so doing she asserts her will to be his equal. For Paul this challenge to man's authority is as much a public disgrace as the unnatural act of cropping or shaving a woman's head.

11:10. Paul sums up his theological argument in this vs. Since woman is created for man she **ought to have a veil** (lit. "authority") **on her head.** The meaning is further obscured for us by the continuation, **because of the angels.** It is perhaps a modernization to say that Paul conceives the veil to be a sign of woman's authority in the sense that it protects her against assault or molestation. Yet this understanding finds support in the ancient interpretation of the passage as an allusion to the "sons of God" who were seduced by the beauty of the "daughters of men" (Gen. 6:1-4). The idea of veiled women exercising authority over angelic powers is found in Jewish apocalyptic writings, but it seems foreign to this context and to Paul's thought generally.

Other passages in the letter provide more probable clues. Paul has affirmed that Christians live at the intersection of 2 ages. The present age is passing and for the short time remaining human affairs are partially dominated by invisible powers (cf. 2:6). Moreover in 6:3 angels are explicitly mentioned as beings not yet judged by men or subjugated to Christ (cf. 15:24). Since therefore for Paul the subordination of woman to man is inherent in the social structure of the present age, he argues that out of deference to the angelic rulers and guardians of this world order Christian women ought not to appear in public assemblies without a veil—the symbol of the authority which men hold over them within this age. Again Paul's expectation of an early end to the present age determines his social conservatism (cf. 7:17-40).

11:11-12. The other side of Paul's belief—viz. that with Christ's present lordship over the church the new and final age has been anticipated—struggles for expression. **In the Lord,** Paul observes, man and woman are not **independent** of each other (cf. 7:4). Nevertheless in this matter Paul's prejudices resist the more important implications of his own revolutionary faith that in Christ there is "neither male nor female" (Gal. 3:28).

11:13. There is a defensiveness in the remainder of the argument. Yet Paul's appeal to his readers' sense of propriety is not without force in view of the prevailing social conventions. Respectable, modest women did not appear in public with their heads uncovered; only women with no proper self-respect, or cult prostitutes, went without veils. The libertines in the church may have argued that the Christian is emancipated from the unwritten laws of society and certainly can express this freedom in church. Paul reasons that women ought not to come before God in a manner considered indecent elsewhere, perhaps thinking of the public suspicions caused by indecorous dress (cf. 5:1; 6:6; 10:27-29).

11:14-16. Possibly Paul's argument from **nature** (vss. 14-15) appeared as weak to his first readers as to later ones. If a woman's **hair** provides a natural **covering,** then why should an artificial one be thought necessary?

It is obvious that Paul throughout this discussion is rationalizing a social custom of which he approves and that in conclusion he resigns himself to the fact that none of his arguments are fully convincing. He falls back on the **practice** of the **churches of God** and will not concede that the Cor. congregation has any freedom in this matter.

11:17-34. Abuses of the Lord's Supper. This passage is esp. important for it contains not only the oldest account of the institution of the Lord's Supper—written as much as 10 years before Mark's—but also Paul's understanding of its significance.

11:17. This statement is set in contrast to vs. 2, but its precise meaning is uncertain because of the ambiguity of the opening phrase in the Greek. It reads lit. "But in instructing this"—which could refer either to the advice about women's veils or to that **following.** The latter meaning seems more likely, and on this assumption we can take the sentence as an important transition. Paul is now ready to discuss at some length 2 disorderly situations affecting the worship services at Corinth far more seriously than the scandal of unveiled women—viz. abuse of the Lord's Supper (vss. 18-34) and contentions over "spiritual gifts" (chs. 12-14). It is because of these problems that Paul seems to be saying: "I certainly cannot commend you, since your gatherings as a church are more harmful than helpful to you."

11:18-19. Some scholars have viewed the **divisions** here as another reference to the partisans of Apollos, Cephas, etc. (cf. 1:10-12). But the following vss. suggest differences of social or economic status among members of the church rather than leadership rivalries. Vs. 19 should be understood in this context (cf. vss. 26-32) as meaning that in the last days **factions** must come to test the genuineness of the Christian's life and work (cf. 3:12-15; Matt. 24:10-14; II Pet. 2:1-3).

11:20-22. Some doubt exists concerning the exact nature of the meetings which have occasioned the abuses implied by Paul's words (cf. vss. 33-34). Evidently the Cors. gather as a church from time to time to share a common meal which is, or which includes, a celebration of the **Lord's supper.** The more prosperous members of the church arrive first, generously supplied with food and drink. The poorer members come later, after longer work hours, with their meager provisions. Unwilling to delay their meal, the early comers eat and drink, some of them to excess, without waiting to partake of the Lord's Supper with their brethren. Rumors of such selfish gluttony and drunkenness have convinced Paul that some of his Cor. converts seriously misunderstand

the meaning of the sacrament and of the **church** as the body of Christ (vss. 20, 22b; cf. vss. 27-29).

11:23a. The Cors. are maintaining the traditional observance (cf. vs. 2) which Paul **received from the Lord**—i.e. through the testimony of Jesus' disciples—and passed on to them. But this very fact turns an otherwise disgraceful church supper into a highly dangerous event. To drive home the fearful consequence of their profanation of the Lord's Supper Paul recalls the solemn circumstances of the original meal.

11:23b-25. Great interest has centered on comparison of Paul's account with the other NT records of the Last Supper: Mark 14:22-26 (cf. Matt. 26:26-29); Luke 22:14-20. The most striking differences are (a) the words **do this in remembrance of me** and (b) the reference to Jesus' **blood** as establishing a **new covenant** (cf. Mark 14:24). Though this account provides documentary evidence earlier than that in the gospels, most scholars consider Mark's the most primitive, on the basis that Paul's tradition reflects the liturgical usage and perhaps the sacramental associations of the Hellenistic churches. On the other hand some have argued for the greater antiquity of Paul's tradition, pointing to the lack of parallelism in the bread and cup sayings in comparison with those of Mark's version, which they judge to be an intermediate step toward the exactly parallel formulas of the 2nd-cent. church. The longer version of Luke's narrative found in most manuscripts includes a passage (Luke 22:19b-20; see RSV footnote) which most scholars consider an interpolation literarily dependent on this account (see comment on Luke 22:14-23), but which may be based on an early independent source reflecting the tradition known to Paul.

Some light on Paul's understanding of the tradition is shed by his rhetorical questions in 10:16, where he refers first to the **cup,** associating it with a genuine **participation in the blood of Christ**—i.e. in the benefits of his death (cf. Rom. 3:25; 5:9)—and then to the broken **bread,** which he associates with a real sharing in the life of the risen Lord of the church. Here the bread saying (vs. 24) may have the same signification: **This is my body which is for you,** i.e. for your salvation now and in the future (cf. Rom. 5:6-11). The cup saying (vs. 25) is tied with the benefits of Christ's passion, as in 10:16, but specifically now with the establishment of the **new covenant.** In Christ's death God sealed with his people a new covenant (cf. Jer. 31:31-34)—once again a covenant ratified by the blood of a sacrifice, as in the days of Moses (cf. Exod. 24:8).

Paul's reference to the Lord's Supper here is too fleeting to provide evidence for a developed theology of the sacrament. Interpreters have persisted in asking what he understood by **This is my body.** In what sense was Christ present, symbolically or realistically, in the bread and the wine? Moreover questions have persisted concerning the nature of the sacramental union of the believer with his Lord. Should one speak of this relationship as mystical or ethical? All efforts to restrict Paul's meaning to one or the other of these may do violence to his comprehension of the relation of Christ to men of faith, a union renewed with each faithful "participation" in the body and blood of Christ.

11:26-32. Paul draws only 2 corollary deductions in his instruction to the Cors.: (*a*) They are reminded (vs. 26) that the Lord's Supper is a memorial of the betrayal and **death** of Christ, which they are to **proclaim** as such—and not with incongruous levity—until his coming, i.e. his final advent. (*b*) They are warned (vss. 27-32) that to partake of the supper in the unworthy manner exhibited by some of them outrages the meaning of Christ's death and incurs his **judgment** (cf. Heb. 6:4-8; 10:26-30). Indeed Paul supposes that God's judgment is already being manifested in cases of sickness and death in the Cor. church. It is clear from other passages (e.g. Rom. 1:18; 2:5-9) that Paul believed that God's judgments fall on men in the present as well as the future, but he seems to attribute these disasters at Corinth to a quasi-physical infection resulting from desecration of the Lord's Supper.

The Cors. must therefore **examine** themselves and take an attitude exactly opposite to that which they are displaying at their suppers. The death they memorialize is at once God's sentence of death on man's sin and the surrendering of Christ's life for man's salvation. Thus whenever Christians receive the bread and cup properly they judge themselves guilty before God, accept afresh his verdict on sin, and in faith receive the divine forgiveness (vss. 28, 31). **Discerning the body** (vs. 29) has been variously understood as having reference to Christ's body present in some sense in the bread and wine, or else to Christ's body the church. In this context both meanings may be implied.

11:33-34. If Christ's broken body were truly being remembered at the Cor. church suppers, as the event constitutive of their community, no one would act greedily or in ways which humiliated fellow members. Paul's conclusion is tantalizing to the reader wishing more light on this subject: further instruction will be given during his visit (cf. 16:5-7).

12:1-11. *Spiritual Gifts.* Chs. 12-14 reveal that there were Christians in Corinth who claimed to speak under the spontaneous inspiration of the Spirit of God, and that those possessing such **spiritual gifts** were provoking rivalries and disorder in meetings of the congregation. It was not altogether clear to the church what were the legitimate claims of these **prophets** (vs. 28) or **spiritual** men (14:37), or what were their respective roles in worship. Apparently some members were making extravagant estimates of the importance of speaking in **tongues,** and perhaps also of **prophecy** (vs. 10). As a consequence some leaders lacking these gifts were being lightly esteemed.

The nature of prophecy in the early church is uncertain, and the testimony of the NT concerning the phenomenon of speaking in tongues, i.e. glossolalia, is equivocal (cf. vs. 28; ch. 14; Mark 16:17; Acts 2:4; 10:46). Some light is shed on glossolalia from the comparative studies of historians of religion and from modern recurrences. In general it may be defined as the ecstatic utterance of emotionally agitated religious persons, consisting of a jumble of disjointed and largely unintelligible sounds. Those who speak in this way believe that they are moved directly by a divine spirit, that their utterance is therefore quite spontaneous and unpremeditated.

12:2-3. Paul reminds his readers that some of the evidences of inspiration in the church at Corinth resemble the religious ecstasy of pagans, that the mere fact of ecstatics in their worship is insufficient evidence of the presence of the Spirit of God. It is necessary to test the spirits, and a rule of thumb, so to speak, is given (vs. 3; cf. I Thess. 5:17-21; I John 4:1). The cry **Jesus be cursed** must allude to an actual occurrence. Various possibilities have been suggested—e.g. a Jewish visitor in the Cor. congregation cursing the Christian Savior above the din of ecstatic speaking, an apostate succumbing to public pressures or disillusionment and renouncing his Lord amid noisy worshipers, or an emotional partisan muttering his contempt for those whom he supposes to be preaching "another Jesus" (cf. 16:22; II 11:4; Gal. 1:6-9). Paul's positive criterion is that any person who exalts Jesus as Lord speaks by the Holy Spirit. It is easy to see that this standard does not eliminate all difficulties, as Paul recognizes elsewhere (cf. Phil. 1:15-18). Moreover in this passage Paul acknowledges that only some persons have the capacity to **distinguish between spirits** (vs. 10) and that this capacity is itself a gift (*charisma,* "grace-gift") inspired by the Spirit of God (vss. 4-6).

12:4-7. In beginning his discussion of God's **gifts** to the church Paul emphasizes (*a*) their variety, (*b*) their single source despite the wide differences in their outward manifestations, and (*c*) their common purpose, viz. the good of the entire community rather than of isolated individuals. Perhaps he stresses variety to teach the Cors. the error of looking for leadership to a few persons whose inspiration is manifested in spectacular behavior. Inspiration within the church cannot be so narrowly defined. The common good is served by the contribution of many different types of persons inspired by the Spirit, each possessing a special gift essential to the life of the church.

12:8-9. It is not surprising in this letter to find that Paul gives pride of place to **wisdom** and **knowledge,** for those gifts were conspicuously absent at Corinth, the claims of the church to the contrary notwithstanding (cf. 2:6-3:4). By **faith** he evidently refers, not to faithful acceptance of the gospel, which is essential for any Christian (cf. Rom. 3:22*b*-25; Eph. 2:8), but to that intensity of faith which some manifest in the church (cf. Rom. 12:3; Mark 9:22-24; Matt. 17:20). Occasionally this intense faith evidences itself in performances of **healing** and other mighty works, explained as the outpouring of God's Spirit in the last days (cf. Gal. 3:5).

12:10-11. It is certainly no accident that Paul ends this list with those gifts of the Spirit most highly prized by his readers. Of course he shows a greater sensitivity than they to the problem of differentiating between genuine and spurious **prophecy** and **tongues.** He admits that God endows some persons with these gifts, but he insists that God provides the church with persons gifted to **distinguish between spirits** and others to make some sense of the utterance of the ecstatics. Paul purposes to discuss the mutual dependence of persons possessing these last 4 gifts (ch. 14), but for the moment he is moved to take up the essentially complementary relationship of the entire membership of the church.

12:12-31*a*. *The Members of Christ's Body.* Cf. Rom. 12:4-5. Students of antiquity have found near parallels to Paul's figure of the body and its members in Greek and in Jewish literature, and there has been much speculation concerning the specific source or sources of his ideas. But in any case the practical application in this context is unique. Just as a living organism depends on the proper functioning of not merely some but all of its parts, so does the church. It cannot thrive if it considers some members—the prophets and the "spiritual"—all-important to its well-being and the rest nonessential.

12:22-27. The import of Paul's idea that the inferior **parts,** i.e. members, are more honorable is not clear. Perhaps his words in 1:26-31 are instructive. What is honored by God and in the church seems foolish to the world, which commonly honors spectacular gifts. In any case Paul's metaphor should not be pressed to the wall; his main idea is evident. In any church, as in the natural body, all parts are necessarily interrelated and function for the common good. If any part should attempt to be the whole, or to exist independently, the life of the organism would be threatened; the many parts together constitute a living whole (vs. 27). Whatever mystical overtones one may discern in Paul's figure of the church as Christ's body, his explicit emphasis in this passage is on the church as a cooperative, working body of Christ.

12:28-31a. Paul's 2nd list of **gifts** differs from his first (vss. 8-10). Special significance is assigned to the services of **apostles ... prophets ... teachers** (cf. Eph. 4:11), but it is unlikely that he enumerates the 3 to signify established orders, i.e. offices with a universal status, distinguishing them from the sporadic ministries of individuals such as **healers, helpers,** etc. Again glossolalia appears last. The differences in the 2 lists support the view that there were no fixed patterns for the church's government and ministry in Paul's congregations.

12:31b-13:13. *The Way of Love.* Since love has not been mentioned as a gift in ch. 12 and since prophecy (12:28-29) as a **higher** gift (12:31a) comes up for consideration at the beginning of ch. 14, some scholars think that this famous hymn extolling love is an interpolation. Few doubt that Paul wrote it, but several point to the abrupt transitions at its beginning and end as enforcing their judgment that it did not originally occupy its present position. That Paul's thought should have taken this turn is not unreasonable, however. He has been emphasizing the special services rendered by many different persons for the common good and has touched on the idea of the church as a community of persons whose fellow feeling leads them to care for and share fully with each other. For him love is the supreme gift of the Spirit which marks the church as the body of Christ (cf. Rom. 12:9-10; Col. 3:12-15). No one person in the church possesses all the gifts earlier noted, but every person can receive this particular gift. Indeed everyone should seek it (14:1), else the special gifts fail their purpose.

13:1-3. Ch. 13 does not stand as an erratic block in its present context, for glossolalia and prophecy remain in the foreground. Paul likens Christians who **speak in ... tongues** yet lack love to a noisy combination of instruments used during pagan festivals (vs. 1). He does not disparage prophecy, any more than intense **faith** (vs. 2; cf. Matt. 21:21) and

self-sacrifice (vs. 3; cf. Matt. 6:2-4); but he considers each of these excellent gifts quite valueless without love. The variant reading "that I may boast" instead of **to be burned** (vs. 3) is well attested in the manuscripts. It may be understood as follows: "If I give away all my goods piece by piece and finally give my body [divesting myself of all security and freedom for the sake of others] so that I may boast, and yet withal lack love, I gain nothing."

13:4-6. Paul finds it easier to write of the attitudes and actions which love avoids than to define its qualities. But beginning positively he joins 2 fruits of the Spirit—patience and kindness—as elsewhere in his letters (e.g. Gal. 5:22). Possibly he conceives of kindness as the active counterpart of patience. Here he must be thinking of a Christian's typical actions as the reflex of God's actions toward all men (cf. Rom. 2:4; 9:22; Matt. 5:43-48). It is unlikely that in these vss. Paul draws an abstract or composite picture of the person possessing love. Many commentators have suggested that the traditions concerning Jesus inspired Paul's portraiture, but this is only a surmise. Rather we may be sure that the disorderly situation in the church at Corinth has influenced Paul, that he has chosen his terms with a view to rebuking the arrogant and self-important persons in the church who are behaving so shamefully toward others.

13:7. The precise connotation of this series is uncertain. The verb rendered **bears** has been used earlier in 9:12b, where it is translated "endure." But its primary meaning is "cover" (cf. I Pet. 4:8); and Paul's thought may be that love is prone to keep confidential the faults or mistakes of others, not wishing to make a public issue of them (cf. Moffatt's paraphrase, "slow to expose"). In the Greek **believes** is the verbal form of "faith," and **endures** has the sense of standing one's ground. The repetitious **all things** can also mean "always," i.e. without limitation. Perhaps, therefore, Paul's meaning is: "Love keeps under wraps shameful deeds [so long as there are possibilities for repentance and forgiveness]; love always possesses faith, always hopes, always remains steadfast."

13:8-11. After his description of love's qualities Paul fixes his thought on the lasting power of love in contrast to the ephemeral forces of **prophecy** and **tongues** and **knowledge.** His first analogy contrasting **imperfect** with **perfect** knowledge, childish with adult behavior, may obscure the meaning of the passage for the modern reader, suggesting a natural development toward maturity. Paul's idea is influenced by his expectation of a new age. Appropriate to the age that is passing (cf. 7:29a, 31b) are the ecstatic phenomena, as well as the inspired but partial knowledge through which Christians perceive imperfectly the ways of God with men. But in the coming age these things will be abolished; the need for them will vanish.

13:12. Paul's view that this expectation is already partially fulfilled is manifested in his 2nd figure. It is uncertain what kind of **mirror** he has in mind, the ordinary polished metal one or the magician's distorting mirror; but the greater value of an encounter **face to face** over the reflected image is obvious. That man's knowledge, i.e. acknowledgment of God results from God's knowledge of man is a common biblical belief altogether congenial to Paul's way of thinking (cf. 8:3; Phil. 3:12).

13:13. The words **So faith, hope, love abide,** i.e. last forever, should rather be rendered: "Now [for the present] faith, hope, love remain," i.e. as esp. important. When sight replaces faith and hope is consummated what need will there be for them? (Cf. II 5:7; Rom. 8:24-25.) Paul appeals to the Cors. to turn from their too exclusive, too acquisitive interest in the spectacular gifts to value the **higher gifts** (12:31a) and above all else to make their aim **the greatest of these . . . love.**

14:1-33a. Prophecy and Glossolalia. Paul now gives his judgment that the gift of prophecy is **greater** than that of glossolalia (vs. 5). The prophet speaks intelligibly to the congregation, benefiting all, whereas the speaker in tongues **utters mysteries** without being understood—in the absence of an interpreter— and benefits only himself in his conversation with God (vss. 1-4). The content of Christian prophecy is not defined, except that it is described as an instruction which encourages and consoles the church (cf. vss. 24-25, 29-32).

14:6-12. Paul illustrates in simple analogies the importance of understandable language in the worship of the church. When music and the spoken word are employed for communication they must convey clear meanings.

14:13. This counsel may be understood in 2 ways: either that the ecstatic **should pray for the power to interpret** his experience to the congregation himself, or that he should recognize that his utterance is of no value to others unless an interpreter is present. The 2nd understanding seems preferable, since Paul elsewhere separates the gifts of glossolalia and interpretation (vss. 26-28; cf. 12:10).

14:14-19. The references to **my spirit** and **my mind** are intriguing, both as an analysis of glossolalia and as a contribution to our understanding of Paul's conception of the nature of man. He does not use psychological terms in a consistent way.

Spirit sometimes connotes man's self-awareness or, as we might say, his consciousness (cf. 2:11; Rom. 8:16). At other times, esp. in rhetorical or liturgical passages. Paul writes "my spirit" or "your spirit" simply as a personal designation (cf. e.g. 16:18; Rom. 1:9; Gal. 6:18; Phil. 4:23). But Paul also writes of a special spirit animating man in his activity and orienting his will; in this sense man's spirit is susceptible to the influence of the divine Spirit (cf. 2:12-13; Rom. 8:4-27; Gal. 5:16-18).

Mind likewise has a complex range of meanings in Paul's letters. Usually it connotes man's capacity for judgment or planning—his intelligent grasp of his experience, which under various influences leads either to good or to evil actions (cf. e.g. 2:15-16; Rom. 8:5-8; 12:2). But in relation to such terms as "heart" or "conscience" Paul uses "mind" with other nuances of meaning, and again one must note the lack of precision in rhetorical passages.

In this passage **my mind** clearly refers to Paul's intelligent comprehension of experience, an understanding which makes possible the articulation of its meaning.

14:20-33a. When inspired by the gift of glossolalia Paul's **spirit** is affected by a power which suspends, or at least seriously diminishes, this capacity for understanding. He is not able—or not willing—by any means to quench the impulse of the divine Spirit in his life or in the lives of others (cf. I Thess. 5:19; Rom. 12:11); nor does he wish to deny that glossolalia is a *charisma,* given on occasions to himself as well as to others in the church. But Paul does not seek this particular gift. His decided preference is that he and his converts may have experiences of divine grace which can be understood and interpreted to others in a rational way.

14:20-25. Such an attitude seems to Paul **mature,** in contrast to the attitude of the Cors., which is that of **children.** He therefore undertakes to instruct them by arguing from scripture (vs. 21, a free rendering of Isa. 28:11-12) that **tongues are a sign** given **for unbelievers** and that in comparison with prophecy the phenomenon holds little value for the corporate life of the church. Even its value for these **outsiders** is dubious when its practical effects are compared with those of prophetic preaching. In vss. 24-25 (cf. vss. 29-32) Paul adds somewhat to our limited knowledge of early Christian prophecy by suggesting that an unbeliever may be **convicted** by the prophet's inspired proclamation of the will of God and that while calling him to account the prophet is able to read the **secrets of his heart,** apparently by clairvoyant power (cf. Acts 11:27-28; 21:9-11).

14:26-33a. Paul imposes a pragmatic curb on the **confusion** at Corinth by demanding that in public worship glossolalia be limited to **two or . . . three** ecstatics, one at a time, and that even these be permitted only if an interpreter is present to explain the meaning of the experience to the whole congregation. Otherwise glossolalia should be a private matter. In public worship the emphasis should rather be on prophecy, and even this should be disciplined. It is interesting to note that Paul believes that the prophet can consciously control the spirit of inspiration and that his revelations are **subject to prophets** —probably meaning that the prophets in the congregation are to evaluate one another's utterances.

14:33b-40. Women at Worship. This passage may seem to be an afterthought; some have conjectured that it is a later interpolation. It is logical, however, that in summing up his instruction on spiritual gifts, with his insistence on decency and order in public worship, Paul should be reminded of the reports of the indecorous behavior of the unveiled Cor. women who have been praying—possibly in tongues —and prophesying in the church (11:2-16). He has just written of the discussions and questionings to be expected as a response to the prophets' utterances. He now presupposes that public discussions during the services are the ordinary practice at Corinth, and he counsels that women **keep silence** at such times. **Let them ask their husbands at home.** Doubtless Paul does not mean to deny to women all opportunities for speaking under the impulses of inspiration (cf. 11:5, 13) or to imply that any speech by women in the church is **shameful.**

14:36. Once again (cf. 11:16) Paul's words reflect his acute sensitivity to the weight of opposition at Corinth to his views of women.

14:37-40. By way of protest Paul provides another rule of thumb for distinguishing genuine from spurious ecstasy: those refusing to heed his instruction cannot be truly inspired. Paul's command silencing women has for us historical interest only, but his principle that all things having to do with the church's worship **should be done decently and in order** transcends the local situation at Corinth.

D. RESURRECTION OF THE DEAD (15:1-58)

15:1-2. *The Gospel Paul Preached.* It cannot be accidental that Paul left until last his teaching concerning the resurrection. This formal introduction of the subject supports the view that he considered the resurrection incomparably important. His awkward style, more evident in the Greek, reflects a heightened consciousness both of his responsibility and of that of the Cors. in giving careful thought to this matter. Paul usually employs the future tense about God's deliverance of men rather than the present tense **are saved.** But the qualification **if you hold it,** i.e. the gospel, **fast** preserves the bipolarity in his conception of salvation as conditionally future as well as presently experienced (cf. e.g. 1:18; 3:15).

15:3-11. *The Resurrection Tradition.* On Paul's having **received** the first and most important truths of the gospel and **delivered** them to the Cors. cf. 11:2, 23. The Christian tradition was older than Paul's preaching which disseminated it (cf. vs. 11). Where in this passage does one locate the division between the tradition Paul received and his own commentary? Probably vs. 5 marks the beginning of Paul's comment, though this also was based on traditional reports.

15:3b-4. The formula **in accordance with the scriptures** expresses an important aspect of earliest Christian proclamation, but one which was by no means always self-evident (cf. 1:18; II Cor. 3:4-18). One cannot be sure whether or not Paul knew a particular story of the finding of the empty tomb, such as those in the gospels. He reports as fact: **he was buried, . . . he was raised on the third day.**

15:5-7. Paul considers the postresurrection appearances of Jesus to be the primary—indeed the indispensable—evidence. It is not possible to harmonize satisfactorily his list of these appearances with the other Easter narratives of the NT. Some consider the reference to **more than five hundred brethren** a variant of the Pentecost tradition (Acts 2); others believe it to report a Galilean appearance otherwise unknown. The appearance to **James** is also generally believed to have occurred in Galilee.

15:8. Paul is convinced that the last of these appearances, the one to him (cf. Acts 9:3-6; 22:6-10; 26:13-18), was not unlike the others (cf. 9:1; Gal. 1:1). **As to one untimely born,** lit. "as to the abortion," refers, not to the lateness of this event, but to Paul's sudden appearance among the company of witnesses, which could be likened to a premature birth. Whether "the abortion" was being applied to Paul as a coarse insult by those who opposed his apostleship cannot be known, but Paul thinks of it as a disparaging term.

15:9-11. In view of his origin Paul considers himself **unfit to be called an apostle,** for he **persecuted the church of God** (cf. Gal. 1:13; Acts 8:3; 9:1-2). But God's **grace** converted him and, supported by this grace, he has persevered (cf. II 1:12; 12:9; Rom. 1:5; Gal. 1:15). Since his credentials are ex-

traordinary, in defense of himself he stresses his energetic labors (cf. II 3:1a-3; 11:21b-29).

15:12-19. *The Resurrection of Christ and of Others.* An important question is raised by the argument here, and throughout this ch.: What are the particular persons and beliefs Paul is opposing? Are members of the church at Corinth, who have accepted the incredible mystery of the risen Christ, finding it impossible to believe in the resurrection of others? Paul assumes that there are some persons who are saying that the resurrection of Christians is an impossibility, for in these vss. he explicitly counters this denial.

But are there still others in the church who are misconceiving Paul's proclamation that believers in Christ are risen with him, who are saying that the Christian's resurrection is a past event? (Cf. II Tim. 2:18.) Are some of the self-styled spiritual men (cf. 3:1-3; 4:8) claiming that they are already reigning with Christ? (Cf. Rom. 6:1-11.) Probably so, but there are elements of conjecture in this conclusion. The popular mystery religions (see "The Greco-Roman Background of the NT," pp. 1037-44) were claiming that their initiates had already overcome death and were living the life of the gods, but one cannot be sure to what extent these ideas influenced Christian conceptions of baptism and the Spirit.

Unquestionably there was enormous resistance among the Greeks to the idea that a man's body should survive death to become the instrument of his immortal spirit or soul. Paul's letter has shown that there were some in the church at Corinth who shared this commonplace contempt for the body (see above on 6:12-20). They believed that the body was unaffected in salvation, a view which was a defense on the one hand for libertine behavior and on the other for asceticism. Of special importance in this connection is Paul's earlier reference in the letter to the Christian's resurrection (6:13b-14).

In this reply to Christians denying that dead men are raised it is important to note the form of Paul's argument. It is a circular one, designed to reduce to logical absurdity the position of his opponents. If the **resurrection of the dead,** i.e. of men, is impossible, then the reports of the resurrection of Christ, who was truly a man, must be false, and belief in these reports vain. But without the reality of Christ's resurrection the Christian faith—the whole of it—is without foundation (cf. Rom. 1:3-4; 10:9). Sad conclusions follow: believers are still **in your sins;** those who have died believing **have perished;** and the deluded Christians, who hope for that which cannot be, **are to be pitied.**

15:20-28. *Christ's Resurrection and the End.* Paul appeals to 2 OT motifs in elaborating the consequence of Christ's resurrection. First this event can be described as the **first fruits.** The first sheaf of the harvest, in Paul's time brought to the temple on the first day following the Passover celebration, represented the entire harvest, given by God and consecrated to him (Lev. 23:10-11). Just so the raising of Christ by God's power portends the resurrection of all persons belonging to him (cf. II 1:22; Rom. 8:23; 11:16; Col. 1:15-23).

15:21-22. The all-comprehensive result of the Easter event leads Paul also to introduce the motif of Adam as a "type" of Christ (see above on 10:1-4;

cf. Rom. 5:12-14). Those who are **in Christ,** i.e. who belong to Christ—in contrast to men who are only **in Adam** and are therefore like him destined to die as a consequence of sin—will share in his victory over death (cf. Rom. 6:20-23).

15:24-28. This "little apocalypse" should be placed alongside I Thess. 5:1-11, but neither of these passages should be separated from others which stress the "already fulfilled" aspects of God's purpose in Christ as well as the "not yet completed." Again we observe Paul's assumption that the world lies under the dominion of angelic or demonic rulers (see above on 2:8)—probably as a result of the sin of Adam, or of man (cf. Rom. 8:19-23). Christ's rule will bring to defeat these powers, who are already "doomed" (2:6), and will vanquish **death**—perhaps personified as Satan.

The language of Ps. 8:6 (vs. 27) introduces the thought of the final subordination of all things to God. It is doubtful that Paul wishes his readers to draw the conclusion which some theologians have drawn from this passage by way of qualifying the divinity of Christ. Paul's thought may be that as the representative of redeemed humanity Christ, the Son of man, acknowledges the sole sovereignty of God. The denial of this supremacy of the Creator constituted Adam's fall (cf. Rom. 1:18-25; 5:10; 6:12-14; Phil. 2:5-11).

15:29-34. *The Need for Belief in the Resurrection.* After sketching briefly the drama of the end, Paul resumes his attack on those denying the possibility of man's resurrection. Scribes and commentators have sought to avoid translating vs. 29 as in the RSV, since it is difficult to think that Paul would approve of baptism by proxy. But at this place he is throwing up questions to expose the illogical nature of the beliefs and practices of those denying the resurrection, and he withholds his personal judgment of baptism **on behalf of the dead.**

15:30-32. If death had the last word, Paul argues, his own courage and that of other Christians would be foolish bravado. **Die every day** (vs. 31) is not merely rhetorical; Paul thinks of the sacrificial pattern of his life as a crucifixion (cf. II 4:8-12; Gal. 6:14, 17). The reference to having **fought with beasts at Ephesus** has provoked speculation. Were there gladiatorial contests at Ephesus? If so, was Paul thrown into the arena? Then how did he escape? Was Paul only threatened with this possibility? The reference seems to be to a specific crisis. But Acts 19 and Paul's catalog of personal crises in II 11:23-29 afford no support to the hypothesis that Paul actually fought against wild animals at Ephesus, and most scholars take the allusion to be figurative. The quotation in vs. 32b is from Isa. 22:13.

15:33-34. Who provide the **bad company** Paul warns against in his quotation from the Greek dramatist Menander (4th cent. B.C.)? Those denying the resurrection? More probably those persons having **no knowledge of God**—as we might say, the materialists in Cor. society. The attitudes of the libertines in the church already reflect such ruinous influences.

Come to your right mind may be rendered: "Become sober [i.e. awake from your drunken sleep] as is fitting." By the use of a common figure of speech Paul appeals once again to the expectation of the Lord's coming at any moment (cf. 16:13; Rom. 13:11-14; I Thess. 5:2-11).

Some commentators have protested that Paul's argument in this passage is not strong, that denial of man's resurrection does not result in cutting the nerve of moral effort, encouraging profligacy, and rendering all **good morals** profitless. But Paul cannot view any man's life which is separated from faith and hope in Christ as other than meaningless (cf. II 5:16-17; Phil. 3:3-11; Eph. 2:12).

15:35-50. *The Resurrected Body.* The burden of Paul's argument in this important passage is that there is both a radical difference and a real continuity between the body that dies and the body that is raised by God's power. He turns here from the fact of the resurrection to a description, insofar as he can give one, of the **kind of body** which survives death.

15:36-41. To those **foolish** men who can conceive of no embodiment of the human spirit other than a grossly material one Paul recalls the miracles of creation—in the transformation of bare seeds into plants (vss. 36-38) and in the great variety of its **bodies,** each possessing a **glory** of its own, appropriate to its function and environment (vss. 39-41). So by analogy one can reflect on the miracles of God's new creation.

15:42-44a. The thrust of these antitheses is that the **spiritual body** that is raised, while linked to the **physical body** as seed to plant, has a unique glory qualitatively superior to the weak body which dies.

15:44b-49. Realizing that arguments based on logical deductions from natural processes are insufficient, and recalling the only adequate basis of the Christian hope, Paul affirms that the paradoxical term **spiritual body** derives its meaning from Christ's own resurrection, that Christians themselves hope to possess such a spiritual body because of their faith in him who as **man**—the Son of man—became for men a **life-giving spirit.** Christ as the **last Adam** (see above on vss. 21-22) marks for Paul the beginning of the new creation. Christians who have borne—and continue to bear—the image of the **man of dust** (cf. Gen. 2:7) **shall also bear the image of the man of heaven** (cf. Phil. 3:20-21). This hope has its present counterpart in Paul's conviction that men in Christ already bear this image, though not visibly (cf. II 3:18; Rom. 8:9-11, 22-25; Gal. 2:20; 4:19; Col. 3:9-10). Note the textual variant in vs. 49 (see RSV footnote). Either reading is compatible with Paul's thought, but the context seems to require the future tense.

15:50. This emphatic statement shows the measure of Paul's agreement with a conclusion commonly held among Greeks; Christian belief in the resurrection is not to be confused with the revivification of the body that is buried.

15:51-58. *The Assurance of Immortality.* Unlike the esoteric truths of the mystery cults Paul's **mystery** is a divine revelation to be published abroad. Change is the dominant idea in this summation of his teaching about the coming day. Not only will the dead undergo transformation in the resurrection, but with the final coming of Christ the living will also be **changed** (cf. I Thess. 4:13-18). His belief in the imminence of the end is further manifested. On the **trumpet** cf. Isa. 27:13.

15:53. Paul's use of the term translated **immortality** must not become a basis for confusing his hope with the immortality of the soul, the survival beyond death of man's disembodied spirit. The whole of Paul's teaching runs counter to this speculation in Greek philosophy. The expression **put on immortality** superficially resembles the language of the mystery religions, but Paul's teaching opposes the ideas of rebirth and deification set forth in the pagan cults.

15:54-57. The exultant cry in vss. 54-55 echoes OT passages (Isa. 25:8; Hos. 13:14) but not the conclusions reached in them; apart from Christ's **victory** no such conclusion is possible. Paul views **sin** as death's weapon to destroy man and the **law** as increasing the power of sin rather than correcting it (vs. 56); this epigrammatic parenthesis becomes intelligible in the light of Romans 7:7-25.

15:58. Some of Paul's contemporaries, and later interpreters, distorted his expectation of the new age into a quietistic, otherworldly hope, but this statement stresses the ethical implications which he drew directly from his belief.

E. FINAL EXHORTATIONS AND PERSONAL NOTES (16:1-18)

16:1-4. *The Offering.* Paul's instructions are concluded on a practical note, but not only so. The **contribution for the saints** was prompted by the material needs of the poor among the Christians in Jerusalem (cf. Rom. 15:26), but also by Paul's desire to manifest the unity of the church. The apostle to the Gentiles was asked by the Jerusalem Jewish Christians to raise money for their needy (cf. Gal. 2:10) and he accepted this mission with enthusiasm, believing that his converts would benefit from it (cf. II 8:1-5). Paul's advice that the money be gathered **every week** may reflect something more than his concern for regularity in giving. He may remember some embarrassment, at Corinth or elsewhere, caused by a single hasty solicitation. Be that as it may, the situation at Corinth warrants his careful plans for the handling of the money.

16:5-9. *Paul's Travel Plans.* Paul's itinerary disclosed here corresponds to the travel notes in Acts 19:21; 20:1-2. He wishes to explain why he is not able to come directly to Corinth. At a later time (II 1:16) he defends himself against the charge that at **Ephesus** he has been "vacillating." At this time, however, an overland trip through **Macedonia** seems necessary. Paul's movements are directed by God's Spirit and not merely by his personal inclinations (vs. 7*b*). Paul's plans were changed at a later time, according to the implications of II 2:1. An emergency situation arose which occasioned a "painful" visit sometime between the writing of this passage and II Cor.

16:10-18. *Requests Concerning Colleagues.* This letter is to arrive at Corinth before **Timothy** (cf. 4:17). Perhaps Timothy already has left for Macedonia en route to Corinth—possibly with Erastus (cf. Acts 19:22; Rom. 16:23). Paul is not certain what sort of reception his emissary will receive. Does he suppose that Timothy's shyness (cf. II Tim.

1:7) may prevent him from carrying out his mission? The Cors. must not discourage Paul's youthful colleague, but speed him on his return.

16:12. Apparently **Apollos** has come back to Ephesus after his work at Corinth (cf. Acts 18:24–19:1). Paul writes as he does concerning Apollos to rid his readers of all suspicion that he opposes Apollos or is jealous of his influence. In the Greek of this vs. the word **God's** does not appear but may be implied; from the construction it is not certain whether it is the **will** of Apollos or of God which has resisted Paul's urging, but Paul is sure that Apollos will return to Corinth sooner or later.

16:13-14. Several ethical injunctions are interposed here. The watchwords of vs. 13 give expression to keen expectation of the end (cf. I Thess. 5:6; II Thess. 2:15; Mark 13:34-37; Rev. 16:15). In view of its imminence these attitudes or responses are enjoined, but in view of ch. 13 there stands fittingly as Paul's "last word": **Let all that you do** (lit. "let all that comes from you") **be done in love.**

16:15-18. The phrase **first converts** is lit. "first fruits" (cf. 15:20). Perhaps the **household of Stephanas** assisted with the offering of vss. 1-4; the Greek word translated **service** here is used to refer to it in II 8:4; 9:1, 12, 13. Paul does not write of Stephanas and his companions as holding an official status in the Cor. church. But he urges an unruly congregation to give deference to men who are qualified by their services to receive its respect.

F. THE CONCLUSION (16:19-24)

16:19-21. *Closing Greetings.* Paul thinks of all the **churches** as forming one church (cf. 1:2, 13; 12:27). It is therefore fitting for congregations in the province of **Asia**, i.e. W Asia Minor, to send greetings to the Cors., along with those from **Aquila and Prisca**, who with Paul founded the church in Corinth (cf. Acts 18:2, 18). Apparently this couple established house churches wherever they lived (cf. Rom. 16:5). The custom of a **holy kiss** arose spontaneously in the early church (cf. II 13:12; I Thess. 5:26; I Pet. 5:14). Later it was a part of the ritual of Christian worship, but it came into disfavor with changing social attitudes. Paul sometimes wished to authenticate his letters by a signature **with my own hand** (cf. Col. 4:18; II Thess. 3:17; Philem. 19).

16:22-24. *Imprecation and Benediction.* Did the thought of sending this letter on its way bring a fleeting premonition of impending crisis? The imprecation in vs. 22 has been compared with the anxious note at the ending of other letters (e.g. Gal. 6:11-17). Some commentators have sought to recover an ancient liturgy from this letter's concluding passage. **Our Lord, come!** translates an old Aramaic phrase, *maranatha*, which most versions of the NT have left untranslated. It could be the indicative form—"The Lord is coming"—thus reflecting a creedal formula of the early church. But the imperative, as an ejaculatory prayer, is more probable (cf. Rev. 22:20). According to an early (*ca.* A.D. 100) book of church order, the Didache (10:6), *maranatha* stood at the ending of the Lord's Supper prayers. After the usual benediction invoking the Lord's **grace**, Paul assures his readers that in spite of their many faults he loves them all.

THE SECOND LETTER
OF PAUL TO THE CORINTHIANS

JAMES L. PRICE

[For introduction see Intro. to I Cor.]

I. EPISTOLARY INTRO. (1:1-11)

1:1-2. Salutation. In resuming his correspondence with the Cors. Paul associates himself with **Timothy,** his emissary to them (cf. I 4:17; 16:10-11); but the personal nature of the things he is now moved to write excludes any contribution to the letter by Timothy. The Roman province of **Achaia,** of which Corinth was the capital, comprised all of Greece S of Macedonia (see color map 16). Paul's greeting joins the blessings of **grace** and **peace from God,** terms which connote for him an objective status—a condition of life—and not merely subjective feelings (cf. Rom. 5:1-11). It also affirms the earliest Christian confessional statement: **Jesus Christ** is the **Lord** of the church.

1:3-7. Thanksgiving for God's Comfort. Paul's thanksgivings—which regularly follow his salutations, as was customary in personal letters of the period—are always directed toward God. But it is noteworthy that here he addresses God as **Father of our Lord Jesus Christ** (cf. Col. 1:3; Eph. 1:3, 17). God's **mercies** and **comfort** have been made known to Paul through his sharing in the sufferings of Christ (cf. 4:10-12; Rom. 8:17; Phil. 3:10-11; Col. 1:24). This could mean simply that his own sufferings resemble those which his Lord endured. But Paul's conviction that faith establishes a vital union between the believer and his Lord—a union which he describes elsewhere as a crucifixion with Christ (Rom. 6:6; Gal. 2:20)—suggests that he is identifying his sufferings with the historical suffering and death of Jesus in a realistic way, that he believes they are in some way a continuation of Jesus' passion. Of course he does not conceive of his sufferings as an apostle as having redemptive value, nor does he believe that the cross of Jesus was somehow an incomplete action of God (cf. I 1:13). But as the founder and father of this church he has been called to bear special affliction on its behalf and also to receive special assurance. From this paradoxical experience of suffering and comfort the church derives special benefit. Also as fellow members of Christ's body the Cors. are themselves liable to share in the sufferings of Christ. In the midst of these they can also share abundantly his comfort. The union of all believers in Christ's crucifixion and resurrection carries with it the inference that those who are Christ's are fully sharing his comfort as they participate in his suffering (cf. I 15:29b-32).

1:8-11. Deliverance from a Deadly Peril. Turning from the general to the specific, Paul recalls a particular **affliction** suffered **in Asia**—i.e. the Roman province comprising W Asia Minor, of which Ephesus was the capital. Evidently his Cor. readers already knew of the incident, since he rehearses no details. Modern readers may recall his allusion to having "fought with beasts at Ephesus" (I 15:32; cf. I 16:9) but still are left in the dark. Acts 19:23-41 reports a riot caused by Paul's preaching at Ephesus but mentions nothing which would cause Paul to feel he **had received the sentence of death** (vs. 9a). This is in fact the first of several dark allusions in this letter to specific events and situations which cannot be recovered. It is evident, however, that deliverance from this crushing experience has imprinted itself vividly in Paul's memory. It affords him a ground for **hope** and confidence which cannot be shaken by subsequent disasters. The Cors. can be expected to share, and to support, Paul's assurance through their **prayers.**

II. REVIEW OF RECENT RELATIONS WITH THE CORS. (1:12–2:17)

A. PAUL'S DEFENSE OF HIS INTEGRITY (1:12–2:4)

1:12-14. Sincerity in Act and Word. Paul is convinced that in his dealings with the Cors. he has been forthright and consistent. His term **boast** and its cognates appear 29 times in II Cor.—always with an apology, for he believes that the Christian has but one cause for boasting, his Lord (cf. I 1:28-31; Rom. 3:27-28). Yet he feels compelled to specify his legitimate claims when they are disputed, and he cannot fail to commend specific actions he has taken when they are being distorted so as to appear vicious. He has written in the same straightforward manner exhibited in his actions. His speech has not been adorned with sophistical rhetoric, so typical of popular teachers of wisdom (cf. I 2:1-5); awareness of the **grace of God** has inhibited such conceit. With the coming of the Lord Jesus the Cors. will justly be proud of him, as he will be of them, though now they suffer him to be maligned. At least their partial understanding gives him confidence that progress in the interim may be expected (cf. Phil. 1:9).

1:15–2:4. Explanation of Changed Plans. Evidently some persons at Corinth have been seriously doubting Paul's integrity. They have been accusing him of disparity between promise and deed, of **vacillating**

813

in decisions and saying **Yes and No at once.** Paul feels these charges so keenly that in setting the record straight he twice takes oath to the truth of his statements.

1:15-17. Paul felt a need for as many visits to this church as possible while he was in the area. To afford a **double pleasure,** he says, he **wanted** to visit Corinth before going to **Macedonia** and then to return there from Macedonia before leaving for Jerusalem (see color map 16). The Cors. were evidently informed of this desire and took it as a promise of an additional early visit not included in the itinerary announced to them in I 16:5-9. But when the time came to leave Ephesus, Paul reverted to his original plan; instead of making the promised visit he set off for Macedonia another way (cf. 2:12). This changing back and forth Paul now defends.

1:18-22. Paul's first oath, **As surely as God is faithful,** leads him to write of Christ as the positive fulfillment of God's **promises** to his people. At first sight one may suppose that Paul digresses aimlessly. But perhaps he wishes to make explicit certain theological motives for his own faithfulness since some in Corinth have their doubts. His fidelity to his calling is grounded in his grateful response to God's work revealed in the gospel of his Son, and in his awareness of his commission as an apostle, which has been sealed by the Spirit. All of his plans and actions relating to the Cors. must be viewed in this perspective. On Silvanus (Silas) **and Timothy** (vs. 19) cf. Acts 18:5. The legal figure of a **guarantee** (vs. 22; cf. 5:5), i.e. the first installment of a payment to be made in full, parallels closely the cultic figure of "first fruits" in Rom. 8:23 (cf. I 15:20). The gift of the Holy Spirit following Christ's resurrection provides a substantial anticipation—a promise and a pledge—of the new age that is to come.

1:23-2:2. Returning to his self-defense, Paul takes a 2nd oath that it was to **spare** the Cors. that he abandoned his plan of going to Corinth on his way to Macedonia. He was determined not to make **another painful visit** to them. The visit alluded to, Paul's 2nd to Corinth (cf. 12:14; 13:1-2), is not mentioned in Acts. Evidently it occurred after the writing of I Cor., though a few scholars have tried to locate it beforehand (see below on 2:3-4). When Timothy returned to Ephesus after his follow-up visit to Corinth (I 4:17; 16:10-11), bringing a report that I Cor. had effected little or no improvement in the situation there, Paul no doubt decided that an immediate personal visit was called for. Accordingly we may suppose that he went directly to Corinth by sea and after the painful encounter returned at once to his work in Ephesus. Such a quick trip might well be omitted by the author of Acts.

2:3-4. After the painful visit Paul wrote a letter to the Cors. **out of much affliction and anguish of heart.** It was a stern letter yet intended not to **cause** more **pain** but to obviate it. A few scholars interpret this as a reference to I Cor., but the description of the letter and of Paul's mood while composing it does not suit the contents of that letter, and the circumstances of its writing seem to call for a later time (see above on 1:23-2:2). On the other hand, many scholars believe instead that a substantial part of this severe letter is preserved in chs. 10-13 (see Intro. to I Cor.).

B. A Plea to Let Bygones Be Bygones (2:5-17)

2:5-11. *Forgiveness of the Offender.* Once again Paul refers allusively to a particular event. The action of some person in the congregation at Corinth **caused pain.** The reference seems to be to a public rather than a private incident; the whole church was pained by someone's defiance of Paul. Those scholars who identify the letter of vss. 3-4 with I Cor. equate this offender with the incestuous man of I 5:1-5. But that offender was to be handed over to Satan, and it is unlikely that that injunction was later revoked, for incest was more serious than personal defiance. Rather Paul must refer here to someone who flouted his authority in the presence of the congregation during his painful visit (vs. 1). In his letter (vs. 9) he demanded this offender's punishment, but now he acknowledges that punitive action has been taken by the church and asks that the offender be forgiven.

2:6-8. The term **majority** might suggest that a recalcitrant minority are still rejecting Paul's authority, but 7:14-15 refers to the church's total obedience. Perhaps the minority are wishing to inflict a more severe punishment and this instruction to forgive is directed esp. to them.

2:9-11. Paul wishes to play down the personal affront (vs. 10), yet in the words which follow it is evident that he does not make light of the offense. When he writes of **Satan** as **gaining the advantage** it is not a mere dramatic figure of speech. The thought that any believer in Christ might be severed from him and delivered to Satan's power for destruction (cf. I 5:4b-5) makes Paul tremble. No doubt it was fear that the Cor. congregation as a whole might succumb to this fate worse than death that so unsettled him in this crisis. In his severe letter he probably laid down an ultimatum, subjecting his church to this final **test:** unless its members repented he would be driven to deliver them all to Satan's power. With an almost inexpressible sense of relief he puts this dreadful crisis behind him. The church has met the test; hopefully its members will continue to do so. Yet the possibility that they may fail cannot be completely dispelled (cf. 13:5-10).

2:12-13. *Anxiety in Troas.* When dispatching his severe letter Paul evidently informed its bearer, **Titus** (cf. Gal. 2:1-3), of his own itinerary in detail, with instructions to meet him and report on the letter's reception as soon as possible. Then Paul himself set out N from Ephesus, probably overland, to **Troas** at the NW tip of Asia Minor near the site of ancient Troy (cf. Acts 16:8-11; 20:5-13; see color map 16). Now he tells the Cors. of his great distress of mind as he vainly hoped that Titus would meet him at this seaport. He was afforded opportunities there for preaching the gospel, but his traumatized emotions kept him from entering this open **door** (cf. I 16:8; Col. 4:3). Therefore he crossed the Aegean to **Macedonia,** probably to Philippi (cf. Acts 16:11-12).

2:14-17. *Triumph in Christ.* Without actually reporting that Titus at length met him in Macedonia with good news (cf. 7:5-16) Paul implies it by interrupting his story with an outburst of thankfulness toward God, thankfulness for the triumphs of Christ in which his apostle shares. Certain scholars find the break so abrupt that they believe a part of a different letter, extending through 7:4, has been interpolated here (see Intro.). Paul is moved to drive home to his readers the true significance of his ministry as an apostle, taking advantage of the wedge which has been fixed by the reinstatement of his authority at Corinth. His journey to Corinth now becomes a victory march. In imagination he sees Christ marching **in triumph,** leading his apostles in his train. He surveys now his ministry as a whole, not just his work in Achaia: everywhere **Christ always leads us in triumph.** The good word from Corinth makes Paul confidently expect this comprehensive victory.

2:14b-16. The gospel of Christ is depicted as the **fragrance** of God's **knowledge,** the apostle as a person deputized to spread the **aroma of Christ.** The precise reference of this latter detail is not certain. Perhaps Paul likens the influence of his ministry to an incense sometimes used in the processions of royalty, or perhaps he thinks of his own life as an aroma of sacrifice (cf. Rom. 12:1; Phil. 2:17; Eph. 5:2; Gen. 8:21; Exod. 29:18). In either case Paul thinks of an apostle of Christ as the messenger both of **life** and of **death,** of salvation and of judgment. Rabbinical scholars have held that the metaphors used by Paul in vs. 15 were common among Jewish writers, who spoke of the Mosaic law as the aroma of life to the good but of death to the evil.

2:17. Before launching on a long digression concerning the source and nature of his ministry Paul again defends himself. In this letter he is unable to forget for long those in Corinth who are impugning his integrity as an apostle. The phrase **like so many** gives the first hint that they include not merely recalcitrant members of the Cor. church but also visiting **peddlers of God's word** who have sought to undermine his influence and draw the congregation into their own orbit (see below on 3:1-3, 7-18; 11:4-6).

III. The Apostle's Ministry (3:1-6:10)

This section is a lengthy digression contrasting, after the manner of rabbinic discourse, the ministries of the Mosaic law and of the Spirit given with the Christian proclamation.

A. Letters of Recommendation (3:1-3)

The implication of a question he has just written (2:16b) holds Paul's attention momentarily. Surely he has been made **sufficient** for his ministry, yet he finds it necessary to commend himself to the Cors. **Again** may refer simply to the earlier self-commendation in this letter (1:12), but it is likely that boasting in the severe letter (cf. 2:3-4) provoked criticism. **Some,** i.e. the rival teachers (see above on 2:17), have brought **letters of recommendation**—from another church or possibly from the apostles in Jerusalem (see below on 11:22-23)—but the only such letter Paul should need is the church members themselves. This letter is written on his own heart—"our" is better attested in the manuscripts than **your** (vs. 2; see RSV footnote; cf. I 9:2). Paul passes up no opportunity to reassure the Cors. of his affection. Moreover the Christians at Corinth are a **letter**

from Christ; i.e. through their thriving, though far from perfect, community they commend the gospel to the world. **Delivered,** lit. "ministered," here probably means "written from dictation"; i.e. the Cor. Christians are a letter of which Christ is the author and Paul is the scribe. This letter has been written, **not on tablets of stone,** like the law in the days of Moses, but on **human hearts** (cf. Jer. 31:33).

B. The Ministry of the New Covenant (3:4-4:18)

3:4-6. Sufficiency from God. Paul's authority and his **confidence** as an apostle are grounded in the fact that God has **qualified** him, lit. "made [him] sufficient," as the minister of a **new covenant** (cf. I 11:25; Jer. 31:31) **in the Spirit.** This contrasts with the old covenant **in a written code,** lit. "in the letter"—i.e. the Mosaic law.

3:7-18. The Splendor of This Ministry. Some interpreters consider that this passage is directed against the visiting teachers alluded to in 2:17; 3:1, whom they accordingly identify as Judaizers, i.e. Jewish Christians seeking to impose on the Cors. the demands of the law (see below on 11:4-6 and Intro. to Gal.). But the thrust of Paul's commentary is not that the gospel abrogates the demands of the law, e.g. circumcision and the food restrictions. Rather he emphasizes here the **permanent,** i.e. new-age, splendor manifested in Christ and in his church, as contrasted with the **fading,** i.e. present-age, splendor of the revelation to Moses.

3:7-11. The word translated **dispensation** in these vss. is lit. "ministry," which is the theme of this section. The rabbis used the narrative of Moses' transfiguration (Exod. 34:29-35) to magnify the lawgiver's lasting glory. Paul uses it to exhibit the limited significance of Moses' ministry of **death** and **condemnation** in contrast with the ministry of the Spirit. Of course he does not wish to deny the glory of Israel's law (cf. Rom. 3:2-3; 7:12; 9:4-5). He is intent only on showing that the transient glory and historical role of the old covenant has been surpassed by the glory of Christ (vs. 10; cf. 4:6).

3:12-13. Paul treats Moses as a "type" (see comment on I 10:1-4) not of Christ but of the apostles and their ministry, which is his main interest in this passage. Their ministry is a manifestation of God's glory and so can be compared with the ministry of Moses. But the apostles' **hope** in the permanent makes them **very bold,** in contrast to Moses, who according to Paul's interpretation used a **veil** to hide the transiency of his ministry.

3:14-16. It is noteworthy that Paul's conception of the gospel as the fulfillment of Judaism is often linked with his consciousness of its rejection by his "kinsmen by race" (Rom. 9:3). In this passage the **veil** of Moses symbolizes for him the blindness of Jews to the divine glory that is Christ's. If only they would turn to **the Lord,** i.e. Christ, this **veil ... over their minds** would be lifted. We may sense the pathos in his development of this figure (cf. Rom. 10:1-17). Paul's phrase **old covenant** (vs. 14) is the source of the Christian name "Old Testament" for the Hebrew Scriptures. The Greek word meant both "covenant" and "testament"; the Latin translators who chose the latter sense in this passage were no doubt influenced by Paul's argument from that meaning of the word in Gal. 3:15-17 (cf. Heb. 9:15-17).

3:17-18. The statement **Now the Lord is the Spirit** provides the most explicit evidence that Paul equated in his thought the risen Lord Jesus and the Holy Spirit. He is able to use "Christ" and "Spirit" interchangeably in his letters; both indwell believers and the church. But it is not correct to say that Paul intends to draw a simple identity, any more than a sharp distinction. Though in this context **we** means the apostles, it is probably that in vs. 18 Paul intends **we all** to apply to all Christians (cf. vs. 16).

4:1-18. *Hope Despite Affliction.* Paul again becomes polemical. The undercurrent of defensiveness, never far beneath the surface of his comforting reassurances in this letter, now erupts vigorously. There is nothing **underhanded,** lit. "hidden," about his ministry!

4:3-6. The imminence of the end, as Paul understands it, explains both the blindness of unbelievers and the undaunted hope of the apostles. In the coming of the Christ the divine glory has been finally manifested; his coming can be likened to a new creation (vss. 4*b*, 6; cf. 5:17; Gal. 6:15; Gen. 1:3). Yet in Paul's view the end of the present age coincides with the beginning of the age to come (see comment on I 10:1-11:1). In the concluding time of the age that is passing (cf. I 7:31) angelic world rulers influence for ill the decisions and actions of men (cf. 2:6; 6:3; 11:10; 15:24). Among these invisible powers is Satan, called here the **god of this world,** lit. "of this age," who has **blinded the minds of unbelievers** to prevent them from perceiving God's **light** in Christ.

4:7-12. The apostles of Christ also contend with Satan, who designs to gain an advantage over them and over their converts (cf. 2:11). Besides this they face all sorts of affliction, carrying **in the body the death of Jesus.** For the present the **treasure** of their apostolic ministry is held in **earthen vessels,** i.e. fragile pots and jars, so that it may be recognized that the **transcendent power belongs to God.**

4:13-18. Paul quotes Ps. 116:10 to confirm that it is **faith** that sustains his preaching. In this faith in a coming salvation he joins with himself his Cor. readers, as fellow members of the body of Christ. Paul is not minded to conceive of his own salvation apart from that of his converts, just as he cannot consider the benefit of his own suffering and consolation apart from them (cf. 1:6-7). With the coming of the end the god of this world and all other powers will be subjugated and God will raise from the dead all those persons who belong to the Lord Jesus (cf. I 15:24-28; Rom. 6:3-5; 8:18-25, 28-30). The thought of God's **grace** abounding for many leads him to be confident of a comprehensive victory in the face of all destructive forces (cf. Rom. 5:19-21).

C. The Hope of an Eternal Home (5:1-10)

5:1-5. *Longing for the Inheritance.* This section has attracted much attention, not only because Paul's hope of life after death possesses an intrinsic interest, but because some interpreters see differences between the hope expressed here and that in I 15:42-53; I Thess. 4:14-17. Paul writes here, not of the immortality of the soul of man, but of the spiritual body of the resurrection, conceived first as a heavenly **house,** then as a heavenly garment. His similitudes are drawn from rabbinical and apocalyptic interpretations of the biblical traditions. The **tent** life of the Israelites during their wilderness sojourn—commemorated in the annual feast of Tabernacles—provides a meaningful context for his gospel of fulfillment (cf. Heb. 11:8-10, 13-16) to his readers of Greek as well as Jewish background.

Paul is contrasting the Christian's present existence with a future mode of existence **prepared** by God (vs. 5). This inheritance is now ready to be possessed by those who have received the Spirit in baptism as a **guarantee,** i.e. down payment (see above on 1:18-22). Therefore Paul can write that we **have** it (vs. 1; cf. Rom. 8:19-25).

Believing that the end will come soon, Paul hopes to inherit his **heavenly dwelling** before having to experience death. By a change of figure he expresses his longing that a new garment may be **put on** over the old one, i.e. that his present body before its dissolution at death may be changed into a spiritual body. The idea of having to exist after death without any body, of being **found naked** at the last day, is abhorrent to him. He is therefore unable to speculate about an intermediate state, and we do not find here material for a doctrine on the nature of a Christian's existence between death and the general resurrection at the last day.

5:6-10. *The Coming Judgment.* Paul is able to persist with **good courage** in the knowledge that he is supported by the Spirit (cf. Rom. 8:22-27). It may seem surprising that he can write of being **away from the Lord** (vs. 6), since he feels so keenly the reality of Christ's presence (cf. e.g. Gal. 2:20). A parenthetical clause (vs. 7) provides a clarification: to be **in the body** does not imply separation from Christ, but the Christian's union with Christ through **faith** is imperfect in comparison with his vision of Christ when hope is fulfilled (cf. I 13:9-10, 12). Consequently Paul longs for the consummation of Christ's kingdom, and indeed for his own death, if by this means he may be **at home with the Lord.** But this outlook does not lead him to otherworldly contemplation. Rather he seeks by every means to **please** his Lord here and now (cf. I 15:58; Phil. 1:21-24).

5:10. Prospect of the full exposure of man's life **before the judgment seat of Christ,** an essential element in Paul's expectation, is not a threat but an encouragement. His conception of salvation includes a belief in the moral accountability of the man of faith. No one is saved by his works, but only by a faithful response to God's grace revealed in Christ (cf. I 3:11-15; Rom. 2:6-11; 3:21-28). Nevertheless **what he has done in the body** must be submitted to Christ's judgment.

D. The Ministry of Reconciliation (5:11-6:10)

5:11-13. *Serving God and the Cors.* While Paul is confident that his aims and motives are manifest to God, the situation at Corinth is not fully predictable. Perhaps his readers will suppose that he is **commending** himself **again** (see above on 3:1-3). The vagueness of the statements in vss. 12-13 suggests that he intends to say more about those in the church priding themselves **on a man's position and not on his heart** as well as to deal more directly with the charge of being **beside ourselves** (cf. chs. 12-13). His concern for the moment is that the Cors. recognize the sober, straightforward way he has dealt with the misunderstandings which arose between them. His actions have sought not personal advantage but the church's good.

5:14-17. *The Love of Christ.* The primary reason Paul cannot live for himself is his keen apprehension of the love of Christ, revealed in his death **for all** (cf. Rom. 5:6-8). The verb translated **we are convinced** recalls a conviction formed in the past. Possibly Paul's first experience of the risen Christ led to the acknowledgment that if Jesus as Messiah brought divine forgiveness to those he gathered around him then the benefits of his death are for all men.

5:14b-15. The meaning of Paul's conclusion **therefore all have died** is not obvious. Does he mean that, since Christ died the death which sinners deserve to die, he died in their stead, in their behalf? Cf. I 11:25; Rom. 5:21; Gal. 3:13-14. Or does he refer here to the death—the crucifixion—which men undergo in giving their faith response to the Cross and in the act of receiving baptism? Cf. Rom. 6:6-11; Gal. 6:14; Col. 3:3. Interpreters are sharply divided. It appears that the context is not decisive, for Paul's concern is not to explicate a doctrine of the Atonement. Rather he is insisting that the consequence of Christ's death and resurrection is that Christians are bound to **live no longer for themselves but for him.**

5:16-17. As a result of this redirection of his own life Paul affirms that he is now unable to judge anyone from a **human point of view,** lit. "according to the flesh." Before his conversion he so regarded all men, even Jesus. He viewed the traditions of Jesus' teaching and claims as blasphemous, and the cross as a shameful thing, God's curse (cf. Gal. 1:13-14; 3:13b). But since becoming a man **in Christ** he has been convinced that God's **new creation** has begun. As he writes elsewhere, those who are in Christ Jesus no longer think or act according to the flesh, but according to the Spirit (Rom. 8:1-8).

5:18-6:2. *The Urgency of Reconciliation.* In the new creation (vs. 17), as in the beginning, all things are the work of God: **in Christ** he was **reconciling the world to himself,** i.e. overcoming the rebellion of his creatures, **not counting their trespasses against them** (vs. 19; cf. 4:6). The initiative of God in the coming of Christ is viewed by Paul against the background of man's revolt. God is the reconciler even though he is the one against whom man sets himself. The gospel of the crucified Christ has revealed to Paul the gravity of man's situation, his hopeless complicity in Adam's sin, his banishment from God's presence, his subjection to God's wrath (cf. Rom. 1:18-32; 5:12-14) as well as the wonder of God's reconciling work in Jesus Christ.

This imagery of enmity and reconciliation, i.e. peace, runs parallel in Paul's thought to his imagery of guilt and justification, i.e. acquittal. This is shown explicitly in Rom. 5:1-11. In his application of the legal or forensic figure of justification by grace Paul emphasizes the wonder of divine forgiveness. In the development of this image of personal relations, the reconciliation of those who are estranged, Paul emphasizes the gracious quality of divine love. The event which determined the appropriateness of these complementary metaphors is for Paul the death of Christ (vs. 21; cf. Rom. 3:24-25; 5:9-10). God's unconditioned forgiveness, his gracious act of reconciliation, were thereby shown to involve great cost to himself.

In referring to the **world** Paul probably has in mind the restoration of all things, i.e. the whole of creation, which he conceives to be "in bondage to corruption"—an opposition to God transcending the rebellion of all mankind "in Adam" (Rom. 5:12-14; 8:19-25). But again we should note that Paul is offering the Cors. no theory of the Atonement. Rather he is proclaiming the way of reconciliation and the imperative need that man accept the way which God has provided.

5:20. God makes his appeal through men who are **ambassadors for Christ.** This term, like "apostle," emphasizes both the representative and the authoritative nature of the work of men so designated to act **for Christ.**

5:21-6:2. Paul returns to the reality which gives content and power to the Christian's proclamation. Vs. 21 is epigrammatic. Paul shares the belief of other NT writers that Jesus **knew no sin,** i.e. never sinned by his own decision or action (cf. Heb. 4:15; I Pet. 2:22; I John 3:5). Yet in some sense God in Christ took on himself the sin of the world (cf. John 1:29-34). This conception lies at the root of all "substitutionary" theories of the Atonement: Christ, though not himself a sinner, identified himself with man in his sin, becoming so involved in it that he shared man's fate and dealt effectively with his predicament. Though this conviction is often held to be intrinsic to Christian faith and hope, and is certainly not unreasonable, Paul resists in principle all claims to rational explanation of it (cf. I 1:21-25, 30; 2:1-5; Rom. 8:3). Rather, conscious of the imminence of the end, he quotes Isa. 49:8 to underscore the urgency of immediate acceptance of God's **grace.**

6:3-10. *Authentication of Apostleship.* Under pressure of deep emotion Paul catalogs the hazardous experiences he has endured (vss. 4-5). There is poetry in the pathos of these torrential words. He has employed no **weapons** in this struggle (vss. 6-7) except those which, under the Spirit's inspiration, support his integrity as an apostle. The paradoxes of his career (vss. 8-10) doubtless refer to abuses suffered at Corinth and elsewhere, but they may also reflect Paul's conviction that in his own life some of Christ's sufferings were renewed (with vs. 10b cf. 8:9).

E. AN APPEAL FOR PERSONAL RECONCILIATION (6:11-7:4)

6:11-13. *Openheartedness.* Paul longs for a more comfortable relation with his **children,** a relation in which both parties can feel and speak freely toward each other. He knows that his authority over this church has been restored as a consequence of his severe letter (see above on 2:3-4, 12-13, 14-17); the impasse in the church has been overcome. But the reconciliation of Christ calls for a more open relation than exists at the moment of writing. Apparently he senses that the relation is still strained by the inhibited **affections** of the Cors.

6:14–7:1. *Avoidance of Unbelievers.* This passage appears as an abrupt change of subject, an interruption in the train of thought. Paul's appeal in 7:2-4 can be read as a logical sequel to 6:11-13. Some scholars, observing in this section a number of words not used by Paul elsewhere, conclude that it was written by someone else and for some unknown reason was later interpolated into II Cor. Recent studies of the Dead Sea scrolls have shown striking affinity between ideas expressed in this passage and ideas taught by the sectarian Jews at Qumran, and **Belial** (6:15) is a common designation of Satan in their writings. Possibly, therefore, some Christian teacher thoroughly imbued with Essene ideals called for this radical separation of the church from unbelievers.

Another hypothesis affirms the Pauline authorship of the passage but claims that it is a fragment of the previous letter mentioned in I 5:9 which was interpolated here by a later editor of the Cor. correspondence. Paul's fleeting description of this earlier letter, which was misunderstood by the Cors., corresponds with the content of this passage. This hypothesis is a popular and not implausible one.

Yet this passage may well be an integral part of II Cor. There are numerous digressions and seemingly irrelevant asides in Paul's letters, esp. in this one. It must be recalled that he dictated his letters and that often he relies on the knowledge of his readers to supply the missing links in his progression of ideas. Having stressed openheartedness, perhaps he realized its possible misappropriation by the Cors. as a careless tolerance of the beliefs and conduct of unbelievers.

The quotation in 6:16c-18 is a conflation of several OT passages: Lev. 26:11-12 (cf. Ezek. 37:27); Isa. 52:11 (cf. Ezek. 20:34); II Sam. 7:14; Isa. 43:6.

7:2-4. *Mutual Confidence.* As long as the Cors. harbor suspicions that Paul has **wronged** some of them, they are restricted in their affections toward the founder of their church. Paul wishes, not to condemn, but to seek reconciliation. He writes out of love rather than bitterness. As he has said before, his heart is wide open toward the Cors. He wishes now to enfold them in his heart, where he would hold them until death. He is therefore able to express his **great confidence** in them. In the midst of affliction—the mark of Paul's apostleship—he experiences **comfort** and joy (see comment on I 1:4-9).

F. The Meeting with Titus (7:5-16)

7:5-7. *Dejection Turned to Joy.* Paul now resumes the account of his travels and of his moods before writing this letter—an account interrupted in 2:14. When he reached Macedonia he was **afflicted** with restless anxiety about the reaction of the Cors. to his severe letter (see above on 2:12-13). Then the news which Titus brought and the contagion of this colleague's assurance brought God's **comfort** to him in the midst of affliction (cf. 1:3-7). Both Paul and Titus were greatly relieved; they experienced a shared joy as they discussed the church's

longing to see Paul and remorse in remembering how he had been treated during his last visit (cf. 2:1). The Christians at Corinth were now zealous to do as Paul commanded, to defend and satisfy him.

7:8-13a. *Effect of the Severe Letter.* There was a time when Paul felt **regret** over the tone of the stern letter he had sent to the Cors. by Titus. He did not wish to grieve those whom he loved. But in view of the outcome Paul confesses that he no longer has this feeling. He draws distinction between **godly grief**—"pain God is allowed to guide" (Moffatt trans.)—and **worldly grief,** a despair which produces spiritual **death.** He can see no reason to regret the letter since the pain it caused has promoted healing. It is noteworthy that Paul does not absolve the Cors. of all blame; he only absolves the guilt of the church's members who supported the individual wronging him. This situation has been a severe test of the relation between him and his church (cf. 2:9).

7:13b-16. *The Joy of Titus.* The recent crisis has had a salutary effect on Paul's colleague. Titus now realizes that Paul's pride in the Cor. church was justified in spite of earlier misgivings. It is unlikely that Titus expected the **fear and trembling with which** the Cors. **received him.** Does Paul find some satisfaction in reflecting that their mood resembled his own when he first came among them (I 2:1-5)? In neither situation can the outcome be explained as the consequence of any man's "plausible words of wisdom," but only as a demonstration of God's Spirit and power.

IV. The Offering for the Poor in Jerusalem (8:1–9:15)

In I 16:1-4 (see comment) Paul directed the Cors. to put aside some money on the first day of every week for the relief of the impoverished Christians in Jerusalem. Similar instructions, he told them, had been given to the churches in Galatia, and on his arrival at Corinth he would make the proper arrangements for delivery of their contribution. Apparently the crisis in the church's relation to Paul frustrated the initial plans for a systematic collection. But now that a reconciliation has been accomplished this project, dear to Paul's heart, receives his attention. The resumption of the offering will do more than substantiate the Cors.' loyalty to him. The satisfactory growth of the church, as of all the Gentile congregations, depends on their rendering this service to the Jewish Christians in Jerusalem (cf. Rom. 15:25-29). More than likely Paul hopes that the demonstration of good will by his Gentile converts will help to reinforce the unity of the body of Christ and allay the deep-seated prejudice of Jewish Christians against the converts' rejection of the Mosaic law.

Paul approaches the subject of this collection with such tact and deliberate restraint that the style of his writing is altered. Observing this, some scholars have concluded that chs. 8–9 were originally a part of another letter, or that they were formed from the fragments of 2 letters. This doubt about the integrity of the passage lacks firm justification. Possibly the change in mood is due to nothing more than a lapse in the time of dictation.

A. EXCELLING IN GENEROSITY (8:1-15)

8:1-5. *The Example of the Macedonians.* Paul is not drawing invidious comparisons in calling attention to the **liberality** of the Macedonians in the midst of their **extreme poverty**—though he is probably not forgetful that some Cors. pride themselves on their so-called riches (cf. I 4:8). It is the **grace of God,** not some superior virtue of the Macedonians, which is responsible for their self-dedication and joy in giving. Nevertheless the generosity of the Macedonians is exemplary.

8:6-15. *Motives for Completing the Collection.* The Cors., who **excel** in so many ways, are urged to take the lead in this also. Paul emphasizes that he is neither commanding that they be generous nor prescribing the amount of their gifts. He calls on them to respond to the **grace of our Lord Jesus Christ,** revealed in the gospel of God's self-giving, as the authentic motive for Christian generosity. It is unlikely, as some have held, that he refers in vs. 9 to the humility of the man of Nazareth; rather, as in Phil. 2:6-11, he is thinking of the voluntary abasement of the preexistent Christ who became man, bringing to the poor the riches of heaven (cf. 5:18-19). It is this divine love in action which provides the believer with the supreme motive for sacrificial giving. Paul sees the proof of genuine love in a Christian's **readiness** to give, not in the amount of the gift. What is important is the intention to offer the gift one desires, without reservations. To support the ideal of equality in Christian sharing Paul cites the experience of Israel with manna in the wilderness (Exod. 16:18).

B. COMMENDATION OF THE EMISSARIES (8:16-9:5)

8:16-24. *Their Character.* Paul is scrupulously tactful in introducing the delegation which is to precede him. These men are coming to Corinth to collect money, and so he assures his readers that they are honorable men of excellent reputation, men of good will who share his confidence in the church. The 2 brothers who are unnamed (vss. 18-19, 22) have provoked unending speculation. It is not possible to identify them certainly with persons known from other NT sources. Paul declares that they are **messengers,** lit. "apostles," **of the churches** (vs. 23), suggesting that both have been formally **appointed** (vs. 19)—which perhaps means "elected." For the moment Paul seems chiefly concerned that his role as administrator of the collection be properly understood (vss. 20-21).

9:1-5. *A Plea to Cooperate with Them.* Here it rather appears that Paul is merely repeating himself. Some, noting this, have conjectured that this is a fragment of another letter addressed to all the churches of **Achaia** (see above on 1:1-2), but this hypothesis has received little attention. It is likely that Paul experienced another interruption and, resuming his dictation, wished to say more about the discussions in Macedonia concerning the **offering,** lit. "ministry," **for the saints.** He wants the Cors. to know that he has spoken confidently to the Macedonians about them. Apparently he wishes also to labor the point made earlier (8:10-11), that the Cors.' **readiness in desiring** should now be matched by a readiness to **complete** their undertaking. Finally

Paul wants to make explicit his decision not to come to Corinth until the mission of the **brethren** has been accomplished. No doubt he is made cautious by the recollection of the humiliation suffered during his last visit (cf. 2:1-11). His presence might make the collection seem a sort of peace offering to him. In this situation he is eager that the church feel no duress but be given every opportunity to respond voluntarily (vs. 5).

C. THE BENEFITS OF GENEROSITY (9:6-15)

9:6-11. *An Abundant Harvest.* From the proverbial wisdom of his people Paul draws the conviction that a truly generous man receives in return gifts from God and men out of proportion to his own giving. He quotes **God loves a cheerful giver** from a line appearing in the LXX of Prov. 22:8 but not in the Hebrew, and vs. 9 is quoted from Ps. 112:9. The prudential motive may seem unworthy to some readers. The biblical writers, however, do not hesitate to employ the sanctions of reward and punishment in moral exhortations, and a recognition of their proper force is inseparable from faith in God's sovereignty in a moral universe. Nevertheless Paul insists that true generosity arises from a free heart that forgets prudential calculations. In his judgment the realization that **every blessing,** lit. "all grace," of God in Christ is undeserved provides the essential motive for Christian generosity.

9:12-15. *A Bond of Thanksgiving.* In conclusion Paul stresses 2 results of liberal giving: (*a*) the needs of worthy persons are met and (*b*) the recipients are led through the gifts to praise God. The collection is now designated as a **service,** lit. "liturgy"— a term which could refer to any voluntary patriotic, charitable, or religious act but was used esp. of worship. Paul envisages here the Jerusalem Christians in their worship remembering the Gentile Christians in the W provinces and withal celebrating the **surpassing grace of God** manifested through their giving. In this thought Paul himself is led to pray (vs. 15).

V. DEFENSE OF PAUL'S APOSTLESHIP (10:1-13:10)

At the beginning of ch. 10 there is again an abrupt change of mood, a discernible difference in approach and style. The break is more marked here than elsewhere e.g. between 2:13, 14 or chs. 7; 8. Esp. evident is the author's rising emotion of hurt and anger. For this and other reasons (see Intro. to I Cor.) many scholars are convinced that 10:1–13:10 was not written as a continuation of the "thankful letter," as they commonly call it, preserved in chs. 1–9. We are introduced here, they say, to a quite different letter, of which the original beginning and perhaps also the ending have been lost. On the one hand some of these scholars hold that this is the substantial fragment of a later Cor. letter, written possibly as late as Paul's Roman imprisonment but more probably following the most recent of the letters preserved in chs. 1–9 by only a short interval during which Paul received a disturbing new report from Corinth. On the other hand an impressive number of scholars have concluded that this is part of the earlier severe letter mentioned in 2:4; 7:8.

The 2nd of these hypotheses has stronger support but falls short of being fully convincing. Rather we can reasonably assume that Paul has resumed dictating his letter after a short delay. His mind is no doubt so preoccupied with his imminent visit to Corinth that he has become tense and jittery. How deep and lasting is the reconciliation brought about by his ultimatum and the assistance of Titus? How influential are the opponents who are disparaging his integrity, impugning his motives, and even casting doubt on his sanity? An undercurrent of anxiety has been evident earlier in the letter (cf. 1:12-14, 17-18, 23-24; 2:17; 3:1, 5; 4:2-3, 5; 5:11-13, 16; 6:3, 8-13; 7:2-3), an anxiety which Paul can never completely suppress even though he devoutly wishes to be rid of it. Now, as he anticipates confronting his detractors, this anxiety and hurt erupts in a torrent of feeling.

A. Refutations of Slanders (10:1-11)

10:1-8. *Worldly and Spiritual Weapons.* Though clearly provoked, Paul makes an earnest entreaty, prompted by the example of Christ (cf. Phil. 2:5-8). His detractors accuse him of **boldness**—at a safe distance. Let them wait and see how a man of authority exhibits boldness when faced with false accusers and unfounded charges. Those who maintain that 10:1-13:10 was written before chs. 1-9 cite Paul's sarcastic use of **confidence** as evidence, saying that it could not have followed 7:16; 8:22. Both of those passages, however, express confidence in the loyalty of the Cor. church, whereas now Paul refers to self-confidence.

10:2. Certain persons at Corinth accuse Paul of **acting in a worldly fashion,** lit. "walking according to the flesh" (cf. 1:17*b;* 5:16). According to one influential view, Paul's principal opposition at Corinth arose from a group of Gnostic libertines whose lawless attitudes and ecstatic behavior reflected their beliefs that they were truly "spiritual" and that they had risen and were reigning with Christ (see comment on I 6:12-20). These, it is said, constituted a schismatic group in the church claiming to belong exclusively to Christ (vs. 7*b;* cf. I 1:12). Some obscure passages in II Cor. may support this theory: In 4:5 Paul refers to the accusation that he is preaching himself. In 11:4 he casts aspersions on those who have received a "different spirit." In 12:1-4 he may be meeting the objection that he has had few if any experiences of the "visions and revelations" vouchsafed to spiritual men, whose ecstasy attests their spirituality (cf. I 14, esp. vss. 6-12, 18-19, 37-38). Perhaps these self-styled "spiritual" men were contending that Paul walked according to the flesh and thus was an ineffectual, worldly-minded man, who must scheme and seek his own advantage, whereas they themselves walked "according to the Spirit" in their freedom from law, in their knowledge and wisdom inspired by their private visionary experiences, and in their possession of spectacular spiritual gifts, esp. "speaking in tongues." This theory is not without merit but it may describe only one group of Paul's opponents at Corinth (see below on 11:4).

10:3-6. Unlike some of the Gnostics, Paul knows that he does **live in the world,** but he does not contend against its forces "according to the flesh." His **weapons** were designed by God and he is enlisted in Christ's service. It is argued that the reference to the church's **obedience** as yet to be given (vs. 6) must have preceded 2:9; 7:15, which say this obedience has been demonstrated. But Paul seems to mean rather that he is **ready to punish every disobedience** caused by his detractors and that at the time of his visit occasion will be given for a further concrete demonstration of obedience.

10:7-8. Some have taken these vss. to indicate that Paul's opponents have created a "Christ party" as a faction in the Cor. church (cf. I 1:12), but this is not clear. Possibly some persons claimed a special relation to Christ through their knowledge of him or of certain traditions from his ministry, but this inference must draw support from other passages (5:16; 11:4-6; 12:11*b*), where allusions to this special advantage are only implicit. It has been said also that Paul's own slogan has been "I belong to Christ." Against this is the plain fact that he nowhere else boasts of an exclusive attachment to his Lord. Paul's **authority** is derived from Christ, but he does not boast of being Christ's favorite (cf. 11:23–12:13; I 3:5-9; 4:1-5).

10:9-11. *Letters and Actions.* The specific nature of the indictment against Paul in vs. 10 is clear though the Greek contains several grammatical difficulties. There are persons in the Cor. church who are making fun of Paul's puny physique and inelegant speech and contrasting his appearance as a man with his presumptuous threats and foolish boasts set forth in **weighty letters.** Paul meets this attack, here as elsewhere, by admitting that he is no superman, no clever rhetorician in the Greek tradition. But wholly unfounded is the charge that he has been unreliable in word and action, inconsistent, indecisive, and vacillating (cf. 2:17-18; 4:1-2; I 1:17; 2:1-5; 3:18-21; 4:9-12, 18-19). It must be acknowledged, however, that Paul's strategy in mission and his changes in plans have given his opponents an entering wedge to further their aim in creating distrust (see comment on I 9:19-23).

B. Claims to Authority at Corinth (10:12–11:21*a*)

10:12-18. *His Pioneer Work.* Paul is incensed that his opponents should take pride in the church at Corinth while daring to revile its founder and true spiritual leader (vs. 14*b;* cf. I 3:6). He can boast justifiably of the Christian mission in Achaia, for he pioneered in this province, a field **apportioned** for his labor (cf. Rom. 1:5; Gal. 2:9; Acts 9:15). While he has imposed a **limit** on his own activity, not wishing to claim credit for **other men's labors** (cf. Rom. 15:20), the conceit of his opponents knows no bounds—they **commend themselves** (vs. 12) and are **boasting of work already done in another's field** (vss. 15-16). It is evident that this reference is not to rebellious members of the Cor. church but to rival missionaries (cf. 2:17; 3:1; see comments on 3:7-18; 11:4), no doubt using their success in Corinth as an argument to convert other churches to their version of Christianity.

10:13-16. In contrast to his rivals Paul does not wish to extend his field of work until the harvest he has sown has been reaped. But of course his pioneering missions among the nations are not yet completed. From Rom. 15:24-29 we learn that his plans for **lands beyond you** include a visit to Rome and work in Spain after delivery of the offering in Jerusalem. It has been argued that this must have been written from Ephesus as part of the severe letter rather than from Macedonia, where chs. 1-9 were written (cf. 2:13; 7:5; 9:2-5; see color map 16). But Paul is thinking here of his mission field, of which Corinth marks the present W limit, and neither he nor his readers would concern themselves with whether at the moment he is E or N of them.

10:17-18. Paul cites Jer. 9:24 to insist that he is not seeking self-glorification in recalling his foundation of the church at Corinth. This work among the Gentiles was commissioned by the Lord, and Paul hopes that the last judgment will bring to him the only commendation that matters (cf. I 3:10, 13; Rom. 15:17-18).

11:1-6. His Concern for the Cors. This section combines biting sarcasm with moving tenderness. So Paul is a fool, is he? Then concede that he is a fool in his love for his converts.

11:2-3. Just as God was jealous of his people Israel, so Paul is jealous of those whom he has begotten (cf. I 4:15; 9:1c). As the father of a daughter, i.e. the church at Corinth, he has **betrothed . . . a pure bride to her one husband,** Christ. Is it surprising that he should long for this bride's single devotion to her betrothed and be alarmed when signs of her corruption appear? In extending this metaphor by an allusion to **Eve** he may be drawing on a Jewish interpretation of Gen. 3 which held that Cain was begotten through her seduction by the **serpent.**

11:4. Some interpreters hold that this vs. suggests simply a hypothetical possibility, that Paul knows of the Cors.' susceptibility to corrupting influences and warns in advance against them. His words here, however, as well as his invective in vss. 12-15 and the hints in 2:17; 3:1; 10:12, 15-16, imply an existing danger caused by the coming to Corinth of visitors preaching a **different gospel.** That they were Jewish Christians is clear from vs. 22. Beyond this the question of their identity and the content of their teaching admits no easy answer. The popular assumption, which some scholars share, is that they were Judaizers such as came to Galatia (see above on 3:7-18). Against this view is the fact that Paul, though ready only a short time later to argue at length against the Judaizers' teachings in Rom., nowhere makes any effort to refute them in his correspondence with the Cors. Other scholars believe rather that the visitors to Corinth were a group who also invaded the church at Philippi and that Paul's attack on them in Phil. 3 (see comment) shows they were Jewish Christians who had Gnostic libertine ideas. Such visitors would of course be warmly welcomed by sympathetic members of the Cor. church (see above on 10:2).

11:5-6. Since in the Greek **these** (vs. 5) is simply "the," the traditional interpretation has been that **superlative apostles** (cf. 12:11) refers to the original 12, or to the leaders among them. This possibility is defended by a few scholars today (see below on vss. 22-23). Most, however, have taken the phrase to be a sarcastic term for the visitors stirring up trouble in the Cor. church. Further support for the view

that they were Gnostics is found in the shift of Paul's thought (vs. 6) to an idea reminiscent of the opening lines of I Cor., viz. that God's foolishness is wiser than men's wisdom (cf. I 1:17, 22-23). Since the Cors. inordinately admire preachers who are clever and elegant in speech and yearn for **knowledge** other than that revealed in the gospel, they have been easily seduced and exploited.

11:7-21a. His Self-Support. It is ironic that Paul's **love** for the Cors., expressed in not wishing to **burden** them financially, has been perverted into evidence that he does not care about them (vs. 11). More than this, his not following the Lord's commandment that "those who proclaim the gospel should get their living by the gospel" (I 9:14) is being used to deny the genuineness of his apostleship. Paul has allowed **other churches,** viz. those in **Macedonia** (cf. 8:2; Phil. 4:14-18), to support his work at Corinth.

11:12-21a. This has become a matter of principle and Paul is determined to adhere to it (cf. 12:13-15). Indeed he will use it to rebut the **false apostles** who boast deceitfully that they work **on the same terms.** His countercharge is that his accusers are preying on the Cors., taking scandalous advantage of them (vs. 20). His judgment of them is most explicit in vss. 13-15, but he does not define their dangerous doctrines. Probably their attacks were concentrated on his person.

C. BASES FOR BOASTING (11:21b-12:13)

11:21b-33. His Sufferings. With withering sarcasm Paul has taunted his readers over their willingness to **bear with fools** (vs. 19). Surely they can give heed to another **fool** when he **dares to boast.**

11:22-23. Vs. 22 makes it explicit that some of Paul's opponents—i.e. evidently the visiting preachers rather than the rebellious members of the Cor. congregation—were Jewish Christians. Were they also emissaries sent from Jerusalem by the original apostles? If so, possibly in these vss. Paul is comparing himself with the senders as well as those sent (see above on vs. 5). It has been forcefully argued that the visiting preachers were at least claiming to represent the 12 and that the fact that Paul was bound to concede the apostles' authority and could only declare himself their equal made this thrust the more insidious. Whether or not Paul's opponents were thus exploiting for their own advantage the unimpeachable authority of the 12, it is obvious that the apostles were not themselves responsible for the situation at Corinth and that Paul harbored no such suspicions (cf. I 15:8-11; Gal. 2:6-10). Moreover, though it is probable that the visitors brought to Corinth letters of recommendation from some Jewish Christian community (cf. 3:1), we cannot be sure that this community was Jerusalem.

11:23-33. Whatever his opponents' credentials, Paul does not permit them to be normative; actions speak louder than words. No man can equal his own ministry—in the hardships, humiliations, and personal indignities he has suffered as a servant of Christ (cf. 6:4-10; I 15:9-10; Rom. 15:18-19). Acts 16:22-23 reports that in Philippi Paul was imprisoned after a beating **with rods**—the Roman practice, whereas the Jewish punishment was 39 **lashes** (see comment on Deut. 25:1-3)—Acts 14:19

tells of his being **stoned** at Lystra, and Acts 9:23-25 (see comment) gives another version of the humiliating escape from **Damascus** (vss. 32-33). Otherwise Paul's list shows up the gaps in the Acts narrative of his career.

12:1-10. *His Strength in Weakness.* Paul's statement in 11:30 stands as the theme of this section. **There is nothing to be gained** by boasting, Paul protests, yet he feels forced by his accusers to write of the abundant experiences of ecstasy which have been granted to him, and esp. to mention one extraordinary vision and audition of the **third,** i.e. highest, **heaven.** His recollection of the specific time, **fourteen years ago,** shows how indelibly this unutterable experience was impressed on his consciousness. It also prevents our equating this vision with his conversion experience, which must have taken place more than 20 years earlier, and which he describes rather as an appearance to him of the risen Lord (I 9:1; 15:8; Gal. 1:15-16; cf. the 14-year interval of Gal. 2:1, which seems to be an unrelated coincidence).

12:5-10. Paul does not wish to offer incommunicable experiences, however important to his own inner life, as evidence of his divine commission (cf. I 14:18-19). His **thorn in the flesh** has been to him a constant reminder that he is not to make capital of spectacular gifts. His testimony is to be the self-evidently meaningful word and deed. To many persons his speech and labor have seemed **weakness** itself (cf. I 1:27-29). In such weakness, however, Christ's grace and power are made perfect.

Speculation has persisted about the specific nature of the **thorn in the flesh**—e.g. malaria, an eye disease, stammering, epilepsy. It was probably some physical malady, chronic and painful (cf. Gal. 4:13-15). Yet many ancient fathers of the church, as well as the Protestant Reformers, held that it was a spiritual affliction, that he was never able to feel himself secure from Satan's wiles and was subject to all the temptations of the flesh in their acute forms (cf. 2:11; I 9:26-27; 10:12-13).

12:11-12. *His Signs and Wonders.* Though the opponents picture Paul as a nonentity, he contends that the standard marks of a **true apostle** accompanied his ministry among the Cors. Patiently he went about his work, and God wrought through him—through his weakness—**signs and wonders and mighty works** (cf. Rom. 15:18-19; Gal. 3:1-5; Acts 14:3). His enemies may distort the facts but they cannot deny them.

D. Plans for a 3rd Visit (12:13–13:10)

The grammatical forms of Paul's references to a **third time** (12:14; 13:1) are ambiguous and can mean either that he is coming to Corinth the 3rd time or that he is making preparations the 3rd time—i.e. that he has planned this visit twice before but postponed it (cf. I 16:7; II 1:15-17, 23). According to the latter interpretation Paul might be writing of preparations for only a 2nd visit to Corinth, and a few scholars have defended this view, largely on the basis that Acts records only 2 visits (Acts 18:1-18; 20:2-3). That the Acts narrative is incomplete, however, is evident from Paul's statements elsewhere (e.g. see above on 11:23-33), and efforts to deny

that a 2nd "painful" visit (2:1) took place have been unsuccessful. Both the context here and other passages in the Cor. correspondence indicate that Paul is now promising the Cors. a 3rd visit.

12:13-18. *Continued Self-Support.* Some have supposed that **Forgive me this wrong** is an admission by Paul that he has wronged the Cors. in accepting no help from them (cf. 11:7-12; I 9:3-18) and thus leaving room for suspicion that he doubts their willingness to support him. It is more probable that the apology is ironical.

12:14-15. However subject to misunderstanding his refusal to live at the expense of the congregation has been, Paul does not intend to abandon this principle on the occasion of his 3rd visit to the church. He desires the love of its members, not their possessions. And it is his prerogative as their father to assume the burden of financial responsibility (vs. 14*b*). It is not possible to know certainly whether the rhetorical question in vs. 15*b* is a plaintive or a barbed appeal, but even if we infer the latter Paul's affection for the Cors. shines through the sternness of his rebuke (cf. 11:1-3, 11). This passage should not be overlooked when contrasts are drawn between the attitudes reflected in chs. 1-7; 10-13.

12:16-17. Paul here shows his sensitivity to a tactic which his opponents may have been using against him. It is perhaps being hinted that though he has not accepted openly the church's support he is craftily pocketing the money ostensibly collected for the saints at Jerusalem. Paul answers this absurd calumny by asking simply whether anyone can produce a shred of evidence that he or Titus has defrauded them.

12:18. There has been much discussion of how this statement about the sending of **Titus** and an unnamed **brother** is related to the recommendation in 8:6, 16-23; 9:3-5 of Titus and 2 "brothers," one perhaps subordinate to the other, who are being sent to complete the collection. The tense of **urged** and **sent** here seems to imply an earlier mission, and the scholars who view chs. 10-13 as part of a letter written at an interval after chs. 1-9 cite this as evidence. On the other hand those who view chs. 10-13 as part of the severe letter preceding chs. 1-9 must assume that Paul sent Titus and a companion on a similar mission once before, presumably when the collection was begun (cf. 8:10; I 16:1). This is of course possible, but the only basis for the interpretation is that the theory requires it.

If this passage and ch. 8 are part of the same letter this is naturally understood as a 2nd reference to the same mission. The tense here is the same as in 8:6 and may properly be rendered: "I have urged Titus to go, and have sent the brother with him." The meaning is probably that Paul has already dispatched them on their journey, which involves collections in one or more other churches on the way, so that they will reach Corinth after the letter commending them has arrived; but it may be that he has simply commissioned them and they will bear the letter when he finishes it. Since only **Titus** is cited in the following question, the unnamed **brother** is evidently not yet known to the Cors.; his commissioning is mentioned to demonstrate that Paul delegates the fund raising to others and never touches the contributions himself.

12:19-21. *A Plea for Complete Repentance.* The apprehension expressed here suggests Paul's painful recollection of his previous visit and its aftermath in spite of the fact that the crisis has passed. The church members must surely understand by this time that he seeks only their **upbuilding**, their welfare, and that it is God's judgment with respect to their relations with Paul that really matters. The contrast between the acknowledgment here of the moral failures of Christians at Corinth and the praise for them in such passages as 1:24; 3:3; 7:4, 11, 15-16; 8:7 has been used as an argument against the unity of II Cor. and for the theory that this passage is a part of the severe letter. But the references to that letter in ch. 2 would lead us to expect fuller criticism than this, including clear reference to the church member whose punishment Paul is commanding and to the church meeting which pained him so. In view of the situation at Corinth a shift of Paul's mood from confidence to **fear** as he looks forward to his imminent visit is understandable.

13:1-4. *A Warning to the Unrepentant.* Possibly at this point Paul had read back to him what he had said since resuming dictation. He may have concluded that he had made large concessions to those who were claiming that his ministry was unimpressive, that as a man he was weak and ineffectual. At any rate he must have realized that he had placed great emphasis on evidences of his apostleship which many would view as weakness and defeat. He had not wished to be overbearing in the exercise of his authority at Corinth. He had not wished to use means other than those which love dictated, which the example of Christ prompted. The Cors., however, must know that he would not hesitate to act with authority if the situation demanded it. If the visiting preachers had persuaded the membership of the church to ask for a sign of his authority the **power of God** must be manifested in judgment.

As he looks forward to the coming visit Paul reiterates his ardent desire to avoid another painful scene, yet he feels it imperative to make clear that he will not come seeking peace at any price. Justice must prevail. Nevertheless he will not act with haste. He will examine **any charge** judiciously, **requiring the evidence of two or three witnesses** (cf. Deut. 19:15; Matt. 18:16). This procedure is to be used with **those who sinned** and are still unrepentant (cf. 12:21); it would scarcely apply, as some have proposed, to the offender whose punishment was demanded in the severe letter (see above on 2:5-11) since his attack on Paul was witnessed by the whole congregation. Some who consider this passage part of the severe letter view 1:23 as an "echo" of **I will not spare them** (vs. 2), but the reverse seems more reasonable—i.e. Paul postponed his visit to spare them for a time, so that they might repent, but now when he actually comes he will not spare those who

have failed to take advantage of the postponement.

13:5-10. *A Plea for Self-Examination.* Because of the subtle influences of his opponents Paul considers that the Cors. may be thinking of examining him when he comes before them. Emphatically he commands them to **examine** and **test** themselves. Like him they live the life of **faith.** Surely there is reason to hope that self-knowledge and final victory will be theirs. If indeed they correct themselves he will have no occasion to provide **proof** (vs. 3) of his apostleship and doubts may never be dispelled. He hopes that he may be vindicated in the eyes of all. But what is more important is that the church **do what is right.**

13:8-10. Assuming, with most commentators, that by the **truth** Paul means the gospel, the implication is that he is determined to assert his personal authority only in order to vindicate the gospel. If the gospel is made effective in Corinth through the power of the indwelling Christ, he will do nothing to show his authority even though by inaction he may appear **weak** and **may seem to have failed** (vs. 7). Like Jeremiah this man of God much prefers to take constructive rather than destructive action (vs. 10*b;* cf. Jer. 1:9-10), but either means is intended for the upbuilding of God's people. Far preferable to **severe . . . use of . . . authority** are stern words of reproof and correction, however subject to misunderstanding and distortion a letter may be (vs. 10*a*). The severe letter was effective; Paul doubtless hopes this one will be also.

VI. CONCLUSION (13:11-14)

13:11-13. *Final Appeal and Greetings.* Some who divide II Cor. into 2 or more letters hold that this ending originally followed 9:15, whereas others keep it as the conclusion to 10:1–13:10. The postscript is too brief to identify related themes or to establish the specific mood of its writer. It is, however, a fitting ending to the letter viewed as a whole. Paul makes a final appeal for self-correction, for loyal submission to his rightful authority, for the members of a divided church to work together for the common good. On **holy kiss** see comment on I 16:19-21. The Christians with Paul in Macedonia send their greeting; Paul has spoken to them of the Cor. brethren (cf. 9:2).

13:14. *Benediction.* This closing prayer is probably the best-known benediction of Paul, no doubt because it mentions Jesus Christ, God, and the Holy Spirit, an association that later found expression in the doctrine of the trinity. It is in keeping with Paul's character for him to think first of the **grace** of Christ —or of the grace of God revealed through Christ— for thereby God's **love** has been apprehended, and therefrom the **fellowship** of the Holy Spirit has become a continuing reality.

THE LETTER
OF PAUL TO THE GALATIANS
Victor Paul Furnish

INTRODUCTION

Character and Significance. In Galatians, as in Rom., we meet many of the weightiest themes of Paul's preaching: justification by faith, life in Christ, the responsibilities of love, the meaning of the Cross, the function of the Mosaic law, and life in the Spirit. In Gal., however, Paul is not as free to develop and comment on these ideas in his own way as he is in Rom. For he is caught up in the heat of controversy—as even the frequently broken syntax of his sentences indicates. He must defend not only the chief points of his gospel but also his apostolic credentials. This is a fervent letter, written with vigor and feeling; but it is also erratic, its argument often hard to follow, its tone frequently harsh, its meaning sometimes obscure, its substantive issues sometimes overshadowed by personal feelings. Yet precisely because Paul here throws himself without reserve into the proclamation of the gospel, the letter has a power unique among his writings and has exerted an influence out of all proportion to its modest size.

The occasion for writing this letter is indicated most succinctly in 1:6-7: Paul's astonishment that the Gals. are turning to a false "gospel," being "bewitched" (3:1) by troublemakers who seek to pervert the gospel of Christ. The specific issue is whether Gentile converts to Christianity must undergo circumcision (6:12-13), but Paul is convinced that this particular question has broader implications. He understands it to involve the very core and substance of the gospel, and to raise the fundamental issue of the Christian's relation to the Law. Because the gospel is in danger of perversion, and because his opponents in Galatia have spared nothing in attacking him personally, Paul in responding is edgy and defensive, frequently to the point of anger.

But it would be wrong to overemphasize the belligerent aspects of this letter. Its power derives primarily from the magnitude of the themes discussed and the vividness with which the crucial points of Paul's preaching are expressed. Its chief importance is theological, not only because it became the scriptural anvil on which the key emphases of Protestantism were hammered out—the "Magna Charta of the Reformation"—but also because it affords an intimate and candid view of Paul's own theological concerns, presuppositions, and methods.

Gal. is important also for what it reveals about the organization and structure of the church in Paul's day. Cephas (i.e. Peter; see below on 1:18-

20), James the Lord's brother, and John are named as Jerusalem apostles (1:18-19; 2:9); we read here of a church council (2:1-10), of an agreement to divide the mission field along ethnic lines (2:9), and of a dispute between Peter and Paul (2:11-14).

Finally, Gal. provides certain valuable data about Paul's own life and ministry. He refers to his past life as a Jew and his persecution of the church (1:13-14), his conversion and call to preach (1:15-16), his visits to Jerusalem (1:18; 2:1), his activity in Antioch (2:11-14), and a bodily ailment suffered in Galatia itself (4:13). Yet it is not part of Paul's purpose to convey autobiographical information as such, and it is only in the course of his total argument that these facts emerge. However important it is for reconstructing the earliest history of the church and the events in Paul's life, the chief significance of Gal. now, as when it was first written and read, is what it declares about the meaning of the gospel for life.

The Address. Gal. was written, not for a single congregation, but for several. The salutation is "To the churches of Galatia" (1:2). Though it is thus a circular letter, intended for more than just local reading, its form and substance indicate that the churches were facing the same problems and being threatened by the same troublemakers (see below). But where were these churches located?

The problem arises because "Galatia" is ambiguous. The name was first used of an area in the central plateau region of Asia Minor inhabited from *ca*. 275 B.C. by a people known as "Galatians." However, after the death of its king, Amyntas, in 25 B.C., the kingdom of Galatia, with its chief cities of Ancyra, Tavium, and Pessinus, was incorporated into a Roman province to which the older territory gave its name. The province included not only certain territorial additions made *ca*. 25 years earlier but also new extensions, esp. to the S, including such cities as Iconium, Lystra, Derbe, and Pisidian Antioch (see color map 16). By Paul's day the province had been further extended to embrace areas in Paphlagonia and Pontus. Hence the question: When Paul addresses himself to the "churches of Galatia" is he using the term to designate congregations in the old kingdom of Galatia or anywhere within the whole Roman province of Galatia? The question is not easily answered, and it has led to the "N Galatia" and "S Galatia" hypotheses.

There is no possibility that Paul addresses churches

in the whole province, for the congregations he writes to were obviously established about the same time and under similar circumstances (cf. 1:6; 3:1-5; 4:12-15, 20). This could not be true were he writing to churches in the entire provincial territory, N and S. In favor of the N view is the fact that when the cities in the S part of the province are named in Acts 13:1–14:28 they are never described as Galatian. Thus when Acts does speak of Paul in Galatia (16:6; 18:23) the reference is probably to the N, the old Galatian kingdom. Moreover, it is argued, the residents of S Galatia would not be likely to think of themselves as Gals., and hence Paul's reference to "foolish Galatians" (3:1) would have no force if addressed to them.

On the other hand nothing is said explicitly in Acts about Paul's founding churches in the N part of the province; he only "went through" (16:6). And in that area his work is described, not as "strengthening the churches," as in Syria, Cilicia, and S Galatia (Acts 15:41; 16:5), but as "strengthening the disciples" (Acts 18:23), perhaps meaning scattered Christians as yet not organized into congregations. Proponents of the S Galatia hypothesis also point out that Paul normally refers to his churches by using the provincial term and that "Galatian" would be the only single word he could use when addressing the churches of Iconium, Lystra, Derbe, etc.

The arguments pro and con are many and complex and it is doubtful whether a clear consensus can ever be achieved. But this does not lessen the importance of the question because a decision on the area to which the letter was sent has a direct bearing on its date.

Date and Place of Composition. If Paul is writing to S Galatia he is addressing congregations founded on his "first missionary journey" (Acts 13, 14) and therefore the earliest possible date is sometime after this first period of his apostolic activity. If on the other hand he is writing to the N areas he is addressing churches founded on the "second missionary journey" (Acts 15:36–18:21), and his letter must be assigned to a later phase in his ministry. But even if a decision on this point were possible we would still have to determine how soon after his "founding visit" Paul wrote the letter. Does the remark that the readers are "quickly" deserting God (1:6) imply that not much time has elapsed since the Galatian Christians were converted? Ought the phrase "at first" (4:13) be interpreted to mean the first of 2 former visits, thus indicating that Gal. postdates not just the founding visit but also a 2nd one? Such questions are not easily answered.

Other approaches to the problem of dating Gal. are also inconclusive. The parallels in content between Gal. and Rom. are striking, but while many commentators agree with J. B. Lightfoot that Gal. stands to Rom. "as the rough model to the finished statue," others are not so sure. Nor is there agreement on whether Gal. was written before or after the "Jerusalem council" (Acts 15), whether it reflects the concerns with which Paul was preoccupied during the period of the Corinthian crisis, or whether Paul's writing a letter rather than going in person to Galatia indicates that this belongs among the "imprisonment letters." There is, then, perhaps a

wider range of possibilities for the dating of Gal. than for any other authentically Pauline letter.

Determination of the place of composition is dependent on the letter's date. Those who believe it was the earliest of Paul's extant letters (48 or 49), written before the council of Acts 15, locate it at Syrian Antioch (cf. Acts 14:26-28). The majority, however, prefer the years when Paul was working in the Aegean area (50-56), and many associate Gal. with the time of the Corinthian correspondence (55-56). Corinth is most often named as the place, but many favor Ephesus, and some have suggested Macedonia. The hypothesis that Gal. was written from prison opens the possibility that it dates from the end of Paul's ministry (57-62) during his imprisonment at Caesarea or at Rome.

The Gal. Troublemakers. Since the letter is occasioned by a threatened, if not actual, apostasy among the Gals., prompted by men to whom Paul refers as "some who trouble you" (1:7), the question of who they are and what they are teaching and doing is crucial. It is commonly held that they are Judaizers—Jewish-Christian legalists perhaps sent by leaders of the Jewish wing of the church to institute among Gentile converts such Jewish rites as circumcision. Those who hold this view regard the warnings about the misuse of freedom (ch. 5) as directed, not at the troublemakers themselves, but at those who might, on the basis of Paul's anti-legalistic emphasis on justification by faith apart from works (3:5-29), fall into the opposite error of libertinism.

To a few commentators it has seemed more plausible that Paul's problem is with 2 different groups: legalists on the one hand and libertinists on the other. Thus he is compelled to fight on 2 opposite fronts at once—a dilemma which explains his own perplexity (4:20) and the apparent shift in emphasis from the dangers of legalism (chs. 1–4) to the dangers of libertinism (chs. 5–6).

A more complicated analysis identifies the troublemakers as Gnostics, i.e. Christians who practice some of the Jewish rites like circumcision but interpret them in mystic, non-Jewish ways and are not legalists in the usual sense (see comment on Phil. 3:1–4:1). This would explain, it is held, the otherwise puzzling comment in 6:13 that "even those who receive circumcision do not themselves keep the law" and other problems which the usual view, that the opponents were Jewish-Christian legalists, leaves unresolved.

There is finally the possibility that Paul himself is not fully informed about the identity of his opponents, their teaching, or even the effectiveness of their mission among the Gals. In 1:6; 3:1 he seems to presume that they have already met with some success, but in 1:7 his saying that they "want to pervert the gospel of Christ" implies that he regards them only as an imminent threat. Because he himself does not have all the details he is forced to launch his counteroffensive in a way which covers various possible dangers.

For Further Study. Commentaries by E. DeW. Burton, 1920; G. S. Duncan, 1934; R. T. Stamm in *IB*, 1953; Ragnar Bring, 1961. Kirsopp Lake, *The Earlier Epistles of St. Paul*, 2nd ed., 1927. J. H. Ropes, *The Singular Problem of the Epistle to the Gals.*,

1929. John Knox, "Gal.," and M. J. Mellink, "Galatia," in *IDB*, 1962.

I. SALUTATION (1:1-5)

Here Paul identifies himself, indicates to whom his letter is sent, and bestows on them an apostolic blessing. One senses immediately his concern to defend his apostolic status in the declaration that his authority derives from no ecclesiastical body and has been mediated to him by no human agent. Rather its source and ground is God the Father through the resurrected Lord (cf. vss. 15-17). Why the emphasis on this point? Is Paul's apostolic authority doubted because it derives from men only, thus requiring a denial? More likely he has been criticized as not having apostolic credentials certified by the church's leaders—a point he himself here confirms (cf. vss. 16c-24) and yet later partially corrects (2:1-10).

1:2. This is the only salutation in which Paul speaks of **all the brethren who are with me,** and it is impossible to know who are in Paul's mind— perhaps the whole congregation from which he is writing, or a small group of companions with whom he is traveling, or possibly those associated with him during a period of imprisonment (cf. Phil. 4:21; see Intro.).

1:3-5. When Paul speaks of Christ's self-giving (vs. 4) he has in mind his death (cf. 2:20; Phil. 2:7-8). There is a certain parallelism here between **our sins** and **the present evil age.** To be rescued from "this age" is to be freed from sin, for sin means bondage to this-worldly values. It is Christ's death which makes possible this freedom, as Paul emphasizes in chs. 5-6 (esp. 6:14).

II. THE OCCASION FOR WRITING (1:6-10)

The most striking feature of the opening of this letter is the absence of Paul's customary "thanksgiving," i.e. a formal paragraph giving thanks to God for the faith and love of his readers (cf. e.g. Rom. 1:8-15; I Cor. 1:4-9). The reason for the omission is not difficult to ascertain: Paul is upset not only with his opponents (vss. 7-9) but with his readers. Hence the thanksgiving is replaced with the blunt words of vss. 6-9. Paul's amazement has a 2-fold cause; that the Gals. would desert God and turn to a **different gospel** and that this would happen **so quickly.** To what interval of time does Paul refer: since his readers' conversion, or since his last visit, or since the arrival of the troublemakers in Galatia? In any case the whole matter has come as a shock to him.

1:6-7. The care to distinguish between a **different gospel** (respecting kind) and **another gospel** (respecting number) is significant in the light of the agreement reported in 2:1-10. As far as Paul is concerned there is only one true gospel—though it may be preached to the circumcised on the one hand, the uncircumcised on the other. Paul's remarks here clarify I Cor. 9:20-23, where he speaks about missionary strategy. Strategic adaptations should not involve theological adaptations in any substantive sense, for in that case, as in Galatia, the one true gospel would be perverted.

1:8-9. In contrast with Phil. 1:15-18, where he rejoices that his opponents are preaching Christ, Paul here shows not the least willingness to be tolerant, and twice invokes divine censure on the preachers of any false gospel. The difference in attitude is due to the difference in the situation. The Philippian opponents preach the true gospel even though they are insincere. These opponents, however, do not preach the true gospel and—whether they are sincere or not, no matter what their personal status and credentials—should be accorded no hearing. Thus the issue Paul addresses in Gal. is the truth of the gospel. The rest of the letter is an attempt to define what this is and to exhort the Gals. to hold it fast without compromise.

1:10. The emphasis falls on the word **now.** Surely the strict words of vss. 8-9 do not support the charge made by Paul's opponents that he has been ingratiating himself to his congregations. Ultimately he is accountable only to the God from whom his apostleship derives.

III. PAUL'S DEFENSE OF HIS APOSTOLIC AUTHORITY (1:11-2:10)

1:11-16b. The Circumstances of His Call. Again (cf. vs. 1) Paul emphasizes the divine origin of his gospel and call, which he says were received, not from men, but through **revelation.**

1:13-14. Paul's reference to his former attainments in Judaism and his persecution of the church (cf. Acts 8:3; 22:3-5; Phil. 3:5-6) is probably in answer to opponents who have been citing his past to support their charges against him. They would find there grounds for doubting Paul's present sincerity, but Paul himself regards the fact of his call from the law to Christ as evidence of its divine origin.

1:15-16b. Paul stresses God's initiative in calling him. Like the OT prophets he regards his call as prenatal (cf. Jer. 1:5; Isa. 49:1) and makes no distinction between his conversion and his commissioning. He was called for a specific task and purpose, to preach the gospel to the Gentiles. It is significant that Paul is not preoccupied with the historical circumstances of his conversion and call. Though in these vss. we have the most explicit reference to the event to be found in his letters, none of the details recounted in Acts (9:1-19; 22:4-16; 26:9-18) are present save, indirectly, in the indication that it occurred near **Damascus** (vs. 17).

1:16c-24. His Independence of the Jerusalem Apostles. Grammatically vss. 15-17 constitute just one sentence, but substantively Paul moves on to a 2nd argument for the validity of his apostleship when he says: **I did not confer with flesh and blood.** It is useless to speculate on what he did in **Arabia,** for his point is only what he did not do after his conversion: he did not **go up to Jerusalem** for instruction, but **went away** without consulting those who were apostles before him. This remark is intended to corroborate the strictly divine origin of his apostleship and his gospel.

1:18-20. Paul further emphasizes his independence. Only after an interval of **three years** did he go to Jerusalem. He remained only a short time, conferred with only one of the apostles, and **saw** only one other. **Cephas** is Aramaic, as Peter (2:7-

8) is Greek, for "rock," the nickname Jesus gave Simon, the leader of the 12 (cf. John 1:42). On **James the Lord's brother** see comment on Acts 12:17. It is impossible to know the reason for Paul's visit with Peter—whether to obtain information, to make an accounting of his ministry, or simply to get acquainted. The last is the most probable, for Paul's main concern is to demonstrate his independence of Jerusalem, and he mentions the visit only to show its insignificance so far as the impetus for and content of his ministry were concerned. The added oath (vs. 20) indicates Paul's defensiveness and perhaps also his knowledge of counterarguments already or likely to be presented.

1:21-24. Leaving Jerusalem, Paul went **preaching the faith** in the regions of **Syria and Cilicia.** Little else is known of this period of his ministry, which Acts appears to skip over (cf. Acts 9:30; 11: 25-26). It has been suggested that Paul means here only that he started out in Syria and Cilicia, and that before revisiting Jerusalem (2:1) he went on from there to Asia, Macedonia, and Greece—travels assigned to a later period in the Acts narrative. Paul's comment that he was **not known by sight** to the Christians of Judea raises some question about the reference in Acts 22:3 to Paul's having studied with Rabbi Gamaliel in Jerusalem. Vss. 23-24 underscore the point already made, that Paul's past life as a persecutor of the church authenticates rather than casts doubt on the divine origin of his apostleship, and add the new point (vs. 24) that opposition to Paul is something recent.

2:1-10. *His Approval by the Jerusalem Apostles.* Paul's 2nd visit to Jerusalem was different in several respects: (*a*) Paul was accompanied this time by **Barnabas,** an apostolic associate (cf. I Cor. 9:6; Col. 4:10, and many passages in Acts) and Titus, to whom Paul elsewhere refers as his "brother" and "partner" (II Cor. 2:13; 8:23). (*b*) The meeting was not with Cephas only, but with the other **reputed . . . pillars** of the Jerusalem church, James (cf. 1:19) and John, as well (vss. 2, 6, 9). (*c*) Paul specifically refers to both the purpose and outcome of this visit. Its purpose was to lay before the pillar apostles the gospel which he had for 17 years been preaching to the Gentiles (vs. 2) and its outcome was an agreement to divide the mission field into work with Jews and work with Gentiles (vs. 9).

Most commentators have regarded Acts 15:1-29 as a parallel, complementary account of the Jerusalem consultation Paul describes here. But there are important differences in the 2 passages, which have led some to believe that this letter must have been written before the meeting of Acts 15 (see Intro.) and accordingly that the consultation Paul tells about is to be identified with his visit to Jerusalem mentioned in Acts 11:27-30 (see comments on Acts 11:27-30; 15:1-35).

2:1-2. Paul is intent on correcting the mistaken notion that he or his gospel was in any sense on trial in Jerusalem. He was not summoned for a public hearing; he **went up by revelation** for a private consultation (vs. 2) only after a long, uninterrupted period of preaching (vs. 1). This emphasis conforms to the point he has already made about his independence of Jerusalem. Conceivably **fourteen years** is reckoned from his conversion (1:16), but more

likely it is reckoned from his first visit to Jerusalem (1:18).

2:3-5. The critical issue for Paul's gospel and ministry concerns the Christian's freedom from the law (vs. 4), and it has been raised in concrete fashion by the dispute over the need for Gentile converts to be circumcised. For this special reason Paul mentions **taking Titus along with me** (vs. 1). Though Titus was an uncircumcised Gentile not even the Jerusalem apostles **compelled** him **to be circumcised** (vs. 3). Some interpreters hold that the emphasis here is on the word "compelled" and that Titus did in fact voluntarily agree to circumcision out of consideration for Paul's total relationship with Jerusalem. According to this view the jumbled syntax of vss. 4-5 reflects Paul's embarrassment about having made such a concession and his eagerness to maintain that it constituted no essential surrender of his position.

On the other hand it is hardly conceivable that the "no compromise" position of 5:2-4 could be so radically stated by one who earlier in the same letter has admitted any kind of concession respecting circumcision, for whatever reason. It is more probable that Titus left the Jerusalem meeting just as he had come to it—an uncircumcised Gentile Christian—and that, therefore, Paul means in the strictest sense what he says about not having yielded submission **even for a moment** (vs. 5). Titus has become a living witness to the approval accorded Paul's gospel by the pillar apostles themselves. Because those to whom Paul refers as having **slipped in to spy out** the Gentiles' **freedom . . . in Christ Jesus** (vs. 4) are called **false brethren,** they are obviously within the church.

2:6-8. Though Paul stresses the recognition accorded his ministry by the Jerusalem apostles, he still guards against the impression that his gospel has been in any detail corrected or supplemented by them. He made no concessions; his preaching after the consultation was different in no respect from what it had been previously (vs. 6). Paul's ministry had its own integrity and authenticity, grounded in a divine call through which he, like Peter, had been **entrusted with the gospel** (vs. 7) and endowed with apostolic **grace** (vs. 9). Nothing is said here about 2 gospels (see above on 1:6-7); there are only 2 ministries of the one true gospel. Yet the significance of the agreement lies, not just in the comity arrangement concluded, but in Jerusalem's recognition of Paul's mission to the Gentiles, which confirms his preaching of freedom in Christ.

2:9-10. Two symbols of the agreement at Jerusalem are mentioned: one, the **right hand of fellowship** (vs. 9), formal and fleeting; the other, an offering from Paul's Gentile churches for Jerusalem (vs. 10), material and continuing. Paul's stress on his own eagerness to raise such an offering may indicate that this agreement too has been held up by his opponents in order to prove Paul's subordination to those who were apostles before him. References to the Gentile offering in his other letters (e.g. Rom. 15:25-32; I Cor. 16:1-4; II Cor. 8–9) indicate the importance he attached to it as a symbol of the unity of the church, the ecumenical scope of the gospel, and the oneness in Christ of both Jew and Gentile.

IV. Paul's Defense of His Apostolic Message (2:11–3:18)

A. Life by Faith Apart from Works (2:11-21)

2:11-14. Peter's Vacillation. Little else than what these vss. tell us can be known about the confrontation of Paul and Peter (Cephas) at **Antioch,** a center of Gentile Christian activity. Neither the occasion of Peter's visit—whether to inspect, to preach, or to confer with Paul—nor the time of it is definitely ascertainable. In 1:18–2:10 events are reported in historical sequence—note **Then** in 1:18, 21; 2:1—but the expression which opens vs. 11 seems to break the sequence. It is conceivable that the Antioch affair actually preceded the Jerusalem consultation (vss. 1-10) and is mentioned after it in the letter only because it is Paul's best evidence for the validity of his mission.

2:12. On his arrival in Antioch, Paul reports, Peter found a Christian congregation already integrated, Jewish and Gentile Christians participating fully together even at the points counter to Jewish law; and he willingly joined their fellowship. But presently **certain men** came to Antioch representing **James** (cf. 1:19; 2:9). Paul does not name them, either because nothing requires it or because he does not wish to accord them even that minimal dignity. Whether he means to identify them with the **false brethren** (vs. 4) is doubtful. In any case their coming caused Peter to withdraw from table fellowship with the Gentile Christians, **fearing the circumcision party,** i.e. those who argued for the necessity of such Jewish requirements as circumcision and the kosher table as conditions for full participation in the gospel and the church. It may be that James and his representatives sought to mediate between these extremists and Paul, but Paul himself gives no clue as to the specific dynamics of this internal struggle.

2:13. Peter and others—**even Barnabas**—were lured into forsaking their own principles in the matter. Paul accuses them, not of a fundamental change of mind about the nature and implications of the gospel, but of acting **insincerely,** i.e. hypocritically, in respect to their own best judgment. And he does not say that Barnabas was persuaded of anything; rather, he, like the others, was **carried away** and deserted his own convictions.

2:14. Discerning that the **truth of the gospel** was endangered by Peter's tactic of retreat and compromise, Paul faced the issue head-on, charging him with hypocrisy. The reference to Peter's living **like a Gentile** must relate to his prior willingness to eat with the Gentile Christians, which had in itself been an affirmation of the truth of the gospel of freedom. It is important for the argument that Peter's subsequent withdrawal from the integrated table be blamed, not on his doubts about the validity of that gospel, but on his acceding hypocritically to the representations of **certain men . . . from James.** It is also important that Paul's readers know Peter was brought to public account for his actions.

Paul's intention in Gal. is not historical but hortatory. He is writing not simply to chronicle the events at Antioch but to address the Gal. Christians with words of warning and instruction. Hence it is impossible to reconstruct those events in detail or to analyze the subtleties of Paul's dispute with Peter. The words Paul says he spoke to Peter are actually directed to the Gals. Paul exhorts them not to forsake the truth of the gospel by acting hypocritically with respect to the freedom Christ bestows on Jew and Gentile alike. This hortatory motive in vss. 11-14 is reflected in the omission of any report about Peter's response to Paul's challenge, and in the way the words addressed specifically to Peter merge into a discussion (vss. 15-21) which far transcends, yet never quite loses sight of, the particularity of the events at Antioch.

2:15-21. Justification by Faith. Paul states without qualification his absolutely fundamental thesis that being **justified,** i.e. man's right relationship with God, is not won by **works of the law** but comes only **through faith in Jesus Christ.** It is this truth he warns the Galatians they dare not in the slightest compromise. Paul describes himself as a Jew **by birth** and then proceeds to affirm that this Jewish heritage is not of itself the way to justification (cf. Phil. 3:3-11). To Jews, Gentiles were *ipso facto* **sinners** because they did not share in the Jewish national heritage of law and covenant. But for Paul all men—Jews as well as Gentiles—are sinners (cf. Rom. 3:22b-23), and all are therefore equally dependent on God's grace, received through faith (cf. Rom. 3:24-25). The posing of faith and works in this antithetical way is a distinctively Pauline contribution to Christian theology. It not only permitted and prompted the church's Gentile mission but also led in due course to its irreconcilable break with the synagogue.

2:17. The Antioch situation is still in Paul's mind. He acknowledges and then dismisses an argument of his opponents against the integrated table: If their doctrine of freedom in Christ leads Jews to break the dietary regulations of the law by eating with Gentiles, then **Christ** has become an **agent of sin!** Paul's response to such logic is emphatic. The objection has no more validity than the prejudicial formula **Gentile sinners** because both identify sin with breaking particular injunctions of the law, while for Paul sin in its most radical dimension is pride and boasting, to which both Jews (cf. Rom. 2:17, 23) and Gentiles (cf. I Cor. 1:19-31) are in bondage.

2:18. Paul seems to ponder the terrible consequences were he to change his tactics and lay on Gentile converts the formalities of the law. These are the **things** that by preaching the gospel he has torn down. Were he now to enjoin them he himself would become a **transgressor** of the true gospel of freedom in Christ.

2:19. Now Paul moves far beyond the previous criticism of works of the law to a criticism of the law itself. He says, not that the law is dead, but that he—his "ego"—is dead to the law, that the law no longer has dominion over him. Paul speaks here of the meaning of the Christian's life, and the passage should not be interpreted in a narrowly autobiographical sense. He stresses the Christian's relationship to God, by which alone one has true life and true freedom. For in dying to that which enslaves—the law—he is authentically free to live in God. Parallel ideas are present in Rom. 7:4, 6, where it is said that one dies to the law "through the body of Christ" (Rom. 7:4), not **through the**

law. Vs. 20*a* shows that these statements involve no essential contradiction, because the law itself plays a role in the death of Christ, through whom freedom is bestowed. Cf. 3:10-14.

2:20. Three essential aspects of the new life are expressed in this vs.:

a) It is bestowed in the 2-fold event of crucifixion-resurrection (cf. Rom. 6:5). By participation in Christ's death one dies to his old self and is freed from the tyranny of the past, the world, and his own ego. And by participation in Christ's resurrection one lives to God and is freed for a life of responsible and grateful obedience. The Christian's life is so invested by the power and grace of God that Paul may say it is not the Christian himself who lives but Christ who lives in him (cf. 4:19).

b) The new life is lived **in the flesh,** i.e. in the world. Paul nowhere suggests that the Christian life requires withdrawal from the world. But it is **by faith,** for thus one participates in Christ's crucifixion-resurrection, dies to his old self, and lives to God in Christ. Faith is man's response to God's saving initiative taken in the cross, openness to the gift of grace, and obedience to the demands of love.

c) Paul defines the object and content of this faith as the **Son of God who loved me and gave himself for me.** The phrase is parallel with the declaration of John 3:16: "For God so *loved* the world that he *gave* his only Son, that whoever *believes* in him should not perish but have eternal life." In each passage it is the whole event of the Incarnation, but esp. the Crucifixion, which is in the author's mind as the decisive act of self-giving love (cf. 1:4). And in each passage the benefits of Christ's passion are said to be received by faith which each writer understands as grateful obedience to the commandment of love (cf. 5:6, 13-25; John 15:9-13). Love is total, unconditional surrender to God's will, the complete giving of oneself to others, as the instance of God's own sacrificial love in the Cross effectively reveals. Hence the appropriation and implementation of this self-giving love is set sharply over against works of law, which require formal and conditional obedience but not the radical and unconditional obedience seen in the Cross.

2:21. This recapitulates the whole preceding argument. Compelling the Gentiles to live like Jews (vs. 14) would in effect reinstitute the statutes of the law as the way of righteousness (vs. 18). But the Christian dies to the law (vs. 19) as he shares in Christ's crucifixion-resurrection (vs. 20), by which the law has been stripped of its power. The affirmation of vs. 21*a* is by intention and in effect an exhortation not to **nullify** God's **grace** by compelling the Gentiles to live like Jews. That would presuppose that righteousness is through law; if that is true, Christ's death was a magnificent but meaningless tragedy.

B. The Authenticity of the Gospel (3:1-18)

3:1-5. *Demonstration from Experience.* Fearing that the Gals. no less than Peter and his group (2:11-14) are in danger of falling away from the truth of the gospel, Paul addresses them with sharp words which imply that they have been distracted from the crucial center of that gospel, **Jesus Christ . . . crucified.** The authenticity of this gospel he seeks to demon-strate first from their own experience. He reminds them that they received the Spirit **by hearing with faith**—lit. "by [the] hearing of faith," which probably means "by the hearing which faith is"—and not **by works of the law.** Faith is "hearing" in the extended sense of surrender, commitment, and obedience (cf. Rom. 10:14-17). The antithesis of faith and works is momentarily transmuted into the corresponding one, **Spirit** and **flesh,** as Paul contrasts worldly "guarantees" of salvation—e.g. circumcision, the kosher table—with the gift of God's Spirit, to which faith alone is the appropriate response. But then (vs. 5) attention is shifted from those who have received the Spirit to the one who supplies it, and to the mighty deeds (**miracles**) which are wrought thereby (cf. I Cor. 12:10, 28-29).

3:6-18. *Demonstration from Scripture.* Scripture itself bears witness to the authenticity of Paul's gospel. The Gal. errorists have evidently argued, on the basis of Gen. 17:10-14, that only those who are circumcised are truly Abraham's **sons** and heirs of the promise of salvation. In response the apostle appeals to 2 other parts of the Abraham story (cf. Rom. 4): (*a*) He cites Gen. 15:6 (vs. 6) and assumes his readers will recognize that the key words are **believed,** i.e. "had faith," and **was reckoned,** as opposed to "earned." Righteousness is not achieved by works of law, but is bestowed as a gift on those who live by faith. (*b*) He quotes Gen. 18:18 (vs. 8) as support for the further claim that, since Abraham's true sons are those who live by faith, Gentiles as well as Jews may share in the promises.

3:10-12. Still more scriptural attestation to the truth of the gospel is available. The law itself (Deut. 27:26) testifies that those who seek to do it are **under a curse** (vs. 10). From Paul's standpoint this is so because the law demands doing, in a formal, legalistic sense, while Abraham's example and Christ's death both demonstrate that righteousness and true life come through believing. Paul's chief criticism of the law is not that its demands are impossible, but that they are superficial and that conformity to them is ineffectual. Faith, in fact, asks far more than conformity to rules of conduct; it asks for the surrender of the whole man, nothing withheld. The law is a curse because it asks for doing and presupposes that righteousness is earned thereby, whereas in reality doing leads to pride in accomplishment, which is the essence of sin. Hab. 2:4, cited in vs. 11, is another favorite Pauline text (cf. Rom. 1:17). Vs. 12 quotes Lev. 18:5.

3:13-14. Redemption **from the curse of the law** comes through Christ (cf. Rom. 7:24-25*a*) in whom the **blessing of Abraham** has been fulfilled. This blessing is identified with the Spirit's coming **through faith** (as in vss. 1-5). The statement that Christ has **become a curse for us** is prompted more by the words of Deut. 21:23, interpreted as a reference to the Crucifixion, than it is by the logic of Paul's own argument in this passage. He probably has in mind the general idea that Christ bore man's sins "in his body on the tree" (I Pet. 2:24; cf. Rom. 8:3).

3:15-16. Here is Paul's chief explanation of how Christ redeems man from the curse of the law. He uses the illustration of a legal testament or **will,** basing his argument on the coincidence that the Greek word used in the LXX for God's covenant with Abraham also had this meaning. That covenant remains valid, he claims, because a will can be neither nullified nor supplemented. In Gen. 12:7, as in Deut. 21:23 cited earlier, Paul finds a reference to Christ. This time he takes advantage of the noun **offspring,** which though plural in meaning is singular in form. The offspring is Christ, in whom is the fulfillment of God's covenant with Abraham, and by whom one is redeemed from the curse of the law.

3:17-18. Paul's employment of OT proofs is continued as he points out that chronologically the **covenant** and its **promise** preceded the giving of the law, and that the law in no way suspends or supplements the prior arrangement. God's covenant is embodied, not in the law, but in the promise fulfilled in Christ. Therefore when the prophet says, "He who through faith is righteous shall live" (vs. 11), he bears witness to the necessity of believing in Christ as opposed to doing works of the law.

V. THE FUNCTION OF THE LAW (3:19-4:7)

3:19-22. *The Definer of Sin.* The question opening this section has been raised by the course of Paul's own argument, which has so far suggested a purely negative evaluation of the law and its works (cf. Rom. 7:7-25). Some proper role for the law in God's plan is presupposed, but his first response—**because of transgressions**—is too compact to suffice without the clarification supplied by Rom. 3:20; 4:15; 5:20. These show that the phrase here means the law's function is to prompt sin into being; it was given "for the purpose of producing transgressions" (Moffatt trans.) and thereby presumably of laying men open to receive the benefits of God's grace. Paul rejects the notion that the law is contrary to God's **promises** (vs. 21). He holds, rather, that its function is to define man's legal standing before God and is therefore incapable of effecting righteousness and transforming one's relationship to God. Righteousness is **given to those who believe** in Jesus Christ (vs. 22). Even as he defines the law's place in salvation, Paul presumes its inferiority to the promises and to the faith. The law is secondary and temporary—**it was added . . . till the offspring should come**—not a gift of God himself, but ordained by angels and offered through an intermediary, i.e. Moses.

3:23-29. *The Restrainer of the Immature.* The crucial word in this passage is **custodian** (vss. 24-25), the translation of the Greek word for a household assistant—usually a slave—to whom the superintendence of a minor child was entrusted. By applying this term to the law Paul stresses 2 points: that the law's function is to impede and hold down, in sin! (cf. Rom. 7:7-25), and that its tenure as an effective instrument of God's plan is limited—until **faith should be revealed** and **Christ came.** Paul may also be thinking of another limitation of the law—that it had its jurisdiction only within Judaism—for he emphasizes that **in Christ Jesus . . . all are sons of God, through faith** (cf. vss. 7-9). Man's relation to God is defined by his humble and obedient openness to receive, not by his prideful eagerness to achieve.

3:27-29. The inclusiveness of the gospel is illustrated by reference to baptism. It is the sign and seal of one's crucifixion and new life with Christ (cf. 2:20) and can thus be spoken of as having **put Christ on** (cf. Rom. 13:14; Eph. 4:24). Since baptism unites all men with Christ (cf. I Cor. 12:13) it unites them with one another, for all are brethren "for whom Christ died" (I Cor. 8:11; cf. Rom. 14:15) and all who believe, without distinction, have one Lord (Rom. 10:12-13; cf. Eph. 2:11-22; Col. 3:11). The description of Christians as **Abraham's offspring** (vs. 29) reflects the argument of vss. 6-18 but also introduces a new element into Paul's development of the custodial function of the law. When sons come of age and pass from life under the law to life in Christ they become full **heirs** of the promises of God (cf. 4:1-7).

4:1-7. *Slavery Under the Law.* This concluding passage on the law has an instructive parallel in Rom. 8:1-17. Man apart from Christ, living under the law, is like a minor **child** for whom the inheritance is only prospective. He is **no better than a slave,** for he is not free to inherit what is promised. Paul avoids saying that men without Christ are slaves to the law; rather they are **slaves to the elemental spirits** (lit. "elements") **of the universe** (vs. 3; cf. vs. 9; Col. 2:20). Commentators interpret this reference in different ways, e.g. as basic religious teachings shared by all men, or as demonic powers which played a role in many ancient religions. In either case Paul is contrasting life in Christ (in freedom) with life under the law (in bondage).

4:4-7. The "fullness of time" (so lit. vs. 4a) is parallel with the **date set by the father** (vs. 2) and expresses the purposefulness of God's sending his Son in fulfillment of the promise made to Abraham (3:14). This is the strongest statement of the Incarnation in Paul's letters, made so by the added phrases **born of woman, born under the law.** But the emphasis here is on the 2-fold purpose of Christ's coming: first, to **redeem** men from bondage; second, to make possible their **adoption as sons** (vs. 5). Redemption (cf. 3:13; Rom. 3:24; 8:23; I Cor. 6:20; 7:23) is the freedom which God's act in Christ makes possible: freedom from the self-defeating struggle for status before God, from enslaving preoccupation with one's own worthiness; and freedom for the full attainment of one's true maturity as an heir of God's promises.

When Paul speaks of **adoption as sons** he is mindful of a 2nd aspect of salvation: the bestowal of full rights as heirs and full access to the Father. Here and in Rom. 8:14-17, 23 he connects adoption esp. with the gift of the **Spirit,** by which one is enabled to place his full confidence in and pledge his total commitment to God the Father. As symbolic of this relationship Paul cites the words by which God is addressed in prayer: **Abba! Father!** That God is thus addressed in both Aramaic and Greek suggests a fixed liturgical form, perhaps the introductory words of a prayer offered by the newly baptized convert expressing the new access to God he finds in Christ. In conclusion (vs. 7) Paul stresses that salvation is from God himself. By God's initiative the **Son** was **sent** (vs. 4) and the Spirit given (vs. 6). The ultimate reference of all preaching and the fundamental object of all faith is God (cf. I Cor. 3:23).

VI. Freedom in Christ (4:8–6:10)

A. The Importance of Freedom (4:8–5:1)

4:8-20. *Another Appeal to Experience.* Paul's concern in this letter is that the Gals. hold to the truth of what the gospel declares about Christian freedom (cf. vss. 1-7; 2:4, 11-21). The "contrary gospel" (1:9) to which the Gals. are being attracted would in fact lead them back into their preconversion bondage, for slavery to the law (vss. 1-3) is essentially the same as their pagan slavery to **beings that by nature are no gods** (cf. Rom. 1:19-23; I Cor. 8:5-6; I Thess. 4:5).

4:9. There is special significance in Paul's preference for the phrase **be known by God** as a description of the Christian life. The knowledge of God about which Paul speaks is love of him, a response to his knowledge, i.e. love, of us (cf. I Cor. 8:2-3). Paul is perhaps seeking to correct the false idea that there is some special mystic knowledge available to the Christian, attainment to which would be a mark of spiritual superiority. On **elemental spirits** see above on vss. 1-7.

4:10-11. It is possible that Paul intended vs. 10, like vss. 8-9, as a question. The effect would then be: "What will you come to next? Once you have deserted the central truth that righteousness is a gift to those who live by faith, and are bewitched by the deceptive notion that performance of good works or religious rites (e.g. circumcision) allows you to make a claim on God, the end can only be a total loss of freedom to become the person God created you to be." This possibility leads Paul to the momentary pessimism of vs. 11 (cf. vss. 15-20; contrast 5:10).

4:12-20. *Paul's Relations with the Gals.* The basis of Paul's entreaty here is neither scriptural nor theological but personal. First (vs. 12) he would have the Gals. follow his example and forsake bondage to the law for a new freedom in Christ (cf. Phil. 3:4-11). As Paul renounced the supposed advantages of Judaism to preach the gospel to the Gentiles (cf. 2:15-16; I Cor. 9:21), so now he asks them to renounce the supposed advantages of the false teaching to become as he is—in Christ. Beyond this is Paul's appeal "for old times' sake." The Gals. gave him warm welcome under very trying conditions (vss. 12b-14) and found his message worthy of their fullest commitment (vs. 15). What the **bodily ailment** was which detained Paul in Galatia (vs. 13) and whether that was his "thorn in the flesh" (II Cor. 12:7) is uncertain. His testimony that the Gals. would have given him their own **eyes** indicates the depth of their former affection for him and the extent of their initial commitment to his gospel.

4:16-19. The relationship between Paul and the Gals. is changed now, because of something he has either said or done (vs. 16; see RSV footnote). The original readers undoubtedly were better able to discern Paul's reference than we are. This is also true of vss. 17-18, the precise meaning of which is now obscure. The motives of the false teachers are here criticized, just as Paul's motives have been called into question by them (see above on 1:10). There is special poignancy in the appeal of vs. 19, though the metaphors are mixed. Paul's mention of his **travail** suggests he is like a mother to them,

even though finally he speaks of Christ's being **formed** in them. The thought is that the new birth effects such a radical transformation of one's whole being that it is no longer he who lives but Christ who lives in him (cf. 2:20).

4:20. Finally Paul frankly admits his perplexity over the Gals. Throughout this letter, as throughout II Cor. 10-13 (cf. esp. 11:4-13), Paul is anxious and upset, worried about his congregation, agitated by troublemakers, frustrated about his inability to rectify the situation, aware of the need to use strong words of rebuke, yet reluctant to use them. He wishes a personal visit were possible, that somehow a mutual understanding could be reached which would allow him to change his tone.

4:21-30. *Another Demonstration from Scripture.* Paul returns to the story of Abraham (cf. 3:6-29) for scriptural evidence concerning the importance of freedom. In rabbinical fashion he allegorizes the account of Abraham's 2 wives (Gen. 16:15; 21:1-21). Sarah was a **free woman** and her son **Isaac** was born **through promise**—a word used earlier to refer to the gospel (cf. 3:8, 14, 16-18). But **Hagar** was a **slave** and her son Ishmael was born **according to the flesh** (vs. 23).

4:24-27. Paul extends the allegory by identifying the 2 women with 2 different **covenants,** presumably an "old" and a "new," and with 2 different Jerusalems—one **present,** earthly, another **above,** heavenly. The passage quoted from Isa. 54:1 (vs. 27) speaks of Jerusalem before and after the Exile. With her people gone into captivity (the **barren** woman) Jerusalem has more cause for rejoicing than before (**she who hath a husband**), for after the ordeal her prosperity will exceed that of former times (**the desolate hath more children**). Thus Paul insists that the new Jerusalem offers far more than the old, freedom far more than slavery, the gospel far more than the law.

4:28-30. The **children of promise** are Abraham's heirs by virtue of belonging to Christ (cf. 3:29). The reference to Ishmael's persecution of Isaac (vs. 29) probably derives from rabbinic elaborations of Gen. 21:9; **so it is now** perhaps alludes to the harassment of the Gals. by the troublemakers. The description of Christians as **born according to the Spirit** recalls 3:2-5, 14; 4:6 and anticipates 5:16–6:10. Paul means the admonition of Gen. 21:10 (vs. 30) to be applied by the Gals. to their own case; they ought to dissociate themselves from the false teachers who seek to lead them back into bondage (cf. 1:8-9).

4:31–5:1. *Exhortation to Remain Free.* The meaning of scripture is plain: to be in Christ is to be free from legalistic constraints of all kinds. Any compromise sullies the integrity of the gospel. To give away one point is to give away all and return to the **yoke of slavery** (cf. 4:8-11). The necessary succinctness of this conclusion accentuates 2 paradoxes which go to the very center of Paul's thought: (*a*) The paradox of indicative and imperative, the event and its demand. **We are . . . children . . . of the free woman; we have been set . . . free.** Therefore **stand fast** and **do not submit** (see below on 5:25-26). (*b*) The paradox of freedom itself. Christ has freed us **for freedom!** It is the meaning of this Christian freedom which is explored in the following section.

B. The Meaning of True Freedom (5:2–6:10)

5:2-15. Faith Rendered Active in Love. The occasion for this letter is the dispute about **circumcision** (see above on 1:6-10) and it is in this connection that Paul writes of freedom. Christians who view circumcision as a necessary requirement are denying the truth of the gospel. Security cannot be attained by the performance of religious or moral duties, but only by faith—surrendering all attempts to win one's own way with God.

5:3-4. One's decision about circumcision has broad implications: to accept circumcision means, in principle, to place oneself under the jurisdiction of the **whole law.** When Paul speaks of being **severed from Christ** he employs the same verb used in Rom. 7:2-6 of the Christian's "discharge" from the law. To be in Christ is to be discharged from the law, and to be under law is to be severed from Christ. The same thought is implicit in **fallen away from grace,** for grace and law are also antithetical concepts (cf. Rom. 6:14).

5:5-6. Justification comes, not by law, but **through the Spirit, by faith;** and it is not an event on which the Christian may look back with pride but a goal to which he looks forward in **hope.** The Christian life permits no complacent contemplation of past attainments but involves ever new commitments (cf. Phil. 3:7-14). This is what Paul means by **wait**—not the purposeless passivity of loitering, but alertness, expectancy, and obedience. The kind of waiting and hoping to which the Christian is called is clarified in vs. 6, one of 3 instances where Paul declares that it is a matter of indifference whether one is circumcised. In I Cor. 7:19 he says what does matter is "keeping the commandments of God," which for him are summarized in the single commandment to love one's neighbor (cf. vs. 14). That comment is parallel with the statement here that what really matters is **faith working through love,** and these 2 illumine the 3rd passage (6:15), which refers to a "new creation." It is possible that here Paul has in mind both God's love and man's: faith is rendered active by God's love, to which it is a response, and finds expression in man's obedience to the commandment of love.

5:7-12. Obedience in love (vs. 6) is also described as obedience to the **truth** of the gospel, from which Paul fears his readers are being distracted. The proverbial saying of vs. 9 is used, as in I Cor. 5:6, to describe the corrupting influence of boastfulness (cf. Matt. 16:6; Luke 12:1). Presumably the false teachers of Galatia are in mind. The mood of vs. 10 is more optimistic than that of 4:11, 16-20, but the words are of course intended as an admonition to cast out (cf. 4:30) the troublemakers. The persecution to which Paul refers (vs. 11) is probably the sharp criticism of his opponents (cf. 4:29); and he cites it as evidence to refute the claim that he himself has been preaching circumcision for Gentiles. That would contradict the gospel (cf. vs. 2) and thus remove the **stumbling-block of the cross.** The partiality of all good works stands under the divine judgment of the totality of God's demand, which the Cross demonstrates. That is why it is a stumbling-block to the Jews esp. (cf. I Cor. 1:23). The invective of vs. 12 is comparable to that of Phil. 3:2.

5:13-15. Freedom is not to be confused with libertinism. Freedom from the legalism of life under the law does not mean release from responsibility but constitutes a summons to the greater responsibilities of life under grace. The gospel asks more, not less; for though it prescribes only one requirement, neighbor-love, that one is unqualified and its implications cannot be specified in advance. The Christian is not deluded by the alleged security of legalism, recognizing that authentic freedom is attained only as he lives in radical dependence on God's grace and in radical obedience to his will. That will is summarized in the commandment of Lev. 19:18b (cf. Rom. 13:8-10). Where freedom is not exercised in love it leads to mutual destruction, the tragedy and violence of which are graphically portrayed (vs. 15).

5:16-26. Life in the Spirit. Just as love is the proper content of freedom (vss. 2-15), so the Spirit is its proper context, that by which love is empowered and guided. In vs. 16, as in Rom. 8:4, Paul uses the phrase **walk by the Spirit** (cf. Rom. 6:4; 13:13; 14:15; II Cor. 5:7; I Thess. 2:12). Vss. 16, 18 express complementary truths about life in Christ and taken together form another instance of the indicative-imperative motif in Paul's thought (cf. vs. 1; see below on vss. 25-26). The reference to being **led by the Spirit** emphasizes God's gift by which one lives; the exhortation to **walk by the Spirit** stresses the attendant demand. The opposite of walking by the Spirit is "walking according to the flesh" (Rom. 8:4; II Cor. 10:2; cf. I Cor. 3:3; II Cor. 4:2; Phil. 3:18), an idea alternately expressed in vss. 16b-17. In the competition for man's life the **desires of the Spirit** are opposed by the **desires of the flesh,** and these latter may be identified with the demands of legalism (cf. 3:2-5) just as surely as with the promiscuities of libertinism. But it is the problem of libertinism which engages Paul's attention here, as the enumeration of a miscellaneous group of typical pagan vices (vss. 19-21) makes clear.

5:22-24. Over against the **works of the flesh** is placed the **fruit of the Spirit.** This fruit (singular) is the "full harvest of righteousness" (Phil 1:11 NEB) bestowed on those who live by faith. It is significant that **love** stands first in the list which describes the content of that life (cf. vs. 6). **Love, joy, peace,** etc. are not to be regarded as separable Christian virtues in the ordinary sense, for man does not achieve them by his own heroic effort, but receives them by faith. By God's grace, in the power of the Spirit, man's whole life is transformed, and these are the marks of that transformation—not to be confused with the "gifts of the Spirit" (I Cor. 12:4-11; cf. 3:5). Life by faith, in the Spirit, is also life in and with Christ, to whom the Christian belongs as his old self is **crucified** (vs. 24; cf. 2:19-21; 3:26-29).

5:25-26. The discussion here is explicitly hortatory; as in vs. 1, the imperative of Christian responsibility issues from the indicative of God's action. This 2-fold aspect of the gospel finds its classical formulation in vs. 25, which may be paraphrased: "Since we are utterly dependent on the power and prompting of God's Spirit, let us live in relation to his purpose." God is known both, and at once, through what he gives and what he demands, through what he bestows and what he claims. He has given life and made it good by endowing it with freedom and purpose, directing and empowering it by his Spirit, and constantly renewing it in love. And he claims the life he has given, for the gift is only fulfilled as the demand is met and as that freedom is used in the service of God who bestows it. But there is no service of God without service of one's brethren, in which the **whole law is fulfilled** (vs. 14).

6:1-10. *Specific Examples.* Paul applies the phrase **law of Christ** (vs. 2) to the central truth of the gospel for which this letter has been a plea: that righteousness is given to those who live by faith. Faith becomes active in love (5:6), in bondage to which one becomes authentically free. Love seeks to reclaim and set right the trespasser by taking unto itself the **burdens** of his sin and guilt. This is the law of Christ, the kind of love revealed in the Cross (cf. I Cor. 9:21-23).

6:3-5. Vss. 3-4 are characteristically Pauline warnings about pride (cf. Phil. 2:3-4). The Christian ought never use the failings of another as an occasion for self-congratulation. All men have sinned and fall short of God's glory (Rom. 3:23); in relation to God's wisdom all men are fools, and in relation to his power all men are weak (I Cor. 1:25; 3:19), really **nothing** (vs. 3; cf. I Cor. 3:7). Vs. 5 does not contradict vs. 2, for the new word **load** refers to one's individual responsibility before God, from which he can never flee—not to his sin and guilt, from which, in the sharing of love, he may be redeemed.

6:6-10. These admonitions are loosely connected with, but not unrelated to, the discussion of life in the Spirit. Though these traditional sayings ought not to be interpreted too specifically with reference to the Gal. situation, each has a certain indirect applicability. Those who receive the gospel become joint shareholders with those by whom it is preached (vs. 6). They are accountable to God for the responsible use of their freedom (vss. 7-8), for its misuse leads to destruction (cf. 5:15, 19-21) but its proper use to eternal life (cf. 5:22-23). There is a play on words in vs. 9 which cannot be reproduced in English, but its effect is suggested by a paraphrase: "Let us not 'go to seed' in our sowing!" In time the harvest shall come, for it is wrought by the Spirit's power (cf. 5:22-23). The admonition to **do good** is synonymous with the command to love. Paul's emphasis on the **household of faith** is of course not meant to be restrictive of love to brethren within the community of the church.

VII. Conclusion (6:11-18)

6:11-16. *A New Creation.* This final paragraph was not dictated to a stenographer but written in Paul's own hand (cf. I Cor. 16:21). It is a summation of the appeal which he has been making throughout: that compromise in the matter of Gentile circumcision would empty the Cross of its power and invalidate the truth of the gospel. The Gal. troublemakers are charged with preaching circumcision only in order to avoid the censure and persecution which might otherwise be incurred (cf. 5:11). Those who are turned away from the true gospel, then, are hypocrites not only with respect to their Christianity (cf. 2:11-14) but also with respect to the law; for the false teachers are not any better Jews than they are Christians (vs. 13). They apparently regard circumcision as a symbol of religious prestige; and here, as in 4:17, that is cause for reproof.

6:14-16. The Christian's **glory,** i.e. boast, is not in himself (cf. vs. 13) but in the **cross of . . . Christ.** To be in Christ is to be completely reoriented in terms of ultimate values and objectives. So total is this reorientation that it may be spoken of as crucifixion of the self—or of the **world.** Justification comes, not through works of the law, but through the Cross, the **law of Christ** (vs. 2), which is the law of love (cf. 5:14). For through the total self-giving of love one's own "ego" dies and Christ lives in him (cf. 2:19-21). Faith is thus active in love, and this is a **new creation** (vs. 15; note the parallelism with 5:6). This total inner transformation (cf. Rom. 12:1-2) is the **rule,** i.e. cardinal principle, of true religion. In form vs. 16 is a benediction but in function it is an exhortation to **walk,** i.e. order one's life (cf. 5:25), according to the guidance of the Spirit. Those who so walk constitute the authentic **Israel of God,** the true sons of Abraham (cf. 3:9, 29).

6:17-18. *Final Plea and Benediction.* Before concluding with his usual benediction (vs. 18) Paul refers to the **marks of Jesus** which he bears. The reference is probably to the scars of his apostolic sufferings (cf. II Cor. 6:4-10; 11:23-29), which mark him as a slave of Christ, just as the identification on Roman slaves and soldiers designated whose men they were and to whom they owed allegiance. What Paul describes as "the daily pressure . . . of my anxiety for all the churches" (II Cor. 11:28) is nowhere better demonstrated than here in Gal., and nowhere is there a more poignant appeal for release from it than in his hope that henceforth **no man** will **trouble** him by wandering from the truth of the gospel to which he has been once converted.

THE LETTER OF PAUL TO THE EPHESIANS

Victor Paul Furnish

INTRODUCTION

Character and Purpose. Ephesians is not a letter in the strict sense, though its opening (1:1-2) and closing (6:21-24) have been designed to make it appear so. Its tone is cool and distant, it nowhere deals with local problems, its author nowhere has in mind a particular group of readers, it is rich with the rhetoric of worship and doctrine, and it deals in a sustained way with a single theme. Moreover manuscript evidence makes it probable that the words "at Ephesus" (1:1, RSV footnote) did not stand in the original document, and as late as the middle of the 2nd cent. the heretic Marcion was identifying this writing as the Letter to the Laodiceans (see comment on Col. 4:15-17).

Various proposals have been advanced about the purpose of Eph. One views it as a circular letter to a group of churches, but since it is not precisely comparable with the other circular letters in the NT (Gal., I Pet.) this hypothesis has not commended itself to many. Another, widely accepted in the English-speaking world, regards Eph. as a compilation of Pauline texts designed specifically to introduce the central themes of Pauline theology. According to this view the author was not Paul himself but an admiring disciple who composed Eph. as a covering letter to be circulated with Paul's collected letters as a kind of foreword. But this view is purely hypothetical: there is no evidence that Eph. ever stood as the opening letter of the Pauline group; there is nothing within the letter itself to indicate that it was intended to introduce Paul's thought; many of the alleged citations of Paul's letters can better be explained by reliance on common liturgical and ethical traditions (see below) rather than by literary borrowing; and the content of Eph. is influenced by a single dominant concern, viz. the unity of the church under the headship of Christ. The purpose of Eph. must therefore be defined in relation to this central theme.

The author's clearest indications of his purpose in writing occur in 2:1-4:16. In this central section he is concerned to emphasize the unity of Jews and Gentiles within the Christian community. His readers, themselves Gentile Christians (cf. e.g. 2:11), apparently need to be reminded that the history of Israel and the inheritance of Jewish Christianity is an essential part of the tradition in which they stand. The development of this theme proceeds on the basis of several significant theological concepts which have given Eph. a place of theological promi-nence not only within the NT but also within the history of Christian doctrine.

Though the author's originality should not be minimized, his indebtedness to various theological, liturgical, and ethical traditions is substantial. Citation from a hymn in 5:14 is the most obvious in-stance of this, but there are others as well—perhaps 1:5-8, 9-12a, 20-23; 2:4-10, 14-17. The author's exhortations, esp. the "household table" (5:21-6:9) and the "armor of God" passage (6:10-17), reveal a similar use of traditional ethical forms and ideas. Numerous and striking points of similarity to the Dead Sea scrolls suggest that the author stands within the general religious tradition now known to us primarily from the writings of the Jewish com-munity at Qumran (see "The Dead Sea Scrolls," pp. 1063-71).

Authorship. The letter purports to be from Paul (1:1; 3:1-13; 6:21-22) writing from prison (3:1, 13; 4:1; 6:20). Accordingly it is traditionally grouped with Phil., Col., Philem. as written from Rome shortly before Paul's death. At a relatively early date the church at Ephesus was regarded as the recipient, though the original text of the letter prob-ably did not indicate this (see above).

Courtesy of Herbert G. May

Ruins at Ephesus showing the paved road leading from the harbor to the theater (see ill., p. 756) flanked by colonnades and shops

Several considerations, however, weigh decisively against Pauline authorship: (*a*) not only is the literary style and vocabulary different from Paul's, but cer-tain key concepts are stated and developed in a non-Pauline way (e.g. "mystery"; see below on 1:9-10);

834

(b) the author accords the apostles a status and role never given them by Paul (see below on 2:20a; 3:5-6); (c) he always uses the term "church" in a universal sense, while Paul applied it to local congregations; and (d) many of the distinctively Pauline theological emphases are reinterpreted, modified, or subordinated to the author's own special interests.

One further characteristic of Eph. also raises difficulties for the hypothesis of Pauline authorship, viz. its close relationship, in form and content, to Col. (see Intro. to Col.). Parallels in subject matter are numerous, ca. a 3rd of the words in Col. are in Eph., ca. a 4th of the words in Eph. are in Col., and 73 of the 155 vss. in Eph. have verbal connections with Col. Thus defenders of Pauline authorship are required to hold that Eph. and Col. were written one after the other while certain thoughts and even phrases were still fresh in Paul's mind. But such a hypothesis raises further difficulties: (a) Why are there crucial differences between Col. and Eph. in the handling of important topics and ideas? E.g. see below on 1:9-10, 23b; 3:5-6; 4:14-16; 5:15-20; 6:18-20. (b) Why in a relatively unimportant passage would Paul slavishly copy 2 sentences from a letter he had written earlier? The similarity of 6:21-22 to Col. 4:7-8 is too precise to be attributed to anything but literary dependence. (c) Why would Paul follow the same pattern and use so many of the same thoughts and phrases in composing 2 writings with decidedly different purposes? Col. is a letter to a specific congregation about a local problem of false teachers (see Intro. to Col.) whereas Eph. is a general essay on the nature of the church.

Many NT scholars today believe, therefore, that the author of Eph. was not Paul but a devoted admirer of Paul who wrote in his name. His literary style, his place in the religious tradition known also from the Qumran scrolls, and his concern to remind the church of its Jewish heritage suggest that he was a Jewish Christian. It is not possible to determine the place from which he wrote, and he addressed himself to no particular congregation or area but to Christendom at large.

Date. Eph. is to be dated in the postapostolic period when the church had become predominantly Gentile and was in danger of losing a sense of its continuity with Israel, when it was looking back on its apostolic heroes and according them special honors, when it had available richly developed liturgical and theological traditions, and when it was conceiving of itself and its mission in boldly universalistic terms. Since Eph. was known to Ignatius and perhaps also to the authors of I Pet. and I Clement, a date before ca. 95 is probable.

Theological Perspectives. The central theme of Paul's preaching, "Jesus Christ and him crucified" (I Cor. 2:2), still survives in Eph. (2:13-16; cf. 1:7; 5:2, 25) but is by no means the determinative element in the author's theological perspective. Rather the exaltation and enthronement of Christ by and with God "in the heavenly places" is given special prominence (e.g. 1:20; 2:4-6). In the preexistent Christ the will of God has been revealed and accomplished: the unity of all things (1:3-10; 3:11) and their subjection to the cosmic Lord (1:19-23). Salvation, then, is understood as that cosmic peace which is established when all things and all men

are reconciled to God and hence to one another through the redemptive deed of Christ (2:11-21).

Salvation is effected for the individual believer as he dies to his old life and is raised to new life through baptism into the church, Christ's body (1:22-23; 2:4-7). The church itself, "the fulness" of Christ (1:23), was in God's purpose from the beginning of creation and therefore has a cosmic status. It is the place where Christ actually reigns (1:22-23; 4:15-16; 5:23-24), where God is praised (3:21), where the Spirit dwells (2:22), where the "mystery" of God's will is revealed to the apostles and prophets (2:20; 3:4-5), where that will is made known to the "principalities and powers in the heavenly places" (3:10), and where the gifts of God's grace are received and expressed in the transformed lives of the members of the one body (4:1-16).

For this author, then, the cosmic reign of Christ and the status of the church as existing in God's purpose from the beginning of creation are definitive and inseparable concepts. The significance of Christ's person and the nature of the church are closely identified. In this he differs from Paul, to whom, however, he is deeply indebted for many of the basic elements of his theology. And yet at other points, as well, Pauline concepts are significantly altered. One example is the concept of salvation by grace apart from works, which, though emphatically stated in Eph. (2:5, 8-10), presupposes that the believer looks back on salvation as a past accomplished event. In Paul's own letters, on the other hand, salvation is regarded as a present and future event. The dimensions of faith and salvation related to an imminent 2nd coming of Christ are almost totally lacking in Eph., and the traces of the earlier Christian expectation which remain are due largely to the author's use of traditional formulas and phrases.

It is primarily because of the original and systematic development of the idea of the church that this anonymous author has a place of special prominence among the theologians of the NT and that his influence in the subsequent history of Christian doctrine has been considerable. In the 20th cent., because of the treatment of such questions as tradition, the ministry, the nature of Christian unity, and the role of the church in God's plan of salvation, Eph. has been one of the basic documents in the continuing ecumenical discussion. Whether this is justified, whether the attempt to formulate the Christian message and tradition in terms of the nature of the church can ever be successful, and whether a doctrine of the church is properly central in the preaching of the gospel are questions with which the interpreter of Eph. is inescapably confronted.

For Further Study. E. F. Scott, *Col., Philem., Eph.,* 1930. E. J. Goodspeed, *The Meaning of Eph.,* 1933; *The Key to Eph.,* 1956. Stig Hanson, *The Unity of the Church in the NT,* 1947. C. L. Mitton, *Eph.,* 1952. F. W. Beare in *IB,* 1953. George Johnston in *IDB,* 1962.

I. SALUTATION (1:1-2)

The letter is opened in a typically Pauline way. It is probable that the original manuscript contained no reference to Ephesus (see Intro.) and was therefore addressed to Christians in general. Here, as in Paul's own salutations, **saints** describes Christians as people called of God and set aside for his service. They are also **faithful,** i.e. believers, **in Christ Jesus,** and it is one of the author's concerns throughout this whole treatise to specify what true belief in Christ, the head of the church, requires.

II. LITURGICAL PREFACE (1:3-23)

The Pauline letters normally include, following the salutation, a section of thanksgiving to God, though in one instance (II Cor.) this section takes the form of a liturgical blessing of God's name. Here both blessing (vss. 3-14) and thanksgiving (vss. 15-19) are used and the whole section is rich in the language of Jewish and Christian worship. It is in fact very likely that the author has taken over and adapted some lines from the Christian hymnody with which he was familiar. These opening paragraphs sing of God's electing purpose accomplished through Christ, his gracious gifts of redemption and forgiveness, his call to praise, and his bestowal of the Holy Spirit as a guarantee of a future inheritance.

A. HYMN (1:3-14)

1:3-8. God's Purpose to Bless. God's blessedness is here described as his gracious bestowal of a **spiritual blessing** on men, not as an abstract quality of his existence. The phrase **heavenly places** occurs nowhere in the NT except in Eph. (5 times), where it is a description of that cosmic sphere where Christ rules and to which the Christian has been raised to new life in him (vs. 20; 2:6). But it is also a realm where the powers of darkness and evil are still active (3:10; 6:12).

1:4-6. The meaning of **spiritual blessing** (vs. 3) now becomes clearer. It refers, first, to God's eternal **purpose.** In love he has willed that man should be **holy and blameless before him** and should attain to his full stature as a son of his heavenly Father. In this context holiness and blamelessness, while not excluding the idea of moral purity, are associated primarily with the believer's election to sonship (vs. 5). The Greek word translated **be . . . sons** lit. means "adoption as sons" and occurs in several significant passages in Paul's letters (Rom. 8:15, 23; 9:4; Gal. 4:5; see comment on Rom. 8:12-15*b*). It emphasizes both God's initiative in establishing a relationship with men and the character of that relationship: God's paternal love and judgment, man's responsibility to obey. In vss. 6, 12, 14 the purpose of this divine election and adoption is formulated in related ways: **to live for the praise of** God's **grace** and God's **glory.** Thus according to this hymn man was created and destined for the service and the praise of his creator.

Throughout the hymn there is emphasis on the sovereign freedom of God, the eternality of his redemptive purpose, and Christ's role as the revealer and mediator of God's grace—the one in whom God's purposes have been set forth and realized. He is the **Beloved** (vs. 6), preexistent (vs. 4) Son through whom God has **freely bestowed** his **glorious grace** (vs. 6), **riches . . . which he lavished upon us** (vss. 7*b*-8). There is a certain baroque quality to these words, crowded as they are one on another

in an attempt to express the superlative blessing of God.

1:7-8. The meaning of this blessing and the function of Christ as its agent are further exhibited in the reference to **redemption through his blood,** i.e. through Christ's life-giving death, the effect of which is the **forgiveness of our trespasses** (cf. Col. 1:14). By the time Eph. was written these phrases had already become a fixed part of the Christian vocabulary, probably associated esp. with the baptismal liturgy. Therefore the author feels no need to elaborate them here or to define the precise way in which Christ's death frees the believer from his sins. For Paul "redemption" meant more than pardon for past offenses; it meant freedom from the power of sin. For him grace itself was a gift of power capable of effecting a total inner transformation. Elsewhere in Eph. Christ's death is mentioned (2:13-16; 5:2, 25), but it does not play the same pivotal role here as in the authentic Pauline letters (see Intro.).

1:9-10. All Things United in Christ. Again God's sovereign freedom and divine initiative in redemption are stressed, and again Christ's role as the agent and means of God's will is prominent. The **mystery of his will** has been revealed in Christ. In this hymn, as elsewhere in the NT, it is not the hiddenness of a mystery but its manifestation which is emphasized. The idea has special importance in Eph., where Christian preaching in general can be described as proclamation of a "mystery" (6:19). The term is also employed in Col., where it refers to Christ himself as the mystery (Col. 1:26-29; 2:2-3). But in Eph., as nowhere else in the NT, this mystery is interpreted specifically as God's purpose, revealed in Christ, that Gentiles as well as Jews should be members of the one body (3:3-6), gathered into one church under one Lord for the common praise of God and a united witness to his word (3:9-13).

1:10. Two related ideas are present here: (*a*) the eternality of God's plan for his church, a **plan for the fulness of time,** and (*b*) the oneness in Christ of **all things . . . in heaven and . . . on earth.** There is repeated stress on the unity of God's creative and redemptive activity. In Eph. these 2 are inseparably related (cf. e.g. vs. 4; 3:9), and therefore the church itself, viewed as the earthly instrument of God's salvation, is accorded a fundamental place in the divine creation. The reference to God's **plan for the fulness of time** recalls the words of Paul in Gal. 4:4-5, but the basic theological perspective is rather different. Paul speaks of the redemptive event of Christ's incarnation—esp. his death and resurrection—which represents God's intervention in history on man's behalf. But here the idea is more of a **plan** for the whole course of human history, culminating in a cosmic unification of **all things** under the sovereign rule of Christ.

1:11-14. All Things Created for God's Praise. God's **purpose** for his creation, his will for men, is that they should **live for the praise of his glory** (vs. 12). This phrase (cf. vss. 6, 14) is probably another of those fixed liturgical and doctrinal expressions which abound in these opening paragraphs. It is characteristic for this author that the church is the place where God is praised—"to him be glory in the church" (3:21). Man was created for the praise of God, and this is fulfilled in the community of those who are united in obedience to the one Lord who is above all (cf. vs. 10; 4:4-16).

1:12. Some commentators have interpreted **we who first hoped in Christ** as a reference to Jewish Christians, among whom the author apparently includes himself (cf. 2:11), in distinction from those of Gentile background—**you also** (vs. 13). Since the arguments for such an interpretation are not conclusive, it is better to regard **we** as including the whole Christian community, as elsewhere in the passage. This writer uses "hope" as a comprehensive term for Christian faith in general (cf. vs. 18; 2:12; 4:4). That Christians have been **destined and appointed** for the service of God does not imply a doctrine of mechanical predestination. Rather it emphasizes the initiative of God in calling men to their proper role as believers in Christ and obedient members of Christ's church.

1:13-14. In contrast to Col., where the Spirit is mentioned only once (Col. 1:8), the **Holy Spirit** holds an important place in the theology of Eph. (cf. 2:18, 22; 3:5, 16; 4:3-4, 30; 5:18; 6:17-18). Here, as in 4:30, **sealed** probably points to Christian baptism as that time when the Christian is inwardly consecrated to the service of God and sacramentally incorporated into the body of Christ, the church. The words are derived from Paul (II Cor. 1:22), for whom God's presence in the Holy Spirit is regarded as a down payment of the promised inheritance. **Inheritance** is for this author a general term which expresses the totality of future blessings to which the obedient Christian may look forward when the "kingdom of Christ and of God" (5:5) is fully present.

B. Thanksgiving (1:15-23)

The liturgical blessing of God's name (vss. 3-14) is followed now by a section of thanksgiving to God for the faith and obedience of the readers, climaxed by a doxological affirmation of the working of God's power in Christ (vss. 20-23). This juxtaposition of blessing and thanksgiving paragraphs never occurs in the other Pauline letters, and its presence here is probably another indication that the author of Eph. is not Paul himself.

1:15-19. *Thanksgiving Proper.* The author acknowledges the Christian loyalty of his readers, which he finds expressed both by their profession of **faith in the Lord Jesus** and by their relationships within the church, **toward all the saints.** As in the Pauline letters the opening words of thanksgiving to God become at once a prayer of petition for the continuing and increasing faith of those addressed—and thereby an indirect exhortation to the readers to discipline themselves in that direction. The author prays that the readers may be given an openness inwardly to apprehend the glory of God, who is himself the **Father of glory,** and to receive what God in his goodness continually offers (vs. 17). The content of this **wisdom** and **revelation** is the **knowledge** of God, understood by this author—as by Paul (I Cor. 13:12)—as a transforming encounter with God himself. Elsewhere in Eph. it is described as attaining "to mature manhood, to the measure of the stature of the fulness of Christ" (4:13), regarded as a gift of God's grace. Similar is the thought of 3:16.

1:18-19. *Eyes of Your Hearts.* The metaphor recalls references to the "eyes of the soul," by which God is "known," appearing frequently in Greek and Hellenistic religious philosophy. But mention of man's heart as the seat and center of his deepest knowledge and experience is particularly characteristic of Hebraic thought, as attested by the many OT occurrences of the metaphor. It refers, not just to some mystic communion of the inner self with God, or to some private display of divine truth, but to an actual transformation of the whole person, accomplished as one is opened to receive the grace of God bestowed in Christ. The author may regard this also as the content of the **hope** and the **inheritance** to which God has called his people, for in the next phrase (vs. 19) he speaks of that divine **power** by which authentic knowledge has been produced, the glorious hope of redemption has been fulfilled, and the riches of the final inheritance have been bestowed.

1:20-23. *Hymnic Conclusion.* The doxological character of Eph. is esp. evident here where the language of petition (vss. 15-19) yields to the rhetoric of praise. God's power has been effectively **accomplished,** i.e. demonstrated and concretely instituted, **in Christ:** in his resurrection **from the dead** (cf. 2:5-6), his exaltation to the **right hand** of God **in the heavenly places** (see above on 1:3-8), and his lordship over all things. These descriptions of Christ's work, common to many parts of the NT, have been influenced by the wording of Pss. 8:6; 110:1. Here the author goes further than Paul in ascribing ultimate authority to Christ. Paul applies the words of Ps. 8:6 to God and specifically says that even Christ is one day to be subjected to the Father (I Cor. 15:25-28; cf. I Cor. 3:23).

1:21. The words translated **rule . . . authority . . . power . . . dominion** would be understood by the first readers of this treatise as referring to those supramundane beings, enthroned in a cosmic hierarchy, who played a great part in certain ancient religions and were often mentioned in late Jewish apocalyptic literature. Here it is affirmed that Christ's universal rule renders impotent every such false pretender to cosmic power. Christ alone, installed by God himself and endowed by him with power, has dominion over all created things. There can be no other claimants to this title, for Christ is **above every name that is named** (cf. Phil. 2:9).

1:22-23. Vs. 22*a* is quoted with only slight variations from Ps. 8:6 LXX. But vss. 22*b*-23 move far beyond the psalmist's perspective and set forth the overall theme of Eph.: God has enthroned Christ as the **head over all things for the church, which is his body, the fulness of him who fills all in all.** This particular statement about Christ's relationship to the church has been framed in a way which leads to profound results for an understanding of the nature of the church.

1:22*b*. It is significant that the same Christ in whom God purposed to unite all things in heaven and on earth (vs. 10), and to whom all claimants to cosmic power have been subjected, has been made **head** over all these things **for the church.** The church is in a sense the locus of Christ's cosmic reign, the focus of his power, the place of his sovereign rule. For this author the church is vastly more

837

than a phenomenon of world history or the result of particular social needs and forces. For him the church was in God's purpose from the beginning of creation and has a cosmic status in the eternal order of things. It is not just a consequence of the gospel, an organization to fulfill the institutional requirements of the Christian mission, but is rooted in the original purposes of God and is part of his **plan for the fulness of time** (vs. 10). This conviction is fundamental to the whole theological outlook and plan of Eph.

1:23a. It is important to note here a further development of the **body** metaphor as applied to the church. Paul speaks of the church as Christ's body insofar as Christians are, "in Christ" (Rom. 12:5), members of one another. He develops this idea esp. in I Cor. 12:12-31, but even there without extending the metaphor to the point of calling Christ the "head" of the body. This identification is made, however, in Col. 1:18; 2:19, and now becomes a key concept in Eph. (cf. 4:15; 5:23). Whereas in the Pauline letters, including Col., the term "body" is used not only of the church but in other ways as well, in Eph. it is employed exclusively of the church. And here, as in Col., the members of the body are understood to bear an organic relationship not only to one another but also to Christ, their head (cf. esp. 4:15-16).

1:23b. Finally to be noted is the striking assertion that the church is the **fulness of him who fills all in all.** Commentators differ in their interpretation of these words, some holding that Christ is regarded as the fullness of the church, others that the church is regarded as the fullness of Christ. In the latter case one would better translate the phrase "the fulness of him who is being fulfilled," meaning that the church's existence is vital and necessary to Christ's functioning as Lord. It seems more likely, however, that the phrase is simply a shorthand expression of the author's later contention that it is Christ's presence and power as head which "fills" the church, builds it up (4:12), makes it one, and nourishes it for growth (4:15-16). In Eph., then, Christ's relationship to the church, its fullness, is described in the terms Col. uses to indicate God's relation to Christ: "in him all the fulness of God was pleased to dwell" (Col. 1:19); "in him the whole fulness of deity dwells bodily" (Col. 2:9).

In Eph. the accent falls heavily on the status and role of the Christian community in God's plan of salvation. For this author the church is one of the primal components of God's creation, its organic integrity is assured by Christ as its head, and its life and growth are sustained by the presence and power of Christ, who is the fullness of its being.

III. THE UNITY OF THE CHURCH (2:1-3:21)

Chs. 2-3 constitute the central theological section of Eph. and emphasize the unity of the church. This unity comes as each believer is united with Christ and becomes one with all who share in the new life God has given (ch. 2). The author interprets Paul's ministry as directed primarily toward the concrete, historical realization of that unity, by which the church truly becomes the church and is enabled to make an effective witness in the world (ch. 3).

A. RESURRECTION WITH CHRIST (2:1-10)

2:1-3. *Spiritual Death.* Apart from Christ one is **dead** in his **trespasses and sins.** This spiritual death involves one's alienation from God, his estrangement from his fellow human beings, the perversion of his divinely bestowed freedom to make responsible choices, and the disintegration of every faculty for wise judgment and moral behavior.

2:2. The metaphor **walked** is employed, as by Paul himself, to depict the style and direction of one's life. Religious mythology current in the author's day spoke of a demonic ruler of the earth whose function was satanic, though the name is not used here for him. He is called instead the **course,** lit. "eon," **of this world** and the **prince of the power of the air.** Formerly the readers were spiritually dead, governed by false pretenders to universal dominion—those powers of this world over whom, in reality, God rules in Christ (cf. 1:20-23).

2:3. Some interpreters believe that **we all** contrasts with **you** (vss. 1-2) and that the Jewish Christian author thus associates himself with his Gentile readers (but see above on 1:12). The moral decadence of life without Christ is further described. It is ruled by human **passions,** guided by nothing surer than the transient **desires of body and mind** and controlled exclusively by temporal, secular goals and values. But man, because of his humanity, because he is a creature of a just and righteous God, stands ever subject to his judgment. **Wrath** therefore connotes, not capricious or vindictive anger, but God's righteous, aggressive judgment of evil wherever found (cf. Rom. 3:21-23).

2:4-7. *God's Saving Love.* In Eph., as throughout the NT, the righteous judgment of God (vs. 3) is not separable from, but in fact presupposes, his loving compassion. The prologue of this letter has already praised God's love and mercy (1:5-8), and that theme now reappears with the heavy rhetorical ornamentation so favored by this author—**rich in mercy . . . great love.** Vss. 4-5 resume the thought of vs. 1a. Even at the very moment when we were most helplessly and hopelessly captured under the dominion of evil powers and pressures (vss. 2-3) God in his love entered into history to save and redeem us. God's grace and love bestowed in Christ have not only brought forgiveness but **made us alive together with Christ.** The parenthetical comment in vs. 5 is the chief topic of vss. 8-10 (see comment).

The believer's new life is **in** and **with** Christ. Three times in rapid succession the author employs words which have the Greek prefix "with": **alive . . . with Christ** (vs. 5) and **raised . . . up with him to sit with him** (vs. 6; on **in the heavenly places** see above on 1:3-8). The first readers of this letter would remember their baptism as the event in which this experience of being in and with Christ was most effectively real. Being in and with Christ is a corporate, not just a private, matter; all believers are **together** in and with Christ. It is Christ's work not only to reconcile men to God but also to reconcile them to one another (cf. vss. 13-22).

2:8-10. *Salvation by Grace.* These vss. develop the thought contained in the parenthesis in vs. 5. The idea of salvation by grace through faith is thoroughly Pauline, but the presupposition that such has already taken place for believers at some time in the past is not to be found in Paul's own letters (cf. Rom. 6:1-23, where resurrection and life with Christ are conceived as still future). Paul's theology has here been distilled into a formula, but in the distillation something important is endangered: his insight that the decision of faith by which God's grace is appropriated must be ever newly actualized in the life of the believer and that for this reason salvation can be sure and complete only in God's own future.

2:8b-9. Here also is a reflection of Paul's theological emphases (e.g. Rom. 3:24; 9:16; I Cor. 1:29, etc.), but again there is a difference, in this instance due to a different historical context. Paul's doctrine of grace was developed in conscious opposition to the Jewish conviction that salvation came by doing "works of the law" (cf. e.g. Gal. 2:16). Here that problem is no longer in sight and the reference is only to **works** in general. This represents a quite proper broadening of Paul's point to apply to all human efforts designed to earn and secure salvation.

2:10. But this author by no means minimizes the importance of good works. They are a necessary part of the Christian life, even though they are not the way to salvation. This point is made in a unique way. Christians are God's **workmanship,** i.e. production, **created in Christ Jesus for good works.** This is part of what their sonship involves (1:5), part of that for which they have been chosen (1:4) and to which they have been called (cf. esp. 4:1-6). The idea that these good works have in fact been **prepared beforehand** by God himself has no NT parallel.

B. Reconciliation in Christ (2:11-22)

The salvation God has effected for believers through Christ involves the oneness of Christ's church. In him Jews and Gentiles have been reconciled to God and therefore to one another. The key word in vss. 11-18 is thus **peace,** which describes this 2-fold reconciliation in Christ. Vss. 19-22 conclude the section with a statement on the nature of the church.

2:11-12. *Grace for the Heathen.* The author here addresses converts from the heathen world, asking them to consider what God's grace (see above on vss. 8-10) has meant to them. The reference to **circumcision** is very Pauline, for Paul repeatedly insists that true circumcision is inward, not outward (cf. e.g. Rom. 2:25-29). Nevertheless the Gentiles did lack certain real advantages enjoyed by the Jews. **Separated from Christ** is used to describe the Gentiles' previous situation generally, and its meaning is defined by the phrases which follow. They were separated from God's people, from God's promises, from the hope of redemption in Christ, and from God himself. The central purpose of Eph. is to admonish the Gentile Christian readers that now, within the church, this Jewish heritage may and must be made their own (see Intro.).

2:13-18. *Christ Our Peace.* The glorious and surprising fact of the Gentiles' redemption is expressed already in the 2 simple words—set over against **at one time** (vs. 11) and **at that time** (vs. 12)—which open vs. 13: **But now . . .** Through Christ's death the Gentiles have been included in the people of

God, their estrangement has been overcome, and they have been **brought near** (cf. Col. 1:20-23). In Judaism the terms "far" and "near" were frequently used of the non-Israelites and Israelites respectively. Here the author seems to have in mind esp. the words of Isa. 57:19, for in vs. 14a he identifies Christ himself as **our peace, who has made us,** Jew and Gentile, **both one** in the church.

2:14b. Moreover Christ **has broken down the dividing wall** between Jew and Gentile. Some commentators believe the metaphor alludes to the wall which was erected in the Herodian temple in Jerusalem to separate the Jewish and Gentile areas. This interpretation, however, is highly conjectural and does not take into account that such an allusion would be lost on the original readers. Others propose a Gnostic background for the metaphor, citing the Gnostic myth of the redeemer's descent, breaking down the wall of separation between the heavenly and earthly realms. Thus the intention here would be to identify that redeemer as Christ and to underscore the cosmic significance of his atoning work (cf. 1:10). In any case the author says that reconciliation with God means reconciliation with one's fellows, that within the community of believers there can be no dividing walls. The church is one because those within it are joint recipients of the saving grace of God in Christ. It is not said that incorporation into Christ somehow erases the differences among men. It is affirmed, however—and this is more important—that for those in Christ such differences no longer alienate men from one another.

2:15-18. The word **flesh** refers to the whole redemptive event of Christ's coming, esp. to his death (vs. 13), by which the power of the Jewish law, with its divisive and hostility-producing **commandments and ordinances,** has been decisively broken (cf. e.g. Rom. 5:1-11). The unity of God's people in the church is further stressed in the vivid picture of the church as a new humanity, **one new man.** Reconciliation does not require the capitulation of one side or the other; it involves the transformation of both. Reconciliation among men always has as its primary dimension their joint reconciliation with God (vs. 16). This is accomplished **in one body,** perhaps a reference both to the crucified Christ, through whose death on the cross reconciliation occurs, and to the church itself as Christ's body, whose life has come through his death. The unity of mankind in the church is further supported in vs. 18 with mention of the **one Spirit** (cf. I Cor. 12:4-27) through whom all **have access** to their common Father (cf. 3:11-12).

2:19-22. *The Church, God's Temple.* The Gentiles are no longer alienated from God's commonwealth (cf. vs. 12) but are now **fellow citizens with the saints.** Whether "saints" refers to the Christian community in general (as in 1:1) or to Jewish Christians in particular depends on whether the phrase **members of the household of God** is strictly parallel in meaning. It probably is, and thus "saints" would refer to all Christians. The word "household" depicts God's church as his family, bound together as one under his paternal will and care.

2:20a. A 2nd metaphor describes the church as a building founded on the **apostles and prophets,** whom this author regards as the certified recipients of God's revelation and official bearers of the Christian tradition (cf. 3:5, which along with 4:11 also shows that Christian prophets are in mind). The contrast with Paul's metaphor in I Cor. 3:10-15 is significant. For Paul, Christ himself is the foundation and the apostles and prophets are only builders on it.

2:20b. This metaphor is expanded by a reference to Christ as one of the vital components of the church's structure. The Greek word used may mean either **cornerstone** (cf. "foundation-stone," NEB) or "capstone." The first meaning refers to the stone situated at the corner of a foundation from which the builders take their bearings for all the other walls. Thus Christ would be presented as the one who by his presence defines the shape and scope of the church, points it in the way it is to go, and enables its sturdy construction. A capstone, or coping stone, on the other hand, is the topmost stone of a wall, the last to be put in place. If this is what the author has in mind—as most recent commentators hold—then Christ is described as both effecting and symbolizing the completion and wholeness of the church, the crowning element under which the structure is united and strong. This latter interpretation accords with the other metaphor of Christ as head of the church, while the former is more in keeping with the immediate context, which speaks of the church's foundation and of its continuing construction.

2:21-22. Whichever interpretation is followed, Christ is here regarded as the one **in whom the whole structure is joined together** (cf. 1:10). Moreover the church is conceived, not as a static mass, but as dynamic and living: the building **grows into**

A leaf from the papyrus codex containing the Pauline Epistles showing Eph. 2:21–3:10

a holy temple in the Lord. The church's true being is a becoming. This author by no means regards the church as still incomplete, for that would contradict his view of the church's eternal status in God's creation (see above on 1:10). Rather he seems to connect the church's growth with the idea of vs. 22 that the believers are together being constantly **built into it for a dwelling place of God in the Spirit.** The **one Spirit** through whom the believer has **access** to God (vs. 18) is thus resident in the church, the all-inclusive body of Christ, the place where God is praised.

C. PAUL'S MINISTRY OF UNITY (3:1-21)

In this section the author (see Intro.) reveals the high regard in which he holds the apostle under whose name he writes. **Paul** is represented as one of the **holy apostles** to whom the **mystery of Christ** has been revealed (vss. 4-5), and whose mission has been esp. to the Gentile world (vss. 1, 2, 6, 8). His is thus a ministry of unity, calling all men unto Christ and into the one church.

3:1-6. *A Steward of God's Grace.* Now the author self-consciously assumes the role of Paul. He considers Paul a missionary of the first rank, one whose imprisonment was specifically for the **Gentiles** (vs. 1). Moreover the grace of God given to Paul involved a special **stewardship,** which was fulfilled in his Gentile mission. This mission was to proclaim the **mystery of Christ** (vss. 3, 4), which was revealed to Paul and the other apostles and Christian prophets as it had not been made known in previous generations (vss. 3, 5).

3:5-6. God's Spirit (cf. 1:13; 2:18, 22) is named as the medium of revelation, and in contrast to Col. 1:26 the circle which receives the revelation is narrowed down from the "saints," i.e. all Christians, to the **holy apostles and prophets.** In vs. 6 the content of the mystery is specified: in the church the Gentiles are "co-heirs, companions, and co-partners" (Moffatt trans.) with the Jews—a compact formulation of the longer discussion in 2:11-22.

3:7-9. *A Minister to the Gentiles.* Here Paul's role as an apostle to the Gentiles is reemphasized (cf. vss. 1-3). Vs. 7 doubtless has his conversion in mind (cf. Gal. 1:15-17). **Though I am the very least of all the saints** (vs. 8) is true to Paul's spirit but betrays the hand of a later author, for even Paul's modesty is intensified, as shown by a comparison with I Cor. 15:9, where he refers to himself as "least of the apostles." **Unsearchable riches of Christ** is simply an alternative designation for the gospel, though like the word "mystery" it suggests that Christian wisdom has depths and dimensions unmatched by any other (cf. **manifold wisdom,** vs. 10).

3:9. Several points made previously are here repeated: (*a*) The gospel is a declaration of God's **plan** for man's salvation (see above on 1:10). (*b*) This plan was once **hidden** but is now revealed; in Christ God's eternal purposes have been set forth and made known through his apostles and prophets in a way hitherto impossible (cf. vs. 5; 1:9). (*c*) The same God who created the world is its redeemer, and since "before the foundation of the world" (1:4) his purpose has been to save.

3:10-13. *The Role of the Church.* The church is the

means by which the **wisdom of God** is cosmically proclaimed and therefore plays a crucial role in God's plan for salvation. That plan involves the proclamation of the riches of God's grace, the revealing of the mystery of Christ, and the subsequent subjection of all men and all powers to him. The church, through the preaching of its apostles and prophets, but no less through its very being—a unity of Jews and Gentiles in Christ and in obedience to him—bears witness to the power of God expressed in his sovereign rule and redeeming grace. The **principalities and powers** are those cosmic deities which, according to the ancient world view shared also by the early Christians, inhabited and ruled the spheres between earth and heaven (on **in the heavenly places** see above on 1:3-8). Col. insists that such authorities are not to be worshiped and are themselves subject to the lordship of Christ in the universe. Here there is an additional emphasis on the church as the means by which this cosmic dimension of Christ's rule is demonstrated.

3:11-13. Whereas it is the church which makes known God's purposes—his **manifold wisdom**—it is Christ himself through whom they are **realized,** i.e. accomplished. More specifically, it is in Christ that the believer has **access** into the presence of God (cf. 2:18). Because of God's forgiving, renewing grace bestowed in Christ, the man of faith can stand before his glorious presence as one "holy and blameless" (1:4; cf. 5:27), with **boldness and confidence** (vs. 12). Neither the relation of vs. 13 to what has preceded nor its precise meaning is certain. It bids the readers not to be discouraged over Paul's afflictions but to know that they serve the cause of the gospel (cf. Col. 1:24; Phil. 1:12-18; II Tim. 2:10) and are esp. efficacious for them.

3:14-19. *Prayer for the Inner Man.* After an interruption (vss. 2-13) the author now resumes the intro. to a prayer for his readers begun in vs. 1. He prays that they may be **strengthened with might through his Spirit in the inner man** (vs. 16). "Inner man" here translates the same words rendered "inmost self" in Rom. 7:22. In both instances man's interior being is meant, his essential personhood, which when yielded to the powerful working of God's Spirit can become thoroughly new (cf. 4:24; II Cor. 4:16). The next phrase of the prayer (vs. 17*a*) elucidates the first. One's inmost self is made new by the Spirit as Christ is received therein (cf. 4:13, 15) and the life which is opened to Christ's presence is **rooted and grounded in love** (vs. 17*b*). This is the widest, longest, highest, and deepest **knowledge** of all (vss. 18-19), the very **fulness of God.**

3:20-21. *Doxology.* This stately doxology brings to a close the most specifically doctrinal section of Eph. The phrase **glory in the church and in Christ Jesus** echoes the author's emphasis on the church as the body of Christ, who is its head (cf. e.g. 1:22-23). The church is the place where God is praised, and to this service of praise man has been appointed since his creation (cf. 1:5, 6, 12, 14).

IV. THE IMPERATIVES OF THE CHRISTIAN LIFE (4:1-6:20)

The 2nd half of Eph. (chs. 4-6), primarily a series of ethical admonitions, differs from the first half in style and content. Yet the 2 sections are closely related, for this author believes that the imperatives of the Christian life are grounded in what God has accomplished in Christ and in what he has intended through the unity of all things in Christ and in the church.

A. THE BASIS FOR CHRISTIAN ETHICS (4:1-16)

Paul's authority is again invoked (vs. 1; cf. 3:1) as the author (see Intro.) begins his exhortations. These are introduced by an appeal to the true basis for Christian ethics: God's call to unity, peace, and love (vss. 1-6) and his bestowal of spiritual gifts for the common good (vss. 7-16).

4:1-6. *God's Call.* Christians have been "destined" as God's sons (1:5), "sealed" by his Spirit (1:13), and "called" to hope (1:18). They have been made "alive" in Christ (2:5) and reconciled to God and to all of God's people in Christ's body (2:11-22). **Therefore** (vs. 1) in their daily conduct they are to show themselves worthy of these riches of grace and manifest them within the life of the Christian community. **Unity,** the hallmark of the church and of all creation, is to be maintained by **love,** expressing itself in **lowliness . . . meekness . . . patience . . . forbearing.**

4:4-6. The slogans in these vss. recapitulate the argument of chs. 1-3 and suggest that the unity of the Spirit is already present, as a gift, in the church. On **one body** cf. 2:16; on **one Spirit** cf. 2:18; on **one hope** cf. 1:18; 2:12; on **one Lord** cf. 2:4-7, 13-22; on **one baptism** cf. 1:13-14; on **one God and Father of us all** cf. 1:5; 3:14-15. **Faith** here, as in vs. 13, refers to the totality of Christian doctrines and practices.

4:7-10. *The Gifts of Christ.* Christian unity is not to be confused with uniformity, for the members of Christ's body have been variously endowed. Whereas Paul speaks of gifts of the Spirit (I Cor. 12:4-11) this author refers to them as gifts of Christ (vs. 7) and endeavors to prove this with a citation from Ps. 68:18 (vs. 8). Rabbinic commentators regularly applied these words to Moses, who ascending Mt. Sinai received the law from God and then gave it as a gift to Israel. Influenced by this rabbinical interpretation, the author of Eph. changes the original verb from "receive" to "give" and then applies the ps. to Christ rather than to Moses. This he seeks to justify in vss. 9-10. An ascent, he argues, presupposes a previous descent, and the ps. must therefore refer to Christ, who was sent from the Father and returned to him (a prominent theme in John, e.g. 3:13). It is probable that the **lower parts of the earth** is a reference not only to Christ's earthly incarnation but to his further descent into Hades to preach to the dead (cf. I Pet. 3:18-22). On Christ as the Lord and fullness of **all things** see above on 1:10, 22-23.

4:11-16. *Specific Gifts.* The author resumes his original point (vs. 7) that Christ has bestowed various gifts on the members of his body. Mentioned first are **apostles** and **prophets,** as in Paul's own list (I Cor. 12:28). But in Eph. these offices are regarded as closed, for the apostles and prophets belong to that select group which formed the foundation of the church (2:20) and were the original guarantors of revelation (3:5). The collective goal of the church's ministries is indicated in vss. 12-16, and all the various phrases and figures pertain to the life of the Christian community, not just to the faith of individual Christians.

4:12-13. Christ's **body** is built up as its members attain **unity** in Christ, founded on a common **faith** in him. It is the church, then, which as a whole—**we all**—attains to **mature manhood, to the measure of the stature of the fulness of Christ** (cf. 1:22-23; 2:15).

4:14-16. The goal of these varied ministries is negatively stated in vs. 14, viz. to prevent the disintegration of the church which occurs when its members are childishly attracted to false **doctrine.** Instead (vs. 15) the church should manifest throughout the **love** of Christ, by which it lives (cf. 1:5; 2:4; 3:19; 5:2). As in 2:21-22 the author implies that there is no life without **growth,** and he reaffirms that this growth comes from Christ, **who is the head** of the **body** (vss. 15b-16; cf. Col. 2:19, where, however, the body is not the church but the whole cosmic order).

B. Exhortations on Personal Morality (4:17–5:20)

The ethical exhortations of this section are not closely tied to a single theme, but they all bear generally on the importance of personal morality. Christians are **children of light** (5:8) and they should **put on the new nature** (4:24) appropriate to their new status.

4:17-24. *Putting Off the Old Nature.* The term **Gentiles** is applied no longer to the Gentile Christian readers of Eph. but to non-Christians in general. A series of phrases describes their moral plight (vss. 17-19; cf. Rom. 1:21-32). Conversion to Christianity ought to mean a radical separation from pagan immorality (cf. 2:1-7). Only in vs. 21 does this author use the term **Jesus** alone, and it may constitute an appeal to the ethical teaching of the historical Jesus as formulated within the church's catechetical tradition. It may also be directed against Gnostic denials of the reality of the Incarnation. The radical newness of life in Christ is emphasized with the metaphor **put off** and **put on** (vss. 22, 24; cf. Col. 3:10; Rom. 13:14; Gal. 3:27), which would recall the total transformation of character symbolized and inaugurated at the time of one's baptism (cf. Rom. 6:2-14; Gal. 3:27). On the other hand the tense of **be renewed in the spirit of your minds,** refers to a continuing experience (cf. II Cor. 4:16).

4:25–5:2. *The New Life of Love.* All the counsels of this section concern one's life within the community and those social responsibilities which contribute to the integrity and stability of the community's life: truthfulness (vs. 25), forgiveness (vss. 26, 32), honesty and philanthropy (vs. 28), and edifying speech (vss. 29, 31). Even more significant is the basis on which these exhortations are founded: the character of God and what he himself has done for men. **For we are members one of another** (vs. 25) alludes to the doctrine of the church as Christ's body. In 4:32b–5:2 the reality of God's love, bestowed in Christ, forgiving men (cf. 1:7) and caring for them as a Father (cf. 1:5; 2:18; 3:14-19), is reaffirmed.

The new life, then, is a life of love, modeled after

God's love revealed in Christ's sacrificial death **for us.** There is no full doctrine of atonement in Eph., and Christ's death is not a central theological concept for this author (see above on 1:7-8). It is enough for him to know that Christ's death has somehow made the church one (2:14-16) and that the love thus revealed and bestowed should form the substance of the church's interior life.

5:3-14. *Walking as Children of Light.* Here the appeal for responsible ethical action is continued and the readers are exhorted to behave in ways appropriate for **saints,** a term which thus begins to take on specifically moral connotations. The vices listed in vs. 4 (cf. Col. 3:8) were also condemned by

Courtesy of Herbert G. May

Ruins of a brothel at Ephesus where prostitutes plied their trade

non-Christian moralists in the ancient world, but the alternative, **instead let there be thanksgiving,** is specifically Christian and conforms to a view of the new life as one lived in the continuous praise of God (cf. e.g. 1:6, 12). Further support for the exhortations comes in vss. 5-6, where disobedience is said to result in exclusion from the future **inheritance** and subjection to God's **wrath.** Only here in the NT does one find the **kingdom** described as belonging to **Christ and . . . God,** and the contrast with Paul's thought (I Cor. 15:23-28) is noteworthy. The admonitions of vss. 6-7 echo Col. 2:4, 8, but here no specific group of false teachers is in mind.

5:8-14. The use of **light** and **darkness** to represent morality and immorality is familiar not only from other NT occurrences but also from the Qumran scrolls and other late Jewish literature. Vs. 10 is an appeal ever to seek out God's will as revealed in Christ, while the words of vss. 11-13 refer to the presumed immorality camouflaged by the cultic rites of secret religious groups. In vs. 14 the author quotes apparently from an early Christian hymn (see Intro.).

5:15-20. *Prudent Living.* The readers are admonished to **understand what the will of the Lord is** and to live as **wise,** i.e. prudent, men in the midst of a perverse world. The striking expression **making the most of,** lit. "buying up," **the time** is borrowed from Col. 4:5, where it is used in an exhortation to pass up no opportunity in bearing witness to those outside the church. Here it is applied in a general way to the whole Christian life. The words against drunkenness (vs. 18) are cited from a Greek version of Prov. 23:31. The exhortation to a Spirit-led life of praise and thanksgiving is simply an alteration of Col. 3:16-17. Again (cf. vs. 16a) the words are disengaged from a specific reference in Col., viz. Christian worship, and extended here to cover the whole Christian life (cf. vs. 4b; 1:6, 12).

C. The Christian Household (5:21–6:9)

This section discusses relationships among members of a household. In both form and content it has many parallels in early Christian literature, esp. Col. 3:18–4:6 (see comment). It is possible to read 5:21 as an introduction to the whole section, for in each relationship the necessity of loyal obedience is emphasized. At no point, however, is servile capitulation in mind, for always the principle of reciprocal responsibility is observed (5:25; 6:4, 9).

5:21-33. Husbands and Wives. These counsels are in Eph. greatly expanded (contrast Col. 3:18-19), doubtless because of this author's overarching concern to define the nature of the church, to which he finds a parallel in the institution of marriage. Thus while this passage is primarily hortatory (vss. 22, 33) it also further expounds the central theme of Eph.

With regard to the marriage relationship itself the author has 2 basic convictions: (a) As declared in scripture (Gen. 2:24) husband and wife **become one.** The reading of many manuscripts, "one flesh," seems likely here because it is equated (vss. 28, 29) with the author's own theological idea of one body. (b) The husband is regarded as the **head** of this body (vs. 23; cf. I Cor. 11:3). The exhortations to each partner are issued in the light of these convictions: the wife is to be obedient and respectful to her husband (vss. 24, 33) and the husband is to love, nourish, and cherish his wife, with whom his own life is completely identified (vss. 25, 28, 29, 33). The analogy drawn between marriage and the relation of Christ to his church provides the exhortations with even deeper dimensions, for Christ is both **head** and **Savior** of the church (vs. 23) and his was a self-sacrificing, sanctifying love (vss. 28, 33). Those who hold that Paul is the author of Eph. must explain the significantly different orientation which characterizes the discussion of marriage in I Cor. 7.

This passage is chiefly important, however, because of what it further reveals about the author's view of the church. The head-body metaphor (cf. e.g. 1:22-23) is repeated, but now it is said also that Christ is the church's **Savior** (vs. 23)—a title used only once by Paul (Phil. 3:20)—the significance of which is not immediately explored. What is stressed is the church's duty of unconditional obedience to Christ (vs. 24), whose authority this author, in contrast to Paul (I Cor. 3:23; 15:20-28), identifies with that of God himself (cf. 1:20-23).

Christ's lordship over the church is closely related to his love for it, exhibited and bestowed in his death (vs. 25; cf. Gal. 2:20). The church is thought of as the "bride" of Christ, to whom she is **presented** properly washed and clothed in matrimonial attire (vss. 26-27). The **washing of water** (vs. 26) is baptism, a sacramental act which is given special prominence throughout Eph. (cf. 1:13; 2:5-6; 4:5). The attendant **word** is probably the baptismal formula ("in the name of . . ."; cf. I Cor. 6:11). By water

and the word Christians individually and in their corporate life as the church are called to the service of God, the "praise of his glory" (1:12, 14; cf. 1:6). It is in this sense that the church is **holy and without blemish** (vs. 27). Reference to Christ's nurture of the church (vs. 29) recalls the figures of 2:20-22; 4:15-16.

Vs. 32a should be translated "This mystery is great," meaning "of great significance." **Mystery** is not used here as it is elsewhere in the letter (1:9; 3:3, 9; 6:19), where it refers specifically to the unity of Jews and Gentiles within the church. Rather it is applied to the figure of the church as Christ's bride, which this author finds presented already in scripture (Gen. 2:24, cited in vs. 30). The emphatic **I take it to mean** indicates that he is offering his interpretation of the OT passage in conscious opposition to others.

6:1-4. Parents and Children. These vss. expand the parallel section in Col. 3:20-21 in 2 respects: (a) The exhortation to children to obey their parents is grounded in the commandment of Exod. 20:12; Deut. 5:16 and reinforced by reference to the **promise** of a long life **on the earth** (adapted from Deut. 5:16). (b) To the admonition to fathers is added the counsel to bring up their children **in the discipline and instruction of the Lord.** Not only are fathers to be reasonable in what they expect of children; they are also to be constructively concerned for their proper nurture. It is perhaps too much to find reference here to Christian education in the home, but it is noteworthy that the same Greek verb used of Christ's relation to the church, and a husband's to his wife ("nourishes," 5:29), is used of a father's responsibility to his children (**bring . . . up**, vs. 4).

6:5-9. Slaves and Masters. As in the instances above, the author seeks a religious basis for the obedience and respect which is to characterize the relationship. He neither condemns nor condones the institution of slavery as such (on the question of Christianity and slavery see Intro. to Philem.). Slaves are reminded that they are also **servants**, lit. "slaves," **of Christ** (vs. 6) and thereby bound to do the will of God, who rewards all good work by whomever done (vs. 8). The relatively inconspicuous phrase **whether he is a slave or free** is of extreme significance. The slave is told that before God there is no distinction; thus his present earthly servitude has been transcended at the point which matters most. Therefore he is to obey **in singleness of heart** (vs. 5), i.e. **from the heart** (vs. 6), and **with fear and trembling** (vs. 5). This latter is a favorite Pauline phrase (cf. e.g. Phil. 2:12) and has reference to man's consciousness that his real **Master . . . is in heaven** (vs. 9). Hence the masters too have a responsibility, for they have that same Master in heaven. Their responsibility, also, is to do the **will of God from the heart.** In their case this means to be patient and forbearing with their slaves.

D. Strength in the Lord (6:10-20)

The exhortations of Eph. conclude with words about spiritual strength. The Christian is to arm himself with the strength God supplies (6:10-17) and to maintain his vigil of prayer both for his own fight against evil and for the apostolic ministry (6:18-20).

6:10-17. *The Armor of God.* These vss. have no parallel in Col., but the imagery of a holy war and spiritual armament is found in many ancient religious texts, including the OT, where God himself is portrayed in armor (Isa. 59:17). The Christian is now admonished to **put on** the Lord's armor, God's strength, to battle the various moral and spiritual foes by whom he is beset (vss. 10-11). The battle is serious, for it is not against human agencies but against the supernatural powers who inhabit the cosmos (vs. 12). The Christian's confidence is made firm in the knowledge that all these are subject to Christ (cf. e.g. 1:21) but the need for moral strength and vigilance is not thereby diminished.

6:13-16. The Christian puts on God's might (vss. 10-11) as he puts on a new nature (4:24), and the various items of spiritual armor are described (cf. I Thess. 5:8). **Righteousness** and **truth** (vs. 14) are also linked together in Isa. 11:5. It is paradoxical that the feet of the Christian soldier are to be shod with the **gospel of peace.** But **above all** ("besides all these," Goodspeed trans.) one must be equipped with the covering **shield** of a protecting **faith.**

6:17. The verb **take** means lit. "accept." The **helmet** and **sword** are to be received as the last and decisive pieces of equipment. The helmet symbolizes **salvation,** here regarded, with faith, as providing the Christian protection. This concept of faith and salvation and the attendant presumption that salvation is an accomplished fact distinguish this writer from Paul. Cf. I Thess. 5:8, where Paul alters the phrase from Isa. 59:17 to read the "hope of salvation."

6:18-20. *The Importance of Prayer.* Strength for the Christian's war against wickedness comes, finally, from prayer (cf. Col. 4:2-4). The call to stay **alert** and persevere is formally parallel to the Pauline exhortations to sobriety and wakefulness (Rom. 13:11; I Thess. 5:6; cf. I Pet. 1:13), which were directly related to Paul's lively sense that the end of all things was at hand. Here that sense is considerably diminished. The open door of Col. 4:3 is interpreted by this author as Paul's **mouth,** hence the request that there be prayers for the apostle's boldness in proclaiming the **mystery of the gospel** (on the meaning of "mystery" see above on 1:9-10). The **saints** (vs. 18) are all other Christians.

V. Epistolary Close (6:21-24)

6:21-22. *The Mission of Tychicus.* These vss. follow closely Col. 4:7-8 and constitute strong evidence against the hypothesis of common authorship. This author is dependent on Col., and by the inclusion of this commendation of Tychicus seeks really to commend his own letter as authentically Pauline. On Tychicus see comment on Col. 4:7-8.

6:23-24. *Apostolic Benediction.* Never does Paul cast his benedictions in the 3rd person as has the author here. **Peace** has been one of the fundamental points of this treatise (cf. 2:14). **Love with faith** is almost an echo of Gal. 5:6, but for Paul himself "hope" is a closely related idea (Gal. 5:5; cf. I Cor. 13:13; I Thess. 1:3). **Grace** is at once the beginning and end of an apostolic letter (cf. 1:2).

THE LETTER
OF PAUL TO THE PHILIPPIANS

LEANDER E. KECK

INTRODUCTION

To the church at Philippi goes the honor of being the first known Christian congregation in what is now Europe. The occasion of its beginning is related in Acts 16:6-40. This account, however, gives no clues for understanding the Letter to the Philippians, since it deals with persons and issues never mentioned in the letter and ignores those which the letter does mention. The interest of the Acts narrative is in Paul, and the founding of a church in the city, though implied (Acts 16:40b), is never described.

Philippi, a Macedonian city located some 10 miles from the Aegean Sea (see color map 16), had been made a Roman colony. The church there appears to have been almost entirely Gentile—note that Jewish sabbath worship took place outside the city and apparently only women attended (Acts 16:13). Despite the unhappy circumstances in which Paul had to cut short his first visit (Acts 16:39b-40) the church took root and became the only congregation that supported his work financially (4:14-16; cf. II Cor. 11:9)—another key fact that Acts ignores. Paul stayed in touch with these friends through their gifts, brought by members such as Epaphroditus (2:25-30), and presumably visited them again (cf. Acts 19:21; 20:1-3). All this took place in the decade beginning *ca.* A.D. 50.

Place and Date of Composition. It is not clear where and when Paul wrote Phil. The traditional view is that he did so at Rome near the end of his life, 3 or more years after his last visit to the church. The author was a prisoner (1:12-13, 17; 2:17, 23), and Paul is known to have been in prison for at least 2 years at Caesarea (Acts 24:27) and then under house arrest for 2 years at Rome (Acts 28:16, 30-31). Although Caesarea has been advocated by a few scholars, more have preferred Rome.

The case for Rome rests largely on the references to the "praetorian guard" (1:13) and to "Caesar's household" (4:22). The praetorian guard was an elite military unit established by Augustus as the emperor's bodyguard. The Greek word elsewhere in the NT is rendered "praetorium" (e.g. Mark 15:

General view of the ruins of Philippi

16; Acts 23:35), meaning a government headquarters building such as existed in many cities of the Roman Empire. "Caesar's household" refers to the official staff—a term used of those in the service of the imperial government both in Rome and throughout the empire. These phrases, then, favor but do not require Rome as the place of writing.

Against both Rome and Caesarea is their remoteness from Macedonia. The references to frequent travel between Philippi and Paul's place of imprisonment in 2:25-30 (see comment) all but exclude Caesarea and cast serious doubt on Rome. Also against both these cities is Paul's promise to visit Philippi on his release (1:26; 2:24). Shortly before the trip to Jerusalem that resulted in his arrest and imprisonment in Caesarea and Rome, he declared that his work in the Aegean area was completed and that he planned to go through Rome and open up a new mission field in Spain (Rom. 15:22-32; cf. Acts 19:21). Dating the letter after that statement requires assuming that Paul not only abandoned his plans for Spain but decided to go back where he had considered his work was no longer needed.

These comments in the letter point rather to a place near enough to Philippi so that continual contact could be easily maintained and to a time when Paul was actively working in that region. During this period Paul stayed longest in Ephesus (Acts 19) and this city seems the most likely place (see color map 16). It is true that Acts says nothing of an imprisonment in Ephesus. A riot in the amphitheater is reported (Acts 19:23-41) but no arrest. The silence of Acts, however, should not be taken to mean that what is not reported did not happen. That the Acts account is incomplete can be seen from Paul's own mention of many imprisonments and of having received 3 times the Roman punishment of beating by rods (II Cor. 11:23-29).

Paul's statement that he "fought with wild beasts at Ephesus" (I Cor. 15:32) is doubtless metaphorical —though some have seen it as referring to an actual narrow escape in the arena—but even so it points to serious difficulties in the city. Further probable evidence of trouble in Ephesus is found in Paul's reference to Prisca and Aquila as having "risked their necks for my life" (Rom. 16:4). This couple met Paul in Corinth and moved with him to Ephesus (Acts 18:1-2, 18-19, 26). Rom. 16 (see comment) is generally recognized as not an original part of Rom. and is probably addressed to the church at Ephesus.

Not to be overlooked is the fact that Colossae was near Ephesus. Since both Col. and Philem. were written in a prison from which Paul was in contact with the Colossian church (which he had not founded), the same imprisonment in Ephesus may be involved. Of course these 2 letters have likewise been traditionally assigned to the imprisonment at Rome, and the question of whether they were written there or at Ephesus is parallel to that regarding Phil. (see Intro. to Philem.).

In sum, then, the case for Rome rests on what we know about Paul's imprisonment from Acts but is undercut by what we may rightly infer from Phil. itself. The case for Ephesus, on the other hand, rests on what we infer from Phil. and other letters but is undercut by the lack of explicit mention in Acts of

an imprisonment there. Scholars are therefore divided in their views on this question. The present writer holds the Ephesian theory.

If Phil. was written from Rome it dates from the end of Paul's career, *ca.* 60-62. If it was written from Ephesus it comes from the midst of Paul's most active period, *ca.* 54-56, when he also wrote I, II Cor. and Gal. (and probably Col. and Philem.). Relating Phil. to these letters, esp. Cor., helps explain the content of all 4 letters, and applying the description of the local situation in 1:12-18 to the church at Ephesus sheds light on Paul's voluminous work during this period in his life.

Unity. Though no one today questions seriously whether Paul wrote Phil. there is renewed debate about the composition of the letter. Every careful reader is startled by the sudden change in tone and topic in 3:1-2. Here the flow of thought is ruptured completely, but is apparently resumed at 4:10. Why should Paul interrupt his expression of gratitude with a sarcastic polemic? To this question 2 kinds of answers have been given.

Those convinced of the unity of Phil. offer psychological theories to explain Paul's abrupt change of mood—e.g. an interval between dictating 3:1 and 3:2 during which he spent a sleepless night or received an unexpected report of difficulty in Philippi which he felt must be treated immediately. Some have minimized the break by stressing the underlying theological continuity—a line of reasoning that would prove the same man wrote chs. 2 and 3 but does not prove that he wrote them in the same letter.

The 2nd type of answer comes from those who seek a literary solution and therefore see here an editorial joining of 2 or 3 separate letters or parts of letters. On this hypothesis various attempts have been made recently to divide Phil. into its constituent parts. All these agree that a 2nd letter begins with 3:2 (or 3:1*b*) but do not agree on where it ends or on whether it is the only other letter. Most who see a 3rd letter find it in 4:10-20, which they view as Paul's thank-you note written immediately after Epaphroditus' arrival with a gift of money from the Phil. church (2:25-26). But 4:10-20 follows naturally after 2:25-30 and before 4:21-23. Probably there were only 2 letters, reconstructed as follows: Letter A, 1:1-2:30; 4:10-23; Letter B, 3:2-4:9 (3:1 may be an editorial splice; no one really knows what to make of it, including those who believe there is only one letter).

Letter A is virtually complete. It was occasioned by the return of Epaphroditus to Philippi following recovery from his illness and contains Paul's interpretation of the partnership symbolized by the gift he had brought. We have only the latter part of Letter B. It was occasioned by an invasion of Paul's churches by Christian teachers who were undermining his interpretation of the gospel (see below on 3:2-4:1). Because this problem grew much more serious in Corinth, what Paul wrote in II Cor. 11–12 helps to explain letter B, which was evidently written during the same period from Ephesus (or Corinth?). Letter A probably came from Ephesus.

For Further Study. E. F. Scott, in *IB*, 1955. F. W. Beare, *Phil.*, 1959. Oscar Cullmann, *The Christology of the NT*, tr. S. C. Guthrie and C. A. M. Hall, 1959, pp. 174-81 (on 2:5-11). Karl Barth, *Phil.*, tr.

J. W. Leitch, 1962. G. S. Duncan in *IDB*, 1962.
R. P. Martin, *Carmen Christi*, 1967 (on 2:5-11).

I. Greeting (1:1-2)

In accord with current style the letter identifies
first its writers, then those addressed, whom it greets
with a wish of **grace** and **peace**.

1:1a. The writers call themselves **servants** (lit.
"slaves") of Christ, for this is the status implied in
having a **Lord** (lit. "master"; cf. e.g. Col. 3:22).
Usually Paul introduces himself with the more authoritative title "apostle" (cf. I, II Cor., Gal., Col.).
Timothy, an associate of Paul's who was with him
when the Phil. church was founded (Acts 16), is
named as a courtesy, but Paul is obviously the sole
author of the letter (cf. vs. 3).

1:1b. Paul designates his readers as residents of
Philippi (see Intro.) and **saints** (lit. "holy") **in Christ
Jesus.** In the NT "saint" refers, not to the elite
Christian, but to the church member. All Christians
are saints, not because they are esp. good, but because the Holy Spirit, whose work is to make life
holy (see comments on I Thess. 4:3-8), is with them.
Bishops (lit. "overseers") **and deacons** (lit. "servers")
has long caused difficulty, for this is the only un-
contested letter from Paul which mentions these
offices in church administration. Rom. 12; I Cor. 12
assume that one's role of leadership is determined
by his gifts, understood as gifts of the Spirit, not by
the office he may hold. Some have therefore portrayed early Christianity as having almost no ordered
responsibility at all. The Dead Sea Scrolls (cf. 1QS
vi. 8-13) have caused the evidence to be reexamined,
however, because the community described in them
had an "overseer." On the other hand Paul's use of
the words hardly proves an early Christian hierarchy;
they must be taken simply in the sense of "overseers
and helpers." (Or is this detail added by the compiler to update the letter?) Precisely what the deacons did is not clear in any case.

II. Partnership in the Gospel (1:3-2:30)

In this section, the bulk of the letter, Paul thanks
his friends for their support and uses the opportunity
to illumine what such partnership in the gospel
means. After the customary thanksgiving paragraph
(1:3-11) he interprets his own current experience
(1:12-26). He asks the readers to live worthily of
the gospel (as he himself has) and suggests the
standards of this mode of life (1:27-2:18) which are
appropriate to their partnership. He then takes up
the immediate situation facing them, viz. the work
of his associates (2:19-30). If Phil. is a single letter,
then at 2:30 the thought is interrupted by chap. 3
and is continued at 4:10; if, on the other hand, Phil.
is composite, mentioning Epaphroditus' work at 2:30
prompts Paul to speak explicitly of the readers' generosity (4:10-20), after which he bids them farewell
(vss. 21-23).

A. The Thanksgiving (1:3-11)

A standard item in all of Paul's letters (and in
those written in his name) is the paragraph of thanksgiving. This sets the direction and tone of the letter
as a whole by speaking of both readers and authors

in ways that are appropriate to the immediate occasion. This thanksgiving quickly moves to a discussion of the basis for Paul's attitude and ends with
a prayer for the life of the church. Throughout, the
double emphasis on Paul and the readers is maintained.

1:3-5. *Gratitude for Partnership.* The thanksgiving
begins by emphasizing the constancy of Paul's gratitude. **All** and **always** should not be pressed, since
they are stylistic elements in a stylized paragraph and
are found regularly in statements of prayer. It is not
a matter of style, however, for Paul to mention **joy**
(vs. 4), for this is a frequent note in the letter.

More problematical is **your partnership in the
gospel** (vs. 5), which is perfectly ambiguous. In
Greek as in English it connotes both fellowship and
financial sharing in a business enterprise. Scholarly
opinion has been divided on whether Paul alludes
here to the money brought from Philippi by Epaphroditus, but he may be speaking of a whole series of
gifts from the Phil. church—at least 4 if we read
4:15-16 together with 2:25-30 and II Cor. 11:7-9.
He interprets these gifts, not as deeds of charity for
a needy apostle, but as tokens of participation in the
gospel enterprise.

In this light the question arises whether vs. 3
should also be translated to reveal the same train of
thought. The 2nd **my** here is not found in the Greek,
which again is perfectly ambiguous; it can mean
either **I thank my God in all . . . remembrance of
you** or "I thank my God for all your remembrance."
This latter sense gives the whole paragraph—and the
whole of Letter A (see Intro.)—a coherence grounded
in a concrete historical situation, viz. the Phil. partnership reaching from the beginning of Paul's European mission until the present.

1:6-8. *Reasons for Gratitude.* Paul shifts to the
rationale behind his thankfulness. He mentions first
his confidence that God will finish his work. This is
a clear expression of the early Christian tension between, on the one hand, the Christian life as
inaugurated by Christ's resurrection and appropriated
now by faith and, on the other hand, the consummation of this salvation. This tension between the
"already" and the "not yet" is expressed by the
phrases **the first day** (vs. 5), i.e. the day the Phils.
first believed in Christ, and **the day of Jesus Christ,**
i.e. the day of consummation (see comment on II
Thess. 2:2). Vs. 7 gives another reason for Paul's
gratitude: the readers remain in his **heart** (another
ambiguity, which can mean that he remains in their
hearts) and are **partakers** (lit. "co-partners"; see
above on vss. 3-5) throughout his recent experience
of **imprisonment** and **defense and confirmation of
the gospel.** Precisely what Paul has been undergoing is not clear (cf. vss. 12-14). Vs. 8 expresses
Paul's deep desire to be with the Phil. church again
(cf. vs. 26).

1:9-11. *A Prayer for the Readers.* Paul prays that
his readers may have increased **love** disciplined by
knowledge and **discernment,** so that they can **approve what is excellent**—better "find out what
is important." Their moral achievement will be
vindicated at the end (vss. 10b-11). All this is for
God's **glory.**

This paragraph of thanksgiving has opened up
themes basic to the whole letter: Paul's situation, the

support of the Phil. church, the need for rectitude among Christians—all set against the horizon of the **day of Christ,** which keeps things in perspective.

B. Paul's Experience Interpreted (1:12-26)

Having emphasized partnership in the gospel, Paul now shares with his readers the meaning of his recent life. The section is framed by the key term translated **advance** at the beginning (vs. 12) and **progress** at the end (vs. 25). The first speaks of the advance of the **gospel** by means of Paul's experience and the 2nd refers to the readers' progress and is a transition to the next topic. The passage asks how the gospel can advance when its representatives are in prison or divided. Has not the end of Paul's freedom ended the advance of the gospel and arrested the progress of his converts? To deal with this Paul speaks first of his own bondage (vss. 12-17; here **my imprisonment,** lit. "bonds," appears 3 times) and then, after a transitional comment (vs. 18), of his response to the imprisonment (vss. 19-26).

1:12-17. The Effect of Paul's Imprisonment. Paul's bondage, he says, has not bound the gospel but in fact advanced it on 2 fronts: government personnel understand his imprisonment and other Christians have more boldness now.

1:13. On **praetorian guard** see Intro. This vs. does not mean simply that the civil servants and military persons have information about Paul the prisoner. Rather it means that they learn how Paul regards his situation—lit. that his "bonds become manifest in Christ." They have come to know that he is Christ's captive whether he is Rome's prisoner or not.

1:14-17. The impact of Paul's fate on the **brethren,** i.e. local Christians, is even more fascinating, for his phrases here imply more than they say. The usual interpretation of vs. 14 is that the example of Paul's fortitude has kindled the courage of the members of the church in the city. Such may have occurred, but this meaning does not fit what Paul goes on to say in vss. 15-17, which should be part of the same paragraph. In these vss. we are plunged into the middle of a discussion of preachers' motives. Paul is not opposing a teaching but is commenting on teachers—not what they say but why, and the fact that they preach at all. The situation described has arisen **because of my imprisonment.** Wherever imprisoned, Paul's arrest suddenly has thrown the full responsibility of leadership on others who respond in differing ways. In some of them **envy and rivalry** have developed. The most intriguing detail is vs. 17b. Is Paul accusing ambitious church members of being **bold** in their preaching with the aim of goading the police into keeping him out of circulation while they seize places of leadership? Whatever the precise circumstances, it is clear that Paul is discussing motives, not as a general problem of Christian ethics, but as part of a power struggle in the church (cf. 2:21) which goes on behind the emboldened preaching of the gospel.

1:18. The One Important Consideration. Paul's attitude toward all this surprises those whose image of him is based on Gal. and II Cor. more than on I Thess. and I Cor. Instead of a torrent of invectives he expresses a "concerned indifference." His sole concern is that Christ be made known, whatever be the motive. Does Paul speak this way because his magnanimity enables him to rise above personal hurt, or because he has learned patience through being in prison, or because he has mellowed with the passing years, or because imprisonment has clarified for him what is important (cf. vs. 10), or because he believes that the nearness of the Day of Christ demands concentration on spreading the gospel? All of these possibilities have been suggested. Whatever the reason, the fact that Christ is proclaimed causes Paul to rejoice in the midst of personal bondage and disappointment. God's word is not dependent on his own freedom any more than it is dependent on the motives of the preachers. Still, a deeper reason for Paul's surprising tolerance appears in the next paragraph.

1:19-26. Paul's Response in His Imprisonment. Quoting Job 13:16a Paul says he is confident of his **deliverance**—a word which can mean either "release" or "salvation." Though some commentators prefer a purely religious meaning, it is probable that Paul is saying he expects to be released from prison (cf. vss. 25-26) yet implying by the ambiguity what he states explicitly in vss. 20-24. His confidence is based on his faith in intercessory prayer. He hopes, however, that both his **life** and his **death** will have integrity so that **Christ will be honored** through him regardless of what happens. What counts is that he be transparent to the gospel.

1:21-24. How seriously Paul means this is shown here. When Paul says **to live is Christ** he affirms that his whole existence is determined and controlled by Christ. In this light **to die** can only bring gain, not loss, because death does not destroy this relationship but leads to its consummation. Therefore he does not know whether he prefers life with **labor** or death with gain. His duty, however, is to live for the sake of the church. Hence he will not try merely to stay alive, nor will he try to die as a glorious martyr in order to secure his reputation before God and man. This passage discloses the mind of Paul as few do. It reveals a man so dominated by his labor and his Lord that in a life-and-death situation he scarcely knows which alternative is to be preferred.

1:23b-24. The chief problem with the passage lies between the lines. Paul assumes his death will result in his departure from the **flesh** and his entry into the presence of the Lord. The problem arises from the fact that in I Cor. 15; I Thess. 4 Paul insists on a resurrection of the dead. If at death one goes immediately to the Lord, why is a future resurrection necessary? No completely satisfactory solution has been found in Paul's writings, though many have speculated about his thinking on an "intermediate stage" between death and resurrection, while others have seen Paul's thought developing in another direction: immediate entry to full salvation. Probably we should recognize that there were 2 streams of thought on the subject of life after death. How Paul related them (if indeed he did) is simply not clear (see comment on I Thess. 4:13-18).

1:25-26. Paul restates his confidence that he will not only be released but see the Phils. again. He views his future relation to the church dialectically: because of *his* return they should **glory** (lit. "boast") **in Christ.** This attitude is consistent with that of I Cor. 1:10-31; II Cor. 11:16–12:10. In this way Paul's whole existence will have integrity appropriate to the gospel, for whether he is released or imprisoned, whether he lives or dies, what happens to him will promote the gospel (cf. vs. 12). The entire passage is a commentary on **for me to live is Christ.**

C. The Readers' Partnership Interpreted (1:27–2:18)

Paul now turns to the other side of the partnership in the gospel and interprets the life of the Phils. The passage is carefully structured: 1:27-30 states the theme, a way of life worthy of the gospel; 2:1-16 develops this with particular emphasis on humility and harmony in the church; 2:17-18 returns to the theme of Paul's possible death.

1:27-30. *Life Worthy of the Gospel.* This thematic statement of the issue is an appeal for a life of integrity in time of difficulty. Having expressed his hope of seeing the Phil. church again (vs. 26) Paul insists that its members develop a **worthy** life, whether or not he comes. He pleads for integrity based on the **gospel,** not on his presence. He asks them to maintain their unified stability and exertion for the gospel. **Faith of the gospel** probably means faith which the gospel elicits. Paul recognizes that this faith, this trust, is not to be taken for granted, esp. in duress, but must be worked for, struggled for.

1:28. If the Phils. achieve such unified struggle they will not be **frightened** by **opponents.** Who these may have been is unknown. This is not yet a martyr situation, for the suffering has not led to death. If the readers adopt the sort of stance Paul counsels, it will be an **omen** of the situation of the Christian in the world—**salvation** (see above on 1:19-26) for the Christian, **destruction** for the opposition. Paul does not develop the idea of destruction (see comment on II Thess. 1:7*b*-10). He is quick to add that this ultimate issue of things is not the achievement of the Phils. but the work of God.

1:29-30. The underlying rationale (a double point) for Paul's attitude is the necessity and the nature of suffering. It does not undermine faith, he holds, nor is it an absurdity that defies theological insight. Instead it is an inherent ingredient of Christian life itself. It is in fact **granted,** i.e. bestowed as a gift or a privilege. **For the sake of Christ,** however, is an absolutely necessary qualification; for not every pain Christians endure falls within the scope of Paul's remarks, but only that suffering in which Christ's cause is involved. Paul is not glorifying suffering as if he were a masochist, but is interpreting the daily meaning of being made participants in the grace of Christ (cf. vs. 7), which centers in the cross.

The 2nd underlying point is that Paul and the Phils. are involved in precisely the **same conflict,** though they are not in the same place or going through the same experiences. Theologically speaking all Christians who stand for the gospel against those forces that oppose it are in the same struggle. This unity of the church transcends regional and theological differences, just as it runs deeper than organizational unifications.

2:1-18. *Christian Unity.* Paul takes up in detail the kind of unity he has called for. Vss. 1-4 spell out the attitudes he sees as appropriate to the gospel; vss. 5-11 highlight this gospel, using an early Christian hymn, while vss. 12-13 draw the basic mandate from it; vss. 14-18 return to the situation of the readers and of Paul and end with the summons to rejoice in the midst of difficulty. A proper understanding of 2:1-18 requires seeing it as a whole and in its setting, as well as its details.

2:1-4. *A Shared Mind-Set.* Carrying forward the concern for unity (1:27) Paul writes a striking sentence. In the Greek the rhetorical effect of the 4-fold conditional clause of vs. 1 is enhanced by the repetition of **if** with every **any.** The resounding "Indeed there is!" which Paul assumes in response to each "if" sets the stage for the central imperative: Set your minds on the same thing. **Being of the same mind** is too weak a translation for the verb Paul uses (of its 22 occurrences in the NT 18 are Paul's). It denotes more than mere thinking or feeling in general; it means to center one's thinking on something and to steer one's actions by this mind-set. It is a key word in this passage. Thus Paul says that if the 4 items of vs. 1 are true the Phils. are to set their minds and to guide their lives by the same thing, to have **the same love.** The opposite of this is stated in vs. 3, while vs. 4 returns to the norm Paul is developing: concern for one another. The partnership in the gospel (1:5) and in grace (1:7) means partnership not only with Paul but with one another.

Having seen where Paul takes the line of thought we can return to the 4 axioms of vs. 1 and their significance for the whole appeal. Paul's basic question is whether there are any norms or goals in Christ for the daily life of Christians. Hence he mentions first **encouragement in Christ.** The word means both comfort and admonition or exhortation. The accent is not on the psychological state of courage but on the basis of action provided in Christ. **In Christ** is to be understood with all 4 items, not merely with the first. Thus, because in Christ are found sharing in the **incentive of love,** sharing in the reality of **the Spirit,** and **sympathy,** Paul can ask that his **joy** be made full by his readers' setting their minds on the same thing.

2:5. *A Mind-Set in Christ.* This single mind-set means, not conformity in thought, but a concentration on the same single norm. That this norm is Christ himself is the point of vss. 5-11. Here, however, we face a lack of clarity in the letter. Because **have this mind** refers to what has already been said (repeating the same "mind-set" verb of vs. 2) what follows carries the same theme forward; this is an important thread for the scope of the whole passage. Every translator of vs. 5*b* must reveal his interpretation, for there is no verb between **which** and **in Christ Jesus** in the Greek text. The RSV supplies **you have.** The NEB sidesteps the question with "Let your bearing towards one another rise out of your life in Christ Jesus," but a footnote has "which was also found in Christ Jesus." Moffatt reads "Treat one another with the same spirit as you experience in Christ Jesus." Beare's commentary suggests "Let this be the disposition that governs in your common life, as is fitting in Christ Jesus." The KJV has "Let this mind be in you, which was also in Christ Jesus" —the poorest of all these efforts, for the point is not to have the same mind that Christ had, not to emulate Christ's thinking or to imitate his acts, but to set the common mind of the church ("you" is plural; cf. RSV **yourselves**) on what one thinks in Christ.

Probably Paul means for his main verb to be understood also with "in Christ Jesus." Thus we may paraphrase: Think among yourselves what you think in Christ—i.e. think of each other the way you think about Christ; regard each other from the same perspective. This interpretation agrees with II Cor. 5:16-17: "We regard no one from a human point of view [lit. "according to the flesh"]; even though we once regarded Christ from a human point of view, we regard him thus no longer." Whatever the precise nuance, the major point is clear: the readers are to act in the light of what and how they think about Christ. The function of vss. 6-11 is to spell out this way of regarding Christ.

2:6-11. An Early Christian Hymn. This passage could hardly have been composed by Paul, for some of its terminology is not Pauline and Paul's characteristic ideas are missing. Its phrases fall into vs. patterns, and it is doubtless a hymn of the early church. In the 19th cent. some thought that an editor added the hymn; now scholarly opinion agrees that Paul quoted it and that the hymn is thus older than the letter. Whether the hymn has 2 or 3 parts is not altogether clear but most prefer to see it in 2 parts divided by the **therefore** in vs. 9. Adapting the RSV we get the following structure:

[Who] though he was in the form of God
Did not count it robbery
To be equal with God

But emptied himself,
Taking the form of a servant,
Coming into existence in the likeness of men;

And being found in human form
He humbled himself
And became obedient to the point of death
[even death on a cross].

Therefore God has highly exalted him
And bestowed on him the name
Which is above every name,

That at Jesus' name
Every knee should bow—
In heaven and on earth and under the earth—

And every tongue confess
"Jesus Christ is Lord"
To the glory of God the Father.

2:6-8. The first half of the hymn begins with God and descends to the low point, **death.** Each of its 3 active verbs focuses on a moment in the deathward movement of obedience.

2:6. The "story" begins with **equality with God,** prior to existence in time-space. Existing **in the form of God** means having divine prerogatives, being God's virtual equal. The word translated **to be grasped** is ambiguous; it can mean either "to be held onto" or "to be achieved by grasping." In the latter sense some have seen reference here to Christ's not acting as Adam did, or as the angels who were tempted into insurrection. But the first meaning, that Christ had equality but did not insist on keeping it, seems much more likely. All attention is concentrated on the free surrender of divine authority; nothing is said about Christ's prior reflecting on this course of action.

2:7. The 2nd verb, **emptied,** is crucial. The 2 phrases help interpret its meaning. "Empty" here means to take the status of a **servant** (lit. "slave") and come into existence as a man. This whole complex of phrases speaks of the incarnation (lit. "enfleshment," a word derived from John 1:14 but never actually used in the NT). The heart of the matter is the change of roles from divine authority to slave status, from the highest thinkable role to the lowest known. "Emptied" must be understood metaphorically, not metaphysically—i.e. it is a poetic way of celebrating the change of status, not a way of talking about the discarding of divine substances or essences (such ideas may lie *behind* the hymn but are not its concern). The hymn makes precisely the same point as II Cor. 8:9.

In **servant** some have seen a reference to the suffering servant of Isa. 53, which Christians early regarded as a description of Jesus' passion. This interpretation is improbable, for the hymn (at least in the first half) uses terms which are generally more at home in Greek than in OT thought. A better clue to what "servant" means is Gal. 4:3, where human existence is described as slavery to "the elemental spirits of the universe"—the invisible hostile powers which were believed to inhabit planets and to control the destinies of men. What the hymn celebrates, therefore, is the movement of Christ from sovereignty over the cosmos to slavery within it.

The next phrase deals with this movement also. **Being born** is an overly free translation. Jesus' birth is not spoken of at all and can be read into the text only by combining it with the Christmas stories. The verb actually means "come to pass" or "happen." The one who pre-existed "came to pass" as a man; he who "is" (as God's equal) "happened"! The **likeness of men** is a way of saying that this one shared the status of man; it falls short of saying he became "just another man," or that "the Word became flesh" (John 1:14; cf. Rom. 5:14; 8:3). The point is that he who was equal with God now became equal with man. The language is hymnic and should not be pressed to mean that the Son of God did not become a real man but only like a man. Such literalism, advocated by some in the 2nd cent., denied the reality of the incarnation and was rejected as heresy, for it turned the intent of the phrase upside down. The point is that God's Son shared man's plight, not that he became a "reasonable facsimile" of man.

2:8. The 3rd verb, **humbled,** speaks of self-humbling as the shape of obedience, obedience to the point of **death.** The phrase **even death on a cross** is apparently Paul's own addition, for it not only disturbs the symmetry of the lines but specifies the particularly degrading character of Christ's death with the typical terminology of Paul. In the self-humbling we should see the sweep of Jesus' life as a whole, not particular incidents in it. It is not clear who is being obeyed here—the cosmic powers or God. Perhaps it is enough to say that he acted as one who was obedient rather than as one who called for obedience to himself, thus taking also this line as an expression of the change of roles. The first half of the hymn celebrates the movement of the pre-existent one (i.e. he **was** before he **became**) from the zenith of authority to the nadir of human subjection. "Pre-existence" is a technical category from the ancient philosophical-theological tradition: it was developed in order to be able to speak of a being who "exists" apart from created time-space and prior to his entry into it. This conception is assumed by the hymn.

2:9-11. The 2nd half of the hymn begins at this low point of self-humiliation, but instead of reversing the downward movement in stages it celebrates the one dramatic act of God—the subject of all action in this half. God **highly exalted him** (NEB "raised him to the heights") **and bestowed on him the name** above all names. These 2 verbs are 2 aspects of the same act. The self-humbling is answered by the exaltation by God, and the role of slave is answered by the role of master. The **name** is **Lord** (lit. "master"). The point is the same as in I Tim. 3:16; Heb. 1:3. "Lord" here means sovereign over the entire cosmos, as the quotations in vss. 10, 11 from Isa. 45:23 make clear. The entire cosmic power structure under whose authority Christ humbled himself now confesses that he is Lord.

This exaltation is the consequence of the Resurrection, though it is not clear whether this means a logical consequence not yet actualized or what has already occurred as a part of the Resurrection itself. Paul himself holds the latter view, if I Cor. 15:20-28 is a valid index; but since Paul is quoting a hymn written by someone else, we should be cautious in interpreting this line. The entire act of God is for his own glory, for the sake of his reputation; his status as God is vindicated by this act which establishes decisively his sovereignty over all cosmic powers. Here there is no cosmic battle, no Armageddon. God's victory over cosmic hostility which tyrannized man and taunted God is achieved solely by the resurrection of Jesus, which made him Lord. This triumph is what the hymn celebrates.

Having analyzed the hymn we may make several overall observations. Though it has been argued that the hymn comes from the Palestinian church and that its intellectual milieu is Jewish, it is increasingly clear that the first stanza at least is really at home in the early Hellenistic church, e.g. at Antioch. It draws on the Palestinian, Christian, and OT tradition, of course, but the basic scheme of a divine being who descends to earth and death to save man is a Hellenistic pattern. Moreover, the key phrases of the first part of the hymn simply will not translate back into Aramaic.

The purpose of the hymn is not to outline the life of Jesus for Christians to imitate, for the movement of the hymn begins with parity with God—where no one else may begin. Paul uses the hymn to remind his readers of the starting point of their own thinking and acting, as vss. 12-13 show. With minds set on such an act of God's Son, implies Paul, you are to act out your partnership in relation to one another.

Since this is a hymn, we must not treat it as if it were a paragraph in systematic theology. Hymns celebrate emphases; they do not analyze. This one holds before the readers the whole sweep of the Christ event, which begins and ends beyond time-space. Therefore it is clearly as mythological as it is historical, for the historical life of Jesus is only one phase in this total event. Thus the hymn poses more theological questions than it answers. It is not designed to analyze Christ's person but to celebrate and proclaim what God's Son has done. Because it

is a hymn it was sung by congregations before it was taken up into Paul's exhortation. By singing this hymn Christians celebrated also their involvement in the Christ event, their being grasped by this movement. Therefore the hymn can become the basis of an appeal by Paul; here worship becomes the basis of action, and praise a motive for ethics. Paul is saying: Act in accord with your praise.

The hymn is nevertheless theological even if it is not a piece of systematic theology. It assumes that man's salvation depends on this invasion of the world's tyrannies. For the hymn man's situation is not ignorance or transgression but bondage epitomized and climaxed by death. Redemption here requires dealing with these tyrannies, which is precisely what the hymn celebrates as having happened.

2:12-13. *Application of the Hymn.* The immediate, ethical mandate from the hymn is stated dialectically: **Work out your own salvation** because **God is at work in you.** Vs. 12*a* picks up the theme of 1:27, showing that 1:27-2:18 must be seen as a whole. The obedience to which Paul refers may be either to himself as founder of the church and pastor in absentia or to the Lord. Actually Paul would not make a sharp distinction, as I Cor. 11:1 shows. At the same time **fear and trembling** is to characterize their attitudes because this is appropriate to the fact that God is at work. Faith does not exclude such fear but actually causes it, because being obedient to the God whose act is celebrated in the hymn makes it impossible to take God's work for granted.

The mandate to work out one's own salvation must not be understood as meaning: "Devise a way to save yourselves as Christ saved himself," but rather: "Bring to pass your own salvation; actualize in your life this lordship of the obedient one." This can be done only because God is at work generating the will and granting the strength to bring it to pass. This is not an easy cooperation, as if Paul were saying, "God will help you with your problems; do what you can and he will do the rest." Rather God's participation is throughout, from the heart's resolve to the final consummation. He who knows that God is at work in him, bringing to pass in his life the salvation grounded in the event celebrated in the hymn, knows that his very life is a hint, a signpost of salvation to come, as 1:28 has already said.

2:14-18. *Specific Applications.* The above is now applied to the specific situation of the readers and of Paul. To begin with, they are to avoid **grumbling** and to strive to be **innocent,** persons of integrity in a culture regarded as **crooked and perverse** (phraseology adapted from Deut. 32:5). Paul calls not only for discontinuity with this culture but also for a creative effort to redeem it (vs. 16). This is an important reminder that Paul's perspective is the life of the church in the world for the sake of the world. Vs. 16*b* shows that Paul has something at stake in the fate of the church at Philippi. If this congregation works out its salvation his labor will not have been for nothing.

2:17. In turn the Phils. have something at stake in Paul's integrity, even in his death. Without speaking of it explicitly, Paul has returned to the theme of partnership in the gospel. The discussion ends with a note of rejoicing, an attitude possible for those who sing the hymn in the midst of a culture not yet redeemed. With such rejoicing the Phils. will set their minds on the one thing, the event of Christ. This will free them from pettiness, for they will be aware that they have been grasped by the grace of God in the world.

D. THE WORK OF TIMOTHY AND EPAPHRODITUS (2:19-30)

2:19-24. Paul's Plans for Timothy. At this point Paul turns to his immediate relation to his readers. He begins with his plan to send Timothy for the express purpose of learning more precisely the state of affairs in the Phil. church. Yet the next vs. suggests Paul's real aim: Timothy is to act in Paul's place as pastor and guide. Paul has **no one** else whom he can send who will be as concerned for the church. Note that the **interests** of Jesus Christ and the **welfare** of the church are 2 ways of saying virtually the same thing—a point more obvious in the Greek. Vs. 22 comments on Timothy's work with Paul; Acts 16:1-3 reports the circumstances in which Timothy joined Paul. Vss. 23-24 return to the plan for sending Timothy and reveal that Paul's fate is still undecided, though he fully expects (**trust in the Lord** expresses confidence rather than mere submission to the divine will) to go to Philippi soon. This expectation offers an important clue to where the letter was written (see Intro.).

2:25-30. Paul's Plans for Epaphroditus. Paul now turns to Epaphroditus, who apparently is about to set out for Philippi, taking the letter. Sometime earlier he brought money from the Phil. church to Paul (4:18) and remained long enough with Paul to become **ill, near to death** (vs. 27). The Phils. **heard** of his illness and were disturbed, and Epaphroditus in turn learned of their anxiety and was **distressed** and probably wanted to return as soon as possible (vs. 26). This return is the immediate occasion of the letter. Timothy is to follow **soon** (vs. 19); then Paul himself will come (vs. 24). All this communication between Paul and the Phils. indicates that Paul's place of imprisonment was fairly near Philippi (see Intro.). Paul speaks highly of Epaphroditus: he is a **brother and fellow worker and fellow soldier** to Paul and in the church a **minister** and **your messenger.** This last word is lit. "apostle"—an indication that for Paul the term was not yet so technical as it became later (cf. Rom. 16:7). If we knew the circumstances of Epaphroditus' **risking his life** to carry out his mission, we could doubtless settle many questions concerning Paul's imprisonment. (See comment at II above for relation of 2:30 to 4:10-20.)

III. TRUSTING RELIGION OR TRUSTING CHRIST (3:1-4:1)

That ch. 3 interrupts the flow of thought and changes the mood is recognized by all interpreters and has convinced many that Phil. incorporates 2 or more separate letters of Paul (see Intro.). If this is true, Letter B begins with either 3:1*b* or 3:2 (see below on 3:1) and continues at least through 4:1 and probably farther. In this passage Paul's pastoral concern issues in a polemic against positions which he considers as alternatives to Christianity even though they may be put forward in the name of Christ.

Against whom is this polemic addressed? Clearly vss. 2-11 are attacking Jews and vss. 17-21 oppose libertines. Most commentators, unable to reconcile these descriptions, have assumed there must be 2 different groups, the 2nd being Gentiles belonging to some sort of religious movement with libertine ethics. Many of them have taken vs. 3 to indicate that the Jews were non-Christian but have judged from Paul's distress in vs. 18 that the Gentiles must be Christians. What is not obvious, however, is which of these 2 groups Paul has in mind in vss. 12-16. More important, nowhere does he give any indication of turning from one group to another. The structure of the passage gives no clear evidence of 2 groups, and it reads more naturally as a unified polemic against a single, though complex, front.

Those who see a single front, however, do not agree on its identity. Some see it as made up of Judaizers—Christian Jews who demanded that all Christians become practicing Jews in order to be the Messiah's people (see Intro. to Gal. and comment on Acts 15). A serious flaw in this theory is that such ardent proponents of the Jewish law could scarcely be described as libertines.

Others maintain that the polemic is aimed throughout at non-Christian Jews and reflects bitter tensions that had already developed between church and synagogue. Since the evidence is that there were virtually no Jews in Philippi (see Intro.) adopting this view would require us to assume that Letter B was addressed to some other city—which is not impossible, for there is no specific reference to the Phil. church or, for that matter, to Paul's imprisonment in ch. 3. It is questionable, however, whether vss. 17-21 would describe loyal members of the synagogue.

A 3rd view, which seems more probable, is that the opponents Paul is writing about were gnosticized Jews who had become Christians—part of the same movement that penetrated his churches in Corinth and Asia Minor (see Intros. to Cor., Gal., Col.). Gnosticism, as known from its serious threat to the church in the 2nd cent., was a syncretistic philosophy which viewed all matter as evil and thus saw the soul as suffering imprisonment in the body—a plight from which it could be saved only through knowledge (Greek *gnosis*) of the self. The ethics resulting from this view of the body tended either toward ascetic efforts to control the imprisoning body or toward libertine excesses intended to demonstrate that the body was really irrelevant to a saved soul. In this ch. Paul may have in mind both these ethical consequences and oppose them both on the basis of God's grace.

Every reconstruction of Paul's opponents is conjectural, of course, since he did not need to describe them to his readers.

The passage consists of the statement of the theme in vss. 2-4*a*, its exposition in vss. 4*b*-16, and its application in vss. 17-21, with a summary exhortation in 4:1 which also introduces the next paragraph. In the middle of the exposition stands an important autobiographical passage (vss. 4*b*-14) in which Paul uses himself as an example to be imitated (vs. 17).

3:1. This vs. is problematical, for it is not clear whether it goes with ch. 2 or 3, or whether vs. 1*a* goes with one and vs. 1*b* with the other. No completely satisfactory solution has been proposed. It is probably at least in part an editor's work. Most of those who defend the unity of Phil. concede that **the same things** cannot refer to anything now in chs. 1–2 and therefore apply it to ch. 3. If we recognize, however, that part of a 2nd letter has been joined on at this point (see Intro.) the phrase can more naturally be understood as referring to what has been lost or omitted from Letter B.

3:2-4b. Warning Against False Teaching. Three staccato commands are followed by a thematic statement, Paul's warning is put in terms of taunt and bitter sarcasm. If we assume a single front, all 3 terms refer to the same opponents. **Dogs** is a common epithet of contempt as in our use of "bitch." **Evil-workers** is so like "deceitful workmen" in II Cor. 11:13 as to suggest that Paul is attacking the same group who infiltrated the Corinthian church—an important clue for identifying them as Jewish Christians with gnostic theology. Paul sees them as undermining the integrity of the gospel as a whole, not just his own ideas about it, as II Cor. 11:3-5 shows.

Those who mutilate the flesh paraphrases a Greek word that puns on "circumcision." Paul uses "circumcision" to speak metaphorically of the Christian's refusal to live "according to the flesh" (cf. Rom. 8); therefore he regards those Christians who require the physical rite as mere mutilators. The readers are to "look out for the mutilators," Paul says, because **we are the circumcision** (the RSV supplies **true** to make the point after the paraphrase). For Paul literal circumcision is only an operation on the body, and so those who insist that it be done are putting **confidence in the flesh** and in what one does with it. For Paul real circumcision means repudiating all *reliance* on the flesh *categorically* and serving God by the Spirit (see RSV footnote) and glorying only in Christ. The opponents required circumcision as a sign of literal repudiation of the flesh, of fleshly existence as such. Paul, however, insists that despite their ideology the fact that they require circumcision at all shows that they trust in a fleshly rite. If flesh were really repudiated, all trust in the meaning of fleshly operations would fall away. Paul centers the issue on where one places his trust, not on the problem of flesh itself.

Paul's Own Life as an Illustration. This is now spelled out. Vs. 4a provides the link by pointing out that Paul himself has achieved this transition. Vss. 4b-6 undergird this by showing that Paul has a perfect score with regard to everything that physical circumcision can mean: the rite itself, family background, participation in the party zealous for the law (cf. Acts 22:3; 26:4-5), zeal in uprooting the new church which seemed to threaten Judaism (cf. Acts 8:1b-3; 9:1-5; 22:3-5; I Cor. 15:9; Gal. 1:11-17), rectitude insofar as this could be measured by what was required (cf. Gal. 1:14). These vss. have no place for the modern view that before his conversion Paul was a Jew who had an uneasy conscience over the stoning of Stephen and a growing dissatisfaction with his own religion. Rather Paul insists that he was a model Jew. All this, he says, was a putting of his confidence in the flesh, in that which he could measure. Everything that the opponents are requiring of Christians he had achieved already before he became a Christian. He can trump anyone's claim (cf. II Cor. 11:21b-22).

3:7-11. Revolution in Values. Paul now explains what his conversion to Christ meant for this entire way of handling one's relation to God. Vs. 7 states the heart of it. The point is that what was **gain** for him suddenly turned into **loss**. Paul does not say that it was lost; he says it was loss. To put it commercially, as Paul does, his profits were discovered to be debts; his money was transformed into IOU's. The long sentence that follows (vss. 8-11) amplifies this.

3:8. Twice in this vs. Paul uses the verb **count;** this means that both phrases make the same point, counting gain as loss and counting it as trash or garbage (**refuse** is too circumspect). For the sake of Christ all standards have been turned upside down, and all religious effort is utterly useless if one is in Christ. Paul renounces his achievements for the sake of **knowing Christ**—a phrase doubtless designed to take the point away from his opponents, who claim to have true knowledge of what Christ means. Paul claims not only to be the true circumcision precisely by this revaluation of the circumcision rite but also to have the true knowledge as well.

3:9. Likewise, precisely because he has the knowledge and has turned his back on literal circumcision as a significant rite, Paul insists that it is not the opponents but he who is **found in him.** In his explanation of what he means by being in Christ the 2 modes of Paul's understanding of Christian salvation come together, a) the legal (man is pronounced to be in right relation to God because he trusts Christ) and b) the mystical (the believer is in Christ and Christ is in him). For Paul, being in Christ means both standing before God on the basis, not of the **law,** but of **faith** only, a standing granted by God because of this faith-trust (the legal mode), and (vss. 10-11) knowing Christ, the **power of his resurrection** and partnership in **his sufferings** (the mystical mode). This is a participative knowing, not data-knowing, just as "I know what war is" does not mean, "I have information about war." Likewise, being a partner with Christ's sufferings means having one's existence shaped by Christ's death in order to reach the resurrection life.

Righteousness (a basic theme of Rom. 1–8) is a key word in this highly compressed statement. Paul uses it in the sense, not of goodness, but of rectitude. Righteousness is a right relation to God. The issue turns on the basis on which one has such a right relation: doing what is required by the law (Paul's Bible, but in a deeper sense the will of God in it) or having faith in Christ (what Christ means for the way God deals with man). The right relation that depends on faith is a relation that comes from God; therefore what Paul *does* has really nothing to do with it, for he cannot compel God to consider him "right" nor earn God's verdict in any way (since then God would be reduced to a guarantor of the efficacy of religious practices). Hence no deed, no doing of God's will, is a credit toward this right relation. If this is the case, then the rite of circumcision and the deeds of religious devotion it represents are as worthless as garbage if one trusts only in God on the basis of Christ. What Paul states briefly here he argues at length in Rom. 1–3, esp. 2:25–3:31.

3:10. This vs. deals with the relation to Christ mentioned in vs. 9 and explains what faith really means. It is not simply an intellectual position, an idea about Jesus, but trust in him to the point of sharing in him. To have faith in Christ is to **know him,** and this knowledge means entering into his radical transformation by death-resurrection. This in turn means having one's own life conform to Christ's death—in the sense of sharing the meaning of his death as the door to freedom from the tyrannies of this world (see above on 2:6-11). The opponents doubtless claimed that circumcision marked their repudiation of the flesh and the world too. Paul insists, however, that the real, radical, effectual dealing with the flesh (matter and death) comes, not at all by rites and religious practices of whatever kind, but only by trusting in the resurrection. Circumcision is a rite of rejecting the flesh; trusting the resurrection is hoping for transformation of the flesh. Here is a radical repudiation of "religion."

3:11. The **resurrection** here is not yet a possession but a promise. This very **if possible** is crucial to the point Paul makes in vss. 12-16 and to the polemic itself, for the opponents were probably claiming that they had attained the resurrection, that they were fully redeemed from time-space. No doubt they practiced circumcision to show their attainment and required it of all who want to claim such perfection too. The same sort of claim to perfection was made in Corinth (I Cor. 4:8-13).

3:12-16. Christian Life as Process. This section develops the tension between having and not having. Paul insists that he has not **obtained this** or appropriated it fully (NEB "got hold of it yet"). The most significant phrase is **am already perfect** (lit. "have already been perfected") since the opponents probably used "perfection" as a slogan. It was an important word in certain forms of Greco-Roman religion, esp. in the gnostic tradition. Paul vigorously insists that perfection is not part of the "already" but belongs to the "not yet."

3:13-14. Paul contends that his life consists of a **straining forward,** that he must **press on** because the **prize** lies ahead. The prize consists, not in a present achievement, but in the **upward call of God in Christ Jesus** (NEB "God's call to the life above.") This may refer to God's call to faith as a summons "upward" or, more probably, to the call into eternal life realized at death, as the NEB suggests. The opponents claimed already to have heeded the "call" (a favorite gnostic expression); Paul insists that this is an ultimate call toward which he presses. Again and again Paul uses the slogans of his opponents to deny them their point. Here he denies that the call to perfection can be "answered" now except as a race, a process, a pursuit which demands that he forget the past—i.e. circumcision as a rite and all that goes with it.

3:15. The word translated **mature** is the adjective form of the verb "have been perfected" of vs. 12 and can mean either "perfect" or "mature." There is a touch of irony here as Paul uses the opponents' self-description to correct their views of perfection: being perfect means struggling throughout life. On this basis **those of us who are mature** (perfect) does not grant that some are in fact already perfected but says in effect, If you want to regard yourselves as perfect you must do so in this way. Therefore vs. 15a sets a requirement for the whole church, not for its elite. In

vs. 15b Paul addresses those who disagree and says that God himself will reveal to them also the point he has been making. (In Greek the **that** of vs. 15b repeats the word translated thus in vs. 15a.)

3:16. In the meantime one is to live according to the degree of perfection he has **attained** in the forward thrust. This whole paragraph is an eloquent statement of life in Christ as progress toward a goal —a process, not an achievement.

3:17-21. Application to the Readers' Situation. Paul intensifies his treatment of the problem of the **brethren** to whom he is writing. He asks that he be imitated (see comment on I Thess. 1:6-7); moreover he appears to ask that the congregation follow those who are already doing this.

3:18-19. Those who live this way are contrasted with the opponents (on the view of many that they are a different group from those attacked thus far see above on 3:1-4:1). Here, as in vs. 2, Paul is sarcastic. He characterizes them **as enemies of the cross,** though they doubtless claimed to understand it rightly— probably as the sign that fleshly existence must be destroyed. **Their end is destruction,** though they doubtless believed it to be perfect salvation here and now. **Their god is the belly** (i.e. physical appetites), though they doubtless claimed to worship a purely spiritual God who had no concern for the flesh. Their **glory** is **their shame,** though they doubtless boasted of their "freedom" from all restraint on their fleshly desires as a sign of spirituality. Their **minds** are **set on earthly things,** though they doubtless claimed to be concerned only with abiding spiritual truths. Paul says he weeps as he writes; the **tears** are clearly bitter ones.

3:20-21. Paul now returns to a positive statement that emphasizes the eschatological nature of Christian perfection suggested in vss. 12-14. By insisting that **our commonwealth is in heaven** Paul maintains that the definitive goal and guide of Christian life lies beyond time-space; thereby he excludes again the opponents' claim to have attained it here and now. When Paul says **we await a Savior** (a word used by Paul only here) he likewise contends that full salvation lies in the future (the NEB catches this: "and from heaven we expect our deliverer to come"). Christ will transform us to be as he now is— a theme elaborated in I Cor. 15:20-57 (presumably this is the "spiritual body") The transforming **power** here is the power inherent in the lordship of Jesus, a sovereignty conferred by God at the Resurrection, according to the hymn of 2:6-11 (cf. I Cor. 15:20-28; I Thess. 4:13-18).

The passage reveals that Paul shares with his opponents, in a sense, the depreciation of the physical body and regards it as the seat (but not the cause) of man's problems (cf. Rom. 7:7-25; Gal. 5:16-17). However, he is too deeply rooted in the OT conviction that God created the body and matter to regard salvation as sheer release from it. Paul's opponents agreed with him that "flesh and blood cannot inherit the kingdom of God" (I Cor. 15:50), but they drew the opposite conclusion: salvation to them was precisely an absolute and ultimate release from the body and from all the influence of matter on the soul. Paul insists that Jesus' resurrection means that salvation will bring not destruction but transformation of bodily existence. In his view "the Lord is for the body" (I Cor. 6:13), and his ethics stand under the mandate "glorify God in your body" (I Cor. 6:20).

4:1. In conclusion Paul counsels the church to **stand firm . . . in the Lord** (see comment on I Thess. 3:8-10).

IV. The Life of the Church (4:2-9)

The several one- and 2-vs. units of this passage show little connection with each other or with other parts of Phil., and the scholars who have tried to analyze the book as a composite work have varied widely in assigning some or all of them to the respective letters (see Intro.). The chief reason for assuming that all of them probably followed 3:2–4:1 in Letter B is the improbability that any of them immediately preceded vss. 10–20 in Letter A (or Letter C; see below on vss. 10-20).

4:2-3. Who **Euodia** and **Syntyche** are is not known, nor is the cause of their disagreement. The identity of the **yokefellow** who is to help them resolve their differences has been the subject of various conjectures, e.g. that the word is a proper name (Syzygus) or that it refers to Lydia (Acts 16:11-15) or to Luke (because in Acts 16:6-10 the author, traditionally assumed to be Luke, shifts to "we" just before Paul's trip to Philippi) or to Epaphroditus (cf. 2:25-30). Some have wanted to identify **Clement** with the author of I Clement, a letter to the church at Corinth written from Rome *ca.* A.D. 96 and included in some early manuscripts of the NT; but that one of Paul's **fellow workers** should be active so many years later is highly improbable. Moreover, Clement was a common name.

4:4. This exhortation to **rejoice** is one of several references to rejoicing (1:18-19; 2:17-18, 28; 3:1; 4:10) and joy (1:4, 25; 2:2, 29; 4:1) often cited as evidence for the unity of Phil. Paul frequently uses these words elsewhere, however, and the only significant parallelism is the appearance of the phrase **rejoice in the Lord** both here and in 3:1 (see comment).

4:5. The significant note of this vs. is that Paul believes **the Lord** is near; by this he means the coming from heaven mentioned in 3:20 and described in I Cor. 15:51-57; I Thess. 4:13-18. Paul clearly expected to see this event in his lifetime (see comment on I Thess. 4:15-17).

4:6-7. Praying is to be done with **thanksgiving** for what has already been received; this will be an effective antidote to **anxiety.** God's **peace** (vs. 7), which transcends comprehension because it is given in the midst of difficulties, just as salvation is begun here and now, will guard the thinking of the readers in Christ, since such peace is grounded in the meaning of the cross.

4:8. This oft-quoted vs. asks the readers to **think about** (NEB "fill all your thoughts with") those things which are worthwhile. The several items were commonplace virtues in Hellenistic morals. Paul takes them up and commends them without explicit Christianization. In this way he shows that Christianity can appropriate sound ethical principles recognized by society in general. A century later, Justin Martyr developed this view: "The truths which men

in all lands have rightly spoken belong to us Christians" (Apol. II 13).

4:9. Paul urges imitation of himself (cf. 3:17). Not the **peace of God** (vs. 7) but the **God of peace** is promised as the accompanying presence.

V. Concluding Thanks (4:10-20)

In this passage Paul, without losing his dignity or independence, expresses in detail his thanks for the gift which the Phils. sent by Epaphroditus (vs. 18; cf. 2:25). Among scholars who consider Phil. a composite work (see Intro.) some have argued that this expression of thanks is a 3rd letter written before the other 2, immediately on Epaphroditus' arrival. The close connection in both subject and mood, however, suggests strongly that it rather belongs immediately after 2:25-30 as the continuation of Letter A following the interpolated Letter B (3:1–4:9).

4:10-13. Paul speaks of a **revived** support from the Phils. after a period of **no opportunity.** What prevented their steady support is not known, and speculation is futile. Vss. 11-12 give an important clue to the attitude of Paul. On the experiences mentioned here cf. I Cor. 4:11-13; II Cor. 11:16-29. Paul knows how to live in such a way that his **circumstances** do not control his inner life. The Greek for **content** (used only here in the NT) is a term from Stoic ethics; for the Stoic, however, it meant, not a freedom in the midst of involvement, but an autonomy which permitted neither participation in the lives of others nor compassion for them, and which resulted in a steely serenity in a troubled world. Paul's **secret** is the empowering from God, which does not simply fortify Paul against difficulty but enables him to live with it creatively. II Cor. 12:1-10 is an important discussion of this power which comes from allowing Christ's strength to be made visible through the way human weakness is borne.

4:14-16. Beginning a new paragraph with vs. 14 (or vs. 15, NEB) is unnecessary, since Paul clearly continues to express his appreciation for support, lest his comments about his freedom suggest that he is not grateful. **Share** and **entered into partnership** translate forms of the word emphasized in chs. 1–2 (see above on 1:3-5). On the help which the Phils. sent see comments on 2:19-30; I Thess. 2:9-12. There is no known reason why only this church supported Paul.

4:17-20. Vss. 17-18*a* use commercial terminology and vs. 18*b* uses the language of religious ritual; both are metaphors, of course. Vs. 19 expresses the same sort of confidence as Jesus expressed in Matt. 6:25-34; by referring to the wealth of God's glory in Christ, Paul speaks of inexhaustible grace through the Cross and the Resurrection. This proviso keeps Paul's statement from being simply a blank check that will not be honored.

VI. Farewell (4:21-23)

On **saint** see above on 1:1*b*. On **Caesar's household** see Intro. Here we learn that some imperial servants have been converted—a fact not mentioned in the previous reference to them (1:13).

THE LETTER
OF PAUL TO THE COLOSSIANS
Victor Paul Furnish

INTRODUCTION

Relation to Eph. Among the NT letters no 2 exhibit such a complex tangle of formal, verbal, and theological agreements and disagreements as Col. and Eph. These writings not only deal with many of the same themes, employ a similar theological vocabulary, and draw on a common fund of Christian hymnody; there are also numerous and impressive instances in which, apparently, there is literary dependence of one on the other (cf. e.g. Col. 1:1-2 with Eph. 1:1-3; Col. 1:23b-29 with Eph. 3:7-9; Col. 3:12-15 with Eph. 4:2-4; Col. 3:16-17 with Eph. 5:19-20; Col. 4:7-8 with Eph. 6:21-22).

On the other hand there are also significant differences. Some of these involve subtle changes of wording, as a careful study of the passages listed will show. It is also noteworthy that, while OT passages are never cited in Col. and there are only a few insignificant allusions to the OT, important OT allusions abound in Eph. and OT texts are sometimes specifically invoked (e.g. Eph. 4:8; 6:2-3). Moreover, while Eph. is dominated by the author's concern to define the true nature of the church, the thought of Col. is controlled by an attempt to counteract some false teaching which has sprung up in Colossae. Thus, while Eph. is a general tractate addressed to the church at large (see Intro. to Eph.), Col. is occasioned by a particular problem and directed to a specific situation.

Many attempts have been made to define the relationship of Col. and Eph., and the variety of current opinions suggests that the question has never gained a definitive answer; but most present views may be grouped into the 3 following: (*a*) Col. and Eph. are both Paul's own, written at the same time, from prison, but for different reasons. (*b*) Only Col. is an authentic Pauline letter; hence the literary dependence is on the side of Eph., written by a Paulinist who in part understood but in part misunderstood —or intentionally modified and adapted—his teacher's views. (*c*) Neither Col. nor Eph. is from Paul himself, though in each some of the authentic Pauline perspectives survive; and Eph. appears to be one step further removed from Paul than Col. in theology and composition. In recent years all discussions of this issue have had to reckon with the possibility that many of the parallels hitherto adduced as instances of literary dependence may in reality reflect a common, independent adaptation of liturgical and ethical materials already formulated and used by the early church. For further comment on this point see Intro. to Eph.

Occasion and Purpose. In contrast to Eph., one can speak of a specific occasion for the writing of Col. If Paul is the author, at least one reason for his writing the letter was his concern about Onesimus, the runaway slave on whose behalf he appeals in Philem. The points of contact between these 2 letters are impressive (see Intro. to Philem.), and considerable attention must be paid to those passages in Col. which may bear on the case of Onesimus (see below on 3:22-4:1; 4:17) and to the fact that Onesimus himself is accompanying the bearer of this letter to Colossae (4:7-9).

Most commentators, however, see Col. as occasioned primarily by the author's concern about the activity of false teachers among the Col. Christians. These teachers are never named, nor are their false doctrines ever specifically labeled, but almost from the beginning the letter is directed against the views they are sponsoring. Their teaching is directly attacked in 2:6-23, but the author's wish to combat it is also reflected in his constant reference to the tradition which the Cols. have received (e.g. 1:3-8, 15-20) and to the apostolic authority which stands behind it (1:24-2:5) and in his exhortations to remain faithful to it (e.g. 1:9-14, 23; 2:6-7). The words of 4:12 provide a succinct statement of the author's objective (see comment).

Colossae and the Errant Teaching. Colossae itself, a city of Asia Minor situated in the valley of the Lycus River 110 miles E of Ephesus (see color map 16), had no special prominence in comparison with the neighboring cities of Hierapolis and Laodicea (cf. 2:1; 4:13, 15-16), and the letter indicates that Paul himself had never been there (1:4; 2:1). The Col. congregation, and probably also those at Hierapolis and Laodicea, had been organized by Epaphras (1:7), himself a native of Colossae (4:12).

It is impossible to reconstruct the details of the false teaching Col. opposes, and it is likely that the author himself had only general information about its doctrines and sponsors. Certain of its features, however, are discernible. It called itself a "philosophy" (2:8) and appealed to some special tradition in support of its teachings (2:8, 22). Its central doctrine concerned the "elemental spirits of the universe" (2:8), probably to be identified with the "principalities and powers" (or "authorities") mentioned in 1:16; 2:10, 15. They were probably regarded as angelic beings who collectively contributed to the "fullness" of God and exercised demonic control over men's lives. This errant teaching probably held that men, to gain freedom from these controlling fates and powers, must pay them homage (2:18). Perhaps for this reason emphasis was placed on the observance of ritual fast days (2:16).

This teaching stressed not only the importance of mystic visions (2:18) but also, more practically, the necessity of adherence to certain regulations (2:16, 20-23). From the remarks of 2:11-15 one may conclude that the rite of circumcision was urged as prerequisite for salvation. Several other passages suggest that the errorists divided men into classes depending on their level of spiritual attainment (1:28; 3:11).

It is apparent that in this teaching various religious mythologies and practices converged. Its speculation about a hierarchy of cosmic powers and its emphasis on a superior "wisdom," or "philosophy," as well as the stress on a special "tradition," is typical of many religious movements in the Hellenistic world. To these particular movements, influenced by oriental religious speculation and mythology, many scholars have applied the term "Gnosticism." Gnosticism as a system was a specifically 2nd-cent. Christian heresy, but gnosticizing tendencies and motifs are identifiable long before. However, one may discern Jewish as well as Gnostic influences—the practice of circumcision, the promotion of dietary laws, and the adherence to statutes and ordinances. Whether one calls the errant teaching a Jewish Gnosticism or a gnosticizing Judaism, it was basically a syncretistic amalgam, typical of its day and not unlike the false teaching propagated among Paul's Galatian churches (see Intro. to Gal. and comment on Gal. 4:8-10). From the way the argument of Col. proceeds it is evident that the false teaching was intended, not to supplant the Pauline gospel, but to supplement it.

Theological Perspectives. The theological position of the author is developed largely in response to the errant teaching which threatens to unsettle the Cols. To make his points against the errorists more effectively he employs some of the very words and concepts used by them, adapting these to his own purposes. But his theological position is also strongly influenced by the traditional language of Christian baptism, for it is to a vital memory of their conversion and incorporation into the church that he wishes to recall his readers.

Because of the nature of the false doctrines the stress is on the role of Christ as sovereign Lord, God's agent in creation and redemption. This view is supported in 1:3-23 chiefly by the quotation of a hymn (1:15-20) which, as adapted, speaks of Christ as preexistent ruler of the cosmos who holds all things together, who is head of the body, the church, and through whose death on the cross all things have been reconciled. Of special importance is the insistence that in Christ alone dwells the fullness of deity (1:19; 2:9; cf. 2:17), that whatever cosmic beings there may be have been disarmed of their power (2:15), and that there is no knowledge or wisdom deeper than that revealed in the "mystery" of the gospel, which is Christ himself (1:26-29; 2:2-3).

The redemptive work of this "cosmic Christ" is interpreted primarily in terms of the forgiveness of sins (1:13-14; 2:13-14) and resurrection to new life in and with Christ (1:21-22; 3:1-4). This is the meaning of Christian baptism, also described as transferral from darkness to light (1:13). The Christian has already been raised to newness of life (see below on 2:12) and "put on the new nature" (3:10).

The believer comes to his fullest "maturity" in Christ (1:28; 2:10) as he is daily renewed in accord with God's own image (3:10). When one holds fast to Christ (2:19) he is sustained and built up in love, the very stuff and substance of new life (2:2; 3:14). Thereby the Christian walks "worthy of the Lord, fully pleasing to him, bearing fruit in every good work and increasing in the knowledge of God" (1:10). Love expresses itself above all in the common life of Christ's body, the church (1:18, 24; 3:15). There all persons, without respect to class, race, nation, or alleged religious attainment (3:11), are united under the rule of Christ (3:15) for mutual service and love (3:12-14) and for the common praise of God (1:12; 2:7; 3:15*b*-17).

Authorship; Date and Place of Writing. Col. purports to be from Paul (1:1, 23, 24-29; 4:7-18), and the majority of scholars accept the letter as his. The close relationship between Col. and Philem.—esp. notable in the lists of greetings (4:10-14; cf. Philem. 23-24) and the references to Onesimus (4:9; cf. Philem. 10-12) and Archippus (4:17; cf. Philem. 2) —would seem, in view of the now unquestioned authenticity of Philem., to confirm this judgment. If so, Col. was evidently written at the same time as Philem., either from Rome shortly before Paul's death *ca.* 59-62 or, as some believe, from an earlier imprisonment at Ephesus *ca.* 54-56 (see Intro. to Philem.).

But the authenticity of Col. has not gone unchallenged. The technical theological terms it employs, its often liturgical style, and the occurrence of many non-Pauline words have all been adduced to support the view that it was written by some later Christian thoroughly at home in Paul's thought. In addition, it has been argued, the Gnostic teaching which the letter combats did not become a problem until the 2nd cent., many years after Paul's death.

These arguments, however, are not decisive. While the fully developed systems of Gnosticism are to be dated only from the 2nd cent., there were Gnostic elements and tendencies in various Hellenistic religions and in Jewish sectarianism even before the Christian era. Moreover, while Col. does employ a technically theological, non-Pauline vocabulary, this could be attributed to the specific polemic needs of the moment. And at least some of the stylistic peculiarities of Col. are due to the use of previously formulated liturgical materials, a phenomenon also present in the indisputably authentic letters (cf. e.g. Phil. 2:6-11).

Insofar as the authorship of Col. remains in doubt, it is because of the theological presuppositions on which it rests and the way in which Pauline motifs are handled or omitted. Virtually all commentators acknowledge a certain theological distance between Col. and indisputably authentic letters like Rom. and Gal.—though not so great as that between Eph. and the Pauline letters. Col. strongly emphasizes the apostolic tradition and ministry as norms for faith; no longer present is Paul's view of salvation as still moving forward to fulfillment, and his doctrine of justification is altogether lacking.

Moreover in numerous smaller ways Pauline ideas as known from the other letters are significantly altered.

To what extent may these points of theological divergence from the incontestably Pauline letters be accounted for by polemic requirements and by a development over the years in Paul's own thinking? The answer is not clear, and it is best to omit Col. from one's list of primary sources for the study of Paul. The commentary which follows attempts to interpret Col. in its own terms and context and in the light of the historical circumstances of its writing rather than in the perspective of Pauline theology as a whole.

If Col. is not authentic, it is probably to be ascribed to a Christian leader in Asia Minor who was strongly influenced by Paul's thought. Being pseudonymous, it must have been written after Paul's death but before the composition of Eph., which seems to be literarily dependent on it. Therefore it can be assigned to a time between 65 and 90, probably closer to the earlier than to the later date.

For Further Study. E. F. Scott, *Col., Philem., and Eph.*, 1930. F. W. Beare in *IB*, 1955. C. F. D. Moule, *Col. and Philem.*, 1957. George Johnston in *IDB*, 1962.

I. Salutation (1:1-2)

The opening of Col. is thoroughly Pauline. The letter is addressed to the Christians of Colossae (see Intro.), most of whom were of Gentile background (2:13; cf. 1:21, 27). They are addressed as **saints,** a term which does not imply perfect moral character but—as the next phrase shows—designates Christians in general as **faithful brethren in Christ,** consecrated to the service of God.

II. Liturgical and Hortatory Preface (1:3-23)

The Pauline letters regularly open with a section of thanksgiving and prayer. This one, unusually rich in the language of praise, is expanded by a hymn to Christ (vss. 15-20) and a concluding exhortation (vss. 21-23). In it the readers are reminded of the essential meaning of their conversion and baptism.

A. Thanksgiving (1:3-8)

1:3-5a. Faith, Love, and Hope. God is thanked for the faith and love manifested in the lives of the congregation. Since Paul himself did not found their church (vs. 7), the author says that he has only **heard** (vs. 4) about the Cols. The supposition that **faith** and **love** are integrally related and that neither is authentic without the other is characteristically Pauline (cf. Gal. 5:6). Faith in Christ is never separable from the love of one's brethren in Christ (**the saints,** vs. 4; see above on vss. 1-2). But **hope** here designates that which is hoped for, an inheritance **laid up . . . in heaven,** and thus does not conform to the general Pauline view of hope as part of the total activity of faith. The author believes that the faith of the Cols. is grounded in their assurance of a heavenly blessing and is expressed in a life of love.

1:5b-7. The Word of Truth. The readers are now reminded of their conversion. Colossae was evangelized by **Epaphras** (vs. 7), apparently sent out by Paul from Ephesus as a missionary to the Lycus Valley (4:13). The author is laying the groundwork for his attack against the false teaching which threatens to unsettle his readers. As opposed to that the gospel delivered by Epaphras is (*a*) the **word of the truth;** (*b*) preached in the **whole world** and therefore not, like the false teaching, a local novelty; and (*c*) **bearing fruit and growing.** Foreshadowed here are some of the appeals the later church was to make in its fight against heresy, appeals to (*a*) tradition, (*b*) catholicity, and (*c*) practical results. The **grace of God** stands parallel with the **word of the truth;** both describe the **gospel.**

1:8. A Good Report. Once more the author stresses the good report he has had from Epaphras about the Cols. If there is any reference to God's **Spirit** in Col. it is here, though some would translate the phrase "in spirit," as in 2:5. In any case the doctrine of the Spirit, so important in Paul's thought as a whole, has no major role in the argument of Col.

B. Prayer (1:9-14)

1:9-11. Petitions. This prayer includes 3 main petitions: (*a*) that the Cols. understand what God's **will** is (vs. 9); (*b*) that they live in a manner befitting their Lord (vs. 10); (*c*) that they be **strengthened with** his **power** for joyful **endurance and patience** (vs. 11). The **knowledge** for which the author pleads (vs. 9) is that insight into truth granted by the powerful working of God (vs. 11) to those who are open to **spiritual wisdom.** This wisdom expresses itself concretely in the life of the believer who increases in knowledge as his life bears fruit "in active goodness of every kind" (vs. 10 NEB; cf. 3:10). In the Greek the phrase used of the gospel in vs. 6, "bearing fruit and growing," is exactly repeated with reference to the believer in vs. 10. The gospel itself bears fruit and grows when those who have been grasped by it bear fruit in their transformed lives and grow in the knowledge of God. The source of this growth, the strength for endurance and patience in obedience, and the ground for joy is God's own power (vs. 11).

1:12-14. Thanksgiving. The petitions of this prayer (vss. 9-11) move without a break into thanksgiving. Three times in Col. God is called **Father,** each time in connection with the thanks due him for his saving action (1:3, 12; 3:17). Here this is specified to be God's call—the essential meaning of **qualified us** (cf. II Cor. 3:5-6)—to participate in the whole company of Christians and the **inheritance** which belongs to them. In vss. 13-14 the readers are reminded of their baptism, which marked their transferral from **darkness** to **light** (cf. vs. 12). The ground for hope is God's own act of deliverance, his own deed of redemption, viewed as the **forgiveness of sins.**

C. Hymn (1:15-20)

Structural, stylistic, and material analyses of this paragraph have revealed it to be a hymn adopted and adapted by the author. There is no unanimity as to its origin, i.e. whether Christian or not, its precise formal structure, or the extent to which it has been modified by the author. Nevertheless 2 parallel stanzas may be discerned with relative ease: (a) Vss. 15-18a, which have undergone extensive modification and expansion in this context, speak of Christ as the agent of **creation.** (b) Vss. 18b-20, somewhat less expanded, present the correlative idea of Christ as the agent of redemption. The hymn is adapted in such a way as to underscore the author's main point: baptism into Christ means deliverance from whatever secondary rulers there may be in the universe and participation in the kingdom of Christ.

1:15-18a. *The Agent of Creation.* The first stanza opens with a reference to Christ as the revealer of God. Christ's cosmic role as the agent of creation is even more explicitly noted when it is said that **all things were created . . . in . . . through . . . and for Christ** (vs. 16). A stronger statement of Christ's cosmic sovereignty is hardly possible, esp. when it is specified—perhaps an editorial expansion of the original hymn—that the existence of every other worldly power is dependent on him. This has particular relevance for the Cols., beset by false teachers insisting on the necessity of paying honor to all the various cosmic potentates (see Intro.).

1:17-18a. The affirmation that Christ is **before all things** and that **all things hold together** in him further supports the point that his authority is primordial, his reign universal, and his power absolute. This is summarized in vs. 18a, which in the original hymn probably said only: **He is the head of the body.** This concept held a place in the pre-Christian cosmogonic mythology which spoke of a "primeval man"—sometimes identified as Adam—who was the "head" of the cosmos, his "body." The hymn apparently draws on this idea, declaring that Christ is this primeval man, the cosmic redeemer, in whom the whole universe finds its being and destiny. In adapting this hymn the author has probably inserted **the church.** In vs. 24 he once more identifies "body" with "church" and then presupposes this identification in 3:15. But it is left to the author of Eph. to develop the concept in his discussion of the nature of the church and its relation to Christ.

1:18b-20. *The Agent of the New Creation.* Vs. 18b is parallel with vs. 15 and opens the 2nd stanza of the hymn. In vs. 15 Christ has been presented as preeminent in creation; now he is declared to be **pre-eminent** in the new creation, **first-born from the dead** (cf. I Cor. 15:20; Rev. 1:5). In Christ these 2 aspects of God's activity are indissolubly bound together, perhaps in specific opposition to the false teachers in Colossae. Moreover this hymn's emphasis on the absolute sovereignty of Christ would be particularly helpful in combating the teaching that other cosmic powers and authorities ought to be worshiped.

1:19-20. The hymn is here further adapted for use in the attack on the errant teachers. **Fulness** was a technical term used by the errorists themselves for the sum of "elemental spirits" which collectively constituted the cosmic deity. The author opposes the idea that cosmic rule is distributed among numerous powers (cf. vs. 16). Christ alone is the world ruler; the fullness of divine power belongs exclusively to him (cf. 2:9-10). Vs. 19 is therefore not primarily a declaration about the Incarnation but an affirmation of the cosmic sovereignty of Christ, effective in redemption as well as creation

(vs. 20). The same Lord who was active in creation is active in renewing that creation and in restoring it to its primeval order and harmony. It is thus **peace** of cosmic dimensions to which the hymn refers, and which is attained as every power of the universe stands in subjection to Christ.

Though these cosmic proportions of reconciliation and peace are never stressed in the unquestioned Pauline letters, to the original hymn the author makes a typically Pauline addition: this peace is made **by the blood of his cross** (cf. Rom. 5:6-11). The cosmic categories of the hymn thus give way to the historical categories of the gospel. The cosmic Lord and Redeemer is identified with the crucified Jesus, and in a later paragraph (2:13-15) the death itself is viewed as both the moment of cosmic victory and the event through which the believer is given new life.

D. Hortatory Conclusion (1:21-23)

1:21-22. *Reconciliation in Christ.* With the perspective of their conversion the readers' pagan past is judged to have been a time of estrangement, hostility, and wickedness. From that moral chaos—analogous to the cosmic chaos which prevails apart from the lordship of Christ (cf. vss. 15-20)—the Christian has been delivered. Being **reconciled** involves a reordering of the context and content of one's life, a restoration and renewal of it. Thus again the author corrects the false view that salvation must achieve separation from the created world, either through mystic visions or by adherence to ascetic regulations (see below on 2:16-19). This renewal of life's wholeness and wholesomeness enables the Christian to stand before God as one **holy and blameless and irreproachable.** And this renewal has been effected by Christ's incarnation and death, concretely and historically real.

1:23. *Steadfastness.* Reconciliation requires fidelity to the tradition—**the faith . . . the hope of the gospel**—which has been **preached to every creature under heaven.** This last phrase underscores the cosmic inclusiveness of God's reconciling activity (cf. **all things,** vs. 20). The mention of Paul at the end of vs. 23 affords the transition to what follows.

III. Paul's Ministry (1:24–2:5)

In the whole liturgical preface (1:3-23), but esp. in his quotation of a hymn in vss. 15-20, the author has appealed to the Christian tradition into which the Cols. were baptized. Later (e.g. 2:9-14) he will return to this theme as he urges them to resist the dangerously false doctrines of errant teachers. Meanwhile another basis for the later arguments is established, viz. the apostolic authority of Paul. Hence the appeal in Col. begins to be to 2 of the bulwarks of faith which the church came increasingly to emphasize in its fight against heresy: the historic tradition and the apostolic office (on the appeal to catholicity and practical results see above on 1:5b-7).

1:24-26. *The Apostolic Office.* Joy in the midst of **sufferings** is a characteristically Pauline emphasis (cf. e.g. Rom. 5:3-11), and the remark opening vs. 24 accords with the claim that Col. is written by Paul from prison (see Intro.). Precisely what it means

859

to **complete what is lacking in Christ's afflictions** is not clear, though it certainly does not mean that Christ's sufferings have in some way been defective in bringing salvation. The general thought is that Paul participates in Christ's sufferings as he endures the trials and afflictions which come to those who preach the gospel. It is not impossible that the author has in mind some "quota" of sufferings which the church must undergo before God's victory is won. But more likely he intends to say only that the sufferings are **for your sake, . . . for the sake of his body**—here, as in vs. 18, identified as the **church**—and that "he brings the work of Christ to a completion, by preaching Christ as a whole, i.e. as crucified and resurrected." Thus, the preaching of the gospel, attended by **afflictions** not unlike Christ's own, "is itself a constituent part of the salvation event" (Hans Conzelmann).

1:25. This idea is now enforced and the **divine** origin of Paul's **office** is emphasized (cf. Gal. 1:1, 11-12). **For you** (repeated from vs. 24) underscores the relationship which exists between apostle and congregation.

1:26. The apostolic office exists to make **fully known** the word of God. That word is a **mystery** (vs. 26), a term which in the NT has a consistently different meaning from that in the ancient mystery cults. In the NT it is always associated with a message publicly proclaimed (on **saints** see above on vss. 1-2), never with a secret reserved for the privileged few (see comment on Eph. 1:9-10).

1:27-29. The Mystery of Christ. The content of the mystery is described as **Christ in you, the hope of glory.** In Col. hope is something prepared and waiting for the faithful Christian (see above on vss. 3-8) and may be used to designate Christian preaching in general (cf. vs. 23). The phrase **Christ in you** must not be read as a mystical formula; it refers to the crucified Christ (vs. 22), presented in preaching and received by faith.

1:28-29. The content of preaching is Christ, and the function of the apostolic office is the presentation of **every man mature in Christ.** The word "mature," a technical term in Hellenistic religion for the fully initiated cult member, may also have been part of the vocabulary of the Col. errorists, for whom there were believers of various ranks. But in Christ **every man** may attain fullness and wholeness of life (see above on vss. 21-22). In him every religious and social barrier dividing men is broken through.

2:1-5. Paul's Relation to the Cols. Paul's labor was for his congregations, even those to whom he was related by letter only (see above on 1:3-8). The wealthy city of **Laodicea** lay 10 miles NW of Colossae (cf. 4:13-16).

2:2-3. In view of the immediate context **encouraged** and **knit together** are better translated as "strengthened" and "instructed." The author is concerned to strengthen his readers in their faith by instructing them **in love**—with patience, tact, goodwill—and thus bringing them to an authentic insight into the true mystery of God, which is Christ (cf. 1:27). All true **wisdom and knowledge**—no matter what the errant teachers say—are in him alone. They are **hid** there only to those who refuse to receive the proclamation of the gospel (cf. 1:25-29).

2:4-5. The readers are warned about the lure of the "smooth talk" employed by the false teachers. Vs. 5b suggests that they have as yet made no substantial progress among the Cols. (cf. 1:3-4).

IV. POLEMIC AGAINST THE FALSE TEACHING (2:6-23)

Earlier paragraphs have attempted to remind the Cols. of the faith into which they were baptized and their commitment to Christ as Lord of all things. Those reminders, as well as the statement about Paul's apostolic authority (1:24–2:5) are in a sense prefatory to this section, in which the false teaching being adopted by some of the Cols. is directly under attack. One meets here the problem which occasioned the writing of this whole letter.

A. FIDELITY TO THE APOSTOLIC TRADITION (2:6-15)

2:6-8. Authoritative Tradition. The author's first argument against the errant teaching is that it departs from the apostolic tradition. **Received** (vs. 6) is a technical term used of that historic, authoritative tradition of formulated doctrines. The whole of this tradition is summarized in the phrase **Christ Jesus the Lord.** The admonition to **live in him** is elaborated in the clauses of vs. 7, which stress the need for an unwavering fidelity to Christ and the church's teaching. **Taught** is here virtually synonymous with **received** in vs. 6, indicating the way in which historic tradition has been delivered to believers. The reference to thanksgiving as a continuing dimension of the Christian's life is characteristic of this whole letter (cf. 1:12; 3:15, 17; 4:2).

2:8a. In sharp contrast with the apostolic tradition stands the teaching of the errorists, specifically branded as **human tradition,** a local novelty without historical roots. The only NT reference to **philosophy** occurs here, where it is equated with **empty deceit.** The writer is concerned lest his readers be duped into accepting and promoting doctrines which have no enduring significance and are not as profound as their exponents pretend.

2:8b. The doctrine of Christ's universal sovereignty is apparently threatened by the errorists' emphasis on the **elemental spirits of the universe** (cf. vs. 20; Gal. 4:3, 9). They are probably regarded as demonic powers which collectively make up the divine **fulness** (cf. vs. 9; see Intro.). But for the Christian, Christ alone is cosmic Lord, the mediator of salvation, and the **fulness of God** (1:19; see comment).

2:9-10. The Fullness of God. The contrast between the **elemental spirits** and **Christ** (vs. 8) leads to a reiteration of Christ as alone God's **fulness** and of his exclusive headship over **all rule and authority** (cf. 1:16). Both ideas were present in the hymn of 1:15-20 (cf. esp. vss. 18-19), and now it is said that God's fullness lives in Christ **bodily.** The word here may simply mean "really" or "wholly"—in contrast to the dispersal of power and divinity among various elemental spirits—or it may be intended to stress the bodily incarnation of deity in the historical Jesus. In either sense it would be in opposition to the false teaching. In vs. 10 the author applies the idea of fullness to the Christians themselves, who in Christ attain their full maturity (cf. 1:28).

2:11-12. Baptism. The contrast between physical and spiritual circumcision is Pauline (cf. Rom. 2:25-

29). The **circumcision of Christ** is Christian baptism, which is first described as **putting off the body of flesh** (vs. 11), i.e. the whole realm of demonic powers to which men, apart from Christ, are enslaved. The act of initiation into Christ and his church frees one from those fateful forces and marks one's transferral into the kingdom of Christ and the forgiveness of sins (cf. 1:13-14).

2:12. The interpretation of Christian baptism as burial and resurrection with Christ is again Pauline, but comparing Rom. 6:3-11 one notes some difference. In Rom. 6:5, 8 resurrection with Christ is still a hope, but here resurrection has already occurred—**you were also raised with him** (cf. vs. 13; 3:1). This has not been accomplished through the rite of baptism itself; for the author, perhaps in contrast with the errorists, does not view baptism as some cultic apparatus for the attainment of salvation. It comes rather through faith in God, who has raised both Christ and the Christian to new life.

2:13-15. *Victory over Cosmic Powers.* The Christian's resurrection is from spiritual and moral death. Baptism marks one's burial and resurrection into new life, and the view that this redemption-resurrection is in its essence forgiveness of sins is now repeated (cf. 1:14). Reference to the **bond . . . against us with its legal demands** (vs. 14) suggests that the false teaching involved some sort of legalistic ordinances, adherence to which was deemed to be essential for salvation. Christ in his death has brought freedom from this enslavement to an external code and the attendant moral guilt.

2:15. Christ's death effects forgiveness and ushers in new life because it establishes God's victory over the **principalities and powers** of the cosmos (cf. 1:16; see Intro.). The false teaching is still in the author's mind, and against the doctrine of diverse cosmic potentates he urges once again the absolute supremacy of Christ. **In him,** i.e. Christ, may also be translated "in it," i.e. the cross. But the meaning is not greatly changed, for the idea is that in Christ's triumphant death on the cross God has conquered the lesser lords of the cosmos; and like a victorious general he has disarmed the pretenders to power, parading them about for all to see their disgrace and impotence.

B. Warning Against False Wisdom (2:16-23)

2:16-19. *Observances and Regulations.* The false teaching abroad in Colossae (see Intro.) apparently stresses the importance of adherence to dietary regulations and a sacred calendar (vs. 16). But these have no essential place in true Christianity (vs. 17). Christ alone—faith in him as sovereign Lord—is sufficient for salvation. Vs. 18 mentions still other aspects of the Col. teaching. **Self-abasement** indicates that certain ascetic regulations are proposed (cf. vss. 20b-22), and the **angels** are probably to be identified with the elemental spirits of the cosmos (cf. vss. 8, 20). The errorists also stress the importance of **visions** and similar unique religious feats. But again these are criticized as having no importance for the authentic Christian life. Those who insist on them are regarded as "bursting with the futile conceit of worldly minds" (vs. 18 NEB).

One here gains the picture of a type of false

Christianity which seeks to establish, through special rules, rites, and religious experiences, a religious elite that thinks to achieve a status of special security before God and an absolute certainty about salvation. The error in this, the Cols. are told, is the tendency to believe that salvation may be secured by one's own religious works, preoccupation with which obscures the primacy of God's act in granting salvation through Christ Jesus.

2:19. Christ is once more (cf. 1:18a) called the **Head** of the **body.** In this instance, however, the author seems to identify the body, not with the church (contrast 1:18a; 3:15; Eph. 4:16), but, as in the popular mythology of his time, with the whole cosmos (see above on 1:17-18a). "Body" here is almost parallel with **all rule and authority** in vs. 10, and the meaning is that Christ is Lord of all things. In him alone is the source of all life and the strength for all **growth.** The author has already asserted that it is love which makes it possible to **knit together** all men in Christ (vs. 2; cf. 3:14).

2:20-23. *Bondage to the World.* For Christians the errant doctrines being sponsored in Colossae ought to hold no appeal, for they have **died to the elemental spirits of the universe.** They know that the power to create and redeem resides solely in Christ, the fullness of God's sovereign rule (cf. vss. 8-9; 1:15-20; etc.). Thus the cosmic hierarchy of beings which play a central role in the false teaching (see Intro.) is to be disregarded; they have been conquered in Christ (vs. 15). The author's worried question, **Why do you live as if you still belonged to the world?** does not accord with his earlier expression of confidence in the Col. congregation (vs. 5).

2:20b-23. Belonging to the world is here understood as bondage to a false religiosity, preoccupation with legalistic statutes designed to secure some special religious status (cf. vss. 16-19). These allegedly religious exercises are in reality only secular, worldly devices of **human** origin. The errant doctrines are again attacked as deviating from authentic apostolic tradition. Both the lure and the perversity of this false teaching reside precisely in its sanctimonious pretensions, in the "air of wisdom" (vs. 23a NEB) it exudes. Such affected piety is but a special form of secularism and self-indulgence (vs. 23b; see RSV footnote).

V. Exhortations to Lead a Christian Life (3:1-4:6)

Thus far the readers have been reminded of their baptismal commitment and admonished to stand firm in their faith despite the lure of certain Christian teachers whom the author regards as dangerous deviators. Their doctrine about elemental spirits and cosmic potentates, the worship of which is necessary for salvation, stands in sharp contrast to the Christian doctrine that Christ alone, God's agent in creation and redemption, is the cosmic Lord. Now the argument becomes more positive and takes the form of exhortations to exemplify in their lives the characteristics appropriate to new life in Christ.

A. The Basis of a Christian Life (3:1-4)

These introductory vss. reaffirm the theological basis for a transformed life. Since the Christian has participated in Christ's resurrection (vs. 1; cf. 2:12-13) and is now free from past enslavement to trespasses and the cosmic powers (vs. 3; cf. 2:12-15, 20), and since true life is to be found in the God revealed by Christ (vss. 3b-4; cf. 1:28; 2:10), the Christian is to see that his whole life is reoriented in terms of the "kingdom of [God's] beloved Son" (1:13). The parallel admonitions **Seek the things that are above** (vs. 1) and **Set your minds on things that are above** (vs. 2) urge in a general way precisely that radically new orientation respecting motives and goals which subsequent paragraphs more particularly specify.

The description of Christ as **seated at the right hand of God** (vs. 1) is frequent in the NT and, in accord with the OT vs. on which it is based (Ps. 110:1), stresses the powerful rule of Christ in God's behalf. The reference to the life **hid with Christ in God** (vs. 3) corresponds with the author's view of a "hope" (1:5) or "inheritance" (1:12) presently laid up in heaven, thus already accomplished but not yet actualized in its fullest sense for the believer. That actualization will occur **when Christ who is our life appears** (vs. 4, cf. I John 3:2).

B. PUTTING OFF THE OLD, PUTTING ON THE NEW (3:5-17)

3:5-8. Earthward Inclinations. Because the Christian's new life in and with Christ is oriented to **things that are above** (vss. 1-2) he is admonished to .put to death his "earthward inclinations" (Weymouth trans.). These are enumerated in 2 groups of 5 each (vss. 5, 8), to which the 5-fold enumeration of virtues in vs. 12 corresponds. Nothing specific about moral conditions at Colossae should be deduced from these lists, for the particular vices mentioned frequently recur in similar lists contained in Hellenistic moral tractates. The author's intention is only to stress the seriousness of the moral degradation of their former life (vs. 7; cf. 2:13). Such immorality in all its various forms stands constantly under God's **wrath** (vs. 6), conceived here, as usually in the NT, not as capricious, vindictive anger, but as his consistent, aggressive judgment of evil.

3:9-11. Renewal unto Knowledge. That the readers have **put off the old nature,** lit. "old man," is parallel with the admonitions of vss. 5, 8 and like them concerns the Christian's yielding his life to Christ, by whose death and resurrection the believer is made free from the power of sin. Though in Gal. 3:27 Paul speaks of "putting on Christ" in baptism, there is more stress here on the new life as an already fully accomplished fact (see above on 2:12).

3:10. But the believer's participation in the resurrected life of Christ does not exclude the need for daily obedience. This is the implication of the striking phrase in vs. 10 which describes the **new** as continuously in the process of renewal—"being constantly renewed in the image of its Creator" (NEB). God's **image** is an allusion to the creation story (Gen. 1:26-27); the author, in opposition to the Gnostic errorists, affirms the essential integrity of God's creating and redeeming activity. The goal of this renewal is the **knowledge** of God—"unto knowledge" is a better translation—a concern which has been present in Col. from the first (cf. 1:9-10). All

true knowledge is in Christ (cf. 2:2-3) and consists in a practical commitment to God, expressed in one's life (see above on 1:9-11).

3:11. Where life has been transformed to accord with the creative-redemptive purposes of God—i.e. for the author in the church, Christ's body—every social, national, racial, and even religious distinction is rendered meaningless—for **Christ is all, and in all.** This conviction is true to Paul's own conception of baptism into Christ as an incorporation into a community of believers where all such barriers have been broken (see comments on Gal. 3:27-29; Philem. 15-19).

Each of the pairs named has contrasting members except **barbarian, Scythian.** The first of these terms would mean to the Cols. "non-Greek," with the slightly derogatory connotation which we usually give to "foreigner." The Scythians were a tribe of Eurasian nomads infamous in antiquity for their allegedly bestial and brutal ways—the most degraded kind of "barbarians." J. B. Phillips' paraphrase "foreigner or savage" is thus true to the author's meaning. The description of Christ as **all, and in all** cannot be too closely analyzed, and is employed only to express Christ's preeminence. Paul uses the phrase of God himself (I Cor. 15:28).

3:12-13. Qualities of the New Nature. In vs. 10 the author has spoken of the **new nature** which the Christian has **put on.** Now in a typically Pauline way he converts the indicative statement into an imperative: **Put on then.** The list of 5 characteristics which follows is meant to contrast with the 2 5-fold lists of vices already presented (vss. 5, 8). They are not proposed as "cardinal virtues" but offered only as typical of the characteristics and attitudes Christianity teaches. While most of the qualities mentioned were widely extolled by non-Christian writers, the word **lowliness** outside of Jewish-Christian circles always conveyed the idea of abject humiliation and was listed among the vices rather than the virtues.

The distinctively Christian element in this passage is not the content of the list but its context. The exhortation has significance because it is addressed to those who have been **raised with Christ** (vs. 1), and whose lives are already being renewed unto knowledge after the image of their creator (vs. 10). Hence the Col. Christians are **God's chosen ones, holy and beloved**—descriptions drawn from the OT, where they are applied to Israel, and found also in Paul's letters. As used here they are virtually synonymous, each referring to the call of God whereby his people are set aside for obedience to his will and the praise of his name.

3:13. All the qualities named in vs. 12 have a bearing on one's relationships with others, and this dimension of the Christian life is here further stressed. The author again provides a specifically Christian basis for his exhortation as he appeals to his readers' experience of the forgiving love of God made real at their baptism.

3:14-15a. The Priority of Love. Love is **above all** the mark of the new life in Christ. It is the bond wherein life has meaning, vitality, and integrity (cf. 2:2, 19). **Perfect harmony** translates a Greek word which connotes wholeness, completeness, and authenticity. Love establishes wholeness not only within the Christian community (vs. 15) but within each participating believer (cf. 1:28, where "mature" translates a linguistically related word) and in the entire cosmos (cf. e.g. 1:17; 2:19).

3:15a. To **put on** this love means (vs. 15) to surrender oneself to Christ's **rule** (cf. 1:15-20). The **peace of Christ** must not be interpreted to mean simply an attitude of inner tranquillity; it is a peace which has cosmic dimensions (1:20), and which is a gift to the whole community of believers, not just a feeling of serenity possessed by individuals. As one is called into the whole **body** of believers he participates in the wonderful reconciliation of all things and all men. Therefore **in your hearts** does not describe the place where Christ's peace rules—for that is in the community, where the Christian's obedience to God is concretely evident. It designates rather the depth and sincerity of commitment to Christ's rule which is to characterize one's new life.

3:15b-17. *Thankfulness.* The author insists that the Christian life ought not be regarded as a burden, or its responsibilities grudgingly borne. The Christian surrenders himself to God, not as a conquered enemy capitulates to the victor; rather his surrender is to take the form of a joyful, grateful presentation of himself to God. Thanksgiving is thus a further characteristic of the new life (cf. 1:12; 2:7; 4:2) and is to express itself both in public worship and in one's daily public life.

3:16. Commentators have variously defined the **word of Christ** as his own preaching, the gospel about Christ, and Christ himself. In any case the idea is that where the church is, God is—working for the mutual upbuilding of all believers. It is not possible to say with certainty whether **psalms and hymns and spiritual songs** represent 3 distinct types of music in the early church. It is clear, however, that a rich hymnody was possessed by the earliest Christians, much of it drawn from or influenced by OT pss., but some of it adapted from nonbiblical sources or newly composed. The NT contains many quotations from this hymnody, an esp. impressive example being found here in 1:15-20.

3:17. The admonition to give thanks is extended to apply to one's whole life and recalls Paul's exhortation to do everything to the glory of God (I Cor. 10:31). One must live in accord with the new life to which he has been raised in Christ, thereby **giving thanks** to God in the only way fully appropriate to the magnificence of the gift which has been bestowed.

C. THE CHRISTIAN HOUSEHOLD (3:18-4:1)

This is perhaps the earliest Christian example of a relatively fixed ethical form which commentators have called a "table of household duties." Other NT examples are Eph. 5:21-6:9; I Pet. 2:13-3:12; Tit. 2:1-10. These tables emphasize the need for mutual respect and consideration among the members of a household. Because their specifically Christian content is minimal, many scholars hold that they have been appropriated from the general ethical teaching of the day and only slightly christianized.

3:18-19. *Wives and Husbands.* Earliest Christianity, in keeping with the prevailing social order, en-

visioned no role for the woman apart from marriage and homemaking. The feminist movement would have seemed as irrelevant in that day as the abolitionist movement (see Intro. to Philem.). Though the husband's authority in the household is not questioned, the command that he should be loving and considerate of his wife injects at least an element of mutuality into the concept of marriage. Cf. I Cor. 7:1-40; Eph. 5:21-33.

3:20-21. *Children and Parents.* Obedience, not just subjection (cf. vs. 18), is expected of the children. The new term connotes an element of instruction and discipline not appropriate in the relationship between husbands and wives. It is this dimension of the parent-child relationship which is emphasized in Eph. 6:1-4, where this section is significantly expanded.

3:22-4:1. *Slaves and Masters.* The exhortations to slaves and masters dominate this household table—(as also that in I Pet.)—perhaps because of the large number of slaves who were members of the various Christian congregations. Most of the specifically Christian elements in the table are present in these vss., viz. the references to **fearing the Lord** (vs. 22), **serving the Lord Christ** (vss. 23-24), and the **inheritance** to be received as a **reward** (vs. 24)—as well as the subtle play running through the whole passage on the word **Lord,** which in Greek is the same as that for a slave's owner. Slaves, then, are admonished to serve their **earthly masters** with fidelity because they can look forward to an inheritance from their heavenly **Master** which will transcend all earthly gains. The masters, on the other hand, are admonished to treat their slaves with justice and equity, knowing that they too have a heavenly Master (see comment on Eph. 6:5-9). On Christianity's attitude toward the institution of slavery see Intro. to Philem.

3:25. Interpretation of this vs. depends on one's judgment about the authorship of Col. If Paul is the author (see Intro.) the whole table should probably be read in the light of the case of the runaway slave Onesimus mentioned in 4:9 as being from Colossae (see Intro. to Philem.). In that event this vs. may be a comment about Onesimus specifically: he is the **wrongdoer** who must pay for what he has done, and his relationship with Paul provides no special favors. If on the other hand the Pauline authorship of Col. is questioned it is likely that the wrongdoer is the master and that slaves are being assured of the impartial administration of justice against all who violate the ordinances of God.

D. CONCLUDING EXHORTATIONS (4:2-6)

4:2-4. *The Importance of Prayer.* Prayer is to be characterized by **being watchful,** which here may have the double meaning of being expectant about salvation (cf. Rom. 13:11; I Thess. 5:6) and alert about one's own moral condition (cf. I Pet. 5:8). Stress on **thanksgiving** as a vital dimension of prayer accords with the author's earlier remarks on the subject (e.g. 3:15b-17) and the request that the Cols. pray for the advance of the apostolic ministry accords with the previous emphasis on the bonds uniting Paul to his congregations (1:23-2:5). **Word** and **mystery of Christ** (see above on 1:26; 2:2-3) are descriptions of the gospel, also called the "word of the truth" (1:5) or the "word of Christ" (3:16).

4:5-6. Conduct in the World. The exhortations which conclude this section deal briefly with the relationship of Christians to persons outside the church. On the one hand by wise and discreet conduct the Christian is to bear witness in the world to his faith, passing up no opportunity (vs. 5; lit. "buying up the time"; cf. Eph. 5:16). On the other hand the Christian needs to be prepared to respond to challenge; his words must be well chosen, temperate yet relevant, and appropriate to each new situation. "Speak pleasantly to them, but never sentimentally, and learn how to give a proper answer to every questioner" (vs. 6, Phillips trans.).

VI. EPISTOLARY CLOSE (4:7-18)

4:7-9. Commendation of Tychicus and Onesimus. Tychicus, named in Acts 20:4 and associated in II Tim. 4:12 with a mission to Ephesus, is represented as the bearer of this letter and is warmly commended (vss. 7-8). With him goes Onesimus, the slave on whose behalf Philem. was written (Philem. 10), and who is here described as himself a Col. (vs. 9). If Col. is authentically Pauline, presumably part of Tychicus' mission was to return Onesimus to his owner, along with the letter (Philem.) dealing with that problem (see Intro.). It is significant that here Onesimus is assumed to have full status as a **beloved brother** in Christ (cf. Philem. 16).

4:10-14. Greetings from Paul's Associates. This list of those who send greetings to the Col. church is almost identical with that in Philem. 23-24 (see comment). Here there is one additional name, **Jesus . . . Justus** (vs. 11), about whom nothing else is known. He, **Aristarchus,** and **Mark** are described as the only Jewish Christians among Paul's associates. They are **fellow workers** with Paul in obedience to the call and claim of God—"in the work of God's realm" (Moffatt trans.).

4:12-13. The founder of the Col. church (cf. 1:7), **Epaphras,** himself a Col., like Paul (1:9-14) labors constantly in prayer on their behalf. The words which identify the object of these prayers summarize the reason for which Col. was written: "that you may stand up fully grown and fully persuaded in everything that God wills" (vs. 12, C. K. Williams trans.). On the one hand Col. admonishes resistance to false teaching, and on the other hand it encourages growth, as individuals and as a community, into the fullness and maturity which is in fact already theirs (cf. e.g. 1:28; 2:2, 10; 3:14-16). Epaphras has also been responsible for the churches in nearby **Laodicea** and **Hierapolis** (vs. 13; see above on 2:1-5).

4:14. Only here in the NT is Luke, to whom the authorship of the 3rd gospel and Acts is traditionally assigned, called a **physician.** According to II Tim. 4:10 **Demas** later deserted Paul's service.

4:15-17. Greetings to Paul's Friends. Now Paul's own greetings are conveyed: to the Laodicean **brethren,** i.e. church, to which this letter is also to be read (vs. 16) and to the church meeting in the house of **Nympha.** The instruction that this letter be shared with the Laodicean church and that the letter to that congregation be read also in Colossae shows how the custom of exchanging apostolic letters must have grown up—leading gradually to their collection and joint circulation and ultimately to their canonization (see "The Letters of Paul," pp. 1136-43, and "The Making of the NT Canon," pp. 1216-24). No letter to the Laodiceans survives, though the 2nd-cent. heretic Marcion identified Eph. as such, and some modern scholars believe it to have been Philem.

4:17. In Philem. 2 **Archippus** is also named. If Col. is regarded as Pauline, this vs. is impressive evidence in favor of the hypothesis that he rather than Philem. was the owner of Onesimus. Thus the **ministry** which Archippus is to **fulfil** may be the freeing—or at least the kind treatment—of his slave, now returning with Tychicus, the bearer of this letter (vss. 7-8). Other commentators have conjectured that this ministry might be to continue the work of Epaphras within the congregation or to assist in the collection of Paul's offering for Jerusalem (cf. e.g. II Cor. 9:1).

4:18. Concluding Apostolic Word. In conformity with Paul's custom the author concludes with a final apostolic certification of the whole letter (cf. I Cor. 16:21; Gal. 6:11), penned by himself and not the scribe to whom the rest has been dictated. As always in the apostolic letters, the last word is one of benediction.

THE FIRST LETTER
OF PAUL TO THE THESSALONIANS

LEANDER E. KECK

INTRODUCTION

Date and Occasion. If the books of the NT stood in the order in which they were written, I Thess. would head the list (only Gal. might compete for this position; see Intro. to Gal.). I Thess. was written by Paul from Corinth *ca.* A.D. 51. This simple conclusion results from interpreting both Acts and I Thess.

According to Acts—the only narrative of Paul's work—Paul, Timothy, and Silas came to Thessalonica (see color map 16) from Philippi. Though the account of their mission there (Acts 17:1-9) speaks of Paul's teaching 3 sabbaths in the synagogue, the whole period was probably longer. The new church they founded was of mixed membership and included prominent Macedonian women (Acts 17:4). Civil disturbances led to a sudden departure by night to nearby Beroea, where their efforts ended when Thess. Jews arrived to stir up opposition (Acts 17:10-13). Paul went on to Athens, accompanied by converts, by whom he sent word back to Beroea for Silas and Timothy to join him as soon as possible (Acts 17:14-15). Then he waited for them at Athens (Acts 17:16).

The letter itself enables us to take up the story at this point. From 3:1-3*a* it is clear that Timothy, at least, met Paul in Athens as instructed and that Paul sent him back from there to Thessalonica to stabilize the young congregation. Later Timothy rejoined Paul, who after hearing his report wrote the letter. This 2nd meeting of Timothy with Paul is evidently to be equated with the arrival of Silas and Timothy from Macedonia after Paul had already moved from Athens to Corinth, which is reported in Acts 18:5. The first meeting in Athens expected in Acts 17:15-16 is missing from the Acts account as is Timothy's resulting trip to Thessalonica. Therefore we may conclude that the letter was written at Corinth. This is confirmed by the implication in 3:1 that Paul was no longer at Athens.

The date of the writing is determined by the time of Paul's work in Corinth. This is known from an inscription found Delphi which reveals that the proconsul Gallio (Acts 18:12-17) took office in the summer of A.D. 51. The letter, then, was written in 50 or 51.

Structure. The letter is simply but carefully constructed. Its 2 sections concern the past work of Paul in Thessalonica (chs. 1–3) and the present issues in the church (chs. 4–5). Because Paul had to leave his converts in haste and was not able to return (cf. 2:18) he found it necessary to discuss extensively the nature of his mission among them, lest they conclude

that he was simply one more traveling huckster of religion. Paul's paragraphs here provide us with the earliest glimpse into a Christian congregation.

The Eschatological Emphasis. The letter is famous, however, mostly for its remarks on the "second coming" of Christ and for its evidence of the tenor of early Christian eschatology. "Eschatology" (lit. doctrine of the end) is a very elastic word that includes all manner of concepts of the future; eschatology is a built-in aspect of all thinking about the life of man and the nature of history. E.g. the Christian eschatology concerns the kingdom of God, the Marxist eschatology concerns the classless society at the end of the historical dialectic, and nihilistic eschatologies speak of the extinction of life on the planet either by uncontrollable technological war or by the disappearance of conditions necessary for life.

In the late literature of the OT (esp. Dan.) we find a special type of eschatological thinking—apocalyptic (from a Greek word meaning "unveiling"; see "The Apocalyptic Literature," pp. 1106-09). Apocalyptic eschatology holds that not only the future is set by God but the schedule as well; therefore history is not a riddle but the working out of a predetermined plan of God which is revealed to the specially chosen spokesman for the sake of the faithful. A constant ingredient is the view that history is accelerating into insurrection (progress in reverse!) which springs from the disobedience of angels before creation and from man's sin since then. History is therefore rushing headlong into a crisis during which God will intervene to set everything right. The Dead Sea Scrolls come from a group that held such views.

Another group holding apocalyptic views was the early church. Early Christians regarded the resurrection of Jesus as the inauguration of the end, and they expected that he would appear soon as final judge and arbiter of history. The 2 Thess. letters, as well as Mark 13 (and its parallels in Matt. and Luke), Rev., and II Pet., show how widespread and persistent such views were. Moreover the trained eye can detect evidences in the NT of the readjustment necessitated by the conversion of Gentiles, who viewed such ideas as strange and peripheral to the meaning of Jesus as they found it, and by the fact that all these hopes were disappointed again and again. The 2 Thess. letters, then, are important documents in the overall story of early Christian apocalyptic eschatology.

A Pastoral Letter. In contrast with Gal. and Col. this letter does not debate theological alternatives,

Top, courtesy of Stella Grobel
Bottom, courtesy of Herbert G. May

Top: Buildings of modern Salonika backdrop an excavation of the palace of emperor Galerius (4th cent. A.D.) located in ancient Thessalonica

Bottom: The arch of emperor Galerius spanning the ancient and famous Via Egnatia (Egnatian Way) with modern Thessalonica (Salonika) in the background; Paul followed the Via Egnatia from Neapolis through Philippi to Thessalonica (see color map 16, sketch map, p. 750 and illus., p. 876)

though it deals with them. In contrast with Rom. it is not a theological essay. In contrast with the Cor. letters it does not deal with a series of crises in the church, though it often seems to touch lightly on some of the same problems. This is a pastoral letter by an apostle who wants to guide the church he has founded but cannot remain with.

For Further Study: Commentaries by J. E. Frame, 1912, William Neil, 1950, Leon Morris, 1959. J. W. Bailey in *IB*, 1955. J. W. Bowman, "Eschatology of the NT"; H. K. McArthur, "Parousia"; F. W. Beare, "Thess." in *IDB*, 1962.

I. Greeting (1:1)

Paul's associates share his greeting, which follows the standard pattern of the Pauline letters. For the circumstances in which **Timothy** joined Paul see Acts 16:1-3; on **Silvanus** (doubtless the same as Silas) see Acts 15:22-41.

II. Thanksgiving for the Reception of the Gospel (1:2–3:13)

All Paul's letters except Gal. open with paragraphs of thanksgiving which orient the letter by mentioning the writer and readers in ways which suggest the themes of the letter as a whole. A distinguishing feature of I Thess. is the extent of its thanksgiving. Not only is 1:6–2:12 an exposition of the theme of thanks as stated in 1:2-5, but 2:13 repeats the statement of thanks so as to shift the discussion from the original work of Paul in Thessalonica to his subsequent relation to the church. In 3:9-10 Paul returns to the theme of thanks, and 3:11-13 is a prayer for the readers, a standard conclusion to the thanksgivings. Thus giving thanks controls the first 3 chs.; the remaining 2 are Paul's exhortation to this church for which he is so deeply grateful.

A. The Thanksgiving Theme (1:2-5)

Vss. 2-3 say *how* Paul gives thanks, while vss. 4-5 say *why*. **Always** ought not to be emphasized because it is a standard item in a thanksgiving paragraph (cf. Rom. 1:9; I Cor. 1:4; Phil. 1:4; Col. 1:3; Philem. 4) and in prayers as well.

1:3. *Faith, Hope, Love.* The famous triad of I Cor. 13:13 appears here in a different order (cf. 5:8; Col. 1:3-5). All 3 phrases must be taken together and in all 3 the word **of** is important. Rather than work inspired by faith, etc., Paul speaks of work as a form of faith, labor as the shape of love, steadfastness as the manifestation of hope (cf. NEB: "how your faith has shown itself in action, your love in labor and your hope . . . in fortitude"). When Paul thinks of this quality of life which the gospel has brought about he gives thanks to God.

1:4. *Election.* Paul believes that his readers are **chosen** by God. This word is a technical term for Paul and the whole Bible. It expresses the belief that in the divine-human relationship the initiative lies with God. Jesus put it tersely: "You did not choose me but I chose you" (John 15:16). Biblical thought holds in tension the choice of God and the choice of man and nowhere does God's choosing take responsibility away from man. Paul's classical treatment of the theme is in Rom. 9–11.

1:5. *Paul's Own Gospel.* Paul knows that God has chosen the readers because his message came with **power,** the **Holy Spirit,** and **full conviction.** This theme will be developed in ch. 2. He speaks of **our gospel** (cf. Rom. 2:16; 16:25; II Cor. 4:3; Gal. 1:8, 11) because for him the gospel is inseparable from his personal conversion and commission to preach. Though in his summary of his gospel in I Cor. 15:1-11 he insists that it is not peculiar to him, nevertheless he had a distinctive grasp of the meaning of Jesus.

Paul declares that his preaching was not "just talk" but an event marked by power, Spirit, and confidence. It is not clear whether **power** refers to healing power such as Acts reports (e.g. Acts 16:16-18; 19:11-20) and as Paul once mentions (II Cor. 12:12) or whether it refers to the ability of the gospel to elicit faith and reshape life. For Paul the **Holy Spirit** was a basic ingredient of Christian life, the "down payment" of salvation (II Cor. 1:22; 5:5).

Though some take this vs. to refer to Paul's own demeanor, it is better to take it as referring to the results of his work, for the text speaks of how the gospel **came to you.** What happened when Paul preached confirms for him that God is at work, "choosing" the church. Paul reckons with the possibility that his message might be only words; but because God was at work as he preached there occurred among the Thess. work, labor, and steadfastness. Remembering this he gives thanks.

B. The Response to the Gospel (1:6-10)

Here Paul states the Thess. response in more detail. What vss. 4-5 said theologically these verses say empirically.

1:6-7. *Imitators and Imitated.* The point here is that the readers became first **imitators** and then became an **example** to be imitated by others (cf. I Cor. 4:16; 11:1; Phil. 3:17; 4:9). Paul did not want to be mistaken as a propagandist of religious ideas; he wanted to be seen as an embodiment of his message of the Cross and the Resurrection. He demanded that his life be transparent enough that his hearers could glimpse the power of the gospel. This transparency is what Paul wants the believers to imitate. The phrase **and of the Lord** is not a correction, as some suggest, but is another way of saying what is said in I Cor. 11:1 (cf. the strong language in Gal. 6:17; Col. 1:24).

What distinguishes Paul from the many hawkers of religion, then and now, is precisely this insistence that his person is inseparable from his message. He did not "sell" the gospel as a commodity external to himself but presented it by word and life (vs. 5*b* is important). The Thess. response in **affliction** (vs. 6) gave Paul evidence that they had indeed imitated him. Because the Corinthians, on the other hand, did not grasp precisely this feature of Paul's gospel, he later expounded fully this point in II Cor. 10–12, the best commentary on this passage.

1:8-10. *The Spread of the Gospel.* That the Thess. response spread **everywhere** is of course a rhetorical exaggeration. Just as Paul's message united his person and his proclamation, so the Thess. response is coupled with **the word of the Lord** (i.e. the gospel) as it spreads.

1:9*b*-10. Because this passage seems to fall into

rhythmical phrases and uses words not common to Paul, it may be quoted from the common stock of early Christian worship material. If so, we should be cautious in using it as a guide to the way Paul actually preached to the Thess. In any case, however, it is an important clue to the themes of early Christian preaching to Gentiles. The call to turn from polytheism to the one God was the core of Jewish preaching to Gentiles. It was taken up by Christians, who added the message about Jesus, here stated in 3 points: the future coming, the identification of the expected one with the resurrected one, and his role as deliverer. This outline assumes more than it says, for it eclipses the whole life of Jesus. The ideas are put into paradoxical form: the heavenly **Son** of God has a historical earthly name, **Jesus;** the one **from heaven** has already been among **the dead,** presumably under the earth; he will deliver **us** who already believe **from the wrath to come.** The emphasis falls on the future. Early Christianity was much more future-oriented and apocalyptically minded than most Christianity today (see Intro.). The Thess. had special problems in this connection (cf. chs. 4-5).

C. Paul as Preacher and Pastor (2:1-12)

This passage, an exposition of 1:5*b*, 9*b*, balances 1:6-10, which has discussed what the Thess. became.

2:1-2. *A Thematic Introduction.* Paul's mission was not in vain. Despite maltreatment in Philippi (cf. Acts 16:16-40) he found courage to preach in Thessalonica, again **in the face of great opposition** (cf. 1:6). The response suggests that God is at work, for it actualizes the meaning of the resurrection in daily life. Acts 17:1-9 does not suggest the steady hostility implied here.

2:3-8. *Paul's Preaching.* Paul makes his appeal in a way that is appropriate to the fact that God entrusted him with the message; therefore he seeks to please him who gave it, not those who hear it (cf. II Cor. 4:1-6). Paul developed the style of his mission so that the meaning of his commissioning was preserved; this left no room for manipulating his hearers.

2:5-8. This is the most personal part of the letter. The ancient world had an ample supply of traveling preachers and promoters of cults and religions, some of whom took advantage of people. The Christian church did not remain free from such abuse (cf. II John 10-11). In contrast Paul emphasizes his integrity (vss. 5-6) and his involvement with the life of his converts (vss. 7-8). Precisely what apostolic **demands** he did not make is unclear, though I Cor. 9 suggests that he means the right to be supported by the church. The entire passage gives us better insight into Paul's mission than anything Acts says.

2:9-12. *Paul's Work as a Pastor.* Paul is proud that he earned his own living (cf. I Cor. 4:11-12; II Cor. 11:27). According to Acts 18:3 he was a tentmaker. Tactfully he ignores the fact that at Thessalonica he received financial help from Philippi more than once (Phil. 4:16); nor does he mention Jason's hospitality (Acts 17:7). In vss. 10-12 he returns to the theme of his solicitous care, now speaking of himself as a **father with his children** (cf. I Cor. 4:15; II Cor. 6:13; Gal. 4:19)—a sterner metaphor than the **nurse** of vs. 7. As father Paul refers to his exhorta-

tions to live a life appropriate to God's call (another way of referring to God's choosing them; cf. 1:4) which they obeyed. **Kingdom and glory** (vs. 12) here mean the complete salvation when the work of God is consummated (cf. Rom. 5:2; I Cor. 15:20-28). Here Christian ethics is not a set of regulations but a mandate to develop a kind of life that is appropriate to the gospel (cf. Phil. 2:1-13).

D. Thanks Restated (2:13)

This gathers up the thrust of the whole discussion so far. Paul calls his message the **word of God.** He recognizes, however, that it is possible to take it simply as the word of a man, as his ideas about Jesus. Yet those who believe it know that Paul's message is the vehicle for God's word. It is the working of this message—its power to elicit the sort of responses Paul has discussed—that convinces the readers that what they have heard and hearkened to is really God's address to them. Their own changed lives (1:2-10) point to the conclusion that God was at work among them.

E. A Polemic Against Jews (2:14-16)

This passage, which interrupts the flow of thought between vs. 13 and vs. 17, contains a vicious attack on unbelieving Jews from a viewpoint unlike that elsewhere in Paul's writings (cf. esp. Rom. 9-11). The final sentence traditionally has been taken to be a reference to the Roman destruction of Jerusalem in A.D. 70, and many scholars consider it an interpolation added after that event (see below on vs. 16*c*). Though most commentators find various arguments to defend Paul's writing of the passage, with or without vs. 16*c*—e.g. a moment of frustration and uncontrolled temper—they are not persuasive; and a number of scholars prefer to regard the whole passage as an interpolation made after the fall of Jerusalem (and after Paul's death).

2:14. *Imitators of Palestinian Christians.* Because the Thess. suffered from their fellow citizens just as Jewish Christians endured much from their compatriots, it is said that they are in effect imitators of the Palestinian Christians. While Paul believed strongly in the unity of the whole church and collected funds from Gentile churches for the needy in Jerusalem to show it, there is no other evidence that he ever regarded Judean Christianity as something to be imitated. The artificiality of this idea supports the view that the interpolation includes all of vss. 14-16, rather than only the polemic of vss. 15-16 as a few have maintained.

2:15-16. *Attack on the Jews.* That the Jews killed the **prophets** is mentioned also in Matt. 23:34-36, 37; Luke 11:47-52 and implied in Matt. 21:33-41. Generally the OT does not say how the prophets died, though intertestamental stories grew up about them (reflected in Heb. 11:37). That many of them were persecuted is clear. According to Matt. 5:11-12; Luke 6:22-23 Jesus himself connected the persecution of his followers with that of the prophets, while according to Matt. 23:37-38; Luke 13:34-35 he made a similar connection regarding his own fate. This text, however, is the only one that connects all 3. Whether **drove us out** refers to Paul himself (cf. e.g. Acts 9:23-30; 17:5-7), to the apostles, or to Christians in general (cf. Acts 8:1*b*-3) is uncertain.

Also unclear is what they were driven out of—the synagogues? or Palestine? The expulsion of Christians from the Palestinian synagogues (reflected in John 9:22; 16:2) did not occur until after A.D. 70. That the Jews **displease God and oppose all men** echoes the anti-Semitic charges of pagans and is difficult to conceive of in the mouth of Paul. That they oppose the spread of the gospel among Gentiles is a possible echo of Acts 13:44–14:20. This opposition is viewed as consummating a sinful history.

2:16c. The phrase translated **at last** can mean either "finally" or "to the end." In either case **wrath** is most naturally understood as an allusion to the destruction of Jerusalem from after the event (see above on vss. 14-16). Those who maintain Paul's authorship of the sentence assert either that he foresaw such a catastrophe or that he refers rather to an apocalyptic day of judgment.

F. TIMOTHY'S VISIT (2:17–3:5)

Following on his 2nd note of thanksgiving in 2:13 (see above on 2:14-16) Paul discusses his relation to the church after he left Thessalonica (cf. Acts 17:1-15). If some are thinking Paul "ran out" on them, he reassures them this is not the case. 2:17-20 states his true attitude and 3:1-5 gives its result: Timothy's trip (see Intro.).

2:17-20. Paul's Attitude Toward the Thess. Paul insists that he himself has wanted to return more than once; of this Acts says nothing. He blames **Satan** for the fact he has not returned. Many interpretations of this have been offered: (a) illness (cf. II Cor. 12:7); (b) the magistrates at Thessalonica (cf. Acts 17:8-9); (c) the Thess. Jews (cf. Acts 17:5-7); (d) problems in Corinth, from where Paul writes (cf. Acts 18:5-17). In any case Paul sees some historical circumstance as part of a cosmic struggle between God and Satanic opposition (cf. II Cor. 2:10-11; 11:12-15). In restating his love for his readers (vss. 19-20) Paul refers for the first time to the **coming** of the Lord (see below on 4:13–5:11) and assures them that they will be his **glory** (i.e. reward) **and joy** on that day. He has not brought about their conversion with its subsequent difficulties only to abandon them.

3:1-5. Timothy Sent to Thessalonica. Paul tells of sending Timothy back from **Athens** to revisit the readers (see Intro.). Why Silvanus (Silas) is not mentioned is unknown; Paul's being **left . . . alone** suggests either that he had stayed on in Beroea (cf. Acts 17:13-15) or that he was sent back with Timothy but to another city in Macedonia (cf. Acts 18:5). The purpose of Timothy's trip was double—to **establish** (i.e. strengthen) the church members in their faith and to **exhort** them so that they would not abandon Christianity in difficulty. Timothy went as theologian and as pastor.

3:3b-4. Paul reinforces Timothy's work by reminding the readers that he foretold the afflictions they have endured. The first 2 uses of **we** in vs. 4 mean Paul and his associates but the 3rd refers to all Christians. That suffering was an inherent part of Christian life was a characteristic emphasis of Paul (e.g. Rom. 5:1-5; 8:18-39; I Cor. 4:9-13; Phil. 3:10-11; Col. 1:24). For him suffering was no threat to the truth of the gospel but a potential confirmation of it.

3:5. Even so, those who do not understand this, or

agree, might fall away from the faith. Hence Paul sent Timothy to determine whether the Thess. were adequately grounded in the gospel, lest **the tempter** (i.e. Satan; **the tempter** is used elsewhere only in Matt. 4:3) seduce them away from Christ and his own work should turn out to have been **in vain.** Paul is a realist; he reckons seriously with the possibility that under pressure Christians might repudiate their faith. He who has been as tender as a nurse (2:7) and as concerned as a father (2:11) is eager to stabilize the church. This is why he sent Timothy.

G. PAUL'S RESPONSE TO TIMOTHY'S REPORT (3:6-10)

Vss. 6-8 state the point and vss. 9-10 return to the theme of thanks, thereby rounding out the entire thanksgiving section (1:2–3:10).

3:6. Timothy's Report. As described here the report was entirely positive, though what follows in chs. 4-5 suggests that Paul's words are too generous. In any case the Thess. church is basically firm in its grasp of the Christian faith and in its regard for Paul. **Brought . . . good news** is the normal Greek meaning of a word that in Christian usage came to mean "preach the gospel"—a development which some have traced to Paul himself. Though Timothy spoke favorably about the Thess.' **faith** and **love,** nothing is said about their hope (see above on 1:3). Hope is a problem discussed in the next section.

3:7-8. Paul's Own Involvement. The news from Thessalonica has comforted Paul in his **distress** in Corinth. Whether this refers to what Acts 18:1-21 tells is unknown. Vs. 8 expresses once more Paul's personal involvement in his church (cf. 2:7-8, 17-20), esp. his concern for the stability of the church (**stand** is Paul's word for "maintain faith"; cf. e.g. Rom. 14:4; I Cor. 15:1; 16:13; Phil. 4:1). Vs. 8 should not be taken lit., though II Cor. 11:28-29 in its context suggests that Paul's involvement in his congregations affected his health (cf. also II Cor. 1:8; 2:4, 13).

3:9-10. A Final Thanksgiving. This concluding mention of the theme of thanksgiving points up the emphasis throughout chs. 1-3. The closing phrase hints the themes of the next section.

H. A TRANSITIONAL PRAYER (3:11-13)

This prayer takes up the relation of Paul to his readers and places it before the will of God. It gathers up themes already discussed and mentions that of the remaining half of the letter, the **coming of our Lord.** In the petition **may God . . . and our Lord Jesus direct our way** the verb is singular. Paul never says how God and Christ work together; such statements as this, coupled with references to the work of the Holy Spirit, pose the problems which are not "solved" until the doctrine of the Trinity is worked out. Paul prays that the result of increasing **love** for all mankind will be increased stability in innocence and in sanctity before God. It is commonly believed that increased **holiness** produces more love; here Paul reverses the process.

III. EXHORTATION: THE DAILY MEANING OF THE GOSPEL (4:1–5:25)

This section begins and ends with miscellaneous exhortations. In the middle, however, 2 specific problems are discussed: the impact of death on Christian faith and the proper attitudes toward the time of the end.

A. GENERAL EXHORTATIONS (4:1-12)

4:1-2. *Learning and Instructions.* Paul begins by tactfully building on the present and past. What he calls for is not a new orientation but a continued effort in the same direction. The passage raises an important historical question: To what extent did Paul's gospel preaching include ethical guidance? This text forbids taking lit. Paul's saying that he preached only Christ crucified (I Cor. 2:2). Besides there is sufficient evidence that Paul did not simply preach the Cross and the Resurrection but included the moral meaning of that theme as the indispensable ingredient of Christian faith as such. All of Rom. makes this point.

Learned (lit. "received") was a technical term for the transmission of tradition (cf. I Cor. 11:23; 15:1). Some think that this passage therefore refers to the transmission of a body of tradition of ethical instruction; e.g. the NEB translates "We passed on to you the tradition of the way we must live." However, this makes Paul's language more technical than it is. Some have even seen here a reference to Paul's transmitting the teachings of Jesus (the gospels were not yet written). This is highly dubious, for even if one can find echoes of Jesus' phrases in the letter, the very fact that they are only echoes and not references shows that Paul did not emphasize Jesus' teachings.

4:2. What **instructions** Paul gave the Thess. is unknown. We can be confident they were not mere general admonitions to "do good" but included specific obligations as well. When he had no tradition to guide him, he trusted his own judgment, as I Cor. 7 shows. In this case, however, he says the instructions were given **through the Lord Jesus.** Paul's ethics were shaped by his Christology, his understanding of the meaning of Jesus in the widest sense, as Phil. 2:1-13 shows. The basis of Christian ethics which he assumes here is not "the good" or "the useful" but that which pleases God. This is the fundamental approach of the Bible. What is good and right is what pleases God; there is no independent good or right according to which one might assess the deed of even God, as in Greek thought. What is good and right is what God wills, not what can be determined rationally or scientifically. Not even Rom. 1-2, which speaks of man's innate ability to discover what is right, eclipses the will of God as the real arbiter of the good and the right. There is no understanding of biblical ethics without seeing this point.

4:3-6. *Sanctification.* Vs. 3a states the theme: God wills **your sanctification** (the translation **the will of God** makes the point too sweeping). "Sanctification" in Greek means, not the process of making holy or the ideal of holiness, but the end product of making holy, the achievement of holiness (cf. Rom. 6:19, 22; I Cor. 1:30). For Paul sanctification is not the result of ritual or of religious experience as such but a matter of ethics. Sanctification—making life holy—is living so as to please God, and is a life-long process, as Rom. 6:19-22 recognizes.

4:3b-6 spells out what Paul has in mind, focusing on 2 problems, sex and greed. Sanctification means abstaining from sexual immorality—lit. "prostitution," but the word had come to mean a variety of sexual sins. Like our own, the Hellenistic world was much more tolerant of all manner of sexual practices than were Paul and the biblical tradition. What Paul demands next is not clear. **A wife for himself** is lit. "his vessel." Since early times many have assumed that Paul speaks of marriage—an interpretation said to be supported by I Pet. 3:7, where woman is "the weaker vessel" (RSV "sex"). Others believe that Paul speaks rather of self-control —that "his vessel" means "mastery over his body" (NEB). That Paul intended the latter sense seems more probable. Vs. 5 reveals Paul's contempt for Gentile sexual ethics and traces it, as Jews commonly did, to idolatry and polytheism (discussed in detail in Rom. 1:18-32). Here Paul draws on Ps. 79:6; Jer. 10:25.

4:6. In vs. 6a the RSV translators have supplied the word **this** on the assumption that Paul is still speaking of sexual immorality; but in Greek usage **matter** had a commercial sense (see RSV footnote), and it seems likely that Paul here brings up dishonesty in business. Vs. 6b returns to the basis of Paul's ethics—the judgment of God. He has already implied it in grounding ethics in God's will, since this commits God to carry out his will and to respond appropriately to opposition to it. For the Bible as a whole, God's vindicating his will corroborates the belief that his will is his commitment and not merely his preference. In Rom. 12:19-21 Paul insists that the vindication of God's will must be left to God, a point not mentioned in this passage and not followed in I Cor. 5:3-5.

4:7-8. *God's Call.* These ethical obligations are tied to theological considerations. What Paul has just discussed is consistent with the goal of God's work with the readers—his call (cf. 1:4; 2:12). Vs. 8 insists that Paul's counsel is not simply his own notion and explains what it means for God to give the **Holy Spirit** to the Christian (cf. 1:5). In this passage the Spirit is not an ecstatic power but a presence which sanctifies because it is the *Holy* Spirit; its work is to elicit the holy life Paul has called for.

4:9-12. *Love and Work.* The phrase **taught by God** may refer either to the lesson taught by God's love in the complex of events summed up in the "Christ event" (in accord with Rom. 5:8) or to the consequence of being granted the Spirit (in accord with Rom. 5:5). **Love of the brethren** was a characteristic of early Christianity (cf. I Pet. 1:22; II Pet. 1:7; I John 2:9-11; 3:14-18; 4:7-12). Perhaps the location of Thessalonica helped this church make contact with other Christians **throughout Macedonia.**

4:11-12. Many commentators have assumed that the Thess. were prone to stop **work** because they were excited over the 2nd coming of Christ, which Paul takes up in his next paragraph. But the connection which the text implies in vss. 10b-12—all one sentence—is a possible abuse of the brotherly love and mutual sharing among Christians. Perhaps some became idlers and busybodies who insisted that their brothers owed them a living. Paul knows (vs. 12) that the character of a Christian's life has an effect on the reputation of the gospel itself. He does not want the church to get the reputation of fostering indolence in the name of religion. The word **nobody** probably should be taken as neuter, i.e. "nothing," so that the 2nd motive Paul suggests for working is not independence of others but to "be in need of nothing." The sharing of goods which early Jerusalem Christians practiced (cf. Acts 2:43-47; 4:32; 5:1-11) was not transplanted by Paul into his churches.

B. Death and Christian Salvation (4:13-18)

This and the following paragraph constitute the hallmark of I Thess. Paul introduces the topic with the same word, **concerning,** which begins each of his answers to a letter from Corinth (I Cor. 7:1, 25; 8:1; 12:1; 16:1). This does not necessarily mean that here too Paul is answering a letter brought by Timothy. Knowledge of what needs to be discussed probably depends on Timothy's report (cf. 3:6). Vss. 13-14 state the basic point; vss. 15-17 amplify it; vs. 18 relates the discussion to the present life of the Christian community.

4:13-14. *Hope in the Resurrection of Jesus.* These vss., along with vs. 18, are important guides to the problem in the church. The **coming** of the Lord is discussed to deal with certain attitudes toward death and toward Christian faith itself—attitudes characterized as the grief of **others . . . who have no hope.** Who are these? Paul is not thinking of the Sadducees (cf. Mark 12:18-23; Acts 23:6-10), for these would not be known in Thessalonica. Probably he has in mind pagans in general, whom he has just described as not knowing God (4:5; cf. Eph. 2:12). He is doubtless aware that many Gentiles believed either in the natural immortality of the soul or in immortality conferred by rites of initiation into the many cults. But for Paul such pagan ideas of life after death are **no hope** at all.

4:14. Hope, as Paul sees it, is grounded in the resurrection of Jesus. His purpose in the discussion, then, is not to assuage normal grief caused by death but to deal with despair. This calls, not for comforting sentiments, but for instruction. What was the problem? The common view that the question was whether at the coming of Christ the Christians who had already died would be on the same level as the living is not convincing. The real problem is the fact that Christians have died at all; some fear that the dead have forfeited their salvation. If this should be true, only those alive at the return of Christ would really be saved; moreover death itself would not really have been dealt with by the resurrection of Jesus, and the Christian message as a whole would be jeopardized. Some may also have thought that baptism into Christ's death and resurrection made them immune to death, immortal as in the rites of the mystery religions.

The heart of Paul's response is that there is an inseparable relationship between Christ and the Christian (cf. Rom. 8:31-39). Hence Paul argues that believing in the resurrection of Jesus means believing also in the participation of the believer in his own exaltation to the heavenly realm. Therefore when Jesus "comes" those who died with him will not be left out. Vss. 15-17 spell this out in detail.

This is one of the few places where the NT says Jesus **rose** (elsewhere only in Mark 8:31; 9:31; 10:34). Usually it says "he was raised"—i.e. by God (e.g. Matt. 16:21; Luke 9:22; Acts 2:32; I Cor. 15:4,

13-19). **Through Jesus** is ambiguous in that it can be taken either with **God will bring,** as in the RSV, or with **those who have fallen asleep,** meaning those who "died as Christians" (NEB). However, there is no reference here to martyrs—those who died because of Jesus. **Bring** can mean bring them to earth with Jesus, or bring them to life, or bring them into participation in the consummated salvation, or bring them back into heaven with the triumphant Lord.

4:15-17. *The End.* These vss. describe the *eschaton* —the end. Paul's purpose in discussing this must not be forgotten (see above on vss. 13-14).

4:15. Paul appeals to the **word of the Lord.** Some think he is referring to a tradition of what Jesus said (the Gospels were written 20-50 years later), while others think he speaks of a special revelation such as he mentions in II Cor. 12:1-9 and such as Acts reports (Acts 9:1-9; 18:9-10; 22:17-21; 27:21-26). Probably Paul is appealing to a tradition of Jesus' words—Matt. 24:30; John 6:40 have often been suggested. It is impossible to reconstruct the saying because the wording is changed—at least **the Lord** and **we** did not belong in Jesus' phrases. This tradition may be otherwise unknown to us. Whether it accurately represented what Jesus said is another matter.

From **we . . . who are left** it is clear that Paul expects to live to see the Lord's coming. Early Christianity generally expected that the Lord would soon consummate his victory over sin and death, which the Resurrection had inaugurated.

The technical term for the arrival of the Lord, **coming** (Greek *parousia*), was used in ordinary speech precisely as our English word is used (e.g. Phil. 1:26). It came to be used in a special sense, however, for the state visits of kings and rulers. From this exalted, official meaning it came into Christian usage, the earliest such being in I Thess. Not until a cent. later (Justin Martyr) is the expression "second coming" found. For the NT period the **coming** was always this imminent, regal arrival of the Lord; the life of Jesus had been far too humble an event to be spoken of as the "first coming." Not until the life of Jesus was glorified, as in John, did one speak of a first and 2nd coming.

Paul insists that those who are alive **shall not precede** the dead. The negative in the Greek is stronger than in this translation. The point is not simply sequence—what would it matter then who came first?—but whether the dead are to be included at all. So strongly does Paul think that the dead will share the event that he says that the living will not even precede them.

4:16. The purpose of this vs. is to show why the foregoing is true. The coming is described as a descent, in keeping with the idea that the Resurrection took Jesus to heaven (only Luke-Acts separates resurrection from ascent to heaven). The descent will be accompanied by the Lord's **command,** the **archangel's call,** and God's **trumpet.** The entire "power structure" of the heavenly court will be involved. These are traditional symbols of divine authority and sovereignty, and it is pointless to speculate about what the Lord will command, the archangel say, or the trumpet play.

That **the dead in Christ will rise first** is the point Paul has been making throughout the passage. The fate of the non-Christian dead is ignored. Another interpretation, however, puts **in Christ** with **will rise** to make the point that all the dead, Christian or not, "will rise in Christ." This interpretation agrees with I Cor. 15:22, where clearly all mankind shares the benefits of Christ's resurrection.

4:17. Those **who are alive** will join the resurrected ones and will be **caught up together in the clouds** for a rendezvous with the Lord in mid-air. There is no mention of the transformation of the living, emphasized in I Cor. 15:50-54; doubtless it is omitted here because this was not a problem in Thessalonica. The goal is **to meet the Lord in the air**—i.e. the realm between earth and the sky. Paul ends the story here, as if to exclude any reference to a continued descent to earth. He may have in mind a triumphal return with all the saints to heaven—a possible meaning of **will bring** in vs. 14. There is no word here, or room, for a millenial rule of the Messiah on earth as envisaged in Rev. 20:4-6.

4:18. *A Basis for Faith.* Paul reminds the readers that his intent is to provide, not a preview of the future, but a basis for **comfort**. The Greek word means not simply emotional consolation but exhortation, counsel, and admonition. The central concern in the whole discussion is to provide the basis for confident faith in Christ in the face of death.

Some general observations about vss. 15-18 are now in order:

a) This is not a complete statement of Paul's ideas of the end. Even when it is joined with I Cor. 15 (esp. vss. 51-56) we do not have a complete picture. Perhaps Paul did not have one either. It is risky, moreover, to fill in the gaps from the rest of the NT or from Jewish apocalyptic literature.

b) The fact that this portrait of the end is not identical with that of Mark 13 or Rev. shows that the early church had a variety of ideas on the subject, just as Judaism did. It is important to let these diversities stand rather than force them into a single, harmonious scheme of the end.

c) This variety suggests that the real intent of all these views is to announce in dramatic form the consummation of God's saving work in Christ. Where this salvation is understood largely in dynamic terms that deal with the release of man from various tyrannies, the consummation is portrayed as a dramatic victory over opposition to God and as a climactic assertion of his sovereignty (cf. II Thess. 2:1-12).

d) It is not clear how this apocalyptic line of thought in Paul (including I Cor. 15) is related to a somewhat different emphasis in II Cor. 5:1-10; Phil. 1:21-23. In those passages being **with the Lord** is an immediate alternative to being alive on earth and does not seem to require a resurrection at all, whereas this passage and I Cor. 15 assume that a resurrection makes being with the Lord possible at the end. Some interpreters have seen in Paul's thinking a later shift away from Jewish apocalyptic views he held at the time of writing I Thess., but this can scarcely be demonstrated convincingly. Hence it is better to recognize the existence of 2 lines of thought in Paul and leave open the question of how he related them—if he did.

e) Whatever one makes of the sequence of events outlined by Paul, it is clear that his scheduling was wrong, that the end did not occur during his lifetime. Hence we cannot avoid asking: In view of his miscalculation of the calendar, is there anything of enduring value here, any transcending truth in what Paul has to say? The answer is that Paul's central point is not when or how the end will come. It is that the prospect of an end to life must not jeopardize one's confidence in Christ, because the relation of the believer to his Lord is indestructible even by death. The real heart of the matter is the confident trust in God stated in Rom. 8:31-39, where there is neither schedule nor trumpet. Paul himself, then, shows how to grasp what is at stake without being confused by the details or the timing of it all.

C. LIFE TODAY IN LIGHT OF THE END (5:1-11)

The 2nd, related, problem that Paul considers is the uncertain time of the end. This paragraph too begins by stating the theme (vss. 1-2) and ends with an admonition (vs. 11). The passage is not a general treatment of a topic but a theological discussion of a pastoral problem. It makes a single point: the suddenness of the end requires an appropriate moral life now.

5:1-2. *Times and Seasons.* Paul begins his discussion of **the times and the seasons** (an expression taken from the OT; cf. Dan. 2:21; Acts 1:7) by pointing out that it is not really needed—probably because of previous instruction. Nevertheless he continues in order to anticipate the problems that may arise and to lead to his major concern, the proper quality of life in the here and now.

5:2. By the **day of the Lord** Paul means the same complex of events discussed in 4:13-18 as the "coming." As a phrase for the end it appeared as early as the 8th cent. B.C. (Amos 5:18) and became common in apocalyptic literature, though not found in the Gospels. Whereas the OT and Jewish literature used it to speak of God, for Paul "Lord" meant Christ, the "Lord Jesus"; elsewhere he speaks of the "day of Christ" (Phil. 1:10; 2:16) and the "day of our Lord Jesus" (I Cor. 5:5; II Cor. 1:14). After Christians called Jesus "Lord" it was easy for them to think "Lord Jesus" as they read of "the Lord" in their Greek OT.

Paul's point is that the day **will come like a thief in the night.** Jesus is recorded as using this simile also (Matt. 24:43-44; Luke 12:39-40, where the one who comes is the Son of man, a phrase Paul does not use). It is uncertain whether Paul had this saying, or a form of it, in mind or whether both he and Jesus took it from the common stock of Jewish ideas. At any rate both Jesus and Paul specify precisely how this coming is to be thief-like. The point of comparison is neither stealth nor stealing but surprise. Just as the thief's coming cannot be reckoned in advance, so the time of the day of the Lord cannot be calculated either. Precisely when least expected it will be here.

5:3. *Suddenness and Surprise.* The sudden arrival will surprise the secure. This unforeseen reversal of circumstances is a theme that pervades the entire apocalyptic tradition; its biblical roots go back at least as far as Amos 5, where precisely this point is made (cf. Matt. 24:36-44; Luke 17:26-30). Similarly, the suddenness will be like the situation of a pregnant **woman** overtaken suddenly by labor pains. Paul's point must not be confused with the Jewish apocalyptic idea of the "birth pangs of the Messiah"—

the conviction that the Messiah would emerge into history only in a time of great distress (taken up in Mark 13:14-37)—for Paul is interested here, not in the difficulty that precedes the end (cf. II Thess. 2), but only in the surprise.

5:4-5. *Light and Darkness.* Paul next develops his admonition based on the contrast of **night** and **day.** Because Christians **belong to the day,** the day that comes will not catch them napping. Paul shifts from simile (the day comes as a thief in the night) to allegory (the night suggests moral darkness). **Darkness** here means not only wickedness but a realm of authority and power to which one may **belong.** Christians (Paul shifts from **you** to **we** in the middle of vs. 5) are **sons of light;** i.e. they belong to this field of force, this realm. Therefore the coming of the day (daylight) will not **surprise** them. By implication the coming of the day will not bring a reversal of their relation to God because as sons of light they are already of the day.

How close this passage stands to Jewish apocalyptic has been demonstrated by the Dead Sea Scrolls (cf. 1QS i.1-15; ii.16; iii.13-iv.26), among which is a document that spells out the final battle between the hosts of good and evil—The War of the Sons of Light and the Sons of Darkness. (See "The Dead Sea Scrolls," pp. 1163-71.) It must not be assumed, of course, that Paul knew or used this document; he simply shared the apocalyptic inheritance from contemporary Judaism.

5:6-7. *Watchfulness.* Paul carries further his allegorical treatment of "night life": Christians are to be alert to the times in which they live and to what they demand. Night and day suggest sleeping and waking; therefore Paul demands wakefulness. Keeping **awake** and going to **sleep** are metaphors of perceptiveness or lack of it (cf. Mark 13:32-37; 14:32-42). Being **sober** (cf. I Pet. 1:13; 4:7; 5:8) makes the same point. Having added sobriety to wakefulness as appropriate acts of daylight, Paul makes the same point in reverse; people **sleep** and **get drunk . . . at night.**

5:8-11. *The Goal of Salvation.* Paul shifts to military metaphors. Here the triad of **faith . . . love . . . hope** (see above on 1:3) is allegorized as defensive armor (cf. Eph. 6:10-17). Having mentioned **salvation** Paul goes on to say that this is the whole point of God's work—our salvation, not **wrath** (i.e. destruction). Vs. 10, however, turns the **wake or sleep** metaphor in still another direction. Returning to the theme of 4:13-18, Paul uses it to say that we will **live** with Christ whether we are dead or alive at the time of his coming. Vs. 11 restates the practical aim of the whole discussion.

The entire paragraph combines rhetorical subtlety with serious pastoral concern. In these 11 vss. Paul has insisted that the end cannot be calculated because it will come suddenly and without warning; this should not catch Christians off guard if they are alert to the ethical obligations of the present. A life of faith, hope, and love, with which the letter began, will be the best preparation for a future that cannot be known in advance. In this way Paul uses apocalyptic terminology and themes to turn back a developing curiosity about the time of the end. Though using apocalyptic tradition, Paul refuses to become an apocalyptic predictor; he remains a pastor.

D. Counsels for the Life of the Church (5:12-25)

This series of unconnected admonitions begins with attitudes toward church leaders and ends with a note of prayer.

5:12-14. *Respect for Church Leaders.* Paul speaks of the congregation and its leaders, addressing first the church as a whole, then the leadership. Significantly, he calls both groups **brethren,** the distinction between them being function rather than ordination. There were, strictly speaking, no laymen in the early church because there were no clergymen either. This is why I Thess. has no technical terms for the various offices, such as we find in Phil. 1:1; Eph. 4:11. The passage is also less specific than I Cor. 12:4-11. The fact that Paul deals with this matter at all suggests that Timothy reported (3:6) that such guidance was needed.

5:12-13. The leaders exercise 3 functions: they **labor** (a semi-technical term for spreading the gospel, as in 2:9), preside, and **admonish** (discipline). The congregation is to respect these men because of their work, their sole claim to authority. Paul's remarks imply that the church had some who, probably in the name of the Spirit, were unwilling to live with any structured responsibility. Paul recognized the need for order, but like the rest of early Christianity he did not know any priesthood or stratified membership in the church. This is markedly different from the community of the Dead Sea Scrolls, which was highly organized into priestly classes, and whose Manual of Discipline spelled out clearly the rights and privileges of the various ranks to which members were assigned. Such an approach to church order was not found among early Christians.

5:14. Many commentators see here 3 distinct groups which are causing difficulties: the **idle** (the word may also mean "disorderly"), explained as excited over the "coming" (see above on 4:11-12); the **fainthearted,** explained as worried about their dead relatives and their own salvation (thus making 4:13-5:11 addressed especially to them); and the **weak,** explained as the morally unstable. All this is possible, but it defines the groups much more clearly than the text warrants. These terms probably reflect not 3 groups, but 3 kinds of problems, here mentioned to balance rhetorically the 3 functions of the leaders. (Paul's style here, as elsewhere, reveals his predilection for carefully balanced sentences, a typical rhetorical touch to facilitate hearing perceptively the letter read orally—cf. vs. 27.) These problems may have resulted from the pressures which the young church has been facing (cf. 1:6; 3:1-5, 7) and the questions about the validity of the gospel which the deaths have raised. In such circumstances Paul urges the congregation to live peaceably and the leaders to be **patient.** The practical, pastoral concern of Paul is clear.

5:15-22. *Bases for Christian Living.* These vss. consist of brief admonitions addressed to the whole church and, though Paul does not say so, show how the church can move forward to actualize the counsels he has just given.

5:15. Paul mentions first the need for a creative response to **evil** deeds. **Seek to do good to one another** is milder than the Greek, which says rather "pursue the good for one another." Paul spells out this same point in Rom. 12:17-21. Here he adds **and to all,** lest Christians do good only to one another. Paul compresses what Jesus said more fully (Matt. 5:38-48); whether he is consciously dependent on Jesus' teaching here is not known.

5:16-18. These 3 admonitions are characterized by the note of constancy: **rejoice . . . pray . . . give thanks.** The **will of God** refers to all 3.

5:19-20. We do not know if Paul is aiming here at particular abuses in the church. Interestingly, he encourages the readers not to **quench the Spirit;** later he will ask the Corinthians to channel the Spirit without despising the ecstatic manifestations of it (I Cor. 12–14, esp. 14:37-40). Vs. 20 makes virtually the same point, since in Paul's view **prophesying** (probably articulating in a coherent and rational way the will of God or the "word" of the Lord, as in I Cor. 14:20-33) is a work of the Spirit.

5:21-22. Vs. 21 reads like a proverb; in this setting it may mean that prophesying is to be tested to determine **what is good** enough to follow. If so, Paul is making the same prudent point as I John 4:1, though Paul does not supply any criterion for testing the Spirit as does John; he assumes that what is good will be self-evident. The demand that Christians keep from **every form of evil** balances rhetorically the previous demand to hold to the good. These directions are designed to furnish the young church with basic moral standards.

5:23-25. *Injunctions to Pray.* Paul closes this section with a prayerful wish for the readers, balanced by the brief request that they, in turn, pray for him and his associates. Vs. 23*a* returns to the theme of sanctification (cf. 4:3), thus setting the whole exhortation section into a framework of sanctification, just as the first 3 chs. were framed with the emphasis on thanksgiving. Vs. 23*b* not only picks up the theme of the coming again, but is the only place in the NT where the triadic nature of man is stated as **spirit and soul and body.** This should not be pressed, since it is not really typical of Paul to divide men into 3 parts, even though he can use these terms. Here the phrase is a rhetorical expression to interpret **wholly;** more than this should not be made of it. Vs. 24 reminds the readers that if the prayer is answered it is because of the faithfulness of God; Paul prays for the end toward which God is working. His prayer makes the same point and serves the same function in the section as the prayer in 3:11-13.

IV. FAREWELL (5:26-28)

The **holy kiss** (vs. 26) apparently was a customary part of early Christian worship, though almost nothing is known of the practice itself (cf. Rom. 16:16; I Cor. 16:20; II Cor. 13:12; I Pet. 5:14). Vs. 27 shows 2 things: (*a*) the seeds of factionalism may have been germinating to such an extent that Paul emphasizes **all the brethren;** (*b*) Paul's letters were intended to be read publicly, doubtless as part of worship, right from the start (cf. Col. 4:16). Vs. 28 is one of Paul's briefer benedictions.

THE SECOND LETTER
OF PAUL TO THE THESSALONIANS
Leander E. Keck

Introduction

Whereas the occasion and purpose of I Thess. are relatively simple to discover, the problems of II Thess. are so complex that no completely satisfactory solution to them has been found though they have been discussed since 1798.

The traditional view is that shortly after Paul wrote I Thess. news reached him that the 2 particular problems to which he had addressed himself—the end of history and the idle Christians—had not lessened but had grown more serious. In response Paul is said to have written II Thess. This traditional view is by far the most widely held. Many see that a strong case cannot be made for it but think that any alternative is even weaker.

The Problematical Relationship Between I and II Thess. There are 5 major issues. (*a*) The eschatology, or doctrine of last things, of II Thess. is crucial because the view of the end set forth in ch. 2 does not appear to agree with I Thess. 4–5. In the latter Paul argues that there is no warning, no hint of when the end will come. II 2, on the other hand, not only tells what signs to look for but also insists that Paul had already discussed this very point when he was in Thessalonica. Many have tried to show that these chs. can be harmonized. However, the real question is whether each ch. assumes what the other chs. say. This commentary does not make this assumption. In any event the material in II 2 is traditional Jewish apocalyptic, which is slightly Christianized and generally ignored in I Thess. (see Intro. to I Thess.).

(*b*) Closely related is a historical issue. 2:3-4 says that the "man of lawlessness" will occupy the temple and claim to be God. If this refers to Caligula's attempt to have a statue of himself erected in the Jerusalem temple in A.D. 40, one could argue that Paul (a decade later) is interpreting either that episode or an interpretation of it as a sign of the times. On the other hand, the passage is clearly related to Mark 13:14-27 (written around A.D. 70 but using older material), and both depend on Dan. (cf. e.g. Dan. 7:25; 8:25; 11:36). Therefore 2:3-4 could simply be using a traditional item in Jewish apocalyptic with no immediate historical referent at all. If so, the reference to the temple does not require a date prior to A.D. 70, when the temple burned.

(*c*) While some are impressed by the problematical contents of II Thess., others focus on the literary relation between the 2 letters. All students are struck by the fact that these 2 letters are more alike in wording and even in sequence of themes than any

2 undisputed letters of Paul (Col. and Eph. are similar, but Eph. is disputed). But they differ precisely where one would expect them to be alike: the relation of Paul to the readers. Whereas I Thess. is warm and personal, II is distant and formal; whereas I Thess. spends 3 chs. dealing with Paul's work in Thessalonica, II ignores this completely, except for 2:5, and has no personal touch. Would the same man write a letter such as II Thess. to the same church soon after he wrote such a letter as I Thess.?

(*d*) The theological teaching in ch. 1 says Christians will escape the judgment of God while unbelievers will be doomed to eternal destruction. In Rom. 14:10-12; II Cor. 5:10, however, Paul speaks of Christians before God's judgment seat. Nowhere else does Paul speak of God's vengeance on unbelievers; this is, however, a basic apocalyptic theme as found in Rev.

(*e*) Finally, there is the issue of pseudepigraphy, or writing in someone else's name. This practice was widespread in the ancient world, and the Christian church followed it rather extensively. II Thess. itself raises the question twice. In 2:1-2 the author mentions a letter claiming Paul as author which holds that the day of the Lord has already come. In 3:17, moreover, the author tries to authenticate his letter by appealing to the handwriting. In I Cor. 16:21 Paul stops dictating to take up the pen to write a personal greeting; yet in this letter, which makes no attempt at authority, he makes no attempt to authenticate the letter, even though I Cor. was written after II Thess. was (if genuinely Pauline) and after it had been circulated. Likewise in Gal. 6:11 Paul calls attention to the size of his handwriting but says nothing about authenticating the letter by this means. Moreover, this external criterion is irrelevant anyway, since all letters were penned by scribes. Besides, II Thess. assumes that no personal messenger brought the letter but that it arrived impersonally, through the mail so to speak, and had to gain acceptance as best it could.

All these considerations taken together persuade this author that the letter is not from Paul. Those who claim II Thess. is genuine must explain why a letter claiming Paul's name would have circulated within weeks after I Thess. was written—or else make Paul speak of a hypothetical letter—and why the readers who had just read I Thess. and who remembered Paul the way I Thess. says would not know how to tell what was Pauline. The advocates of the traditional view seem to have failed to do this.

These 5 arguments, then, make a compelling case against the genuineness of II Thess. as a Pauline letter. If we had either I or II Thess. alone, there would be no problem; it is precisely our having them both that makes the problem acute, and it is precisely the fact that I Thess. is genuine that shows that II is not.

Purpose, Place, and Date. Why then was II Thess. written? The clue is 2:1-4—a letter had circulated which claimed that Paul taught that the day of the Lord had already come. II Thess. opposes that letter by arguing that Paul did not hold this view because the necessary preliminary events of which he spoke had not yet occurred. The author wants to provide a definitive Pauline rebuttal for a misrepresentation of Paul. II Thess. reflects the struggle of the later church for a correct understanding of Paul. The author used as a model the one letter of Paul's which contained apocalyptic material and which was not as well known as I Cor., viz. I Thess. II Thess. really has nothing to do with the church at Thessalonica—unless it was written there. The exact time and place of writing are unknown; A.D. 75-90 seems adequate. The letter was accepted as genuine from the time it was circulated. No one in the ancient church questioned it. This does not prove it is Pauline, as many think, but only that the author succeeded in what he set out to do.

Arguments for Pauline Authorship. Those who hold the letter to be genuine either take the traditional view (see above) or one of the following variants: (a) Silas wrote it, having been told generally by Paul what to discuss. This is really a way of saying yes and no at the same time. (b) Paul wrote II Thess. to Jewish Christians in the church but I Thess. to the Gentile wing. This view is discredited because

Top: Buildings of modern Salonika with the arch of emperor Galerius immediately to the left (*cf.* ill. p. 866)

Bottom: Ruins of the ancient marketplace of Thessalonica with buildings of modern Salonika in the background

Paul would never have founded a segregated church (cf. Gal. 2). (c) II Thess. was sent to Beroea. This is possible but without any evidence whatever. (d) II Thess. was sent to Philippi. Evidence for this is too slight to be persuasive. (e) II Thess. was written first, then I Thess. This fails to account for the fact that I Thess. is more personal.

These varying suggestions actually support the view that II Thess. is not genuinely Pauline, for they all show that the traditional view cannot account for the phenomena of I and II Thess. The real test of the view advocated here is whether the letter makes sense on the assumption that it was written in the name of Paul but not by him. The value and insight of II Thess. of course do not depend on whether or not Paul was the author.

For Further Study: Commentaries by J. E. Frame, 1912, William Neil, 1950, Leon Morris, 1959. J. W. Bailey in *IB*, 1955. J. W. Bowman, "Eschatology of the NT"; H. K. McArthur, "Parousia"; F. W. Beare, "Thess." in *IDB*, 1962.

I. Greeting (1:1-2)

This greeting is very similar to that of I Thess., on which it is modeled.

II. The Thanksgiving (1:3-2:17)

The author follows Paul's structure of I Thess., in which the thanksgiving forms the bulk of the letter (cf. I Thess. 1:2-3:13). Just as I Thess. 2:13 repeats the thanksgiving formula of 1:2, so II 2:13 restates 1:3. There are 2 differences however. (a) The thanksgiving of I Thess. moves back and forth between statements about the readers and those about the author. This gives the letter its personal tone. In II, however, the thanksgiving has few personal touches and says nothing which has not already been said of the readers in I Thess. (b) In contrast with I Thess., the apocalyptic material has been moved from the 2nd section of the letter to the middle of the thanksgiving (2:1-12). No other Pauline thanksgiving is used as a setting for straightforward theological exposition. Apparently I Thess. was the model for II, but the writer abandoned his pattern at just those points where he was out of touch with the living situation of the historical Paul (see Intro.).

The thanksgiving may be divided into 3 parts: (a) After a brief reference to the church's founding, attention shifts to the impending punishment for those who are not Christians, 1:3-12. (b) The signs of the times are taken up in 2:1-12. (c) The section closes with another statement of thanks, followed by a prayer for the readers—standard elements in Pauline thanksgivings—2:13-17.

A. Gratitude for the Church's Fidelity (1:3-12)

The structure of the thanksgiving is obscured by the RSV, which begins a paragraph at vs. 5, and by the NEB, which begins one at vs. 6, perhaps because each phrase of the long sentence (in Greek, vss. 3-10 are one sentence) leads into another set of ideas. The whole sentence draws heavily on OT ideas and phrases.

1:3. The formality of the letter is seen in that whereas I Thess. 1:2 says, "We give thanks to God always," II says, **We are bound to give thanks,** and adds, **as is fitting.** Instead of Paul's immediate response of thanks, the author speaks of a judicious, proper act of thanks because **faith** and **love** are growing (cf. I Thess. 1:2-3).

1:4. The church is lauded for its character in persecution. If II Thess. were a genuine letter from Paul, this would be the oldest reference to the persecution of Christians; **afflictions** and difficulties are mentioned in I Thess. 1:6; 3:3, but not persecution (assuming I Thess. 2:14-16 is an interpolation; see comment). II Thess., then, is to be seen as part of early Christian literature of persecution situations. This gives an urgency to the argument. It also points to a date later than A.D. 51, when I Thess. was written.

1:5-7a. The Judgment of God. This section interprets the persecution situation, while vss. 7b-10 describe in detail what has been asserted theologically. The real point of vss. 5-7a is that this persecution situation demonstrates the **righteous judgment of God;** the passage, then, is a kind of theodicy—a rationale for the justice of God. In keeping with the biblical view, the justice of God's ways is vindicated at the end of history rather than by arguing the rightness of things now.

The **evidence** of the righteous judgment of God which the author sees is probably the whole situation, not merely Christian fortitude. Being related to the kingdom brings the **suffering** which in turn makes one **worthy of the kingdom.** This is one side of the situation; vss. 6-7a give the other. The righteous judgment of God will afflict the afflicters and relieve the **afflicted.** Because the judgment of God reverses the present, the future lies with those who are presently persecuted. Hence being made steadfast in persecution is a sign of the righteousness of God, a hint of what God's judgment will do. Such an attitude toward suffering is rooted in the martyr theology of Dan., reaffirmed by Jesus (Matt. 5:10-12) and ratified by the cross and Resurrection.

1:7b-10. The Revelation of the Lord Jesus. These vss. spell out the time and character of the future judgment in which the roles of the afflicted and the afflicters are reversed. They speak in turn of the time, the event, and the persons involved (both non-Christian and Christian) and their respective destinies, and then return to the theme of the indefinite time when these things will happen.

1:7b. The time will be at the "revelation," or as the RSV translates, **when the Lord Jesus is revealed from heaven,** a reference to the "coming" (2:1; cf. I Cor. 1:7; I Thess. 2:19; 3:13; 4:15-18; 5:23; I Pet. 1:7, 13). Speaking of the end events as the "revelation" implies that matters are decided already; that history as we see it contradicts, in part, the existing lordship of Christ which will be finally unveiled then. The awesome character of this disclosure, or revelation, of Christ is conveyed by the 3 phrases that define it: **from heaven,** with **angels,** in **flaming fire** (a standard element for divine judgment in apocalyptic literature).

1:8-10. Whom this act of God will affect and what it will be are dealt with in these vss. The unbelievers are described as those **who do not know God** and **who do not obey the gospel.** The 1st phrase (cf. Jer. 10:25) was a standard Jewish designation for

Gentiles (cf. I Thess. 4:5); the 2nd is found only in Rom. 10:16 and thus is used to defend the Pauline authorship of II Thess. The 2 phrases probably do not refer to 2 groups (Gentiles and unbelievers) but to 1 group: the non-Christians. Their fate is **eternal destruction.** This destruction is **exclusion from the presence of the Lord.** The author is in the Hebrew tradition (he borrows from Isa. 2:10), in which being related to God and being in his presence express fulfilled existence. One cannot be cut off from God without being annihilated, for God makes existence possible.

Precisely what will be the destiny of the believers is not stated; by implication theirs is the opposite of destruction (salvation). God will be **glorified in** them and **marveled at** by them. This can only occur if they are in the presence of God (opposite of being cut off). Here it is God who will be glorified, not the believers. The time of this reversal will be **on that day,** a phrase which the Greek text leaves dangling at the end to show that the whole complex of events stands in the indefinite future, an important hint of the emphasis of ch. 2.

1:11-12. *Prayer for God's Blessing.* These vss. complete the first section of the thanksgiving by picking up the theme of the readers' "worthiness" of God's action toward them (cf. vss. 3, 5). The **call** refers to their coming to **faith,** not to death by martyrdom (see comments on I Thess. 1:4; 4:7-8). The author asks that God bring to fulfillment their **every good resolve and work of faith** in the midst of persecution, so that Christ and Christians will **be glorified** in one another. The norm of God's activity toward man is the **grace** of Christ, a standard emphasis in the Pauline tradition.

This complex paragraph uses Jewish apocalyptic tradition to illumine a situation of a persecuted church. It encourages Christians by setting their present moment against the horizon of God's future.

This is a stern comfort, for God's vindicating act is said to be vindictive. Nothing is said of the positive, constructive function of God's wrath, nor are Christians summoned to a creative response to suffering.

B. EVENTS OF THE END TIME (2:1-12)

The purpose of the letter is revealed in this passage. It is not an easy passage to understand because its argument is obscure, the terms vague, and the grammar not clear. The passage has no evident relation to what precedes or what follows, though it discusses "when he comes" (1:10). Vss. 1-2 state the problem; vss. 3-4 make the rebuttal; vss. 5-12 develop the rebuttal. The entire discussion concentrates on a single point: the time of the end. The passage is not really an apocalypse, however, but uses apocalyptic material to defend orthodox eschatology. Though vs. 5—which says Paul had already taught all this—is questionable, it is at least clear that the author assumes the readers know the apocalyptic tradition.

The passage must be seen as a whole. The author uses apocalyptic ideas to oppose the radical anti-apocalyptic teaching circulating in Paul's name. In a sense the author does not really deal with the problem, for he requires the readers to agree with his conception of **the day of the Lord** before they can discuss whether or not it has come. But if a different understanding of the day is itself at issue, then his argument does not touch the matter. On the other hand, at a deeper level he does deal with the question because he insists (only implicitly, of course) that what the opposing view means by the day of the Lord is not the day of the Lord but only the present Christian anticipation of it. He holds that whatever is the richness of the present life in Christ, one must not restrict the meaning of salvation to believers only or to the present. Such a view of salvation severely limits the lordship of Jesus. This lordship, however, must eliminate all resistance to God sometime or else remain unfulfilled.

This passage has endured much at the hands of interpreters. The ancient church allegorized the **temple** (vs. 4) as the church and therefore saw the rebellion as heresy. The Protestant Reformers saw the **lawless one** as the Pope. Premillennialists down through the years have identified the lawless one with the political or religious opponent of the moment.

Historical-critical study of this passage, however, insists that it be read together with all apocalyptic literature and that it be regarded as a distinctive theological interpretation of God, the cosmos, and Christ. However, many do not see that this makes it unnecessary to ask whether the author meant the restrainer (vs. 7) to be the Roman Empire, as many think—or even Paul's mission to the Gentiles, as a few hold. The terms of the passage belong to the "furniture of apocalyptic." This passage is not an apocalyptic allegory of a historical moment in the life of Paul or the early church; rather it is a theological interpretation of the problem of history seen in the light of Christ's lordship and the oneness of God. This interpretation is made in the apocalyptic mode of thought and designed to displace an alternative. Pursuing questions about what historical contemporary figures the text may refer to not only is beside the point but leads away from it.

2:1-2. *Statement of the Problem.* These vss. state the problem and set the tone: the author wants to prevent confusion in the church over a point of view. Four things may be noted. (*a*) The author states a double problem: the **coming** (cf. I Thess. 4:13-18) and **our assembling to meet him.** "Assembling" here is a technical term (as is the verb in Mark 13:27). In apocalyptic literature it refers to the final gathering together of Israel out of the dispersion (cf. II Macc. 2:7); here it is applied to Christians. This theme can be fitted into I Thess. 4:13-18, though Paul neither mentions nor implies a Christian gathering together just prior to the coming. In any case, having stated these topics, the author ignores them; instead he deals with what might happen first.

(*b*) The controversial teaching holds **that the day of the Lord has come.** This must not be weakened to "the day of the Lord is near." Apparently this teaching held the same view combatted in II Tim. 2:18. Early Christianity generally existed in a tension between the salvation already accessible here and now through Jesus' resurrection and the gift of the Spirit (this is why Paul speaks of the Spirit as a down payment, II Cor. 5:5), and the full salvation when all history and all the cosmos would be redeemed and God's kingship fulfilled. This was a tension between the "already" because of Christ's resurrection and the "not yet" until his coming.

The teaching combatted here apparently dissolved the above-mentioned tension by holding that full salvation was available here and now and dismissing the future categorically. This view, probably some form of gnosticism, may have emphasized the sacraments as means of grasping complete salvation now. Based partly on ancient Greek philosophy and partly on Near Eastern mythology, gnosticism was a movement whose adherents claimed to have saving *gnosis,* or knowledge, from Christ. It invaded the Christian churches and became a major threat in the 2nd cent. (see "The Greco-Roman Background of the NT," pp. 1037-44). Because this was a movement and a mood more than a rival organization or church, it had many forms and interests. Thus it is difficult to trace with certainty today.

The movement opposed by II Thess. was a radical transformation of the gospel in which the future redemption of the whole world was given up for the sake of the present salvation of the believers. This new teaching in effect repudiated not merely a future consummation but the redemption of history as a whole and of nature as such. Instead it championed full salvation here and now for those saved individuals who partook of the sacramental means. On this basis Jesus is not the Lord of the cosmos nor of history but only of the saved souls.

(*c*) How might one come to such a position? Vs. 2 mentions 3 possibilities: **spirit, . . . word,** or **letter.** The RSV and NEB assume that **from us** goes only with the letter; it might also go with all 3. Here **spirit** does not refer to speaking in tongues (as in I Cor. 14) but to prophecy (as in I Thess. 5:19-20). If Paul's authority stands behind this too, then someone claims that by inspiration Paul said that the day of full salvation is here, but if Paul's authority is claimed only for the letter, then some other teacher claims that the Spirit led him to precisely this point, that the present ecstatic experience makes the future irrelevant. **Word** can mean either a tradition or an argument. For the problem of the **letter** see the Intro.

2:3-4. *Rebuttal of a False Teaching.* Here is the heart of the rebuttal: the end cannot be here because the 2 things that must happen 1st have not happened: the **rebellion** and the rise of the **man of lawlessness.** "Rebellion" became a technical theological term (*the* rebellion) for the consummation of the cosmic opposition to God which began, in apocalyptic thought, with the revolt of the angels before creation. The text thus refers to the general widespread repudiation of religion which the anti-God forces will bring about just before the end (cf. II Tim. 3:5; Rev. 13:3-4; Didache 16:3-4). This conception of accelerating opposition to God which issues in a cosmic Armageddon was standard in Jewish apocalyptic tradition. The author stands in this tradition and claims that because the rebellion has not yet occurred the end cannot have come. He also speaks of the anti-God person, commonly referred to as "antichrist" (named only in I John 2:18, 22; 4:3; II John 7; cf. Rev. 13, where he is called simply "the beast"). The text gives him a double name: **man of lawlessness** (some manuscripts read "man of sin") and the **son of perdition.**

2:4. Because the enemy **opposes and exalts himself,** he is the paragon of sin as the Bible understands it. His self-exaltation goes against everything religious, i.e. he opposes religion as such. He does it, however, in the name of religion; the capstone of his work is his self-enthronement in the **temple.** Irreligion will take over the worship of God; here is the utter nadir of God's sovereignty. Not until then can the end come. At the lowest point, however, God will assert himself so as to make his triumph clear and complete.

2:5-12. *Development of the Rebuttal.* The exposition of this answer to the false teaching (not attributed to the enemy as in I John) tells of the **coming of the lawless one** (vs. 9) and the purpose of his coming.

2:5. This vs. is transitional, claiming that Paul had already taught all this (see Intro.).

2:6-7. Vs. 6 explains why matters are not yet as bad as they will be—the restrainer is at work too. The way the text shifts from **what is restraining him** (vs. 6) to **he who now restrains** (vs. 7) is intriguing. The readers are expected to know what and who are being discussed, if indeed it is anyone in particular. The restrainer holds the rebellion in check until the enemy is **revealed in his time.** That forces and persons have their times allotted to them is a fundamental claim of apocalyptic. If the enemy is being checkmated, he must **already** be **at work,** as vs. 7 actually says in speaking of the **mystery of lawlessness.** Hence the impending revolt will actually bring into full tide the forces already at work but now checked.

2:8-10. These vss. deal with the climax of the struggle. Vs. 8 picks up the note of the revelation of the antichrist as stated in vs. 6 but insists immediately that **the Lord Jesus will slay him.** The **breath of his mouth** (cf. Isa. 11:4) probably means that a mere breath will be sufficient. Here is another title for the enemy: **lawless one,** who works by Satan's power (the enemy is not **Satan** himself but his earthly agent). Significantly in vs. 9 the lawless one will have his **coming** just as Christ will have his (vs. 8). Satanic power will support the lawless one by spurious miracles (vs. 9) and moral **deception** (vs. 10) which will lead followers to death. The writer sees that miracles in themselves have nothing to do with the truth. This double stratagem of false **signs** and deceit will work because those who are already under the sway of death will grasp for it, not perceiving the deception. They cannot distinguish truth from falsehood because they do not **love the truth** (cf. John 3:19).

2:11-12. Ultimately this failure to understand is traceable to God himself. Here the relationship between the culpability of man and the sovereignty of God is at its sharpest: God causes man to be misled so that those who are misled **may be condemned** (vss. 11-12). A similar relationship is argued by Paul (Rom. 9–11; esp. 9:6-32, where Pharaoh is as much the instrument of God as is Moses).

We may shrink from such theology until we see that a strict monotheistic faith compels such a conclusion, for if God alone is finally responsible for the whole of human history, he cannot share ultimate responsibility with anyone else, including Satan. If opposition to God were not traced in some logical way to God himself, it would be traced to a counter-god. There is no completely satisfactory answer to such problems. The least objectionable view holds that God, the one ultimately responsible, tolerates evil for the sake of some degree of freedom of choice for man. Since the text speaks of the final conquest of **Satan,** it must also grant that Satan has no ultimate independent existence (lest he be made into a 2nd god) but actually maintains his revolt only as a parasite whom God has tolerated for his allotted time. The Lord at *his* coming will annihilate the opposition and thereby consummate the sovereignty of God.

C. Thanks Restated (2:13-17)

2:13. The transition from vs. 12 is abrupt. Vs. 13 begins precisely as 1:3—the readers are called **beloved by the Lord** (cf. I Thess. 1:4). The phrase is interpreted immediately: being beloved by God means being chosen by him for salvation. On the sanctifying work of the **Spirit** see the comment on I Thess. 4:3-6. The **belief in the truth** (vs. 13) apparently intends to be a contrast with the unbelievers in vs. 10.

2:14. This vs. restates vs. 13*b,* this time speaking of God's saving work as his calling (see comment on I Thess. 2:9-12). That God's call is through the gospel is never said by Paul, though he doubtless assumed it. Whereas the goal of God's choosing in vs. 13 is salvation, in vs. 14 it is restated as the achievement of the **glory of Christ** (cf. I Thess. 4:7-8).

2:15. Here the need to cling to the tradition of what Paul has taught, a basic theme of the letter, is repeated. Once more the author refers to the Pauline authority of **word** or **letter.** Had Paul written this, he probably would have referred more clearly to "my former letter" or some such phrase. The text refers to Paul's letters much more generally, however, and so implies that the readers know of more than one. This was the case in the post-Pauline period in which the letter was written.

2:16-17. These vss. end the 1st section with a prayer just as I Thess. 3:11-13 ends the 1st section of that letter (see Intro.). Here God, who has already **loved** and given **eternal comfort and good hope,** is also asked to encourage and strengthen in **work and word.**

III. Exhortation (3:1-15)

This section reads almost as if it were a farewell; actually it is a transition to the major problem of the ch. There is no real unity of thought in these vss. but rather a series of ideas.

A. Request for Prayer (3:1-5)

3:1-2. Vss. 1-2 begin as I Thess. 4:1 begins, but whereas I Thess. puts the request for prayer for Paul at the end of the letter (I Thess. 5:25), this author not only moves it forward to this point but also spells out the aim of the prayer: continued success of the gospel (**the word of the Lord;** cf. I Thess. 1:8) and the rescue of Paul **from wicked and evil men.** What the 2nd point actually means is not clear. Those who assume II Thess. is from Paul think he is speaking of the Jews who opposed him

(cf. Acts 18:5-17). Actually the text is much too general to be certain of any identification. If Paul did not write the letter, then the phrases reflect the author's attempt to create the appearance of genuineness, just as vs. 17 does. Vs. 2*b* reveals this artificiality, since Paul himself would scarcely have grounded the need for deliverance in such a truism as this.

3:3. Here the author shifts to the readers and picks up the last word of vs. 2 to contrast the faithfulness of God with the lack of faith among men. The RSV is uncertain whether the text speaks of "evil" or of "the evil one" (NEB). The latter is preferable. This vs. may have in mind the Lord's Prayer (Matt. 6:13). If this is the case, as is probable, we may see here the influence of Christian worship. The author promises no escape from the evil one but defense against him. It is precisely here that the fidelity of the Lord (presumably Lord Jesus) is actualized.

3:4-5. Vs. 4 expresses the author's **confidence** that the readers will respond to what is being written, though vss. 14-15 reveal a more realistic picture. Vs. 5 asks that the Lord guide the readers' wills (**hearts**) to the **love of God and to the steadfastness of Christ.** It is not clear whether in these 2 phrases **of** refers to God's love or man's love for God on the one hand, or to Christ's endurance or the human endurance generated by Christ on the other.

B. The Idle (3:6-15)

This section deals with a problem discussed briefly in I Thess. 4:11-12; 5:14. If II Thess. were genuinely from Paul, one would conclude that the problem in Thessalonica grew much worse in a short time. On the other hand, if II Thess. is not from Paul but from a follower of his, this section reveals either the persistence of a problem into later decades or the author's efforts to imitate Paul. Probably both are at work here. This section calls for disciplining the idle by ostracism. Vs. 6 states the point (restated in vss. 14-15); vss. 7-10 deal with Paul's prior work in Thessalonica; vss. 11-13 give positive counsel.

3:6. The author points out that what follows has the authority of Christ behind it. Whereas I Thess. 5:14 asked the church to admonish the idlers, here the text calls for dissociation from them. However they are not to be excluded or condemned as the man in Corinth (I Cor. 5:1-5), for this action is intended as an admonition to a brother (vs. 15). The object of this action is **any brother who is living in idleness.** The word lit. means "disorderly," but the discussion as a whole shows that the disorderliness consists in refusing to work for a living, with the common result that idle hands make mischief (vs. 11). As throughout II Thess., the problem is traced to a disregard for Paul's teaching, here spoken of technically as **the tradition that you received from us.**

3:7-10. The explanation of this tradition begins by calling attention to the need to imitate Paul, but in contrast with I Thess. 1:6 (see comment) what is to be imitated here is Paul's manual **labor**—the author is trying to write like Paul, but he changes Paul's meaning! Vs. 8 refers to the labor and independence of Paul while in Thessalonica, while vs. 9

says Paul gave up his **right** to be supported by the church (cf. I Cor. 9) so that he might be independent and set **an example.** The wording of vs. 8 depends on I Thess. 2:9 (see comment); that of vs. 9 is entirely the author's own idea. The **command** of vs. 10 sounds like a proverb. The origin of vs. 10 is unknown.

3:11-13. These vss. address the idlers themselves and ask them to go to work. The author's pun is caught by the Moffatt translation: "Some . . . are loafing, busybodies instead of busy." Vs. 13 is general advice whose precise point is not clear in this context.

3:14-15. Cf. Matt. 18:15-17.

IV. Farewell (3:16-18)

The final prayer (vs. 16) echoes I Thess. 5:23. **Peace** is emphasized here because it is the fitting alternative to the disorders which have just been discussed. For vs. 17 see the Intro. The benediction (vs. 18) repeats (except for **all**) that of I Thess.

THE FIRST LETTER
OF PAUL TO TIMOTHY

Eric Lane Titus

Introduction

I, II Timothy and Titus have been known as the "Pastoral epistles" since the early part of the 18th cent. The name is appropriate, for the letters obviously were written by a pastor to pastors. However, they are not pastoral in the sense that they cover the wide range of church affairs. Rather, like all NT books, they grow out of the immediate and pressing problems of their time and speak to those problems. This means that the number of "pastoral" problems dealt with is limited and determined by the situation confronting the readers for whom they were intended.

Historical Situation and Purpose. A number of problems posed for the early church are reflected in the Pastorals. There is some indication of pressure from the state; e.g. II 4:6-8 presents the language of martyrdom: "For I am already on the point of being sacrificed." But the threat of persecution is not a pervasive theme. Rather one has a sense of "the church against the world," the world—or this "present age"—being decidedly hostile. The world is the "enemy" (I 5:14); Demas has fallen in love with "this present world" (II 4:10); Christians stand in sharp contrast to the world, since they are God's people (Tit. 2:14). On the other hand at certain points Christians are to adjust to the world: Slaves are to be submissive and obedient to their masters (Tit. 2:9-10); Christians are likewise to be obedient to "rulers and authorities" (Tit. 3:1). In both cases obedience is held up as exemplary conduct befitting a Christian. The Pastorals also reflect problems with respect to the customs of the time—e.g. the subordination of women—and with respect to morals.

The overarching concern of the Pastorals, however, is with certain heretical teachings which have invaded the church. These teachings had their source in oriental dualism which flowed into the Mediterranean world and united with Hellenistic thought to produce a diffuse and complex movement known as Gnosticism (see "The Greco-Roman Background of the NT," pp. 1037-44). The movement, at first fluid and unstable, by the middle of the 2nd cent. A.D. became systematized in great Gnostic systems. The Pastorals view the impingement of this movement on the church as a severe threat to Christianity.

Until recently knowledge of Gnosticism was available solely through Christian sources, esp. Irenaeus' great work Against Heresies (*ca.* 180). But in 1946 there was discovered at Nag Hamadi in Upper Egypt a library of 49 Gnostic writings, including the now famous Gospel of Thomas. These documents give firsthand materials on Gnosticism and show more clearly the nature of the movement, which evidently posed a considerable threat to Christianity in the early cents. The degree of development represented by the Gnosticism reflected in the Pastorals is a good question; but certainly the letters reflect the basic dualism of the Gnostic position, in which matter was considered evil and spirit good. This position led naturally into a view that the material universe, including human beings clothed in flesh, was evil. It led in actual practice in either of 2 directions, asceticism or libertinism.

Salvation in Gnosticism was dependent on a special kind of revealed knowledge; in a sense it was self-knowledge, the knowledge of man as spirit as he was before his imprisonment in flesh. Salvation was accomplished through the descent from heaven of a savior or redeemer who brought knowledge of the heavenly or spiritual world and thereby enabled men to escape the prison house of flesh.

Since the major concern of the Gnostics was the problem of evil, they addressed themselves to the question of creation: How could a good God create an evil world? Some held that the universe was created by an inferior deity, the Demiurge, identified by Marcion as the god of the OT. The Gnostic view of matter as evil also created a problem with respect to Jesus. Since flesh as matter was evil, Jesus, they argued, could not have possessed a material body. Consequently Jesus' body of flesh only *seemed* to exist; it had no concrete reality. Those who held this view were the Docetists.

It would appear that this kind of philosophical-religious viewpoint lies behind the polemic of the Pastorals. By the middle of the 2nd cent. it had taken specific forms, as in the system of Valentinus. But before that time, undoubtedly, its various elements impinged forcibly on the Christian church. Insistence on one God (I 2:5), on the goodness of things created by God (I 4:4), on Christ "manifested in the flesh" (I 3:16), on the status of the OT as scripture (II 3:15-17), on opposition to "what is falsely called knowledge" (I 6:20) points to Gnosticism as the crisis which prompted the writing of the Pastorals. This accounts too for the strong emphasis on true doctrine. This doctrine, and its expression in high moral living, is contrasted with the "godless chatter" (I 6:20) and moral laxity of the Gnostics.

Authorship. The Pastorals claim Paul as their author (I 1:1; II 1:1; Tit. 1:1). And indeed Pauline authorship has been maintained by the church since the 2nd half of the 2nd cent.—at that time by Theophilus of Antioch, Irenaeus, and the Muratorian Canon. Before then the evidence is uncertain. Tertullian says that Basilides and Marcion rejected the Pastorals, but the meaning of this is unclear; it may mean no more than that they were not acquainted with the letters.

Doubt of Paul's authorship of the Pastorals was first expressed by biblical scholars at the beginning of the 19th cent. The position that the letters are pseudonymous, i.e. written under an assumed name, has become increasingly accepted so that today in scholarly circles Pauline authorship is rarely advanced. This position grows out of the following considerations: (*a*) Relating the historical situation of the Pastorals with the career of Paul as set forth in Acts and in admittedly genuine letters of Paul is difficult. (*b*) Church organization seems to be more advanced than that reflected in Paul's letters, esp. with respect to church orders. (*c*) Gnosticism—and possibly Marcionism—seems far more in evidence than anything of the sort reflected in Paul's letters. (*d*) The great and characteristic Pauline doctrines have little or no place in the thought of the Pastorals. (*e*) Differences in style between the Pastorals and Paul's letters are notable; e.g. Paul finds difficulty in making the form of his writing conform to the spontaneity of his thought, but the sentences of the Pastorals are precise and their thoughts are matter-of-fact. (*f*) The vocabulary is not the vocabulary of Paul. (*g*) The formality of the letters is inconsistent with the close personal relation between Paul and his 2 associates.

These points taken cumulatively have to be considered in making a judgment on the question of authorship, and the problems involved in defending Pauline authorship in the face of them are very great. Most NT scholars today agree that the Pastorals are pseudonymous, that they represent important teachings of a date later than the time of Paul, and that they were written in the name and supposedly the spirit of the great apostle. Who the author was we cannot now know. What we can know of him must be derived from these 3 letters. In them he appears as the champion of a practical and well-disciplined religion of "works" which are in harmony with true doctrine. He might be characterized as the champion of orthodoxy in contrast to the dynamic religion of the Spirit which was characteristic of Paul. Yet when his orthodoxy is seen against the Gnostic danger which threatened Christianity, we must pay him a tribute for the service he rendered the Christian church.

It is possible that the Pastorals, though pseudonymous, contain genuine Pauline fragments, as a number of scholars believe. One of these has isolated 5— (*a*) Tit. 3:12-15; (*b*) II 4:13-15, 20-21*a;* (*c*) II 4:16-18*a;* (*d*) II 4:9-12, 22*b;* (*e*) II 1:16-18; 3:10-11; 4:1-2*a*, 5*b;* 4:6-8; 4:18*b*-19, 21*b*-22*a*—and integrated them into an intelligible relationship with Paul's career. Perhaps the reconstruction is too detailed, esp. the last list. But the possibility of the inclusion of some genuine fragments, esp. in II 4:9-18, remains strong.

Date of Composition. Since the situations mentioned in the letters cannot be fitted into the Acts account of Paul's career, those who maintain Pauline authorship generally assume that after 2 years of Roman imprisonment (Acts 28:30) he was released and returned to the E for a further period of ministry there, after which he suffered a 2nd imprisonment and martyrdom at Rome. According to this hypothesis the 3 letters were written during this post-Acts period and their date would be *ca.* 63-67.

When the letters are recognized as pseudonymous their date becomes problematical, and scholars have proposed dates all the way from soon after Paul's death to 180.

Some have argued that the martyr theme (II 4:6-8) indicates a time relatively late in the 2nd cent., in the reign of Antoninus Pius (138-61) or Marcus Aurelius (161-80); but it should be noted that the martyr theme is found as early as the gospels and Acts (e.g. Acts 7:54-60; 20:17-38). Stronger support for a late date might be suggested by the concern of the letters with the acute danger from a Gnostic heresy, which has been assumed to be close to the advanced system of Valentinus represented in his writings published early in the 2nd half of the 2nd cent. But the difficulty is that we cannot discern from the letters just how systematized and how advanced the Gnostic heresy they attack actually was. Gnostic elements were present in the environment of the early church long before the emergence of the great Gnostic systems (see comment on Phil. 3:1–4:1).

Some scholars believe that the warning against "contradictions," Greek *antitheseis*, in I 6:20 refers to Marcion's writing with this title published *ca.* 140. If so, a date for the Pastorals *ca.* the middle of the 2nd cent. would seem likely. Aside from this one passage, however, there is little in the Pastorals that appears directed against the distinctive emphases of Marcion.

An important consideration is the similarity of certain phrases in the Pastorals and in the epistle of Polycarp, bishop of Smyrna, to the church at Philippi. This epistle has generally been dated *ca.* 115, but a significant study of it has produced evidence that a major part of the content was not composed till *ca.* 135. Scholars are not agreed, however, on whether the alleged parallels indicate literary dependence or, if so, which depends on the other.

Another factor that has been much studied is the status of the office of bishop revealed in the Pastorals in comparison with the rather detailed portrait of that office in the 7 epistles of Ignatius, bishop of Antioch, written *ca.* 115. Since the Pastorals seem to show a more primitive stage of development than appears in the Ignatian letters, some date them a decade or more earlier, *ca.* the turn of the first cent. But can we assume that the development of church orders was in a straight line from Paul through the Pastorals to Ignatius, or that it went forward at the same pace in the various parts of the Mediterranean world?

It is therefore impossible to pinpoint the date when the Pastorals were written. Among the possibilities a general period within the first half of the 2nd cent. may be ventured with most confidence; and if Polycarp shows dependence on the Pastorals—for which among the several proposed evidences of date the strongest case can be made—the time can perhaps be narrowed to a few years earlier than 135.

Place of Composition. On the assumption that Paul wrote the letters, the place for II Tim. would be a prison in Rome (cf. 1:8, 12; 2:9; 4:6-7) and for I Tim. probably Macedonia (cf. 1:3). The locale of Tit. is uncertain, but Paul's plan to spend the winter in Nicopolis (3:12) might suggest a place somewhere in Achaia or Macedonia.

Some who consider the Pastorals pseudonymous, esp. those who view them as directed against Marcionism, have regarded Rome as their place of origin. Syria has been suggested but is only a possibility. The most likely place seems to be Ephesus, where Tim. is represented as being addressed (I 1:3), or some other place in Asia Minor, in view of the intense interest in this area shown in the documents themselves. It is probable that the author wrote out of concern for the situation in the churches with which he was personally acquainted and gave his work a geographical background to appeal to the readers he esp. had in mind.

The Question of Sequence. It cannot be assumed that the traditional order of the letters found in the NT today reproduces the sequence in which they were written. Naturally the 2 letters to Tim. are grouped together, leaving Titus to complete the whole. In general scholars have advanced 2 possibilities as to the original sequence of writing: (a) I, Tit., II; (b) II, Tit., I. The first order is held by those who accept Pauline authorship, and by some who do not, since it permits accommodation to the alleged 2nd Roman imprisonment and martyrdom of Paul—note the position in this sequence of II 4:6-8. The 2nd position is championed by the majority, who point to such matters as the development of church polity which this arrangement provides, the notable increase in the intensity of opposition to heresy, and a lessening of the personal elements—a feature natural to pseudonymous writings. Some scholars maintain that all the material was composed and published at one time as a single work in the form of 3 letters, but the more common view is that the author wrote 3 successive letters separated by intervals of time.

Pseudonymity in Antiquity. Ancient pseudonymous writing should not be equated with forgery. The numerous examples of this method in antiquity indicate that it was entirely acceptable and apparently frequently desirable. There are many Jewish examples (see "The Intertestamental Literature," pp. 1110-15) and the practice was current among Christians as well (see "Noncanonical Early Christian Writings," pp. 1144-49). Perhaps the desire for the authority attached to a great name was the paramount motivation. But it is also true that the author thought of himself as writing in the spirit of the earlier person and so did not consider his thoughts as a perversion of those of his hero. This is certainly true of the author of the Pastorals. Paul is his idol; Paul's position represents the true doctrine of the church; Paul is the supreme example of heroic living and dying; in the face of dangerous views and practices the church must be confronted with a norm of orthodoxy, and Paul provides the norm.

Recently it has been suggested that the reason the Pastorals were published under the name of Paul is that his letters were being assailed by Jewish Christians on the one hand and on the other were being suspected by some Gentile Christians because they were looked on with favor by the Gnostics. The Pastorals, speaking in Paul's name, become his defense, so that the influence of his writings should not be lost to the orthodox church by default.

It should be kept in mind that in addressing Tim. and Titus the author is writing to church leaders who are his contemporaries. These are not necessarily specific individuals but rather pastors who hold responsible positions in the churches of Asia Minor. The letters were written by a pastor for pastors, and through them to the church.

For Further Study. P. N. Harrison, *The Problem of the Pastoral Epistles,* 1921. E. F. Scott, *The Pastoral Epistles,* 1936. B. S. Easton, *The Pastoral Epistles,* 1947. F. D. Gealy in *IB,* 1955. J. C. Beker in *IDB,* 1962. C. K. Barrett, *The Pastoral Epistles,* 1963. J. N. D. Kelly, *The Pastoral Epistles,* 1963; maintains Pauline authorship.

I. Epistolary Intro. (1:1-7)

1:1. Salutation. The epistle leaves no doubt at the start that it speaks with the authority of an **apostle** and that that apostle is no less than **Paul** himself. Paul's apostleship, it declares, was instituted at the **command of God . . . and of Christ Jesus.** The claims of the historical Paul as to the legitimacy of his apostleship are reflected here (cf. Gal. 1:1, 11-12, 15). Ordinarily the NT speaks of Christ as **Savior,** but of course it assumes that God stands behind the saving event of Christ. **Hope** was an important concept for Paul and was basic to his eschatology, i.e. his doctrine of last things, in that for him salvation was eschatological. The eschatological element is in the Pastorals also, though it has lost some of the urgency found in Paul's letters; salvation seems to be both present and future.

1:2a. The letter is directed to **Timothy,** described as Paul's **true child in the faith** (cf. I Cor. 4:17). Acts 16:1, which refers to Tim. as already a disciple when found by Paul, seems to rule out the idea that he was Paul's "child" in the sense of convert. The general impression in the Pastorals is rather that Paul is an older man talking down to a younger man for whom he nevertheless has great respect. Perhaps this accounts for the "distance" between them; the author finds it a useful teaching device— the venerable Paul writing to the inexperienced Tim. Yet the element of mere age may be overstressed. Rather Paul speaks out of superiority of office; he is an apostle while Tim. is a subordinate. In any case Tim. is a devoted follower of Paul and in that sense his "child in the faith."

1:2b. The salutation closes with the familiar Pauline triad **grace, mercy, and peace.** In this setting they probably do no more than give the impression of Pauline authenticity; the typical theology of Paul, in which these elements form so important a part, is virtually missing in the Pastorals.

1:3-7. Charge to Tim. The historical note in vs. 3 serves 2 purposes: (a) to connect the letter with Paul's activities, though in a very general way (see

Intro.), and (*b*) to address it to **Ephesus,** probably the true center of intended readership (see Intro.), as instruction against heretical teachings.

These vss. set forth the real concern of the Pastorals, viz. deviations from the normative doctrine of "Paul," i.e. that embraced by the author himself. Precise identification of the heretical group or groups is impossible. Judaizing Christianity, Gnosticism, and Marcionism are possibilities. It is probable that elements found in all of these were present in the situation.

The reference to **myths and endless genealogies** is not given precise content in these letters. The author may have in mind the complex system of emanation from deity characteristic of Gnosticism. But it is notable that myths are closely related to Jewish law (cf. Tit. 1:14), and the same may be said for genealogies. The situation here is probably a syncretistic movement in which Gnostic and Jewish elements are intermingled. Over against this **different doctrine** the author urges **sound doctrine** (vs. 10) and **love that issues from a pure heart and a good conscience and sincere faith** (vs. 5). It is Tim.'s task, then, to guard the true faith in the presence of heretical threats.

II. Knowledge of the Truth (1:8–2:15

1:8-11. *Function of the Law.* The historical Paul's problem with the law is reflected here (cf. Rom. 7:12) but a different function for the law from that advanced by Paul is introduced. It is **not laid down for the just, but for the lawless and disobedient** people specified in the long list (vss. 9-10). The thought is that true Christians do not need the law—they stand above it—but the law holds evil men in check.

1:12-17. *Paul the Great Example.* These vss. turn the light on Paul himself as the perfect example of the faithful. He is pictured as the **foremost of sinners** (vs. 15), a reference to his pre-Christian days when he **acted ignorantly in unbelief** (vs. 13). Christ's saving power is fully exemplified in Paul, because in Paul's transformed life Jesus Christ displays his **perfect patience for an example to those who were to believe in him for eternal life** (vs. 16).

1:17. This doxology is intended to stress that God alone is supreme. The heretic Marcion held that the god of the OT was not the God of Jesus but an inferior deity. If the Pastorals are in part directed against this teaching, the emphasis on the sole sovereignty of God takes on added meaning. **King of ages** means that God is King both now and in the future; he is the eternal King. This stress on the one high God stands in marked contrast to the complex system of divine beings or emanations from deity advanced by the Gnostics.

1:18-20. *The Prophetic Utterances.* Tim. is charged by Paul to **wage the good warfare, holding faith and a good conscience.** But he does this in accordance with and inspired by the **prophetic utterances** (vs. 18), a reference no doubt to the activity of Christian prophets. Perhaps the author thinks of the appointment of Tim. to his work as having taken place in some such manner as described in the "setting apart" of Paul and Barnabas in Acts 13:1-4,

where prophets are present. The Greek word rendered **charge** is intended to stress Tim.'s appointment as not arbitrary but in accordance with God's purposes as made known through the prophetic utterances. Perhaps the meaning is that the prophetic utterances marked out Tim. for the work and that Paul's recognition of him as called of God came at that time. The reference may well be to the occasion of Tim.'s ordination.

1:19*b*-20. In contrast to the steadfastness of Tim. 2 men, **Hymenaeus** (cf. II 2:17) and **Alexander** (cf. II 4:14), have fallen away from the faith. The seriousness of their apostasy is evident; Paul has **delivered** them **to Satan** (see comment on I Cor. 5:5). In this paragraph, then, the author includes an example of heroic and steadfast faith and an example of the failure of faith and its dire consequences.

2:1-7. *Inclusiveness of Christian Prayer.* The position of Christians and the church in the 2nd cent. was in certain ways precarious. While as yet they were not persecuted simply for being Christians, they were undoubtedly looked on with suspicion by the authorities, and any deviation from established custom might easily lead to serious trouble (cf. Rom. 13:1-7; I Pet. 4:14-16). This situation seems to lie behind the author's concern that **prayers . . . be made for . . . kings and all who are in high positions** and his urging that Christians **lead a quiet and peaceable life, godly and respectful in every way.** But there is another thought here, viz. that kings and lesser officials of government are themselves recipients of God's favor (vs. 4). **Christ Jesus . . . gave himself as a ransom for all** (vss. 5-6), including the emperor and his subordinates. It is of interest that at this point the author, in the manner of Paul in Gal. 1:20, feels called on to assert in strong language the reason for his appointment as **preacher and apostle . . . , a teacher of the Gentiles** (vs. 7). As such his concern reaches beyond the masses to those in places of governmental responsibility. It should be added that good and stable government was a condition for the spread of Christianity in the empire.

2:8-15. *Men and Women at Public Worship.* The author carries forward the subject of prayer. **Lifting up holy hands** is of special interest; it gives the normal posture for prayer common among Christians and Jews at the time. In the art of the Christian catacombs the praying figure always stands with uplifted arms rather than kneels. **Holy hands** might suggest ceremonial washing, but there is here no hint of this. To have holy hands is to be free of **anger or quarreling;** i.e. the thought is ethical and not ceremonial.

2:9-15. The rest of the passage deals with the conduct of **women** at public worship. They are to dress **modestly** and **adorn themselves** with **good deeds.** They are to be submissive and never exert **authority over men;** they must be **silent** (cf. his fears for the younger widows in 5:11-15). He supports his position by an appeal to the story of Adam and Eve: Adam was the first to be created, but Eve was the first to sin (cf. Gen. 2:7, 21–3:6). Yet woman will be **saved,** by childbearing and by abiding in **faith and love and holiness, with modesty**—a peculiar approach to salvation.

III. STANDARDS FOR CHRISTIAN OFFICERS (3:1-13)

3:1-7. *Qualifications of Bishops.* This passage raises the difficult question of church offices as reflected in the Pastorals. The titles **bishop** (*episkopos*, lit. "overseer") and "elder" (*presbyteros*) here seem interchangeable (cf. Tit. 1:5-7) and it is highly doubtful that they represent 2 clearly distinct offices such as are evident in the Ignatian letters (see Intro.), where the bishop has monarchical authority. The closest approximation to that here is in the implied offices of Tim. and Tit., who appear to stand apart and above the elders. It has been suggested, therefore, that in Tim. and Tit. the Ignatian bishops are present in all but title. According to this view bishop in this passage means the same as elder, so that, apart from the implied offices of Tim. and Tit., the Pastorals deal with 2 major groups, elders and deacons.

This section describes the personal qualifications of the bishop. The list suggests the importance attached to the ministerial office. In general the thought is clear, though **married only once,** lit. "a husband of one wife" (vs. 2), poses a special problem. Since the context does not elaborate, it is possible to see this as forbidding: (*a*) a 2nd marriage after the death of the first wife, (*b*) the practice of polygamy, (*c*) concubinage, or (*d*) remarriage after divorce. It is impossible to be sure which of these is meant. But the import is plain: the bishop must be free of any suspicion of loose sexual relationships; he must be above reproach as the exemplar of family integrity. Vs. 4 makes clear that the author does not advocate celibacy for the clergy; instead it is taken for granted that the bishop has his own household and that his wise management of it demonstrates his ability to care for God's church. Conversely inability to do so disqualifies him for the office of bishop.

3:8-13. *Qualifications of Deacons.* The description of a bishop's qualifications is now followed by a similar one for **deacons** (*diakonos*, lit. "servant"). Acts 6:1-6 relates the appointment of 7 deacons who would relieve the apostles of the necessity to "serve tables" and would care for the needs of widows of the Hellenists who were being "neglected in the daily distribution." Here the close connection of deacons with bishops and the similarity of qualifications suggest the importance of the office. It is probable, though not specified, that their duties included care of the poor.

Qualifications for deacons generally parallel those for bishops, stress being placed on **married only once,** and on the good management of **their households** (vs. 12). In both cases, moreover, special mention is made of the temperate use of **wine** (vs. 8; cf. vs. 3). Nowhere, however, does the author advocate total abstinence. Indeed in 5:23 he urges Timothy to "use a little wine" for medicinal purposes. This together with other emphases, e.g. a generally positive attitude toward marriage, even for the clergy, indicates that the author was no advocate of asceticism (see below on 4:1-5).

IV. THE TRUE FAITH (3:14–4:16)

3:14-16. *The Christian Mystery.* The letter, which is explained as a substitute for a personal visit that may be **delayed,** contains **instructions** on how to **behave in the household of God,** i.e. the **church of the living God,** described in turn as the **pillar and bulwark of the truth.** In his discussion of bishops and deacons the author has emphasized the importance of their being managers of their own **household** (3:5, 12). This term is now applied to the church, and Tim. is to behave in—not manage—the church in strict accordance with Paul's **instructions.** The church is the custodian of Paul's, i.e. the true, religion.

3:16. This **religion** is a **great . . . mystery** and is set forth in the form of a liturgical confession which undoubtedly the author is quoting from some source. The meaning of the hymn is difficult because it has been removed from its original context. However, it seems to emphasize Christ's incarnation, the vindicating power of his resurrection, his exaltation to heaven, and the spread of his gospel in the world. The simple formula stands in stark contrast to the elaborate system of eons advanced by the Gnostics. Moreover its insistence on the reality of the Incarnation is a refutation of the Gnostic view of flesh as evil, which denied the real humanity of Jesus.

4:1-5. *Deviations from the Faith.* The author's concern for sound doctrine in the face of heretical views is sounded in his words **Now the Spirit expressly says . . .** It is unnecessary to ask where it says this; it was generally understood that demonic activity would characterize the **later times** preceding the end of the age. The role which the author attributes to the Spirit is quite different from that found in the genuine letters of Paul. There the Spirit is a vital, energizing, creative power; here it is the custodian of the true doctrine, speaking out against departures from the faith (cf. II 1:14). That faith includes a positive attitude toward **marriage** and the recognition of **foods** as good because they were **created by God.** The author consequently condemns those who teach celibacy and abstinence. This is undoubtedly a reaction to Gnostic tendencies toward asceticism in the church.

4:6-10. *The Minister and the Faith.* Tim. is enjoined to instruct the church in Paul's teaching on these matters. If he does so, he will be a **good minister of Christ Jesus** (vs. 6). The word translated "minister" is *diakonos* (see above on 3:8-13). If "deacon" in the official sense is intended this vs. places Tim. in that class. As such he becomes representative of the whole group, i.e. of those deacons who are **nourished on the words of faith and of the good doctrine,** and who reject the **godless and silly myths** of the Gnostics. The Christian life, so conceived, calls for discipline in the same way that the athlete disciplines his body (cf. II 4:7-8). But training in godliness far surpasses in importance **bodily training,** for it prepares not only **for the present life** but **also for the life to come,** the goal toward which **we toil and strive.**

4:11-16. *The Example of Tim.* These vss. contain admonitions to Tim. He is to **teach** the things of which Paul has written. Even though young he is to be an example for believers in **speech . . . conduct . . . love . . . faith . . . purity.** He is to attend to the ministry of the church: **public reading of scriptures,** i.e. the OT, **preaching,** and **teaching.** The practices of the church in public worship are reflected here. He is urged to employ the gift given when the **elders laid their hands** on him, i.e. at ordination. **Prophetic utterance** was the guide to the selection of Tim. for ordination (see above on 1:18-20). He is to **practice** with diligence the duties laid on him at that time and to guard his character and **teaching.** By doing so he will save himself and those under his pastoral care.

V. CONDUCT OF TRUE CHRISTIANS (5:1–6:10)

5:1-2. *Treatment of Others.* Here we have specific exhortations about the pastor's personal relationships placed between advice about pastoral duties and about the treatment of widows. The addition of **in all purity** with respect to **younger women** betrays an anxiety regarding relations between the sexes in the church. But the author nevertheless refuses to advocate asceticism, as did many 2nd-cent. Christian writers.

5:3-16. *Widows in the Church.* The phrase **real widows** (vss. 3, 5, 16) suggests a problem in selection based on qualifications for the "office." What the author has in mind is indicated in vss. 11-13, where **younger widows** are described as having a tendency to **grow wanton** and to become **gossips and busybodies.** These women are not to be enrolled as widows. There is a question, moreover, about widows who have **relatives** capable of giving financial support (vss. 8, 16). The probability is that vs. 5a defines the "real widow"; she is one who is **left all alone,** i.e. has no source of financial help outside the church itself. As such she **continues in supplications and prayers night and day;** she devotes herself exclusively to the practice of religion.

5:9-10. Certain qualifications are made quite specific. The real widow must be over **sixty** and married only once (see above on 3:1-7). The minimum age limit would limit the number of women qualifying for the office; it would also provide a long period of testing in terms of character and **good deeds.** In general it reinforces the stringency of qualifications for the office. **Hospitality** was important in the spread of the Christian movement. The privilege of staying in Christian homes rather than in the highly undesirable inns facilitated the work of the missionary considerably. There is no reason to think of **wash the feet of the saints** as referring to an established ritual of the church like the Lord's Supper. "Saints" means simply Christians, and the expression has reference to the task, ordinarily that of a slave, of washing the feet of the traveler—a possible reference to the itinerant missionary. The true widow must not be above the most menial task and must pass the demanding tests of humility.

5:11-16. The **younger widows** are not real widows; they must not be enrolled. They tend to **desire to marry.** The author has no aversion to marriage, however, for he states his wish that they should marry. The point is that they do not qualify for the order of widows. Apparently there was some justification for this opinion in the situation (vs. 15).

5:17-22. *Pay and Discipline of Elders.* The author has already dealt with the qualifications for the office of bishop, which apparently he equates with that of **elder** (see above on 3:1-7). He now proceeds to deal with 2 specific problems of this office: ade-

quate remuneration and proper disciplinary action for those who have failed its high calling.

5:17-18. Evidently the task of the elder does not include **preaching and teaching.** Those who do preach and teach are **worthy of double honor**— i.e. in the light of the context additional pay, perhaps lit. double pay. The right of elders to an adequate wage is supported by an appeal to the OT (Deut. 25:4; cf. I Cor. 9:9) and to Christian tradition (cf. Matt. 10:10; Luke 10:7; I Cor. 9:14). It may be that the author thinks of his source for the 2nd saying as **scripture** also; since the exact words appear in Luke 10:7 some interpreters believe that he knew that gospel as scripture.

5:19-22. Vs. 19 introduces the question of proper procedure in dealing with elders against whom some **charge** has been laid. The author seems to apply the general legislation of Deut. 19:15 specifically to the trial of an elder. That matters of discipline earlier began to be hedged about with legal processes is evidenced by Matt. 18:15-17, where indeed the appeal is also to the evidence of **two or three witnesses.** Elders who **persist in sin** are to be publicly, i.e. before the whole church, rebuked—a procedure again reminiscent of Matt. 18:17. The seriousness with which the author views this problem is indicated by his charge to carry out this procedure without **partiality.** Moreover the **laying on of hands,** i.e. the ordination of new elders—or possibly restoration of elders who have sinned—is to be conducted only after due deliberation; otherwise Tim. will be party to the **sins** of defective elders.

5:23. *Use of Wine as Medicine.* This oft-quoted vs. possibly should be understood against vs. 22b— purity does not mean total abstinence. More esp. it should be viewed with reference to Gnostic asceticism. While the author warns against drunkenness by bishops (3:3) and instructs deacons not to be "addicted to much wine" (3:8), he forthrightly proclaims that "everything created by God is good" (4:4). Since he is no ascetic, he does not reject the use of wine but recommends it for the **stomach,** i.e. for medicinal purposes. Here, as elsewhere, he urges a counsel of moderation.

5:24-25. *Revelation of Character.* The parallelism of these 2 vss. is striking. Perhaps the author is drawing here from current moralizing tradition. The connection with the context is uncertain, unless he is referring to the conduct of the elders who persist in sin (vs. 20). The thought seems to be that men will ultimately be revealed for what they are, good or evil.

6:1-2b. *Deportment of Christian Slaves.* Slavery was an established legal institution in the Roman Empire. When the slaveholder and/or his slave became Christian, special problems naturally arose in their relationships (cf. e.g. I Cor. 7:21-23; Eph. 6:5-9; Col. 3:22-25; Philem.). This passage urges that Christian slaves treat their non-Christian **masters** with complete respect; to do otherwise would defame the **name of God** and the **teaching.** Similarly they must be respectful toward Christian masters because they are **brethren,** i.e. in Christ. Indeed when the master is a Christian the slave must render him superior service.

6:2c-10. *Failures of False Teachers.* These vss. deal with 2 issues: heretical teachings and the dangers of riches. It is probable, however, that the discussion of wealth is not a general statement on the subject but an outgrowth of problems posed by heresies. Vs. 5*b*, with its reference to **godliness as a means of gain,** leads into the discussion on riches and ties the 2 sections together.

6:3-5. While the nature of the heresy or heresies against which the author speaks is not specified, the teaching evidently is at variance with what the author considers normative. **Sound words of our Lord Jesus Christ** does not necessarily indicate that the author had a collection of sayings of Jesus before him; more likely it means that the true **teaching,** i.e. Paul's teaching as interpreted by the author, stems ultimately from Jesus. It would be equal, then, to "words of the faith" and "good doctrine" (4:6). By contrast **morbid craving for controversy and for disputes about words** is the same as the tendency which produces "godless and silly myths" (4:7). This repetition of subject matter betrays the author's major interest. But he goes on to suggest that the evil of departure from true doctrine is evident in the character and conduct of those involved (vss. 4*c*-5). This of course gives the author's estimate of the heresy but does not provide a description of its content.

6:6-10. Seizing on a tendency by the heretics to exploit people in the name of religion (vs. 5*b*), the author turns to the **craving** for **money** that causes men to leave the **faith.** By contrast the true Christian must realize that **godliness** brings **contentment,** that **food and clothing** constitute the only essentials of the journey between birth and death. The **desire** for riches causes men to **fall . . . into a snare** and leads in turn to other desires which **plunge** them **into ruin and destruction.** The emphasis here on desire for money, rather than money itself, as evil may reflect Stoic thought, for Stoicism numbered desire among the 4 emotions—the other 3 being pleasure, grief, and fear—which must be mastered. In general, however, this passage adds to the long list in early Christian literature which take a strongly negative view toward wealth (cf. e.g. Matt. 6:19-21; 19: 23-24; Mark 10:17-22; Luke 12:13-21; Jas. 2:1-7).

VI. FINAL CHARGES (6:11-21)

6:11-16. *The Good Fight of the Faith.* In contrast to the lovers of money Tim. is a **man of God,** a term apparently used here in a special sense as related to his particular calling and probably to his being set apart by his ordination. He is exhorted in somewhat Johannine language to **take hold of the eternal life** to which he was called in making the **good confession** before **many witnesses.** The language sounds like that of martyrdom; indeed vs. 13 looks to Jesus himself, who made the good confession **before Pontius Pilate.**

Is this a reflection of the actual martyrdom of Tim.? It is noteworthy that the tradition in the Acts of Tim. has him martyred during the reign of Nerva (96-98). Though the author's reference may be simply to his ordination or to his baptism, the similarity to the language of II 4:6-8, which certainly refers to Paul's martyrdom, reinforces the interpretation that the historical Tim. has already suffered martyrdom and that the author is holding him up as an example to his readers.

6:14-16. Tim. is now charged to **keep the commandment,** i.e. the true Pauline doctrine, **unstained.** He must remain faithful to this trust until the appearing of Christ. The sense of urgency characteristic of an earlier period has now grown weak; the church has settled down to the task of finding its place in the world. Nevertheless the idea of the coming last day is maintained; God will usher in that day through the appearance of Christ at the appointed time. The titles of God in vs. 15 are reminiscent of Rev. (e.g. 17:14; 19:16) and may, as in Rev., be written against the powerful claims of emperors. Vs. 16 takes on the lofty language and to some extent the form of a doxology. The idea of the sovereignty of God sounds Jewish, while the language of vs. 16 sounds Hellenistic. **Whom no man has ever seen** is reminiscent of John 1:18.

6:17-19. *The True Riches.* The author now returns to the theme of wealth (cf. vss. 6-10). The passage assumes the presence in the church of wealthy persons. While they are not condemned for their riches, they are not to become **haughty** on account of their wealth. Rather they are to set their hopes on God, the source of all good (cf. 4:4). They are to engage in sound ethical conduct, which is true riches. Their **good deeds,** done in a liberal and generous spirit, will reap abundance in the **future** in terms of true **life.**

6:20-21. *Warning Against False Knowledge.* These vss. have frequently been cited as identifying the heretical group against which the Pastorals were written. The word translated **contradictions** is the title, usually transliterated "Antitheses," of a book by the heretic Marcion (*ca.* 140; see Intro.) and is therefore possibly a specific reference to that work. **What is falsely called knowledge** makes the theory more attractive, since Marcion was in some sense a Gnostic; i.e. he claimed revealed knowledge for himself and his followers. But whether or not the reference is to Marcion remains uncertain.

The benediction at the end is extremely simple. It is Pauline in that it employs Paul's great word **grace,** but here it is little more than a convention. The plural form of the personal pronoun **you** is used, whereas in a letter to Tim. we should expect the singular. This is a good indication of the pastoral nature of this letter, in fact addressed, not to a certain individual, but through the pseudonymous Tim. to the church.

THE SECOND LETTER
OF PAUL TO TIMOTHY

ERIC LANE TITUS

[For introduction see Intro. to I Tim.]

I. EPISTOLARY INTRO. (1:1-7)

1:1-2. *Salutation.* The letter is written in the name of **Paul,** whose authority is expressed in the title **apostle of Jesus Christ** but rests ultimately on the authority of God himself. It is written, then, with full and complete authority, **according to the promise of the life which is in Christ Jesus;** i.e. life in Christ provides the norm by which true apostleship must be judged. Life here must be thought of as present as well as future. It is the Christian life in harmony with the true doctrine which the author espouses. Like I Tim., the letter is addressed to **Timothy,** characterized as Paul's **beloved child** (see comment on I 1:2*a*).

1:3-7. *The Faith of Tim.* Except Gal. the unquestioned letters of Paul consistently include a thanksgiving. Following that pattern the author introduces a passage of thanksgiving at this point, whereas I Tim. and Tit. do not include one. The highly personal character of II Tim. makes its appearance here seem perfectly natural. If, as most scholars believe, II Tim. had chronological priority over I Tim. and Tit. (see Intro.), the thanksgiving may have been introductory to all 3.

1:3-5. The author draws a parallel between the faith of Paul and of Tim.: Paul serves God **with a clear conscience** like his **fathers;** Tim. possesses a **sincere faith** like his **grandmother Lois and his mother Eunice.** It is doubtful that the historical Paul could have made this claim for his fathers; it is more likely the pseudonymous author referring to his own Christian fathers. As for Tim.'s forebears, nothing is known of his grandmother Lois apart from this passage. His mother is mentioned, though not by name, in Acts 16:1, where she is described as a "Jewish woman who was a believer" though her husband was a Greek. The impression in vs. 5 is that Christianity is now a matter of at least 3 generations and Tim. is the fine product of a long history of sincere faith.

1:6-7. Tim.'s strong Christian background, however, does not guarantee the continuance of a resilient faith. He must not allow the fire of faith, originally bestowed by the **laying on of my hands,** i.e. the rite of ordination, to smolder; rather he must stir it so that it becomes a blaze. For Tim. is twice blessed: he is the product of a Christian home, and he is the recipient of the **gift of God,** officially and supernaturally bestowed by the act of ordination. This divinely touched inner spirit should be characterized, not by **timidity,** but by **power and love and self-control** (cf. I John 4:18). Power by itself is not enough; it must be balanced by the warmth of love and by personal discipline.

II. TESTIFYING TO THE LORD (1:8–2:7)

1:8-14. *Suffering for the Gospel.* Suffering—possibly martyrdom—is part of the Christian's testimony to his Lord. Like Paul, the Lord's **prisoner,** Tim. is not to be **ashamed** to suffer **for the gospel.**

1:9-10. The Christian's **holy calling** is to a consecrated life, dependent not on **works,** but on the eternal **purpose** of God, and manifested in the appearance of Christ. The **gospel,** then, is far more than an arbitrary historical occurrence; it is rooted in the **grace** of God.

1:11-12. The suffering of Paul is integral to his divine appointment as **preacher and apostle and teacher.** Thus it is not something to be **ashamed** of but an honor and a privilege. His assurance is that God is trustworthy and will be able to safeguard till **that Day,** i.e. the end of the age, the priceless deposit of the gospel—as understood by the author—proclaimed by him as preacher, apostle, and teacher.

1:13-14. Tim. is exhorted to **follow** Paul's example and **guard the truth,** lit. "good deposit," by the power of the **Holy Spirit.** This Spirit **dwells within us.** The plural may refer either to Christians generally or to those specially ordained—probably to the former.

1:15-18. *The Household of Onesiphorus.* The first 2 persons mentioned, **Phygelus and Hermogenes,** are included as a foil for the loyalty and kindness of Onesiphorus. Just as these 2 **turned away** from Paul, so Onesiphorus turned toward him to refresh him during his imprisonment. None of these persons is known apart from this epistle. It appears that Onesiphorus is dead; the prayer is first for his family (cf. 4:19) and then that he may **find mercy from the Lord on that Day.** If, as some believe, this is a fragment of genuine Pauline correspondence, perhaps it speaks to a recently bereaved family. In any case its inclusion here serves to underscore the preceding injunction for loyalty.

2:1-7. *Unreserved Devotion.* Tim. is now enjoined to **be strong in the grace that is in Christ Jesus.** The letter has already made clear that he has received a "spirit of power" (1:7); now it uses 3 analogies to illustrate the strength of the true Christian: (a) he must suffer **as a good soldier of Jesus Christ** with single-minded dedication to his Lord (vs. 3); (b) he must strive in the Christian life as an **athlete** who **competes according to the rules** (vs. 5); (c) he must be like the **hard-working farmer** who receives the **first share of the crops** as his reward (vs. 6). Devotion that is unreserved is of course the point in all of this. The admonition in vs. 2 brings to a culmination the call to loyalty of 1:3–2:2. The reference seems to be to a responsible line of descent of the Pauline tradition from Paul down to and through the author, who is writing in Paul's name to still others.

III. APPROVED WORKMEN (2:8-26)

2:8-13. *Remembering Jesus Christ.* This section begins with what must be considered an early Christian creed: **Jesus Christ, risen from the dead, descended from David.** This is advanced as **preached in my gospel;** i.e. it contains constituent elements of Paul's gospel. Certainly the doctrine of the Resurrection was central in the historical Paul's thought. But **descended from David** appears only in Rom. 1:3 and seems peripheral. Its inclusion here may be for the purpose of refuting the Docetic element in Gnosticism (see Intro.) since it tends to emphasize the humanity of Jesus. In any case it is for this gospel that Paul was imprisoned **like a criminal.** But unlike Paul, the **word of God,** i.e. the word or gospel which Paul preached, is free. The **elect,** i.e. the chosen people of God, is a term now applied to the Christians as it was to Israel in the OT. The suffering of Paul, and by extension the suffering of all Christians, advances the purpose of God with respect to the **salvation . . . in Christ Jesus.**

2:11-13. This relation between endurance in suffering and salvation is reinforced by appeal to a "sure saying." The balanced structure of the lines, together with the intro., indicates a quotation from a Christian hymn or creedal confession, most likely sung or recited at baptism. The conditional **if we endure** relates it securely to **I endure everything** in vs. 10. Endurance in suffering on behalf of the gospel is the main theme of the section.

2:14-19. *God's True Workman.* The author now turns to a familiar theme, viz. the problem of heretical teachers. Their teachings are characterized as **disputing about words** (vs. 14) and **godless chatter** (vs. 16). Some of them, including Hymenaeus (cf. I 1:20) **and Philetus** (vs. 17), are teaching that the **resurrection** has already taken place. The precise implications of this teaching are not specified; but since the doctrine of the resurrection held so central a place in early Christianity it is natural that groups within the church, both "heretical" and "orthodox," would give a great deal of attention to it. In response to the heresy the author exhorts Tim. to strive to handle the **word of truth,** i.e. the gospel given to him through Paul, with correctness. This means in this context that he is to preach and teach it faithfully and exemplify it in his conduct.

2:18b-19. In spite of unorthodox, and therefore untrue, teachings which are **upsetting the faith of some,** the author asserts that **God's firm foundation stands** and supports this by an appeal to scripture (apparently Num. 16:5; Isa. 26:13).

2:20-26. *Pastor of Good and Bad.* This section is an elaboration of the ideas expressed in vss. 14–19. While it is true that men like Hymenaeus and Philetus are in the church, God knows **those who are his** (vs. 19). Now, using the analogy of a **great house,** the author points out that as there are in the house objects for both **noble** and **ignoble** use so it is in the church. Timothy is therefore to avoid the ignoble people who deal in **senseless controversies** (vs. 23) and **shun youthful passions** (vs. 22). He must correct **his opponents with gentleness** (vs. 25a). The hope is that they will turn from their perverse ways (vss. 25b-26). The main thrust of the passage is directed toward the fact of the mixture of good and bad people within the church. Tim., as a leader, stands in relation to this situation both as ideal ethical example and as teacher.

IV. INSTRUCTIONS FOR THE LAST DAYS (3:1–4:18)

3:1-9. *Signs of the Last Days.* The end of the age was expected to be preceded by terrible conflict, by intense last-ditch efforts of Satan to gain control over the cosmos, and by devastating upheaval in nature (cf. Mark 13; Matt. 24; Luke 21). While the doctrine of the end of the age—in vs. 1 called the **last days**—has here lost some of the sense of urgency characteristic of Paul himself, the author uses it to show that the activity of the heretical teachers is not something to occasion surprise.

3:2-5. The list of vices set forth in vss. 2-4 is undoubtedly a conventional catalog in common usage and does not necessarily provide a precise description of the heretical teachers. It is likely, however, that vs. 5 does characterize them—**holding the form of religion but denying the power of it.** In view of the earlier reference to the resurrection (2:18) it is possible that the author sees the heretics' position as denying the power of the Resurrection; power and resurrection are commonly associated in early Christian writings.

3:6-9. The author feels that **weak women**—lit. "little women," a diminutive of contempt—are esp. susceptible to the perverse doctrines of these aggressive heretics. But their **folly** will be made **plain,** like that of **Jannes and Jambres,** who **opposed Moses.** These names, while not mentioned in the OT, appear in nonbiblical early Jewish and Christian literature as Egyptian magicians in the court of Pharaoh (cf. Exod. 7:11).

3:10-17. *Paul the Great Example.* Paul is now held up as the great example of the **life in Christ Jesus.** His life is characterized by **faith . . . patience . . . love . . . steadfastness.** No doubt both the author and his first readers were quite familiar with the Acts account of his **persecutions . . . at Antioch, at Iconium, and at Lystra,** from which **the Lord rescued** him (cf. Acts 13:14–14:20). Indeed persecution is seen as the lot of true Christians, while **evil men** and those who pose as Christians but are not will **go on from bad to worse.**

3:14-17. But Tim. is to remain steadfast in the faith, having been instructed by Paul and **from childhood** solidly grounded in the scriptures. The **Sacred writings** certainly mean the OT but may also embrace the letters of Paul. In II Pet. 3:15-16 Paul's letters are considered as scripture, and it is unlikely that so ardent a Paulinist as the author of the Pastorals would consider them less authoritative. In any case **all scripture** (vs. 16) would certainly include the OT. If Marcion and his work lie behind the Pastorals (see Intro.) the reference to the function of scripture as **reproof . . . correction, and . . . training in righteousness** would constitute a rebuke to his rejection of the OT.

4:1-5. *Tim.'s Responsibility.* Tim. is now charged to **preach the word,** i.e. in this context the true doctrine, **in season and out of season,** i.e. when the times are favorable and when they are adverse. Presumably they were adverse at the time of writing. The solemnity of the charge is underscored by vs. 1. Tim. is ultimately responsible to God, and he must appear before Christ, who will **judge the living and the dead.**

4:3-5. Vss. 3-4 refer to the present state of affairs. **The time is coming** is future with reference to the historical Paul but present for the pseudonymous author. Some have turned aside from the **sound teaching** of Paul and **accumulate for themselves teachers** (Goodspeed: "overwhelm themselves with teachers") who say what they want to hear. They **wander into myths** (vs. 4), i.e. into the extravagant and untrue doctrines of the heretics. In contrast to these fickle people (vs. 5) Timothy is to remain **steady** and in all ways to discharge faithfully his responsibility as a minister.

4:6-8. *Imminent Martyrdom of Paul.* Here Paul, the great example of Christian fidelity, is **on the point of being sacrificed.** He compares himself to the disciplined athlete. He has **fought the good fight;** i.e. like the contestant in the arena he has done his best. He has **finished the race**—suggesting both the heroic struggle in the race Paul has run and the imminence of its completion. He has **kept the faith,** i.e., in keeping with the athletic figure, adherence to the rules of the game, but also the Pauline religion advocated by the author. Just as the athlete gains his reward by receiving the victor's wreath, so Paul need only await the **crown of righteousness,** to be bestowed by Christ himself at **his appearing.**

4:9-18. *The Loneliness of Paul.* Some scholars believe this section to be a fragment or fragments of genuine correspondence of Paul (see Intro.). The persons mentioned are all friends of Paul except **Demas** and **Alexander the coppersmith** (vs. 14; cf. I 1:20). Demas was apparently a co-worker (cf. Philem. 24; Col. 4:14) but for some reason not specifically stated left Paul, and perhaps Christianity itself, and became enamored with **this present world,** i.e. perhaps business pursuits.

The section reflects the mood of loneliness.

Crescens has gone to Galatia—or, according to some manuscripts, Gaul; the reading Galatia is to be preferred, esp. if the historical Paul is the author. **Titus** has gone to **Dalmatia** and **Tychicus** to **Ephesus** (vs. 12; cf. Acts 20:4; Col. 4:7; Eph. 6:21). Paul is left alone except for **Luke** (cf. Col. 4:14; Philem. 24). He apparently expects a visit from Tim. in prison, for he instructs him to bring **Mark** also with him (vs. 11). What specifically is meant by **for he is very useful in serving me** is not clear; perhaps he would act as a secretary or simply lend support to Paul's ministry (cf. Col. 4:10-11; Philem. 24). Such added support would strengthen Paul in his hour of extreme loneliness.

This theme of loneliness carries into vs. 16 in an allusion to Paul's preliminary hearing before the court. Though forsaken by men, he was not forsaken by God, who delivered him from death. Rescue **from the lion's mouth** (vs. 17) is probably to be taken figuratively and simply means deliverance from death.

Mention of the **books** and **parchments** (vs. 13) suggests a situation quite different from that indicated in vss. 6-8, where Paul anticipates imminent martyrdom. Here he looks forward to a considerable future in which the documents would serve a useful function. The same point is suggested by the request for Tim. to bring the **cloak,** a heavy outer garment important for warmth during the coming winter. This break in thought has seemed to some to support the theory that vss. 9-18 constitute a genuine Pauline fragment which the author has incorporated in his letter. On the other hand the author may have drawn heavily on the genuine Pauline letters (cf. e.g. Col. 4:7-17) for references to persons engaged with Paul in the work of the church.

V. FINAL GREETINGS (4:19-22)

4:19-21. *Personal Greetings.* The final greeting is typical of Paul's letters and is imitated here (cf. Rom. 16:21-23; I Cor. 16:19-20; II Cor. 13:13; Phil. 4:22; Col. 4:10-17). On **Prisca and Aquila** cf. Acts 18:2-3, 18-19, 26; I Cor. 16:19; Rom. 16:3. On the **household of Onesiphorus** see above on 1:15-18. On **Erastus** cf. Acts 19:22. On **Trophimus** cf. Acts 20:4; 21:29. Of the others we know nothing. The greeting is an expression of Christian fellowship and solidarity. As used by the author it serves the purpose of giving an authentic Pauline touch to his letter.

4:22. *Benediction.* For the combination of the 2 elements in the Pauline benediction cf. Gal. 6:18; Phil. 4:23; Philem. 25. For the shortened form cf. I 6:21; Tit. 3:15; Col. 4:18.

THE LETTER
OF PAUL TO TITUS

Eric Lane Titus

[For introduction see Intro. to I Tim.]

I. Epistolary Intro. (1:1-16)

1:1-4. Salutation. The characteristic salutation of a Pauline letter is emulated here by the author. The statement is carefully worded to stress that Paul's message is not his own but is grounded in: (a) his **servant** relationship to God, (b) his office as an **apostle of Jesus Christ,** (c) the divine promises given **ages ago,** and (d) the commandment of **God our Savior.** Paul's task as servant and apostle is to **further the faith of God's elect and their knowledge of the truth.** The devotion of the author to Paul's doctrine is thus seen as more than personal admiration; he is convinced that that doctrine represents the due manifestation of the promise of the ages. It did not originate with Paul but was mediated through him to the church.

1:4. Whereas the other 2 Pastoral epistles are addressed to Timothy, this one is addressed to **Titus.** That Tit. should be so honored by a devout Paulinist is understandable in view of the nature of the relationship between him and Paul shown in genuine Pauline letters. It is evident from II Cor. that Tit. effected reconciliation between Paul and the Corinthian church after a serious rift had occurred (cf. II Cor. 7:6-7, 13-14). This historical situation thus provides a fitting background for the choice of Tit., Paul's **true child in a common faith** (see comment on I Tim. 1:2a) as the recipient of a letter. For now, in the new church situation, a problem has arisen comparable to that which earlier existed at Corinth and Tit. must provide a solution.

1:5-16. The Task of Tit. Quite in keeping with his ability to solve problems in church relations, Tit. has been left behind among the difficult Cretans to **amend what was defective** and to **appoint elders** in accordance with Paul's directive. The elders—apparently indistinguishable from the **bishop** (see comment on I Tim. 3:1-7)—must be men of high character (vss. 7-8) and be able to **give instruction in sound doctrine** (vs. 9), i.e. in Pauline doctrine as understood by the author.

1:10-16. The author has a low view of Cretan society. Quoting the Cretan Epimenides (6th cent. B.C.) with approval, he characterizes Cretans as **liars, evil beasts, lazy gluttons** (vs. 12). The point, of course, is that false doctrines have grown up in the church in Crete; certain people are insubordinates, **empty talkers and deceivers**—probably a reference to the **Jewish myths** of vs. 14—who are disrupting church family life. Moreover they are utterly immoral (vss. 15-16). Tit. must minister to this difficult situation.

II. Sound Doctrine (2:1-14)

2:1-10. Tit. as Teacher. Quite in contrast to the perverted ideas of the Cretans with their consequent immorality, Tit. is to **teach what befits sound doctrine** (vs. 1). Along with this normative Pauline doctrine he must instruct the church in moral and practical matters. The **older men** must be instructed in sobriety, **in faith, in love, and in steadfastness.** The **women** are to be instructed in **reverent behavior** and to carry on domestic duties faithfully, to be **submissive to their husbands** and to be **chaste.** The **younger men** must be taught to **control themselves.** The **slaves** are to be **submissive to their masters**—a thoroughly typical NT teaching (cf. I Cor. 7:21, 24; Col. 3:22; Eph. 6:5-8; I Pet. 2:18). A conscience on slavery had not yet arisen (see Intro. to Philem.). Indeed the slaves' obedient conduct will **adorn the doctrine of God our Savior** (vs. 10).

Tit. must himself be a **model of good deeds** and of sound teaching (vs. 7). His very deportment will **put** the enemies of the truth **to shame** and Christianity will be protected from slanderous charges.

2:11-14. The People of God. The reason for the radical difference between the opponents of the church and the Christians is that the **grace of God has appeared** and is **training** the Christian in a new way of life which stands in sharp contrast to the way of irreligion. It is the Christian's responsibility to live the upright life while awaiting the appearing of Christ. The work of Christ has a 2-fold meaning: (a) it redeems **from iniquity** (vs. 14a) and (b) it separates from the world a people who belong to Christ (vs. 14b; cf. I Pet. 2:9-10).

It is to be observed that a great deal of stress on **good deeds** characterizes the Pastorals in general and Tit. in particular. This makes it evident that, while the author uses the conventional vocabulary of Paul for the **grace of God,** the profound meaning of the term as used by Paul has largely been lost. It is therefore likely that its occurrence in vs. 11 means no more than that the true doctrine has been given (as in 1:1-3) and transmitted by Paul, servant and apostle of Jesus Christ.

2:15. The Authority of Tit. Here the authority of Tit. is strongly emphasized. It is grounded in his church office, but it is derived also from his authoritative message. His message, the true doctrine, has been transmitted to him from Paul, and Paul has directed him to carry out certain duties in Crete (1:5). In a certain sense, then, the work of Tit. is but an extension of that of the great apostle himself.

III. Christian Conduct (3:1-11)

3:1-8a. Contrast with Non-Christians. Christians are to present themselves blameless before the world. They are to obey the civil **authorities,** engage in **honest work,** be prudent in speech, and display gentleness and **courtesy** in human relations. The conduct of Christians in the days before they experienced the **goodness and loving kindness of God our Savior** (vs. 4) was like that of the rest of men in its sin. Now it is different, and the reason for the difference is God's saving act in Christ. The thought resembles that of the historical Paul. The author throws the weight of the saving act on the fact of God's mercy and **not because of deeds done by us in righteousness** (vs. 5a).

3:5b-8a. The conclusion **The saying is sure** (vs. 8a) suggests that the material preceding it is a quotation, possibly from a Christian baptismal formula. Precisely how much of vss. 1-7 should be included in the quotation remains problematical, but it may well be that the peculiarly Pauline ideas, as distinct from the thought of the Pastorals in general, should be attributed to this source. To be sure, the phrase **washing of regeneration** does not appear in Paul. However, since the formula was the common property of the church, there is no reason to expect strictly Pauline language to dominate it.

Washing of regeneration refers to baptism, which results in a permanent change of life. The Greek word translated **regeneration** occurs in Matt. 19:28, where it refers to the "new world," the transformed messianic age of the exalted Son of man and of the 12. The idea here is also transformation, but transformation of the individual through baptism. The radical change produced at baptism has some affinity with the sacramental changes effected in the Hellenistic mystery cults but is more nearly paralleled by the historical Paul's view of "newness of life" set forth in Rom. 6:4.

3:8b-11. Insistence on Good Deeds. The stress on the conduct of Christians as that of good, loyal, law-abiding, industrious citizens (vss. 1-2) seems characteristic of the period. This may be the point of the insistence on good deeds in this section. The status of Christianity with respect to the state was precarious; exemplary conduct by Christians was therefore most important. It was quite possible for Christians, with their consciousness of themselves as God's chosen people (cf. 2:14; I Pet. 2:9), to feel themselves above the mundane concerns of citizens of this world. Or it might be that the **factious** and quarrelsome activity of some Christians would throw suspicion on the church generally (cf. I Pet. 2:13-17; 4:12-19). The author therefore exhorts Tit. to insist that Christians **apply themselves** to **good deeds** (vs. 8b) and **avoid** conduct that does not befit the new life in Christ (vs. 9). Severe disciplinary measures are to be used when anyone persists in his factious ways (vss. 10-11).

IV. Final Charges (3:12-15)

3:12-14. Personal Instructions. Tit.'s work in Crete must be well on its way to completion, for Paul asks him to meet at **Nicopolis,** probably the city of this name on the Adriatic coast of Greece (see color map 16). Nothing is known of **Artemas.** On **Tychicus** see comment on II Tim. 4:12. Nothing further is known of **Zenas** than that he was a **lawyer** (vs. 13). This may mean a lawyer in the sense of a (former?) Jewish scribe, or it may refer to the profession of law in the Greek or Roman sense. **Apollos** (vs. 13) almost certainly refers to the great Alexandrian Christian mentioned in Acts 18:24–19:1; I Cor. 1:12; 3:4-6, 22; 4:6; 16:12. Zenas and Apollos are to be speeded **on their way** by Titus, who is to **see that they lack nothing.** Presumably their mission has to do with the furtherance of the gospel, though this is not said. If Apollos is the eloquent preacher of Acts and I Cor., the reference is probably to a mission of preaching.

3:14. This seems to follow up the injunction to Titus to make provision for their physical needs on their journey. Christians in Crete are to be generous in this respect. One of the **cases of urgent need** would be the support of the mission of Zenas and Apollos. But the vs. may have a more general application as well.

3:15. Greetings and Benediction. The letter ends with greetings from Paul and his companions to Tit. and to **those who love us in the faith,** i.e. all loyal Christians. Since the "you" in **Grace be with you all** is plural the brief benediction means at least that grace is sent to the whole church, perhaps even that the import of the letter is to be shared by the total church. It must be said, however, that the benediction may be largely conventional, copying general Pauline usage.

THE LETTER
OF PAUL TO PHILEMON

Victor Paul Furnish

INTRODUCTION

Character and Purpose. Philem. deals with a single issue. In it Paul is concerned to aid Onesimus, a runaway slave whom he has met while in prison—how is never revealed—and whose master was probably one of Paul's converts (vs. 19). Onesimus is returning to his master, evidently bearing Paul's letter; and its appeal is not just that he be treated gently but that he be released into Paul's continuing custody for the service of the gospel. Nowhere in the letter is this latter request explicitly made, but it is implicit throughout.

Even though Philem. was written for a very particular reason, it would be misleading to describe it as a purely private document. While its central appeal is directed to an individual (vss. 4-22), the opening salutation (vss. 1-3) and concluding benediction (vs. 25) presuppose a Christian congregation, a "house church" (vs. 2). Moreover Col. may have been written to this same congregation at the same time, at least in part to bolster the appeal of this letter (see below). Therefore in this as in his other letters Paul speaks as an apostle mindful of a whole community of Christian brethren, and everything he says presupposes that wider context.

The owner of Onesimus is generally assumed to be Philem. (vs. 1), but the theory that the owner is Archippus (vs. 2) has been adopted by some scholars (see below on vss. 1-3 and on Col. 4:17). In light of the close relationship between this letter and Col., the remark to the Colossians that Onesimus is "one of yourselves" (Col. 4:9), and the inclusion of greetings from Epaphras (vs. 23), evidently the founder of the Colossian church (Col. 1:7-8; 4:12-13), the place of Philem.'s residence has usually been regarded as Colossae (see below on vss. 1-3).

Place and Date of Composition. Philem. is one of Paul's imprisonment letters (vss. 1, 9, 10, 13, 23), but nothing in the letter indicates the prison's location. Traditionally the place has been assumed to be Rome (cf. Acts 28:16-31), and on this basis the letter is to be dated *ca.* 59-62. Caesarea (cf. Acts 23:33-24:27; esp. 24:23) has also been suggested but is not generally favored because it seems unlikely that Onesimus would flee to that place. The hypothesis has been advanced that Paul also suffered imprisonment in Ephesus (see Intro. to Phil.), and a number of scholars regard that city's proximity to Colossae as making it a likely spot for Onesimus to meet Paul. If the letter was written from Ephesus the date would be *ca.* 54-56, near the time of the Corinthian correspondence.

Relation to Col. Significant relationships between this letter and Col. are easily recognized: both are written from prison; Onesimus is mentioned in Col. 4:9 and described as being from Colossae; Archippus is mentioned in both letters (vs. 2; Col. 4:17); and in each letter greetings are sent from the same 5 persons—Epaphras, Mark, Aristarchus, Demas, and Luke (vs. 23; Col. 4:10-14). Moreover among the household duties discussed in Col. 3:18-4:1 the relationships of masters and slaves receive the most attention (3:22-4:1). Formerly doubts about the authenticity of Col. sometimes raised corresponding doubts about this related letter. Today, however, no serious questions about the authenticity of Philem. remain, and it is more common to view the close relationship of the 2 letters as lending support to the authenticity of Col.

If Col. is a genuine letter of Paul, as the majority of scholars hold, then it may be regarded as intended, at least in part, to support and strengthen the appeals Paul makes in Philem. Further, if the real owner of Onesimus is Archippus, as some believe, Paul's urging of the Colossians to see that Archippus fulfills his service (Col. 4:17) is a specific reference to the whole issue discussed in this letter.

Paul and Slavery. Though Paul's objective seems to be the release of Onesimus from his master, one must not regard Philem. as an abolitionist tract. Neither here nor in I Cor. 7:20-24 does Paul question the rightness or wrongness of slavery as an institution. For Paul, as for early Christianity in general, the institution of slavery was regarded as a fixed part of society, and there is no writer within the NT who envisions a social order without this institution. On the other hand slavery is never expressly condoned or given theological sanctions. What, then, may one conclude about Paul's view of slavery?

Paul viewed all human institutions as features of a temporary worldly order which was in the process of "passing away" (I Cor. 7:31). Because he shared the conviction of earliest Christianity that the last days were at hand, the reform of social institutions would have seemed to him irrelevant and superfluous. Moreover slave labor was basic to the whole economic structure of the Roman Empire. The abolitionist would have been at the same time an insurrectionist, and the political effects of such a movement would have been unthinkable. The situation of the freedman was often more difficult than that of a slave, because of the abundance of slave labor and the scarcity of work for others.

While Paul is no sponsor of social reforms, his letters do emphasize those aspects of the Christian gospel which, freed from the first-cent. expectation of the early dissolution of the social order, and provided with more appropriate socioeconomic conditions, were destined to support and encourage the abolitionist cause. The substance of Paul's appeal in Philem. absolutely excludes the idea that Onesimus should be punished, though Roman law allowed the owner of a runaway slave almost unlimited privileges of punishment—on occasion even execution. In I Cor. 7:20-24 the point is established that true freedom is achieved as one surrenders himself to the service of God, and that such freedom is more significant than whether one was born free or a slave. Yet this remark to the Corinthians should not be interpreted as implying that Paul and earliest Christianity regarded only inner freedom as important and had no concern for its outer manifestations. For, perhaps most important of all, the actuality of even the slave's freedom in Christ was made concrete in the life of the Christian community. Paul himself emphatically declared that all men, regardless of their worldly stations, could be baptized into Christ and into the brotherly communion of believers in Christ (Gal. 3:27-28).

Considered in this perspective, Philem. may legitimately be regarded as an eloquent witness to the brotherly status of all persons in Christ, a plain testimonial that for the church to be the church—the community of baptized brethren—it must manifest in its life and labor the way in which the social barriers dividing men are not just transcended but actually broken through. Paul therefore bids Philemon receive Onesimus back as "more than a slave, as a beloved brother" (vs. 16).

For Further Study. M. R. Vincent, *Phil. and Philem.*, 1911. E. F. Scott, *Col., Philem., and Eph.*, 1930. John Knox in *IB*, 1955; *Philem. Among the Letters of Paul*, rev. ed., 1959. W. L. Westermann, *The Slave Systems of Greek and Roman Antiquity*, 1955. C. F. D. Moule, *Col. and Philem.*, 1957. Theo Preiss, *Life in Christ*, 1957. M. E. Lyman in *IDB*, 1962.

COMMENTARY

Vss. 1-3. Salutation. Paul writes from prison (see Intro.) and addresses 3 persons specifically, of whom only **Archippus** is named elsewhere in the NT (Col. 4:17). Most interpreters presume that **Philemon** and **Apphia**, like Archippus, are members of the Christian church at Colossae (see Intro. to Col.), that Philem., named first, is probably the one primarily addressed, and that the church which Paul has in mind meets in Philem.'s house. It is possible, however, that Archippus is the one to whom the letter is primarily directed, and that the church meets in his house (see comment on Col. 4:17).

Vss. 4-7. Thanksgiving. In the Pauline letters a paragraph giving thanks to God for the love and faith of those addressed regularly follows the salutation. Here, and throughout most of the rest of the letter, **you** is singular, indicating that Paul is writing to one person esp., probably Philem. It is characteristic that the thanksgiving sections in Paul's letters foreshadow subsequent themes and appeals, and

that is true here. He refers to Philem.'s **love** (vss. 5, 7) and then makes his appeal on that basis (vs. 9); he refers to Philem.'s **sharing of . . . faith** (vs. 6) and later appeals to him as a **partner** (vs. 17); he speaks of **the good that is ours in Christ** (vs. 6) and presently expresses concern that Philem.'s **goodness** be of his own **free will** (vs. 14); and after a reference to the **hearts of the saints** which Philem. has **refreshed** (vs. 7) he requests that his own **heart** be refreshed in Christ (vs. 20).

Throughout this letter Paul places extraordinary emphasis on the brotherly relationship which exists between himself and Philem. (cf. e.g. vss. 1*b*, 17, 20), esp. so in this paragraph of thanksgiving. Moreover Philem. is commended as an edifying member of the church (**the saints**), in which he is apparently a leading participant (vss. 5, 7).

Vss. 8-14. Appeal on Behalf of Onesimus. Paul here shows remarkable restraint in exercising his apostolic authority, but this is due not so much to the need for tactfulness as it is to his understanding of the nature of ethical decisions. This letter is concerned with a particular ethical question: Onesimus, the slave of a Christian master, has run away, somehow fallen in with Paul, and served him with distinction (vss. 10-11). Legally Paul should return the slave to his owner and make full restitution. But in this case the owner is one of Paul's Christian brethren, and the runaway slave has been extraordinarily **useful** as an apostolic helper. Here there is a play on words, for the name Onesimus is related to the Greek word "useful."

How does Paul solve the question of right and wrong in this kind of situation? (*a*) He is concerned to fulfill his legal obligation; he is returning Onesimus to his owner (vs. 12) and offers to reimburse Philem. fully for any financial losses (vs. 19). (*b*) He lets it be known that, were the final decision his, Onesimus would be retained for the service of the gospel in which he has already been so valuable (vss. 11, 13). The affection Paul feels for Philem. is hardly more than that he feels for Philem.'s slave (vss. 10, 12), and this is said rather explicitly (vss. 16, 17). (*c*) He makes it clear that, so far as Onesimus is concerned, the responsibility and decision are with Philem. alone (vs. 14). Paul does not directly ask Philem. to free Onesimus, nor even to deal gently with him. Rather he praises Philemon for his love, reminds him of his partnership in faith, informs him of Onesimus' usefulness to the gospel, and charges him with making his own decision in the matter.

This whole appeal is made on the basis of love (vs. 9; see above on vss. 4-7). Paul does not spell out in particular what is required of Philem. His appeal is made with the assurance that those who are partners in one faith and one Spirit also share the common directives of love by which their common life in Christ finds expression. The word which actually stands in vs. 9 is "old man" (see RSV footnote), but since the addition of just one letter would form the word **ambassador** and thus conform to the thought of II Cor. 5:20 (cf. Eph. 6:20) many commentators and translators have adopted the conjectural form as the original. Though Paul nowhere in Philem. refers to himself as an "apostle," an appeal to his apostolic authority is nonetheless present.

Vss. 15-19. Christian Brotherhood. Before his

escape Onesimus did not measure up to his name —"useful." In fact he was **useless** (vs. 11). But since his meeting with Paul that has changed. Perhaps, then, there was a constructive purpose for this whole incident (vss. 15-16), and Paul hopes that Philem. will receive Onesimus back as **more than a slave, as a beloved brother, . . . both in the flesh and in the Lord** (vs. 16). Philem. and Paul are brothers (vss. 7, 20). Paul and Onesimus are on the one hand like father and son (vs. 10) and on the other also beloved brothers in Christ (vs. 16). Therefore in Christ the relationship between Philem. and Onesimus ought now to be transformed. Paul is not a social reformer (see Intro.), but the seeds of social reform are certainly present here: in Christ men are bound together in ways which transcend and in fact —**in the flesh** (vs. 16) —overcome the barriers of race, class, and position. This unity in Christ is constantly stressed in Paul's letters (cf. e.g. Rom. 10:12; Gal. 3:28; Col. 3:11) and is summed up in the word *koinonia,* which in its various forms Paul frequently uses, and which is variously translated **sharing** (vs. 6; II Cor. 1:7; Gal. 6:6; Phil. 3:10), **partnership** (vs. 17; II Cor. 6:14; 8:23; Phil. 1:5; 4:15), "participation" (I Cor. 10:16; Phil. 2:1), and "fellowship" (I Cor. 1:9; II Cor. 13:14; Gal. 2:9).

Vss. 17-19. Onesimus, then, is to be welcomed back even as Paul himself would be received—a Christian brother free to come and go when the tasks of his ministry may require (vs. 17), in fact a **guest** in Philem.'s house (vs. 22)! The pledge to make restitution for any losses Philem. may have incurred (vs. 18) is certified in Paul's own handwriting (vs. 19; cf. I Cor. 16:21; Gal. 6:11). He probably does not expect Philem. to demand payment, for the slave owner's debt to Paul is infinitely greater —a remark which suggests that Philem. was one of Paul's converts. Since Paul himself has never been to Colossae, Philem.'s home, their meeting must have occurred elsewhere—perhaps Ephesus.

Vss. 20-22. *Onesimus' Future Service.* In vs. 20 the term **benefit** is a form of the name Onesimus (see above on vss. 8-14) and thus with this play on words Paul indicates his actual intent for Onesimus. In the 2nd part of the vs. **heart** also has a double significance, recalling the earlier remarks that (*a*) Philem. has refreshed the **hearts of the saints** (vs. 7) and (*b*) Onesimus himself is Paul's **heart** (vs. 12). These expressions show that Paul appeals to Philem. not just to forgive Onesimus but to receive him back as a free man, a Christian brother, an apostolic delegate, and then return him to Paul's service. Paul expresses confidence that Philem. will act with a Christian conscience in this matter, doing **even more** than would be normally required (vs. 21). These 2 words constitute a simple yet profound summary of Paul's understanding of the Christian's ethical responsibility. True Christian obedience is not legalistic conformity to prescribed rules but the surrender of one's whole life to the unconditional demands of love. Love always asks "even more" than what "normally" would be **required** (vs. 8) or expected.

Vs. 22. Though Paul is writing from prison (see Intro.) he anticipates release and the opportunity to visit Philem. in Colossae.

Vss. 23-25. *Greetings and Benediction.* The appeal of this letter has been addressed to just one man (vss. 4-22); and though Paul makes it in the context of an address to the whole Christian community of which Philem. is a part (vss. 2, 25), closing greetings are directed to him alone—**you** in vs. 23 is singular. These are from **Epaphras,** who has been an evangelist in Colossae, Laodicea, and Hierapolis (Col. 1:7; 4:12-13), and from his other **fellow workers,** viz.: **Mark,** to whom the earliest gospel is ordinarily assigned; Aristarchus (cf. Acts 19:29; 20:4; 27:2); Demas (cf. II Tim. 4:10); and Luke, to whom the 3rd gospel and Acts are ascribed, the "beloved physician" (Col. 4:14). Greetings from these same men are conveyed in Col. 4:10-14, though there the name of "Jesus who is called Justus" (4:11) also occurs. Its absence here is inexplicable.

THE LETTER
TO THE HEBREWS

Warren A. Quanbeck

Authorship. A very old tradition, preserved in the Vulg. and in the KJV, ascribes Hebrews to Paul. When we examine the book itself, however, and the testimony of ancient writers to it, we discover that its authorship is uncertain and that we know very little about its origin, destination, and date. It is difficult to determine even why the letter was written, and modern interpreters differ on this question.

The earliest known quotation from the book appears in a letter of Clement of Rome usually dated *ca.* A.D. 96. From this and other citations we learn that in the W part of the church it was known very early but was not ascribed to Paul until the 4th cent. The story is different in the E. Here it was ascribed to Paul as early as the 2nd cent., though scholars in Alexandria, esp. Origen, had their doubts about Pauline authorship because it differed from the Pauline letters in literary style and theological language.

Detailed study in modern times has led to almost unanimous agreement that the language, style, and ideas differ so markedly from those of Paul that it is almost inconceivable that he could have been the author. Origen long ago observed that who the author was God alone really knows. Modern scholarship has been unable to improve on this verdict, though it has examined with care the credentials of those who have been nominated for the honor, including Barnabas, Apollos, and Clement.

The book itself tells us a good deal about the kind of person the author was. He had an excellent command of Greek, writing with a refined and elegant style which no translation conveys adequately. He read his OT in Greek, for he always quotes the LXX, the Bible of Greek-speaking Jews and Christians. His world of thought was dominated by the tradition of worship, and he saw Jesus Christ as the fulfillment of the sacrificial system. He also knew the speculations of the Alexandrian Jewish philosopher Philo but did not follow him in fitting biblical ideas into the Hellenistic thought world. He quarried his materials from thinkers like Philo but fitted them into an architecture of biblical origin— e.g. the distinction between the shadow world of matter and the real world of spirit, which he set in the framework of the history of salvation. He therefore refused to discount the created world of time and space. Instead of the allegorical interpretation of the OT favored by Philo and others he preferred the typological—i.e. finding in the ancient stories "types" or analogies of truths fully revealed in Christ (see "The History of Biblical Interpretation," pp. 971-77).

Though a subtle, profound, and at times abstruse theologian, the author shows himself as practical. The preacher in him takes over frequently and in intermittent passages of exhortation seeks to apply the truth of theology to the situation of his readers. His combination of literary skill and pastoral concern has produced some of the most eloquent and moving passages in the NT. People who have no detailed acquaintance with the book still know such expressions as "since we are surrounded by so great a cloud of witnesses" (12:1), "Jesus Christ is the same yesterday and today and for ever" (13:8), "we have no lasting city" (13:14), and the glowing benediction of 13:20-21.

Origin, Destination, and Date. While the book tells us something about its author, it gives us virtually no information about where it was written and to whom it was addressed. The closing greeting from "those who come from Italy" (13:24) has been commonly interpreted as a message sent home by Italians who were with the author and thus as evidence that the book is a letter written from a place outside Italy and addressed to a group inside Italy, probably at Rome. The fact that the first known citation of the work is by Clement of Rome lends some support to this theory. On the other hand the Greek phrase translated as above is ambiguous (see below on 13:24) and may mean simply "Italians"—e.g. native members of a church in Italy as distinguished from visiting missionaries.

Furthermore it is not certain that this greeting was an original part of the work. Though traditionally designated a letter on the basis of the final paragraph (13:22-25) and the personal request for intercessory prayer (13:18-19), the book actually has more the literary character of a treatise or a homily, a sermonic exhortation. For this reason some have suggested that an editor, noting the popularity of Paul's letters, composed an epistolary ending after the Pauline pattern (cf. II Cor. 1:11-12; Phil. 2:19, 23-24; 4:20-22) and added it in the hope of attracting more readers by giving the impression of a letter. In fact there has been much discussion on whether all of ch. 13 may be an addition, since it obviously does not fit into the close-knit structure of chs. 1-12. If a 2nd author produced it, however, he was clearly one who shared the same world of ideas,

897

and was trained in the same school of rhetoric, for both thought and style are similar to those of the original author. It seems more probable, therefore, that ch. 13—or at least vss. 1-17—was composed by the same author as chs. 1-12, either as an original part of the work for the purpose of including some practical afterthoughts, or possibly as a later supplement to commend it to a new group of readers, or even as a separate writing which was joined to the longer work by an editor. Nevertheless it must be admitted that assuming all of ch. 13 to be an original part of the work gives us little help in identifying either the place of writing or the readers to whom it was addressed.

If the book was intended as a letter, it perhaps originally had an epistolary introduction which became lost in transmission or was dropped by an editor seeking to circulate it beyond the group addressed. If so, it is barely possible that the title "to the Hebrews" had some basis in the text. Otherwise it must be viewed as an editorial interpretation of the content and thus gives little clue to the original address. In any case the phrase is not very specific; it could mean either Jews or Jewish Christians, and the latter designation might apply to many different communities in the early church. Though some scholars in recent times have defended the title "to the Hebrews" in the sense of Jewish Christians, most have challenged it and shown how little support the text provides. They see the arguments of the book as aimed at Gentile Christians, or at Christians in general, who are well acquainted with the LXX, which was the Bible of the early church, but know little or nothing of contemporary Judaism.

Nor can the date be fixed with precision. The citation of the work by Clement *ca.* 96 indicates that it was in circulation by that time. The lack of any reference to the destruction of the temple has been urged as evidence that it originated before 70. But inasmuch as the author is interested in the tabernacle rather than the temple, this argument from silence is of doubtful significance. In fact it has been suggested that the author avoids mentioning the temple because he was writing after it had been destroyed. More significant are the exhortations in the text to endurance and discipline (e.g. 3:14; 10:23, 36; 12:1-11; cf. ch. 11) which may imply that the readers face the threat of persecution, and esp. the mention of "former days" (10:32-34) when the readers suffered a period of persecution. Earlier commentators interpreted these as evidence the book was written during or shortly before the persecution of Roman Christians by Nero in 64-67; assuming the readers to be Jewish Christians in Rome, they took the "former days" to be the period when Claudius banished the Jews from the city (Acts 18:2). Recent interpreters, however, have been more inclined to take the persecution of "former days" as that under Nero and the present threat as either a danger that faced a particular Christian group thereafter or a general persecution of Christians believed to have occurred in the reign of Domitian (81-96).

Significant also are the evidences that the readers are Christians of the 2nd or 3rd generation (e.g. 2:3; 5:12; 6:1). Some scholars have found what they claim to be signs that the author was acquainted with a number of Paul's letters. Since it appears that these letters were not generally circulated until after the publication of Acts, such clues, if valid, would date the book in the last decade or so before its citation by Clement. If the reference to Timothy (see below on 13:23) is an original part of the book, however, it suggests that the author had some contact with the missionary circle gathered by Paul, in which no doubt many of the apostle's ideas and expressions long persisted in preaching and teaching. Thus there seems to be no sure foundation for fixing a more precise date than sometime during the period between *ca.* 60 and 96.

Purpose. On the traditional assumption, expressed in the title, that the book was addressed to Jewish Christians the author's purpose has commonly been described as strengthening the faith of readers about to abandon their commitment, perhaps under pressure of persecution, and return to the religion of the synagogue. Close study of the text, however, shows that it fails to deal with the real issues between the early church and the synagogue. Modern scholars who defend the traditional address, therefore, see a somewhat different purpose. E.g. one suggests that those addressed are members of a community of conservative, legalistic bent, interpreting the gospel within the framework of Judaism rather than as fulfillment of the old covenant. The author's purpose then is to win them to an understanding of the gospel along the lines of Stephen or of Paul, a gospel which sees the dynamic and creative elements set in motion by Jesus Christ and grasps the missionary, expansionist character of Christianity.

If the view of a majority of modern interpreters may be accepted—that the book is addressed to Christians whose "Hebrew" background is limited to the LXX—then the author's purpose may best be seen in his exhortations. These he aims at readers whom he views as in danger, not of apostasy, but of inattention, complacency, and drifting into unbelief. He is seeking not so much to strengthen the commitment of new converts as to reawaken the lost zeal and fervor of longtime Christians. Thus in his writing he combines theological argument and homiletical exhortation in order that he may both inform his readers and persuade them to perseverance, self-discipline, and mutual love. The understanding of the role of Christ which he presents is intended not merely for contemplation but for appropriation and action.

Distinctive Features. One of the most prominent elements in the book—and one of the most puzzling to the modern reader—is the use made of OT quotations. One trained in contemporary literary and historical method may suspect the author of unhistorical, allegorical, and arbitrary interpretations and thus discount his argument. For him and for his readers the LXX was the authoritative Bible, and critical problems concerning its accuracy did not occur to them. We use an English text translated from the Hebrew, and at times it does not seem to support the author's point. In at least one case (Ps. 104:4) the LXX reading is one of several possible translations of a difficult passage but differs from the choice in the English text.

In some cases (1:5-13; 5:5; 6:14) the author uses the OT as though it were a direct quotation from God himself. Examination of these passages in their original setting shows that he has grasped the main thrust of most of them. The divergence from modern interpretation is not so great as one at first supposes. In 2 instances (2:12; 10:5-7) he uses the OT as a quotation from the preexistent Christ. These are hardly persuasive to a modern reader, but it should be noted that the author's christological convictions do not rest solely on these passages. On the basis of many converging testimonies he has come to his faith that Jesus is Lord and Son of God. In these 2 passages he finds a confirmation which seems to him remarkable and to us accidental. His convictions, however, are not threatened if the witness of these passages is withheld.

Much has also been made of the presence of Platonic ideas in the book. The contrast of the earthly tabernacle as copy or shadow with the heavenly sanctuary as exemplar and reality is basic to the argument. The death of Christ is seen as first of all an event in the eternal world of God, the self-giving of God to his creatures; but it is also an event in human history, the Crucifixion. This may be a derivative from the Platonic philosophy common in the first cent. The ideas of Alexandrian Jews such as Philo have undoubtedly influenced the author. But their Platonic character is often overstated and their constant connection with the biblical history of salvation overlooked or underestimated.

The idea that Christ has offered the true and complete sacrifice and that he now ministers as priest in the real, the heavenly, sanctuary is certainly basic to the book. The interpretation of the fulfillment of the OT, the old covenant, the sacrificial cultus, and even prophetic ethics all depend on it. But these ideas are set in the midst of a dynamic historical understanding of the unfolding purpose of God. Also permeating the book are ideas of eschatology —i.e. the anticipation that God will soon catastrophically bring the present age to an end and inaugurate a new age. Examples are the world to come (2:5), the urgency of today (3:7, 15), the present era as the last time (1:2; 3:14; 6:11), and the stress on the once-for-all character of Christ's offering (7:27; 9:12; 10:10). Even the idea of perfection may be wrongly read as a Platonic term, overlooking its eschatological character as applied to Christ (cf. 2:10; 5:9; 7:28) and to the Christian (cf. 10:14; 11:40; 12:23). The eschatological ideas are indeed remarkably similar to contemporary developmental ideas in taking seriously the notions of time, movement, and growth.

For Further Study. James Moffatt, *Heb.*, 1924. T. H. Robinson, *Heb.*, 1933. William Manson, *Heb.*, 1951. A. C. Purdy in *IB*, 1955. Antony Snell, *The New and Living Way*, 1959. Erich Dinkler in *IBD*, 1962.

I. THE THEME (1:1-4)

This opening statement (all of vss. 1-4) is a single long, sonorous sentence in elegant Greek. It introduces the theme of the work, connects it with the religious traditions of the immediate past, and in a few pregnant phrases indicates the central significance of Jesus Christ in the working out of the purpose of God.

1:1. *God's Revelation to Men.* The author assumes that his readers share his attitude toward the reli-

gious traditions of Israel. God has spoken **to our fathers** at various times and in **various ways.** This is a real and effectual revelation of God to men. What the prophets spoke and wrote was the word of God, i.e. God's own address to his creatures. This is not only information about God but a personal word spoken by God to men. In this speech God opens himself to men, admits them to his presence, bestows himself on them in fellowship. The prophetic tradition knows itself in awed humility as the bearer of the wonderful gift of the knowledge of the God who made and sustains the world. He has established a covenant with Israel, granted them the knowledge of his love for all mankind, and called them to be the servants of his mercy.

1:2-4. *Jesus as God's Ultimate Revelation.* In view of this lofty estimate of the traditions of Israel, what the author has to say about Jesus Christ is quite moving in its impact. He regards Christ the Son as the bringer of fulfillment of the purposes of God and ascribes to him a series of titles and accomplishments. **These last days** refers to the time of fulfillment of the purpose of God spoken of in the OT. The climax and culmination of God's working in history has appeared in the career of the man Jesus of Nazareth. His life and mission, his death and resurrection comprise God's final speech to men. What he began to say through the prophets of Israel he has now brought to completion in this person. God has condescended to use human language in order to speak to his creatures; what he has to say finally could not be expressed in words alone but took the form of a human life, a life whose obedience and dedication mark the turning point of human history and embody the love of God for men. The decisive revelation of God is given, not in a document, but in a person; who this person is unfolds in the remaining clauses of vss. 1-4.

1:2a. The term **Son** has acquired metaphysical overtones in the course of theological controversy. These are defensible in their theological context, but ought not to be read into this passage. The meaning here is that of the OT tradition: one who has a unique relationship to the Father, one who carries out the will and purpose of the Father, and who therefore has a unique and supreme revelatory function. But it should be noted that though the author applies very exalted titles to the Son, he also maintains the distinction between Father and Son and indeed consistently subordinates the Son to the Father. The titles and activities ascribed to the Son in the following vss., however, certainly strain this OT language to its uttermost limits and push strongly in the direction of the language of the Nicene Creed, in which the 4th-cent. church declared the Son to be "very God of very God, . . . of one substance with the Father."

1:2b. Because he is the Son, he is also **heir of all things.** The promise of the royal pss. (cf. e.g. Ps. 2:8) finds fulfillment in the work of the Son. All human wisdom, wealth, and glory are properly his. All human suffering, defeat, and disgrace he also makes his own. It is the teaching of the gospels that the way to honor is the way of the cross.

1:2c. Late Jewish theology saw wisdom as the power of God and the agent of creation. In Hellenistic Christianity the Son was identified as the Logos, or Word, of God, **through whom . . . he created the world** (cf. John 1:3).

1:3a. The Greek word translated **reflects** may mean also "radiates," which would imply a more active role; whereas "reflects" suggests that "the Son can do . . . only what he sees the Father doing" (John 5:19). More important, the NT gives new content to the word **glory.** Secular conceptions of glory are equivalent to fame or good report, but new content is invested in this term when it is seen in the light of the Son's obedience unto death. It is the special glory of God that he gives himself in the service of his creation. The image in **bears the very stamp of his nature** is of the impress of a seal in wax or clay. As the impression of the signet testifies to the origin of a letter, so the mission of the Son shows its derivation from the will of the Father. When one encounters the Son, one observes the sign of the Father's activity. **Upholding the universe** expresses the OT idea of creation as that of a continuous work of God. He has not only made the world; he supports and sustains it. God's relationship to the world is through **his word of power.** He is not merely the first mover, but one whose relationship to the world is personal, taking the form of speech.

1:3b. The central theme of the entire work appears for the first time in a subordinate clause— **when he had made purification for sins.** The author seeks to show how Jesus Christ fulfills the Levitical priesthood, thus bringing to light the reality which the priesthood symbolizes or foreshadows. But in this passage his chief concern is to assert the glory of Christ. When he finished his work of purification, he achieved authority and power, symbolized by the image of **the right hand of the Majesty** (cf. Phil. 2:9).

1:4. The assertion that the Son is **superior to angels** and the following paragraph make little sense to us because angels play no significant role in our thought. But for the first cent. reference to angels was not speculation about heaven's population; it was concern for revelation. God was so remote and exalted that revelation became possible only if heavenly messengers were at hand to convey God's message to men. In the thought of the rabbis, angels were the intermediaries who brought the law (cf. Gal. 3:19). It is in this light that we must see the author's concern. Jesus is greater than the angels; he has a **name . . . more excellent:** the Son. He does a more perfect work: the fulfillment of OT prophecy, including the prophetic institution of sacrifice. He brings the perfect and complete revelation, the disclosure of God's love in the cross.

II. The Identity of Jesus Christ (1:5–4:13)

After the eloquent statement of his theme, the author moves into a lengthy theological statement (1:5–10:18) consisting of 2 main sections, each having passages of exhortation which apply the message to the life and situation of the readers. This first main section deals with the question: Who is Jesus Christ? The author has already indicated his convictions on this question in the series of ascriptions contained in the opening thematic statement. He now proceeds to support and defend these claims by comparing Jesus first to the angels, the heavenly beings who are the bearers of divine revelation, and then to Moses, the mediator of the covenant given by God to Israel after the exodus deliverance. His practical interests appear clearly in the way he makes an application of his theological statement in 2 sections of exhortation (2:1-4; 3:6b–4:13), which contain practical reflections on the meaning of Christ's preeminence to the believer.

A. Superiority to the Angels (1:5–2:18)

This first section has 3 parts: a demonstration from scripture that Jesus is superior to the angels (1:5-14), an exhortation to take this fact seriously (2:1-4), and a summary discussion of Jesus' work in salvation (2:5-18).

1:5-14. Demonstration from Scripture. The superiority of the Son over the angels is shown by 7 quotations from the OT: 5 of them assert the preeminence of the Son in his unique relationship to the Father; the other 2 stress the servant function of the angels and their obligation to worship the Son.

1:5a. The first quotation, Ps. 2:7, is from a "royal" ps., a song used in the enthronement of a king in Israel. **"Thou art my Son, today I have begotten thee"** was a legal formula used in the ceremony of adoption in ancient Semitic countries. The father pronounced the formula to the child whom he was adopting, with witnesses present to certify the act. The child thus became the son and heir of his father; in ancient law no distinction was made between natural and adopted children. The use of the formula in the enthronement ceremony stressed such a relationship between the covenant God and the king. Here the author sees the ceremony of enthronement as a prophetic event pointing forward to the coming of the true King and the words of the hymn as supremely fitting in the enthronement of the Messiah. In the Lukan tradition (Luke 3:22) the baptism of Jesus is interpreted as a coronation.

1:5b. The 2nd quotation is from II Sam. 7:14, the prophecy of Nathan concerning the establishment of David's kingdom. David was the king par excellence for the Jews and a favorite prophetic symbol. He had been called from his tasks as a shepherd to become the shepherd of his people, and God had promised that his throne would be established forever. From the long and moving speech of Nathan the author chooses the words that assert the father-son relationship of God and the Davidic king. Here David is treated as a prophetic figure who finds his true place as a preparation for the great King, "great David's greater Son."

1:6. The 3rd quotation does not appear in the Hebrew text but comes from a LXX expansion of the conclusion to the Song of Moses (Deut. 32:43). In the best LXX manuscripts the reading is "God's sons," but texts with "God's angels" may have been in use by early Christians (cf. the LXX rendering of Ps. 97:7c, "Worship him, all his angels"). In the LXX context **him** clearly means God, but here the author views it as referring to the Son.

1:7. Ps. 104:4 lauds the greatness of God, who uses his creation as royal regalia, making "winds thy messengers, fire and flame [i.e. lightning] thy ministers." The Hebrew text is ambiguous, however, and capable of at least 2 other translations, one of which, as found in the LXX, is followed here. The author uses this quotation as a kind of stepping-stone to the last 3 citations. The meaning is: this is what God says about the angels, his messengers, but what he says about the Son is far greater.

1:8-9. Ps. 45:6-7 (see comment) is another of the royal pss. declaring the honor and favor of God to the anointed king of Israel. This ps. stresses the permanence of the **kingdom,** the king's love of **righteousness,** and the consequent graciousness of God, who bestows preeminent favor on him.

1:10-12. The quotation from Ps. 102:25-27 is notable in that the ps. is addressed to Yahweh, the God of the covenant, but the regular LXX translation of this divine name by a word meaning "Lord" enables the author to apply the text to Jesus, who is the Lord from the Christian viewpoint. Thus understood, the passage asserts Jesus' activity in the creation of the world and adds that the creation is transient but the creator is eternal. It should be noted that the early Christian conviction that Jesus is Lord does not rest solely on such debatable interpretations of the OT but on a total interpretation of what he did, what he said, and what he was. Many different lines of OT interpretation converge on this conviction. This passage did not create the conviction, but once the conviction of Christ's lordship existed, it was natural that passages like this should be used to expound the meaning of his status as Lord.

1:13-14. Ps. 110:1 (see comment), another of the royal pss., forms the climax of the series of quotations. It speaks of the exaltation of the king to the **right hand** of honor, power, and majesty. Though the ps. was used in the enthronement of kings of Israel, it was historically true of none of them. Its truth is prophetic: in the victory of Jesus the Son the validity of earlier enthronements is established. Through his obedience to death he won a victory over his **enemies** and now reigns. By way of contrast the angels, great and powerful as they are, have been sent forth as servants **for the sake of those** whom God seeks to save.

2:1-4. *An Exhortation.* Ch. 2 opens with one of the several sections of exhortation which punctuate the book. The author evidently fears that his readers are in danger of drifting away from the message concerning Jesus Christ and urges them to hold fast to it for 2 reasons: (*a*) because of the judgment that awaits those who neglect it and (*b*) because the message has been **declared . . . by the Lord** himself and affirmed **by signs and . . . miracles** worked by God.

2:2-3. The **message** of the old covenant **declared by angels was valid.** Everyone who transgressed it came under the judgment of God. This is the premise which the author and his readers share. But if this message is valid and brings judgment to those who disobey it, how much more serious it is to ignore the message brought by the Son! This message was given by Jesus himself. He is the greatest of the prophets and speaks the word of God with authority, not simply as one who hands on a tradition. **Those who heard him,** i.e. the apostles, transmitted his message through their preaching, bringing it to people like those addressed here.

2:4. Their testimony was not by words alone, however, but was accompanied by miracles and **by gifts of the Holy Spirit.** The early church did not regard miracles as objects of faith or as ends in themselves but as corroboration of the testimony given by Christ and his apostles. The object of faith is Christ himself; the miracles are signs which command attention but point beyond themselves to the person whose message and mission they accompany and celebrate.

The danger of the people addressed here is not heresy or immorality but neglect and carelessness. They are in peril of drifting away from the word of God. Judgment will overtake them, not because of gross wickedness, but because they **neglect** the salvation offered them in Jesus Christ.

2:5-18. *Jesus' Work in Salvation.* The author now resumes his theological argument. The superiority of Christ to the angels is urged not only because scripture testifies to it (1:5-14) but also because of what Christ was and did during the days of his flesh.

2:6-9. Ps. 8 speaks of the wonder of **man** as compared with the majesty of the heavens; God has made him but little less than divine and subjected all things to him. In quoting the LXX of Ps. 8:4-6 (see comment) the author underlines the point that there are no exceptions to this statement; **nothing** is **outside his control.** But, he adds, human experience shows us that actually not everything is in subjection to man. The fulfillment of this statement is therefore to be sought, not in the lives of men, but in the career of **Jesus.** The Son was indeed **made lower than the angels** for a time, but **because of the suffering of death . . . for everyone** he is now **crowned with glory and honor.** The mission of Jesus is thus seen as the fulfillment of the prophecy of Ps. 8, with the implication that he is the man of whom the psalmist writes, the true man whose career calls forth the wonder of the prophet. By his self-humiliation he identifies himself with mankind so that he becomes a representative man and what he undergoes becomes the experience of the human race. What does not normally happen to men occurs in the person of Jesus. Through God's goodness mankind has in its representative, Jesus Christ, the experience of God's crown of glory and honor.

2:10-11. The thought just intimated is now developed. Christ is the pioneer of human **salvation.** He has gone out into the wilderness alone and broken the trail. This he has done by his identification of himself with men: **he is not ashamed to call them brethren.** But 2 other important ideas are also expressed. God's initiative in human salvation is solemnly emphasized. The Creator brings **many sons to glory** by making the Son **perfect through suffering.** Man's **origin** in God is also affirmed. Christ, **who sanctifies,** and men who are sanctified by his work come from God. It is important to note that this author who stresses the defilement of sin and the resulting separation from God also emphasizes man's origin in God and the kinship of Christ with sinners.

2:12-13. The use of OT quotations (Ps. 22:22; Isa. 8:17-18) is again interesting and instructive. Jesus Christ, as the fulfillment of God's revelation, is seen as the speaker of the prophetic word through the psalmist and the prophet. An interpreter today would begin with an examination of the passage in its literary and historical context and be concerned to note first what the words meant to their first readers. The author by contrast has a vivid sense of being confronted by God's address both in Christ and in the OT and therefore regards it as proper to read the word of prophecy in the light of its fulfillment. When he listens to the prophetic word of the OT it is really the voice of Christ that he is hearing. Thus he sees the prophet's identification of himself with the people of God as a prediction of Christ's identification of himself with men in his incarnation.

2:14-18. Because those whom God seeks to save are **flesh and blood,** the Son takes the **same nature** on himself to enter into battle on behalf of his brothers and **deliver** them from **fear** and **bondage.** For men of the first cent. man's plight in the world was seen as bondage to alien spirits. An important part of early Christian preaching portrays Christ as the one who overcomes the demonic host and their chief. His power to cast out demons, heal the sick, and cleanse lepers was seen as assurance that he had both authority and power to overcome the forces which held man in slavery. The same imagery is used here, in a way which assumes that the language is familiar to the readers. The stress, however, is not so much on the victory of Christ as on the way he conformed himself **in every respect** to his brothers, sharing their plight in order that he might **make expiation for the sins.** As high priest he not only represents God's purpose in rescuing his creation but has undergone temptation and suffering and thus **is able to help** men who are subject to these afflictions.

B. Superiority to Moses (3:1-6a)

The blend of theological exposition and exhortation which characterizes this book is well illustrated in this section. Its purpose is to complete the demonstration of Christ's superiority to the law by showing that he is not only greater than the angels, the heavenly mediators of the law, but also greater than Moses, God's human instrument in the giving of the law. The opening vs., however, has the hortatory tone, which is picked up again in vs. 6b and continued to 4:13 in a lengthy homily.

3:1. In this vs. the author reminds his readers that they are **holy,** not through self-purification, but through their relationship to Jesus Christ. They **share in a heavenly call;** the real center of gravity of their existence is not in their earthly circumstances but in God's will for their **glory.** They are reminded to **consider Jesus,** who is both **apostle and high priest.** As apostle he represents, not his own interests, but those of the one who sent him—here again the divine initiative in salvation is stressed. As high priest he mediates between God and man, bringing God's will to men and interceding for men in the divine presence.

Our confession does not refer to confession of sins, or to confession of faith in the sense of affirming a creed. The central reference of the term "confession" in the NT is rather doxological; it is praise of God. It is the Christian's recognition that his proper attitude toward God is adoration and praise. Man's failure and his misery is that he is bound up

in himself and gives no thought to his creator. In Christ he recovers the proper dimensions of his existence and finds his proper place in creation by joining in the chorus of praise ascending to God. The Christian is first of all a worshiper; his activity as theologian, as man of affairs, or as one ethically concerned flows properly from his life of praise to God.

3:2-6a. Num. 12:7 in the LXX speaks of "my servant Moses" as "faithful in all my house." Alluding to this, the author says that Christ was like Moses except that, instead of being a **servant,** he **was faithful over God's house as a son.** Therefore Christ is worthy of greater honor. Moses testified to matters which **were to be spoken later.** Christ is the content of these matters.

C. Exhortation (3:6b–4:13)

The exhortation compares the readers to Israel in the wilderness and suggests that their lukewarmness will cause them **to fall away from the living God** and miss their deliverance.

3:6b-11. *The Household of God.* The author begins by recalling to his readers what they are—the **house,** i.e. household, of God. This is one of the common biblical pictures of the people of God, the church. It emphasizes God's role as father, his protective and nurturing care of his family, the discipline which he imposes on his children, the love and affection which he displays, and the intimate relationship which they enjoy. They exist, not as slaves or as servants but as members of the family; they move about in the home with confidence and freedom.

3:6b. A conditional clause is a reminder that the family relationship is not automatic or to be presumed on. It is only as we **hold fast our confidence and pride in our hope** that we remain God's household. **Confidence** implies the confident boldness of children in their own home. **Pride** might be expressed rather as exultant rejoicing or even boasting. God has provided his church with great riches, but the church can experience poverty if it becomes absentminded and overlooks what God has done. The author seeks to rouse his readers to a state of confident boldness in which they will rejoice in what God has done for them.

3:7-11. This quotation from Ps. 95 invites God's people to come into his presence to worship. It reminds them that God is the creator of all things and that the whole creation lives by his bounty but, most important of all, that he is their God and they are his people, the sheep of his pasture. It is only after this recital of the goodness of God and the invitation to worship that the solemn warning is given. Israel **in the wilderness** was surrounded by the evidences of God's goodness and care, and yet many of the people missed the encounter with God. Their problem was not the gross carnal appetites but "hardness of heart" or, as we might render it, insensitivity. They simply had too many things on their minds to give heed to the presence of God among them.

3:12-19. *The Failure of Israel.* The exhortation becomes specific. Be alert lest history repeat itself. The essence of sin is idolatry, the refusal to worship the true God. This is also the **deceitfulness of sin.** As long as we avoid the more dramatic sins and crimes we consider ourselves sound. But the subtlety of sin is that it puts something—sometimes something good—in the place of God. Man's "original" sin is to put his own preferences before the will of God, and as a result all the structures of his life are distorted and misshapen. The congregation here addressed was most likely an orderly and respectable group, unmarred by crimes or vices. But in their complacent respectability they are in danger of losing God. What they need most of all is the recovery of a sensitivity to God's work and presence among them.

3:14. The implication of **for we share in Christ** is that an action in the past has made us effectual partakers of Christ **if only we hold . . . firm** the solid foundation we have been given. The Christian's standing is not the product of his decision, his obedience, or his theological insight. He stands on the basis of God's deed in Jesus Christ and God's act in uniting him to Christ. He can render this ineffectual for himself by drifting away from it through preoccupation or carelessness. But even the one who has drifted can recover the center again. He can find anew the great event that gives meaning and perspective to his life and build again on the foundation laid by God.

3:16-19. Three rhetorical questions focus the author's concern: Who **heard and yet were rebellious?** With whom was God **provoked forty years?** Whom did God forbid to **enter his rest?** It was the very people who experienced the deliverance of the Exodus, the notable sign of God's love and care. The parallel is an instructive one for early Christians. For Israel the great emblem of God's mercy was the Exodus. Here was the ground of their assurance that God had called them to be his people. For Christians the decisive act of God is Jesus Christ, who is the sign of God's mercy to his creatures. But the exodus generation contrived to drift into **unbelief** and lost the promise. It is equally easy for Christians to miss the significance of Christ and to idle away into unbelief. That the author regarded this as a real possibility for his contemporaries is shown by the fact that he continues his exhortation for most of the next ch.

4:1-10. *The Danger of Failure Today.* In 3:18 the sabbath **rest** has been mentioned, a theme which is now picked up and developed. The sabbath was central to Jewish piety both in Palestine and among those who lived in the Gentile world. It was a sign with both backward and forward reference. It looked back to the creation of the world and was an enduring reminder to Jews that their God was no provincial deity but the God of the entire earth. It also served as a memorial of the covenant and recalled to the Jews their vocation as the people of God and their destiny to bring the knowledge of his name to all peoples. It looked forward to the rest that God promised to his people. Its weekly observance was a reminder that though Israel was small, little regarded among the nations, often despised and persecuted, its future was with God. And just as **God rested** from his labors on the sabbath, so a weary and discouraged Israel should one day enter into God's rest. The Promised Land seemed to one generation the fulfillment of the hope of rest, but the people were unwilling to take the risk of trusting God and for their lack of faith lost the promise.

Underlying the thought of this section is the idea that the sabbath is prophetic in character. Its meaning is not exhausted in the backward reference to creation and the covenant; it has also a forward reference to a yet unfinished work of God. Jesus Christ is the realization of this forward thrust; the prophetic work of God comes to completion in him. Those who are in him, those who have faith, therefore already take part through this faith in God's sabbath rest. And faith is decisive. Its presence means a real participation in the fulfillment of God's plan. Its absence makes the message of no benefit to those who hear because they do not receive it with faith. And here is the throbbing concern of the book. Good news came to Israel but because faith was lacking there was no entry into **God's rest.** The abiding peril of the Christian church is the same: the good news is proclaimed, but unless it is received by faith the promise remains ineffectual. Israel's history is one of God's goodness and man's disobedience. But God speaks of another day and in Christ offers once more the gift of rest to those who believe. **There remains a sabbath rest for the people of God** and those who have faith in Christ enter into that rest.

4:11-13. *The Word of God.* The exhortation comes to an eloquent climax. **Let us . . . strive to enter that rest,** that no one repeat the history of Israel's **disobedience.**

Faith is the active thing it is partly because that which calls it forth, the **word of God,** is also **living and active.** Since the invention of printing there has been the constant temptation to think of the word of God as a deposit of doctrine or a book. For the Scriptures the word of God is the word which God addresses to his creation. It is the word which he speaks through the prophet, making his will known to his people. It is the word of power by which he created and sustains the world. It is the word of apostolic preaching, declaring the good news of what God has done in Jesus Christ. It is Christ himself as the sum and substance of God's speech to man. In all of these usages it is the personal encounter with the God who honors his creatures by addressing himself to them in the demand for responsibility and the offer of life.

The word which God addresses to man establishes effective communication. It penetrates into the innermost recesses of the personality, **piercing to the division of soul and spirit,** and leaves no place to hide from his presence. The prophets impressed their contemporaries in this way. An encounter with Jesus Christ was for many a similar experience of being opened up to oneself and to his searching eyes. One reason that unbelief remains so constant a threat in the Christian community is man's insistent tendency to live in his self-chosen deceptions. But man cannot hide from God. The peril of man's encounter with God is that of being stripped of all evasions and defenses and of being compelled to see himself with clarity and candor.

III. The Accomplishment of Jesus Christ (4:14–10:18)

The 2nd main section of the book discusses what Jesus Christ accomplished in his mission. Exposition and exhortation are mingled, with the preacher following hard on the heels of the theologian. The author first sets out his view that Christ is priest after the order of Melchizedek (4:14–5:10), then enters on a lengthy exhortation in which rebuke, warning, and encouragement are mingled together (5:11–6:20), next asserts the superiority of the priesthood of Jesus to that of the Levites (7:1-28), and finally offers a summary discussion of Jesus' ministry as high priest (8:1–10:18).

A. High Priest After the Order of Melchizedek (4:14–5:10)

4:14-16. *A Transition.* These vss. summarize the preceding exhortation and lead into the new section, which discusses the priestly activity of the Son.

4:14a. The high priest in the old covenant **passed through** the veil separating the holy place from the holy of holies once each year as he made atonement for the sins of the people. Christians have a **great high priest,** a high priest beyond compare, **who has passed through the heavens,** fulfilling what is symbolized in the entry of the holy of holies and coming into the presence of God. He is identified explicitly as **Jesus, the Son of God.** This identification holds the earthly and the heavenly names together and points to the fact that he combines in this remarkable way an ordinary life as a human being with an extraordinary calling as God's high priest.

4:14b-15. As our personal history involves this great event and includes the person of Jesus, the great high priest, we should **hold fast our confession.** At once this is a testimony before men of our faith in and loyalty to God and also a paean of praise to God for his marvelous acts of redemption. The readers are characteristically urged to remember the meaning of their experience and not to lose it through inattention or neglect. The author supports his exhortation with a reason: our high priest is not inaccessible, above man's struggle, but one who has endured the vicissitudes of a human life, who knows what temptations human beings face and can therefore be sympathetic to their problems. His sinlessness is not the spotlessness of an object sealed from traffic or contamination but a human achievement. Jesus was really **tempted** but remained in obedience and fellowship with the Father and is thus without sin.

4:16. Because he has shared our experience we can have **confidence** as we approach the **throne,** a symbol of his triumph and authority. It is moreover the throne of **grace;** the chief characteristic of the rule of Christ is that it is gracious. He rules, not through the power of armies, but through the power of grace. God is strong enough and secure enough in his rule that he can show graciousness even to his enemies, even to enemies who respond with a crucifixion. Because the throne is occupied by one whose strength is his graciousness, those who draw near may confidently expect **to receive mercy . . . in time of need.**

5:1-10. *The Priestly Qualifications of Jesus.* Priests are chosen from among men **to act on behalf** of their fellows. They have the responsibility **to offer gifts and sacrifices** to God for both their own sins and those of others. Because they know what human

life is like they should be able to deal sympathetically with others, even with those who are **ignorant** or are wandering astray. The position is not one which men seek for themselves; the priest should be **called by God, just as Aaron was.**

5:5-6. Jesus fulfills the above qualifications. He did not seek the position but held it by divine appointment. His appointment came in the divine declaration of 2 royal pss. (2:7; 110:4). How these vss. gave Jesus the assurance of his calling to be high priest is not indicated. The Synoptic tradition quotes the first as a part of Jesus' experience at his baptism, and it may be that the author assumes the knowledge of traditions such as this among his readers. His use of the passages suggests his conviction that the voice of God speaking in the psalmists reaches its proper objective in the person of the man Jesus, who thus recognizes himself as the one divinely appointed to the task of high priesthood. Our more consistently historical approach to the OT and our preoccupation with psychological questions such as the way Jesus came to know himself as Messiah and high priest raise for us questions which occurred to neither the author nor his readers. It was enough for them that God spoke in the OT and that his message was delivered to the right person in reaching Jesus, who did not aspire to the duties of high priest, but accepted them when he was named by God.

5:7. The qualification of identity with the people was fulfilled by Jesus in his life of temptation and prayer. His fellowship with God and obedience to his will were not given at the outset and hermetically sealed throughout his life. They were achieved through strenuous effort and acceptance of suffering. **Loud cries and tears** may be a reference to the Passion, but shows at least the Semitic coloration of the account. Compared with the composure of Socrates in face of death or the Stoic fortitude so much admired in the W tradition the man of the Middle East is far less restrained in the expression of his emotions. Jesus wept as he contemplated Jerusalem (Luke 19:41); he showed anger at the harshness of his opponents (Mark 3:5); in Gethsemane he manifested strong emotion (Mark 14:33); but he also showed remarkable self-control in the face of the disbelief of his disciples (Mark 5:31), the crowd (Mark 5:40), and the authorities (Mark 14:61). The main point, however, is not that Jesus was exposed to great strains and sufferings but that in them he turned in prayer to God. **He was heard for his godly fear** and received deliverance from his afflictions, not the deliverance of escape, but the power to endure that came upon him.

5:8-10. Even though **he was a Son,** Jesus **learned obedience** in the school of suffering and through it **became the source of eternal salvation.** The language echoes that of Phil. 2:9 and stresses again the initiative of God in the work of Jesus Christ: he was heard, **being made perfect,** being designated by God a high priest. It is the Son who obeys, who suffers, but his obedience is the expression of the Father's will that men should be redeemed. The perfection mentioned here is not that of a painting or statue which satisfies all the criteria of artistic excellence but the perfection of that which is adapted to its purpose. The author's stress is not on the moral excellence of Jesus but on the fact that he submitted to whatever was necessary for the accomplishment of his work.

The use in this passage of chiasmus, rhetorical crisscrossing, is an interesting example of attention to style. In vss. 1-4 the priest's sympathetic sharing with men comes first, then the importance of being called by God. In vss. 5-10 the order is reversed, giving both literary elegance and the desired stress on the importance of Jesus' submission to suffering and its resultant exaltation to honor.

B. EXHORTATIONS (5:11-6:20)

5:11-14. *A Rebuke.* The previous section concludes with a 2nd reference to priesthood **after the order of Melchizedek** (cf. vs. 6), a figure mentioned only in passing in the OT and one of perplexity to us. It apparently perplexed people in the first cent. too, for the author acknowledges that he has **much to say** on the subject and great difficulty in making it clear. He opens a long section of exhortation by asserting that the difficulty lies, not in the expositor, but in the deficiencies of his readers, who **have become dull of hearing.** They ought by now to be teaching others, but are in need of learning the ABC's of God's word. At a time when they should be eating **solid food** they are still behaving like infants and living on **milk.** They have not yet acquired the ability to distinguish between good and evil and therefore cannot be dealt with as mature people.

This section adds to our knowledge of both the readers and the author. We can again see that the peril of those here addressed is not immorality or heresy. They are simply inattentive—Christians taking themselves for granted, neither anxious nor excited, but nevertheless in danger of losing their faith. They have not advanced in their understanding of the gospel, nor has Christian service equipped them to discriminate among values. They present the embarrassing sight of adults who are still bottle fed, an image with just enough humor to ease the bite of the rebuke it conveys. The author shows himself again as a theologian who is also a preacher. The interweaving of theology and exhortation throughout the book shows that his exposition is for the sake of obedience. Clarification is never enough; he insists on involvement. His intense moral earnestness is barely relieved by the seasoning of humor, which, however, is not permitted to disturb the exalted and elegant style.

6:1-8. *A Warning.* Rebuke is followed by warning. Complacency and indifference will end in the judgment of God. Proper and respectable churchmen do not realize the seriousness of their situation. They are actually on the verge of nailing Christ to the cross all over again.

6:1-3. The opening vss. are tantalizing in their vagueness. It is clear that the ABC's are to be left behind for growth toward **maturity;** it is clear that the list comprises a kind of catechism. But the context that would enable us to grasp the meaning and relationship of the terms is not supplied. The list is apparently given as elements familiar to the readers, elements which they are inclined to interpret as the whole of the Christian religion. Some of the terms offer no difficulty. **Repentance from dead works** (i.e. works which have no life-giving power) . . . **faith**

toward God . . . resurrection of the dead . . . eternal judgment sound like familiar elements in Christian teaching to us. But **ablutions,** lit. "baptisms" (note the plural), sound more like the ceremonial lustrations of Judaism than anything familiar in the Christian tradition. **Laying on of hands** too is a familiar Jewish practice and was taken over by Christians in connection with the forgiveness of sins, healing, and the bestowal of the Holy Spirit. But whatever the details may mean, the bearing of the total passage is clear. Christians must move on from beginnings to maturity. Here the author identifies himself with his readers: **this we will do if God permits.**

6:4-6. The danger of not moving on to maturity is that of sliding into **apostasy.** Here are some of the sharpest and most solemn words of the letter, indeed of scripture as a whole. The denial of the possibility of a 2nd **repentance** has troubled many readers, causing some to refuse the right of lapsed believers to be reinstated in the church and leading others to question the apostolic authorship of the letter. It is not clear whether the reason a 2nd repentance is deemed impossible is theological, i.e. the will of God or psychological, i.e. the hardening of the human heart. The distinction is indeed one which would not occur to the author but one which for modern readers is inevitable.

Tasted the goodness of the word of God (cf. Ps. 34:8) implies, not sampling, but a genuine experience of the reality. **Powers of the age to come** is common language in the early church, which believed that in Jesus Christ and his church the powers of the age to come were already at work, as evidences of the realism and earnestness of God in his redeeming work. God's future is already present where the gospel is preached and believed. Apostasy is to **crucify the Son of God.** Those who have once bowed before him in worship now join in encompassing his death and offering him to the **contempt** of bystanders.

6:7-8. The image of the cultivated field is common among the OT prophets. Israel is God's farm or vineyard, and he expects a harvest for all his work. The field which does not bring a harvest is worthless; its yield of **thorns and thistles** is only fit **to be burned.**

6:9-12. *Encouragement.* The warning is followed by words of encouragement. The solemn warning was necessary: apostasy follows complacency. But the author holds out **better things** for his readers, for God will not **overlook** the evidences of genuine faith among them—faith shown in their **work,** in their past and present deeds of mercy to his **saints,** and in the **love** which motivated these acts.

Confidence can repose in the sovereign goodness of God, who has brought **salvation** in Christ and has also awakened faith among men. If matters depend on men, the doom portrayed above would be the outcome. But since matters depend rather on God, there is ground for hope for the future of his children. And here again is the paradox. Because salvation is God's work, therefore do not be **sluggish** but hold your **hope** firmly to **the end** and become **imitators of those who through faith and patience inherit the promises.** Human cunning says: if it is all of God, then man can relax. Faith says: since it is all God's work, therefore hang on patiently to the end. Note the interesting succession: not faith and patience earn their reward, but faith and patience inherit the promises. One inherits what someone else has toiled to amass. The promise is a free and generous offer, not the result of haggling.

6:13-20. *Assurance.* Encouragement is followed by assurance. The deeds of God are recounted as a basis for the confidence just expressed. Our hope is not in the voltage generated by our faith, nor in the reputation earned by our good works, but solely in the character of the one who has made the promise. **God made a promise to Abraham** and confirmed it by an **oath.** He had made the promise earlier, and when Abraham was willing to offer up even his son at God's command, the promise was confirmed (Gen. 22:16-17). God condescends to man's craving for assurance and gives **two unchangeable things,** his word of **promise** and his **oath,** thus making his will toward men unmistakably clear and firm. It is interesting to note the difference of accent in Paul's reading of this same passage (Gal. 3:6-9). Paul stresses that the old covenant was also a religion of grace, that Abraham obtained the promise through faith. Here the emphasis falls on the faithfulness of God, a faithfulness underlined by his oath.

6:19*a*. After this rather involved analogy the long exhortation moves to its close with a pair of vivid pictures. Since God cannot lie we refugees have strong encouragement to grasp firmly the hope which has been extended to us. God offers the hope to us; inasmuch as he is dependable we ought to reach out and take it. This hope is a **sure and steadfast anchor of the soul**—i.e. for our life, for **soul** in the Bible is not some ethereal substance within man, but a way of expressing what we call person, or personality. The Christian's hope keeps him securely anchored in port. It gives him stability, poise, confidence, and it does this because of the surpassing reliability of the one who holds out the hope.

6:19*b*-20. The 2nd image is taken from the tabernacle. The Christian's **hope** does not linger in its outer courts; it enters into the holy of holies, **the inner shrine . . . where Jesus has gone** to be our **forerunner.** This is not the tabernacle in the wilderness nor the later temple but their counterpart in heaven, of which they are only shadows. The Christian hope, being fixed in Christ, enters with him into the realm of the real. Hope is thus a kind of participation in the reality hoped for because of the steadfastness of him who guarantees the hope. With the closing phrase the exhortation comes to a well-turned conclusion, which both reasserts the subject previously discussed and resumes the argument interrupted by the hortatory section.

C. The Superiority of Jesus' Priesthood to the Levitical Priesthood (7:1-28)

The closing words of ch. 6, a quotation from Ps. 110:4, reintroduce the figure of Melchizedek (cf. 5:6, 10), who is mentioned elsewhere in the OT only in Gen. 14:17-20. That such a shadowy figure should serve in a theological argument seems strange to us, and even stranger is the way the OT reference to him is interpreted. But unfamiliar as the interpreta-

tive principles may be to us, the argument of the ch. is clear. There is a priesthood older than that of Levi (vss. 1-3), and in the encounter of Abraham and Melchizedek it is also established as superior (vss. 4-10). Since the Levitical priesthood is plainly inadequate the priesthood is changed (vss. 11-14). Christ appears in the line of Melchizedek and introduces a better hope (vss. 15-19), which is guaranteed by an oath (vss. 20-22). This priesthood is permanent (vss. 23-25) and the sacrifice of Christ is offered once for all (vss. 26-28).

7:1-3. *An Older Priesthood.* The elements of the story in Gen. 14 are summarized briefly, with stress on the fact that Abraham gave a **tenth** of the plunder to Melchizedek. The significance of his name and title is then pointed out, relating him to the story of salvation as **king of righteousness** and **king of peace.** Finally rabbinic principles of interpretation are applied to stress his resemblance to the **Son of God.** For one trained in modern historical scholarship vs. 3 is only an argument from silence, and not particularly persuasive. But to the rabbis it was not only what God said in scripture that was to be noted but also what he did not say. The absence of vital statistics and of reference to parents is therefore used to heighten the mysterious significance of Melchizedek in the unfolding of salvation history. But having made his point the author leaves it quickly, since his interest is not so much in Melchizedek as in the priesthood which he represents.

7:4-10. *A Superior Priesthood.* Melchizedek blessed Abraham and received tithes from him. Since the greater blesses the lesser, Abraham concurred in the superiority of Melchizedek. Levi, whose descendants exact tithes from the people of Israel in accordance with the Mosaic law, actually offered **tithes** to Melchizedek in the person of his great-grandfather Abraham—an argument less cogent to us than to a people who stressed the continuity between generations and the subordination of the younger to the older. Vs. 8 reasserts the point of vs. 3. Since nothing is said in scripture about the death of Melchizedek the ancient interpreter can conclude that the silence is deliberate and meaningful: Melchizedek still lives; he continues a priest forever.

7:11-14. *The Priesthood Changed.* That Jesus is high priest has already been shown (4:14-5:10). But why another priesthood in the order of Melchizedek if the Levitical priesthood was adequate? The fact that another priestly order has been established shows that the priesthood of Aaron and his descendants did not achieve perfection. But a **change in the priesthood** means also a **change in the law.** This becomes clear when it is recalled that Jesus the high priest comes from the tribe of **Judah,** and that **Moses said nothing** authorizing priests from that tribe. Thus from the change of priesthood the author argues back to a change in the law which establishes the priesthood. All of this argumentation seems to us involved and obscure because we do not share the presuppositions about covenant, law, priesthood, and sacrifice which underlie it. Further, the logical progression seems to us not direct but crablike, sidling from one point to another.

7:15-19. *Christ in the Line of Melchizedek.* It is encouraging for us to note that even the author's contemporaries may have had difficulties with the paragraph above. To make matters clearer to them he introduces 2 illustrative parallels. The high priest is here. He is Jesus Christ. He has become priest, not by birth into the priestly tribe, but by virtue of a **life** which has overcome death. His high priesthood is established by his fulfillment of a priestly mission and confirmed by the prophetic word in Ps. 110:4. Thus the career of Jesus and the testimony of the scripture converge on the conclusion that he is God's high priest, not in the order of Levi, but in that of Melchizedek.

7:18-19. The 2nd illustration is an appeal to experience. The law was weak and useless and failed to bring about perfection; therefore it has been **set aside.** In its place a **better hope is introduced** which enables men to come into the divine presence.

7:20-22. *An Oath as Guaranty.* Another distinctive mark of the new covenant is that an oath accompanied its establishment. Priests in the Levitical order **took their office without an oath.** The high priest of the new covenant **was addressed with an oath.** Through the prophetic scriptures God assured him that his appointment was firm and unchangeable. God is not going to **change his mind.** Jesus is therefore the **surety of a better covenant** because behind him and his mission stand the determination of God himself, who has bound himself with an oath and thereby firmly established his promise to men.

7:23-25. *A Permanent Priesthood.* The numerous priests of the old covenant died and had to be replaced. But Christ lives **for ever** and therefore **holds his priesthood permanently.** At this point the preacher breaks through the involved chain of theological reasoning with a homiletical point. Because Christ lives forever he exercises his intercessory mission permanently and therefore **is able for all time to save those who draw near to God through him.** Christ's victory over death is an event in the temporal and eternal worlds; it is a theological affirmation with manifold consequences, one of which is stressed here. The Christian does not need many deliverers. Christ is quite adequate **since he always lives to make intercession for them.**

7:26-28. *A Sacrifice Once for All.* An earlier passage emphasized Christ's human experience, which equipped him to deal sympathetically with weakness. Here a complementary aspect of his career is stressed. He is the exceptional one—consecrated to God, beyond reproach, without stain, by the quality of his life effectively set apart from sinful men, through his victory over death **exalted above the heavens.** His uniqueness sets him apart from other high priests. They must **offer sacrifices daily,** for their own sins before those of others. Christ's sacrifice is a once-for-all offering of himself to God. Others are appointed high priests by the law in their human **weakness;** he has been appointed as **a Son ... made perfect for ever.** With this catalog of qualities in view it is important to note that he is our high priest. Great and wonderful as he is, it is the more remarkable that he is God's gift to us.

D. The Ministry of Jesus as High Priest
(8:1-10:18)

The 4th section interprets the work of Jesus as high priest in the heavenly sanctuary (8:1-5), im-

plying a new covenant (8:6-13) and offering a new sacrifice (9:1-14) which fulfills the promise of the new covenant (9:15-10:18). Its thought is a combination of Platonic ideas, in which the reality of the heavenly is contrasted with the shadowy character of the earthly, and biblical ideas which stress the forward movement of the purpose of God toward fulfillment. Thus ideas taken from the world of space are combined with those derived from the realm of time in a remarkable theological synthesis.

8:1-5. *Jesus' Ministry in the Heavenly Sanctuary.* The author seems aware that his previous argument is difficult and complex and so proceeds to restate it in a summary way. The word translated **point** can also be rendered "pith" or "substance." We have a high priest who possesses power, and he ministers in the tabernacle established by God, not by men. The risen and regnant Jesus has not gone into retirement but continues to serve as high priest in the heavenly sanctuary. The author marshals an array of images from Jewish theology. **Seated at the right hand** is not to be read lit.; the Jew of ancient times was well aware that his scriptures were permeated with images or metaphors. The right hand is the place of honor, preferment, and power. The joining of this image with that of the **throne of the Majesty** stresses again that the power of Jesus is derivative from God the Father and that it is his through his carrying out of the Father's purpose. **Majesty** reflects the Jewish reluctance to pronounce the name of God, a custom rooted in profound reverence for the transcendent God. A similar usage is reflected in expressions such as "kingdom of heaven" (Matt. 5:3) and "right hand of Power" (Matt. 26:64).

8:2. The reference to the **true tent** suggests that the author is not interested primarily in the Jerusalem temple but in its predecessor, the tabernacle. He may share the idea of Stephen (Acts 7), who regarded the building of the temple as a mistake; the tabernacle in the wilderness seems to him a better symbols of the voluntary relationship of God to his covenant people, as well as the character of the people as pilgrims. Or he may be writing at a time (see Intro.) when emotions aroused by mention of the temple destroyed by the Romans might divert readers from his argument. Whether we think of tabernacle or temple, we are concerned with an earthly structure which symbolizes a heavenly reality. Jesus, the great high priest, serves, not in an earthly shrine, but in the very presence of God.

Since this is true, the earthly sanctuary with its rituals and sacrifices is no longer important. There was a time when men related themselves to God through tabernacle or temple. The ministry of Jesus, however, has changed that situation. Men now should relate themselves to God through the new way opened to them through Christ's high-priestly work. Life in Christ opens new possibilities, a better covenant, better promises, through the man who lives forever.

8:3-5. What follows seems difficult to us, partly because the author's logic differs from ours, but more because we do not share his presuppositions about worship and sacrifice. High priesthood is established for the offering of **gifts and sacrifices;** so Christ as priest should also have an offering to make. We expect now a discussion of Christ's sacrificial activity;

instead it is postponed until 9:11, and a new line of argument appears in its place, pointing out the imperfections and inadequacy of the covenant with Israel. It is introduced by pointing out that if Christ **were on earth, he would not be a priest at all.** The earthly sanctuary had priests of the house of Levi appointed to serve. Jesus was not even of the priestly family. But the sanctuary which they served is not the true sanctuary. It is rather a **copy** of it, an earthly **shadow** cast by the heavenly reality. The quotation from Exod. 25:40 is used to prove the imitative or secondary character of the tabernacle. Moses' instructions were to follow the **pattern** disclosed to him on Mt. Sinai. We tend to read this text as meaning Moses was shown plans for the tabernacle; the author reads it to mean that Moses was given a glimpse of the heavenly reality and instructed to pattern the earthly sanctuary after it.

8:6-13. *The New Covenant.* The ministry of Christ is **more excellent** than the ministry of the old covenant because it mediates a better covenant and is based on **better promises.** Here we return to the groundwork laid in the opening chs. Jesus is the Son, and he is high priest in the distinctive order of Melchizedek. Without further argument on this point or additional buttressing with scripture the author now turns, not to the superiority of the new, but to the inferiority of the old—a point which he establishes with a quotation from Jer. 31:31-34 (see comment). Scripture itself testifies to the imperfections of the old covenant and looks longingly toward a future day when God will establish a new and better relationship. If the old covenant had been perfect, there would have been no reason for another.

8:8-13. The passage from Jer. makes clear that it was not the covenant that was to blame. God **finds fault** with his people. Israel's disobedience and waywardness were the ruin of the old covenant. Therefore God has to take other measures to achieve his goal of fellowship with his people. He will put his **laws into their minds** and **hearts,** so that all will be full of the knowledge of his will. In the light of this vision the old covenant is seen as inadequate, even **obsolete, . . . ready to vanish away.** At this point we return from examination of the old to an exposition of the offering brought by Jesus the priest.

9:1-14. *Old and New Sacrifices Contrasted.* The old may be obsolete, but it still has continuity with the new, and as copy or shadow it offers itself for edifying comparisons, which are drawn in meticulous detail. Vss. 1-10 discuss the earthly priesthood, describing the place where it functions (vss. 1-5), its way of approach to God (vss. 6-7*a*), its sacrifice (vs. 7*b*), and an evaluation of its work (vss. 8-10). Vss. 11-14 set forth somewhat more briefly the priesthood of Christ, following precisely the same pattern: the place of his ministry (vs. 11), his way of approach to God (vs. 12*a*), his sacrifice (vs. 12*b*), and an evaluation of his work (vss. 12*c*-14).

9:1-5. The description of the tabernacle is quite detailed, but it differs significantly from the account in Exod. 25:10-40 (see comment), which does not locate Aaron's rod or the urn containing the manna within the **Holy of Holies.** Whether another tradition is being followed here, or the details are altered for symbolic reasons, or the author is not esp. concerned about exact correspondence with the Exod.

account is not possible to say. He sketches the 2 main parts of the tabernacle clearly and mentions the chief furnishings, **lampstand** and **table** in the **Holy Place** and in the **Holy of Holies** the **altar of incense** and **ark of the covenant** containing the memorials of the exodus deliverance, with the figures of the **cherubim** above it.

9:6-7*a*. The approach to God is now presented. The priests are busy with their prescribed duties each day in the **outer tent.** The inner tent, however, is entered **but once a year** and only by the high priest in the offering for the sins of the people. This stresses the difficulty of access to God under the old covenant and the importance of the priestly office, without which expiation of sins is impossible.

9:7*b*. In the mention of the sacrifice 3 points may be noted:

a) The priest offers **blood,** which for Hebrew thought is the seat of life. For us it may suggest that in sacrifice the guilt of the worshiper is transferred to an animal which is put to death in his place. But biblical thought sees sacrifice rather as the offering of one's own life, symbolized by the identification of the worshiper and the sacrifice in the laying on of hands. When the prophets inveigh against the abuse of sacrifice it is the misunderstanding that they attack, the notion that man can barter with God or buy him off. Understood in the context of prophetic religion, sacrifice is a profound expression of man's basic relationship to God, his recognition of God's ultimate claim on him, and his way of offering his life to God.

b) The priest offers sacrifice **for himself** as well as the people. He does not stand aside from the people but in their midst, and his priestly character is enhanced by his awareness that he shares the frailty of his fellows. This aspect has been stressed previously (5:1-10) in outlining the credentials of Jesus as high priest.

c) The priest offers for the people's **errors.** This is a reminder that in the old covenant there was no way to expiate deliberate sins, e.g. apostasy. Sacrifice provides a way of atonement for sins of weakness but not for sins done "with a high hand." Sacrifice is efficacious for those who live within the covenant. It is only for those who stand before God as his people. It is not an automatic or magic device to provide cleansing for the impious or careless. Even in the old covenant man's relationship to God was personal and responsible.

9:8-10. This evaluation of old covenant sacrifice stresses 2 things: (*a*) the symbolism of the holy of holies as witness to the remoteness and inaccessibility of God and (*b*) the importance of sacrifice as the way of expiation of sins. Against the vegetation religions, which insisted on a natural relationship with God through the performance of prescribed ritual, the religion of Israel insisted that God can be known only as he makes himself known, and approached only in the way that he has provided. Israel was a testimony to the grace of God, for it showed how God revealed himself and opened up an avenue by which man can enter his presence. Compared with vegetation religion the old covenant is the offer of life. Compared to the new covenant it is a reminder of God's remoteness and the tragic difficulty of the human problem.

Courtesy of the University of Michigan Library

Papyrus leaves of the "Pauline Epistles" dating *ca.* 300 A.D.; left is Heb. 9:10-16; right is Heb. 9:18-26; the source of these writings is unknown (see Intro.)

9:11-14. The priesthood of Christ is now contrasted to the priesthood of the old covenant. The language used is a combination of time language and space language. The space language, usually referred to by commentators as Platonic language, contrasts the place of Christ's function with that of the Levitical priesthood. They functioned in the earthly tent which is a copy and shadow of the real. He functions in the **greater and more perfect tent (not made with hands).** This language, which courses through the entire book, contrasts the perfection, permanence, and fullness of the heavenly priesthood to the imperfection, temporary character, and incompleteness of the earthly priesthood. The career of Jesus represents the intersection of the heavenly with the earthly, the perfect with the imperfect, the eternal with the temporal. It is not a bolt of lightning from beyond, but was prepared in the royal priesthood of Melchizedek (7:1-18). It comes thus as the fulfillment of a process within history, and it is in this way that time and space vocabularies come together in the book.

9:11. The aspect of fulfillment is stressed by the use of the word **appeared,** which might well be rendered "has come," and by the mention of the **good things that have come.** Christ is the bringer of the new age foretold by the prophets. In him the new day breaks in on man, the new eon of God's gracious work in his creation. This line of thought relates to the interpretation of the miracles in the Synoptic gospels, to the understanding of demon

exorcism (cf. Mark 3:23-27), and to the emphasis on the new age in Paul's letters. What has been true of God from all eternity, what the prophets pointed to as the purpose of the covenant God, this has now broken into the world in the life and ministry of Jesus.

9:12a. The Levitical priesthood approached God through the services of the tabernacle. The great high priest approaches God by entering **once for all into the Holy Place.** Here again time and space vocabularies are interwoven. The death of Christ is an event within earthly history, taking place, as the creeds identify it, "under Pontius Pilate." But it is also an event in eternity, the once-for-all entry of the Son, the great high priest, into the presence of God. His death is the true fulfillment of the sacrificial system, for he offered, not the blood of an animal, but his own. His death is the climax of a life offered freely in obedience to the will of God and is thus a working out in human experience of the inner meaning of tabernacle worship, the offering of one's own life to God. And inasmuch as he is not only a man, the son of Mary, but also the Son, his life is at once the offering of God himself to men in his Son and also the act of true human obedience which at once fulfills and demonstrates the meaning of human existence.

9:12b. Christ's approach to God is by his self-offering as sacrifice, an act in which eternity intersects time. In the Cross God provided the sacrifice and showed what sacrifice really means—not man's

909

attempt to placate a threatening deity but God's provision of a means by which rebellious and runaway sons may be restored to the father's house.

9:12c-14. The result of Christ's sacrifice is an **eternal redemption.** The old sacrifices were effectual; they provided a way of **purification of the flesh.** But the sacrifice of Christ is more effectual; it not only cleanses the body but grants release to **conscience** so that it may be dedicated to the service of God. The paradoxical character of the self-offering of Christ is asserted in the words **through the eternal Spirit he offered himself.** His life is God's entry into human affairs. It is also Jesus' offering of himself **without blemish to God**—a human achievement, the outcome of a disciplined and dedicated human career. We find it difficult to hold the 2 elements together; either all is of God or man's work is everything. Here the 2 are in closest relationship. The self-offering of Christ is a magnificent human achievement; it is accomplished "through the eternal Spirit." The result of his work is a new era in human life. Those who live in Christ are already taking part in the messianic age; they experience the powers of the age to come; they live in the Spirit. United with Christ in his self-offering the Christian shares in true worship, which is the dedication of himself to God's service in union with Jesus Christ.

9:15-22. *The Meaning of Christ's Death.* Because of his self-offering Christ has become the **mediator of a new covenant.** Moses served as mediator of the old covenant, which was ratified by animal sacrifices and the sprinkling of blood on the **people,** the **book** of the covenant, the **tent,** and all the paraphernalia of **worship.** Indeed, the author summarizes, under the old covenant **almost everything is purified with blood, and without the shedding of blood there is no forgiveness of sins.**

9:15. Through the offering of blood, i.e. the life, the old covenant prefigures the self-giving of Jesus Christ. His **death,** as the fulfillment of sacrifice, **redeems** men from **transgressions.** There is a shift here from the language of sacrifice to that of the commercial world. Redemption is the recovery of an article given in pledge or the purchase of a slave in the slave market. The ideas are closely related in the OT and used in equally close connection in the NT. As God purchased Israel out of slavery in Egypt so in Christ he buys his people from their bondage in sin and death. Commercial language is accompanied by that of the lawyer, the language of wills and inheritances. The death of Christ procures for those called by God the **promised eternal inheritance.** It is not something that they have earned or accumulated for themselves; it comes to them from the bounty of a generous benefactor.

9:16-17. The confluence of sacrificial, commercial, and legal language leads to another emphasis on the death of Christ. The reference to **covenant** and **will** is for us obscure, and we need to be reminded by a footnote that the same Greek word is used to express both ideas. This verbal coincidence provides basis for the argument that the death of Christ was necessary to the establishment of the new covenant. Here, as in some of the OT quotations, the argument seems to us lacking in persuasiveness. In this case, however, it is like erecting a supporting scaffold around a tower which is quite capable of standing

by itself. The self-offering of Christ is the entry of God's will for human salvation into the course of human history. As such it establishes the new covenant.

9:23-28. *Cleansing of the Heavenly Sanctuary.* Sacrificial rites in the old covenant were effective in cleansing the tabernacle and the furniture of worship. If this is true of the copy it is true also of the heavenly pattern. But whereas the blood of calves and goats was sufficient to cleanse the earthly shrine, the heavenly tabernacle requires **better sacrifices.** And this is the significance of Christ's self-offering. He does not minister in the earthly shrine (cf. 8:4), a **copy of the true one,** but has entered heaven itself and there appears **in the presence of God on our behalf.** Moreover he does not perform this sacrifice **repeatedly,** as the high priest did annually in Israel, but has accomplished it **once for all at the end of the age to put away sin.**

Here again we encounter the Platonic space vocabulary combined with the eschatological time vocabulary. The contrast between the earthly and heavenly shrines, between the temporary and eternal, is joined with the biblical sense of God's purpose moving toward a goal. The goal, or end, appears in the middle of history in Jesus Christ. Thus the author can speak of Christ's coming **at the end of the age.** But Christ still has his people on earth and therefore there is still movement toward the goal in the life of the church. Thus the author can speak of Christ's appearing **a second time,** this time **not to deal with sin**—his sacrifice—but to accomplish salvation for **those who are waiting for him.**

Throughout the NT we encounter a perplexing duality of language. The kingdom has come in Jesus Christ and yet it is still future. The old age has come to an end with the cross and resurrection of Christ, and the new age has come into being. Yet the old age remains alongside the new, and the Christian experiences the tension between the ages, between the realm of the Spirit and the realm of the flesh. He lives in the age to come, possesses the earnest money of the Spirit, and yet awaits the fullness of the inheritance. He exists in the tension between the now and the not yet, between the present reality of the work of God and its future fullness. Attempts are frequently made by theologians to resolve the tensions by stressing only present realization or future completion, but the NT writers hold the 2 together.

9:27-28. These vss. offer another analogy. Men **die once** and then come before God's **judgment.** Christ also has been **offered once**—note the stress on his death as the act of God—and also appears **a second time,** not, however, to be judged but to be savior of his people. It is often noted that this is the only explicit reference in the NT to a 2nd coming of Christ. Elsewhere the writers speak of his *parousia*—his "coming" or "presence," i.e. manifestation. But it would be a misplaced emphasis to stress **a second time** in this text. The words appear in the completion of the analogy and the accent falls, not on the word "second," but on the fact that both the death and the reappearance of Christ are distinctively different from those of others. Christ died, but not as a hapless victim. He offered up his life in freedom, and his death has a sacrificial and redemptive character. When he appears at the judgment he does not join the long line awaiting assessment but is Lord of the judgment and savior and deliverer of those who are waiting for him. He voluntarily shared our human experience and the outcome of his life and death is the transformation of the human situation. Death once meant only judgment. Those who are Christ's now can look beyond death to the deliverer.

10:1-18. *Contrast of Old and New.* The theological argument of the book comes to its conclusion in this section, which repeats many of the ideas previously presented but emphasizes different aspects. The fundamental thesis is by now a familiar one: the worship of the old covenant is a copy of the heavenly pattern, a shadow of the eternal reality; the worship of the new covenant is an entry into the eternal reality.

10:1. Because it has only the **shadow of the good things to come** the law cannot **make perfect** those who approach God through its institutions. Its sacrifices are **continually offered year after year,** serving thus as a reminder of sin but making no permanent purification. The author adds 2 arguments, persuasive enough to those who share his point of view about eternal and temporal realities in worship, but hardly persuasive to those within the Jewish community of worship and service. This is one of the considerations which make modern interpreters question the view that the book was written to Jewish Christians who were considering a return, under pressure of persecution, to the religion of the old covenant (see Intro.).

10:2-4. A Jew would have no difficulty answering the question in vs. 2: **Otherwise would they not have ceased to be offered?** His reply would be the simple one that the sacrifices continued because men continued to sin and therefore were in constant need of atonement and forgiveness. The Jew would also object to the flat assertion that **it is impossible that the blood of bulls and goats should take away sins.** Anyone aware of the prophetic interpretation of sacrifice would recognize that the blood of sacrificial animals had something to do with expiation of sins, not because of powers inherent in the blood, but because God had established the institution of sacrifice to enable sinners to draw near to him and respond to his grace by the offering of themselves. From the standpoint of the author, however, the work of Christ has fulfilled sacrifice. Christ has entered the divine presence, and the preparatory prophetic institutions recede into the background. He recognizes their usefulness to remind one of sin and to afford expiation under the old covenant, but they pale before the glory of Christ's accomplishments.

10:5-7. The quotation of Ps. 40:6-8 introduces a new emphasis. The author interprets the ps. as being the words of the Messiah and sees in it Christ's interpretation of his own mission. He has not come simply to participate in the worship of the old covenant. He does this, but he does more. He accepts the **body,** the life, that God has **prepared** for him, and through it he accomplishes the will of God, as the **roll of the book** has predicted. The language of the ps., **sacrifices and offerings thou hast not desired,** is to be read, not as a rejection of the sacrificial cultus as such, but as the prophetic condemnation of externalized worship, the understanding of covenant religion as a barter transaction with God. It is not the offering of gifts God desires but the offering of self which the offering symbolizes.

10:8-10. Ps. 40 speaks of one who has grasped the prophetic character of covenant religion and sees his life as committed to God, set aside for his will. In the career of Jesus Christ the inner meaning of the sacrificial cultus is lived out in dedication to God and sacrifice is thereby fulfilled. Here is the realization that it is not only the hours on the cross or the week of the Passion that represent the fulfillment of sacrifice. The entire life of Jesus was a life of commitment and dedication. The Cross is the climax, the culminating expression of a life wholly concentrated on the will of God. Sacrifice is therefore abolished, not in the sense that it never had usefulness or that it represented a misunderstanding, but rather in the sense that scaffolding is taken down when the building is completed, or temporary approaches removed when a bridge is finished.

Sacrifice had its valid role in preparing a people for God. Its role is now taken up into the career of Christ, who is the new humanity, the people of God. Sacrifice is abolished because the will of God for man's salvation has now been established in Christ. His self-offering is the consecration of all humanity to God, and through the deed of the true man all men are now dedicated to God.

10:11-12. The contrast concludes with reference to the frequency of the offering. The priest of the old covenant attends to his work each day, **offering repeatedly the same sacrifices.** But Christ has made **for all time a single sacrifice for sins.** The work of the priest in the old covenant is ineffectual, for he needs constantly to repeat his offerings. But the work of Christ is perfect and complete. When he had made sacrifice for sins he took his place at **the right hand of God,** the place of rule, authority, and power. It could be argued that the ineffectual quality of the old sacrifices is overstated; they did, after all, grant assurance of forgiveness to worshipers. It could also be pointed out that Christ's triumph seems to be lacking something, inasmuch as he awaits the subjugation of **his enemies** (vs. 13). Both illustrate the taste for hyperbole which is characteristic of the Hebrew tradition, and which cannot properly be accused of distortion or exaggeration, since the exception to the rule is so promptly added.

10:13-14. The reference to subjugation of **enemies** introduces again the duality of the language of biblical eschatology. Christ has already won his battle and is exalted to power. Yet the final manifestation of his conquests remains in the future. The decisive battle of the war has been fought and the enemy's back has been broken. But the fighting continues; the enemy continues to resist desperately. Nevertheless the Biblical writers are confident that with the death and resurrection of Christ the victory is secure, and however fierce the struggle what remain are the mopping-up operations. The final outcome cannot be changed. God's verdict is in. Those who are set aside for God in Christ have been **perfected for all time** by the single offering of Christ.

10:15-18. Jeremiah's vision of the new covenant (31:33-34) is recalled at the end of the discussion. The point that the author urges as the conclusion of his argument is also affirmed by the **Holy Spirit** speaking through the prophet. When God establishes his new covenant he makes religion a matter of inwardness, putting his laws in men's **hearts.** But even in the age of inwardness and spontaneity forgiveness is a necessity and is announced as the climax of the prophetic proclamation. Where forgiveness is operative offering for sin is past. With this the author brings his argument to a conclusion and turns to the closing section, composed of exhortations and greetings.

IV. ENCOURAGEMENT: MAINTAIN YOUR FAITH (10:19–12:29)

A. AN EXHORTATION TO HOLD FAST (10:19-39)

The 3rd main part of the letter begins with exhortation. In stately, moving language it proceeds through 3 stages: a reminder of what the Christian has received through the work of Christ (10:19-25), a warning of the dangers of drifting into unbelief (10:26-31), and an invitation to recall past encounters with God as a motivation for endurance (10:32-39).

10:19-25. *Response to Christ's Sacrifice.* The exhortation begins by recalling what Christ has accomplished and what the Christian should do in response. It uses the language of worship, adapting the terminology of the tabernacle to the new world of realities inaugurated by the sacrifice of Christ. The impulse to worship has a 2-fold source: the **confidence** made possible by Christ's self-giving, and the living presence of the **great priest** who presides over God's house. The traditional language of OT worship is given heightened meanings in this paragraph as the author summarizes his theological argument. The **sanctuary** is the true sanctuary, the presence of God. The **blood of Jesus** is his self-offering as a sacrifice for sin. The **new and living way . . . through the curtain** means that access to God is now the prerogative of every Christian, and that it has been won for him through the obedience of Christ in offering up **his flesh,** i.e. his life. Since the conditions of worship have now been transformed by the work of Christ, 3 exhortations follow:

10:22. (*a*) **Let us draw near.** The language is again the language of the tabernacle cultus. To "draw near" is the technical term for approaching God in worship. It is possible to do so with sincerity in confident **faith** because **hearts** have been **sprinkled** and **bodies washed.** The reference to sprinkling recalls the OT sacrifice in which the blood was sprinkled on the altar. The sacrifice which cleanses the Christian is of course that of Christ. The washing of bodies may be a reference to the ceremonial ablutions of Jewish religion, in which an external ceremonial cleansing symbolized accomplishment of inner purity. It is at least very likely that a reference to the cleansing of baptism is intended here.

10:23. (*b*) **Let us hold fast the confession of our hope.** Confession is the NT technical expression for the praise of God. The reader is urged not only to maintain his creed but also to keep a firm grip on the worship of God, which is the content of confession. The characteristic NT emphasis on the close interconnection of divine and human activities is also present here. The ground of our worship is the faithfulness of God. We can hold our confession **without wavering** because underneath and behind us is God's covenanted reliability.

10:24-25. (*c*) **Let us consider how to stir up one another to love and good works.** The experience of worship is a community affair. We do not respond automatically to the full meaning of worship; we need to be stimulated. Even in the apostolic age there were people who were **neglecting to meet together** in worship and needed encouragement. The expectation of a short interval between the Cross and the **Day** of the return of the victorious Christ supplies such a stimulus. The enduring value of this hope is its motivation to life in the spirit of Christ.

10:26-31. *A Warning Against Apostasy.* Like the earlier passage on the impossibility of a 2nd repentance (6:4-8) this warning is expressed in strong language. The analogy of the old covenant is the starting point. **Sacrifice** expiated only sins of ignorance; there was no atonement for sins committed **deliberately.** Apostasy is no less perilous in the new covenant. If death was the lot of one who **violated the law of Moses** (cf. Deut. 17:2-6), how much worse will be the fate of one **who has spurned the Son of God,** treated the **blood of the covenant** as a common thing, and **outraged the Spirit of grace?** God is indeed gracious, but he remains God and is not to be taken lightly. His mercy draws men back to his purpose; it does not license them to do as they will. He who does not respect the grace of God will discover that God judges his people (cf. Deut. 32:35*a,* 36*a*) and that it is a frightful thing to meet him apart from Jesus Christ.

10:32-39. *The Need for Endurance.* This passage of encouragement also echoes an earlier discussion (6:9-12). The author seeks to stir his readers from their complacency by reminding them of more heroic times in their own history. They once endured **sufferings . . . abuse. . . affliction.** They helped others in such trials, showed mercy to **prisoners,** and **accepted** the loss of their **property.** They were able to do so because they were convinced that in faith they had a **better possession**—one that endured. Since that time their **confidence** in God has been neglected, and the author warns them not to **throw** it **away,** for it promises a **great reward.** They have real need of staying power so that they may **do the will of God** and receive the promised inheritance. The exhortation concludes with a quotation from the LXX of Hab. 2:3*d*-4—preceded by a phrase appearing in Isa. 26:20—in which the order is transposed so that it appears to be the **righteous one** who **shrinks back.** The author identifies himself with his readers in expressing assurance that they will not be such drop-outs but will maintain faith and **keep their souls.**

B. THE TRIUMPHS OF FAITH (11:1-40)

The exhortation of ch. 10 climaxes in the appeal for steadfast and loyal faith. The power and wonder of faith is now exalted in a rapturous hymn. It has six parts or movements: (a) a definition of faith with a brief summary of its past and present benefits (vss. 1-3); (b) a review of what faith accomplished from Abel to Abraham and Sarah (vss. 4-12); (c) a recapitulation of the pilgrim character of faith (vss. 13-16); (d) a recalling of what faith accomplished from Abraham to the settlement in the Promised Land (vss. 17-31); (e) a summary of what people have been able to accomplish through faith (vss. 32-38); (f) a transition concerning the communion of believers (vss. 39-40).

11:1-3. A Definition of Faith. The description of faith in vs. 1 shows the same characteristics of language noted earlier—a combination of space (Platonic) with time (eschatological) vocabularies. Faith is seen in both dimensions. **Assurance** is used in ancient commercial documents in the sense of "title deed." Faith as title deed of good things to come combines the elements of hope, confidence, and trust and parallels Paul's understanding of the presence of the Spirit as "earnest money" guaranteeing the inheritance or "first fruits" assuring the imminence of the harvest. By faith the believer has title to good things to come and also a solid conviction of the reality of the divine realm.

11:2-3. In the past faith brought the **divine approval** to the men who trusted God. In the present it enables us to understand that the things we see and touch are actually dependent on what is invisible to us. Faith is the encounter with God in which a taste of his goodness enables us to trust in him even without the evidence necessary to convince a skeptic. By faith we can understand life as God's gift and see the world about us as his creation.

11:4-16. Early Witnesses to Faith. The patriarchs were asked to trust God without much supporting evidence, and by the courage and confidence of their faith they still speak encouragement to us. **Abel** perceived that the deepest meaning of **sacrifice** is trust in God. The common interpretation of Gen. 5:24 as meaning that **Enoch** did **not see death** appears in the LXX translation **taken up** (cf. Ecclus. 44:16); **pleased God,** the LXX rendering of "walked with God," testifies to Enoch's faith. **Noah** endured the mocking of his contemporaries to obey God's commandment. **Abraham** went out into a **foreign land** at God's command, giving up the securities of family, home, and religion and risking everything at the word of one he had not previously encountered. **Sarah** in a situation which was humanly speaking impossible trusted in God's faithfulness.

11:13-16. All these people died without seeing the fulfillment of **what was promised** and thus might seem vulnerable to the reproach that faith was in vain. But they looked forward in hope to God's promise, rejecting the temptation to turn back. Their lives show that they were concentrating on a **better country, that is, a heavenly one.** Therefore God is **not ashamed** to be identified with them and **has prepared for them a city.** The vision of the city as an ordered civilization, secure against its enemies, prosperous and peaceful, has been a favorite image of religious thinkers in many traditions.

11:17-31. More Witnesses to Faith. The succession of heroes of faith continues, resuming with **Abraham** and moving forward in time to the Exodus and settlement in Canaan. Abraham showed the quality of his faith when God asked for the sacrifice of his son. Though **Isaac** was the heir through whom the **promises** were to be fulfilled, he obeyed in the belief that God would still find some way to keep his word. The other patriarchs are listed as examples of faith, and then **Moses** is considered. He found life through the faith of **his parents,** who trusted God and defied the **edict** of Pharaoh. By faith he chose to share the fate of his countrymen and led them out of **Egypt** and through the **Red Sea.** By faith **Jericho** was conquered by a method that seemed futile by military standards, and **Rahab** was spared the fate of her fellow citizens.

11:32-38. Summary of Faith's Accomplishments. The rhetorical question **And what more shall I say?** suggests that the story could be continued indefinitely, but the catalog of heroes comes to an end and another method of summation is employed. Instead of enumerating heroes of faith up to the era of the gospel, the author lists instead the achievements of believers—temptations overcome, persecutions endured, life won from the jaws of death. It is an eloquent and impressive account of steadfast faith in the presence of disaster, of men who had their hope fixed on the promise of God and could be diverted by neither persuasion nor threats—men **of whom the world was not worthy.**

11:39-40. The Communion of Believers. Vs. 39 seems a disappointing ending to so heroic an account, until we realize the use the author is making of his catalog. These giants of faith, however great their achievement, **did not receive what was promised,** not because God failed to keep his word, but because he willed that believers of all times should share in the joy and triumph of the new age inaugurated by the coming of Christ. If faith could win such victories under conditions so difficult and unpromising in the old covenant, how much more will faith accomplish in the new age—lived in the sure knowledge of God's favor in Jesus Christ, possessed of the gifts of the Spirit, having tasted the powers of the age to come! The preacher skillfully conceals a rebuke beneath an inspirational account of past heroes and seeks to move his readers to ask themselves, "If they did so much with so little, what will be expected of us who live in the day of fulfillment?" The faithful of other generations do not reach their destiny alone; it is in fellowship with contemporary believers that they are **made perfect.**

C. Therefore Take Courage! (12:1-29)

12:1-2. The Race of Life. The 3rd stage brings the exhortation to a close. The heroes of the past have been reviewed, and they stand by watching anxiously to see how God's people fare. This calls to mind the image of an Olympic contest, the stadium filled by past generations, the generation now living on the field. Since we have such a distinguished **cloud of witnesses** let us thrust aside our anxieties and cares, let us put off the sin that besets us, and **let us run with perseverance.** The **race** is a long run, where speed may be of less importance than endurance. If the witnesses do not stimulate us to effort there remains one motivation —the example of **Jesus.** He is **the pioneer and perfecter of our faith,** who needed the utmost of courage and stamina for his strenuous ministry. He has broken the trail for us, and he also enables us to follow his path. His mission in life required great personal effort. He needed motivation, even as we do. His motivation was the joy of doing God's will. He **endured the cross, despising the shame;** thus he won the victory and now shares the **throne** of the universe.

12:3-11. *Consideration of the Life of Christ.* Whatever the readers have undergone, they cannot seriously maintain that their **struggle against sin** has brought them **to the point of shedding . . . blood.** Christ's obedience was unto death; he has not promised to let his disciples off more easily. Their trials, moreover, are sent, not to discourage, but to **discipline,** as illustrated by Prov. 3:11-12. This is a sign that **God is treating us as sons.** The father who does not discipline his sons does not thereby demonstrate his love but treats them as **illegitimate children,** in whom he has no pride. Two other analogies occur to the author: (*a*) We have endured the discipline of **earthly fathers;** how much more that of the **Father** of all the living! (*b*) Earthly fathers discipline us only during our childhood and may be erratic and arbitrary about it. God **disciplines us for our good, that we may share his holiness.** The final remark of the section reminds that all discipline is hard and **painful.** It can be appreciated only in its outcome, **the peaceful fruit of righteousness.**

12:12-17. *An Admonition to Respond.* The exhortation becomes specific. The problem of the readers is evidently not overwhelming difficulties but lack of resolution. They have simply not planned intelligently or worked with energy. **Peace** and **holiness** will not drop on them like snow from heaven. They must **strive** for them. The center of the problem (vs. 15), as intimated in earlier exhortations (2:1; 3:6; 5:11-14), is that they do not appropriate the **grace of God.** They apparently expect God to do everything and fail to understand that he has done his work and now awaits the response of the believer. Those who like to hear about God's goodness and never exert themselves become a **root of bitterness** (Deut. 29:18), a source of contention, which then infects an entire community with bickering and jealousy. The outcome of this is shown in the experience of **Esau,** who in his impatient appetite **sold his birthright for a single meal.** When he later came to his senses and claimed the **blessing,** it was too late, and even his **tears** were of no avail —another somber warning about the problem of a 2nd repentance (cf. 6:4-8; 10:26).

12:18-29. *The New Accessibility of God's Holiness.* The awful and frightening events which accompanied the giving of the old covenant are contrasted to the graciousness and tenderness of God's love in Christ. Sinai is portrayed in heightened language: **fire . . . darkness . . . gloom . . . tempest . . . sound of a trumpet . . . a voice** so terrifying that those who heard it were appalled. But the same God who disclosed himself as dread mystery at Sinai now invites our approach to a **heavenly Jerusalem,** to

angels in festive array, to an **assembly** of the elect, to God the **judge,** and to **Jesus, the mediator of the new covenant.** An examination of the details shows how carefully the section has been constructed to contrast 2 dramatic scenes of revelation, both awesome but quite different in total impression. The approach to Sinai suggests an experience so intense as to be emotionally disintegrating. The approach to heaven itself has potential to be even more awesome, but the author manages to make it sound hospitable, the kind of environment in which humans can feel at home even though it is unsettling in its overpowering graciousness and its suggestions of the renewal of the human person.

12:25-29. This contrast gives the setting for listening to the gospel. When God spoke **on earth** his warning was awesome and no one who refused him could escape. But now in Christ God has spoken **from heaven.** How **much less shall we escape** if we reject him! At Sinai **his voice . . . shook the earth.** The voice from heaven **will shake not only the earth but also the heaven** (Hag. 2:6). When this happens all that is changeable will be removed so that **what cannot be shaken may remain.** The exhortation ends on a positive note, not frightening or threatening. For this reason the Christian can be grateful—he has received **a kingdom that cannot be shaken.** And he can **offer to God acceptable worship, with reverence and awe.**

This closing section well illustrates the remarkable capacity of the author to combine the numinous and gracious elements in the Christian religion in an impressive synthesis. Few writers excel him in presenting the awful majesty and holiness of God. Not many succeed as well in presenting the approachability and graciousness of God in Christ. Fewer still keep the 2 together in such close and living connection in their teaching.

IV. EPILOGUE: EXHORTATIONS, BENEDICTION, GREETINGS (13:1-25)

This closing ch., which may be an addition to the original work (see Intro.), has 5 sections: (*a*) exhortations concerning the conduct of Christians (vss. 1-6); (*b*) urgings for respect toward leaders (vss. 7-17); (*c*) an appeal for intercessory prayer (vss. 18-19); (*d*) benediction (vss. 20-21); (*e*) greetings (vss. 22-25).

13:1-6. *Exhortations on Conduct.* The first section urges **brotherly love** and **hospitality,** compassion for prisoners and sufferers, respect for the purity of **marriage,** and freedom from covetousness. The exhortation to hospitality recalls the experience of Abraham (Gen. 18:1-8; 19:1-3). The reference to being **in the body** would be construed as a reference to the church as body of Christ if it occurred in a Pauline letter. Here it is probably no more than a reminder that the readers too live on the physical level and should therefore be sympathetic to those who suffer. God's faithfulness and care is urged as the ground for avoiding covetousness.

13:7-17. *Respect for Leaders.* This section suggests that there have been tensions between the leaders and the people, perhaps over questions of doctrine and ascetic practices. The assimilation of Jesus Christ into the circle of leaders is somewhat surprising but quite appropriate. It recalls that Christ is also one of us, that he has shared our human experience, which thereby makes him accessible to us as an example. It also reminds the leaders that they are to be conformed to Christ. He won his leadership of God's people by submission to the cross. There is no other pattern for his followers.

13:9-14. The **strange teachings** referred to here are difficult to identify. The reference to **foods** suggests that it involved a form of asceticism or abstention from certain foods. The teaching, whatever it was, is rejected for 2 reasons: (*a*) The proper nourishment of man is the **grace** of God (cf. Deut. 8:3; Matt. 4:4). Therefore distinction of foods has no significant place in the religion of the gospel. (*b*) **We have an altar,** the eternal one in heaven, from which the priests **have no right to eat.** Even in the old covenant the flesh of the animal offered in the sin offering was not used in a sacrificial meal but was **burned outside the camp** (Lev. 16:27). In the new covenant **Jesus . . . suffered outside the gate.** The argument seems to be that foods cannot be brought into the center of Christian worship, i.e. in relation to the experience of forgiveness and life with God. Even in the old covenant food was separated from the ritual of atonement. In the new the atoning sacrifice itself takes place, not in the sanctuary, but on a hill outside the city. The Christian therefore leaves the sanctuary with its ritual requirements and goes with his Lord **outside the camp,** sharing his humiliation. **Here we have no lasting city,** no permanent community with its rules and regulations. Christians are a pilgrim community on the way, seeking a settled life to come.

13:15-16. The worship that we offer God is therefore not the worship of a legally regulated ritual, but the **sacrifice of praise . . . , the fruit of lips that acknowledge his name.** The word "name" here, as elsewhere in the Bible, is a shorthand expression for all the deeds of God by which he discloses himself to men. To **acknowledge his name** is therefore more than giving a passing gesture of recognition. It is to relate oneself seriously to God's self-disclosure, to accept Jesus Christ as God's definitive word to men. This worship is moreover not limited to what we designate as liturgical acts. It is liturgy in the older sense, the worship and praise of God which includes acts of mercy, kind-

ness, love, and service; **such sacrifices are pleasing to God.**

13:17. Readers are reminded of their obligations to their leaders. The author suggests with almost humorous irony that leaders be permitted to work out their responsibilities **joyfully, and not sadly.** After all, sadness does not benefit the congregation.

13:18-19. *An Appeal for Intercessory Prayer.* The references to a **clear conscience** and to acting **honorably in all things** may imply that the author is in prison, in circumstances which might be embarrassing to his readers. His wish to be restored to them may be read as supporting this suggestion, but other explanations are also possible.

13:20-21. *Benediction.* This beautiful benediction and doxology contains one of the few references to the Resurrection in the book. It also sums up ideas expressed at greater length earlier: the sacrifice of Christ, the establishment of a new covenant, and the life of the Christian as at once the work of God and a matter of his own exertions.

13:22-24. *Greetings.* The closing lines appeal for receptivity, offer an item of news about a co-worker, express the author's hope to visit his readers, and conclude with greetings.

13:23. Though no doubt there were a number of early Christians bearing the same name, **our brother Timothy** is generally assumed to refer to the well-known associate of Paul (cf. II Cor. 1:1; Col. 1:1; I Thess. 3:2; Philem. 1). This reference may have been largely responsible for the attribution of the book to Paul, and some suspect that it was added to the work specifically to give such an impression. On the other hand Timothy was apparently quite young when he joined Paul (cf. Phil. 2:22; I Tim. 4:12) and thus may have continued to be an active leader in the church throughout the remainder of the first cent. There is no reason to doubt that he could have been known both to the author of this book and to the readers he addressed (see Intro.).

13:24-25. The author concludes with **greetings** to both **leaders** and **saints,** i.e. church members, and his wish that the favor of God may be with them. **Those who come from Italy** is lit. "they from [or "of"] Italy"—an ambiguous phrase that might mean Italians either at home or abroad and therefore offers no clue as to the whereabouts of the author and his companions (see Intro.).

THE LETTER OF JAMES

RICHARD L. SCHEEF, JR.

INTRODUCTION

To benefit from the letter of James, the reader must first understand the kind of book he is reading. It would be a mistake to look into Jas. for profound theology. The letter is no such theological treatise. It is rather a collection of moral exhortations (see below on 1:1). The practice of the Christian life is the author's subject. To this end he compiles a collection of teachings to give specific directions to Christians: things they should do or not do, attitudes they should adopt, and others they should reject. The mood of the letter is imperative, its tone hortatory, and its purpose practical.

In collecting such teachings as these the author was following a practice already established by other early Christian writers. E.g. Paul joined a collection of practical instructions to his letter to the Romans (chs. 12–15; cf. the lists of household duties in Eph. 5:21–6:9; Col. 3:18–4:1; I Pet. 2:18–3:7). A comparison of the collections of ethical instructions within the NT reveals many similarities of subject matter, style, and mood. This has led many scholars to conclude that the churches of NT times borrowed previously existing traditions of moral instruction from Jewish and Greek philosophical or religious sources and incorporated them in the Christian teaching.

It is important to notice how each NT author relates his moral teaching to the Christian gospel, which has its center in the person of Jesus Christ. E.g. one exhorts his readers to follow the example of Christ in patience and suffering (I Pet. 2:21-24; 4:1); another, to be "imitators of God" and to "walk in love, as Christ loved us and gave himself for us" (Eph. 5:1-2). In each case the moral exhortation is based upon some aspect of the life and work of Jesus Christ.

The author of Jas. does not state his christological foundation for ethical exhortation. Rather he assumes it and proceeds into the moral teaching itself. This has led some students of the NT to regard Jas. as inferior to other books in the canon. They assign to it a "subcanonical" status. The well-known example of this attitude is Martin Luther's designation of Jas. as an "epistle of straw" because it did not witness to Christ in the Pauline manner.

In this light, Jas. *is* inferior to the letters of Paul. On the other hand, if one simply lets the author speak his own mind in his own way and to his own purpose, then the book can be appreciated for what it really is. What does a Christian *do* about his faith (2:14-26)? What should be his attitudes toward the rich and the poor in his own congregation (2:1-7), or his thought as he contemplates a journey (4:13-15)? These are the kinds of questions helpfully answered in the letter.

If Jas. is primarily a collection of practical instructions, is it really a letter in the usual sense of that term? Outside the opening salutation (1:1) there is little in the book to indicate that it was intended as a personal communication. Instead the author has merely collected and edited traditional materials for circulation among churches throughout the world (see below on 1:1).

Authorship. The author of the letter identifies himself in 1:1 as "James, a servant of God and of the Lord Jesus Christ." He tells us little else about himself except that he is a teacher (3:1). He sends no greetings to his readers at the end of the letter, and there is no formal closing which would give any clue about either the writer or the recipients of the letter (cf. Rom. 16; Gal. 6:11-18; I Pet. 5:12-14). Thus we have only the name James to tell us who wrote the letter. But who is James?

The traditional view is that the author is James the Lord's brother, the leader of the Jerusalem church. He was in contact with Paul (cf. Gal. 1:19; 2:9, 12; Acts 15:13) and could have written to correct a false view of Paul's teaching on faith and works (cf. 2:14-26).

Many scholars, however, find reasons for questioning this tradition: (*a*) The letter does not seem to have been known in early Christian churches until the time of Origen at the close of the 2nd cent. A document composed by a person as prominent as James of Jerusalem would certainly have been widely circulated and known before that time. (*b*) There is nothing in the letter itself to indicate a close relationship between the author and Jesus. Though some passages make allusions to the teachings of Jesus, the author uses Hellenistic and Jewish traditions as his primary sources. A person in the position of James of Jerusalem would probably not compile such traditions. Rather he would write on his own authority and on the basis of the Lord's teachings. (*c*) The author uses excellent Greek. Such facility would be unlikely in an Aramaic-speaking Jew of Jerusalem.

Though none of these arguments is conclusive evidence against the traditional view, their cumulative effect makes it hard to believe that James of Jerusalem is the author. Rather it seems more probable that someone compiled a set of Christian teachings and sent them out to the churches of the world under the name of the Lord's brother.

The name the author chose had meaning for his readers in another way. "James" is the English translation of the Hebrew and Greek "Jacob," which immediately suggests the father of the 12 tribes of Israel. The author or editor probably selected this name to suggest that now the church as the new Israel has a new patriarchal authority in the person of James ("Jacob") of Jerusalem (see below on 1:1).

The Readers. Jas. is addressed to Christians scattered throughout the world rather than to the members of a particular local congregation (see below on 1:1). Though the opening verse suggests that both author and addressees were Jewish Christians, the teachings of the letter are not exclusively Jewish nor are they addressed to Jews alone. These are moral teachings applicable to Jews and Gentiles alike. The intended recipients of the letter, therefore, could be Christians anywhere who need moral instruction in the specific duties of practical Christianity.

Thus Jas. is written for all Christians who claim to believe but do not act (2:14-26), who let their partiality go unchecked (2:1-7), who blame God for their temptations (1:13), who fail to control their tongues (3:2 ff.), who let strife run wild (4:1 ff.), etc. All such attitudes and actions make a mockery of true religion. Against this kind of sham the author urges his readers to embrace pure religion in which belief and conduct, words and deeds form a unified and beneficial whole.

Date of Composition. If Jas. is a compilation of traditions and moralistic instructions, the formation of these traditions could have taken place quite early. E.g. a recent study claims that what is reflected in Jas. is a simple and undeveloped piety which might have been employed in the Galilean ministry of Jesus.

While the teachings of Jas. do in some respects echo those of Jesus, the variety of the collection shows that the author gathered his material from no single source. Probably he collected some Jewish, some Greek, and some Christian teachings and put them all together in his letter. Some of these traditions might even be older than the time of Jesus, e.g. those which seem to parallel the OT, esp. Prov. On the other hand, some might have originated later than the missionary work of Paul, e.g. on faith and works in 2:14-26.

The question remains: When was the collection made and put into its present form? On the supposition that the letter was composed to combat a corrupted and misinterpreted form of Paul's teaching it must be dated sometime after the major work of Paul, i.e. past the middle of the first cent. Further, on the supposition that Paul's teaching was not too widespread until after his letters were collected about A.D. 95 the final composition of Jas. must then be dated about 100-125.

Status in the NT. As already noted, some theologians and scholars like Luther have assigned to Jas. an inferior status among the documents of the NT. This opinion has some foundation in the early history of the book among NT writings. The first Christian writer to accept it as canonical was Origen at the close of the 2nd cent. Origen, who probably brought it with him from Caesarea to Alexandria, is responsible for its acceptance in that city as a work of James the Lord's brother.

Meanwhile, in the churches of the W, Jas. remained relatively unknown. Jerome's including it in the Vulgate (*ca.* A.D. 382) probably led to its eventual acceptance as a canonical book in the W. Following Jerome, Augustine (*ca.* A.D. 354-430) also accepted it as canonical, and it was similarly accepted in the councils of Hippo in 393 and Carthage in 397 and 419.

Thus Jas. was viewed with some doubts from the beginning and, even though eventually accepted as canonical, has always had a hard time winning its way to an authentic status among the letters of the NT. Nevertheless, because of its down-to-earth teaching and quotable maxims, the letter enjoys wide popular appeal.

For Further Study: J. H. Ropes, *A Critical and Exegetical Commentary on the Epistle of St. James,* 1916; a scholarly commentary based on the Greek text. Alexander Ross, *Commentary on the Epistles of James and John,* 1954; a conservative commentary, thorough and scholarly. E. C. Blackman, *The Epistle of James,* 1957; the best popular commentary in recent years. Bo Reicke, *The Epistles of James, Peter and Jude,* 1964. B. S. Easton in *IB,* 1957. A. E. Barnett in *IDB,* 1962.

I. SALUTATION (1:1)

Following the customary form for letters in his day, the author names himself, designates the addressees, and greets them. **James** is the English translation of the Greek and Hebrew name "Jacob," the father of the 12 sons representing the tribes of Israel (see Intro.). The name itself would immediately suggest to the original readers that the author is following an OT model of some kind. In Gen. 49 there is a collection of blessings in poetic form pronounced by the aged Jacob upon each of his 12 sons. Though the letter has little more than a general resemblance to these blessings, the similarity hints at intentional connection. Perhaps the author wants to suggest that, just as Jacob of old addressed himself to his 12 sons representing the tribes of Israel, so now a "Christian patriarch" of the same name writes to the church as the new Israel.

Twelve tribes would be clearly understood by the original readers as an allusion to the whole nation of Israel. The **dispersion,** or Diaspora, was also currently understood to designate the Jews who were scattered in various parts of the world outside their homeland of Palestine. To Christians, however, **the twelve tribes in the dispersion** would clearly mean that the letter is addressed to the church as the new Israel and to all the followers of Christ scattered throughout the world (cf. I Pet. 1:1-2). For this reason the letter has sometimes been classified with others like I, II Pet. and Jude as general, or catholic, epistles.

Outside the opening vs. there is little in this "letter" which looks like a personal communication. The author does not seem to know his readers personally; nor does he speak of the problems or concerns of Christians in a particular place, as Paul, e.g. addresses himself in a personal way to his fellow Christians of Corinth, Thessalonica, or Philippi. Rather the collection of teachings reflects generally accepted moral principles which might be applied in any church.

II. GENERAL EXHORTATIONS (1:2-18)

The first major section consists of a collection of miscellaneous exhortations. The subjects of the various teachings gathered here seem to be unrelated to each other and are loosely organized. The author moves abruptly from one subject to another without apparent transition. Yet there are "tag words" which serve as connecting links between some of the varied subjects, e.g. **steadfastness** in vss. 3-4, **lacking** and **lacks** in vss. 4-5, **ask** in vss. 5-6, etc. This suggests that the collection was put together in oral form in which the tag words aided memory and recitation.

1:2-4. Through Trials to Full Life. The church in the dispersion was made up of people who found themselves in an alien and sometimes hostile world. That they endured **trials** or persecution which tested their faithfulness is evident throughout the NT. Rather than let these adversities defeat them, the readers of this letter are to rejoice because such trials provide the testing which strengthens faith and leads to full and meaningful life. Cf. the similar description in Rom. 5:3-5, where Paul traces the movement from suffering to hope; also I Pet. 1:6-7, where the trials of Christians are likened to the refiner's fire.

Faith (vs. 3), in contrast to its meaning in 2:14-26, means not mere belief but faithfulness. What is being tested is not a body of doctrine but fidelity in action. Such a testing **produces** (lit. "works out") **steadfastness,** or endurance, as Paul calls it in Rom. 5:3 (cf. Heb. 10:36; Rev. 2:2-3). Such steadfastness has **its full effect** in the long-range result that the Christian **may be perfect and complete, lacking in nothing.** These last terms define each other. **Perfect** denotes, not absolute sinlessness, but wholeness, the kind of life which is filled with meaningful purpose and which leaves nothing to be desired. Because their life has this meaning and goal, Christians can and should **count it all joy** when confronted with various trials (cf. Rom. 5:3; I Pet. 1:6).

1:5-8. Pray in Faith. The main point of the next teaching is that God gives freely in answer to prayers made in faith. **Wisdom** (vs. 5), essential to the full Christian life, is a gift of God and will be discussed more fully in 3:13-18 (cf. Prov. 2:1-15). Anyone who lacks this virtue should **ask God who gives to all men generously** (vs. 5; cf. Gen. 1:29; Matt. 7:7-11; Rom. 8:32; Eph. 1:6). God gives **without reproaching,** i.e. without condescension which spoils the gift. **Faith** (vs. 6) is the opposite of doubt. It is firm trust in God like that of Abraham, who did not waver in unbelief (cf. Rom. 4:18-21; also the teaching of Jesus on faith and effective prayer in Matt. 21:21-22; Luke 17:6). Like a wind-driven wave, the person who doubts is **unstable in all his ways** (vs. 8). His **double-minded** wavering permeates all his attitudes and actions and destroys the relationship of full trust in God. The person who lacks faith cuts himself off from God and **will receive nothing from the Lord.**

1:9-11. Riches Pass Away. Although these verses contrast lowliness and riches, the main thrust is against riches as in 2:5-9 and 5:1-6. The **lowly brother** may **boast** or rejoice **in his exaltation** because in actuality he is rich in faith and an heir of God's kingdom (cf. 2:5; Matt. 6:19-21; Luke 6:20, 24; 14:11). On the other hand, the **rich** man and his riches will pass away **like the flower of the grass** (cf. Isa. 40:6-7).

1:12-15. Blessed Trials and Ruinous Temptations. Vs. 12 picks up the theme of **trial** from vss. 2-4 and adds a new dimension to the happiness of the man who endures: **He will receive the crown of life** (cf. I Cor. 9:24-25; II Tim. 4:8) guaranteed to those who love God.

1:13-15. In Greek the same word means both "trial" and "temptation." In vs. 13 there is a switch to the verbal form of the 2nd meaning—to "lure" or "entice." Such enticements do not come from God. Since he is only good, he is beyond temptation and **he himself tempts no one.** A person cannot blame God for his temptations since they arise from **his own desire** or lust (cf. Matt. 15:11). Illicit desires, when allowed to run their course, give rise to **sin.** In this letter sin means the failure to do right or the neglect of good deeds (cf. 2:9; 4:17). The disastrous consequence of sin is that, like a malignant growth, it brings death (cf. Rom. 5:12-21; 6:20-23; 7:8-11).

1:16-18. All Good Gifts Come from God. To say, "I am tempted by God" (vs. 13), is to deceive oneself (vs. 16). On the contrary, God gives only good and perfect gifts. He is **the Father of lights,** who is light and who creates light and the heavenly bodies (cf. Gen. 1:3; Ps. 136:7-9). With God **there is no variation or shadow due to change.** Though the exact meaning of this last phrase is not clear (and the reading of some ancient manuscripts as indicated in the RSV footnote is even less clear), the purpose is probably to contrast the unchanging light of God with that of heavenly bodies which do change (cf. I John 1:5).

1:18. Cf. the use of **word** here with the meanings in the following passage, vss. 21-23. The **word of truth** here refers to God's creative power by which we were made **first fruits** of all created things and beings. In Christian usage, however, it may mean God's creative power which continues to regenerate us through the gospel, that we might be the first fruits of the new age in Christ (cf. Rom. 8:19-23; I Cor. 15:20; Rev. 14:4).

III. THE WAY TO PURE RELIGION (1:19-27)

Hear and do. These are the ingredients of true piety. The way to pure religion is to receive the word and to apply it in concrete deeds of charity.

1:19-21. Receive the Saving Word. The imperative **know this** engages the reader's attention and marks the beginning of a new section dealing with the author's practical concept of true religion. This begins with receptivity: **Be quick to hear** not only the **word** (vs. 21) but also whatever is said. The ability of Christians to help one another often begins with the willingness to listen to each other. The attentive listener will be **slow to speak.**

1:20. The religious person will be **slow to anger,** for anger does not bear the fruit of true piety. **The righteousness of God,** a profound and dynamic concept in Paul's thought (cf. Rom. 1:16-17; 3:21), has a practical meaning here—viz. the good deeds which God requires.

1:21. The path to true religion is obstructed by **filthiness** and **wickedness.** The Christian must put aside these evils and receive the **implanted word** of the gospel, which is able to save the soul. True religion has an inner core which is the source of piety and action. To the author this center is the **implanted word,** which is Christian teaching, **the law of liberty** (vs. 25), and **the royal law** (2:8).

1:22-25. *Doing the Word.* True religion begins by receiving the word, but hearing alone would be an empty and meaningless thing. The word must lead to deeds (vs. 22). The author's insistence on good deeds anticipates his teaching that faith without works is dead (2:14-26).

1:23-24. A person who hears but does not do the word is like one who casually looks at himself in a **mirror** and then at once turns away without further thought. Nothing happens to change him or his ways.

1:25. But he who looks into the **perfect law** and does not forget but perseveres and acts—this person **shall be blessed in his doing.** The law of God was already thought of as the perfect law in OT times (cf. Pss. 19:7-14; 119). To the author of Jas. the perfect law, like the implanted word of vs. 21 and the royal law of 2:8, is the law of God as understood in the OT and as interpreted by Jesus in the gospels. By calling it the **law of liberty** he reflects the then current Jewish teaching that obedience to the law is true freedom.

1:26-27. *Pure Religion.* It has already been said that the religious man is "slow to speak" (vs. 19). More than that, he must **bridle his tongue** (vs. 26); cf. 3:3). The person who **thinks he is religious** and does not control his tongue deceives himself. Such religion is merely an empty form.

1:27. Ritual purity and spotlessness, universally required in all ancient religions, was insisted on by pious Jews and Pharisees in NT times (cf. Mark 7:3-4). Only the **pure and undefiled** is acceptable to God. Such pure religion is defined as (*a*) **to visit orphans and widows,** i.e. to work the works of justice and charity (cf. Mic. 6:8); and (*b*) **to keep oneself unstained from the world** by avoiding involvement in the wickedness which inevitably surrounds Christians scattered abroad in the world (cf. I John 2:15-17).

IV. Partiality Is Sin (2:1-13)

Ch. 2 is less miscellaneous than ch. 1. It is organized around 2 major themes: partiality (vss. 1-13) and faith and works (vss. 14-26). Moreover, the style of ch. 2 differs from that of ch. 1. Instead of collecting various exhortations strung together by means of tag words as in ch. 1, the author now employs the style of the diatribe. This was a technique of oral discourse used by Greek Stoic and Cynic philosophers in which the speaker acted as if he were carrying on a dialogue with an imaginary person. One characteristic of this style which appears frequently in ch. 2 is the use of rhetorical questions (e.g. vss. 4, 5, 15-16, 20).

2:1-7. *No Partiality in Church.* Partiality, i.e. regard for outward appearance, is incompatible with Christian faith (vs. 1). God himself does not look on outward appearance (cf. I Sam. 16:7). Jesus obviously did not cater to the rich or powerful, but humbled himself and associated with ordinary people. The one who is **the Lord of glory,** who reflected the power and presence of God, humbled himself and appeared in the form of a servant (cf. Phil. 2:6-11).

2:2-4. Nor should partiality ever find its way into the Christian **assembly** (lit. "synagogue," but vs. 1 makes clear that a Christian congregation is meant). The example of partiality is obvious: do not favor the rich and well-dressed man by offering him a seat while at the same time providing no seat at all for the poor man or letting him sit on the floor. The persons who make such **distinctions** set themselves up as **judges** with ulterior motives (vs. 4).

2:5-7. Such distinctions are contrary to the fact that God himself has **chosen those who are poor in the world** (vs. 5) to receive his blessings (cf. 1:9-11; Luke 6:20; I Cor. 1:26-31). To favor the rich would dishonor the poor man (vs. 6a), the very one whom God would exalt. In addition there is little to be gained by favoring the rich. They are the very ones who **oppress** Christians and **drag** them **into court** (vs. 6b). The author seems to have in mind rich outsiders who are unsympathetic to Christians and who also **blaspheme** or despise the very **name** of God by which his people are called (vs. 7; cf. Deut. 28:10; Isa. 63:19; Jer. 14:9).

2:8-13. *Partiality Is Against God's Law.* The **royal law** (vs. 8), like the "perfect law" in 1:25, refers to the whole law of God revealed in the OT and interpreted by Jesus and in Christian tradition. The law is summed up in the commandment to **love your neighbor** (cf. Lev. 19:18b; Rom. 13:8), and the Christian will do well to comply with it—even with respect to the rich.

2:9-11. On the other hand, partiality is a violation of another part of the law (cf. Lev. 19:15). To break any part of the law is to **commit sin** (vs. 9); for whoever breaks one part of the law is **guilty of all of it** (vs. 10).

2:12-13. The Christian is to obey the whole law of God in all its parts, for only full obedience achieves freedom and makes it a **law of liberty** (cf. 1:25). The teaching of Jesus clearly shows that mercy will not be given to the person who shows **no mercy** (Matt. 18:23-35), yet **mercy triumphs over judgment** in the sense that the one who shows mercy will receive it (Matt. 5:7).

V. Faith Produces Works (2:14-26)

This passage is probably the most famous of all in Jas. **Faith apart from works is dead** (vs. 26) is an oft-quoted maxim. It has wide popular appeal because it makes good common sense. The author is obviously correcting a false notion about faith. Some people apparently thought that faith was mere belief in certain doctrines like the unity of God. Such belief is not faith, for **even the demons** can believe that much! (vs. 19). True faith, rather, is the kind of belief which produces good works.

Where did such false conceptions of faith arise? Our lack of complete knowledge of the circumstances in which the letter was composed prevents us from answering this question with certainty. Yet the fact that "faith alone" was a cardinal doctrine of Paul suggests that 2:14-26 was directed against a distorted form of Paul's teaching (cf. II Pet. 3:15-16). The fact that Abraham, one of Paul's favorite OT characters (cf. Rom. 4), is used to illustrate the point gives added weight to this supposition.

This observation indicates that though the author differs with Paul on the meaning of faith and its relationship to works, the apparent conflicts are not irreconcilable. To Paul faith is the deep personal relationship of trust in Christ in which the believer receives God's grace. Faith is a living relationship in which the believer is re-created and empowered to live the Christian life as described by Paul in Rom. 5-8. Surely the notion that faith is mere belief which excuses a person from action and responsibility is far from Paul's understanding.

The author tackles this heresy by affirming the necessary relationship between faith and works. Belief becomes faith only when it produces action. To be sure, he lacks Paul's profundity; for he, unlike Paul, does not think of faith as a living relationship between the believer and Christ. Rather to him faith is sincere belief which is accompanied and validated by good works.

2:14-17. Faith Without Works Is Dead. Consistency of belief and action constitutes true faith. Contrariwise, belief without action is of no profit and cannot save a person. An obvious example (vss. 15-16) makes the point: Mere words cannot clothe or fill a person in need. Without the articles of clothing and food such words are hollow sounds. Similarly belief alone **is dead** (vs. 17); i.e. such supposed "faith" is not faith at all.

2:18-19. The Unity of Faith and Works. Faith and works are 2 sides of the same reality. Faith is the inner side of action; works are the outward expression of faith. Even **demons** can believe in the unity of God—and **shudder** in their fear of him. But obviously such belief which has no fruition in good works is vain.

2:20-26. Abraham's Works and Faith. The point of the interrelationship between faith and works is now illustrated. The rhetorical question is hurled at an imaginary **foolish fellow** (vs. 20), who is foolish to twist Paul's teaching into such an obvious error.

2:21-24. To understand the point here, cf. the thought in Rom. 4. Paul bases his doctrine of "faith alone" on Abraham's complete trust in God (Gen. 15:1-6). The stress here is on the deeds of Abraham, specifically the sacrifice of Isaac (vs. 21; cf. Gen. 22:1-19). The point is that Abraham's faith was not mere belief. His **faith was active along with his works,** and it **was completed by works** (vs. 22). It is this kind of faith, evinced and completed by good deeds, which counts as **righteousness** (vs. 23). In Rom. 4 Paul thinks of righteousness as the gift of right relations which God bestows on the person who receives it in faith. Here, however, the righteousness which counts, and is therefore valid, is reckoned to the person who combines belief with action.

2:25. Even a **harlot** (cf. Josh. 2:1-21) can be **justified**—i.e. acquitted, excused, and made right—by actions which demonstrate true faith.

2:26. The conclusion is obvious: Faith and works, like **body** and **spirit,** are bound together. Faith without works, like a corpse without spirit, **is dead.**

VI. CONTROL THE TONGUE (3:1-12)

The opening vss. of ch. 3 turn to a new subject without apparent transition from ch. 2. Although the author has previously mentioned controlling the tongue in 1:19, 26, he now develops and applies the theme more fully. His main point is: control the tongue, for through it you also control the whole person. The 2nd part of the argument (vss. 6-12) is entirely negative. Not only is the tongue practically

impossible to control, but the unbridled tongue leads to great disaster and self-perpetuating evil.

3:1-5. The Tongue Controls the Person. A widespread tendency is for people to appoint themselves as **teachers** (vs. 1) and give advice to others. To be sure, there was need for teachers to instruct members of the church in NT times (cf. Acts 13:1; I Cor. 12:27-30; Eph. 4:11). Yet not all are qualified to teach, and here those who would teach are reminded that they have the greater responsibility since they will **be judged with greater strictness.**

3:2. The warning is particularly appropriate, for all people—teachers included—**make many mistakes.** On the other hand, the person who does not make mistakes in his speech is a mature person. The Greek words for **perfect man** can mean either a flawless person or a complete or whole person, i.e. one who is mature (cf. Eph. 4:13). Such maturity is shown in one's ability to control his speech and **to bridle the whole body** as well.

3:3-4. Two obvious examples illustrate how the tongue, though small, is related to the control of the whole person. A bridle bit in the mouth of a horse controls his actions. Similarly the small rudder of a great ship guides its direction at **the will of the pilot.**

3:5. The transition to the following discussion about the inability of man to control his tongue is formed by the warning that a **small fire**—e.g., in modern times, a match or lighted cigarette carelessly thrown away—can set a whole **forest . . . ablaze.**

3:6-12. The Problem of the Tongue. This passage points out the problem of the tongue, which is as deep as sin (though this word is not actually used). The difficulty is due to man's inability to control the tongue and his consequent impotence to control himself. The author offers no solution to the problem except to exhort his readers, **This ought not to be so** (vs. 10).

3:6. The tongue, like a fire, rages with its evil effects in all members of the **body.** In turn this fire is fed by the evil depths of man's sickness. Hence it is perpetuated by the deep resources of **the cycle of nature;** i.e. it sets in motion the force of man's nature which is already sick and breeds corruption. (The exact meaning of the text here is not clear. The alternate in the RSV footnote, **wheel of birth,** could mean the force of heredity, not unlike "original sin.") The flame is further nourished by the **fire of hell.** The Greek word for "hell" here is *Gehenna,* the city dump of Jerusalem, which with its perpetual blaze was a vivid reminder of the condemnation in the final judgment. In these references to the deep resources of evil the author is moving close to a doctrine of original sin and Paul's analysis of sin's power (cf. Rom. 7).

3:7-8. The point here is obvious. The tongue, as related to the self, is man's worst enemy. Wild beasts can be tamed; but man's own tongue, and consequently his self, cannot be brought into subjection.

3:9-12. Further evidence of man's lack of self-control is the pouring forth from his mouth of both blessings and curses (vs. 9). These obvious contradictions indicate that something is radically wrong. In nature a **spring** does not yield both **fresh water** and **brackish,** nor does a **fig tree** bear **olives.** Only man has such a curious and disastrous contradiction in his nature. Thus the point of the exhortation remains: **This ought not to be so.**

VII. The Meaning of Wisdom (3:13-18)

The emphasis in this passage is on the meaning of true **wisdom,** which **comes down from above** (vss. 15, 17). True wisdom stands in stark contrast to supposed earthly wisdom, which manifests itself in **jealousy and selfish ambition,** leading to **disorder** and evil deeds (vs. 16).

The key word of the passage is **wisdom,** an important concept throughout the Bible and related writings, especially the so-called "wisdom literature" (see pp. 1101-05) such as Prov., Wisd. Sol., and Ecclus. The word is frequently used with a wide variety of meanings. Sometimes it is used to designate prudence or worldly wisdom. Such earthly wisdom is often described in a bad sense and is contrasted with the wisdom of God, e.g. by Paul in I Cor. 1-4, and in this passage.

3:13. True wisdom is a divine gift (vss. 15, 17). Like faith, it is manifest in **good** patterns of **life,** in good **works,** and in virtues like **meekness** and those mentioned in vs. 17.

3:14-16. The opposite of true wisdom is self-centeredness characterized by **bitter jealousy and selfish ambition,** qualities of character which are nothing to boast about and are contrary to **truth** (vs. 14). Such supposed wisdom is earth-bound and even **devilish** or demonic (vs. 15).

3:17. Following a widespread custom of his day, the author lists the virtues which characterize the wisdom from above (cf. Paul's contrast between works of the flesh and fruits of the spirit in Gal. 5:19-23).

3:18. This verse appears to be a teaching independent of its context. **Righteousness,** which to James means right conduct and piety (cf. 1:19-21; 2:21-23), is the fruit of **peace.** Seen in the context of the following passage, peace is the opposite of hostility and strife.

VIII. Submission to God (4:1-17)

Even though this ch. covers a wide range of subjects and appears to be loosely organized, the basic theme running throughout is submission to God. This thought is brought into clear focus in vss. 7-10, with the accent on God's exaltation of the humble in vs. 10. In 2:14-26 the exhortation was aimed at those who think that religion consists in mere belief without good deeds. Ch. 4 is directed against those who are morally lax and still hold to worldly pleasures.

4:1-3. *Passions and Strife.* The strife mentioned in vss. 1-2*ab* stands in contrast to righteousness and peace in 3:18. The author uses strong words to make his point: **wars, fightings,** and even **kill.** The root of these external ills is in the **passions** which rage in the **members** of the body. Such unchecked desires may lead to murder (cf. Matt. 5:21-24, 27-28), and unquenched covetousness leads to conflict.

4:2c-3. It has already been said that God freely bestows gifts on those who ask in faith (1:5-6; cf. Matt. 7:7-8). Now the negative form of that teaching is stated: No one who asks **wrongly,** i.e. simply to gratify his **passions,** can receive anything. Here it is not lack of faith but wrong intention which cuts off the receiver from the gift (cf. 1:8).

4:4-6. *Love of the World Is Enmity with God.* The relationship between God and his people through-

out the Bible is based on a covenant of mutual fidelity (cf. Exod. 19; 24; Mark 14:24; Heb. 9:15). Vss. 4-10 seem to follow a 3-fold covenantal form: (*a*) warnings and curses against those who are unfaithful (vss. 4-5), (*b*) blessings of grace to those who submit to God (vs. 6), and (*c*) obligations of the covenant people (vss. 7-10).

4:4. The key to these vss. is in the opening words, **unfaithful creatures.** Marital infidelity is the accusation, for the Greek word means "adulteresses." The infidelity of God's people is compared to adultery in Hos. 3:1 (cf. Jer. 3:9; Ezek. 16:30-43), and Jesus denounced his generation as adulterous and sinful (Mark 8:38). Here there is assumed a covenantal relationship of faithfulness between God and his new people in Jesus Christ. Hence **friendship with the world** can only mean a breach of covenant and **enmity with God.** The "world" is everything which is corrupted by sin and hence opposite, at enmity, with God (cf. 1:27; John 8:23; I Cor. 5:9-10; I John 2:15-17).

4:5-6. These vss. are obscure and hard to interpret. **The scripture** (lit. "writing") can refer to a noncanonical work as well as the OT. The quotation in vs. 5 is not found in the OT and has not yet been found in other extant writings. The Greek can mean either "Yearns jealously for him the spirit . . ." or **He yearns jealously over the spirit . . .** The latter seems to fit the context better. **The spirit which he has made to dwell in us** is probably an allusion to Gen. 2:7 and God's desire for fellowship with man. The quotation in vs. 6 is from the LXX of Prov. 3:34. It serves as a text for the emphasis on **grace,** i.e. God's benevolent gifts and help to those who are humble.

4:7-10. *God Exalts the Humble.* The imperatives of this passage are vigorous in moral fervor. Self-mortification (in contrast to passions and friendship with the world in vss. 1-4) includes not only cleansing from sin and purification of the heart but also **mourning** and **dejection.** Only those who thus **humble** themselves will be exalted by God (vs. 10).

4:7-8a. Because God **gives grace to the humble** (vs. 6), the reader may well ask, "What shall we do?" The answer is, **Submit yourselves to God.** The meaning of submission is spelled out in the following vss. That the **devil** (the personification of temptation to evil) **will flee** from those who resist him is spiritually and psychologically true (cf. Testament of the Twelve Patriarchs, Naphthali 8:4; Simeon 3:5; Benjamin 5:2; also I Pet. 5:8). Those who have broken an undesirable habit, e.g. smoking or drinking, know that temptations weaken with persistent resistance. Divine aid is available in the struggle against evil, for God **will draw near** to those who come to him. (For other examples of ways God or Christ helps the believer against sin cf. Rom. 6:1-11; Eph. 6:11-13; Heb. 2:18; 4:15-16).

4:8b-10. The injunction to **cleanse your hands** refers to ritual washing (cf. Mark 7:1-8), and it is ethically interpreted in Isa. 1:16-17 to mean changing from evil deeds to good and justice. "Clean hands and a pure heart" are combined in Ps. 24:4 as the prerequisite for approaching God. **Sinners** are **men of double mind** who would try to love both the world and God (vs. 4; cf. 1:8). To the author repentance means that worldly pleasure and wickedness must be rejected and the Christian must mortify himself so that his **laughter** turns to **mourning** and his **joy to dejection** (vs. 9; cf. Luke 6:25). These disciplines, however, are not ends in themselves; for God exalts those who thus **humble** themselves (vs. 10; cf. vs. 6).

4:11-12. Judge Not. That the Christian should not **speak evil against . . . another** or judge a brother is a universal NT teaching (e.g. Matt. 5:21-22; 7:1-5; Luke 6:37; Rom. 2:1-3; 14:3-4). The author points out how this practice amounts to opposing **the law** (here, as in 1:25 and 2:8-12, the law of God revealed in the OT and interpreted by Jesus and Christian tradition), for in this way the judge places himself above the law.

4:12. Where the law of God is concerned, there is but **one lawgiver and judge,** God himself, who has the will and power **to save and to destroy.** Though the author does not quote the words of Jesus, he echoes the Lord's teaching (Matt. 10:28).

4:13-17. Living Under Providence. Under normal circumstances life appears to have a certain permanence. A businessman (vs. 13) comes to assume that tomorrow he can buy, sell, and travel just as he did today. Such confidence is unfounded. It is like that of the man with a bumper crop who plans to build bigger barns to store his grain that he may rest in his assumed security; his assumption is false, and he is a fool (Luke 12:13-21). Such a man does not realize that his life is but a **mist** (vs. 14), like a breath on a cold morning which appears for less than a second. The realization of the conditional nature of human life—**if the Lord wills** (vs. 15)—is the beginning and constant state of living under God's care.

4:16. The recognition of life's conditional nature excludes **boasting** (cf. Paul's affirmation that faith excludes boasting, Rom. 3:27). All such **arrogance,** like worldliness (vss. 1-9), is **evil.**

4:17. The name which might be given to all forms of evil in this chapter is **sin.** The definition here is thoroughly practical and has to do with deeds: to know the right and to fail in doing it is sin. This practical concept of sin is less profound and dynamic than that of Paul, who understands the deepest dimensions of the biblical view. For Paul sin is a power operative in every man so that only God's miraculous deliverance in Christ can liberate and enable him to live a new kind of life (Rom. 7).

IX. AGAINST RICHES AND INJUSTICE (5:1-6)

Throughout the letter the author has opposed the rich and favored the poor. He has warned the wealthy that life is transient and that riches will pass away (1:9-11). He has accused the rich of oppressing Christians and of blasphemy (2:6-7). Here he expands on these themes in two ways, by showing that the rich (*a*) are headed for miseries, especially those of the last days, and (*b*) have gained their wealth by committing injustice, particularly against agricultural workers.

5:1-3. Wealth Is Corrupted. Probably the **rich** are not members of Christian congregations, but the indictment is general and is hurled at the rich as a class. They are warned to **weep and howl** because of the **miseries** about to come upon them. These are signs of the coming judgment and the **last days** (vs. 3; cf. Isa. 13:6; Ezek. 21:12; Amos 8:3; Rev. 6:15-17).

5:2-3. The verbs **have rotted, are** (lit. "have become") **moth-eaten,** and **have rusted** are in the perfect tense to show that though these corruptions are still in the future their effects are as good as already accomplished. The last days have already begun. Even the most permanent forms of earthly wealth, like **gold and silver,** have no eternal value. Looked at from the viewpoint of the last days, they too are subject to corrosion. Far from having real value, these precious metals stand as **evidence** (lit. "witness") against the rich who have failed to care for the poor as prescribed in Deut. 15:7-8 (cf. Luke 16:19-31), and probably have gained their wealth through injustice (cf. vss. 4-6; Wisd. Sol. 2:6-20). Riches alone cannot satisfy; consequently the person who seeks wealth for its own sake finds that its corruption will consume him—**will eat your flesh like fire.** Most versions punctuate vs. 3 with a period after **fire,** leaving the following sentence fragmented and obscure. The RSV footnote indicates an alternate translation: "will eat your flesh, since you have stored up fire for the last days." This makes clear that the fire is that of the final judgment which the rich store up for themselves. The rich man is headed for disappointment in this life and judgment in the life to come (cf. Matt. 6:19-20).

5:4-6. Injustice Cries Out. From ancient times down to the migratory workers and sharecroppers of the modern American era, agricultural laborers have been among the most exploited of peoples. Deuteronomic legislation in the OT insisted that workers be paid promptly and with fairness (Deut. 24:14-15) lest injustice against laborers **cry out** to the **Lord of hosts,** the avenger of the poor (vs. 4; cf. Lev. 19:18; Deut. 32:35).

5:5. Those who in this life live in **luxury and pleasure** simply fatten themselves like cattle (cf. Amos 4:1) for the **slaughter,** i.e. the judgment, which is at hand.

5:6. The rich and the powerful **have condemned** and **have killed the righteous man.** In Wisd. Sol. 2:6-20 there is a vivid portrayal of ways the rich exploit the poor. The **righteous man** is identical with the poor (cf. Amos 2:6-7; 5:12; 8:4) who does not resist injustices against him because it would be folly for him to do so.

X. PATIENT WAITING FOR THE LORD (5:7-12)

5:7-11. Patience and Steadfastness. From the threat of judgment against the rich in vss. 1-6 the author now turns to exhort the **brethren** of the Christian fellowship to be patient while awaiting the **coming of the Lord** (vss. 7-8). The *parousia,* or arrival, of the Lord was expected in the immediate future in early NT times; and the apparent delay in his return caused some problems of impatience and misunderstanding among Christians (cf. Matt. 24:3-6; I Thess. 4:13-18; I John 2:28).

5:9. The period of waiting may try the patience of some and tempt them to **grumble** or blame each other for their troubles. Since they may thus fall into judgment, they are warned that the Lord who comes is like a judge who stands at the door.

5:10-11. Further examples of **suffering and patience** are found in the **prophets** who, because they **spoke for the Lord,** were persecuted (cf. Matt. 5:12; Acts 7:52; Heb. 11:32-33). Similarly **Job** was steadfast, even when tried with severe pain and great losses. Yet in the final outcome, as portrayed in Job 42:10-16, God did show him mercy and compassion. Such an end is a token of God's purpose, an additional incentive for waiting with patience.

5:12. Do Not Swear. This vs. is a detached teaching without any apparent connection with the preceding or following passages. The injunction against oaths is found in the teaching of Jesus (Matt. 5:33-37) and often in Jewish parallels. The point of the saying is simply that the Christian should always speak the truth; both his **yes** and his **no** should mean what they say. No oath can or should make a Christian truthful, nor can the lack of an oath permit him to lie. With anything less than the truth he falls into **condemnation.**

XI. MINISTERING TO EACH OTHER (5:13-20)

This is one of the most positive sections in the whole book. In the language of the modern church the passage describes the "priesthood of all believers," showing ways in which Christians minister to each other. Specific practices in the modern church may differ from those of NT times, but the concern of Christians to serve one another in the fellowship of the church is the same.

5:13-15. The Service of Prayer. In the rounds of life's experiences Christians know **suffering** or trouble (cf. vs. 10) as well as good times when they can be **cheerful.** In all circumstances of life they can and should turn to God. In suffering Christians should **pray;** in fortunate circumstances they should **sing praise** (cf. Phil. 4:10-13).

5:14-15. In vs. 14 **sick** refers to illness rather than to suffering or trouble as in vs. 13. When a church member is sick, he is to **call for the elders of the church.** Undoubtedly the organizational structure of early Christian communities was patterned after that of the Jewish synagogues. The office of **elder** has a long history in Judaism, and in NT times each Jewish community had its council of elders. The references to elders in the church of Jerusalem (Acts 11:30; 15:2, 4, 6, 22-23; 16:4; 21:18) suggest that they functioned much in the usual pattern of elders in Jewish communities. Distinctive in this passage, however, is the fact that the elders perform a ministry of prayer and anointing for the sick. They are assumed to be not simply governing authorities or organizational leaders but functioning ministers to members of the congregation.

The elders are to **pray** over the sick man, i.e. at his bedside, and they should anoint him **with oil in the name of the Lord.** Since Mark 6:13 is the only other place in the NT which mentions anointing as a religious rite in healing, the practice was probably not widespread among the churches. Vs. 14 recommends both prayers of the elders and their anointing the sick man; but vs. 15 stresses the **prayer of faith,** i.e. offered without doubt (cf. 1:6), as the element which will **save the sick man** or heal him from his sickness (cf. vs. 20, **will save his soul**) because **the Lord will raise him up.**

Restoration to physical health alone, however, falls short of real cure. The forgiveness of sins is necessary for the total well-being and wholeness of the person (cf. Mark 2:5). The healing ministry of the church has as its objective the cure of souls, the restoration of health to the whole person.

5:16-18. Confession and Intercession. In the ongoing ministry of the church the elders do not function alone. Rather Christians minister to one another and are urged to **confess** their **sins** to each other (vs. 16). But there is an immediate return to prayer, the dominant theme of the passage. In the context of mutual confession and prayer, healing takes place in the fellowship of the church.

5:17-18. To illustrate his conclusion in vs. 16 the author cites the example of Elijah (I Kings 17:1; 18:1, 42-45), who prophesied to King Ahab that rain would cease until the word of the Lord would command it to fall again. The rain did cease and only began again when Elijah bowed himself down to the earth. Interestingly, the author cites the incident of the drought rather than Elijah's healing of the widow's son (I Kings 17:17-24) and he does not mention the healing miracles of Jesus. His main point is that Elijah, a mere man—**of like nature with ourselves**—prayed and his prayers were answered. If the prayers of this righteous man effected a drought, how much more will the prayers of Christians avail for health and salvation.

5:19-20. Bring Back Wanderers. In primitive Christianity when doctrines were not fully defined, and when Christians were subject to severe trials (1:2-4) and temptations to worldliness (4:1-10), the tendency to wander from the truth was a real problem. To bring back such wanderers was part of the church's ministry. The person who **brings back a sinner from the error of his way,** back into the fellowship and life of the church as described in vss. 13-18, **will save his soul from death and will cover a multitude of sins** (cf. the familiar saying in I Pet. 4:8 that "love covers a multitude of sins"). The meaning of this is ambiguous. Will the person who brings back the wanderer save his *own* soul and thus cover a multitude of his own sins? Or will his corrective action save the soul of the wanderer and cover his sins? Probably the latter is correct, for the wanderer can be made whole when he comes back into fellowship with the church, where he can join again in confession and prayer (vs. 16).

The author does not mention the atoning work of Christ which covers sins. Rather his focus is on the church where that atoning work is known and shared. The church knows the forgiveness of sins in a fellowship of confession and prayer (vss. 15-16). The return of the wanderer **will cover a multitude of sins**—his own, those of the man who brings him back, and those of the whole Christian fellowship, where forgiveness of sins is a shared reality.

THE FIRST LETTER OF PETER

Claude Holmes Thompson

INTRODUCTION

This vigorous letter has long been a favorite in the church. Addressed to Christians in Asia Minor, it sought to encourage them as they faced scorn from their neighbors and, to some extent, persecution from the government. Authorship, date, purpose, and theology are all bound up together.

Authorship. Though the text designates Peter the apostle as the author, serious questions have been raised against this claim. It is said that (a) the rugged Galilean fisherman could not have written the exquisite Greek of this letter; (b) it refers to persecutions more intense than any which took place by the time of Pet.'s death ca. A.D. 64; (c) it relies too heavily upon the Pauline letters, which allegedly were not circulated extensively until after Pet.'s death; (d) it bears little evidence of the personal acquaintance Peter had with Jesus.

In reply, several points must be considered. (a) The excellent Greek may be due to Silvanus, the "Silas" of Acts and the Silvanus of II Cor. 1:19; I Thess. 1:1; II Thess. 1:1. This responsible member of the mother church in Jerusalem, a Roman citizen (Acts 16:37) and fellow missioner with Paul, could have written the letter as Pet.'s amanuensis, as stated in 5:12.

(b) The persecutions need not refer to those under Trajan in A.D. 111-112. Very early the church was mistreated for bearing the name "Christian" (Acts 5:41; 9:16; 21:13), and by ca. A.D. 50 Paul met trouble in Thessalonica (I Thess. 2:14-15). The report in this letter could reflect the gathering storm under Nero. As William Barclay says, "The persecution situation in *First Peter* does not in any way compel us to date it after the life time of Peter himself."

(c) As for the influence of Paul, much of this was common property of the Christian community before he began to write in ca. A.D. 51. Pet. had access to the same data, and he likely had seen Paul's letter to Rome, written perhaps between A.D. 53-58.

(d) As to the absence of firsthand knowledge of the life of Jesus, this seems overstated. The author claims to have seen Jesus (1:8) and to have witnessed his sufferings (5:1), and the Master's teachings echo in various places in the letter (1:13, 17; 2:12; 3:9, 14; 4:5, 14; 5:2, 6-7)

Yet different judgments remain concerning authorship. Ten years ago 2 equally distinguished scholars published commentaries almost simultaneously. One dates the letter no earlier than 112 with author unknown; whereas the other regards it as basically Petrine, written from Rome no later than 64. The

case against Pet. as the author has not been established. If we accept the contribution of Sylvanus, the view that Pet. produced the letter may be accepted.

Date and Place of Composition. If the letter was the joint work of Pet. and Silvanus, it may be dated ca. 64, not long before Pet. lost his life and shortly before the outbreak of the persecution under Nero. Since loyalty to the emperor is urged (2:13-17), doubtless that persecution, while anticipated, was not yet actual.

An early date is suggested also by the absence of technical language pertaining to church organization. The only term referring to church officials is "elder" (5:1). Not even the familiar terms "deacon" and "bishop" are used.

There seems no reason to reject the traditional view that this letter was written from Rome, referred to as "Babylon," a term recognized among Christians as the designation of the capital city of the empire (5:13; cf. Rev. 14:8; 16:19; 17:5; 18:2, 10, 21).

Purpose. I Pet. appears to have one major purpose with several subsidiary, though closely related, emphases. The basic theme is to provide encouragement now that persecution seems imminent. Even in so brief a letter persecution is mentioned at least 4 times (1:6-7; 3:16-17; 4:12-19; 5:9). One element of encouragement is the promise of the return of Christ. This is referred to quite vividly (1:5, 7, 13; 2:12; 4:13, 17; 5:1, 4). The purpose is to keep hope alive at any cost, but it is hope which only God can vindicate.

There seems to be some liturgical purpose in the letter, especially in reference to baptism and the Holy Communion. It may be that 1:3–4:11 is a manual of instruction for new converts, with 2:4-10; 3:18-22 included as hymns of encouragement. At least the author intends to instruct his readers in the faith.

There is also an ethical purpose. The new life through baptism is a radical departure from the old patterns of conduct. Not only are there specific instructions for husbands, wives, and servants; there is clear evidence that the believers in Christ are to be obviously different from their pagan neighbors (1:14; 2:1, 9, 11-18; 3:1, 7; 4:3-6, 15).

But the total purpose of the letter involves the certain grace of God as available for any need (5:12).

Theology. God is the "faithful creator" (4:19) who is likewise "the God and Father of our Lord Jesus Christ" (1:3). His gracious care extends to all people (5:7, 10), but he is righteous in all his judgments, since his judgments rest upon his own holy character (1:14-17). Thus he is both "for" the righteous and "against" the wicked (5:5), yet his patience in dealing with the wicked demonstrates the quality of holy compassion (3:20). While his people may endure suffering here on earth (3:17; 4:19), they are to submit to him, knowing that he will give strength for the day and assurance of final victory for the future (5:6, 10).

The doctrine concerning Christ is related also to this certainty of suffering (1:11), but these sufferings are redemptive (3:18). While Christ is set forth as an "example" (2:21), he is likewise to be worshiped as "Lord" (3:15). Pet. here reflects the earliest creed of the church as seen also in Paul (cf. Rom. 10:9; 14:9; I Cor. 12:3; Phil. 2:11). As Lord he is the standard for final judgment (2:7-8; 4:5). This lordship is more than the portrait of a good man committed to his ideals; Jesus is seen as a redeeming sacrifice, unique and solitary in human history.

While the word "church" is not in the letter, 3 definitive ideas of the church are present: "spiritual house" (2:5), "God's own people" (2:9), and "flock of God" (5:2).

The whole theology is primitive, i.e. centered in the earliest proclamation of the gospel. All the elements in the *kerygma,* or proclamation, are found clearly stated, but there is also the clearly defined *didache,* or instruction in Christian living. Thus here is the earliest stratum of Christian witness.

For Further Study: E. G. Selwyn, *The First Epistle of St. Pet.,* 1946. F. W. Beare, *The First Epistle of Pet.,* 1947. A. M. Stibbs, *The First Epistle General of Pet.* ("Tyndale NT Commentaries"), 1959. William Barclay, *The Letters of James and Pet.,* 2nd ed., 1960. C. E. B. Cranfield, *Pet., I and II, and Jude,* 1960.

I. GREETING AND PRAISE (1:1-9)

1:1-2. *The Author's Greeting.* By identifying himself as **Peter, an apostle of Jesus Christ,** it is obvious that the author intended to include himself among the 12. In Aramaic, the dialect spoken by the Jews of the time, Pet.'s name was Simon Bar-Jona, or Simon son of John. But Jesus had given him the additional name of Cephas, or "Rock," which was to convey a symbolic meaning later in the life of this yet unsteady disciple. Since this letter is addressed to Greek-speaking Jews, it is natural that it should carry the Greek form of the name, Petros.

In a sense Pet. is his Christian name. Just as Paul does not use his original name of Saul in his letters, so Peter uses this distinctive Christian form to refer to himself.

The language of the opening phrase could simply mean one sent on a special mission. But here it obviously is used to designate Pet. as an authentic apostle, an originally appointed member of the 12. Though at times Paul had to defend his apostleship against those even within the church, Pet. apparently feels his clear claim to this authority will be accepted by his readers.

To the exiles of the dispersion in Greek actually reads, "to the elect strangers of the Dispersion." The idea of election, once held to refer to Israel alone, now is applied to all the redeemed under the new covenant of grace (cf. 2:9 with Deut. 7:6).

The term "diaspora," technically referring to Jews living outside Palestine, is here used not only to designate Christians alienated from their native land but also to indicate the temporal nature of this exile. Thus while the Christians were the new Israel, they were also the new dispersion.

Pontus, Galatia, Cappadocia, Asia, and **Bithynia** are districts in N Asia Minor (see color map 16). They were important in early Christianity, especially in the ministry of Paul and in Rev. (cf. Acts 2:9; 16:6-7; 18:2; I Cor. 16:1; Gal.; Rev. 1-3). It is significant that within *ca.* 3 decades of the Crucifixion the church was sufficiently strong in this remote area of the Roman Empire to warrant this letter.

1:2. Lit. **destined by God the Father** is "according to the foreknowledge of God the Father." Apparently many translators have felt that the stronger terms, "destined," or "predestined," are implied in the Semitic idiom, where "to foreknow" is substantially equivalent to "to determine" or "to decide." This idea, coupled with the previous term, "elect," underscores the peculiar divinely chosen mission of these believers. If they were mostly slaves, as seems possible, this must have given to them an exciting sense of dignity.

This divine election is the 1st of 3 definitive elements of Christian living set forth. The 2nd is that of being **sanctified by the Spirit.** Basically this ministry of the Holy Spirit is 3-fold: to purify the church redeemed by Christ, to set it apart as a distinct fellowship of believers, and to empower it to continue to witness to the ministry begun by Christ and consummated by his death and resurrection. The 3rd element refers to the purpose of this divine election and sanctification: **for obedience to Jesus Christ and for sprinkling with his blood.** Here the inauguration of the new covenant through Christ is seen in the light of the old covenant made at Sinai (Exod. 24:7-8).

The trinitarian form of these expressions—**Father . . . Spirit . . . Jesus Christ**—has been mentioned by various writers. Though we must not read back into this letter the doctrine of the Holy Trinity, which was formulated in the midst of later controversy, yet this is what has been called a "trinity of experience."

The salutation concludes with words almost identical with those used by Paul: **May grace and peace be multiplied to you.** Grace is God's suffering love in action to redeem sinful men who do not deserve this unmerited gift, and peace is practically identical with the idea of salvation, where reconciliation between God and man, past, present, and future, is already an accomplished fact.

1:3-9. *The Doxology of New Life.* Two ideas dominate these vss.: a doxology for the risen Savior and the certainty of new life in Christ. Writing to frightened people whom he knows face trials, Pet. gives encouragement through praise to God. The touchstone of the Christian's strength is the power of the resurrection of his Lord—now available for him. **Blessed** is not used in the same sense as in the Beatitudes (Matt. 5; Luke 6). In the Sermon on the Mount the word describes the happiness, the bliss, of the man in communion with God. But here the word is used in prayer addressed to God. The simplest Jewish prayer, "Blessed art Thou, O God," becomes, **Blessed be the God and Father of our Lord Jesus Christ!** Yahweh, somewhat remote, even austere, is now intimate and personal in Jesus Christ.

1:3. The theme of rebirth is a major message of the NT. Nicodemus needs to be "born of the Spirit" (John 3:6); the believer walks in "newness of life" (Rom. 6:4); the Christian is a "new creation" (II Cor. 5:17); while once we were dead in sin, we have now been "made . . . alive together with Christ" (Eph. 2:5). The **living hope** to which Peter refers is rooted in **the resurrection of Jesus Christ from the dead.** His resurrection not only guarantees our resurrection but also keeps hope fresh and alive until we join him in the life beyond the reach of death. The certainty of the resurrection of Christ from the dead was the central theme of all preaching in the early church.

1:4-5. But this hope is nurtured by **an inheritance . . . imperishable, undefiled, and unfading.** In the LXX "inheritance" refers to Canaan, the land of promise (cf. Deut. 15:4; 19:10). Peter uses the same word here. Thus this inheritance is **kept in heaven for you,** i.e. as a kind of heavenly Canaan. But since the Christian is to "seek the things that are above, where Christ is" (Col. 3:1) and since **the last time** has already entered history in the incarnate ministry of Christ, who "was made manifest at the end of the times" (1:20), the Christian already has a foretaste, installment, pledge, guarantee (cf. II Cor. 1:22; 5:5; Eph. 1:14) of this blessed hope. This inheritance is reserved **in heaven** untouched by earthly changes, and those who are to receive it are **guarded through faith** until its final possession.

1:5-9. A definitive NT word, **Salvation** is used to indicate divine action in the past, man's present experience, and the future hope. Since the Christians were already living **in the last time,** they could **rejoice** in spite of impending trials. Suffering is the lot of the faithful, as of the Lord himself. Yet this only serves to distinguish genuine faith from sham. Pet. contrasts his own experience of having known Jesus "in the flesh" with his readers who were not so privileged. Yet so authentic was Jesus' mission they could still love him and believe in him (cf. John 20:29*b*).

II. A Living Hope (1:10-25)

1:10-12. *From the Prophets to the Gospel.* The Bible for the first Christians was the OT, and the importance of the prophets can hardly be overstated. The early church saw the uncompleted hopes of the prophetic movement, and thus it was inevitable that these OT writers should be read so as to foreshadow the coming of the Messiah. This is a common NT theme (cf. e.g. Luke 24:25-27; John 5:39, 45-47; Acts 2:15-36; 7:52; 8:30-35). Jesus said that the prophets looked for the day which Pet. is describing "and did not see it" (Matt. 13:17).

Four things seem significant in this relation of the gospel to the prophetic insights: (*a*) The **prophets** were not passive recipients of an imposed message— **they searched and inquired about this salvation.** (*b*) It was **the Spirit of Christ within them,** i.e. the secret both of the ministry of Jesus and of the prophets was the Spirit of God (cf. Rom. 8:9; I Cor.

10:4). (*c*) Christ is understood as the Suffering Servant. The early Christians understood that Jesus identified his ministry with that of the Suffering Servant of 2nd Isaiah (cf. Luke 22:37 with Isa. 53:12; Acts 8:32-33 with Isa. 53:7-8; Heb. 9:28 with Isa. 53:12). (*d*) They knew their vision was not for their own day but for the time of fulfillment. That time had now come.

1:13-21. *An Admonition.* Pet. now turns to the consequences in Christian living. As the oriental workman wearing the flowing robes of his land must tuck up the loose ends under a belt, or girdle, so in Christian living there must be no frazzled ends, no fuzzy thinking—Christians must **gird up** their **minds. A** modern metaphor might be: "Roll up your sleeves."

Be sober is a warning not to panic even though trouble does come. Strenuous discipline is required of the believer. But what is the basis of this appeal? Five elements seem apparent.

1:14-16. (*a*) First is the call to sanctity. As God is **holy,** so must be his children. Pet., appealing to Lev. 11:44-45, sets the standard as conformity to the character of God. This is both negative—**do not be conformed** to the old way (cf. Rom. 12:2)—and positive—**be holy yourselves in all your conduct.** In an age of moral laxity and ethical relativism, then and now, the demand for the standard for Christian living is still holiness of character and conduct.

1:17. (*b*) Second, there is the judgment of God. **Conduct yourselves with fear,** since we now live in **exile** on earth. The reference is to the impartial judgment of God upon the children of Israel during their stay in the wilderness.

1:18-21. (*c*) Third is the tremendous cost of redemption. **The precious blood of Christ** is responsible for this rescue from bondage. **Blood** here refers to the poured out, or spilled, blood, as in ceremonial sacrifices (cf. Exod. 12:5; Lev. 22:19, 20; Deut. 15:21). Here Christ is seen as the Passover Lamb slain from **before the foundation of the world** (cf. Acts 2:23; 4:28; Eph. 1:4-10; Heb. 4:3; 9:14; Rev. 13:8).

1:20. (*d*) Fourth, an idea expressed in vs. 5—"revealed in the last time"—is given somewhat fuller treatment: **He was . . . made manifest at the end of the times.** The coming of Christ has been the beginning of the end. With the Incarnation the kingdom has been inaugurated; the final stage of the history of man under God is on its way. There will still, however, be a final consummation in the "revelation of Jesus Christ" (vss. 7, 13). But these 2 ideas are inseparable.

1:21. (*e*) Finally, the appearance of Christ on earth produces faith, but especially so since God **raised him from the dead.** The life, death, and Resurrection constitute what is sometimes spoken of as "the Christ-event." No creation by an adoring church is this faith, and no mythological Jesus can account for it.

1:22-25. *Brotherhood of the New Birth.* There is community through social or political structures as within a state. There is community through natural generation as in a family. But here Pet. describes a community through divine grace, i.e. by rebirth into the family of God.

1:22-23. Pet.'s reference to **obedience to the truth** is regarded as referring to baptism, initiation into the

Christian way. It results in moral sanctification which in turn is seen as Christian love within the fellowship. But this love is not simply good will; it comes from the completely transformed life which Pet. refers to as being **born anew.**

1:23-25. This new life comes through **imperishable** divine **seed** which is identified with **the living and abiding word of God** (cf. Luke 8:11). Thus those so reborn become "partakers of the divine nature" (II Pet. 1:4). But this word of God is no mere collection of written documents. It is God's message of salvation declared for all men. Pet. contrasts the transitoriness of life through natural descent with the permanence of this divine rebirth. "That which is born of the flesh is flesh" (John 3:6) and hence is subject to decay, but "that which is born of the Spirit is spirit" (John 3:6) and hence **abides for ever.**

III. NEW LIFE IN CHRIST (2:1-12)

2:1-3. *New Birth Means New Life.* "Love of the brethren" (1:22) requires the elimination of characteristics of the old life. Some of these well-known evils are stated, and Pet. indicates that new life cannot continue along with these death-producing practices. They must be stripped off with relentless severity.

2:2-3. But positively, this new life needs nourishment. An automatic function of the newly born infant is eating. The word here for **newborn babes** refers to infants in arms, hence the metaphor is appropriate. Does this suggest that the readers were recent converts? Perhaps. A similar idea is used by Paul regarding the Corinthian Christians (I Cor. 3:1-2), and the writer to the Hebrews blames the people for their continued infancy (Heb. 5:12-14). But here Pet. sees this healthy appetite as a good thing, provided it is satisfied with proper food (cf. Ps. 34:8).

2:4-10. *The New People of God.* The new people were not merely individual Christians; they were the church. By the use of figures of speech, OT references, and personal appeals, the origin, nature, and function of the church are set forth.

The origin is Christ, **in Zion a stone, a cornerstone** (cf. Isa. 28:16). Though **rejected by men** (vs. 4), he **has become the head of the corner** (vs. 7; cf. Ps. 118:22), since he was divinely **chosen.** This divine choice brings judgment, since he is **a stone that will make men stumble, a rock that will make them fall** (cf. Isa. 8:14). This stumbling comes from disobedience to the will of God.

The nature of the church is suggested in the metaphor of the **spiritual house** constructed of the **living stones** of believers. But this spiritual house is further described as a **race, . . . priesthood, . . . nation, . . . people** (vs. 9). This is one of the most meaningful interpretations of the church in the NT. Note that all terms are corporate; to be a Christian is to live within the community of God's people.

These descriptive terms all come from the OT. As with Israel, the church is the new race to inherit the role of the elect people (cf. Isa. 43:20*b*-21; Col. 3:12; Tit. 1:1). As Jesus is the Messiah, king of the new kingdom, his subjects are a priesthood continuing the role of Israel as the priestly people

(cf. Exod 19:6; Deut. 7:6; Gal. 6:16). The word *laos,* from which comes laity, refers to all the people who belong to God, as distinct from all others. These were the new people of the new covenant.

The function of the church is to **declare the wonderful deeds** (vs. 9) of God's redeeming love by offering **spiritual sacrifices acceptable to God through Jesus Christ** (vs. 5).

Three contrasts should be noted in this discussion of the church: (*a*) Though Christ was rejected by men, he was divinely chosen (vs. 4). This same idea is seen in Pet.'s sermon at Pentecost. (*b*) God called his people **out of darkness into his marvelous light** (vs. 9). The conflict between light and darkness is a common NT theme (cf. John 1:5; 12:35; Acts 26:18; Eph. 5:8; Col. 1:13-14), and a similar idea is found in the Dead Sea Scrolls. (*c*) There is a contrast between **no people** and **God's people** (vs. 10). This is an obvious reference to Hos. 1:6, 9; 2:23 (cf. Rom. 9:25).

2:11-12. *Pilgrims Among Pagans.* These words introduce a discussion concerning the Christian's conduct within a pagan society. Pet. had warned against sins of the inner life. Now he speaks of **passions of the flesh.** While these may be crude physical practices, they are primarily the perverted condition of man's life, the "fallenness" of unredeemed human nature, the self twisted inward and away from God. Thus there is warfare between the old life and the new. This is a common theme in Paul's writings (cf. Rom. 7:7–8:14; Gal. 5:6-25; cf. also Jas. 1:14-15; Jude 16, 18).

Like the children of Israel before him, the Christian knows he is an alien and an exile on earth, but he is not thereby excused from noble conduct. Negatively, there is the demand to avoid the desires of the flesh, the lower nature. Positively, behavior must be such as to impress even the pagans with the excellence of the Christian way. **So that . . . they may see your good deeds** seems an obvious reference to the saying of Jesus: "Let your light so shine before men, that they may see your good works and give glory to your Father who is in heaven" (Matt. 5:16).

IV. CHRISTIAN RELATIONSHIPS (2:13–3:17)

2:13-17. *Church and State.* The Christian may not ignore his responsibility as a citizen. This section regards the state as a divine institution, designed to protect the weak, punish the unruly, and devise welfare for all. Life is to be an ordered society, not chaos.

2:16. Acting as **free men** and at the same time as **servants of God** constitutes the paradox of Christian living within the state. Freedom does not mean unrestrained liberty to do as one may please. Rather it is freedom to do the will of God.

2:17. The author issues 4 short commands for Christians to follow in their relationships with one another and with non-Christians. (*a*) They must **honor all men,** for every man is a person for whom Christ died. No man is cheap; not one of the 60 million slaves of Rome. This idea was a breath of fresh Christian air in a land where multitudes were exploited. (*b*) Christians must **love the brotherhood.** Within the Christian fellowship is born a new relationship which reflects the kind of God-caring love (*agape*) which led Jesus to die for sinners. (*c*) They must **fear God**—fear in the sense of reverence, awe, worship (cf. Prov. 1:7; 24:21). (*d*) Finally they must **honor the emperor.** If this emperor was Nero, Pet. calls for an attitude toward him by the church which even some Romans could not endorse.

2:18-25. Suffering Servants. The word for **servants** employed here by the author refers to household, or domestic, servants. Slavery was a recognized fact in the early church. Many Christians were slaves, but in spite of this there is no evidence that the gospel sought the destruction of this social system. It was accepted *de facto*, and directions were given for its operation. Slaves were often people of culture and education, at times superior to their masters. Doctors, librarians, teachers, musicians, and secretaries were among them. A slave had no legal rights at all—he was not a person; he was a thing. Sooner or later the implicit freedom for every man would emerge, but when Pet. wrote this letter, this was far in the future.

2:18-20. Servants are to obey, not only when masters are considerate, but also when they are cruel. Thus if these servants could not please their perverse masters, they at least could please their God, who understood their plight. Their motive of service, therefore, was not to curry favor with these masters, but to **have God's approval.** God honors **suffering** which comes **unjustly.** On the other hand, pain which comes from wrongdoing is simply what is deserved.

2:21-25. But why is suffering meritorious? **Because Christ also suffered for you, leaving you an example, that you should follow in his steps.** These vss. should be read in the light of Isa. 53, where the figure of the Suffering Servant is seen. Cf. esp. parallel expressions in Isa. 53:5-6, 9, 12. This messianic passage, long understood in the church to portray the divine purpose in the death of Christ, sees Christ's death as God's answer to human sin.

The significance of this message for slaves must not be overlooked. Christ's suffering is not only redemptive; it is an **example** which even slaves are to imitate. His patience under mistreatment, suffering without threats, death in behalf even of enemies, could not fail to impress those called to endure unjust treatment. God would bring justice to cruel masters. It was enough that the death of Christ was a healing to those who had to suffer as well as the means of bringing the straying ones to the **Shepherd** who would forever be the **Guardian of** their **souls.** The word used here for "guardian" is often translated "bishop," but apparently Pet. reserves it for the peculiar ministry of Christ to protect his chosen ones. It has no reference to ecclesiastical office.

3:1-7. Wives and Husbands. In this section there are 98 words (in Greek) in 6 vss. (1-6) for instruction to wives, 25 words (in Greek) in 1 vs. (7) for husbands. **Wives,** like servants, had little standing in the ancient world, hence the need for more detailed directions concerning their conduct. Husbands, when they became Christians, took their wives with them into the fellowship of the church; but if wives became Christians, their husbands did not necessarily follow them. Thus there was need for special care in their manner of life. They are to be obedient even

to a pagan husband. This may lead to the conversion of the husband, but even if it does not, they must still be obedient. Pet. appeals to the example of **Sarah,** who **obeyed Abraham,** in support of his directive for submission (vs. 6).

3:2. The standard of chastity, **chaste behavior,** is of special significance. It has been said that the one unique virtue which Christianity contributed to the ancient world was chastity. There was a single pattern for Christian conduct for men or women—moral purity (Jas. 1:27).

3:3-6. As for dress, Pet. warns against luxury, show, and even excessive attention given to the **hair** styles currently in vogue.

3:7. Husbands too have a responsibility: not to exploit their superior physical powers but to recognize that along with their wives they share a common life within the grace of God. This has been referred to as spiritual equality (cf. Eph. 5:25-33; Col. 3:19). Pet. in addition suggests that unless husbands recognize this **joint** participation of both sexes in a spiritual fellowship, a meaningful prayer life is impossible.

In the ancient world, even within Judaism, a woman had an inferior position. She, like the slave, was not a person but a thing, a piece of property. Theoretically, Christianity changed all this by destroying the inferior status of women.

Likewise, at a time when questions had been raised concerning the wisdom of marriage at all in view of the shortness of the time (I Cor. 7:7-8, 20, 26-27), Pet. exalts the relationship of husband and wife as a noble expression of Christianity at its best.

3:8-12. Christian Action and Attitude. Herein are presented Christian attitudes which promote Christian conduct. Christian **unity** leaves no place for quarrels, schism, unholy divisions. This is a basic NT idea. Jesus prays for it (John 17:21-23; the church early experienced it (Acts 4:32); Paul repeatedly urges it (Rom. 12:4-5, 16; I Cor. 1:10-15; 3:3-9; 12:12-31; Phil. 1:27; 2:2; 4:2). This is not to be a flat and uncritical uniformity in which personal differences are erased; it is rather the disposition to fellowship beyond these differences.

3:8. A close relation exists between **sympathy** and **love of the brethren.** We have to love for one another (cf. John 13:34) which will express itself in a suffering concern, a sympathy which has no room for selfishness (cf. Rom. 12:15; I Cor. 12:26). **A tender heart** means compassionate concern for the suffering people of the world. **A humble mind** suggests teachableness, but it also refers to the kind of humility seen in Jesus in both precept and example (Matt. 11:29; 23:12). Pet. must have written these words with painful memories of his own weaknesses yet with humble gratitude for God's mercy.

3:9-12. Forgiveness, the refusal to pay back **evil for evil,** means there is no place for retaliation in the Christian life. Vss. 10-12 are based on Ps. 34, which is used freely to show the contrast between the man who merits God's approval and the one who does not.

3:13-17. The Christian in Trouble. Does Pet. here also recall the words of Jesus: "Blessed are those who are persecuted for righteousness' sake, for theirs is the kingdom of heaven" (Matt. 5:10)?

3:15-16. To **reverence Christ as Lord** reflects

the earliest Christian creed, "Jesus is Lord" (cf. Rom. 10:9; I Cor. 12:3; Phil. 2:11). "Lord" is used in the LXX for God, and here the divine title is assigned to Jesus. This confession provides a freedom from fear of suffering, but it also provides a basis for witness. So often suffering and a **defense** of the faith go together. This confession, however, must be made **with gentleness and reverence,** no arrogance or abuse. After all, the best evidence is **good behavior in Christ.**

3:17. Sometimes this witness brings pain, but while suffering for wrong is the consequence of faulty living, suffering for the right may indeed be the **will** of God.

V. CHRIST THE SAVIOR (3:18–4:19)

3:18-20. *The Suffering Savior.* This passage requires careful attention. Several themes are crucial:
3:18. (*a*) The first of these themes reveals the meaning of the death of Christ. The cosmic character of that death is seen in his passion on earth, his ministry among the departed spirits beyond death (vs. 19), and his consequent authority in heaven (vs. 22). Whatever else he thought of Christ, the author could never understand him as only a man among men. And even if vs. 18 reads "suffered" instead of **died,** as some manuscripts have it, the context carries the same redemptive meaning for all men. His death was exclusive, unique, **once for all,** never requiring repetition (cf. Rom. 6:10; Heb. 7:27; 9:28; 10:10).

Again, it was death **for sins,** i.e. it was a divine atonement to restore a broken relationship between man and God (cf. I Cor. 15:3; Gal. 1:4; Heb. 10:12; I John 2:2). Likewise, it was vicarious, **the righteous for the unrighteous.** It removed the barrier between sinful man and the holy God—**that he might bring us to God**—since "through him we . . . have access in one Spirit to the Father" (Eph. 2:18).

The expression, **being put to death in the flesh but made alive in the spirit,** probably refers to death to the earthly, perishable flesh which Jesus took in the Incarnation and to the quickening of his own self (spirit) for his continued ministry beyond the Resurrection.

3:19-20. (*b*) The 2nd theme is Christ's ministry to the dead. These vss., with parallel thoughts in 4:6 (cf. Jude 6), suggest that Jesus, after crucifixion and before resurrection, proclaimed the gospel to those who had died before his time. Thus in Hades, the Hebrew designation for that existence between death and final destiny, even the departed souls are confronted by the claims of Christ. This passage lies back of the expression in the Apostles' Creed, "He descended into hell."

3:20-22. (*c*) The 3rd theme concerns Christ's ministry in heaven. These vss. tie together a series of ideas: (i) Noah was rescued from an evil people **through water.** (ii) Water suggests **baptism,** the saving sacrament for the Christian. (iii) Baptism is meaningful only because **through the resurrection of Jesus Christ** the believer is raised to new life. (iv) Resurrection has led to Christ's priestly function **at the right hand of God.** Thus the authority of Christ extends from before the covenant with Abraham to his final rule in **heaven.**

4:1-6. *Through Death to Life.* This section now

returns to the thought in 3:18. As Paul indicates in Rom. 6:3-14, baptism is seen as a dying to the sin of the present life to live in the new life in Christ (cf. Rom. 8:10-13). The new life and the old are contrasted as **human passions** and **the will of God.** These are the alternatives which are spelled out quite vividly. Cf. the specified evils with Paul's list of the "works of the flesh" in Gal. 5:19-21. The lofty ethical standards of the Christian community stood in contrast to the sordidness of the time. This is seen as an eschatological judgment since God **is ready to judge the living and the dead** (vs. 5). The final judgment between right and wrong has come in Christ; it is now about to be seen within the Christian community.

4:7-11. *The Beginning of the End.* There is a persistent note in the NT of something just about to happen. The Christian always lives on the edge of the end. If the existentialist insists upon the "isness of the was," the bringing up into the present of the meaning of the redemptive past, we must also insist upon the "isness of the shall be," i.e. the final judgment as having already come. There is no judgment more final than the entrance of Christ into history.

The sanity, sobriety, prayerfulness, **love,** and **hospitality** with joy referred to in these vss. are the qualities of Christian life at the beginning of **the end.** In light of the shaky minority of the Christian community these characteristics become not only right but imperative. Notice 2 things: preaching and ministering—**whoever speaks . . . whoever renders service.** Communal worship—a community of service—how better to describe the Christian fellowship in any age!

4:12-19. *A Further Admonition.* The purpose of the letter is now obvious: to encourage believers when trouble comes. Trouble is certain; thus it must be met not with surprise but with glory to God. Actually, persecution can bring us into a more intimate fellowship with Christ in his sufferings (cf. Rom. 8:17; Phil. 3:10; II Tim. 3:11). Suffering can not only bring **glory** to God; it can bring glory to the Christian.

The eschatological mood enters into this suffering: **when his glory is revealed, . . . the time has come.** It was an ancient idea that the people of God would be the first to suffer the judgment of God (vs. 17; cf. Amos 3:2; Isa. 10:12; Jer. 25:29; Ezek. 9:6).

VI. CLOSING COUNSELS (5:1-14)

5:1-4. *A Message to Elders.* Elders had been officials in the synagogue. Here, however, the word refers to local officials in the Christian community whose function is the care of **the flock.** Paul had designated elders in the cities where he preached (Acts 14:23; cf. Tit. 1:5). While Pet. as an apostle possessed an authority by virtue of his personal relation to Christ, here he identifies himself as **a fellow elder.** Such ministry entails the added role of suffering. Again, pastoral care is set in the context of pain—mutual pain within the community of faith.

Christ as **the chief Shepherd** directs the ministries of the undershepherds. Notice the repeated contrasts: not by compulsion—but gladly; not for **gain**—but with eager zeal; not in lording it over the church—but as an example in holy living.

5:5-11. *Final Exhortations.* Again cf. the contrasts: **humility** under God leads to victory (cf. "Whoever loses his life for my sake, he will save it," Luke 9:24). Undue anxiety is to be surrendered, since God is in charge (cf. Matt. 6:25-34). Be **sober** (clear-headed, cool) and alert since **the devil prowls** about **to devour** (cf. "Resist the devil and he will flee from you," Jas. 4:7*b*).

5:10-11. Again this theme of suffering is used to show how it can be God's sanctifying medium to establish and strengthen the believer. This is the painful price to be paid for the **glory** to come. Thus to God **be the dominion for ever and ever.**

5:12-14. *Conclusion.* Silvanus—Silas—apparently is the same person who aided Paul with I and II Thess. and who accompanied him on various journeys (Acts 15:40; 16:19, 25, 29; 17:4; 18:5); a prominent member of the church at Jerusalem (Acts 15:22, 27, 32), he was associated with Paul in preaching the gospel (II Cor. 1:19).

5:13. Babylon doubtless refers to Rome, a title not intended to be complimentary (cf. Rev. 14:8). Mark, the John Mark of Acts 12:12, 25; 13:5, 13; 15:37, was the cousin of Barnabas. He is also mentioned in Col. 4:10; II Tim. 4:11; Philem. 24. Tradition has associated him with Pet. as his interpreter, and the 2nd gospel bears his name.

5:14. The **kiss of love,** practiced in the early church, has been replaced in our time by the handshake.

THE SECOND LETTER OF PETER

CLAUDE HOLMES THOMPSON

INTRODUCTION

This letter, which has led to much academic discussion, is concerned with vital issues for the Christian church. The author stoutly defends the orthodox faith of the apostolic community, perhaps overstating it at one point, viz. the parousia, or 2nd coming of Christ. Likewise, he vigorously combats the threat which jeopardized the moral excellence of the Way (cf. Acts 9:2). Faith and life, doctrine and deportment—each is exceedingly important.

Authorship. While the letter bears the name of Simon Peter, hardly any scholar today, or even in the early church, regards it as having come from the apostle. Several reasons may be given for this judgment: (a) Early Christian writers give scant reference to Pet. as the author. This is in contrast to I Pet., which has good attestation. (b) The author uses Jude, but Jude could hardly have been written early enough to have been known by Pet. before his death. (c) The criticism of the denial of the parousia (3:1-4; see above) suggests a late date. Nowhere else in the NT are there any such denials, and it is not likely that they arose before the destruction of the temple in A.D. 70—Pet. is thought to have died before this. (d) There are clear differences between II Pet. and I Pet. in vocabulary, ideas, and use of the OT. These differences were pointed out in the early church. (e) The Hellenistic mood of the letter is not found in I Pet. nor in the life of Pet. which we see in the gospel and the sermons in Acts. (f) The author refers to a collection of Paul's letters as "scriptures" (3:15-16), certainly a collection which had not been made during Pet.'s lifetime.

But what must be said when the letter itself claims to have come from Pet. (1:1)? For one thing, the practice of writing under the name of another person was not uncommon in the ancient world. Jewish apocalyptists often wrote under the name of some revered person long dead, as e.g. documents purported to have come from Enoch, Moses, Ezra, Solomon, Daniel, Isaiah. Such writings were called "pseudonymous." This does not mean that they were false or forged. There are such writings bearing the name of Pet.: the Gospel of Peter, the Acts of Peter, the Apocalypse of Peter, the Preaching of Peter (see "Noncanonical Early Christian Writings," pp. 1144-49). While these writings were known to the church in the 2nd cent., none of them won sufficient approval to be placed in the canon. We may never know why II Pet. was so honored, but it was not simply because it bore the name of the apostle.

II Pet. and Jude. No less than 19 of the 25 vss. of Jude are incorporated into or used in some manner by II Pet. (II Pet. 2:1-3:3). In addition there are other parallel ideas. Scholars substantially agree that II Pet. used Jude rather than vice versa.

Date and Place of Composition. There seem to be good reasons for dating this letter about the middle of the 2nd cent., or possibly as early as 125. Paul's letters had been collected and were regarded as "scripture" (3:15-16). The heretics who twisted Paul's letters "to their own destruction" (3:16) could have been followers of Marcion, ca. 140. The apostles are clearly men of the past (3:2, 4). Finally, it was the middle or late 2nd cent. before other writers explicitly referred to this letter at all. Perhaps this is as near as we can date II Pet., the last NT book to be canonized.

As for the place of composition, various suggestions have been made: Rome, Palestine, Asia Minor, Egypt. If the influence of I Pet. is seen, perhaps this letter also came from Rome; but if Jude is from Palestine, as some believe, it is difficult to rule out this possibility.

Message. The author is disturbed over the threat to both the Christian ethic and doctrine by certain "lawless men" (3:17). The faith is in jeopardy. Aware of the passing of the original leaders of the Christian movement, this author feels a special urgency to call the church back to the purity of faith and practice that characterized its beginnings. Several elements are found in the message: (a) The standard for Christian living is the prophetic and apostolic witness (1:19; 3:2). The convergence of the message of the prophets with the "commandment of the Lord and Savior through your apostles" (3:2) identifies the faith with that of the primitive Christian community. (b) False teachers have arisen even within the fellowship (2:1). This was no casual difference on the surface; it threatened to destroy the very foundation of Christianity, even to the repudiation of Jesus himself. (c) Central in this heresy was the denial of the return of Christ (3:3-7). Such a denial was essentially a denial of the promise of God to complete his redemptive action begun in Christ. (d) False teaching tended to result in false conduct (ch. 2). It is possible that the author's attention was directed first of all to the lowering of morality as evidence of perverted teaching. This ethical section of the letter is severe in its description of immorality. (e) Two elements enter into a new devotion to the

931

faith. First, attention should be given to Paul's letters, since these convey the authentic gospel (3:15-18). Second, a true knowledge must replace false teaching (1:2-3, 5-6, 8, 20; 2:20-21; 3:3, 17-18).

With all the uncertainties surrounding this letter, it still retains an urgent call to devotion to the classic expression of the gospel. It is a clear voice in that period between the production of the major portions of the NT and the 2nd-cent. defenders of the faith, such as Justin Martyr, Irenaeus, Aristides, Tertullian.

For Further Study: J. W. C. Wand, *The General Epistles of St. Pet. and St. Jude* ("Westminster Commentaries"), 1934. A. M. Hunter, *Interpreting the NT, 1900-1950,* 1951. William Barclay, *The Letters of James and Pet.,* 2nd ed., 1960. C. E. B. Cranfield, *Peter, I and II, and Jude,* 1960.

I. LIFE AND GODLINESS (1:1-11)

1:1-2. *Salutation.* The best manuscripts use "Symeon" rather than **Simon Peter** in 1:1. This is the only place in the NT, except in Acts 15:14, where Pet. is given the name Symeon. Most often he is referred to as Pet., the name assigned to him by Jesus. The terms **servant** and **apostle** indicate that the author has been influenced by both I Pet. and Jude.

1:1*b.* The **faith of equal standing with ours** designates the apostolic nature of that faith which rests not on human achievement but on **the righteousness of our God and Savior Jesus Christ.** This at once discredits the "false prophets" (2:1), claims the authority of the primitive Christians as the standard for the faith, and identifies the author with this standard.

1:2. On **grace and peace** see comment on I Pet. 1:2. Grace, as God's free forgiveness of sinners, brings peace as the assurance of divine favor. Here the author adds **knowledge.** This is not academic information, nor is it initiation into a mysterious religious experience; it is personal acquaintance with Jesus as Lord. The reference to Jesus as Lord is an echo of the earliest creed, or confession of faith, viz. "Jesus is Lord" (cf. Rom. 10:9; 14:9; I Cor. 12:3; Phil. 2:11).

1:3-4. *Divine Provision for Human Need.* This true knowledge is the **divine power** which enables one to live the godly life, and the source of this power is Jesus the Risen Lord. This life was concretely demonstrated in his earthly ministry. He was no mythical character created by an adoring church. **His own glory and excellence,** i.e. his presence among men as revealing the purpose of God, is the pattern of the offer for us to **become partakers of the divine nature** (cf. John 17:3; Rom. 5:2; II Cor. 3:18).

1:4. It is no wonder that the author refers to this life as available through **his precious and very great promises.** Yet it is a promise, an offer, a gift which may be rejected. Received, it leads to full Christian faith and life.

1:5-11. *The Call for Response.* These vss. contain what has been called "the ladder of virtues" and also the consequences, pro and con, of our response to the divine promise. When one responds in a faith-surrender, he receives the divine gift of new life, but this involves strenuous moral endeavor. Beginning with **faith** there is added a series of qualities of character: **virtue, . . . knowledge, . . . self-control, . . . steadfastness, . . . godliness, . . . brotherly affection, . . . love.** Cf. this list with the "fruit of the Spirit" named by Paul in Gal. 5:22-23.

II. THINGS TO REMEMBER (1:12-21)

1:12-21. *A Pastor's Concern.* The author is sure of 2 things. First, while the gospel is "good news," it is not "new news." Thus the witness is not to astonish his hearers with something they have never heard but **to remind them of these things** they already know. Second, they cannot learn the gospel so well as to be beyond danger of its loss, thus the necessity that they be constantly reminded of God's grace.

1:14-15. There is a tenderness in the pastor's concern to establish his readers in the faith—since his own days are numbered. His body he compares with a tent (vs. 14; see RSV footnote), even as Paul does in II Cor. 5:4. **The putting off of** his **body will be soon.** This common reference in the early church suggests the temporary nature of this life. The Christian attitude toward death is seen in the confidence that Jesus is Lord both of the present and the future.

1:16-21. *The Apostolic Witness.* Here the author contrasts the true gospel with the fables of the false teachers. He claims the authority of an eyewitness, assuming that his readers know the account of the Transfiguration (Matt. 17:1-8; Mark 9:2-8; Luke 9:28-36). II Pet. emphasizes the **majesty** of Jesus which was then revealed and which will again be known at his return in glory. Thus when false teachers deny the 2nd coming, they actually attack the majesty of Christ. This the author cannot tolerate.

Thus the gospel does not rest on fables, but on the validity of God's action in history, revealed in Jesus of Nazareth (vs. 16). The Transfiguration itself was a kind of foretaste of the 2nd coming and as such validated the apostolic witness on the plane of history just as the prophetic faith had been declared within the framework of actual events on earth. The author here also claims that this **prophetic word** points to the mission of Christ. Men are **to pay attention to this until . . . the morning star rises in** their **hearts** (vs. 19).

1:20-21. These vss. refer to the need for inspiration in interpreting the scriptures. Private opinions must be met by revelation of the Holy Spirit. The Bible is a book of the Christian community and must be interpreted within that community, the peculiar sphere where the Holy Spirit operates. In prophecy **men moved by the Holy Spirit spoke from God.** Thus the apostles as successors to the prophets were the special agents operating under the Spirit both to write and to interpret the scriptures. The same Spirit who inspired men of old to write also inspired persons within the church to understand the meaning. This is the protection against false teaching.

III. HINDRANCES TO THE FAITH (2:1-3:13)

2:1-3. *False Prophets—False Teachers.* This ch. should be studied in the light of Jude, esp. vss. 4-16,

18. Characteristics of false prophets and teachers are described: They work **secretly,** under cover. Their deception cannot bear the full light of the truth (cf. John 3:19-21). They promote **destructive heresies,** i.e. ideas of their own, private opinions which replace the judgment of the church. They deny **the Master who bought them** (cf. I Cor. 7:23; Gal. 3:13; Rev. 5:9), not by outright rejection, but by immoral influences upon the faithful. Their doom is sure since they seduce others into sin and hence become victims of their own evil. **In their greed** they disguise the truth and bring the faith into disrepute.

2:4-11. *Judgment and Deliverance.* The author cites examples of God's judgments: **the angels** (cf. Gen. 6:1-4), **the ancient world** (cf. Gen. 6:5-7), **Sodom and Gomorrah** (cf. Gen. 19:24-25). But he also shows how **Noah** (cf. Gen. 6:8-22; 8:20-22) and **Lot** (cf. Gen. 19:15-23) were rescued. Thus God saves the righteous in the midst of trouble while the wicked are condemned in terms of their own sins (vs. 9). Two evils are cited: **the lust of defiling passion** and the act of despising **authority,** perhaps against angels or heavenly beings (vs. 10). This may seem obscure, but it portrays those evil persons who live for only one world with disdain for the realm of spiritual authority.

2:12-16. *The Evil That Men Do.* This sustained picture shows in detail the crass evil of these impostors. The author, in brilliant defiance, scorns the immoral conduct which threatens the people of God.

2:12-14. Evil men are worse than brutes since they disregard intelligence and hence live **like irrational animals.** But as the beasts are destined for capture and death, so destruction awaits these perverters of goodness. No longer do they seek the cover of darkness; they blatantly sin **in the daytime** and gloat in their persistent **adultery,** i.e. they see in every woman the possibility of seduction. This is no occasional lapse; this is a calculated plan to express unbridled passion—and that upon **unsteady souls.**

2:15-16. The author refers to the story of **Balaam** (cf. Num. 22–24), who corrupted his prophetic office by covetousness and cowardice and hence turned Israel into sinful ways. The irony of this old story is that the performance of the ass was more intelligent than the conduct of the prophet.

2:17-22. *When Freedom Becomes Bondage.* In the name of emancipation there is a threat of new slavery. Paul warned against a false view of liberty turned into an occasion for indulgence (Gal. 5:13). This freedom is a freedom only to sin—with consequences of utter moral ruin. How can these false teachers **promise . . . freedom** when they themselves are **slaves of corruption?** And the tragedy is that they once knew the way of the Lord but now have returned to **the defilements of the world.**

2:22. The author combines a reference to Prov. 26:11 and one to the Story of Ahikar (see "Noncanonical Early Christian Writings," pp. 1144-49) to give the picture of the **dog** and the pig both returning to filth of their own making.

3:1-4. *Scoffers of Christ's Return.* A warning is raised against the scoffers of the return of Christ (cf. I Pet. 1:3-7; 4:5-7, 13; 5:4, 10). Both prophets and apostles had declared Christ to be the final judge and savior of men. But now, in the 2nd or 3rd genera-

tion of Christians, nothing had happened. Things remained pretty much the same **from the beginning of creation;** thus, **"Where is the promise of his coming?"** This was obviously asked in scorn.

3:5-13. *The Scoffers Answered.* While in an earlier age scoffers derided Noah, still the world was destroyed **by . . . water.** Created **out of water,** the earth is not impervious to ruin. This time the **destruction** will be by **fire.** This is the only NT reference to destruction of the earth by fire, but the idea is persistent in nobiblical sources—Hebrew, Greek, and Roman. There is no built-in assurance of the claim that everything has remained the same since creation. If it was destroyed once, it will be destroyed again. (The present stockpile of atomic devices gives a touch of realism to this passage.)

3:8-13. But again, God does not measure time by a clock or a calendar. The author employs Ps. 90:4 to help us see time as God sees it. God is in no hurry. Nor is his delay evidence of dilatoriness. Indeed, it is divine patience, since it is his will **that all should reach repentance.** But God will act in his time with a suddenness of divine doom upon the wicked. Thus the Christian is to be engaged in watchful waiting, busy and eagerly desiring the day which will not be a terror but a joy. For vs. 13 cf. Isa. 65:17; 66:22; Rom. 8:21; Rev. 21:1.

The idea of the parousia was deeply embedded in the life of the primitive church. Possibly some scholars have overemphasized the sense of an immediate expectation shortly following Jesus' death. There is some question whether Jesus intended to leave an impression of such nearness, though some of his followers apparently did get this idea. Yet there seems little evidence that the church as a whole was confused by the nonreturn of Jesus. The fact that the author can reaffirm the certainty of this return **like a thief** suggests that neither the doctrine nor the delay greatly troubled the church. It may be that the scoffers and some overly eschatological NT scholars have made more ado over it than the rank and file of believers.

IV. Final Admonitions (3:14-18)

3:14-17. *A Call for Zeal.* The writer is convinced that the hope of the return of Christ is needed to assure moral stability. In the meantime the task is to **wait** even as God waits. Even the divine patience, **the forbearance of our Lord,** is itself **salvation** in action; judgment is delayed to provide opportunity for response. **Paul** is appealed to in support of this patience. Divine forbearance, however, must not encourage moral laxity. Thus these scoffers twist Paul's idea of freedom to promote license. While there may be things in Paul's letters **hard to understand,** perhaps in relation to freedom from the law or the idea of unmerited grace freely provided for the sinner, yet Paul may not be cited to promote immoral living.

3:15b-16. The reference to Paul's writings as scripture relates them to the OT, **the other scriptures.** Likely a collection of Paul's letters was known by *ca.* A.D. 90, and perhaps it is this collection to which the author refers.

3:17-18. *God's Gift of Grace.* Being forewarned by Paul's witness and by the author of II Pet., Christians provided protection against (*a*) **the error of lawless men,** i.e. the perversity of evil men, and (*b*) the loss of their **own stability,** i.e. the inner foundation of a committed life. There is one security against this threat from without and within: **grow in the grace and knowledge of our Lord and Savior Jesus Christ.**

3:18*a*. Grace, that magnificently complex word, refers to the undeserved gift of God's love which can never be known or experienced save by the surrender of all trust in human skills and ability and the surrender to Jesus as Lord. **Knowledge** is instruction in the truth of the Christian tradition. Both grace and knowledge come from Christ and characterize the growing Christian experience and life.

3:18*b*. The only proper response to such a lofty conception of Christian living is a doxology, here addressed directly to Christ (cf. Jude 25).

THE FIRST LETTER OF JOHN

Massey H. Shepherd, Jr.

Introduction

Form of the Letter. Since the later years of the 2nd cent. I John has been accounted one of the Catholic, i.e. general, letters of the NT canon. Yet it lacks the customary address and greetings of a letter. Hence many interpreters have described it as a sermon, such as Jas., which has an introductory address but no closing greetings, or as a treatise, such as Heb., which contains no opening address but has a doxology and greetings at its close. Letter, sermon, or treatise—the writing is addressed to a specific group of Christian believers, whether of one or of several congregations. These include persons young and old, either in age or in their Christian experience (cf. 2:12-14), who remain steadfast in the "truth," in contrast to others who "went out" (cf. 2:18-27) from the "fellowship" that was "from the beginning." Those who do abide faithful and obedient to the true testimony of God in his Son Jesus Christ and remain in his communion are given exhortation and encouragement by the author.

Authorship. Most students of the letter have been persuaded that the author is the same person who wrote the gospel of John. The same style, the same vocabulary, the same themes are in the two writings. Both documents appear to have been published, circulated, and first cited at approximately the same time, the 2nd quarter of the 2nd cent., and in the same locale, the Roman province of Asia, i.e. W Asia Minor (see color map 16), whose capital was Ephesus. But the identity of this author has been much disputed (see Intro. to John). The preface of the letter (1:1-4) certainly links the author with the gospel, both its beginning (John 1:1-14) and its ending (John 20:19-29). Whether it presents the author as a personal eyewitness of Jesus or a disciple of one who was a companion of the Lord depends on the way one interprets the phrase "word of life" (1:1).

There are significant differences between the letter and the gospel. Stylistic differences are more apparent in the original Greek, but any reader can detect a more abstract and a less vivid and dramatic character in the writing of the letter. It overworks certain constructions, e.g. conditional sentences, antithetical sentences, sentences beginning with a demonstrative pronoun, and rhetorical questions. The letter has none of the Semitic coloring of the gospel; and singularly, among writings of comparable length in the NT, it contains no quotation from the OT. Maxims such as "God is light" (1:5) and "God is love" (4:8, 16) are peculiar. Other biblical books, including the gospel, employ more personal, less abstract ways of conveying "ideas" about the nature of God. On the other hand there are many expressions common to letter and gospel, e.g. "born of God," "do the truth," "walk in darkness," overcome the world," and "keep the commandments."

The letter lacks certain fundamental keynotes of the gospel: the Resurrection, the judgment, the kingdom; glory, grace, and peace. Some distinctive words and concepts in the letter are not found in the gospel: "fellowship," "anointing," "antichrist," and the denoting of Christ's redemptive work as an "expiation for our sins" (2:2, 4:10). A notable difference concerns the "advocate" (Paraclete): in the gospel he is the Holy Spirit (John 14:16-17, 26; 15:26; 16:7); in the letter he is "Jesus Christ the righteous" (2:1).

All these contrasts of style and interest may be, and have been, explained with reference to the different form, purpose, and time of writing of the letter and the gospel. If indeed the gospel betrays indications in its appendix (John 21:23-24) of having been shaped and edited by a "witness" of an earlier apostle or disciple of Jesus, we may attribute to this same person the composition of I John. He may well be the "elder" who has left us the more personal and individual notes of II, III John (see comments). Some scholars believe that I John was written as an intro. to the gospel; others believe it was composed some years after the gospel, by one whose advanced age shows signs of a weakening capacity for dramatic expression.

Date. The earliest citation of I John occurs in a letter of Bishop Polycarp of Smyrna to the church in Philippi (cf. 2:22; 3:8; 4:2-3 with Polycarp Phil. 7), written shortly before 117. Eusebius of Caesarea in his Church History (iii.39.17), tells us that a contemporary of Polycarp, Bishop Papias of Hierapolis, also cited "testimonies" from the letter. In the last decade of the 2nd cent. Irenaeus, bishop of Lyons and a pupil in his early years of Polycarp, referred the letter to the apostle John. So also did his contemporary Clement of Alexandria. But certain contemporaries of Irenaeus and Clement, who rejected the Johannine writings as nonapostolic, attributed them to one Cerinthus, a Jewish-Christian heretic who taught in Asia Minor in the early years of the 2nd cent.

No scholar today takes seriously the authorship

of the letter by Cerinthus. On the contrary the letter, as also the gospel, is perhaps best understood, in its immediate situation, as an answer to the teaching of Cerinthus. According to Irenaeus, Cerinthus was one of the first Gnostics. He taught that the world was made, not by the supreme God, but by an inferior power who was ignorant of the Father. Jesus was a man born as other men, but because of his righteousness, prudence, and wisdom the heavenly "Christ" descended on him at his baptism, whereupon he proclaimed the "unknown Father" and performed miracles. But the Christ departed from him before the crucifixion and ascended back to the Father. Thus Cerinthus distinguished between "Jesus" and "Christ," and denied the unity of his person in the Incarnation, Atonement, and Resurrection.

Other early church writers tell us that Cerinthus was also a "Judaizer"—i.e. he insisted on obedience to the Jewish law of circumcision and sabbath—and that he favored the conception of a millenium of feasting and pleasure at the end of the present age when the righteous, including Jesus, would be raised from the dead. In the light of such teaching one appreciates the story told by Irenaeus (Against Heresies iii.3) that on encountering Cerinthus in the public baths at Ephesus the apostle John exclaimed: "Let us flee, lest the bathhouse collapse, because Cerinthus the enemy of the truth is within!"

Teaching of the Letter. The author treats the immediate, crucial issue of heresy against a broad background of boldly sketched strokes contrasting the true nature of Christian faith and life over against error and sin. It is difficult to give a logical outline of his thought. Just as in the gospel, the letter throws out key words and phrases which recur again and again in similar but subtly altered contexts. The argument moves, as many have noted, not so much in a straight line as in a "spiral" of revolving, cumulative effects. The whole presentation is held together by the striking contrasts that mount one on another almost as synonyms: light, darkness; truth, lie; keeping the commandments, sin; love, hate; of the flesh, of the world; him from the beginning, the evil one.

For Further Study. Commentaries: A. E. Brooke, 1912; C. H. Dodd, 1946; A. N. Wilder in *IB*, 1957; Neil Alexander, 1962. Expositions: Robert Law, *The Tests of Life*, 1909; Charles Gore, *The Epistles of John*, 1920. G. B. Caird in *IDB*, 1962.

I. Preface (1:1-4)

The author's theme is the **word of life,** viz. Jesus Christ. He is a truth about God, the ultimate reality, and a mediator of personal relationships that bring complete and perfect joy. He is himself a gospel, i.e. "good news." He was a real man, who was actually **heard** and **seen** and **touched** by other men. He was also a revelation from God, with whom he shares eternally a life such as a father shares with a son. This same life he came to share with men. With the company of those who saw and heard him **from the beginning** the author associates himself, and hands on to his readers their testimony. The Christian gospel is both a message of truth and a **fellowship** of persons. It reconciles and unites God with men, and men with their fellowmen. The Gnos-

tic teachers, such as Cerinthus, separated God from his world, the divine Christ from the human Jesus, and the favored few who had a secret knowledge about God and themselves from the many who had no hope of fellowship in perfect joy.

It is typical of the rich texture of language and thought in the Johannine writings that words and phrases suggest more than one meaning. Thus the **word of life** is also the Word of Life—not only a **that which,** a message of truth proclaimed, but a living person, concretely individual, who enters fully into the sense relations of our human community. Similarly the phrase **from the beginning** may refer to Christ's eternal existence with his Father, or it may point to the historical beginning of his appearing as man on earth. This preface recalls, without actually quoting, the prologue of the gospel: "In the beginning was the Word. . . . In him was life. . . . And the Word became flesh and dwelt among us . . . ; we have beheld his glory." (John 1:1, 4, 14.) Likewise it reminds one of the resurrection scene when "he showed them his hands and his side" and "the disciples were glad when they saw the Lord" (John 20:20).

Hence it is not possible to tell with certainty whether the author was an actual eyewitness of Jesus or a believer in the testimony of eyewitnesses. In either case the fellowship with the Father and the Son is one and the same, unbroken and inseparable.

II. The Nature of Christianity (1:5-2:17)

1:5-10. *Fellowship with God.* The author's initial message would strike many chords in his readers: **God is light and in him is no darkness.** Ever since Plato, Greek philosophers used the imagery of light to describe the goodness and truth of ultimate reality. The religion of Zoroaster, stemming from Persia and increasingly influential in the Roman world, divided all reality into a mighty conflict of 2 opposing realms of light and darkness. The Gnostics made much of the idea. One of their earliest writings, The Gospel of Truth, says:

> Ignorance of the Father has brought anguish and fear; and the anguish has become dense like a fog, so that none can see. . . . Through the mercies of the Father has been revealed the secret mystery, Jesus the Christ, through whom it has enlightened those who were in darkness because of forgetfulness. It (He) enlightened them and gave them a way. . . . As ignorance melts away when one gains knowledge, as darkness melts away when light appears, so incompleteness melts away in Completion."

No doubt the Gnostic author has in mind, as does the author of I John, the revealer of light, Jesus Christ, who is the light that "shines in the darkness, . . . the true light that enlightens every man . . . , the light of the world" (John 1:4, 9; 8:12). But in the Johannine writings this light is not a merely abstract, metaphysical principle of ultimate reality, of truth over against error and ignorance. It is a principle and guide of daily life that illumines personal relationships and creates fellowship of men with God and with one another. Light is the way of righteousness; sin is the way of darkness (cf. 2:8-11; John 3:19-21; 11:9-10). Light as a way of life is the OT view, which the Johannine authors follow.

It is to **walk** in the path of righteousness that God illumines (cf. e.g. Pss. 27:1; 36:9; Isa. 9:2).

2:1-6. Fellowship with Christ. The fundamental difference between Gnostic teaching and that of apostolic witness **from the beginning** had to do with the nature of evil. For the Gnostics evil was simply error and ignorance, a misfortune for which man was not responsible. Christ came into the world to bring man knowledge (*gnosis*) of the truth. Hence man needs only illumination, not forgiveness.

But NT writers see the root of evil in **sin**—a deliberate rebellion against, and willful disobedience to God's **commandments.** All men the **whole world** over are sinners; to deny this fact is the real lie against truth. Men need to be cleansed from sin, and this they cannot do for themselves. To say **I know him** and remain in sinful disobedience to God is a contradiction. How then does man extricate himself from this dilemma?

Ancient man, whether Jew or pagan, conscious of his sin and alienation from God, sought to do this by a sacrificial offering of **expiation,** usually by way of a living, i.e. bloody, animal who was costly and hence in some degree a substitution for his own life. But as Heb. points out, such a manner of expiation—to "cover" or "blot out" sin and restore divine favor—was essentially ineffective. The victim was unwilling; the offerer in fact, if not in intention, was unrighteous. It is God himself who resolves man's dilemma by sending his Son to be the **expiation for our sins** (cf. 4:10). Not only was the **blood of Jesus** (1:7) offered willingly; he was also, as offerer, perfectly righteous. He is our **advocate** (see comment on John 13:31–16:33), who pleads our cause and intercedes for us. Therefore by his act we may be assured that when we confess our sins God forgives us. But our confession is real only if we **keep his commandments** and his **word.** We must abide in him and **walk** in his **way,** if our **love** and fellowship with God are to be **perfected.**

The Gnostic had no answer, despite his claim to superior knowledge. He ignored the fact of sin—for which he substituted mere ignorance. He also denied the reality of Christ's suffering and death; for to him the "blood of Jesus" had no significance, since he separated the human Jesus from the divine Christ.

2:7-17. Fellowship with the Brethren. The author is always insistent that theological truth can never be separated from ethical demand. If we accept God's forgiving love for Christ's sake, we must love one another as he loved us. The **commandment** of love is the summary and fulfillment of all commandments—**from the beginning.** Yet Jesus gave it a new form: "This is my commandment, that you love one another as I have loved you" (John 15:12). By the fruits of love one may know whether he is in **light** or in **darkness.** Love for one's brother and neighbor, not theoretical knowledge, is the only true test of Christian discipleship. It embraces all men of all ages—children, the young and the old.

Love is not the principle of life in the **world.** In the Johannine writings the term "world" does not mean, as with the Gnostics, the material creation of God as such, but those who are alienated from God by setting their ultimate values and ends on the **things in the world** and following the tempt-

ing example of the **evil one.** E.g. Cerinthus stressed the coming millennium as a time devoted to sensual pleasures. Darkness has blinded the eyes of such persons. They do not realize that Christ in his temptation conquered the world, the flesh, and the devil (cf. Matt. 4:1-11)—the selfish **lust** and **pride** of self-centered existence. Nor do they see that Christ is at work now in the world, as ever new disciples **overcome the evil one,** and that thereby a process is taking place by which **the darkness is passing away and the true light is already shining.**

III. The Crisis of Christianity (2:18-4:6)

2:18-27. The Coming of Antichrist. Jesus viewed his coming into the world as prelude of the final crisis of history—**the last hour**—the inauguration of the kingdom of God. In this crisis the forces of evil would marshall all their powers in an attempt to defeat God by troubling and deceiving his righteous ones—through wars, tumults, and persecutions, schisms and divisions, and "false Christs and false prophets" (Mark 13:22) who perform wondrous miracles. In the Synoptic gospels these signs are presented in apocalyptic form (cf. Mark 13; Matt. 24; Luke 21:5-36)—as also in Rev. 12-13, where they are symbolized in the monster figures of the dragon (Satan) and his blasphemous beast who would usurp the worship of Christ the Lamb. The same crisis is predicted in the gospel of John (e.g. 15:20–16:11), though in less flamboyant imagery; and its whole message is pervaded by Jesus' pronouncements of a coming "hour" which will be decisive.

Quite likely the author of I John invented the symbol of **antichrist** as a sign of this **last hour.** He sees its appearance first of all in the schism produced in the church by the teaching of a false Christ—viz. the doctrine, e.g. that of Cerinthus, that Jesus and the Christ are not one and the same **Son** of the **Father,** and therefore that Jesus Christ did not "come in the flesh" (cf. 4:2-3; II John 7). Presumably these early Gnostic groups **went out** of the church voluntarily, but the elder in II John 10 advises a more positive policy of excluding them.

The author makes an interesting play on the word **anointing.** *Christos* is the Greek equivalent of the Hebrew word transliterated Messiah, the "Anointed One." In the OT kings, priests, and prophets were consecrated in their office by a ceremony of anointing. So the true Messiah, Jesus Christ, fulfills these roles by his anointing with the Holy Spirit (cf. Acts 4:27; 10:38). Those who abide in him have received his anointing (cf. II Cor. 1:21) and become in him a "royal priesthood" (I Pet. 2:9; cf. Rev. 1:6). Thus they are all initiated into his truth and need no further teaching.

The Gnostics with their superior knowledge of the heavenly *Christos* made much of this anointing as the imparting of their more advanced truth. It was linked with the "chrism" or oil used in the ceremonial anointing of the head of initiates immediately following their baptism in water. The Gospel of Truth speaks of how Christ "will anoint them with the ointment. The anointing is the mercy of the Father who will have mercy on them. But those whom he has anointed are perfect." A document of the Gnostic sect known as Naassenes also refers to "Christians who alone of all men are those whom the mystery . . . has made perfect, and anointed there with the ineffable ointment from the horn, such as that with which David was anointed." (See Hippolytus, *Refutation of All Heresies*, 5:9.)

2:28–3:12. Children of God and of the Devil. The separation of the true **children of God** from those of the **world** is also a sign of the **last hour.** The difference will be manifest for all to see at Christ's 2nd coming. The righteous will be revealed **like him** —pure, loving, obedient in keeping God's commandments. This is their confidence and their hope.

The bold metaphors of begetting and birth used in the gospel of John, both of Christ's intimate relation with God the Father and of the Christian believer's with the Father and the Son (cf. John 1:12-13, 18; 3:3-16), were much exploited by the Gnostics. In their interpretation "seeds" of the divine Being were scattered among men in this world, and Christ came to collect and return them to God by way of his revealing knowledge. A man's moral condition and behavior had nothing to do with this predestined return of the seed to its divine source. Irenaeus (Against Heresies i.31) records a Gnostic sect of "Cainites," who, to both his and our way of thinking, read the OT in reverse—i.e. **Cain** was from the good God, Abel from the **evil one** (cf. vs. 12), and so on—but the existence of this sect in the time of the author of I John cannot be established.

The author does not flinch from using language as astonishing as that of his opponents: **No one born of God commits sins; for God's nature,** lit. "seed," **abides in him** (vs. 9). But he controls his statement by the context. He does not mean to say that the new birth demanded by Jesus in the Gospel produces a man who is sinless (cf. 1:10). Rather the man who is born of God is set in the right direction —of doing what is right and of loving his brother. Sin is a matter not of nature but of conduct. Love is the test of those who are truly born of God. Cf. I Pet. 1:23, which in turn probably goes back to the interpretation of the parable of the weeds (Matt. 13:37-38).

3:13-24. Persecution. Jesus predicted that the **world** would hate his disciples, as it hated him, even to death (John 15:18–16:4). Out of hatred comes the impulse to kill. Indeed Jesus equated hatred with murder (Matt. 5:21-22, 43-45) and warned his disciples strictly against the temptation to strike back. Love knows no enemies, and least of all any person in need.

When I John was written persecution of Christians by the Roman state was already a constant menace, even though it was not persistently pursued. In Asia Minor it appears to have been esp. grievous, as we know from I Pet. and Rev. for the decade of the 90's, and from the correspondence of Pliny, the Roman governor of Bithynia, with the Emperor Trajan in 112. It is ironic that the Roman historian Tacitus (55-120) should sum up the opinion which the pagan populace had of Christianity as "hatred of the human race" (Annals xv.44.5). The Christian's only consolation in his sufferings was the assurance that he was following Christ's example, and the confidence of a good conscience before God. Cf. I Pet. 2:21-25; 4:12-19.

4:1-6. Contradiction of Prophetic Spirits. In the apostolic age prophecy was accounted one of the highest gifts of the Spirit of God to his church. Yet even Paul, who held this gift in utmost esteem, realized that not all **spirits** spoke the truth (cf. I Cor. 12:3; II Cor. 11:4). Jesus warned his disciples about **false prophets** (Matt. 7:15) and predicted their appearance, with their deceiving signs and teachings, as indicative of the last times (Matt. 24:11, 24; Mark 13:22). The testing of prophets was no light matter, however, for it might be a presumptuous testing of God. This passage offers 2 basic criteria for the test: (*a*) doctrine, esp. the prophet's teaching about the nature and person of Jesus; and (*b*) manner of life, whether the prophet is **of the world.** Contemporary documents offer similar tests: for doctrine, cf. I Tim. 4:1; II Pet. 2:1; for behavior cf. Didache 11-13; Shepherd of Hermas, Mandate xi: "Test the man who has the divine spirit by his life."

IV. THE VICTORY OF CHRISTIANITY (4:7–5:17)

4:7–5:3. In Perfect Love. In the preceding sections the author has developed his themes with reference to the dictum **God is light.** He has reiterated that the truth of God and knowledge of him cannot be separated from the character of daily living in obedience to his righteous commandments. Now in conclusion he turns the same arguments around, with reference to the dictum **God is love.** All he has said about truth is now said about love. For Christian belief and Christian life are inseparably linked. As a man believes, so he lives. As a man lives, so is his real belief. The initiative is always from God. He loved first. He sent his Son to expiate our sins, to be our Savior. He has given us his Spirit. So if we believe in him, confess him, and show our love for him by loving our brethren, we may confidently face the coming **judgment** without **fear.** To live in love is to live victoriously over all error and all anxiety.

5:4-12. In the True Faith. Just as the Christian overcomes the external **punishment** of the world and the internal **fear** of his heart by love; so he overcomes the falsehoods, lies, and disbelief of the world, and any inner doubts in the testimony of his own belief by **faith.** It is remarkable that only here (vs. 4) in the Johannine writings do we find the word, so common in all the other NT documents. It has therefore a climactic force. But though the noun "faith" is rare in Johannine usage, the related verb "believe," i.e. "have faith," is a principal thread that runs through all the writing, and in every nuance of grammatical construction, and not least in this passage: (*a*) Believe God (vs. 10, verb with dative)—i.e. accept his word, trust him to be credible. (*b*) Believe in God's witness concerning his Son (vs. 10, verb with preposition)—i.e. live in full confidence and reliance on his revelation. (*c*) Believe that . . . (vs. 5; cf. vs. 1; verb with subordinate clause)—i.e. acknowledge as true that which God reveals.

Thus the Johannine writers have a much deeper insight into faith than the Gnostics. Christianity is much more than a system of belief and knowledge of a revealed doctrine—though this is important too, viz. right belief about God's revelation in Christ.

Christian faith reaches down to the very basis and ground of life—our deepest convictions about God and about his relation to us and to the world, and the way these convictions manifest our trust, and witness to this trust, in the everyday issues of our life.

Faith is grounded in the **witness** of God, first of all. We can only testify and proclaim what we have seen and heard from him (cf. 1:2; John 3:31-36). And God's witness is the whole life and death of his Son, the incarnate Jesus Christ. His birth, his baptism, his ministry, his perfect obedience, his bloody death, his resurrection were all wrought by the power of God's Spirit. Without the witness of that Spirit—the Spirit of **truth,** who guides us in all truth (cf. 4:13; John 16:13)—his baptism in **water** and his death in **blood** (cf. John 19:34) would be only that of an ordinary man, not of the Son of God, in whom and by whom we have **eternal life.**

The **three witnesses** of vs. 8—**the Spirit, the water, and the blood**—may be an allusion to the church's sacramental rites of initiation, viz. confirmation, baptism, and Eucharist, in the form and order observed in the churches of Asia Minor at the time of writing of I John. During the controversies of the 4th cent. over the doctrine of the Trinity the text was expanded—first in Spain *ca.* 380, and then taken up in the Vulg.—by the insertion: "There are three that bear record in heaven, the Father, the Word, and the Holy Spirit: and these three are one." A few late Greek manuscripts contain the addition. Hence it passed into the KJV. But all modern critical editions and translations of the NT, including the RSV, omit the interpolation, as it has no warrant in the best and most ancient manuscripts or in the early church fathers.

5:13-21. *In Answer to Prayer.* "Whatever you ask in my name, I will do it" (John 14:13-14; cf. Matt. 7:7; 18:19). So Jesus promised his disciples. To pray in his **name,** to pray as he prayed, is to offer perfect prayer, for it is prayer that is always according to God's will. Such prayer is always answered, though the answer may be different from our expectations. This assurance that God **hears** and answers our prayer is for the Christian the final confidence in victory—that he is guarded by God, and no power of sin or of the devil can ultimately claim him.

There is in this final summation of the author, however, a disturbing note—the suggestion that there is an evil, a **mortal sin,** over which no prayer can prevail. It is possible that the author has in mind the Gnostics, who repudiated the fact of sin and consequently had no need in their scheme of things for repentance and forgiveness. More probably he subsumes them within a larger category of all who deliberately commit apostasy.

Jesus gave solemn warning of the fateful judgment, with eternal consequences, of those who openly denied him before men (Matt. 10:32-33; Mark 8:38; Luke 9:26; 12:8-9). And another tradition of his sayings recorded the unpardonable sin of blasphemy, viz. the lie given to God's Spirit by attributing his work to Satan (Matt. 12:31-32; Mark 3:28-29; Luke 12:10). Such a lie is indeed the antichrist (cf. 2:22)—a mortal sin that goes beyond all will and capacity to distinguish right from wrong. The early church was most severe in its judgment on the willful perversity of deliberate apostasy by any of its members (cf. Heb. 6:4-6; 12:16-17). It offered no hope of reconciliation; for there can be no accommodation between worship of the one true God and any other substitute for God, which is idolatry. Hence the final warning of the letter: **keep yourselves from idols.**

THE SECOND LETTER OF JOHN

Massey H. Shepherd, Jr.

Authorship. II John is a specific illustration and application of the concerns of I John. The similarity of thought and expression in the 2 letters makes obvious an identity of authorship.

Who then is the **elder** (vs. 1)? The word in Greek, as in English, lit. means an "old man." In Jewish communities from ancient times (cf. Num. 11:16; Josh. 24:31; Ruth 4:2) a council of elders supervised the administration and interpretation of the law. In NT times these councils were no doubt modeled on the great Sanhedrin in Jerusalem with its "chief priests, scribes, and elders." At the synagogue assemblies the elders were given seats of honor (cf. Matt. 23:6; Luke 11:43; Rev. 4:4; 11:16).

The church in apostolic times took over the institution. The apostles and elders of the church in Jerusalem (cf. Acts 11:30; 15:2-29; 16:4; 21:18) served as model for the elders of local Christian communities (cf. Acts 14:23; 20:17). The term was broad enough to include all leaders who exercised oversight and pastoral care in the congregations (cf. I Pet. 5:1; Jas. 5:14; Titus 1:5-6). Here the elder speaks with authority—in the singular, not as a member of a council group—but his personal identity and rank and the basis of his authority are not clear.

The Address. The letter is a message from one Christian congregation to another, either in Ephesus or in the province of Asia (see Intro. to I John). The gracious figure used to describe the 2 churches in this exchange—**the elect lady and her children** (vs. 1), **the children of your elect sister** (vs. 13)—has a parallel in I Pet. 5:13, which was also written by an apostle-elder. **Elect** is not merely honorific but indicative of those who are esp. "chosen" of God (cf. Matt. 22:14; Eph. 1:4; I Pet. 2:9). The figure of the church as a **lady** derives from the

bridegroom-bride, husband-wife imagery common in the OT to express the loving relation of God to Israel (cf. e.g. Isa. 62:5; Jer. 31:32; Hos. 2:16) and in the NT of Christ to his church (cf. Matt. 9:15; 25:1-13; II Cor. 11:2; Eph. 5:23-25; and in the Johannine writings John 3:29; Rev. 21:2, 9).

The Situation. The themes of **truth** and **love** to which the elder points are bases of his warning to the **lady**—i.e. the congregation meeting in the **house** (vs. 10). At this period the churches met in private homes offered in hospitality to Christian brethren for their instruction and worship. They were often edified by wandering prophets and teachers, visiting preachers and lecturers. But by the latter years of the first cent. many of these visitors were **deceivers** (vs. 7). The elder is concerned lest the Christian virtue of hospitality be used as a cover for these intruders of false teaching.

He has in mind the same heretics who are combated in I John—the early Gnostics, e.g. Cerinthus (see Intro. to I John). They claim to have a more advanced teaching than what has been handed down **from the beginning** (vs. 5), esp. suited for one who **goes ahead** of his Christian brethren (vs. 9). Thus they divide the fellowship, not following the **commandment** to **love one another** (vs. 5). Their doctrine is nothing less than a sign of Satan himself—**the deceiver and the antichrist** (vs. 7). For they do not acknowledge that the Christ, the Son of the Father, was truly incarnated in the humanity of Jesus. By their false division of the man Jesus and the divine Christ these heretics split every fellowship and every communion, by which the Father **abides in** the Son, and Jesus Christ the Son **abides in** his Father and in us, and we **abide in** him and in one another.

940

THE THIRD LETTER OF JOHN

Massey H. Shepherd, Jr.

Authorship and Address. In contrast to II John (see comment) this letter of the **elder** is personal, not an exchange between churches. Its recipient **Gaius**—a common name in the Roman world—is otherwise unknown, as are also the other persons named in the letter. Nor is it at all certain that the church congregations of the 2 letters are the same. In both letters the elder writes briefly—and for us today somewhat cryptically—in view of an impending visit and meeting **face to face** (vs. 14). Personal interviews are more effective than **pen and ink** in resolving problems of broken relationships and misunderstandings.

The Situation. It is tempting to see the situation in Gaius' church as comparable to that of the congregation addressed in II John. For the elder takes pains to stress the **truth** which Gaius follows and the **love** which he practices. In both letters the question of Christian hospitality is raised.

Yet in fact the situation indicated in the 2 letters seems to be reversed. In II John, the elder warns the church not to give hospitality to deceiving teachers. But in this letter the elder's friends, who have received hospitality from Gaius, have been rejected and put out of the church by one **Diotrephes** (vs. 9), who is presumably a local church authority. What position **Demetrius** (vs. 12) holds is not clear. He may be the leader of the visiting brethren whom Diotrephes has refused to **welcome.**

It should be noted that the elder accuses Diotrephes, not of false teaching and heresy, but of resistance to the elder's authority. It is possible of course that their differences are doctrinal. But some interpreters think not. They see in Diotrephes an emerging leader—perhaps bishop—of a local church who is concerned to keep his church free from outside interference. It often happens that younger leaders in the churches find difficult, and at last unbearable, the dictatorial ways of older persons who set themselves up as authorities, even with the best of intentions and out of considerable experience.

Hospitality may also become burdensome by repeated and unnecessary visits of **strangers.** But throughout the NT it is stressed as a primary virtue of Christian love (cf. Matt. 10:40-42; 25:34-40; Rom. 12:13; Heb. 13:2; I Pet. 4:9).

THE BOOK OF JUDE

Claude Holmes Thompson

Introduction

For Further Study: James Moffatt, *The General Epistles* ("Moffatt NT Commentary"), 1928. J. W. C. Wand, *The General Epistles of St. Peter and St. Jude* ("Westminster Commentaries"), 1934. William Barclay, *The Letters of John and Jude*, 1961.

Introduction

Reference has been made to this letter in the study of II Pet. (see p. 931). The fiery denunciations of Jude were used in II Pet. in an attack upon the enemies of the faith (cf. vss. 4-16, 18 with II Pet. 2). Thus the 2 writings have much in common as they face a dual threat to the church: antinomianism (see below on vs. 4) and some form of Gnosticism, a heresy within the early Christian church which claimed to have special knowledge (*gnosis*) concerning salvation and which considered all matter evil. The latter view led either to asceticism on the one hand or to complete moral license on the other.

Author and Date. The author calls himself Jude (Judas), the "brother of James," who apparently is to be identified as the "brother of the Lord" (cf. Mark 6:3; I Cor. 15:7; Gal. 1:19; 2:9; Jas. 1:1). But this close relationship with Jesus is doubtful. "The faith which was once for all delivered to the saints" (vs. 3) seems to be a 2nd-cent. expression. The era of the apostles is apparently well in the past (vs. 17). The letter condemns the Gnostic heresies which arose late in the 1st cent. (see "The Early History of the Church," pp. 1045-53).

While most scholars feel it was written in the 2nd cent., hence not by Jude the brother of Jesus, the question has been raised as to why a pseudonymous author would have used the name of such an undistinguished and almost unknown brother of the Lord. Apparently the purpose was to establish his message as in harmony with the apostolic gospel— which he sought to defend.

A "General" Epistle. From *ca.* the 4th cent. 7 letters of the NT have been known as "General" or "Catholic" epistles: Jas.; I, II Pet.; I, II, III John; and Jude. Although II, III John are specifically directed to persons, all 7 have borne this title, meaning that they have been addressed to the whole Christian community. Jude simply says, "To those who are called"—about as general a designation as could be found. It has been suggested, however, that perhaps this letter was written to Jewish Christians, since there are repeated references to the OT and other Jewish writings (vss. 9-15). Yet the evils portrayed suggest the sexual irregularities which Paul met in Gentile communities (cf. I Cor. 6:12; Gal. 5:13). Could the readers have been Jews of the Diaspora who knew both cultures? As for the place of composition, discussion to date has been of little help.

Message. The book was produced in a crisis to defend the Christian faith against ungodly persons who threatened it by corrupt doctrine and practices.

I. Introduction (vss. 1-4)

Vss. 1-2. Salutation. Lit. "slave," **a servant of Jesus Christ** was not an uncommon designation of an author (cf. Rom. 1:1; Phil. 1:1; Jas. 1:1; II Pet. 1:1). It suggests a special devotion to Jesus as Lord. In the words **called, beloved,** and **kept** note the strength of the believer's relation to God. Those who respond are kept through love for Christ, perhaps implying a security until the final judgment.

Vss. 3-4. The Reason for the Letter. A threat developed which endangered the Christian movement; thus the author proceeds to defend **the faith.** This faith was not restricted to saving faith, as in Paul (cf. Rom. 3:21-31). Nor was it mere trust in God's protection (cf. Matt. 6:25-34). It was not even an assurance of a blessed future (cf. Heb. 11:1). The faith now had become clearly defined doctrine as well as a way of life.

While the author is diverted from writing concerning the **common salvation,** i.e. the salvation belonging to all Christians, this vigorous defense of the faith is of immediate concern. Believers are the custodians of the faith given **once for all.** The fact that the author simply refers to it is evidence that it was well known and carefully defined. While it was not a fully developed system of theology, it did articulate the redemptive action of God in Christ as the inauguration of man's salvation. This salvation was not a human achievement; it was divine action. This message is found at every level of NT witness and may be assumed to be substantially identical with the *kerygma,* or proclamation of the gospel.

Vs. 4. The emergency is urgent since **ungodly persons** have become part of the community of faith. They not only deny Jesus Christ as Lord; they even exploit his gracious love as an opportunity for immorality. The danger from this evil was that it was within the church. While their ultimate doom was sure, something had to be done about these persons lest the whole community be contaminated (cf. I Cor. 5). Such evil could not be harbored within the fellowship.

Apparently the evil here is a form of antinomianism, i.e. the teaching that a person living within the faith is free from observing the law. This perversity has a long history. Paul met it (cf. Rom. 3:8; 6:1, 15). It erupted within the Reformation in the 16th cent. Some early Methodists claimed to be above the necessity of keeping the moral codes, only to be positively repudiated by John Wesley. It has again become known in our time under the popular idea of "once saved, always saved," or the dangerous teaching of the eternal security of believers. It likewise underlies the current plea for a "new morality" which appears suspiciously similar to the old immorality.

II. The Heretics and Their Punishment (vss. 5-16)

Vss. 5-7. *God's Punishment of Sinners*. Our current tendency to think that God is too nice to punish evildoers would have been utterly unacceptable to the author of Jude. Just as the church received the perpetually valid faith, never needing repetition, so it also learned **once for all** of God's judgment. Examples are given to show that God takes an active role in the punishment of sinners: unbelievers in Israel en route from **Egypt** to Canaan, the unfaithful **angels** in heaven, and **Sodom and Gomorrah,** all experienced divine rejection. The unbelief of Israel fares no better than the crude and lustful immorality of the Sodomites (cf. Num. 13-14). Even the ambitious angels in heaven were put into **eternal chains in the nether gloom until the judgment of the great day.** The reference comes from the pseudepigraphic book of Enoch, chs. 6-16; 21; 54; 64; 67 (see "The Intertestamental Literature," pp. 1110-15). The fate of Sodom and Gomorrah was well known. It is used extensively to illustrate divine judgment (cf. Gen. 19:12-28; Deut. 29:23; 32:32; Isa. 1:9; 3:9; 13:19; Jer. 23:14; Amos 4:11; Matt. 10:15; 11:24; Luke 10:12; 17:29; Rom. 9:29; II Pet. 2:6; Rev. 11:8). The warning here is of alarming urgency since it illustrates God's severe judgment upon those who turned from an earlier privileged position in faith.

Vss. 8-10. *Sin Unmasked*. Three manifestations of evil are particularly repugnant to the author: defilement of **the flesh,** rejection of **authority,** and scorn of **the glorious ones.** These evils are the result of what is called **dreamings,** a sort of reverie in fantasy. This likely refers to claims of special revelation or inspiration which release the visionaries from the normal demands of common decency. Hence the Gnostic and antinomian tendency: the flesh being evil, what one does with it carries no moral significance. Thus the instincts of the body may be given full license. Likewise, since God's grace covers everything, sin is merely the occasion for a fuller expression of divine mercy. No wonder authority is rejected. It interferes with unchecked sexual indulgences.

Vss. 8-9. As for scorn of **the glorious ones,** this is a bit obscure, possibly indicating mockery of the divine glory to which a multitude of angels bore witness. A vivid illustration is given from a Jewish writing, the Assumption of Moses, where **the archangel Michael** does not even rebuke **the devil** as he greedily seeks **the body of Moses.** Only God is adequate for such judgment. Yet these false leaders of Jude's day presume to act even against God himself.

Vss. 11-13. *Unrelieved Doom*. Three examples of severe judgment are now cited: **Cain** (Gen. 4:3-16) is more than a murderer; he typifies the man who exists in a living judgment of self-seeking, greed, and treachery. He is always running away—from everything except himself. **Balaam** (Num. 22-24; cf. II Pet. 2:15-16) is the covetous false prophet who taught Israel to sin, thus compounding the collective guilt of the community. **Korah** (Num. 16) was disobedient, resisting the divinely appointed authority of Moses so needed for consolidation of the nation. Basically all 3 are examples of the danger which the author of Jude saw as the rejection of the way of God and the indulgence in self-seeking.

Vss. 12-13. A series of vivid metaphors pictures the fate of these perverse souls: (*a*) **Blemishes,** blots **on your love feasts**—erring Christians selfishly consume the food provided at their love feasts with no thought for its sacramental significance and hence render holy observances times of revelry (cf. I Cor. 11:20-34). This sort of conduct destroyed the very idea of Christian love in the feast. (*b*) **Waterless clouds, carried along by winds,** mock the parched fields—the erring ones have become impostors, useless and empty. (*c*) They are like **fruitless trees in late autumn, twice dead, uprooted;** at the time of harvest they merely clutter the ground. (*d*) Like **wild waves of the sea,** they cast **up the foam of their own shame,** mere bubbly froth which does not even make a noise when it disintegrates. (*e*) They may desire to shine as **stars** in the heavens, but they become flaming meteors burning themselves away to nothingness.

Vss. 14-16. *Judgment Foreseen*. The author quotes from the book of Enoch, which he erroneously attributes to **Enoch in the seventh generation from Adam**—it actually appears to have been written in the 1st cent. B.C.—to show that this form of godlessness had been foreseen in the distant past. So serious is the evil that God alone is able to manage the situation; hence he sends **his holy myriads** in judgment.

Vs. 16. Three final characteristics of these false leaders are described: (*a*) They are **grumblers,** full of surly discontent. (*b*) They are **malcontents,** complaining that their lot in life is unfair; hence they want to express **their own passions** to escape their drab existence. (*c*) As **loud-mouthed boasters,** they arrogantly flout their own importance and flatter other people only to exploit them.

III. The Foundation of Faith (vss. 17-23)

Vss. 17-19. *The Witness of the Apostles*. The actual source of the words in reference to **scoffers** and those who follow **their own ungodly passions** has not been found within apostolic documents. But present research into the "twilight period," A.D. 30-60, of the oral tradition discloses an element of apprehension of danger to the faith. This oral tradition was part of the preaching of the church before the writing of the NT. And the evidence for the moral content of instruction of the converts to the faith is quite convincing. The Christian community of faith could never compromise with ethical relativism. There is a remarkable compilation of instructions, even to detailed regulations, in the NT. We may assume this is but representative of the larger body of teaching.

Vss. 20-23. *The Basis of Positive Goodness.* Goodness can never be merely negative. However skillful one may be in refuting evil, more than this is required. Again the basis is the author's insistence upon the faith, **your most holy faith.** That faith is a divinely given deposit, the only foundation for Christian living. Faith and practice, theology and life, doctrine and conduct are inseparable.

Vss. 20-21. But this faith is no static thing. There must be progress, development, even in its practice. Specific directions are given for: (*a*) Prayer—life in which **the Holy Spirit** resides is the true pattern of Christian living, and prayer is inspired by the Holy Spirit (cf. Rom. 8:26). (*b*) Active obedience— while the gift of **the love of God** is a divine activity, without the corresponding human response in devoted obedience, this gift will be lost. (*c*) Patient expectation—since the faith is **unto eternal life,** the present distress requires the long look and the hope that even evildoers may be brought to repentance.

Vss. 22-23. In an epistle of such fierce denunciations against evil it is healthy to find judgment relieved by hope. Perhaps the false leaders may be saved. Clear reasoning has its place; doubters are to be confronted by intelligent persuasion. Others must be rescued from the very brink of ruin. But even this rescue mission has its dangers. Perhaps the thought is that sin must not be minimized or condoned lest the salvation be only apparent. But it is likely that some are beyond redemption; and while compassion must always be a Christian virtue, it still includes **hating even the garment spotted by the flesh.**

IV. The Benediction (vss. 24-25)

Vs. 24. *Sustained Aid from God.* After all the trouble described in this brief letter, this moving benediction is like a breath of fresh air. Though one may live in the midst of sin, God **is able to keep him from falling.** This is no temporary aid; it will be sustained until we stand **before the presence of his glory.**

Vs. 25. *Salvation Through Christ.* Salvation is regarded as God's gift, but the bestowal of the gift is accomplished **through Jesus Christ,** whom the church accordingly confesses and obeys as **Lord** (cf. Rom. 10:9; Phil. 2:11), since he alone effectively acts for God.

THE REVELATION TO JOHN

S. MacLean Gilmour

Introduction

Literary Affiliation. The Revelation opens with what was probably its original title: "The revelation of Jesus Christ, which God gave him . . ." The word "revelation" translates a Greek original that is transliterated "apocalypse." Though so far as we know Rev. was the earliest writing to employ this word as a title, apocalyptic or revelation literature had long been familiar to both Jews and Christians (see "The Apocalyptic Literature," pp. 1106-09).

Even at early levels in its development nearly every religion has some eschatology, i.e. doctrine of last things, that leans in the direction of apocalyptic ideas. There are passages in Amos, Mic., Isa., and Jer. which prepared the way for the later Jewish apocalyptists, esp. those passages in which the prophets reflected popular speculation about the coming "day of Yahweh." This apocalyptic tendency in the literature of the OT was heightened in postexilic times. The imagery and symbolism of Ezek., Joel, Isa. 24–27, and Zech. 9–14 are apocalyptic in character and prepared the way for their full-blown emergence in Dan.

Jewish apocalyptic had its roots, then, in OT prophecy, but its development was in the main the consequence of alien influence. The literature of Babylonia and of Iran reveals at an earlier date than does the OT the chief apocalyptic traits: a pronounced dualism the doctrine of the 2 ages, the ideas of a resurrection and a final judgment, and an imagery of the catastrophic events that will mark the end of the present age and inaugurate the new. It is no accident that apocalyptic ideas became naturalized within Judaism after the exilic period, for it was then that the Jews were vassals of the Persians. It was almost inevitable that a view of history which dominated the thought of the great power that was Judaism's political overlord should leave its mark on postexilic Jewish writing.

The earliest and most influential of the extant Jewish apocalypses is Dan., written in 165-164 B.C. during the Maccabean revolt against Antiochus Epiphanes of Syria. Apocalyptic literature flourished in Judaism for the next cent. and a half, until the destruction of Jerusalem by the Romans in A.D. 70 and for a time thereafter. Among the scores of Jewish apocalyptic books that are known in whole or in part are the various writings ascribed to Enoch (notably I Enoch), the Testaments of the 12 Patriarchs, the Jewish Sibylline Oracles, the Ascension of Moses, the central section of II Esdras (chs. 3–14), often known as IV Ezra, the Apocalypse of Baruch, and the "War Scroll" found at Qumran.

Apocalyptic literature reflects the historical situation at the time of writing. The various apocalyptic books were tracts of their times—one might even say tracts for bad times. Within a general framework of ideas, details differed according to the interest and emphasis of the individual author. In some the chief interest lay in the extraordinary events that would herald the end of the present age. In others it was religious: How would God vindicate his justice? In some the Messiah was the central figure. In others he was not even mentioned. In some God's kingdom would be established on this earth. In others God would reign in a re-created heaven and earth. In some all Jews would be raised from the dead at the end of the present age and would inherit the new age of God's rule. In others only a remnant would share in the good time coming. In still others the redeemed would consist only of those Jews who would be alive at the last day.

With all its variety and flexibility Jewish apocalyptic literature shared a number of leading ideas:

a) Time is divided into 2 ages. The present age is evil. It is dominated by Satan and his demonic hosts. But the coming age is at hand, the age in which God alone will reign. Satan and his demonic powers will be destroyed, their allies on earth will perish, and the elect in Israel will enjoy prosperity and peace on a transformed earth or in a new heaven and a new earth.

b) The end of the present age is to come with dramatic suddenness. God will intervene suddenly and catastrophically in the processes of history and his purposes will be accomplished.

c) The end is expected almost immediately. It is not a far-off divine event toward which creation is moving but a consummation that is anticipated in the immediate future. The author of Daniel and many of his successors make various estimates of the time of the end that have engrossed the interest of innumerable readers to this day, but in no case do they think of the end as more than a few months or a few years distant.

d) The end of the present evil age is to be marked by a period of extreme distress. "The woes of the Messiah" is a term occasionally used to describe the events of this premessianic tribulation. Natural catastrophes, a breakup of the cosmic order, plagues, famines, wars, internecine strife—such are the hor-

945

rors on which the authors love to dwell. The idea behind such speculation is that the worse will have to come to the worst before God can intervene. But apocalyptic writers always believe that they live in the last days. The end is at hand!

Christian Apocalypses. The extent to which Jesus was influenced by apocalyptic ways of thought is still a matter of debate. It would appear that he took over many apocalyptic categories of thought that his day and age provided but at the same time interpreted the apocalyptic scheme in such a way that his thought became virtually independent of it. E.g. the apocalyptic doctrine of the 2 ages was basic to his teaching about the kingdom of God, but the evidence of the gospels supports the conclusion that he modified it in a radical fashion. The full accomplishment of God's rule belonged to the future. Only then would the kingdom "come with power." In his own ministry, however, what belonged to the end was already manifesting itself among men. The new age of God's rule had already broken in on history before the old age had completely run its course. The kingdom of God was more than a hope; it was a new order already in process of realization.

However we may understand Jesus' thought of the future, it is clear that the early church lived in an atmosphere of apocalyptic expectation. Early Christians thought in terms of the imminent return of Christ as the vicegerent of God and expected that the new age of God's rule would be inaugurated in dramatic fashion with that return. Believers, declared Paul, were those who had "turned to God from idols, to serve a living and true God, and to wait for his Son from heaven" (I Thess. 1:9-10). Parts of the NT that conform to the apocalyptic scheme include Mark 13 (and its parallels in Matt. and Luke); I Cor. 15:20-28; II Cor. 5:1-3; I Thess. 4:15-17; II Thess. 2:1-12; Heb. 12:22-23. Christians early appropriated many Jewish apocalypses and edited and adapted them, e.g. IV Ezra, the Testaments of the 12 Patriarchs, and the Ascension of Isaiah. Early in the 2nd cent. such Christian apocalypses were written as the Apocalypse of Peter and the Shepherd of Hermas. But the first and most important of the specifically Christian apocalypses is Rev.

Variations of Rev. from the Apocalyptic Norm. One feature of Jewish apocalypses is their pseudonymity. They claim to have been written by some great figure of a remote era—e.g. Daniel, Ezra, Moses, Enoch, Noah. The fact that the book has remained unknown for so long is often accounted for by the statement that the seer was ordered to hide or "seal" his revelation until the last days, and the assumption is that it has been "found" when the generation at last has come to which the revelation applies.

Rev. is not a pseudonymous book. Its author writes under his own name: "I John [of Patmos], your brother, who share with you in Jesus the tribulation and the kingdom and the patient endurance" (Rev. 1:9). His message is the "revelation of Jesus Christ" and is imparted under his own authority.

Claiming to be the work of ancient seers, Jewish apocalypses also purport to be visions of the future set in the framework of the distant past. Daniel or Noah or Enoch is made to predict situations and

developments that are contemporaneous with the author and with the times with which the book's first readers are concerned. Such proleptic vision enables the apocalyptist to speak to the present with all the authority of hoary antiquity.

John of Patmos does not locate his visions in the distant past. They apply to the immediate future. The "revelation of Jesus Christ" is to show God's servants "what must soon take place" (1:1). An angel bids the seer: "Do not seal up the words of the prophecy of this book, for the time is near" (22:10; cf. 1:3).

Finally, in contrast to Jewish apocalypses Rev. has the format of a letter. Chs. 1-3 consist of a covering letter followed by letters to 7 churches, and the epistolary form is superimposed on the whole by delaying the benediction to the very end: "The grace of the Lord Jesus be with all the saints" (22:21). 1:3 makes clear that John expects the book to be read aloud in the various congregations, much as Paul at an earlier time intended his letters to be presented to assembled bodies of Christians.

Occasion, Date, Address. The occasion of Rev. was an attempt by the Roman imperial authorities to revive and enforce the cult of emperor worship. John pictures the Roman Empire as a 7-headed beast rising out of the sea (13:1). The imperial priesthood is represented as a 2nd beast, having 2 horns like a lamb (simulating the Messiah) but with the voice of a dragon (betraying its Satanic origin). Working great signs and imposing economic sanctions, it endeavors to enforce the universal observance of Caesar worship (13:11-17). The Christians at Smyrna are warned that persecution for their faith is at hand (2:10). Christians at Philadelphia are told that the hour of trial is about to come upon the whole world (3:10). Reference is made to many who have been slain for their faith (6:9) and to one martyr by name (2:13).

In the early 60's A.D. Nero instituted a violent persecution of Christians at Rome, but it was restricted to Rome and had nothing to do with the issue of emperor worship. The first emperor who appears to have tried to compel Christians to participate in Caesar worship was Domitian (81-96). The earliest reference to the date of Rev. is by Irenaeus, ca. 180, who placed the composition of the book toward the end of Domitian's reign (Against Heresies 5.30.3), and most scholars today agree that the internal evidence supports a date during the early 90's.

If we could solve the puzzles involved in the number of the beast in 13:18 and in the mysterious reckoning in 17:9-12 we might be more certain of the date of the book. Unfortunately we do not have the "mind with wisdom" that no doubt most of John's first readers possessed. It may be that 13:3 is an allusion to the widespread belief that Nero did not commit suicide in 68 and would later return to afflict the Rome he had ruled as a tyrant, that this belief in a Nero come to life again was combined with the doctrine of the Antichrist in 13:8, and that some belief in Domitian as the reincarnation of Nero underlies 17:11. But all this, however attractive, remains hypothetical. Rev. probably comes from the later years of the reign of Domitian, but an earlier or later date cannot be ruled out of consideration.

Some scholars view 6:6 as a protest against, or at any rate a reference to, a change of agricultural policy by Domitian (see comment). If this interpretation is correct, Rev. might be dated *ca.* 93.

The address in 1:4, 11 to the 7 churches in the Roman province of Asia (W Asia Minor; see color map 16) and the 7 letters that follow in chs. 2-3 indicate that the intended readers were the Christians of the Asian churches. From extrabiblical notices it appears that the cult of emperor worship was enforced with particular zeal in the province of Asia and that a new temple for the worship of Caesar was erected at Ephesus during Domitian's reign.

Authorship. The author refers to his own name on 4 occasions as John (1:1, 4, 9; 22:8). As early as the middle of the 2nd cent. Justin Martyr (Dialogue with Trypho 8.1.4) identified the author with John the son of Zebedee. Though this identification was challenged late in the 2nd cent. by Christian heretics and early in the 3rd also by many orthodox leaders in W Christendom, the view ultimately prevailed and in the 4th cent. was more in-

First cent. jar from Qumran (the Dead Sea sect) inscribed with the name "John"

strumental than anything else in determining the final acceptance of Rev. by the church as a canonical book.

Early in the 3rd cent. Dionysius, bishop of Alexandria, held that John the son of Zebedee, since he had written the gospel and the letters that bear his name, could not have written Rev. because its style, vocabulary, and ideas differ so greatly. This is a judgment in which most scholars today concur, though there are some who hold that, if any of the

NT writings can be ascribed to the apostle John, Rev. has a better claim than any other.

John himself tells us that at the time of the first vision he records he "was on the island called Patmos on account of the word of God and the testimony of Jesus" (1:9). Patmos is off the coast of Asia Minor W of Miletus. The meaning may be simply that the author was engaged in missionary work there; but since the island is known to have been the site of a Roman penal colony, the traditional view that he was imprisoned there for his activities as a Christian missionary is probably correct. In 1:1 he speaks of himself as a "servant" of God, or of Jesus Christ; in 1:9 he describes himself as a brother and companion of Asian Christians in their tribulation and endurance; and in his letters to the 7 churches and throughout the book he writes with a sense of commission and authority. This implies that he himself belonged to the province of Asia, that he was well known to the readers of his book, and that he exercised some measure of jurisdiction over Asian churches. His imperfect command of Greek and the many Semitisms that occur in his writing support the assumption that he was a Jewish Christian who still thought in Aramaic. With these facts about the John of Rev. we must needs be content.

The Message. John's revelation is primarily an appeal for stanch resistance to all demands and encroachments of the cult of emperor worship. The glories and privileges of martyrdom are extolled throughout the book. The souls of those who have been slain are sheltered beneath the heavenly altar and their prayers for vengeance on the non-Christian world have been heard. Martyrs have already been granted their spiritual bodies and are assured that soon their predestined number will be filled (6:9-11). A voice from heaven declares blessed all who will die as Christians (14:13). The author sees them standing by the glassy sea in heaven, singing a song of praise to God as Moses and his followers did after their sea passage (15:2-4). They participate with the Lamb in the last war against paganism (19:14); they reign with him for the millenial interregnum as judges, priests, and kings; and they escape the 2nd death (20:6).

The author is certain that the Roman Empire and the cult of emperor worship are shortly to be destroyed. The demonic plagues that are to come upon the empire are portrayed in lurid colors. Rome is symbolized as a great harlot seated on many waters and drunk with the blood of the saints and martyrs of Jesus (17:1-6). John beholds the city wasted in civil strife (17:16). An angel foretells its doom (18:1-3). Christians are urged to forsake its precincts lest they share the impending disaster (18:4) and the "saints and apostles and prophets" in heaven are proleptically exhorted to gloat over the judgment God has wrought (18:20). Merchants, shipowners, and mariners, whose prosperity depends on their Roman trade, will view the disaster with amazement and despair (18:11-19). An angelic host in heaven sings a hymn of praise that God has avenged his servants and has passed judgment on the city, which by its imperial cult has corrupted the earth with idolatry (19:1-2). An anticipated 8th emperor and his supporters will be conquered by the Lamb

Courtesy of Herbert G. May

View of the island of Patmos showing the harbor; the island lies *ca.* thirty-seven mi. W-SW of Miletus and is *ca.* ten mi. long (N to S) and *ca.* six mi. at its greatest width; the island was one of several in the Aegean used by the Romans to banish political prisoners

and his called, chosen, and faithful followers (17:14). In the end the emperor and his false prophet—the representative of the cult of Caesar worship—will be cast alive into the fiery lake of brimstone; and their allies, the kings of the earth and their armies, will be slain by the sword of the Lamb (19:19-21).

The Church. Christians form a community of redeemed people, purchased for God from every linguistic, racial, and national group by the sacrificial death of Christ. They will be protected by the seal of God on their foreheads from the demonic plagues which will afflict the pagan world (7:3). Under the symbolism of 144,000 drawn in equal numbers from the ideal 12 tribes they are pictured as the true Israel of God which is to be saved from the eschatological woes shortly to be unloosed (7:1-8). In a succeeding vision the same community appears as an innumerable multitude from all nations. They will constitute the ultimate society of those who have been redeemed from the "great tribulation." John proleptically beholds them praising and serving God day and night in his temple, shepherded, guided, and comforted by Christ (7:9-17). They are "those who are invited to the marriage supper of the Lamb" (19:9). In the new Jerusalem they will see God's face, bear his name on their foreheads, and worship him as his servants (22:3-4).

The true church for John is made up of all who have refused or will refuse to worship the statue of the emperor. Those who suffer captivity or martyrdom are predestined to do so (13:10). In fact all who will inherit the new Jerusalem have had their names "written in the Lamb's book of life" (21:27). Martyrs constitute a preferred group within the true church, but John believes that all Christians in the evil period of intensified conflict he anticipates will suffer martyrdom (13:15). The faithful of earlier days who have died a natural death will join them in the new heaven and the new earth after the resurrection and the judgment that are to follow the millenial age (20:11-15).

Some General Observations. Rev. is drama of a high order set on a cosmic stage. Despite its author's faulty Greek his book rises again and again to heights of sublimity and grandeur that have inspired some of the world's greatest literature, poetry, and art. Though he has drawn heavily on OT symbolism and imagery and occasionally on pagan mythology (cf. ch. 12), he has made this borrowed material his own and has created a work of singular vividness, power, and intensity.

The God of Rev. is represented as a heavenly oriental king. His righteous judgments will fall on his enemies and on the oppressors of his faithful people. But he is not just a God of wrath and retribution. He is also a God who can enter into tender relations with his people. He will wipe away every tear from their eyes in the day that sorrow and death will be no more. He will make them kings and priests, and they will serve him every day in his temple.

The Christ of Rev. shares the throne with God. He is a divine being, and titles ascribed to him are often not to be distinguished from those applied to God. He holds the "keys of Death and Hades" (1:18). He is "Lord of lords and King of kings" (17:14). He is "the Alpha and the Omega, the first and the last, the beginning and the end" (22:13). His most characteristic title is the "Lamb," or "Lamb of God," which refers in part to the significance of his death—he was the sacrificial victim by whose blood the faithful are redeemed—and in part to his role as vicegerent, or agent, of God. In this latter sense "Lamb of God" is interchangeable with "Lion of Judah."

We are reminded incidentally that Jesus Christ was descended from David (22:16), that he was of the Jewish race (5:5), that he was crucified (11:8), and that he rose from the dead. That is virtually all that is left of the gospel portrait. In its place is that of a divine warrior who will overcome all his enemies. Seated on a white horse, clad in a robe dipped in blood, and followed by heavenly armies, he will triumph at last in the hard-fought battle (19:11-16).

John represents Christianity as a moral religion. He condemns idolatry, theft, uncleanness, and falsehood, and he stresses the virtues of chastity, loyalty,

948

patience, endurance, faith, and zeal. But the reader will note that there is in the book scarcely an echo of the Sermon on the Mount. Nothing is said of love for one's enemies. On the contrary there is hatred, bitter and unalloyed. The situation for which the book was written in part accounts for this bitterness, though it cannot condone it.

As an apocalypse Rev. is concerned with the events of its own time and with those that its author expected to take place in the immediate future. We can understand its message to the extent that we keep its literary and theological affiliation in mind and to the extent that we can relate it to the historical and religious situation in the Roman Empire and esp. in the province of Asia toward the close of the first cent.

Apocalypses in general were not written for a world or a people or a church hundreds or thousands of years later than their time of writing. They were written for their own day and generation. Like other apocalyptic seers, John believed that history had about run its course. It was about to be interrupted by the dramatic and catastrophic intro. of the kingdom of God. The message of Rev. for the reader today is therefore indirect rather than direct. Perhaps it may be expressed in the words of James Russell Lowell:

Though the cause of Evil prosper, yet 'tis Truth alone is strong.
. . . .
Truth forever on the scaffold, Wrong forever on the throne,—
Yet that scaffold sways the future, and, behind the dim unknown,
Standeth God within the shadow, keeping watch above his own.

For Further Study. I. T. Beckwith, *The Apocalypse of John*, 1919; for advanced students. R. H. Charles, *Rev.*, 2 vols., 1920; for advanced students. Martin Kiddle, *Rev.*, 1940. E. F. Scott, *The Book of Rev.*, 2nd ed., 1949. T. S. Kepler, *The Book of Rev.*, 1957. Martin Rist in *IB*, 1957. T. F. Torrance, *The Apocalypse Today*, 1959. C. M. Laymon, *The Book of Rev.*, 1960. J. W. Bowman in *IDB*, 1962.

I. Prologue (1:1-3)

Probably the original title of the work was this entire prologue, or possibly its opening words: **The Revelation of Jesus Christ.** "The Revelation of John" (e.g. ASV, NEB; cf. KJV) and **The Revelation to John** are variant translations of a 2nd cent. superscription. In the prologue the author wishes to stress that the revelation to follow was given by **God** to **Jesus Christ** and mediated by the latter to the author through the agency of an **angel.** He expects the **words of the prophecy** to be read **aloud** in congregational assemblies and pronounces a blessing on the reader and on the listeners provided they pay attention to **what is written therein.**

II. Exhortation to the Asian Churches (1:4–3:22)

A. A Covering Letter (1:4-20)

A covering letter is prefixed to 7 letters (chs. 2–3) to churches in the Roman province of Asia (see

Intro.)—possibly congregations under the author's special oversight.

1:4-8. Salutation and Ascription. At the very beginning we are introduced to the sacred number **seven,** the symbol of wholeness or perfection which determines so much of the structure of the book. As in Paul's letters, **grace** is substituted for the secular "greetings," and **peace** carries overtones of the Semitic word for "salvation." The greetings come from 3 sources. He **who is and who was and who is to come** is probably an expansion of God's name as given in Exod. 3:14: "I AM WHO I AM." The reference to the **seven spirits who are before his throne** may have been influenced by the idea of 7 archangels in late Jewish angelology, but the number corresponds also to the 7 spirits of Persian Zoroastrianism. The word for **witness** can also mean "martyr," and in its present reference to **Jesus Christ** should probably be so rendered.

1:5b-8. Vss. 5b-6 refer of course to Christ. Vs. 7 draws on the imagery of Dan. 7:13 but reinterprets the passage to apply to Christ and his imminent 2nd coming (see below on vss. 12-13a). God is represented as the speaker in vs. 8 (cf. 21:6). **Alpha** and **Omega** are the names of the first and last letters in the Greek alphabet, and the clause is synonymous with "the first and the last, the beginning and the end," as appears from its application with the latter to Jesus in 22:13.

1:9-20. The Commission to Write. John presents his credentials as a prophet and seer. He claims to be, not an apostle, a bishop, or an elder, but only a **brother** who shares in the persecution, the fortitude, and the triumph that are the lot and the privilege of his fellow Christians. On **Patmos** see Intro. Assuming the usual interpretation that John is a prisoner, his statement that he is on the island **on account of the word of God and the testimony of Jesus** means that he has been banished because of his loyalty to the Christian cause—he has refused to deny Christ and worship the emperor.

1:10-11. The vision described took place, according to John's claim, when he was in a mystical trance **on the Lord's day.** Here is the first reference in literature to the first day of the week as the Christian holy day. As in Paul's description of the appearance of Christ in the last days (I Thess. 4:16), John's heavenly Lord speaks to him with a **loud voice** that sounds like **trumpet** blast. **Book** should probably be translated "scroll" here as it is in chs. 5; 10, though it is just possible that the codex, i.e. book, form for written communications of some length had already been introduced as early as the author's day (see "Writing in Biblical Times," pp. 1201-08).

1:12-13a. John's loose Greek in vs. 12a justifies the NEB translation "I turned to see whose voice it was that spoke to me." The **seven golden lampstands** are identified in vs. 20 as symbolic of the 7 churches. The phrase **one like a son of man** is used in Dan. 7:13 for the faithful remnant of the Jewish people—or possibly for some representative of the nation, conceivably its patron angel Michael. In various intertestamental writings, however, notably the central section of I Enoch (The Similitudes of Enoch), "son of man" is the designation of God's heavenly vicegerent in the last days. It is this latter usage that is characteristic of the title in the Synoptic

Mediterranean Sea

gospels and that determines its content in John's revelation.

1:13*b*-16. The portrayal of the heavenly Christ as one **clothed with a long robe and with a golden girdle round his breast** was suggested by the description of the angel in Dan. 10:5-6, as were also the references to **his eyes** as a **flame of fire** and **his feet . . . like burnished bronze.** That **his head and his hair** are **white as white wool** is drawn from the description of God as the "ancient of days" in Dan. 7:9. **Many waters** is appropriately rendered "rushing waters" by the NEB. **In his right hand** the heavenly Christ **held seven stars,** identified in vs. 20 as the angels of the 7 churches but also symbolizing Christ's power over the 7 planets that in popular astrology determined the destinies of men. The **sharp two-edged sword** proceeding **from his mouth** suggests both a warrior who smites his foes and a judge who annihilates them with his sentence of judgment. The simile of Christ's countenance as the **sun shining in full strength** is probably drawn from Judg. 5:31. Some interpreters hold that John's composite imagery is also intended to portray Christ in terms to surpass a current description of the sun god Mithra.

1:17-18. Prostration as a consequence of the manifestation of the supernatural is a familiar feature of accounts of visions and is usually followed by some word of reassurance (cf. e.g. Ezek. 1:28–2:1; Dan. 8:17; 10:9-11; Matt. 17:6-7; Acts 26:13-14). It was probably Dan. 10:9-11 that the seer had esp. in mind. **I am the first and the last** (cf. vs. 8) is derived from Isa. 44:6; 48:12, where the clause is used by God as a self-designation. Here it is expanded in light of the Crucifixion and Resurrection and used by the heavenly Christ of himself, as also in 2:8 and, in part, in 22:13. **Hades** for this author is

not the Greek place of punishment but the Hebrew Sheol (see comments on Pss. 6:4-5; 18:7-18), thought of as a subterranean pit where the souls of both good and evil dwell after death. **Death** is the state and **Hades** is the place of the dead, and both are personified in 6:8; 20:13. Since they have been overcome by Christ, he can be pictured as holding the **keys** with which at the time of the end he can release his faithful followers.

1:19-20. Vs. 19 resumes and amplifies the order given in vs. 11. The **seven lampstands** (cf. vs. 12) are identified with the **seven churches** that are to be addressed, and the **seven stars** are said to represent their guardian **angels.** As nations have their special angelic patrons (cf. Dan. 10:13, 20-21), so have the 7 congregations of the province of Asia.

The covering letter appears to end without the benediction customary in other NT writings that are in letter form, but John may think of the letter as superimposed on the whole book and as concluding with the grace in 22:21.

B. LETTERS TO 7 CHURCHES (2:1–3:22)

2:1-7. *Ephesus.* In the first cent. Ephesus was the 4th largest city in the Empire and capital of the province of Asia. Located on the Aegean coast at the mouth of a small river, it served as the W terminus of a long caravan route from the far E by way of Palestine and Syria (see color map 16). It was "temple keeper of the great Artemis" (Acts 19:35), the goddess whose Ephesian shrine was one of the wonders of the World, and also a major center for the promotion of emperor worship. In the early 50's Paul had founded the church in the city and had ministered there longer than anywhere else. The fact that the Ephesian congregation is named first among the 7 indicates its importance in John's day.

2:1*b*-5. The letter contains a mixture of praise and criticism. The church is commended for its vigorous action against **false** teachers and its fortitude under suffering, but blamed for having lost the earlier warmth of its **love**—probably referring to brotherly love rather than to devotion to Christ.

2:6-7. Censure is tempered by acknowledging the hatred of the Ephesian Christians for the practices of the **Nicolaitans,** probably the false **apostles,** i.e. itinerant missionaries, of vs. 2, whose special vices are condemned in vss. 14-15. From late 2nd-cent. times the Nicolaitans were believed to have been followers of Nicolaus, the proselyte of Antioch who was early made a deacon of the church (Acts 6:5). Vs. 7*a* is a formula in all the letters and relates each to the readers of the whole book. According to 22:2 the **tree of life,** the symbol of immortality, stands in the street of the heavenly Jerusalem, for which the **paradise of God** is therefore a synonym.

2:8-11. *Smyrna.* The city of Smyrna was N of Ephesus, at the head of a deep gulf of the Aegean and at the end of a road leading across Lydia from Phrygia and the E. Long an ally of Rome, it dedicated a temple to the goddess Roma as early as 195 B.C. and in A.D. 23 was granted the right to erect a temple to the Emperor Tiberius. When or by whom the church at Smyrna was founded is not known. A mid-2nd-cent. writing tells of the martyrdom at Smyrna of Polycarp, an aged bishop of the church.

2:8b-9. For this congregation this 2nd letter has nothing but praise. Though they are persecuted and poverty-stricken from the confiscation of their property, these Christians can still be described as **rich** in spiritual possessions. The reference to false **Jews** (vs. 9; cf. 3:9) is usually understood as a bitter comment based on the church's claim to be the true Israel, but there is another possibility. Jews were exempted by Rome from participating in emperor worship, and this may be John's condemnation of Christians who seek to escape persecution by claiming to be Jews.

2:10-11. The seer predicts that the church is about to suffer a brief but still more violent affliction and anticipates that it may lead to martyrdom for many. The ultimate power behind the persecuting Roman state is the **devil.** The Christian's reward for martyrdom is a **crown of life,** a metaphor borrowed from the wreath awarded to a victor in competitive games and symbolizing immortality. Martyrs are to be spared the **second death,** which is explained in 20:14-15; 21:8 as the eternal death of those condemned at the last judgment.

2:12-17. *Pergamum.* To the NE of Smyrna, Pergamum had long been the capital of the province of Asia when Augustus moved the seat of government to Ephesus. It was noted as a religious center, with shrines to Zeus, Athena, Dionysus, and Asclepius, the Greek god of healing. More esp. it was also the major center in Asia of the cult of emperor worship. In 29 B.C. it dedicated a temple to the "divine Augustus and the goddess Roma," and this symbolized for Christians the threat to the existence of the church and no doubt explains the reference to **Satan's throne** (vs. 13).

2:12b-13. The congregation is praised for its loyalty and esp. for its steadfastness when a certain **Antipas** was put to death. Throughout his apocalypse John anticipates that many believers will suffer martyrdom, but Antipas is the only one he cites as having already died for his faith.

2:14-17. Praise is coupled with a warning. There are those in the church **who hold the teaching of Balaam.** On the basis of Num. 31:16 Balaam had long been regarded as the prototype of corrupt teachers. Here the Balaamites are closely linked with the **Nicolaitans,** and both may be understood as meaning "destroyers of the people." They are accused of sexual immorality and of eating meat sold on the market after the animal was sacrificed to pagan gods. If they persist in their practices, they are threatened with destruction at Christ's imminent return. On the other hand those who remain faithful will be fed in the new age with **manna,** as the Israelites were after their deliverance from Egypt (cf. Exod. 16), and will be given an amulet, or charm, to protect them against every evil. The **new name** is probably that of Christ or God (cf. 3:12; Isa. 62:2) but some interpret it as a secret name given to the victor himself.

2:18-29. *Thyatira.* Ca. 40 miles to the SE of Pergamum, Thyatira was unimportant as a political and religious center; yet it was a prosperous industrial town, noted among other things for the manufacture and dyeing of woolen goods (cf. Acts 16:14). In his opening description of the **Son of God** (cf. 1:13b-16) John may be contrasting him with the sun god Apollo, the special deity worshiped at Thyatira.

2:19-23. While commending the congregation for its **patient endurance** under persecution, John blames it for tolerating a false **prophetess,** to whom he gives the symbolic name **Jezebel,** after Ahab's immoral and idolatrous queen (cf. I Kings 16:31; 18:13; 19:1-2; 21:1-16). Her teachings and example are similar to those of the Nicolaitans (cf. vss. 14-15). John forecasts her punishment as a warning to **all the churches.** The reference to **her children** and their fate is probably to her followers rather than to any adulterous offspring.

2:24-29. Those unaffected by this woman's vicious belief and behavior are urged to **hold fast.** It is uncertain to what **deep things of Satan** refers. Early heretics known as Gnostics claimed to have access to depths of knowledge denied the uninitiated, and some interpreters believe that John has replaced "of God" with "of Satan." Others believe that, since the whole phrase is said to be in current use, those concerned maintained that they were capable of probing the depths of evil without thereby contaminating themselves. Still others relate the phrase to John's overriding horror of emperor worship, whose devotees could be described as having plumbed Satanic depths. The faithful are promised a share in Christ's final victory. To what the gift of the **morning star** refers is not certain. At any rate it is intended to symbolize the immortal life that the faithful are to receive from Christ.

3:1-6. *Sardis.* Ca. 30 miles SE of Thyatira, Sardis was the former capital of the ancient kingdom of Lydia and reached the peak of its prosperity during the reign of the fabulous Croesus (*ca.* 560 B.C.). Under Persian rule it fell into decline, but recovered some of its earlier importance under the Romans. Devastated by an earthquake in A.D. 17 and rebuilt through the generosity of Tiberius, it competed for the honor of erecting a temple to the emperor, but lost out to Smyrna. Early Greek historians accused the citizens of Sardis of luxury and immorality.

3:1b-3. In John's day the church has fallen into a state of apathy, and he charges it with being spiritually **dead.** In words that recall admonitions credited to Jesus in the gospels (e.g. Mark 13:33) he summons the Christians at Sardis to recall what they have **received and heard,** to hold that fast, and to **repent** forthwith. If they are not on the watch, Christ's 2nd coming will overtake them as a **thief** in the night (cf. Matt. 24:43-44; I Thess. 5:2-4).

3:4-5. Yet, with all the church's lethargy, there are still a **few** at Sardis who have kept themselves free of the prevailing immorality and who are promised a fitting reward; they are to be Christ's companions in the messianic kingdom. They will be robed **in white garments** as a symbol of their purity, an idea conventional in ancient thought (cf. Ps. 104: 2, where God is said to clothe himself "with light as with a garment"). Some interpreters hold that the author had in mind some such notion of the resurrection body as that to which Paul refers in II Cor. 5:4. The names of the victors will be preserved in the **book of life.** The belief that God keeps a heavenly register has been traced by some to the influence on Jewish thought of astrological speculation. However that may be, the concept is a familiar one in the OT (Exod. 32:32; Ps. 56:8; Neh. 13:14; Mal. 3:16), in intertestamental literature, elsewhere in the NT (Luke 10:20; Phil. 4:3; Heb. 12:23), and often in this book (13:8; 17:8; 20:12, 15; 21:27).

3:6. In words that sound like a reminiscence of the saying in Matt. 10:32; Luke 12:8 the heavenly Christ assures him who is victorious in his life of Christian loyalty that he will be acknowledged as a follower before God and the angelic hosts in the day of judgment.

3:7-13. Philadelphia. A city ca. 30 miles to the SE of Sardis, Philadelphia was of more recent foundation and of commercial rather than of political importance. It suffered like Sardis from the earthquake of A.D. 17 and was also given a generous donation from imperial funds to assist in rebuilding.

3:7b-9. The letter, like that to Smyrna, is one of praise and encouragement, with no element of censure. While the **key of David** points back to 1:18, together with what follows it is also a quotation from Isa. 22:22. As Eliakim during the reign of Hezekiah had authority to open and shut the house of David, so the heavenly Christ can open and shut the door of God's kingdom. The **open door** over against the Philadelphian Christians may refer to one of opportunity for missionary work, but more probably it is an assurance of entrance into the new age. On vs. 9 see above on 2:8b-11.

3:10-13. Despite their numerical weakness the Philadelphians have shown fortitude under persecution and will be brought safely through the **hour of trial** that is shortly to beset all non-Christians. He who remains faithful will be made a **pillar** in God's temple. Since the language is metaphorical, there need be no inconsistency between this statement and the declaration in 21:22 that God and the Lamb are to be the only temple in the heavenly Jerusalem. Christ will imprint a **name** on the victor (cf. 2:17; 14:1; 22:4)—God's and Christ's because he is their possession, and that of the **New Jerusalem,** the messianic city that is to descend after the last judgment and the creation of the new heaven and the new earth (cf. 21:1-2). According to 19:12, 16 Christ's **new name** will not be revealed until his 2nd coming and will be "King of kings and Lord of lords."

3:14-22. Laodicea. Situated ca. 50 miles SE of Philadelphia in the valley of a tributary of the Meander River called the Lycus, Laodicea was an important commercial, banking, and medical center. The congregation at Laodicea, together with those at nearby Colossae and Hierapolis, had already been founded as early as Paul's day (cf. Col. 2:1; 4:13-16) and Paul intimates that he wrote it a letter (Col. 4:16). This has either been lost or, as some believe, is the little letter known as Philem. (see Intro. to Philem.).

3:14b-18. It is the apathy of the entire congregation, unrelieved as at Sardis by notable exceptions, which troubles the seer, and to which he directs the censure of the heavenly Christ. Christ is given the title **the Amen,** as is God in the Hebrew text of Isa. 65:16, and is called the **beginning of God's creation,** a phrase that probably recalls the "first-born of the dead" in 1:5 rather than some doctrine of his preexistence as in Col. 1:15. The loyalty of Laodicean Christians is scathingly characterized as **lukewarm,**

their complacency in their material well-being is ridiculed, and they are counseled to purchase true spiritual riches. Many interpreters see in vss. 17-18 references to Laodicean wealth based on banking and the manufacture of woolen goods and to a popular eye medicine known as "Phrygian powder" that was used in the Laodicean medical school.

3:19-22. The tone of the letter now changes abruptly from censure to appeal. The bitter words were utterances of reproving and chastening **love.** But the summons to repentance is urgent. Christ's 2nd coming is at hand. In language that recalls such passages as Mark 13:29; Luke 12:36 the heavenly Lord declares: **I stand at the door and knock.** The idea that the new age of God's rule would be inaugurated with a banquet at which the redeemed would feast together with the Messiah is a familiar one in Jewish intertestamental literature. It is also reflected in Jesus' words as reported in Luke 12:35-38; Mark 14:25. The thought of the heavenly Christ on a **throne** occurs also in other NT writings (e.g. Matt. 19:28; Heb. 1:8). The seer depicts the fulfillment of Christ's promise to the faithful that he will **sit with me on my throne** when he speaks in 20:4 of the martyrs reigning with Christ for a thousand years.

III. THE REVELATION OF THINGS TO COME (4:1–22:5)

The letters of chs. 1–3 have sought to fortify and encourage Christians who have experienced or are about to experience persecution for their Christian faith, in part by threats to apostates of fearful punishment and in part by promises to the faithful—esp. to those who will suffer martyrdom for their loyalty—of glorious immortality with Christ in God's kingdom. The 2nd major division of the book now depicts how these threats and promises are to be fulfilled. The benediction in 22:21, with which the epilogue concludes, was evidently intended to give an epistolary format to the whole work. Only chs. 4–22 are apocalyptic—"revelation of things to come" —in the strict sense of the word, but the material in ch. 1 gives such a setting to the letters also.

A. PRELUDE IN HEAVEN (4:1–5:14)

Chs. 4–5 consist of visions of God enthroned in heaven, surrounded by his worshiping hosts and angelic attendants, and of God's giving the book of his will to Christ, the Lamb. The scenes are an assurance to Christian readers that God and Christ are shortly to intervene in the affairs of this age and to deliver the faithful from the domination of Satan and his demonic powers, both superhuman demons and the demonic forces embodied in the Roman state and the priesthood of the imperial cult.

4:1-11. Vision of God on His Throne. The formula **After this I looked, and lo** is the seer's way of introducing a new vision (cf. 7:1, 9; 15:5; 18:1). In terms of the cosmology of antiquity John thinks of a solid vault arching over the flat earth, with heaven located above the vault and Hades a pit below the earth. While the notion of 7 heavens occurs in much Jewish intertestamental writing, in this book there is only a single heaven. The seer, who has heretofore been on earth, is admitted to **heaven** by an **open door** in the sky. The **first voice** that bids him **come**

up is presumably Christ's as in 1:10. The feat of levitation is accomplished in a state of spiritual ecstasy or trance. As often in Jewish and Christian literature, and as customarily in this book, God is represented as **seated on the throne.** No attempt is made at direct description. John views only the splendor of light encircling the throne, which he compares to that of precious stones passing through a cloud and emerging as a **rainbow** of **emerald** green.

4:4. The **twenty-four elders** on their several **thrones** are God's heavenly court. Some interpreters believe they represent angelic kings, though such a hierarchy in this precise form and number is not mentioned in Jewish literature. Others trace their origin in the seer's thought to astrological speculation of 24 stars outside the circle of the zodiac, stars that functioned as judges of the world. Another, and possibly more attractive, guess is that they are the heavenly counterpart of the 24 groups, or "courses," of priests and the 24 details of Levites who ministered in turn in the temple in Jerusalem. Still others think that John's reference to **thrones** and **white garments** and **crowns** means that he has Christian martyrs in mind.

4:5-6a. The description of God's manifestation of himself to the seer is resumed with imagery often used in the book (8:5; 11:19; 16:18) to suggest God's awful power and majesty. The **seven torches of fire** that burn before the throne, probably suggested to begin with by the 7 planetary gods of popular astrology, are identified as the **seven spirits of God,** mentioned in 1:4, and in 3:1 said to belong to Christ.

4:6b-8a. The **four living creatures** are visualized for the most part after the manner of the cherubim of Ezek. 1, but John's description has also been influenced by Isaiah's vision of the seraphim in Isa. 6. They represent the highest order of angels for this NT writing. The concept of the cherubim as 4-winged guardian powers with faces of a **lion,** an **ox,** a **man,** and an **eagle** was derived originally by Jews from Babylonian sources and is ultimately dependent on the 4 signs of the zodiac in astral speculation. The seraphim with **six wings** of Isaiah were angelic representations of lightning or fire. The reference to **eyes all round and within** is borrowed from Ezekiel, who had in mind, not the creatures themselves, but wheels that accompanied them in flight. Here "within" probably means on the under side of the wings. The plethora of eyes symbolizes the all-seeing intelligence of the creatures.

4:8b-d. The song of these creatures, with its thrice-holy designation of deity, is of course the hymn of the seraphim in Isa. 6:3, with modifications that introduce attributes of God that John stresses throughout his book: **the Lord God Almighty.** It may be that the seer delighted in this name because it overshadowed the title "Our Lord and God" which had been assumed by the Emperor Domitian, and which John would regard as blasphemous. However that may be, it asserts John's conviction of the ultimate triumph of righteousness. The latter half of the song reproduces the title already given to God in 1:4.

4:9-11. Whereas the praise of the living creatures has been said in vs. 8 to be continuous, it is now represented as breaking forth at intervals (cf. 5:8, 14; 11:16; 19:4). But this is a minor inconsistency in

an imposing and magnificent scene. **Glory and honor and thanks** summarize the praise of the living creatures, at which the 24 elders prostrate themselves, and to which they make their antiphonal response. When they **cast their crowns before the throne** they acknowledge that all their kingly dignity is derived from and subordinate to God. It may be assumed that their hymn to the glory of God as creator, poetic in content, rhythm, and balance, belonged already in John's time to the liturgy of the church.

5:1-5. *Vision of the Sealed Scroll.* The seer's attention is now directed to a sealed **scroll** (see above on 1:10-11) that lies in God's **right hand.** The scroll is written both on the recto, the side on which the narrow strips of papyrus were laid crosswise, and on the verso, the side on which they were arranged lengthwise. Since in a rolled scroll only a portion of the outside or verso writing is visible, the conclusion that it holds writing also on the inside, however obvious, can be only an assumption. It is not clear how John thinks of the scroll as **sealed with seven seals**—the perfect number again—whether the entire roll cannot be opened until all 7 seals are broken or, more probably, in some way each of the scroll's 7 sections is separately sealed. As in Dan. 8:26, the book of destiny has been sealed to keep its contents secret until the time of revelation should come. John may have drawn his imagery in part from such passages as Isa. 29:11; Dan. 8:26, but it is dependent largely on Ezek. 2:9-10.

5:2-5. The scroll contains God's judgments and counsels that John is to reveal in the following visions. The **angel** is described as **strong** because his appeal for someone **worthy to open the scroll** is uttered in a **voice** that can penetrate to the farthest limits of **heaven** and **earth** and **under the earth,** i.e. Hades. The seer reports that he **wept** because there appears to be no one in the whole of God's creation whose rank and office gives him the right to open the scroll, so that the promise of a revelation to him of what is to take place (4:1) will remain unredeemed. But **one of the elders** assuages his grief. There is one uniquely qualified by his office to **open the scroll** and to break **its seven seals**—the Messiah, the Christ. The victor is described as the **Lion of the tribe of Judah** in dependence on a messianic interpretation of Gen. 49:9, "Judah is a lion's whelp," and as the **Root of David** in dependence on the indubitably messianic meaning of Isa. 11:1: "There shall come forth a shoot from the stump of Jesse, and a branch shall grow out of his roots." The Davidic descent of Christ may be presupposed in 3:7, but is explicitly mentioned elsewhere in this book only in 22:16. In each instance it belongs to the liturgical inheritance of the church rather than in any particular sense to John's own doctrine.

5:6-14. *Vision of the Lamb.* In this passage the **Lamb** is introduced as another name for the risen Christ. It occurs a total of 29 times in this and the succeeding chs. and is therefore John's characteristic title for the heavenly Lord. In this respect Rev. and the Gospel of John have a christological element in common, though the respective presentations of it differ in detail.

Nowhere in the use of the title in Rev. is there an allusion to any idea of Christ's meekness or gentleness. In this ch. the Lamb is the object of the worship offered by the hosts of heaven and earth. In ch. 6 he opens the book of destiny. In 7:9-11 he is enthroned with God and receives the praise of a host that no man can number. In 13:8; 21:27 he has charge of the book of life. In 14:1 he stands on Mt. Zion with the 144,000 of the redeemed. In 17:14 he is the victor over the armies of the Antichrist. In 19:7 the multitude of the redeemed celebrate his marriage to the glorified church. In 21:22-23 the Lord God and the Lamb are the temple of the new Jerusalem and the Lamb is the lamp by which God's glory illuminates the city. In 22:1 the water of the river of life in the new age issues from the throne of God and of the Lamb.

But the term designates not only the conquering and triumphant Christ but also one "with the marks of slaughter upon him" (NEB; cf. 13:8). The portrayal of the Messiah under the figure of a lamb is found occasionally in Jewish intertestamental literature, but the inclusion here and in the Gospel of John (cf. also Acts 8:32; I Pet. 1:19) of the idea of a redeeming sacrifice is due no doubt to a messianic interpretation of Isa. 53:6-7: "All we like sheep have gone astray; . . . and the LORD has laid on him the iniquity of us all. . . . Like a lamb that is led to the slaughter, . . . so he opened not his mouth."

5:6. The position of the Lamb is in immediate proximity to the **throne,** "inside the circle of living creatures and the circle of the elders" (NEB). It is useless to try to harmonize the various metaphors used by John for the celestial Lord: the Lion of Judah, the Root of David, and the **Lamb . . . with seven horns and with seven eyes.** The terms are symbolic rather than representative. The Lion of Judah and the Root of David designate Christ as the expected Davidic Messiah. Since the horn is a common OT symbol of power, his **seven horns** suggest power that is full and complete. His **seven eyes,** identified with the **seven spirits of God sent out into all the earth,** symbolize his omniscience. All this is combined with the thought of Christ's self-sacrifice on the cross as the avenue to that full power and knowledge, much as Paul does in Rom. 1:3-5; Phil. 2:5-11.

5:7-8. By virtue of his adequate office the Lamb takes the scroll of destiny (cf. vss. 1-5), and the heavenly court of angels and representatives of God's people respond with homage and adoration. The **harp,** lit. "lyre," is the instrument of praise. The **golden bowls full of incense** that they hold in their hands are equated with the **prayers of the saints,** the supplications of God's people on earth for the speedy consummation of his will.

5:9-10. In possible dependence on Isa. 42:10 the seer speaks of a **new song,** of the heavenly court that praises the Lamb as **worthy** to open the scroll and avenge God's people, worthy because his death has purchased men **for God from every tribe and tongue and people and nation**—in itself a description of the multiracial church of John's day. As in 1:6, the promise is that faithful Christians will exercise sovereignty and serve God as **priests,** a promise whose fulfillment in the millennium is further predicted in 20:6.

5:11-14. The adoration of the Lamb by the 4 living creatures and the 24 elders in vss. 8-10 is fol-

lowed by that of countless hosts of angels in vss. 11-12 and by all God's creation in vs. 13. The ch. ends with the response of **Amen** by the creatures and with an act of homage and worship by the elders.

B. The 7 Seals (6:1-8:1)

In this section the Lamb breaks the seals of the book of destiny one by one and the events recorded in it are dramatically enacted. Nothing is said of reading the document. Its contents are made known by visual fulfillment. Some interpreters have looked for clues to the various woes in historical events that may be presumed to have taken place during John's lifetime. Others have tried to understand them as an adaptation of ancient themes of oriental mythology. Still others have found references in some of the 7 to great empires of the past. Most students of this material agree that John's imagery is based on the apocalyptic tradition reflected in Mark 13; Matt. 24; Luke 21: war, international strife, famine, pestilence, persecution, and evidences of cosmic collapse. Whether he knew the gospels themselves may be questioned, but the tradition behind these passages belonged to the common property of apocalyptic thought.

The underlying idea was that the coming of the end would be presaged by evidence that evil was rampant—evil in international affairs, in social life, and in the very structure of the universe. God would not intervene until the worst had come. Many authors, e.g. of the Jewish sections of the Sibylline Oracles and of II Esdras, took manifest pleasure in detailing the disasters to come. Though John has made use of the more or less stereotyped predictions of his predecessors, he has given them his own special arrangement and highly individual treatment. All this does not rule out the possibility that he has been prompted in some of his predictions by memories or experiences of historical events.

6:1-2. A White Horse and Its Rider. The ordinal numbers in vss. 3, 5, 7 suggest that both occurrences of **one of** in vs. 1 should be translated "the first of." The opening of the first seal is accompanied by a thunderous command of the first of the 4 living creatures of the heavenly court: **"Come!"** Then a white horse appears, on which a crowned rider sits holding a bow. The imagery of this and of the 3 succeeding woes has evidently been suggested by the colored horses of Zech. 1:8; 6:1-8, but John transforms the functions of the OT figures. What Zech. represented as God's messengers to the 4 quarters of the heaven with a mission to patrol the earth now become God's agents of destruction. The imagery of vs. 2, its armed horseman presented with a **crown,** is clearly a personification of conquest. Whether it is conquest in general or conquest of the Roman Empire by hordes of Parthian horsemen, of which many at that time stood in dread, is a matter on which interpreters differ. The **bow** is known to have been the special weapon of the Parthians, but the frequent mention in the OT of the bow as the emblem of the warrior may be all that John has in mind.

6:3-4. A Red Horse and Its Rider. With the opening of the 2nd seal a 2nd living creature issues the order and a 2nd rider appears on a red horse. He is given a **sword** and **permitted to take peace from**

the earth. The color of the horse, the sword, and the mission clearly symbolize war. If the first episode symbolizes a war of conquest, the words **so that men should slay one another** suggest civil strife. Those who see an allusion to the Parthians in vss. 1-2 sometimes see one in these vss. to Rom; but the crown, bow, and sword are stereotyped symbols. The first rider is given a crown to symbolize conquest and the 2nd a sword to foment civil strife.

6:5-6. *A Black Horse and Its Rider.* When the 3rd rider appears, mounted on a black horse and holding a **balance,** i.e. a pair of scales, a voice announces: **A quart of wheat for a denarius . . .** The measure translated **quart** held enough grain to feed one person for a day. Though a **denarius** had a silver content of only about 20 cents, it represented a day's wage (cf. Matt. 20:2). With grain selling at such a price, the scene symbolizes the apocalyptic woe of famine. In the interests of Italian winegrowers Domitian issued an edict in 92 restricting the cultivation of vineyards in the provinces but was compelled to revoke it because of opposition in Asia Minor. Some scholars see a reflection of this event in the final clause of vs. 6.

6:7-8. *A Pale Horse and Its Rider.* The opening of the 4th seal is introduced by the now familiar formula. **Pale** represents a word translated "green" in 8:7 (cf. Mark 6:39), but the Moffatt translation "livid" suits the context better. **Death** and **Hades,** i.e. the Hebrew Sheol (see above on 1:17-18), are personified (cf. 20:13-14) and are represented apparently as riding on the same beast. It has been suggested that originally John described a single rider, death in the sense of pestilence—the usual sequel to war, internal strife, and famine—who was **given power over a fourth of the earth,** and that an editor influenced by 1:18; 20:13-14 added Hades and the summary concluding vs. 8.

6:9-11. *Lament of the Martyrs.* The opening of the 5th seal is followed by a vision of a different sort. The seer views the **souls** of the faithful Christians who have already suffered martyrdom in safekeeping beneath the **altar** in the heavenly temple, where they cry aloud for God's avenging judgment on the pagan world. They are told to wait in patience until the persecutions still to come fill up the roll of their fellows. The idea that the end will not come until the predestined number of martyrs is **complete** has anticipations in earlier Jewish literature, and in ch. 7 the seer declares that the number is 144,000.

6:12-17. *Shaking of the Universe.* The opening of the 6th seal is followed by a **great earthquake,** an eclipse of the **sun,** and other appalling portents of cosmic collapse. Terror-stricken men of every degree interpret them as signs that the last **day . . . has come,** though the seer thinks of them only as forerunners of the ultimate calamities. The language and imagery are familiar from Mark 13; Isa. 34:4; Joel 2, and elsewhere. The statements in vs. 14 that **every mountain and island was removed** and in vs. 16 that the refugees call on the **mountains** to **fall on us** illustrate the author's use of hyperbole.

7:1-8. *Sealing of the Redeemed.* There is now a pause in the fearful succession of plagues. All that has gone before is preparatory to the breaking of the 7th seal, the event that will precipitate the awful final drama of the world's history. During this dramatic interlude the 144,000 of the spiritual Israel are **sealed** for their protection against demonic powers. John thinks of the earth as a vast square, as in Isa. 11:12; Ezek. 7:2, with **four angels** at its **four corners** restraining the **four winds** that are to destroy it. The fact that no reference is made later in the book to these apocalyptic agencies is one of several indications that in this section the author is adapting material to his purpose from some source, clearly Jewish.

7:2-3. An **angel** rises out of the E bearing God's **seal,** i.e. signet ring, to imprint, with the help of others, God's name or mark on the **foreheads** of those whose faithfulness is to be demonstrated by their martyrdom. Various prototypes may have influenced the author at this point. In Exod. 12 the firstborn of the Jews are protected against the destroyer by blood sprinkled on the doorposts of Jewish homes. In Isa. 44:5 it is said that converts to Judaism will write God's name on their hands as evidence that they belong to him. The closest approximation in the OT is in Ezek. 9:4, where one is to go "through Jerusalem, and put a mark upon the foreheads of the men who sigh and groan over all the abominations that are committed it it." Here the sealing of the redeemed on earth anticipates the reference to God's name on their foreheads in 22:4.

7:4-8. The **number of the sealed** is 144,000 (cf. 14:1), drawn in equal numbers from **every tribe of the sons of Israel.** If the surmise that John is editing Jewish material is correct, his source thought of the true Israel as a core of the Jewish faithful of all the ideal tribes, but he interprets it to refer to Christians of every racial origin (cf. e.g. Rom. 2:29; Jas. 1:1; I Pet. 1:1). Some have construed vss. 1-8 as referring to Jewish Christians and vss. 9-17 to their Gentile counterparts, but there is no ground for this; both passages designate the same vast company. The square of 12 multiplied by 1,000 is to be taken symbolically, no doubt representing the completeness and perfectness of God's people. According to one count the Bible enumerates 20 different arrangements of the Jewish tribes, and this one agrees with none of them. The author puts **Judah** first in his list because elsewhere he traces Christ's descent through that patriarch (5:5). Curiously the tribe of Dan is omitted. Irenaeus, writing toward the end of the 2nd cent., asserted that the omission was due to the belief that the Antichrist would come from that tribe. John fills the gap left by the exclusion of Dan with **Manasseh,** the name of one of Joseph's sons.

7:9-17. *The Martyrs Before God's Throne.* The 2nd vision in this interlude is not intended as a contrast to the first. The 144,000 symbolize the church as the true Israel while still militant on the earth. The **great multitude which no man could number** from all national, racial, and linguistic groups is the church triumphant in heaven, the company of the glorified and victorious faithful awaiting the final consummation of God's purpose. The vision is recounted by the seer to inspire the communities to which he is writing. The vast throng in heaven are those who will remain loyal despite the pressures of persecution and the threats of death. They stand in the presence of God and Christ, clothed as martyrs in **white robes** and carrying **palm branches** as symbols of thanksgiving and victory (cf. John 12:13). The theme of their praise is **salvation**—properly translated into our idiom in this context by the NEB as "victory"—which they joyously ascribe to **God** and the **Lamb,** for neither they themselves nor any earthly powers could have overthrown the demonic hosts opposed to them.

7:11-12. The seer enumerates the concentric ranks of spiritual beings about the **throne,** from the outermost to the innermost, about whom the innumerable host is presumably ranged. The various heavenly orders prostrate themselves in homage to God and make an antiphonal reply to the doxology of the church with their own 7-fold paean of praise (cf. 5:12). The first **Amen!** is a response to the song of the church. The 2nd is the liturgical conclusion to the doxology of the heavenly court.

7:13-14a. Serving as an "interpreting angel," **one of the elders** engages the seer in a dialogue—often in the OT a formula for explaining a vision (cf. e.g. Amos 7:8). **Sir,** lit. "my lord," represents the original meaning of the Greek term used of God and Christ. The seer cannot answer the elder's question until the identity of the heavenly company with that of the 144,000 is revealed.

7:14b. Since the visions in this ch. are in preparation for all that follows the breaking of the last seal, the reference to the **great tribulation** through which the company has passed must be a proleptic reference to all the woes that are still to be described rather than to one specific calamity. The statement that **they have washed their robes and made them white in the blood of the Lamb** asserts that deliverance and victory have been made possible because Christ, the first martyr, won that victory through his death.

7:15. The Greek verb translated **serve** means to perform the ritual service of the temple. The heavenly sanctuary will disappear at the final consummation, for in the new heaven and the new earth God and the Lamb will be the only temple (21:22); but in the one that now is (chs. 4-5) all Christians are priests (1:6; 5:10). In turn God **will shelter them with his presence.** The Hebrew word lying back of this last Greek phrase is *shekinah.* In Jewish literature *shekinah* meant the direct presence of God among men, in the tabernacle or temple, in Jerusalem, or immediately overshadowing and protecting his people. Hence this text declares: "God will cause his *shekinah* to dwell upon the church in heaven."

7:16-17. The concluding vss. of the scene are based in part on Isa. 49:10. The thought of the Lamb as the shepherd of the church triumphant may well have been suggested by a memory of Ps. 23, and the words with which the interpreter ends, the wonderful promise that **God will wipe away every tear from their eyes,** may have been prompted by Isa. 25:8.

8:1. *A Half-Hour Silence in Heaven.* With the opening of the 7th seal there is an end to the praises and thanksgiving in heaven. The **silence** implies no interruption in the revelations given the seer. Possibly, as has been suggested, it is enjoined on the heavenly hosts so that the prayers of the suffering saints on earth, which concern God more than the praises of the angelic orders, may be laid before him (vss. 3-5). Probably, however, the dramatic interest of the author is enough to explain the introduction of the scene. The pause is an ominous prelude to the calamities that are to ensue. No satisfactory explanation of the **half an hour** length of the heavenly silence has been advanced.

C. THE 7 TRUMPETS (8:2–11:19)

In a 2nd group of 7 the seer lists the 7 catastrophes that follow the opening of the last of the seals, the 7 plagues released by blasts of the trumpets of doom.

8:2-6. *Fire Flung on the Earth.* Though **the seven angels who stand before God** may be the 7 spirits mentioned in 1:4; 4:5; they more probably are thought of as a new and distinct group who reflect the idea in late Jewish angelology of 7 archangels. In I Enoch they are listed as Uriel, Raphael, Raguel, Michael, Sariel, Gabriel, and Remiel. In Jewish literature they are often called the "angels of the presence." Raphael speaks of himself in Tobit 12:15 as "one of the seven holy angels who present the prayers of the saints and enter into the presence of the glory of the Holy One" and in Luke 1:19 the angel who appears to Zechariah identifies himself as "Gabriel, who stand in the presence of God." Here the 7 are God's ministering angels who carry out his commands. The trumpet, i.e. the ram's horn *shophar,* as an instrument to announce God's judgment is familiar in intertestamental literature and in such OT passages as Isa. 27:13.

8:3-6. Before the 7 trumpets are blown the interlude of the **incense** offering is introduced. A nameless **angel** mixes the **prayers of all the saints** with **much incense** to offer them on the **altar** in the heavenly throne room. The scene is reminiscent of that portrayed in 5:8. Like the prayers of the martyred souls under the altar (6:10), they are pleas for God's judgment. Once the prayers have ascended with the smoke of the incense to God, the angel employs the **censer** in a new role—to hurl **fire from the altar . . . on the earth.** The act is followed by natural portents (cf. 4:5) which imply that God has heard the intercessions and will speedily furnish an answer. The 7-fold woe that issues from the 7th seal is about to break, and the 7 angels prepare to sound their 7 trumpets.

8:7. *A Shower of Bloody Hail and Fire.* Various OT passages have suggested the author's images. In Joel 2:30 (cf. Acts 2:19) **blood** and **fire** are among the portents of the day of Yahweh, and **hail** mixed with fire is one of the plagues brought on Egypt preceding the Exodus (Exod. 9:24)—a series that esp. serves as a model for the disasters to the oppressors which are now to precede God's deliverance of his people. After each of the first 4 and the 6th trumpet blasts a **third** of the objects affected are injured or destroyed.

8:8-9. *A Fiery Mountain Cast into the Sea.* In this 2nd plague the turning of the sea into **blood** and the destruction of the fish are features taken from the first of the plagues in Egypt (Exod. 7:14-25), while the ideas of a flaming mountain hurled into the sea and the wreck of a **third of the ships** are contributed by the seer. On the basis of a passage in I Enoch some interpreters believe the mountain of this woe and the star of the next represent wicked angels cast out of heaven to wreak destruction on the world.

8:10-11. *Pollution of the Waters.* The blast of the 3rd trumpet is followed by the fall of a torchlike **star,** i.e. meteor, from the sky on a **third of the rivers** and the **fountains of water.** The scene is similar to the preceding, and the idea of the corruption of the water is likewise taken from the first Egyptian plague. The name given to the blazing star is a puzzle. No star, meteor, or fallen angel is called **Wormwood** in any other ancient writing known. It may have been suggested by Jeremiah's use of this bitter plant as a symbol of divine punishment (Jer. 9:15; 23:15). That the **waters became wormwood** means that they were impregnated with the juice of the plant. Wormwood is not a poison, but John was not concerned with such fine distinctions.

8:12. *A Partial Eclipse.* The blowing of the 4th trumpet results in a darkening of a **third** of the **light** of the **sun** and the **moon** and the **stars.** The consequence, curious and illogical, is a diminution not of the intensity but of the duration of the light. There is darkness for a **third of the day** and for a **third of the night.** The author is intent on describing the awesome effect of the scene as a whole, without concerning himself overly much with realistic detail. However startling he may have thought it, this plague does not match the others in the severity of its effects. The 9th Egyptian plague of darkness (Exod. 10:21-23) was probably in his mind.

8:13. *An Eagle's Triple Cry of Woe.* The seer again makes effective use of the device of an interlude. The woeful cry of an eagle in **midheaven** separates the first 4 trumpet visions, which have involved upheavals of nature, from the final 3, which bring direct attacks on men. Of the 3 woes announced by the eagle the first is identified in 9:12 with the result of the 5th trumpet blast and the 2nd is identified in 11:14 with that of the 6th. The 3rd is probably the whole series of the plagues of the 7 bowls narrated in ch. 16.

9:1-12. *A Horde of Demonic Locusts.* With the blast of the 5th trumpet John describes the fall of a **star** from the sky to **earth.** The star is personified and represents an angel. **Fallen** means not that the angel is a wicked one, cast out of heaven, but merely "descended." The angel is an agent of God sent from heaven to carry out the divine will. He is **given the key to the shaft of the bottomless pit,** and later we are told that he retains that key (20:1).

Bottomless pit translates a single Greek word that has been anglicized as "abyss." It is not to be confused with Hades (Sheol), which is the temporary residence of the souls of men after death (see above on 1:17-18). Rather this abyss is a place of punishment which burns with **smoke like the smoke of a great furnace** and thus resembles the "hell," lit. "Gehenna," of the gospels (see comment on Mark 9:43-47) and the horrible waterless, fiery chaos described in I Enoch 18:12-16; 19:1-2; 21:1-6. John distinguishes 2 such places: (*a*) the bottomless pit, the temporary prison of the fallen angels, the demons, the beast, the false prophet, and esp. Satan,

who is confined there for 1,000 years (11:7; 17:8; 20:1-3); and (*b*) "perdition" (17:8, 11) or the "lake of fire and brimstone," the final and unending place of punishment of all these and also of the men whose names are not written in the book of life (19:20; 20:10, 14-15). See further below on vss. 11-12.

9:3-6. Out of the smoke of the bottomless pit comes a swarm of **locusts** with **power** to torment **mankind.** Locusts are the 8th of the Egyptian plagues (Exod. 10:4-15), but these locusts are demonic rather than earthly (cf. Joel 1-2). They do no damage with their mouths, as do ordinary locusts. In fact they are expressly forbidden to touch **any green growth.** They have **stings** like a **scorpion,** and it is with these that they inflict **torture,** but a torture short of death. From this demonic torment the 144,000 who have the **seal of God upon their foreheads** (cf. 7:4-8) are protected. The limitation of the torture to **five months** was no doubt suggested by the fact that the natural locust is born in the spring and dies in the early autumn and thus lives for a period of *ca.* 5 months. Vs. 6 is a vivid description of the agony suffered by all exposed to the torture.

9:7-10. The seer expands his description of the locusts, drawing in part on material in Joel 1-2: they appear like war **horses** (cf. Joel 2:4); **crowns of gold** mark them as a conquering horde; their antennae give the appearance of **hair;** their **teeth** are like those of a lion (cf. Joel 1:6); their thoraxes suggest **iron breastplates;** and the loud rushing **noise** made by their **wings** is like that of **many chariots rushing into battle**—a comparison adopted directly from Joel 2:5.

9:11-12. The locusts' **king** is the ruler of the **bottomless pit** and the demonic powers incarcerated it it. The **Hebrew** name **Abaddon,** lit. "destruction," appears in the OT (e.g. Job 26:6; Ps. 88:11; Prov. 15:11) as a poetic designation of Sheol, the subterranean abode of the dead. **Apollyon,** lit. "destroyer," is the **Greek** equivalent. One of the symbols of the Greek god Apollo was the locust, and to him plagues and destruction were sometimes attributed. Those who see back of John's thought a symbolism derived ultimately from Persian Zoroastrian religion have identified Abaddon-Apollyon here with Ahriman (see below on 12:1-6), who after being cast out of heaven dwelt in the abyss as lord of all evil spirits, hurtful beasts, scorpions, and snakes. On vs. 12 see above on 8:13.

9:13-21. *Demonic Horses.* The blast of the 6th trumpet has as its consequence the release of a horde of demonic horses—a scene that appears to be a variant of the preceding plague of the 5th trumpet. The author uses the familiar imagery of the onslaught in the last days of a fierce host of **cavalry** (cf. e.g. Jer. 4:13; Ezek. 26:11) but transforms the horses into fiendish monsters, as he has already done with the locusts, and represents them as the instruments of God's wrath on the enemies of his people.

9:14*b*-15. The **Euphrates** was the easternmost limit of the Roman Empire, and fears were constant during the imperial era of an invasion by the dreaded Parthian cavalry across that river boundary. But the thought of a Parthian invasion is not uppermost in John's mind. The invasion is demonic, not natural. It is the monstrous horses that are the threat, not the horsemen. The **four angels . . . bound at the great river** are presumably other than the 4 who in 7:1-3 are represented as standing at the 4 corners of the earth and holding back the 4 devastating winds. John can vary and multiply comparable symbols. Though they play no part in what follows, the angels are evidently thought of as the leaders of the invading host of demonic horses, **held ready,** John says, **for the hour** when they should slay a **third of mankind.** It was a familiar doctrine in apocalyptic that God had fixed the precise time for every event, and John took over that determinism.

9:16-19. The vast number of 200,000,000 demonic horses is in accordance with John's use of hyperbole and the superlative. The brilliant armor of the **riders** is mentioned, but the stress is all on the fiendish horses. With **heads . . . like lions' heads** (cf. the locusts with **teeth like lions' teeth** of the preceding vision), they belch **fire and smoke and sulphur . . . from their mouths** and do harm also with their **tails,** which look **like serpents, with heads.** Probably the seer's own fancy is responsible for this imagery, though some have pointed to the representation on Greek vases and coins of the chimera, a fire-spouting monster whose fore part was a lion and whose hinder part was a serpent.

9:20-21. Despite the devastation of a 3rd of mankind outside the church by these plagues, **the rest . . . did not repent.** Though the punitive effect of the plagues is John's main concern, he holds also that they could have given men cause for repentance (cf. Joel 2:12-14). Those who might have done so, however, do not desist from the **immorality** of every description which, John holds, is the inevitable consequence of the worship of **demons and idols.** His ridicule of idolatry is based on Dan. 5:23.

10:1-11. *The Angel and the Little Scroll.* The first 6 trumpet visions following one another in rapid succession have ended. Before the 7th, as before the opening of the 7th seal (ch. 7), the author introduces another dramatic interlude to serve as a preparation and a prelude or overture for it. The seer has evidently changed his station from heaven (4:1) to earth, though he makes no reference to this shift of place. A **mighty angel**—possibly Gabriel is meant—descends **from heaven** (vs. 1) and the seer is addressed by a **voice from heaven** (vs. 4).

Much of John's vision is dependent on scenes from the opening chs. of Ezek. The angel comes **wrapped in a cloud** (cf. Ezek. 1:4), with a **rainbow** and **fire** (cf. Ezek. 1:26-28). He holds a **little scroll open in his hand** (cf. Ezek. 2:9-10). A **voice . . . from heaven** orders the seer to **take the scroll,** and the angel bids him **eat** it, warning that it will be **sweet as honey** in his **mouth** but **bitter** to his **stomach** (cf. Ezek. 3:2-3). After eating the scroll the seer is told to **prophesy about many peoples and nations and tongues and kings** (cf. Ezek. 3:1).

Other elements in John's vision are drawn from Dan. The angel has **legs like pillars of fire** (cf. Dan. 10:6). The angel raises his **right hand** and swears **by him who lives for ever and ever . . . that there should be no more delay** (cf. Dan. 12:6-7). The seer is commanded to **seal up** what he has heard (cf. Dan. 12:4, 9).

The **seven thunders** (vs. 4; cf. 8:5; 11:19; 16:18) may recall the 7-fold description of the voice of Yahweh in Ps. 29:3-9 as sounding like thunder and shaking both sea and land.

Virtually all the material in this scene, therefore, is borrowed from OT sources, but John interweaves and adapts it to his own dramatic and artistic purpose. The angel bestrides **sea** and **land** and cries with a **loud voice** because his message is addressed to the whole world. The words which John hears but is forbidden to **write** are a foreboding of judgments about to break with the blowing of the 7th trumpet. Then the **mystery of God,** i.e. God's whole purpose with respect to the world, will finally be accomplished. John's finding the little scroll with its undisclosed contents sweet in his mouth but bitter in his stomach means that the initial reception of the revelation brings joy but the later realization of its awful consequences brings grief and dismay.

11:1-14. *The 2 Heavenly Witnesses.* It is widely held that in this 2nd interlude John has adapted earlier Jewish apocalyptic material to his use and that this reworking of an older source is responsible for much of the difficulty in understanding his message. The reference to the temple in Jerusalem (vss. 1-2) indicates that the source was composed before the destruction of the city and the burning of the temple in 70.

11:1-2. This opening scene, in which a command is given to the seer to **measure the temple of God,** is modeled on Ezek. 40-43, though there the measurement was preparatory to the temple's restoration and rebuilding, whereas here its purpose is to protect those who worship in the temple. Probably the seer thinks of the incident as comparable to the sealing of the 144,000 (ch. 7). The church is to be guarded against the onslaught of demonic powers. The outer **court**—i.e. the Court of the Gentiles, to which non-Jews were admitted—and the **holy city** will be devastated **for forty-two months,** the conventional period of 3½ years that in Daniel and in this apocalypse limits the duration of the power of evil. As the Roman army under Titus trampled Jerusalem, so Satan through the agency of the Roman Empire holds sway over the world in which Christians are set.

11:3-4. The seer passes to the prophecy of the **two witnesses.** God will give them **power to prophesy** throughout that calamitous period—1,260 days equal 3½ years. They are first described with imagery adapted from Zech. 4:1-14, where **two olive trees,** apparently representing Zerubbabel and Joshua and symbolizing the channels through which God's power becomes effective, pour their oil into a single lampstand located between them. In John's use of the images both the olive trees and the **two lampstands** symbolize the witnesses.

11:5-6. John does not identify the witnesses by name, but this description of their activities makes clear to whom he is referring. Elijah is said to have called down **fire** on the messengers of King Ahaziah (II Kings 1:9-16) and Moses brought a plague of hail mixed with fire on the Egyptians (Exod. 9:23). The **power to shut the sky** and prevent rainfall was given to Elijah (I Kings 17:1). Though according to the OT the drought during Ahab's reign lasted for less than 3 years (I Kings 18:1), in the form of the tradition reflected here (cf. Luke 4:25; Jas. 5:17) the period was extended to 3½ years to conform to the conventional symbol for the duration of calamity.

The **power over the waters to turn them into blood** is that granted to Moses for the first plague afflicting the Egyptians (Exod. 7:20). Elijah ascended to heaven (II Kings 2:11) and according to Jewish tradition (Assumption of Moses) Moses too was taken up from the earth by physical levitation. Mal. 4:5-6 predicts the return of Elijah before the expected day of Yahweh, and this became the ground for a widely held belief that he would return as a forerunner of the Messiah (cf. Mark 6:15). In some quarters the prediction in Deut. 18:15 that God would raise up a prophet like Moses led to the belief that Moses also would return before the Messiah's advent. In the account of the Transfiguration (Mark 9:2-8 and parallels) the inner circle of the disciples sees Moses and Elijah standing with Christ on the holy mount.

11:7-10. The witnesses are secure from all attacks by enemies while they perform their mission, but they fall as martyrs when the **beast that ascends from the bottomless pit** overcomes and kills them. Though the relation of this beast to the 2 beasts of ch. 13 is unclear—perhaps it is meant to be the same as the 2nd beast, which rises from the earth (13:11-17)—it obviously shares their character as Antichrist (cf. I John 2:18), the enemy of God, Christ, and the Christians. The **dead bodies** of the prophets are left unburied for the symbolic period of **three days and a half,** the objects of rejoicing and derision on the part of non-Christians. Most interpreters conclude that Jerusalem is meant by the **great city which is allegorically called Sodom and Egypt** but some recent writers maintain that it means neither Jerusalem nor Rome but the great city of this world order in contrast to the coming heavenly and eternal one. It is in this world city that Jesus was crucified, Christians are persecuted, and Moses and Elijah in their reincarnation will be killed by the Antichrist.

11:11-14. The witnesses, now become martyrs, are restored to **life** and reascend **to heaven** in response to a heavenly voice that bids them **"Come up hither!"** A great earthquake destroys a **tenth of the city** and the **rest** of its inhabitants are filled with fear. They acknowledge the might of the **God of heaven** without, however, changing their ways. On vs. 14 see above on 8:13.

John has no expectation that the pagan world will be converted. Its only fate is destruction. The passage as a whole is intended to encourage readers with the thought that their martyrdom, like that of the witnesses, will be followed by God's vindication. Elijah and Moses in their reincarnation, like Jesus himself (cf. 1:5), are prototypes of the victorious martyr. This, rather than the more common understanding of the material as an assurance that the majority of the Jews in the last days will be converted to Christianity, is probably the right interpretation of what is one of the most difficult passages in the entire book and under any interpretation bristles with unresolved problems.

11:15-19. *Voices and Visions in Heaven.* The blast of the 7th trumpet, delayed by the interludes described in 10:1–11:14, is followed by an outburst of joy in heaven and responses to it in heaven and in the world of nature (vs. 19). There are similarities between this scene and those described in 4:8-11; 7:10-12. Here no particular class of the heavenly court is named as those who sing the hymn of praise. It proclaims that the **kingdom of the world,** i.e. the rule of Satan, has ended and given place to the eternal **kingdom of our Lord and of his Christ.** It declares in anticipation that God's sovereign rule over the world is to be completely established.

11:17-18. The anthem of praise with which the **twenty-four elders** respond is an expansion of the preceding. God has now taken the power that he permitted Satan to exercise, and the time has come to judge the **dead,** to recompense the **saints,** and to destroy the **destroyers of the earth**—viz. Rome, Satan, Antichrist, and the false prophet, whose destruction is portrayed in the chs. that follow.

11:19. When God's heavenly sanctuary is opened, John views the **ark of his covenant,** which disappeared at the destruction of the first temple, and which Jewish tradition held would reappear at the Messiah's coming. Terrible natural phenomena suggest the awful events still to happen.

D. The Dragon and the Lamb: Warfare and Victory (12:1–14:20)

12:1-6. *The Heavenly Mother and Her Child.* Various myths of the ancient world portrayed the escape of a divine child from a superhuman enemy at birth, and in this passage the author draws on some formulation of them. According to a Greek myth the goddess Leto, with child by Zeus, was pursued by the dragon Python. She was brought by Boreas to the sea and handed over to Poseidon, who gave her a place of refuge on an island. There she was safely delivered of the god Apollo. According to Persian mythology Ormazd, the supreme spirit of good, fought with Ahriman (see above on 9:11-12), the supreme power of evil, for possession of the "great royal Glory." Ahriman sent a dragon with 3 heads to capture it, but it fled to a lake and found refuge and nurture with a water spirit and thus foiled the dragon's purpose. According to Egyptian mythology Isis, the mother of the gods, was persecuted by a dragon but fled to an island, where she reared her child Horus. Horus later slew the dragon by his magic arts.

From some such source, no longer identifiable, the apocalyptist has edited and incorporated this account of a **male child** born of a **sun** goddess, persecuted by a 7-headed **dragon,** and miraculously taken up to the **throne** of God. The purpose of the narrative, of course, is to declare that all the devices of Satan to destroy the Christian Lord were foiled. No parallels between the gospel accounts of the birth of Jesus and this myth are to be noted or looked for. The myth is related as a **portent,** or sign, for the encouragement of Christians under persecution.

12:1-4*a*. The **woman** is not Mary but a sun goddess, with the **moon under her feet** and the 12 constellations of the zodiac as her **crown,** symbolizing her power over the destinies of mankind. The 7-headed **great red dragon** is the devil, or Satan (cf. vs. 9). The **ten horns** are a symbol of his power as prince of this world, and the detail is taken from a description of the one-headed beast of Dan. 7:7. The casting down of a **third of the stars of heaven** may be a reference to the fall of angels who are to assist Satan in his evil purposes.

12:4b-6. Satan wishes to destroy the child that is about to be born lest it should later destroy him, as Apollo destroyed Python and Horus destroyed the dragon of Egyptian mythology. But the Messiah is **caught up to God and to his throne.** In language adapted from Ps. 2:6 the Messiah is described as one destined to **rule all nations with a rod of iron.** The woman, described in vs. 17 as the church, the heavenly mother of all Christians, is protected and **nourished** in a **place prepared** for her for 1,260 days, the 3½ years that are symbolic of the period of calamity.

12:7-12. *Michael's Victory over the Dragon.* The preceding passage has described an incident **in heaven** (vss. 1, 3), not on earth. The present one gives a version of the conflict by which Satan was expelled from heaven. In Dan. 10:21 the archangel **Michael** is called the patron, or "prince," of Israel, and in Dan. 12:1 he is Israel's defender in the troubles of the last days. As Michael has **his angels,** so too has the **dragon,** for the name "angels" can be ascribed to both good and evil supernatural beings. The war between the 2 representatives of good and evil is not described; only its consequences are noted. Satan and his minions are not destroyed but **thrown down to the earth**—supporting the apocalyptic belief that this age is under Satan's control and is irretrievably evil and corrupt.

12:10-12. The expulsion of Satan assures his ultimate overthrow and calls forth an outburst of praise (cf. 7:14-17; 11:17-18) that celebrates the future triumph as already present. The singers are not identified. If they are angels, they describe faithful Christians on earth as **our brethren.** If they are martyrs, they refer in these words to their fellow servants of God on earth. The defeat of Satan in heaven is an assurance that the **kingdom of our God and . . . of his Christ** is at hand. This will be brought about by Christ's death and also by the faithfulness of the martyrs in preferring **death** to the disloyalty involved in worshiping the emperor. But the hymn has also an anticipation of foreboding. It bewails Satan's increased rage in the persecution of the faithful. **His time is short** both accounts for that rage and encourages those who suffer under it.

12:13-17. *The Dragon's Pursuit of the Woman.* Since John is using mythological material from some source and adapting it to his purpose, we cannot press his version of it for consistency. In vss. 1-6 the woman is **in heaven.** With this shift in scene she is on **earth** and the dragon, now too of course on earth, resumes his pursuit of her. In several respects this section parallels the earlier one, and some interpreters see in this an indication that John is using 2 parallel sources. Probably his wish to reiterate is enough to explain the similarities.

12:13-16. Again the woman escapes to the **wilderness** for safety, this time with the aid of **two wings of the great eagle,** and in this place of safety she is again **nourished** for the 3½ years that are the conventional symbol of the time of calamity.

Since the woman symbolizes the church, the true Israel, John may have in mind the words of God to the Israelites in the desert: "I bore you on eagles' wings and brought you to myself" (Exod. 19:4). The dragon, now also called the **serpent,** tries to inundate the woman with a flood of **water** spewed from its **mouth.** Some interpreters see in this a reflection of an Egyptian myth in which a personification of the Nile attempts to engulf the goddess Isis (see above on vss. 1-6) with a flood, from which she is saved by the earth, which swallows the water. Whatever its origin, the scene symbolizes the protection of the church, providentially saved from the onslaughts of Satan.

12:17. Foiled in his attempt on the church, the dragon now turns to the **rest of her offspring,** who are identified as the whole body of faithful Christians, those who hold fast to God's **commandments** and **bear testimony to Jesus.** The reading **And he stood** is found in the earliest papyrus manuscript (3rd cent.) and in what are usually regarded as the best of the parchment texts. On the strength of this reading it is the dragon who stands on the shore, there to summon the beast from the sea as his agent in the war to be carried on. Some editors prefer the reading "And I stood," referring to the seer, which they believe makes for a better connection with 13:1. Probably it was to make this easier transition that the reading was originally introduced into some Greek texts.

13:1-10. *The Beast from the Sea.* The beast of this passage clearly symbolizes the Roman Empire. The description of it is similar to that of the dragon in 12:3, but here the **horns** are mentioned before the **heads** and the **diadems** are on the horns. In Dan. 7:6 the 4 heads of the beast representing Persia symbolize Persian kings. Here the **seven heads** represent Roman emperors, as is explicitly stated in 17:10. The **blasphemous name** must refer to some divine title assumed by the emperors, possibly *divus,* "divine," or Augustus, lit. "reverend." The description in vss. 1-2 combines into one beast features of the 4 beasts of Dan. 7—the lion, the bear, the leopard, and the monster with 10 horns. It is implied that the beast rises from the sea at the summons of the dragon, i.e. Satan, who delegates **his power and . . . throne and . . . authority** to it. The hated Roman Empire is Satanic in origin.

13:3. The head that bears the marks of a **mortal wound** but has been **healed** probably reflects the myth that Nero did not actually commit suicide in 68 but took refuge in the E and would return at the head of Parthian kings for the destruction of Rome. At some point in early Christian tradition this expectation that Nero would return was combined with the idea that the Antichrist would rise up with demonic powers from the abyss to persecute the church. The non-Christian **world** is filled with **wonder** at this marvelous revivification of Nero.

13:4. This is a direct reference to the cult of emperor worship. Worship of the emperor was predicated on the claim that he was divine; John holds that this worship is actually directed to Satan, who has invested the **beast** with his **authority.** The non-Christian world, awed by the extent of the power and rule of the empire, is persuaded that it is invulnerable. The Christian community, however, would be assured that this embodiment of demonic might is shortly to be overthrown by the heavenly Christ.

13:5-10. As the author of Dan. spoke of the incarnation of evil in his time, Antiochus Epiphanes (Dan. 7:25), so this author speaks of the Roman incarnation of Satanic power: he will speak **haughty and blasphemous words** against God and **those who dwell in heaven** and will prevail for 3½ years, the period predicted in Dan. for Antiochus' supremacy. From the point of view of a resident of the Mediterranean world the Roman Empire could be thought of as embracing the whole earth—**every tribe and people and tongue and nation.** Since emperor worship was enforced on all but Jews, it could be said that **all who dwell on earth** would worship the deified Roman ruler. The only exceptions to the universality of Satan's sway through the emperor cult are the faithful Christians. Their names have been entered before the beginning of time in the heavenly register, the Lamb's **book of life.** As in the letters to the 7 churches (chs. 2-3) the significance of what has been said is to be impressed on all readers. The fatalistic refrain that follows is almost a paraphrase of Jer. 15:2. The passage ends with a summons to **endurance** and **faith,** the virtues that mark and support the martyr.

13:11-17. *The Beast from the Land.* A 2nd beast appears, this one from the **earth.** According to ancient tradition there were 2 monsters, Leviathan dwelling in the sea and Behemoth on the dry land. John may think of the beast from the land as the one already mentioned in 11:7, the beast who ascended from the bottomless pit to kill the 2 heavenly witnesses. He is called the false prophet in 16:13; 19:20; 20:10. He simulates the Christ but reveals himself to the discerning as Satanic, for his voice is like that of a **dragon** (cf. Matt. 7:15).

13:12. This 2nd beast represents the priesthood of the imperial cult. The priests use their delegated **authority** to enforce the worship of the emperor, **the first beast, whose mortal wound was healed.** Vs. 3 has spoken of the fatal wound of one of the heads of the beast, but here the reference is widened to apply to the beast itself, who is thus identified with Nero come back to life.

13:13-17. According to Mark 13:22; II Thess. 2:9 **great signs** were expected of the Antichrist. The special miracle in vs. 13 recalls that of Elijah (I Kings 18:38). The priests of the imperial cult command the non-Christian world to **make an image for the beast** and establish the fearful alternative of worship or death. To escape death all are required to bear a **mark** showing that they have rendered worship, and economic sanctions are imposed as a further lever of enforcement on all who do not exhibit the mark. During Trajan's reign, early in the 2nd cent., Pliny's correspondence shows that death was inflicted on those who refused to worship the emperor at the bidding of the imperial priesthood, and it may be assumed that such punishment was already in force in Domitian's reign.

13:18. *The Number of the Beast.* John now makes a cryptic identification of the first beast. His reference is apparent, he says, to those who possess the requisite **wisdom.** To interpreters who are no longer within John's frame of reference the meaning is not so clear. In fact any resolution of the enigma remains at best a controlled guess. Some think the explanation is that the thrice-repeated **six** is meant to symbolize the apotheosis of evil, since 6, falling just short of 7, the perfect number, might carry the sense of imperfection. More usually the number is regarded as an example of gematria, i.e. the practice of giving letters of a word or name their numerical equivalent—possible in either Hebrew or Greek, since both used the letters of their alphabets as numbers. The most attractive of the many solutions put forward is that the name is the Greek form Neron Caesar, which when transliterated in Hebrew characters adds up to 666. If the Latin spelling Nero is used, the sum in Hebrew transliteration is 616, which might account for the variant in some Greek mss. (see RSV footnote).

14:1-5. *The Bliss of the Redeemed in Heaven.* This scene, with its description of Christ and his followers, stands in dramatic contrast to the preceding. The **Lamb** is set over against the beast, and Christ's faithful with his name and that of his Father **on their foreheads** over against those who bear the beast's mark. The vision anticipates the end, when the faithful will receive their reward. The 144,000 are probably those already spoken of in 7:1-8 rather than a select class of God's people. **Mount Zion** was traditionally the site where God or his Messiah would summon the faithful Israelites (cf. Mic. 4:6-8). In this scene John probably thinks of it as located in heaven, though some interpreters believe the seer is envisaging the time when Christ will establish his millennial kingdom on earth.

14:2-5. A **voice from heaven** is heard, sounding like **many waters** and **loud thunder** and **harpers playing on their harps** (see above on 5:7-8). The singers of the **new song** are not identified. Probably John has an angelic chorus in mind rather than the redeemed, for he says that only they can **learn** the song. In vs. 4a the redeemed are described as celibates. Taken lit. this might distinguish them from the group of 7:1-8, but the meaning may be figurative—martyrs who have not yielded to idolatry (cf. e.g. vs. 8; 17:1-2). They **follow the Lamb wherever he goes.** They are described as **first fruits** because, like the first fruits of the harvest, they are wholly consecrated to God. Their virtues of truthfulness and chastity are emphasized.

14:6-20. *The Doom of Worshipers of the Beast.* The first of several angels announces that God's eternal purpose is about to be fulfilled, that **judgment** is at hand, and that God the Creator and God alone should be worshiped. A **second** angel follows, pronouncing doom over Rome: **Fallen, fallen is Babylon the great** (cf. Isa. 21:9). The rest of vs. 8 is based on the condemnation of Babylon in Jer. 51:7. **Her impure passion** refers to her idolatry.

14:9-11. In view of the coming judgment a **third** angel utters a warning of the terrible punishment that must fall on those who worship the beast. They will **drink the wine of God's wrath,** wine that is undiluted. Isa. 34:8-10, describing the punishment of Edom, may have been in John's mind when he wrote that the worshipers of the beast will be **tormented with fire and brimstone . . . and the smoke of their torment goes up for ever and ever.**

14:12-13. Vs. 12 repeats most of 13:10c, with

the additional description of the **saints as those who keep the commandments of God and the faith of Jesus.** The steadfastness to which the saints are summoned must involve martyrdom for many of them. With this in view the vision now brings assurance that martyrs who perish as a consequence of their loyalty to their faith during the interval before the final judgment are the objects of God's love and grace. The beatitude is declared by a **voice from heaven** and then echoed by the **Spirit**—the same Spirit who has warned and exhorted the readers of the 7 letters (chs. 2-3). Their martyrdom will bring surcease from trials and sufferings—no doubt **labors** refers to their activities as Christian witnesses—and their obedience and faith will be remembered at the last judgment. Here, as in 2:23; 20:12-13; 22:12, John stresses the importance of Christian "works" as a manifestation of loyalty and devotion.

14:14-16. The seer now returns to the impending doom of the worshipers of the beast. As in 1:13, the heavenly Christ at his 2nd advent is described as **one like a son of man**—the phrase borrowed from Dan. 7:13. The **golden crown** symbolizes his regal authority, and the **sharp sickle**—elsewhere the instrument of his wrath is a rod of iron or a sharp sword that projects from his mouth—fits the metaphor of the harvest that follows. In vss. 6-9 3 angels have proclaimed the imminence of the judgment. Now **another angel** issues an order to the heavenly Christ that the judgment should be executed. As in 6:9, heaven, God's dwelling place, is portrayed as a **temple.** The angel is thought of as God's messenger to the Messiah, and the command is not the angel's but God's. It is God alone who sets the time of judgment (cf. Matt. 24:36). The reaping of the harvest both here and in vss. 17-20 appears to be based on Joel 3:13.

14:17-20. Some interpreters hold that the harvest of vss. 15-16 is general, that it portrays the whole judgment as it affects both the righteous and the wicked, and thus Christ can be represented as God's emissary. This vintage harvest, on the other hand, pictures God's vengeance on the wicked, and an **angel** with a **sharp sickle** is made the divine agent of wrath. It is not clear that John intended such a distinction. More probably both are parallel representations of the same event, and in both the wicked are the objects of the judgment. If so, an angel fulfills the function here that was ascribed in vss. 15-16 to the heavenly Christ, and to him **another angel** conveys God's command to begin gathering the **vintage of the earth.** The angel who issues the order is described as one who **came out from the altar,** possibly the same angel who in 8:3 mingles the prayers of the saints with the incense on the golden altar before God's throne. That he has **power over fire** is perhaps an allusion to 8:5, where he is said to have filled the censer with fire from the altar and flung it on the earth. The symbolism of the judgment on the wicked as the treading of grapes in a **wine press** is probably derived from Isa. 63:1-6. No doubt **outside the city** means "outside Jerusalem," in whose vicinity apocalyptic writers often placed the final overthrow of God's enemies (cf. e.g. Ezek. 39:1-11; Dan. 11:45; Zech. 14:1-5). The lifeblood flowing from the wine press will make a

river of about 200 miles in length. If John intended symbolism by his use of 1,600, it is obscure. On **stadia** see "Measures and Money," pp. 1283-85.

E. The Seven Bowls (15:1-16:21)

15:1. *The Last Series of Plagues.* This vs. introduces still another sign or **portent,** viz. **seven angels with seven plagues**—the **seven bowls of the wrath of God** (16:1) that are to be poured on those who bear the mark of the beast. Probably John thinks of this series as the "third woe" announced in 11:14. It resembles the plagues of the 7 seals (6:1-8:1) and of the 7 trumpets (8:2-11:19) and, like the 2 earlier series of calamities, is a manifestation of the **wrath of God** on his enemies. This is the 3rd and last series of 7, but the final destruction of Rome (ch. 17) and the final judgment on the beast and the dragon (19:11-20:10) are still to follow. The **seven angels** no doubt are the traditional 7 archangels of late Jewish angelology (see above on 8:2-6).

15:2-16:1. *The Temple in Heaven.* The **sea of glass** has already been mentioned (4:6) as standing before God's throne in heaven. Here there is the added detail **mingled with fire.** The saints who have triumphed over the beast are pictured as standing by the shore of this heavenly sea, holding **harps of God,** i.e. for his worship (see above on 5:7-8).

15:3-4. The saints sing a hymn of praise to God for his mighty acts, anticipating the final victory and the execution of God's righteous judgments. **Song of Moses** may be an allusion to Exod. 15:1-18, where Moses and Israel sing a song of deliverance after having passed through the sea, but some interpreters think that John has in mind Deut. 32:1-43. It is true that the hymn of the saints has no resemblance to that in Exod. 15, but contacts with that in Deut. 32 are also few and remote. More important is its designation as the **song of the Lamb,** who has effected the deliverance of the Christian victors. Parallels between several phrases of the hymn and passages in various pss. can be noted: with **Great and wonderful are thy deeds** cf. Pss. 111:2; 139:14; with **Just and true are thy ways** cf. Pss. 145:17; 119:151; with vs. 4 cf. Ps. 86:9-10; also Jer. 10:7.

15:5-16:1. The phrase **temple of the tent of witness** presents difficulties, for there is no exact equivalent to the term elsewhere in biblical usage; but it would appear to be synonymous with the **temple** of vs. 6. From God's dwelling place issue the **seven angels with the seven plagues.** They are arrayed in **pure bright linen** and like the heavenly Christ (1:13) are **girded with golden girdles.** From **one of the four living creatures** they receive the **seven golden bowls full of the wrath of God,** bowls which are about to be poured out on God's enemies. The **smoke** that fills the temple is a symbol of God's **glory** and **power** (cf. Isa. 6:4). God's majesty is so awesome that **no one could enter the temple** until the series of calamities is complete. The **loud voice from the temple** that orders the **seven angels** to inflict the impending punishments is no doubt the voice of God, for the seer has just recorded that the temple is unapproachable for the duration of the 7 plagues.

16:2. *A Plague of Ulcers.* The first plague is like

the 6th Egyptian plague of boils (cf. Exod. 9:10). The victims of the **foul and evil sores** are the **men who bore the mark of the beast and worshiped its image.**

16:3. *The Sea Turned to Blood.* The 2nd plague turns the sea into coagulated blood, and all marine life is destroyed. Like the 2nd of the trumpet plagues (8:8-9), this calamity has been adapted from the first Egyptian plague (Exod. 7:14-25), by which the Nile was turned to blood and all fish in it were destroyed.

16:4-7. *Fresh Waters Turned to Blood.* The 3rd plague turns all drinking water into blood. This has a parallel in the 3rd trumpet plague (8:10-11), where a 3rd of the waters become wormwood and cause "many men" to perish. It corresponds also to part of the first Egyptian plague as described in Exod. 7:19, where all the waters of Egypt, including the water in household utensils, are turned to blood. As the 4 winds of the earth have their angels (7:1) and as fire has its angel (14:18), so there is also a guardian **angel of water.** In words that echo phrases from the song of 15:3-4 the water angel praises God's justice and holiness in this act of judgment: **It is their due!** In vs. 7 the **altar** is given the power of speech and reiterates the truth and justice of God's **judgments.** The prayer of the martyrs in 6:10 for vengeance on the pagan world has been answered.

16:8-9. *The Sun's Scorching Heat.* The 4th plague causes the sun to inflict a scorching heat on the wicked. Though they recognize that God is the source of this and the other plagues, worshipers of the beast do not **repent.** On the contrary **they cursed the name of God.**

16:10-11. *Darkness on the Kingdom of the Beast.* The 5th plague envelops the **throne of the beast,** i.e. Rome, and the whole Roman Empire in a pall of supernatural darkness. No doubt John has the 9th Egyptian plague in mind, the plague by which all of Egypt was covered with darkness for a period of 3 days (Exod. 10:21-29). Though grievously tortured by their **pain and sores** the worshipers of the beast persist in their blasphemy and impenitence. They **cursed the God of heaven . . . and did not repent of their deeds.**

16:12-16. *The Euphrates River Dried Up.* The 6th plague dries up the Euphrates to facilitate an invasion of the Roman Empire by Parthian **kings from the east.** The plague has some resemblance to the plague of the 6th trumpet (9:13-21), which releases a horde of demonic horses to cross the Euphrates and slay a 3rd of mankind. Both passages may draw on the widespread belief that a reincarnate Nero would lead the enemies of Rome in a final invasion that would devastate the city over which the hated emperor once exercised his tyrannical rule.

16:13-14. The vision here looks forward to the final battle of the **dragon,** the **beast,** and the **false prophet** and their allies with the heavenly Christ (19:11-21). Three demons in the form of **frogs** issue from their mouths. Like the beast out of the earth (13:13-14) they perform **signs** to deceive men. They gather the **kings of the whole world**—no longer just the Parthian kings—in preparation for the **battle on the great day of God the Almighty.**

16:15. This warning and beatitude interrupts the flow of the narrative but need not be a displacement or an interpolation. It is a dramatic declaration of the suddenness of the end and an assurance that those Christians who are ready for Christ's return, who are clothed with **garments** of immortality, are blessed.

16:16. The 3 demons assemble the forces of the Antichrist **at the place which is called in Hebrew Armageddon.** The site of the assembly is doubtless the one that John thinks of as the scene of the last great battle between the Antichrist and the Messiah, to be described in 19:11-21. Like the number 666 (13:18) the meaning of Armageddon is obscure. It may be a purely imaginary designation of the scene of the final battle. The name does not occur elsewhere in the Bible or in other earlier literature. It is usually interpreted as a compound of the Hebrew word *har,* "mountain," and the name Megiddo. Megiddo was a stronghold guarding the pass across Mt. Carmel into the Plain of Esdraelon, sometimes also known as the Plain of Megiddo (see color map 5). By the "waters of Megiddo" Barak and Deborah defeated Sisera and the Canaanites (Judg. 5:19-20). The difficulty with this explanation is that there is no evidence of a mountain named Megiddo and the supposition that the term refers to some mountain in the neighborhood of Megiddo is not wholly satisfactory.

16:17-21. *Storm and Earthquake.* The 7th and last of the bowl plagues affects the **air. A great voice** from the **temple** and the **throne**—the voice of God himself—declares **It is done!** The stage is set for the climactic events of the end. The **loud noises, peals of thunder, and a great earthquake** (vs. 18) have also accompanied the 7th trumpet plague (11:19), and the **hail** mentioned in the earlier passage is also brought into this picture (vs. 21). The earthquake of this plague is described as the most disastrous in the history of mankind. The city of Rome, referred to (vs. 19) as the **great city** and as **great Babylon,** is **split into three parts,** and the other cities of the empire are utterly destroyed. In this catastrophic manner God vents on his enemies the full **fury of his wrath,** and the predictions of 14:8, 10 are fulfilled. As a further consequence **every island fled away, and no mountains were to be found,** a detail that has already formed part of the disasters following the breaking of the 6th seal (6:14). Though enormous **hailstorms** fall on them **from heaven,** the enemies of God and of the church remain impenitent (cf. vss. 9, 11) and respond to the plague only with blasphemy.

F. THE FALL OF BABYLON (17:1–19:10)

17:1-18. *Judgment on Babylon.* An angel, **one of the seven angels who had the seven bowls,** offers to serve as the seer's guide and interpreter. An interpreting angel is a familiar figure in apocalypses (e.g. Dan., Enoch, Baruch), and in 1:1 John has avowed that his entire series of revelations was communicated to him by an angel. The **great harlot** on whom the judgment is to be meted out is clearly identified in vs. 18 as Rome. The city is described as a harlot because it has seduced mankind by its cult of emperor worship. Babylon was located on a network of canals that distributed the Euphrates through the surrounding country and is described by Jeremiah as "you who dwell by many waters" (Jer. 51:13). Since Babylon for this author is Rome, he transfers the description even though it is inept.

17:2-6. The rulers and inhabitants of the Roman world have participated in emperor worship and are described as drunk **with the wine** of that **fornication.** As in 1:10; 4:2; 21:10, John speaks of himself as **in the Spirit.** In a change of imagery the harlot is now viewed as seated **on a scarlet beast.** In earlier descriptions the adjective "scarlet" has not been applied to the beast, though the dragon in 12:3 is described as "red." The **blasphemous names** which cover the beast refer no doubt to the various titles of divinity assumed by the emperors (cf. 13:1). According to vss. 9-12 its **seven heads and ten horns** symbolize the 7 hills of Rome and 10 kings. In vs. 4 the harlot's garish garments and luxurious ornaments are described. The detail of the **golden cup** which she holds may be derived from Jer. 51:7 (see above on 14:6-20). It is **full of abominations and the impurities of her fornication,** i.e. the idolatry of the imperial cult. As the scarlet beast is covered with blasphemous names, so the scarlet woman bears a name **on her forehead.** It is mysterious and calls for interpretation. It is clear that **Babylon the great** means Rome, the city that for the Christian seer is the source and origin of the idolatrous worship of Caesar. In the course of propagating this worship Rome has inflicted martyrdom on Christians who have refused to deny their God. Consequently she can be described as **drunk with** their **blood.**

17:7-8. Now the angel volunteers an explanation of the phenomenon of the scarlet **woman** and the scarlet **beast.** He begins with the beast. Vs. 8*a* is almost certainly a reference to the expectation that Nero would reappear in a new incarnation. His rule over Rome, his death, his imprisonment in the abyss, his anticipated return, and his ultimate destruction form the content of the angel's reference. The vs. proceeds to refer to the astonishment of the non-Christian world at the reappearance of the feared and hated emperor.

17:9-11. The explanation becomes more detailed and at the same time, to the modern reader at least, more enigmatical. Not only are the **seven heads** the **seven hills** of Rome; they are also **seven kings.** If it were possible to solve the puzzles of vss. 10-12 we might be surer of the date of the book. From whom do we reckon the 7 kings? If we start from Augustus and omit the 3 emperors who ruled only a few months during the interim between Nero and Vespasian, the 6th would be Vespasian (69-79). Titus would then be the 7th, and an anticipated 8th emperor (Domitian) would be represented as a reincarnation of Nero. If this supposition is correct—and it is problematical at best—and if Rev. comes from the reign of Domitian, the only conclusion that the interpreter can draw is that John has worked material from the reign of Vespasian into his vision without making it entirely consistent. His own special contribution would then be the identification of Domitian with the reincarnate Nero (vs. 11).

17:12-14. There is also no certainty that we can any longer identify the **ten kings,** rulers who have not yet assumed regal authority and who the seer

declares are represented by the **ten horns** of the beast. They may refer to governors of the provinces of the empire. More probably John has Parthian satraps in mind, anticipated associates and allies. They will cede **their power and authority** to the Antichrist in his effort to destroy the heavenly Messiah. But their attempt will be frustrated. It will be the **Lamb** who will emerge victorious, aided as he will be by an army of Christian martyrs. The conquering Christ is given the title **Lord of lords and King of kings,** as in 19:16—but there in reverse order. Vs. 14 anticipates the final great battle to be described in 19:11-21.

17:15-18. As the angel proceeds with his interpretation, John is told that the **waters** on which the **harlot** is **seated** represent the **dwellers on earth** (vs. 2) who have paid Rome homage and worship and who have been described as drunk with the wine of her fornication. Before the final battle against the Lamb, the Antichrist and his associates will turn on the harlot and utterly destroy her. Here again the seer thinks of a reincarnate Nero, aided by his Parthian allies, as ravaging the city of Rome. In vs. 17 the angel asserts that in inflicting this destruction Nero and the kings from the E are actually carrying out God's purpose. The ch. concludes with a clear identification of the great harlot of the vision as the city of Rome.

18:1-24. *Dirge over Babylon.* John views **another angel**—"another" in contrast to that of ch. 17—who descends **from heaven** and lights all the **earth** with **his splendor.** With a **mighty voice** he sings a dirge over the city of Rome as though it had already been destroyed. The song begins with the words already used in 14:8, **Fallen, fallen is Babylon the great!** which echo the taunt of Isa. 21:9. The language with which the city's desolation is portrayed in vs. 2 recalls Jer. 50:39. In vs. 3 the reasons for Rome's ruin are briefly stated. The city has seduced the peoples of the empire with the worship of the emperor, and all the rulers of the world over which she has imposed her sovereignty have participated in the cult. Furthermore her demand for luxuries has enriched the **merchants of the earth,** who thereby shared in her **wantonness.**

18:4-5. Vss. 4-8 are represented as the utterance of **another voice from heaven.** No doubt God himself is thought of as the speaker, since what is said is directed to **my people.** Christians are bidden to forsake the city of Rome lest they be tainted by **her sins** and become involved in her punishment. The enormity of the city's sins is stressed as well as the fact that her punishment is to be a divine visitation.

18:6-7*b*. The law of revenge is again enunciated. Rome's punishments are to be in retaliation for her treatment of Christians, a repayment that is to be **double for her deeds.** A draught that is twice as deadly as that which she has prepared for others is to be made ready for her. Her torment and grief will correspond to her impious pride and luxury. In her confidence and arrogance she cannot foresee the doom that awaits her.

18:7*c*-8. Vs. 7*cd* appears to be based on Isa. 47:8-9, which is directed against Babylon. The plagues that are to be visited on Rome will come suddenly, catastrophically, **in a single day,** and will include **pestilence and mourning and famine** and devastation **with fire.** All these judgments are inescapable, for they are the work of the **Lord God.**

18:9-10. Here the **kings of the earth** who have participated in the cult of emperor worship and have shared Rome's luxury utter their dirge over the devastated city, much as the princes of the sea in Ezek. 26:16-17 come down from their thrones and utter their lamentation over Tyre. In a single hour God's judgment has been visited on **Babylon** (Rome), that **great** and **mighty city.**

18:11-17a. The **merchants of the earth** are pictured as joining in the lamentation, for with Rome's destruction their trade has come to an end. The catalog of merchandise imported by Rome in vss. 12-13 is based on the more detailed and elaborate list of the world's trade with Tyre in Ezek. 27:5-24. Rome's imports include the necessities of life but also feature luxuries of the most varied kind, as well as **slaves.** The couplet in vs. 14 is presumably the utterance of the merchants. The luxuries in which Rome delighted are now lost to it forever. The lamentation of the merchants is phrased in vss. 16-17a. Rome's vast and spectacular **wealth** has been destroyed in a single hour.

18:17b-20. Vss. 17b-19 constitute the lament of the mariners and all who do business **on the sea.** In a dirge parallel to those of the kings and of the merchants, the mariners bewail the sudden destruction of great Rome. John has drawn here from Ezek. 27:25-34, where seafarers lament the destruction of Tyre. Vs. 20 is punctuated in the RSV as belonging to the mariners' lament, but it can hardly be so interpreted. It is probably the seer himself who calls on **heaven** and its company of Christian martyrs to rejoice over the **judgment** that God has executed on the pagan and persecuting city of Rome.

18:21-24. This is still another dirge. By a symbolic act a **mighty angel** predicts the destruction of Rome and accompanies his prediction with a song. Both the symbolism of a great **stone** hurled **into the sea** and the content of vs. 21bc are suggested by Jer. 51:63-64. OT phrases are also adapted and built into much of the rest of the song; e.g. with vs. 22ab cf. Ezek. 26:13; with vss. 22e-23d cf. Jer. 25:10. With all his borrowing, however, John has woven his material into a structure that is poetic in its own right. The song ends (vss. 23e-24) with 3 reasons (cf. vs. 3) why Rome has been visited with destruction: (a) the power of her **merchants;** (b) the deception she has imposed on **all nations** by her **sorcery,** probably meaning the propagation of the imperial cult; and (c) the martyrdom she has inflicted on Christians.

19:1-10. *Jubilation over Babylon's Fall.* The scene shifts from earth to **heaven** and a vast heavenly chorus sings a song that celebrates God's justice in destroying Rome and avenging the martyrdom of faithful Christians. The song has some similarities to that of Moses and the Lamb in 15:3-4 but is esp. reminiscent of the hymns in ch. 5—antiphonal responses, the higher and lower orders of heavenly beings, the prostration before God's throne of the 24 elders and the 4 living creatures, and their response to the chorus. **Hallelujah** is a Hebrew doxology that means "Praise Yahweh!" It occurs often in the Pss. (e.g. 111-113, 146-150), but in the NT only in this ch. With vs. 1b cf. 12:10; with vs. 2a cf. 16:7; with vs. 2bc cf. 17:1-6.

19:3-4. Vs. 3 is another brief song of praise. Its one line is a virtual quotation from the description of the burning of Tyre in Isa. 34:10. In vs. 4 the **twenty-four elders** and the **four living creatures,** last mentioned in 14:3, are brought again—and for the last time—into the author's vision. They prostrate themselves and worship before God's heavenly **throne** (cf. 4:10; 5:8) and respond to the chorus of the heavenly host with **Amen. Hallelujah!** (cf. 5:14).

19:5. The **voice** that comes **from the throne** can scarcely be the voice of God, for the doxology it speaks refers to **our God** and **his servants.** Whether the seer thinks of the singer as one of the living creatures or as the Lamb is uncertain. **Praise our God** is a translation of the Hebrew "Hallelujah." The song is a combination of Pss. 134:1; 115:13.

19:6. The fourth song to begin with "Hallelujah" or its Greek translation is now introduced. The vast **multitude** that sings the song is not identified but is presumably an angelic throng. The description of their singing is reminiscent of that applied to the angelic chorus in 14:2. The opening line of the hymn in the 18th cent. became the inspiration of Handel's "Hallelujah Chorus." It recalls the words of the 24 elders in 11:17. In both passages the celebration of God's victory and of the inauguration of his kingdom is anticipatory.

19:7-8. The description of the new relationship between God and his people as a **marriage** is an occasional image in the OT (cf. e.g. Isa. 54:1-6; Jer. 31:32; Ezek. 16:8), and the image is also applied to Christ and his church in the NT (cf. e.g. Mark 2:19; Matt. 25:1-10; II Cor. 11:2; Eph. 5:22-32). The entrance of God into his eternal reign and the marriage of Christ and the church are parallel ways of expressing the same grounds for joy and exultation. In vs. 8b the seer explains that the **fine linen** with which the church is clothed is the **righteous deeds of the saints.**

19:9. The opening words of this vs. read lit.: "And he said." No doubt the RSV translators are correct in regarding this as a reference to the "interpreting angel" of ch. 17. He bids the seer write a blessing on **those who are invited to the marriage supper of the Lamb** and bears testimony to the truth of the beatitude. It was a familiar idea in late Jewish literature that the messianic age would be inaugurated with a banquet (cf. 3:20; Matt. 22:1-14; 25:1-13).

19:10. The angel rebukes the seer when he is about to pay him homage. Worship belongs to God alone. Perhaps, as some interpreters hold, this vs. and the comparable passage in 22:8-9 are John's protest against a tendency in Asia Minor to angel worship (cf. Col. 2:18). The meaning of **For the testimony of Jesus is the spirit of prophecy** is obscure. It may be a reference to the seer's experience of being "in the Spirit" as he is called and fulfills his mission.

G. The Coming of Christ to Culminate God's Purposes (19:11–22:5)

19:11-21. *Christ's Triumphant Appearance.* In this great passage the seer comes at last to the event that has frequently been anticipated—esp. in the harvest and the vintage (14:14-20), the battle of Armageddon (16:12-16), and the conflict of the beast and his allies with the Lamb and his army of martyrs (17:12-14). It is an account of the last great battle between the Christ and the Antichrist, of the victory of the former and of the overthrow of the latter. Once again, as in 4:1; 11:19; 15:5, John views **heaven opened.** The heavenly Christ is seen seated on a **white horse,** the color symbolizing his anticipated victory (cf. 6:2). As in 3:14, he is described as **Faithful and True.** John's words about Christ's righteous judgment echo Isaiah's description of the Messiah in Isa. 11:3-5.

19:12-13. Repeating a phrase already used in 1:14; 2:18, John describes Christ's **eyes** as **like a flame of fire.** As **King of kings and Lord of lords** he is crowned with **many diadems**—cf. the dragon (12:3) with 7 diadems and the beast (13:1) with 10. The **name** unknown to all but the heavenly Christ is obscure (cf. 2:17; 3:12; 14:1). Presumably it is other than the 3 listed in this paragraph (vss. 11, 13, 16). Some interpreters hold that the author has the name Jesus in mind (cf. Phil. 2:10), though it is difficult to think of this as a "secret" name. The **blood** with which his **robe** is drenched (cf. Isa. 63:1) probably is that of his enemies slain in battle. When John gives the heavenly Christ the title **The Word of God** he indicates familiarity with the concept in the prologue to the Gospel of John but reveals no understanding of the religious and philosophical background of the "Logos" idea.

19:14-16. The heavenly hosts that follow the heavenly Christ are probably not angels but Christian martyrs (cf. 17:14). Their **white horses** symbolize the victory they are to gain. The description in vs. 15 is compiled from earlier statements in 1:16; 12:5. The picture of Christ's coming victory as the treading of the **wine press** of God's **wrath** is repeated from 14:19-20. The title **King of kings and Lord of lords** has already appeared in reverse order (17:14).

19:17-21. The course and outcome of the climactic battle are now briefly described. Carrion **birds** are summoned to gorge themselves on the bodies of those to be slain, much as the prophet Ezekiel is bidden by God to summon the birds and the beasts to feed on the bodies of Gog and those who are to be killed with him (Ezek. 39:4, 20). The **great supper of God** stands in gruesome contrast to the marriage feast of the Lamb (vs. 9). The enemies of Christ and of the martyrs are enumerated as **the beast and the kings of the earth with their armies** (vs. 19). The beast, i.e. the satanic Roman empire (cf. 13:1-8), and the **false prophet,** evidently to be identified with the 2nd beast of 13:11-17, symbolizing the priesthood of the imperial cult, will be taken prisoners and hurled alive into the place of everlasting punishment, the **lake of fire that burns with brimstone** (see above on 9:1-12). Their followers will be **slain by the sword** issuing from the mouth of the heavenly Christ and carrion birds will gorge themselves on **their flesh.**

20:1-10. *The Millennial Reign.* It has been evident that God's judgments in this book are frequently carried out by some representative of the angelic host. The unnamed **angel** of this vision holds the **key of the bottomless pit** and carries a **great chain.** Satan, variously described as the **dragon,** the an-

cient serpent, and the **Devil,** is bound, thrown into the pit, and confined in this abyss for a **thousand years.** His power to deceive mankind is thus terminated, though the warning is added that, at the end of the millennium, he is to be **loosed for a little while.**

20:4-6. With the casting of the 2 beasts into the brimstone lake and the imprisonment of Satan, the power behind them, the stage is now set for the 1,000-year reign of Christ. The company of Christian martyrs is raised from the dead to share this reign **with Christ.** Since the **rest of the dead**—both the righteous and the unrighteous—are not to be raised until after the millennium, the raising of this select group of martyrs can be described as the **first resurrection.** Those who share in it are declared **blessed and holy.** Their millennial rule with Christ is a foretaste of their eternal felicity, for they will not die at the end of that era.

The idea of an interim messianic age is not original with John. Among other Jewish writings it appears in II Esdras 7:26-30, where the Messiah's reign is said to last for 400 years, and in II Baruch 39-40. In I Cor. 15:23-28 Paul seems to presuppose something similar. The most probable suggestion is that it was an attempt to combine 2 basically disparate conceptions. The prophets thought of a Messiah who would exercise his rule over a purified remnant of Israel on earth. The apocalyptists despaired of any such hope; the present age seemed irredeemably evil and must give way in dramatic fashion to the new and eternal age of God's rule. The doctrine of the interim messianic rule preceding the eternal kingdom preserves the prophetic hope within the framework of the apocalyptic conception.

20:7-10. The last great conflict between Satan and Christ and the final commitment of Satan to the place of eternal punishment are now related. With the end of the millennial age Satan is released from imprisonment. He gathers a vast army of followers from all parts of the earth for a final assault. **Gog and Magog** are personifications of Satan's hosts based on various references in Ezek. 38-39. The assault is made on Jerusalem, which is clearly regarded as the encampment of Christ and his martyrs. The destruction of Satan's army in the end is the work of God himself. The devil is then cast into the **lake of fire and brimstone** (see above on 9:1-12), to be tortured forever with the **beast** and the **false prophet,** who have preceded him to that place of torment (cf. 19:20). After all the plagues that had been inflicted on the enemies of God and his people, on Satan, on the Roman Empire, and on the priesthood of the imperial cult, those enemies are finally and eternally eliminated.

20:11-15. *The Last Judgment.* God alone is the judge at the Last Assize. He sits on a **great white throne,** emblematic of his power and purity. All but the martyrs, who have been raised in the first resurrection (cf. ch. 7), all dead, both just and wicked, stand before the Judge. They are judged from the heavenly records that have been kept, the **book of life** for the faithful (cf. 3:5) and other **books** for the wicked and idolatrous. Their recorded works are the basis of their acceptance or rejection. A general resurrection is presupposed in vs. 12 but not actually mentioned until vs. 13. The bodies of those who have been drowned are given up by the **sea** —its continued existence when all other creation has passed away is an inconsistent note in the account—and the bodies of those who have died in other ways are yielded by **Death and Hades** (see above on 1:17-18). All whose names are not inscribed in the **book of life** are committed to the **lake of fire** (cf. 19:20; 20:10; see above on 9:1-12), and this for them can be described as the **second death.** Such a description, however, seems hardly appropriate when referred to the fate of Death and Hades, who also are cast into the same place of fiery torment.

21:1-8. The New Heaven and New Earth. The seer views a new creation. All that God made in the beginning is removed. With the coming of a new heaven and a new earth John adds that the **sea was no more.** This may be a reflection of Jewish awe and dread before the mysteries and dangers of the vast deep. The **new Jerusalem** descends and is personified as a **bride** made ready for Christ (cf. 19:7-9). It is to be the eternal dwelling place of the church, the redeemed community. **God himself** will dwell with men, will comfort them, will support them. Grief, pain, and death **shall be no more.** All this belonged to the former dispensation and has no place in the new. God will **wipe away every tear from their eyes** (cf. 7:17c; Isa. 25:8).

21:5-7. God reiterates his intention to **make all things new** and affirms the trustworthiness and truth of his assurance—probably the affirmation relates also to the whole book. **It is done!** God's words have come to pass. His purposes have been accomplished. God speaks of himself as **the Alpha and the Omega,** as in 1:8, but now adds that this title, the first and last letters of the Greek alphabet, means that he is **the beginning and the end** (cf. 22:13). In 7:17 the martyrs have been assured that the Lamb would "guide them to springs of living water." In vs. 6b (cf. 22:17b) the promise is repeated **to the thirsty,** i.e. to those who yearn for communion with God, with the added assurance that the life-giving **water** will be provided **without price** (cf. Isa. 55:1). In vs. 7 the promise is articulated in still another form. **He who conquers,** a title that the seer has applied to Christian martyrs in the concluding sections of the letters to the 7 churches (chs. 2-3), will be given the status of God's **son**—a relationship that Paul declares (Rom. 8:17; Gal. 4:7) is already the possession of the Christian as a result of the work of the Holy Spirit.

21:8. The lot of the wicked is contrasted with that of Christian martyrs. Variously described as apostates, persecutors of the church, and adherents of the cult of emperor worship, these followers of Satan are to suffer everlasting punishment (see above on 20:11-15).

21:9-22:5. The Heavenly Jerusalem. With images drawn in large part from Ezek., John describes the new Jerusalem, already existing in its perfection and splendor in heaven and ready to descend on the new earth. The seer's guide, though reintroduced, is presumably the same angel who has been his interpreter since 17:1. The vision has been anticipated in vs. 2.

21:10-11. Vss. 10-17 are based mainly on Ezekiel's vision of the new temple in Ezek. 40-48. As Ezekiel in a state of ecstasy was set on a high mountain that he might see the new temple of the restored community (Ezek. 40:2), so this seer is borne **in the Spirit** to a lofty eminence whence he can view the descent of the heavenly city. The new Jerusalem has the **glory of God** (cf. Ezek. 43:5); God's presence manifests itself in an effulgence of marvelous light, comparable in its brightness and clarity to that emitted by a precious **jewel.**

21:12-14. The picture of a walled city **with twelve gates,** 3 on each of its 4 sides, each inscribed with the name of one of the **twelve tribes of the sons of Israel,** is taken over directly from Ezek. 48:31-34, to which John adds the detail of the **twelve** guardian **angels.** Here, as in 7:1-8, the 12 tribes symbolize the whole company of Christian martyrs, the new Israel which is assured access to the heavenly city. On the 12 **foundations** to the city's wall, each bearing the name of one of the **twelve apostles,** cf. Eph. 2:19-20; also Matt. 16:18; I Pet. 2:5.

21:15-17. The heavenly city is described as a vast cube, each side measuring **twelve** times a **thousand stadia,** ca. 1,500 miles. The imagery of measurement, including the detail of the angel with a **measuring rod,** was suggested by the measurement of the temple in Ezek. 40-42. **A hundred and forty-four cubits** (12 times 12, ca. 216 feet; see table, p. 1285) almost certainly refers to the thickness of the wall (cf. Ezek. 40:5; 42:20), since a wall 216 feet high would be out of proportion to a city 1,500 miles high. **A man's measure, that is, an angel's** probably means that angelic standards of measurement are the same as those employed by men.

21:18-21. The precious materials of which the city is constructed are now named. The **wall** is made of **jasper,** the **city** of translucent **gold,** the **foundations of the wall** of 12 different precious stones, the **twelve gates** of twelve **pearls,** and the **street** of gold. For this description John draws on the account of the ornamentation of Aaron's breastplate in Exod. 28:17-21; 39:10-14, and perhaps also on the list in Ezek. 28:13 of the jewels that adorned the dress of the king of Tyre. The identifications of **agate,** of **onyx,** and of **carnelian** are doubtful.

21:22-27. In earlier passages John has anticipated a **temple** in the heavenly city (cf. 3:12; 7:15). Now, however, he states that the city will have no temple, for the presence of **the Lord God the Almighty and the Lamb** will make any other sanctuary superfluous. He adds that their **glory** will also make all other sources of illumination unnecessary, whether they be **sun or moon** or **lamp.** The **nations** of the earth will pay God homage (cf. Isa. 60:3), entering by **gates** that are always open (cf. Isa. 60:11). The continued existence of the Gentile nations after the establishment of the new era of God's rule was presupposed by the author from whom John was borrowing, and his use of this source material without adaptation creates an inconsistency. According to 19:21; 20:7-10; 20:12-15 none but faithful Christians will survive the events of the last days and the final judgment. But John often did not exert himself to remove inconsistencies. With vs. 27 cf. 22:14-15. According to vs. 8 those who practice **abomination or falsehood** cannot enter the city because they are in the lake of fire. **Only those who are written in the Lamb's book of life** (cf. 3:5; 13:8; 17:8; 20:12, 15) will share in the new age of God's rule.

22:1-2. For the **river . . . of life** and the **tree of life** in the new Jerusalem the river that flowed out of the garden of Eden (Gen. 2:10) and Eden's tree of life (Gen. 2:9) are no doubt the ultimate source. But the immediate source is Ezek. 47:1-12, where a river, issuing from under the temple and with fruit trees on both banks, flows to make the waters of the Dead Sea fresh. John's river of life flows **from the throne of God and of the Lamb.** His tree of life is used collectively, for like Ezekiel's trees it can be described as on **either side of the river.** Also like Ezekiel's trees it bears **fruit each month** and its **leaves** are **for the healing of the nations.** Probably **twelve kinds of fruit** is John's interpretation of Ezekiel's "fresh fruit every month" and means 12 different kinds in succession rather than at the same time. Since Ezekiel speaks of the fruit as "for food," it is probable that John also thinks of it as nourishment for the dwellers in the heavenly city. The reference to the nations appears to repeat the inconsistency of 21:27.

22:3-5. No person or thing will be permitted in the city that would desecrate it. **The throne of God and of the Lamb** will be there, and God's **servants** will **worship him** and **see his face,** i.e. experience his immediate presence. They will bear **his name . . . on their foreheads** (cf. 3:12; 14:1). With vs. 5 cf. 21:23, 25*b*. The prophecy that the Lord God himself will illuminate the saints in the new age and that they will **reign** with God and his Christ **for ever and ever** marks the climax of the visions and brings them to an end.

IV. Epilogue (22:6-21)

22:6-7. The speaker in vs. 6 is presumably the interpreting angel of 17:1 and of the preceding section. He reiterates the assurance of 21:5*b* that **these words,** i.e. the revelation vouchsafed to John, **are trustworthy and true.** With vs. 6*b* cf. 1:1. **God** is the source, an **angel** is the medium, and faithful Christians are the recipients of a revelation that pertains to the immediate future. The speaker in vs. 7, who stresses the imminence of his advent, is almost certainly Jesus Christ himself. Perhaps some indication of a change of speaker has been lost in transmission, or possibly John intended for vs. 6 to be understood as spoken by Christ also. The beatitude in vs. 7*b* reiterates 1:3*b* and is intended to underscore the seer's authority.

22:8-9. The author once more identifies himself as a certain **John,** as in 1:9. Clearly he was well known to the book's first readers. As in 19:10 he is reproved for attempting to worship his angelic mentor. Only **God** is to be worshiped.

22:10-11. The angel is still the speaker and bids the seer: **Do not seal up the words of the prophecy.** The revelation applies to the immediate future. The command reverses the words of Dan. 8:26; 12:4, 9, where Daniel is ordered to keep his book hidden until the distant "time of the end." Vs. 11 is reminiscent of Dan. 12:10. While it is hopeless to look for any change in the wicked (cf. 2:21; 9:20; 16:9, 11), the **righteous** can be exhorted to remain steadfast.

22:12-13. Jesus Christ is again the speaker. Once more (cf. vs. 7*a*) he stresses the nearness of the end and the certainty of reward and punishment. In vs. 13 he applies to himself the titles that God has used of himself in 21:6, with an additional designation, **the first and the last,** which he has used of himself in 1:17 (cf. 2:8). In this book God and Christ tend to merge.

22:14-15. This final beatitude pronounces a blessing on the Christian martyrs. They will be allowed to eat of the **tree of life** and will be granted entrance into the **city.** According to some Greek texts we should read "do his commandments" instead of **wash their robes.** With the former cf. 12:17*b;* 14:13*b;* with the latter cf. 3:4; 7:14. According to 21:8 the wicked have been consigned to the lake of fire, but in vs. 15 John appears to forget this and picture them as debarred from the city's gates. Once more we should remind ourselves not to demand too great an interest in consistency from an apocalyptic seer.

22:16. Christ is once more the speaker and rephrases the assurance of vs. 6 (cf. 1:1). He identifies himself as the **offspring of David** (cf. 5:5) and the **bright morning star**—anticipated in 2:28, where it refers to the gift to be granted to the martyrs of Thyatira and appears to symbolize immortality.

22:17. The **Spirit,** speaking through the seer, and the church, designated as the **Bride** (cf. 19:7), join in a prayer for the speedy advent of Christ; and those who hear the prayer read in Christian assemblies are invited to join in it also. Those who are spiritually athirst are summoned to partake of the gift of the **water of life** promised them in 21:6.

22:18-19. The speaker is probably the author. His solemn warning against any changes by addition or omission may be modeled on Deut. 4:2; 12:32.

22:20-21. Christ's assurance of vss. 7*a,* 12*a* that he is **coming soon** is repeated, but this time in a quotation from him rather than directly. **Amen,** lit. "so be it," is part of the seer's response to Christ's promise of his speedy advent. **Come, Lord Jesus** translates a Greek ejaculation that Paul quotes in its original Aramaic form, Maranatha (I Cor. 16:22). Vs. 21 (cf. I Cor. 16:23-24) provides the concluding epistolary benediction that was missing from the 7 letters of chs. 2-3 and gives an epistolary form to the whole book.

GENERAL ARTICLES

THE HISTORY
OF BIBLICAL INTERPRETATION

GEORGE W. ANDERSON

I. THE NECESSITY AND NATURE OF INTERPRETATION

Any great work of literature needs to be interpreted, even to the author's contemporaries. The need is all the greater when the reader belongs to an age, a country, and a cultural tradition different from those in which the work originated. The problems of interpretation are accentuated when the text is fragmentary or composite, and when it has to be translated from a language other than that of the reader. The attempt to determine the date, origin, background, and literary character of a document establishes limits within which the task of interpretation may properly be carried out.

The attempt to translate the document into a language other than the original is in some measure an interpretation of it. In that initial stage of interpretation the sense which was originally expressed in one language is rendered into another. It may be followed by a further stage in which the meaning of the text is apprehended, analyzed, and re-presented in such a way that obscurities which might have baffled the reader are explained and his attention is drawn to elements in its content of which he might otherwise have been unaware. When the text is a religious one, the unfolding of the meaning will normally lead to its application to the life of the individual reader and the community.

In the interpretation of the Bible 2 other factors must be reckoned with: (*a*) The Bible is neither a single document nor a literary anthology but a collection of writings which have been produced, assembled, and transmitted within the community life of ancient Israel, Judaism, and the Christian church. Within the life of the community the collection speaks with authority; it constitutes a canon (see "The Making of the OT Canon," pp. 1209-15; "The Making of the NT Canon," pp. 1216-24). The canonical status of the biblical writings has profoundly affected their interpretation. They are thought of as having a special relation to each other, as forming a unity. The way this relation and unity is understood influences their interpretation. (*b*) Though fashions and methods have changed over the cents., the interpreter who himself participates in the life of the religious community can hardly avoid being influenced in some measure by traditional interpretations. It is not simply that there is a history of interpretation of the Bible—as there is of any great literary classic—so that the interpreter may learn from both the discernment and the errors of his predecessors. Its interpretation has been an integral part of the continuing life of the religious community. The sense in which earlier generations understood particular passages has been transmitted in the language of liturgy and sacred song and in the symbolism of sacred art, which continue to influence all who share this devotional heritage.

II. INTERPRETATION WITHIN THE BIBLE

Within the Bible itself there is the recognition of the need for interpretation and the attempt to supply it.

In the OT, prophecies from earlier times are interpreted afresh (e.g. Dan. 9:2). It is also recognized that certain communications of divine truth, such as dreams, need interpretation if they are to be rightly understood (e.g. Gen. 40; 41; Dan. 2; 5). Particularly within the prophetic records there are instances of interpretation which is direct and of immediate application—as when Nathan interprets his parable about the rich man's theft of the poor man's ewe lamb, saying bluntly, "You are the man" (II Sam. 12:7), or when Isaiah unfolds and drives home the meaning of the Song of the Vineyard as an indictment of Israel's unrighteousness (Isa. 5:7).

In the NT too it is recognized that religious teaching may need to be interpreted. Some of the parables of Jesus are supplied with interpretative comment or application, e.g. the parable of the sower (Mark 4:13-20; Matt. 13:18-23; Luke 8:11-15); and it is evident that the Pauline writings were felt to call for elucidation (e.g. II Pet. 3:15-16). Running throughout the NT are varied yet interwoven strands of interpretation of the OT. Its authority is both recognized and qualified. It is seen both as pointing to the meaning of the life, death, and resurrection of Jesus and as being itself illumined by them.

Jesus himself presupposed and reaffirmed the validity and enduring worth of OT teaching (e.g. Mark 10:17-22; Matt. 19:16-22; Luke 18:18-23). He set aside or treated as of only temporary application some elements in it (e.g. Mark 10:2-9; Matt. 19:3-9), and he challenged the views of the Pharisees and scribes by his own interpretation of particular passages (e.g. Mark 2:23-28; Matt. 12:1-8; Luke 6:1-5; Mark 12:35-37; Matt. 22:41-46; Luke 20:41-44). But he also indicated in various ways during his earthly ministry that his own coming and work were the fulfillment of OT prophecy (e.g. Mark 1:15; Luke

4:16-21; Matt. 11:4-5; Luke 7:22), and after his resurrection he affirmed that the OT foreshadowed and illumined his death and resurrection (Luke 24:25-27, 44-47).

This thought of the fulfillment of prophecy in the person and work of Jesus is basic to Paul's understanding of the OT (e.g. Rom. 1:1-4; I Cor. 15:3-4; II Cor. 1:20). Even when he is emphasizing the newness of the gospel he bases his arguments on the OT and draws his illustrations from it (e.g. Rom. 4; 9–11). He asserts that its essential meaning is opened up to Christians but unconverted Jews fail to discern it (II Cor. 3:14-18). Yet his own interpretation of some passages recalls the exegetical methods of the rabbis in its emphasis on verbal minutiae (e.g. Gal. 3:16). In contrast with such literalism he can also import into his exposition ideas not found in the original text (e.g. I Cor. 10:1-5) or ascribe to it a sense which would have surprised the original authors (e.g. I Cor. 9:9-10).

Paul avowedly resorts to *allegorical* interpretation, i.e. finding in the text a meaning other than the literal sense of the words (e.g. Gal. 4:22-26). This method had already been applied to the Greek myths and has had a long and influential history in the subsequent interpretation of the Scriptures. He also anticipates later developments of *typological* interpretation, i.e. seeing in the OT "types" of elements in the Christian message (e.g. Rom. 5:14; I Cor. 10:6, 11). This method takes the literal sense of the text as its basis, but it finds a connection between that sense and realities later revealed. The connection is one of both correspondence and difference, e.g. between the first Adam and Christ (Rom. 5:14-21; I Cor. 15:22, 45-49; cf. 2nd Isaiah's description of the return from Babylonian exile as a new Exodus, Isa. 51:10-11; 52:12). But far more important than Paul's exegetical methods is the revolution which was brought about in his understanding of the OT by his encounter with Christ and his life in Christ.

The double theme that the OT points forward to Jesus Christ and that in him the true meaning of the ancient Scriptures is made plain appears with varying emphasis in other parts of the NT, e.g.: Matt.'s frequent allusions to the fulfillment of prophecy (1:22-23; 2:5-6, 15, 17-18, 23; etc.); the opening chapters of Luke, where the citations and echoes of the OT are no mere literary adornment; the apostolic preaching in Acts, which declares the saving events of the life, death, and resurrection of Jesus to be in accordance with the Scriptures (2:14-36; 3:12-26; etc.); the recurring parallels in I Pet.; and the detailed typological argument of Heb.

III. EARLY JEWISH INTERPRETATION

The Rabbis. During the cents. immediately preceding the rise of Christianity, Judaism had increasingly become a religion based not only on the Scriptures but also on the tradition by which they were supplemented, interpreted, and applied. It was held that Scriptures and tradition alike had been revealed to Moses on Sinai and had been faithfully handed on ever since. The term *halakah* was applied to traditional teaching when it related to conduct, making plain how the Law was to be obeyed in situations and conditions which were often very different from those of OT times, or supplementing in specific detail what the written Law enjoined in general terms. The term *haggadah*, on the other hand, denotes an expository amplification of the OT text (often with the addition of legendary or fictitious detail) in the interests of edification and inspiration. Though much of this traditional material (both *halakah* and *haggadah*) seems artificial to the modern W reader, it was not simply arbitrary. Rules of interpretation were formulated to govern the deductions which were made from the text of scripture. Rabbi Hillel the Elder (a somewhat older contemporary of Jesus) formulated 7 such rules, presumably based on principles already recognized and practiced. Over a cent. later these were expanded to 13 by Rabbi Ishmael ben Elisha, though with little real addition in substance.

There are obvious and even striking similarities in phraseology and method between rabbinic exegesis and the use of the OT which we find in the NT, but there is also the distinctive difference that in the NT the OT is interpreted in the light of a new and decisive revelation.

The Qumran Sectaries. In spite of differences of opinion about the identity of the religious community which produced the Dead Sea Scrolls (see pp. 1063-71) there can be no question that it sought to base its common life on the Scriptures and that the transmission and interpretation of the OT was one of its central preoccupations. Among the documents found in the Qumran caves are fragments of commentaries on various OT books, of which the best known is that on Hab. It is evident that the men of Qumran, like the early Christians, found in the OT predictions the unfolding of God's purpose in their own time. In what the modern exegete regards as allusions to nations and events in the prophet's own age they saw veiled references to nations and persons contemporary with themselves, to events already experienced or impending, and to a supreme climax still to come. But they provide no counterpart to the NT concentration on the person and work of Jesus Christ as the fulfillment of the ancient Scriptures.

Philo. Yet another variety of early Jewish interpretation is seen in the writings of Philo of Alexandria, a contemporary of Jesus and Paul. His work is important because it reveals the confrontation between Jewish and Hellenistic thought and also because it influenced the great Christian teachers of Alexandria some 2 cents. later. The devotion of the Alexandrian Jewish community to the OT is evidenced by the LXX, by which the Hebrew Scriptures were made accessible to Greek-speaking Jews and later to Greek-speaking Christians.

In contrast to both the NT and the Qumran authors Philo was concerned, not with fulfillment of the OT in events of his time, but with general spiritual truths and speculations. He sought to expound the Hebrew Scriptures in such a way as to demonstrate that they both included and transcended the highest wisdom found in Greek philosophy. This involved him in a massive task of reinterpretation, for which his principal tool was an elaborate allegorical method. He distinguished between the plain sense of scripture and the allegorical. Sometimes he acknowledged the value of the literal meaning, though he urged the reader not to be content with it but to look beyond it. In other passages, however, he held that the literal meaning was absurd or objectionable and only the allegorical or figurative sense was valid. By such an approach he sought to remove features which raised theological difficulties (e.g. anthropomorphisms) or involved seeming contradictions. More positively he sought to lay bare the hidden riches of the text, which he, as surely as the rabbis and the Qumran sectaries, held to be of divine origin and authority. To this end he brought to bear on its minutiae all the resources of a formidable ingenuity.

IV. Early Christian Interpretation

The development in the church of its own growing collection of sacred writings, which came to be recognized as authoritative and combined with the LXX to form the Christian Bible, sharpened the problem of interpreting the OT in its relation to the gospel. The 2nd-cent. heretic Marcion held that a consistent belief in the gospel entailed rejection of the OT. But to maintain this view consistently he was obliged to base his exposition of Christian truth on only some of the books which came ultimately to be recognized as the NT canon, and to omit parts even of those books which he retained. He was, moreover, ruthlessly literal in his interpretation of the OT. Orthodox writers who attacked Marcion, e.g. Justin Martyr, made use of both allegorical and typological interpretation. At this period the interpretation of the Scriptures was closely related to the twin tasks of presenting an apologia for the Christian faith to its critics and refuting the doctrines of heretics. The outstanding figure during the 2nd cent. was Irenaeus, who, while he condemned the heretics' irresponsible exegesis, maintained the unity of the Scriptures by a moderate use of typology and allegory and by his insistence that true interpretation is that which is in accordance with the tradition of the church. But within the church itself there continued to be marked diversity of exegetical method, exemplified by the schools of Alexandria and Antioch.

The School of Alexandria. The most notable representatives of the Alexandrian school were Clement (active *ca.* 200) and Origen (185-254). Their interpretation of the Bible has obvious affinities with that of Philo, but they also inherited that wider Alexandrian tradition of scholarship which had made important contributions to the textual and philological study of classical Greek authors. In Clement's treatment the allegorical method serves not only to remove difficulties but also to unfold hidden truths which, according to Clement, underlie the plain sense of the text. Alike when he allegorizes the details of the patriarchal narratives and when he finds symbolic meanings in the gospel miracle stories, it is evident that Clement is using such methods of interpretation to elicit teaching which he already holds to be true.

A more thoroughgoing and systematic application of these methods is to be found in the work of Origen. Book IV of his On First Principles, a comprehensive statement of his theology, contains a general statement of the principles of biblical interpretation which he applied in detail in his many commentaries and homilies. Corresponding to the 3-fold constitution of human nature as body, soul, and spirit, he found in scripture 3 senses: literal, moral, and spiritual. The literal sense is what is understood by the ordinary, unenlightened Christian. The higher senses, the moral and spiritual, are appropriate to those further advanced in understanding and insight, though none can fathom the ultimate divine mystery concealed in scripture. Although the literal sense is often to be accepted as valid, in many passages it is absurd or impossible (e.g. the statement in Gen. 1 that there were 3 days before the creation of sun, moon, and stars). Such difficult or offensive elements in the text were put there by God to incite the reader to search for the higher meanings. The moral sense is related not only to duty and obedience but to the entire range of the soul's experience. The spiritual sense conveys the divine nature and purpose.

It is evident, therefore, that Origen's methods of interpretation were aimed not merely at the removal of difficulties which puzzled the believer or evoked criticism from the unbeliever but also at extracting from the text an ampler measure of spiritual teaching. His choice and use of those methods undeniably reflect a defective sense of history and lead to some distortion of the gospel. In spite of the fact that his theology was held to be tainted by heresy, his influence on biblical interpretation was deep and lasting.

The School of Antioch. A markedly different type of interpretation is seen in the work of the school of Antioch. Its earliest known exponent was Theophilus, bishop of Antioch in the latter part of the 2nd cent., but the greatest representatives of the school were active during the late 4th and early 5th cents.: Diodorus of Tarsus, Theodore of Mopsuestia, and John Chrysostom. Their exegesis was based on careful grammatical treatment of the text, close attention to and strong emphasis on the literal sense, and understanding of each passage in relation to its context. The emphasis on the literal sense did not exclude figurative or allegorical meanings where it was evident that the biblical authors intended such meanings. But the Antiochenes recognized the importance of the historical element in the Bible and were able in some measure to see its teaching in historic perspective. They drew attention to differences between the testaments and sought to avoid reading a NT sense into OT passages. In particular they rejected the messianic and christological interpretation of many OT passages, holding that OT prophecy was for the most part fulfilled within the history of the Jews. Whereas in Alexandrian biblical interpretation the influence of Greek philosophy (esp. Platonism) is evident, there can be little doubt that the Antiochene fathers owed much to the influence of the synagogue.

Jerome. Jewish influence is also manifest in the work of Jerome (*ca.* 340-420). In carrying out the immense task entrusted to him by Pope Damasus of revising and editing the Latin Bible he acquired a more extensive knowledge of Hebrew than any other of the fathers, and of necessity he acquired it from Jewish scholars. Not only did he go behind the various Greek translations of the OT to the Hebrew text, but he came to lay great emphasis on the literal sense as the basis of sound interpretation. In this

973

he was the heir of the school of Antioch. Not that he excluded a higher and spiritual sense or discarded allegorical methods of interpretation, but he took the literal sense seriously as a guide to a deeper understanding of the text. It is not difficult to convict him of inconsistency in his views about scripture, but his legacy to the church was his monumental work as translator and editor of the biblical text.

Augustine (354-430) was inferior to Jerome as a biblical scholar but surpassed him as a theological interpreter of scripture. Since it was the allegorical method of interpretation as exemplified in the sermons of Bishop Ambrose of Milan that made it possible for him to accept orthodox Christianity, it is not surprising that he gave particular attention to principles of interpretation and also to the character of the interpreter himself. Like Origen he was deeply influenced by Neoplatonist philosophy and, like him, put the higher, spiritual sense above the literal —the written word was the sign which betokened the higher reality. But for Augustine certain factors operated as safeguards against arbitrarily fanciful exegesis. He emphasized the necessity of careful and scholarly study of the text. Further, the interpreter must control his exegesis by reference to the rule of faith, the orthodox teaching of the church. But the supreme test was that interpretation must conform to the 2-fold norm of love to God and love to one's neighbor.

V. The Middle Ages

During the cents. which followed the patristic age and preceded the Reformation the activity of Christian expositors produced an extensive literature in the field of biblical interpretation. Generalization about so vast an area is hazardous, but it may fairly be said that a dominant feature of that literature is the conservation of tradition. This is exemplified in 2 types of compilation produced to help the student of scripture: the *catena*, a "chain" of excerpts from patristic commentaries and expositions; and the *gloss*, an agglomeration of miscellaneous comments in the margin and between the lines of the text.

In what was taken over from earlier authorities throughout this period the Alexandrian tradition predominated over that of Antioch. The recognition of lower and higher senses was applied in accordance with a 4-fold division into the literal, allegorical, moral (or tropological), and mystical (or anagogical). This is aptly summed up in the Latin verse:

> *Littera gesta docet, quid credas allegoria,*
> *Moralis quid agas, quo tendas anagogia.*

"The letter teaches what happened, the allegory what you must believe, the moral sense what you must do, the anagogical sense whither you must journey." The name "Jerusalem" provides the clearest and most frequently quoted example of this 4-fold interpretation: literally it signifies the earthly city, allegorically the church, tropologically the soul, anagogically the heavenly city.

Medieval Jewish Exegesis. From quite early times there had existed in rabbinical treatment of scripture the double strain of literal interpretation and more fanciful homiletical exposition. In the work of the influential exegete Saadya (892-942) there be-

gan a new emphasis on the plain sense and on rational interpretation. His most important work was his translation of the Hebrew Scriptures into Arabic, one of the great versions of all time. Though his life's work was done in Egypt, Palestine, and Babylonia, his true heirs were in the W, in the Jewish communities of Muslim Spain, where rigorous philological study provided a basis for exegesis, but where there also arose a tradition of exegesis based on speculative philosophy.

A reaction against the speculative approach is seen in the work of Abraham ibn Ezra (*ca.* 1100-1167), the author of a famous commentary on the Pentateuch. He has been called "the father of higher criticism"—e.g. he seems to have been the first to hold that Isa. contains the work of two prophets. His work was continued by Joseph Kimchi and his sons Moses and David. David Kimchi (1160-1235) exercised through his writings a profound influence on Christian study of the OT at the time of the Reformation.

In the work of Maimonides (Moses ben Maimon, 1135-1204), a native of Cordova who finally settled in Egypt, medieval Jewish scholarship reached its finest expression. Whereas Philo had earlier sought to demonstrate the essential harmony between Platonism and the divine revelation in the Jewish Scriptures, Maimonides interpreted the Scriptures and rabbinic teaching in terms of Aristotelianism as he had learned it from Arabic sources. He recognized a higher or esoteric sense in the Scriptures, but for him reason was the master key to their meaning. The influence of his work was profound, not only among Jews but on Christian writers, notably Thomas Aquinas.

At a somewhat earlier date there arose in N France—independently of the Spanish communities of Jewish learning—a school of interpretation which concentrated on the plain sense of scripture and sought to expound it with the utmost clarity and simplicity. Its founder was Solomon ben Isaac (1040-1105), commonly known as Rashi (RA*bbi* SH*elomoh* I*z*chaki), the author of a masterly commentary on the Talmud. His commentary on the Pentateuch is of special importance. In principle his method of literal interpretation differs from both the *halakic* and the *haggadic* traditions, but his work does not represent an overt revolt against either. A more thoroughgoing application of the method was carried out by Rashi's successors, of whom Samuel ben Meir (Rashbam) and Joseph Kara were the most noted.

The Victorines. Biblical interpretation naturally played an important part in Christian homiletical and devotional literature. Bernard of Clairvaux (*ca.* 1091-1153) was both an eloquent preacher and the supreme exponent in the Middle Ages of the application of the Scriptures to mystical experience. Above all in his homilies on the Song of S. he extracted from the text (or imposed on it) a wealth of allegorical and mystical meaning concerning the relation between Christ and the church and between Christ and the individual soul. During Bernard's lifetime there was founded at Paris the Abbey of St. Victor, which became the home of a school of interpretation in which a new emphasis on the literal sense was basic. This is already evident in the work of Hugh of St. Victor (*ca.* 1097-1141). He recognized 3 senses: literal, allegorical, and tropological. The first 2 are related to scientific and doctrinal knowledge respectively, the 3rd to virtue. This bracketing of the literal with the allegorical in the domain of knowledge served to enhance the importance of the literal sense. Hugh's work was carried further by his disciples, Richard (d. 1173) and Andrew (d. 1175), who is the more representative. The Victorine school has obvious affinities with Jewish exegesis, particularly with the contemporary school of Rashi. Both Hugh and Andrew acknowledged their debt to Jewish scholarship. Of particular interest is Andrew's citation of Jewish interpretations of the controversial passages about Immanuel (Isa. 7:14-16) and the "man of sorrows" (Isa. 53).

Thomas Aquinas. Though Aquinas (*ca.* 1225-74) was primarily a philosophical theologian, his system was intimately related to the text of scripture. He discussed and sought to justify the 4-fold scheme of interpretation in such a way as to emphasize the basic importance of the literal sense. In this he followed the lead of his teacher, Albertus Magnus (1193-1280). Both were indebted to Jewish scholars, particularly Maimonides, and both were imbued with Aristotelianism. In this setting Aquinas stressed the distinction between words and things found in the teaching of Augustine. Words are used by the human authors to convey their meaning; God also uses "things" (i.e. events recorded in scripture) to express his meaning, which is the higher or spiritual sense. But the literal sense is the solid rock on which spiritual exposition must be built.

VI. THE REFORMATION AND AFTER

The question of the authority of scripture and its relation to ecclesiastical authority was central to the Reformation. It is a drastic and misleading oversimplification, however, to assert that only at long last was the authority of the Bible being enunciated. Its authority is presupposed throughout the history of biblical interpretation sketched above. Nevertheless it is true that Augustine stated he would not believe the gospel were he not moved to do so by the authority of the Catholic Church. In the conflicts with heretics the orthodox maintained that the sense extracted from the text of scripture must be controlled by the tradition of catholic teaching. This in turn was linked with the hierarchical succession. The Bible was the quarry from which came the stones to buttress the citadel of the faith, but the shaping of the stones and the layout of the citadel were the concern of ecclesiastical masons and architects.

Martin Luther (1483-1546) had been trained in traditional methods of interpretation and had himself employed them in his lectures on Pss. (1513-16), but he came to reject these methods as a result of the new light which he received as he studied Rom. God's word had come to him through the Bible. He could no longer treat scripture as a text which should be made to yield those meanings determined by ecclesiastical authority and by traditional methods of interpretation. The Bible was prior to the church and superior in authority to the church and its ministers. In order to hear God speak in scripture the reader must look for the plain sense. Such direct and straightforward apprehension of the literal sense is open to the ordinary believer. This conviction was the driving force behind Luther's enterprise in translating the Bible into German. For those who viewed it as a source book for theologians or professional ecclesiastical interpreters it might reasonably be left in a language not understood by the ordinary believer, but for Luther it was a book in which the believer who read with faith and prayer might hear the living word of God.

Though Luther sometimes seems to equate God's word with the written text of the Bible, the true Word for him is Christ, to whom both OT and NT witness. It is this witness to Christ which constitutes the unity of the Bible. This, and this only, is its essential meaning. What matters in the Bible is what "urges Christ." Luther therefore does not hesitate to express his preference for some books (notably Pss., John, Rom., Gal., Eph.) and a lower estimate of others (e.g. Jas., Rev.). A theological systematizer reading the Bible as a doctrinal source book might find such varying estimates embarrassing. But Luther was not a systematizer. For him the Bible was not a dead, impersonal code but a living testimony through which, by the power of the Holy Spirit, the believer might share the experience of the men and women of the Bible and hear God speak to him now.

John Calvin (1509-64) exhibits a more systematic approach to the Bible. The logical and orderly cast of his mind is exemplified supremely in his *Institutes of the Christian Religion,* the first part of which deals with the knowledge of God. It is from the Scriptures alone that we learn clearly what we need to know about God. To acquire this knowledge the reader must study them with faith. The authority of scripture is not dependent on that of the church but is attested by the witness of the Holy Spirit. On the other hand the written word remains as an eternal standard. Accordingly Calvin is hostile to allegorical interpretation except as it is required by the text itself. It is the plain and natural meaning of the written word that the reader must seek. Though he thus rejects allegorical interpretation, Calvin makes use of typology in establishing the relationship between the OT and the NT.

Ulrich Zwingli. The supremacy of the Bible was also maintained by the great Swiss reformer Zwingli (1484-1531). He had received humanist as well as theological training, and in his expositions of the faith his first concern was to present rational grounds for belief in God. But it is in the Scriptures, he maintained, that the true nature of God is disclosed, and it is through them that man may come to a personal apprehension of God by the inner operation of the Holy Spirit.

Whatever differences of emphasis there may have been among the reformers in their doctrine and interpretation of scripture, their rediscovery of its power and their conviction about its authority are amply testified by the sustained courses of expository preaching and by the torrent of biblical commentaries they produced. As the humanist scholars of the Renaissance rediscovered the literature of classical antiquity, so the reformers rediscovered the biblical literature.

The Post-Reformation Period. The eruptive period of the Reformation was followed by one of conserva-

975

tion and consolidation. On the one hand the Council of Trent (1545-63) affirmed for Roman Catholics the infallibility of the Bible, together with the unwritten traditions of the church, and laid it down that interpretation of scripture in matters of faith and morals must accord with ecclesiastical teaching. Thus the general position of the reformers was rejected and the older methods of interpretation safeguarded.

Within the Protestant churches there followed a period of what has been termed "Protestant scholasticism." The Bible was regarded as an infallible standard, produced by a process of inspiration which overrode the personalities of the human authors and amounted to divine dictation. The interpretation of the inerrant text must be on the basis, not of ecclesiastical tradition but of scripture itself, passage being compared with passage to elucidate obscurities. There were of course differences of emphasis between the various traditions within Protestantism. In some quarters an extreme literalism was adopted; in others the interpretative operation of the Holy Spirit was so understood as to leave the way open for highly arbitrary interpretations.

Rationalism. The biblical scholarship of the Reformation period owed much to the Renaissance. The period of Protestant scholasticism may seem to represent a divorce between biblical interpretation and other fields of knowledge. But in fact there were already at work forces of a generally rationalist character which presented a challenge to traditional attitudes to scripture, Catholic and Protestant alike. Incipient changes in the intellectual climate were brought about on the one hand by advances in scientific knowledge and the application of the scientific method and on the other hand by the philosophic rationalism which stemmed from the work of Descartes (1596-1650).

Thomas Hobbes (1588-1679) approached the problems of biblical authority and interpretation from the standpoint of political philosophy. He treated the Bible as the record of revelation rather than as itself revelation. The position which he adopted was in fact a rejection both of the traditional modes of interpretation current in the Roman Catholic Church and of thoroughgoing Protestant biblicism. His prime concern was to find in the Bible a satisfactory basis for political authority.

In the work of the Dutch Jew Baruch Spinoza (1632-77) the question of the authority and interpretation of the Bible are discussed within the context of a general philosophical argument. Spinoza held that the teaching of scripture relates to the moral life, and therefore that scientific inquiry and philosophic reasoning may proceed without being in any way embarrassed by or embarrassing the essential message of scripture—in his own words "the Bible leaves reason absolutely free." But the Bible must be interpreted, not in accordance with tradition and ecclesiastical authority, but on rational and scientific principles: (a) by applying a knowledge of the original languages, (b) by grouping passages according to subject matter, and (c) by taking into account the historical situations in which the various scriptural authors wrote.

A similar but more positive attitude to the Bible is found in the work of another 17th-cent. philoso-

pher, John Locke (1632-1704). Though he acknowledged the presence in the Bible of revealed doctrines as well as moral teaching, he was critical of the detailed theological niceties which ecclesiastics had extracted from the biblical text. It is of a piece with his rationalism that he held that the revelations imparted in scripture were vouched for by the "visible signs" or miracles which accompanied them. His attempts to relate reason to revelation and to apply rational methods to the interpretation of scripture, like those of Spinoza, were aimed against both the persecuting zeal of traditional orthodoxy and the vagaries of irresponsible sectarian fantasy.

VII. The Modern Period

The Critical Movement. The rationalist approach to the evaluation and interpretation of scripture was exemplified by a variety of 18th-cent. authors, but the situation was again changed by new trends of thought. A departure from a narrowly dogmatic or an aridly rationalist treatment of the biblical text is represented by the influential work of the Englishman Robert Lowth (1710-87) and the German Johann Gottfried von Herder (1744-1803), who inaugurated a new era in the understanding of Hebrew poetry. Friedrich Schleiermacher (1768-1834), whose influence on theological thought generally has been deep and far-reaching, also inaugurated a new phase in interpretation by his fusion of rationalism with the subjectivism of romanticism. He saw the work of the interpreter as more than the formal analysis of the linguistic and literary features of a text; it was necessary to penetrate to its inner truth and to the mind of the author, and further still to the entire literary and historical process of which the work formed a part.

Already in the work of some 17th-cent. pioneers (e.g. Spinoza and Hobbes) the unity and Mosaic authorship of the Pentateuch had been questioned. From then on—at first fitfully, then with increasing momentum—there developed that critical approach to the biblical literature which has come to exercise so profound an influence on exegesis. After the first questionings about the integrity, authorship, and date of the Pentateuch there followed a variety of hypotheses, culminating in the 3rd quarter of the 19th cent. in the theory associated with the names of Karl Heinrich Graf (1815-69) and Julius Wellhausen (1844-1918). This involved not only a literary analysis of the Pentateuch and a reconstruction of its growth (see "The Compiling of Israel's Story," pp. 1082-89) but also a new perspective on the history of Israel's religion; it thus radically affected the entire interpretation of the OT.

In the NT field we may note the remarkable impact of the skeptical *Life of Jesus* by D. F. Strauss (1808-74) and the influence of Ferdinand Christian Baur (1792-1860) and the Tübingen school, who sought to explain the emergence of the church as the outcome of a conflict between Jewish Christianity and Gentile Christianity—i.e. a thesis and antithesis which resulted in the synthesis of Catholic Christianity. As the Pentateuch and other OT books had been analyzed into strata of differing date, so the gospels were dissected (see "The Literary Relations Among the Gospels," pp. 1129-35) and both the traditional theological interpretation of the gospel narrative and its very historical basis were challenged. One line of interpretation resulted in the "liberal portrait" of Jesus, which represented him as an inspiring human teacher and leader; another emphasized the eschatological character of his teaching.

Into all the ramifications of critical scholarship we cannot attempt to explore. It must suffice to notice that amid all varieties of critical opinion there was the determined attempt to see the biblical documents in their historical setting and perspective. Not unnaturally there were many who held that the presupposition of this attempt was that the biblical documents did not differ essentially from other ancient literature, and that the task of the interpreter was complete when he had analyzed them and shown their significance for the situation in which they were produced.

Contemporary Trends. In the present cent. the heirs of 19th-cent. criticism have moved to new positions. In the study of both OT and NT much attention has been given to the study of the literary forms, their setting in life, and their history, and to the creative influence of the worship of ancient Israel and the early church on the biblical documents. But above all there has been a new preoccupation with problems of interpretation. Karl Barth, the greatest modern exponent of biblical theology, in his commentary on Rom. presented with challenging emphasis the authority of the Bible as no mere collection of writings from another age but a genuine unity, bearing witness to Jesus Christ, a book in which God speaks to men today. More recently Rudolf Bultmann has summoned the biblical interpreter to the task of interpreting to the modern man, living in an age profoundly different from that of the biblical authors, the truth enshrined in the "mythological" language of the Bible, and to present it in such a way that it speaks to man's present vital need. The debate continues, and it is futile to seek to assess its present significance except in the light of the entire history of interpretation.

For Further Study. C. W. Dugmore, ed., *The Interpretation of the Bible*, 1944. J. D. Wood, *The Interpretation of the Bible: A Historical Introduction*, 1958. R. M. Grant, *A Short History of the Interpretation of the Bible*, rev. ed., 1963. D. E. Nineham, ed., *The Church's Use of the Bible*, 1963.

THE HISTORICAL
STUDY OF THE BIBLE

S. Vernon McCasland

Historical study of the Bible means reading it in the light of the times in which it was written and of the readers for whom it was intended. This approach is based on recognition that our Scriptures were written for people of antiquity, who lived in other lands than ours, and whose ways of life and thought were often unlike our own.

The Bible is not a single book in the sense that it was all written by one author and at the same time. Rather it is a collection of writings, known as "books," though no one of them is long enough to be called a book as we ordinarily use the term. Since many of the books are compilations of older materials, it is difficult to say how many authors had a part in writing our Bible.

Some of the stories and poems may have been written down as long ago as 1200 B.C. Indeed some of these must have existed first in oral form and been handed down by memory for cents. before they were put into writing. The latest books are from the early part of the 2nd cent. A.D. Thus the biblical literature spans a period of at least 13 cents., and in oral form much longer than that. As these writings have come down to us, they are a collection of books which the Hebrews first and early Christians 2nd selected from all those available among them at the time, and which they saved because they considered them worthy of preservation.

The closest parallel in our time to such a compilation is an anthology—especially the kind used in high school and college courses in English literature. Such a volume begins with early writers, such as Caedmon and Chaucer, and includes selections from the classic writings in the English language down to our own time. To be a more exact parallel such an anthology should include law codes, a hymnal, and a prayer book. In order to understand this type of collection the student must read it with reference to the times when the individual pieces were produced. In a similar way this is what we mean by the historical study of the Bible.

I. Principles

The People of the OT. Historical interpretation of the OT is based on the insight that it is composed of the literature of a real ancient people (see "The Hebrew Community and the OT," pp. 1072-76). These people lived around the fringes of Arabia, then in Mesopotamia and Egypt, and finally established themselves as a nation in Palestine. About 4 cents.

later they were conquered by the great powers of the ancient world, and many of them were carried away into exile. A few were able to return to Palestine from time to time, but most of the exiles had to adjust to life among alien peoples, far from the land of their fathers.

The various writings of the OT were produced at different times during this long period. Some were written in Palestine, the Hebrew homeland; others were written in strange lands of their conquerors. Some reflect the pride and joy of independence and prosperity; others reveal the nationalism which caused the division of their nation into 2 small and weak kingdoms standing side by side. Their literature also describes the sufferings of these small kingdoms as hostile powers ravaged first one and then the other and finally destroyed them.

The Hebrews knew how to celebrate their happiness in the picturesque festivals of their villages, vineyards, and shrines. They joined processions of joyful pilgrims going up to the great temples. Young people knew play and courting and love, and adults were devoted to their families. No people ever took greater pride in children.

A good understanding of the OT places every single document into the very time, place, and activities which caused it to be written. By means of his learning and imagination the interpreter must be able to reconstruct these historical situations.

The People of the NT. The NT, like the OT, was written by real people (see "The NT and the Christian Community," pp. 1116-23). The first Christians were Jews, but as the new faith spread beyond the frontiers of Palestine the churches soon gathered into their membership more Greeks and Romans than Jews.

It is fully as necessary to re-create the historical situations of the NT as it is of the OT. The difference is that now we must learn the geography, the government, the religions, the philosophies, and the general culture of the Hellenistic world (see "The Greco-Roman Background of the NT," pp. 1037-44). Nothing short of this can ever lead to full enjoyment of the literature of the NT. The Greeks and Romans were different from the Hebrews. They spoke their own languages; they had their own literatures, their own philosophies, their own forms of art. The Hebrews had no sculpture, no painting, no drama, no theater; these things were associated in their minds with pagan gods. But the new world in which Christianity emerged excelled in all these expressions of culture, and we must know this Hellenistic life if we would understand our NT. We must read the Greek philosophers, also their geographers and historians—perhaps most of all their poets and dramatists.

While it is necessary to know the cultures of Hebrews and Christians, it is equally necessary to know the various peoples with whom they were associated. The life of any people is to some extent a response to the stimulation which comes from both friendly and hostile cultures. Thus we should know the cultures of Mesopotamia, Abraham's first homeland, and the peoples of Syria, Phoenicia, Canaan, and the other small nations adjacent to them. Especially we ought to know ancient Egypt and follow its history all the way down to the times of Cleopatra, Antony, and Octavius, better known as Augustus, who was reigning over the Roman Empire when Jesus was born. The gospels, letters of Paul, general letters, and especially Revel. can be understood only in the perspective of this Roman period.

The Period Between the Testaments. As the OT
does not mention Pharisees, Sadducees, and Zealots—groups well known to every reader of the NT—these names will remain shadowy unless we know the Jewish history of the last 2 cents. before Jesus was born. We must know about the Essenes too, another Jewish group of real importance at the time, although they are not mentioned in the Bible. Scholars have long known something of the Essenes from references by first-cent. writers—Josephus, a Jewish historian who wrote at Rome; Philo, a Jewish philosopher of Alexandria; and Pliny, a Roman scientist. Pliny vividly describes an Essene community by the Dead Sea—apparently the Qumran settlement which owned the manuscripts discovered since 1947 (see "The Dead Sea Scrolls," pp. 1063-71). These Essene writings throw light on John the Baptist, Jesus, and the early Christians. No student can ignore these people and do his duty as an interpreter of the NT.

While the background of John and Jesus and the early disciples lies mainly in the OT, it also includes the Maccabean struggle for national independence. When Pompey annexed the Jewish state to the empire of Rome in 63 B.C., the independence movement was forced to go underground, but it did not die. During the days of Jesus its adherents were known as the Zealots—the agitators who finally aroused the Jews to rebel against Rome in the disastrous war of A.D. 66-70. Whatever John and Jesus said about a Messiah, a king, and a kingdom of God found a ready audience in these nationalistic circles; and it was the suspicion that John and Jesus were involved in this movement that led to their executions by Herod Antipas and Pontius Pilate.

Much of the Jewish history of this period has to be derived from the OT Apoc. and from contemporary writings known as Pseudepigrapha (see "The Intertestamental Literature," pp. 1110-15). Some of the ideas can be found only in the obscure and little-known books under the name of Enoch. Especially in I Enoch can much be learned about the "Son of man," an expression often used by Jesus. Unless an interpreter knows this material many sayings of Jesus will remain unintelligible. These now unfamiliar writings form a bridge between much in the OT and the NT.

Other Tools of Study. Archaeology has now be-
come one of the most useful tools of historical study (see "Archaeology," pp. 1054-62). A thorough familiarity with the results of excavation of biblical sites has now become one of the elementary principles of historical interpretation.

Another equally indispensable tool is a knowledge of the geography of the biblical world. All history is rooted in the lands where people live (see "The People of the OT World," pp. 1005-17). Culture has much to do with the size, climate, fertility, and location of a land. Palestine is a tiny country—only 150 miles from Dan to Beer-sheba—bordered by sea on one side and largely by deserts on the others. It is a land of hills and valleys. Much of the soil has been washed from the hillsides, and the valleys have often been eroded into deep gorges. It is a land of limited resources. The literature of the Bible reflects and records these natural phenomena, and it can only be understood by reference to them. Like the people and the nation, the land itself was a religious concept. It was part of the covenant God made with Abraham. They loved its wind and rain, its brooks and springs, its withering heat, its rainy seasons, the penetrating cold of its winters, its cedars, cypresses, oaks, olives, and grapes, especially the spring flowers on its hillsides. God was in all these things.

The mountains, the plains, the rivers, the deserts, and the rocks with which ancient Hebrews and Christians were familiar are still there. Many a biblical sentence is clarified as soon as we see the geographical site to which it refers. Present cities like Jerusalem and Damascus—with their walls still around them, houses crowded together, narrow streets through which only people, donkeys, and camels can pass, shoppers and merchants bargaining over prices in the bazaars—are living museums of ancient biblical life. All of these are "principles" of historical interpretation.

Even the biblical vocabulary is rooted in Hebrew history. One does not read far in the gospels without discovering that the language of Jesus makes frequent use of "Messiah" and "kingdom of God" (or "kingdom of heaven," which means the same thing). It is true that Jesus does not give these idioms the meanings they have in the minds of the nationalists. The Messiah of whom he speaks is not a David conquering a kingdom for himself nor a Solomon enrolling his subjects in army units or labor battalions. That is not the sort of kingdom Jesus has in mind. But we cannot understand his words without beginning with their elementary and traditional meanings.

Yet historical study of the Scriptures must not be taken to exclude other essential types of study. One of the most basic is textual criticism. A scholar must secure the most accurate text available—a large task, since no autograph of any biblical writing has survived, and we are dependent on copies. As new copies were made, either by accident or on purpose scribes introduced variant readings. It is difficult to choose between them. There is also the problem of translation. Most readers today have to pursue their studies in their own mother tongue, but a scholar must learn the original languages of the Bible—Hebrew, Aramaic, and Greek. The Bible is also a great literature, using both prose and poetry, and its writers often adorned what they wrote with colorful figures. They were masters of fiction as well as factual historical style. An interpreter must be able to recognize all of these literary forms and their embellishments (see "The Literary Forms of the OT," pp. 1077-81; "The Literary Forms of the NT," pp. 1124-28).

Historical study depends on other forms of study, but it insists that we must always begin with the author himself, the people he was talking to, and what he was trying to say to them. He was talking to them, not to us. We are obligated to discover what a writer meant to say to the people he was addressing at the time; and we have no right to introduce into a biblical document any idea which the original author did not have in his own mind.

The Bible has been accepted as sacred scripture. It is therefore regarded as a revelation of God's will (see "The Word of God," pp. 994-98). This means that not only in parts of the Bible but in all of it God is revealing himself to man. At the same time the historical point of view holds that God's revelation in the Bible is always expressed through a particular culture. God speaks first of all to one age and one generation in its own vernacular speech and forms of thought, its own experience and life, through the joys and sorrows, successes and failures, the life and death of its people. Historical study means to express that emphasis.

II. OT Examples

Now let us illustrate some of the principles of the historical study of the Scriptures by showing how they apply to a few well-known passages from the Bible.

Lamech's Retaliation. First is a very simple example, the boast of Lamech in Gen. 4:23-24:

Adah and Zillah, hear my voice;
  you wives of Lamech, hearken to what I say:
I have slain a man for wounding me,
  a young man for striking me.
If Cain is avenged sevenfold,
  truly Lamech seventy-sevenfold.

Lamech is presented here as a vindictive, cruel man, hardly an example of what we consider Christian morality. But if we set this poem—for that is what it is—in its true historical context, Lamech appears in a more favorable light. First of all, of course, he practiced polygamy, a form of marriage now considered not only immoral but illegal. Lamech, however, lived in an ancient period of frontier tribal life when the urgent need for more children made this type of marriage moral as well as lawful. It was common practice.

Lamech's seemingly bloodthirsty nature has a similar explanation. In the simple life of his time there was no national government to provide justice; there were no police, no sheriff with his deputies, no soldiers, no courts. The only justice meted out to a criminal was that which a man himself could administer. Lamech was like our own ancestors on the American frontier. They carried knives and guns even while they worked in the fields, and did not hesitate to use them in self-defense. When a man attacked Lamech, he retaliated immediately

with vigor. The essence of what Lamech affirms in his boastful way is that he proposes to enforce justice.

Sisera's Death. The killing of Sisera, a Canaanite general, by Jael, the wife of Heber the Kenite, is recorded first in Judg. 4:17-22. According to this prose account Jael flagrantly violated the custom of hospitality which required one to give food and shelter even to an enemy. She murdered Sisera in cold blood after he had drunk his fill of milk and then fallen asleep on a rug in her tent. But the poetic account of the same incident in the Song of Deborah (Judg. 5:24-27) presents Jael in a more favorable light:

Most blessed of women be Jael,
  the wife of Heber the Kenite,
  of tent-dwelling women most blessed.
He asked water and she gave him milk,
  she brought him curds in a lordly bowl.
She put her hand to the tent peg
  and her right hand to the workmen's mallet;
she struck Sisera a blow,
  she crushed his head,
  she shattered and pierced his temple.
He sank, he fell; . . .
  where he sank, there he fell dead.

According to the poem, which is far older than the prose, Sisera was still standing upright when Jael shattered his skull with one mighty blow. Her deed must be judged as an act of war. Sisera made the mistake of assuming that she, a foreigner, would be hostile to the Hebrews. To say the least, she was a courageous woman. Striking down a soldier while he is standing upright is very different from killing him after he has fallen asleep. Indeed it is doubtful that from Jael's point of view she violated the law of hospitality.

An Elegy of the Exile. Ps. 137:1-6 reads:

By the waters of Babylon,
  there we sat down and wept,
  when we remembered Zion.
On the willows there
  we hung up our lyres.
For there our captors
  required of us songs,
and our tormentors, mirth, saying,
  "Sing us one of the songs of Zion!"

How shall we sing the LORD's song
  in a foreign land?
If I forget you, O Jerusalem,
  let my right hand wither!
Let my tongue cleave to the roof of my mouth,
  if I do not remember you,
if I do not set Jerusalem
  above my highest joy!

Every reader should see at first glance that this poem must be set in its historical context. The situation is of course the Babylonian exile, which followed the fall of Jerusalem in 586 B.C. The sorrowing prisoners are taunted by their arrogant captors. The exiles are no longer able to sing; their hearts will not let them forget their lost homeland. Neither the poet's name nor the exact date of the poem has survived. Since the author writes in the past tense, he may have returned to Jerusalem, as some of the exiles did after the Persians conquered Babylon in 539. On the other hand the bitterness the poet feels toward Babylon (cf. vss. 8-9) may indicate that he wrote even before that infamous city fell.

An Oracle About Edom. Obad., a short prophetic book of only 21 verses, is an oracle denouncing Edom. The Edomites were a fierce people supposedly descended from Esau, Jacob's erratic brother. They lived in the almost barren canyons and hills S of the Dead Sea. Their main fortress was Sela, a city cut from the rock walls of the almost inaccessible Wadi Musa. From this retreat Edomite bandits made raids into S Judah, carrying off flocks and herds and terrifying the population. The bitter resentment of the Jews is reflected in numerous passages in the OT (e.g. Isa. 34; 63:1-6; Jer. 49:7-22; Ezek. 25:12-14; 35; Amos 1:11-12; Mal. 1:2-5).

The modern name of the ancient capital of Edom is Petra, the Greek word for "rock." Its picturesque houses carved from the solid rock of the canyon walls may still be seen by tourists. Obad. 3, probably written about 550 B.C., reflects the ancient cliff dwellings:

> The pride of your heart has deceived you,
>   you who live in the clefts of the rock,
>   whose dwelling is high,
> who say in your heart,
> "Who will bring me down to the ground?"

The Punishment of Achan. Unacceptable ideas of God which we sometimes encounter in the OT often become more intelligible when considered in the light of the time when they were held. Viewed in this way they become interesting milestones along the way over which Hebrew spiritual insight passed before their high and mature monotheism was finally attained. The episode of Achan, who appropriated certain articles from the spoils of Jericho, illustrates this point. Josh. 7:24-26 records the LORD's judgment on him thus:

And Joshua and all Israel with him took Achan the son of Zerah, and the silver and the mantle and the bar of gold, and his sons and daughters, and his oxen and asses and sheep, and his tent, and all that he had; and they brought them up to the Valley of Achor. And Joshua said, "Why did you bring trouble on us? The LORD brings trouble on you today." And all Israel stoned him with stones. . . . And they raised over him a great heap of stones that remains to this day; then the LORD turned from his burning anger.

What startles us in this story of Achan is the execution of the sons and daughters and even the animals for Achan's crime. The LORD's burning anger did not turn away until this was done. The idea here is that guilt is a contagion which affects all members of a family; one member of the family could bring guilt upon the whole group, even on the animals.

A closely related case was recorded about King David and the people of Gibeon in II Sam. 21:1-14. Saul, David's predecessor, had brought bloodguilt on himself and his house by putting to death some of the Gibeonites. In order to remove this bloodguilt from Saul's house—long after Saul was dead—and to pacify the Gibeonites, David turned over to them 2 of Saul's sons and 5 of his grandsons, and the Gibeonites "hanged them on the mountain before the LORD." The story about Achan relates an incident said to have occurred about 1200 B.C. The episode of Gibeon was some 200 years later.

But this concept of bloodguilt is by no means the last word on guilt as the Hebrews understood it. After perhaps 3 more cents. Deut. repudiated the earlier view. This book is a revision of the older law codes, bringing them into harmony with some of the ideas of the great prophets who had lived by that time. Thus in Deut. 24:16 we have Moses himself represented as saying, "The fathers shall not be put to death for the children, nor shall the children be put to death for the fathers; every man shall be put to death for his own sin." Deut. is therefore one of the most outstanding landmarks in the development of Hebrew law. At the same time it shows the new concept of a just God, which was one of the contributions of the prophets beginning with Amos. This view that justice is an individual matter appears also in Jer. (31:29-30), a prophet who was probably in his early years in 621 B.C. when a copy of Deut. was found in the temple and published by the king's command (II Kings 22:3-23:3; II Chr. 34). But this high concept of justice was given fullest expression by Ezekiel (18:1-32), who was Jeremiah's younger contemporary.

David's Census. The account of David's registration of the manpower of the nation (II Sam. 24:1-25; I Chr. 21:1-27) is another illustration of the necessity of setting scriptures in their historical contexts. David's object was no doubt 2-fold: first to provide a steady supply of recruits for his armies; but 2nd and probably far more objectionable, to draft men into labor battalions to carry on his public works programs, a practice carried further by Solomon (I Kings 5:13-18). The list of David's cabinet in II Sam. 20:23-26 names Adoram, who was in charge of the forced labor. This practice was obnoxious to the Hebrews and was one of the main causes of the division of the kingdom when Solomon died (I Kings 12:1-18).

The author of the story in II Samuel can account for David's action only on the assumption that God himself caused the king to do it (24:1). Then he relates that as soon as David had performed the sinful deed God turned and punished him for doing it. But the author of I Chr. changes this theory. He says it was Satan who incited David to commit the sin and that God punished him for it—a view which reflects the change in theology brought about by the prophets who had lived between the time of the earlier author and his own time. When the account in II Sam. was written the Hebrews had no concept of Satan. God was regarded as the cause of all that happened to man, whether prosperity or adversity. He was not subject to the moral code man lived by. But as thinking about God's nature developed, Satan was introduced to account for tragic things in life, the suffering of innocent persons—a view which the Chronicler held.

III. NT EXAMPLES

The historical approach is fully as important in the study of the NT.

The Choice of Barabbas. Consider this well-known passage in Mark 15:6-7:

Now at the feast [the governor] used to release for them any one prisoner whom they asked. And among the rebels in prison, who had committed murder in the insurrection, there was a man called Barabbas.

Then Mark says that Pilate gave the crowd the choice between Barabbas and Jesus and they chose

Barabbas. In its historical setting this was a natural choice. The Jews were resentful of the presence of Roman officials and soldiers, who reminded them of the fact that since 63 B.C. their nation had been a vassal of Rome. This resentment was incited by the Zealots, whose agitation finally led to the tragic rebellion of A.D. 66-70. Barabbas was probably one of the Zealot leaders who had the misfortune to fall into the hands of the hated Romans. He was well known to the people and a hero. They had no hesitation in calling for his liberation in preference to that of Jesus.

A Voice in the Wilderness. The historical approach to the Bible as a principle of interpretation is demonstrated by study of Mark 1:3 (Matt. 3:3; Luke 3:4):

> The voice of one crying in the wilderness:
> Prepare the way of the Lord,
> make his paths straight.

This passage from Isa. 40:3 is quoted to explain the appearance of John the Baptist in the Judean wilderness preaching a baptism of repentance. That John identified himself as "the voice of one crying" (John 1:23) shows that he found himself in this scripture that had been spoken some 570 years before his time about the expected return of the Hebrews from their exile. But John was not the first person of his generation to make such an interpretation of this passage. The Essenes of the Qumran community quoted this same vs. to explain why they had established themselves in the forbidding wilderness by the Dead Sea. They believed that their life there was "the way of the Lord." John may have learned to use the passage from them, but he went beyond them in finding himself personally in the poetic words. Moreover, it appears that Jesus, in finally accepting the messianic destiny, saw himself as the Lord for whom a way was being prepared.

The Gallio Inscription. Acts 18:12 further illustrates the value of archaeology in interpreting the Scriptures historically:

> But when Gallio was proconsul of Achaia, the Jews made a united attack upon Paul and brought him before the tribunal.

This passage came to life some years ago when fragments of an inscription containing a reference to "Gallio proconsul of Achaia" were found at the historic Greek city of Delphi. The inscription is a letter from the Emperor Claudius to the people of Delphi. From statements it contains this letter can be dated A.D. 51-52. As Paul had been in Corinth about a year and a half before the episode mentioned in Acts 18:12, it is probable that he arrived there in A.D. 50, hence also that he wrote I Thess. in that year. This is the most certain date in the life of Paul; from it we can begin to construct a chronology of his career. Indeed this date is probably the most certain in all the NT.

Slavery in the NT. The ownership of slaves by many early Christians has its natural setting in the history of the times. That the author of I Pet. 2:18-25, writing to Christians in the Roman provinces of Asia Minor, devotes a considerable space to slaves indicates that many were found in the churches of that area. He urges slaves to be submissive not only to kind masters but also to the cruel. Paul also addresses slaves (Col. 3:22-4:1; cf. Eph. 6:5-9). His letter to Philemon is concerned with Onesimus, a runaway slave who wishes to return to his master. In no place does Paul attempt to abolish slavery, but he does say that in Christ there is neither slave nor free (Gal. 3:28). These passages show that slaves and masters were fellow Christians; they were brothers in Christ. Thus the worst features of slavery must have been somewhat ameliorated.

Slavery existed in all the cultures of that period. Hebrews had owned slaves from earliest times, both Hebrew and foreign; but their laws gradually improved the lot of slaves, especially those of Hebrew blood, with the intention that these would eventually be set free (Exod. 21:2-11; Lev. 25:39-46; Deut. 15:12-18). The main source of slaves was prisoners taken in war. Hundreds of thousands of slaves resulted from the Roman conquests. Josephus declares that no less than 97,000 were taken by Titus when Jerusalem fell in A.D. 70. Another source of slaves, especially female, was the Greek and Roman custom of discarding unwanted babies. These were often picked up by slave dealers and converted into prostitutes. Strabo reports that at one time the temple of Aphrodite at Corinth had 1,000 prostitutes. Whether this practice was still going on at Corinth in Paul's time we do not know, but this attitude toward sex is in the background of many things Paul says concerning the moral life of his Greek converts.

The Word of God. A more subtle application of the historical principle is necessary to understand Heb. 4:12-13:

> For the word of God is living and active, sharper than any two-edged sword, piercing to the division of soul and spirit, of joints and marrow, and discerning the thoughts and intentions of the heart. And before him no creature is hidden, but all are open and laid bare to the eyes of him with whom we have to do.

The key to this passage is "the word of God." The Greek term for "word" is *logos,* which at the time was widely applied in the Stoic philosophy as the all-pervading reason, or intelligence, or mind of the universe. If in translating this passage we substitute "mind" for "word," we immediately see what it means. It would then go, "For the mind of God is living and active . . ." In that sense the passage is easily understood.

In a similar way almost every page of the NT is vastly illuminated if we read it with a moderate knowledge of the geography, the government, the economic and social life, the morality, the arts, the philosophies, and the religions in the midst of which early Christians lived.

For Further Study: E. C. Colwell, *The Study of the Bible,* 1937. M. S. Enslin, *Christian Beginnings,* 1938. R. H. Pfeiffer, *Intro. to the OT,* 1941; *History of NT Times,* 1949. Jack Finegan, *Light from the Ancient Past,* 1946. S. V. McCasland, "The Greco-Roman World" in *IB,* 1951; *The Religion of the Bible,* 1960; *The Pioneer of Our Faith: A New Life of Jesus,* 1964. E. G. Kraeling, *Bible Atlas,* 1956. R. M. Grant, *A Historical Intro. to the NT,* 1963.

THE THEOLOGICAL STUDY OF THE BIBLE

G. ERNEST WRIGHT

I. THE PROBLEM

How can the religious faith of biblical writers be interpreted and expounded in our time? The attempt to answer this question is the task of the theological study of the Bible. The church's struggle with this concern constitutes the primary ingredient of church history, theology, and Christian proclamation.

The Protestant reformers were "biblical theologians" in the sense that they endeavored to use the Bible rather than current philosophies as the primary source of the categories or themes which they expounded. By the 18th cent., however, several lines of influence—including a rapid growth in the number of denominations, each of which claimed biblical truth for itself—led to a movement toward a more intensive study of the Bible for its own sake, as distinct from its confessional use in relation to faith and religious practice. During the 19th cent. the rapidly developing disciplines of history and comparative religion were extended to biblical study, and to them have been added, particularly in this cent., archaeology and increasing attention to the character and use of language. As a result of vast labor by many scholars in the past cent. we are now able to present biblical history and to expound biblical theology with greater historical accuracy than ever before.

This is to say that the primary emphasis in biblical study today is a critical and historical one. We want to "get back there," to do away with the temporal and cultural gap so that we may stand with them in the first cent., or in the 8th cent. B.C. Yet here we encounter problems. Biblical literature has a history and a great variety in type and viewpoint. How can one systematize it in a theology? Perhaps, then, biblical theology is an impossibility. Excellent scholars both in the last generation and in this have been inclined to such a view and to insist that the best we can do is to write a history of biblical religion.

A modification of this position is to define biblical theology as the examination of the religious viewpoints of the compilers of the great collections of historical traditions and of the various "schools" of thought which already in biblical times show a variety of interest and interpretation. Thus in the OT we can point to the old epic sources in Gen.; Exod.; Num., to the Deuteronomic school responsible for Israel's history in the Promised Land (Deut.–II Kings), to the Jerusalem priesthood and the compiler of I-II Chr.; Ezra-Neh., and to the prophets, psalmists, and wise men. In the NT we have the "school" of Matt., the author of Luke–Acts, the Johannine literature, Heb., Paul, etc.

If one desires something more than this, then he may attempt to use a major concept, such as covenant or kingdom of God, as an organizing theme. It must be admitted that no single theme is sufficiently comprehensive to include within it all varieties of viewpoint. There are central thrusts in emphasis, however, and one must attempt an analysis of what they are and particularly what it is that characterizes the Bible as a whole in the world of religions—what holds it together so that its various parts may be seen as belonging within one particular movement rather than to "religion in general" or to another religious movement.

The historical emphasis, however, raises more problems (see "The Historical Study of the Bible," pp. 978-82). After having worked so hard and faithfully to "get back there," how do we return to our own world with anything of basic importance for faith? Is the solution to the present problems of faith and life a kind of primitivism wherein we suppose that merely by going back into scripture we can find the answer to every present and future problem? Or does not historical study tend to show us how different were biblical people and the biblical world so that it is impossible for us to believe just as they did? In NT times there was a heaven above and a hell below and on earth demons and angels were fighting for the souls of men. In our world we have a different geography of space, and demons and angels are more often referred to in poetic ways rather than in direct prose assertion.

The task of theology in every age has been to interpret the Scriptures meaningfully, struggling to see what can be regarded as centrally important and what can be seen as time-bound and not transferable to another age. Today the tension and distance between the Bible and our time has been keenly felt. This tension has given rise, particularly among NT scholars, to a fresh struggle with "hermeneutics," i.e. the theological effort to "translate" the biblical message into the context of our time or, as some say, to "demythologize" it by peeling off the ancient thought forms in which it is expressed in order to reveal its essential meaning.

Some scholars would consider biblical theology as involving both the description of the past faith and life and the hermeneutics involved in making it contemporary. I.e. biblical theology from this viewpoint is the enterprise of a believing community whose heritage of faith or "tradition" will influence what is considered of central importance for our time. Others, however, more wisely insist on the Bible as a revelation external to themselves and to their community of faith, and therefore on the necessity of "getting back there" in their attempt to understand it. I.e. biblical theology is properly a descriptive and historical discipline.

It has been the church's teaching and her actual experience that this type of biblical study when done with reverence even in a critical spirit can have the effect of enlivening those who undertake it because of the contemporary work of the Holy Spirit. Put differently, the function of biblical study is to provide the point of view and the spectacles wherewith we face our own historical situation. The "prophetic" attitude of expectancy and the seriousness with which we examine the signs of our own times form the context in which the Bible "comes alive" by the action of the Spirit. Yet insofar as it is humanly possible we should separate the question, "What does the Bible say and mean?" from the question, "What can I believe?" sufficiently long to make sure that we answer the first properly, using all the tools of historical research which are necessary.

II. The Central Content of the Bible

From the standpoint of comparative religion modern commentators have been led to emphasize as of central importance the seriousness with which most of the biblical writers have taken history and historical tradition. This is a unique phenomenon among the religions of the world. Certain actual and datable happenings among a particular people in the ancient Near East have been interpreted as the special activity of the God who otherwise to that world was the unknown God. It is by these events that God introduces and identifies himself, and it is around them that biblical literature takes form.

The manner of God's self-disclosure primarily by means of events instead of by means of a system of doctrine, teaching, ritual, or oracles is of special importance. Teachings, forms used in worship, and prophetic oracles are all present, but they receive their context in, and are secondary to, the historical. The theology of Israel was such as to make her the first people in the world who seriously collected her historical traditions. For her to do so was an act of testimony to the wonder, power, and glory of God and as well the means of her self-identity and of her confession. Purpose was set within time so that the past was remembered and rehearsed as of crucial importance in the present, and beyond both was a future in which God's self-disclosure in judgment and mercy would dramatically occur. While the other gods of the time were identified as primarily the forces and powers experienced in nature, the biblical God revealed himself as the Lord of time and event who had chosen the forms of history as the manner of his self-disclosure.

The biblical event was *a happening in time* deemed of special importance because God's word was present within it, interpreting it as such. I.e. certain events were selected as especially "newsworthy" because by them God revealed himself in a specially clear manner. The historical happening and its interpretation, the deed and the word of God as its commentary—these constitute the biblical event.

The centrality of events further furnishes the particular biblical mode by which the knowledge of God is conveyed. An event is expressed by means of a noun subject conjugating a verb predicate. Neither the subject nor the predicate will be analyzed as an entity in itself; it is the noun realizing itself through the verb, giving to the verb its tense, its time. Thus an event is an attribute of an active subject which reveals itself only to the degree that inferences can be properly deduced from what it does. Since in the Bible God is the central subject, there is no attempt to penetrate what he is in himself. There is only the testimony of what he has done, together with the body of "inferences" or assumptions as to what may be deduced from the events. Thus a happening or tradition about a happening may be charged with meaning. The event may have, as it were, an electric field around it which contains an inexhaustible source of energy as worshipers recall it in their own particular historical situations.

The exodus of Israel from Egypt can thus be recalled in a variety of ways depending on one's situation. The basic interpretation is that God delivered Israel from slavery. This interpretation can be seen to point to the power and glory of God as the reason for praise. It can be seen as the portrayal of the righteousness of God which is the ground of present hope. It shows the content of God's grace or love as ultimate power reaching into history to save the weak, the poor, the lost; thus worshipers will be reminded that they are the poor and the needy and only as such will enter the kingdom (Matt. 5:3). The narration of the event can be done in such a way as to contrast the grace of God with the faithlessness of his people and thus to transform sin into guilt, or betrayal of relationship. People in any variety of circumstances can rehearse the exodus story and find in it a word of God for their own situation.

In other words the event-centered character and manner of God's revelation cannot be systematized. It includes both the telling and the meaning for faith of what God has done in history to save men as these are understood in the worshiping community of believers. This is the primary nature and substance of biblical theology.

III. God's Saving Events

Modern biblical scholarship has shown that the chief events in the OT which form the central elements of professed belief are God's call to Abraham and his promises to him and the fathers of Israel, God's deliverance of Israel from slavery in Egypt, and his gift of the Promised Land. Behind these lie the prehistorical traditions and the creation of the world, viewed as the first of God's mighty acts, in which he created heavens and earth, placed man in time, and gave him his vocation under the divine sovereignty. An additional event which played an increasingly significant role as time went on was God's choice of and promises to David. Around these the theology of government in Jerusalem took form. Here the hope for the coming of the Messiah, the new David and God's king in the eschatological age at the end of time, burned ever more brightly in Jerusalem and Judah as the centuries passed.

In the NT the proclamation centers in the life, death, and resurrection of Jesus. As a background for this most of the OT was read and interpreted as prophetic literature filled with statements regarded as fulfilled in Christ. As saving event, however, the Jerusalem proclamation of the faith saw the advent of Jesus the Christ as the culmination of God's saving acts in Israel, beginning wtih Abraham and ending with David. The record of Paul's sermon at Antioch in Pisidia contains an excellent summary of the proclamation in this form (Acts 13:16-23). I.e. the interpretation of the meaning of Jesus Christ is that he was "sent" by God as the climax of God's mighty acts, for which what had gone before was a preparation.

In Matt. and Luke, though only here, this meaning is further accentuated by the virgin birth traditions. On only 2 other occasions in the Bible is so much space given to the story of a birth—the birth of Moses (Exod. 2) and the birth of Samuel (I Sam. 1). In each case a critical moment in the affairs of Israel is at hand and God's intervention to save his people begins with the raising up of his representative. The birth stories accentuate the importance of the event and of the representative, and are a sign that God was at hand with power to act and to save. The birth stories in Matt. and Luke serve a comparable purpose. The advent of Jesus of Nazareth is a special action of God, a "salvation which thou hast prepared in the presence of all peoples, a light for revelation to the Gentiles, and for glory to thy people Israel" (Luke 2:30-32; cf. Isa. 42:6; 49:6).

The immediate purpose of these actions of God was the formation of the congregation, the church, the people of God. One of the primary inferences or deductions from the exodus event was that Israel had been saved by God and formed into a special nation with a special status before God. This is generally referred to as the doctrine of Israel's "election," of her being the *chosen* people (though the word "choose" in this connection first appears in an 8th-7th-cent. passage, Deut. 7:6, the conception is implicit in Israel's earliest poetry, e.g. Exod. 15:13-16; Num. 23:21-23; Deut. 33:3-5). The aim of God to bring Israel into being as his special people was used also as one element in the interpretation of the patriarchal traditions in Gen. Abraham was called out of the nations and given the 3-fold promise: (a) from his progeny a great nation would be formed, (b) in whom all nations would bless themselves, and (c) to whom would be given the land of Canaan (Gen. 12:1-3, 7).

God's actions in the promises and in the exodus deliverance created a bond between himself and his people of a special type. A superior showed a kindness that was unexpected, and the recipient was thus drawn to him. The gracious action of the giver pulled from the recipient a response and created a special relationship. "We love, because [God] first loved us" (I John 4:19) is a basic characteristic of biblical religion, and it has its primary setting in the saving acts of God. The goodness of God will thus be the first and primary conviction Israel will have about God, and even his "wrath" will be suffered in the sure knowledge that his goodness and graciousness will prevail. This faith together with the promises of old led to another basic biblical theme: the promises point forward and the future becomes a time of fulfillment.

The specific identity of the people of God at a given time was always somewhat ambiguous, particularly as Israel's prophets sought to distinguish those of the true Israel who by their faith and faithfulness were called to stand over against current national policies. In the NT the people of God, the true Israel, was being reconstituted in Christ, though, as Paul argued, by faith rather than by birth or national origin (Gal. 3:7). The controversy over the question of the Jewish law in relation to Gentiles was settled in line with Paul's interpretation with the result that no specific identification as a Jew was required for entrance except faith in the God of Abraham and in Jesus Christ whom he had sent.

In the Bible as a whole, then, the primary focus of attention is not simply individuals alone. Rather it is God's creation of a people to serve him, to proclaim his name and identity in the world and to exhibit in their corporate life their knowledge of him. It was characteristic of their worship of him that they should "remember" and not "forget" his mighty acts, his power used in their salvation and creation as his people, that they should praise, magnify, and eulogize him for what he had done.

Within the context of the community the individual found his life as a vocation and a service. His dignity, worth, and creativity had their setting within the community's vocation wherein each heard himself singled out and addressed personally. He was both the servant of his Lord and the ruler over God's creation with responsible charge over it (Gen. 1:27-28; Ps. 8:3-8). Yet his true selfhood and individuality were fulfilled only within the new community which God had brought into being. This balance in conception between individual and community is one of the remarkable characteristics of the Bible. Neither the one nor the other should be so emphasized as to throw it out of focus. When a man is summoned to stand alone over against his people and all mankind, as was Jeremiah, it is something distinctly unusual that is required by the special circumstances of his calling among a sinful and disloyal people.

IV. Covenant

The dominant language used to describe God's acts to save men is drawn from human society, with the political sphere of life providing the basic metaphors which give structure to the whole. God is the Lord of all his creation, the suzerain who actively rules over nature and history. His purposes give meaning to history, and his active direction of human life is grasped in terms of a divine government. His is a benevolent and redemptive power understood as operating dynamically from the heavenly seat of government. He can be seen as the monarch who is leading his forces against his enemies, thus giving ground for human hope that the evil in man will not prevail. He is also the monarch who judges the world; when all men acknowledge his sovereignty and bring their disputes to him, then and only then will the weapons of war be converted into the tools of agriculture and fear be eliminated from the human heart (Isa. 2:2-4; Mic. 4:1-4).

Ancient monarchs were generally viewed in a pastoral and paternal capacity as they ruled over their people. So too the thought of God as Father and as the Good Shepherd introduced nonpolitical metaphors to portray his benevolent relationship to his people. Yet behind all was the picture of the world ruler whose work is to be seen in human affairs as the primary clue to their meaning and whose purpose gives history its direction. The human problem is at root a political one, a refusal to acknowledge God's sovereignty. The direction of God's activity is to turn the whole world into his kingdom, i.e. to win an acceptance and acknowledgment of his sovereignty in the hearts of all men. Consequently the concepts of covenant and kingdom have generally been taken as the primary unifying factors between the OT and the NT, the term "testament" being derived from a Latin translation of the Greek word for "covenant" (see "The Unity Between the Testaments," pp. 989-93).

The primary structuring concept in the OT by which Israel interpreted her existence in relation to God and the purpose for which he created her is the Mosaic covenant. A covenant is a pact or treaty between 2 parties which is sealed by a vow. Israel's particular type of covenant has been shown by recent scholarship to have been derived from international suzerainty treaties of the 2nd millennium B.C. wherein a great king or emperor attempted to bind a vassal to himself in ties of affection. Such a document begins with the king's presentation in first-person narrative of his benevolent acts or those of his dynasty toward the vassal. Only after this declaration does the king give expression to the stipulations of the covenant, the obligations which he would have the vassal assume. Witnesses to the vows of the vassal are then listed, consisting of all the known divine powers in heaven and earth. I.e. the sanctions of the treaty are solely religious.

This form of treaty was understood to portray the relationship between God and Israel, and the following were some of the results of the concept: (a) God is the world's sovereign and Israel became his special vassal, his servants having a service to perform for him. The basic language of Israel's faith took shape around this picture. (b) God's wondrous acts of goodness toward Israel were tied closely to the obligations which in gratitude to him she vowed to assume. The primary expression of these obligations was the 10 Commandments. They alone were separated from other law and given a special name, the "words" (i.e. of God), to which the people vowed obedience (Exod. 20:1; 24:3-8; Deut. 5:22). They formed the legal policy within which the covenant people were to live. All other law, of complex formal background, was called "ordinances" (Exod. 21:1; 24:3), which were mediated to Israel through Moses or in special cases through Aaron. (c) The concept of treaty furnished a major element in worship; the recital of God's mighty acts was tied closely to covenant renewal and to repentance for faithlessness. (d) It also furnished the Deuteronomic historian and the preexilic prophets their central theme — God's legal case or "controversy" with his people for their

breach of the pact. Israel's tragic involvement in Assyrian and Babylonian imperialisms thus found justification. Israel was tried in God's heavenly court, found guilty, and sentenced. The prophet was the official of the court who made known to Israel the news of the terrible decision.

So confident were the prophets in the goodness of God, however, that punishment was not the last word. The valley of death was the road to hope. Two other covenants in the OT, the promises to Abraham and to David (Gen. 15; 17; II Sam. 7:8-17; 23:5), were understood as commitments which God would not break. In the crisis of destruction and reconstruction these promises were the sure anchor in the heaving sea (cf. Ps. 89:3, 19-37, 49). They were God's "everlasting covenant," and in their context the hope for the new David, the Messiah, whom God would provide in the coming age burned brightly (e.g. Isa. 9; 11; Mic. 5). Less frequently one could express the hope in a "new covenant" of the Mosaic type which would be written on men's hearts so that they could and would keep it (Jer. 31:31-34).

It is the task of the theological study of the Bible to penetrate within the thought world just outlined and to follow numerous lines of study deep within the biblical world of faith and its expression. In the NT the study must follow among others particularly the concepts of covenant, church, and kingdom. When we do so, however, we are faced with many problems, differences of opinion among scholars, and a new, fresh, and very creative atmosphere. While it is the function of the past to provide the forms by which the present is interpreted, it is also true that the new, dramatic, creative event will initiate a fresh interpretation of old symbols and create a new language of its own.

The NT, or New Covenant, was the term used by the church for the new body of Christian literature appended to the Old Covenant. The primary source for this interpretation in the literature itself is to be found in passages describing the Lord's Supper as the "new covenant" (I Cor. 11:25) or covenant in Christ's blood (Mark 14:24; cf. Matt. 26:28; a reference to Exod. 24:8). The new covenant in Christ is referred to also both by Paul (II Cor. 3:6) and by the author of Heb. (e.g. 7:1-22; 8:1-13). Yet since in NT times "covenant" had come to mean almost exclusively obedience to the Jewish law, one can observe that NT writers were not comfortable with the term, except to point out that the covenant in Christ was not of law but of faith or of the Spirit.

Paul uses the covenant with Abraham as a better model of life in Christ than that at Sinai (Gal. 3:16; 4:21-28). The applicability of the term to Christianity, therefore, can only be in the general sense of the new community of God's people who in Christ are heirs of the promises of old, who have taken on themselves the obligation of discipleship and look forward to the "banquet" of the kingdom with Christ at the head of the table. It preserves the sense of the *community* of God's people, the new people of God, the church.

Thus to find further evidence of the influence of the OT covenant conception on the NT would require a searching investigation of the meaning of the church in the light of its background in Israel, in Judaism, and in the Hellenistic world. The new community was a new creation by God's Spirit which could be depicted by a great variety of organic and social metaphors—e.g. the new Israel, the progeny of Abraham by faith, the household of God, the bride of Christ, the company of the forgiven, heirs of the kingdom empowered by the Spirit to live in the world with love and joy. I.e. God's purpose in the creation of old Israel is now seen fulfilled, for a central fact in both testaments, celebrated in worship, is the divine creation of a new community which is intimately tied into God's whole universal program for the world's redemption.

The significance of Israel's use of political language as the manner in which God's work in his creation was understood and expressed in the NT is to be seen in the central place occupied by the conception of the kingdom of God (see "The Kingdom of God in the OT," pp. 1159-66; "The Kingdom of God in the NT," pp. 1176-86). As in the OT, the expression primarily signified, not a realm, but rather an acknowledgment of God's sovereignty. Judging from the frequency of occurrences of the kingdom in recorded sayings of Jesus, we must assume that it was a central concept in his teaching.

According to Mark 1:14-15 Jesus began his ministry with the proclamation that God's "time" of preparation "is fulfilled, and the kingdom of God is at hand." So imminent is the advent that some who hear him will see it come with power (Mark 9:1). At the Last Supper Jesus explained to the disciples that the next time he drank of the fruit of the vine it would be in the kingdom (Mark 14:25). "As my Father appointed a kingdom for me, so do I appoint for you that you may eat and drink at my table in my kingdom, and sit on thrones judging the twelve tribes of Israel" (Luke 22:29-30). In the "Lord's Prayer" he taught his disciples to pray, "Thy kingdom come" (Matt. 6:10; Luke 11:2).

The kingdom thus is an eschatological concept in that it refers to a fulfillment at the end of the age. Jesus refers to the new age about to dawn when all the conflicts of the present will find resolution in the new heavens, new earth, and new humanity. Precisely when this final consummation is to come is unknown (Mark 13:32), but it nevertheless is imminent. Elsewhere in the NT the life, death, and resurrection of Jesus is proclaimed as the sign that the kingdom has actually come, though its consummation must be awaited until Christ returns. Only in the Johannine literature does there appear to be a reinterpretation of the significance of Christ so that the concept of the kingdom is replaced by one of eternal life. When the kingdom is referred to by Nicodemus (John 3:3, 5) it is coupled with being born again. Yet the life present in believers now who are "in Christ" suggests that the kingdom into which one is born again is conceived more as a present reality than as a future promise.

V. JESUS CHRIST

The central content of the NT is its testimony to the meaning, the exaltation, the lordship of Jesus as the Christ (see "The NT Interpretation of Jesus," pp. 1167-75). As indicated above, God sent him into the world for the salvation of man. One statement of this is given in Matt. in a reflection on the meaning of the name "Jesus" as involving the salvation of

people from their sins (1:21). A Pauline statement of the same theme reads: "But when the time had fully come, God sent forth his Son, born of woman, born under the law, to redeem those who were under the law, so that we might receive adoption as sons" (Gal. 4:4-5). The close relation between Jesus and God is given expression in the filial term "Son." The emphasis on "born of woman" is to testify, on the other hand, that he was really a human being, not a purely spiritual or otherworldly event. The expression "born under the law" affirms the fact that he was a Jew to whom God had given the law as the primary religious obligation.

Theological penetration within the NT has the task of investigating the nature of God's saving work in Christ. A variety of language is used, all with one object: to speak of the release of man from the burden and estrangement of his sin and guilt, from his alienation and hopelessness without God in the world (Eph. 2:12). Christ came to seek out and to save the lost, and in so doing he lost his life at the hands of sinners. Following the image of the ancient sacrifice, Christ's self-giving on the cross was described as an offering which bore the sins of many (Heb. 9:28). He "bore our sins in his body on the tree" (I Pet. 2:24). He was the Passover lamb by which Christians celebrated their deliverance from bondage to the powers of darkness, as in the Passover Jews celebrate their deliverance from the power of Pharaoh (I Cor. 5:7). As a sacrifice he could also be referred to as the "Lamb of God, who takes away the sin of the world" (John 1:29, 36). Like a sacrifice his death has the function of propitiation, expiation, or means of reconciliation with God (Rom. 3:25; Heb. 2:17; I John 2:2). The meaning of the event, expressed in another way, is given by Paul in the well-known vs.: "God was in Christ reconciling the world to himself" (II Cor. 5:19; cf. Phil. 2:5-11). He has opened up a fresh access to God, the way to which, however, is by faith (Rom. 3:25; Eph. 3:12).

A key passage on the atoning work of Christ is: "For the Son of man also came not to be served but to serve, and to give his life as a ransom for many" (Mark 10:45; cf. I Tim. 2:5-6). The language of ransom and redemption is deeply set within the OT, where, when the action is God's, all thought of payment is left in abeyance and the concentration of thought is on the setting free. In similar manner the meaning of this saying is simply: "I have come to give my life for the liberation of many." Back of it is the deep biblical sensitivity to slavery, which in the NT contexts is a slavery, not primarily to an earthly power, but to sin itself and to its deep spiritual and virulent background which can be described as Satan or the principalities and powers of darkness (Acts 26:18; Eph. 6:12; cf. Rom. 8:38).

The whole of the OT was searched for appropriate language to express the manner in which Jesus fulfilled his mission. The main religious offices of Israel —prophet, priest, and king—were all applied to him. None of them was complete expression in itself. Indeed, while the early church freely applied the concept of the Messiah (Christ), or the new David, to Jesus, the concept was modified from its OT form by Isa. 53. His kingship was from the heavenly throne only after his resurrection; in his life he was the suffering servant of the Lord who "was wounded for our transgressions," who "bore the sin of many, and made intercession for the transgressors" (Isa. 53: 5, 12). Indeed, in his life it does not appear that he willingly or clearly accepted the title "Messiah," unless he modified it sharply with the teaching that he must suffer (cf. Mark 9:12; 15:2-5; Luke 23:1-4; John 18:33-38).

A special term used by Jesus himself and by the evangelists for his mission is "Son of man." In many passages the meaning is unclear because it was an old way of saying simply "man." Yet in such passages as Mark 8:38; 13:26; 14:62; John 6:27; Acts 7:56 a different meaning, developed in inter-testamental Judaism, seems apparent. That is the Heavenly Man, the prototype of earthly man. Its use in the NT is clearly modified by the concepts of both the Messiah and the suffering servant in Isa. 53. The exaltation of the Son of man will come only after his resurrection. This concept, however, could be used to speak of the "preexistence" of Christ, a way of asserting that he was always a part of the plan and purpose of God. The "Logos," or Word of God, in the OT which became flesh in Jesus Christ was another way of expressing a similar thought (John 1).

Theological study of the Scriptures must also survey the particularity of each of the writers and schools of thought in the NT and early church in the attempt to understand what each is saying about the work of Christ and of the past, present, and future of God's work. The authors of Mark, Matt., and Luke-Acts, the Johannine authors, Paul, the author of Heb. and the rest—all have their own ways of testifying to God's climactic event and what it means. While a unity is given them by the event and its Israelite and Jewish background, there is also great variety of perspective. The truth proclaimed is too great to be confined to one theology or manner of expression. The NT's great variety will become source of later variety in the church. At different times and in different groups one emphasis and then another will be made, in part because particular experience, background, and need lead one to draw different things from the almost inexhaustible richness of the biblical events. Yet the event and its total biblical setting will always be the judge and critic of its interpretation.

VI. Worship and the Common Life

In this brief summary of some of the chief topics which constitute the theological study of the Bible

much has been omitted, including treatments of such important themes as God and his creation, God and the gods of mankind, man and his history, the law, right and wrong, duty, and worship and the spiritual attitudes in which it is set, such as faith, hope, love, patience, watchfulness, a passion for justice, etc. The problems of relating the OT and the NT, of what is meant by the "resurrection," of the new age, and of apocalypticism or the hidden mystery of the future —all must be studied in their biblical setting. Particularly important is the manner in which the interpretation of God's saving events gave form to the common life and common worship of the new community of Israel, how the forms differed from those in other religions, and how they came to give birth to 2 differing religious communities in Judaism and Christianity.

Although the central task of the biblical theologian is analytical and descriptive, his work is not finished until he begins to build some bridges to the modern world. He must show how it is possible to find in the Bible the symbols of faith which have been able to restructure the lives of people in ages very different from those of the Bible. I.e. the theological study of the Bible must relate itself, however briefly or allusively, to other Christian disciplines and to the world in which we now live. A religious past or, for that matter, any past, remains an archaism without some such assessment of its contemporary meaning or relevance.

For Further Study: The 2 most important works on OT theology are Walther Eichrodt, *Theology of the OT*, tr. J. A. Baker, vol. 1, 1961; Gerhard von Rad, *OT Theology*, tr. D. M. G. Stalker, 2 vols., 1962-65. Their counterpart for the NT is Rudolf Bultmann, *Theology of the N.T.*, tr. Kendrick Grobel, 2 vols., 1951-55.

Less comprehensive are Edmond Jacob, *Theology of the OT*, tr. A. W. Heathcote and P. J. Allcock, 1958; F. C. Grant, *An Intro. to NT Thought*, 1950; Ethelbert Stauffer, *NT Theology*, tr. John Marsh, 1955.

See also: R. H. Strachan, "The Gospel in the NT" and C. T. Craig, A. N. Wilder, W. R. Bowie, "The Teaching of Jesus" in *IB*, 1951. G. Ernest Wright, "The Faith of Israel" in *IB*, 1952; *God Who Acts*, 1952; *The Biblical Doctrine of Man in Society*, 1954. Otto Betz, "Biblical Theology, History of" and Krister Stendahl, "Biblical Theology, Contemporary" in *IDB*, 1962.

THE UNITY BETWEEN THE TESTAMENTS

Floyd V. Filson

The church through the centuries has affirmed that there is a basic unity between the OT and he NT. It has set aside these 2 groups of books as its canon because these books have a common message and when properly used have authority for Christians.

I. The Church's Canon of Scripture

It should be noted that the church has always had a Bible, a canon of scripture. Jesus and the apostles accepted the canon which first-cent. Judaism held to be scripture. The apostolic church found that these books, which included almost exactly the books we have in our OT, were in harmony with the gospel message. These writings were seen to point clearly to the life and work of Jesus Christ and to the work of the Spirit in the apostolic church. There was thus an essential unity between the OT (as we call it) and the apostolic witness to Jesus Christ, his work, and the gift of the Spirit. This was felt so strongly that the church at first saw no need of adding new Christian writings to the canon. The OT was the church's book; it pointed to Christ; it gave the church guidance for worship, witness, and life.

An Early Challenge to the Unity. This viewpoint was challenged about A.D. 140 when Marcion arrived in Rome and began to assert that the OT told of a God different from the God and Father of Jesus Christ. Marcion refused to regard the OT as Christian scripture; he formed a new canon, consisting of Luke and 10 letters of Paul. But to make these writings support his views he had to "correct" them; he cut out passages not in agreement with his views, especially those which accepted the OT as scripture, and claimed that they were not part of the original writings of Luke and Paul.

The teaching of Marcion was a part of the Gnostic movement that developed in the 2nd cent. and constituted a real challenge to the church. Gnosticism, as the Greek word *gnosis* ("knowledge") shows, claimed a special revealed knowledge. Prominent in this teaching was a tendency to regard matter as inherently evil, from which followed the idea that the creator of the material world could not be the true God. The OT as the witness to God the creator was thus suspect to the Gnostics. This entire movement either belittled the OT or rejected it outright.

It is highly probable that even before Marcion appeared the church was at work to form the NT.

Paul's letters had been collected, the 4 gospels probably were already combined in a 4-fold witness to Christ, and the need of an authoritative collection of Christian writings was becoming clear. Some scholars think that Marcion's action is setting up his own canon first suggested to the church that it should form a NT. But it is much more likely that Marcion prompted the church to speed up a process that was already under way before he appeared.

The Church Affirms the Unity. The effect of Marcion's attempt was 2-fold: the church reaffirmed that the OT was scripture, and it went on to form a more inclusive NT than the collection of 11 writings which Marcion had chosen. In so doing the church consciously and emphatically chose to combine in one canon both the OT and the NT. It sensed and affirmed the unity between the testaments and declared them both to be part of the total Christian scripture.

Since the Reformation certain small groups have been ready to discount or discard the OT and be content with the NT as the sole Christian scripture. Individuals have maintained that the OT is antiquated or sub-Christian and so is no legitimate part of the church's scripture. Such views imply that there is no essential unity between the testaments and that the NT alone forms the Christian canon. The church as a whole has always rejected such proposals. It has included both testaments in the Bible and found a deep unity between them.

This church position has roots in the NT itself. Not simply by quoting the OT as scripture but also by continually accepting and reasserting OT content and ideas the NT attests the unity between the testaments. To reject the OT or to deny its basic unity with the NT not merely casts doubt on the OT but also charges the NT with being deeply in error, for to the NT writers the OT is truly scripture; to them it is an indispensable witness to God, his work, and his will for men. These NT writers think that their message is in basic accord with the OT.

II. Historical Study of the Bible

In recent generations this long-standing view of the church has been questioned in a variety of ways. Judaism, free to present its case, has claimed that the OT is rightly understood by Jews apart from the NT. Prior to and during World War II the Nazis, moved by rabid anti-Semitism, opposed the Jews, the OT, and the Christian conviction that the church has its real roots in the OT and thus in God's dealings with Israel.

A quite different development in scholarship tended to promote the idea that the OT and the NT should be kept separate. In recent generations scholarly study of the Bible has tended to be divided into 2 parts, one concentrating mainly on the OT and the other focusing attention almost entirely on the NT. This division, though natural in many ways, has seemed to imply that the 2 areas have no basic unity and that each can best be understood separately.

The Challenge of the Historical Method. But the real challenge to the unity between the testaments arose from the development of independent historical study. The Bible consists of ancient writings. Their setting differs from that in which we live. They were written over a period of about 1,000 years. To understand them, this method of historical study has insisted, we must refuse to let church dogmas settle historical questions. We must develop methods of free historical study which examine what happened, what the setting of that ancient history was, and what stages of development the biblical people went through. Each biblical writing must be studied in its ancient setting. The historian must work on the basis of the evidence and continually ask what the events meant to the men of that time.

This view studies all ancient documents for whatever they can tell us of the ancient history and teaching. It recognizes that the books in the canon have had a special history in later centuries, but in writing the history of the ancient period from which these books come it makes no distinction between canonical and noncanonical writings. It tends to regard the OT as rather separate from Christian history; it usually connects the OT with Judaism rather than with the church. The setting of the NT is sought in the Greco-Roman world as much as in the OT. This method of study sharpens attention to the diversity not only between the 2 testaments but also between books within each testament. The things that distinguish each writing and each group of writings from other writings tend to receive emphasis.

The Essential Role of Historical Study. It would be easy to point out faults and limitations in the way this method has been used in the study of the Bible. It often has concentrated on the human and naturalistic area and has excluded the question whether the Bible's central message about God and Christ is true. In so doing it either has suggested that this basic question is not vital or has actually expressed a skeptical attitude. At times it has not been able or willing to recognize limitations and flaws in its work.

Nevertheless the historical method, rightly used, is indispensable, and it must be accepted as a constructive tool in biblical study. It makes a contribution by barring the way to any simple but misleading statement of the unity between the testaments. It shows that each writing has its own characteristics and thus forces us to recognize the rich diversity present in the biblical writings. In particular it makes clear that the situation of the OT authors is different from that of the NT authors who wrote after the life and work of Jesus Christ. No valid statement of the unity of the Bible can ignore this rich diversity.

The historical method of study also sets us free from modern prejudices and misconceptions and enables us to grasp better the situation and mind of the ancient writers. To transcend our own limitations and enter as far as possible into the actual setting and mental outlook of the biblical writers is a great gain. It gives us the understanding to use in testing whether there is a basic unity of content and message between the 2 testaments. The study of the question of unity must accept as an important tool the historical method of study.

III. Wrong or Inadequate Statements of Unity

The problem the church has faced in recent decades has been to recognize the diversity which historical study has taught us to see in the various writings of the Bible and yet to discern and state the unity that the church senses to be present in the entire book. It may clear the way for the best possible answer to this problem if we first examine ways of stating the unity which would be wrong or inadequate.

Persons. We do not find that unity between the testaments in a special type of person who always appears as the actor or author. In each testament a great variety of personalities appears; in each testament we find individuals, such as Isaiah and Ezra and Peter and Paul and James, who though they are alike in being men of faith and active faithfulness are each of them unlike any other actor or spokesman in the biblical story.

Social Pattern. The 2 testaments are not bound together by a consistent and controlling pattern of organization and life. In fact the lack of a fixed pattern of religious and social life is the common characteristic of the 2 testaments. For one thing no common political structure exists; this aspect of social life is not a factor in the early church. A still more important fact is that no authoritative priesthood gives the biblical pattern of religious life. In the OT the priesthood is often prominent but frequently under criticism, while in the NT, although Christ is spoken of in Heb. as the great high priest and Christians are (rarely) described as a holy and royal priesthood (I Pet. 2:5, 9), the life of the church is not in the hands of a priesthood formally set apart for that purpose. No common political, social or religious pattern of organization marks the 2 testaments or binds them together.

There is more to say. The biblical leader who appears prominently and decisively in both testaments and is not really paralleled in any other religious movement is the prophet. Even Jesus (Matt. 21:11; Luke 4:24), Paul (Acts 13:1), and other NT leaders are so described. It belongs to the very essence of the prophet's role that he speaks for God without and often in spite of the official approval of his people's leaders. Amos appears without any previous hint that he would be called to act as God's prophet (Amos 7:14-15); Saul of Tarsus, who was not one of the 12 or a disciple of the earthly Jesus, is stirred to speak and act for the risen Christ. The one type of leader who binds the 2 testaments together is not the king or the priest but the prophet. God's unexpected challenge of men by spokesmen not appointed by men is a prominent feature of the life of the people of God in both testaments.

Literary Form. The 2 testaments do not express their unity in a common literary form or in a common group of such forms. Within each testament there is a remarkable variety of literary forms, and it is noteworthy that the NT was written mainly in forms not known in the OT: gospels, the apostolic witness to Christ (Acts), and letters to churches or to the church. Both testaments have a variety of literary forms—either unique forms or known forms used with distinctive freshness and effectiveness.

Law and Gospel. A partial but inadequate way to state the unity between the testaments is to say that the OT gives the law of God while the NT offers the gospel. On this view the OT is preparatory; it states God's will, depicts man's sin, and shows man's need of God's grace. The NT then gives the answer to man's dilemma; in the life and work of Jesus Christ, proclaimed in the apostolic witness, it presents the gospel of God's redeeming grace.

There is truth in this position; the OT does present God's will and man's sin, and the NT presents the gospel offer of salvation effected by God and made available to men through faith. But this view does not do full justice to either testament. The OT has also the note of grace and forgiveness; e.g. it is the God who has redeemed Israel from Egypt who then as Israel's redeemer gives his people the Ten Commandments (Exod. 20:1-2). And the NT, both in the teaching of Jesus and in the letters, insistently presents the will of God as obligatory on all Christians; it presents God's demand for obedience and brands as sham a faith that does not work through love (Gal. 5:6; Jas. 2:14-26).

Basic Ideas. The unity between the testaments is not merely a sharing of common basic ideas. The 2 testaments do indeed share a common fund of great and crucial ideas and teaching. In what they teach of God's holiness and demand for obedience, of his covenant with his people, of helpfulness to others as an integral part of the life of faith, of God's grace, of the triumph of suffering love, and of the final victory of God's purpose—in all this the 2 testaments have a common mind and a unity which set them apart from other writings of the biblical period. Moreover this common biblical mind constitutes a standard of judgment which condemns the thinking and customs of later times. This then is one way to state an important part of the unity between the testaments.

But the Bible is more than a storehouse of great ideas. Its claim is not simply that it records the most profound and creative thinking that men have produced. In the biblical view man's basic problem is not ignorance; his basic need is not for more and clearer ideas. His trouble is not primarily in his thinking but in his will and action. Man is a moral failure. He needs a remedy that will break the grip not merely of wrong thinking but even more of evil action. His problem is sin, and he needs a power to break its grip, free him from its guilt, and give him the power to live as he should. He needs a power not his own; he needs the power of God to step in and do for him what he cannot do for himself. The Bible speaks to this need. How are we to grasp and state the common message of the 2 testaments on this crucial problem?

Allegory. One falsely attractive way is by the use of allegorical interpretation which finds the entire gospel message stated as fully in the OT as in the NT. This method finds behind the literal meaning of a book a 2nd (and sometimes even a 3rd) meaning; it finds, not simply isolated examples of such a 2nd meaning, but a network of such meanings. It can find the entire message of salvation through Christ taught in the OT as clearly as in the NT. To state the extreme form of this view; the OT pictured completely what Jesus would be like and what God would do in the entire plan of salvation; the NT needed only to identify Jesus of Nazareth as the one of whose work the OT gave such a complete account.

An obvious fault of this way of relating the testaments to one another is that it takes no account of the newness, the uniqueness, and the decisiveness of the coming and work of Jesus. It ignores the fact that God led his people by stages and prepared them for the coming of their Messiah. And it reads into the OT more than is clearly meant there; it gives to the fancy of the modern interpreter a wide field to read into the OT his own understanding of the gospel. To avoid capricious and partisan interpretation of the Bible it is necessary to keep attention on what the original author intended and to beware of letting fertile fancy find in his writing a grasp of history and ideas which the author did not possess.

Typology. A less fanciful way of stating the unity is the study of parallel persons and actions known as "typology." It takes the OT history as actual history and sees in its leading figures and events "types" of NT figures and events. E.g. Abraham as a man of faith may be the type of the Christian believer; Joseph, persecuted and suffering but saving the lives of his brothers in Egypt, may be the type of Jesus Christ the crucified Savior of his fellow men; Moses as the giver of God's law may be the type of Jesus the preacher and teacher of the full will of God. Such parallels show the common ideas and types of leaders in the 2 testaments. They do not obscure the literal meaning and actual teaching of the OT.

But we may question the adequacy and correctness of this method of relating the 2 testaments to each other. Between the OT and the NT leaders and ideas there are not only similarities but also differences. Moreover, when Jesus says, "You have heard that it was said to the men of old. . . . But I say unto you" (Matt. 5:21-22 etc.), he indicates that the NT message constitutes a real advance. The NT leaders and teaching are not limited to the points of exact parallelism with the OT ones. The OT leaders had a real message and ministry in their own day, but their characteristics and methods did not have to be exactly paralleled by those of the NT leaders. The 2 testaments are bound together by something more than parallel types.

One form of typology has been called "homology." In this not only do the 2 testaments present various parallel types but also the basic divine action in the 2 testaments falls into a parallel series of events. In each testament a "divine pattern" controls the history and religious life; it consists essentially of redemption from bondage, consecration of the people of God by covenant, and the gift of the inheritance. This view has some value. God's deliverance of the people of Israel from Egypt, his establishment of the covenant with them at Mt. Sinai, and his giving to them of the promised land of Palestine form a central pattern in the OT which has a parallel in the NT.

But this parallel pattern does not work out in detail, and God's help to enslaved Israel was not an adequate picture of man's need and of the full work of redemption provided by Christ and the Spirit.

Promise and Fulfillment. The recently emphasized pattern of promises and their fulfillment throws much light on the relation between the testaments and helps to state their unity. The OT is an unfinished story. There is still need of a leader who will be the servant of God's people (Isa. 52:13–53:12; Ezek. 37:24-28), of a new covenant to be written on men's hearts (Jer. 31:31-34), and of the gift of God's Spirit to give the power of new life to his people (Joel 2:28-32). The OT often speaks, especially in some of its later writings, of the coming fulfillment of God's promises and purpose. The NT picks up this note and presents the NT gospel as the fulfillment of what has been promised in the OT. This view rightly emphasizes the sense of newness and creative event in the gospel of the NT and yet it sees that there is a close link between the OT history and writings and the NT history and message.

This promise-fulfillment scheme is instructive as long as it is clear that it does not do full justice to either testament. In the OT there is much more than promise. God is with his people; even in the OT he acts to deliver, help, judge, and restore them; there is already a degree of fulfillment even in the OT itself. In the NT there is indeed a fulfillment of OT promises, but it is a partial fulfillment, and the NT looks forward still to a complete fulfillment for which believers hope but which they do not yet see.

Historical Continuity. One prominent attempt to state the unity between the testaments emphasizes the historical nature of the essential biblical story. It thinks of a continuous history of God's people as the common mark of both testaments. History is prominent in the Bible, which is a story of God's action in history to redeem his people. Something vital is lost whenever the gospel is stated as a set of ideas or a system of doctrine. Unless the ideas and doctrine come from the right understanding of this special history, the gospel is misunderstood.

But this special biblical history is not a continuous human history. For some parts of the history of Israel the OT offers but a meager account. Only at special points do the OT writers see something crucial and decisive, and the action at those points is not the result of human development and achievement but is the purposeful action of God to fulfill his purpose for his people. Most striking of all is the great gap between the end of the historical narrative of the OT in the 5th cent. B.C. and the coming of Christ in the first cent. A.D. Note the pattern of the sermon summaries in Acts (e.g. 7:1-53; 13:16-41). They tell of the history of Israel in sketchy form down to the time of David or Solomon, with rare and brief mention of the Exile; then they leap over several centuries to tell how God fulfills the OT history and promise in Jesus Christ and the church. Obviously the aim of the Bible is not to recount a continuous story. And the motivation of the history is not essentially in men.

A Book About God. The unity between the testaments thus results, not from the agreement of men in their ideas, or from their common purpose and action, but from the fact that the Bible is concerned throughout with God and with his dealings with mankind. It is one and the same God who is present and active in the history of Israel, in Jesus Christ, and in the Spirit-led life and witness of the apostolic church. The Bible essentially is a book about God and it is rightly understood only when it is seen to witness primarily to the one true God.

God's Plan and Purpose. The unity between the testaments is found not so much in the harmony and consistency of the ideas God makes known to men as in his persistent plan for men and his ongoing action to realize his purpose. The unity of the Bible is the unity of God's saving plan and purposeful action. It is the story of his purpose for men, his actions to achieve that purpose, and the way men find their place and their blessing in that ongoing plan.

Focus on Jesus Christ. The unity between the testaments puts the central focus on God's action in Jesus of Nazareth, who is the central figure of the story. The OT tells of the history of Israel; it prepares for and leads up to the coming of Jesus as the Christ of Israel and the Savior of all men. The NT witnesses to the life and work of Christ and offers salvation through him. This is all the doing of God (II Cor. 5:18), and it has its center in Christ. The OT points to him; his coming and work is the focal center of the entire story; and the apostolic witness in the NT proclaims him and interprets God's saving purpose as realized and to be realized through him.

The unity between the testaments thus is understood only when Christ is taken as the interpreting center of the entire biblical story. The OT when truly understood points to him. His coming and work is the main clue to what the OT wants men to grasp and accept. In this sense the OT is an incomplete book. It points ahead; the Jews say that it points ahead to rabbinical Judaism and the modern synagogue, but the church confesses that what the OT pointed to was given by God in Jesus Christ and is now offered to men in the gospel. Thus the OT must be read as the preparation for and the advance witness to what God did in Christ. The OT belongs in the church's canon only because it is a preparation for Christ and a witness to him.

The NT is the apostolic witness to Christ by the generation which had just experienced his coming and his work. These writings were gathered into the NT because they were felt by the worshiping church to be the necessary witness to the central redeeming work of God in his Son Jesus Christ. They are concerned to lead the church to worship, live, and witness in the light of God's central action in his Son. The work of Christ is continued in the work of the Holy Spirit, whose gift to the church results from the central work of Christ and whose witness continually confirms the gospel message of God's saving action in Christ.

IV. The Unity Grounded in God's Action

This last characteristic of the Bible points us to the real center and source of the deep unity that links the 2 testaments.

V. Unity Discerned by Faith

It is indeed true that the unity between the testaments is found in God, in his historical action, and centrally in his historical action in Jesus Christ to give the needed gospel to sinful men. But this fact, while not closed to reason, is grasped essentially, not by human brilliance, but by faith. As the Christian lives in faith in the fellowship of the church, as he worships with his fellow Christians and gratefully dedicates his life to God, who in the gospel has offered him the divine grace, as he reads and studies the Bible in obedience to Christ and in loyalty to Christ's church, he knows that these testaments taken together give an essentially unified witness to the God he worships and the gospel he has accepted in faith. In the true and full sense it is only as he shares in the worship, fellowship, witness, and service of the church that he knows this unity between the 2 testaments which make up his one Bible.

For Further Study: C. H. Dodd, *The Apostolic Preaching and Its Developments,* 1936. A. G. Hebert, *The Throne of David,* 1941. Robert M. Grant, *The Bible in the Church,* 1948. H. H. Rowley, *The Unity of the Bible,* 1953. Raymond Abba, *The Nature and Authority of the Bible,* 1958. Oscar Cullmann, *Christ and Time,* rev. ed., 1964.

THE WORD OF GOD

L. Harold DeWolf

Should we speak of the Bible as "the word of God"? Precisely what should this phrase mean to an instructed Christian today? Let us see, first of all, how the Bible itself uses the phrase and the idea it represents.

I. BIBLICAL MEANINGS OF "THE WORD OF GOD"

Concerning OT Revelation. When the writers of the OT tell of God's disclosures of truth, or of himself, to his people, they often speak about "the word of God," or "the word of Yahweh" (usually translated "the LORD"). Indeed the phrase "word of Yahweh" occurs more than 200 times in the OT. In addition there are many other appearances of "word" with possessive pronouns or other words referring to God. In few of these instances does the phrase appear to mean a writing. Much more often it refers directly to a personal experience of a man in which God gave to him a truth or a vision of himself.

E.g.: "After these things the word of the LORD came to Abram in a vision, 'Fear not, Abram, I am your shield' " (Gen. 15:1). "And the LORD appeared again at Shiloh, for the LORD revealed himself to Samuel at Shiloh by the word of the LORD" (I Sam. 3:21). "But that same night the word of the LORD came to Nathan, 'Go and tell my servant David, "Thus says the LORD" ' " (II Sam. 7:4). Worthy of special notice is the interpretation of Joseph's bitter experiences in slavery in the statement: "Until what he had said came to pass the word of the LORD tested him" (Ps. 105:19). On the other hand in Ps. 119 "thy word" means the law, understood of course as divinely revealed.

It is in some of the literary prophets that the phrase "word of the LORD" comes to its highest and also most frequent use. It appears in nearly all the prophetic books. Amos not only uses the phrase but gives us the memorable statement: "The lion has roared; who will not fear? The Lord GOD has spoken; who can but prophesy?" (3:8). Hos. is introduced with the words: "The word of the LORD that came to Hosea" (1:1). The beginnings of Joel, Jonah, Mic., Hag., Zech., and Mal. are similar. Isaiah warns: "Hear the word of the LORD, you rulers of Sodom!" (1:10). The unidentified prophet of the Exile whose work is combined with Isaiah's writes: "The grass withers, the flower fades; but the word of our God will stand for ever" (Isa. 40:8). Jer. opens in a way suggesting the truth about the entire Bible: "The words of Jeremiah, the son of Hilkiah, . . . to

whom the word of the LORD came" (1:1-2). Throughout Jer. the phrase "word of the LORD" is used more frequently than in any other book of the Bible, although Ezek. is not far behind.

In Creation. "By the word of the LORD the heavens were made, and all their host by the breath of his mouth," cries a psalmist (Ps. 33:6). So in the great creation story of Gen. 1 we read: "And God said, 'Let there be light'; and there was light" (1:3). Every stage in the creation is described similarly as the speaking of God. In this way the writers teach us how powerful and different from our human speech is the word of God. When we speak we may be "just talking," but when God speaks great events occur.

Speech is the most direct and clear expression of human thought. So the purposive thought of God himself is expressed in his creation of the world. It is no accident that in Gen. and also in Ps. 33 the creation is attributed both to the speech and to the breath of God (cf. Gen. 1:2; 2:7; Ps. 33:6). The Hebrew word for "breath" is the same as the word for "spirit." So it is also in Greek and in many other languages, ancient and modern. The breath is, in the Hebrew view, the very life of a man; and it is no wonder that in speech it expresses his innermost thought and feeling. Thus God puts his own inner power and meaning into his creation and something of his own life into man.

Of Christ. The NT continues in places the usage of the OT, particularly that of the prophets. John the Baptizer is placed firmly in the succession of the prophets when Luke writes that "the word of God came to John the son of Zechariah in the wilderness" (3:2). As the phrase "word of the LORD" in the OT sometimes refers to the Mosaic law, so in the NT "the word of God" sometimes refers to the gospel, the good news of Christ (e.g. Acts 4:31; 13:46; 17:13; Col. 1:25). Often the same message is called "the word of the Lord," the phrase then meaning the good news concerning Christ the Lord (e.g. Acts 15:35; 19:10; cf. 15:7). In places "the word of God" means the promises of God to his people (e.g. Rom. 9:6). One writer says: "By faith we understand that the world was created by the word of God" (Heb. 11:3).

However, the most distinctive idea of "the Word" in the NT occurs in the prologue of the 4th Gospel (John 1:1-18). The English translation inevitably fails to bring out the whole meaning of the original Greek in this passage. "Word" in the English is a literal translation of the Greek *Logos,* it is true. But *Logos* means much more. It means also the thought behind the word, the organizing of thought for expression and hence reason. It commonly appears in the writings of the Greek philosophers and of the Church fathers of the 2nd cent. and is usually there translated "reason."

The prologue provides a marvelous bridge of thought between both the Greek culture and the Hellenistic Jewish culture of the day on the one hand and the gospel of Christ on the other. We have already seen how prominent a place the word of God holds in the OT, representing as it does both the outgoing, purposive, creative power of God and his disclosure of himself and his truth to men. On the other hand, in Greek philosophy the word meant not only reason in the minds of men but also the rational order in or behind nature—the order which makes natural science possible—and the structure of truth itself which men discover in mathematics and logic. Some philosophers, especially the great Hellenistic Jew Philo, who was an older contemporary of Jesus, combined the 2 traditions by explaining the reason in men's minds, in nature, and in all truth by a reason (*logos,* or "word") which came out, or "emanated," from the mysterious God.

When John tells us, "In the beginning was the Word, and the Word was with God, and the Word was God" (1:1), he is saying that the reason for everything is not something which has been derived from God. The reason has always been in God, indeed was God himself—God's own reason or meaningful purpose. It is this outgoing, purposive thought of God that has made all things (John 1:3), even as Gen. 1 has declared.

"And the Word became flesh and dwelt among us, full of grace and truth; we have beheld his glory, glory as of the only Son from the Father" (John 1:14). If you would see the reason for everything, the purpose or thought of God in all creation, then behold Jesus! He is the embodiment of God's own creative purpose, the perfect revelation of God himself.

Not only did Jesus speak the truth. He *was* the truth (John 14:6), himself the supreme revelation of God to men. Hence "the name by which he is called is The Word of God" (Rev. 19:13).

In good biblical language, therefore, a Christian may properly speak of Jesus' teaching as "the word of God" (Luke 5:1; cf. John 5:24; 8:43; 12:48), or he may call Jesus himself "the Word of God." Some passages in the NT use the phrase "word of life" (Phil. 2:16; I John 1:1), referring either to Jesus or to the gospel message through which we come to faith in him.

Revelation. All the biblical testimonies concerning the word of God, then, refer to God's revelation or disclosure of himself and his instruction to men. His purposive, powerful acts of creation, his showing of his power and will to the prophets, his giving of the righteous law, his supreme self-disclosure in Jesus Christ, and his own good news concerning Christ— every one of these or all together may properly be called "the word of God."

Now we look again at that suggestive opening of Jer. "The words of Jeremiah . . . to whom the word of the LORD came" (1:1-2). Should we call Jer., and likewise the whole Bible, itself "the word of God"? Or are these writings the "words of Jeremiah" and

other human writers *about* the word of God which came to them in various ways and supremely in Jesus Christ? We must not answer too hastily, for both may be true in different perspectives. We must pursue the question further, looking next at the nature of revealed religion and of revelation itself.

II. REVELATION AS DIVINE COMMUNICATION

God as One Who Speaks. God is known to Jews and Christians as personal. This does not mean that he is reduced to the form or limits of human beings. The God who created us and all things and who reigns over all is obviously not a big man, in the sky or elsewhere. Besides being invisible to our eyes he has powers beyond all our imagination and understanding. Yet with all his unmeasured mystery he is one who thinks, acts with purpose, and loves. He is not a mere blind force but the Father who has made himself known.

"God is love" (I John 4:8). Because love is of his very nature he has sought to communicate with those of his creatures which possess a little power to understand, to love, and to share his purpose. It is his communication with human beings that we call revelation.

Man as One Who Hears. Man is able to hear the word of God because he is made "in the image of God" (Gen. 1:27). God made us for a personal relationship with him and so gave us a power which stones and trees do not have, the power to receive and understand his communication of his word to us. A brilliant scientist and self-confessed atheist said publicly that he found rather attractive and believable the Jewish and Christian idea that a great rational Mind governed the universe. But he could not see, he said, any more reason why there should be communication of any kind between that Mind and a man than between a man and one of his shoelaces. There is a good answer: my shoelace does not share with me the power to give and receive communication, while God and I do both possess that power, thanks to his sharing it with men in his creation.

Every kind of communication has 2 sides, one giving and one receiving. Revelation is no exception. God's word is actually communicated to men only when men receive it. No matter how good a radio station is, a poor radio receiver may bring into my living room a garbled and senseless program. In the process of revelation God's own word is always perfect, but our receiving of that word is limited by our own poor attunement to God. The bias of our expecting to hear what our selfish desires, our limited instruction, and our faithless fears dictate distorts our hearing to some extent even when we are at our best.

Infallible Word Fallibly Received and Reported. Men of old who received and reported God's revelations to them and to their people were, like us, sinful, fallible men. Consequently they often failed to grasp the whole meaning of God's word to them. Later, when they set down in writing their reports of the revelations they had received, their expressions of their understanding—though often exalted and marvelous—were still human and sometimes ambiguous or even misleading. In view of these human limitations Jeremiah's description of his own writing takes on deep significance, both concerning that book and concerning the Bible as a whole. He wrote "The words of Jeremiah . . . to whom the word of the LORD came" (Jer. 1:1-2). The Bible is literally the words of men seeking to express the word of God which had come to them.

III. THE MESSAGE OF THE WORD OF GOD

God Himself Revealed. Of all the contents revealed by God the most important by far is God himself. There is no thought or true proposition man may know which can be compared in importance to a personal meeting with God himself.

Everyone has seen a youth growing into manhood, confused about himself, insecure, troubled. Many people give him good advice and much of it he recognizes as good and true. Yet his anxious, troubled search for self-understanding and self-acceptance continues. Then one day a certain young woman appears on the scene and the personal acquaintance with her transforms him into a confident, effective personality.

Nothing which God said to Moses at the burning bush would have changed his life and world history if Moses had not received all this from the experienced presence of God himself. The greatest thing which ever happened to Isaiah was that, as he tells it, "in the year that King Uzziah died I saw the Lord sitting upon a throne, high and lifted up; and his train filled the temple" (Isa. 6:1).

The most important revelation reported in the Bible is God's own meeting with men. Even more valuable than any teaching of Jesus was men's confrontation of God's own spirit and power in Jesus.

The Word Communicating Truth. To confront a person and recognize him as the person he is, is to know some truth as well as to meet that person. It is to know something about his appearance, spirit, or manner—perhaps all these. How much more an encounter with God gives a man knowledge of truth! There is no other truth so important to learn as truth about the character and attitude of the sovereign God on whom the meaning and future of our existence depend.

Moreover, in God's experienced presence his people have often learned much more. He puts everything in a new perspective. Ps. 73 tells of such a change. The writer was "envious of the arrogant" and bitter about "the prosperity of the wicked," while he himself, trying hard to be clean and obedient, "all the day" has "been stricken, and chastened every morning." Continuing, he says, "But when I thought how to understand this, it seemed to me a wearisome task, until I went into the sanctuary of God." Then, however, all was changed. In God's presence he saw the longer and deeper view. Soon he was praising God. Indeed the psalm as a whole is expressing the poet's gratitude for his having been saved from the sinful envy into which he had been slipping.

Often when God makes himself known it is with the purpose of filling the mind and heart of a man with a message or with the understanding of his will. It is in this way that the prophets were impelled to warn the people of their sins, encourage them in adversity, and direct them into ways of righteousness. So Jesus teaches all his disciples about the reign of God and his will for us.

Often in the biblical accounts of such revelations there are descriptions of accompanying wonders—such as the burning bush, the writing on tables of stone, or a voice from heaven. Many of these marvels are fitting symbols of the greater marvel that God was present in overwhelming power. Some were visible only to eyes of faith. Some may have happened quite literally as described—for God is not a helpless prisoner in the world which he has made. Some may be concrete symbols of spiritual realities which witnesses found to be altogether beyond their powers of literal description. In every instance it is important that we not miss the essential message through undue preoccupation with the forms in which its coming is described.

IV. THEN AND NOW

The Word Came in Ancient Times. The books of the Bible tell how, long ago, revelations of God came at many times and places to many persons. But more than that they tell how a single cumulative stream of revelation rose and fell through many centuries until it reached a mighty climax in Jesus Christ, then spread from him far out around the Mediterranean basin. Although this stream includes a great variety of ideas, and as reported some are in irreconcilable conflict, nevertheless it all belongs together in one story—a story of a single subject, the Word of God. Indeed, as we often call a book by its subject matter—as when a schoolgirl says, "I dropped my geography on the sidewalk"—so in that sense we may call the Bible "the word of God."

How the Word Comes Through the Bible to Us Today. It is possible to read the Bible today without finding the word of God. Many people, of course, simply lack understanding to comprehend passages which they read—and some passages are far from being easy. But learned scholars too may read through the pages of scripture, and even carefully study them for many years, without discovering the word of God. Some read it as a source of information about customs in ancient times; e.g. Acts 27 is one of the most important sources of information we have about sailing ships in the first cent. Others read it to enjoy the beauty of its great literature. Argumentative people sometimes look for material by which to humiliate their neighbors.

Occasionally readers who are only seeking information or practicing a language are drawn into a new kind of quest and soon find themselves confronted by the commanding presence of God himself. However, there are ways by which one is more likely to discover the divine word and to distinguish that word from the erring words of men in which it comes to us. One of these men said, "But we have this treasure in earthen vessels" (II Cor. 4:7). If we are to find the treasure and not merely the clay jar in which it comes, we need to be prepared in mind and heart.

In order to discover the revealing word we need to read in the following ways:

In Context. In most versions of the Bible which we read the text is divided by numbers into short vss. for convenience of reference. This purely artificial division leads many readers to think that each vs. is supposed to stand alone and convey its meaning without regard to the words which precede or follow it. Perhaps this supposition is further encouraged by the practice of using a single verse as text for a sermon (see "The History of Biblical Interpretation," pp. 971-77).

The general practice of reading single vss. in isolation, however, is likely to lead to serious misunderstanding. Some sayings do stand forth clear and strong by themselves. Indeed many vss. of Prov. are in themselves complete proverbial sayings, and throughout the Bible many other vss. are similarly independent in meaning. However, more often a vs. belongs thoroughly to the passage of which it is a part and, when a reader is seeking understanding of it, should be examined as part of the whole. Later, when its meaning has been securely grasped, it may of course be repeated by itself or be made to stand alone as text of a sermon.

In Historical Perspective. Every passage of the Bible was originally written in a time very different from our own. Often it is impossible to catch its full force or even to gain elementary understanding of it without some knowledge of the historical situation in which it was written. Since we cannot all be specialists in the study of the historical events that provided the background of each book, the historical articles and the introductions to the various books in a commentary like this are invaluable resources for improving our understanding (see "The Historical Study of the Bible," pp. 978-82).

In Relation to Other Knowledge. Truth is one. God does not reveal to us through the scripture what is known through the sciences to be in error. When we read the Bible we should bring to it our best knowledge and intelligence. When the words on the page of scripture say to us what is contrary to scientific teaching, we can be sure that the scientific teaching is mistaken—and hence probably has already been or will soon be corrected by other scientific study—or that we are misunderstanding the biblical passage, or that the biblical idea here is simply a bit of the common human understanding at the time of writing and does not belong to the revealed word of God. It is part of the "earthen vessel," not of the divine "treasure."

Under the Lordship of Jesus Christ. The supreme revelation of God is Jesus Christ. It is to God as we know him in Christ that we owe our loyalty. Whether in life or thought, what is contrary to Christ we must as Christians discard. Much of ancient pagan culture in Athens or Rome we may acknowledge as beautiful, and we may be grateful for the ennobling and good influence of a Plato or a Seneca in his own time and place. Much more we may be grateful for Moses and Isaiah, through whom came into human history not only much good influence for their own times but also much preparation for the coming of Jesus Christ. In the teachings of all these men there are ideas which are in harmony with Christ and with all we know today. All such thoughts we welcome as truth for ourselves as well as good for men of old. But when their teachings conflict with Christ, even though we find those teachings in the Bible, we acknowledge the Lordship of Christ by declining to accept as true for us anything contrary to him.

Jesus himself gives us an example when he says, "You have heard that it was said, 'An eye for an eye and a tooth for a tooth.' But I say to you, Do not resist one who is evil. But if any one strikes you on the right cheek, turn to him the other also." (Matt. 5:38-39.) Despite the fact that "an eye for an eye and a tooth for a tooth" is given as God's command in 3 books of the OT (Exod. 21:24; Lev. 24:20; Deut. 19:21) we cannot so accept it. It represents a partial understanding of God's will and was doubtless good in its own time since it pointed away from the older law of the jungle which exacted a life for an eye and a life for a tooth, and it pointed toward the mercy and love of Christ. But we have been given the revelation of God in the Word made flesh, and in him the old law is found wanting.

Watching for the Forward Thrust of Revelation. In the time when any writing occurred there were many beliefs and practices which were common in the writer's nation and often also among neighboring peoples. The appearance of such customary ways of thinking and acting in the biblical writings is as natural as the use of the Hebrew language or of the Greek by people who spoke those languages. Such elements are no part of the unique illumination of God's revealing word, although of course some of them are true, and may afford useful means by which the revelation may be expressed.

E.g. the belief that the earth was flat, with the realm of the dead beneath it, was part of the popular science in the ancient world. So likewise was the description of many diseases as due to possession by demons. Such ideas are found in the Bible, not because it is a record of revelation, but because it was written when such ideas were taken for granted.

If we would find the element of revealed truth in the Scriptures we must give special attention to teachings which differentiate the scriptural writings from others current in the same periods of time.

In Christian Community. Every Christian belongs to a special community, known as the universal or catholic church of Jesus Christ, or "God's own people" (I Pet. 2:9). The Christian life has been brought to him by the actual historical stream of the Christian community, which in turn sprang from the people of the Old Covenant, the congregation of Israel. The stream tends continually to be corrupted by influences from the sinful world. The Bible is read to cleanse this stream, recovering the purity and power of God's own word by which our spiritual community was created and to which we owe our own existence as Christians.

The Bible was produced by the communities of the Old and New Covenants and preserved by them for community use. When a solitary individual reads it alone, he is in danger of losing its proper perspective. The individual needs the perspective and mutual correction of understanding which are provided by the Christian community. One person sees what another fails to discover. Indeed the people of one organized denomination may become prisoners of their own tradition, so that they fail to discern what is clear and precious to the people belonging to another branch of the church. Christians profit much by studying the Bible together in groups in order that together they may discover the word of God through the written words.

Indeed one great value of a commentary like this volume is that scholars of many backgrounds and traditions contribute to the reader corrections and insights from many perspectives. Together they represent not only important kinds of specialized learning but also a broader and more diverse cross section of the church than most individuals could possibly hope to know in person. Studying the Bible with constant help from such a commentary is an important way of reading in community. If along with such study the reader also participates in the studying, worshiping, working life of a local church, he truly meets this requirement for finding the word of God.

Prayerfully. If one reads the Bible only to learn some facts of ancient history he needs only the appropriate human intellectual equipment. If, however, he is seeking the word of God to him, then he needs to pray that God himself will cleanse him of his guilt and every obstructing desire and will illuminate in his heart and mind the word which God would have him receive at this time. An essential interpreter of the ancient word of God to the present reader of scripture is the Holy Spirit himself.

Expectantly. If a reader has little faith he is not likely to find the life-giving word to himself. Expecting little he will find little. On the other hand, encouraged by the lives of multitudes who have found in the Bible the divine word of forgiveness, life, truth, and victory, despite all odds, we have a right to approach our reading with high expectation. He who takes pains to learn the right techniques for his study and then makes a practice of reading with prayerful expectancy will not always be rewarded at the time, but now and then he will be surprised by the unexpected ways in which God will speak to him out of the sacred page.

Obediently. The Bible is not a book for the idly curious but for the earnest seeker. God does not illuminate the minds of people who are not concerned with walking in the way he shows to them.

According to the 4th Gospel Jesus said, "If any man's will is to do his will, he shall know whether the teaching is from God or whether I am speaking on my own authority" (John 7:17). So an eagerly obedient mind is sensitive to recognize among the human words of the Scripture the word of God to him for his own need.

Then, having found that word, the reader must follow it obediently, else the search will have been in vain. "But be doers of the word, and not hearers only" (Jas. 1:22).

For Further Study: C. H. Dodd, *The Authority of the Bible,* 1929 (now in paperback); a plainly worded book by an internationally famous NT scholar; recommended as at once scholarly and spiritually helpful. Karl Barth, *The Doctrine of the Word of God,* 1936; translation from the German of a Swiss theologian discussed throughout the world in the past 40 years. Benjamin B. Warfield, *The Inspiration and Authority of the Bible,* 1948; an able, recently reprinted defense of a very conservative view, opposing historical criticism. Alan Richardson and Wolfgang Schweitzer, eds., *Biblical Authority for Today,* 1951; a symposium. John Baillie, *The Idea of Revelation in Recent Thought,* 1956; solid book by an able Scottish theologian.

THE FERTILE CRESCENT AND ITS ENVIRONMENT

Herbert G. May

The term Fertile Crescent was first used by the noted orientalist James Henry Breasted to designate the generally more fertile lands which encircle the N end of the Arabian and Syrian deserts. The outer edge of this roughly crescent-shaped fertile area (see color map 2) is bordered on the E and N by the great highland belt of the mountains of Iran, Armenia, and Asia Minor and on the W by the Mediterranean, with Sinai and Egypt touching the SW tip. The crescent itself consists of Mesopotamia as the center and E horn and Syria-Palestine as the W horn.

The OT world was centered in the Fertile Crescent, and from that center went out the movement that produced the NT. Some knowledge of the geographical features of the Fertile Crescent and of its environs is therefore essential for understanding the Bible.

I. The Lands Around the Fertile Crescent

Iran. The great Iranian Plateau, the homeland of the Medes and Persians, is separated from the E horn of the Fertile Crescent by the Zagros Mountains and their W foothills (see color map 2). Here on the W slopes of the plateau was Elam, with its capital at Susa (cf. Ezra 4:9). The plateau extends E to the Indus River valley and to the Himalaya Mountains, of which it is a part. It is bordered on the N by the Alborz Mountains along the S end of the Caspian Sea, and farther E by the mountains of Koppeh Dagh. On the S are the Persian Gulf and the Gulf of Oman. The Alborz Mountains rise to more than 18,000 feet and the Zagros Mountains to more than 14,000 feet. Between these ranges in E Iran are the great salt deserts of Dasht-e Kavir and Dasht-e Lut.

Across this immense plateau into the Fertile Crescent moved commerce and culture. Archaeological evidence even for the prehistoric period links the Indus Valley and Mesopotamian cultures. The Elamites and the Medes were significant factors in Mesopotamian life, and from Iran came the Achaemenid rulers of the line of Cyrus, who in the 6th cent. and after shook to its foundations the life and culture of the Fertile Crescent. A main route between Mesopotamia and the Iranian highlands led up the Diyala branch of the Tigris River through the mountains to Ecbatana, the capital of ancient Media (cf. Ezra 6:2). It passed by Bisitun (Behistun; see color map 10), where Darius the Great memorialized on the dizzy heights of the cliffs in 3 languages the conquest of his enemies near the beginning of his reign (see ills., p. 224). In SW Iran in the province of Fars—Old Persian *parsa,* whence Persia and Persians—was Persepolis, glorified by Darius and his son Xerxes as the capital of the Persian Empire. It was burned and pillaged by Alexander the Great when he was en route all the way to the Indus River. In the next cent. the Parthians under the Arsacid dynasty set up an empire which eventually reached from the Euphrates to the Indus River and held the Romans at bay, even working with the Jews against Rome.

Armenia and Asia Minor. On the N of the Fertile Crescent the Armenian Mountains rise at times to more than 16,000 feet. This area is the Ararat of the OT (Gen. 8:4; II Kings 19:37; Jer. 51:27-28), the equivalent of Urartu in the records of Assyrian kings who made inroads beyond their N border. Two lakes, Urmia and Van, nestle in the rugged hill country, the latter in its geographical center. It is here in the Armenian highlands that the Tigris and Euphrates rivers have their origin.

Asia Minor is to the W of Armenia. Here the Halys is the most important of the rivers which flow from the mountain highlands to the Black Sea. Within its bend lay Hattusa, the capital of the Hittite Empire of patriarchal times (see color map 2). Later it formed the E boundary of the great Lydian Empire, which fell to Cyrus the Persian in 546. On the S border of Asia Minor are the Taurus Mountains, from which the Pyramus (Ceyhan) and the Saros (Seyhan) rivers flow into the fertile Cilician coastal plain by the Gulf of Issus at the NE corner of the Mediterranean. Through the Taurus Mountains the pass known as the Cilician Gates (see color map 12) gives entrance into the Cilician plains. Between Cilicia and Syria are the Amanus Mountains, really a part of the Taurus chain; and another pass, the Syrian Gates, leads across them to Antioch on the Orontes River in Syria.

Something of the complexity of racial and political conditions in Asia Minor throughout its history is suggested in the article on "The People of the OT World" (pp. 1005-17) and by color maps 2, 9, 10, 12, 16. Paul's journeys took him through Roman provinces in this area. Here was the province of Asia with its 7 churches (Rev. 1-3; see color map 16). W Asia Minor must be included in the Grecian

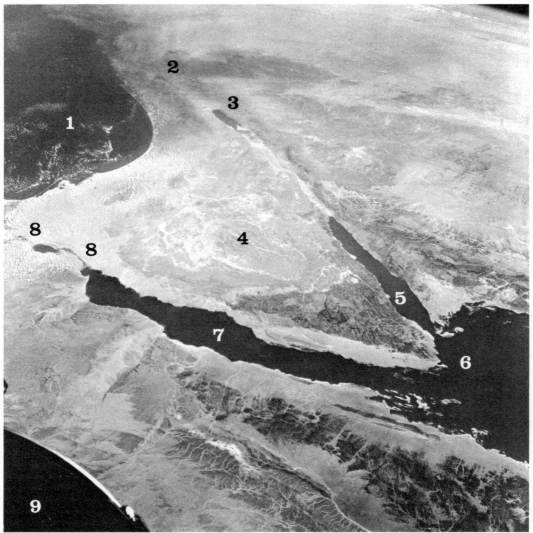

Courtesy of the National Aeronautics and Space Administration

The Sinai Peninsula and related areas, looking N: (1) Mediterranean Sea; (2) Sea of Galilee; (3) Dead Sea; (4) Sinai Peninsula; (5) Gulf of Aqaba; (6) Red Sea; (7) Gulf of Suez; (8) Suez Canal; (9) Space capsule

world, for here was Ionia, which with Greece proper formed the 2 mainlands of Greek life. The Greek world extended all the way from W Asia to Sicily and S Italy, which the Greeks colonized.

Egypt. Several trade routes through Palestine linked the Fertile Crescent with Sinai and Egypt. The most direct was the "way of the land of the Philistines" (Exod. 13:17; see color map 4), which kept close to the coast across N Sinai, leading from Egypt into the Philistine plain. This much-traveled route thence continued up the coast of Canaan, a branch of it cutting across Mt. Carmel through the Megiddo Pass to the Plain of Esdraelon. Another road, the "way to Shur" (Gen. 16:7), passed through the Wilderness of Shur in the Sinai Peninsula E of the Delta and continued up through the central highlands of Palestine, past Beer-sheba, Hebron, Jerusalem, and Shechem, to the Plain of Esdraelon. Another important route into the Fertile Crescent

led from the head of the Gulf of Aqaba, the E arm of the Red Sea, through Edom, Moab, and Transjordan up to Damascus and thence to Mesopotamia; in the OT it is known as the King's Highway (Num. 20:17; 21:22; cf. Deut. 2:27). In the 2nd cent. A.D. this road was rebuilt by the Emperor Trajan after his defeat of the Nabateans, who had occupied the region since early postexilic times; and Roman milestones may still be found here and there along the road.

Egypt is a narrow strip of fertility on each side of the Nile in the desert of NE Africa. Its life and culture were a gift of the Nile. One is impressed by the sharply outlined border between the desert and the sown, between the unfertile red lands and the fertile black lands. There are 2 natural divisions: the fan-shaped Delta of Lower Egypt, with its branches of the Nile, and the long ribbon of Upper Egypt. The latter, OT Pathros (Isa. 11:11; Jer. 44:1, 15; Ezek.

29:14), from one to 24 miles wide, extended from the apex of the Delta to the First Cataract at Syene —modern Aswan, where the new high dam is built (see color map 10). There a great granite ridge formed a natural boundary with the country to the S, biblical Ethiopia (Cush). The pharaoh of Egypt was the "Uniter of the 2 Lands," wearing the double crown of Upper and Lower Egypt.

Memphis, near the point of the Delta, S of modern Cairo, became the first capital of united Egypt early in the 3rd millennium. Near it the early kings built the pyramids as their tombs. But during the times of Egypt's greatest magnificence, beginning in the 11th and 12th dynasties (ca. 2000), the capital was at Thebes in Upper Egypt, some 400 air miles from the Mediterranean coast. It was the city of the god Amon, and the ruins of the great temples at present-day Luxor and Karnak on the E bank of the Nile witness to the glory of its past. On the W side of the Nile, since the land of the dead was in the W, were the tombs of the kings, queens, and nobles, and their mortuary temples and monuments. For ca. 2 cents. (18th-16th) the foreign Hyksos ruled from a capital at Avaris in the E Delta—a site later rebuilt as Raamses by Hebrew slaves (Exod. 1:11) and still later renamed Zoan (cf. e.g. Num. 13:22). In the 14th cent. the reformer king Akh-en-Aton built a new capital halfway between Memphis and Thebes and named it Akhet-Aton (now Tell el-Amarna), but it was destroyed by his successors.

In the heights of equatorial Africa the Nile has its source in 2 rivers, the Blue Nile and the White Nile, which meet at Khartoum, to flow for 1,900 miles to the Mediterranean. The Nile is navigable to the First Cataract, and river travel was an important factor in the life of Egypt. The annual flooding of the Nile (cf. Amos 8:8; 9:5), bringing rich sediments from its highland sources, reaches its height in Sept. A complicated and extensive irrigation system is necessary to hold back the waters as long as possible. Waterwheels lift the water from lower- to higher-level canals (cf. Exod. 7:19; Isa. 19:6). The celebration of the cresting of the Nile has been a cents. old festival in Egypt. Water use and conservation, inevitably a public works project, was a major motivation of unified government in Egypt.

The Nile provided the basis of Egyptian agriculture and dictated the mode of travel and commerce. Barges on the Nile carried the stones from the quarries for the public buildings and monuments of its cities. The rose granite of Aswan was transported widely down to the sea and thence to distant countries. But the Nile could be a capricious river, and variations in its crest, either too high or too low, could be disastrous. There are few clouds in the Egyptian sky, and the Nile and the sun were understandably prominent in Egyptian religious symbolism. The sun, rather than the rain god, was the chief god of Egypt, as also in Mesopotamia. Rainfall in Egypt is negligible.

Arabia. One is always conscious of Arabia in Palestine. Its desert encroaches on the cultivable lands of Transjordan. From it come the sand-laden winds to bring distress on the population and ruination to their crops. In the OT the E wind is properly the instrument of Yahweh's wrathful judgment (cf.

e.g. Isa. 27:8; Jer. 4:11-12; 13:24; Ezek. 17:10; 19:12; Hos. 13:15). The Arabian Desert covers an area of nearly a million square miles (see color map 7). The Arabian Peninsula is bounded on the W by the Red Sea, on the S by the Indian Ocean, and on the E by the Persian Gulf and the Gulf of Oman. Its N triangular section adjoining the Fertile Crescent is the rocky plateau of the Syrian Desert. In antiquity Arabia provided gold, associated esp. with Ophir and Havila (cf. e.g. Gen. 2:11-12; 1 Chr. 29:4; Job 22:24). From Arabia also came the much prized frankincense, myrrh, and spices, as well as precious stones (I Kings 10:2; Ezek. 27:22).

The highlands on the W of Arabia in Syria and Transjordan and on the W and S coasts of the peninsula provide a barrier and make for a paucity and irregularity of rain in the interior. There are 2 great sandy deserts in the heart of the Arabian Peninsula. That in the S—"The Empty Quarter" according to its Arabic name—is the largest continuous sandy area in the world. Only in SW Arabia, where there arose such kingdoms as Saba and Hadramaut (Hazarmaveth, Gen. 10:26), and in the SE by the coast of the Gulf of Oman was there sufficient rain for extensive regular cultivation. Saba and its people the Sabeans are in all probability to be associated with Sheba, from whence came the queen of Sheba to Solomon (I Kings 10:1-10). In these areas settled life could be supported, but the steppe-desert areas with a minimum of rainfall supported a predominantly nomadic and seminomadic population. The rains are sporadic and evaporation rapid, with little penetration into the ground. The daytime temperatures are usually over 100° F., though the night temperatures may at times be 50° cooler than at noon.

II. MESOPOTAMIA

Having surveyed the surrounding lands, we turn now to the Fertile Crescent itself and consider first its larger E and N area, Mesopotamia (see color map 2). Egypt is a land of one river and Mesopotamia of 2 rivers, the Tigris and Euphrates, which originally flowed independently into the Persian Gulf. Mesopotamia, using the term more generally, may be regarded as divided into 2 parts, indicated in the roughly hourglass-shaped territory between the Tigris and Euphrates, with Babylonia to the S and Assyria to the N. It is this N section which is more properly Mesopotamia; Assyria was located in the E part of it, along the Tigris River, on which lay such important cities as Nineveh, Calah, and Asshur.

The Tigris and Euphrates both originate in the highlands of Armenia. A number of tributaries flow into the Tigris from the adjoining mountains to the E: the Great or Upper Zab, the Little or Lower Zab, the Adhaim, and the Diyala (see color map 9). Two tributaries, the Balikh and the Khabur, join the Euphrates in upper Mesopotamia. On the Balikh is Haran in Paddan-Aram, the home of Abraham and his kindred (Gen. 11:31; 24:4, 10), where Jacob also sojourned and found his wives (Gen. 28-31). The Khabur is the OT Habor in the territory of Gozan, where some of the Israelites were exiled (II Kings 17:6; 18:11).

Babylonia was located in the alluvial plain which extends from N of present-day Baghdad to the Persian Gulf. It was here that the civilizations of Sumer and Akkad arose. The Euphrates has changed its course here through the cents., moving away from some sites which used to be on the river. Also the expansion of the alluvial plain S has resulted in separating some cities from their original position on the Persian Gulf. The Tigris, unlike the more sluggish Euphrates, was navigable for a long distance and was a river of commerce.

Like Egypt, Babylonia was dependent on the annual inundations. They resulted from the melting of the snows in the Armenian highlands, and flood stage was reached on the plains in Apr., with the lowest levels in Sep.-Oct. As in Egypt, the problem of storing and controlling the water was imperative and was a government function. In the alluvial plains the elaborate canal systems needed frequent renewing. Without effective government control the alluvial plains reverted to unfertile sands.

III. SYRIA-PALESTINE

Unlike Mesopotamia and Egypt, Syria-Palestine has no unified river system. There is some relation between this fact and the economic and sociopolitical lag in its development. Likewise its position as a corridor between the 2 great cultural areas hampered its political development, for both its neighbors wanted to control it and were loath to see a strong power develop within it. Into and through this area marched the armies of Egypt and Mesopotamia in their struggles to dominate it and each other. Egyptian, Babylonian, and Assyrian conquerors marched along the Phoenician coastal road and left their inscriptions on cliffs where the mountains come down close to the shore, and under which the modern coastal road is now tunneled. Certain common geographical features characterize this area, but more often they serve to divide rather than to unite. A neat thumbnail description of the Promised Land occurs in Deut. 8:7-9: "A land of brooks of water, of fountains and springs, flowing forth in valleys and hills, a land of wheat and barley, of vines and fig trees and pomegranates, a land of olive trees and honey, . . . a land whose stones are iron, and out of whose hills you can dig copper."

The Great Rift. The main geographical features of Syria-Palestine run in N-S zones (see color map 1). Most notable is the geologic depression which begins in N Syria below the Amanus-Taurus range and extends as a great trough down between the Lebanon and Anti-Lebanon mountains to become the valley of the Jordan and its S extension into the Gulf of Aqaba and the Red Sea. In it lie the Sea of Galilee, its surface 695 feet below sea level, and the Dead Sea, 1,280 feet below sea level—figures which must be increased as modern irrigation techniques are reducing the amount of water that flows into the Jordan and hence into the Dead Sea, to be lost through evaporation. The Jordan Valley and its waterless S extension are designated the Arabah, and the Dead Sea in the OT is the Sea of the Arabah or the Salt Sea. Today this great depression as it passes through Palestine is called the Ghor, i.e. Rift. Its deepest section, the flood plain of the Jordan River, separated from the upper level by marl terraces, is called the Zor. The tamarisk thick-

ets beside the Jordan are the biblical "jungle of the Jordan" (Jer. 12:15), formerly the habitat of wild animals (cf. ill., p. 613).

The Jordan River has its sources at the foot of Mt. Hermon, the S-most peak of the Anti-Lebanon range. To the N the fertile valley or plain between the Lebanon and Anti-Lebanon mountains is the biblical Valley of Lebanon (Josh. 11:17) or Valley of On (RSV Aven, Amos 1:5). It is today known as el-Biqa', "the Valley." It is drained by the Leontes River, which flows into the Mediterranean above Tyre. The N-most part of the depression between the Syrian plateau and the coastal range is drained by the Orontes River, which flows into the sea near Antioch. Near the watershed of these 2 rivers, some 3,300 feet above sea level, is modern Baalbek, the Heliopolis of the Roman period, and the On of OT times, which gave its name to the plain. Here also is the "entrance to Hamath," the N boundary of Israel at its greatest expansion (I Kings 8:65; II Kings 14:25). Hamath, along with Kadesh and Riblah, were important cities on the Orontes River (see color map 9).

The W Highlands. W of this great depression are the W Highlands, which include the Central Highlands of Palestine and the Lebanon Mountains to the N. The Lebanon Mountains form a backdrop for the Phoenician cities on the coastland. Their forest-covered slopes provide a commodity in demand not only in Mesopotamia and Palestine but also in Egypt. The cedars and cypresses of Lebanon in the days of Hiram of Tyre furnished materials for Solomon's building projects; a part of Solomon's palace was called the House of the Forest of Lebanon (I Kings 7:2-5). The hill country of Palestine was much more wooded than at present, but its forests could not compete with those of Lebanon. The Lebanon ridge is more than 6,000 feet above sea level, and its snow-clad slopes in the winter today provide resorts for skiing. The highest peak of the Lebanons is Qurnat el-Sauda, a little over 11,000 feet above sea level.

The Central Highlands of Palestine are the continuation of the W Highlands. They rise highest in Upper Galilee, where Jebel Jermaq reaches almost 4,000 feet (see color map 1). Upper Galilee is sharply differentiated from Lower Galilee with its more rolling hills, amid which lies Nazareth. The Central Highlands are interrupted by the E-W fertile Plain of Megiddo–Valley of Jezreel depression, which provides not only a granary for Palestine but a route from the Mediterranean coast to Transjordan. The Kishon River drains the Plain of Megiddo (Esdraelon), flowing through the narrow pass which separates Mt. Carmel from the Lower Galilee foothills, to issue out through the Plain of Acco to the Mediterranean. The rains made this quiet stream a raging torrent disastrous to the Canaanite chariotry in the days of Deborah (Judg. 5:19-22). The plain is bordered on the S and SW by the hills of Manasseh and the ridge of Mt. Carmel. The Central Highlands continue on through the Hill Country of Ephraim and the Hill Country of Judah, and then on into the Negeb, the steppe-desert area S of Beer-sheba. In the Hill Country of Ephraim on either side of Shechem are Mts. Gerizim and Ebal, elevation 2,889 and 3,083 feet respectively. In the Hill Country of Judah is Jerusalem, *ca.* 2,500 feet above sea level.

The Wilderness of Judah. The E slopes of the Central Highlands drop down quickly to the Jordan Valley. E of the watershed of the Judean hills lies the Wilderness of Judah (Judea), extending S into the Negeb. The Wilderness of Judah is a barren land of limestone ridges, narrow gorges, and desolate vistas. In it were mountain fortresses of Herod the Great—Hyrcania, E of Bethlehem; Herodium, where Herod was buried, to the NE of Tekoa; and Masada, the last stronghold of the Jews against Rome in A.D. 73, *ca.* 10 miles S of En-gedi (see color map 14). It was here in the Wilderness of Judah that David fled before Saul and that John the Baptist preached, and this was the scene of the temptation of Jesus. Even here in the wilderness there may be some greenness of vegetation when the winter rains irregularly and niggardly cross beyond the central ridge.

The Coastal Plain. The coastal plain toward the N, the Plain of Phoenicia, is narrow, with the Lebanons coming close to the shore. With the mountains at their back and with an irregular shoreline providing excellent harbors, the Phoenician cities looked toward the sea. This is not to imply that they ignored inland trade. The excavations at Tyre, Sidon, and Gebal, or farther N at Ugarit, evidence the cosmopolitan character of these seacoast cities. Ezek. 27 illustrates the complex international character of the trade of the city of Tyre. In considerable contrast with the Phoenician coastland was the relatively straight shoreline of Palestine S of the Plain of Acco and the Mt. Carmel promontory. Here the narrow Plain of Dor fans out into the luxuriant Plain of Sharon and the low rolling hills of the Plain of Philistia. The last extends E *ca.* 20 or more miles from the shore before reaching the Shephelah, the foothills of the Hill Country of Judah, which forms a distinct topographical feature of Palestine. Before the time of Herod the Great the only really good harbor of Palestine was at Acco, renamed Ptolemais in the 3rd cent. B.C. Dor and, farther to the S, Joppa were significant but 2nd-rate harbors. Joppa, whose rocky reefs are appropriately identified by tradition with the remains of the dragon slain by St. George, served as a port of Jerusalem at the time of Solomon; through it the cedars, floated down from the north, were taken up to Jerusalem (II Chr. 2:16). Not until NT times were more adequate harbor facilities made available through the construction of the harbor and city of Caesarea by Herod the Great.

The E Highlands. The Anti-Lebanon Mountains and the Transjordan tableland lie E of the Great Rift. From the Anti-Lebanons flow the Abana and Pharpar rivers to provide water for the city and plain of Damascus. The pass of the Abana River forms the only route over the E slopes of the mountains. At the S end of the Anti-Lebanons Mt. Hermon rises to more than 9,000 feet above sea level, and its crown is snowcapped most of the year. S of Hermon and the Damascus Plain lie the fertile plains of Bashan and the Hauran. Farther S in Gilead the Transjordan tableland rises at times to 4,000 feet. It drops toward the E to merge with the Arabian steppes only some 25 to 30 air miles from the Jordan.

Four main rivers cut spectacular clefts into the Transjordan plateau to exit into the Arabah. The N-most of these, the Yarmuk, entering the Jordan *ca.* 5 miles S of the Sea of Galilee, is unmentioned in the biblical text. Separating N and S Gilead (Deut. 3:12, 16), the Jabbok River flows into the Jordan near ancient Adam (see color map 5). One of its fords on the King's Highway was the scene of Jacob's night adventure with an angel (Gen. 32:22-32). The Jabbok marked the boundary between the kingdoms of Sihon king of the Amorites and Og king of Bashan (Num. 21:24; Judg. 11:22). Its S bend formed the W boundary of Ammon, and its source was a spring near Rabbath-ammon, the capital of the Ammonites—renamed Philadelphia in the Hellenistic-Roman period and now Amman, the capital of present-day Jordan. The Arnon River flows through one of the most spectacular of the many gorges of Transjordan to issue into the Dead Sea. The city of Aroer sat on the rim of the gorge, whose steep sides rise to more than 4,000 feet above the level of the Dead Sea. The Arnon formed the boundary between Moab and the kingdom of Sihon (Num. 21:13). To the S the Brook Zered, which served as boundary between Moab and Edom, empties into the Arabah at the S end of the Dead Sea. It falls almost 4,000 feet in its 35-mile length.

Climate. The latitude of Palestine is roughly that of the state of Georgia. Because it is near the desert on the one hand and the Mediterranean on the other, because its main geographical features run N-S while the prevailing winds come from the W and NW, and because it varies so greatly in elevation, Palestine has an incredible variety of climate and scenery. There are the occasional snows of winter in the highlands and the near-tropical climate of the Dead Sea; there are the pleasant rolling hills of Lower Galilee and the stark desert ridges of the Wilderness of Judea; there are the fertile plains of Esdraelon and the coastlands and the dry desert-steppes of the Negeb; there are rainless summers and wet and stormy winters.

The rainless summer lasts *ca.* May-Sept. The "heat of the day" (Gen. 18:1) of this time of year is tempered by the W breezes which reach Jerusalem before noon to produce the "cool [lit. "wind"] of the day" (Gen. 3:8). The first and last of the winter rains are called the "former," i.e. autumnal, and "latter," i.e. spring, rains. The biblical writer describes Palestine as "a land of hills and valleys, which drinks water by the rain from heaven," and properly contrasts it with the land of Egypt (Deut. 11:10-12). Here, unlike Egypt and Mesopotamia, it was not the sun god who held the chief position in the pantheon of gods, but rather the storm god, Baal. Here the rain clouds are important for the life of the country (cf. I Kings 18:41-46). Both Baal and Yahweh were described as riders on the clouds (Canaanite texts; Pss. 68:4; 104:3; cf. Ps. 18:10-15). Baal and Yahweh hurled thunderbolts. A significant cloud symbolism is associated with God in the Scriptures (Ezek. 1:4). The rain and the dew were both important for the crops; the summer dews came from the moist air when the land cooled rapidly at night (Gen. 27:28; Judg. 6:37-40; Ps. 133:3; Isa. 18:4) and were important for the preservation and ripening of the crops during the heat of the summer.

With the beginning of the rains in the autumn the agricultural processes could start, and understandably in this part of the world there was an autumnal New Year. The prevailing winds came from the Mediterranean, and the clouds dropped their waters on the W slopes of the central hills and across the gorge of the Jordan on the Transjordan plateau. Palestine is the recipient of the heavier rains, and the areas of considerable rainfall are much larger there than in Transjordan. The plateau of Transjordan is at points higher than the Central Highlands, so that there can at times be heavier rains there; there was obviously more rain in Moab than in Judah when Naomi and her husband fled from famine in Judah to sojourn in Moab (Ruth 1:1). Generally, however, Moab's rainfall is much less than that of the Jerusalem-Hebron area.

In Palestine the rainfall decreases from N to S, and it is less near the coast than in the highlands. In Upper Galilee it may reach 47 inches a year, while below Hebron it may be only 12 inches, and in the Negeb S of Beer-sheba it is only 5 inches a year. It becomes still less as one moves farther S. The annual rainfall at Jerusalem in the Judean hills is 26.1 inches, in contrast with 5.5 inches at Jericho and 3 inches or less at the Dead Sea. At Joppa on the coast the rainfall is 21 inches a year. Occasionally there may be snows in the Central Highlands

in the winter, as at Jerusalem. It may rain on both sides of the Rift of the Jordan while the sun is shining in the Jordan Valley. On rare occasions, however, even heavy rains may reach into the Jordan Valley; in Dec. 1966 the Jordan Valley became temporarily a muddy morass with its roads nearly impassable, and the waters of the Jordan inundated a police post beside the bridge. Generally, however, the Jordan Valley must depend on irrigation for water for agriculture—as it must have at the time of Lot, when it was "well watered everywhere like the garden of the LORD" (Gen. 13:10). Today portions of the Jordan Valley again flourish as a result of the East Ghor Canal leading from the Yarmuk River and wells producing water for irrigation in the Jericho area. The temperature variant between the Central Highlands and the Jordan Valley is considerable; the mean annual temperature is 14° lower at Jerusalem than at the Dead Sea.

For Further Study: D. Baly, *Geography of the Bible,* 1957; *Geographical Companion to the Bible,* 1963. Y. Aharoni, *The Land of the Bible,* 1967, translated by A. F. Rainey, pp. 3-72. G. E. Wright and F. V. Filson, eds., *Westminster Historical Atlas to the Bible,* rev. ed., 1956, pp. 17-20. H. G. May, R. W. Hamilton, G. N. S. Hunt, *Oxford Bible Atlas,* 1962, pp. 9-15, 48-53. C. C. McCown, "Palestine, Geography of," *IDB,* vol. III, 1962, pp. 626-39.

THE PEOPLE
OF THE OLD TESTAMENT WORLD

Herbert G. May

I. Introduction to the Biblical World

Understanding the Biblical World. The biblical world is the world disclosed in the Bible. It is also the larger world, often known primarily from non-biblical sources, in which the Bible arose and which provides background for understanding the Bible better.

The Bible is concerned with an immense span of time and a wide area of space. In time it begins with creation and ends within the Roman Empire. The legends of the patriarchs contain reminiscences of the early 2nd millennium B.C., and the ultimate sources of the myths in Gen. 1–11 go back at least a millennium earlier. The latest of the NT writings belong to the early 2nd cent. A.D. The geographical perspective of the Bible extends from India (Esth. 1:1) to Spain (Rom. 15:24, 28; the Tarshish of the OT is perhaps to be located in Sardinia or Spain; see comment on Jonah 1:3) and from Italy, Greece, and Armenia in the N to Arabia and Ethiopia in

the S. The biblical revelation took place in the arena of history, and while it is the events recorded which are significant, these cannot be understood apart from some appreciation of the places involved.

To understand the Scriptures better one must set the biblical events in their larger backgrounds, using all available pertinent nonbiblical sources. Thus, to appreciate the events of the enslavement of Israel in Egypt, the exodus from Egypt, and the conquest and settlement of Canaan by Israel, it helps to be familiar with something of the history of Egypt during the 18th-20th Dynasties, when these events were taking place, and particularly with the role played in his age by Pharaoh Ramses II, who was most probably the ruler of Egypt at the time of Moses. Inscriptions found in Egypt, written by Canaanite kings and others to 2 pharaohs of the 18th Dynasty (the Tell el-Amarna letters) throw significant light on the social and political situation in Canaan before the time of Moses in the 14th cent. From the same period in Canaan cuneiform alphabetic inscriptions

Tablets with inscriptions in cuneiform characters in the Assyro-Babylonian language; two letters to the King of Egypt (Akhnaton); *left*, from King Ashur-uballet of Assyria stating that the ambassador who bears it is sent bringing greetings and a gift of one splendid chariot, two horses and lapis lazuli (semi-precious stone of rich azure blue similar to a sapphire); the letter concludes with a statement that the embassy is not to make a long stay in Egypt; *right*, from Abi-mili, ruler of Tyre, stating that he has carried out the king's commands and that the whole region is in fear of the king's army; he says that he has sent ships for the use of the king's army and that he is protecting the city

from a temple library at the N Canaanite city of Ugarit disclose much about the religion of the Canaanites and throw into perspective some of the problems encountered by the invading Israelites. Egyptians, Assyrians, Babylonians, Phoenicians, Arameans, Greeks, Romans, and others were much involved in the events described in the Bible. Sometimes the records of these peoples refer to specific events mentioned in the Bible and give further data on them. Two volumes by James B. Pritchard (see the suggestions for further study below) witness how much the inscriptions, reliefs, statues, etc. from throughout the ancient Near East illumine biblical backgrounds.

The article "Archaeology" (pp. 1054-62) is part of the story of the discovery of the biblical world. The toil and romance of the struggle of mankind through the hundreds of millennia of the Old Stone (Paleolithic) Age, the Middle Stone (Mesolithic) Age, the New Stone (Neolithic) Age, and the Copper-Stone (Chalcolithic) Age into the Bronze and Iron ages and the Hellenistic and Roman times are revealed by archaeology in Palestine, Iraq, Iran, and other parts of the Middle East and in the Mediterranean area. This all belongs to the story of the larger world into which the biblical record must be set. Anthropologists, historians, philosophers, theologians, linguists, and others assist in interpreting these data. The discovery of the Dead Sea Scrolls in the Wilderness of Judea has highlighted for many the importance of the work of the archaeologist, as they have thrown light on the sectarian life of Judaism in the NT world.

The Expanse of the Biblical World. Something of the world-wide perspective of the biblical writers may be seen in the remarkable table of nations in Gen. 10, where the peoples and nations are listed in a genealogical tree of 3 main branches as descendants of Japheth, Ham, and Shem, the 3 sons of Noah. There are inner inconsistencies in this genealogy, due in part to variant sources, but it is an important first attempt at such a comprehensive classification. Despite the fact that it is not a scientific racial, geographical, linguistic, or ethnic classification, it combines ethnic, national, and political criteria; and the presumed genealogical relationships of the nations and peoples reveal much about the viewpoints of the authors. In this table are peoples of Anatolia and Armenia, Media and Persia (Iran), Mesopotamia (Iraq), Syria and Palestine, Arabia, Egypt and Ethiopia and Libya, Greece and the Grecian isles, and even distant Tarshish. Some of the names were only names to biblical scholars until they were found in nonbiblical records, which have often made possible more definite identification and location (see comment on Gen. 10 and color maps 2, 7, 9).

Another good example of Israelite awareness of the "outer world" is the list of countries and their products involved in the trading activities of the city of Tyre in Ezek. 27. Materials from Syria, Palestine, Cyprus, and Egypt went into the making of Phoenician ships. In Tyre's army were men of distant Persia, Lydia (Lud) in Asia Minor, and Cyrenaica (Put) in N Africa. Among those who traded with Tyre were Tarshish, Greece (Javan), Asia Minor (Tubal, Meshech, Beth-togarmah), Rhodes, Edom, Judah, Syria (Damascus, Helbon), Arabia (Uzal, Dedan, Kedar, Sheba, Raamah), and Mesopotamia (Haran, Eden, Asshur, Chilmad). A list of products from the various places is given, and it is evident that the ships and shops of Tyre must have carried a very cosmopolitan inventory.

Ezekiel knew well the intricacies of Phoenician commerce. The perspective of the prophets extended to the pagan nations, and their oracles indicate no little familiarity with them. Though there were no newspapers to keep them informed, the Israelites were acquainted with the larger world around them. Palestine's position as a corridor through which passed the commerce and armies of many nations preserved it from a narrow provincialism.

The story of the journeys of Abraham from Ur to Haran, from Haran to Canaan, from Canaan to Egypt, and then back to Canaan illustrates something of the mobility of people in the biblical world, which was accustomed to many and distant migrations of peoples (see color map 2). The missionary journeys of Paul, who was born at Tarsus in Asia Minor, educated in Jerusalem, and converted on the road to Damascus, took him over wide areas of the biblical world—to Antioch in Syria, to Perga and Attalia in Pamphylia, to Antioch in Pisidia, to Iconium, Lystra, and Derbe in Lycaonia, to Patara in Lycia, through Galatian Phrygia to Troas, Miletus, and Ephesus in Asia (i.e. the Roman province in the W part of Asia Minor), to Neapolis, Philippi, Thessalonica, Amphipolis, Apollonia, and Beroea in Macedonia, to Athens and Corinth in Achaia, and to the Greek isles of Samothrace, Cyprus, Rhodes, Cos, Chios, Samos, and Lesbos. His fateful trip to Rome, which began at Caesarea, took him to Sidon, to Myra in Lycia, off the S of Crete and on to the islands of Malta and Sicily, and thence to Puteoli in Italy and to Rome (see maps, pp. 745, 746, 750, 752, 754, 766, and color map 16). Though it is uncertain, Paul may have visited Spain before his death, as he hoped to do (Rom. 15:24, 28).

In NT times the Jewish dispersion was widespread, and when the Jews returned to Jerusalem for the festivals, it became indeed a cosmopolitan city. In Acts 2:5-11 we are told there were dwelling in Jerusalem at Pentecost "devout men from every nation under heaven," a statement which is about as inclusive of the biblical world as we can get! Moving from the E ends of the biblical world westward, they are listed as Parthians, Medes, Elamites, dwellers in Mesopotamia, Armenia (with some authorities, instead of Judea), Cappadocia, Pontus, Asia, Phrygia, Pamphylia, Egypt, and Cyrene of Libya, and visitors from Rome, both Jews and proselytes, Cretans and Arabians.

For Israel the Promised Land was the center of the biblical world; "This is Jerusalem; I have set her in the center ["midst"] of the nations, with countries round about her" (Ezek. 5:5). The returned exiles are described as dwelling "at the center [lit. "navel"] of the earth" (Ezek. 38:12). Cf. how for the Greeks Delphi was the navel of the earth, and for the Romans it was Rome. In the OT the emphasized direction is more from outside toward the Promised Land, e.g. from Ur and Haran to Palestine, from Egypt to Palestine (the Exodus), from the lands of the dispersion to Palestine (the return from exile). In the NT, though the center of the biblical world is still Palestine, as the gospels witness—and the traditional spot of the geographical center of the world is now shown to Christian pilgrims in the Church of the Holy Sepulcher—yet the emphasized direction of movement is from Palestine to the outlying nations. The scene shifts from Jerusalem to the churches of the Gentile world. Paul's journey from Palestine to Rome may be taken as symbolic of this. Yet the importance of Palestine and Jerusalem for Christianity must not be minimized.

II. Ethnic Classification of the Peoples of the Biblical World

Hamites and Semites. The biblical world presents a very complicated picture of peoples, nations, and languages. Peoples who belong to the same general racial group may speak different languages, and a people moving into a new area may adopt the language of that area and give up its more native tongue. Race has no necessary relation to culture. The same general physical types may be found in many different peoples. One does find in the Middle East 2 general types to which we shall find it convenient to refer: one which the anthropologists call dolichocephalic, or longheaded, and the other brachycephalic, or broadheaded. The latter type may be associated more particularly with certain peoples of the highlands of Anatolia and Armenia, and the term Caucasic or Armenoid is sometimes applied to them. As far as language is concerned, we shall find a number of languages which as yet defy classification with other well-known families of languages.

A general classification of the peoples of the biblical world may be made in terms of Hamites, Semites, Indo-European, and others, the "others" being no less important than the first 3. The Hamites are named after Ham, one of the 3 sons of Noah, and they include the Egyptians, Ethiopians (Cushites), and Libyans. The Semites are designated after the name of another son of Noah, Shem, and they include, linguistically and ethnically speaking, the Assyrians and Babylonians (Akkadians), the Canaanites and Phoenicians, Amorites, Arameans, Hebrews, Moabites, Ammonites, Edomites, and the Arab groups. The table in Gen. 10 classifies the Canaanites and Phoenicians (Sidon) as descendants of Ham, but does so probably on the basis of political and geographical considerations and understandably hesitates to make the Hebrews and Canaanites descendants of the same son of Noah. The Hamitic and Semitic languages have enough similarities that a common origin is sometimes posited, possibly in N Africa, or they are explained as a result of early invasion of N Africa by the Semites. Both Hamites and Semites generally belong to the dolichocephalic (longheaded) type, rather than the brachycephalic type, although, as e.g. in Mesopotamia and Canaan, the Semitic-speaking peoples may be of mixed types as a result of invasions from the N.

Indo-Europeans. The Indo-Europeans in the biblical world include many peoples, such as the Greeks, Romans, Lydians, Cimmerians (Gomer), and also the Medes, Persians, and Scythians (Ashkenaz), who are Indo-Iranians. The language of the older Hittite inscriptions is Indo-European, imposed by foreigners on the non-European (Armenoid) population of the area. A different Indo-European tongue

is found in later Hittite inscriptions at various sites in S Anatolia and N Syria. In the neighboring region the Armenoid population of the kingdom of Mitanni was similarly ruled by Indo-Iranians (Indo-Aryans) belonging to the Indo-European family. The Philistines who came from Caphtor (Crete) were in all probability Indo-Europeans. In the table of nations Gomer, Madai (the Medes), Ashkenaz, and Javan (Greeks) are in the line of Japheth, Noah's 3rd son, while the Caphtorim (Philistines) and Ludim (Lydians) are descendants of Ham, and Lud (also Lydia?) is a descendant of Shem.

Other Peoples. Among the other peoples of the biblical world are the Hurrians (Horites), Urartians (people of Urartu, biblical Ararat), Hittites, Elamites, and Kassites. The first 3 of these, at least, may be ultimately Caucasic in origin and belong to the broadheaded type. The Hittites and Urartians were located in central Anatolia and the Armenian highlands, respectively, and the Hurrians in the nearby upper Tigris-Euphrates area. The Hurrians formed the basic population of the kingdom of Mitanni (see color map 2). They were also dispersed through other areas, being found prominently in Canaan. They are known by the equivalent term "Horites" in the OT, which associates them peculiarly with Edom. One authority has plausibly argued that they were apparently also known in the OT as Hivites, Jebusites, and Perizzites and has identified their language as belonging to the Caucasic group, its only known relative being Urartian. The language of the "native" Hittite population is called Hattic or proto-Hittite or proto-Hattic; it is unlike any other language and is of course different from the official language of the Hittite Empire in the inscriptions, which was Indo-European.

In the table in Gen. 10 the Elamites, who occupied the slopes of the Iranian plateau E of the Babylonians (see color map 2), are ascribed to the line of Shem. The Elamite language has no known relatives. The Kassites, another unassignable group, earlier located in W Iran (see color map 7), became the rulers of Babylonia for several centuries in the period which followed the fall of the First Dynasty of Babylon. With the Kassites is to be related the Cush of Gen. 10:8-12—a portion of the table from a different source from the preceding vss., in which Cush means Ethiopia.

Among the more important peoples of the biblical world are the Sumerians, of whom no hint is given in the table of nations—or elsewhere in the Bible, for that matter. They inhabited Sumer, the lower Tigris-Euphrates alluvial valley, from late in the 4th millennium to the early 2nd millennium and laid the foundations for much of the later Mesopotamian cultures, influencing indirectly a great deal of the ancient Near East. They are linguistically and ethnically a people separate from all the rest. Their language resembles no known speech.

III. The Peoples and Nations of the Biblical World

Some background of knowledge of the peoples of the biblical world is imperative for an understanding of the Bible. Since the purpose here is to give perspective on the peoples of the biblical world rather than to present a digest of the history of the ancient world, the outline followed is more geographical than chronological. We begin with the Sumerians and their successors in Mesopotamia and then turn to the Egyptians. After this we move to the peoples of Asia Minor and their Hurrian neighbors, and then to the Medes and Persians of the Iranian plateau. Next we consider some of the peoples adjoining Canaan, including those of Arabia, and finally those whom the Israelites encountered in Canaan and the Hebrews themselves.

A. THE PEOPLES OF MESOPOTAMIA

The Sumerians and Akkadians. What was probably the earliest system of writing in the world was not, as used to be thought, the Egyptian but rather that invented in Mesopotamia during the 4th millennium, *ca.* 3300 B.C., with clay tablets used as writing material. It began as a pictographic (picture) script, but it became conventionalized, with the signs made up of wedge-shaped marks produced by a stick or stylus in the soft clay; hence it is called "cuneiform" (wedge-shaped) writing (see "Writing in Biblical Times," pp. 1201-08). The baked clay tablets proved to be almost imperishable, and thanks to this fact the inscriptions could be preserved until today (see ill., p. 1005).

It was most probably the Sumerians who invented this style of writing, although it is possible that when they migrated into Mesopotamia from some unknown area they adapted the already existing pictographic script to their own language. In the 3rd millennium it was adopted from the Sumerians by the Semitic Akkadians, centering around Akkad just to the N of Sumer, who were the predecessors of the Babylonians and Assyrians. The invention of writing thus may have been one of the many "firsts" of these remarkable Sumerians, who built a high civilization with impressive art, architecture, music, literature, and science (particularly mathematics). From thousands of cuneiform tablets, coming largely from the early 2nd millennium, the literary works of the Sumerians are known; they include myths, hymns, proverbs, fables, love lyrics, lamentations, and epic tales. It was they who told and probably originated the story of the Flood that lies behind the later Babylonian and Hebrew tales. In Gen. 11:1-9, the Tower of Babel story, the great tower referred to is probably the 7-staged ziggurat, or temple tower, at Babylon; such towers were earlier characteristic of Sumerian cities (see ill., p. 10).

The first great period of Sumerian development is designated the Early Dynastic period (*ca.* 3000-2300), when Sumer was ruled successively by royal dynasties from such cities as Kish, Erech, Ur, Lagash, etc. (see color map 2). Something of the culture of the period is dramatically illustrated by the wealth of treasures recovered in the excavations of the royal tombs at Ur. One of the notable kings of the Early Dynastic period was Urukagina of Lagash, famous for his social reforms.

The Semitic Akkadians took over the rule of Sumer about 2300, when Sargon established a famous dynasty and extended his power to Syria and into Asia Minor and possibly even to Egypt, Ethiopia, and Cyprus. His capital city was at Agade, or Akkad ("Accad" in Gen. 10:10), which gave its name to

the region to the N of Sumer for many succeeding cents. A later Assyrian king of the time of Hezekiah and Isaiah (Isa. 20:1) honored himself by taking the name of Sargon.

The dynasty of Sargon of Agade was short-lived, although Sargon himself had a long rule. The Guti, barbarians invading from the mountains of Iran, brought this Old Akkadian period to an end. The rule of the Guti lasted until a revival of Sumerian power and culture *ca.* 2100-1720. The city of Ur again came to the forefront when Ur-nammu established there the 3rd dynasty of Ur about the middle of the 21st cent. Ur-nammu is especially to be remembered for his code of laws. Bronze statues of his prosperous son and successor, Shulgi, were found in the excavations of the temple at Nippur, the religious center of Sumer. The Elamites destroyed Ur, and Semitic nomads called Amurru ("Westerners," the biblical Amorites) came into the country.

The First Dynasty of Babylon. After a struggle for power in which control was first in the hands of the city of Isin and then Larsa, Babylon became dominant. The 6th king of the First Dynasty of Babylon, Hammurabi, defeated Rim-Sin of Larsa and became master of Sumer and Akkad around the middle of the 18th cent. He is particularly famed for his law code, the most influential legal code in the ancient Near East. His was an Amurru (Amorite) dynasty, as was the contemporary dynasty at Mari on the middle Euphrates, where King Zimri-Lim ruled. Thousands of tablets found in the Mari excavations throw much light on Amorite institutions and religion of the patriarchal period. That the power of Hammurabi extended to Syria and as far as Hazor in Canaan may help explain the influence which his legal code seems to have had on the Israelites, perhaps through the medium of the Canaanites.

The First Dynasty of Babylon and the Old Babylonian period came to an end with the conquest of Babylon by the Hittites. Mesopotamia was then invaded from the E by the non-Semitic Kassites, who ruled Babylonia for nearly 4 cents. during what has been called the Dark Age. The Kassite period came to an end in the middle of the 12th cent., when the Elamites attacked Babylon and took to Susa as booty the stele on which Hammurabi had inscribed his code of laws. The Hammurabi stele now stands in the Louvre in Paris as one of the great documents of antiquity (see ill., p. 19).

The Assyrians. The Assyrians to the N of Babylonia in the 13th cent. conquered Babylon and helped hasten its downfall. Tiglath-pileser I (*ca.* 1100), who hunted elephants in the upper Euphrates area, extended Assyrian rule toward the W as far as Tadmor (Palmyra; see color map 9). His later successors were much involved with the Hebrew monarchies, as Assyria was destined to become the dominant nation in the Near East. Shalmaneser III's campaigns westward culminated in the great battle at Qarqar on the Orontes River in N Syria in 853, where he met a coalition which included armed forces of the kings of Kue (Cilicia), Damascus, Hamath, Ammon, and Israel. This was when Ahab was Israel's king. Shalmaneser's claim to complete victory must be discredited, for he had to retreat. However, Hazael of Damascus, without his allies, was later defeated by Shalmaneser; and Jehu, now king of Israel, along with Tyrians and Sidonians, had to pay tribute to the victor. The scene of Jehu's submission is depicted on the monument known as the Black Obelisk, which was found at Calah (Nimrud) and is now in the British Museum (see ill., p. 1061).

The involvement of the grand succession of Assyrian monarchs Tiglath-pileser III, Shalmaneser V, Sargon II, Sennacherib, and Esarhaddon in the affairs of Israel and Judah in the golden age of Assyria's expansion in the last quarter of the 8th cent. and the first half of the 7th cent. is related on p. 1024. Tiglath-pileser III carved most of the kingdom of Israel into Assyrian provinces, and Shalmaneser V and Sargon II effected its complete demise in 722. Sennacherib's armies invaded Hezekiah's Judah, and Esarhaddon carried King Manasseh temporarily into exile. Even Egypt and Ethiopia became a part of the Assyrian Empire. The last great king of this succession was Ashurbanipal (668-629), whose library at Nineveh was discovered in the excavations. The combined onslaughts of the Medes and Babylonians resulted in the destruction of the capital city of Nineveh in 612. The Assyrians made a brave but futile attempt to carry on at Haran with the aid of the Egyptians, but the defeat of the Egyptians and Assyrians at Carchemish by the Babylonians in 605 was finally decisive (Jer. 46).

The Babylonians. The Assyrians were succeeded by the Babylonians as masters of a large portion of the Near East. Nabopolassar was the first king of the Chaldean dynasty of this Neo-Babylonian period, and his son Nebuchadrezzar (spelled Nebuchadnezzar in some books of the Bible) ascended the throne in 605, his first official regnal year being reckoned from the spring month of Nisan 604. The Chaldeans lived in the swampy lake area between the Persian Gulf and the southernmost cities of Babylonia, called Kaldu in Assyrian records from the 9th cent. on. An independent, tribal-organized Akkadian people, they provided the rulers of the Neo-Babylonian Empire.

New light has been shed on this period by the translation and publication of the tablets found at Babylon containing the chronicles of the Babylonian kings. The chronicle of Nebuchadrezzar relates how in his 7th year in the month of Chislev (Dec. 598), he marched against Hatti-land and encamped against the city of Judah (Jerusalem); he took it on the 2nd day of the month of Adar (Mar. 16, 597), captured its king (Jehoiachin), and set a king of his own choice (Zedekiah) on the throne. After a siege of 1½ or 2½ years Jerusalem again fell to Nebuchadrezzar in 587 or 586, and the kingdom of Judah came to an end. Nebuchadrezzar's son and successor Amel-Marduk (Evil-merodach) honored the exiled Jehoiachin (II Kings 24-25).

The last king of the Neo-Babylonian period was Nabu-naid (Nabonidus), who was defeated by the Persians in 539, when Babylon and the Babylonian Empire fell into the hands of Cyrus the Great. Nabu-naid is not mentioned in the Bible, but his son Belshazzar, who was for a time coregent with him, appears in Dan. 5, where the folktale tradition makes him the son of Nebuchadnezzar (Nebuchadrezzar).

B. THE EGYPTIANS

In the table of nations in Gen. 10 Cush (Ethiopia) is one of the brothers of Egypt (vss. 6-7). Cush was to the S of Egypt, below Syene, which marked the S border of Egypt at the First Cataract (see color maps 2, 4, 7, 9). Syene was located at modern Aswan, the site of the great new dam which means so much to the economy of Egypt, and which posed for archaeologists a vast problem of saving the antiquities which would be covered up by the waters behind the dam. In the OT the expression "from Migdol to Syene" (Ezek. 29:10; 30:6) indicates the length of Egypt. Migdol is located in the fanlike delta area of Egypt, which was known as Lower Egypt, with Memphis its chief city. S of the Delta to Syene was known as Upper Egypt, and its chief city was Thebes. To the W of Egypt were Libya and Put, the latter represented as a brother of Egypt in the table of nations (vs. 6) and the former possibly appearing as a son (Lehabim, vs. 13). Two other sons of Egypt may allude to Lower and Upper Egypt, viz. Naphtuhim ("those of the Delta"? vs. 13) and Pathrusim ("those of Pathros," i.e. Upper Egypt, vs. 14).

The Old Kingdom. Pharaoh Menes (ca. 3000) is credited traditionally with uniting Upper and Lower Egypt and founding the First Dynasty, with the capital at Memphis. Shortly before, perhaps as a result of influence from Mesopotamia, the Egyptian pictographic ("hieroglyphic") script had begun to appear. The hieroglyphic writing was usually found on stone inscriptions. A more cursive script, "hieratic," was very early developed for writing on papyrus, which was the characteristic writing material of Egypt (see "Writing in Biblical Times," pp. 1201-08). Later a still more abbreviated form of the script, "demotic," was made and used for letters and business documents.

The first 2 dynasties were the prelude to the first of 3 great periods of early Egyptian history: the Old Kingdom (ca. 2700-2200), the Middle Kingdom (ca. 2000-1800), and the New Kingdom (ca. 1570-1090). The Old Kingdom comprises the 3rd-6th dynasties. It was during the 3rd dynasty that the great stepped pyramid at Saqqarah was built as a tomb for Pharaoh Zoser and that the 3 great pyramids at Gizeh were built as tombs for Khufu (Cheops), Khaf-Re (Chephren), and Men-kau-Re (Mycerinus). The pharaoh was regarded as a god with absolute power. In the 5th and 6th Dynasties there was an increasing decentralizing of the state. The Pyramid Texts inscribed on the walls of the chambers of the pyramids of these 2 dynasties provide important information on the cult of the hereafter.

The Middle Kingdom. A period of disintegration after the 6th Dynasty, the First Intermediate Period, was followed by a revival in the 11th and 12th Dynasties, particularly the latter, with the capital now at Thebes. This Middle Kingdom period was one of great prosperity, also characterized by unusual literary activity. Among the more important compositions are the Prophecy of Neferti, the Wisdom of Amen-em-het I, and the story of Si-nuhe. It was a period of considerable democratization in Egyptian religion and ethics and of search for social justice. The Pyramid Texts developed into the Coffin Texts, inscribed on the inside of coffins. The story of Si-nuhe has been popularized in our day in a historical novel by M. Waltari, *The Egyptian*. From the end of the 12th or the beginning of the

13th Dynasty come a number of pottery bowls and figurines inscribed with curses against the enemies of the state; these were ceremonially broken to bring about the defeat of the enemies. Known as Execration Texts, they give us information on Canaan, for among the names given are rulers of Acco, Ashkelon, Achshaph, Beth-shemesh, Jerusalem, Shechem, and Tyre.

The New Kingdom. The 2nd Intermediate Period, which began *ca.* 1750, is the era when Egypt was ruled by the Hyksos (lit. "rulers of a foreign country"). These invaders introduced many new elements into Canaan and Egypt, including the horse and chariot, new weapons, and new fortification techniques. Their capital was Avaris (Tanis) in the Delta. Scholars disagree whether Abraham is to be placed within the period of the Middle Kingdom or within this 2nd Intermediate Period, or later. Some scholars think the evidence points to a 20th-cent. date for him, but others think he was more probably at least a near contemporary with Hammurabi and that his descent into Egypt may have coincided with the Hyksos age. Some would even date him as late as the Amarna age in the 14th cent. In any case Abraham had a number of associations with Egypt and married an Egyptian girl (Hagar). The date of Joseph's entry into Egypt and the descent of Jacob and his family there is also not without question.

The beginning of the New Kingdom was marked by the expulsion of the Hyksos from Egypt and the capture of Avaris by Ah-mose I, at the beginning of the 18th Dynasty (*ca.* 1570-1305). Among the most notable pharaohs of this dynasty were Queen Hatshepsut (1486-1468), Thut-mose III (1490-1439), Amen-hotep II (1439-1406), Amen-hotep III (1398-1361), and Amen-hotep IV, or Akh-en-Aton (1369-1353). Thut-mose III made 17 campaigns into Canaan and Syria; in the first in 1468 he defeated at Megiddo a coalition of 330 princes and brought Palestine and Syria within the Egyptian Empire. This is the earliest record of many important battles to be fought at Megiddo on the Plain of Esdraelon, the place selected in Rev. 16:16 as the site of the final battle (Armageddon, i.e. "Mt. Megiddo").

To the reigns of Amen-hotep III and Akh-en-Aton belong the Amarna letters, diplomatic correspondence mostly in Babylonian cuneiform on clay tablets, the majority of which came from city kings in Syria and Palestine. They were found at Akhet-Aton (modern Tell el-Amarna), the capital city of Egypt under Akh-en-Aton. They illuminate the situation in Canaan in the first part of the 14th cent. In them are references to a group of people called "Habiru" (or "Hapiru"), who, as they appear in these records (they are known elsewhere), probably bear some relation to the Hebrews. This information has to be taken into consideration in reconstructing the story of the Hebrews in Canaan, as will be discussed below. The Habiru were threatening the security of Egypt's vassal kings in Canaan. Akh-en-Aton, whose religious reforms must be considered in any history of monotheism, imposed on Egypt the cult of the sole god Aton in a remarkable renaissance of art, architecture, and religion. He was so busy at home with internal affairs that his Asiatic empire was allowed to collapse. The bust of his beautiful wife Nefert-iti is one of the most familiar objects of Egyp-

Courtesy of the Oriental Institute, University of Chicago

Cast of a bust of Queen Nefert-iti, wife of Egyptian King Akh-en-Aton (original in Berlin Museum)

tian antiquity. Something of the artistic glories of Akh-en-Aton's kingdom are known as a result of the recovery of the tomb furnishings of his son-in-law, Tut-ankh-Amon, in the Valley of the Kings W of the Nile opposite Thebes.

The 19th Dynasty (1303-1202) saw the rebuilding of the empire, particularly under the rule of Seti I and Ramses II. The latter, whose mammoth statue recovered from Memphis today gazes in majesty over the main square at Cairo, and whose mummy is in the museum at Cairo, was a truly great monarch and an indefatigable builder of monuments and temples. He fought the Hittites at Kadesh on the Orontes River in Syria and carved his relief on the cliffs beside the Dog River in Phoenicia. Both he and Seti I left inscribed monuments at Beth-shan in Canaan. It was Ramses II (1290-1224) who used Israelite slaves to build the cities of Pithom and Raamses (Exod. 1:11) and was probably the pharaoh of the Exodus. In an inscription of his son and successor Mer-ne-Ptah (1224-1214) appears the first nonbiblical use of the word "Israel." Ramses III (1195-1164) of the 20th Dynasty defeated by land and sea the Sea Peoples, among whom were the Philistines.

The Later Dynasties. Egypt's glory soon waned, and the last kings of the 20th Dynasty and those of the 21st were weak. It was during the latter dynasty that Solomon married the daughter of an unnamed

Courtesy of the Oriental Institute, University of Chicago

Triumphal relief of Shishak (Sheshank I) found on wall of Amon temple at Karnak; bottom center are prisoners with upraised hands; surrounding a figure of Shishak are names of Palestinian and Syrian towns he captured

pharaoh (I Kings 3:1-2). The founder of the 22nd Dynasty (ca. 940-745), Shishak (Sheshank I), a Libyan general, invaded Judah and Israel in the 5th year of the reign of Rehoboam (I Kings 14:25-28) and left a record of it engraved on the temple wall at Karnak. The 23rd and 24th Dynasties were insignificant.

A revival came with the 25th and 26th dynasties. The 25th was an Ethiopian dynasty, and to it belonged Pharaoh Tirhakah (689-664) mentioned in II Kings 19:9; Isa. 37:9. The 26th Dynasty (663-525) marked a movement to recover the past glories of Egypt's art and literature. Pharaoh Neco in 609 fought, defeated, and mortally wounded Josiah, Judah's king, on the Plain of Megiddo (II Kings 23:29-30; II Chr. 35:20-24); then in 605 Neco was decisively defeated at Carchemish by Nebuchadrezzar. In 588 Pharaoh Hophra offered unsuccessful aid to Judah against the Babylonians, and in his reign some of the Judeans sought political asylum in Egypt (Jer. 37:5-10; chs. 42-44). In these ways and others did the paths of Egypt and Israel cross.

The 26th Dynasty came to an end when in 525 Cambyses, son of Cyrus the Great, conquered Egypt and made it a part of the Persian Empire. Egypt fell into the hands of Alexander the Great in 332, and the city of Alexandria was founded to become a center of commerce and Greek culture. After the death of Alexander, Ptolemy I became the founder of the Ptolemaic dynasty (305-30). The Ptolemies claimed and controlled Palestine until a Seleucid king, Antiochus III, was victorious over Ptolemy V at Paneas in 199. The efforts of Antiochus IV (Epiphanes) to rule Egypt were frustrated by the Romans in 169. Julius Caesar came to Egypt in 48, and Mark Antony in 41. With the defeat of Mark Antony by Octavian (Augustus) at the battle of Actium in 31 and the suicide of Antony and Cleopatra the following year, Egypt became a Roman province.

C. Peoples of Asia Minor, Armenia, and N Mesopotamia

Despite their distance from Palestine the peoples of Asia Minor were involved in its affairs—and in the affairs of the Fertile Crescent generally. There were Hittites in Canaan from the patriarchal period, and objects of Hittite origin have been found in the excavations at Ugarit, Megiddo, and elsewhere. The famous narrow defile through the Tarsus Mountains called the Cilician Gates on the route between the interior of Asia Minor and Cilicia-Syria provided an important entry into the Fertile Crescent. Asia Minor also provided the bridge between the Fertile Crescent and Europe; the swift but narrow Hellespont was both a link and a dividing line between Asia and Europe. Across it the Indo-European "Hittites" and other Indo-European peoples came into Asia Minor. By this route the Greeks under Alexander the Great moved eastward to become the masters of the Near East. In reverse direction the Persian armies had invaded Greece.

The Hittites. In central Anatolia lived the native Hittites, a Caucasic, non-Indo-European, brachycephalic people, who came to be ruled over by Indo-Europeans invading Asia Minor perhaps near the beginning of the 2nd millennium. Here in the highlands of Asia Minor, in the bend of the Halys River, lies the present-day village of Boghazköy, the site of the capital city of the Hittites, Hattusa (see color map 2). Before excavations the magnitude and splendor of the ancient city which stood there were obvious from the extent of the ruins and the 2 great gates of the fortification wall. In 1906 Hugo Winckler, a German archaeologist, began excavations there. Under the palace were discovered the royal archives, some 10,000 clay tablets written in Babylonian cuneiform, many in Akkadian, but some in the Indo-European tongue (Nesian) of the ruling caste.

Here in the Old Hittite Empire (*ca.* 1600-1500) ruled Labarnas, Hattusilis I, and Mursilis I, and it was under the last of these that the Hittites destroyed the city of Babylon (*ca.* 1550). After a period of eclipse by Mitanni, the New Hittite Empire arose (*ca.* 1375-1200) under its first great king, Suppiluliumas, who conquered Mitanni, as well as Aleppo and Carchemish, and extended his rule to the borders of Babylonia. He was one of the correspondents whose letters were found at Tell el-Amarna, and the widow of Pharaoh Tut-ankh-Amon asked for one of his sons in marriage. His most worthy successor was Mursilis II. It was in the reign of the latter's son, Muwatallis, that the wars with Egypt climaxed in the great battle with Ramses II at Kadesh in 1286. The New Hittite Empire disintegrated when Indo-European folk invaded from across the Aegean Sea, and it was replaced by many small kingdoms in Anatolia and N Syria, such as Malatya, Samal (Zinjirli), Cilicia (Kizzuwatna), Aleppo, Hamath, and Carchemish. To these belong the Hittite hieroglyphic inscriptions, in a different Indo-European language from that of the earlier cuneiform texts.

The Hittites appear frequently in the OT. The table of nations in Gen. 10 makes Heth (Hittites) a son of Canaan and brother of Sidon, perhaps because of the proximity of the later small Hittite states to Phoenicia. Abraham bought as a burial place the field containing the cave of Mach-pelah from Ephron the Hittite (Gen. 23), and Judith and Basemath (Adah), daughters of Hittites, were married to Esau (Gen. 26:34; 36:2; cf. 27:46). The Hittites are listed among the several "nations" occupying Canaan before the conquest (Gen. 15:20; Exod. 3:8, 17; Num. 13:29; etc.). The Hittites were perhaps more localized in the southern hill country of Palestine (cf. Num. 13:29). Consonant with this is Ezekiel's description of the mother of Jerusalem as a Hittite (Ezek. 16:3, 45). Solomon married Hittite wives (I Kings 11:1), and Ahimelech and Uriah were Hittites in David's army (I Sam. 26:6; II Sam. 11:3 ff.).

Solomon sold horses and chariots to the kings of the Hittites and the kings of Syria (I Kings 10:29), and in the Elisha tale (II Kings 7:6) the king of Israel is reported to have hired against the Syrians the kings of the Hittites and the kings of "Misraim" —the usual word for Egypt, but possibly a reference to the kings of Musri, a land in Asia Minor mentioned in the cuneiform inscriptions. These and II Sam. 24:6 are references to the later Hittite states.

The Lydians. There were numerous states, peoples, and districts in Asia Minor in various periods of the biblical world. In SW (?) Asia Minor lay Arzawa, to which 2 letters in the Amarna correspondence are addressed, and which is mentioned in the Hittite inscriptions. Also in the Hittite inscriptions appears Assuwa in W Asia Minor, from which the name "Asia" may be derived. Contemporary with the Hittites was the kingdom of Kizzuwatna in what was later E Cilicia. There were also the Phrygians who came into Asia Minor, perhaps from Thrace.

A special word should be said about the Lydians. In the table of nations of Gen. 10 Lud (Lydia) appears as a son of Shem in one source (vs. 22) and Ludim as a son of Egypt and grandson of Ham in another (vs. 13). The capital of Lydia was Sardis in the Hermus Valley (see color map 10). Of more ancient origin, the Lydians flourished as a kingdom within the first millennium. The founder of the important Mermnad Dynasty was Gyges (*ca.* 685-652), whose name has been questionably associated with Gog of Magog in Ezek. 38-39. He defeated the Cimmerians (biblical Gomer), perhaps with the help of the Assyrian king Ashurbanipal, and later the Cimmerians ransacked Lydia. After the reigns of kings Ardys and Sadyattes, under Alyattes the Halys River became the E border of Lydia by treaty with Cyaxares of Media.

Alyattes' successor was the rich Croesus (560-546), the most famous king of Lydia. His kingdom came to an end when Cyrus the Persian in 546 took Sardis after previously defeating Croesus at the Halys River. Lydia became a satrapy (province) of the Persian Empire and fell to Alexander the Great at the battle at the Granicus River in 334. After a period under the Seleucids it went to Rome in 133, to become part of the province of Asia (see color map 16). As the excavations dramatically illustrate, Sardis was extensive and prosperous under the Romans, and the large Jewish community there is evident from the extensive remains of a magnificent synagogue uncovered by the archaeologists.

The Urartians. To the E of the land of the Hittites was Urartu in Armenia, in the mountainous country in the area of Lake Urmia and Lake Van (see color map 2), a kingdom frequently in conflict with Assyria. This is the biblical Ararat, in whose mountains the ark of Noah is reported to have landed (Gen. 8:4), and it was into Ararat that the sons of the Assyrian king Sennacherib fled after they had murdered their father (II Kings 19:37; Isa. 37:38). In Jer. 51:27-28 the kingdom of Ararat, along with Minni (S of Lake Urmia, the Manneans of the Assyrian records) and Ashkenaz (the Ashguza of the Assyrian records, the Scythians), is summoned to destroy Babylon. An important Urartian king was Rusa I, a contemporary of Sargon of Assyria. Urartu's allies against Assyria were Tabal (biblical Tubal) and Mushki (biblical Meshech). In the 6th cent. Urartu was conquered by the Medes.

The Hurrians (Horites). A neighbor bordering on the territories of the Hittites and Urartians was Mitanni in N Mesopotamia, a Hurrian or Horite kingdom (see color map 2; for other peoples in this area see the discussions of Assyrians, Amorites, and Arameans). Mitanni, one of the great kingdoms of the biblical world, flourished *ca.* 1500-1370 between the Old Hittite Kingdom, for the downfall of which it was responsible, and the New Hittite Empire, by which it was overrun. Its aristocracy was E Indo-European (Indo-Aryan), but its basic population was Armenoid Hurrian. A letter in Hurrian written by Tushratta, king of Mitanni, was among the Amarna correspondence, and texts written in Hurrian come from Hattusa and also from Ugarit, where a Sumerian-Hurrian vocabulary ("dictionary") was found. The language is related to Urartian, sharing features with the Caucasic languages.

The center of Mitanni was in the area of Haran, described in Gen. 24:4 as Abraham's country and place of his kindred. Here Isaac and Jacob secured their wives (Gen. 24; 29), and here the Israelite "tribes" (the sons of Jacob, save Benjamin) were born (Gen. 29-30). Inscriptions from Nuzi, E of the upper Tigris River, from the 15th-14th cents., when the area was a province of Mitanni, throw much light on the social customs of the patriarchal period as reported in the Bible and also assist in understanding the problem of the Habiru (mentioned above).

Though in the OT the name Horite is used for the early inhabitants of Seir (Edom, Gen. 14:6; Deut. 2:12, 22) there were Horites in Canaan itself. This is evident from the fact that Egypt in the New Kingdom designated Palestine as Huru. In Gen. 34:2; Josh. 9:7 the LXX reads Horites for Hivites. These Hivites, who appear frequently in lists of peoples inhabiting Canaan, are found in central Palestine and at the foot of Mt. Hermon and in Mt. Lebanon (Gen. 34:2; Josh. 9:7; 11:3; Judg. 3:3). It has been suggested that the term Hivites came to be applied to the Horites, since the name Horites came to be preempted for the pre-Edomite population of Edom. The name of the king of Jerusalem in the Amarna period (Abdu-Hepa) honors the Hurrian mother goddess. The name of Uriah, the Jebusite husband of Bathsheba, is a form of the Hurrian word for "lord."

D. PEOPLES OF IRAN

Elamites and Medes. The highland belt of Asia Minor and Armenia continues into the Iranian plateau, an incredibly rugged country with a vast salt desert in the central eastern part. Toward the S on the W slope of the plateau and E of the Tigris Valley was Elam, object of a prophetic oracle (Jer. 49:34-39), with its capital at Susa (see color map 9). It was much involved in Mesopotamian history, sometimes raiding and conquering and sometimes being conquered, finally becoming a part of the kingdom of the Medes and Persians.

Media, with its capital at Ecbatana (see color map 10), under Cyaxares (ca. 625-585) extended its rule to the Halys River in Asia Minor and successfully made common cause with Babylonia against Assyria. When Cyaxares' successor, Astyages (585-550), met defeat at the hands of Cyrus in 550 Media became a part of the Persian Empire.

The Persians. Cyrus the Persian had been king of Anshan, which had earlier been a part of Elam, and his defeat of Astyages was followed by his conquest of Lydia in 546. His victorious armies entered Babylon in 539, and the next year he was crowned king there, with all Babylonia's empire in his hands. Second Isaiah looked on Cyrus as the Lord's anointed to free the Jews from exile (Isa. 44:28; 45:1), and in accord with a decree issued by the new ruler the first return took place. The son of Cyrus, Cambyses, in 525 incorporated Egypt into the Persian Empire.

Darius the Great acceded to the throne in 522; his first official year was reckoned from 521. The main route from Babylon to Ecbatana passes by the great rock cliffs of Behistun, and here in relief Darius carved a picture of himself. His foot is on a prostrate rival who tried to claim the throne, and standing before him are 9 other bound rebels; an inscription in 3 languages tells the story. Darius extended his rule E to the Indus River in India and expanded his empire W into Europe by adding Thrace. It was his armies which were defeated at Marathon in 490. Haggai and Zechariah began to prophesy in his 2nd year (520).

Darius' successor, Xerxes I, marched into Greece and burned Athens, but was defeated at the naval battle at Salamis (480) and in a decisive land battle at Plataea (479), so that the Persians had to retire from Greece. He is the Ahasuerus of Esth.

Xerxes' son Artaxerxes I in his 20th year (445) gave Nehemiah permission to go from Susa to Jerusalem and as governor repair the city's defenses. According to the natural interpretation of the text the same king in his 7th year (458) commissioned Ezra to lead a group to Jerusalem. Many scholars believe this event must have occurred instead in the 7th year of Artaxerxes II (397).

The last king of the Persian Empire was Darius III, who began to reign in 336/35. His armies were defeated by Alexander the Great at the river Granicus in 334, at Issus in 333, and at Gaugamela near the ruined site of Nineveh in 331. In the same year Alexander sacked the capital, Persepolis, which Darius the Great had made a city of splendor. Then Alexander, like Darius, extended his march to the Indus River.

After Alexander's death Iran eventually came under the control of the Seleucid Empire. About the middle of the 3rd cent. the Parthians (cf. Acts 2:9) of central Iran secured their independence, and the Parthian rulers, known as Arsacids after Arsaces, the founder of the dynasty, built an empire that reached from the Euphrates to India, with its capital at Ctesiphon on the Tigris (see color map 12). The Parthians were involved in wars with Rome and sided with the Jews against the Romans, giving support to Jerusalem when it was under siege by Titus in A.D. 69-70.

E. SOME CLOSER NEIGHBORS OF THE HEBREWS

The Amorites. The term "Amorites" is applied in the OT both generally to the pre-Israelite population in Canaan and specifically to one of several peoples of Canaan (Gen. 15:16, 19-21). Special attention is given to 2 Amorite kingdoms in Transjordan: that of Og king of Bashan in the N, and that of "Sihon king of the Amorites" from the Jabbok to the Arnon rivers in the S (Num. 21:21-35; see color map 3). The Amorites are also found much more widely, and the term is to be related to the cuneiform "Amurru" (Westland, Westerners). They originated as seminomadic folk on the desert edges of the

Fertile Crescent. Their presence in Mesopotamia is attested for the late 3rd and early 2nd millennia, and by the 18th cent. they had established dynasties at Mari and Babylon, as noted above, and also at Larsa and Asshur, as well as in Aleppo and other places in N Syria. Haran was also at one time an Amorite state. In the Amarna period the Amorites under Abdi-Ashirta were threatening Phoenicia and collaborating with the Habiru.

The arrival of the nomadic Amorites in Canaan during the 23rd-19th cents., the Intermediate Early-Middle Bronze period of the archaeologists, has been thought by some to be illustrated archaeologically, particularly by the excavations at Jericho by the great English archaeologist Kathleen Kenyon. There is evidence of an essentially nomadic people who did not build walled towns or even houses at first, but camped on the mound, and who left a distinctive pottery and disclosed burial customs of the type which might be more expected of nomads.

The Arameans. Aram (RSV "Syria") was the land of the Arameans. Their main territory extended from the area of the upper Euphrates and Balikh rivers to Damascus and northern Transjordan (see color map 9). Here they were able to control key caravan routes of the Fertile Crescent. In the Euphrates-Balikh region, in which lay Haran, is to be located Beth-eden, an Aramaic city state mentioned in Amos 1:5 and the Bit-adini of the Assyrian records. It is also the Eden of II Kings 19:12; Ezek. 27:23. In this area also is Paddan-aram or Aram-naharaim (lit. "Aram of the Two Rivers," RSV "Mesopotamia"), the home of the patriarchs (Gen. 24:10; 25:20; 28:2; 48:7; see comment on 11:28-32). When Jacob is called "a wandering Aramean" (Deut. 26:5), the allusion is to his associations with this area, although the Aramean control of it probably came after patriarchal times. As already noted, the Hurrians of Mitanni and the Amorites were earlier in this area.

Aram-zobah or Zobah, an Aramean kingdom lying between the Lebanon and Anti-Lebanon mountains, was the center of a federation of Aramean and non-Aramean states, including Damascus, Syria, and Transjordan. Its king, Hadadezer of the dynasty of Beth-rehob, called in by the Ammonites, was defeated by David, who thereafter controlled the Aramaic states up to the border of Hamath (II Sam. 8:3 ff.). Rezon of Zobah fled from Hadadezer and became king of Damascus and an adversary of Solomon (I Kings 11:23-25). Aram-maacah or Maacah was an Aramean state E of the Jordan, close to Mt. Hermon (Deut. 3:14; Josh. 12:5; 13:11-13); and S of it was the kingdom of Geshur, whose princess David married (II Sam. 3:3). Among other Syrian states were Samal, Hamath, Arpad, and Aleppo.

Aram-Damascus, however, was most directly involved in the affairs of Israel and Judah. Near the end of the reign of Solomon, Damascus under Rezon got its independence from Israel. Beginning with the middle of the 9th cent. it became the metropolis of a great empire. The kingdoms of Israel and Aram-Damascus had competing claims for northern Transjordan. Asa of Judah called in Ben-hadad of Damascus for help against Baasha of Israel (I Kings 15:16-21). Ahab of Israel fought 3 wars with Damascus (I Kings 20; 22), in one of which Ben-hadad had 32 kings in his army, satellite rulers of Syria and Transjordan. The Elisha stories tell of wars between Israel and Damascus. Israel was allied with Damascus against the Assyrians in the battle at Qarqar in 853. Of special import is the Syro-Ephraimite War of 734, when Rezin of Damascus and Pekah of Israel united against Ahaz of Judah—providing the setting for Isaiah's Immanuel oracle (II Kings 16:5-9; Isa. 7).

The Arameans were a Semitic people. Gen. 10:22-23 makes Aram a son of Shem, but in Gen. 22:21 Aram is a grandson of Nahor, Abraham's brother; and this is perhaps the older genealogy. The Arameans are first mentioned outside the Bible in the inscriptions of Tiglath-pileser I (*ca.* 1100), where they are called Akhlami-aramaya, i.e. Aramean Bedouin. They occupied territories in Syria after the end of the Hittite Empire, their expansion through the Fertile Crescent beginning at the end of the 2nd millennium.

The Aramaic language may have been developed in the middle or upper Euphrates area by Bedouins from the Syrian desert who settled there. It became widely used in the Near East. It was an official tongue in the Assyrian Empire (II Kings 18:26) and became a secondary language throughout the Persian Empire. Among the Aramaic papyri from the Jewish colony at Elephantine in Egypt is an order issued by the authority of Darius II in 419 for the celebration of the Feast of Unleavened Bread. Ezra 6:3-5 may be the Aramaic form of a decree of Cyrus. In the following cents. Aramaic came to be the common language of Palestine and was the tongue of Jesus and his contemporaries (see "The Languages of the Bible," pp. 1194-1200).

The Arabians. There are 2 specific references to Arabia in the NT (Gal. 1:17; 4:25) and one to the Arabians (Acts 2:11). The kings of Arabia sent tribute to Solomon (I Kings 10:15) and are mentioned in Jer. 25:24. Arabia's extensive trade with Tyre is listed in Ezek. 27:19-22, and one of Isaiah's oracles was against Arabia (Isa. 21:13-17). Geshem the Arab, who appears in nonbiblical records as the king of Kedar, was one of the opponents of Nehemiah (Neh. 2:19; 6:1-2, 6).

There are many biblical references to places and peoples of Arabia (see color map 7). In the table of nations of Gen. 10 various places in Arabia are named according to one source as descended from Ham as sons of Cush (Ethiopia), viz. Seba, Havilah, Sabtah, Raamah, Sabteca, with Sheba and Dedan sons of Raamah (vs. 7); while according to another source some of the same and others are descendants of Shem as sons of Joktan (vss. 26-29). In Gen. 25:1-4 a number of Arab groups are descendants of Abraham by Keturah; here Sheba and Dedan are sons of Jokshan the son of Abraham. The descendants of Ishmael in Gen. 25:13-14 (Nebaioth, Kedar, Adbeel, Dumah, Massa, Tema, etc.) are references to N Arabian places and persons. The Midianites, Ishmaelites, Amalekites, and "people of the East" (which would also be translated "sons of Kedem," Judg. 6-7) were among the N Arabian groups. Seba refers to a kingdom in SW Arabia, roughly corresponding to modern Yemen, and Sheba usually to a settlement of Sabeans in N Arabia, although the queen of Sheba (I Kings 10:1-13) was obviously from S Arabia. The Kedarites appear in the Assyrian records as Qidri, and others are also known from the cuneiform records. In Isa. 60:6-7 Midian, Ephah, Sheba, Kedar, and Nebaioth are involved in bringing tribute to Israel in the new age.

Among the more important Arab groups of NT times were the Nabateans, whose king, Aretas IV (*ca.* 9 B.C.–A.D. 40), appears in II Cor. 11:32 (cf. I Macc. 5:25; 9:35). Their civilization is dramatically illustrated in the remains of their capital city of Petra and by recent archaeological explorations in Edom, Moab, the Arabah, and the S part of the Negeb. They were the only N Arabians who developed a civilization comparable to that of the S Arabians. In S Arabia in classical times there were 4 kingdoms, Minaean, Sabean, Qatabanian, and Hadramauti. The recovery of the Sabean civilization began with 18th- and 19th-cent. explorers; in this cent. excavations have been carried out near Marib, the ancient capital of Seba.

The various Semitic peoples have their ultimate origins in Arabia. The Akkadians, Amorites, Arameans, Canaanites, Edomites, Ammonites, and others were the result of the penetration of Semitic nomads from Arabia.

The Philistines. We now turn to the neighbors of Israel in Canaan and begin with the Philistines. They were among the Sea Peoples mentioned in the inscriptions of the pharaohs Mer-ne-Ptah and Ramses III. They raided the African coast and Palestine, and against them Ramses III fought land and sea battles, depicted on his palace walls at Medinet Habu at ancient Thebes. According to Amos 9:7 they came from Caphtor, and in Jer. 47:4 are called "the remnant of the coastland [or "isle"] of Caphtor." They are designated as Caphtorim in Deut. 2:23, and in the table of nations the Philistines and Caphtorim are mentioned together (Gen. 10:14)—probably originally synonymously. Caphtor is Crete, and the southern Philistine coastland of Canaan is called "the Negeb of the Cherethites," i.e. Cretans (I Sam. 30:14). Philistines and Cherethites occur in parallelism in Ezek. 25:16; Zeph. 2:5.

The Philistines settled on the S coastland of Canaan, and their territory was called Philistia, from which the name Palestine is derived. They had a Pentapolis, a confederation of 5 cities: Ashkelon, Ashdod, Gaza, Gath, and Ekron (see color map 5). Their pottery, distinctive in form and decoration, has analogies with 13th-cent. Mycenean wares in the Greek islands. The characteristic feathered helmet of their warriors appears in Egyptian depictions of the Sea Peoples. An analogous helmeted head is a hieroglyph on an inscription from Phaistos in Crete. The Philistines entered Canaan at the beginning of the Iron Age (*ca.* 1200), and they seem to have had a monopoly on that metal (I Sam. 13:19-22). Smelting furnaces for iron have been excavated in their territory. Indo-European in origin, they adopted the Canaanite gods and language.

The Philistines first appear at the time of the judges, although there are anachronistic references to them from the patriarchal period (Gen. 21; 26). The early judge Shamgar slew 600 Philistines with an oxgoad (Judg. 3:31). They play an important role in the Samson story (Judg. 14–16). They won an important battle against Israel at Ebenezer in the time of Samuel (I Sam. 4–6). The Hebrew mon-

archy was in part an answer to the threat from the Philistines. King Saul engaged them in battle, and eventually he and 3 sons lost their lives fighting against them on Mt. Gilboa (I Sam. 13; 14; 17; 28–31). At the death of Saul the Philistines controlled Beth-shan at the intersection of the Jezreel and Jordan valleys. At that time David was bodyguard for Achish, king of Gath. Later as king of Israel and Judah he defeated the Philistines at Baal-perazim near Jerusalem (II Sam. 5:17-25). Cherethites (Cretans) and Pelethites (perhaps Philistines) were in David's personal army as mercenaries (II Sam. 8:18; 20:23; etc.). After the division of the kingdom Israel engaged in border fights with the Philistines (I Kings 15:27; 16:15). The control of Judah over the Philistines varied during the monarchy; sometimes the Philistines raided Judah.

Assyrian kings on several occasions conquered and controlled Philistia, as reported in the records of Tiglath-pileser III, Sargon II, and Sennacherib. In 712 Sargon's soldiers captured Ashdod and made it into an Assyrian province (Isa. 20:1); in the excavations at Ashdod parts of Sargon's victory monument were recovered. Sennacherib tells how in 701 Padi king of Ekron refused to join in the revolt against Assyria and was sent by his own subjects to Hezekiah for confinement. After Sennacherib's victories in Philistia and the capitulation of Hezekiah, Padi was returned and Ekron's citizens were cruelly punished. The Philistines lined up with Egypt against the Babylonians, but Nebuchadrezzar in 604 attacked Ashkelon and turned it into a heap and carried away its king, who had written a letter to the pharaoh for help. This letter, in Aramaic, was found in Egypt at Saqqarah in 1942.

The Canaanites. Canaan consists generally of Palestine W of the Jordan and parts of Syria, including the Phoenician coastland. In the table of nations Canaan is the son of Ham, and the firstborn of Canaan is Sidon. The name "Canaan" may be of Hurrian origin. It is found first in the records of Amen-hotep II (15th cent.) and in the Amarna letters of the following century. Its meaning is probably "red purple," and in this sense its Akkadian equivalent occurs in the Nuzi tablets. "Phoenicia" has been taken as a Greek rendering of the meaning of "Canaan," formed by an assimilation of the Greek *phoinix*, meaning "red purple," with a similar Egyptian word meaning "woodworker." It would thus have reference to common products of the country used in international trade, the purple-red dye and cloth and wood from the famed cedars of Lebanon. The dye was produced by the large sea snail murex. Large shell mounds still exist at Tyre and Sidon, and the discarded shells were also found at Ugarit. In the light of this it is not surprising that "canaan" could also mean "trader," as in Zech. 11:7, 11 ("those who trafficked," "traffickers") and Isa. 23:8 ("merchants" of Tyre).

Much is known about the early cultures of Canaan as a result particularly of the excavations of remains of the Old Stone (Paleolithic) Age and the Middle Stone (Mesolithic) Age at Wadi el-Mughara at Mt. Carmel and the Neolithic (New Stone) Age at Jericho. The first occupation at Jericho was marked by a sanctuary (?) with a wall of stones and wooden posts of the late Middle Stone Age; a carbon-14 test provided a date of 7800 B.C. The beginnings of agriculture lie in this period. It was in the Neolithic Age that the first houses appeared at Jericho, and here in the pre-pottery era of the Neolithic Age were found the earliest city wall and a great stone tower which still stands to a height of some 30 feet, dated to *ca.* 7000. Uncovered in a trench at the site, it stands as a marvel to archaeologists and tourists. The first pottery makers at Jericho arrived from outside the country already knowing the technique.

The Neolithic was followed by the Chalcolithic (Copper-Stone) Age; a most important light on this period comes from Teleilat el-Ghassul NE of the Dead Sea in the Jordan Valley, where frescoed plaster walls appear; at Tell Abu Matar S of Beersheba, where the inhabitants lived in artificial cave dwellings connected by galleries; and at Hederah on the coastal plain, where the bones of the dead were put in pottery ossuaries, some of which had the form of model houses. This "Ghassulian" culture belongs to the first half of the Copper-Stone Age, in the early 4th millennium. In the last 3rd of this millennium invasions of new groups took place, evident in new types of pottery and tombs. Now first occur tombs cut in the rock with multiple burials and with offerings for the dead in pottery vessels. The Early Bronze Age (*ca.* 3100-2300) marked the beginning of the historic period (with written records) in Egypt and Mesopotamia and in Palestine witnessed an increasing development of city life. The Early Bronze Age came to an end apparently with an invasion of nomads, perhaps to be identified with the Amorites. It has been suggested that the culture introduced in Palestine at the beginning of the Middle Bronze Age (*ca.* 1900), perhaps from an amalgamation of the Amorite and the earlier more civilized populations, should be called Canaanite and originated in coastal Syria.

Archaeological data make it clear that Canaan was early subject to periodic settlement by peoples of diverse origins. Even in the prehistoric period the population of Canaan was very mixed, although by at least *ca.* 3000 it consisted generally of Semitic-speaking peoples. This is evident from the Canaanite loan words in Egyptian and from the names of many ancient towns—though not all the older names are Semitic. In this period the population was generally longheaded, and in the following periods the broadheaded types begin to be more common.

The cosmopolitan character of the Canaanite population is evident from the biblical lists of "nations" who occupied Canaan at the time of Israel's conquest. There are more than a score of such lists, ranging from 2 (Canaanites and Perizzites, Gen. 13:7; 34:30) to 10 (Kenites, Kenizzites, Kadmonites, Hittites, Perizzites, Rephaim, Amorites, Canaanites, Girgashites, and Jebusites, Gen. 15:19-21). The number most commonly given is 6 (e.g. Exod. 3:8). In Deut. 7:1; Josh. 3:10; 24:11 the following 7 are listed: Hittites, Girgashites, Amorites, Canaanites, Perizzites, Hivites, Jebusites. Either "Amorites" or "Canaanites" may be used to designate all the population of Canaan (e.g. Gen. 15:16; Josh. 24:15, 18).

A number of these peoples have already been discussed, viz. Hittites, Amorites, Hivites, and Jebusites, the last 2 being perhaps Horite or Hurrian. And there were, of course, the Ammonites of E

Transjordan, the Moabites E of the Dead Sea, and the Edomites between the Brook Zered and the Gulf of Aqaba, who possessed rich copper resources (see color maps 4, 5). The Ammonites and Moabites are deprecated by being given an origin in incest as sons of the daughters of Lot (Gen. 19:30-38), and the Edomites are pictured as descended from the uncouth brother of Jacob, Esau. Expelled from their homeland by Arab (Nabatean) invaders, the Edomites moved into S Palestine to become the Idumeans of Maccabean and NT times. They were forcibly converted to Judaism *ca.* 120 B.C., and Herod the Great issued from them.

The Phoenician area of Canaan lay N of Mt. Carmel and did not come under Israelite domination. The Phoenicians were great sea traders and were noted also for their export of cedars, which were in demand in Egypt, Mesopotamia, and Israel. The cosmopolitan character of their cities is evident from the excavations at Ugarit, Gebal, Tyre, and Sidon. Egyptian objects appear at Gebal (Byblos) as early as 3000, and a pharaoh of the 4th dynasty tells of bringing to Egypt 40 ships laden with cedar logs from Phoenicia. The victory of Thut-mose III at Megiddo gave the Egyptians a hold on Phoenicia, and in the Amarna letters Rib-addi of Gebal, Abimilki of Tyre, and other Phoenician kings acknowledge vassalage to Pharaoh. The 2 greatest cities were Tyre and Sidon, and in the OT "Sidonians" is used to mean Phoenicians. Hiram of Tyre provided cedars for Solomon's buildings and sailors for his ships on the Red Sea. By the 11th cent. the Phoenicians had founded trading colonies around the Mediterranean islands. Assyrian armies were often in Phoenicia, and it took Nebuchadrezzar a 13-year siege to make Tyre capitulate. Phoenicia fell to the Persian Empire, and Alexander the Great took Tyre following his victory at Issus in 333. Phoenicia lay within the Seleucid Empire, and in 64 B.C., with Pompey's victories, it came into the Roman Empire.

F. The Hebrews

The origin of the Hebrews is treated in the article "The History of Israel" (pp. 1018-25) but may be considered briefly here in the light of the materials presented above. The sons of Jacob, except Benjamin, are said to have been born to Jacob in Paddan-aram (Gen. 29–30). Their names, except Joseph, are the names of tribes. We have seen how the Paddan-aram area, in which was Haran, successively was subject to the invasion of the Amorites, was within the Hurrian state of Mitanni, and then became Aramean—whence the designation Paddan-aram, the area forming the Aramean state of Beth-eden. Probably Haran rather than Ur was the homeland of Abraham (see comments on Gen. 11:20-32). The Haran area was in the hands of the Semitic Amorites at the time of Abraham. Jacob is designated as an Aramean (Deut. 26:5), and so are Laban, the father of Rachel and Leah (Gen. 25:20; 31:20, 24), and Bethuel, Laban's father (Gen. 25:20; 28:5; contrast Gen. 22:20-24).

In vs. 21 of the table of nations in Gen. 10 Shem is called "the father of all the children of Eber" (the name ancestor of the Hebrews); but in vss. 22, 24 Aram (i.e. the Arameans) is the brother of Arpachshad, which may be a Hurrian name form, and Eber is descended from Arpachshad. The prominence of non-Semitic Armenoid types among the Hebrews could be explained both in terms of Haran origins and by the prominence of Horite elements in the population of Canaan. The majority of the Canaanites were eventually absorbed into the invading Hebrews. The situation at Jerusalem is clear; the Jebusites, probably Hurrian or Horite, were not killed by the Israelites who conquered the city at the time of David but were doubtless absorbed by them. All this suggests a very cosmopolitan origin of the Hebrews.

The word "Hebrew" itself, in the Bible first applied to Abraham, bears some relationship to the cuneiform Habiru (Egyptian Apiru), which in origin is not an ethnic or racial term but probably refers to a social class. References to Habiru occur as early as the 3rd dynasty of Ur (*ca.* 2050), over a wide area in the Hammurabi period, and on tablets from Mari, Alalakh, Nuzi, Hattusa, Amarna etc. If the Hebrews are to be related in some way with the Habiru of the Amarna period, then it would seem that the entrance of Hebrew tribes into Canaan under Joshua was not the only such occurrence and that there were Hebrew tribes in Canaan earlier, as Gen. 34 and other evidence may indicate. The biblical text represents 2 tribes, Ephraim and Manasseh, as "born" in Egypt to the daughter of an Egyptian priest (Gen. 41:50-52) and one tribe, Benjamin, as born in Canaan (Gen. 35:16-18). The problem is complex, and numerous solutions have been offered. We can be certain that the course of events was at least as complex as the biblical text itself hints, despite the overly simplified sacred history theme that 70 persons went down into Egypt with Jacob and that in the 3rd generation the exodus of the 12 tribes took place (Gen. 46:8-27; Exod. 6:18-20).

Conclusion. This has been a cursory survey of the biblical world and its people. Not only must the history of Israel be viewed within its larger setting, but also the religion of Israel can better be understood against the background of the religions of the biblical world. We have only here and there touched on this last point. Additionally, the myth, ritual, and symbolism and the literary forms and institutions of the religion of Israel can better be understood and appreciated against the background of the religions of the biblical world. The biblical scholar must be something of a historian of the religions of the biblical world. This will be evident in the articles "The Religion of Israel" (pp. 1150-58) and "The NT and Christian Origins" (pp. 1187-93).

For Further Study: E. A. Speiser, *Mesopotamian Origins*, 1930. W. F. Albright, "The Old Testament World," 1952; S. V. McCasland, "The Greco-Roman World" in *IB*, 1951. J. B. Pritchard, *The Ancient Near East in Pictures Relating to the OT*, 1954; *Ancient Near Eastern Texts Relating to the OT*, 2nd ed., 1956. C. W. Ceram, *The Secret of the Hittites*, 1956. G. E. Wright and F. V. Filson, eds., *Westminster Historical Atlas to the Bible*, rev. ed., 1956. J. W. Swain and W. H. Armstrong, *The Peoples of the Ancient World*, 1958. S. Moscati, *The Semites in Ancient History*, 1959. In the series "Ancient Peoples and Places": C. Aldred, *The Egyptians*, 1961; D. Harden, *The Phoenicians*, 1962; J. Gray, *The Canaanites*, 1964. A. L. Oppenheim, "Assyria and Babylonia"; A. Haldar, "Canaanites"; J. A. Wilson, "Egypt"; F. C. Grant, "Greece"; E. A. Speiser, "Man, Ethnic Divisions of"; M. J. Dresden, "Persia"; R. M. Grant, "Roman Empire"; S. N. Kramer, "Sumer" in *IDB*, 1962. H. G. May, R. W. Hamilton, and G. N. S. Hunt, eds., *Oxford Bible Atlas*, 1962. Kathleen M. Kenyon, *Amorites and Canaanites*, 1966.

THE HISTORY OF ISRAEL
Part I. From the Beginnings to the Exile

Harrell F. Beck

The biblical documents, our primary sources for the history of Israel, are interpretations of historical events by members of a community of faith. In these biblical accounts history and faith are intimately related. The nature of Israel's history is grasped in the OT in terms of the nature and purposes of Israel's God. He is a covenant God and the OT is a covenant history, the record of a God who creates, reveals, sustains, judges, and redeems. Uninterpreted event—even without faith—is largely meaningless; faith unrelated to event is neither relevant nor persuasive.

Israel's great leaders and teachers remind us of this intimate bond between faith and history. In the acute, crucial moments of history where they are personally involved these biblical personalities discern the word of God and find the ability to proclaim, "Thus says the Lord." It is their faith that distinguishes these leaders, and insofar as we have their biographies, it is only to demonstrate how they received and attested their belief in God.

Faith and history, event and interpretation, these do not result in a hodgepodge of narratives and proclamations. The OT reflects Israel's belief that God is at work in the life of his chosen people. The God who *created* at the beginning *sustains* his people now in order that they may, in the fullness of time, be *redeemed*. The freedom and joy which characterized life in the garden called Eden will be recovered in the garden called Paradise. The domain of harmony and prosperity memorialized in the myths of Gen. 1; 2 will be recreated in the prosperity and peace of the kingdom of God which is to be. God is the beginning and the end, Alpha and Omega. Biblical thinking, then, moves from beginning to end in terms of the old covenant and the new, the old creation and the new heaven and the new earth, the promises made to Abraham (Gen. 12:1-4) and those promises fulfilled.

The essential character both of rabbinic Judaism and of Christianity is fixed in this linear view of history. Differ as they do in many essentials, each regards itself as a continuation and fulfillment of the covenant history portrayed in the OT. Interpreters of the biblical text are obliged to seek not only its original and intended meaning but also its place in this overarching biblical perspective and its subsequent use in biblical thought and the life of the believing community.

I. The Patriarchal Age

The history of Israel properly begins with the saga of the patriarchs (Gen. 12–50), from whom traditionally the 12 tribes of Israel were descended. In the OT these patriarchal stories are preceded by a series of creation and origination traditions (Gen. 1–11), which span the period from Creation to the patriarchs, providing genealogies from Adam to Abraham. However valuable they may be in the study of biblical thought, it is evident that these early traditions are not materials that provide assistance to the scientific historian as he compiles the history of Israel.

Regarding the patriarchal traditions, themselves, however, scholars differ widely in appraising their historical value. Some have held that they provide us, not with historical knowledge of the patriarchs and their times, but with opinions about them held cents. later when the stories were put together and written down. Others admit the antiquity of the traditions but see the patriarchs as personifications of tribes and the stories about them as reflecting tribal relationships rather than individual experiences, with such mixture of mythical and legendary elements that the underlying historical events cannot be distinguished.

In recent years, however, there has been increasing reluctance to regard the difficulties as grounds for denying at least some reliable historical value in the patriarchal traditions. Even if we allow that many of the stories were tribal experiences originally —and certainly not all were—they still have historical value. Archaeology has shown that some of the customs attributed to the patriarchs belong to the times and places in which the stories are set but not to the later times in which they were written down. It is fair to assume that traditions which have preserved customs accurately have also transmitted much of the essential content of the narratives.

With reasonable confidence, therefore, we may view at least Abraham, Isaac, Jacob, and Joseph as historical individuals, even though we must recognize their family relationship as probably a construction of those who gathered the traditions for the purpose of fostering national unity. To be remembered so long, each of them must have been an outstanding leader of his day among the nomadic ancestors of Israel, and it seems likely that each was a religious leader. We cannot dismiss the recurring references of the Mosaic and later ages to the God of Abraham, of Isaac, and of Jacob. Though there is no secure basis for determining the nature of their faith, its existence and lasting influence are evident not only from such references but also from the shrines at various places in Palestine which were remembered as founded by one or another of the patriarchs.

In the traditions of the patriarchs' geographical movements we may understand the migrations not merely of their own households but probably of sizable bodies of nomads who followed their leadership. Thus in the tradition of Abraham's coming to Canaan (Gen. 11:26–12:9) we may trace the origins of a group of Israel's ancestors to Babylonia. This is supported to some extent by the similarities of early OT stories to Babylonian myths of Creation and the Flood—though the religious views of the Babylonian and biblical stories differ significantly. According to the tradition Abraham's father, Terah, lived in or near Ur, a Babylonian city (see color map 2), from which he and Abraham set out for Canaan. They settled first in the NW Mesopotamian city of Haran, and there Terah died. Later Abraham and Lot, his nephew, moved on to Canaan. That the connections of Israel's ancestors with NW Mesopotamian culture remained strong is shown by the traditions that the wives of both Isaac and Jacob came from Haran.

The Joseph tradition indicates that later, in a time of drought and famine in Palestine, some of Israel's ancestors migrated to Egypt and settled in the E Delta region. Israelite historians assumed that all their 12 tribes were descended from the sons of Jacob who went to Egypt at this time and that all later came out together, but there are various clues in the traditions to suggest that most of the tribes either remained in Canaan throughout the Egyptian sojourn of the Joseph tribes or else entered the land for the first time during this period. Thus it is likely that the traditions of the patriarchs associated with specific shrines in Palestine were preserved through the cents. by an unbroken succession of worshipers at those places.

II. The Exodus

"Now there arose a new king over Egypt, who did not know Joseph" (Exod. 1:8). In this sentence we pass from the era of Joseph's leadership and his people's prosperity in Egypt into a period of slavery under an oppressive pharaoh.

The chronology of the Exodus, like that of the patriarchs, is an extremely complicated matter. Biblical and extrabiblical evidence, while not in full agreement, seems to suggest a 13th-cent. date for the Israelite conquest of Canaan under Joshua. This is supported by archaeological evidence of the destruction of such Palestinian towns as Bethel, Debir, and Lachish during this time. The earliest mention of Israel outside the Bible is on a stele (victory tablet) of Pharaoh Mer-ne-ptah which dates from *ca.* 1220. In his hymn of triumph he lists the "people of Israel" among those whom he conquered during a military campaign in Palestine. Exod. 1:11 states that the Israelites in Egypt "built for Pharaoh store cities, Pithom and Raamses," sites in the E Delta (see color map 4). The fact that Egyptian kings of the 18th dynasty ruled from Thebes in Upper Egypt while rulers of the 19th dynasty (from 1310) built their capitals in the Delta is important. This move was undertaken as a part of their plan to reconquer their Palestinian empire and to protect the Delta from attack from Asia. Taken together, these evidences seem to support the view that the Exodus occurred early in the 13th cent. and that Ramses II (1290-1224) was the pharaoh of the Exodus (see also Intro. to Exod.).

The migration of Asiatics and bedouins across the peninsula of Sinai and into Egypt, esp. in periods of drought, is mentioned frequently in Egyptian sources. It would appear that the Israelites were a part of this nomadic population of the Delta. Apparently at most times relations between these nomads and the Egyptian officials were cordial. The Joseph stories, which are regarded by many as historically substantial, record a time when one of these Asiatics, a Hebrew, exercised considerable authority on behalf of a pharaoh in governing Egypt. Such resident aliens became a ready source of forced labor for pharaohs of the 19th dynasty in building their new capital and the store cities and in carrying on military campaigns in SW Asia.

The story of Moses in Egypt cannot be regarded as historically accurate in every detail. Some scholars view the narratives of Moses and the Exodus as a work of faith having little historical value. Yet it cannot be denied that our knowledge of the Near Eastern world in the 13th cent. provides a suitable context for the biblical narratives in which Moses is presented. In that context events of lasting religious significance unfolded.

The exodus from Egypt was the moment of Israel's birth as a people, and Moses dominates the exodus traditions. He is unique among his people, clearly the most important figure in the history of the Jews and the most frequently mentioned OT figure in the NT. The Bible is our only source of information for his life and work.

The story of Moses' birth (Exod. 2:1-10) is told in folkloristic themes common in the ancient Near East and designed to foretoken his achievements. An attempt is made in the record (Exod. 2:1) to associate Moses with the priestly tribe of Levi. The story suggests a connection between Moses and the Egyptian court and implies that he was educated in court circles.

According to tradition Moses sought refuge in Midian after he killed an Egyptian taskmaster and had to flee from Egypt. There he found employment and a wife in the house of a priest of Midian whom the traditions variously name Reuel, Jethro, or Hobab (Exod. 2:18; 3:1; Num. 10:29). Some scholars hold that this man played a decisive role in the religious life and thought of Moses.

It was while tending his father-in-law's flock on Mt. Horeb (or Sinai), according to the tradition (Exod. 3–4), that Moses received his commission to return to Egypt and deliver Israel into freedom, to bring a people to God. God disclosed himself to Moses in the symbols of the burning bush, the holy ground, and the new divine name Yahweh. Though frightened at the prospect of carrying out a divine commission, Moses could not refuse. He returned to Egypt, declared to Hebrew and Egyptian alike the commission which he had been given, and proceeded to carry it out by securing from the pharaoh the release of his people.

The actual exodus from Egypt is described as preceded by a cultic celebration in which the later Israelite rites of Passover, dedication of the firstborn, and the feast of Unleavened Bread are rooted. The drama of Moses' leadership, begun in his confrontation with Yahweh and then with Pharaoh, now continues. He delivers his people at the sea crossing, orders their communal life in the wilderness, ordains a priesthood and cultic rites and procedures, and mediates the revealed law at Mt. Sinai. Through it all Moses makes it clear to his people that Yahweh is the Great Protagonist in this unfolding drama. It is he who offers to enter into covenant with his people. He has saved them, nurtured them, and tested them. He alone can deliver (Exod. 14:1-4); he alone claims the exclusive allegiance of his people. He chose to deliver them from bondage and to give them the gracious gift of the law. Now he wills to be the Lord of Israel's life and calls for her obedience. It was to this divine will and power that Moses bore matchless and memorable witness among his people.

In Moses and the Exodus the foundations of Israel's faith were laid. Subsequent generations in the biblical tradition point to this Mosaic age and the Exodus as the time of Israel's emergence as a people and of Yahwism as her way of life. In Israel's legal tradition Moses is the celebrated lawgiver, in her prophetic tradition the greatest of the prophets (Deut. 34:10), and in her cultic life the great mediator.

Moses was not permitted to enter the promised land but he set that dream in his people's heart and so disciplined and consolidated them as to make that divine promise a reality.

III. The Settlement in Canaan

The Conquest. Joshua is portrayed in the OT as the principal figure in the invasion of Canaan during the 2nd half of the 13th cent. He appears first as an Israelite general (Exod. 17:8-16), as an assistant to Moses (Exod. 24:13), and as one of those sent to spy in Canaan (Num. 14:6-10) before being commissioned by Moses to be his successor (Deut. 31:7-29).

Joshua's role in the invasion of Canaan centered in his leadership of the Joseph tribes and others who had come up from Egypt. They secured a foothold in the central part of the country around Shechem (see color map 5). Following further campaigns into the N and S of Canaan, he settled in a town near Shiloh, where he died (Josh. 24:29; Judg. 2:8).

Apparently Joshua's reputation grew as Israel's literary tradition expanded. At many points his relationship to Yahweh parallels that of Moses as does his authority among the people (cf. Josh. 3:7; 4:14). His figure as regal leader, judge, priest, and servant of Yahweh (Josh. 24:29) is endued with honor and authority in subsequent OT and intertestamental writings.

In the book which bears his name Joshua is portrayed as the leader of a united Israel, a commander given the task of conquering Canaan (chs. 1-12) and dividing the land among the tribes (chs. 13-24). A number of the battle accounts were brought together, perhaps by a 6th-cent. Judean theologian known as the Deuteronomist, and shaped into the narrative we have in Josh. 1-12. In the process the whole account was edited to show that it was Yahweh himself who gave the victory, that the conquest was not Israel's triumph but Yahweh's, the result of his intention to give his people a land. In contrast Judg. 1, a fragment of a more objective account, credits the incomplete conquest to tribal groups—the total conquest eventually to be completed by David. This account is nearer the truth, for there is strong reason to believe that the actual appropriation of the territory took place over a period of several cents.

While Joshua led the Joseph tribes in establishing a stronghold in the central highland, S tribes, who sensed a kinship with the Joseph tribes even though they had not gone into Egypt, pressed N. Tradition says that Transjordan was conquered by Israel during the lifetime of Moses. The Joseph tribes carried the battle from their stronghold in the hill country of Ephraim toward the coast, where later there were to be military encounters with the Greek migrants whom we know as the Philistines. The hill country remained the bastion of Israelite rule for centuries and the center of her major shrines. Certain prized territories, the great fortress cities of the plain of Esdraelon as well as its fertile lands, were not to be wrested from Canaanite hands until the reign of David.

The occupation of Canaan brought both blessings and problems to Israel. Apparently the covenant proclaimed by Moses prospered in these cents. and fostered a stronger sense of kinship and unity than ever the idea of a common ancestry had. A significant number of leaders and people in Israel affirmed the belief that they had been called to serve one God and to become one people in covenant with him.

But strife and disunity also characterized relations among several of the tribes. In this incomplete conquest the Israelites also found themselves living among the highly civilized Canaanites, whose religion and culture many of the Israelites found immensely attractive.

The Age of the Judges. The settlement of Israel in Canaan did not mean that a national state had been established. Rather, between the entry into Palestine (late 13th cent.) and the unification of the people under one ruler (ca. 1033) Israel seems to have lived in tribal units which came together primarily for mutual defense in times of crisis. The leaders of these often isolated groups are known as "judges," though it is not certain that this title was used during their own lifetimes (see Intro. to Judg.). They were men who felt themselves called by Yahweh to assume leadership of his people. In times of crisis they gathered the men of their own and neighboring tribes around them and led such troops against the invading forces. Thereafter some of them, at least, continued their leadership as administrators and judges.

In Judg. we have biographies of several of these judges—though surely by no means all of them. This document is uniquely important for the study of political, social, and religious conditions in the period immediately following the settlement. There was little cohesion among the Israelite tribes except when they were threatened by external enemies. At such times appeals for unity were almost always sent forth in the name of Yahweh. Some scholars believe that the Israel tribes—or more probably clusters of them—formed an amphictyony, i.e. an association of neighboring communities for the purpose of protecting a common religious center, and that they bound themselves by a religious pledge which was confirmed at the amphictyonic shrine at the center of such a confederation. Several such shrines are mentioned in Judg.

The leaders whom we confront in this book are presented by the Deuteronomist editor in the framework of a distinctive, if somewhat artificial, philosophy of history, which he describes in his preface to the stories (Judg. 2:6–3:6): (a) Israel forgot the demands of Yahweh; (b) as a consequence she was oppressed by foreign troops; (c) under such oppression she repented and cried out to Yahweh for help; (d) then Yahweh raised up a leader who judged the people, put down the oppressor, and restored peace and prosperity. On the death of the judge Israel again forgot her God and began to serve the Baals and the cycle was under way again.

With one exception the enemies recorded in Judg. were invaders who came from outside the borders of Canaan. That exception was the Canaanite confederation under Sisera, whose defeat by Deborah and Barak is celebrated in Judg. 4–5. Among the external enemies were Moab (Ehud, 3:12-30), Midianite raiders from E of the Jordan (Gideon, chs. 6–8), Ammon (Jephthah, ch. 11), and the Philistines, Greek migrants moving into the E Mediterranean, who carved out a home on the coastal plain of Palestine beginning ca. 1200. Israelite resistance to these invaders in the age of the judges is epitomized in the Samson stories (chs. 13–16). The age ends with Philistine dominance in W Palestine. The military and political threat that these skillful and cultured people posed against the increasingly unified tribes of Israel made a strong central government imperative.

IV. The Rise of the Monarchy

Philistine domination of the hill country of Ephraim, the central highland of Palestine, led to the establishment of the monarchy in Israel. The central highland had been the stronghold of Israelite settlement and more than any other region had succeeded in resisting absorption into Canaanite cultural and religious practices. But in the time of the priest Eli the Philistine forces defeated the Israelite army in the battle of Aphek, captured the ark, which had been carried into battle from the shrine at Shiloh, and destroyed the shrine itself.

Saul. The need for a strong central military force was apparent. And with the need came the warrior in the person of Saul the Benjaminite. Saul's rise to preeminence as Israel's first king (ca. 1033-1011) reflects not only his prowess as a military commander but also his charismatic religious leadership; he was summoned to his task through the phenomenon of prophetic inspiration. The leader most directly involved in the anointing of Saul as king

was Samuel. Two accounts of the rise of the monarchy are combined in the biblical record, but both make it clear that Samuel—seer, prophet, priest, and judge—anointed Saul in the name of Yahweh to lead Israel against the Philistine forces (I Sam. 9:1-10:16).

Saul's military leadership was established in his initial successes against the Ammonites, who threatened Jabesh-gilead in Transjordan (I Sam. 11:1-11; see color map 6). In due course he led a major Israelite uprising against the Philistines (I Sam. 14:1-46), driving them out of the highland. Thus he established his authority over the highland and Transjordan, though his armies never secured the coastal regions or the plain of Esdraelon. For a number of years he repulsed Philistine attempts to attack the hill country from the W. Finally the Philistines undertook to approach that region from the N, and in the tragic battle of Gilboa they succeeded in killing Saul and several of his sons and in reasserting their control over the territory W of the Jordan (I Sam. 31:1-7).

Saul's treatment of David, his insanity, and his tragic death should not be allowed to obscure our appreciation for the purity of his political motives or his significant role in the unification of the tribes of Israel.

David. Among Saul's warriors was David the Bethlehemite, about whom we have more biographical details than about any other OT personality. His military successes as one of Saul's commanders aroused the jealousy of the king, and David was obliged to leave the country. He entered the service of the Philistine king of Gath and from that vantage point gained considerable popularity in the S and also gathered around himself an army of refugees from Israel (I Sam. 27).

At the death of Saul his youthful son Ishbaal (called Ish-bosheth in II Sam.; see comment on 2:8-11) succeeded to the throne, making his headquarters in Transjordan, where his father's authority had also been most secure. There is no evidence that Ishbaal exercised any significant influence W of the Jordan, where the Philistines had reasserted their dominance. David established his authority in Judah, where he was soon proclaimed king (ca. 1010). War between his forces and those of Ishbaal became inevitable. Through a series of events, involving some intrigue, Saul's son was murdered, and David was declared king of all Israel (ca. 1003-971/70). The Philistines, who to this point had been content to observe Israelite fighting Israelite, were now themselves faced with the strong military and political leadership of David and an increasingly unified Israelite people.

David's first military stroke, however, was not against Philistine power but against an ancient Canaanite fortress that had held out between N and S Israelite territory, viz. the Jebusite city of Jerusalem. This stronghold he captured with characteristic aggressiveness (II Sam. 5:6-8) and made it his new capital. From Jerusalem David directed a series of accomplishments which led later generations to regard his reign as the golden age of Israel's history and the pattern for Israel's later dreams of a messianic order.

Early in his reign David reasserted Israelite control over the central highland, took the plain of Esdraelon, and established Israelite authority far to the N between the Lebanon ranges. Except for the Philistine city-states in the SW, the land W of the Jordan was united for the first time under a strong Israelite ruler.

With the aid of Joab, his longtime military commander, David then proceeded to conquer the nations surrounding Israel in order that they might serve as buffer states for the protection of her borders. The defeat of Edom, Moab, Ammon and the Aramean tribes to the N, coupled with the decline of the Philistine power and the promulgation of a treaty of friendship with Phoenicia, served to strengthen Israel's security in an unusual interlude when the E Mediterranean region was free from domination by imperial powers.

David's external military consolidation was matched by skillful internal administration. He brought the ark of Yahweh to Jerusalem thus proclaiming the religion of Yahweh as the foundation of national unity and strength. He also took financial advantage of the fact that the great trade routes of the Near East ran through his territory, no doubt gaining profits for the crown by provisioning and protecting caravans. David's skill as an organizer was reflected in the internal political organization of Israel, in the expert use of a militia drawn from among the Israelite people primarily for use in foreign wars, and in the establishment of a royal bodyguard made up largely of foreign soldiers.

Notwithstanding these successes David's reign was not entirely peaceful. Two revolts against his rule are mentioned in the biblical record, one led by his son Absalom, who was supported by dissidents from David's own tribe of Judah, and the other emanating from the tribe of Benjamin, of which Saul had been a member. The burdens of foreign wars and of a permanent military establishment, as well as the forced labor which David required of his subjects, undoubtedly aroused resentment. In the final years of his reign the court of David would seem to have taken on many of the characteristics commonly associated with ancient oriental potentates. Nevertheless David's faults should not blind us to his greatness. We have reason to share the views of David's objective and impartial biographer—the author of II Sam. 9-20; I Kings 1-2, a historical masterpiece of the OT—who portrayed him as a man of heroic chivalry, a champion of justice, and a devout servant of Yahweh.

Solomon. David's son Solomon (971/70-931/30) acceded to the throne of Israel long after the last of the foreign wars of his father, yet his reign was not a time of genuine peace in Israel. He came to the throne as the result of a palace revolution and at his death the kingdom fell into division. Born to the purple, Solomon seems to have been unmindful of the circumstances and problems faced by the majority of his subjects.

David's oldest surviving son, Adonijah, expected to succeed his father and was supported in his claim by Joab, David's commander, and Abiathar the priest. But Nathan the prophet and Solomon's mother, Bathsheba, conspired in David's last days to see that Solomon was proclaimed king by his father.

As king, Solomon proved selfish, unbelievably pretentious, and inconsiderate of the personal values prized by his subjects, to say nothing of their wellbeing. His reputation for wisdom seems to have resulted from the resplendence of his court, his cleverness as a judge, and a certain verbal or literary skill (cf. I King 3-4).

Solomon's reign was characterized by extensive building projects, for which he levied burdensome taxes and required forced labor both from his own people and from foreign subjects. At one time, it appears, every Israelite peasant was required to give a 3rd of each year to the crown. Disregarding tribal boundaries, he divided the kingdom into 12 administrative districts, each of which was charged with the responsibility of maintaining the court for a month each year. The most famous of his projects was the building of the temple, as the royal shrine, in which the ark of Yahweh was housed (I Kings 6-8). For this building, as well as the royal palace and other shrines, he imported workmen and the best of costly materials, esp. from Phoenicia. He established chariot depots around the country as well as stables for horses, which were imported from Egypt and perhaps other lands. Solomon outfitted a fleet of vessels which sailed from Ezion-geber on the Gulf of Aqaba through the Red Sea, probably as far as India, carrying on trade and bringing great profits to the monarch (see color map 7). Modern archaeology has brought to light copper mines near Ezion-geber which were worked during this reign. Heavy tolls continued to be levied on the caravans which passed through Israel's territory.

Despite extensive sources of income, and even though Solomon carried on no costly foreign wars during his reign, the royal treasury was often depleted and the king could not pay his bills. At one point he ceded a part of his territory to the king of Tyre, Hiram, in order to raise funds (I Kings 9:10-14). In such circumstances Solomon's recourse was to increase taxes and to levy even greater demands for forced and unpaid labor against his people.

Though his troops were splendidly equipped with chariots and horses, Solomon showed no interest in military activity even when it would seem to have been called for—a fact which has led some commentators to charge Solomon with cowardice. When Edom revolted against Israelite dominion and the Arameans established an independent state in Damascus, Solomon apparently did nothing to hold them.

Alliances with Tyre and Egypt involved the king's marriage to foreign princesses; easy access was thereby provided for foreign cultural and religious influences to come into Jerusalem. It was to these acts of disloyalty to Yahweh that later historians credited the division of the kingdom after the death of Solomon (I Kings 11).

V. THE DIVIDED KINGDOM

The Division. Given the popular dissension and resentment of the last years of Solomon's reign, it is surprising that he did not have to face widespread rebellion by his subjects. If they did initiate any significant insurrection during his reign, record of it has been omitted from the accounts. We have evidence, as already noted, that the neighboring states which David had brought under Israelite control began to reassert their independence. In addition we also have the record that the prophet Ahijah (I Kings 11:29-40), who was critical of Solomon's extravagance and his patronage of foreign gods, encouraged Jeroboam, an officer in charge of the king's forced labor program, to lead the 10 tribes of the N in revolt. When the matter was reported to Solomon, Jeroboam fled to Egypt, where he remained until Solomon's death (I Kings 12:1-20). Ahijah's prediction that only 2 tribes would remain loyal to Solomon's heirs was soon to become a reality.

Rehoboam (931/30-913), the son of Solomon, was accepted in Judah as his father's successor. Judging from I Kings 4:7-19 Judah had been excused from many of Solomon's demanding levies and may therefore have been less resentful against the royal family. When Rehoboam went to Shechem to accept the loyalty of the tribes gathered there and establish a covenant with them, they made reform a condition of their acceptance of the new monarch (I Kings 12:1-20). His incredibly arrogant answer to their demands led to a revolt, and the tribes of the N proclaimed Jeroboam king.

While Rehoboam's answer seems indefensible and a cause for anger, there is reason to conclude that division might have come whatever his response, if not immediately at least soon. A number of circumstances indicate that the new monarch had inherited a difficult situation. Longstanding differences existed between Judah and the Joseph tribes. Reform would have involved cutting back taxes and the forced-labor schemes and subsequently lowering the standard of luxury to which court and ruling class had become accustomed. Beyond these problems was the serious fact that neither Rehoboam nor his advisers were well enough informed to know they should take the complaints of the N tribes seriously.

Inevitably war followed as Rehoboam attempted to hold his father's domain together. In time Sheshonk of Egypt entered the battle against Jerusalem (I Kings 14:25-28), forcing Rehoboam to capitulate and pay a heavy indemnity.

The separation of N and S which followed the revolt of Jeroboam continued until the fall of the N (Samaria) to the Assyrians in 722. Save for a brief interim the S was ruled by the Davidic dynasty while the N underwent frequent changes of ruling dynasty.

Among the most obvious signs of disruption was Jeroboam's proclamation of the ancient shrines at Dan and Bethel as national centers for the worship of Yahweh. A golden bull was enshrined in each of these places—some scholars say as a symbol of Yahweh while others believe as a throne for the invisible God. The later editor of Kings was sharply critical of Jeroboam for establishing these shrines, presumably because they diverted the N worshipers from the Jerusalem temple, which he considered the only legal sanctuary. Solomon's Temple, however, was built as a royal sanctuary and was not intended as the only legal place of worship. That view of it did not evolve until the Deuteronomic reform in 622.

Despite this political separation both N and S

seem to have envisaged a time when the 12 tribes would be unified. They shared a common religious tradition, and that tradition prospered in the N. We cannot dismiss lightly the fact that great religious leaders like Elijah, Elisha, and Hosea were from the N while Amos, though a Judean, prophesied and preached in the N.

Indeed the influential role of the prophets began to emerge clearly in these times of political turmoil. Actually the prophets were interested in political power only insofar as it was influential in maintaining or corrupting the religious purity of the people of Jahweh. They intentionally and boldly incited rebellion against a king when they felt that his policies were oppressive and the people were suffering social injustice, or when under his leadership Israel's participation in international affairs threatened Yahwism. The prophets were entirely willing to bring down kings or dynasties and to call for disruption in order to foster that religious purity which they believed would one day make Israel into one people, the servant of one God.

From Jeroboam to Ahab. While the house of David remained a symbol of political stability in Judah, Israel was governed by a series of dynastic families, many of whom came to the throne through revolution and violence. Jeroboam (931/30-910/9), who ruled from Shechem, asserted the religious and political independence of the N. He was succeeded by his son Nadab (910/9-909/8), who was soon murdered and replaced by a military commander, Baasha (909/8-886/85), who moved the capital to Tir-zah (see color map 8). His son in turn suffered early assassination, and the land was thrown into some years of civil conflict.

During these years not only was Rehoboam of Judah unwilling to accept the division of the kingdom, but his son Abijam (913-911/10) and his grandson Asa (911/10-870/69) also fought against the ruling house of Israel. It was not until Jehoshaphat (870/69-848) came to the Judean throne that that country's efforts were directed toward strengthening the Judean economy and reconquering the trade routes through Edom.

The winner of the civil war in Israel, Omri (880-874/73), was an able ruler. He attracted international attention, and his dynasty is mentioned in ancient Assyrian records. He recaptured Israel's military strongholds and built Samaria as his capital. Under Omri Moab was again brought under Israel's submission and an alliance was drawn up with the Phoenician king of Tyre. This alliance was confirmed by the marriage which was arranged between Omri's son, Ahab, and Jezebel, the princess of Tyre.

Jezebel was a worshiper of the Tyrian god Baal. When Ahab became king (874/73-853) his willingness to support the temple and priests and prophets of Baal was the occasion for Elijah's protest (I Kings 17-19; 21). The career of Elijah during the reign of Ahab heralds the beginning of a long-lived prophetic protest against the worship of gods other than Yahweh in Israel, and against social injustice by monarch and nobility.

During his reign Ahab engaged in war with the Syrians, whose leader, Ben-hadad, set siege against Samaria *ca.* 857. The following spring at Aphek E of the Sea of Galilee Ahab defeated the Syrians, thus reasserting Israelite authority over certain N border areas and securing trade rights in Damascus. During this time the Assyrian Empire began to emerge in the W under a strong new leader, Shalmaneser III. From its center in N Mesopotamia this militant and often cruel people pushed W, theatening the independence of the small kingdoms of the E Mediterranean world. This threat led Ahab and Ben-hadad to join forces against their common enemy. These kings, together with other local rulers, met and turned back the Assyrians at Qarqar on the Orontes (see color map 9) in 853, as described in Assyrian records. Hardly had the victory been won when Israel and Syria took up arms against each other, and Ahab was killed in battle at Ramoth-gilead.

The Revolt of Jehu. Ahab's son and successor Ahaziah (853-852) died from a fall and was succeeded by a 2nd son of Ahab, Jehoram, or Joram (852-841). Joram was soon confronted with a revolt by his vassal Mesha of Moab, as described on the famous Moabite Stone erected by Mesha (see comment on II Kings 3:4-27). Later Joram renewed the attack on the Syrians—now under Hazael, who had usurped the throne of Ben-hadad—and succeeded in taking Ramoth-gilead; but while recovering from a wound he was slain in a revolt by one of his generals, Jehu.

Jehu's insurrection was sponsored and supported by Elisha and a religious sect known as the Rechabites as a protest against the Baal worship of Ahab's household. It was a bloody uprising in which Jehu's followers murdered Jezebel, 70 of Ahab's sons, many Baal worshipers, and a number of princes of the house of David who were making a royal visit to Israel.

At the very beginning of his reign (841-814/13) Jehu was threatened with a new invasion of the W by Shalmaneser III and had to pay tribute to that Assyrian monarch, as pictured on Shalmaneser's Black Obelisk (see ill., p. 1061). In addition Jehu had little success in defending his territory against Hazael of Damascus and lost all of Transjordan to the Syrians. Under his son Jehoahaz (814/13-798) the situation grew worse and Israel was reduced to military impotence. As Assyrian power began to increase again Damascus was obliged to think of her self-defense and her attention was turned to the E. Under these circumstances Jehoahaz' son Jehoash (Joash, 798-782/81) was able to regain some of Israel's lost territory.

The revolution of Jehu in Israel was paralleled by a countermovement in Judah. Athaliah, a daughter of Ahab and Jezebel, had become queen of Judah through her marriage to Jehoram (Joram, 848-841). Their son Ahaziah, who succeeded Jehoram, was killed within a few months in the revolt of Jehu. In reaction Athaliah murdered other claimants to the throne and ruled Judah for 6 years (841-835). The Jerusalem priests finally brought her 7-year-old grandson, Jehoash (Joash, 835-796), out of hiding, proclaimed him king, and killed the queen on grounds that she was an idol worshiper.

The son of Jehoash of Judah, Amaziah (796-767), stirred up a quarrel with Jehoash of Israel that resulted in war between the 2 kingdoms. Judah was defeated in battle and Jerusalem was despoiled.

For a time, Judah fell to the status of a vassal state under Israel.

The Fall of Samaria. The first half of the 8th cent. was a time of general peace in the Near East. Egypt had fallen into decline. Assyria was not yet ready to undertake the building of a new empire—though strong enough to hold the attention of Damascus and turn it away from Israel. In such circumstances Jeroboam II (782/81-753) was able to reestablish international trade in Israel and wealth began to pour into that country. It was during the last years of Jeroboam's prosperous reign that Amos came from the S to announce the imminent downfall of Israel. His proclamation was based on the conviction that greed and social injustice were about to bring God's judgment on Israel. He deplored the concentration of wealth in the hands of monarch, nobility, and upper classes and lamented the poverty and injustice which prevailed among the masses.

In 745, under the strong rule of Tiglath-pileser III, the Assyrians began their move W in search of empire. Out of theconfusion following the death of Jeroboam II, Menahem (752-742/41) gained political control in Israel. When the Assyrian forces moved S along the Mediterranean, he temporarily saved his country from invasion by paying tribute to the Assyrian emperor. Menahem was succeeded by his son Pekahiah (742/41-740/39), who was slain by Pekah (740/39-732/31). The new king of Israel joined with Rezin of Syria in an attempt to stop Assyrian encroachment on their territories. The 2 tried unsuccessfully to force Ahaz of Judah to join them, but the whole resistance effort failed and Ahaz subsequently appealed to the Assyrian emperor for protection. Tiglath-pileser captured Damascus in 732 and established sovereignty over Galilee and Transjordan.

The Assyrians supported Hoshea (732/31-723/22) in his bid for the Israelite throne. After killing Pekah he became the last king of Israel, as a puppet of Tiglath-pileser III and then of Shalmaneser V. When he joined a plot with Egypt against Assyria, the new Assyrian ruler retaliated with vigor and besieged Samaria for 3 years. Scholars differ on whether the city actually fell to Shalmaneser in 723/22, as implied in II Kings 17:3-6 (see comment), or to his successor, Sargon II, in 721, as claimed by Sargon in a later inscription. At any rate Sargon followed up the capture by scattering a large part of the population of Israel—the "10 lost tribes"—among other provinces of Assyria and in their place settled Assyrians and others from his empire.

The Decline of Judah. The prosperous reign of Jeroboam II in the north was paralleled by the long rule of Amaziah's son Azariah, or Uzziah, in the S (792/91-740/39; see "Chronology," pp. 1271-82). His successors were Jotham (740/39-732/31) and Ahaz (732/31-716/15). Apparently Ahaz assumed the actual rule of Judah in 735, while his father was still living, and as already noted was confronted with the demand of Pekah and Rezin that Judah join Israel and Syria in resisting Assyria. Ahaz refused and unhappily sought the protection of the Assyrian monarch. Later, after the fall of Israel, Ahaz was obliged to pay annual tribute to the Assyrian ruler, though officially the Judean kingdom retained its independence.

Ahaz was succeeded by his son Hezekiah (716/15-687/86), whom we know rather well in connection with the ministry of Isaiah. Hezekiah joined other rulers in a widespread Near Eastern revolt against Assyrian authority. In response Sennacherib, who succeeded Sargon as Assyrian emperor in 705, began to stamp out the rebellion. His forces marched across Judah, captured 46 of her cities, and set siege to Jerusalem itself in 701. Apparently a plague among the Assyrian troops forced their withdrawal and Jerusalem was spared, though much of the Judean wealth had already been taken.

Assyrian imperial power reigned triumphant for the next 75 years. Under Esarhaddon (680-669) and Ashurbanipal (668-*ca.* 626) Assyrian influence dominated the political and the religious life of the Judeans. Manasseh (687/86-643/42) and his son Amon (643/42-641/40), rulers of Judah, were obliged to promote the worship of the gods of the Assyrians even in the temple of Yahweh in Jerusalem.

The Fall of Jerusalem. From about 630 Assyrian power declined rapidly. Scythians and Medes moved against her from the N and the E, and the Babylonians from the S. In 612 the Babylonians captured Nineveh, the Assyrian capital.

In Judah, Josiah (641/40-609), Amon's son and successor, undertook a series of reforms, beginning in 622, in an attempt to bring Judah back to the worship of Yahweh and to reassert Judean political independence (cf. II Kings 22–23). Josiah destroyed Assyrian idols and pagan shrines throughout Judah and declared the temple at Jerusalem the only legitimate center for offering sacrifices to Yahweh, the God of Israel.

The fall of Assyria seemed to Pharaoh Neco of Egypt to be an opportunity to reassert Egyptian control over SW Asia; undoubtedly he was also troubled over the rapid rise of Babylonian power. In 609 when Neco marched N toward Syria he was confronted at Megiddo by Josiah, who was killed there in the ensuing battle. One of Josiah's sons, Jehoiakim (609-598/97), was put on the throne at Jerusalem by Neco; another, Jehoahaz, whom the Judeans had crowned, was carried captive into Egypt.

Predictably Babylonian and Egyptian forces joined battle at Carchemish on the upper Euphrates (see color map 9) in 605. Nebuchadrezzar defeated Neco, and Babylon became mistress of the Near East. Shortly thereafter Jehoiakim of Judah, confident that Egypt would support him, led a revolt against Nebuchadrezzar. The Babylonian king marched against Jerusalem, and Jehoiakim died, perhaps slain by his own men. Nebuchadrezzar's forces captured Jehoiachin, son of Jehoiakim. He and a number of other Judean princes, numerous priests, military officers, and artisans, and significant elements of the upper classes of Judean society were carried off to Babylon. Zedekiah (597-586), a 3rd son of Josiah, was made puppet king in Jerusalem.

In due course Zedekiah also rebelled against Babylonian authority. Nebuchadrezzar retaliated with fury. The major fortresses of Judah were captured and burned. For 30 months (588-586) the Babylonians besieged Jerusalem, and the city suffered tragically (cf. the descriptions in Lam.). When the Babylonians finally broke into the city they leveled the walls and palaces and razed the temple to the ground. Zedekiah's sons were slain in front of him, and he himself was blinded and carried to Babylon in chains. The greater part of the population of Jerusalem was taken into exile with him. Thus the kingdom of David came to a tragic end.

For Further Study. H. H. Rowley, *From Joseph to Joshua,* 1950. J. B. Pritchard, ed., *Ancient Near Eastern Texts Relating to the OT,* rev. ed., 1955. G. E. Wright and F. V. Filson, *The Westminster Historical Atlas to the Bible,* rev. ed., 1956. W. F. Albright, *From the Stone Age to Christianity,* 2nd ed., 1957. John Bright, *A History of Israel,* 1959. Martin Noth, *The History of Israel,* 2nd ed., 1960. H. G. May, ed., *Oxford Bible Atlas,* 1962. G. E. Wright, *Biblical Archaeology,* rev. ed., 1963.

THE HISTORY OF ISRAEL
Part II. From the Exile to the Second Revolt Against Rome

Jonas C. Greenfield

I. The Return from Exile

The Exile. The fall of Jerusalem in 586 left political, social, and religious life disrupted throughout Judah. The temple was destroyed, all of the fortified cities were razed, and the ruling class and most artisans were taken into exile. Judah was reorganized into a province of the Babylonian Empire and a certain Gedaliah was appointed governor. After ruling from Mizpah, *ca.* 8 miles N of Jerusalem (see color map 11), for 2 or 3 years he was killed by a tool of the king of Ammon (II Kings 25:22-25). Thereupon many Jews fled to Egypt, taking Jeremiah with them against his will (Jer. 43:5-6). The Judean colonies in Egypt had begun in the 7th cent. and were greatly augmented by refugees from the Babylonian assaults.

The deportees from Judah were settled in various parts of Babylonia and were in all likelihood conscripted into public works, draining the land and building dams. Though many Jews adopted Babylonian names, we know from texts of the Persian era that Hebrew names were preserved among them, a clear sign of religious and national identification. It is quite possible that the varied commercial and agricultural activities in which the Jews are known to have engaged during the Persian era had their beginning in this period.

During the reign of Amel-Marduk (Evil-merodach, 562-560), Nebuchadrezzar's successor, Jehoiachin, the Judean king exiled in 597, was granted a regular dole from the royal treasury (II Kings 25:27-30). The beginnings of the Diaspora—i.e. the dispersion of Jews among the nations—are to be traced to this period, with Jews settled in the countries near Judah and along the Mediterranean coastline. The Edomites, taking advantage of the situation, moved into much of S Judah (see Intro. to Obad.).

The Return to Zion. The Neo-Babylonian Empire came to an end under Nabonidus (555-539), who neglected the security of the country and entrusted the actual rule to his son Belshazzar. Cyrus, the head of the Persian confederation, conquered Babylon in 539 and without difficulty annexed most of the Babylonian Empire. In 538 he issued an edict for return of the Jewish community to Judah and the rebuilding of the temple in Jerusalem (Ezra 1:1-6). We know little of the initial return under Sheshbazzar, a member of Jehoiachin's family, except that the rebuilding of the temple was begun (Ezra 1:7-11). He was followed as governor by his nephew Zerubbabel, grandson of Jehoiachin (Ezra 3:1-7). The prophets Haggai and Zechariah greeted him as a scion of David.

Cambyses II (530-522), who succeeded his father Cyrus, spread Persian rule to Egypt in 525. When he died, a period of unrest and upheaval began in the empire, and a pretender who claimed to be a son of Cyrus seized the throne. But Darius I (522-486), a member of the royal family, took control of the army and after much struggle was established as ruler. With his permission the rebuilding of the temple was continued. It was dedicated with great rejoicing in 515.

Almost nothing is known of the Jews in Palestine under Xerxes I (486-465) or the first part of the reign of Artaxerxes I Longimanus (465-424) except that friction between the Jews and the neighboring Edomites, Arabs, and the officialdom of Samaria had developed (cf. Ezra 4:6-22). It is also clear that only a few Jews had returned and a viable state had not developed.

II. Nehemiah and Ezra

Nehemiah. According to the account written by Nehemiah himself, he was serving as an officer in the court of Artaxerxes I when a delegation of Jews led by his brother Hanani informed him of conditions in Jerusalem (Neh. 1). In 445 Nehemiah received royal permission to go to Jerusalem and rebuild its walls. He was also appointed governor of Judah, a small district of about 1,000 square miles centering primarily about Jerusalem. On arriving he discovered powerful foes, including Sanballat, governor of the province of Samaria to the N, and Tobiah, governor of the province of Ammon to the E. Both had strong ties with the influential priestly families of Jerusalem (Neh. 2). Geshem, an Arab chieftain to the S, was allied with them in trying to frustrate Nehemiah's plans. Nevertheless Nehemiah was able to rebuild the walls and also to institute economic reforms in the country (Neh. 5-6). He persuaded the people to accept a covenant in which they undertook to live according to the Mosaic law—specifically to observe the sabbath, enter into no more marriages with non-Jews, keep the sabbatical year, and support the temple and its priesthood (Neh. 10; 13:10-31).

Nehemiah returned to the Persian court in 433. After a time he came back to Jerusalem and, finding that his enemies Tobiah and Sanballat had achieved influential positions in the city again, drove them out along with their relatives, including a grandson of the high priest Eliashib (Neh. 13:4-9, 28). The beginnings of the breach between Jews and Samaritans must be traced to this period. Hanani may have succeeded his brother (cf. Neh. 7:2), but by 410 a Persian named Bagoas was governor.

Ezra. The dating of Ezra's coming to Jerusalem "in the seventh year of Artaxerxes" (Ezra 7:7) has traditionally been taken to refer to Artaxerxes I, making the date 458 and placing Ezra in the city at the time of Nehemiah's arrival. Many scholars, however, have found reasons to believe that the reference is to Artaxerxes II rather than to Artaxerxes I and that therefore Ezra did not come to Jerusalem till 397, some years after the time of Nehemiah (see Intro. to Ezra).

According to Ezra 7 the Persian king, addressing Ezra by the official title "scribe of the law of the God of heaven," authorized him to lead a body of Jews resettling in Judah, make inquiry into religious conditions in the province, and institute the "law of your God" as the law of the land. Soon after his arrival Ezra assembled the people of Jerusalem to read to them from the "book of the law of Moses" (Neh. 8) and secured their acceptance of it. Many scholars believe that the law presented by Ezra was the Torah, i.e. the Pentateuch, in essentially complete form and that its canonization dates from this time or soon afterward. Ezra proceeded to concern himself with the problem of mixed marriages that had become prevalent among the people, including members of the high-priestly family (Ezra 9–10). Going beyond Nehemiah, he insisted on the divorce and banishment of all foreign wives and their children.

Jews in Egypt. Much information about the life of Jews in Egypt during this period has been revealed by the discovery of many papyrus manuscripts on the Nile island of Elephantine near Syene (modern Assuan; see color map 10). One of these, written in 401, is a letter addressed to Bagoas, the Persian governor of Judah mentioned above, asking him to help the Jews of that community get permission to rebuild their temple, which had been built before Cambyses conquered Egypt in 525 and had been destroyed in 410. From the papyri we can trace the well-organized life of this Jewish military garrison during the 5th cent. and study the social, legal, religious, and communal institutions. Though their religious institutions were Israelite and holidays such as Passover were observed, we find some traces of syncretism. The fate of the Elephantine colony is unknown.

The Rest of the Persian Period. During the greater part of the 4th cent. we know only that Judah was a semiautonomous commonwealth ruled by the high priests, who levied taxes for the temple and were also allowed to mint coins. These coins bear the inscription *Yehud.* Handles of vessels used for collection of various levies, with *Yehud, Yerushalem,* and other inscriptions on them, have been found in increasing numbers in recent excavations. Aramaic was the official language of the country as part of the Persian empire, and the old Hebrew script was gradually replaced during this period by the Aramaic letters from which the modern Hebrew alphabet was developed.

III. UNDER GREEK RULE

Alexander the Great. A decisive turning point in Judean history came with the victory of Alexander of Macedon over Darius III Codomannus at Issus in 333. The Persian Empire lay open before him for conquest. He marched victoriously down the Syrian-Palestinian coast, conquered the area, and met with resistance only in Tyre and Gazara (Gezer).

The Samaritans were granted permission to construct a temple on Mt. Gerizim; but after they rebelled in 331 Alexander returned from Egypt, quelled the revolt, and resettled the city of Samaria as a Macedonian colony. Shechem, at the foot of Mt. Gerizim, now became the center of a Samaritan confederation, and excavations have traced its occupation from the last 3rd of the 4th cent. into the late 2nd cent. The coin finds reflect Ptolemaic control in the 3rd cent. and Seleucid control in the 2nd.

After the death of Alexander (323) his empire was divided among his generals. Syria and Mesopotamia came under the control of Seleucus I while Palestine fell first to Ptolemy I of Egypt. After it changed hands five times from 323 to 301, the Ptolemies ruled over Palestine until 198, when the Seleucid ruler Antiochus III succeeded in joining it to his realm.

Under the Ptolemies. Judea, still limited in size, remained a self-governing unit, and there was no royal governor in Jerusalem though troops were garrisoned in the country. Internal administration lay in the hands of the high priests and a council of elders composed of laymen and priests.

Judea was part of the planned economy developed by the Ptolemies. Movable property and cattle had to be declared for taxation, and tax farming was introduced. This was usually in the hands of the priestly aristocracy, headed by the house of Onias. In the last third of the 3rd cent. the Tobiads, who governed Transjordan and were intermarried with the high priestly family, became the tax-farmers for Judea. The house of Tobias rivalled the house of Onias for rule in Judea.

Many Judeans had been taken to Egypt as prisoners of war by Ptolemy I, and many more emigrated to Egypt during the 3rd cent. Large settlements developed in Alexandria and other cities, and the Jews lived in their own communities and enjoyed a degree of self-rule. Greek papyri attest to Jews serving in the army, engaged in agriculture as military settlers, lease holders, field hands, and also in commerce and the handicrafts. In all likelihood the Greek translation of the Torah which came to be known as the LXX was undertaken, with the sponsorship of Ptolemy II, *ca.* 280-250.

Antiochus III. The conquest of Palestine by Antiochus III brought Judea under Seleucid rule. Antiochus reaffirmed the rights of the Jews, exempted the elders and priests from taxes, and remitted the taxes of Jerusalemites for three years. He was defeated by the Romans at Magnesia in 190, and decline set in for the Seleucid Empire. His death in 187 was followed by dynastic conflict that strongly affected the Judean state.

Seleucus IV followed his father on the throne, but his reign was short (187-175) and his brother Antiochus IV Epiphanes (175-163) seized the throne.

1027

In Jerusalem conflicting views over the future of Judaism in general and over the role of the high priest in particular had developed. A party of members of highly placed priestly families favored the hellenization of Jerusalem, which included the establishment of a Greek community in Jerusalem and the creation of a gymnasium. Antiochus IV deposed Onias III from the high priesthood and gave the position to Onias' brother, who was called by the Greek name Jason (175-172). He then sold the position to Menelaus (172-162) and exiled Jason. To safeguard his position Menelaus contrived the murder of Onias III (cf. II Macc. 4).

The Maccabean Revolt. In 168 Antiochus had a citadel, called the Acra, built on the hill opposite Mt. Zion and manned it with Seleucid forces. This took the legal place of the city of Jerusalem; an earlier edict of Antiochus III establishing the Torah as the law of the city-state was thus abolished, and Hellenism spread among the upper classes. The service of the temple was fitted to Hellenistic concepts. By decree of Antiochus IV in Dec. 167 the Jerusalem temple was desecrated by the sacrifice of a pig and by the introduction of the cult of Zeus Olympius. Mosaic law was proscribed—observance of circumcision, of the Sabbath, and of holidays meant death. Altars to Greek gods were erected throughout the countryside, and the populace at large was expected to worship at them.

Resistance centered about Mattathias, of the priestly family of Hasmon, who with his sons left their home in Modein for the Judean desert. There they gathered followers and mounted an offensive against the pagan altars and the apostates. The mass of the rural population followed Mattathias and after his death rallied about his son Judas Maccabeus. In Dec. 164 Judas conquered Jerusalem, purified the temple, and restored the daily sacrifice—an event celebrated by the festival of Hanukkah ("Dedication").

Judas was now master of all Judea except for the Acra. Soon afterward Antiochus IV died on an expedition to Persia, and his young son Antiochus V (163-162) was made king with Lysias as regent. Lysias launched a massive campaign against Judas and was about to recapture Jerusalem when word reached him of a rival claimant to the regency. In haste to return to the Seleucid capital and protect his position, he made terms with Judas and agreed to the reestablishment of the dominion of the Torah over the Jews. New trouble soon came, however, when a son of Seleucus IV, Demetrius I (162-150), killed Antiochus V and Lysias and seized the throne. An aspirant to the high priesthood, Alcimus (Yakim), incited the new king to send an army under Nicanor to put down the rebels. In Mar. 161 Judas won a great victory over Nicanor, the anniversary of which was celebrated by the Jews for many years. But the triumph was short-lived, for the Seleucid government reacted with strength, and in 160 Judas fell in battle. His brother Jonathan took over the leadership but was forced to make peace with Demetrius.

In 152 there appeared a pretender to the Seleucid throne, Alexander Balas. In the face of this threat Demetrius sought the support of Jonathan and placed him in charge of Jerusalem. But Alexander outbid Demetrius by offering Jonathan the high priesthood.

When the 2 rivals met in battle, Demetrius was killed and Alexander became king (150-145). Thus the Maccabees at last came into power.

The Maccabean house which was to rule over most of Palestine for almost a cent. had its real start with Jonathan. Though not a member of the Zadokite high-priestly family he became high priest. Though a member of the family that led the revolt against the hellenizers he became a Seleucid official, designated a provincial governor and awarded the purple reserved for the "king's friends." Before being murdered in 143 Jonathan was able to expand the borders of Judea. Not all Jews rejoiced to see the high priest become a military and political leader. Some, perhaps during the time of Jonathan or perhaps later, went so far as to withdraw into the wilderness and form the Qumran community (see "The Dead Sea Scrolls," pp. 1063-71).

IV. SELF-GOVERNMENT

A 3rd son of Mattathias, Simon, followed the example of his brother Jonathan, carefully playing Seleucid king against counter-king. He succeeded in expanding Judea to include the plain, the seacoast from Joppa to Ascalon, and Hebron to the S of Jerusalem. In 141 he was able to win the Acra and expel its pagan inhabitants. In 140 in a great assembly of "priests and people, princes of the nation and elders" he was appointed hereditary high priest and ethnarch by an unalterable decree.

John Hyrcanus. Simon was murdered in 134 and was succeeded by his son John Hyrcanus I (134-104). Though at first the new ruler suffered reverses he took advantage of the Seleucid successional quarrels to strengthen his position. To organize a professional army he recruited foreign mercenaries and levied troops among his people. In the course of his reign he raised Judea to the most important power in Syria and extended his realm to include Galilee in the north, the Carmel region on the sea coast, and Idumea in the south. He forced the Idumeans, the descendants of the ancient Edomites, to accept circumcision and to become Jews. He also conquered Shechem and Samaria and destroyed the hated sanctuary on Mt. Gerizim. His coins read "Yohanan [John] High Priest and the Council of the Jews."

John Hyrcanus faced a certain amount of dissension within the country with the rise of a popular religious and political party, the Pharisees, in opposition to the established priesthood and landed aristocracy, the Sadducees. He at first favored the Pharisees but broke with them and thereby aroused widespread antagonism. For this reason some scholars consider him the "Wicked Priest" who persecuted the "Teacher of Righteousness" in the Qumran literature.

Alexander Janneus. John Hyrcanus' son Aristobulus I reigned only one year (104-103) and was succeeded by his brother Alexander Janneus (103-76). His coins contain the legends "Jonathan the King" in Hebrew and "of King Alexander" in Greek—the first known use of the title "king" since the end of the Davidic monarchy. He married his brother's widow, Salome Alexandra—an act which was not in consonance with his position as high priest. The Pharisees were his enemies throughout his reign.

Janneus' defeat at the hands of the Nabateans in 90 led to 6 years of civil strife. The Pharisees even sided at first with Demetrius III, who successfully invaded the country, but later they joined Janneus in driving out the Seleucid king. He then crucified many of them—an outrage which is possibly alluded to in the Qumran fragment of a commentary on Nah. Because of this and other like cruelties some scholars view him as the "Wicked Priest" of Qumran. Despite frequent setbacks the boundaries of the country at the time of Janneus' death included most of the ancient kingdom of David and took in almost all the Philistine coast to Gaza and parts of Transjordan. Though he wore the raiment of the high priest he was first and foremost a Hellenistic king.

Hyrcanus II and Aristobulus II. Salome Alexandra became queen of Judea (76-67) after her husband's death and appointed her older son, Hyrcanus, to the office of high priest. Effective rule over the country passed into the hands of the Pharisees. Her younger son, Aristobulus, sided with the Sadducees and became the leader of the opposition even before his mother's death. When she died in 67, Aristobulus with the help of the Sadducees forced Hyrcanus to renounce the throne and began to rule as Aristobulus II (67-63). Hyrcanus, instigated by Antipater the Idumean, father of Herod, sought the aid of the Nabateans. In the spring of 65 he besieged Aristobulus in the temple mount with their help. Both brothers also laid their case and their promise of money before the Roman general Scaurus, Pompey's legate, in Damascus. When he decided in favor of Aristobulus, the Nabateans raised their siege and abandoned Hyrcanus.

When Pompey arrived in Damascus in 63, 3 Jewish parties appeared before him—Hyrcanus, Aristobulus, and a delegation from the people, who wanted neither of the brothers and wished to return to the older form of priestly government. Pompey's final decision was to occupy Jerusalem. Aristobulus again fortified himself in the temple mount; but with the help of Hyrcanus the city was captured, a terrible massacre took place, and the temple was taken. Though priests were struck down at the altar and Pompey and his cohorts entered the Holy of Holies, the temple was not plundered and the sacrificial cult was soon resumed.

V. Under Roman Rule

With the coming of Roman dominion Judea was reduced to limited size and heavily taxed. Hyrcanus II was at first allowed to rule as high priest; but when Alexander, a son of Aristobulus II, tried to seize power in Jerusalem the country was placed under the direct rule of Gabinius, Roman governor of Syria. Gabinius' division of the land into five districts was to have lasting consequences. When Julius Caesar's power became felt in Syria, Hyrcanus and Antipater the Idumean supported his cause. In reward Hyrcanus was given the hereditary high priesthood and the title of ethnarch while Antipater was designated as Roman procurator over Judea. Political power was now in the hands of an Idumean. Antipater gave control over Jerusalem to his son Phasael and over Galilee to a 2nd son, Herod.

By a variety of acts Herod ingratiated himself with the Roman governor of Syria, but he antagonized the Jews despite the fact that he was married to Mariamne, a granddaughter of Hyrcanus. After the murder of Julius Caesar (44) and the victory of Mark Antony and Octavius the Jews sent delegates to hail the new leaders and to complain against Antipater and his sons (42). Herod, skilled in diplomacy, won the confidence of Antony and Octavius and in 40 was proclaimed king of the Jews by the Roman senate. But at that time the Parthians occupied Syria and helped Antigonus, son of Aristobulus II, to establish his rule over Jerusalem (40-37). With Roman help Herod drove out Antigonus and his followers and was established as king of the Jews in Judea. At Herod's insistence Antigonus was killed by the Romans at Antioch even though he had surrendered unconditionally. With his death the Maccabean dynasty came to an inglorious end.

The Reign of Herod. Herod's long rule over Judea (37-4) may be characterized as a period of growth and repression. Though he had supported Mark Antony he was able to win Octavius Augustus' favor and to keep his throne (34). He remained a faithful vassal of Augustus all of his life. Judea was limited in size when he assumed the throne, but he added to its size and in the course of time came to rule over almost all of Palestine—including the coastal cities—and parts of S Syria (see color map 14). He undertook an extensive building program which included such cities as Sebaste (Samaria) and the great seaport of Caesarea, both named in honor of Augustus. He fortified Machaerus and Masada near the Dead Sea. Excavations at Masada have revealed his extensive work there. Jerusalem was entirely rebuilt, and in the year 20 he began work on the renewal of the temple complex.

Though Herod greatly expanded the temple and glorified it, his essential attitude toward it was contemptuous. He meddled with the high priesthood, made and deposed high priests, and even had one, Aristobulus, a Maccabean relative of his wife, killed. He slaughtered most of the remaining members of the Maccabean family including his mother-in-law Alexandra, his wife Mariamne, and his own children by her.

To increase his prestige Herod presented Hellenistic cities with gifts and buildings. He was intensely disliked by the Jews of all parties not only because of the heavy burden of taxation but because of his tyranny and brutality. Even though such great teachers as Shammai and Hillel lived during his rule, the power of the Sanhedrin, the high court, was greatly reduced.

When he died in 4 B.C., the leaders of the Jewish community sent a deputation to Augustus to ask him to put an end to the rule of Herod's family and to restore their former independence. Augustus, however, following Herod's will, gave Judea to his son Archelaus along with Idumea and Samaria and appointed him ethnarch; he appointed 2 other sons of Herod as tetrarchs over the rest of Palestine.

With the integration of Palestine in the Roman Empire under Pompey and the tolerant attitude of Julius Caesar and Augustus toward the Jews, the Diaspora communities grew. The Jewish communities in Rome, in Antioch, and throughout Asia Minor prospered. The community in Alexandria and other parts of Egypt also grew, but friction was developing among the citizens, the natives, and the Jews.

The Rule of the Procurators. In A.D. 6 a delegation of Jews and Samaritans went to Rome to lodge strong complaints against Archelaus. Unable to refute the charges, he was banished. Judea, Samaria, and Idumea were incorporated into the empire and made a province whose governor had the status of procurator, with his seat in the city of Caesarea. He was responsible for taxation and maintaining public order, but internal administration was given to the Sanhedrin, the procurator reserving the right to pass death sentences.

Herod's son Herod Antipas (4 B.C.-A.D. 39) was made tetrarch over Galilee and Perea. He ingratiated himself with the Romans and founded a city on the W side of Lake Gennesaret which he called Tiberias after the Emperor Tiberius. He married the Maccabean princess Herodias; it was she who had John the Baptist put to death (cf. Mark 6:17-28). Philip, Herod's third son (4 B.C.–A.D. 34), was made tetrarch over parts of Transjordan. He died childless. In 37 when Caligula became emperor he gave Philip's territory to Herod Agrippa I, a grandson of Herod the Great, added to it territory in Syria, and granted him the title of king. Caligula deposed Antipas in 39 and gave Galilee and Perea to Agrippa. In 41 Claudius, after the murder of Caligula, added Judea to Agrippa's realm. He now had under his scepter most of the territory of his grandfather. Agrippa tried to please the Jews, supported the Pharisees, and endowed the temple. He also attempted to refortify Jerusalem and used his influence with Claudius on behalf of the Jews of Alexandria (41). He died in 44 (cf. Acts 12:20-23).

The Romans on the whole respected the religious sensitivities of the Jews, but a series of cruel and venal procurators made their rule hated. Between 4 and 66 (except 41-44) 14 procurators ruled. Of these Pontius Pilate (26-36) was particularly known for his cruelty and the arbitrariness of his death sentences. Jesus' life falls within the reigns of Archelaus, Herod Antipas, who ruled over Galilee, and the procuratorship of Pilate. It is not possible to ascertain the year of Jesus' appearance in Jerusalem. He was tried on charges of blasphemy and sedition and sentenced to death by Pilate.

The First Revolt. With the death of Agrippa I in 44 Judea became just another minor Roman province. The Jews became restive and increasingly hostile to Roman rule. The numerous excesses committed by the procurators, their interference with internal affairs, and their meddling with high priesthood, including the murder of the high priest Jonathan by Felix (52-59), fanned the spirit of revolt. Even the granting to Agrippa II (cf. Acts 25:13–26:32) a son of Agrippa I, of supervision over the temple did not ease conditions. Brigandage and assassination spread through the country.

Two extreme nationalist groups, the Zealots and the Sicarii, came to the fore with the goal of driving out the Romans from the country. Most of the Pharisees and the Sadducees were in favor of a peaceful solution to the crisis. The last procurator, Gessius Florus (64-66), however, by plundering the land and violating the temple treasury in May 66 brought the insurrection to a head. He also allowed the Roman troops in Jerusalem to murder and plunder in the city. The revolt broke out in Jerusalem and spread through most of the country.

We are well informed about the revolt by Flavius Josephus, whose Antiquities of the Jews (ca. 93) is the chief source for Jewish history of the Greek and Roman periods. At the outset of the revolt he was in charge of Jewish forces in Galilee and then surrendered to the Romans. Soon after the conflict ended he wrote a detailed if somewhat biased account of it, The Jewish War.

The Jews were at first successful, but when Vespasian was sent by Nero to quell the insurrection the tide turned against them. By 68 the battle was limited to Jerusalem and its environs though the Zealots also held the fortresses of Herodium, Machaerus, and Masada. The Essene center at Qumran was destroyed by the Romans at this time. In Jerusalem internal disputes that weakened the defense of the city were taking place. The Zealots, headed by John of Gischala and Simon bar Giora, seized control and held Jerusalem.

Vespasian was proclaimed emperor in 69 and went to Rome to take the throne. His son Titus was put in charge of the siege and in Jul. 70 was able to penetrate the city. In Aug., after severe fighting, he set fire to the temple area and conquered the city. The Romans set up their standards and sacrificed before them. Herodium and Machaerus were easily conquered, but Masada resisted for another 3 years and fell only in 73. After setting fire to Herod's palace the defenders took their own lives; excavations have uncovered grim evidence of their last days.

To commemorate Titus' victory, coins with the legend "Judaea Capta" were struck, and a triumphal arch depicting sacred objects captured from the temple was erected in Rome. Jews throughout the Roman Empire now had to pay the former temple tax of a half-shekel to a fund for the support of the Capitoline Jove, but Judaism remained a permitted religion.

Reconstruction and the Second Revolt. A new center of religious and cultural leadership developed at the city of Jamnia near the coast (see color map 15) under the leadership of Johanan ben Zakkai and other rabbis. The house of Hillel, represented by Gamaliel II, also played a prominent role in the formulation of policy and religious decisions. The council in Jamnia interpreted the law, served as a supreme court, and took the lead in restoring internal order. Such matters as the biblical canon and the establishing of the text were given priority.

Under Trajan (98-117) a series of uprisings against Roman rule flared up in Cyrene, Egypt, and Cyprus in 115 when he was engaged in war in the E against the Parthians. The uprisings were quelled with great loss of life; it is not clear if Judea was also involved in the revolts.

The second Jewish revolt took place under Hadrian (117-138), who was dedicated to an ideal of pagan homogeneity in his empire. It is difficult to ascertain the direct cause of the revolt, but strongly contributing factors were Hadrian's decision to found the Roman city of Aelia Capitolina on the site of Jerusalem with a shrine to Jupiter on the site of the temple and the banning of castration, which included circumcision.

The revolt broke out in 132, led by Simon ben Koseba—called also both bar Kocheba, "son of the star," and bar Kozeba, "son of the lie"—who had the backing of the illustrious Rabbi Akiba. The revolt was at first successful. Jerusalem was liberated and made the capital. Coins were issued bearing the name of "Simon, Prince of Israel" and celebrating the liberation of Israel. It is possible that the sacrificial cult was also reestablished. Archives from this period containing letters from ben Koseba have been found in caves near the Dead Sea. A strongly aug-mented Roman army under Julius Severus suppressed the revolt after a final struggle at the town of Bether 6 miles SW of Jerusalem. Thus ended the last semblance of Jewish independence in ancient Judea.

For Further Study. S. W. Baron, *A Social Religious History of the Jews,* 2 vols., 1952. John Bright, *A History of Israel,* 1959. Victor Tcherikover, *Hellenistic Civilization and the Jews,* 1959. Martin Noth, *The History of Israel,* 2nd ed., 1960. F. M. Cross, Jr., *The Ancient Library of Qumran,* 1961. H. J. Leon, *The Jews of Ancient Rome,* 1961. Elias Bickerman, *From Ezra to the Last of the Maccabees,* 1962. Yigael Yadin, *Masada,* 1966.

GREECE AND ROME
IN THE BIBLICAL WORLD

Herbert G. May

I. Greece and the Near East

Early Contacts. Neither Greece nor the Near East lived in a vacuum, and commercial contacts and cultural influences existed between the 2 areas from an early period. Trade relations between Grecian lands and Phoenician cities existed in the 3rd millennium B.C., and Cretan goods found their way to Phoenicia and Egypt in the days of the Minoan civilization of Crete, before 1400 and contemporary with the Hebrew patriarchs. One scholar has even maintained that the Minoan civilization of Crete was predominantly Phoenician in character before 1500 and that the language of the so-called Linear A tablets from Crete (17th-16th cents.) is W Semitic of the Phoenician type. Mycenaean wares from Greek lands appear in Phoenician and Canaanite excavated sites dated to the 14th-13th cents. An obvious influence of Phoenicia on the Greeks is evident in their adoption of the Phoenician alphabet in the 8th or early 7th cent.

Peoples from Grecian lands came spectacularly into the Near East with the invasion of the Sea Peoples. They attempted invasion of Egypt in the 8th year of Ramses III (*ca.* 1190), and are depicted on the wall of the great temple of this pharaoh at Medinet Habu across the Nile from Luxor, ancient Thebes. Among the Sea Peoples were the Pelast or Philistines. According to Amos the origin of the Philistines was in Crete (9:7; cf. Jer. 47:4). Repulsed from Egypt, they settled on the coastland of Canaan below Joppa and eventually gave their name to the entire country in the form Palestine. The S part of the Philistine coastland is called the "Negeb of the Cherethites," i.e. of the Cretans (I Sam. 30:14). The descendants of these folk from Grecian lands played a large role in Israel's history.

The table of nations in Gen. 10 lists the nations of the world as known to Judeans in the middle of the 7th cent. Greece is included in it under the name Javan (vs. 4), the etymological equivalent of Ionia, i.e. W Asia Minor, which was one of the 2 Greek mainlands. Among Javan's "descendants" are the Greek lands of Elishah (probably part of Cyprus), Kittim (Cyprus), and Dodanim (perhaps Rhodes). Greek contacts in the reign of Josiah are evident from large quantities of Ionian pottery found at an excavated Judean fortress today called Mesad Hashabyahu on the coast between Ashdod and Joppa. A Greek mercenary garrison force may have been stationed here. Kittim—perhaps Cypriote

mercenaries serving in the Judean armies—are mentioned as recipients of provisions in important letters inscribed on potsherds found in the excavations at Arad in S Judah (see color map 5), to be dated just before Nebuchadrezzar's capture of Jerusalem.

The Persian period, beginning in the middle of the 6th cent., brought the Greeks and the Near East into violent military conflict when the kings of Persia waged war against the Greeks. This was followed in the latter part of the 4th cent. by Alexander the Great's conquest of Persia and its empire, which spread Hellenistic, i.e. postclassical Greek, culture throughout the Near East. Pottery imported from Greece into W Asia gives evidence of continuing contacts with Hellenistic culture before Alexander's conquest. So also do the early coins found in the area. The earliest Greek coin discovered in Palestine is from the 6th cent. and came from N Greece. There are 5th-cent. coins with the goddess Athena and her symbol, the owl. From the later 5th and early 4th cents. come coins with the name Yehud (Judah) and the Athenian owl, and one coin has on it a head with a crested Corinthian helmet. In a cave N of Jericho were found clay sealings originating in Samaria which were impressed with designs showing Attic Greek influences, as well as a tetradrachmon of the time of Philip II, father of Alexander the Great. Trade relationships of Tyre with Javan are mentioned in Ezek. 27:13 (cf. Isa. 66:19), and the Greeks appear in the postexilic prophetic books in Joel 3:5; Zech. 9:13.

The Persian Invasion of Greece. The Ionians on the W coast of Asia Minor in the 6th cent. were vassals of King Croesus of Lydia (see color map 10). His own hellenization is highlighted by his consulting in a time of crisis the famed oracle at Delphi, to be told that if he crossed the Halys River he would destroy a great empire. He did—his own; in 546 Cyrus the Persian captured his capital, Sardis. The Ionian cities, placed by Cyrus under Greek governors, thrived; and in this period the early Greek philosophers, nourished in Ionian culture, flourished.

Persian armies were soon to be in Greece. In 513 Darius the Great crossed the Bosporus and conquered Thrace. The Ionian cities, under the leadership of Aristagorus of Miletus, revolted against Persian rule and, aided by the Athenians, who landed with a fleet at Ephesus, attacked and burned Sardis in 498. But the Persians crushed the Ionian allies near Ephesus and brought the revolt to an end. To avenge the burning of Sardis they captured and sacked Miletus.

In 490 the Persians crossed the Aegean from Samos and landed on the Marathon Plain to face an army of some 10,000 Athenians. The battle on the plain of Marathon was disastrous for the Persians, who lost 6,400 men. The 200 Greek heroes who fell that day lie buried beneath a mound on the plain.

At the urging of its archon, Themistocles, Athens prepared an adequate fleet against possible Persian invasion. In 480 the great army of Darius' son Xerxes I took 7 days and nights to cross the Hellespont on boat bridges under the lash. The army moved through Thrace and into Macedonia and Thessaly. Victory seemed within its grasp. King Leonidas with 300 of his Spartans and a few allied contingents gave their lives to the last man at the pass of Thermopylae. In such acts of heroism Sparta found its memorial, rather than in sculptured stone and temples; the Athenians found it in both. Several oracles from Apollo of Delphi promised hope in wooden walls and help from the winds. The Acropolis of Athens, defended by a few zealots behind wooden barricades, was burned and its defenders

Courtesy of H. Thomas Frank

View of the ruins of the Acropolis of Athens seen from the Areopagus (Mars Hill, but see comment on Acts 17:19-21); tradition holds that the Council of Athens met on the Areopagus; note evidence of rock-hewn benches in center foreground (cf. ills., p. 752); the Persians attacked the Acropolis ca. 480 B.C., breached the defensive wooden barricades, killed its defenders, and set fire to the buildings

were killed; but other Athenians in wooden ships brought disaster to the Persians. This was the great naval battle at Salamis, dramatically described by the contemporary Greek dramatist Aeschylus in The Persians, and today reproduced in "Sound and Light" for tourists at the Acropolis. Mute witness to the destruction of the Acropolis buildings are the drums of the old temple of Athena reused in the later rebuilding of the Acropolis fortification wall.

But the Persian advance was checked. Actually more decisive were the simultaneous defeat of the Persians by the Athenians and Spartans in the battle of Plataea and the Persian defeat and the burning of their ships at Mycale in 479. Soon the Persians withdrew and the ambitions of Xerxes for Greece were finished.

Greece in the Age of Pericles. The Athenians under Themistocles rebuilt their burned city and fortified the harbor of nearby Piraeus. They organized and controlled the confederacy centered in the shrine of Apollo on the island of Delos, and the Delian League became essentially the empire of Athens. Athens broke with weakened Sparta, and the Peloponnesian League was deserted under Pericles, the new leader of a new age for Athens. War with Sparta ended in a truce in 445, and the next 14 years were Athens' proudest.

It was now that the Parthenon, whose glory still elicits awe and admiration, was built on the Acropolis. To the same era belong also the columned entrance or Propylea of the Acropolis, the temple of Hephaestus overlooking the Agora, the temple of Poseidon on the promontory at Sounion, the new Hall of Mysteries or Telestrion at Eleusis, the majestic and lonely temple of Apollo on the mountaintop at Bassae, and other monuments. It was Iktinos, architect par excellence of Athens' age of glory, who built the Parthenon and Bassae temples. It was the master sculptor of the period, Pheidias, who produced the 40-foot high gold and ivory image of Athena Parthenos, i.e. the Maiden, for the Parthenon; who supervised the making of its sculptures; and who, inspired by Homer, made the great gold and ivory statue of Zeus for the temple of Zeus at Olympia. The workshop of Pheidias in which he made the Zeus statue may be seen today at Olympia, built over by a Byzantine church. The Parthenon was 2,400 years old in 1964; after being for almost a thousand years the home of Athena it became for another thousand the Church of the Virgin and then for almost 4 cents. a Muslim mosque.

The age of Pericles knew the great dramatists Sophocles and Euripides. Socrates was challenging the young men with his gadfly dialogue and Herodotus was preparing his great history. The patron of the philosopher Anaxagoras was Pericles himself.

The last years of the rule of Pericles witnessed the beginning of a bitter and crippling war between Athens and Sparta. Pericles was humiliated in the trial of Aspasia, a cultured Miletus girl he had taken into his house after his divorce, but whom he could not marry since she was an alien. He died in 429 during the plague which harassed Athens. But classical Greek culture continued to flourish, with such greats as the historian Thucydides, the physician Hippocrates, and the dramatist Aristophanes.

Over in the following cent. Plato established his Academy and later Aristotle, one of its members, became Greece's universal scholar, logician, philosopher, natural scientist, political scientist, and much else—and was selected as tutor of Alexander by his father, Philip II, king of Macedonia.

Alexander the Great. Philip, founder of the city of Philippi which was named after him, succeeded in spreading his kingdom into the neighboring territories. He was assassinated in 336 before he could realize his dream of the conquest of Persia. Alexander brought Greece effectively under control, and in 334 he crossed over into Asia Minor. His victories against the Persian armies at the Granicus River in 334 and at Issus in 333 presaged the inevitable end of the Persian Empire, now under Darius III. Alexander moved down the E coast of the Mediterranean and Marathus, Byblos, and Sidon submitted. In 332 Tyre fell after a 7-month siege when Alexander built a mole connecting the island city with the mainland. It had taken Nebuchadrezzar 13 years to force capitulation of Tyre. In the same year Gaza held out vainly for 2 months, and Jerusalem capitulated without opposition. In 331 Egypt fell to Alexander; and in that year, after Darius was defeated at Gaugamela, Babylon surrendered and then Susa, the old capital of Elam, and Ecbatana, the capital of Media. Soon Alexander was in wealthy Persepolis, the Persian capital, which he plundered and burned. His path of conquest led him all the way to the Indus River by 326. But with the ancient world at his feet he died in Babylon in 323, at the age of 33.

The Ptolemies and Seleucids. Confusion and struggles for power followed Alexander's death. A compromise which gave the rule to Alexander's half-brother and his son, Alexander II, born after his death, proved futile. The empire disintegrated and fell to his generals, and it eventuated that Antipater and then Cassander ruled Macedonia, Ptolemy Egypt and southern Syria, Lysimachus Thrace, and Antigonus Asia Minor. Antigonus was defeated in the battle at Ipsus in 310; and Seleucus, who had been commander of Alexander's footguards, by this time having possession of Babylonia, secured Asia Minor and Syria. Ptolemy established the Ptolemaic dynasty and Seleucus became the first of his dynasty to rule the Seleucid Empire (see color map 12).

The conflicts between the Ptolemies and Seleucids are reflected in Dan. 11. An attempt to unite the 2 empires through marriage, when Berenice, daughter of Ptolemy II, married Antiochus II of the Seleucid Empire, only resulted in bitter warfare (cf. Dan. 2:43; 11:6). As a result of victories over Egypt at Gaza in 200 and at Paneas in 199 (Dan. 11:15-19) the Seleucids secured control of Palestine.

In the meantime the process of hellenization of large areas conquered by Alexander went on apace. It is of more than a little significance that the Pentateuch was translated into Greek in Egypt *ca.* the middle of the 3rd cent., both for the famous library at Alexandria and for the Greek-speaking Jews in Egypt. Long before Alexander there had been Jewish colonies in Egypt (cf. Jer. 43-44). One of the most notable, on the island of Elephantine opposite Syene at the First Cataract, was there already in the late 6th cent. when the Persians under Cambyses conquered Egypt. An edict of the Roman emperor Tiberius on behalf of the Jews of Alexandria describes them as joint inhabitants with the Alexandrians in the earliest times. In the first cent. A.D. Philo of Alexandria, of whose extensive writings much has been preserved, stands out as an important source of information about the influence of Hellenism on Judaism.

Just how important the numerous cities established by Alexander or the settlements of his mercenaries far from home were for the spread of Hellenism is difficult to estimate. The Seleucids and Ptolemies built in Palestine Greek cities. Two of these, Pella and Dion, to judge from their Macedonian names, may have been settled by Alexander's veterans. The Romans continued this policy, and the Decapolis, a federation of 10 such cities, is mentioned in the gospels (Matt. 4:25; Mark 5:20; 7:31). The Ptolemies and Seleucids fostered the hellenization of Palestine. Greek religion and culture were attractive to many Jews, but quite the contrary to others. The Seleucid king Antiochus IV Epiphanes tried to unify his subjects with Greek culture. It was this attempt that brought on the revolt by the Jews, led by Mattathias and in turn by his three sons, Jonathan, Judas Maccabeus, and Simon, which resulted at length in an independent Jewish state ruled by Simon and his descendants, the Hasmoneans (see "The History of Israel," pp. 1027-28, and Intros. to I, II Macc.).

II. ROME AND THE NEAR EAST

The E March of Roman Power. During the 3rd cent. B.C. the city-state of Rome extended its control to the entire Italian Peninsula and eliminated the threat of conquest by Carthage in N Africa. At the beginning of the 2nd cent., therefore, Roman leaders were ready to turn to the E, seeking Greek culture perhaps as much as power and material gain. First they freed Achaea, i.e. S Greece, from Macedonian domination (cf. I Macc. 8:5; see color map 12) and drove out the invading Seleucid king Antiochus III. Then in a follow-up they crossed the Aegean and under Lucius Cornelius Scipio decisively defeated Antiochus at Magnesia in 190, releasing most of Asia Minor from his control (cf. Dan. 11:18; I Macc. 8:6-8), requiring a large annual tribute (cf. II Macc. 8:10, 36), and taking his son back to Rome as a hostage (cf. I Macc. 1:10). Later this son, reigning as Antiochus IV Epiphanes, was frustrated by the Roman legate Popilius Laenas in an attempt to conquer Egypt—and no doubt was moved thereby to vent his anger on the Jews (cf. Dan. 11:30). When Epiphanes' nephew Demetrius, another hostage at Rome, escaped and wrested the Seleucid throne from the boy Antiochus V (I Macc. 7:1-4) Judas Maccabeus sent an embassy to Rome to make an alliance (I Macc. 8; cf. II Macc. 11:34-38). After Judas' death his brother Jonathan is reported to have sent envoys to Rome to confirm and renew friendship (I Macc. 12:1-4); so also his brother Simon (I Macc. 14:16, 24; 15:15-24).

During the period of the Hasmonean dynasty in Judea (see "The History of Israel," pp. 1028-29) events perhaps made it all but inevitable that Rome should take over one by one the lands to the E—first Macedonia and Achaea, then Asia Minor and

Syria. Thus when 2 Hasmonean brothers, Aristobulus II and Hyrcanus II, battled for the succession, it was to the Roman commander Pompey in Damascus that both went to seek recognition. Pompey chose to attack Jerusalem; he laid siege for 3 months against those holding out on the temple hill, and they succumbed with terrible slaughter. From that time (63) Judea was in the hands of the Romans.

Julius Caesar in 48 defeated Pompey, who was subsequently assassinated. He appointed Antipater, an Idumean, as procurator of Judea. The last of the Ptolemies was Cleopatra. Her brother Ptolemy XIII had deposed her but Caesar made her ruler of Egypt. Caesar died in 44 in the conspiracy of Brutus and Cassius. The 2 committed suicide after their defeat by Mark Antony and Caesar Octavian, great nephew of Julius Caesar, at Philippi. After the death of Antipater 2 of his sons were appointed tetrarchs by Antony. One of them, Herod, went to Rome and secured from the Senate appointment as king of Judea. War broke out between Octavian and Antony, and Antony was defeated in the crucial battle at Actium in W Greece in 31. Octavian invaded Egypt, and Antony and Cleopatra committed suicide in 30.

Augustus and the Empire. Octavian was now ruler of the Roman world. He was voted the title Augustus, i.e. "exalted, revered," in 27 and declared *princeps,* Rome's chief magistrate, and early bore the title *imperator,* which later came to mean emperor. The republic became the empire. After the battle at Actium, Herod appeared before Octavian at Rhodes, and Octavian confirmed his kingship over Judea. Herod later visited Octavian again in Egypt and received further territories (see color map 14). He rebuilt the city of Samaria and named it Sebaste, Greek for Augustus. He also rebuilt Strato's Tower and named it Caesarea, making it an important seaport. The remains of Herod's building activities at both cities are strikingly revealed by the excavations there. He is the Herod of the birth stories of Jesus (Matt. 2; Luke 1:5) and is known as Herod the Great.

The empire flourished under the rule of Augustus. He provided an improved administration for the provinces. After A.D. 6 he placed Judea under procurators. This was the golden age of Roman literature; to it belong the historian Livy and the poets Virgil, Ovid, and Horace.

Tiberius. Augustus was succeeded by Tiberius Claudius Caesar (A.D. 14-37), who was 55 years old. His divorced mother Livia had married Augustus; and he himself had married the licentious, twice-divorced Julia, Augustus' daughter, at Augustus' insistence. Augustus had adopted Tiberius as his own son. Tiberius proscribed the observance of Jewish law in Italy, and many Jews who would not give up their religion were forced to leave. The Jewish historian Josephus reports that Tiberius ordered all Jews to leave Rome, and relates how Tiberius brought misery on the best families in Rome and used the death penalty for small offenses. Tiberius is the Caesar of the gospels (cf. esp. Luke 3:1). It was he who appointed Pontius Pilate as procurator of Judea.

The city of Tiberias on the Sea of Galilee (see color map 15) was built by Herod Antipas and named for the emperor. Herod Philip had earlier raised Beth-saida across the lake to the status of a city and named it Julias, after Julia. The Sea of Galilee, or of Gennesaret, came to be called the Sea of Tiberias (John 6:1; 21:1) after the city built by Antipas. Herod Agrippa was brought up in Rome with Drusus, Tiberius' son. Six months before his death Tiberius put Herod Agrippa into bonds for voicing the hope that Tiberius would soon go off the stage and leave the government to Caligula.

Caligula. Tiberius was succeeded by his great-nephew Gaius, nicknamed Caligula (37-41), said to have been regarded by Tiberius as a potential murderer and capable of losing the Roman Empire. Caligula released Herod Agrippa from prison and gave him the tetrarchy of Philip with the title of king. He ignored the Senate and ruled as absolute monarch, claiming divinity. He was ruthless and irresponsible. Josephus comments that he filled the whole habitable world with false accusations and miseries. His successor called him mad. He confiscated property ruthlessly on charges of treason. But for the entreaties of Herod Agrippa I and the stalling tactics of the legate of Syria, Caligula would have placed a statue of himself as god in the Jerusalem temple itself. He was assassinated in a conspiracy.

Claudius. The uncle of Caligula, Claudius (41-54), now succeeded to the throne. He extended Roman citizenship readily to provincials. He personally led the troops in a conquest of Britain, which he made a new province. He married the promiscuous, twice-married Agrippina, and adopted her son by her first marriage, who was to be known as Nero. He expelled the Jews from Rome, and it was at this time that Priscilla and Aquila, whom Paul met at Corinth, were banished (Acts 18:2). He died of poisoned mushrooms fed to him by Agrippina when Nero was 16 years old.

Nero. Nero (54-68) was the great-great-grandson of Augustus. His mother, Agrippina, was unable to be the power behind the throne that she had hoped. Nero had her assassinated. His wife Octavia was banished and later murdered, and Poppaea, his mistress, became his wife. He was a licentious and vain youth. In Jul. 64 fire broke out in Rome, and some whispered that it was set by Nero. He made the Christians the scapegoat, and there were many martyrs. Some were set on fire as torches for the nocturnal games in the imperial gardens. I Clement indicates that it was at this time that Peter and Paul were martyred. Nero, like Caligula, murdered people for their wealth, and he became a ruthless despot. He loved to take part in competitions; on a trip to Greece he took 1,808 first prizes, some in contests in which he did not participate. His reign of terror ended in revolts, and the Senate declared Nero an enemy of the state. He died ignominiously at the hands of another when he could not bring himself to commit suicide.

It was in his reign that Felix was procurator of Judea (52-60). Paul appeared before Felix in Caesarea (Acts 24). Felix was followed by Festus (60-61), and Paul defended himself before him and appealed to Caesar, i.e. to Nero (Acts 25). Near the end of Nero's reign, in 66, a revolt started in Judea (see "The History of Israel," p. 1030). Vespasian led the Roman armies against Jerusalem until 69; his son Titus completed the siege of the city and razed it to the ground in 70—a victory commemorated by the Arch of Titus in Rome.

From Galba to Vespasian. Confusion followed Nero's death. Galba, a man of 73, was recognized as emperor in 68. In 69 Otho, who had been Poppaea's husband, was proclaimed emperor by the troops, and Galba was murdered. Otho became a suicide and was followed briefly by Vitellius, a governor in Spain. Vespasian (69-79), returning from the war in Judea, now founded a new dynasty and brought an era of peace and prosperity and an improvement in morals. He built the Colosseum at Rome, which was finished by Titus. He was a responsible ruler, and there was a long-overdue new aristocracy. He improved the finances and revenues of the empire and was a good administrator. His son Titus was made coregent in 71.

Titus and Domitian. Titus (79-81) was a popular emperor. It was in his reign that there occurred the eruption of Mt. Vesuvius which destroyed Pompeii and Herculaneum.

Titus was succeeded by his younger brother Domitian (81-96). The latter years of Domitian's reign were a time of terror, though the empire flourished and the frontiers were defended. He had extensive building programs. He secured monies through expropriation and judicial murder, false charges, and banishment. Senators, governors, philosophers, astrologers, and actors were the object of his wrath. He elicited rebellion and hatred. He investigated the Jews to enforce their paying of the temple tax to Rome rather than to the temple. Rev. was written during his reign; the heads of the beast in 13:1-10 are the Roman emperors; Babylon is Rome and the Roman Empire, and its fall is predicted (cf. 16:17-20). Pergamum, the provincial center of the imperial cult, is pictured as Satan's throne, the place where Satan dwells. Here Christians were persecuted and one Antipas died a martyr (Rev. 2:12-17). Domitian claimed to be master and god. He was murdered in a palace intrigue in which his wife participated.

Nerva and Trajan. Domitian left no heir and was followed by the senator Nerva (96-98), who put an end to the law of treason and the reign of terror. He returned those banished and restored confiscated properties. He was the first of a series of rulers called the "good emperors."

Nerva adopted as his son and coregent Trajan (98-117), who became a just and capable emperor. Trajan extended the boundaries of his empire and annexed Arabia Petrea to the S and E of Palestine, which included Sinai, Edom, Moab, and E. Transjordan, and which had been a client kingdom ruled by the Nabateans. He conquered territory N of the Danube and E of the Euphrates. He died on his way home from the attempted conquest of the Parthians. His were the days of the historian Tacitus and of Pliny the Younger, governor of Bithynia, who reported on the investigation and trials of Christians.

Hadrian. Hadrian (117-38) was the adopted son of Trajan. He spent much time in the provinces, and his footsteps in NT sites may be traced by his buildings all the way from Pergamum to Jerusalem. He was in Arabia in 129-30, visiting Petra and spending the winter at Gerasa in Transjordan (see color map 14). In 130 he crossed into Palestine. Jerusalem was in partial ruins, and the builder emperor planned to rebuild it, no longer as a Jewish but as a Grecianized city, a Roman colony. This desecration of the city sparked the 2nd Jewish Revolt of 132-35 (see "The History of Israel," pp. 1030-31). After the rebellion was put down Jerusalem was rebuilt as Aelia Capitolina. At the temple site, which was left outside the new city, a temple of Jupiter Capitolinus was built, and a temple of Venus was placed at the site of the tomb of Jesus. The main columned street of Jerusalem led from N to S, where today the Damascus Gate is located. Excavations below the gateway level in 1966 revealed the side arch of the gate of Herod Agrippa I, rebuilt by Hadrian. Above it is the inscription AELIA CAP D D. An E gate of Hadrian's city exists at the so-called arch of Ecce Homo, "Behold the man." A great triumphal arch of Hadrian stands today in Transjordan at the S approach to Gerasa. Hadrian also built a temple to Zeus on Mt. Gerizim, where the Samaritans earlier had a temple. Its remains have been uncovered, along with traces of the 1,500 steps which led up to it. It can be found represented on contemporary coins. These represent only a few of Hadrian's activities in this part of the empire.

For Further Study: T. R. Grover, *The Ancient World*, 1935. R. H. Barrow, *The Romans*, 1949. R. H. Pfeiffer, *History of NT Times, with an Intro. to the Apoc.*, 1949. S. V. McCasland, "The Greco-Roman World," in *IB*, 1951. F. C. Grant, *Hellenistic Religions*, 1953; *Ancient Roman Religion*, 1957; "Greece" in *IDB*, 1962. R. M. Grant, *The Sword and the Cross*, 1955; "Roman Empire" in *IDB*, 1962. S. H. Perowne, *The Life and Times of Herod the Great*, 1956; *The Later Herods*, 1958; *Hadrian*, 1960. Michael Grant, ed., *Roman Readings*, 1958. R. M. Cook, *The Greeks Until Alexander*, 1962. A. R. Burn, *The Pelican History of Greece*, 1966. Bo Reicke, *The New Testament Era*, trans. by D. E. Green, 1968.

THE GRECO-ROMAN
BACKGROUND OF THE NEW TESTAMENT
David Stanley, S.J.

I. The Cultural Milieu of the NT Authors

While the unique character of the Christian revelation is universally admitted by those who subscribe to the Christian faith, it should not be forgotten that this revelation was necessarily communicated to mankind through the medium of a specific culture and hence makes its appearance in history bearing the imprint of a particular civilization. Culture is to be distinguished from civilization in that it is involved with the things of the mind, whereas civilization refers to the entire area of material progress—the effect of human culture. The necessity of such a distinction is due to the fact that man on the material side of his personality exists in the world and in history, while at the same time man is able because of the spiritual dynamism of his mind to assimilate and grasp the material universe in which he exists.

It is a basic tenet of both the Israelite and the Christian faiths that God has spoken to man through history and that the Bible is the particular record of that divine communication to man. Yet the paradoxical character of the assertion that the Bible is the "word of God" ought to escape no one (see "The Word of God," pp. 994-98). The Bible was written in human language by human beings. God, on the other hand, does not speak in human speech, nor does God write books. To refer to the literary collection held sacred in the Judeo-Christian tradition as the "word of God" is to state that its authors were, because of a special insight into the divine action in history, constituted the privileged witnesses of God's self-revelation to mankind.

This compelling testimony of the biblical author, the fruit of his extraordinary intuition of the sacral significance of history together with his own personal reaction of faith, is written in the words by which he relates his experience and judgments of the divine reality in history for the men of his age and culture. If we are to comprehend what the biblical author is attempting to say, we must appreciate the cultural milieu out of which he speaks and recognize the peculiar nature of his native language, its idioms, and its patterns of thought (see "The Languages of the Bible," pp. 1194-1200). Above all we must possess some acquaintance with the forms of literature current in his world (see "The Literary Forms of the NT," pp. 1124-28). Otherwise there is a grave danger of misconstruing his words and misunderstanding his message by forcing it into categories familiar to us but unknown to the ancients, separated as they are from us both by history and esp. by culture.

Since the NT authors were almost without exception of Jewish origin, it is obvious that the greatest influence on their thought and expression comes from the OT and from the Judaism in which they were born with its legal, liturgical, and historical institutions as well as its traditions and practices. On the other hand it must be borne in mind that the NT belongs to Greek, not Semitic, literature. Accordingly the importance of that Hellenistic culture which influenced its creation cannot be overlooked. The Greco-Roman background of this sacred library of Greek writings is a factor of paramount importance in any attempt to understand and assess the contribution of the Christian writers of the apostolic age. Indeed since the discoveries at Qumran (see "The Dead Sea Scrolls," pp. 1063-71) it has become clear that the Judaism contemporary with the writing of the NT had already undergone considerable influence from Hellenistic culture (see "The Intertestamental Literature," pp. 1110-15).

Moreover the presence in the early Christian community of a group characterized as "Hellenists" by the author of Acts (6:1) provides a plausible explanation of the Hellenistic orientation of the apostolic preaching summarized in that book (see "The NT and Christian Origins," pp. 1187-93; "The NT and the Christian Community," pp. 1116-23). Finally, by the very fact that the apostolic church entered the field of Greek literature through the creation of the NT, it is clear that those members of the church who composed it were faced with the problem of addressing themselves to the Greek reading public of their day, not only to narrate the unique history of Jesus of Nazareth but also to express through the categories of Greek thought certain essentially Christian concepts. Such a task could be successfully accomplished only by creating an almost totally new Christian vocabulary, while respecting the genius of the Greek language and without doing violence to the transcendent novelty of the gospel.

II. History of Hellenism

The term "Hellenism" denotes the impact of Greek culture on the civilizations of the ancient world located in the Mediterranean basin. The scope of its influence may be defined geographically by the boundaries of the Roman Empire at the height of its extent, for the culture of imperial Rome was thoroughly Hellenistic.

The rise of Hellenism corresponds with the decade of Alexander's conquest of the ancient Near East (334-323 B.C.). Alexander the Great, tutored by Aristotle and familiar with the achievements of the Golden Age of Greece in art, as well as literature, philosophy, and political thought, gave the initial impetus to the spread of Hellenistic culture. The first phase of the resultant civilization inspired by the Greek spirit coincided with the rise of several dynasties founded by the generals of the dead Alexander: the Ptolemies in Egypt, the Seleucids in Syria, and the Antigonids in Macedonia. These Hellenistic kingdoms ruled the E Mediterranean world for nearly 3 cents., until the E thrust of Roman imperialism under Augustus eventually put an end to them. Far from terminating Hellenism, however, the Roman conquest merely caused it to enter a 2nd phase, which may be said to date from the battle of Actium (31 B.C.). The Roman conquerors were impregnated with the Hellenistic spirit, and until the fall of the Roman Empire Hellenism was the culture and civilization in the ancient world of E and W.

Though the term "Hellenism" is found neither in the LXX nor in the NT, the negative reaction to the hellenizing of the Jewish people in the first half of the 2nd cent. B.C. under Antiochus Epiphanes IV, the Seleucid monarch of Syria, is recorded in I, II Macc. (see Intros.). The Maccabean revolt succeeded, to a degree, in resisting the anti-Jewish religious influences generated by certain devotees of Hellenism, and it was followed by nearly a cent. of political independence for the Jews (see "The History of Israel," Part II, pp. 1028-29). The cultural aspects of Hellenism, however, left their mark on Judaism, esp. among the Jews of the Diaspora, i.e. the Jewish settlers throughout the Mediterranean world. This is attested by the literary remains of such Jewish authors of the first cent. A.D. as the philosopher Philo of Alexandria and the historian Josephus, as well as by the paintings of the 3rd-cent. A.D. synagogue at Dura-Europos on the Euphrates and in the Jewish catacombs of Rome.

In Christianity there was not the same opposition to Hellenism as in Judaism, except perhaps for the difficulty which appears to have arisen in the primitive community of Jerusalem between "Hebrews" and "Hellenists" (Acts 6:1-6). The "Hebrews," i.e. Aramaic-speaking natives of Palestine, were Jews of the conservative type, who took refuge from the liberal, humanistic influences of Greco-Roman culture behind the fence of the law. The Hellenists were also Jews, but they had been broadened in outlook by contact with the Hellenistic civilization in the various parts of the Mediterranean world where they had lived and so were inclined to be more progressive.

Acts presents Stephen as the outstanding representative of the Hellenists, both by natural endowments of temperament and character which made him a leader and by the grace of the Holy Spirit— "a man full of faith and of the Holy Spirit" (Acts 6:5). He appears to have been the first in the Jewish Christian community to create a theology of history by rereading the OT in the light of the function of Jesus Christ. On his view sacred history is the result of 3 movements: (a) the divine attempt to enter history by the gift of the holy land, the legal and cultic institutions of Israel, and the preaching of the prophets; (b) man's opposition to this divine plan; and (c) God's ultimate triumph over human perversity by the seeming paradox of the death and resurrection of his incarnate Son. Stephen had the ability to see, perhaps more clearly than any of his Jewish Christian contemporaries, that the Christian community must stand forth in history independent of the Mosaic institutions as the church, a visible sign to men of God's offer of redemption. He was able to perceive the basic incompatibility between Christianity and the ancient religion in which it had been born, and he foresaw clearly the inevitability of a clash between the 2.

Stephen, by his teaching and still more by the witness of his death, made it clear to his fellow believers that the time between the first and 2nd comings of Christ was the "time of the church," during which she had a mission to carry the Christian message to all mankind. Hence she could not afford to await the ingathering of the Dispersion and the Gentiles on the holy mountain of Zion, as the primitive Jewish Christian community of Jerusalem is represented as doing in the early chs. of Acts. Instead she must go forth to "preach the gospel to the whole creation" (Mark 16:15). This spirit of universalism, exhibited by Stephen, was a reflection of the cosmopolitan attitude characteristic of Hellenistic culture. This same spirit communicated itself to many of Stephen's Hellenist disciples, represented in Acts as attempting in the Christian community of Antioch an entirely new experiment (Acts 11:19-26). These Hellenist missionaries broke with the customary methods of evangelizing only the Jews and proclaimed the good news also to the pagans (Acts 11:20). This novel departure had most felicitous results, and the upshot was the creation of a fully integrated Christian community involving both Jews and Gentiles in the capital of Syria. Here for the first time the disciples appeared as a group distinct not only from the pagans but also from the Jewish colony in that city, and it was not accidental that the name "Christian" was originally given to the Christian community at Antioch (Acts 11:26).

The mother church of Jerusalem, disturbed by the unprecedented nature of this Jewish-Gentile church, sent Barnabas to look into the genuineness of this utterly new type of Christianity. Barnabas, a Cypriot, came from a Hellenistic background himself. He liked what he found at Antioch so well that he decided to remain on as a member of the church, later bringing Saul of Tarsus to work there with him for a full year (Acts 11:26). The result was the efflorescence of a genuine missionary spirit. Antioch became a center from which radiated groups of evangelists like Barnabas and Saul (Acts 13:1-3) throughout Asia Minor. The pattern thus invented was to be followed throughout his preaching career by Paul, apostle to the Gentiles. We are reminded several times in Acts of the presence of a typical phenomenon of Hellenistic civilization which either helped or hindered the progress of the gospel: the influence of socially prominent women (Acts 13:50; 17:4).

The unfavorable reaction of certain Christian Pharisees to the Antioch experiment (Acts 15:1-5) was in its origins probably a specific instance of the rejection by Judaism of Hellenistic culture, as during the Maccabean rebellion almost 2 centuries earlier. This opposition to the presence of Gentiles within the church quickly led to a "judaizing" movement, with which Paul was to contend throughout his apostolic life. It had the unhappy result, as Paul saw so clearly in writing to the Galatians (Gal. 5:2-6), of producing an unorthodox view of the universal redemptive power of Jesus' death. For the movement was inspired by the conviction that in addition to faith in Jesus Christ it was necessary for salvation that Christians of pagan background adopt circumcision and observe the prescriptions of the Mosaic religion (Acts 15:1). Once again it was the liberalizing spirit, present in Hellenistic culture, which helped Christian thinkers like Paul to discern and express the fundamental Christian truth that all men are called by the gospel to saving faith in Christ.

III. Hellenistic Greek Language

We can scarcely overestimate the significance for the orientation of apostolic Christianity of the Greek tongue in the spoken and written forms in which it had evolved as a consequence of its spread throughout the ancient world toward the beginning of the Christian era. It is certainly no accident that the entire collection of Christian sacred writings, adopted by the church as the necessary and sufficient rule of faith, were written in Hellenistic Greek or, as it is more commonly called, the Koine or "common," i.e. universal, Greek vernacular (see "The Languages of the Bible," pp. 1194-1200). Moreover we cannot ignore the fact that from the earliest years it was the Greek (LXX), not the Hebrew, Bible which was taken over by the Christians from the legacy of Israel as part of their own sacred literature.

The Attic dialect had been adopted already in the 5th and 4th cents. B.C. in diplomacy and commerce beyond the borders of Attica as the result of the growth of the great commercial and political empire of Athens. The greatest impetus to the spread of Attic Greek among the "barbarian," i.e. non Greek-speaking, nations of the E was given by the conquests of Alexander and those who succeeded to his empire. The consequence of this wide use of the Greek tongue was its evolution from what is regarded as the "classical" form into the Hellenistic language. By the beginning of the Christian era this Greek had become the universal language of the then known civilized world, and its universality may be rightly regarded as part of that preparation for the gospel referred to so frequently by the Greek church fathers.

This common tongue developed by the breaking down of the more formal, sophisticated Attic dialect into a freer, simpler, less rigid language. It acquired new color and vitality from its adoption by peoples of such varying cultures as Syrians, Egyptians, Romans, Macedonians, and the inhabitants of Asia Minor. Obviously a distinction must be made, as in other languages, between the literary and the spoken usage. The literary Greek of the Hellenistic age was produced by those educated in classical Greek, who attempted, with a certain artificiality and ultimately without much success, to return to the forms and the idiom (Atticisms) of a bygone era. Scholars today are unanimous, however, in considering NT Greek as closer to the simple popular "common" language.

Koine Greek as found in the NT possesses despite variations among authors of different personality and cultural background, 3 general characteristics: (a) a tendency toward grammatical simplification, (b) a trend in the direction of colloquial and conversational idiom, and (c) a definite Semitic stamp, the result of its adoption by men who spoke Aramaic. This last peculiarity is merely a specific instance of a more general tendency of the language to adopt loan words and phrases from the cultural milieu in which it was spoken.

The cultural syncretism of the Greco-Roman world, if not its philosophical-religious syncretism, played a positive and major role in fashioning the presentation of the gospel to those peoples who had adopted and adapted Hellenistic civilization. The fluidity, novelty, and vitality of Koine Greek, symbolic of the spirit of the Hellenistic era, struck a sympathetic note with the developing Christian church, whose newfound faith demanded a malleable idiom for the expression of so many utterly new religious concepts. The popular character of this language made it an invaluable instrument for reaching the various social classes to which Christianity made its appeal.

Certain NT writers, e.g. Luke and the author of Heb., at times write in a language which approximates in style and vocabulary the literary manner of the period; yet they never appear to lose sight of their primary purpose in writing, the promulgation and defense of Christianity. Paul condemns as empty and irreverent the pretensions of the professional rhetoric and sophistry of his pagan Greek contemporaries; yet he can do so in a manner which betrays a fair competence in the very arts and disciplines which he treats so disparagingly (cf. I Cor. 1:18-2:16). The author of John, who manages to write a fairly correct Greek flavored with an undeniably Semitic mode of thought, is capable of prefixing to his work a hymn in honor of Jesus Christ as the Logos who is the incarnate Son of the Father. This openness to the influences of Hellenistic culture reveals the truly universalist concern of these primitive Christian writers and accounts to a certain extent for the wide appeal of their writings throughout the ancient world.

IV. Greek Thought

Philosophy. The Hellenistic age has been compared to our own with a certain justification. The general effect of Alexander's conquests, with the consequent destruction to a large degree of the old Greek ideal of the city-state, was to give rise to a new view of life, cosmopolitan and universalist and at the same time intensely individualistic. There was a marked tendency toward skepticism prevalent also in the contemporary world view. The philosophies which won most adherents in the Hellenistic age were the Epicurean and the Stoic.

The older schools of Greek philosophy, the Academy of Plato and the Lyceum (Peripatetics) founded by Aristotle, gradually succumbed to decadence. The Academy degenerated into sophistry, interesting itself mainly in dialectics and the critique of other philosophies. The Lyceum became absorbed in descriptive work in the natural sciences, and one of its members founded the great library or cultural center of Alexandria, celebrated as a seat of research and learning in antiquity. Literary and textual criticism, as well as botany and zoology, was carried on with considerable success in Alexandria.

The Cynic philosophers, a series of challenging eccentrics beginning in the 4th cent., did not form a school but continued the work of Socrates. They were represented by Antisthenes and Diogenes, who was given the nickname "cynic," doglike, because of his unconventional behavior. The Cynics challenged their contemporaries to seek wisdom and shun hypocrisy, and their method of using the diatribe, or prolonged discussion, was taken over by Stoicism together with their insistence on virtue as the sole good for man. While it is commonly claimed that the literary form of the diatribe was passed on by Stoicism to Paul and other NT writers, who employed it for apologetic or ethical instruction, it may well be that this NT dialogue form was inherited from Jewish synagogue practice.

Epicurus (342-270 B.C.) founded a school of philosophy which held that pleasure in its nobler forms is the purpose of man's existence. Only a life of virtue provides the happiness which man is bent on seeking. If Epicurus and his immediate disciples lived a fairly austere life, there were those among the Romans esp. who interpreted his teaching as a license for unrestrained sensual pleasure. Epicurus followed the atomistic views of the physical universe propounded by Democritus, and this materialism provided a basis for his denial of any divine direction or intervention in the world. It may be that certain Corinthians' views expressed in the slogan "All things are lawful for me" (I Cor. 6:12) betray a certain exaggerated Epicureanism.

The most influential philosophy in Hellenistic culture was undoubtedly that which emanated from the Stoa, or "painted porch" in the agora of Athens, where its founder, the Cypriot Zeno, had lectured during the 3rd cent. B.C. The very nobility of the Stoic ideal, its immense popularity, esp. among the cultured, and its religious character made of Stoicism the foremost adversary to the preaching of the gospel in the Gentile world. When Paul condemns the "wisdom of this age" (I Cor. 2:6) he may well be thinking of certain popular forms of Stoicism. The Stoic ideal was to live in accordance with reason (logos), which was actually a kind of world soul, or a god, or destiny, or providence. By a rigid asceticism the Stoic sought the complete discipline of his passions and emotions, and the resulting "apathy" made him indifferent to sickness or health, good fortune or ill. Hence he attained a "self-sufficiency" by his own efforts which made him immune to pain or pleasure or any of life's vicissitudes. It is not difficult to see how such wisdom, acquired solely through human effort, was diametrically opposed to the Pauline insistence that the Christian should "boast of the Lord" (I Cor. 1:31), and is "justified by faith apart from works of law" (Rom. 3:28). The pantheistic nature of the Stoic deity was openly contradicted by the whole Judeo-Christian tradition of a personal God. Moreover the Stoic belief in a universal conflagration in which the cosmos was to perish can hardly be reconciled with the Pauline view of the cosmic redemption of even the material universe (Rom. 8:19-22).

Religion. In the classical Greek city-state religious sentiment was closely allied with patriotism. Fidelity to the gods of the fatherland was the mainstay of devotion to one's city-state as it was of family piety. The imperial conquests of Alexander began the dissociation of religion and patriotism, and Rome's enforced unification of the Greco-Roman world made the divorce permanent. The dissolution of national and city boundaries encouraged the fusion of various cults and religious beliefs, a phenomenon known as Hellenistic religious syncretism. There was a tendency to identify the gods of the E with the ancient Greek or Roman deities. E.g. Zeus was considered to be the same as the Roman Jupiter, the Egyptian Serapis and Amon, and Baal-Shamem of Syria, while Astarte, Isis, and Hestia were regarded merely as other names for Artemis. The emigration of Near Eastern deities to the W was an increasingly common occurrence in the Hellenistic age, which became by the time Christianity made its appearance one of the most religious eras in history.

If widespread interest in religious novelties made the spread of the gospel easy in one sense, it also proved to be a constant threat to the purity of Christian faith. Witness Peter's experience with Simon Magus in Samaria (Acts 8:9-24) and Paul's polemic against a kind of Gnostic cult in Col. Indeed in any attempt to assess the influences of the Hellenistic religious spirit on the Jewish Christian missionaries and writers of the primitive church it should not be forgotten that to the eyes of a man like Paul the whole Greek world view must have appeared fundamentally irreligious, despite the diplomatic overtures ascribed to him by the author of Acts in the celebrated Areopagus discourse (Acts 17:22). His own reaction of abhorrence is faithfully reflected in his reminiscences of this soul-searing experience at Athens (I Cor. 2:1-5).

The Hellenistic mentality with its intellectual curiosity, its instability and love of novelty, its passion for rhetorical argument, its skepticism and intellectual independence, was something which the religiously inclined Semite could scarcely comprehend. The Greek intoxication with the beauty of form must have appeared a blasphemous affront to the one God worshiped without images in Judaism. It is as difficult to imagine Paul succumbing to the charm of Hellenistic humanism as to see him or any other Christian thinker attempting to reconcile the Greek "nothing to excess" with the preaching of the folly of the cross (I Cor. 1:18).

Though the educated man no longer believed in the traditional gods of Greece in the Hellenistic age, there was a great revival of the public cult of the old gods paralleling attempts to restore the city-state system. However, the likelihood is that the vast program of temple building characteristic of this period witnesses rather to civic prosperity and pride than to genuine religion. The Parthenon at Athens, renowned as one of the world's masterpieces of architecture, was used more as a public treasury than as a temple.

Throughout the Hellenistic world religious festivals were popular, e.g. the Panathenean and Dionysiac festivals at Athens. The imported worship of the Greek deities refashioned Roman religion in the image and likeness of Greek cultus. Alongside this public worship, which did not express anything like real religion, the age was characterized by the growth of private associations, or guilds, honoring various gods—an attempt to foster a more personal religious spirit. Many of these religious fraternities were dedicated to the worship of foreign gods like Serapis and Isis (Egypt), Adonis (Phoenicia), or the Great Mother (Phrygia). In most Hellenistic cities Christianity was probably tolerated as such a religious brotherhood. At the same time the close connection between these pagan associations and various trades or professions must have made it difficult for Christian converts to pursue their work as artisans and yet avoid trade-union obligations of assisting at ritualistic gatherings (cf. I Cor. 10:14-22).

One of the most notable features of the Hellenistic period was the universal popularity of oriental religions, which had invaded Greece and Rome and won many devotees. Paul expressed his surprise—and undoubtedly concealed his horror—at the multitude of gods worshiped in Athens (Acts 17:16, 22). The author of Rev. expresses the Christian attitude to the famous altar to Zeus at Pergamum, erected by Attalus I, by calling it "Satan's throne" (Rev. 2:13). At Ephesus the Anatolian worship of the Great Mother flourished as the endemic cult of Artemis (Acts 19:23-41), and her orgiastic religious revels became very popular in the W Roman world at a later date. Astrology was widespread in Hellenistic civilization, having been transmitted from Babylonia to the W through Syria. Persian Zoroastrianism provided certain elements in the religious thought of late Judaism—e.g. angels, demons, resurrection—which in turn passed on into Christianity. The radical dualism so characteristic of Iranian religion was rejected uncompromisingly by the theologians and writers of NT times, and it was to survive only in certain Gnostic or proto-Gnostic sects.

The Hellenistic mystery religions were a survival from earlier Greek religion. They spread rapidly throughout the ancient Greco-Roman world, since they promised immortality and provided, through artificially induced ecstatic states, an experienced participation in the life of the deity. These fanatic and orgiastic rituals were shrouded in secrecy; they could become a threat to human sanity. Paul's concern over the possible confusion at Corinth between such phenomena and certain genuine manifestations of the Spirit, e.g. speaking with tongues, shows the danger which the mysteries presented to developing Christianity (I Cor. 12:1-3).

The Hellenistic age was marked in addition by the growth of worship offered to rulers, promoted by Alexander after his visit to the oracle of Amon in Egypt. Though it met at first with opposition from the Greeks, the successors of Alexander were accorded divine honors after death. By the time of Ptolemy Philadelphus and his consort Arsinoe, this worship was paid to living rulers. Among the Syrian Seleucids Antiochus II spoke of himself as a god, and Antiochus IV claimed to be a manifestation—hence his title "Epiphanes"—of a deity. The Roman policy of toleration for local religions among conquered peoples had the disadvantage of depriving the imperial government of one of its most powerful allies, religion. Accordingly the Roman state decided to deify itself and employ the cult of the goddess Roma as well as emperor worship to consolidate the empire.

Domitian was the first emperor seriously to decree divine honors for himself during his lifetime, though Julius Caesar had after his death been apotheosized almost a century earlier. Henceforth impiety to the gods ranked as treason to the state, and this liaison between religion and patriotism in the later empire was to cause a terrible crisis of conscience for the young Christian church, esp. in Asia Minor, where such imperial worship flourished. This conflict between the church and the state forms the dramatic theme of Rev. It was not mere persecution or the danger of adoring Caesar which anguished the early Christians; for Jesus himself had foretold the one, and the other, ruler worship, any believer could not but reject. It was rather the meaning and the outcome of this struggle which tortured the suffering Christians of Asia Minor. To reply to such questions was the dominant purpose of Rev.

V. Roman Institutions

Religion. By NT times Roman religion had been refurbished through Greek and oriental influences and even more effectively perhaps by the demands of Roman imperialism. Primitive Roman religion is said to have been ritualistic without any theology or authorized beliefs. The Roman genius for legalism, to which Paul pays tribute (Rom. 7:1), inspired the ritual and the formulation of prayers. The public cult was, like other Roman institutions, efficiently organized under the pontifical college, whose presiding officer was called pontifex maximus. This college occupied itself with divination and the interpretation of the Sibylline books in addition to the regulation of public cult. Thanks to constant interference by officials of the government, public worship received a bad name, and in the era of decadence into which Roman religion fell in the first cent. B.C. the invasion of foreign deities easily succeeded in dominating whatever religious feeling survived among the Romans. During the NT period, however, occult practices, astrology, and mystery cults were not permitted any wide dissemination.

Though there have been some who maintained that Christianity borrowed from the mystery cults, most scholars today agree that there is no evidence in the NT that Christian liturgy or Christian beliefs were in any way influenced by the oriental or Greek mystery religions. Paul indeed uses the term "mystery" not infrequently (e.g. Rom. 11:25; 16:25; I Cor. 2:7; 15:51; Col. 1:26), but the word never means a rite in Pauline or other NT literature. It invariably denotes some doctrine or belief, most commonly the revelation of God's plan for the salvation of mankind. It is fair to say that Roman religion as such—like Greek religion for that matter—had no direct or positive influence on Christianity in the apostolic age. It has been suggested that the primitive Christian creed "Christ is Lord" may have been formulated in reaction to the blasphemous credo enforced throughout Asia Minor esp. in the name of the emperor cult, "Caesar is Lord."

Government. In NT times the Roman Empire had been extended to include, in addition to the Mediterranean world, the lands from Britain to Morocco and E to Arabia. This vast conglomeration of peoples was held together by the *pax Romana,* inaugurated under Augustus and protected by forts and over 25 legions of mercenaries (6,000 constituting the full complement of the legion). It was of paramount importance for the spread of Christianity that piracy was put down, public order enforced, and international communications improved by a network of good roads and unimpeded sea travel.

Judea became a province of the empire in A.D. 6, governed by an official—called a "prefect" until the time of Claudius, after which the title "procurator" was employed—who had full judicial powers like a Roman magistrate. He could deal with serious criminal, administrative, or political matters involving non-Roman citizens. The prefect or procurator conducted judicial trials, assisted by his council, charges being usually initiated by private prosecutors. Recent historical studies in Roman provincial jurisprudence tend to confirm the historical character of the gospel narratives of the trial of Jesus. Acts contains accurate references to various forms of civil administration throughout the Greco-Roman world: proconsuls in the senatorial provinces (Gallio for Achaia, Sergius Paulus for Cyprus), procurators in procuratorial provinces (Felix and Festus for Judea), and "generals" in the Roman colony of Philippi.

Tax collection in the provinces was in the hands of companies of "publicans" under the supervision of the procurator. Abuses in this matter were frequent. The uniform system of imperial coinage contributed to the unity of the empire. The basic silver coin, the denarius, was maintained on a par with the drachmas of E lands.

During NT times Roman citizenship, originally closely restricted and highly prized as a privilege, was gradually extended. Acts suggests 2 of its advantages for its holder: immunity from scourging (Acts 16:37; 22:25) and the right to appeal for trial to the imperial tribunal (Acts 25:11). It is probable that, as in the case of enfranchised soldiers, some sort of identity card was given in proof of Roman citizenship; one who was born a Roman citizen could produce a birth certificate.

Apart from the few scattered references to Roman provincial government and the narrative of Jesus' trial before Pilate, the gospels are singularly silent, esp. in the Galilean sections, about Roman administration. Given the agrarian character of life in Galilee and its remoteness from all large cities, even Jerusalem, this silence is not surprising. The great events of the Greco-Roman world of the first century left this small segment of the empire singularly untouched.

The Latin Language. Though as a Roman citizen Paul probably knew some Latin—as did the disciple Matthew, who was a customs officer for Herod Agrippa (Matt. 9:9)—the only noticeable influence of this language on the NT is the presence of certain Latinisms. These, however, are not nearly as strongly represented as the Semitic element. Terms like praetorium, legion, centurion are borrowings from military parlance; census, colony, title come from administrative terminology; and there are other loan words for measures, coinage, and commercial transactions. In addition we find a number of Greek translations for Latin official titles like proconsul, procurator, legate of Augustus, prefect, tribune, lictor, cohort, patron. There are also certain Latin idiomatic phrases lit. translated into Greek: e.g. "settle" (Luke 12:58), "wishing to satisfy" (Mark 15:15), "took counsel" (Matt. 27:1). It is highly doubtful if Jesus knew any Latin, though he may have had enough Greek to respond to questioning, e.g. at his trial before the Roman procurator.

VI. The Septuagint

Perhaps the most important formative factor in the creation of NT literature was the Greek translation of the Hebrew scriptures, of which the most significant example is the LXX. For probably the majority of Christians of the apostolic age—certainly for the NT authors—the LXX was regarded as "the Scriptures." Three other versions may be mentioned: that by Theodotion, sometime during the 2nd cent. A.D., whose translation of Dan. replaced the LXX version; a very literal rendering by a Jew named Aquila (*ca.* A.D. 130); and one toward the end of the 2nd cent. A.D. by Symmachus, an Ebionite Christian.

The Pentateuch was the first part of the OT to be rendered into Greek in the LXX, *ca.* the middle of the 3rd cent. B.C. The Greek translator of Ecclus. claimed that by 132 B.C. the whole Hebrew canon already existed in Greek, hence his translation of his grandfather's Hebrew book. The LXX, the work of many hands, varies in accuracy and in the quality of the Greek. The Pentateuch, part of Josh., Isa., and I Macc. are judged to be good Koine Greek; the poorest parts, so far as an understanding of the Hebrew text is concerned, are probably Isa. and the minor prophets. The LXX is of great value for OT textual study, as it exemplifies a text at variance at many points with the traditional Masoretic text found in the Hebrew manuscripts. The text from which the LXX was translated is witnessed to by some manuscripts found among the Dead Sea scrolls.

The great significance of the LXX for the creation of NT literature lies in the fact that these Jewish translators had already performed the difficult task of rendering the Hebrew sacred writings into Greek. Thus they provided a most helpful example to the NT authors faced with the similar problem of transposing the teachings of Jesus and Christian theological conceptions, which had been expressed in Semitic idiom and bore the imprint of Hebraic culture, so alien to Hellenistic, into the Greek language. It should not be forgotten, moreover, that these NT writers had been steeped in the language of the LXX translators. They were also accustomed to their theological viewpoint, which had undergone a certain hellenization. The OT anthropomorphisms, characteristic of prophetic writings—such personification of the deity underscored the personal nature of the God of Israel—were soft-pedaled in the LXX.

By the time the LXX was translated Jews no longer pronounced the ancient covenant name of Israel's God, Yahweh; instead they substituted a title. Accordingly the LXX translators rendered the unpronounceable name by a Greek equivalent of the substitute, *Kyrios,* "Lord." This provided the NT writers with the means of expressing their Christian faith in the divinity of Christ. The hymn quoted by Paul in Phil. 2:6-11 exemplifies this "name" theology: "Therefore God has highly exalted him and bestowed on him the name, which is above every name" (vs. 9). Here it is the confessing of the divine name *Kyrios* by the Father which gives dramatic expression to the belief in Jesus' divine sonship. In Acts references to the "name" recur like a litany. By the invocation of the name comes universal salvation (Acts 2:21); faith in the name effects miracles of healing (Acts 3:6; 3:16; 4:10) and evokes the recurrence of the original Pentecostal phenomena to strengthen the community in time of persecution (Acts 4:31). Profession of faith in the name is so characteristic of the Christian initiation rite that it is most commonly designated as baptism "in the name of Jesus Christ" (Acts 2:38; 8:16; 10:48; 19:5; 22:16).

In the opening chs. of Rom. Paul employs the Greek term for "justice" in his celebrated description of the justice of God in the sense which that word frequently had in the LXX, esp. in the version of 2nd Isa. This divine justice has nothing to do with the classical Greek notion of "rendering each his due"; rather it connotes God's redemptive activity, whereby he makes good his OT promises of salvation. The author of John uses the substantive "glory" in the technical sense given it by the Greek translator of the Pentateuch, where it is the equivalent of the Hebrew word used of the tangible manifestation of the protective presence of Yahweh, without relation to the classical Greek sense of "opinion." The LXX translator of Isa. 7:14 rendered the Hebrew word *almah* (maiden) by the Greek *parthenos* (virgin); it is in this sense that Matt. 1:23 cites this text. These examples provide some idea of how greatly the NT writers are indebted to their predecessors, the Alexandrian Jews, who translated the Hebrew scriptures into Greek.

VII. Creation of Christian Literary Forms and Vocabulary

Not only did the Christian writers of the apostolic age attempt to forge a Christian vocabulary out of the language of the Hellenistic world by their borrowings from the phraseology of the LXX. In certain ways they created a new medium out of Hellenistic Greek to present various facets of the Christian message in their books.

First a word must be said about the literary forms which the NT authors employed. The letter as well as the epistle was commonly employed in the Greco-Roman world—the letter being written to specific individuals or communities, the epistle being a treatise or exhortation addressed to the general public. Paul's writings are genuine letters, clearly recognizable as such by a comparison with the great store of ancient Hellenistic Greek letters on papyrus which have survived esp. in Egypt. Paul follows the conventional letter form, length being the principal dif-

ferentiating feature of his documents—90 words constituted the average papyrus letter. Other NT documents, though cast in epistolary form, are really tracts (Heb.) or sermons (I Pet.) or apocalyptic (Rev.).

The written gospels exemplify a type of literature which is unique and as such appears to owe nothing to Hellenistic literary forms. The gospel form grew out of the apostolic preaching but differs from it in aim and scope. The preaching was the proclamation to the non-Christian world of a message bringing hope of salvation through the death and resurrection of Jesus Christ; its purpose was conversion to the Christian faith. The written gospel presents this apostolic testimony to the believing community in order to provide a deeper insight into the significance of the events of Jesus' earthly career. Its purpose is not biographical, or even primarily historical, but christological: it presents the various facets of the Christian mystery. Hence its basic literary form, like the life of Jesus which is its theme, is unique in Hellenistic literature. Subordinate to the general gospel form are many literary forms, which, however, come out of OT literature—e.g. parable, genealogy, wisdom sayings.

Luke is perhaps the only evangelist who has cast much of his materials in the form of the travel story, a type of literature which enjoyed great popularity in the Greco-Roman world. The whole movement of his gospel is from Galilee to Jerusalem, and this direction is underscored by the considerable space and emphasis which the author gives to Jesus' last journey from the Galilean theater of his public ministry to the Holy City (9:51–19:27). In this section of his book Luke has inserted all the traditions unearthed by his personal research. Luke's 2nd volume, Acts, is also a travel story, one which narrates the trends in the development of the apostolic church away from the city of Jerusalem, through Syria, Asia Minor, and the Greek mainland until, in the person of Luke's hero, Paul, Christianity reaches the capital of the world empire, Rome—symbol of that universalism which the author considers the hallmark of the new religion.

The Hellenistic influences discernible in John have been mediated by Hellenistic Judaism of the type seen in the Qumran literature, and echoes of the vocabulary and the thought patterns of the Dead Sea scrolls have been noted by contemporary Qumran scholarship. The Johannine use of the term logos in the hymn which forms the prelude to the gospel probably owes as much to rabbinic Judaism and to OT wisdom literature as to popular Hellenistic philosophical thought.

Heb. perhaps more than any piece of NT writing betrays the influence of Hellenistic thought. Its author is considered by some scholars to have been a pupil of Philo of Alexandria, the cultured Jewish contemporary of Jesus who made it his vocation to demonstrate how congenial was the Mosaic religion to the world of Platonism. Heb. contrasts the excellence of Christianity with the imperfect, relative character of Israelite religion by opposing the heavenly sanctuary and the celestial sacrifice of the exalted Christ with the earthly sanctuary and its ritual, which are merely the "copies of the heavenly things" (Heb. 9:23); for "the law has but a shadow of the good things to come instead of the true form of these realities" (Heb. 10:1).

Perhaps nowhere so clearly as in the Pauline writings can we perceive the effort to create a Christian vocabulary capable of expressing the NT faith out of the old language of the Hellenistic world. Paul does not recommend "virtue," a Greek term prominent in Stoicism, without qualification (Phil. 4:8). He does not hesitate on the other hand to employ a Stoic term like "forbearance" (Phil. 4:5), i.e. equanimity in confronting life's vicissitudes; but he gives the word an entirely new connotation by providing Christian motivation for the practice of such an attitude—the 2nd coming of Christ.

To express the central event of Christian sacred history, the death and resurrection of Christ, Paul employs the terms "redeem" and "redemption," familiar to his Greek readers from their use in connection with the Hellenistic ritual for the freeing of slaves. By a legal fiction the god in whose temple the price of the slave's freedom was deposited—to be given by the priests to the master—was considered to "buy back," i.e. redeem, the slave from the owner. The freedman was thus considered to have passed from the service of his master to that of the god. Yet though this Hellenistic connotation of the Pauline word "redeem" cannot be entirely excluded,

it is much more likely that its meaning derives principally from OT usage, where "redemption" is a technical term for Yahweh's great saving event in favor of his people, the exodus from Egypt.

As a general conclusion it may be said that the Hellenistic world has unquestionably left its imprint on NT literature and on the formulation of Christian belief to an even greater extent than it did on Palestinian Judaism. For at a very early date in the history of the church, while it was still in a formative stage, Christianity through its preachers and writers made a successful bid to enter the Greco-Roman world of the first cent.

For Further Study. G. A. Deissmann, *Bible Studies,* 1901; *Light from the Ancient East,* 1910. S. Vernon McCasland, "NT Times: The Greco-Roman World" in *IB,* 1951. Gregory Dix, *Jew and Greek,* 1953. C. H. Dodd, *The Bible and the Greeks,* 1954. H. J. Cadbury, *The Book of Acts in History,* 1955. F. C. Grant, *Roman Hellenism and the NT,* 1962. F. W. Beare, "Greek Religion and Philosophy," E. C. Colwell, "Greek Language," F. C. Grant, "Greece," "Roman Religion," R. M. Grant, "Roman Empire," J. W. Wevers, "Septuagint," in *IDB,* 1962. A. N. Sherwin-White, *Roman Society and Roman Law in the NT,* 1963. A. D. Nock, *Early Gentile Christianity and Its Hellenistic Background,* 1964.

THE EARLY HISTORY OF THE CHURCH

Frederick Abbott Norwood

After the stirring events of the Crucifixion and the Resurrection the followers of Jesus, esp. the apostles, had to face facts. Most of these were unpleasant. The leader, the beloved rabbi, was gone. The Jesus they knew had died the death of mortal men in a most humiliating fashion. Many followers had quailed before the wrath of the Jews and the power of Rome and now had their consciences to live with. Even the sturdy Peter had in a crucial moment faltered. The one bright note of joy was the experience of the Resurrection.

The number of those who gathered together was indeed small. It was so small that neither the Jews of the city nor the Roman authorities took notice of a curious development which, if they could only have known, contained the seeds of a power far greater than anything they represented. This tiny thing was the event which took place on the day of Pentecost (Acts 2:1-4). It marks the beginning of the Christian church as a community of the people of God in whom dwells the Holy Spirit as power and guide.

I. Growing in the Apostolic Age and After

Jewish Christians. Today we would be inclined to call it First Church, Jerusalem. Galileans might complain (cf. Mark 16:7); but the earliest organized congregation, which quickly assumed leadership of the movement, was in the ancient capital. There, surrounded by the powerful reminders of ancient splendor, the followers of the "Way" were accustomed to gather in a part of the temple court known as Solomon's Portico. They continued as a matter of course many of the Jewish practices on which they had been nurtured. Paul, a good Jew himself, discovered this when he visited the brethren in Jerusalem and was immediately required to prove his loyalty to the temple and its ceremonies (Acts 21:20-24). That his attempt to do so resulted in his arrest only emphasized the point.

These primitive Christians continued to observe the Sabbath like other Jews. They fasted, like them, on Monday and Thursday. Their baptism was derived from John. Their meal of communion was a remembrance (*hosanna!*), a fellowship (*koinonia*), and an expectation (*maranatha*, "our Lord, come!"). The "elders" of whom we hear at Jerusalem were leaders whose title and office followed Jewish practice.

And yet from the very first forces of change were at work. Before long, even among these strictly

Jewish Christians, the "Lord's Day," Sunday, supplanted the old Jewish sabbath observance (I Cor. 16:2; Acts 20:7). As the Epistle of Barnabas (*ca.* A.D. 131) explains, Sunday was the day of resurrection and therefore most appropriate for Christian worship. By like token Friday, the day of crucifixion, became the standard day of fast, along with Wednesday, when the passion began. Thus, simply as a matter of physical necessity, one could not remain a practicing Jew, fasting on Monday and Thursday, while at the same time observing Christian devotion by fasting on Wednesday and Friday.

It is most significant that James the brother of Jesus soon came to the position of leadership. Though Acts speaks of the prestige of the 12, increasingly the real power in Jerusalem was exerted by the elders under James. Perhaps the best explanation of the situation is that, while Peter's prestige continued preeminent as leader of the Christian mission in the world, James became the focal point of authority in the mother church at Jerusalem, which claimed and received honor and support from all the churches, even those most loyal to Paul. Between Paul, the advocate of free spread of the gospel emancipated from the bonds of Judaism, and James, the strict defender of the Jewish tradition carried over, Peter stood more or less in the middle, deferring now to the position of James and the elders, moving then to a broader vision not far from that of Paul.

Besides these elders and apostles other officers arose, e.g. teachers and prophets. Of special interest is the appearance of the office of deacon, as reported in Acts 6:1-6. Deacons originally represented the Hellenistic branch of Jewish Christians, those who had escaped from the narrow confines of Jewish culture to live in the wider world of Greek influences. This passage from Acts hints at much more than it says and indicates the existence of many tensions in the early Christian community. One must keep in mind the various levels of culture in which early Christianity moved: Palestinian Jews, Hellenistic Jews, Palestinian Jewish Christians, Hellenistic Jewish Christians, and Greek (i.e. non-Jewish) Christians, all living in the midst of a vast pagan society. Stephen, who undoubtedly would have been one of the most influential leaders of the church had he escaped untimely martyrdom (Acts 7:54-60), was spokesman for the Hellenistic Jewish Christians.

Many of these tensions came into the open at an apostolic council held in Jerusalem *ca.* 49, which is reported not only in Acts 15 but also in Gal. 2:1-10, with some interesting differences (see comments) which show that not all the tensions were resolved. Here Paul made his famous plea for freedom of the gospel as related to non-Jewish converts. After considerable hesitation James and the elders agreed, but to what extent is uncertain. Paul may have left the council under the impression that he had gained more than he really had.

At any rate the strong tension between strict Jewish Christians and those of the Hellenistic world continued right down to the fall of Jerusalem in 70, which marked the end of the original but abortive Jewish Christian community. When the Roman Emperor Titus, after a war which lasted 4 years, finally entered Jerusalem in triumph, many if not most of the Christians died in the ensuing massacre. How many actually departed before the climax to take refuge in Pella across the Jordan, as reported by the 4th-cent. church historian Eusebius, cannot be known.

Gentile Christians. Paul and the Gentile mission are fully discussed in the Intros. to Acts and his several letters and in "The Letters of Paul," pp. 1136-43. A good way to visualize the wide range of his activity is to trace his missionary journeys on the maps in the comments on Acts. For proper balance, however, we must remember that he was not the only effective missionary. He stands out because of the fortunate preservation of his letters. The NT preserves many instances of the natural spread of Christianity which resulted from the dual forces of persecution and trade. E.g. Acts tells us that "those who were scattered because of the persecution that arose over Stephen traveled as far as Phoenicia and Cyprus and Antioch, speaking the word to none except Jews" (Acts 11:19). As a result the church was extended before the end of the first cent. to the important centers of life in the Roman world.

Almost everywhere questions arose concerning the relations of Christians to the synagogue on the one hand and to the Gentile population on the other. Peter learned a lesson regarding the inclusion of Gentiles that needed to be learned over again presently in his encounter with Cornelius the centurion (Acts 10). Paul made a decisive move at Pisidian Antioch when he found the Jews unwilling or unable to accept the gospel. "Since you thrust it from you, and judge yourselves unworthy of eternal life, behold, we turn to the Gentiles" (Acts 13:46). He continued, however, to minister to all sorts whenever possible. In the long course of history his decision to serve the Gentiles and to answer his "Macedonian call" (Acts 16:9) determined in large measure whether Christianity would remain an insignificant and probably ephemeral sect of Judaism or would become a world-shaking force.

Before the end of the 2nd cent. the faith was expanding into every province of the Roman Empire and outside to Mesopotamia. By this time it was also penetrating every social class. Long before this the apostles had disappeared. That is the word for it. We know very little about the later careers of those who followed the Lord in the days of his earthly life. All sorts of legends about them arose to fill in the blank places left by solid history. It was said they parceled the "world" among them and

dispersed each to his assigned area. It was said they got together one day and composed the "Apostles' Creed," each in turn contributing a phrase or 2. Apocryphal "gospels" attributed to them and "acts" describing their miracles and martyrdoms appeared out of nowhere from the 2nd cent. on. Peter did make his way to Rome and Paul was brought there for trial; both probably died there as martyrs. John the son of Zebedee may possibly have lived to a ripe old age and been known to Polycarp; more likely he also met martyrdom earlier. Maybe Thomas got to India and founded there the Christian community now known by his name, but there is only later legend to vouch for it.

Whatever happened to the apostles happened during a crucial but murky period in the latter half of the first century. It was crucial because the original apostolic leadership was replaced by various forms of enduring institutional authority, because the domination of the Jerusalem church ended with the death of James the Lord's brother and the fall of Jerusalem, and because Paul's letters gained circulation and the gospels were written. It was murky because almost no historic record, apart from the NT itself, has been preserved. From the mist of the subapostolic age the church emerged transformed, a Gentile institution whose many new features reached across the empire. Of the mother church in Jerusalem there remained scarcely a trace. Her robust children, however, were ready to face the pagan world. They soon had occasion to call on all their strength.

II. Achieving Self-Consciousness in the 2nd Cent.

Weaning from Judaism and Pagan Rivals. The first step in the growth of Christianity was its weaning from Judaism. So much had been inherited from the parent. Almost every aspect was colored by a precedent or promise made in the OT. God, creation, man, sin, fall, providence, Holy Spirit, revelation, judgment, mercy, redemption, history, hope—these were only a few of the many treasures common to both. The OT and NT were at one even on the central doctrine which ultimately brought division—the Messiah. The difference, at first at least, was a matter of tense. And yet, as has been seen, the separation came in the first cent. It was already well developed by the time of the fall of Jerusalem, when the temple was destroyed. The infant had no choice but to stand on its own feet. It desperately needed self-understanding as it proclaimed God's new word to men through Jesus Christ. It needed to define its role in a world still dominated by the powerful Roman Empire and still crowded with competing religions.

Thus 2 directions were given to the development of the Christian church as it struggled from infancy to self-consciousness and self-understanding: (*a*) relation to the world at large and the empire in particular, and (*b*) inner awareness of the truth of God's revelation through Christ and of the church as the body of Christ. The first involved a struggle against rival religions and persecution by the state. The 2nd involved a struggle against heresy within.

Christianity had to make its way as a tiny movement among powerful rivals. These rivals were accustomed to the competition of many religions in the syncretistic atmosphere of the empire. Two things might happen, both bad. On the one hand Christianity might simply get lost before anyone had a chance to hear about it, destroyed while still in infancy. On the other hand it might be taken up into the deadly embrace of one or another popular religion or philosophy. It could easily have disappeared in the powerful attraction of the Great Mother or the Mithra cult. All these faiths were tolerated by the authorities as long as they did not threaten the public peace. Christianity could have become another mystery religion, but it would thereby have ceased being Christian. Against this threat the group of writers called the "apologists" directed part of their effort.

The Imperial Threat. In many ways the Roman Empire was a good thing for the church. The public peace maintained in the days of Augustus and his successors did much to provide the civilization in which the gospel could flourish. Law and order prevailed everywhere, and trade flourished along the excellent sea and land routes. Great cities like Rome, Antioch, and Alexandria were centers of culture.

A strong Christian tradition emphasized the duty of obedience to the established government, i.e. Rome. Jesus had said people ought to render to Caesar what was his (Mark 12:17), and Paul taught obedience to the higher powers which are ordained of God (Rom. 13:1). Later writers down through Eusebius in the 4th cent. insisted that Christians could and ought to be loyal citizens.

And yet there was trouble, serious trouble. The root of it lay in the non-Christian character of the state. Though in some ways the aims of the church and the state coincided, conflict arose over the fundamental question of final loyalty. Peter defied the authorities: "We must obey God rather than men" (Acts 5:29). There really was an irreconcilable conflict on crucial matters. The result was persecution of Christians by those in authority, first the Jewish rulers and then the Romans.

The Roman persecution began almost by chance during the reign of the Emperor Nero (54-68). In the summer of 64 this unworthy ruler lighted on the Christians as a convenient scapegoat for his own errors and excesses. The spectacle of Christians dragged to execution or immolated as torches in Nero's garden marked the beginning of a long period of sporadic persecution in which the Christian faith possessed no legal standing in the empire. Until 250 the persecutions were not general, nor did they last very long. Violence against the leaders and members of the church would break out in one province for a brief period, then subside. It was sometimes bad enough while it lasted.

The correspondence of the able provincial officer Pliny with the Emperor Trajan in the early 2nd cent. throws some light on the actual status of Christians. Pliny was frankly puzzled as to the proper procedure. He recognized various situations of age and involvement and wondered whether the mere profession of Christianity was to be punished or only crimes associated with the profession. He made it easy for Christians to escape punishment; all they had to do was curse Christ and burn incense before statues of the emperor and the Roman gods. True Christians, he had learned, could not be made to do

this. The emperor's reply was full of approval of the policy followed by his lieutenant. He directed that Christians were not to be sought out—no "heresy hunts." But if they were denounced and arrested they must be tried and, if found guilty, punished. "However, accusations presented anonymously must not be admitted, no matter what the charge is. They follow a very bad example which is not of our age." The same requirement was imposed on Justin, known as the "Martyr." This admirable example of the early apologists stood firm in spite of the most diligent efforts to turn him from his faith.

Local and sporadic persecution went on till the middle of the 3rd cent., when Emperor Decius ordered the first empire-wide effort to eradicate Christianity. By this time those charges against Christians which were *half* true—otherworldliness, uncooperative spirit in civil affairs, a higher loyalty than Caesar, etc.—were mingled with a large body of pure rumor based on ignorance and fear. There were charges that Christians murdered little children, drank blood, held secret orgies, and "hated the human race."

The Apologists. Against the dangerous rivalry of other religions and the equally dangerous opposition of the state some leaders of the church tried to defend Christianity by setting forth the truth as they understood it. In the process they presented a valuable picture of the nature of the church and its faith.

Some of the attacks were scurrilous and not worthy of reasoned answer. Such was the cartoon which ridiculed the faith by showing a believer worshiping before a cross on which hung a donkey. The caption read "Alexamenos worships his god." More subtle was the criticism by a man named Celsus, who wrote *ca.* 180. Starting with the proposition that human nature cannot be changed, he denied the process of conversion. Christianity did not make sense, he argued, and all the apostles were incompetent scoundrels. The Resurrection was a fraud. Jesus, failing to get a congregation on earth, sought one in hell. More serious, Celsus charged that Christians had no answer to the problem of evil.

Serious attacks like these, together with the overt persecution by the state, called forth "apologies," or defenses, with the dual purpose of justifying the faith to pagans and claiming the right of toleration from the state. One of the most effective of these was the work of Justin Martyr, mentioned above, which he addressed to the emperors Antoninus Pius and Marcus Aurelius. Christianity, he maintained, is the true philosophy, better than anything the Greeks produced. He used the term *Logos* ("Word") for Christ and explained that this meant both the word of revelation from God and true reason in philosophy. Thus he sought to bring together the truth of Christian revelation and the wisdom of the Greeks. In the end, however, he barely made a beginning, because he made no real connection between his faith and his philosophy. Other apologists took a different line. Tatian, a Syrian who hated Greek culture, claimed that Moses was the first to produce true philosophy and the Greeks merely plagiarized Moses. The anonymous "Letter" to Diognetus charmingly described the spiritual citizenship of the Christian, who has all the virtues and none of the faults of ordinary citizens.

In various ways the apologists sought to justify the faith to pagan minds and to claim a place of toleration in society. When they were dealing with the problems of persecution they argued that Christians were the most valuable and reliable citizens, people of integrity, honesty, sobriety, and industry, always ready to pray for the welfare of the state. When they were defending the faith against rival religions they pointed out the obvious moral failings of the mystery cults and ridiculed the superstitious belief in many gods and goddesses, some of whose morals were no better than those of their worshipers. Against the philosophers they tried to show that Christianity was worthy of serious thought, the finest of all philosophies. Through it all, however, there ran an undercurrent, which sometimes came to the surface, of independence of all earthly powers. Christians in their final loyalty were citizens of heaven, not Rome. God would take care of superstitious and immoral pagan cults. God's foolishness is higher than the wisdom of the Greeks. "What," asked Tertullian *ca.* the end of the 2nd cent., "has Jerusalem to do with Athens?"

The Peril of Heresy. It was one thing to deal with challenges to the faith from outside the church. These could be identified and combated. But what about the peril within, the insidious danger of confused thinking, wrong belief? What about new and strange ideas introduced in the name of Christianity? These were a problem from the beginning. The NT itself makes frequent allusion to false prophets and dangerous teaching. Paul fought against the Judaizers, those who would compromise the new covenant by combining it with the Jewish frame of law. To say that Jesus was only a good rabbi or brave prophet was to him a great heresy. Jesus was manifestly the Christ, the Son of God.

Another very primitive heresy went to the opposite extreme, by denying the reality of Christ's earthly life and insisting on his full divinity. The Son of God, they said, only "seemed" to be a human person, had only the appearance of human life. Actually he remained the pure divine Son of God and never really lived, suffered, and died on the cross. These were the Docetists, so called from the Greek word meaning "seem." Even as the Judaizers denied Christ's divinity, the Docetists denied his humanity.

Much of simple Docetism entered into the complex systems which go under the name of Gnosticism, derived from the Greek word for "knowledge." This was a far more serious threat because it embodied the Christian message in a form which was alien to its central meaning. It could plausibly claim to be a Christianity of a higher order while in reality destroying it. It replaced the new birth by faith through the grace of God working in Jesus Christ with a system of "knowledge" which would itself bring eternal life. Basilides (mid-2nd cent.) described the Most High God as the unbegotten Father, living alone and ineffable, and Nous (Understanding) as a divine being begotten of the Father. Basilides identified other gods and goddesses in the first of the 365 heavens. The Father sent his Son (Nous) as Christ to save men. The Docetic influence is seen in his teaching that on the way to the cross Nous changed bodies with Simon of Cyrene and thus only an in-

significant human body suffered on the cross. Another Gnostic, Valentinus, had a system of male and female deities, all of them rays or emanations from the prime Father, the Most High God, with his female consort, Ennoia. Recent discoveries in Egypt, esp. the hitherto unknown Gospel of Thomas and Gospel of Truth, are adding much to our understanding of early Gnosticism.

Gnosticism was the most dangerous inner threat to the integrity of the faith because it was so appealing to the mind of the ancient world and because it could appear to be really Christian. The language, if not the spirit, of Gnosticism entered into the NT, esp. in the writings of Paul and the 4th Gospel. Gnostics called attention to Paul's antithesis of flesh and spirit (Rom. 8:4-5) and to his "principalities and powers" who are "world rulers of the present darkness" (Col. 2:15; Eph. 6:12). The Johannine concept of the preexistence of Christ (John 17:5) also lent itself to Gnostic use.

If Gnosticism had prevailed it would have destroyed Christianity by absorbing Christ into the system of "knowledge." The historic roots of the faith would have been wiped out. There was in it no real incarnation or resurrection. God the Father of Christ was not the creator god of the OT. The life of the spirit had nothing to do with the life of the flesh. The only escape from flesh to spirit was through secret "knowledge," known only to a few. By this way the Christian church would have become nothing more than a secret lodge.

Gnostic elements played a strong part in the life and work of Marcion, who enjoys the distinction of being the first to make a formal list of scriptures for a NT. He also lived in the middle of the 2nd cent., the crucial time of the Gnostic crisis. His main teaching was that the creator God of the OT had nothing to do with Christ or the High God who begot him. He considered the creator god an incompetent troublemaker who was responsible for man's fall into sin. The law of the OT was well meant but wrongly applied, with impossible demands and retaliation. Christ abolished this law and along with it the whole OT. Then he revealed the unknown High God. Marcion took his theme from his hero Paul in II Cor. 4:4: "The god of this world has blinded the minds of the unbelievers." His Bible therefore was the product of radical surgery. The entire OT was out. Paul's letters, expurgated, and a purified Luke became the NT.

Obviously something had to be done if the Christian movement was to be kept on the main track. Apologists could defend the faith against external threats, but who would protect it from dangers within? Who could say what was truth and what was falsehood? In response to these many challenges, both without and within, defenses were developed which offered both assurance against heresy and a basis for new growth. These included an authoritative leadership, a formal canon of scripture, and a systematic theology. The result was the institution of the ancient catholic, i.e. universal, church.

III. BUILDING INSTITUTIONAL DEFENSES

Church and Ministry. Among the chief instruments for preserving the unity of the faith were the offices of the ministry. These were principally 3: deacon (*diakonos*, lit. "servant"), elder (*presbyteros*), and bishop (*episcopos,* lit. "overseer"). The first has already been noted in connection with Stephen. Presently it lost part of its original significance and became subordinate to the office of elder. Already during the first cent. local churches in cities were governed by "colleges," or committees, of elders. Sometimes the elder who conducted the service was called the bishop. This was true even of Rome in mid-2nd cent., where the bishop and deacons were special officers assigned special duties. But by the end of the cent. the Roman bishop controlled there.

The early leader whose testimony is most important for tracing the development of the bishop is Ignatius, bishop of Antioch in the early 2nd cent. His letters constitute one of the most precious nonbiblical sources on primitive Christianity. In them we learn that the bishop was assuming powers of leadership in local areas. Each sizable church had its own bishop, who ruled over his city and its environs. Generally there was a college of elders who assisted in administration. Though the NT and early nonbiblical writings do not emphasize the authority of the bishop, that is exactly what Ignatius does. The bishop, he says, stands in the church in the place of Christ himself. "Do nothing without the bishop." He is the chief bulwark against heresy and schism. Ignatius was the first to list clearly 3 separate orders of the ministry—bishop, elder, deacon. The only element of a classical doctrine of the episcopacy lacking in Ignatius is that of apostolic succession—i.e. the assertion that the bishops enjoy their peculiar authority as a result of direct succession from one or another of the apostles.

Only Alexandria, Antioch, Jerusalem, and Rome possessed lists of bishops supposedly starting from apostles. Of these Rome was unique in her claim to both Peter and Paul and in her undisputed leadership of the church in the W, to say nothing of her situation in the capital. The early names on the list were uncertain as to identity, sequence, and date. Irenaeus compiled a list in 180 that contained 16 names. The considered judgment of many scholars is that the earliest names represent simply leading members of the ruling college of elders. This view of course is vigorously disputed by traditional Roman Catholic interpretation, though few would argue that the traditional list is accurate in historical detail. In the E the attiude toward Rome was one of mixed deference and independence. In Alexandria the college of elders continued to govern.

By the middle of the 3rd cent. the bishop had become the key figure. Cyprian, bishop of Carthage in N Africa, clearly set forth the doctrine of apostolic episcopal authority. He said that the episcopacy belongs to the very essence (*esse*) of the church, not merely to her well-being (*bene esse*). "The bishop is in the church and the church in the bishop." Those who are not with the bishop are not in the church. And outside the church is no salvation. Thus the strong catholic doctrine of the church began to take form. On the other hand, said Cyprian, all bishops are equal, and none may stand in judgment on another. There is no such thing as a "bishop of bishops." Thus Cyprian rejected the growing claims of Rome to precedence in the order of bishops.

Worship and the Bible. The unity of the church was further symbolized by the ordering of forms of worship, the sacraments, and the definition of the canon, i.e. the official list of accepted books of the Bible. The Didache, a valuable document of the early 2nd cent., throws much light on early forms. This work, discovered only in 1873, contains material that goes back to the first cent. It describes worship on the Lord's Day, when Christians gathered to break bread, give thanks, and confess their sins. Esp. interesting is the evidence on the sacraments. Baptism was a rite which followed instruction of catechumens (candidates), was performed by immersion or pouring, preferably but not necessarily in running water, and was accompanied by the formula "in the name of the Father, Son, and Holy Spirit." The directions on the Lord's Supper employed both bread and wine, but in reverse order. Curiously there is no specific reference to the body and blood of the Lord. A long eucharistic (thanksgiving) prayer was included.

After Marcion had performed his destructive work on the sacred Christian books it became all the more important to define clearly the canon of the NT (see "The Making of the NT Canon," pp. 1216-24). The earliest nonbiblical writers, e.g. Clement of Rome, used the writings of the church freely but did not regard them as uniquely inspired. The Shepherd of Hermas and the Epistle of Barnabas were sometimes considered as holy scripture; on the other hand Heb., Rev., and II Pet. were long held in doubt. By the time of Irenaeus (late 2nd cent.) the canon was nearly fixed.

Theological Definition. Finally, in the process of strengthening the church against outward and inward perils, the faith was defined, systematized, and formalized. Esp. important were the efforts of Irenaeus, a Greek Christian transplanted to Gaul; the 2 major Alexandrian theologians, Clement and Origen; and the "father" of Latin theology, Tertullian of N Africa.

Irenaeus' significance can scarcely be exaggerated. He stood at the fountainhead of thought both E and W. He helped lay the foundation of authority in his 3-fold emphasis on (*a*) reason as common sense in the use of the mind, (*b*) the Bible as an authoritative standard, and (*c*) the tradition of the church in the pronouncements of the bishops and councils. He was already, at the end of the 2nd cent., talking about "ancient" authorities. His doctrinal formulations were elaborate and well advanced. Esp. he had much to say about the place of Christ in salvation. The Son of God became man in order that men might be redeemed from their sins and achieve incorruptibility. In Christ the whole divine plan of salvation was summed up. Through the sacraments the church offers salvation to men. God became man in order that men might become godlike. All this suggests only a few of the incisive contributions. Though he by no means worked out a full systematic theology, he started many new lines of thought for later development and helped provide a meaningful theological language.

In N Africa Tertullian at the end of the 2nd cent. and the beginning of the 3rd created ecclesiastical Latin as a language for theological expression. His lively style added much to the effectiveness of his writings. Largely as a result of his own conversion his view of Christianity centered on the way of moral rebirth. Many of the terms that came to mean so much—trinity, person, and substance, or essence—were introduced by him.

The 3rd cent. brought to prominence 2 theologians of Alexandria, the famous Hellenistic city of Egypt. The origin of Christianity here is uncertain. By the early 3rd cent., however, the Christian school at Alexandria was world famous. Clement, and then Origen, carried theology to new heights. The main significance of both is that they were completely at home in the environment of Hellenistic culture. Here were Christians who could speak directly to the "Greeks." In a great trilogy of works Clement laid the foundations for an interpretation of the faith suitable for all men, from mere catechumens through the most advanced thinkers. He skirted close to Docetism and Gnosticism but came down on the Christian side of that thin line dividing orthodoxy and heresy. He made free use of allegorical interpretation of the Bible and employed this method as a weapon against the real Gnostics, who were also great allegorizers.

Origen built further on the work of Clement. His was one of the most brilliant minds in the history of the church. His life was filled with tremendous enterprises in theology and biblical study. He prepared a whole series of biblical commentaries, most of which are now lost. He wrote a long treatise against the incisive attacks of Celsus. He worked out the first systematic theology in his classic On First Principles. His most massive work was the Hexapla, a multicolumn edition of the Bible in which the original Hebrew of the OT was placed side by side with various Greek translations, including the LXX. Before it was lost Jerome made use of it in the library of Caesarea as he prepared his Latin Vulg. In his biblical study Origen gave strong support to the allegorical method. He believed that the words of scripture were susceptible of various levels of meaning—the literal, the moral, and the allegorical or spiritual. Though modern Christians do not respond readily to such methods, they were admirably suited to the needs of his day and were effective in refutation of pagan criticisms and heresies. He was a persuasive and very popular teacher whose disciples dominated the theological controversies of the 3rd and 4th cents.

Development of the Creed. The 6th-cent. legend, falsely attributed to Augustine, that on a day the apostles gathered together and one by one contributed the phrases of the Apostles' Creed has no foundation in fact. And yet the creed is apostolic. All the ideas represented in the various articles are to be found in the NT, though not in any one place. It developed over 2 cents. along 2 more or less separate lines. The first provided the main frame of 3 paragraphs on Father, Son, and Holy Spirit. The original formula was extremely simple: "Jesus is Lord" (Rom. 10:9), or "Jesus is the Christ" (I John 2:22), or "You are the Christ" (Mark 8:29). The next step was to relate Father and Son, as in I Cor. 8:6: "one God, the Father, from whom are all things and for whom we exist, and one Lord, Jesus Christ" (cf. Rom. 4:24; I Tim. 6:13). The reference to the Holy Spirit rounded out a 3-clause affirmation (cf. Matt. 28:19; I Cor.

12:4; II Cor. 13:14; I Pet. 1:2). In this way the framework for the creed was found in the NT itself.

The 2nd line went straight to the heart of the gospel—faith in Christ. The more fully developed christological section is anticipated in the almost liturgical psalmlike passage in Phil. 2:5-11, in which Christ is presented as the God-man who "emptied himself" to become man and suffer on the cross and be exalted—wherefore men "confess that Jesus Christ is Lord, to the glory of God the Father." Ignatius already has the ingredients of the middle section of the creed:

> Be deaf when anyone speaks to you apart from Jesus Christ, who was of the stock of David, who was from Mary, who was truly born, ate and drank, was truly persecuted under Pontius Pilate, was truly crucified and died in the sight of beings heavenly, earthly, and under the earth, who also was truly raised from the dead, his Father raising him. (Trallians 9:1-2.)

Note the unremitting emphasis throughout, including the birth from Mary, on the importance of Jesus' humanity. The creed in question form appears in Hippolytus (early 3rd cent.) as a baptismal interrogation:

> Do you believe in God the Father Almighty? Do you believe in Christ Jesus, the Son of God, who was born of the Holy Spirit from the Virgin Mary and crucified under Pontius Pilate and died and was buried and was raised again on the third day, living from the dead, and ascended into the heavens and sat at the right hand of the Father, and will come to judge the living and the dead? Do you believe in the Holy Spirit, the holy church, and the resurrection of the flesh?

When the long christological formula was inserted in the short trinitarian framework, sometime in the 3rd cent., the Apostles' Creed in its original form—called the Old Roman Symbol—was completed. Though its final form is found no earlier than the 8th cent., it was almost complete from the 4th cent. on. It is easily the most ancient and most universal of the creeds. Cast in the times of its origin, it appears as a firm rejection of Docetic and Gnostic elements and a powerful affirmation of the humanity, as well as the divinity, of Christ—born of this woman, executed under that procurator, really died and was buried. Later additions only clarified intended points —God the creator, descent into hell, holy catholic (i.e. universal) church, eternal life as well as resurrection.

By the time the church had weathered the storm of persecution and received toleration in the empire, it already possessed the forms of an enduring institution—strong leadership in a structured ministry, an authoritative standard in the canon of the Bible, and a reasoned and systematic theology and creed.

IV. Winning the Victory of Christianity

The Final Struggle. In the year 250 Emperor Decius, a strong military ruler who insisted on unity of purpose in the Roman state, determined to wipe out the (to him) insidious infiltration of Christians into all ranks of society. An edict was issued which required of all citizens an act of veneration of the image of the emperor as a symbol of political loyalty. Every citizen was expected to possess a certificate, signed and sealed, to the effect that he had sacrificed as required. It was widely understood that Christians would not perform such an act of worship because of their peculiar monotheistic prejudices. In this way disloyal Christians could be ferreted out and punished.

The plan worked rather well. Many Christians were exposed, arrested, and punished with either imprisonment or death. Others became refugees in the mountains or across the seas. Some, however, managed to evade discovery and punishment through subterfuge. They perhaps had friends who were able to secure properly attested certificates for them even though they had not made any act of veneration. Others simply compromised under pressure and performed the required act. The death of Decius on the field of battle soon ended this persecution, at least for the time being. Life returned to normal. Then the Christians who had sacrificed and those who had secured falsely attested certificates came back to church. There were those who said they could not come in because they had sinned mortally in betraying the faith. This was the issue that led to the Donatist movement in N Africa, which grew over the years until it became a major threat in the time of Augustine. These people quoted the perfectionist passages of the NT and identified apostasy as the unforgivable sin. Esp., they said, an unworthy priest cannot perform valid sacraments, nor can an unworthy bishop ordain truly.

A few years later another persecution spread briefly. In it Cyprian, bishop of Carthage, was arrested and condemned. He had escaped arrest in 250 by flight—for which he had been roundly censured by the perfectionists. But after this the church was left almost at peace for nearly a half cent., long enough for people to forget the rigors of persecution. Then when Diocletian, the last of the great pagan emperors, instituted a general and intensive persecution in 303 the results were disastrous. When pressure is off it is easy to relax. Relaxed Christians are not ready to resist sudden temptation. Church buildings were ordered destroyed and sacred books burned. Christians were ousted from places of responsibility. Christian servants were enslaved. Then came orders to imprison church leaders, to excuse former Christians who would sacrifice to the gods, to submit others to torture. The hunt, which spread over the whole empire, lasted a decade or more. In Britain Alban died a saint. In Asia Minor an entire Christian town was burned to the ground together with its inhabitants. Many Christians faltered. Others became refugees for conscience' sake. Still others, though not in excessive numbers, were executed.

At this juncture Constantine appeared on the scene, the finally victorious leader among many rivals for the mantle of the great Diocletian. He started as a "caesar" (junior emperor) in the W regions. By a process of elimination he arrived at the imperial throne in 312, when he defeated his immediate rival, Maxentius, at the famous battle of the Milvian Bridge. On this occasion he professed to have seen a vision in the sky promising him victory under the sign of the cross. Thus when he consolidated his control over the empire he issued an edict of toleration by which Christianity was placed on a par with the other religions. Increasingly he favored the new faith, protecting its rights under the law, restricting pagan religions, building new churches, and even taking direct part in the deliberations of the church.

Church and State in the 4th Cent. Under the successors of Constantine the church prospered as never before. Now finally the upper classes entered in large numbers. No longer did Christians suffer persecution and privation. No longer was the church a small movement among the lower classes. No longer was the faith disdained by supercilious pagans. Now it was their turn to plead for the return of the old ways of Roman virtue associated with the ancient pagan deities. In vain did they request the reestablishment of the altar of victory in the senate. The Christian church was now dominant under the aegis of imperial favor.

But that was the source of a new uneasiness among some earnest Christians. They were of the opinion that Constantine had no right, unbaptized catechumen that he was, to make decisions on ecclesiastical, even theological, matters. His laws against the Donatist "heretics" were welcomed as a defense of the church by most leaders, but others with foresight observed that such laws could cut both ways and might be used against the truth as well as for it. The symbolic significance of Constantine's role in calling together and presiding over a general council of the bishops of the church was not overlooked. The question inevitably arose of the proper relation of church and state. Should one or the other predominate? Should they be equal but separate? The stage was set for a long medieval struggle over political and spiritual authority.

With the unique exception of Julian (361-63), who tried unsuccessfully to bring back pre-Constantinian paganism, the rulers aided the church. More than once, however, they favored a position identified later as heretical. This was esp. true of Constantine's son Constantius in the Arian controversy over the status of Christ in relation to God.

A decisive crisis arose in the time of Theodosius (379-95) that involved defiance of the emperor by the famous bishop of Milan, Ambrose, then the most influential prelate in the W. He had been elected bishop in 374 while yet a catechumen. In 8 days he was baptized and processed through the orders to be consecrated bishop. He had already come into conflict with the Arianizing empress, Justina, who wanted an Arian chapel in Milan. Ambrose refused on the ground that "what belongs to God is outside the emperor's power." In the subsequent struggle he preached a sermon in which he compared Justina with Eve, Jezebel, and Herodias. Then occurred a tragedy in Thessalonica, where Theodosius took revenge on the rioting populace by luring them into the hippodrome and massacring them. When he returned to Milan, Ambrose met him at the church door and prevented his entry until he had confessed his enormous sin like any ordinary Christian. Theodosius laid aside the robes of office and confessed publicly. Only then was he absolved and allowed to share in the sacrament.

This same Theodosius completed the process of establishing the Christian church by issuing orders in 391 which proscribed all pagan religions and permitted thenceforth only the worship of the God of Moses and Jesus Christ. From this time on the church was in a position, if it so desired, to persecute those who formerly had persecuted the church. Unfortunately in the Middle Ages it so desired.

Institutions and Worship. In the 4th cent. ecclesiastical forms matured. Evolving slowly from the primitive practices reflected in the NT, the catholic church became a formal institution, complete with a hierarchy of priests, ordered liturgy, and creedal structure. This was not yet the Roman Catholic Church or the Eastern Orthodox Church as we know them today, but the process of institutionalization was moving in that direction.

The clergy were now definitely set apart from the laity by the sacrament of ordination to the priesthood. The hierarchy was structured, from the lower orders through deacons and presbyters (elders) to bishops. Certain metropolitan centers enjoyed the prestige of being the seat of an archbishop, whose province extended over several dioceses. Some of the more important of these had the title "metropolitan." Finally there existed 5 patriarchal sees, one in the W at Rome and 4 in the E at Jerusalem, Antioch, Alexandria, and Constantinople. The patriarchs claimed more general authority for their sees on 2 grounds: they were of apostolic origin, each cherishing legends of one or another of the apostles; and they centered in most important cities of ancient prestige. Constantinople did not quite qualify on either of these grounds, because foundation by Andrew was difficult to establish and because the place was new, refounded by Constantine, after whom it was named. But its immense prestige as the new capital of the Roman Empire and its favored location at the meeting of E and W, Asia and Europe, assured it a high place in ecclesiastical affairs. The papacy in Rome was already claiming precedence over the other patriarchates, theoretically on the ground of its dual foundation by Peter and Paul, practically on the ground of its monopoly of religious affairs in the W.

Worship. Forms of worship also matured in the 4th cent. The Church Order of Hippolytus (*ca.* 250), the catechisms of Cyril of Jerusalem, the Apostolic Constitutions, and some Egyptian prayers, together with some fragments illustrating comparable practice at Rome, reveal a richly developed liturgy. The main service, generally held on Sunday, consisted of 2 distinct parts—the public service and the believers' service. In the former the order consisted of prayers, scripture reading, and sermon. The reading of scripture, now formalized, included the OT, Pss., epistle, and gospel. The priest read the gospel from the ambo, or pulpit, the people standing. After the sermon the catechumens, the sick, and the penitents departed, leaving the believers to join in the observance of the Lord's Supper. This began with the ancient cry *Kyrie eleison*, "Lord, have mercy." After a symbolic washing of hands the bread and wine were carried to the altar by the deacons. The bishop then, with the presbyters, blessed the congregation with the responsive "Lift up your hearts." A long formal eucharistic prayer followed, after which the elements were consecrated and distributed to the people kneeling at the altar. The service ended with a prayer of thanksgiving and benediction. In this central service 2 features mingled: the communion as the Lord's Supper and the eucharist as the cult sacrifice. The original simple meal of fellowship and remembrance increasingly became a reenactment of the sacrifice of Christ recapitulated in the eucharistic prayer. The ordained priest alone had power to conduct this act of worship, in which the elements became the body and blood of the Lord.

Along with the main worship other forms developed. Vestments and holy vessels became important. Processions took place for carrying the gospel or the elements or, soon, holy relics. Sometimes the Lord's Supper was observed daily, but generally weekly on Sunday. Secondary services were set for daily devotion—lauds in morning and vespers in evening. Hippolytus already in mid-3rd cent. suggested 7 canonical hours. In addition vigils—esp. in the E—and pilgrimages became popular. Easter, of course, was universally observed, though not at the same time in E and W. Observance of Lent was also general, but its duration was not yet fixed. In the 4th cent. both Epiphany (esp. E) and Christmas (esp. W) were observed.

Theological Interpretation. Purely by coincidence the achievement of toleration and the Nicene definition of the Trinity came at the same time. In the 2nd half of the 3rd cent. certain questions had been raised in Alexandria about the relation of God the Father to Christ the Son. Both sides liked to quote Origen in defense of their positions. In the midst of the debate appeared a talkative presbyter named Arius. He undertook to set everybody straight on relationships in the Godhead. All agreed that "God himself became man for our salvation." The question was how this could be and still maintain a difference between Father and Son. None of the orthodox wanted to say that the Father himself came down incarnate and suffered, as the Patripassians had claimed, or that God only seemed to become flesh, as the Docetists had said. Arius explained the relations as follows: The Father and the Son are both divine. But the Father is superior to the Son; he is alone the "genuine" (original) God. The Father created the Son out of nothing. Therefore the Son is limited, cannot fully know the Father, and "there was a time when he was not." There is a Trinity of 3 persons, but they are of unequal status.

This laid the ground for the Arian controversy, which was dealt with but not settled by the First Ecumenical Council of Nicaea in 325. Many leaders believed that the persons of the Trinity must be recognized as coequal members of the Godhead. They said the Word (*Logos*) was eternally begotten and that Son and Father are equal. The Son was "begotten," not made.

The 2 sides squared off in this council, called by authority of the emperor himself. Constantine actually presided and took part in the debates, though he was only a layman. This large gathering was the most formidable voice in the early church. It was the first council since Jerusalem (Acts 15) that could claim to be representative of the whole church. About 300 bishops attended, including just 7 from the W. After considerable maneuvering it became clear that a purely scriptural definition of the Trinity would not distinguish the issue raised by the Arians. Hence the term *homoousios*, "of the same substance," was introduced, though it was not scriptural, to make quite clear—it was hoped—the equality of Father and Son except that the Son was begotten. Thus the

Nicene Creed incorporated this curious and unprecedented term to assert that the Son is "of the same substance" with the Father. Most of the phrases of the Creed were directed against the Arians.

Unfortunately it did not succeed. The Arians continued to urge their position and found ways of adjusting to the definitions of Nicaea. They received support from some of the imperial successors of Constantine. In this 2nd phase of the conflict the famous trinitarian champion, Athanasius, bishop of Alexandria, who had participated vigorously at the Council of Nicaea, continued to be active. Throughout a lifetime of alternate victory and exile he forged a doctrine of the Trinity that finally became normative for Christians almost throughout the world.

Problems, however, continued. It is very difficult to define a trinitarian relationship without falling into monarchianism (one unitary God), ditheism (2 separate Gods), tritheism (3), or subordinationism (Son inferior to the Father, or a secondary God). The Council of Constantinople (381) further defined the orthodox position on the Trinity, and the Council of Chalcedon (451) defined the 2 natures, divine and human, in Christ. But the issues remained alive for future controversy. Out of the early conflicts came a few splinter churches, some of which survive to this day—the Nestorians and the Monophysite (one divine nature) Syrian Jacobites, Egyptian Copts, and Arminians.

By the time of Augustine (d. 430) and Jerome (d. 420) the church as an institution in society, as a community of faith, as a worshiping congregation, and as an authority on orthodoxy had come of age. Augustine summed up the wisdom of the ancient church, E and W, on the deep matters of faith. Jerome provided the W church with a reliable Latin version of the Bible, sufficient for the needs of the next thousand years. E and W churches continued to diverge until in the 11th cent. they split into 2 catholic churches, the one which became the Roman Catholic Church of the W and the other which gave rise to a number of E catholic, or Orthodox, churches. The Roman Empire, which had unwittingly and unwillingly nurtured the new faith, disappeared. The Christian church was well on the way toward dominating history so completely that each new year still gives witness to the power unleashed in the "Christian era."

For Further Study. A. C. McGiffert, *A History of Christian Thought*, 2 vols., 1932. K. S. Latourette, *The First 5 Centuries*, vol. I of *A History of the Expansion of Christianity*, 1937. Hans Lietzmann, *A History of the Early Church*, 4 vols., 1937; reissued in 2 vols., 1961. James Stevenson, *A New Eusebius*, 1957; source readings in English translation. Williston Walker, *A History of the Christian Church*, rev. ed., 1959; a standard text; W. H. C. Frend, *The Early Church*, 1965.

ARCHAEOLOGY

James B. Pritchard

Archaeology has added new dimensions to the study of the Bible. For many centuries students were limited in their resources to the written text itself and to the reports of travelers on what they had been told as they visited the sacred sites of Palestine. Now, thanks to recent exploration in the lands of the Bible and the excavation of numerous biblical cities, the modern reader has available a wealth of illustrations for places and things mentioned in the text. The biblical record has been supplemented frequently by new data on many aspects of ancient life that were so well known in the writer's day that they were taken for granted. Archaeology has also provided new data on biblical history, enriching immeasurably the accounts of historical events found in biblical books. While the religious truths for which the Bible is cherished are by their very nature beyond the scope of archaeological research, their significance has been brought into sharper focus by contrasts with the ideas of other religions of the ancient Near East as they have been recovered through archaeology.

The Science of Archaeology

Scientific archaeology is a relatively new discipline. The more than a hundred excavations in Palestine have all been made since 1890. The Bible lands of Mesopotamia, Syria, and Anatolia have yielded significant light for the Bible over a somewhat longer period, since the 1840's.

Tells. Archaeologists working in these Bible lands are concerned principally with mounds of ancient debris called "tells," which contain the remains of the cities of biblical times. Hundreds of these artificial mounds dot the landscape of the modern Near East. A tell is readily distinguished from a natural hill because of its steeper sides and the presence of bits of broken pottery strewn on the top and sides, sherds which have been washed or plowed out from the debris of ancient occupation. The sides are held up by the remains of ancient city walls buried within; these act as retaining walls and have prevented erosion (see ills., pp. 126, 192, 484, 697).

The formation of a tell is a long process that involves the founding and the abandonment of cities at the same place over a long span of centuries or even millenniums. The first inhabitants settled beside a spring of water and fortified their houses by means of an encircling city wall. When the first city was destroyed—laid waste by a hostile army or decimated by plague or famine—the new settlers who came to take advantage of the local water supply and other natural resources found the debris of their predecessors a decided asset. The height of the refuse and ruins of the earlier occupation augmented by sand blown in during the period of desertion, afforded a measure of protection, since the newcomers did not have to build their city wall as high as did the first settlers. Furthermore building materials of stone could often be salvaged from the ruins for new construction. Older buildings were leveled and the remnants of the first human occupation at the site became sealed below the floors and streets of the newer settlement.

Through the centuries the process of destruction, abandonment, and rebuilding was repeated time and time again. In addition to the practical considerations of water and defense people were drawn to the formerly inhabited site by the well-attested conservatism which impels them to a familiar place for building their homes and place of worship even after a violent destruction (cf. Jer. 30:18). So the tell grew in height with each new building level, or "stratum" as it is called by archaeologists. E.g. at Megiddo (see color map 8 for this and other ancient Palestinian places except as otherwise noted) a cut into the tell has disclosed no less than 20 different strata of occupation during the several thousand years of the city's history. From the record lying within these strata it is possible for the archaeologist to learn the relative sequence of habitation in a particular place.

Tombs. Throughout biblical times—and long before—people were generally buried with pots, jewelry, weapons, and other artifacts of daily life. These relics, which serve to illustrate life in biblical times, have survived better in tombs than they have in houses, most of which have been subjected to violent destruction or long abandonment. Tombs, containing as they generally do objects that are contemporaneous, document the styles of pottery and other manufactured objects current at the particular time of the burial. While time moves as it were through a succession of strata on a tell, it stands still in the collected artifacts of a tomb. Obviously burials supply information on the beliefs about life after death as well as reveal the material culture of the time.

Recording and Interpreting Data. Archaeology is both a science and an art. It makes use of scientific precision in recording accurately every detail of the destruction which is the inevitable consequence of digging ancient remains. Since the excavation of a building, floor, or tomb is an experiment which can never be repeated, more than ordinary care must be exercised in recording by drawing, diagram, measurement, and photograph the exact location of all objects, even though the significance of the data is not apparent at the time.

It is not enough, however, merely to record the data observed. The ultimate aim of archaeology is to know the people who lived at an ancient site. This search for the human past requires disciplined imagination; in the interpretation of archaeological data the practice of art comes into play. Without scientific discipline speculations about life in biblical times are valueless; yet recorded data, no matter how thoroughly the record is made, are dull and meaningless without the breath of life given them by reconstruction and interpretation.

Methods of Excavation. Two general methods have been employed for digging an ancient tell. One is to cut a trench or trenches through the layers of accumulated deposits. The sides of the cut—or "balks" as they are called—give a good synopsis of the history of occupation, and the pottery and other datable objects found sealed between the floors provide a chronological sequence for the settlements. This method of excavation involves drawing a vertical section of the trench and labeling all the distinctive objects which come from each stratum. It has the advantage of economy and of a sure control over the record of the arrangements of strata in the balks of the trench.

The other method for getting the history of a tell is to strip off each layer of occupation—or a sizable portion of it—in turn until the earliest is reached at the bottom. This procedure has an advantage over the trenching method in that complete plans of houses and streets emerge. Yet it is costly, so costly in fact that only one mound in Palestine, the relatively small and low Tell en-Nasbeh, identified by many scholars with Mizpah of Benjamin, has been completely excavated. More generally the practice in recent years has been to combine the two methods and to limit severely the area of the mound that is stripped off.

The most valuable relic of ancient life is pottery. Unlike wood and metal, pieces of pottery are virtually indestructible and retain their characteristic forms, decorations, and textures by which styles can be recognized. Pottery was relatively inexpensive and was continually being broken in use. Thus new styles and types were made at short intervals to replace the older forms.

The dates for certain characteristic types of pottery have been determined by the fortunate discovery of such datable objects as inscriptions or imports of known date sealed within the same stratum. These fortuitous discoveries along with the relative sequence of superimposed strata have provided a chronological scale for the occurrence of certain forms of pottery which is the chief basis for the dating of archaeological strata. Not only pottery, but other objects— e.g. toggle pins, fibulas, tools and weapons, beads, ivory carvings, and other objects of daily life—display types that are important for fitting into the time scale the discoveries made in a stratified tell.

Major Periods of Archaeological History. The major periods of the archaeological history of Palestine during the biblical period are the following:

Early Bronze	3100-2100 B.C.
Middle Bronze I	2100-1900 B.C.
Middle Bronze II	1900-1500 B.C.
Late Bronze	1500-1200 B.C.
Iron I	1200- 900 B.C.
Iron II	900- 539 B.C.
Persian	539- 332 B.C.
Hellenistic	332- 63 B.C.
Roman	63 B.C.–A.D. 323

THE DEVELOPMENT OF ARCHAEOLOGY

Early Scientific Exploration. Important for the rise and development of biblical archaeology were the surface explorations of Edward Robinson in 1838. Unlike the pilgrims who for centuries before him had visited Palestine and returned home to publish uncritically the identifications of ancient places told them by local guides and monks, Robinson was skeptical of traditions which had attached themselves to the holy places. He devised a new principle for ascertaining the ancient names of modern sites, a principle which has since proved to be remarkably useful. Ancient place names tend to preserve themselves, Robinson contended, even though peoples and languages change. In the modern Arab name of el-Bireh he could hear an echo of the ancient Beeroth of the Bible; in Anata, Anathoth; in Beitin, Bethel; in el-Jib, Gibeon. By the use of this method, combined with a thorough knowledge of the geographical sources in the Bible and other ancient writings, Robinson was able to identify over a hundred ancient sites and thus lay the foundation for the first scientific map of ancient Palestine. His researches were given more precision in 1880 when the Palestine Exploration Fund published its one-inch-to-one-mile map of W Palestine, on which there were fixed by careful survey *ca.* 9,000 names.

A further step in the making of an archaeological map of Palestine came with the discovery of dating ancient remains by pottery washed out of tells. In the 1920's and 30's William F. Albright retraced many of Robinson's steps looking for pottery to confirm or disprove the identifications based on modern place names. A biblical site must have sherds from biblical times. Following the methods of surface prospecting for pottery developed by Albright, Nelson Glueck worked in the desert of Transjordan between 1932 and 1947, visiting and collecting evidence from more than a thousand ancient settlements. Surface exploration, though obviously not as precise as excavation, has served to fix with a high degree of probability the identification of a great many historical sites.

The Beginnings of Excavation. The first important excavation of a biblical city took place in 1890, when Flinders Petrie made a cut into Tell-el-Hesi in S Palestine, probably ancient Eglon (see color map 5). The excavation is important because Petrie was the first to see the value of pottery for dating the layers of occupation within a tell. Though there had been soundings at Jericho and at Jerusalem and 2 important inscriptions had been found, Petrie's introduction of a method for establishing chronology marks the starting point for Palestinian archaeology as a reliable discipline.

From Petrie's beginning till World War I there were some important excavations. Gezer (see color map 5) was dug by R. A. S. Macalister in 1902-9 and the results published promptly in 3 vols. by the Palestine Exploration Fund. Ernst Sellin worked at Taanach in 1901-4; Schumacher cut trenches at Megiddo in 1903-5; Jericho was dug by a German-Austrian expedition in 1907-9; and the first excavations at Samaria were begun in 1908 by George A. Reisner for Harvard University. Of these 5 sites all but one have been more extensively excavated by later missions. Thus in the first quarter cent. for Palestinian archaeology some of the important mounds were probed and enough of the artifacts published to form a base for the typology of characteristic forms.

Later Development. Between the World Wars archaeology made great advances, measured both in improvement in technique and in a series of remarkable discoveries in several major excavations. Most noteworthy were the University of Chicago's excavation at Megiddo during 1926-39, the University of Pennsylvania's work at Beth-shan in 1921-33, the Pacific School of Religion's exhaustive excavation of Tell en-Nasbeh, the work of Haverford College at Beth-shemesh, and the American School of Oriental Research–Pittsburgh-Zenia Theological Seminary expeditions at Tell Beit Mirsim (probably ancient Debir of Judah; see color map 5), a basic site for the study of strata of the biblical periods. The British were active in the further diggings at Samaria and Jericho and were responsible for the spectacular discovery at Lachish of 21 ostraca (i.e. potsherds bearing writing). In addition to these major efforts there were many less ambitious but by no means insignificant excavations at such sites as Shechem, Ai, and Bethel in central Palestine; Beth-zur near Hebron; Tell el-'Ajjul, Tell Jemmeh, and Tell el-Far'ah (S) S of Gaza; and Ezion-geber (Tell el-Kheleifeh) at the head of the Gulf of Aqaba (see color map 4). The 2 decades between the wars were years of large-scale projects, ambitious in their scope and enormously productive not only in their quantity of data but in well-stratified material useful for establishing a relative chronology of biblical periods.

After World War II archaeological work did not get under way to any marked degree until after the troubles of 1948, when Palestine was divided. Since 1950 Yigael Yadin has conducted a major excavation at Hazor in the N; Benjamin Mazar has worked at Tell el-Qasile N of Tel-Aviv; Y. Aharoni has excavated at Ramat Rahel, probably ancient Beth-haccherem, near Jerusalem; and other competent archaeologists have dug at scores of biblical sites when modern road building and other projects of reconstruction have made excavations imperative. Roland de Vaux has led expeditions of the French School at Tell el-Far'ah (N), probably ancient Tirzah, and at Khirbet Qumran. American expeditions have gone to Dibon in Moab, Herodian Jericho, Shechem, Gibeon, Dothan, Zarethan (Tell es-Sa'idiyeh: see color map 6), and the Nabatean capital of Petra S of the Dead Sea (see color map 12).

The British have been responsible for spectacular results in the early levels at Jericho and for new excavations in Jerusalem.

WRITINGS RELATING TO THE BIBLE

Of all the things found in the course of excavation surely written material is the most useful to the student of the past. Except for the rare phenomenon of the Dead Sea Scrolls (see pp. 1063-71) ancient documents of leather and papyrus, the most common writing materials of biblical times, have not survived in the damp climate of Palestine. Yet enough writing on stone, clay, and pottery has been found in the course of exploration and excavation to bear independent witness to words, names, grammar, and the history in the Bible. Documents written in Hebrew, Aramaic, Ugaritic, Akkadian, Egyptian, Greek, and Latin have come to light.

Early Discoveries. The longest single text yet discovered for the OT period is a slab of black basalt with 34 lines of a boastful inscription of Mesha king of Moab. This commemorative stele, written in a script similar to archaic Hebrew, begins with an account of Mesha's victories over the house of Omri of Israel (cf. II Kings 3:4-27). Mesha recounts how his god Chemosh (cf. e.g. I Kings 11:7, 33) commanded him to "go take Nebo from Israel." Not only Chemosh but also the Israelite God Yahweh is mentioned in this inscription, which was discovered in 1868 at the modern Dhiban (Dibon) E of the Dead Sea and now stands in the Louvre Museum.

Another text linked with biblical history is the Siloam inscription, discovered accidentally in 1880 at the lower entrance to the tunnel of Hezekiah S of the temple area in Jerusalem. Its 6 lines describe the cutting of the tunnel from the spring at the N to the reservoir at the S for a distance of 1,200 cubits, a truly remarkable engineering feat. The tunnel in which the inscription was found is surely to be identified with the conduit by which water was brought into the city in the days of Hezekiah (II Kings 20:20; II Chr. 32:30; see also ills., p. 218).

Other Archaic Hebrew Inscriptions. Smaller inscriptions in Hebrew include a limestone plaque engraved with a calendar for farmers found at Gezer and a collection of 63 ostraca found at Samaria. The most impressive ostraca are the 21 letters in biblical Hebrew discovered by J. L. Starkey in 1935 and 1938 at Lachish. These letters, written in 589, just before the Babylonians besieged Lachish, reflect the background of the time of Jeremiah both in their language and in their mood of crisis and fear. Extra-biblical evidence for the earlier attack of Nebuchadrezzar on Jerusalem has recently come to light in the form of a Babylonian cuneiform inscription dated in his seventh year (598/97). It states that his army encamped against the city of Judah "and seized the town on the second day of the month Adar. He captured the king. He appointed there a king of his own choice. He took much booty from it and sent (it) to Babylon." Cf. II Kings 24:10-17.

An ostracon found in 1946 at Tell el-Qasile NE of Tel-Aviv, reads "Ophir gold to Beth-horon, thirty shekels" (cf. e.g. I Kings 9:28; Isa. 13:12). In almost every excavation of remains from the period of the divided monarchy there have come seals, stamps, and impressions of stamps on clay containing personal names, most of which are either biblical or contain elements which are authentically Hebrew. It is possible to compile a list of almost 400 of these names from such materials found in Palestine or the adjacent regions.

Cuneiform Inscriptions. That Akkadian (i.e. Mesopotamian) cuneiform was used in biblical Palestine is evident from the discovery of 20 cuneiform tablets or fragments of tablets, most written in the 15th and 14th cents.: 12 tablets or fragments found at Taanach, of which 4 are important letters to a prince of this city named Rewashsha; a tablet containing 26 lines discovered at Tell el-Hesi in 1892; 3 tablets found at Gezer, 2 of which seem to be of the Assyrian period; at Megiddo a fragment of the Babylonian Gilgamesh Epic recently found by chance; at Shechem 2 tablets found in 1926; and one small and badly mutilated tablet discovered at Jericho. A fragment of an Assyrian inscription carved in limestone was discovered at Samaria, and 3 fragments of a stele that probably belonged to Sargon II have been recently found at Ashdod. While the harvest of cuneiform from Palestine is small when compared to that found in Mesopotamia, it is sufficient to prove that this script was used, esp. for diplomatic correspondence. Many of the cuneiform letters found at Tell el-Amarna in Egypt in 1887 originated in Palestine during the early part of the 14th cent. and are valuable for a knowledge of political conditions in the land during this disturbed period.

The discovery of inscriptions has been an important factor in the identification of ancient sites. E.g. an Egyptian stele of Seti I found at Beisan contains the name of the biblical city of Beth-shan, and the name Lachish appears in the text of one of the 6th-cent. letters found at Tell ed-Duweir. Though these discoveries do not prove identifications of the places where they were found with the biblical cities, they do, when taken with other evidence, strengthen the cases for them. On the outskirts of Tell el-Jazari there were discovered boundary stones inscribed with the name Gezer. At the modern village of el-Jib, long thought to be the site of ancient Gibeon on the basis of the similarity of the names there were found 31 wine jar handles inscribed with the name Gibeon in archaic Hebrew script. This discovery seems to establish beyond question the validity of the earlier guess.

Inscriptions in Other Scripts. In addition to the materials in archaic Hebrew script and in Akkadian cuneiform there have been found in Palestine 2 short inscriptions written in the alphabetic cuneiform script of Ugarit (Ras Shamra) in Syria: a tablet of clay from Beth-shemesh and a bronze knife blade of the 14th or 13th cent. found E of Mt. Tabor. Clay tablets found at Ugarit have provided a sizable collection of myths and epics of the Late Bronze Age (15th cent.) that makes explicit some of the veiled allusions to Canaanite beliefs in the OT. The poetic form of parallelism, so widely used in the Pss., is a characteristic of Ugaritic poetry. Canaanite deities long known from references in the OT—e.g. Baal, Asherah, El, Anath, Astoreth, Dagon, the legendary Daniel (cf. Ezek. 14:14), and the mythological Lothan (cf. Leviathan, Ps. 74:14; Isa. 27:1)— play their parts in the mythological drama of

Ugarit. More specifically there have been found parallels in thought and phrasing to passages in Pss. E.g. Ps. 92:9 reflects 3 lines from the poems about Baal and Anath:

> Now thine enemy, O Baal,
> now thine enemy wilt thou smite,
> now wilt thou cut off thine adversary.

Of the many Greek inscriptions found in Palestine the stone slab discovered by M. Clermont-Ganneau in Jerusalem in 1871 is one of the most important. It was a poster in the temple of Herod reading: "No foreigner is to enter within the balustrade and enclosure around the temple. Whoever is caught will render himself liable to the consequent penalty of death" (cf. Acts 21:27-40). Silver and bronze coins inscribed with Hebrew and Greek are numerous, esp. in the Roman period, and serve to date buildings and other remains when they have been found in context.

RELIGIOUS BUILDINGS AND ALTARS

Temples and Altars. Excavations have disclosed a series of temples from the major archaeological periods in the history of Palestine. At the beginning of the Early Bronze I period (*ca.* 3100) there was a broad-room type of temple at Megiddo measuring 13 by 10 feet, with an entrance on the long side. Opposite the entrance there was a rectangular altar *ca.* 18 inches high. Later temples and a stone altar measuring *ca.* 7 by 7½ feet were found in the Megiddo of the Middle Bronze Age (19th-18th cent.).

Late in the Middle Bronze period (1650-1550) a fortress-temple was erected at Shechem, which with alterations was used down to the time of the judges (cf. Judg. 9). The stone building with walls 17 feet thick measured 86 feet long by 70 feet wide and stood on an earthen embankment specially built for the temple.

From the Late Bronze Age, just before the conquest of Palestine by the Hebrews, there has been discovered a square building at Lachish, measuring *ca.* 33 feet on each side, built of rough stones. The contents of the building included an altar, a platform of mud bricks with steps leading up to it, and clay benches which possibly once held offerings dedicated to the Canaanite deity. Other temples of this period have come to light at Beth-shan and at Megiddo.

At Hazor a Canaanite temple of the Late Bronze period, measuring 81 by 55 feet and consisting of 3 chambers—a porch with 2 round basalt bases, a main hall, and a holy of holies—is similar in plan to the temple of Solomon as described in I Kings 6. The equipment of the inner holy of holies consisted of an incense altar made of basalt and decorated with the design of a 4-pointed star, bowls of stone and pottery, offering tables, a statue of a man sitting in a chair and holding a goblet in his right hand, cylinder seals, beads, and a scarab carved with the name of Amen-hotep III (1413-1377). An excavation at Tell Tainat in Syria has disclosed a chapel, dating to the 8th cent., that has a ground plan remarkably similar to that described for the temple of Solomon. Recent excavations at Zarethan have disclosed cast bronze vessels of the 12th cent. which illustrate the tradition that Solomon had the bronzes for his temple cast in the Jordan Valley between Succoth and Zarethan (I Kings 7:45-46).

Objects of Religious Practice. Most of the objects to which have been assigned religious functions have been found in Canaanite levels. In addition to the incense altar and offering tables at Hazor mentioned above there have been found pottery stands used to support incense bowls. At both Megiddo and Bethshan were discovered elaborately decorated pottery stands for incense or other offerings. These were frequently decorated with such symbolic representations as the serpent, the bird, or even the human figure. Statuettes of a seated Canaanite god made of bronze and covered with a thin layer of gold or silver have been found at several sites. The god sits on his throne, wearing a high conical headdress and dressed in a long robe.

The most common "likeness of anything that is in heaven above, or that is in the earth beneath," prohibited by Hebrew law, is the clay plaque or figurine of a nude female figure standing only 5 to 8 inches high. Hundreds of these crude representations have come from strata which can be dated from the 18th to the 6th cents. B.C. They have come mostly from houses and only rarely from temple areas or from tombs. While they may have been intended to represent a goddess who was prominent in Canaanite religion, it is more likely that they were used as charms to assist women in childbirth or as an aid to fertility. They are certainly not works of art to be valued for their beauty; they must be interpreted as belonging to the magical or religious system of the peoples of ancient Palestine.

Throughout the long archaeological history of Palestine burial customs changed with regard to the method of burial, the position of the body, and the general type and plan of the tomb; yet one feature remained constant: the dead were almost always buried with articles of everyday life. This custom suggests a belief that the life after death required food, drink, light, and the other necessities of earthly life. Burial deposits include storage jars, dishes, jugs and juglets, weapons, beads, jewelry, lamps, and occasionally wooden furniture and cosmetic containers of ivory.

DISCOVERIES RELATED TO BIBLICAL HISTORY

Assyrian Records. The principal bits of evidence for confirming, supplementing, and correcting biblical history have come from excavations of sites lying outside Palestine itself. The account of the fall of Samaria to the Assyrians in II Kings 17:5-6 (see comment) is confirmed by a detailed account in an inscription of Sargon II discovered in his ancient capital Khorsabad. The Assyrian account in cuneiform is more explicit than that in the Bible in that the number of the captives is recorded as 27,290. Similarly the account of Sargon's attack on Ashdod is given in greater detail in his Display Inscription than in the biblical account in Isa. 20:1. Excavations in 1962-63 by David N. Freedman and M. Dothan at Ashdod have disclosed 3 pieces of a stele of black basalt on which there are portions of an account of Sargon's victory there.

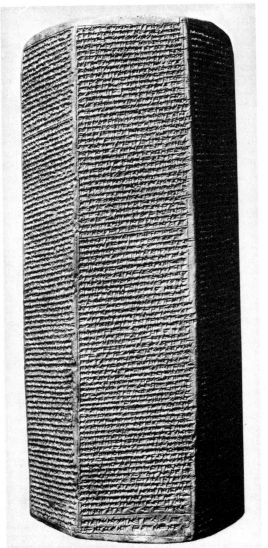

Courtesy of the Oriental Institute, University of Chicago

Sennacherib's prism, a hexagonal clay cylinder on which the Assyrian monarch recorded his various campaigns, including one against Hezekiah of Judah; the middle column pictured contains the reference to Hezekiah quoted in the text

The famous siege of Jerusalem by Sennacherib in 701 recorded in II Kings 18; Isa. 36 is reported also in Sennacherib's own account of this 3rd campaign. About one of the rebels against the Assyrian yoke the scribe wrote in the cuneiform record: "As to Hezekiah, the Jew, he did not submit to my yoke, I laid siege to 46 of his strong cities. . . . Himself I made a prisoner in Jerusalem, his royal residence, like a bird in a cage. . . . Hezekiah himself . . . did send me, later, to Nineveh, my lordly city, together with 30 talents of gold, 800 talents of silver." In the account of the same event in II Kings 18:14-16 the tribute is 300 talents of silver and 30 talents of gold.

When Lachish was excavated in the 1930's it was discovered that the city had been surrounded by 2 lines of defense, both with recessed panels, with a free standing bastion at the SW corner. When the plan recovered by archaeologists is compared with the bas-relief of the capture of Lachish by Sennacherib discovered by A. H. Layard at Nineveh, it is clear that these significant features of the city's defenses are all to be found in the Assyrian artist's portrayal of this important campaign of his royal patron. In the ashes of the destruction of the city of Lachish there were found arrowheads, sling stones, a spear point, and a bronze holder for the plume of an Assyrian soldier—all mute testimony to the event described in the Assyrian relief.

In addition to these striking parallels to biblical history there is the mention by name in Assyrian annals of such kings of Israel as Omri, Ahab, Jehu, Menahem, Pekah, and Hoshea. Occasionally these Assyrian accounts of contact with ancient Israel have brought to light events which, for one reason or another, are not mentioned by biblical writers. One such account is the battle of Shalmaneser III with Ahab and his allies in 853. In the 6th year of his reign Shalmaneser III is said to have left his capital city of Nineveh and marched W. In the region of Hamath near the river Orontes he was met by a coalition of enemies including the king of Israel, Ahab, who had 10,000 foot soldiers and 2,000 chariots.

These and other accounts of Assyrian campaigns in biblical lands have made it possible to tie biblical chronology to dates for the campaigns of Assyrian kings that have been established astronomically. Furthermore the literary references to devastations meted out to Palestinian cities by the ruthless Assyrian armies have provided an identification for certain levels of destruction found in the course of excavation.

Light on the Patriarchal Age. Though archaeology has as yet produced no specific evidence for the individual patriarchs Abraham, Isaac, and Jacob of biblical saga, it has supplied data for the history and geography of the first half of the 2nd millennium, in which they have generally been placed. Names found on tablets from Mari, a city on the Euphrates excavated by A. Parrot, and social customs and legal precedents described in tablets from the city of Nuzi in the upper Tigris region point toward Mesopotamia as the probable source for the Hebrew patriarchs. The prevailing opinion in scholarly circles of biblical studies is that these unique sagas, passed along by a long process of oral tradition, have preserved hints of an origin in the lands of Mesopotamia and N Syria.

Scholarly opinion is sharply divided on the question of the relevance of archaeological discoveries for the historicity of the patriarchal material. E.g. in 2 histories of Israel published a year apart one author, Martin Noth, contends that the Gen. narratives are primarily theological and supply virtually no evidence "for making any definite historical assertions about the time and place, presuppositions and circumstances of the lives of the patriarchs as human beings," whereas the other, John Bright, looking at the same evidence asserts that "the Bible's picture of the patriarchs is deeply rooted in history."

Excavations in Egypt have provided little to confirm or to supplement the biblical accounts of the sojourn in and the exodus from Egypt. From what

evidence is available it seems that while the Exodus was epochal in importance for the Hebrews it left little impression on those who were responsible for writing Egypt's history. The stories about Joseph bear unmistakably the imprint of Egyptian customs and a number of biblical names from this period and that of the Exodus (including the name of Moses himself) are clearly Egyptian. Israel is mentioned only once in Egyptian records; in a hymn of Pharaoh Mer-ne-Ptah, dated *ca.* 1230, there is the line "Israel is laid waste, his seed is not."

DISCOVERIES RELATED TO DAILY LIFE

The City. Compared with modern cities, biblical cities were small indeed. They consisted of small houses, made of stone or mud brick, built close together with only narrow passageways for traffic and drainage between them. E.g. the famed Jerusalem covered only 11½ acres, Megiddo 13, Lachish 18. Hazor, with 175 acres, was by far the largest city in ancient Palestine.

The one feature that all biblical cities up until Roman times had in common was the city wall. It was this defensive measure, rather than size, that made a settlement of people a city. City walls were built of mud brick or stone or sometimes of a combination of the two. Within the biblical period the width of these walls ranged from *ca.* 6 to 19 feet; how high they stood is unknown since the top of a city wall has not as yet been discovered. As much as 20 feet of the city wall at Tell en-Nasbeh was found standing. An economical type of construction called a "casemate" was popular in the period of the united kingdom and the early part of the divided kingdom in Israel. This casemate wall consisted of 2 shells, a thicker one on the outside and a thinner one within, strengthened by cross walls at right angles at regular intervals. Generally the space between the shells and ribs of this structure was filled with rubble to provide added strength, but occasionally the space between was utilized for storage. This casement type of fortress appears at Gibeah, Debir, Megiddo, Gezer, Hazor, and later at Samaria.

The City Gate. The city gate was more than an entrance into the walled city; it was the meeting place for the elders (cf. Ruth 4:1-2) and a place for transacting legal business (cf. II Sam. 15:2). Gates have been found in each of the major excavations.

Throughout the biblical period they consisted of a line of piers which jutted out at right angles to the city wall. The space between the piers served as rooms for the guards. The well-preserved gateway to Tell en-Nasbeh, though not typical in its plan, is instructive. Here the city wall coming from the N overlapped the wall coming from the S for *ca.* 40 feet; the space between them was also *ca.* 40 feet, leaving an open space of *ca.* 40 by 40 feet. Toward the inside of the city was the gate proper, consisting of 2 sets of gate piers with an opening of 14 feet between them. Two leaves of a wooden gate swung on stone sockets and were bolted by a beam which fitted into a slot to provide security in time of attack.

Tunnels. Another civil defense measure was the water tunnel which made it possible for the inhabitants to have access to fresh water in times of

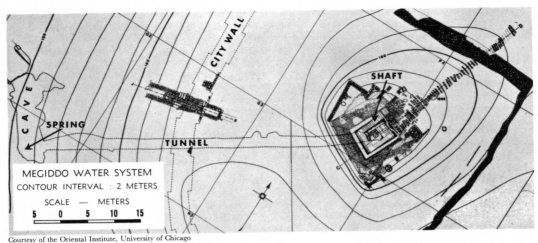

MEGIDDO WATER SYSTEM
CONTOUR INTERVAL : 2 METERS
SCALE — METERS
5 0 5 10 15

Courtesy of the Oriental Institute, University of Chicago

Plan of the Megiddo water system

Courtesy of the Oriental Institute, University of Chicago

Tunnel of the Megiddo water system looking toward the shaft entrance (see plan of the system, above)

attack when the city gates were shut and barred. Examples of this device have been found at Megiddo, Ibleam, Gezer, Gibeon, and Zarethan. At Gibeon there were 2 separate means of access from within the city to the water table under the hill on which the city was built. One was a circular stairway built around a cylindrical cutting in the rock, 37 feet in diameter. By means of 79 steps Gibeonites could reach fresh water 33 feet below the surface. It is possible that this pool-stairway cut from hard limestone was indeed the landmark referred to in II Sam. 2:13 as the "pool of Gibeon" (see ill., p. 171). The other device was a tunnel with 93 steps cut through the solid rock of the hill downward to the spring which flows all year from the base of the hill on the E. The lower entrance to this tunnel could be blocked with huge stones in time of emergency to provide a protected access to the spring.

The massive city walls, the strong city gates, and these costly measures to insure the supply of water in time of siege underline the need for security of the inhabitants of Palestinian cities in biblical times.

Industries and Crafts. For the major occupation of biblical Palestine, farming, archaeology has produced both plows (bronze and iron) and sickles. For the making of wine the evidence is more explicit. At Gibeon have been found 63 vats for the storage of wine, cut into the limestone of the hill, which could accommodate in excess of 25,000 gallons and keep the temperature at 65 degrees. In addition there were wine presses, storage jars, jars with labels for the export of the product, and funnels for the filling of the jars. It would seem that in the 7th cent. the major industry of this city, situated just 8 miles N of Jerusalem, was the manufacture and export of fine wine.

Other cities specialized in the weaving and dyeing industry. In an 8th cent. stratum at Debir were found a number of dye vats of stone which had once belonged to an industry in the production of cloth. Loom weights found in almost every major excavation bear witness to the use of the vertical loom; and spindle whorls illustrate the method used in the making of thread to be woven into cloth. Copper ores were smelted in a refinery found by Nelson Glueck at Ezion-geber. Pottery seems to have been made in almost every city, as well as imported from Syria and Cyprus, esp. in the Late Bronze period. Ivory carving is known from Megiddo, Samaria, Zarethan, and other sites. Many of the examples come from inlay in walls and furniture (cf. Amos 3:15; 6:4).

Weights and Measures. Many inscribed weights have come from excavations and the approximate values of the shekel and its fractions and multiples have been determined, though there is considerable variation in the actual values (see tables 4, 5, p. 1285). One weight inscribed with the word *pim* has solved a problem of translation in I Sam. 13:21 (see comment). The commonly accepted value of the cubit, 17.49 inches (see table 1, p. 1285), is derived from the figure of 1,200 cubits in the Siloam inscription for the length of the tunnel, which measures 533.1 meters.

Dress and Personal Adornment. Information on the details of dress and costume in biblical times comes largely from those paintings and reliefs within Egyptian tombs on which foreigners from Palestine-Syria are pictured. The earliest is a scene on a wall painting of about 1890 found at Beni Hasan that shows Ibsha leading a caravan of 37 Asiatics bringing eye paint to Egypt. Garments of colored, woven material are worn by both men and women. The women and those men who wear more than a simple kilt generally have on a garment that covers the left shoulder but leaves the right arm and shoulder free. Other representations record the customs in dress of the peoples of Palestine-Syria down to the time of Ramses III (1194-1164). Characteristic is a long-sleeved garment that extended almost to the ankles, frequently with a cape over the shoulder.

From excavations in Palestine there have come earrings of gold and bronze, finger rings, anklets, beads and pendants, toggle pins, fibulas (the precursors of safety pins)—all of which illustrate the styles in personal adornment (cf. Isa. 3:18-21 for an inventory of the finery worn by the ladies of Jerusalem). Numerous examples of decorated palettes for grinding eye paint have been found, as have the bronze spatulas for applying the paint. Ivory boxes and unguent bottles or tubes attest the use of cosmetics by the ladies of biblical times. Mirrors in bronze, once highly polished, were generally used, to judge from examples which have been found in tombs.

THE WORLD OF THE ANCIENT NEAR EAST

Mention has already been made of the discovery of cuneiform texts in Mesopotamia which throw light on the history of Israel in the time of the divided monarchy. A wealth of information on ancient Near Eastern mythology, law, and literature has been gleaned from thousands of tablets in the Sumerian and Akkadian languages, and these comparatively recent discoveries have illuminated details in the prehistory of Gen. 1–11 and in Hebrew laws found in the Pentateuch. Comparisons have also been made with profit between the wisdom literature of Egypt and that found in the Bible. Even Hittite mythology and law has been found to have significant points of contact with biblical material. Thus it is now apparent, after the discovery of many facets of life in the ancient Near East, that there was a certain common denominator in the life and thought of that world. The peoples of the Bible, while in many ways significantly different from their neighbors, shared with them certain basic concepts.

This participation in the larger contemporary world of the ancient Near East is apparent in the realm of crafts and techniques of everyday life. Inventions and ideas spread rapidly through conquest and commerce. Much can be learned about life in biblical times from the bas-reliefs of Assyria, in which royal scribes and artists left records of Assyrian invasions to the W. Our only picture of a king of Israel is the relief on the Black Obelisk of the kneeling figure of Jehu (see ill., below).

For Further Study: W. F. Albright, *The Archaeology of Palestine,* 1949, rev. ed., 1960; an excellent survey. G. E. Wright, *Biblical Archaeology,* 1957, abridged ed., 1960; a detailed account of the impact which

Courtesy of the Oriental Institute, University of Chicago

A cast of the Black Obelisk of Shalmaneser III of Assyria; in the second panel from the top Shalmaneser receives tribute of "Jehu, son of Omri," king of Israel, who is on his hands and knees, his face to the ground

archaeology has made on the study of the Bible. J. B. Pritchard, *Archaeology and the OT*, 1958; an introduction to the relevance of the results of ancient Near Eastern archaeology for the OT; *The Ancient Near East: An Anthology of Texts and Pictures*, 1958; selected translations of ancient Near Eastern texts related to the OT and a collection of pictures which illustrate it. K. M. Kenyon, *Archaeology in the Holy Land*, 1960; a well-illustrated summary of the results and methods of Palestinian archaeology by an outstanding British archaeologist. D. N. Freedman and G. E. Wright, eds., *The Biblical Archaeologist Reader*, 1961; essays on various subjects reprinted from the journal *The Biblical Archaeologist*. G. W. Van Beek, "Archaeology" in *IDB*, 1962; includes references to related articles on particular aspects of the subject.

THE DEAD SEA SCROLLS

Edward P. Blair

The Dead Sea Scrolls are widely recognized as "the greatest manuscript discovery of modern times." The excitement they have aroused is due, not so much to the fact that they are older than many manuscripts from antiquity, but to the flood of light they throw on the Bible and on the 2 religions most closely associated with it, Judaism and Christianity. The excitement is thus an indirect testimony to the widespread conviction concerning the importance of our Judeo-Christian heritage.

I. The Discovery

The first group of 7 literary compositions—contained on 11 rolls—came to the attention of scholars in Jerusalem late in 1947 and in the opening months of 1948. At that time they were shown to persons associated with the Hebrew University and the American School of Oriental Research by antiquities dealers and monks from the Syrian Convent of St. Mark. It was eventually learned that they had come from a cave high in the cliffs along the NW shore of the Dead Sea which had been located by a Bedouin goatherd.

Four of the 7 compositions were purchased by the head of the Syrian Convent of St. Mark and the other 3 by the Hebrew University. The group of 4 was secretly brought to the United States and finally sold here to the state of Israel for $250,000. All 7

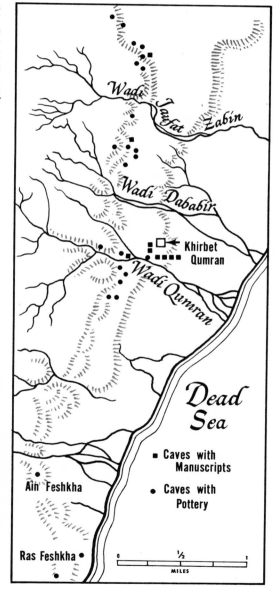

Courtesy of Jay and Mary Smith

Bedouins on the desert; a young Bedouin tribesman, searching for a lost goat in 1947, discovered the first of the Dead Sea Scrolls

1063

now rest in a specially constructed exhibition building at the Hebrew University in Jerusalem.

In 1949 the cave from which the manuscripts had come, now known as Cave I, was carefully investigated by archaeologists. Several hundred manuscript fragments, pieces of linen scroll wrappers, and many broken pottery jars were found. The large number of jar fragments led the investigators to believe that the cave once contained 150 or more manuscripts.

Between 1951 and 1956 the cliffs and the marl plateaus S of Cave I were thoroughly explored by bedouin and archaeologists. More than 200 caves were located in the vicinity of Cave I, 11 of them containing manuscripts or at least fragments (see map, p. 1063). In addition, at Wadi Murabba'at (see color map 15) *ca.* 11 miles SW of Cave I Bedouins found 2 huge caves which contained a group of manuscripts unrelated to the finds from the region around Cave I and somewhat later in date of writing. Still other manuscripts were found at a place known as Khirbet Mird, 9 miles SE of Jerusalem. These too were unrelated in date and content to the manuscripts from Cave I and environs.

The chief archaeological project of 1951-56 centered in the excavation of Khirbet Qumran, a ruined settlement on a spur of the plateau along the shore of the Dead Sea, *ca.* a half mile S of Cave I (see map, p. 1063, and color map 15). This ruin had long been

Courtesy of Herbert G. May

Excavations at Qumran

thought the site of ancient Gomorrah or a Roman military camp. On a surmise that there might be a connection between the ruin and the cave deposits, the site was excavated and found to consist of a large fortified monastery. Some of the pottery fragments uncovered were identical in type with those found in Cave I. The complex of buildings comprising the monastery covered an area *ca.* 260 feet square (see plan, p. 1065). It was found that the spot had been occupied from the 8th cent. B.C. to about A.D. 135, but the period of its principal use fell between the last half of the 2nd cent. B.C. and A.D. 68, when the buildings were destroyed by the Romans. Numerous coins, as well as pottery types and architectural styles, helped to date the history of the settlement.

The main structure consisted of 2 stories and was protected at its NW corner by a 3-storied defensive tower. In this building were found the scriptorium where the scrolls were written (including plastered

tables perhaps used in the writing operation and 2 inkwells, see ill., p. 1208), rooms for study and perhaps for community records, a kitchen and storage rooms, a cistern and facilities for washing, a dyer's shop, and a large court.

Adjacent to the main building on the S was a large meeting hall, measuring *ca.* 72 by 15 feet. Its floors and walls were plastered and pillars supported its roof. At one end of the hall stood a podium, probably for a reader, an expounder of the Scriptures, and a presiding officer. A pantry attached to the hall yielded nearly 1,100 pottery plates, bowls, cups, wine flasks, and other eating ware. In this hall the meals of the community were eaten.

Secondary buildings and courtyards to the W contained workshops, stables, storage rooms, and cisterns. An elaborate system of aqueducts brought water from a dam at the foot of a waterfall in the Wadi (Gorge) Qumran to 7 cisterns scattered over the community center. There were few, if any, sleeping accommodations in the complex of buildings. The inhabitants apparently slept in caves and huts in the vicinity. A cemetery containing about 1,100 burials lies outside the wall of the monastery.

Most scholars have concluded that the people who lived here from the 2nd cent. B.C. to A.D. 68 were the Essenes—or a branch of that sect—known to us from the writings of Josephus, Philo, and Pliny the Elder. Not all of them lived at Qumran; settlements of Essenes were scattered among the cities and towns of the E Mediterranean world. Their teachings were written down in sacred books, *ca.* 600 of which are now known in whole or in part, thanks to the discoveries in the caves. How they came to be deposited in caves is not certainly known. The most likely explanation is that they were hidden there by their owners shortly before, or at the time of, the Roman conquest of the Jordan Valley in A.D. 68, when it seemed certain that the community center would be destroyed. The fact that no manuscripts were found in the center itself would indicate that a systematic attempt was made to hide them from the invaders. Most of them were thrown into Cave IV, which lay at the edge of the marl terrace on which the monastery was situated (see ill., below).

In 1963 Israeli archaeologists excavated the great rock fortress built chiefly by Herod the Great at Masada on the W shore of the Dead Sea (see color

Courtesy of Jay and Mary Smith

Cave IV; prominent hole in the face of the bluff was cut by archaeologists; two openings at top were original entrances

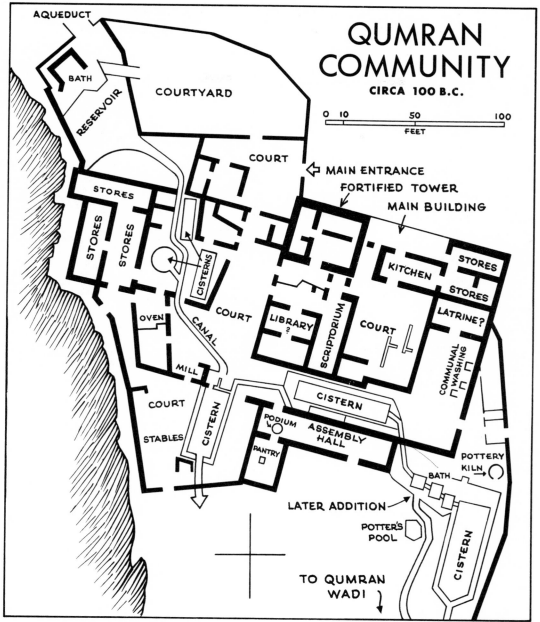

QUMRAN
COMMUNITY
CIRCA 100 B.C.

0 10   50   100
FEET

AQUEDUCT
BATH
RESERVOIR
COURTYARD
COURT
⟵ MAIN ENTRANCE
FORTIFIED TOWER
MAIN BUILDING
STORES
STORES
STORES
CISTERNS
KITCHEN
STORES
STORES
OVEN
CANAL
COURT
LIBRARY ?
SCRIPTORIUM
COURT
LATRINE?
MILL
COMMUNAL WASHING
COURT
CISTERN
CISTERN
STABLES
PODIUM
PANTRY
ASSEMBLY HALL
POTTERY KILN
BATH
LATER ADDITION ⟶
POTTER'S POOL
CISTERN
TO QUMRAN WADI ↓

map 14). They found Qumran-like documents in a
room believed to have been occupied by the Jewish
defenders of Masada at the time of the Roman siege
in A.D. 73. One fragment deals with liturgy related to
sabbath sacrifices and uses the special Qumranic
solar calendar. Other fragments are biblical (Pss. 81:
3–85:10; Lev. 4:3-9; Gen. 46:7-11); one is from an
unidentified apocryphon; and several are pieces of
papyrus letters. It is likely that some, at least, of
these documents were carried to the fortress by
Essenes who fled to the great rock for a last-ditch
stand, along with the Zealots, against the Romans.
This discovery is important, for it is the first time
Qumran-type scrolls have been found outside the
environs of Qumran and not in a cave.

II. The Library at Qumran

About a dozen complete or fairly extensive compositions have been discovered, most of them from
Caves I and XI. Fragments run into tens of thousands, varying from a column or 2 of text to tiny
pieces containing a single letter of the alphabet. The
fragments are being sorted and classified in the Palestine Archaeological Museum in Jerusalem. About
600 manuscripts have been identified thus far.

Biblical Texts. Approximately a 4th of the manuscript finds are copies of the text of the Hebrew
Scriptures. Two of the scrolls from Cave I are copies
of Isa., one in an excellent state of preservation. It is
24 feet long and *ca.* a foot wide, with 54 columns of

Scroll of Isaiah found at Qumran opened to Isa. 38:8–40:28; the scroll was copied with carbon ink *ca.* 100 B.C. and is the oldest complete biblical manuscript known to exist; the marginal line to the upper right of the bottom line in the right col. indicates the beginning of chapt. 40 and was probably a guide for public reading; note editorial insertions

text. The whole of Isa. as we know it is preserved, with certain significant textual variations. Every OT book except Esth. is represented among the manuscript discoveries, some in a number of copies, the most popular at Qumran being Pss., Isa., and Deut.

Of books of the Apoc. fragments of Tobit, Ecclus. and the Letter of Jeremiah were found.

Commentaries, Anthologies, and Paraphrases. The remainder of the manuscript discoveries contain material representing the point of view of the sectarians at Qumran, or at least acceptable to them. It is difficult, if not impossible, to classify these works. Closest to the strictly biblical manuscripts are the commentaries on biblical materials, e.g. on Hab., Nah., Isa., Hos., Mic. Zeph., and several pss. These commentaries quote successive passages of scripture with an interpretation of each. The interpretation, as well as the scripture interpreted, is said to have come by divine revelation. The objective is mostly to show that OT prophecy has been fulfilled in events of the interpreter's time.

Some manuscripts contain collections of OT passages which set forth the basis of the community's hopes for the future. These are sometimes immediately followed by an interpretation (in the Florilegium, or anthology) or compiled without interpretation (in the Testimonia).

Related to biblical materials, but a step farther away, are works that virtually rewrite OT materials for the sake of stressing theological interpretations, worship practices, legal regulations, etc. which are dear to the interpreter's heart and regarded by him as divinely authorized. These often follow the order of the biblical text but paraphrase, omit objectionable material, supplement with new data, reinterpret theologically, and sometimes deliberately alter the text. Of such kind are the Gen. Apocryphon (from Cave I) and the Book of Jubilees (previously known), both rewritings of the text of Gen. The Targum of Job, a translation into Aramaic of the Hebrew text of Job, from its surviving parts shows only a slight tendency to modify the text in the direction of sectarian interests. The Sayings of Moses, a paraphrase of portions of Deut., is drawn up to lay emphasis on the importance of appointing special interpreters of the law.

Apocalyptic Works. Books that unveil the future (see "The Apocalyptic Literature," pp. 1106-09) were popular at Qumran, as indicated by the considerable number of fragments of Dan. and the presence of nonbiblical apocalypses, e.g. I Enoch, the Testaments of Levi and Naphtali, the Book of Mysteries, the Description of the New Jerusalem, and the War Scroll.

The War Scroll (from Cave I) deals with the final 40-year war which the Essene community ("the sons of light") is to wage with the wicked nations round about ("the sons of darkness"), who are identified as the Edomites, Moabites, Ammonites, Philistines, and "Kittim"—perhaps a general designation of all nations which are enemies of the people of God, though sometimes used specifically for the Seleucids of Syria and the Romans. The stages of the war, the organization of the army, the weapons to be used, the banners to be carried, the infantry and cavalry maneuvers, the trumpet signals, the role of the priests and the Levites, the assistance of angelic powers—all are dramatically set forth. The war is cosmic, with God, the angels, and the righteous fighting against Belial, the evil spirits, and the wicked nations. The final victory will end the period of great tribulation and the dominion of evil and will introduce the eternal rule of light and goodness.

Pss. and Hymns. Another important scroll from Cave I is the Thanksgiving Pss. Because of the fragmentary condition of the manuscript the exact number of poems it contained cannot be determined. A recent translator identifies 25. Originally there perhaps may have been as many as 40. Fourteen times the phrase "I thank thee, O Lord" appears. There are strong similarities in these pss. to those of the canonical Psalter, after which they seem to be modeled. But the differences in language, content,

Courtesy of John C. Trever and the Israel Department of Antiquities and Museums

Qumran Cave I exhibit in the Palestine Archaeological Museum showing jars, Hellenistic lamps, fragments of manuscripts and linen cloth discovered in Feb., 1949

and poetic structure are striking. A number of them have a strongly autobiographical flavor, reflecting the sufferings of a leader of the community who is abandoned by his friends and abused by his enemies. It has been suggested that the author of these psalms is the Teacher of Righteousness (perhaps the title should be translated "Right Teacher" or "Righteous Teacher"), the founder or consolidator and guiding genius of the sect. The pss. thank God for salvation from pollution and transgression, for understanding of the divine mysteries, for the gracious help of God extended to a creature of clay, a mere worm, who cannot attain to perfection of way by his own efforts.

An important pss. scroll, found in Cave XI, contains 44 pss., of which 36 are in the Hebrew canon. The rest are biblical-type pss. glorifying David, wisdom, and Zion and praising the Creator of all. It is evident from these 2 major pss. scrolls and from additional fragments that the men of Qumran possessed a rich hymnody of their own. These hymns may have been chanted individually or collectively at the community meetings and used as the basis of individual meditation.

Liturgical Works. Several liturgical pieces have been found. The Words of the Heavenly Lights contains a collection of prayers apparently intended for the days of the week. In them God's gracious election

of Israel, his righteous punishment of the fathers for their sins, and his merciful forgiveness are made the basis of an appeal for present deliverance from trouble and distress. In the Angelic Liturgy the 7-word blessings of the righteous by the 7 chief angels of God—that they may obtain everlasting peace—are celebrated. In a collection of Blessings the overseer of the community is represented as successively blessing the righteous, the high priest, the sons of Zadok (the priests of Qumran), and the Prince of the Congregation (the political messiah). A Prayer for the Feast of Weeks, perhaps part of a collection of prayers for festival occasions, makes mention of the renewal of the covenant, which, it appears, was celebrated at that festival. Other liturgical materials of importance have been found.

Writings About the Community. The most important documents for an understanding of the beliefs and practices of the Qumran community are the Manual of Discipline (or Order of the Community, from Cave I and the Damascus Document (fragments from three caves), of which medieval copies, sometimes called the Zadokite Fragments, have been known to scholars since 1910. On the same roll with the Manual of Discipline were 2 other pieces of material, the Rule of the Congregation and the Blessings.

The contents of the Manual of Discipline may be briefly outlined: (*a*) initiation into the community, including the vows to be taken, the ritual of initiation, and the standards of admission; (*b*) a brief summary of its beliefs; (*c*) its rules; (*d*) a hymn on its doctrines and practices. The whole seems to be a manual for the leaders of the community and for initiates, so that the latter might be properly instructed and inducted into the life of the community.

The Damascus Document consists of (*a*) a long exhortation to obedience to the laws of God, based on a review of Israel's history, and (*b*) a summary of the community's regulations. The community is regarded as God's righteous remnant, which will experience his magnificent blessings in the coming messianic age if it wholeheartedly obeys his laws as interpreted by the community's great Teacher. The most solemn warnings against apostasy are uttered.

Exactly who the first readers of the Damascus Document were is not known. A reference is made in it to certain men of Israel "who went out of the land of Judah to sojourn in the land of Damascus." Since the Qumran discoveries scholars have proposed 3 possible interpretations of this: (*a*) some members of the sect actually migrated to Damascus or its environs; (*b*) "Damascus" is a symbolic name for Qumran; (*c*) at the time the community was founded the territory in which Qumran lay had been taken from the Jews by the Nabateans whose kingdom included Damascus and areas south of it. Though comparison with the Manual of Discipline reveals some important differences in the structure of the community as reflected in the 2 works, it is evident from the number of fragments of the Damascus Document found at Qumran and the general character of its theology and legal matter that its readers belonged to the same group—that segment of Judaism known as Essene.

The Copper Scroll. The most enigmatic and tantalizing discovery of all is the one text written on metal, inscribed on 3 thin sheets of copper riveted together to form a scroll. As found in Cave III it was so badly oxidized that it had to be cut into strips to be read. It lists over 60 hiding places where great quantities of treasure are alleged to be buried. Attempts to identify the spots have been fruitless. Scholars have conjectured that the treasure either belonged to the temple treasury in Jerusalem or represented the funds held in common by the Essenes. Possibly it is legendary, like much folklore about buried treasure, though why such folklore would be put on expensive copper is hard to see. If the treasure was real, this record of its location was put in the cave at a time of crisis—perhaps *ca.* A.D. 68—to make possible its recovery when the danger was past.

III. The Community at Qumran

Its History and Organization. It is impossible to date accurately the founding of the community at Qumran and the precise stages of its history, including the period when its great Teacher lived. The death of the community *ca.* A.D. 68 is archaeologically established. It is clear from the coins found at Qumran—the earliest from the reign of John Hyrcanus I (135-104 B.C.) and the latest from *ca.* A.D. 68—that the community was in operation by the last quarter of the 2nd cent. B.C., when perhaps its principal buildings were erected. But the creation of a center of the size found at Qumran would hardly be possible at the very beginning of a new community's life and would seem to force us to look back at least a generation for its inception. Whether the Teacher was the founder or a later consolidating and organizing genius is debated, though it is more likely he was the founder.

Three main hypotheses have been advanced for the date of the Teacher and the Wicked Priest who chastised him, drove him into exile, harassed him at his place of exile on the day of atonement, and possibly brought about his death. These are the periods of (*a*) Antiochus IV (Epiphanes) and Demetrius I (*ca.* 175-160 B.C.), (*b*) Jonathan and Simon Maccabeus (*ca.* 152-134 B.C.), (*c*) the later Hasmoneans, esp. Alexander Janneus (103-76 B.C.) or Aristobulus II (*ca.* 67-63 B.C.). Of these the 2nd seems most convincing. Attempts to identify the Teacher and the Wicked Priest by name have brought forth many possibilities but no consensus of opinion.

Not all "men of the covenant" lived at Qumran. Many lived in cities and towns and were organized into local units around a minimum nucleus of 10 men. It has been estimated that the community at Qumran numbered about 200 males. Those not living at Qumran probably were married. It is likely that at least once a year—at the feast of weeks (Pentecost)—all members were expected to meet at Qumran for the renewal of the covenant, the admittance of initiates, and the reassessing of status within the hierarchical structure of the sect.

The membership comprised 4 groups: priests (sons of Aaron), Levites, men of Israel, proselytes. The last are mentioned only in the Damascus Document and probably made up only a minor element in the membership.

The priests exercised commanding leadership, though the laity were full participants in the plenary

Excavations at Qumran showing a stepped cistern (a baptistry?)

sessions and outnumbered the priests in the "council of the community." This council, whose duties embraced among other things the fixing of penalties for infractions of community regulations, consisted of 12 laymen and 3 priests (or the 12 may have included the priests). The Damascus Document refers instead to a court of 10 judges—4 priests and Levites and 6 laymen.

A pastor and administrator, called the "overseer," instructed initiates, enforced the community's regulations, administered the funds of the common treasury, supervised business and other relations with outsiders, and in general acted as shepherd of the flock.

Strong gradations of rank were maintained within the community. Two years of probation preceded full membership, and periodic advancement was possible according to one's individual attainments. Strict penalties were administered to any who did not respect the rights of persons of higher rank.

Its Theology. Of first importance is the community's self-understanding. It saw itself as the only truly faithful and righteous religious group in the nation. Its members were "sons of light"; all others, inside and outside Judaism, were "sons of darkness." This differentiation rested on the belief that God, who had given his law to Israel at Sinai and who had spoken to the prophets, had revealed the true meaning of that law and of the words of the prophets to the community's great Teacher. He in turn had taught this revelation to his followers. They alone knew how to live in a way fully pleasing to God and in harmony with their high destiny. They saw themselves as the faithful remnant of Israel, the heirs of the promises God had made to the fathers, the community of the messianic age, which they believed was about to dawn.

The community called itself by various names, which in translation may be rendered: "unity" (or "community"), "congregation," "council," "assembly," "the covenant" or "the members of the new covenant," "sons of light," "the men of God's lot," "the house of truth in Israel," etc. By radical repentance and absolute obedience to God's laws, as understood by the Teacher of Righteousness, the members believed that they would come to perfection in the "way" individually and collectively required of the true Israel. Thus would atonement be made for themselves and for the nation.

Once a year, on the occasion of the feast of weeks (Pentecost), a renewal of the covenant was carried out in solemn liturgy. Confession of sins, vows of obedience to the law of Moses as interpreted within the community, baptism of initiates (and possibly ceremonial lustration of all members of the community, see ill., p. 1068), blessings and curses by the priests and the Levites—all combined to make the members realize once more their solemn responsibility and high privilege as the community of the covenant (or new covenant).

The monastery in the wilderness of Judea symbolized both the separateness of life expected of members and the glorious future anticipated for the community. The covenanters, as evidenced by their fondness for Isa. 40:3, were attempting to prepare there the way of the Lord. In the light of the predictions of the glorious future of this desolate region —the spring from under the altar in the temple would fructify the entire area, turn the Dead Sea into a body of fresh water swarming with fish (Ezek. 47: 1-12), and "make the Valley of Achor a door of hope" (Hos. 2:14-15)—it is not difficult to see that the Essenes of Qumran expected the new Garden of Eden to appear in the barren area where they lived.

It may be said that life and thought at Qumran centered on the law of Moses and the words of the prophets, on the present will of God for his people and on the future he had marked out for the remnant. It was believed that God had revealed to the Teacher of Righteousness exactly what Moses meant in the multitudinous prescriptions of the law and precisely how they should be observed, and that he also had shown the Teacher how the predictions of the prophets were being fulfilled in the events and personages of the community's life.

The interpretation and application of the law was more rigid and rigorous at Qumran than elsewhere in Judaism. Pharisaic rabbis e.g. allowed for differences of interpretation and practice and in fact quoted one rabbi against another. But for the men of Qumran only one interpretation was possible, that revealed by God to their Teacher. In general the Mosaic demand was intensified rather than relaxed. This may be seen in their sabbath regulations and in their marriage laws. The Pharisees apparently allowed the rescue of an ox or an ass from a well on the sabbath (cf. Matt. 12:11; Luke 14:5), but the Damascus Document forbids the lifting of a newborn animal from a cistern or pit on that day. In Lev. 18:13 marriage with an aunt is forbidden; in the Damascus Document the prohibition is widened to include also marriage of a man with his niece. Violation of the law of Moses as understood and practiced by the sect involved the most extreme penalties, even expulsion from the community. Promotion to higher ranks or stages in community life was dependent on strict obedience.

Much of the theology of the sect can be seen in its view of the future as willed and executed by God. God, the majestic and glorious creator of the heavens and the earth and all beings and objects therein contained, rules according to his sovereign pleasure. From the beginning he ordained the nature and course of all things, so that nothing can happen apart from his will. In fact God's eternal decrees concerning the life and destiny of all beings and things were written down before the creation on heavenly tablets. The movements of the sun, moon, and stars, the alternation of day and night, the change of the seasons—all follow a pattern established by God at creation. The times for the observance of religious festivals are grounded in this pattern and are therefore unchangeable.

This omnipotent God called the fathers and gave his law to Moses as the basis of a covenant relationship with Israel. But Israel again and again was disloyal. Yet God mercifully left a remnant of righteous souls in Israel. The "men of the covenant" at Qumran are the remnant of the end time. To them God will show his bounteous goodness in the gift of 2 messiahs and the age of glory. God is ceaselessly at work in history in accordance with his preordained plan.

The content of his plan is a "mystery" to most men, though it has been written down to some extent in the words of the prophets. Only the Teacher of Righteousness has understood the oracles of the prophets. In the Hab. Commentary it is said that God made known to the Teacher "all the secrets of the words of his servants, the prophets." Only in the community is it known that God will soon judge and destroy the "sons of darkness" through the instrumentality of the elect, who have loyally kept his commandments.

God's plan is conceived of as involving a cosmic struggle between opposing forces: God, the angels, and righteous men on one side; Belial, the evil spirits, and wicked men on the other. It is stated flatly that God is the creator of the spirits both of truth and of error. He allows these 2 spirits to have dominion over a "lot" or band of followers. Each group works to win adherents from the opposing one. Yet it is held that one's position in either camp is predetermined by God. Predestination and free will are both asserted in the texts. Even though God created the evil spirit, he hates him and all his works. At the appointed time the evil spirit and his wicked followers will be destroyed by God, the angels, and the righteous in a great 40-year war, and then the new age will dawn. The elect will become the instrument of his judgment on the nations. All evil will be annihilated forever.

The leaders of the new age are called "the anointed ones of Aaron and Israel." Two messiahs are predicted, one priestly, the other political. The priestly Messiah will officiate in the temple of the last days, have fellowship with the holy angels, and be a light for the entire world. It is possible that he is to be identified with the high priest who, according to the War Scroll, will bless and strengthen the sons of light in the final great war. The political messiah is to be a descendant of David, a mighty warrior and righteous ruler. With his sword the nations will be judged.

A 3rd figure of the end time is a prophet, whom the men of Qumran found predicted in Deut. 18:15, 18. It was believed that he would settle difficult questions concerning the law and perhaps function in some way as forerunner of the messiahs. Some have thought that he is to be identified with the Teacher of Righteousness, who (on this view) would have to rise again and return before the end. But this identification is unlikely.

The wonder of election to the community of salvation is emphasized repeatedly in the Thanksgiving Pss. That God should be gracious to weak, sinful, mortal, and worthless man is marveled at again and again. God's call, enlightenment, cleansing, and strengthening for faithful service in the community of the elect lead to the privileges of fellowship with the holy angels, not only in the future but also in the present moment. There is a marked note of joy in the theology and piety of Qumran.

IV. The Significance of the Scrolls for Study of the Bible

The OT. The scrolls are offering significant information concerning the original text of books of the OT. They show that in pre-Christian cents. several important textual traditions existed. One may have had its home in Babylonia, another in Palestine, and a 3rd in Egypt. While most of the Qumran manuscripts reflect the Palestinian tradition (including the Samaritan) some stand close to the text underlying the LXX, the Greek translation made in Egypt between *ca.* 250 and 100 B.C.

At many places the wording of the LXX departs markedly from the Masoretic text (see below). This has presented a problem of explanation to scholars. Some have thought that the Greek translators exercised great freedom in handling the Hebrew text they used. It now appears that they simply translated as best they could the text before them, which often represented a tradition different from that which became the Masoretic text. This Egyptian tradition must now be taken seriously in any attempt to get back to the original wording of OT books.

The Masoretic text appears to have arisen *ca.* the middle of the first cent. A.D. and to have displaced rival texts in the interval between the 2 Jewish revolts against Rome. It has been argued recently that this text is based on Babylonian textual tradition in the Pentateuch and the Former Prophets and on Palestinian tradition in the Latter Prophets. The Qumran documents show no influence of this standardized text or of the Babylonian tradition on which it is so largely based.

The net result of the discovery of the scrolls for the textual criticism of the OT is that we can reach much farther back in the history of the transmission of the text than heretofore. Thus we are in a better position to sift the variant readings presented by the several lines of textual tradition and assess their witness to the original text.

The historical criticism of the OT has also been advanced by study of the scrolls. Some scholars have argued that the Prophets, both Former and Latter, received additions to their texts as late as the 1st cent. B.C. This is now seen to be extremely unlikely. Qumran copies of some of these books, dating to the 2nd cent. B.C., include the alleged late additions. Eccl., sometimes dated as late as the 2nd or 1st cent. B.C., is now known from a Cave IV manuscript—obviously not the autograph—which comes from the first half of the 2nd cent. B.C. A manuscript of canonical pss. copied in the 2nd cent. B.C., though fragmentary, seems to rule out the possibility that some of the pss. were composed in Maccabean times (2nd and 3rd quarters of the 2nd cent. B.C.) and adds

to the evidence that the latest canonical pss. come from the Persian period (538-331 B.C.). A study of the many pss. and hymns composed by the Qumranians reveals linguistic, stylistic, and theological characteristics which argue for a much later date of composition than the canonical pss. The story of Nebuchadnezzar's 7-year illness in Dan. 4 has received important correction from the Prayer of Nabonidus found at Qumran. This document reflects a Jewish tradition independent of Dan. and correctly assigns the 7-year illness to Nabonidus, the father of Belshazzar.

The NT. The background and content of the NT is strikingly illuminated by the scrolls. NT hymnody shows strong resemblances to the hymns and pss. of Qumran and can now be adequately studied. The use of the OT at Qumran helps us to understand its use in the early Christian church. The concept of the community in relation to the purpose of God in history, as spelled out in the scrolls, shows similarities to the NT view and assists in its comprehension. The messianic hope and eschatology (study of last things) in general, as understood by the Qumranians, illuminates these themes in the NT. The dualism of the scrolls, the concept of predestination, the doctrine of man, the grace and righteousness of God, conceptions of atonement, attitudes toward the law, and many other theological perspectives offer significant comparisons and contrasts with the theology of the NT. It is obviously of inestimable value to have a vast body of Jewish literature from the time of the rise of Christianity against which to see the language, the theology, the rituals, the forms of organization, and the pattern of everyday life of the primitive church.

It has been argued that Jesus was strongly influenced by the sectarians of Qumran and their brothers in the towns and villages of Palestine. While his teachings show similarities to those contained in the scrolls, most scholars feel that the resemblances are outweighed by the differences. The Qumranians were strict legalists; he was liberal to the point of radicality in stressing the principles behind the law and freedom in its application to life. They were ascetic in their manner of living; he spent time at banquets and in the free and happy fellowship of normal social relationships. They were a closed, secret community, exclusive in spirit; he welcomed all to the fellowship of his followers and delighted in spreading the truth to everyone who would listen. They were priestly ceremonialists, stressing sacred days, seasons, strict conformity to the solar calendar, and ritual ablutions; he subordinated the ceremonial to the moral and spiritual. They taught hatred of enemies; he enjoined and practiced love of enemies. They were militaristic in spirit to the point of thinking of themselves as God's army in the 40-year war of the end time; he refused to be drawn into a military contest with Rome and eschewed the sword. Such striking and basic differences do not argue for close contacts with the Qumranians.

The closest similarities between the scrolls and the NT are to be seen in the teachings and ministry of John the Baptist, in Acts, in the letters of Paul, and in the Johannine literature.

John the Baptist, like the Essenes, was preparing in the wilderness by repentance, baptism, and radical dedication to the will of God a highway for the Lord leading to the messianic age. His manner of life was ascetic. Yet he also differs from the Essenes. He was more missionary-minded than they and apparently not so legalistic. His once-for-all baptism is unlike the repeated lustrations of Qumran. It has been contended that he was reared by the Essenes at Qumran, became dissatisfied, and launched a ministry of his own. But this falls short of proof.

The church in Acts exhibits characteristics that remind one of the community at Qumran. The full members of both are called the "many." In both communities an inner circle of 12 exercises important functions and seems to be thought of as pillars who by their blameless life and activities participate in God's work of atonement for the sins of men. The overseer at Qumran is at least partly paralleled by Peter and later by James in the Jerusalem church. The Lord's Supper, as a liturgical anticipation of the messianic banquet, bears points of similarity to the sacred meals of Qumran, as well as differences—at Qumran there was no memorializing of the death and resurrection of Jesus, of course. The sharing of goods in both communities, while voluntary in the church and mandatory at Qumran, highlights the strong communal attitude of each.

Paul resembles the Qumranians at several points: the stress on the divine mystery, long hidden but now revealed to God's people through his elect servants; the doctrine of man, particularly the emphasis on the weakness, sinfulness, and unworthiness of man individually and collectively; the divine righteousness and grace which rescue helpless man in a radical conversion and gift of the Holy Spirit; the stress on perfection of life in the community of the saints; the dualistic outlook; etc. But similarity does not prove actual firsthand contact. The central point of Pauline theology—salvation through the death and resurrection of Jesus, God's end-time deliverer who has already appeared—has no parallel to anything in the thought of Qumran.

The terminology and theology of John and the Johannine letters are often strikingly reminiscent of the language and thought of the scrolls—e.g. the strong dualism of both (God and the devil, light and truth as opposed to darkness and error, the children of God and the children of the devil); the interplay between determinism and free will in both, logically resolved in neither; the common emphasis on love within the brotherhood of faith; the use of the metaphor of a spring (or well) of water (at Qumran it is the law as interpreted by the Teacher, but in John it is Jesus Christ).

In short, the person of Jesus Christ—the quality of his spirit, the nature of his activity, the character of his teaching—and the growing faith of his followers in his deity and in the atoning significance of his ministry, death, and resurrection constitute the crucial difference between the Christian and the Essene communities. Much that they have in common was drawn by each from the OT and the common reservoir of ideas and terminology of intertestamental Judaism. Some Essenes undoubtedly joined the Christian church and carried into it their background of terminology and beliefs. But Christianity is certainly not, as has been alleged by some, a later version of Essenism. Both were creative redemptive movements, born of the same mother and growing up side by side for a period. To both we owe significant insights into God's saving truth.

ADDENDUM

As a result of the Six Day War of 1967, there came into the hands of the Israelis the longest Qumran scroll yet discovered (over 28 feet), containing 66 columns of text, dating probably from the 1st cent. B.C.

It has been called "The Temple Scroll," since about half of the document deals with prescriptions for building the temple and procedures for celebrating the various festivals there. The rest of the contents offer many rules (*halakhoth*) on various subjects such as ritual cleanness, an enumeration of the sacrifices and offerings according to the several festivals, and directions for protecting the king and the land of Israel from falling "into the hands of the Gentiles."

For Further Study: Millar Burrows, *The Dead Sea Scrolls,* 1955; *More Light on the Dead Sea Scrolls,* 1958. F. M. Cross, Jr., in *IB,* 1957; *The Ancient Library of Qumran and Modern Biblical Studies,* rev. ed., 1961. Geza Vermes, *The Dead Sea Scrolls in English,* 1962. Otto Betz, in *IDB,* 1962. Helmer Ringgren, *The Faith of Qumran,* 1963. T. H. Gaster, *The Dead Sea Scriptures,* rev. ed., 1964.

The Making of the Literature

THE HEBREW COMMUNITY AND THE OLD TESTAMENT

John L. McKenzie, S.J.

I. Literature in the Ancient Near East

Literature and History. The literature of a people is not its history. Literature is one of the sources of history; the history of those peoples who have not produced a literature is obscure. Literature arises within history and under the influence of history. The literature and the history of a people interpret each other. Literature which hangs isolated from its historical background is a voice crying in a wilderness; it is like overhearing one end of a telephone conversation or a casual remark on the street—we recognize the words, but we go on our way wondering what the remark meant. History without literature is inarticulate; it is a silent moving picture without subtitles; it is men in action seen from a great distance with no clear vision of what they are doing—their external movements can be seen, but their minds and intentions are hidden.

Definition of Literature. What is literature? The question has been asked and answered many times and in many different ways. To the historian literature is all the written records of a people, including such things as lists and receipts. To the student of the humanities literature is creative writing, or at least writing which attempts to be creative. To the philosopher literature is the history of ideas. To the sociologist literature is the product and the expression of a social structure. Thus literature can be viewed and can be studied under several approaches, none of which are exhaustive. For the present purpose a more basic definition which does no more than identify the material object will suffice: literature is the record of speech. When one writes he thinks of himself as speaking and recording what he says. He addresses himself to others and imagines their reaction and replies. This makes literature a kind of dialogue.

The Spokesman of the Community. The ancient scribe, far from desiring to speak his own mind and feelings before all else, appears to have desired to speak the mind and feelings of the community in which he wrote. He was not his own spokesman; he was the spokesman of the group. The excellence of his work, as far as we can judge, was measured by a standard which is the reverse of our own; the best work was the work in which the individual artist submerged himself and let the mind of the community appear. All literature which has universal appeal has it because the literature says what is in the minds of its readers and gives their unvoiced thoughts articulate expression; the ancient Near Eastern scribes, consciously or unconsciously, aimed at this end.

Most early writing was done on commission. The chief sponsors of literary production were the king and the temple; the scribal centers in any city were found in the palace and the temple. Society was a community ruled by its god and its king. Only through these did the society express itself at all. In the hymns and mythological recitals of the temple, in the inscriptions and annals which recorded the victories and the building enterprises of the king, the community spoke to its gods and narrated its achievements. The king "wrote" the annals just as the king "fought" the battles; for the king was the people.

Literary Forms. What determined the writer to produce one type of literature rather than another? It is not beside the point to note that the origins of literary forms are almost always obscure. We cannot tell who "invented" the epic or tragedy or lyric or other forms, and "invent" is not the word to designate the process. If anything can be called the result of social evolution it is literary forms; they arise from social forces just as political forms do. They are not solely the work of the individual genius, even if the anonymous individual genius must be assumed. The literary form must be accepted by the society in which it arises; and the acceptance of the society modifies the form continually. The society permits the author to speak only in those forms which the society makes its own, and the author who departs from conventional forms risks losing his readers almost as much as he would if he wrote in a foreign language (see "The Literary Forms of the OT," pp. 1077-81).

Israelite Literature. These considerations are presented in general as a background for the topic under discussion, which is Israelite literature and the Hebrew community. The general considerations are modified when they are applied to any particular case, and they are modified for Israel. The fact that Israelite literature did not arise in isolation from general Near Eastern culture takes nothing away from the originality of Israelite literature. Where the Israelites borrowed forms they modified them, and they created entirely new forms. The explanation of this originality lies in the peculiar dynamism of Israel; thus we find ourselves thrown into contact with the forces of Israelite society.

II. ORAL TRADITION

We must first turn our attention to a factor of fundamental importance in the formation of Israelite literature—the factor of oral tradition. It is generally accepted that no Israelite literature was written extensively before the reign of David. It is altogether unlikely that much of the prophetic literature was composed in writing. The later historical books, the Former Prophets, contain extensive passages which must have been formed in oral tradition before writing. Our questions about literature in society must recognize that the things written were composed and retained orally before their writing, and in some instances they were retained in oral tradition for several cents.

Oral tradition arises and endures only within the community to which it belongs. We must ask what were the sources of oral tradition in early Israel, or—what amounts to the same question—who produced oral tradition? This question will be answered more fully below. Here we observe at once that one must be cautious about speaking of "Israelite" tradition. Before we can do this, we must be sure that there was an "Israel" which could be the subject of tradition. The most recent studies of earliest Israel cast some doubt on this probability. We can be sure that we have the traditions of clans and tribes; we are less certain that we have many traditions of Israel. The generalization of particular traditions into traditions of all Israel is a social development of the literature.

Forms of Oral Tradition. One thing which is clear for oral tradition in general is that it likes fixed forms in which individual variations are freely permitted as long as the form remains. The form, among other things, is an aid to the memory. It also authenticates the story; popular tradition seems to have much in common with the children's story, and children are very tenacious of the form. In oral tradition it is often clear that the group did not wish to hear something new. It wished more than anything else to have something which it knew very well repeated, and the wishes of the group thus imposed themselves on the form and content of the tradition. The speaker re-creates the story anew each time he tells it, but limits are set to the originality of his treatment by the conventional and well-established forms.

The formation of a piece of popular oral tradition is far more properly a dialogue than the written composition can ever be. The speaker addresses a live and present audience whose response is immediately apparent in their external attitude. More than that, such popular pieces are often couched in a dialogue form; the listeners respond to the speaker, and they take part in the recital. Each member of the community thinks of the composition as his own; it says what he wants to say. Each one can tell it in his own way, and as such a piece circulates through a group and is learned and retold by succeeding generations, how can it be determined what particular form is official, or "canonical"? Who ultimately is the author of such a piece, if not the group which possesses it?

The clan or tribe group which we envisage is not a numerous group. All or most of its members are known personally to each other and are united by tribe or clan kinship. The spokesman is not in the position of a modern author publishing a book or an article or of a professional entertainer on the stage. The control which the group exercises over his work is much more rigorous than the modern audience and reviewers would wish to exercise. There is not the slightest chance that the spokesman would feel alienated; as much as anyone else, he is perfectly identified with the community. It is his perfect identity which qualifies him as spokesman. He has a finer perception for the mind and sentiment of his group than his fellows. In him the group finds its voice and discovers its identity, even when the spokesman, like the prophet, stands in opposition to the expressed mind and attitudes of the community.

Function of Oral Tradition. Why do such traditions arise? Even in illiterate societies the community spokesmen are found. They supply a need, and the need is greater than the need to express oneself. Man has the power of speech and an irresistible urge to employ it, but the need for such spokesmen of the community does not arise from the personal drive of individual men. The need is a social need and it is vital, for such spokesmen are one of the components which keep the group united.

How does a group achieve and retain awareness of its distinct identity? How does it recognize that it is different from other groups with similar social and political structures, related ancestry, similar needs and ambitions, similar skills and techniques? Certainly one of the factors here is the group's assertion of itself in its popular traditions. These relate its present to its past, give expression to its thinking and its ideals and preserve its memory of its achievements. The group knows itself as the individual person knows himself, in that the same group which has experienced its remembered past now experiences its present. Its knowledge of itself equips it to meet the present and the future.

In a simple society with no literature its oral traditions are invested with tremendous importance. In a much more complex modern society literature produced by self-conscious individual writers is still the voice of the people, even if not in the same way as popular tradition is the voice of simpler peoples. We still expect our writers to assert the identity of our society, and if they begin to speak only for themselves, the society becomes decadent.

Traditions of the Pentateuch. Against this general background we can examine some of the literature of the OT in particular. The Pentateuch (see "The Compiling of Israel's Story," pp. 1082-89) includes some of the oldest traditions of Israel as well as some of her later literary compositions. The early traditions are of the highest importance for our purpose here, for these are the traditions of the origins of Israel. Any historical account of Israelite origins must first reckon with Israel's own account of her origins. The modern historian may advance beyond the Israelite account to modify it or supplement it at certain points; but it is no longer possible to dismiss it, as interpreters once did. Whenever and however Israel became Israel, it was unified about the historical and legal traditions which we find in the Pentateuch; and there is no doubt that it united about these traditions before the traditions were reduced to writing.

Covenant Traditions. Whatever theory one may maintain about the origins and composition of early Israel, it must be taken as established that earliest Israel did not include all the 12 tribes. The traditions of the Pentateuch to a large extent, which cannot now be determined, are tribal traditions in the sense that they were traditions of particular tribes before they became the traditions of all Israel. Wherever we locate these traditions as original—a task which is both impossible and unnecessary here—they are the traditions of the covenant of Israel with Yahweh. This is the feature of Israelite society which makes it not only distinctive but unique in the ancient Near East. Every people, we have noticed, asserts itself in its traditions; Israel asserted itself as the people of Yahweh. The Israelite league was not first formed and then equipped with the traditions of the covenant; the covenant is the essence of the league. The institutions of the covenant are law and cult; these appear in the Pentateuch. It is as near a constitution with a historical preamble—actually interspersed in the constitution—as we can find in the Bible, and no similar document is found elsewhere in the ancient Near East.

The Liturgical Factor in Oral Tradition. The document as we have it is a literary work of great complexity, and the pieces from which the literary document was compiled must have exhibited the dominant themes before they were reduced into single documents. Such a unity of theme is unlikely to have been preserved in scattered songs and ballads, which we must assume to have existed, and some of which have been preserved. Scholars have recently assigned a situation in life to these early traditions which was certainly a factor of great importance, even if the degree of importance is uncertain. This is the liturgical factor.

In a society as simple as the society of early Israel we can assume no centers like palaces and temples with their scribal offices. What we can and must assume is the liturgical celebration of the great events in Israel's past. These festivals included a liturgical recital of the event which the feast commemorated; such recitals are prescribed in the Israelite ceremonial laws. The assumption that this was the earliest form in which the traditions of the covenant were preserved has much in its favor, esp. the fact that no other carrier of the traditions can be discovered.

The further assumption that the more extended narratives which we have were expanded from the liturgical recitals is again no more than an assumption, but it also has much in its favor. The Song of Moses (Ex. 15:1-18; see comment) in its present form cannot be early; but if the oldest part of it is to be dated as early as some scholars have recently proposed, it may be the oldest surviving account of the events it celebrates. It would then also be a sample of liturgical recital from which the prose narratives of the Pentateuch were developed.

Exodus and Passover. That Israelite festival which commemorates the greatest of the saving events in the history of Israel is the Passover. It is impossible here to explore the complex history of the Passover, or even to review the wide variety of scholarly opinion on the original character of the festival. In the final form of the festival which is described in the OT the Passover is a domestic celebration which includes a recital performed by the head of the family. It is not difficult to suppose that these recitals early reached a standardized form which permitted variations. It is less easy to suppose that a fixed form which excluded variations arose early. The variations which appear in the text of Exod. are no more than scattered samples of the exuberance of early popular tradition. No individual can be identified as the author of these traditions. They are Israel's collective memory of the experience which made her the people of Yahweh. Until this memory was put in writing it was a living memory, and as living it experienced constant growth and change.

Traditions of Law. The traditions of early Israel were traditions of covenant as well as recitals of the saving acts of Yahweh. The Pentateuch includes virtually all the Israelite laws which remain, and they are attributed to Moses the lawmaker. This attribution is historically impossible. It is evident from an examination of Israelite law that it has much in common with the common law of custom of the ancient Near East as this law is set forth in Mesopotamian collections. That these are common laws is not important in Israelite legal traditions. Israel has its way of life determined by its covenant with Yahweh; its law is a stipulation of the covenant and has thereby a unique sanction.

As early Israel developed from a simple pastoral society to an agricultural and commercial society ruled by a monarchy, many questions arose about the manner in which the covenant way of life was to be harmonized with such cultural changes. These questions were answered by the application of the covenant traditions to specific situations, and a corpus of legal traditions arose, created by the elders and judges of the Israelite towns and villages. One scholar has with good probability suggested that there was an official "law-reciter" who uttered legal decisions at the festivals when the tribes came together. Such an office did not take law away from the community in which it grew.

Early Israelite law was the response of the community to the covenant in the affairs of its daily life. It is not a mere historical accident that royal legislation is rarely mentioned in the OT, though law was one of the 2 functions of the ancient Near Eastern king. Law was an operation of the covenant; and it was Israel, not the king as an individual, who stood in a covenant relation with Yahweh.

III. UNIFICATION OF ISRAELITE LITERATURE

The Yahwist. The Israelite monarchy, however, was responsible for a step of incalculable importance in the history of Israelite literature. It seems impossible to speak of "Israelite" literature in the proper sense of the term before the unification of Israel and Judah under David. This political unification furnished a situation in which Israelite literature could arise under royal sponsorship, and in turn unification of popular local and tribal traditions into a normative document for all Israel contributed greatly to the unity which David wished to foster.

The first Israelite historical work, the Yahwist (J) document (see "The Compiling of Israel's Story," pp. 1082-89), should probably be dated in the reign of David or of Solomon. Here for the first time scattered traditions of Israel and even of Israel's ancestors were arranged in a continuous account. That the royal scribes generalized particular traditions is clear, though the analysis of traditions in detail is always difficult and often impossible. E.g. the cycles of Abraham and of Jacob can scarcely belong to the same clan or tribal groups, and the 2 have been linked by the shadowy figure of Isaac. The royal scribes "yahwized," so to speak, the entire traditions of pre-Israelite times, even into the prehistoric period. Indeed it is the "yahwization" of the traditions which gives them their literary unity in the J document.

The J scribes are the creators of salvation history, an entirely original theological and literary form. Their work gave the new nation a common tradition for all the tribes, whether the tribes had been a part of these traditions or not. The historical reality of Israel which issued from the J document outlived the political unity of the monarchy which had sponsored the document. The theological conceptions of the Yahwist become the basic conceptions from which later Israelite thought develops and expands.

The Elohist. Modern critical analysis of the documents of the Pentateuch finds the J source ambiguous on the Sinai narratives; these episodes are not prominent in J, and some critics believe that J did not include anything of the Sinai traditions. This again is scarcely an accident; the theology of the covenant is not combined easily with the royal theology of Jerusalem. The covenant theology of the Pentateuch is a theme of the Elohist (E) document, which probably was set down a cent. or more after the J source.

E is the work of the scribes of N Israel, where the original Israel was to be found, and where the monarchy never became a theological factor. From N Israel also come most of the traditions of covenant law. E, less well preserved than J, is also a history of Israel and a statement of the national consciousness. The 2 documents reflect a schism in the soul of Israel, a schism which was explicit in the political division of the monarchies and implicit in the encounter of Israel with Canaanite civilization.

The Prophets. The prophets appear in Israel at the time when the schism in the soul was leading to a crisis in the life of the nation. With the prophets we meet individual spokesmen. The prophets, unlike the earlier anonymous reciters and scribes, could be considered isolated individuals, alienated from their group. They themselves would never have accepted this idea of their position. Had they been able to grasp the question in these terms, they would have answered that it was not they but Israel who was alienated. They and they alone were the spokesmen of the nation; the charismatic officers, king and priests, had lost any power to represent Israel. For Israel was the people of Yahweh, and this not by her own choice. One who represented Israel as anything else had cut himself off from the community of Israel. The prophets and those who followed them might constitute no more than a remnant, but that remnant was the only genuine Israel.

Compilation of Prophetic Books. The prophets before the exile were speakers, not writers. The books of the prophets are compilations like the historical books, and most of them include the words of other

men than those whose names appear as the titles of the books. Most of the prophets, like the scribes, are anonymous. There are numerous indications that the prophets were associated with groups somewhat improperly called "schools." These groups of disciples and assistants wrote and preserved the words of their venerated leaders, and they did not hesitate to add to them. A search for the exact words of Isaiah or the other prophets of the 8th cent. is not a rewarding search. The prophets inspired a movement, and the books of the prophets are the products of this movement.

The Prophets and Early Traditions. The books of the prophets exhibit very little awareness of the written traditions of J and E. The conclusion that the prophets were entirely original and independent of the traditions would be superficial. Only a few generations ago it was nearly a dogma of critical interpretation that the prophets were the creators of ethical monotheism — i.e. of Israelite religion specifically as such. This view was superficial and has properly been abandoned. It reposed on a bookish conception of Israelite tradition and assumed that what was not written was not said.

We are now aware of the vitality of Israelite oral tradition, which did not die with the composition of J and E. The earliest prophets, Amos and Hosea, are keenly aware that Israel's identity is rooted in her past; they know the traditions of the Exodus and the Conquest, though we cannot be sure that they knew them in the form in which we now have them in the OT. They do not speak of the relationship of Israel with Yahweh as a covenant, even as the other 8th-cent. prophets do not. The covenant reappears in the 7th cent. with Deut. But the absence of the word does not imply a totally different idea of the relationship. The prophets did not create the belief that Israel was the people of Yahweh; they found it and reaffirmed it. The reaffirmation was uttered in a national crisis in language suited to the crisis. Had the prophets not built on the collective memory of Israelite traditions, they could not have spoken as they did.

The Prophets and Political Crisis. It is not too much to attribute the preservation of Israel in her political crisis to the prophets. There was nothing in the political resources of Israel which would have guaranteed that she should be preserved any more than the kingdoms of Damascus, Ammon, and Moab. All these were swept away by the whirlwind of Mesopotamian power. Israel as a political entity perished with them. That there was still a group which could justifiably call itself Israel after the conquests of Assyria, Babylon, and Persia is a fact without precedent or parallel. Israel knew what she was, and other peoples did not know what they were. In the crisis even Assyria disappeared. It was a matter not of power but of self-knowledge. Israel's knowledge of herself was a knowledge of Yahweh also, and Israel passed through her period of crisis with the knowledge of Yahweh and of herself which the prophets had communicated.

IV. The Survival of Israel

The Israel which survived was not the same as the Israel which had entered her period of testing.

The living tradition of old Israel did not endure through the terrible disasters of the Assyrian and Babylonian conquests. When an Israelite community reappeared in the territory of Judah it was not much larger than the population of Jerusalem and the villages in its neighborhood. It had no life of its own; it was merely one small province of a vast empire. The Persian Empire succeeded better than its predecessors in achieving a cultural leveling of the peoples whom it ruled. Its broad tolerance of native languages and customs was not enough to counteract the weight of political power; neither Israel nor other subject peoples had that self-consciousness which peoples have only when they believe that they make their own national decisions. The restored Israel was, as Mohammed called Judaism many centuries later, a people of a book. Israel survived as Israel because she possessed Israelite literature.

The Law in the Restoration of Israel. The history of the restoration is preserved only in fragments, and these fragments are disarranged. We cannot be certain who came first, Ezra or Nehemiah, though the opinion that Nehemiah came first, rather than Ezra as the order of the books suggests, has the greater probability in its favor (see Intro. to Ezra). But the course of events can be reconstructed. The first community in rebuilt Jerusalem was a temple community. The accounts of the restoration indicate that this community was not sure enough of itself to remain Israelite; the issue of mixed marriages was only one facet of the problem of assimilation.

The community was not definitely and permanently established until it was founded on the written document that Ezra imposed, which was evidently the Torah, i.e. the Pentateuch, in substantially complete form. The Torah gave Israel her own way of life, a statement of her faith in her traditions and her laws, and a new knowledge of Yahweh, the God of Israel. Around the Torah were collected other monuments of Israelite literature—the traditions of Israelite history, the collections of the schools of the prophets, the sayings of the wise, and the literature of the cult. These acquired an entirely unique value and esteem (see "The Making of the OT Canon," pp. 1209-15). The Israel of the restoration could read and study the literature of Israel's past; but by a process of thought which we cannot reconstruct the restored Israel did not believe it could continue to produce such literature. The traditions, once put in writing, soon became fixed. But because Judaism possessed and treasured this literature it knew what it was and how it could remain what it was, in spite of the forces of assimilation.

Judaism and Hellenism. Judaism needed this strength that came through the realization of its identity; for it had yet another crisis to face which threatened it with extinction. The crisis was not purely political, though the Jewish scribes who wrote its history, like most historians, could understand and report a political crisis better than they could handle more subtle and more fundamental issues. The political power of the Seleucid kingdom of Antioch was not to be compared with the power of Assyria or Babylon; the Jews faced a moribund kingdom. But behind the Seleucid kingdom was the vast cultural force of Hellenism, which had smothered the civilizations of the Near East less by arms than

by seduction. Hellenism as an expression of Greek culture was a force of such vitality that it could be resisted only by an equally vital culture. Its literature and art, its superior mastery both of ideas and of material goods gave it an attraction which needed no political and military support.

Against this force the Jews mustered all their resources, and of these the greatest was the faith enshrined in their literature. They knew what they were and what they believed because they could read it in books which by this time had become sacred. Without knowing why, they were aware that if they became hellenized they ceased to be Jews and thus ceased to be the people of Yahweh. The military resistance was the least important and the least successful part of the whole resistance. To the Hasmoneans the resistance was a merely political operation (see "The History of Israel," Pt. II, pp. 1028-29). Those who knew the literature of Israel knew that Israel could never engage in a purely political operation. Had the entire Jewish community accepted the Hasmonean victory, the Jews would have lost the cultural and religious struggle; and the political victory would have been meaningless.

Israelite Society and Literature. In discussing the relations of the literature of the OT to the society in which it was produced and read we should hesitate to use such a term as "folk creation," since it implies a background of theory which is not entirely acceptable. But when we deal with the OT we encounter problems which cannot be solved as they are solved in dealing with more recent literature. It is the product of a society in a way in which Greek or French or English literature is not, and if this imposes such terms as "folk creation" then we shall have to live with these terms. If we ask for the author of English literature, we are answered by an enumeration of the men whose names appear in handbooks of English literature; to say that England is the author of English literature can have no more than metaphorical significance. If we ask for the author of Israelite literature, we can be answered Israel in a way which is more than metaphorical. The difference lies in the relation of the individual Israelite to his society, a relation which we have not yet exactly formulated. But we know that we cannot simply and without modification apply our own conception of the individual and the group to ancient societies.

Israelite literature is better understood if its social implications are grasped. We know that man in ancient society neither had nor desired that personal independence which we prize so much. He could conceive no activity or survival which was possible in solitude; in all he did and in life itself he thought of himself as associated with his fellows, depending on them and serving them as they served him. And if he could not live except as a member of a community, it follows that he could not speak except as a member of a community. He needed to feel the power of the community behind him before he could open his mouth.

For Further Study. Aage Bentzen, *Intro. to the OT*, 1949, I, 102-264. W. A. Irwin, "The Literature of the OT," in *IB*, 1952. B. W. Anderson, *Understanding the OT*, 1957, pp. 154-82. Artur Weiser, *The OT: Its Formation and Development*, 1961, pp. 11-68.

THE LITERARY FORMS
OF THE OLD TESTAMENT
Dorothea Ward Harvey

For many of us the OT is a puzzling book to read. The language is often striking in its beauty and power, and we find ourselves gripped by an atmosphere or by a clarity of insight or description, so that we know we must continue to read. But when we do, we are often perplexed by unexpected changes in style, mood, continuity, or even details of the events. Here there seems to be much we do not understand, and here an awareness of literary form is the key to understanding.

As we approach the English Bible, it is obviously a single volume, translated for us into our language, waiting to be read. We soon find, however, that we are actually browsing, not in one book, but in a library of writings with variety of literary forms. As we come to understand these literary forms, we discover that they themselves are only one phase of a long development of oral tradition coming out of many different situations in the lives of people. And as we become better informed, we learn that these were Hebrew people, with their own sense of language and literature, their own understanding of life and culture, living in the actual world of the ancient Near East. If we read the OT, therefore, with an awareness of its own approach to literature, it can open up a new world of thought, attitude, and use of language, as well as of understanding of God.

I. Poetry

The Form of Hebrew Poetry. One of the first things a reader needs to determine is whether he is reading poetry or prose. To take a poetic figure literally, or for that matter to take a literal statement figuratively, is to fail to grasp its original intent. The distinction between poetry and prose was the starting point for the modern literary study of the OT. As early as 1753 Bishop Robert Lowth of Oxford identified the basic formal principle of Hebrew poetry, viz. parallelism. Hebrew poetry makes almost no use of rhyme and no direct use of meter in the sense of regularly recurring accents. Its formal characteristic is a balance of ideas, with the units of thought in each line of the poem enhanced, compared, or emphasized by their relationship to those in a parallel line.

Ps. 1 illustrates the 2 basic types of this balance of ideas. In vs. 2 the same thought is repeated in 2 lines of "synonymous" parallelism:

> but his delight is in the law of the LORD,
>> and on his law he meditates day and night.

The man who delights in God's law is the man who gives time to meditation on that law. The 2nd line repeats and reinforces the first.

In vs. 6 the 2 lines are in contrast with each other, in "antithetic" parallelism:

> for the LORD knows the way of the righteous,
>> but the way of the wicked will perish.

In this ps. the principle of antithetic parallelism is evident also in the poem as a whole. The righteous man, securely rooted and prospering, described in the first stanza (vss. 1-3), is contrasted with the wicked man, driven away like chaff, in the 2nd half of the poem. Groups of lines or complete stanzas can also be in parallelism with each other.

Variety is given by a 3rd type of relationship, usually called "synthetic parallelism," intermingled with the 2 types of balanced ideas. In this the 2nd line is not actually parallel to the first but expresses an extension of the thought or a comparison with it.

> One thing have I asked of the LORD,
>> that will I seek after;
> that I may dwell in the house of the LORD
>> all the days of my life (Ps. 27:4).

Here the 2nd line gives an incomplete repetition of the thought of the first—a variety of synonymous parallelism. The thought of the 4th line, however, extends rather than parallels that of the 3rd and thus is in synthetic relationship. Often synthetic parallelism is combined with synonymous or antithetic parallelism so that the thought is both repeated or contrasted and extended (e.g. in Ps. 1:2, 6 quoted above).

> Ascribe to the LORD, O heavenly beings,
>> ascribe to the LORD glory and strength.
> Ascribe to the LORD the glory of his name;
>> worship the LORD in holy array. (Ps. 29:1-2.)

In this passage there is repetition of thought, in exact words and in a synonym in the last line, combined with synthetic extension of thought by a new element added in each of the 2nd, 3rd, and 4th lines. This type of continuing extension is called "cumulative" or "stair" parallelism. It is found in some of the most ancient poetry in the OT (e.g. Judg. 5) as well as in Canaanite poetry of the 2nd millenium B.C.

> As a hart longs
>> for flowing streams,

> so longs my soul
> for thee, O God (Ps. 42:1).

Here a simile brings out the comparison. Almost endless variations of extension or comparison are possible.

One of the joys of Hebrew poetry is the balance it maintains between the inherent structure of its parallelism and its delight in variation from this structure. The very nature of the structure, with its emphasis on units of thought, tends to support this balance between pattern and freedom.

The meter of Hebrew poetry is relatively free. Such rhythmic patterns as occur grow out of the parallelism, which requires that each line be a thought unit of approximately the same weight. Thus the successive lines regularly contain the same number of stressed words—usually 3, sometimes 2, rarely 4, with an alternation of 3 followed by 2 as a special form. Since the unstressed syllables fall into no pattern, however, there is no such thing as a Hebrew iambic pentameter, i.e. no meter of either the ancient Greek or the modern European sort.

Songs and Poems. The principle of parallelism can be seen in poems of all kinds, in various poetic types of wisdom literature, and in the sayings of the prophets—in fully a 3rd of the literature of the OT in fact. The earliest examples of literature in the Bible are poems. Lamech's song of boasting against his enemy shows clear parallelism:

> Adah and Zillah, hear my voice;
> you wives of Lamech, hearken to what I say:
> I have slain a man for wounding me,
> a young man for striking me.
> If Cain is avenged sevenfold,
> truly Lamech seventy-sevenfold (Gen. 4:23-24).

Other early poems are songs of victory (Exod. 15:21; Judg. 5), a song sung for the digging of a well (Num. 21:17-18), a taunt song over Moab (Num. 21:27-30), and 2 examples of dirges, David's laments over the deaths of Saul and Jonathan (II Sam. 1:19-27) and of Abner (II Sam. 3:33-34). Also a kind of song in parallel form is the short, repeated victory chant for Saul and David:

> Saul has slain his thousands,
> And David his ten thousands (I Sam. 18:7).

Songs intended for use in public worship were collected in Pss. Of these the hymn is one of the most common types. Ps. 113 illustrates the form of the hymn. Beginning with a call to sing to God or to praise him,

> Praise the LORD!
> Praise, O servants of the LORD,
> praise the name of the LORD,

it continues with the reason for the praise, i.e. a statement of what God has done,

> He raises the poor from the dust,
> and lifts the needy from the ash heap (vs. 7),

and it concludes with a further call to praise,

> Praise the LORD! (vs. 9.)

Such hymns were evidently part of public services of worship, with choirs and instrumental music (cf. e.g. Pss. 100; 106; 135; 145-150). I Chr. 23:5 speaks of Levites ready to "offer praises to the LORD" with musical instruments, and II Chr. 5:13 gives the words of a song raised "with trumpets and cymbals and other musical instruments, in praise to the LORD."

The other most common type in Pss. is the individual lament, probably intended to accompany a guilt offering in the temple. It expresses a cry for help in illness or other danger,

> Consider and answer me, O LORD my God;
> lighten my eyes, lest I sleep the sleep of death (13:3),

and normally concludes with a brief hymn of thanksgiving for the saving help God has given in the past and is expected to give now,

> I will sing to the LORD,
> because he has dealt bountifully with me (13:6).

The laments are thus typically related to the thanksgiving pss., probably composed to be used with a purification or thank offering in the temple after an illness or other danger was past (e.g. Pss. 30; 92). A declaration or recital to the congregation of God's act of deliverance is often mentioned (e.g. Pss. 26:6-7; 40:9-10; 51:14-15), sometimes accompanying the offering of a sacrifice of thanksgiving or the payment of vows to God (cf. e.g. 22:22-25; 107:17-22).

Other types of pss. include national laments (e.g. Pss. 44; 74; 79) and thanksgivings for harvest (e.g. Ps. 67) or victory (Ps. 124); occasional poems for the king's coronation (e.g. Pss. 2; 110) or marriage (Ps. 45); liturgies for public worship (e.g. Pss. 80; 134; 136); a special group of hymns celebrating God's kingship or enthronement (Pss. 29; 47; 93; 95-99); and poems in the tradition of wisdom literature (e.g. Pss. 1; 37; 73). See further Intro. to Pss.

Poetry in Wisdom Literature. Much of the thought of the wise men (see "The Wisdom Literature, pp. 1101-05) was expressed in poetic form—e.g. the wisdom pss. just mentioned. Job, except for its prose prologue and epilogue (chs. 1-2; 42:7-17), is poetry unsurpassed in any literature.

The simplest and most common form of wisdom teaching is the single proverb—a brief, striking example or statement of some observation on life. In its original form the proverb was probably a popular saying, citing a well-known example (e.g. "Like Nimrod a mighty hunter before the LORD," Gen. 10:9; cf. I Sam. 10:12) or making a general observation (e.g. "Out of the wicked comes forth wickedness," I Sam. 24:13; cf. I Kings 20:11; Jer. 23:28; 31:29).

The Hebrew word for proverb means "likeness" or "comparison" and often the parallelism is of this type:

> Like clouds and wind without rain
> is a man who boasts of a gift he does not give (Prov. 25:14).

The likenesses may be piled up in one proverb:

> Like vinegar to the teeth, and smoke to the eyes,
> so is the sluggard to those who send him (Prov. 10:26).

Or the comparison as a whole may be set in parallelism with a contrasting line:

> It is like sport to a fool to do wrong,
> but wise conduct is pleasure to a man of understanding (Prov. 10:23).

Often a vivid example used to illustrate the point has the effect of a comparison:

> The wise of heart will heed commandments,
>> but a prating fool will come to ruin (Prov. 10:8).

Sometimes the comparison is stated as "better than"; in Prov. 16:16 2 of this type are combined in synonymous parallelism:

> To get wisdom is better than gold;
>> to get understanding is to be chosen rather than silver.

Comparisons like these are combined with others in a more extended description of the happiness of the wise man in a longer poem in Prov. 3:13-18. For other longer wisdom poems cf. Prov. 7–9; 31:10-31.

The riddle is very similar to the proverb and is also connected with the wisdom tradition. Samson proposed a riddle to a group gathered to enjoy a feast (Judg. 14:14) and the answer was returned to him in the form of another riddle,

> What is sweeter than honey?
> What is stronger than a lion? (vs. 18),

which could also be answered if desired. But riddles were not only for enjoyment. Solomon's wisdom was partly that he could answer "hard questions," as the same word is translated in I Kings 10:1. The wise man is the one able

> to understand a proverb and a figure,
>> the words of the wise and their riddles (Prov. 1:6).

In Ps. 78:2 parables and "dark sayings" are associated with each other and with the wisdom of the past. The man who understands the proverb or the riddle has access to the hidden wisdom of the ages.

The numerical proverb (Prov. 6:16-19; 30:15-31) is a wisdom form which seems to have elements of both the riddle and the proverb. Though not phrased as a question, the first 2 lines imply a riddle, which is then answered in the succeeding lines—e.g.:

> Under three things the earth trembles;
>> under four it cannot bear up:
> a slave when he becomes king,
>> and a fool when he is filled with food;
> an unloved woman when she gets a husband,
>> and a maid when she succeeds her mistress (30:21-23).

Poetry in Prophetic Literature.
The books of the "writing" prophets—Isa., Jer., Ezek., and the minor prophets—are for the most part not writings but collections of sayings. The basic form is not a sermon, in the sense of an extended composition, but rather a short oracle, or word spoken directly to the situation, with the intensity of poetic speech.

The imagery of prophetic poetry is often striking. Isaiah pictures the proud kingdom of Israel as about to be swallowed up by Assyria

> like a first-ripe fig before the summer:
>> when a man sees it, he eats it up
>> as soon as it is in his hand (28:4).

Both imagery and parallelism are sometimes important for the meaning of a prophetic saying. Amos' indictment against the nations begins

> For three transgressions of Damascus,
>> and for four, I will not revoke the punishment (1:3),

lit., "I will not turn it back" (see comment). The poetic imagery seems to portray God's hand raised in judgment and not to be turned aside until it strikes its intended object. In parallelism a number in one line is often balanced by another number in the next. Thus 4 is the normal poetic parallel for 3 (cf. e.g. Prov. 30:21) and 7 for 6 (cf. Prov. 6:16). Amos' 3 and 4 are not so much a numerical progression as an expression of poetic intensity by repetition, combined with a strong prophetic sense of the specific. To read the oracles of the prophets as poetry, aware of the emphasis or contrast effected by parallelism, and of the imagery, is to read with new pleasure and understanding.

The spoken aspect of prophetic poetry is also important. Writing in the ancient world was useful more as a record, esp. of business transactions, than as a means of communication. Communication itself was from person to person. Inflection, rather than grammar or punctuation, was the primary way to convey question or exclamation; and the speaker's inflection is sometimes necessary to the meaning. E.g. Isaiah's

> Though your sins are like scarlet,
>> they shall be as white as snow (1:18)

was probably spoken as a biting satirical question.

The prophets use many different types of poetic speech and many variations of these types. Often an invective or a specific warning to the people of their wrongdoing is followed by "therefore" and the brief poetic word of God's judgment. Isaiah's series of woes against the people's reversal of true judgment (5:18-24) ends with a woe against those who "acquit the guilty for a bribe" and the concluding judgment:

> Therefore, as the tongue of fire devours the stubble,
>> and as dry grass sinks down in the flame,
> so their root will be as rottenness,
>> and their blossom go up like dust.

Prophetic warnings are often expressed in the traditional form of a taunt song against an enemy, like the ancient poem in Num. 21:27-30 gloating over the destruction of Moab's cities, a destruction terrible enough to be a byword for ballad singers. In similar fashion Isa. 37:22 describes Jerusalem as taunting Assyria:

> She despises you, she scorns you—
>> the virgin daughter of Zion;
> she wags her head behind you—
>> the daughter of Jerusalem.

For other examples cf. Isa. 23:1-12, 16; 47; Jer. 48–51. The place of the ancient taunt songs in actual wars against the enemies of the nation makes the prophets' use of them against Israel herself unusually awesome (cf. e.g. Jer. 15:4-9).

The prophets also adopt the typical form of the lament or dirge to announce God's dread judgment against Jerusalem:

> How we are ruined!
> We are utterly shamed,
> because we have left the land,
>> because they have cast down our dwellings. (Jer. 9:19.)

David's lament over Saul and Jonathan contains the similar phrase "How are the mighty fallen!"

(II Sam. 1:25, 27; cf. Amos 5:2; Ezek. 19; 26:17-18). A lament sung over a still proud enemy has the force of a taunt, and the 2 forms are combined in Isa. 14:4-21; Ezek. 27:2-9; 28:12-19; 32:2-8. Outside the prophetic books the lament form is preserved in Lam., the laments collected for use on annual days of mourning for the fall of Jerusalem.

II. Poetic Prose

If the recognition of poetry is helpful for an understanding of the OT, an awareness of nonliteral prose is equally important. To treat parable, myth, drama, or fiction as literal prose is to miss the depth of its meaning. The distinction between the literal and the poetic is not always easy to make in another culture. This is perhaps esp. true for us in Hebrew, where expression of thought is more by example than by general category or abstract term. The vivid comparison of the poetic proverb is natural in Hebrew. In poetic prose the parable, allegory, and fable are the comparable forms.

Parable. The contrast in Prov. 6:6-11 between the industrious ant and the sluggard man is a parable in poetry. Nathan's comparison of David to a rich man who took a poor man's one ewe lamb (II Sam. 12:1-7) is an equally effective parable in the form of a prose story. The wise woman of Tekoa told her parable to David partly by telling her story, partly also by acting out her role (II Sam. 14:1-17). A prophet told his parable to Ahab by similar means (I Kings 20:35-42). Isaiah's word and act connected with the birth of Maher-shalal-hash-baz (Isa. 8) follows in this same tradition. The Hebrew sense of the identity of word and deed carries parable well beyond a literary form in this and other symbolic acts of the prophets (e.g. Isa. 20; Jer. 13; 32; Ezek. 4–5). The acts have a significant power to bring about the judgments, just as the taunt can be an actual weapon against the enemy.

Allegory. The allegory is another literary form of the comparison or proverb. It could almost be described as an extended prose riddle, for it has much the same significance of hidden and revealed wisdom. Ezekiel is told to "propound a riddle, and speak an allegory" to Israel in describing 2 eagles breaking off the top of a cedar and planting and transplanting the seed (Ezek. 17). His comparison of the vine is proposed as a riddle and interpreted as an allegory (Ezek. 15). The allegorical interpretation of visions and of all the strange apocalyptic symbolism (see "The Apocalyptic Literature," pp. 1106-09) follows in the same tradition of riddles and wisdom. Zechariah, when he saw a "man riding upon a red horse" with horses of other colors in the background, asked an angel who was with him to explain what these things meant (Zech. 1:8-9). An angel acting as an interpreter is fairly typical in apocalyptic visions (cf. e.g. Zech. 1–6; Ezek. 40:3-4; Dan. 7:16; 8:15-17; 10:10–11:1). The angel, or sometimes the "God . . . who reveals mysteries" (Dan. 2:28), gives man the key to these ultimate riddles of history.

Fable. A simpler form of comparison, the fable is a tale about plants or animals told to illustrate some aspect of human life. Jotham tells a fable about trees who went out to choose a king and found

that only the worthless bramble would serve (Judg. 9:7-15). This story is similar to Ezekiel's riddle-allegory about the vine, and both belong to the wisdom tradition. King Jehoash of Israel answers the request of the king of Judah with a fable about a thistle and a cedar (II Kings 14:8-10). Among the examples of Solomon's wisdom the mention of his ability to speak about trees and beasts (I Kings 4:33) may refer to skill in telling fables.

Myth. A myth is a symbolic story that develops among a people to explain origins, both of the natural world and its features and of customs and ideas. E.g. the story of Adam and Eve in Gen. 2:4b-3:24 explains not only the creation of the earth, plant and animal life, and mankind but also the causes for such things as dislike of snakes, pain in childbirth, and toil in agriculture. More deeply it interprets everyman's experience of human responsibility as essentially related to his awareness of guilt, judgment, and grace. In the Hebrew this universal dimension of the myth is emphasized in the name Adam, which means "mankind."

The Semitic peoples of the ancient Near East, to which the Hebrews belonged, shared a considerable mythology. Discovery of records of some of the myths of these peoples, esp. the Babylonians and Canaanites, has shed much light on certain passages of the OT, not merely by elucidating the meaning of common elements but even more by revealing the distinctive interpretation Israel has given such stories in adapting them to her understanding of the nature of her God Yahweh. E.g. an ancient Semitic myth saw the origin of heaven and earth as the result of a primeval warfare between the chaos-dragon force of water and a god of order. Traces of this myth appear in a number of OT poetic passages (e.g. Pss. 74:13-14; 89:10; Isa. 27:1; 51:9-10), and the author of Gen. 1:1–2:4a seems to have borrowed parts of the Babylonian version of it in composing his own account of creation by the power and purpose of the one universal God. The brief story of the origin of the "mighty men . . . of old" (Gen. 6:1-4) seems to be a fragment of ancient myth, and the following flood story (Gen. 6:5-9:29) is full of mythological motifs which may be compared with those of the flood stories in the Babylonian epics.

Short Story. Storytelling was an art among the ancient Hebrews, and biblical stories are known for their perfection of this art. No art is included in the OT for its own sake, however, and every story has its significant point. Ruth is an excellent example of the short story in its characterization, narrative movement and suspense, and direct use of the simplest and most effective language. It makes the point of respect for the foreigner by bringing to life an incident from the traditional history of King David's family. Other OT short stories are Jonah, which shows the absurdity of provincialism, and Esth., which defends religious freedom in the face of persecution and gives the traditional basis for the observance of Purim.

III. Historical Traditions

Legends. When poetry and poetic prose merge with history the poetic element is still present. Ruth has become a part of the traditional history. The stories of Balaam's ass (Num. 22:21-35) and of Joseph and Potiphar's wife (Gen. 39), which has its parallel in an Egyptian tale, have found their place in the history of Israel's origins. The legend is the literary form in which the tale and history meet. The legends of Samson's encounters with the Philistines (Judg. 13-16) have some of the motifs of hero tales but are also connected with historical wars between the Danites and their neighbors. The stories of Gideon (Judg. 6-8), Jephthah (Judg. 11-12), and David's killing of Goliath (I Sam. 17) belong to this same type.

The sacred legends recounting the origins of sanctuaries represent another type, and seem to come from the earliest times. Jacob's dream at Bethel (Gen. 28:10-22) is now associated with Yahweh, the God of Israel; but the name of the city, Bethel, "house of El," shows that the place was originally a cultic center of the pre-Israelite Canaanite god El. The sacred legend was no doubt adopted by Israel and told and retold as long as worship continued at Bethel. The form in which we have the story, a conflation of 2 strands of tradition (see comment), probably represents a late stage in this process of retelling.

History. Israel's sense of the importance of history is evident in the proportion of OT literature recounting her historical traditions. The court history of David in II Sam. 9-20; I Kings 1-2 is one of the important historical writings of the ancient world, dating well before the work of the Greek historians and very different from the self-glorifying monuments set up by contemporary Near Eastern kings. In these chs. we have an accurate account of David's reign, probably written soon after the events occurred. Other eyewitness accounts are Nehemiah's memoirs (most of Neh. 1-7; 11-13) and Baruch's biography of Jeremiah (Jer. 26-29; 32-45).

In most other historical narratives in the OT, however, there is much more evidence of oral tradition and its influence. The scope of the earliest account of the origins of Israel (J; see "The Compiling of Israel's Story," pp. 1082-89), from the time of Abraham through the establishment of the nation in its land according to the blessing and purpose of God, requires an amazing sense of history. Here, however, we are dealing with traditions handed down orally for centuries, and certainly shaped by the telling. In the tales of origins and of the deeds of patriarchs and heroes the poetic and symbolic elements are apparent. Our awareness of Israel's respect for history combines with our modern desire to separate "what really happened" from these ancient accounts, and we tend to be confused by this material. But such a separation has no meaning in Israel's ancient oral culture. It is the writer who wants an accurate historical source in the modern sense. The teller or the listener wants the meaning of the event, the significance of the names, the right word to express the sense of the occasion. In the hearing and telling of stories the symbolic has no less meaning than the literal, in fact more. Poetry is present as well as history. If we read these stories with a sense of their being told, we can appreciate both their history and their poetry.

IV. Law

One other major form of OT literature is law (see "The Law Codes of Israel," pp. 1090-94). Here again the oral process is important. Decisions were transmitted and instructions recited by priestly groups. Such teaching—*torah,* usually translated "law," lit. means "teaching"—is often in the apodictic, i.e. absolute form (e.g. "You shall not wrong a stranger," Exod. 22:21) as distinguished from the casuistic, i.e. case law (e.g. "If a man steals an ox . . . , he shall make restitution," Exod. 22:1), which is common in the law codes of the ancient Near East. The case-law form is predominant in Exod. 21:1–22:17, and many of these laws are found also in the great Babylonian law code of Hammurabi, dating from the early part of the 2nd millenium B.C.

V. Oral Tradition

It is the awareness of oral transmission—the shaping of accounts and traditions by their telling and by the occasions on which they were told—which has had the most important recent influence on the study of the literary forms of the OT. Hermann Gunkel first applied this approach, known as form criticism, in his brilliant commentary on Gen. (1901), and students of both the OT and the NT are still gaining new understanding from his methods. Everything said above about the origins of literary types in oral forms shows the influence of form criticism.

The majority of these literary types were already present in the literature of the ancient Near East. Gunkel emphasized this common heritage in his analysis of the literary forms of the OT, and this aspect of biblical study has become increasingly important with the continued discovery and decipherment of ancient texts. Israel's distinctive contribution to thought and literature can be seen clearly only against this background of the literary and cultural traditions she held in common with her neighbors.

There is of course written literature in the OT, but it belongs within the larger oral tradition. E.g. the developed themes of Isa. 40-55, the extended dramatic treatment of wisdom poetry in Job, and the essay treatment of prose wisdom forms in Eccl. seem to be the culmination of earlier oral forms. The literary forms we have are almost all integral parts of a long and changing process of oral tradition. Songs of joy and grief, hymns and liturgies for worship, wisdom meditations, proverbs, riddles, prophetic oracles, parable, allegory and apocalyptic, fable, myth, short story, historical tradition, legend, and law—all have their place in actual occasions in the life of a people. This variety of form is a delight to the reader who encounters in it Israel herself, in all the various aspects of her life.

For Further Study. E. G. King, *Early Religious Poetry of the Hebrews,* 1911. G. B. Gray, *The Forms of Hebrew Poetry,* 1915. Aage Bentzen, *Intro. to the OT,* 1948. J. B. Pritchard, ed., *Ancient Near Eastern Texts Relating to the OT,* 1950; an anthology of many forms of literature of Israel's neighbors. S. H. Blank, "Fable," "Proverb," "Riddle," T. H. Gaster, "Myth, Mythology," N. K. Gottwald, "Poetry, Hebrew," Sigmund Mowinckel, "Legend," "Literature," Lucetta Mowry, "Parable," W. F. Stinespring, "Irony and Satire," in *IDB,* 1962.

THE COMPILING OF ISRAEL'S STORY

J. Philip Hyatt

The telling of Israel's story comprises a large part of the OT, approximately a 3rd of the whole. This is characteristic of the Israelites, for they placed great emphasis on history. Theirs was a historical religion, both in the sense that it had a history and in the sense that they viewed the acts of their God in the ongoing events of their life as very important. Their God Yahweh was not for them primarily a nature deity, but one who at a certain time had chosen, had made a covenant with them, and then had been in control of their history. He revealed himself by what he did for them over a long span of time.

Thus we should not be surprised that the Israelites wrote the first genuine history in antiquity—and did it some 400 or 500 years before Herodotus, the Greek author generally reputed to be the "father of history." Only 2 nations in antiquity had a strong sense of history, Greece and Israel, and the latter nation developed it first.

Israel told her story in various forms: in poetry, in legends of various types, and in narrative history. The earliest recitals of their story, or of outstanding moments in it, were doubtless in poetic form, handed down orally. Two of the earliest poems in the OT are recitals of such outstanding events: the Song of the Sea in Exod. 15:1-18 (of which vss. 1-12 are the oldest part) tells how Yahweh saved his people as they left Egypt, and the Song of Deborah in Judg. 5 recounts the victory which Yahweh won for Israel near Megiddo. Legends passed through an oral stage before they were written down. The subject of the various literary forms and their transmission is dealt with in the article "The Literary Forms of the OT" (pp. 1077-81). The present article is concerned with the various historical books of the OT —how they were composed, edited, and put into the form in which we now have them, and their nature and value.

I. The Pentateuch

The first 5 books of the OT are variously known as the 5 Books of Moses, the Pentateuch, or the Torah. The last is the Jewish designation. "Torah" is often translated as "The Law," but the word means far more than that. It means "instruction" or even "revelation." The Torah contains both legal prescriptions and narratives which instructed the Israelite in what he should do and what he should know concerning his early history. Much of it is taken up with legal prescriptions (see "The Law Codes of Israel," pp. 1090-94). We are here concerned with the narratives of the Pentateuch, within which the laws were placed.

Though these books are often referred to as the 5 Books of Moses, scholars long ago proved that Moses is not their author. This is clearly shown by the presence of strikingly different styles and vocabularies in various parts, anachronisms, duplicate or even triplicate narratives of the same incident, evidence of developing theological concepts and legal requirements, and outright disagreements in the laws and narratives that would not have existed if they had come from the pen of one man. OT scholars believe that the Pentateuch is the result of a process of composition and editing that extended over some 5 cents. This makes the work far more valuable as a historical source than it would be if it had been composed by Moses.

There are in the Pentateuch 3 interwoven strands of material, known by the symbols J, E, and P, and one large block, known as D, comprising most of Deut. Some scholars prefer to speak of the composition of the Hexateuch, the first 6 books of the OT, because they believe that the 3 strands extend through Josh. It is very doubtful, however, that P extends into that book, and we cannot be certain that J and E do.

The Yahwist Strand. The earliest strand is the Yahwist, or J. The symbol J is derived from the first letter of the divine name "Jahveh," now usually spelled "Yahweh" to accord with its pronunciation, which this narrative employs in Gen. "Yahweh" may be recognized in the RSV, KJV, and most other English translations by the small capital letters in "the LORD" or, when following the Hebrew word for "Lord," "GOD." This account specifically says that in the time of Adam's grandson Enosh "men began to call upon the name of the LORD," i.e. worship Yahweh (Gen. 4:26). The symbol J reminds us also that this narrative was written in Judah. However, there is not much in it that is specifically Judean. It was written at a time when Israel was united, very probably in the era of Solomon (*ca.* 950).

The Yahwist—as we may call the individual chiefly responsible for the J strand—was a literary genius and one of the most creative authors in the history of Israelite literature. He wrote an epic of monumental proportions. Beginning with the account of the creation of man and the animals (his first words now preserved being in Gen. 2:4b) he extended his story to the conquest of Canaan. He may have begun with the creation of the universe, but if so his account of it has been omited in favor of the P account (Gen. 1:1–2:4a).

In the early chs. of Gen. the Yahwist told of the first sin and the expulsion of Adam and Eve from Eden, the first murder, the beginning of arts and crafts, the Flood, and the tower of Babel. Then he related the story of the patriarchs, beginning with the significant promise to Abraham: "I will make of you a great nation, and I will bless you, and make your name great, so that you will be a blessing. . . . By you all the families of the earth will bless themselves" (Gen. 12:2-3). He related the descent into Egypt of Jacob and his sons, the oppression there, the exodus from Egypt, the covenant at Sinai, and the wandering in the desert.

It is very probable that the Yahwist also told of the conquest of Canaan, but only fragments of his account of it have survived. They are outside the Pentateuch, in Josh. 13:13; 15:13-19, 63; 16:10; 17:11-18; 19:47 and Judg. 1. Some scholars believe that the Yahwist continued his narrative even down through the time of David and the coronation of Solomon—i.e. to the verge of his own era.

There are some inconsistencies in the J narrative. As a consequence some OT scholars subdivide it into J^1 and J^2 or the like, assigning J^1 to one author and J^2 to another author at a later date. While we must recognize that J does contain inconsistencies, so that some parts of it appear to be more primitive than others, we can account for them by viewing the Yahwist as a collector of traditions who did not always trouble himself to reconcile them. He gathered his traditional materials from many different sources —Canaanite legends, Israelite legends, and possibly written records. He put them into a sequence and conceived the epic which we now have.

The Yahwist wrote in a lively style that is simple but very effective. He could characterize individuals in a few sentences and tell a story with a minimum of words. He was somewhat pessimistic about man and his own nation Israel, but he had great faith in the promises of Yahweh and his ability to fulfill them. His story is about how the purposes of Yahweh triumphed over all the obstacles of stubborn and rebellious men, both in Israel and in other nations. His conception of Yahweh is not of a highly "supernatural" deity who works through miracles and unusual irruptions into history. Yahweh works through persons and through what appear to be almost natural events of everyday life. The Yahwist believed that Yahweh was Isarel's only God, the only deity that the people needed to take into account.

The Yahwist provided the basic and fundamental narrative of Israel's story from creation to the conquest of Canaan (if not beyond). Others were to add to it, but they did not alter it substantially.

The Elohist Strand. The next strand is the Elohist, or E. The name is derived from the fact that this strand uses the divine name "Elohim," translated "God," until after the revelation of the name "Yahweh" to Moses in Exod. 3:15. The symbol E can also be associated with Ephraim, a name used for the N kingdom, whose traditions this narrative repre-

sents. The date is usually thought to have been in the 8th cent. Some scholars, however, think of E as being chronologically parallel to J rather than its successor.

E is not as well preserved as J. As it is usually analyzed, E begins in Gen. 15 in the story of Abraham and goes to the conquest of Canaan, but in the latter part of the history E and J are frequently difficult to disentangle. Because of its fragmentary nature some scholars even doubt that E ever existed as a separate document, seeing the E material rather as a series of additions to J or else attributing it to the other narratives. However, there are enough sections that are significantly different from J to justify belief that E should be considered as a separate narrative. Some of its characteristic features may be seen in Gen. 20, which is the E parallel to the J story in Gen. 12:10-20; in Gen. 22, the story of the intended sacrifice of Isaac; in much of the Joseph story, for Joseph was a hero of the N tribes; and in Exod. 3:6, 9b-15, 19.

The style of the Elohist author or authors is more elaborate and usually contains more detail than that of the Yahwist, and the theology seems to be somewhat more advanced. God often appears in dreams and visions rather than directly, and the ethical standards represented by E are a little higher than those of J, as in the patriarchal narratives. Moses is a more heroic figure, and the miraculous is more evident in some of the stories.

Deuteronomy. The D material comes next chronologically. However, it is not a strand in the Pentateuchal narrative but a book included all in one piece, now found as most of Deut. It will be discussed in detail in the next section. D is mostly law of a special type. Here it may be noted that Deut. 1–3 contains a summary of events from Sinai to the arrival at the point from which Moses is assumed to be speaking in D. Deut. 34 relates the death and burial of Moses; part of this is from the J strand.

The Priestly Narrative. The final strand of the Pentateuch is that symbolized by P, derived from the fact that it was written by priestly authors after the Babylonian exile, probably *ca.* 400. P begins with the majestic, noble account of the creation of the universe and of man in Gen. 1:1–2:4a and continues almost as far as J (we cannot now identify a P account of the conquest of Canaan). The Pentateuch contains a very large block of P material, Exod. 35:1–Num. 10:11, which is mostly of a legal nature. P is interested mainly in setting forth the priestly law regulating the ritual of the temple, the priesthood, the festivals, etc. Insofar as P relates history, the principal interest is in showing the origin in history of the various religious institutions and practices. Gen. 17 (the rite of circumcision) is a good example of the P style and interest.

P divides history into four eras, each of which began with a divine revelation, the 2nd and 3rd being marked by a covenant: (*a*) From Adam to Noah. God instituted the sabbath, and man was vegetarian. (*b*) From Noah to Abraham. A covenant was made with Noah: man was allowed to eat meat, but without blood, and murder was prohibited. The rainbow was a sign of this covenant. (*c*) From Abraham to Moses. God was revealed as God Almighty, and a covenant was made with Abraham, of which circumcision was the sign. (d) Beginning with Moses, to whom God's name Yahweh was first revealed (Exod. 6:2-3). P does not tell of a covenant with Moses, perhaps because that with Abraham was considered sufficient as the covenant with the Israelite people. P conceives of religious progress in terms of insistence on the divine election of Israel and the disapproval of intermarriage with outsiders. This concept of history is suggested even in J, but P makes it explicit.

While the P authors could occasionally write prose that is exalted and inspiring, as in the first ch. of Gen., their style is often monotonous and detailed, frequently given over to genealogical lists, series of numbers, and elaborate ritualistic details. The style and vocabulary of P are very easy to distinguish from J and E, whereas J and E cannot always be distinguished from each other with certainty.

The P narrative sometimes incorporates old material that may be authentic, but in general it is not as valuable for the reconstruction of the actual history of Israel as J and E. This can be readily explained by its late date and its special interests.

The 4 groups of material J, E, D, and P were combined by redactors (i.e. editors) in 3 principal stages: (a) J and E were put together, probably in the first half of the 7th cent., by a redactor or redactors identified by the symbol R^{JE}. He, or they, did not work in a slavish or mechanical manner. Sometimes he preserved part of one intact and omitted the corresponding portion of the other; sometimes he preserved duplicate stories from both; sometimes he rewrote both (particularly in Num.), and occasionally he made additions or changes to harmonize the 2 or bring them up to date. (b) JE was subsequently combined with D by a redactor or redactors symbolized as R^{JED}. In the process he made some judicious additions to JE in order to bring it into accord with D ideas. This redactor was probably the same person or persons who edited the D histories to be discussed in the next section, ca. 550. (c) Finally, JED was combined with P by the redactor or redactors known as R^{JEDP}. He preserved both JED and P almost intact and made only a few editorial additions. Some scholars think, however, that P never existed as a separate document but was composed as a supplement to JED. When JEDP was at last produced, probably in the 4th cent., the Pentateuch was complete, except for very minor changes or additions made prior to the crystallization of the OT canon (see "The Making of the OT Canon," pp. 1209-15).

II. THE DEUTERONOMIC HISTORIES

The Pentateuch, which we have just surveyed, is partly legal material, and partly narrative that is a combination of legend and history. The books which we consider now are most often referred to as "historical books." The Jewish canon calls them the Former Prophets. They comprise the books of Josh., Judg., I-II Sam., I-II Kings. The history which they cover extends from the choice of Joshua to succeed Moses as leader to the time in 561 when the exiled Judean king Jehoiachin was released from prison in Babylon (II Kings 25:27). While these books contain some legendary stories, they were compiled and edited in a time when the writing of genuine history was possible.

These books must be considered as a great block of historical narrative that was brought together by an editor or, more probably, a group of editors known as the Deuteronomists. Most scholars agree that, whatever may be the origin of the sources used by these editors, all of the books show marks of their editing. Since the nature of the editing differs in the various books, it seems likely that more than one person was involved, i.e. a school of editors. Their date was ca. 550, though, as noted below, in II Kings there is evidence for dating 2 periods of editing.

The editors are called Deuteronomists and designated as D because they show great affinity in both style and ideas with the D material of Deut. In fact it is well to think of Deut. as introducing this large corpus of historical narrative. In order to understand the historical books we must first consider Deut. and the religious reformation which was based on it.

Deut., or its original nucleus (probably Deut. 5-28), is believed by most critical OT scholars to be the "book of the law" or "book of the covenant" which was found by Hilkiah the priest in the Jerusalem temple in 622 and was made the basis of far-reaching religious reforms by King Josiah (II Kings 22:8-23:25). In these reforms the king purified the worship in the Jerusalem temple, destroyed the various local sanctuaries, abolished divination and various superstitious practices, and held a great celebration of the passover. Deut. is considered to be that book because it is the only part of the OT which appears to prescribe the reforms made by Josiah. In addition to prescribing the purification and centralization of worship, Deut. sets forth many social regulations for commerce, administration of justice, family life, etc., in which prophetic principles were incorporated.

It was the discovery of Deut. and the resulting reformation which undoubtedly stimulated the D editors to compile the historical books as a demonstration of the working out of the principles of Deut. in the history of Israel. In joining their work to Deut. they added before its original introduction, chs. 5-11, a new introduction, chs. 1-4, to the whole corpus consisting of Deut., Josh., Judg., Sam., and Kings. Since the last 2 originally were single books, we may think of the 5 as comprising a D "Pentateuch."

The D historians edited these books in accordance with certain general principles based on Deut. which they employed in selecting their materials, rewriting old materials, composing new sections, and passing value judgments on various persons and events. Three principles were of paramount importance to them: (a) The principle of the single sanctuary: Yahweh should be worshiped only at the central sanctuary in Jerusalem after it had been built by Solomon, and there only with a pure form of worship. This represented cultic orthodoxy to D. (b) The principle of divine retribution: God rewards those who are righteous and obedient to his will and punishes those who are disobedient and wicked. (c) The principle of God's fulfillment of his word, usually given through a prophet. We should add to these principles the fact that the D historians had an interest in chronology and attempted to put into these books a chronological scheme that shows an interest in history writing.

The intros. in this volume to the individual books of the corpus discuss details of their composition and editing, but we may here survey briefly the way in which the D historians edited their books and the nature of the sources on which they worked.

Josh. relates the conquest of Canaan, the division of the land among the tribes, and the renewal of the covenant by Joshua and the people at Shechem. Some scholars believe that the J and E sources of the Pentateuch continue through this book. It is very difficult, however, to separate the 2, and it seems very probable that the D historians rewrote the story in order to make it appear to have been a quick and complete conquest by the united tribes under Joshua. They used older sources which may have included J and E.

As indicated above, there are traces of a J account of the conquest in scattered passages in Josh. 13–19. It is almost inconceivable that J should not have told of Canaan's conquest, since this narrative constantly looks forward to Israel's receiving the Promised Land. Josh. 24 is usually assigned to E. The division of the tribes in Josh. 13–21 has often been assigned to P, but it is likely that these chs. also are from the D editors, who wrote them on the basis of official lists of the S tribes of the 7th cent. and older traditions of the N tribes. If this is true, we may conjecture that the J and E narratives continued into the period of the conquest, but not P. In its present form, however, Josh. is a D book, and precise identification of its sources throughout is impossible.

Judg. opens with a summary of the conquest, relates the history of the various judges who ruled Israel between Joshua and Samuel, and closes with 2 stories about the migration of Dan and the war against Benjamin. Here the D editors have employed a different method from that used in Josh. They have taken a group of traditional stories about heroes who lived in the period of the settlement in Canaan (which may be J or E narratives, but are more likely not), and provided for them a historical framework. In this framework we see the D conception of the nature of this period: it was a continuous series of cycles of apostasy from Yahweh, oppression by a foreign enemy because of Yahweh's anger, outcry of the people for help, and deliverance by a judge who saved them from oppression and then ruled over them for a period of time, after which a new cycle began. The D philosophy of history is well summarized in Judg. 2:11-23. The D editors are responsible also for the chronological scheme in which the judges are presented.

The D edition of Judg. probably included only the central core of the book, 2:6–16:31, without the stories of the "minor" judges in 3:31; 10:1-5; 12:8-15. It almost certainly did not contain the summary account of the conquest in 1:1–2:5 (which is based largely on J material), and it may not have included all of the Samson stories and the stories about the Danites and Benjaminites. However, it is somewhat difficult to believe that the unsavory stories at the end of the book were added in late times, when there was a tendency to idealize the past.

I-II Sam., originally a single book, relate the history from Samuel's birth to just before David's death. This was the extremely important era when the monarchy was formed and the first 2 kings ruled.

These books show clear traces of composition from differing sources or traditions. E.g. in I Sam. 9:1–10:16 Saul is secretly anointed to be king by Samuel at the express direction of Yahweh, but in I Sam. 8:1-22; 10:17-27 Samuel reluctantly consents to anoint Saul and declares the people's demand for a monarchy to be a rejection of Yahweh. There are a number of duplicate accounts in the book—e.g. the origin of the proverb "Is Saul also among the prophets?" (I Sam. 10:9-12; 19:18-24), and David's flight from Saul (I Sam. 19:11-17; 20:35-42). Some scholars believe that the book is composed largely of the combination of 2 documents, which they call the Early Source and the Late Source. The former is friendly to the monarchy and on the whole a very reliable historical document; the latter is opposed to the monarchy and often is more homiletical than historical. In the opinion of a few scholars these 2 sources are continuations of J and E of the Pentateuch. Some who subdivide J see 3 sources continued here.

More recently several scholars have denied that we can identify only 2 or 3 sources. They see in Sam. a series of independent units that were subsequently placed together and expanded at various points, the major units being a legend of the infancy of Samuel, the story of the ark, a history of the monarchy that was favorable to its establishment, an unfavorable history of the establishment of the monarchy, and a history of the reign of David in Jerusalem. The last is sometimes called the Court History of David, or the Story of the Throne Succession of David (II Sam. 9–20; I Kings 1–2, to which the original portion of II Sam. 7 is often prefixed).

Whatever position one takes concerning these sources, we must recognize that Sam. contains unusually objective and authentic history, especially in the Court History of David. For the first time we have the writing of what can be called history in the usual modern sense of that word. The Court History was obviously written by either an eyewitness of the events or one who had firsthand information about them. He writes a straightforward narrative with a minimum of moralizing. While he sees the hand of Yahweh in the events, he thinks of Yahweh as working through persons and through the occurrences of secular life rather than in a miraculous manner. In the opinion of some scholars the author of this Court History was absolutely the first historian in antiquity; other scholars give this honor to the author of the Early Source, or to the Yahwist, if they conceive of his work as extending through the time of Samuel.

The D editors did not work extensively on Sam., probably because they saw little in it that needed modification. They did not choose to magnify David or to eliminate the accounts which attributed sin to him. They very probably composed, or revised, the speech of Samuel in I Sam. 12; it expresses clearly the D principle of divine retribution. They may have contributed a few other passages, e.g. I Sam. 2:27-36; 3:12-14 and some vss. in II Sam. 7. It is not probable, as some scholars have suggested, that they wrote the long antimonarchic sections.

I-II Kings, also originally a single book, relate the history of the Israelite monarchies from the death of David to the release of King Jehoiachin from prison.

This writing is our principal source of information for 4 cents. of Israel's story and an excellent example of the D. work. In it the editors had a good opportunity to show the importance and interrelationship of 2 of their basic principles: cultic orthodoxy and divine retribution.

We are told the names of some of the sources employed by the D historians. At the end of the reign of Solomon we read: "Now the rest of the acts of Solomon, and all that he did, and his wisdom, are they not written in the book of the acts of Solomon?" (I Kings 11:41). This book, which they undoubtedly used, must have been not simply a bare chronicle or annalistic account of Solomon's reign but a mixture of legends and of history which told of his activities and wisdom. Similarly we read of the "Book of the Chronicles of the Kings of Israel" (I Kings 14:19 and 16 other places) and the "Book of the Chronicles of the Kings of Judah" (I Kings 14:29 and 14 other places). These were perhaps official annals kept by scribes at the 2 royal courts. In addition they apparently used other sources, including the end of the Court History of David (I Kings 1–2); popular narratives concerning Elijah, Elisha, and possibly other prophets; a description of the Jerusalem temple, or possibly a history of it; and special narratives concerning particular periods or persons (e.g. Ahab and Isaiah the prophet) of this long span of time.

The task of the D editors was to select the materials which they wished to use, provide the whole with a chronological framework, and compose some sections, especially those in which they passed judgment on the various kings. A fine example of a long D composition is Solomon's address to the people and prayer to Yahweh at the dedication of the temple (I Kings 8:15-53).

The D editors of Kings made a bold effort to provide a chronological framework by an elaborate system that includes not only the lengths of the reigns of the successive kings but also synchronisms between the kings of Israel and Judah. These figures are very valuable for the modern student but involve difficulties because totals for the 2 kingdoms do not match. The discrepancies have generally been thought due to errors in transmission of the text, but recently many scholars have accepted a theory that attributes them to different methods of calculating accession dates in the respective kingdoms, complicated by coregencies of some of the kings with their successors (see "Chronology," pp. 1271-82).

The D editors passed judgment on the Hebrew kings on the basis of their view that legitimate worship of Yahweh could take place only in the Jerusalem temple and that Yahweh always rewards obedience and punishes evil. Thus they condemn all of the kings of the N kingdom because they permitted worship in N sanctuaries and explain the fall of that kingdom as punishment for its people's sins (cf. II Kings 17:7-18). Among the kings of Judah they have unqualified words of praise for only Hezekiah and Josiah. They give qualified approval to 5 others, but in each case point out that they did not remove the high places and permitted the people to worship at them.

It seems very likely that there were 2 D editions of Kings. There are passages in the book which appear not to know of the destruction of Jerusalem and

the temple (I Kings 8:8; 9:21; 11:36; II Kings 8:19), whereas others indicate knowledge of this disaster and of the exile of the Jews (I Kings 8:46-53; 9:6-9; II Kings 21:11-15; 22:16-17; chs. 24–25). Some scholars interpret the prediction in II Kings 22:20 as indicating that the authors of the first D edition were unaware of the violent death of Josiah at Megiddo and thus wrote shortly before that event. Other scholars interpret it as the actual words of Huldah the prophetess, which were quoted accurately even though unfulfilled, and date this edition just before the fall of Jerusalem and the beginning of the Babylonian exile.

The 2nd group of D editors must have lived after 561, the date of Jehoiachin's release from prison. Thus they are ordinarily placed ca. 550. It was probably this 2nd group, living in the middle of the 6th cent., who edited Josh., Judg., and Sam., wrote II Kings 24–25, and made some editorial additions to earlier parts of Kings.

Writing in the middle of the 6th cent., after the Exile had begun, these editors lived in a time of pessimism and of resignation to divine retribution. Their work is thus somewhat gloomy, and it shows little or no feeling for the mission which Israel was given among the nations of the earth. The books do not end on a note of hope, though some scholars have taken the release of Jehoiachin from prison as a faint glimmer of hope for the renewal of the Davidic dynasty. Yet the accomplishments of the D editors in compiling their books of history were monumental, and they deserve the deep gratitude of every reader of the Bible.

III. The Chronicler's History

I-II Chr., Ezra, and Neh. are included in English Bibles among the historical books, but in the Jewish canon they are found in the division known as the Writings. This fact is of significance and can give us a clue to the time of their writing, for this 3rd division was the latest to be canonized and generally includes books written relatively late (see "The Making of the OT Canon," pp. 1209-15).

We may consider I-II Chr., Ezra, and Neh. together as a single work, for critical study has shown that they are from the same author-editor, usually called simply the Chronicler. This is evident from several facts: the last 2 vss. of II Chr. are repeated as the opening vss. of Ezra; the style and vocabulary of the editorial parts of these books are very similar; the same interests and ideas are generally found throughout.

Taken as a whole, these books cover a very long span of history—from Adam to Ezra and Nehemiah, i.e. from creation to ca. 400 B.C. or later. This period is covered, however, in various ways. The long era from Adam to Saul is quickly dispensed with in the first 9 chs. by a long list of genealogies, with very little narrative. The Chronicler dismisses Saul as an unfaithful king in a single ch. that tells of Saul's death. Then he devotes a long section (I Chr. 11–29) to the reign of David, emphasizing his role as the one who made all the plans and preparations for the building of the temple and the organization of its clergy. In II Chr. the first 9 chs. describe the reign of Solomon and the remaining 27 cover the 2 kingdoms of Israel and Judah and the Babylonian exile. Little space is given to the N kingdom but much to Judah. The book ends with Cyrus' decree permitting the Jews to return to their homeland.

Ezra and Neh. relate the return of Jews to the land of Judah, the rebuilding of the temple and its rededication, and the activities of Ezra and Nehemiah. These books are clearly from the same hand, but in their present form a number of sections are disarranged. The modern reader must rearrange the 2 books in order to read the account in chronological order (see Intro. to Ezra and Neh.).

This is obviously a long and ambitious work. It is our primary source of information about the return from exile and the early postexilic period. However, Chr. covers almost the same span of history as the Pentateuch and the D histories. Careful study has shown that the Chronicler knew and made use of the OT books from Gen. to Kings (except Judg. and Ruth), esp. Sam. and Kings. Approximately half of Chr. is taken from other OT books, often verbatim. We are therefore immediately faced with the question of why the Chronicler wrote a history about a long period which had already been dealt with in biblical narratives. Did he have additional sources of information? Or did he wish to rewrite history because he wanted to make emphases not found in the earlier books and express ideas in which he had a special interest?

The answer to our basic question is found in the latter suggestion. It cannot be proved that the Chronicler had better sources of information than the earlier historians (though he may have had at some points), but we can show that he had special interests and wanted to set forth emphases that prevailed in the time when he lived.

The large space which he devotes to David gives a clue to one of his interests. He wished to picture David as the founder of the temple and of its ritual and clergy. He omits the scandalous story of the adultery of David and Bathsheba and its consequences. His David is an ideal king, the founder of the temple cult.

The Chronicler was interested in showing the legitimacy of the holy community in Judah after the Exile, and of its temple and priesthood. This is one reason for the large amount of space he devotes to genealogies. He wants to show that David and his dynasty were the legitimate possessors of royal authority in Israel. He writes a history of the dynasty of David in terms primarily of its contributions to religion and specifically to the temple cult. The Chronicler shows a special interest in the position of the Levites and of the temple singers. Some scholars have suggested that he was himself a Levitical singer in the postexilic temple.

If the Chronicler is responsible for the stories of Ezra and Nehemiah, he must have written after the time in which they lived. The chronology of these 2 persons and their relationship to each other have been much debated. The most likely date for the first trip of Nehemiah to Jerusalem is 445, the 20th year of Artaxerxes I, and for Ezra 397, the 7th year of Artaxerxes II. The genealogy of the Davidic line in I Chr. 3 is carried to 6 generations beyond Zerubbabel, who lived ca. 520. These and other considerations point to a date in the 4th cent.—or possibly early in the following cent., as some scholars maintain—for the writing of the chronicler's history.

As noted above, one of the sources used by the Chronicler consisted of earlier canonical books, esp. Sam. and Kings. Anyone who makes the comparison will see that he sometimes omitted important portions that did not agree with his purposes, made deft changes here and there, and sometimes made additions that are not found elsewhere in the Bible.

The Chronicler frequently refers to books which he seems to have known and may have used as sources, e.g.: "Book of the Kings of Judah and Israel" (II Chr. 25:26) and a similar work for Israel alone (I Chr. 9:1); "Chronicles of the Kings of Israel" (II Chr. 33:18); "Commentary on the Book of the Kings" (II Chr. 24:27); "Chronicles of Samuel the seer," of "Nathan the prophet," and of "Gad the seer" (I Chr. 29:29); "history of Nathan the prophet," "prophecy of Ahijah the Shilonite," and "visions of Iddo the seer" (II Chr. 9:29); "chronicles of King David" (I Chr. 27:24); and "Laments" (II Chron. 35:25). He refers altogether to nearly 20 such writings.

It is difficult to determine just what is meant by these references. The royal histories may be the canonical books or the chronicles on which they depended. The writings attributed to various prophets and seers probably are portions of the canonical books which were known by such names. The reference to the "Commentary on the Book of the Kings" is esp. puzzling. Was this an expanded edition of Sam. and Kings from which the Chronicler drew much of his material?

In the opinion of many scholars the Chronicler's additions to Sam. and Kings must be looked on with suspicion. E.g. the portrait of David as the one who prepared all of the materials, architectural plans, and organization for the temple is greatly overdrawn; obviously it was inspired by the Chronicler's theological interests. Thus he was capable of rewriting history in his own way to illustrate his own themes. Yet we cannot be dogmatically sure that he did not have some authentic sources of information which were not available to the earlier historians.

In Ezra and Neh. the Chronicler had some valuable source materials. One was the memoirs of Nehemiah, from which he quoted long sections. This was apparently a diary-like composition made by Nehemiah that is authentic and valuable. The Chronicler may also have used Ezra's memoirs, but this is much less certain, for the passages supposedly from these memoirs are in the style of the Chronicler. A few scholars have even gone so far as to declare that Ezra never lived but is a fictitious character invented by the Chronicler. On the other hand a few have said that Ezra himself was the Chronicler.

Even if we are inclined to doubt the dependability of the Chronicler's history of the period covered in Sam. and Kings, we can look on Ezra and Neh. as sources of information that, though sometimes difficult to interpret, are most valuable. In his whole writing we can see many reflections of the consuming interests of the postexilic community in Judah— esp. the concern to prove the claims of its members to be the lineal descendants of ancient Israel, and the legitimacy of the city of Jerusalem, its temple, and the temple worship. For the study of the period in which it was written his history is invaluable.

IV. History in Narrative and Poetry

In the English Bible 2 additional books are usually counted as historical books: Ruth, which is placed immediately after Judg., and Esth., which comes after Neh. In the Hebrew canon these 2 books are included in the 3rd division, the Writings. Specifically they are 2 of the group of books called the 5 Scrolls, which are read by the Jews on special occasions—Ruth at the feast of weeks, and Esth. at the feast of Purim.

Ruth is a classic example of the storyteller's art. It is placed immediately after Judg. because the story it relates is supposed to have taken place in the time of the judges. Yet in its present form Ruth is almost certainly from the postexilic period; the nature of the Hebrew used as well as some other features of the book require such a dating. In the view of many scholars this story of a Moabite great-grandmother of David was written to oppose by adroit indirection the narrow exclusiveness of Ezra and Nehemiah, who forced Jews to divorce non-Jewish wives (Ezra 10; Neh. 13:23-31). It is in any event a wonderful story of human kindness and fidelity that transcend the ordinary limits of self-interest and national loyalty. Many scholars consider it to be historical fiction. It is impossible to determine whether it is pure fiction or rests on an old story, handed down for many generations in oral form, that contained some genuine historical reminiscences.

Esth. is a most unusual book in that it never mentions the name of God and is completely secular. It purports to tell of events in the Persian period and does display some accurate knowledge of Persian customs and names. On the other hand some of the details are either inaccurate or most improbable (see Intro. to Esth.). Like Ruth, this book may rest on a small core of historical verity, or it may be entirely fictional. Its purpose was no doubt to explain the origin of the feast of Purim and probably also to commend its observance.

Pss. It is worth noting that several of the poems in the Psalter are summaries of the history of Israel, or of some significant portion of it. Among these may be listed esp. Pss. 78; 105; 106; 135; 136. The longest, Ps. 78, summarizes the longest span in history. It portrays the disobedience and ingratitude of Israel in spite of God's mighty acts on her behalf. The same mood is found in Ps. 106. On the other hand Pss. 105; 136, express joyful gratitude to God for his wondrous acts in the past. Pss. 135; 136 praise God both for his control over nature and for his control over history. In sections of other pss. we find references to Yahweh's mighty deeds in history, sometimes coupled with his act of creation, as in Pss. 74:1-17; 77:5-20. These pss. show the great importance which the Israelites attached to history and how in their worship they sometimes recited Yahweh's glorious deeds of the past.

V. The Nature of Israel's History Writing

When we use the word "history" we customarily have in mind one of 2 different meanings: (a) We may refer to a series of past events which cluster about some specific interest, such as a nation, an era, a department of culture, an institution, a person, or a group of persons. Those events throw light on the character and significance of the particular interest under consideration. (b) We may refer to a systematic, written account of such events, usually with an interpretation which seeks out causes, influences, and patterns that enable the reader to understand them. If we want to be strict, perhaps we should refer to the first as history and the 2nd as history writing, but such a distinction would be pedantic and is sometimes difficult to make.

Using the word in its first sense, Israel's attitude toward history belongs properly in a discussion of her religion or theology. As already noted, this was a historical religion. It may be added here that the Israelites affirmed the reality of history and of the time process; their religion was never a mysticism which sought to escape from history into a timeless realm of being. Furthermore, they were conscious of the great importance which the past had for their present and their future. They were aware of a yesterday as well as of a today and a tomorrow. That is one of the reasons why they were the first to write history in the 2nd sense.

If we look at the whole of Israel's story as it is presented in the great blocks of narrative discussed in this article, we find that it consists of 3 types of material: (a) origin stories, (b) legends, and (c) history (in the 2nd sense, or closely approaching it). These 3 types cannot always be neatly distinguished, and students of the Bible disagree on the category to which certain parts of the OT should be assigned. Yet it is worth while to characterize each type and show where in general it is to be found.

Origin Stories were told primarily in order to show the origin of some particular thing—a place, a name, a custom, an institution, or a phenomenon of some kind which is found in the world as man knows it. The most striking examples are the stories regarding the primeval beginnings in Gen. 1-11. There we are told of the origin of the universe, of man, of sin, of the various arts, of certain customs and laws, of languages, etc. Origin stories are found in later chs. of Gen. and in some of the later books. E.g. the story in Gen. 32:22-32, which describes Jacob's wrestling with the angel at the Jabbok, is intended to explain the origin of the name Israel, of the place name Peniel, and of a Hebrew dietary custom (vs. 32).

Some scholars call these stories "myth." But they are not myths like those found in classical literature—stories about the conduct and attitudes of the gods in their dealings with one another and sometimes with men. There are occasional fragments of myths in this sense, as in Gen. 6:1-4, but they are not frequent. Furthermore the word "myth" suggests to the popular mind a story that is essentially fictitious and untrue, whereas these origin stories in the OT convey very profound and important religious truths. We may call them myths only if we are very careful to define the term and make sure that it is not misleading.

These origin stories are not historical in the ordinary sense. By their very nature they lie beyond the possibility of historical verification. Yet they are vehicles of great truth and should be read as such.

Legends differ from the preceding in that they usually have a nucleus of historical "happening," though that nucleus is very often difficult or impossible to recover with confidence. Legends were frequently told about heroes of the past, important ancestors of the Israelites who accomplished great feats of deliverance (as the judges did) or were bearers of the promise made by God (as the patriarchs were). Legends are found in Gen. 12–50 and in Josh. and Judg. We should not suppose that these legendary stories are unhistorical. They may rest on historical events and reflect authentic movements. But legends are frequently bound together only loosely, and it is difficult to assess their authenticity and thus their significance for historical reconstruction.

History Writing appears first in Sam. and is found in the succeeding books discussed above. As already noted, genuine history—or history writing proper—made its first appearance in Israel, as well as in human culture, in the Court History of David or perhaps in the Early Source of Sam. It apparently was written in the era of King Solomon.

History writing developed at this time for several reasons. One was that Israel was now a nation immersed in the stream of international life of its day. Only a nation that had made history could write history. Israel had been in existence long enough, first as a people then as a nation, to have developed a consciousness of its own past and of its dependence on that past. In the reign of Solomon, when there was peace and prosperity and literary endeavors were promoted, there were persons capable of collecting the traditions, putting them in order, and writing excellent narrative.

Another factor was that the idea of causality had been developed. I.e. there had developed in Israel an awareness of cause-and-effect sequences in human life, apart from the belief in divine causation which was widely prevalent in the ancient world. Some scholars believe that Israel may have been influenced in this by the Hittites, whose annals and prayers show such a sense of causality.

We can see this factor at work e.g. in the life of David. After he became king he had a large harem, with children by various wives. Conflicts arose among the children, and David in his indulgence took no steps to settle them. Also he refused to make provision for his successor. These factors led to the revolt of Absalom, who drove David out of Jerusalem. But even in his time of retreat David shrewdly took steps to foil the revolutionaries, and in time the revolt was ended and the king returned to Jerusalem. Here the reader sees the effects of a series of human causes, and little emphasis is placed on the ultimate divine cause.

The Israelites did not tell their story in the manner of a modern professional historian. The historian today searches for all possible primary source materials and then exercises critical scrutiny in using them. He tries to distinguish the authentic from the spurious; he selects certain events and factors for emphasis, omitting or placing small stress on others. He wants to discover "what actually happened." He offers his interpretation of past events, movements, and personalities, trying to ferret out causes and influences. He searches for trends and tries to fit the whole into a pattern if possible. Yet the modern historian is inevitably a child of his own time. He is influenced by the intellectual environment in which he has been trained and in which he lives. He has

his own philosophical presuppositions and personal prejudices, of which he may or may not be aware. The best he can do is to try to recognize his presuppositions and prejudices and strive for "objectivity." History must continually be rewritten.

The writers of Israel's story were not completely different from the modern historian. They had to be selective in using their sources, and they wrote in the light of their controlling principles and presuppositions. Yet they were not critical in the modern sense in their use of sources, and they probably were not consciously aware of their presuppositions. They were not so concerned to record "what actually happened" as to present the message of the event.

Looking on Israel's story as a whole we may call it didactic history—i.e. history that was told for the purpose of teaching the readers what they should know. Or we may call it kerygmatic history, history that was told in order to proclaim Israel's faith in God and in what he had done in the course of the past for Israel and for the nations. Their history proclaimed Yahweh as the God who had created the world and had guided the course of their history. He performed mighty acts of deliverance and salvation (esp. in the exodus from Egypt), but also made demands on Israel, punishing her for disobedience and holding out the hope of reward for obedience.

In presenting Israel's story the successive authors and editors had their own presuppositions and emphases. At times these coincided with, or supplemented, one another, but at times they conflicted. They did not always agree concerning details.

All of this means that the modern student of the historical books of the OT may read them for 2 different purposes.

On the one hand he may read them seeking to learn the actual course of events and what the personalities involved in them were and did. These can be learned only through careful, critical study, and biblical scholars often disagree in their reconstructions of the history of Israel. This is inevitable. Historians in any field do not agree completely in their interpretations of the past, and the nature of the OT narratives places added burdens on the modern historian. The fact that the OT is part of a sacred book makes the task doubly difficult. Sometimes we must conclude that we cannot with confidence discover "what actually happened."

On the other hand the modern student can read the historical books of the OT to discover how, at successive periods, the Israelites interpreted their own history. He can see the faith concerning it that they held and wished to teach or proclaim to others. We have the materials for the study of the history of the traditions of Israel concerning her own past, and this is often of great value. We can know the history of Israel's faith, even if we cannot always know the course of events as well as we might wish.

For Further Study: Intros. to the OT, e.g. by S. R. Driver, 9th ed., 1913; W. O. E. Oesterley and T. H. Robinson, 1934; A. Bentzen, 2nd ed., 1952; R. H. Pfeiffer, rev. ed., 1953. C. R. North, *The OT Interpretation of History,* 1946. H. H. Rowley, ed., *The OT and Modern Study,* 1951, chs. III, IV. R. C. Dentan, ed., *The Idea of History in the Ancient Near East,* 1955. John Bright, *Early Israel in Recent History Writing,* 1956. D. N. Freedman, "Pentateuch" in *IDB,* 1962.

THE LAW CODES OF ISRAEL

Norman K. Gottwald

To understand Israelite law we should first place it in the context of other Near Eastern laws, then examine its forms ranging from the separate prescriptions through the smaller and larger collections, and finally consider its origin, development, and religious import.

I. Ancient Near Eastern Law Codes

Our knowledge of Near Eastern law, apart from the Bible, has been notably though unevenly extended during the last cent. Laws from Mesopotamia (Sumerian, Old Babylonian, Assyrian) and from Asia Minor (Hittite) are available in some fullness; to date Canaanite (except for a few valuable priestly lists) and Egyptian laws have not been uncovered.

In probable chronological order the collections known to us, with their approximate dates, locales (see color map 2), and contents, are as follows:

Ur-Nammu Code, 2040-2027, from Sumerian Ur: a prologue and 22 laws in fragmentary state.

Bilalama Code, 1930, from Akkadian Eshnunna: a preamble, identifying the lawgiver, city, and date, and 59 laws.

Lipit-Ishtar Code, 1864-1854, from Sumerian Isin: a prologue with the lawgiver's credentials, approximately 38 laws partially preserved, and an epilogue recounting the erection of a stele bearing the text of the laws.

Hammurabi Code, 1728-1686, from Amorite Babylon: an adulatory prologue, 282 laws governing a wide range of economic and social relations and transactions, and an admonitory epilogue (similar in character to that of the Lipit-Ishtar Code). This code is both more inclusive and more complex than any of the preceding, but that it is built on them or on similar preceding codes is evident.

Hittite Laws, 1400-1200, from Hattusa: 200 laws, without prologue, epilogue, or king specified as the codifier.

Middle Assyrian Laws, 1114-1076, from Asshur: 116 laws, some in very fragmentary form, without prologue or epilogue. The text dates from the time of Tiglath-Pileser I but the laws may be cents. older.

Neo-Babylonian Laws, 626-539, from Babylon: 9 laws surviving out of an original 13, without preface or conclusion.

We may call the first 4 of the above legal compilations "codes" in the sense that their accompanying prologues and epilogues indicate that their publication was the work of particular kings. That the re-maining 3 do not give such information may be due to the accidents of textual transmission, since it is likely that all the collections were issued under royal directives.

The term "code" should be used, however, with considerable caution. We do not have in view systematic publication of an entire body of civil law, as in the codes of Justinian and Napoleon. More properly the ancient Near Eastern code is a modest attempt to sum up and bring some order into the growing body of common law. Such codes are less a matter of exhaustive prescriptions than of illustrative precedents. Old and new materials stand side by side and the order of the laws often lacks discernible rationality.

The Near Eastern law collections show emphatic parallels to Israel's laws—e.g. the Hittite treatment of rape, the Assyrian preservation of the practice of levirate marriage (see comment on Deut. 25:5-10), and such features in the Hammurabi Code as a trend toward the substitution of fines for the death penalty in cases of theft, the principle of retaliation, similar punishments for similar crimes, and the oath of purgation before God.

It is extremely doubtful, however, that Israel ever borrowed directly from these codes, for the differences are more pronounced than the similarities. The parallels may rather be explained as due to (*a*) a common Semitic (and perhaps partly Indo-Aryan) legal heritage, conserved by the codes in varying ways, which may have been brought by the Hebrews from Mesopotamia, may have been mediated to Israel through Canaan, or may have come through some combination of these 2 processes, and (*b*) certain socio-cultural and legal tendencies which would affect legal materials similarly even in widely separated cultures.

The ancient Near Eastern codes are valuable, therefore, in illuminating the background, process of formation, and sometimes even the details of Israelite law. To date, however, they have not been helpful in showing the origin of particular Israelite laws.

II. Basic Units of the Law in Israel

It is essential to examine the basic building blocks of Israelite law. The single laws have particular forms. These, in turn, are gathered into a number of collections or codes. The chronological order and literary relationships of these collections are matters of continuing discussion. They are unfortunately not dated in the text and usually their headings are of the briefest sort. Before considering the complicated questions of the development and interrelations among the respective codes we need to identify and characterize the chief types of single laws and the main collections: decalogues, dodecalogues, and codes.

Single Laws. The laws of ancient Israel were constructed stylistically in a number of ways.

Very frequent is the *conditional* statement that announces a general type of case (e.g. release of a Hebrew slave) and under that stipulates certain subsituations (e.g. if the slave is single or married, if he does or does not wish to go free in the sabbath year). Most of the conditional laws impose fine or compensation rather than death. This type of law has commonly been called "casuistic," since it calculates in terms of the qualifying circumstances in given cases.

The conditional or casuistic law is illustrated by the following:

> *When* you buy a Hebrew slave, he shall serve six years, and in the seventh he shall go out free, for nothing. *If* he comes in single, he shall go out single; *if* he comes in married, *then* his wife shall go out with him. *If* his master gives him a wife and she bears him sons or daughters, the wife and her children shall be her master's and he shall go out alone. But *if* the slave plainly says, "I love my master, my wife, and my children; I will not go out free," *then* his master shall bring him to God. . . . (Exod. 21:2-6a.)

The *categorical* statement is of an altogether different type stylistically, and perhaps also functionally and ideologically. It simply declares that something is not to be done or that an offender of a certain type is not to live. This has been known technically as "apodictic" law from a Greek term meaning "proving" or "demonstrative."

The categorical or apodictic law is usually either in a participial form (e.g. "Whoever strikes [lit. "one striking"] his father or his mother shall be put to death," Exod. 21:15) or in the form of the imperfect (jussive) verb with a negative, which becomes in effect an imperative (e.g. "You shall not wrong a stranger or oppress him," Exod. 22:21a). When a penalty is stated, normally it is death.

Occasionally the 2 types of laws are found together, as when a categorical statement is qualified by conditional subtypes:

> Whoever strikes a man so that he dies shall be put to death. But if he did not lie in wait for him, but God let him fall into his hand, then I will appoint for you a place to which he may flee. But if a man willfully attacks another to kill him treacherously, you shall take him from my altar, that he may die. (Exod. 21:12-14.)

As to length, the laws may range from 2-word categorical commands (e.g. *lo tirtsah*, "You shall not kill!") to fairly elaborate conditional statements that require 6 or 8 sentences—and even to paragraphs of hortatory expansion. The types are intermixed in an often inexplicable way—a fact which suggests that the present form of the laws is far from the original one or, at any rate, that considerations other than style have determined the order.

It has been noted that the laws which are most

frequently and closely paralleled outside Israel are the conditional or casuistic laws, whereas the categorical or apodictic laws are seldom or never (the point is disputed) paralleled elsewhere. It is perhaps then legitimate to look to the categorical laws for the most direct and powerful influence of Israel's religion and ethos. This may be only partly true, however. The uniqueness of Israelite categorical law may have less to do with the content of the law than with its form and life setting. Laws that everywhere else in the Near East seem to have come under the aegis of the king remained the prerogative of priests in Israel. In that situation the direct and emphatic character of the categorical law expresses the absolute sacral demand as against the more rationalistic royal secular formulations. It is at any rate clear that the religious spirit of Israelite law is not confined to the categorical laws but also infects and colors the conditional laws.

Smaller Collections: Decalogues and Dodecalogues. The briefer law compilations in the OT tend to occur in units of 10 (decalogues) and 12 (dodecalogues). Uncertainty about the precise demarcation of the collections and of proper division of units in the collections makes for some doubt on this point.

A clear instance of a unit of 10 is the familiar 10 Commandments or "Ethical Decalogue" of Exod. 20:1-17, which prescribes:

1. Singular worship of Yahweh
2. Prohibition of images
3. Sanctity of the divine name
4. Sabbath observance
5. Honor of parents
6. Prohibition of murder
7. Prohibition of adultery
8. Prohibition of theft
9. Prohibition of false witness
10. Prohibition of covetousness

The same provisions appear in Deut. 5:6-21, with minor variations, esp. in the motivations.

The claim that Exod. 34:12-26 forms a "Ritual Decalogue" accords with the view of the author of vs. 28, who speaks of the foregoing "ten commandments." Yet it is not easy to make a separation of the component laws. They may be seen as from 10 to 12 in number, or even somewhat more or less, depending on the analysis. In any case the form and style are not sufficiently clear to permit a confident reconstruction.

By way of contrast, Deut. 27:15-26 gives a table of 12 curses on particular sins which are to be pronounced by the Levites, with the people responding to each with an emphatic "Amen."

Lev. 18; 19 contain laws some of which closely parallel those in the above-mentioned collections. In its present form, however, each ch. contains considerably more than 10 or 12 elements, and the variegated style and length of the provisions suggest more kinship to Exod. 34:12-26 than to the 10 Commandments and the 12 curses of Deut. 27:15-26.

Thus the attempt to find collections of a particular number of components does not yield uniform results. In considerable measure this is probably due to subsequent editing which obscured earlier forms and sequences. It is at least clear that the final editor of the laws did not see fit to adhere rigidly to a scheme of 10 or 12. Insofar as the pattern does appear it may most naturally be explained as an aid to memory in oral recitation.

Possibly more significant than the number pattern is the distinction to be drawn between the 10 Commandments as a fundamental statement of the interests of Yahweh to be protected by all Israel and the other shorter collections cited, in which more particular laws of a cultic and civil nature are joined. Apparently the programmatic character of the 10 Commandments was influential in penetrating other collections and leading to mixtures such as in Exod. 34:12-26; Lev. 19. The fact remains that this great decalogue retains its distinction as a relatively unitary statement of the fundamental requirements of Yahwism. This is true whether or not it can be traced back to Moses. An illuminating way of thinking about the relationship is to regard it as high-level "policy" while the remainder of OT law is lower-level "technique" for implementing the policy from time to time and from case to case.

Larger Collections: "Codes." With the exceptions of Lev. 18; 19 the smaller collections discussed above stand outside the framework of the major OT legal codes. The 3 most clearly discernible codes are the Covenant Code (Exod. 20:22-23:33), the Deuteronomic Code (Deut. 12-26), and the Holiness Code (Lev. 17-26). In addition large sections of the P stratum of the Pentateuch (see "The Compiling of Israel's Story," pp. 1082-89) contain legal materials which may be loosely, but somewhat misleadingly, characterized as the Priestly Code. Ezek. 40-48 presents a plan for the reconstruction of the Jerusalem temple in the literary form of a vision narrative. The details are so doctrinaire and impractical that they were never implemented. But, as with other segments of Ezek., the temple plan has important affinities with the ideas of holiness in Lev. 17-26.

Covenant Code (Exod. 20:22-23:33; some limit it to 21:1-23:19). The body of this code, characterized by the heading "the ordinances" (21:1), consists of 41 laws: 20 on crimes against person and property; 13 on cultic practices; 2 each on slavery, judicial proceedings, and resident aliens; and one each on usury and aid to an enemy.

The topical order of the laws is reasonably coherent in the section 21:1-22:17, which deals with slavery and crimes against person and property in that order. The remainder of the code, 22:18-23:19, is less homogeneous, laws of cultic practice being interlarded with other types in a seemingly random manner. In addition 20:22-26 comprises 2 cultic laws which amount to an intro. to the code and precede the caption "These are the ordinances" (21:1).

Very approximately we may say that the first of these sections is "civil" in character and the 2nd is "cultic," but this is only a rough distinction. It is interesting that the conditional form predominates in the "civil" section (18 laws to 4) whereas the categorical form predominates in the "cultic" section (17 to 2). There is thus some ground for believing that the 2 sections were originally separate. It may be, as some have claimed, that the conditional laws of the first section reproduce an old Canaanite civil code taken over by Israel and that the categorical laws of 21:12-17 and all of the 2nd section are miscellaneous Israelite laws added to it at the time it

was placed in the present narrative framework. Similarly it may be assumed that the narrative suture in 20:21-22a permitted the insertion of the cult laws in 20:22b-26.

Deuteronomic Code (Deut. 12-26). This code is introduced (chs. 1-11) and concluded (chs. 27-33) by a lengthy speech of Moses and is headed by the caption "These are the statutes and ordinances which you shall be careful to do" (12:1). The laws are approximately 78 in number but the length of the code is almost 4 times that of the C Code.

The provisions of the D Code coincide at some points with those of the C Code, but not all the laws of one appear in the other. The D Code in particular concerns itself with centralization of worship and profane slaughter, prophecy, kingship, cities of refuge, holy war, mixtures of dress and seed, and divorce—none of which occurs in the C Code.

Some of the D laws are straightforwardly categorical or conditional without adornment. Many others are greatly expanded, e.g. those on centralization of worship and prophecy. The expansions include appeals for radical obedience which are extremely inward, so that in effect law here becomes moral exhortation. It remains a question how much of the D law was in fact ever strictly enforced.

As in the C Code, it is not possible to find an orderly sequence to the laws in Deut. There is evidence of topical subgroups concerning protection of marriage, entrance requirements to the cultic assembly, holy war, etc.; but not all the laws on a topic are necessarily gathered at a single point in the text. The dislocations suggest that a number of originally independent subgroups were combined and that either some elements were shifted from the topical clusters or else some were added somewhat randomly because they had never belonged to such topical clusters. The oral and literary complexities of the code are patent but the reconstruction of the stages of growth remains beyond our grasp.

Holiness Code (Lev. 17-26). This code is embedded in the larger P stratum. It is nearer to the D Code than to the C Code in length, variety of literary forms, and hortatory expansion. Its treatment of sex crimes and of priestly regulations is fuller than in either of the 2 preceding codes.

The H Code stands out from the surrounding material by a subscription that reads: "These are the statutes and ordinances and laws which the LORD made between him and the people of Israel on Mount Sinai by Moses" (26:46). The collection is particularly motivated by the desire for divine holiness to be reciprocated in the holiness of people and priesthood: "You shall be holy; for I the LORD your God am holy" (19:2). Holiness in this context, while possessed of a moral quality, is more nearly a matter of *distinction*—the distinctness of a deity who asks for a distinct moral and cultic life from his worshipers. Israel is to be metaphysically stamped as God's distinct people but the form of imprint is in a particular historical style of life.

The contents of the code are at points built up rather clearly of blocks of topical clusters: sacrifice laws (ch. 17), sex laws (ch. 18), laws about priestly defilements (ch. 21), appointed feasts (ch. 23), sabbath years and jubilee year (ch. 25), and concluding admonition and warning (ch. 26). The entire code, however, cannot be accounted for by the simple juxtaposing of topical clusters.

The complexities of the H Code are evident in such points as the following: (a) There are 2 tables of the prohibited degrees of sexual relations—one in categorical form (18:6-18), the other in conditional (20:10-21). (b) Ch. 19 is an ethical and cultic complex formed out of interlarded categorical and conditional prescriptions. Within the complex it is tempting to posit an original decalogue or dodecalogue of a fundamental theological and ethical character amounting to a "policy" statement on the order of the 10 Commandments. (c) In its present form 24:10-22 provides a narrative setting for the policy that "you shall have one law for the sojourner and for the native"; but within the unit are included specific provisions—for blasphemy, murder, killing of an animal, and disfigurement of persons—in which the issue is not whether the offender is native or foreign but whether the crime merits death or only compensation.

Priestly Code. This term refers, not to a single entity with anything like the precision of the above codes, but rather to all the remaining legal prescriptions in the P stratum of the Pentateuch. These include Exod. 12:1-27; 13:1-16; 25–31; 35–40; Lev. 1–16; 27; Num. 1:1–10:10; 15:1-31; 18–19; 27:1-11; 28–30; 35–36.

P Code provisions are rich in cultic directives and are especially diverse in literary form. Frequently they are so conditioned by the narrative setting that it is difficult to judge whether they did in fact ever govern cultic life or were either entirely figments of the narrator's imagination (which is not probable) or were simply ad hoc practices which quickly died out but have been dressed up as binding law by the P authors. Num. 1–4 looks like just such a learned construction, composed of operative elements at certain stages in the cult but also embroidered by imagination as needed to complete the picture. The same seems to be true of the directives for the construction of the portable shrine or tabernacle and its cult objects, including the ark (Exod. 25–31) as well as the consequent repetitious account of the actual construction (Exod. 35–40). Research suggests that certain features of the shrine possess some historical probability, but that the present form of the account ever served as a blueprint for the cult is highly doubtful.

Even those sections of the P Code that seem to treat the cult prescriptively are often in narrative form. The laws of the passover and of the firstborn are grounded in events at the departure from Egypt (Exod. 12–13). The same characteristic may be observed in Num. 8:6-13; 15:32-36; 27:1-11; 31; 36:1-12. In fact it has been noted that the tendency to link laws with past events or to cast the very form of the law into narration is more prevalent in P than in J, E, or D.

III. Origin, Development and Religious Import of the Laws

The law codes of the OT, in the form we possess them, are a product of the Jewish religious community of postexilic Jerusalem.

It is evident, however, that much older material

has been included in the late editions and that the laws have undergone cents. of development. In principle it should be possible to reconstruct the stages of the development, but widely varying reconstructions have been offered and only the very sketchiest kind of consensus is presently possible.

How far back can the laws be carried? Tradition says that they are the work of Moses, and it is very likely that one of the functions of the historical Moses was to regulate the collective life of the clans or tribes in his keeping by means of law. A key issue in evaluating the tradition of the Mosaic origin of the laws is the question of the level of socio-cultural life reflected in them. It is widely assumed that most, if not all, of the OT laws reflect sedentary life dependent on agriculture and therefore could not have come from Moses. It is not clear, however, that Moses was merely a nomad; Israelite life was at least seminomadic in his age, and even the wandering in the wilderness appears to allow for a long period of settlement at Kadesh, at whose oases limited agriculture could have been carried on.

So it is altogether possible that some of the individual laws go back to Moses, and a good case can be made for the view that the 10 Commandments, at least in their short form, stem from him. At all events the great bulk of the law has been formulated and reshaped during many subsequent stages of Israel's life. It has been a flexible instrument of national life, serving various interests and situations. Its very literary chaos is an expression of the law's organic relevance.

What precisely can be said about the course of the law's development? It is standard to regard the C Code as the earliest of the major codes and attributable to the E stratum of the Pentateuch in the 9th or 8th cents. Next the D Code has been identified as sparking Josiah's reformation in 622. The H Code, in close association with Ezek. 40–48, is normally located in the 6th cent., and the remainder of the P Code is placed in the late 6th or early 5th cent.

For the finished forms of the respective codes the assigned dates are probably still acceptable, but they do not tell us much about the age of the various elements gathered into the codes. On the basis of our widening knowledge of legal theory and practice, and especially of the Near Eastern environment of Israel, it is precisely this open-ended oral and written "snowballing" of traditions which interests us today. E.g. it seems entirely reasonable to believe that some of the elements of the P Code are as ancient as the early materials in the C Code.

As a result we now view the legal codes as having developed along somewhat parallel but often independent lines. We cannot posit simple unilinear development from one code to the next. It is not certain, e.g., that the compiler of the D Code was familiar with the C Code—much less that he sought to replace it.

Some of the differences in the codes may be due not to differing times but to differing locales. There are certainly clear signs that the D Code, or an earlier version of it, was recited at the sanctuary at Shechem in N Israel. The C Code has also been connected with N Israel, possibly at Bethel or again at Shechem. If the latter should be true, then affinities between the C and D codes could be explained by common rootage in a Shechemite tradition which differing traditionists have preserved and supplemented in 2 variant forms. The Ritual Decalogue of Exod. 34:12-26, probably preserved by J, may be attached to some S site such an Hebron. The H and P codes have been identified with Hebron or Shiloh by some scholars. We are very far from being able to reconstruct a sketch of the parallel and successive legal traditions in their proper locales. We do see enough, however, to suggest that the present Jerusalem imprimatur on all the laws was achieved by drawing law complexes from various sanctuaries in Israel in much the same way that David made Jerusalem cultically central by bringing separate tribal symbols such as the ark, the ephod, and the brazen serpent to his new capital.

Easily the single most important feature of OT law is the way that it is tied into events and linked literarily with the narratives. In part this is strictly a literary phenomenon. In the main the blocks of law seem to have been incorporated in the strands of narrative material before the individual strands were joined in the present arrangement. This has resulted in their being scattered rather disjointedly throughout the final narrative. Law in and of itself was never dealt with by the Israelite traditionists; it was always a particular law in a particular context. The resulting arrangement is markedly arbitrary and casual.

At base, however, this somewhat leisurely and casual literary process reflects the cultural and theological values of Israel. For Israel law was primarily a description of what had happened before and thus should happen in a given case, or else it was what God's will directly called for at the present moment. Legal theory and practice alike were tailored to particular cases and to particular sensitivities to the divine will. The sense of the law as an eternal and absolute good was built up only slowly out of a sense that the sum total of the laws had a cumulative binding effect. As such a sense of the law's absoluteness arose it became necessary to harmonize the discrepancies and eventually to extrapolate new laws for situations not covered in the old laws.

But the law devotion of the postexilic period was not characteristic of earlier times. Laws throughout most of Israel's history were precedents or admonitions; they described and they appealed. They were rich with exhortation and they were earthy in their situation-centeredness. Many situations are not touched on at all in the present form of the law; e.g. there are virtually no commercial or marriage laws in the OT.

For the greater part of her early life Israel saw law as one aspect of God's instruction, as a continually plastic body of historical precedents and recorded commands that remained ever-growing and open-ended. When that open-endedness ceased and the laws became simply the law a new era had arrived. Yet even at that later stage the historic process by which the various laws had become the law was still attested to in the conglomeration of narratives and laws within the great corpus called Torah.

Study of the dynamic development and religious dependency of the laws of ancient Israel may serve contemporary Jews and Christians in their endeavor to make creative use of religious traditions and institutions without being strangled by them either because of hyperorthodoxy or because of lethargic acquiescence to the status quo.

For Further Study: T. Meek, "The Origin of Hebrew Law," *Hebrew Origins*, rev. ed., 1950. G. Mendenhall, *Law and Covenant in Israel and the Ancient Near East*, 1955. J. B. Pritchard, ed., *Ancient Near Eastern Texts*, 2nd ed., 1955. H. Schrey, H. Walz, W. Whitehouse, *The Biblical Doctrine of Justice and Law*, 1955. W. J. Harrelson, "Law in the OT" in *IDB*, 1962. A. Alt, "The Origins of Israelite Law," *Essays in OT History and Religion*, 1966. M. Noth, "The Laws in the Pentateuch: Their Assumptions and Meaning," *The Laws in the Pentateuch and Other Studies*, 1966.

THE PROPHETIC LITERATURE

Charles T. Fritsch

The prophetic literature of the OT includes 16 books—popularly classified as 4 major (i.e. longer) prophets, Isaiah, Jeremiah, Ezekiel, Daniel, and 12 minor prophets, Hosea, Joel, Amos, Obadiah, Jonah, Micah, Nahum, Habakkuk, Zephaniah, Haggai, Zechariah, Malachi. These books originated over a period of *ca.* 600 years, beginning with Amos in the middle of the 8th cent. B.C. Though Dan. is included among the prophetic books in Christian Bibles, in the Hebrew Scriptures it is placed among the Writings rather than the Prophets; and it actually belongs to the apocalyptic literature (see "The Apocalyptic Literature," pp. 1106-09) which flourished in Judaism from *ca.* 200 B.C. until after the Roman destruction of Jerusalem in A.D. 70. The main period of OT prophecy extended from the time of Amos to the anonymous prophet of the Exile whose writing appears in Isa. 40–66 (*ca.* 540). Hag. and Zech. (520), Mal. (*ca.* 450), and probably Joel and Jonah belong to the declining period of prophetic activity.

Most of the prophetic books as we know them today are compilations of spoken oracles delivered on special occasions. Though these oracles may have been handed down orally over a period of time, we know that some were preserved, presumably in written form, by the prophet's disciples (e.g. Isa. 8:16), while others were written down by an amanuensis (Jer. 36). There is evidence that some of the prophetic oracles were later expanded (cf. Amos 2:4-5), reused (cf. Isa. 2:3-4 with Mic. 4:2-3), and even reinterpreted (cf. Isa. 2:3-4 with Joel 3:10; Jer. 29:10 with Dan. 9:24). Historical sections derived from other sources were incorporated into prophetic writings (cf. Isa. 36–39 with II Kings 18:13–20:19), and the works of later anonymous authors were attached to earlier prophetic works (e.g. Isa. 40–66 to 1–39; Zech. 9–14 to 1–8). The final stage of the editorial process is represented by the superscriptions found at the beginning of most of these books (Isa. 1:1; Jer. 1:1-3; Hos. 1:1) and by the last vs. of Hos. (14:9), which is a later summation of the prophet's message in language associated with the wisdom school.

I. History of Prophetism

Prophecy as a religious phenomenon flourished in Israel long before the days of Amos. Traces of prophetic activity are found as early as Mosaic times (cf. Num. 11:26-30), but not until the end of the 11th cent. does prophecy emerge in the life of Israel as a recognized institution. At that time 2 distinct types of prophet appear: the ecstatic groups of prophets, like those who met Saul on the way to Gibeah (I Sam. 10:5-13; cf. also 19:18-24), and the lone seer type, represented by Samuel (I Sam. 9:5-10:8).

The ecstatic bands of prophets in the Saul narrative are associated with the sites of Gibeah and Ramah. The group at Ramah seems to have been under the direction of Samuel (I Sam. 19:20). These men, who had the gift of prophecy, lived together in communities of spiritual fellowship where they cultivated their own spiritual lives and whence they went forth in companies to instruct the people and revive the Yahwistic faith in the land. Their prophetic ecstasy was aroused, or at least accompanied, by the playing of musical instruments (I Sam. 10:5), and their contagious enthusiasm affected certain people who came in contact with them (cf. I Sam. 10:10; 19:20-23).

Nearly 200 years later prophetic communities reappear in the N kingdom under the leadership of Elijah and Elisha. These groups were associated with the cultic sites of Bethel, Jericho, and Gilgal, whose notorious pagan practices they no doubt openly opposed. They also actively supported Elijah, their champion, in his constant fight against the evils of Baal worship. There is no evidence that these communities existed after the days of Elisha.

Samuel, who is called both a "seer" (I Sam. 9:11, 18-19) and a "prophet" (I Sam. 3:20), stands at the threshold of a new era in OT prophecy. As a "man of God" who had supernatural powers to reveal secrets and foretell future events (I Sam. 9:6), he represents the popular "seer" type of prophecy so common in the ancient world. But as a "prophet of the LORD" he went from place to place reviving and strengthening the people's faith in Yahweh (I Sam. 7:15-17). Rejecting the priestly system at Shiloh, he closely associated himself with the ecstatic prophets (I Sam. 19:20) and fostered the religion of Yahweh at the local sanctuaries. He preached and taught the word of Yahweh (I Sam. 12) and advised the king in spiritual matters (I Sam. 13:8-15*a;* 15:17-31). By his emphasis on the word of Yahweh as the important factor in Israel's history and his insistence on obedience rather than sacrifice Samuel set the course for OT prophecy for cents. to come. His unique position in the history of prophetism is also shown by the fact that from this time on he who had been called a "seer" was called a "prophet"

(I Sam. 9:9). We can therefore appreciate why the later prophetic tradition ranks Samuel with Moses (cf. Jer. 15:1; Hos. 12:13, where the prophet by whom Israel "was preserved" is probably Samuel).

For the next 2 cents. the prophetic office was centered in charismatic individuals who were closely associated with the political life of Israel. Undeterred by political pressure and utterly fearless in the face of persecution, these messengers of God stood before kings to pronounce judgment on their personal lives, to give advice concerning national policies, and to predict the outcome of events. Some well-known prophets of this period are Nathan and Gad, who served in David's court; Ahijah, who advised Jeroboam I; and Elijah and Micaiah, who prophesied in the time of Ahab.

From the 8th cent. on prophecy flourished for the most part in times of great national crisis. Amos, Hosea, and Isaiah, at least in the early part of his ministry, warned the people that Assyria was the rod of God's anger, and that her armies would destroy Israel if she did not repent of her evil ways. Israel refused to heed the warning, and the Assyrians took the N kingdom into captivity in 722.

The climax of OT prophecy is reached in the period just before and after the fall of Jerusalem to the Babylonians in 586. Once again God raised up his messengers, the prophets, to warn the people of Judah of impending doom unless they repented. Jeremiah, Zephaniah, and Habakkuk bravely tried to avert the tragedy with their powerful preaching and persuasive pleading, but to no avail. After the fall of Jerusalem Ezekiel comforted the exiles in Babylonia with his message of a restored nation in Palestine, worshiping in a new and glorious temple. New elements appearing in his prophecy led ultimately to apocalypticism on the one hand and to institutional Judaism on the other (see "The Religion of Israel," pp. 1150-58). He was followed within a generation by the greatest poet-theologian among the prophets. II Isaiah, the anonymous prophet of the Exile, proclaimed to his people the good news of imminent release from the Babylonian captivity.

With the fall of Babylon to Cyrus of Persia in 539 came freedom for exiles to return to their ancestral homelands. The small group of Jews that returned to Palestine soon fell on hard times. Crop failures, abject poverty, the hostility of their neighbors, esp. the Samaritans, and spiritual indifference reduced the morale of the community to a dangerously low point. Even the rebuilding of the temple, which was the only rallying point of the people, was abandoned. There was real danger that the restoration might fail altogether and that God's redemptive purpose might be thwarted. At this critical time (520) God raised up two prophets, Haggai and Zechariah, to revive the hopes of his people and to urge them to finish the temple. Though their messages lacked the dynamic power and theological dimensions of the earlier prophets, the people responded to their pleas and completed the work in 515. The "remnant of Israel," which now became identified with the worshiping community in the restored temple, was saved again.

The prophetic office now fell into disrepute (cf. Zech. 13:2-6) and, with the exception of Malachi (*ca.* 450) and probably Joel and Jonah, disappears from the scene. The Chronicler (*ca.* 400 or later) still remembered the halcyon days of Israel's prophets and recognized the important role they had played in times long past. But the prophetic figures which populate his history are mere shadows of those spiritual giants of long ago, and their stereotyped messages are a far cry from the thunderous denunciations of an Amos or the impassioned pleadings of a Jeremiah.

It was not until 200 years later, when the culture and religion of the Jews were again seriously threatened, that a new phase of prophetic activity, known as apocalypticism, arose. Some of its literary and theological characteristics (see "The Apocalyptic Literature," pp. 1106-09) are already perceptible in Ezek. and Zech. 1-8. Joel and Zech. 9-14, and possibly Isa. 24-27, are definitely assigned to this category. But it is Dan., written during the Maccabean crisis of 168-165 b.c., which is the classic representative of this type of literature in the OT canon.

II. The Role of the Prophet

The prophetic movement is the most astonishing phenomenon in the history of Israel—in fact it has no real parallel anywhere in human history. To be sure, there were prophets in Mari on the Euphrates in the 18th cent. who brought messages from the deity to the king; in Byblos in the 10th cent. an ecstatic youth instructed the king to give audience to the Egyptian ambassador, Wen-Amon; and in 8th-cent. Syria a king received word from the deity through seers and diviners that he would be victorious over his enemies. But nowhere do we find such a succession of creative personalities whose message was both relevant to the needs of the moment and of enduring value to men of all ages.

The origins of Israelite prophecy are difficult to determine from the sources at our disposal. That ecstatic prophecy was present among the Israelites in Mosaic times seems to be indicated from the account in Num. 11:16-30. Balaam's prophecies (Num. 22-24), accompanied by sacrifices and certain acts of divination, reveal an early link between the Israelite seer and his Near Eastern counterpart. With the coming of the monarchy under Saul the charismatic leadership of the tribal confederacy gave way to the new office of prophet, which was founded by Samuel.

Called by God to proclaim the divine word to Israel, the prophet was completely independent of hereditary ties or royal appointment. Uninvited and undaunted, he stood alone before king and people as God's messenger of weal or woe. The best description of the prophetic office and its meaning is found in Deut. 18:15-22. After condemning the heathen practices of sorcery, divination, necromancy, etc. (vss. 9-14), the writer continues, "I will raise up for them a prophet like you from among their brethren; and I will put my words in his mouth, and he shall speak to them all that I command him" (vs. 18).

The immediacy of the relationship by which the prophet received the divine communication to give to Israel is graphically described in the Micaiah episode recorded in I Kings 22:13-28. Yahweh presides over the heavenly council, with all the host of heaven standing beside him (cf. Isa. 6). The prophet shares in this higher fellowship as an earthly representative. He hears what goes on, is appointed the messenger of the verdict, and expounds it to the people. No doubt Amos had a scene like this in mind when he wrote: "Surely the Lord GOD does nothing, without revealing his secret to his servants the prophets" (3:7).

The prophet was also a "political" figure in that he played a leading role in the formation of the kingdom—Samuel anointed both Saul and David—and as interpreter of the divine will in the subsequent affairs of the nation. Until the time of Amos the prophetic office was held by charismatic messengers who stood in direct line of communication between God and his representative on earth, the king. Through the prophet the divine word of judgment was communicated to the ruler, usually in a face-to-face encounter. The dramatic confrontations of Nathan and David (II Sam. 12:1-15a) and Elijah and Ahab (I Kings 17:1; 18:17-19) and Ahijah's condemnation of the sins of Solomon (I Kings 11:31-33) belong to this phase of OT prophecy.

From Amos on, however, the controversy of God is with the nation and not simply with the kings. To be sure, Isaiah encountered Ahaz "at the end of the conduit of the upper pool" and gave him a sign from the Lord (Isa. 7:3-17) and Jeremiah spoke harsh words concerning Jehoiakim (Jer. 22:13-19) and counseled frequently with Zedekiah. But the main concern of the classical prophets was the chosen people who had sinned against God and were under divine judgment until repentance (cf. e.g. Amos 3:1; Isa. 1:4; Mic. 1:5; Jer. 7:2; Ezek. 3:4-7).

In recent times OT prophecy has been studied from the psychological point of view in order to ascertain the nature of prophetic inspiration. The prophet has been subjected to all kinds of psychological tests, and his oracles have been interpreted as mere ecstatic utterances. Much has been learned about OT prophecy from these investigations, but they have failed to give us the clue to the unique character and role of the prophet of Israel. Others have stressed the cultic role of the prophet, comparing it with that of the cultic prophets of Babylonia and Canaan. But nowhere in the OT is there any evidence that the prophets of Israel were officially connected with particular shrines or that their message was determined by cultic or ritual patterns. They were deeply interested in the cult and, like Samuel and Elijah, were closely associated with local sanctuaries or, like Isaiah and Jeremiah, with the temple in Jerusalem. But one could hardly attribute a cultic role to the prophet in the technical sense of that term.

The prophet was not a mere officeholder, bound by ancient traditions or cultic pattern. He was chiefly a representative of the heavenly court, divinely appointed to proclaim the living word of God to the chosen people. He sought no royal or ecclesiastical favors, since his life was completely directed and dominated by the divine Suzerain. As spokesman for God to the covenant community he advised kings and exhorted the nation to obey the laws of God and live in accordance with his will.

III. THE CALL OF THE PROPHET

The call of the prophet was a basic and fundamental experience in his life, for it gave legitimacy to his office, authority to his message, and urgency to his preaching. The divine compulsion to preach the word of Yahweh is well described by Jeremiah:

> If I say, "I will not mention him,
>   or speak any more in his name,"
> there is in my heart as it were a burning fire
>   shut up in my bones,
> and I am weary with holding it in,
>   and I cannot." (Jer. 20:9.)

That which distinguished the true prophet from the false was the validity of his call. In Jer., where false prophets so often oppose the divinely appointed messenger of God, it is stated several times that they were not commissioned by Yahweh, and that their words were not from him (e.g. 14:14; 23:21-22; 28:15). The call for the prophet was the valid expression of God's will in his life, the certain assurance that God had reached down to take hold of him and make him aware of his mission.

This was not a mystical experience primarily but a convulsive moment which changed the prophet's whole life. By this divine intervention the prophet was set apart from other people and brought into special relationship with God in order to serve as the medium of the divine word to the nation. The divine call implied the consecration of the person to God and his service. More particularly we hear about the mouth or the lips or the ear of the prophet being specially anointed or cleansed or opened to receive the word of Yahweh.

The prophets evidently responded in different ways to the call as far as we can tell from the few accounts that have come down to us. Jeremiah, like Moses, was reluctant to accept the divine commission because he was a mere lad and did not know how to speak (1:6). On the other hand Isaiah accepted his vocation with alacrity as the glory of Yahweh overwhelmed him (6:8).

In no case, as far as we can tell, was the individuality of the prophet lost, or his personality submerged, because of this experience. The austerity of desert life passed over into the message of Amos; Isaiah remained the aristocratic city man; both Hosea and Jeremiah brought to their ministries deeply sensitive hearts and a concern for the personal aspect of religion. Neither did the prophets become mere automatons without freedom of thought and action. Habakkuk was bold enough to question the righteous character of God in the light of oppression by a "bitter and hasty nation," whose "horses are swifter than leopards, more fierce than the evening wolves" (1:6, 8), and Jeremiah even dared to accuse Yahweh of deceit and treachery (15:18; 20:7).

A brief review of the recorded prophetic calls reveals the rich variety of ways in which God claims men for his service. The story of Samuel's call (I Sam. 3) is cast in the mold of the classical prophetic tradition of later times. The word of Yahweh, which was rare in Samuel's day, is once more heard in the sanctuary at Shiloh. Yahweh speaks directly to Samuel of the coming judgment on the house of Eli, and Samuel, as the divinely appointed messenger, communicates the word of judgment to Eli. From now on the word of Yahweh is emphasized as the mode of revelation in the prophetic tradition (cf. vs. 21).

The account of the call of Amos (7:14-15), which is the essence of simplicity, is set in the context of a most dramatic scene. Amaziah, the priest of Bethel, has just ordered Amos out of the country because of his excoriating words against Israel. Amos, unperturbed because of this attack, tells Amaziah that "the LORD took me from following the flock, and . . . said to me, 'Go, prophesy to my people Israel.'" As one who has been present in the heavenly council where God reveals his secrets to his prophets (3:7) he has received a message for Israel and no human agent can prevent him from proclaiming it:

> The lion has roared;
>   who will not fear?
> The Lord GOD has spoken;
>   who can but prophesy? (3:8.)

Hosea receives his call in quite a different way. From the bitter experience of a shattered home and a faithless wife, whom he loves nevertheless, Hosea comes to understand God's deep love for faithless Israel. Even as God forgives Israel and woos her back to the relationship of wilderness days to marry her again "in righteousness and in justice, in steadfast love, and in mercy" (2:19), so Hosea forgives Gomer and takes her back to himself (chs. 1-3). From this experience, which we may interpret as his call, Hosea learns the deeper meaning of love and forgiveness which is the heartbeat of his message.

Isaiah's call took place during a service in the temple in Jerusalem (ch. 6). It is one of the most elaborate of the prophetic calls, as well as one of the most dramatic. The sense of God's presence in the temple leads to the prophet's confession of his sin and unworthiness before the "King, the LORD of hosts." On confession of his guilt his lips are touched with a burning coal, and his sin is forgiven. When the call comes from the Lord, "Whom shall I send, and who will go for us?" Isaiah immediately accepts the challenge and receives the message which he is to proclaim to the sinful people of Israel.

The account of Jeremiah's call (1:4-10) is less detailed than that of Isaiah's. Several new aspects appear here. Yahweh has appointed Jeremiah a prophet before he was born; his mission is not just to Israel alone but to the nations (vss. 5c, 10); and his hesitancy to accept the appointment is overcome by the assurance that God will be with him to deliver him. The actual commissioning is described in simple terms: "The LORD put forth his hand and touched my mouth; and the LORD said to me, 'Behold, I have put my words in your mouth'" (vs. 9). The message of the prophet has little to do with human reflection or speculation; what he speaks comes from God, not from himself.

The description of Ezekiel's call (1:1-3:21) is the most ornate in the prophetic literature of the OT. The prophet's ecstatic vision of God seated on his throne, which is borne aloft by four living creatures, is triggered by a mighty storm cloud, flashing bolts of lightning as it sweeps across the sky. Having fallen down in awe before this manifestation of the divine glory, Ezekiel is raised up by the Spirit to receive the divine message which is written on a scroll. The command to eat the scroll once again emphasizes the objectivity of the prophetic word.

These examples show that the divine call was one of the most characteristic features of the prophetic consciousness. This unique experience was an impelling force in the life of the prophet, giving urgency to his message and confident assurance in the face of hostile opposition.

IV. THE TEACHINGS OF THE PROPHETS

To deal adequately with the teachings of the OT prophets in a brief survey would be difficult, not only because of the vast scope of the subject, but also because of the different historical backgrounds and theological emphases at different times. It should be helpful, however, to consider a few of the major themes found in the prophetic corpus. We must keep in mind that the prophets, who always spoke to a particular situation, never presented a philosophy of history or a theological system. Their central message, however, was always the same, though its application changed from time to time in varying historical circumstances.

God. The basic characteristic of OT prophecy was the centrality of God. For the prophet God was everywhere—in his life, in his message, and in history. God had personally called him and was with him at all times to strengthen him for his tasks and to protect him in time of trouble. With the eyes of faith he saw the reality of God in all that happened. Because of this prophetic insight historical events acquired religious significance. Catastrophes, as prophesied, were punishments inflicted by Yahweh because of the wickedness of Israel; deliverance from danger, as prophesied, was the result of divine intervention because of Yahweh's love for Israel. The historical event, therefore, becomes a theophany, a manifestation of God's presence for judgment or salvation.

But the prophet also saw God's hand in the history of other nations. Amos reminds his hearers that God brought "the Philistines from Caphtor and the Syrians from Kir" (9:7); Jeremiah can call Nebuchadnezzar, the conqueror of Jerusalem, the "servant" of Yahweh (25:9); and II Isaiah gives the pagan ruler Cyrus the honorific title of God's "anointed" (45:1). As the prophet views things, all history is under the direction of God. He initiated the historical process by a uniquely creative act (Isa. 42:5); he supervises its unfolding throughout the ages; and he will bring it to a close by establishing a new age. The prophet saw unity and purpose in history because he saw God in it from beginning to end.

The Word. The message of the prophet is the living word of God. This above all differentiates him from the priest and the wise man. According to Jer. 18:18 law (*torah*, which basically means "teaching" or "instruction") belongs to the priest and counsel to the wise man but the word of God belongs exclusively to the prophet. From the very beginning to the end of the prophetic movement in Israel God revealed himself to the prophet through his word. "The LORD revealed himself to Samuel at Shiloh by the word of the LORD" (I Sam. 3:21). To Elijah at Horeb the divine revelation was mediated, not through wind, earthquake, and fire as in Moses' day, but through a "still, small voice" (I Kings 19: 11-12). "Thus says the LORD," "the oracle of the

LORD," and other comparable phrases which are the earmark of the prophetic tradition indicate the divine source of the prophet's message.

This divine word which the prophet proclaimed was active and powerful, creating and destroying, comforting and disquieting. It was continually creating history, for that which God spoke through his prophets came to pass. It also was a destructive force, even against Israel (Isa. 9:8-10). In time of utter desolation and despair it was the only source of hope and consolation (Isa. 40:6-8). But it also troubled the sinner's soul and made him feel uneasy (I Kings 17:1; 18:17-18).

The success of this word, as it is communicated by the prophet, is assured by God himself:

So shall my word be that goes forth from my mouth;
   it shall not return to me empty,
but it shall accomplish that which I purpose,
   and prosper in the thing for which I sent it." (Isa. 55:11.)

Ethics. According to prophetic teaching Yahweh, who is holy, just, and righteous, demands that his people be holy, just, and righteous. Ethics for the prophet is rooted and grounded in God, whose holy will is expressed in justice and righteousness, and who is the defender of all that is right and good. The prophets were the first to preach that morality is of prime importance, since God places moral righteousness above cultic purity. The pleas of the 8th-cent. prophets for mercy and charity to the poor and oppressed, as well as their strong condemnation of the greedy oppressor and religious hypocrite, are well known. "Let justice roll down like waters, and righteousness like an ever-flowing stream," cries Amos (5:24), while Hosea states that God desires of his people steadfast love and saving knowledge rather than meaningless sacrifices offered in the temple (6:6). In contrast to the pagan philosophy of sacrifice—the bigger and more precious the gift the more easily the offerer will be able to manipulate the deity—the offering that Yahweh requires is justice, mercy, and humility (Mic. 6:8). A later prophet defines religion simply in terms of love for one's fellow man. In speaking of the good King Josiah, Jeremiah says:

He judged the cause of the poor and needy;
   then it was well.
Is not this to know me?
   says the LORD. (22:16.)

Knowledge of God, according to the prophet, is measured by the love one has for the poor and needy. Jesus himself cannot improve on this high ethical view of the prophets (cf. Matt. 25:31-46).

The Ultimate Victory. Even though the prophets were mainly concerned with interpreting the divine will for their own day, they believed that the climax of history lay in the future, when God would destroy evil and bring in the age of bliss. This hope of a golden age was not the result of human speculation but was rooted and grounded in Israel's faith in a God who was guiding history to a divinely appointed goal. Belief in God's ultimate victory over evil and the establishment of his kingdom on earth is found throughout the prophetic literature, beginning with the 8th-cent. prophets and reaching its climax in

postexilic times. The "day of the LORD" about which Amos spoke with new insight had evidently been in the popular mind long before his time. Men had believed this was a day on which God would scatter his foes and deliver Israel in a miraculous way. Amos, however, interpreted it as a day of darkness (5:18), on which God would judge Israel for her sins. It was not an ordinary day but a time when God would break into history in a spectacular way in order to accomplish his purpose. Later prophets elaborated on this theme (cf. Joel) and broadened its scope to include God's judgment on all the nations of the world (cf. Zeph. 1:14-18).

Another related motif is the idea of the "remnant," which appears first in Isaiah's writings. This important concept is already hinted at in the inaugural vision of the prophet (6:13); it is announced in the name of his son Shear-jashub, which means "a remnant shall return" (7:3); and it is fully expressed in 10:20-23 (cf. 28:5; 37:32). The faithful ones of Isaiah's time, perhaps the small group of his disciples (8:16), point forward to this remnant who will be saved at the last day to form the new community in the new age.

This new age, which God alone can bring about (Isa. 65:17), will be accompanied by blessings too numerous to count. It will be a time of peace and prosperity (Isa. 2:4; Mic. 4:3-4); the wild beasts will be tamed (Isa. 11:6-9); justice and righteousness will prevail everywhere (Isa. 11:3b-5; Jer. 23:5); the breach between the kingdoms of Judah and Israel will be healed (Hos. 3:5; Jer. 3:18; 31; Ezek. 37:15-28); and all nations will enjoy the divine blessings (Zeph. 3:9-11; Jer. 16:19, 21; Zech. 8:22-23).

Associated with the coming of the new age is the messianic figure of the Davidic leader. According to Isaiah the scion of David's line will rule with equity and justice in the coming kingdom (9:6-7; 11:1-5). Another description of the ideal ruler is quite similar (Mic. 5:2-4). The same motif appears in the prophecies of Jeremiah (23:5; 33:14-18) and Ezekiel (34:23-24). In Zech. 9:9-10 stress is laid on the humility of Jerusalem's king in the golden age, whose dominion will be worldwide.

A somewhat different figure appears in Dan., where the seer sees in a night vision "one like a son of man" coming with the clouds of heaven, "and to him was given dominion and glory and kingdom, that all peoples, nations, and languages should serve him; his dominion is an everlasting dominion" (7:13-14). This figure is not the same as the Davidic leader, since he is not of the line of David—in fact is not born as a human being but comes down from the sky. The character of his kingdom, however, is similar to that of David's scion. In vs. 18 the son of man figure seems to be interpreted as the "saints of the Most High," who will "receive the kingdom."

Completely different is the figure of the suffering servant in II Isa., who brings true religion to the ends of the earth and instructs all men in God's law. Unlike the other 2 figures, he accomplishes his mission through suffering and dying for others so that they may be justified (50:6; 52:13–53:12). Similarly in II Zech. mention is made of one whose death is associated with the coming of the new kingdom (12:10; 13:1). All these figures, each in his own way, are linked with the coming of the time when men's hearts will be changed and brought into harmony with God's will, and peace and righteousness will cover the earth as waters cover the sea.

For Further Study. Alfred Guillaume, *Prophecy and Divination*, 1938. R. B. Y. Scott, *The Relevance of the Prophets*, 1944. J. P. Hyatt, *Prophetic Religion*, 1947. Martin Buber, *The Prophetic Faith*, 1949. Curt Kuhl, *The Prophets of Israel*, 1960. A. J. Heschel, *The Prophets*, 1962. Johannes Lindblom, *Prophecy in Ancient Israel*, 1962. B. D. Napier, "Prophets" in *IDB*, 1962. N. K. Gottwald, *All the Kingdoms of the Earth*, 1964.

THE WISDOM LITERATURE

Edward Lee Beavin

Job, Prov., and Eccl. are the wisdom books of the OT; but wisdom literature is found also in the Pentateuch, the historical and prophetic books, Pss., and Dan. In addition even a brief list of Israel's wisdom materials must include Wisd. Sol. and Ecclus. of the Apoc.

I. Solomon's Wisdom

The OT records the ancient, enduring tradition of King Solomon as the preeminent sage in Israel, the wisest of the wise.

And God gave Solomon wisdom and understanding beyond measure, and largeness of mind like the sand on the seashore, so that Solomon's wisdom surpassed the wisdom of all the people of the east, and all the wisdom of Egypt. For he was wiser than all other men . . . and his fame was in all the nations round about. (I Kings 4:29-31.)

Scattered references in the early chs. of I Kings relate that Solomon's wisdom was a gift of God, bestowed on him in answer to his prayer for "an understanding mind to govern" and to "discern between good and evil" (3:9). By this wisdom he is able to try the case of the child of disputed parentage and to render a decision so wise that all Israel stands in awe (3:16-28). By it also he utters 3,000 proverbs and 1,005 songs, speaking of trees, beasts, birds, reptiles, and fish (4:32-33). Through his wisdom he gains an international reputation and is visited by kings and commoners from other lands (4:34; 10:23-25). Hiram king of Tyre knows of his wisdom (5:7), and the queen of Sheba, who comes "to test him with hard questions," sees her original skepticism transformed into positive, boundless admiration when she hears his replies (10:1-9).

Certainly it would be naïve to assume the wholesale historical accuracy of these accounts in I Kings, just as it would be naïve to credit with literal accuracy the superscriptions which claim Solomonic authorship for a major portion of Prov., Eccl., Wisd. Sol., and even the Song of S. The passages in I Kings convey an unmistakable aura of folk legend, and the ascriptions of authorship of the wisdom books are to be taken in the sense that these materials are of the type generally associated with Solomon.

On the other hand it would be equally unrealistic to deny that Solomon occupied an important place in the origins of Israel's wisdom movement and to state categorically that nothing in the wisdom books originated with him. The truth is simply that we do not now understand Solomon's precise role in the emerging wisdom movement and that, while some of the materials, esp. in Prov., may have originated with him, no such particular passage can now be confidently identified.

The passages in Kings are important for 2 reasons: (a) They show that Solomon was the focus of Israel's own understanding of her wisdom movement, as Moses was of the law and David the pss. (b) The content of these passages suggests some of the central features of OT wisdom, features which are discussed under the various headings below.

II. The International Character of Wisdom

Wisdom occupied a primary place in Israel. Popular wisdom, professional wise men, and a highly developed wisdom literature influenced her society and were in turn influenced by it. But wisdom was not limited to Israel, nor did it originate there. The survival of a number of non-Hebraic wisdom texts, principally from Egypt and Mesopotamia, demonstrates conclusively that wisdom belonged to the entire ancient Near East, indeed was one of the major facets of Near Eastern culture. Hebrew wisdom developed within this broader milieu.

One witness to the international nature of wisdom is the frequent allusion in the OT to the wisdom and the wise men of other lands: of Canaan (Judg. 5:29; II Sam. 20:18), of Phoenicia (Ezek. 28:2, 6; Zech. 9:2), of Edom (Obad. 8), of Syria (II Kings 6:8, 11-12), of Babylonia (Isa. 47:13; Jer. 50:35; and often in Dan.), of Persia (Ezra 7:14-15; Esth. 1:13-22), and of Egypt (Gen. 41:8, 39; Exod. 7:11, 22; 8:7, 18-19; Isa. 19:11-13). Jer. 10:7 summarizes this with a reference to "all the wise ones of the nations." That these passages often speak disdainfully of the wisdom of other nations is doubtless an expression of Israel's national pride. But it is interesting to observe that their wisdom is criticized for its low level of achievement, not generally because it differs in type from Israel's wisdom.

The international character of wisdom is also shown in that at least twice the OT seems to have recorded non-Hebraic wisdom, identifying, if only vaguely, its source. Prov. 30 is purportedly the words of Agur son of Jakeh—not Hebrew names—and Prov. 31:1-9 the words of Lemuel. Both are said to have been "of Massa," generally taken as a reference to a N Arabian tribe (cf. Gen. 25:13-14). Thus here Prov. records brief excerpts of Arabian wisdom.

Unquestionably OT wisdom has been influenced by non-Hebraic wisdom, in at least one case directly, far more often indirectly, though the sources are not explicitly identified in the text. The Wisdom of Amen-em-Opet certainly underlies one section of Prov. This ancient, extant Egyptian wisdom book was organized into 30 chs. which have been borrowed as the "thirty sayings" of Prov. 22:17–24:22 (cf. 22:20). This is not to suggest a simple translation of the Egyptian into Hebrew. The Hebrew wise men recast what they borrowed in terms of their Palestinian perspectives and their faith in Yahweh, but in no other case is the non-Hebraic original more apparent than in this passage.

Some scholars have suggested that other parts of Prov. were taken directly from the Aramaic Wisdom of Ahikar, which is of Mesopotamian origin and may be called an Assyrian wisdom book. This view is not widely accepted, nor is the inverse suggestion that Prov. has influenced Ahikar, since the parallels are not at all certain. Perhaps their similarity lies only in some general wisdom sayings which both include, or possibly both may have utilized some unknown 3rd source.

In another case OT wisdom may embody a non-Hebraic source. The prose prologue and epilogue to Job may preserve an original Edomite tale which the Hebrew author has reworked and expanded by the insertion of the long poetic section (3:1–42:6).

Aside from the relation of Prov. to The Wisdom of Amen-em-Opet and these other more dubious cases, the impact of Near Eastern wisdom on Israel was general, not specific—general in that Israel's wisdom shared with it similar moods, forms, and subject matter.

III. LITERARY TYPES OF WISDOM

The Mashal. The basic literary unit in OT wisdom is the *mashal*, usually translated "proverb," though used in numerous senses. While the original meaning of the word is not certainly known, at least 2 attempts to trace its etymology deserve attention. Some believe that it is derived from a verb meaning "rule," so that the *mashal* was originally "a ruling saying," an authoritative word. This seems appropriate in that it is often a statement which conveys the wisdom of the ages in capsule form and as such commands assent.

A more widely held view is that *mashal* derives from a verb meaning "be like," and thus originally meant a "likeness" or "comparison." This verb occurs several times in the OT and has cognates of similar meaning in other Semitic languages. Such proverbs as "Like mother, like daughter" (Ezek. 16:44) and "Like vinegar to the teeth, and smoke to the eyes, so is the sluggard to those who send him" (Prov. 10:26) explicitly convey the notion of comparison, as does "Like Nimrod a mighty hunter before the LORD" (Gen. 10:9), which is clearly a *mashal*, though the text does not identify it as such. In the popular proverb "Is Saul also among the prophets?" (I Sam. 10:11) the point is simply that Saul's behavior resembles that of the ecstatics. To be sure, in the majority of instances the *mashal* does not carry the connotation of likeness, but this does not necessarily deny such etymology. It indi-

cates rather that this word, like so many others both ancient and modern, passed through an extensive development of meaning in which the original connotation was obscured or altogether lost.

Often the *mashal* is a short popular saying. These are widely scattered through the OT. In addition to those quoted above, other well-recognized examples are: "The fathers have eaten sour grapes, and the children's teeth are set on edge" (Ezek. 18:2; cf. Jer. 31:29); "Out of the wicked comes forth wickedness" (I Sam. 24:13); and "The days grow long, and every vision comes to naught" (Ezek. 12:22). In Luke 4:23 Jesus refers to the familiar proverb "Physician, heal yourself."

Scholars have come increasingly to recognize that many passages in the historical and prophetic books may contain popular proverbial sayings. Some of the most likely of these are: "What has straw in common with wheat?" (Jer. 23:28); "The fool speaks folly" (Isa. 32:6); and "Let not him that girds on his armor boast himself as he that puts it off" (I Kings 20:11).

Preponderantly, however, the *mashal* is the polished aphorism, the product of the wise men's skill. Extensive collections of these are found in Prov. 10:1–22:16; 25–29; Eccl. 9:17–10:20. The difference between these and the folk proverb mentioned above is basically a matter of literary form. The "professional" proverb customarily occurs as a distich in synonymous, antithetic, or synthetic parallelism; i.e. it consists of 2 lines of which the 2nd repeats the meaning of the first, offers a counter proposition, or completes its meaning.

Sometimes the *mashal* is a taunt or taunt song—a word of mocking, scornful derision directed against those who have justly received punishment from Yahweh (cf. Isa. 14:4-20; Mic. 2:4; Hab. 2:6-8). Again, it is a byword, a reproach against those who have turned away from Yahweh and thus have made themselves a horrible example to others (cf. Deut. 28:37; I Kings 9:7; Pss. 44:14; 69:11; Jer. 24:9; Ezek. 14:8). Three times in Ezek. the *mashal* is an allegory. The story of meat boiling in a cauldron (24:3-14) is introduced as a *mashal;* that of the eagle and the plants (17:2-10) is called a riddle and an allegory; and when God instructs Ezek. to preach destruction to the S in the figure of a flame consuming the forest he complains, "Ah Lord GOD! they are saying of me, 'Is he not a maker of allegories?'" (20:45-49).

Elsewhere the *mashal* is a more lengthy saying or discourse. The discourses of Balaam (Num. 23:7, 18; 24:3, 15, 20, 21, 23) are so called, as are the speeches of Job (Job 27:1; 29:1). In Ps. 49:4, where the RSV translates *mashal* "proverb," as in Ps. 78:2 where it translates "parable," the word suggests the oracle or longer discourse.

Fables. In addition to the *mashal* there are several other literary types of wisdom. The reference to Solomon's speaking of trees, beasts, birds, etc. probably means that he was a maker of fables. Unfortunately none of his fables survive. Nevertheless the story of the trees' attempt to anoint a king over them (Judg. 9:8-15) and the tale of the thistle and the cedar of Lebanon (II Kings 14:9) are good examples of the fabulists' art.

Riddles. The queen of Sheba comes to test Solomon with riddles (I Kings 10:1; RSV "hard questions") and he answers them all (10:3). Recent scholars are probably correct when they assert that riddles played a more important role in early wisdom than is now apparent in our text. Judg. 14 records Samson's famous riddle—the only fully developed riddle in the OT. But other passages may have been riddles originally, e.g. the Song of the Vineyard in Isa. 5:1-7 and the numerical proverbs of Prov. 30:15-31. This type of wisdom is referred to in Num. 12:8; Prov. 1:6; Ezek. 17:2; Dan. 5:12 and elsewhere.

The Wisdom Address. Finally there is the longer wisdom address, not specifically called *mashal,* but similar in style to the discourses mentioned above. Most of Job is of this type and such longer treatments are found in Prov. 1-9 and in Eccl. Related to this type also are the wisdom pss., e.g. Pss. 1; 37; 73 and the beautiful wisdom poem of Job 28.

IV. The Wise Men and Their Wisdom

In the OT a variety of persons are called wise. Sometimes the term is used in a popular sense, at other times technically. Too strict or narrow a classification would be a distortion. Presented here is a description of some of the major groups of wise men.

Craftsmen. Artists and craftsmen are called wise men, and their wisdom consists in their ability to do their jobs well. The metalworkers, stonecutters, woodcarvers, embroiderers, and weavers who work on the tabernacle (Exod. 31:2-6; 35:30-33, 35) have wisdom (RSV "ability"), as do the tailors who work on Aaron's priestly garments (Exod. 28:3). Hiram of Tyre, whom Solomon employs in the construction of the temple, is wise in that he is a skilled bronze worker (I Kings 7:13-14). Ship pilots and ship builders are wise men (RSV "skilled men"; cf. Ezek. 27:8-9). Even the foolish craftsmen who make idols are men of wisdom (Jer. 10:9; Isa. 40:20, RSV "skilful"). In Jer. 9:17 the wise women are artists at mourning, and in Prov. 30:24-28 the ants, badgers, locusts, and lizard are called wise because of their special talents.

Royal Counselors. The OT designates as wise those who exercise shrewd native intelligence. They provide sound judgment concerning practical problems of life, and possess political sagacity. They give counsel. Almost all of these are introduced in some connection with kings or members of the royal family. Hushai and Ahithophel, whose counsel is "as if one consulted the oracle of God," are counselors to David and his son Absalom (II Sam. 15:31–17:23). Jonathan, David's uncle, is "a man of understanding and a scribe" (I Chr. 27:32). David's son Amnon follows the counsel of Jonadab, "a very crafty man" (II Sam. 13:3). Joab sends to David a wise woman from Tekoa to intercede for Absalom (II Sam. 14:2-20); and the wise woman of Abel, remembering the ancient custom of those who used to "ask counsel at Abel," advises Joab against destroying the city (II Sam. 20:14-22). At a much earlier time the professional wise women in Sisera's court use their wisdom to comfort Sisera's mother, who is distraught over the failure of her son to return from battle (Judg. 5:28-30).

Solomon himself is the outstanding example of a royal figure whose wisdom is the exercise of shrewd native intelligence. His ability to answer the riddles of the queen of Sheba shows astuteness of mind, and his success in deciding to which woman the infant belongs illustrates his adeptness at common-sense psychology. His prayer for wisdom to discern between good and evil is not a request for keen moral sensitivity but for the ability to make beneficent decisions. It is ironic that for all his reputation for wisdom Solomon's foolishness led to the destruction of the united monarchy in Israel.

Occultists. Another group of wise men stand in bold contrast to those discussed above. These are the occult persons—sorcerers, magicians, and astrologers. In the OT Joseph, Moses, Aaron, and Daniel are wise men of this type. Joseph's wisdom is his God-given ability to interpret dreams. He interprets the dreams of the Egyptian butler and baker (Gen. 40) and in competition with the magicians and wise men of Egypt the dream of Pharaoh (41:1-36). Pharaoh proclaims, "There is none so discreet and wise as you are," and makes Joseph the chief administrator in Egypt (41:39-45).

A strikingly similar portrait is given of Daniel, who vies with the wise men of Babylon. Daniel, it is said, has "understanding in all visions and dreams" (Dan. 1:17), and he and his 3 Hebrew companions are "in every matter of wisdom and understanding concerning which the king inquired of them . . . ten times better than all the magicians and enchanters that were in all his kingdom" (1:20).

Moses and Aaron have to compete with the Egyptian "wise men" and "sorcerers" and "magicians" who practiced "secret arts" (Exod. 7:11), but by their wisdom they are triumphant (cf. Exod. 8:18; 9:11).

In numerous references the OT speaks disparagingly of the occult wisdom of other nations, but such wisdom was not prominent in Israel. One would be tempted to regard these references to Joseph, Moses, Aaron, and Daniel as expressions of national pride—"Our wise men are better than yours!"—and write off this kind of wisdom altogether in Israel were it not for Isaiah's statement that in 8th-cent. Judah the wise men included, along with the elder and the counselor, "the diviner . . . , the skilful magician and the expert in charms" (Isa. 3:2-3).

The Wise Men of Prov. With reference to OT wisdom literature the most important group of wise men were the professional sages who produced Prov. They recorded, organized, and preserved ancient wisdom sayings, doubtless wrote much themselves, and served as wisdom teachers. As a professional group they occupied a place in Israelite society alongside the priests and prophets. Their importance, as well as their distinctive interest, is indicated in Jer. 18:18, where the people say: "The law shall not perish from the priest, nor counsel from the wise, nor the word from the prophet."

Some scholars believe that the sages were cultic figures, associated with the priests in the cultus of the Jerusalem temple. This could explain why the prophets were sometimes hostile to them (cf. Isa. 29:14; Jer. 8:8-9). But this view overlooks the crucial fact that the wise men show no interest in cultic matters. It is much more probable that this group evolved from the earlier royal scribes and served at first as teachers of the aristocratic youth. Their association with the court could be the grounds for the prophet's criticism of them and the explanation for the "upper class" background which some of their teachings reflect. It may be assumed that after the destruction of the monarchy the wise men became an independent group and their teaching less class conscious.

On the whole the teaching of the wise is for all men. They seek to answer the question "How can the good life be achieved?" and their teachings form virtually a manual of good conduct. Their interests are man-centered; their approach is highly practical. Instead of priestly revelation, prophetic oracle, or vision they stress common sense as gained through practical experience. Their ethical standards are praiseworthy. Family life is to be marked by respect toward parents and by fidelity. Loyalty and righteousness are everywhere upheld, and laziness, drunkenness, gluttony, theft, and oppression of the poor are denounced. The contrast is often drawn between the wise and the foolish—not the ignorant, interestingly—who are equated with the righteous and the wicked.

For the sages the goal and consequence of such ethical living are the rewards which come to the individual. These rewards are prosperity, general well-being, and most esp. long life. Conversely the wicked inevitably suffer misfortune, misery, and early death. This doctrine, often called the doctrine of retribution, is a primary feature of Prov.

In their ethical aphorisms, extensive collections of which are found in Prov. 10:1–22:16; 25–29, the wise men assume that wisdom is man's means of achieving the good life. Human experience discloses basic moral patterns, and man's responsibility is to learn these and conform to them by self-discipline. But in Prov. 1–9, which is clearly the latest section of the book, a quite different concept of wisdom appears. First there is a sharpened awareness that to be wise basically means recognizing God as the ultimate source of all wisdom:

The fear of the LORD is the beginning of knowledge;
fools despise wisdom and instruction (1:7).

For the LORD gives wisdom;
from his mouth come knowledge and understanding (2:6).

The fear of the LORD is the beginning of wisdom,
and the knowledge of the Holy One is insight (9:10).

But then wisdom is also personified in this section. She is presented as a woman who stands in the streets, calling her invitation to men to follow her and partake of her instruction (1:20-33; 3:15-18; 8:1-21, 32-36; 9:1-6).

Finally she is spoken of as the first work of God, present with him in creation:

The LORD created me at the beginning of his work,
the first of his acts of old.
Ages ago I was set up,
at the first, before the beginning of the earth.

When he established the heavens, I was there,

when he assigned to the sea its limit,

when he marked out the foundations of the earth,
then I was beside him, like a master workman;
and I was daily his delight,
rejoicing before him always,
rejoicing in his inhabited world
and delighting in the sons of men.
(Prov. 8:22-31; cf. 3:19-20.)

This portrayal of wisdom as God's agent is carried even further in Wisd. Sol. 7–9, where wisdom is said to be

a breath of the power of God,
and a pure emanation of the glory of the Almighty;

a reflection of eternal light,
a spotless mirror of the working of God,
and an image of his goodness (7:25-26).

These passages cannot but suggest the Logos doctrine of John 1 and Paul's equation of wisdom and Christ in I Cor. 1:24, 30.

Job and Eccl. These books grew out of the wisdom movement, but their authors were independent thinkers who could not accept the naïve, complacent optimism of Prov. To them the nature of God and his plan for the world were not so easily known as the sages of Prov. had assumed, and they believed that the doctrine of retribution failed to take account of the harsh realities of life.

Two assumptions underlie the belief in individual retribution: God is characterized by justice, and his justice is manifest in human affairs. That is why the righteous are rewarded and the wicked punished; the justice of God could not let it be otherwise.

Even so, Job suffers, though he is "blameless and upright, one who feared God and turned away from evil." He suffers as a consequence of his many losses. He loses his wealth, his children, and his health. Worst of all, he loses his God, as he and his friends conceive God to be. The more the friends argue the various facets of the doctrine of retribution, the greater Job's despair, and he is led to explore the depths of religion. Finally, through the climactic confrontation of God (chs. 38–41), which Job has alternately longed for and dreaded, Job comes to see that he can no more understand God's ways in the world than he can comprehend God's power and wisdom as shown in creation. God's crucial question "Will you even put me in the wrong? Will you condemn me that you may be justified?" (40:8) demands that Job either turn from God altogether or abandon his limited understanding of justice. So Job repents in dust and ashes (42:6).

The unknown author of Eccl., who wrote under the name Koheleth, concludes after a vigorous and thorough investigation of life that all is meaningless. "I have seen everything that is done under the sun; and behold, all is vanity and a striving after wind" (1:14). The values which men cherish, whether pleasure (2:1-2), material gain (2:4-8; 5:13-17), or wisdom itself (2:15), turn out to be nothing. The best one can hope for is "to eat and drink and find enjoyment in all the toil with which one toils under the sun" (5:18).

But Koheleth's skepticism is basically religious. He clearly recognizes that God is the creator who directs men and the world as he sees fit. Indeed God so orders and controls all things that man can do nothing to change what is fixed (1:15; 3:14; 7:13-14), nor can he understand it (8:17; 11:5). Man is helpless just because the rule of God is so pervasive.

Koheleth may not have been a great thinker—certainly he was neither systematic nor consistent—but he was refreshingly honest. With all its limitations his book is a wholesome rebuke of all forms of narrow self-assurance.

V. The Theology of Wisdom

In the OT there is a central ambiguity concerning the source and nature of wisdom. At times wisdom is presented as a human achievement the concerns of which are the attainment of well-being in life. But elsewhere wisdom is thought of as ultimately derived from God and as concerned with understanding God and the divine plan for the world. Some scholars believe that this difference can be explained by recognizing that early wisdom was secular in character but began to take on a new religious dimension which gradually increased until the full flowering of religious wisdom late in the postexilic period. Other scholars even distinguish distinct wisdom schools: an earlier "secular school," whose wisdom was humanistic and utilitarian, and a later "religious school," which accepted the wisdom of the former, but modified it by adding appropriate religious elements, and whose own wisdom was theocentric.

While we might, with most scholars, doubt the existence of sharply defined wisdom schools, nonetheless there is much to be said for this general explanation. A similar description of the developing concept of wisdom has been given above. Yet one question remains. Was Israel's wisdom "secular," even in the earliest period, as this view maintains, or was the religious element present even then, albeit in less prominent degree? There are good reasons for doubting that Israel's wisdom was ever secular. Would a distinction between secular and religious even have been understood in early Israel? Was not life regarded as a whole? No such distinction was drawn in any other aspect of Israel's life. Is it not unnatural to assume that *all* the religious references in the early wisdom materials—Solomon's prayer to God for wisdom, all references to Yahweh in the early section of Prov., etc.—were later interpolations? Was not the early search for wisdom a search for meaning in life, and is not that itself religious by definition? Even if, as some have suggested, Near Eastern wisdom moved from the secular to the religious—a view which is still subject to dispute—would this necessitate a similar development in Israel, esp. since such a transition, even if it took place elsewhere, was already accomplished before that wisdom began to influence Israel?

Should we recognize, however, in light of these and other objections that Israel's early wisdom was not altogether devoid of religious content, the problem would not yet be completely solved. The further question suggests itself: Granted that there was a religious element, what kind of religion was it? The greater part of OT wisdom makes little or no use of those features which elsewhere in the OT are readily assumed as characteristic of Hebrew religion. In wisdom literature where are the law, the prophet, the priest, the temple with its ceremonies? Where are the national consciousness, the election, the covenant? Where are references to political and social events? Where are the messianic hope and missionary imperative? For the most part these are absent.

Recent scholars have succeeded in identifying the major theological strands which pervade the OT: the history of salvation as it was made known through the mighty acts of God, election faith, covenant faith, the cult with its interest in institutions. Wisdom literature emphasizes none of these. To be sure, ben Sira equates all wisdom with the law (Ecclus. 24:23) and in general brings wisdom into closer accord with the basic elements of Hebrew faith, but this is a late development.

There is another major theological theme in the OT with which the wisdom literature in all its stages seems to be in fullest accord. That is the creation faith. The affirmation that this is the primary theological perspective of wisdom necessitates an earlier dating for the emergence of creation faith than has customarily been assumed, but this is not an insurmountable obstacle and is the surest ground for integrating wisdom literature into the theology of the OT.

Of course the wise men were not exponents of "natural theology" as distinct from "revealed theology," nor did they equate God with nature. They did, however, take creation seriously as the form of Yahweh's self-revelation, and they sought to live by what it taught them.

For Further Study. O. S. Rankin, *Israel's Wisdom Literature*, 1936. J. C. Rylaarsdam, *Revelation in Jewish Wisdom Literature*, 1946. William A. Irwin, "The Wisdom Literature," in *IB*, 1952. Charles T. Fritsch, "Prov.," in *IB*, 1955. S. H. Blank, "Wisdom," in *IDB*, 1962.

THE APOCALYPTIC LITERATURE

Morton S. Enslin

I. The Meaning of Apocalyptic

"Apocalypse" as the term for a writing of a distinctive and popular type which flourished in both Judaism and early Christianity comes from the opening phrase, "the apocalypse of Jesus Christ," of one such work which now stands as the last book of the Christian Bible. The word means simply "revelation"—most English versions so translate it in Rev. 1:1—and its derivative "apocalyptic" means "revealed." These terms are appropriately descriptive of the contents of the writings, which claim to be revelations of future events which God made to eminent persons—e.g. Enoch, Abraham, Moses, Daniel, Ezra, John. Since each apocalypse except Rev. itself purports to date from a time long past, it explains its newness by the inclusion of an instruction that it is to be kept hidden from those unprepared to receive it. Therefore an earlier name for writings of this type was "apocrypha," i.e. "things hidden."

Purpose. Much confusion has been caused by these terms. Actually such books were not written, as has been often assumed, as puzzles for the curious, to afford glimpses of history still far in the future. Rather they were intended as sources of strength and confidence for contemporaries of the author who were in a period of crisis and needed encouragement to stand firm in the testing days immediately at hand. Their message is that despite the machinations of wicked men and nations shameless in their opposition to God and his chosen people —and each author seems convinced that the last and superlative act of outrage has just then been perpetrated—God's purpose cannot be stayed or thwarted. Now, at this very instant, after so long a time of misery and degradation, the final glorious victory is to be achieved. In this time of crisis—one might better say of "destiny"—men are to stand firm, to gird up their loins and meet the final onslaught. In a word, this type of writing may properly be styled a shot of adrenalin to nerve those who well might falter in despair just as the glorious day was about to dawn. Attempts to turn these practical calls to arms against a present foe in the authors' own day into timetables of events cents. distant have totally misinterpreted them.

Pseudonymity. The chief reason for confusion is that regularly these writings are pseudonymous, i.e. written under another's name. They purport to be from the pens of heroes of the past who are foretelling what must come to pass in the real author's

own day. This author is convinced that he stands at the very end of history. The bell has sounded. At any moment the long-expected day will dawn. Thus for him the future is to be very brief. But since he is writing in the name of one long dead, he must make his hero predict the whole period to elapse between that day and the expected climax. Most apocalypses therefore contain a quick review of history from the purported author's day to that of the actual author followed by a fuller but usually far less accurate forecast of the short period still to come. In consequence it is often comparatively easy to date the particular writing, viz. between the last correct historical allusion and the first error.

Extant Apocalypses. We have 3 apocalyptic books in the Bible: Dan. in the OT, II Esdras in the Apoc., and Rev. in the NT. In addition we have what seem to be fragments of others, notably the "Little Apocalypse" which many scholars see lying behind the words of Jesus "as he sat on the Mount of Olives opposite the temple" as preserved in Mark 13 and the parallels in Matt. 24; Luke 21. Joel and certain later additions to other OT prophetic books—Isa. 24–27; Ezek. 38–39; Zech. 9–14; and other shorter passages—are of a not dissimilar nature.

These, however, are but a few of the writings of this sort which were produced. Many, but far from all, have been preserved: Enoch, the Secrets of Enoch, the Apocalypse of Baruch, the Assumption of Moses, to mention only the more conspicuous.

II. The Historical Background

For the most part the apocalyptic writings come from a definite era in history of almost exactly 300 years, 165 B.C.–A.D. 135. These years extend from the rise of Judas Maccabeus in opposition to the persecutions of the Seleucid king Antiochus Epiphanes to the final subjugation of the nation by Rome after the 2nd futile attempt against the oppressor in the days of the Emperor Hadrian (see "The History of Israel," pp. 1030-31).

For cents. Israel had been subject first to one foreign oppressor then another. Dreams of a restoration after the Babylonian captivity had proved disillusioning. Persian policy permitted Jewish exiles to return to Jerusalem and rebuild the temple but speedily squelched efforts to restore the kingdom. The Jews were forced to change from a nation with its own king to a religious community with a priest at its head.

Persian Influence. Though the years of Persian control stifled hopes of a national restoration, they did not hinder the practice of Jewish religion but even proved conducive to its development. Persian religion was congenial to Judaism. Both Persian and Jew worshiped one supreme God; both had a bitter hatred of idolatry; both looked for a coming glorious age. Thus the Jewish guard was down. During the 2 cents. of Persian rule Judaism underwent many very real changes through the unconscious stimulation of ideas that were in the air. Gradually they entered her thinking and easily came to seem a part of her own uniquely glorious heritage.

The Persian belief in a future life with recompenses and penalties seemed an apt and necessary answer to the growing Jewish emphasis on the individual evidenced in the words attributed to Jeremiah and Ezekiel:

In those days they shall no longer say:
"The fathers have eaten sour grapes,
and the children's teeth are set on edge."
But every one shall die for his own sin (Jer. 31:29-30; cf. Ezek. 18).

It is not surprising that the borrowed idea that the individual is rewarded or punished after death came to replace the older Jewish view that "there is no work or thought or knowledge or wisdom in Sheol, to which you are going" (Eccl. 9:10; see comment on Ps. 6:4-5).

Persian thought was definitely dualistic. The powers of good, personified in the supreme being Ormuzd (Ahura Mazda), were in ceaseless clash with the forces of evil under their prince Ahriman (Angra Mainyu). At the end of a 12,000-year struggle between these 2 would come Shaoshyant, the last of the Persian saviors, who would prepare men for a new age utterly different from the present evil age, rouse the dead, and preside over a final judgment. By the time Jewish apocalyptic literature began to be produced similar ideas were firmly, if not always clearly, held by many orthodox Jews.

Greek and Roman Rule. Alexander the Great brought the Persian control to its end, but the Jews soon discovered that the expectations aroused by his conquest were once more mistaken. God had not raised up Alexander to restore their long-promised dominion. Instead they found themselves in a new vassalage to his successors, first to the Ptolemies in Egypt and then *ca.* 200 to the Seleucid kings of Syria. Unlike the Persians the latter overlords sought to force Greek culture and religion on all their subjects. Antiochus Epiphanes (175-163) attempted to blot the Jewish religion from the earth by defiling the Jerusalem temple and its altar, forbidding the proud badge of circumcision, and making even possession of the sacred law punishable by death. It was this crisis that produced the first true apocalyptic writing, Dan.

The successful revolt led by Judas Maccabeus and his brothers soon restored religious freedom for the Jews and eventually gained political independence— for the first time in 500 years. For *ca.* 80 years the Jews were a free nation, ruled by their high priest-kings Hyrcanus, Aristobulus, and Alexander Janneus and by a queen, Alexandra. Yet for most Jews the restoration of the kingdom brought little of the peace and well-being of which they had dreamed for so long. The period was one of continual strife, not only with outside enemies but even more among factions within the nation. To many of the faithful there seemed every reason to believe that the world had fallen wholly under the control of evil. From these dark days came the writing of Enoch, the most influential of the noncanonical apocalypses, as shown by the allusions to it in the NT.

Then, dashing any remaining hopes, came the Romans to strip the nation of its independence again. In 63 B.C. Pompey and his army marched into Jerusalem and into the temple, and once more the Jews were subject to a foreign empire. The oppressions of Roman rule gave rise to a number of apocalypses. E.g. there can be little doubt that the Little Apocalypse known to us in a later and greatly altered form in Mark 13 was inspired by the rumor that spread *ca.* A.D. 41 of a plan of the Emperor Caligula to set up his statue in the sacrosanct Holy of Holies. In the latter part of Nero's reign Jewish resentment broke into open revolt that eventuated in the destruction of Jerusalem and the temple in 70. The core of II Esdras is the most important of the Jewish apocalypses written during the aftermath of this disaster. It was as a result of the persecutions in the final years of the reign of Domitian (81-96) that the Christian Rev. was written.

III. CHARACTERISTICS OF APOCALYPTIC WRITINGS

Prophecy and Apocalypticism. The apocalyptic writings have often been styled the "new prophecy." In but a limited degree is this characterization warranted. The contrasts between them and the pre-exilic prophetic writings are far more striking than the similarities—and would be even more noticeable if traces of this later outlook had not been inserted in the books of the prophets as they have come down to us. Prophecy as seen in an Amos, Hosea, Isaiah, or Jeremiah came at a time when the nation was, at least superficially, free and prosperous. As spokesmen for God the prophets were concerned to castigate the nation for its sins. They protested against the greed and cruelty of the powerful, against the outrages so evident on every hand—e.g. selling the "needy for a pair of shoes" (Amos 2:6)—and against the blindness to the divine demand of justice and of loyalty to God alone. They declared that this flagrant flouting of God could and would lead to but one result, complete destruction. To this extent they foretold the future, but only as they saw the inevitable consequence of present sin.

These prophets were outspoken proclaimers of doom. They seemingly had no expectation that men would heed their calls to repent and therefore they had no hope for the future. In our present texts of their books there are occasional passages predicting a happy future for Israel, but these contradict the prophets' own passionate concern and are patently later insertions. The prophets themselves rebuked the nation personally, speaking boldly before rulers and people. It was only later that their messages were written down and compiled into books by disciples. In the process the starkness of their declarations of doom was often diluted by the revisions and additions of editors.

In contrast stand the writings of the apocalyptists.

They are indeed writings, literary productions, rather than records of spoken messages; and, far from being personal, they are presented under the names of persons of another time. In one sense the apocalyptists may be considered more pessimistic than the prophets, in that they view the present evil age as so utterly wicked and corrupt that nothing men could do would redeem it. But the evil age is momentarily to end. The forces of evil are rampant but it is they who are doomed. Whereas the prophet denounced, the apocalyptist encourages. "Stand firm," he says, "for the time of evil is soon to end." Thus his is a word of lively optimism.

Underlying this difference in expectation is a different view of the nature and source of the present evil. The word of the prophet was essentially, almost exclusively, moral. He denounced sin, the viciousness and disobedience of men, and saw it as the sole cause for their certain doom. Though the apocalyptist does not deny the awful consequence of sin, for the individual at least, he sees the fate which has befallen Israel as due rather to the machinations of evil spirits who have plunged the world into its sorry state. What is going on here on earth is simply the consequence and reflection of what is going on above, the bitter struggle between the hosts of evil and those of good. Thus the apocalyptist exhorts men to stand firm amid this interplay in which they are enmeshed—the invisible but tremendously potent war among the angels, some with, some against God. His basic confidence is that the coming victory, with the end of the present evil age and the advent of its entire opposite, the age to come—in the language of the gospels the kingdom of God—is to be achieved, not by human valor or even goodness, but by direct divine intervention. Though God is in contact with the present evil age, it is actually under the control of demons (cf. Paul's casual reference to the "god of this world," II Cor. 4:4), who are working its ruin, a ruin now near at hand. This note, so different in essence from that of the 8th- and 7th-cent. prophets, is to be seen in all these writings. It is esp. evident in Dan. and the Assumption of Moses.

Symbolism and Imagery. To many casual readers the most characteristic feature of apocalyptic writings is their free use of symbols and fantastic imagery. Grotesquely malformed wild beasts represent the wicked nations; domestic beasts or human figures represent Israel and individual leaders. Horns and stars abound, along with a veritable phantasmagoria of angels. This potpourri of imagery provides the apocalyptic "stage properties," for it is utilized over and over again by the different authors.

Visions. Regularly the author has his visions, often of essentially the same sort his fellow author has had. It is not too much to say that the visions which he reports having seen he did not see with his own eyes, be they of body or of mind. I.e. "vision" and "seeing" are as conventionalized for the apocalyptist as "Thus says Yahweh" for the prophet. What he wishes to express he reports as having "seen." Thus the author of Rev. can see a scroll that is rolled up and sealed with seven seals, yet can see that it is "written within and on the back" (5:1). He can turn around to see the voice which is

talking to him (1:12) and see the Son of man holding 7 stars in his right hand yet placing that same right hand on the author's head (1:16-17). He can see the new Jerusalem in the form of a perfect 1,500-mile cube (21:16). Failure to understand this convention of apocalyptic imagery has led to most unwarranted conclusions; e.g. because several Jewish apocalyptists had occasion in the course of their personally conducted tours of heaven to "see" the Messiah, some scholars have assumed that they shared the Christian idea of a preexistent Messiah.

Adaptation. The imagery is used again and again in the various writings, often with very different interpretations. E.g. Daniel, in his vision (Dan. 7) sees 3 beasts successively appear. Then comes a 4th, before whom the first 3 fall. On his head is a "little" horn in which are "eyes like the eyes of a man, and a mouth speaking great things." The heaven is opened, with a vision of God worshiped by the angelic host. Judgment is set—an indispensable scene in this type of writing—and Israel, seen as a "son of man," i.e. a human being, in contrast with the awesome wild beasts which represent Babylon, Media, Persia, and Greece, appears before the Ancient of Days and receives an "everlasting dominion, which shall not pass away." In this apocalypse, which depicts the Maccabean struggle in the form of a prophecy by the ancient hero Daniel, the 4th beast is clearly Greece, i.e. Alexander the Great's Seleucid successors, esp. Antiochus Epiphanes, the "little horn." In succeeding cents., however, Rome became the special and final abomination. Thus in later apocalypses, notably Rev. and II Esdras, the 4th beast comes to be interpreted as Rome, e.g.:

This is the interpretation of this vision which you have seen: The eagle which you saw coming up from the sea is the fourth kingdom which appeared in a vision to your brother Daniel. But it was not explained to him as I now explain or have explained to you. (II Esdras 12:10-12.)

Similarly the 70 years which Jeremiah predicted as the length of Babylon's sway over Israel (Jer. 25:11-12; 29:10), though a prophecy that numerically failed to "come to pass" (cf. Deut. 18:22; Jer. 28:9), were not forgotten. Dan. utilizes them but transforms them into 70 weeks of years (490 years), of which 69½ have already passed, with a half week (3½ years) yet to come (ch. 9). In Enoch the 70 years are interpreted as the length of the rule of 70 patron angels, and the current age is placed in the hands of the 70th angel—i.e. the end is at hand. In II Esdras Dan.'s 70 weeks are naturally recast to include Rome.

Sealed Books. Regularly apocalyptic writings carry the word that their content is to be sealed up. So to Daniel comes the injunction: "Shut up the words, and seal the book, until the time of the end" (Dan. 12:4; cf. vs. 9). In II Esdras 14 Ezra is commissioned to restore the scriptures destroyed in the fall of Jerusalem to Nebuchadrezzar and is inspired to dictate to his 5 secretaries "everything that has happened in the world from the beginning" (vs. 22). He dictates in 40 days 94 books: the 24 canonical books of the OT and 70 others. While all men may read the 24, the 70 are to be reserved, hidden from all save those competent to use them, "for in them is the spring of understanding, the fountain of wisdom, and the river of knowledge" (vs. 47).

This innocent fiction, which led to the earlier designation of apocalypses as "apocrypha," i.e. hidden books, was the natural consequence of the regular practice of ascribing them to authors in the distant past. The sealing would explain why they were hitherto unknown. Now that the end is imminent their seals are broken. This, not the notion that the authors did not desire a wide reading public, is the obvious reason for this constant emphasis. Actually the use of the names of past heroes may well have been a direct bid for public attention which a recently written book might not achieve.

In Rev. it is to be observed that this traditional touch is retained but reversed: "Do not seal up the words of the prophecy of this book, for the time is near" (22:10). The reason for the change is obvious. If the author is writing in the name of another, viz. John the apostle, his purported author has but shortly died. Thus there is no need for the long time of silence, as in the case of an Adam, Enoch, Moses, Daniel, or Ezra.

IV. The Influence of Apocalypticism

At least in the form in which we know it from the extant writings, apocalypticism is definitely a Jewish product. That it developed in Judaism unaided, however, would appear most unlikely, despite the occasional previews of it in some of the OT writings mentioned above. Rather it would seem to be the product of long and significant contact with Persian thought. It was from this source that the distinctive ideas—the basic dualism, the lush angelology, the expectations of a resurrection and final judgment—are to be seen coming. Earlier Judaism did not originate it but came to adopt, adapt, and develop it. It might even be conjectured that the conspicuous traces of it in the prophets (notably Isa. 24–27; Ezek. 38–39; Zech. 9–14) are to be seen as reflections of this later type of thinking included by postexilic editors to whom the form of thought had become natural.

Popularity. That the apocalyptic writings were popular or at least highly regarded in some circles of Judaism is certain. They never seem to have appealed to what has been styled "normative Judaism," which was to produce the rabbinical writings we know as the Talmuds, Mishnahs, and Midrashes. Here they are never mentioned. Despite their claims to antiquity and authorship by revered heroes of the past, only one of them found a place in the OT canon. This exception, Dan., finally was accepted and now stands in the Hebrew Scriptures, not among the Prophets, as in the Christian Bible, but in the 3rd section of the canon, the Writings.

This silence is not surprising. In the type of Judaism evidenced by most of the Pharisees there was no place for this sort of revelation. God had revealed his whole will through the Mosaic law. This was his medium of revelation. This same attitude—the consequence of the centrality given to written scripture—had earlier meant the end of prophecy. Nor is it surprising that the more rigidly staid conservatives, of whom the Sadducees may be seen as examples, had no time for this new development, which

they properly failed to find in the Scriptures, and which was cluttered with angels and such nonscriptural aberrations as resurrection. What was good enough for Moses was good enough for them.

In Christian circles the apocalypses were highly popular from the start—suggesting that appreciation for them was no new Gentile importation but a carry-over from popular Judaism and those of the Pharisees who appear to have found this type of thinking congenial. Nor did this popularity cease in Christian circles, as in Judaism after the rebellion in the days of Hadrian. Many more such writings were produced, e.g. apocalypses of James, of Paul, of Peter, of Stephen, of Thomas, and of the Virgin.

It is probably safe to say that had it not been for Christian use none of the Jewish apocalypses except Dan. would have been preserved. As it is, none but Dan. has come down to us in its original Hebrew or Aramaic text, and no other gained a permanent place in the Greek OT. Most are known to us only in other languages into which they were early translated—e.g. Enoch in Ethiopic, the Secrets of Enoch in Slavonic, and the Apocalypse of Baruch in Syriac. One—in very faulty Latin translation, with a late intro. and later conclusion, both palpably from Christian pens—came to be added as an appendix in some manuscripts of the Vulg. and thus got to be the solitary example of this wildfire prose in the Protestant OT Apoc. under the caption II Esdras.

Yet that all the early Christians shared the apocalyptic viewpoint is most unlikely. At precisely the moment when the author of Rev. was dipping his pen in gall and vitriol to compose his diatribe against Rome and her godless emperor worship, another Christian may well have been writing an epistle in which he insisted, as Paul had before him: "Honor all men. Love the brotherhood. Fear God. Honor the emperor" (I Pet. 2:17).

Abiding Values. The apocalyptic writers erred in thinking they had heard the heavenly trumpet sounding the last hour. They may also be criticized for overstressing the catastrophic, for finding a too easy explanation of the chaos on earth as a mere shadow of the greater chaos in the invisible realm above, for minimizing the responsibility of men to work out their destiny, for encouraging their readers to wait for divine intervention. However their confidence, fanatic though it may by some be styled, that in the end right will prevail is not to be overlooked. Thus these men made a real contribution at a time when courage in many was ebbing low. To many modern readers these writings may seem outdated, repellent, actually repulsive, with their lush imagery and nightmarish visions. Nevertheless it may be pondered if a new apocalyptic, phrased in an imagery as natural in this day as theirs was in that day, is not a compelling need.

For Further Study. F. C. Porter, *The Messages of the Apocalyptic Writers,* 1905. R. H. Charles, *The Apoc. and Pseudepigrapha of the OT,* 1913. F. C. Burkitt, *Jewish and Christian Apocalypses,* 1914. G. F. Moore, *Judaism,* 1927. M. S. Enslin, *Christian Beginnings,* 1938, pp. 351-72. H. H. Rowley, *The Relevance of Apocalyptic,* rev. ed., 1946. R. H. Pfeiffer, "The Literature and Religion of the Pseudepigrapha," in *IB,* 1952. Martin Rist, "Apocalypticism," in *IDB,* 1962.

THE INTERTESTAMENTAL LITERATURE

Lucetta Mowry

The 2 cents. between the rise of the Maccabean family to political power (*ca.* 165 B.C.) and the period of Roman control of Jewish political life in Palestine under the procurators when the Christian church had its beginning presents the historian with a complex yet fascinating series of events. The persons who took part in these events and indeed were in large measure responsible for them have been familiar figures throughout history—e.g. Judas Maccabeus, Pompey, Antony, Cleopatra, Herod the Great, Pontius Pilate, Hillel, Shammai, John the Baptist, and Jesus himself. Not only the Jews of Palestine but also those settled in other lands were caught up in tensions created by these persons and by others unnamed and forgotten. No area of life was free from the necessity of adjusting to the various forces, political, social, economic, and religious, which pressed on men from every quarter.

The religious parties within Judaism and the individual religious leaders reflect in their teachings and writings the chaotic uncertainty of the times. What makes this period so intensely interesting is the variety of answers given to those searching for a way of deliverance, a way of salvation or redemption. Some Jews, valuing the tradition of their fathers, tried to ignore the changes in their world. Others, while cherishing the tradition, were willing to accommodate its values and ideals to those of the Gentile world. Still others preferred to abandon the ancient ways of thought and action because of their apparent lack of relevancy.

The Jewish writings of this period comprise an extensive literary output of great variety. They have been somewhat artificially classified as Apoc. and Pseudepigrapha, to which we may now add certain other writings, esp. those of the Qumran sectarians discovered among the Dead Sea scrolls. The recognition that Dan. was written *ca.* 165 and Esth. perhaps even later, whereas several of the Apoc. apparently must be dated earlier, e.g. Ecclus. *ca.* 180, and that II Esdras comes from the end of the first cent. A.D., after many of the NT books were written, requires that the customary designation "intertestamental" be understood rather loosely.

I. The Apocrypha

The 15 books which in Protestant usage are know as the Apoc. are those found in the LXX and Vulg. versions of the OT but not in the Hebrew.

They were set off separately by the Protestant reformers, but in Roman Catholic editions all except I, II Esdras and the Prayer of Manasseh are interspersed among the books of the OT. As arranged in Protestant editions the Apoc. are: I, II Esdras, Tobit, Judith, Additions to Esth., Wisd. Sol., Ecclus., Baruch, Letter of Jeremiah, Prayer of Azariah and Song of the Three Young Men, Susanna, Bel and the Dragon, Prayer of Manasseh, I, II Macc.

The term "Apocrypha," lit. "hidden," is often taken to mean "spurious" and therefore of little value. Less frequently it is understood as referring to the esoteric and profound, which is to be withheld for the edification of those already familiar with the canonical documents.

Historical Writings. There are 3 histories: I Esdras, I, II Macc. Of the 3 I Macc., which narrates the Jewish struggle for political and religious liberty under the first generation of the Maccabean family, is the document most accurately designated as historical. Though the authors of the other two documents have based their works on historical events, they have been so eager to dramatize these events (II Macc.) or to use the material for didactic purposes, ethical or religious (I Esdras), that their reports must be taken with critical caution.

Fictional Writings. Five of the books are works of fiction: Tobit, Judith, Additions to Esth., Susanna, and Bel and the Dragon. The Additions to Esth. have little meaning unless read along with the canonical book. In contrast the following 2 books are additions to Dan. which can stand independently as short detective stories. They effectively and vividly point out on the one hand the rewards of traditional Jewish piety and moral rectitude and on the other the futility of false pagan religious beliefs and ethical practices. Similarly the authors of Tobit and Judith use fictional narrative as a didactic means to show how God guides his loyal and law-abiding devotees through all sorts of disasters and ultimately bestows upon them appropriate rewards.

Didactic Writings. Ecclus. and Wisd. Sol., though quite different in character, are significant works in the tradition of Israel's wisdom literature. Ecclus. is more traditional in character isofar as it stresses the true nature of wisdom in its practical and social aspects. While the author of Wisd. Sol. reflects his training in the conventional piety of orthodox Judaism, he very effectively combines this tradition with Greek philosophical thought current in Alexandria during the first half of the first cent. B.C. By this combination he is able to set forth a telling apologetic for Judaism against idolatrous paganism.

The Letter of Jeremiah stresses this same theme in a polemic rather than apologetic vein. Baruch, Jeremiah's secretary, is indicated as the author of a 2nd work associated with the prophet. The book, however, is clearly composite in character. It contains a brief account of events taking place in Babylonia in the 5th year after the fall of Jerusalem which includes prayers of confession for divine mercy. There follows a poetic section on wisdom, i.e. the law, which God gave to Israel alone, and words of comfort and exhortation.

Apocalyptic Writing. The Jewish portion of II Esdras (chs. 3-14; see Intro.) reflects the sense of tragedy experienced by the Jews as a result of the destruction of Jerusalem in the war with Rome (A.D. 70; see "The Apocalyptic Literature," pp. 1106-09). Bizarre and fantastic as the apocalyptic visions are, the author is nevertheless struggling with a difficult question: If God is merciful and just, how could this disaster have befallen us when pagan cities continue to flourish and prosper?

Devotional Writing. The Prayer of Manasseh is an outstanding prayer of confession, matched in the OT only by Ps. 51 with its expression of hope for redemption from a personal sense of guilt. The prayer in a remarkable way reflects the depth of feeling of the penitent and the hope that God with his infinite mercy will redeem those who are of contrite and lowly heart.

II. The Pseudepigrapha

The term "pseudepigrapha," lit. "false writings," originally was used of certain Jewish works pretending to have been written by famous biblical characters of much earlier times. In time it came to be extended to all the Jewish writings outside the canonical OT and the Apoc. which were valued and preserved by various branches of the early church, even though some of them were anonymous rather than pseudonymous. In this respect the term is unfortunate since it implies that all the Pseudepigrapha are spurious and the canonical and Apoc. books by contrast are genuine, whereas some of the latter are actually pseudonymous also, e.g. Eccles., Dan., Wisd. Sol. Roman Catholics call these books Apoc. using the word in the sense of "spurious."

A precise list of the works included in the Pseudepigrapha has not become established, though most of the books have long been included in this category. In 1913 R. H. Charles published a collection which made this literature familiar to most biblical scholars. In it he placed IV Ezra, i.e. the Jewish portion of II Esdras (see Intro.), among the Pseudepigrapha rather than the Apoc.—a classification in which a number of scholars have followed him—and included 3 works not found in earlier lists: Sayings of the Fathers, a wisdom work which later became a tractate of the Mishnah, the earlier portion of the Talmud; Ahikar, a non-Jewish Aramaic work probably written in Assyria in the 5th cent. B.C. (see Intro. to Tobit); and Fragments of a Zadokite Work, also known as the Damascus Document, which the Dead Sea scrolls have identified as a writing of the

Qumran sect. In 1945 C. C. Torrey, who lumped the Apoc. and Pseudepigrapha together under the term Apoc., omitted Charles's 3 additions from his list but added instead the Lives of the Prophets and the Testament of Job. To these may now be added also the Paralipomena (lit. "omitted acts") of Jeremiah, which has come to be recognized as basically a Jewish work with later Christian additions.

Most of these writings seem to have originated in Palestine in either Hebrew or Aramaic, but the Semitic originals have been lost except for some fragments found among the Dead Sea scrolls. They were translated into Greek at the great Greek-speaking center of Judaism in Alexandria, where the works composed in Greek probably originated. Even the Greek versions of many of them did not survive, however, and they have become known only in translations made from the Greek into other ancient languages. All of them seem to date from a period of 3 cents. between 165 B.C. and A.D. 135.

Apocalyptic Writings. Both the Jews of Palestine and to a lesser extent those of Alexandria found the apocalyptic form useful for expressing their religious aspirations and hopes for a new age. Though Pharisaic Judaism tended to ignore and discourage this type of visionary fantasy, nevertheless apocalyptic literature flourished during the intertestamental period in certain circles of Judaism. Because of the pseudonymity characteristic of such writings it is difficult to determine the precise origin of each document.

The largest and most influential of these apocalyptic books is Enoch, actually a compilation made during the first cent. B.C. of several different and often contradictory works claiming authorship by the patriarch supposedly translated to heaven (Gen. 5:21-24; cf. Heb. 11:5). It was composed in Hebrew or Aramaic or both but is extant as a whole only in Ethiopic, though parts of the Greek version have been found. Several NT authors seem to show acquaintance with Enoch, and Jude 14-15 quotes from it. Jude 9 is identified by early Christian commentators as a reference to another apocalyptic work, the Assumption of Moses, which dates from Jesus' lifetime; but the passage referred to is not in the portion extant in a Latin version. The Apocalypse of Baruch, or II Baruch, attributed to Jeremiah's secretary, was written after the Roman destruction of Jerusalem (A.D. 70), probably in Hebrew; it is extant only in Syriac. In addition to these Palestinian works there are 2 late apocalypses composed in Greek: Slavonic Enoch, II Enoch, or Secrets of Enoch, extant only in Slavonic; and III Baruch, or Greek Apocalypse of Baruch, which has been preserved in the original language.

It is interesting to note that sections of one of these apocalyptic works, Enoch, have been discovered in the remains of the library of the Qumran sect. Yet the most important section of this apocalypse, the Similitudes of Enoch (chs. 37-71), has not turned up there—quite understandably. In this section the apocalyptic visionary of the future portrays the messianic deliverer as the pre-existent, transcendental Son of Man. This view must have come from some other group, as yet unidentified, for it could in no way be tenable for the Qumran sect with its expectation of 3 messianic figures, the eschatological prophet and the 2 Messiahs of Aaron and of Israel. It would seem, then, that the apocalyptic form of expression satisfied the spiritual needs of a number of groups or individuals, including NT authors. Inspired by Dan., they found this genre commendable for encouraging the oppressed adherents of the faith to maintain their loyalty in the assurance that God's righteousness would ultimately manifest itself on their behalf.

Historical Legends. Seven Palestinian works and one Alexandrian may be classified as historical legends. Recent discoveries in the caves of Qumran indicate that 2 of these are to be associated with the monastic community which produced the Dead Sea scrolls: Jubilees and at least sections of the testaments of Levi and Naphtali from the larger work known as the Testaments of the 12 Patriarchs. Because of this association it is no longer possible to claim with as much confidence as formerly that these works were written by Pharisees.

The extant Greek manuscripts of the Testaments of the 12 Patriarchs contain so many Christian elements that some scholars have maintained that only the parts represented by the Qumran fragments are Jewish and that the work as a whole should be dated in the 2nd cent. A.D. or later. On the other hand many of the allegedly Christian moral counsels are equally characteristic of the Qumran sectaries. Thus the more general view is that the basic work was composed in Hebrew in the 2nd cent. B.C.

The structure of this document is an interesting literary development of Jacob's deathbed blessing of his sons (Gen. 49:1-27). Inspired by this earlier poem, the author has each of Jacob's 12 sons deliver on his own deathbed a testament which combines pseudo history, wise counsels, and prophecies. Each includes a legendary narrative of the patriarch's life, his words of wisdom on a characteristic vice or virtue —with frequent stress on God's delight in the unity of the brothers based on love and on conflict against the evil one, Beliar—a prophecy regarding his posterity, and a concluding account of his death and burial.

Throughout the series Levi assumes a position of importance, stressed esp. in his own testament. It opens with the declaration that, having always enjoyed good health, he has needed a special revelation that his death is imminent. He dutifully calls in his sons and recounts to them his sins, for which he has been duly repentant. Then he describes how an angelic guide took him through the 7 spheres of heaven and revealed the divine plan for his own mission on earth: not only to reveal God's mysteries to men but also to serve as the great priestly model for Israel until God comes to Jerusalem to reign as sovereign over his nation. It is further revealed to Levi that his descendants will disgrace the high office of the priesthood. Counsels of wisdom appropriately find their place in his pseudo-historical account of the events by which it is to reach the nadir of corruption and degeneracy. At this lowest point in Israel's religious life Levi prophesies that during the last generation of men God will raise up a new priest from his descendants to rule over Israel, to remove darkness from the world, to bring peace to the earth, and to open the gates of Paradise for the saints (18:2-14). In this testament, as in others, it is clear that the Messiah from Levi's line is superior to the kingly Messiah from the line of David, a doctrine esp. suitable for the disaffected and disillusioned priestly monastics at Qumran.

Of Jubilees the only complete manuscript is in Ethiopic, though part of it is found also in Latin. Evidently it was originally written in Hebrew in the latter half of the 2nd cent. B.C. Because of the ideas it expresses as well as the discovery of the cave fragments it is now considered a writing of the Qumran sectaries rather than the Pharisees.

The book takes its title from the author's precise dating of the events narrated in Gen. 1–Exod. 12— retold in a version purportedly revealed to Moses on Mt. Sinai—according to a chronological scheme of "weeks" of years composing 49-year cycles, with a jubilee year marking the end of each (see comment on Lev. 25:8-12). Recently scholars have directed attention to the book's unusual annual religious calendar, which it claims to be divinely ordained and therefore the one and only valid calendar. Clearly one of its main objectives is to stress the sanctity of the Qumran festival calendar. This emphasis must reflect a bitter dispute in which the Qumran sectaries were engaged with the temple authorities at Jerusalem. According to the book their calendar is the one decreed by God, written on "heavenly tablets" like the law, and followed by the patriarchs and Moses. Obviously if the rites in the Jerusalem temple were performed according to a calendar influenced by Greek paganism it would be utterly impossible for the Qumran purists to worship there. Their withdrawal to the desert on the NW shore of the Dead Sea was thus in part necessitated by the controversy over the calendar.

Another ritual practice stressed in Jubilees is the importance of a particular annual festival, the feast of weeks, i.e. Pentecost. Not only, it declares, did significant events occur on this day during the patriarchal period but esp. on this day Moses received God's gift of the law on Mt. Sinai. The document therefore gives a great deal of information about how and why the Qumran sectaries rewrote the biblical narrative. Their legendary additions gave support to their religious beliefs and practices.

A 3rd historical legend, the Martyrdom of Isaiah, has certain features which some scholars believe point to an origin in the Qumran community, though no evidence of it has as yet been found among the cave fragments. This work is extant only in an Ethiopic text, where it is combined with 2 Christian works under the title Ascension of Isaiah. According to the Jewish story Isaiah predicts to King Hezekiah that his son Manasseh will give himself so thoroughly to the control of Beliar, i.e. Satan, that he will reign as one of the most evil kings in Israel's history. One of his wicked deeds will be the persecution of God's loyal worshipers, including the execution of Isaiah himself. This prediction does indeed come to pass, through the machinations of a false Samaritan prophet. Isaiah is sawed in 2 (cf. Heb. 11:37) with a "wooden saw"—evidently a translator's misinterpretation of "wood saw"—but in a state of ecstasy he miraculously feels no pain. The story closes with the comment: "He neither cried aloud nor wept, but his lips spake with the Holy Spirit until he was sawn in twain" (5:14, trans. R. H. Charles).

This story illustrates the type of legend found in such works. It is retold in the Lives of the Prophets, which includes legendary biographies of all the prophets to whom OT books are attributed and also a number mentioned in Kings and Chr. Other writings in this category are the Paralipomena of Jeremiah, Testament of Job, and Life of Adam and Eve. The last is known in 3 widely differing versions, Greek, Latin, and Slavonic; and the Greek has often been referred to as the Apocalypse of Moses because erroneously so identified by the 19th-cent. editor who first published it. Whereas these Palestinian legends deal with OT characters, an Alexandrian legend, III Macc., tells of an alleged victory of Egyptian Jews over persecutions of Ptolemy IV Philopator (221-203 B.C.). Its author imitates II Macc., or its source, but makes no mention of the Maccabees, and its title is apparently due to scribal error.

All of these writings enhance the miraculous element, and most of them in their extant forms have further wondrous happenings added from Christian circles. Even more than the apocalypses they indicate that at least certain pious groups were unable to cope with the problems of the day in a tough-minded, realistic manner and sank to such a level of credulity that their faith must be nourished primarily by this kind of literature.

Pss. The collection of hymns known as the Pss. of Solomon are a valuable addition to the range of literature produced in the intertestamental period. While liturgical poetry is to be found in such books as Tobit and Judith, this collection and the recently discovered Pss. of Thanksgiving among the scrolls of the Qumran community are unique. Its 18 pss. follow the literary forms and character of the canonical Pss., but none of them measures up to the quality of the best in the earlier collection. One reason for this failure may be the psalmist's involvement in the immediate political situation. The intensity with which he felt the specific pressures of his day may have prevented him from creating an immortal expression of the soul's triumphant aspirations and hopes. At any rate his concern with the issue of power politics is indicated by the references to abuses practiced by the party in control of the nation's life.

The specific situation reflected in these hymns, so it seems, is the tyranny of the Hasmoneans, the high priest-kings of the Maccabean line. Because they have harmfully ruled the nation they will receive in due course their just punishment. In ps. 8 Pompey is regarded as the instrument to be used for their defeat. The ultimate answer to the political problem, however, is not Pompey, who is said to have met his end in Egypt (2:30-31), but the Davidic Messiah. In ps. 17, which is undoubtedly the most important of the entire collection, the poet revives this ancient messianic hope. God will raise up for the nation Israel one from the line of David who will shatter the wicked rulers, cleanse Jerusalem from the Gentiles, drive out evil men from the land, and crush the arrogant "like the vessels of the potter." When he has conquered Israel's enemies he will rule his kingdom with righteousness. The messianic figure here differs markedly from those mentioned earlier in the Testament of Levi and the

Similitudes of Enoch. The psalmist looks forward to a national leader rather than to an inspired priest or a supernatural deliverer.

Propaganda Literature. The Alexandrian Jews not only produced literature of the types familiar in Palestine, as already mentioned, but also created new types needed to communicate Jewish ideals and beliefs to the larger Greco-Roman world. Among these was pseudonymous literature for propaganda purposes attributed to Gentiles, represented by the Letter of Aristeas and the Sibylline Oracles. Though quite different in literary form, both were designed primarily to prove the superiority of Jewish wisdom over Greek philosophy and of Jewish religion over pagan beliefs and practices.

The Letter of Aristeas, probably written near the end of the 2nd cent. B.C., is a narrative in the form of a purported letter of a Greek official of Ptolemy II Philadelphus (283-247). It seeks to prove 2 points: (a) the Greek version of the OT is no distortion of the original Hebrew text and (b) the Mosaic law provides more satisfactory answers on philosophical, ethical and political issues than does Greek philosophy. The evidence for the first point is a story that verges on the miraculous—at least to those acquainted with the history of translation committees from the KJV on—how 72 expert linguists, 6 from each of the 12 tribes of Israel, translated all 5 books of the Law in 72 days and ended in unanimous agreement about the accuracy of the new version. The 2nd point is proved by a debate in which the 72 Jews triumph over their opponents because of their greater skill and knowledge.

The historical basis for the story, which is certainly legendary in character, is that sometime during the 3rd or possibly 2nd cent. B.C. the Alexandrian Jewish community found it necessary to translate the Pentateuch and eventually the entire OT from Hebrew into Greek in order to read and understand it. From this story or, more likely, from a tradition lying behind it that the Pentateuch translation was made or sponsored by a body of 70 (cf. Exod. 24:1, 9-10; Num. 11:16-17, 24-25) the Alexandrian version came to be known as that of the *septuaginta*, Greek for 70. It became the OT of the early Christians, who therefore highly valued Aristeas as a witness to the reliability of their scriptures.

The Sibylline Oracles propagandized Judaism effectively in the Greco-Roman world in quite another way. Boldly an Alexandrian Jew of the 2nd cent. B.C. appropriated a literary form popular among the pagans—obscure and often ambiguous Homeric hexameters attributed to a figure of Greek tradition, the ancient prophetess Sibylla. Incorporating some of the pagan vss., he composed others in the same style to communicate the truths of Judaism, esp. monotheism and the Mosaic law, and to narrate the chief events of Hebrew history. Other Jews and later Christians added oracles until *ca.* the 4th cent. A.D. to make a total of 15 books, of which almost 12 survive.

Popular Philosophy. Finally the Pseudepigrapha include a work which skillfully combines Greek philosophical thought and Hebraic religious views in the form of a diatribe or well-organized treatise. IV Macc. dates from the early part of the first cent. A.D. and was composed in Greek, probably at Alexandria, though some scholars favor Antioch. Quite clearly its author was reared in the synagogual school and deeply revered the tradition of Judaism. At the same time he was learned in Greek philosophy, esp. that taught by Zeno and his school of Stoics, which had become dominant in the Greco-Roman world of his day. His writing shows that he loves the one and respects the other and may therefore wish to equate these 2 world views. Nevertheless he tends in actual fact to make Moses Zeno's teacher.

The thesis of his work is that reason triumphs over passions. After defining his terms he proves his point in 2 ways, by philosophical argumentation and by examples of how it has worked out in the lives of heroic individuals. He defines reason as follows:

> Reason I take to be the mind preferring with clear deliberation the life of wisdom. Wisdom I take to be the knowledge of things, divine and human, and of their causes. This I take to be the culture acquired under the Law, through which we learn with due reverence the things of God and for our worldly profit the things of man (1:15-17, trans. R. B. Townshend).

In his philosophical discussion (1:13-3:18) he states that wisdom is demonstrated in the 4 Stoic virtues, prudence, justice, courage, and temperance. This argument is interspersed with several brief examples of OT heroes who nobly endured anguish of heart and is followed by a lengthy account (3:19-7:24) of the Maccabean martyrs Eleazar and the 7 brothers and their mother, adapted and expanded from II Macc. or its source, in which harrowing details of their fortitude in enduring torture are cited as illustrations of the thesis. One of the most interesting doctrines in this document is that the death of the martyr can in some way ransom the nation and purify it of its sin (6:29; 17:21).

III. The Dead Sea Scrolls

The probability that certain of the Pseudepigrapha are products of the Qumran sectarians has already been mentioned. It suggests that some or even all of their writings discovered among the Dead Sea scrolls were likewise circulated outside their own monastic community. Certainly this supposition is supported by the fact that parts of the Damascus Document, the Fragments of a Zadokite Work of the Charles collection, which deals with their own organization and rules, were found earlier in the remains of a medieval synagogue. These Qumran documents are discussed in a special article in this volume (see "The Dead Sea Scrolls," pp. 1063-71) but for comparison the several literary types may be noted here. There are essentially 4 types: (a) Biblical paraphrases and commentaries, on Gen., Pss., Isa., Hos., Mic., Nah., Hab., Zeph. These are significant because of the sect's exegetical procedure in interpreting OT documents. (b) Apocalyptic writings, esp. the War of the Sons of Light and Sons of Darkness, an imaginative description of the battle preceding the final triumph of God, and the Apocalypse of the New Jerusalem with its picture of a purified temple. (c) Handbooks of the sect, e.g. the Damascus Document and the Manual of Discipline, containing rules of the order to prepare the members

for entry into the new age. (d) Devotional literature, including prayers and esp. the Pss. of Thanksgiving, which though perhaps not equal to the best of the OT Pss. in beauty of style and structure are moving expressions of trust in God's unfailing power to deliver his faithful followers from doubt, adversities, and calamities.

IV. Other Intertestamental Literature

It may be conjectured that the extant writings named above represent only a fraction of the Jewish literature produced during the intertestamental period. Of the quantity and character of that published but not preserved in Palestine, where seemingly anonymous and pseudonymous authors won lasting readership more often than those who laid claim to their works, we have little information. But in the larger Greco-Roman world authorship often brought some measure of fame if not wealth, and thus a number of Hellenistic Jews identified themselves in their writings and achieved mention and even quotation in later literature. Most of these wrote histories, presumably of the same legendary character as those described above; but some ventured into the forms and meters of Greek poetry to produce epics, e.g. glorifications of Jerusalem and of Shechem, and dramas, e.g. one in the style of a classic tragedy based on the Exodus. In contrast to the unknown and barely known are 2 major literary figures, Jewish authors whose writings in Greek have been recognized as highly significant since their first appearance.

Philo. Among the large Jewish population of the great cultural center of Alexandria there arose a school of Hellenistic-Jewish metaphysical thought that reached its climax in Philo, whose activity covered most of the first half of the first cent. A.D. He was not only a prolific and profound author but also an active participant in the political affairs of his people and on one occasion headed a delegation to Rome on behalf of religious freedom for the Jews. His most ambitious literary effort was his allegorical commentary on Gen., a monumental work in which he endeavored to reinterpret the ancient traditions and esp. the Mosaic law in the light of Greek philosophy and thus commend them to the intelligentsia of his day. Some NT authors have been thought to show acquaintance with Philo's writings.

Josephus. Though sometimes not included among the intertestamental literature because of their date near the end of the first cent. A.D., the writings of Josephus (37-ca. 100) deserve mention if only because some scholars have suspected that certain passages in Luke-Acts reflect acquaintance with them. In any case they are our chief source for Jewish history during the intertestamental period. A Palestinian, indeed a priest, Josephus won the patronage of the emperors Vespasian, Titus, and Domitian, whose family name Flavius he adopted, and did his writing in Rome. His first work was an account of the Jewish War of 66-70, in which he had fought, told in 7 books, of which the first reviews Jewish history from Antiochus Epiphanes (ca. 175 B.C.) to the beginning of the war. His major work is Antiquities of the Jews, published in 93. Of its 20 books the first 11 retell the story in the OT and the rest give a fuller account, with some discrepancies, of the history in the first book of his earlier work. In addition he wrote an autobiography and an apology for the Jews known as *Against Apion*. All are extant and remain a valuable resource in biblical studies.

Oral Tradition. In surveying the literature of the intertestamental period we must take into account a development which, though not literature in the sense of being written, was of equivalent significance. In Palestine, as in Egypt, there was a need for translation of the OT. During the last cents. B.C. Hebrew was almost entirely disappearing as a spoken language and was being replaced by Aramaic. In the synagogues it became the custom, therefore, to have an interpreter stand beside the reader of the Hebrew text to translate the passages selected from the Law and the Prophets. Though rules controlling these translations were rather strict, nevertheless it is possible that there was little discrimination between translation and preaching. It seems likely that this oral development of interpretation and exposition during the intertestamental period led to the creation of the literary monuments of normative Judaism, the Mishnah and the Targums, beginning *ca.* A.D. 200.

Finally, a survey of the intertestamental literature leads one to make 2 conclusions: (*a*) It is obvious that in the various circles of Jewry, whether Palestinian or Hellenistic, the Mosaic law had a position of supreme and central importance. Wherever the Jew might find himself, it provided the common bond which united him with his fellows. Even for the Hellenistic Jew who attempted to reach out to the pagan and to communicate to him by use of Greek words and ideas the truth of the law, it still set him apart from the world of paganism. (*b*) Though the law was the focal point of Jewish life, various groups differed radically in their interpretation of its meaning. The writings from these religious movements are indicative of the dynamic character of Judaism in this period. Jews were struggling to understand the full significance of the law as a guide and norm for life. What they wrote in the attempt is a testimony to the vitality of Judaism.

For Further Study. R. H. Charles, ed., *The Apoc. and Pseudepigrapha of the OT*, 1913. W. O. E. Oesterley, *An Intro. to the Books of the Apoc.*, 1935. C. C. Torrey, *The Apocryphal Literature: A Short Intro.*, 1945. R. H. Pfeiffer, *History of NT Times, With an Intro. to the Apoc.*, 1949; "The Literature and Religion of the Apoc.," "The Literature and Religion of the Pseudepigrapha," in *IB*, 1951. B. M. Metzger, *An Intro. to the Apoc.*, 1957. C. T. Fritsch, "Apoc.," "Pseudepigrapha"; Judah Goldin, "Josephus, Flavius"; E. R. Goodenough, "Philo Judeus," in *IDB*, 1962. H. H. Rowley, *The Relevance of Apocalyptic*, rev. ed., 1964. See also under "The Dead Sea Scrolls," pp. 1063-71.

THE NEW TESTAMENT
AND THE CHRISTIAN COMMUNITY

Sherman E. Johnson

I. The Community and the Literature

The NT, or properly speaking the books of the New Covenant, emerged out of the life of the Christian community. The process of making the NT was approximately complete in the late 4th cent. The community had become the Catholic Church, whose outward unity was symbolized by the councils of bishops, beginning with Nicaea (A.D. 325). But there were some bishops and congregations who were rejected by the "orthodox," and there had previously been disputes and schisms in the community. More were to come. Though the most influential leaders of the time stood for our present 27 NT books, the Council of Laodicea in 367 still rejected Rev. Meanwhile Egypt had a larger NT and the Syriac-speaking church a much smaller one (see "The Making of the NT Canon," pp. 1216-24).

Thus more than 300 years after the Crucifixion neither the community nor the NT can be defined with absolute precision. What, then, were they?

As at the beginning, the community was a collection of groups that found their relationship to God and to one another through the personality, the deeds, and the sayings of Jesus of Nazareth. Even when they disagreed and rejected one another it was because of this bond; otherwise they would not have cared deeply enough to differ and might have ignored one another. The majority accepted the OT as a true revelation of God. But all Christians, from the 2nd cent. on, had some kind of NT and relied on it.

The NT was a collection of collections. Its nucleus consisted of 4 gospels, the letters of Paul—eventually including the "Pastorals" (i.e. I, II Tim., Tit.) and Hebrews—and the book of Acts binding them together. Soon a collection of "Catholic" (i.e. general) epistles, partly modeled on Paul's letters, began to emerge. At one time there was a tendency toward a collection of apocalypses, but only one, that bearing the name of John, maintained its position.

The real, almost unconscious, criterion of selection was the value to the community of the individual book. To us there may seem little reason to choose Jude and II Pet. instead of I Clement, but the former bore apostolic names. Otherwise the selection was almost inevitable. An apostolic name may have helped the 4th gospel to be established, but it was no doubt the theological and devotional power of the book that insured it a place in the canon. Gospels bearing the names of Peter, Andrew, James, and Thomas were rejected.

II. Variety of Early Christianity

The community that produced the NT can be described only from the NT itself; apart from a few slighting or hostile references, pagan and Jewish sources tell us almost nothing about it.

One who penetrates beneath the surface of the NT is immediately struck by the variety of the thought and life of early Christianity. This was partly due to its wide geographical distribution. In Palestine the church was predominantly Jewish, though it included Samaritans. Antioch, the 3rd largest city of the empire, contained both Jews and Gentiles. Philippi was a Roman colony, Corinth a cosmopolitan port where goods were transshipped across the isthmus, and Ephesus a rich Greek city almost fanatically devoted to the empire. Colossae, far inland in Asia Minor, had a peculiar spiritual life of its own in which Jewish and Hellenistic elements were mingled. Rome, we may imagine, was open to every type of influence that existed in the early church.

Individual personalities counted for much. Paul, who is best known to us, was an oriental Jew of stormy temperament and strong will. He was eloquent in Greek and had an original and creative mind. While Paul in his letters emphasizes man's powerlessness to save himself, the author of Jas. teaches a simple religion of obedience to the moral law. Luke, often thought to have been Paul's disciple, was polished, thoughtful, and sympathetic, with a special interest in the history of the Christian movement and no particular attachment to Paul's specific theology. Matthew, with his concern for community life and the new law of Christ, is a personality, entirely different from the 4th evangelist, who emphasizes the spiritual life of the individual. A church that read and valued Rev., with its proclamation of the near end of the age, would have an outlook different from one that read Luke and John, which expected an indefinitely long continuation of church life and the preaching of the gospel.

Above all, the interplay of the new and the old made for variety. Just how radical was the break with the old religion? How much was Christianity a continuation of the OT tradition and how much a new faith? Various answers were given.

III. THE OLD AND THE NEW

The problem arises at the very beginning in the tradition of Jesus' deeds and words. We read: "Think not that I have come to abolish the law and the prophets; I have come not to abolish them but to fulfill them. For truly, I say to you, till heaven and earth pass away, not an iota, not a dot, will pass away from the law until all is accomplished" (Matt. 5:17-18). "The scribes and the Pharisees sit on Moses' seat; so practice and observe whatever they tell you" (Matt. 23:2-3). On the other hand the gospels contain such words as these: "The law and the prophets were until John; since then the good news of the kingdom of God is preached and every one enters it violently" (Luke 16:16)—a saying followed immediately by one on the permanence of the law. Again, "Can the wedding guests fast while the bridegroom is with them? . . . . No one sews a piece of unshrunk cloth on an old garment. . . . No one puts new wine in old wineskins" (Mark 2:19, 21-22).

Jesus must have appeared to his contemporaries as an unofficial teacher of the law and as a prophet. He approached the OT more freely than did the rabbis of the time. Both realized that one provision in the law might override another, but Jesus seems clearly to have gone behind the letter of the OT to its spirit. His point of view was not far from that of Paul: "The written code kills but the Spirit gives life" (II Cor. 3:6). The gospels portray him as specially endowed with the Holy Spirit (Mark 1:10; Luke 4:1, 14), and at least once he claimed to be acting by the Spirit (Matt. 12:28; cf. Mark 3:29; Luke 4:18). More often he claimed no authority except the transparent truth of his words.

In Judaism the categories of law and prophecy were not regarded as in opposition. Moses was considered a prophet (Deut. 18:15), while the Jews thought of the prophets as upholders and transmitters of the written and oral law. The Christian church from the beginning appealed to 3 sources of truth and authority: the OT, the tradition of Jesus' words and deeds, and the Holy Spirit present in the community. Christian prophets continued to arise until the 2nd cent., when because of the apocalyptic movement known as Montanism the great church became suspicious of prophecy. Rev. and the letters of Ignatius bear witness to the work of prophets.

Jesus shifted the balance between the legal tradition on the one side and prophecy and the Spirit on the other. The problem of the early church was: How new is the gospel, and how old? The leaders of Judaism had rejected Jesus, but he had not forsaken his own people and the old religion. Though he had interpreted the law with prophetic freedom, he had lived as a Jew. With very few exceptions the early Christians joyously claimed spiritual descent from the old stock. Paul emphasized his Judaism again and again; Luke, who was a Gentile, dwelt lovingly on the religious life in which Jesus was born and nurtured. One of the themes of the 4th gospel is that the Hebrew scriptures must be read in a Christian light, and Rev. says that the non-Christian Jews are no true Jews at all (Rev. 2:9; 3:9). The implication is that the genuine Jews are Christians.

Stephen is pictured as more radical than others; he held that the Jews, save for a small remnant, had always gone wrong (Acts 7:35-53). Certain sections in the gospels—Mark 7:1-13; Matt. 23:1-36; John 7-8—take almost as strong a position. These passages, sometimes extremely bitter, may come out of controversies with non-Christian Jews. There is of course evidence of persecution of Christians by the synagogue (I Thess. 2:14-16; John 16:1-3). In turn the Christians called Jews "hypocrites." Heb. goes still further: the OT ordinances were no more than types and shadows of the true sacrificial worship.

Yet the church was slow to go beyond the bounds of Judaism and to appeal to Samaritans and Gentiles. The conservatives—and there were Christians who claimed to be Pharisees (Acts 15:5)—followed the tradition that restricted Jesus' work to his own people (cf. Matt. 10:5-6). But there were also records of his occasional friendly contact with Gentiles and Samaritans; Luke-Acts and John esp. emphasize the Samaritan mission (Luke 9:51-56; 10:30-37; Acts 8:4-25; John 4:1-42). Actual preaching to the Gentiles probably began with the Hellenists of Antioch (Acts 11:19-26) and was soon carried forward by Paul.

Only after much controversy and searching of heart was the Gentile mission finally accepted. This theme dominates Gal. and part of Acts and is responsible for most of the ideas of Rom. It has been suggested that Paul may have based his rejection of circumcision on the decisive fact that baptism makes one a member of Christ. The author of Eph., whether Paul or someone else, can look back on the division between Jew and Gentile as something in the past (Eph. 2:11-22).

After the fall of Jerusalem in A.D. 70 the Jewish wing of the church ceased to be influential. The triumph of the Gentile mission was so complete that all of the NT comes to us in Greek and bears much of the stamp of Greek thought. By sometime in the 2nd cent. Christians had come to look on themselves as a 3rd and new race, distinct from Jews and Gentiles (see "The Early History of the Church," pp. 1045-53).

IV. THE TRADITION OF JESUS' LIFE AND TEACHING

In the NT we see the foundations of a completely new culture. Early Christians may not have been altogether conscious of this. At least they did not set out to organize a church that would endure for many generations. They lived at the turn of the ages and often in the belief that the end was near. Yet for the interim, however short it might be, they ordered their community life and integrated their children and the new converts into it. Paul's letters and Acts bear witness to this, and much more can be read between the lines of the gospels and other NT books.

Persecution and the sense of aloneness in the world further stimulated this development. If Christians were not to be absorbed into conventional Judaism or relapse into paganism, they had to live with one another in community. This was the more possible because national groups—esp. the Jews—often maintained their individuality in the Roman Empire. And the Christians developed a distinct culture, with their own worship, literature, community organization, and discipline.

The Gospel. One of the first problems of the new community was to determine its identity, and this was linked to its primary reason for existence, viz. to proclaim the good news. There were 2 parts of this which shaded into each other. Jesus had preached the coming kingdom of God and the signs of its penetration into the world. The church saw Jesus as part of the gospel. He had not merely announced the kingdom; he had inaugurated it. His work in the world and his death and resurrection were themselves good news. The gospels and the materials underlying them were formulated to tell this 2-fold story. Because early Christians were convinced that both parts were true, it is very difficult—and for most Christians quite unnecessary—to disentangle the actual words of Jesus from the interpretations placed on them by Christian teachers.

Nevertheless historical study cannot avoid this task. The type of gospel study known as "form criticism" attempts to understand the development of the oral tradition behind the written gospels and their sources. Form critics generally assume that the gospels were written, not to record history, but to propagate the faith. They are therefore direct sources for our knowledge of the community's life. The various stories and sayings once circulated independently. Thus little weight is to be placed on the editorial passages that link them together. Each unit should be examined to discover its "situation" or "setting in life" to see whether it reflects primarily the Hellenistic or Palestinian church or the situation of Jesus' ministry and whether earlier stages of tradition can be distinguished. Form critics generally classify the materials according to their forms, assuming that each form had a particular function in the community's propaganda and developed according to definite tendencies of oral tradition. This last point is more debatable than the others (see "The Literary Forms of the NT," pp. 1124-28).

Influence of Christian Faith. In a few cases we can see clearly the interests of the community at work. When Jesus spoke the parable of the great supper he was trying to make just one point, found in Luke 14:21: he has offered the message to the "good" people of the land who might be expected to hear it, but they were busy with other concerns, and he has gone to those who will listen—the "poor and maimed, and blind and lame." Luke expands this to tell of 2 sendings, one to the Gentiles (vss. 22-24) as well as to the Jews, while Matthew develops the parable into an allegory which deals with the destruction of Jerusalem and adds another section affirming that one must put on the "wedding garment" of righteousness in order to enter the great banquet (Matt. 22:11-14).

But how is one to deal with the saying "for my sake and the gospel's" (e.g. Mark 8:35)? Jesus' activity was clearly concentrated on the message, but did he demand allegiance to himself? Even in John there are indications that he did not seek his own

glory. Recently some scholars have concluded that, while he was relatively unconcerned for his own position, he exercised a unique authority over his disciples, and that it was his bearing, his sense of inner authority, and his emphasis on his vocation, rather than anything he taught formally about it, that led his disciples—and all other believers—to give him that honor that is due to God alone.

This helps to explain the function in Mark of the story of Jesus' suffering and death. The basic account is very straightforward and contains very little theological interpretation, but its solemn simplicity and prominence show that to early Christians it had supreme religious significance. It is more than the story of a martyr.

The gospels give various titles to Jesus, and in all cases they describe the early Christian faith in him. He may well have referred to himself as Son of man (cf. e.g. Luke 9:58), and the church immediately understood this title as referring to his coming to judge the living and the dead (Mark 13:26; Matt. 25:31-46). Whether or not he referred to himself as Son of God (cf. e.g. Matt. 11:25-30), he had a strong sense of his filial relation to God, though there was a sense in which all true followers were sons of God (Matt. 5:9, 45). He acted as a prophet and was recognized as such (Luke 7:16), but just as certainly he was reluctant to claim the prerogatives of the Messiah (Mark 8:29-33), except perhaps at the end (Mark 14:62). "Lord" is a title that others ascribe to him.

In the thinking of the early church the meaning of all these titles was transformed; they meant all that Jesus was and did. Thus *Christos,* the Greek translation of Messiah, no longer refers to the typical Jewish Messiah but to the Son of God, the heavenly judge, the new prophet like Moses. In John this development in thought about Jesus is complete; the terms are almost interchangeable, and Jesus is pictured as teaching the church's fully developed Christology. But the process was well under way in the Synoptic gospels. E.g. the Son of man is master of the sabbath and has power to forgive sins (Mark 2:10, 28), and Matt. 9:8 understands that this power is now given to other humans, specifically to the church. The gospels dwell on the divine signs of the truth of his person and words, and when Matthew and Luke rewrite Mark they eliminate whatever might seem derogatory to Jesus' perfection (cf. e.g. Mark 10:17-18; Matt. 19:16-17; see "The NT Interpretation of Jesus," pp. 1167-75).

Criticisms to which replies are made are sometimes thought of as directed against Jesus' disciples rather than their master (e.g. Mark 2:18, 24; 7:2; Luke 5:30; cf. Mark 2:16). This is a sign that the church is in controversy with the synagogue. Sometimes the evangelists picture Jesus as giving private teachings to an inner group of disciples (Mark 4:10, 33-34; 7:17; 9:28; 10:10; 13:3-4). While this may partly reflect the actual situation, it is also the way in which the church suggests that some reliable traditions have come down through only a few witnesses.

The ideal Christian teacher is pictured in Matt. 13:51-52 as a scribe who brings out of his treasure house things new and old, and it has been suggested that Matt. originated in a Christian scribal school. Guidance for the community through use of Jesus' teachings can be illustrated in several ways. Often sayings that did not originally belong together were combined (e.g. in Matt. 5, vss. 21-22 with vss. 23-26 and vss. 27-28 with vss. 29-30). The parables of the weeds and the dragnet (Matt. 13:24-30, 47-50, with the interpretation, vss. 36-43) warned Christians against being too eager to excommunicate sinners. The rule for church discipline in Matt. 18:15-20 with its parable of unlimited forgiveness (vss. 21-35) is consistent with this.

In contrast with these evidences of the influence of the interests of the community the evangelists record many traditions that fit perfectly into the Palestinian background of Jesus' work and teaching. One may mention most parts of the passion narrative and also Luke 13:10-17; 14:1-10, 12-13; 15:1-32; Matt. 20:1-15. Many of Jesus' sayings go against known community tendencies—e.g. the teachings that no sign will be given this generation (Luke 11:29; Mark 8:12), that one can expect no reward (Luke 17:7-10), and that it is almost impossible for a rich man to get into the kingdom of God (Mark 10:25).

V. Worship

Worship is the most characteristic activity of any religious community. Much of early Christian practice must have been built on the foundations of the synagogue. Except on the great festivals there seems to have been little Jewish corporate prayer before the time of the Maccabees, but in the critical times of the first cent. A.D. it may have come to a great flowering. To this the early Christians added a note of joy and triumph.

Christian festivals such as Easter and Pentecost were directly derived from Judaism, and Christmas later developed as a solstice festival parallel to Hanukkah. It has been suggested that the gospel form itself is an extension of the Passover exposition and that the paschal liturgy is related to Rev. The Lord's Day (Sunday) soon took precedence over the sabbath, though the latter was also observed for some time. Attempts have been made to show that the Christian calendar influenced the structure of the gospels, but this is by no means certain.

The relation between Christian worship and literature is still very obscure. But the NT contains elements of hymnody—e.g. Eph. 5:14, the canticles in Luke 1-2, and the choruses in Rev.—and the Lord's Prayer (Matt. 6:9-13; Luke 11:2-4) has contacts with parts of the synagogue service.

It is not certain whether synagogue worship followed a fixed routine in the time of Jesus, but it is likely that elements from the temple service were incorporated into the synagogue after the destruction of the temple. In any event Christians exercised full freedom to develop new forms. The worship in Corinth, pictured in I Cor. 14, is an extreme example of this, and a more regular order may have been followed elsewhere.

In the Lord's Supper the "words of institution" may have been a fixed element; at least the evidence of Mark 14:22-24; Luke 22:17-20; and I Cor. 11:23-25 suggests this. The story of the miraculous feeding of the 5,000, combined with the walking on the water, in Mark 6:30-52, and still more in John 6:1-59, shows the influence of the church's observance of the Lord's Supper. If Jesus can multiply the loaves he can be present with his people whenever and wherever they need him.

The account of Jesus' baptism (Mark 1:9-11) provided a precedent for the Christian rite. The Christian goes through the same experience as his Lord in the symbolic death and revivification (cf. Mark 10:38-40 with Rom. 6:3-11; Col. 2:11-15). The evangelist also recognizes a connection with the work of the forerunner, John the Baptist. The tradition was not quite certain whether Jesus had personally baptized anyone (John 4:2), but Christian baptism was in any case more than John's rite (Mark 1:8; John 3:3-7; Acts 19:1-5). Finally, Jesus' baptism was a sign that God had claimed him as his unique Son, and in union with him the believer also became a son of God by adoption (Gal. 4:1-7). This tended to strengthen his moral obligation to behave like a son (cf. Matt. 5:45).

VI. Poverty and Wealth

The earliest Christian fellowships were mainly made up of poor villagers, workers, and lower middle-class people (I Cor. 1:26), though it was not long before some relatively rich members joined the movement (Jas. 2:2-7; Mark 4:18-19). Jesus addressed his beatitudes to the poor, meek (or gentle), mournful, hungry, merciful, pure in heart, peacemakers, and persecuted (Matt. 5:3-12). It was these, who expected the coming of the Son of man (Luke 6:22) and were as candid and unsophisticated as children (Mark 10:14-15), who were fit for the kingdom of God. To such people, exposed like himself to the chances and changes of this mortal life, he addressed the command not to be distracted by care (Matt. 6:25-33; Luke 12:22-31). Jesus at first spoke to small groups of obscure people; he said that what was spoken in the ear would later be proclaimed on the housetops (Matt. 10:27; Luke 12:3). His true kinfolk were those who heard the word of God and kept it (Mark 3:31-35; Luke 11:27-28).

Jesus was concerned for suffering humanity, but he did not need to dwell on this, for in his day rich and poor lived side by side and no one was insulated from the hard facts of life. Instead he emphasized the spiritual need of the fortunate. For their very salvation they needed to give (Mark 10:21) and to be neighbors to those in trouble (Luke 10:29-37). Many would be astonished at the day of judgment; they had not known that they were serving the Son of man (Matt. 25:31-46).

Jesus and his disciples lived a life of communal sharing (Luke 8:1-3), and this naturally carried over into the Jerusalem church (Acts 4:32-37). Though this was natural in the Jewish world, it was esp. characteristic of Jesus, whom Paul sees as the pattern of practical Christian love (I Cor. 13; I Thess. 4:9). Rom. 16 and Philem. give vivid pictures of the warm intimacy of the churches. Mark 10:29-30 promises that those who have given up everything will have support in the Christian fellowship, and Paul's journey to bring relief money to Jerusalem illustrates this (Acts 11:27-30; I Cor. 16; II Cor. 8-9). To Paul thinking and believing rightly and participating in the collection were both part of the right understanding of Jesus.

The early church did not doubt that the widow's mite was entirely acceptable to God (Mark 12:41-44), but it was not prepared to reject the generous rich, and Zacchaeus could be cited as an example of Jesus' acceptance (Luke 19:1-10). A rich man, like everyone else, could be saved only by the grace of God (Mark 10:26-27).

VII. Christian Behavior

Christians were in daily contact with outsiders; they could not depart from the world (II Cor. 6:14-7:1). Yet such a church, conscious of being chosen by God beyond any deserving, stood in danger of spiritual pride. Paul found that the Thessalonians did not always work quietly and steadily and behave well toward non-Christians (I Thess. 4:11-12; 5:14). He thought it scandalous that others went to law against one another in a pagan court (I Cor. 6:1); they should instead settle their differences within the community. In their public life he expected them to conform to the standards of society. Evidently a decent woman did not go unveiled in Corinth (I Cor. 11:2-6), and if a Christian flouted this convention it brought discredit on the community. Members of the church were taught to pay taxes (Mark 12:13-17; Matt. 17:24-27) and to pay proper respect to rulers (Rom. 13:1-7; I Pet. 2:13-17).

As in Judaism, women had a higher position than in the ancient world generally. Paul is quite clear that the sexes are equal in their relationship to God (Gal. 3:28), and Luke dwells affectionately on the part played by women in Jesus' ministry and in the early church (Luke 8:1-3; 10:38-42; Acts 9:36-43; 12:12-17; 16:14-15).

The basic ethical standard was the law of love, and it is possible to argue that Jesus tested the OT law by what was really love to God and neighbor (Luke 13:10-17; 14:1-6; Mark 7:9-13). But his teaching regarding the law is difficult to reconstruct, and some early Christians must have thought that where he did not modify the law they must keep it strictly; otherwise there would have been no Christian Pharisees (Acts 15:5).

Paul, however, put the principal emphasis on love (Rom. 13:8-10; I Cor. 13), and in this he was followed by the 4th evangelist (John 15:12-17) and his school (I John 4:7-21). But Paul was under no illusions. Unacceptable behavior, esp. sexual looseness, was completely intolerable (I Cor. 5:1; 6:15-20; I Thess. 4:3-8). The famous passage on the fruits of the Spirit and the works of the flesh (Gal. 5:16-24) gives Paul's corrective to the doctrine of Christian freedom. There are even directions for the behavior of various groups in the community (Col. 3:18-4:1). Mark gives a catalogue of vices (Mark 7:21-22). In general Paul and other early Christians accepted the moral commands of the OT and the best standards of Jewish and pagan ethics, even as they claimed theoretical freedom from all external rules.

VIII. Church Discipline and the Ministry

Authority. But how free were Christians in their personal lives? Did they have to obey God—as they understood his commands—or a church? The answer as found in the NT is not quite certain. Jesus gave no directions for the founding of a new church. The word "church" occurs in the gospels only in Matt. 16:18; 18:17, even though it is a favorite word of Paul's and though John 13-17 obviously deals with the church's future destiny. Yet in a true sense the authority of the old Israelite community was felt as having passed to the new church, and both were under the word of God—as spoken in the past through Moses and the prophets, through Jesus, and now in the new age by Christian prophets. The early church did not behave as though it were a collection of individuals. It was under discipline.

Apostles certainly exercised authority. One strand of Mark's sources deals with the 12—the number, more or less, of Jesus' original intimate disciples. At one point they were expected to be the judges of Israel in the coming age (Matt. 19:28; Luke 22:30), and this expectation may explain why Matthias was chosen to replace Judas Iscariot (Acts 1:15-26) though there was apparently no attempt later on to preserve a college of 12.

Both Acts and Paul speak of apostles, i.e. traveling missionaries, one of whose functions was to be witnesses of the Lord's resurrection (Acts 13:30-31; I Cor. 9:1). Paul regards at least some of the 12 as apostles (I Cor. 9:5; Gal. 1:19), but the term includes others (Rom. 16:7; Acts 14:14). An apostle, like a prophet or teacher, seems to have been appointed directly by God.

It is esp. in Luke-Acts that the 12 are regarded as the original apostles (Luke 6:13; 24:10; Acts 1:26). Peter is one of the inmost group in all the gospels, and in Matt. he has a unique place: he is the rock on which the new church is founded (Matt. 16:17-19). As the church's typical rabbi he is often given special instruction (Matt. 17:24-27; 18:21-35). Even John, in which the Beloved Disciple is the hero, assigns to Peter a unique role (John 20:6-7; 21:15-19).

Yet there are traditions that Jesus gave no special rank to any follower, and even Matthew speaks of the equality of all Christians (Matt. 23:7-12). Because of this variation one can understand why Paul had to compete with "superlative apostles" (II Cor. 11:1-12:13) whose authority he did not acknowledge. In another generation or 2 Christians had a well-defined ministry claiming to rest on apostolic foundations, but in Paul's time there was no fixed definition of power.

Apostles and Followers. Paul behaved as the supreme authority under God and Christ for the Gentile churches. His rule of excommunication (I Cor. 5:3-5; II Cor. 2:5-11; 7:8-13) rests on the practice of the synagogue. He introduces an exception to the divorce rule on his own authority as an apostle (I Cor. 7:12-16), whereas Matt. 5:31-32 (cf. 19:9) tries to trace another type of exception to Jesus himself. In both cases we see an attempt to adapt Jesus' principles to concrete situations.

From early times the ministry of Jesus must have been a pattern both for leaders and for Christians generally. All were expected to proclaim the gospel, to give a good answer when challenged, and to endure persecution (for an old formulation, see Luke

12:2-9). Matthew, by prefixing the healing stories to his mission discourse (10:1-40), seems to show that the ministry of healing was one of the "signs of an apostle" (II Cor. 12:12). Though Jesus cast out demons, and so did later Christians, this activity may not have been part of the original commission. In Luke 10:17-20 the disciples seem amazed that they have this power.

Support of Apostles. It was assumed that one who preached the gospel should live by the gospel (I Cor. 9:3-14; I Tim. 5:18), and some apostles traveled with their wives (I Cor. 9:5). Paul was an exception. Evidently he maintained his independence by supporting himself, so that no one could say that he worked for his own profit (II Thess. 3:8-9; I Cor. 9:12; II Cor. 11:7-10). He accused some others of deceit and craft (I Thess. 2:3), lording it over the people and taking their money (II Cor. 11:20). He took the precaution of having ambassadors appointed by the churches to carry the collection to the poor in Jerusalem so that no one might question his honesty (I Cor. 16:1-4; II Cor. 8:16-24). Yet he accepted help from the church in Philippi, with which he had warm relations (II Cor. 11:9; Phil. 4:15-16) and evidently hoped that the church in Rome would help him journey on to Spain (Rom. 15:23-29).

Congregational Autonomy. Paul personally and closely directed his churches, with the help of fellow workers who visited them (I Cor. 16:10-18; Phil. 2:25-30; Col. 1:7; 4:7-9). But he had great difficulty with rivals who invaded his field and with recalcitrant factions within the churches. Matthew seems to picture congregational meetings in which the local church directed its own affairs (Matt. 18:15-20), and the situation must have been similar in Corinth. Faced with revolt, Paul had only spiritual weapons—persuasion by letter or personal visit, and the threat of excommunication.

Gentile Churches. Gentile Christians posed special problems. The Greeks had only recently turned from idols (I Thess. 1:9), and despite their first enthusiasm they did not have the background of the Jewish moral tradition. Corinth in particular was a seaport city with a rootless cosmopolitan population. There Paul had to deal constantly with factionalism and with "spiritual" people who pretended to superior wisdom (I Cor. 3:1-3).

The Galatians were all too easily persuaded that to be proper Christians they must also become Jews, and Colossae was open to high-flown speculations, partly Jewish and partly pagan. No wonder, then, that Paul urged his people to keep the traditions they had received (II Thess. 2:15; 3:6) and follow the leadership of steadier members (I Cor. 16:15-18). Every one of his letters contains moral admonitions, and a Christian system of practical morality can be seen developing in the Pastoral and Catholic letters. The gospels often warn against false prophets (e.g. Matt. 7:15, 22); at the same time no one wished to silence true prophecy (I Thess. 5:19-21).

Foods led to special problems in the Gentile world. Paul apparently abrogated the Jewish dietary laws for his churches, but there was the question of whether Christians might purchase and eat meat that had been sacrificed to a pagan god. A Christian dared not be involved with idolatry (I Cor.

10:6-22). On the other hand a pagan god did not really exist, and eating the food did not in itself make one an idolator (I Cor. 8:4-6). Paul ruled practically on this problem: a Christian must behave so as not to upset the faith of weaker brethren (8:7-13; 10:23–11:1). In Rome the situation was somewhat different; here apparently some were vegetarians with scruples about the eating of any meat (Rom. 14). We can see from Col. 2:16 Paul's general principles regarding taboos on food, as well as special days in the calendar.

IX. THE POSTAPOSTOLIC AGE

As the original apostles began to die, the 2nd generation produced special problems. Matthew speaks of the love of many growing cold (Matt. 24:12), while Heb. recalls the great leaders of the past (13:7) and the former days when Christians endured persecution (10:32-34). Even Mark knows of the word's being choked by the cares of the world and the delight in riches (Mark 4:19). Books written in the postapostolic period are marked by an appeal to apostolic example and teaching; they attempt to revive the hope of Christ's early coming (e.g. II Pet.), warn against false teachers, and emphasize God's purpose for the unity of the church. Heb. and I John assert that apostasy or grievous sin after baptism will lead to spiritual death with no hope of repentance and forgiveness. The church later modified this stern rule, beginning with the Shepherd of Hermas, a 2nd-cent. writing that teaches that a Christian may have a 2nd chance of repentance, but no more than that.

In this period the ordained ministry was beginning to take on fixed forms. Paul once mentions bishops and deacons (Phil. 1:1), while the Pastorals mention elders (presbyters) also, but in such a way that they may be identical with bishops (Tit. 1:5-7). Acts pictures Paul as appointing elders in each city, and they are once called bishops (Acts 20:28; the RSV translates "guardians"). The idea that a spiritual gift is imparted at ordination first appears in I Tim. 4:14; II Tim. 1:6, while the late first-cent. I Clement (42:4-5) is the first to teach that the apostles appointed their successors (see "The NT and Christian Origins," pp. 1187-93).

The NT contains much evidence of how the communities wrestled with the intellectual problems of their faith. Paul stands out as the first great theological thinker, who dealt with the relation of the new faith to the old, the basis on which man is accepted by God, the nature of Christ, and the meaning of baptism and the Lord's Supper. The Synoptic gospels were later to reflect Christian thought on some of these themes. The process reached its high point in John, which might almost be described as a creed in gospel form.

John understands Christ as the eternal Son of God, the Logos, or Word, through whom the world was made, and who not only creates but also reveals and redeems. He looks back at the story of Jesus from the vantage point of the church's experience of the risen Christ, who has returned to his people through the Holy Spirit, leading them into the full truth.

In this way John seeks to protect the developing

church from error and from the attacks of its opponents. Once the community emerged from Judaism and had to stand on its own feet, it faced the dangers inherent in freedom. On the one hand there was always a tendency to return to the synagogue, while in the other direction Christians were influenced by a Hellenistic-oriental way of thinking that later developed into Gnosticism. This was a speculative philosophy which taught revelation and redemption—but a redemption of only the divine spark in man, not the world or man's physical life. Gnostics believed that one was saved by learning his true nature and destiny, viz. to leave the evil created world and be absorbed into the godhead. This teaching was surrounded by elaborate speculations that dazzled the half-educated and even captured some brilliant minds. Sometimes Gnostics taught a high ethic; often they were ascetic. But some teachers scoffed at ordinary Christian morality: "spiritual people" were supposed to be beyond such conventions. Against such thinking John affirmed that he who created the world is also its redeemer and that the highest morality is that same practical love that Jesus and Paul taught.

X. Personal Religion and the Community

The Earliest Tradition. The earliest gospel tradition bears on the problems of the individual's inner experience. E.g. the stories of Jesus' temptation (Matt. 4:1-11; Luke 4:1-13) suggest that one who is tempted shares the experience that Jesus had just after his baptism and, like Jesus, can remember words of scripture to gain strength. Peter's denial of Jesus and its sequel (Mark 14:66-72; Luke 22:31-34; John 21:15-19) reminded everyone that the wavering apostle had become a rock. Still more poignant is the picture of Jesus in Gethsemane (Mark 14:32-42); since he was not spared this experience he can give his followers the strength they need (Heb. 2:18; 5:7-10).

The Synoptic gospels emphasize faith and prayer (cf. Mark 11:23-24 with vs. 25, and note the addition of vs. 26 in some manuscripts; cf. also Mark 9:29; Luke 11:5-13; 18:1-8). As the tradition develops, watching and fasting become increasingly prominent (Mark 13:32-37; 14:37-38; Matt. 6:16-18; Acts 13:2-3). Luke and Matt. put a little more weight on poverty and celibacy than does Mark (Matt. 19:10-12, 21; Luke 2:36-37; Acts 4:32-37; 21:9). Here one recalls Paul's bent toward asceticism and the possibility that "spiritual marriages" were contracted in Corinth (I Cor. 7:1-7, 36-38).

Paul's Personal Religion. Paul's own piety, which has been permanently influential, has two sides. On the one hand his approach is objective: the great event has occurred, independently of anything that man might do or think. Justification is a fact, not merely a subjective experience. From this springs a hearty confidence. The Corinthians are already saints, washed and justified (I Cor. 6:11). This explains the assurance with which he expects that ethical directions can be obeyed. The Christian is transformed, not conformed to this world (Rom. 12:2). The old law was impossible to keep, but under the new order one need not remain in sin (Rom. 6:1-14; 8:12-13; I Cor. 6:11).

It is often argued that Rom. 7 pictures the Christian, even after his conversion, as torn in 2 directions. But this ch. deals with the man who lives by the law—the non-Christian or the Christian who has fallen back into bondage (Gal. 4:1-7; 5:1; Col. 2:6-3:11). Paul himself is a man of strong conscience; while he does not claim to be perfect, he knows exactly where he is going (Phil. 3:4-16). He has found a new freedom from sin, death, and the law, and he expects his converts to imitate him in this.

This belief in an objective fact has intense emotional consequences. Paul describes his vivid religious experience as being "in Christ Jesus." But this is a 2-fold concept, and he finds his strength in 2 ways which can be separated only in theory. He is in individual union with Christ, but also in union with him through the community. He describes his personal experience in various ways. Christ called him directly to be an apostle (Gal. 1:11-17; cf. 2:2). When caught up to the 3rd heaven he received visions and revelations (II Cor. 12:2-4). Looking into the face of Christ he sees the glory of God, and like Moses he reflects this light. As a result he is crucified, dying, and living anew with Christ, transformed into that which he sees (II Cor. 3:4-5:21; Gal. 2:19-20; Phil. 1:21). As a spiritual person to whom the depths of God are revealed he can be judged by no one else (I Cor. 2:15).

We would probably know little about this experience if there had not been revolts in Corinth and Galatia against Paul's authority. The "spiritual" people in Corinth claimed to have as much experience and authority as Paul. Paul and the "spirituals" are in fact 2 sides of the same coin. Paul, like his opponents, has a strong drive to exert authority and express himself. The difference seems to be that he is the founder of the church, not they, and that unlike them he recognizes the spiritual problem in his own "boasting" and fights against it. The difference between mature or spiritual people on the one hand and the "animate" or fleshly on the other does not depend on some innate distinction in human nature but on whether they exercise ethical love. Paul is imperfect as a pastor, but he has been trying to learn the painful lesson of humility through the insults heaped on him by the Corinthians and through the thorn in the flesh (II Cor. 12:7). This is part of his dying with Christ.

Thus Paul's very existence depends on his relationships with his churches and not just on individual union with Christ. The man is never separated from the apostle, nor does he think that any Christian can live apart from the community.

What Paul says elsewhere about the religious life is suffused with his warm friendship and concern. The gospel itself is an objective power to salvation (Rom. 1:16). The grace of God leads man to repentance (Rom. 2:4); in fact what does anyone have that he has not received (I Cor. 4:7)? If man knows God, it is because God first knew him (Gal. 4:9). Man's response to the gospel is faith and obedience (Rom. 1:5), and Christians mutually strengthen and encourage one another in their faith (Rom. 1:12). On the other hand Christ and the Holy Spirit give strength (I Cor. 1:8; Phil. 1:19; I Thess. 1:5). God the Father comforts humans in their trials (II Cor.

1:3-7). Tribulation leads to endurance, tested character, and hope (Rom. 5:3-4), and indeed there is no temptation without the strength to overcome it (I Cor. 10:13). Even in his inarticulate attempts at prayer man is assisted by the Holy Spirit (Rom. 8:26-27; Gal. 4:6).

Life is in fact an athletic struggle (I Cor. 9:24-27). Paul has reached the stage of self-sufficiency in which possessions or the lack of them mean nothing to him (Phil. 4:10-13), but in a spirit of thanksgiving somewhat different from that of the Stoics. He himself feels no need to marry, but he corrects the tendency to make celibacy a general rule (I Cor. 7). The end result of Christian nurture is to make a man "mature" (Phil. 3:12-16; Col. 1:28). In Paul's religious life the prevailing tone is joy, and this comes out even in some of the darker passages.

Spiritual Life in the 4th Gospel. It is of course John that deals most directly and fully with the spiritual needs of the individual, esp. in chs. 13–17.

Many themes from earlier Christian writings reappear in John in a new form. Instead of the crisp sayings in the other gospels or the arguments of Paul we find discourses of a meditative nature attributed to Jesus. Here the process by which a believer comes to mature religious life and salvation is an organic whole. Salvation can be analyzed into several factors: (*a*) "believing," the verb, rather than Paul's noun, "faith"; (*b*) "abiding" in the "true vine," the "flock," i.e. the church looked at as a religious unity (though the word "church" is not used); (*c*) seeing and knowing; (*d*) participation in baptism and the Lord's Supper; and (*e*) keeping the commandment of love.

The result of the process is that the believer is in Christ and Christ in him, just as the Son is in the Father and the Father in him. Such Christians will follow the path that Jesus has trodden out and will have eternal life in the many rooms in the Father's house. Because they are in complete union with Jesus, all their prayers will be answered.

Throughout Christian history misunderstandings of John's thought have arisen because of a tendency to dissolve this complex and concentrate on isolated ideas. Thus in John the sacraments have no independent meaning apart from the church, faith, and the commandment of love. Nor does the bread of the Lord's Supper become the flesh of Jesus, the "bread of life," in a magical sense. The words that Jesus speaks are spirit and life; the truth of the sacrament depends on his words and is not to be separated from his teaching. Love has no meaning apart from the community. The church is not an external institution but the community in which all the other elements inhere. There is no true believing without abiding and love.

Certainly in the teaching of Jesus and in the NT generally the individual and his religious life come to a new stature and importance. Every soul is the object of God's direct care and concern, and his spiritual development to maturity is his birthright as a son of God. But the individual cannot find his true meaning except in community. Though Paul and John are often said to exhibit what has been called a "Christ mysticism," the NT contains no mysticism in the sense of a "flight from the alone to the alone." Here and there in later Christianity appears a mysticism divorced from history and ordinary human contacts. But the NT is a literature of a community, and the community is always one dimension of its religion.

For Further Study. Ernst von Dobschütz, *Christian Life in the Primitive Church*, 1904. F. C. Grant, ed., *Form Criticism*, 1934. Martin Dibelius, *From Tradition to Gospel*, 1935. Johannes Weiss, *The History of Primitive Christianity*, 2 vols., 1937; reissued as *Earliest Christianity*, 1959. Hans Lietzmann, *The Beginnings of the Christian Church*, 2nd ed., 1949. A. E. Welsford, *Life in the Early Church A.D. 33 to 313*, 1953. P. H. Menoud, "Church, Life and Organization of," in *IDB*, 1962. C. F. D. Moule, *The Birth of the NT*, 1962.

THE LITERARY
FORMS OF THE NEW TESTAMENT

R. McL. Wilson

Every literature has its characteristic forms and modes of expression. Speaking generally, we may make a broad distinction between poetry and prose, and within this broader division we may further distinguish various subdivisions—e.g. in prose the essay or the novel, in poetry the epic or the lyric, the ode or the sonnet. Each has its place and function, and as a rule the form adopted is one appropriate to the author's purpose. Likewise our standards of criticism for assessing the quality of a literary composition must be appropriate to the type of literature with which we are dealing.

This must be borne in mind when we turn to the literature of the NT. Our critical standards must be those appropriate to the literature at hand. Moreover we must remember that the NT is not literature in the strict sense, comparable to the classical literature of Greece or Rome or of more modern cultures. Only Luke-Acts and Heb. show any pretensions to style in the literary sense. The NT authors wrote for purposes of their own, and it is in the light of these purposes that their work must be examined.

Within the NT we may broadly distinguish 4 main types of composition: apocalypse, epistle, theological history, and finally a new literary genre which is distinctively Christian, the gospel. Some of these are the subject of more extended treatment elsewhere in this vol. (see "The Apocalyptic Literature," pp. 1106-09; "The Letters of Paul," pp. 1136-43; "The Literary Relations Among the Gospels," pp. 1129-35). Here we are concerned chiefly with general considerations of literary form.

I. Apocalypses

Under the head of apocalyptic writing we have to consider not only the Jewish tradition of the inter-testamental period and Rev. but also elements in the Synoptic gospels, esp. Mark 13 and its parallels, and in I, II Thess. Its general characteristic is that it is literature for a time of stress and crisis, intended to confirm its readers in their faith and point them beyond their present trials and hardships to the expected consummation. Jewish apocalyptic presents world history as the battleground of good and evil and looks for the final triumph of the good. Rev. consists largely of visions intended to encourage persecuted Christians in their resistance to idolatry and worship of the Roman emperor. Thus 2 characteristic marks are a visionary element and a strain

of cosmic dualism. A 3rd is a conviction of the imminence of the end, of the climax of all history—e.g. Mark 13 is introduced by the disciples' question "When shall these things be?" A 4th feature is the use of cryptic imagery which cannot be understood without the necessary key. Christian apocalyptic is further marked by an expectation of the return of Jesus. Jewish apocalyptic commonly looked for the coming of a Messiah, but for the Christian authors it is Jesus who will come again, this time in glory with the heavenly angels.

II. Epistles

Among the letters of the NT we have not only those of Paul but also the Catholic, i.e. general, epistles—Jas., I, II Pet., I, II, III John, Jude—and Heb., sometimes considered less a letter than a homiletic treatise. The usual pattern is a salutation in the form "A to B greeting," followed often by a prayer or thanksgiving and then by the main body of the letter, the whole rounded off by more or less personal messages.

Material for comparison here is provided by the letters found among the papyri and by the correspondence of such classical authors as Cicero, but there are also differences to be noted. The papyrus letters on the one hand are often brief personal notes about the everyday concerns of the correspondents, who never dreamed of their publication. On the other hand the "letters" of some classical writers were consciously written with an eye to publication.

Paul's letters, at any rate, are genuine letters, ranging from the personal note to Philemon to the longer letters addressed to churches. All are designed specifically to deal with problems arising in the life of the churches and, in the case of Rom., to prepare the way for Paul's coming in person. Apart from Philem. and the Pastoral epistles—I, II Tim., Tit.—all the NT letters are addressed, not to individuals, but to communities, and were intended to be read to the assembled congregation of the church to which they were sent. This to some extent sets them apart from the personal letters of the papyri, but they do not thereby become merely impersonal circulars. E.g. the warmth of Paul's relationship with the churches he founded is abundantly evident.

Older Material in the Epistles. Embedded in these letters are elements of older material—hymns, confessions of faith, creedal formulas. It was at one time customary to regard the parallels between Paul's letters and other NT documents as evidence of Pauline influence on their authors; but it is now increasingly recognized that Paul himself, for all his originality and creative power, was greatly indebted to his Christian predecessors, and that there is much in his theology which is in fact not specifically "Pauline" but common and apostolic.

Paul himself, indeed, expressly says that he "received" the tradition which he handed on. If in I Cor. 11:23-25 he adds that he received it "from the Lord," this does not necessarily imply that it was by the medium of a special revelation, since the Markan account of the Last Supper, despite the differences, is so similar as to suggest that both versions go back to a common origin. The point is that Paul is thinking of the risen and exalted Lord as the real author of the church's tradition, whatever the medium by which it was transmitted. Again, in I Cor. 15:3-5 he presents a succinct summary of the basic Christian beliefs, and in vs. 11 states that this is what all the apostles preach.

The Preaching Element. The substance of the early apostolic preaching (Greek *kerygma*) has been the subject of much research. In the speeches in Acts we can trace a regularly recurring pattern, a basic outline of early Christian preaching which underlies them all: The OT prophecies have been fulfilled and the new age has dawned. The Messiah, long awaited, has now come. He is Jesus of Nazareth, who by the power of God did mighty works, died for our sins, was raised from the dead, is now exalted at the right hand of God, and is to come again to be the judge of all mankind. Therefore let all who hear repent and be baptized for the forgiveness of their sins.

Elements of this pattern may be found in the epistles (e.g. I Cor. 15:3-5), not in isolation but grouped together so as to form as it were the rudiments of a creed. Indeed it is possible to trace the sequence of development from these beginnings to the more elaborate and comprehensive creeds of later generations.

The Liturgical Element. A second such element of older tradition found in the epistles is represented by the early hymns which Paul quotes (e.g. Phil. 2:5-11; Col. 1:15-20). Not all scholars agree that these are in fact pre-Pauline rather than his own composition, but that they are really hymns is shown by their rhythmical structure and by the fact that they can be analyzed into strophes or stanzas. Study of the vocabulary in these sections shows the use of words which Paul does not normally employ and suggests that he is taking over older compositions by other authors.

Other liturgical elements have been detected in the NT documents. E.g. in Rev. it has been suggested that the author has projected into the heavens a reflection of the Christian worship of his own day. The narratives of the Last Supper also have probably a liturgical background in the early Christian communion services, in which these narratives would be recalled in remembrance of the crucified and risen Lord. Some view I Pet. as largely based on a baptismal liturgy. Matt. may be regarded from one point of view as an adaptation and expansion of Mark for use in the church's worship, and indeed it is a measure of the author's success that his work has remained the basic document for this purpose ever since.

The importance of this liturgical element is therefore evident, but at the same time caution is required. The investigation of these various elements—creed, liturgy, preaching, or teaching—is both necessary and valuable, but concentration on any one to the exclusion of the others entails a failure to comprehend the full richness of the life and worship of the early church.

The Teaching Element. A 3rd feature common to many of the NT documents is the presence of catechetical material, i.e. material appropriate for the instruction of catechumens, new converts. It was necessary not only that these converts should know the doctrines of the Christian faith, the facts of the life of Jesus, and the significance of these facts, but also that they should have some guidance in matters of conduct. This was esp. true of those who entered the church from paganism and had no background in the ethical tradition of Judaism.

It is characteristic of Paul that he never fails to bring out the ethical implications of the gospel, either by a special section (e.g. Rom. 12-13, Gal. 5:13-6:10) or by exhortation interwoven with the discussion in the main body of his letter. The transition is marked with special clarity in Rom., where after devoting 11 chs. to exposition of the gospel and of the purpose of God he proceeds: "I appeal to you therefore, brethren, by the mercies of God, to present your bodies as a living sacrifice, holy and acceptable to God, which is your spiritual worship" (12:1). Unlike some of his successors in all ages, Paul did not divorce the worship and service of God from the practical demands of the Christian life in the world of daily living. Nor did such a writer as the author of I John. For them, as for the NT authors generally, religion is not something apart from daily life but integral to it, indeed its inspiration and control.

Much of Paul's hortatory material—the catalogues of vices to be shunned and virtues to be embraced; the tables of household rules (*Haustafeln*) for the relationships of husband and wife, master and slave; the injunctions to brotherly love, humility, hospitality, and general well-doing—much of this is common not only to Paul's letters but to other parts of the NT also. In the days when Pauline influence was thought to be all-pervasive, these passages were claimed as evidence. Correspondingly, when parallels were found in Stoicism or in other Hellenistic sources, they were claimed as evidence for Hellenistic influence on the NT. Paul was influenced by his Hellenistic background and environment and all the others were influenced by Paul. Today the picture is different. We have come to ask if such an explanation is really adequate, and it is now possible to discern more clearly the common pattern of this early Christian teaching. Elements there are from the Hellenistic popular philosophy, elements also from the Jewish tradition; but it is always a question how far such elements are derivative and indicate dependence and how far they merely reflect the popular ethical wisdom common to all peoples and basic to all cultures. In any case, whatever their origin, whatever the medium—e.g. Hellenistic Judaism—

through which they passed into Christianity, these diverse elements have been welded into a Christian tradition.

Consideration of these and other factors serves to show that the NT authors were guided not merely by the conventions of contemporary letter writing but also by the common tradition of the early church, from which they drew in their several ways according to the purposes which their letters were intended to serve. One of the great services of recent scholarship has been to restore these documents to their proper context in the ongoing life of a vital and active community.

III. THEOLOGICAL HISTORY

The one real historical composition in the NT is Acts. The other writings are of course historical documents in that they provide the materials for historical study; but as a historical composition, an attempt to present and interpret history, Acts stands by itself. The gospels also, it is true, present and interpret history, but they belong rather to a distinct and separate category.

With Acts again we must consider the author's aim and purpose if we are to understand his work. To apply the standards of modern scientific history would be an anachronism. Nor is it altogether accurate to think in terms of the classical Greek historians. E.g. Thucydides frankly declares that where he knew the substance of a speech he recorded it and that where he did not he set in the mouth of the speaker such words and reflections as he himself considered appropriate to the occasion. By this standard the speeches of Acts would in the main be the author's own composition and worthless as evidence for an earlier period. It has already been noted, however, that these speeches preserve the outlines of the primitive apostolic preaching, and indeed it has been claimed that one of them presents the most primitive Christology of all.

Again we must consider the author's use of older sources: one at least, possibly Aramaic, for the early period in Jerusalem; others for the Pauline mission, apparently including his own travel diary, as is shown by the "we sections" (see Intro. to Acts), but not Paul's letters. Since, as the prologues of the 2 books show, Acts is a continuation of Luke, we can form some estimate of the author's aim and methods from his use of Mark as a source.

A certain apologetic interest is evident in the way the author handles Paul's relations with the authorities. It is commonly Jewish hostility, or the envy and opposition of those with vested interests, which is the source of conflict. The Christians themselves are neither antisocial nor disloyal. On the other hand Acts is not a complete and exhaustive history. Peter disappears from the scene halfway, and some of the other apostles are scarcely even mentioned; whereas Stephen, Philip, and later Paul, none of whom belonged to the original apostolic college, play a prominent, indeed in Paul's case a dominating, part. I.e. the book is not a comprehensive survey but a selective history, concentrating on those points which serve the author's purpose. Part at least of this purpose was to show the development of the Christian mission—how under the guidance of the Holy Spirit

the gospel was carried from Palestine through Asia Minor into Greece and finally to Rome itself, the very heart of the empire. The author's interest in the Spirit is indeed such as to justify the description of the book as the "Acts of the Holy Spirit."

This means that our standards of judgment here cannot be purely historical. Though the author shows accurate knowledge of geography and of the details of provincial administration and local government, his book is not pure history. The true standard of comparison is provided, not by modern historical research or by the classical Greek historians, but by the historical books of the OT, in which we can see the same kind of theological interpretation, the same recognition of the working of the Spirit of God in the affairs of human history.

IV. THE GOSPELS

The gospel is a new and distinctively Christian literary form. We have, of course, examples of biographical writing from the same period in Plutarch's Lives and the Agricola of Tacitus, and a closer parallel in Philostratus' Life of Apollonius of Tyana from the early 3rd cent.; but comparison only serves to point up the differences. The gospels in fact are not biographies at all. They tell us practically nothing of the youth and upbringing of Jesus, his education, or the influences which molded his attitude and outlook. Even the material they do record is only a selection (cf. John 20:30; 21:25). This does not mean that the early church had no biographical interest in the life of Jesus, as is sometimes assumed; it means only that the biographical interest was not primary. Here again we must consider the purpose of the author, which in one case is expressly stated: "These are written that you may believe that Jesus is the Christ, the Son of God, and that believing you may have life in his name" (John 20:31).

Purposes of the Gospel Authors. It was at one time customary to distinguish between John and the Synoptic gospels, the 4th gospel being held to present a theological interpretation whereas the others, esp. Mark, supplied the unvarnished facts of history. This we now know to be erroneous; even in Mark there is theology. All 4 are the product of the life and mission of the early church and present the church's tradition of the events which gave it birth—the tradition of the early apostolic preaching modified, pruned, and adapted in the light of Christian experience.

At some points it is possible to recognize the motives which prompted the preservation of an element in the tradition, the interest which made it important for the life of the early church—e.g. the questions of prayer and fasting, sabbath observance, tribute to Caesar, the temple tax. The OT quotations, again, may belong, not to the most primitive stratum, but to a later but still very early stage at which the church was striving to attain a better understanding of its place and function in the light of the Jewish Scriptures. Even in Mark some sections seem to be grouped under a common theme—suggesting that they may already have been brought together for catechetical purposes in the early tradition. Each of the evangelists has made his own selection from the material available, Matthew and Luke both building on the work of Mark but at the same time modifying it to suit their own purposes. Scrutiny of these modifications, and examination of the several gospels generally, reveals to us something of the outlook and the theology of the authors.

It is sometimes suggested that we can get back only to the early church and no further, that the 19th-cent. "quest of the historical Jesus" was misguided, doomed to failure from the outset. But this is too radical and too skeptical; indeed the latest trend in gospel criticism is a new quest for the historical Jesus. It is true that all our information has been mediated through the early church, but this is not to say it was invented by the church. If there has been modification, adaptation, expansion, development, interpretation, the fact remains that our earliest gospel was written within little more than a generation from the date of the Crucifixion. We may have our doubts as to the value of the oral tradition which after a full cent. Papias is reported to have preferred to written gospels, and it is certainly unlikely that the Gnostic and apocryphal gospels of even later times preserve anything really reliable. But in the earliest days the tradition was not allowed to develop without control. There were people who could from their own recollections vouch for the truth of a story or refute what was manifestly false. The problem for the NT scholar is to determine what is solid historical fact and what the accretion of pious reflection. That there is a solid basis of historical fact is a presupposition without which his study of the gospels would be pointless.

Form Criticism of the Gospels. Scholarly study of the gospels in the 19th cent. established 2 main conclusions: (*a*) the priority of Mark and (*b*) the existence of a sayings source, commonly designated Q, from which Matthew and Luke derived the material common to their gospels but not found in Mark (see "The Literary Relations Among the Gospels," pp. 1129-35). Generally speaking, these conclusions still hold, though not all scholars today are convinced that Q was a single document and there is not complete agreement as to its exact limits. This period of research reached its climax in 1924 with B. H. Streeter's endeavor to enlarge the "2-document hypothesis" into a 4-document theory, postulating a special source (M) for Matt. and another (L) for Luke. That the 2 authors had access to special sources is clear enough, since each presents material peculiar to his gospel; but whether these were written sources and whether each was a single document is by no means so certain.

Even before Streeter a fresh approach had been inaugurated in Germany: *Formgeschichte,* usually translated "form criticism." In the earliest period the gospel material was transmitted by word of mouth, and it was only with the expansion of Christianity in the wider world and the gradual passing of the eyewitnesses that their testimony came to be fixed in writing. Form criticism attempts to get back to this oral tradition that lies behind the documentary sources. Its basic assumption is that the gospel material originally circulated orally as independent pericopes, i.e. units. It is therefore legitimate and proper to isolate these pericopes and examine them independently, to classify them according to their form and character, and to draw the appropriate conclusions. The terminology varies with different

form critics, but the chief classifications may be described as:

a) Narratives which culminate in a significant saying of Jesus—e.g. the paralytic (Mark 2:1-12), the man with the withered hand (3:1-5), the blessing of the children (10:13-16), the tribute money (12:13-17). The story is simply a setting for the saying and only the essential points are related. The interest lies, not in the story, but in the saying which forms its climax.

b) More detailed narratives in which the teaching element is almost completely absent from any words of Jesus that they contain, and in which the center of interest is commonly a miracle, the story being told with greater detail and more vivid coloring—e.g. the storm on the lake (Mark 4:35-41), the Gadarene demoniac (5:2-20), the feeding of the multitude (6:31-44).

c) Such narratives as Jesus' baptism and temptation, his transfiguration, Peter's confession, and the passion story generally.

d) The sayings and parables.

That some of the sayings are differently grouped in different gospels suggests that they were originally independent. The same explanation may also account for certain doublets, where the same saying, or one very similar, appears at 2 different points. An evangelist may have found the same saying in 2 different contexts in the tradition as it came down to him and made use of both, or different evangelists may have received slightly different versions. Some of the differences between Matt. and Luke probably go back to different Greek versions of the same Aramaic original.

The connecting links between the stories are sometimes merely conventional, and moreover they sometimes differ from one gospel to another. This suggests that the evangelists either did not know or simply did not care about the exact details of time and place, the precise historical situation of any particular saying or event. This in turn leads to the further question whether we have in fact a connected account of the ministry of Jesus. Some scholars have maintained that the framework of the gospel narrative is actually an artificial construction composed by the evangelists themselves, and the question has been much discussed. Perhaps the most satisfactory answer is that the framework was composed by Mark on the basis of a general knowledge of the course of the ministry of Jesus, such as he might have gained from his association with Peter. This would mean that although it is dangerous to press the details in terms of precise chronological development we should still be able to assume the historical accuracy of the story as a whole. The Coptic Gospel of Thomas, a 2nd-cent. Gnostic work discovered in Egypt in 1946, here provides food for thought. It contains a miscellaneous collection of sayings without any real connecting thread running through them. To produce so coherent and realistic a narrative as Mark from such a "heap of unstrung pearls" without the aid of some general outline of the story would be an almost incredible achievement.

Having thus isolated and classified the material, removing the connecting links and any later supplements, the form critic proceeds to locate the units in the tradition. He seeks to relate them to the life of the early church and thus to recognize the motive or interest which led to the formation or preservation of each element in the tradition. Thus he can detect modifications to the tradition. E.g. the parables can sometimes be shown to have direct relevance to situations in the life and ministry of Jesus, but sometimes it is clear that the early church has given them new applications and interpretations in the context of its own life and mission.

Form criticism has aroused much controversy. That the gospel material originally circulated in the form of separate units may be readily admitted; over the greater part of the gospels it is possible still to detach these pericopes from their context, complete and self-contained. The classification of the material and its investigation in the context of the life of the early church has much to teach us about the growth and development of the tradition in its earliest period, and from detailed scrutiny and comparison we can learn a great deal about the motives and interests of the several evangelists. Some of the leading form critics, however, have been overly skeptical of the historicity of the gospel accounts, and the terminology they have employed in classifying the material sometimes has been tendentious—e.g. "myth" and "legend." According to the chief exponent, Rudolf Bultmann, form critics do not deny the possibility that the church preserved genuine historical material in the tradition, but his own work makes very little allowance for it. There has been a tendency to treat the preservation and molding of the tradition as if these terms were synonymous with "formation" and so to conclude that the early church invented much of the material. In other fields where form criticism has been applied the oral tradition has lasted perhaps for cents., and here obviously there was ample scope for invention and modification. When, however, the tradition was committed to writing within the lifetime of eyewitnesses it is quite another matter.

With the passing of time it has become clear that form criticism has a genuine contribution to make and that it is possible to employ the method without going to extremes of historical skepticism. Much of the work on the kerygmatic, liturgical, and catechetical elements in the epistles has in fact been an application of form criticism. The study of the oral tradition behind the gospels takes us back to a "twilight period" of early Christian history and enables us to realize how much the life and worship of the early church contributed to the preservation and development of the tradition. The NT literature is the product of the life and faith of the early church and bears witness to the things in which that church believed. If it was early Christian faith that created the gospel record we must also ask what created that early faith. Behind it is no mere figment of the imagination, but the living reality of the Christ who "died for our sins in accordance with the scriptures."

For Further Study. B. H. Streeter, *The Four Gospels,* 1924. C. H. Dodd, *The Apostolic Preaching and Its Development,* 2nd ed., 1944. A. M. Hunter, *Interpreting the NT, 1900-1950,* 1951. F. C. Grant, *The Gospels: Their Origin and Growth,* 1957. C. F. D. Moule, *The Birth of the NT,* 1962. H. J. Cadbury, "Acts of the Apostles," Kendrick Grobel, "Gospels," Martin Rist, "Apocalypticism," O. J. F. Seitz, "Letter," in *IDB,* 1962. On form criticism: Vincent Taylor, *The Formation of the Gospel Tradition,* 1933. Martin Dibelius, *From Tradition to Gospel,* 1935. E. B. Redlich, *Form Criticism,* 1939. Rudolf Bultmann and Karl Kundsin, *Form Criticism,* 1962. Kendrick Grobel, "Form Criticism," in *IDB,* 1962. Rudolf Bultmann, *History of the Synoptic Tradition,* Eng. trans., 2nd ed., 1968.

THE LITERARY
RELATIONS AMONG THE GOSPELS

Floyd V. Filson

The gospels come to us as part of the Bible. Because the entire NT centers in Jesus Christ and he is the central figure of the entire Bible, we may not realize how unique the gospels are. They are not biographies. They tell how God provided the one effective way of salvation through the life, teaching, and work of Jesus Christ. They summon the reader to believe in and obey Christ as Lord. Ancient literature prior to his lifetime contains nothing like them. Later centuries have produced nothing to rival them; the pale imitations in later apocryphal gospels dating from 2nd cent. A.D. down to modern times are inferior works and are indebted to the NT gospels for the literary form in which they are written. The NT gospels are thus unique and outstanding literary achievements. Their real aim was not to earn such literary recognition. They were composed to serve the church in its worship, life, and teaching and to challenge other people to faith and obedience. But their unique literary form and religious message set them apart and call for special attention.

I. Each Gospel Separate and Complete

It is not enough to study the 4 gospels as a group. Each one of them was written to be read by itself. Each was one Christian's presentation of the gospel story. He no doubt knew more about Jesus than he put into his gospel. E.g. Luke 1:1-4 indicates that the author knew more than he could use and that some things had been written which needed correction. John 20:30 states that the author knew much more than he thought it necessary to include (cf. 21:25). Each of the 4 authors selected what he thought essential to an effective gospel. We must remember that when first written each was the only gospel that most of its first readers and hearers knew. The author had to keep his work within manageable length and at the same time write so that his gospel by itself would give an intelligible and useful witness to the life and work of Christ.

Thus we must first try to understand each gospel and recapture what it had to say to its first readers and hearers (it would be read aloud: most people could not read). To do this we must first of all read each gospel in its entirety and read it by itself, as though we had no other. How does it start? How does it end? What is its outline? What aspects of the life, teaching, and acts of Jesus does it emphasize? What use does it make of the OT? Does it give any clues as to what readers it has in mind: Christians?

Non-Christians? Jews? Gentiles? Church teachers? Ordinary church members? Where do the events take place? When did all this happen?

All this does not mean that it is wrong to compare the gospels. The question is simply what to do first. The first task is to realize that each gospel was written as an independent work which was meant to give to its readers and hearers the essential gospel story. Once we have paid attention to what each gospel says and aims to do, it is not only proper but even necessary to compare them. This can help us to understand each one still better, and it will give us a fuller and surer grasp of what the gospel story really is.

II. Similarities and Differences

The 4 gospels in our NT are alike in many ways. In each Jesus is the central figure and interest centers on him almost continuously. No other person remotely rivals him in importance. In large part the lesser figures in the story are the same. Among secondary figures the prominence of John the Baptist is 2nd only to that of Peter. The 12 appear in all 4 (though not listed in John). Judas the traitor plays his dark role in them all. In all 4 the chief priests and Pilate take leading roles in the arrest, trial, and execution of Jesus. Above all, each of these writings has the literary form of a gospel. Each tells how Jesus Christ was sent by the Father to fulfill God's promises to Israel and how through his ministry, with its preaching, teaching, healing, and suffering, he confronted men with God's claim and offered them forgiveness and new life.

But while all 4 gospels are alike in many ways, the similarities among Matt., Mark, and Luke are much greater than those between John and any of the other 3. Ca. 95% of Mark is paralleled in either Matt. or Luke or both; 65% of Matt. is paralleled in either Mark or Luke or both; and 53% of Luke is paralleled in either Matt. or Mark or both. Thus each of the 3 shares most of its material with one or both of the other 2. This is why these 3 gospels are called the Synoptic gospels. The word "synoptic" means here "giving a common view" of the gospel story in which Jesus is the central actor.

John does not have such extensive parallelism with the 3 Synoptics. It has the same general outline of the gospel story but is remarkably independent in its choice of material. It has been estimated that only *ca.* 8% of its material is paralleled in any of the

Synoptics. Its prologue about the divine Word (Logos) who became flesh is unique (1:1-18). Its picture of a Judean and Jerusalem-centered ministry of Jesus is quite different from the Galilee-centered ministry in the Synoptics. It concentrates attention on Jesus as the Christ, the Son of God, and on faith in him as the way to eternal life. Instead of centering the teaching of Jesus, as the Synoptics do, on the theme of the kingdom of God ("of Heaven" in Matt.) John focuses on the theme of eternal life through faith in Christ (explicitly stated in 20:31). Jesus' washing of the disciples' feet and his extended farewell teaching at the Last Supper (John 13-17) is without real parallel in the first 3 gospels. The author of John obviously had an independent mind and possessed a special tradition which he used to present the gospel story.

Comparison of the Synoptics. The percentages of common material given above show that most of the material in each Synoptic gospel is paralleled in one or both of the other 2. We do not know exactly how long the public ministry of Jesus lasted, but it seems to have been at least more than a year and probably more than 2 years. In that time Jesus uttered hundreds of thousands of words and did many thousands of acts. Yet out of all those teachings and events these 3 gospels choose for the most part the same material. It is not a large amount of material; all of Jesus' teaching reported in any one gospel can be read aloud in less than 2 hours, and all the deeds could have been done in a few dozen days. Yet these 3 gospels direct our attention mainly to the same sayings and actions.

More than that, they follow to a great extent the same order in presenting the events. Each author has arranged his material with some freedom; but when 2 or all 3 report the same event, Mark is usually one of the group and the order of Mark is usually followed. In such cases, with one exception in which all 3 locate the incident differently, either Matt. or Luke agrees in order with Mark; Matt. and Luke never agree against Mark in the order of events.

Furthermore there is a notable amount of agreement in wording. Each Synoptic author has his own style and favorite words, but there is so much agreement in actual wording as to suggest that either these 3 gospels are dependent on a common oral or written source or else one or 2 of them are dependent on the other. This suggestion cannot be refuted by saying that they all simply report faithfully what Jesus did and said. If they wrote independently they would report the same events in different words. Moreover the agreements in order and wording are not in Aramaic, the language in which Jesus and his first disciples taught, but in Greek. No 2 authors, working independently, would ever translate line after line of Aramaic into the same Greek. Some kind of common source must be found for these agreements in Greek.

To satisfy himself of the facts and see the need of an explanation, the student of the gospels should get a "harmony" (or "synopsis") of the Synoptic gospels, in which the 3 are printed in parallel columns. With a red pencil he should underline every word found both in Mark and in one or both of the others—an unbroken line when exactly the same word is used and a broken line when essentially the same word is used but in a different number or tense. This will show how many words in Mark occur in one or both of the other 2 gospels. But there are a great many passages, totaling about 200 vss., where the Mark column is blank but Matt. and Luke have common words; these consist mostly of sayings of Jesus. The student should underline these common words in blue, using unbroken and broken lines in the same way. To do this carefully will call attention to the similarities and differences and show clearly what is found in one gospel alone.

Such a visual test of the similarities and differences forces us to ask: How did it happen that out of all the remembered deeds and sayings of Jesus these 3 gospel authors chose much the same material and presented it in much the same order and to a considerable extent in much the same wording—a wording that comes to us, not in the Aramaic in which Jesus regularly spoke, but in Greek? The same problem can be stated from the other side: How did it happen that these authors of the first-cent. church, dealing with the gospel story, with material of the utmost importance to every Christian, continually show striking agreements and tantalizing differences in material selected, order used, and wording? This combination of similarities and differences is called the Synoptic problem.

Unsatisfactory Solutions. Certain attempts to solve this problem have been advanced often but fail to fit all the observed facts:

a) God dictated the gospels. Multitudes of Christians have held that the Spirit of God dictated to each author exactly what to write. Each gospel therefore must be fully accurate; no problem exists. But why should the Spirit dictate a saying of Jesus to one gospel author in one wording and to another author in another wording? The human activity and freedom of each writer must be taken into account.

b) Jesus had his disciples memorize his sayings, which he formulated in compact wording easy to remember. Two things are wrong with this idea: it does not explain why the gospels differ in their wording of the same saying; and it explains neither the agreements in selection of material and order nor the agreements of wording in the narrative passages.

c) The apostles established a fixed and comprehensive oral tradition which all teachers and church leaders learned and used, and from which the gospel authors drew their material. But no one in the ancient church mentions such a fixed oral tradition. Moreover, because the agreements we find are in Greek, this theory would require assuming not only that there was originally a fixed oral tradition in Aramaic but also that a fixed oral translation of that tradition into Greek was soon made and that this translation was accepted and followed by all. There is no trace or evidence of such a fixed oral tradition in Greek. Since each gospel author has used independence in selecting, arranging, and wording his material, we must seek an answer which allows more human freedom in the handing on of the tradition.

III. The Period of Oral Tradition

Jesus never wrote a book. Nothing suggests that his disciples took notes as he taught or even wrote down his words and deeds soon after his death. It probably was many years, perhaps 20, before the gospel tradition began to be written down. This is not surprising. The traditions of the rabbis, which were later codified and written down in the Mishnah *ca.* A.D. 200, most probably were oral when Jesus and his apostles lived. To be sure, the Dead Sea Scrolls show how a monastic group in Jesus' day carried on intensive study of the OT and wrote down their rules and interpretations of scripture (see "The Dead Sea Scrolls," pp. 1063-71). Other related Jewish sects may have written down their studies and traditions. But the rabbinical tradition was kept in oral form. The group Jesus gathered together were not scholars; and their aim, like that of Jesus, was not to write books but to preach urgently and widely in order to lead people to believe in Christ.

Thus the tradition was oral at first. It was a message preached and taught to win and guide disciples. The words and deeds of Jesus were remembered and used in evangelism, worship, and life guidance and in answering opponents or sincere inquirers. The disciples were not a bookish group but in loyalty to Christ were enthusiastically concerned to preach of him as widely and promptly as possible. For years after Jesus' death the gospel story was an oral tradition.

For nearly half a cent. now the method of gospel study known as "form criticism" has directed attention to this oral stage of tradition. It assumes that the early church selected, remembered, and used the tradition to meet its own needs. The church was guided, not by historical or scholarly interest, but by urgent practical concerns. It paid no attention to the order in which Jesus said or did things or to the exact wording of his sayings. Individual items were recalled, used, shaped, and adapted to meet the needs of the worshiping, witnessing, teaching, developing church. The process was controlled by the church, which used the tradition to meet its needs.

Form criticism has helped us understand better the gospels and the early church. It accents important truths: the gospel tradition at first was kept in oral form, was preserved largely in the form of separate incidents and sayings, and was used for the practical needs of the church, and was so told and shaped as to fit those needs best. Each of our gospels bears the stamp of an individual author, but his writing bears the marks of the church's early, oral, practical use of the tradition (see "The Literary Forms of the NT," pp. 1124-28).

But form critics often have gone to extremes. The evidence does not support some who deny that the church had a historical interest. It preached that Jesus had come in history; his ministry, teaching, death, and resurrection were facts on which faith takes its stand. The evidence also is against those who deny that the basic chronological outline of the gospels is reliable. To be sure, a large proportion of the gospel events and sayings cannot be dated or placed in chronological order, but some elements cannot be doubted: The opening phase is introduced by John the Baptist and includes Jesus' baptism, temptation, first preaching, first disciples, and the first opposition. Then follows a Galilean ministry, Peter's confession that Jesus fulfills the Jewish messianic hope, Jesus' decision to carry his appeal to

Jerusalem, his warning of impending death, his final appeal, arrest, condemnation, execution, and resurrection. This basic chronological structure should not be ignored or rejected.

The early church had a real historical concern and competence and for many years was helped in this by the presence of eyewitnesses. This early oral period is crucial; if the tradition was distorted or largely created in that period, we can know little of what Jesus did and said. But in fact there is no reason for the excessive skepticism which some form critics have expressed.

IV. The Use of Written Sources

As time passed the church spread, eyewitnesses died, and the need of writing down the gospel tradition was increasingly felt. We do not know exactly when the gospel story or part of it was first written down. It could hardly have been later than A.D. 50 and could have been earlier. Such writing did not end at once the use of oral tradition. It continued to be used even as late as *ca.* A.D. 135, when Papias is quoted in Eusebius' Church History (*ca.* A.D. 325) as having written that he preferred oral tradition to written documents—though how he meant this is not clear since other quotations show he was not hostile to written gospels. But once the gospel story began to be written down, oral tradition became less important, and the church soon depended mainly on written gospels.

What were these first written accounts of the gospel tradition?

OT Prophecies. One view is that the first documents the church produced were collections of OT passages which the church saw had been fulfilled in the coming and work of Jesus. From the first the church held that he had fulfilled the OT messianic prophecies, and the Dead Sea Scrolls found at Qumran show that it was a Jewish practice to collect passages which contained messianic promises. In the NT such OT passages are quoted. Christian leaders used such scripture passages as a starting point for preaching (e.g. Philip, Acts 8:35). Since a handwritten copy of the entire OT was very expensive, short collections of messianic passages must have been made to help preachers and teachers explain how Jesus fulfilled God's promises to Israel. But how early this began we cannot say.

The Passion Story. It can be argued that the story of Jesus' arrest, condemnation, execution, burial, and resurrection was the first part of the gospel narrative to be written down in a connected form. Christians had to explain how Jesus, if he was God's Messiah and guilty of no crime, was seized and put to death by the official action of Jewish and Roman leaders. The Last Supper, Cross, and Resurrection were central in the Christian message from the start. A single incident would not establish the Christian position; what was needed was a connected story. The great importance which the church gave to this part of the gospel story is shown by the large amount of space given to it in the gospels. Each gospel gives 25% or more of its total space to the last week of Jesus' life. This part of the gospel story may well have been the first part written down for preachers, teachers, and worshiping congregations to use.

Jesus' Teaching. Sooner or later collections of certain areas of Jesus' teaching were made. Perhaps one early document was a collection of his parables. Mark 4:1-34, paralleled in Matt. 13; Luke 8, shows what such a collection could have been. Perhaps someone collected "controversies," situations in which Jesus defended himself against Jewish leaders; with such a collection Christians could appeal to Jesus' example in their later disputes with Jewish opponents. One suggestion is that Mark 2:1-3:6; 11:15-17, 27-33; 12:13-40 formed such a written collection of controversies. Another possible early document may have been a collection of teaching about the end of the world (Mark 13 and parallels in Matt. 24; Luke 21).

It is widely agreed that one early document was a larger collection of Jesus' sayings. We have noted about 200 vss., almost entirely sayings of Jesus, which are found in both Matt. and Luke but not in Mark. Did Matt. and Luke take them from a written document? This is a reasonable suggestion, although the document no longer survives. Luke 1:1 proves that several documents of gospel tradition had been written before the writing of Luke. Among the Coptic manuscripts found at Nag-Hammadi in Egypt a collection of Jesus' sayings is found in the so-called Gospel of Thomas. It probably was written originally in Greek in the 2nd cent. and then was translated into Coptic and revised about the 4th cent. It contains about 114 sayings or incidents in which a saying of Jesus occurs. We may reasonably suppose that a still earlier collection was made by the middle of the first cent., before the Synoptic gospels were written. Eusebius quotes Papias as writing of the *Logia* ("oracles" or "sayings") of Matthew. This may refer to our First Gospel, or to a collection Matthew made of fulfilled scripture passages, or to a collection of Jesus' sayings.

These possible written documents we do not possess. If they existed, they were not so satisfactory as the NT gospels and so were not preserved by the later church. But, as Luke 1:1 shows, there were some such written documents as those suggested above.

Ancient Use of Written Sources. If such documents existed, one or more of them can have been used as sources by the authors of the Synoptic gospels. In our day an author who uses another writing must show by quotation marks, footnotes, and preface just what he has done. That was rarely done in ancient times. Josephus in the latter part of the first cent. A.D. used written sources in writing his history of the Jews. In the OT Apocrypha the author of II Macc. states (2:23) that he has condensed and rewritten Jason of Cyrene's account of the early Maccabean struggle. It is widely recognized that the writers of the Pentateuch and the books of Sam., Kings, and Chr. used written sources. For a gospel writer to use another man's writing without naming his source was in line with the literary methods of ancient times.

To some Christians it belittles the gospels to say that their authors used written sources. There is no need to think this. In fact, since use of such sources means that the gospel tradition had a definite written form even earlier than the date our Synoptic gospels were written, it gives added assurance that the tradition was well preserved. The nearer such written sources take us to the days of Jesus' ministry, the more likely they are to be essentially dependable witnesses to what he did and said.

One caution is in place. We have no copy of such early sources back of our gospels. We cannot reconstruct them in any definite way. All we can hope to do is to discern their existence and something of what they contained. This will be a real help, but it remains a fact that all we actually have is the 4 gospels. No conjectured source approaches these gospels in importance. We know what they say; our early manuscripts of them differ in minor details, but on the whole they are the solid bases for our study in a way that no lost source can ever be.

Theories of Written Gospel Sources. There have been many theories as to exactly what sources lay behind the Synoptic gospels. One older suggestion was that back of them lay an early written gospel longer than any of them, and that each Synoptic author drew from that longer work what he needed to write the kind of gospel which he thought most helpful. But we find no mention or trace of such a larger gospel; had it existed, we could expect some ancient mention of it.

Another older suggestion was that the gospels have many agreements because the first to be written was used by the author of the 2nd and then one or both of the earlier 2 were used by the 3rd author. On one view Matt. was written first, then Mark was constructed as an abridged edition of Matt., and Luke was based on Matt. or on Matt. and Mark. This does not explain why Luke has so much new material, nor does it do justice to the evidence given by patient study that Mark was the earlier gospel and that in Matt. and Luke much of Mark's material is shortened or compressed to leave room for a good deal of new material, especially teaching, which these 2 authors wanted to include.

The solution most widely held today is as follows: Mark wrote the earliest gospel. Back of Matt. lie 2 written sources: Mark as the basic narrative source and a collection of Jesus' sayings, which for convenience is called "Q" (from the German *Quelle*, "source"). Luke had the same 2 written sources, Mark and Q, but used them independently of Matt. This is known as the "2-document theory." Developments of it have proposed additional documents as sources for the unique portions of Matt. and Luke but without substantially modifying their basic use of the 2 written sources Mark and Q.

The chief rival to the 2-document theory is the theory that Matt. in some form was the first and basic gospel—the official Roman Catholic view, and that of a few Protestant scholars. According to this theory Mark was a shortened edition of Matt., and Luke was written with the use of Mark and Matt. Chief objections to this theory are: (*a*) Mark seems not only more vivid and original but usually more detailed than its parallels in Matt. and Luke. It is hard to imagine why the author of Mark should omit so much of Matt. and yet expand in small details what he is supposed to have taken from that source. Some have tried to explain this by supposing that Mark used a first draft of Matt. that was later expanded; but there is little evidence for such a first draft, as contrasted with many passages where Mark appears the more likely original. (*b*) When 2 gospels agree with each other but differ from the 3rd about the order of events, they are always Matt. and Mark or Mark and Luke, never Matt. and Luke. It is hard to explain how Luke could have used Matt. as a source for so many of Jesus' sayings without being influenced by Matt.'s order of events.

Taking the 2-document theory as a basis, therefore, let us look in more detail at the origin and character of each of the Synoptic gospels.

V. Mark, the First Complete Gospel

It appears highly probable that Mark was the first complete gospel produced in the church. There may have been written sources before this gospel. Among them, as already noted, may have been a collection of scripture passages seen to be fulfilled in the gospel story, a collection of parables, a collection of controversies Jesus had with opponents, a collection of Jesus' sayings about the end of the age, and a passion narrative. If Mark did use one or more such sources, he so used them as to produce one complete gospel.

Mark set the pattern for the written gospels. He began with John the Baptist, pointed out that the gospel story fulfilled God's OT promises, and told of Jesus' baptism, first preaching, first disciples, Galilean ministry, final journey to Jerusalem, appeal to his people in their temple, arrest, condemnation, execution, burial, and resurrection. This was the gospel pattern, found with variations of detail and accent in all of the 4 NT gospels. Whatever Mark's sources, oral or written, he used them to produce a powerful document for the worship, teaching, and guidance of the church.

In ancient tradition Peter is named as the source of Mark's information about Jesus. Eusebius quotes Papias as writing that Mark in his gospel faithfully reproduced Peter's teaching about Jesus. Most scholars today accept the tradition that John Mark, originally from Jerusalem (Acts 12:12), wrote this gospel (but see Intro. to Mark). As I Pet. 5:13 indicates, Mark knew Peter and so knew what Peter taught. But Mark's gospel does more than report Peter's teaching; it collects from various oral and written sources what Jesus did and said, arranges the essential material effectively, and in so doing created a new literary form.

Mark probably wrote *ca.* A.D. 65-70, and he most likely wrote at Rome. The Roman church had just suffered terrible persecution by Nero. During this persecution, it appears, Paul and Peter had been martyred. Shaken by persecution and deprived of apostolic leadership, the harassed Roman Christians needed a written gospel story to steady and guide them. From Mark's gospel they could learn that, just as their Christ had had to suffer, so their faith had to be ready to face hostility and mistreatment. Mark had no idea of writing great literature; he wrote primarily to meet the need of the church at Rome. In doing so he created a new literary form and his work has proved to be one of the notable writings in the world's literature.

VI. The Writing of Matt. and Luke

Features Common to Matt. and Luke. When we compare Matt. and Luke with Mark we see that in general they follow the pattern of Mark, though Matt. agrees with Mark more than does Luke. In both, however, the agreement in events, order, and wording is sufficient to support the view that both used Mark as a written source.

But in addition to Markan material Matt. and Luke both have a considerable body of tradition, mostly sayings of Jesus, which they report to a notable extent in the same words (e.g. Matt. 12:41-45; Luke 11:32, 31, 24-26). As already mentioned, some have thought that Luke copied from Matt. at these (and other) points, but more likely both gospels used a written source, Q, containing mainly sayings of Jesus. That the authors of Matt. and Luke used not only Mark but also Q as written sources on which they drew in writing their gospels is a part of the 2-document theory.

Matt. and Luke share other features not in Mark. Each begins with birth and infancy narratives (Luke even has such a narrative about John the Baptist as well as about Jesus). Each has a genealogy of Jesus. But the content and style of both the birth and infancy stories and the genealogies differ greatly; they did not come from a common written source. They show that these matters had begun to arouse great interest in the church, that more than one local church center had a tradition about them, but that the tradition on these items still varied greatly from place to place. Matt. and Luke also have more resurrection stories than does Mark. The authentic text of Mark as we now have it ends at 16:8. Perhaps, as certain scholars claim, this was where Mark ended his gospel. But probably Mark's original ending has been lost and so we cannot say how much Matt. and Luke added to Mark's resurrection narrative. It appears likely that to some extent Matt. and Luke did add resurrection stories to give increased testimony that the resurrection of Jesus really occurred.

The Writing of Matt. In Matt. we find considerable gospel tradition not found in either Mark or Luke. Of Mark's 665 vss. all but 31 have a parallel in Matt. or Luke or both, but 370 of Matt.'s 1,072 vss. are peculiar to Matt. For comparison, of the 1,150 vss. in Luke 535 are peculiar to Luke. Obviously the authors of Matt. and Luke had other sources of information in addition to Mark and Q. Matt. has a special form of the genealogy and birth and infancy stories; he also quotes more OT passages as fulfilled in Jesus' ministry, gives greater attention to Jesus' views on Jewish leaders and teaching, and puts greater emphasis on the church and relations among disciples.

This gospel evidently was written by a Jewish Christian teacher for use particularly in a Jewish Christian area. The ties with Judaism are quite clear, but the gospel is not narrow in outlook. From the coming of the Magi (2:1), who represent the world's coming to Christ, to the Great Commission, Jesus' final word to preach the gospel to all nations (28:19), the author presents the gospel as worldwide in its outreach. The use of Mark as a source suggests that the author was not the Matthew who was one of the 12 but a brilliant Christian teacher concerned to provide other Christian teachers with a well-arranged account of Jesus' life and words (see Intro. to Matt.).

What sources did this author have to use in writing? Apart from Mark and Q he may have had oral tradition he knew and trusted. But much of his additional material he may have found in one or more shorter documents such as we have reason to believe existed in the first-cent. church. If he took this added material from one main source, we may call it "M" and say that in writing Matt. the author used Mark as basic and used in addition Q and M (and any small items of oral tradition he chose to include).

There is no way to date Matt. with exactness and certainty. Our knowledge of the history of the church in the last 3rd of the first cent. is so sketchy that we have no basis on which to build a chronology of the later gospels and the non-Pauline letters. A date about A.D. 80-90 may well be near the truth.

The Writing of Luke. It is erroneous to think of Luke merely as a gospel. It does follow the gospel pattern; it tells the gospel story from John the Baptist to the resurrection of Jesus. Even as a gospel, however, it differs in important respects from the other gospels. It is the only one of the 4 gospels to begin with a literary preface (1:1-4). It has birth and infancy stories not only about Jesus, as does Matt., but also about John the Baptist (1:5-25, 36-80); the narratives include several hymns or poetic passages (1:14-17, 46-55, 67-79; 2:14, 29-35). It traces Jesus' genealogy back not merely to Abraham (cf. Matt. 1:1) but to Adam (and God! Luke 3:38). In this and in other details it accents the universal outreach of the gospel as a message for Gentiles as well as for Jews.

In Luke, Jesus starts his final journey to Jerusalem, not in the latter part of the gospel, but at 9:51. The extensive material in 9:51-19:27 is reported as events which occurred on this final journey. In this section Luke places much material which he alone reports; this includes such noted parables as the good Samaritan (10:25-37) and the lost sheep, the lost coin, and the lost son (ch. 15).

The most original feature of Luke, however, is not merely its new material or its distinctive arrangement but the fact that this gospel is only half of a 2-part work. It was the conviction of Luke, who, as the united tradition tells us, was the author of the gospel, that the full gospel message must include not only Jesus' ministry, teaching, death, and resurrection but also the gift of the Holy Spirit and the Spirit's witness in the apostolic age to both Jews and the Gentile world. Luke-Acts is one work in 2 parts, and Luke's insight into the importance of the apostolic witness led the church to include in the NT not only the gospels but also Acts and the letters of early Christian leaders (see Intro. to Luke).

From what sources did Luke get the material he included in his gospel? He claims that he made diligent search for it for some time before he wrote (1:3). The "we" passages in Acts, in which the author implies that he was present at those times (16: 10-17; 20:5-16; 21:1-18; 27:1-28:16), probably point to Luke. If so, 21:17; 27:1 indicate that he was in Palestine—at Jerusalem and Caesarea and perhaps other places—for over 2 years until he sailed for Rome with Paul the prisoner. In that period he could have made many inquiries about Jesus' ministry and teaching and could have learned much from oral traditions circulating in Palestine. One prominent scholar argued that Luke first wrote a document (we may call it "L") to preserve information not found in Mark or Q, that he then combined L with

Q to form a "Proto-Luke," and that finally he combined this document with Mark to produce our present form of Luke. This theory cannot be proved, but it is reasonable to think that in Palestine Luke gathered added material and wrote it down. Thus this gospel could have resulted from a combination of Mark, Q, and L, plus a few other oral or written items of tradition, including the birth and infancy narratives, which were probably not found in L.

Opinions differ concerning the date of Luke. Some date it *ca.* A.D. 60 and think that it (with Acts) was written to be used at Paul's trial in Rome. It would show that Christianity was not a revolutionary movement against Rome and that Paul had committed no crime against the state. This probably dates Luke too early; it would require that Mark be written some years before A.D. 60, which is unlikely. Other scholars think Luke-Acts was written *ca.* A.D. 95, after Josephus published his Antiquities of the Jews (which a few scholars think Luke used in his writing). A more likely date for Luke is *ca.* A.D. 85.

Conclusions. Following an early period in which the tradition was almost if not entirely oral, the writing of short documents of gospel tradition began. Mark wrote the first complete gospel *ca.* A.D. 65-70. Matt., written *ca.* A.D. 80-90, shows interest in the developing church. Its sources were Mark, Q, and special traditions from a broadminded Jewish Christian area of the church. Luke expanded the scope of his writing to include not only the gospel story as Mark and Matt. had told it but also the witness of the apostolic age, in which the church spread and became a world church. His gospel dates from *ca.* A.D. 85, and his gospel sources were Mark, Q, special material called L, and still other oral or written gospel material. Each of the 3 authors so used his sources as to produce a powerful and original literary composition. Their work did not put an end to oral traditions about Jesus, but they gave a dependable and permanent form to the essential tradition which the church needed for its worship, preaching, teaching, and life guidance.

VII. JOHN AND THE SYNOPTIC GOSPELS

It is often noted that John is quite different from the Synoptic gospels. Only *ca.* 8% of it is parallel to these other gospels, and even then no such word-for-word parallelism occurs as we find among the Synoptics. If the author of John used written sources, he used them so freely that he puts the stamp of his own vocabulary and style on the material. Some have thought that he knew and used all 3 Synoptics. Indeed Clement of Alexandria, writing *ca.* A.D. 200, says he did. Others think that he knew only one or 2 of the Synoptics. No such theory of dependence on written sources can be proved. This author presented the gospel story in his own way; his gospel is an independent witness to Christ. It has the basic marks of a gospel, but it is no mere imitation of earlier gospels.

John is marked by its continual blending of interpretation with historical tradition. The author wants the reader to see the meaning of the coming and ministry of Jesus. To do this he selects fewer events and teaching themes and brings out their meaning in discourses. To him a miracle story really happened, but his main concern is to bring out the truth it symbolizes. E.g. the new wine (2:1-11) points to the new life and energy which the gospel brings; the feeding of the multitude teaches that Jesus is the bread of life (ch. 6), the healing of the man born blind symbolizes the fact that Jesus is the light of the world (ch. 9), the resurrection of Lazarus expresses the truth that Jesus is the resurrection and the life (ch. 11). This gospel, strongly marked by interpretation, centers attention throughout on Jesus. It says little of man's obligations in various situations of life; it focuses on what is basic: "Jesus is the Christ, the Son of God," and all who believe in him have eternal life. This is the substance of the gospel, as the author says plainly in the original conclusion of his work (20:31; ch. 21 is an appendix added later).

Unlike the Synoptic gospels John is Jerusalem-centered. In the Synoptics, Jesus' ministry is in and near Galilee until he goes to Jerusalem in the closing days just before his arrest and crucifixion. But in the 4th Gospel Jesus spends little time in Galilee; only 2:1-12; 4:45-54; 6:1–7:9 are laid there. This author knew that Jesus ministered in Galilee, but to him Jesus' ministry in and near Jerusalem, in touch with the temple and the Jewish leaders, was crucial. He concentrated mostly on Jesus' challenge to Judaism at its center.

This gospel was written about the last decade of the first cent. It does not name its author (the headings of the books of the NT were added long after the works were written; they represent church tradition); but the appendix in ch. 21, added several years after chs. 1–20 were written, says that the disciple whom Jesus loved wrote it (21:20-24; cf. 13:23; 19:26; 20:2; 21:7). According to the dominating tradition this disciple was John the son of Zebedee, one of the 12, who plays a rather prominent part in the Synoptics but is never named in this gospel (cf. 21:2). It is hard to believe that John the Galilean fisherman was author of this Jerusalem-centered, interpretative gospel. Therefore most scholars who accept the traditional identification assume that there was another actual author who was somehow associated with John the apostle in his later years. On the other hand the clues in the gospel itself as to the identity of "the disciple whom Jesus loved" point rather to Lazarus, the one man mentioned by name whom

Jesus is said to have loved (11:3, 5, 11, 36). Lazarus was a resident of Bethany, a suburb of Jerusalem; and if this gospel records his witness to Christ, this would explain why the gospel is so Jerusalem-centered. Moreover, the resurrection of Lazarus is an acted parable of the gospel's theme of new life through Christ. For other suggested identifications of the beloved disciple see Intro. to John.

However this may be, this gospel is unique in blending historical tradition with Christian interpretation of what Jesus' coming and ministry means for Christian faith. All 4 gospels were written by men of faith to further faith, worship, and Christian living. But John accents interpretation to a unique degree. The Synoptics give far more details of what Jesus did and said. For them too the gospel message grows out of this history, but we go to John for the fullest interpretation of the gospel story.

VIII. FOUR GOSPELS WITHOUT RIVALS

Occasionally it is suggested that these 4 gospels are not outstanding. There were other gospels, and we are told we should listen also to them. But if a gospel ever existed that could rival any of the four NT gospels, it has disappeared without a trace. Fragments of other early gospels survive, but none of them, it seems, dates as early as the 4 (the Synoptic sources were probably not complete gospels); none matches in quality the NT gospels; and the still later apocryphal gospels are pitifully inferior to the NT works they try to imitate (see "Non-Canonical Early Christian Writings," pp. 1144-49). At one point in history, between A.D. 65 and 100, 4 gospels were written which have never been matched either by predecessors or by successors. The unique gospel message and the urgent need of the church for a competent and trustworthy written record of the gospel story led men whose main interest was not literary to produce 4 of the world's notable literary works.

For Further Study: B. H. Streeter, *The Four Gospels: A Study of Origins,* 4th ed., 1930. Vincent Taylor, *The Gospels: A Short Intro.,* 6th ed., 1948. F. C. Grant, *The Gospels: Their Origin and Their Growth,* 1957. C. F. D. Moule, *The Birth of the NT,* esp. pp. 4 ff., 86 ff., 185 ff., 223 ff., 1962. R. M. Grant, *A Historical Intro. to the NT,* chs. 7-12, 1963.

THE LETTERS OF PAUL

S. MacLean Gilmour

I. Paul's Letters in the NT

Development of the Canon. Almost all manuscripts of Paul's letters since the 4th cent. contain 14 letters —the 13 that are ascribed to Paul in their addresses and the anonymous Heb.—and almost all present the letters in the sequence familiar to us from the English translations: Rom., I, II Cor., Gal., Eph., Phil., Col., I, II Thess., I, II Tim., Tit., Philem., Heb. In this order the letters addressed to churches were placed first, arranged according to length; those addressed to individuals followed, again in order of length; and Heb. was attached as an appendix.

This scope and this sequence were determined in part by long custom and in part by the decisions of the great councils of the W church which *ca.* the end of the 4th cent. fixed the canon of the NT (see "The Making of the NT Canon," pp. 1216-24). They do not correspond, however, to those of the earliest collection known to us. This was the one made *ca.* A.D. 140 by the anti-Jewish heretic Marcion, who compiled a canon consisting of an edited version of Luke and 10 letters of Paul to replace the LXX as scripture for the unorthodox churches that followed his leadership. Marcion's set of letters began with Gal.—presumably because he regarded it as Paul's most anti-Jewish writing —and continued, according to length, with I, II Cor. (treated as one letter), Rom., I, II Thess. (also treated as one letter), Eph. (which he called "Laodiceans"; cf. Col. 4:16), Col., Phil., Philem. He made no place for the Pastorals (I, II Tim., Tit.) or Heb., either because he did not know them or because he questioned their authenticity or—probably at least in the case of Heb.—because he disliked their theology.

After Marcion's time the order of the collection was changed and its scope was gradually and variously enlarged. *Ca.* 200 the church at Rome, whose canonical list is preserved in the Muratorian fragment, included the Pastorals but not Heb. On the other hand the papyrus codex P⁴⁶ (see "The Transmission of the Biblical Text," pp. 1225-36) from about the same period but representing another church or group of churches, almost certainly in Egypt, includes Heb., placed immediately after Rom., but not the Pastorals, II Thess., and Philem.

The earliest complete text of all the NT letters ascribed to Paul is found in the Codex Sinaiticus, written in Egypt early in the 4th cent. The equally early Codex Vaticanus, also Egyptian, unfortunately now lacks Heb. 9:14*b* to the end, the Pastorals, and Philem.

The Authenticity of Paul's Letters. Heb. was assigned to Paul and placed among the canonical books of the NT by the E church as early as the 2nd cent., but it was accepted as Pauline and canonical only slowly and hesitantly by the church in the W. This was not because the W church regarded Heb. as unorthodox but because the epistle made no claims to apostolic authorship—which had become an important criterion of canonicity and because all claims advanced in the E that it was Pauline were held to be suspect. In terms of style, vocabulary, philosophical background, and theological ideas Heb. differs markedly from the Pauline norm (see Intro. to Heb.). Various names of possible authors have been put forward in ancient and in modern times— e.g. Barnabas, Apollos, Prisca—but these, however interesting, are no more than guesses.

From the end of the 2nd cent. the church both in the E and in the W included the Pastorals among the Pauline letters; but since early in the 19th cent. their Pauline authorship has been questioned because of differences from the admittedly genuine letters of Paul in vocabulary, style, theological ideas, and the historical and ecclesiastical situation presupposed (see Intro. to I Tim.). The difficulties in the way of maintaining their Pauline authorship are so great that often even conservative scholars ascribe them to Paul only in part or indirectly. E.g. it has recently been urged that several of the personal references, esp. in II Tim., stem from genuine Pauline fragments or memorabilia.

Marcion's most famous writing was known as the *Antitheses,* "Contradictions," and his theology was lumped by the early fathers with others that professed to reveal *gnosis,* "knowledge." In light of this the author of the Pastorals may have been attacking Marcion and Marcionism when he wrote: "Avoid the godless chatter and *contradictions* of what is falsely called *knowledge*" (I Tim. 6:20). If so, they must be dated at least as late as 140.

Of the 10 remaining letters in the NT ascribed to Paul only Rom., I, II Cor., and Gal. were accepted by a group of radical German scholars, known as the Tübingen School, who in the 19th cent. debated matters of authenticity. Traces of their skepticism survive both in Europe and in America. In 1963 their approximate conclusion was revived when Angus Q. Morton, a Scottish minister-mathematician, announced the results of 7 years of research with a computer. On the assumption that Gal. is unquestionably genuine Morton recorded in the computer's memory the typical word patterns and sentence lengths of that letter. He then fed into the machine the other 13 letters. The machine found only Rom., I, II Cor., and Philem. sufficiently close to Gal. to be regarded as genuine. Stylistic criteria, however, cannot be ultimately determinative, for any writer may show some variation—even great variation—in style. Other factors, esp. those concerned with the life setting and with theological points of view and emphases, cannot easily be measured by a mechanical device. On such bases most NT scholars judge that not only the 5 letters supported by the computer's calculations but also Phil. and I Thess. can be accepted as genuine letters of Paul.

The 3 that remain are much debated. Among those who weigh the criteria of historical and literary criticism the balance of judgment is against the authenticity of Eph. and for that of II Thess. and Col. The arguments against Eph. as a Pauline letter are based on style, on its doctrines of the church and of the work of Christ as compared with those in admittedly genuine letters, and on the fact that it seems to be dependent on Col. and probably also on other letters (see Intro. to Eph.). Objections to the authenticity of II Thess. are grounded mainly on its similarity to I Thess. in structure and in content and on the peculiar and—it is claimed—un-Pauline character of the references in ch. 2 to the imminent coming of the Lord, and esp. to the "man of lawlessness" and "what is restraining him now" (see Intro. to II Thess.). These objections are real but fall short of convincing most scholars. Objections to Pauline authorship of Col. are based largely on the contention that its doctrine of the person and work of Christ is more advanced than that in Rom., Gal., or I, II Cor. and shows more influence of Gnostic and related ideas (see Intro. to Col.). Again most scholars seem to find that the hypothesis of Pauline authorship raises fewer difficulties than any alternative.

To sum up: (a) Heb. and the Pastorals are clearly not Paul's letters; (b) Rom., I, II Cor., Gal., Phil., I Thess., and Philem. are almost certainly genuine; (c) the balance of evidence is against the authenticity of Eph. and (d) in favor of the authenticity of Col. and II Thess.

Noncanonical Letters Ascribed to Paul.

In addition to the 14 letters ultimately accepted by the church as Paul's 4 other letters circulated in ancient times as Pauline and were the occasion of much debate among churchmen: (a) In Col. 4:16 Paul bids his Colossian readers to "read also the letter from Laodicea." On the strength of this reference a "Letter to the Laodiceans" was constructed in the 4th cent. out of phrases taken from Paul's canonical letters and was included in many Latin manuscripts of the NT to the end of the Middle Ages. (b) A "Letter to the Alexandrians" that purported to be by Paul circulated in the 2nd cent. among Marcionite churches and according to the Muratorian fragment was branded uncanonical by the orthodox church of Rome. (c) What claimed to be an exchange of letters between Paul and the Corinthians originally formed part of the "Acts of Paul." It was adopted as "III Cor." into the canon of the Syrian church as early as the 3rd cent. and passed from the Syrian canon into the Armenian, only to be excluded in the 5th cent. from the former and somewhat later from the latter. (d) Correspondence between Paul and the Stoic philosopher Seneca was fabricated in the 4th cent. but, though widely circulated, was never given canonical status by any branch of the church.

The Collection of Paul's Letters.

As already observed, Marcion *ca.* 140 published a collection of 10 letters of Paul as part of his canon of Christian scriptures. It is clear, however, that he was not the first to issue such a collection, for there is evidence that one had already been made and was in circulation before the end of the first cent. The author of I Clement, writing at Rome *ca.* 96, was certainly familiar with not only Rom. but also I Cor. and possibly other letters of Paul. The letters of Ignatius, written *ca.* 25 years later, show evidence of acquaintance with several of Paul's letters, as does Polycarp's letter to the Philippians about the same time. The author of II Pet., writing probably *ca.* 150 (see Intro.), must have known an extensive collection, for he refers to the wisdom that Paul manifested "in all his letters" (II Pet. 3:16).

It has commonly been supposed that from very early days congregations founded by Paul or by his disciples exchanged copies of letters in their possession and that the collection known in the 2nd cent. was the product of a gradual process of accumulation. According to this hypothesis, which is still widely current, one cannot give any precise date to the collection, speak of any single cause of it, or hold any single individual or group responsible for it. All that can safely be hazarded is that all extant manuscripts go back ultimately to the text of the codex or roll that contained the oldest collection.

This assumption is challenged by the lapse of 30 to 45 or more years between the writing of the various letters and the first evidence that any one of them was known to a Christian group other than the congregation to which it was addressed. Esp. striking is the absence in Acts, over half of which is devoted to a narrative of Paul's career, of any sign that the author had ever read one of Paul's letters. Early in the 1930's Edgar J. Goodspeed proposed an explanation of this phenomenon that has appealed to many scholars and been variously supported and developed. According to this hypothesis it was the publication of Luke-Acts in the mid 80's that prompted someone to visit the centers of Paul's missionary activity named in this work and secure copies of his letters that remained in the various church archives. The compiler then wrote Eph., which textual evidence indicates was originally not addressed to a specific church, as a covering letter or introduction, producing a collection of 7 letters—reckoning I, II Cor., I, II Thess., and Col.-Philem. each as one letter. To this hypothesis John Knox added identification of the collector as Onesimus, the slave for whom Paul pleads in Philem. (see Intro.), and who in Knox's view later became the Bishop Onesimus of Ephesus mentioned in Ignatius' letter to the Ephesians.

The Goodspeed-Knox hypothesis gives a plausible explanation for the apparent heavy dependence of Eph. on Col. and to a lesser degree on all the extant genuine letters of Paul, for the ignorance of Paul's letters shown by all Christian writers before the time of Clement of Rome (*ca.* 96), and for the wide acquaintance with a collection of them after that time. It can be objected, however, that there is no manuscript or other evidence that Eph. ever stood at the beginning of the Pauline collection or that there was ever a collection of Paul's letters that was limited to 7.

II. THE FORM OF PAUL'S LETTERS

Letter Writing in Paul's Time. Thousands of letters or fragments of letters from ordinary folk to relatives, friends, or business associates have come to light among papyri discovered in Egypt since 1896. In recent years a few from late pre-Christian and early Christian times have also been discovered in Palestine. These show that the writing of many different types of letters was common practice in Paul's time. E.g. letters of recommendation have been found. In II Cor. 3:1 Paul alludes to letters of recommendation used by his opponents at Corinth, and he himself incorporates recommendations of his co-workers in his letters (I Cor. 16:10-11; II Cor. 8:16-24; Phil. 2:19-23). A special letter of recommendation to introduce a certain Phoebe, a former deaconess of the church at Cenchreae, the Aegean seaport of Corinth, is now appended as ch. 16 to Rom. but probably was originally a separate letter addressed to the church at Ephesus (see comment on Rom. 16).

None of the books of the OT is cast in the form of a letter, but no less than 21 of the 27 books of the NT have this form—a witness to the popularity of the letter as a literary vehicle in the Hellenistic world. "Epistles"—i.e. literary letters intended for publication and reading by the general public—were known in the ancient world from at least the 4th cent. B.C. in Greece and the 2nd cent. B.C. in Rome. E.g. the epistles of Seneca, the Roman patrician and philosopher, date from the time of Paul.

Paul's Letters as Letters. It is now generally agreed that Paul's letters are true letters rather than epistles. Of course when they were collected and published and read by the whole church as vehicles of a message for all men they came to be considered literature, in time Holy Scripture (cf. II Pet. 3:15-16); but Paul himself had no inkling of these developments. He wrote to meet specific needs of specific groups at specific times, and it was only when the universal and timeless significance of what he had written was perceived by the church that his letters became "epistles" and therefore "literature."

Apart from Paul's letters there are no other true letters in the NT, with the possible exception of the letters to the 7 churches in Rev. 2-3. The Catholic, or General, epistles (Jas., I, II Pet., I-III John, Jude) are epistles rather than letters, as are Heb. and the Pastorals. As already noted, Eph. was originally an encyclical—a message for a number of persons or groups—and is closer to an epistle or a homily than to a letter.

Paul's letters are true letters, but there appear to be no private letters in our NT collection. Philem. was addressed not only to Philemon, Apphia, and Archippus but also to the "church in your house" (Philem. 1-2).

Since Paul's letters were intended to be read aloud in a service of public worship they partake also of the character of an address, and the fact that their author wrote with apostolic authority (cf. e.g. I Cor. 7:40; Gal. 1:1) lifts them out of the class of letters as we ordinarily understand them and justifies the title "mandatory addresses" that a German scholar has recently given them.

According to Col. 4:16 Paul wished Col. to be read also to the Laodicean congregation and a letter that church had received (possibly Philem.) to be read also in Colossae. Phrases in I Cor. 1:2; II Cor. 1:1 imply that these letters were intended also for a wider constituency than the church at Corinth, but they may well be interpolations added when the letters were published as part of a collection to be read by all Christians.

Because of the hortatory and argumentative character of Rom. some interpreters are inclined to classify it as an epistle rather than a letter. It is true that a version circulated as early as the 2nd cent. without the address (1:7, 15) and without ch. 16 (see Intro. to Rom.). There is reason to believe, however, that the form with which we are familiar, possibly without ch. 16, is the original; and 15:22-29 demonstrates that Rom. is a letter in the true sense.

Characteristics of Paul's Letters. The letter style of the day determined the basic structure of Paul's letters, but he introduces characteristic variations into the Hellenistic formula. He usually asserts his apostolic authority in the prescript. Instead of the customary "greeting" he uses another word that in Greek sounded much the same but had a rich content for the Christian believer, "grace." To this he adds "peace," the translation of a Hebrew word which carried a meaning very close to "salvation." Then follows a prayer of thanksgiving which also explains in part why the letter came to be written (cf. e.g. Rom. 1:8-12) and includes a petition for its recipients (cf. e.g. Phil. 1:3-11). A departure from this norm is in II Cor. 1:3-11, where Paul expresses thanks for his own rescue from some mortal peril at Ephesus. Another is in Gal., where Paul is so wrought up that after the prescript he plunges immediately into his quarrel with his readers.

After the thanksgiving there sometimes follow some personal references (cf. e.g. Phil. 1:12-26). Then comes the body of the letter. Toward the end Paul adds hortatory material of general or specific application. His letters usually close with a list of those to whom he wishes greetings extended and a brief wish for the welfare of the recipients—a Christian development of the pagan formula—or a list of those who wish to join him in greeting the congregation. Rom. ends with a doxology and the other letters end with a grace or benediction (cf. e.g. II Cor. 13:14, which is familiar from its present-day liturgical use)—material which has no parallel in ancient letters and is appended by Paul as an appropriate conclusion to a message which he expects to be read aloud in the church's service of worship.

Since dictation in antiquity was a time-consuming

process, it was a common custom for the letter writer to let a secretary jot down mere notes of his ideas on blocks of wood covered with wax and then develop them into a complete letter on parchment or papyrus (see "Writing in Biblical Times," pp. 1201-08). It has occasionally been maintained that this was Paul's practice, but it can hardly have been so. The genuine letters have a similarity of style and a unity of ideas that must stem from Paul himself. The numerous breaks in sentence structure, parentheses, and diatribes, i.e. presentations in debate form, show that, however long it might take—possibly several sittings for the longest letters—Paul must have dictated his letters verbatim. Rather than employing professional scribes he no doubt called on members of his own circle for assistance. In Rom. 16:22 the scribe even interjects his own greeting.

It was also a custom in antiquity for the author to append his signature to a dictated letter as a guarantee of authenticity. Since Paul's letters were to be read to a congregation he often emphasized at the end that his signature was in his own handwriting (I Cor. 16:21; Gal. 6:11; Col. 4:18; II Thess. 3:17; Philem. 19).

Letters in imperial times were commonly dated by reference to the year of the reigning emperor (cf. Luke 3:1). No doubt such dates once were attached to Paul's letters but unfortunately were dropped by copyists before the time of our earliest manuscripts.

There was a postal service for official mail, but private letters had to be delivered by special messengers. II Cor. 8:16-18 may indicate that Titus was to be the bearer of the letter Paul was then writing. Phil. 2:25 seems to imply that Epaphroditus was the intended letter carrier. Col. 4:7-8 points to Tychicus as the messenger, and it may be inferred that he was also to deliver Philem. Presumably the Corinthian delegation mentioned in I Cor. 16:17 had brought a letter from the Corinthians to Paul and would carry back Paul's reply.

The unity of certain of the letters as now included in the NT has been seriously questioned. As already noted, it is probable that Rom. 16 was originally a separate letter to Ephesus to introduce the deaconess Phoebe. There are strong reasons for believing that II Cor. (see Intro. to I Cor.) is made up of at least 3—or parts of 3—separate communications (6:14-7:1; 10-13; 1-9), and there is some reason to believe that chs. 8; 9 were also originally separate letters or parts of letters. Some scholars are convinced that I Cor. (see Intro.) is also composite, and a greater number view Phil. (see Intro.) as composed of 2 or 3 originally independent writings; but the case for the unity of these 2 letters as we have them seems the stronger.

Col. and Philem. were written to congregations that Paul had not personally founded and to whom he was not known "after the flesh." This is true also of Rom. The other letters continue and reinforce a ministry the apostle had begun at some previous time.

Much of the material in Paul's letters may already have been in some form before he incorporated it —i.e. he had already worked over or prepared it for some other purpose. This hypothesis commends itself esp. as applied to: I Cor. 13, the hymn to love;

Phil. 2:5-11; Col. 1:15-18, hymns to Christ; Col. 3:18-4:1, an adaptation of a Stoic "table of household duties"; Rom. 1:28-32; Gal. 5:19-24, catalogs of vices and, in the latter case, also of virtues; Rom. 1:3-4, possibly an early Christian baptismal confession; Rom. 13:1-7, an adaptation of Jewish-Hellenistic wisdom teaching. No doubt many of the exhortations with which Paul was accustomed to end his letters were committed to writing from his oral teaching.

Paul often includes others with himself in the prescripts to his letters: Timothy in II Cor., Phil., Col., and Philem.; Silvanus and Timothy in I Thess.; and Sosthenes, according to Acts 18:17 a onetime "ruler" of the Corinthian synagogue, in I Cor. Some have maintained that these associates are included in the addresses because they had some part in the composition of the respective letters. More probably they are mentioned only as an act of courtesy— because they are well known to the readers. At any rate by mentioning them Paul implies that they are in basic agreement with what he is writing; e.g. in Gal. 1:2 he would have his readers know that in defending himself he has the support of "all the brethren who are with me."

III. The Churches to Which Paul's Letters Were Addressed

Asia Minor. Long before the Christian era Asia Minor (Anatolia; see color map 16) was an important meeting place and melting pot of oriental and occidental civilizations, connected as it was with Mesopotamia by the Tigris and Euphrates rivers, with Egypt by a caravan route that ran along the Palestinian coastal plain, and with Macedonia and Greece by various sea lanes. Even in very ancient times—with the decline of the Hittite empire (12th cent. B.C.)—Greek colonists settled along the Anatolian coast, and these Greek settlements increased in size and number after the conquests of Alexander the Great (333 B.C.). During the Roman era, in Paul's day, order was established, good roads were built, commerce was encouraged, the arts flourished, and the diverse communities prospered in security and peace.

The Galatian Churches. *Ca.* 280 B.C. Gauls from W Europe (modern France) invaded the Balkans, pushed on into Asia Minor, and established a small kingdom about Ancyra (now Ankara, the capital of Turkey). In 25 B.C. this kingdom of Galatia was overrun by the Romans, who organized it, together with slices of Phrygia and Lycaonia to the S, into the province of Galatia. The Galatians of Paul's day therefore included the Galatians proper to the N and many Phrygians and Lycaonians to the S.

Many scholars believe that Gal. is addressed to Galatian communities in the N, around Ancyra, which Paul first visited apparently no earlier than his "2nd missionary journey" (Acts 16:6). More commonly, however, the "S Galatian" hypothesis is assumed—i.e. that Gal. is addressed to the churches at Antioch in Pisidia and at Iconium, Lystra, and Derbe in Lycaonia, towns that Paul evangelized during his "first missionary journey" (Acts 13-14) and revisited during his 2nd tour (Acts 16:6). Since Gal. 4:13 implies that Paul has visited the communities more than once, if the latter assumption is correct, the letter was probably written during his long stay in Corinth (Acts 18:1-11) in 50 or 51 and is thus one of the earliest of his letters which have been preserved. Because of the similarity of the subject matter to that of Rom., however, some scholars prefer a later date for Gal. and therefore place it after the visit to Galatia mentioned in Acts 18:23 and during Paul's residence in Ephesus or in Corinth (see Intro. to Gal.).

None of Paul's letters is so full of emotion and passion as Gal., and in none is the language so strong or the tone so intense. Much of the letter is Paul's defense of his interpretation of the gospel as good news to all men, regardless of race or former religious association. In chs. 1-2 he gives an illuminating review of his own record before and after he became a Christian, and in chs. 3-6 he works out his understanding of the gospel. Nevertheless, despite the turbulence of its mood, the letter is rich in passages of lyrical cadence and spiritual insight (cf. e.g. 2:20; 5:22; 6:2).

Ephesus. In Paul's day Ephesus was a bustling cosmopolitan city—next in size in the Roman Empire to Rome, Alexandria, and Antioch, and the capital of the Roman province of Asia. It was located on the Aegean coast at the mouth of a small river, the Cayster; but much of its prosperity was due to a larger river nearby, for the bulk of the busy freight and passenger traffic from the hinterland down the Maeander was transported over a height of land to Ephesus rather than taken down the long arm of the river parallel to the coast. The city was also the terminus of the long caravan route from the far E by way of Palestine and Syria. The port of Ephesus was therefore the main point from which goods and produce were shipped from Asia to Greece and Italy.

According to Acts, Paul paid his first visit to Ephesus while en route from Corinth to Jerusalem and to Antioch in Syria (Acts 18:19-21)—probably late in the autumn of 51—but on this occasion he deliberately postponed any vigorous program of evangelization until his projected return. Instead we are led to believe that Prisca (Priscilla in Acts) and Aquila, former residents of Rome whom Paul had met at Corinth, and who at this time accompanied him to Ephesus and resettled there, laid the foundations of the Ephesian church. Among their converts Acts 18:24-26 tells of an Alexandrian Jew, Apollos, whose own later ministry at Corinth is mentioned both in Acts 18:27-19:1 and in the opening chs. of I Cor. In Rom. 16:5 Paul refers to a certain Epaenetus as the first Christian convert in the province of Asia, and we may assume that he was an Ephesian.

Paul returned to Ephesus, probably in the autumn of 53, and spent the greater portion of his "3rd missionary journey" there, until the summer of 56. In I Cor., which was written from Ephesus, he declares that the city presented many difficulties but at the same time a "wide door for effective work" (16:9). His words "humanly speaking, I fought with beasts at Ephesus" (I Cor. 15:32) may only be a metaphorical way of describing some of the difficulties, but it is also possible that he was actually arrested and compelled to fight with wild animals in the civic arena. If so, his somber remarks in II Cor. 1:9-10 take on added meaning. Many scholars are convinced Paul's difficulties in Ephesus included a period of imprisonment, during which he wrote some or all of the letters in which he mentions being in prison, viz. Phil., Col., and Philem.

As already noted, Rom. 16 in the judgment of many scholars was originally a separate letter that Paul wrote to the church at Ephesus to introduce and recommend the deaconess Phoebe, who was moving there from Cenchreae. From the list of individuals and groups of individuals to whom he sends greetings in this ch. it would appear that in Ephesus, a city the size of Baltimore or Boston, Paul's converts after almost 3 years of labor (Acts 20:31) could not have numbered many more than 150.

Sometime early in the history of its transmission an encyclical letter originally addressed to the "saints who are also faithful in Christ Jesus" came to be credited to Paul and labeled as "to the Ephesians." Whether it was actually written by Paul or by some unknown but brilliant disciple remains a matter of debate; but the ideas that it develops are Paul's, esp. that of the church as the body of Christ, the community through which Christ carries on his work in the world.

Colossae and Laodicea. Ephesus was a center from which Christian missions could easily be extended to various inland towns. Paul himself did not visit Colossae, a city on a tributary of the Maeander called the Lycus; but one of his associates, a certain Epaphras, founded the congregation there (Col. 1:5-8). Paul's letter to this congregation is concerned in large part with combating doctrines of a sort that he regarded as dangerous, doctrines akin to those held by Gnostic sects.

It would appear from Col. 4:16 that Paul also wrote a letter to the church in the neighboring city of Laodicea. Many scholars believe that some or all of the addressees of Philem., viz. Philemon, Apphia, and Archippus (Philem. 1; cf. Col. 4:17), were residents of Laodicea and that Philem. is therefore the "Letter to the Laodiceans" that has been commonly assumed to have been lost.

Col. and Philem. were written during a period of imprisonment (Col. 4:18; Philem. 1, 9). According to Acts, Paul was imprisoned for 2 years at Caesarea before his appeal to Caesar's tribunal, and there have been some who would place his "imprisonment letters" during this period. No imprisonment at Ephesus is recorded in Acts, but various notices in the letters (I Cor. 15:30-32; II Cor. 1:8-10; Rom. 16:3-4, 7), at least some hints in later Christian literature, and various more or less probable deductions have made the hypothesis that one occurred there attractive. Consequently there are those who regard Col. and Philem. as written from Ephesus, perhaps in 56. The older, conventional, and possibly most attractive hypothesis is that all the imprisonment letters come from the period of imprisonment at Rome—sometime after 60—and therefore can be termed Paul's "later" letters.

Macedonia. The N part of what is now Greece, Macedonia was a land of rugged mountains interspersed with fertile plains. Bounded on the N by Illyria and Thrace and on the S by Achaia, it stretched from the Adriatic to the Aegean, with its leading towns on or near the latter's coast. Its heyday as a world power was during the latter part of the 4th cent. B.C. when the Macedonian king Alexander the Great imposed his rule from his native highlands to the Indus River in the far E and to the upper reaches of the Nile in the deep S. On his death in 323 Alexander's sprawling empire became the scene of a struggle for power by some of his former generals; and ultimately Macedonia came under the control of the descendants of a certain Antigonus, who ruled over it as an independent kingdom until it was conquered by the Romans and organized by them in 148 B.C. as an imperial province.

During his first European journey, conventionally called his "2nd missionary journey," and in the course of a later tour Paul established and revisited congregations at Philippi, Thessalonica, and Beroea. Possibly he worked also at still other centers such as Apollonia on the Aegean and Amphipolis. These and the other leading Macedonian communities were linked by a famous road, the Via Egnatia, a highway almost 500 miles in length that the Romans had constructed in the 2nd cent. B.C. It extended from 2 points of departure on the Adriatic across the mountains to Thessalonica and on to Thrace. No doubt this was the road that Paul and his companions traveled from the time they landed at Neapolis.

Philippi. So far as we are aware the church that Paul founded at Philippi was the first European congregation of Christians, though it is barely possible that the new religion had been introduced into Rome earlier.

The city had once been known as Krenides; but in the 4th cent. B.C. it had been fortified by Philip, the father of Alexander the Great, and renamed in his own honor. After defeating Brutus and Cassius in a battle near Philippi in 42 B.C. Mark Antony and Octavian settled the city with some of their veterans and granted it the status of a Roman colony —i.e. gave the Philippians Roman citizenship and modeled their city government on that of Rome.

Paul arrived at Philippi in 50, and though his first stay in the city was brief (Acts 16:12-40) it was long enough to lay the foundations of a strong and vigorous congregation. In the later stages of his "3rd missionary journey" (56-57) he called again at Philippi, both going to and returning from Corinth (Acts 20:1-6).

Phil. was written from prison (1:7, 13-14, 17). If it was composed during an Ephesian imprisonment, as some scholars maintain (see Intro. to Phil.), it belongs to the years 53-56 with the Corinthian correspondence and possibly Col. and Philem. If it was written from the Caesarean prison, it is later than Rom. If it was sent by Paul when he was awaiting trial at Rome, as seems probable, it may be the last letter we have from his pen. The letter makes it clear that Paul continued to cherish an especial affection for the first congregation he had established on European soil. The Philippians on their part retained a deep interest in and concern for the welfare of the apostle who had converted them to faith in Jesus Christ. Theirs was the only congregation from which he accepted gifts of money (Phil. 4:15). While he was in Thessalonica the Philippians twice forwarded help (Phil. 4:16). When he was in Corinth and his funds ran low Christians from Macedonia— no doubt including the Philippians—supplied his needs (II Cor. 11:9). Finally they sent him still further bounty while he was in prison, commissioning a certain Epaphroditus to deliver what Paul terms "a fragrant offering, a sacrifice acceptable and pleasing to God" (Phil. 4:18).

Thessalonica. Following the route of the Via Egnatia, Paul and his companions traveled through Amphipolis and Apollonia to Thessalonica (the modern Salonika). This city was founded in the 4th cent. B.C. and named after a sister of Alexander the Great. In Paul's day it was not only the capital of the province of Macedonia but also its most populous city and its leading seaport.

According to Acts 17:2 Paul and his company stayed in Thessalonica on his first visit for a little over three weeks. But Paul's own words (I Thess. 2:9), probably written from Corinth a few months later, during the autumn of 50, seem to imply a longer period of ministry, as does also his statement (Phil. 4:16) that he accepted financial aid from his congregation at Philippi on at least 2 occasions during his Thessalonian mission.

Soon afterward Paul while at Athens sent Timothy back on a special mission to Thessalonica (I Thess. 3:1-5). Later Timothy rejoined him at Corinth (Acts 18:5), bringing him good news of the faith and love of the Thessalonian Christians, of their kindly remembrance of him who had first brought them into the church, and of their longing to see him again (I Thess. 3:6; cf. 1:6-8).

But not all the news that Timothy brought was good, and some of the problems caused Paul to write I Thess. He learned that at Thessalonica he had been subjected in absentia to personal abuse (2:1-8), and against such slander he defends himself (2:17-20). Later in the letter he seeks to correct several misinterpretations of his teaching that some Thessalonians have come to accept. There are some who continue to behave like pagans, on the assumption that morality has no necessary connection with religion, and he attacks this intolerable misapprehension (4:3-8). In expectation of the imminent end of the present age and of the return of Christ some have given up all productive labor, and he rebukes these (4:9-12). Some are in despair at the death of certain members of their fellowship, and he seeks to comfort them with the assurance that, when the Lord descends from heaven, those believers who have died will actually be at an advantage over those who have remained alive (4:13–5:11).

On the assumption that II Thess. is a genuine letter of Paul we must conclude that it was written a few months after I Thess., probably late in 50 or early in 51, also from Corinth. By letter or oral report Paul learned that the situation at Thessalonica had deteriorated. Persecution of the Christian community had increased since he last wrote; expectation that the end of the present age was immediately at hand had grown more intense; and increasing numbers of Thessalonian Christians were using their doctrine of last things as a theological justification of parasitic indolence. Paul wrote II Thess. to comfort converts in persecution, to caution enthusiastic waiters for the coming of Christ against drawing too hasty conclusions from what they believed to be "signs of the end," and to renew in more vigorous terms his earlier condemnation of idlers.

Corinth. In early Greek times Corinth was a great and wealthy commercial center and played an important role in city-state politics. In the 2nd cent. B.C. it headed a revolt against Rome and was destroyed in 146. It lay largely in ruins for a cent. and then was rebuilt as a Roman colony by Julius Caesar. In 27 B.C. the Romans made it the capital of the province of Achaia.

Courtesy of Stella Grobel

Closeup of massive columns of the temple of Apollo at Corinth; columns are *ca.* 24 ft. high and 6 ft. in dia.; *cf.* ill., p. 803

Because of its strategic location Corinth was a great center of transit trade. It lay on a chief sea lane between Ephesus to the E and Rome to the W. To escape the dangerous voyage around the Peloponnesus ships often called at either the E or W port of Corinth and transhipped their cargoes across the narrow isthmus.

In Paul's day Corinth was a city to which Egyptians, Syrians, Jews, and other orientals had been attracted, and to which they had brought their diverse cultures, their distinctive social customs, and their differing religious beliefs and practices. It was also a city that had become notorious for its lax morality, even in an age when moral standards everywhere were low.

The first contact of the Jewish community in Corinth with the troublesome Christian sect was in 49, when the tentmakers Prisca (Priscilla) and Aquila came to the city after an edict of the Emperor Claudius had compelled all Jews to leave Rome

(Acts 18:2). Sometime the following year this Christian couple opened their Corinthian home to an itinerant evangelist of the same trade and faith.

Acts 18:11 estimates that Paul spent 18 months in Corinth during his first visit, and it may be inferred that he left the city late in 51 or early in 52. I Cor. was written to the Corinthian congregation from Ephesus *ca.* 4 years later.

In I Cor. 5:9-11 Paul refers to an earlier letter, and some scholars believe that a fragment of this is now embedded in II Cor. 6:14–7:1. As already noted,

Courtesy of Stella Grobel

In south stoa at Corinth; these ruins date *ca.* fourth cent. B.C.; destroyed in 146 B.C. Corinth was later restored by the Romans; this area is believed to have been used as an inn and tavern

I Cor. was in part a reply to a letter Paul received at Ephesus from the church at Corinth—a letter that asked questions about marriage (ch. 7), meat sold in the public market after having been sacrificed to pagan gods (chs. 8–10), and spiritual gifts (chs. 12–14). Paul not only answered these inquiries but also made observations and issued instructions on a number of other problems.

Because of the variety of matters with which it deals I Cor. is one of the most illuminating documents in the NT. It casts a flood of light not only on many aspects of Paul's thought but also on typical problems that emerged in Gentile churches. 11:23-26 is our earliest account of the celebration of the Lord's Supper and, chronologically speaking, the earliest account of the words Jesus used at the Last Supper. 15:3-11 is the earliest detailed account of the resurrection appearances of Jesus. And the hymn to love in ch. 13 is perhaps the most familiar and most beloved passage in Paul's writings.

I Cor. was probably written late in the winter of 55-56. According to 16:5-9 Paul's plans at the time were to leave Ephesus after Pentecost and journey through Macedonia to Corinth, with the intention of spending the following winter there. In II Cor., but not in Acts, there are indications that these travel plans were altered. Paul made a hasty trip from Ephesus to Corinth during the late spring or early summer of 56. The visit proved an unhappy one (II Cor. 2:1), and on his return he wrote a stern letter in the hope of correcting the situation (II Cor. 2:3). Many scholars believe that II Cor. 10–13 is at least part of this "painful letter."

Leaving Ephesus, Paul went to Troas and then on to Macedonia (II Cor. 2:12-13), where he tells us that he was torn with anxiety lest the Corinthians should reject his appeal (II Cor. 7:5). Then the arrival of Titus with the good news of a radical change of heart in Paul's beloved Corinthians transformed his whole mental attitude (II Cor. 7:6-7). As a result he wrote a letter of reconciliation that is found in II Cor.—either the whole letter as it appears in the NT or, as many scholars now believe, chs. 1–9.

Rome. Acts 20:1-3 tells us that Paul, after passing through Macedonia and encouraging the Christians there, came again to Greece, where he spent 3 months. The date was probably late in 56 and most of the time was no doubt spent at Corinth. During this period Paul wrote Rom. (see Intro.). At the end of this final visit, probably in the spring of 57, he left Corinth by way of Macedonia for Jerusalem.

In the form that we have Rom.—a short edition is known to have circulated also in the early church, one that omitted chs. 15–16 and the references to Rome in 1:7, 15—it is addressed "to all God's beloved in Rome" (Rom. 1:7). From 15:22-29 we learn that Paul at the time of writing had never visited Rome, but that he hoped shortly to do so on the way to a new field of missionary endeavor in Spain, since he considered his work in the E practically at an end. His immediate plans were to journey to Jerusalem, deliver the offering for the Jerusalem poor that had been collected among the congregations of Macedonia and Achaia, and then proceed to Rome to be sped further on his way "once I have enjoyed your company for a little."

Probably Christianity reached Rome very early in the apostolic age. Early converts to the faith would find their way from Palestine or elsewhere by natural migration to the hub of the known world. According to Acts 2:10 "visitors from Rome, both Jews and proselytes," were among those who witnessed the event of Pentecost and who listened to Peter's sermon. One 3rd-cent. tradition claims that the Roman church was founded by Barnabas, another that Christianity was first introduced in Rome by Peter; but both traditions are too late and too unsubstantiated to command much credence.

It is clear that when Paul wrote the Roman church was already well established. He declares that he has often entertained the wish to visit the congregation (1:13-15) and speaks of the reputation it enjoys in terms that sound extravagant but no doubt are sincere (1:8).

At this time it is clear that the Roman church was predominantly non-Jewish (1:5-6, 13; 11:13), but it also included among its members many who had formerly been Jews. The argument in 2:1-3:20 would carry little conviction unless addressed to readers whose religious heritage was Jewish. Though most Roman Christians had formerly been pagans, some at any rate could associate themselves with Paul when he spoke of Abraham as "our forefather according to the flesh" (4:1).

Rom. states its theme in 1:16-17: "The gospel . . . is the power of God for salvation to every one who has faith, to the Jew first and also to the Greek. For in it the righteousness of God is revealed from faith to faith." Paul then declares that apart from the gospel all men stand under the wrath of God (1:18-3:20) and that all, both Jew and Gentile, are offered the righteousness of God by faith in Jesus Christ (3:21-4:25). He then describes the new being in Christ (5:1-8:30), discusses the question raised by the unbelief of the Jews (chs. 9-11), gives a series of both general and specific exhortations (12:1-15:21), and concludes with an account of his travel plans (15:22-33). Ch. 16, as already noted, was probably originally a little letter to the Ephesians.

Someone has said that every great movement in Christian thought since apostolic times has stemmed from a rediscovery of Rom. Such names as Augustine, Luther, Wesley, and Barth can be cited in support of this generalization. But Rom. is for the run-of-the-mill Christian as well as for the theologian, and Rom. 8 is every bit as important as Rom. 7.

As the earliest known documents of the Christian church all the letters of Paul are invaluable as sources for a study of the preaching of the early church that Paul shared with those who were "in Christ" before him, and to a lesser extent of the teaching of Jesus; of the history of early Christianity, and to a lesser extent of the life of Jesus; and of the life, order, and worship of the early church. More important than their historical value, however—great as that is—is the power they still possess to convict us of sin, to lift us in Christ to God, and to help us to say with their author: "In all these things we are more than conquerors through him who loved us" (Rom. 8:37).

For Further Study. G. A. Deissmann, *Bible Studies*, 1901, pp. 1-59, 217-38. E. F. Scott, *The Literature of the NT*, 1932, pp. 107-15. E. J. Goodspeed, *An Intro. to the NT*, 1937, pp. 210-21. W. H. P. Hatch, "The Life of Paul," P. S. Minear, "Paul the Apostle," in *IB*, 1951. C. L. Mitton, *The Formation of the Pauline Corpus of Letters*, 1955. John Knox, *Philem. Among the Letters of Paul*, rev. ed., 1959. O. J. F. Seitz, "Letter," A. C. Purdy, "Paul the Apostle," in *IDB*, 1962.

NONCANONICAL
EARLY CHRISTIAN WRITINGS

Lucetta Mowry

At the end of the NT period (*ca.* 96-138) certain developments encouraged the production of an extensive Christian literature. Whereas the absolutist desires of the Emperor Domitian (81-96) had led to harsh repressive measures against the church, liberalism in imperial policies returned with the accession of Nerva (96-98), who discouraged informers and sedition trials. Trajan (98-117) continued these policies toward Christians. His official attitude is set down in the famous correspondence with Pliny, the governor of Bithynia. Pliny had not been certain about how to try Christians under his jurisdiction and inquired of the emperor. In reply Trajan stated that they were not to be disturbed unless formally accused by personal testimony and when charged should be tried by due process of law. This policy, though it did not prevent occasional martyrdoms, e.g. Ignatius and Polycarp, tended to leave the Christian communities generally undisturbed. At the same time another imperial policy favored the development of the Christian movement. Military campaigns and colonial enterprises began to make the empire more aware of the E. As an E religion Christianity was benefited by the beginning of this outlook.

Within the church conditions were also favorable. Christianity had come through a period of severe testing with its local communities intact in Syria, Egypt, Asia Minor, Greece, and Italy. These communities had by now fixed patterns of worship, the elements of organization, a distinct heritage in terms of local traditions, and esp. books, letters, and other written records of their past. They had a consciousness of their inherent character and were now in a position to produce a generation of indigenous believers who would be firmly established in the life of the church and would begin to mold and develop it both internally and in its relation to its wider environment.

This advance is evident in the reappearance of forceful and vivid personalities among the leaders of the church, men who could write on the authority of their own names. It is a striking fact that all the Christian literature of the previous period except Rev. was either anonymous or pseudonymous. Such works continued to appear, e.g. the latest books of the NT; but among the Apostolic Fathers, as the earliest noncanonical Christian authors have come to be called, a number name themselves in their writings because they were able to speak from recognized positions of leadership in the church.

It is significant that the Apostolic Fathers and their successors down to the time of Irenaeus (*ca.* 180)—the period surveyed in this article—show their familiarity with the literary types found in the NT, viz. letters, gospels, acts, and apocalypse. To these they add one new form, the apology, which proved valuable for defense of Christian beliefs and practices against the accusations of opponents in the wider cultural environment of the Roman Empire. Some of the latest NT books were written during this same time and similarly imitate the form of earlier NT books. The writings to be considered here are therefore some which might have become a part of the NT, and indeed were in some cases viewed as scripture by certain groups for a time, but for varying reasons failed to achieve the distinction of being finally accepted into the canon.

I. Letters

Paul, the earliest Christian author whose writings are extant, wrote letters of such vigor and effectiveness that for a period of nearly a cent. after *ca.* 90, when they began to be generally circulated among the churches, churchmen found the "letter" a most serviceable vehicle for religious and ethical instruction. During this period of Christian thought and life the primary centers from which these letters were sent were those established during the NT period, all in the Mediterranean basin: Antioch, Ephesus, Smyrna, Alexandria, Rome.

I Clement. Toward the end of the first cent. distressing news came from Corinth to the church at Rome. A revolt against the elected clergy entrusted with the performance of spiritual and practical duties had involved the Corinthian church in a bitter dispute. Paul in his time had struggled with factionalism there, and now the church was in danger of being fragmented again. The authority, competence, and character of the local bishops and deacons was being questioned by some who wished to oust them. Having recently gone through such party strife itself, the Roman church knew the danger and wrote the Corinthians to plead for unity in their church and respect for those bearing the heavy burden of responsibility for their welfare. Though the letter mentions no individual author, early tradition which there seems little reason to doubt identifies him as Clement, a bishop of the Roman church.

The lengthy letter exhorts the Corinthians by reminding them of the detrimental effects of divisiveness as recorded in the OT, by upholding the Christian virtues of kindness, peaceableness, sincerity, humility, faith, and love, by supporting the authority of elected bishops, and by asking for God's blessing on the Corinthian church. Two elements in the letter seem to be of major significance: the role of leadership in the life of the Christian community and the bond of love which unites all its members from the smallest to the greatest. "Love admits no schism, love makes no sedition, love does all things in concord. In love were all the elect of God made perfect. Without love is nothing well-pleasing to God." (49:5, trans. K. Lake.) In fact we are received by God because Christ, motivated by love, gave his life for us.

The Letters of Ignatius. Arrested and sent to Rome to die, Ignatius, bishop of Antioch in the early years of the 2nd cent., was persuaded while stopped in Smyrna on his journey to write letters to 3 nearby Christian communities at Ephesus, Magnesia, and Tralles and also to the church at Rome. From a later stop at Troas he wrote back to Polycarp, bishop of Smyrna, and also to the church there and to that in Philadelphia. Shortly after his death Polycarp secured copies of the other letters and sent the collection of 7 to Philippi as requested by the church there.

The letters show that to Ignatius on his way to martyrdom 3 concerns were of utmost importance: (*a*) that his own church at Antioch be given aid and be remembered in the prayers of other churches, (*b*) that heretical views be stamped out, and (*c*) that each Christian community live in peace and love under the leadership of the clergy. He supported the divinely ordained authority of the bishop because he believed that the holder of that office was the only figure powerful enough to stand against the infiltration of heretical doctrines and to prevent the Christian communities from breaking into schismatic factions. The collection of his letters is of great importance as a source for the history of the Christian movement because of what it reveals about developments during this period in both doctrine and organization of the church.

The Letter of Polycarp. Along with the request for Ignatius' letters the Philippian church asked Polycarp to write his own thoughts on the subject of righteousness. The reason was apparently concern about an elder named Valens who had proved to be avaricious and dishonest. In response Polycarp states that the Christian way of life must be characterized by love for one's fellow men, obedience to God's commandments, loyalty and perseverance in the faith, virtue and forgiveness, confession that Jesus Christ has come in the flesh, and belief in the Resurrection. He urges that Valens and his wife be regarded, not as enemies, but as straying members of the church for whom God's gift of repentance is to be sought. The letter is chiefly important for the evidence it shows of the use of the NT documents for guidance in solving the problems of local church life.

The Martyrdom of Polycarp. Many years later, in Feb. 155 or 156, Polycarp himself in his old age died as a martyr. Soon afterward an anonymous account in the form of a letter was widely circulated. The author uses restraint in telling the story and stresses the idea of steadfast loyalty to Christ under extreme torture. The scene in which the aged man is urged by the Roman proconsul to save his life by reviling Christ but instead affirms his faith is most moving. This letter begins a new type of Christian writing, "acts" of martyrs.

The Letter of Barnabas. A religious tract in the form of a letter which in its present form claims authorship by Paul's companion Barnabas actually seems to have been written anonymously *ca.* 130 by a Christian teacher who admired the kind of allegorical interpretation of scripture found in the works of Philo of Alexandria (see "The Intertestamental Literature," pp. 1110-15), in Heb., and occasionally in Paul's letters. The first 17 chs. deal allegorically with the OT but the last 5 brief chs. set forth a doctrine of 2 ways, of light and of darkness. The latter section recalls the manual form of instruction found in the Essene library of Qumran, esp. the Manual of Discipline, as well as the Christian manual called the Didache. The longer first section seeks to show how the covenant of Jesus superseded the Mosaic covenant, the promises of the OT being fulfilled in the appearance of Christ and the Christian community, and strongly condemns Judaism. Many OT passages are interpreted as allegories; e.g. the prohibition of eating pork means that one should not associate with the ungodly.

II. Gospels

The gospel is a distinctive literary form presumably invented by the author of the first extant example, Mark. That this first attempt was a success is indicated by the use made of it by other Christian authors. In Matt. and Luke not only the form is taken from Mark but also a large percentage of the content. In John the same form is used but with different content which is actually a theological treatise.

The term "gospel" originally meant the message of these writings, the "gospel of Jesus Christ," as announced in the opening phrase of Mark. In this sense there was only one gospel and the several books were merely different witnesses to it. Thus to these documents titles were superscribed to identify the witnesses as known from tradition—According to Matt., According to Mark, etc. By the latter half of the 2nd cent., however, when the 4 we know as canonical had come to be recognized as authoritative, the word "gospel" was applied not only to the message itself but also to the document in which it was expressed. Thus the accepted 4 came to be called gospels, and so also did the works of other Christian authors who had already recognized and were continuing to recognize the usefulness of this literary form as an instrument to express their particular views regarding the significance of Jesus for the lives of men. Later when the 4 became a closed canon, the rejected gospels came to be called "apocryphal." Lit. this means "hidden" or "secret" and perhaps it was first applied because their circulation was limited to the small groups whose faith was nourished by them. Soon, however, the term came to mean "spurious."

Early Noncanonical Gospels. A considerable number of apocryphal gospels are mentioned and sometimes quoted by later Christian authors, usually in order to point out their errors. Scholars have studied these carefully in hope of finding possible independent traditions of Jesus' life and teachings, but with rare exceptions these fragments seem to be based on one or more of the canonical gospels.

Among the earliest of these works, apparently dating from *ca.* mid-2nd cent., are the Gospel According to the Hebrews and the Gospel According to the Egyptians. Probably these titles are not those by which the writings were known to most of their readers but rather designations given them by critics identifying them with the particular groups where they originated and were used. Both seem to have come from Egypt, "Hebrews" apparently referring to a group of Jewish Christians there and Egyptians to a Gentile group. These were both in Greek, whereas a work from which Jerome quotes a number of times, calling it the Gospel According to the Hebrews, seems rather to have been an Aramaic version of Matt. in which the translator took some liberties of interpretation. Perhaps it was the same as the gospel said by another author to have been used by a group of Jewish Christians in Syria known as Nazarenes. Some scholars believe that the Gospel According to the Hebrews should be identified rather with the gospel used in another part of Syria by a sect of Jewish Christians called the Ebionites, who denied Jesus' virgin birth and maintained instead that he became the Christ at his baptism.

Other apocryphal gospels are referred to by names which indicate that they attempted to enhance the value of their contents by claiming apostolic authorship—either by all of the 12 or by a particular one. Of these all have become lost except a few which give legendary expansions at 2 points where the canonical narratives apparently did not satisfy popular demand—Jesus' birth and childhood and his appearances following his resurrection. Of the first type is the Gospel of Thomas, which relates a series of miracles performed by Jesus as a boy—e.g. correcting Joseph's mistake of sawing a beam too short by pulling it to its proper length, and bringing clay pigeons to life. Another, the Protevangelium of James, tells the story of Mary from her birth to the birth of Jesus. These 2 seem to have originated in the latter part of the 2nd cent., and later works of this kind are derived from them. An example of the 2nd type is the fragmentary Gospel of Peter, which begins with the handwashing episode at Jesus' trial and breaks off with what seems to be the beginning of an unusual resurrection experience.

Such documents, differing as they assuredly do from the canonical gospels, are yet in many respects comparable to them. It should be noted that the authors of Matt. and Luke did not hesitate to change the account they found in Mark and felt free to interpret material. By adding stories about Jesus' birth and childhood and about his resurrection they also give evidence in at least some degree to a greater biographical interest. On the other hand there is a great contrast in that the apocryphal gospels show scarcely any restraint in the addition of legendary embellishments. Thus these narratives make the account of Jesus' words and works more and more grotesque. Clearly the unknown areas of Jesus' life kindled the imagination, and popular piety demanded more biographical material. We can be grateful to the church fathers for admitting only the 4 gospels to the canon.

Gnostic Gospels. Among the series of almost incredible discoveries of ancient manuscripts in recent years one of great significance is the finding of a number of papyrus volumes in the ruins of a monastery near ancient Chenoboskion, not far from the modern town of Nag Hammadi in Upper Egypt. The importance of this discovery lies chiefly in its making available for the first time actual writings of Christianized Gnosticism, a powerful rival of orthodox Christianity which previously was known almost entirely from the works of apologists attacking it. Though the early stages of the church's encounter with Gnosticism are still obscure, these works now make possible a more precise understanding of the variety and complexity of Gnostic thought from the middle of the 2nd cent. on.

As now seen, the basic doctrine of Gnosticism was that there is a true, perfect, and unknown God, who has no contact with this imperfect world, which was created by a lesser imperfect God. Man's proper abode is with the perfect God, but he is now trapped in the imperfect world. It is by knowledge, *gnosis*, of his essentially perfect nature that man can escape the world of imperfection and achieve his essential and true divine nature.

Among the Gnostic books discovered are 3 which are called gospels: the Gospel of Thomas, which is entirely different from the work of that title mentioned above, the Gospel of Philip, and the Gospel of Truth. In all 3 of these the authors have attempted to assimilate their Gnostic views with the doctrines characteristic of more orthodox Christian writings. They do this primarily by indicating how Jesus could be thought of as a redemptive figure within the Gnostic scheme. Their ideas vary considerably, but a typical syncretistic view can be illustrated briefly from the opening words of the Gospel of Thomas, which hint at the use made of canonical gospel materials as well as the modification required by the new point of view:

> These are the secret words which Jesus the Living spoke and (which) Didymus Judas Thomas wrote. And He said: He who will find the interpretation of these words will not taste death. Jesus said: Let him who seeks not cease in his seeking until he finds; and when he finds, he will be troubled, and if he is troubled he will marvel, and will be a king over the All. (Trans. by W. R. Schoedel.)

This initial section makes clear that Jesus through his teaching rather than his acts is the unique revealer of secret wisdom and saving truth. Further on in the gospel he is spoken of as the light over everything and the All from which all has gone forth and returned. He appeared in the flesh, though not born of woman, to give those who had come from the realm of light the true knowledge of their origin. Having understood this secret knowledge, the redeemed Gnostic will reject the world as unworthy of the enlightened sons of the living Lord. Even this brief statement makes clear some of the Gnostics' perversions of NT thought. They deny the value of the world, of actions and events, and of such fundamental Christian doctrines as those of sin and forgiveness, repentance and grace.

Though none of these noncanonical gospels provide us with any dependable information about the words and deeds of Jesus, they have value in the study of the history of Christian thought. They were obviously written to serve the needs of certain Christian communities which were no longer in the main stream of the developing Christian tradition. On the one hand there were the pious who demanded that their faith be bolstered by popular tales of miraculous events. On the other hand there were heretical groups such as the Gnostics who used the gospel form as a means of communicating their peculiar views regarding the significance of Christ and of the church.

III. ACTS

The canonical Acts of the Apostles leaves even greater gaps in the story of Christianity's expansion than do the canonical gospels in the life of Jesus. Thus it is not unexpected that apocryphal "acts" came to be written to supply in the form of imaginative fiction the stories of the pioneers of the faith which had not been transmitted in the tradition.

A reader of Acts might well get the impression that only 2 apostles, Peter and Paul, played any outstanding role in the missionary movement of the church. To correct any such misconception, probably soon after the middle of the 2nd cent. an author took such clues as are to be found elsewhere in the NT and built on them to create an Acts of John. The extant portion begins with his departure from Patmos and tells of the remainder of his life in Ephesus, including many miraculous deeds, a reminiscence of his experiences with Jesus, and finally his death in old age—the only apostle not said to have been martyred.

Perhaps not too long afterward one who found even the emphasis of the canonical book deficient produced the Acts of Paul. This narrative recounts the apostle's adventures from his arrival at Pisidian Antioch to his death at Rome with many added fictional details, mostly series of miracles at one town after another. Certain parts of this work were so popular that they were used separately: (a) the Acts of Paul and Thecla, telling of a young woman converted by Paul and sent out as a missionary (contrast I Cor. 14:34-35); (b) III Cor., a purported additional letter quoted in the book; and (c) the Martyrdom of Paul, an account of his execution at Rome.

A reader of the Acts of Paul, probably before the end of the 2nd cent., composed a similar Acts of Peter to relate what is missing from the canonical book about the latter part of this apostle's career. It tells of his coming to Rome and of his martyrdom there, a story that has become well known.

These 3 works and 2 of similar character probably written in the 3rd cent., the Acts of Andrew and the Acts of Thomas, were substituted for the canonical Acts of the Apostles by the Manicheans, adherents of a syncretistic Persian religion that arose during this cent. Orthodox critics mistakenly attributed all 5 of them to one author, a certain Leucius, otherwise unknown, and denounced them vehemently. The Acts of Thomas narrates this apostle's missionary work in India, where a Christian sect today claims him as founder. In this work appears a song allegedly composed and sung by Thomas that has become known separately as the "Hymn of the Soul" or "Hymn of the Pearl." Actually it appears to be an earlier Gnostic poem which the author incorporated in his narrative. Simply but movingly it tells the story of the soul's, or pearl's, redemption by the Prince, i.e. the Gnostic redeemer. Though originally divine and perfect and part of the All from which all is derived, the soul has become lost in the imperfect world of darkness and of cosmic existence. For its salvation the redeemer from the perfect supernatural world divests himself of his divine qualities to undergo the same fate. Since in the Gnostic scheme the soul is a part of the All, the redeemer in a sense seeks that lost element of his own being.

Acts of the other apostles were added after these, as well as a number of new versions of those already narrated. Obviously all these apocryphal acts have little if any historical merit; and on the whole, even though they have been better preserved, they seem to have had less influence on Christian thought than have the apocryphal gospels.

IV. APOCALYPSES

The NT apocalyptic materials, Mark 13 and Rev., are so closely related to Palestinian ideas of an end to the present age and the beginning of a new age that the later Christian writers from a non-Jewish background found it necessary to make more or less radical modifications in this traditional literary type. They were able to use the form, that of the vision, but were compelled to alter the content within that form.

The most significant noncanonical Christian apocalypse is the Shepherd of Hermas, said to have been the brother of a Roman bishop who wrote ca. 140, though some scholars believe that parts of the work originated very early in the cent. It was highly valued in the early church, being considered inspired scripture by many, and is generally included among the Apostolic Fathers. The work is divided into 3 parts, called Visions, Mandates or Commandments, and Similitudes or Parables. For the most part it is cast in the traditional apocalyptic mold, but the content concerns everyday ethical problems rather than a coming new age. According to current doctrine in Rome one who sinned after baptism could not hope for forgiveness and consequent salvation. The main purpose of the writing is to counter this idea and emphasize instead the necessity for repentance.

Probably from about the same time comes the Rev. of Peter, which shows its indebtedness to the canonical Rev. but is concerned simply with portraying the delights of heaven and the tortures of hell. Several later apocalypses of this character are attributed to other apostles. The desire of some groups for this type of literature was also met by taking over Jewish apocalyptic works and christianizing them—interpolating into the visions predictions of Jesus, e.g. in I, II Enoch, II, III Baruch, and adding new visions, e.g. in II Esdras (see Intro.) and the Sibylline Oracles (see "The Intertestamental Literature," pp. 1110-15).

The Apocryphon of John from the library of

Chenoboskion illustrates the use made of this modified literary type by the Gnostics. Since they regarded knowledge of salvation as secretly revealed, they found the vision form of the apocalypse eminently appropriate, but not its hope for coming redemption of the world along with man. They were concerned with man's destiny as were the apocalyptists, but their understanding of man's nature differed so radically from that of the Jews and Jewish Christians that their whole scheme of salvation bore no resemblance to that of Jewish and Christian apocalypticism.

In the Apocryphon of John the essential problem concerns imperfect man's relationship to a perfect divine being. To explain man's sense of relatedness to and separation from this perfect God the author sets forth an elaborate doctrine of man and the world which involves a struggle between tremendously powerful spiritual forces. Jesus' place in this struggle is merely that of a revealer of knowledge which will bring man's salvation. Redemption from this evil and imperfect world will belong to the one who understands the true nature of the universe, of God, and of himself. The world, as a creation of an evil power, has somehow entrapped man. Fortunately there is latent within man life and light so that he can respond to the Spirit sent from God and thus overcome the world. If man does not respond to this knowledge there are 2 possible fates: he may be reincarnated and in due course understand the meaning of saving knowledge, or he may refuse ever to respond and be condemned to eternal torment.

V. APOLOGIES

The NT contains an occasional apologetic element but no example of an apology, or defense of the faith, as such. A number of works of this literary type, however, were written during the first half of the 2nd cent., as is known from references and quotations found in later Christian writings. They include: the Preaching of Peter (*ca.* 110), an attack on certain Jewish and Greek beliefs and practices; the Apology of Quadratus (*ca.* 125), an appeal to the Emperor Hadrian for the recognition of Christianity as a legitimate religion; the Dialogue Between Jason and Propiscus Concerning Christ by Aresto of Pella (*ca.* 140); and the Apology of Aristides (138-47), a defense of Christianity before the Emperor Antoninus.

The earliest extant Christian apology may be the Letter to Diognetus, which has been included in most editions of the Apostolic Fathers on the assumption that it comes from the first half of the 2nd cent. Some scholars believe, however, that it should be dated in the 3rd cent. or later. The unknown author shows unusual skill in rhetoric, and certain passages are often quoted today; but no references to the work have been convincingly identified in any ancient writings.

With more assurance we can turn to the well-known apologies of Justin, who earned the surname Martyr *ca.* 165. His 2 major works, written at Rome between *ca.* 150 and 160, are: the Apology, addressed to the Emperor Antoninus, a defense of Christian beliefs and practices against accusations by opponents; and the Dialogue with Trypho, in the form of a debate in which the author argues with a Jew that OT prophecies of the Messiah and the covenanted community have been fulfilled in Jesus Christ and the church. Another extant early apology is Athenagoras' Plea Regarding Christians, addressed to the Emperor Marcus Aurelius in 176-77.

The adoption of this type of literature is significant for our understanding of the Christian tradition because it gives additional insight into the church's development both internally and in its relation to its wider environment. On the one hand the church is being recognized as an expanding force which must be dealt with by the more established religious traditions. On the other hand the facing of opposition is aiding the church to clarify its own distinctive nature.

VI. OTHER WRITINGS

While most early Christian authors tended to follow the patterns of literary form outlined above, there are a few works that took other forms and must be considered individually.

The Teaching of the 12 Apostles, more often called the Didache, Greek for "teaching," is a manual of instruction for the Christian community, setting forth rules for the conduct of the laity and the clergy and regulations for services of worship. Chs. 1–6 present moral precepts in a formulation of the 2 ways of light and darkness similar to that in the last part of the Letter of Barnabas; the relationship is not clear but probably indicates a common source. Some or perhaps most of the content may come from the beginning of the 2nd cent. or even earlier, but the work appears to be composite and may not have reached its present form until mid-cent. Part at least stems from Jewish-Christian circles in Syria, but the work seems to have taken final shape in Alexandria.

The Odes of Solomon is a collection of 42 hymns, of which portions have been found in Coptic and Greek but the whole only in Syriac, which may have been the original language. These unique survivals of early Christian hymnody probably date from the middle of the 2nd cent. and originated in Jewish-Christian circles, perhaps in Mesopotamia, which were influenced by Gnostic thought.

A major work of scripture commentary is the Interpretations of the Sayings of the Lord, in 5 vols., composed by Papias *ca.* 140. A considerable number of fragments of it have survived in quotations by various later authors. Since in one of these Papias expresses a preference for oral tradition over written gospels, it might be supposed that his work contained a treasure of sayings of Jesus not reported in the NT. The fact that no such sayings are quoted from him by the later authors, however, seems to indicate that the oral tradition sought by Papias failed to produce anything beyond what is preserved in the canonical records.

II Clement takes its name from being in ancient times attributed to the same author as I Clement, but clearly it is the work of a different hand and from a later time, probably early in the latter half of the 2nd cent. It has the form of a letter but is actually a sermon intended to stir the reader to repent with a sincere heart and do the will of God so that he may escape the terrors of a fiery judgment and gain the rewards of life eternal.

This survey has brought us down to Irenaeus, bishop of Lugdunum (Lyons) in Gaul, whose great work Against Heresies, directed primarily against Gnosticism, was published *ca.* 180. The most important of his successors among Christian authors of the 3rd-4th cents. are mentioned in the articles on "The Making of the NT Canon" (pp. 1216-24) and "The Early History of the Church" (pp. 1045-53).

The examination of the growing literary output of the early church indicates 2 major interests: (*a*) Churchmen had to deal with problems of church life, esp. organization and the issue of heresy. (*b*) Now clearly established in the Roman world, the church felt a greater need than in former years to interpret the Christian tradition for non-Christian groups. Powerful Christian centers responded in varying ways. The Roman church was inclined to stress the practical, ethical issues while the churches of Greece, Asia Minor, and Egypt tended to take a more mystical and speculative approach. As time went on the church found it necessary to set the norms for distinguishing the orthodox from the heretical response to this larger cultural environment. In so doing it eventually selected 27 books to constitute the canon of the NT and virtually consigned the rest of its early literature to oblivion. Some of the books quite rightly belong there, but others deserve a better fate.

For Further Study: Kirsopp Lake, *The Apostolic Fathers,* 2 vols., 1919; Greek texts and trans. M. R. James, ed., *The Apoc. NT,* 1924; trans. of collected texts. E. J. Goodspeed, *A History of Early Christian Literature,* 1942. Hans Jonas, *The Gnostic Religion,* 1958. H. C. Puech et al., *The Gospel According to Thomas,* 1959. Jean Doresse, *The Secret Books of the Egyptian Gnostics,* 1960. R. M. Grant, *The Secret Sayings of Jesus,* 1960; "Gnosticism" in *IDB,* 1962. K. M. Grobel, *The Gospel of Truth,* 1960. W. C. Van Unnik, *Newly Discovered Gnostic Writings,* 1960. M. S. Enslin, "Apoc., NT"; M. H. Shepherd, Jr., "Apostolic Fathers," in *IDB,* 1962. E. Hennecke, W. Schneemelcher, R. McL. Wilson, eds., *NT Apoc.,* 2 vols., 1963; trans. of collected texts. R. McL. Wilson, *The Gospel of Philip,* 1963.

THE RELIGION OF ISRAEL

Samuel Terrien

The religions of the ancient Near East and of classical antiquity have not outlived the nations which gave them birth. The religion of Israel constitutes a single exception, for the reality which is represented by Yahweh, the God of Israel, has remained identified with the faith of contemporary Judaism and Christianity. For this reason alone the religion of Israel possesses an element of distinctiveness which is without parallel in the Mediterranean world.

It used to be said dogmatically that the religion of Israel was unique among the religions of mankind because the only true God chose the Hebrews as the exclusive vehicle of his revelation among men. Such a view, shared by traditional Jews and Christians alike, was linked with rabbinical beliefs in the Mosaic authorship of the Pentateuch and in the divine dictation of the law on Mt. Sinai.

Literary and historical criticism in the 19th cent. exploded the possibility of accepting the validity of these beliefs with intellectual honesty. At the same time archaeological discoveries brought to light an enormous amount of artifacts, inscriptions, and literary texts, which show beyond question that the Hebrews were indebted in many ways to their Semitic and Egyptian neighbors. At the beginning of the 20th cent. the German school of the comparative study of religions pointed out religious as well as other similarities which bound Israel to her cultural environment. Many scholars looked at the God of Israel as one deity among others and at the religion of Israel as one form of the general cultic pattern of the classical Orient.

In the middle 20's the British and Scandinavian schools of "myth and ritual" approached the study of Israel's religion not only in the light of the ancient Near Eastern culture but also from the perspective of international, esp. Norse, folklore. Numerous parallels of cultic rites and mythical patterns were discovered among the Hebrews, Mesopotamians, Egyptians, and esp. Phoenician-Canaanites. In the 30's and 40's the early Phoenician religious texts of Ugarit Ras Shamra (modern) provided for a time an added impetus to the thesis of oriental patternism, and the originality of the religion of Israel was widely underestimated. According to this trend of opinion, which still prevails in some quarters, Israel conformed to the general culture of the ancient Near East in her religious beliefs and practices as well as in her political, legal, and technological modes of existence.

Since the 2nd World War the situation appears to have altered considerably. A sober assessment of the many data available to contemporary scholarship, together with the definite progress in textual criticism, form-critical and literary, and traditio-historical analysis, has compelled empirical historians to face the enigma of Israel's religious specificity. The mystery of Hebrew faith is no longer only a presupposition of Jewish or Christian dogma. It has become evident as a result of historical observation. Considerable doubt remains, however, concerning an accurate picture of the religion of the patriarchs.

I. The Religion of Israel's Ancestors

While the traditions of Gen. were not written before the time of David and Solomon (10th cent.), it is now admitted that they reflect tribal memories of an earlier age. Since the narratives reflect accurately the sociological and legal customs of W Semites in the 2nd millenium, some historians find no cause to question the validity of the biographical and theological framework in which these tribal memories were preserved. Nevertheless no archaeological evidence has been so far discovered which may tend to support the biographical character of such figures as Abraham, Isaac, Jacob, and Joseph and his brothers. For this reason, and also because of the numerous examples of contradiction, anachronism, addition, selection, elimination, and conflation or reorganization of heterogeneous details, many interpreters who pay meticulous attention to the method of traditio-historical criticism are unable to offer any precise description of the Hebrew cult and beliefs in the patriarchal age.

There is general agreement, of course, on the polytheistic background of Israel's earliest ancestors (cf. e.g. Josh. 24:2, 14). These men probably worshiped a form of the moon god in Ur and Haran (cf. the names Terah and Laban, which are associated with lunar worship.

One of them, Abraham, migrated W and S along the Fertile Crescent, probably early in the 18th cent. Tradition at a later age was unanimous in ascribing this move to a religious experience, the story of which is now embedded in the narrative of Abraham's call (Gen. 12:1-6).

Whether or not Abraham was the father of Isaac and the grandfather of Jacob must remain a matter of uncertainty. There are numerous reasons to suppose that the scheme of the 12 sons of Jacob, born through 2 Aramean wives and 2 Canaanite concubines, represents a symbolic way of portraying the origin of Israel's tribal league as it was formed at Shechem late in the 13th cent. (Josh. 24).

It is not even possible to say whether the Hebrew ancestors worshiped Yahweh, for the N tribal memories (Elohist) explicitly related the disclosure of the divine name to Moses (Exod. 3:13-15), whereas the S, Judahite memories (Yahwist) kept alive the idea that men began to worship Yahweh in the remotest antiquity (Gen. 4:26).

Nevertheless even the N traditions pointed out that there was an element of continuity between faith in the God of the Exodus and the worship of the ancestral deity (Exod. 3:6). In all probability the Hebrew fathers invoked their family gods, known sometimes as the Shield of Abraham (Gen. 15:1), sometimes as the Kinsman (or possibly Fear) of Isaac (Gen. 31:42), and again as the Mighty One of Jacob (Gen. 49:24). These clan deities may have been conceived as various forms of the same divine power, revealing themselves at specific shrines or watering places. The word *el,* "god" as a generic term, was combined with other words in such designations as *El Olam,* "God of Ages" (Gen. 21:33), *El Shaddai,* "God of the Fruitful Mountain" or possibly "God of the Breast" (Gen. 17:1; cf. 49:25-26), *El Elyon,* "God of High Heaven" (Gen. 14:18), and *El Bethel,* "God of the Divine Tent" (Gen. 31:13). In some instances *El* may have been a proper name, e.g. in *El Elohe Israel,* "El the God of Israel" (Gen. 33:20), and *El Elohe Abhika,* "El the God of Your Father" (Gen. 46:3).

It is significant that these clan deities were also conceived as high gods, endowed with a cosmic character not unlike that of the supreme god El in the Ugaritic pantheon. The story of Abraham and Melchizedek, king of Salem (Jerusalem?), shows that El Elyon, like the Ugaritic El, was worshiped as the creator of heaven and earth (Gen. 14:19).

Israel remembered that her ancestors were Aramean nomads, perishing of thirst and exhausted from wandering (Deut. 26:5). Her historical existence was explained as an act of divine intervention. Thus the figure of Abraham, having abandoned the comforts and the security of a settled civilization for the risks of obedience to a divine vision, became the model of her faith (Gen. 15:6).

In the course of time, to be sure, Hebrew religion learned of shrines, of dynasties, of hierarchies, and of complicated rituals which led to a sharp distinction between clergy and laity, the sacred and the secular. Yet the traditions concerning Israel's ancestors spoke only of a familiar though bewildering God, intervening at the most unexpected moments and entering with simple men into a dynamic rapport for the sake of a distant goal, the unity of mankind (Gen. 12:1-6).

It was the dream of a blessing for all nations that the narratives depicted as controlling the patriarchs' separation from their cultural environment. Abraham, Isaac, and Jacob appeared already as a "peculiar" people (Exod. 19:5-6 KJV), as "a people dwelling alone, and not reckoning itself among the nations" (Num. 23:9). They were aliens passing through the land, in quest of some sort of inaccessible permanence.

The storytellers may well have oversimplified the religious complexity of those distant times. E.g. it seems that the pillar of stone which Jacob erected at Bethel (Gen. 28:22) was not clearly distinguishable from the phallic symbols of the Canaanite cultus. Nevertheless Israel's ancestors seem to have kept themselves by and large from conforming to the ways of their nature-worshiping neighbors. For a small elite, at least, neither earth with its fertility nor sky with its sun, moon, and star symbols of sexuality could be confused with the divine ruler of nature. Such a theological element pervades the Hebrew traditions and is found nowhere else in the religious literatures of the ancient Near East. Magical techniques by which man deludes himself into attempting to control the forces of his natural environment or himself again and again fascinated the Hebrew masses, but they were consistently rejected by their leaders. The idea of God was not to be identified with either nature or man.

Hence Israel's ancestors were never idealized into heroes. Abraham was portrayed as a coward and a liar as well as a model of trust and prayer. Jacob was viewed as a cheat and a thief as well as the father of Israel. Neither ancestral worship nor the hero-making process seems to have molded the narratives. On the contrary belief in a transcending yet proximate Deity dominates all the scenes. The God of the fathers possessed qualities of holiness, of ineffability, and of elusiveness which did not exclude the intimacy of his approach to the men of his concern. He promoted at once the sense of comforting presence and of demanding ultimacy (cf. esp. Gen. 12:1-6; 15:1-6; 22:1-18; 28:17; 32:24-30).

At the fringe of the desert Israel's ancestors accepted the gift of life and the challenge of a historical mission. Under the sign of a nature-transcending God they discerned a proper scale of human values. When Moses came on the scene he was probably able to draw on this tribal inheritance of religious peculiarity.

II. The Exodus and the Covenant

Traditio-historical analysis of the narratives preserved in Exod., Num., Deut., Josh. and of numerous allusions in other books of the OT shows that only a few Hebrew nomads, from a group which may be called the Joseph tribes, went to Egypt. The Exodus and the Sinai covenant did not at first concern "all Israel," but it was through these momentous events and the ritual memory of their tradition in the cultic festivals that the various ethnic groups became conscious at Shechem under Joshua of forming a new nation.

The God of Moses. The figure of Moses is intimately interwoven with the stories of the Exodus and Sinai. Legendary processes appear to have been at work on the circumstances of his birth and of his dealings with the Egyptian king, but on the whole the early traditions (Yahwist and Elohist) preserved a remarkably sober picture of the founder of Israel's religion. As with the patriarchs, the early Hebrew theological mind, thoroughly captured by faith in a God who transcends the world of nature and of men, avoided the pitfalls of a later age. Hero-worship developed with the birth of Judaism during the Exile, when the Jerusalem priestly traditions, which provided the structural framework of the Pentateuch, began the trend of Mosaic exaltation that led to the glorification of the law in Hellenistic and Roman times.

The earliest memories of Moses describe him as a member of the Joseph tribes, brought up in the Egyptian culture, who associated at some time in his youth with the Kenites, a nomadic group of the Sinai Peninsula. After a religious experience of determinative proportion, described in the scene of the burning bush (Exod. 3:1-4:18), Moses became the reluctant leader of a revolt among the Hebrew slaves near the NE border of the Nile Delta. He successfully led them out of Egyptian territory, across a momentarily dried body of water, and into the wilderness of Sinai. There at the foot of the "mountain of Elohim," he persuaded the fugitives to bind themselves solemnly by a ritual of "covenant" to the God who had saved them from political oppression and apparent death. Critical examination of the narratives of Exod. has led modern scholars to accept substantially the historical validity of the events described therein.

It appears most probable that Moses learned from the Kenites to worship the God with the ineffable name Yahweh. This is indicated by the part played by Jethro, the Kenite priest of Yahweh, in the ceremonies of the covenant (Exod. 18) and by the later devotion of Kenites to the pure desert form of Yahwism (cf. e.g. Judg. 4:17-22; II Kings 10:15; I Chr. 2:55; Jer. 35). At the same time the memory of the faith of the Hebrew ancestors (Exod. 3:13), together with the psychological impact of the experience of Moses at the burning bush, profoundly transformed the Kenite religious heritage.

The divine name revealed to Moses (Exod. 3:14) probably means "I cause to be whatever I cause to be." The traditional rendering "I am who I am" is certainly erroneous. It is based on a late Jewish reading which seems to reflect philosophical speculations on "being" in Alexandria in the 3rd cent., when Jews were translating the LXX. The interpretation of the 4 consonantal letters YHWH as "he causes to be" is confirmed by Hebrew morphology and syntax, by the reading "Yahweh" supported by the Greek magical papyri of Egypt, by the tradition collected by Jerome, and by the immediate context of the use of the name both in Exod. and in Pss. and the prophetic literature.

According to this hypothesis the God of Moses is not a localized mountain spirit but a cosmic actor and doer, not only the self-contained and free agent who brings the cosmos into existence at creation but also the faithful sustainer who keeps the world in order through his provident care. It is this God who can cause a simple shepherd and outlawed alien like Moses to become a prophet and a political leader. It is this God who can transform a herd of unorganized, dispirited Hebrew slaves in Egypt into a dynamic, closely knit organism. We discern in the Mosaic vision and in the theological interpretation provided by its narrative the main characteristics of Israel's faith: the reality of a divine presence which creates a peculiar people for the sake of a universal mission in history.

The Covenant. These characteristics are made explicit and effectual in the Sinai covenant. The covenant ritual and its formulation appear to have been influenced in part by the sovereign-vassal treaties which were apparently contracted among some W Semites in the 2nd millenium, and which are known to modern scholarship through the Hittite documents of Asia Minor. The originality of Moses appears in the startling fact that he borrowed those forms of political alliance between a king and his satellites and applied them to an entirely different relationship—the alliance between a divine sovereign, Yahweh, and a nomadic society in which no social, political, economic, or clerical class hierarchy was tolerated. The covenant society envisaged by Moses appears like a prophetic utopian theocracy, without the intermediary of royal or ecclesiastical clericalism.

The covenant was God-initiated. It provided for a constitutional structure of society, not only for the generation of Hebrew slaves who were delivered in the Exodus, but also for their descendants.

The archaic formulation of the covenant ceremony (Exod. 19) discloses the primacy of the theological motif of divine presence as the basis of sociological homogeneity and ethical solidarity. It makes corporateness and community organization dependent on a specifically religious response to the acceptance of transcending grace, unexpected, unrequested, unmerited. "You have seen what I did to the Egyptians, and how I bore you on eagles' wings and brought you to myself" (Exod. 19:3).

The covenant, however, must be viewed, not as a mystical fusion, but as a reasoned and structural union between God and man. The covenant formula confirms the narrative of the disclosure of the divine name. Yahweh, unlike the other deities of the ancient Near East, is neither a deified force of nature nor a local desert demon or spirit. "All the earth is mine" (Exod. 19:5). He is the creator God, whose sway comprehends the universe and "all the nations."

The covenant inaugurates the corporate consciousness of Israel, as the solidarity of the social body which it promotes transcends the generations. It contains within itself the principle of historical continuity which in turn prefigures an expectation of future completeness. The reason for Israel's existence is related to a hope of the end of history which is not terminal and negative but germinal and positive. Through the covenant Israel becomes aware of time, not as the unfolding of a perfect past, as in the mythical golden age, but as the preparation of a perfect future—a theme to be developed by the prophets in the myths of the divine kingdom, the new earth, and the Messiah.

The Hebrews of the Exodus and, even more, the Israelites of the Shechem tribal federation in the post-Mosaic generation, belonged to various ethnic elements. In the language of a later era they were "a no-people." But they became united among themselves because they were united to the same God, Yahweh, the creator of nature and history. Their social and political bond depended, not on the normal sociological factors of the ancient Near East —royal or imperial dynasties, priestly hierarchies attached to special shrines and giving religious support to engineering teamwork necessary for flood control or military defense—but on the disclosure and the proximity of a passionately purposive God.

It may be said that the introduction of a theological form of covenant by Moses represented a new stage in the history of religions as well as in the history of human association. It also provided for later Judaism and Christianity a unique characteristic which is reflected in the traditional designation of the divisions of the Bible as the old covenant and the new covenant (see comment on Gal. 3:15-18).

By creating a union between Yahweh and Israel, however, the covenant separated the new people from all other nations. The price of the sense of mission and awareness of theological election was cultural isolation, with the risks of national arrogance. The union between Yahweh and Israel meant a setting apart from the corruptions of agrarian and technological civilization. The religion of Israel tended to remember desert nomadism as a mode of existence superior to the sedentary life of farming and commerce. The covenant theology of Moses paradoxically contained the seeds of both worldwide parliamentarism and utopian perfectionism, reactionary sectarianism, and esoteric separatism. The sect of the Pharisees (lit. "separated ones") in Roman times illustrates both the ethical sensitivity and the danger of self-righteous aloofness which were inherent in the covenant form of Israel's religion.

The element of particularism was strongly counteracted by the sense of universal mission. The covenant had meaning only in the light of the whole history of man. Renewing the motif of God's promise to Abraham, whose posterity would become a blessing for all the families of the earth, the Mosaic formulation offered a perspective which even today is futuristic in the light of all the nationalisms and imperialisms of past and present history.

"You shall be to me a kingdom of priests and a holy nation" (Exod. 19:6). This terminology is the more remarkable because it is derived from the cultic language of the ancient world, and it applies the reality of cultus to the reality of universal responsibility. It transforms the realm of priesthood from a privileged class to a whole people for the sake ultimately of all men.

Israel was called to become the world's priest, the agent through whose sacrificial mediation the union of God with man was to be accomplished. On the one hand the covenant formula attempted to translate into reality the vision of Abraham, and on the other hand it already bore the sign of 2nd Isaiah's theology of the servant of Yahweh (Isa. 53). Israel was the light, the priest, and the sacrificial victim offered for the sins of all peoples.

The purpose of the covenant, therefore, was to reveal effectively the presence, the will, and the beneficence of Yahweh to the noncovenant nations through the activity of the covenant people. In ancient religions a priest opened the shrine and through ritual brought the worshipers into the presence of deity. In Israel's covenant religion—as differentiated sharply from the later theology and practice of postexilic Judaism—the notion of priesthood was boldly transferred from its lit. and localized sense to a metaphorical, historical, and universal significance.

The covenant, however, was conditional. It confronted Israel with the awful obligation and responsibility of obedience to the divine word—"if you will obey my voice and keep my covenant" (Exod. 19:5). Yahweh out of pure grace had elected Israel to complete within history the work of cosmic creation. But the covenant must be kept. It was not in itself eternal. It might be annulled.

In the religion of Israel the will of Yahweh was always expressed in a word. "God spoke all these words, saying" (Exod. 20:1). Thereupon follows in the present text the Decalogue, or Ten Commandments.

Scholars have scrutinized the problems of the origin of the Decalogue. In its pithy or stone-tablet form—i.e. the "ten words" of Exod. 20 or Deut. 5, without the later elaborations (see comments)—it may well represent the earliest code of covenant obligation known to Israel. Adapted to the simplicity of nomadic existence, it contrasts sharply with the cultic dodecalogue (12 words, Exod. 34:11-27) which reflects, like the Covenant Code (Exod. 20:23-23:19), the agrarian and industrial civilization of Israel after the conquest of Canaan. It contrasts even more with the elaborate ritual that dominates the Priestly Code, traditionally associated with Moses but representing on the whole the Jerusalem priesthood of early Judaism.

Mosaic Cultus. While the Decalogue stresses the purity of a nomadic and family cult, without images, which translates itself into the purity of family and clan relationship, there is no doubt that Moses instituted—or perhaps inherited from Kenite Yahwism as well as from the Joseph tribes themselves—a ceremonial of festivals with sacramental meals of sacrificial communion, at least at the spring and autumn seasons. Moreover he provided the ark, a concrete symbol of the presence of Yahweh in battle (Num. 10:35-36; cf. Josh. 3:13-17; I Sam. 4:3-11). While the ark appears to have been associated with the "wars of Yahweh," another cultic object, the tent of meeting (Exod. 33:7-10), seems to have answered the popular need for spatial localization of the same presence in time of peace. The awful experience of the descent of Yahweh's manifestation in "thick darkness" (Exod. 20:21) on Mt. Sinai was necessarily limited in time and in space. The ark and the tent of meeting provided educational and ritual means of perpetuating the mystery of divine proximity.

It was in the tent of meeting that the early traditions described Moses in conversation with Yahweh, "face to face" (Exod. 33:11) or even "mouth to mouth" (Num. 12:8). After the temple of Jerusalem was destroyed by the Babylonians in 586 the Jerusalem priests and their descendants described their architectural plans for a new temple in a new Zion under the model of a tabernacle built by order of Moses in the wilderness (Exod. 35:4-36:38).

There seems to have been no priesthood in the time of Moses, except through the prophetic function of Moses himself, who was remembered as a prophet (Hos. 12:13)—in fact the stories of his intimate encounters with Yahweh depict him as the preeminent prophet (Deut. 34:10).

Israel's religious consciousness arose during the destitute wilderness existence. Her faith was molded in burning wind, in glittering spaces, in boundless expanses of sand and pebbles. Economic poverty was endured as the price of freedom from political tyranny. Could the sons of Israel, when they became proprietors of a land, survive the risks of cultural compromises and remain free from the tyranny of national and religious selfhood?

III. YAHWEH AND THE GODS OF CANAAN

The conquest of the land, beginning under Joshua, continued during the period of the judges and was not completed until the time of David and Solomon. The descendants of the Joseph tribes, who had wandered with Moses in the wilderness of Sinai for two generations, began to infiltrate the mountain ranges of Canaan in the latter part of the 13th cent. Probably they found and allied with other Hebrew tribes that had been in the land all along. The Song of Deborah (Judg. 5) shows that the covenant faith was powerful enough to unite most of the clans of Israel for a moment of military crisis. However, their political structure and religious homogeneity were still tenuous.

Influence of Baalism. As the sons of the Hebrew shepherds had to learn from the Canaanites the difficult art of farming, they inevitably borrowed from their teachers the rituals which enabled them to enlist or palliate the fertility powers of the soil. Conquest of city-states which worshiped a deified nature undermined the Hebrew faith in Yahweh. As the baals, i.e. "lords," of the field had to be won over and pacified, the specific qualities of the covenant theology were diluted into the surrounding cultural patterns of the Fertile Crescent. The gods of Canaan "baalized" the God of the wilderness. Concern for real estate conquered the conquerors' religion.

To be sure, some devotees of Yahweh resisted the corrupting influence of Baalism (cf. e.g. Gideon's name Jerubbaal, "let Baal contend," Judg. 6:28-32), but reforms were short-lived. One of the sons of Saul was named Ishbaal, "man of Baal" (see comment on II Sam. 2:8-11) and a grandson Meribaal, "hero of Baal" (see comment on II Sam. 4:4). Baal, "Lord," may not have been used to designate a god distinct from Yahweh, but here is precisely the sign of the depth of the religious confusion. The word was probably applied as a common appellative to Yahweh himself. In a similar fashion the synonym Adon, "Lord" (cf. the Greek Adonis, borrowed from the Phoenician pantheon), was used at a later age by the Jews in its superlative form, Adonai, as a euphemism for the ineffable name Yahweh. It was the mixture of the sacred consonants YHWH with the vowels of Adonai in the medieval manuscripts which led to the mistaken reading "Jehovah." In any case the popular mind was not able to differentiate between the God of the covenant and the lords of the fields.

The Canaanite influence perverted the Yahwist faith the more easily since the Hebrews took over not only the fortresses but also the sanctuaries of Canaan.

At the ancient shrine of Shechem the sons of Israel could remember their ancestors—Abraham under the oak tree and Jacob at the well. Several Hebrew clans had probably been participating in rites there throughout the cents. of the Joseph tribes'

Egyptian sojourn. There Joshua renewed and enlarged the Sinai covenant (Josh. 24) and provided a cultic structure for a new tribal league which attempted to gather various ethnic groups. Such a feat could be more easily accomplished since at Shechem the Canaanites honored Baal-berith (lit. Lord of the Covenant, Judg. 8:33; 9:4).

It was most likely at Shechem also that the "book of the covenant" (Exod. 20:23-23:19; 24:7), the Covenant Code, with its relatively high ethical standards, was slowly compiled and published. During the agrarian festivals—the spring feast of Unleavened Bread, the early summer ceremony of Weeks, and the autumn celebration of Ingathering or Booths (Exod. 23:14-17)—the people heard and recited the cultic, criminal, and civil legislation which regulated the life of their society.

Other sanctuaries were likewise taken over from the Canaanites, esp. Gilgal and Bethel in the N, Hebron and Beersheba in the S. The seasonal devotion was popular, but religion appears to have consisted chiefly in some forms of ecstatic techniques designed to attune the worshipers to the exuberance of sexuality and fertility.

Priests did not form a class of clergy apart from the people, nor were they confined to any hereditary family such as the Levites in later times (e.g. Micah's son, Judg. 17:5, and Samuel were Ephraimites). They were merely the sextons of the shrines and the teachers of the correct rites and formulas.

The Institution of the Monarchy. The process of religious compromise with environmental paganism was considerably accelerated by the founding of the monarchy by Samuel and Saul.

During the cents. of the conquest many invaders threatened to engulf the Israelite footholds from without, just as the Canaanite survivors continued to menace them from within. A series of holy men of war, leaders of uncommon magnetism who were known as "judges," were momentarily capable, in the name of the faith in Yahweh, to unite groups of neighboring clans against common enemies. Their efforts, however, were always localized and short-lived. An attempt by Abimelech to create a hereditary monarchy at Shechem failed, for it represented clearly a departure from the old tribal independence of the covenant confederation (Judg. 9).

In the 11th cent. the Philistines became an unprecedented threat to the very life of Israel. In the face of impending disaster the prophet Samuel yielded to popular demand and Saul of Benjamin was anointed king—not without bitter protest (I Samuel 10:27). Samuel himself attempted to guard against the risks of tyranny by creating a constitutional monarchy (I Sam. 10:25). The dynasty of Saul came to a tragic end in defeat by the Philistines and intertribal strife within Israel.

David of Bethlehem, leader of Judah in the S, succeeded in winning the support of all the tribes. To cement the union he captured for himself a new capital, Jerusalem, by taking it from the Jebusites, a Canaanite clan that up till this time had held this fortress between the N and S tribes of Israel. David brilliantly reversed the military situation and created a dynasty that was to last more than 4 cents. (*ca.* 1005-586).

Thus a paradoxical situation ensued. On the one

hand the victories of David insured the survival of Israel; on the other hand they set the stage for the extravagance and callousness of his son Solomon, which precipitated at his death the secession of the N tribes (931) and aggravated the processes of religious and ethical decadence in the divided nation.

The institution of kingship profoundly altered the religion of the fathers. In the ancient Near Eastern cultures the person of the king was endowed with a sacred and sometimes even divine character. While the Yahwist theologians attempted to oppose a similar belief in Israel, they did not really succeed. Kings assumed priestly functions, becoming intermediaries between God and the common people. The old religious immediacy was destroyed. In addition the royal family, the court, the foreign diplomats, the public servants—in fact the whole apparatus of the state administration—formed a privileged class, and the rich began to oppress the poor.

The Jerusalem Temple. The erection of the temple in Jerusalem introduced still another factor of paganization. The former Canaanite fortress could not easily become the capital of a united Israel without becoming at the same time the covenant shrine, as Shechem and later Shiloh seem to have been in the time of the judges. To Jerusalem David brought the ancient symbol of nomadic Yahwism, the ark, and sheltered it in a tent outside of the city (II Sam. 6:1-19). When he attempted to erect for the ark a permanent shrine similar to other temples of the Fertile Crescent, he was stopped by prophetic opposition. The language is of extreme significance for the development of Israel's religion: "Thus says the LORD: Would you build me a house to dwell [lit. "sit"] in? I have not dwelt in a house since the day I brought up the people of Israel from Egypt to this day, but I have been moving about [lit. "have walked"] in a tent" (II Sam. 7:5-6).

Under the naïveté of the language a profound theological concept was at stake. The presence of Yahweh cannot be attached to space, lest the God of Israel be mistaken for the gods of the nations, who were more or less at the disposal of the temple functionaries. Yahweh does not "sit" in a temple; he "walks." The nomadic image disclosed the sense of transcendence. The covenant God was present in the midst of his people, but even the people of the covenant could not possess or manipulate him. David bowed to the objections of the prophet Nathan, but Solomon apparently brushed them aside. To be sure, his formula at the dedication of the new temple indicates that he attempted to pacify the theologians of transcendence. He referred explicitly to the sovereignty of Yahweh over nature and pointed out the elusiveness of divine presence by using the word "thick darkness," which alluded directly to the wonders of Mt. Sinai (I Kings 8:12; cf. "thick darkness," the same Hebrew word, Exod. 20:21). Nevertheless he also added his conviction that the new temple would be a house for Yahweh "to dwell ["sit"] in for ever" (I Kings 8:13).

The new edifice had been conceived and constructed by Phoenician architects. All its features—orientation, plan, decoration, and cultic objects, esp. the "molten sea" (I Kings 7:23-26), a symbol of the cosmic ocean—pointed to the worship of the sun deity. Subsequent history shows that sexual mysteries

were again and again celebrated within its precincts. In the course of time the religion of Judah came to be centered around the myth of Zion, the sacred space, which was similar to pagan beliefs about the navel of the earth.

Nevertheless the deterioration of the covenant faith was partly arrested through the intervention of a few prophets of Yahweh.

IV. THE PROPHETIC VISION

Early Prophets. The origins of the Hebrew prophets are complex and obscure. As has been seen above, Moses was remembered in the traditions as the preeminent prophet (Deut. 34:10). His sister Miriam, who composed the earliest song of deliverance at the sea crossing, was known as a "prophetess" (Exod. 15:20). One of the inspired leaders of Israel during the conquest of Canaan was Deborah, a "prophetess" (Judg. 4:4). Samuel, the last judge, was brought up in the sanctuary of Shiloh as a priest, but he was called a "seer" or a "prophet" (I Sam. 3:20; 9:19) and appears to have founded a prophetic guild (I Sam. 19:20-21).

The ancient shrines of the Fertile Crescent were centers of divination. The earliest prophets of Israel appear to have been official or unofficial diviners who interpreted the will of Yahweh for kings and people. Some of them stood out as religious personalities of exceptional magnitude.

The prophet Gad was an adviser to David who organized sacred music and wrote a history of the reign (I Sam. 22:5; II Sam. 24:11-25; I Chr. 29:29; II Chr. 29:25). The prophet Nathan rebuked the king on the temple project (II Sam. 7:2-17) and for the affair with Bathsheba which led David to treachery and homicide (II Sam. 12:1-15).

In addition to the professional diviners and royal advisers a special prophet seems to have officiated at the yearly ceremonies of covenant renewal as the successor of Moses (see Intros. to Deut., Pss.). It is not unlikely that these were the occasion for preserving many of the historical memories of Israel now found in the OT. Some scholars suggest that Nathan was the first publisher of the Yahwist (J) epic which provided the earliest stratum of traditions in the Pentateuch (see "The Compiling of Israel's Story," pp. 1082-89). One can imagine the significance of the story of the man and the woman in the garden (Gen. 3) against the background of life at the court of David in Jerusalem. In a time of economic and political prosperity a shallow form of religious nationalism took hold of Israel—as it generally does in similar situations in history—and a prophetic voice arose to show the dangers of Canaanite syncretism and the theological meaning of human pride. "You are dust, and to dust you shall return" (Gen. 3:19).

The schism of Israel from Judah was partly supported by a N prophet, Ahijah of Shiloh (I Kings 11:29-39). A cent. later Ahab maintained at his court a large number of professional prophets (I Kings 18:17-20; 22:6). Against them a man from the Transjordan desert, Elijah, stood alone as the champion of Yahwism.

More significant by far than the legendary account of his victory over the prophets of Baal on Mt. Carmel (I Kings 18), is Elijah's vision of Yahweh on Mt. Horeb (i.e. Sinai, I Kings 19:8-18), which closed an era and opened a new period in the history of Israel's religion. From the time of Elijah on, the mode of divine disclosure was no longer to be sought in the wonders of Mt. Sinai. In a "sound of complete silence"—rather than a "still small voice" (I Kings 19:12)—the prophet discerned the momentous destiny of a spiritual society of the faithful (I Kings 19:18). On that day the idea of a "church," as distinguished from state and nation, appeared in the history of mankind.

Elijah, the last representative of the Mosaic covenant, was the forerunner of the great prophets, and through them he became a link between the faith of Abraham and a universal religion.

The Great Prophets. That a handful of Judahites survived the destruction of the kingdoms of Israel and Judah to become the Jews was largely due to the great prophets. Without them the exile in Babylon would have been a terminal disease. On account of them the faith of Abraham, Moses, and Elijah could preside over the birth of Judaism. They were men possessed by the vision of the sovereignty of Yahweh over the whole of mankind, even at the expense of the destiny of Israel as a nation.

It is not correct to state that the great prophets initiated the monotheistic faith of Israel, for such a faith was implicit in the religion of Moses. But the prophets understood with tragic seriousness the implications for individual and society of the absolute demands of the covenant God. According to them, monotheism is not mere belief in one God. It means the total devotion of man to that God. He must love God with the whole of his being, in deed as well as in thought and in heart (Deut. 6:5). The prophets applied to their contemporaries the principle of covenant conditionalism which appeared in the original ceremony on Mt. Sinai (Exod. 19:5-6). They hailed with gratitude the election of Israel. "You only have I known of all the families of the earth," exclaims the God of Amos (3:2a), but a unique relation is inseparable from a unique mission and therefore a unique responsibility. The failure to fulfill the unique commitment means national doom. "Therefore I shall requite the depth of your guilt upon you" (Amos 3:2b).

Alone among the religionists of the ancient Near East the prophets maintained that the Deity is not dependent on the welfare of a dynasty or a nation. They took the universal quality of Yahweh's rule so seriously that they did not hesitate to show Israel's bitter enemies, the Philistines and the Syrians, or the most distant peoples like the Ethiopians, as living under the embrace of divine creation and providence. They destroyed forever the idea of a national God.

The prophets also discerned that the holy could not be equated only with the sacred in cultic ritual. Holiness for them must be translated into social decency. This extraordinary conviction not only enabled them to see the corruption of worship but also to revive the immediacy of the God-man communion which characterized the religion of the fathers and of Moses.

Appalled by the blindness of nationalistic piety, they saw no alternative to the prospect of divine judgment and interpreted the signs of the times in the light of their theological vision. "Ah, Assyria, the rod of my anger!" (Isa. 10:5). Such was the summons hurled by Yahweh at monstrous Nineveh. A cent. later, when the threat was no longer Assyrian but Babylonian, Jeremiah did not hesitate to call Nebuchadrezzar the "servant" of Yahweh (Jer. 25:9). Yet it was that tyrant who was about to destroy the temple, decimate the people, deport the elite of the nation, and devastate the land. No more "subversive" interpretation of religion has ever been made.

Amos apparently did not believe that Israel could ever repent, and neither did Hosea, Isaiah, or Jeremiah. Amos, however, differed from his successors in that his view of divine justice and human inability to repent led him to announce without qualification the end of the nation and perhaps of the whole of history (Amos 9:1-8).

Some scholars have maintained that Amos proposed the idea of a righteous "remnant," but it is clear from his own words that he envisaged the possibility of divine forgiveness only after the conditions of repentance had been met (Amos 5:15). The successors of Amos, however, predicted that at the end of history, Yahweh would establish a peaceable kingdom in a new earth.

Hosea deepened the theological notion of justice by developing for the first time in history what was called later the concept of self-giving love. Through his own life of pathos he discovered an element of suffering and forgiveness at the core of the divine reality, and he understood that by his love God himself could and would create in man the ability to return to him and to be transformed (Hos. 2:13-20; 3; 11:8-9).

Isaiah resolved the tension between the demands of divine justice and the corruption of society by developing the notion of the "remnant." He saw that Judah, like Israel, would be removed from the face of the earth, but that a few men, perhaps led by his own disciples (Isa. 8:16), would form the nucleus of a new society and provide a historical link between the present and the future kingdom. He expressed hope that a descendant of David, a humble shepherd king, would be the agent of divine rule among a reconciled humanity (Isa. 9:1-7; 11).

More directly than any other prophet Jeremiah made the survival of Judaism possible, for his faith in the universal sway of Yahweh over all mankind led him to renounce the theology of a presence which was spatially located in the temple of Jerusalem. To the first exiles (597), who were in danger of losing their faith and disintegrating sociologically in the hardships of the Babylonian deportation, Jeremiah wrote a letter which deserves to be called the key document of universal religion (Jer. 29:1-9). The prophet advised them to adapt themselves to living in a foreign land under a foreign yoke, to "seek the welfare" of Babylon, and even to "pray . . . on its behalf." I.e. Jeremiah took the opportunity to put into practice the principle of religious universalism. He knew that Yahweh could be present everywhere.

By proclaiming the coming of a new covenant (Jer. 31:31-34) Jeremiah also developed the revolutionary principle of the renewal of the human will. It must be noted, however, that his expectation probably referred, not to the normal conditions of history as we know it, but to life in a new earth, after the end of the present economy of historical existence.

THE BIRTH OF JUDAISM

Many nations of the ancient Near East which had been uprooted from their lands by Nebuchadrezzar were soon absorbed in the great racial and cultural melting pot of the Babylonian Empire. Only the Judahites retained their cultural, sociological, and religious identity.

The birth of Judaism resulted from a meeting of complex factors. On the one hand Jeremiah was able to convince the Babylonian captives that Yahweh was the Lord of all and that nothing could separate him from his people. On the other hand Ezekiel, the son of a Jerusalem priest, kept alive among them the hope of a return to a new Zion. Like Jeremiah, however, he expected this event to take place in a suprahistorical mode of existence. In anticipation of the day of Yahweh's advent he wrote an architectural blueprint for the new temple, from which would flow a river of the waters of grace (Ezek. 47:1-12).

As a prophet who was also a priest, Ezekiel explained the fall of his nation not only by the moral corruption of the covenant people but also by the contamination of ritual impurity, esp. through contacts with foreigners. His disciples prepared for the new era by formulating an intricate set of laws, which are now assembled in the Holiness Code (Lev. 17-26). The next generation of priestly legislators went even further. They made official a large number of rites, the purpose of which was to keep the new Israel in the restored Zion completely separated from all possible risks of ritual impurity, esp. through contacts with pagans, corpses, and women. It was because of this stress on ritual cleanliness that Judaism, unlike the Hebraism of old, developed a fear of sexuality and consequently was led to lower the status of womanhood.

At the same time the oral traditions of the national past were written down. Thus the books of the Pentateuch were slowly edited into a monumental corpus which formed an expansion of the ancient laws of Moses. In the course of the cents. the diversity of their origins was forgotten and the entire Pentateuch as a block became revered as "the Law."

Ca. 545 Cyrus the Persian began to conquer the Babylonian Empire. The anonymous prophet known as 2nd Isaiah (Isa. 40-55) interpreted the military events as the signs of the imminence of the coming of Yahweh on earth. Soon the work of creation would be fulfilled. The old things were passed away. Behold the good tidings (gospel) of the coming of the Lord! The words of comfort to Jerusalem (Isa. 40:1-11) stirred an immense hope among the Jewish exiles. Israel was still the servant of Yahweh. Through national death and resurrection Israel might truly become "a light to the nations" as well as the sacrificial lamb, an atoning victim for the sins of the world (Isa. 42:6; 49:3; 52:13–53:12).

For generations the Jews expected the coming of their Lord, but the divine advent was always postponed. In this delayed eschatology (i.e. doctrine of the last things) appears to lie the final secret of Israel's religion.

When Cyrus conquered Babylon (539) and allowed the Jews to return home (Ezra 1), most of them had adapted themselves so well to their alien environment that they remained in their homes of adoption. Through the cents. of the Persian Empire (538-333) and of the following Hellenistic and Roman times their descendants formed numerous communities. They gathered on the sabbath around their "houses of prayer" (synagogues). Thus arose the Judaism of the Dispersion (Diaspora).

A handful of the descendants of the Jerusalem priests, however, inspired by the Zion-centered ideal of Ezekiel, returned to their ruined homeland and rebuilt a temple in Zion (520-515). Palestinian Judaism was born when the vision of Ezekiel for a new temple at the end of history was translated into an actual edifice within history. A ceremonial which had been aimed at regulating the priestly community in the kingdom of God on a new earth was now enacted on the same old earth. History was continuing.

For a long time the restored Zion barely managed to exist. At last a Jewish official of the Persian court, Nehemiah, became governor of Judah (445) and rebuilt the walls of Jerusalem. A priest of the Babylonian Dispersion, the scribe Ezra, whose family had remained in Mesopotamia, was moved by the news of the plight of the Palestinian Jews. He returned to Jerusalem at the head of a new contingent of immigrants and reformed the life of the Zionist community. Ezra was the true founder of the Judaism of the law, for it was probably he who read for the first time the Pentateuch in its final form during a solemn celebration of the feast of the new year in 397 (see Intro. to Ezra).

Under the prescriptions of the law the Jerusalem Jews lived in the shadow of the temple. Their life was ruled by a high priest through a priestly hierarchy. A sharp distinction arose between clergy and laity. To keep the community ritually pure strict marriage laws were enforced and foreign wives were divorced.

The historian should not oversimplify the wide range of diversity which characterized the religious life of the Jews during the Persian and Hellenistic times. The universalism of the great prophets still continued to exercise a powerful influence on many minds. E.g. the story of Ruth makes the point that an ancestress of David was a Moabitess, like some of the wives whom Ezra compelled his fellow Jews to repudiate. The story of the prophet Jonah taught the breadth of divine mercy, including even the men and beasts of Nineveh (Jonah 4:11). A disciple of the prophet Zechariah maintained a tension between the Zion-centered hope of the priestly school of Ezekiel and the worldwide dream of Jeremiah and 2nd Isaiah: "On that day living waters shall flow from out Jerusalem. . . . And the LORD will become king over all the earth; on that day the LORD will be one and his name one" (Zech. 14:8-9). Such a vision can be seen at the core of the poetic themes of the psalmists, whose hymns and prayers from older times offered a musical and theological interpretation of the priestly ceremonies of the Jerusalem temple. While the psalmists never tired of singing about the love of Yahweh for Israel, they too were waiting for the day when

> The princes of the peoples gather
> as the people of the God of Abraham.
> (Ps. 47:9.)

Another evidence of the variety of the religious heritage of early Judaism appears in the wisdom poetry of Israel. The public servants and diplomats of the kings of Judah, from Solomon (10th cent.) to Hezekiah (8th cent.) and Josiah (7th cent.), were internationally cultured. They looked at human character, not in terms of special people or ceremonial purity, but in the light of a worldwide humanism. Egyptian proverbs were translated into Hebrew and some of them are now preserved in Prov. The wise saw that the fear of Yahweh could inspire broad attitudes of respect for one's neighbor, whoever he might be, of concern for the poor and the oppressed, and even, cents. before Jesus, of hospitality toward one's enemies (Prov. 25:21-22).

In the depth of despair and of hatred brought about by the razing of the temple by the Babylonians in 586, a poet of genius meditated on the meaning of pure religion without the hope of any reward. He used the ancient folktale of Job, a foreigner, symbol of complete destitution, who revolted against his fate and attacked the justice of God in history but ultimately discovered the white-hot faith of immediate presence (Job 42:5-6).

The heights of sublimity were reached in Israel's religion when the Jobian poet refused to condemn God (Job 40:8), when the prophet Habakkuk expressed his exultation even if the fig tree would fail to blossom (3:17-19), and when the psalmist, sorely buffeted, asked for nothing else on earth than communion with the divine (Ps. 73:21-26).

After the conquest of the ancient Near East by Alexander the Great (333-323) Jews prospered almost everywhere. Under the Ptolemies of Egypt and after 198 under the Seleucid kings of Syria even the Jerusalem high priests learned Greek ways, language, and customs. The sectarianism of the Ezra reformation was in danger of cultural dilution.

The Maccabean War (167-164) abruptly reversed the hellenizing trend. Once again fighting for their survival, the Jews of Palestine revived their hopes for a suprahistorical salvation—notably expressed in an apocalypse, Dan., written in the midst of the conflict (see "The Apocalyptic Literature," pp. 1106-09). This new outburst of eschatological fever practically never let up during the next 3 cents. In the intensity of their suffering many Jews of the Maccabean and Roman times found comfort in the apocalyptic visions of the last judgment, when their oppressors would be exterminated by God's general-in-chief, the Messiah, i.e. "the Anointed One" (in Greek, *Christos*).

An alternative hope in the final intervention of God in history was not forgotten. An obscure Jew rose under the reign of Tiberius Caesar and discovered in the Prophets the motto of his own ministry:

The Spirit of the Lord is upon me,
because he has anointed me to preach good
news to the poor.
(Luke 4:18; cf. Isa. 61:1.)

VI. The Peculiarity and the Universality of Israel's Faith

The religion of Israel in OT times represents 12 or more cents. in the life of a few men and women, striving, sometimes boasting and carousing, usually hungering and dying at the hands of innumerable persecutors.

The spring of this religion is intricately bound, therefore, to history. Only the most serious respect for the changes and relativity in the formulations of religious truth through the ages will prevent the student of Hebrew faith from stressing one aspect at the expense of the others. Nevertheless a common thread appears from generation to generation.

The people of the covenant were at once unfaithful and yet faithful in a strange way to the absolute demands of the love of their God. They were aware of the cardinal pitfall of their distinctiveness—pride over their election, their temple, and their law. A "people holy to the LORD" (Deut. 7:6), they knew full well they were a "stubborn people" (Deut. 9:13). The paradox of their historical destiny lies in the ambivalence of their obedience to a law which culminated in the love of God but also in the exclusivism of circumcision, sabbath, and sectarianism. Without these restricting factors, however, they would never have preserved their religious and sociological identity.

One theme dominates the religion of Israel more than any other, and on it all the others depend. It may be called the determined and even obstinate will to live in the presence of the holy God. Israel was the people of the covenant, and the covenant was maintained by a difficult and even frantic attempt to fulfill the ceremonial and moral aspects of the Law. A few men within Israel learned that the presence of the holy was never at the disposal of man, even and esp. moral man, legally obedient man, religious man. In this respect the religion of Israel came to transcend religion.

Israel, the light to the nations, had to become the sacrificial lamb whose mission was to atone for the crimes of humanity. Israel, who could not be the slave of any potentate, because she was the slave of Yahweh alone (Lev. 25:42), was brought to ask, "My God, my God, why hast thou forsaken me?" (Ps. 22:1). Israel, the religious nation, came to her highest hour when she lost the sense of the presence.

The theme of the presence motivates the call of Abraham, the deliverance from Egypt, the total demand of the First Commandment, the absolutism of the Shema (Deut. 6:4-5), the ceremonial of the temple, and the expectation of the day of Yahweh.

It was the theme of the presence, overcoming the restrictions of ritual peculiarity and seeking to embrace all the races of men, which explains the birth of that Jewish sect, the Christian church.

For Further Study. James Muilenburg, "The History of the Religion of Israel," in *IB*, 1952. Edmond Jacob, *Theology of the OT*, 1958. T. C. Vriezen, *An Outline of OT Theology*, 1958. Walther Eichrodt, *Theology of the OT*, 2 vols., 1961-67. Roland de Vaux, *Ancient Israel: Its Life and Institutions*, 1961. John Bright, "Hebrew Religion," in *IDB*, 1962. Gerhard von Rad, *OT Theology*, 2 vols., 1962-65. Walther Zimmerli, *The Law and the Prophets*, 1965. G. W. Anderson, *The History and Religion of Israel*, 1966. Henricus Renckens, *The Religion of Israel*, 1966. Helmer Ringgren, *Israelite Religion*, 1966.

THE KINGDOM OF
GOD IN THE OLD TESTAMENT

Robert C. Dentan

I. Introduction

The unifying theme of the Bible is the kingdom of God—God's perfect and undisputed rule over all that he has created. The word "kingdom" as used here means "kingly rule" or "reign" rather than "territory ruled by a king."

From Creation to the End Time. The OT begins with the story of creation, which tells how God out of formless chaos brought the universe into existence and declared that it was "very good" (Gen. 1:31). At that moment, ideally speaking, the kingdom of God was established. But the OT goes on almost immediately to describe how that kingdom was disrupted through the disobedience of man (Gen. 3), who was the summit of God's creation, formed in God's image (Gen. 1:27), honored with a share in God's rule (Gen. 1:28; Ps. 8:6-8), and furnished with free will so that he could serve God joyfully and without compulsion. These opening chs. of Gen., although they are obviously not to be taken as a record of historical events, are essential for understanding the rest of the Bible story, which deals with the process by which God has ever since been reasserting his royal and loving rule over wayward man and the other recalcitrant forces in his creation.

It is against this background that one must understand the words of Jesus which in effect open the NT story: "The kingdom of God is at hand" (Mark 1:15). With these words, however, the final ch. is only begun; the last page is still in the future. The end of the story is pictured poetically, in anticipation, in the last book of the Bible, where the heavenly chorus proclaims, "The kingdom of the world has become the kingdom of our Lord and of his Christ, and he shall reign for ever and ever" (Rev. 11:15).

Thus the theme of the kingdom—its founding, disruption and restoration—is like a great arch which extends from the first chs. of the Bible to the last; all the other elements in the Bible story must find their places beneath it. The separate incidents of the story are meaningful because they are part of a continuous history which runs from the account of the disruption of God's original kingdom by man's disobedience to its final, triumphant reestablishment.

It is this conception of the kingdom, and the story of God's work in history to establish it, that gives unity to the Bible and significance to its various parts. Obviously the OT is integral to the scheme, since the NT proclamation of the imminence of the kingdom makes no sense except as seen against the background of the OT account of creation and the fall of man and the first mighty steps that God took to reassert his dominion when he set up the old Israel as his royal vanguard. The first Christians saw their own story simply as the climax and conclusion of the history of God's kingdom which had begun in the OT.

Questions to Consider. Thus far we have been looking at the subject only in a general way and from the standpoint of a developed Christian theology. Although this view is undoubtedly correct, it is the result of a long process of intellectual development, of Israel's growing reflection on the meaning of her election and her covenant with God. Let us turn, then, to historical, less theological examination of the process itself. Where did the conception of God's rule as a "kingdom" come from? At what point did it enter into Hebrew thought?

While both the idea and the terminology of the kingdom of God are certainly to be found in late OT writings, it is fairly certain that the terminology at least was not a part of Hebrew thought from the start. Thus we must make a distinction between 2 quite different questions. There is to begin with the simple question of when God's claim to be absolute ruler of his people was first acknowledged. This is a substantive question, and the answer to it is obvious: there was never a time in OT history when Yahweh was not regarded as the ultimate source of all authority—at least in theory. The 2nd and much more difficult question is: "When did the people of Israel first begin to conceive of God as a "king" and of his rule as a "kingdom"? This question has to do with the imagery in which the faith of Israel was clothed, and the answer to it is far from clear.

Two further questions must also be asked: (*a*) What, at different periods of Israel's history, was conceived to be the extent of Yahweh's dominion (whether called a "kingdom" or not)? Was it only over the nation of Israel, over mankind in general, over other gods, or over the created universe? (*b*) When men living in different periods spoke of God's kingdom (or kingship) did they think of it as something that had been established in the past, existed in the present, or was yet to be achieved in the future? These are complex problems and the answers are not certain.

II. In the Period Before the Monarchy

It is a commonplace of present-day scholarship that Israel before the rise of the monarchy was organized in the form of an amphictyony—sacred confederacy of tribes constituted for the purpose of supporting a religious shrine. While this is merely a theory, based primarily on the analogy to the Greek amphictyonies, and the evidence is indirect and not necessarily conclusive, it may be accepted as a working hypothesis. What is perfectly certain is that the bond of unity among the Hebrew tribes was a religious one; their association was based, not on common "nationality" or the occupation of a common territory, but on a common devotion to the God Yahweh.

In a profound sense the Israelite confederacy was the first historical manifestation of the kingdom of God. From this small group of relatively uncultured tribes, united solely by their loyalty to Yahweh, there ultimately developed the hope of God's one day bringing the whole disordered universe into conformity with his will. On the level of historical fact the original nucleus of the idea of the kingdom is to be located here; on the level of Christian faith we see here not merely the beginning of the *idea* of the kingdom but also *the inception of the actual historical process* in which God has ever since been at work to establish his kingdom.

Possible Clues to Early Ideas. Many scholars would deny that the Hebrews thought of God as a king or of his rule over them as a kingdom during the period of the confederacy in Palestine (the age of the "judges") or the preceding period of life in the desert. It is argued that the theology of a group is at least partly conditioned by its social institutions and that the idea of a "Kingdom of God" could not have originated before the establishment of a "kingdom of Israel." These scholars also point to the fact that references to God as king are very rare in literary material dealing with the premonarchical age and that even these references may in fact be retrojections of the viewpoint of a later age.

The principal references in support of the view that Israel thought of God as king in the period of the confederacy are: "The LORD will reign for ever and ever" (Exod. 15:18); "You shall be to me a kingdom of priests" (Exod. 19:6); "The LORD their God is with them, and the shout of a king is among them" (Num. 23:21); "The LORD became king in Jeshurun" (Deut. 33:5); and Gideon's refusal to become king because, he says, "the LORD will rule over you" (Judg. 8:23). Though the word for "king" does not appear in the last passage, Gideon's speech is of particular importance since it seems to express a theological antipathy to the idea of a human monarchy. The people of Israel should have no earthly king, he seems to say, because God is their king. Similar ideas are found in I Sam. 8:7; 12:12, which are connected with the founding of the monarchy.

If these passages could be firmly dated in the period which they describe, they would provide incontrovertible evidence that a developed conception of the "kingdom of God" existed as early as the time of the judges. But claims for such early dating have found little acceptance among scholars. Most would probably think that the Gideon and Samuel passages reflect the antimonarchical reaction which set in under the influence of the prophets rather than the religious and political philosophy of the age of the judges. Most would also date the poetical passages from the Pentateuch quoted above no earlier than the reign of David. It seems unlikely that the concep-

tion of the kingdom of God in the sense of political rule over Israel existed at this early period.

The King of the Gods. There is a growing disposition among scholars to feel on general grounds that Israel in the period of the judges was probably acquainted with the idea of God's kingship in the special sense of rule over the gods. From her earliest entry into Palestine she was certainly aware of the common Semitic practice of designating high gods as "king." That the practice was current among the Canaanites is evident from proper names preserved in scripture which incorporate the word for "king," *melech*, e.g. Abimelech, Melchizedek. It is evident also from the designation of El as king of the gods in the Ras Shamra texts found in the excavation of ancient Ugarit in Syria, a city occupied from before 3500 to 1200 B.C. It would have been strange if the Israelites had not adopted this terminology also, considering its appropriateness to their conception of Yahweh.

While no certainty is attainable as to the views of this early period, then, it may be accepted as likely that Israel in the time of the judges already thought of Yahweh as king of the gods. This idea of his kingship is most clearly expressed in a late passage from the Pss., "The LORD is a great God and a great King above all gods" (Ps. 95:3). Such a conception was a distinctly limited one, but it provided the nucleus around which could grow the (probably) much later idea that Yahweh was king over his people Israel and was destined ultimately to be acknowledged as king over all other nations as well.

III. DURING AND AFTER THE MONARCHY

The establishment of the kingdom of Israel under Saul, David, and Solomon provided the political and cultural background that made possible in the long run the flowering of the idea of the kingdom of God. Even so, there is no indisputable evidence that the early years of the monarchy saw any fundamental change in the conception that prevailed in the previous period. Insofar as Yahweh was given the title of "king," it was probably only as king of the gods or of the forces of nature rather than as heavenly monarch of an earthly realm. Actually the first direct evidence of even this idea of kingship comes from Isaiah in the latter part of the 8th cent., nearly 3 cents. after the monarchy had been founded. There is nevertheless little doubt that the title was used. Some scholars believe that there was an elaborate cult in the preexilic temple centering around the concept of Yahweh as king of creation, but the existence of such a cult is purely hypothetical.

Attitude Toward the Monarchy. The influence of the monarchy on the idea of the kingdom of God was chiefly felt after the monarchy itself had disappeared. When there was no longer a human king sitting on the throne it became natural for men of Israel to begin to think of God as their king. The passing of the earthly monarchy would incline them to think more favorably of the idea of a heavenly monarchy.

Tendencies toward thinking of God's kingship in this analogical fashion may have appeared during the declining years of the kingdom of Judah, or even earlier (cf. I Sam. 8:7; 12:12, date uncertain); but they were always held in check by Israel's traditional suspicion of monarchical institutions, a suspicion that had both political and theological roots. Monarchy was an alien importation into Israel, where from the earliest days the political temper had been tribal and democratic. This is evident from Jotham's fable (Judg. 9:7-15), Nathan's parable (II Sam. 12:1-6), the story of Naboth's vineyard (I Kings 21), and Samuel's antimonarchical speech (I Sam. 8:11-18), at whatever period it may be dated. On the theological side, which is not of course to be strictly separated from the political, Israel was always somewhat uneasy about the secular monarchy because of the not unjustified fear that it might take to itself the honor and authority that belonged only to Israel's God. At the beginning there seems to have been some reticence even about using the title "king" for the earthly ruler, partly because it was a Canaanite term and partly also, it may be, because of a feeling that it was a title that belonged to Yahweh alone as king of the gods. The earliest stories about Saul call him "prince" rather than king (I Sam. 9:16; 10:1) and the same term is also sometimes preferred for David (e.g. I Sam. 13:14; 25:30).

The creation of the monarchy in Israel had been due to the exigencies of history, not to religious motives, and it was always going to be difficult for at least some of the people to harmonize the fact that they were now a nation like other nations with their firm conviction of being a unique community under the control of Yahweh. That this harmony was never in fact achieved is clear from the frequent conflicts between prophets and reigning monarchs and from the final Deuteronomic attempt to reduce the king, at least in theory, to "a first among equals" whose sole function was to administer the law of God (cf. Deut. 17:14-20). When finally the monarchy was abolished by the Babylonians in 586 B.C., it was the prophetic, theocratic idea that triumphed, although in a form greatly affected by Israel's long experience with the monarchy. The secular monarchy enriched the conceptual framework of Israel's faith far more in death than in life.

God's Rule Over Israel. The contribution of the kingdom of Israel to the idea of the kingdom of God is to be seen particularly in 2 areas. In the first place the kingship of God came naturally to be thought of as earthly and social rather than as merely celestial or cosmic. Israel's religion had always been of a strongly social character, i.e. it was a religion concerned with the life of the group rather than with the life of individuals. To put it more accurately, it was concerned with individual life only as seen in the context of a particular society—Israel. The idea of the kingdom of God is one way of expressing this sense of man's social relationship to God. Once her members knew what it meant to live under the rule of a human king, they must have found it logical to conceive Israel's polity, even on its purely spiritual, non-political, "churchly" side, as analogous to that of a monarchy. She was a kingdom under the dominion of Yahweh, seen no longer merely as king in heaven but as king of Israel. The full-blown idea of "the kingdom of God" as we meet it in the NT and later parts of the OT can hardly be explained just as an extension of the idea of Yahweh's heavenly kingship; it is reflection of Israel's experience as an earthly monarchy under the rule of an earthly king.

The Concept of the Messiah. The 2nd contribution of the kingdom on earth was the figure of the Messiah, the "Anointed One." In adopting the title "king" for her ruler Israel of necessity took over with it a whole complex of associated ideas from neighboring and alien cultures. Among these was the belief in the deity or divinity of kings. While in view of Israel's commitment to the ultimate and absolute claims of Yahweh it seems unlikely that she accepted this idea in an uncritical way, there can be no doubt that the king of Israel was regarded, at least in court circles, as a superhuman figure. One isolated passage possibly even calls the king "god" (Ps. 45:6; see comment). At any rate he was God's adopted "son," charged with carrying out God's will (II Sam. 7:14; Pss. 2:7; 89:27; cf. Ps. 110). There was about him the aura of the invisible world; he was more than human though less than divine, a supernatural mediator, a sacramental channel through whom the prayers of the people ascended to God and God's blessings flowed to the people (II Sam. 14:17; 23:4; Ps. 72:6; Lam. 4:20). His most characteristic and instructive title was "the anointed of the LORD," which asserted on the one hand that he possessed a divine charisma through the act of anointing (I Sam. 10:1; 16:13) but made it evident on the other that his authority was dependent on the election and favor of Yahweh. It was this conception of kingship that provided the soil from which the idea of the Messiah was eventually to grow.

A Kingdom to Come. The Messiah is the divine, or semidivine, king transferred from the field of present experience to that of future expectation. Even the most extreme partisans of the divinity of kings must have found it difficult to believe in the divine character of many of the monarchs—misfits and worse—who sat on the throne of David. The failure of successive kings to fulfill the promises given in such grandiloquent language at their birth or coronation (note e.g. the high-flown court style of such passages as Pss. 2; 45; 72; 110; Isa. 9:6-7) and the gradual decline in the power and prosperity of the Hebrew kingdoms led to a tendency for the nation to transfer its hopes to an ideal king of the future. This tendency was finally crystalized by the extinction of the earthly monarchy in 586 B.C.

Since David was the first real king in Israel (Saul's reign being merely transitional) and since David's family continued on the throne of Judah until its final catastrophic overthrow, there arose a special mystique around him and his dynasty. Several passages testify to the particular importance of the idea, not merely of kingship, but of Davidic kingship (II Sam. 7:8-16; 23:1-7; Ps. 89:19-37). So the future ideal king, the Messiah as he would one day be called, was necessarily conceived both as a member of the Davidic family—thus fulfilling God's promise that David's house should be "sure"—and as also a "new David," exhibiting once again the piety and wisdom that tradition ascribed to the historical David (I Kings 15:3-5; Ezek. 34:23-24; 37:24-25).

In Chr., written toward the end of the OT period, the monarchy (which had long passed away) was pictured in idealized form as a kind of prototype of the future messianic kingdom. Significantly it is here we meet for the first time the actual phrase "the kingdom of God" (or "the LORD"), although not in the familiar sense. I Chr. 28:5 has David say, "He has chosen Solomon my son to sit upon the throne of the kingdom of the LORD over Israel." This passage, like the whole of the Chronicler's narrative, illustrates how closely interwoven is the rise of the monarchical institution in Israel with the development of the idea of the kingdom of God. But it also illustrates how easy it must have been sometimes to confuse the kingdom of God with the kingdom of Israel (cf. II Chr. 13:8). In Chr. the danger was mostly theoretical, but in the days of the Hebrew kingdoms it was a very real one.

If the idea of the kingdom of God was to become an adequate framework for supporting the truths of biblical religion, the notion of divine rule would somehow have to be disentangled from all national, territorial, and dynastic limitations. To effect such a disentanglement was the special function of the great radical prophets.

IV. IN THE GREAT PROPHETS

The first occurrence of the idea that God is king which can be dated with certainty is in Isa. 6:5, where the prophet declares: "My eyes have seen the King, the LORD of hosts!" According to one theory theological emphasis on Yahweh's kingship dates only from this time, originating partly, it may be, in a polemic against other gods who were called king, especially Molech (an intentional distortion of Melech, i.e. "King"; cf. I Kings 11:7; II Kings 23:10), and partly because the bare proper name "Yahweh" was losing some of its primitive force and a need was felt to strengthen the idea of God by the use of descriptive epithets. However this may be, it is certainly primarily in the books of the great prophets, from Isa. on, and in their successors, the apocalyptic writers, that we must trace the full development of the idea of the kingdom of God.

The Preexilic Prophets. Before the Exile prophetic designation of Yahweh as king remains infrequent. Isaiah connects neither the noun nor its related verb with God in any other certainly authentic passage. Thus the conception cannot be regarded as basic to his thought, being perhaps merely a reflection of ideas current in his age and specifically in circles connected with the Jerusalem temple. The words are not used at all by Amos and Hosea, the prophets of the N kingdom. In Mic. 2:13 the thought of God's kingship appears, but the passage is viewed by most scholars as an interpolation from the postexilic age. The same judgment is commonly made of Zeph. 3:15, where Yahweh is called "the King of Israel." The noun is found in Jer. 6 times, but only in 8:19 can the use be attributed with any confidence to the prophet himself. Of the other instances, 10:7, 10 come from a passage that is almost universally regarded as later, while 46:18; 48:15; 51:57 belong to passages so regarded by many scholars.

The last 3 examples cited above contain repetitions of the formula, "says the King, whose name is the LORD of hosts." Although some scholars regard "hosts" as referring to human armies, the more likely view is that it means subordinate divinities. If so, its use provides significant support for the view that Yahweh's kingship was originally conceived as purely celestial and "mythological." It is striking that in Isaiah's vision, as in these 3 vss. "the King" is identified as "the Lord of hosts" and is represented as surrounded by heavenly attendants. It must be noted, however, that in Jer. 8:19 Yahweh is, on the contrary, described as King of Zion. The conception of God's kingship seems as yet undeveloped and imprecise.

It is evident from the infrequent use made of the idea of Yahweh's kingship in the preexilic prophets (perhaps only Isa. 6:5; Jer. 8:19) that there was still a certain hesitation about using it. This may have been due in part to a fear of somehow involving the rule of Yahweh too closely in the corrupt and finally disastrous administration of the Judean state. The idea of kingship would become far more attractive after the Exile, when it could be viewed as a theological ideal, abstracted from uncomfortable reality. Nevertheless, despite the apparent misgivings of the preexilic prophets about embracing the ideology of kingship in the theological realm, one can hardly exaggerate their importance in preparing the way for its ultimate adoption.

It was these prophets who first made clear that God's rule is not to be confused with the fortunes of the Israelite kingdoms. It is a natural human tendency to believe that one's own way of life is God's way, and this was particularly a danger in the ancient world, where the worship of the deity was so inextricably tied up with the life and mores of a particular social group.

What the preexilic prophets accomplished, first of all, was the assertion that only through *moral* obedience can a nation claim to be under the rule and protection of its God. The extension of his sway is not to be identified with the enlargement of national borders, nor is the diminution and even obliteration of those borders to be taken as an indication that he has lost his power. This step was necessary to prepare the way for a moral understanding of the kingdom of God. Only with such an understanding can one say that "thy kingdom come" means "thy will be done" (Matt. 6:10) and that the kingdom of God means, not "food and drink," not wealth and political power, but "righteousness and peace and joy in the Holy Spirit" (Rom. 14:17).

The prophets' 2nd achievement was to make clear that God's rule (or kingdom) is not only moral but also *universal.* Although they made no abstract claims for his universal sovereignty, there can be no doubt that a God who sits in judgment over neighboring peoples (Amos 1:3-2:3; cf. 9:7) and summons at his will the mighty rulers of Assyria (Isa. 10:5-6) and Babylonia (Jer. 25:9) is, if a king at all, a universal king and not merely king of Israel.

The Exilic and Postexilic Prophets. With the destruction of the kingdom of Judah all the rich vocabulary and imagery that had grown up in connection with the secular monarchy could now be used in glorifying the rule of God without fear that the divine kingdom would somehow be contaminated by association with the merely human. It was only after the Exile that the idea of the kingdom of God became a commonplace of OT thought. The imagery connected with God's kingship was given extension and precision in 2 directions.

In the first place, in accordance with a tendency already noticed above in connection with the monarchy, the *earthly and social* conception of the kingdom became predominant. Even under the monarchy

Yahweh's kingship had been understood chiefly as his heavenly dominion over other gods or celestial beings. This idea was of course not lost in the exilic and postexilic periods; but men of these later times, influenced by the recollection of their vanished human monarchs, liked to think of God as "King of Israel" (Isa. 44:6) and, at least potentially, as "king over all the earth" (Zech. 14:9). Thus the kingdom of God came to be regarded as a vital, active factor in human history rather than as a transcendental, abstract, purely theological idea.

In the 2nd place, since it was obvious that God's rule was not universally acknowledged, even among the people of Israel, the belief in a full realization of the kingdom was transferred to a later date, when a new act of God would establish it. I.e. the idea of the kingdom became primarily *eschatological*—looking toward the final end of history. For the most part it is this earthly, social, and eschatological conception that we meet in the NT.

For 2nd Isaiah it was Yahweh the king who was directing the movements of human kings and their armies so that he could lead his people back to the land of Israel (Isa. 43:15 in the context of vss. 14-21; cf. Mic. 2:13). This conception is not strictly eschatological because the events it celebrates are to take place on the plane of history, but it is moving in the direction of genuine eschatology in the sense that it is concerned with the future unfolding of God's plan for his people—with their coming deliverance from oppression and the reestablishment of their national life under ideal and presumably permanent conditions (cf. Isa. 51:11; 55:12-13). In some of the other exilic and postexilic prophets the conceptions are more precisely eschatological, and they constantly tend to become more so. I.e. they are concerned not so much with events that will occur within history as with events that will mark the end of history. Admittedly the line of demarcation between the 2 points of view is often difficult to draw.

The various pictures that the prophets give of the realization of God's purpose and the future blessedness of his people, whether using the image of "kingship" or not, are so varied that we can do no more than give here a few examples:

a) Some passages, taking over the message of the great preexilic prophets (e.g. Isa. 2:6-21; Zeph. 1:2–3:11), speak of a coming *judgment of the wicked* as a prelude to the establishment of God's righteous rule (e.g. Isa. 33:7-16; 66:15-16; Ezek. 38–39; Joel 3:9-15, 19; Mal. 3:1-5).

b) According to Zech. 2:10-11; 8:20-23 the recognition of Yahweh's goodness will be widespread among the Gentiles, so that many will join themselves voluntarily to the people of Israel (cf. Isa. 2:1-4, which may also be postexilic) and God will have *universal dominion* (e.g. Isa. 45:23; 56:7).

c) In the part of Jer. written after the Exile had begun there is the promise that God will base his rule on a *new covenant* (Jer. 31:31-34; cf. I Cor. 11:25).

d) Ezek. 36:26-27; Joel 2:28 speak of the eschatological *outpouring of the Spirit* (cf. Acts 2:16-21).

e) Isa. 33:17-24 describes the perfect *peace* of God's people in that future time, blessed with the vision of "the king in his beauty" (vs. 17), who will dwell among them "in majesty" (vs. 21) as judge and ruler (vs. 22).

f) Finally, 3rd Isaiah promises that there will be a *new creation,* for God will "create new heavens and a new earth" where life will be lived under idyllic conditions (Isa. 65:17-25).

In the prophetic books these are only scattered, unsystematized, half-poetic glimpses of a better world to come. As time passed, however, there was a tendency to reduce them to a system and to arrange them in a kind of tentative program for the coming of the kingdom of God.

One isolated and highly mysterious conception from this period—one that was never integrated into the final pattern—is that of the *suffering servant* of Yahweh (Isa. 42:1-4; 49:1-6; 50:4-9; 52:13–53:12). The servant is, in some sense, a "historical" figure and can be connected with the OT hope for the kingdom only in the most general way, as being God's agent to bring "justice" and "law" to the earth (42:4), "light to the nations" (49:6), and through his death justification to "many" (53:11-12). In the NT, nevertheless, he is identified with the Messiah and the Son of man (e.g. Mark 10:33-34, 45), both of whom the OT explicitly connects with the establishment of the eschatological kingdom.

In Ezek. 34:15-22 Yahweh declares that he himself is going to become king in Israel to punish the rapacious and to protect the helpless. Though the word "king" does not occur in the passage, the word "shepherd" is its equivalent, as the context shows. The rule of the former kings, the bad shepherds (vss. 1-6), is to be followed by the rule of God, the Good Shepherd. But now there appears a seeming anomaly which runs through much of the later thinking about the kingdom, for in vs. 23 (and 37:24-25) it appears that the new kingdom is to be ruled also by a human figure ("David"), who will be himself a shepherd as well as prince (vs. 24) and king (37:24).

This figure of *the Messiah* (who is never actually called by that name in the OT) is also found in other exilic and postexilic pictures of the kingdom. Jer. 30:9; 33:14-26 speak of him soberly in much the same spirit as Ezek., but Isa. 11:1-9 (probably a postexilic passage, though some scholars continue to attribute it to Isaiah) presents a much more exuberant picture of the Messiah as a figure of superhuman powers and the messianic age as one of supernatural righteousness and peace. Other important passages are Mic. 5:2-4; Zech. 9:9-10.

We have previously seen how the messianic hope represented the projection into the future of the idea of divine kingship that had at one time been associated with the historical kings of Israel and Judah. Those who accepted this hope of a future ideal king of David's line were unable, however, to harmonize it fully with other conceptions of the kingdom. Consequently in the OT there are some passages that see the Messiah as an integral element in the establishment of the kingdom, while there are others that see the kingdom as established by the activity of God alone, unaccompanied by the presence of any human king. These 2 apparently incompatible ways of picturing the rise of the kingdom persisted in later Judaism, though eventually an attempt was made to bring them into harmony by reducing the messianic age to a merely preliminary status (as in II Esdras 7:28-29). For men of the later OT period it must have seemed more important to hold fast the hope of the kingdom than to concern themselves with the precise manner of its coming. Most of the language describing it is to be understood as poetic and emotional rather than literally descriptive.

V. IN THE CANONICAL APOCALYPTIC WRITERS

It is impossible to make a rigorous distinction between the later prophets and the apocalyptic writers (see "The Apocalyptic Literature," pp. 1106-09). Apocalyptic is an outgrowth of prophecy but is distinguished from it, at least in part, by its diminished interest in the ethical and its preponderant concern for the predictive, the schematic, the supernatural, and the fantastic. No one questions that Dan. 7-12 is apocalyptic, in the same sense as Rev. in the NT. Isa. 24-27; Zech. 12-14 should be included, though some would deny them the title since they do not exhibit one of the characteristic marks of developed apocalyptic, viz. the division of history into precisely marked periods. These writings are among the most difficult for a modern reader to understand or read sympathetically, but they are among the most important for study of the idea of the kingdom of God since they show it in its latest OT form and cast the most illumination on the concept in the NT.

The Zech. Apocalypse. Zech. 12:1-13:6; 14:1-21 are probably 2 different accounts of the eschatological events that introduce the kingdom of God. The first of these makes no explicit use of the concept of kingdom and is concerned largely with the judgment that prepares the way for it. It describes an eschatological battle in which "all the nations of the earth" (12:3) are supernaturally defeated in a great battle against the city of Jeruslem (cf. Ezek. 38-39). Some kind of "messianic" figure is present (vs. 8), but his role is not clear. After a period of mourning for an act of treachery (vss. 10-14) Yahweh proceeds to purify the land from sin, idolatry, and superstition (13:1-6).

Ch. 14 begins again with a picture of all nations laying siege to Jerusalem (vs. 2). They are once more defeated by the direct intervention of Yahweh, although in a fashion quite different from that of ch. 12. He stands on the Mount of Olives, which splits in 2 beneath him (vs. 4). Then the regular alternation of the seasons and of day and night comes to an end and a great river of water begins to flow from the city toward the Dead Sea and the Mediterranean (vs. 8, cf. Ezek. 47:1-12; Joel 3:18; Rev. 22:1-2). At this moment the kingdom of God will be established "and the LORD will become king over all the earth." There will be no other gods, for "on that day the LORD will be one and his name one" (vs. 9). The rest of the ch. describes the supernatural transformation of the land and the punishments with which all nations will be afflicted who fail to come year by year to Jerusalem at the feast of Booths to honor "the King, the LORD of hosts" (vss. 16-17). As in other apocalyptic writings the cruel and ugly features of this picture are probably a reflection of the cruel and unjust sufferings of the Jewish people in a period not too long before the beginning of the Christian era. What is more worth noticing is the fact that under these grotesque features there is preserved a vivid faith in the final establishment of God's kingly rule and a belief that all nations will somehow participate in it.

The Isa. Apocalypse. Isa. 24-27 begins with a picture of a universal judgment (ch. 24) which involves not only the inhabitants of earth but all the powers of the cosmos (vss. 21-22). This will result in the setting up of God's universal kingdom with its center at Jerusalem (vs. 23: "the LORD of hosts will reign on Mount Zion and in Jerusalem"). A remarkable feature of this picture of the end time is the great feast that God will prepare for all nations on his holy mountain (25:6)—the first appearance of the so-called "messianic banquet" that became a stock feature in later pictures of the messianic age. Death and sorrow will be abolished forever (25:8) and, if the customary translation of one difficult passage is correct, the dead will rise from their graves (26:19). The theme of resurrection seems to appear here in Jewish literature for the first time (Ezek. 37:1-14 has to do with the nation, not individuals). The apocalypse also speaks, though perhaps not in chronological sequence, of the slaying of Leviathan, the primeval monster of chaos (27:1; cf. Ps. 74:14; Rev. 20:2), the blowing of a trumpet (27:13; cf. Rev. 8:6), and the return to Jerusalem of the Jews of the Dispersion (27:12-13).

The Dan. Apocalypse. The most important of the apocalyptic accounts of the establishment of the eschatological kingdom is that found in Dan. 7:9-27. It is generally agreed that this account in its present form comes from the time of the persecutions under Antiochus Epiphanes (168-165 B.C.; I Macc. 1-4). In this ch. we find for the first time the schematization of history that is so characteristic of the developed apocalyptic style. Before the end time there will appear 4 kingdoms having the characteristics of wild beasts, says the seer (represented as speaking toward the end of the Babylonian exile), of which the last (the Greek) will be the worst of all (vss. 1-8). Just at the moment when this kingdom reaches its acme of arrogance (vs. 8) God, "the ancient of days," will appear on his throne and pass judgment on all the former bestial kingdoms (vss. 9-12). Then will come "with the clouds of heaven" one who is "like a son of man"; and he will receive the final, universal, and imperishable dominion (vss. 13-14; on this whole eschatological program cf. 2:31-45).

In the following section (vss. 15-27) it is explained that the "one like a son of man" (which in Aramaic idiom means "one in human form") is merely a symbol of "the people of the saints of the Most High," i.e. the faithful Jews (vs. 27). Many scholars believe that the explanation (vss. 15-27) is secondary and the story reflects a legend in which the leading role was originally played by a messianic figure of heavenly origin. However this may be, there can be no doubt that the "son of man" was later understood in an individual sense (cf. Enoch 46:1-6) and that the belief in this form has profound significance for the interpretation of the NT (cf. e.g. Matt. 16:27-28; 24:30; 26:64).

There is much more in Dan. that is relevant to the coming of the kingdom, but here it is enough to mention only 2 additional elements: "the abomination that makes desolate," which will be set up before the end time (11:31; cf. Mark 13:14; see comments); and the resurrection of "many" of both the righteous and the wicked dead (12:2), set forth in much clearer language than in Isa. 26:19.

It is in the apocalyptic literature that the concept

of an eschatological kingdom of God becomes an article of OT faith. The beginnings of this tendency, of course, are found in the later prophets; but with them it tended to be general, vague, poetic, and homiletical. The apocalyptic writers, who were active in times of persecution, made the hope of the kingdom a sure anchor to which men could cling when faced with temptation to apostasy or unbelief. The preexilic prophets anchored Israel's faith chiefly on God's saving work in the past (e.g. Amos 2:9-11; Hos. 11:1-2; Jer. 2:1-7). It was the apocalyptic writers who finally succeeded in turning the eyes of the men of the old Israel with equal intensity toward the future. It is largely in this latest form that the idea of the kingdom of God became basic to the thought of the new Israel.

VI. IN THE PSALMS

The idea of the kingdom plays an important role in the Psalter, but its function there is primarily devotional—i.e. to provide images suitable for praising God—and the conception is much more fluid than in the prophets and apocalyptic writers. Sometimes Yahweh is spoken of as king of the gods (e.g. 95:3; cf. 82:1), sometimes as king of all nations (e.g. 47:2, 7, 8); sometimes only as king of Israel (e.g. 149:2). In one psalm his kingship may, as many scholars suppose, be associated especially with the ark (24:7-10). It is of interest that here, as in Isa. 6:5; Jer. 46:18 etc., it is connected also with the mysterious title "the LORD of hosts," though one can only speculate as to the reason for the connection. These different ways of conceiving the kingship of Yahweh are not, of course, essentially contradictory, even though each has a separate history behind it. To those who wrote and sang the psalms they would have seemed only descriptions of different aspects of God's unitary rule. In some instances the title "king" is no doubt simply an honorific emotional epithet without precise intellectual content (e.g. 5:2; 84:3).

More important than the question of the extent of God's kingdom in space is the question of its location in time, whether it is to be regarded as a present fact or as a future expectation. In developed Jewish and Christian thought the idea of the kingdom is used in both senses. Because God is the omnipotent creator of all he must even now—at least potentially —be the king of all. But since at present his sovereignty seems to be widely flouted there is another sense in which he will ascend the throne of his kingdom only in the future.

A further complication has been added to the picture by the theory that in certain of the psalms the proclamation that God is king was a feature of an annual feast of Yahweh's enthronement, celebrated in preexilic Israel, during which God was believed ceremonially to reenact the drama of creation and each year reascend the throne of the universe for the coming 12 months (see Intro. to Pss.).

The question of *when* God is king arises particularly in connection with the so-called enthronement psalms (47; 93; 95–99), where God's kingship is the major theme. Ps. 47 provides the best support for the enthronement-festival theory, since the prima-facie meaning of vs. 5 is that a ritual act of some kind has just taken place ("God has gone up with a shout"). In the other psalms the situation is more ambiguous and the precise meaning of the Hebrew clause translated "The LORD reigns" (93:1; 96:10; 97:1; 99:1) is uncertain. Grammatically any of 3 translations of this clause is possible: "The LORD has [just now] become king"; "The LORD is [always] king"; "The LORD will become king." One's understanding of the words and his interpretation of the psalms in which they appear will be determined by his theory as to the purpose for which these psalms were composed. In any case, however, Pss. 96:10c, 13; 98:9 are clearly eschatological, and regardless of the original setting of the enthronement psalms they were undoubtedly understood in the postexilic period as expressions of faith in God's eschatological reign.

While the thought of God's enthronement in a ritual act, if it ever existed, eventually disappeared, except perhaps as a poetic fancy, the 2 ideas of God's present kingdom and his future kingdom remained vital elements in the faith of both Israel and the Christian Church. This is shown e.g. by 2 clauses of the Lord's prayer: the petition "thy kingdom *come*" and the liturgical ascription "Thine *is* the kingdom." It is faith in God's present kingship that makes possible belief in his future kingship. Because he is now—at least potentially—king of Israel, of the gods, and of the universe, one cannot doubt that someday his sovereignty will be manifest to all and that he will come to rule the earth in fact and "judge the world with righteousness, and the peoples with equity" (Ps. 98:9).

VII. SUMMARY

When we speak of the kingdom of God in the OT we cannot be tied too closely to precise terminology. The exact phrase "kingdom of God" nowhere occurs in the canonical books (I Chr. 28:5 comes closest). Its first appearance is in Wisd. Sol. 10:10, where, however, it means nothing more than "God's heavenly court"!

The use of the title "king" for God is a more significant clue to follow. As we have seen, the evidence for its early use is tenuous and its meaning uncertain. By the end of the OT period, however, the thought of God's kingship not only had acquired the eschatological reference in which the student of the NT is specially interested but could be used also to express the whole range of Israel's faith. It was connected with the Creation (Ps. 93:1-4), God's ongoing care for his world (I Chr. 29:11-12), the Exodus (Exod. 15:18), the founding of the covenant (Deut. 33:5), the constitution of the monarchy (I Chr. 17:14), the return from exile (Mic. 2:13), the future hope (Dan. 2:44), and even the individual's sense of his personal relationship to God (Ps. 84:3). In the hymns of this late period the kingship of God had become a comprehensive term to describe his universal control over heaven and earth, over angels and men (Pss. 103:19; 145:11-13; Dan. 4:3). This conception in all its richness is a part of the Christian church's heritage from the OT and is deeply significant for her theological, liturgical, and devotional life (cf. I Tim. 1:17; 6:15-16; Rev. 15:3).

A 2nd basic clue to be followed is that of Israel's life as a community constituted by God's act and pledged to absolute obedience to his will. From the beginning OT religion was corporate in character;

it was never concerned with the salvation of individuals in isolation. Though the form of the community underwent several notable changes—from tribal confederacy to monarchy to postexilic priestly theocracy to something in the nature of a church—it remained a community of men who regarded themselves as under God's control and as the principal instrument for bringing the world into subjection to his rule. It was ultimately seen that the most adequate image for expressing this social conception of Israelite man's relation to God was that of a kingdom under the rule of a divine king. The confederacy at Sinai was, at least retrospectively, pictured as "a kingdom of priests" (Exod. 19:6; cf. I Pet. 2:9), Yahweh's divine rule in Israel as "the kingdom of the LORD" (I Chr. 28:5), and God's final triumph over all opposing forces as his reign in the kingdom of "the people of the saints of the Most High" (Dan. 7:27; cf. Isa. 24:23; Zech. 14:9).

In the latest period of OT thought the idea of the kingdom of God had developed to the point where it could carry the full weight of thought expressed at the beginning of this article. The hope of the *future* "kingdom of God" had become the concentrated focus of Israel's expectations, and it is to this hope in particular—modified and enriched, of course, by developments in the intertestamental period—that the good news of the NT was to attach itself (e.g. Matt. 3:2; 4:17; 6:10; Luke 13:18, 20; Gal. 5:21; Rev. 11:15; 12:10; see "The Kingdom of God in the NT," pp. 1176-86).

For Further Study: J. Bright, *The Kingdom of God*, 1953. S. Mowinckel, *He That Cometh*, 1954. T. C. Vriezen, *An Outline of OT Theology*, 1958. O. E. Evans, "Kingdom of God" in *IDB*, 1962. R. Schnackenburg, *God's Rule and Kingdom*, 1963. G. von Rad, "Basileia" in G. Kittel, ed., *Theological Dictionary of the NT*, 1964.

THE NEW TESTAMENT
INTERPRETATION OF JESUS

CHARLES M. LAYMON

The person of Jesus dominates the entire NT. Whether he is presented as the Jesus of history or as the living, transcendent Lord in whose authority and power lies the destiny of men and nations, he is preeminent throughout its 27 books. Although many subjects are considered in these writings—including earthly goods, the state, marriage, divorce, proper foods, war, forgiveness, death, immortality, and the end of the world—whatever the subject under consideration Jesus is involved either directly or indirectly.

The reason for this centrality of the person of Jesus in the NT is that his life, death, resurrection, and continuing lordship came to be regarded as matters of salvation among his followers. As we shall examine more closely later, to them he was more than rabbi or teacher; he was also their *Lord*. They believed that there was a meaning in his person and career that extended beyond the segment of time when he lived among men in Palestine. What had happened was "salvation history." It required the perspective of the centuries within Israel before his coming to understand him. And only in the light of the eternal purpose of God could his full significance be known and related. His role in the future would show him to be "King of kings and Lord of lords" (Rev. 19:16); at his name every knee would bow, above, on, and under the earth, and every tongue confess him Lord to God's glory (Phil. 2:10-11).

When we inquire as to how the early church, whose views are found in the NT, came to think of Jesus in this exalted manner, we are brought face to face with the fact that all this did not occur in a vacuum. First of all the person of Jesus as one of their contemporaries made a transforming impression on his immediate followers. Even those who view the account of Jesus in the gospels with historical skepticism of varying degrees are today disinclined to deny the reality of the life that led men to write about him in this manner. And whether one concludes that the gospel authors are presenting myth (see "The Literary Forms of the NT," pp. 1124-28), kerygma (a preaching message), or history, the fact remains that there is a figure behind the portrayal —a figure of such character that they found it necessary to write about him in such transcendent terms.

In the 2nd place the NT authors were not writing in a world that was insulated from the thought currents of their own time. Even the members of the Dead Sea community who produced the scrolls in their ascetic seclusion were touched with Hellenism, or Greek thought. How this reached them is difficult to determine, whether through Judaism or by some other indirect contact (see "The Dead Sea Scrolls," pp. 1063-71). The influence of Hellenism also on the author of John and of Platonic thought on the author of Heb. are widely accepted today by biblical scholars likewise.

Another contact that determined what the early church felt, thought, and wrote about Jesus was Judaism. Jesus himself was a Jew who was represented as saying that he came to fulfill the Law and the Prophets. Many of his followers were Jews. Paul, one of his most vocal interpreters within the NT, was a Pharisee. It fell to his lot preeminently to take the gospel to the Greco-Roman world, and in this endeavor he preached to Hellenistic Jews abroad as well as to Gentiles. His personal experience and understanding of God had been Jewish before he was converted, and as such a one he came to know and, as mentioned above, to proclaim Jesus as Lord.

All of this is to say simply that Jesus was experienced, interpreted, and presented within a real life situation. And in doing this the early church through its leaders and writers spoke within the framework of their time (see "The Greco-Roman Background of the NT," pp. 1037-44). They laid hold of ideas and forms of thought and expression that were at hand, those which best interpreted the meaning of the new life that they had found in Jesus.

It is sometimes difficult in assessing the NT interpretation of Jesus to distinguish between the form in which it is presented and the reality at its core. E.g. when the Christian of NT times said, "Jesus is the Messiah," he meant more than to assert that Jesus was simply the messianic figure depicted variously in the OT. And when the author of John stated that Jesus is "the Word made flesh," even though he may have used an expression from Philo, he was not limiting his interpretation to the view of that Jewish philosopher who had made the idea of the word (logos) significant in his thinking. In cases such as this we must always ask what the NT authors were *intending to say* about Jesus when they used literary forms and expressions contemporary to their day, formulated their accounts, and proclaimed the kerygma. This process is sometimes referred to as demythologizing the NT writings. Thus the eternal message is separated from its passing form in the enlightenment and deepening of the faith today.

It would be erroneous to hold, however, that NT thought about Jesus is nothing more than a syncretism made up of concepts and ideas borrowed from the environment of that day. That these were at hand and that they were helpful in formulating the conclusions of Christian thinkers as they sought to interpret and explain their experience of Jesus is rather obvious to the informed reader. But to say that the NT view of Jesus is just a mosaic of Hebrew, Greek, and oriental ideas is misleading, for it misses the originality and uniqueness of what is being said.

In any interpretation, then or now, one must engage in conceptual thinking and employ the ideas at hand, currently used and understood. A writer has no other choice if he is to communicate with others about Jesus. And this is what the NT authors did in their presentation of Jesus. It was a procedure that led to great insights, even though in other circumstances and places the basic truth in some instances would possibly have been expressed differently. The question to ask is always "Why do men write as they do? What are they attempting to say?"

Sometimes the thought forms and concepts of any given age are incapable of carrying the full definitive meaning that a writer has to communicate. New truth may burst the bonds of the tools of thought at hand. It must be expressed in a variety of ways, even though it may require the use of a new vocabulary to do so.

More than this, different individuals will express the same truths differently. A glance at the editorial page of any newspaper will bear this out. And a thoughtful reading of the NT as its authors sought to explain Jesus to their readers will likewise confirm it. Heb. does not read at all points like John, just as the Rev. does not sound like Jas. Yet each in its own way is interpreting Jesus in exalted terms to its readers.

These considerations account for both the variety and the unity in the NT portrait of Jesus Christ. Both aspects must be stressed as its several writings are interpreted or a truncated and one-sided reading will result. Each author in his own way, to meet his specific situation, and to speak a word in season has sought to present Jesus to the first-cent. world —Jew and Gentile, bond and free, male and female —so that his true character as eternal Lord will be grasped.

It would be misleading to assert and insist that each NT author sees and understands Jesus from a single perspective. At the same time it would be unwarranted to seek to arrive at a lowest common denominator by trimming away the individual insights and delineations of each so that a kind of static uniformity would result. A more fruitful approach would be to seek to discover what the NT *as a whole* says about Jesus. There is to be found here, amid all the variety, a consensus of conviction, intellectual and spiritual, where Jesus is concerned. This includes what is written in the gospels, as well as in the letters and the apocalyptic Rev.

The NT does not present numerous Christs. Through all its variety of approaches there emerges but one Lord Jesus, (*a*) whose origin was in God, (*b*) through whom God created the world, (*c*) whose coming was foreseen and prophesied in the OT, (*d*) who was incarnate in human flesh, (*e*) who in his role as the Messiah proclaimed the kingdom of God, performing "signs and wonders," (*f*) who according to the Scriptures died for man's sins, (*g*) who was raised from the dead and ascended in glory to God's right hand as Lord, (*h*) who was present through the Spirit to bring eternal life to his followers here and hereafter, (*i*) who established, indwelt, and guided the church, (*j*) who at the end of the age would return to bless, judge, and overcome all evil in men, nations, and the spirit world, and (*k*) who finally would reign with God in an eternal kingdom.

A. The Preexistence of Jesus Christ

The idea of preexistence is not limited to the NT interpretation of Jesus. There were also expressions in rabbinic and Talmudic times in which the Jews ascribed this characteristic to Jerusalem, the law, the sabbath, and the tabernacle. Basic to this ascription, in part, was the conviction that there was a divine revelation in these religious realities. Did they not reveal the eternal God? Must they not therefore be eternal?

Perhaps it was in this same vein that the early church came to regard Jesus Christ as eternal, since he brought to man an eternal salvation and revealed the eternal God in his transcendent power and glory. This was an intuitive conclusion, to be sure, but it was in line with the new life that had come to them through Christ.

Another factor that contributed to the church's thought of Jesus as preexistent was Paul's probable identification of him with the eschatological "Son of man," an apocalyptic figure mentioned in the Similitudes of Enoch (I Enoch 46:2-8). Jesus himself may also have thought of his own person in these terms when he called himself the Son of man. This one was presented in the Similitudes as an individual figure who would at the judgment pass on men and nations. Of heavenly origin, the Son of man stands in the presence of God, "the Lord of Spirits," where his uprightness is forever, and he shall control the destiny of kings. If Jesus is identified with this exalted being, the reality of his preexistent life is a logical conclusion.

The Jews sometimes also wrote of wisdom in preexistent terms, asserting its role in the act of creation. And Paul in Col. 1:15-17 associates Christ with this divine wisdom of the OT. The implication for his preexistence is present in this reference, even as it is when he is associated with the divine glory (I Cor. 11:7; Eph. 1:17).

Yet another view that was current in Paul's day and which may have turned his thoughts toward the idea of the preexistence of Jesus was the current Hellenistic myth of the origin of man. Originally a Persian conception, it interpreted man's origin in terms of the descent from heaven of a Primal Man. We can only speculate concerning Paul's familiarity with this teaching, but it was being taught at this time and carried overtones of preexistence that could have influenced the apostle's thinking about Jesus. Paul did teach that Jesus was the "last Adam" or a 2nd Adam creating a new humanity (I Cor. 15:45), and this is not unrelated to the above.

In discussing the NT's teaching concerning the preexistence of Jesus his identification with the divine Logos in the prologue to the 4th Gospel is pivotal. Here it is stated: "In the beginning was the Word [Logos] and the Word was with God, and the Word was God" (John 1:1). It is also said here in reference to Jesus: "The Word became flesh and dwelt among us, full of grace and truth" (John 1:14).

It is usually thought that the author is here identifying Jesus before his advent with the logos of Hellenistic-Jewish thought as once taught by the Stoics and then taken up by Philo. In the latter's hands the logos stands for the *rational principle*, or *reason*, through which God created the universe. The point for consideration is that such identification expressly proclaims the preexistence of Jesus as the Word.

These many possibilities as a background for the NT's assertion of the preexistence of Jesus make it abundantly clear that there were numerous teachings abroad in that day which were congenial to the idea of preexistence. And in view of the quality of Jesus' life, the experience by his followers of his resurrection, and the exalted character of their fellowship with him as their Lord—in view of all of this his preexistence seemed a logical, if not actually an inevitable, conclusion.

The preexistence of Jesus in the NT, however, is not simply a philosophical or theological idea which the church held in an abstract sense. At the hands of Paul it became a motive for Christian living in the highest sense.

Such is the case in his christological passage in Phil. 2:5-11. He is seeking here to shame the church because of its pride. To do this he points to the preexistence of Jesus and contrasts its glory with the coming to earth in lowly form:

> Have this mind among yourselves, which you have in Christ Jesus, who, though he was in the form of God, did not count equality with God a thing to be grasped, but emptied himself, taking the form of a servant, being born in the likeness of men. And being found in human form he humbled himself and became obedient unto death, even death on a cross. (Phil. 2:5-8)

Paul does not speculate as to the manner in which Christ previously lived "in the form of God." He did not do so probably because he could not; he did not know how to delineate it. But the reality of the Lord's preexistent life which he relinquished by coming to earth is definitely asserted.

It is implied also when Paul urges Christians to realize the extent of "the grace of God" (II Cor. 8:1) and the need to show love that is genuine:

> For you know the grace of our Lord Jesus Christ, that though he was rich [in his preexistent life], yet for your sake he became poor, so that by his poverty you might become rich. (II Cor. 8:9.)

B. THE AGENT OF CREATION

Another feature in the portrait of Jesus Christ as interpreted in the NT is that he is presented as the agent of creation (John 1:3; Col. 1:16; Heb. 1:2; 2:10). Modern man with his scientific approach to the universe may find it difficult to grasp the significance of this idea. There were reasons for it, however, in terms of first-cent. thought that help us to understand why this reference was included.

In the first place it gave meaning to his preexistence. There was something that he performed. In the 2nd place the conception of Christ as an agent of creation was an expression of his relation to God. "The Word [Logos] was with God, and . . . was God" (John 1:1). And in the 3rd place it assigned to him a significant place in the cosmos. Had he not through his signs and wonders among men indicated such power over nature as to suggest his supremacy over it? And was it not, along with their total experience of the exaltation of Christ, but a little distance to the idea that he actually participated in the creation of nature itself? All these are possible explanations of the teaching that he was the agent of creation.

There is yet a 4th approach to the inclusion of this idea in the NT, one that grows out of the philosophical background of the day. An incipient Gnosticism being taught at this time claimed that between heaven (God) and earth there existed a host of intermediary beings as emanations of deity. These were regarded as necessary in connection with the creation of matter. Matter was considered to be evil, and pure deity therefore could not be conceived as having contact with it, such contact as creation would involve. Accordingly the Gnostics taught that it was through the agency of these intermediary beings that the earth was made.

Into this picture Paul stepped and with one great intellectual judgment swept away these intermediaries. He asserted that there were no such "aeons" at all. Christ was the sole mediary between God and man. It was through Christ that the world was created. His place between heaven and earth is thus unique and unshared.

Here we see an illustration of the way the thought world of the first cent. provided a framework of reference within which to interpret the significance of Jesus Christ. What was at stake was his uniqueness. Modern man might have said it differently but in the light of his day Paul could hardly have said it more effectively.

There is yet another influence that probably caused the church to regard Christ as the agent of creation. People of the first cent. believed that there were in the universe many hostile forces—demons, powers, and principalities—which threatened their lives constantly, bringing them misfortune, sickness, and death. But they were convinced that Christ had overcome them. In his ministry he had cast out demons and in his resurrection he had triumphed over them. He had reconciled "to himself all things, whether on earth or in heaven" (Col. 1:20). Thus his cosmic significance had been demonstrated. Should not such a one have had a part in creation itself? Christ is preeminent as the agent of creation of all that is.

C. THE ADVENT WAS PROPHESIED

The attitude of NT authors toward prophecy reflected the thinking of the church concerning the advent of Jesus. They held that in their own time prophecy was still active among the believers in Christ. The ability to prophesy was regarded as one of the charismatic gifts given to certain individuals by the Holy Spirit. Paul lists it among others (I Cor. 12:10, 28; cf. Eph. 4:11).

It is not surprising, therefore, to discover their conviction that the advent of Jesus was prophesied in the OT, as were certain events in his life, including his death for sin (I Cor. 15:3) and his resurrection (Acts 2:24-31). God's work in Christ was considered to be a part of his redeeming activity begun in Israel.

In identifying the events in Jesus' life which had been prophesied or foreshadowed in the OT, sometimes even the slightest similarity between the OT statement and the NT event was regarded as indicating a prophecy-fulfillment relationship. Matt. in particular leans in this direction. Along with other instances, he views the flight of Mary and Joseph with the baby Jesus into Egypt (Matt. 2:14-15) as fulfilling Hos. 11:1, which in its original context clearly refers to the deliverance of Israel under Moses. In this same vein the anguish caused by Herod's killing of the babes (Matt. 2:16-18) is connected with Jer. 31:15, which speaks of "Rachel weeping for her children" who have been carried away in the Exile.

Jesus' death on the cross provided a particular incentive for interpretation in the light of earlier scriptures. This no doubt gave needed ballast for stabilizing the church as it faced this tragic event. What had probably at first been seen as a dire blow to the faith of his followers now came to be regarded as within the purpose of God (Mark 14:21), a purpose that had been made known in the OT itself. E.g. his arrest must not be interrupted (Matt. 26:53-56; cf. Pss. 22; 69), and the 30 pieces of silver which Judas returned were used to purchase a potter's field (Matt. 27:3-10; cf. Zech. 11:13)—each in fulfillment of prophecy.

A particularly significant illustration of this approach to the events in the last days of Jesus' life is found in Acts 8:30-35, where Philip discovers the Ethiopian eunuch reading the passage from Isa. 53:7-8 concerning the suffering servant. When the eunuch professes his inability to understand the words he is reading, Philip "beginning with this scripture . . . told him the good news of Jesus." The death on the cross by this time had come to be interpreted in the light of Isaiah's portrayal of the suffering servant.

It is possible that Jesus himself may have viewed the Cross in the light of Isaiah's words here, although there are no specific places in the record where he is said to have done so. In any case the church may be here seen to be finding an answer to the tragedy of the Cross. Hanging on a tree was regarded as a curse by the Jews (Deut. 21:23); thus for Jewish Christians the Crucifixion was a double stumbling block. Not only was there the awful suffering it involved with its cruelty and repugnant exhibition, but there was also the curse of the law. If the Crucifixion, however, is viewed in the light of Isaiah 53, the sting is removed and a divine meaning crowns the event.

Although the coming of the Spirit at Pentecost did not occur during Jesus' earthly life, it was associated with his anticipated advent because it was seen as an outgrowth of it. When the charge was made that the Spirit-filled followers of Jesus were intoxicated, Peter arose and denied the allegation. What was taking place before their very eyes, he asserted, was a fulfillment of the prophet Joel's anticipation of the coming of the day of the Lord (Joel 2:28-32; Acts 2:14-21).

Other instances could be given to indicate the NT's understanding of the prophecy-fulfillment relationship in the events associated with the advent of Jesus and the outcome of his life, death, and resurrection (cf. e.g. Matt. 2:5-6, 18; Luke 2:25-26; 2:36-37; Acts 3:11-13; 13:17-23). Undoubtedly some of the authors, such as Matt., took this legalistically. What was basic throughout the NT, however, was the conviction that what had taken place in Jesus Christ's coming was part and parcel of God's continuing purpose for mankind, first expressed and revealed in Israel (Heb. 1:1-2). God's will from all eternity was to save men in love, and Christ was the full and absolute manifestation of that love, by which a new people of God came into being.

D. INCARNATE IN HUMAN FLESH

What we refer to as the incarnation is perhaps best expressed in the NT in the prologue of the 4th Gospel: "And the Word became flesh and dwelt among us, full of grace and truth; we have beheld his glory, glory as of the only Son from the Father" (John 1:14). Another Johannine passage, I John 1:1-2, expresses this same truth. Here the author claims to have seen and touched the "word of life." He states that he is proclaiming to his readers "the eternal life which was with the Father and was made manifest to us." Since he says that this word of life existed "from the beginning," he is probably referring to its preexistence, even as this view is propounded in the prologue to the 4th Gospel. Another less likely possibility is that he is referring to the gospel as "the word of life."

The point being stressed above is that the Word had actually been incarnate in human flesh. The importance of this emphasis at this particular time was the emergence of a docetic view of the person of Christ. Among the Gnostics it was held that Jesus' life in the flesh was unreal. He only *seemed* to be flesh of our flesh, they taught. Some held that his entire physical life was unreal; others would include only certain aspects of it, particularly his death. Not all Gnostics held this view, but probably all of the Docetists were Gnostics (see "The Greco-Roman Background of the NT," pp. 1037-44).

Why did the church at this time insist on the reality of the life of Jesus in the flesh? According to the Docetists it was unworthy of God to suffer and feel pain—to die on the cross as in the case of Jesus. Matter and that which went with it was essentially evil to them. Therefore Jesus Christ only *seemed* to experience the cross; the divinity in him had left his body just prior to the Crucifixion, if his body had been real at all throughout his ministry.

To conclude that Jesus' death on the cross was unreal was to remove from the gospel its chief illustration of the love of God that would go to such lengths to save man. As Paul put it in a passage already examined, Christ Jesus, "being found in human form, . . . humbled himself and became obedient unto death, even death on a cross" (Phil. 2:8). Because of this—suffering, death, and all—God exalted him and gave him a position preeminent in the universe (vss. 9-11).

The question of the historicity of the gospel records of Jesus is not immediately pertinent here, except to the extent that they assume a genuine historical existence for him. In fact it is interesting to note that the other NT writers make little use of the details of the gospels, although they show some knowledge of them. Nevertheless they base their interpretations of Jesus on the basic assumption that he actually lived as a figure of history. Even Heb. makes certain general references to the reality of Jesus' life in the flesh when it refers to his "suffering of death" (2:9), to the children sharing with him "in flesh and blood" (2:14), his being tempted (2:18), and his offering up of "prayers and supplication with loud cries and tears" in the "days of his flesh" (5:7).

Finally, the accounts of the virgin birth of Jesus in Matt. 1:18 ff. and Luke 1:26 ff. assume that he was born into a genuine historical existence. His mother Mary was an actual person even as he entered the world as an actual infant. The shepherds and wise men came to worship a real baby in the manger.

E. Jesus Is the Messiah Who Performs Messianic Signs and Wonders

In the NT interpretation of Jesus the teaching that he is the Messiah runs throughout the entire collection of writings as a unifying theme. Not every writer understands or expresses Jesus' messiahship in the same way, but the basic idea of his vocation and person in these terms prevails in all these writings, whether they are gospels, letters, or apocalyptic.

The question whether Jesus regarded himself as the Messiah is a separate one to which various answers have been given by different scholars. The NT authors, it would seem, were convinced that his own view of his calling and person was in line with theirs. In their own minds they were not "creating" a messiah but reporting and interpreting one.

Some scholars today conclude that Jesus' life and work when considered in terms of traditional messianic ideas was not messianic. It was the church that regarded him as the Messiah following the Resurrection. Others hold that, though he thought of himself as the Messiah, he did not present any messianic claims. God would do this on his behalf when he intervened to establish the kingdom. Still others insist that he began to fulfill his mission with a prophetic consciousness that became messianic as his work continued. And in addition there are those who believe that the NT when referring to Jesus in messianic terms is reflecting his own conviction that he was the Messiah, an office which he claimed to fill in his own lifetime and would further express in the final coming of the kingdom.

In spite of the variety of interpretations of scholars as to whether Jesus regarded himself as the Messiah, almost all would assert that the NT presents him as such. In the birth stories the angel announces to Mary that God will give to her son "the throne of his father David," saying that "he will reign over the house of Jacob forever; and of his kingdom there will be no end" (Luke 1:32-33). And in Matt.'s genealogy he is called the "son of David" (1:1). The voice of God at Jesus' baptism points him out as the Messiah by referring to him as the "beloved Son" with whom he is "well pleased" (Luke 3:22). Even though among the Jews this designation was not messianic, the NT authors interpreted it that way.

Again, the temptation of Jesus in the wilderness that followed his baptism is regarded in the Synoptic gospels as a struggle between the Messiah and Satan from which Jesus the Messiah emerged as victor (Mark 1:12-13; Matt. 4:1-11; Luke 4:1-13). This accomplishment foreshadowed his continuing lordship over evil that was finally brought to a climax in his death and resurrection.

In his healing ministry involving "signs and wonders" the gospels likewise present Jesus as the Messiah who overcame Satan's grip on mankind. They have been called "the messianic signs." Through them Satan was being cast out as "by the finger of God," and the kingdom of God was in these events coming upon those present (Luke 11:20). We are to see here more than examples of humanitarian concern for the afflicted. They are this, to be sure, but more significantly they are expressions of the coming of the day of the Lord to which prophets in the OT pointed. Isa. 29:18 had already spoken of the day when the deaf would hear and "out of their gloom and darkness" the eyes of the blind would see.

As the record of the ministry of Jesus is continued in the gospels, Jesus applied one of the servant passages from Isa. to himself with messianic implications in the synagogue at Nazareth (Luke 4:16-21); Peter confessed Jesus to be the "Christ" at Caesarea Philippi (Mark 8:27-30); the voice from heaven once more proclaimed Jesus to be the beloved Son at the Transfiguration (Mark 9:2-8); the Triumphal Entry is presented as a messianic visitation (Mark 11:9-10; Matt. 21:9; Luke 19:38); and the title "King of the Jews" seems to have been accepted by Jesus when he stood before Pilate (Mark 15:2; Matt. 27:11; Luke 23:3).

The above references come from the Synoptics. John is no less definite in ascribing messiahship to Jesus. Here he is the Christ, the Son of God, and all who believe in him shall find life (20:31). He revealed himself openly as the Messiah (a procedure not followed in the Synoptics except at the end) to the Samaritan woman (4:25-26), as well as to the man born blind (9:35-38), and claimed in this capacity to do both the will and the work of God (10:25). Messiahship here is not simply the traditional son of David or earthly ruler concept. As the Messiah, Jesus is the bringer of light and life to the world (6:35; 8:12; 10:9; 10:14; 11:25; 14:6; 15:5). As a king he comes "to bear witness to the truth" (18:33-38).

In reporting Jesus' frequent use of the term "Son of man," which he applied to himself and his office, the gospels further reflect the conviction of the early church that Jesus was the Messiah. Reference has already been made to this expression as it occurs in I Enoch. The term also is found in Ezek. 2:1 etc., where it is a designation of the prophet, and again in Dan. 7:13-14, where it may refer to a heavenly being but more probably signifies the messianic reign of Israel. On the lips of Jesus it was capable, therefore, of several interpretations, suggesting humility or exaltation (or both), and likewise not necessarily implying an earthly, Davidic royal ruler.

In the primitive church Acts depicts Peter on one occasion addressing the Jews. He refers to Jesus as "the Holy and Righteous One" (Acts 3:14). Again, in his Pentecost sermon he says that God has made the crucified one "both Lord and Christ" (Acts 2:36). The expression "Righteous One" suggests Isa. 53:11*b* in the suffering servant passage, while the term "Christ" is the Greek equivalent for Messiah. In both instances, therefore, Jesus' messianic office is implied.

Paul also refers to Jesus in messianic terms. He knows him as the "Son, who was descended from David according to the flesh and designated Son of God in power according to the Spirit of holiness by his resurrection from the dead, Jesus Christ our Lord" (Rom. 1:3-4).

In Heb., where Jesus' sonship is also stressed, we have once again a messianic implication. The author regards Jesus as superior to both Moses and Joshua (3:1-4:13) since he "was faithful over God's house as a son" (3:6). No angel was ever told, says the writer, "Thou art my Son, today I have begotten thee"; and to none other did God say that he would "be to him a father, and he shall be to me a son" (1:5). In interpreting the word "son" here the messianic overtones should not be missed.

One more example of the messianic interpretation of Jesus should be sufficient to indicate how widespread was this understanding of his mission. This time we turn to Rev., where Jesus is presented as the warrior Messiah. The author is depicting in apocalyptic fashion the final death struggle between the forces of evil and of righteousness. He does this in terms of a battle at "the place which is called in Hebrew Armageddon" (16:16). Here the issue is to be drawn. As head of the opposition to evil Jesus rides a white horse, leading an army of heavenly martyrs arrayed in pure white linen. He proves to be supreme over Satan's agents, the beast and his forces. The names given to the warrior Messiah are "Faithful and True," "the Word of God," "King of kings, and Lord of lords" (19:11-16). He rules with a rod of iron and treads "the wine press of the fury of the wrath of God the Almighty." His victory is immediate and final. At the end of time no person or thing can withstand him.

F. JESUS CHRIST'S DEATH FOR SIN

It is difficult to determine how soon after Jesus' crucifixion his death was interpreted in relation to the forgiveness of sins. That it was shortly afterward, however, seems probable. An early example of Christian kerygma, or preaching message, may well be found in the account of Peter's sermon at the home of Cornelius (Acts 10:34-43). It makes reference, as it proceeds to enumerate the events in his ministry, to his death by hanging on a tree (vs. 39). And at its close it states that "every one who believes in him receives forgiveness of sins through his name" (vs. 43).

Even more direct is one of the statements of Paul to the Corinthians (I Cor. 15:3 ff.). He is listing for them the things he considers of first importance and refers to these as *what he received*. By this he probably has in mind the early tradition concerning Jesus that has been handed down to him. At the heart of this listing he says that "Christ died for our sins in accordance with the scriptures" (vs. 3). He does not elaborate further in this statement by indicating what scripture reference he has in mind or how it is that Christ's death is related to the forgiveness of sins.

Paul, however, treats this theme more fully elsewhere in his letters. In one instance he speaks of "Christ Jesus, whom God put forward as an expiation by his blood, to be received by faith" (Rom. 3:24-25). The meaning here is rooted in the area of religious sacrificial systems, which were found among both Jews and Gentiles. "Expiation" in this passage is joined with "faith" so that it is removed from the realm of the strict sacramentarian. Neither is it to be regarded as propitiating or placating an angry god. This is pagan rather than biblical. Man is delivered as he responds by faith to Christ crucified.

Christ "died for all," Paul declares (II Cor. 5:15). He represents all humanity, and men by faith enter into his death on their behalf. The ancient's view of group solidarity whereby the act of one represents the entire body of persons provides the background for understanding this reference. Christ's faith and obedience become man's when he is in union with him.

There are numerous other passages which refer to Christ's death for sin and sinners in the NT (e.g. Rom. 6:4; I Tim. 1:15; I Pet. 1:2; 2:21-24). Sometimes the idea of his achieving on man's behalf a victory over evil cosmic forces is present (Col. 2:15); again it is to ransom men (I Tim. 2:6); yet again it is "to redeem us from all iniquity" and to produce purified people "zealous for good deeds" (Tit. 2:14).

In the Gospel of John the author sees the Crucifixion as Jesus' special "hour" (7:30; 8:20; 12:23-27; 13:1; 17:1); it is the occasion not of defeat but of his glorification (12:28; 13:31). As a result he will draw all men to himself (12:32). Like a seed that falls into the ground and dies in order to bear fruit (12:24), so his death will bear an abundant harvest. Indeed, if he is "lifted up," whoever believes in him shall have eternal life (3:14-15). Against the background of the paschal lamb (Exod. 12:21-27) and also of the suffering servant (Isa. 53:12) John the Baptist points out Jesus as the "Lamb of God, who takes away the sin of the world!" (1:29, 36). And, as a final indication of the meaning of his death for sin, Jesus is represented as being crucified at the very hour when the paschal lamb is being killed for the Passover meal (19:14).

In Heb. the relationship between Jesus' death and forgiveness is delineated with a studied deliberateness. In his crucifixion the author sees the provision of a "better" sacrifice, one that supersedes that which was based on the old covenant (8:6). Jesus is both the eternal high priest and the sacrifice who offered, not the blood of goats and calves, but his own instead. And this brings a "better" salvation,

for if the sprinkling of defiled persons with the blood of goats and bulls and with the ashes of a heifer sanctifies for the purification of the flesh, how much more shall the blood of Christ, who through the eternal Spirit offered himself without blemish to God, purify your conscience from dead works to serve the living God (9:13-14).

Christ offered himself (9:25), once and for all (9:26), rather than like the high priest who had to enter the Holy Place on the Day of Atonement yearly.

In the face of these numerous references to the death of Jesus Christ for sin we should focus our thought finally, not on the terms in which this relationship is interpreted as it is presented, but on what lies behind them, viz. the experience of Christians as they contemplated the cross. Here they found life-giving renewal; here the cleansing love of God laid hold of them.

G. Resurrected and Ascended Lord

The NT in its entirety was written within the perspective of the Resurrection. When telling the story of Jesus the gospel writers knew the outcome of the account before they recorded it. In fact it was this outcome that provided the incentive to write. No author in the NT wrote of a dead Jesus. They were so sure of this event that they allowed differences in detail within the record to remain. In one sense the very existence of the NT itself is a witness to the reality of the Resurrection.

It is not the bare fact alone of the Resurrection that concerns the NT authors. Of equal importance is its meaning. Here was an event that was prophesied to occur, said Peter at Pentecost (Acts 2:24-31). It was therefore according to God's purpose. They were witnesses that God had raised him up (Acts 2:32). Paul later also stated that it was God who raised Jesus; he did not raise himself: "For he was crucified in weakness, but lives by the power of God" (II Cor. 13:4). The Resurrection was therefore no less than an act of God.

Not only was Jesus resurrected; he also ascended to heaven (Acts 1:9-11). Henceforth they were to think of him as their living Lord, the exalted "Son of man standing at the right hand of God." Thus Stephen saw him in his vision (Acts 7:55-56). As "Lord," Jesus called forth from his followers an allegiance and dependency all but equal to that which they gave to God. He came to have for them the religious value of God as they looked to him in faith and loyalty.

The NT followers of Jesus regarded his relation to God as utterly unique, unshared by any other. They went so far as to address prayers to him, e.g. when Paul said in Aramaic, "Maranatha," translated as "Our Lord, come" (I Cor. 16:22), and when Stephen prayed while he was being stoned (Acts 7:59). Even so it is not likely that they identified him fully with the being of God. The quotation from Ps. 45:6 which Heb. 1:8 uses in relation to Jesus, the Son, that opens with "Thy throne, O God," should probably be thought of, not as equating Jesus with God, but as pointing to his uniqueness. Similarly, Paul's statement in Rom. 9:5 sounds in the KJV as if he is calling Jesus "God," but the RSV has translated this differently so that it refers to the praising of God.

But although they did not call Jesus God, they did refer to him as "Lord." Some scholars hold that "Lord" as a title came from Hellenistic cult sources and was late in its use, while others see it as early in the life of the church, noting Paul's employment of it in the Aramaic *Maran* ("Our Lord"), mentioned above. The translation of the Hebrew *Adonai* as "Lord" in Jesus' day when referring to God also suggests the possibility of an early Palestinian use of "Lord" when speaking of Jesus. In any case, early or late, Hellenistic or Hebraic, Jesus as *Lord* was both served and worshiped.

It was as resurrected Lord that Jesus sent the Holy Spirit at Pentecost (Acts 2:33). In his victory over death he also overcame cosmic evil forces that were believed to have a hold over men. As Lord he "disarmed the principalities and powers and made a public example of them, triumphing over them in him [God]" (Col. 2:15). Again it was as resurrected Lord that he gave the great commission to evangelize all nations, promising to be with them until the end of the age (Matt. 28:19-20). Thus an eschatological dimension is present.

In addition to being known as "Lord," Jesus is referred to in numerous ways and by various titles in the NT. Briefly, he is called rabbi (John 3:2), master (Mark 9:5), prophet (Mark 8:28), teacher (John 13:14), Messiah (John 1:41), servant (Acts 3:26), Son of man (Mark 8:38), savior (Acts 5:31), mediator (I Tim. 2:5), high priest (Heb. 4:14), judge (Acts 10:42), Son of God (Gal. 2:20), Word (John 1:1), and King of kings and Lord of lords (Rev. 19:16). These are more than names and titles; they represent what he does for men.

H. Present Through the Spirit and Bringing Eternal Life

The full presentation of Jesus Christ in the NT is, as we have seen, many-sided. Yet another facet in this interpretation is its teaching that he is not only alive and not only the exalted Lord; he is also present in the Spirit in the Christian fellowship and at work in the lives of his followers bringing them eternal life. He bestowed the Spirit on the church at Pentecost (Acts 2:33), even as he had promised in the Upper Room discourses (John 16:7).

Of particular significance here is the fact that in the coming of the Spirit the church experienced the presence of Jesus himself. The Spirit dwelt within the lives of the Christians, even as Christ (John 14:17-18). He taught them and recalled to their minds the words of Jesus (John 14:26), even revealing to them the future, which during the days of his flesh they were too immature to grasp (John 16:12-13). In addition to this he convinced the world of sin, righteousness, and judgment (John 16:8-11).

There is yet a further aspect to the indwelling of Christ through the Spirit. The Spirit of Jesus and the Holy Spirit, in experience, became one reality. The terms are used interchangeably as Luke describes Paul's guidance on the 2nd missionary journey (Acts 16:6-7). And Paul himself, in explaining the new life in the Spirit, equates the Spirit of Christ, the indwelling Christ, and the Spirit of God:

> But you are not in the flesh, you are in the Spirit, if the Spirit of God really dwells in you. Any one who does not have the Spirit of Christ does not belong to him. But if Christ is in you, although your bodies are dead because of sin, your spirits are alive because of righteousness (Rom. 8:9-10).

In spite of the above references it would be misleading to conclude that Paul actually comes to the position that the Spirit of God and the Spirit of Christ represent a single being. There is still a distinction between them, although to experience each is to experience in that same moment the other. This conclusion should hold even though Paul once says, "The Lord is the Spirit, and where the Spirit of the Lord is, there is freedom" (II Cor. 3:17).

The believing Christian is frequently referred to by Paul as one who is "in Christ." It has been estimated that this expression and its cognates appear

164 times in his writings, without including Col., Eph., I-II Tim., and Tit. To be in Christ is to be united to him both mystically and ethically, a union in which the identity of each is retained. Some have regarded this union as pantheistic absorption, but others conclude that this is not what Paul actually has in mind. It is a mysticism that prenames the "I-Thou" relationship.

The new life "in Christ" is probably to be regarded as a foretaste of the fullness of life that will come at the end of the age. In John it is referred to as eternal life, which Jesus Christ gives here and now to him who believes, but which continues forever (John 3:15-16, 36; 4:14; 6:27, 40, 47, 54; 10:28).

I. CHRIST AND THE CHURCH

In the NT interpretation of Jesus his relation to the church is another basic consideration. The question as to whether before his death he actually founded the church in the sense of establishing it, leaving it a blueprint for organization, and setting up offices and officers should be answered negatively in the light of our data in the NT. The familiar "You are Peter, and on this rock I will build my church" (Matt. 16:18) permits different interpretations. The Roman Catholic view stresses the person of Peter in his office as the foundation of the church, while the Protestant emphasis is usually placed on the witness of Peter that Jesus is the Christ, which he had just made, as being the foundation.

The resurrection fellowship that resulted in the drawing together of those who had known this experience should probably be pointed out as the dynamic basis of their first union as a worshiping community in Christ. This was welded into a closer communion as the Spirit entered its life at Pentecost, empowering it for its future. And, as we have already noted, Peter's sermon on this occasion reflects the view of the church that Jesus, now raised up by God, had sent the Spirit to them (Acts 2:33).

Following the account of Pentecost in Acts we are given a picture of the early church as it discovers itself and learns step by step what it is to do. At one point certain church officers are selected to administer the care of the poor and widows, thus freeing the apostles to bear their witness in preaching (6:1-6). At another the new community in Christ faces its responsibility toward Gentiles in admitting them to its fellowship, even to considering the terms of admission (Acts 10-11; 15). Still later a deliberately planned missionary venture is undertaken under the urging of the Holy Spirit (Acts 13:1-4). All this is an account of the enlargement of the life of the church.

Paul, who became a part of this development and spearheaded its first major missionary thrust, in time undertook to phrase an understanding or doctrine of the church as he wrote to the new communities that had come into existence through his missionary preaching. Thus a more doctrinal conception of the church was formalized.

Paul understood the church as "the body of Christ" (I Cor. 12:27). This refers, not simply to an aggregation or association of individual parts, but to an organic entity which is metaphysically as real as an individual existence is real. The solidarity here is mystical and spiritual, to be sure, but no less genuine.

To the extent that the church is regarded as an entity, the body of Christ, it may be said to be an extension of the person of Christ. And yet Christ is more than the church. Just as individuals within the church maintained their individual existence, so Christ maintained his own identity apart from the church. While some would make the identification complete, it seems more accurate to interpret Paul's view as outlined above, even though it involves a paradox. The conception is mystical and Paul grasps it intuitively. He does not spell it out completely.

Again, Paul refers to Christ as the head of the body, the church (Col. 1:18). As its head he is its most important member, giving direction to the whole. He has an organic relationship to the church in this sense. To inquire how he could be the body and the head also at one and the same time is to press for a logic that goes beyond the nature of Paul's thought here. Fact precedes formulation; actually it directs it, but it is not always possible to be wholly logical in such instances.

Paul also regards Christ as the indwelling divine presence within the church, thinking of it in this sense as the temple of God (II Cor. 6:16). In addition he establishes a new covenant for the church, regarding it as the new people of God (II Cor. 5:17; Gal. 6:15; cf. I Pet. 2:9-10).

J. THE RETURN OF CHRIST

The return of Christ is usually referred to as the Parousia or sometimes as his Second Coming. That in the NT he was expected to return soon after his resurrection and ascension is a widely accepted conclusion by scholars. Pentecost itself was regarded as an eschatological event that looked toward the last days. Jesus had sent the Spirit; he would return to bring to its fullness the ecstatic life of the New Age. Even the Lord's Supper was anticipatory of his return, proclaiming "the Lord's death until he comes" (I Cor. 11:26).

Paul seems to have expected the return of Jesus Christ within his own lifetime. This hope provides a background for his advice concerning marriage (I Cor. 7:26, 29-31). Within an end-of-time perspective marriage did not seem to Paul to be as necessary as otherwise. In his later writings he does not give the return the same emphasis in his thought, but he does not surrender it altogether as a misleading hope. Col. 3:4 and Phil. 3:20-21 are references to it. The latter in particular reveals Paul's outlook:

> But our commonwealth is in heaven, and from it we await a Savior, the Lord Jesus Christ, who will change our lowly body to be like his glorious body, by the power which enables him even to subject all things to himself.

It is clear above that the Parousia is not simply a return to the days of Jesus' ministry but an eschatological establishment of the kingdom. At this time "God's righteous judgment will be revealed" (Rom. 2:5). The "things now hidden in darkness" will be brought to light, as will "the purposes of the heart" (I Cor. 4:5). Men will be judged, all men, at this time as they stand "before the judgment seat of Christ" (II Cor. 5:10). He will be acting in his capacity as Lord "both of the dead and of the living" (Rom. 14:9).

Paul usually does not draw pictures of this final

event by way of describing the nature of Jesus' return. In his earlier letters (I Thess. 4:13-18; II Thess. 2:1-12) he presents some description, but such attempts are given up in his later writings. He is not like the typical apocalyptists in this regard. The Thessalonian portrayals involve the rising of those already "dead in Christ" first of all, followed by a meeting with him in the air of those who are alive. They also speak of a restraining power that at present is holding back the events which must precede it.

The historical question whether Jesus himself anticipated his return is not the issue in this present discussion. His followers believed that he did, and there are numerous references to it in the Synoptic Gospels. The 4th Gospel stresses instead the present return of Jesus in the Spirit as a fact of personal experience (John 14:16-22). The major references to the return of Jesus in the Synoptics are found in the 3-fold apocalyptic tradition of Mark 13; Luke 21; Matt. 24. In their present form these chs. probably represent the use of earlier Jewish apocalyptic materials into which words of Jesus have been interspersed. From our standpoint, however, the question is not whether Jesus spoke them as reported but the fact that the NT attributes them to him as his own views.

References to the return of Jesus are found in other places in the NT also. Heb. 9:26 implies to the end of the age, and 9:28 more specifically speaks of Christ's appearing "a second time . . . to save those who are eagerly waiting for him." Jas. indicates that "he is soon to return" (5:7) and that as the Messiah he is the Judge who is already "standing at the doors" (5:9). II Pet. is much concerned with urging this belief also, even attempting to encourage those who assert that there has been too great delay by pointing out that "with the Lord one day is as a thousand years, and a thousand years is as one day" (3:8).

Finally Rev. makes the return of Jesus its chief concern, expecting it to take place shortly (1:1; 22:7, 10, 20). It is associated with the overthrow of evil men and nations (19:11-21), the final judgment (20:11-15), and the beatific blessing of the faithful in a new heaven and a new earth (21:1-22:5).

K. Christ Reigns in an Eternal Kingdom

The NT is interested in time as a part of its view of history. There were the events before the advent of Jesus and there were the events after his coming. These latter looked toward an end-time; there was thus an eschatological perspective within the purview of the church. Not only would Jesus Christ return (Mark 13:26; Luke 21:27; Matt. 24:30); he would return as Lord, the role which his followers had assigned to him and in terms of which they were related to him since the Resurrection.

As a part of this expectation Paul saw a universal acclaim of Jesus as Lord. God had given him a name above all other names. Therefore in worship and recognition "every knee should bow, in heaven and on earth and under the earth, and every tongue confess that Jesus Christ is Lord, to the glory of God the Father" (Phil. 2:10).

Before such universal acclaim can be realized there will be the overthrow of evil men and nations referred to in the previous section when Christ has put all enemies under his feet. Then even Christ himself shall become subject to God, "that God may be everything to everyone" (I Cor. 15:28). In both this passage and the previous one it is God who ultimately reigns as supreme at the same time that Christ reigns with him. It is in Christ that God wins the victory. Although Christ is a divine being, the ultimate unity is found in God. It was from such convictions as this that the doctrine of the Trinity developed.

The reign of Christ is not a solitary experience as the NT depicts it. Those who are his followers reign with him. This is expressed with particular pointedness in II Tim., where the author writes in what almost appears to be a credal formula with liturgical overtones, perhaps baptismal:

If we have died with him, we shall also live with him;
if we endure, we shall also reign with him;
if we deny him, he also will deny us;
if we are faithless, he remains faithful.
(II Tim. 2:11-13.)

Rev. has numerous references to the triumphant company of the redeemed who share in Christ's reign. Here we see great multitudes beyond our power to enumerate "from every nation, from all tribes and peoples and tongues." Clothed in white, they stand before the throne of God and before the Lamb crying, "Salvation belongs to our God who sits upon the throne, and to the Lamb [Christ]!" (7:9-10).

In addition to this, Rev. interrupts the progress of judgment to introduce a millennial reign of Christ with the martyrs. These are "priests of God and of Christ" (20:4-6). Millennial periods of high blessing are also found in Persian and Egyptian thought, but they are often sensuous in their representation, while that of Rev. is highly moral and spiritual, centering as it does in Christ. The martyrs have their day of glory while all history awaits the final consummation.

It is in the new heaven and the new earth of this same apocalypse, however, where we see the eternal reign of Christ with his own depicted in its most glowing tones. After an elaborate description of the external aspects of the new Jerusalem (21:5-21), we are given the inner aspects of its life (21:22-22:5). There is no temple because all is temple, the temple of the Lord God the Almighty and the Lamb. There is no night there; it is forever day since God is its light and the Lamb is its lamp. Here those in Christ shall reign with him as they worship him "for ever and ever."

For Further Study: John Knox, *Christ the Lord,* 1945. A. E. J. Rawlinson, *The NT Doctrine of the Christ,* 1949. Rudolf K. Bultmann, *Theology of the NT,* tr. Kendrick Grobel, 2 vols., 1951, 1955. Floyd V. Filson, *Jesus Christ the Risen Lord,* 1956. Archibald M. Hunter, *Introducing NT Theology,* 1958. John Knox, *The Death of Christ,* 1958. Charles M. Laymon, *Christ in the N.T.,* rev. ed., 1958. Oscar Cullmann, *The Christology of the NT,* tr. Shirley C. Guthrie and Charles A. M. Hall, 1964. Articles: "Jesus Christ," F. C. Grant in *IDB,* vol. 2. "Christology," F. D. Gealy in *IDB,* vol. I. "The Gospel in the N.T.," R. H. Strachan in *IB,* vol. 7. "The Life and Ministry of Jesus," Vincent Taylor in *IB,* vol. 7.

THE KINGDOM OF GOD
IN THE NEW TESTAMENT

G. W. H. LAMPE

The phrase "kingdom of God," or its reverential paraphrase "kingdom of heaven," appears often in the gospels but is relatively rare elsewhere in the NT. Nor is it a common expression in the OT, though it acquires some importance in the later canonical books and in late Judaism. Nowhere is any precise definition of it offered, and even the inherent ambiguity of the meaning of "kingdom" is usually not explicitly clarified. According to the context it may cover a wide range of meaning, including "sovereignty," "kingship," "exercise of royal authority," "reign," "territory ruled by a king."

The NT writers give the impression that they assume the term is familiar to their readers. In the light of its rarity outside the gospels this may suggest that it was deeply rooted in the earliest Christian tradition because it actually was found in the teaching of Jesus. If so, it could well be alluded to by the evangelists and occasionally by other early Christian writers as a term which would present no puzzle to the reader. For us, however, the fact that the phrase is used without precise explanation, that it can embrace a wide range of meaning, and that its content is by no means uniform in the NT means that in every instance its significance has to be inferred from its immediate context and from what can be discovered about the characteristic usage of the author.

I. THE OLD TESTAMENT BACKGROUND

Yahweh as King. In the OT God is frequently spoken of under the imagery of kingship. Yahweh is King of Israel. He is the Lord who chose his people by an act of sovereign grace, requires from them obedience to the laws which he has decreed, and can be relied on to protect and champion them against foes and oppressors (Num. 23:21; cf. Deut. 33:5).

Israel is marked out from other nations, according to the Deuteronomic tradition in I Sam. 12:12, by the fact that Yahweh exercises kingship over the people directly and uniquely; hence the demand by the nation for an earthly king is almost an act of apostasy. On the other hand, in the tradition which emphasizes the covenant with David, God's rule is mediated through the Davidic monarch. He exercises the divine sovereignty as one who has been chosen to "sit upon the throne of the kingdom of the LORD over Israel" (I Chr. 28:5).

The Future Divine Rule. God's reign over Israel is a present reality. His rule is everlasting (Exod. 15:17-18), and it is exercised from his temple in the midst of his people. It is there that Isaiah is granted his vision of Yahweh seated upon his throne. Yet his royal glory transcends the earthly sanctuary; he is revealed to the prophet as the King who is Lord of the heavenly hosts (Isa. 6:5). This transcendence implies both God's providential ordering of history and his judgment on Israel's human kings (I Kings 22:19). Yet the sovereignty of God is also—and this becomes ever more strongly emphasized—an object of future hope. This is necessarily so, since it is not yet acknowledged by the other nations and even in Israel its full authority, with its accompanying blessings, is frustrated by the people's faithlessness and disobedience.

Thus the kingdom of God in the sense of God's reign becomes the content of Israel's eschatological hope, i.e. the hope of an end to the present age and the inauguration of an age of blessing and the fulfillment of God's promises that will bring restoration and renewal for the afflicted and downtrodden (Mic. 4:6-7).

The 2nd Isa. (52:7) sees the future in a foreshortened perspective. The imminent deliverance from the Exile is to inaugurate the reign of God. The announcement of the approaching redemption of Jerusalem is described in terms of bringing good news, and the content of the good news is "peace" and "salvation." Here is a fundamentally important passage for the understanding of the meaning of the kingdom of God in the NT. It is echoed in Mark's account of the opening of Jesus' proclamation of the near approach of the kingdom (Mark 1:15) and in the association in other NT passages of salvation, peace, and joy as the effects of the reign of God.

God's Universal Rule. Hopes such as these unite with a deepening realization of the implications of God's present rule over Israel to enable the prophets and psalmists to acknowledge God as King of the whole world. The redeemer of Israel is no less than the universal Creator (cf. Isa. 43:14-15). The King of Israel is the first and the last, beside whom there is no God (Isa. 44:6), the everlasting King, the Lord of the nations and the Creator who established the world by his wisdom (Jer. 10:7, 10). Mal. 1:14 presses this universalism so far as to assert that the name of God, as a great King, is actually feared among the foreign nations while it meets with profanation in Israel.

The thought of the universal sovereignty of God in the realms of nature and human history is esp. prominent in the pss.

Ps. 146:6-9 sums up the effects of God's everlasting reign thus: He keeps faith forever, executes justice for the oppressed, gives food to the hungry, sets the prisoners free, opens the eyes of the blind, lifts up those who are bowed down, loves the righteous, watches over the strangers, supports the widow and the orphan, and brings the way of the wicked to ruin. This is perhaps the fullest statement in the OT of what it means to say that Yahweh is King, and it ranks with Isa. 52:7 as a key to the significance of the kingdom of God as this was proclaimed by Jesus in word and in action. At the same time it is to be noted that the pss. sometimes address God as king in a more personal and individual way; the God who is Israel's King and the Creator-King of the universe may also be addressed in private devotion as "my King" (Pss. 5:2; 84:3; 145:1; cf. Ecclus. 51:1; Tobit 13:6, 10, 15).

The Word "Kingdom" in OT and Apoc. In all the passages so far discussed God is called King or is said to reign. In the light of these the meaning of the few passages which speak of God's "kingdom" becomes clearer. They occur in the later OT books. Ps. 22:28 expresses the thought of God's rule over all the nations and the worship of him by the entire world. Ps. 103:19 similarly speaks of his supremacy over the universe, and Ps. 145:11-13 of his providential care, justice, and mercy. Justice and mercy are also the characteristics of his kingly rule in Tobit 13:1-2; omnipotent sovereignty and righteousness in Dan. 4:34-35, 37.

Thus in the OT the kingdom (i.e. the rule or sovereignty) of God denotes his almighty power, ordering the created world and establishing within it righteousness and justice, the vindication of his people, and mercy and deliverance for the fallen and the oppressed. Though his kingly rule is everlasting, its full manifestation belongs to the day when God will reveal his glory in saving Israel:

> Then the eyes of the blind shall be opened,
>   and the ears of the deaf unstopped;
> then shall the lame man leap like a hart,
>   and the tongue of the dumb sing for joy.
>   (Isa. 35:5-6b.)

The Alexandrian Judaism of Wisd. Sol. adds 2 further concepts foreign to the canonical OT: the equation of the kingdom of God with the knowledge of God's holy things (10:10) and the thought of God's reigning over the souls of the righteous in the life hereafter (3:8). In the former passage God's kingdom means the sphere of his self-revelation. Its identification with knowledge plays little part in NT thought. The transposition of the corporate hope of Israel into terms of individual life after death becomes more important and leads to the later Christian tendency to identify the kingdom of God with "heaven." A combination of the corporate and the individual is characteristic of apocalyptic (see "The Apocalyptic Literature," pp. 1106-09), with its concern about the destiny of men in the world to come and its hope for the manifestation of God's universal reign in the new world which will be inaugurated

when Satan has been destroyed and sorrow and evil abolished (cf. Assumption of Moses 10:1).

Late Judaism lays more stress on the personal and individual aspects of the kingdom of God than we commonly find in the OT. The term itself is relatively rare in the rabbinic literature. It occurs in the context of the hope of the age to come, but also in that of the acceptance by converts of the obligations of Judaism. To accept the yoke of the kingdom of God is to accept the Jewish faith; indeed it is to recite the Shema (Deut. 6:4-5) and thus to submit to the law. The kingdom is thus an object of present decision: the choice of receiving or rejecting the divine sovereignty.

II. The Kingdom of God in Mark

In the light of this background we can approach the meaning of the kingdom of God in the gospels. Here too it signifies God's reign of righteousness and of salvation for his people. Its effects are the blessings of deliverance from oppression by the devil and from sin, so that forgiveness is of central importance, and of healing and restoration. It is the object of eschatological hope—i.e. it is to be manifested in its completeness at the end of history— and thus is equivalent to the age to come, the final age of blessedness. Yet individuals, and the group of Jesus' followers, are called within the present age to enter it or receive it, through faith and obedience. This is made possible because Jesus stands in such a relation to it that men's response to him is decisive for their entry into it. The future kingdom is already being presented to men, challenging them to a decisive choice, in the mission of Jesus through which the effects of the kingdom are being made present by anticipation.

To determine which of these 2 interrelated aspects predominates in any particular passage is extremely difficult, for in the nature of the case the eschatological concept and the recognition that the kingdom has already begun to manifest its effects in the mission of Jesus overlap and are held together. Furthermore it is impossible to determine whether any particular passage reflects the meaning which Jesus himself gave to the term. We can do no more than recognize that certain passages about the kingdom in the gospels clearly reflect the situation of the post-Resurrection church. This is especially true of the evangelists' explanations of certain parables of the kingdom which may have been intended to convey a different meaning. Accordingly the viewpoint of the evangelist is a vital factor in interpreting each passage, and we must consider the presentation of the kingdom of God by each of them in turn. Since according to the most widely accepted critical view Mark was the earliest and Matthew and Luke used his gospel and a 2nd source known as Q (see "The Literary Relations Among the Gospels," pp. 1129-35) we begin with Mark.

Jesus' Proclamation of the Gospel. The opening of Jesus' ministry in Mark is summed up thus: "Jesus came into Galilee preaching the gospel [good news] of God, and saying, 'The time is fulfilled, and the kingdom of God is at hand; repent, and believe in the gospel'" (1:14-15). The proclamation of good news recalls Isa. 40:9, where the message is of the coming of Yahweh with power to rescue his people and as a shepherd to tend his flock, i.e. to exercise kingly rule over Israel. It is also reminiscent of Isa. 52:7, where the good news is of peace, salvation, and the coming reign of God as King, and of Isa. 61:1, where the prophet is sent to announce good news of healing, release, comfort, and the restoration of Israel as God's people.

The "good news" is that the manifestation of God's rule on the plane of human history is no longer merely an object of eschatological hope. The future age of blessedness has drawn near. The meaning of the Greek verb translated "is at hand" has been much discussed; it has been interpreted by some to mean "has arrived" in this passage. This is unlikely to be correct; for it normally (perhaps always) has the meaning "approach" rather than "arrive," as shown by the fact that Matthew can ascribe the same proclamation to John the Baptist (Matt. 3:2). The kingdom is announced, not as having actually come, but as being imminent and about to dawn.

This is "the good news of God." A fairly strongly supported variant reading is "the good news of the kingdom of God." This reading is probably due to assimilation to the text of Matt. 4:23. Nonetheless Matthew in expanding, as he probably has, this passage of Mark interprets his phrase "the good news of God" rightly. It is good news of the kingdom of God, for the message is that the kingdom is imminent. If Mark 1:1-4 implies that John's proclamation of a baptism of repentance was the beginning of the gospel, then this implies also that the imminence of the kingdom demands repentance with a view toward remission of sins. The same demand is made by Jesus (Mark 1:15); the near approach of God's kingdom means that men must respond with repentance and with faith in the good news.

"The time is fulfilled" means that, though the kingdom has not yet arrived, it is now at hand. Its approach is directly related to Jesus' own person, as Mark shows in his subsequent treatment of the content of the good news. Jesus is not merely a prophet who announces the kingdom's imminent coming. His mission is to bring men into that relationship to God (of faith and repentance) which the coming kingdom demands. This is effected through a relationship of faith and discipleship toward himself. Insofar as the kingdom meets with this response its coming is anticipated. Jesus is not merely its messenger; he is also the agent through whom God is already beginning to make his future rule effective in the present time. He is the bearer and communicator of the kingdom itself and not merely of an announcement about it.

Jesus' Mission. What this kingdom means Mark soon goes on to show, but not until he has related the call of the first disciples to follow Jesus and be made fishers of men (1:16-20). Thus he indicates that it is by being brought into a personal relationship with Jesus that men are enabled to respond with faith and repentance to the near approach of the kingdom. The meaning of the kingdom is then disclosed in the unfolding of the course of Jesus' mission.

Jesus teaches with an authority which amazes his hearers by its contrast with scribal expositions (1:21-22). This authority is demonstrated (1:27) in a series of works of power in which Jesus, as "the Holy One of God" (i.e. consecrated, like a prophet or like Aaron, Ps. 106:16; cf. the prophet anointed with God's Spirit in Isa. 61:1), subdues demons (1:24-27, 32, 34, 39), raises up the sick (1:31), heals diseases (1:34), and cleanses a leper (1:42). In this work of healing and exorcism the expected blessings of God's future reign are beginning to appear. They are to be found in the rescue from demonic foes rather than in the ancient hope of deliverance from national enemies. The series of works of power accompanied by preaching (1:38-39; 2:2) culminates in the declaration to a paralytic of that forgiveness of sins which is the prerogative of God but which the Son of man has authority to exercise on earth (2:1-12). The paralyzed man's spectacular arising and walking is a confirmatory sign which causes the crowd to glorify God for the advent of a new state of affairs never before experienced.

Response to the Kingdom. The kingdom has not yet, however, come in its full manifestation, for it is at present only partly accepted with faith. It also partly meets with rejection and hostility. Hence the mission of Jesus presents men with a crisis of decision and it is on their attitude to him that the coming of the kingdom depends. Therefore the next section of Mark is chiefly concerned with the growing conflict between Jesus and official Judaism.

Opposition has already found expression in the indignant reaction of the scribes to Jesus' assumption of authority to forgive sins; their charge of blasphemy anticipates the final verdict of the sanhedrin (2:7; 14:63-64). It develops when the call to follow Jesus is addressed to and answered by tax gatherers and sinners and when Jesus makes it clear that his mission is not to call the righteous but sinners (2:14-17). Opposition to Jesus further develops when his presence as the bridegroom is shown to require a total renewal of the old religion and its practices (2:18-22) and when this renewal is declared to involve a changed attitude toward the law, esp. in regard to the sabbath (2:23-3:5). That this opposition culminates in the plotting of Pharisees and Herodians to destroy Jesus (3:6) indicates that the full manifestation of the kingdom must lie beyond the Cross. The other side of the conflict is seen at the same time in the coming of great crowds to Jesus, his healing of many, his recognition as Son of God by evil spirits, and his choice of the 12 so that they may share in his mission of proclamation and his authority to cast out demons (3:14-19).

This calling of the 12 indicates that, though the proclamation of God's good news and the application to men of the healing power of God's sovereign rule are uniquely the work of Jesus, he will give a share in this work to his disciples. It also suggests that Jesus is creating a community to be the sphere in which and through which the coming kingdom is to begin to operate—a community of those who have faith, who carry out God's will, and who receive the blessings of his rule. The significant number 12 suggests that Israel is to be reconstituted on the basis of Jesus' call to discipleship, beginning with 12 new "patriarchs." Such a society is the true family of Jesus (3:34-35), as opposed to his actual relatives, who apparently try to deflect him from his mission (3:31-32) and may even consider him to be mad (3:21). Rejection of his authoritative proclamation is carried even further by the Jerusalem scribes; they ascribe his exorcisms to the devil. Yet his works prove that Satan is being defeated and that to attribute them to the devil is the unforgivable blasphemy against the Holy Spirit (3:22, 27-29).

Jesus' Teaching. At this point Mark, who has often mentioned the teaching of Jesus, gives some information about its content. It is in the form of parables about the proclamation of the kingdom and the conflicting responses which it evokes. As Mark interprets the tradition, the parables are intended to conceal the truth from all except those who are "about him, with the twelve" (4:10-12), i.e. the Christian society. They thus register the fact that the rejection of Jesus is divinely determined: his disciples have been given "the secret of the kingdom of God," while the rest have been made blind toward it in accordance with God's purpose.

The Parable of the Sower. The disciples, however, have been granted insight into the mystery, i.e. the revelation of what has hitherto been God's secret. This secret is that in the mission of Jesus the eschatological kingdom of God is beginning to take effect; God's plan for bringing in his kingdom is known to them. Mark 4:11 suggests that the author understands the parable of the sower to be about the kingdom of God. If so, he probably equates the present operation of the kingdom with the preaching of the word of the gospel (4:14-20) and its acceptance by faith. Vss. 17-19 indicate that Mark has in mind the effective spreading of the gospel in the church's post-Resurrection mission. His thought thus resembles Luke's reinterpretation of a nationalist concept of the kingdom in terms of the worldwide witness of the church to Jesus as the glorified Lord (Acts 1:6-8). If this is correct, Mark's interpretation of the parable is certainly not derived from Jesus himself. But, even so, the original point of the parable may not have been very dissimilar, viz. that despite opposition and indifference the mission of Jesus will be fruitful in bringing the kingdom to men. What the kingdom means is intended in God's ultimate purpose to be made known to all men (4:21-23), though whether through the disciples' preaching or at the return of Jesus is not clear. The important thing is that the disciples should listen to the parables with an insight which will bring them reward (4:24-25).

The Parable of the Growing Seed. The parable of the seed growing secretly (4:26-29) is announced as a parable of the kingdom of God, but its meaning is obscure. In the first part of it the emphasis lies on the fact that the harvest grows without any need for activity by the farmer. The meaning may be that God, having planted the seed of the kingdom through the mission of Jesus, will bring it to fruition when the time is ready, despite all the apparent failure of men to respond. In the 2nd part the farmer's seeming neglect of the sown seed gives place to instant and decisive action at the moment when the grain is ripe. God will bring in his kingdom without fail at the right time. Joel 3:13, which is alluded to in the description of the reaping (vs. 29), refers in its context to God's eschatological judgment of the nations. Here it may suggest that

the final manifestation of the kingdom will involve the ultimate judgment.

The Parable of the Mustard Seed. A somewhat similar point is made by the parable of the mustard seed (4:30-32). It begins with the statement that the kingdom of God is like a seed of mustard, but there is in fact no direct comparison. The meaning probably is that, just as the very small seed turns into a great plant, so the obscure and seemingly insignificant seed of the kingdom, implanted by the mission of Jesus, will in due time bring about the kingdom's full realization. There is an OT allusion here which may be significant; the reference in vs. 32 to the branches and the birds is reminiscent of Dan. 4:21 and perhaps is intended to indicate that the nations of the whole world will be brought within God's rule.

Wonder Deeds and Miracles. Mark 4:35-41 tells of Jesus' performing an act characteristic of God as Creator-King. He rebukes the wind and "muzzles" the sea (cf. e.g. Pss. 89:10; 104:7; Isa. 51:9-10). The power of Jesus corresponds to the completeness of his faith in God, in contrast to the disciples' lack of trust. He is thus by faith the agent of God's sovereign rule even over the elements which typify unruly chaos.

In the same way the episode of the Gerasene demoniac (5:1-20) illustrates Jesus' power as the agent of the mercy and beneficence of God the Savior-King. This is made clear in the deliberate equation of "how much the Lord has done for you" with "how much Jesus had done for him" (5:19-20).

To recognize the wisdom of Jesus in his words and his works of power—2 more of which are related in 5:25-43, the 2nd being no less than a raising of the dead—as being the wisdom and power of God operating through him is virtually equivalent to acknowledging him as the bearer of God's kingdom. This is what the people of Nazareth fail to do (6:2-6). They do not discern the source of his authority, because they lack the faith necessary to perceive the sovereign rule of God and accept it.

The Future Kingdom. In the accounts of the miraculous feedings another theme related to the kingdom is introduced and developed: the anticipation by Jesus of the eschatological feast—an image under which the future age of salvation and the reign of God has already been depicted (e.g. Isa. 25:6). The feedings of the 5,000 in 6:30-44 and 4,000 in 8:1-10 should therefore, if rightly understood, be the key to the meaning of Jesus' mission (8:17-21). At Caesarea Philippi what was hinted at in the saying that the bridegroom would be taken away (2:20), in the conspiracy by Jesus' opponents (3:6), and in the death of the forerunner (6:16-29) is at last made clear. The mission of Jesus must involve the suffering and death of the Son of man, and to follow him means taking up the cross (8:31-35). If men are ashamed of Jesus and his words in the present evil time, the Son of man will be ashamed of them when he comes in his Father's glory as the agent of God's judgment—i.e. the final vindication of the righteous (8:38).

This coming of the Son of man in glory for the final judgment, which is to be the outcome of the paradoxical suffering and death of the Messiah–Son of man in the present age, is virtually equated with the coming of the kingdom of God in power, i.e. in its full and final manifestation (9:1). This coming of the kingdom will be within the lifetimes of some of those present. Mark no doubt believed in its near advent, and there is no good reason to deny that Jesus may have done the same. It is therefore unnecessary to suppose that Mark identifies the "coming in power" with the Transfiguration or the Resurrection. Neither should it be concluded that the tense of the participle "has come" implies that Mark is thinking of the speedy conversion of individuals who will then realize that the kingdom did actually come in Jesus' mission though they did not recognize it at the time. No such realization could be described as the coming of the kingdom with power or as the final judgment.

A prediction that the kingdom will come soon in its fullness does not contradict the ignorance of Jesus about the precise time of the end (13:32-37). It is true, however, that the Transfiguration (9:2-8) is related to this passage. It is an anticipation in the present time of the future glory of the Son of man, to which the Cross is the appointed way (9:9-13).

Receiving the Kingdom. Yet the kingdom of God may be already "received" in the present age, as the obscure and perhaps composite narrative of the blessing of the children indicates (10:13-16). To receive it one must have the receptiveness of a child who lacks self-consciousness and is content to accept what is given, for the kingdom is a gift and not an achievement by man. The child here typifies the true disciple. To be willing to receive the kingdom is to enter it.

Some see a turning point in Mark's presentation of the idea of the kingdom of God at Caesarea Philippi. Before Peter's confession there the kingdom is proclaimed as imminent; afterward it becomes a present reality to be taken or entered. But the idea of entering or receiving the kingdom is implicit in the earlier part of Mark; and though the relation of Jesus' coming death to the kingdom becomes clearer from Caesarea Philippi on, Peter's confession of Jesus as Messiah is scarcely a great positive turning point in Mark.

As opposed to disciples who possess the humility and trust of children there stand the rich (10:24) or, as a variant has it, those who trust in possessions. These cannot accept the kingdom as a gift, like children. They cling to the security of possessions and so cannot meet the demand of the kingdom for total self-commitment. Hence it is easier for a camel to go through a needle's eye than for a rich man to enter the kingdom of God which confronts him in the present time in the call and demand of Jesus (10:17-26). Here the kingdom is equivalent to "life." The questioner asks Jesus how he may inherit eternal life, and because he does not have the empty-handed receptiveness of the child-disciple of 10:15, his question evokes the comment, "How hard it will be for those who have possessions to enter the kingdom of God." Eternal life, or the kingdom of God, is then further identified with "being saved," i.e. the attainment of final blessedness, entrance to which is conditional on faith and self-surrender to the present demands of Jesus.

The Christian disciple's sacrifice, not only of property but also of all human ties—Mark is thinking

of the persecuted church of his own day—will be rewarded now by new human relationships in the Christian fellowship and by eternal life in the age to come. This surrender is required for the sake of Jesus and the gospel (10:29); thus a man's response to Jesus determines his relationship to the future kingdom. Indeed in Mark's great stress on the suffering of the Son of man and on Christian leadership as consisting in service and humility (10:32-45) the kingdom is implicitly equated with the future glory of Jesus himself, to be won through giving his life as a ransom for many.

The Last Week. After his exercise of judgment on Jerusalem (symbolized by the fig tree) and on the temple, made possible by faith and prayer (11:12-24), Jesus ascribes his authority to God (11:27-33). Like John's baptism it is "from heaven," for, as Mark has often shown, Jesus is the agent of God's sovereignty. In contrast to the opposition of the Jewish leaders, variously portrayed in 12:1-27, the sincere question of a scribe and his acceptance of the obligation of obedience to the basic principles of the law gain the commendation "You are not far from the kingdom of God" (12:34). True obedience to the law, rightly understood, sets a man in close relationship to God's rule as a present reality. The law may bring one near to the kingdom, but the hypocrisy and shallowness of the lawyers are contrasted with this saving obedience (12:38-40).

Mark 13 speaks of the future glorification of the Son of man and his gathering in of the elect after troubles in which Christian disciples are to share. The kingdom is not explicitly mentioned here, but it is implied, and the glorification of the Son of man is to usher in its sudden and catastrophic manifestation, for which Christians must constantly be on the watch.

This consummation lies beyond the death of Jesus. At the Last Supper the cup of wine is made a sign that his death has a sacrificial character, instituting a covenant or new relationship between God and the disciples, who by sharing in the cup enter this covenant and receive its blessings (14:24). Communion with Jesus in a new covenant relationship to God points forward to the kingdom of God, depicted as the eschatological feast (14:25). It is a pledge that this communion will be renewed and fulfilled when, in consequence of Jesus' sacrificial death, the kingdom of God is manifested in its fullness.

The only remaining allusion to the kingdom of God in Mark is in the description of Joseph of Arimathaea as one who was "looking for the kingdom of God" (15:43). Mark may mean that he was a disciple of Jesus, and Matt. 27:57 so interprets it. The phrase could denote a pious Jew awaiting the age to come and the salvation of Israel, but to Mark the kingdom of God is always associated with the mission of Jesus. Only through that mission does the future kingdom draw near to men in the present age.

III. THE KINGDOM OF GOD IN MATT.

Generally speaking, Matthew reproduces, with certain modifications, the Markan concept of the kingdom of God. He usually prefers, however, the more Jewish-flavored "kingdom of heaven." For him too it is the age to come, already making its blessings apparent in the mission of Jesus and demanding a decisive response from those who encounter Jesus.

It is thus surprising that the opening proclamation of Jesus in Mark (reproduced in Matt. 4:17) is ascribed in identical words to John the Baptist (3:2; cf. Mark 1:15). For Matthew, John is so much the forerunner of Jesus that his mission is virtually part of that of Jesus. He can proclaim the imminence of the kingdom because his essential function is to point to the approach of the "stronger one" who will carry out the divine task of judgment (3:11-12), whom John already knows to be Jesus (3:14). Matthew inserts this proclamation of the kingdom by John in place of Mark's statement that John proclaimed a baptism of repentance for remission of sins. He is ready to describe John's baptism as "for repentance" (3:11), but forgiveness of sins is reserved for Jesus himself to bring about (9:2; 26:28).

Jesus' mission is summed up (4:23) as teaching, proclaiming the good news of the kingdom, and healing every disease and infirmity. At this stage disciples have already been associated with the mission, as in Mark. The 2 aspects of the proclamation of the good news of the kingdom are then elaborated in turn.

The Sermon on the Mount. First is the teaching, collected into the Sermon on the Mount. This begins with a proclamation of the blessings of the age to come, for the poor, the mourners, the meek, the merciful, etc. Two groups are specially assured that the kingdom of heaven, i.e. the age of blessedness, is given to them: the poor in spirit, i.e. those who are humble, not self-seeking, and willing to receive the gift, like Mark's "children" (5:3); and those who, in the church of Matthew's day, suffer persecution for righteousness' sake (5:10).

The whole "sermon" is an exposition of the blessings of the kingdom and the discipleship which it demands. One very difficult passage (5:17-20) sets the kingdom in direct relation to the law. Anyone who practices and teaches the dissolution of the law, even in its least important injunctions, will be called least in the kingdom of heaven; one who does the contrary will be called great in the kingdom of heaven. The kingdom probably here means the final judgment in the age to come. If so, the "great" will mean those who are rewarded at the judgment and the "least" those who are condemned—for the context scarcely permits us to suppose that the kingdom means the age of blessedness and that the great and the least are both admitted to it but at different levels. This interpretation involves giving a different meaning to the phrase "in the kingdom of heaven" from that which it bears in the apparently similar passage, Matt. 11:11. Yet it is preferable to the alternative, which is to take the kingdom of heaven here to mean the community of Jesus' disciples or the Christian church; for the context seems to require an eschatological reference. To enter the kingdom demands a higher righteousness than that of the scribes and Pharisees (5:20). This involves the observance of the law in its most profound and challenging sense, as opposed to the superficial casuistry of Pharisaism (5:21-48).

The Lord's Prayer. The kingdom, though imminent, remains future. The prayer must be "Thy kingdom come" (6:10), for the coming of the kingdom in its fullness still lies within the secret counsel of God. Its coming is associated with God's demonstration to all the world that his name is holy and with his establishment on earth of his sovereign will. These are familiar OT ideas, but "Give us this day our daily bread" (or perhaps "our bread for the morrow," 6:11) may pray for the anticipation in the present age of the eschatological feast in the future kingdom.

These themes are partly echoed in 6:33-34. God's kingdom is to be sought—in prayer and expectation—with a single-minded devotion which is not distracted by self-centered anxieties. This passage is common to Matt. and Luke, but it is characteristic of Matthew that he alone equates the kingdom with God's righteousness, i.e. the manifestation of his righteous will. Thus he brings this saying into line with his inclusion in the Lord's Prayer of the clause "Thy will be done in earth as it is in heaven" and with his insistence that entry into the kingdom is conditional, not on a merely formal acknowledgment of Jesus as Lord, but on the performance of his Father's will (7:21).

The "sermon" ends with a note of Jesus' supreme authority. This is based on the opening of Mark's record of Jesus' mission to proclaim the approach of the kingdom (Mark 1:22). Matthew has given a detailed account of the teaching of Jesus to which Mark alludes only in general terms.

Acts of Power. Matthew now proceeds to describe the other aspect of Jesus' proclamation of the good news of the kingdom (Matt. 4:23)—his work of healing. This he does by reproducing (in a different order) and supplementing Mark 1–2, adding passages about the cost of following Jesus (8:18-22) and about Jesus' power over winds and sea. This section on healing culminates, like the section on teaching, with a note of the supreme authority given to Jesus and thus "to men" (9:8). This expression probably indicates that Jesus' disciples, and thus the church, are associated with him in proclaiming the kingdom through acts of power.

Within this section on the power of Jesus the kingdom of heaven appears as the future age of blessedness (8:11), symbolized by the gathering in of the nations from E and W (cf. Ps. 107:3) to recline at the eschatological feast with the patriarchs of Israel. The Jews, the proper heirs ("sons") of the kingdom, will be excluded through their lack of faith in Jesus (8:10, 12; partly paralleled in Luke).

In 9:9-34 Matthew, like Mark, steadily introduces the theme of conflict with opponents. Then, before the calling and giving of authority to the 12, Matthew repeats in 9:35 the summary of Jesus' mission from 4:23: teaching, proclaiming the good news of the kingdom, and healing. The 12 share this mission: to proclaim that the kingdom of heaven has drawn near and to perform the works in which the age to come is already operative (10:7-15). Their mission involves suffering and persecution; Matthew interprets the instructions given to them in terms of the missionary experience of the church.

In 11:3-5 John the Baptist's question whether Jesus is the coming one is answered by reference to his works of power which fulfill the promise of the age to come (Isa. 29:18-19; 35:5-7; 61:1) and are thus signs that the kingdom is dawning in Jesus' mission. John himself, though greater than any prophet, belongs to the age of expectation; in the kingdom of heaven (here, the age of fulfillment; contrast 5:19) even the least important person is greater than John (11:11). John's work marked the transition from preparation to fulfillment. From his days till now the kingdom of heaven has begun to break in on men with violence, and men of violence, i.e. men of courageous decision and revolutionary outlook, seize on it to win it for their possession. This difficult passage (11:12) might also be rendered "the kingdom . . . suffers violence [at the hands of opponents] and violent men plunder it." This suits the Greek better, and it might be true of the situation in Matthew's day if the kingdom of heaven is here equivalent to the church. But it gives the wrong sense in the context in which Matthew or his source has placed the saying. It is the growing triumph of the new order which is being emphasized, not its oppression by external enemies.

In 12:28 the kingdom of God—not "heaven"; the phraseology of a source may be reproduced—has come into the present time; the age to come is, by anticipation, a contemporary reality because Jesus is here and now casting out demons by the Spirit of God—not, as his opponents suggest, by the devil.

Parables of the Kingdom. Matt. 13 reproduces Mark's parable of the sower and its interpretation. In a striking agreement with Luke against Mark, Matt. 13:11 has, "To you it has been given to know the secrets of the kingdom of heaven," where Mark has "To you has been given the secret . . ."; i.e. Matthew's thought is of a revelation of the conditions or means of receiving the kingdom rather than of a revelation of the fact that the kingdom is operative in Jesus' mission. The seed in the parable is said to be "the word" in Mark; in Luke "the word of God"; in Matt. it is "the word of the kingdom" as the subject of Jesus' proclamation.

In place of Mark's parable of the seed growing secretly Matthew has the parable of the weeds (13: 24-30). It is a parable of the kingdom of heaven and may perhaps have originally referred to the fact that the final separation of those who reject the kingdom from those who accept it will surely come but the ministry of Jesus is not the appointed time. However, Matthew's explanation (13:37-43) focuses attention on the final judgment rather than on its postponement. The "sons of the kingdom" (vs. 38) are not the Jews as in 8:12. They are faithful Christians, who belong to the kingdom just as the unrighteous belong to the devil. At the end of the age the Son of man will cast the unrighteous out of *his* kingdom, but the righteous will shine like the sun in *their Father's* kingdom (vss. 41-43). This unusual passage suggests that the kingdom, the coming age, is to be administered by the Son of man until the judgment is performed, after which it will become the Father's. If so, the thought is parallel to I Cor. 15:24-28.

Matthew then has the parable of the mustard seed (13:31-32), with the same point as in Mark. The parable of the leaven (13:33) also means that the apparently insignificant beginning of the kingdom's advent in Jesus' mission will have a great result.

Though this is so, the kingdom has to be sought out by men, and when found it demands a total response. This is shown in the parables of the hidden treasure and the pearl (13:36-46), in which the kingdom is a present reality to be discovered. However, the parable of the net (13:47-50) speaks of final judgment. The eschatological kingdom involves the separation of the evil from the righteous, which will not happen until the end of the age. Possibly both here and in the parable of the weeds Matthew identifies the kingdom, as the *sphere* of God's rule, with the church and applies the parables to church discipline. The context in Matt., however, is against this supposition. Matthew ends this section with what may be a self-portrait—the "scribe who has been trained for the kingdom of heaven," i.e. who has learned to find the kingdom through discipleship to Jesus (13:52).

The Kingdom and the Church. At Caesarea Philippi (16:13-20) Matthew, unlike Mark, enlarges on Peter's quasi-creedal confession that Jesus is "the Christ, the Son of the living God," as the foundation of the church. To Peter are given the keys of the kingdom of heaven, i.e. he is given authority to admit men into it. This probably means that Peter is entrusted with the leadership of the church's mission, which rests on and spreads abroad the faith which he has been the first to profess. By proclaiming the gospel Peter admits into the future kingdom those who accept it with faith and repentance, and he excludes those who reject the gospel. Admission means forgiveness for sinners; those who are excluded are condemned. Thus Peter has authority to "bind" and to "loose," for the impact of the gospel produces in men positive or negative decisions which will be ratified at the judgment. Peter's mission, like that of Jesus, may bring forgiveness or condemnation (cf. John 20:21-23).

It is possible, however, that "binding" and "loosing" refer to the enactment of, and dispensation from, rules. If so, the passage alludes to church teaching and discipline (cf. 18:18). The kingdom will then be virtually equated with the church as the sphere of God's rule, but this is improbable in the context and in relation to the general concept of the kingdom in Matt.

This section ends with the Markan saying that within the lifetimes of some present the kingdom will be seen to have come, but it is reinterpreted as "until they see the Son of man coming in his kingdom" (16:28), i.e. his coming in glory as the judge. The thought is similar to that of 13:41.

The perplexing episode of the temple tax (17:24-27) apparently means that Jesus and his disciples are sons of God the King, and since secular taxes are not levied on citizens (the "sons" of kings)— the poll tax was levied on provincials—they should be exempt from the tax due to God because they are citizens of his kingdom. Matthew corrects any misunderstandings about this in his exposition of Mark's story of the quarrel of the disciples about who should be the greatest (Matthew adds "in the kingdom of heaven"). He introduces here the lesson from Mark 10:15 that one must become like a child

(Matthew adds "unless you turn," i.e. "are converted") to enter the kingdom (18:3). The quality in children that is to be imitated is humility (18:4).

More Parables of the Kingdom. Matthew's parable of the unmerciful servant (18:23-35) is presented as a parable of the kingdom. Its coming means judgment. Paradoxically this takes the form of forgiveness, which in turn demands a readiness to forgive others; otherwise God's forgiveness will be canceled. The parable echoes the link made in the Lord's Prayer between the future coming of the kingdom and the present forgiveness of offenses.

The addition in Matt. to Mark's saying on divorce (19:10-12) indicates that the demands of the kingdom of heaven may include celibacy. This might refer to the pressing urgency of the missionary task, requiring the surrender of all human ties. More probably the demand relates to the near approach of the end of the age and the dissolution of the institution of marriage (cf. I Cor. 7:29-31).

Matt. 19:14, 23-30 reproduce Mark's sayings about the kingdom belonging to those such as children and the difficulty for the rich to enter it. The parable of the laborers (20:1-16) is another parable of the kingdom. It is given equally to all who respond to the call of Jesus, not in proportion to merit but as a gift of grace. The implication may be that Gentiles are to be admitted on equal terms with Jews. A rather similar point is made in the parable of the 2 sons (21:28-32), though here tax gatherers and harlots enter the kingdom of God (cf. the terminology of 12:28) before Israel's leaders because their faith is greater—they were willing to repent at the summons of John. More difficult is the addition of Matthew, or his source, to Mark's parable of the wicked farmers (21:43). The kingdom of God will be taken from the leaders of Israel and given to a nation that produces its fruits. If the kingdom is something that these leaders already possess (since they are to lose it), it may be equivalent to the covenant with Israel. But though this would fit the figure of the vineyard, Matthew cannot have identified the kingdom with the old covenant. For him the kingdom is future and is anticipated only in the work of Jesus. We should probably paraphrase: "The promise or assurance of the kingdom of God will be taken from you and given to a nation that produces the fruits of repentance and faith [cf. 3:8] which are the condition of receiving it." The nation is probably the true Israel of the Jewish and Gentile church.

The meaning of the above will be rather like that of the wedding feast (22:2-14)—another parable of the kingdom. Those originally invited, who have insulted their king, will be destroyed with their city; the Christian mission brings in all kinds of men, good and bad, to take their place at the eschatological feast, but the new guests must wear the garment of righteousness which repentance procures.

As for the scribes and Pharisees, their self-conceit, inflated through petty legalism (23:3-13), makes them the antithesis of the "poor in spirit" to whom the kingdom belongs (5:3). Hence they incur a "woe" (23:13) which is the reverse of the first beatitude. Their attitude debars them from entering the kingdom, and their legalistic tyranny prevents others

from doing so. They "shut the kingdom of heaven against men," the kingdom here signifying the right relationship that God is beginning to establish with men through Jesus. The universal mission of the church, which is to be completed before the end, is the proclamation of the good news of the kingdom of heaven (24:14, expanding Mark's "gospel"). This mission is thus seen as the continuation of that of Jesus (9:35).

The parable of the 10 virgins (25:1-13) is again a parable of the kingdom, here depicted as the eschatological event which may be delayed but must still be awaited with vigilance and preparation. It is virtually identified with the return of the Son of man (cf. 24:27, 37), here pictured under the ancient imagery of the bridegroom. In 25:34 the kingdom is the eschatological reward which the righteous "inherit," prepared for them from eternity and bestowed on them by the Son of man as king. In this sense it is equivalent to "eternal life" (25:46).

Matthew reproduces Jesus' saying over the cup at the Last Supper (26:29), but he makes him speak of drinking wine, not in the kingdom of God, but, more personally, "in my Father's kingdom." He also characteristically associates the disciples with Jesus' participation in the heavenly feast by adding the words "with you."

IV. THE KINGDOM OF GOD IN LUKE-ACTS

Luke adds certain distinctive emphases to the material which he copies from Mark and to that which he has in common with Matthew. For him the kingdom of God remains the future age of blessedness which is already taking effect in the work of God in Christ. But he lays special stress on this work of God in the post-Resurrection mission of the church. The gospel event comprises the whole period from the birth of the forerunner, John the Baptist, to the unhindered proclamation of the kingdom of God in Rome. The end is not yet; the age of the Spirit in the church has first to be fulfilled, and during this intermediate period the kingdom is preached and its effects are manifested in the apostolic mission.

Jesus' Announcement of His Mission. Like Mark and unlike Matthew, Luke does not include the advent of the kingdom in John's preaching. In a dramatic prologue (4:16-30) to the gospel and Acts he makes Jesus announce his mission in terms of the Spirit-possessed prophet of Isa. 61:1-2. "Good news," "release," "recovering of sight," proclamation of God's "acceptable year"—these are the content of Jesus' mission, and so of the kingdom which his mission signalizes. This is indicated in 4:43, where Jesus declares that he has been sent (i.e. by God; contrast Mark 1:38, "I came out") to proclaim the good news (cf. 4:18) of the kingdom of God "to the other cities also" (besides Capernaum, his headquarters). This phrase may hint at the later extension of the preaching to the world outside Jesus' homeland, just as 4:25-30 foreshadows the rejection of the gospel by Jesus' own nation and its acceptance by Gentiles.

The Kingdom in Luke's Earlier Chs. Explicit references to the kingdom of God are rare in the earlier chs. of Luke. In 6:20 he includes the blessing on the poor—i.e. Matthew's "poor in spirit," the humble and faithful—and in 7:28 the saying that the least in the kingdom is greater than John. In 8:1 he repeats his description (4:43) of Jesus' proclamation of the kingdom of God, and here associates with Jesus in this preaching the 12 and some women who assisted them with funds or provisions. Thus the mission of the post-Resurrection church is foreshadowed, with its ministry of the word and its church offices (cf. Acts 6:1-7).

In the parable of the sower and its explanation (8:4-15) Luke speaks of the "secrets" (plural) of the kingdom as given to the disciples to know (vs. 10; cf. Matt. 13:11; contrast Mark 4:11). For Luke these secrets, i.e. the ways of receiving the kingdom, comprise the hearing of the word of God, which in Luke is represented by the seed in the parable, and the reception of it with faith and assurance—"that they may . . . *believe and be saved*" (vs. 12; cf. vss. 13, 15). Failure to believe is due to the action of the devil (vs. 12) and not, as in Mark 4:12, to Jesus' own purpose in using parables. Luke lays great stress on faith as the means by which salvation is received (cf. 5:34; 7:50; 8:50; 10:52; 17:19; Acts 14:9; 16:31) and on the word of God, both as the message of Jesus about the kingdom (5:1; 8:21; 11:28) and as the preaching of the apostles (frequently in Acts). This is given added emphasis by the setting in this context of the saying that the true family of Jesus are those who hear the word of God and do it (8:21; cf. Mark 3:35; Matt. 12:50).

The Disciples and the Kingdom. In 9:2 the 12 are commissioned to proclaim the kingdom of God and to heal. Here Mark and Matt. have no direct mention of the kingdom, but Mark says that the 12 preached repentance; Luke may interpret this as meaning the proclamation of the kingdom. Here again Luke is looking forward to the apostolic mission to be described in Acts. Teaching about the kingdom of God is made the setting of the feeding of the crowd (9:11), where Mark does not specify the content of the teaching and Matthew mentions healing alone.

In 9:27 Luke has only "before they see the kingdom of God" in place of Mark's "the kingdom of God come with power," and Matthew's "the Son of man coming in his kingdom." Perhaps Luke means that within the lifetimes of some of those present the kingdom will be manifested in the post-Resurrection mission. Every disciple is called to proclaim the kingdom of God (9:60, 62, Luke alone referring to the kingdom). The 70 also are charged to preach that the kingdom "has come near to [lit. "upon"] you" (10:9), where Luke's addition of "upon you" suggests that he thinks of the coming of the kingdom chiefly in terms of men's personal acceptance of it in the hearing of the word. When the word is rejected, on the other hand, it is still true that the kingdom "has come near," but not "upon" the hearers (10:11).

The Holy Spirit. The Lord's Prayer in Luke 11:2-4 has the textual variant "May thy Holy Spirit come upon us and cleanse us" in place of "Thy kingdom come." It has slight manuscript attestation, but it is commented on by Gregory of Nyssa and Maximus Confessor and is at least as old as Marcion, who, however, seems to have read it in place of the pre-

ceding clause. If it should possibly be authentic, Luke may have identified the coming of the kingdom "upon" men with the action on them of the Holy Spirit.

In view of Luke's interest in the inward reception of the kingdom by men it may be significant that 11:52 speaks of the lawyers' having "taken away the key of knowledge," where Matt. has "shut the kingdom of heaven." It is hardly likely, however, that Luke simply identifies the kingdom with knowledge. More probably he means that the scribes, by their legalistic distortion of the true meaning of the Scriptures, have prevented men from understanding that they point to Jesus and the kingdom (cf. 24:27).

In 12:31 Luke speaks in similar terms to Matthew's of the need to seek the kingdom rather than to satisfy earthly requirements, but he adds an assurance that it is the Father's will to give the kingdom to the "little flock" of disciples, i.e. the church (vs. 32). Their response to this must be to acquire heavenly treasure by selling their possessions and giving alms, a theme developed in Acts 2:44-45; etc.

Parables and Sayings. Luke places the parables of the mustard seed and the leaven (13:18-21) in the context of a condemnation of Israel's leaders for their narrow legalism. This may suggest that Luke here comes close to identifying the kingdom with the church, whose growth and transforming power are contrasted with Pharisaic Judaism. It might be said that the church is regarded as the instrument by which the kingdom takes effect. In this context too there stands the picture of the feast in the kingdom to which all nations enter with the patriarchs of Israel, whereas the leaders of Judaism are excluded (13:28-29). The gathering into the kingdom of the outcasts from Israel is also depicted in the parable of the great supper (14:16-24), spoken in reply to the exclamation "Blessed is he who shall eat bread in the kingdom of God!"

More difficult is Luke's use in 16:16 of the saying paralleled in Matt. 11:12-13. Here he clarifies what was implied in 3:3—that John did not proclaim the coming of the kingdom. He belonged to the age of preparation; the preaching of the kingdom is the work of Jesus. Since John's day, by responding to the gospel everyone—for the ultimate scope of the kingdom is universal—is forcing his way into it.

In the following saying, that the law stands in its entirety (16:17), Luke probably means that though John the Baptist belongs to one age and Jesus to another, there is continuity between the 2; the law is not annulled by the gospel, and it does not belong to the "abomination" of Pharisaic legalism (16:15).

The succeeding saying on divorce and adultery (16:18) may mean in this context that, despite the coming of a new order, God's old covenant with Israel stands. God will not abandon his marriage bond with them and leave them to find another god. On any other interpretation the abrupt introduction of a saying on divorce into this context, in which it is irrelevant, would be inexplicable. But 16:17 has seemed to many to be so extreme a statement of the immutability of the whole law, so much at variance with the outlook of Luke, that it has been taken as an ironical saying. As such, however, it too would be out of place in the context.

Still more difficult is 17:21: "The kingdom of God is in the midst of [or "within"] you." The Pharisees ask when the kingdom is coming. This shows their total failure to perceive that it is actually coming, by anticipation, in the words and deeds of Jesus. They are told that it does not come while they are watching for it. When it comes, those who have realized the significance of Jesus' mission will have no doubt where it is to be found; for the kingdom of God is already within the grasp of these Pharisees if they will but accept it.

In 18:24-25 Luke reproduces the saying in Mark about the difficulty for those who have possessions to enter the kingdom. In 18:29 the Markan saying about abandoning family and possessions for the sake of Jesus and the gospel appears in the form "for the sake of the kingdom of God," here equated with the church's mission to preach the kingdom.

Luke is anxious to explain that it is a mistake to suppose that the kingdom's full manifestation was intended to come when Jesus approached Jerusalem (19:11). It is, in fact, still long delayed, as the parable of the pounds indicates (19:12-27; cf. Matt. 25:14-30). Jesus must ascend to heaven to receive his kingdom. Until his return his church has to administer his property through the spreading of the gospel. Meanwhile the leaders of Israel reject the gospel and so refuse to prepare for the return of their king. The result will be the destruction of the nation. Here the kingdom of God is identified with the return and so with the royal glory of Christ. Nevertheless, though delayed, the manifestation of the kingdom will be near when the final woes and the return of the Son of man begin to come about (21:31).

The Apostolic Mission. At the Last Supper Luke makes the actual passover, as well as the Markan cup of wine, a prefiguration of the eschatological feast in the kingdom of God (22:16). Meanwhile the kingdom which the Father has appointed, or covenanted, to Jesus is in turn covenanted to his apostles. They are promised that they will share in the heavenly feast with Jesus and judge the tribes of Israel (22:29). Thus they are associated with his kingdom as being administrators on his behalf (cf. the parable of the pounds), and they fulfill this office through their mission of witness to the end of the earth (Acts 1:6-8), by which a kingdom of Israel, conceived in political terms, is replaced.

This reinterpretation of the kingdom in which the apostles were promised a share is prefaced by the risen Lord's speaking to them of the things concerning the kingdom of God (Acts 1:3). In the remainder of Acts the kingdom of God is the subject of the apostolic preaching, usually in very close association with the proclamation of Jesus as the Messiah whose lordship has been declared by God's act in raising him from the dead. He is both the agent of the kingdom and the object of the faith by which men are brought within the sphere of the kingdom.

Luke mentions this interpretation in connection with the preaching by Philip at Samaria (Acts 8:12), where the kingdom is linked with the "name" of Jesus Messiah, the name being the sign of the lordship of the exalted Christ over the mission of the church on earth. It is also found in Paul's speeches

at Ephesus (Acts 19:8; 20:25) and in conjunction with preaching about Jesus as Messiah by Paul at Rome in the triumphal conclusion of Luke's work (Acts 28:23, 31). One aspect of discipleship seems to strike Luke with particular force: that it is through much tribulation, i.e. persecution, that he and his fellow Christians have to enter the kingdom of God (14:22).

V. THE KINGDOM OF GOD ELSEWHERE IN THE NT

Paul uses the phrase rarely. In Rom. 14:17 the kingdom of God is the new relationship with God established through Christ, into which men enter by faith. This means a righteousness which is God's gift through Christ, peace with God, and the joy which, esp. according to Paul and Luke, is the special characteristic of the presence of the Spirit. This is the sign of the new age and the guarantee that it will be brought to fulfillment at the return. Hence rules about eating and drinking have no relevance to the kingdom. At the present time the kingdom of God is manifested in God's power displayed in the mighty acts which accompany the Christian mission (I Cor. 4:20).

In I Cor. 6:9-10; 15:50; Gal. 5:21, however, the kingdom of God is the future state of blessedness and is equivalent to the resurrection life after death —the reward of the righteous (cf. Eph. 5:5). Flesh and blood cannot participate in the kingdom, for the corruptible body must first be transformed into the "spiritual body." This means participation in the glory of God (I Thess. 2:12), and it is for this that the Christians now endure suffering (II Thess. 1:5).

A similar thought is expressed in Heb. 12:28 in the Christians' assurance of a kingdom that cannot be shaken, and in Jas. 2:5, where the kingdom is the inheritance promised to those who love God. In such passages the kingdom of God is taking on its usual later meaning of the bliss beyond the grave, or "heaven." The 4th Gospel, however, at a deeper level, equates seeing the kingdom of God with entering into eternal life through the new and heavenly birth which is conferred by the indwelling of the Spirit and is focused in Christian baptism (John 3:3-5).

In Rev. the kingdom is the reign of God which is to replace "the kingdom of the world" (11:15), and which is associated with the final manifestation of God's saving power in the overthrow of Satan (12:10).

VI. THE KINGDOM AS THE KINGDOM OF CHRIST

Prominent in the infancy stories is Jesus' messiahship—his reign as the promised son of David (Luke 1:32-33; cf. 2:11) and king of the Jews (Matt. 2:2). Luke is clear that this kingship belongs to Jesus from his birth, though only at his glorification does he receive the full possession of lordship and messiahship (Acts 2:36) and obtain his kingdom. In Mark this theme is absent except for the cry of the crowd at the entry to Jerusalem, "Blessed be the kingdom of our father David that is coming!" (11:10) and the narrative of the trial before Pilate, which turns on an implicit charge of political messianism

1185

(Mark 15:2, 9, 12, 18, 26, 32). Luke is very frank in admitting that Jesus was greeted as king at the entry into the city (19:38) and in giving in full the charge before Pilate that is only implied in Mark: "saying that he himself is Christ a king" (23:2). He is equally concerned to show, however, that the charge failed and that Pilate formally acquitted Jesus. The 4th Gospel develops this point theologically in the saying of Jesus to Pilate that his kingdom is not of this world (John 18:36).

Christ's Kingdom and His Return. In another sense Christ's kingdom is his reign which will begin at his 2nd coming. Thus in Mark 10:37 James and John ask to sit on either hand of Jesus in his glory; in Matt. 20:21 this becomes "in your kingdom." Matthew repeats this theme frequently. The kingdom of the Son of man will be inaugurated at his appearance in glory. This is the general "rebirth" or "renewal" (Matt. 19:28). The return of the Son of man is a "coming in his kingdom" (Matt. 16:28), and as king the Son of man will execute the final judgment (Matt. 25:34), a concept which owes much to the picture of the Son of man in Dan.

Christ's Kingdom and the Church. Only in 13:41 does Matthew suggest that the kingdom of the Son of man is an intermediate state before the final manifestation of God's reign and that it may perhaps be identified with the period of the church.

In Luke 22:29 the heavenly feast is at the table of Jesus in his kingdom, and the relation of this passage to Acts 1:6-8 suggests that this eschatological kingdom is already being administered by the apostles in the course of the church's witness to the world. The eschatological kingdom of Jesus is acknowledged by the penitent thief (Luke 23:42), and it is identified with the return and the final judgment by Christ in II Tim., where also it is the blessed reward of the righteous (4:1, 18), as it is in II Pet. 1:11.

Col. 1:13 presents the kingdom of the Son of God's love as the rule of Christ over his church: the sphere of Christian obedience and discipleship contrasted with the authority of darkness over the world outside.

In I Cor. 15:24 this kingdom is an intermediate age; it is the time of Christ's victory over all hostile powers, including ultimately death itself. When his conquest is complete, the kingdom is to be handed over to the Father.

Elsewhere in the NT, however, the kingdom of Christ and the kingdom of God are so closely linked to each other as to be virtually identified—Christ rules on the Father's throne. The phrase which expresses this is "the kingdom of Christ and of God" (Eph. 5:5; cf. Rev. 11:15).

For Further Study. C. T. Craig, "The Proclamation of the Kingdom," in *IB*, 1951. H. Roberts, *Jesus and the Kingdom of God*, 1955. W. G. Kümmel, *Promise and Fulfilment* (trans. D. M. Barton), 1957. O. E. Evans, "Kingdom of God, of Heaven," in *IDB*, 1962.

THE NEW TESTAMENT
AND CHRISTIAN ORIGINS

James C. G. Greig

I. Scope

The Gospels. Pagan authors of the first and early 2nd cents. have little to tell us about the origins of the Christian movement; no consistent picture of the face the church presented to the world can be built up from their evidence. We learn simply of an uproar affecting the Jewish population at Rome in the reign of Claudius (Suetonius), or of Nero's blaming the Christians for the fire there in A.D. 64 (Suetonius, Tacitus), or of a "depraved . . . superstition" in which hymns were sung to Christ as to a god, and which had been emptying the pagan temples in Bithynia (Pliny the Younger).

Reliable Jewish evidence is even harder to come by. There are a few references in the Talmud to Jesus' execution (one makes him a sorcerer and lawbreaker), to some disciples by name (only occasionally easy to identify), and to the Christians as a group; but deductions are hard to make from such material.

We therefore turn to the NT for the earliest picture of the church and so must remember that while this gives us the advantage of inside information it can tell us only very indirectly what was the sociological impact of the church in the first-cent. world.

In all the NT writings, of whatever kind, the person of Jesus is the focus for anything they have to say about the origins of the movement to which their authors belonged. Some of them in addition are at pains to draw attention—albeit implicitly more often than overtly—to the setting in history for Jesus' activity and its outcome. Thus the work of John the Baptist, the Crucifixion, and the Resurrection provide points of reference which are anchored in the civil history of Galilee and Judea under the Romans, and under Pontius Pilate (A.D. 26–36) and Herod Antipas (4 B.C.–A.D. 39) in particular.

This almost involuntary dependence of at least the first 3 gospels—and with a different emphasis also the 4th Gospel—on the externals of history is esp. interesting because the authors' primary aim was theological; none of them set out to write a record of the past even in the sense of a commemorative biography. The gospels were affirmations of the impact of the character of Jesus on the church. These affirmations were made by drawing from the fund of material about Jesus that was available in primitive Christian circles. Selection varied with the theological inheritance and intention of each author. But so too did the traditions on which he drew.

As in the discussion of other NT subjects, therefore, we have to ask ourselves in studying references to Christian origins in the gospels how far the situation in which the author wrote has led him involuntarily to distort his picture of the evolution of the church. The gospels, in fact, report on Christian origins with the bias of at least one generation's Christian experience.

When we remember the literary interdependence of at least the first 3 gospels (see "The Literary Relations Among the Gospels," pp. 1129-35) we see all the more clearly the extent to which norms for the interpretation of the intentions of Jesus may be said to have been established even before they were written. We see also that it is imperative to try to understand the minds of the primitive Christians in regard to truth and history. Otherwise we may utterly fail to see the point of gospel references to the Christian community.

The Letters. Study of the NT letters, many of which come from the 50's of the first cent., will help us here. The letters comment on problems facing the church and its leadership at this time—or later, e.g. in Hebrews, I, II, III John, and the Pastorals (I, II Tim., Tit.). The solutions offered to the problems raised therefore reflect, even where the problems were new, the considered judgments of at least some 20 years' experience from the Crucifixion onward and, like the gospels, are a pointed commentary on the state of the churches at the time of writing.

A good example of this is to be seen in I Cor. 15, where the topic of resurrection is raised as one of several affecting the Corinthian converts. Here Paul seeks to vindicate his authority as an apostle by an appeal to what he himself "received" as an established tradition from people, one supposes, of the caliber of Peter and James. This may be set alongside Gal. 2, where Paul concedes that he submitted his version of the gospel to be reviewed by the "pillars" of the church at Jerusalem lest he should have "run in vain."

As the letters are the work of men in a missionary situation it may be that we should take special note of the tensions that can be seen in them between established patterns of belief and the very different and previously unrelated life situation of the new converts. The problems the letters tackle are for our purposes more important than the solutions they offer; for the solutions set a standard for the future, whereas the problems tell us something about the past—except, of course, that the solutions, as previously noted, also took the form they did because of the past experience of the apostles.

Rev. This writing has the appearance of an anthology of correspondence and theological comment addressed to a group of churches suffering political persecution. It adopts a traditional Jewish literary form—apocalyptic, i.e. pseudo prophecy of an imminent and decisive divine intervention in history written in the guise of a vision granted to an eminent figure, usually of the distant past (see "The Apocalyptic Literature," pp. 1106-09)—in order to relate church life on the E shore of the Aegean Sea to the 2nd coming of Jesus and the associated judgment of God. In passing it gives us some information about church organization; but this is of less significance than the light it throws on the concern of the early church with eschatology, i.e. its thought about the end of history, and on the liveness of Jewish ways of looking at history for Christians far from Palestine at the end of the first cent.

Acts. In this book we have a devotional history of the expansion of the church throughout the Roman world. It may be dated anywhere between the 60's of the first cent. and the early 2nd cent., but it purports to carry us back to the ascension of Jesus. Though it may draw on early sources it exhibits considerable artificiality in its use of language (e.g. Greek OT style); and over against its accuracy in historical externals—not in fact uniformly maintained—we may set its somewhat uncritical use of sources resembling the Jewish devotional tale rather than sober history.

The usefulness of Acts is reduced by its concentration in the 2nd half on Paul in such a way that we gain no impression of the work done by others after Peter's escape from Jerusalem to "another place" (12:17). Though the author seems to have planned his picture of the church's progress with the deliberateness of a literary artist, his promise outreached his performance; for the reader's horizon is progressively narrowed to the immediate environment of Paul in such a way as to make it at least plausible to maintain that Acts is primarily a brief for Paul's defense at his trial in Rome, whatever broader apologetic motifs and motivations may also underlie it. Alternatively we may think of it as Pauline propaganda belonging to a somewhat later period. At all events it must be used with extreme caution, for its "apostolic" speeches may well be subapostolic and its record of the growth of the church be little more than pious fiction. Furthermore it is intrinsically extremely hard to interpret at crucial points, e.g. chs. 10; 11; 15.

Background Material. All the NT material we have mentioned is in debt to "both Greeks and barbarians"; i.e. the authors were open to the influence of Hellenistic culture and to that of Judaism. Hellenistic culture, too, is an umbrella term sheltering among many other elements various types of "colonial" Judaism, and even some elements of Palestinian Judaism in which foreign fashions blended with the native way of life.

The Greek of the NT most obviously illustrates this indebtedness. In the realm of ideas we may cite John's concept of the Word (*Logos*, John 1:1) and Paul's notion of the body of Christ (Rom. 12:4-5;

I Cor. 12:12-13; Col. 1:18) as 2 subjects that can be understood only by taking into account both the Jewish and the pagan background of early Christianity. After all, even a rabbi like the famous Gamaliel was at home in Greek literature; Jewish prohibition of Greek studies belonged to a later date.

While approximately contemporary literature has little or nothing to say about the church it has much to say about Jewish and pagan religious institutions and ideas. Since the Christian community lived in this atmosphere such literature and relevant archaeological material may teach us much about its attitudes, if not about its organization.

The harnessing of biblical scholarship to ecumenical discussion has been helping to substitute sober analysis for a denominational apologetic; and independently of ecclesiastical considerations academic scholarship has been led by study of the methods and implications of biblical interpretation to pose the question of how far the "quest of the historical ministry and sacraments" will ever be able to yield a new doctrine to be the basis of a permanently united church. Detailed analysis of the text and background of scripture leads to increasing awareness of the ambiguity and incompleteness of the evidence. Every page of the Dead Sea scrolls, every hint about the existence of a Gnostic movement in the early years of the church is open to a variety of interpretations, as is the NT itself.

It is with this admonition in mind that we therefore turn to consider some of the main aspects of Christian origins to which all such sources allude.

II. THE QUEST OF THE INTENTION OF JESUS

Eschatology in the Early Church. There is abundant evidence that the early church interpreted the life of Jesus and its own life in the language of Jewish eschatology (cf. esp. Mark 13; I Cor. 15; I, II Thess.; Rev.). Jesus was its Messiah, but a crucified Messiah who, though in their eyes "risen" and in Paul's eyes "in" the Christian (Gal. 2:20), was not in the normal empirical sense present with his followers. He would, however, come again (II Thess. 1:7); it was set forth that he had said so himself (e.g. Mark 8:38; 13:26; cf. John 21:22; see comments). This 2nd coming was associated with the day of the Lord, the climax of history in which the "saints," i.e. Christians, would judge the world (I Cor. 6:2-3).

Attempts to represent some or all of such language as merely figurative are hard to accept in their entirety both for contextual reasons and because of our knowledge of first-cent. Jewish sectarianism. It can be arguable without great difficulty that Jewish eschatological language was understood lit. and fell out of favor only when the church, having expanded into the Gentile world, had to make a reappraisal of Christian teaching in the light of the failure of a cataclysm to materialize.

In saying this, however, we must bear in mind the great variety in the language of eschatology, from the simple equation of historical events with OT proof texts to the complex approach to history discernible in the apocalyptic literature attributed by literary convention to ancient patriarchs and sages. We must also make allowances for variety in the interpretation of it among the early Christians.

Jesus and Eschatology. It has been suggested that insofar as Jesus may have used the language of apocalyptic at all he used it only figuratively—e.g. to hint at his vindication by God and at a judgment on those who rejected him. It can also be argued that he used the OT to show his own mission as the fulfillment of history rather than to emphasize an interim period between his crucifixion or resurrection and his return. But it is difficult to exclude altogether some future reference by Jesus. An attempt to show that a nonapocalyptic outlook of Jesus was superseded by an apocalyptic phase among his followers, at its height when I, II Thess. were written and dwindling thereafter, is not entirely convincing. The leap from a Jesus little interested in conventional eschatology to a church for which eschatology and in particular apocalyptic was the lifeblood demands further explanation if it is to be accepted.

While we can with varying degrees of probability write off some aspects of the NT records as natural and gradual accretions from the thought world of 2nd-remove writers, we still find ourselves with a mass of varied material belonging to a recognizable pattern of Jewish thinking—an eschatological and apocalyptic one—and since Jesus was himself a Palestinian Jew there is the presumption that many factors contributing to the emergence of this pattern could have originated with him as easily as with his followers.

Organization and Eschatology. If both Jesus and the church which produced the material later taken into the NT belonged to the same eschatological thought world, what we learn about the relationship of church order to eschatology may be informative about Jesus' original intentions insofar as the evidence is not intrinsically ambiguous.

E.g. as early as the 50's the Pauline letters allude to the existence of house churches, hint at something like synagogue organization, and recognize special apostolic authority. Their concerns are their relationship to Jesus, as the risen Christ, and to Israel, esp. with reference to the last days, the resurrection of the dead, and the age to come. I.e. the church of Paul's day saw itself as an eschatological community with Jewish roots, Jewish institutional leadership, and a belief that Jesus was the Messiah of the Jews—it cannot be seriously contended that for Paul "Christ" was a mere surname.

We cannot offer sufficient evidence to show that the details of organization were everywhere the same, but we need have no hesitation in maintaining that the church was a Jewish organization and had Jewish precedents. Again, there is no hint that a particular mode of organization was ordained by Jesus to cover every particular of church life. There is fair evidence, however, that a junta of church leaders who had been his close associates were purveyors of acceptable traditions (cf. I Cor. 9; 11:2; 15:1-11; II Cor. 10-13; Gal. 2). This suggests that what was not their own interpretation of events and intentions, or else the common stock of Judaism, can very well be consistent with and derived from Jesus' own views. Only we cannot say from the Pauline letters how far Jesus had already contemplated creating an institution.

In comparison with the Pauline letters as a source

of information Acts is secondary, and we have seen that it should be used with some care. Bearing this in mind we may note that Acts 1:15-26 gives the impression that in the period before the first Pentecost after the crucifixion the church had an organization which required a special "college" of 12 at its head. These 12 were to be knowledgeable from personal experience about the beginnings of the Christian movement in the days of John the Baptist. The author, moreover, still thinks it important to note that, though their understanding of Jesus' intentions may have been faulty, some of these leaders, as he believed, expected the immediate restoration of the "kingdom" to Israel, and Jesus did not contradict them in principle but only in regard to the eschatological schedule.

Whatever was sacrosanct about the authority of the 12 in Acts, it was not that they were the only "apostles." Usage of this term is loose. The practical needs of the church are shown as permitting the development too of new officials, again probably with Jewish models in mind. The rounded picture is of a sectarian synagogue with a distinctive eschatological schedule. The author, writing late, may have read into his sources ideas and practices of his own day; nevertheless these ideas and practices must have had a history within the Christian community before he inherited them. His text certainly does not oblige us to drop the notion that the rudiments of a Christian society were consciously planned by Jesus, even if it does nothing to demonstrate its veracity.

Limitations of the Quest. To the evidence of the letters and Acts we may add in particular that of the gospels, the reliability of which rests on the reliability of the collective memory of the churches that accepted them. We cannot guarantee that the church as a whole was capable of being an effective censor of misleading reports on Jesus' intentions, but neither can we demonstrate which reports if any are indeed tendentious.

When therefore we read in Matt. 18:15-20 of Jesus' concern for church discipline we cannot confidently say that not he but the church so spoke or that the church claimed his authority for its own practice. We can merely note that the Qumran community had similar provisions in its Manual of Discipline (see "The Dead Sea Scrolls," pp. 1063-71) and that Jesus, as an eschatologically self-conscious leader, could quite well have made such provision for his followers. A similar approach to the status of Peter in Matt. 16 would be in order.

Taking into account the relative lateness of the gospels in their finished form, it can be argued that such features were retained disinterestedly as material that was reckoned to be primitive. There is no need to see in it a contrived apologia for certain ecclesiastical claims chiefly challenged in any event only much later. The authoritativeness of such material for today is of course a completely separate question.

We see, then, that the quest of the intention of Jesus must be carried on with material none of which takes us assuredly back behind the 50's, much of which either may or may not reflect his own views, and all of which show us a church looking to a leader and founder whose Palestinian background would make it easy for him to hold both the eschatological and the organizational views discernible in this later material.

III. NT DESCRIPTIONS OF THE CHURCH

Theological and Nontheological Factors. The primitive Christians used language very flexibly to describe the organization by which they hoped to transform the world. We are not here concerned primarily with factual description of a body of people in a certain building performing certain acts, except insofar as these physical circumstances point toward theological attitudes. Our principal interest is in the language used to express the "ideology" (in the popular sense) of the church.

The word "church" in the English NT translates *ekklēsia*, the Greek term for any body of people called together—e.g. the Ephesian mob of Acts 19: 28-41. In ancient Greece it developed a special constitutional sense. Among the Jews it was used in the LXX to describe the congregation of Israel. It seems to have been used also for more local assemblies such as would be found in a synagogue. The Greek word transliterated "synagogue" also could mean a "gathering" of people, and it came to mean in addition the place where they were gathered together. In Jas. 2:2 it is used of a Christian assembly but elsewhere in the NT is reserved for the Jewish assembly or its meeting place.

"Church" (*ekklēsia*) in the NT frequently has the sense of the local congregation but is also used with the general sense of the "congregation of the new Israel," or as an abstraction. In Matt. 16:18 the church to be built on the rock (of Peter's faith?) is the new, true Israel standing over against the temple associated with the rock of Mt. Zion. In this sense the passage agrees with other NT material which speaks of the church as a spiritual temple or of its members as stones in a living temple (I Pet. 2:5), the cornerstone of which is the Messiah himself. Sometimes he himself indeed seems to be identified with the temple, its high priesthood, or its sacrifices. These are all ways of asserting the adequacy of the church as an eschatological community over against Judaism, which in A.D. 70 saw its temple razed by the Romans. At the same time the debt to Judaism in the use of such language is evident.

The Qumran community also saw itself as *the* eschatological representative of the true Israel and used similar though not identical terminology derived from knowledge of and respect for the OT. The Christians, however, had a focus for their use of such terminology in the person of Jesus, whom they took to be the Messiah, whereas the Qumran group appears to have been convinced that the last days were upon them without reaching the point of identifying the Messiah(s) they expected with any one historical character such as their Teacher (see "The Dead Sea Scrolls," pp. 1063-71).

The Christian focus on the person of Jesus comes out in the description of the church as the bride of Christ (cf. e.g. Matt. 25:1-13; Rev. 21:9) or the body of Christ (cf. e.g. Col. 1:18). The figure of the bride goes back to OT references to Yahweh as Israel's husband. That of the body may be connected with a Jewish myth known from later material—that all humanity are the limbs of Adam (Christ is the new or 2nd Adam in I Cor. 15:22; cf. Rom. 5:12-14—but it may also have pagan philosophical antecedents. Assuming the Jewish influence to predominate, we may sum up by asserting that confession of faith in Jesus as Messiah meant readiness to be incorporated by baptism into the new Israel whose representative he was (cf. Rom. 6:1-11; Col. 2:12). It is hardly necessary to reaffirm after this the importance of understanding the role of eschatology in the development of the thinking of the church.

Flexibility of Language. It is important not to build the varied concepts related to the church too readily into a system. We have to think first of the way an immediate situation would draw forth an allusion to this myth or that OT quotation. The unifying force behind such usages is that complex of ideas centered in the belief in a coming, latter-day Messiah.

In the NT writings and in the later growth of church doctrine we see a gradual transmutation of such ideas into Christian metaphysics. Descriptions of the church which individually are suggested by an immediate relationship of the believer to Christ (i.e. Messiah), though obviously capable of discussion in terms of the church's nature, are made part of such a discussion only after the key to their being used at all has been lost. It is like sailing inside a lagoon of iceberg peaks and supposing them all originally joined together by a wall of ice above the water, without ever suspecting the existence of a quite different underwater base.

Interpretative Method. We should tackle New Testament descriptions of Christian origins psychologically, sociologically, and historically rather than metaphysically. This particular community used that particular language to describe the church because it was captivated by the idea of a nation chosen by God, punished in the past for its unworthiness, but destined to be "saved" and to lead others to salvation through a special servant of God whose immediate followers would be a righteous remnant to found a new Israel (cf. e.g. Rom. 11:5; Gal. 3:29).

The validity of the primitive Christians' interpretation of their life situation is a separate question, but it should be said that there was perhaps nothing inevitable about their choice of language.

IV. SACRAMENTS

"The Body of Christ." The link between the church and the Lord's Supper is perhaps at its most intriguing in I Cor. 10-11. These rich chapters suggest that already by Paul's time the tendency to view Jesus' death as a sacrifice fulfilling if not eclipsing the intention of Jewish sacrifice had led to an equation of Christian participation in the Lord's Supper with the principle behind the cultic activity of ancient Israel. Consistently with this, Paul could have easily regarded his application of the term "body of Christ" to the church itself as a legitimate "function" of its use in relation to the Lord's Supper. The extent of his consciousness of this connection, however, remains a matter for debate, as does the legitimacy of later ecclesiastical deductions from such NT material concerning the prerequisites for the proper celebration of the sacrament.

The "Sufferings of Christ." Another aspect of the sacraments may be seen in Col. 1:24, where the suffering of the church is related to this by virtue of her supposed "incorporation" into Christ. At this point we may observe that though the Qumran community thinks of itself as having an atoning function, its literature's references to congregational meals with a messianic setting fail to make a connection between these and the sacrificial system, or between them and the misfortunes of the community and its leaders or founder. Pauline "Christ mysticism" provides us with a much more highly developed sacramental theology than that of Qumran. This does not mean that Paul had to go outside the Jewish circle of thought to construct it; if the Hellenistic mystery religions (see "The Greco-Roman Background of the NT," pp. 1037-44) play a part in Christian sacramental thinking, it is through the medium of ideas already circulating in some Jewish quarters. Much of this may be due to the rationale of the Crucifixion which early Christianity had to have, and which e.g. Gal. 3 supplies. Qumran does not seem to have had to answer the question: How can your hero be the Messiah though crucified?

Baptism. Gal. 3 achieves this rationale by subordinating the Jewish law to what is taken to be a promise of God antedating that law and to Abraham's faith in that promise (Gen. 15:6). This leads to the doctrine of a new spiritual Israel, access to which involves union with Christ by baptism (Gal. 3:27-29).

The stages by which baptism became normative for admission to the Christian community are difficult to trace. Various rites involving the use of water were practiced in the Palestinian area in NT times. In particular baptismal rites existed at Qumran. The novitiate there could gain access to this type of "baptism" only after certain set conditions had been met.

In the NT and in the writings of the Jewish historian Josephus the concern of the desert preacher John for baptism is indicated by his being surnamed "the Baptist." He seems to have been capable of causing a commotion in political circles and to have had a highly charged eschatology (cf. e.g. Mark 1:4-8; Luke 3:7-17). Jesus' movement arose in John's environment and Jesus was baptized by John. John's baptism is stated to have been one "of repentance for the forgiveness of sins." Between the beginning of Jesus' ministry and its close virtually nothing is heard of the practice of baptism in the earliest Christian circles. Thereafter it is mentioned in Paul and in Acts and elsewhere, in some instances in terms very similar to those used of the baptism of proselytes, i.e. converts to Judaism, in the rabbinic literature.

It is still debated whether proselyte baptism antedated John's and how the 2 are to be related. But even if John was connected rather with sectarian Judaism than with orthodoxy, Pauline interpretation of baptism could certainly be understood as importing a ready-made terminology from proselyte baptism. Indeed the NT makes better sense on this assumption or a similar one than it does if we suppose it to have no antecedents in this subject matter. The Christian's "burial" with the Messiah (Christ) in baptism becomes understandable if it is seen as his incorporation into a latter-day spiritual Israel by analogy with the proselyte's incorporation into an Israel that still awaited its Messiah. Certainly at some stage in Jewish history the proselyte was regarded as one risen from the dead, or as a newborn child—terms relevant also to Christian baptism (cf. e.g. John 3; Rom. 6). It is difficult to conceive of Jewish borrowings from Christianity in this situation. Paul's silence on Jewish proselyte baptism when he deals with the theology of circumcision may therefore be more apparent than real—and apparent at all only insofar as he is allusive rather than direct in his references.

Among the Christians baptism superseded circumcision. Its sectarian and eschatological nature together with the antilegalistic strain in the teachings of Stephen and Paul, would be enough to make it a symbol of Christian liberty. Subtle adaptation of the language of proselyte baptism to the Christian teaching on the crucifixion and resurrection of Jesus as the rallying points for Christian conduct would make such a symbol all the more forceful. Without the precedent of proselyte baptism, or the like, however, the Pauline terminology seems unnecessarily strained and fancifully metaphorical.

The Christian, then, seems to be viewed in the NT as the "new Israelite"; he is "in" the community, and since Christ is the 2nd Adam, whose limbs men are, he is "in" Christ. But Christ died and rose again; therefore at least spiritually and by extension physically (I Cor. 15) the Christian by baptism dies and rises again *in principle*. He is incited to do so spiritually in practice (Rom. 6) by the constant reminder of what happened to Jesus, interpreted as having saving significance and indeed judging significance (Rom. 3:21-26; Heb. 9:27-28).

The Lord's Supper. The sacrament which has this quality of calling Christ to mind is the Lord's Supper. The Hebrew is often appealed to to suggest that e.g. in I Cor. 11:24 something more than mere factual reminiscence is intended—something like "re-presentation" or "realization" of Christ in the sacrament. This mode of reasoning is acceptable insofar as one can say that Jesus is to be remembered *for a purpose*. To think of him is to say something about what he did and why he was thought to have done it (I Cor. 11:26). It is dangerous, however, to use the Hebrew background of the term to support some ontological view of the elements in the Lord's Supper in relation to the "Body of Christ."

Whether the original meal took place before or as the Passover meal, it was held in the atmosphere of the festival, and the words attributed to Jesus in the gospels suggest as so often in the NT an understanding by the church or by him of his career as a fulfillment of Judaism. This time it is the notions of covenant and sacrifice (cf. Exod. 24:8; Jer. 31:31; Zech. 9:11) that are uppermost.

As used in the gospel accounts of the Last Supper the direct identification of the term "body" with the church is most difficult to make. It is also difficult to know whether Jesus, or the church, had anything more in mind than the feeling that at succeeding Passovers his act of self-sacrifice, as later understood, should be purposefully remembered. For the author of Luke-Acts the stress on fellowship in meals seems to point to something more.

V. Ministry

From what has already been said it will be clear that while the primitive church may have been institutional by design from the first it was, as an eschatological phenomenon, the institution to end all institutions. Yet its discrimination in its teaching and traditions, esp. sacramental traditions, and its concern for liturgical propriety point to tight rather than loose control by a governing ministry, so far as the essentials were concerned. We conclude therefore with a brief account of the origins of the ministry.

Commissioning of the Disciples. The gospels tell of the dispatch of Jesus' disciples on missions during his ministry. The scope of this work was ostensibly comparable to that envisaged as Jesus' farewell commission to the 11 (Mark 16:15-18), just as the scope of the disciplinary powers of the 12 in Matt. 18:15-20 bears an interesting resemblance to the power to forgive or "retain" sins granted in John 20:22-23. With what justice we know not the church writers of the first cent. are attributing to Jesus the desire to create a corps of plenipotentiaries whose number and whose instructions alike imply that he was very much at home in the world of Jewish eschatology.

The Inner Circle. From a variety of sources it is evident that only 3 of this group of 12 had anything like full access to Jesus' confidences. It is instructive, though probably not capable of showing us where the Christian organization had its archetype, to note that the Qumran community had a council of 12 and 3 priests—possibly included in the 12—at its head. More to the point is to note the bearing of the existence of this oligarchy on the transmission of Christian doctrine. Even Paul is dependent on these "pillars" of the church (Gal. 2:9; cf. I Cor. 9:1-27; 15:1-11; Mark 8:29-33; 9:2-8; 14:32-42). The lateness or secondary nature of Acts and the Pastorals unfortunately makes it hard to say how far in the earliest period a wider group could influence the activity of the "pillars."

The Timetable. There is adequate evidence in the NT to suggest that the primitive Christian leaders expected a speedy climax to history in the shape of a 2nd coming of Jesus. It might therefore be fair to say that the immediate purpose of their ecclesiastical authority was simply preparative for this return, and that there is no telling how their authority and responsibilities were intended to be carried out in any sequel to this winding-up of history. The decease of certain members of the apostolic band may have raised questions about Jesus' own intention for them in this respect, and Mark 10:39-40; John 21:20-23 look like attempts to answer these on the basis of available traditions. We have already discussed the difficulty of determining the validity of these traditions for a picture of Jesus' mind.

The Easter Event. It is still conceivable that Jesus envisaged no long interval between his death and his vindication and that the most primitive sources emphasized the fulfillment achieved by his ministry more than a future return. In fact concrete pictures of a return may have been a natural compensation for the sensed inadequacy of the vindication—cf. e.g. the explanation of the absence of the "historical" Jesus from the community by means of a formal picture of his ascension and of the gift of the Spirit in Acts 1-2.

The dependence of the list of resurrection appearances in I Cor. 15:1-7 on the oligarchy and the lateness of the gospel accounts of the Resurrection make it extremely perilous to reconstruct the state of mind in which the primitive leaders came to speak of Jesus as vindicated and risen. The lateness of the present setting of the apostolic speeches in Acts also compels us to observe similar caution there.

Such diffidence is the natural parent of existential interpretations of the Easter event in which tales of the empty tomb etc. are considered unimportant—whatever the extent of their historical and symbolic content—over against the claim that in the preaching of the gospel Jesus is "really present." This makes the gospel message "eschatological" as the word of Jesus. In effect, however, it begs the question of the motivation for the continued preaching of Christ as risen. The preaching task of the Christian leaders was made more difficult, not less, by the Crucifixion. If they could not have a resurrection to rely on, they must have had recourse either to Jesus' interpretation of scripture or to their own and constructed quite ingenuously a resurrection belief of their own. In this light the importance for their own psychological development of insisting on the messiahship of the crucified Jesus is very relevant to a discussion of their standing as ecclesiastical functionaries.

Apostles and Elders. The scope of the word "apostle" varies in the NT (cf. e.g. Luke 6:13; Acts 9:27; 14:4; Rom. 16:7; Heb. 3:1). Decidedly wider than the oligarchy, it is still sometimes limited to the 12, but can also cover, it seems, a wider group, perhaps overlapping with the eldership.

The term "apostle" seems to have connections with a Jewish word for a plenipotentiary and in later Judaism, if not already in Jesus' day, official functionaries existed with such a designation. The Christian usage may or may not have had an intrinsic eschatological force—may or may not imply a view of the primitive community as a dissident synagogue. But together with the use of the term "elder" it shows how indebted to its Jewish seedbed the Christian movement was. Similar indebtedness may be traced in the development of the Christian practice of ordination and its relationship to the gift of the Spirit. Whether one can go further and claim that the primitive Christians established a dissident high priesthood under James the Lord's brother remains uncertain.

Bishops. The related question of ecclesiastical hierarchy and succession cannot be adequately treated from the NT alone. The Qumran community had functionaries who exercised oversight, but nothing can be read from this into the oversight exercised by Christian ministers. NT usage is meager and not specific. The 2nd-cent. Christian manual known as the Didache speaks somewhat loosely of apostles, prophets, and teachers and esp. commends the ecstatics of the church. On the other hand it mentions the election of bishops and deacons as "your dignitaries together with the prophets and teachers." In the letters of Ignatius (early 2nd cent.) the monarchical bishop is more easily to be discerned, and in I Clement (late first cent.) there is a famous passage that can be understood either as implying an apostolic succession in the episcopate or as recording the establishment of a regular episcopal succession as something other than the apostolate.

The emergence of such an episcopal pattern of church government, linked to the notion of the gifts of the Spirit, follows without too much difficulty from the kind of situation we may discern behind such a passage as the list of church functionaries in I Cor. 12:28-30; but it tells us nothing about what is necessary for the church today. Besides being a ripe field for the scythe of conjecture it is properly handled only when one keeps in mind the extent to which Jewish—and, later, Hellenistic—precedent and practical needs were determinative. This is true even when dogmatic interpretations of the action taken appear to be cited as the reason for such action.

VI. The Relevance of the Study

The ecumenical concern of the 20th cent. has been responsible for a concentrated study of Christian origins such as might provide a secure scriptural basis for forms of ministry and interpretations of the sacraments that could be used in a united church.

Modern biblical principles of interpretation, however, raise the question whether firm answers to such studies can ever become available in the dogmatic field. Moreover, behind the question "What was intended?" lurks the supplementary "Why was this rather than something else intended?" And this must be largely answered by endeavoring to establish ever more clearly the antecedents of the Christian movement in the life of its time and, a tantalizing task, the psychology of its exponents.

In this situation the value of an existentialist approach to church, ministry, and preaching should be apparent. It helps us to see in the NT a crystallization of a response to basic religious challenges, uttered in the language of that time. The propriety of the response must be adjudged by each for himself. It amounted to an acceptance of the need for a new spiritual motivation for humanity, but it sought to fulfill that need by dragooning humanity into an institutional new Israel because its leaders had inherited the pretensions of the old Israel to be God's chosen people. The longer this lasted the more institutional it became, even when the explicit Jewish framework was transcended. In this there may be a lesson for tomorrow as well as a comment on yesterday.

For Further Study. E. F. Scott, W. H. P. Hatch, P. S. Minear, M. H. Shepherd, Jr., "The History of the Early Church," in *IB*, 1951. G. B. Caird, *The Apostolic Age*, 1955. J. A. T. Robinson, *Jesus and His Coming*, 1957. P. S. Minear, *Images of the Church in the NT*, 1960. Edouard Schweizer, *Church Order in the NT*, tr. Frank Clarke, 1961. W. D. Davies, *Christian Origins and Judaism*, 1962. R. H. Fuller, *The NT in Current Study*, 1962. P. H. Menoud, "Church, Life and Organization of," in *IDB*, 1962. Werner Foerster, *From the Exile to Christ*, 1964.

THE LANGUAGES OF THE BIBLE

Kendrick Grobel

"What was originally expressed in Hebrew does not have exactly the same sense when translated into another language." So in the 2nd cent. B.C. an Egyptian Jew prefaced his Greek translation of his grandfather's book (Ecclus.). He was speaking of 2 unrelated languages, as utterly unlike as English and Japanese; but what he says applies in some degree to all translation, even though the 2 languages may be close sisters, e.g. French and Spanish. Parallel expressions in different languages inevitably have different connotations; in each there is a plus of associations, a fund of submeanings, not shared in the other, so that apparent equivalents do not carry quite the same freight. Thus for a text of much length and depth of meaning a translation can never be more than an approximation. The good translator aims at bringing the reader as close as possible, not to the wording of the original, but to its intent.

Most of us know the Bible best in some version, perhaps that in which we first read it in childhood. For us this version is our Bible, but we need to remember that it is a translation and not *the* Bible. Some who forgot this have engaged in violent debates about "what the Bible really says" on the basis of details not found in the original text. The student of the Bible unable to read the original languages is therefore wise to make a practice of comparing different translations, observing the footnotes in which translators explain their choices, and taking advantage of the information offered by commentators. In such study it is helpful to know some of the general characteristics of the languages in which the Bible was written.

Much the greater part of the Bible's bulk was composed in Hebrew—all the OT except a very few passages, totaling *ca.* 10 chs., which are in Aramaic. The NT is all in Greek. The books of the Apoc. have all come down to us in Greek—except II Esdras, extant only in several ancient translations, the most important of which is the Latin—but Hebrew and Aramaic originals seem to underlie a number of them. Thus there are 3 biblical languages, Hebrew, Aramaic, and Greek.

I. The Semitic Languages

Hebrew and Aramaic belong to the family of languages known as Semitic. This name was invented by a linguist in the late 18th cent. who observed that the sons of Shem (Gen. 10:21-31), spelled Sem in the Vulg., were the peoples who spoke these related languages. In one respect the name is unfortunate, for Gen. speaks of the sons of Shem as related by blood, whereas peoples of quite diverse stock often adopt related languages—cf. e.g. those who now speak English.

Today Semitic languages of some kind, mostly Arabic, are spoken in larger and smaller patches in a great band reaching from the W coast of Africa through Indonesia and from the Caucasus Mountains to the equator. But at the dawn of written documents the family was confined to the Near East—more specifically to the area extending from the E coast of the Mediterranean E through the valley of the Tigris and Euphrates and from the Caucasus S through the Arabian Peninsula, with probably an extension from its SW corner to the opposite African coast.

The Semitic language family hangs together both in vocabulary and in characteristic formal devices for connection, shades of meaning, and derivatives. A considerable dictionary could be made—indeed several have been—composed of recognizably identical words shared by 2 or more Semitic languages. All of them show a great preference for word roots consisting of 3 consonants to which various vowels may be added to form related words. The personal pronouns are recognizably the same throughout the family, and in all the languages verbs are conjugated by the addition of shortened forms of these pronouns as prefixes or suffixes. The Semitic verbs have no tenses to indicate time but instead have 2 forms, sometimes called tenses, to distinguish complete and incomplete action. In addition a verb may occur in up to a dozen different forms which indicate shades of meaning, e.g. intensity, reciprocity, causality.

It was the structure of the Semitic languages that led to one of the greatest inventions of all time, the alphabet. The earlier systems of writing, cuneiform in Mesopotamia and hieroglyphic in Egypt (see "Writing in Biblical Times," pp. 1201-08), used signs to represent whole syllables and thus had to have hundreds of them. Somewhere along the Mediterranean coast or in the Sinai Peninsula *ca.* 1600 B.C. a Semitic-speaking people, probably the Canaanites, thought of a much simpler way. Since the distinctive feature in most words of their language was a cluster of 3 consonants, they recognized that showing the consonants would provide enough identification for readers to fill in the vowel sounds. They found that only 20-odd signs would suffice for all the consonant sounds of their language. The set they chose became the first alphabet, the source from which all true alphabets of the world are derived. When after many cents. Greek traders learned of it, they adapted it to their language by putting the signs for some Semitic consonants they did not need to a new use—to represent vowels, which they had to include to identify Greek words. Further modifications by the Etruscans and Romans resulted in our own alphabet, whose descent from the original Semitic alphabet is recognizable both in its order and in the forms of a number of the letters.

The languages of the Semitic family are classified by linguists into subfamilies. The South Semitic subfamily, represented by pre-Arabic inscriptions, Arabic, and Ethiopic, shows enough differences from the rest that some divide the whole family into only North and South Semitic. It is more common, however, to divide into 4 subfamilies: South, Northwest, North, and East Semitic. NW Semitic is Canaanite in its various forms; they include Hebrew, along with Moabite, Edomite, Phoenician, Punic, and Ugaritic. N Semitic is essentially Aramaic and falls into 2 groups: Western Aramaic, which is that found in the Bible and the Targums, i.e. Aramaic translations of the OT, and the Palestinian Gemara in the Talmud, and includes Samaritan and Nabatean; and Eastern Aramaic, which is represented by the Syriac translations of the Bible, Christian writings in Syriac and Mandean, and the Babylonian Talmud. The 4th subfamily, E Semitic, includes Akkadian and its daughters, Assyrian and Babylonian.

II. HEBREW

No biblical author writing in Hebrew ever calls his language by that name, doubtless because it was not yet so called. For it was not the ancestral language of the Hebrew people but one they had adopted. Abraham and his clan are said to have come originally from Ur of the Chaldees in S Mesopotamia (Gen. 11:31; see color map 2), where they would naturally have spoken the local language, probably some form of E Semitic, i.e. Akkadian. But before entering Palestine they are said to have settled for a time in Haran in NW Mesopotamia among Arameans (cf. Deut. 26:5) whose N Semitic speech, Aramaic, they undoubtedly adopted. In the story of Jacob's parting agreement with Laban, whose branch of the clan had stayed in Haran, it is told that Laban called the pile of stones Jegar-sahadutha, Aramaic for "heap of witness," but Jacob called it Galeed (Gen. 31:47). His name meant the same thing in the NW Semitic language his branch of the clan had adopted from the people dwelling in the land to which they had migrated. It was correctly called the "language [lit. "lip"] of Canaan" (Isa. 19:18), not simply because it was the language which Hebrews were then speaking in Canaan, but because it was the language their ancestors had found the Canaanites already speaking there when they arrived.

The alphabet as it developed in Hebrew usage had 22 letters though some of them had alternate sounds, depending on the neighboring sounds (cf. our *c* and *g*). All were consonants, though in time certain of them came to be used sometimes to indicate long vowels (cf. our *w* and *y*). The vowels were not fully indicated till the 5th or 6th cent. A.D. and then not as letters but as little dots and dashes below or above the preceding consonants. Some of the Hebrew consonant sounds do not exist in English, or at least are not recognized as distinguishing words. E.g. the first letter, *aleph*, represents what is almost no sound at all as a transition from one vowel sound to another in the following syllable or word, while *ayin* represents such a transition with a catch in the throat which might be noticed in someone's pronunciation of an English word but would not affect its meaning. In precise transliterations these letters are usually indicated by apostrophes, aleph normal (') and ayin reversed ('). Some of the Hebrew guttural and hissing sounds are also not found in English. Whereas we have only *s* and *z* as sibilant letters, Hebrew has 5. Originally they must have been all distinct to the ear, but local variations—cf. the shibboleth password (Judg. 12:5-6)—and the changes of time broke down some of the distinctions, as evidenced by later confusions in writing them.

The differing sounds of the languages were a problem to the LXX translators as they tried to represent the OT names in Greek. Some of their attempts, after an intermediate transcription into Latin, became familiar to our English ancestors in forms that are far from representing their original pronunciations. E.g. our way of saying Jacob has become so embedded in the language that it cannot be displaced, but Ya'aqobh—the *bh* indicating a *v* pronounced with the lips in the position for *b*—would more nearly show the original sound. Similarly Solomon might better be represented by Shlomo, Isaiah by Yesha'yahu, and Jeremiah by Yirmeyahu. In those names we keep at least some of the original sounds, but consider what has happened to the name the Hebrews pronounced Chawwah—with *ch* as in German *ach*. In its transmittal to us through not only Greek and Latin but also French it became Eve, which has neither a consonant nor a vowel sound of the Hebrew name.

In Hebrew, as in all languages, a proper name when originally given had a meaning that was apparent to all. Often that meaning has become lost in the mists of time. In other cases the name has importance only for its meaning—e.g. the threat of national doom that Isaiah proclaimed in the name of his son, Maher-shalal-hashbaz (Isa. 8:1-3; for its meaning see RSV footnote) and the symbolic names Hosea gave his children (Hos. 1:8-9; 2:23; for the Hebrew forms see KJV or ASV). Some strands of the traditions about early Hebrew history show a lively interest in the meaning of names. We may suspect that some of the stories of their origins are folk explanations that arose during the period of oral transmission. E.g. Adam is explained as coming from *'adamah*, "earth" (Gen. 3:19); Chawwah (Eve) from *chay*, "living" (Gen. 3:20); Ya'aqobh (Jacob) from *'aqebh*, "heel" (Gen. 25:26); Yehudah (Judah) from *hodeh*, "praise" (Gen. 29:35; 49:8). Many such stories are told of the names of places.

As in most other languages, the verb in Hebrew is the most complicated and most interesting part of speech. E.g. let us take a common verb root, *MLK*, a characteristic cluster of 3 consonants which form the backbone of a whole series of words associated with the idea of reigning or ruling as a king. The simplest form of the verb is the 3rd person masculine singular of the perfect, i.e. the form denoting completed action, *MaLaK,* which unless a subject is expressed means "he ruled"—or "has ruled," "had ruled," "will have ruled," or even "rules" or "will rule" so long as the action is conceived as completed. With different vowels the word is a noun, *MeLeK,* "king," or, as pronounced by a neighboring people, *MoLeK,* the title, "King," of a pagan god which most English versions spell Molech or Moloch.

Of course all 3 of these words would be written simply *MLK* and the reader would have to recognize the right one from the context; but other forms of the verb, as well as derivative nouns, being constructed by adding prefixes or suffixes containing consonants, would usually be recognizable when written without vowels. E.g. adding abbreviated forms of the pronoun "you" as suffixes gives the 2nd person of the perfect: *MaLaKta,* "you ruled," and its plural, *MaLaKtem.* On the other hand adding a simplified pronoun as a prefix produces the imperfect, e.g. *eMLoK,* "I am ruling." Adding another sort of prefix gives a special form expressing causation that requires 2 verbs in English, *hiMLyK,* "he made . . . to rule." The *y* here represents a long vowel that came to be denoted by inserting the consonant *yodh* for this nonconsonantal service; without it the word might be read as the corresponding passive, *hoMLaK,* "he was made to rule." This verbal root lacks other such derived forms which express passive, reflexive, and intensive meanings of many other verbs; but it has the usual imperatives, infinitives, and participles, as well as the derivative nouns *MaLKah,* "queen," *MaLKuth,* "kingdom," and *maMLaKah,* "sovereignty."

As already suggested, the perfect and imperfect "tenses," as they are sometimes called, do not indicate time as do our tenses. Rather one chooses between them according to whether he thinks of the verb's action as complete or incomplete. Either sense may refer to past, present, or future; the time must be understood from the context rather than from the form of the verb. This creates much less chaos than a stranger to it might expect, but there are occasional ambiguities which have resulted in some differences of tense among the English versions.

In Hebrew nouns come from verbal roots much more often than verbs come from nouns. There are only 2 genders, as in French; there is no neuter gender. Not only are males named with masculine nouns and females with feminine nouns—often formed by adding a feminine ending to the masculine —but unsexed things are all either masculine or feminine. The gender distinction extends even to the 2nd person, though not the first, of pronouns and verbs. On the other hand there are 3 numbers, not only singular and plural but also dual; but use of the dual is limited to things that generally are found in pairs.

There is evidence that at one time Hebrew nouns had case endings, but before the written stage they gave way to dependence on word order and particles, just as most Anglo-Saxon case endings dropped out in English. Nevertheless the Hebrew noun has what is called the construct form, a lightened or reduced form of singular or plural by means of which it is propped against a following noun that governs its

meaning. Cf. e.g. *debhar,* "word," and *debhar elohim,* "word of God," and their plurals, *debharim* and *debhare elohim.* The small superior *e*'s represent the neutral unstressed vowel sound common in unaccented syllables of ordinary English speech, which most recent dictionaries denote by the phonetic symbol ə. In general, the construct form requires no stress so that the accent can be given to the following noun. Thus the phrase might be said to form a compound noun, with the stress on the 2nd element, in keeping with the Hebrew tendency to throw the accent toward the end of a word. In such a compound in English we would usually reverse the order to put the accent first and say "God-word."

Hebrew adjectives follow their nouns and agree with them in gender and number, which are indicated by the same endings. The language is relatively poor in true adjectives, and it makes up for this lack in 2 ways: (*a*) Many verbs have meanings that we would express by "be," "become," or "make" followed by an adjective; e.g. our own verb "blush" means "become red," and "flatten" means "become or make flat." (*b*) In a phrase using the construct form the 2nd noun often has the force of an adjective; e.g. "spirit of holiness" means "Holy Spirit," "man of words" means "eloquent man," "men of name" means "famous men," and "son of death" means "doomed man." This childlike yet strong construction makes translations from Hebrew seem poetic even when they are rendering ordinary prose.

The Hebrew adjective has neither a comparative nor a superlative form, but certain constructions can suggest ideas so similar that an English comparative or superlative is required to translate them. E.g. when 7 of Jesse's 8 sons have passed in review before Samuel and the father says that there is still "the young one" (I Sam. 16:11) he is clearly referring to the youngest. The same meaning is also expressed by "the little of his sons" (II Chr. 21:17). Another substitute for the superlative is provided by the singular of a noun or adjective in the construct form with its own plural; e.g. "king of kings" means the kingliest king, "song of songs" the most melodious song, and "holy of holies" the most holy place.

Instead of the missing comparative Hebrew uses the simple adjective followed by "from" and the person or thing surpassed. E.g. Deut. 1:28 lit. speaks of a people "great and high from us"; i.e. with us as a standard they are great and high, and the translation "greater and taller than we" is justified. But "great from us" can also mean "greater than we can deal with," i.e. "too great for us," and perhaps this is the meaning in Deut. 1:28. Certainly "too . . . for" rather than "more . . . than" is the meaning in the lit. "such knowledge is wonderful from me" (Ps. 139:6). Thus the construction is somewhat ambiguous, and the comparative sense must be determined from the context.

The remaining words in Hebrew are lumped together as "particles." They include exclamations like "oh," "ah," "alas," adverbs like "now" and "soon," the definite article, and the prepositions and conjunctions, both of which are mostly single letters that must lean against the following word. The few conjunctions are overworked and have to carry a bewildering number of implications. The commonest is *w,* which is prefixed to the following word with an intervening vowel sound that varies according to the initial consonant. Its primary sense is "and"; but the context often shows that it means rather "but," "whether," "while," "because," "although," "in order that," "with the result that," "so," "then," or other shade of connection. Unlike Greek, Latin, and English, Hebrew does not favor long complex sentences with several dependent clauses along the way; rather its usual style is a series of independent clauses strung together with "and . . . and . . . and." Since in English composition such a style is considered childish or awkward, translators largely disguise it by varying the conjunctions or dividing into simple sentences.

Because the Hebrews were in constant contact with neighbors on all sides, their language contains many borrowed words from a dozen languages, some Semitic, some belonging to utterly foreign language families.

Old Egyptian, which was not a Semitic language, contributed a good many words to Hebrew. The most easily noticeable is "Pharaoh," the title of the Egyptian king. It was originally 2 Egyptian words, "house" and "great," usually meaning "palace." Quite a number of Egyptian nouns came into Hebrew as the names of commodities imported from Egypt, e.g. "ebony" (Ezek. 27:15), "fine linen" (Ezek. 16:10), "amethyst" (Exod. 28:19), and "fine gold" (Ps. 45:9). A word for "ivory" (I Kings 10:22; II Chr. 9:21) combines the Hebrew for "tooth" with the Egyptian for "elephant." Beside such nouns there is a considerable number of verbs very close in sound and meaning. Many if not most of these are probably borrowed, but which language was the borrower can seldom be determined. Some may even go back to a very remote prehistoric and only conjectural language that was in some sense a parent of both families. To this class may belong the pronoun for "I," in Hebrew and other Canaanite dialects *anoki*, in Old Egyptian *ink*.

Among words from languages to the N are probably those for "iron" and "helmet," both quite likely Hittite. Words for "coat of mail" and "jasper" may be Hurrian. The word *seren*, used only of the Philistine lords, is evidently borrowed from the Philistines. It is believed to be another form of the Greek word we know as "tyrant," which was probably adopted by the Greeks from a language of Asia Minor, perhaps Phrygian or Lydian. The Hebrew and Greek words for "concubine" are nearly the same, and the Hebrew word is not Semitic; either Hebrew borrowed it from Greek or both Greek and Hebrew happened to borrow the same word from an unknown 3rd language.

The Semitic languages to the E contributed many terms to Hebrew, esp. in the fields of government, the army, and law—primarily because the Mesopotamians blossomed into organized and literary civilization earliest of the Semitic-speaking peoples. But suspected borrowing cannot always be proved; the word may be a common Semitic heritage.

Most interesting of all are the words borrowed from the non-Semitic languages farther E, Persian, Sanskrit, and the Dravidian family of S India. The Persian word *pairidaeza* has become our English word "Paradise," even though in Persian, Hebrew, and Greek it was not a proper name but meant simply "garden of trees" or "park." The Hebrew borrowing, *pardes*, is used only in Neh. 2:8; Eccl. 2:5; Song of S. 4:13 and is there respelled in the LXX as *paradeisos*. But in Gen. 2:8, where the Hebrew text has an entirely different native Hebrew word for "garden," the LXX translators also use *paradeisos*. By way of the Latin our ancestors therefore took over "Paradise" as the name for the Garden of Eden.

Persian is so foreign to Hebrew that its words were violently adapted, often beyond recognition. It is hard to see any relation of Ahasuerus, the Persian king in Esth., to Xerxes. In fact it was impossible to equate them till Old Persian was deciphered in the 19th cent. Then it became apparent that the Greeks were even more puzzled than the Hebrews over how to transcribe the Persian name Khashayarsha. Most of the Persian words are in writings of the period when Israel was under Persian domination and refer to governmental matters, e.g. *achashdarpan*, "satrap" (Esth. 3:12), from the Persian *khshatrapan*.

Rare and precious imported articles bear names from still farther E. Several words, with varying degrees of probability, may be of Sanskrit origin as names of articles imported directly or indirectly from India. E.g. *karkom*, "saffron" (Song of S. 4:14), may come from Sanskrit *kunkuma*—akin to Greek *krokos* and Latin and English "crocus"—as the name for the essence distilled from the autumn crocus which gives all Indian curries their yellow color and a bit of their fragrance. Sanskrit terms may also lie behind the words translated "topaz" (Exod. 28:17), "aloes" (Song of S. 4:14), "fine cotton" (Esth. 1:6), "sapphire" (Exod. 24:10), and "ape" (I Kings 10:22). The word for the last exotic import of Solomon's fleet, translated "peacocks" (I Kings 10:22; II Chr. 9:21), may come from one of the Dravidian languages of S India—probably Malayalam, if the fleet touched the Kerala coast, or Tamil, if the trading was with Ceylon. Hebrew, like every other language, shows in its vocabulary a record of the peoples with whom it has been in contact.

III. Aramaic

After the Exile the everyday language of the Jews came to be Aramaic, but it must not be thought that it developed out of Hebrew, like Italian out of late Latin. Rather Aramaic was a sister language that engulfed them politically and culturally until they succumbed to its pressure. At first they added it to their own Hebrew speech and then gradually they gave up Hebrew except in worship.

The oldest inscriptions in Aramaic are of the same age as the oldest in Hebrew (*ca.* 10th cent.). Before that time the development of the 2 languages was perhaps more or less parallel. But in the following cents. Aramaic grew to be the official language of the successive great Assyrian, Neo-Babylonian, and Persian empires. It served them as administrator's Latin did the Roman Empire and as pidgin English does today in the former colonial areas of Asia and Africa. When the Assyrians began their conquests of the Near Eastern world they found Aramaic dialects spoken over so many of the conquered areas that they began to use a simplified form of the language for administrative, military, and business communication. The sands of Egypt have preserved for us many fragments of such correspondence on otherwise perishable papyrus. When the Chaldeans and later the Persians took over the power they continued this practice. Even under the successors of Alexander the Great, Greek only slowly pushed back but did not eliminate Aramaic as the universal language of the Near East. Consequently inscriptions in Aramaic have been found from Greece to Pakistan and from Egypt into what is now S Russia.

In the original text of the Bible as we now know it there is no whole book in Aramaic, though some scholars believe that our supposed original Hebrew and Greek texts of certain books are actually translations of Aramaic originals. Our OT contains 4 inlays of Aramaic in books otherwise in Hebrew: Ezra 4:8–6:18; 7:12-26; Jer. 10:11; Dan. 2:4b–7:28. One of these (Ezra 7:12-26) is a decree of a Persian emperor addressed to a subject people on the edge of his empire and thus is quite properly in the official language in which such decrees were regularly written. Another (Ezra 4:8–6:18) also contains official correspondence with the Persian court that makes the language appropriate. For the shift in languages in the other 2 passages, however, no convincing explanation has been found.

Much of what is said above about Hebrew is also true of Aramaic. Many words are identical in the 2 languages, and many more can be converted by the systematic exchange of one letter for another. The Aramaic verb has the same alternative forms to express complete and incomplete action, but in addition a widely used participle construction practically results in a present tense equivalent to our "he is doing." As in Hebrew, nuances of the verb are expressed by special forms developed from the verbal root, but these use different affixes from those in Hebrew and are more numerous. Some of these Aramaic formations spill over into the Hebrew of the latest books of the OT. Aramaic knows the method of propping a noun in construct form against the following noun to get a phrase, but it also has a much-used preposition for "of" which is lacking in Hebrew.

The later Aramaic found in the Talmud became very hospitable to Greek and Latin loan words. A few such are found in biblical Aramaic, e.g. the Greek musical terms in Dan. 3:5. As might be expected there are also Persian loan words, mostly from the governmental vocabulary.

The NT also contains precious bits of Aramaic embedded in its Greek. Wherever the traditions have preserved the precise words spoken by Jesus (Mark 5:41; 7:34; 15:34) they are in Aramaic, which was the everyday language of Palestine in his time. Such sentences do not indicate that the gospels were first written down in Aramaic and then translated into Greek; it seems certain now that the translation took place while the stories were still circulating only by word of mouth. Nevertheless the Semitic coloration of many of the Greek sentences forces us to think them back into Aramaic, from which we can sometimes arrive at a probable translation which was only awkwardly or ambiguously expressed by the Greek. Paul repeats what must have been a common 2-word Aramaic prayer, *Marana tha!*—

"Our Lord, come!"—in a letter to Greek converts (I Cor. 16:22) and many names of both places and persons throughout the NT are Aramaic. Unfortunately the Aramaic-speaking wing of the church disappeared so early that it left us not a single document in its own language.

IV. GREEK

Whereas the Semitic languages Hebrew and Aramaic are completely foreign to English, except as some of their vocabulary and idiom have entered our everyday speech from the translated OT, Greek is our own kind of language. Along with English it is a member of the great Indo-European family, which today includes most of the languages of N India and Europe and in ancient times included such languages as Sanskrit, Persian, Hittite, and Latin. This is not to say that English and Greek are closely related, like Hebrew and Aramaic; but the Proto-Germanic language that must be assumed to lie behind Anglo-Saxon and the other Germanic languages shared a common ancestry with Greek and other ancient members of the Indo-European family.

There are hundreds of words in English and Greek which have a common origin. This is not to speak of such borrowings as "psychology," "esthetics," "athlete," and "music" which we have adopted along with Greek culture. Rather the shared words that prove kinship are those of everyday usage which are the warp and woof of both languages. Separate development for thousands of years makes most of the similarities recognizable only by experts, but there are some which anyone can see. Cf. e.g. "me" with *me*, "am" with *eimi*, "is" with *esti*, "three" with *treis*, "father" with *pater*, "daughter" with *thugater*, "work" with the root *werg*, and the old verb "wit" with the root *weid*. Even more important are the shared structure and machinery by which thoughts are conveyed. Greek verbs have tenses and moods like ours, including others which English has dropped but other languages of the family still retain. Other parts of speech are the same and are similarly used—e.g. a wealth of adjectives and adverbs, as well as prepositions to express relationships. Complex sentence structure is available for emphasizing the chief thought and subordinating contributory elements. All these are a common family heritage.

Greek literature is vast and rich. Though much of it got lost forever during the centuries before the revival of learning and the printing press we still have hundreds of volumes that were composed before the NT. Furthermore from then to now Greek has always remained both a spoken language and a literary medium. Its ancient literature was consciously and triumphantly artistic. Any list of the world's great literature must draw from it at least the Iliad and the best of the Greek dramas, and its treasures include almost all the classifications of a modern library: poetry, philosophy, history, oratory, literary criticism, grammar, mathematics, medicine, mechanics, botany, geography, essays, novels, and many more. No ancient literature is richer in content or more varied in form.

In addition to literary works we now have a vast body of Greek inscriptions impressed or painted on stone, clay, pottery, metal, wood, or ivory. They have been found in countless places, from far up the Nile to N Germany, and from Spain to India. Hundreds of clay tablets from Crete and the mainland have shown that an early form of Greek was already being written in a syllabary as early as the 15th cent. B.C.

By the time the Greek of the Bible came to be written the classic period of Greek literature was long past. The golden age of Greece was the 6th-4th cents. B.C., the period of Aeschylus and Sophocles, of Plato and Aristotle. The following 6 cents. were its silver age, known as the Hellenistic period. It was a time when Greeks were meeting and being influenced by non-Greek cultures and languages. It was also a time when non-Greeks—orientals, Egyptians, Romans—were irresistibly attracted by things Greek and did their best to learn the Greek language as a linguistic window and door to the larger world.

It could hardly be expected that the Greek language resulting from such intermingling would be up to the standard of the golden age, or for that matter that it would always be worthy even of a silver age. Scholars of that time condescendingly spoke of it as the *koine*, i.e. "common," dialect as distinguished from the recognized old dialects, Ionic, Attic, Doric, and Aeolic; and scholars of our time have adopted this name for it. Koine had contributions from most of the old dialects but esp. from Attic, which completely overshadowed the others because of the political ascendancy of Athens and the talent, power, and inventiveness of her writers. It was a form of Attic that Alexander the Great, a Greek-educated Macedonian, spread into Egypt, Palestine, Syria, Persia, and clear on to India. After his early death his successors ruled this vast area for cents., gradually making a knowledge of some kind of Greek a necessity for the man who aspired to anything more than local influence or importance. The kind of Greek available was Koine.

Just such non-Greeks who had learned the language were the authors of the NT. Probably most if not all of them were Jews. The Greek which they all spoke and wrote was Koine. Like every living language, however, Koine was not just one language. The speech of a construction worker on the job and of a Supreme Court justice giving an opinion are both English yet remarkably different. Perhaps each of the men can understand the other, but neither can speak the other's special language. Even so there was an everyday Koine spoken in the marketplace and the dockyard. We know it from ancient messages scratched on walls and from hundreds of ordinary letters, receipts, and memoranda that have turned up in the dry rubbish heaps buried under drifting Egyptian sand. It was a simple, artless language for saying simple, artless things. Its grammar was often not correct according to the classic rules, though it had its own habits that were grammatical rules when consistently followed. Its spelling was apt to be phonetic as heard by an ear accustomed to non-Greek sounds. At the same time there was a literary Koine, in which many ambitious writings have survived. Its authors attempted, with greater or less success, to imitate the models of the golden age, yet at the same time they used words and forms from the spoken Koine.

The Greek of the several NT authors falls at various points between the literary Koine and that of the marketplace, without quite reaching either extreme. Rev. is at the bottom of the scale, nearest to the careless Koine of the street. Its eloquence in translation conceals a multitude of barbarisms and grammatical errors. In contrast the gospel and letters of John display a very different language, simple and without stylistic ambitions, yet correct, so that as early as the 3rd cent. a Christian scholar noted the striking contrast and recognized that Rev. could not be by the same author. Only a little above Rev. on the scale is Mark; it is interesting to observe Matt. and Luke correcting Mark's rough language, both often finding the same expression in need of improvement.

At the other end of the scale among NT writings is Heb. Not a few of its sentences are really literary Koine, though so much of it is quoted from or influenced by the LXX that ancient critics would scarcely have so rated the book as a whole. Next lower on the scale but still near the top are Luke-Acts and Jas. Paul comes somewhere in the middle, with a talent for moving toward either the popular speech or the literary as the occasion required.

Compared to English, Greek is a compact language, one that can say much in a few words. A great factor in this is its flexible verb, a heritage from the ancestral Indo-European speech which English has largely lost. At the peak of its development each Greek verb could have more than 500 forms, each a little sentence in itself. Among these are 11 infinitives and 11 participles, each with its own shade of meaning; contrast our one simple infinitive and 2 simple participles, which require auxiliaries for multiplication to the forms needed. Contrast also our one imperative with the Greek 6, each of which once had 6 forms, in the Koine reduced to 4, for different numbers and persons. Where we must often use auxiliaries for subjunctive ideas Greek has a whole set of one-word forms for this mood, and in addition an optative mood to express desire or possibility. Where we must use auxiliaries even for the passive voice Greek has not only one-word passive forms but also a middle voice to express reflexive action. Speakers of the popular Koine tended to simplify their language by ignoring some of these verbal resources, esp. the optative mood and the middle voice, for which the NT authors often substitute less compact expressions.

Yet the advantage here is not entirely with the Greek. While Greek has a few verbs that act like our modal auxiliaries, English by necessity has developed them to such an extent that their use can sometimes express more subtle nuances than the Greek tenses, moods, and voices. Thus the NT author who relies too much on the form of his verb may be somewhat ambiguous—cf. e.g. several versions of John 8:32, where the differing combinations of English auxiliaries express distinctions that can only be guessed at in the original text. More often, however, it is the Greek which makes distinctions that are difficult and unwieldy to express in English.

Like most members of the Indo-European family Greek kept the case endings for nouns, which English has dropped except for the possessive form. There are 5 cases, distinguished according to 3 different declensions, i.e. sets of endings; and each set has endings for singular and plural but in Koine usage no dual number. In addition each noun has its gender. Though words for males are always masculine, a few words for females are neuter, and beyond this nouns have genders for which we can no longer even guess the reasons—e.g. why "sea" is feminine, "wine" masculine, and "milk" neuter. Every adjective, including the definite article "the," is declined in all 3 genders and must agree with its noun in gender as well as case and number.

All this is a great nuisance for one learning the language—in ancient times as well as today—but it is a boon to the author seeking effective expression of this thought. Since the case endings show the relationships within the sentence he can vary the order to emphasize the words he wishes without risk of being misunderstood. Furthermore he can safely separate an adjective from its noun by many words if only he is careful to avoid another noun of the same gender, case, and number in the context. The words that belong together are tied by their endings even though far apart in the sentence; even the definite article can point ahead over the backs of a dozen words to its coming noun. Participles follow the pattern of adjectives yet retain their verbal force, and the rich supply of them encourages quite involved constructions. A variety of conjunctions also invites the use of dependent clauses and often results in long complex sentences; some in the NT recent translators have found necessary to break up into half a dozen English sentences.

Another boon to the Greek author is the ease with which a word root can be converted to various parts of speech—verb, noun, adjective, adverb—or, with the addition of one of a number of prefixes, to a derivative word with more or less related meaning. Such a combination might often acquire an entirely new meaning yet retain a suggestion of the original sense as an overtone because the common root remained obvious to both ear and eye. This flexibility allows puns and other word plays, as well as ironic statements and half-whimsical deductions that can only occasionally be suggested in translation.

Even more than the languages of the OT, the NT Koine preserves souvenirs of the languages it has met in the form of borrowed words and expressions. Many Hebraisms are present in the numerous quotations from the LXX as well as in new composition in the style of the LXX (e.g. Luke 1-2). Also many Aramaisms show through from the Aramaic speech of Jesus and his earliest followers and from the Aramaic-Greek bilingualism of most of the NT authors. Often an effect might come from either Hebrew or Aramaic and thus must be labeled simply a Semitism.

A few borrowings from other E languages show up. Mention has already been made of the word "tyrant," taken probably from Lydian or Phrygian, which is found in the name Tyrannus (Acts 19:9), and of the Persian word "paradise," which in the NT is used of heaven (Luke 23:43; II Cor. 12:3; Rev. 2:7). A word used for the temple "treasury" (Mark 12:41) is a hybrid of a Persian word meaning "treasure" and a Greek word for "keeper." In Jesus' saying about the 2nd mile (Matt. 5:41) and the incident of Simon of Cyrene (Mark 15:21) there

appears a verb that is a borrowed Persian military term for a soldier's right to squeeze service to himself from a civilian. A word for palm branches (John 12:13) comes from Coptic, the native language of Egypt in that period. In addition to the title "Pharaoh," coming from Old Egyptian by way of the OT, an exactly similar title from still farther S survives in the supposed name Candace (Acts 8:27). From hieroglyphic records we now know that it was the title of every Ethiopian queen, and though the NT author may have thought it was an individual name, the NEB is right in rendering it "the Kandake, or Queen, of Ethiopia."

Jesus, the early church, and all the NT authors lived within the Roman Empire. E of the Adriatic the imperial government wisely and indeed necessarily let the current Koine continue and made the local officials adopt it as the language of their administration. Even in Rome itself Koine was widely spoken—by the upper classes in an aping of Greek culture and by the lower classes because so many of them were immigrants from the E—and for at least 2 cents. it remained the language of the Roman church. Yet the native tongue of the Romans, including those sent as soldiers and governors, was Latin. As in any occupied country, many of their military, monetary, and administrative terms jumped the language barrier into Koine. In translation we can recognize some of them which also came over into English—e.g. praetorium, legion, centurion, colony, mile, denarius, triumph—and one who can distinguish them in the Greek text finds many others, as well as occasional Latin idioms. Even many of the names—e.g. Paul, Mark, Luke—come from Latin.

In addition to its influence on the Koine of the NT text, Latin has had a tremendous effect on the whole Bible as we know it in English through the Vulg., which remained the Bible of W Europe for over a thousand years. The earliest English translations were from the Vulg., including the first complete one, John Wycliffe's in the 14th cent. When in the 16th cent. William Tyndale and others began to translate from the original languages, they were much influenced by familiarity with the Vulg. In the names long known in Latin they made only minor changes, e.g. Solomon and Isaiah instead of Salomon and Isaias; and they kept many of the distinctively biblical terms that had long been adapted rather than translated from the Latin, e.g. firmament, tabernacle, temple, sacrifice, testament, consecration. Even those today who attempt fresh translations from the original languages cannot avoid using the many words which the Latin version of the Bible has contributed to our everyday speech.

For Further Study. H. H. Rowley, *The Aramaic of the OT,* 1929. C. H. Dodd, *The Bible and the Greeks,* 1935. D. W. Thomas, "The Languages of the OT," in H. W. Robinson, ed., *Record and Revelation,* 1938, pp. 374-402. B. M. Metzger, "The Language of the NT," in *IB,* 1951. N. H. Snaith, "The Language of the OT," in *IB,* 1952. C. F. D. Moule, *An Idiom Book of NT Greek,* 1953. Matthew Black, *An Aramaic Approach to the Gospels and Acts,* 2nd ed., 1954. G. R. Driver, *Semitic Writing from Pictograph to Alphabet,* 2nd ed., 1954. E. C. Colwell, "Greek Language"; Arthur Jeffery, "Aramaic," "Hebrew Language," "Languages of the Ancient Near East," in *IDB,* 1962.

WRITING IN BIBLICAL TIMES

John C. Trever

Writing was invented by the people of the Near East long *before* the beginning of biblical history. It was long *after* the beginning of biblical history, however, when the Israelites began to record their thoughts and experiences. This paradox of biblical history is one on which much light has been cast through discoveries in the lands of the Bible during the past cent.

I. The Earliest Writing

Sumerian. To the best of our present knowledge it was among the ancient Sumerian invaders of S Mesopotamia (see "The People of the OT World," pp. 1005-17) during the 4th millennium B.C.—

A	B	C	D	E
Original pictograph	Pictograph in position of later cuneiform	Early Babylonian	Assyrian	Original or derived meaning
1				bird
2				fish
3				donkey
4				ox
5				sun / day
6				grain
7				orchard
8				to plow / to till
9				boomerang / to throw / to throw down
10				to stand / to go

Courtesy of the Oriental Institute, University of Chicago

Table showing development of cuneiform script

probably *ca.* 3500—that writing began. The earliest examples of what may clearly be called writing have come from ancient Uruk—biblical Erech (Gen. 10:10), modern Warka—S of Babylon in the Tigris-Euphrates Valley. There over 1,000 clay tablets have been found on which pictographs, i.e. simple pictures representing words, were inscribed when the clay was soft. At first they were written like Chinese in vertical columns from the upper right corner down. Some 900 different pictographs have been identified on these earliest tablets. How much earlier the Sumerians, or perhaps even some neighboring people, invented the system of writing in pictures remains a mystery, for perishable materials may have been used for the first attempts.

Through the subsequent cents. gradual modifications of the original pictographs and their use were introduced—e.g. arranging them horizontally from left to right; using ideograms, i.e. pictures to stand for ideas as well as objects; and speeding up the writing by making most of the pictures so stylized that they lost their original identity. A radical change occurred *ca.* 3200 when it was found that pressing the strokes into the soft clay with a stylus with a triangular end was easier than scratching them with a pointed stylus. Thus cuneiform, i.e. wedge-shaped, writing continued as the medium of Mesopotamia for more than 3,000 years (see ill., at left).

Semitic Cuneiform. When the Akkadians, a Semitic people who came up out of Arabia, conquered the Sumerians *ca.* 2500, they soon adapted the cuneiform writing to their own language, and thus the basis for Babylonian cuneiform was established. Despite its refinement of Sumerian, it still included more than 600 symbols. During subsequent cents. the Elamites, Hurrians (Horites), Mitannians, and Hittites also adapted the cuneiform to their languages; and eventually the art of cuneiform writing reached its height of perfection among the Assyrians.

Babylonian cuneiform became the lingua franca, or diplomatic language, of the Near East. While the patriarchal ancestors of Israel were wandering tribesmen and traders in Mesopotamia *ca.* 2000-1700 the Babylonians were using cuneiform copiously in business and literature, thus providing a priceless, almost indestructible, literary heritage to be deciphered in the 19th and 20th cents. of our era. In the great city-states of Mesopotamia, with their urban wealth and stable civilization, scribal schools developed to train the specialists needed to use the complicated wedge-form writing, and historical records and a literature developed. For illiterate seminomads like Abraham, Isaac, and Jacob, however, this elaborate writing had no meaning or use, except perhaps for an occasional business transaction. For Abraham to carry a literature on cuneiform tablets in his donkey saddlebags would be most impractical. For him traditions, stories, and events were remembered and shared by word of mouth, much as they are among the bedouins of the Near East today.

Egyptian Hieroglyphics. Across the Arabian and Sinai deserts to the SW of Mesopotamia, in the land of the Pharaohs, another great writing tradition began developing not long before 3000. Egyptian hieroglyphics also began with pictographs, but by the time from which our earliest examples come (*ca.* 2900) modifications had already taken place and ideograms had developed. They remained essentially unchanged for 3,000 years, though modified scripts, called hieratic and demotic, were developed later for less formal writing.

Courtesy of the Oriental Institute, University of Chicago

Cast of the Rosetta Stone (original in the British Museum); the chance finding of this text written in hieroglyphic Egyptian, Demotic and Greek enabled scholars to decipher hieroglyphic script

When the Hebrew patriarchs entered Egypt, perhaps *ca.* 1700, they were no doubt impressed by the elaborately carved hieroglyphic inscriptions on granite monuments already cents. old. Likewise they probably saw some of the magical formulas, incantations, prayers, and other writings on papyrus which the Egyptians customarily buried with their dead in pyramids and tombs. But the task of eking out a meager existence in the land of Goshen on the Nile delta left little incentive for these shepherds to ponder the mysteries of writing, which was used by kings, princes, and priests and was unintelligible even to most of the Egyptian natives. Later Moses (13th cent.) may have dabbled in the art of writing by this complex method during his youth in Egypt; but for the Midianites, among whom he dwelt for many years, and for the illiterate crowd of depressed, toiling slaves whom he led out of Egypt reading and writing still held no value.

II. THE ORIGIN OF HEBREW WRITING

The Canaanite Alphabet. The language in which the earliest biblical records finally came to be written was none of those so far mentioned, as far as any evidence reveals. The Hebrew that the people of Israel came to use was a language adopted from the Canaanites of Palestine, among whom they settled sometime after 1250. Evidence has only recently become available to show that the Canaanites were developing their written language during the very time when the Hebrews were in Egypt. No Canaanite inscriptions have appeared from as early as the patriarchal period, when the ancestors of Israel were mingling with the Canaanites in Palestine.

It was probably during the 17th cent. that some genius among the peoples of Palestine or Syria made the greatest invention for written communication that the world had yet seen—the alphabet. Whether it was an individual or a group who made this startling breakthrough we may never know, but it was indeed a tremendous step forward for civilization. Unlike the cumbersome systems of Mesopotamia and Egypt, with their multitude of syllabic, ideographic, and determinative symbols, the alphabet began with 2 dozen or so simple pictures each representing one basic consonantal sound. The symbols were chosen by the acrophonic principle—e.g. a house, *bayt* in Canaanite, was drawn to stand for the sound "B," a wavy line representing ripples on water, *maym* in Canaanite, to stand for the sound "M," etc.

The earliest evidence of this alphabetic script is on a fragment of pottery containing 3 characters scratched in the clay before it was fired *ca.* 1600 or a little earlier, judging by the nature of the pottery. The piece was found at Gezer W of Jerusalem on the road to Joppa. Other examples dating from the following 2 cents. have been found at Shechem, Lachish, and Beth-Shemesh, all cities in Palestine. Judg. 8:14 mentions a 12th-cent. Canaanite who could write.

Proto-Sinaitic Script. A similar alphabetic script, perhaps influenced by the Palestinian Canaanite alphabet as well as by the Egyptian hieroglyphics, was in use by Egyptian turquoise miners on the W coast of Sinai around Serabit el-Khadim—perhaps the Dophkah of Num. 33:12-13—during the 15th and 14th cents. This Proto-Sinaitic script, as it is called, seems to be the ancestor of still another alphabetic script, S Arabic, the earliest example of which comes from the 8th cent. It is unlikely that the seminomadic Midianites, among whom Moses spent his early life, practiced writing at so early a time—no evidence of it has been found. If they had done so, it would probably have been a modified form standing between the Proto-Sinaitic and the S Arabic scripts.

Alphabetic Cuneiform. These alphabetic scripts were still in their formative stages when Israel was emerging under the leadership of Moses. It should not be presumed, therefore, that an extensive literature was written with them. There is one notable exception, however, viz. the alphabetic cuneiform of ancient Ugarit, of which numerous examples were discovered in 1929 at the site of Ras Shamra on the N coast of Syria. In the 15th-14th cents. the large and affluent city of Ugarit apparently was a key Canaanite center of industry, trade, and culture. Closely associated with this city's prominent temples of Baal and Dagon, important deities of the extensive Canaanite pantheon of gods, were priest-scribes who ingeniously adapted the Canaanite alphabet to the cuneiform medium and recorded a copious literature on clay tablets. A library of these documents was discovered in the home of the high priest of Ugarit. Many of them contain the mythology of the early Canaanites in a language clearly related to the Hebrew in which the OT was written. Ugaritic has in fact shed considerable light on the Hebrew of the Bible. A few of these early alphabetic cuneiform inscriptions have been discovered in Palestine.

Early Hebrew. Even though the Hebrews were surrounded by civilizations in which writing was being used for business and literature, there is no reason to assume that they were writing down their own traditions during these early periods. Written languages, without exception, developed among peoples who had already achieved the level of urban civilization, where trade and industry demanded recording of information and the emergence of an affluent culture stimulated literature. We should therefore not expect to find a literature or copious written records among the Hebrews much before the time of the united kingdom of Saul, David, and Solomon (*ca.* 1033-931), when their secular culture became more like that of the Sumerians, Akkadians, and Canaanites.

How early, then, did the Hebrews actually begin to write down their traditions and experiences? The evidence is inconclusive, to be sure. To suggest that it was before or during the time of Moses, however, seems unlikely. Tradition has long asserted that Moses wrote the first 5 books of the Bible, but the accumulated evidence to the contrary is overwhelming. On the basis of the epigraphic, i.e. inscriptional, evidence and in view of the social circumstances of the Hebrews at that time, it is even doubtful that Moses put anything into writing, even the 10 Commandments (to note the confusion in the tradition cf. Exod. 34:27-28 with Exod. 34:1; Deut. 10:1-4). That he established the foundation for Hebrew law with a basic group of remembered commandments there can be no doubt. But what need was there to write when no one would be able to read? Or why inscribe commandments on stones to be put in a sacred box (Deut. 10:5) which no one could touch, let alone read from? When the traditions of Israel's history finally came to be written down (see "The Compiling of Israel's Story," pp. 1082-89), it was natural for the scribes to assume that writing had been practiced by their ancestors. The earliest references in the Bible to writing (Exod. 17:14; 24:4; 39:30; Num. 33:2) may therefore well be a reading back into the tradition of a later development rather than evidence of historical fact.

A similar observation may be made regarding the references to writing in Josh. 8:32-35; 18:4-9, though the origin of the covenant in the form of written laws doubtless should be placed quite early in the history of Israel. It is only conjecture, to be sure, but perhaps it was as early as the period of the Conquest and Settlement (*ca.* 1250-1033) that some Israelite priest who had mastered the Canaanite alphabetic script recorded the first code of laws. Such important sacred centers as Shechem or Shiloh are likely places where such writing may have been done in that early period. Nevertheless not a fragment of Hebrew writing has yet been recovered from before the 10th cent.

Reference in Num. 21:14 to the "Book of the Wars of the LORD" suggests that a collection of early war ballads was written down in this period (*ca.* 1100?). It may have included the Song of Deborah (Judg. 5), the Song of Miriam (Exod. 15:21), and other early ballads, some of which were later copied into Israel's early literature. Josh. 10:13; II Sam. 1:18 mention another such collection, called the "Book of Jashar" ("upright"?), which may have circulated *ca.* 1000.

That Hebrew writing was used extensively during the 10th cent., however, there is no doubt. In that time Israel reached her golden age, and writing for business and official documents was necessary. For this period the OT first refers to persons whose duties included writing. David appointed Jehoshaphat as "recorder," lit. "remembrancer" (II Sam. 8:16; 20:24; I Chron. 18:15), whose duties probably included the keeping of court records or at least the overseeing of those who were capable of writing such records. Also in David's court Seraiah is mentioned as "secretary" or "scribe," who very probably was skilled in writing (II Sam. 8:17). Doubtless scribal schools existed by this time in Israel.

It was probably Solomon's reign that produced the first great epic of Israel's ancestral traditions, commonly called "Yahwist" (J), which was later incorporated into Gen., Exod., Num., and possibly other books. From this same time comes also the intimate eyewitness story of David's court now found in II Sam. 9-20; I Kings 1-2.

Despite all this scribal activity, only one Hebrew inscription from the 10th cent. has been discovered —the Gezer calendar. Inscribed on soft limestone, it may be a schoolboy's practice tablet for learning the art of writing in a scribal school. Comparison with Canaanite inscriptions of the same period from Byblos and elsewhere in Syria shows that the alphabetic script had by then become fairly stabilized. This paucity of epigraphic evidence suggests a word of caution in drawing conclusions about the growth of biblical literature. The percentage of epigraphic evidence recovered by archaeology in Palestine is no measure of the degree of literary activity. It merely suggests that the materials used were of a perishable nature.

Beginning in the 10th cent. the Paleo- (i.e. early) Hebrew script was used extensively by scribes, who wrote down the thoughts of Israelite priests, prophets, and historians for their copious historical records and literary compositions. After the Exile (6th cent.) this early script fell into disuse as the Aramaic square script was adopted for both sacred scriptures and daily use. The Paleo-Hebrew script lingered on, however, or was revived periodically, esp. during periods of conservative reaction, as its appearance among some of the Dead Sea scrolls and on Maccabean and Jewish revolt coins demonstrates.

Epigraphic material is now available to show the appearance of Paleo-Hebrew in each of the cents. of its use in Israel. The 10th-cent. Gezer calendar has been noted already. From the 9th cent. comes the famed Moabite Stone with its lengthy inscription paralleling the record in II Kings 3. From the 8th cent. we now have numerous business ostraca, i.e. writings in ink on broken pieces of pottery, from Samaria, mostly wine receipts. From the end of that cent. comes the Siloam inscription, which tells how Hezekiah's water tunnel was dug under Jerusalem between the Gihon spring and the Siloam pool when the Assyrians threatened siege in 701. Most important are the Lachish ostraca, some 25 pieces of pottery with notes sent to the commander of the Judean forces defending Lachish against the Babylonians in 589/88. From Tel Arad south of Hebron have now come 17 more ostraca from the same period, and from Mezad Hashavyahv further west have come three more, one of which is quite large and may date from the late 7th cent. From these and the later Dead Sea scrolls we can now visualize the manuscript which Baruch prepared for Jeremiah in 604 (Jer. 36). In addition to these few inscriptions numerous inscribed stamp seals, like the famed jasper lion seal of Jeroboam II's official at Megiddo, have come from various excavations in Palestine and illustrate the writing of these latter cents.

Considering the vast literature of prophecy, history, poetry, and wisdom which developed during those cents. in Palestine, these epigraphic remains seem paltry indeed, but they are at least instructive. It must be remembered that repeated invasions and strife in Palestine, which lay like a bridge between the imperialistic nations of Mesopotamia and Egypt, doubtless account for the destruction of most of that literature which was copied on perishable leather and papyrus. What war did not destroy the climatic conditions of most of Palestine disintegrated in time. Unfortunately the Israelite scribes did not use the Ugaritic method of writing on clay tablets. The Dead Sea scrolls illustrate graphically both these means of destruction. Only by the good fortune of the particular location of the caves by the Dead Sea was it possible for so much of the writings of ancient Qumran to be preserved. Many of the fragments reveal the ravages of moisture and insects as well as destruction from war—some show signs of deliberate violent abuse.

Scholars disagree over the dating of the Paleo-Hebrew fragments of Lev. and Exod. found in Qumran Caves I, II, IV during 1949-52. Some believe that their script represents a continuation of the older script among conservative Jews and thus date the fragments in the 4th or 3rd cent. Others consider them to be a revival of that script during the first cent. B.C. by the men of Qumran for their most sacred law scrolls. Such a revival may have been inspired by the successful Maccabean revolt, as inscriptions on the Maccabean coins imply. If the earlier dating is correct, these fragments represent the earliest known examples of any part of the Bible.

III. ARAMAIC SQUARE SCRIPT

During the exile of the Jews in Babylonia (6th cent.) they found that Aramaic had already become the common language of international communication. As early as the 8th cent. scribes in Mesopotamia had begun to add notes in Aramaic on clay cuneiform business documents. The Aramaic script was an adaptation of the Canaanite alphabet in a somewhat cursive, or less angular, direction. By the 6th cent. it began to displace the unwieldy cuneiform throughout the Near East. The Jews tended to adopt this script as they began to learn the Aramaic language, which by the beginning of the 5th cent. became the lingua franca of the Near East.

From the late 6th and the 5th cents. we now possess a considerable correspondence on papyrus from the Jewish colony on the island called Elephantine in the Nile River close by Syene (modern Aswan) in S Egypt. We have also a number of letters on skins, probably written in Babylon or Susa ca. 410 by the Persian satrap Arsham. These documents were all written in the early Aramaic script. Other papyri and ostraca from the 5th-3rd cents. —mostly from Egypt but including a few ostraca from S Palestine—have helped to round out our knowledge of the development of the square Aramaic script down to the Dead Sea scroll materials. Then in 1962 came the discovery of 40 fragmentary Samaritan business documents on papyrus deep within a huge cave called Mughâret Abu Shinjeh in the Wadi Daliyeh 9 miles N of Jericho. They supply illustrations of this script from Palestine which can be specifically dated from 375 to 335. These are now the oldest manuscripts yet to appear in Palestine. They provide an important link in the history of the square Aramaic writing between the Elephantine papyri and the earliest of the Dead Sea scrolls.

The rapidity with which our knowledge of the development of Hebrew writing has been accumulating during the mid-20th cent. is almost overwhelming, largely as a result of the numerous cave discoveries in Palestine beginning in 1947. From 11 Qumran caves near the NW shore of the Dead Sea have come ca. 600 different Hebrew and Aramaic manuscripts from among thousands of fragments written mostly on skins. Among these fragments have been identified scripts ranging from ca. 250 B.C. to ca. A.D. 60, the earliest being a fragment of Exod. in an Elephantine-type square script. Fragments have been discovered also at Masada, where the Zealots made their last stand against the Romans in A.D. 73; and manuscripts found in the Wadi Murabba'at and Nahal Heber caves in the S wilderness of Judea carry the evidence down to the 2nd revolt against Rome in 132-35. From these discoveries it is now possible to trace the development of the square script as used for sacred scriptures from the 3rd cent. B.C. to its formalization in the late first cent. A.D.

IV. THE BEGINNING OF CHRISTIAN WRITING

Whether or not the early Christian apostles wrote anything down in their native Aramaic language is still an intensely debated question. No fragment of any Christian writing in Aramaic—or any language—from the first Christian cent. is yet known to exist. Had any of the gospels been written in Aramaic, we now at least know what they would have looked like as a result of the discoveries at Qumran. The Genesis Apocryphon from Cave I, though badly disintegrated over most of its 22 columns, preserves 3 columns written by a scribe at Qumran in an elegant square Aramaic character and language probably from the very lifetime of Jesus.

In evaluating the problem of writing among the first-cent. Palestinian Christians, we need to remember that the focus of their gospel preaching was on a firm belief in the immediate return of Christ. What need would there be for writing in the new age as they conceived it? Most of those Christians could not read anyway. Unlike the Qumran community, which concentrated on written scriptures, the earliest Christian community was a fellowship of preachers.

When in the middle of the first cent. Christianity moved out into the Greek-speaking world among the Jews of the Diaspora, i.e. those outside Judea, and the Gentiles, written communications became necessary. Thus it is probable that the first Christian writings were letters in Greek, such as Paul's letters to his churches. The earliest of Paul's letters were doubtless written sometime during A.D. 49-52. It is presumed that near this same time a collection of the sayings of Jesus was recorded for use with Christian converts in the Gentile world. Papias, a leader of the church in the 2nd cent. A.D., is reported to have said that Matthew wrote down the "sayings" (*logia*) of Jesus "in Hebrew"—probably meaning Aramaic—but there is no evidence to confirm this statement.

The Greek language had already been in use by the Jews of the Diaspora, esp. in Alexandria, Egypt, as early as the 3rd cent. B.C., when they began to translate their Hebrew scriptures into Greek, which was by then their native tongue. These Greek translations of the OT and the Apoc., called the LXX, became the Bible of the early Christian church. Most of the quotations from the OT in the Christian writings are from the LXX.

There is an interesting relation between the early Greek and the Hebrew writing in the fact that the early Canaanite alphabet, as developed by the Phoenicians *ca.* the 10th-9th cents. B.C., was adopted and improved by the Greeks for their writing—most notably by the adaptation of some of the characters to represent vowels. This Greek-improved Canaanite alphabet became the basis of all the scripts of W civilization. By the time the Greek language returned to Palestine with the invading armies of Alexander the Great in 331 B.C.—and with Phoenician traders even before that—the individual developments of the Greek and the Hebrew scripts had obscured almost all the similarities except the names of some letters and the general order of their alphabets.

The earliest known example of NT writing is a small fragment of a papyrus leaf, barely 2½ by 3½ inches, which is believed to have been copied *ca.* A.D. 125. Inscribed on both sides with portions of John 18, it is also the earliest example of a biblical codex, i.e. a book with leaves. All earlier biblical fragments are from scrolls or single sheets.

About the turn of the 20th cent. a flood of papyrus manuscripts came from the sands of Egypt, esp. near the Faiyum. Consisting mostly of Greek business documents and some classical literature, they provide ample evidence for the nature of writing during the earliest Christian period. The character of the language on these documents, called Koine Greek, has shed much light on the text of the NT, which we now know was also composed in the Koine Greek of the first cent.

V. Materials Used for Writing

Clay. The oldest preserved writing was done on clay tablets in S Mesopotamia by the Sumerians, who found the alluvial soil of the Tigris-Euphrates Valley esp. suited to a writing medium. It was abundant and cheap. Tablets of many different shapes and sizes have been discovered in numerous mounds of ancient Mesopotamian cities. Most are flat on one

Courtesy of the Oriental Institute, University of Chicago

Clay tablet from ancient Nuzi (*ca.* 1500-1400 B.C.) inscribed with list of personal names, plus seal impressions

side and convex on the other for ease in holding, the writing beginning on the flat side and often continuing on the convex side. Often the tablets were merely dried or sunbaked, but for more permanent preservation occasionally some were baked in a furnace like pottery. Most of those discovered today have to be baked very carefully in electric furnaces to assure their preservation and to permit necessary cleaning. Sometimes letters or legal documents were encased in a thin layer of clay to make an envelope on which the essential information of the contents was repeated.

The Bible makes no reference to the use of clay for writing, though a number of cuneiform tablets have been found in the mounds of ancient Palestinian cities and many originating in Palestine and Syria during the 14th cent. were recovered at Tell el-Amarna (ancient Akhetaton) in Egypt.

Octraca. Clay was used in all ancient countries for pottery utensils. Potsherds, i.e. broken pieces of pottery, were therefore readily available to write on. The Hebrews found that potsherds were useful for scribal practice, notes, receipts, brief letters, and other inscriptions. Inscribed potsherds, called "ostraca" (Greek for "potsherds"), have been found in the mounds of Palestine—e.g. Lachish, Samaria, Eziongeber, Masada—the Jewish colony at Elephantine in

Courtesy of John C. Trever and the Israel Department of Antiquities and Museums

Potsherd on which appears the Hebrew alphabet (beginning from lower right) dating *ca.* 31 B.C.; this ostracon was found in a dump just N of the Qumran settlement and is thought to have been the practice work of a student scribe

Egypt, and most Near Eastern countries. References to potsherds are found in the Bible but with no mention of their use for writing.

Stone. Egyptian hieroglyphics, Akkadian cuneiform, early Canaanite, Moabite, Hebrew, and many other languages of the ancient world frequently were incised on stone monuments. The number is esp. great in Egypt as a result of its ancient reverence for the dead as well as of the abundance of available stone. Ancient Egyptian reliefs in pink granite, alabaster, and limestone are still among the wonders of the ancient world. Mesopotamia has many fewer because of its alluvial soil. The code of Hammurabi and the Black Obelisk of Shalmaneser III, both with cuneiform chiseled in black diorite, are among the notable stone monuments from ancient Mesopotamia. The early laws of the Hebrews are said to have been inscribed on stone (Exod. 24:12; 34:1; Deut. 4:13; Josh. 8:32). The earliest known Hebrew inscription, as already mentioned, was the limestone Gezer calendar. The Mesha and Siloam inscriptions were likewise on stone. During the first cents. B.C. and A.D. the Jews gathered the bones of their deceased into limestone bone chests, called "ossuaries," and often the name of the person was incised or painted thereon.

Metal. Inscriptions in gold, silver, copper, bronze, and even lead have been found in excavated cities, though not often. I Macc. 8:22; 14:18, 27, 48 refer to bronze plaques, and the copper scrolls from Qumran Cave III are well known. There is a reference to inscribing gold in Exod. 28:36. One of the earliest alphabetic inscriptions found at Lachish was on a bronze dagger.

Wood. The use of wood in the form of tablets for writing was apparently common throughout the Near East in Bible times. Though none have been preserved from Mesopotamia, references to them and pictures on reliefs make clear that they were used. In Egypt the carving of reliefs with hieroglyphs on wooden statues and panels was common. Clay- and perhaps wax-coated tablets were employed for practice in the schools, a stylus being used to scratch the surface for writing lessons. The diptych, consisting of 2 tablets laced together to form a hinge, is known to have existed as early as 700 in Mesopotamia and a cent. later in Greece. It appears to have been the prototype of the papyrus or parchment codex and the modern book.

Num. 17:2-3 mentions inscribed "rods" in the tent of meeting, and Ezek. 37:16-17 suggests the use of the diptych. In Isa. 8:1; 30:8; Hab. 2:2 there are 2 different Hebrew words which seem to refer to wooden tablets. The tablet on which Zechariah wrote the name of John (Luke 1:63), to judge from the Greek, was the waxed wooden tablet, a common item in ancient Greek and Roman schools.

Papyrus. The manufacture of papyrus for letters, business documents, and books was a major industry and export item for ancient Egypt from a very early time. Its invention must go back to around 3000, for examples of it are known from the first dynasty shortly thereafter. The earliest inscribed example, however, comes from *ca.* 2400. Until the 10th cent. A.D., when paper finally supplanted it, papyrus was one of the most common media used for writing.

The papyrus plant grew abundantly in the marshes of the Nile delta. The pithy stalks of the reed were slit with a sharp instrument to produce thin strips. These were laid side by side; then a similar layer was laid horizontally on them with some kind of adhesive, the nature of which is unknown. The resulting crisscross was pressed firmly, dried, and trimmed to form a sturdy sheet, usually about 10 by 12 inches. Sheets could be glued together to produce a roll of varying length. Though the average book roll was *ca.* 30-35 feet long, a few scrolls have been found more than 100 feet long, and the Great Harris Papyrus is 133 feet long. Writing was done on the horizontal stripped side in most cases, using a reed pen and ink. The text was arranged in neat columns of a convenient width.

Though the papyrus plant is referred to several times in the OT (Exod. 2:3; Job 8:11; Isa. 18:2; 35:7) its use in documents and scrolls is not specifically mentioned. The scroll of Jer. 36, however, was doubtless a papyrus roll, for King Jehoiakim would hardly have tolerated the stench of a burning leather scroll (vss. 22-23) in his winter palace. Many manuscript fragments among the Dead Sea scroll discoveries are on papyrus, esp. those from Cave VI, though the men of Qumran used skins primarily for their manuscripts.

That the first NT books were written on papyrus seems clear (cf. II John 12). All the earliest copies are of this material. About the beginning of the Christian era it was found that several sheets of papyrus could be placed one on top of the other, then folded in the middle to make a quire of several pages, thus utilizing both sides of the papyrus sheets. The codex was thus introduced for lengthy documents. Thus early Christians seem to have adopted the codex form for their scriptures by the beginning of the 2nd cent.

Leather, Parchment, and Vellum. That tanned leather was used in Bible times is clear from references to it in Exod. 25:5; 26:14 (cf. Num. 31:20; II Kings 1:8), but no biblical reference implies its use as a writing material. Jewish rabbinical tradition specifically requires that Torah scrolls used in synagogues be written on specially prepared skins, a custom which continues in Judaism today. An early Jewish legend, in fact, testifies to the custom as early as the 3rd cent. B.C. From the late 5th cent. B.C. we have a group of letters on skins written in Persia and Babylonia to officials in Egypt.

Use of skins for writing in Babylonia and Persia is also attested by literary remains and in Assyria by some reliefs. In Egypt the evidence suggests their use as early as 2500; in fact the earliest preserved inscribed skin, a 6th dynasty scroll, dates from *ca.* 2350.

The discovery of the Qumran scrolls has revealed that the use of animal skins for manuscripts may have been far more common in Israel than previously believed. Animal skins perhaps were so abundant that they were cheaper to use for writing than papyrus imported from Egypt. At least this seems to have been true for the men of Qumran. Remains of buildings discovered in 1958 2 miles S of the community center led the excavators to believe that skins were prepared there, though no evidence for the practice of tanning was found. Skins used for manuscripts, it seems from all the evidence available, were not tanned but treated by scraping and rubbing, an early stage of the development of parchment.

Tradition has long claimed that Eumenes II, king of Pergamum (197-159 B.C.), invented parchment when the supply of papyrus rolls from Egypt was cut off. It is more likely, however, that there was merely a refinement of the use of skins for writing about that time. Soaking the skins of various animals in limewater, rubbing with pumice stone, and stretching them on a frame were found to produce a finer quality writing surface. Tradition required the Jews to use animal thongs to join the sheets for synagogue rolls, but at Qumran linen thread was used.

By the 4th cent. A.D. Christians adopted the parchment codex for their best scripture copies. The Codex Sinaiticus and Codex Vaticanus, the 2 earliest complete Bibles yet discovered, are on a fine quality of parchment, or vellum, the distinction between which is not always clear. Vellum is technically a finer quality parchment made from calfskin.

VI. Equipment for Writing

Pens. The tool used for writing depended on the nature of the material on which the writing was to be done. For clay a stylus was made of a reed such as grew abundantly along the riverbanks. The end was squared off in a triangular shape to punch the wedge marks. A pointed end was used for earlier pictographs and potters' marks. The stylus could also be made of wood or bone. For signatures on letters and legal documents, stamp or cylinder seals, usually beautifully cut from precious stones, were pressed into the clay or rolled over it while it was still soft. A metal stylus or chisel of course was necessary for stone inscriptions or for engraving metal (cf. Job. 19:24; Jer. 17:1).

On potsherds a pen was used with ink. The reed was ideally suited for this purpose. The pointed end was apparently frayed somewhat, producing a brush-like stroke. Papyrus required a similar pen, but on skin a sharper pointed pen could be used to produce a finer stroke. A sharp knife was needed by the scribe to keep his pens in proper shape, for they

Courtesy of the Oriental Institute, University of Chicago

Portrait statuette of an Egyptian scribe

would tend to wear out rapidly (cf. Ps. 45:1). During the Greek period a reed pen with a sharp point that was split to form a nib came into use. This kind of pen was esp. useful for writing on parchment.

To carry his reed pens the scribe had a rectangular reed case with slots to accommodate several pens, and on one end were depressions for the ink cakes (cf. Ezek. 9:2-3, 11). Many examples of such cases have been recovered from the tombs of Egypt. The earliest found was made from a larger hollow reed to which were attached with leather thongs a flat pottery rectangle with 2 depressions to hold red and black inks and a small pottery jar to hold water for dissolving the inks.

Ink. The Egyptians discovered the means for producing ink very early, before 3000. Pure carbon was produced from lampblack gathered from bottoms of cooking pots and mixed into a solution of gum and water. The solution was then dried to produce small round cakes which looked like children's watercolors today. The scribe moistened the cake to get his ink for writing. Thus a small jar of water was a part of his equipment, as early examples show. Later inks made of metallic compounds were sometimes used, esp. for color. At Qumran 3 ink wells were discovered in the scriptorium, one containing some dried ink. There ink was probably used in solution, much as today. Exod. 32:33; Num. 5:23; Ps. 69:28; Jer. 36:18 imply an ink which could be washed off, suggesting a pure carbon ink. Erasures in the Dead

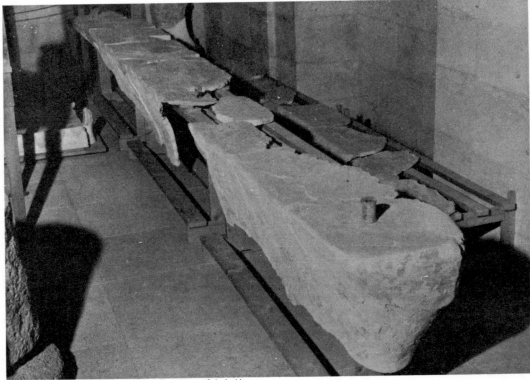

Courtesy of John C. Trever and the Israel Department of Antiquities

Table and bench with ink wells from the "Scriptorium" at Khirbet Qumran

Sea scrolls appear to have been made by scratching with the scribe's knife.

VII. THE WRITING CRAFT

Writing was a specialized craft in biblical times. The involved cuneiform and hieroglyphic characters required highly trained experts. Even the alphabetic writing seems to have been mastered only by a few, so that scribal schools early became a necessity throughout the Near East. The scribes therefore were an honored class of men. The appearance of many clay tablets, stone inscriptions, and papyrus and leather manuscripts indicates that these men were indeed skilled in their craft.

Jer. 36 tells of the preparation of a scroll. The prophet did not do his own writing but employed Baruch, who was evidently a trained scribe as well as a loyal companion. Baruch probably sat on a low bench with the roll of papyrus on his lap and a small table close by to hold the pen case with its ink cakes, cup of water, extra reed pens, and other scribal needs. Careful measurement of the benches and tables in the Qumran scriptorium has shown that the scribes there must have worked in this posture, just as did Egyptian scribes when writing on scrolls began (see ill., p. 1207). Baruch wrote in Paleo-Hebrew characters, like those on the Lachish ostraca, as Jeremiah dictated his thoughts aloud. His angular letters followed one another from right to left, the words separated only by dots or short slanting strokes.

For a legal document, e.g. the deed for the pur-chase of a piece of property described in Jer. 32:9-14, a single sheet of papyrus would be used, not unlike those discovered at Elephantine in Egypt. The professional scribe wrote the agreed terms and description of the property, probably at the dictation of the contracting parties. With the official document completed, the scribe handed a pen to the parties and witnesses for their signatures. These appear quite crude beneath the artistic lettering of the scribe, as several examples show. The deed was folded and tied with thongs, and the knots were covered with clay, which was flattened and inscribed by a stamp seal.

Paul's letters were dictated in Greek. Gal. 6:11; Col. 4:18; II Thess. 3:17 indicate that when he took the papyrus from the scribe he wrote more than just his name. His agitation over the Galatian problem prompted him to add a paragraph (Gal. 6:11-18). His scribes were probably not professionals but fellow missionaries or church members. In at least one case (Rom. 16:22) the scribe added his own greeting to the greetings at the close of the letter.

For Further Study. Edward Chiera, *They Wrote on Clay*, 1938. David Diringer, *The Alphabet*, 1947; *The Hand-produced Book*, 1953; *Writing*, 1962. F. G. Kenyon, *Books and Readers in Ancient Greece and Rome*, 2nd ed., 1951. F. M. Cross, Jr., "The Development of the Jewish Scripts," in G. E. Wright, ed., *The Bible and the Ancient Near East*, 1961. J. P. Hyatt, "The Writing of an OT Book," C. C. McCown, "The Earliest Christian Books," in D. N. Freedman and G. E. Wright, eds., *The Biblical Archaeologist Reader*, 1961. T. O. Lambdin, "Alphabet," R. J. Williams, "Writing and Writing Materials," in *IDB*, 1962.

THE MAKING
OF THE OLD TESTAMENT CANON
Lou H. Silberman

I. The Holy Scriptures of the Synagogue

Names. The traditional collection of the Holy Scriptures of Judaism has been designated by many names. The most general and perhaps the earliest is simply the Hebrew word for "books." In Dan. 9:2 this word is used to refer to the sources—among them Jer.—which Daniel consulted. In later Jewish writings, as well as in the NT (e.g. Gal. 3:10; Luke 4:17), it is used without an adjective. Only in medieval times was it necessary to add the modifier "holy" to distinguish this collection from other books. An earlier differentiation of nonscriptural books was made by adding the modifier "outside," or "extraneous," to indicate books not included in the recognized collection.

Another designation is a Hebrew word meaning "that which is read," indicating the cultic-liturgical role the collection played. The term most frequently used in the NT—"scripture" (e.g. John 2:22; Acts 8:32), "scriptures" (e.g. Mark 12:24; I Cor. 15:3-4), "holy scriptures" (Rom. 1:2), "writings" (John 5:47), "sacred writings" (II Tim. 3:15)—as well as in the works of Hellenistic writers such as Philo and Josephus, reflects another Hebrew term meaning "that which is written."

The Hebrew word *torah*, often translated "law" but more accurately "teaching," is used to designate the whole collection, though often restricted to a portion of it, the Pentateuch. In an extended sense, however, "Torah" covers the entire range of authoritative Jewish teaching. The abbreviation TNK, composed of the initial letters of the Hebrew words designating the 3 major divisions of the collection and read as a word, "Tanakh," is yet another traditional term. The common expression "Old Testament" is of course a Christian term, but contemporary Jewish scholars use it without accepting its theological implications.

Divisions. The synagogal collection consisted of 24 books—Sam., Kings, Chr., Ezra-Neh. each being a single book and the "minor," i.e. shorter, prophets composing the one "Book of the 12." The Jewish historian Josephus (late first cent. A.D.) mentions but 22 "justly accredited" books, apparently combining Ruth with Judg. and Lam. with Jer. The reason for this enumeration may have been to parallel the number of books with the 22 letters of the Hebrew alphabet. It is possible, however, that there is no discrepancy between the 2 counts, 22 indicating the number of scrolls and 24 the number of books.

The books are divided into 3 groups: (*a*) The Torah, often translated "Law," consisting of the 5 books attributed to Moses, i.e. the Pentateuch: Gen., Exod., Lev., Num., Deut.; (*b*) the Prophets, subdivided into the Former Prophets: Josh., Judg., Sam. Kings, and the Latter Prophets: Isa., Jer., Ezek., and the 12; and (*c*) the Writings: Pss., Prov., Job, the 5 Scrolls (Song of S., Ruth, Lam., Eccl., Esth.), Dan., Ezra-Neh., and Chr. It will be recognized at once that this division and order is different from that found in both Protestant and Roman Catholic texts. In these Ruth follows Judg. and Lam. follows Jer., as apparently in Josephus, and Dan. is included among the prophets. Further the remaining books of the Writings intervene between the Former Prophets and the Latter Prophets, so that a 3-fold division is not preserved.

How early this division may have been made is not certain. Some scholars interpret the references to Ezra's bringing the "law of your God" from Babylonia with official Persian approval (Ezra 7:14) and gaining the people's acceptance of it after a public reading (Neh. 8:1-12) as describing the separation of the Pentateuch from other books and its recognition as holy scripture. But there is no way to identify the "law" presented by Ezra, and in fact details of the account suggest that it was a more limited document than the Pentateuch. The acceptance by the Samaritans of the Pentateuch and Joshua only points to the fixing of the Torah tradition before the final rupture between that community and the Jews.

The earliest clear evidence we have comes from Jeshua ben Sira, the author of Ecclus. (*ca.* 180 B.C.). In his praise of the great men of Israel (chs. 44–49) he mentions them in a sequence that reflects the order of books in the Torah and the Prophets. In addition he knows the writings of the minor prophets as a collection under the heading "the twelve prophets" (49:10) and cites (48:10) the final vss. of Mal. (4:5-6), which are thought to be an editor's addition to indicate the conclusion of the 2nd division, the Prophets. Ben Sira shows also knowledge of some of the Writings, but not all; Eccl., Esth., and Dan. were not in his collection. His grandson, who translated his book into Greek (soon after 132 B.C.), 3 times mentions in his preface the 3-fold collection of "the law and the prophets and other books."

Sequence. The Babylonian Talmud, an extensive

1209

compilation of Jewish tradition completed *ca.* A.D. 500, says of the sequence of the books: "Our Rabbis taught: The order of the Prophets is, Joshua, Judges, Samuel, Kings, Jeremiah, Ezekiel, Isaiah and the Twelve" (Baba Bathra 14*b,* Soncino trans.). The discussion at this point makes it clear that the principle applied here was not chronological but involved other factors. Though Hosea was considered the first of the literary prophets and hence should have preceded all the others in order, his work was copied with that of those who came later, lest being on a separate scroll and small in compass it be lost. Here we see the principle of size at work, a principle that played an important role in the division of traditional materials into books. The same principle is to be recognized in the order Jer., Ezek., Isa. Here too size is determinative of the order.

The present sequence Isa., Jer., Ezek. represents a chronological order. This same principle makes itself evident from Gen. through Kings, i.e. the history of Israel from creation to the Babylonian exile. However, the way this continuous narrative is divided into books suggests that the principle of size along with concern for content may also have played a role. E.g. Sam. and Kings are about equal in size. The point of division between them, while not indefensible in terms of content, is not the most pertinent. The further division of each of these 2 books into 2 more or less equal sections supports such a contention.

The same Talmudic text also reports the sequence of the Writings: Ruth, Pss., Job, Prov., Eccl., Song of S., Lam., Dan., Esth., Ezra-Neh., Chr. This, in traditional terms, represents a quasi-chronological ordering, with Ruth, ending with the Davidic genealogy, serving as an introduction to the Davidic book Pss. Job is apparently out of place in this sequence, intervening between Davidic and Solomonic writings. Its location may be explained on formal grounds as being written with the same poetic structures as the books preceding and following it, though size may have played a role since Job is slightly larger than Prov.

In this sequence, and that found in modern Jewish texts, the chronological principle is ignored at the end by the reversal of Ezra-Neh. and Chr. It seems certain that originally these 2 comprised one work (see Intro. to I Chr.) written on 2 scrolls, as the repetition of the 2 concluding vss. of Chr. in the first 3 vss. of Ezra indicates. The division point was chosen on the basis, not of size, but of pre- and postexilic history.

It is possible that the division of Pss. into 5 books had as its model the Pentateuch. The reason for the division may have been to make the material more easily accessible for liturgical use.

The sequence Lam., Dan., Esth. may as well be thought of as being chronological within the exilic period; the reversal of Ezra-Neh. and Chr. to make the former follow Esth. may have occurred to preserve this order.

It is quite certain, however, that there was no absolute sequence in either the Prophets or the Writings until after the invention of the printing press. The Venice ed. (1517-48) of the Hebrew text was the first to divide Sam., Kings, Ezra-Neh., Chr.

into 2 separate books each. Elijah Levitas (16 cent.) reported that among the Spanish-Portuguese Jews the sequence Isa., Jer., Ezek. was observed, while among the German and French Jews the sequence given in the Talmud was followed. In the Writings the Spanish-Portuguese had the sequence Chr., Pss., Job, Prov., Ruth, Song of S., Eccles., Lam., Esth., Dan., Ezra-Neh.; while the Germans had Pss., Prov., Job, Song of S., Ruth, Lam., Esth., Dan., Ezra-Neh., Chr. In the latter sequence the 5 Scrolls follow the order in which they are read during the synagogal year: Song of S. at Passover, Ruth at Pentecost, Lam. on the 9th of Ab, Eccl. at Tabernacles, Esth. at Purim.

The ordinary sequence found in Christian texts is chronological from Gen. through Esth., from Job —traditionally placed in the patriarchal period— through Dan., and within the 12.

History. Traditional Jewish literature from the early rabbinic period (first 6 cents. A.D.) contains no direct report about the process by which books were included in the collection of Holy Scriptures, though there is a discussion about keeping in the collection certain books previously included. The passage in the Babylonian Talmud from which a sentence was quoted above is taken by some to be a description of the process of canonization, but it proves on closer scrutiny to be no more than a report on the authorship of certain books as related to their being written down, i.e. edited and published.

Moses wrote his own book and the portion of Balaam [Num. 23–24] and Job. Joshua wrote the book which bears his name and the last eight verses of the Pentateuch. Samuel wrote the book which bears his name and the Book of Judges and Ruth. David wrote the Book of Psalms, including in it the work of the elders. . . . Jeremiah wrote the book that bears his name, the Book of Kings, and Lamentations. Hezekiah and his colleagues . . . wrote Isaiah, Proverbs, the Song of Songs and Ecclesiastes. The Men of the Great Assembly wrote . . . Ezekiel, the Twelve Minor Prophets, Daniel and the Scroll of Esther. Ezra wrote the book that bears his name and the genealogies of the Book of Chronicles up to his own time. (Baba Bathra 14*b,* Soncino trans.)

This passage reflects the rabbinic theory of what was included in the sacred collection, but it offers no evidence for the process by which the works mentioned were included. Perhaps, indeed, the whole question of how or when this happened was irrelevant to the rabbis of the period.

The same is true of another passage in the Babylonian Talmud:

For in the ancient times when the Torah was forgotten from Israel, Ezra came up from Babylon and established it. It was again forgotten and Hillel the Babylonian came up and established it. Yet again was it forgotten and R. Hiyya and his sons came up and established it. (Sukkah 20*a,* Soncino trans.)

Basically this passage is a glorification of Babylonian Jewry—a well-known tendency in this source—which is held to be the preserver of the traditional teachings of Judaism, and it has nothing to do with the establishment of the collection of Holy Scriptures. It is paralleled in II Esdras 14, which describes the renewal of the 94 lost books, 24 public and 70 private, through Ezra. Such other passages from early rabbinic sources as are educed to prove that the Jewish tradition viewed the canonization of scripture as an activity of Ezra, when examined, turn out rather to emphasize his care for and interest in scripture and can be used for the former purpose only on the basis of an already developed thesis.

The 16th-cent. Jewish scholar mentioned above, Elijah Levitas, in discussing the use of certain Hebrew consonants as vowel signs, argued against those who held that the decision about these usages was the action of Ezra and his companions—in the Jewish tradition the Men of the Great Assembly. He claimed that in the Torah the tradition about the usage went back to Moses. He further argued that insofar as autographs of prophetic books and the other writings were available to Ezra and his companions they merely copied the traditions. Only in cases where the tradition was uncertain did they collate texts and follow the majority. To explain why there should be any uncertainty about some texts he offered the theory that at that time all of the books had not been collected and arranged in order. This allowed for the possibility that some texts could have variants in orthography.

This discussion led Levitas to the side remark that part of the activity of Ezra and the Men of the Great Assembly was the collecting of the books and the dividing of them into 3 parts:

The 24 books had not been collected together, so they gathered them and divided them into 3 parts, Torah, Prophets, and Writings. The Prophets and Writings they arranged in an order different from that given in the Talmud.

Again it is clear that the interest of this author was in the redactional problems but not in the question of canon. Indeed, as suggested above, the interest of the rabbis was primarily that of explaining the source of authority for the books included in the synagogal collection. Viewed from that position, the question of when a book became canonical was irrelevant, for if it fulfilled the proffered definition it was canonical from the moment it came into existence. In terms of that definition the entire sacred collection was from the traditional point of view merely arranged, not begun or established, in the days of Ezra.

Canon and Authority. It would be a grave mistake to equate canonical status of a book with authority, for to do so would be to import distinctions based on other points of view. Judaism with its concept of the double nature of Torah—viz. written, i.e. scripture, and oral, i.e. tradition—did not permit a distinction between the authority of the 2; hence the status of scripture could not be determined on that basis.

The Talmudic passage quoted above once again offers a clue to the status of scripture in the synagogue. In it we have seen that the authorship as well as the editing or publishing of the various books was reported. A scrutiny of the reported authors as contrasted with editors indicates that in terms of the synagogal tradition all were prophets. E.g. Job is credited to Moses, Ruth to Samuel. David and Solomon too are considered prophets in the rabbinic tradition, as was Ezra, who was identified with Malachi. The one book whose prophetic pedigree was in doubt was Esth.; therefore in some rabbinic sources Esther's cousin Mordecai was designated a prophet.

All of this indicates that from the rabbinic point of view the special status of scripture derived from its having been composed by prophets, i.e. those under the influence of the Holy Spirit. This was the position of Josephus, who said that from the time of Artaxerxes I onward "the complete history has been written, but has not been deemed worthy of equal credit with the earlier records, because of the failure of the exact succession of the prophets" (Against Apion I.8). In a rabbinic source a similar statement is made: "When Haggai, Zechariah, and Malachi died, the Holy Spirit left Israel" (Tosefta Sotah 13:2).

From this we may conclude that scriptures were books composed under divine inspiration and committed to writing. From them, or from the legal sections, i.e. from the laws in the Pentateuch, other legal prescriptions could be derived that were equally authoritative for the Jewish community, being considered implicit in scripture, hence divine in origin. In addition there was according to rabbinic Judaism a body of legal tradition also divine in origin and equal in authority with the scriptures though it had not been put down in writing but was transmitted orally. This is the meaning of the frequently quoted passage from Pirke Aboth 1:1 that traces the transmission of Torah, in the broadest sense, from its divine origin on Sinai through Moses, Joshua, the elders, the prophets, and the Men of the Great Assembly to the rabbinic teachers.

Thus the peculiar status of the Holy Scriptures did not reflect their exclusive authority—which they did not possess—but rather the fact that they had been reduced to writing. The rest of the tradition was equally authoritative, coming as it did from the same divine source, but was not written down; indeed its being written down had been prohibited. The Holy Scriptures were therefore that part of the total revealed tradition that had been committed to writing.

The status of these writings is expressed in rabbinic sources by the strange-sounding phrase "render the hands unclean." The reason for this usage is not clearly understood nor is it relevant here. What is important is our understanding that it is intended to be complimentary. In rabbinic sources it is used as the term that points to the way a distinction may be made between Holy Scriptures and other books. In short it equals the Christian term "canonical" devoid of any other particular implication that word may have.

Ecclus. In a rabbinic source (Tosefta Yadayim 2:13) it is stated that "neither the book of Ben Sira nor any of the books written thereafter render the hands unclean"; i.e. they are not Holy Scriptures. Later writers from the same period went further than this and seem even to have prohibited the reading of this book. However, since it is occasionally quoted in other places in the Babylonian Talmud, even with the honorific introductory phrase reserved for quotations from the Writings, an absolute prohibition cannot have been intended.

It has been suggested that all that is really meant is that Ecclus. was not to be read in such a way as to allow the impression to arise that it was on the same level as Holy Scriptures. That would seem to mean that it was not to be read in a formal fashion publicly. This meaning seems certain from a statement in an interpretation of "My son, beware of anything beyond these" (Eccl. 12:12), which reads: "He who brings more than 24 books into his house brings confusion. Thus, the books of Ben Sira or Ben Tigla [?] may be read, but not to 'weariness of flesh' [i.e. not deeply or seriously]." The exclusion of Ecclus. is clearly not because its content was unsuitable but because it was written later than the period in which the Holy Spirit was believed to have inspired prophets. It is important to note that this is the only book included in the Apoc. that is discussed in the rabbinic sources.

Ezek. The Babylonian Talmud (Hagigah 13a) reports that in the generation before the fall of Jerusalem in A.D. 70 a discussion arose about Ezek. It involved, not the scriptural status of the book, but only the question of the continuation of its reading in public. There were apparent contradictions between its description of the temple service and that found in the Torah which, it was held by some, would tend to confuse the unlearned. However, the interpretation provided by the sage Hananiah ben Hezekiah made this withdrawal from public reading unnecessary. Another report indicates that the reason for the suggested withdrawal centered around the vision of the chariot in ch. 1. This ch. was used in later time for Gnostic speculations, so that the suggestion Ezek. be withdrawn from public reading may reflect a controversy over such interpretations.

Eccl. and Song of S. More serious was the conflict over Eccl. and Song of S. The report is as follows:

All Holy Scriptures make the hands unclean. The Song of Songs and Ecclesiastes make the hands unclean [i.e. they are Holy Scriptures]. Rabbi Judah says: The Song of Songs makes the hands unclean, and about Ecclesiastes opinions are divided. Rabbi Jose says: Ecclesiastes does not make the hands unclean and about the Song of Songs opinions are divided. Rabbi Simeon says: Ecclesiastes is one of the things on which the School of Shammai took the laxer view and the School of Hillel the stricter. Simeon ben Azzai says: I received it as a tradition on the authority of the seventy-two elders on the day on which they installed Rabbi Eleazer ben Azariah in the presidency that the Song of Songs and Ecclesiastes make the hands unclean. Rabbi Akiba says: God forbid! no man in Israel was ever of the opinion about the Song of Songs, holding that it does not make the hands unclean. For the whole age altogether is not equal to the day on which the Song of Songs was given to Israel; for all the Hagiographa [i.e. the Writings] are holy, but the Song of Songs is holy of holies. If there was a division of opinion, it was only about Ecclesiastes. Rabbi Johanan ben Joshua, son of Rabbi Akiba's father-in-law says: It is as ben Azzai says: so they were divided and so they decided. (Mishnah Yadayim 3:5, Danby trans.)

An analysis of this passage is most revealing, for it discloses that even after the 2nd Revolt (after A.D. 135) there was still controversy over these 2 books. The argument about Eccl. went back to the period before the First Revolt (before A.D. 68) and even the discussion of the rabbinic scholars at Jamnia ca. A.D. 85 did not, as has been pointed out, bring the matter to an end. Even as late as Jerome (end of 4th cent.) echoes of the controversy were heard.

Esth. From the discussions of 2nd-cent. rabbis it is evident that some controversy surrounded Esth. The question was even raised whether it should have been written at all. A 3rd-cent. teacher is reported to have declared that it "does not render the hands unclean," i.e. it is not canonical. Synagogal usage of the time, however, makes it clear that for practical purposes, whatever theoretical objections were raised, Esth. was accorded the dignity of scripture.

Conclusion. From the above discussion it may be concluded that, though theoretically rabbinic Judaism viewed the collection of Holy Scriptures as having been completed by Ezra and the Men of the Great Assembly, questions about the status of some of the Writings continued to be asked by individual scholars on into the 3rd cent. A.D. Nonetheless to all intents and purposes Judaism possessed its collection of writings, accompanied by its growing body of oral tradition, by the end of the first cent. A.D.

II. THE OT CANON OF THE CHURCH

The term "OT" makes sense only within the context of the Christian church, in which a distinction between an old and a new covenant is made. Thus the question arises: What is the relation between the Holy Scriptures of Judaism and the OT? Are they the same? As a corollary to this question it may be asked: How did the church acquire a collection of books called the OT that has in some fashion a normative status?

The answer to the first question, about the relation between the Holy Scriptures of Judaism and the OT must be a qualified negative. They are not always the same. Of course the churches in the Reformed tradition and, with some variation, the Lutheran churches do have as their OT a different arrangement of the Jewish Holy Scriptures. Luther himself, however, did not altogether dismiss those books that were not part of the Jewish collection, the so-called Apoc. preserved by the church. The Roman Catholic Church, on the other hand, has included such books and additions to books in its OT canon, though it makes a distinction between proto- and deutero-canonical books. The Orthodox churches have not established a single collection but have various collections. Thus the question about the OT canon of the Christian church turns out to be a question about its several canons, and the corollary question must concern itself with how the several canons arose and what they have meant for the church.

In the NT. That the Holy Scriptures of Judaism played an important role in the life of Jesus and of the early church is evidenced by the profusion of quotations found throughout the NT. The references to "the law and the prophets" and to "the law of Moses and the prophets and the psalms," while not necessarily evidence for the exact scope of the Holy Scriptures at that time, indicate general knowledge and acceptance of the collection. Whatever other books the NT authors knew—e.g. Jude contains a quotation from Enoch and an allusion to the Assumption of Moses; some scholars also assume a knowledge of Wisd. Sol. by Paul—the Jewish Scriptures seem to have been their scripture as well.

The controversy about the role of the Scriptures connected with the heretical bishop Marcion reached its climax in the middle of the 2nd cent. in the attempt to repudiate the OT; but it was both preceded and followed by other tendencies within various churches to differentiate the contents of the collection. Thus there was, in addition to total repudiation, a scale running from partial to complete recognition. The triumph of the orthodox party, however, made it necessary for the churches to determine the scope of what had been accepted.

The Search for the OT Canon. Uncertainty about the scope of the OT was a continuing problem for the church. In A.D. 170 Melito of Sardis traveled to Palestine to discover the answer to it. He found the Jerusalem church in possession of the Jewish Scriptures without Esth. This collection became the canon for Asia Minor. It was as well the canon of the Egyptian church as the Easter Letter of Athanasius (367) indicates, though Esth., Wisd. Sol., Ecclus., Judith, and Tobit were permitted public reading.

In Palestine there seems not to have been unanimity. Cyril of Jerusalem in his catechism of 348 indicated the canon of the OT to be the Jewish Scriptures in the order found in the LXX with the addition of Baruch and the Letter of Jeremiah. In Palestine, as in Egypt, other books were permitted public reading, though the scope of such permitted works varied. It included in various combinations II, III Macc., Wisd. Sol., Pss. and Odes of Solomon, Ecclus., Esth., Judith, Tobit, and Susanna.

The situation of the Syrian churches was entirely otherwise. Here, in spite of considerable variation, it seems certain that the OT canon included without distinction all of the books permitted public reading elsewhere and others as well, i.e. the so-called deutero-canonical books of the Roman Catholic Church. It was this enlarged collection that was accepted by the African churches at the synods of Hippo (393) and Carthage (397) and from there traveled to Rome, where it was accepted over the cents. Its final formal authorization as the canon of the Roman Catholic Church took place only at the 4th session of the Council of Trent, Apr. 8, 1546.

As pointed out above, the Protestant churches rejected this canon and in its place accepted only the Scriptures of Judaism. Nevertheless the role of the Apoc. continued to agitate the Anglican Church until the 19th cent., when the practice of printing it together with the OT and the NT was largely discontinued.

The Role of the OT in the Church. The OT was for the church a witness to the mighty acts of God fulfilled in the person of Jesus Christ. Therefore this specific function of witnessing provided the standard, i.e. the canon, by which writings were to be judged. Thus viewed, the OT canon of the church was not necessarily coincident with the Holy Scriptures of the synagogue. Yet the 4 chief forms of the canon all contain, except for variations with regard to Esth., the Palestinian Jewish Holy Scriptures, no matter what other books were added. In other words the Christian church took this as the "witnessing" collection par excellence, though various churches found in other writings the same inner motif. It was only with the Protestant Reformation that Lutheran orthodoxy and esp. the Reformed churches, limited the canon, i.e. the witnessing collection, to the Hebrew text.

The Meaning of the Word Canon. In classical Greek the word "canon"—perhaps derived from a Semitic root—meant "straight rod" and then, as emphasis was placed on the adjective, "measure" and "balance beam." Carried over into the intellectual realm it came to mean that which was artistically, scientifically, or ethically normative. This latter is the use made of the word in Gal. 6:16: "this rule." In the 4th cent. the plural "canons" was used for ecclesiastical rules and for the decisions of church councils. Thus what was originally called in the NT "scripture" came to be designated "canonical [i.e. normative] scripture." The earliest evidence for this usage is in the 59th canon of the Council of Laodicea (360), followed by the Easter Letter of Athanasius (367). This indicates the process by which the synagogal collection became the OT canon.

The Jewish writings read publicly in accordance with apostolic usage were declared to be normative for the church. The meaning of normative in this situation may of course have had overtones pointing to other matters of belief and practice, but the crucial test was the church's conviction that these texts contained the promise it believed was fulfilled in Jesus Christ. Thus, while there was unanimous agreement that the Holy Scriptures of Judaism—granting some ambiguity to the position of Esth.—met this test, there were in addition claims brought forward by various churches on behalf of one or another or several or many other writings. Such claims were definitively accepted by one part of the Christian church in the 16th cent., and as conclusively rejected then by others.

The Scope of the OT Canon. The scope of the OT canon varies, therefore. In Protestant versions it adheres strictly to the synagogal collection, in the order: Gen., Exod., Lev., Num., Deut., Josh., Judg., Ruth, I, II Sam., I, II Kings, I, II Chron., Ezra, Neh., Esth., Job, Pss., Prov., Eccl., Song of S., Isa. Jer., Lam., Ezek., Dan., Hos., Joel, Amos, Obad., Jonah, Mic., Nah., Hab., Zeph., Hag., Zech., Mal.

In the Roman Catholic version it follows the same order except as follows: "I, II Sam. and I, II Kings are called I-IV Kings; I, II Chron. are called I, II Paralipomenon; Ezra and Neh. are called I, II Esdras—not to be confused with I, II Esdras of the Apoc. Following the latter 2 books Tobias (Tobit) and Judith are inserted. Esth. has the Additions found in the LXX. Pss. has 9-10 of the Hebrew text joined into Ps. 9 and divides the Hebrew text of Ps. 147 into Pss. 146; 147. Song of S., called Canticle of Canticles, is followed by Wisd. Sol. and Ecclus. Inserted between Lam. and Ezek. is Baruch. Inserted in Dan. are the Song of the Three Children, Susanna, and Bel and the Dragon. Following Mal. are added I, II Macc.

III. THEORIES ABOUT THE PROCESS OF COLLECTING SCRIPTURES

The later part of the history of the OT canon or, strictly speaking, the entire history of the OT canon insofar as its formation is to be thought of as an activity of the Christian church, has already been briefly sketched. Basically the church has applied to a generally well-established collection and to some more or less widely circulated and variously considered books its standard of judgment. The application of this standard was not a once-and-for-all procedure but itself has had a long and varied history that may not as yet be completed, as some contemporary discussions indicate.

We are left, however, with the problem of determining something about the history of the process by which that part of the OT canon that comprises the 3-fold collection of the synagogue was brought into being. The synagogal definition of its Holy Scriptures, viz. those books composed under the inspiration of the Holy Spirit and committed to writing, does not shed any light on the way in which those writings as completed entities were brought together. The history of such a process is by no means to be equated with the literary history of individual books, but presupposes the existence of the books and asks the questions: On what basis were they given special status? How were they formed into collections, and finally into a collection defined as the synagogue defined it? The most the synagogal tradition discloses is that it saw Ezra playing an important role and his period crucial in the process.

The Canon as Inspired Literature. The traditional answers, both Jewish and Christian, to the above questions, that such books, i.e. written works, were included as were produced under divine inspiration, can be transposed into a critical theory that accounts for the formation of an authorized collection. Such a theory sees the canon as having its origin in a collection of the statements of those believed by their community to have spoken or taught under divine inspiration—a prophet, an oracular priest, a sage. The primary collection would then have been of prophetic speeches such as are gathered in the books of the major and minor prophets. Other materials were then added in some derived fashion. As we have seen, the rabbinic tradition proceeded in such a manner and was able to include all the other books, on their face not prophetic utterances, by claiming prophetic authorship for them when their authors were not known, or by asserting prophetic status for their authors when they were.

Such a procedure is of course unavailable to those who are committed to any of the contemporary critical approaches to biblical literature. This gives rise to a crucial question with regard to such a theory. A considerable part of the Scriptures is, as has been pointed out, not prophetic utterance. Further, it was not the prophetic books that in the pre-Christian period were the center of interest. The Samaritans did not include them in their canon, and Alexandrian Judaism, which produced the LXX, devoted its primary interest to the Pentateuch and only then to those portions of the prophets used in public worship. Such considerations make it open to question whether the dynamic of the process is to be found in the idea of inspired, i.e. prophetic, utterances.

Canon as Law. The fact of the primary concern for the Pentateuch, the Torah, has suggested another theory, viz. that the basis for inclusion in the sacred collection lay in the legal character of the material.

From this point of view the origin of the canonical collection is to be found in one of 2 events: (a) the acceptance of the book of law (torah) found in the temple in Jerusalem (II Kings 22) and considered by contemporary scholarship to have been the book of Deut. in some form or another; or (b) the acceptance by the community of the book of the law of Moses (torat Mosheh) read by Ezra (Neh. 8). In either case canonicity is equated with legal obligation.

An attempt has been made to combine this with the preceding theory by suggesting that the basic nature of a canonical book was that of a law book approved by a prophet (cf. II Kings 22, where Huldah the prophetess sanctions the book of law found in the temple). Related to this is the theory that the temple book was intended by its author to be accepted as a prophetic utterance of Moses but was misunderstood and accepted as a law book, thus making its legal contents rather than its prophetic source the basis of its authority.

The difficulty with such theories is that they assume that torah means "law," so that the acceptance of a book of torah means acquiescence to a legal code. Thus the norm for the canonical status of a book is assumed to be its legal content. However, torah cannot be made to conform to such a narrow definition, for it means far more than law, being the entire range of religious teaching that includes but is not limited to rules, regulations, and prescriptions for group and individual behavior. More than that, such theories do not make clear how books with contents remote from law receive canonical status if legal content is crucial. In other words, in neither of the above positions and their variations is it possible to apply a single standard (canon) that will define the whole range of material.

Canon as Cult Recital. To meet such objections a 3rd position has been offered. It is based on the argument that the function of the canonical books was their public recital as part of the cultic act of the community. The inclusion of books in the collection used for such recitals was determined by their exposition of a fundamental motif, the acts of Yahweh in a structure characterized by struggle and victory.

This of course provides a far wider definition than do the other positions mentioned. However, the attempt to find everywhere the presence of the fundamental motif of struggle and victory with Yahweh as the protagonist often requires forced explanations and torturous interpretations. Further, while the function of public reading seems most suggestive in providing the purpose for a canon, it is not applicable to the 3rd section of the synagogal canon, the Writings, where there is no evidence for such use of Prov., Job, Dan., Ezra-Neh., I, II Chr. Further, it is just in this section that the so-called fundamental motif is noticeably absent.

Canon as Process. This latter position, despite its difficulties, is helpful in suggesting the way in which the problem may be approached. The statement of Josephus mentioned earlier (Against Apion I.8) about the nature of the sacred collection suggests that he understood it to be the "record of all time." In it are to be found "books of Moses, comprising the laws and the traditional histories from the birth of man down to the death of the lawgiver" and the "history of the events" subsequent to Moses, written by the prophets. In addition it contains "hymns to God and precepts for the conduct of human life." If we understand this history as having been thought of as divine, i.e. as being the activity of Yahweh, then the motive for its collection and preservation becomes clearer.

The original brief recitations of Yahweh's acts that, according to contemporary scholars, were regular parts of the cult and served as the nuclei around which larger units were gathered, may well have bequeathed to these larger sections in which they were merged the status of public recitation. These finally became formalized into the triennial and annual cycles of Pentateuchal readings in the synagogue and the accompanying readings from the Former Prophets (histories) and the Latter Prophets. The division of the collection into 3 sections, i.e. the addition of books that did not conform to recitations of the sacred history, may again reflect certain other practices of public reading. This seems indicated by the placing of Ruth, Esth., and Lam. in the 3rd section together with Song of S. and Eccl. in a sequence that followed the order of their annual public reading in the synagogue. Dan. and Ezra-Neh. may have been drawn together by the occurrence in them of lengthy passages written in Aramaic, and the use of that language may have militated against their public reading and occasioned their relegation to the 3rd section. Job's place may have been determined, as pointed out above, by its structural affinity to Pss. and Prov.; or a theological motive may have placed it contiguous to its incompatible neighbor, Prov., in order to correct the latter's opinions or to be corrected by it. At any rate it would appear that the inclusion of various books in the Writings cannot have been determined on the basis of a single factor or of the same factor that determined the inclusion of books in the first and 2nd divisions.

Again, the claim that the division between the Pentateuch and the Prophets was made on the basis of the superior status of law and the role of this kind of material in the formation of the canon is called into question by the problematic nature of this definition of *torah*. It may well be, as in the case of Josephus, that the distinction was chronological, between Mosaic and post-Mosaic. Under the circumstances, it is foolhardy to insist on a uniform explanation for the inclusion of various books in the sacred collection.

Viewed from the standpoint of function, it seems evident that an important motive for the creation of a sacred collection, i.e. the Holy Scriptures, was the public recitation of the mighty acts of God in the history of Israel. Once this process got under way, and its origins seem very old, the materials increased in scope. Eventually some writings were drawn into the orbit of this public function as they were adapted by means of an interpretative process to the original intent of public reading. Thus Song of S. found its place in the collection because it was susceptible of an allegorical interpretation as the description of the relation between God and Israel, and the reference to the spring season (2:11-13) could provide it with a historical locus, the Passover season. It thus became a reading for the sabbath during the Passover festival.

In conclusion, the specific function a book performed may well be the clue to the reason how and why it was included in the sacred collection. This function is most clearly seen in the first 2 divisions of the synagogal collection. The books included in the 3rd division do not disclose their reasons for finding a place in the collection so easily, but this does not mean that such reasons cannot be discovered if they are looked for in the correct way without dogmatic presuppositions to obscure the search.

For Further Study. G. F. Moore, "The Definition of the Jewish Canon and the Repudiation of Christian Scriptures," in *Essays in Modern Theology and Related Subjects*, 1911. Solomon Zeitlin, "An Historical Study of the Canonization of the Hebrew Scriptures," in *Proceedings of the American Academy for Jewish Research*, III, 1931-32. Gunnar Ostborn, *Cult and Canon*, 1950. Arthur Jeffery, "The Canon of the OT," in *IB*, 1952. R. H. Pfeiffer, "Canon of the OT," in *IDB*, 1962. Ludwig Blau, "Bible Canon," in *The Jewish Encyclopedia*, 1964.

THE MAKING
OF THE NEW TESTAMENT CANON

Albert C. Sundberg, Jr.

The story of when and why Christian writings came to be regarded as scripture and compiled into an authoritative collection to which nothing could be added and from which nothing could be subtracted is an important part of the history of Christendom. It needs to be retold because recent discoveries in biblical research have brought to light information that significantly alters our understanding of the development of the Christian canon of scripture.

I. THE INHERITANCE: THE JEWISH SCRIPTURES

Christianity arose within Judaism. The earliest Christians were Jews who believed that God had raised Jesus from the dead and thereby declared him to be the Messiah, i.e. Christ, through whom Jewish hopes and expectations would be fulfilled. These hopes and expectations were embodied in the Jewish Scriptures already in hand when the Christian faith arose, and it was to be expected that those writings would continue to be the scriptures of the Christian movement as it gradually became distinguished and separated from Judaism. Consequently the story of the making of the NT canon cannot be told apart from the context of the inheritance of the Jewish Holy Scriptures (see "The Making of the OT Canon," pp. 1209-15).

Since the earliest Christians continued to use and regard the Jewish Scriptures as they had before the birth of their Christian faith, the Jewish view of scripture passed into early Christianity along with the writings themselves. This view of scripture probably formed the earliest basis for the evaluation of Christian writings when such documents came to be written and circulated. This has been a basic assumption of scholarly histories of the NT canon and it is a valid one. However, a radical revision of our understanding of the history of the OT, i.e. the Jewish Scriptures, within the Christian church has recently been demonstrated; and this revised history significantly alters the consequent relationship between the OT of the church and the growth of the NT canon.

Until now, historians of the making of the NT canon have assumed that the church received a closed canon of scripture from Judaism. Even though they recognized that the Jewish canon was not closed until near the end of the first cent. A.D.—at Jamnia ca. 85-90—they assumed that it had been closed in practice since before the days of Jesus. Since the NT writings and other early Christian

literature used a larger collection of Jewish scripture than the Jamnia canon, a theory was proposed, first by J. E. Grabe (1720) and again independently by J. S. Semler (1771), that a larger Jewish canon was to be found in the LXX, the Greek translation of the OT made at Alexandria, which circulated generally throughout the Jewish dispersion. This theory came to be generally accepted by the last quarter of the 19th cent. Since the NT writings and the other early Christian literature were composed in Greek, and since after the destruction of Jerusalem in 70 Christianity became increasingly Gentile and non-Palestinian, it has been assumed that it was this LXX or Alexandrian canon that passed into the church as its OT.

It has now been shown, however, that no such larger LXX or Alexandrian canon, i.e. one including more books than were accepted in Palestine, ever existed. Rather it has become clear that Jews in Palestine as well as in the dispersion had and used as scripture the 2 closed collections of Law and Prophets and also a 3rd unnamed and undefined group of books which included not only those that later came to be called Writings but the Apoc. and Pseudepigrapha and other books as well.

No closed canon of scripture existed in Judaism when Christianity arose and became separated from it. There is no evidence of any attempt to limit the scope of scripture in Judaism until after the catastrophe of 70. The Jewish doctrine limiting inspiration to the time from Moses to Ezra is first encountered in writings dating *ca.* 90. Before that time the Jewish concept of scripture was a very open one. A wide religious literature, defined only by production and popularity, circulated throughout Judaism as scripture, and there was no doctrine that would prohibit contemporary works from achieving this stature. Since this was the circumstance that existed in Judaism when Christianity arose, this was the concept of scripture that passed into early Christianity.

Thus in the history of the NT canon, as in the history of the OT, it is necessary to distinguish between the terms "scripture," meaning writings which are held in some sense as authoritative for religion and "canon," meaning a defined collection that is held to be exclusively, i.e. with respect to all other books, authoritative. What the church received from Judaism, then, was a collection of scripture and not a canon. To be sure, the Law and the Prophets were closed collections in Judaism and passed as such into

Christianity. But by the time a concern for Christian scripture and canon arose within the church these Jewish divisions were forgotten or ignored in Christendom. Consequently when we compare the use of Christian writings within the early church with the use of the OT, the results inform us, not about NT canon, but about NT scripture.

In view of the concept of scripture in Judaism that passed, together with the Jewish Scriptures, into Christianity, one would expect that Christian writings would come to be regarded as authoritative, i.e. scripture. At the same time one would not expect to find predetermined criteria for canonicity, since the church received none from Judaism. Thus stages in the making of the NT canon come to light, and the history of the NT can be divided into 3 main steps: (a) the rise of Christian literature to the status of scripture, to be treated as in some sense authoritative, a step for which there appear to have been no criteria other than circulation and authority parallel to that of the OT; (b) the conscious grouping of Christian writings into closed collections such as the 4-fold gospel, the Pauline collection, and the Catholic letters; (c) canonization proper, wherein the concern is not simply the acceptability of particular books but the formation of a NT list, a closed canon.

II. Christian Writings as Scripture

The rise of Christian writings to a position of scripture, so that they came to be regarded as in some sense authoritative and were cited and appealed to on an equal basis with the OT, must certainly have been an unconscious process in the church. No NT author wrote as a contributor to the NT. No NT canon, or in most cases even a NT scripture, was in mind when the NT books were written. Whatever concept of authority may have been envisioned by the authors—such as Paul's sense of apostolic authority (cf. e.g. Rom. 1:1; 11:13; I Cor. 1:1; 9:1; Gal. 1:1) or the authority of apocalyptic revelation (cf. Rev. 22:18-19)—it was related to the content of the particular writing at hand and was not related to any body of scripture. The exceptions to this, of course, are the pseudonymous writings—e.g. I, II Tim., Tit., and II Pet. (see Intros.)—but even in these it was not the authority of the writings of Paul or Peter that was sought but the personal authority of the apostles themselves.

In the proclamation of the gospel and other activities from the early beginnings (cf. Acts 2; John 20:22-23) the Christians felt themselves possessed by the same Spirit that had inspired the prophets (cf. e.g. Acts 2:16-21; 15:28; I Cor. 2:4). This sense of inspiration in word and deed carried over to Christian writings. So Paul could commend his instruction to Corinthian Christians by saying, "And I think that I have the Spirit of God" (I Cor. 7:40b). By the end of the first cent. a leader of the church at Rome could write to the Corinthians:

Take up the epistle [I Cor.] of the blessed Paul the apostle. ... With true inspiration he charged you . . . (I Clement 47:1-3, trans. K. Lake).

He also could refer to his own letter as "written through the Holy Spirit" (63:2). Early in the 2nd

cent. Ignatius, bishop of Antioch in Syria, wrote to the church at Philadelphia in Asia Minor on his way to martyrdom in Rome:

I cried out while I was with you; I spoke with a great voice, with God's own voice . . . the Spirit was preaching and saying this (7:1-2, trans. K. Lake).

That Polycarp, bishop of Smyrna martyred *ca.* 155, was regarded as inspired is evident from the statement in the Martyrdom of Polycarp:

For every word which he uttered from his mouth both was fulfilled and will be fulfilled (16:2, trans. K. Lake).

Irenaeus, bishop of Lyons in Gaul, in his Against All Heresies (*ca.* 180) applies to his own writing, as well as Paul's, the words "we know in part and prophesy in part" (I Cor. 13:9; Heresies 2:28:9; cf. 3:24:1) and directly affirms:

But we do now receive a certain portion of His Spirit, tending towards perfection, and preparing us for incorruption, being little by little accustomed to receive and bear God (5:8:1, trans. Roberts and Donaldson).

In the Epistle to Diognetus (probably early 3rd cent.) we read:

And if you [the reader] do not grieve this grace you will understand what the word says through the agents of his choice, when he will. For in all things which we were moved by the will of him who commands us to speak with pain, we become sharers with you through love of the things revealed to us (11:7-8, trans. K. Lake).

The presence and inspiration of the Spirit is a continuing doctrine in the church; it is not possible to separate it from the Christian writings. Since the early Christians regarded themselves as possessed by the same Spirit that inspired Moses and the prophets, it was to be expected that their writings would come to be regarded as possessing an authority similar to that of the OT. In the early period no other credential was required than that of inspiration for a writing to come to be regarded as scripture; breadth of circulation, i.e. popularity, was the remaining determinative feature. It is only on this basis that we can understand how some writings, e.g. I Clement and the Shepherd of Hermas, which clearly did not fit the later criteria of canonicity, attained the status of scripture in the earlier period. Hence the story of the rise of Christian writings to scripture is largely that of the circulation of these writings and acquaintance with them in the early church.

The Gospels. It is usually said that from the start the sayings of Jesus were authoritative in the church. This seems obvious to us, and we are quite unprepared for the scanty attention to the sayings and doings of Jesus in the earliest Christian writings. Paul, whose letters are the earliest we possess, gives us but a minimum of information about Jesus of Nazareth, and the rest of the epistles are similarly reticent. No doubt one reason for this was that authority for the earliest Christians was found in the word of the risen Lord immediately available through inspiration and revelation (cf. Gal. 1:11-12). The memory of Jesus was the immediate living voice of the new covenant, the fulfillment of the written promise of the old. Consequently our problem is not why the epistles and Rev. and Acts say so little about Jesus but why gospels ever came to be written at all.

Even after gospels were written—usually Mark is dated *ca.* A.D. 64-65 and Matt., Luke, John *ca.* 80-110—their portrayal of the words and doings of Jesus did not become immediately authoritative, as is shown by their infrequent use in Christian writings continuing into the 2nd cent. Occasional passages begin to appear toward the end of the first cent. and are quoted authoritatively, e.g. the saying of Jesus in Acts 20:35 introduced by "remembering the words of the Lord Jesus, how he said" (cf. I Clement 13:1; 46:7-8). Ignatius seems to have ranked the gospel above the OT. Replying to those who would not believe in the gospel unless they could find it in the "documents" —presumably meaning the OT—he writes:

But to me the charters are Jesus Christ, the inviolable charter is his cross and death and resurrection, and the faith which is through him (Philadelphians 8:2, trans. K. Lake).

But it is evident that the gospel authority for him was in the events of the gospel themselves and their recounting rather than in any written form in which they were preserved. It has been shown that the material about the life and teaching of Jesus in the letters of Ignatius and other writings of this period is more probably derived from sources similar to those from which our gospels were compiled than from the gospels themselves. Thus until well into the 2nd cent. we find words of Jesus quoted infrequently, with little or no evidence of the use of written gospels.

Papias, bishop of Hierapolis in Asia Minor (*ca.* 130), is the first person known to name a gospel. His famous statement, preserved in the Church History (*ca.* 325) of Eusebius, bishop of Caesarea, reads:

"Mark became Peter's interpreter and wrote accurately all that he remembered, not indeed, in order, of the things said or done by the Lord. For he had not heard the Lord, nor had he followed him, but later on, as I said, followed Peter, who used to give teaching as necessity demanded but not making, as it were, an arrangement of the Lord's oracles, so that Mark did nothing wrong in thus writing down single points as he remembered them. For to one thing he gave attention, to leave out nothing of what he had heard and to make no false statements in them." This is related by Papias about Mark, and about Matthew this was said, "Matthew collected the oracles in the Hebrew language, and each interpreted them as best he could" (3:39:15-16, trans. K. Lake).

From this statement it is clear that Papias knew and approved of Mark. He also knew a Hebrew, i.e. Aramaic, collection of sayings of Jesus attributed to Matthew. But nothing identifiable remains of this collection. Neither particular of Papias' description fits the canonical Matt. (see Intro.) and we have no information about any connection between these sayings and the gospel, though it is possible that Matt. received its name from Papias' statement. It is gratuitous to assume from Papias' words that he also knew Luke and John. So far as our information goes he knew only one gospel, Mark, and a Matthean sayings collection in Aramaic.

Clearly Papias was defending Mark, but against what attacks: that its chronology was garbled? that it was not in Hebrew? or that it was written? Elsewhere Papias declared his preference for the "living and surviving voice" concerning the Lord Jesus recounted by the followers of the apostles above "that information from books," though he did append his own collection of gospel stories to his Interpretation of the Oracles of the Lord (Eusebius History 3:39:2-3).

Thus, though the first to name a known gospel, Papias preferred oral tradition. The intimations that Eusebius gives concerning the gospel traditions that Papias preserved give no hint of dependence on Mark. His gospel material was in no sense limited to the materials known in our NT. While he knew of a written gospel (or gospels) he appears not to have regarded it as authoritative or scripture.

It is evident, therefore, that throughout the first half of the 2nd cent. the words and doings of Jesus were regarded as authoritative but their authority was vested in the oral form of their transmission and was not yet applied to written gospels. With the passage of time an increasing amount of gospel material was cited. In this material parallels to Matt. and Luke predominate with indications of a possible combination of Matthean and Lukan materials. Even where there is virtual verbal identity with a gospel passage, however, there is no attempt to identify the citation with the written gospel. While it becomes increasingly clear that written gospels are known, there is no appeal to their authority and their material is used tacitly as oral tradition. Alongside such material there is a significant amount of material that is cited with like authority but does not appear in the 4 gospels of the NT.

Amid such circumstances it is not surprising that new gospels continued to come into existence. It is not possible to date them with precision since, like the gospels of the NT, they are cited a considerable time after their writing. Some—e.g. the Gospel according to the Hebrews and the Gospel according to the Egyptians—probably were not to be distinguished in their teaching from what may be called the normative Christianity of their time. Others—e.g. the Gospel of Peter, the Gospel of Thomas, the Gospel of Truth, and the Gospel of Philip—seem to be related in varying degrees to the form of Christianity known as Gnostic that flourished esp. in N Africa during the 2nd cent. (see "The Early History of the Church," pp. 1045-53). In most instances it probably was not the intention of the authors of these variant gospels to break away from normative Christianity and the members of variant groups usually remained within the church until they were expelled from it. Their writings should most probably be understood as based on the ordinary Christian usage of their times in the places in which they wrote.

Justin Martyr, the most important of the Greek apologists of the 2nd cent., came from Palestine to Rome, where he founded a school and was martyred *ca.* 165. He marks an important transition in the use of the gospel materials. Whereas there is no direct appeal to written gospels in earlier Christian writings, Justin does appeal directly to them. He says that Christ sent 12 men into all the world to teach the word of God (I Apology 39) and that it is in the "memoirs" which were written by his "apostles and those who followed them" that his sayings and doings are recorded (Dialogue 103). Justin refers to gospel material as from "our writings" (I Apology 28) and says that "the apostles, in the memoirs composed by them, which are called Gospels, have thus delivered unto us what was enjoined upon them" (66) and that "on the day called Sunday . . . the memoirs of the apostles or the writings of the prophets are read" to the assembled Christians (67, trans. Roberts and Donaldson).

The passages which Justin cites indicate that he probably knew the 4 gospels of our NT. In Dialogue 106 he cites material found only in Mark 3:16-17 and says that it is written in the memoirs of Peter, indicating that he was acquainted with the Papias tradition about Mark. He also frequently cites gospel material not found in the NT, showing that he was acquainted with a wider gospel tradition. It is clear that for him the authority of these "memoirs" or gospels was the authority of Jesus Christ, who sent out the apostles to preach his gospel. But it is also clear that Justin located the authoritative words and doings of Jesus in written apostolic gospels. Here for the first time the concept of apostolic writings clearly emerges. And since here the words and doings of Jesus are of like authority with the OT —if not greater—we may recognize Justin as the first to regard written gospels as scripture.

Tatian, a Syrian, probably was converted to Christianity after coming to Rome, where he became a pupil of Justin. Ca. 172 he returned to the E and became the founder of the Encratites, a sect stressing asceticism. His importance for the making of the NT is that he combined 4 gospels into one, which he called the Diatessaron. While this work has not survived, quotations from it in the writings of later church fathers show that it was made up from the 4 gospels of the NT. It is erroneous, however, to suppose that this shows that these 4 were already canonical in his day. In fact Tatian's compilation of the 4-in-1 gospel parallels what we know of earlier gospel construction. Each of the 4 evangelists utilized the gospel material at his disposal when compiling his book, and it is not surprising that Tatian should do the same. His use of our gospels does show, however, that these 4 either were the only gospels known to him or were gaining a position of preeminence in his day. The position of these 4 was not so secure, however, that they could not be displaced by the Diatessaron, which continued as the gospel in the Syriac church for almost 2 cents.

By the end of the 3rd quarter of the 2nd cent., then, the written gospels had come to a position of authority paralleling the OT and could properly be deemed scripture. By that time the 4 gospels later to be defined as the gospel collection of the NT were probably the gospels that circulated most widely and hence had become the most influential gospels in Christendom.

The Pauline Letters. It is an anomaly that other Christian writings were more readily accepted as authoritative in Christian communities. The reason for this appears to be that written gospels arose in competition with an authoritative oral gospel tradition, whereas the letters of an apostle—or writings purporting so to be—stood alone as the word of that apostle. Hence already by the end of the first cent.

letters of Paul were appealed to as authoritative. As already noted, after citing examples from the OT and the "words of the Lord Jesus," I Clement refers to I Cor. as written "with true inspiration" (47:3). The inspiration attributed to Paul parallels the inspiration of the OT (cf. e.g. 13:1; 16:2). This shows that at least I Cor. was already known by Christians in Rome and that Paul's authority could be appealed to alongside that of the OT.

The first clear implication of a collection of Paul's letters appears early in the 2nd cent. Ignatius writes to the church at Ephesus that Paul "in every epistle makes mention of you in Christ Jesus" (12:2). Though it is not certain how many letters of Paul were known to Ignatius, various passages reflect at least I and perhaps II Thess., I Cor., Rom., Col., and Eph.

A similar situation obtains for Polycarp. In his letter to the Philippians 11:2 f. he quotes Paul specifically (I Cor. 6:2) and then makes 2 allusions to his letters—to Phil. 4:15 and to either Phil. 2:16 or more probably II Thess. 1:4, applying it to the Philippians. It seems certain that he knew also Rom., Gal., Philem., and Eph., and he may have known Col.

The pseudonymous author of II Pet. (125-50) clearly knew a collection of Paul's letters since he says:

So also our beloved brother Paul wrote to you according to the wisdom given him, speaking of this as he does in all his letters. There are some things in them hard to understand, which the ignorant and unstable twist to their own destruction, as they do the other scriptures (3:15b-16 R.S.V. trans.).

What he means by the "other scriptures" is not clear, but it is usually thought that he refers to the OT. If so, then he regarded Paul's letters as of equal authority with the OT and therefore scripture.

By 140 Marcion published in Rome his own edited version of 10 letters of Paul, which he arranged in the order Gal., I, II Cor., Rom., I, II Thess., Laodiceans (probably Eph.), Col., Phil., Philem. Since these 10 letters of Paul were known in Rome at that time, it is probable that they were then or shortly thereafter generally accessible.

The Pastoral Epistles. I, II Tim., and Tit. have been called "Pastoral" epistles since the 18th cent. Certain passages of Polycarp seem to indicate that he knew I, II Tim., though some scholars attribute the similarities to common tradition (see Intro. to I Tim.). There is no other sign of early acquaintance with the Pastorals. They were not included in Marcion's collection of Paul's letters, probably because he did not know them rather than because he rejected them, as was later charged (Tertullian Against Marcion 5:21). The writings of Justin Martyr show traces of most of Paul's letters but none of the Pastorals.

In the last quarter of the 2nd cent. evidence of familiarity with the Pastorals becomes frequent. Tatian is reported to have rejected some of Paul's letters but recognized the authenticity of Tit. (Jerome On Tit., Preface). There appears to be an allusion to I Tim. 2:1-2 in Athenagoras' Apology 37:2-3 (ca. 177). Irenaeus opens his Against All Heresies (ca. 180) with an allusion to I Tim. 1:4, and he argues from II Tim. 4:10-11 that Luke was the constant companion of Paul (3:14:1). His frequent quotations from the Pastorals are their first extensive use. Thereafter they are often quoted and used as the work of Paul. It appears probable, however, that they were not included in the missing portion of the 3rd-cent. manuscript of Paul's letters known as the Chester Beatty Papyrus (P[46]).

The Catholic Letters. As distinguished from Paul's letters, which had local addresses, the other NT letters were regarded as encyclical in character, intended for the church universal, and thus came to be called "Catholic." The earliest author known to use the term is Apollonius (*ca.* 197), who says that the Montanist Themiso, "dared, in imitation of the apostle, to compose an epistle general, to instruct those whose faith was better than his" (Eusebius, History 5.18.5, trans. K. Lake). Writers of the Alexandrian school applied the term to I John and I Pet. in the first half of the 3rd cent. (Eusebius, History 7:25:7-10; Origen, Commentary on John 6:18) and later it was used of all the non-Pauline letters.

These 2 letters, I John and I Pet., came to relatively early recognition. Similarities to I Pet. are found in writings from early in the 2nd cent., but these may be explained as derived from common Christian teaching. However, Eusebius says that Papias "used quotations from the first epistle of John and likewise also from that of Peter" (History 3:39:17). He also says that the ancient elders of the church used I Pet. in their writings (3:3:1) and that Polycarp employed testimonies from I Pet. in his letter to the Philippians (4:14:9), as is confirmed by that letter.

Traces of I Pet. have been noticed in Gnostic writers—e.g. Basilides (*ca.* 125) and Theodotus (*ca.* 160), a disciple of Valentinus.

Irenaeus has a single quotation from I Pet. (1:18), introduced with the words "Peter says in his epistle" (Heresies 4:9:2). Clement, head of the Christian school at Alexandria (190-202), has a number of allusions to I Pet. and once cites a quotation from it as a word of Peter (Miscellanies 4:7:6). Tertullian of Carthage while trying to reconcile orthodoxy and Montanism (*ca.* 203-7) once cites I Pet. with the intro. "Peter said to the Pontians" (Scorpiace 12). Thus soon after 200 I Pet. was known as a work of the apostle, though it was not frequently used.

Polycarp is the first to show acquaintance with I John (Letter to the Philippians 7). Papias, according to Eusebius (History 3:39:17), quoted from it a number of times. Irenaeus quotes from I and II John as though they were a single letter and ascribes them to John the apostle (Heresies 3:16:5, 8). Clement of Alexandria makes frequent use of I John, calling it John's "larger epistle" (Miscellanies 2:15:66), implying that he knew at least one other letter attributed to John. There is no mention of III John in the 2nd cent.

The earliest evidence of Jude is in II Pet., where it constitutes the large part of ch. 2. Clement of Alexandria quotes it as the work of Jude (Instructor 3:8), as does Origen, his successor as head of the Alexandrian school (203-32). It is also mentioned by Tertullian.

The first explicit reference to II Pet. is by Origen, and then only once, with the comment that it is of doubtful authenticity (Commentary on John 5:3).

Other Writings of the NT. Rev. had a somewhat checkered history in the church. It is just possible that it was known to Hermas (early 2nd cent.) since in the Shepherd his imagery of the church as a woman and its enemy as the beast is parallel to the Rev. imagery. Reportedly it was known also to Papias (according to Andrew of Caesarea *ca.* 500). Justin Martyr is the first to refer to it by name, saying:

And further, there was a certain man with us, whose name was John, one of the apostles of Christ, who prophesied, by a revelation that was made to him, that those who believed in our Christ would dwell a thousand years in Jerusalem (Dialogue 81, trans. Roberts and Donaldson).

It is likewise named and used by Irenaeus (e.g. Heresies 5:26:1; 30:3).

Heb. has its earliest witness in I Clement. Allusions to Heb. are found throughout the first half and ch. 36 is made up almost entirely of echoes from it, but there are no allusions or echoes in the remainder. It is possible that Hermas knew Heb. (cf. Shepherd, Vision 2:3:2 with Heb. 3:12). Polycarp almost certainly knew it since he used the characteristic phrase "the eternal high priest" for Christ, and his letter to the Philippians 6:3 seems to allude to Heb. 12:28. Allusions are also found in Tatian and the apology of Theophilus, bishop of Antioch (*ca.* 175). According to Eusebius (History 5:26) Irenaeus mentioned Heb. and quoted from it in a little book on various discourses not now extant. According to Stephanus Gobarus (6th cent.), however, Irenaeus rejected the Pauline authorship of Heb., as did Gaius of Rome (*ca.* 200).

Irenaeus and the early church believed that Acts was written by Luke, the author also of a gospel. Like Mark, Luke was not an apostle but a follower of an apostle. Hence Irenaeus finds it desirable to offer special pleading for the acceptance of Acts. His argument (Heresies 3:14:1–15:1) runs as follows: Luke was inseparable from Paul, as is shown in the "we" passages in Acts (see Intro. to Acts). He was not merely a follower but also a fellow laborer with the apostles and esp. with Paul, as Paul notes—here Irenaeus cites II Tim. 4:10-11 and Col. 4:14. Moreover Luke was entrusted to hand down to us a gospel. The apostles delivered what they had heard from the Lord and Luke delivered what he had learned from them. Hence if anyone were to set Luke aside as one who did not know the truth, he would be rejecting the gospel of which he claims to be a disciple. But Luke's gospel cannot be set aside because there are many important items of the gospel that are known only from that written by Luke.

Indeed it may be [concludes Irenaeus] that it was with this view that God set forth very many Gospel truths, through Luke's instrumentality, which all should esteem it necessary to use, in order that all persons following his subsequent testimony, which treats upon the acts and the doctrine of the apostles, and holding the unadulterated rule of truth, may be saved. His testimony, therefore, is true, and the doctrine of the apostles is open and steadfast, holding nothing in reserve (trans. Roberts and Donaldson).

The Apostolic Fathers. That the argument of Irenaeus concerning the status of Acts pertains as well to other hearers of the apostles—i.e. the Christian authors contemporary with the later NT authors known since the 17th cent. as "apostolic fathers"— is indicated by Irenaeus' subsequent statement about the "elders" (presbyters):

> For Peter, and John, and Matthew, and Paul, and the rest successively, as well as their followers, did set forth all prophetical [announcements], just as the interpretation of the elders contains them. For the one and the same Spirit of God, who proclaimed by the prophets what and of what sort the advent of the Lord should be, did by these elders give a just interpretation of what had been truly prophesied; and He did Himself, by the apostles, announce that the fulness of the times of the adoption had arrived (Heresies 3:21:3-4, trans. Roberts and Donaldson).

Also Irenaeus warns against heretical writing's being mistakenly received "as coming from a presbyter" (Fragment 51) and links the testimony of the gospel and "all the elders" (Heresies 2:22:5). It appears, therefore, that the status of the apostolic fathers in the early church deserves more attention in the history of the making of the NT than is usually accorded.

The writing known as I Clement, sent from the church in Rome to the church at Corinth *ca.* 95 and traditionally ascribed to Clement of Rome, was already used extensively by Polycarp. Irenaeus says concerning this writing and its supposed author:

> In the third place from the apostles, Clement was allotted the bishopric [of Rome]. This man, as he had seen the blessed apostles, and had been conversant with them, might be said to have the preaching of the apostles still echoing [in his ears], and their traditions before his eyes. Nor was he alone [in this], for there were many still remaining who had received instructions from the apostles. In the time of this Clement . . . the Church in Rome despatched a most powerful letter to the Corinthians, . . . declaring the tradition which it had lately received from the apostles (Heresies 3:3:3, trans. Roberts and Donaldson).

Clement of Alexandria has several quotations from the letter and calls the author the "Apostle Clement" (Miscellanies 4:17). Origen refers to him as a "disciple of the apostles" (First Principles 2:3:6). Eusebius identified him with Paul's fellow worker mentioned in Phil. 4:3 (see comment), saying that the letter is recognized and has a long-standing tradition of being read publicly in many churches (History 3:15-16) and also that Clement of Alexandria used testimonies from it but that its status is still under dispute (6:13:6).

The letters of Ignatius are first mentioned by Polycarp, who gives an interesting insight into the circulation of early Christian writings in naming them. Writing to the Philippians just before Ignatius' martyrdom, which Eusebius (History 3:36) dates in the reign of Trajan (98-117), Polycarp says:

> Both you and Ignatius wrote to me that if anyone was going to Syria he should also take your letters. . . . We send you, as you asked, the letters of Ignatius, which were sent to us by him, and others which we had by us. These are subjoined to this letter, and you will be able to benefit greatly from them. For they contain faith, patience, and all the edification which pertains to our Lord (13:1-2, trans. K. Lake).

Irenaeus quotes Ignatius' letter to the Romans 4:1, with the intro.: "As a certain man of ours said,

when he was condemned to the wild beasts because of his testimony with respect to God" (Heresies 5:28:4, trans. Roberts and Donaldson). Origen cites his letter to the Ephesians 19:1 and says that he was the 2nd bishop of Antioch after Peter (Homily 6 on Luke).

Eusebius counts Ignatius as one of the apostolic men, saying:

> It is impossible for us to give the number and names of all who first succeeded the Apostles. . . . It was, therefore, natural for us to record by name the memory only of those of whom the tradition still survives to our time by their treatises on the Apostolic teaching. Such writings, of course, were the letters of Ignatius, of which we gave the list. (History 3:37:4-38:1, trans. K. Lake).

In listing the letters Eusebius says that Ignatius warned the Christians in the cities in which he stayed on his way to Rome "to be on their guard against heresies, . . . and exhorted them to hold fast to the tradition of the Apostles, to which he thought necessary, for safety's sake, to give the form of written testimony." He wrote letters to the churches at Ephesus, Magnesia, Tralles, and Rome from Smyrna. From Troas he wrote letters to Philadelphia and both the church at Smyrna and its bishop, Polycarp, whom he knew as an "apostolic man" (History 3:36:5-11).

The Epistle of Barnabas gained recognition in Alexandria. It was quoted as the words of the apostolic Barnabas (cf. Acts 4:36-37; 9:27; 11:22-30; 13-15; Gal. 2:1-13) by Clement of Alexandria (e.g. Miscellanies 2:6; 7:5; 20). As late as Eusebius it was still among the disputed books (History 3:25:4; 6:14:1) and Jerome, though counting it apocryphal, recognized that it was read by some in his day (*ca.* 400, On Illustrious Men 6).

Irenaeus cites Papias as an apostolic man, a "hearer of John and companion of Polycarp," saying that he wrote books (Heresies 5:33:4). Eusebius, to the contrary, while giving Irenaeus' account, says for himself that it was John the Elder whom Papias heard, citing Papias' own account that he was not a hearer of apostles (History 3:39:1-13).

Polycarp also was regarded by Irenaeus as an apostolic man (Heresies 3:3:4) and Eusebius confirms that he was a "companion of the apostles" (History 3:36:1) and calls him the "apostolic presbyter" (History 5:20:6-7; 24:16).

The writing called the Shepherd of Hermas was highly regarded in the early church in both E and W. Irenaeus cited it with approval; Clement of Alexandria regarded it as divinely spoken and by revelation; Origen thought it was divinely inspired and attributed it to the Hermas greeted by Paul in Rom. 16:14, though he was more reserved in his later writings. Tertullian used it as scripture before his conversion to Montanism (*ca.* 207); after that he spoke of it as the "book that loves adulterers" and said that even the Synod of the Orthodox counted it spurious, but there is no confirmation of this. Probably it was the strong influence of Montanism in the E that caused the book to be called into question. Roman contemporaries of Cyprian of Carthage (martyred 258) cited it as divine scripture and as a recognized book of teaching.

Other than being rejected by Tertullian for doctrinal reasons, the Shepherd of Hermas was not seriously questioned until the 4th cent. Eusebius seems to mark the turning point. He notes that some take it to be the work of the Hermas mentioned in Rom., but he thinks it should be known that the book is rejected by some. Hence some would place it among the accepted books while others reserve it for use with those needing elementary instruction. Eusebius says that he has found it quoted by some of the most ancient writers and that it has been used in public in churches. However, while initially placing it among the "divine writings which are disputed," he later places it among the ungenuine books (History 3:3:6-7; 25:4). Thus Eusebius apparently marks the period of its transition from an accepted book into the category of the rejected. Following Eusebius the Shepherd of Hermas finds no place in NT lists.

It is clear from the foregoing that certain of the apostolic fathers play an important role in the story of the making of the NT. During the 2nd and 3rd cents. these writings of apostolic men were placed alongside the writings of the apostles themselves as records of the apostolic teaching. Probably they should be included in the general category of scripture during this period.

Thus a large body of Christian writings, extending markedly beyond the bounds of the NT as later defined, came to be regarded as in some sense authoritative in the Christian church, and therefore as scripture. That the list could be further extended, by other books accepted by one or another faction or place of the church, is certain. This discussion has been limited to those books that came into widest circulation and therefore had the greatest likelihood of being included in the NT.

III. Closed Collections of Christian Scripture

The 2nd stage in the formation of the NT was the recognition of closed collections of Christian writings. This stage, to be sure, began concurrently with the later phases of the rise of Christian writings to authoritative recognition, so that there was overlapping in what we recognize as different phases. Likewise, inasmuch as the final NT was a collection of books considerably fewer than the total number of Christian books that came to authoritative status, it becomes immediately evident that one of the most significant factors in the making of the NT was the process of selection by which some books were retained and others excluded from the final NT. It is from *ca.* the middle of the 2nd cent. that we find the beginning of this selective process.

Marcion. A wealthy shipowner of Sinope in Asia Minor, Marcion *ca.* 139, came to Rome, where he joined himself to a Christian congregation. Apparently haunted by the problem of evil and suffering, he began proclaiming a doctrine of sharp dualism which contrasted the OT God of this world with a loving God, the father of Jesus. His rejection of the God of the OT necessitated his rejection of the Jewish Scriptures and of all the heritage of Judaism. It may be that his desire to find an effective substitute for the OT that caused him to form what he promoted as an authoritative collection of Christian writings.

Since almost nothing has survived of Marcion's own writings, it is impossible to say with any accuracy what Christian writings he consciously rejected. It is known, however, that those he chose were writings related to Paul, whom he regarded as the only apostle who rightly understood the gospel. His collection was divided into 2 parts: (*a*) the "gospel," an abridgment of Luke, according to early Christian tradition derived from Paul; and (*b*) the "apostle," 10 letters of Paul, edited to exclude any pro-Jewish elements. It may be that he regarded his own writing, Antitheses, as similarly authoritative. Thus it is probable that Marcion created the first NT canon, i.e. closed collection of Christian writings.

It has been widely held that Marcion's collection provided the impetus for orthodox Christianity to form its authoritative collection of scripture, but Marcion probably did not have such a definitive influence in the church. Justin Martyr, who knew Marcion's position well, significantly fails to make any mention of his "Christian scripture." The next earliest evidence for a closed collection of Christian writings was not a response to Marcion's gospel and apostle but rather a closed collection of gospels.

The 4-fold Gospel. We have noticed above that Justin was the first extant writer to appeal to written gospels as having authority and that the basis of this authority was that in the gospels the apostles had delivered what was enjoined on them by Jesus Christ. Thus for Justin the gospels contained and preserved the gospel of Jesus.

This doctrine was further developed by Irenaeus and crystallized into belief in a closed collection of 4 gospels. Employing a fanciful numerology for support, he declared that there could be only 4 gospels, no more, no less. And it was our 4 gospels that he included in his gospel canon—though in his writings he has 3 citations from other gospels. His argumentation shows that his definition of a gospel canon was directed against the Gnostics and their Gospel of Truth; but it is also clear that he was defending Luke, which was in jeopardy because of its use by the Marcionites—a situation indicated by Tertullian as well.

This 4-fold gospel canon first defined by Irenaeus soon made its impact in Christendom. Clement of Alexandria states that the church accepts only 4 gospels (Miscellanies 3:13)—though this recognition resulted in only a temporary restriction in his use of a far wider gospel tradition. With Tertullian and Origen, however, the 4-gospel canon becomes secure, though Origen's usage is not entirely confined to it. However, as late as 220 we find Hippolytus of Rome contending with a certain Gaius, who rejected John—as did the Alogi (*ca.* 175), who would use no Johannine writing.

The shift of the basis of authority between Irenaeus and Origen, however, is quite as important as the 4-gospel canon accepted by them. Irenaeus argues at length that the oral tradition of the gospel, preserved in all the apostolic churches throughout the world, exactly parallels the gospel recorded in the 4-fold gospel; but he argues from the accepted authority of tradition for the authority of the 4-fold gospel. Thus we find in Irenaeus the transition in authority from oral to written gospel. In Origen this transition has been accomplished. For him it is the 4-fold gospel that is authoritative and no question of oral tradition appears as an alternative authority. This transition is of primary importance in the development of a concept and doctrine of canon.

Paul: From Collection to Corpus. We have seen that an interest in collecting Paul's letters existed in the church at least since the last decade of the first cent. However, while an open collection of Paul came to be regarded as scripture, the question of a defined corpus is intrinsic to the development of a canon. Whereas the definition of a closed gospel collection occurred *ca.* the end of the 2nd cent., apparently no attempt to define the extent of the Pauline corpus was made until the 3rd cent. Marcion's use of 10 letters of Paul probably indicates the extent of the literature he knew attributed to Paul. As already noted, the Pastorals appear not to have been included in the Pauline collection until the last quarter of the 2nd century at the earliest.

Heb. appears as the critical issue in defining the Pauline corpus. Despite its early acceptance in E and W, its status came under attack in the W in the 3rd cent. As a result its position did not become assured until late in the 4th cent. The issue ostensibly was that of authorship. However, that Heb., which taught a rigorous doctrine of no sin after baptism, should come under attack in the W just when the Shepherd of Hermas, teaching the new liberalism of forgiveness of one sin after baptism, was enjoying widespread popularity there was hardly coincidental. And that the issue was innocent of any recognized criteria of apostolicity is shown by the fact that Tertullian, who vigorously defended Heb., fully expected that his argument that it was written by an apostolic man, Barnabas, would settle the issue for its authority. That Tertullian should argue this way shows the novice state of discussion on canon in the early 3rd cent. Tertullian knew of no criterion of apostolicity, but he did know of an attack on the status of Heb. Thus the literary analysis of Heb., showing that it was not written by Paul, must have been handmaiden to other considerations. But it launched the question of apostolic authorship that previously had been applied only against heretical books.

Collections in Origen. Eusebius has preserved Origen's comments on accepted NT books (History 6:25); and since he presents several of these in succession, his arrangement gives the appearance of a canonical list. The comments, however, are collected from 4 separate writings of Origen. Originally these comments were related to collections, and there is no evidence that Origen ever thought of a NT list. His terminology of "accepted," "disputed," or "false" books must therefore be understood within the context of the collections he is discussing and are not to be related to classifications in a canonical list.

Origen's first collection is the 4 gospels. He knows Paul's letters but does not enumerate them. He recognizes one acknowledged letter of Peter and knows a 2nd that is disputed. Of Johannine writings he names the gospel, Rev., one letter, and possibly 2 others not considered genuine by all. Heb. he recognizes as written in a style not Paul's; he attributes the thoughts to Paul, but who the composer was God knows. These observations apart, Origen also uses

Jas., II, III John, Jude, II Pet., the Epistle of Barnabas, and the Shepherd of Hermas. He also uses gospel material not found in the 4-fold corpus. This shows that while Origen's use of Christian literature was not as broad as that of Clement of Alexandria it nonetheless was not different in kind.

Like Origen, his Roman contemporary Hippolytus (*ca.* 235) used Heb., the Shepherd of Hermas, the Revelation of Peter, II Pet., the Acts of Paul, and Jas.

In the face of this lack of conformity it is impossible to believe that the canonical list of NT books known as the Muratorian Fragment could have been promulgated by the Roman church at the date usually assigned to it, viz. *ca.* 200—in the time of Irenaeus. Rather it must come from the period, more than a cent. later, when its interest in defining a canon is paralleled in the writings of the church fathers; and some of its concerns appear elsewhere only in the context of the E church. At the end of the 2nd cent. and through the first half of the 3rd there is no evidence among the fathers of a need for, or interest in, defining a canonical list of NT books. While their writings reflect a common situation with respect to the status of Christian scriptures, the variety in the books they use suggests that they are guided by other factors than any promulgated authoritative list or concern for canonical definition. Through Origen we are still in the period of scripture rather than canon, though the general use of a closed corpus of 4 gospels and the attacks on Heb. in the W raising the question of apostolicity forecast the development to come.

IV. THE NT CANON

Early Canonical Lists. With Eusebius the stage of canonization proper begins. In his Church History, completed *ca.* 325, he shows a concerted interest, when recounting the contributions of the church fathers, in itemizing their opinions about the Christian scriptures. And he does not hesitate to express his own opinions on the matter. Like Origen he notes that books are "acknowledged" or "disputed" and divides the latter into those he accepts and those he rejects. In the summary in 3:25 the accepted books include the 4 gospels, Acts, the letters of Paul, I John, I Pet., and "if it seem desirable" Rev. Disputed books "known to most" include Jas., Jude, II Pet., and II, III John, "which may be the work of the evangelist or of some other with the same name." Books "not genuine" are the Acts of Paul, the Shepherd of Hermas, the Revelation of Peter, the Epistle of Barnabas, the Teaching of the Apostles (Didache), and Rev. "if this view prevail." Some have also counted the Gospel According to the Hebrews. Heretical books include gospels of Peter, Thomas, Matthias, and others, and acts of Andrew and John and others. In 2:23:25 Eusebius mentions that there are 7 Catholic letters and notes that the authenticity of Jas. and Jude has been denied, though they are used publicly in most churches. The Revelation of Peter and the Epistle of Barnabas, while placed among the rejected books in the list above, are called disputed in 6:14:1. Probably Heb. is to be understood as included in the references to the letters of Paul since Eusebius accepted its Pauline authorship.

Thus, while Eusebius expresses a concerted interest in determining a list of NT books that were authoritative in the church, he himself was equivocal about the acceptance of some. Of note is his indecision concerning Rev. Previously Dionysius, who succeeded Origen at the Alexandrian school, had evaluated the language, style, and thought of Rev. as compared with the 4th Gospel and I John and concluded that Rev. could not have been written by the apostle John but must be by another man with the same name. Here again the questioning of apostolicity arose as a means to another end—combating apocalyptic fervor. Eusebius' uncertainty about Rev. marks a continued antiapocalyptic mood.

The criteria by which Eusebius constructed his list include universal acceptance, evaluation of the content on doctrinal grounds, and the claim to apostolicity. However, these theoretical criteria may have been the rationalization for more practical concerns in the church, as illustrated above by Heb., the Shepherd of Hermas, and Rev.

In the Codex Clarmontanus, a 6th-cent. manuscript of Paul's letters, a scribe included a Latin list of the books of the OT and NT which appears to date from *ca.* 300. It includes the 4 gospels, 10 letters of Paul—apparently inadvertently omitting Phil., I, II Thess., and probably Heb.—I, II Pet., Jas., I, II, III John, Jude, the Epistle of Barnabas, Rev., Acts, the Shepherd of Hermas, the Acts of Paul, and the Revelation of Peter.

Athanasius, bishop of Alexandria, promulgated a canonical NT list in his Easter letter of 367. This list is famous as the first to include just the books found in our NT today. But he also added a list of books to be read by those being instructed in Christianity. Christian writings included in this category of quasi-canonicity are the Teaching of the Apostles and the Shepherd of Hermas. The fact that Athanasius had used Hermas in his earlier writings as authoritative shows that the definition of his list of 367 was not of long standing and was not completely integrated into his practice. His inclusion of Heb. as written by Paul and exclusion of Hermas as not apostolic shows an interesting reversal of the apparent intention when apostolicity was first argued as a criterion, viz. to remove Heb., possibly in favor of Hermas.

Similar to the attempt to exclude Heb. in the W was the later dissatisfaction with the Catholic epistles in the E. Though I Pet. and I John were initially accepted, there arose a movement that brought all the Catholic letters into question. Some E writings accepted none of them whereas others accepted I Pet. and I John only. However, by the beginning of the 6th cent. there was acceptance not only of all the Catholic letters but of Rev. as well, as is shown by the Syriac translation made *ca.* 508.

In the W at mid-3rd cent. Cyprian of Carthage excluded Heb., Jas., II Pet., II, III John, and Jude and did not mention Philem. However, toward the end of the 4th cent. Latin writings had accepted them all. This is indicated in the actions of church councils in N Africa at the end of the 4th cent. and the beginning of the 5th. A council at Hippo in 393 enacted a NT list which included just the 27 books of our NT but separated Heb. from Paul's letters.

The Synod of Carthage (397) also issued a NT list paralleling ours but providing that martyrdoms were permitted to be read on the anniversary of the martyrdom. The 419 Carthaginian Council repeated the list of the previous council but shifted Heb. into the Pauline collection.

The Authority of the NT Canon. When the OT canon was defined within Judaism at the end of the first cent. A.D. a doctrine of inspiration was promulgated that made the Jewish canon coextensive with inspiration. No similar doctrine, however, was promulgated in the early church when the canonical lists of the Christian OT and the NT were developed. Indeed such a doctrine would have been antithetical to the content of the NT since the doctrine of the presence of the Holy Spirit in every Christian is frequently encountered within its writings. That Christians in the early period of Christian history so understood their experience and writing has been illustrated above. Similar expression of a sense of being inspired can be found among Christian writers throughout the period of the development of the NT canon. Thus Irenaeus speaks of the presence of the Spirit in the Christian as to "bear God." Origen uses language closely paralleling his description of the inspiration of I, II Macc. when describing his own writing. And the Passion of Perpetua and Felicitas, perhaps compiled by Tertullian, speaks unequivocally of its inspiration (Preface 6). It continued to be so highly regarded in the Church that Augustine found it necessary to warn that it was not canonical (On the Soul and Its Origin 1.10.12).

It is evident, therefore, that the definition of a NT canon was not accompanied by any restriction to it of the understanding of inspiration in the church. To be sure, the books of the NT canon were regarded as inspired, and orthodox writers attacked the writings of heretics as uninspired. But the NT canon was not regarded or defined as the exclusively inspired writings in the church. When the Shepherd of Hermas came to be questioned as an authoritative writing, it was not its inspiration that was questioned but its apostolicity. No attempt to make the NT the sole inspired writing was made in the church in the W until early Calvinists appropriated the Jewish doctrine of the coextensiveness of inspiration with canon as their doctrine.

It is evident, therefore, that the making of the NT canon in the church was the definition of a standard of inspiration rather than a restriction or limitation of it. Thus the activity of the Spirit in the church was not regarded as restricted to the books of the canon; rather the books of the canon defined what was of the Spirit in the church.

For Further Study. E. J. Goodspeed, *The Formation of the NT*, 1926; *The Meaning of Eph.*, 1933; "The Canon of the NT," in *IB*, 1952. John Knox, *Marcion and the NT*, 1942; *Philemon Among the Letters of Paul*, rev. ed., 1959. E. C. Blackman, *Marcion and His Influence*, 1948. R. P. C. Harron, *Origen's Doctrine of Tradition*, 1954. R. M. Grant, *The Letter and the Spirit*, 1957. R. M. Grant, *The Formation of the NT*, 1965. Kurt Aland, *The Problem of the NT Canon*, 1962. F. W. Beare, "Canon of the NT," in *IDB*, 1962. A. C. Sundberg, Jr., *The OT of the Early Church*, 1964.

THE TRANSMISSION
OF THE BIBLICAL TEXT

John Reumann

Almost 2,000 years separate us from the NT events, and more than 3,500 from the earliest in the OT. Over these cents. the biblical witness has been transmitted to us, first by word of mouth, then in writing; first in small units, then in individual books, eventually in collections of books, and finally in the canon we know today. Composed originally in Hebrew, Aramaic, or Greek (see "The Languages of the Bible," pp. 1194-1200), this material has been translated into over a thousand tongues. Its home, within which it has been handed down, has been a religious community, the Jewish synagogue or the Christian church. The story of transmission of the biblical text encompasses this span, from the time when a prophet or apostle spoke till today.

I. THE STUDY OF THE BIBLICAL TEXT

Scope. The history of text transmission properly includes (*a*) composition, (*b*) canonization, (*c*) standardization, and (*d*) transmittal of the text in manuscripts and then in printed form. For the oral period before material was written down there is a special method of investigation called "form criticism." Each biblical book has its own story of how its sources were transmitted and how it was composed. These earliest stages are prior to the concern here. Canonization, though always intertwined with text transmission, must also be dealt with separately (see "The Making of the OT Canon," pp. 1209-15, and "The Making of the NT Canon," pp. 1216-24). Ancient versions, i.e. translations made before *ca.* A.D. 1000, are an essential part of transmission history, but not translations into modern languages (see "The Bible in English," pp. 1237-42, and "The Bible in Every Tongue," pp. 1243-47). The study of transmission history requires not only the exacting technical disciplines of textual criticism but also familiarity with the sweep of theology and history. It is an art as well as a science. Today there is increasing interest in this study, with greater awareness that its goal is not merely recovering the presumed "original" text but also understanding how the scriptural witness has been handled from age to age.

The Need for Study. No longer can we read directly from a manuscript which Jeremiah or Paul wrote —or rather dictated to a scribe (cf. Jer. 36:4, 32; Rom. 16:22). The autographs, written on none too durable material, wore out long before they became canonical. We have copies of copies of copies—all

of which differ. In all biblical manuscripts variations appear. Already in a copy of John transcribed *ca.* A.D. 200 the writer has crossed out some words and corrected them with others. As soon as one sees the mass of manuscript evidence he grasps the need for textual study to ascertain the best form of the biblical text.

The approach to this study can be either backward through the cents., in light of the material extant today, or forward from the beginning, in an attempt to see what happened in each cent. The 2 methods are interdependent. A survey of the cents. depends on the materials available today and so must contain many gaps and guesses; conversely, all newly discovered materials must be fitted into place with what is already known. Because of new finds, e.g. the Dead Sea scrolls, and new observations about earlier discoveries all summaries must be rewritten every generation or so.

Terminology. In textual study the word "manuscript" (MS, plural MSS) refers to a handwritten document by which the text was transmitted before the invention of printing. Greek and Latin MSS are classified by their script. Earlier letters were square or rounded, mostly similar to those carved on stone monuments of classical antiquity, from which modern capital letters are derived. They are called "uncial," from the Latin for "inch," apparently because of a sarcastic comment of Jerome, translator of the Vulg., about the size of the letters made by scribes of his day. From the 9th cent. on, most scribes used a "cursive" ("running") script with "minuscule" ("rather small") letters which are the prototypes of modern lowercase letters. Besides this major difference MSS show gradual developments in the script by which most can be dated within half a cent.

MSS may also be classified by the material on which they are written: papyrus ("paper," II John 12), made from the stem of a reed; or the skin of an animal treated to make leather, parchment, or vellum (see "Writing in Biblical Times," pp. 1201-08). Being expensive, parchment or vellum was sometimes scraped of its writing and used again. Such a MS is called a "palimpsest." Much of the original writing still shows faintly, and by modern technological processes it can be almost completely recovered. Sheets of the writing material were at first fastened end to end to form a "scroll" or "roll" up to *ca.* 40 feet long—enough for Isa. in Hebrew or Acts in Greek, which took up more space because of including vowels (see "The Languages of the Bible," pp. 1194-1200)—and later were folded and sewed as in a modern book to form a "codex" (plural "codices"). The codex begins to appear in the late first cent. A.D. and, if not a Christian invention, was soon adopted by Christians for convenience and economy and to distinguish their writings from those of Jews and pagans.

A "version" is a translation of some part of the Bible into a language other than the original, e.g. the OT in Greek, the NT in Latin. A "recension" is a text revised by a specific editor or body of editors.

Causes of Variants. The Bible mentions several ancient documents which have been lost—e.g. the Book of the Wars of the Lord (Num. 21:14-15), the Book of Jashar (Josh. 10:13; II Sam. 1:18), various court chronicles (e.g. I Kings 14:29; I Chr. 29:29), Paul's initial letter to Corinth (cf. I Cor. 5:9), and probably his letter to Laodicea (Col. 4:16). Doubtless these are only a tiny fraction of the writings that once existed but were destroyed by war or disaster or rotted away in storage. Only those have come down to us that were valued enough to be copied and recopied as earlier copies wore out in use. In this process of repeated copying every document has suffered corruption.

That there are variants in our biblical text can be seen by anyone who studies it closely. Literary forms are often disturbed, a poetic rhythm or acrostic marred. Small differences show up clearly in OT "doublet" passages, which should agree (cf. e.g. II Sam. 22 with Ps. 18; II Kings 18–20 with Isa. 36–39; Ps. 40:13-17 with Ps. 70).

Many variants in MSS are unintentional, unconscious changes, often of a quite mechanical sort. Sometimes they are errors of the eye—misreadings of the exemplar being copied which result in omissions, repetitions, and transpositions of letters, words, or lines. Such misreadings were inevitable, not only because of the copyist's lapses in attention, but also because certain Hebrew consonants look much alike, as do some Greek uncial letters, esp. when carelessly written, and because the exemplar was often so worn as to be illegible.

If the eye skips over a letter, word, or line or 2, the error is known as "haplography" ("single writing"); if it sees something twice, the error is dittography ("double writing"). E.g. in I Thess. 2:7 the difference between "we were gentle" and "we were babes" (RSV footnote) is whether one or 2 *n*'s belong in the Greek. In Matt. 27:17 the insertion in a few MSS of the name "Jesus" before "Barabbas" (RSV footnote, NEB) may stem from dittography of the last 2 letters of the Greek word for "for you," which form the regular abbreviation for "Jesus"; or haplography may have caused its omission in all other MSS. If the confusion is due to similar endings on 2 words or lines, so that intervening words drop out, the error is "homoeoteleuton" ("similar ending"); it is "homoeoarcton" if "similar beginnings" are responsible. A clear case of homoeoteleuton is found in I Sam. 14:41, where several clauses dropped out in the Hebrew (cf. KJV) between 2 occurrences of the word "Israel," as is evident from the LXX and from the Vulg., which seem to have preserved the original reading.

Unintentional variants may also result from errors

of the ear—mishearings as the exemplar is read aloud. E.g. in Rom. 5:1 "we have peace" and "let us have peace" (RSV footnote) sounded the same in first-cent. Greek, and the confusion between them could go back even to Paul's original scribe. In the Hebrew such errors seem less likely, as there are no rabbinic references to a practice of reading an exemplar to a copyist; but Christians sometimes used the mass-production method of dictating to several copyists at a time.

There are also errors of the mind—failures in judgment by the copyist. He may misinterpret the abbreviations often used in MSS, esp. terms like "God" and "Christ," which were regularly abbreviated. The variants in I Tim. 3:16, "who," "which," and "God" (see RSV footnote), involve this point. Or a copyist may wrongly divide the words. Greek uncials and sometimes Hebrew were written continuously, and a scribe introducing word divisions had to make his own. Occasionally a double sense was possible, as in the famous English example GODISNOWHERE—"nowhere" or "now here"? In Amos 6:12 the RSV has divided the text to get a better sense than the KJV has. Since punctuation was uncommon in ancient times, later transcribers had to settle sentence divisions. E.g. is Rom. 9:5 one sentence or two? On the answer depends whether or not Paul called Christ God (see RSV footnote).

Liturgical instructions have sometimes been copied into the text—e.g. "Selah" in Pss. and Hab. 3, and Acts 8:37 (see RSV footnote), which probably reflects the baptismal confession in the church of some 2nd-cent. copyist. Marginal glosses also seem to have been copied into our text—e.g. "the king of Assyria" in Isa. 7:17, and the explanation in II Kings 9:4 (see RSV footnote) to make utterly clear that the "young man" is the "prophet." In I Cor. 4:6 the cryptic phrase paraphrased "to live according to scripture," lit. "not above what is written," seems to stem from a copyist's including in the text an earlier copyist's note to clarify a mistake by a still earlier copyist.

Intentional, deliberate variants were often introduced in all sincerity, to show the copyist's faith and make scripture speak more pertinently to the needs of his day. "Changing scripture" may horrify us, but ancient copyists sometimes made changes precisely for religious reasons, seeking not necessarily the original reading, but what seemed to them the "true" one. Piety was behind the practice in the Hebrew Scriptures of altering proper names compounded with the name of the Canaanite god "Baal" by substituting the word *bosheth,* "shame," e.g. in Ishbosheth (see comment on II Sam. 2:8-11; cf. I Chron. 8:33). A similar feeling produced in Gen. 18:22 the reading "Abraham still stood before Yahweh," where the original text undoubtedly said "Yahweh stood before Abraham"—this might imply that God served Abraham. Christian copyists—as well as English translators—often changed the unfortunate wording in Luke 23:32, lit. "two other malefactors," to avoid implying Jesus was a malefactor too.

Scribes often followed the human urge to replace rare words with familiar ones. E.g. the unusual verb in Mark 6:20, Herod "was perplexed," was changed in later MSS to "did" (cf. KJV). Sometimes a copyist tried to clarify a verse. E.g. in Mark 4:12 "lest

... it be forgiven them" (lit.) becomes in certain MSS "their sins should be forgiven them." John 5:3*b*-4 (RSV footnote) is an early insertion to explain the conversation which follows. In Matt. 5:22 "without cause" is an attempt to "explain" one of Jesus' "hard sayings." On occasion scribes corrected obvious errors, e.g. the reference to Jeremiah in Matt. 27:9, where the quotation is mainly from Zech., and that to Isaiah in Mark 1:2, where Mal. is quoted first. No doubt they also believed they were correcting an error when they changed a passage to agree with another part of the Bible, e.g. the OT with the NT or one gospel with another.

Insertions often reflect the growing tradition of later cents. E.g. the copyist of one Old Latin MS doubtless felt he was rendering a service by providing the names of the 2 thieves in Mark 15:27 as Zoathan and Chammatha. In some cases the transcriber desired to harmonize what he was copying with the worship he was accustomed to—e.g. the doxology to the Lord's Prayer in Matt. 6:13 in some MSS doubtless reflects Jewish-Christian practice—or with the theology of his day. E.g. devout copyists sometimes omitted the words "nor the Son" in Matt. 24:36 so as not to impugn Jesus' omniscience. I John 5:7 in the KJV was a late effort, introduced into Latin MSS, to get support in the NT for the doctrine of the Trinity. The reading of some MSS in Heb. 2:9, that Jesus died "apart from God," may well be original (cf. Mark 15:34) but too strong for early scribes, who accordingly changed it to "by the grace of God." John 1:18, where Christ is called either "the only Son" or "the only God" (RSV footnote), varied with the Christology of the copyist.

II. MSS OF THE OT

Beginnings. The earliest Hebrew traditions were oral, but a written literature began at least by the 10th cent. B.C.; our sources refer to "secretaries" and "recorders" at that time (cf. II Sam. 8:16-17; 20:24-25). Oral and written materials must then have existed side by side, with a shift to written literature by the 7th cent. At first the writing was in the Old Hebrew (Paleo-Hebrew) or Phoenician alphabet, a script which was used for some purposes down to A.D. 135. After the Exile, however, a new alphabet developed under the influence of Aramaic, which became the vernacular of the Jews. This new "square script," or "book hand" or "Assyrian script," came to dominate by the first cent. B.C. The transition from one alphabet to the other must have been a source of confusion in the copying of MSS.

In the Hebrew canon the Law, or Torah (Gen.-Deut.), was the first part counted authoritative; its text was being fixed and more carefully transmitted at a date before the other parts were so handled. The Prophets came next, and the Writings last of all. But in all cases the sacred text was fixed in distinct stages: (*a*) the consonantal text, developed in pre-Christian times and certainly established by the 2nd cent. A.D.; (*b*) the vowel points, dots and dashes added above or below the consonants to show the pronunciation, work on which began before the time of Christ, but which were finally systematized only in the early Middle Ages (A.D. 500-950); and (*c*) the diacritical markings to insure correct reading, chanting, and interpretation, details of which were not completed till the invention of printing. The really significant work was finished, however, by about A.D. 150, and from then on the story is a less eventful one. Unfortunately many details in this early period are far from clear. Textual work on the canonical books could have begun in several places—in Babylon or Alexandria, both centers of large Jewish colonies, or in Jerusalem.

The Sopherim. Traditionally the authorities in text transmission were the scribes or "bookmen," called "Sopherim because they used to count [*saphar*] all the letters in the Torah." Such scribes emerged during the Exile as professional theologians as well as copyists. They flourished esp. during the 5th and 4th cents. B.C., with Ezra as their archetype. In the synagogues there was need for many copies of the Torah and other scriptures, and the Sopherim began to work out a standardized text.

Their activity was continued by the later Sopherim on into the first cent. A.D., esp. during the Maccabean period (164-63 B.C.). The Jewish rulers then collected MSS to replace those lost in persecution and war (cf. I Macc. 1:56; II Macc. 2:14). Rabbinic sources speak of a temple library and of "correctors" who determined the proper forms from 3 authoritative scrolls kept there. The scribal scholars employed some of the same markings used by the Greek grammarians at Alexandria to call attention to possible textual disorders, "unexpected" (i.e. odd, if not wrong) forms, omissions, and emendations of the "bookmen." Best known of these are places where the *kethibh*, "what is written," i.e. the consonantal text, is accompanied by vowels and a note indicating that something else is to be read, the *qere*, "what is read." Piety was often a motive for these changes —"Better that one letter be removed from the Torah than that the Divine Name be publicly profaned." The scribes' work reached its acme in the 2nd cent. A.D., when the Masoretes took up the task and established the Masoretic ("traditional") text (MT) which we have today.

Evidence from Qumran. The biblical documents found in the Qumran caves (see "The Dead Sea Scrolls," pp. 1063-71) show, however, that in the last 2 cents. B.C. no one Hebrew recension, even at the Jerusalem temple, dominated to the exclusion of all others. Instead sharply differing text traditions existed side by side. True, the Qumranites were not an orthodox party, but their scrolls help us reconstruct a picture of text transmission in this period.

Some OT books, edited during the Exile, were carried back to Palestine in the 6th and 5th cents. This text type, the Old Palestinian Recension, was current in Palestine from the 5th cent. on. The "A" copy of Isa. from the 2nd-first cent. B.C. found in Cave I at Qumran reflects such a background, for the Babylonian names in it are quite correctly represented. There seems to have been another Hebrew text edited in Egypt in the 5th and 4th cents., from which the LXX translation was made in the 3rd and 2nd cents. This Egyptian text seems allied also with one in Palestine used by the Chronicler *ca.* 400 and reflected in Hebrew MSS at Qumran of Sam. and Kings. Finally it appears that textual work in Babylon continued and resulted also in a late Palestinian text introduced in the Hellenistic period, a Hebrew text so much like that later adopted by the Masoretes that it can be called Proto-Masoretic. Proto-Masoretic readings are found in the "B" copy of Isa. from Cave I a cent. later than the "A" copy.

This means that at least 3 recensions of the Hebrew OT existed at Qumran, an Old Palestinian, the Egyptian (LXX-like), and the Proto-Masoretic. To this list can be added a revision that was akin to the Samaritan text, a form close to the Proto-Masoretic but also in agreement with the LXX at times. No one of these text types was necessarily "superior" to the others; they were simply different editions of the Hebrew, all in use at Qumran. Throughout this period editorial refinement was constantly going on, pruning and shortening a text into which accretions had entered, just as was occurring at this same time among the Greeks with the text of Homer. Some scholars think that the Samaritan is an unpruned, rather full, "popular" text, the Egyptian a more edited one, and the Proto-Masoretic a still more edited, "official" text.

The Masoretes. It was this latter text type which the scribes of the Pharisaic party perpetuated after the fall of Jerusalem in A.D. 70 as the standard for rabbinic Judaism. Fixed in its details over the following cents., it became the MT. The other text types disappeared, neglected or suppressed, though traces of them linger on in some Hebrew MSS. Note that the Masoretes, the Jewish scholars after 70, did not thus create, but rather chose and transmitted an existing text form. Rabbi Akiba (ca. 50-135) and his colleagues did not invent a text tradition but established one which they had received. How firmly established the MT was by the time of Akiba's death is indicated by the Hebrew MSS discovered at Murabba'at. Deposited during the 2nd Jewish revolt of 132-35, these MSS do not exhibit the varying text types of Qumran but the orthodox, rabbinic MT.

It remained now to fix this MT as securely as possible in all details. The Masoretes built a fence of tradition (*masorah*) around the text, "traditions around the Tradition." The Jewish dispersion after 135 led to slightly differing lines of development among the Masoretes of the E in Babylon, and the Masoretes of the W, who labored at Jamnia in Judea from 70 to 135, and then in Galilee, esp. at Tiberias. Their work involved vocalization of the consonantal text, and other marks and notes to fix the tradition as surely as possible.

In the cents. B.C. a consonant had sometimes been inserted in the text to indicate a vowel, e.g. *y* for *i;* but the real work of vocalization was accomplished only by the Masoretes. There were celebrated debates over how some words should be pointed; e.g. in Deut. 25:19 should it be *zekher,* "remembrance," or *zakhar,* "male"? Three methods of pointing developed: (*a*) Babylonian and (*b*) Palestinian systems, with dots and dashes written above the consonants, and (*c*) a Tiberian system, written below the consonants, created by the Masorete families in Tiberias 780-930, the form handed down to the present. But even in Tiberias there was conflict over details between 2 Masoretic families, ben Asher and ben Naphtali. The ben Asher text won out, esp. because of support from the rabbinic philosopher Maimonides (died 1204), but traces of the ben Naphtali recension have infiltrated most ben Asher MSS. Thus the Hebrew text printed in the 15th cent. was a composite, the vowel pointing of which had been fixed only in the 10th cent. (see Table I, p. 1235).

Extant Hebrew MSS. Some 2,000-2,500 MSS of the Hebrew Scriptures are now known, the vast majority in the uniform MT tradition. Few were copied before 1000. The oldest and most significant are of the ben Asher type (see Table I). In 1890 a hoard of some 200,000 MS fragments, dating from as early as the 6th cent., was discovered in an old *geniza,* a storeroom for worn-out synagogue MSS, in Cairo. The evidence of this find is still under study. There have been few papyrus finds for the OT; the Nash Papyrus, at Cambridge University since 1902, is unusual—a scroll fragment from the first cent. B.C. or A.D. containing the 10 Commandments and the Shema (Deut. 6:4-5).

The Dead Sea scrolls are therefore of immense importance textually. From Qumran have come complete MSS and fragments of varying text types written 10 cents. or more before the ben Asher MT, from the very period when the OT was going through crucial stages in its transmission. From Murabba'at have come fragments deposited A.D. 132-35 of the Pentateuch and Isa., almost uniform with the MT.

Samaritan Pentateuch. The Samaritan text of Gen.-Deut., written in a form of the Old Hebrew script, differs from the later MT in some 6,000 places. Some variants stem from Samaritan religious beliefs; e.g. in Exod. 20:17 a command is added to build a sanctuary on Mt. Gerizim (cf. John 4:20-21) and in Deut. 27:4 "Gerizim" is substituted for "Mount Ebal." But other variants reflect a text different from the Proto-Masoretic, akin to the LXX, and now attested at Qumran (4QExod[a]). The Samaritan text has usually been dated at the time of the schism from Judaism in the 4th cent. B.C. but is now placed by some scholars in the early Maccabean period. Most MSS are from the 13th cent. A.D. or later; even the great Abisha Scroll exhibited at Nablus seems a patchwork from medieval MSS.

Greek Versions. The Letter of Aristeas (ca. 130 B.C.) describes how ca. 280 B.C. 72 Jewish scholars translated the Pentateuch into Greek at Alexandria. From this and from other traditions of 70 translators arose the name Septuagint, Latin for "70," abbreviated LXX. Later accounts applied the term to the Greek translation of the entire OT, completed ca. 130 B.C. Much in Aristeas is legend, but it is likely that a Greek OT did take shape at Alexandria in the 3rd and 2nd cents. B.C., though Jews elsewhere, e.g. in Ephesus or Palestine, may have produced other local renderings. This Alexandrian LXX became the Bible of the early Christian church. Heb. and Acts regularly, and Paul and the evangelists frequently, cite it rather than the MT. Passages like Matt. 1:23 (cf. Isa. 7:14); Acts 15:16-18 (cf. Amos 9:11-12); Heb. 10:5-7 (cf. Ps. 40:6-8) are possible only on the basis of the LXX.

The LXX contained some poor translations and was based on a Hebrew text which differed from the emerging MT in content and arrangement. Attempts were therefore made to bring the Greek translation into conformity with the Masoretic standard. A leather scroll from a site near Murabba'at preserves portions of the Minor Prophets written 50 B.C.–A.D. 50 in a revision of the LXX approximating the emerging MT. After A.D. 70 at least 3 efforts at a revised translation appeared. Aquila, a proselyte from Christianity, produced a fearsomely literal translation following the text and principles of Rabbi Akiba *ca.* 130. Theodotion (*ca.* 130-80) revised the LXX along the lines of a translation common in the Ephesus area; his revision of Dan. was so superior that it ousted the LXX form in most MSS. Symmachus, perhaps a Jewish-Christian Ebionite, *ca.* 180 created yet another OT version in Greek.

Readings from all these efforts unfortunately were mixed together in the MSS. In a huge undertaking, the Hexapla (230-40), the greatest Christian scholar of the day, Origen, working at Caesarea in Palestine attempted to turn this chaos into order. In 6 parallel columns he listed word by word for the entire OT: the Hebrew, a Greek transliteration of the Hebrew, Aquila, Symmachus, the LXX, and Theodotion. For some books he also included 3 other Greek versions he knew. Through careful text markings Origen tried to indicate the "true Hebrew" OT for Greek-speaking Christians. His parallel columns, however, simply made it easier to conflate the various Greek renderings.

In the 4th cent. other editors tried to smooth out the textual snarl. Three recensions came into circulation: (*a*) the Hexaplaric, from Origen, in Palestine; (*b*) one at Antioch by Lucian, martyred in the final wave of persecution in 311; and (*c*) that attributed to a Bishop Hesychius in Egypt. Today more than 1,500 Greek OT MSS exist. Through their maze of readings scholars seek to work back to the presumed Hebrew original.

Aramaic Targums. Aramaic became the common language in the near East from the Persian period onward. As early as Ezra's day (cf. Neh. 8:8 RSV footnote) paraphrases in Aramaic known as "targums" were given after the Hebrew verses were read. In time conventional renderings were agreed on. By NT times these were written down. There are targums for most OT books except Dan. and Ezra-Neh., portions of which were in Aramaic to begin with. These paraphrases show how the OT was being interpreted in their day. They tend to avoid the name of God, substituting "the Word," and shun all anthropomorphic expressions; e.g. "the LORD came down" becomes "the Word revealed himself."

OT translations into other languages generally came under Christian auspices as part of versions of the entire Bible and therefore may be considered along with versions of the NT.

III. MSS OF THE NT AND OF THE COMPLETE BIBLE

Beginnings. The story for the NT is in some ways clearer than for the OT because we have more MS variants as evidence. Again there was an initial oral period. The earliest written documents extant today are Paul's letters, written *ca.* 50-62. The rest of the NT literature was written by 150.

An important stage in transmission, increasingly under study today, is the period when early Christian editors were assembling the NT documents. E.g. II Cor. and Phil. are each believed by some scholars to be a compilation from 2 or more letters by Paul (see Intros.). They and other letters of his were assembled in a Pauline corpus, probably *ca.* 90-95. Each of the 4 gospels is the product of a final editor-evangelist. These gospels circulated separately at first, then were gathered *ca.* 140 into a 4-fold gospel collection. This editorial arrangement caused problems by splitting Luke-Acts, which had been designed as a 2-vol. work. After Luke became attached to the gospels collection, it had a separate history textually from Acts.

For a time each NT book has a transmission history of its own. By *ca.* 100, individual books are being gathered into larger collections. The most common type of collection includes only the gospels; *ca.* a 3rd of our NT MSS contain only the Pauline letters and Heb.; Rev., the book least copied, usually circulated alone. Eventually these little collections come together into the NT canon we know, but this canon, though taking shape in the late 2nd cent., emerges clearly only in the 4th.

The Crucial Period. The 2nd cent. is crucial for transmission of the NT text, as for the OT. Except for one tiny fragment, however, our MS evidence begins only after 200. There is thus a "tunnel period"—*ca.* 180 years between Paul's death and the earliest extant copies of his letters, 100-200 years between our gospels and the earliest extant copies of them. Variants and errors may thus go back to a period before our oldest MSS. Within this period some scholars suspect a "splurge of deterioration." When one recalls such difficulties as persecution, poverty, and lack of library facilities, as well as greater interest in the OT than in the new Christian writings and expectation of the Second Coming any day, it is not surprising that the text of the emerging NT took varied forms.

The original "apostolic" text likely moved along several lines of descent. Different text types appeared. Already *ca.* 140 there existed the "Western" text, a rather longish recension with many interesting details not in the "Egyptian" text, also circulating then. In the 2nd cent. translations of the NT were being made into Latin and Syriac. Though known to us only from MSS of later cents. the Old Latin and Old Syriac versions are witnesses to the NT text in this tunnel period.

There were also heretical movements like Gnosticism and Montanism which could affect the text. Tatian, a Syrian Christian, *ca.* 170 combined the 4 gospels into one account, the Diatessaron (one "through 4"). Later he was declared heretical and his Diatessaron was hunted down and destroyed, but his work seriously affected the Syriac text tradition of the gospels. Marcion, a wealthy leader from Pontus in N Asia Minor, came to Rome and in 144 put forth his own canon, consisting of Luke and 10 Pauline letters expurgated of any "Jewish" ideas. Scholars today are still debating how much his work may have influenced our text of Luke.

During the 3rd cent. text types identified with local Christian centers further developed and mingled. At Caesarea, as already noted, Origen devoted himself to bringing the LXX into conformity with the MT. How much work he did on the NT text is unclear, but a "Caesarean" text type has been identified. In Alexandria scribes reflecting an increasing Christian concern with culture revised the Egyptian text type to conform with the "purer" standards of classical Greek, thus producing an "Alexandrian" text. It is from this cent. that papyrus MSS preserve rather sizable portions of the Greek NT, but in most cases their text is "mixed," i.e. adhering now to the W text type, now to the Caesarean or Egyptian. Thus by 300 the gospels, Acts, and Pauline letters might be transmitted in a single MS collection, but each book or section would have a distinct ancestry. The situation has aptly been likened to a mixture of freight cars from various lines put together to make up a train.

Standardization. In the 4th cent. the text began to be standardized. State support of Christianity now made it possible to produce handsome uncial codices like Vaticanus and Sinaiticus (see Table II), which some think were among the 50 copies of the Bible that the Emperor Constantine enjoined

Codex Vaticanus (fourth century A.D.) stands as one of the most important witnesses to the text of both the LXX and the NT; *left:* John 7:3-32*b; right:* Luke 24:32 to end and John 1:1-14*a*

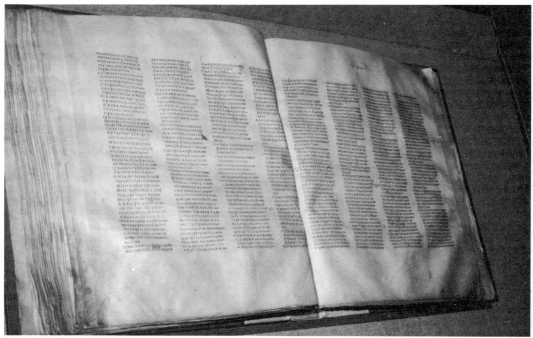

Codex Sinaiticus (fourth century A.D.) the only early Greek MS containing the entire NT; sheets are of high quality vellum, probably made from antelope skins

Eusebius to have prepared in 331. Textually, as noted above for the OT, a series of 3 recensions resulted—the Caesarean, growing out of the earlier work of Origen, and those of Lucian at Antioch and Hesychius in Egypt. From Lucian's Antiochian recension there developed an "ecclesiastical text" adopted by the state church, sometimes called the Syrian or Byzantine or Constantinopolitan text. Many of its readings can be traced back to the 2nd cent.; but it assumed its particular, conflate form in the 4th, and developed over the next 5 cents. as the dominant text type in the Middle Ages. Most later MSS conform to this standard.

From 400 on the NT text was thus more stabilized. It circulated in several text types, the W, Egyptian, Alexandrian, Caesarean, and Syrian, with the Syrian increasingly holding sway. MS copies became more numerous, reaching peak production perhaps in the 13th cent. Minuscule MSS begin to replace uncials in the 9th cent. It is amazing, though, how little the Greek and Hebrew originals were known during the Middle Ages in the W. By and large medieval W Christendom subsisted on the Vulg. The Hebrew OT was being transmitted in Jewish circles, of course, and the Greek OT and NT in the E and in a few monastic libraries and writing rooms. But the texts, frequently conflated, were corrupt heirs of the Byzantine tradition.

Extant Greek MSS. The very magnitude of the Greek evidence complicates the textual problem. There are nearly 5,000 Greek MSS and thousands of biblical quotations in the writings of the church fathers—a transmission history more intricate than for any other ancient documents. Early in the 20th cent. Hermann von Soden printed evidence on 45,000 NT variants. To put this in proper perspective, however, we should note that many of these are of a minor nature, and no denominational dogmas seem to have been revamped because of textual criticism. Indeed the very amount of evidence shows the concern of Christians with transmission of the sacred text. By contrast the poems of Catullus and Tacitus' Annals are preserved in only one Latin MS each, and even of Homer's Odyssey there are only some 100 MSS. Plato is extant chiefly in 13th-cent. MSS, and few classical authors are preserved in MSS copied before 1000, but NT uncials go back to the 4th and 3rd cents.

Besides 25 ostraca, i.e. potsherds, and 9 talismans, or amulets, with NT material inscribed, which are of no textual significance, the Greek material falls into 5 categories:

a) The papyri have brought significant recent advances. A cent. ago none were known; now 77 have been catalogued, though some are only fragments. Papyrus texts are denoted by the letter P followed by an officially assigned number. Among the most important are: (*a*) P[52], the John Rylands fragment of John 18:31-34, 37-38 in Manchester, England, dated *ca.* 125, a generation after the gospel was composed. (*b*) The Chester Beatty papyri: P[45], fragments of the gospels and Acts, 3rd cent.; P[46], Rom., Heb., I, II Cor., Eph., Gal., Phil., Col., I Thess. in that order, early 3rd cent.; and P[47], Rev. 9–17, late 3rd cent. (*c*) The Bodmer papyri: P[66], much of John 1:1–14:26, *ca.* 200; P[72], Jude, I, II Pet., from the 3rd or

4th cent.; and P[75], parts of Luke and John, early 3rd cent.

b) Uncial MSS were written on parchment or vellum between the 4th and 11th cents. They have commonly been denoted by a letter of the alphabet in English, Greek, or Hebrew. Since *ca.* 250 uncials are now known, however, scholars have evolved a system for identifying them by a zero prefixed to an officially assigned number. The most noteworthy uncial MSS are listed in Table II.

c) Minuscule MSS, in a cursive hand with letters linked together, total over 2,500, written between the 9th and 17th cents. Many contain only the gospels. Nine out of 10 are Byzantine in text. They are designated simply by a number. Around MSS 1 (12th cent.) and 13 (13th cent.) distinct family clusters of minuscules have been identified.

d) Lectionaries are service books for liturgical use containing NT readings for Sundays or weekdays in the church year. Almost 2,000 have been catalogued, 4 times as many for the gospels as for Acts and the letters combined. Not all the NT is included. Some readings appear twice in the course of the year. Most are minuscules. They are indicated by the letter *l* and a number. Their study has been taken up only in recent years.

e) Quotations from the Bible in writings of the church fathers can provide an extremely early witness to the text and also help fix geographical localities for text types, e.g. Irenaeus *ca.* 180 in S France. However, this patristic evidence is made difficult to use by the fact that a father may quote the same vs. in several forms, even loosely from memory—as we often do. Furthermore the document containing his words runs all the hazards of MS transmission too.

Latin Versions. Translation of the Bible into Latin began in the late 2nd cent., first in N Africa, then in Italy. Old Latin translations were the work of many hands. As part of the 4th-cent. trend toward standardization Jerome undertook their revision, beginning with the NT in 382. In 384 he is said to have overhauled an Old Latin translation of Pss. on the basis of the LXX, producing a version traditionally but wrongly identified with the "Roman Psalter." In 386-87 on the basis of Origen's Greek text he rendered a 2nd version of Pss., the "Gallican Psalter." In 392, after learning Hebrew in Palestine, he translated Pss. a 3rd time. Thereafter he followed the Hebrew rather than just the LXX or Old Latin for the rest of the OT.

Jerome's Bible was finished in 405 but met much opposition before it caught on. In time, however, it became the Vulgate ("common") Bible of W Europe, even though its readings often suffered corruption in transmission. The Council of Trent in 1546 decreed the Vulg. the official version for the Roman Catholic Church, and the Rheims-Douay translation (1582-1610) and that of Ronald Knox (1944-50) are based on it. A 1943 encyclical of Pius XII seems, however, to assign the Vulg. "juridical" rather than "critical" authority in Roman Catholic Bible study.

Syriac Versions. The Old Syriac translation stems from the 2nd cent. and is attested for the gospels by the 4th-cent. Sinaitic Syriac MS, discovered in the St. Catharine monastery at Mt. Sinai in 1892, and by a 5th-cent. MS edited by Cureton in 1858. The text is W in type. Tatian's Diatessaron had great influence in the Syriac-speaking world. OT work may have been begun by Jews. In the 5th cent., Bishop Rabbula of Edessa and others produced a standardized text, the Peshitta—meaning either the "common" translation or the "simple" one, i.e., without variants. Later revisions were undertaken by Philoxenus in 508 and Thomas of Heraclea in 610 or 616. Paul of Tella made a copy of column 5 in Origen's Hexapla, including all his critical markings, and this Syro-Hexaplar is a prime source for recovering Origen's work.

Other Versions. Ancient translations exist for various national Christian churches, made usually from the LXX rather than the Hebrew. In Egypt translations were made in the 3rd-4th cents. into the Coptic dialects, notably Sahidic and Bohairic. Many of the Bodmer papyri and the Gnostic documents like the Gospel of Thomas found at Nag Hammadi in 1945 are in these Coptic dialects. Bishop Ulfilas (310-83) invented an alphabet for the Visigoths and translated the Bible into Gothic. Mesrop and Sahak in the 5th cent. did the same thing in Armenian. Georgian, Ethiopic, and Arabic translations developed between the 5th and 10th cents. There were also Anglo-Saxon and Old Church Slavonic renderings.

Courtesy of James M. Robinson

Site of the discovery of the Gospel of Thomas at Nag Hammadi; the books were found in the remains of a Greco-Roman cemetery in the foreground; slight hillocks among the tufts of grass mark the grave sites and the contrasting dark soil is the topsoil sought by natives when they dug and found the books; cliff in the background locates the site of Sixth Dynasty tombs later used as private cells by monks who prepared the gospel

IV. THE PRINTED BIBLE

The invention of the printing press opened a new era by making possible the multiplying of hundreds of copies of the same text. It thus spurred scholars to seek out the best text. Gutenberg's first printed book (*ca.* 1455) was a Vulg. Bible. Oddly, the much longer Hebrew Scriptures were in print under Jewish auspices 25 years before Christians published a Greek NT—in part because of the dominance of the Vulg. in the Christian mind.

Early Printed Hebrew Scriptures. As early as 1477 the Psalter was printed, the Pentateuch in 1482, the entire OT in the MT by 1488 at Soncino, near Milan, Italy. Only in 1516-17 did a Christian, Felix Pratensis, the converted son of a rabbi, publish a Hebrew OT, at the famous press of Daniel Bomberg in Venice. From this press came a 2nd ed. in 1524-25, destined to be the standard printed Hebrew Scriptures. Its 4 vols. were edited by Jacob ben Chayim, who used a few late MSS of the ben Asher type. In spite of the limited sources consulted, the 1524-25 Bomberg ed. became the foundation for most later printed Hebrew Scriptures until 1937, when Paul Kahle in the 3rd ed. of Kittel's *Biblia Hebraica* went behind these late MSS used by Chayim to a ben Asher codex written in 1008 (see Table I).

Early Printings of the Greek NT. A significant step came with production of a 6-vol. Bible, the Complutensian Polyglot, in Hebrew, Greek, Aramaic, and Latin at Alcalá, Latin "Complutum," in Spain. Cardinal Jiménez, often latinized as "Ximines," and 8 associates worked on it for over 15 years. The NT part was printed by 1514, the entire Bible by 1517; but a papal permit came only in 1520, and circulation began only in 1522. Meanwhile Erasmus had scooped the world by getting a Greek NT on the market in 1516. But the Polyglot served dramatically to direct attention away from the Latin column to the Hebrew or Greek it printed alongside.

Erasmus, most renowned Greek scholar of the day, had been persuaded by the Basel printer Froben, who held exclusive rights from the pope to publish the Greek NT for 4 years, to rush through the Greek NT of 1516. He consulted only 6 late minuscules, and at times sent one of these directly to the printer to be set in type. When he found Rev. 22:16-21 missing from all his exemplars he boldly translated from Latin back into Greek himself.

Opponents were outraged that the dominant Latin was now challenged by the Greek. Stunica, one of the Polyglot editors, attacked the omission of the vs. about the Trinity in I John 5:7 (KJV)—missing even in the late Greek MSS consulted by Erasmus. Rashly Erasmus agreed to insert the vs. if a single Greek MS with it could be found. One turned up, apparently written for the purpose by a Franciscan at Oxford in 1520, and so Erasmus put the spurious vs. into his 3rd ed. of 1522, whence it entered subsequent Greek NT's and the KJV. It is a Latin gloss, found in no MS before the 12th cent.

Erasmus' text went through many reprintings, often blended with the Complutensian NT. The 1550 ed. by Stephanus—a learned printer who in 1551 first added numbered vs. divisions to the ch. divisions which Stephen Langton had introduced into the Vulg. in the 13th cent.—became standard in Great Britain and provided the basic Greek text for the NT of the KJV of 1611. The similar Elzevir edition of 1633 in Holland became standard on the Continent and came to be called the *Textus Receptus* (TR) from a blurb in the preface describing it as the "text received by everyone." The Greek NT was now being circulated widely in print, but in a form based on only *ca.* 25 late MSS.

The Collection of Evidence. In 1628, 17 years after the KJV was published, Codex Alexandrinus (see Table II) arrived in England. The readings of this 5th-cent. MS suggested that the accepted text contained many errors. In Paris *ca.* 1700 a palimpsest was discovered containing, under a commentary by the Syrian theologian Ephraem copied in the 12th cent., a 5th-cent. Greek Bible, which was accordingly named Ephraemi Rescriptus (see Table II). Other MSS, previously known but unused, were now examined, including 2 bilinguals (Greek-Latin) from the 6th cent. (see Table II). Evidence from the Latin, Syriac, Ethiopic, Arabic, and Persian versions was also studied.

During the 17th and 18th cents. progress on the Hebrew OT was slow, but for the NT variants piled up increasingly. John Fell of Oxford in 1675 listed readings from *ca.* 100 Greek MSS plus the Coptic and Gothic. By 1707 John Mill, also of Oxford, listed 30,000 variants in his Greek NT. But when he dared to correct the TR 31 times great controversy arose; his work was deemed a menace to Christianity.

Leadership in textual study now passed to Germany. J. A. Bengel of Tübingen in his NT of 1734 presented many variant readings he judged preferable to the TR—but only in footnotes, lest traditionalists be too disturbed. He also began to classify MSS into families and formulated principles to guide the text critic, e.g. "The difficult is to be preferred to the easy reading"—since copyists are likely to ease a difficult phrase. J. J. Wettstein in his NT of 1751-52 raised the total of MSS collated to 225. At the end of the cent. J. J. Griesbach, professor at Jena, laid out some 15 canons of text criticism and analyzed the MSS and versions into 3 main families, Western, Alexandrian, and Constantinopolitan. Most important, at many points he disregarded the TR and printed the results of his own study of the evidence.

Development of a Critical NT Text. By 1830 *ca.* 600 Greek MSS had been examined. Methods had been worked out in classical studies. It was the professor of classical philology at Berlin, Karl Lachmann, who in 1831-50 undertook reconstruction of the NT text of the 4th cent. based solely on early Greek MSS, as if the TR had never existed. In Britain S. P. Tregelles proceeded along similar lines in his NT eds. of 1857 and 1872. Striking confirmation of Lachmann's reconstructed text came when Konstantin von Tischendorf published 2 great 4th-cent. MSS., Sinaiticus in 1862 and Vaticanus in 1867—though a fully satisfactory reproduction of the latter was published only in 1890. Tischendorf found and published more uncials than any other man in history and edited over 20 eds. of the Greek NT. His 8th major ed. of 1869-72 (reprinted 1964) is still a standard because of its extensive and precise citations. His

dramatic story of rescuing part of Sinaiticus from being burned as trash and 15 years later, as he was about to end his 3rd visit to the monastery of St. Catharine at Mt. Sinai, discovering the greater part of it, including the complete NT, caught the public mind and roused the desire for a better, i.e. older, text.

Two Cambridge scholars, B. F. Westcott and F. J. A. Hort, climaxed almost 30 years of work with publication in 1881 of *The NT in the Original Greek,* in which they sought, behind even the 2 great uncials of the 4th cent., an earlier text. Their working principles took into consideration: (*a*) the internal evidence for each reading, on the basis of "intrinsic probability" ("Which variant makes the best sense?") and of "transcriptional probability" ("Which reading will explain all the others which have evolved in the history of transmission?"); (*b*) internal evidence for each document, e.g. the date and credibility of a MS; (*c*) "genealogical evidence," whereby a "family tree" of readings is constructed and the trunk is preferred to the later branches; and (*d*) the internal evidence of groups of MSS and versions, wherein relationships among text families are evaluated.

Westcott and Hort outlined 4 text types. Though they made no claim to have reconstructed the apostolic autograph, they saw this autograph handed on most faithfully in what they dubbed the "Neutral Text," an early, if not the original, form from the 2nd cent., witnessed to esp. by the 2 4th-cent. codices. A later offshoot of this Neutral Text was the "Alexandrian Text," a polished, "classical" reediting in the 3rd cent. The "Western Text" they regarded as a 2nd-cent. reworking of the NT, marked by paraphrase, interpolation, and harmonization of readings. The "Syrian Text" was the product of 4th-cent. editors, who conflated readings and smoothed out rough spots; the TR was a later development of this. They preferred the Neutral Text—as their question-begging name suggests. Their reconstructed text had wide use and became in its own way a new "critical TR." Goodspeed's NT translation is based on it.

Later NT Text Criticism. Discoveries and investigations since 1881 have rolled back the evidence another full cent. and challenged much in the Westcott-Hort theory. Esp. exciting are the Greek papyrus codices recovered from the sands of Egypt; containing portions of both OT and NT from the 3rd cent. Most of these early MSS exhibit "mixed" texts. Since the Old Syriac version of the gospels in the 4th-cent. Sinaitic Syriac MS, discovered in 1892, was made in the 2nd cent., it offered evidence older than any Greek MS then known. James Moffatt and a footnote in the 1952 revision of the RSV NT, soon deleted, gave credence to its much-debated reading in Matt. 1:16, "Joseph . . . was the father of Jesus."

Among the uncial discoveries Codex Washingtoniensis (see Table II), a 5th-cent. MS which came to light in 1906, is noteworthy for its blocks of text, first Byzantine, then Western, then "Caesarean," then Alexandrian in type; it seems to go back to a MS pieced together from various gospel MSS after Diocletian's attempt to destroy Christian books. Codex Koridethi, rediscovered in 1901, was copied only in the 8th or 9th cent.; but its unusual text in Mark, B. H. Streeter decided, was used by Origen and Eusebius at Caesarea in the 3rd and 4th cents.

Such finds led scholars to rework the Westcott-Hort reconstruction considerably. In 1924 Streeter posited a theory of "local texts" at each great center of Christianity: Alexandria, Antioch, Caesarea, Carthage and Rome, and later Constantinople with its Byzantine text. Gone was the assumption of a superior "Neutral" Text. Streeter's most significant contribution, to call attention to a Caesarean form, has been much analyzed; but there does seem to be a group of distinct readings allied with Codex Koridethi—esp. in certain families of minuscules which have been isolated—readings connected with Origen and Caesarea.

NT textual criticism in the 20th cent. has reconsidered even some of the principles of Westcott and Hort. Their genealogical method was further developed, but in time its limitations became apparent too. The Western Text, which they probably held in too low esteem, has been variously reassessed.

Other editors have tried their hand at editing the NT. The most elaborate effort was doubtless that of Hermann von Soden, who between 1902 and 1913 worked out his own system of MS symbols, theory of text history, and critical text. Generally the results of his immense labor have not found scholarly approval, though Moffatt based his English translation on this text. Among half a dozen other Greek NT's the series of eds. from 1898 on by Eberhard Nestle, his son Erwin, and more recently Kurt Aland—a composite of the opinions of great editors since Tischendorf—has long been a standard for students. In 1966 the American Bible Society and its counterparts in Great Britain, Germany, and the Netherlands published a new ed. of the Westcott-Hort text as modified from more recent discoveries and editors. Intended esp. to aid translators, it presents a critical apparatus, i.e. listing of variants and the witnesses to them in order of probability, only for variants which affect the meaning. An ambitious International Greek NT Project is under way to publish in 8 vols. the TR, the text of the majority of Greek MSS, with as full and accurate an apparatus as possible. Both the RSV and the NEB are eclectic and follow no one editor.

OT Text Study in Modern Times. Until recently scholars had to work from the rather limited evidence in the MT tradition and the versions. The 19th cent. was therefore a time of elaborate theories—e.g. that of Paul de Lagarde (1827-91), who argued with great brilliance that all existing Hebrew MSS were descended from an archetype *ca.* A.D. 130 and that we must work back to earlier forms through the LXX—and of text emendations, in which the scholars presumed to rewrite Hebrew better than the biblical authors did.

More recently recovery of the cognate, i.e. other Semitic, languages—esp. Ugaritic, a form of Canaanite found on many tablets at Ras Shamra in N Syria in 1929—and certain archaeological discoveries have unlocked the meaning of obscure phrases in the MT and heightened respect for its transmission over the cents., curbing the itch to emend. The fragments from the Cairo Geniza, masterfully interpreted by Paul Kahle, have given evidence concerning Masoretic transmission several cents. earlier than data previously available. The Qumran (2nd cent. B.C.—first cent. A.D.) and Murabba'at (deposited A.D. 132-35) finds have given us MSS in Hebrew, Aramaic, and Greek not only 1,000 years older than the MT MSS but also Proto-Masoretic and non-Masoretic. They have vaulted us behind the barrier of the 2nd cent. A.D. to the time of variant Hebrew texts that underlie our existing text and versions. Only through these finds is the survey outlined above possible, and it is subject to further modification as new texts become available.

V. Methods and Problems in Textual Study Today

With so much objective material available textual criticism should be the most scientific area in biblical studies. Because both testaments have been transmitted primarily within believing communities, however, the investigator is immediately confronted with the history and beliefs of the synagogue and the church as influential factors in text development. Careful subjective judgment is often called for. Work must be carried on as an integrated part of Bible study and theology as a whole. Numerous problems arise.

The Texts We Seek. Textual critics once assumed their task was simply to recover the "original" text. Scholars today recognize the need of historians and theologians to know the scriptures that guided the synagogue and the church at each stage of their development. E.g. they must seek not only what Jeremiah dictated to Baruch *ca.* 600 B.C. but also its form in the Proto-Masoretic and other early, Maccabean recensions, the consonantal text fixed under Akiba early in the 2nd cent. A.D., and the developed MT of ben Asher in the 10th cent. For the NT the goal is not only what Paul dictated in the middle of the first cent. but also the form it took in the collection of his letters which inspired later NT writers at the end of that cent., in the local recensions of the 2nd cent., in the uncial MSS read by the church fathers of the 3rd and 4th cents., and in the TR used by translators in the 16th cent. It is the duty of textual scholars to collect all readings and evaluate them and try to reconstruct not only the autographs but the texts in use throughout the cents.

The investigator is always limited by the sources at his disposal. In Martin Luther's day the text available was that of the late Middle Ages. By the 19th cent. knowledge of the NT text had been rolled back to the 4th or 3rd cent. More recent discoveries take us back to A.D. 200 for some parts of the NT and back to the 2nd cent. B.C. for parts of the OT. But experts have no illusions that "originals" are in sight of recovery, in spite of recent momentous finds.

Methodology. How can we reverse the flow of history and work back from our sources toward the earliest forms? In the 19th cent. textual criticism developed a number of rules and "assured results." Some of these have been brought into question, e.g. the Westcott-Hort analysis and the genealogical method. The "family tree" approach is still widely used but has its limitations, because a "mixture" of NT text types already existed in the 2nd cent. and because a 2-branched family tree no longer fits the complex evidence. Some textual critics prefer the

TABLE I. OLDEST MSS OF THE MASORETIC TEXT

Designation	Date	Contents	Location	Other Information
Or. 4445	820-50?	Gen. 39:20–Deut. 1:33	British Museum	Text of Aaron ben Asher
Cairo Codex (C)	895	Former and Latter Prophets	Karaite Synagogue, Cairo	Copied by Moses ben Asher
Petersburg Codex (P)	916	Former and Latter Prophets	Public Library, Leningrad	Ben Asher text, but with earlier "Babylonian" vowel pointing
Aleppo Codex	900-950	Complete	Hebrew Univ., Jerusalem	Vocalization and masorah by Aaron ben Asher; used by Israeli scholars as basis for new ed.
Leningrad Codex B 19*a* (Leningradensis, L)	1008	Complete	Public Library, Leningrad	Copied from MSS written by Aaron ben Asher; used in 1937 as basis for Kittel-Kahle *Biblia Hebraica,* third ed.

TABLE II. CHIEF UNCIAL GREEK PARCHMENT MSS

Number	Letter	Name	Cent.	Contents	Location	NT Text Type	Discovery
01	א (*aleph*)	Sinaiticus	4th	Last half of OT; all NT	British Museum; 43 OT leaves in Univ. Library, Leipzig	Alexandrian with Western touches	By Tischendorf at Mt. Sinai 1844, 1859
02	A	Alexandrinus	5th	Almost complete	British Museum	Alexandrian but gospels Byzantine	Gift to king of England from patriarch of Constantinople in 1627
03	B	Vaticanus	4th	Most except Gen. 1:1–46:28; Heb. 9:14–13:25, Pastorals, Philem., Rev.	Vatican Library	Alexandrian	In Vatican Library since before its first catalog in 1475 but opened to scholars only in latter half of 19th cent.
04	C	Ephraemi Rescriptus	5th	Palimpsest of scattered parts of OT & NT	National Library, Paris	Mixed, mostly Byzantine	Noted *ca.* 1700; deciphered by Tischendorf, 1840-45
05	D	Bezae	5th/6th	Greek & Latin of Gospels, Acts	Cambridge Univ. Library	Western	At Lyons in 1562
06	D^p	Claromontanus	6th	Greek & Latin of Pauline letters, Heb.	National Library, Paris	Western	At Clermont, France
032	W	Washingtoniensis	5th	Gospels	Smithsonian Inst., Washington, D.C.	Mixed	Egypt, 1906
038	Θ (*theta*)	Koridethi	9th	Gospels	Georgian Museum, Tiflis, U.S.S.R.	Caesarean in Mark, elsewhere Byzantine	In a monastery at Koridethi, Georgia (Russia) 1853, but later lost and rediscovered in 1901

analogy of clusters or constellations of MSS instead of a tree.

There is agreement, in varying degree, that the decision among variant readings cannot be made on the basis of the family tree alone, or of past custom or tradition (the TR), or majority vote (MSS must be weighed, not counted), mere age (the oldest MSS are not necessarily the best), geographical spread, patristic usage, "quality" (as if some "model" could be selected), or even the computer method of ascertaining the author's "style."

Those in the forefront of textual study follow an eclectic method which takes into consideration (a) external factors, e.g. date, genealogy, and geographical distribution of MSS supporting a reading, and (b) internal evidence, e.g. context and "transcriptional probability," and allows (c) conjecture on occasion. There are canons of criticism which can be applied with discrimination to decide which reading makes the best sense in a passage: e.g. we should prefer the shorter reading, the more difficult one (though not so difficult as to defy all sense), the reading characteristic of the author generally, the one which explains all other (later) variants. Shrewd conjectures, i.e. guesses, not necessarily based on any MS evidence, are allowed in rare cases—2 or 3 in a NT edition—but nothing on the scale practiced in the 19th cent. They are more justified in books like the Catholic epistles or Rev., where MS evidence is less good. E.g. conjectures which enjoy some current support include "with trembling kiss his feet" (Ps. 2:11b-12a; see comment) and "Enoch went and preached even to those spirits that were in prison" (I Pet. 3:19 Goodspeed; cf. Moffatt; see comment).

Use of the versions is a "must" but demands great caution. Each version is an interpretation as well as a translation and has its own history of transmission and inner corruptions. Before an investigator can use a version, he must get the "feel" of it. But, such warnings heeded, the LXX esp. is of tremendous importance for the simple reason that it antedates our MT and ties in with Hebrew recensions now being recovered at Qumran. In the RSV it has been used to fill some gaps in the Hebrew, e.g. in Judg. 16:13-14; I Sam. 12:3, 6, 8, 9. Some other versions, it may be noted, are not independent witnesses, since they derive from the LXX.

Problems. The Bible reader is confronted with innumerable specific textual problems, with which the commentator must deal. In many passages, e.g., Rom. 8:28; I John 4:19, changes in the RSV from the KJV are to be explained solely on the basis of better, earlier MS evidence which has come to light since 1611. The fact that OT quotations in the NT do not accord with those in our OT today is often explainable by the NT author's use of the LXX whereas our OT translates the MT—e.g. cf. Matt. 12:18-21 with Isa. 42:1-4. The Western readings in Luke-Acts provide an excellent illustration of a problem confronting even the casual reader. The MSS and versions in the Western text tradition omit certain vss. in Luke and add some striking details in

Acts, contrary to all other text types. The omissions include Luke 22:19b-20; 23:34; 24:12, 40, 51b; Acts 15:20, 29; 21:25; some of the additions occur in Luke 22:43-44; Acts 8:37; 15:34; 19:9; 24:6b-8a; 28:29 (see RSV footnotes). Experts have taken differing views on these readings, but they are primitive, and some may have a claim to originality, as RSV adoption of them shows.

We must constantly be aware of our ignorance about many matters in transmission history, e.g. the state of Babylonian Jewish textual work from the 5th cent. B.C. to the 2nd A.D., or the cross-currents in 2nd-cent. Christianity. Extrapolation, i.e. expanding our theories too universally on the basis of too meager evidence, is a continual temptation. There is always danger that historical accident, i.e. what has survived and what has been discovered at a given time, will wrongly dictate our overall picture of development.

In all of this we need to recognize the basic trustworthiness of our Bible text compared with other documents transmitted from antiquity. Orthodox theology has often spoken of the Bible's significance in terms of its inspiration. It should now be clear that any doctrine of inspiration, if it is to be meaningful, ought to reckon with the Spirit at work in transmission of the text. The church fathers tended to subsume the long story of transmission of the Bible under the providence of God, and some schools of recent theology see it as an ongoing part of the history of salvation. Regardless of the exact view one takes, believers have cherished the text they transmitted over the cents. because they found here the Word of God, though in a servant's form, speaking to their day. It is this action of the Word and the Spirit which gives the transmitted Scriptures their life-giving quality.

For Further Study. Arthur Jeffery, "Text and Ancient Versions of the OT," E. C. Colwell, "Text and Ancient Versions of the NT" (esp. methods), in *IB*, vol. 1, 1952; K. W. Clark, "The Transmission of the NT" (esp. history), J. C. Trever, "Illustrated History of the Biblical Text" (27 color photos), F. M. Cross, Jr., "The Dead Sea Scrolls," in *IB*, vol. 12, 1957. H. G. C. Herklots, *How Our Bible Came to Us,* 1954; a reliable popular account. F. G. Kenyon, *Our Bible and the Ancient MSS,* rev. ed. by A. W. Adams, 1958; a standard handbook of the Bible text in its original languages, ancient versions, and English translations, with halftone illustrations of MSS and early printings. F. M. Cross, Jr., *The Ancient Library of Qumran and Modern Biblical Studies,* rev. ed., 1961; esp. pp. 161-94; the best survey of OT transmission in the light of the Qumran finds. B. J. Roberts, "Text, OT," M. M. Parvis, "Text, NT," B. M. Metzger, "Versions, Ancient," in *IDB,* 1962; all excellent surveys. B. M. Metzger, *The Text of the NT,* 1964; now the definitive treatment, full of engaging facts. B. J. Roberts, "The Transmission of the Text, OT," Nigel Turner, "The Transmission of the Text, NT," in *A Companion to the Bible,* ed. by H. H. Rowley, 2nd ed., 1964.

THE BIBLE IN ENGLISH

Clyde L. Manschreck

The greatest single factor in the shaping of English thought and culture in the past 4 cents. has been a translation from foreign literature. The English Bible is the book of books in our heritage. As the historian G. M. Trevelyan has remarked, no other literary or religious movement has so profoundly affected the character, imagination, and intelligence of the English-speaking people.

I. Early English Translations

The Bible in Old English. Before the time of John Wycliffe in the 14th cent. the only translations of the Bible into the vernacular of England consisted of metrical paraphrases and manuscript glosses from the Latin Vulgate, which was the Christian Bible of W Europe throughout the Middle Ages. According to the Venerable Bede (d. 735) Caedmon, a laborer in the monastery at Whitby, with the aid of the monks there paraphrased and sang metrical versions of stories from the OT. Eadfrith (d. 721), bishop of Lindisfarne, and Aldhelm, the first bishop of Sherborne, are supposed to have translated some parts of the Bible; but these traditions are not substantiated by extant copies.

Two of the oldest known Bibles in Old English are manuscript glosses, more or less word-for-word translations like a schoolboy's crib in a textbook, used largely in the monasteries for instruction of those who did not understand Latin. The British Museum's Vespasian Psalter (9th cent.) has the Pss. in Latin with a literal translation just above each word. The Paris Psalter from the time of King Alfred (871-901) has a gloss in parallel columns of 50 pss. in Anglo-Saxon prose and the others in Anglo-Saxon verse. Alfred may have been the author of this early monument in Old English. He is known to have incorporated the 10 Commandments and extracts from Exod. 21–23 into his code of laws.

In the 10th cent. 3 notable glosses appeared. One was the Lindisfarne Gospels. The Latin manuscript was written by Bishop Eadfrith *ca.* 700, and *ca.* 950 a monk named Ealdred made an interlinear literal translation in the Northumbrian dialect. A 2nd was the Rushworth Gospels written originally in Latin by an Irish scribe. Three of the Rushworth Gospels were virtually the same as the Lindisfarne gloss, but the Matt. gloss was an independent work in the Mercian dialect by a priest named Faerman. A 3rd, toward the end of the century, was the W Saxon Gospels with parts of the first 7 books of the OT

as well as some homilies on Kings, Esth., Job, Dan., and Macc.; these were translated by Abbot Aelfric.

The Middle English Period. The early forms of the Bible in Old English were virtually eclipsed in 1066 when the Norman Conquest of William I brought the tongue of Bede and Alfred into disrepute. French became the language of the gentry and nobility, and Latin the language of the clergy. Old English was disparaged as peasants' jargon. Even so Old English was interlined in some Bible manuscripts during the 11th and 12th cents. But gradually the language evolved into what is called Middle English, a developed form of the dialect of the E Midlands which was spoken in London, Oxford, and Cambridge. This was the English of Chaucer's *Canterbury Tales* and Wycliffe's Bible, enriched by the addition of many French words and made more flexible by the loss of many clumsy constructions. By the 14th cent. Middle English predominated as the grass-roots language in England and was rapidly challenging Latin and French. Popularized and dignified by Chaucer and Wycliffe, it emerged in Tudor times as the standard King's English, the immediate ancestor of Modern English.

During the Middle English period (1100-1500) glosses, paraphrases, and translations of the Bible were few. A poetical version of the gospels and Acts was done by the Augustinian monk Orm about 1200; rhyming versions of stories in Gen. and Exod. and metrical pss. appeared in 1250; and 2 Psalters were written in the middle of the 14th cent.—one in the W Midlands dialect with the Latin text and English alternating, the other embedded in a commentary done by Richard Rolle, a hermit of Hampole.

Two events combined with a hatred of the Norman conquerors to nourish a renaissance of the English of the common man: the Hundred Years' War, which began in 1338, made French unpatriotic; and in 1348-49 the Black Death spread its devastation throughout the land, bringing laborers a new status because of the increased demand for workers. In 1362 Parliament was officially opened in English, and John of Trevisa reported in 1385 that French was declining.

The Version of John Wycliffe. An Oxford theologian, John Wycliffe (1330?-1384) chose Middle English for the first complete Bible in English. Wycliffe appealed to the authority of scripture to combat the corrupted papal control of his time. His protest came during the Babylonian Captivity (1309-1378), when the papacy was held "captive" by the

1237

French in Avignon, and the Great Schism (1378-1417), when popes sat in both Rome and Avignon, each claiming to be the apostolic successor of Peter. Wycliffe demanded a priestly stewardship worthy of stewards of the sovereign Lord of all. All things, all offices, all powers are bestowed by God, he said; if men do not use them as good stewards should, then the unfit stewards should be removed. Since such stewards should know God's will, Wycliffe undertook to translate the Latin Vulgate into the language of the people. The NT was finished *ca.* 1380, the OT in 1382. Wycliffe may actually have done only a few portions, but the entire work was his inspiration. The OT and Apoc. were translated by Nicholas of Hereford, an ardent follower of Wycliffe. After Wycliffe's death John Purvey, another disciple, carried on, achieving for the first time a truly idiomatic English translation. His literary revision appeared in manuscript between 1388 and 1395.

The impact of the Wycliffe Bible was immediately felt as copies were circulated by Wycliffe's followers, known as Lollards. Vernacular translations were prohibited, however, and both John Purvey and Nicholas of Hereford eventually suffered imprisonment and had to abjure their Wycliffite principles. In 1382 Archbishop Courtenay, with the sanction of the king, took stern measures against the followers of Wycliffe, forcing Lollardy to become an underground movement. The statute *De heretico comburendo* (1401) caused many Lollards to be burned as heretics, but eventually anticlerical sentiment against the suppressors became so widespread that a saying went abroad, "If Abel had been a priest, Cain would have been acquitted by a jury of London citizens."

II. The Reformation Century

In 1453 Constantinople fell to the Turks, causing a dispersal throughout Europe of Greek scholars who stimulated renewed interest in Hellenism and Christian beginnings. John Colet, Desiderius Erasmus, and Sir Thomas More were the mentors of the "new learning" in English universities. They boldly attacked clerical obscurantism and stultifying church practices, and in 1516 Erasmus published his Greek NT so that scholars might check the sources. But, even more important, about 1455 Johann Gutenberg of Mainz invented the printing press. Thousands of copies of books were now possible in the time formerly taken to produce only a few manuscript copies. Yet so successful was the control of the church in England that no English translation of the Bible was printed until 1526, no complete Bible before 1535, and no printing was made in England before 1537. France, Germany, Italy, Spain, and Bohemia all had vernacular editions before the time of Henry VIII.

Tyndale's Translation. William Tyndale (*ca.* 1492-1536) first printed the NT in English "because I had perceaved by experyence how that it was impossible to stablysh the laye people in any truth, excepte the scripture were playnly layde before their eyes in their mother tonge." This resolve was made in 1522, the year of Luther's German NT. Failing to find a position in the patronized circle of Cuthbert Tunstall, bishop of London, Tyndale journeyed to Hamburg, probably visited Luther in Wittenberg, and then went to Cologne to publish the NT which he had

William Tyndale's translation of the NT

translated into admirable English. When the printing was only partially finished Tyndale and his helpers had to flee to Worms, where another printing in a smaller octavo size was completed in 1526. Both the Cologne sheets and the Worms edition circulated in England, but the church authorities pressed their ban with spectacular burnings at St. Paul's Cross, London, and other places, so that only a few copies have survived.

Tyndale's NT would not stay suppressed. Three surreptitious editions appeared in the next 2 years; and in 1534 George Joye, a former friend, issued an altered edition that so displeased Tyndale that in 1534 and 1535 he himself published revised editions. In addition he worked steadily on controversial treatises and the OT Pentateuch, which he had ready in Jan. 1530. Copies of it were seized and burned just 4 months later. How much further he got with the OT is questionable.

Tyndale's tragic martyrdom began when he was enticed to leave the free city of Antwerp. He was immediately seized by Roman Catholic authorities, imprisoned for 16 months at Vilvorde, and finally strangled and burned at the stake there on Oct. 6, 1536. His last words were, "Lord, open the king of England's eyes!" Ironically, King Henry VIII of England was interceding for Tyndale, for reasons of political expediency, but his plea was hardly heeded by the Emperor Charles V, whose aunt Henry had divorced. Fully a 3rd of the great KJV of 1611 is based directly on Tyndale's magnificent achievement.

The Coverdale Bible. Miles Coverdale (1488-1569), an Augustinian friar who left his order in 1528 and fled to the Continent for safety, figured prominently in the next 3 English Bibles. His early work paralleled that of Tyndale, and like Tyndale he did much of his translating outside England; but how much contact he had with Tyndale is not certain. In Oct. 1535 his Bible was printed, the first complete printed Bible in English. It was dedicated to Henry VIII as the defender of the true faith of Christ.

Coverdale used Tyndale's translation of the Pentateuch and NT but changed elements which had aroused particular objections. For the rest, knowing little or no Hebrew and Greek, he translated from Latin and German versions. He included ch. summaries and marginal notes but avoided controversial comments. He introduced Luther's separation of the Apoc. from other OT books—a practice still followed by most Protestant translations if the Apoc. is included.

In contrast to the Tyndale translation Coverdale's Bible was imported and circulated without official hindrance. This reception was a historical fortuity. In 1534 the Convocation of Canterbury had requested that the king authorize a Bible in the English tongue, and so Henry had commissioned Archbishop Thomas Cranmer and his bishops to prepare a satisfactory translation. As a result of disagreements among the bishops, however, Cranmer had made little progress when Coverdale's Bible appeared. Because there was demand for an English Bible, therefore, and Coverdale's appeared likely to arouse no fresh controversies, and perhaps because the new queen, Anne Boleyn, was pleased with the beautifully bound copy presented to her, Henry raised no objection to its circulation. Two additional printings were made in 1537, of which the 2nd claimed to be "sett forth with the Kinges moost gracious license," though no other record of this license is known.

The Matthew Bible. Meanwhile another translation appeared from the Continent in 1537, under the name of Thomas Matthew. This seems to have been the pen name of John Rogers, an associate of Tyndale. At any rate this Bible reproduced not only the published Tyndale translations with few revisions but apparently also the manuscript of Tyndale's unfinished OT, perhaps as far as Chr. For the remainder of the OT it largely copied Coverdale. The volume contained copious Protestant notes of controversial character, many of which were Tyndale's.

Whether Cranmer failed to recognize the Tyndale elements or chose to ignore them is uncertain, but he gave the new version his endorsement. He sent a copy with a letter to King Henry's vicegerent, Thomas Cromwell, recommending the translation as the best yet made and asking that it be licensed for general use until he and the bishops could provide the translation assigned to them. The license was quickly granted. Thus it came about that within a year Tyndale's dying prayer was answered by the king's consent to circulation of not one but 2 English Bibles incorporating his translations.

The Great Bible. Cromwell shared Cranmer's desire that an English Bible be made accessible to every parishioner in every parish church. Yet neither available version suited this purpose. The Matthew Bible was clearly the better translation, but its controversial features were already offending many. Rather than wait longer on the bishops, Cromwell arranged for Coverdale to make a revision of the Matthew Bible.

Because no press in England was large enough for the desired page size Coverdale journeyed to Paris to do the printing. There he encountered the inquisitor general, who arrested the printer and impounded all paper and type. Coverdale and an assistant escaped to England, and soon the press was shipped there. Meanwhile the officer charged with destroying the impounded materials sold some of the printed sheets as scrap paper to a haberdasher, who proceeded to pass them on to friends of Coverdale for transport to London. There Coverdale resumed printing and was able to complete the work in 1539.

A few months earlier Cromwell had issued in the king's name an injunction to the clergy calling for "one boke of the hole bible of the largest volume in englyshe" to be placed in every parish church so that the people might "most commodiouslye resorte to the same and reade yt." The Great Bible, as it came to be called because of its size, was approved as the volume to be used for this purpose and thus became the first "authorized version." At the 2nd printing a note was added on its title page: "This is the Byble apoynted to the use of the churches." It was received by the people with enthusiasm and quickly went through 7 editions.

The woodcut on the title page of the Great Bible pictured King Henry VIII giving the Bible to his subordinates to transmit to the people, but it proved true only in part. In 1539 Henry reversed his Protestant overtures and proclaimed his 6 Articles, the "whip with six strings" which scourged the evangelicals. In the following year he turned against Cromwell and let him be executed for treason. Henry's act of 1543 forbade the public reading and explaining of the Bible by an unlicensed person and even forbade private reading among the lower classes. Yet when Henry died in 1547 the Great Bible was still required in every parish church in England, and the promise Cromwell had issued in his name of the "free and lyberall use of the bible in oure oune maternal english tonge" had been fulfilled.

The Geneva Bible. During the brief reign of Edward VI (1547-53) Cranmer vigorously promoted the Reformation in England, only to have his efforts reversed and to suffer martyrdom during the Roman Catholic restoration under Queen Mary (1553-58). An average of 56 Protestants died for each year of Mary's reign, and thousands of others sought safety on the Continent. The refugees who fled to Geneva included John Knox, William Whittingham, and Miles Coverdale. In exile they prepared the translation that became the household Bible of the English people, the Geneva Bible of 1560, "translated according to the Ebrue and Greke, and conferred with the best translations in divers languages." It carried a flattering dedicatory epistle to Queen Elizabeth, the rebuilder of "the ruins of God's house."

This Geneva Bible was essentially a revision of the Great Bible and Whittingham's NT of 1557. It was marked by a combination of Calvinistic Puritanical fervor and excellent scholarship. Though it carried the Apoc. as an appendix to the OT, the translators carefully pointed out that some heroes in the Apoc., as well as some in the canonical books, were not to be imitated. Its abundant, decidedly Calvinistic notes helped make Puritanism the strong religion that it became. It was the first English Bible to divide the text into vss. It became so popular that

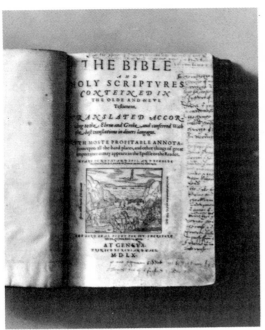

Courtesy of the American Bible Society

The Geneva Bible of 1560

printed so that the reader might skip them if he so chose. The Bishops' Bible was ready in 1568, and in 1571 the Convocation of Canterbury ordered every bishop to possess a copy and every cathedral and church to make it available. For use in the churches it prevailed for more than 40 years, but it did not displace the Geneva Bible in the homes.

The Rheims-Douai Bible. Meanwhile English Roman Catholics sought to counteract the influence of the Geneva and Bishops' Bibles with a version of their own, based on Jerome's Latin Vulgate, the official text as decreed by the Council of Trent (1545-63). In 1568 William Allen, who despised Elizabeth's *via media*, established an English college at Douai in Flanders to train priests. There a biblical translation was undertaken by Gregory Martin, who was joined by Richard Bristow when the college moved to Rheims in 1578. The NT was published in 1582 at Rheims and the OT in 1609-10, after the college had returned to Douai. This translation, commonly called the Rheims-Douai (or Douay) Bible, is in no wise the equal of the KJV, primarily because the Vulgate had to be the controlling source. Bishop Richard Challoner of London assisted in a revision of the NT in 1738 and made extensive revisions of the

Courtesy of the American Bible Society

The Rheims-Douai Bible

it went through more than 100 editions, often with the Prayer Book and metrical Pss. appended, though it was never adopted by the Church of England. The Scottish edition of the Geneva Bible in 1579 was the first Bible ever printed in Scotland. Long after the KJV was published the Geneva Bible was still popular. *The Souldiers Pocket Bible* of 1643, used by Oliver Cromwell's army, was extracted from it.

The Bishops' Bible. With the accession of Elizabeth I in 1558 England returned to royal supremacy over the church and the uniformity of the *via media*. Elizabeth would not tolerate deviation toward either evangelical Protestantism or Roman Catholicism. When the feudal chiefs of N England marched under the banner of the 5 wounds of Christ, tearing up the Bible and Prayer Book in Durham Cathedral and hoping to reinstate the Mass, Elizabeth did not hesitate to kill off 800 of the feudal tenantry. The Ridolfi Plot (1572), the Babington Conspiracy (1586), the intrigues of the Jesuits, and the launching of the Spanish Armada (1588) turned her solidly against the Roman Catholic recusants. On the other hand she did not hesitate to execute many of the Puritan nonconformists for not complying with the laws establishing the *via media*.

Because the Geneva Bible was too Calvinistic to suit Elizabeth, even though her privy council continued to license its publication, in 1563 Elizabeth authorized Matthew Parker, archbishop of Canterbury, to organize a revision of the Great Bible of 1539 by "able bishops and other learned men." An editorial committee of high churchmen, mostly bishops, parceled out portions of the Bible to various scholars with the general rule that the common English of the Great Bible should be retained if not in conflict with the Hebrew and Greek texts. Caustic notes were eliminated, obscenities glossed over, controversial passages left unmarked, and genealogies

whole Bible in his 1749-52 editions, introducing many phrases and words from the KJV. This Rheims-Douai-Challoner Bible was authorized for use in America in 1810.

The King James Version. In 1611 all the previous translations were superseded by the justly famous KJV, known in England as the Authorized Version. The newly crowned King James I, who had been reigning as James VI of Scotland, objected to the sharply Calvinistic notes in the Geneva Bible. Accordingly in a conference of high and low church parties at Hampton Court in 1604 he agreed that a uniform translation minus notes should be made by the best men from the universities. Strict rules for translating were adopted and 6 panels of translators (47 men in all) divided the work—3 panels for the OT, 2 for the NT, and 1 for the Apoc. Every portion was carefully scrutinized, and the entire draft was reviewed by a committee selected from the panels. Some passages were revised 17 times before being passed. The translators, who paid special praise to King James for his active role, were so successful that for more than 2½ centuries no other authorized version was made. It is aptly called "the noblest monument of English prose," and its revisers in 1881 paid tribute to "its simplicity, its dignity, its power, its happy turns of expression, . . . the music of its cadences, and the felicities of its rhythm." The KJV of the Bible has had an incalculable influence on the culture of the English-speaking peoples.

Inclusion of the OT Apoc. in the KJV caused heated protests from the Puritans. The Apoc. had been officially adopted by the Roman Catholics at the Council of Trent, but the Protestants, along with the orthodox Jews, regarded these books as inferior. The Calvinistic Synod of Dort (1618-19) specifically rejected them, and as early as 1629 a KJV was printed without the Apoc. The Puritan-dominated Long Parliament in 1644 declared that only canonical books of the Bible could be read in the churches, and in 1646 the Westminster Assembly branded the Apoc. an uninspired collection. After a vigorous controversy originating in Scotland the British and Foreign Bible Society in 1827 ceased printing Bibles with the Apoc. The Church of England, however, has continued to accept these books "for example of life and instruction of manners" but not "to establish any doctrine." When Edward VII was crowned in 1901 the Church of England refused to use the "mutilated" coronation Bible presented by the British and Foreign Bible Society.

III. Recent Versions

Since its acceptance in the 17th cent. the KJV has been the English Bible to most people—and perhaps still is today. Nevertheless throughout this period many have undertaken to revise it, or to produce new translations, principally in order to modernize the language and to correct its inaccuracies. E.g. John Wesley in 1755 wanted to simplify some portions of the NT and conform others to their Greek sources; Edward Harwood in 1768 sought to introduce contemporary idioms; and Samuel Sharpe in 1865 desired to bring it into conformity with Griesbach's critical Greek text.

The Revised Versions: English and American. The advance of biblical scholarship and the discovery of many more ancient texts prompted the Convocation of Canterbury in 1870 to call for a revision of the KJV. Eminent scholars from other countries and communions were to be invited to participate. Among these were John Henry Cardinal Newman, the leading English-speaking Roman Catholic, who did not accept, and G. Vance Smith, a prominent Unitarian scholar, who did. They were not to change the KJV without "decidedly preponderating" evidence and were to make a marginal indication of any alteration. The archaic language was not to be modernized. The Revised Version NT appeared in May 1881 and the OT in May 1885. American scholars aided the venture but reserved the right to publish after an agreed interval a revision incorporating their own preferences; this was issued as the American Standard Version in 1901. The English completed a revision of the Apoc. in 1895; the American revisers did not include the Apoc.

The publication of the NT of the Revised Version caused much excitement in England and America. Though its textual accuracy was superior, the marginal notes on some of the changes and omissions created an uproar, for the revisers questioned the genuineness of some passages on which doctrinal arguments had been based. It did not displace the centuries-old KJV in general use.

Translations in Modern Speech. If because of the rationalistic and scientific trends of the 20th cent. the Bible has tended to lose some of its cultural force, this is not due to any lack of new translations, most of which have tried either to express its original meaning in the speech of modern man or to reach a special group of readers. *The Twentieth Century NT* (1899-1901), based on the Greek text of B. F. Westcott and F. J. A. Hort, led the way. More than 30 ministers, laymen, and others, but no outstanding linguistic experts, participated and kept their identity a secret until the last survivor died in 1933. They were remarkably successful in catching the spirit of the original sources. This was followed by Richard Francis Weymouth's *NT in Modern Speech* in 1903, his purpose being simply to render the Greek into good modern English. Subheadings made the basic passages easier to grasp.

Ferrar Fenton, a businessman who believed he was "the only man who has ever applied real mental and literary criticism to the Sacred Scriptures" and that he had rediscovered "the Hebrew laws of Syllabic verse," also published *The Holy Bible in Modern English* in 1903, the NT having appeared previously in 1895. He transliterated names the way they sound in Hebrew, e.g. "Aisebal" for Jezebel; and he placed John and I John at the beginning of the NT because he thought they were earlier than the other books and belonged together. Despite its limitations Fenton's Bible has commanded a wide circulation; as late as World War II it was still being reprinted.

In 1913 James Moffatt's NT appeared, followed in 1924 by the OT. Both were combined in one volume, *The Holy Bible: A New Translation,* in 1926. The flowing, flowery freedom which he introduced in his translation was an attempt to reproduce something of the effect felt by those who read and heard the original. Varying styles of type were used to indicate passages derived from different documentary sources. Many grateful readers have indicated that he succeeded; others have felt that he took too many liberties and detracted from the dignity of the Scriptures, as when he made the Song of Songs so secular.

Edgar J. Goodspeed brought out *The NT: An American Translation* in 1923, and J. M. P. Smith and others followed with the OT in 1927. Goodspeed provided the Apoc. in 1938, and *The Complete Bible: An American Translation* appeared in 1939. This joint translation not only displayed scholarship that won it wide use in colleges but achieved a clarity and freshness of expression that endeared it to millions of general readers for whom it was intended.

The astounding task of translating the Bible into Basic English, using only about 1,000 words, was attempted by S. H. Hooke, who produced the NT in 1941 and the whole Bible in 1949. Though limited in vocabulary, especially in verbs and adjectives, this translation proved unusually good and useful to people with little knowledge of English. Something of the same goal was in the mind of Charles Kingsley Williams when in 1952 he published a translation of *The NT in Plain English.* Having taught in Ghana and Madras, he used about 1,700 words to convey the insights of the Bible to people whose native tongue was not English but who had to have it to communicate and compete in modern culture.

In America in 1937 Charles B. Williams published *The NT in the Language of the People*, still another attempt to communicate plainly the exact meaning of the original languages. So also was *The Amplified NT* (1958) by a committee of 12 in California who added materials in parentheses and brackets to make the meaning clearer. Arthur S. Way in his *Letters of St. Paul* (1901) filled in "gaps" which supposedly resulted from Paul's dictating to a secretary. *St. Paul from the Trenches*, done by Gerald Warre Cornish during World War I, also expanded Paul's words in order to bring out the inner sense. It was not published until 1937 and proved to be very popular, but hardly as successful as was J. B. Phillips' *Letters to Young Churches* (1947), designed to make Paul's writings appealing to people who had come to regard the Bible as dull and irrelevant. Other portions by Phillips followed, with the complete *NT in Modern English* appearing in 1958, and parts of the OT thereafter. The immense popularity of these translations is an index of their achieved goal, although they are frequently regarded as paraphrases rather than translations.

Even the Roman Catholics were caught up in the translating trends, and 2 unofficial translations appeared: in 1941 the NT sponsored by the Episcopal Committee of the Confraternity of Christian Doctrine and, published serially between 1913 and 1935, the *Westminster Version of the Sacred Scriptures* under the editorship of Cuthbert Lattey, S.J. But the only official translation was that of Msgr. Ronald A. Knox, the NT in 1945 and the OT in 1950. Though it has built-in limitations because the Vulgate is not the best text, still it achieved a freedom and exactness of meaning that many have come to admire.

The Revised Standard Version. The translation that brought a storm of criticism and yet is likely to be the most enduring of all the translations in the 20th cent. is the RSV. The International Council of Religious Education, representing most of the major Protestant denominations of the U.S.A. and Canada, authorized revision of the ASV of 1901, stressing that the revision was to make use of the best of modern scholarship and to preserve "those qualities which have given to the King James Version a supreme place in English literature." In 1937 a committee of 32 scholars along with a board of 50 representatives from various denominations undertook the task. In 1946 the RSV of the NT was published and in 1952 the whole Bible. A smaller committee worked on the Apoc., which was published in 1957.

The RSV takes into consideration vast amounts of newly discovered biblical material, advances in biblical languages, and historical criticism. Grammar and vocabulary have been modernized, although

prayers retain "thee" and "thou" and the corresponding verbs. Quotation marks indicate direct speech, and poetry is printed in poetical form. Some passages are printed in italicized footnotes to show that they were not in the best early texts. Certain changes—e.g. the substituting of "young woman" for "virgin" in Isa. 7:14 and the dropping of "through his blood" in Col. 1:14—engendered objections in conservative quarters. Copies of the RSV were publicly burned, and pamphlets denounced it as the product of Antichrist, blasphemy, atheism, and communism. Nevertheless the RSV has commended itself to millions of readers around the world.

The New English Bible. In England 2 Bible societies, the Church of Scotland, the free churches, and the Church of England undertook an entirely new translation resulting in the publication of the NT section of NEB in 1961. The work was begun in 1947, 3 panels of prominent biblical scholars being chosen to work respectively on the OT, Apoc., and NT., and a 4th composed of some of the country's foremost poets and authors to give literary advice. Vividness of expression and flashes of meaning, in addition to textual accuracy and modern speech, are characteristic of this newest version.

Conclusion. This long history of the Bible in English is not without occasional humor. The Geneva Version acquired the nickname "Breeches Bible" because it said Adam and Eve sewed themselves "breeches" from fig leaves (Gen. 3:7). Very early printings of the KJV are distinguished as "He" and "She" Bibles by the pronoun in Ruth 3:15c, which soon settled down to "and she went into the city." An edition in 1631 was called the "Wicked Bible" for omitting "not" in the 7th commandment. The "Vinegar Bible" of 1717 was so called because of a misprinting in the heading over the parable of the vineyard (Luke 20), and the "Murderers' Bible" of 1795 rendered "Let the children first be killed" instead of "filled" in Mark 7:27 and "murderers" for "murmurers" in Jude 16.

The story is not ended, not just because no translation has achieved the finality of perfection, but because man's world, knowledge, and language are constantly changing while the human needs to which the Bible speaks remain. For the Bible is not just any book; it peculiarly embodies God's word for man.

For Further Study. J. Baikie, *The English Bible and Its Story,* 1928. H. Guppy, *Miles Coverdale and the English Bible, 1488-1568,* 1935. C. C. Butterworth, *The Literary Lineage of the KJ Bible,* 1941. Hugh Pope, *English Versions of the Bible,* 1952. I. M Price, *The Ancestry of Our English Bible,* 3rd rev. ed., 1956. T. L. Leishman, *Our Ageless Bible,* 1960. F. F. Bruce, *The English Bible,* 1961. J. H. Reumann, *Four Centuries of the English Bible,* 1961. S. L. Greenslade, ed., *The Cambridge History of the Bible,* 1963.

THE BIBLE IN EVERY TONGUE

ROBERT G. BRATCHER

Nowhere is the missionary spirit of the Christian religion more evident than in the endeavor from the very beginning to make the Scriptures, both OT and NT, available to all peoples everywhere in their own native language.

I. ANCIENT VERSIONS

Greek. The first known written translation of the Scriptures was the Greek version of the Hebrew OT which came to be known as the Septuagint (LXX), from the tradition that it was produced by 70, or 72, translators. The Pentateuch, at least, was translated into Greek in Alexandria during the reign of Ptolemy Philadelphus (285-246 B.C.).

Aramaic. Before this, however, the Palestinian Jews had already provided an oral paraphrase in the Aramaic vernacular of the Hebrew Scriptures read in synagogue worship for the benefit of those who were more and more becoming unfamiliar with biblical Hebrew. These paraphrases, known as targums, were later reduced to writing. The extant

Palestinian Pentateuch Targum

copies, the oldest of which is the Palestinian Pentateuch Targum, date from originals made as early as the 2nd cent. A.D. The Samaritan Pentateuch was not strictly a version, since it was only the Hebrew Pentateuch written in Samaritan characters. Early in the Christian era, however, it was translated into the Aramaic dialect used by the Samaritans.

Syriac. It is probable that the earliest translation of the NT was into Syriac, the Aramaic dialect of NW Mesopotamia. The Old Syriac version of the gospels was produced sometime in the latter half of the 2nd cent., perhaps in Edessa (see color map 16). Tatian, a disciple of Justin Martyr, prepared in Syriac a combined version of the gospels, the Diatessaron, *ca.* A.D. 170.

Latin. It was in this general period also that the Scriptures were first translated into Latin. There may have been a development parallel to the Aramaic Targums, with an oral translation in public worship for the benefit of converts and interested listeners who could not understand Greek. The specific date, locale, and identity of the translators are unknown; but it is probable that Latin translations of parts of the NT first appeared during the latter half of the 2nd cent. in N Africa—though Antioch of Syria and Rome are other possibilities. These Old Latin translations, esp. of the NT, were long copied and used; there are manuscripts of the complete NT made as late as the 13th cent. In the 4th cent., however, Jerome was commissioned by the pope to revise the Latin Bible; and his translation, of which the OT was made from the Hebrew, came to be accepted as the standard Latin text and called the Vulgate, i.e. "common," version.

Other Ancient Versions. In the 3rd cent. versions began to appear in different dialects of Coptic in Egypt: Sahidic, Bohairic, Achmimic, sub-Achmimic, Middle Egyptian, and Fayyumic. The Gothic version (4th cent.) is the earliest whose translator is known. Ulfilas (*ca.* 311-381), consecrated at the age of 30 as bishop of the "Christians in Gothia," devised a Gothic alphabet and translated most of the Bible. The extant remains of his version—most of the NT and a few fragments of the OT—constitute the oldest surviving literature in any Teutonic language. The Armenian version (5th cent.) was the work of Mesrop, who devised the alphabet, and Sahak. According to tradition Mesrop also devised the Georgian alphabet, but the translator of the Georgian version (5th cent.) is not known. The brothers Cyril and Methodius of Thessalonica (Salonika) missionaries in the Balkan peninsula in the latter half of the 9th cent., translated portions of the Bible into what is now known as Old Church Slavonic, using an alphabet devised by Cyril.

Medieval Versions. Before the invention of printing (mid-15th cent.) the Bible had been translated in whole or in part into 33 languages, of which 22 were European, 7 Asiatic, and 4 African. Besides those already mentioned the list includes: Ethiopic (4th or 5th cent.); Anglo-Saxon (7th cent.); Arabic (8th cent.); Bohemian (9th cent.); German and Low German (11th cent.); Dutch, Provencal, Romance, French, Icelandic, Italian, and Spanish (12th-13th cents.); Catalan, English, Norwegian, Persian, Polish, and Vaudois (14th cent.); Hungarian and Swedish (15th cent.).

II. THE AGE OF PRINTING

The first printed Bible was an edition of the Vulg. produced by Johann Gutenberg *ca.* 1450-56 at Mainz, Germany.

Courtesy of the American Bible Society

Page of the Gutenberg Bible showing parts of Acts, chapters 23 and 24

Early Printed Scriptures. From the invention of printing until the beginning of the 19th cent. the number of languages into which the Bible was translated grew from 33 to 71, of which 50 were in Europe, 13 in Asia, 4 in Africa, 3 in the Americas (Massachusetts, Mohawk, Arawak), and 1 in Oceania.

The 2nd printed Bible, and the first in a modern language, was the German Bible published in 1466 in Strassburg by Johann Mentelin. There were 14 printed Bibles in High German and 4 in Low German before Martin Luther's translation of 1534, which was the first complete Bible in a modern language translated from the original languages. The Italian Bible of 1471 (Venice) was the 3rd printed Bible; it was a translation from the Vulg. by Nicolo di Malherbi (Malermi). The Catalan Bible of 1478, by the brothers Bonifacio and Vicente Ferrer, of which only one page has survived, was the 4th complete printed Bible. The Czech Bible of 1488 (Prague) was the 5th printed Bible.

By the end of the 16th cent. entire Bibles had been printed also in Dutch (1526), French (1530), Swedish (1541), Danish (1550), Polish (1561), Spanish (1569), Slavonic (1581), Icelandic (1584), Slovenian (1584), Welsh (1588), and Hungarian (1590). Many of these were the work of scholars and churchmen commissioned by reigning monarchs. E.g. in Denmark the king's secretary, Hans Mikkelsen, with the aid of Kristian Winter, translated the NT in 1524 by order of King Christian II; and the whole Bible was commissioned by King Christian III. In Sweden the archbishop of Uppsala, Laurentius Petri, and his brother Olaus, who had issued the first NT in 1526, produced the whole Bible in 1541.

The first printed translation of the NT into Spanish was done by Francisco de Enzinas (known in England as Dryander, the Grecized equivalent of Enzinas) while he was living in the home of his teacher Melanchthon, in Wittenberg, Germany, and was printed in Antwerp in 1543. The OT, printed in 1553, was a revision of an old Jewish version made from the Hebrew which had existed previously in manuscript form; it was published in Ferrara, Italy. The first complete Bible in Spanish was the work of the reformer Cassiodoro de Reina, published in Basel in 1569. The first NT in Portuguese, published in Amsterdam in 1681, was the work of Lisbon-born João Ferreira de Almeida, a minister of the Dutch Reformed Church in the East Indies. The whole Bible was published in Batavia (Jakarta) in 1753, a revision and completion of Almeida's work by Lutheran missionaries of the Danish mission in Tranquebar, India.

The first Bible in a language of the W Hemisphere was the Mass. Bible of 1663 (NT in 1661), translated by John Eliot, the Cambridge-trained pastor of the small Puritan parish of Roxbury and missionary to the Indians, who arrived in the Mass. Bay Colony just 11 years after the first Pilgrims. This Bible, which was the 22nd complete Bible, is known as the earliest example of the translation and printing of the entire Bible into a new language as a means of evangelization.

The first translation into a language of Oceania was the work, not of a biblical scholar or minister, but of a Dutch trader of the Dutch East India Co., Albert Cornelisson Ruyl, who in 1629 translated Matt. and later Mark into Malay. Ruyl's work is the earliest example of the translation and printing of a book of the Bible in a non-European language as a means of evangelization. Another merchant, Jan van Hasel, translated the other 2 gospels in 1646. The whole NT, by Daniel Brouwerius, was printed in 1668 in Amsterdam, the first NT in a language of Oceania.

The first language of India to have the NT was Tamil. Bartholomäus Ziegenbalg of the Danish Lutheran Mission completed the NT in 1715; and the whole Bible, revised and completed by Benjamin Schultze, appeared in 1727, being the 4th complete Bible printed in an Asian language. During this period Dutch traders began translation into Formosan Chinese; Matt. and John were translated by Daniel Gravius and published in 1661 in Amsterdam. Dutch traders were also responsible for the first translation into Sinhalese (Ceylon), Willem Konijn translating the 4 gospels in 1739.

The 19th Cent. This period, known as the "missionary cent.," saw a remarkable increase in the number of languages into which the Bible was translated. In the first 30 years alone 86 languages were added to the list, of which were non-European: 43 in Asia, 10 in the W Hemisphere, 7 in Africa, and 6 in Oceania. This was the time of Robert Morrison in China (Bible in 1823), Adoniram Judson in Burma (NT in 1832, Bible in 1835), Samuel Brown in Japan (NT in 1879), John Ross in Korea (NT in 1887), and Henry Martyn, who in 6 short years (1806-12) completed the translation of the NT into Urdu, Persian, and Arabic. Supreme among missionary translators is William Carey of India, who with his companions in the Serampore mission, William Ward and Joshua Marshman, was responsible for publications in 44 languages.

This was also the time of the founding of the British and Foreign Bible Society (1804), the Netherlands Bible Society (1815), the American Bible Society (1816), and the National Bible Society of Scotland (1861)—all of which greatly contributed to the increase in both the translation and the distribution of the Scriptures.

It is estimated that during the 19th cent. a total of 500 languages and dialects received the Scriptures for the first time, making a grand total of 571 at the close of the cent.

III. THE MODERN ERA

In Every Tongue. By the end of 1969 the number of languages into which at least one book of the Bible was translated had grown to more than twice what it was at the beginning of the cent., reaching a total of 1413. This number includes the entire Bible in 244, the NT in an additional 324, and at least one book in another 845 languages. It is estimated that over 90% of the world's population has the entire Bible, while over 97% has at least one book of it. Mark is the most widely translated book in the world; it is found in at least 800 languages and dialects.

Yet there remain well over 1,000 mutually unintelligible languages and dialects which have nothing of the Scriptures. E.g. in Africa it is calculated that there are 700 spoken languages; yet the whole Bible is available in only 82, and there are 11 countries which do not have an entire Bible in any of the vernacular languages.

To supply this need and to carry on the endless task of revision there are about 3,000 people who give their time in something like 130 countries to the work of Bible translation in over 500 languages. Every year from 16 to 20 new languages and dialects are added to the list. E.g. in 1967 complete Bibles appeared for the first time in Kurundi (Central African country of Burundi) and Nama (South-West Africa).

There are many missions and boards engaged in translation work, such as the New Tribes Mission, the Overseas Missionary Fellowship, the Christian and Missionary Alliance, and the Wycliffe Bible Translators (Summer Institute of Linguistics). The last named, dedicated exclusively to the translation of the Scriptures into languages and dialects which have nothing of the Bible, has a corps of over 1,500 members who work among 330 different tribes in 16 countries.

In addition to new translations there is the work of completing the translation of the NT and of the entire Bible in languages which have only portions of them, and the task of revising existing translations. Revisions are needed because of rapid changes in languages, better and older biblical manuscripts from which to work, the deficiency of earlier translations, and a better understanding of the purpose and nature of translation. It is also recognized that major languages require more than one standard version, and increasingly there is the desire to provide at least 3 versions: (*a*) one of a traditional and conservative orientation for the majority of Bible readers, (*b*) one based on critical texts and provided with helps for more sophisticated readers, e.g. students and ministers, and (*c*) a "simple-language" translation for the newly literate and for those who are reading an acquired language.

Translation Problems. The modern translator faces innumerable problems posed by the differences, sometimes very great, between the language and culture of the intended readers and those of the biblical authors. The problems become even more acute where there is no history and tradition of the Christian religion in the tribe or society for which the Scriptures are being translated.

On the cultural side the translator encounters some relatively simple problems. E.g. to translate "your sins . . . shall be as white as snow" (Isa. 1:18) where snow is unknown he must find the equivalent standard of whiteness, or purity, in that culture and thus may have to translate "as white as an egret's feather." In the S Toradja language of Indonesia wolves in sheep's clothing (Matt. 7:15) become "crocodiles in human form," while "grapes gathered from thorns, or figs from thistles" (Matt. 7:16) becomes "bananas from thorn trees, guavas from cane." In a landlocked tribe on the edge of the Sahara which knows nothing of large ships and anchors, what is a translator to do with "hope . . . as a sure and steadfast anchor of the soul" (Heb. 6:18-19) or with "shipwreck of their faith" (I Tim. 1:19)? Or in the rain jungles of the Peruvian Amazon, where the unceasing rain is a curse rather than a blessing, how can he urge men to imitate "your Father who . . . sends rain on the just and on the unjust" (Matt. 5:45)?

The translator may choose sometimes deliberately to introduce a "zero" word into his text with an explanation in a footnote, or else he may use a descriptive phrase. In most cases, however, he tries to find a functional equivalent. E.g. the yoke is unknown in the Navaho culture. In translating "Take my yoke upon you . . ." (Matt. 11:29-30) a transliteration of the word "yoke" would be meaningless, while a descriptive phrase would be too long and cumbersome—e.g. "a heavy bar of wood resting on the necks of 2 oxen, with attached curved pieces enclosing their necks." Therefore the functional equivalent was used: "As two horses work, being harnessed side by side, so you, having been harnessed, work with me. . . . For work done with my harness goes well . . ."

Preciseness. Some languages are far more explicit and precise than the biblical languages. E.g. the Zulus of Africa have 120 words to describe different ways of walking; in the Nupé language of Nigeria there are 100 words for "greatness" and 60 for "long"; in Otetela (Congo-Leopoldville) there are 7 words for "there," each with its own specific aspect; and the Agatu in Nigeria have different words for 7 ways of deceiving. The Guaicas of Venezuela attach to almost every principal verb one of 3 suffixes which will specify whether the speaker (*a*) saw what he is relating, (*b*) heard it on good authority, or (*c*) is simply reporting a legendary event. In many languages one cannot refer simply to a brother or sister; one must specify whether he or she is younger or older, and whether he or she is the son or daughter of the same father or mother or both. For Lazarus, Martha, and Mary, for Peter and Andrew, for James and John these specific relationships must be made clear in translation, for they are obligatory, not optional, in those languages.

In some languages one cannot simply say "bear his own cross" (Luke 14:27). How? In the arms? On the shoulder? Across the back? On the head? The Zapotecs of S Mexico have 4 different and mutually exclusive ways of asking a question. In Mark 6:24, where the daughter of Herodias says, "What shall I ask?" the translator must decide whether the girl (*a*) knew and asked as a mere formality, (*b*) did not know and wanted information, (*c*) had once known but had forgotten, or (*d*) had once known but had forgotten some of the details. The Akha language in N Burma is specific as to the exact direction of all movements. In translating "They were sawn in two" (Heb. 11:37) the translator had to answer the question, "Which way, lengthwise or across?"

Exclusive Versus Inclusive. One very common category in many languages is the distinction between the exclusive and inclusive first person plural pronoun—i.e. whether the person addressed is excluded or included. Early missionaries in Melanesian languages in the S Pacific, unaware of this distinction, used the inclusive in the Lord's Prayer, "Forgive us our trespasses," thus including God. In another case the exclusive was used in quoting Rom. 3:23, "All of us have sinned and fall short of the glory of God," thereby excluding the hearers.

In Mark 9:5 the translators must decide whether Peter excluded or included Jesus and the heavenly visitors when he said, "Master, it is well that we are here; let us make three booths." The same decision must be made in Mark 4:38: "Teacher, do you not care if we perish?" When the Jewish elders speak to Jesus of the Roman centurion, they say,

"He loves our nation and he built us our synagogue" (Luke 7:5). It is probable that the first "our" should be inclusive (Jesus was a fellow Jew) but that the 2nd should be exclusive (Jesus was not a citizen of Capernaum).

Passive Verbs. Many languages lack the passive voice of the verb; every verb must be in the active voice and the subject specified. In translating Mark 2:5, "My son, your sins are forgiven," the verb "forgive" must be made active and the subject ("God"? "I"?) named. An apparently simple description such as "the Son of the Blessed" (Mark 14:61) cannot be literally translated. "The Blessed," of course, is a typically Semitic circumlocution for the divine name; but even if the translator uses "the Blessed God" he must deal with the passive participle and define who it is that "blesses" God.

Figures of Speech. These pose special problems of their own. Jesus refers to Herod Antipas as "that fox" (Luke 13:32). The translator may change this metaphor to a simile, use a substitute metaphor, or eliminate the metaphor altogether. The comparison of the devil to a "roaring lion" (I Pet. 5:8) appears in the Mid-Waria language of New Guinea as "like a champing wild boar." In Matt. 10:16 sheep and wolves, serpents and doves, stand for weakness and violence, cunning and innocence; but in many cultures the proper animals for these comparisons may be altogether different. In each instance the natural functional equivalent must be found. In the Chol tribe of Mexico bread is known, not as a staple, but as a delicacy used for dessert only on special occasions. Had the translation of "I am the bread of life" (John 6:35) used the Chol word for "bread," the message would have been completely distorted, for Jesus would have been reported as saying that he is desirable, but not absolutely indispensable, for man's life. The functional equivalent of the biblical "bread" in Chol is *waj*, the thin corn cake eaten daily.

Rhetorical Questions. These may mislead the translator, for in some languages questions are asked only for the purpose of eliciting information. A question such as "Do you not say, 'There are yet four months, then comes the harvest'?" (John 4:35) cannot be translated as a question, but only as a statement of fact. The same applies to the question in John 7:51: "Does our law judge a man without first giving him a hearing and learning what he does?" In some languages, like the Huixteco of Mexico, a question may be rhetorical only in a context where the answer is obviously negative. Therefore, to translate John 6:70 as a question would be to imply that Jesus did not choose the 12 and that one of them was not a devil. The same negative implication would be present in Matt. 6:25-26 if translated as a question: "Is not life more than food, and the body more than clothing? . . . Are you not of more value than they?"

Psychological Terms. Where the Bible may speak of the heart or the bowels as the center of love, pity, or tenderness, many cultures will locate these emotions in the abdomen, others the liver, others the throat. Among the Anuak in Ethiopia many psychological attitudes and patterns of behavior are described in terms of the liver: to have a good liver is to be generous, and to have a bad liver is to be bad or unsociable; to have a shallow liver is to be angry, and to have a heavy liver is to be sad; a white liver stands for kindness, a cold liver for politeness. The Shilluk of the Sudan describe a stingy man as having a big heart and the generous man as having a small heart—on the excellent assumption that one who gives everything away will have a small heart, and one who keeps everything for himself will have a large heart.

Grammatical Difficulties. Such things as emphasis, shift of word classes, relationships between words, and the total complexity of clauses and sentences are only some of the difficulties the Bible translator encounters. Rarely will the grammatical structure of the language with which he is working match that of the biblical languages. An early translation of Ps. 23:1 in the language of the Tlingit Indians of Alaska misrepresented the possessive in "The LORD is my shepherd," so that the readers understood the phrase to mean, "The Lord is the one who takes care of my goats" ("goats" being the functional equivalent of the biblical "sheep").

The whole structure of clauses, sentences, and even of paragraphs must often be recast, with a corresponding shift in word classes, to make the meaning of the passage clear to new readers. Much of what is implicit in the biblical text must be made quite explicit, since the modern readers, so far removed in time, culture, and experience, cannot come to the passage with the same wealth of information that enabled the original readers to understand the written message. Much that is expressed succinctly must be expanded and explicitly stated in detail in translation.

In Mark 1:4 the author states that John the Baptist preached a "baptism of repentance for the forgiveness of sins." It will often be necessary (a) to show the proper sequence of the events referred to in the words "baptism," "repentance," "forgiveness," and "sins"; (b) to clarify relationship between these events, which in English is conveyed by the prepositions "of " and "for"; and (c) to use verbs or even complete sentences rather than nouns in order to show in each instance the subject and the object of each of the events. In many languages, therefore, the translation will read: "John preached to the people: 'Change your bad ways and I will baptize you, so that God will forgive the bad things that you have done.' "

Helps. Under the aegis of the United Bible Societies, the different national Bible societies are providing aids for translators all over the world in addition to the individual help and guidance provided for particular translation projects. A series of commentaries for translators is in preparation, of which the commentary on Mark has already been published, as well as other specialized helps. The quarterly journal *The Bible Translator* provides exegetical, translational, and linguistic materials for translators. Beginning in 1962 in Upper Volta, month-long translators' conferences have been held, usually 2 a year, in which anywhere from 50 to 100 translators, missionaries and nationals, working in related languages in a given area of the world, come together for intensive study in biblical, translational, and linguistic courses, with lectures, workshops, individual conferences, and examination of translations.

For Further Study. E. M. North, *The Book of a Thousand Tongues,* 1938. E. A. Nida, *God's Word in Man's Language,* 1952; *Bible Translating,* 1961. E. E. Wallis and M. A. Bennett, *Two Thousand Tongues to Go,* 1959. B. M. Metzger, "Versions, Medieval and Modern (Non-English)," in *IDB,* 1962. S. L. Greenslade, ed., *The Cambridge History of the Bible,* 1963. E. J. Eisenhart, *Scriptures of the World,* 1965.

THE IMPACT
OF THE BIBLE ON HISTORY

Arnold B. Rhodes

Sometimes the impact of the Bible on history has been so direct that it can be easily identified; at other times it has been more indirect and general. Here "history" is taken to be the story of the human past. In whatever manner the Bible's impact may be conceived, it has been so potent and so widespread that this presentation can be merely suggestive.

The Bible has an inherent relation to history. It is the book of revelation—God's making himself and his will known to men—and the most crucial unit of revelation is the interpreted event. Jesus was crucified under Pontius Pilate. This is one of the best-attested facts of history, accepted as such by the believer and nonbeliever alike. But the believers who wrote the NT did not stop there. They maintained that through this event God redeemed men from sin. This is interpretation.

Not only are historical events interpreted in the Bible, but also the literature which composes the Bible is set in an overall framework of history, albeit history as viewed through the eyes of faith. Fundamentally speaking, animals live in nature. Though man is also a creature within nature, his distinctive realm is history. The Bible has come to men through history and is designed to speak to men in history. It is to be expected, then, that the Bible should exert a dynamic impact on history.

Even as the materials which were to compose the Bible were in the process of coming into being they began their impact on history. E.g. Deut., or part of it, is usually regarded as the "book of the law" which was found in the temple in the time of Josiah (622 B.C.). Though it did not save Judah from the Babylonian Exile (586 B.C.), it did undergird Josiah's reformation (II Kings 22–23). Moreover Josiah's acceptance of the book as an authoritative standard set the precedent for succeeding steps in the formation of the canon (see "The Making of the OT Canon," pp. 1209-15; "The Making of the NT Canon," pp. 1216-24).

Our major concern, however, is with the impact of the Bible as such on history. We pursue this concern by a consideration of representative areas in which this impact has been felt: language and literature, the fine arts, and personal and social life.

I. Language and Literature

The impact of the Bible on language has been varied. In some cases the Bible has given people a literary language for the first time. Words such as the following have come from the Bible: angel, devil, manna, paradise, sabbath, scapegoat, and shibboleth. Various biblical expressions have entered into our literature and speech: e.g. a soft answer, a mess of pottage, the shadow of death. The Bible has also supplied a host of proper names. And it has stimulated a comparative study of languages.

The Bible is a library of many kinds of literature and has called libraries of literature into being. The translation of the Bible into a multitude of languages is both a witness to and a channel of its impact. The story of translation is told elsewhere in this volume (see "The Bible in English," pp. 1237-42; "The Bible in Every Tongue," pp. 1243-47), and attention is called here only to the impact of a few versions. Ulfilas (*ca.* 311-381), bishop of the Goths, created an alphabet for the Germanic languages out of existing alphabets, esp. the Greek, and translated most of the Bible into Gothic. Jerome's Latin Vulg. has had a lasting impact on theological terminology, the production of Latin literature, other translations of the Bible, and the development of the Romance languages.

While the Bible as a whole and in parts had been translated into both High and Low German before the time of Luther (1483-1546), no translation had really captivated the hearts of the German people. But Luther's translation did this at once. It helped to overcome his people's dialectal disunity and continued to mold their language. German grammar of the 16th century was based on it. It played a major role in the translation of the Bible into various languages, has been revised repeatedly, and has exerted a profound effect on German literature. Such literary figures as Klopstock, Wieland, Herder, Goethe, and Schiller cut their teeth on Luther's German. In time the KJV was to do for the English-speaking world something of what Luther's translation did for Germany.

The Bible is not only literature that has been translated; it is also literature that has been interpreted (see "The History of Biblical Interpretation," pp. 971-77; "The Historical Study of the Bible," pp. 978-82; "The Theological Study of the Bible," pp. 983-88). Throughout the centuries, beginning in biblical days, both Christians and Jews have produced many different kinds of aids to Bible study.

Wherever the Bible has gone it has entered into the literature of the country. Shortly after NT times no writer stands out more clearly than Augustine (354-430). While the Bible was not the only instrument in his conversion it was a major one. One reason he hesitated to receive Christian baptism was the temptation to sexual incontinence, but Rom. 13:13-14 helped him to make the decision to become a Christian. His most famous writings are his *Confessions* and *City of God.* The former reflects his experience of conversion, his study of the Bible, and the evils of his time. Augustine stressed original sin and salvation by God's grace alone. Pelagius became his antagonist, maintaining that man himself, without the help of God's grace, took the first steps toward his salvation. The *City of God* is a Christian philosophy of history and is therefore greatly dependent on the Bible. A popular theme for writers in the early church, the creation and fall, reflected the controversy between Augustine and Pelagius.

Dante (1265-1321) symbolizes Italian writers of the Middle Ages whose works show the influence of the Bible. His *Divine Comedy* is indirectly dependent on the Bible. Victor Hugo (1802-85) may well represent French writers whose works give evidence of dependence on the Bible. The best representatives of Russian authors who have been influenced by the Bible are Dostoevski (1821-81) and Tolstoi (1828-1910).

The early translations and paraphrases of parts of the Bible into Old English helped to make the English a Bible-loving people. In the Middle English *Canterbury Tales* Chaucer (*ca.* 1340-1400) demonstrates a detailed knowledge of the Bible at specific points. The principal Bible used by Shakespeare (1564-1616) seems to have been the Geneva Version. Though the extent of his knowledge of the Bible has been debated, he probably knew it well. It is interesting that 2 of his daughters, Susanna and Judith, were named after characters in the Apoc.

John Milton (1608-74) grew up with the Bible. English life of his day was permeated with it. Milton read from the Bible every morning, sometimes in the Hebrew. He was a linguist, and his study of the Scriptures was carried on in various languages. Moreover it was supported by wide reading in interpretations of the Bible and a thorough knowledge of the classics. So far as we know, his first literary attempt was the versification of Pss. 114; 136 at the age of 15. At the age of 43 he was totally blind; the sonnet "On His Blindness" makes use of the parable of the talents (Matt. 25:14-30). His major works—*Paradise Lost, Paradise Regained,* and *Samson Agonistes*—are all based on the Bible.

In contrast to the widely read Milton stands John Bunyan (1628-88), whose "library" was the Bible with only a few other books. Thus his thought was biblically saturated. Among English-speaking people his *Pilgrim's Progress* has probably been the most widely circulated religious book other than the Bible itself. George Fox (1624-91), founder of the Society of Friends, placed emphasis on both the Bible and the Inner Light in his *Journal.* Perhaps the best place to see Robert Burns's acquaintance with and appreciation of the Bible is in "The Cotter's Saturday Night" (1785), where he pictures the Scottish father leading his family in worship as he reads a passage from each testament. In his writings Sir Walter Scott (1771-1832) quotes or alludes to not less than 30 of the biblical books as well as to certain of the Apoc.

Many of the poems of Robert Browning (1812-89) deal with biblical themes, and it has been claimed that there are 500 biblical expressions or allusions in *The Ring and the Book* alone. While Thomas Carlyle (1795-1881) has been likened to an OT prophet, Charles Dickens (1812-70) has been likened to a prophet of the NT. He is noted for his love of children and for his frequent mention of Christ's placing a little child in the midst of his disciples. The impact of the Bible on Tennyson (1809-92) is reflected in his style, expression, and thought. *In Memoriam* is regarded by many as his greatest work. As he grapples there with the problem of death, he recalls the angels' song from Luke 2:14, the raising of Lazarus, and God's dealings with Israel at Sinai.

As a child Robert Louis Stevenson (1850-94) was nourished on the Bible and the Shorter Catechism. His favorite biblical passage was Isa. 58. Though the Bible does not seem to be regarded as a source of his *Dr. Jekyll and Mr. Hyde,* the student of the Bible is struck by the similarity of its theme to Paul's doctrine of the conflict between good and evil within a man (cf. Rom. 7). Of course the influence of the Bible on English literature has continued to be felt in the 20th cent., e.g. in the work of T. S. Eliot (1888-1965).

When the land which was later to become the U.S.A. was being settled in the 17th cent. there was comparatively little literary production. That which was produced, however, was mostly religious and biblical—often in the form of diary. In the next cent. Jonathan Edwards (1703-58), Calvinistic preacher and theologian, was one of the most prominent writers. Among the 19th-cent. American writers who made use of the Bible were Nathaniel Hawthorne (1804-64) and Herman Melville (1819-91). Hawthorne was familiar with the Bible, esp. valuing Job, but generally used it without making direct reference to it in his writings. Melville, on the other hand, made extensive use of biblical characters and episodes, not so much treating the characters and episodes in their original setting and with their original meaning, but rather reworking the biblical material and giving it a symbolic meaning.

II. THE FINE ARTS

Drama. Though the Bible itself contains no book which can be called a drama in the strict sense of the word, it does contain much dramatic material —Job being the most conspicuous example. Biblical drama as such did not flourish in the ancient world. In the latter part of the Middle Ages, however, "miracle" plays became very popular. The earliest of these plays were written in Latin and centered about the themes of Christmas, Good Friday, and Easter. In them the biblical narratives were presented by the clergy in the form of dialogue. Soon such plays were presented in the vernacular of several European countries. The famous Passion Play of Oberammergau, Germany, is a descendant of these early miracle plays. Sometimes the presentation would consist of a series of plays extending over several days and covering much of both testaments. Obviously these plays had a part in the development of the later drama.

From the time of the Middle Ages to the present such biblical themes and personalities as the following have been communicated in the form of drama: creation, Adam and Eve, Cain and Abel, Noah and the Flood, Abraham, Jacob, Joseph, Moses, Jephthah, Saul, David, Solomon, several of the prophets, Job, Ruth, Esther, Daniel, Mary Magdalene, Pilate, and the prodigal son. Among the characters of the Apoc. the following have been popular with the dramatists: Judith, Judas Maccabeus, Tobit, and Susanna.

A few authors and titles of dramas based on the Bible or the Apoc. are: George Peele, *The Love of King David and Fair Bethsabe* (1599); Byron, *Cain* (1821); Longfellow, *Judas Maccabaeus* (1872); Christopher Morley, *East of Eden* (1924); Clemence Dane, *Naboth's Vineyard* (1925); Marc Connelly, *The Green Pastures* (1929); and Archibald MacLeish, *J. B.* (1958).

Today drama, some based on the Bible, is being used increasingly in the church. Guilds of players travel here and there to put on religious plays. Radio, television, filmstrips, and motion pictures are all being used by the church for dramatic productions. The motion picture industry itself occasionally produces a film which is based on the Bible—e.g. the productions of Cecil B. DeMille.

Music. The impact of the Bible on music is found among various musical forms: pss., hymns, gospel songs, folks songs, motets, cantatas, anthems, masses, operas, and oratorios. Many if not all of the OT pss. were sung in the temple and are still used in the synagogue. The hymn which Jesus and his disciples sang at the Last Supper was probably the final part of the Hallel (Pss. 115–118). Pss. were chanted in the church from the earliest times. They were arranged in meter to be sung as hymns at the time of the Reformation and soon became very popular. *The Bay Ps. Book* (1640) was used widely by the early settlers of New England, and pss. are still sung today. Hymns are frequently based on pss. and other parts of the Scriptures.

Many of the same biblical subjects are present in musical works as are found in dramas, though the prophets as a whole have not inspired many musical compositions. Only a few of the master composers can be recalled here:

The Italian Palestrina was the most renowned composer of the 16th cent. Among his works are some 93 masses and 250 motets.

Much of the vocal music of the German master J. S. Bach (1685-1750) and the Anglo-German master Handel (1685-1759) is a setting for biblical words. Bach's *St. Matthew Passion*, using the text of the gospel story of Jesus' crucifixion, and his *Mass in B Minor* are regarded as the greatest choral music ever composed. Handel is esp. known for his numerous oratorios, biblical materials arranged for singing in concert form. Among them are: *Esther, Deborah, Saul, Israel in Egypt, Samson, Belshazzar, Judas Maccabaeus, Joshua, Solomon, Jephtha,* and *Joseph.* In *The Messiah,* which is sung far and wide, esp. near Christmas and Easter, Handel quotes from no less than 14 biblical books.

F. J. Haydn (1732-1809), an Austrian, known as the "father of the symphony," completed his oratorio *The Creation* in 1799. The words were adapted by friends from the Bible and Milton's *Paradise Lost.* Mozart (1756-91), also an Austrian, in a tragically short career composed an almost unbelievable number of masterpieces, many of them using biblical texts. One of his last undertakings was his famous *Requiem,* which had to be completed by one of his pupils.

Beethoven (1770-1827), the "Shakespeare of music," composed an oratorio, *The Mount of Olives.* Among other major German composers Mendelssohn (1809-47) is known for his oratorios *Elijah* and *St. Paul,* and Brahms (1833-97) himself selected a variety of scripture passages for his great *German Requiem.*

In the 20th cent. such eminent composers as Igor Stravinsky and Benjamin Britten have set many biblical selections to music.

Of all the American folk songs the Negro spirituals are the most significant. Among the best examples are "Go Down, Moses," "Roll Jordan, Roll," "Dry Bones," and "Swing Low, Sweet Chariot."

In recent years biblical motifs have played a part in the idiom of jazz, including traditional jazz, folk masses, and rock 'n' roll. E.g., Joseph Wise has produced a jazz arrangement of the Lord's Prayer, and Geoffrey Beaumont has composed "The Folk Mass."

Visual Arts. Visual arts include symbols, painting, sculpture, architecture, stained glass, tapestry, and work in metal. In spite of the fact that there have been disagreements among the churches about the role of these arts, the Bible has consistently made its impact on them.

The Bible had both a negative and a positive effect on the development of the visual arts in Judaism. The negative effect arises from the commandment "You shall not make yourself a graven image, or any likeness" (Exod. 20:4). Such a command was a wholesome restriction on the ancient Israelites, who lived in the midst of polytheistic peoples; and something of its effectiveness is seen in the fact that archaeologists have discovered no representation of Yahweh. The primary intent of the commandment seems to have been the prohibition of idolatry, for the temple had figures of cherubim in the Holy of Holies and 12 metal bulls under the molten sea.

On the positive side, in the Jewish catacombs there are representations of the 7-armed lampstand, the scroll of the law, and the ethrog—the fruit of the citron used with the palm branch in celebration of the feast of Booths. A synagogue discovered at Dura-Europos on the Euphrates has mural frescoes from the middle of the 3rd cent. A.D. These frescoes, which include such scenes as Abraham's sacrifice of Isaac, episodes from the life of Moses, the exodus from Egypt, and Ezekiel's vision of the valley of dry bones, raise the question of earlier works of art among the Jews. Regardless of the manner in which this question is answered, however, there was but little Jewish art before the 19th cent.

More evidence is available for the development of art in the early church. A prominent symbol in the Christian catacombs is the fish. The letters of the Greek word for "fish" are initials of a phrase meaning "Jesus Christ, Son of God, Savior." The shepherd with a lamb on his shoulders in earlier cultures designated a worshiper bringing his animal for sacrifice, but in Christian art this figure represents the Good Shepherd, who restores his lost sheep. Among the most popular themes for painting in the catacombs are Noah and the ark, Abraham's sacrifice of Isaac, the gift of water in the wilderness, the story of Jonah, the young men in the fiery furnace, Daniel in the lions' den, the visit of the wise men, the baptism of Jesus, the healing of the paralytic, the healing of the woman with the flow of blood, the Samaritan woman at Jacob's well, and the raising of Lazarus.

At Dura-Europos there has also been discovered a house church which is dated in the same general period as the synagogue mentioned above. Scenes from both testaments are painted on its walls. These paintings were designed to point to the victory of God's saving power.

Art was expressed in various media even in the early church: stone, marble, mosaic, ivory relief, painting, and metal. Stone coffins often had sculptured friezes which told biblical stories. Illustrative paintings were sometimes included in manuscripts of the Bible. Throughout all the art of the early church the emphasis was placed on message rather than appearance.

Art flourished from the 5th to the 15th cents. in the Byzantine Empire, located in S Europe and W Asia with its capital at Byzantium (Constantinople). Though early Christians often met in homes, many church buildings were erected in this period. Churches in the shape of a Greek cross were popular, and they were decorated with biblical paintings and mosaics known as icons. Emphasis was placed on the transcendence of Christ, who was called Pantocrator, "Ruler of All." As a part of this theological emphasis more attention was given to the Virgin Mary and to saints. The last judgment was brought into Christian art with stress on the horrors of the damned.

The Middle Ages in W Europe had their own distinctive characteristics in art. Illustrated manuscripts of the Bible and parts of it continued to serve the purposes of education and inspiration. Book covers were sometimes decorated with biblical scenes in ivory relief—e.g. the Crucifixion. The Romanesque church plan was often in the shape of a Latin cross. Tapestries and murals, some in the form of frescoes, were sometimes based on paintings found in illustrated Bibles. In the Gothic cathedrals, thought to represent the heavenly Jerusalem, stained glass came into its own. Various forms of art were concentrated on the life of Jesus, esp. on his birth and passion. The time came when great stress was also placed on the representation of the Virgin Mary. The theme of the last judgment remained popular, but it came to be handled in such a way as to emphasize God's salvation.

The age of the Renaissance and Reformation was a time of illustrious names in art: Ghiberti (Italian), Donatello (Italian), Masaccio (Italian), van der Goes (Dutch), da Vinci (Italian), Dürer (German), Cranach (German), Michelangelo (Italian), Titian (Italian), Grünewald (German), and Raphael (Italian). All of these men made use of biblical subjects at least some of the time. E.g. Ghiberti's bronze doors on the baptistery in Florence show among other scenes the meeting of Solomon and the Queen of Sheba. Da Vinci's most famous work is his painting of the Last Supper in the refectory of Santa Maria delle Grazie, Milan. Dürer's greatest masterpiece is his portrait of 4 apostles, John, Peter, Mark, and Paul. Cranach tried to develop a distinctive Reformation art. One of his themes is Jesus blessing little children. Michelangelo, a genius in several of the arts, was influenced by the teachings of Savonarola and perhaps by the reformers of his own day. Multitudes of people know at least something of his paintings of prophets and biblical scenes on the altar wall and the ceiling of the Sistine Chapel in Rome. Grünewald's painting of the Crucifixion on the Isenheim altarpiece is noteworthy.

From the Reformation to the present time many artists have been stimulated by the Bible, but special notice may be taken of 3: Rembrandt (1606-69) has the reputation of being the greatest painter of religious themes in Protestantism. His work embraces some kind of illustration of almost every book in the Bible and the Apoc.; in fact his work is largely biblical. In keeping with his Protestant outlook is his emphasis on the preaching of Jesus. Among the works for which William Blake (1757-1827) is remembered are his illustrations of Job and his painting of the Ascension. Finally mention may be made of "The Raising of Lazarus" by Vincent van Gogh (1853-90). Today some of the most creative work in the visual arts is to be found in sculpture and church architecture.

III. Personal and Social Life

The biblical writers were concerned about man's relation to God and man's relation to man. They knew that faith should be expressed in action. Though there has been variety in the understanding of biblical ethics, ethical concern based on the Scriptures has never been completely lost. Under the influence of such calls for self-denial as Matt. 19:21, 29 some have tried to escape life's problems by an ascetic withdrawal from the world, but for the most part those who have based their lives on the Bible have sought to work toward the solution of the world's problems.

In spite of their extremes the Puritans had a valid desire to keep faith and conduct united. Moreover their excesses in moral strictness must be viewed against the background of their own time. On the whole their impact on society was healthy; they gave men spiritual muscle and moral backbone. The transforming effect of the Bible on multitudes of individuals and through them on society is too great to measure. The human conscience could not be what it is apart from the influence of the Bible. Jesus' identification of the neighbor in the parable of the good Samaritan (Luke 10:25-37) will not let man's moral sensitivity rest.

The Family. The Bible has greatly influenced marriage and the family. Jesus taught the sanctity of marriage and the value of every person, including women and children. In early Roman society divorce was very easy, but the church set its own standard of marriage according to its understanding of the Bible. The church fathers denounced the exposure of infants, a practice of frequent occurrence in the Roman world. Much of the concern for little children today goes back to Jesus' love of children. Certain passages in the Bible have been used to thwart the cause of women's rights, but repeatedly the truth of its message of the worth of every person has prevailed in support of the cause.

Education. Public education originated under religious auspices and was originally designed to serve a religious purpose. Basic school texts in the colonial days of America were the *New England Primer*—which contained biblical and theological materials—the Psalter, and the Bible. Grammar school children were required to report on the Sunday sermon. In 1642 the Puritans of Mass. passed a law requiring that children be taught to read. Colleges were Bible and theological institutions. The process of secularization of education began about the middle of the 18th cent. and has continued to the present time. Nevertheless the impact of the Bible is still felt to some extent in institutions which are not church-related, through Bible and theological courses and through denominational foundations near college and university campuses.

Service Organizations. The Bible has provided at least a part of the motivation for such service organizations as hospitals, the YMCA, the YWCA, the Red Cross, the Salvation Army, the Volunteers of America, and philanthropic foundations. Christian hospitals were established as early as the 4th cent. In the Middle Ages church institutions specialized in meeting the needs of particular groups: the aged, the poor, the sick, and orphans. Various types of reform movements have been rooted in the Bible.

Politics. Religion and politics have of necessity been closely associated in the life of men and nations. This is at once obvious in reading the OT. Jesus' "Render therefore to Caesar the things that are Caesar's, and to God the things that are God's" (Matt. 22:21) and Paul's injunctions in Rom. 13 still play their part in the discussion of the relation between church and state. Charlemagne (742-814) based his government on the OT and thought of himself as a new Davidic king. Cents. later the divine right of kings was promoted by rulers in various monarchies.

At the time of the opening up of the new world many changes began to take place in politics. It is claimed that Columbus was encouraged to make his famous adventure by passages in Isa. and by a statement in the Apoc. (II Esd. 6:42) that when creating the earth God left only a 7th of it covered with water. It was shortly after this that the reformers did their work. Calvinism played a major role in developing what has been called a "nonconformist conscience," though various ecclesiastical groups made contributions to the democratic and representative elements in the politics of the U.S. to be. The Puritans believed that all men are equal before God, for they read in their Bible that "God is no respecter of persons" (Acts 10:34 KJV; cf. Rom. 2:11; Col. 3:25).

No nation was ever founded by so many Bible-believing people as the U.S., even though these people differed considerably in their interpretation. The Declaration of Independence was signed by men of varied theological persuasions. But, among other things, these men agreed that "all men are created equal" and that "they are endowed by their Creator with certain unalienable Rights." Many of our national leaders have drunk deeply from the biblical stream. It is widely known that the Bible was one of a small group of books in the "library" of the young Abraham Lincoln. He sometimes quoted the Scriptures in his public addresses. E.g. in a speech in 1858 he reflected the words of Jesus in saying, "A house divided against itself cannot stand."

Law. The Mosaic law exercised a measure of influence in the Roman Empire as early as the 4th cent. A.D., but for the most part the law of the empire was Roman. Constantine (*ca.* 280-337) abolished the branding of the human face because man is made in God's image, made remarriage culpable unless the partner was guilty of adultery (Matt. 5:31-32), required at least 2 witnesses to a crime (Deut. 17:6; 19:15), constituted Sunday a holiday, and humanized law in general. Theodosius (*ca.* 346-395) put a Bible in every courtroom. The OT was used by Charlemagne as a basis for persecuting heretics as well as for prohibiting interest on money (Deut. 23:19).

The laws of Puritan New England were heavily indebted to the OT. Somewhere along the line the Puritans learned the principle of equality before God and the law (cf. Deut. 1:17). Their observance of Sunday by the rules of the sabbath had antecedents in the Middle Ages. The strictness of their observance was a reaction against the dissipation often associated with the day. Puritans are recorded as having executed so-called witches on the authority of Exod. 22:18. It should be remembered, however, that witch hunting was practiced by others as well, that some of the best educated men of the time believed in the existence of witches, and that many Puritans did not hunt for them.

The Bible has had and is having a part in solving the problems of human relationships. Though it has been misinterpreted in the defense of slavery and racial discrimination, the Bible is playing a far more potent role in the cause of freedom at the present time than is evident to the superficial eye. Moreover it is having a constructive influence on the controversy about capital punishment. Men are beginning to realize that the message of the Bible as a whole, rather than the words of a proof text alone, must be brought to bear on a particular problem in relation to its total contemporary situation. With regard to war both the Christian pacifist and the Christian nonpacifist see that they are called by Christ to be peacemakers.

Economics. The Bible enjoins a healthy materialism, but not a materialism which puts things on the throne of God. It acknowledges God as the creator of all and men as his stewards. This stewardship was given a variety of concrete expressions in Israel. The early Jerusalem Christians participated in a program of voluntary sharing for a time (Acts 2:43-47; 5:4), but this was not Marxian communism. It was religiously motivated. Experiments, more or less similar, have been carried out in various places from time to time. These experiments, for the most part, have been communal in the consumption of products but not in their production.

Conflicting attitudes have been held concerning

the relationship between the Bible and society. In the latter half of the 19th cent. a movement known as the "social gospel" arose as a reaction to the problems created by modern industry. While the movement was concerned with the application of the gospel to the whole of life, it showed a special concern for employer-employee relations. Names associated with it include Washington Gladden and Walter Rauschenbusch. Among the resources of the proponents of the social gospel were the teachings of Jesus and the prophets. Of course there were more conservative and more radical reformers both within the ranks of the social gospelers and outside their ranks. There was a tendency among the advocates of the social gospel to think that the economy of the nation was more distant from the kingdom of God than the other areas of life. But the social gospel movement failed to take human sin and divine judgment seriously enough. Among others Reinhold Niebuhr has sought to work out a more realistic doctrine of man than that of the earlier liberals as a basis for personal and social life.

Even a brief study reveals that the Bible has had a greater impact on the story of man than any other book and suggests that its impact will continue into the future. Though it has been used superstitiously, has been abused by its friends and its foes, and has often been misused, its overall impact when properly interpreted has been creative and redemptive.

For Further Study. Ernst von Dobschütz, *The Influence of the Bible on Civilization*, 1914. P. M. Simms, *The Bible in America*, 1936, ch. XIV. M. B. Crook, ed., *The Bible and Its Literary Associations*, 1937. W. L. Nathan, *Art and the Message of the Church*, 1961. S. L. Greenslade, ed., *The Cambridge History of the Bible*, Epilogue, 1963.

THE BIBLE AND PREACHING

George Arthur Buttrick

The title of this article in a Bible commentary implies a blood bond between the Bible and the sermon. But the world to which the preacher now speaks sees no bond. Modern man after 4 cents. of growing skepticism does not believe in God and grants no primacy to the Bible. So biblical preaching addresses itself not only to ignorance of the Bible but to outright unbelief. The Bible is "old stuff," or at best another book.

Were we to tell the world that the Bible is not a unified book but a collection of 60 or 80 books written over a period of about 1,000 years, the latest of them nearly 2,000 years old, contemporary man would be doubly baffled. "Then why the Bible?" he would ask. He might then dismiss the church as exhibit A of life before the Flood. Surely relevant preaching could better concern itself with the new psychology, the new science, the new drama, or with the newspaper and what is happening in our tumultuous world.

I. God and Man in the Bible

But the church has said for centuries that all true preaching is biblical because the Bible is inspired; i.e. God the Creator is self-revealed in and through the Scriptures. This claim is the crux of the issue. The inspiration is not literal in the sense that every phrase is scientifically and factually "true." Such an assumption would have us believing in a flat earth, in the burning of witches, and in racial segregation:

> What damned error, but some sober brow
> Will bless it and approve it with a text.
> (Shakespeare, *The Merchant of Venice*)

Besides, the assumption runs foul of the fact of transmission: which manuscript of thousands is the one that is factually "true"? We could speak perhaps of literal mechanization—of God's turning men into dictation machines to speak his literal word, though he never so degrades men whom his love has fashioned—but not of literal inspiration.

We have thus raised the real question: What is truth? It is not a "philosophy of life," despite the jargon of our times, for philosophy is largely an affair of *our* mind, a realm of concepts which are soon remote from life. Truth is not a scientific formula, though modern man is reluctant to make that admission, for science uses only one level of mind (the analyzing mind) addressed to only one aspect of the world (the quantitative world measured by the senses). There is little chance that truth can find us through philosophy or science, though both are valid quests in man's total range of interest. Truth is that which stands over against our finitude. Truth says, "Time is swift, and you must soon die." Truth asks, "What now will you do?" Truth beckons, "Here am I!" The NT word for truth is at root the negative of "concealment"; it deeply means the unveiling of the Mystery in whom our life is held.

So truth is in and through event. How else? Events are surprise, for they are only partly in man's control. Events are invasive, as witness the Alaskan earthquake or Luther's "Here stand I." Events are from the totality, the spear thrust of the mystery of existence. That is why the Bible is neither philosophy nor science but a book of events. The Scriptures are onset, beyond our human control, within our life but over against our life. They tell us flatly that our days are precarious, that our attempt to be our own salvation in our anxiety-pride only doubles our dilemma, that egocentricity first distorts and then destroys all man's works, and thus wrings from us the cry, "Is there any word from the LORD?" (Jer. 37:17). Then the Bible speaks precisely that word: "By grace you have been saved through faith; and this is not your own doing, it is the gift of God—not because of works, lest any man should boast" (Eph. 2:8-9).

Bible events, sacred history as the core of all history, are thus a dialogue between God and man. There are echoes within the dialogue, a harking back to that which has already happened, as in any dialogue; and there are startling newnesses. The dialogue comes to climax in one event—the event of Christ. It is a 4-fold event—his life, his death, his resurrection, and his granted Spirit. *He* is truth. This is the "scandal" of the Bible: truth is not in concepts but in a person, not in scientific "laws" but in particularity. But what else could be true except that ultimate onset? The life of Christ leads to his death, for only the Cross can condemn our "success" and redeem our broken pride. The death of Christ leads to his resurrection, for without that victory we would be obliged to say that the best in our earth is finally at the mercy of the worst. The resurrection of Christ leads to Pentecost, the bestowal of the Holy Spirit, without whom the Bible would be of the past, by whom the Bible becomes the present word. In this deep sense the Bible is inspired, breathed-into of God. If modern man still asks "Why?" there is no answer in logic, for there are no arguments for God. The Bible answers, "Confront me, and then confront your own alienation." The Bible can wait. It is the only book not caught in surprise by our present world. It looks at us and asks, "What did you expect?"

II. The Herald and the Proclamation

Now we can inquire again about the Bible and preaching. There is no true preaching except biblical preaching, for only in the Bible—the book of God-informed events and of the Event—does God centrally speak in human history; and only in and through the Bible does his Spirit centrally work. So to avow is not to deny that God is everywhere present or that his secret and open witness is found in every place. It is simply to admit that our finite lives are met in finite terms, in focal and determinative events on which history turns. Always our pride of mind seeks refuge in vague universals; always God brings us back to what has happened, is now happening, and shall happen. Because of the "human situation," the plain fact that man cannot live by his own poor mortal powers, and that he wickedly tries even while he knows his creaturehood, the only true preaching is the preaching of "justification by faith"—viz. that man's salvation is of God, as God, by the total event of Christ, has made common cause with our loss and shame to open for us "a new and living way" to himself.

Preaching is therefore just what the word implies. It is heralding: "Make straight in the desert a highway for our God" (Isa. 40:3c). It is proclamation: "The saying is sure and worthy of full acceptance, that Christ Jesus came into the world to save sinners" (I Tim. 1:15). Thus there is a blood bond between the Bible and preaching. For the good news, God's self-disclosure in Christ, is null and void without a proclaimer of the news. The Bible proclaims the news, the new age ushered in by Christ, the new being whom he quickens in mortal man; and therefore the Bible is one with the news, and what we find in the Bible is always word-event. Furthermore—such is the joy and burden of preaching—the preacher becomes one with the news.

Why and how? Herbert Farmer in his *The Servant of the Word* has called attention to the fact that a newspaper may be called "The Daily News." Strange title, for the paper is manifestly not the news. The print on the page is not an earthquake in Japan or election returns in the United States. Yet these events would not be known except for the newspaper, or for the slower or swifter method of word-of-mouth testimony. Thus the newspaper becomes one with the news and may rightly name itself "The Daily News." By the same bond the preacher, the proclaimer of the news, becomes one with the news—yes, and with the power and grace of God who sent his Son into the world that all who courageously respond to his Spirit's beckoning shall be saved.

Always in the Bible there is an unbreakable hyphen between event and word. In OT thought a word was not simply sounds and syllables from a man's lips, but an invasive energy. Perhaps the translation should not be, "God said, 'Let there be light'; and there was light" (Gen. 1:3), but rather, "God spoke light and there was light." In the NT

Christ is "the Word" (John 1:1), not simply in the sense of God's speaking to men through him, but rather as the outthrust of God's creative might and love: "All things were made through him, and without him was not anything made that was made" (John 1:3).

Thus the preacher's word, if his preaching is truly biblical, is not merely sounds or speech. Because he is one with the good news, his word is the outgo of God's grace and power. "As the Father has sent me," said Christ to his disciples, "even so I send you" (John 20:21)—with the same energy of the Spirit! Even on the human level words are not just words, and the motto "Deeds, not words" brings no deep conviction; for words *are* deeds, the action of a man's lips as surely as the making of a table is the action of his hands. The preached word is far more powerfully deed, because the preacher, the proclaimer of good news, is now one with the news, i.e. with the invasion of God in the event of Jesus the Christ. The preacher himself becomes word-event.

III. The "Way" of Biblical Preaching

Now we must ask how preaching becomes truly biblical. Obviously the preacher should know the Book, preferably in its original tongues, though that learning should not obtrude, much less become a pride. Because the Scriptures are inspired they have their own doctrine of history, not to be confused with current doctrines which men eagerly read; their own doctrine of human nature, which makes both American optimism and existential despair seem half-baked; their own doctrine of science, which grants man the right to "name" all things (cf. Gen. 2:19-20), i.e. to enter into their secret and exercise their power, but to do this as trustee, never as owner; their own doctrine of ethic, a doctrine so revolutionary that in the NT it disavows the law and makes decision by the spirit of Christ as he lights life's ever-changing context; their own doctrine of nature, which is never our popular nature worship but a discovery in nature of the faithfulness and terror and gentleness of the Eternal; and, above all, their own doctrine of God, viz. that the love found in Christ is the burning heart of the Abyss.

The preacher who is under the authority of the Bible will not succumb to either the blandishments or the threats of present culture. On the other hand he will not condemn the fashion of the times, however much he may feel stranger to it. He will know that every culture is under both the judgment and the mercy of God's word in Christ, the Christ who came "not to condemn the world, but that the world might be saved through him" (John 3:17). The biblical preacher, then, will be at home in the vast and quickening world of the Bible. That world is more than Copernican: all its occasions and all the ranges of its life revolve around a Throne on which a Lamb is "slain from the foundation of the world" (Rev. 13:8 KJV). The preacher must have the Book by heart so that its truths and its Truth occur and re-occur to him under all the onsets of daily life.

But how shall the preacher use the Bible? We might better ask how shall he gladly and freely let the Bible use him? He will be an expository preacher in the sense that he will always expound the truth of scripture. But there is exposition and exposition. If the sermon is strictly exposition and no more, preaching will be little else than a study in semantics. The proverbial "dull as a sermon" describes such preaching. "The hungry sheep look up and are not fed" (John Milton, "Lycidas"). The preacher should know the meaning of words and phrases, but these must be regarded only within the purport of the whole passage. It is boon to the preacher that the Scriptures come in nubs and pericopes. That last word means "cut around." The revised versions rightly offer paragraphs, not the unjustified "verses" of the older versions. Only in rare instances has the preacher the right to "lift" a text out of context, even though preaching has been under that misconception, not to say sin, for many generations.

As for exact meanings, "the simplicity that is in Christ" (II Cor. 11:3 KJV) is not basis for a sermon on the simplicity of life of those who live in Christ, even though such simplicity is required, for the word "simplicity" is rightly translated as "a sincere and pure devotion to Christ" (RSV).

As for texts held in their context, that honesty will know that the 10 Commandments is not a list of moralistic injunctions but rather a setting forth of man's response to the asonishing covenant of faithfulness and mercy which God proposed: "I am the LORD your God, who brought you out of the land of Egypt, . . . showing steadfast love to . . . those who love me and keep my commandments" (Deut. 5:6, 10). Here is another double instance: in Phil. 4:8 the phrase "whatsoever things are of good report" (KJV), should be translated "whatever is gracious" (RSV); but the whole passage should be treated as a unit. Who could rightly claim that his "thinking on these things" has proved his salvation, or even that he is able to control his thoughts in our distraught and distracting time? The passage on thinking harks back to the preceding pericope, "The peace of God . . . will keep your hearts and your minds in Christ Jesus" (vs. 7); and it looks forward to the last line of its own paragraph: "and the God of peace will be with you" (vs. 9).

But it is not enough to expound the pericope, for each unit of scripture must be set within its book, and each book must be viewed within the total witness of the Bible. The need to keep the book in mind is particularly required in preaching from the 4 gospels, for each author has his own angle of vision and his own purpose, even though the thought of all has been made captive to Christ. Consider the miracle of the stilling of the storm. Mark's account records the fear of the disciples as almost an upbraiding of Christ, "Teacher, do you not care if we perish?" (Mark 4:38); but Matt.'s version is, "Save, Lord; we are perishing" (Matt. 8:25). Which account is true? Which is earlier? Almost certainly the Markan rendering is original. Then why the Matthean change? The major purpose, the date, and even the locale of each gospel are now involved; and the study of the Synoptic problem and of form criticism, far from "rending the Scriptures" as the timid maintain, becomes for the preacher the means of clearer and richer interpretation (see "The Literary Relations Among the Gospels," pp. 1129-35).

The plea that each book should be held in the total witness of the Bible gives no warrant for "reading Christ" into every OT passage—the tree cast into the bitter waters of Marah (Exod. 15:23-25) was not the cross of Christ or even its prototype, and the angel who wrestled with Jacob (Gen. 32:24-30) was not the NT Messiah—but it does mean that the preacher may not preach on the 10 Commandments as if the "new commandment" in Christ's love had never been given.

Biblical preaching not only honors the meaning of scripture and its immediate context, the book in which the word occurs and the total witness of the Bible, but acknowledges also the *mood* of the passage. "My God, my God, why hast thou forsaken me?" (Matt. 27:46; Mark 15:34), however it be interpreted, whether as quotation from Ps. 22:1 in victorious trust or as "cry of dereliction," is certainly no permit for a sermon on the rival doctrines of the atonement, much less an opening for the preacher to air his own theological preferences. The mood of Ps. 23 is not that of the parable of the 2 houses with its crashing crescendo, "It fell, and great was the fall of it" (Matt. 7:24-27; Luke 6:47-49). The story of the Emmaus road (Luke 24:13-35) hangs in the light of all golden sunsets; but "the wages of sin is death" (Rom. 6:23), even though that clause should not be "lifted" from the whole paragraph, is in another mood.

This plea for fidelity to the mood is not fastidiousness, but rather indicates a door through which the gospel may be addressed to the changing moods of human nature. The Bible is omnific: all the griefs and gladnesses of daily life, all its horror and hope, all its dearth and destiny there break into speech. The preacher who is sensitive to the moods of scripture is well armed to contend for the faith.

IV. The Bible and the Modern Mind

But expository preaching, however well informed and however faithful, is not enough; for the Bible confronts the world, as the preacher necessarily confronts his world. The Bible has its own history, which is faith-history (there is no "objective" history), and it has its own language, which now in phrase after phrase has become the treasure of our common speech. But Bible language in its own time was not esoteric. How could it be in a book which is not philosophy or science, but history, drama, story, person, and community? We need not regret the fact that the NT is written in koine Greek, the common language of colloquial cast which was spoken across the world of Christ's time from Spain to N India. Yes, our knowledge of that fact has robbed us of the majestic cadences of the KJV (except as we rightly use them as commentary and for devotion), but it has brought us nearer to the common life. Rev., and in places even Mark, break grammar in some passages, though for compensation Heb. verges in its language on classical Greek. Our plea is that biblical preaching will do what the Bible has done: speak to its age in the language of the age.

Thus we confront the problem of "communication." Rudolf Bultmann holds a brief for "demythologizing." His contention raises huge questions. What is meant by "myth"? Is the NT myth or history-and-myth? Is *our* idiom that which he proposes, viz. the existentialism of Martin Heidegger? Why is he so gentle to the "scientific world view" at the very time when that approach to life shows signs of bankruptcy? As each generation proclaims the gospel in its own "tongue," how can successive demythologizings be held together except by devotion to the biblical witness? But beyond all these questions Bultmann has recalled us to a central verity: the gospel can be proclaimed to our world only in the thought forms and language which our world understands, and in which indeed it lives its strange life.

Despite our use of the word "relevant" applied to modern preaching, relevance is not enough, and could even betray the word-event of the Bible. "Relevant" meant originally the "raising up" of an order of life and now means "applied to" or "pertinent to." But is this enough? The gospel in stance after stance goes clean counter to our modern life. If history is not ended by atomic blight, a gentler time than ours will wonder how the followers of Christ could unconcernedly drive to work from comfortable suburbs through rat-infested slums. Relevance may be another word for surrender.

But the Bible itself claims of the preacher that he *enter into dialogue* with his world, using its thought forms and speaking its language, while never betraying the sovereignty of scripture. This task involves far more than a knowledge of the world's idiom: it means some knowledge of its mind by the reading of its novels and drama, by exposure to its music and its art. How else could a dialogue proceed? Modern man has discarded the Bible and its language. So the preacher must speak in the idiom of his time. Presumably this is what Karl Barth intends when he says that the preacher must have the daily paper in one hand and the Bible in the other.

Thus preaching in our time *cannot be argument.* It never could in any age: when does the Bible logicize? Argument itself rests back on axioms and thus is at best a feeble reed. Pulpit argument gives the congregation no chance to reply and thus seems coercion. Besides, the preacher's arguments invite the congregation to treat the gospel on that level, the level of debate, and so to evade the gospel's onset, whereas the gospel never argues the truth, but offers the truth to challenge our response in brave faith. Besides, the existentialist is surely partly right in his doctrine of "absurdity," at least in his plea that our world cannot be constrained into any completely rational pattern, because the "irrational" (which is not necessarily the untrue) always breaks our neat formulas. There should be provision for dialogue between preacher and congregation, but biblical preaching is not argument. It is existential in the best sense of the word. It is addressed more to the dynamics of the subconscious—to man's ultimate concern—than to his neat rationalisms.

Biblical preaching is *not moralism,* even though moralism rests like a blight on the American pulpit. Moralism (not morality) is the censoriousness whose stock in trade is a list of "thou shalt not's." It is not the preacher's job to tell people what to do, and even more decidedly not his job to tell them what not to do. Clinical psychiatry has shown beyond cavil that such an approach in parents is outright threat to the mental health of children. Modern drama is in many an instance the messy record of

frustration—Why not, when modern man, playing his own God, finds himself in a dead-end street?— but it is right in its near contempt for pulpit moralism. Life cannot be governed by 2 columns: "This is always right; that is always wrong." Indeed the gospel has delivered us "from the curse of the law, [Christ] having become a curse for us" (Gal. 3:13). Ethical decision is always ambiguous: suppose the money on the collection plate could speak, saying, "If you only knew where I've been!" Strict moralism might not allow any church to accept any money! Pulpit moralism is destructive domination. Besides it is ethical pride and therefore sinful self-deception. Biblical preaching does not tell people what not to do, but what God has already done in Jesus Christ in judgment and mercy—for both preacher and congregation.

Preaching is *not dogmatism* in the modern constricted sense of the word, though it is dogmatism in the word's original meaning: that which is *right* because inwardly attested age on age. Biblical preaching is under the mystery, the height and abyss of God, who is always being revealed by his grace, but whose Godhead is never resolved by man's theologies. Yes, Christ is God's very word, but the heavens were not emptied when Christ came. I.e. biblical preaching does not presume to give complete and final answers; the preacher's mind is still a finite mind. There are no "objective certainties" in Christian faith; there is a much more wonderful gift, viz. final certitudes prompting a final venture of faith: "I know whom I have believed and I am sure that he is able to guard until that Day what has been entrusted to me" (II Tim. 1:12). Real knowing is not a knowing of dogmas, but a knowing of God through Christ. Biblical preaching does not coercively tell people what to believe, but persuasively shows them whom they already believe and whom they may know "unto salvation."

It must be added that biblical preaching *cannot be merely the "individual gospel."* When is the Bible merely "individual" in its approach? In the OT it is in the best sense a national faith and is constantly exercised about God's will for other nations. In the NT its concern is for the beloved community of the church as it confronts the world which "God so loved." A man's life is never merely individual, but a paradox of individual-social. A man is not a "soul" to be saved, but a body-psyche, so that his body— and the daily work of his hands—is precious in the sight of God. We see in Russia and Germany in the near past the failure of the church to protest giant wrongs, with resultant tragedy, but we deny the right of the church to make the proper protest in America. When was Jesus concerned only for the individual? He addressed his nation, and he defied rulers.

Yet biblical preaching *is* individual, because only the individual can view his own life, and therefore only the individual can speak the prophetic word. So biblical preaching focuses on the individual to confront man's life in its whole paradox and in its world concern.

In short, biblical preaching stands on the borderline between the Bible and the present world. It uses the idiom of the world—how else could the world hear?—yet never forgets the language of the Book. Nay, it alternates in its proclamation between present-world idiom and Bible-world idiom, so that the world knows that the Bible is more sharply contemporaneous than any newspaper. It addresses man's lostness and insecurity, but never allows that these are ultimate issues, for the ultimate question in the midst of our clutter of proximate questions is God's dealings with us in the mystery of our life in the "scandalous" clarity of Christ. Biblical preaching does not try to "fit" the needs of modern man, much less to give him "peace of mind," for the gospel does not fit our culture; it confronts it in love with the proffer of eternal life.

V. "Finally, Brethren"

There has been little discussion here of the various types of sermons. That consideration would have gone far beyond the bounds of a topic already too vast. Suffice it to say that doctrinal preaching is included under the word "biblical," for the gospel proclaims the true nature of both God and man. "Life-situation" preaching is also gathered in, for the gospel is addressed to our life in its total situation—though we should add that pulpit psychology, even if it has skill to heal the mind, may easily forget that the mind thus healed must still make the ultimate decision in ultimate concern. Topical preaching is likewise granted passport, but only if its topics are related to the final assurance of the gospel, and only if they are at home in the biblical witness—otherwise they are only the preacher's notions and may belong in the trivia displayed on the department store counter labeled "notions." The Holy Spirit is made known in his energies through the word-events of the Bible, and through the Word-Event. Every type of preaching is under challenge: "Is it biblical, and does it proclaim in man's helplessness and sin the eternal grace of God in Christ?"

This article has not dealt with the need for biblical teaching, or for biblical and sacramental worship, for these issues also are "out of bounds" of our assigned topic. But the study of the Bible by groups such as those in the new "house churches" (with the proper questions asked: "What does this mean? What does it mean to me? What does it mean to the culture in which I live?") is perhaps the only way in which the preacher can be rescued from an outright wilderness. As for biblical worship, how else shall the "household of faith" know the Book (which is the very stuff of worship) or understand the proclamation of the Word? The church needs renewal, for in many a place it is hardly distinguishable from the world, and is herself unaware of that guilty sameness. Perhaps the church must now "wait," in the biblical sense of that tremendous word, until she is made new in the biblical faith.

Preaching is essential in that quickening, for the good news is still unknown without the teller of the news. "Jesus came . . . preaching the good news of God." (Mark 1:14). It is the preacher's terrible joy to follow in his steps, proclaiming the kingdom which has so already come that all man's kingdoms fall on chaos without him, the kingdom which now is and which shall be "world without end." The preacher is not asked to "succeed"—"success" is a dubious word. Did Christ "succeed" in his preaching? Yes, but only by way of the Cross. Maybe preaching is always cruciform. In any event the preacher is asked only to be a faithful herald. Then he can say: "That I may know him and the power of his resurrection, and may share his sufferings" (Phil. 3:10). Thus the preacher may in God's providence bring resurrection to our dying age.

For Further Study. Paul Scherer, *The Word God Sent*, 1964. Kee and Young, *Understanding the NT*, 2nd ed., 1965. B. W. Anderson, *Understanding the OT*, 2nd ed., 1966. Dwight Stevenson, *In the Biblical Preacher's Workshop*, 1967.

TEACHING THE BIBLE TO CHILDREN
FRANCES EASTMAN

I. INTRODUCTION

Ever since the closing decades of the 19th cent. words like the title phrase of this article have conjured up in the minds of the general public pictures of telling Bible stories to boys and girls of all ages, at home or at church, and exhorting them to memorize Bible vss. In the popular mind these activities constituted the heart of both teaching and knowing the Bible.

Past Assumptions and Practice. To those persons more immediately engaged in Christian education more carefully structured goals and more varied methods were employed in introducing children to the Bible. Yet through the years, whatever the specific approach, a similar assumption undergirded much of the use of the Bible with children. This was an assumption that teaching means to transmit certain prescribed knowledge or information *about* something and that learning means to take such knowledge or information into our *minds* for retention, recall, and possible action on it, either now or in the future.

In terms of teaching the Bible to children this assumption meant making boys and girls familiar with Bible stories and a variety of Bible passages. Stories from the early OT and the gospels were great favorites; selected psalms and teachings from both testaments were widely chosen. A child was considered to know the Bible when he could recite biblical materials from memory or retell the substance of the biblical narratives. Familiarity with the *words* of the Bible, it was frequently taken for granted, would insure proper behavior, or would provide precepts and rules for determining one's conduct, or would be valuable for recall in time of future need. The 10 Commandments and Jesus' teachings were lodestars of the first magnitude. The life and customs of Bible times were increasingly employed as background for teaching.

Thus knowledge of biblical content for its own sake or for its value in eliciting moral behavior was a primary factor in "teaching children *about* the Bible," as the phrase was frequently worded.

Changes and New Directions. Familiarity with biblical content will always be a goal of Christian education, including the religious education of children. Mid-20th-cent. developments in biblical scholarship and biblical interpretation and the profound shift in theological emphasis, however, have brought about significant changes in what we understand the Bible to be and what its meaning for us

is. In addition new findings in the fields of human personality development and the nature of learning (and therefore of teaching) have contributed other dimensions. All these, coupled with the insights of biblical studies and theology plus the demands of life in these times, have produced new directions in teaching the Bible to persons of all ages. Quite naturally teaching the Bible to children has been affected by these changed approaches and the new orientation.

II. THE BIBLE: AN ADULT BOOK

What the Bible Is. What we consider the Bible to be determines our stance in teaching it. Popular opinion of the past has thought of the Bible as containing "nice stories for children" and beloved devotional passages for adults. Mature biblical scholarship has always held otherwise, that the Bible is a book for adults. Both biblical research and biblical interpretation of recent years have stressed the unity of the Bible and the theology of its central message or themes. Contemporary faith, and therefore contemporary Christian education, insists strongly that the Bible is far more than a book of information, rules for living, or history—though it may contain these. Contemporary faith and scholarship insist that the Bible is more than a body of knowledge or compendium of truths—though it may also contain these.

The Bible is a book of faith. It is the scriptures of the people whom God has called to serve him and make his name known to all men. It is the account of God's dealings with men and their response to him, the account of God's mighty acts in history which reveal what God has done, is doing, and stands ready to do for men. The Bible is a channel through whose pages and words God, in the mystery of his providence, comes to men to speak his word to them, to disclose his will, and to offer salvation and redemption. The Bible is, in short, a channel of God's revelation.

Those who read the Bible must respond to this revelation, not just with their minds but with their whole being, with their lives. Their response may be to accept or to reject God's revelation, to believe or to disbelieve, or, more characteristic of human nature, to respond with a mixture of belief and disbelief. But whatever the response it is a personal response.

The Bible, therefore, is a living book. God acting

in men's lives—not just announcing ideas—stands at the heart of the events recorded in the Bible. The same God continues to stand at the heart of men's lives today. He is still calling us to trust him, to enter into faithful relationship with him. He is still summoning us to put him at the center of our lives, not at the fringes.

Why We Study the Bible. We study the Bible, then, in the hope and expectation of coming to know God and be known by him. This is quite different from studying the Bible in order to find precepts or ideals which we, of our own strength, will "live up to." We study the Bible, not alone to learn words by which we can guide ourselves, but to discover what may be disclosed through the words of God and his purposes for us. Insight and illumination may come while we are actually reading or at some other time, but such revelation comes because we have pondered thoughtfully some portion of the Bible and its meaning for us.

We study the Bible in search of a deeper relationship to God, a renewed sense of belonging to his people, a better understanding of what our faith has to say to the day's work or the decision we must make.

The Bible and Life Experience. The Bible, then, deals profoundly with our life experiences. But we must be clear that it is the God who discloses himself to us in and through the Bible who makes the Bible relevant to experience. We are not here talking about some vague "inner glow" or "uplifted feeling" which comes after reading some familiar Bible passage; this is not what is meant by experience. Nor are we referring to application of codes of external conduct as norms by which "our religion" is to be judged—the moralizing or legalisms which are so often called religious experience.

Experience here refers to our living of life, how we handle all the involvements, problems, and events that come our way. As we reflect on what we know of God through the biblical record, and at the same time look on our day-to-day life as the scene of this God's activity, we find meaning, guidance, and significance which we would not otherwise know. The Bible deals with the total range of men's experiences—from the most intimate personal ones to the vast panorama of world history and God's final victory—in the light of God working through all such experiences to accomplish his good purposes. Our day-to-day lives and our time in history belong to that range of men's experiences.

In the light of this view of the Bible how do we "teach it" to children? What is there, indeed, in the Bible for children? There are positive answers to these questions, and their substance leads us to the new orientation and changed approaches referred to earlier.

III. CHILDREN AND THE BIBLE

One fundamental principle in teaching the Bible to children is this: We seek to find out what the Bible is saying concerning God and man—i.e. what the original writers were saying—rather than seek to extract from it points we wish to uphold. This cardinal principle is true for any age, but esp. for work with children because in the past we have been prone to twist biblical materials to suit our own purposes when we were selecting them for use with children. This has been true because so comparatively few of the materials of the Bible are within the scope of children's experience.

E.g. for decades the story of Noah and the ark has been told to 3- and 4-year-olds because children like the animals—yet the narrative deals fundamentally with man's sin and God's judgment. Daniel's refusal to eat Babylonian food has been interpreted to children as an example of the value of eating good food. Jesus' visit with the elders in the temple at the age of 12 has been used as an illustration of disobedience to parents. Countless other distortions of biblical materials to provide moralisms or to support nonbiblical points could be cited. They are not examples of teaching the Bible, for they have not taught the essential meaning of the particular biblical passage. Mere use of materials from the Bible is no guarantee that the biblical message concerning God will be taught. All teachers should be well aware of this distinction.

Choosing Biblical Materials. Only a relatively small portion of the total content of the Bible is within the scope of children's comprehension or experience. Therefore passages must be chosen carefully. The child's age is a key to selection because it offers some clue to what his significant life experiences and language skills may be, and therefore to what passages may meaningfully be within his interest and comprehension.

This does not, however, mean choosing only passages that children will "fully understand." No one of any age fully understands the meaning—in terms of our relationship to God—of most biblical passages. Rightly taught, passages will have ever enlarging meaning as persons grow and their life experiences broaden. But some Bible passages are best reserved for older years because of the difficulty of their language and meaning rather than used with children whose experience and language skill is limited.

E.g. the wonder of the Nativity and Incarnation can be conveyed to 6- and 7-year-olds through the story in Luke 2:1-20 whereas the profundity of John 1:1-18 belongs to more mature years. In similar vein the OT story of Joseph can have considerable meaning for 8- and 9-year-olds, who frequently experience problems of rivalry with brothers and sisters, and who are also old enough to achieve an elementary grasp of how God can bring good out of what was meant for evil. But the true meanings of the story of Noah and the flood are probably best reserved for at least the teens, when young people, like adults, are more consciously raising questions about the meaning of judgment and God's dealing with man's sin. Children aged 10 and 11 thoroughly relish the prophet Amos, his dramatic appearances, the uncompromising nature of his message. The prophet Hosea, on the other hand, can be more adequately and appropriately understood by older teens and adults, to whom his personal experiences and message for life have greater reality than for children.

When Jesus is portrayed to children as a fully human being who came to do a unique work for God—or whatever phraseology is selected to describe his divinity to children—highlights of his entire life, from birth through resurrection, can be presented as a single narrative even to kindergartners. Without such a framework—which is of course supplied in the gospels—Jesus is reduced to another man and distortion of biblical materials results. Younger children can know that Jesus helped and healed people whom God loved but whom others neglected. Older children can ponder the mystery of details of the miracles as signs of God's activity among those whom Jesus encountered, rather than promptly assume that the miracles can't be "true" because they can't be proved scientifically today.

Age Level Selections. Curriculum and resource materials produced by denominations which use sound biblical scholarship make careful choices of biblical passages for use with children of various ages. Wise teachers and parents will follow their recommendations. The following sketch may suggest a progression in graded selections:

Age 3 (nursery): Only a very few Bible vss., mostly NT, referring to God's love and forgiveness. A few stories of Jesus, showing him both as baby and as grown man.

Age 4-5 (kindergarten): Stories of Jesus and how he came to help people and show them God. A few OT stories and passages which show a high level of love and desire to serve God.

Age 6-7: More stories of Jesus and his work, his death, why it occurred, and the fact of the Resurrection. Additional OT stories revealing how God works in people's lives. Other passages significant for Christian life and heritage, e.g. the short form of the 10 Commandments and some of Jesus' sayings.

Age 8-9: More of the structure of the Bible and a beginning understanding of how it was written. Biographical treatments of OT and NT people, showing them as human beings who struggled with faith, not as whitewashed heroes. A continuing study of Jesus. Some stories of the early leaders of the church. More basic passages, e.g. parables and some psalms, including memorization.

Age 10-11: Previous emphases continued. A clear picture of Jesus, his mission and his impact on men. Some picture of the beginning of the church and of the relationship of NT days to OT days. A beginning acquaintance with Paul and his work. Familiarity with major biblical passages from both testaments and memorization of a number of them.

These age divisions are only suggestive, not arbitrary. There will be many variations between individuals at any one age level and across age levels. Every teacher will want to help each child according to his own capacities and needs. It is exceedingly important that all children *not* be marshaled into uniformity of performance. Rather, if the Bible is to speak to each child, or God to speak through it, each must be encouraged to find his own best level in using and responding to it. Here the newer findings of learning theory and human development coalesce with theological concerns for the person's relationship to God.

Experience Can Be Biblical. It has been previously suggested that use of materials from the Bible is no guarantee that the teaching will be truly biblical, i.e. a channel for God to speak to men and men to respond to God. By the same token resource materials for teaching do not have to come from the pages of the Bible in order to be biblical in spirit. It has

already been said that God acts today in the lives of men. So it is that contemporary experiences, either children's or adult's, or experiences and events of the postbiblical past, can be objects of study and, if viewed as opportunities for God meeting man and man responding, may reveal God's purposes for us. From consideration of an extrabiblical experience a teacher can lead children to consider Bible passages which deal with the same issue or problem.

Day-to-day experiences, in the classroom or elsewhere, are particularly fruitful for use in teaching the Bible to children. E.g. a 3-year-old can understand very few words of the Bible. But when he has upset a class because of a temper tantrum and is sorry, he can feel the forgiveness of the teacher who holds him gently until he quiets down and then leads him back to his interest corner again. Such an experience is essentially biblical in quality, for—without trying to play God—this teacher is exemplifying the forgiveness of which Jesus spoke. The child has a foundation in experience of forgiveness that is valuable now and also prepares him for a more mature understanding of it. Esp. for younger children the quality of relationships existing among children and between children and teacher are important opportunities for biblically rooted teaching.

By the same token contemporary experiences of children in narrative form can be studied for what they reveal of such biblical matters as love, guilt, sin, alienation, forgiveness, mercy—even though these words may not be used by the children. E.g. 3rd- and 4th-graders found it enlightening to study a series of stories about Joey and his "mean feelings" about himself, his family, his friends, almost everybody. With Joey they found what it was to secure release through an understanding and forgiving older person. Subsequently they experienced a sense of empathy with the biblical Joseph, recalled the contemporary Joey, and were able to see how God can and does work through people.

Such use of contemporary experience is not intended to show "black and white" moralisms about conduct as the goal of teaching. Rather this use of experience aims to help children begin to look on life here and now from a biblical stance. It also aims to make Bible materials themselves seem of vital importance now because they deal with men's experiences and God, even though the Bible is written in unfamiliar terms and is set in an unfamiliar world.

Children and the Biblical World. In an age of science the biblical world poses special difficulties, esp. with children and young people who are being reared in faith in science. It is not easy to get to the heart of the biblical message in terms which will seem sensible to children.

God was viewed in the biblical world as acting directly on his creation. Even where God is acknowledged as creator today, our scientific knowledge somehow removes him from the immediacy assumed by the Bible. The biblical universe was a 3-storied structure. Our universe seems to be forever expanding. God was definitely in control of the biblical universe. Man acts as though he is in control of today's universe, and no venture seems too daring or hazardous for him to think about undertaking.

The Bible lands are a part of the world that is comparatively little known to us, even though it appears frequently in the news. Customs and ways of thinking are different from our modes of behavior and thought. Even the history of which Bible people were a part is comparatively little studied in school, and certainly not at children's levels.

These strangenesses, coupled with children's innate lack of a sense of time and space, pose real problems in teaching the Bible to children. Not until the late years of childhood do they have a developing sense that a thousand years ago is very much different from a hundred years ago or, when they are very young, from yesterday. By age 10 or 11 children do have some sense of time and an interest in that which is different or past, and the Bible world can take on considerable reality for them. But what of earlier years?

It is during the earlier years especially that teachers must be concerned to lay foundations such as described above. Without the sense that from the Bible we learn of God and that God is at work in life today too, children will tend to think of the Bible as largely a book of the past and of its events and persons as hopelessly long ago and far away. Without this sense they will be slow to recognize themselves as heirs and spiritual descendants of the people of God in the Bible. God as the center of the world of the Bible and the world of today must be the focal point of teaching the Bible to even the youngest child.

It is of course highly desirable to explain Bible customs to children. Younger boys and girls enjoy the fun of making Palestinian houses, wearing Palestinian costumes, creating Palestinian home scenes. Older children can take an interest in archaeological discoveries, compare past and present Near Eastern settings, dramatize customs. These are important teaching activities, but only because they are contributory to making clear the meaning of biblical events and passages. They are a means of clearing away some of the underbrush which obscures the real world of the Bible, as it were. They help to clarify obscurities or confusions, but they are not the essence of teaching the Bible.

IV. THE TEACHER AND TEACHING

Both Learner and Teacher. Any person who would teach the Bible to children must himself be one who is studying the Bible as a learner. Only the person whose life is open to God's further speaking and leading can effectively help children explore the Bible as a channel through which God may speak to them. The good teacher does not have to know all the answers—but he must know some and be seriously engaged in seeking to find more. He must be interested enough in studying the Bible for himself that he will be able to look for what he does not know.

E.g. a mother who had never gone to Sunday school as a child herself was called on to teach a class of 5th-graders. Only a year previously she had joined a church discussion club with her husband and had been spurred into study of what she believed when she could not tell a sectarian evangelist who called at her door why she did not agree with his tracts. This woman began her church school teaching by entering on some earnest Bible study of her own. She used the Bible passages suggested in the class's course of study as springboards for more

extensive study of her own. The total experience became an exhilarating one for her, and a rewarding one for both teacher and pupils.

In this case the children sensed that their teacher took the Bible seriously. They sensed that she took God seriously. The teacher's own attitude communicated itself to the pupils and spoke far more effectively than a dozen lectures on the importance of the Bible.

To say that the teacher need not know all the answers, however, is not to say that he need not know much of anything. The teacher must know far more of the Bible and Bible backgrounds than he can ever use in a class session. He must teach out of the fullness of his knowledge rather than on the basis of barely filling in the time. Most good resource materials provide special background enrichment in Bible study which the teacher will never plan to use in class; but this background provides the extra understanding, the additional information, the special interpretation which may be the answer to some child's special query or need. This fullness of knowledge is the extra margin on which the teacher who is genuinely a learner in the area of the Bible relies.

Not only must the teacher be a learner and one who has "spare knowledge"; he must also be one who ponders the meaning for his pupils of what he is studying at his own level. He may not plan to use what he has been learning of Jeremiah's suffering, but there may come an unexpected protest from justice-minded 11-year-olds who resent mistreatment of leaders in a civil rights demonstration. The teacher who has thought about Jeremiah may then be able to help children face up to the realities of what can be involved in being faithful to a cause and to God's will. At the same time he may be able to point them toward the kind of strength and ultimately the joy that comes with faithfulness. Children may not be able to comprehend all these meanings, but they will be able to sense the quality of life that is involved. They themselves will have been helped to think more deeply about the meaning of life, even as they may also be acquiring certain information and answers.

If the Bible is to be anything more than a book of information and stories to children, it must be taught to them by teachers who take joy in being students of the Bible themselves.

The Art of Teaching. It has already been suggested that basic foundations of teaching the Bible to children are (a) the teacher's own devotion to Bible study and (b) the exemplification in the teacher's relationships with pupils of God's love and concern with which the Bible deals.

On these foundations the teacher may then build his skills in working with whatever age his pupils are. Specific methods of teaching are numerous, and their precise form varies with the age of the child: storytelling, conversation, drawing and painting, play (for younger children), role playing, creative dramatization, construction of various kinds, writing, singing, reading, memorizing, etc. Almost any sound teaching method may be useful in teaching the Bible, provided the goals for use of the Bible are sound. Most curriculum and resource materials give adequate guidance in the use of specific methods.

Children below the 3rd grade usually cannot read well enough to be able to read from the Bible itself.

Therefore teachers will probably tell stories or pupils will read story versions from their own readers. Some Bible vss. may be read from charts or reading books or learned from memory by repeated use. The Bible itself should be used or referred to frequently by teachers so that children, especially preschoolers, will become familiar with its appearance.

After children are able to read from the Bible they should be encouraged to do so. Selections chosen should be within their reading comprehension. Many a child has been discouraged from reading the Bible by being told to start with Gen. 1:1 and read straight through. Interest soon lags in the face of difficult selections and even more difficult meanings. Children should have their own Bibles, with type large enough that it is easy to read, preferably in an edition designed for children. The teacher, however, should not employ "round robin" reading of Bibles in class situations. This is a tedious procedure. Rather one pupil should read a passage, or all pupils should be asked to read a given portion silently; then discussion may follow. Guidance on what to look for in reading a passage should also be given, so that the child reads purposefully, enjoying the experience.

Children enjoy memorizing and should be encouraged to do so. The teacher should not take advantage of their facility in memorizing, however, by making quantity of vss. learned or winning a reward the motive for memorization. Portions of the Bible chosen for memorization should be included in regular study. Memorizing through familiarity or frequent use is a better method than by rote. Most curriculum materials point out which passages are to be memorized so that over a period of several years a number of basic biblical passages will be learned in meaningful fashion.

Worship and the Bible. Worship is not a method of teaching, but there is a genuine place for use of the Bible in children's worship.

Portions of the Bible studied in class are particularly meaningful when used in worship. Vss. from a psalm may be used as a call to worship or a prayer. A story may be recalled. An appropriate memory passage may be recited as a scripture reading. Whatever the selection employed, it should contribute to worship and not be introduced as one more means of teaching.

The devotional use of the Bible should also be encouraged, particularly with older children.

For Further Study. Suzanne de Dietrich, *The Witnessing Community,* 1958; a study guide on the people of God as a witnessing community. *Bible Readings for Boys and Girls,* ill. Lynd Ward, 1959; selections from the RSV chosen to introduce junior age children and older to a direct and somewhat consecutive reading of the Bible, with references to point readers to the full passages. Iris V. Cully, *Children in the Church,* 1960; a general treatment which has a sound theological annotation to its understanding of teaching children.

TEACHING
THE BIBLE TO YOUTH AND ADULTS

FRANCIS E. KEARNS

Doing God's work in the world is the mission of the church. Among the several ministries which the church must undertake if it is to fulfill this mission the most significant are worship, preaching, witnessing, serving, and teaching. It is with the teaching ministry that we are concerned here. In his final commission to his disciples Jesus said: "Go therefore and make disciples of all nations, . . . teaching them to observe all that I have commanded you" (Matt. 28:19-20).

The church teaches through its total life. The ideas, attitudes, and patterns of behavior which prevail in the lives of the members of the congregation may either further or thwart the purpose of Christian teaching. The church also teaches through the home, where the genuineness of the parents' commitment registers in the lives of the family members. The ministry of teaching is the responsibility of the entire church and to be effective needs to be planned in the light of the total mission of the church.

I. CALLED TO TEACH

There can be no higher honor than to be called to be a participant in the teaching ministry of the church. In the true sense it is not a responsibility which we undertake because we feel that we ought to do it or because there is no one else to do it. Rather it is a commitment which we make in response to what God has done for us.

Our participation in the ministries of the church is in response to the command of Christ: "You shall be my witnesses in Jerusalem and in all Judea and Samaria and to the end of the earth" (Acts 1:8b). We are called to be teachers. Through a grateful and devoted response to this call we become partners with Christ in inspiring and helping others to grow toward Christian maturity.

As we respond to the call to teach the Christian faith, we are following in the footsteps of the Master Teacher. Jesus was known to his contemporaries as a teacher. The gospels record "Teacher," sometimes translated "Master," as the title by which he was usually addressed. Whether Jesus was teaching or preaching, he was always open to questions from his hearers and in turn propounded questions which motivated them to think and to make decisions. In his approach he always insisted that the vital questions of daily life should be honestly and helpfully discussed.

Inspired by Jesus' example, the church has been engaged in the task of teaching through the cents. As soon as the primitive church was born the apostles became teachers; we are told that the new converts "devoted themselves to the apostles' teaching and fellowship" (Acts 2:42a). During the Middle Ages schools grew up in the cathedrals and monasteries. With the coming of the Reformation new catechisms were written and classes were held to instruct prospective church members in the tenets of their faith. The first Sunday School was started by Robert Raikes in 1780. The church saw great possibilities in this movement and continued to expand its areas of participation to include weekday classes, vacation church schools, and week-night adult study groups.

II. THE TASK OF TEACHING

The relevance of the Bible to daily life makes teaching it an exciting adventure. Our teaching of the Bible is dynamic and meaningful as it guides persons into an understanding of God's approach to man and man's response to God and into the commitment of their lives to God as he has disclosed himself in Jesus Christ. As our teaching reveals the creative and redemptive activity of God in the history of the Hebrew people and in the story of Christ and the early Christian community, it makes the Bible live and shows its relevance to similar situations which we confront today.

Our task as teachers in the church has to do with people and our effectiveness as teachers will depend on our knowledge of who people are and why they act as they do. It is here that the findings of the sciences such as psychology, sociology, and anthropology are helpful. There are many factors, both conscious and unconscious, which enter into the development of a person. Therefore it is important in Christian teaching to remember that the individual reacts as a whole person, including the physical, mental, emotional, and spiritual. As teachers of the Bible we must seek to bring to the learners the resources of Christian truth so that they will understand what God is doing with them in the whole of their experience.

Learning involves change. This means not only the change that comes from the accumulation of knowledge, but also changes in attitude and behavior, changes in ways of believing, thinking, acting, doing, responding. God does not change, but as we come to an understanding of him through his disclosure of himself in the Bible, esp. in Jesus Christ, and respond in faith and love, we are changed. Our aim is that those who participate in the teaching-learning process will change in the direction of Christlikeness.

The learner should be encouraged to search behind the words of the Bible to discover what God is saying to him. In this way the impact of the Bible is immediate and personal. One of the most effective methods of teaching is to engage the learner in a dialogue with the Bible. In his study he should be encouraged to ask such questions as: Is what the Bible says really true? What does the Bible say to me about my relationship with God? What does it say to me about the way I am to live with other persons? What changes will I need to make in my motives and actions if I try to live this biblical truth in my life? There is no substitute for personal encounter with God as disclosed in the Bible to show the relevance of the Bible to daily living.

III. Qualifications for Teaching

Effective teaching begins with the teacher. This is esp. true in teaching the Bible. Certain qualifications are necessary if a person would be an effective leader of those who are seeking to understand the Bible and discover its meaning for their lives.

Since the primary responsibility of the teacher is to help persons learn, he should understand the learner—his interests, the motives operative in his decisions, his needs, the environment in which he lives. A knowledge of how persons grow is also an invaluable asset for one who is striving to relate the insights of the Bible to the development of personality.

A teacher needs a competent knowledge of the Bible combined with the ability to use creatively the basic knowledge which he has. This does not mean that he must be a specialist or that he will have all the answers. Honesty in acknowledging that he is not familiar with certain information requested can be a wholesome experience. Resources are available, however, and when additional facts or interpretations are needed in the teaching-learning situation, the teacher should be able to refer to sources where such information can be found.

Creative teaching moves in the direction of helping the members of the group to accept responsibility for their own learning. Teacher and class members alike are involved in the learning process. A knowledge of how learning takes place and how persons interact with each other is very important. For this reason a teacher should be flexible, open to the opinions of others. He should respect the judgments of the class members and always encourage them to participate and give free expression of their ideas. Whatever the idea expressed, he should be "shock-proof." In such a climate the learners will feel free to express their thoughts and feelings and to experiment with new ways of thinking and doing. The role of the teacher is not to furnish all the answers but to stimulate independent thought and action, to encourage persons to explore and discover for themselves.

An important qualification, which is not a substitute for the others already mentioned but in a true sense the crown of them all, is the personality and total life of the teacher who bears witness to God's word as disclosed in the Bible. Personal witness is a potent force in the learning situation. Thus the creative teacher of the Bible will be a person who is wholeheartedly committed to God and who practices spiritual discipline in living and study. His witness will be persuasive, not just because of what he says, but because of what he is.

IV. The Focus of Teaching

Our aim in teaching the Bible is not just to impart information but to help young people and adults to become witnessing disciples to their faith in all the relationships of their lives. With this as our aim what should be at the center of our attention, determining our purpose and methods? Let us look briefly at various approaches which are made in teaching the Bible.

Content-centered. In this approach the focus of attention is on the quantity of the Bible's content which can be transmitted to the minds of the persons being taught. Effective teaching is often judged by the ability to repeat many vss., to find passages quickly, to tell stories and answer questions about the books or personalities. The weakness of this approach has been the assumption that a person who knows the content of the Bible has all he needs for being a Christian. The method of stressing Bible content has frequently been too mechanical and consequently has failed to produce results in day-by-day living.

This does not mean that knowledge of Bible content is unimportant. Great passages stored in the memory may serve as a rich treasure house from which to draw in daily living—for strength, for guidance, for comfort, for courage. However, ideas encountered in the Bible will be effective in the shaping of attitudes and the making of decisions only if they are taught with "purposeful awareness" of the life situations being confronted by the learner.

Life-centered. When the weakness of the content-centered approach became evident, the emphasis of teaching changed from Bible content to the pupil as the center. "Learning to live by living" became the watchword, and the central concern was shifted from "things learned" to "character achieved." The life of the learner, including his felt needs and interests, was the determining principle. There was a concentration on character education to the neglect of the deep biblical foundations necessary to undergird it.

The distinct task of Christian education is to help persons grow in Christian faith and life. This makes Christian education different from all other education. Theological foundations are significant. Christian teaching is concerned with the meaning and purpose of life as disclosed in the Bible, esp. in the person and work of Jesus Christ. Such teaching must be done within the framework of life situations where motives are operative, decisions are being made, growth is taking place.

Church-centered. The church is a community of believers. It is a living organism in which Christ lives and through which he acts. The church is the extension of Jesus' spirit, Jesus' life, and Jesus' work in the world. The aim of the church is to introduce persons into the life and mission of the community of the Christian faith and to help them to become responsible participants.

Christian teaching is the work of the Christian community—not of one segment of the community but of the whole community. Nearly all Christian teaching is planned and promoted by organized churches. This is true even when the teaching is done in the homes. The church is a meaningful community and is the natural environment for Christian nurture.

The danger in the church-centered approach is that the deeper meaning of the church may be lost sight of and the institution itself become the focus. It is easy for the church to center its attention on its own life rather than lose itself in its ministry of witnessing and serving, in the fulfillment of the will and purpose of God for his world.

God-centered. None of the above approaches are mutually exclusive. Each has a contribution to make in the teaching of the Bible to young people and adults. However, if our aim is to help persons become aware of and grow in their understanding of God and to respond in faith and love, then the center on which we focus will be God as he has revealed himself in Jesus Christ. The Bible is an account of the mighty acts of God with men in creating and sustaining the community of faith of which we are a part.

The teacher will first of all seek to relate his own life to God in a glad, obedient faith. Then he will strive to bring those for whom he is responsible into the experience of commitment to and fellowship with the God who forgives, transforms, commands, strengthens, and judges. Out of such a living relationship with God is born the desire to witness and the concern to serve. Our human relations never can be made right apart from God. Amid all the tangled complexities of modern life Christian teaching strives to bring guidance so that the insights of the Bible, the mind and spirit of Christ, will be brought to bear on them.

There will always be a place for content in the creative teaching of the Bible. All effective teaching will be done within the framework of life situations and life experiences. The church as the community of believers is responsible for Christian nurture. But central to all of these approaches is teaching our Christian faith in God.

V. Age Levels in Teaching

In group study of the Bible an attempt is made to relate its message to the persistent lifelong concerns of persons—e.g. interpersonal relations, self-image, sense of destiny, sex, security, power, authority, trust, love, forgiveness, reconciliation. These concerns are present on all age levels. For this reason the educational process should be seen as a whole embracing the life span from birth to death. It must always be recognized, however, that what is being taught must be graded to the learner's level of readiness for appropriation. Our concern here is with youth and adults.

Junior Highs. These young people are searching to discover themselves and to relate creatively to an enlarging world and to their growing faith. Central to their search is the question Who am I? The teacher should strive to understand and interpret physiological growth and its bearing on social and religious development. Areas of interest at this age level would include: God and our relationship to him, a Christian understanding of oneself as a free and responsible person, what the church is and does, the meaning of commitment which leads to discipleship, meaningful participation in the life and ministries of the church, achieving Christian maturity, accepting Christian responsibility.

Senior Highs. Young people in the middle teens have their own needs as they face their enlarging experience. They are becoming acquainted with the wide world of history, science, and public affairs. At this age there is an interest in broadening friendships, esp. in relation to the opposite sex. They are beginning to see before them the years of adult responsibility. Personality conflicts as a result of the growing-up experience are numerous. In the process of maturing the adolescent must break ties which hold him too close to parents or teachers. He is seeking to find a balance between authority and freedom, and in so doing he sometimes becomes defiant to all discipline and clamors for full adult privileges. This is an age of deep perplexity and disturbance.

Teaching the Bible to teenagers requires a great deal of patience and understanding. What the young people need is a counselor and friend. Underneath all the outward demonstrations of rebellion and frivolity there is a desire to discover the meaning of life at a deeper dimension. In making the Bible attractive to young people the teacher will appeal to their depth of yearning for God, their capacity for heroic courage, and their response to the call for sacrifice.

College Age. The teacher working with persons who have finished high school and are entering on adulthood discovers that their study of the Bible must be based on interests and needs. They are capable of a more mature type of Bible study since their reflective capacities are coming to fuller development. Hence they are more philosophical and capable of more sustained interest in content studies and cultural pursuits.

The teacher who would deal effectively with persons of this age must first make an honest effort to understand them. Their interests include: preparation for life work either through study in a college or university or through beginning the first serious fulltime job, economic independence, independence from parents, marriage, the assumption of civic and social responsibilities. The role of the teacher is to be a mature and responsible friend to members of the group and to provide helpful counsel. He will encourage the group members to develop their own leadership skills. The teacher's responsibility becomes that of a resource leader. His use of the Bible will be to show how it provides a framework of reference that can add perspective to their thinking and moral purpose to their decisions.

Adults. The teacher of an adult group should look on himself as a counselor and resource person. The more he can stimulate the class members to participate and to develop their own skills, the more effective he will be as a leader. A knowledge of group techniques to encourage participation is an invaluable asset. The class members will show greater interest if they are given the opportunity to share in the choice of the areas to be studied—e.g. the nature of

God as Creator, Redeemer, life-giving Spirit; the new man in Christ; the kingdom of God; Christian ethics and social relations; the vocation of the Christian; Christian family living; the stewardship of life and work; the nature and mission of the church; the history and use of the Bible.

VI. Procedures for Teaching

Methods are helpful when looked on as means for the achieving of an end. They are never ends in themselves. Variety in methods of teaching is necessary to stimulate persons to explore new ideas and to reach out for new experiences. Let us look briefly at some of the methods which may be used effectively in teaching the Bible.

Storytelling. Jesus' consuming desire to help people in their struggle for abundant living prompted him to begin with basic foundations in their thought and experience. Hence he told parables which had to do with the ordinary routine of daily living. The strength of a Bible story lies in its capacity to identify the listeners with biblical ideas and with the characters which are portrayed. Thus religious truth can readily be translated into contemporary life.

Audio-visual Materials. Pictures, maps, and diagrams when used as background materials help to stimulate questions and to encourage conversation. Motion pictures, filmstrips, and tape recordings can be used effectively to motivate and guide group discussion.

Drama. In creative drama the participants translate a particular biblical event into their conception of what occurred and how the people involved reacted. There is a personal identification with the characters involved and the causes served. Extra benefits come when the participants are encouraged to select their own themes, make up their own dialogue, and interpret the characters.

Role Playing. In this informal type of drama the participants extemporaneously assume roles in a prescribed situation and try to react as the persons involved would react. Thereby they gain insight into how others feel and think. This is a splendid method for identifying with biblical characters and seeing them as real people. Such a procedure is stimulating both to the participants and to those who are observing. It should be followed by a group discussion.

Forum. A speaker presents his findings on a particular subject. This is followed by a question-and-answer period in which all the group members are encouraged to participate. A brief summary should be presented at the close.

Symposium. Several speakers present prepared statements on various phases of a given theme. Their presentation is followed by group participation in which the members address questions to particular speakers and offer general comments.

Seminar. A broad topic or problem is broken down into smaller themes, which are assigned to individuals for research. The results of the research are presented to the entire group for their questions and additional suggestions. This method is esp. effective in applying biblical principles to social concerns— e.g. racial integration, crime and delinquency, war and peace, alcoholism, labor-management relations.

Debate. This is a more formal type of presentation.

The debaters take sides on some significant issue. After careful preparation each presents his case to the group. Significant insights are brought to light which are helpful to all in clarifying the areas of agreement and disagreement.

Discussion. The members of a group under the leadership of one of their own number discuss an issue that is of interest and significance to all. There is wholesome exchange of ideas and feelings, with a demand on the reasoning powers of the participants. The leader should encourage all persons to express their views and should keep the comments focused on the objective.

Panel Discussion. Two or more persons discuss an issue and share their ideas before the group. Afterward the members of the group are invited to ask questions and make further comments. This method is esp. helpful in dealing with controversial issues. It is democratic in procedure and helps the members of the group to see that people may be sincere and still have opposite views.

Conversation. Two or more persons may be invited to engage in conversation on a particular theme. After they exchange their ideas, attitudes, and feelings, other members of the group are invited to share their reactions. This is a useful method to open up areas of new information or to clarify ideas, and helps to unify the group into a fellowship. The teacher must seek to guide the conversation toward the desired objective.

Buzz Groups. After announcement of a topic the group is broken up into smaller groups of 6 to 8 persons, each of which chooses a leader and a reporter and then engages in discussion. The topic should be relevant to the interests of the entire group, and everyone should be encouraged to take part in discussing it within his buzz group. Each reporter takes careful notes and summarizes for the larger group the ideas developed in his buzz group. The value in this procedure comes from every member's having an opportunity to contribute toward the insights discovered.

Huddle Groups. The group is divided into discussion units of 10 or 12 under leaders who have been assigned topics for preparation in advance. Each huddle group takes one phase of the total theme. The findings are shared with the entire group and a general discussion follows.

Good teaching calls for a variety of methods to broaden the appeal to more individuals and to enrich the Christian experience of all. The end is to guide and inspire the individual so that God's revelation may become meaningful to him.

VII. Resources for Teaching

Many resources are available to aid in teaching the Bible.

Versions. Translation of the Bible into the language of the people has been a continuing challenge to biblical scholars. The KJV (1611) has been a favorite in the English-speaking world because of its simplicity, directness, and beauty of English style. Its revision in the ASV (1901) was used widely until the appearance of the RSV (NT 1946, OT 1952, Apoc. 1957). In translating the Bible there is room for freedom of expression to make the language more familiar and meaningful to the reader. Hence the British churches sponsored an independent translation rather than a revision, and as a result the NEB (NT 1961) has created great interest throughout the church because of its use of colloquial language. Among the translations by individual scholars some that have proved esp. helpful in communicating the biblical message are: *The NT in Modern Speech* by R. F. Weymouth (1903), *The Bible: A New Translation* by James Moffatt (NT 1913, OT 1924), *The Complete Bible: An American Translation* by E. J. Goodspeed and J. M. P. Smith (NT 1923, OT 1927, Apoc. 1938), *The NT in Modern English* by J. B. Phillips (1947-58). See also "The Bible in English," pp. 1237-42).

Synopses and Harmonies. A synopsis of the gospels contains the Synoptic gospels, i.e. Matt., Mark, Luke, arranged in columns with the parallel passages side by side. In this arrangement materials common to 2 or to all 3 can be readily distinguished, as well as those which are unique in each gospel. In a harmony the parallel columns are arranged with the aim of presenting a continuous narrative and may include all 4 gospels. A harmony offers the opportunity to compare the same events or teachings as they appear in the several gospels. Thus it is possible to follow the changes resulting from the transmission and to observe the individual interests of the several authors.

Commentaries. Interpretations of the biblical text are perhaps the oldest of basic tools devised for the study of the Bible. Among the Jewish writings there are interpretative treatments of the tradition. In the gospels the authors often attempt to interpret the material which they are editing (cf. e.g. Luke 18:1). The church fathers had a keen interest in biblical interpretation, which has continued to the present day.

Interpretation of the biblical text involves both "exegesis," i.e. analysis of the meaning, and "exposition," i.e. elaboration of the thought by comparison and application. Every commentary contains both these elements, usually in combination, but some emphasize one more than the other. In addition most commentaries contain intros. to the biblical books, giving information about such matters as authorship, date, and circumstances of their writing. Many separate intros. to the Bible and its books are also available.

Concordances. A biblical concordance lists in alphabetical order the words, including names, used in a version of the Bible and indicates under each all the vss. where it appears. In the large editions a part of the context is quoted for each occurrence. Concordances are available for the RSV and the Moffatt translation, as well as in a number of older editions for the KJV. Some editions of the Bible include an abridged concordance, limited to important words and references, along with other helps in an appendix. A concordance is most often used to locate a partly remembered vs. but is even more valuable in finding new passages that bear on a particular line of study. E.g. by arranging all the references to a certain term in chronological order one can trace the changes in its meaning and the development of thought thus revealed.

Dictionaries. A biblical dictionary defines terms as they are used in the Bible and also identifies the persons and places named in the text. The larger dictionaries are actually encyclopedias, containing comprehensive articles about important topics, including some terms not specifically mentioned in the Bible but relevant to its interpretation. Such a dictionary is valuable not only for clarifying the meaning of unfamiliar terms but also for securing a concise summary of all the information from both biblical and extrabiblical sources that scholars have been able to assemble about a given topic.

Atlases. The maps and pictures provided in a biblical atlas serve as a valuable tool in Bible study and teaching. This is esp. true today when young people in school receive part of their instruction through audio-visual materials and when television is looked on as a necessity in so many of our homes. It is interesting to locate a biblical event on a map, but more important to understand the geographical factors which contributed to the experiences described in the biblical record. Properly used as supplemental material, maps and other geographical resources help interpret biblical information in terms of actual situations and human relationships.

Archaeological Reports. Biblical archaeology has made rapid strides in recent years (see "Archaeology," pp. 1054-62) and has greatly aided and enriched our understanding of the Bible message. Evidence concerning the customs of the people in biblical times and the situations in which they lived enables us to picture them as real persons akin to us in their struggles and conflicts. Archaeology has rendered a service to our appreciation of the Bible through its confirmation of the accuracy of the record at many points. Fortunately the teacher does not need to be a specialist in order to share the benefits of archaeological findings. There are many books which point up their significance for Bible study and interpretation.

In using the many resources which are available for the study and teaching of the Bible we must always remember that they are not ends in themselves. Such tools should not become a substitute for the Bible itself. Rather their use should stimulate deeper study of the biblical text and broader application of its insights to Christian living today.

The central concern in teaching the Bible to young people and adults is to help persons to become aware of and grow in their understanding of God, esp. as he has disclosed himself in Jesus Christ, so that they will make the total commitment of their lives to him and will strive to fulfill his will and purpose for them in the world. This is a growing experience in which we are constantly committing our lives to God at a deeper dimension as we increase our understanding of him. The goal ever beckoning us onward is that we may attain "to mature manhood, to the measure of the stature of the fulness of Christ" (Eph. 4:13).

For Further Study: J. D. Smart, *The Teaching Ministry of the Church*, 1954. D. C. Wyckoff, *The Task of Christian Education*, 1955. E. F. Zeigler, *Christian Education of Adults*, 1958. R. E. Koenig, *The Use of the Bible with Adults*, 1959. C. M. Laymon, *The Use of the Bible in Teaching Youth*, 1962. L. C. Little, *Wider Horizons in Christian Adult Education*, 1962. Bruce Reinhart, *The Institutional Nature of Adult Christian Education*, 1962. R. R. Boehlke, *Theories of Learning in Christian Education*, 1963. L. H. DeWolf, *Teaching Our Faith in God*, 1963.

CHRONOLOGY

MEASURES and MONEY

INDEX of SCRIPTURE REFERENCES

MAPS

INDEX of SUBJECTS

CHRONOLOGY

Gordon B. Duncan

The accompanying table includes both precise dates—some quite certain and others less provable which may be a year or 2 off—and round numbers, indicated by italic type, which indicate general periods or approximations. To this italic class must belong most of the dates included for the biblical and other books. For further information about these see the respective Intros. and the articles "The Compiling of Israel's Story," "The Interestamental Literature," and "Noncanonical Early Christian Writings." Explanations of some of the other dates follow.

CHRONOLOGICAL TABLE

Dates in italics represent periods rather than exact years. Names of persons mentioned in the Bible are printed in boldface type at their first appearance.

B.C. *The Background of the Patriarchs*

8000 Stone Age inhabitants of Palestine leave evidences of village life and agriculture.

5500 Pottery invented.

4500 Use of metals begins with gold and copper.

3500 Sumerians settle in S Mesopotamia and develop complex civilization, including pictographic writing.

3300 Bronze is discovered as harder metal for tools and weapons.

3200 Sumerians adapt pictographs to cuneiform system of punching syllabic characters into clay tablets.

3000 Egyptians become united under first dynasty and develop advanced civilization. They adapt pictographs to hieroglyphic writing, invent papyrus.

2300 Sargon, a Semite, conquers Sumer and builds vast Akkadian empire. His people learn Sumerian arts and culture.

2000 Ur-Nammu, Sumerian king of Ur, gains control of all Sumer and Akkad, issues earliest known code of laws.

1900 **Abraham** migrates to S Palestine. Sodom and Gomorrah destroyed.

1750 Hyksos invaders seize control of Palestine and Egypt. Hammurabi, Semitic ruler of first Babylonian Empire, issues elaborate law code. Kings of Mari preserve archive of cuneiform tablets which reveal customs like some in Gen. stories and mention Habiru (Hebrews?) and Benjaminites.

1650 Alphabet invented, probably by Canaanites.

1570 Ahmose I of Egypt expels Hyksos, destroying many Palestinian cities.

1468 Thutmose III of Egypt reconquers Palestine, establishes empire soon reaching the Euphrates.

1400 At Nuzi, Hurrians (Horites) leave cuneiform tablets revealing customs like some in Gen. stories and mentioning Habiru. At Ugarit (Ras Shamra) in N Syria, Canaanites leave tablets, esp. of Baal myths, in a language much like Hebrew.

1360 Palestinian vassals ask Pharaoh Akhenaton, in cuneiform letters preserved at his capital, Akhetaton (Tell el-Amarna), for protection against Habiru, apparently Hebrew tribes entering Palestine, possibly with **Jacob** as a leader. Perhaps it is under Akhenaton that **Joseph** holds office and some Hebrew tribes settle in Egypt.

The Exodus and Settlement in Palestine

1302 Seti I accedes in Egypt, revives empire in Palestine, and undertakes to drive Hittites from Syria.

1290 Ramses II succeeds Seti, continues his father's military campaigns in Syria-Palestine, begins extensive building projects in Delta region with enforced labor that includes Apiru, i.e. Habiru or Hebrews.

1250 **Moses** leads exodus of Hebrews from Egypt.

1225 Hebrew tribes under **Joshua** destroy a number of major Canaanite cities.

1220 Merneptah, Ramses' son and successor, erects victory stele naming Israel among peoples defeated in Palestine.

1200	Iron comes into use.	*850*	**Elisha** succeeds Elijah as influential prophet of Yahwism in Israel. King **Mesha** of Moab erects stele to commemorate his winning independence from Israel.
1188	Invasion of Egypt by Sea Peoples is turned back. Part of them, the Philistines, settle on the S Palestinian coast.		
1120	N Israelite tribes join in defeating **Sisera.**	848	Jehoshaphat dies; Jehoram (Joram) sole ruler in Judah.
1100	**Abimelech** destroys Shechem.	841	**Ahaziah** succeeds Jehoram in Judah. He and Jehoram of Israel are killed in revolt of **Jehu.** Assyrian obelisk shows Jehu as king of Israel paying tribute to Shalmaneser III. **Athaliah** seizes rule in Judah.
1075	Gibeah destroyed in intertribal war against Benjamin.		
1050	Philistines destroy temple at Shiloh, also other Israelite and Canaanite cities.		
		835	Athaliah killed; **Jehoash** (Joash) enthroned in Judah.

The United Kingdom

1020	**Saul** unites Israelite tribes as first king.	*830*	Yahwist revival in Israel stimulates collection and writing of traditions of judges and beginning of monarchy.
1009/8	Saul dies. **David** is chosen king of Judah in Hebron.		
1002/1	David is anointed king of Israel, captures Jerusalem and makes it his capital.	814/13	**Jehoahaz** (Joahaz) succeeds Jehu in Israel.
990	David's interest in poetry stimulates written collections of old poems as well as new compositions.	798	**Jehoash** (Joash) succeeds Jehoahaz in Israel.
		796	Jehoash of Judah assassinated; **Amaziah** succeeds.
970/69	**Solomon** anointed king. David dies.	793/92	**Jeroboam** II coregent with Jehoash in Israel.
965	Building of temple is begun in Apr./May.		
959	Temple completed in Oct./Nov.	792/91	War between Israel and Judah results in capture of Amaziah of Judah. **Azariah** (Uzziah) is enthroned in his place.
950	Solomon encourages collection and composition of wisdom sayings. Literature flourishes, e.g. stories of Saul and David and the basic J material of the Pentateuch (Gen.-Deut.).		
		782/81	Jehoash of Israel dies; Jeroboam II sole ruler. He frees Amaziah, who resumes rule in Judah.
		767	Amaziah assassinated; Azariah sole ruler in Judah.

The Divided Kingdoms

931/30	**Rehoboam** succeeds Solomon. N tribes secede, choose **Jeroboam** king of Israel.	*755*	**Amos** is banished from Bethel. **Hosea** begins to prophesy. E material of Pentateuch collected and written, perhaps also nucleus of D Code.
926/25	Egyptian invader **Shishak** (Sheshonk I) despoils Jerusalem, destroys several cities of both Israel and Judah.		
920	Gezer calendar, earliest example of written Hebrew yet found.	753	**Zechariah** succeeds Jeroboam II in Israel.
		752	Zechariah killed; **Shallum** usurps, reigns one month; **Menahem** usurps.
913	**Abijam** succeeds Rehoboam in Judah.		
911/10	**Asa** succeeds Abijam in Judah.	750	**Jotham** coregent in Judah when Azariah becomes leper.
910/9	**Nadab** succeeds Jeroboam in Israel.		
909/8	Nadab killed; **Baasha** usurps in Israel.	742/41	Menahem of Israel pays tribute to **Tiglath-pileser** III of Assyria. **Pekahiah** succeeds Menahem.
886/85	**Elah** succeeds Baasha in Israel.		
885/84	Elah killed by **Zimri,** who reigns 7 days. **Omri** and **Tibni** lay rival claims to throne of Israel.	740/39	Pekahiah killed in Israel; **Pekah** usurps, dates reign from 752. Azariah dies in Judah; Jotham sole ruler. **Isaiah** called to prophesy.
880	Omri overcomes Tibni, builds Samaria as his capital.		
874/73	**Ahab** succeeds Omri in Israel.	735	**Ahaz** coregent with Jotham in Judah.
873/72	**Jehoshaphat** coregent with Asa in Judah.	734	Syro-Ephraimitic War sets Israel and Syria (Aram-Damascus) against Judah. Ahaz asks help from Tiglath-pileser.
870/69	Asa dies; Jehoshaphat sole ruler in Judah.		
865	Prophet **Elijah** sparks revival of Yahwism in Israel.	733/32	Tiglath-pileser invades Israel, seizes Galilee and Transjordan, exiles many of inhabitants.
854/53	**Jehoram** (Joram) coregent with Jehoshaphat in Judah.		
		732/31	Pekah of Israel is killed; **Hoshea** usurps as Assyrian vassal. Jotham of Judah dies; Ahaz sole ruler.
853	Assyrian record of Shalmaneser III mentions Ahab of Israel at Battle of Qarqar. **Ahaziah** succeeds Ahab.		
		725/24	Hoshea revolts. **Shalmaneser** V of Assyria besieges Samaria. **Micah** prophesies the city's destruction.
852	**Jehoram** (Joram) succeeds Ahaziah in Israel.		
		723/22	Fall of Samaria brings end to N kingdom, exile to many Israelites.

The S Kingdom Alone

716/15	**Hezekiah** succeeds Ahaz in Judah.
710	Hezekiah encourages immigration of N Yahwists who escaped exile. They bring traditions and documents, which stimulate literary activity, e.g. probably compiling of core of Deut. and combining of J and E.
701	Assyrian record of **Sennacherib** reports his siege of Jerusalem.
697/96	**Manasseh** coregent with Hezekiah.
687/86	Hezekiah dies; Manasseh sole ruler. As Assyrian vassal he promotes Assyrian cults, represses Yahwism.
663	Ashurbanipal (**Osnappar**) destroys Thebes and adds Egypt to the Assyrian Empire, bringing it to its widest extent.
643/42	**Amon** succeeds Manasseh.
641/40	**Josiah** succeeds Amon.
630	**Zephaniah** prophesies.
628/27	**Jeremiah** called to prophesy.
623/22	Law scroll found in temple is made basis for drastic Yahwist reform. Josiah extends rule to N as Assyrian power is weakened by revolts.
615	Editors under influence of Deut. compile historical records of Israel to demonstrate D ideas.
612	**Nahum** prophesies destruction of Assyrian capital, Nineveh, which is accomplished by Cyaxares, king of Media.
609	Josiah killed in Jun./Jul., as indicated by Babylonian record of expedition of **Pharaoh Neco** to support Assyrian forces holding out in W. **Jehoahaz** succeeds, is deposed by Neco after 3 months. **Jehoiakim** is enthroned as Egyptian vassal.
607	**Habakkuk** begins to prophesy.
605	**Nebuchadrezzar** defeats Neco and Assyrian remnants at Carchemish in May/Jun., takes Palestine from Egypt. In Sep. he accedes as Babylonian king.
604/3	Jeremiah dictates oracles to **Baruch** in Dec./Jan.
601	Nebuchadrezzar suffers heavy losses in attempt to invade Egypt. As a result Jehoiakim withholds tribute.
598/97	**Jehoiachin** succeeds Jehoiakim in Dec./Jan., *ca.* when Nebuchadrezzar besieges Jerusalem.
597	Babylonian Chronicle dates Nebuchadrezzar's capture of Jerusalem Mar. 16. Jehoiachin and many leading citizens exiled; **Zedekiah** made regent as Babylonian puppet.
593	**Ezekiel** called to prophesy Jul. 31.
589	Pro-Egyptian party forces Zedekiah to revolt.
588	Nebuchadrezzar besieges Jerusalem Jan. 15. Later the siege is lifted for a time as the Babylonians drive back invasion of Palestine by **Pharaoh Hophra.**
586	Wall of Jerusalem breached Jul. 18; Zedekiah flees and is captured. Destruction of city and temple begins Aug. 14 or 17. Many more are exiled.

The Exile and Persian Rule

562	**Evil-merodach** succeeds Nebuchadrezzar in Sep.
561	Jehoiachin released from prison Mar. 31 or Apr. 2.
555	D editors revise and complete history of Israel to form Deut.–II Kings, perhaps with JE as intro. Obad. composed.
550	**Cyrus** the Persian gains control of Median Empire.
546	Cyrus conquers Lydia in Asia Minor.
540	Second Isaiah prophesies Cyrus will free exiles for return to Jerusalem.
539	Cyrus' army takes Babylon without a battle.
538	Cyrus authorizes return to ancestral lands of displaced peoples. **Sheshbazzar** leads a body of Jews to Jerusalem.
530	Cambyses succeeds Cyrus.
525	Cambyses adds Egypt to Persian Empire.
522	**Darius** I overcomes rival to secure Persian throne.
520	**Zerubbabel** begins rebuilding of temple in Aug./Sep. at urging of **Haggai** and **Zechariah.**
515	Temple completed Mar. 12.
486	Xerxes I (**Ahasuerus**) succeeds Darius.
480	Xerxes attempts conquest of Greece.
470	Basic P material of Pentateuch composed.
465	**Artaxerxes** I succeeds Xerxes.
450	Mal. composed.
445	**Nehemiah** appointed governor of Judea, plans rebuilding of walls of Jerusalem.
433	Nehemiah ends first term as governor.
410	Editors combine P with JED and put the Pentateuch into substantially final form.
404	Accession of **Artaxerxes** II.
397	**Ezra** brings the Law, probably the completed Pentateuch, to Jerusalem and gains its acceptance as the constitution of the Jewish state.
380	I, II Chr., Ezra, Neh., Joel composed.

Hellenistic Rule and the Maccabean Revolt

334	**Alexander** the Great begins his conquest of the Persian Empire.
332	Alexander conquers Syria-Palestine, taking Tyre by a 7-month siege.
331	Alexander conquers Egypt, founds Alexandria.
323	Alexander dies, leaving his empire for his generals to squabble over. Ptolemy, founder of the Ptolemaic dynasty, gets control of Egypt, claims but is unable to hold Palestine.
312	Seleucus, founder of the Seleucid dynasty, gets control of Babylonia. He dates his

reign, on which the Seleucid Era is based, from Oct.

301   Seleucus adds Syria to his realm. Ptolemy secures firm hold on Palestine.

300   Seleucus founds Antioch in Syria as his capital.

250   LXX, Greek translation of the Law (Pentateuch), is made in Alexandria, followed in time by translation of other books. In Palestine editors compile the Prophets. Regular readings in the synagogues accord them wide familiarity and acceptance.

198   Seleucid **Antiochus** III, the Great, takes Palestine from Ptolemy V.

190   Romans defeat Antiochus the Great at Magnesia, remove Asia Minor from his control, impose heavy tribute and hostages.

187   **Seleucus** IV succeeds his father, Antiochus the Great.

180   **Jeshua ben Sira** writes Ecclus.

175   **Antiochus** IV **Epiphanes** succeeds his brother, Seleucus IV. He deposes the Jewish high priest, **Onias** III, appointing **Jason.**

172   **Menelaus** outbids Jason for the high priesthood.

169   Antiochus invades Egypt. Jason makes armed attack on Jerusalem. Antiochus brings army to quell revolt, enters temple, takes some of its treasures.

168   Roman ultimatum halts Antiochus in another invasion of Egypt.

167   Antiochus bans Jewish religious practices, desecrates temple on Dec. 6.

166   **Judas Maccabeus** takes lead in Jewish revolt, organizes guerrilla force.

165   Antiochus sets out on campaign in E, leaves **Lysias** in charge of Syria and Palestine. Dan. is written.

164   Judas defeats Lysias, enters Jerusalem, rededicates the temple on Dec. 14.

163   Antiochus IV dies in the E. His young son, **Antiochus** V **Eupator,** succeeds with Lysias as regent.

162   **Demetrius** I, son of Seleucus IV, seizes the throne.

160   Judas killed in battle. His brother **Jonathan** takes command of the revolt.

152   **Alexander Balas,** pretender to the Seleucid throne, appoints Jonathan high priest.

150   Qumran community formed. Judith, Testaments of the 12 Patriarchs written.

143   Jonathan murdered. His brother **Simon** takes over.

Judean Independence and Conquest by Rome

142   Simon secures from **Demetrius** II recognition as high priest and ruler of an independent state of Judea.

134   Simon murdered; his son **John** Hyrcanus I succeeds.

130   Jeshua ben Sira's grandson translates Ecclus. into Greek.

120   Jubilees written.

110   Hyrcanus conquers most of Palestine, forcibly proselytizes many. Pharisees gain wide following as opponents of aristocratic Sadducees. **Simon of Cyrene** writes 5-vol. history of Maccabean revolt.

104   Aristobulus I succeeds Hyrcanus, conquers Galilee.

103   Alexander Janneus succeeds his brother Aristobulus, issues coins with title "king," completes conquest of Palestine.

100   I Macc. written.

90   Pharisees lead 6-year revolt against Janneus, ended by his crucifying 800 rebels.

80   Epitomist condenses Simon of Cyrene's history to form II Macc. Main part of Enoch written.

76   Janneus dies; his widow, Alexandra, rules as queen, favors Pharisees.

67   Alexandra dies, bequeathing rule to her elder son, Hyrcanus II; but the younger, Aristobulus II, backed by the Sadducees, seizes it by force.

65   Hyrcanus is incited by Antipater, an Idumean, to besiege Jerusalem. Both parties seek Roman support.

63   Pompey captures Jerusalem, brings Palestine under Roman rule, appoints Hyrcanus II high priest.

50   Wisdom. Sol. written.

48   Julius Caesar defeats Pompey, becomes absolute Roman ruler. Antipater appointed governor of Palestine.

44   Caesar assassinated by Brutus, Cassius, and others. Palestine comes under control of Cassius.

42   Mark Atony and Octavius Caesar defeat Brutus and Cassius. Palestine under Antony.

40   Parthians invade Palestine, help Antigonus, son of Aristobulus II, to seize control. Roman Senate proclaims **Herod,** son of Antipater, king of the Jews.

37   Herod defeats Antigonus, establishes himself as king.

31   Octavius defeats Antony, becomes master of Roman world.

27   Octavius proclaimed **Augustus** Octavianus, Roman emperor.

20/19   Rebuilding of temple begun.

The Life of Jesus

7   **Jesus** is born.

4   Herod dies in Apr. His realm is divided among 3 sons: Judea, Samaria to **Archelaus;** Galilee, Perea to **Herod** Antipas; NE region to **Philip.**

A.D.

6   Augustus deposes Archelaus, puts Judea under Roman prefect.

14   **Tiberius Caesar** succeeds Augustus Aug. 19.

25   Philo of Alexandria writes to harmonize Judaism and Greek philosophy.

26   **Pontius Pilate** becomes prefect of Judea.

28   **John** begins baptizing in 15th year of Tiberius.

30   Jesus crucified Friday, Apr. 7.

The Career of Paul

33   **Paul** is converted, goes into Nabatean Arabia.

36   Paul visits Jerusalem, goes to Syria and Cilicia. Pilate replaced as prefect of Judea.

37   Caligula succeeds Tiberius Mar. 16.

41   **Claudius** succeeds Caligula Jan. 25. **Herod Agrippa I** appointed king of Judea, executes **James,** imprisons **Peter.**

44   Herod Agrippa dies. Judea put under procuratorship (formerly prefectship; see "The Greco-Roman Background of the NT," p. 1042) again.

47   Paul and **Barnabas** begin "first missionary journey," to Cyprus, S Galatia.

49   Paul confers with apostles in Jerusalem, wins approval of Gentile mission. He and **Silas** begin "2nd missionary journey," going overland through Asia Minor and crossing to Macedonia. Claudius expels Jews from Rome.

50   Paul works in Macedonia, Athens. He arrives in Corinth, meets **Aquila** and **Prisca,** recent refugees from Rome, writes I Thess.

51   Paul is haled before proconsul **Gallio** after 18 months in Corinth.

52   Paul leaves Corinth, sails for Ephesus, then Syria.

53   Paul arrives at Ephesus on "3rd missionary journey," beginning 3-year residence there.

54   Nero succeeds Claudius.

55   Paul perhaps writes Phil., Col., Philem. while imprisoned for a time in Ephesus.

56   Paul writes I Cor. He makes a brief "painful" visit to Corinth, returns to Ephesus, writes a "severe" letter to the Corinthians (II Cor. 10–13 in the view of some scholars). Perhaps at this time he writes Gal., Phil. 3. He goes to Macedonia, where he writes part or all of II Cor. He begins 3-month stay in Corinth.

57   Paul writes Rom. at Corinth, spends Passover at Philippi, arrives at Jerusalem for Pentecost. He is arrested and sent to the procurator **Felix** at Caesarea.

59   **Festus** replaces Felix as procurator. Paul appeals to Caesar, is sent to Rome.

60   Paul arrives in Rome, perhaps writes Phil., Col., Philem. while imprisoned there. I Pet. written *ca.* this time if by Peter.

64   Fire destroys much of Rome in Jul. Christians are blamed and persecuted. Perhaps Peter and Paul are among the martyrs.

The Period of the Later NT Books

66   Jews revolt against Rome.

68   Nero commits suicide; Galba succeeds. Roman troops destroy Qumran community.

69   Galba succeeded by Otho, Vitellius, and finally Vespasian, the general besieging Jerusalem.

70   Vespasian's son Titus takes Jerusalem in Aug., destroys temple and razes city.

73   Last Jewish rebels commit suicide at Masada.

75   Mark written. Josephus writes an account of the war in Aramaic, later translates it into Greek.

79   Titus succeeds Vespasian.

81   Domitian succeeds Titus.

85   Matt. written.

90   Luke-Acts written. Rabbis at Jamnia close Hebrew canon.

92   Paul's letters collected and circulated together.

93   Josephus writes his Antiquities of the Jews.

95   Heb., Rev. written.

96   Nerva succeeds Domitian. I Clement written, perhaps also I Pet. if pseudonymous.

98   Trajan succeeds Nerva.

100   John, Jas., and main part of II Esdras written.

110   Letters of John written.

115   Letters of Ignatius and Polycarp written.

117   Hadrian succeeds Trajan.

125   Jude written. Oldest extant NT manuscript copied—a papyrus fragment of John.

130   Pastorals, Letter of Barnabas written.

132   Hadrian's plan to rebuild Jerusalem as Roman colony incites 2nd Jewish revolt, led by Simon ben Koseba.

135   Romans put down revolt, proceed to build Aelia Capitolina on site of Jerusalem.

138   Hadrian succeeded by Antoninus Pius.

140   Shepherd of Hermas written.

144   Marcion promotes his expurgated version of Luke and Paul's letters to replace the OT in Christian usage.

150   II Pet., Teaching of the 12 Apostles (Didache) written.

The Patriarchs. That the social customs depicted in the stories of the patriarchs belong to the early and middle 2nd millennium has been revealed by records of this period, esp. the stores of cuneiform tablets found at Mari (18th-17th cents.) and at Nuzi (15th-14th cents.). Both Mari, on the middle Euphrates, and Nuzi, in NE Assyria, had close relations with the Haran region in upper Mesopotamia, the center of Hurrian population, which in at least one of the Gen. sources is the ancestral home of the patriarchs. The traditions are thus confirmed as coming down from this general period, but there is little basis for more specific dating of the individual tribal leaders to whom they refer.

Abraham is often dated during the upheaval of the Hyksos invasion in the mid-18th cent. on the basis of the names of the invading kings in Gen. 14:1 (see comment), at least 2 of which appear linguistically equivalent to names of kings of that period mentioned in the Mari tablets. Since the tablets provide no evidence that these kings might have joined in an invasion of Palestine, however, it is possible that the biblical reference is to similarly named kings of another time. If Gen. 14 contains a genuine tradition of a historical event, a more reliable clue to its date would seem to lie in the identification of the 5 Palestinian cities attacked—Sodom, Gomorrah, Admah, Zeboiim, and Bela—for it must have occurred before the natural disaster which permanently destroyed at least the first 4 of them (Gen. 19; cf. e.g. Deut. 29:23; Isa. 13:19; Hos. 11:8; Amos 4:11). Even if both the story of Gen. 14 and Abraham's part in the story of Lot (Gen. 13; 18-19) are regarded as later elaborations, they may well be based on a tradition that Abraham settled in S Palestine when these chief cities of the region were still standing, and perhaps that their destruction occurred during his lifetime.

Though direct archaeological evidence for the date of the catastrophe is lacking, since the sites of these "cities of the valley" are apparently under the S end of the Dead Sea (see color map 3), there are significant indirect clues. Surface survey has shown that the surrounding area—including on the E the lands which later became Moab and Edom and on the W the Negeb of Palestine, i.e. the arid region around Beer-sheba and on to the S—was well settled during the 21st-20th cents. but unoccupied except for nomads during the 19th-14th cents. More specifically, near the probable underwater sites are the remains of a cultic center to which the citizens apparently made seasonal visits for festivals. The evidence that the center was abandoned *ca.* 1900 points to this date for the catastrophe and for Abraham's residence near Hebron.

Isaac appears mostly as either Abraham's son or Jacob's father—a family structure imposed on the traditions much later. As an individual he seems to be associated with Beer-sheba (Gen. 26:23-33; 28:10) and Beer-lahai-roi (Gen. 24:62; 25:11), sites in the Negeb region which, as noted above, had no settled occupation during the 19th-14th cents. Otherwise there is no clue to his date.

Jacob represents a combination of traditions. The oldest of these are folktales of a clever young shepherd who tricks his brother and his employer, and the social customs reflected in them show that they originated in the period recorded in the Mari and Nuzi tablets. Other traditions concern a tribal hero associated with shrines in Transjordan and central Palestine, apparently a leader of Hebrew tribes migrating into these areas. Though such migrations no doubt occurred at various times, the relations with the Edomites (Esau) and the Arameans (Laban) suggest esp. the inroads of Habiru mentioned in the Amarna letters, since both these groups seem to have been in Transjordan at this time.

Joseph is often assumed to have risen to high office under one of the Semitic Hyksos rulers *ca.* 1600 or earlier. But the silence of the traditions about events in Egypt between Joseph and Moses and indeed the lack of evidence of any significant influence of Egyptian culture on the Hebrew tribes point to a much shorter interval. The revolutionary reign of Akhenaton (1369-1353), who rejected the established Egyptian priesthood and nobility and set up a new government in a new capital, seems a likely time for an able foreigner to reach high office. The picture in the Amarna letters of Habiru on the move in Palestine suggests that at the same time some of them may have sought a home in Egypt.

The Exodus and Settlement in Palestine. On the possible dates for the Exodus and the reasons for considering the middle of the 13th cent. most likely see Intro. to Exod. Archaeological evidence of the destruction of such Canaanite cities as Bethel, Debir, Lachish, and Hazor during the 2nd half of the 13th cent. indicates that the Hebrews who left Egypt spent much less than the conventional "forty years" (cf. e.g. Exod. 16:35; Num. 14:33-34; Deut. 8:2) on the journey to Palestine. Similar intervals in Judg. (cf. e.g. 3:30; 6:1; 8:28) are equally unreliable, and we must look to archaeology for such dating of events of the period as is possible. Excavation at the site of Megiddo has shown that this great fortress guarding the pass into the valley of the Kishon River was unoccupied *ca.* 1125-1075. The nearby battle between Israelites led by Deborah and Barak and Canaanites under Sisera must have occurred during this time (cf. esp. Judg. 5:19), presumably near the beginning of it. The uncovering of 11th-cent. levels at the sites of Shechem and Gibeah has confirmed the biblical traditions of disasters at these places (Judg. 9:45-49; 20:37-40) and supplied their approximate dates.

The destruction of Shiloh and Eli's temple there —strangely omitted from the account in I Sam. but mentioned in Ps. 78:60; Jer. 7:12; 26:6—evidently followed soon after the Philistine capture of the ark (I Sam. 4). After 7 months (6:1) the Philistines are said to have returned the ark, which was then kept in the "house" of Abinadab at Kiriath-jearim (7:1) until David brought it to Jerusalem (II Sam. 6). Since the time of its stay there must include a period of Philistine domination during which the young Samuel grew "old" (I Sam. 8:1) and also the reigns of Saul and of David in Hebron, an editorial guess of "some twenty years" (I Sam. 7:2), if intended to cover the whole period, is clearly too short. If we understand the unfortunate Uzzah and his brother to be descendants of Abinadab rather than lit. "sons" (II Sam. 6:3) the other biblical data fit with the archaeological evidence that Shiloh was destroyed *ca.* 50 years before David established his capital in Jerusalem.

The United Kingdom. The notes that the temple was begun "in the fourth year of Solomon's reign" (I Kings 6:1, 37) and completed "in the eleventh year" (vs. 38) illustrate the common method in the ancient Near East of dating events by the monarch's regnal years. These were calendar years; i.e. they were counted, not from the actual day of the king's accession, but from the new year's day preceding or following. In this passage the explanations that Ziv (Apr.-May) is the "second month" and Bul (Oct.-Nov.) the "eighth month" would seem to put the new year in the spring, but obviously these are editorial notes added after the names Ziv and Bul had become obsolete. Actually as originally recorded the dates were probably based on a fall new year. On a fall basis the building time is 6½ years, on a spring basis 7½ years; that the former would be counted as "seven years" (vs. 38) seems more likely. More significant is the evidence of the synchronisms from the period of the divided monarchy, as will appear below, that Solomon's successors in the Davidic line counted their regnal years from a fall new year.

When one king succeeded another there were 2 ways of dating the year of change. In Assyria, Babylonia, and most other parts of the ancient Near East it was usually reckoned as the last regnal year of the deceased king and the accession year of the new king, whose first regnal year would then begin with the following new year. This is known as the "accession-year" or "postdating" method. In contrast to this is the "non-accession-year" or "antedating" method, used esp. in Egypt, whereby a new king counted his first regnal year as beginning with the new year's day preceding his accession, even though this made it coincide with the last regnal year of his predecessor. Since, as will appear below, the kings of the Davidic line in Judah used the accession-year method except during the latter half of the 9th cent., it is likely that Solomon's first regnal year began with the fall new year's day following the death of David.

It must be noted, however, that Solomon was anointed king while David was still living (I Kings 1:39, 47-48) and thus was coregent with his father for a time. The evidence from later cases of coregency shows that ordinarily the son's regnal years were counted only following the death of the father but after the son's death the years of his coregency, including the year of his appointment, were added to his regnal years for the total length of his reign.

The length of "forty years" reported for Solomon's reign (I Kings 11:42) has often been dismissed as another of the editor's conventional round numbers like those in Judg., but in this case most evidence points to its being approximately correct. In fact the citation of a written source, the "book of the acts of Solomon" (vs. 41; cf. e.g. I Kings 14:29; 15:31) suggests that it comes from a contemporary official record and is a precise figure. If so, we may count back from Solomon's death in 931/30 and place the beginning of his coregency in 970/69.

The source which describes in detail Solomon's anointing and David's death (I Kings 1–2) does not indicate the interval between them, but it implies that little time elapsed. Most likely, therefore, David died before the end of 970/69, so that Solomon's first regnal year was 969/68, his 4th was 966/65, and his 11th was 959/58.

For the reign of David no official contemporary written source is named; therefore suspicion that the 40 years attributed to him is a conventional round number is justified. On the other hand there are reasons for suspecting that despite the coincidence it may be a precise figure: (a) Most evidence points to its being at least approximately correct. (b) The breakdown of the total (II Sam. 2:11; 5:4-5; cf. I Kings 2:11) suggests that David's 7½ years at Hebron as king of Judah are actual elapsed time whereas the 33 years "at Jerusalem . . . over all Israel and Judah" are regnal years. It is not un-likely that sometime during his reign David adopted the system of dating by regnal years which his successors continued, and that he discreetly began his count with the year he became king of Israel as well as Judah. (c) Inclusion of a "recorder" and a "secretary" among David's chief officials (II Sam. 8:16-17; 20:24-25) indicates a concern for keeping records, which of course would have to be dated.

If David's 33rd regnal year was 970/69 his first was 1002/1. Since he had no immediate predecessor, allowance of an accession year was unnecessary. Thus this first year was no doubt that in which he became king of Israel (II Sam. 5:3). His capture of Jerusalem (vss. 6-8) seems to be dated the same year (vs. 5). Measuring back 7½ years brings us to a time between the spring of 1009 and the spring of 1008 for his becoming king of Judah in Hebron.

The text giving the length of Saul's reign (I Sam. 13:1) is defective, with only the final digit 2 in the number of years, and the notice itself may be a late addition with no valid basis. If any reliance is to be placed on the digit it must point to a reign of 12 years for Saul. At Michmash (I Sam. 14) near the beginning he is old enough to have a son who is an able warrior, yet in the final battle on Mt. Gilboa he is not too old to be an active warrior himself. Other events told of his reign can be fitted into a 12-year interval.

The Divided Kingdoms. The chronology of the kings of Israel and Judah in the table is adapted from S. J. De Vries, "Chronology of the OT" in *IDB*, 1962, which is in turn based on the chronology of Edwin R. Thiele in *The Mysterious Numbers of the Hebrew Kings*, 1951 (rev. ed. 1965, Wm. B. Eerdmans Publishing Co.). It assumes that the chronological data about them in Kings are derived from authentic contemporary annals of the respective kingdoms. The validity of this assumption is confirmed by the consistency with which the many apparent discrepancies in the figures are resolved when differences in calendars and methods of counting regnal years are recognized.

As already noted (see above on Solomon), the kings of the Davidic line in Judah continued observance of a new year in the fall. In establishing the N kingdom of Israel, however, Jeroboam I made changes in the calendar (cf. I Kings 12:32-33) which included beginning the year in the spring. Because of this difference the dates during the period of the 2 kingdoms can be fixed as falling between spring and fall (e.g. 913 for Abijam's accession) or between fall and spring (e.g. 911/10 for his death).

For nearly a cent. the 2 kingdoms differed also in the point from which a king's first regnal year was counted. Judah continued to use the accession-year method (see above on Solomon), but in Israel each new king claimed the remaining fraction of the year of his accession as his first regnal year, thus adding an extra year to the recorded length of his reign. In the middle of the 9th cent. Judah changed over to the system used in Israel; then at the beginning of the 8th cent. both kingdoms changed to the former system of Judah and continued to use it from that time on.

In calculating synchronisms the annalists of each kingdom recognized the calendar of the other but followed their own method of counting or not counting accession years. E.g. for Rehoboam, who succeeded Solomon soon after the fall new year of 931, the Judean annalists considered the period from then till the next new year as his accession year and numbered his regnal years from the fall of 930. Since Rehoboam's death in the summer of 913 fell in his 17th regnal year, they recorded his reign as 17 years (I Kings 14:21). At the same time they recognized Jeroboam's first regnal year as beginning 6 months earlier, with the Israelite spring new year in 930. Therefore their record that Rehoboam's son Abijam began to reign in Jeroboam's 18th year (15:1) does not mean that his succession was delayed.

On the other hand the Israelite annalists made no allowance for an accession year. Instead they counted the short period between Jeroboam's coronation and the spring new year of 930 as his first regnal year—a year earlier than the Judeans were counting. On that basis his death in the winter of 910/9 fell in his 22nd year and a reign of 22 years was attributed to him (14:20) though he actually outlived Rehoboam by only *ca.* 3½ years.

In recording at this time the succession of Jeroboam's son Nadab the Israelite annalists synchronized it with what they counted as the 2nd year of the Judean king, Asa (15:25). In Judah this was only the beginning of Asa's first year, for the preceding year, during which he had succeeded Abijam, had been considered his accession year. To the Israelite annalists this was also Nadab's first year; and the following year, in which Nadab was assassinated, was his 2nd and Asa's 3rd. Therefore they recorded that Nadab reigned for 2 years between the 2nd and 3rd years of Asa (15:25, 33).

Omri. That the chronological notices in Kings come from annals recorded at the time of the events is shown by inconsistencies in data from different times now appearing in the same sentence. Such a combination represents that Omri reigned 12 years beginning in the 31st year of Asa (I Kings 16:23), but it is contradicted by the record that Ahab succeeded Omri in Asa's 38th year (vs. 29). Omri's accession was recorded when he overcame Tibni in 880 after *ca.* 4½ years of civil war (vss. 21-22). Once on the throne he no doubt asserted his claim to have been the rightful ruler since 885/84 by so numbering his regnal years. On this basis at his death in 874/73 his reign was recorded as 12 years long.

Jehoshaphat and Jehoram of Judah. A similar inconsistency in I Kings 22:41-42, if not an error, reveals a coregency like that of David and Solomon which is not otherwise mentioned. Apparently it was occasioned by Asa's illness (I Kings 15:23; cf. II Chr. 16:12). Jehoshaphat's years as coregent with his father—presumably calculated without allowance of an accession year, since there was no predecessor to be credited—were counted in his total reign at his death, but I Kings 22:51; II Kings 3:1 suggest that they were not counted as regnal years during his lifetime.

That Jehoshaphat in turn appointed his son Jehoram coregent, probably when leaving for the battles of 853 (cf. I Kings 22:2-4; see comment), is shown by the duplicate synchronisms in II Kings 1:17; 3:1. It may also be hinted in "Jehoshaphat being king of Judah" in the Hebrew text of 8:16 (omitted in the LXX; see RSV footnote), but it is not taken into account in the length of Jehoram's reign reported in vs. 17. Evidently the annalists who recorded the reigns of Jehoshaphat and Jehoram had different views about coregencies. Both the synchronism in vs. 16 and the length in vs. 17 show that Judah changed here to the Israelite non-accession-year method—no doubt as a result of the close relations with Israel evidenced by Jehoram's marriage with Ahab's daughter (vs. 18).

Synchronism with Assyrian Records. The Assyrians kept track of their years, which began in the spring, by naming each in honor of a prominent official, who became the *limmu* of that year. The complete limmu list for 892-648 is known and is synchronized with dates B.C. by reference to an eclipse identified by astronomers as having occurred Jun. 15, 763. Shalmaneser III of Assyria twice mentions Israel in records which can thus be dated: (*a*) during a W campaign begun the 14th of Ayaru (Apr.-May) 853 Ahab was among the W allies he fought at Qarqar; (*b*) in 841/40 Jehu paid him tribute. The biblical records report that the reigns of 2 sons of Ahab, Ahaziah's of 2 years (I Kings 22:51) and Jehoram's of 12 years (II Kings 3:1), intervened before Jehu's revolt. Each of these reigns, being calculated by the non-accession-year method, actually lasted a year less, so that the total of the 2 was 12 years. This harmonizes with the Assyrian records only if Ahab died in the year he fought at Qarqar and Jehu paid tribute to Assyria in the year he revolted. Since Ahaziah of Judah also was killed in the revolt (II Kings 9:27-28) the records of the 2 kingdoms here coincide for the first time since the division. Calculated from this common point the synchronisms show that both Ahab's death and Jehu's revolt must have occurred between Israel's spring new year and Judah's fall new year. Therefore the dates 853 for the former and 841 for the latter are established and provide reference points for the preceding and following chronological notices about both the kingdoms.

Ahaziah of Judah, it is said, reigned one year beginning in the 12th year of Joram, i.e. Jehoram, of Israel (II Kings 8:25-26); but a misplaced duplicate notice (9:29) dates his accession in Joram's 11th year. His father, Jehoram of Judah, is recorded as having reigned 8 years beginning in Joram of Israel's 5th year (8:16-17)—figures which, as already noted, do not include a coregency and are counted for the first time in Judah by the non-accession-year method. The father thus died in the 12th year of Joram of Israel, i.e. after the spring new year of 841. Ahaziah therefore ruled less than 6 months, but by the non-accession-year method the brief period was counted as his first regnal year and was recorded as a reign of one year. The duplicate dating of it in Joram's 11th year, if not an error, may reflect a parallel record kept by Judah's former accession-year method.

The Early 8th Cent. The discrepancy in the reports that Jehu's son Jehoahaz reigned 17 years beginning in the 23rd year of Joash, i.e. Jehoash, of Judah (II Kings 13:1) and that Jehoash of Israel succeeded in Joash's 37th year (vs. 10) is to be resolved by recognizing that with the latter reign Israel changed to the accession-year method. Apparently the Israelite annalist felt free to recalculate the Judean Joash's regnal years by the new method but did not venture a corresponding reduction in the length of Jehoahaz' reign. Soon afterward Judah also changed to the accession-year method with the reign of Amaziah. From this time on both kingdoms used this method without further change.

The threat of war with Judah perhaps was the occasion for Jehoash of Israel to make his son coregent. A long coregency before Jeroboam II began his sole reign in the 15th year of Amaziah must be assumed to accommodate the 41 years recorded (II Kings 14:23). That Jeroboam counted this coregency in his regnal years during his lifetime is indicated by the synchronism in 15:1.

The war resulted in victory for Jehoash and humiliating defeat for Amaziah. Though the account is not clear, it appears that from early in his 5th year Amaziah was held a captive in Samaria for *ca.* 10 years and his son Azariah (Uzziah) ruled in his place (14:13). On the death of Jehoash he was evidently released and lived 15 more years (vs. 17). That he resumed the rule of Judah, no doubt with his son as coregent, is suggested by his being assassinated (vs. 19).

The implication in 14:21; 15:1-2 that Azariah was only 16 at his father's assassination in the 27th year of Jeroboam II is misleading. Actually his reign largely coincided with Jeroboam's. It was when his father was taken captive, *ca.* a year after Jeroboam became coregent, that Azariah was made king at 16 (14:21), and from this time he reigned 52 years. That he himself numbered his regnal years on this basis is indicated by the synchronisms in 15:8, 13, 17, 23, 27. Since there was no assurance Amaziah would ever be freed from captivity, the young Azariah was no doubt considered his father's successor and the year of the capture was counted as his accession year.

Jotham and Ahaz. The 2nd year of Pekah in II Kings 15:32 refers to the start of Jotham's coregency in 750 because of the leprosy of his father, Azariah (vs. 5)—an innovation, since heretofore the accession notice has dated the start of the king's sole reign. Because Jotham's regnal years were counted from his coregency without an accession year (see above on Jehoshaphat) the first half of his 20th year overlapped the last half of Pekah's 20th (vss. 27, 30).

The contradictory record that Jotham reigned only 16 years (vs. 33) combines with the evidence that his son Ahaz led Judah in the Syro-Ephraimitic War (II Kings 16:5-9; Isa. 7:1-17) to indicate that in 735 he effectively ceased to rule even though he lived on for *ca.* 3½ years. It has been suggested that he was deposed by a pro-Assyrian faction in an internal conflict that precipitated the war. Support for this conjecture is possibly to be found in the aim of Israel and Syria to make the son of Tabeel king of Judah (Isa. 7:6), which might be based on the existence of substantial opposition to Ahaz within Judah. But if some were denying the legitimacy of Ahaz' takeover, why would they not try to restore Jotham rather than back another claimant? Perhaps Jotham, like his father, had to commit the rule to his son because of illness.

As in the record of Jotham, the synchronism dating Ahaz' accession (II Kings 16:1) refers to the beginning of his coregency. No doubt the annalist who made this entry viewed the son's assumption of authority in 735 as bringing the father's rule to an end and therefore recorded Jotham's reign as lasting 16 years. On the other hand after Ahaz' death another annalist evidently took a different view of his coregency. From the Assyrian record of Sennacherib's invasion of Judah in Hezekiah's 14th year (18:13) we know that the date was 701 and therefore that Hezekiah succeeded Ahaz in 716/15. The length of 16 years recorded for Ahaz' reign thus assumes his accession in 732/31, the 20th year of Jotham (15:30). Evidently Jotham died in that year and Ahaz' 16 years count only his sole reign. Thus the period when Jotham and Ahaz were coregents seems to have been credited to neither father nor son.

The Last Years of the N Kingdom. Since the accession of Zechariah, the last of the dynasty of Jehu, came in Azariah's 38th year (II Kings 15:8), i.e. before Judah's fall new year of 753, the notice that he reigned only 6 months probably means that Shallum's usurpation occurred before Israel's spring new year of 752. It is certain that Shallum's brief reign ended after the new year because Menahem's reign from the 39th year of Azariah (vs. 17) to the 50th (vs. 23) was counted as only 10 years. In all likelihood, therefore, the new year began during Shallum's one month.

The 52nd year of Azariah (vs. 27) dates Pekah's reign as beginning after his assassination of Menahem's son Pekahiah (vss. 23-25) in 740/39, but the length of 20 years and the synchronisms in vs. 32 and 16:1 show that his regnal years were numbered on the basis that his accession year was 752/51. Evidently, like Omri (see above), Pekah claimed to have been king of Israel for some years before his actual rule began. Whether he claimed to be the successor to Shallum or to Zechariah depends on when Shallum's one-month reign began. Since it probably began before 752/51 Pekah apparently was a partisan of Shallum who denied the legitimacy of the reigns of Menahem and Pekahiah. If the synchronism in vs. 32 with his 2nd year was recorded at the time Jotham began to rule, his claim must have been asserted near the beginning of Menahem's reign and recognized then by Judah. Against this assumption, however, is the reference to Pekah as an officer of Pekahiah (vs. 25).

Pekah's claim caused confusion in ancient times as well as today. Vs. 30 gives the correct date of Hoshea's usurpation but the synchronisms in 17:1; 18:1, 9-10 all place his reign 12 years too late. No doubt they are the work of an editor who assumed that Pekah's 20 years all followed the 52nd year of Azariah.

That Samaria fell to Shalmaneser V of Assyria, who died in 722, is indicated by II Kings 17:3-6 and partially confirmed by Assyrian records of Shalmaneser's siege and capture of a city whose name is missing. The annals of Shalmaneser's successor, Sargon II, mention only building projects as accomplishments of his early years; but an inscription in the palace he built late in his reign boasts of his capture of Samaria during his accession year (see comment on II Kings 17:1-6). Because of this inscription some scholars date the fall of Samaria 721, but Sargon's claim seems more open to suspicion than the other evidences pointing to 723/22.

The S Kingdom Alone. Sennacherib, as already noted, establishes for us the date 701 for his siege of Jerusalem in Hezekiah's 14th year. The Babylonian Chronicle records a siege of Haran by Pharaoh Neco in the summer of 609, thus establishing the date of his killing of Josiah at Megiddo on his N journey (II Kings 23:29; II Chr. 35:20-24). An excess of 10 years in the total regnal years reported between these dates apparently indicates a coregency of Manasseh with Hezekiah. The son's appointment as coregent at the age of 12 (II Kings 21:1) was no doubt occasioned by the father's illness (cf. 20:1).

The account of Josiah's reform shows that Judah's observance of a fall new year continued at least through this reign, for the finding of the book of the law in his 18th year (II Kings 22:3) is followed by a passover in the same year (23:23). Since Josiah's death occurred in his 31st year (22:1) in the early summer of 609, his 18th year was 623/22 rather than 621 as often stated on the basis of former estimates that he died in 608. In fact, since the events related in chs. 22-23 would seem to occupy several months, the finding of the law book probably occurred in the fall of 623.

The Fall of Jerusalem. The dating of the destruction of Jerusalem and the temple and the beginning of the Exile depends on whether the regnal years of Zedekiah in II Kings 24-25 (cf. II Chr. 36; Jer. 39; 52) are based on a fall or a spring new year. The Babylonian Chronicle records that in Chislev (Dec./Jan.) of his 7th year (598/97) Nebuchadrezzar invaded Judah and on the 2nd of Adar (Mar. 16) took Jerusalem, captured the king (Jehoiachin), and appointed a new king of his choice (Zedekiah). If, then, Zedekiah's first regnal year began in the fall of 597, the beginning of the siege in his 9th year (25:1) was on Jan. 15, 588, the breach of the wall in his 11th year (vss. 2-4) occurred on Jul. 18, 586, and the destruction of the city and temple (vs. 8) began on Aug. 14, 586, or perhaps Aug. 17 (Jer. 52:12) or 16 (see comment on Ezek. 33:21-22).

On the other hand if the data are based on a spring new year the exact date of Zedekiah's appointment becomes significant. Most scholars who favor a spring new year have assumed that Nebuchadrezzar completed his arrangements during the month Adar and that Zedekiah's first regnal year began in the spring of 597. On this basis the siege in Zedekiah's 9th year would begin on Jan. 15, 588, but last only 18 months, so that the capture and destruction in his 11th year would occur in Jul.-Aug. 587. However, the statement that Nebuchadrezzar made Jehoiachin a captive in his 8th year (II Kings 24:12) suggests that he may not have set Zedekiah on the throne till after the beginning of the Babylonian spring new year. This may be supported by II Chr. 36:10, where "in the spring of the year" is lit. "at the turn of the year," and possibly by Ezek. 40:1, where "on that very day" is taken by some scholars as referring to the anniversary of "our exile" on the 10th day of the first month. If most of 597/96 was considered Zedekiah's accession year and his first regnal year did not begin till the spring of 596, then the siege of his 9th year did not begin till Jan. 5, 587, and the catastrophe of his 11th year would be dated in the summer of 586.

The date 586 is indicated by the 19th year of Nebuchadrezzar in II Kings 25:8, which is supported by the synchronism of his 18th year with Zedekiah's

10th in Jer. 32:1. On the other hand 587 is indicated by the 18th year in Jer. 52:29. Various attempts have been made to reconcile these contradictory figures on the basis of different methods of calculating Nebuchadrezzar's regnal years from his accession in the late summer of 605, but none are convincing.

The account of Josiah's reign in II Kings 22-23 assumes a fall new year, as noted above. The question is therefore whether this calendar is continued in chs. 24-25. In 25:27 the phrase translated "in the year that he began to reign" is most naturally interpreted as referring to Evil-merodach's accession year, 562/61, the remainder of Nebuchadrezzar's 43rd year. If the first year of Jehoiachin's captivity is counted as ending in the fall of 597 his release in the spring of 561 comes in the 37th year as stated. Reckoning this by a spring new year would require assuming that the first year of the captivity was counted as ending in the spring of 597, a few weeks after the surrender of the city—an assumption that cannot be reconciled with the dating by years of the captivity in Ezek., where the first year is clearly 597/96 (cf. esp. 24:1).

Most scholars who defend a spring new year in chs. 24-25 count the first year of Jehoiachin's captivity as 597/96 and interpret 25:27 as referring rather to Evil-merodach's first regnal year, 561/60. As evidences for a switch to a spring new year after the reign of Josiah they cite: (*a*) the numbering of the months on this basis in Jer. and Ezek., (*b*) the obvious use of a spring calendar in Jer. 46:2 and an implication of its use in Jer. 28:17, and (*c*) the probable spring basis of the dates of Ezek. But the weight to be given these is questionable:

a) With the Exile the Jews adopted the Assyrian-Babylonian calendar with its spring new year and after a time assumed it had been theirs from the beginning (cf. Exod. 12:2, P). The only evidence of resistance to it is the use of numbers for the months rather than names—no doubt because their derivation from the pagan cult was recognized. Later this resistance died away and the names were adopted (cf. e.g. Ezra 6:15; Neh. 1:1; Esth. 2:16; Zech. 7:1; I Macc. 1:54). If the month numbers in Jer. and Ezek. are original—rather than editorial as some scholars believe—the Assyrian-Babylonian calendar was being used in Judah (see Intro. to Ezek.) before the Exile. This might mean it was imposed officially by Jehoiakim when he became a vassal of Nebuchadrezzar ca. 604, but more probably it had been around a long time as a result of international trade. Its commercial and popular use would not necessarily conflict with official use of the traditional regnal and religious calendar, which we know continued through the reign of Josiah (see above). There seems little evidence here for a change in the counting of regnal years thereafter.

b) Jer. 46:2 is probably an editor's annotation. "The same year" in Jer. 28:17 implies one that began in the spring but may indicate merely such popular use of the Assyrian-Babylonian calendar as has just been noted. There is stronger counter evidence that Jeremiah and Baruch observed a fall calendar in Jer. 25:1, 3; 36:1, 9. It has been claimed that 25:3 is based on a spring calendar, but this assumes that Jeremiah counted the years of his ministry like regnal years; being a prophet rather than a king he more probably counted the anniversaries of his call and described the actual elapsed time. If so, his figures are based on a fall calendar. In 36:1, 9 an interval of *ca*. 3 months possible with a fall calendar is more likely than one of over 9 months by a spring calendar.

c) If we assume that Ezekiel was a Palestinian prophet (see Intro. to Ezek.) his use of a spring calendar is still not incompatible with an official fall calendar, as indicated above. In fact his "twelfth year" in 33:21, if the text is correct, shows he is using a different calendar from that in II Kings 24–25. That "twelfth" is original is likely, for later scribes unaware of the difference in calendars would be tempted to harmonize it with "eleventh."

The date in Nebuchadrezzar's 18th year in Jer. 52:29 thus remains the only clear evidence for a date of 587, and this seems to be overweighed by the evidence in II Kings for 586.

After the Exile. The Persian Empire adopted the Assyrian-Babylonian calendar, and so apparently did the Jews. The seeming assumption of a fall new year in Neh. 1:1; 2:1 is thus so surprising that many scholars suspect some error. Scholars are divided on whether Ezra is to be dated in the 7th year of Artaxerxes I (458) or II (397), or possibly in the 37th year of Artaxerxes I (428). On this question see Intro. to Ezra. From this time until the Maccabean Revolt we have little information about Jewish history.

The years of the Seleucid era in the dates of I, II Macc. were officially counted from Oct. 312 by the Hellenistic calendar, which began the year in the fall. The Jews, however, continued to observe the spring calendar they had been using since the Exile. In II Macc. the dates all seem to be Hellenistic, but in I Macc. dates of both kinds are found, evidently reproduced from different sources. The dates of the Seleucid kings and their doings presumably follow the official calendar and are counted from the fall of 312; but the dates of events among the Jews, which are generally quite specific, seem to be based on their own calendar. Scholars are divided on whether the Jewish years were antedated to the spring of 312 or postdated to the spring of 311. The former places the desecration of the temple in 168, the latter in 167, with other dates varying correspondingly. Either choice results in inconsistencies, but there seem to be somewhat fewer if the Jewish dates are 6 months later than the Hellenistic.

The precise days of the month shown in the table for some Maccabean dates are based on the known Babylonian dates for this period. Since the Jews fixed the exact day of beginning a new year by observation of the new moon rather than by advance calculation, their dates may have varied slightly from those of Babylon.

The Life of Jesus. The nativity stories of both Matt. and Luke say Jesus was born during the reign of Herod the Great (Matt. 2:1; Luke 1:5) and Matt. 2:16 implies that Jesus approached the age of 2 while Herod was still ruling. Since Herod died shortly before the passover of 4 B.C. our Christian era, calculated in the 6th cent., begins several years too late.

Luke 2:1-2 places Jesus' birth at the time of a census ordered by Augustus Caesar when Quirinius was governor of Syria. Such a census was taken in A.D. 6/7 following the transfer of Judea from the rule of Herod's son Archelaus to that of a prefect under Quirinius, and it touched off a revolt (cf. Acts 5:37). Many scholars believe that this was the first census in Judea and that it is erroneously associated with Jesus' birth. Others, however, point to some evidences that Augustus inaugurated a census policy for his empire, with a 14-year interval as found in Egypt at a later time, that the first census thus may have been taken in 7 B.C., and that Quirinius then may have been associated with Saturninus, who is recorded as governor of Syria at that time. See comment on Luke 2:1-20.

Luke 3:1 dates the start of the ministry of John the Baptist in the 15th year of Tiberius. By the official Roman count this was the year beginning Aug. 19, A.D. 28, the anniversary of his succeeding Augustus. The Jews, however, may have counted it to coincide with their year beginning in the spring of 28, and some scholars have suggested that the author may have followed the Hellenistic calendar and antedated it to the fall of 27. The gospels give no indication of how long John had been preaching when he baptized Jesus, but their concern with the relationship between the 2 shows that John's movement was still active when they were written (cf. Acts 18:25; 19:3-4) and therefore that his ministry must have lasted long enough to win a considerable following.

Some passages say that Jesus' ministry began only after John's ended (Matt. 4:12; Mark 1:14) but this may be an error arising from the Christian conception of John as Jesus' forerunner. Luke 7:18-23 tells of John's sending 2 of his disciples to check on what he has heard of Jesus' work. In the parallel in Matt. 11:2-6 he is said to be in prison at the time, but this may be an addition of the author, for John's imprisonment was in the fortress of Machaerus, where access by his disciples would seem questionable. John 3:22-24 also describes Jesus and John as active at the same time. Some overlapping is therefore probable.

John 2:20 reports that at the passover at the beginning of Jesus' ministry Herod's temple, which was still incomplete, had taken 46 years to build. Since it was begun in 20/19 the date indicated is 28.

The common idea that Jesus' ministry lasted 3 years is derived from a literalistic interpolation of the events described in the Synoptics into the chronological framework of John, but the accounts differ too much for valid harmonizing. John refers to a series of feasts that bring Jesus to Jerusalem, including 2 passovers before that at which he was crucified (2:13; 6:4). A ministry of a little over 2 years is therefore assumed. In the Synoptics, Jesus' ministry is all in Galilee until his final journey to Judea. Most scholars find this Synoptic portrayal more plausible, though many believe that the one visit to Jerusalem lasted longer than a single week. In the account of the feeding of the 5,000 the mention of green grass (Mark 6:39) dates the event in early spring, presumably a year before Jesus' crucifixion. Preceding this is the story of the disciples' plucking grain on the sabbath (Matt. 12:1-8; Mark 2:23-28; Luke 6:1-5). If this order can be trusted the harvest time *ca*. 10 months earlier is indicated. Thus the Synoptics also suggest a ministry of *ca*. 2 years.

The most certain chronological information in the NT is that Jesus was crucified on a Friday at the passover season. The fixing of the date is complicated by a difference in the Synoptics and John (see comments on Matt. 26:17-29; Mark 14:12-16; John 13:1) and by the Jewish custom, mentioned above, of postponing the beginning of the new year for a day if witnesses failed to report seeing the new moon. Nevertheless astronomy provides us with 4 possibilities: April 11, 27; Mar. 18, 29, probably a month too early for passover; Apr. 7, 30; Apr. 3, 33. Of these the most widely accepted among scholars is Apr. 7, 30, which fits most easily with the usual chronology for Paul. On the other hand Apr. 3, 33, is not impossible in relation to Paul; and in relation to the 15th year of Tiberius, i.e. 28/29, it allows more time for John's ministry before his baptism of Jesus.

The Career of Paul. The major chronological problem for Paul is the adjustment of the story in Acts to his own account in Gal. 1-2. Whereas he swears that he has visited Jerusalem only twice since his conversion, Acts tells of 3 or perhaps 4 visits before the time when other evidence would seem to date the letter. Though several theories have been advanced, the equation of the conference of Acts 15 about Paul's Gentile mission with the 2nd visit he describes seems most favored (see comments on Acts 11:27-30; 15:1-35; 18:22-23; Gal. 2:1-10).

An inscription dug up at Delphi shows that Gallio's term of one year as proconsul at Corinth began in the early summer of 51 and thus dates Paul's arraignment before him (Acts 18:12-17). From this fixed point the dates of the preceding events of Paul's missionary career according to the order in Acts and the intervals of Gal. 1-2 can be calculated, and the dates of subsequent events may be estimated by the account in Acts and certain references in I, II Cor., Rom. An important question is whether, as some scholars believe, Paul suffered a period of imprisonment during his long stay in Ephesus *ca.* 53-56, during which he wrote some or all of his prison letters (Phil., Col., Philem.), traditionally assigned to his later stay in Rome (see Intro. to Phil.).

The replacement of the procurator Felix by Festus (Acts 24:27) might be expected to fix the date for Paul's 2 years in prison in Caesarea, but unfortunately the reports of this event are inconsistent, so that it may be placed as early as 55 or as late as 61. A late source gives some basis for 59, which seems to fit the Acts chronology well.

The chronology of Paul shown in the table is accepted, with variations of a year or 2, by many scholars. A few, however, have undertaken to derive a chronology primarily from the data Paul himself gives in his letters and have arrived at a somewhat shorter career for him. If the Acts order for the conference of Gal. 2:1-10 is dismissed, most of Paul's missionary work can be fitted into the 14-year interval preceding this 2nd visit to Jerusalem. Following it there need be only some 2 or 3 years during which he collected the offering for the Jerusalem poor (cf. Rom. 15:25-31; I Cor. 16:1-4; II Cor. 8-9; Gal. 2:10) and then delivered it on his final visit, when he was arrested. One chronology dates the conversion in 34, the first visit in 37, the conference in 51—following his appearance before Gallio during a later visit to Corinth rather than the first—and his final visit to Jerusalem and arrest in 53 or 54.

For Further Study: John Knox, *Chapters in a Life of Paul,* 1950. G. A. Barrois, "Chronology, etc." in *IB,* 1952. R. A. Parker, W. H. Dubberstein, *Babylonian Chronology 626 B.C.–A.D. 75,* rev. ed., 1956. E. F. Campbell, Jr., "The Ancient Near East: Chronological Bibliography and Charts"; D. N. Freedman, "OT Chronology"; G. E. Wright, "The Archaeology of Palestine," in G. E. Wright, ed., *The Bible and the Ancient Near East,* 1961. G. B. Caird, "Chronology of the NT"; S. J. DeVries, "Chronology of the OT," in *IDB,* 1962. E. R. Thiele, *The Mysterious Numbers of the Hebrew Kings,* rev. ed., 1965.

MEASURES AND MONEY

GORDON B. DUNCAN

A Canadian motorist visiting the U.S. finds that more gallons are needed to fill his tank, and a pharmacist or jeweler soon learns that the ounces on his scales are heavier than those at the post office. Ancient people also had to take different standards for measures into account (cf. e.g. Gen. 23:16; Exod. 30:13; Deut. 3:11; II Sam. 14:26; II Chr. 3:3; Ezek. 40:5). Archaeological discovery of inscribed weights and containers from biblical times shows further that there was considerable tolerance in the standards, for no 2 examples have been found in agreement; evidently the repeated injunctions against false measures (e.g. Lev. 19:35-36; Deut. 25:13-15; Prov. 20:10; Amos 8:5) were aimed at rather gross deviations. That the values varied at different periods would seem almost certain (cf. II Chr. 3:3), and that some of the relations stated in the Bible (cf. esp. Ezek. 45:11-15) and other ancient writings are later harmonizings of systems originally independent is to be suspected.

In spite of much scholarly study, therefore, calculations of biblical measures are at best approximate. For convenience the equivalents in the tables given here have been chosen as "round" numbers. Though obviously not exact, they lie within the limits indicated by the varying data and in view of the uncertainties may sometimes be as close as other computations to several decimal places.

I. LENGTHS AND AREAS

The measure of length most often mentioned in the Bible is the **cubit**, which originated as the distance from elbow to tip of middle finger. The **span,** originally the distance between the tips of thumb and little finger of the outstretched hand, came to be considered half a cubit. Various archaeological data —e.g. the inscription stating the length of Hezekiah's conduit (cf. II Kings 20:20)—point to a usual cubit of 17½-18 inches, so that the convenient equivalents of Table 1 are fairly close.

In the vision of the restored temple in Ezek. 40-48 the dimensions are given in cubits described as a handbreadth longer than usual (40:5; 43:13). Probably this represents a return to a standard known or at least believed to have been in use when Solomon's temple was built (cf. II Chr. 3:3). Egyptian and Mesopotamian analogies suggest that the longer cubit contained 7 handbreadths, equaling 20-21 inches, though it is not certain that handbreadths under the 2 standards were identical. Apparently the span of Ezek. 43:13 is intended to be equal to the half cubit of vs. 17 and thus in this system contained 3½ handbreadths.

In the NT **fathom** translates a Greek measure based on the distance between fingertips of the outstretched arms, *ca.* 6 feet. It was used for land as well as water. **Mile** in Matt. 5:41 is probably the Roman mile of 1,000 paces (double steps), standardized at *ca.* 58 inches each, or a total of *ca.* 1,618 yards. Elsewhere in the RSV miles are conversions into modern terms of Greek distances in stadia, the stadion being 400 cubits, *ca.* 200 yards. Similarly **hundred yards** (John 21:8) is a conversion of 200 cubits.

A **sabbath day's journey** was the distance scribal interpretation permitted one to go from his home on the sabbath without violating the injunction of Exod. 16:29. Most evidence indicates it was 2,000 cubits, *ca.* 1,000 yards (cf. Josh. 3:4). **Day's journey** was apparently not a standardized distance.

Area, when not indicated by dimensions in cubits, was measured by the "yoke," translated **acre**—i.e. the land a yoke of oxen could plow in a day, perhaps *ca.* .6 acre like the corresponding Roman term —or else by the amount of grain needed to seed the plot (cf. Lev. 27:16; I Kings 18:32).

II. VOLUMES

The units in Tables 2 and 3 are classified as dry or liquid measures on the basis of their use in the Bible. Possibly some were used for both kinds of materials, but all except the largest may represent containers—pots and perhaps baskets—of standardized shapes esp. suited for one or the other. In the description of a vision of a woman in an **ephah** (Zech. 5:6-11) the vessel is evidently so identified because of its form rather than its size. Here a lead cover is needed to keep the woman inside; contrast the excavated specimens of jars inscribed **bath,** which have small mouths. The demand that ephah and bath be "of the same measure" (Ezek. 45:11) thus may be an effort to standardize the capacities of vessels of similar size but differing shapes.

The derivation of the name **homer** shows that originally it was an assload of grain, which would be carried in a large sack (cf. Gen. 42:27). No doubt the quantity early became standardized along the trade routes, and at various places local smaller

1283

measures came to be adjusted to convenient fractions of this major unit. The series in Table 2 may represent a combination of 2 or more systems that developed in this way. The **cor,** originally a Sumerian measure, is used in reports of large quantities of grain (cf. e.g. I Kings 4:22; 5:11; Ezra 7:22). Whether it was equivalent to the homer is not entirely certain because of the corrupt text in Ezek. 45:14, and because of the corruption here and in I Kings 5:11 (cf. II Chr. 2:10) there is question whether it was ever used of liquids. The **lethech,** originally Canaanite, is mentioned only once, and the value given by the later rabbis may be merely a guess.

Measure is the regular RSV translation for seah (Gen. 18:6; Ruth 3:15, 17; I Sam. 25:18; I Kings 18:32; II Kings 7:1, 16, 18; Matt. 13:33; Luke 13:21; see footnotes) and is used in Isa. 40:12c for the lit. "third," which presumably means a seah pot as a 3rd of an ephah. It is also occasionally the translation for ephah (Deut. 25:14-15; Prov. 20:10; Mic. 6:10), bath (Luke 16:6), and cor (Luke 16:7). In Bel and the Dragon 3 **bushel** translates a Persian measure adopted in Egypt which was probably equivalent to *ca.* 1.8 U.S. bushels, but **fifty gallons** is a conversion into modern terms of the lit. "six metretes." Probably this Greek measure was equivalent to *ca.* 10 U.S. gallons, so that the total should be 60 gallons, corresponding to the conversion in John 2:6, where the lit. "two or three metretes" becomes "twenty or thirty gallons." In Matt. 5:15; Mark 4:21; Luke 11:33 "bushel" probably refers to a Roman measure equivalent to *ca.* a U.S. peck. **Quart** (Rev. 6:6) denotes a Greek measure equivalent to *ca.* a U.S. dry quart.

III. WEIGHTS AND WEIGHED MONEY

Most references to weights in the OT concern precious metals used as money. Until the intro. of coins into Palestine during the Persian period pieces of gold, silver, and bronze used in exchange had to be valued by weighing in balances.

All the biblical data about relationships among weights are found in connection with the **shekel of the sanctuary,** specified repeatedly in the P legislation (e.g. Exod. 30:13-14; Lev. 5:15; Num. 3:47-48) as the standard for offerings, esp. the contribution of a half shekel, or **beka** (Exod. 38:24-26), required yearly of each adult male. In several of the passages the sanctuary shekel is defined as containing 20 **gerahs,** evidently in distinction from a shekel containing another number, probably that referred to elsewhere in P (Gen. 23:16) as "according to the weights current among the merchants," i.e. the commercial standard. Calculation from the figures in Exod. 38:24-26 shows that there were 3,000 sanctuary shekels in a **talent.** Ezek. 45:12 states the relation of the sanctuary shekel to the **mina,** but the text is in doubt. On the basis of the LXX the RSV says 50 shekels to the mina, but the Hebrew text seems to indicate 60.

The repeated insistence of the P legislation on the sanctuary standard might suggest that it was heavier than the commercial standard, and this has often been assumed. On the other hand the reference in Neh. 10:32 to the yearly temple contribution as a 3rd of a shekel, presumably commercial, implies otherwise. If the same amount as half a sanctuary shekel is intended, the commercial shekel would be heavier by a ratio of 3 to 2. Other evidence, however, suggests a lesser difference. In Babylonia the shekel contained 24 gerahs, a relation that may well have been customary in Palestine also, even though the values were probably different. Evidence indicates that the Canaanites counted 50 shekels to the mina and 50 minas to the talent, in contrast to Babylonian ratios of 60 each; and thus it is likely that by the Palestinian commercial standard there were 2,500 shekels in a talent. If so, 2,500 24-gerah shekels by the commercial standard would make a talent of the same weight as the 3,000 20-gerah shekels by the sanctuary standard indicated in Exod. 38:24-26. Probably, therefore, the sanctuary standard differed from the commercial by having a shekel a 6th lighter. No doubt the name "beka"—derived from a root meaning "split"—was used for a half of either shekel.

Archaeological support for this assumption is perhaps to be found in the inscribed weights from preexilic times which have been uncovered in Palestine. Among these the largest number are labeled "netseph," a word not appearing in the OT. The ratio of the average of these weights to the probable weight of the commercial shekel is close enough to 5 to 6 to suggest that "shekel of the sanctuary" may be a postexilic designation for the netseph. In fact the inclusion of what may be an abbreviation for "shekel" on one of the netseph weights may indicate that this unit was sometimes called a shekel in preexilic times. If the P legislation was based on an older custom of contributing half a netseph, the renaming would be aimed at maintaining this equivalent of 10 gerahs rather than a 3rd of a commercial shekel, equivalent to only 8 gerahs. If, on the other hand, the contribution was a postexilic innovation, the legislation might be an effort to raise the requirement. In either case the repeated emphasis on the lighter standard becomes understandable as the basis for a higher actual rate.

Tables 4 and 5 display the assumed relations and equivalents of the OT weights according to the sanctuary and commercial standards as explained above. The **pim** is included on the basis of excavated weights so inscribed. No example has been found, however, of the **qesitah** (Gen. 33:19; Josh. 24:32; Job 42:11; see RSV footnotes) and its value and relations are unknown.

In the NT weights are specified only in John 12:3; 19:39, where **pound** probably means the Roman pound of *ca.* 11½ ounces, and Rev. 16:21, where **hundredweight** is a translation of "talent." Elsewhere in the NT both "pound" and "talent" refer to sums of money (see below).

IV. COINED MONEY

Coins seem to have been invented in Asia Minor or Greece in the 7th cent. B.C., and some of them soon found their way into Palestine, as revealed by excavations. The first coins officially used there, however, were the Persian gold **darics** issued by Darius the Great (522-486). Sums in darics appear in Ezra-Neh.; a reference to them in the time of

David (I Chr. 29:7) is of course an anachronism. The Persians also issued silver **shekels,** valued at 20 to the daric, which weighed only half a shekel by the Palestinian commercial standard. Whether a tax of 40 shekels which Nehemiah mentions (5:15) refers to these coins or to weighed silver is uncertain.

Alexander the Great introduced Greek **drachmas** throughout the Near East. In the Greek monetary system, which had developed in Asia Minor under Babylonian influence, the terms **mina** and **talent** were used for larger sums, mina meaning 100 drachmas and talent 60 minas, so that a talent was 6,000 drachmas. Since the drachmas issued by the Ptolemies in Egypt in the 3rd cent. approached the weight of half a sanctuary shekel, the LXX translators in some of the passages translated "shekel of the sanctuary" as "didrachma," i.e. 2-drachma coin. For "gerah" they used "obol," the smallest Greek silver coin, which was actually a 6th of a drachma rather than a 10th.

Later the drachma was devalued so that a talent became 100 minas or 10,000 drachmas, while silver shekels minted in the Phoenician coastal cities of Tyre and Sidon followed a heavier standard than that of Table 5. Thus in NT times the shekel was equated with the tetradrachma, i.e. 4-drachma coin. In the RSV of Matt. 17:24 **half-shekel tax** is an interpretation of the lit. "didrachma," and **shekel** in vs. 27 stands for "stater," here meaning a tetradrachma. The lost coin in Luke 15:8-9 is a drachma, and the **pounds** in the parable of Luke 19:11-27 represent minas. The payment to Judas, lit. "thirty of silver" (Matt. 26:15), means 30 shekels as in the corresponding Hebrew phrase in Zech. 11:12. Since the Jews first minted shekels during their revolt against Rome in A.D. 66-70, the coins given Judas would have to be Phoenician shekels or else tetradrachmas counted as shekels.

The money most often mentioned in the NT is the **denarius,** a Roman silver coin bearing the "likeness and inscription" of the emperor (Matt. 22:20; Mark 12:16; Luke 20:24). Though slightly lighter than a drachma, it was valued more highly because officially required for paying taxes (cf. Matt. 22:19). The implication that a denarius was a normal day's wage for a field laborer (Matt. 20:2; cf. Tobit 5:14, where a drachma is the daily wage for a guide and bodyguard on a long journey) provides a basis for judging the actual value of money in ancient times. Perhaps the suggestion that 200 denarii would buy a minimum meal for 5,000 (Mark 6:37, 44) gives a clue to its purchasing power.

Penny as a price for sparrows (Matt. 10:29; Luke 12:6) refers to the assarion, a bronze coin issued by local rulers as an approximate equivalent for the official Roman bronze as, which was valued at a 16th of a denarius. Elsewhere (Matt. 5:26; Mark 12:42) "penny" stands for the quadrans, the smallest Roman bronze coin, worth a 4th of an as. The smallest Greek bronze coin, the lepton, is represented by the **two copper coins** contributed by a poor widow, which together are said to equal a quadrans (Mark 12:42).

For Further Study. G. A. Barrois, "Chronology, Metrology, Etc.," in *IB,* 1952. Herbert Hamburger, "Money, Coins"; O. R. Sellers, "Weights and Measures," in *IDB,* 1962.

Table 1. Lengths

UNIT	RELATION TO CUBIT	APPROXIMATE EQUIVALENT
finger	÷24	.75 in.
handbreadth	÷6	3 in.
span	÷2	9 in.
cubit		1.5 ft.

Table 2. Dry Volumes

UNIT	RELATION TO EPHAH	APPROXIMATE EQUIVALENT
kab	÷18	.89 qt.
omer	÷10	1.6 qt.
seah	÷3	.67 pk.
ephah		.5 bu.
lethech	×5	2.5 bu.
homer	×10	5 bu.
cor	×10	5 bu.

Table 3. Liquid Volumes

UNIT	RELATION TO BATH	APPROXIMATE EQUIVALENT
log	÷72	.56 pt.
hin	÷6	3.33 qt.
bath		5 gal.
cor	×10	50 gal.

Table 4. Weights, Sanctuary Standard

UNIT	RELATION TO SHEKEL	APPROXIMATE EQUIVALENT
gerah	÷20	.017 oz.
beka	÷2	.17 oz.
shekel		.33 oz.
mina	×60	1.25 lb.
talent	×3,000	62.5 lb.

Table 5. Weights, Commercial Standard

UNIT	RELATION TO SHEKEL	APPROXIMATE EQUIVALENT
gerah	÷24	.017 oz.
beka	÷2	.2 oz.
pim	÷1.5	.267 oz.
shekel		.4 oz.
mina	×50	1.25 lb.
talent	×2,500	62.5 lb.

INDEX OF SCRIPTURE REFERENCES

Reader note: General references are often cited followed by more detailed references. E.g., Gen. 1:1–11:32 is followed by Gen. 1:1-8. This is in keeping with the arrangement and presentation of material within the Commentary.

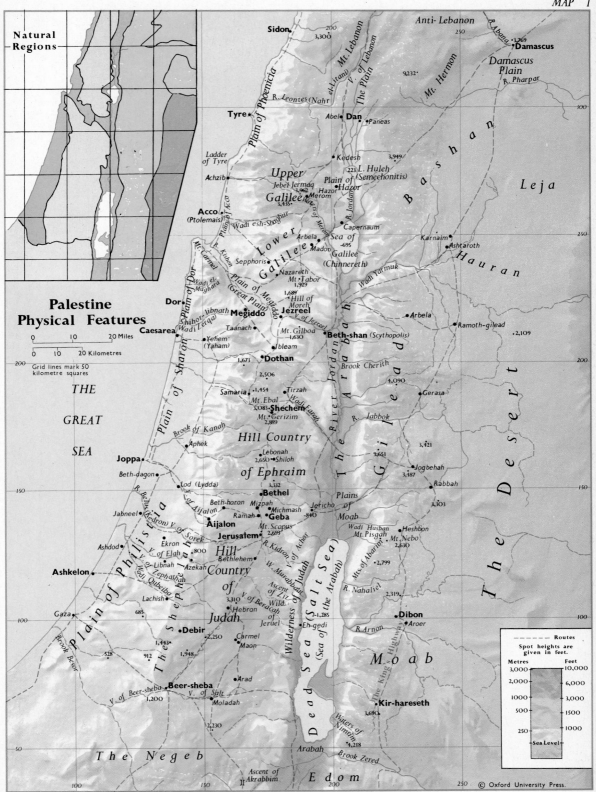

MAP 1

Natural Regions

Palestine Physical Features

Grid lines mark 50 kilometre squares

0 10 20 Miles
0 10 20 Kilometres

THE

GREAT

SEA

Anti-Lebanon

Sidon •
3,300

Mt. Lebanon
V. of Lebanon
The Plain

R. Abana • 3,769
• Damascus

9,232 •

Damascus Plain
R. Pharpar

R. Leontes (Nahr el-Litani)

Plain of Phoenicia

Tyre •

Abel • Dan •
• Paneas

Ladder of Tyre

Mt. Hermon

Bashan

Leja

Achzib •

Upper

Galilee

• Kedesh
3,949

223 L. Huleh (Semechonitis)

Jebel Jermaq 3,962

Plain of Hazor

Hazor •

Merom •

Plain of Acco

Acco (Ptolemais) •

3,435 •

Waters of Merom
R. Jordan

Capernaum •

Karnaim •
• Ashtaroth

Wadi esh-Shaghur

Lower

Arbela •
Madon •

Sea of Galilee (Chinnereth)
−695

Hauran

Sepphoris •

Galilee

Nazareth •

Mt. Tabor
1,929

Wadi Yarmuk

• Arbela

R. Kishon

Mt. Carmel

Dor •

Wadi el-Mughara

Plain of Dor

Plain of Megiddo (Great Plain)

1,689
• Hill of Moreh

Ramoth-gilead •

• 2,109

Caesarea •

Shihor-libnath (Wadi Zerqa)

Megiddo •

• Jezreel

V. of Jezreel

Taanach •

Mt. Gilboa
1,630

Beth-shan (Scythopolis)

Gilead

Yehem (Yaham) •

Ibleam •

Dothan •
1,673

Brook Cherith

4,090

• Gerasa

2,506 •

Plain of Sharon

Samaria •
1,454

Mt. Ebal
3,083 Shechem
Mt. Gerizim
2,889

Tirzah •

Wadi Farah

R. Jabbok

3,421 •

THE

Brook of Kanah

Hill Country

Joppa •

Aphek •

R. Jabbok

3,651

• Jogbehah
3,487

Beth-dagon •

Lebonah
2,650 • Shiloh

of Ephraim

Rabbah •

Lod (Lydda) •

3,332

Plains of Moab

3,303

Beth-horon • Mizpah •
Ramah •

Bethel •

Jericho •
−840

Jabneel •

R. Belus (Kedron) V. of Aijalon

Michmash •

Aijalon •

Geba •

Mt. Scopus
2,693

Wadi Husban
Mt. Pisgah

Heshbon •

Ekron •

V. of Sorek

Jerusalem •

Mts. of Abarim

Mt. Nebo
2,630

Ashdod •

V. of Elah
800

Hill

R. Kidron

• 2,799

Libnah •

Bethlehem •

Country

W. Murabba'at

R. Nahaliel

Ashkelon •

Wadi Qubeiba
Azekah •

V. of Zephathah

of

Ascent of Ziz

2,319 •

Lachish •

3,310

Wilderness of Judah

Dibon •
• Aroer

Gaza •

685

Judah

Hebron •
Wilderness of Jeruel

Dead Sea (Salt Sea) (Sea of the Arabah)

R. Arnon

Debir •

1,443 • 2,250
Carmel
Maon •

En-gedi •
−1,285

Moab

528 •
912

1,948 •

• Arad

Kir-hareseth •

The King's Highway

Beer-sheba •
1,200

V. of Salt

Moladah •

3,690

The Negeb

2,230 •

Arabah

Waters of Nimrim
−4,218

Brook Zered

Edom

Ascent of Akrabbim

Brook Besor

The Shephelah

Plain of Philistia

The Arabah

The River Jordan

The Desert

Routes
Spot heights are given in feet.

Metres   Feet
3,000   10,000
2,000   6,000
1,000   3,000
500   1500
250   1000
Sea Level

© Oxford University Press.

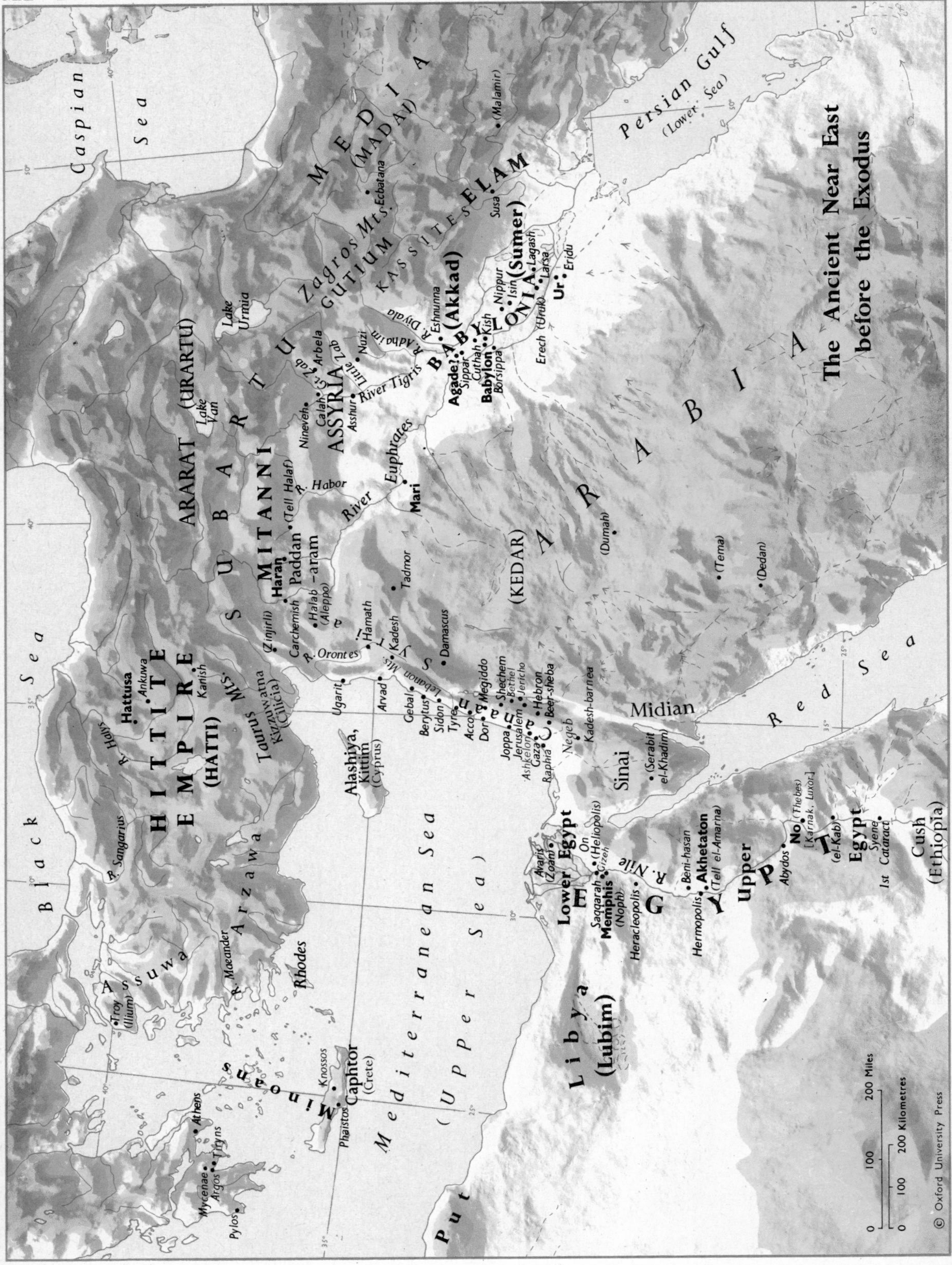

MAP 2

The Ancient Near East
before the Exodus

Caspian Sea

Black Sea

Mediterranean Sea
(Upper Sea)

Persian Gulf
(Lower Sea)

Red Sea

MEDIA (MADAI)

ELAM

GUTIUM

KASSITE

SUMER (Sumer)

BABYLONIA (Akkad)

ARARAT (URARTU)
Lake Van

Lake Urmia

Zagros Mts.
Ecbatana

Malamir

Susa
Isin
Nippur
Lagash
Larsa
Ur (Ur)
Erech (Uruk)
Eridu
Kish
Borsippa
Babylon
Cuthah
Sippar
Agade
Eshnunna
R. Adhaim
R. Diyala

SUBARTU

MITANNI

ASSYRIA

Nineveh
Calah
Asshur
Arbela
Z. Zab
Nuzi
Little Zab
R. Habor
Paddan-aram
Haran (Tell Halaf)
Carchemish
Halab (Aleppo)
Zinjirli
Mari

Euphrates River

River Tigris

Tigris

ARABIA

(KEDAR)

(Dumah)

(Tema)

(Dedan)

Tadmor

SYRIA

Kadesh
Hamath
Damascus
R. Orontes
Lebanon Mts.

Ugarit
Arvad
Gebal
Berytus
Sidon
Tyre
Acco
Dor
Megiddo
Shechem
Bethel
Jericho
Jerusalem
Hebron
Joppa
Ashkelon
Gaza
Raphia
Beer-sheba
Negeb
Kadesh-barnea

Alashiya, Kittim (Cyprus)

HITTITE EMPIRE (HATTI)

Hattusa
Ankuwa
Kanish
R. Halys
R. Sangarius
Troy (Ilium)
R. Maeander
Assuwa
Arzawa
Taurus Mts.
Kizzuwatna (Cilicia)

Rhodes

Minoans
Caphtor (Crete)
Knossos
Phaistos

Mycenae
Argos
Tiryns
Pylos
Athens

Midian

Sinai
(Serabit el-Khadim)

Lower Egypt
On (Heliopolis)
Avaris (Zoan?)
Gizeh
Saqqarah
Memphis (Noph)
Heracleopolis
Beni-hasan
Hermopolis
Akhetaton (Tell el-Amarna)

Upper Egypt
Abydos
No (Thebes)
[Karnak, Luxor]
(el-Kab)
Syene
1st Cataract

Cush (Ethiopia)

EGYPT

R. Nile

Libya (Lubim)

Put

200 Miles
200 Kilometres
0   100   200
0   100   200

© Oxford University Press

MAP 3

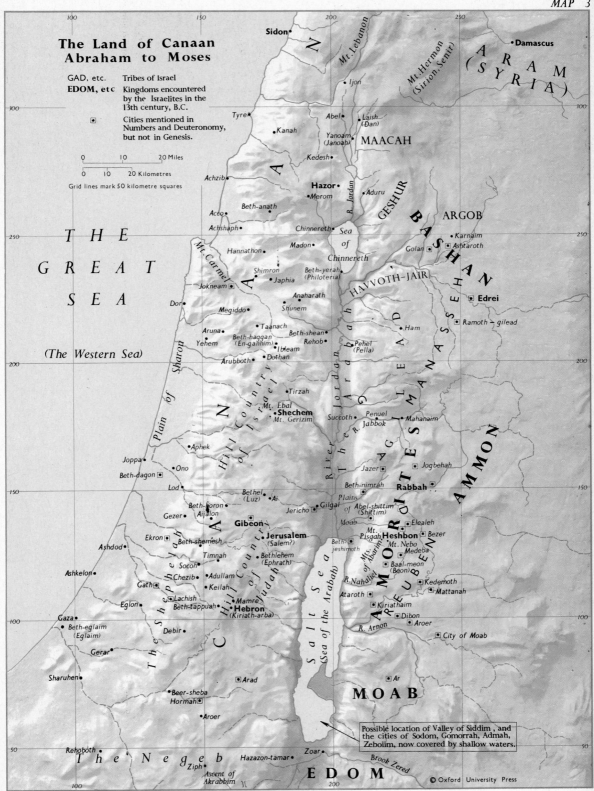

The Land of Canaan
Abraham to Moses

GAD, etc.   Tribes of Israel
EDOM, etc   Kingdoms encountered
            by the Israelites in the
            13th century, B.C.
     ▣   Cities mentioned in
            Numbers and Deuteronomy,
            but not in Genesis.

0   10   20 Miles
0   10   20 Kilometres
Grid lines mark 50 kilometre squares

THE
GREAT
SEA

(The Western Sea)

Sidon

Damascus

Mt. Lebanon

Mt. Hermon
(Sirion, Senir)

A R A M
(S Y R I A)

Ijon

Tyre

Abel

Laish
(Dan)

Kanah

Yanoam
(Janoah)

MAACAH

Kedesh

Achzib

GESHUR

Aduru

ARGOB

Beth-anath

Hazor

Merom

R. Jordan

Acco

BASHAN

Achshaph

Chinnereth

Sea
of
Chinnereth

Karnaim

Golan

Ashtaroth

Hannathon

Madon

Mt. Carmel

Jokneam

Shimron

Japhia

Beth-yerah
(Philoteria)

HAVVOTH-JAIR

Edrei

Dor

Megiddo

Anaharath

Shunem

Aruna

Taanach

Beth-shean

Ham

Ramoth - gilead

Plain of Sharon

Yehem

Beth-haggan
(En-gannim)

Rehob

Pehel
(Pella)

Arubboth

Dothan

Ibleam

G I L E A D

Tirzah

M A N A S S E H

Mt. Ebal

Shechem
Mt. Gerizim

Hill Country of Israel

Aphek

Succoth

Penuel

Jabbok

Mahanaim

River Jordan

River Arabah

Joppa

Ono

Jazer

Jogbehah

AMMON

Beth-dagon

Lod

Bethel
(Luz)

Ai

Beth-nimrah

Rabbah

Beth-horon

Jericho

Gilgal

Plains
of
Moab

Abel-shittim
(Shittim)

Gezer

Aijalon

Gibeon

Moab

Elealeh

Ekron

Beth-shemesh

Jerusalem
(Salem?)

Mt.
Pisgah

Heshbon

Bezer

Ashdod

Timnah

Socoh

Bethlehem
(Ephrath)

Beth-
jeshimoth

Mt. Nebo

Medeba

Ashkelon

Chezib

Adullam

Mamre

Baal-meon
(Beon)

A M O R I T E S

Gath

Keilah

Hebron
(Kiriath-arba)

Kedemoth

Mattanah

Eglon

Lachish

Beth-tappuah

R E U B E N

Gaza

Debir

Kiriathaim

Beth-eglaim
(Eglaim)

Atarbth

Dibon

Aroer

Gerar

R. Arnon

City of Moab

Sharuhen

The Shephelah

Hill Country of Judah

Salt Sea
(Sea of the Arabah)

Arad

Ar

MOAB

Beer-sheba

Hormah

Aroer

Possible location of Valley of Siddim , and
the cities of Sodom, Gomorrah, Admah,
Zeboiim, now covered by shallow waters.

Rehoboth

The Negeb

Ziph

Hazazon-tamar

Zoar

Brook Zered

Ascent of
Akrabbim

E D O M

© Oxford University Press

MAP 4

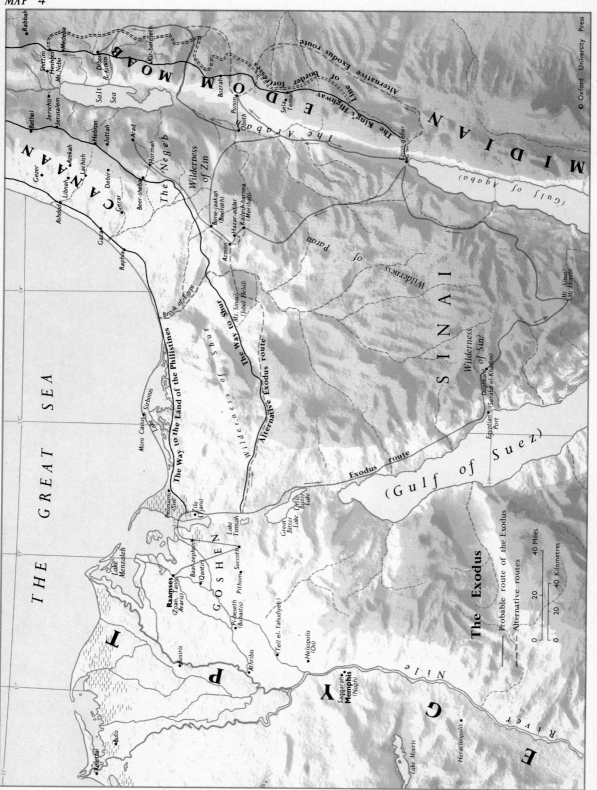

The Exodus

Probable route of the Exodus
Alternative routes

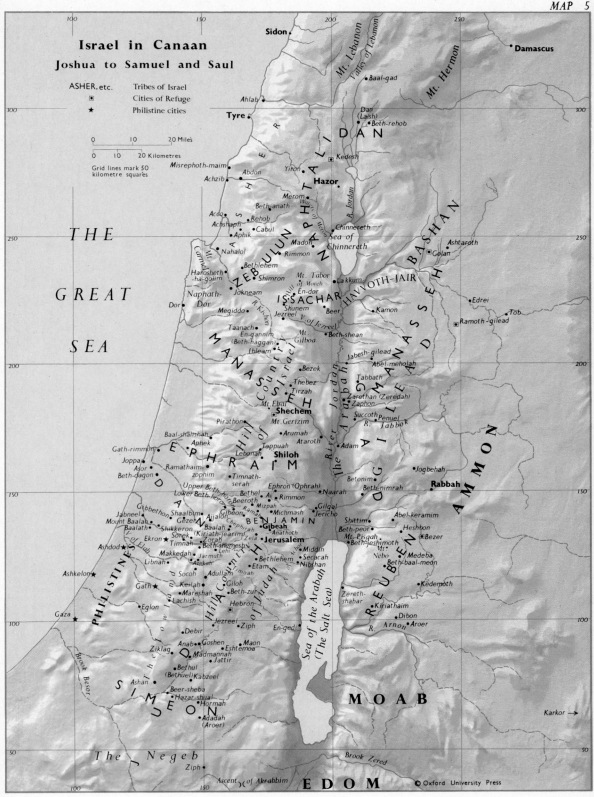

MAP 5

Israel in Canaan

Joshua to Samuel and Saul

ASHER, etc.   Tribes of Israel
⊡   Cities of Refuge
★   Philistine cities

0   10   20 Miles
0   10   20 Kilometres
Grid lines mark 50
kilometre squares

THE

GREAT

SEA

Sidon

Damascus

Mt. Lebanon
Valley of Lebanon

Baal-gad

Mt. Hermon

Ahlab

Tyre

Dan
(Laish)
Beth-rehob

N A P H T A L I   D A N

Kedesh

Misrephoth-maim

Yiron

Hazor

Abdon

Achzib

Merom

R. Jordan

Waters of Merom

Beth-anath

Acco
Achshaph
Aphik
Rehob
Cabul

Madon

Rimmon

Chinnereth —
Sea of
Chinnereth

Ashtaroth

Golan

B A S H A N

Nahalol

Bethlehem

Shimron

Mt. Tabor

Harosheth
-ha-goiim

Jokneam

ZEBULUN

Mt. Tabor
Hill of Moreh
En-dor

Lakkum

HAVVOTH-JAIR

Edrei

Tob

Naphath-
Dor

Dor

Megiddo

R. Kishon

ISSACHAR
Shunem
Jezreel
V. of Jezreel
Beer

Kamon

Ramoth-gilead

Taanach

En-gannim
(Beth-haggan)

Mt.
Gilboa

Beth-shean

M A N A S S E H   I N   G I L E A D

Ibleam

Jabesh-gilead

Abel-meholah

Bezek

Tabbath

THE   Country   of   Israel

Thebez

Tirzah

Zarethan (Zeredah)
Zaphon

Mt. Ebal
Shechem
Mt. Gerizim

Succoth
Penuel
R. Jabbok

Pirathon

Arumah

G A D

Baal-shalishah

Aphek

Ataroth

Gath-rimmon

Tappuah

Adam

Joppa
Azor
Beth-dagon

E P H R A I M

Lebonah

Shiloh

Jogbehah

Ramathaim-
zophim

Timnath-
serah

Ephron (Ophrah)

Naarah

A M M O N

Rabbah

Betonim
Beth-nimrah

D A N

Upper Beth-horon
Lower Beth-horon

Bethel
Ai
Rimmon

Gibbethon
Shaalbim
Gezer
Aijalon
Chephirah
Gibeon
Ramah

Mizpah

Michmash

Gilgal
Jericho

Abel-keramim

Jabneel
Mount Baalah
Baalath
Shikkeron
Sorek
Timnah
Zorah

Baalah
(Kiriath-jearim)
Anathoth
Zela

BENJAMIN
Gibeah

Jerusalem

Beth-peor
Mt. Pisgah
Beth-jeshimoth
Mt.
Nebo

Heshbon

Bezer

Medeba
Beth-baal-meon

R E U B E N

Ekron ★
Beth-shemesh
Lehi
Makkedah
Libnah
Jarmuth
Azekah

Middin
Secacah
Nibshan

Bethlehem
Etam

Ashdod ★

Hill   Country   of   Judah

Kedemoth

Socoh
Valley of Elah
Adullam
Keilah
Mareshah
Lachish
Eglon

Giloh
Beth-zur

Zereth-
shahar

Kiriathaim

Dibon

Ashkelon ★

Gath ★

Hebron

Aroer

The Shephelah or Lowland

R. Arnon

Gaza ★

Jezreel
Ziph

En-gedi

PHILISTINES

Debir

Anab
Ziklag
Madmannah
Jattir

Goshen
Eshtemoa
Maon

Sea of the Arabah
(The Salt Sea)

Brook Besor

Bethul
(Bethuel)
Kabzeel

M O A B

Ashan
Beer-sheba
Hazar-shual
Hormah

S I M E O N

Adadah
(Aroer)

Karkor →

The   Negeb

Ziph

Brook Zered

Ascent   of Akrabbim

E D O M

© Oxford University Press

The   River   Jordan

The   Arabah

Mt.
Carmel

MAP 6

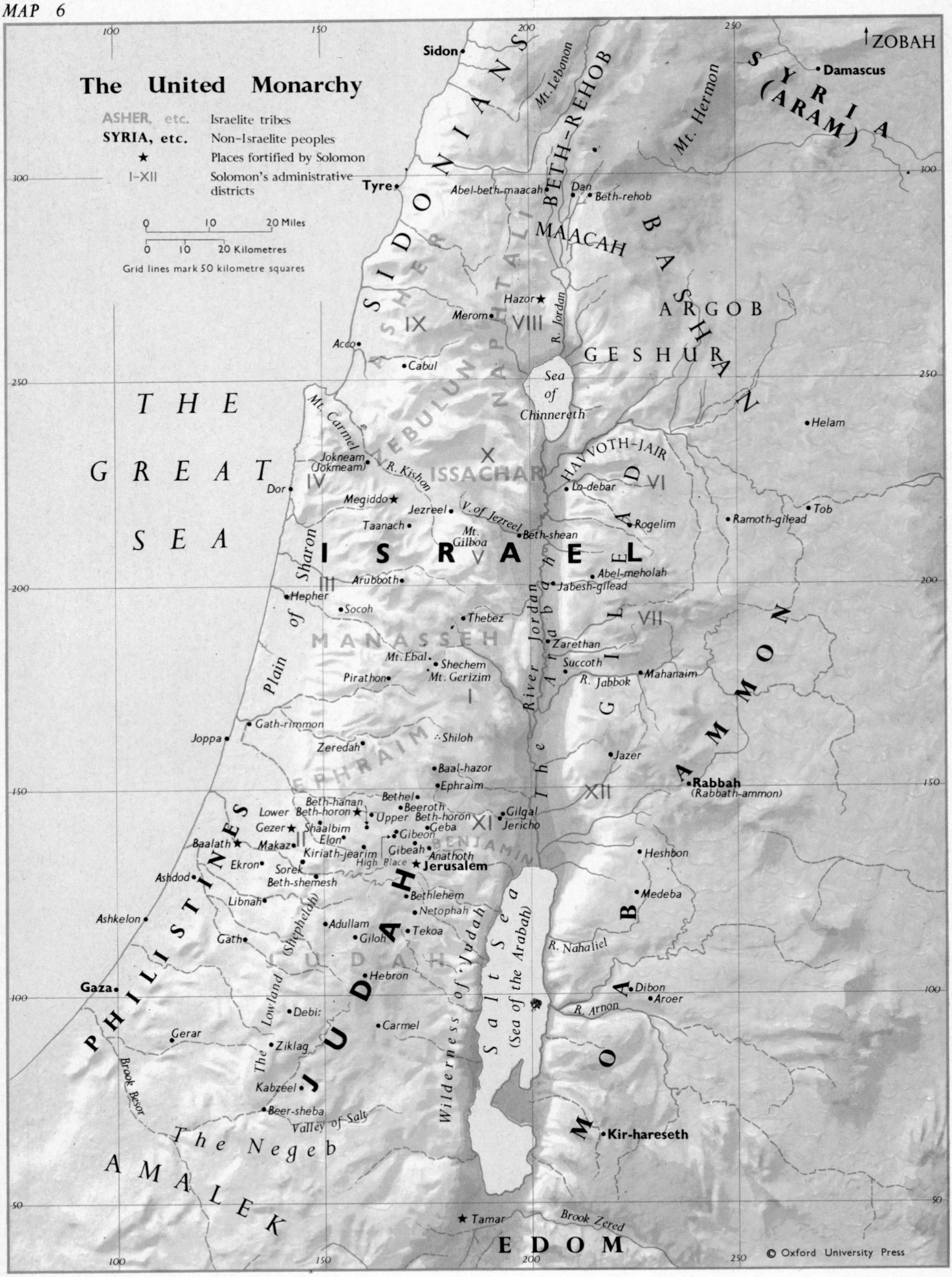

The United Monarchy

ASHER, etc.   Israelite tribes
SYRIA, etc.   Non-Israelite peoples
★   Places fortified by Solomon
I–XII   Solomon's administrative districts

0   10   20 Miles
0   10   20 Kilometres
Grid lines mark 50 kilometre squares

100   150   200   250

↑ZOBAH

Sidon
• Damascus

S Y R I A
(A R A M)

Mt. Lebanon

Mt. Hermon

BETH-REHOB

Tyre
Abel-beth-maacah
Dan
Beth-rehob

MAACAH

B A S H A N

A R G O B

Hazor ★
Merom •
IX
VIII
R. Jordan

GESHUR

Acco •
• Cabul

Sea of Chinnereth

• Helam

THE
GREAT
SEA

Mt. Carmel
Jokneam (Jokmeam)
R. Kishon
Dor •
IV
Megiddo ★
Taanach •
Jezreel •
V. of Jezreel
Mt. Gilboa
Beth-shean •
Lo-debar •
X
ISSACHAR
HAVVOTH-JAIR
VI
Rogelim •
Ramoth-gilead •
• Tob

I S R A E L

Plain of Sharon
III
Arubboth •
• Hepher
• Socoh
MANASSEH
• Thebez
Abel-meholah •
Jabesh-gilead •
GILEAD
Zarethan •
Succoth •
VII
R. Jabbok
Mahanaim •

Mt. Ebal
Shechem •
Pirathon •
Mt. Gerizim
I

Joppa •
• Gath-rimmon
Zeredah •
⁖ Shiloh
EPHRAIM
• Jazer

• Baal-hazor
• Ephraim
Bethel •
Beth-hanan
Lower Beth-horon ★
Gezer ★
Shaalbim
Makaz •
II
Beeroth •
Upper Beth-horon ★
Geba •
Gibeon •
Elon
XI
Gilgal
Jericho
XII
• Rabbah
(Rabbath-ammon)
A M M O N

Baalath ★
Ekron •
Sorek
Kiriath-jearim
Gibeah •
Anathoth
High Place
★ Jerusalem
BENJAMIN

Ashdod •
Beth-shemesh •
Libnah •
The Lowland (Shephelah)
Bethlehem •
Netophah •
• Heshbon

Ashkelon •
Gath •
Adullam •
Giloh •
• Tekoa
Salt Sea
(Sea of the Arabah)
Medeba •

R. Nahaliel

J U D A H
Wilderness of Judah
Hebron •

P H I L I S T I N E S

Gaza •
• Debir
Carmel •
• Dibon
• Aroer
R. Arnon

Gerar •
Ziklag •
The Negeb
Kabzeel •
M O A B

Beer-sheba •
Valley of Salt
• Kir-hareseth

A M A L E K

★ Tamar
Brook Zered

Brook Besor

E D O M

© Oxford University Press

250   300   250   200   150   100   50

50   100   150   200   250

MAP 7

Pergamum
Sardis
Smyrna
Samos
Chalcis
VAN
Rhodes
Caphtor
(Crete)
The Great Sea
IBYA
IBIM)

LYDIA
(LUD)
HITTITES
ARARAT
(URARTU)
Caspian Sea

Meshech
Kue Tubal
Iconium
Kanish
Melid
L. Van
Van
Tabriz

HORITES
L. Urmia

Markasi
Samal
Gurgum
Kummukhu
Amida
MEDIA

Tarsus
Adana
Yaudi
Carchemish
Haran R. Khabur
Gozan
Singara
Nineveh
Arbela

Alalakh
Halab
ASSYRIA
Calah

Posidium
Hittites
Tiphsah
Asshur
Nuzi
Arrapkha
Ecbatana

Ugarit
Hamath
Qatna
Tirqa
Mari
R. Euphrates
Eshnunna
Susa

Alashiya
Arvad
Homs
Tadmor
BABYLONIA

Kittim
(Cyprus)
Gebal
Berytus
Damascus
Babylon
Nippur

Sidon
Tyre
Lebanon
Hazor
Bashan
Bozrah

Acco
Dor
Megiddo
Samaria
Shechem
Gilead
Rabbah
Ammon

Joppa
Ashkelon
Gaza
Judah
Israel
Jerusalem
Moab
KEDAR

Kenite
Seir
Nebaioth
Ur

Pharos
Naucratis
Shur
Sela
Edom
Dumah

Memphis
(Noph)
Heliopolis
(On)
Sinai
Ezion-geber
Buz
Sealand

Akhetaton
(T.el-Amarna)
EGYPT
Midian
Ephah
Tema
Persian Gulf

Oasis
Myos Hormos
Dedan
Dilmun

Thebes
(No)
R. Nile
Leuke Kome
Khaibar

Syene
Berenike
Yathrib

Buhen
ETHIOPIA
(CUSH)
Red Sea
ARABIA

R. Nile
JOKTAN

Napata
?OPHIR

Meroe

Ancient Trade Routes

Approximate line of principal
trade routes

0   100   200 Miles
0   100   200 Kilometres

© Oxford University Press

Adulis
?OPHIR
PUNT
Uzal
Marib
Shabwa
SHEBA
Timna
HAZARMAVETH
Canneh
Muza

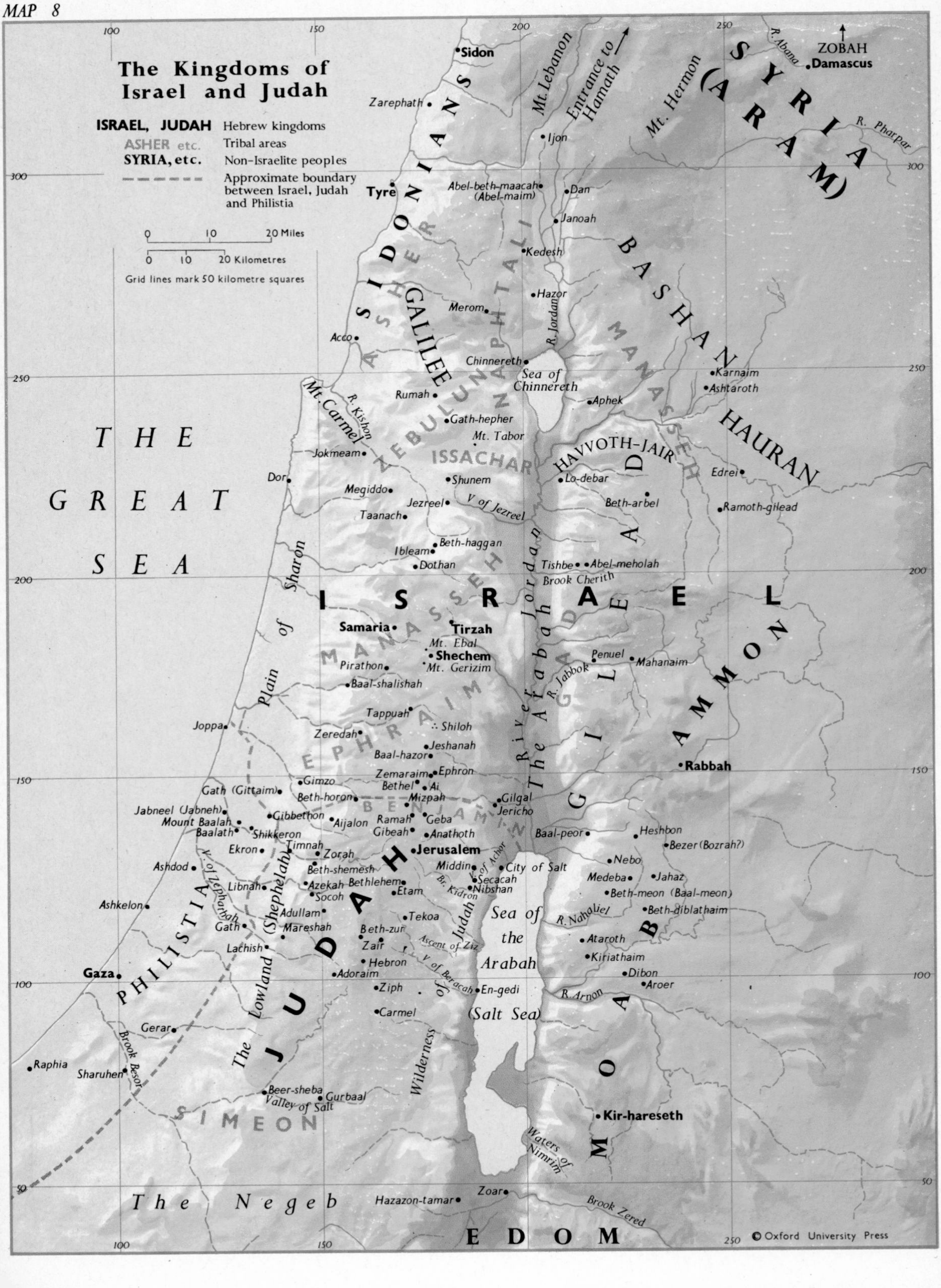

MAP 8

The Kingdoms of Israel and Judah

ISRAEL, JUDAH Hebrew kingdoms
ASHER etc. Tribal areas
SYRIA, etc. Non-Israelite peoples
— — — Approximate boundary between Israel, Judah and Philistia

0   10   20 Miles
0   10   20 Kilometres
Grid lines mark 50 kilometre squares

SYRIA (ARAM)

ZOBAH
•Damascus
R. Abana
R. Pharpar

•Sidon
Zarephath•

Mt. Lebanon
Entrance to Hamath
Mt. Hermon

SIDONIANS

•Ijon

Abel-beth-maacah (Abel-maim)
•Dan
•Janoah

Tyre
•Kedesh

BASHAN

•Hazor
Merom•

ASHER
GALILEE

R. Jordan

Acco•

•Karnaim
•Ashtaroth

ZEBULUN
NAPHTALI

Chinnereth•
Sea of Chinnereth
•Aphek

HAURAN

Mt. Carmel
R. Kishon
Rumah•

MANASSEH

Gath-hepher•
Mt. Tabor

ISSACHAR

HAVVOTH-JAIR

•Edrei

Jokmeam•

•Lo-debar
•Ramoth-gilead

THE

Dor•
Megiddo•
Shunem•
V. of Jezreel
Jezreel•
Beth-arbel•

GREAT

Taanach•

GILEAD

Ibleam• Beth-haggan
•Dothan
Tishbe• •Abel-meholah
Brook Cherith

SEA

Plain of Sharon

ISRAEL

The River Jabbok
The River Jordan
The Arabah

Samaria •Tirzah
Pirathon• Mt. Ebal
•Shechem
Mt. Gerizim

AMMON

•Baal-shalishah

Penuel•
•Mahanaim

MANASSEH

Joppa•

EPHRAIM

Tappuah•
Zeredah• •Shiloh
Baal-hazor•
Jeshanah•

•Rabbah

Gimzo• Zemaraim• Ephron•
Gath (Gittaim)• Beth-horon• Bethel• •Ai
Jabneel (Jabneh)• •Mizpah
Mount Baalah• Gibbethon• Aijalon• Ramah• Geba•
Baalath• Shikkeron• Gibeah• •Anathoth
Ekron• Timnah• Zorah• **Jerusalem**

BENJAMIN

Gilgal•
•Jericho
Baal-peor•
•Heshbon
•Bezer (Bozrah?)

Ashdod• Beth-shemesh• Middin• •City of Salt
Azekah• Bethlehem• Secacah• •Nebo
Libnah• Socoh• Etam• Nibshan•
Ashkelon• Adullam• Br. Kidron •Jahaz
Gath• Mareshah• Tekoa• •Beth-meon (Baal-meon)
Lachish• Zair• Sea of •Beth-diblathaim
Gaza Beth-zur• the R. Nahaliel
•Adoraim Arabah •Ataroth
Gerar• •Hebron •Kiriathaim
•Ziph En-gedi• •Dibon
•Adoraim R. Arnon •Aroer

JUDAH

PHILISTIA
The Lowland (Shephelah)
V. of Sorek
V. of Elah
Br. Kidron
Ascent of Ziz
V. of Beracah

(Salt Sea)

MOAB

•Carmel
Raphia•
Sharuhen•
Brook Besor
Beer-sheba• Gurbaal•
Valley of Salt
Wilderness

•Kir-hareseth

SIMEON

Waters of Nimrim

The Negeb
Hazazon-tamar• Zoar• Brook Zered

EDOM

© Oxford University Press

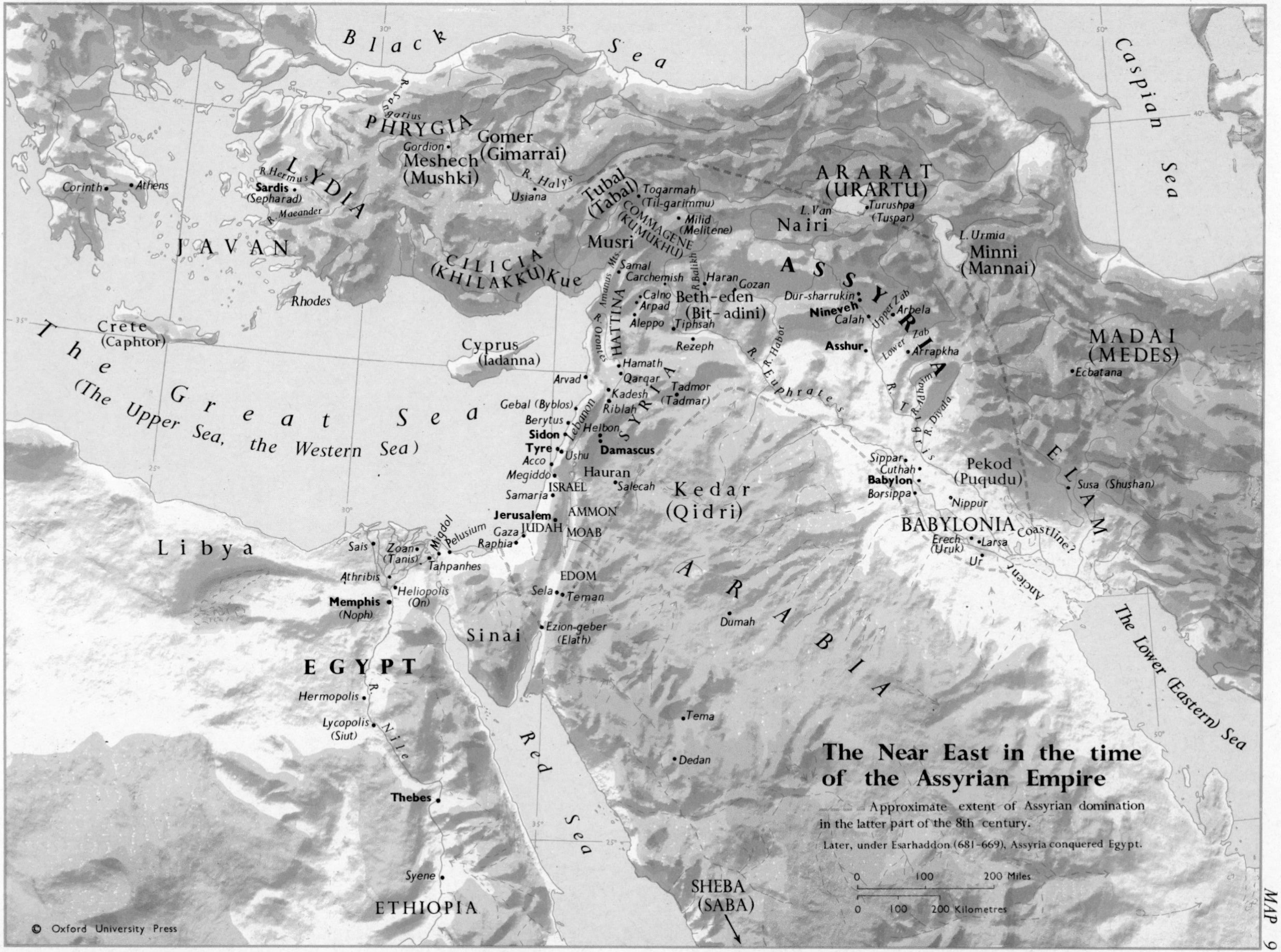

MAP 9

The Near East in the time of the Assyrian Empire

Approximate extent of Assyrian domination in the latter part of the 8th century.

Later, under Esarhaddon (681–669), Assyria conquered Egypt.

200 Miles
200 Kilometres
0 100
0 100

Caspian Sea

Black Sea

MADAI (MEDES)
•Ecbatana

ELAM
Susa (Shushan)•

The Lower (Eastern) Sea

BABYLONIA coastline?
Larsa• Ur•
Erech (Uruk)•

•I. Urmia
Minni (Mannai)
ARARAT (URARTU)
•Turushpa (Tuspa?)
L. Van
Nairi

A S S Y R I A
Dur-sharrukin• •Arrapkha
Nineveh• •Arbela
Asshur• Upper Zab
Calah Lower Zab
R. Tigris

Nippur•
Sippar Cuthah•
Babylon• •Borsippa

Pekod (Puqudu)
R. Diyala

A R A B I A

SHEBA (SABA)

Togarmah (Til-garimmu)
Milid (Melitene)
COMMAGENE (KUMMUKHU)
Musri Gozan
Harran
Carchemish Beth-eden (Bit-adini)
Calno Arpad
Aleppo Tiphsah
HATTINA
Rezeph
Hamath Tadmor (Tadmor)
Qarqar Kadesh
Riblah
Helbon• Damascus
Hauran Salecah (Salhad)
K e d a r (Qidri)
Dumah•
•Tema •Dedan

PHRYGIA
Gomer (Gimmirai)
Meshech (Mushki)
Gordion•
R. Halys
CILICIA (KHILAKKU) Kue
Cyprus (Iadanna)

Tubal (Tabal)
Mts. Amanus
R. Orontes
Arvad•
Berytus
Gebal (Byblos)
Sidon• Tyre•
Acco Ushu
Megiddo Samaria
ISRAEL
Jerusalem JUDAH AMMON
Gaza Raphia MOAB
EDOM
Sela• •Teman
Ezion-geber (Elath)•

T h e   G r e a t   S e a
(The Upper Sea, the Western Sea)

Rhodes•

LYDIA
Sardis• (Sepharad)
R. Hermus• •Maeander
JAVAN

Crete (Caphtor)
Corinth• •Athens

R e d   S e a

Sinai

Migdol
Pelusium
Zoan (Tanis) Tahpanhes
Heliopolis (On)
Sais• •Athribis
Memphis (Noph)

E G Y P T
Libya
R. Nile
Hermopolis•
Lycopolis (Siut)•
Thebes•
Syene•
ETHIOPIA

© Oxford University Press

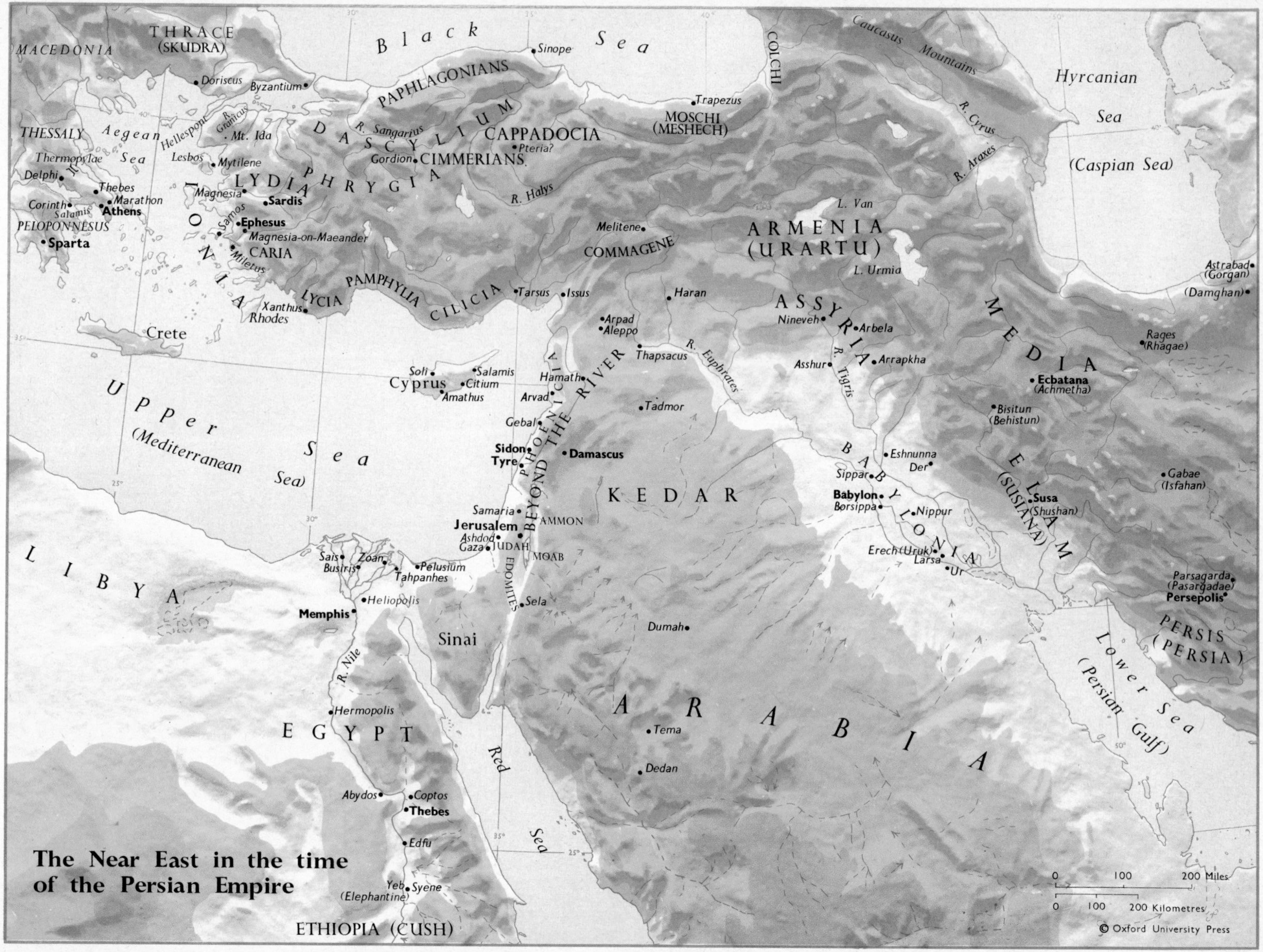

MAP 10

**The Near East in the time
of the Persian Empire**

© Oxford University Press

THRACE (SKUDRA)
MACEDONIA
Doriscus
Byzantium
PAPHLAGONIANS
Sinope
Trapezus
MOSCHI (MESHECH)
COLCHI
Caucasus Mountains
Hyrcanian Sea (Caspian Sea)
Astrabad (Gorgan)
(Damghan)
Rages (Rhagae)
MEDIA
Ecbatana (Achmetha)
Bisitun (Behistun)
ELAM (SUSIANA)
Susa (Shushan)
Gabae (Isfahan)
Parsagarda Pasargadae
Persepolis
PERSIS (PERSIA)
Lower Sea (Persian Gulf)
200 Miles
100   200 Kilometres
ARMENIA (URARTU)
L. Van
L. Urmia
R. Cyrus
R. Araxes
ASSYRIA
Nineveh
Asshur
Arbela
Arrapkha
R. Tigris
Eshnunna
Der
BABYLONIA
Sippar
Babylon
Borsippa
Nippur
Erech Uruk
Larsa
Ur
Haran
R. Euphrates
Thapsacus
Tadmor
KEDAR
Dumah
Tema
Dedan
ARABIA
Arpad
Aleppo
Melitene
COMMAGENE
Hamath
Issus
Tarsus
CILICIA
PAMPHYLIA
CAPPADOCIA
CIMMERIANS
Pteria?
Gordion
R. Sangarius
R. Halys
PHRYGIA
LYDIA
Sardis
Magnesia-on-Maeander
Magnesia
CARIA
LYCIA
Xanthus
Rhodes
Miletus
Ephesus
IONIA
Mt. Ida
Lesbos
Mytilene
Cyzicus
Hellespont
Aegean Sea
THESSALY
Thermopylae
Delphi
Thebes
Marathon
Corinth
Salamis
Athens
PELOPONNESUS
Sparta
Crete
Upper Sea (Mediterranean Sea)
Black Sea
DASCYLIUM
Soli
Salamis
Citium
Amathus
Cyprus
Arvad
Gebal
Sidon
Tyre
Damascus
PHOENICIA
BEYOND THE RIVER
Hamath
Samaria
Ashdod
Jerusalem
Gaza
JUDAH
AMMON
MOAB
Sela
EDOMITES
Red Sea
Sinai
Pelusium
Tahpanhes
Zoan
Bubastis
Heliopolis
Saïs
Memphis
Hermopolis
Abydos
Coptos
Thebes
Edfu
Syene
Yeb (Elephantine)
R. Nile
EGYPT
LIBYA
ETHIOPIA (CUSH)
LYDIA

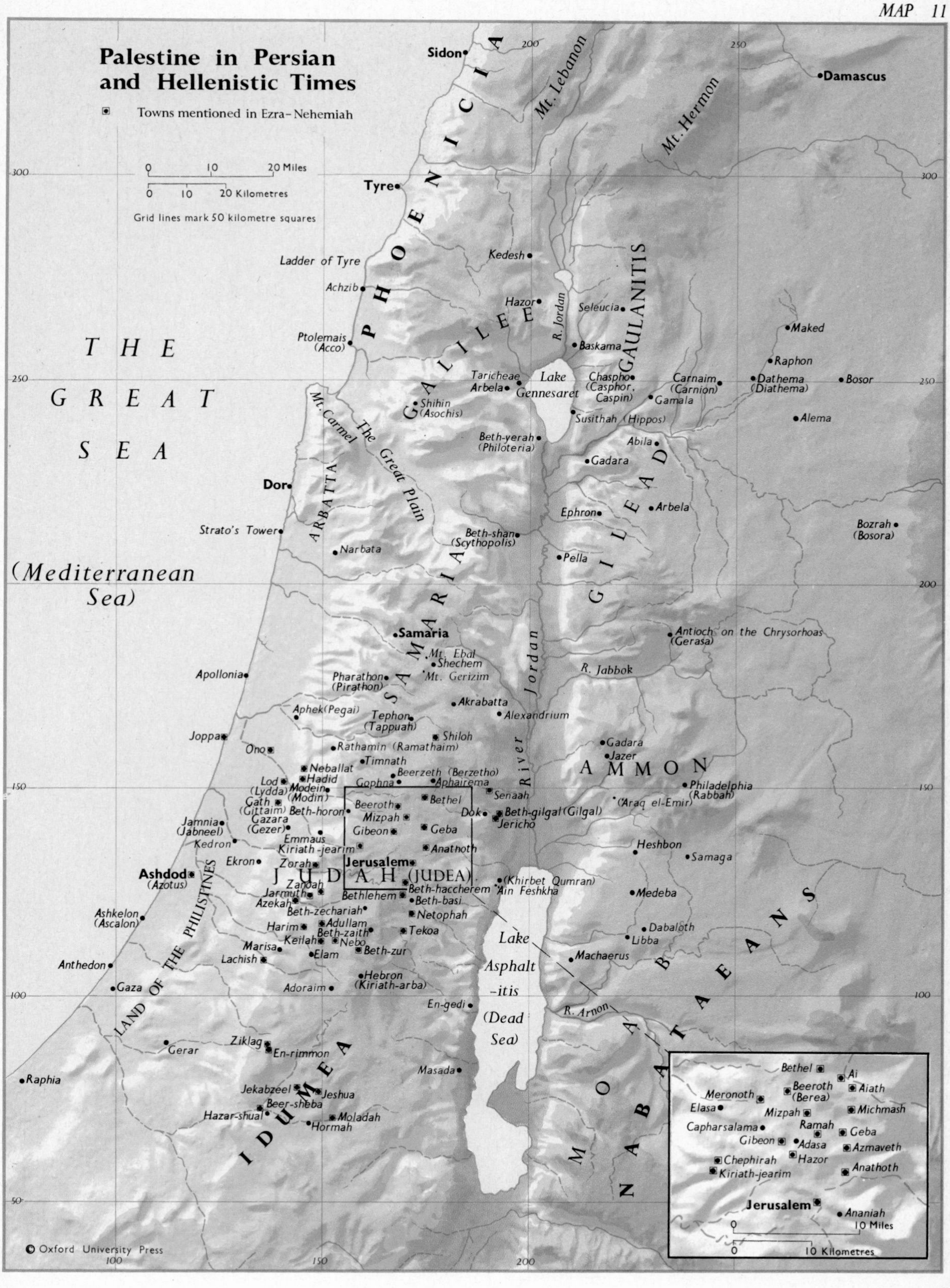
Palestine in Persian and Hellenistic Times
Towns mentioned in Ezra–Nehemiah
0 10 20 Miles
0 10 20 Kilometres
Grid lines mark 50 kilometre squares
THE GREAT SEA
(Mediterranean Sea)
PHOENICIA
GALILEE
GAULANITIS
GILEAD
SAMARIA
ARBATTA
JUDAH (JUDEA)
LAND OF THE PHILISTINES
IDUMEA
AMMON
MOAB
NABATAEANS
Mt. Lebanon
Mt. Hermon
Mt. Carmel
The Great Plain
R. Jordan
River Jordan
R. Jabbok
R. Arnon
Lake Gennesaret
Lake Asphaltitis (Dead Sea)
Sidon
Damascus
Tyre
Ladder of Tyre
Achzib
Kedesh
Hazor
Seleucia
Ptolemais (Acco)
Baskama
Maked
Raphon
Taricheae
Arbela
Chaspho (Casphor, Caspin)
Carnaim (Carnion)
Dathema (Diathema)
Bosor
Shihin (Asochis)
Gamala
Susithah (Hippos)
Alema
Beth-yerah (Philoteria)
Abila
Gadara
Dor
Ephron
Arbela
Strato's Tower
Beth-shan (Scythopolis)
Bozrah (Bosora)
Narbata
Pella
Samaria
Antioch on the Chrysorhoas (Gerasa)
Mt. Ebal
Shechem
Mt. Gerizim
Apollonia
Pharathon (Pirathon)
Akrabatta
Aphek (Pegai)
Tephon (Tappuah)
Alexandrium
Joppa
Shiloh
Ono
Rathamin (Ramathaim)
Gadara
Jazer
Timnath
Neballat
Beerzeth (Berzetho)
Lod (Lydda)
Hadid
Gophna
Aphairema
Philadelphia (Rabbah)
Modein (Modin)
Senaah
Gath (Gittaim)
Beeroth
Bethel
Beth-horon
Dok
Beth-gilgal (Gilgal)
'Araq el-Emir
Jamnia (Jabneel)
Gazara (Gezer)
Mizpah
Jericho
Gibeon
Geba
Emmaus
Kedron
Kiriath-jearim
Anathoth
Heshbon
Ekron
Samaga
Ashdod (Azotus)
Zorah
Jerusalem
(Khirbet Qumran)
Zanoah
Beth-haccherem
'Ain Feshkha
Jarmuth
Bethlehem
Medeba
Azekah
Beth-basi
Ashkelon (Ascalon)
Beth-zechariah
Netophah
Adullam
Harim
Beth-zaith
Tekoa
Dabaloth
Keilah
Nebo
Libba
Marisa
Beth-zur
Elam
Machaerus
Lachish
Anthedon
Hebron (Kiriath-arba)
Gaza
Adoraim
En-gedi
Ziklag
En-rimmon
Gerar
Raphia
Masada
Jekabzeel
Jeshua
Beer-sheba
Hazar-shual
Moladah
Hormah
Bethel
Ai
Meronoth
Beeroth (Berea)
Aiath
Elasa
Mizpah
Michmash
Capharsalama
Ramah
Geba
Gibeon
Adasa
Azmaveth
Chephirah
Hazor
Kiriath-jearim
Anathoth
Jerusalem
Ananiah
0 10 Miles
0 10 Kilometres
© Oxford University Press

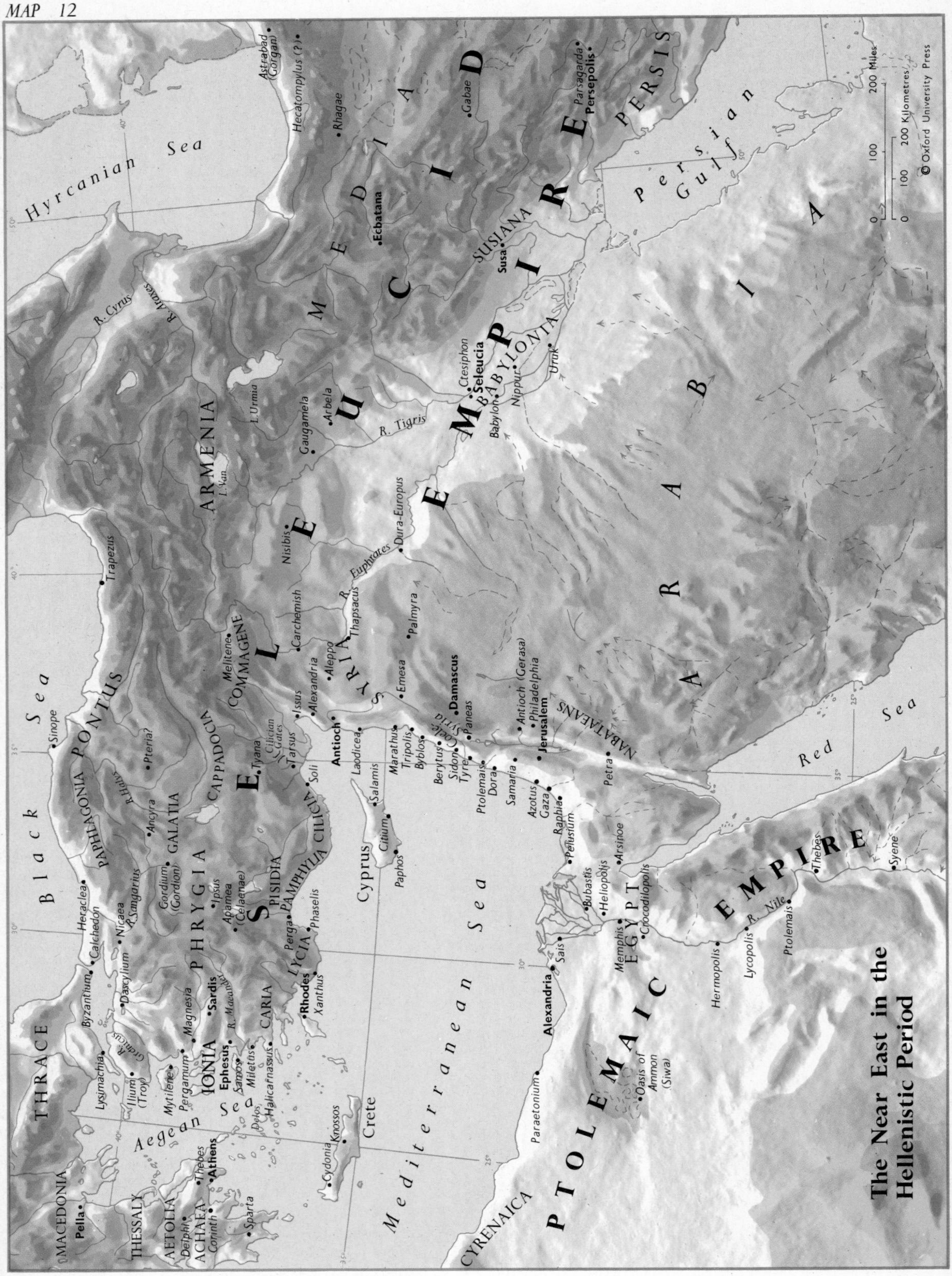

MAP 12

**The Near East in the
Hellenistic Period**

200 Miles

100   200 Kilometres

© Oxford University Press

Hyrcanian Sea

M E D I A

Astrabad
Gorgan?

Hecatompylus (?)

Rhagae

Gabae

Ecbatana

PERSIS

Parsagarda
Persepolis

Persian Gulf

SUSIANA

Susa

R. Cyrus

R. Araxes

ARMENIA

L. Urmia

L. Van

S E L E U C I D   E M P I R E

Ctesiphon
Seleucia
Babylon
BABYLONIA
Nippur
Uruk

R. Tigris

Gaugamela

Arbela

Nisibis

Carchemish

Dura-Europus

Euphrates

R. Euphrates

Thapsacus

Palmyra

A R A B I A

Trapezus

Black Sea

Sinope

PONTUS

PAPHLAGONIA

Heraclea
Byzantium
Calchedon
Nicaea
Dascylium

Ancyra

GALATIA

R. Sangarius

R. Halys

CAPPADOCIA

Pteria?

Gordium
(Gordion)

PHRYGIA

Apamea
Celaenae

Tyana

Melitene

COMMAGENE

SYRIA

Alexandria
Aleppo

Issus
Alexandria

Tarsus
CILICIA
Soli
Cilician
Gates

PISIDIA

Perga
PAMPHYLIA
Phaselis

LYCIA
Xanthus

CARIA

Sardis
IONIA
Ephesus
Magnesia
R. Maeander
Miletus
Samos
Halicarnassus

Pergamum
Ilium
(Troy)
Mytilene
Lysimachia

THRACE

MACEDONIA
Pella

THESSALY
AETOLIA
Delphi
ACHAEA
Corinth
Thebes
Athens
Sparta

Aegean Sea

Delos

Cydonia
Knossos
Crete

Mediterranean Sea

Rhodes

Cyprus
Salamis
Citium
Paphos

Laodicea
Marathus
Tripolis
Byblos
Berytus
Sidon
Tyre
Paneas
Damascus
Emesa

Antioch (Gerasa)
Philadelphia
Jerusalem

NABATAEANS

Petra

Dora
Samaria
Azotus
Gaza
Raphia
Pelusium

Ptolemais

Antioch
Laodicea

Red Sea

EMPIRE

Thebes
Syene

Ptolemais

Lycopolis

Hermopolis

Crocodilopolis
Heliopolis
Bubastis
Arsinoe
Memphis
EGYPT
Sais
Alexandria

P T O L E M A I C   E M P I R E

Paraetonium

Oasis of
Ammon
(Siwa)

CYRENAICA

R. Nile

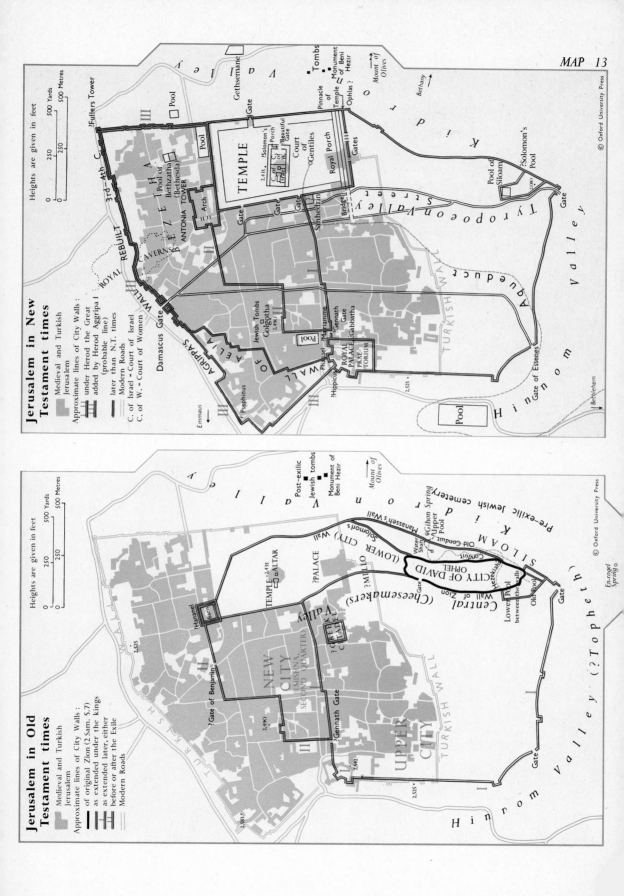

MAP 13

© Oxford University Press

Jerusalem in New Testament times

Medieval and Turkish Jerusalem

Approximate lines of City Walls:

under Herod the Great

added by Herod Agrippa I (probable line)

later than N.T. times

Modern Roads

C. of Israel = Court of Israel
C. of W. = Court of Women

Heights are given in feet

0   250   500 Yards
0   250   500 Metres

?Fullers Tower

Gethsemane

Gate

Tombs

Monument of Beni Hezir

Pinnacle of Temple

Ophlas?

Mount of Olives

Bethany

?Solomon's Porch

?Solomon's Pool

III

BEZETHA

?Pool of Bethzatha (Bethesda)

Pool

TEMPLE

2,416

C. of Isr.

C. of W.

?Solomon's Porch

?Beautiful Gate

Court of Gentiles

Royal Porch

Gates

Pool of Siloam

2,080

Gate

ANTONIA TOWER

CAVERNS

ROYAL REBUILT

3rd-4th C.

Arch

II 11

Gate

Gate

Gate

Sanhedrin

Bridge

Tyropoeon Street

Tyropoeon Valley

Kidron Valley

Aqueduct

TURKISH WALL

WALL III

ROYAL

Damascus Gate

AGRIPPA'S

OF

FELIX

WALL

Jewish Tombs

Golgotha

?Gennath Gate

Maramme

?Gabbatha

ROYAL PALACE PRAE- TORIUM

?Phasael

?Hippicus

II

2,490

Pool

2,525

Pool

Gate of Essenes

Gate

Hinnom Valley

Bethlehem

?Psephinus

III

Emmaus →

Jerusalem in Old Testament times

Medieval and Turkish Jerusalem

Approximate lines of City Walls:

of original Zion (2 Sam. 5,7)

as extended under the kings

as extended later, either before or after the Exile

Modern Roads

Heights are given in feet

0   250   500 Yards
0   250   500 Metres

© Oxford University Press

Post-exilic Jewish tombs

Monument of Beni Hezir

Mount of Olives

Kidron Valley

Pre-exilic Jewish cemetery

Gihon Spring

Upper Pool

Old Conduit

Conduit

?Hananel

Baris

TEMPLE

2,416

ALTAR

?PALACE

Solomon's Wall

(LOWER CITY)

OPHEL

CITY OF DAVID

Water Shaft

?Hezekiah

Central Wall of Zion (between the walls)

SILOAM

Lower Pool

Old Pool

Manasseh's Wall

MILLO

(Cheesemakers)

Valley

NEW CITY (MISHNA, SECOND QUARTER)

2,490

?Gate of Benjamin

II

TURKISH WALL

2,581

?Gennath Gate

II

2,490

CITADEL

?CASTLE

UPPER CITY

2,542

2,525

I

Gate

Gate

En-rogel Spring

Hinnom Valley (?Topheth)

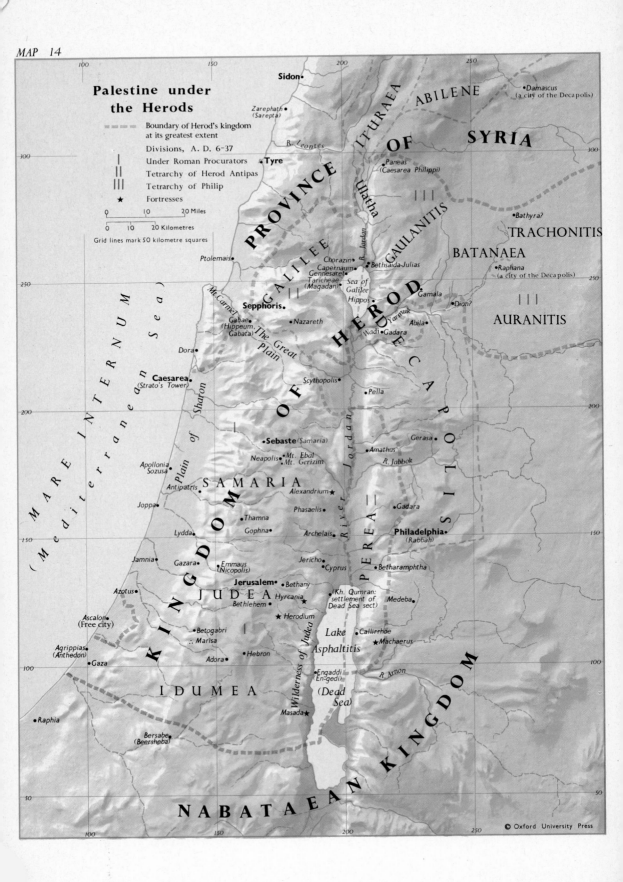

MAP 14

Palestine under the Herods

- - - - Boundary of Herod's kingdom
at its greatest extent
Divisions, A.D. 6-37
I   Under Roman Procurators
II Tetrarchy of Herod Antipas
III Tetrarchy of Philip
★ Fortresses

0   10   20 Miles
0   10   20 Kilometres
Grid lines mark 50 kilometre squares

Sidon•

•Damascus
(a city of the Decapolis)

Zarephath
(Sarepta)

PROVINCE

R. Leontes

ITURAEA

ABILENE

OF

SYRIA

•Tyre

Paneas
(Caesarea Philippi)

III

Ulatha

Ptolemais•

GALILEE

Chorazin•
Capernaum•
Gennesaret•
Taricheae
(Magadan)•

Bethsaida-Julias•

GAULANITIS

BATANAEA

•Raphana
(a city of the Decapolis)

Sea of
Galilee

R. Jordan

Hippos•

Gamala•

•Dion?

TRACHONITIS

•Bathyra?

Sepphoris•

Mt. Carmel

Gabae
(Hippeum,
Gabata)•

The Great
Plain

Nazareth•

HEROD

Wadi •Gadara

Abila•

Yarmuk

AURANITIS

III

Dora•

MARE INTERNUM

(Mediterranean Sea)

Caesarea
(Strato's Tower)•

Plain of Sharon

Scythopolis•

•Pella

OF

DECAPOLIS

Amathus•

Gerasa•

Sebaste• (Samaria)

Neapolis•

•Mt. Ebal
•Mt. Gerizim

R. Jabbok

KINGDOM

SAMARIA

Apollonia
Sozusa•

Antipatris•

Joppa•

Alexandrium ★

Phasaelis•

River Jordan

PEREA

•Gadara

Lydda•

Thamna•
Gophna•

Archelais•

II

Philadelphia•
(Rabbah)

Jamnia•

Gazara•

Emmaus
(Nicopolis)•

Jericho•
•Cyprus

Azotus•

JUDEA

Jerusalem

•Bethany
Hycania•
Bethlehem•

Betharamphtha•

(Kh. Qumran:
settlement of
Dead Sea sect)

Medeba•

Ascalon
(Free city)

I

★Herodium

Lake
Asphaltitis

•Callirrhoe

•Machaerus★

Agrippias
(Anthedon)•

•Betogabri
∴ Marisa

Hebron•

Adora•

Wilderness of Judea

Engaddi
(En-gedi)•

R. Arnon

•Gaza

IDUMEA

(Dead
Sea)

•Raphia

Masada ★

Bersabe
(Beersheba)•

NABATAEAN

KINGDOM

© Oxford University Press

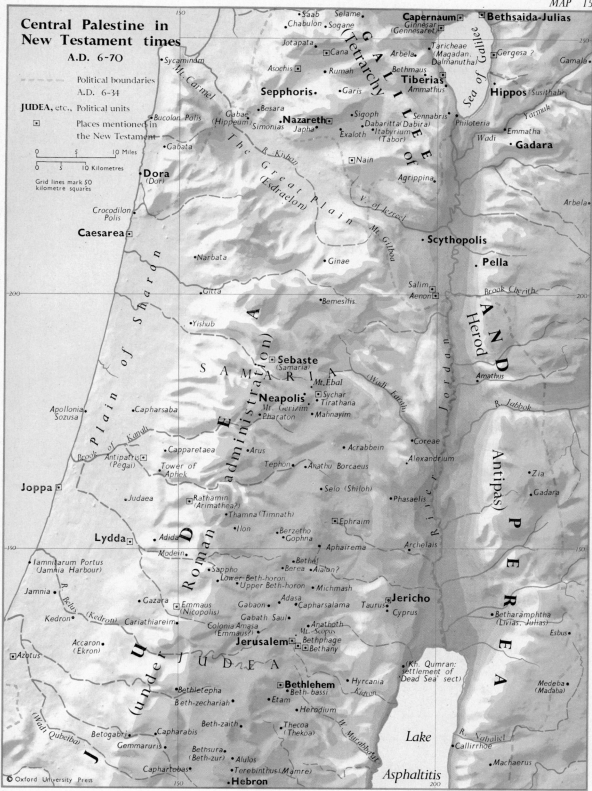

MAP 15

Central Palestine in New Testament times
A.D. 6-70

Political boundaries
A.D. 6-34

JUDEA, etc., Political units

⊡ Places mentioned in
the New Testament

0   5   10 Miles
0   5   10 Kilometres

Grid lines mark 50
kilometre squares

© Oxford University Press

•Saab Selame
•Chabulon Sogane •Ginnesar **Capernaum**⊡ ⊡**Bethsaida-Julias**
(Gennesaret)
•Jotapata •Taricheae •Gergesa ?
Arbela• (Magadan, Gamala
•Cana Dalmanutha)
Asochis⊡ •Rumah Bethmaus **Hippos** (Susithah)
Bethmaus **Tiberias**
Ammathus Yarmuk
Sepphoris• •Garis Sennabris Emmatha
•Besara Sigoph Philoteria Wadi
•Gabae **Nazareth**• Dabaritta (Dabira) • **Gadara**
(Hippeum) Japha • Itaburium
•Simonias Exaloth (Tabor)
•Bucolon Polis R. Kishan ⊡•Nain
•Gabata Agrippina
Dora V. of Jezreel
(Dor) Mt. Gilboa
Scythopolis
•Narbata **Pella**
Crocodilon •Ginae
Polis
Caesarea⊡ Salim Brook Cherith
•Gitta Aenon⊡
•Bemesitis
•Yishub **Herod** Amathus
SAMARIA ⊡**Sebaste**
(Samaria)
Apollonia •Capharsaba Mt. Ebal •Coreae
Sozusa **Neapolis**• ⊡Sychar
Mt. Gerizim •Tirathana
Brook •Pharaton •Alexandrium •Zia
Antipatris•⊡ •Arus Mahnayim •Gadara
(Pegai) Tephon• •Anathu Borcaeus
Tower of •Acrabbein
Aphek •Selo (Shiloh)
Joppa⊡ •Phasaelis
•Judaea Rathamin •Thamna (Timnath)
(Arimathea?) ⊡Ephraim Archelais
Lydda⊡ •Adida •Ilon •Berzetho Aphairema•
Modein• •Gophna **PEREA**
•Iamnitarum Portus •Bethel Betharamphtha
(Jamnia Harbour) Sappho• Berea Aialon? (Livias, Julias)
Jamnia• •Lower Beth-horon •Michmash Esbus
Kedron• Gazara• Upper Beth-horon **Jericho**⊡
⊡Azotus Emmaus Gabaon• Adasa Cyprus• •Betharamphtha
(Nicopolis) Capharsalama Taurus⊡
•Accaron Gabath Saul• •Anathoth Medeba
(Ekron) Colonia Amasa Mt. Scopus (Madaba)
Cariathiareim (Emmaus?) ⊡Bethphage
Jerusalem⊡ ⊡Bethany
JUDEA (Kh. Qumran:
settlement of
Bethlehem⊡ 'Dead Sea' sect)
•Bethletepha •Beth-bassi Hyrcania Machaerus
Beth-zechariah• •Etam Kidron
(Wadi •Herodium **Lake**
Qubeiba) Beth-zaith R. Vahaliel
Betogabri• •Capharabis Thecoa •Callirrhoe
Gemmaruris• (Thekoa)
Bethsura **Asphaltitis**
Caphartobas• (Beth-zur) •Alulos
•Terebinthus (Mamre)
Hebron

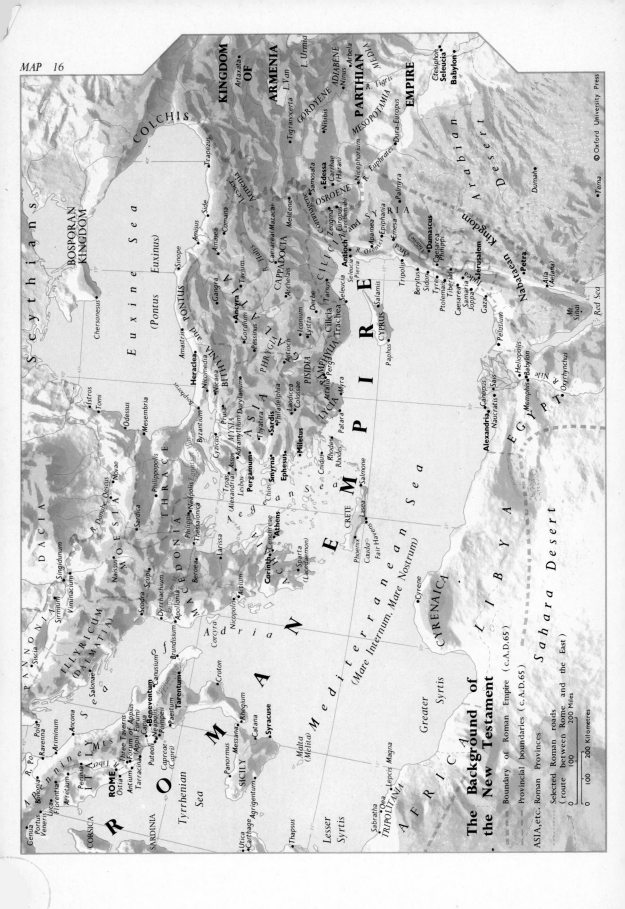

MAP 16

© Oxford University Press

KINGDOM OF ARMENIA

COLCHIS

L. Urmia

MEDIA

L. Van

ADIABENE

GORDYENE

PARTHIAN EMPIRE

Ctesiphon
Seleucia
Babylon

Artaxata
Arbela
Ninus

MESOPOTAMIA

R. Tigris

Tigranocerta

Nisibis

Nicephorium

Dura-Europus

R. Euphrates

Palmyra

Dumah

Tema

Arabian Desert

BOSPORAN KINGDOM

Scythians

Euxine Sea

(Pontus Euxinus)

Chersonesus

Sinope

Amisus

Amisus

Anisea

Trapezus

Lesser Armenia

Lesser Armenia

Comana

Samosata

Melitene

Edessa

Carrhae
(Haran)

OSROENE

Commagene

Zeugma

Europus

(Carchemish)

A (Carchemish)

Apamea

SYRIA

Emesa

Epiphania

Damascus

Caesarea
Philippi

Tiberias
Galilee

Samaria
Judea

Jerusalem

Petra

Nabataean Kingdom

Mt. Sinai

Red Sea

Aila
(Aelana)

PONTUS

BITHYNIA and PONTUS

Amastris

Heraclea

Nicomedia

Nicaea

Prusa

Byzantium

Bosphorus

Gangra

Ancyra

Tavium

GALATIA

Pessinus

Gordium

PHRYGIA

CAPPADOCIA

Archelais

Caesarea (Mazaca)

R. Halys

CILICIA

Tarsus

Seleucia

Seleucia

Antioch

R. Orontes

Pieria

Tripoli

Berytus

Sidon

Tyre

Ptolemais

Caesarea

Joppa

Gaza

Pelusium

Istros

Tomi

Odessus

Mesembria

R. Danube

Oescus

Novae

Philippopolis

Sardica

THRACE

Neapolis (Apolli)

Byzantium

Cyzicus

Lampsacus

Assos

Adramyttium

Dorylaeum

MYSIA

Thyatira

Sardis

Philadelphia

ASIA

Laodicea

Colossae

Iconium

Antioch

PISIDIA

Lystra

Derbe

LYCAONIA

Apamea

Pergamum

Ephesus

Miletus

Smyrna

Chios

Lesbos

Troas
(Alexandria)

Philippi

Thessalonica

Beroea

MACEDONIA

Larissa

ACHAIA

Corinth

Cenchreae

Athens

Sparta
(Lacedaemon)

Nicopolis

Actium

Apollonia

Dyrrhachium

Scodra

ILLYRICUM
(DALMATIA)

Salonae

e Salonae

PANNONIA

Siscia

Sirmium

Singidunum

Viminacium

Naissus

MOESIA

DACIA

Aegean Sea

Cnidus

Rhodes

Rhodes

Patara

Myra

Attalia
Perga

PAMPHYLIA

LYCIA

CILICIA Trachea

Salmone

Salamis

CYPRUS

Paphos

CRETE

Phoenix

Lasea

Fair Havens

Cauda

Mediterranean Sea

(Mare Internum, Mare Nostrum)

ROMAN EMPIRE

Adria

Corcyra

Croton

Brundisium

Tarentum

Canusium

Beneventum

Capua

Neapolis

Pompeii

Paestum

Puteoli

Caprea
(Capri)

ROME

Ostia

Antium

Tarracina

Three Taverns

Forum of Appius
(Appii Forum)

Forum of Appius

R. Tiber

Antium

ITALY

Arretium

Florentia

Perusia

Luca

Bononia

Genua

Portus Veneris

Pola

Ravenna

Ariminum

Ancona

Apennines

R. Po

R. Arno

CORSICA

SARDINIA

Tyrrhenian Sea

Panormus

SICILY

Messana

Rhegium

Catana

Syracuse

Agrigentum

Malta
(Melita)

Carthage

Utica

Thapsus

Hadrumetum

Lesser Syrtis

Greater Syrtis

Sabratha

Oea

Lepcis Magna

TRIPOLITANA

AFRICA

Cyrene

CYRENAICA

LIBYA

Sahara Desert

EGYPT

Alexandria

Naucratis

Sais

Canopus

Heliopolis

Memphis

Babylon

R. Nile

Oxyrhynchus

The Background of the New Testament

Boundary of Roman Empire (c.A.D.65)

Provincial boundaries (c.A.D.65)

ASIA, etc. Roman Provinces

Selected Roman roads (route between Rome and the East)

100   200 Miles

100   200 Kilometres

0

0

INDEX OF SUBJECTS

Where page numbers are followed by an italicized *a* or *b*, the letters refer to left and right-hand columns respectively on a page. Where page numbers have no *a* or *b*, reference is to a complete article or to the author of an article.

A

Aaron, 38*a*, 49*b*, 51*b*, 59*a*, 59*b*, 64*b*, 65*b*
  authority of, authenticated, 91*b* f
  confrontation of, with Pharaoh, 40*b*, 42*a*
  death of, 92*b*, 120*a*
  death of sons of, 74*b*, 75*a*
  Ezra descended from, 225*a*
  genealogy of, 42*a*, 211*a*
  and the golden calf, 64*a*
  as mediator between God and people, 91*b*, 289*b*, 548*b*
  mission of, 42*a*
  Moses' association with, 40*a*, 40*b*, 45*b*, 572*b*
  praised by ben Sira, 572*a* f, 575*b*
  as priest, 74*a*, 78*a*, 82*a*
  rebellion of, 88*b* f
  sacrifices offered by, 74*b*
Aaronic priesthood, 61*b*, 62*a* f, 63*a*, 74*a*, 133*a*, 213*a*
Abaddon, 248*a*, 312*a*, 957*b*
  See also Sheol
Abana River, 199*a*
Abarim, 106*a*, 387*b*
Abba, 689*b*
Abba, Raymond, 993*b*
Abdon, 146*a*
Abednego, 439*a*, 581*b*, 582*a*
Abel, 321*a*, 638*b*, 913*a*
Abel (town), 179*a* f
Abel-Shittim, 96*b*
Abiathar, 61*b*, 158*a*, 162*b*, 166*b*, 169*a*, 173*a*, 175*a*, 183*a*, 184*b*, 210*b*, 375*a*
  demotion of, 184*a*
Abib (month), 44*b*, 46*a*
Abigail, sister of David, 178*a*
Abigail, wife of David, 167*a* f
Abihu, 59*a*, 59*b*, 65*b*
  sin of, 74*b*, 77*b*, 78*a*
Abijam (Abijah), 191*b* f, 215*b*

Abilene, 677*b*
Abimelech, 17*b*, 136*b*, 143*b*, 144*a* f
  Abraham's covenant with, 18*a*
  death of, 144*a*, 144*b*
  revolt against, 144*b*
Abi-mili, 1005
Abinadab, 163*a*
Abiram, 278*b*
  rebellion of, 91*a*, 91*b*
Abishag, 183*a*, 184*a*
Abishai, 168*a*, 171*b*, 172*a*, 175*a*, 177*b*, 178*a*, 179*a*, 180*a*
Abishalom, 191*b*
Abner, 163*a*, 166*a*, 168*a*, 171*a*
  attempt of, to fulfill oath, 172*a*
  murder and burial of, 172*a*
  quarrel of, with Ishbaal, 171*b* f
Abraham, 10*b* f, 32*a*, 38*b*, 355*a*, 355*b*, 1276*a*
  and Abimelech, 18*a*
  allegory of wives of, 831*b*
  ben Sira's mention of, 572*a*
  and covenant of circumcision, 16*a* f
  death of, 20*a*
  descendants of, 20*a*, 209*b*
  faith of, 776*b* f, 913*a* f, 920*a*
  God and, 16*b* f, 362*a*, 582*a*, 737*a*
  God's covenant with, 14*a* ff, 291*b*, 777*a* f, 906*a*
  and Hagar, 15*b* f
  as historical person, 1018*b* f
  and Isaac's marriage, 19*b* f
  and Ishmael, 17*b* f
  and the life of faith, 3*a*
  and Melchizedek, 293*a*, 906*b*
  migration of, to Canaan, 12*a* f
  and proposed sacrifice of Isaac, 18*a* f, 128*b*, 913*b*
  purchase of grave for Sarah by, 19*a* f
  recognized by wisdom, 547*b*
  redemption of, 349*a*
  and rite of circumcision, 126*b*

Abraham—*cont.*
  and Sarah, at Gerar, 17*b*
  separation of, from Lot, 13*a*
  story of, in Genesis, 11*b* ff
  victory of, 13*a* ff
  visit of, to Egypt, 13*a*
Abraham ibn Ezra, 485*b*, 974*b*
Abram (Abi-ram). *See* Abraham
Abron (brook), 537*b*
Abronah, 98*b*
Absalom, 183*a*
  death of, 156*b*, 178*a* f
  nonrecognition of, at court, 177*a*
  rebellion of, 177*a*
  revenge of, for rape of Tamar, 176*b*
Abyss, 551*b*, 957*a*, 957*b*
Acacia tree, 77
Acacia Valley, 464*b*
Accad, 10*a*
Acco, 1003*a*
Achaemenid dynasty, 999*a*
Achaia, 813*a*
Achan (Achar), 58*a*, 128*a*, 210*a*, 981*a*
Achior:
  confirmation of, 541*a* f
  history of Jews of, 538*b* f
  punishment of, 539*a*
Achish, 166*b*, 168*a*, 168*b* f, 184*a*
Achor, Valley of, 128*a*, 370*b*, 454*a*
Ackroyd, Peter R., 329
Acra, citadel in Jerusalem, 595*a*, 597*b*, 598*b*
Acrocorinth, 795*a*
Acrostic poems (psalms, hymns), 254*a*, 264*a*, 306*b*, 319*b*, 491*a*, 491*b* f, 576*a*, 576*b*
"Acts," apocryphal, 1147*a* f
Acts of the Apostles, 729 ff
  authorship of, 729*a* f
  date and place of composition of, 729*b*
  history of church growth and organization in, 1188*a*, 1189*b*

1297

Boaz, 116*a*, 150*a*, 152*a* ff, 365*a*
Boaz (temple pillar), 186*b*, 214*b*
Bochim (Bethel), 138*a*
Body:
    resurrection of, 810*b*, 811*b*
    sanctity of, 801*a* f
    transformation of, and salvation, 854*b*
    See also Dualism
Boehlke, R. R., 1268*b*
Boghazköy, 1012*a*
Boils, plague of, 43*a*
Boleyn, Anne, 1239*a*
Bones:
    desecration of, 468*a*
    Ezekiel's vision of, 430*b*
Booths, feast of. *See* Feasts
Booths, sabbatical, 119*b*
Bornkamm, G., 610*b*
Borrowing and lending, 566*a* f
Bougaean, 544*a*
Boundary markers:
    law against removal of, 113*a*
    respect for, 315*b*
Bowie, W. R., 988*b*
Bowls, seven, in Revelation, 962*b* ff
Bowman, J. W., 867*a*, 877*a*, 949*a*
Bowman, R. A., 221*a*
Box, G. H., 522*a*, 551*b*
Bozez, 162*b*
Bozrah, 351*b*, 400*b*, 467*b*
Brahms, 1250*b*
Branscomb, B. H., 645*a*
Bratcher, Robert G., 1243
Bread:
    of heaven, 716*b* f
    holy, 166*a*
    leavened, for thanksgiving, 81*b*
    for peace offering, 73*a*
    of the presence, 69*b*, 82*a*, 166*a*
    staff of, 292*a*, 416*b*
    symbolism of, 640*b*
    unleavened, feast of, *see* Feasts
Breasted, James Henry, 999*a*
"Breeches Bible," 1242*b*
Bribes:
    and gifts to avert anger, 315*a*
    taking of, 313*a* f
Brickmaking in Egypt, 40*b* f
Bride-price, 57*b*
Bride-sister motif, 326*b*, 327*a*
Bright, John, 124*b*, 137*a*, 157*a*, 183*a*, 375*a*, 483*b*, 1025*b*, 1031*b*, 1059*a*, 1089*b*, 1158*b*, 1166*b*
Bring, Ragnar, 825*b*
Bristow, Richard, 1240*b*
Britten, Benjamin, 1250*b*
Brockington, L. H., 587*b*, 591*a*

Bronze altar, 203*b*
Bronze pillars and objects in temple, 186*b* f, 187*b*, 204*a*, 214*b*
    breaking or looting of, 207*b*
    melted and sent to Assyria, 203*b*
Bronze serpent, 54*a*, 94*a*, 713*b*
Brooke, A. E., 936*a*
Brotherhood:
    of all men, 513*b*
    Christian, 784*a*, 895*a*, 895*b* f
    covenant of, 165*a*, 165*b*, 166*a*, 170*a*, 467*b*
    demonstrated in parables, 437*b*
    of the new birth, 926*b* f
Brouwerius, Daniel, 1244*b*
Brown, R. E., 709*b*
Brown, S. L., 452*a*
Brown, Samuel, 1245*a*
Browning, Robert, 1249*b*
Brownlee, William Hugh, 411, 601*a*
Bruce, F. F., 730*a*, 1242*b*
Buber, Martin, 1100*b*
Bul (month), 186*a*
Bull:
    images of, 63*b*, 64*a*, 457*a*, 470*a*, 475*b*
    as symbol of Baal, 142*b*
Bullough, S., 477*b*
Bultmann, Rudolf, 709*b*, 977*b*, 988*b*, 1128*a*, 1128*b*, 1175*b*, 1256*b*, 1257*a*
Bunyan, John, 591*a*, 1249*a*
Burial:
    of executed criminals, 113*b*
    proper, 529*b*, 530*b*, 569*b*, 620*a*, 642*b*
Burkill, T. A., 551*b*
Burkitt, F. C., 1109*b*
Burn, A. R., 1036*b*
Burnet, J., 710*a*
Burney, C. F., 183*a*
Burning bush, 39*a*
Burns, Robert, 1249*a*
Burnt offerings, 55*b*, 62*b*, 67*b*, 69*a* f, 71*b*, 72*b*, 446*b*, 473*a*
    altar of, 67*b*, 223*a*
Burrows, Millar, 1071*b*
Burton, E. DeW., 825*b*
Business:
    dishonesty in, 565*b*, 870*b*
    ethics in, 314*b*
    pointlessness of, 321*a*
Butterworth, C. C., 1242*b*
Buttrick, George A., 1254
Buz, 389*a*
Buzz groups, 1267*b*
Byron, 1250*a*
Byzantine churches, 1251*a*

C

Cabul, 187*b*
Cadbury, Henry J., 673*b*, 730*a*, 1044*b*, 1128*b*
Caedmon, 1237*a*
Caesar:
    Paul's appeal to, 762*b*
    tribute to, 637*b*
    worship of, 946*b*, 947*a*; *see also* Emperor worship
Caesarea, 741*b*
    Paul in, 754*a*, 760*b* ff, 845*b*
    Peter in, 742*b*
Caesarea Philippi, Peter's confession at, 628*b*, 658*b*, 687*a*
Caiaphas, 641*b*, 668*a*, 677*b*, 678*a*, 720*b*, 721*a*, 733*a*
Cain, 6*a* f, 209*b*, 943*b*
Cain (Byron), 1250*a*
Cainites, 938*a*
Caird, G. B., 157*a*, 936*a*, 1193*b*, 1282*b*
Cairo, Hebrew texts of Ecclesiasticus from, 550*b*
Calcol, 210*a*
Caleb, 89*a*, 89*b*, 90*b*, 97*a*, 105*b*, 138*b*, 210*a*
    inheritance of, at Hebron, 131*b*
    Negeb territory of, 169*a*
    praised by ben Sira, 572*b* f
Calebites, 167*b*
Calf cult, 63*b* f, 529*a*
Caligula, 744*a*, 1035*b*
Calkins, Raymond, 501*b*, 504*b*
Calmness:
    health through, 312*a*
    in speech, 313*b*
    of spirit, 313*a*
Calneh (Calno), 473*b*
Calvin, John, 975*b*
Calvinism, 1252*a*
Cambyses, 501*a*, 1011*a*
Camels, 13*a*
Campbell, E. F., Jr., 1282*b*
Cana, Miracles at, 712*a* f, 715*a*
Canaan:
    Abraham's migration to, 12*a* f
    age of the judges in, 1020*b* f
    allotment of land in, 131*a* ff, 266*a*
    attempt to enter, 105*b*
    enigma of Israel's presence in, 104*a* f
    Israel to be tested by abundance in, 108*a*
    Israel's conquest of, 113*a* f, 123*b* f, 124*b*, 172*b* f, 281*b*, 282*a*, 1020*a* f
    Jacob's return to, 24*b*
    as land of promise, 39*a*

Children:
behavior of, and implications for training, 314*b*
and the biblical world, 1261*b* f
blessings of, 313*a*
born of an adulterous relationship, 563*b*
choosing biblical materials for, 1260*b* f
discipline of, 555*b*, 562*b*, 566*b*, 843*b*, 863*b*
education of, 311*a*, 311*b*, 315*a*, 315*b*
giving of, to Molech, 79*a*, 79*b* f
of harlotry, 452*b* ff
immortality in, 293*b* f, 310*b*
Jesus and, 662*a*
and the kingdom of God, 633*b*, 662*a*, 697*a*
many, to be desired, 297*a* f
many, as reward for righteousness or to be despised, 546*b*
naming of, in Hosea, 452*b* ff
quality of, better than quantity, 559*b*
rebellious, 113*b*
relationship of parents and, 843*b*, 863*b*
sacrifice of, 79*a*, 112*b*, 127*b*, 203*a*, 423*b*, 425*b*
as symbolic of Israel, 656*b*
teaching the Bible to, 1259 ff
unwanted, exposure of, 420*b*, 421*a*
worship for, 1263*b*
Chileab, 156*b*, 171*b*, 177*a*, 210*a*
Chilion, 151*a*
Chimham, 179*a*
Chislev (month), 227*a*, 507*a*
Chloe, 797*a*
Choaspes (Karkheh) River, 537*a*
Christ:
the title, 658*b*
See Jesus Christ
Christ-event, 926*b*
Christ mysticism, 1123*b*, 1191*a*
Christian II; Christian III of Denmark, 1244*b*
Christian life:
brotherhood of, 895*a*, 895*b* f
conduct in, 887*a* ff, 893*a* f, 914*b*, 1120*a*
consequences in, 926*b*
contrasted with that of non-Christians, 893*a*
discipline in, 886*b*
mutual ministry of, 923*a* f
practice of, 916*a*
qualities of, 929*b*
relationships in, 927*b* ff

Christian life—*cont.*
responsibility in, 892*b*
and the Spirit, 782*a* ff, 832*b* f
and the world, 882*a*, 1120*a*
Christianity:
apocalyptic-mindedness in, 868*a*
assimilation of God's promise to Israel by, 365*a*
crisis of, 937*b* ff
and doctrine of the cross, 658*b*, 659*a*
doctrines of, 664*a*, 664*b*, 665*a*
early, variety of, 1116*b*
early biblical interpretation in, 973*a* ff
early creed of, 890*a*
ethics in, 788*b* ff
as heir of OT faith, 766*b*
hindrances to, 932*b* ff
importance of martyrs in, 600*b*
influence of, 1118*a* ff
Jewish and Gentile, 645*a*, 656*b*, 658*b*, 659*a*, 666*b*, 748*a*, 766*b*, 828*a*, 834*a*, 837*a*, 976*b*, 1045*a* ff, 1121*a* f, 1216*a*
and Judaism, incompatibility of, 637*b*, 638*b*, 649*b*, 656*b*, 725*a*, 1117*b*, 1118*b*
Judaizing form of, 708*a* f, 715*b*
life and godliness in, 932*a* f; *see also* Christian life
and the literature, 1116*a* f
Luke an apology for, 672*a*
mystery of, 886*a* f
nature of, 936*b* ff
persecution of, 898*a*, 928*b* f, 929*b*, 938*a*, 946*b*, 1047*a* f, 1050*b* f
personal, and the community, 1122*a* ff
postapostolic, 1121*b* f
and poverty and wealth, 1119*b* f
qualities taught by, 862*b* ff
in Revelation, 948*b* f
spread of, among the Jews, 609*a*
and tradition of Jesus' life and teaching, 1117*b* ff
in transition from Semitic to Gentile culture, 644*b*, 748*a*
as true Israel, 664*a* f, 886*a* ff
understanding of Jesus by, 644*b*
understanding of Song of Solomon by, 324*b*
victory of, 938*b* ff, 1050*b* ff
worship in, 1119*a* f
See also Church

Christology: in Acts, 734*a*
and ideas expressed in Wisdom of Solomon, 546*a*
Logos, 547*b*
and OT scriptures, 591*a*
Son of God, 658*b*
"wisdom" in development of, 305*a*
See also Jesus Christ
Chronicler, 208*a* ff, 220*b*, 221*a*, 519*a*, 587*a*
Chronicles, Book of the (royal annals of Persian court), 230*b*, 234*b*
Chronicles, First and Second Books of, 208 ff, 519*a*, 1086*b* ff
content and purpose of, 208*a* f
date and sources of, 209*a*
name of, and place in the canon, 208*a*
Chronology, biblical, 1271 ff
Church:
admission into, 732*a*
at Antioch, 743*b* f, 745*a*, 747*b* f, 828*a*
and apocalyptic expectation, 865*b*, 946*a*
apologists for, 1047*b* f
apostolic leadership of, 739*a* f
art in, 1250*b* f
Asian, Revelation's exhortation to, 949*a* ff
beginning of, in Jerusalem, 730*b* ff
beginning of judicial procedure in, 632*a*
Bel and the Dragon used in, 585*a*
as body of Christ, 789*b*, 807*b* f, 1174*a*, 1190*b*
Byzantine, 1251*a*
canon of scripture of, 989*a* f; *see also* Canon, NT, *and* Canon, OT
Christ and, in NT, 1174*a* f
Christ as head of 837*a*, 837*b*, 843*a*, 861*b*, 1174*b*
Christ as Savior of, 843*a*
as Christ's bride, 843*a*, 843*b*
in Colossae, 895*a*
a community of faith, 630*a*
conduct of, 887*a* ff
conduct of Christians outside of, 864*a*, 882*a*
and conference at Jerusalem, 748*a* ff
conflict of, with Judaism, 637*b*, 638*b*, 649*b*, 656*b*, 725*a*, 1117*b*, 1118*b*

David:
  and Abigail, 167a f
  and Absalom, 176b ff, 178b
  Ammonites conquered by, 467b
  anointing of, as king, 156b, 164a, 170b, 172b, 211b
  ark brought to Jerusalem by, 65a, 212a
  and Bathsheba, 175b f, 183a
  brigand band of, 166b
  campaigns and chief officials of, 174b f, 179b, 213b
  capture of Jerusalem by, 421a
  care of, for Jonathan's son, 175a
  census of, 212b f, 981b
  Chronicler's special concern for, 208a, 208b
  conquest of Edom by, 21a
  descendants of, 210a
  desire of, to build a temple, 212a f
  family struggles of, 176a ff
  as first real king, 162a
  flight of, to Gath, 166a f
  flight of, from Jerusalem, 177a f
  genealogy of, 154b
  and Gibeon, 981a
  God's promise to, 174a f, 180a, 182b, 187a, 216b, 267b, 287a f, 298a, 365b
  God's spirit in, 164a
  Goliath slain by, 164b f
  at Hebron, 212a
  and Hiram, 212a, 467b
  and his court, 175a ff
  as ideal king, 338b
  as instrument of God, 164b, 284b
  introduction of, 164a ff, 212b
  Jesus born of lineage of, 611b, 638a, 663a, 665a, 679a, 699b, 718a
  and Jonathan, 165a, 165b f, 167a, 170a
  at Keilah, 166b f
  as king of Judah, 170b ff, 211b, 1021b f, 1277a f
  lamentation of, 170a
  last words of, 180a, 183b f, 213b
  at Mahanaim, 178a
  marriage of, to Michal, 165a
  military victories of, 172b f, 212b
  Moabite ancestry of, 150b, 151a, 154b, 342b
  at Nob, 166a
  oath of, 298a
  praised by ben Sira, 573a

David—cont.
  as preparation for the great King, 900b
  preparations of, for the temple, 213a f, 298a
  psalms attributed to, 253a, 259b, 260b, 320b
  references to life of, in psalms, 260a
  rescue of captives at Ziklag by, 169a
  restoration of line of, 338b, 340a f, 394a, 476b, 486a, 487a ff, 503b
  returned to power, 178b f
  rise of, to power, 164a ff
  and Saul, 164a, 164b, 165a ff, 170a
  Saul's attempts to kill, 165b
  senility of, 183a, 213b
  service of, to Philistines, 168a
  sharing of spoils by, 169b
  solving of dilemma of, 168b f
  sons of, 171b
  stories about, in Samuel, 156a f
  and temple personnel, 222b
  as true shepherd, 430a
  at the well at Bethlehem, 152a, 180a
  and Yahweh, 156b, 157a, 165b, 167b, 187a
Davies, Gwynne Henton, 68b
Davies, W. D., 1193b
da Vinci, 1251a, 1251b
Day of the Lord, day of Yahweh, 334a ff, 336b, 351b, 406b f, 462b, 463a ff, 465b, 472b, 475a f, 478b, 479a f, 484a, 499a f, 509b, 511b, 872b f, 878a f, 1099b
  See also Judgment
Day and night:
  creation of, 3b, 4a
  for waking and sleeping, 873a
Day Star:
  as Lucifer, 342a
  name for a tyrant, 341b
Deaconesses, 793b
Deacons in early church, 793b, 847a, 886b, 1045b, 1049a
  qualifications of, 886a
Dead, Book of the (Egyptian), 239a, 249a
Dead Sea, 50a, 105b, 121a, 130b, 279b, 326a
Dead Sea scrolls, 83a, 232b, 496, 527a, 550b, 593b, 610a, 617a, 847a, 873a, 1056b, 1063 ff, 1204b, 1205a, 1207a, 1228a, 1228b

Dead Sea scrolls—cont.
  discovery of, 1063a ff
  four types of, 1114a f
  and Qumran community, 1068a ff
  and Qumran library, 1065b ff
  significance of, 1070a ff
Death:
  Babylonian lord of, 254b
  better than chronic sickness, 566b
  Christian attitude toward, 932b
  and Christian salvation, 871a ff
  covenant of, 559a
  desirability of, 321b
  as early punishment for adultery, 308b
  of family for offense of one member, 128a
  freedom from, 274b f, 778b ff
  horror of, 278b
  inevitability and finality of, 570b
  isolation of priest from, 80a, 80b
  judgment after, 542b, 546b f, 587b
  lament in the face of, 263a
  or life, choice of, for Israel, 471b f
  life after, 816a f
  life's meaningless movement toward, 321b
  new life through, 929a f
  as only certainty, 323a
  for Paul, 779a
  as penalty for disobeying parents, 113b
  as penalty for murder, 56b
  as penalty to rebels, 125a
  as penalty for sorcery, 58a
  premature, 312a
  as separation from God, 6a
  and sin, 546b, 783a, 812a
  spiritual, 838b
  termination of man's relationship with God through, 287a
  uncleanness from contact with, 92a, 530a
  universality of, 277a, 788b f, 783a
  way of, 350a f
  wealth no security against, 557b
  word of, 348a f
  as work of the devil, 546a, 546b
Debate, in Bible teaching, 1267a f
Debir, 35b
Deborah, 529a

Farming—*cont.*

for security, 317*b*

used as metaphor, 458*a*

Fasting, 621*a*

of Esther, 235*a*, 237*b*

followed by feasting, 507*a* f

ineffectiveness of, 507*a*

of Jesus, 679*a*

Jesus' words on, 617*a* f, 649*b*

true, 366*b* f

Fat:

offering of, 70*a*

prohibition against eating of, 73*b*

Fathers: duties of, 555*b*, 567*b* f, 843*b*

the patriarchal family, 114*a*

rights of, 55*a*, 57*b*

Fear:

conquest of, 270*b* f

overcome by trust, 278*b*

of retribution, 317*b*

Fear of (reverence for) God, 262*b*, 273*a*, 297*b*

as essential nature of wisdom, 551*a*, 551*b*, 772*b*

understanding founded on, 293*b*

Feasts:

of booths (tabernacles, in-gathering), 66*a*, 66*b*, 81*b* f, 86*b*, 111*a*, 117*a*, 119*b*, 223*a*, 229*b* f, 255*a*, 340*b*, 434*a*, 510*b*, 529*a*, 571*a*, 717*b*

day of atonement, 81*b*

of dedication of temple, 187*b*

enthronement of the Lord, 255*a*, 268*a*, 269*b*, 271*a*, 276*b*, 289*b* f, 298*a*

of lights (Hanukkah), 590*a*, 594*a*, 719*b*

new year, 81*b*, 254*a* f, 255*a* f, 272*b*, 276*b*, 277*a*, 285*a*, 286*a*, 336*a*, 510*b*

passover, 111*a*, 255*a*, 434*a*, 571*a*, 640*b*, 701*a*

Pentecost (weeks), 529*a*, 529*b*, 731*a* ff

of unleavened bread, 44*b*, 46*b*, 66*a*, 81*a*, 111*a*, 225*a*, 255*a*, 529*a*, 640*b*, 701*a*

of weeks (harvest), 58*b*, 66*a*, 81*a*, 110*b*, 111*a*, 117*a*, 255*a*, 529*a*, 529*b*, 731*a* ff

See also Festivals

Feeding of the multitudes, 627*a*, 655*a* f, 657*b*

Felix, Antonius, 761*a*, 761*b* f, 769*b*

Fell, John, 1233*a*

Fenton, Ferrar, 1241*b*

Ferrer, Bonifacio and Vicente, 1244*b*

Fertile Crescent, 1001*b* ff

climate of, 1003*b* ff

lands around, 999*a* ff

Mesopotamia, 1001*b* f

Syria-Palestine, 1002*a* ff

Fertility-cult interpretation of Song of Solomon, 324*b*, 325*a*, 325*b*, 326*a*, 326*b*, 327*a*, 327*b*

Fertility god, 254*b*, 281*a*

Fertility rites, 64*a*, 149*b*, 452*b*, 455*b*, 457*a*, 484*b*, 488*a*, 499*a*

failure of, 457*b* f

Fertility symbols, 62*a*, 278*a*, 352*a*, 380*a*, 470*a*

Festivals:

of new moon, 475*b*

poetic art in, 254*a* f

See also Feasts

Festus, Porcius, 762*a* ff, 763*b*, 769*b*

Feudal culture, Canaanite, 123*a*

Feuillet, André, 709*b*

Fictional writings in intertesta-mental literature, 1110*b*

Fidelity, 552*a* f

in friendship, 554*b*, 565*b*

to mood of the Bible, 1256*b*

See also Faithfulness

Filson, Floyd V., 581*b*, 583*b*, 591*a*, 610*b*, 730*a*, 796*b*, 989, 1004*b*, 1017*b*, 1025*b*, 1129, 1175*b*

Final age of judgment and promise, 330*b*, 343*b*, 347*b*; *see also* End time, Judgment, *and* Eschatology

Finegan, Jack, 982*b*

Fire:

adversity as, 582*a*

baptism with, 612*b*

called down by Elijah, 958*b*

contained in cloud, 74*b*

destructive, from presence of God, 74*b*

of the Lord, 74*b*, 88*a*, 474*b*

ordeal by, 203*a*

pillar of, 47*b*

three young men in, 440*b* f, 581*b* ff

Firmament, creation of, 3*b* ff, 571*a*

Firstborn:

dedication and redemption of, 45*a*

J ordinance of the, 46*b*

law of, 489*a*

males, count of, 86*b*

P ordinance of the, 46*a*

Firstborn—*cont.*

right of, 113*b*

substitute sacrifice for, 46*b*

First fruits:

offering of, 66*b*, 69*b*, 110*b*, 116*b* f, 308*a*, 388*b*

of the Spirit, 783*b*, 784*a*

Firstling, given to God, 84*b*, 110*a*, 111*a*

Fish:

as Christian symbol, 627*a*, 1250*b*

in story of Tobit, 531*b*

Fish Gate, 228*a*

Flavian emperors, 524*b*

Fleece, used for oracles, 142*b*

Flies, plague of, 43*a*

Flood narrative, 7*b* ff, 365*a*

Florus, Gessius, 1030*a* f

Flute, 400*a*

Foakes-Jackson, F. J., 730*a*

Foerster, Werner, 1193*b*

Folly, contrasted with wisdom, 309*b* f

See also Fools

Food:

clean (*kosher*), 540*b*

cult, of worshipers, 454*b*

for demons, 805*a*

of exile, 457*b*

holy, eating of, 80*b*

for man and beast, creation of, 291*a*

offered to idols, 803*a* ff

problem of, for Gentile Chris-tians, 1121*a* f

regulations about, 66*b*, 75*b*, 78*b*, 110*a*, 438*a* ff

ritually unclean, 656*b*

scarcity and defilement of, 416*b*

strange teachings about, 915*a*

Fools, 306*a*, 313*b*, 316*b*, 318*a*

dreams of, 568*a*

and the law, 567*b*

speech of, 562*a*, 562*b*

talking with, 315*b*

and wise men, 310*a* f, 562*b* f

Foot washing by Jesus, 722*a* f

Forced labor:

of Canaanites, 132*a*

of Hebrews, 37*a* f

revival of, 387*b*

and Solomon's building of the temple, 185*a*, 187*b* f

Foreigners:

changing status of, in Ruth, 150*a* f

charging interest of, 115*a*

oracle of third Isaiah on, 365*b* f

See also Sojourner

Foresight, 561a

Forgiveness:
in the Christian life, 928b
in Jesus' death, 1172a f
Jesus' power of, 648b, 649a, 684b f
Joseph as exemplar of, 316b
prayer for, 269b f, 814b
promise of, to Israel, 333a f
repentance and, 272a f, 277b, 297b, 560b f
sin, faith, and, 695b f
unlimited, 632b

Form criticism, 1081b, 1118a, 1225a
of the gospels, 1127a ff, 1131a

Former Prophets, 155a, 181a, 526b, 529a, 1084a, 1209b, 1215a

Forum of Appius, 766a

Forum method of Bible teaching, 1267a

Fosbroke, H. E. W., 465b

Fountain for cleansing, 509b

Fountain Gate, 227b, 228b

Fox, George, 1249a

Fox tails, 147b

Frame, J. E., 867a, 877a

Freedman, David N., 1058a, 1062b, 1089b, 1208b, 1282b

Freedmen, 736b

Freedom:
from anxiety, 617b f
cause of, and the Bible, 1252b
of choice, as essence of human existence, 522a, 524a, 785b
of choice, given men by God, 448b
Christian, 803b, 804a, 828a, 828b f, 831a ff
derived from wisdom, 323a
of exiles, see Exile, return from
false view of, 933a
importance of, 831a f
from law, 780b ff
of religion, after Maccabean Wars, 606b
and repentance, 647a f
from sin and death, 778b ff
from slavery, 368a
true, 828b f, 832a ff, 895a, 918a
voluntary limitation of, 805a

Freewill offering, 73a, 278a, 471a

Frend, W. H. C., 1053b

Frescoes, 1250b

Friendship:
among neighbors, 317a
choosing friends, 554b, 568b
covenant of, broken, 278b
false and true friends, 554b, 563a

Friendship—cont.
fidelity in, 554b, 565b
moderation in, 316b
one of life's highest values, 313b, 565b
preservation of, 563a
with the world, as enmity with God, 921b

Fritsch, Charles T., 208, 214, 220, 227, 307a, 519, 1095, 1105b, 1115b

Frogs, plague of, 42b

Frost, Stanley Brice, 438a, 577, 579, 587

Fruit trees, preservation of, 113b

Fuller, R. H., 1193b

Funerary laws, 110a; see also Burial

Furnace, smelting:
analogy of, for purifying Jerusalem, 425a
and the three young men, 440b f, 581b ff

Furnish, Victor Paul, 824, 834, 856, 894

Future:
of the disciples, 723a, 728a f
justice to reign in, 338b
not to be counted on, 316b

G

Gaal, 144b

Gabael, 531a

Gabatha (Bigthan), 544a

Gaber, 222a

Gabriel (angel), 447a, 448a, 533b, 674a, 674b, 956b

Gad, Gadites, 31b f, 106a, 125a, 132b, 138a, 400a
allotment of land to, 131a
sons of, 210b

Gad (a deity), 370b

Gadara, demoniacs at, 620b, 653b; see also Gerasene demoniacs

Gaius a convert, 794b

Gaius of Derbe, 756a

Gaius an opponent of Hippolytus, 1222b

Gaius of III John, 941a

Galatia, 749b f, 1139b
churches of, 824b f, 1139b f

Galatians, Letter of Paul to, 824 ff
address of, 824b f
benediction of, 833b
character and significance of, 824a f
date and place of composition of, 825a f

Galatians—cont.
the Galatian troublemakers, 825b, 832a, 833b
occasion for writing, 826a f
salutation of, 826a

Galba, 1036a

Galeed, 23b

Galerius, 866, 876b

Galilee:
captured by Assyria, 203a
Jesus' instructions to return to, 642b
Jesus' ministry beyond, 658a ff
Jesus' ministry in, 614a f, 647a ff, 648b ff, 679b ff
Jesus' woes on cities of, 623b
Maccabean victories in, 594b f
overrun by Tiglath-pileser III, 210b
women from, at the tomb, 642b

Gallican Psalter, 1231b

Gallienus, 525b

Gallim (stone heaps), 459a

Gallim (town), 167b

Gallio, 753b, 795b

Gallio inscription, 982a

Gamad, 427a

Gamaliel the Pharisee (Rabbi), 713a, 735b, 827a

Gangsterism, warning against, 307a f

Gardner-Smith, Percival, 709b

Garrulity, warning against, 311a

Gashga (Gaga), 431a

Gaster, T. H., 1071b, 1081b

Gatekeepers, temple, 211a f, 222b, 226b

Gath, 158b, 184a, 201b, 467a, 473b, 485a
David's flight to, 166a f
David's services offered to, 168a

Gath-hepher, 202b

Gaumata, 224a

Gaza, 138a, 185a, 426b, 467a, 739b
captured by Neco, 399a
Samson at, 147b

Gazara (Gezer), 593b, 598b, 604b

Gealy, F. D., 884b, 1175b

Geba, 161b, 162b, 171b, 173b, 192a, 510b

Geba (town near Dothan), 538a

Gebal (bedouin tribe), 285b

Gebal (Byblos), 185a

Geber, 184b

Gedaliah, 373a
as governor of Judah, 207b, 390b, 396b
murder of, 396b

Gnosticism—cont.

beliefs of, 1122a, 1170b

and creation of matter, 1169b

gospels of, 1146b, 1147a

salvation in, 882b

threat of, to church, 1048a f

Gob, 179b

God:

and Abraham, 14a ff, 16a ff, 355a, 362a, 582a, 777a f, 906a

action of, and unity between the Testaments, 992a f

adultery hated by, 583a, 583b

alienation from, 6a, 6b, 262b, 268b, 272a, 301a, 838b

all nations to come to, 365b

and Amos, 465b ff, 475a

as arbiter of good and right, 870a, 870b

armor of, 844a

assurance of, to Hebrews, 41b

attitude toward name of, 54b

authority of, 267b f, 299a, 301b

Bible a book about, 992b

Bible teaching centered in, 1266a

Bildad's concept of, 243b

blessing of, 581b, 582b, 593b, 640b

call of, 870b

call to Israel to become a nation by, 12a, 446a

centrality of, in OT prophecy, 1098b

chosen people of, in the new age, 347a f

church the temple of, 839b ff

concept of, as higher than all human reckoning, 247a

concept of, in Joshua, 124a f

confidence in, 540a

continuing presence of, 64b, 65a

covenant against, 285b

covenant of, with Israel, see Covenant

covenant of, with Noah, 8a, 8b f

creation to be ended by, 523a f

creation of social distinctions by, 315a

as creator, 3b ff, 272b f, 290b ff, 302a, 308a, 560a f

as creator and sustainer of nature, 354a ff, 472a, 551a, 571a f

Cyrus as instrument of, 355b, 356a, 358a f, 360a

God—cont.

Daniel as instrument of, 583a, 584b

and David, 174a f, 216b, 284b, 287a f, 298a, 365b

day of judgment of, 334a ff, 369a, 484a

death as separation from, 6a

deeds of, 284a, 291b f, 301b, 302a, 367b, 488b f, 489b, 570a, 582a, 984b f

of deliverance, 262a, 265a, 267a, 268b, 273a, 274b

departure of, from his people, 455b, 485b f, 511b, 512a

devotion to will of, 615a

and dignity of man, 251a

doctrine of, in Scripture, 1255b

dwelling of, in Jerusalem (Zion), 276a, 280b, 281b, 284b, 298b, 302a, 333b, 464b

Elihu's depiction of, 249b ff

as enemy, 243b, 244a, 245b f

enjoyment bestowed by, 321a

Ezra's intercessory prayer to, 225b f

faith grounded in witness of, 939a

fatherhood of, 458b, 513b, 546b, 830b, 858b, 914a

fear of (reverence for), 262b, 273a, 293b, 297b, 481b

fear of, as beginning of wisdom, 551a, 551b

festival of enthronement of, 255a, 268a, 269b, 271a, 276b, 289b f, 298a

foreign nations used as instruments of, 336a, 339a ff, 341a f, 637a

forgiveness by, 482a, 490b, 554a, 554b, 560b f, 817a f

four people hated by, 319a

freedom of choice given men by, 448b

fulfillment of purpose of, 617a

fullness of, 860b

gifts from, 918a, 918b, 933b ff

God Almighty, 16a, 41a, 256a

grace of, 490a, 504b, 514b, 634b, 778a, 832b, 840b, 841a, 892b

graciousness of, 349b f, 369b, 371a

in history, 255b, 261b, 276b, 285a, 291b f, 298b f, 341a f, 342b f, 347a, 356a, 358b, 469b, 505a, 836b, 1160a

holiness derived from, 78b

God—cont.

holiness of, 49b, 289b f, 332b, 335b, 336a, 336b, 355b, 431b, 914a f

of hosts, 256a, 269b, 471b

household of, 902b

increasing distance between man and, 505a

independence of, from man, 250a

inscrutability of ways of, 323a

Isaiah commissioned by, 336a

and Israel, Song of Solomon an allegory of, 324b

Israel as chosen people of, 52a f, 53a, 54a, 104a, 104b, 108a f, 338a, 355a f, 356b, 357a f, 358a, 360b f, 363a ff, 370a, 409a, 458b, 469b, 488b, 512a f, 968a f

Israel's destinies directed by, 547b ff

Israel's rebellion against, 456b f

Jesus as revealer of, 623b, 899b f

Job and, 241a, 243a, 243b, 245b f, 246b, 247b f, 249a f, 251b, 252a, 252b ff

judgment of, 313a, 445b, 560b, 877b

justice and righteousness of, 240b, 247a, 250a, 255b f, 263b, 264a, 277a f, 278a, 279a, 281b, 283b, 285b, 289a, 289b, 293b, 295a f, 296a f, 300b, 301a, 301b f, 306b, 308a, 312a f, 314a, 314b, 356a f, 422a, 477b, 511b f, 514a, 514b f, 523b, 548a, 568b, 771b, 774a, 775a, 782b

kingship of, 885a, 1160b, 1161a, 1162b

knowledge of, 300a, 300b, 307b, 455a, 456a f, 772a

and the law, 274b

as the light of his people, 368a

of the living, 637b

love and faithfulness of, 54b, 255b, 262b, 263a, 271b, 273b, 275b, 277b, 278a, 279a, 281a, 287b, 288b, 289b, 290b, 291b, 294a, 294b, 295a, 299a f, 365a, 369a, 408a, 412b, 422a, 438a, 447b, 452b, 454b, 456a, 458b ff, 512a f, 581b, 617a, 638a, 778a, 784b, 814a, 838b, 934a f

loyalty of, to his "word," 103b

Hazeroth, 88b

Hazor (center for Arabian tribes), 400b

Hazor (in N. Galilee), 35b, 130a f, 466a

"He" and "She" Bibles, 1242b

Headlam, A. C., 770a

Healing:

anointing in, 923a

by disciples, 732a f, 734b, 739a, 741a, 747a, 765b

by Jesus, 614b, 619b f, 620b, 621a f, 627b, 628a, 631a, 635a, 647b f, 650a, 654a, 657a, 658a, 660a f, 663a, 680b f, 681b, 683b ff, 686a, 692b f, 696a, 697b, 715a f, 718b f, 1179b, 1181b f

in ministry of church, 923a f

Health:

better than wealth, 566b

kind words and, 311b

through calmness, 312a

through cheerfulness, 312b

Heathcote, A. W., 988b

Heaven, 3b, 476a

bliss of redeemed in, 961b

Christ's ministry in, 929a

entrance into, 618b, 633b ff

God's throne in, 371a

a half-hour of silence in, 956a f

king above, 293b f

kingdom of, 614b, 618b, 1176a; see also Kingdom of God

new, and new earth, 370b, 967a

organization of, 291a

prelude to apocalypse in, 952b ff

scorn in, 379a f

temple in, 962b

voice from, 613a, 646b, 678b, 740a, 961b, 962a

war in, 448b

Heavenly beings, 285a f, 336a, 803b, 805a

judgment of, 346a

See also Angels

Heber, 139b

wife of, 140a

Hebert, A. G., 993b

Hebrew canon. See Jewish canon

Hebrew (language), 239a, 1194a

alphabet, 525b

Baruch in, 577a

Daniel in, 436a, 437a

development and structure of, 1195a ff

Ecclesiasticus in, 550a, 550b

of II Esdras, 521b

Hebrew—cont.

extant MSS in, 1228b

Judith in, 536a

Letter of Jeremiah in, 579a

for I Maccabees, 588b

origin of, 1202b ff

replaced by Aramaic, 1115a

scriptures printed in, 1232b

Tobit in, 527a

Hebrews, 10a, 162b

beginning of nation of, 123b

connotations of term, 27b

desert wandering of, 49b f

Egyptian pursuit of, 48a

first appearance of word in OT, 13b

forced labor of, 37a f

God's assurance to, 41b

and Hellenists, 1038a

in hill country of Canaan, 124b

history of, in Egypt, 33b ff

identified with Habiru, 13b f, 34b, 35a, 37a, 40b, 56a, 123b, 129a, 144a, 1010a, 1017a

journey out of Egypt by, 46b ff

killing of infants of, 37b

land of Canaan promised to, 39a

memorials of deliverance of, 44a ff

and the OT, 1072 ff

oppression of, in Egypt, 34b, 35a, 36a ff, 40b f

origin of, 1016b ff

poetry of, 253b f, 364a, 415a, 422b, 423a, 541b f, 645b, 1077a ff, 1088a

preparation for departure of, from Sinai, 64b

rescued at the sea, 46b ff

some close neighbors of, 1013b ff

a term of contempt, 162a

a term for Israelites used by outsiders, 540b

wisdom literature of, 305a f

See also Israel and Jews

Hebrews, Gospel According to the, 646b, 1146a, 1218b

Hebrews, Letter to the, 546a, 897 ff

authorship of, 897a f, 1136b, 1223a

distinctive features of, 898b f

epilogue of, 914b ff

origin, destination, and date of, 897b ff

purpose of, 898b

Hebrews—cont.

references to Maccabean exploits in, 593a

theme of, 899a ff

Hebron, 19a, 170b, 477a

Absalom at, 177a

Caleb's inheritance at, 131b

David at, 156b, 210a, 212a

Hedonism, 546b

Heidegger, Martin, 1256b

Helam, 175b

Helbon, 427b

Helech, 427a

Heliodorus, 445a, 449a, 601b, 602a

Heliopolis, 344a, 397b, 1002b

Hellenism:

Greek language of, 1039a f

history of, 1037b ff

influence of, on church, 1167b

influence of, on NT writers, 1188a

and Hebrews, 1038a, 1273b a

and Judaism, 708a, 1076a f

philosophy of, 1039b ff

religion of, 1040b ff

Hellenization, 448a, 449a, 602b, 1034a f

Antiochus' program of, 437a, 439a, 444a, 535b, 590a, 591b, 592a

of Menelaus, 604b

Heman, 210a, 210b, 213a, 213b, 222a

psalms attributed to, 259b

Hennecke, E., 1149b

Henry VIII of England, 1238b, 1239a, 1239b

Heraclitus, 710a

Herbert, A. G., 32a

Herbert, A. S., 3b

Hercules, 146b, 147a

worship of, 602a

Herder, Johann Gottfried von, 976b

Heresy, 878b, 882a, 885a, 931b

appeal of, to weak women, 890b

perils of, for early church, 1048a f

problem of, 890a, 936a

punishment for, 943a f

warning against, 794b

See also Gnosticism

Hereth, forest of, 166b

Héring, Jean, 796b

Herklots, H. G. C., 1236b

Hermeneutics, 983b; see also Biblical interpretation

Hermogenes, 889b

J

Judah, tribe of—*cont.*
  primacy of, 25*b*, 26*a*, 29*a*, 31*b*,
    279*b*, 284*b*
Judah, Wilderness of, 151*b*, 1003*a*
Judaism:
  Antiochus' attempts to destroy,
    528*a*, 536*b*, 538*a*, 590*a*
  apocalypticism in, 945*a* f,
    1109*a*
  arrogance of, 773*a*
  attitude of, to law and
    prophets, 1117*a*
  birth of, 1157*a* ff
  calendar followed by, 98*a*
  Christianity the fulfillment of,
    815*b*
  confidence of, in God's victory,
    508*a*
  conflict of Christian church
    with, 637*b*, 638*b*, 642*b*, 643*a*,
    725*a*, 1117*b*, 1118*b*
  defense of, in Wisdom of Solo-
    mon, 546*a*
  early biblical interpretation in,
    972*a* ff
  failure of, to perceive true
    nature of Jesus, 659*b*
  forced conversion to, 236*b*
  and Hellenism, 1076*a* f
  holy days of, 232*b*
  importance of written word in,
    533*b*
  influence of, on early church,
    1167*b*, 1188*a*
  Jesus' rejection by, 626*b*, 627*a*
  Matthew's repudiation of,
    627*b*
  medieval exegesis in, 974*a* f
  moral earnestness of, 579*b*
  official acceptance of Purim
    by, 237*b*
  "otherness" of God in, 533*b*
  Paul on, 773*a* ff
  for Paul and Luke, 1117*b*
  and Persian religion, 1107*a*
  as personal religion, 528*a* f
  preserved by a remnant, 441*a;*
    see also Remnant
  profession and practice in, 773*b*
  rejection of gospel by, 784*b* ff
  religious thought in, 600*b*
  sabbath observance by, 365*b*
  teachings of, 528*a* f, 530*b* f
  theology of, 534*a*
  and true circumcision, 773*b* f
  use of divine name avoided in,
    235*b*
  visual arts and, 1250*b*
  weaning church from, 1046*b* f

Judaizers, 825*b*, 852*b*, 936*a*,
  1048*a*
Judas Barsabbas, 749*a*, 749*b*
Judas the Galilean, 735*b*
Judas Iscariot, 622*a*, 717*b*, 721*a* f,
  723*a*
  betrayal of Jesus by, 640*a*,
    640*b*, 641*b*, 666*b*, 667*b*,
    701*a*, 702*b*
  death of, 731*a*
Judas Maccabaeus (Handel), 1250*a*
Judas Maccabaeus (Longfellow),
  1250*a*
Judas Maccabeus, 437*a*, 446*b*,
  447*a*, 449*b*, 536*a*, 590*a*,
  600*a*, 719*b*
  alliance of, with Rome, 596*a*
  death of, 590*b*, 596*a*
  dream of, 606*a*
  Nicanor killed by, 593*a*, 596*a*
  ode in honor of, 592*b* f
  opposition to, in Jewish ranks,
    595*a*, 595*b*
  rededication of temple by,
    538*a*, 594*a*, 601*a*, 601*b*
  resistance under, 592*b* ff
  as sole hero of II Maccabees,
    600*a*, 601*a* ff
  victories of, 593*a*, 593*b*, 594*b* f,
    602*a* ff
Judas the son of James, 682*b*
Judas the son of Simon Maccabeus, 599*b*
Jude, Book of, 931*a*, 942 ff
  author and date of, 942*a*
  as a "general" epistle, 942*a*
  message of, 942*a*
  II Peter and, 931*b*
  reason for, 942*b*
  salutation of, 942*b*
Judea, 437*a*, 448*b*, 536*a*, 538*b*,
  589*a*, 674*a*, 711*a*
  absorbed into Roman Empire,
    599*b*, 604*b*
  and the Maccabean Wars,
    591*b*, 592*a* ff, 599*a*, 1028*a* f
  political change and religious
    crisis in, 591*a* ff
  revolts of, against Rome,
    1030*a* ff
  self-government for, 1028*b* f,
    1274*a* f
  under the Ptolemies, 1027*b*
  under Roman rule, 1029*a* ff,
    1042*a*, 1274*b*
Judea, wilderness of, 592*a* f,
  612*a*, 679*b*
Judge, office of, 111*a*
Judge River, 283*b*, 294*a*

Judges:
  age of the, 1020*b* f
  Israel's deliverance by, 138*b* ff
  minor, 135*b*, 146*a*
  period of, as setting for Ruth,
    150*a*, 150*b*
  praised by ben Sira, 573*a*
  Samuel as last judge, 159*a*
  tribal leaders as, 136*b*
Judges, Book of, 100*a*, 135 ff,
  1085*a*
  D introduction to, 138*a* f
  and history of Israel, 136*a* f
  literary history of, 135*a* ff
  prologue to, 137*a* ff
  religious outlook of, 136*b* f
Judgment:
  of apostasy, 366*a* f
  for Babylon, 341*a* ff
  breastpiece of, 62*a*
  certainty of, 560*b*, 691*a* f
  confession and, 367*a* f
  curse in, 346*a*
  day of, *see* Day of the Lord
  decree of, on Nebuchadnezzar,
    441*b* f
  and deliverance, 933*a*
  on dishonesty, 734*a* f
  to early church, 734*a* f
  of Edom, 477*b* ff
  exile as, 353*b*
  final, 346*a*, 475*a* f, 622*a*, 630*b*,
    743*a*, 966*b* f; *see also* End
    time
  of God, 277*a* f, 278*a*, 313*a*,
    370*b* ff, 445*b*, 514*a*, 560*b*;
    see also Day of the Lord
  God's purpose in, 428*a*
  Hall of, 186*a*
  of the heavenly beings, 346*a*
  holiness as ground of, 428*a*
  hope in, 335*a*, 339*b*
  Hosea's word of, on Israel,
    456*a*
  on images, 402*a*
  on Israel, 456*a*, 468*a* ff
  on Judah and Jerusalem, 336*b*,
    499*a* f, 500*b*
  of mankind, 334*a* ff
  of the nations, 351*b* f, 355*a* ff,
    357*a*, 463*b* f, 466*b* ff, 479*a*,
    499*b* f
  premature, 561*b*
  and promise, 338*a* f
  of Samaria, 348*a*
  summons to, 488*b*
  universal, 346*a*, 389*a* f
  of women, 334*b* f, 350*b*
Judith:
  blessing of, 541*b*

Neil, William, 461*b*, 867*a*, 877*a*

Neo-Babylonian Empire, 207*a*, 438*b*, 440*a*, 443*a*, 445*a*

Neo-Babylonian Laws, 1090*a*

Nephilim, 7*b*, 89*b*, 542*a*

Nergal, 204*a*, 288*a*, 414*b*

Nergal-sharezer, 207*b*

Nero, 898*a*, 924*a*, 946*b*, 960*b*, 964*a*, 1035*b*

Nerva, 888*b*, 1036*a*, 1144*a*

Nestle, Eberhard and Erwin, 1234*a*

"Neutral Text," 1233*b*

New age, hope and promise of, 350*b*, 370*a* f

New England Primer, 1252*a*

New English Bible, 1242*b*, 1268*a*

New Jerusalem Scroll, 435*b*

New Testament:

apocalypses in, 1124*a* f, 1188*a*

authority of canon of, 1224*b*

beginning of study of, 1229*a* f

Christ as central theme of, 987*a* ff

and the Christian community, 1116 ff

and Christian origins, 1187 ff

chronology of period of, 1275*b*

covenant in, 986*b* f

crucial period in transmission of, 1229*b* f

cultural milieu of authors of, 1037*a* f

descriptions of the church in, 1190*a* f

development of critical text of, 1233*a* f

early canonical lists for, 1223*b* f

examples of historical study of Bible from, 981*b* ff

extant Greek MSS of, 1231*a* f, 1235

foundations of a new culture in, 1117*b*

the gospels, 1126*b* ff, 1187*a* f, 1218*b*, 1222*b* f

Greco-Roman background of, 1037 ff

and Greek thought, 1039*b* ff

and Hellenism, 1037*b* ff

and inheritance from Jewish scriptures, 1216*a* ff

interpretation of Jesus in, 1167 ff

later text criticism of, 1233*b* f

Latin versions of, 1231*b*

letters in, 1124*b* ff, 1187*b*, 1219*a* f, 1223*a*

literary forms and vocabulary of, 1043*a* ff, 1124 ff

New Testament—*cont.*

making of canon of, 1136*a*, 1216 ff, 1223*b* ff; *see also* Canon, NT

and the ministry, 1192*a* ff

and OT, intertestamental literature between, 1110 ff

and OT, period between, 979*a*

and OT, unity between, 989 ff

OT canon in, 1212*b* f

and OT tradition, 1117*a* f

the Pastoral epistles, 1219*b* f

Paul's letters in, 1136 ff

people of, 978*b* f

printed in Greek, 1232*b* f

Resurrection the perspective of, 1173*a* f

and Roman institutions, 1041*b* ff

and the sacraments, 1190*b* ff

the Septuagint, 1042*b* f; *see also* Septuagint

significance of Dead Sea scrolls for study of, 1070*b* ff

standardization of, 1230*b* f

Syriac versions of, 1231*b* f

theological history in, 1126*a* f

and tradition of Jesus' life and teaching, 1117*b* ff

and Wisdom of Solomon, 546*a*

NT, The: An American Translation (Goodspeed), 1241*b*

NT in the Language of the People, The (Williams), 1242*a*

NT in Modern English (Phillips), 1242*a*, 1268*a*

NT in Modern Speech (Weymouth), 1241*b*, 1268*a*

NT in the Original Greek, The (Westcott and Hort), 1233*b*

NT in Plain English, The (Williams), 1241*b*

New year, observance of, 81*b*, 98*a*, 254*a* f, 272*b*, 276*b*, 277*a*, 285*a*, 286*a*, 336*a*

Newman, John Henry (Cardinal), 1241*a*

Newman, Murray, 86*a*

Nibhaz, 204*a*

Nicaea, Council of, 1052*b*, 1116*a*

Nicanor, 593*a*, 595*b*, 596*a*, 600*a*, 603*b*, 605*b* ff

Nicene Creed, 1052*b* f

Nicholas of Hereford, 1238*a*

Nicodemus, 651*a*, 713*a* f, 726*a* f, 926*a*

Nicolaitans, 950*b*, 951*a*

Nicolaus, 950*b*

Nida, E. A., 1247*b*

Niebuhr, Reinhold, 1253*b*

Nile River, 15*b*

annual flooding of, 475*b*, 476*a*, 1001*a*

dragon of the, 428*a*, 428*b*

drying up of, 343*b*

pollution of, 42*b*

Nimrod (Assyrian Empire), 10*a*

Nineham, D. E., 977*b*

Nineveh, 10*a*, 372*a*, 480*a*, 481*b*, 529*a*

conversion of, 480*a*, 482*a*

fall of, 491*a*, 492*a* ff, 526*a*, 534*b*, 1009*a*

God's pity for, 482*b*

taunt against, 500*a*

Tobias' return to, 533*a* f

Tobit's advice to leave, 534*b*

Ninib, 414*b*

Ninurta, 10*a*

Nisan (month), 44*b*, 227*a*, 230*a*

Nisroch, 205*b*

Noah, 7*a*, 420*a*, 531*a*, 913*a*

descendants of, 209*b*

and the Flood, 7*b*, 8*a* f

God's covenant with, 8*a*, 8*b* f, 365*a*

mentioned by ben Sira, 572*a*

the name, 7*b*

Noah the discoverer of wine, 9*a* f

Nob, 61*b*

David at, 166*a*

priesthood at, 375*a*

Saul's revenge on priests of, 166*b*

Nobah, 98*b*

Nock, A. D., 1044*b*

Noncanonical early Christian writings, 1144 ff

"acts," 1147*a* f

apocalypses, 1147*b* f

apologies, 1148*a* f

gospels, 1145*b* ff

letters, 1137*a* f, 1144*b* ff

other works, 1148*b* ff

Noninvolvement, 316*b*

Nonretaliation, 799*a*

North, C. R., 332*b*, 1089*b*

North, E. M., 1247*b*

Norwood, Frederick Abbott, 1045

Not my people (name of child of Hosea), 453*b*

Not pitied (name of child of Hosea), 453*a* f

Noth, Martin, 36*a*, 68*b*, 124*b*, 137*a*, 157*a*, 183*a*, 1025*b*, 1031*b*, 1059*a*, 1094*b*

Numbers, Book of, 85 ff

sources of, 85*a* f

theological significance of, 85*b*

Numerical proverbs, 306*b*, 310*a*, 318*b*, 319*a*, 1079*a*

"Nunc Dimittis," 676*b*
Nuzi, 68*a*, 71*b*, 1275*b*
Nympha, 864*b*

O

Oaths:
  of clearance, 117*a*
  formula for, 335*b*, 370*b*
  of innocence, 262*b*, 263*a*, 270*a* f
  Jesus' words on, 616*a* f
  making of, 57*b*, 563*b*
  of purgation, 249*a*, 266*b*
  warning against, 923*a*
  of Yahweh, 473*b*, 475*b*
  See also Swearing
Obadiah, 193*b*
Obadiah, Book of, 477 ff, 981*a*
  authorship and date of, 477*a*
  structure of, and relation to
    other books, 477*a* f
  theological viewpoint of, 477*b*
Obed, 154*a* f, 217*a*
Obed-edom, 173*b*
  ark in the house of, 212*a*
Obedience:
  to covenant, 66*a*
  to food laws, 438*a* ff
  to God, 5*b*, 16*a*, 18*b*, 261*a*,
    334*a*, 489*b*, 514*b*
  to the law, Moses' call to,
    106*a* f, 107*a* ff
  the only true worship, 379*b*
  preferred to sacrifice, 380*b*
  rewards of, 346*b* f, 365*b* f
  true, 366*b* f
  way of, 360*a*
  and wisdom, 295*b*
Oboth, 94*b*
Obscene language, 563*a* f
Occultists, 1103*b*
Ocina, 537*b*
Octavian (Augustus), 611*b*,
    1011*b*, 1035*a*, 1141*a*
Odenathus, 525*b*
Odes of Solomon, 1148*b*
Oesterley, W. O. E., 261*a*, 307*a*,
    522*a*, 528*b*, 551*b*, 588*a*,
    1089*b*, 1115*b*
Offerings:
  brought to Jerusalem, 109*b*
  burnt, 62*b*, 67*b*, 69*a* f, 71*b*,
    72*b*, 223*a*, 446*b*, 473*a*
  cereal, 62*b*, 69*b*, 71*b*, 72*b* f,
    473*a*
  daily, 62*b*
  at dedication of altar, 87*a*
  eating of, 75*a*, 110*b*, 269*a* f
  of fat, 70*a*
  of first fruits, 66*b*, 69*b*, 110*b*,
    116*b* f, 308*a*, 388*b*

Offerings—*cont.*
  of firstling, 84*b*, 110*a*, 111*a*
  freewill, 60*a*, 73*a*, 223*a*, 278*a*,
    471*a*
  guilt, 71*a*, 71*b* ff, 73*a*, 76*b*,
    158*b*
  holy and most holy, 69*b*, 71*a*,
    72*b*, 73*a*, 80*b*, 82*a*, 432*b*
  initiatory, of priests, 74*a* f
  of money, 71*b*, 72*a*
  of oil, 489*a*
  peace, 55*b*, 69*b* f, 72*b*, 73*a* f,
    78*b*, 187*b*, 471*a*, 473*a*
  for poor at Jerusalem, 793*a*,
    812*a*, 818*b* ff, 827*b*
  propitiatory, 90*b*
  public and private, 70*a* ff, 73*a*,
    97*b* f
  purification, 70*b*, 72*a*, 73*a*
  by royalty, 489*a*
  sin, 62*b*, 70*a* ff, 73*a*, 78*a*
  thank, 269*a*, 292*b*, 294*b*, 471*a*
  votive, 73*a*
  See also Sacrifice
Og, 95*a*, 104*a*
  defeat of, 106*a*
Oholah, 425*a* f
Oholiab, 67*a*
Oholibah, 425*a* f
Oil:
  beneficial to hair, 298*b*
  for a constant light, 61*b*
  healing by anointing with, 655*a*
  as sacrifice offering, 489*a*
  a symbol of rejoicing, 288*a*
Old age:
  blessings of, 313*a*
  description of, in Ecclesiastes,
    323*b*
  in the wicked, 547*a*
  wisdom in, 564*b*
Old Egyptian language, 1197*a*
Old English, Bible in, 1237*a*
Old Gate, 228*b*
Old Kingdom of Egypt, 272*b*,
    1009*b*
Old Latin:
  for Bel and the Dragon, 585*a*
  for Tobit, 527*a*, 533*a*
Old Testament:
  apocalyptic in, 1106 ff
  Aramaic targums, 1229*a*
  background for kingdom of
    God in, 1176*a* ff
  based on Mosaic covenant,
    986*a* f
  beginnings of, 1227*a* f
  as Bible of first Christians, 926*a*
  as canon for church, 1212*b* ff
  the Chronicler's history,
    1086*b* ff

Old Testament—*cont.*
  compiling of, 1082 ff
  the Deuteronomic histories,
    1084*a* ff
  evidence of, from Qumran,
    1227*b* f, 1228*b*
  examples of historical study of
    Bible from, 980*a* ff
  extant Hebrew MSS of, 1228*b*
  fulfilled in Jesus Christ, 610*a*
  Greek versions of, 1228*b* f,
    1235
  Hebrew community and,
    1072 ff
  historical traditions in, 1080*b* f
  history in narrative and poetry
    in, 1088*a*
  as inspired word of God, 591*a*
  law codes in, 1093*a* ff
  law as literary form in, 1081*b*
  literary forms of, 1077 ff
  making of canon of, 1209 ff
  MSS of, 1227*a* ff
  Masoretic, 1228*a*, 1235
  the name, 815*b*
  nature of history writing in,
    1088*a* ff
  and NT, intertestamental lit-
    erature between, 1110 ff
  and NT, period between, 979*a*
  and NT, unity between, 989 ff
  and oral tradition, 1081*b*
  the Pentateuch, 1082*a* ff; *see
    also* Pentateuch
  people of, 978*a* f
  people of the world of, 1005 ff
  poetic prose of, 1080*a* f
  poetry in, 1077*a* ff, 1088*a*
  prophecies in, and the gospels,
    1131*b*
  prophetic literature of, 1095 ff
  quotations from, in Hebrews,
    898*b* f, 901*b* f
  role of, in the church, 1213*a*
  Samaritan Pentateuch, 1228*b*
  search for canon of, 1213*a*
  significance of Dead Sea scrolls
    for study of, 1070*a* f
  text study of, in modern times,
    1234*a* f
  wisdom literature of, 1101 ff
  word of God in, 994*a* f
  the word "kingdom" in,
    1177*a* f
Olives, Mount of, 177*b*, 206*b*,
    510*a*, 635*a*, 698*b*, 701*a*,
    730*b*
  Jesus' prayer on, 702*a* f
Omer, 50*b*
Omri, 111*b*, 191*b*, 488*b*, 489*b*

Omri—*cont.*
destruction of house of, 200*b*
reign of, in Israel, 192*b*, 1278*a*
Samaria built by, 470*a*
On (Heliopolis), 28*b*, 91*a*, 1002*b*
On First Principles (Origen), 973*a*
Onan, 27*a*, 30*a*
O'Neill, J. C., 730*a*
Onesimus, 856*b*, 863*b*, 864*a*, 864*b*, 894*a* ff, 982*b*
Onesiphorus, 889*b*
Onias I, 598*a*
Onias III, 448*a*, 449*a*, 575*b*, 591*b*, 601*b*, 602*a*
Ono, 229*a*
Openheartedness, 817*a* f
Ophel mount, 222*b*
Ophir, 189*a*, 555*b*
Ophrah, 25*b*
Oppenheim, A. L., 1017*b*
Oppression:
complaint of, 495*a*, 495*b*
economic, 496*a*
political, taken for granted, 322*a*
of the poor, 248*a*, 472*a*, 511*b*
of the sojourner, 425*a*
Oracles: acted, 383*a*, 386*a*, 390*b*, 393*b*, 402*b*, 416*a* ff, 419*a* f, 424*a* f, 430*b*
against Judah's religious leaders, 348*a*
against the nations, 330*b*, 331*a*, 341*a* ff, 350*a* ff, 374*a*, 389*a* f, 398*a* ff, 413*a*, 426*b* ff, 466*b* ff, 499*b* f, 981*a; see also* Oracles on the nations and cities, *below*
against tyrants, 341*b* f
ambiguity in, 200*a*
of assurance, 271*a*, 409*b*
of Balaam, 96*a* f
to Baruch, 398*a*
on beasts of the Negeb, 349*b*
before battle, 142*b*, 149*b*, 169*a*, 195*a*, 268*a*
of blessing, 492*a*
on bloodguilt, 179*b*
of the coming of the Messiah, 508*a* ff
consultation of, 162*b*, 173*a*
to the Danites, 148*b*
on David's dynasty, 174*a* f
doom, 195*a*, 197*a*, 199*b*, 392*a*
of Ezekiel, 419*a* ff, 426*b* ff
fleece used for, 142*b*
on foreigners, 365*b* f
formulas for, 466*b*
on Gog of Magog, 413*a*, 431*a* f

Oracles—*cont.*
on Habakkuk, 495*a* f
of Haggai, 501*a*
of Hosea, 455*a* ff
of hope and restoration, 391*b* ff
by Isaiah, 205*a*
of Jeremiah, 397*a*
on Jerusalem, 205*a*, 333*b*, 509*b* ff
on Joseph, 32*a*
of lament, 381*b*
of Malachi, 514*a* ff
priestly, 52*a*, 61*b*
prophetic, 185*b* f, 191*a*, 192*a*, 199*b*, 201*a*, 206*a*
in prophetic literature, 1079*a*, 1079*b*
of rejection, 163*b*
of salvation, 257*b*, 259*b*
of Second Isaiah, 330*b*
Sibylline, 945*a*, 1113*b*
silent, 163*a*
of theocracy, 506*b* f
of Third Isaiah, 365*b* ff
threat, 385*b*
the word, 512*a*
of Yahweh, 20*b*
in Zechariah, 505*b*, 506*a*, 506*b*, 508*a* ff
to Zedekiah, 394*a*, 394*b*
of Zephaniah, 498*b*, 499*a* ff
See also Miracles
Oracles of the Lord (Papias), 708*b*
Oracles on the nations and cities:
Ammon, 400*a*, 466*b*, 467*b* f, 500*a*
Arabia, 344*b*
Assyria, 342*a*, 351*b*
Babylon, 341*a*, 401*a* ff
Damascus, 343*a*, 400*b*
Edom and Arabia, 344*b*, 351*b*, 352*a*, 400*b*, 426*b*, 466*b*, 467*b*, 981*a*
Egypt, 343*a* ff, 350*a*, 398*a* ff, 426*b*, 428*b*
Elam, 401*a*
Israel, 31*a* ff, 424*a*, 466*b*, 468*a* ff
Judah, 330*b*, 468*a*
Kedar, 400*b*
Moab, 342*a* f, 346*b*, 399*a* ff 426*b*, 466*b*, 468*a*, 500*a*
Philistia, 342*a*, 399*a*, 466*b*, 467*a*
Phoenicia, 345*a* f
Sidon, 427*b* f
Syria, 466*b*, 467*a*
Tyre, 345*a*, 413*a*, 426*b* ff, 466*b*, 467*b*

Oral law, 536*a*, 539*b*, 556*a*, 627*b*
Oral tradition, 627*b*, 1073*a* ff, 1075*b*
of the covenant, 1074*a*
exodus and Passover in, 1074*a* f
and form criticism, 1081*b*
forms of, 1073*a* f
function of, 1073*b*
and the gospels, 1130*b* ff
liturgical factor in, 1074*a*
of the Pentateuch, 1073*b*
and translation of Hebrew, 1115*a* f
Oreb, 143*a*, 285*b*
Ordeal, trial by, 87*a*, 203*a*, 283*b*
Ordination, 736*a*, 745*b*, 887*b*, 889*a*
offering of, 73*b*
ram of, 62*b*, 74*a*
Origen, 546*a*, 633*b*, 897*a*, 897*b*, 973*a* f, 1050*a*, 1220*a*, 1221*a*, 1221*b*
collections in, 1223*a* f
and four-gospel canon, 1222*b* f
Hexapla of, 1229*a*, 1232*a*
Spirit inspiration of, 1224*b*
translation of LXX by, 1229*b*
Origin stories, 1088*b*
Original sin, doctrine of, 522*b*, 903*a*
Orlinsky, H. M., 601*a*
Orm, 1237*b*
Ornaments, discarding of, 64*b*
Ornan, 180*b*
Orontes River, 1002*b*
Oropherenes, 535*b*, 537*a*
Orpah, 150*b*, 151*a*, 151*b*
Orphans, special consideration for, 58*a*
Orthodox churches, canons of, 1212*b*
Orthodoxy, 320*a*, 320*b*, 321*a*
of wisdom teachers, 304*b*, 306*a*
Osiris, 398*b*
Osnapper (Ashurbanipal?), 223*b*
Ostborn, Gunnar, 452*a*, 1215*b*
Ostentation, 311*a*, 311*b*, 557*a*
of Pharisees, 638*a*
Ostraca, 1204*a*, 1205*b* f
Othniel, 138*b*
Oversimplification of human character, in Proverbs, 306*a*
Ox:
goring by, 57*a*
unmuzzled, 115*b*

P

P (Priestly) Code (tradition, source), 1*b*, 2, 33*a*, 33*b*, 34,

Parallelism—*cont.*
in poetry, 1078*a,* 1079*a* f
in psalms, 253*b,* 276*a*
synonymous, 1077*a* f
synthetic, 306*b,* 1077*b*
of Tirzah and Jerusalem, 324*a,* 327*a*
Paran, Mt., 120*b*
Paran, wilderness of, 167*b,* 190*a*
Parchment, used for writing, 1206*b* f, 1225*b*
Parents:
and children, relationship of, 843*b,* 863*b*
disrespect for, 56*b*
duty to, 555*b*
education of youth by, 307*a,* 319*b*
honor for, 552*b* f, 566*b,* 623*a,* 627*b*
penalty for disobeying, 113*b*
Paris Psalter, 1237*a*
Parker, Matthew, 1240*a*
Parker, R. A., 1282*b*
Parousia, 871*b,* 910*b,* 922*b,* 933*b,* 1174*b* f
Parrot, André, 481*a,* 491*b,* 1059*a*
Parsin ("halves"), 443*a*
Parthians, 1013*b*
Particularism, 1153*a*
Parvis, M. M., 1236*b*
Pashhur the son of Immer, 386*a,* 387*a*
Pashhur the son of Malchiah, 386*b*
Passion of Jesus, 637*a,* 640*a* ff, 666*a* ff, 721*a* ff, 1180*b,* 1192*a* f
prediction of, 630*a,* 631*a,* 634*b,* 658*b,* 660*b,* 662*b*
writing down of, 1131*b*
Passion of Perpetua and Felicitas (Tertullian), 1224*b*
Passion Play of Oberammergau, 1249*b*
Passover, 44*a* f, 81*a,* 111*a,* 255*a,* 434*a,* 571*a,* 640*b,* 677*a*
celebrated at temple in Jerusalem, 207*a,* 217*b,* 218*b,* 225*a*
etymology of, 45*a*
at Gilgal, 127*a*
J ordinance of, 45*b*
Jesus' "signs" at, 710*b*
and Last Supper, 666*b,* 701*a,* 722*a*
and oral tradition, 1074*a* f
P ordinance of, 44*b* f, 46*a*
regulation of, 44*b* ff, 66*b*
Song of Solomon associated with, 324*b*

Passover—*cont.*
supplemental, 87*b*
true, and moral purity, 800*a*
Pastoral epistles, 882*a* ff, 1219*b* f
Patara, 757*b*
Paterson, John, 261*a*
Pathros, 397*b*
Patience, exhortation to, 922*b* f
Patmos, 948
seer of, 708*a*
Patriarchs:
age of, 1018*b* f
archaeological discoveries pertaining to, 1059*a* f
chronology of, 1271*a* f, 1275*b* ff
genealogies of, 209*b*
history of, 11*a* f, 1018*b* f
as models for prophets and anointed kings, 291*b* f
See also Abraham, Isaac, Jacob, *and* Joseph
Patriarchs, Twelve, Testament of the, 638*a,* 665*a,* 945*a,* 1112*a*
Paul the apostle:
accepted into church, 740*b*
on advantages of being single, 633*a*
answers of, to questions from Corinth, 801*b* ff
in Antioch, 828*a,* 890*b*
in Antioch of Pisidia, 745*b* ff
on the apostle's ministry, 815*a* ff
apostleship of, 770*b*
arrests, trial, and imprisonment of, 758*b* ff, 761*a* ff, 883*b,* 890*a,* 894*a*
in Athens, 751*b* f, 865*a*
attitude of, toward Thessalonians, 869*a*
authority of, 820*b* f, 826*b* ff
and baptism, 47*a*
basis of ethics of, 788*b* f
in Beroea, 751*b*
bodily ailment of, 822*a,* 831*a*
in Caesarea, 754*a,* 760*b* ff, 845*b*
on Christian life and brotherhood, 841*a* ff, 855*a* f, 861*b* ff, 895*b* f
chronology of, 1275*a,* 1282*a* f
church unity as theme of, 834*a,* 838*a* ff, 840*b* f
from collection to corpus, in NT canon, 1223*a*
concern of, for Corinthians, 821*a* f
on congregational meetings, 805*a* ff
conversion of, 740*a* ff, 763*b*

Paul—*cont.*
in Corinth, 753*a* f, 754*b,* 795*a* f, 796*b,* 865*a,* 982*a*
creation and Creator in thought of, 548*a*
on Davidic descent of Jesus, 611*b,* 663*a*
on divine righteousness, 775*a* ff
and the doctrine of the elect, 665*b*
effect of imprisonment of, 848*a*
in Ephesus, 753*b* ff, 795*b,* 813*b,* 846*a,* 894*a,* 1140*a* f
on ethics, 788*b* ff
experience of, on the road to Damascus, 646*b,* 740*a* f
experience of, interpreted, 848*a* f
on faith, 771*b,* 776*a* ff
on false teaching, 860*b* ff
farewell of, at Miletus, 756*b* ff
on forgiveness, 814*b*
on freedom in Christ, 831*a* ff
on function of the law, 830*a* f
future plans of, 793*a,* 812*a,* 821*a,* 822*a* ff, 846*a*
gospel demonstrated in experience of, 829*a* ff, 831*a*
as great example, 853*a* f, 884*a,* 885*a,* 890*b,* 891*a*
Hebrews (book of) ascribed to, 897*a*
in Iconium and Lystra, 747*a* f, 890*b*
on idol meats, 803*a* ff
on idolatry, 772*a* ff
importance of, in early church, 1116*b*
and Jeremiah's understanding of God, 381*b*
and the Jerusalem apostles, 826*b* ff
at the Jerusalem conference, 748*a* ff
on Jesus as "first fruits," 642*b*
on the Jews, 868*b* f
Joel quoted by, 463*b*
journey of, to Rome, 755*b* ff
on Judaism, 773*a* ff, 784*b* ff
and Judaizing Christianity, 708*a*
on justification by faith, 18*b,* 832*a*
letter of, to Colossians, 856*a* ff
letter of, to Ephesians, 834*a* ff
letter of, to Galatians, 824*a* ff
letter of, to Philemon, 894*a* ff
letter of, to Philippians, 845*a* ff
letter of, to Romans, 768*a* ff
letter of, to Thessalonians, 865*a* ff

Phillips, J. B., 862*b*, 1242*a*, 1268*a*

Philo of Alexandria, 589*b*, 660*a*, 661*b*, 710*b*, 731*b*, 897*a*, 979*a*, 1167*b*
  biblical interpretation by, 972*b* f, 974*b*
  and *logos*, 995*a*, 1169*a*
  reconciliation of Judaism with Greek philosophy by, 546*a*, 804*b*

Philosophy:
  Cynic, 1040*a*
  Essene, 536*a*
  foreign, in Israel, 305*b*
  Platonic, 547*a*, 547*b*, 548*a*, 589*a*, 710*a*, 899*a*, 910*b*
  of Proverbs, 306*a* f
  of the Pseudepigrapha, 1113*b* f
  Socratic, 589*a*
  Stoic, 546*b*, 547*a*, 710*a*, 752*a*, 773*b*, 792*a*, 855*b*, 888*a*, 982*b*, 1040*a* f
    See also Syncretism
  and intertestamental literature, 1114*b*

Philoxenus, 1232*a*

Phinehas, 42*a*, 133*b*, 134*b*, 284*b*
  praised by ben Sira, 572*b*, 575*b*
  zeal of, 97*a*

Phoebe, 793*b*

Phoenicia, 434*b*, 467*b*, 519*b*, 1003*a*
  influence of, on Proverbs, 305*b* 309*b*
  Omri's alliance with, 192*b*
  oracle against, 345*a* f
  as setting for Song of Solomon, 327*a*

Phoenicians, 131*a*

Phoenix, 764*b*

Phrygia, 749*b* f

Phrygian powder, 952*b*

Phygelus, 889*b*

Phylacteries, 46*b*

Physician:
  consultation of, 569*a* f
  honoring of, 569*a*

Pictographs, 1201*a*, 1201*b*

Piety:
  mocked, 282*a* f
  symbolized by the poor, 682*b*

Pi-hahiroth, 48*a*

Pilate, Pontius, 668*b*, 677*b*, 704*a*, 981*b*, 1030*a*
  Jesus' trial before, 641*b* f, 703*b*, 724*b*, 725*a*

Pilgrim psalms, 259*a*

Pilgrims:
  memories of Jerusalem of, 296*a*
  murder of, 396*b* f
  priestly blessing on, 297*a* f

Pilgrim's Progress (Bunyan), 1249*a*

Pillar of cloud and fire, 47*b*

Pillars:
  bronze, in temple, 186*b*
  cult, 22*a*, 130, 487, 488*a*
  graven, as idols, 84*a*
  Hall of, 186*a*
  of sanctuary court, 61*b*

Pim (weight stones), 162*a*

Pisgah, 106*a*

Pishon River, 5*a*

Pithom, 35*a*, 36*a*, 37*b*

Pity, as new attribute of religion, 440*a*

Pius XII, Pope, 1231*b*

Plague(s), 97*a*, 212*b*
  brought by the hand of God, 158*b*, 288*a*
  of Egypt, 42*a* ff, 45*b*, 548*b*
  of mice attacking Sennacherib's army, 205*a*
  of Revelation, 954*b* ff, 962*b* ff

Platonic philosophy, 547*a*, 547*b*, 548*a*, 589*a*, 710*a*, 899*a*, 910*b*

Play on words, 39*b*, 375*b*, 377*b*, 387*b*, 401*b*, 415*b*, 443*a*, 446*b*, 459*a*, 463*a*, 463*b*, 467*a*, 467*b*, 470*b*, 475*a*, 485*a*, 487*b*, 490*b*, 530*b*, 544*b*, 555*b*, 573*b*, 629*b*, 652*a*, 773*a*

Pledges:
  good faith in, 57*b*
  on loans, 115*a*, 115*b*
  and unpaid loans, 496*a*

Pliny, 755*a*, 938*a*, 961*a*, 979*a*, 1047*a*, 1144*a*

Plumb line, Amos' vision of, 474*b*

Poetic justice, 280*b*, 383*b*, 585*b*

Poetry:
  acrostic, 306*b*
  in Baruch, 577*b*
  in Ecclesiasticus, 576*a* f
  of Ezekiel, 412*b*, 415*a*, 416*a*, 416*b*, 419*b*, 420*b*, 422*b*, 423*a*, 424*b*, 426*a*, 427*a*, 427*b*, 430*a*
  forms of, 1077*a* ff
  of Habakkuk, 495*b*
  Hebrew, 253*b* f, 364*a*, 415*a*, 422*b*, 423*a*, 541*b* f, 645*b*, 1077*a* ff, 1088*a*
  history in, 1088*a*
  imagery in, 1079*a*
  in Isaiah, 331*a*
  in Judith, 535*b*, 541*b* f
  in Maccabees, 588*a*, 592*b* f
  of Nahum, 491*a*, 491*b*, 492*a*, 492*b* ff
  OT, 1077*a* ff, 1088*a*

Poetry—*cont.*
  poetic prose, 1080*a* f
  in prophetic literature, 1079*a* f
  of Proverbs, 304*a*, 306*b* f
  of psalms, 253*b* f
  religious, of Egypt, 254*a*
  of Song of Solomon, 322*b*, 323*a*
  in Tobit, 534*a*
  Ugaritic, 1057*a* f
  in wisdom literature, 306*b* f, 1078*b* f
  in Zechariah, 507*b*
  of Zephaniah, 499*a*, 499*b*, 500*a*

Politics:
  despotism in, 439*b*
  failure of leaders in, 348*a* f
  faith and, 337*a* f
  Jeremiah's comments on, 383*a* f
  Judah's infidelity in, 377*a*
  oppression of, taken for granted, 322*a*
  power, 337*a* f
  religion and, 1252*a*
  role of prophets in, 1075*b*
  use of marriage in, 440*a* f

Poll tax, 63*a*

Pollution of water, 42*b*

Polycarp, 708*a*, 708*b*, 935*b*, 1220*a*, 1220*b*, 1221*a*, 1221*b*
  letter of, 883*b*, 1137*b*, 1145*a*, 1219*b*
  martyrdom of, 950*b*, 1145*a* f, 1217*b*
  and the Spirit, 1217*b*

Polycrates, 709*a*

Polygamy, 565*a*, 661*b* f

Pomegranate, as fertility symbol, 62*a*

Pompey, 979*a*, 1113*a*

Poor:
  care of, 312*a*, 313*a*, 315*a*, 317*b*, 318*a*
  gifts to, on Purim, 237*b*
  gleanings for, 115*b*, 116
  incompatibility of rich and, 558*b*
  of Jerusalem, offering for, 812*a*, 818*b* ff, 827*b*
  kingdom to be possessed by, 633*b*
  land of exiles given to, 419*a*, 429*b*
  misfortunes of, 311*b*
  neglect of, 421*b*
  persecution of, 248*a*, 472*a*, 511*b*
  relief of, 229*a*
  and righteousness, 922*b*
  in spirit, 615*a*
  symbolic of pious of Israel, 682*b*

Pope, Hugh, 1242*b*

Pope, M. H., 241*a*
Popilius Laenas, 449*b*
Population spread, 6*a* ff
Porcius Festus. *See* Festus, Porcius
Porter, F. C., 1109*b*
Postal system of Persia, 235*a*
Postapostolic age, 1121*b* f
Post-Reformation biblical inter-
　pretation, 975*b* ff
Pot, corroded, Ezekiel's allegory
　of, 418*b*, 425*b* f
Potiphar:
　Joseph sold to, 27*a*
　wife of, and Joseph, 27*b* f
Potiphera, 28*a*
Potsherd Gate, 386*a*
Potsherds, 1250*b* f, 1207*a*
Poverty:
　preferred to wealth, 312*b*, 317*b*
　and wealth, in early Christi-
　　anity, 1119*b* f
　　See also Poor
Powerful man, warning against,
　558*b*
Practical jokes, 316*b*
Praetorium, 845*b* f
Praise:
　call to, 294*b*, 302*b*
　of famous men, 571*b* ff
　of a girl's beauty, 327*a* f
　in heaven and earth, 302*a*
　hymns of, 441*b*, 442*a*, 444*a* f,
　　490*b*, 541*b* f
　liturgy of, 294*a* f
　of the Lord of nature, 571*a* f
　men worthy of, 564*b* f
　psalms of, 340*b*, 346*b*, 356*b*,
　　368*b*, 570*a*
　universal song of, 587*b*
　of wisdom, 308*a* f, 316*a*
Pratensis, Felix, 1232*b*
Prayer:
　against the nations, 279*b*
　as antidote to anxiety, 855*a*
　asking favors, 318*b*
　Christian, inclusiveness of, 885*b*
　combined with fasting and
　　thanksgiving, 533*b*
　and the coming of the Spirit,
　　678*b*
　compulsion to, 274*a* f
　of confession, 459*b* f, 577*b* f,
　　587*b*
　of confidence in God, 346*b* f
　danger averted through, 548*b*
　of Daniel, 447*b*
　defined, 259*b*
　for deliverance, 257*a*, 266*b*,
　　267*a*, 275*a*, 282*a*, 295*b*, 347*a*
　doubtful value of, 322*a*
　in early church, 783*a*

Prayer—*cont.*
　of Elijah, 923*b*
　of Esther, 544*a*
　and faith, 918*a*
　faithfulness in, 444*a*
　for forgiveness, 269*b* f
　for God's blessing, 878*a*
　of gratitude, 532*b*
　for guidance, 262*b* f, 269*b* f
　of Habakkuk, 496*b* ff
　of Hannah, 556*a*
　for hearing, 270*b*, 271*a*
　High Priestly, of Jesus, 724*a* f
　in illness, 569*a*
　importance of, 844*b*, 863*b*
　for the inner man, 841*a*
　intercession of the Spirit in,
　　784*a*
　intercessory, 915*b*
　for Israel, 568*b*
　for Jerusalem, 395*b*
　of Jesus, on Mt. of Olives,
　　702*a* f
　in Jesus' name, 939*b*
　Jesus' words on, 617*a* f
　of Judith, 540*a* f
　for justice, 265*b*
　the Lord's, 617*a*, 667*b*, 689*a* f,
　　1181*b*, 1184*a*
　of Manasseh king of Judah, 587
　of Mordecai, 544*a*
　of Paul, 847*b* f, 858*b*, 869*b*
　Paul's injunction to, 874*a* f
　of penitence, 587*a*
　people's lament and, 369*a* ff
　petitionary, 858*b*
　for pity, 369*b*
　posture for, 540*b*
　prophet's pledging himself to,
　　368*b*
　for protection from temptation,
　　300*b*, 563*a*, 617*b*
　of Raguel, 532*b*
　request for, 880*a* f
　for restoration of Israel, 299*b*,
　　410*b*
　ritual, 462*b*
　for the ruler, 578*a*
　service of, 923*a* f
　of Tobias and Sarah, 530*a* f,
　　532*b*
　of Tobit, 530*a*
　for vengeance, 266*b*, 282*a*,
　　282*b*, 285*b*, 300*a*, 301*a*
　for victory, 268*a*
　and victory of Christianity,
　　939*a* f
　for vindication, 270*b*, 273*b*,
　　275*b*
　and word of God, 998*a* f

Prayer of Azariah, 436*b*, 441*a*,
　447*b*
Prayer of Azariah and the Song
　of the Three Young Men,
　581 f
　additions to Daniel, 581*a*
　date and composition of, 581*a* f
　teachings of, 581*b*
　theological significance of, 582*a*
Prayer shawl (tallith), 91*a*
Preacher, the (Ecclesiastes), 320*a*,
　320*b*
Preaching:
　biblical, the "way" of, 1255*b* ff
　Christian leaders' task of,
　　1192*b*
　and dialogue, 1257*a*
　dogmatism to be avoided in,
　　1257*b*
　expository, 1255*b* ff
　false, 485*b*
　to Gentiles, prohibited, 622*a*
　of the good news, 368*a*, 678*b*,
　　1258*b*
　of Haggai, 502*a*
　as heralding and proclamation,
　　1255*a* f
　of Jesus, 614*a* ff, 661*a* ff,
　　717*b* ff, 1181*a*
　"life-situation," 1258*a*
　and moralism, 1257*a* f
　need for, 787*a*
　in NT letters, 1125*a*
　pain of, to Ezekiel, 415*b*
　of Paul, 745*b* ff, 747*b*, 752*b*,
　　754*b*, 756*a* ff, 816*a*, 867*b*,
　　868*a*, 873*b*
　of Peter, 731*a*, 731*b*, 732*b* f,
　　735*a* f, 742*b* f
　prophetic, 430*b*
　topical, 1258*a*
　and way of the cross, 659*a*
Preaching of Peter, 1148*a*
Predestination, 747*a*, 784*b*, 785*a*
Pre-existence:
　concept of, 850*b* f
　of Jesus Christ, 850*b* f, 1168*b* f
　of soul, 547*a*
　of wisdom, 1168*b*
Prejudice:
　against the Jews, 522*b*, 624*a*,
　　633*a*, 637*a*, 642*a*, 725*a*, 989*b*
　Haman the prototype of, 233*a*
Premillennialists, 878*b*
Pesumptuousness, warning
　against, 555*a* f
Price, I. M., 1242*b*
Price, James L., 795
Pride:
　afflictions brought by, 553*a* f
　before a fall, 428*b*

Righteousness—*cont.*
fate of, 523*b* f
gates of, 295*a*
of God, *see* God, justice and righteousness of
grace, 787*b*
hatred of, by the wicked, 318*a*
human and divine, 408*b*
humility and, 552*b*
inclusive of both Jew and Gentile, 792*a*
of Joseph, 292*a*
joy of, 263*a*
life of, in the light, 308*a* f
as life's ultimate aim, 311*a*
and peace, 921*a*
of the poor, 922*b*
problem of, 17*b*
reward of, 264*b* f, 274*a*, 288*a*, 293*b*, 297*a*, 306*a*, 334*b*, 367*a*, 514*b* ff, 546*a* ff
and right relation to God, 853*b*
self-control in, 313*a*
as source of security, 317*a* f
suffering of, 570*a*, 578*a*
survival of, 420*a* f
Teacher of, 463*a*
thirst for, 615*a* f
of the true Israel, 296*b*
and truth, 844*a*
universal, 523*b*
versus wickedness, 310*a* f
way of, 261*b*
as the will of God, 408*a*
zeal for, 613*a*
Rimmon, 199*b*, 470*b*, 510*b*
Rimmon-perez, 98*b*
Ring and the Book, The (Browning), 1249*b*
Ringgren, Helmer, 1071*b*, 1158*b*
Riphath, 209*b*
Rissah, 98*b*
Rist, Martin, 949*a*, 1109*b*
Rithmah, 98*b*
Ritual Code, 33*a*, 34, 50*b*, 55*a*, 55*b*, 66*a*, 457*a*
Ritual ordinances, 53*a*, 55*b*, 58*a* f, 62*b* f, 71*b*, 77*b* f, 78*b* ff, 87*a*, 90*b* f
Ritual uncleanness, 70*b*, 73*b*
purification of, 75*a* ff, 92*a*
Rizpah, 172*a*, 179*b*
Roberts, B. J., 1236*b*
Roberts, H., 1186*b*
Robinson, Edward, 1055*b*
Robinson, H. W., 241*a*, 452*a*, 1200*b*
Robinson, J. A. T., 709*b*, 1193*b*
Robinson, T. H., 899*a*, 1089*b*
Rogelin, 178*a*

Rogers, John, 1239*a*
Role playing in Bible teaching, 1267*a*
Rolle, Richard, 1237*b*
Roman Catholic Church:
and additions to Daniel, 581*a*
and Additions to Esther, 543*a*
Apocrypha accepted by, 1241*a*
canon of, 1212*b*, 1213*a*, 1213*b*
councils of bishops and, 1116*a*
modern translations of the Bible and, 1242*a*
teaching of, on consummation of marriage, 661*b*
teaching of, on perpetual virginity of Mary, 652*a*
Vulgate and Rheims-Douai Bibles used by, 1231*b*
Roman Empire:
citizen's duty to, 790*a* f
destruction of, predicted in Revelation, 947*b*, 963*b* ff
emperors of, 1035*a* ff
government in, 1042*a*
growing power of, 604*b*
influence of Mosaic law in, 1252*b*
institutions of, 1041*b* ff
Jewish revolt against, 721*a*
Judea ruled by, 604*b*, 1029*a* ff, 1274*b*
Latin language in, 1042*a* f
and the Near East, 1034*b* ff
persecution of Christians by, 525*b*, 938*a*, 946*b*, 1047*a* f, 1050*b* f
picture of, in Revelation, 946*b*, 961*a*
religion of, 1041*b* f
represented by eagle, 524*b*
slavery in, 894*b*
See also Rome
Romanesque churches, 1251*a*
Romans, Letter of Paul to, 768 ff, 1143*a* f
addendum to, 793*b* ff
authenticity and integrity of, 769*b* f
the church at Rome, 769*a*, 1143*a* f, 1149*a* f
date and place of composition of, 769*a* f
new theology in, 768*b* f
occasion and purpose of, 768*a* f
salutation of, 770*a* ff
Rome:
break of, with Simon Maccabeus, 599*a*
church in, 769*a*, 1143*a* f, 1149*a* f

Rome—*cont.*
determined to execute all Jewish nationalists, 642*a*
as instrument of God's judgment on Israel, 637*a*
Jerusalem destroyed by, 521*b*, 522*b*, 524*b*, 577*a*
Jews expelled from, 769*a*, 795*b*
Maccabean alliance with, 596*a*, 597*b* f
Paul in, 766*b* f, 845*b*, 883*b*
Paul's journey to, 755*b* ff, 764*a* ff
Paul's letter to the church in, 768 ff
subjugation of Israel by, 522*a*, 523*a*, 1107*b*, 1274*b*
See also Roman Empire
Ropes, J. H., 825*b*, 917*b*
Rosetta Stone, 1202*a*
Rosh Hashanah, 490*b*
Ross, Alexander, 917*b*
Ross, John, 1245*a*
Rothenberg, Benno, 36*a*
Rowley, H. H., 151*a*, 325*b*, 375*a*, 438*a*, 495*a*, 993*b*, 1025*b*, 1089*b*, 1109*b*, 1115*b*, 1200*b*, 1236*b*
Royal counselors, as wise men, 1103*a* f
Royal psalms, 258*a* f
Rufus, son of Simon of Cyrene, 669*a*
Rusa I, 1012*b*
Rushworth Gospels, 1237*a*
Ruth:
and Boaz, 116*a*, 152*a* ff
and Naomi, 150*b*, 151*a* ff
son of, 154*a* f
Ruth, Book of, 150 ff, 342*b*, 365*a*, 1088*a*
date of composition of, 150*b* f
place of, in the Bible, 151*a*
purpose of, 150*a* f
Ruyl, Albert Cornelisson, 1244*b*
Rylaarsdam, J. C., 36*a*, 1105*b*
Rylands, John, 1231*a*
Ryle, H. E., 3*b*, 587*b*
Ryle, H. W., 221*a*

S

Saadya, 974*a* f
Sabbath:
controversy over, 623*b* f
disdain for, 425*a*
humanitarian explanation of, 58*b*
importance of, to Jews, 903*a* f

Transjordan—*cont.*
overrun by Tiglath-pileser III, 210*b*
progress through, 94*a* f
seminomadism in, 123*b*
settlement of tribes of, 98*a* f, 125*a*
tribes of, dismissed, 133*a*
Translation problems, 979*b*, 1245*b* ff
exclusive or inclusive pronouns, 1246*a* f
grammatical difficulties, 1247*a* f
helps with, 1247*b*
passive verbs, figures of speech, and rhetorical questions, 1246*b*
preciseness, 1246*a*
psychological terms, 1246*b* f
Transportation, miraculous, 412*b* f, 413*b*, 415*b*, 417*b*, 433*a*
Tree(s):
fruit, preservation of, 113*b*
of life, in temple area, 434*b*
messianic, 421*b* f
Pharaoh as, 428*b*
symbolism of, 278*a*, 441*b*
waker (almond), 375*b*
Tregelles, S. P., 1233*a*
Trent, Council of, 976*a*, 1213*a*, 1231*b*, 1240*b*, 1241*a*
Trevelyan, G. M., 1237*a*
Trever, John C., 1201, 1236*b*
Trial(s): endurance of, 552*a* f
by fire, 440*b* f
by ordeal, 87*a*, 283*b*
Tribute:
to Caesar, 637*b*
paid to Assyria, 204*b*, 456*b*, 458*a*, 486*a*
question of, 699*b*
Trinity:
doctrine of, 869*b*, 925*b*, 939*a*, 1053*a*
Godhead as Unity in, 724*a*
names of, 643*b*
persons of, 1052*b*
Tripolis, 605*b*
Troas, 750*a*, 756*b*, 814*b*
Trogyllium, 757*a*
Trophimus, 756*a*, 758*b*
Trumpets:
ram's horn (*shophar*), 83*a*, 87*b*, 276*b*, 285*a*, 289*b*, 302*b*, 956*b*
seven, in Revelation, 956*b* ff
silver, made in Sinai, 87*b*
Trust:
breach of, 57*b*
false, in magic, 359*b*

Trust—*cont.*
fear overcome by, 278*b*
in God, 255*a*, 265*b*, 268*b*, 270*b*, 271*a*, 274*a*, 278*a*, 318*a*, 371*b*, 440*b* f, 489*b* f, 552*b*, 872*b*
of Job, in God, 246*b*
in man or in God, 385*a*
and mistrust, 349*a* ff
position of, and dependability, 311*b*
security in, 287*b* f, 318*a*
support for, 280*a*
versus envy, 273*b* f
in wealth, futility of, 277*a*
Truth:
and beauty, 307*a*, 412*b*
Christ as, 1254*b*
communicated by word of God, 996*a* f
conveyed by a midrash, 437*b*
efforts to define, 1254*a* f
knowledge of, 885*a* f, 934*b*
limits to claim to, 321*a*
of a man's word, 311*a*
no compromising of, 323*b*
oneness of, 997*a*
presented in myth, 448*b*
and righteousness, 844*a*
sources of, for church, 1117*a*
Spirit of (Paraclete), 723*b* f
Truth, Gospel of, 708*a*, 936*b*, 937*b*, 1146*b*, 1218*b*
Trypho, 598*a* f; *see also* Dialogue with Trypho
Tubal, 371*b*, 427*b*
Tübingen School, 1136*b*
Tudhalias (Tidal), 13*b*
Tukulti-Ninurta I, 10*a*
Tunnels, 1059*b* ff
Turahi (Terah), 10*b*
Turner, Nigel, 519*b*, 522*a*, 1236*b*
Tur-Sinai, N. H., 240*a*, 241*a*, 249*a*, 250*a*
Tut-ankh-Amon, 1010*b*
Twelve Apostles, Teaching of the, 701*b*, 1224*a*; *see also* Didache
Twelve Patriarchs, Testament of the, 638*a*, 665*a*, 945*a*, 1112*a*
Twelve Prophets, Book of the, 451*a*, 477*b*, 574*b*
Twentieth Century NT, The, 1241*b*
Two-document theory, 1132*b*
Tychicus, 756*a*, 844*b*, 864*a*, 864*b*, 1139*a*
Tyndale, William, 1238*a* f, 1239*a*
"Typology," 804*b*, 810*b* f, 815*b*, 897*a* f, 972*a*

"Typology"—*cont.*
and unity between the Testaments, 991*b* f
Tyrannus, hall of, 754*b*
Tyre, 180*b*, 390*b*, 399*a*, 537*b*, 628*a*, 744*b*
church in, 757*b*
downfall of, 508*a*
oracles against, 345*a*, 413*a*, 426*b* ff, 466*b*, 467*b*
siege and recovery of, 345*b*

U

Ucal, 318*b*
Udugs, 268*b*, 288*a*
Ugarit, 68*a*, 420*a*
Ulai Canal, 446*a*, 446*b*
Ulfilas, 1232*a*, 1243*b*
Unborn, protection of life of, 56*b*
Unchastity, 114*a*, 633*a*, 749*a*
Uncial script, 1225*b*, 1231*b*
Uncleanness:
in animals, 75*a* ff, 110*a*
from childbirth, 76*a*
from contact with the dead, 92*a*, 530*a*
from eating carrion, 78*b*
of food, 656*b*
from genital discharges, 77*a*
laws of, 75*a* ff
ritual, 70*b*, 73*b*, 110*a*, 579*b* f
of Samaritans, 502*b*
from skin diseases, 76*a* f
from touching a dead animal, 75*b* ff
Understanding:
found in reverence for God, 293*b*
limits of, in humans, 320*a*, 322*b*, 523*a*
the man of, 557*a*
and obedience, 295*b*
of others, 314*a*
of self, 268*a*, 314*b*, 882*b*
of what is good and right, 307*b*
of the world of the Bible, 1005*a* ff
See also Knowledge *and* Wisdom
Underworld, entrance to, 292*b*
See also Sheol
Unfilial man, 319*a*
Unger, E. and H., 403
Unity, Christian, 812*a*, 812*b*, 813*a*, 827*b*, 834*a*, 838*a* ff, 840*a* f, 928*b*, 1048*b* ff
Unity between the Testaments, 989 ff
affirmed by church, 989*b*

Designer:	*David Dawson*
Jacket Designer:	*Harry Towns*
Sketch Maps:	*Cliff Johnston*
Printing:	*Parthenon Press*
	Text: One Color Offset
	Maps: 4 Color Offset
Textpapers:	*S. D. Warren Co.*
	Text: 45 # Warren's Commentary Offset
	Maps: 70 # Warren's Dull Coated Enamel White
Endsheets:	*S. D. Warren Co.*
	80 # Warren's Endsheets Printed 3 Colors Offset
Binding:	*Holliston's Roxite Tan*
Bound By:	*Parthenon Press*